Printed in the United States of America

The GREEK TESTAMENT

WITH A CRITICALLY REVISED TEXT, A DIGEST OF VARIOUS READINGS, MARGINAL REFERENCES TO VERBAL AND IDIOMATIC USAGE, PROLEGOMENA, AND A CRITICAL AND EXEGETICAL COMMENTARY

by

HENRY ALFORD, D.D.

with revision by

EVERETT F. HARRISON, Th.D., Ph.D.

Two double volumes

Volume I
THE FOUR GOSPELS

Volume II
ACTS, ROMANS, CORINTHIANS

(Table of Contents for Vol. II follows page 924)

MOODY PRESS
CHICAGO

PUBLISHER'S PREFACE

The value of Dean Alford's work is proved by the frequent reference to it in the Biblical literature of our day, the recommendation of it in the classroom, and the avid search of students for used copies. More than a mere reprint is needed, however. Since Alford's day the discovery of the papyri has been made and the science of papyrology developed. A new standard Greek lexicon has been published. New information has changed some interpretations. Therefore, this edition is published with revisions.

The present edition is based on Alford's seventh edition of volumes one and two and his fifth edition of volumes three and four. He never completed revision of the set. In order to put the set within financial reach of the student and at the same time to permit the student to have Alford's work in his possession, the entire original has been reproduced here. Whenever a revision is made, an asterisk (*) appears in the margin. Such revisions appear at the end of each double volume.

INTRODUCTION

Some men have their memorial in stone; others in the hearts of those who have known and loved them; still others live on in the institutions they have founded and shaped. But among the most fortunate of mortals are those who remain contemporary by the continuing influence of their literary works. Such a man is Henry Alford. It is now 112 years since this Anglican clergyman conceived the plan of *The Greek Testament* associated with his name. Like many another writer, his original intentions were modest. As he discussed the matter with his publisher, he expressed the thought that the whole work would be embraced in two thin octavo volumes, and that the task could be finished in a year. Little did he realize that the work would extend to the four large volumes that have become familiar to students of the New Testament in many lands.

To appreciate this commentary, it is well to know something of the author. The main facts of his life are chronicled for posterity in *The Life of Henry Alford, D.D.*, by his widow, published by J. B. Lippincott and Co., Philadelphia, 1873. His father turned from the law to the ministry when Henry was only an infant, so his own desire to serve the Church is easily understood. In 1828, at about eighteen years of age, he entered Cambridge, where he enjoyed the association of several of the most brilliant minds of his generation. Yet he was never swept off his feet by the sheer impact of the academic. In that first year at the university, after completing a reading of the New Testament, he wrote in his journal, "Always estimate men in proportion as they estimate this Book."

As for his interest in Greek, we are told that he was determined to impart some knowledge of the language to his cousin Fanny, and to this end composed a grammar which he wrote and sent to her a few pages at a time. During his ministry at Quebec Chapel in London he taught Greek to a class of ladies, and in the course of one year conducted them through several chapters of John, patiently explaining every word grammatically. At about the same time (1854) he noted in his journal that he would soon be having a class in Greek at the Young Men's Christian Association.

His knowledge of the language bore fruit in his preaching. At Quebec Chapel he promoted an afternoon service which drew people from various parts of the city at a time when they had no commitments in their own churches. "The consequence of all this was, that the Sunday afternoon congregation at Quebec Chapel was of a high order; members of Parliament, eminent lawyers, and other representatives of the intellectual classes were always to be found there." At such times his messages were expository and extemporaneous, drawing deeply upon the treasures he had amassed from the study of the original text.

By no means should Henry Alford be thought of merely as a learned ecclesiastic. He was a poet and a musician as well. At least two of his hymns still find a place in most modern collections: "Come, Ye Thankful People, Come," and "Ten Thousand Times Ten Thousand." He had a keen interest in art, and loved to relax by sketching scenes which attracted his attention during his travels. Toward the end of his life he served as editor of the *Contemporary Review*. To this must be added his valuable service on the committee for revision of the King James Version.

It cannot be said in all fairness that Alford was brilliant as a scholar. He did not stand at the head of his class in the university. But one of his fellows gave a judicious appraisal of him as he recalled their student days together. "His versatility was wonderful. Outdone by many of his competitors in each department, he could do more things very well than any of them, and succeeded accordingly."

He had a breadth of spirit which made him impatient of little ideas and little men. His love of truth led him to be less interested in the source of material than in its intrinsic worth. His sense of fairness and his catholicity constrained him to adopt a sympathetic attitude toward nonconformists which was somewhat rare for one in the established church. His ecclesiastical outlook may be judged from a letter which he wrote to one who might assist him in locating a curate to help him in his parish work. Among other things he said, "I want him to preach and teach Jesus Christ, and not the Church; and to be fully prepared to recognize the pious Dissenter as a brother in Christ, and as much a member of the Church as ourselves."

This has an important bearing on *The Greek Testament*, for the reason that this very openness of attitude led him to welcome the contribution of scholars who were not of his communion or his theological persuasion. If he felt that they had something to teach him, he was prepared to listen. In 1849 he wrote to an archdeacon as follows: "I am fully prepared, however unworthy, to cast in my lot among those who are digging in the soil of Scripture for the precious truth that lies beneath; and I cannot feel grateful enough to those German writers who have done so much of the heaviest earthwork before me—some, I own, in the wrong direction and leading only to disappointment; but some also in the right one, and that one untried before. I have been painfully struck, as I have advanced in my work, with the dishonesty of our English commentators in concealing difficulties, or solving them in a manner which must be even to themselves unsatisfactory."

It was with the purpose of being able to read the German expositors more readily that Alford went to Bonn in the summer of 1847 and secured the services of a German tutor and mingled in the society of the place. This experience gave him a freedom in the use of German which he had not acquired on English soil, and it proved an invaluable aid to him in the preparation of his *magnum opus*.

The Greek Testament project was launched when Alford was at Wymeswold, was continued during his stay at Quebec Chapel, and completed during his incumbency as Dean of Canterbury. Together with his work on *The New Testament for English Readers* which was based on his *Greek Testament* and was always considered by him as part of one great enterprise, his labor covered a period of more than tweny-four years.

One of his first moves was to write to Archbishop Trench and confide in him, setting forth the main lines of the project and seeking his counsel. The letter deals with three things, discussing first the question of the Greek text to be employed. He proposed to follow closely the text of Lachmann and Buttmann. Next he indicated his plan to supply a system of references "to Hellenistic constructions and usages of words." Finally, he proposed to make his commentary "rather referential and suggestive than complete in itself."

Volume I appeared in the year 1849. Three years later Volume II was released, bearing evidence of much greater skill and independence in the handling of textual materials. In 1854 a second edition of Volume I was called for, and it was a thorough revision. Its popularity was demonstrated by the necessity for a third edition in the following year, as well as a second edition of Volume II. In 1856 Volume III came out, and in 1859 and 1860 Volume IV was released in two parts. The author was kept busy with the task of revision. Volumes I and II, at least, attained as many as seven editions.

One of the most important aspects of revision was the gradual abandonment of the received text in favor of the improved text such as the Revisers used a few years later. Alford lived in that time of transition between the two when some men remained inseparably wedded to the old, but he had the courage to endorse the superiority which he saw in the improved text, particularly in the work of Tischendorf. With his characteristic readiness to embrace that which commended itself to his judgment, he committed himself to adherence to the older manuscripts even though they were fewer in number.

Later editions witnessed changes in the comments also, as further study or the arguments of his contemporaries convinced him that he should make alterations. A good example is Luke 10:18, where, in commenting on the words of the Saviour, "I beheld Satan fall as lightning from heaven," Alford wrote that this "refers to the original fall of Satan, when he lost his place as an angel of light, not keeping his first estate . . . and this ἐθεώρουν belongs to the period before the foundation of the world when He abode in the bosom of the Father." This was maintained as late as the third edition, but ultimately it was modified by an added note, as follows: "I would not altogether erase the foregoing interpretation: but surely it is grammatically more correct, with Bleek, to refer the imperfect to the time just past—to the Lord's prophetic sight at the time of the ministering of the Seventy."

Reactions to *The Greek Testament* were somewhat mixed. Ellicott wrote a rather severe indictment of it in the *Christian Remembrancer,* objecting that Alford did not adhere closely enough to standard interpretation guided by patristic exegesis, but inclined to novelty, particularly in his espousal of the views of rationalistic interpreters such as the German critics Meyer and DeWette. This criticism was a bit unfair, especially in its insinuation that Alford had imported the views of the German writers without acknowledgment. As a matter of fact, the Prolegomena to

The Greek Testament took full cognizance of the author's debt to foreign theology. Furthermore, one can find scores of places where Meyer, for example, is cited, and exception is taken to his position. So it is apparent that Alford's dependence on such sources was far from slavish. He wrote in reply to Ellicott a pamphlet of some fifty-five pages.

Alford was psychologically prepared for attacks on his work. On the eve of the publication of his first volume he wrote to his father: "Then comes the struggle with I expect almost every party and party organ in the country. . . . So that it will be well if the English Church does not cast off her recreant son, and put my book into an *Index expurgatorius*, thickening up the gloom of the approaching November, not, however, without brighter spots of consciousness that I have humbly and earnestly laboured at God's Word, in God's strength, and of hope that those few among us who really are students of Scripture may give me quarter, and regard my book as a contribution, however humble, to the understanding of it." His temperament was such that criticism did not unduly disturb him, for he lived in serene assurance that he was doing the will of God. A friend of long standing wrote after Alford's death, "I really think he was morally the bravest man I ever knew. His perfect purity of mind and singleness of purpose seemed to give him a confidence and unobtrusive self-respect which never failed him. I never heard one murmur from him, I never saw him despond, I never knew him look about anxiously for the means of bettering and advancing himself. His mind seemed at perfect peace, as one well assured that his work was appointed him, and that he was doing it."

Others besides Ellicott were inclined to be negative in their estimate of *The Greek Testament*. L. E. Elliott-Binns tells us that, "Gwatkin used to say that when he began to take pupils he bought a copy of Alford to see where all their mistakes came from" (*Religion in the Victorian Era*, p. 293). The compendious Swete, when still a student at Cambridge, wrote to a friend, "You have heard doubtless of Alford's promotion (to Canterbury). What a nice couple—Dean Trench and Dean Alford! I hope Alford will make use of the leisure and means thus consigned to him to bring out his next volume more carefully."

A writer who reviewed Volume I in the *Edinburgh Review*, July, 1851, found considerable fault with Alford's handling of textual problems, yet his over-all verdict was far from adverse.

"We cannot but think, that, whatever errors of detail Mr. Alford may be chargeable with in the course of his commentary, they are much more than made up for by the truthful and earnest spirit which prevents him from ever patching up the difficulties which occur to him; and, although we do not go with him in his extreme suspicion of the statements which have come down from Christian antiquity, we entirely share his antipathy for the arbitrary proceedings of modern harmonists. He has done good service by giving, we hope, the *coup de grace* to a system which is productive of more mischief to the cause of true religion than the efforts of any one open enemy of Christianity that ever lived."

A. P. Stanley, writing in the *Contemporary Review,* Volume 16 (1871), shortly after Alford's death, commented as follows: "Many objections, both general and in detail, may be brought against his edition of the Greek Testament. But its great merit is, that it was done at all; and, being done, although far from reaching the ideal of such a work, and inferior in execution and conception to that which is displayed in particular portions of the Sacred Writings as edited by others, it remains, confessedly, the best that exists in English of the whole volume of the New Testament."

The same writer adds an intensely interesting sidelight which reveals the powerful influence of Alford's work upon theological students. "It had fallen to the lot of an Examining Chaplain in an important diocese to put, year after year, to the candidates for ordination, the question which, perhaps, of all others, is the readiest test for distinguishing between an educated and a half-educated or an uneducated clergyman—'What is to be said of the authorship of the Epistle to the Hebrews?' Year after year he received the same stereotyped, traditional reply—'It is by the apostle St. Paul.' At last he suddenly found a change. The whole conditions of the problem, as known to scholars, were, with more or less perspicuity, put forth in almost all the answers. The cause of this new appreciation of so elementary a fact of Biblical knowledge was simple but instructive. It was, that in the interval Dean Alford's fourth volume had appeared, with the Prolegomena to the Epistle to the Hebrews, describing (with perhaps more than his usual vivacity and clearness) the exact state of the case. This was probably one example only out of many which might be adduced as indicating the amount of enlightenment which this hard-working student had incidentally communicated to his brother clergy."

No doubt it is a testimony to the worth of Alford's work that the scholarly Frederick Field, in his *Notes on Select Passages of the Greek Testament* (1881), later expanded into his *Notes on the Translation of the New Testament* (1899), makes such frequent references to his comments, not always in agreement with them, to be sure, but indicating that they were always to be reckoned with.

A fair and succinct appraisal of Alford is found in Canon Fremantle's article in *The Dictionary of National Biography*, as follows: "His work forms an epoch in Biblical studies in England; and, though separate portions of the Greek Testament have since been more fully dealt with by others, it is as yet unapproached as a whole." This statement was published in 1908, some years after Alford's death.

The Greek Testament attracted international attention. A review in the *Presbyterian Magazine*, Vol. 9, 1859, made this observation: "So far as we have examined the Commentary, we have been pleased with its frank, outspoken utterance, its condensation, its originality of suggestion, its learning, its elevation of thought, and generally successful exposition." The reviewer is bothered somewhat by Alford's criticisms of the received text, his rejection of the close of Mark's Gospel and the passage in John 8:1-11, and his conclusion that the final chapter of John's Gospel is an appendix added by the writer in the decline of life. In all these positions, of course, Alford has long since been vindicated by the progress of study.

A distinctly favorable review appeared in the *Congregational Quarterly* (Boston), in the year 1859. Commenting on Volume I, the reviewer said: "This will take rank at once here, as it has in England, as *the* critical edition of the sacred original. In the most condensed and convenient form, it furnishes a complete critical apparatus; showing the discrepancies of the manuscripts and furnishing the data for estimating the exact position of every disputed reading and doubtful passage. Brief, yet most useful comment is added on every page, while a very thorough collection of parallel passages is noted in the margin."

In the same year the *American Theological Review* of New York carried the following book notice on Volume I. "This is an admirable edition of a work which is indispensable to a critical study of the Gospels. No one who has used it will part with it. It is to the English student what DeWette and Meyer are to the German. The critical apparatus is full and minute. The notes are concise and to the point." Later in the year a reprint of the same volume called forth this comment. "Upon the whole it is the best critical work on the Gospels which England has yet produced. It unites in a rare degree the learning of the German with the strong, practical, historical sense of the English school of sacred philology. It does not bring forward a philosophical hypothesis about the universe to alter the meaning of a plain text. Incidentally, the work is a perpetual vindication of the Gospels against both the rationalistic and the mythical theories as to the origin and the character of the four Evangelical records."

Along the same line is the brief word of appreciation which appeared in *Bibliotheca Sacra.* Vol. 11, 1854: "For theological students and ministers we consider this, on the whole, the most valuable Testament extant."

The learned Philip Schaff also indicated his high esteem of this work.

On French soil, a cautious appraisal appeared in Vigoroux's *Dictionnaire de la Bible.* "Despite a certain propensity for liberal views, he holds himself to Anglican orthodoxy. His work, so carefully prepared, has had an extraordinary success, and his fellow countrymen consider even today (this was published in 1912) his Greek Testament as being, on the whole, the best commentary which exists in their language."

This consensus means, among other things, that Alford's work was regarded as superior to the similar projects by Bloomfield and Wordsworth which belong to the same general period.

We note, finally, the verdict of a great preacher. After speaking in his *Commenting and Commentaries* of Alford's work as "an invaluable aid to the critical study of the text of the New Testament," Spurgeon ends up by saying, "all critics speak of Alford with respect, though they consider that something better than his Greek Testament is still needed. He is, for the present at any rate, indispensable to the student of the original. With some faults he has surpassing excellencies."

It is well to emphasize here certain features of Alford which characterize his work as a whole. One is his method of handling difficulties, particularly in the Gospels. In a note on John 6:5 he writes: "Here there is considerable difficulty, on account of the variation from Matthew, Mark, and Luke, who relate that the disciples came to the Lord after He had been teaching and healing the multitudes, and when it was now evening, and asked Him to dismiss the multitudes, that they might buy food; whereupon He commanded, 'Give ye them to eat'; whereas here apparently, on their first coming, the Lord Himself suggests the question, how they were to be fed, to Philip. This difference is not to be passed over, as it has usually been by English commentators, without notice. Still less are we to invent improbable and hardly honest harmonistic shifts to piece the two narratives together. There can be no doubt, fairly and honestly speaking, that the narratives, *in their mere letter*, disagree. But those who are not slaves to the mere letter will see here that inner and deeper accordance of which Augustine . . . speaks in commenting on this passage . . . I repeat the remark so often made in this Commentary, that if we were in possession of the facts as they happened, there is no doubt that the various forms of the literal narrations would fall into their places, and the truthfulness of each historian would be apparent: but as we cannot at present reconcile them in this way, the humble and believing Christian will not be tempted to handle the word of God deceitfully, but to admire the gracious condescension which has given us the evidence of so many independent witnesses, whose very difference in detail makes their accordance in the great central truths so much the more weighty." In line with this general outlook is Alford's contention that the Evangelists wrote independently of one another, without acquaintance with the wording of the other accounts. This opinion is rarely if ever voiced in scholarly circles today, but it is a natural concomitant of Alford's rejection of the harmonizing method.

As a result of his attitude toward verbal differences in the accounts of Scripture, Alford felt that he could not accept the theory of verbal inspiration of the Bible. Under Acts 9:7 he speaks of it as a "suicidal theory." His friend Vaughan, looking back over his association with the Dean, remarked on his position as follows: "He dreaded theories of Inspiration; but no man ever lived and studied under a deeper conviction that every part of Scripture was given by inspiration of God, and expressed a wisdom which no human mind could exhaust."

Enough has been said to convey the impression that in the broad sense, Alford took a generally conservative view of Scripture. It must be pointed out in passing, however, that he seems to have allowed himself, in one place, to take a lower view of the Person of Christ than orthodoxy maintains. In his comments on Hebrews 1:4 he makes a rather sweeping statement about the laying aside of the divine nature in the Incarnation which precise exegesis will not validate.

In his viewpoint on prophecy, Alford took a firm millennial position and went on record in regard to predictions concerning Israel in these terms: "I firmly believe in the literal accomplishment of all the prophecies respecting them as a nation" (see under Acts 15:16-18).

On the more technical side, Alford needs some correction because of his limited appreciation of the New Testament as written in the language of everyday life. In this he is not to be blamed, for he lived before the day when Deissmann made his great discovery and reinforced it by the study of hundreds of papyri which illuminated the vocabulary of the New Testament. It is impossible to insist today, as Alford did, that the conjunction ἵνα always denotes purpose in greater or lesser degree. He is much too rigid in rendering the Greek aorist into English. Some correction of his treatment of prepositions is called for here and there also. These things are pointed out in the notes.

For the limited revision which has been attempted here, the seventh edition has been employed. No effort has been made to consider Alford's views on matters relating to New Testament Introduction. One will find them discussed in the Prolegomena to each volume. To treat such matters here would require too much space. The reader will do well to check questionable positions in one or more of the leading works on Introduction now available.

The demand for the reprinting of Alford's *Greek Testament* is in itself a magnificent tribute to this man who wrought so faithfully a century ago. May his mantle fall on a new generation of students of the Word who crave his critical discernment so finely blended with a meek and devout spirit.

—EVERETT F. HARRISON

THE

GREEK TESTAMENT

VOL. I

THE FOUR GOSPELS

CONTENTS OF THE PROLEGOMENA.

CHAPTER I.

ON THE THREE FIRST GOSPELS GENERALLY.

CHAPTER II.

OF THE GOSPEL ACCORDING TO MATTHEW.

CHAPTER III.

OF THE GOSPEL ACCORDING TO MARK.

CONTENTS OF THE PROLEGOMENA.

CHAPTER IV.

OF THE GOSPEL ACCORDING TO LUKE.

CHAPTER V.

OF THE GOSPEL ACCORDING TO JOHN.

CHAPTER VI.

OF THE ARRANGEMENT OF THIS EDITION.

CHAPTER VII.

APPARATUS CRITICUS.

PROLEGOMENA.

CHAPTER I.

ON THE THREE FIRST GOSPELS GENERALLY.

SECTION I.

GENERAL CHARACTERISTICS OF THE THREE FIRST GOSPELS.

1. On examining the four records of our Lord's life on earth, the first thing which demands our notice is the distinctness, in contents and character, of the three first Gospels from the fourth. This difference may be thus shortly described.

2. Matthew, Mark, and Luke, in relating His ministry, discourses, and miracles, confine themselves exclusively to the events which took place in Galilee, until the last journey to Jerusalem. No incident whatever of His ministry in Judæa is related by any of them[1]. Had we only their accounts, we could never with any certainty have asserted that He went to Jerusalem during His public life, until His time was come to be delivered up. They do not, it is true, *exclude* such a supposition, but rather perhaps imply it (see Matt. xxiii. 37; xxvii. 57, and parallels: also Matt. iv. 12 as compared with iv. 25; Matt. viii. 10; xv. 1); it could not however have been gathered from their narrative with any historical precision.

3. If we now turn to the fourth Gospel, we find this deficiency remarkably supplied. The various occasions on which our Lord went up to Jerusalem are specified; not indeed with any precision of date or sequence, but mainly for the purpose of relating the discourses and miracles by which they were signalized.

[1] The reading Ἰουδαίας in Luke iv. 44 (to the authorities for which, the Codex Sinaiticus must now be added) would seem to introduce an exception. But the notice of a ministry in Judæa would even thus be merely incidental and general: and no visit to Jerusalem is implied.

4. But the difference in *character* between the three first Evangelists and the fourth is even more striking. While their employment (with the sole exception, and that almost exclusively in Matthew, of the application of O. T. prophecies to events in the life of our Lord) is *narration without comment*, the fourth Evangelist speaks with dogmatic authority, and delivers his historical testimony as from the chair of an Apostle. In no place do they *claim* the high authority of eye-witnesses; nay, in the preface to Luke's Gospel, while he vindicates his diligent care in tracing down the course of events from the first, he implicitly *disclaims* such authority. This claim is, however, advanced in direct terms by John (see below, ch. v. § ii. 1). Again, in the *character of our Lord's discourses*, reported by the three, we have the same distinctness. While His sayings and parables in their Gospels almost exclusively have reference to His dealings with *us*, and the nature of His kingdom among men, those related by John regard, as well, the deeper subjects of His own essential attributes and covenant purposes; referring indeed often and directly to His relations with His people and the unbelieving world, but usually as illustrating those attributes, and the unfolding of those purposes. That there are exceptions to this (see e.g. Matt. xi. 27: Luke x. 22) is only to be expected from that merciful condescension by which God, in giving us the Gospel records through the different media of individual minds and apprehensions, has yet furnished us with enough *common* features in them all, to satisfy us of the unity and truthfulness of their testimony to His blessed Son.

5. Reserving further remarks on the character of John's Gospel for their proper place (see ch. v. of these Prolegomena), I further notice that the three, in their narration of our Lord's *ministry*, proceed in the main upon a common outline. This outline is variously filled up, and variously interrupted; but is still easily to be traced, as running through the middle and largest section of each of their Gospels. From this circumstance, they are frequently called *the synoptic Gospels:* and the term will occasionally be found in this work.

6. Besides this large portion, each Gospel contains some prefatory matter regarding the time before the commencement of the Ministry,—a detailed history of the Passion,—fragmentary notices of the Resurrection, and a conclusion. These will be separately treated of and compared in the following sections, and more at large in the Commentary.

SECTION II.

THEIR INDEPENDENCE OF ONE ANOTHER.

1. Having these three accounts of one and the same Life and Ministry of our Lord, it is an important enquiry for us, *how far they may be considered as distinct narratives,—how far as borrowed one from another.* It is obvious that this enquiry can only, in the absence of any direct historical testimony, be conducted by *careful examination of their contents.* Such examination however has conducted enquirers to the most various and inconsistent results. Different hypotheses of the mutual interdependence of the three have been made, embracing every possible permutation of their order[2]. To support these hypotheses, the same phænomena have been curiously and variously interpreted. What, in one writer's view, has been a *deficiency* in one Evangelist which another has supplied,—has been, in that of a second writer, a *condensation* on the part of the one Evangelist of the full account of the other;—while a third writer again has seen in the fuller account the more minute depicting of later tradition.

2. Let us, however, observe the evidence furnished *by the Gospels themselves.* Each of the sacred Historians is, we may presume, anxious to give his readers an accurate and consistent account of the great events of Redemption. On either of the above hypotheses, two of them respectively sit down to their work with *one, or two, of our present narratives before them.* We are reduced then to adopt one or other of the following suppositions: Either, (α) *they found those other Gospels insufficient, and were anxious to supply what was wanting;* or, (β) *they believed them to be erroneous, and purposed to correct what was inaccurate;* or, (γ) *they wished to adapt their contents to a different class of readers,* incorporating at the same time whatever additional matter they possessed; or (δ) *receiving them as authentic, they borrowed from them such parts as they purposed to relate in common with them.*

[2] 1. That Matt. wrote first—that Mark used his Gospel—and then Luke both these. This is held by Grotius, Mill, Wetstein, Townson, Hug, &c., and Greswell, who advances, and sometimes maintains with considerable ingenuity, the hypothesis of a *supplemental* relation of the three taken in order.

2. Matt., Luke, Mark.—So Griesbach, Fritzsche, Meyer, De Wette, and others.

3. Mark, Matt., Luke.—So Storr and others, and recently, Mr. Smith of Jordanhill.

4. Mark, Luke, Matt.—So Weisse, Wilke, Hitzig, &c.

5. Luke, Matt., Mark. So Büsching and Evanson.

6. Luke, Mark, Matt.—So Vögel. See reff. to the above in Meyer's Commentary, vol. i. Einleitung, pp. 30, 31.

3. There is but one other supposition, which is plainly out of the range of probability, and which I should not have stated, were it not the only one, *on the hypothesis of mutual dependency*, which will give any account of, or be consistent with, the various minute discrepancies of arrangement and narration which we find in the Gospels. It is (ε) *that* (see last paragraph) *they fraudulently plagiarized from them, slightly disguising the common matter so as to make it appear their own.* One man *wishing to publish the matter of another's work as his own*, may be conceived as altering its arrangement and minutiæ, to destroy its distinctive character. But how utterly inapplicable is any such view to either of our three Evangelists! And even supposing it for a moment entertained,—how imperfectly and anomalously are the changes made,—and how little would they be likely to answer their purpose!

4. Let us consider the others in order. If (α) was the case, *I maintain that no possible arrangement of our Gospels will suit its requirements.* Let the reader refer to the last note, and follow me through its divisions. (1), (2), (5), (6) are clearly out of the question, because the *shorter* Gospel of Mark follows upon the *fuller one* of Matthew, or Luke, or both. We have then only to examine those in which Mark stands *first.* Either then *Luke* supplemented *Matthew*— or *Matthew, Luke.* But first, both of these are inconceivable as being *expansions of Mark;* for his Gospel, although shorter, and narrating *fewer* events and discourses, is, in those which he does narrate, the fullest and most particular of the three. And again, Luke could not have supplemented Matthew; for there are most important portions of Matthew which he has altogether omitted (e. g. ch. xxv. much of ch. xiii. ch. xv.);—nor could Matthew have supplemented Luke, for the same reason, having omitted almost all of the important section, Luke ix. 51—xviii. 15, besides very much matter in other parts. I may also mention that this supposition leaves all the difficulties of *different arrangement* and *minute discrepancy* unaccounted for.

5. We pass to (β), on which much need not be said. If it were so, nothing could have been done *less calculated to answer the end*, than that which our Evangelists have done. For in no material point do their accounts differ, but only in arrangement and completeness;—and this latter difference is such, that no one of them can be cited as taking any pains to make it appear that his own arrangement is chronologically accurate. *No fixed dates* are found in those parts where the differences exist; no word to indicate that any other arrangement had ever been published. *Does this look like the work of a corrector?* Even supposing him to have suppressed the charge of inaccuracy on others,—would he not have been precise and definite in the parts where his own corrections appeared, if it were merely to justify them to his readers?

6. Neither does the supposition represented by (γ) in any way ac-

count for the phænomena of our present Gospels. For,—even taking for granted the usual assumption, that Matthew wrote for Hebrew Christians, Mark for Latins, and Luke for Gentiles in general,—we do not find any such consistency in these purposes, as a revision and alteration of another's narrative would necessarily presuppose. We have the visit of the Gentile Magi exclusively related by the Hebraizing Matthew;—the circumcision of the child Jesus, and His frequenting the passovers at Jerusalem, exclusively by the Gentile Evangelist Luke. Had the above purposes been steadily kept in view in the revision of the narratives before them, the respective Evangelists could not have omitted incidents so entirely subservient to their respective designs.

7. Our supposition (δ) is, that receiving the Gospel or Gospels before them as authentic, the Evangelists borrowed from them such parts as they purposed to narrate in common with them. But this *does not represent the matter of fact.* In no one case does any Evangelist borrow from another any considerable part of even a single narrative. For such borrowing would imply verbal coincidence, unless in the case of strong Hebraistic idiom, or other assignable peculiarity. It is inconceivable that one writer borrowing from another matter confessedly of the very first importance, *in good faith and with approval,* should alter his diction so singularly and capriciously as, *on this hypothesis,* we find the text of the parallel sections of our Gospels altered. Let the question be answered by ordinary considerations of probability, and let any passage common to the three Evangelists be put to the test. The phænomena presented will be much as follows:—first, perhaps, we shall have three, five, or more words *identical;* then as many *wholly distinct;* then two clauses or more, expressed in the *same words* but *differing order;* then a clause *contained in one or two,* and *not in the third;* then *several words identical;* then a clause not only *wholly distinct* but *apparently inconsistent;*—and so forth;—with recurrences of the same arbitrary and anomalous alterations, coincidences, and transpositions. Nor does this description apply to verbal and sentential arrangement only;—but also, with slight modification, to that of the larger portions of the narratives. Equally capricious would be the disposition of the subject-matter. Sometimes, while coincident in the things related, the Gospels place them in the most various order,—each in turn connecting them together with apparent marks of chronological sequence (e. g. the visit to Gadara in Matt. viii. 28 ff. as compared with the same in Mark v. 1 ff. and Luke viii. 26 ff.; and numerous other such instances noticed in the commentary). Let any one say, divesting himself of the commonly-received hypotheses respecting the connexion and order of our Gospels, whether it is within the range of probability that a writer should thus singularly and unreasonably alter the subject-matter and diction before him, having (as is now supposed) *no design*

in so doing, but intending, fairly and with approval, to incorporate the work of another into his own? Can an instance be any where cited of undoubted borrowing and adaptation from another, presenting similar phænomena [3]?

8. I cannot then find in any of the above hypotheses a solution of the question before us, *how the appearances presented by our three Gospels are to be accounted for*. I do not see how any theory of mutual interdependence will leave to our three Evangelists their credit as *able* or *trustworthy writers*, or even as *honest men*: nor can I find any such theory borne out by the nature of the variations apparent in the respective texts.

SECTION III.

THE ORIGIN OF OUR THREE GOSPELS.

1. It remains then, that the three Gospels should have arisen *independently of one another*. But supposing this, we are at once met by the difficulty of accounting for so much common matter, and that narrated, as we have seen, with such curious verbal agreements and discrepancies. Thus we are driven to *some common origin* for those parts. But of what kind? Plainly, either *documentary*, or *oral*. Let us consider each of these in turn.

2. *No documentary source could have led to the present texts of our Gospels*. For supposing it to have been in the Aramaic language, and thus accounting for some of the variations in our parallel passages, as being *independent translations*,—we shall still have no solution whatever of the more important discrepancies of *insertion*, *omission*, and *arrangement*. To meet these, the most complicated hypotheses have been advanced [4],—all perfectly capricious, and utterly inadequate, even when

[3] The examples cited from modern historians by Mr. Smith of Jordanhill, are not in point. In almost every one of those, reasons could be assigned for the adoption or rejection by the posterior writer of the words and clauses of the prior one. Let the student attempt such a rationale of any narrative common to the three Gospels, on any hypothesis of priority, and he will at once perceive its impracticability. If Matthew, Mark, and Luke are to be judged by the analogy of Suchet, Alison, and Napier, the inference must be, that whereas the historians were intelligent men, acting by the rules of mental association and selection, the Evangelists were mere victims of caprice, and such caprice as is hardly consistent with the possession of a sound mind.

[4] It may be worth while, as an example, to state the nature of Bp. Marsh's hypothesis of the origin of our three Gospels. He supposes, 1) א, the original Hebrew Gospel, 2) א a Greek version of the same. 3) $\aleph + \alpha + A$, a volume containing a copy of the Hebrew original Gospel, accompanied by lesser (α) and greater (A) additions. 4) $\aleph + \beta + B$, another copy of ditto, accompanied by *other* lesser (β) and greater (B) additions. 5) $\aleph + \gamma + \Gamma$, a third copy of ditto, accompanied by *a third* set of lesser

apprehended, to account for the phænomena. The various opponents of the view of an original Gospel have well shewn besides, that such a Gospel could never have existed, because of the omission in one or other of our three, of passages which *must necessarily have formed a part of it;* e.g. Matt. xxvi. 6—13 (*see there*) omitted by Luke[5]. I believe then that we may safely abandon the idea of any single original Gospel, whether Aramaic or Greek.

3. Still it might be thought possible that, though *one* document cannot have originated the text of the common parts of our Gospels, *several documents*, more or less related to one another, may have done so, in the absence of any original Gospel. But this, it will be seen, is but an imperfect analysis of their origin ; for we are again met by the question, *whence did these documents take their rise?* And if they turn out to be only so many modifications of a received oral teaching respecting the actions and sayings of our Lord, then to that oral teaching are we referred back for a more complete account of the matter. That such evangelical documents *did exist*, I think highly probable ; and believe I recognize such in some of the *peculiar* sections of Luke ; but that the *common* parts of our Gospels, even if taken from such, are *to be traced back further*, I am firmly convinced.

4. We come then to enquire, whether the *common* sections of our Gospels could have originated from a *common oral source.* If by this latter is to be understood,—*one and the same oral teaching every where recognized*, our answer must be in the negative : for the difficulties of verbal discrepancy, varying arrangement, insertion, and omission, would, as above, remain unaccounted for. At the same time, it is highly improbable that such a course of oral teaching should ever have been adopted. Let us examine the matter more in detail.

(γ) and greater (Γ) additions. 6) ב, a Hebrew gnomology (collection of sayings of the Lord), varying according to different copies.

Hence he holds our Gospels to have arisen : viz. the *Hebrew Matthew*, from א + ב + α + A + γ + Γ:—*Luke*, from א + ב + β + B + γ + Γ + א̅:—*Mark*, from א + α + A + β + B + א̅: the Greek *Matthew*, to be a translation from the Hebrew Matthew, with the collation of א̅, and of Luke and Mark. This is only *one* of the various arrangements made by the supporters of this hypothesis. For those of Eichhorn, Gratz, &c., see Meyer's Comment. vol. i. Einleitung, pp. 25—27.

[5] Those who maintain the anointing of Matt. xxvi. 6 to be the same with that of Luke vii. 36, forget that it is incumbent on them in such cases to shew *sufficient reason* for the inversion in order of time. It is no reply to my argument, to say that Luke omits the anointing at Bethany, *because he had related it before in ch.* vii. Had he *not had Matthew's Gospel before him*, it is very likely that he may have inserted an incident which he found without date, in a place where it might illustrate the want of charity of a Pharisee : but *having* (on their hypothesis) *Matthew's Gospel before him*, and the incident being there related in strict sequence and connexion with our Lord's Death, it is simply inconceivable that he should have transposed it, and obliterated all trace of such connexion, deeply interesting and important as it is.

5. The Apostles were *witnesses of the resurrection of the Lord Jesus.* In this consisted their especial office and work. Others besides them had been companions of our Lord :—but peculiar grace and power was given to them, by which they gave forth their testimony (Acts iv. 33). And *what* this testimony included, we learn from the conditions of apostleship propounded by Peter himself, Acts i. 21, 22 : that in order to its being properly given, an Apostle must have been an eye and ear witness of what had happened *from the baptism of John until the ascension :* i. e. during the *whole official life of our Lord.* With the *whole of this matter,* therefore, *was his apostolic testimony concerned.* And we are consequently justified in assuming that the substance of the teaching of the Apostles consisted of their *testimony to such facts,* given in the Holy Ghost and with power. The ordinary objection to this view, that their extant discourses do not contain Evangelic *narrations,* but are hortatory and persuasive, is wholly inapplicable. Their extant discourses are contained in the Acts, a second work of the Evangelist Luke, who having in his former treatise given all which he had been able to collect of their *narrative* teaching, was not likely again to repeat it. Besides which, such narrative teaching would occur, not in general and almost wholly apologetic discourses held before assembled unbelievers, but in the building up of the several churches and individual converts, and in the catechization of catechumens. It is a strong confirmation of this view, that Luke himself in his preface refers to this original apostolic narrative as the source of the various διηγήσεις which many had taken in hand to draw up, and states his object in writing to be, that Theophilus might know the certainty (ἀσφάλειαν) of *those sayings concerning which he had been catechized.*

It is another confirmation of the above view of the testimony of the apostolic body,—that Paul claims to have received an independent knowledge, by direct revelation, of at least some of the fundamental parts of the gospel history (see Gal. i. 12 : 1 Cor. xi. 23 ; xv. 3), to qualify him for his calling as an Apostle.

6. I believe then that the Apostles, in virtue not merely of their having been eye and ear witnesses of the Evangelic history, but especially of *their office,* gave to the various Churches their testimony in *a narrative of facts :* such narrative being modified in each case by the individual mind of the Apostle himself, and his sense of what was requisite for the particular community to which he was ministering. While they were principally together, and instructing the converts at Jerusalem, such narrative would naturally be *for the most part the same,* and expressed in the same, or nearly the same words : coincident, however, *not from design or rule,* but because the *things themselves were the same,* and the teaching naturally fell for the most part into one form. It would be easy and interesting to follow this cycle of narratives

of the words and deeds of our Lord in the Church at Jerusalem, with regard to its probable origin and growth for both Jews and Hellenists,—the latter under such teachers as Philip and Stephen, commissioned and authenticated by the Apostles. In the course of such a process some portions would naturally be written down by private believers, for their own use or that of friends. And as the Church spread to Samaria, Cæsarea, and Antioch, the want would be felt in each of these places, of similar cycles of oral teaching, which when supplied would thenceforward belong to and be current in those respective Churches. And these portions of the Evangelic history, oral or partially documentary, would be adopted under the sanction of the Apostles, who were as in all things, so especially in this, the appointed and divinely-guided overseers of the whole Church. This *common substratum of apostolic teaching*,—never formally adopted by all, but subject to all the varieties of diction and arrangement, addition and omission, incident to transmission through many individual minds, and into many different localities,—*I believe to have been the original source of the common part of our three Gospels.*

7. Whether this teaching was wholly or in part expressed originally in *Greek*, may admit of some question. That it would very soon be so expressed, follows as a matter of course from the early mention of Hellenistic converts, Acts vi., and the subsequent reception of the Gentiles into the Church ; and it seems to have been generally received in that language, *before any of its material modifications arose.* This I gather from the remarkable *verbal coincidences* observable in the present Greek texts. Then again, the *verbal discrepancies* of our present Greek texts entirely forbid us to imagine that our Evangelists took up the usual oral teaching at one place or time ; but point to a process of alteration and deflection, which will now engage our attention.

8. It will be observed that I am now speaking of *those sections which our Gospels possess* IN COMMON, and WITHOUT REFERENCE TO THEIR ORDER. The larger additions, which are due to peculiar sources of information,—the narratives of the same event which have not sprung from a common source,—the different arrangement of the common sections, with all these I am not now concerned.

9. The matter then of those sections I believe to have been this generally-received oral narrative of the Apostles of which I have spoken. Delivered, usually in the same or similar terms, to the catechumens in the various Churches, and becoming the text of instruction for their pastors and teachers, it by degrees underwent those modifications which the various Gospels now present to us. And I am not now speaking of any considerable length of time, such as might suffice to deteriorate and corrupt mere traditional teaching,—but of no more than the transmission through men apostolic or almost apostolic, yet of independent

habits of speech and thought,—of an account which remained in substance the same. Let us imagine the modifications which the individual memory, brooding affectionately and reverently over each word and act of our Lord, would introduce into a narrative in relating it variously and under differing circumstances :—the Holy Spirit who brought to their remembrance whatever things He had said to them (John xiv. 26), working in and distributing to each severally as He would ;—let us place to the account the various little changes of transposition or omission, of variation in diction or emphasis, which would be sure to arise in the freedom of individual teaching,—and we have I believe the only reasonable solution of the arbitrary and otherwise unaccountable coincidences and discrepancies in these parts of our Gospels.

10. It might perhaps be required that some presumptive corroborations should be given of such a supposition as that here advanced. For the materials of such, we must look into the texts themselves of such sections. And in them I think I see signs of such a process as the latter part of paragraph 9 describes. For,

11. It is a well-known and natural effect of oral transmission, that while the *less prominent* members of a sentence are transposed, or diminished or increased in number, and *common-place expressions* replaced by their synonymes, any *unusual word*, or *harsh expression*, or *remarkable construction* is *retained*. Nor is this only the case, such words, expressions, or constructions, *preserving their relative places* in the sentences, —but, from the mind laying hold of them, and retaining them at all events, they are sometimes found preserved *near their original places*, though perhaps with *altered relations* and *import*. Now a careful observation of the text of the Gospels will continually bring before the reader instances of both of these. I have subjoined in a note a few, more to tempt the student to follow the track, than to give any adequate illustration of these remarks [6].

[6] Of unusual words, &c., retaining their places in the parallel sentences:—*ἀπαρθῇ*, Matt. ix. 15 : Mark ii. 20 : Luke v. 35 ;—*κατέκλασεν*, Mark vi. 41 : Luke ix. 16 ;—*ὀπίσω μου*, Matt. xvi. 24 : Mark viii. 34 : Luke ix. 23 ;—*δυsκόλως*, Mark x. 23 : Luke xviii. 24 ;—*συνθλάω* and *λικμάω*, Matt. xxi. 44 : Luke xx. 18 ;—*κολοβόω*, Matt. xxiv. 22 : Mark xiii. 20 ;—*συλλαβεῖν* (whereas they generally use *λαμβ.* simply), Matt. xxvi. 55 : Mark xiv. 48 ;—*διαβλέπω*, Matt. vii. 5 : Luke vi. 42 ;—*γεννητοὶ γυναικῶν*, Matt. xi. 11 : Luke vii. 28.

Of unusual words, expressions, or constructions, found at or near their places in parallel passages, but *not in the same connexion*:—*ἀπέχω*, Matt. vi. 2 al. : Luke vi. 24 ;—*χρείαν ἔχω*, Matt. xiv. 16 : Luke ix. 11 ;—*εἰς*, Mark viii. 19, 20 : Luke ix. 13 : John vi. 9 ;—*σκύλλω*, Mark v. 35 : Luke viii. 49 ;—*εἶτα*, Mark iv. 17 : Luke viii. 12 ;—*βασανίζω*, Matt. xiv. 24 : Mark vi. 48 ;—*πῶς*, Mark v. 16 : Luke viii. 36 ;—*ἀνασείω*, Mark xv. 11 : Luke xxiii. 5 ;—*ἦλθεν* (of Joseph of Arimathea), Matt. xxvii. 57 : Mark xv. 43 : John xix. 38 ;—*περιτίθημι*, Matt. xxvii. 28 : Mark xv. 17 ;—*προσφωνέω*, with dative, Matt. xi. 16 : Luke vii. 32

12. With regard to *those parts of our Gospels which do not fall under the above remarks*, there are various conceivable sources whence they may have arisen. As each Evangelist may have had more or less access to those who were themselves witnesses of the events, whether before or during the public ministry of our Lord, or as each may have fallen in with a more complete or a shorter account of those events, so have our narratives been filled out with rich detail, or confined to the mere statement of occurrences :—so have they been copious and entire in their history, or have merely taken up and handed down a portion of our Lord's life. These particulars will come under our notice below, when we treat of each Gospel by itself.

13. The above view has been impugned by Mr. Birks (Horæ Evangelicæ, &c. Lond. 1852), and Mr. Smith of Jordanhill (Dissertation on the Origin and Connexion of the Gospels: Edinb. 1853). While maintaining different hypotheses, both agree in regarding 'oral tradition' as quite insufficient to account for the phænomena of approximation to identity which are found in the Gospels. But both, as it seems to me, have forgotten to take into account the *peculiar kind* of oral tradition with which we are here concerned. Both concur in insisting on the many variations and corruptions to which oral transmission is liable, as an objection to my hypothesis. But we have here a case in this respect exceptional and sui generis. The oral tradition (or rather ORAL TEACHING) with which we are concerned, formed the substance of a deliberate and careful testimony to facts of the highest possible importance, and as such, was inculcated in daily catechization : whereas common oral tradition is careless and vague, not being similarly guarded, nor diffused as matter of earnest instruction. Besides which, these writers forget, that I have maintained the probability of a very early collection of portions of such oral teaching into documents, some of which two or even three Evangelists may have used ; and these documents or διηγήσεις, in some cases drawn up after the first minute verbal divergences had taken place, or being translations from common Aramaic sources, would furnish many of the phænomena which Mr. Smith so ingeniously illustrates from *translation* in modern historians and newspapers. I have found reason to infer, Vol. II., Prolegg. ch. ii. § ii. 17 *β*, that St. Luke was acquainted with Hebrew ; and he would therefore be an independent translator, as well as the other two Evangelists.

14. For the sake of guarding against misunderstanding, it may be well formally to state the conclusion at which I have arrived respecting the origin of our three first Gospels : in which, I may add, I have been much confirmed by the thorough revision of the text rendered necessary in preparing each of these later editions, and indeed by all my observation since the first publication of these prolegomena :

That the synoptic Gospels contain the substance of the Apostles' testimony, collected principally from their oral teaching current in the Church,—partly also from written documents embodying portions of that teaching: that there is however no reason from their internal structure to believe, but every reason to disbelieve, that any one of the three Evangelists had access to either of the other two Gospels in its present form.

SECTION IV.

THE DISCREPANCIES, APPARENT AND REAL, OF THE THREE GOSPELS.

1. In our three narratives, many events and sayings do not hold the same relative place in one as in another: and hence difficulties have arisen, and the faith of some has been weakened; while the adversaries of our religion have made the most of these differences to impugn the veracity of the writers themselves. And hence also Christian commentators have been driven to a system of harmonizing which condescends to adopt the weakest compromises, and to do the utmost violence to probability and fairness, in its zeal for the veracity of the Evangelists. It becomes important therefore critically to discriminate between *real* and *apparent* discrepancy, and while with all fairness we acknowledge the former where it exists, to lay down certain common-sense rules whereby the latter may be also ascertained.

2. The *real* discrepancies between our Evangelistic histories are very few, and those nearly all of one kind. They are simply the results of the entire independence of the accounts. They consist mainly in different chronological arrangements, expressed or implied. Such for instance is the transposition, before noticed, of the history of the passage into the country of the Gadarenes, which in Matt. viii. 28 ff. precedes a whole course of events which in Mark v. 1 ff. and Luke viii. 26 ff. it follows. Such again is the difference in position between the pair of incidents related Matt. viii. 19—22, and the same pair of incidents found in Luke ix. 57—60. And such are some other varieties of arrangement and position, which will be brought before the readers of the following Commentary. Now the way of dealing with such discrepancies has been twofold,—as remarked above. The *enemies of the faith* have of course *recognized* them, and pushed them to the utmost; often attempting to create them where they do not exist, and where they do, using them to overthrow the narrative in which they occur. While this has been *their* course,—equally unworthy of the Evangelists and their subject has been that of those who are usually thought the *orthodox Harmonists*. They have usually taken upon them to state, that such variously placed narratives *do not refer to the same incidents*, and so to save (as they imagine) the credit of the Evangelists, at the expense of

common fairness and candour. Who, for example, can for a moment doubt that the pairs of incidents above cited from Matthew and Luke are identical with each other? What man can ever suppose that the same offer would have been, not merely twice made to our Lord in the same words and similarly answered by Him (for this is very possible), but actually followed *in both cases* by a request from *another* disciple, couched also in the very same words? The reiterated sequence of the two is absolutely out of all bounds of probability:—and yet it is supposed and maintained by one of the ablest of our modern Harmonists. And this is only one specimen out of very many of the same kind, notices of which may be seen in the following Commentary.

3. The fair Christian critic will pursue a plan different from both these. With no desire to create discrepancies, but rather every desire truthfully and justly to solve them, if it may be,—he will candidly recognize them where they unquestionably exist. By this he loses nothing, and the Evangelists lose nothing. That one great and glorious portrait of our Lord should be harmoniously depicted by them,—that the procession of events by which our redemption is assured to us should be one and the same in all,—is surely more wonderful, and more plainly the work of God's Holy Spirit, *the more entirely independent of each other they must be inferred to have been.* Variation in detail and arrangement is to my mind the most valuable proof that they were, not *mere mouthpieces or organs* of the Holy Spirit, as some would suicidally make them, but holy *men*, under His inspiration. I shall treat of this part of our subject more at length below (in § vi.):—I mention it now, to shew that we need not be afraid to recognize real discrepancies, in the spirit of fairness and truth. *Christianity never was, and never can be the gainer, by any concealment, warping, or avoidance of the plain truth, wherever it is to be found.*

4. On the other hand, the Christian critic will fairly discriminate between real and apparent discrepancy. And in order to this, some rules must be laid down by which the limits of each may be determined.

5. *Similar incidents must not be too hastily assumed to be the same.* If one Evangelist had given us the feeding of the *five* thousand, and another that of the *four*, we should have been strongly tempted to pronounce the incidents the same, and to find a discrepancy in the accounts:—but our conclusion would have been false:—for we have now *both events* narrated by each of two Evangelists (Matthew and Mark), and formally alluded to by our Lord Himself in connexion. (Matt. xvi. 9, 10: Mark viii. 19, 20.) And there are several narrations now in our Gospels, the identification of which must be abstained from; e.g. the anointing of our Lord by the woman who was a sinner, Luke vii. 36 ff., and that at Bethany by Mary the sister of Lazarus, in Matt. xxvi. 6 ff.: Mark xiv. 3 ff.: John xi. 2; xii. 3 ff. In such cases we must judge fairly and according to

probability,—not making trifling differences in diction or narrative into important reasons why the incidents should be different;—but rather examining critically the features of the incidents themselves, and discerning and determining upon the evidence furnished by them.

6. *The circumstances and nature of our Lord's discourses must be taken into account.* Judging *à priori*, the probability is, that *He repeated most of His important sayings many times over, with more or less variation, to different audiences, but in the hearing of the same apostolic witnesses.* If now these witnesses by their independent narratives have originated our present Gospels, what can be more likely than that these sayings should have found their way into the Gospels *in various forms*,—sometimes, as especially in Matt., in long and strictly coherent discourses,—sometimes scattered up and down, as is the matter of several of Matthew's discourses in Luke? Yet such various reports of our Lord's sayings are most unreasonably by some of the modern German critics (e. g. De Wette) treated as discrepancies, and used to prove Matthew's discourses to have been mere arrangements of shorter sayings uttered at different times. A striking instance of the repetition by our Lord of similar discourses, varied according to the time and the hearers, may be found in the denunciations on the Scribes and Pharisees as uttered during the journey to Jerusalem, Luke xi. 37 ff., and the subsequent solemn and public reiteration of them in Jerusalem at the final close of the Lord's ministry in Matt. xxiii. Compare also the parable of the *pounds*, Luke xix. 11 ff., with that of the *talents*, Matt. xxv. 14 ff., and in fact the whole of the discourses during the last journey in Luke, with their parallels, where such exist, in Matthew.

SECTION V.

THE FRAGMENTARY NATURE OF THE THREE GOSPELS.

1. On any hypothesis which attributes to our Evangelists the design of producing a *complete history* of the life and actions of our Lord, and gives two of them the advantage of consulting other records of the same kind with their own,—the *omissions* in their histories are *perfectly inexplicable*. For example,—Matthew, as an Apostle, was himself an eye-witness of the Ascension, an event holding a most important place in the divine process of the redemption of man. Yet *he omits all record or mention of it*. And though this is the most striking example, others are continually occurring throughout the three Gospels. Why has there been no mention in them of the most notable miracle wrought by our Lord,—which indeed, humanly speaking, was the final exciting cause of that active enmity of the Jewish rulers which issued in His crucifixion?

Can it be believed, that an Apostle, *writing in the fulness of his knowledge as such, and with the design of presenting to his readers Jesus of Nazareth as the promised Messiah*,—should have omitted all mention of the *raising of Lazarus*,—and of the *subsequent prophecy of Caiaphas*, whereby that Messiahship was so strongly recognized? The ordinary supposition, of silence being maintained for prudential reasons concerning Lazarus and his family, is quite beside the purpose. For the sacred books of the Christians were not published to the world in general, but were reserved and precious possessions of the believing societies : and even had this been otherwise, such concealment was wholly alien from their spirit and character.

2. The absence of completeness from our Gospels is even more strikingly shewn in their *minor* omissions, which cannot on any supposition be accounted for, if their authors had possessed records of the incidents so omitted. Only in the case of Luke does there appear to have been any design of giving a regular account of things throughout: and from his many omissions of important matter contained in Matthew, it is plain that his sources of information were, though copious, yet fragmentary. For, assuming what has been above inferred as to the independence of our three Evangelists, it is inconceivable that Luke, with his avowed design of completeness, ch. i. 3, should have been in possession of matter so important as that contained in those parts of Matthew, and should deliberately have excluded it from his Gospel.

3. The Gospel of Mark,—excluding from that term the venerable and authentic fragment at the end of ch. xvi.,—terminates abruptly in the midst of the narrative of incidents connected with the resurrection of our Lord. And, with the exception of the short prefatory compendium, ch. i. 1—13, there is no reason for supposing this Evangelist to be an abbreviator, in any sense, of the matter before him. His sources of information were of the very highest order, and his descriptions and narratives are most life-like and copious; but they were confined within a certain cycle of apostolic teaching, viz. that which concerned the official life of our Lord : and in that cycle not complete, inasmuch as he breaks off short of the Ascension, which another Evangelistic hand has added from apostolic sources.

SECTION VI.

THE INSPIRATION OF THE EVANGELISTS AND OTHER N. T. WRITERS.

1. The results of our enquiries hitherto may be thus stated :—That our three Gospels have arisen independently of one another, from sources of information possessed by the Evangelists :—such sources of

information, for a very considerable part of their contents, being the narrative teaching of the Apostles; and, in cases where their personal testimony was out of the question, oral or documentary narratives, preserved in and received by the Christian Church in the apostolic age;—that the three Gospels are not formal complete accounts of the whole incidents of the sacred history, but each of them fragmentary, containing such portions of it as fell within the notice, or the special design, of the Evangelist.

2. The important question now comes before us, *In what sense are the Evangelists to be regarded as having been inspired by the Holy Spirit of God?* That they *were so, in some sense*, has been the concurrent belief of the Christian body in all ages. In the *second*, as in the *nineteenth* century, the ultimate appeal, in matters of fact and doctrine, has been to these venerable writings. It may be well, then, first to enquire on what grounds their authority has been rated so high by all Christians.

3. And I believe the answer to this question will be found to be, *Because they are regarded as authentic documents, descending from the apostolic age, and presenting to us the substance of the apostolic testimony.* The Apostles being raised up for the special purpose of *witnessing to the gospel history*,—and these memoirs having been universally received in the early Church as embodying that their testimony, I see no escape left from the inference, that they come to us with *inspired authority.* The Apostles themselves, and their contemporaries in the ministry of the Word, were singularly endowed with the Holy Spirit for the founding and teaching of the Church : and Christians of all ages have accepted the Gospels and other writings of the New Testament as the written result of the Pentecostal effusion. The early Church was not likely to be deceived in this matter. The reception of the Gospels was *immediate* and *universal.* They never were placed for a moment by the consent of Christians in the same category with the spurious documents which soon sprung up after them. In external history, as in internal character, they differ entirely from the apocryphal Gospels ; which, though in some cases bearing the name and pretending to contain the teaching of an Apostle, were *never recognized as apostolic.*

4. Upon the authenticity, i. e. the *apostolicity* of our Gospels, rests their claim to inspiration. Containing the substance of the Apostles' testimony, they carry with them that special power of the Holy Spirit which rested on the Apostles in virtue of their office, and also on other teachers and preachers of the first age. It may be well, then, to enquire of what kind that power was, and how far extending.

5. We do not find the Apostles transformed, from being men of individual character and thought and feeling, into mere channels for the transmission of infallible truth. We find them, humanly speaking, to have been still distinguished by the same characteristics as before the

descent of the Holy Ghost. We see Peter still ardent and impetuous, still shrinking from the danger of human disapproval;—we see John still exhibiting the same union of deep love and burning zeal;—we find them pursuing different paths of teaching, exhibiting different styles of writing, taking hold of the truth from different sides.

6. Again, we do not find the Apostles *put in possession at once* of the divine counsel with regard to the Church. Though Peter and John were full of the Holy Ghost immediately after the Ascension, neither at that time, nor for many years afterwards, were they put in possession of the purpose of God regarding the Gentiles, which in due time was specially revealed to Peter, and recognized in the apostolic council at Jerusalem.

7. These considerations serve to shew us in what respects the working of the Holy Spirit on the sacred writers was analogous to His influence on every believer in Christ; viz. in the retention of individual character and thought and feeling,—and in the gradual development of the ways and purposes of God to their minds.

8. But their situation and office was *peculiar* and *unexampled*. And for its fulfilment, peculiar and unexampled gifts were bestowed upon them. One of these, which bears very closely upon our present subject, was, the *recalling by the Holy Spirit of those things which the Lord had said to them.* This was His own formal promise, recorded in John xiv. 26. And if we look at our present Gospels, we see abundant evidence of its fulfilment. What unassisted human memory could treasure up saying and parable, however deep the impression at the time, and report them in full at the distance of several years, as we find them reported, with every internal mark of truthfulness, in our Gospels? What invention of man could have devised discourses which by common consent differ from all sayings of men—which possess this character unaltered, notwithstanding their transmission through men of various mental organization—which contain things impossible to be understood or appreciated by their reporters at the time when they profess to have been uttered—which enwrap the seeds of all human improvement yet attained, and are evidently full of power for more? I refer to this latter alternative, only to remark that all considerations, whether of the Apostles' external circumstances, or their internal feelings respecting Him of whom they bore witness, combine to confirm the persuasion of Christians, that they have recorded as said by our Lord *what He truly did say*, and not any words of their own imagination.

9. And let us pursue the matter further by analogy. Can we suppose that the light poured by the Holy Spirit upon the *sayings* of our Lord would be confined to such sayings, and not extend itself over the other parts of the narrative of His life on earth? Can we believe that those

miracles, which though not uttered in words, were yet *acted parables*, would not be, under the same gracious assistance, brought back to the minds of the Apostles, so that they should be placed on record for the teaching of the Church?

10. And, going yet further, to those parts of the Gospels which were wholly out of the cycle of the Apostles' own testimony;—can we imagine that the divine discrimination which enabled them to detect the 'lie to the Holy Ghost,' should have forsaken them in judging of the records of our Lord's birth and infancy,—so that they should have taught or sanctioned an apocryphal, fabulous, or mythical account of such matters? *Some account* of them must have been current in the apostolic circle; for Mary the Mother of Jesus survived the Ascension, and would be fully capable of giving undoubted testimony to the facts. (See notes on Luke i. ii.) Can we conceive then that, *with her among them*, the Apostles should have delivered other than a true history of these things? Can we suppose that Luke's account, which he includes among the things *delivered by those who were eye-witnesses and ministers of the word* from the first, is other than the true one, and stamped with the authority of the witnessing and discriminating Spirit dwelling in the Apostles? Can we suppose that the account in the still more immediately apostolic Gospel of Matthew is other than the same history seen from a different side and independently narrated?

11. But if it be enquired, *how far* such divine superintendence has extended in the *framing of our Gospels as we at present find them*, the answer must be furnished by no preconceived idea of what ought to have been, but by *the contents of the Gospels themselves*. That those contents are *various*, and *variously arranged*, is token enough that in their selection and disposition we have human agency presented to us, under no more direct divine guidance, in this respect, than that *general leading*, which in main and essential points should ensure entire accordance. Such leading admits of much variety in points of minor consequence. Two men may be equally led by the Holy Spirit to record the events of our Lord's life for our edification, though one may believe and record, that the visit to the Gadarenes took place before the calling of Matthew, while the other places it after that event; though one in narrating it speaks of two dæmoniacs,—the other, only of one.

12. And it is observable, that in the only place in the three Gospels where an Evangelist speaks of himself, he expressly lays claim, not to any supernatural guidance in the arrangement of his subject-matter, but to a diligent tracing down of all things from the first; in other words, to the care and accuracy of a faithful and honest compiler. After such an avowal on the part of the editor himself, to assert an immediate revelation to him of the *arrangement to be adopted* and the *chronological*

notices to be given, is clearly not justified, according to his own shewing and assertion [7]. The value of such arrangement and chronological connexion must depend on various circumstances in each case :—on their definiteness and consistency,—on their agreement or disagreement with the other extant records ; the preference being in each case given to that one whose account is the most minute in details, and whose notes of sequence are the most distinct.

13. In thus speaking, I am doing no more than even the most scrupulous of our Harmonizers have in fact done. In the case alluded to in paragraph 11, *there is not one of them who has not altered the arrangement*, either of Matthew, or of Mark and Luke, so as to bring the visit to the Gadarenes into the same part of the evangelic history. But if *the arrangement itself* were *matter of divine inspiration*, then have we *no right to vary it* in the slightest degree, but must maintain (as the Harmonists have done in other cases, but never, that I am aware, in this) *two distinct visits to have been made at different times, and nearly the same events to have occurred at both*. I need hardly add that a similar method of proceeding with all the variations in the Gospels, *which would on this supposition be necessary*, would render the Scripture narrative a heap of improbabilities ; and strengthen, instead of weakening, the cause of the enemies of our faith.

14. And not only of the *arrangement* of the evangelic history are these remarks to be understood. There are certain minor points of accuracy or inaccuracy, of which human research suffices to inform men, and on which, from want of that research, it is often the practice to speak vaguely and inexactly. Such are sometimes the conventionally received distances from place to place ; such are the common accounts of phænomena in natural history, &c. Now, in matters of this kind, the Evangelists and Apostles were not supernaturally informed, but left, in common with others, to the guidance of their natural faculties.

15. The same may be said of citations and dates from history. In the last apology of Stephen, which he spoke being full of the Holy Ghost, and with divine influence beaming from his countenance, we have at least two demonstrable historical inaccuracies. And the occurrence of similar ones in the Gospels does not in any way affect the inspiration or the veracity of the Evangelists.

16. It may be well to mention one notable illustration of the principles upheld in this section. What can be more undoubted and unani-

[7] To suppose St Luke to have written ἔδοξεν κἀμοί, κ.τ.λ. if he were under the conscious inspiration of the Holy Spirit, superseding all his own mental powers and faculties, would be to charge him with ascribing to his own diligence and selection that which was furnished to him independently of both. Yet to this are the asserters of *verbal* inspiration committed.

mous than the testimony of the Evangelists to THE RESURRECTION OF THE LORD? If there be one fact rather than another of which the Apostles were witnesses, *it was this*:—and in the concurrent narrative of all four Evangelists it stands related beyond all cavil or question. Yet, of all the events which they have described, *none is so variously put forth in detail*, or with so many minor discrepancies. And this was just what might have been expected, on the principles above laid down. The great fact that the Lord *was risen*,—set forth by the ocular witness of the Apostles, who had seen Him,—became from that day first in importance in the delivery of their testimony. The *precise order* of His appearances would naturally, from the overwhelming nature of their present emotions, be a matter of minor consequence, and perhaps not even of accurate enquiry till some time had passed. Then, with the utmost desire on the part of the women and Apostles to collect the events in their exact order of time, some confusion would be apparent in the history, and some discrepancies in versions of it which were the results of separate and independent enquiries; the traces of which pervade our present accounts. But what fair-judging student of the Gospels ever made these variations or discrepancies a ground for doubting the veracity of the Evangelists as to the fact of the Resurrection, or the principal details of the Lord's appearances after it?

17. It will be well to state the bearing of the opinions advanced in this section on two terms in common use, viz. *verbal* and *plenary* inspiration.

18. With regard to *verbal inspiration*, I take the sense of it, as explained by its most strenuous advocates, to be, that every word and phrase of the Scriptures is absolutely and separately true,—and, whether narrative or discourse, took place, or was said, in every most exact particular as set down. Much might be said of the à priori unworthiness of such a theory, as applied to a gospel whose character is the freedom of the Spirit, not the bondage of the letter: but it belongs more to my present work to try it by applying it to the Gospels as we have them. And I do not hesitate to say that, being thus applied, its effect will be to destroy altogether the credibility of our Evangelists. Hardly a single instance of parallelism between them arises, where they do not relate the same thing indeed in substance, but expressed in terms which if literally taken are incompatible with each other. To cite only one obvious instance. The *Title over the Cross* was written in Greek. According, then, to the verbal-inspiration theory, each Evangelist has recorded the *exact words* of the inscription; *not the general sense*, but the *inscription* itself,—not a letter less or more. This is absolutely necessary to the theory. Its advocates must not be allowed, with convenient inconsistency, to take refuge in a common-sense view of the matter wherever their theory fails them, and still to uphold it in the

main [8]. And how it will here apply, the following comparison will shew:—

Matt., οὗτός ἐστιν ἰησοῦς ὁ βασιλεὺς τῶν ἰουδαίων.
Mark, ὁ βασιλεὺς τῶν ἰουδαίων.
Luke, ὁ βασιλεὺς τῶν ἰουδαίων οὗτος.
John, ἰησοῦς ὁ ναζωραῖος ὁ βασιλεὺς τῶν ἰουδαίων.

19. Another objection to the theory is, that if it be so, the Christian world is left in uncertainty what her Scriptures are, as long as the sacred text is full of various readings. *Some one manuscript must be pointed out to us*, which carries the weight of verbal inspiration, or *some text whose authority shall be undoubted*, must be promulgated. But manifestly neither of these things can ever happen. To the latest age, the reading of some important passages will be matter of doubt in the Church: and, which is equally subversive of the theory, though not of equal importance in itself, there is hardly a sentence in the whole of the Gospels in which there are not varieties of diction in our principal MSS., baffling all attempts to decide which was its original form.

20. The fact is, that this theory uniformly gives way before intelligent study of the Scriptures themselves; and is only held, consistently and thoroughly, by those who have never undertaken that study. When put forth by those who have, it is never carried fairly through; but while broadly asserted, is in detail abandoned.

21. If I understand *plenary inspiration* rightly, I *hold it to the utmost*, as entirely consistent with the opinions expressed in this section. The inspiration of the sacred writers I believe to have consisted in the fulness of the influence of the Holy Spirit specially raising them to, and enabling them for, their work,—*in a manner which distinguishes them from all other writers in the world, and their work from all other works.* The men were full of the Holy Ghost—the books are the pouring out of that fulness through the men,—the conservation of the treasure in earthen vessels. The treasure is ours, in all its richness: but it is ours as only it can be ours,—in the imperfections of human speech, in the limitations of human thought, in the variety incident first to individual character, and then to manifold transcription and the lapse of ages.

22. Two things, in concluding this section, I would earnestly impress on my readers. First, that we must take our views of inspiration not, as is too often done, from à priori considerations, but ENTIRELY FROM THE EVIDENCE FURNISHED BY THE SCRIPTURES THEMSELVES: and secondly, that the MEN were INSPIRED; the BOOKS are the RESULTS OF THAT INSPIRATION. This latter consideration, if all that it implies be duly weighed, will furnish us with the key to the whole question.

[8] This has been done, as far as I have seen, in all remarks of verbal-inspirationists on this part of my Prolegomena.

SECTION VII.

IMPRACTICABILITY OF CONSTRUCTING A FORMAL HARMONY OF THE THREE GOSPELS.

1. From very early times attempts have been made to combine the narratives of our three Gospels into one continuous history. As might have been expected, however, from the characteristics of those Gospels above detailed, such Harmonies could not be constructed without doing considerable violence to the arrangement of some one or more of the three, and an arbitrary adoption of the order of some *one*, to which then the others have been fitted and conformed. An examination of any of the current Harmonies will satisfy the student that this has been the case.

2. Now, on the supposition that the three Gospels had arisen one out of the other, with a design such as any of those which have been previously discussed (with the exception of ϵ) in § ii. 2, 3, such a Harmony not only ought to be *possible*, but should *arise naturally* out of the several narratives, without any forcing or alteration of arrangement. Nay, on the *supplementary* theory of Greswell and others, the *last written Gospel should itself be such a History as the Harmonizers are in search of.* Now not only is this not the case, but their Harmonies contain the most violent and considerable transpositions:—they are obliged to have recourse to the most arbitrary hypotheses of repetition of events and discourses,—and, after all, their Harmonies, while some difficulties would be evaded by their adoption, entail upon us others even more weighty and inexplicable.

3. Taking, however, the view of the origin of the Gospels above advocated, the question of the practicability of harmonizing is simply reduced to one of *matter of fact:—how far* the three Evangelists, in relating the events of a history which *was itself one and the same*, have presented us with the *same side* of the narrative of those events, or with fragments *which will admit of being pieced into one another.*

4. And there is no doubt that, as far as the *main features* of the evangelic history are concerned, a harmonious whole is presented to us by the combined narrative. The great events of our Lord's ministry, His baptism, His temptation, His teaching by discourses and miracles, His selection of the Twelve, His transfiguration, His announcement of His sufferings, death, and resurrection, His last journey to Jerusalem, His betrayal, His passion, crucifixion, burial, and resurrection,—these are common to all; and, as far as *they* are concerned, their narra-

tives naturally fall into accordance and harmony. But when we come to range their texts side by side, to supply clause with clause, and endeavour to construct a complete history of details out of them, we at once find ourselves involved in the difficulties above enumerated. And the inference which an unbiassed mind will thence draw is, that as the Evangelists wrote with no such design of being pieced together into a complete history, but delivered the apostolic testimony as they had received it, modified by individual character and oral transmission, and arranged carefully according to the best of their knowledge,—so we should thus simply and reverentially receive their records, without setting them at variance with each other by compelling them in all cases to say the same things of the same events.

5. If the Evangelists have delivered to us truly and faithfully the apostolic narratives, and if the Apostles spoke as the Holy Spirit enabled them, and brought events and sayings to their recollection, then we may be sure that *if we knew the real process of the transactions themselves, that knowledge would enable us to give an account of the diversities of narration and arrangement which the Gospels now present to us.* But *without such knowledge*, all attempts to accomplish this analysis in minute detail must be *merely conjectural:* and must tend to weaken the evangelic testimony, rather than to strengthen it.

6. The only genuine Harmony of the Gospels will be furnished by the unity and consistency of the Christian's belief in their record, as true to the great events which it relates, and his enlightened and intelligent appreciation of the careful diligence of the Evangelists in arranging the important matter before them. If in that arrangement he finds variations, and consequently inaccuracies, on one side or the other, he will be content to acknowledge the analogy which pervades all the divine dealings with mankind, and to observe that God, who works, in the communication of His other gifts, through the medium of secondary agents—has been pleased to impart to us this, the record of His most precious Gift, also by human agency and teaching. He will acknowledge also, in this, the peculiar mercy and condescension of Him who has adapted to universal human reception the record of eternal life by His Son, by means of the very variety of individual recollections and modified reports. And thus he will arrive at the *true harmonistic view of Scripture;* just as in the great and discordant world he does not seek peace by setting one thing against another and finding logical solution for all, but by holy and peaceful trust in that Almighty Father, who doeth all things well. So that the argument so happily applied by Butler to the *nature of the Revelation* contained in the Scriptures, may with equal justice be applied to *the books themselves* in which the record of that Revelation is found,—that "He who believes the Scriptures to have proceeded from Him who is the Author of nature, may well expect

to find the same sort of difficulties in them as are found in the constitution of nature."

CHAPTER II.

OF THE GOSPEL ACCORDING TO MATTHEW.

SECTION I.

ITS AUTHORSHIP.

1. THE author of this Gospel has been universally believed to be, THE APOSTLE MATTHEW. With this belief the contents of the Gospel are not inconsistent; and we find it current in the very earliest ages (see testimonies in the next section).

2. Of the Apostle Matthew we know very little for certain. He was the son of Alphæus (Mark ii. 14), and therefore probably the brother of James the less. His calling, from being a publican to be one of the Twelve, is narrated by all three Evangelists. By Mark and Luke he is called Levi; in this Gospel, Matthew. Such change of name after becoming a follower of the Lord, was by no means uncommon; and the appearance of the apostolic, not the original name, in the Gospel proceeding from himself, is in analogy with the practice of Paul, who always in his Epistles speaks of himself by his new and Christian appellation. (On the doubts raised in ancient times respecting the identity of Matthew and Levi, see note on Matt. ix. 9.)

3. The Apostle Matthew is described by Clement of Alexandria[9] as belonging to the ascetic Judaistic school of early Christians. Nothing is known of his apostolic labours out of Palestine, which Eusebius mentions generally (ἐφ' ἑτέρους, Hist. Eccl. iii. 24). Later writers fix the scene of them in Ethiopia, but also include in their circle Macedonia, and several parts of Asia (Rufin. Hist. Eccl. x. 9: Socr. Hist. Eccl. i. 19). Heracleon, as cited by Clement of Alexandria, Strom. iv. 9, p. 525, relates that his death was natural. This is implicitly confirmed by Clement himself, and by Origen and Tertullian, who mention only Peter, Paul, and James the greater, as *martyrs* among the Apostles.

[9] Ματθαῖος μὲν οὖν ὁ ἀπόστολος σπερμάτων κ. ἀκροδρύων κ. λαχάνων ἄνευ κρεῶν μετελάμβανεν, Ἰωάννης δὲ ὑπερτείνας τὴν ἐγκράτειαν ἀκρίδας κ. μέλι ἤσθιεν ἄγριον. Pædag. ii. 1, p. 174-5.

SECTION II.

ITS ORIGINAL LANGUAGE.

1. It has been much disputed among biblical scholars, whether this Gospel was originally composed in HEBREW (i. e. Syro-chaldaic, the vernacular language of the Hebrew Christians in Palestine) or in GREEK. I shall state the principal arguments on both sides, and give my own judgment on them.

A. Those who maintain a HEBREW original rest on the evidence of the early Church. And this evidence was unanimous. It mainly consists of the following testimonies :

(*a*) PAPIAS, bishop of Hierapolis in Phrygia in the beginning of the 2nd century. Eusebius thus describes him (H. E. iii. 36),—Παπίας, τῆς ἐν Ἱεραπόλει παροικίας καὶ αὐτὸς ἐπίσκοπος, ἀνὴρ τὰ πάντα ὅτι μάλιστα [1] λογιώτατος καὶ γραφῆς εἰδήμων. He wrote five συγγράμματα, entitled λογίων κυριακῶν ἐξηγήσεις (ib. iii. 39) ; as Irenæus also states (Hær. v. 33, p. 332),—where he calls him Ἰωάννου μὲν ἀκουστής, Πολυκάρπου δὲ ἑταῖρος γεγονώς, ἀρχαῖος ἀνήρ. It is true that Eusebius asserts him, with reference to his adoption of chiliastic opinions, to have been σφόδρα σμικρὸς τὸν νοῦν (H. E. ibid.) : but this, it is alleged, cannot be brought to bear on the validity of his testimony to a matter of fact ; being only said controversially, and with regard to the adoption by Papias of apocryphal stories, and his belonging to a particular school of interpretation, from which Eusebius dissented. His testimony runs thus : **Ματθαῖος μὲν οὖν ἑβραΐδι διαλέκτῳ τὰ λόγια συνετάξατο· ἡρμήνευσε δ' αὐτὰ ὡς ἐδύνατο** (or **ἦν δυνατὸς**) **ἕκαστος.** That Papias meant by τὰ λόγια the Gospel of Matthew, not merely a collection of discourses, is probable, from his calling Mark's Gospel (apparently), σύνταξις τῶν κυριακῶν λογίων (Eus. ib.) : and from the title of his own work (see above). It would seem from the latter words of the above testimony, that Papias was not,

[1] The author of the article on the first edition of this vol. in the Edinburgh Review, July, 1851, would render ἀνὴρ λογιώτατος "a man full of anecdotes," and thereby disparage Papias' testimony. But not to mention how inconsistent this is with the whole tenor of the passage in which the term occurs, which goes to *exalt* that testimony, the usage of λόγιος by Eusebius himself is decisive against the Reviewer. See, e. g., H. E. vi. 15 (of Origen), διανείμας τὰ πλήθη, τὸν Ἡρακλᾶν τῶν γνωρίμων προκρίνας, ἔν τε τοῖς θείοις σπουδαῖον, καὶ ἄλλως ὄντα λογιώτατον ἄνδρα κ. φιλοσοφίας οὐκ ἄμοιρον, κοινωνὸν καθίστη τῆς κατηχήσεως : ib. 20,—ἤκμαζον δὲ κατὰ τοῦτο πλείους λόγιοι κ. ἐκκλησιαστικοὶ ἄνδρες, . . among whom he enumerates Beryllus of Bostra, Hippolytus, Gaius (λογιώτατος ἀνήρ) : cf. also v. 16 (init.), vii. 7 (αὐτὸς οὗτος λόγιός τε καὶ θαυμάσιος). See Heinichen's note on the word in the passage cited in the text.

at all events, aware of any authoritative contemporaneous version in Greek.

(β) IRENÆUS, Hær. iii. 1, p. 174 : ὁ μὲν Ματθαῖος ἐν τοῖς Ἑβραίοις τῇ ἰδίᾳ διαλέκτῳ αὐτῶν καὶ γραφὴν ἐξήνεγκεν εὐαγγελίου, τοῦ Πέτρου καὶ τοῦ Παύλου ἐν Ῥώμῃ εὐαγγελιζομένων καὶ θεμελιούντων τὴν ἐκκλησίαν. Not a word is here said of Papias : indeed, by the last clause, this testimony, it is said, manifestly rests on independent ground. That such a note of time should have been, as has been supposed (Edin. Rev. July 1851, p. 38), a calculation of Irenæus himself, is inconceivable.

(γ) EUSEBIUS, H. E. v. 10, relates of Pantænus, ὁ Πάνταινος καὶ εἰς Ἰνδοὺς ἐλθεῖν λέγεται, ἔνθα λόγος εὑρεῖν αὐτὸν προφθάσαν τὴν αὐτοῦ παρουσίαν τὸ κατὰ Ματθαῖον εὐαγγέλιον παρά τισιν αὐτόθι τὸν χριστὸν ἐπεγνωκόσιν, οἷς Βαρθολομαῖον τῶν ἀποστόλων ἕνα κηρύξαι, αὐτοῖς τε Ἑβραίων γράμμασι τὴν τοῦ Ματθαίου καταλεῖψαι γραφήν, ἣν καὶ σώζεσθαι εἰς τὸν δηλούμενον χρόνον. This tradition recognizes a Hebrew Gospel according to Matthew, and thus agrees with the testimonies before cited.

(δ) ORIGEN, Comm. in Matt. tom. i., preserved in Eus. H. E. vi. 25, describes himself as ἐν παραδόσει μαθὼν περὶ τῶν τεσσάρων εὐαγγελίων ἃ καὶ μόνα ἀναντίῤῥητά ἐστιν ἐν τῇ ὑπὸ τὸν οὐρανὸν ἐκκλησίᾳ τοῦ θεοῦ, ὅτι πρῶτον μὲν γέγραπται τὸ κατὰ τὸν ποτὲ τελώνην, ὕστερον δὲ ἀπόστολον Ἰησοῦ χριστοῦ, Ματθαῖον, ἐκδεδωκότα αὐτὸ τοῖς ἀπὸ Ἰουδαισμοῦ πιστεύσασι γράμμασιν ἑβραϊκοῖς συντεταγμένον.

(ε) EUSEBIUS, Hist. Eccl. iii. 24: Ματθαῖος μὲν γὰρ πρότερον Ἑβραίοις κηρύξας, ὡς ἔμελλε καὶ ἐφ' ἑτέρους ἰέναι, πατρίῳ γλώττῃ γραφῇ παραδοὺς τὸ κατ' αὐτὸν εὐαγγέλιον, τὸ λεῖπον τῇ αὐτοῦ παρουσίᾳ τούτοις ἀφ' ὧν ἐστέλλετο διὰ τῆς γραφῆς ἀνεπλήρου. With this may be compared another passage of Eusebius (Ad Marin. quæst. ii., vol. iv. p. 941) : λέλεκται δὲ ὀψὲ τοῦ σαββάτου παρὰ τοῦ ἑρμηνεύσαντος τὴν γραφήν· ὁ μὲν γὰρ εὐαγγελιστὴς Ματθαῖος ἑβραΐδι γλώττῃ παρέδωκε τὸ εὐαγγέλιον. This last passage shews that Eusebius *himself believed* the Gospel to have been written in Hebrew.

(ζ) EPIPHANIUS, Hær. xxix. 9, vol. i. p. 124, says of the Ebionites and Nazarenes, ἔχουσι δὲ τὸ κατὰ Ματθαῖον εὐαγγέλιον πληρέστατον ἑβραϊστί. παρ' αὐτοῖς γὰρ σαφῶς τοῦτο, καθὼς ἐξ ἀρχῆς ἐγράφη ἑβραϊκοῖς γράμμασιν, ἔτι σώζεται. And again, Hær. xxx. 3, p. 127, καὶ δέχονται μὲν καὶ αὐτοὶ τὸ κατὰ Ματθαῖον εὐαγγέλιον . . . καλοῦσι δὲ αὐτὸ κατὰ Ἑβραίους, ὡς τὰ ἀληθῆ ἐστιν εἰπεῖν, ὅτι Ματθαῖος μόνος ἑβραϊστὶ καὶ ἑβραϊκοῖς γράμμασιν ἐν τῇ καινῇ διαθήκῃ ἐποιήσατο τὴν τοῦ εὐαγγελίου ἔκθεσίν τε καὶ κήρυγμα.

(η) JEROME, Præf. to Matt,, vol. vii. pp. 3, 4 : "*Matthæus . . Evangelium in Judæa Hebræo sermone edidit ob eorum vel maxime causam qui in Jesum crediderant ex Judæis.*" Also De Viris Illustr. 3, vol. ii. p. 833 : "*Matthæus, qui et Levi, ex publicano Apostolus, primus in Judæa propter eos qui ex circumcisione crediderant, Evangelium Christi Hebraicis literis verbisque composuit, quod quis postea in Græcum transtulerit, non satis certum est. Porro ipsum Hebraicum habetur usque hodie in Cæsariensi bibliotheca, quam Pamphilus martyr studiosissime confecit. Mihi quoque a Nazaræis qui in Berœa urbe Syriæ hoc volumine utuntur, describendi facultas fuit. In quo animadvertendum, quod ubicumque Evangelista, sive ex persona vera sive ex persona Domini Salvatoris, veteris scripturæ testimoniis utitur, non sequatur LXX translatorum auctoritatem, sed Hebraicum, e quibus illa duo sunt: 'Ex Ægypto vocavi filium meum:' et, 'Quoniam Nazaræus vocabitur.'*" Also, In Quatuor Evv. ad Damasum præfatio, vol. x. p. 527, Migne: "*De novo nunc loquor testamento, quod Græcum esse non dubium est, excepto Apostolo Matthæo, qui primus in Judæa Evangelium Christi Hebraicis literis edidit.*" Again, Ep. (xx.) Damaso de Osanna 5, vol. i. p. 68: "*Matthæus, qui Evangelium Hebraico sermone conscripsit, ita posuit* osanna berama, *id est,* Osanna in excelsis," &c. Again, Ep. (cxx.) Hedibiæ, quæst. viii. 1, p. 831: "*In Evangelio autem*" (*Matthæi,* from context), "*quod Hebraicis literis scriptum est, legimus, 'non velum templi scissum, sed superliminare templi miræ magnitudinis corruisse.'*" Again, Comm. in Hos. xi., vol. vi. p. 123, in treating of the words, 'Out of Egypt have I called my son,' he says, "*Hunc locum in septimo volumine Julianus Augustus quod adversum nos, i.e. Christianos, evomuit, calumniatur et dicit, quod de Israel scriptum est, Matthæus Evangelista ad Christum transtulit, ut simplicitati eorum qui de gentibus crediderant illuderet. Cui nos breviter respondebimus:* 1°, *Matthæum Evangelium Hebræis literis edidisse, quod non poterant legere nisi hi qui ex Hebræis erant: ergo non propterea fecit ut illuderet ethnicis.*" Jerome refers also to the tradition mentioned under (γ) above, and says, "*Reperit (Pantænus) in India Bartholomæum de duodecim Apostolis adventum Domini nostri Jesu Christi juxta Matthæi Evangelium prædicasse, quod, Hebraicis literis scriptum, revertens Alexandriam secum detulit*" (De Viris Illustr. 36, vol. ii. p. 876).

(θ) Gregory Nazianzen, Chrysostom, Augustine, Isidorus Hispalensis, Theophylact, Euthymius, and others, assert the same.

B. Those who maintain a GREEK original, rest principally on the internal evidence furnished by the Gospel itself. But they also *demur to the sufficiency of the external evidence above cited.* They object,

I. (ι) That the testimony of Papias, on which much of this evidence rests, is unsatisfactory, as having proceeded from a man of weak judgment.

(κ) That there appears to have been some confusion between the (supposed) Hebrew original of St. Matthew, and the heretical 'Gospel according to the Hebrews.' Jerome, de Viris Illustr. 3, says (see above, (η)) that he had seen the Hebrew original of Matthew at Berœa by favour of the Nazarenes, and had copied it. But further, in his Commentary on Matt. xii. 13, vol. vii. p. 77, he says, "*In Evangelio quo utuntur Nazaræi et Hebionitæ, quod nuper in Græcum de Hebræo ser-*

mone transtulimus, et quod vocatur a plerisque Matthæi authenticum," &c. And the Commentary on Matthew was written some years after his treatise De Viris Illustr. Again, still later, Dialog. adv. Pelagianos, lib. iii. 2, vol. ii. p. 782 : "*In Evangelio juxta Hebræos, quod Chaldaico quidem Syroque sermone, sed Hebraicis literis conscriptum est, quo utuntur usque hodie Nazareni, secundum Apostolos, sive ut plerique autumant, juxta Matthæum, quod et in Cæsariensi habetur bibliotheca, narrat historia*" (then follows an apocryphal anecdote).

Now let these notices be compared with his assertion above, that the Hebrew original of Matthew related "*superliminare templi miræ magnitudinis corruisse,*" and it will appear,

1. That Jerome once believed the Hebrew MS. in the Cæsarean library to be the original Gospel of St. Matthew.

2. That he believed this original to be different from our present Greek Gospel : for he quotes from it things not found there.

3. That in subsequent years he modified his opinion that this document was the original Hebrew text of St. Matthew, and took refuge under "*quod vocatur a plerisque,*" and "*secundum Apostolos, sive ut plerique autumant,*" &c.

(λ) Light is thrown on this uncertainty by the assertion of Epiphanius (above, (ζ)), which clearly shews that he was misled by the Nazarenes and Ebionites to believe their Gospel to be the genuine Gospel of Matthew.

II. But the advocates of the Greek original rest mainly on the *phænomena of the Gospel itself.* They maintain,

(μ) That the present Greek text stands on precisely the same footing as that of the other Gospels : is cited as early, and as constantly as they are.

(ν) That the hypothesis of a translation from the Hebrew altogether fails to account for the identity observable in certain parts of the text of the three synoptic Gospels. For the translator must either have been acquainted with the other two Gospels,—in which case it is inconceivable that in the midst of the present coincidences in many passages, such divergences should have occurred,—or unacquainted with them, in which case the identity itself would be altogether inexplicable.

(ξ) A further observation of the coincidences and divergences is said to confirm the view of a Greek original. The synoptic Gospels mainly *coincide* in the *discourses and words of our Lord,* but *diverge* in their *narrative portions;* and while verbal identity is found principally in the former, the latter present the phænomena either of independent translations from the same original, or of independent histories.

(ο) Again, whereas the Evangelists themselves, in citing the O. T., usually quote from the Hebrew text, our Lord in His discourses almost uniformly quotes the Septuagint, even where it differs from the Hebrew.

This is urged as tending to establish the Greek original of St. Matthew: for if the Gospel were really written in Hebrew for the use of Jews, it is not conceivable that the citations would be given in any but the Hebrew text: and equally inconceivable that the translator would have rendered them into the language of the LXX in our Lord's discourses, while he retained the Hebrew readings in the narrative.

(π) But the same fact would also tend to establish that our Lord *spoke usually in Greek*[2],—that Greek was the language commonly used and generally understood by the Jews of Palestine,—and consequently, that the composition of a Hebrew Gospel for the early Judæo-Christians would be unnecessary, and in the last degree improbable.

C. (ρ) It would exceed the limits of these Prolegomena to argue the question at length. I can only state my own judgment on the point in debate. In the first edition of this work, I acceded to what appeared to me the irresistible weight of testimony of antiquity. But I have since then studied very closely the text itself, especially with reference to its revision in those passages which find parallels in the other Gospels: and I am bound to say that my view of the Hebrew origin is much shaken.

(σ) Besides which, it certainly appears to me, that the testimonies of Epiphanius and Jerome go to shew that they believed the so-called *Gospel to the Hebrews* TO BE THE VERITABLE ORIGINAL of St. Matthew: that *so believing*, Jerome copied and translated it, and quoted from it: but subsequently found reason to doubt this, and gradually modified his former assertions. Strange as this may be, I do not see how we can deny it as the result of combining the above extracts from his writings.

(τ) On the whole, then, I find myself constrained to abandon the view maintained in my first edition, and to adopt that of a Greek original.

(υ) We thus have to consider the first Gospel on the same ground, and to judge it by the same rules, as the second and third Gospels.

[2] This has been maintained (by the late Duke of Manchester) in 'A Chapter on the Harmonizing Gospels,' printed at the University Press, Dublin, 1854. See also Hug, Einleitung, ed. 4, vol. ii. pp. 27—49, on the ordinary language of Palestine when Matthew wrote his Gospel: and Discussions on the Gospels, by Alexander Roberts, D.D., 2nd edn. pp. 26—316; and on the general subject of this section, ib. pp. 319—448.

SECTION III.

FOR WHAT READERS AND WITH WHAT OBJECT IT WAS WRITTEN.

1. The statements in several of the testimonies above cited, shew the prevalence of a general opinion that Matthew originally drew up his Gospel for the use of the Jewish converts in Palestine. And internal notices tend to confirm this inference. We have fewer interpretations of Jewish customs, laws, and localities, than in the two other Gospels. The whole narrative proceeds more upon a Jewish view of matters, and is concerned more to establish that point, which to a Jewish convert would be most important,—*that Jesus was the Messiah prophesied in the Old Testament.* Hence the commencement of His genealogy from Abraham and David; hence the frequent notice of the necessity of this or that event happening *because it was so foretold by the Prophets;* hence the constant opposition of our Lord's spiritually ethical teaching to the carnal formalistic ethics of the Scribes and Pharisees.

2. But we must not think of the Gospel as a systematic treatise drawn up with this end continually in view. It only exercised a very general and indirect influence over the composition, not excluding narratives, sayings, and remarks which had no such tendency, or even partook of an opposite one.

3. *Grecian readers* were certainly also in the view of the Apostle; and in consequence, he adds interpretations and explanations, such e. g. as ch. i. 23; xxvii. 8, 33, 46, for their information.

4. In furtherance of the design above mentioned, we may discern (with the caution given in 2) a more frequent and consistent reference to the Lord *as a King*, and to his Messianic kingdom, than in the other Gospels. Designing these Prolegomena not as a complete Introduction to the Gospels, but merely as subsidiary to the following Commentary, I purposely do not give instances of these characteristics, but leave them to be gathered by the student as he proceeds.

SECTION IV.

AT WHAT TIME IT WAS WRITTEN.

The testimony of the early Church is unanimous, that Matthew wrote *first* among the Evangelists. Clement of Alexandria, who dissented from the present order of our Gospels, yet placed those of Matthew and Luke first: προγεγράφθαι ἔλεγε τῶν εὐαγγελίων τὰ περιέχοντα τὰς γενεαλογίας (Eusebius, Hist. Eccl. vi. 14). Origen's testimony see above (§ ii. 1, δ). And Irenæus (see above, ibid. β) relates that Matthew wrote his Gospel while Peter and Paul were preaching and founding the Church in Rome[3]. Without adopting this statement, we may remark that it represents a date, to which internal chronological notices are not repugnant. It seems, from ch. xxvii. 8, and xxviii. 15, that some considerable time had elapsed since the events narrated; while, from the omission of all mention of the destruction of Jerusalem, it would appear that the Gospel was published *before* that event. All these marks of time are, however, exceedingly vague, especially when other notices are taken into account, which place the Gospel eight years after the Ascension (Theophyl. and Euthym.);—fifteen years after the Ascension (Niceph. Hist. Eccl. ii. 45):—at the time of the stoning of Stephen (Cosmas Indicopleustes, Fabricius, Bibl. Gr. iv. 5).

SECTION V.

ITS STYLE AND CHARACTER.

1. The Gospel of Matthew is written in the same form of diction which pervades the other Gospels, the Hebraistic or Hellenistic Greek. This dialect resulted from the dispersion of the Greek language by the conquests of Alexander, and more especially from the intercourse of Jews with Greeks in the city of Alexandria. It is that of the LXX version of the Old Testament; of the apocryphal books; and of the writings of Philo and Josephus. In these two latter, however, it is not so marked, as in versions from the Hebrew, or books aiming at a Hebraistic character.

2. Of the three Gospels, that of Matthew presents the most complete example of the Hebraistic diction and construction, with perhaps the exception of the first chapter of Luke. And from what has been above said respecting its design, this would naturally be the case.

3. The internal character of this Gospel also answers to what we know of the history and time of its compilation. Its marks of chronological sequence are very vague, and many of them are hardly perhaps to be insisted on at all. When compared with the more definite notices of Mark and Luke, its order of events is sometimes superseded by theirs. It was to be expected, in the earliest written accounts of matters so

[3] The Edinburgh Reviewer blames it in me as an instance of carelessness, that I have here combined a passage relating to the *existing Greek* Gospel, with one referring to the *hypothetical Hebrew* one. But I own I am unable to see why the view of the early Church, as to a matter of *date*, may not be gathered from both, irrespective of the question of a Hebrew or Greek original.

important, that the object should rather be to record the *things done*, and the *sayings* of our Lord, than the *precise order* in which they took place.

4. It is in this principal duty of an Evangelist that Matthew stands pre-eminent; and especially in the report of the *longer discourses* of our Lord. It was within the limits of his purpose in writing, to include all the descriptions of the state and hopes of the citizens of the kingdom of heaven which Jesus gave during His ministry. This seems to have been the peculiar gift of the Spirit to him,—to recall and deliver down, in their strictest verbal connexion, such discourses as the Sermon on the Mount, ch. v.—vii.; the apostolic commission, ch. x.; the discourse concerning John, ch. xi.; that on blasphemy against the Holy Ghost, ch. xii.; the series of parables, ch. xiii.; that to the Apostles on their divisions, ch. xviii.; and in their fulness, the whole series of polemical discourses and prophetic parables in ch. xxi.—xxv.

5. It has been my endeavour in the following Commentary, to point out the close internal connexion of the longer discourses, and to combat the mistake of those critics who suppose them to be no more than collections of shorter sayings associated together from similarity of subject or character.

6. On the connexion between the Epistle of James and some parts of this Gospel, see the Prolegomena to that Epistle, § iv. 2, note.

CHAPTER III.

OF THE GOSPEL ACCORDING TO MARK.

SECTION I.

ITS AUTHORSHIP.

1. As in the case of the two other Gospels, we are dependent entirely on traditional sources for the name of the author. It has been universally believed to be *Marcus:* and further, that he was the same person who, in Acts xii. 12, 25; xv. 37, is spoken of as Ἰωάννης ὁ ἐπικαλούμενος (ἐπικληθείς, καλούμενος) Μάρκος: in xiii. 5, 13, as Ἰωάννης: in xv. 39, as Μάρκος: also in Col. iv. 10: 2 Tim. iv. 11: Philem. 24. The few particulars gleaned respecting him from Scripture are, that his mother's name was Mary (Acts xii. 12); and that she was sister to the Apostle Barnabas (Col. iv. 10); that she dwelt in Jerusalem (Acts, ibid.); that he was converted to Christianity by the Apostle Peter (1 Pet. v. 13); that he became the minister and companion of Paul and Barnabas, in

their first missionary journey (Acts xii. 25); and was the cause of the variance and separation of these Apostles on their second (Acts xv. 37—40),—Barnabas wishing to take him again with them, but Paul refusing, because he had departed from them before the completion of the former journey (Acts xiii. 13). He then became the companion of Barnabas in his journey to Cyprus (Acts xv. 39). We find him however again with Paul (Col. iv. 10), and an allusion apparently made in the words there to some previous stain on his character, which was then removed: see also Philem. 24: 2 Tim. iv. 11. Lastly, we find him with Peter (1 Pet. v. 13). From Scripture we know no more concerning him. But an unanimous tradition of the ancient Christian writers represents him as the 'interpres' of Peter: i. e. the secretary or amanuensis, whose office it was to commit to writing the orally-delivered instructions and narrations of the Apostle. See authorities quoted in § ii. below.

2. Tradition (Eusebius, Hist. Eccl. ii. 15) brings him with Peter to Rome (but apparently only on the authority of 1 Pet. v. 13); and thence to Alexandria. He is said to have become first bishop of the Church in that city, and to have suffered martyrdom there. All this however is exceedingly uncertain.

SECTION II.

ITS ORIGIN.

1. It was universally believed in the ancient Church, that Mark's Gospel was written under the influence, and almost by the dictation, of Peter.

) Eusebius quotes from Papias (Hist. Eccl. iii. 39), as a testimony of John the presbyter, Μάρκος μὲν ἑρμηνευτὴς Πέτρου γενόμενος, ὅσα ἐμνημόνευσεν, ἀκριβῶς ἔγραψεν, κ.τ.λ.

(β) The same author (Hist. Eccl. v. 8) says Μάρκος ὁ μαθητὴς καὶ ἑρμηνευτὴς Πέτρου, καὶ αὐτὸς τὰ ὑπὸ Πέτρου κηρυσσόμενα ἐγγράφως ἡμῖν παραδέδωκε. This he quotes from Irenæus (iii. 1, p. 174); and further that this took place μετὰ τὴν τούτων (i. e. τοῦ Πέτρου κ. τοῦ Παύλου) ἔξοδον.

(γ) The same author (Hist. Eccl. ii. 15) relates, on the authority of Clement (Hypotyp. vi.) and Papias, that the hearers of Peter at Rome, unwilling that his teaching should be lost to them, besought Mark, who was a follower of Peter, to commit to writing the substance of that teaching; that the Apostle, being informed supernaturally of the work in which Mark was engaged, ἡσθῆναι τῇ τῶν ἀνδρῶν προθυμίᾳ, κυρῶσαί τε τὴν γραφὴν εἰς ἔντευξιν τῆς ἐκκλησίας. This account is manifestly inconsistent with the former.

(δ) In Hist. Eccl. vi. 14, Eusebius gives yet *another* account, *citing* the very passage of Clement above referred to: that Peter, knowing of

Mark's work when it was completed and published, προτρεπτικῶς μήτε κωλῦσαι μήτε προτρέψασθαι.

(ε) The same author, in his Demonstr. Evang. iii. 5, vol. iv. p. 122, says Πετρος δὲ ταῦτα περὶ ἑαυτοῦ μαρτυρεῖ· πάντα γὰρ τὰ παρὰ Μάρκῳ τοῦ Πέτρου διαλέξεων εἶναι λέγεται ἀπομνημονεύματα.

(ζ) Tertullian (Cont. Marcion. iv. 5, vol. ii. p. 367) relates : "Marcus quod edidit Evangelium, Petri adfirmatur, cujus interpres Marcus."

(η) Jerome (Ad Hedibiam (Ep. cxx.), quæst. xi., vol. i. p. 844) writes : "Habebat ergo (Paulus) Titum interpretem, sicut et beatus Petrus Marcum, cujus Evangelium *Petro narrante* et *illo scribente* compositum est."

2. The above testimonies must now be examined as to how far we are bound to receive them as decisive. We may observe that the matter to which they refer is one which could, from its nature, have been known to very few persons ; viz. the private and unavowed influence of an Apostle over the writer. (For I reject at once the account which makes Peter *authorize* the Gospel, from no such authorization being apparent, which it certainly would have been, had it ever existed.) Again, the accounts cited are most vague and inconsistent as to the *extent* and *nature* of this influence,—some stating it to have been no more than that Peter preached, and Mark, after his death, collected the substance of his testimony from memory ; others making it extend even to the dictation of the words by the Apostle.

3. It is obvious that all such accounts must be judged according to the phænomena presented by the Gospel itself. Now we find, in the title of the Gospel, a presumption that no *such* testimony of Peter is here presented to us, as we have of Matthew in the former Gospel. Had such been the case, we should have found it called the Gospel according to *Peter*, not according to *Mark*.

4. If again we examine the contents of the Gospel, we are certainly not justified in concluding that Peter's hand has been directly employed in its compilation in its present form. The various mentions, and omissions of mention, of incidents in which that Apostle is directly concerned, are such as to be in no way consistently accounted for on this hypothesis. For let it be allowed that a natural modesty might have occasionally led him to omit matters tending to his honour,—yet how are we to account for his omitting to give an exact detail of other things at which he was present, and of which he might have rendered the most precise and circumstantial account ? This has been especially the case in the narrative of the day of the Resurrection, not to mention numerous other instances which will be noticed in the Commentary. Besides, the above hypothesis regarding his suppressions cannot be consistently carried out. A remarkable instance to the contrary may be seen, ch. xvi. 7, where εἴπατε τοῖς μαθηταῖς αὐτοῦ καὶ τῷ Πέτρῳ stands for εἴπατε τοῖς μαθηταῖς αὐτοῦ in Matthew.

5. We are led to the same conclusion by a careful comparison of the contents of this Gospel with those of Matthew and Luke. We find that it follows the same great cycle of apostolic teaching;—that its narratives are derived in many cases from the same sources;—that it is improbable that any individual Apostle should have moulded and fashioned a record which keeps so much to the beaten track of the generally-received evangelic history. His own individual remembrances must unavoidably have introduced additions of so considerable an amount as to have given to the Gospel more original matter than it at present possesses.

6. But while unable to conceive any influence *directly* exerted by Peter over the compilation of the Gospel, I would by no means deny the possibility of the derivation of some narratives in it from that Apostle, and recognize in such derivation the ground of the above testimonies. The peculiarly minute and graphic precision (presently, § viii. to be further spoken of) which distinguishes this Evangelist, seems to claim for him access in many cases to the testimony of some eye-witness where the other two Evangelists have not had that advantage. I have pointed out these cases where they occur, in the Commentary; and have not hesitated in some of them to refer conjecturally to Peter as the source of the narration.

7. The inference to be drawn from what has preceded is, that,—the general tradition of the ancients, which ascribed to Mark a connexion with Peter as his secretary or interpreter, being adopted, as likely to be founded on fact,—yet the idea of any considerable or direct influence of Peter over the writing of the Gospel is not borne out by the work itself. We may so far recognize in it one form of the probable truth;—it is likely that Mark, from continual intercourse with and listening to Peter, and possibly from preservation of many of his narrations entire, may have been able, after his death, or at all events when separated from him, to preserve in his Gospel those vivid and original touches of description and filling-out of the incidents, which we now discover in it. Further than this I do not think we are authorized in assuming; and even this is conjectural only.

SECTION III.

FOR WHAT READERS AND WITH WHAT OBJECT IT WAS WRITTEN.

1. Internal evidence is very full as to the class of readers for whom Mark compiled his Gospel: *the Gentile Christians* are clearly pointed out by the following indications:—

(*α*) The omission of all genealogical notices of our Lord's descent.

(*β*) The general abstinence from Old Testament citations, except in reporting discourses of our Lord (ch. i. 2, 3 is the only exception, xv. 28 being rejected as spurious).

(γ) The appending of interpretations to the Hebrew or Aramaic terms occurring in the narrative (ch. v. 41 ; vii. 11, 34).

(δ) The explanations of Jewish customs, as for example ch. vii. 3, 4.

(ε) Remarkable insertions or omissions in particular places : as, e. g. *πᾶσιν τοῖς ἔθνεσιν*, ch. xi. 17, which words are omitted in Matthew and Luke :—no mention of the *Jewish law* :—omission of the *limitations* of the mission of the Apostles in Matt. x. (common, however, also to Luke).

2. It is true that too much stress must not be laid on single particulars of this sort, as indicating *design*, where the sources of the Gospels were so scattered and fragmentary. But the *concurrence* of all these affords a very strong presumption that that class of readers was in the view of the Evangelist, in whose favour all these circumstances unite. See Prolegg. to Matthew, § iii. 2.

SECTION IV.

AT WHAT TIME IT WAS WRITTEN.

1. The most direct testimony on this head is that of Irenæus, iii. 1 (see above, § ii. 1, β), that it was after the deaths of Peter and Paul. This would place its date, at all events, *after the year* 63 (see Prolegg. to Acts, chronological table). But here, as in the case of the other Gospels, very little can be with any certainty inferred. We have conflicting traditions (see above, § ii.), and the Gospel itself affords us no clue whatever.

2. One thing only we may gather from the contents of the three first Gospels,—that none of them could have been *originally written* after the destruction of Jerusalem. Had they been, the omission of all allusion to so signal a fulfilment of our Lord's prophecies would be inexplicable. In the case indeed of Luke, we can approximate nearer than this (see below, ch. iv. § 4) ; but in those of Matthew and Mark, this is all which can be safely assumed as to the time of their first publication ;—that it was after the dispersion or even the death of most of the Apostles, and before the investment of Jerusalem by the Roman armies under Titus in the year 70.

SECTION V.

AT WHAT PLACE IT WAS WRITTEN.

Of this we have no trustworthy evidence. Most ancient writers (Clement, Eusebius, Jerome, Epiphanius, &c.) mention *Rome;* but apparently in connexion with the idea of Mark having written under the superintendence of Peter. Chrysostom mentions *Alexandria;* but no Alexandrine writer confirms the statement. In modern times, Storr has advanced an hypothesis that Mark wrote at Antioch, which he grounds, but insufficiently, on a comparison of ch. xv. 21, with Acts xi. 20.

SECTION VI.

IN WHAT LANGUAGE IT WAS WRITTEN.

1. There has never been any reasonable doubt that Mark wrote in *Greek.* The two Syriac versions contain a marginal note, that Mark *preached in Rome in Latin:* and four mss. (Centt. X.—XIII.) enumerated by Scholz, prolegg. p. xxx, append a notice, *τὸ κατὰ μάρκ. εὐαγ. ἐγράφη ῥωμαϊστὶ ἐν ῥώμῃ μετὰ ἔτη ιβ τῆς ἀναλήψεως τοῦ κυρίου.* This statement, however, is destitute of probability from any external or internal evidence, and is only one more assumption from the hypothetical publication in Rome under the superintendence of Peter, and for *Roman* converts.

2. Many writers of the Romish Church have defended the hypothesis of a Latin original, being biassed by a wish to maintain the authority of the Vulgate: and a pretended part of the *original autograph* of the Evangelist is still shewn in the Library of St. Mark's church at Venice; which, however, has been detected to be merely part of an ancient Latin MS. of the four Gospels,—another fragment of which exists, or existed, at Prague,—formerly preserved at Aquileia.

3. If Mark wrote in Latin, it is almost inconceivable that the original should have perished so early that no ancient writer should have made mention of the fact. For Latin was the language of a considerable and increasing body of Christians,—unlike Hebrew, which was little known, and belonged [but even this is doubtful] to a section of converts few in number:—yet ancient testimony is unanimous to Matthew's having written in Hebrew,—while we have not one witness to Mark having written in Latin.

SECTION VII.

GENUINENESS OF THE GOSPEL.

1. This has never been called in question, till very recently, by some of the German critics (Schleiermacher, Credner:—which last however (see Meyer, Com. ii. 9, note) has since seen reason to abandon his view,—and more recently still, Grimm) on, as it appears to me, wholly insufficient grounds. They allege that the testimony of Papias (see

above, § ii. 1, *a*) does not apply to the contents of our present Gospel, but that some later hand has worked up and embellished the original simple and unarranged notices of Mark, which have perished.

2. But neither do the words of Papias imply any such inference as that Mark's notices must have been simple and unarranged; nor, if they did, are they of any considerable authority in the matter. It is enough that from the very earliest time the Gospel has been known as that of Mark; confirmed as this evidence is by the circumstance, *that this name belongs to no great and distinguished founder of the Church*, to whom it might naturally be ascribed, but *to one, the ascription to whom can hardly be accounted for, except by its foundation in matter of fact.*

3. On the genuineness of the remarkable fragment at the end of the Gospel, see notes there.

SECTION VIII.

ITS STYLE AND CHARACTER.

1. Of the three first Gospels, that of Mark is the most distinct and peculiar in style. By far the greater part of those graphic touches which describe the look and gesture of our Lord, the arrangement or appearance of those around Him, the feelings with which He contemplated the persons whom He addressed, are contained in this Gospel. While the *matters related* are *fewer* than in either Matthew or Luke, Mark, in by far the greater number of common narrations, is the most *copious, and rich in lively and interesting detail.*

2. In one part only does Mark appear as an abridger of previously well-known facts; viz. in ch. i. 1—13, where,—his object being to detail the official life of our Lord,—he hastens through the previous great events,—the ministry of John, the baptism and temptation of Christ. But even in the abrupt transitions of this section, there is wonderful graphic power, presenting us with a series of life-like pictures, calculated to impress the reader strongly with the reality and dignity of the events related.

3. Throughout the Gospel, even where the narratives are the most copious, the same isolated character of each, the same abrupt transition from one to another, is observable. There is no attempt to bind on one section to another, or to give any sequences of events. But occasionally the very precision of the separate narratives of itself furnishes accurate and valuable chronological data:—e. g. the important one in ch. iv. 35, by which it becomes evident that the whole former part of Matthew's Gospel is out of chronological order.

4. Mark relates but few *discourses.* His object being to set forth

Jesus as the SON OF GOD (see ch. i. 1), he *principally* dwells on the *events* of His official life. But the same characteristics mark his report of our Lord's discourses, *where he relates them*, as we have observed in the rest of his narrative. While the sequence and connexion of the longer discourses was that which the Holy Spirit peculiarly brought to the mind of Matthew, the Apostle from whom Mark's record is derived seems to have been deeply penetrated and impressed by the *solemn iterations of cadence and expression*, and to have borne away the *very words themselves* and *tone* of the Lord's sayings. See especially, as illustrating this, the wonderfully sublime reply, ch. ix. 39—50.

5. According to the view adopted and vindicated in the notes on ch. xvi. 9—20, the Gospel terminates abruptly with the words *ἐφοβοῦντο γάρ*, ver. 8. That this was not intentionally done, but was a defect,—is apparent, by the addition, in apostolic times, of the authentic and most important fragment which now concludes the narrative [a].

6. I regard the existence of the Gospel of Mark as a gracious and valuable proof of the accommodation by the Divine Spirit of the records of the life of our Lord to the future necessities of the Church. While it contains little matter of fact which is not related in Matthew and Luke, and thus, generally speaking, forms only a confirmation of their more complete histories, it is so far from being a barren duplicate of that part of them which is contained in it, that it comes home to every reader with all the freshness of an individual mind, full of the Holy Ghost, intently fixed on the great object of the Christian's love and worship, reverently and affectionately following and recording His positions, and looks, and gestures, and giving us the very echo of the tones with which He spoke. And thus the believing student feels, while treating of and studying this Gospel, as indeed he does of each in its turn, that,—without venturing to compare with one another in value these rich and abiding gifts of the Holy Spirit to the Church,—the Gospel of Mark is at least as precious to him as any of the others; serving an end, and filling a void, which could not without spiritual detriment be left uncared for.

[[a] Since the above was written an important book has been published on this subject, "The Last Twelve Verses of the Gospel according to St. Mark," by the Rev. J. W. Burgon. Oxford, 1871. Mr. Burgon makes it appear that the numbers of Ammonius and Eusebius would have been more accurately designated the numbers of Eusebius, and that the patristic evidence against the passage ought to be limited to that of Eusebius, whose language has been adapted, or even literally copied, by the later authorities. All the Fathers, moreover, who are usually cited against these verses, treat them as part of the Gospel record; and as such they are recognized in the following Commentary; while Victor of Antioch expressly states *ἡμεῖς ἐξ ἀκριβῶν ἀντιγράφων ἐν πλείστοις εὑρόντες αὐτά, καὶ κατὰ τὸ Παλαιστιναῖον Εὐαγγέλιον, ὡς ἔχει ἡ ἀλήθεια Μάρκου, συντεθείκαμεν . . ., μετὰ τὸ* **ἐφοβοῦντο γάρ**, *τουτέστιν ἀπὸ τοῦ* **ἀναστὰς δὲ** . . . *καὶ καθ' ἑξῆς, μέχρι τοῦ* **διὰ τῶν ἐπακολουθούντων σημείων.** *Ἀμήν.*]

CHAPTER IV.

ON THE GOSPEL ACCORDING TO LUKE.

SECTION I.

ITS AUTHORSHIP.

1. ALTHOUGH the Author of this Gospel plainly enough speaks of himself in his Introduction, and in that to the Acts of the Apostles, we are left to gather his *name* from tradition. Here, however, as in the case of Mark, there seems to be no reasonable ground of doubt. It has been universally ascribed to *Lucas*, or *Luke*, spoken of Col. iv. 14, and again Philem. 24, and 2 Tim. iv. 11.

2. Of this person we know no more with any certainty than we find related in the Acts of the Apostles and the passages above referred to. From Col. iv. 11, 14, it would appear that he was *not born a Jew*, being there distinguished from οἱ ὄντες ἐκ περιτομῆς. It is, however, quite uncertain whether he had become a Jewish proselyte previous to his conversion to Christianity. His worldly calling was that of a *physician;* he is called ὁ ἰατρὸς ὁ ἀγαπητός by Paul, Col. iv. 14. A very late tradition (Niceph. Hist. Eccl. ii. 43), generally adopted by the Romish Church, makes him also to have been a *painter;* but it is in no respect deserving of credit. His birthplace is said by Eusebius (Hist. Eccl. iii. 4) and Jerome (De Viris Illustr. 7, vol. ii. p. 840) to have been Antioch, but traditionally only, and perhaps from a mistaken identification of him with Lucius, Acts xiii. 1 (Lucas = Lucanus, not Lucius). Tradition, as delivered by Epiphan. (Hær. li. 11, vol. i. p. 433), Pseudo-Origen, Theophylact, Euthymius, &c., makes him to have been *one of the seventy*, Luke x. 1 ; but this is *refuted by his own testimony*, in his preface,—where he by implication distinguishes himself from those who were eye-witnesses and ministers of the word. It seems to have arisen from *his Gospel alone containing the account of their mission.*

3. Luke appears to have attached himself to Paul during the second missionary journey of the Apostle, and at Troas (Acts xvi. 10). This may be inferred from his there first making use of *the first person plural* in his narrative; after saying (ver. 8) κατέβησαν εἰς Τρωάδα, he proceeds (ver. 10), εὐθέως ἐζητήσαμεν ἐξελθεῖν εἰς τὴν Μακεδονίαν. He thence accompanied Paul to Macedonia, remaining perhaps at Philippi (but see below, § iv. 3) until Paul returned thither again at the end of his

second visit to Greece, after the disturbance at Ephesus. Thence (Acts xx. 5) we find him again accompanying Paul to Asia and Jerusalem (xxi. 17); being apparently with him at Cæsarea during his imprisonment (xxiv. 23); and travelling with him to Rome (xxvii. 1—xxviii. 16). There we also find him remaining with the Apostle to a late period, very nearly till his martyrdom (see 2 Tim. iv. 11).

4. Of the time and manner of his death nothing certain is known, and the traditions are inconsistent one with another: some, as Greg. Naz., alleging him to have suffered martyrdom, while the general report is that he died a natural death.

SECTION II.

ITS ORIGIN.

1. A plain statement of the origin of this Gospel is given us by the Author himself, in his preface, ch. i. 1—4. He there states that many had taken in hand to draw up a statement, according to the testimony of those who were from the beginning eye-witnesses and ministers of the word, of the matters received (or fulfilled) among Christians; and that it therefore seemed good to him also, having carefully traced the progress of events from the first, to write an arranged account of the same to his friend (or patron) Theophilus.

2. From this we gather, (1) that Luke was *not himself an eye-witness, nor a minister of the word* (ὑπηρέτης τοῦ λόγου) *from the beginning*; (2) that he compiled his Gospel *from the testimony of eye-witnesses and Apostles*, which he carefully collected and arranged. For (1) he implicitly excludes himself from the number of the αὐτόπται κ. ὑπ. τ. λόγου: and (2) by the κἀμοί he includes himself among the πολλοί who made use of autoptic and apostolic testimony.

3. I have before proved *generally* that the Gospels of Matthew and Mark *cannot have been among the number of these* διηγήσεις *of which Luke speaks.* I may now add to those proofs, that if Luke had seen and *received*, as of apostolic authority, either or both of these Gospels, then his *variations from them* are, on his own shewing, unaccountable; if he had seen them, and *did not receive them*, his *coincidences with them* are equally unaccountable. The improbabilities and absurdities involved in his having either or both of them before him and working up their narratives into his own, I have before dealt with, in the general Prolegomena to the three Gospels.

4. Judging entirely from the phænomena presented by the Gospel itself, my conclusion with regard to its sources is the following:—that Luke, under the guidance of the Holy Spirit, drew up his Gospel inde-

pendently of, and without knowledge of, those of Matthew and Mark;—that he fell in with, in the main, the same cycle of apostolic teaching as the writers of those Gospels placed on record, viz. that which embraced principally the *Galilæan* life and ministry of our Lord, to the exclusion of that part of it which passed at Jerusalem before the formal call of the twelve Apostles;—but that he possessed other sources of information, not open to the compiler of Matthew's Gospel, nor to Mark.

5. To this latter circumstance may be attributed his access to (I believe, from its peculiar style and character) a *documentary* record of the events preceding and accompanying the birth of the Lord, derived probably from *her* who alone was competent to narrate several particulars contained in it:—his preservation of the precious and most important cycle of our Lord's discourses and parables contained in that large section of his Gospel, ch. ix. 51—xviii. 15, which is mostly peculiar to himself:—numerous other details scattered up and down in every part of his narrative, shewing autoptic information:—and, lastly, his enlarged account of some events following the Resurrection, and the narration, *by him alone*, of the circumstances accompanying the Ascension.

6. A tradition was very early current, that Luke's Gospel contained the substance of the *teaching of Paul*. Irenæus, Hær. iii. 1, p. 174, states: Λουκᾶς δὲ ὁ ἀκόλουθος Παύλου τὸ ὑπ' ἐκείνου κηρυσσόμενον εὐαγγέλιον ἐν βιβλίῳ κατέθετο[4]. See also Tertullian, cont. Marc. iv. 5, vol. ii. p. 367. But this is contradicted by the implicit assertion of the Evangelist himself in his preface, that the Gospel was compiled and arranged by himself from the testimony of those who ἀπ' ἀρχῆς, '*from the beginning of our Lord's ministry*,' *were eye-witnesses or ministers of the word*[5]. Among these it is not, of course, possible to reckon Paul.

7. It is however an interesting enquiry, how far his continued intercourse with the great Apostle of the Gentiles may have influenced his diction, or even his selection of facts. It is a remarkable coincidence, that the account of the institution of the Lord's Supper should be nearly verbatim the same[6] in Luke xxii. 19, and in 1 Cor. xi. 23,—and that Paul claims to have received this last *from the Lord*[7]. For we know

[4] Origen, Eusebius, and Jerome go so far as to understand the expression τὸ εὐαγγέλιόν μου, Rom. ii. 16, of the *Gospel of Luke*. But this is contrary to the usage of the word εὐαγγέλιον in the N. T.: see notes there.

[5] The Edinburgh Reviewer denies this. But it is implied by the ἡμῖν and ἔδοξεν κἀμοί. Had Paul been the source of his information, he would surely have expressed himself otherwise in his preface, and not have so plainly classed himself among those who were dependent for their information on the αὐτόπται and ὑπηρέται τοῦ λόγου.

[6] Even after conforming the texts to the best MSS. Cf. the two passages.

[7] It is impossible, with the Edinburgh Reviewer, to regard ἀπὸ τοῦ κυρίου here as

that to compensate to Paul in his apostolic office for the want of autoptic authority, and to constitute him a witness to the truth of the gospel, a revelation was made to him,—to which he refers, Gal. i. 12 : Eph. iii. 3 : 1 Cor. xi. 23 ; xv. 3,—embracing at least the leading facts of the evangelic history. And this circumstance may have acted imperceptibly on the mind of Luke, and even shaped or filled out some of his narratives, in aid of direct historic sources of testimony.

8. There is *very little trace of Paul's peculiar diction*, or *prominence given to the points which it became his especial work to inculcate* in the Gospel of Luke. Doubtless we may trace a *similar cast of mind and feeling* in some instances ; as e. g. Luke's carefulness to record the sayings of our Lord which were assertive of His unrestricted love for Jew and Gentile alike : Luke iv. 25 ff. ; ix. 52 ff. ; x. 30 ff. ; xvii. 16, 18. We may observe too that in Luke those parables and sayings are principally found, which most directly regard the great doctrine of man's free justification by grace through faith : e. g. ch. xv. 11 ff. ; xvii. 10 ; xviii. 14, in which latter place the use of δεδικαιωμένος (see note there) is remarkable. These instances, however, are but few,—and it may perhaps be doubted whether Commentators in general have not laid too great stress upon them. It would be very easy to trace similar relations and analogies in the other Gospels, if we were bent upon doing so.

SECTION III.

FOR WHAT READERS AND WITH WHAT OBJECT IT WAS WRITTEN.

1. Both these questions are formally answered for us by the Evangelist himself. He states, ch. i. 3, that he wrote primarily *for the benefit of one Theophilus*, and *that he might know the certainty of those accounts which had formed the subject of his catechetical instruction.*

2. But we can hardly suppose this object to have been the *only* moving cause to the great work which Luke was undertaking. The probabilities of the case, and the practice of authors in inscribing their works to particular persons, combine to persuade us that Luke must have regarded his friend as the representative of a class of readers for

spurious. The variations are otherwise accounted for: παρά, by παρέλαβον preceding ;—θεοῦ, by the invariable practice of noting in the margin, where ὁ κύριος occurs, θεός, or χριστός, by way of explanation. And if it be genuine, then Paul did certainly receive *matters of fact* by special revelation. The idea of the facts of the gospel history having been "familiar to Paul when he was a persecutor" is too absurd to require refutation, as will at once appear from applying it to such a fact as this very one, viz. the institution of the Lord's Supper.

whom his Gospel was designed. And in enquiring what that class was, we must deal with the data furnished by the Gospel itself.

3. In it we find *universality* the predominant character. There is no marked regard paid to Jewish readers, as in Matthew, nor to Gentiles, as in Mark ; if there be any preference, it seems rather on the side of the latter. In conformity with Jewish practice, we have a genealogy of our Lord, which however does not, as in Matthew, stop with Abraham, but traces up his descent even to the progenitor of the human race. Commentators have noticed that Luke principally records those sayings and acts of our Lord by which God's mercy to the Gentiles is set forth : see ch. xv. 11 ff. ; xviii. 10 ; xix. 5 (but see notes there) ; x. 33 ; xvii. 19 ; ix. 52—56 ; iv. 25—27. Such instances, however, are not much to be relied on ;—see above, ch. i. § ii. 6 ;—to which I will add, that it would be easy to construct a similar list to prove the same point with respect to Matthew or John [8];—and I therefore much prefer assigning the above character of *universality* to this Gospel, which certainly is visible throughout it. That it was constructed for Gentile readers as well as for Jews, is plain; and is further confirmed from the fact of its author having been the friend and companion of the great Apostle of the Gentiles.

4. I infer then that the Gospel was designed *for the general use of Christians*, whether Jews or Gentiles ; and, subordinately to this general purpose, for those readers whose acquaintance with Jewish customs and places was sufficient to enable them to dispense with those elucidations of them which Mark and John have given, but which are not found in Matthew or Luke.

5. The object of the Gospel has been sufficiently declared in Luke's own words above cited,—*that the converts might know the certainty of those things in which they had received oral instruction as catechumens ;* in other words, that the portions of our Lord's life and discourses thus

[8] e.g Matthew relates the *visit of the Magi*, ch. ii. 1 ff. ; refers to *Galilee of the Gentiles* seeing a great light, ch. iv. 15, 16 ; 'Many shall come *from the East and West*,' &c. ch. viii. 11 ; '*Come unto Me, all ye that labour*,' ch. xi. 28 ; the *Syrophœnician woman* (*not related by Luke*), ch. xv. 21 ff. ; 'The Kingdom of God shall be *taken from you*, and *given to a nation*,' &c. ch. xxi. 43 (*omitted by Luke*) ; 'the *elect from the four winds of heaven*' (*not in Luke*), ch. xxiv. 31 ; *the judgment of πάντα τὰ ἔθνη*, ch. xxv. 31—46 ; '*Make disciples of πάντα τὰ ἔθνη*,' ch. xxviii. 19.—Again, John relates the *visit to the Samaritans*, ch. iv. ; 'the *other sheep not of this fold*,' ch. x. 16 ; '*not for that nation only*, but that he should gather together in one *the children of God that were scattered abroad*,' ch. xi. 52 ; the *request of the Greeks* at the feast, ch. xii. 20, &c. &c. See the view, that Luke wrote for *Greeks* principally, ingeniously illustrated in the lecture prefixed to this Gospel in the first volume of Bp. Wordsworth's Greek Testament : which however, like the other notices of this learned writer, is written far too strongly in the spirit of an advocate, who can see only that which it is his aim to prove.

imparted to them might receive both permanence, by being committed to writing,—and completion, by being incorporated in a detailed narrative of His acts and sayings.

SECTION IV.

AT WHAT TIME IT WAS WRITTEN.

1. We are enabled to approximate to the time of the publication of this Gospel with much more certainty than we can to that of any of the others. The enquiry may be thus conducted.—We may safely assume that the '*former treatise*' of Acts i. 1, can be no other than this Gospel. And on that follows the inference, that the Gospel was published *before the Acts of the Apostles.* Now the last event recorded in the Acts is an interview of Paul with the Jews, shortly after his arrival in Rome. We further have the publication of the Acts, by the words of ch. xxviii. 30, postponed *two whole years* after that arrival and interview ; but, I believe, *no longer than that.* For had Paul continued longer than that time in his hired house before the publication, it must have been so stated ; and had he left Rome or that house, or had any remarkable event happened to him before the publication, we cannot suppose that so careful a recorder as Luke would have failed to bring his work down to the time then present, by noticing such departure or such event. I assume then the publication of the Acts to have taken place *two years after Paul's arrival at Rome:* i. e. according to Wieseler (Chron. des Apostolischen Zeitalters, pp. 117, 118 : see chronological table in Prolegg. to Acts, Vol. II.), in the spring of A.D. 63.

2. We have therefore a fixed date, before which the Gospel *must have been published.* But if I am not mistaken, we have, by internal evidence, the date of its publication removed some time back from this date. It is hardly probable that Luke would speak of, as ὁ πρῶτος λόγος, a work in which he was then, or had been very lately, engaged. But not to dwell on this,—even allowing that the prefatory and dedicatory matter, as is usually the case, may have come *last* from the hands of the author,—I find in the account of the Ascension, which immediately follows, a much more cogent proof, that the Gospel had been some considerable time published. For while it recapitulates the Gospel account just so much that we can trace the same hand in it (compare Acts i. 4 with Luke xxiv. 49), it is manifestly a *different account*, much fuller in particulars, and certainly *unknown to the Evangelist when he wrote his Gospel.* Now, as we may conclude, in accordance with the παρηκολουθηκότι πᾶσιν ἀκριβῶς, of Luke i. 3, that he would have carefully sought out every available source of information at the time of writing his Gospel,—this becoming acquainted with a new account of the Ascen-

sion implies that in the mean time fresh sources of information had been opened to him. And this would most naturally be by *change of place*, seeing that various fixed cycles of apostolic teaching were likely to be current in, and about, the respective mother churches. Now the changes of place in Luke's recent history had been,—two years before, from Cæsarea to Rome, Acts xxvii. 1 ff.; two years and a half before that, from Philippi to Jerusalem, Acts xx. 6; xxi. 15 ff.,—and Cæsarea. This last is left to be inferred from his leaving Cæsarea with Paul, ch. xxvii. 1;—at all events he was during this time in Palestine, with, or near Paul. I shall make it probable in the Prolegomena to Vol. II. that during this period he was engaged in collecting materials for and compiling the Acts of the Apostles; and by consequence (see above), that in all probability the Gospel had been then written and published. This would place its publication before A.D. 58;—consequently, before the traditional date of the Gospel of Matthew,—see above, ch. ii. § iv.

3. Tracing Luke's history further back than this,—it has been thought that he remained at Philippi during the whole time comprised between Acts xvii. 1 and xx. 6, because he disuses the first person at the first of those dates, at Philippi,—and resumes it also at Philippi, at the second. Now this was a period of *seven years:* far too long for such an inference as the above to be made with any probability. During this time he *may* have travelled into Palestine, and collected the information which he incorporated in his Gospel. For that it was collected *in Palestine*, is on all accounts probable. And that it should have been published much before this, is, I think, improbable.

4. My reasons are the following:—I have implied in the former part of these Prolegomena, that it is not likely that the present evangelic collections would be made until the dispersion of all or most of the Apostles on their missionary journeys. Besides this, the fact of numerous διηγήσεις having been *already drawn up* after the model of the apostolic narrative teaching, forbids us to suppose their teaching by oral communication to have been in its fulness still available. Now the Apostles, or the greater part of them, were certainly at Jerusalem at the time of the council in Acts xv. 1—5 ff., i. e. about A.D. 50. How soon after that time their dispersion took place, it is quite impossible to determine:—but we have certainly *this date* as our *terminus a quo*, before which, as I believe, no Gospel could have been published.

5. After this dispersion of the Apostles, it will be necessary to allow some time to elapse for the διηγήσεις of which Luke speaks (ch. i. 1) to be drawn up;—not less certainly than one or two years, or more; which would bring us just about to the time when he was left behind by Paul in Philippi. This last arrangement must however be, from its merely hypothetical grounds, very uncertain.

6. At all events, we have thus eight years, A.D. 50—58, as the limits within which it is probable that the Gospel was published. And, without pretending to minute accuracy in these two limits, we may at least set it down as likely that the publication did not take place much before Luke and Paul are found together, nor after the last journey which Paul made to Jerusalem, A.D. 58. And even if the grounds on which this latter is concluded be objected to, we have, as a final resort, the fixed date of the *publication of the Acts* two years after Paul's arrival at Rome, *after which*, by internal evidence, *the Gospel cannot have been published.*

SECTION V.

AT WHAT PLACE IT WAS WRITTEN.

1. Our answer to this enquiry will of course depend upon the considerations discussed in the last section. Adopting the view there taken, we find Luke in Asia Minor, Syria, or Palestine (probably) previously to his first journey with Paul A.D. 51 ; and from that time till his second journey A.D. 58, perhaps remaining in Greece, but perhaps also travelling for the sake of collecting information for his Gospel. At all events, at the latter part of this period he is again found at Philippi. We need not then dissent from the early tradition reported by Jerome (Prolog. in Matt. vol. vii. pp. 3, 4), that Luke published his Gospel "in Achaiæ Bœotiæque partibus," as being on the whole the most likely inference.

2. The inscription in the Syriac version,—and Simeon Metaphrastes in the tenth century,—report that the Gospel was written at Alexandria, but apparently without any authority.

SECTION VI.

IN WHAT LANGUAGE IT WAS WRITTEN.

There never has been any doubt that Luke wrote his Gospel in Greek. His familiarity with Greek terms and idioms, and above all, the classical style of his preface, are of themselves convincing internal evidence that it was so[9].

SECTION VII.

GENUINENESS OF THE GOSPEL.

1. It has been generally and almost unanimously acknowledged that the Gospel which we now possess is that written and published by Luke.

[9] See the lecture above referred to, prefixed to St. Luke in Wordsworth's G. Test. vol. i.

2. Whatever doubts may have been raised by rationalistic Commentators as to the genuineness of the *two first chapters*, have been adopted in aid of their attempts to overthrow their *authenticity* (on which see the next section); and have rested on no sufficient ground of themselves. Their principal appeal is to Marcion, who notoriously mutilated the Gospel, to make it favour his views of the Person of Christ.

3. On the genuineness of ch. xxii. 43, 44, see various readings and notes there.

SECTION VIII.

THE AUTHENTICITY OF THE TWO FIRST CHAPTERS.

1. If the view maintained above of the probable time of the publication of the Gospel be adopted,—and its later terminus, the publication of the Acts two years after Paul's imprisonment at Rome began, is, I think, *beyond question*,—I cannot see how any reasonable doubt can be thrown upon the authenticity of this portion of the narrative. For there were those living, who might have contradicted any false or exaggerated account of our Lord's birth and the events which accompanied it. If not the Mother of our Lord herself, yet His brethren were certainly living: and the universal reception of the Gospel in the very earliest ages sufficiently demonstrates that no objection to this part of the sacred narrative had been heard of as raised by them.

2. The ἀκριβῶς παρηκολουθηκότι of Luke forbids us to imagine that he would have inserted any narrative in his Gospel which he had not ascertained to rest upon trustworthy testimony, as far as it was in his power to ensure this: and the means of ensuring it must have been at that time *so ample and satisfactory*, that I cannot imagine for a moment any other origin for the account, than *such testimony*.

3. If we enquire what was probably the *source* of the testimony, I answer, that but one person is conceivable as delivering it, and that person the Mother of our Lord. She was living in the Christian body for some time after the Ascension; and would most certainly have been appealed to for an account of the circumstances attending His birth and infancy.

4. If she gave any account of these things, it is inconceivable that this account should not have found its way into the records of the Lord's life possessed by the Christian Church, but that instead of it a spurious one should have been adopted by two of our Evangelists, and that so shortly after, or even coincident with, her own presence in the Church.

5. Just as inconceivable, even supposing the last difficulty sur-

mounted, is the formation of a mythical, or in any other way unreal account of these things, and its adoption, in the primitive age of the Church. For the establishment of this I refer to the late Professor Mill's able tract, On the Mythic Interpretation of Luke i.;—in which he has stated and severally refuted the arguments of Strauss and the rationalists.

6. I infer then that the two first chapters of this Gospel contain the account given by the Mother of our Lord, of His birth, and its prefatory and attendant circumstances; of some of which circumstances that in Matt. i. 18—25 is a more compendious, and wholly independent account.

SECTION IX.

ITS STYLE AND CHARACTER.

1. We might have expected from Luke's name and profession, that he was a man of education, and versed in the elegant use of the Greek, which was then the polite language in the Roman empire. We accordingly find that while we have very numerous Hebraisms in his Gospel, we also have far more classical idioms, and a much freer use of Greek compounds than in the others. By consulting the marginal references in this edition it will be seen that the number of *ἅπαξ λεγόμενα* in Luke is very great, far exceeding those in any other Gospel; and that very many of them are classically-authorized compound words.

2. The composition of the sentences is more studied and elaborate than in Matthew or Mark;—the Evangelist appears more frequently in the narrative, delivering his own estimate of men and things—e. g. ch. xvi. 14; vii. 29, 30; xix. 11 al.;—he seems to love to recount instances of our Lord's tender compassion and mercy;—and in *the report of His parables*, e. g. in ch. xv., is particularly simple in diction, and calculated to attract and retain the attention of his readers.

3. In narrative, this Evangelist is very various, according to the copiousness or otherwise of the sources from which he drew. Sometimes he merely gives a hasty compendium: at others he is most minute and circumstantial in detail, and equally graphic in description with Mark: see as instances of this latter, ch. vii. 14; ix. 29. It has been remarked (see Olshausen, Bibl. Comm. i. p. 20) that Luke gives with extreme accuracy not so much the *discourses*, as the *observations* and *occasional sayings* of our Lord, with the replies of those who were present. This is especially the case in his long and important narrative of the journey up to Jerusalem, ch. ix. 51—xviii. 14.

4. On the question how far those doctrines especially enforced by the

great Apostle of the Gentiles are to be traced, as inculcated or brought forward in this Gospel, see above in this chapter, § ii. 7.

5. In *completeness*, this Gospel must rank first among the four. The Evangelist begins with the announcement of the birth of Christ's Forerunner, and concludes with the particulars of the Ascension: thus embracing the *whole great procession of events by which our Redemption by Christ was ushered in, accomplished, and sealed in heaven.* And by recording the allusion to the *promise of the Father* (ch. xxiv. 49), he has introduced, so to speak, a note of passage to that other history, in which the *fulfilment of that promise*, the great *result* of Redemption, was to be related. It may be remarked, that this *completeness*,—while it shews the earnest diligence used by the sacred writer in searching out, and making use of every information within his reach,—forms an additional proof that he can never have seen the Gospels of Matthew and Mark,—or *he would* (to say nothing of the other difficulties attending this view, which have before been dealt with in ch. i.) *most certainly have availed himself of those parts of their narratives, which are now not contained in his own.*

6. The chronological notice, on the discovery, by the younger Zumpt, that Quirinus was twice governor of Syria, and the light thus thrown on Luke ii. 2, inserted here in the third edition, is now incorporated in the notes ad loc.

CHAPTER V.

THE GOSPEL ACCORDING TO JOHN.

SECTION I.

ITS AUTHORSHIP.

1. The universal belief of the Christian Church has ascribed this Gospel to the Apostle John. I shall not here anticipate the discussion respecting its genuineness (see below, § vi.), but assume that it has been rightly so ascribed.

2. John was son of Zebedee and Salome, and younger (?)[1] brother of James. His father was a Galilæan, and by occupation a fisherman on

[1] This is by no means certain. While Matt. and Mark always write 'Peter, James, and John'—Luke, in ch. ix. 28 and Acts i. 13 (not in rec.), has 'Peter, John, and James;' although in the other catalogue of the Apostles, Luke vi. 14, he keeps the usual order. It is impossible to say whether the order arose from any account at all being taken of mere seniority.

the lake of Galilee. Where he resided, is uncertain—perhaps at Bethsaida: but the circumstance of Simon Peter, who was of that place, being (Luke v. 10) partner in the fishing trade, or perhaps, in that particular expedition only with the sons of Zebedee, is no proof as to *their* residence there also.

3. The family of John seems not to have been one of the lowest class: we find *hired servants* in the ship with Zebedee, Mark i. 20; their mother Salome was one of those women who came with Jesus from Galilee, and ministered to Him of their substance, Luke viii. 3; xxiii. 55, compared with Mark xvi. 1; the same Salome was one of those who bought sweet spices and ointments to anoint Him (Mark, ibid.); and, John xix. 27, we find John himself taking the mother of our Lord εἰς τὰ ἴδια, which though (see note there) it *need not* imply that John had *then a house at Jerusalem,* certainly denotes that he had some fixed habitation, into which she was received. If, as is most likely, John be meant by the ἄλλος μαθητής of ch. xviii. 15, he was personally known to the High Priest Caiaphas. From all these facts the inference is that his family belonged to the *middle class of society;* the higher grade of those who carried on the by no means despised or ungainful business of fishermen on the sea of Galilee.

4. If (see note on John i. 41) the second of the two disciples who heard the Baptist's testimony to Jesus, and followed Him in consequence, was John himself,—we have his acquaintance with our Lord dating from the very beginning of His ministry. And to this agree the contents of chapters ii. iii. iv. v., containing particulars of the Ministry at Jerusalem and in Galilee which happened previous to the commencement of the official record of the other Evangelists. It seems that John accompanied our Lord to Jerusalem,—with perhaps those of the Apostles already called,—and witnessed those incidents which he has related in that part of his Gospel.

5. In the intervals of our Lord's first circuits and journeys, the Apostles seem to have returned to their families and occupations. Thus in Luke v. 1—11, we find the sons of Zebedee, as well as Simon Peter, again engaged in fishing, and solemnly and finally summoned by Jesus to follow Him;—an incident which, as Lücke acknowledges (Comm. in Joh., Einleitung, p. 12), would be inexplicable even by the miracle, unless there had been a previous acquaintance on their part with our Lord.

6. From that time John belonged to that chosen number known as 'the Twelve,' who were nearest to the Person of Jesus during His ministry. And of that number, he seems to have been the most personally beloved by our Lord. For the assumption that he is the author of our Gospel, also identifies him with 'the disciple whom Jesus loved,' so often mentioned in it (see ch. xiii. 23; xix. 26; xx. 2; xxi. 7, 20, 24). He, together with his brother James, and Peter, was witness of the

raising of Jaeirus's daughter, Mark v. 37; also of the transfiguration, Matt. xvii. 1 ff.; and of the agony in Gethsemane; he lay on the bosom of Jesus at the last supper; and was recognized by Peter as being the innermost in His personal confidence, John xiii. 23. To him was committed the charge of the mother of Jesus, by Himself when dying on the Cross, John xix. 26, 27.

7. And to this especial love of the Redeemer John appears to have corresponded in devoted affection and faithfulness. He fled, it is true, with the rest, at the dark hour of the capture of Jesus: but we find him, together with Peter, soon rallying again,—and from that time, John xviii. 15, 16, even to the end, xix. 25 ff., an eye-witness of the sufferings of his Divine Master. In John xxi. we find the same personal distinction bestowed on the beloved disciple by our Lord after His Resurrection.

8. In the Acts of the Apostles, John comes before us but very seldom, and always in connexion with and thrown into the background by Peter. See Acts iii. 1 ff.; viii. 14—25. The history leaves him at Jerusalem: where however he appears *not to have been on Paul's first visit to Jerusalem*, Gal. i. 18 ff., A.D. 38—40 (see chronological table in Prolegg. to Acts, Vol. II.), for he states that he saw *none of the Apostles save Peter and James*. On his second visit, Acts xi. 29, 30, cir. A.D. 43 (see as above), we have no intimation whether John was there or not. If the journey to determine the question about circumcision, Acts xv. 1, was identical with Paul's third visit, Gal. ii. 1 (which I have maintained in Prolegg. to Acts, Vol. II., note 1 to Chron. Table), then at that date (i. e. cir. A.D. 50) John was in Jerusalem. After this time, we lose sight of the Apostles, nor can we with any approach to certainty point out the period of their final dispersion. It took place probably some time between this council and Paul's last visit to Jerusalem, Acts xxi. 18 (cir. A.D. 60), when we find only James resident there.

9. For the after-history of John, we are dependent on tradition. And here we have evidence more trustworthy than in the case of any other Apostle.

(α) It is related by Polycrates, Bishop of Ephesus at the end of the second century,—in his Epistle to Victor Bishop of Rome on the keeping of Easter,—that John, whom he numbers among the great lights (στοιχεῖα, see Eusebius, iii. 31, and Heinichen's note) of Asia, died and was buried (κεκοίμηται) in Ephesus.

(β) Irenæus also,—the scholar of Polycarp, who himself was a disciple of John,—relates that John remained in Ephesus till the times of Trajan (Adv. Hær. ii. 39, p. 148; iii. 1 and 3, pp. 174, 178, cited also by Eusebius, iii. 23). To the same effect testify Clement of Alexandria (Euseb. ibid.), Origen (Euseb. iii. 1), Eusebius (ibid.), and Jerome (De Viris Illustr. c. 9, vol. ii. p. 845).

10. But assuming as a fact the long residence and death of the Apostle at Ephesus, we in vain seek any clue to guide us as to the time when, or the place whence, he came thither. The Asiatic Churches were founded by St. Paul, who made it a rule not to encroach on the field of labour of any other Apostle, Rom. xv. 20:—who never, in his Epistles to the Asiatic Churches, makes any mention of nor sends any salutation to John :—who, in his parting speech to the Elders of the Ephesian Church at Miletus (Acts xx.), certainly did not anticipate the coming of an Apostle among them. So much then we may set down as certain, that the arrival of John in Asia must have been after the death of Paul.

11. We may perhaps with some appearance of probability conjecture that the dangers which evidently beset the Asiatic Churches in Paul's lifetime,—and to which Peter in his First Epistle, written to them, not indistinctly alludes (see 1 Pet. i. 14 ; ii. 1, 2, 7, 8, 12, 16 al. fr.),—had taken so serious a form after the removal of Paul their father in the faith, that John found it requisite to fix his residence and exercise apostolic authority among them. This is supposed by Lücke, Einl. p. 24, and Neander, Leitung u. Pflanzung der Kirche, 4th edition, p. 614.

12. But we are as far as ever, even if this conjecture be adopted, from arriving at any method of accounting for the interval between John's leaving Jerusalem, and his coming to Asia Minor : a period, on any computation, of nearly six years, A.D. 58—64. It is not necessary, however, as Lücke also observes, to reject a tradition so satisfactorily grounded as that of John's residence and death at Ephesus, on this account ;—especially when we consider that we seem compelled to interpose some influence corresponding to that of John, between the state of the Asiatic Churches as shewn in the Pauline Epistles, and that in the time of Polycarp, who immediately followed the apostolic age. See Neander, Leitung u. Pflanzung, 4th edition, p. 615. I reserve the discussion of the other element of uncertainty in this matter,—the possible confusion of two persons named John, the Apostle and the Presbyter, for the Prolegomena to the Second Epistle of John, in Vol. IV.

13. I mention here,—reserving its discussion for the Prolegomena to the Apocalypse, Vol. IV.,—the tradition universally received in the early Church, which records that the Apostle John was exiled under Domitian to the island of Patmos. *Assuming the Apocalypse to be his work, the fact of such an exile is established*, see Rev. i. 9,—but the time left uncertain. But even those who do not ascribe the Apocalypse to him, relate this exile, e. g. Eusebius, Hist. Eccl. iii. 20.

14. It is also related (Euseb. ibid.) that he returned under Nerva to Ephesus, and that his death (under Trajan, see above) took place (in what manner is uncertain, but probably not by martyrdom) in extreme old age. It would be out of place here to recount the other traditions, some of them highly interesting, which are extant. See one of them in

note on 1 John iii. 18, and the whole recounted and commented on in Stanley's Sermons and Essays on the Apostolic Age, pp. 275—289.

SECTION II.

ITS SOURCES.

1. In several places the Author of this Gospel plainly declares or implies that he relates what he had seen and heard. See ch. i. 14; xiii. 23; xviii. 15; xix. 26; xx. 2, and especially xix. 35 [2]. Also xxi. 24.

2. And with this declaration the contents of the Gospel agree. Amidst the entire disregard of minute specifications of sequence or locality as a general rule, in almost every narrative we have undoubted marks of autoptic testimony.

3. The only question which arises on receiving this as the fact, has reference to the *diversity of style observed in the discourses* of our Lord as related by the three other Evangelists, and as related by John. In their more or less common report, a certain similarity of style is supposed to be observable throughout the parables and sayings of Jesus, which is wholly absent from them in John's Gospel. Let us examine this matter more closely.

4. In order to form a satisfactory judgment on this point, it would be necessary to be in possession of some *common matter reported by both.* But such common matter, in any sufficient quantity for this purpose, *we do not possess.* No one discourse is reported by all four. Certain insulated sayings are so reported: e.g. compare John ii. 19 with Matt. xxvi. 61 and Mark xiv. 58; John vi. 20 with Matt. xiv. 27 and Mark vi. 50; John xii. 7, 8 with Matt. xxvi. 10, 11 and Mark xiv. 6, 7; John xiii. 20 with Matt. x. 40 and Luke x. 16; John xiii. 21 with Matt. xxvi. 21 and Mark xiv. 18; John xiii. 37, 38 with Matt. xxvi. 33 and ||; John xx. 19 with Luke xxiv. 36. Now in these common reports, amidst much variety in verbal and circumstantial detail, such as might have been expected from independent narrators, there is *no such differences of style observable.*

5. We have then the following remarkable phænomenon presented by the two classes of narrators: that the sayings of our Lord reported by the one are *different from,* and *exclusive of* those contained in the other. And this must very much modify our view of the subject in question.

[2] On the futility of the attempt to shew from this verse, on account of κἀκεῖνος, that the eye-witness spoken of is a different person from the writer of the Gospel, see note on the usage of ἐκεῖνος by our Evangelist, John vii. 29.

6. It would be in the highest degree probable that our Lord would discourse mainly and usually on *two great branches of divine truth:* one of these being, the *nature and moral requirements of that kingdom which He came to found among men*, which would embrace the greater part of His discourses to the multitude,—His outer or popular sayings,—His parables and prophecies:—and the other, *the deeper spiritual verities relating to his own Divine Person and Mission.* Of these latter, there would be two subdivisions: one class of them would be spoken in the gracious condescension of love to His own disciples when conversing privately with them, and the other in the fire of holy zeal when contending against His bitter adversaries, the rulers of the Jews.

7. Now of the two greater classes just mentioned, let us enquire which would most naturally form the matter of the oral apostolic teaching to the Churches in the first age. Let it be remembered that that teaching was mostly elementary,—matter of catechization;—selected for the edification of those who were to be built up as Christian converts. Would it not unquestionably be *the first?* Granted, that some few of those deeper sayings (deeper, I mean, in their very *form* and *primary reference*) might occasionally find their place in the reports of longer discourses (see e.g. Matt. xi. 27: Luke x. 22), yet I cannot imagine the main stream of oral apostolic teaching to have been otherwise composed than as we find it: viz. of the popular discourses and parables of our Lord, to the exclusion for the most part of His inner teaching and deeper revelations respecting his own Divine Person. These, in case the Apostles had been suffered by Providence to carry on systematically their testimony to the Church, might have followed after: but certainly they would not be likely to form the *first* subject of their oral teaching.

8. But that they would dwell powerfully on their minds, and in proportion to their individual receptivity of the Spirit and Person of their Lord, is most evident. And this consideration, united with that of the very nature and purpose of the apostolic office, and with the promise specially recorded that the Spirit should bring to their minds all things which He had said to them, will fully account for there arising, late in the apostolic age, so copious and particular a report of these inner and personal discourses of our Lord.

9. That such a report should be characterized in some measure by the individual mind which has furnished it, was to be expected, on any view of spiritual guidance. But that this individuality has in any considerable degree modified the report, I think extremely improbable. Taking the circumstances into consideration, the relation of John to his Divine Master, the employment and station from which he was called, and the facts also which have been noticed respecting the sayings reported by all in common, I think it much more probable, that the character and diction of our Lord's discourses entirely penetrated and

assimilated the habits of thought of His beloved Apostle; so that in his first epistle he writes in the very tone and spirit of those discourses; and when reporting the sayings of his own former teacher the Baptist, he gives them, consistently with the deepest inner truth of narration (see note on ch. iii. 31), the forms and cadences so familiar and habitual to himself.

10. It belongs to the present section of our subject, to enquire how far it may be supposed that John had seen or used the synoptic Gospels. I confess myself wholly unable to receive the supposition *that any of them, in their present form, had ever been seen by him.* On such a supposition, the phænomena presented by his Gospel would be wholly inexplicable. To those parts of it which he has in common with them, the reasonings of the former part of these Prolegomena will apply. And though these are not so considerable in extent as in the case of the three Gospels, yet they are quite important enough to decide this question. The account and testimony of the Baptist in ch. i.;—the miraculous feeding in ch. vi.;—the whole history from ch. xii. 1, in its subject-matter, will come under this description. Let any *common passages* be selected, and tried by the considerations above advanced, ch. i. § ii.,—and our conclusion must be that the report is *an independent one, not influenced or modified by theirs.* Of those parts of his Gospel which are peculiar to himself, I will speak in another section.

11. It is, however, an entirely distinct question, how far John had in his view the generally received oral teaching from which our three Gospels are derived. That he himself, answering so strictly to the description in Acts i. 21,—laying so much weight as he does on *testimony*, ch. i. 19; xix. 35; xxi. 24,—bore his part, and that no inconsiderable one, in the Apostles' witness to the facts of the evangelic history,—I take for granted. It will follow that he was aware of the general nature and contents of that cycle of narratives and discourses of our Lord which became current at Jerusalem from his own testimony and that of the other Apostles. Accordingly we find him in his Gospel *assuming as known, certain facts contained in that cycle.* See ch. vii. 41, and note,—ch. xi. 1,—also ch. i. 40, where *Simon Peter* is referred to as *one known*, before the giving of the latter name is related.

12. I can hardly however suppose, that John wrote with any fixed design of filling up by a supplementary Gospel the deficiencies of the generally-received oral account. Sometimes, e. g. ch. vi. 1—14; xviii. xix., he goes over *the same ground* with it: and in no part can it by the most ingenious application of the supplementary theory be shewn, that he in any respect produces or aims at the effect of a work designed to fill up and elucidate those which have gone before. This point will be dwelt on more at length in the next section.

13. I have no hesitation, therefore, in receiving as the true account

of the source of this Gospel, that generally given and believed;—viz. *that we have it from the autoptic authority of the Apostle himself.*

SECTION III.

FOR WHAT READERS AND WITH WHAT OBJECT IT WAS WRITTEN.

1. This Gospel presupposes readers already Christians, and was written to build them up and confirm them in the faith. (See ch. xix. 35; xx. 31.) It is, as Lücke remarks (Einl. p. 185), neither complete enough, nor elementary enough, for the *first founding* of a belief in Christ in the mind. This must have been, even as early as the apostolic times, the work of no written Gospel (see Luke i. 1—4), but of the oral preaching of the word.

2. Being written then for Christian readers, the *main and ultimate* purpose as regards them is sufficiently declared in ch. xx. 31,—ταῦτα γέγραπται ἵνα πιστεύσητε ὅτι Ἰησοῦς ἐστιν ὁ χριστὸς ὁ υἱὸς τοῦ θεοῦ, καὶ ἵνα πιστεύοντες ζωὴν ἔχητε ἐν τῷ ὀνόματι αὐτοῦ.

3. This purpose however, as it would be common to all the sacred writings of the New Testament more or less, in no way accounts for the *peculiar cast of the Gospel*, or the portions of the Christian's faith which are most prominently brought out in it. These will require closer examination.

4. It will at once appear, that *some especial occasion* must have induced John to write so pointedly as he has done on certain doctrines, —and to adopt, in doing so, a nomenclature unknown to the rest of the New Testament writers. Some state of opinion in the Church must have rendered it necessary for the Apostle to state strongly and clearly the truth about which error was prevalent, or questions had been raised: the method of speaking which even *he*, under the guidance of the Spirit, adopted to convey that truth, must have become familiar to and valued by the educated and philosophic minds in the Christian community.

5. It may be well to set down the opinions of the ancients on this, before we enter into the matter itself.

Irenæus states that John wrote his Gospel to controvert the errors of Cerinthus, and before him the Nicolaitans[3]. Tertullian (De Præscript. adv. Hær. 33, vol. ii. p. 46) in the main agrees with this. Epiphanius

[3] "Hanc fidem annuntians Johannes Domini discipulus, volens per evangelii annuntiationem auferre eum qui a Cerintho inseminatus erat hominibus errorem, et multo prius ab his qui dicuntur Nicolaitæ, qui sunt vulsio ejus, quæ falso cognominatur scientia,—ut confunderet eos et suaderet quoniam unus Deus qui omnia fecit per verbum suum, ... sic inchoavit in ea quæ est secundum evangelium doctrina, &c." Adv. Hær. iii. 11, p. 188.

(Hær. li. 12, vol. i. p. 434) and Jerome[4] repeat it as a certain fact, that John wrote against Cerinthus, but instead of the Nicolaitans, they mention the Ebionites. Those who assert him to have written against Valentinus or Marcion are evidently chronologically in error.

6. Several of the ancients give in substance, the *supplementary* view of the design of John's Gospel. Clement of Alexandria, as cited by Eusebius, Hist. Eccl. vi. 14, related, τὸν Ἰωάννην ἔσχατον συνιδόντα ὅτι τὰ σωματικὰ ἐν τοῖς εὐαγγελίοις δεδήλωται, προτραπέντα ὑπὸ τῶν γνωρίμων, πνεύματι θεοφορηθέντα, πνευματικὸν ποιῆσαι εὐαγγέλιον. Eusebius in another place (Hist. Eccl. iii. 24) states, that whereas the other Evangelists wrote the history of the official life of our Lord subsequent to the imprisonment of the Baptist, John, wishing that there should be a complete account, gave in his Gospel the particulars *preceding* that event. The same is repeated almost verbatim by Jerome, ut supra. Later authors (see Lücke, Einleitung, p. 189) reproduced the conjectures of their predecessors as being traditions of the Church ; and for the most part united the *polemical* with the *supplementary* theory[5].

7. None of the above-cited authors appeal to any *historical* or *traditionary* fact, as the ground of their own statements. Those statements have therefore for us *no authority ab extra*, and must be judged by their own intrinsic probability or otherwise, as established by the contents of the Gospel, and the state of the Church at the period of its publication. In modern times, these last considerations have given rise to several opinions, which I shall now briefly state ; acknowledging, throughout this part of the section, my obligations to Lücke, whose facts and remarks I have for the most part borrowed.

8. Grotius, and some of the Socinian commentators, supposed,—on account of the contrast strongly drawn in the prologue, ch. i. and elsewhere, between Jesus Christ as the true Light, and the Baptist as only having come to bear witness of that Light,—that the Evangelist wrote against the so-called *disciples of John*, who held the Baptist to have been the Messiah. Others (as Herder, Overbeck, Ziegler) thought that the *Sabæi*, who combined gnostic errors with an overweening estimation of John the Baptist, were principally aimed at. Others, not finding in

[4] "Joannes Apostolus novissimus omnium scripsit evangelium, rogatus ab Asiæ episcopis adversus Cerinthum aliosque hæreticos et maxime tunc Ebionitarum dogma consurgens, qui asserunt, Christum ante Mariam non fuisse." De Viris Illustr. c. 9, vol. ii. p. 843. But he also gives in the same place another reason : see in the text below.

[5] For an instance of the kind of use which is made of these notices in Eusebius and others by the advocates of the supplementary theory, see Wordsworth's note introductory to St. John : where such parts of them as suit that theory are strongly affirmed as fact, and called "the uniform consent of antiquity concerning the design of St. John's Gospel in relation to the other three," while the part not suiting it is hushed up under "for *other* reasons of a doctrinal nature."

this a sufficient account of the peculiarities of the Gospel, supposed this or other polemic aims, to have been united with the supplementary one. Of this last number are Storr, Wegscheider, Hug, &c. Others again (as Paulus) finding in the Gospel no sufficient evidence either of a polemical or a supplementary intention, fell back on the didactic aim set forth ch. xx. 31. This view, however, was never found satisfactory to explain the *peculiar phænomena* of the Gospel.

9. Meantime, however, the critical study of the other Gospels had so far advanced, that it became more and more clearly seen, that the hypothesis of John having been acquainted with, and having wished to complete or correct them, was *entirely untenable.* Again, not finding traces of a *polemical* design sufficiently prominent in the Gospel, some critics, slightly altering the term, have supposed it to be *apologetic* in its character (Hemsen, Seiffarth, Schott). Some, lastly, pronounced it unworthy of the Apostle to follow any secondary designs, considering his own avowal in ch. xx. 30, 31 (Credner). But, as Lücke remarks, even granting this, it may still be a lawful enquiry, *What peculiar circumstances led to his realizing this his great design in the present peculiar form of composition?* The synoptic Evangelists had, he says, beyond question, *the same great design*, and yet have followed it in a very different manner. Something of this may doubtless be explained by the individual character of the writer's mind, but clearly *not all:* and that character itself was modified by surrounding events. We are driven therefore to the special circumstances under which the Gospel, but especially *the prologue*, which in this matter rules the Gospel, was composed.

10. Into these Lücke enquires under two heads: (1) the relation of John's Gospel to the other three; (2) the character of the age and section of the Church in which the Evangelist lived. In treating the first of these he disproves, much in the same manner as has been done in these Prolegomena, the probability that John intended to supply, or had ever seen, our present Gospels; and maintains that an acquaintance on his part with the general stream of oral testimony from which they were derived, will sufficiently account for the relations observable between him and them. His inference is, that if his Gospel (as undoubtedly is the case) sometimes supplies and gives precision to theirs, this has been only the *result*, but could in no way be the *aim* of his writing; the peculiarities and object of which must be altogether accounted for from considerations belonging to the other head of the enquiry.

11. In pursuing this, he distinguishes three classes of writings likely to arise in the apostolic age: (*a*) the simple committal to paper of the cycles of oral narration, with a view to fixing them for the general and continued edification of the readers. To this class he refers the Gospels

of Matthew and Mark. (β) Writings compiled with a more set purpose of giving a *complete* account, *in order*, of the events of our Lord's life on earth. In this division he classes the Gospel of Luke. (γ) The third class would arise from the growing up of the faith, which at first was a simple historical belief, into the maturer γνῶσις of doctrinal system. In the course of this progress, various questions would arise respecting the life and teaching of the Lord Jesus, which the generally-received oral narration was not competent to answer. And these writings would be composed to satisfy such enquirers by presenting such an apologetic view of the Lord's life, and such a doctrinal account of His teaching, as might tend to set their questionings at rest. To this class he supposes *may* have belonged some of the gnostic apocryphal writings; and to this class certainly does belong the Gospel of John.

12. At the time of its composition, many questionings were already raised between the believing and unbelieving, and among the believing themselves. Traces of such we find even in the Pauline Epistles, 1 Cor. i. 23 ; xv. 1. Lücke instances some of these questions which this Gospel was well adapted to answer. (α) The rejection of the Lord Jesus by His own people the Jews, was an event likely to prove a stumbling-block, and to be used by unbelievers against our religion. To the elucidation of this,—the tracing its progress, step by step,—the shewing its increasing virulence amidst the blameless innocence and holy words and deeds of the Redeemer,—does John especially devote the middle and principal section of his Gospel. He shews that thereby His enemies were fulfilling the divine purpose, and that they were even forewarned of this by one among themselves, ch. xi. 51, 52. (β) We may evidently see, from the diligence with which John accumulates autoptic evidence on the subject of the actual death of Christ, and His resurrection, that he has in this part also some in view, who did not receive those great events as undoubted facts, but required the authority of an Apostle to assure them of their truth. (γ) The way also in which he relates the testimonies of our Lord respecting the manner, results, and voluntary nature of His own death,—that it was His true glorification,—that it was undertaken freely, but in complete accordance with the Father's will,—seems to point to doubts as to the character of that event, which the Evangelist meditated removing. (δ) It was certainly, later (see Origen against Celsus, quoted in note on Matt. ix. 9—13), a reproach against the Apostles, that they were low-born and ignorant men. In the case of Paul, we find very early a disposition on the part of some in the Churches, to set aside apostolic authority. And those who were so disposed might perhaps appeal to the oral narrative which forms the foundation of the synoptic Gospels, to prove that the Apostles often misunderstood the sayings of the Lord, and might from thence take occasion to vilify their present preaching as resting on

similar misunderstanding. John,—from his relating so much at length the discourse of our Lord in which He promised the Comforter to guide them into all the truth, and bring to their minds all that He had said to them, and from noticing (ch. xii. 16; xx. 9) that they understood not certain things at first, which were made clear to them afterwards,—seems to be guarding the apostolic office and testimony from such imputations.

13. But all these designs, possible as they may have been, do not reach so far as to give any account of the very remarkable cast and diction of the *prologue*. This opening gives a tone to the whole Gospel, being no less than a compendium or programme of its contents, gathered up and expressed according to a nomenclature already familiar to certain persons within the Church. The fact of John having been led to adopt the gnostic term λόγος as the exponent of his teaching respecting the person of our Lord, would of itself make it probable that he had the combating of *gnostic error* in his view; or perhaps, speaking more accurately, that he was led to take advantage of the yearnings of the human desire after an universal and philosophic religion,—by grasping and lifting upward into the certainty of revelation the *truth* which they had shaped to themselves,—and thereby striking off and proscribing their manifold and erroneous conceits. But neither the language of the prologue itself, nor any prominence given to antagonistic truths in the Gospel, justify us in ascribing to the Evangelist a position directly polemical against the peculiar tenets of Cerinthus[6]. The stand made in the Gospel, is *against gnosticism in the very widest sense:* in its Ebionitish form, as denying the Divinity and pre-existence of Christ,—and in its Docetic, as denying the reality of His assumption of the Human Nature.

14. While, however, John contends against false γνῶσις, he is, in the furtherance and grounding of the true γνῶσις, the greatest, as he was the last, of the spiritual teachers of the Church. The great Apostle of the Gentiles, amidst fightings without and fears within, built in his argumentative Epistles the outworks of that temple, of which his still greater colleague and successor was chosen noiselessly to complete, in his peaceful old age, the inner and holier places. And this, after all, ranging under it all secondary aims, we must call the great object of the Evangelist;—to advance, purify from error, and strengthen, that maturer Christian life of *knowledge*, which is the true development of the teaching of the Spirit in men, and which the latter part of the apostolic period witnessed in its full vitality. And this, by setting forth the Person of the Lord Jesus in all its fulness of grace and truth,

[6] For an account of them, see Neander's Church History, Rose's translation, vol. ii. p. 49.

in all its manifestation in the flesh by signs and by discourses, and its glorification by opposition and unbelief, through sufferings and death [7]. That he should have been led to cast his testimony into a form antagonistic to the peculiar errors then prevalent,—that he should have adopted the thoughts and diction of previous seekers after God, so far as they were capable of serving his high purpose and being elevated into vehicles of heavenly truth,—these are arrangements which we may not, because they are natural and probable, the less regard as providential, and admirably designed for that which especially was his portion of the apostolic work,—the PERFECTING OF THE SAINTS [8].

[7] I cannot here forbear from referring to an important work on the Gospel of St. John, Luthardt's Das Johanneische Evangelium nach seiner Eigenthümlichkeit geschildert und erklärt, Nürnberg, 1853, 2 voll. The reader will find all the preliminary matter copiously and ably handled in vol. i.,—and vol. ii. contains a running commentary in which many striking ideas are suggested. Without subscribing to all Luthardt's views, I cannot but think his book a most valuable contribution to a right understanding of our Gospel. The greater part of the new matter in my notes on St. John is derived from this source. Note to 2nd edition. (I may now say, that having since used Luthardt's book during a continuous pulpit exposition of the earlier part of St. John, I have ever found more and more reason to value it. No such attempt to give a general account of the aims and characteristics of the Gospel has ever before been made. A good translation of it could not fail to bring about in England a worthier appreciation of this wonderful Gospel.—Note to 3rd edition.) (The above opinion remaining in its full force, I may now add, that the second edition of Stier's Reden Jesu notices and reviews throughout the remarks of Luthardt, and forms a very valuable corrective to the sometimes overwrought views of that earnest and delightful writer.—Note to 4th edition.)

[8] It will be hardly necessary to state, but I do so in order to bring down the views respecting the Gospels advocated in these Prolegomena expressly to the date of this last (the fifth) edition, that additional study, and subsequent reflection, convince me more and more of the untenableness of the ordinary harmonistic theories, and of that which attributes to St. John the design of supplementing the rest. I need only ask any student, who shares with me the same general idea of the fair and ingenuous principles which should rule our enquiries respecting this subject, to consult the introductions to the Gospels in Bp. Wordsworth's Greek Testament; and I feel assured he will derive similar confirmation, as far as it is gathered from seeing to what shifts the advocates of the procrustean theories are driven. Witness e. g. the objection (1) and answer, p. 206: where those who doubt, as matter of fact, the communication of the three Gospels to St. John, are charged with disbelief in Inspiration, and are refuted by an à priori decree of Bp. Wordsworth's as to what was "morally certain" to have been the procedure of the Holy Spirit. And this is really but a fair sample of the way in which every received theory of the patristic and middle ages is advocated, and enforced by strong anathemas, in that and similar works. I may also mention, that the remarks in a work entitled "The Gospel of St. Mark, in the Authorized Version, arranged in Parts and Sections, with Titles and Summaries of Contents, Marginal Notes of Time and Place, and a Preface; to which are appended, Cautions against the Greek Testament of Dean Alford, and the Hulsean Lectures of Dean Ellicott. For the Use of Schools and Young Students. By the Rev. J. Forshall, M.A., F.R.S., formerly Fellow of Exeter College, Oxford," have not induced me to modify any of the statements or expressions in these Prolegomena. (1863.)

SECTION IV.

AT WHAT PLACE AND TIME IT WAS WRITTEN.

1. These two questions, as relating to John's Gospel, are too intimately connected to form the subject of separate sections.

2. The most ancient testimony, that of Irenæus, relates that it was published *at Ephesus*[9]. This testimony is repeated by Jerome[1] and others, and is every way consonant with what we have above (§ i.) related of the history of the Apostle its author. Some later writers have reported that it was published from *Patmos*, during John's exile; some have combined the two accounts, and made John dictate the Gospel in Patmos, and publish it at Ephesus after his return. But of these the only account which from its date and character deserves attention, is that of Irenæus.

3. The Gospel itself furnishes only negative or uncertain evidence on this point. From the manner in which the sites and habits of Palestine are spoken of[2], it seems evident that it was composed at a distance from that country. If again we regard the peculiar nomenclature of the prologue, and enquire to what locality this points, two places occur to us where it would be likely to have been adopted; one of these, Alexandria,—the other, Ephesus. The first of these cities was the home and birthplace of the gnostic philosophy; the other (Acts xviii. 24) was in communication with, and derived its philosophic character from Alexandria[3]. Now as no history gives us any account of the Apostle having laboured or ever been at Alexandria, this consideration also forms a presumptive confirmation of the tradition that the Gospel was written at Ephesus.

4. If so, we have some clue, although but an indirect one, to the time at which it was published. If John cannot be supposed to have come thither till some time after the ultimate disappearance of the Apostle Paul from Asia Minor[4], then we have obviously a time specified, before which the Gospel cannot have been published.

5. The voice of tradition on this point is very uncertain. Irenæus states that this Gospel was the latest written of the four: which, as he places Mark's and Luke's after the deaths of Peter and Paul (but see

[9] Ἰωάννης ὁ μαθητὴς τοῦ κυρίου, ὁ καὶ ἐπὶ τὸ στῆθος αὐτοῦ ἀναπεσών, καὶ αὐτὸς ἐξέδωκε τὸ εὐαγγέλιον, ἐν Ἐφέσῳ τῆς Ἀσίας διατρίβων. Adv. Hær. iii. 1, p. 174; cited also by Euseb. H. E. v. 8.

[1] Prologue to Matthew, vol. vii. pp. 5, 6.

[2] See ch. ii. 6, 13; iii. 23; iv. 4; v. 2; vi. 4; x. 22; xi. 18, 49—51, 54, 55; xviii. 1, 13, 28; xix. 13, 31.

[3] See note on John i. 1 (I. ϵ).

[4] See § i. of the present chapter, paragraph 10.

Prolegg. to Luke, § iv.), would bring us to a similar date with that pointed out in the preceding paragraph[5]. As usual in traditional matter,—on our advance to later writers, we find more and more particular accounts given:—the year of John's life, the reigning Emperor, &c., under which the Gospel was written[6]. In all such cases the student will do well to remember, that *such late traditions are worthless exactly in proportion to their particularity of detail.*

6. But we have thus no direct indication, at what date to place the Gospel. On examining its contents, we find no such indication given by them. It is true that the Evangelist speaks in ch. v. 2 of the pool of Bethesda in the *present* tense as being near the sheepgate, and thence it might seem as if he wrote before the destruction of Jerusalem:—but such indications are confounded by the fact that he alone of the Evangelists speaks of places near Jerusalem, which would remain after the destruction, in the *past* tense (ch. xi. 18), which seems to shew that no stress is to be laid on such expressions, which were perhaps used by him according to the cast of the particular narrative which he was then constructing, without any reference to the existing state of things at the time of his writing[7]. See, however, note on ch. xi. 18.

7. It has been variously inferred,—from ch. xxi. 18, 19,—that the Gospel must have been published *during the lifetime* of Peter;—for that, had the Lord's prophecy been fulfilled before the account was written, some notice would have been taken of such fulfilment;—and from ch. xviii. 10, that it cannot have been published till *after his death,*—for that Peter's name would not have been mentioned, had he been still living. But it is plain that we might just as well argue for ch. xxi. 18, 19, being written *after* Peter's death, on account of the definiteness of the interpretation there given to the prophecy; and I have shewn in my note on Matt. xxvi. 51, that no stress can be laid on the other inference.

8. Nor do we find any more certain indication by comparison of the Gospel with the First Epistle, or with the Apocalypse. The dates of both these are very uncertain;—and it has been disputed whether their contents presuppose the Gospel or not. Such expressions as ὁ λόγος τῆς ζωῆς, ἡ ζωὴ αἰώνιος, ἥτις ἦν πρὸς τὸν πατέρα καὶ ἐφανερώθη ἡμῖν, 1 John i. 1, 2, and similar ones, make it at least probable, that the Epistle was written after the Gospel (see Lücke, iii. 21 ff.). But *how long after*, we have no means of even conjecturing. And with regard to the Apocalypse, if we assume the Domitianic date (95 or 96 A.D.), up-

[5] Similarly Clement of Alex., Origen, and Eusebius: see Eus. H. E. v. 8; iii. 24.

[6] ἐπὶ τῇ γηραλέᾳ αὐτοῦ ἡλικίᾳ, μετὰ ἔτη ἐννενήκοντα τῆς ἑαυτοῦ ζωῆς, μετὰ τὴν αὐτοῦ ἀπὸ τῆς Πάτμου ἐπάνοδον, τὴν ἐπὶ Κλαυδίου γενομένην Καίσαρος. Epiphan. Hær. li. 12, vol. i. p. 434.

[7] See also ch. xviii. 1; xix. 41.

held in Prolegg. to Revelation, § ii., we yet get no trustworthy points of comparison whereby to infer the date of the Gospel.

9. Our only resource then must be, the space included between the very wide limits above indicated. The final departure of Paul from Asia Minor, and indeed his death, must be supposed to have happened some time;—this, such as it is, will be our *terminus a quo*;—and our *terminus ad quem, the probable duration of John's life*, or more properly speaking, *of his power of writing as we find him writing in this Gospel.* And as antiquity testifies that he lived to a great age, and survived his vigour, this latter terminus will be even less definite than the former.

10. One consideration, however, may tend somewhat to narrow its limits. I have argued in the Commentary, that ch. xxi. is a genuine addition by the hand of the Apostle himself, probably in the decline of life, some years at least, from internal evidence of style, after the Gospel was completed. Add to which, as hinted above, that the style of the Gospel is, as Lücke has also remarked, that of a *matured*, but *not of an aged* writer.

11. Whether then we set the death of Paul with Wieseler in A.D. 64, or, as upholders of a second Roman imprisonment, in A.D. 68, we perhaps must not in either case allow our *terminus a quo* to be placed much earlier than 70: nor, supposing John to have been a few years younger than our Lord, can we prolong our later limit much beyond A.D. 85. We should thus have, but with no great fixity either way, *somewhere about fifteen years*,—A.D. 70—85, during which it is probable that the Gospel was published.

SECTION V.

IN WHAT LANGUAGE IT WAS WRITTEN.

1. The testimony of antiquity is unanimous that John wrote in Greek. (See Lücke, Einleitung, § xi.) Nor is there any reason to doubt the fact. If he lived and taught in Asia Minor, he must have been familiar with the Greek language.

2. Some among the moderns (Salmasius, according to Lücke, the first) have held an Aramaic or Hebrew original. They seem to ground this principally on the citations from the Old Testament being from the Hebrew, not from the LXX. But this latter is by no means without exception: see ch. i. 23; ii. 17; vi. 45; x. 34; xii. 14, 15, 38; xv. 25; xix. 24, 36. That we find other citations (xii. 40; xiii. 18; xix. 37) after the Hebrew solely or principally, was to be expected from the Apostle's personal history, as a Jew of Palestine who had been brought up in the knowledge of the Hebrew original: and is a confirmation of the genuineness of the Gospel. See below in the next section, and Bleek, Beiträge zur Evangelien Kritik, p. 87.

SECTION VI.

ITS GENUINENESS.

1. It would enlarge these Prolegomena too much, to give a detailed history of the recognition of this Gospel, and its impugners, in ancient times. It may suffice to refer to such works as Lücke's Einleitung, where this history will be found. The result of his researches on the subject is, that down to the end of the second century the Gospel was by all recognized and attributed to the Apostle whose name it bears, with the sole exception of the Alogi, an unimportant sect in Asia Minor, who, from excessive opposition to the heresy of Montanus, rejected both the Apocalypse and Gospel of John, as favouring (according to them) some of the views of that heretic. Such an exception rather strengthens than weakens the general evidence of ancient Christendom in its favour.

2. Equally satisfactory is the testimony of the Fathers after the close of the second century. The citations by Irenæus from this Gospel are very frequent, and express, both as to its canonicity and the name of its Author. And his testimony is peculiarly valuable, because (1) he was an anti-gnostic : (2) his acquaintance with the whole Church, Eastern and Western, was greater than that of any other ecclesiastical writer : and (3) in his youth he had conversed with Polycarp, himself a disciple of the Apostle John. Theophilus of Antioch, Tertullian, Clement of Alexandria, Hippolytus, Origen, Dionysius of Alexandria, Eusebius,—the ancient Syriac version, the Peschito,—the adversaries of Christianity, Porphyry, and Julian,—all these refer to the Gospel as without doubt the work of the Apostle John.

3. We may then, *as far as antiquity is concerned*, regard its genuineness as established. But there is one circumstance which has furnished many modern writers with a ground for doubting this. Neither Papias, who carefully sought out all that Apostles and apostolic men had related regarding the life of Christ,—nor Polycarp, who was himself a disciple of the Apostle John,—nor Barnabas, nor Clement of Rome, in their Epistles, nor lastly Ignatius (in his genuine writings), makes any mention of, or allusion to, this Gospel. So that in the most ancient circle of ecclesiastical testimony, it appears to be unknown or not recognized.

4. But this circumstance, when fairly considered in connexion with *its universal recognition by writers following on these*, rather serves for a *confirmation of the genuineness* of this Gospel. It confessedly was written *late in the apostolic age*. As far then as silence (or apparent silence) can be valid as an argument, it seems to shew that the recognition of

this Gospel, as might have been expected, was *later than that of the others*. And it is some confirmation also of this view, that Papias, if Eusebius (iii. 39) gives his testimony entire, appears *not to recognize Luke's Gospel*, but *only those of Matthew and Mark*. It is remarkable, however, on the other hand, that Papias (Eusebius, ibid.) recognizes the *First Epistle* of John, which, as remarked in § iv., was probably written after the Gospel. This would seem to make it probable that we have not in Eusebius the whole testimony of Papias given; for it would certainly seem from internal grounds that the First Epistle and the Gospel must stand or fall together.

5. It is evident that too much stress must not be laid on the silence of Polycarp, from whom we have one short epistle only. He also (apparently) was acquainted with the First Epistle of John[8]. But he wrote with no purpose of giving testimony to the sacred books, and what reason therefore have we to expect in his Epistle, quotations from or allusions to any particular book which did not happen to come within his design, and the subject of which he was treating?

6. The same may be said of the silence of Barnabas, Hermas, and Ignatius. Had any intention existed on the part of the primitive Christian writers of informing posterity what books were counted canonical in their days, their silence would be a strong argument against any particular book:—but they had no such intention: their citations are fortuitous, and most of them loose and allusory only. So that we cannot argue from such silence to the recognition or otherwise of any book, unless it be universal and continuous, which is not the case with regard to this Gospel.

7. Again, the *kind of testimony* furnished by Irenæus is peculiarly valuable. He does not relate *from whom* he had heard that John wrote a Gospel, but he treats and quotes it as a well-known and long-used book in the Christian Church. What could have induced Irenæus to do this, except *the fact of its being thus known and used?* So that this character of his testimony virtually carries it back farther than its actual date. Besides, when one who has had the means which Irenæus had of ascertaining the truth in a matter, asserts things respecting that matter,—the ordinary and just method is to suppose that he *draws his information from his superior opportunities of gaining it*, even though he may not expressly say so: so that when Irenæus, who had conversed with Polycarp himself, the friend of the Apostle John, quotes this Gospel as the work of that Apostle, we may fairly presume that he had assured himself of this by the testimony of one so well capable of informing him.

[8] πᾶς γὰρ ὃς ἂν μὴ ὁμολογῇ Ἰησοῦν χριστὸν ἐν σαρκὶ ἐληλυθέναι, ἀντίχριστός ἐστι. Ch. vii. p. 1012, ed. Migne: compare 1 John iv. 3.

8. Another historical argument used against its genuineness is,—that in the dispute about the time of keeping Easter between Polycarp and Anicetus bishop of Rome about the year 160, the former defended the practice of the Asiatic Churches,—which was to keep their Christian passover at the time of the Jewish passover, the evening of the 14th of Nisan, by what he had learned from John and the other Apostles (Eusebius, Hist. Eccl. v. 24). But, say the opponents, John himself in his Gospel clearly relates that our Lord instituted the Lord's supper on the evening of the 13*th of Nisan, and was crucified on the* 14*th.* Therefore either Polycarp falsely appealed to John's authority, which is not probable, or John did not write the Gospel which bears his name. But, as Lücke has shewn, this argument is altogether built on the assumption that the Christian passover must necessarily coincide with *the time of the institution* of the Lord's supper; whereas such a coincidence does not appear to have entered into the consideration of the litigants in this case, but merely the question, whether the Churches should follow the Jewish calendar, or an arrangement of their own. Even in the later dispute between Polycrates bishop of Ephesus and Victor (Eusebius, ut supra), on the same point, *this question was not raised*, but the matter was debated on other grounds.

9. The last historical objection which I shall notice is, that this Gospel was first circulated by the Gnostics, and therefore is to be looked on with suspicion. But Lücke has shewn (Einl. p. 119) that this was not the case : that *unquestionable traces of catholic reception of it are found before it was received by them :* and that, at all events, Irenæus recognized and used it contemporaneously with the Valentinians. The known opposition between the catholic Fathers and the Gnostics furnishes a sure guarantee, that, *had they first promulgated the Gospel, it never would have been received into the Canon of the catholic Church.*

10. The modern opponents of the genuineness and canonicity of this Gospel have raised two arguments against it upon *internal* evidence. The first of these rests upon the assumed radical diversity between the views of the Person and teaching of Christ presented to us by John, and by the synoptic Evangelists. On this point I have said nearly all that is necessary in § ii. ; and I will only now add, that supposing the diversity to be as unaccountable as it is natural, it would of itself serve as a strong presumption that the Gospel was not the work of a forger, who would have enlarged and decorated the accounts already existing, but a genuine testimony of one who was not an imitator of nor dependent on those others.

11. The second endeavours, by bringing out various supposed inconsistencies in the narration, to shew that the Apostle John cannot have been the Author. Such are,—imagined want of connexion in certain

parts (ch. iv. 44 ; xiii. 20 ; xiv. 31, where see notes) ;—an imputed inconsistency in the character and development of the treachery of Judas (see note on ch. vi. 64) ;—the not naming once in the Gospel of his own brother James (which, as Lücke remarks, is far easier to account for on supposition of its genuineness than on that of its spuriousness[9]) ;—the supposed want of accurate information with regard to the geography and customs of Judæa. But again, the passages cited to support this, involve only geographical and archæological *difficulties*, such as would never have been raised by an impostor;—and one in particular (ch. vii. 52: see note there) is chargeable, not on the Evangelist, but on the Sanhedrim, who were likely enough to have made the mistake, or purposely overlooked the fact, in their proud spirit of contempt for Galilee. The other objections derived from internal considerations are hardly worth recounting. They are fully stated and answered by Lücke, Einleitung, pp. 136—140.

12. An hypothesis was advanced by Eckermann, Vogel, and Paulus, and brought to completeness by Weisse, founded on a compromise between the evidence for and against the Gospel : that it is *partly genuine*, and principally in the didactic portions, which are veritable notices from the Apostle John : but that a later hand has wrought upon these, and added most of the narrative portions. But first, ecclesiastical tradition gives no countenance to this, always citing the Gospel *as a whole*,—and dropping no hint of any such distinction between its parts ;—and secondly, it is quite impossible to draw any line in the Gospel itself which shall separate the original matter from the supposed additions. There certainly is a marked distinction in diction and style between the rest of the Gospel and ch. xxi. (of ch. vii. 53—viii. 12, I do not now speak ; see notes there) :—which I believe to be accounted for by that chapter being a later addition by the Author himself : but farther than this, no such distinction can, even by the most fanciful analogies, be established. The same spirit pervades the form of the narrative and didactic parts : and so strongly, that the impugners of the Gospel have made this very circumstance an argument against the authenticity of the latter ;—how unjustly, I have shewn above in § ii. :—but the fact of the objection having been made is important, as fatal to Weisse's hypothesis.

13. The principal arguments against the genuineness of the Gospel have been repeated and elaborated by Baur (in Zeller's Theologisches Jahrbuch, 1844, 1. 3. 14), who tries to shew that the whole is apocryphal,

[9] James, the son of Zebedee, though one of the favoured Three, comes forward no where personally in the Gospels, nor in the Acts; and vanishes the first of all the Apostles from the historic field of view. It is very unlikely that John would have introduced mention of him merely because he was his brother. He has not named several others of the Apostles. See ch. xxi. 2, and note.

—and has arisen from a pious fraud of an author in the latter part of the second century. I mention this attempt because an admirable answer to it has appeared, by Ebrard, Das Evangelium Johannis und die neueste Hypothese über seine Entstehung, pp. 217. Zurich, 1845. In this work he has gone over carefully all the arguments treated in the preceding sections, and shewn their entire untenableness. Luthardt also, in the work above referred to, has treated at length of the view of Baur and his school, vol. i. pp. 230—237.

14. Our conclusion then from internal as well as external evidence, must be that the Gospel is what it has generally been believed to be,—*the genuine work of the Apostle John.* And this result has been obtained by rigid criticism, apart from all subjective leanings either way. To dilate on the importance of this conclusion, does not belong to these Prolegomena; but I cannot avoid pointing it out, in an age when on the one hand the historic truth of our scriptural accounts is being again boldly denied;—and on the other, we providentially stand at a point in the progress of criticism, where none but the most rigid trial of them,—none but the fairest and most impartial judgments,—can or ought to satisfy us.

SECTION VII.

ITS STYLE AND CHARACTER.

1. This is the only one of the four Gospels to which a *pre-arranged and systematic plan* can with any certainty be ascribed. That such does not exist in the other three, any farther than the circumstances under which they were each respectively written have indirectly modified their arrangement, has been already shewn. But that such a plan is proposed and followed out by the Writer of this Gospel, will become evident by an examination of its contents.

2. The prologue contains *a formal setting forth of the subject-matter of the Gospel:*—'that the Eternal Creator Word became Flesh, and was glorified by means of that work which He undertook in the flesh.' This *glorification of Christ* he follows out under several heads: (1) the testimony borne to Him by the Baptist; (2) His miracles; (3) His conflict with the persecution and malice of the Jews; (4) His own testimony in His discourses, which are very copiously related; (5) His sufferings, death, and resurrection. And this His glorification is the *accomplishment of the purpose of the Father, by setting Him forth as the Light and Life of the world,—the One Intercessor and Mediator, by whose accomplished Work the Holy Spirit is procured for men;* and through whom all spiritual help, and comfort, and hope of glory, is derived.

3. Several subdivisions of the Gospel have been proposed, as shewing its arrangement in subordination to this great design. The simplest and most satisfactory is that adopted by Lücke: (1) the prologue, ch. i. 1—18; (2) the first main division of the Gospel, i. 19—xii. 50; (3) the second main division of the Gospel, xiii. 1—xx. 31; (4) the appendix, ch. xxi.

4. Of these divisions, I. the prologue, contains a general statement of the whole subject of the Gospel. II. The first main division treats of the official work of the Lord in Galilee, Judæa, and Samaria, His reception and rejection, and closes with the general reflections of the Evangelist, ch. xii. 37—43, and summary of the commission of Jesus, ib. 44—50:—its foundation in the will of the Father, and purposes of grace and love to men. III. The second main division may be subdivided into two parts, (1) the inner glorification of Christ in His last supper and His last discourses, (2) His outer and public glorification by His Sufferings, Death, and Resurrection. Then IV. the appended chapter xxi. relates, for a special purpose, an appearance of the Lord, after His resurrection, in Galilee: see notes there.

5. In all these, except the last, the great leading object of the Gospel is kept in view, and continually worked out more fully. After having stated it in the prologue, he relates the recognition of Christ's glory by the testimony of the Baptist;—then by the disciples on their being called;—then the manifestation of that glory by His miracle in Cana of Galilee,—by His cleansing of the temple,—by His declaration of Himself to Nicodemus,—and so onwards. But the more this is the case, the more is He misunderstood and withstood: and it becomes evident by degrees, that the great shewing forth of His glory is to be brought about by the result of this very opposition of His enemies. This reaches its height in the prophetic testimony of Caiaphas, ch. xi. 47 ff.; and the voice from heaven, xii. 28, *ἐδόξασα καὶ πάλιν δοξάσω*, seems to form the point of transition from the manifestation of His glory by His acts, discourses, and conflict with the Jews, in Part I., to that by His Sufferings, Death, and Resurrection in Part II. Thus, as Lücke remarks, these words form the ground-tone of the whole Gospel,—"The public working of Christ manifested His glory; but at the same time led on to His Death, which Death again manifested His glory."

6. In the course of the Gospel the Evangelist steadily keeps his great end in view, and does not turn aside from it. For its sake are the incidents and notices introduced, with which his matter is diversified; but for its sake only. He has no chronological, no purely historical aims. Each incident which is chosen for a manifestation of the Lord's glory, is introduced sometimes with very slight links, sometimes with altogether no links of connexion to that which has preceded. So that while in the fulfilment of its inner design the Gospel forms a closely

connected and perfect whole, considered in any other view it is disjointed and fragmentary [1].

7. With regard to the style of this Gospel, it may be remarked—(1) that Dionysius of Alexandria, as cited by Eusebius, Hist. Eccl. vii. 25, remarked the purity of its Greek as compared with that of the Apocalypse. *τὰ μὲν γάρ* (the Gospel and First Epistle) *οὐ μόνον ἀπταίστως κατὰ τὴν τῶν Ἑλλήνων φωνήν, ἀλλὰ καὶ λογιώτατα ταῖς λέξεσι, τοῖς συλλογισμοῖς, ταῖς συντάξεσι τῆς ἑρμηνείας γέγραπται. πολλοῦ γε δεῖ βάρβαρόν τινα φθόγγον, ἢ σολοικισμόν, ἢ ὅλως ἰδιωτισμὸν ἐν αὐτοῖς εὑρεθῆναι.* (2) That without subscribing to the whole of this eulogy, if classical authors are to be the standard of comparison, the same will hold good of this Gospel as compared with the other three. (3) That the greater purity of its Greek is perhaps mainly owing to its far greater *simplicity of style*. While the deepest truths lie beneath the words, the words themselves are almost *colloquial* in their simplicity; the historical matter

[1] Luthardt's division is:

I. JESUS THE SON OF GOD: ch. i.—iv.
  1. The Christ: ch. i. 1—18.
  2. The introduction of Jesus into the world (i. 19—ii. 11) by the testimony (a) of the Baptist (i. 19—40); (b) of Himself (i. 41—ii. 11).
  3. First revelation of Himself as the Son of God (ii. 12—iv. 54)—(a) in Jerusalem and Judæa (ii. 12—iii. 36), (b) in Samaria and Galilee (iv. 1—54).

II. JESUS AND THE JEWS: ch. v.—xii.
  1. Jesus the Life. Opening of the conflict: ch. v. vi. (a) His divine working as Son of God—beginning of opposition (v. 1—47); (b) Jesus the Life in the flesh,—progress of belief and unbelief (vi. 1—71).
  2. Jesus the Light. Height of the conflict: ch. vii.—x. (a) He meets the unbelief of the Jews at Jerusalem (vii. 1—52); (b) opposition between Jesus and the Jews at its height (viii. 12—59); (c) Jesus the Light of the world for salvation, and for judgment (ix. x.).
  3. The delivery of Jesus to death is the Life and the Judgment of the world: ch. xi. xii. (a) The raising from the Dead (xi. 1—57); (b) prophetic announcements of the Future (xii. 1—36); (c) final judgment on Israel (ib. 37—50).

III. JESUS AND HIS OWN: ch. xiii.—xx.
  1. Jesus' Love and the belief of His disciples. (a) His Love in condescension (xiii. 1—30); (b) His Love in keeping and completing the disciples in the faith (xiii. 31—xvi. 33); (c) His Love in the exaltation of the Son of God (xvii.).
  2. Jesus the Lord; the unbelief of Israel, now in its completion; the belief of His own: ch. xviii.—xx. (a) His free self-surrender to His enemies, and to the unbelief of Israel (xviii. 1—xix. 16); (b) His self surrender to Death, and divine testimony in death (xix. 16—42); (c) His manifestation of Himself as passed from death into liberty and life, and the completion of the disciples' faith worked thereby (xx. 1—29).

The APPENDIX: ch. XXI. The glimpse into the future. (a) the symbolic draught of fishes (1—8); (b) the symbolic meal (9—14); (c) the calling and its prospect (15—23); (d) conclusion.

These leading sections he follows out into minor detail in other subdivisions of much interest.

is of small amount as compared with the dialogue. (4) That while the language is for the most part unobjectionable Greek, the cast of expression and thought is Hebraistic. "Sermo quidem Græcus sed plane adumbratus ex Syriaco illius sæculi" (Grotius). There is, both here and in the Epistle, very little unfolding or deducing one proposition from another: different steps of an argument, or sometimes different conclusions from mutually dependent arguments, are indicated by mere juxtaposition;—and the intelligent reader must be carrying on, as it were, an undercurrent of thought, or the connexion will not be perceived. (5) That in this respect this Gospel forms a remarkable contrast to those parts of the New Testament written by Hellenistic Christians,—e. g. the Epistles of Paul, and that to the Hebrews; in which, while external marks of Hebraistic diction abound, there is yet an internal conformation of style, and connexion of thought, more characteristic of the Grecian mind:—they write more in periods, and more according to dialectic form. In observing all such phænomena in our sacred writings, the student will learn to appreciate the evidence which they contribute to the historic truth of our belief with regard to them and their writers:—and will also perceive an admirable adaptation of the workman to his work, by Him whose one Spirit has overruled them all.

8. The reader will find a very elaborate and detailed account of the peculiarities of diction and style of this Gospel in Luthardt's work referred to above, vol. i. pp. 21—69.

CHAPTER VI.

ON THE ARRANGEMENT OF THIS EDITION.

SECTION I.

THE TEXT.

1. In order to set clearly before the student the principles on which the text has been revised, it may be well to premise a short account of what has been hitherto done towards its revision in modern times.

2. The *received text* of the Greek Testament is that of the second Elzevir edition, published at Leyden in 1633, and founded on a collation of the third edition of Robert Stephens (1550),—which itself was founded on the fifth edition of Erasmus (1535),—with Beza's editions. The term '*received text*' appears to have originated in an expression used by the Elzevirs in their preface—"Textum ergo habes nunc *ab*

omnibus receptum, in quo nihil immutatum aut corruptum damus." (For particulars respecting the previous editions of the Greek Testament, see Wetstein, prolegg. pp. 116 ff.: and Tregelles, Printed Text of the Greek Test.)

3. The critical authority of the received text is very feeble.—The fifth edition of Erasmus mentioned above was nearly a reprint of his fourth, which was founded on his former editions corrected by the Complutensian[2], which had just been published at that time. But neither Erasmus nor the Complutensian editors had before them any sufficient critical apparatus whereupon to construct their text;—nor did the latter use faithfully even that which they had. Wetstein has shewn that their text is singularly corrupted and inaccurate. Erasmus also, besides committing numerous inaccuracies, tampered with the readings of the very few MSS. which he collated[3]. Stephens has given but a very vague account of the additional MSS. to which he had access, and the work appears to have been done with levity and carelessness. The Elzevirs differ from Stephens's third edition in about 150 readings only. (Tischendorf, ed. 7, p. lxxxv.)

4. The first systematic attempt to revise the received text which I shall notice here, as embracing in itself some previous partial ones, is that of J. J. Griesbach, whose edition (complete) appeared in 1796—1806. He collected and systematized the previous labours of Mill and Wetstein, adding to them very many collations of his own. His theory of various recensions of the Greek text apparent in the different classes of MSS., although arbitrarily carried out by him and those who have adopted it from him, has certainly a foundation in truth, and corresponds in the main to the phænomena:—but it misled him in the recension of the text. Nor has he been sufficiently careful in his collation of the principal MSS., nor consistent in the application of his own critical rules. Besides which, the number and complexity of his symbols indicating his judgment on the quality of the readings, form an objection to his edition as furnishing a text for general use.

5. The next considerable attempt to revise the text is found in the edition of Dr. Scholz, late Roman Catholic professor of sacred literature at Bonn. In his extensive travels undertaken in pursuance of his work,

[2] Published at Alcala (Complutum) in Spain, under the superintendence of Cardinal Ximenes. This edition was ready in 1514, two years before Erasmus published his first edition; but from various delays, not published till 1522, after Erasmus had published his *third*.

[3] "Ut jam non repetam, quod Erasmus lectionem eorum quos habebat codicum Evangeliorum, Actorum et Epistolarum aliquoties temere mutaverit, cujus rei vestigia adhuc dum in ipsis codd. manifesta conspiciuntur, præter loca supra p. 44 allata. Quin neque ipse diffitetur, ultro ad amicos scribens 'se codices suos præcastigasse.'" Wetst. prolegg. p. 127.

he discovered, and cursorily collated very many MSS. unknown before :—and in this, the pioneering department of criticism, his services were considerable. But the theory which he upheld with regard to the recension of the text is as untenable, as his own departure from it is manifest. He adopts, in the main, Griesbach's classification of MSS., arranging them however in *two* great families or recensions, the Alexandrine and the Constantinopolitan. Of these he holds that the latter contain the true original text of the sacred books, the former having been altered and corrupted by transcribers and grammarians. But notwithstanding this, he continually receives into his text, in almost every page, Alexandrine readings, against the nearly unanimous testimony of the Constantinopolitan MSS.[4] In fact, his is a text constructed in spite of, not according to, his theory. Besides which, with all respect for Dr. Scholz's labours in the cause of biblical criticism, it must be confessed that the extreme inaccuracy of his edition of the New Testament renders it almost unfit for the use of the scholar [5].

6. In 1831 a stereotype edition of the New Testament appeared, followed in 1842 by a first part, containing the Gospels, of a larger edition with various readings and the Latin Vulgate annexed, by C. Lachmann. The view with which he reconstructed his text is explained at length in his prolegomena to the edition of 1842. He professes to give the text as it was received in the East in the fourth century. To this end he cites as his authorities *entirely the older* MSS.[6], A B C P Q T Z in the Gospels as of primary, and D as of secondary authority : neglecting altogether the other uncial MSS. and all the cursive mss. :—of the versions he lays most stress (and properly) on the ancient latin, represented by its most important MSS., *a*, *b*, *c*, D-lat., but to the entire neglect of the important syrr., copt., æth., arm., sah.[7] Of the Fathers, in the Gospels he cites Origen only as of primary authority,—Irenæus, Cyprian, Hilary, and Lucifer as of secondary ;—and lastly, the vulgate of Jerome. But this rejection of the greater part of the witnesses for the text has reduced him, in a very considerable part of the New

4 Dr. Scholz himself informed me in 1847, not long before his death, that if he lived to bring out another edition of his Gr. Test., he should transfer into the text most of the Alexandrine readings which now are noted in large type beneath it. And the same intention is alluded to in an academical prolusion published by him in 1845.

5 So viel aber ist entschieden daß man den Angaben dieses Kritikers nimmer mit Zuversicht vertrauen kann, und daß seine Arbeiten, die denen welche sich damit befassen nur vergebliche Mühe und Zeit kosten, als völlig unbrauchbar möglichst bald der Vergessenheit überliefert werden sollten. Es gibt wenig Zeilen im Vol. 1. dieses N. T. worin sich nicht irgend eine Incorrectheit nachweisen ließe. Schulz, cited by Tischendorf, ed. Lips. 2, prolegg. p. xxxix,—who adds: "Quod D. Schulz testatus est; Es gibt wenig Zeilen u.s.w.: id majorem in modum in vol. ii. quadrare quævis pagina docet."

6 See catalogue of MSS. below, ch. vii. § i.

7 See, for all these catalogue of versions below, ch. vii. § ii.

Testament, to implicit following of one MS. only (e. g. A does not contain Matt. i.—xxv. 6, besides other lacunæ; B does not contain the Epistles to Timothy, Titus, and Philemon, nor the Apocalypse; and the lacunæ in C are large and frequent). Besides which, he has not consistently followed his own system, as Tischendorf, ed. Lips. 2, prolegg. p. xlv, has shewn by many instances. And he has not taken the pains which he should have done to obtain the best collations of the Vatican MS. (B), by far the most important for his work [8]; having neglected altogether that of Bartolocci, which was known and accessible to him;—nor of the Parisian Codex Ephremi (C), which was also accessible to him, but which he has taken from the imperfect collation of Wetstein.

7. These defects necessarily take off considerably from the otherwise valuable services of Lachmann to N. T. criticism. And it is much to be lamented that, owing to the nature of his plan, and the fact of its never having been thoroughly carried out, his work has ever been very generally and fatally misunderstood, and its readings cited by ignorant persons as if they were the result of the Editor's deliberate judgment. All this ought in fairness to be recognized, when we discuss the residuum of value which Lachmann's provisional labours now possess for the biblical student. It is undoubtedly true, as Dr. Tregelles has observed,—Printed Text of the Greek Test., p. 113,—that, "let any objections be raised to the plan, let inconsistencies be pointed out in the execution, let corrections of varied kinds be suggested, still the fact will remain, that *the first Greek Testament, since the invention of printing, edited wholly on ancient authority, irrespective of modern traditions, is due to* CHARLES LACHMANN." At the same time the student must take care to keep this high praise in its proper place. Lachmann's was the work of a pioneer, not that of a builder. It was not in his design, *in the work which we now possess*, to give us a critical and trustworthy text. This he might have done, had he lived, and had he not been deterred and discouraged by the general misunderstanding of what he had done. His real service to the cause of sacred criticism has been, the bold and uncompromising demolition of that unworthy and pedantic reverence for the received text, which stood in the way of all chance of discovering the genuine word of God; and, the clear indication of the *direction* which all future sound criticism must take, viz. a return to the evidence of the most ancient witnesses. For the firm hold which this latter principle has taken, for the comparative absence of blind fautorship of the received text, in spite of repeated attempts to shake the one and to re-establish the other, we have mainly to thank Lachmann: and this,—even in the midst of all conceded objections to

[8] See below, ch. vii. § i., catalogue of MSS. under B.

his plan, to his carrying it out, and to his tone and temper,—is surely no mean eulogy.

For further and full description of his Edition, see Tregelles, Printed Text, &c., pp. 97—115.

8. Dr. Tischendorf has published at Leipzig several editions of the Greek Testament. I shall speak here of two only: the second, which appeared in 1849, and the seventh, in 1859[9]. In his revision of the text, as explained in his prolegomena to the edition of 1849, he has followed the *most ancient* MSS., not however disregarding the testimony of the later ones and of versions and Fathers, where the former disagree, or where the readings of the elder MSS. have apparently sprung from corruption of the text. And to judge of this last, he lays down the following rules:—Readings are to be suspected,—1. which are peculiar to one or other of the elder MSS., or which savour strongly of the character of some one class of recensions, and have therefore probably proceeded from some corrector;—2. which although supported by many MSS., have manifestly or probably sprung from the error of a copyist;—3. which have sprung from a desire to assimilate citations from the Old Testament to the text of the cited passage, or parallel places in the Gospels to one another. In such cases (unless there be strong cause to the contrary) the discrepant reading is to be preferred to the accordant one. 4. A reading is to be preferred, which appears to furnish a clue to the others, or to contain the elements of them in itself. 5. The usage of the New Testament writers in general, and of each one in particular, is to be regarded in balancing readings with one another. For the discussion of these rules, I refer the student to the work itself. The theory of them is unobjectionable; it will be by the practical carrying out of them that the New Testament editor must be judged. And on the whole his principles appear to have been boldly and consistently carried out; and the text of this edition of 1849 is, in my view, very far superior to any which preceded it. The fact of my never having adopted it myself, will shew that I do not consider this praise to be in all cases deserved. The edition is very unequal in its various parts. His design grew on him as he advanced, and he did not re-write the earlier portion to correspond with the later. In the Epistles, he gave in full the authorities for the reading which he adopted, as well as those for that which he rejected: in the Gospels, *very rarely the latter*,—sometimes *neither*. Indeed the digest, in the early Gospels, was miserably meagre. Full one-third of the readings of D were omitted, as well as many others of importance. Compare only, e. g., the various readings of Matt. xii.

[9] While this edition has been preparing, a portion of an 8th edition has been published, and has been consulted where it was available. It is by no means free from inaccuracies, both in the compilation and in the printing.

1—8 with those in Lachmann. And the same is true of almost every page. His adoption of readings was not always distinguished by watchfulness to detect trips of transcribers, as e.g. in John vi. 51, where the homœoteleuton δώσω—δώσω was obviously the first source of confusion: see also Luke xxiv. 51, 52. But, allowing for such imperfections, and for instances of carelessness such as are incident to all who undertake a work of this kind, I cannot but regard Tischendorf's 2nd edition as the most valuable contribution, at the time of its appearance, which had been yet made to the revision of the text of the New Testament. And I believe that all future texts arranged on critical principles, will be found to approach very closely to his. Such has been the case with my own, although in every instance of correction or re-arrangement I have been led, not by him, but as the careful reader may see, by the rules which he and I have followed in common. And it will be found by any who will take the trouble to compare our texts, that the differences between us are both numerous and important.

9. Tischendorf's *seventh* edition is a far larger work, and, on account of its many departures from the second and subsequent ones[1], requires special notice.

As far as regards uniformity of plan and execution, this edition is certainly superior to the second. The array of witnesses cited for and against the text adopted is every where as copious as circumstances would admit. But it may be doubted whether in point of text the later edition is any advance on the former. While professing the same critical principles as before, the Editor has involved himself far more in subjective speculations, the tendency of which has been to lead him away in very many instances from the safe path of the consensus of our most ancient evidence, into the defence of a speculative text, respecting which arbitrary opinion may be as strongly pronounced on one side as on the other. This habit has resulted in a going back in a number of passages to the received text: so much so, that the defenders of that text against ancient evidence have claimed this edition of Tischendorf's as a victory on their side[2]. So that, on all sound critical principles, it must be regarded, as far as its text is concerned, as a retrogression, rather than an advance, since that of the edition of 1849.

[1] This term must, in Tischendorf's case, be taken with some qualification. His various editions do not represent successive deliberate recensions of his text and digest, nor do they embrace the same design, as in most other works: but they are merely, for the most part, varying *forms* under which he has issued his text, with or without an abbreviated digest of various readings. Properly speaking, we have had but *three* complete *editions* from him: the first in 1841, the second in 1849, and the third in 1857-9. It may be mentioned, that in his *eighth* edition [1864 &c.], many places are conformed to the readings of the Codex Sinaiticus.

[2] So, e.g., Bp. Wordsworth, Preface to his Greek Testament, vol. i. p. xiv.

10. It is much to be regretted that in many particulars Tischendorf's digest should still present so many marks of inaccuracy ; and that, where not borne out by others, so little reliance can be placed upon its citations of versions and Fathers. This is the universal testimony of those who have taken the pains to compare his citations with the originals : and I can add to it from my own experience. When I have had occasion to search the works of a Father to discover the real bearing of a passage which has been obscured by being partially extracted in his notes, I have, at least as often as not, found that it ought not to have been alleged as evidence.

11. And the complaints made with regard to the versions are even more loud and general. The charges are made against Tischendorf, that he has referred very carelessly to the Curetonian Syriac : that in the case of the important Syriac version (Peschito) he relies on the Latin translation of Leusden and the very unsatisfactory edition of Schaaf: and it would appear certain from his silence (prolegg. edn. 7, p. xix) that he has neglected the much more important editions of Widmanstadt and Lee (see Tregelles, Horne's Introd. to N. T. vol. iv. p. 260). He has passed over in silence the edition of the Coptic (Memphitic) version of the Acts and Epistles by Dr. Paul Bötticher—which, though not perfectly satisfactory, should still not have been left unconsulted by a professed critical editor—and has relied on the very incorrect Latin of the older edition of Wilkins. Again, in the case of the Armenian version, he has trusted wholly to the incorrect and partial collations (Tregelles, ib. p. 311) which were made for the N. T. edited by Scholz. It is also not unjust to say, that I have been informed by a friend who has some knowledge of the original languages, that in the case of other versions, where Tregelles and Tischendorf differ in their statement of the readings adopted and the impressions given by an ancient version, the English Editor is commonly right, and the German Editor commonly wrong. Several of these defects appear to have been remedied in his eighth edition.

12. Still, with all these faults, Tischendorf's book is indispensable to the thorough biblical scholar. Its research, and accumulation of testimonies are wonderful, considering that they are the work of one man : and the digest contains what must necessarily form the materials for all future revisions of the N. T. text. It is all the more to be regretted that such a work should be disfigured by blemishes so considerable, and should not have been carefully kept free from those elements of untrustworthiness, which its Author was so ready to point out and insist on in his predecessor, Dr. Scholz.

13. In 1857, Dr. Tregelles published the first part of his edition of the Greek Testament, containing the Gospels of St. Matthew and St. Mark : and in 1861, the second part, containing the Gospels of St. Luke

and St. John. The ends which he proposes are thus stated in his introductory notice :—

I. To give the text of the New Testament on the authority of the ancient witnesses, MSS., and versions, with the aid of the earlier citations, so as to present, as far as possible, the text best attested in the earlier centuries.

II. To follow certain proofs when obtainable, which carry us as near as possible to the apostolic age.

III. So to give the various readings, as to make it clear what is the evidence on both sides : and always to give the whole of the testimony of the ancient MSS. (and of some which are later in date but old in text), of the versions as far as the seventh century, and the citations down to Eusebius inclusive.

In order to accomplish this end, Dr. Tregelles has himself spent much time on the labour of collating and re-collating, and has availed himself of trustworthy materials before collected by others.

14. It will be superfluous, to those who are acquainted with the character of Dr. Tregelles's previous biblical labours, to say that his work has been done with scrupulous fidelity and accuracy. And it is on this ground principally that his edition is so peculiarly valuable : that we every where are assured of the ground on which we stand; and are not left to the fallacious influence of vast catalogues of authorities on which we know not whether we can fairly depend.

15. It was perhaps to be expected, that Dr. Tregelles, approaching biblical criticism from the side of faithful research and thorough assurance of his ground, should be somewhat more dependent than others on mere diplomatic evidence, and less alive to the necessity of judicially estimating, and in some cases even putting aside, the evidence of our oldest MSS. And if Tischendorf has run into a fault on the side of speculative hypotheses as to the origin of readings found in those MSS., it must be confessed, that Tregelles has sometimes erred on the (certainly, far safer) side of scrupulous adherence to the mere literal evidence of the ancient MSS. I shall elsewhere try to shew, that to accept *merely* such literal evidence, is, in fact, to shut our eyes to very much of the *real evidence* which due study of the habits of the MSS., and consequent intelligent judgment *on* that literal testimony, might set before us [3].

16. Believing this, I cannot concur with Dr. Tregelles in his view of the conclusion to be arrived at from the evidence in many disputed places. My reasons will be stated at length in the subsequent paragraphs. Meantime I would beg my readers to carry away in their

[3] See below, parr. 38 ff.

minds the impression, not of my dissent from Dr. Tregelles in regard to such passages, but of my thorough concurrence with his principles on the whole, and of my great value for his biblical labours, and for the spirit of painstaking and accuracy, and reverence, which every where distinguishes them. My *personal* obligations to him in the preparation of this edition will be acknowledged under their proper heads [4]. No one among those interested in the elucidation of the sacred text can more heartily wish than I do, that he may have health and eyesight spared him to complete the important work which he has so faithfully and worthily begun.

17. It remains now that I should explain in detail the principles on which I have revised the text.

18. The text which I have adopted has been constructed by following in all ordinary cases the united or preponderating evidence of the most ancient authorities: in cases where the most ancient authorities do not agree nor preponderate, taking into account later evidence; and in cases where the weight of diplomatic testimony is interfered with by adventitious circumstances (such as parallelism or the like), applying those principles of criticism which appear to furnish sound criteria of a spurious or genuine reading. The object of course is, in each case, *where evidence is divided*, to mount up, if possible, to the *original reading from which all the variations sprung:* in other words, to discover some word, or some arrangement, which shall account for the variations, but for which none of the variations will account.

19. The carrying out of this primary object will lead to several critical maxims, more or less applicable under varying circumstances. These have been for the most part so well detailed long ago by Griesbach, that I shall need no apology for transferring to my pages his important paragraphs on the subject:—

"1) *Brevior lectio*, nisi testium vetustorum et gravium auctoritate penitus destituatur, *præferenda est verbosiori.* Librarii enim multo proniores ad addendum fuerunt, quam ad omittendum. Consulto vix unquam prætermiserunt quicquam, addiderunt quam plurima: casu vero nonnulla quidem exciderunt, sed haud pauca etiam oculorum, aurium, memoriæ, phantasiæ ac judicii errore a scribis admisso, adjecta sunt textui. In primis vero brevior lectio, etiamsi testium auctoritate inferior sit altera, præferenda est—

a) si simul durior, obscurior, ambigua, elliptica, hebraizans aut solœca est,

b) si eadem res variis phrasibus in diversis codicibus expressa legitur,

c) si vocabulorum ordo inconstans est et instabilis,

[4] See below, in the list of MSS.

d) in pericoparum[5] initiis,

e) si plenior lectio glossam seu interpretamentum sapit, vel parallelis locis ad verbum consonat, vel e lectionariis immigrasse videtur.

"Contra vero pleniorem lectionem breviori (nisi hanc multi et insignes tueantur testes) anteponimus—

α) si omissioni occasionem præbere potuerit ὁμοιοτέλευτον,

β) si id quod omissum est, librariis videri potuit obscurum, durum, superfluum, insolens, paradoxum, pias aures offendens, erroneum, aut locis parallelis repugnans,

γ) si ea quæ absunt, salvo sensu salvaque verborum structura abesse poterant, e quo genere sunt propositiones, quod vocant, incidentes, præsertim breviores, et alia, quorum defectum librarius relegens quæ scripserat haud facile animadvertebat,

δ) si[6] brevior lectio ingenio, stylo aut scopo auctoris minus conveniens est,

ε) si[6] sensu prorsus caret,

ζ) si e locis parallelis aut e lectionariis eam irrepsisse probabile est.

"2) *Difficilior et obscurior lectio anteponenda est ei, in qua omnia tam plana sunt et extricata, ut librarius quisque facile intelligere ea potuerit.* Obscuritate vero et difficultate sua eæ potissimum indoctos librarios vexarunt lectiones—

a) quarum sensus absque penitiore græcismi, hebraismi, historiæ, archæologiæ, &c. cognitione perspici non facile poterant,

b) quibus admissis vel sententia, varii generis difficultatibus obstructa, verbis inesse, vel aptus membrorum orationis nexus dissolvi, vel argumentorum ab auctore ad confirmandam suam thesin prolatorum nervus incidi videbatur.

"3) *Durior lectio præferatur ei, qua posita, oratio suaviter leniterque fluit.* Durior autem est lectio elliptica, hebraizans, solœca, a loquendi usu græcis consueto abhorrens aut verborum sono aures offendens.

"4) *Insolentior lectio potior est ea, qua nil insoliti continetur.* Vocabula ergo rariora, aut hac saltem significatione, quæ eo de quo quæritur loco admittenda esset, rarius usurpata, phrasesque ac verborum constructiones usu minus tritæ, præferantur vulgatioribus. Pro exquisitioribus enim librarii usitatiora cupide arripere, et in illorum locum

[5] In the beginnings of the ecclesiastical portions we often find a word or a clause supplied,—the proper name of the agent or speaker, or the like.

[6] Both these must be applied with caution: the first, because it is quite possible that an intelligent librarian might correct *to* the well-known expression of his author: the second, because that which on a mistaken conventional view of a passage, seems without sense, often acquires an admirable sense when the true context is discovered.

glossemata et interpretamenta (præsertim si margo aut loca parallela talia suppeditarent) substituere soliti sunt.

"5) *Locutiones minus emphaticæ*, nisi contextus et auctoris scopus emphasin postulent[7], *propius ad genuinam scripturam accedunt*, quam discrepantes ab ipsis lectiones quibus major vis inest aut inesse videtur. Eruditul enim librarii[8], ut commentatores, emphases amabant ac captabant.

"6) *Lectio, præ aliis sensum pietati* (præsertim monasticæ) *alendæ aptum fundens, suspecta est*[9].

"7) *Præferatur aliis lectio cui sensus subest apparenter quidem falsus*, qui vero re penitus examinata verus esse deprehenditur.

"8) *Inter plures unius loci lectiones ea pro suspecta merito habetur, quæ orthodoxorum dogmatibus manifeste præ cæteris faciet.* Cum enim codices hodie superstites plerique, ne dicam omnes, exarati sint a monachis aliisque hominibus catholicorum partibus addictis, credibile non est, hos lectionem in codice, quem quisque exscriberet, obviam neglexisse ullam, qua catholicorum dogma aliquod luculenter confirmari aut hæresis fortiter jugulari posse videretur. Scimus enim, lectiones quascunque, etiam manifesto falsas, dummodo orthodoxorum placitis patrocinarentur, inde a tertii sæculi initiis mordicus defensas seduloque propagatas, cæteras autem ejusdem loci lectiones, quæ dogmati ecclesiastico nil præsidii afferrent hæreticorum perfidiæ attributas temere fuisse[1].

"9) Cum scribæ proclives sint ad iterandas alieno loco vocabulorum et

[7] But it is evident that this exception requires the utmost caution in its application.

[8] "Librarios enim dicimus, et hic et alibi criticos simul ac codicum possessores intelligi volumus, qui in suis libris, e quibus alii deinceps exscripti sunt, vel ipsum textum immutarunt, vel margini saltem qualescunque suas animadversiones et emendationes illeverunt." (not. Griesb.)

[9] Thus, e. g., in Rom. xiv. 17, where the kingdom of God is said to be not meat and drink, but δικαιοσύνη κ. εἰρήνη κ. χαρὰ ἐν πν. ἁγίῳ, the ms. 4 inserts after δικαιοσύνη, καὶ ἄσκησις. In some portions, such interpolations and corrections abound. Cf. as an example 1 Cor. vii. with the var. readd.

[1] This rule, sound in the main (and hardly to be cited, as Scrivener, p. 375, would wish me to do, without its concluding sentence), must be applied with the following discrimination :—If the passage is of such a nature, that, *whichever reading is adopted, the orthodox meaning is legitimate*, but *the adoption of the stronger orthodox reading is absolutely incompatible with the heretical meaning*,—then it is probable that *such stronger orthodox reading was the original.* For while the heretics would be certain to annul the expression offensive to them and substitute the weaker one, the orthodox, on the above hypothesis, would have originally no motive for alteration.—A case in point is the celebrated τὴν ἐκκλησίαν τοῦ θεοῦ, Acts xx. 28. Had θεοῦ been the original, it would have been certain to be altered by the heretics: had κυρίου been the original, no reason can be assigned why the orthodox should have tampered with it. It is probable therefore, as far as *this* consideration is involved (see note in loc.), that θεοῦ was the original word.

sententiarum terminationes easdem, quas modo scripsissent aut mox scribendas esse, præcurrentibus calamum oculis, prævidérent, *lectiones ex* ejusmodi *rhythmi fallacia facillime explicandæ, nullius sunt pretii*[2].

"10) Hisce ad peccandum illecebris similes sunt aliæ. Librarii, qui sententiam, antequam scribere eam inciperent, totam jam perlegissent, vel dum scriberent fugitivo oculo exemplum sibi propositum inspicerent, sæpe ex antecedentibus vel consequentibus literam, syllabam aut vocabulum perperam arripuerunt, novasque sic lectiones procuderunt. Si v. c. duo vocabula vicina ab eadem syllaba vel litera inciperent, accidit haud raro, ut vel prius plane omitteretur, vel posteriori temere tribueretur, quod priori esset peculiare. Ejusmodi hallucinationes vix vitabit, qui libello paullo verbosiori exscribendo operam dat, nisi toto animo in hoc negotium incumbat: id quod pauci librarii fecisse videntur. Lectiones ergo, quæ ex hoc errorum fonte promanarunt, quantumvis vetustæ ac consequenter in complures libros transfusæ sint, recte rejiciuntur, præsertim si codices cæteroqui cognati ab hujus labis contagio puri deprehendantur[3].

"11) E pluribus ejusdem loci lectionibus *ea præstat, quæ velut media inter cæteras interjacet;* hoc est ea, quæ reliquarum omnium quasi stamina ita continet, ut, hac tanquam primitiva admissa, facile appareat, quanam ratione, seu potius quonam erroris genere, ex ipsa cæteræ omnes propullularint.

"12) *Repudiantur lectiones glossam seu interpretamentum redolentes,* cujus generis interpolationes nullo negotio emunctioris naris criticus subolfaciet.

"13) *Rejiciendas esse lectiones, e Patrum commentariis aut scholiis vetustis in textum invectas,* magno consensu critici docent. (He proceeds at some length to caution against the promiscuous assumption of such corruptions in the earlier codices and versions from such sources.)

"14) *Respuimus lectiones ortas primum in lectionariis,* quæ sæpissime in anagnosmatum initiis ac interdum in clausulis etiam atque in medio contextu claritatis causa addunt, quod ex orationis serie sup-

[2] See a curious instance, among many others, of mechanical repetition of a phrase from association, 1 Cor. xiv. 18: and Rom. viii. 1.

[3] The vast number and extent of mistakes of this kind are only known to those who have carefully observed the phænomena of the later and usually less regarded mss. There is hardly an opportunity presented by similar endings of words, of which the fertile genius of error has not availed itself. And even in our most ancient MSS., these occur not unfrequently. A remarkable instance is found in A, 1 Cor. vi. 2—6, where because ἐλαχίστων ends ver. 2, and ἀπίστων ends ver. 6, the whole lying between is omitted, the transcriber's eye having passed on from the first -ιστων to the second; and another in B, Matt. xii. 46—48, where the whole ver. 47 is omitted between λαλῆσαι and λαλῆσαι.

plendum esset, resecantque vel immutant, quod, sejunctum ab antecedentibus aut consequentibus, vix satis recte intelligi posse videretur. (Similar cautions are here added against assuming this too promiscuously.)

"15) *Damnandæ sunt lectiones e latina versione in græcos libros invectæ.* (Cautions are here also inserted against the practice of the earlier critics, who if they found in the græco-latin MSS. or even in those of high antiquity and value, a solitary reading agreeing with the Latin, hastily condemned that codex as latinizing.)"

20. Having reprinted for the use of students these excellent rules of Griesbach's, I must be contented to refer for their ampler illustration to the prefaces of his and other editions, especially that of the 7th Leipzig edition of Tischendorf, pp. xxvii ff.

21. It is mainly in accordance with these rules that my text has been arranged. Every various reading has been judged with reference to external manuscript authority and internal probability combined,—and that reading adopted, which on the whole seemed most likely to have stood in the original text. Such judgments are of course open to be questioned, and in many cases the reading will perhaps never be completely agreed on; but I do not know that this should deter successive editors from using all means in their power to arrive at a decision in each case, and conscientiously discharging their duty by the sacred text[4].

22. The reader will expect to find a statement, how far, in the later Editions of the present volume, I have remained firm to the principles enunciated in the earlier ones, and how far increasing experience, and the labours of others, have modified the manner in which I have aimed at reaching the end above enounced.

23. The tendency of any change which time has brought about in my critical views, may be described as twofold; both branches being consistent and concurrent.

24. FIRST, I have become disposed, as research and comparison have gone on, to lay more and more weight on the evidence of our few most ancient MSS. and versions, and less on that (in its present state at least) of the great array of later mss. which are so often paraded in digests as supporting or impugning the commonly received text.

25. It is but due from me to render a reason for an assertion apparently so much at variance with some passages in the Prolegomena to the Second Edition of this volume, and in the Prolegomena to the earlier Editions of Vol. II.

[4] In this part of my work I have found of especial service the critical notices prefixed to each chapter in Meyer's Commentary, and the similar discussions of readings in the text of that of De Wette: and have consulted whatever else I have been able to find on the more important and celebrated varieties of reading.

I am still willing to endorse what was said there, Vol. II. ch. v. § i. par. 5 (Third Edition):—

"With regard to manuscript testimony, it has been my endeavour to *combine*, as far as possible, that furnished by the *later* MSS. with that of the more ancient, and to give them, as well as the others, due weight in the determination of readings. The great thing required, in weighing the testimony of MSS., is a knowledge of the habits of various classes of correctors and transcribers. Long before the date of our earliest MS., a systematic course of correction had begun, and there existed errors of transcription of considerable standing. The earlier those corrections or errors originated, the more extensively would they be spread among our present families of manuscripts, and the more likely are they to have found their way into the generally received text. Also, I need hardly say, the more difficult are they of detection. The only sure way to detect them, is by intimate acquaintance with the general phænomena of manuscripts, the cursive as well as the uncial. Such acquaintance will enable us at once to pronounce a reading to be spurious, which yet has a vast array of MS. authority in its favour: just because we know that it furnishes an instance of a correction or of an error commonly found in other places."

26. But it is in the very course of applying this in practice, that difficulties have sprung up, of a nature so formidable, as to produce in me an oscillation back towards the purely diplomatic principle, as after all the only trustworthy one under our present circumstances.

27. For let us consider, the remarks above cited being taken as substantially correct, how we are to proceed. We find a certain number of MSS. and versions respecting which our knowledge is definite and reliable: whose date we can determine within very narrow limits of deviation. So far, as to external evidence, we are safe. We cannot arrive by their means at the original sacred text, for the reasons stated in the paragraph above quoted: viz. because, before they were written and made, a course of correction, and a series of mistakes in transcribing, had taken place: but we can arrive at a result of which we know the value: we can ascertain, in the main, what was the text of the times to which that body of evidence belongs: and we can then, under safe caution, apply to that text the above canons of subjective criticism: of which application I shall speak by and by. We now come to the great mass of cursive mss., written in later ages. That some of these possibly may be transcripts of texts of at least as much value as those of our more ancient MSS., hardly admits of a doubt: and in some few cases it has been ascertained that it is so. But in the great majority of cases, where are we now, as to definiteness of evidence? What do we know of the character of the texts which we are citing? Even supposing that our collations have been

thoroughly made, as in the case of the mss. examined by Mr. Scrivener, how can we be sure that many of our witnesses ought not to be reduced to one, as being mere transcripts of one and the same text? Here all is uncertainty; all is vague, and liable to wide mistake. In this field it is, that the strong assertions may be safely made, which we so constantly find in the pages of those who would uphold the received text at all hazards: who tell us again and again that "*four or five* MSS. *only*" read this or that, and "*all the rest agree with the received text:*" when perhaps those "four or five" are just the consensus of our most ancient and venerable authorities, and "all the rest" may, for aught we know, be in many cases no more worthy to be heard in the matter, than so many separate printed copies of the present day.

28. The tendency of these remarks has been to shew, that though there may yet lie hid, among the mass of cursive mss., texts of great value and of independent ancient origin, we must be contented to take, as our basis of revision of the sacred text, such ancient texts as can, at each period of revision, be definitely pointed out to us; and we must not assume at random that because the mass *may* contain more of such, therefore it is to be regarded as made up of them. Future researches will very probably bring to light more such trustworthy witnesses: as this happens, let them be admitted into our list, as has been already done in the case of the mss. 1, 33, 69, and some others. And let the existence of any remarkable readings in the other cursive mss. be carefully noted, that their value and position may be by degrees ascertained. But it is high time that it should be acknowledged, with humility and ingenuousness, that we of this age, when sacred criticism is yet in its infancy, must be contented with a provisional text, founded on such data as are well assured and defined for us: and must leave it to other times, and more complete states of our manuscript evidence, to approximate closer and closer to what may be presumed to be our ultimate best text.

29. It is considerations such as these which have led me to banish from my digest the long processions of cursive mss. of which I have been speaking[5]: and to base my revision only on those witnesses respecting which I am able to speak with something like certainty.

30. SECONDLY, experience has brought about some change in my convictions with regard to the application of canons of subjective criticism to the consensus of ancient MSS. In proportion as I have been led severely to examine, how far we can safely depend on such subjective considerations, I confess that the limits of their applicability have become narrowed. In very many cases, they may be made to tell with

[5] The main reason for inserting the evidence of cursives has been, the fact of their supporting or illustrating readings found in one or two only of the uncial MSS.

equal force either way. One critic adopts a reading because it is in accord with the usage of the sacred writer; another holds it, for this very reason, to have been a subsequent conformation of the text. One believes a particle to have been inserted to give completeness: another, to have been omitted as appearing superfluous.

Now doubtless the statement of such uncertainties as these will lead mere reviewers, and those who like them only skim the surface of the subject, to cast contempt on all application of subjective considerations. But such ought not to be its result, and will not be, on any critical mind. The limits of such application will become narrowed: but by that very contraction it will become safer and more certain. It is manifest that we ought, in every case where it seems to be called for, to look at and weigh both sides: where the probabilities appear to be balanced, we are bound, in fair dealing with the sacred text, to leave on the mind of the critical reader the impression of that equilibrium, and for the general reader, *who must be furnished with a text*, to give the ancient witnesses the benefit of the doubt;—where the preponderance appears to us to be clear (a matter which I will presently illustrate) against the ancient MSS. and versions, we ought not to adhere stiffly and formally to diplomatic conformity, but boldly to reject them in this case, as we boldly follow them in others.

31. And as to this latter, I do not know that the difference between the principles of intelligent critics is very great. Certainly, as before remarked, Tischendorf, in his 7th edition, committed himself to subjective speculations of a vague and untrustworthy kind: but they were violations of his own principles. The difference with which I am mainly here concerned on this point, is that between the practice of Dr. Tregelles, and my own. In order to set this clearly before the reader, I will cite some of the principles which he has enounced in the Introductory Notice to his Greek Testament.

32. He says,

"(3.) If the reading of the ancient authorities in general is unanimous, there can be but little doubt that it should be followed, whatever may be the later testimonies: for it is most improbable that the independent testimony of early MSS., versions, and Fathers, should accord with regard to something entirely groundless."

And,

"(6.) The readings respecting which a judgment must be formed, are those where the *evidence* is really divided in such a way, that it is needful to enquire on which side the balance preponderates. In such cases, it is not enough to enumerate authorities: they must be examined point by point. OTHER THINGS BEING EQUAL, (*a*) an early citation will sometimes be *decisive*, especially if it is given in express terms. (*b*) Also if one reading accords with a parallel passage and the other does not: (*c*) or if one introduces an amplification given elsewhere: (*d*) or if one seems to avoid a difficulty which the other does not: (*e*) or if there is *one* well-attested reading, and *several* others which may probably have been taken from it: (*f*) or if the one reading might be easily accounted for on principles connected with the known origin of variations; in such cases it is not difficult, on the whole, to form a judgment as to what was probably the original reading. It is quite true that at times it may be very doubtful whether the quantity of direct evidence may not overbalance all modes of procedure derived from the application of a principle, and as to *which* of two seemingly conflicting considerations ought to have most weight."

33. Now with the whole of these statements I accord in the main, and it is only on a certain portion of frontier ground, so to speak, that I have any difference with Dr. Tregelles: on that namely which lies *between* the cases described in these two paragraphs of his. Where ancient evidence is *vastly preponderant* in favour of some reading, but at the same time we have very strong reasons for suspecting that reading, it is in these cases, which I am bound to say very seldom occur, that I sometimes feel bound to go one way and Dr. Tregelles goes the other.

34. There is one element, implied perhaps in his case (*f*), but not explicitly stated, which in such cases deserves more weight than he has given to it. It is this: the known habits of early copyists, and of the particular MSS. with which we are dealing. All biblical critics know, that certain ways of writing, e. g. αι for ε and vice versa, η for ει, ει for ι, υ for οι, &c., prevail to such an extent as to form a subject for discrimination, entirely separate from that of various readings. One MS. reads εταιρε, another ετεραι: but we hardly as much as notice this at all[6]. We call it *itacism*, the name by which such *normal enormities* are known: and no further notice is taken of it. Of these Tregelles himself says, Horne, vol. iv. p. 51, "Such interchanges as these are frequent even in the oldest MSS. extant: and their occurrence belongs rather to the head of orthography than to that of various readings in the proper sense of the term. In general, they may and ought to pass unnoticed: but when they happen to form an actual word it may require some consideration to determine *what* was the word intended. . . . The sense and meaning must determine: for the spelling has no authority at all between εσται and εστε, εχετε and εχεται, and similar words. Even if every MS. should agree in one spelling, there would be no liberty taken by any who read the other: since these vowels and diphthongs are used indiscriminately."

[6] I believe that on one occasion or other, specimens of all these 'monstra' will be found noticed in the digest; but no point has been made of inserting them throughout.

35. Now there are *other variations* in our ancient MSS., not quite of the same character, but very nearly approximating to it, which ought whenever they occur, to be taken *cum grano salis*, bearing in mind the entire uncertainty whether they ought really to be reckoned as various readings or not.

36. To give but one instance, that of the convertible use of the long and short vowels. A reads ζονην for ζωνην Mark vi. 8; λαμβανωμεν for λαμβανομεν 1 John iii. 22 : Bℵ read εχωμεν for εχομεν Gal. vi. 10 : C reads ζησωμεν for ζησομεν Rom. vi. 2, and συνζησωμεν for -ομεν ib. 8 : D reads χειρων σχισμα γινεται Mark ii. 21 : AB read διωκομεν for διωκωμεν Rom. xiv. 19 : AC read εισερχωμεθα for -ομεθα Heb. iv. 3 : AD read προσευξωμαι twice for -ομαι in 1 Cor. xiv. 15. Dr. Tregelles attempts (Horne, ut supra) to clear the most ancient MSS. from the charge of this confusion : but in vain ; they are amenable to it in common with, though not to such an extent as, the later ones.

37. With these facts before us we come to such a reading as the εχωμεν of Rom. v. 1. Here we have certainly not one or two ancient MSS., but the consensus of all, together with the oldest versions and Fathers. And I own to having been so far shaken in the trustworthiness of subjectivities, that in the Fourth Edition of my Second Volume, I edited εχωμεν, as matter of strict duty. But I feel that my confidence in it, as the original word of St. Paul, was very much diminished owing to the practice of the MSS. of interchanging ο and ω.

38. But let us descend from this almost irrefragable diplomatic ground to the far more common case, where perhaps, first-rate evidence being but scanty to begin with, all that exists in the particular case presents just such a reading as the mistakes or corrections of copyists are constantly bringing before us : where, without that balance of evidence which Tregelles seems to require as the condition for the exercise of critical judgment, some one of his six considerations might in most minds carry conviction as to the original reading ; are we to abstain, in such a case, from sitting in judgment on the reading, and on the authority of two, or even but one, of our early uncials, to carry into our text what we are all but sure is not part of it, or leave out of it that which we are nearly certain belongs to it ?

39. The question which I have just asked applies to the majority of passages where my readings differ from those of Dr. Tregelles. It would lead us too far, in these prolegomena, to examine them one by one ; but if the reader, who follows my text and digest, notes the passages where I have been led, not by the weight of ancient external testimony, but by some one of the above-stated principles which seems to me to establish the text in spite of it, he may be nearly sure that in those Tregelles and I diverge.

40. The principal matter in which our great MSS. are at fault in

the three Gospels, is, the piecing one Gospel from another in parallel places. The observation of a close student of the text will not fail to convince him, without "assuming that in every passage where there is variety of reading, the probability that two Evangelists did not use the same words exceeds all other probabilities[7]," that in even the earliest MSS. there has been constant tampering with the text of one Gospel to conform it to that of another. And surely, such being a patent fact, nothing can justify us in lending ourselves to sanction such a practice by adopting it in our text, nor ought we to follow the multitude, whether it be of moderns or of ancients, in thus doing evil; but, even with the possibility of mistake in judgment, to avoid the almost certainty of mistake in fact. These cases require a discrimination which we can hardly expect in any critic to be faultless: but I submit that they *do peremptorily* require it; and I cannot believe that it will be found entirely wanting to those who with the human appliances of study of the sacred text, and ripened caution, unite that spirit of conscientious reverence, without which all biblical labour is in vain.

41. It remains that I should say something of the principles of recension of the text enounced and defended by Mr. Scrivener, in his edition of the Codex Augiensis, and now more elaborately in his "Introduction to the Criticism of the N. T."

42. From what has preceded, it will be clearly seen that I cannot consent to the course which he would prescribe for us, that of seeking our readings from the later uncials, supported as they usually are by the mass of cursive mss.: for to this his practice really amounts, after all the explanation which he has given of it in the work last cited. Nor can I conceive a time when examinations of texts, whose character is now latent, should lead scholars to such a procedure. For what right have we to set virtually aside these two wonderful facts: First, *the agreement in the main of our oldest uncials, at the distance of one or two centuries*,—of which, owing probably to the results of persecution, we have no manuscript remains,—*with the citations of the primitive Fathers, and with the earliest versions?* I say, the agreement *in the main:* for Mr.

[7] So Mr. Hort, in an able notice of Tischendorf and Tregelles in the Journal of Philology for March, 1858, expresses himself, charging us with making the assumption. But surely this is not quite fair. We do not *assume* this, *all other things being equal;* but we are led to *conclude this to have been so in the particular case,* other things being *unequal,*—e. g. where one Gospel is undisputed in the use of some particular word or phrase, and where in the parallel place in the others this word or phrase is found as the reading of one or more (perhaps all that happen to be present, in case of defect of one or more) of our great MSS., against the concurrence of the later uncials. It is obvious that in such a case as this we make no assumption such as that with which Mr. Hort charges us.

Scrivener's instances of discrepancy [8] are in vain used by him to produce an impression, which we know would be contrary to the fact in the majority of instances [9].

43. Secondly, *the very general concurrence of the character of text of our earliest* MSS., *versions, and Fathers, with that text which the soundest critical principles lead us to adopt.* This surely invests the authority of those early witnesses with a claim upon us which can never be set aside: whereas on the other hand, the fact, that the character of the text generally received, depending as it does in the main on our later uncials and on the mass of the cursive mss., instances so much more frequently the violation of sound critical principles, does seem to me to detract from the weight of those later witnesses in a measure which no mere concurrence of numbers can ever fill up.

44. If this were reversed; if we found, the earlier we mounted up, the Gospels more conformed, instead of more divergent; easy readings abounding instead of difficult ones; if we found that the text at present received differed from that of the early ages in being more harsh, more apparently discrepant from itself, more difficult and startling: then indeed we should have good reason to cling pertinaciously to it, and to believe, in spite of history, that the vigilance of the Church over the sacred word had been ever on the increase, at a period in her history when all her other graces were on the decline: then we should be compelled to take as truth the plaint of the old tragedian, ἄνω ποταμῶν ἱερῶν χωροῦσι παγαί [1], and to accept for once the prodigy, that "the *further from* the source the clearer the stream." The fact that all this is undeniably the other way; that the process by which the present received text has been attained has been that of crumbling down salient points, softening irregularities, conforming differences, favouring prevalent doctrines [2],—forms what will ever prove to me an insuperable

[8] Mr. Scrivener, no doubt without designed unfairness, but very unfortunately, chose for his field of comparison the Gospel of St. Mark, in which we have not the Curetonian Syriac, on the testimony of which Tregelles very much relies.

[9] It would be impossible here to range over such a number of examples as would prove this to the reader. But Mr. Scrivener himself furnishes a comment which may at least tend to relax the stringency of his own conclusion from those which he adduces: "I am fully aware that in a field so wide as the criticism of the N. T., those who dexterously select their examples may prove just what they will." It is true he has avoided the imputation of "dexterous selection" in those now brought forward by him (Introd. &c. pp. 401-2): but may not almost the same be said of any limited selection of examples as set against the great prevailing currents of manuscript evidence? The dissidence of ancient testimony is, I own, more valuable to me than the concurrence of that which is later. The study of the various readings in parallel places in the Gospels will, I should imagine, bring most minds to the same conclusion.

[1] Eur. Med. 414.

[2] Mr. Scrivener says (Introd. p. 406), "I am sorry he should think it right to add,

barrier against accepting the principles so ably advocated by Mr. Scrivener.

45. Of course it will be inferred that still less can I accede to the principles of recension enounced by another school of critics, e. g. by a writer in a number of the British Quarterly. I need but mention these principles by way of illustrating by antagonism those which I believe more and more to be the only sound ones. They seem to be nearly as follows:

1. That the received text requires alteration in comparatively few passages.
2. That in making alterations, the earlier MSS. should have much less authority yielded to them than critical editors have hitherto assigned.
3. That the *context* ought to have great weight in determining the true reading.
4. That ancient versions, Fathers, and such known facts as corruption from parallel passages, should only be used in subordination to the mass of mss. and considerations derived from the context.

46. In fact, to dwell but on one point here put forward, the consideration of the "*context*" is the very last that should be allowed by a critic to be present in his mind as an element of his judgment. I do not say that in some extreme cases it may not have to be introduced, as perhaps (but I should now speak doubtfully even in this case) in Rom. v. 1, where there are so many confusing considerations arising from the habits of the MSS.: but certainly we may say, that it is by this very consideration of the context, and of N. T. usage, that our deteriorated Textus Receptus has in many instances arisen[3], and that the general

'favouring prevalent doctrines.' Why should any one be backward in stating that which is a notorious fact?" Mr. S.'s two next pages are very instructive as to the difference in view between him and myself as regards the dissidence of ancient, and concurrence of later evidence. The challenge which he there throws out to me, to "illustrate the next edition of my text of the Gospels with a further accession of various readings from the best cursive codices," is one which I of all men should be most ready to accept, if, on the one hand, my digest were to be taken for more than a compendium of various readings: and if, on the other, I could find that the character of the text of the various cursives had been sufficiently studied to be accurately ascertained.

[3] See two notable instances of these, 1) in a note of Dr. Bloomfield's on John vi. 69—where the ancient reading ἅγιος is rejected, because the expression ἅγιος τοῦ θεοῦ does not elsewhere occur except in the confession of the dæmoniacs, and χριστός, ὁ υἱὸς τοῦ θεοῦ frequently occurs in the N. T. (!) A purer piece of arbitrary subjectivity can hardly be imagined. And 2) in Bp. Wordsworth's note in loc., in which he retains τοῦ ζῶντος in the text, against BCDL (A being deficient, which he does not state) 1. 33, all the old latin versions except ff_2, the vulg. copt. arm. Cyr. al., as being "*very expressive and relevant to this place in connexion with* ῥήματα ζωῆς, *ver.* 68."

adoption of it as a critical gnomon would be the worst imaginable retrograde step in sacred criticism.

47. I am very anxious, in concluding this section, not to leave the impression on the reader that my present text differs from the former ones, or from those of Tischendorf and Tregelles, *more than is really the case.* In fact, with regard to the principles which regulate the decision in by far the greater number of differing readings, we are all in accord. It is but seldom, in most parts of the N. T., that those passages occur where our reasons of divergence come into play. And the same caution should be carried yet further. When it is objected by such writers as the critic in the British Quarterly, that "the texts in the modern critical editions are not even substantially the same," let the reader not hastily take this for granted, but carefully examine for himself how far it is true. He will find, that while in some passages differing views as to the comparative value of mere diplomatic evidence and of subjective considerations have led modern critical editors to different results, in the great mass of cases they are in accord. And let him hence learn to estimate the real gain which has accrued to our knowledge of the sacred text from that modern criticism which it is now becoming the fashion to despise : the positive progress which has been made in all those places where the ancient MSS. are unanimous against our received text : and the more satisfactory state of our knowledge by means of more collations, and the exercise of critical judgment, even in those places where the true reading is, and perhaps must ever remain, a matter of doubt.

48. It now remains to give a brief account of the *method of spelling* adopted in the text which I have edited. It has been taken, like the text itself, from the testimony of our most ancient existing MSS.

The following table is intended to bring into one view the main outlines of the course pursued in this volume, and to aid in freeing the digest as far as possible from all purely orthographical details :—

ἁλεεῖς, Mark i. 16, 17, AB^1[C also in 17]. (*ἁλιεῖς* has been retained in Matt. iv. 18, 19 (*αλεεις* B^1(since ascertained) Cℵ^1) and Luke v. 2 (*αλεεις* ACQℵ^1). In Mark i. 16, C def.; ℵ has *αλιεις* ver 16, *αλεεις* ver 17.)

ἀλλ' for **ἀλλά** (or *vice versa*). Whenever weighty testimony necessitates a change in the ordinary text, the chief witnesses for the form adopted are given as briefly as possible in the digest *ad loc.* Similarly with all other cases of elision or non-elision.

ἀνάγαιον ABCD[PR]ℵ. (Mark xiv. 15 : Luke xxii. 12.)

ἀνάπειρος AB^{1}DRℵ. (Luke xiv. 13, 21.)

ἀντιπέρα ABDRΞℵ. (Luke viii. 26.)

ἀποκτέννων AC, and sometimes Dℵ.

βαθέως ABCDℵ. (Luke xxiv. 1.)

βαλλάντιον ABDℵ, supported also by CQTΞ.

βεελζεβούλ ACDR (Luke xi. 15, &c.), also ℵ in Mark iii. 22. Elsewhere ℵ reads *βεεζεβουλ* with B.

Βοανηργές ABCℵ. (Mark iii. 17.)

Βοός, Luke iii. 32, ABDℵ[3a] and C(def. in Luke) Matt. But we read **Βοές** with Bℵ in Matt. i. 5.

Γεθσημανεῖ (-νει) ABCDℵ. (Matt. xxvi. 36: Mark xiv. 32.)

γένημα ABCDℵ. (Compare under Ἰωανάν below. Similarly ρ for ρρ, e.g. **ἐριμμένοι** B[1]Cℵ, Matt. ix. 36: **ἐράπισαν** ABCDZℵ, Matt. xxvi. 67; *προsέρηξεν* (not edited) BDℵ[1], Luke vi. 48; and B[1] has *παρησίᾳ* Mark viii. 32, *διαρήξας* Mark xiv. 63, *et similia.*)

Δαυείδ ABCDℵ. So also LTΞ of Gospp., E of Acts, and (always) D of Epistles. The abbreviated form δᾱδ is exclusively used in FKN P[also P of Acts Epp. Apoc.] QRU XZΓΔ[Π] 33. 69; it is also found in ACEGHLMΛΞℵ 1, E of Acts, F of Epistles. The word is found at full length in BD always; in A, Luke iii. 31; in C, Heb. iv. 7; in ℵ, Matt. i. 6. See Tregelles' digest on Luke iii. 31, from which this is partly taken. Δαυίδ is read in B[2]EMVΓΛ, and in F of Epistles; but Δαυείδ is supported by overwhelming manuscript authority and is the form adopted by Lachmann, Tischdf., Tregelles, and Westcott.

ἐδύνατο and **ἠδύνατο**. The best MSS. have the one almost as often as the other. When a consensus of MSS. leads to a form different from that found in the *textus receptus* the authority for our text is given in the digest.

[**-ει-** and **-ι-**. See under Λευεί.]

εἱλκωμένος ABDPℵ, Luke xvi. 20. (Cf. ἀνάπειρος.)

ἑκατοντάρχης BCℵ[1], Matt. viii. 13. (AD def.) But ἑκατόνταρχος Matt. viii. 5, 8 (read by BC notwithstanding the -χῃ in ver 13); xxvii. 54 (-χης Dℵ); Luke vii. 6 (-χης BL); xxiii. 47 (-χης Bℵ[1]).

Ἐλίσαιος ABDℵ, Luke iv. 27. (Cf. γένημα, above.)

ἔνατος ABCDℵ. But in Matt. xxvii. 46 [and xx. 5] D has εννατ., in ver 45 εvατ. (ἐνενήκοντα is also read in BDℵ [and all the other uncials]. Cf. γένημα.)

ἕνεκα BZℵ, Matt. xix. 5. But elsewhere in Gospp. ἕνεκεν is retained. Except Luke vi. 22, where most agree in ἕνεκα; and **εἵνεκεν** Luke iv. 18, in which the uncials agree. (B has ενεκα in Matt. v. 10, 11: Mark xiii. 9;—[Dℵ in Matt. xix. 29;—] D, in Mark x. 29: Luke xxi. 12. Bℵ have ειvεκεν Luke xviii. 29.)

ἐπροφήτευσα B[1]CD [L(exc Matt. xi. 13) T_cZ] ℵ[exc Luke i. 67, ℵ[3a]], and sometimes A.

ἐραυνᾶν B[1]ℵ, John v. 39 al.

ἐρρήθη B[b] D. (AC def. in Matt. v. 21, 27, 31, 33, 38, 43.) In Rom. ix. 12, 26 AB[1] have **ἐρρέθη**, and so also Cod. Clarom. 1. m.,—and ℵ throughout (Rev. vi. 11, ἐρέθη).

ἔσθειν Bℵ in Mark i. 6; BD in Luke vii. 33; x. 7; xxii. 30. In other places **ἐσθίειν** as rec.

εὐδόκησα and **ηὐδόκησα**; **εὐλόγησα** and **ηὐλόγησα**; **εὕρισκον** and **ηὕρισκον**; *et similia*, treated as ἐδύνατο and ἠδύνατο, *q. v.*

εὐθύς, BCℵ every where in Mark (except i. 18; where, however, Lℵ have εὐθύς).

ἐχθές, John iv. 52, AB[1]CDℵ.

ἠρώτουν, Matt. xv. 23, BCDℵ. (So also Cℵ in Mark iv. 10, where ABD and the text have -των.)

Ἱεροσόλυμα, Mark xi. 1, BCDℵ. This is the form used in all other places in Matt., Mark, and John (Gosp.), except Matt. xxiii. 37, where there is clearly special reason for the Hebrew form found alike in the ancient MSS. and in the ordinary text.

Ἱερουσαλήμ, Luke xviii. 31, BDRℵ. This is the form found in all places in Luke (Gosp.) except ii. 22; xix. 28 (Ιερουσαλημ D); xxiii. 7.

Ἰωανάν (for Ἰωαννά) AB ℵ-corr[1·3], Luke iii. 27 (ℵ[1] ιωναν, C def., D has a different genealogy). Similarly B generally reads Ἰωάνης, which Tregelles has edited: so does ℵ-corr[1] in Mark xiii. 3, ℵ[1] in Luke i. 13. But B has Ἰωάννης Luke i. 60, 63

[[b] Tischdf. gives ἐρρέθη as the reading of B[1], taking the correction to ἐρρήθη as made sometimes appy by his B[2] (= our B[1]-corr), sometimes by B[3] (= our B[2]).]

[and B[1] (Tischdf.) ib. ver 13]: Acts iv. 6, 13, 19, where Vercellone (similarly Tischdf.) states expressly, "*ita cod. cum duplici ν.*" In the other great MSS. the double ν holds its ground.

κἀγώ, κἀμοί, κἀμέ, κἄν, κἀκεῖ, κἀκεῖθεν, κἀκεῖνος, or their respective uncontracted forms, edited according to the preponderance of the early testimony briefly given in the digest. Variation only noticed when this consensus differs from the *textus receptus.*

Καφαρναούμ BD[RT]Zℵ [also in C Luke x. 15; John iv. 46, vi. 59; C[1] Luke vii. 1]. (The received Καπερ. is found in A C[sometimes] NP.)

κράβαττος ABCD, so ℵ in Acts v. 15. (B[1] has κραββαττος (not as Tischdf.) in Mark ii. 9, 11, 12, and only there; κραβαττος in ver. 4; also in Mark vi., John v. &c. In Mark ii. vi. and John v., ℵ has κραβακτον: so ℵ[1] in Acts ix.)

λεγιών BDℵ[1]. So also C in Mark v. 9, but in v. 15 -ε-; -ε- has been retained in this edition in Matt. xxvi. 53: Luke viii. 30. λεγειων is the form in D Matt. xxvi. 53: in the MSS. ει and ι are constantly confounded; this is therefore equivalent to λεγιών, as λεγαιων (D[2], Luke viii. 30; so B[1](perhaps) ℵ[3a]) is to λεγεών.

Λευεί ABℵ, Luke iii. 29. Similarly Λευεί Heb. vii. 5 (BCD[1]ℵ); Λευείς Heb. vii. 9 (BC[1]ℵ[3]), Luke v. 27, 29 (ABC (D[-ει]) RΞℵ); Λευείτης Luke x. 32 (BD), John i. 19 (Bℵ); Λευειτικός Heb. vii. 11 (BDℵ). In all places B has -ει-, but as it is certainly a special characteristic of B to substitute ει for ι (e. g. γεινομαι, γεινωσκω, κρεινω, μεισω, τειμω), it has not been followed in Λευεί or Λευείς (except when further supported, as above), Ηλειας, Ιερειχω, Γαλειλαια, Ελεισαβετ. It is fair to remark that ει is not *invariably* found in B, e. g. κρινῶ is spelt with ι; κρίνω, with ει: we find also (and have edited) Ἐζεκίας, Ζαχαρίας, Ἀβιά, Ἱερεμίας, Ἰεχονίας, Λυσανίας. The tendency in C was rather to substitute ι for ει; but in Matt. xxviii. 3, we have ventured to reject ειδεα though supported by ABCD ℵ-corr[1], and in Mark i. 5 Ιεροσολυμειται (ABDℵ). There is no doubt that some names should be written with ει which it has been customary to spell with ι, but about many others there is an uncertainty which it has been thought best that the text of this edition should reflect. The following names, occurring for the most part in the genealogies of Matt. i. and Luke iii., have been edited with -ει-: —Ἀμειναδάβ B (Matt. i. 4, D def.) D (Luke iii. 33, an omission in B), **Ἐσλεί** ABℵ, **Ἡλεί** ABℵ, **Ἰωσείας** B[1]Dℵ[1], **Μελχεί** ABℵ, **Νηρεί** ABℵ, **Νινευεῖται** ABC(D)ℵ, in Matt. xii. 41 (but Νινευῖται Luke xi. 30, with AC against Bℵ, D omitting the ver.), **Ὀζείας** BD, **Χοραζεῖν** ABCΞℵ.

λήμψομαι ABCDNQRT[Θ]ℵ. So also in all compounds. Similarly **ἀνάλημψις** ABCDℵ (Luke ix. 51), **λῆμψις** ABD[1]ℵ (Phil. iv. 15, C def.)

Μαριάμ and **Μαρία**. The leading MSS. do not seem to be uniform in their practice. All agree in Μαριάμ Luke i. 27, and in making the genitive case Μαρίας (it occurs 7 times). In the dative, there is no reason to depart from the received reading Μαριάμ Luke ii. 5 (D alone reading Μαρίᾳ), Μαρίᾳ τῇ Μαγδ. Mark xvi. 9 (C has Μαριάμ). In the accusative, there is sufficient authority throughout the Gospels for editing Μαριάμ; rejecting the received Μαρίαν in John xi., on the authority of BC, and sometimes A: but Μαριαν is read in B Matt. i. 20; in D, Luke ii. 16; and in ABC, Rom. xvi. 6. (For variations between μ and ν, compare **Ἰωανάμ** and **Καινάμ** (Luke iii. 30, 36) where μ has been edited with Bℵ: similarly in ver. 27 for **Ἰωανάν**, Ἰωανάμ is read in ℵ.)

Μαθθαῖος B[1]D, and, in Matt. ix. 9 and Luke vi. 15, ℵ. This form has been adopted by Lachmann, Tischdf., and Tregelles. The received Ματθ. is supported by AC &c., and, in Mark iii. 18, by ℵ. Similarly **Μαθθάν** (Matt. i.) and **Μαθθάτ** in Luke iii. 29, but **Ματθάτ** (so even B) in Luke iii. 24.

μαχαίρῃ, Matt. xxvi. 52 (AB[1]Cℵ), Luke xxii. 49 (B[1]DTℵ). Similarly **πλημμύρης** B[1]Ξℵ (Luke vi. 48).

Μωϋσῆς B[not Luke xvi. 31; John ix. 28] D[not Luke xxiv. 27] and, at least sometimes, RΞא; so also occasionally A (Rev. xv. 3) C ([Luke v. 14, ix. 30; John i. 17;] Heb. iii. 2, 5). In the dative Μωυσει is the form generally found in BDא, but B¹Cא have -ση in Mark ix. 4. The accusative occurs only once in the Gospels (Luke xvi. 29), and there all the uncials agree in the received termination -σεα. In the Acts and Epistles (4 places), however, there seems to be a similar agreement in favour of -σην.

ν ἐφελκυστικόν uniformly added, except where manuscript testimony is overwhelming against it.

Ναζαρέθ, Ναζαρέτ, and **Ναζαρᾶ**. Some of the second and third-rate uncials have adopted *one form throughout:* thus L always has Ναζαρετ; and HMUVΛ, Ναζαρεθ. But in our earliest and best MSS. we find no such artificial uniformity. A has Ναζαρατ 4 times, Ναζαραθ twice, and Ναζαρετ 3 times; B, Ναζαρετ 6 times (besides 3 times *secunda manu*), Ναζαρεθ 4 times, and Ναζαρα twice; C, Ναζαραθ 3 times, and Ναζαρεθ 4 times; Ξ, Ναζαρετ, Ναζαρεθ, and Ναζαρα, each once; א, Ναζαρετ 6 times, Ναζαρεθ 4 times, and Ναζαρα once (besides once *secunda manu*); D, however, has Ναζαρεθ 7 times, Ναζαρετ and Ναζαρεδ each once. We have then four or five forms, each of which has strong claims to be considered as the ancient or even the original reading in one or other of the twelve passages in which the word occurs. In Acts x. 38 and Matt. xxi. 11 we have no difficulty in adopting Ναζαρέθ: in the former case on the authority of BCDEא against AGH, and in the latter on that of BCDXא &c. against FGL[MNS]Γ. With as little hesitation we are bound to accept Ναζαρέτ in John i. 46, 47, with ABLXא against EFGHMUVΛ[KSΓ(Δ)Π]. In Matt. iv. 13, a third form, Ναζαρᾶ, establishes itself, on the authority of B¹Zא² 33 Orig., supported as they are by B¹Ξא in Luke iv. 16, lat-*e* in John i. 46, and Eus. (teste Scholz) in Matt. ii. 23: see also Griesbach's fourth Canon. In Luke ii. 39, 51, the agreement of B¹ with D &c., confirmed in ver. 39 by Ξ, establishes the form Ναζαρέθ (B²א however reading Ναζαρετ). The five remaining cases admit of considerable doubt, and in fact it is almost impossible to come to any steady decision upon them: for in Matt. ii. 23, Ναζαρεθ is supported by C &c., Ναζαρετ being the reading of B(sic) DLא; in Mark i. 9 Ναζαρετ is supported by BLΓΔא, Ναζαρατ by AP, and Ναζαρεθ by DFHKMUVΠ; in Luke i. 26, we have Bא for Ναζαρετ, C for Ναζαρεθ, and A for Ναζαραθ; in Luke ii. 4 Ναζαρετ is supported by BEKLΞ, Ναζαρεθ by DFGHMU ΓΛא, and Ναζαραθ by ACΔ; lastly, in Luke iv. 16, we have every variety—A has Ναζαρατ; B²KL, Ναζαρετ; EFGHMUVΓΛ, Ναζαρεθ; Δ, Ναζαραθ; D, Ναζαρεδ; and B¹(Tischdf., expr.) Ξא, Ναζαρα,—which last ought to be read. (We may mention here that Γεννησαρέτ, though it only occurs three times, and then with preponderating authority for the usual form, is still, in one or two uncial MSS., varied in a manner similar to Ναζαρέτ. Thus we find Γεννησαρεθ, Γεννησαρατ, Γεννησαρεδ (D, Luke v. 1), and even (in D¹ [so also latt Syr syr-cu, Matt. xiv. 34; Syr syr-jer Luke v. 1]) Γεννησαρ.)

Ναιμάν ABC(D)א, Luke iv. 27.

οὕτως before a consonant, edited uniformly. So, but with occasional exceptions, ABCDא &c.

παραδοῖ, e. g. Mark iv. 29 BDא¹. Similarly **γνοῖ**, e. g. Mark v. 43 ABD.

πεῖν B¹CD(א), John iv. 7, 9, 10. (א has πιν, so A ver. 9.)

πραΰς BCDא. Similarly πραΰτης in the Epistles.

ῥαββεί ABCDא, Mark ix. 5; xi. 21 [not A]; xiv. 45. But **ῥαββί** retained in all other places, though in most, if not all, Bא read ραββει.

ῥαββουνί ABCא and all other uncials (Mark x. 51 and (rec. also) John xx. 16). (B has -νει.)

Σολομῶνος (Gospels) BDΞא¹ and som times AC. Similarly **Σολομῶνα**.

σπεκουλάτορα AB(D)א &c. (Mark vi. 27, C def.)

συνζητεῖν AB¹CDא. Adopted by Lachmann, Tischendorf, and Tregelles. (But in the following cases the ordinary form has been retained: ἐγκακεῖν,—ενκ- AB¹DQא (Luke xviii. 1, C def.); παλιγγενεσία,—παλινγ- B¹CDZא Matt. xix. 28; συγκαθῆσθαι,—συνκ- AB¹CPא (Mark xiv. 54, *var. lect.* in D); συγκαλεῖν,—συνκ- Dא and sometimes ABC; συλλαλεῖν,—συνλ- BD א(*var. lect.* in Mark ix. 4) and, twice, C (συλλ. A and, once, C); συμμαθητής,—συνμ- A B¹(Tischdf.) CDא John xi. 16. συλλαμβάνειν holds its ground in B,—συλλ- is read 11 times, συνλ- only once (Phil. iv. 3, where 2. m. has συλλ-); in א συλλ- is read 10 times, συνλ- twice (Luke v. 7: Phil. iv. 3). The same is the case with συλλέγειν: συλλ- all 7 times in B, 6 times in א (συνλ- א in Luke vi. 44, D in Matt. xiii., the only place in that MS. where the word occurs).

συνλυπεῖσθαι B¹CDΔא. (Mark iii. 5.)

συνπαραγίνεσθαι AB¹CDPQRא. (Luke xxiii. 48.)

συνπνίγειν AB¹CDא.

συνπορεύεσθαι AB¹Cא. (Mark x. 1, *var. lect.* in D.)

συνσταυροῦν AB¹א. (Matt. xxvii. 44 (C def., D *var. lect.*): John xix. 32 (CD def.).)

ταμεῖον BDא (-μιον Dא), Matt. vi. 6. (All agree in this form in the 3 other passages.)

τεσσεράκοντα AB¹CPא. (C contains only one of the 4 places (Matt. iv. 2) in the Gospels in which the word is found.) But τέσσαρες in B throughout the Gospels; τεσσερες in א (John xi. 17; xix. 23); τεσσαρ- 5 times in A, τεσσερα once (John xix. 23). So also ἐκαθερίσθη has been edited in Mark i. 42 with A B¹(sic) C; but ἐκαθαρίσθη in the 7 other places, in 6 of which B has -θαρ-, in Matt. viii. 3 -θερ-, 1. m.

χρεοφειλέτης ABDI$_e$PRΞא. (Luke vii. 41; xvi. 5. C def. in both.)

49. The conflicting claims of ἄν and ἐάν have in general more the character of various readings than of mere orthographical variations. But the habit of B and many other MSS., and also of the printed text from the *Textus Receptus* to that of the present volume, brings before us many cases in which ἐάν must be looked upon merely as a popular corruption for ἄν. The following is a list of certain of these, compiled by Kuenen and Cobet (*N. T. ad fidem Cod. Vat. præf. p.* lxxiii), in which B has εαν. Matt. v. 19 (once); xi. 27; xii. 32 (once)*; xv. 5 (once); xvi. 19 (once), 25*; xviii. 5, 18 (once), 19; xx. 4; xxii. 9*; xxiv. 28; xxvi. 13: Mark iii. 28*; vi. 10; viii. 35 (once)*; x. 35; xiii. 11; xiv. 9*: Luke vii. 23; ix. 48 (once), 57*; xvii. 33 (once)*: Acts ii. 21*; viii. 19. On looking out these places in critical editions, we find that in every one of them D has αν. In those marked with an asterisk the text of this edition differs from the received. In the rest, the received, as well as our text, has the form found in B. The other instances in the Gospels and Acts included in Cobet's list are:—Matt. viii. 19, where, D being deficient, there seems to be no variation from the reading ἐάν; and Luke x. 35, where B stands alone.

50. One other matter, referred in the digest to the Prolegomena, must be treated of here. We have to decide in some way or other between the readings Γαδαρηνων, Γερασηνων, and Γεργεσηνων in the parallel passages of the three synoptical Evangelists (Matt. viii. 28: Mark v. 1: Luke viii. 26, 37). There being strong ancient evidence for each of these words,

and each occurring in all three Gospels, how are we to find out which of them belongs properly to any one of the three? The ancient versions are here of little assistance: for Syr syr-txt uniformly adopt Γαδαρηνων; latt, Γερασηνων; copt æth arm, Γεργεσηνων. We have endeavoured then to assign the proper reading to each Gospel by weighing MS. against MS. in the light of the principle called 'corruption from parallel passages.' In *St. Matthew*, we have BC^1 (ℵ^1 Γαζαρ-) for Γαδαρηνων; against D for Γερασηνων (A being here defective), and we therefore adopt Γαδαρηνῶν. Again in *St. Luke*, we have Γερασηνων, supported by BC^{1}D; against Γαδαρηνων, which is the reading of AR &c., and Γεργεσηνων which is read by ℵ &c.; we therefore place Γερασηνῶν in the text of St. Luke. Lastly, in St. Mark's Gospel, we find that BDℵ^1 are arrayed against AC; the former supporting Γερασηνων, which we have already accepted as St. Luke's word, the latter supporting Γαδαρηνων, which seems to be the right reading in St. Matthew. ℵ alone seems to keep a distinction between the Gospels:—Matt. Γαζαρ-, Mark Γερασ-, Luke Γεργεσ-; but ℵ^{3a} has reduced all to a level by reading Γεργεσ- in Matt. and Mark,—though he strangely puts Γαδαρ- in Luke viii. 37, restoring however the original text. What is to be done in this division of the best MSS., joined as it is to the high probability that there has been corruption in C from ∥ Matt., in BD from ∥ Luke? At this juncture, the second-rate MSS. come to our aid, supported by other considerations of importance: Δ reads Γαραδηνων in St. Matt., Γαδαρηνων in St. Luke, but Γεργεσηνων in *St. Mark;* U deserts the class with which it is usually found, to support the same reading, which is moreover the only one found in the three places in L(ℵ^{3a}) 1.33 copt æth arm, is the reading of PΞ in St. Luke (the only one of the three passages in which they are extant), of X elsewhere, of Epiphanius, of ev-y, and (though in other places it has Γερασηνων) of the margin of the later Syriac.

51. The punctuation of the text in this and my other editions has been revised on the principle which as far as I know Lachmann was the first to apply to the N. T., viz. the dropping of commas wherever they were unnecessary, i. e. wherever the sense of itself sufficiently indicates the break: and the frequent substitution of commas or periods for the colons so plentifully scattered in the received text: of commas, where the sense flows on, and the colon hindered it; of periods, where the sense is entirely broken, and the colon seemed to connect it. Almost all printed books are sadly over-punctuated. There is no greater hindrance to the flow and connexion of thought in the mind of a reader than that festooning off words and clauses by commas, of which many modern typographers are so fond. And if the getting rid of them is desirable in other books, it becomes a duty in our treatment of the sacred text. All stops in it are purely human inventions: and though some are absolutely necessary for the guidance of the general reader,

they should be as few as possible and only those positively required. Among other services which modern criticism has rendered to the sacred text, this, though it may seem one of the least, is no mean one, that it has cleared it from the exegetical obscuration of many thousand commas.

SECTION II.

THE VARIOUS READINGS.

1. The digest of various readings in the Fourth Edition of this Volume was entirely re-written. In the Fifth Edition the whole was carefully revised and the processes mentioned in the next paragraph carried out more thoroughly and consistently than in the previous Edition. This labour was undertaken and carried through, under my own superintendence, by the Rev. A. W. Grafton, now Prebendary of Wells.

2. The particulars in which these Editions differ from their predecessors may be thus stated :

a) The weeding out of matter untrustworthy, or irrelevant, or not properly belonging to a work whose *main* purpose is philological and exegetical.

β) The insertion of valuable additional matter which has chiefly accrued by the labours of collators during the years 1856—April, 1863.

3. With reference to the former of these, I may remark that experience has shewn great numbers of the cursive mss. commonly cited for or against readings in the sacred text, to be evidence of the most uncertain and questionable kind. Their readings have been very imperfectly collated: their individual character is little known : the impression given by a long array of them on one side is most fallacious, for we know not whether an equally long array might not be mustered on the other, had they been more thoroughly collated. This remark applies to very many readings which are commonly supposed to rest on the almost unanimous testimony of the later mss. The whole reasoning founded on them has been loose and baseless. We know not the stability of our ground.

4. It seemed therefore in re-arranging the digest for the Fourth Edition, that it would be best to banish from it all uncertain and ill-assured evidence, and to construct our text out of that only, on which we could entirely depend. The abbreviations 'al_{20} Sz,' 'al_{180} Tischdf,' and the like, no longer appear, since, in our entire ignorance of any definite particulars, such statements tend only to mislead. A summary of the evidence of the cursive mss. is given in passages where they have been really examined. We have been able to place on our margin and cite systematically three of the most important and most thoroughly

collated of the cursive mss. Others have been occasionally cited, chiefly with the view of shewing something of the relation which they bear either to our more ancient mss. or to the *Textus Receptus*.

5. As respects the omission of irrelevant matter, it may be remarked, that at the same time with the long lists of cursive mss., has vanished from our digest the pretension of being a *complete* account of all various readings. And since no such complete account could be given, it became a question whether it were really answering any worthy purpose to encumber our pages with numerous insignificant readings of later mss., or versions which could not under any circumstances enter into consideration in editing the text. And the reply to this question has been, the exclusion as a general rule of all readings which are not supported by at least some one MS. as old as the sixth century. Even with respect to these, mere variations in orthography and alteration of grammatical forms were in the Fifth Edition to a great extent omitted. The list given above, pp. 94 *et seq.*, is intended as a summary account of such matters. In a manner similar to that which is there described (under ἀλλά, κἀγώ, &c.) we have treated the frequent substitution of the first aorist εἶπα for the second εἶπον; 1 aor. ἔδωκα, for perfect δέδωκα; and the like.

6. The additional MSS., &c., incorporated in the digest in this Edition, will be found specified in detail in the enumeration of the Apparatus Criticus.

7. I have given, in almost all cases, the authorities both for and against the text which I have adopted; and have, where it seemed requisite, inserted in the digest, in brackets and in italics, the reasons which influenced my judgment[4].

8. In some cases I have found it impossible to decide between two conflicting readings. When it seemed to me more than usually doubtful whether one or more words ought to be inserted or omitted, they have been printed in the text, but marked by square brackets. In more complex cases, where this expedient could not be used, one of the two readings stands in the text itself, the alternative one in the digest, but with accents and *in the same type as the text*, the attention of the reader being called to the fact by asterisks both in the text and in the digest.

9. I would recommend to the student, though it may seem irksome at first, the diligent study of the digest of various readings. It is of the first moment, to become familiar with the criticism of the sacred text: to be able to decide for oneself in each case, or at all events to be acquainted with the reasons on which others have decided. Charges of rashness are often brought against us as editors, by persons totally unacquainted with the science of criticism: and nothing short of a patient

[4] Where only one or two MSS. are cited for a particular variation from the edited text, and none in support of that text, it is to be concluded that at least the remaining MSS. indicated on the margin contain the reading adopted.

examination of classes of various readings will prevent students from being misled by such easy and random verdicts.

10. In the digest I have used the following *signs* and *abbreviations:*

aft, after.

al, alii = some cursive mss.

appy, apparently.

ast, asterisk. 'w-ast,' marked with an asterisk or asterisks: see note on 'ob' below.

bef, before.

beg, beginning.

comm, commentary—when appended to the name of a Father denotes that the reading referred to is found in the body of his commentary, and not in the text printed at the head of the commentary. This last is often very much tampered with.

corr, corrector. corrd, corrected.

def, defective.

ed, edition.

elz, elzevir edition of the Greek Test.

e sil, e silentio collatorum.

ev, evangelisterium, i.e. a copy of the Gospels arranged for church use.

ev-eb, Ebionite Gospel.

exc, except.

expr, expressly.

Fd, Field.

gr, greek—when appended to a letter denoting a Græco-latin MS. means that the reading of the Latin text differs from that of the Greek:—when followed by 'ff,' the Greek Fathers. Similarly 'lat' in both applications.

ins, insert. 'ins καὶ AB' means that the MSS. A and B insert καὶ.

marg, margin. 'marg-eccles' denotes that the reading cited is given on the margin as an alteration to be made in reading the passage in church, e. g. the name of our Lord, where the pronoun would otherwise stand, at the beginning of a 'Gospel for the day.'

Mey, Meyer.

ob, obelus. 'w-ob,' marked with an obelus or with obeli. This abbreviation and 'ast' are principally used with reference to the later Syriac version [5].

[5] On these marks Tregelles observes: "The asterisks and obeli shew points of similarity to the Syriac version of the Old Test. made from the Hexaplar text of the LXX as revised by Origen. As that translation employs those marks, borrowed from the Greek text, to indicate variations from the Hebrew, so too here, they seemed to be used in a similar manner; they thus point out respectively additions, and words which are marked as if they should be omitted. It looks, therefore, as if in revising, additions had been introduced marked with an asterisk, and that whatever was or was deemed redundant was marked with an obelus." (Treg. in Horne, vol. iv. p. 272.)

om, omit. 'om και AB' means that the MSS. A and B omit the και given in the text or inserted by other MSS.

pref, prefix. e. g. 'aft τι ins και A : pref C :' 'pref' means that C inserts και before τι instead of after it as A does.

rec, the *Textus Receptus*, or received text of the Greek Testament. Used in this Edition when elz and Steph agree

rel, reliqui—means that all the other manuscripts named on the margin have the reading to which this is appended.

simly, similarly.

Steph, Stephens' Greek Testament.

Sz, Scholz.

Tischdf, Tischendorf.

transp, transpose.

Treg, Tregelles.

txt, text—when followed by a list of MSS., versions, &c., means that the reading adopted in this Edition is supported by those MSS., versions, &c.

ver, verse.

vss, versions.

vv, verses.

Wetst, Wetstein.

The figures 2, 3, &c. inserted *above* the line to the right hand, imply a *second*, third, &c. hand in a MS. Thus B^1 means the original scribe of B; C^2 the first corrector of C; C^3, the second; D^r, a recent corrector of D; and so on. A^1-corr denotes a correction by the original scribe of A; the same thing is sometimes expressed by 1. m. or *eadem manu*. In D and ℵ where the various hands have been minutely distinguished, ℵ-corr^1 means ℵ as corrected by the contemporary διορθωτής, ℵ^2 the second corrector, ℵ-corr$^{1.3}$ implies that the correction of the διορθωτής has been repeated by the third corrector, ℵ-corr^1(?)^3 that the correction may have been made by the διορθωτής but certainly by the later corrector, &c.: see below in the list of MSS.

The same figures *below* the line, imply *recurrence* of the reading, 2, 3, &c. times in the author or the evangelisterium mentioned; e. g. Aug_1, $Orig_5$, Bas_3, ev-H_1.

(But ff_1 means (see p. 135) that Corbeian MS. which is cited by Scholz, &c. as "Corb. 1."

ff_2, Corb. 2: $ff_{1.2}$, Corb. 1 and 2. Similarly in the cases of g_1, g_2, $g_{1.2}$.

$ff_2{}^1$, means the original scribe of Latin MS. ff_2.

$ff_1{}^2$, means the corrector of ff_1.

f^1, the original scribe of MS. *f*.

ev-$H^1{}_1$, one occurrence in ev-H *prima manu*.)

See further the note on the list of Fathers below.

SECTION III.

THE MARGINAL REFERENCES.

1. The references in the margin of this edition of the Greek Testament are not those usually printed in other editions. Those are references to the *subject-matter* of the text: and are most useful and necessary to every biblical student. As however they are now to be found in many editions of our English Bible, it seemed unnecessary to reprint them here. Instead of them, I have drawn up a body of references *to verbal and idiomatical usages*, which I hope will be found an addition to our apparatus criticus, as tending to exhibit, simultaneously with the text itself, the peculiarities and ἅπαξ λεγόμενα of the passage under consideration.

2. The materials for constructing such a body of references have of course been principally found in the various Greek Testament Lexicons, aided by personal study of the text in matters of which Lexicons do not treat. I have also used with profit, but not extensively, Grinfield's Editio Hellenistica Novi Testamenti, and take this opportunity of acknowledging my obligations to that work.

3. The hindrances, as well as the helps, to such a compilation, should be mentioned. They mainly consisted in the almost uniform *inaccuracy in the references in the existing Lexicons.* In Schleusner and Parkhurst, little more than half of the passages referred to were to be found. Their citations are *copied without verification.* In Wahl, this was not the case, nor are the inaccuracies so many; but the errors in printing have introduced far more than were compatible with a profitable use of his very laborious and copious work. An honourable exception to the general inaccuracy of our Lexicon references I found in Robinson's Greek and English Lexicon to the New Testament, edited by Dr. Bloomfield. I was however constrained principally to use Wahl, from his greater copiousness in detail. I cannot omit to mention the very complete and accurate Concordance of Bruder, as saving the scholar very much of the complication of lexical arrangement, and giving freer scope for the exercise of his own judgment. I only wish I had been acquainted with it when I began to compile these references : as I might have been saved many a weary hour's search.

4. In the present work, *no reference has been inserted which has not been verified*[6]*:* and I trust that the accuracy of the printing has corresponded to my earnest desire that the whole may be found correct. In the course of so many thousand citations, I cannot expect but that errors will occasionally have crept in: and I shall still be obliged to any

[6] An exception to this has arisen : as experience has approved the almost unexceptionable accuracy of Bruder's Concordance, I have generally cited from him in the later additions to my references, without verifying.

reader who may discover mistakes, to communicate with me (addressed at Messrs. Rivingtons', Waterloo Place) that they may be corrected.

5. The sources whence the references have been drawn have been :—(1) *the text of the Greek Testament itself*, as affording instances of similarity of usage or construction,—of use of the same or different words in parallel passages of the Gospels,—or of tacit reference to the words and acts of our Lord in the Epistles;—(2) *the Septuagint version*[7] of the Old Testament; as being, from the place and time of its publication, its use by the New Testament writers, and its similarity of style and diction, so full of interest in the elucidations of the sacred text ;—(3) *the Apocrypha*, which approaches even more nearly than the canonical LXX to the peculiar Hellenistic style of the New Testament; —(4) in the case of words not occurring in the LXX, the fragments of the other Greek interpreters in Origen's Hexapla[8],—and (5) the works of Josephus, Philo-Judæus, and the Apostolic Fathers, who occasionally are found using expressions and constructions similar to those in our text. To these may be added, (6) a few instances from the classic writers, especially Xenophon, justifying or elucidating New Testament words or constructions.

6. For convenience in arranging this body of references, it has been found necessary to use some few signs and abbreviations, which will here be explained.

(α) When a reference is preceded by the sign (=), it is indicated that the word which is the subject of reference is used, in the passage referred to, *in the same sense* as in the text.

(β) When, in the Gospels, and in the Evangelic statement, 1 Cor. xi. 23—25, the sign (‖) occurs in a reference, it is signified that the word occurs *in the parallel place* in the other Gospels, which will always be found indicated *at the head of the note* on the paragraph. When the sign (‖) is *qualified*, thus, '‖ Mk.,' or '‖ Mt. Mk.,' &c., it is signified that the word occurs *in the parallel place in that Gospel or Gospels, but not in the other or others.*

(γ) When the words 'here only,' or in such and such places 'only,' occur in a reference, they are always to be understood as meaning that the word occurs in that place or those places only *of the New Testament;* and as having *no reference* (unless so implied by their following citations from the LXX) *to its occurring in the LXX or elsewhere.*

[7] In references to the LXX,—'Ed-vat.' appended signifies the common Roman edition; 'B,' the readings as far as ascertained of the Codex Vaticanus; 'Ald.,' 'compl.' the Aldine and Complutensian editions; 'Alex.,' 'F.' the editions of the Codex Alexandrinus by Grabe and Field respectively; and 'A' the readings of the MS. itself.

[8] Of these, 'Aq.' appended to a reference signifies Aquila, 'Symm.' Symmachus, 'Theod.' Theodotion, 'alius' or 'incert.' an unknown interpreter.

(δ) When a reference is followed by the sign (†), it is indicated that the word *does not occur in the* Canonical *Septuagint version of the Old Testament*, though it may occur in the Apocrypha.

(ε) When a reference is followed by the sign (‡), it is indicated that the word *does not occur in the* Canonical *LXX in the same sense* as in the text.

(ζ) The abbreviation 'constr.' occurring before a reference, indicates that it is the *construction* of the clause or sentence which is referred to.

(η) Other abbreviations will be understood from the context: e. g. 'trans.' or 'intrans.,' that the verb is used *transitively*, or *intransitively* in the passages referred to: 'gen.,' 'dat.,' 'acc.' that the verb or preposition governs these cases respectively in those passages: so of 'act.,' 'pass.' &c. &c. 'v. r.' added to a reference implies that the word or construction is found in the passage referred to, not in the text adopted in this Edition, but in some generally well supported *various reading* recorded in the digest.

(θ) In *one only case* are the references not to verbal or idiomatical usage, but to *subject-matter*. Where the text contains a *citation from or reference to* the Old Testament, or to an earlier place in the New Testament, the place of that citation or reference is indicated in the margin, but *in small capitals*: thus, 'Isa. liii. 5.'

7. The student is requested not to consider the references in any instance as embracing *the whole number of times* where a word occurs in the New Testament,—*unless it be expressly so stated.* In by far the greater number of cases, they consist merely of a selection, at discretion, from an abundance of similar instances. At the same time considerable pains have been now taken to make some one set of references in each volume *exhaustive;* which one has then been used as the *stock* reference for that particular word or construction.

8. To avoid mistakes, I think it well to advertise the student, that when the references extend *below the text*, they are to be read *in single lines* across the page.

9. In the Fifth Edition, the whole body of references was gone over, and many corrections and insertions made. The object proposed in doing this was, to supply a more complete account, both of ἅπαξ λεγόμενα and of peculiar usage of words and constructions, in the sacred Writers, however common such words or constructions may be in ordinary Greek: to add, in very many instances, references to the LXX: and to bring the former portion of my work, in which the design of the body of references had less opened before me than it afterwards did, into harmony with the subsequent volumes. In this part of the work, I had the valuable co-operation of the Rev. Robert Hake, M.A., Minor Canon of Canterbury, without whom it would have been impossible that it should have been accomplished.

CHAPTER VII.

APPARATUS CRITICUS[9].

SECTION I.

MANUSCRIPTS OF THE GREEK TESTAMENT REFERRED TO IN THIS EDITION.

Manuscripts written in the capital, or uncial character.

(The names of MSS. as old as the sixth century are printed in small capitals.)

A. The MS. referred to by this symbol is that commonly called the Alexandrine, or CODEX ALEXANDRINUS. It once belonged to Cyrillus Lucaris, patriarch of Alexandria and then of Constantinople, who in the year 1628 presented it to our King Charles I. It is now in the British Museum. It is on parchment in four volumes, of which three contain the Old, and one the New Testament, with the Epistle of Clement to the Corinthians. This fourth volume is exhibited open in a glass case. It will be seen by the letters in the inner margin of this edition, that the first 24 chapters of Matthew are wanting in it, its first leaf commencing ὁ νυμφίος, ch. xxv. 6:—as also the leaves containing ἵνα, John vi. 50,—to καὶ σύ, viii. 52. It is generally agreed that it was written at Alexandria;—it does not, however, *in the Gospels*, represent that commonly known as the Alexandrine text, but approaches much more nearly to the Constantinopolitan, or generally received text. The New Testament, according to its text, was edited, in uncial types cast to imitate those of the MS., by Woide, London, 1786, the Old Testament by Baber, London, 1819: and its N. T. text has now been edited in common type by Mr. B. H. Cowper, London, 1861. The date of this MS. has been variously assigned, but it is now pretty generally agreed to be the *fifth century*.

B. The CODEX VATICANUS, No. 1209 in the Vatican Library at Rome; and proved, by the old catalogues, to have been there from the foundation of the library in the 16th century. It was apparently, from internal evidence, copied in Egypt. It is on vellum, and contains the Old and New Testaments. In the latter, it is deficient from Heb. ix. 14 to the end of the Epistle;—it does not contain the Epistles to Timothy, Titus, and Philemon;—nor the Apocalypse. An edition of this celebrated codex, undertaken as long ago as 1828 by Cardinal Angelo Mai, has since his death been

[9] For a more complete account of the subject of this chapter, I would refer the reader to Tregelles' vol. iv. of the new edition of Horne's Introduction, p. 152 ff., and to Scrivener's Introduction to N. T. Criticism, p. 76 ff.

published at Rome. The defects of this edition are such, that it can hardly be ranked higher in usefulness than a tolerably complete collation, entirely untrustworthy in those places where it differs from former collations in representing the MS. as *agreeing with* the received text. An 8vo edition of the N. T. portion, newly revised by Vercellone, was published at Rome in 1859 (referred to as 'Verc'): and of course superseded the English reprint of the 1st edition. Even in this 2nd edition there were imperfections which rendered it necessary to have recourse to the MS. itself, and to the partial collations made in former times. These are—(1) that of Bartolocci (under the name of Giulio de St. Anastasia), once librarian at the Vatican, made in 1669, and preserved in manuscript in the Imperial Library (MSS. Gr. Suppl. 53) at Paris (referred to as 'Blc'); (2) that of Birch ('Bch'), published in various readings to the Acts and Epistles, Copenhagen, 1798,—Apocalypse, 1800,—Gospels, 1801; (3) that made for the great Bentley ('Btly'), by the Abbate Mico,—published in Ford's Appendix to Woide's edition of the Codex Alexandrinus, 1799 (it was made on the margin of a copy of Cephalæus' Greek Testament, Argentorati, 1524, still amongst Bentley's books in the Library of Trinity College, Cambridge); (4) notes of alterations by the original scribe and other correctors. These notes were procured for Bentley by the Abbé de Stosch, and were till lately supposed to be lost. They were made by the Abbate Rulotta ('Rl'), and are preserved amongst Bentley's papers in the Library of Trinity College, Cambridge (B. 17. 20)[1]. The Codex has been occasionally consulted for the verification of certain readings by Tregelles, Tischendorf, and others. A list of readings examined at

[1] During the printing of the present Edition, has appeared "Novum Testamentum Vaticanum: post Angeli Maii aliorumque imperfectos labores ex ipso Codice edidit C. Tischendorf." This edition has been consulted, especially in its prefatory part, noticing the differences between previous collators and Prof. Tischendorf. With reference to the notices therein contained of my own collations, I may observe, that Prof. Tischendorf had not seen those collations when the text of his work went to press: and that in several instances where he assumes the accuracy of his own account of disputed readings as against mine, I am prepared, from having *traced* the Codex, to vindicate my own report. It is no inconsiderable drawback to the value of Prof. Tischendorf's work, that *hardly more than one-third of the text* is really taken from the MS. itself. Before he had finished the Gospels, the MS. was taken from him. In the subsequent part he was only allowed to consult it where discrepancies existed. I may also add, without pretending to have examined his work throughout, that it appears not to be free from some grave inaccuracies: e. g. on Matt. xxv. 15, in his "Commentarius," he says, "in codice est: ιδιαν δυναμιν απεδημησεν,"—whereas his text in the body of the volume gives ιδιαν δυναμιν και απεδημησεν. But however this may be, there can be no doubt that this edition is a great advance on our previous knowledge of the Codex. [This note refers to the Sixth Edition.]

Rome by the present editor (Feb. 1861), and by the Rev. E. C. Cure, Fellow of Merton College, Oxford (April 1862), will be found at the end of these prolegomena. A description, with an engraving from a photograph of a portion of a page, is given in Burgon's "Letters from Rome," London 1861. This most important MS. was probably written in the *fourth century* (Hug, Tischendorf, al.).

C. The CODEX EPHRAEMI, preserved in the Imperial Library at Paris, MS. Gr. No. 9. It is a Codex rescriptus or palimpsest, consisting of the works of Ephraem the Syrian written over the MS. of extensive fragments of the Old and New Testaments[2]. It seems to have come to France with Catherine de' Medici, and to her from Cardinal Nicolas Ridolfi. Tischendorf thinks it probable that he got it from Andrew John Lascaris, who at the fall of the Eastern Empire was sent to the East by Lorenzo de' Medici to preserve such MSS. as had escaped the ravages of the Turks. This is confirmed by the later corrections (C^3) in the MS., which were evidently made at Constantinople[3]. But from the form of the letters, and other peculiarities, it is believed to have been written at Alexandria, or at all events, where the Alexandrine dialect and method of writing prevailed. Its text is perhaps the *purest* example of the Alexandrine text,—holding a place about midway between the Constantinopolitan MSS. and most of those of the Alexandrine recension. It was edited very handsomely in uncial type, with copious dissertations, &c., by Tischendorf, in 1843. He assigns to it an age at least equal to A, and places it also in the *fifth century*. Corrections were written in, apparently in the sixth and ninth centuries: these are respectively cited as C^2, C^3.

D. The CODEX CANTABRIGIENSIS, or BEZÆ,—so called because it was presented by Beza in 1581 to the University Library at Cambridge; where it is now exposed to view in a glass case. He procured it in 1562, from the monastery of St. Irenæus at Lyons. It is on parchment, and contains the Gospels and Acts, with a Latin version. Its lacunæ, which are many, will be perceived by the inner marginal letters in this edition. It once contained the Catholic Epistles: 3 John 11—15 in Latin is all that now remains. It was edited with very accurate imitative types, at the expense of the University of Cambridge, by Dr. Kipling, in 1793. A new edition carefully revised and more generally accessible was published by

[2] The extent of these fragments being indicated in every case by the notes in the inner margin of the text, I have not thought it necessary to swell the Prolegomena by also specifying them here. The same remark applies to the lacunæ in the other MSS.

[3] The general reader may be advantageously referred to the careful and accurate account of this MS. given in the Christian Remembrancer for October, 1862, vol. xliv. p. 273 et seq.

Mr. Scrivener in 1864, and has been collated for this Edition. In the introduction some ten or twelve correctors are distinguished, whose readings are found in the notes at the end of the volume. The text of the Codex Bezæ is a very peculiar one, deviating more from the received readings and from the principal manuscript authorities than any other. It appears to have been written in France, and by a Latin transcriber ignorant of Greek, from many curious mistakes which occur in the text, and version attached. It is closely and singularly allied to the ancient Latin versions, so much so that some critics have supposed it to have been altered from the Latin: and certainly many of the phænomena of the MS. seem to bear out the idea. Where D differs in unimportant points from the other Greek MSS., the difference appears to be traceable to the influence of Latin forms and constructions. It has been observed, that in such cases it frequently agrees with the Latin codex *e* (see the list further on). Its peculiarities are so great, that in many passages, while the sense remains for the most part unaltered, hardly three words together are the same as in the commonly received text. And that these variations often arise from capricious alteration, is evident from the way in which the Gospels, in parallel passages, have been more than commonly interpolated from one another in this MS. The concurrence with the ancient Latin versions seems to point to a very early state of the text; and it is impossible to set aside the value of D as an index to its history;—but in critical weight it ranks the lowest of the leading MSS. Its age has been very variously given: the general opinion now is that it was written in the *latter end of the fifth or the sixth century.*

E. The Codex Basileensis (Public Library at Basle, formerly B. vi. 21; now K. iv. 35). Contains the four Gospels with some considerable lacunæ. Collated by Tischendorf and Tregelles. Said to be of the middle of the *eighth century.* [Burgon gives the press-mark as A. N. iii. 12; and assigns the MS. to the *seventh* century.]

F. The Codex Boreeli, once possessed by John Boreel, Dutch ambassador in London under James I. It was lost for many years, till found at Arnheim by Heringa, a professor at Utrecht. It is now in the public library at the latter place. Heringa wrote a dissertation on it, so copious as to serve for an edition of the codex itself. This dissertation was published by Vinke in 1843. Contains the four Gospels with many lacunæ, which have increased since Wetstein's time. Tischendorf in 1841 examined the codex and compared it with Heringa's collation. Tischendorf assigns it to the *ninth century:* Tregelles, to the *tenth.*

G. The Codex Harleianus, 5684, in the British Museum, brought by Andrew Seidel from the East. Contains the Gospels with many lacunæ. Collated by J. C. Wolf, to whom it once belonged, and recently by Tischendorf and Tregelles (known as Seidelii I., or Wolfii A). Ascribed to the *ninth* or *tenth century*.

H. The Codex Wolfii B, now in the Public Library at Hamburg. Its history is the same as that of the last MS. Its contents, the Gospels,—with many lacunæ: its assigned date, about the end of the *ninth century*. It was collated by Wolf, Tregelles, and Tischendorf.

I. FRAGMENTA PALIMPSESTA TISCHENDORFIANA (or Codex Tischendorfianus II.). "Certain portions of the New Test. in Greek, under Georgian writing. The parts appear to vary from the *fifth* to the *seventh century*. Examined by Tregelles, and since edited by Tischendorf in his Monumenta Sacra, [vol. i.] 1855." (Tregelles.) The volume is now in the Imperial Library at St. Petersburg. Tischendorf states that he can distinguish the remains of seven different MSS. The three most ancient of these he considers quite equal to C or A both in age and in purity of text. The first of these (cited in this edition as I_a) contains: John xi. 50—xii. 9; xv. 12—xvi. 2; xix. 11—24. The second (I_b), 1 Cor. xv. 53—xvi. 9: Titus i. 1—13: Acts xxviii. 8—17. The third (I_c), Matt. xiv. 13—16, 19—23; xxiv. 37—xxv. 1; xxv. 32—45; xxvi. 31—45: Mark ix. 14—22; xiv. 58—70. These are all ascribed to the *fifth century*. The fourth fragment (I_d) contains Matt. xvii. 22—xviii. 3; xviii. 11—19; xix. 5—14: Luke xviii. 14—25: John iv. 52—v. 8; xx. 17—26. The seventh (I_e), Luke vii. 39—49; xxiv. 10—19. These two are assigned to the *sixth century* and compared with Cod. P. The two remaining fragments, Tischendorf's fifth and sixth, contain portions of the Acts and are ascribed to a century later than the two preceding.

K. The Codex Cyprius, brought from the island of Cyprus to Paris, and now in the Imperial Library there (MS. Gr. 63). Contains the Gospels (entire), memoirs of the saints of the Greek Church, and the canons of Eusebius. Collated by Tischendorf and Tregelles. Its text is peculiar and *sui generis*; and is consequently of much value. Assigned to the *ninth century*.

L. The Codex Regius Parisiensis (Bibliothèque Impériale Manuscrit grec, No. 62 [olim 2861 and 1558]), contains the Gospels with some lacunæ. Edited by Tischendorf in his Monumenta Sacra, 1846, pp. 57—399. Its text, both in various readings and in grammatical forms, is of the kind which has been called Alexandrine, and is very nearly related to that of B. From the careless positions of the accents, Scholz and Griesbach think it to have been copied from some more ancient MS. which had no accents. Ascribed by Tischendorf to the *eighth century*; by Tregelles and others, to the *ninth* [4].

[4] Griesbach describes this MS. as "incredibili cum venerandis illis exemplaribus quæ Origenes olim suis manibus versavit consensu insignem."

M. The Codex Campianus (Paris: Bibl. Imp. MS. Gr. 48). Presented to Louis XIV. by the Abbé des Champs, in 1706. Contains the Gospels, with notices of the saints of the Greek Church, the Canons of Eusebius, and much inserted matter betokening late date. Its text is irregular in character, and has some readings common only to itself and K. Assigned to the latter part of the *ninth* or beginning of the *tenth century*. Collated by Tregelles, and copied by Tischendorf.

N. CODEX PURPUREUS. "These fragments (of the *sixth century*) are found in three places: four leaves are in the British Museum (Cotton. C. xv.), denoted J or I by Wetstein and others; two are at Vienna (Imperial Library, Cod. Theol. Gr. num. 2 Lambec.), to which the notation N was formerly restricted; and six in the Vatican (No. 3785), called by Scholz Γ. Edited by Tischendorf in his Monumenta Sacra, 1846." (Tregelles.) To these must now be added some further fragments collated by Tischendorf for his eighth edition.

P. Q. By these symbols are designated the portions of two ancient MSS., discernible (as also are fragments of Ulphilas' gothic version) under the later writing of a volume known as the Codex Carolinus in the Ducal Library at Wolfenbüttel. P (GUELPHERBYTANUS A) contains fragments of each of the Gospels. Q (GUELPH. B) fragments of Luke and John. Both are probably of the *sixth century*. They were edited by F. A. Knittel in 1762; and, more thoroughly, by Tischendorf in 1860 [1869], Monumenta Sacra, vol. iii. [vi.]

R. CODEX NITRIENSIS. A palimpsest in the British Museum (Additional MS. 17211): the same volume which contains the palimpsest Homer. Brought from a Nitrian monastery. Contains large fragments of St. Luke's Gospel. Edited by Tischendorf in 1857, Monumenta Sacra, vol. ii. Tregelles had however previously collated it, and has given several corrections of Tischendorf's edition; these are noticed in their proper places in the digest. This MS. is ascribed to the *sixth century*.

S. The Codex Vaticanus 354, contains the Gospels entire, with the canons of Eusebius. Written by Michael, a monk, in the year 949. Collated by Birch, whose collation Tregelles and Tischendorf have used; hence when quoted as agreeing with the received text, its testimony is only 'e silentio Birchii,' except in those cases in which express testimony has been obtained from Tischendorf, who has collated this MS. and the preceding for his eighth edition.

T. CODEX BORGIANUS 1, in the Library of the Propaganda at Rome, of the *fifth century* (probably). Contains fragments of Luke and

John with a Sahidic version. The portions John vi. 28—67; vii. 6—viii. 31 were published by A. A. Georgi, at Rome, in 1789: and examined by Tischendorf. This Græco-Egyptian MS. also contains a portion of St. Luke, ch. xxii. 20 to xxiii. 20, which was first brought to my notice by Dr. Tregelles, as being mentioned by Zoega in his "Catalogus Codicum Copticorum MSS. qui in Museo Borgiano Velitris adservantur." My brother, the Rev. Bradley H. Alford, happening to be at Rome, was fortunate enough to obtain permission to collate this ancient fragment, and sent me the collation, from which the readings were, in Edn. 4 of this Volume, first published. Two other portions of the same MS. were once in the possession of C. G. Woide and were published by Ford in the Appendix to the Codex Alexandrinus, Oxford, 1799. They comprise Luke xii. 15—xiii. 32 : John viii. 33—42.

[T_b. CODEX PETROPOLITANUS. *Sixth century.* John i. 35—42; ii. 9—17; iii. 8—iv. 14; iv. 34—38, 42—50.]

T_c. CODEX PORPHYRIUS PETROPOLITANUS. Matt. xiv. 22—xv. 8. *Sixth century.*

T_d. [Fragmentum Borgianum Græco-Ægyptiacum. *Seventh century.*] Mark xii. 35—37 [John xix. 23—27; xx. 30, 31]. The readings of these and other fragments have been introduced from Tischendorf, N. T. edn. 8.

U. The Codex Nanianus 1, in St. Mark's Library at Venice ([Gr. Class.] I. viii.), contains the Gospels entire, with the canons of Eusebius. It has been collated by Tischendorf and Tregelles. Assigned to the *tenth century.*

V. A MS. in the Library of the Holy Synod at Moscow. (No number, referred to as "in a box.") Contains the Gospels,—as far as John vii. 39, in uncial letters of about the *ninth century* (Tischendorf);—after that, in cursive characters of the thirteenth century. Collated by Matthæi.

X. The Codex Monacensis, formerly Ingoldstadiensis. [It is a folio in two columns, and was presented by Gerard Vossius (1577—1641) to Ingoldstadt, transferred with the University to Landshut in 1803, to Munich in 1827.] (University Library, Munich, I. 26.) Contains the four Gospels with numerous lacunæ. [Burgon states that it does not contain Matt. vi. 6—10, but vv. 6, 10, 11. Mark xiv. 61—64; 72—xv. 4 has perished; xv. 32 (latter half)—xvi. 8 (former half) has nearly perished.] It is accompanied by an interspersed commentary [that on Matt. and John abbreviated from Chrys.: on Luke from Titus (not Bostr., but rather later). There is no comm. on Mark]. Ascribed to the end of the *ninth*, or beginning of the *tenth century.* Collated by Tischendorf and Tregelles.

Y. A fragment, No. 225, in the Barberini Library at Rome. Contains

John xvi. 3—xix. 41. Assigned to the *eighth* or *ninth century*. Edited by Tischendorf, Monumenta Sacra, 1846, pp. 37—50.

Z. The CODEX RESCRIPTUS DUBLINENSIS, in the Library of Trinity College, Dublin. Contains, of the N. T., the Gospel of Matthew. It was discovered (under the cursive writing of a copy of Chrysostom de Sacerdotio, extracts from Epiphanius, &c.) by Dr. Barrett, who published all that he could read in not very exact copper-plate facsimile at the expense of the college in 1801. Tregelles, in 1853, by the aid of a chemical mixture was able to decipher the portions which had baffled Barrett, and carefully recollated the whole. It has many lacunæ, which will be seen by the letters in our inner margin. The date assigned to it is the *sixth century*.

Γ. Codex Tischendorfianus IV. A MS. brought by Tischendorf from the East, and now in the Bodleian Library (Auct. T. Infra II. 2). It contains portions of St. Matthew and St John, the greater part of St. Mark, and the whole of St. Luke. Collated by Tischendorf and Tregelles. In 1859, Tischendorf procured 99 more leaves of the same MS.; these are now at St. Petersburg, and contain Matt. i. 1—v. 31; ix. 6—xii. 18; xiv. 15—xx. 25; xxiii. 13—xxviii. 20, and the whole of John minus the two portions (vi. 14—viii. 3; xv. 24—xix. 6) preserved in the Bodleian. Ascribed to the *ninth century*.

Δ. The Codex San-Gallensis, in the Library at St. Gall. Contains the Gospels entire, except John xix. 17—35, with a Latin version. Edited in lithographed facsimile by Rettig, at Zurich, in 1836. This MS. and Cod. Boernerianus (G of St. Paul's Epistles: see Prolegg. Vol. II.) are of the same country and date (i. e. Switzerland, in the latter part of the *ninth century*), and originally formed part of the same volume.

Θ.[5] The Codex Tischendorfianus I., brought by Tischendorf from the East, now in the Library of the University at Leipsic. It consists of four leaves, containing a few fragments of Matthew: xiii. 46—55 (but this almost illegible); xiv. 8—29; xv. 4—14. Of the latter part of the *seventh century*. Edited by Tischendorf, Monumenta Sacra, 1846, pp. 1—10.

Λ. Codex Tischendorfianus III., now in the Bodleian (Auct. T. Infra I. 1). Contains the whole of the Gospels of St. Luke and St. John. Collated by Tischendorf and Tregelles. Ascribed to the *eighth* or *ninth century*. An early cursive copy of Matt. and Mark taken by Tischendorf to St. Petersburg, in 1859, is said by him (Notitia Cod. Sinaitici, p. 58) to be part of the same codex.

[[5] Θ_a Θ_b &c. see p. 117, note 7.]

Ξ. CODEX ZACYNTHIUS. Edited by Tregelles, London, 1861, with the types cast for printing the Codex Alexandrinus. The following is an abridgment of his account of the MS.: "On the 11th of August, 1858, I received a letter from Dr. Paul de Lagarde of Berlin, informing me that a palimpsest MS., hitherto unused, containing a considerable portion of St. Luke's Gospel, with a Catena, was in the library of the British and Foreign Bible Society. It is noted in the Catalogue, and on the back, '24, *Greek Evangelisterium. Parchment.*' In many parts the ancient writing is illegible, except in a very good light. The later writing is a Greek Lectionary from the Four Gospels, and belongs, I suppose, to the thirteenth century. The elder writing must have been part of a volume of large folio size; for the leaves are now folded across, the later writing running the other way. The text is in round full well-formed uncial letters, such as I should have had no difficulty in ascribing to the *sixth* century, were it not that the Catena of the same age has the round letters (ϵΘOC) so cramped as to make me believe that it belongs to the *eighth century*. Besides the ordinary *κεφάλαια* or *τίτλοι*, this MS. contains also the same chapters as the Vatican MS., similarly numbered. The only other document in which I have ever seen this *Capitulatio Vaticana* is the Vatican Codex itself; nor do I know of its being found elsewhere. Occasionally the same portion of Scripture occurs twice, when accompanied by a different Patristic extract."

Π. Codex Petropolitanus (Tischendorf, N. T. edn. 8). Of the *ninth century*. The readings of this MS. were not available [for the sixth Edition] at the beginning of St. Matthew, nor for Luke i. 30—viii. 3, nor beyond xviii. 9. [Def. John iii. 5—39: xxi. 22—end supplied by a later hand.]

א. The CODEX SINAITICUS. Procured by Tischendorf, in 1859, from the Monastery of St. Catherine on Mount Sinai. The Codex Frederico-Augustanus (now at Leipsic), obtained in 1844 from the same monastery, is a portion of the same copy of the Greek Bible, the 148 leaves of which, containing the entire New Testament, the Ep. of Barnabas, parts of Hermas, and 199 more leaves of the Septuagint, have now been edited by the discoverer. A magnificent edition prepared at the expense of the Emperor of Russia appeared in January, 1863, and a smaller edition containing the N. T. &c., has been published by Dr. Tischendorf. The MS. has four columns on a page, and has been altered by several different correctors, one or more of whom Tischendorf considers to have lived in the sixth century. The work of the original scribe has been examined, not only by Tischendorf, but by Tregelles and other competent judges, and is by them assigned to the *fourth century.* The internal character of the text agrees with the external, as the student may judge for himself from the readings given in the digest. The principal correctors as distinguished by Tischendorf are :—A, of the same age with the MS. itself, probably the corrector who revised the book, before it left the hands of the scribe, denoted therefore by us ℵ-corr^1 ; B (cited as ℵ^2), who in the first page of Matt. began inserting breathings, accents, &c., but did not carry out his design, and touched only a few later passages ; C^a (cited as ℵ^{3a}) has corrected very largely throughout the book. Wherever in our digest a reading is cited as found in ℵ^1, it is to be understood, if no further statement is given, that C^a altered it to that which is found in our text ; C^b (cited as ℵ^{3b}) lived about the same time as C^a, i. e. some centuries later than the original scribe. These are all that we need notice here[6].

Frag. Ath$_a$. A fragment (7 folios) at the Monastery of St. Dionysius, Mt. Athos, collated by P. E. Pusey, Esq., M.A. It contains John ii. 17—iii. 8, and forms the cover of a MS.

Frag. Ath$_b$., for a transcript of which I have also to thank Mr. Pusey, consists of 3 folios, containing John iv. 9—14. It forms part of a MS. at Ch. Ch. Oxford (Abp. Wake's Gr. MSS. 2), and is assigned by Mr. Coxe to the [latter half of the] *tenth century.* It is apparently part of the same MS. with the above, and perhaps with Frag. Mosq. below.

Frag. Cant. (W^d in Tischendorf, edn. 8.) Fragmentum Cantabrigiense. Now preserved in a frame between pieces of glass in the Library of Trinity College, Cambridge. Ascribed to the *eighth century.* The scraps of which this fragment is made up were discovered in 1861 by Mr. H. Bradshaw, Fellow of King's Coll. Camb., in the binding of a copy of Gregory Nazianzen formerly brought from Mt. Athos. It contains portions of Mark vii. viii. ix. The text is very peculiar and interesting. The readings have been inserted from a photograph.

Frag. Mosq. (Called O by Tischendorf.) Fragmentum Mosquense. A Codex of the Holy Synod at Moscow, No. 120 (now 119). From the Monastery of St. Dionysius, at Mt. Athos. It

[6] It may be well here to mention, that the Rev. E. H. Hansell has published at the University Press, Oxford, a useful edition of the New Testament exhibiting the entire texts of the earliest known MSS. in parallel columns. Vol. i. contains the Gospels from ABCD and (in St. Matthew) Z. Vol. ii. contains the Acts from ABCDE, the Catholic Epistles from ABC, the Pauline Epistles from ABCD^{ep}, the Apocalypse from AB^{ap}C. Vol. iii. contains notes stating the alterations made by later hands in each MS., a collation of the Codex Sinaiticus, a general account of the plan of the work, facsimile plates, &c. The Rev. F. H. Scrivener also has published "A Full Collation of the Codex Sinaiticus with the Received Text of the N. T.," in a very handy little volume which has deservedly reached a second edition.

consists of 8 leaves, bound up with a MS. of Chrysostom, and contains John i. 1—4; xx. 10—13, 15—17, 20—24,—with catena. Edited by Matthæi, in one of the Appendices in his N. T. Appears to be of the *ninth century* (Tischendorf, *eighth* according to Matthæi).

Frag. Neap. (W^b in Tischendorf.) Fragmentum Neapolitanum rescriptum. Naples Library, II. C. 15 (LXXIX.). Contains beneath more recent (fourteenth century) ecclesiastical writing of the Greek Church, twelve or fourteen leaves of an ancient MS. of the Gospels, probably of the *eighth century.* In his N. T. edn. 8 Tischendorf has readings of this MS. from Mark xiii. 21—xiv. 66 [Luke iv. 1—19].

Frag. Nitr. (N^b [I^b (ed. 8)] in Tischendorf.) FRAGMENTUM NITRIENSE. A few verses of the xiiith and xvith chapters of St. John's Gospel deciphered by Tischendorf under Syriac writing in a British Museum MS. (Additional, 17136) brought from the Nitrian valleys. Edited by Tischendorf in Mon. Sacra Nov. Coll. vol. ii. Tischendorf ascribes these fragments to the *fifth* or even to the *fourth century.*

Frag. Par. (W^a or W in Tischendorf.) A fragment in the Imperial Library at Paris, attached to MS. Gr. 314, containing only two leaves, Luke ix. 35 (ακουετε)—47; x. 12—22. Edited by Tischendorf in Mon. Sacra, 1846, pp. 51—56. Ascribed to the *eighth century.*

Frag. Sang. (W^c in Tischendorf, edn. 7.) Fragmentum San-Gallense. Three leaves published by Tischendorf, Mon. Sacra, vol. iii. Contains Mark ii. 9—16: Luke i. 20—32, 64—79. Ascribed to the *ninth century.*

Cod. Guelph., Cod. Bodl., Cod. Veron., Cod. Turic., and [Cod. Sang.] are MSS. at Wolfenbüttel, the Bodleian, Verona, Zurich, and [St. Gall,] respectively, which contain one or more of the hymns in Luke i. ii. Tischendorf calls them O^a, O^b, O^c, O^d, [O^e,] and ascribes the first two to the *ninth*, the third to the *sixth*, the fourth to the *seventh* [and the last to the *ninth*] *century.*

Coisl.-oct.-marg., or Coisl.-LXX-marg. (F^a in Tischendorf.) On the margin of the great Coislinian Octateuch of the Septuagint several texts from the N. T. are written in uncial characters of the *sixth* or *seventh century.* The following are the passages from the Gospels: Matt. v. 48; xii. 48; xxvii. 25: Luke i. 42; ii. 24; xxiii. 21: John v. 35; vi. 53, 55. The whole are published by Tischendorf, Mon. Sacra, 1846, p. 400[7].

[7] The readings when available of certain Uncials given by Tischendorf in his 8th edition have been cited in the digest of this Edition when their testimony has appeared important. They are—

Θ (or $Θ_a$, Tischdf.). Codex Tischdf. Lips., *Cent.* vii. Matt. xv. 4, 6. [OVER

Manuscripts written in cursive letters.

(I.) *Scrivener's Manuscripts*[8].

a. Lambeth 1175. Brought from the Greek Archipelago by Professor Carlyle. "Very few rare or noticeable readings will be found in this document, which approaches as nearly to the received text as many of a much lower date." Probably of the *eleventh century.*

b. Lambeth 1176. "Well merits Burney's commendation, 'eximiæ notæ.'" About the *twelfth century.*

c. Lambeth 1177. "Written with irreverent and scandalous negligence, but abounding with remarkable readings frequently countenanced by more ancient authorities." Probably of the *twelfth century.*

d. Lambeth 1178. *Tenth* or *eleventh century.*

e. Lambeth 1179. Many lacunæ. Possibly of the *tenth century.*

f. Lambeth 1192. Of very little critical value. Of the *thirteenth century.*

g. Ephesius, Lambeth 528. (71 of critical editions of the N. T.) Brought to England in 1675 by Traheron. Dated A.D. 1160.

h. British Museum, Arundel 524. About the *eleventh century.*

i. Trinity College, Cambridge, B. x. 17. Brought from Mt. Athos. Belonged to Bentley. Assigned to the *thirteenth century.*

k. British Museum, Additional MS., 11300. Came from the library of the Bishop of Cæsarea Philippi at the foot of Lebanon. *Eleventh century.*

l. Codex Wordsworth. In Bp. Wordsworth's possession. *Thirteenth century*[9]. (= g in Acts and Epistles.)

Θ_b. Cod. Petrop., *Cent.* vi. Matt. xxii. 25—28; 30—xxiii. 14: Mark iv. 21—27, 29—35.

Θ_c. Cod. Petrop., *Cent.* vi. Matt. xxi. 22—24 [John xviii. 29—35].

Θ_d. Cod. Petrop., *Cent.* viii. Luke xi. 40—42.

Θ_e. Cod. Porph. Petr., *Cent.* vi. Matt. xxvi. 3—7, 9.

Θ_f. Cod. Porph. Petr., *Cent.* vi. Matt. xxvi. 59—61; xxvii. 44—55: Mark i. 34—ii. 12.

[Θ_g. Cod. Porph. Petr., *Cent.* vi. John vi. 13, 14, 22—24.]

Θ_h. Cod. Porph. Petr., *Cent.* ix. Matt. xxv. 9—16, 41—44.

[8] These mss., none of which (except ev-y) have as yet been shewn to be of any great critical value, have been occasionally cited in the present Edition (as Scr's a, Scr's b c d, and the like); especially in those places where their evidence may help to point out the time at which the more modern of the received readings arose. 'Scr's-mss,' appended to any reading in the digest, means all the mss. in this list which contain the passage, with the exception of any (Scr's c g, or the like) expressly cited for some opposing reading. The remarks given above are extracted from Scrivener's own description.

[9] "I regard codices m n as representatives of the ordinary Greek copies in general

m. (Scholz's 201) British Museum, Additional MS. 11837. Contains the whole New Testament. (See 201 below). Formerly at Florence. Purchased for the Brit. Mus. from the heirs of Dr. Sam. Butler, Bp. of Lichfield. Dated A.D. 1357.

n. British Museum, Burney 18. Contains the Gospels and two leaves of the Ep. to the Hebrews (ch. xii. 17 to end). Dated A.D. 1366.

o. British Museum, Burney 19. Belonged in 1809 to the Library of the Escurial. Possibly one of the mss. numbered 226—233 below. Assigned to the *tenth* or *eleventh century*.

p. British Museum, Burney 20. Written by a monk named Theophilus, A.D. 1285.

q. Codex Theodori. When collated by Mr. Scrivener it was the property of Pickering the publisher. Written by Theodore, A.D. 1295.

r. British Museum, Burney 21. Written by Theodore, A.D. 1292. Text very similar to that of q.

s. British Museum, Burney 23. Very much mutilated in Luke. Ends at John viii. 14. Written in the *twelfth century*.

t. Lambeth 1350. St. John's Gospel appended to Damasc. de Fide. Written about the *fourteenth century*.

u and *v*. Once formed part of the Carlyle collection, but were returned in 1817 to the Patriarch of Jerusalem. u badly collated in Matt. and Mark for Carlyle. *v* collated in Mark i. 1—iv. 16 : John vii. 53—viii. 11 by Dr. Burney. The readings from these collations, and from his own accurate collations of mss. a to h and k to t published by Scrivener in "A full and exact Collation of about 20 Gr. MSS.," 8vo, Cambridge, 1853.

v. The readings of this ms. are given (with those of i and w, and the evangelisteria H, P and Z) in the Appendix to Scrivener's Codex Augiensis.

w. Trinity College, Cambridge, B. x. 16. Written in A.D. 1316. (= l in Acts and Epistles.)

ev-y. Brit. Mus. Burney 22. Dated 1319, but Scrivener thinks this was added some time after the writing of the ms. and that it really dates from the *twelfth century*. The text is a very important one.

use for two centuries before the invention of printing. The connexion between m and n is too close to be accidental, and I can only conjecture that they were written in the same monastery, though by different hands. Nearly as they approach the standard or printed text, they still exhibit some remarkable and rare readings." (Scrivener.)

(II.) *Cursive Manuscripts contained in the lists of Scholz and others.*

	Identification.	Date.	Collator. Remarks.	Paul.	Acts.	Apoc.
1	Basle, K. iii. 3 (late B. vi. 27 [1]).	X. [XII. or XIII.?]	Wetstein, Tregelles, and Roth [2].	1	1	—
2	Basle, B. vi. 25 (now? [A. N. iv. 1]).	XV. [XIII. or XIV.?]	Used as the copy for Erasmus' edition of the Gospels. Bengel's Bas. β.	—	—	—
3	Vienna, Theol. 5, Kol.	XII.	Alter. Known as *Corsendoncensis*. (Forlos. 15.)	3	3	—
4	Paris, 84.	XII.	Stephens' γ'. Scholz (Matt., John). Defective Matt. ii. 9—20: John i. 49—iii. 11.	—	—	—
5	Paris, 106.	XII.	Stephens' δ'. Scholz.	5	5	—
6	Paris, 112.	XIII. (or XI.)	Stephens' ε'. Scholz (Matt.: Mark i.—iv.: John vii. viii.).	6	6	6
7	Paris, 71.	XI.	Stephens' ς'. Scholz (Mark i.—vi.: John iii.—viii.).	—	—	—
8	Paris, 49.	XI.	Stephens' ζ'. Scholz (John).	—	—	—
9	Paris, 83.	1168.	Stephens' ιβ'. Küster's *Par.* 3. Scholz (Matt. i.—viii.: Mark i.—iv.: John iv.—viii.).	—	—	—
10	Paris, 91.	XIII.	Küster's *Par.* 1 [3]. Inspected by Griesbach. Scholz (Mark i.—iv.: John v.—viii.). [Formerly belonged to the Canons Regular at Verona.]	—	—	—
11	Paris, 121, 122.	XII.	Küster's *Par.* 4. Scholz ("denuo").	—	—	—
12	Paris, 230.	XI.	Scholz (Mark [with Victor's comm.], Luke, John). (Wetstein gives, under this number, readings from mss. 119, 120, and from another which has not been identified, all mixed together.)	—	—	—
13	Paris, 50.	XII.	Küster's *Par.* 6. Griesbach. Begtrup (in Birch and Schulz's Griesbach). Defective Matt. i. 1—ii. 21; xxvi. 33—53; xxvii. 26—xxviii. 10: Mark i. 2—45: John xxi. 2—end. A very valuable ms.; text closely allied to that of mss. 69, 124, 346.	—	—	—

[1] Delitzsch, Handschriftliche Funde ii. 24, gives A. N. iii. 12 as the press-mark of this ms. [Burgon gives A. N. iv. 2; having identified iii. 12 as Codex E. Much of the information inserted in square brackets in this section is derived from "Manuscript Evangelia in Foreign Libraries," in letters to the Rev. F. H. Scrivener by the Rev. J. W. Burgon, published in the *Guardian* newspaper, 1873-4.] The particular form of the figure '1' is used to distinguish this MS. from 'Scr's 1.'

[2] "There are uncial MSS. of the Gospels more recent than this cursive copy; but none of the later MSS. of that class is comparable to this, as to the goodness of the text in the Gospels." (Tregelles.)

[[3] Burgon explains that this statement arose from a mistake of Griesbach's: see ms. 285 below.]

	Identification.	Date.	Collator. Remarks.	Paul.	Acts.	Apoc.
14	Paris, 70.	964 [4].	Küster's *Par.* 7. Scholz (Matt. vii.—xxi.: Mark i.—vi.: Luke iii. iv. ix. xi.: John iii.—ix.). [Mutilated Matt. i. 1—9; iii. 16—iv. 9.]	—	—	—
15	Paris, 64.	X.	Küster's *Par.* 8. Scholz ("maximam partem Matt., Mar., Joh.").	—	—	—
16	Paris, 54.	XIV.	Wetstein. Scholz (Mark). The Latin Vulgate in parallel column. Defective Mark xvi. 6—20.	—	—	—
17	Paris, 55.	XVI.	Wetstein. Griesbach. Scholz (Mark). Accompanied by the Latin Vulgate. Written by Hermonymus. ["This assertion is manifestly incorrect." Burgon.]	—	—	—
18	Paris, 47.	1364. [1368.]	Scholz (Gospp. and Acts). Additional readings in Reiche.	133	113	51
19	Paris, 189.	XII.	Scholz ("integre"). Catena on John and scholia on the other Gospels. [That on Mark ascribed to Victor.]	—	—	—
20	Paris, 188.	XI.	Scholz ("longe maximam partem"). Scholia. [Corresponds with mss. 215 (see there) and 300, to which last it has been corrected. Victor's comm. on Mark is claimed for Cyril.]	—	—	—
21	Paris, 68.	X.	Scholz (Matt. i.—xi.: Mark: John iv. v. vii. viii.).	—	—	—
22	Paris, 72.	XI.	Very imperfectly collated by R. Simon (in Mill and Wetstein) and Scholz. Defective Matt. i. 1—v. 25 (or ii. 2 as Sz.). John xiv. 22—xvi. 27.	—	—	—
23	Paris, 77.	XI.	Simon and Scholz, as before. With Latin Vulgate. Defective Matt. i. 1—17: Luke xxiv. 46—John ii. 20: John xxi. 24, 25.	—	—	—
24	Paris, 178.	XI.	Simon. Scholz. With a commentary. Defective Matt. xxvii. 20—Mark iv. 22.	—	—	—
25	Paris, 191 [formerly Colb. 2259: 1880].	X.	Simon. Scholz. Defective Matt. xxiii. 1—xxv. 42: Mark i. 1—vii. 36: Luke viii. 31—41; ix. 44—54; x. 39—xi. 4: middle of John xiii. to end of Gosp. Scholia.	—	—	—
26	Paris, 78.	XI.	Simon. Scholz. With a comm.	—	—	—
27	Paris, 115.	XI.	Larroque in Mill (*Colb.* 1). From John xviii. 3 to end supplied by a later hand in cent. XIV.	—	—	—
28	Paris, 379.	XI.	Larroque in Mill (*Colb.* 2). Scholz. Defective Matt. vii. 17—ix. 12; xiv. 33—xvi. 10; xxvi. 70—xxvii. 48: Luke xx. 19—xxii. 46: John xii. 40—xiii. 1; xv. 24—xvi. 12; xviii. 16—28; xx. 20—xxi. 5; xxi. 18—25.	—	—	—

[[4] Burgon shews this to be a mistake, adding, "The exquisite writing cannot be of nearly the antiquity claimed for the ms."]

	Identification.	Date.	Collator. Remarks.	Paul.	Acts.	Apoc
29	Paris, 89.	XII.	Larroque in Mill (*Colb.* 3). Scholz (Mark i.—v.: John v.—viii.). Some leaves supplied in cent. XV.	—	—	—
30	Paris, 100.	XVI.	Readings from 1st chapters of Matt., Larroque in Mill. Cited with 31 as *Colb.* 4. Inspected by Scholz. Written by Hermonymus.	—	—	—
31	Paris, 94	XIII.	Readings from Matt., Mark, Larroque in Mill. Cited with 30 as *Colb.* 4. Inspected by Scholz.	—	—	—
32	Paris, 116.	XII.	Readings from Matt., Larroque in Mill (*Colb.* 5). Defective Matt. i. 1—x. 22; xxiv. 15—30: Luke xxii. 35—John iv. 20. Inspected by Scholz.	—	—	—
33	Paris, 14 (Colb. 2844).	XI.	Tregelles. Called the Queen of the cursive mss.	17	13	—
34	Paris, Coisl. 195.	XI.	Cursorily collated by Wetstein and Scholz. Catena [that on Mark claimed for Victor]. From Mt. Athos.	—	—	—
35	Paris, Coisl. 199.	XI.	Cursorily collated by Wetstein and Scholz.	18	14	17
36	Paris, Coisl. 20.	XI.	Cursorily collated by Wetstein and Scholz. Commentary [Victor's on Mark]. From Mt. Athos.	—	—	—
37	Paris, Coisl. 21.	XII.	Cursorily collated by Wetstein and Scholz. [Commentary. Victor's on Mark.]	—	—	—
38	Paris, Coisl. 200.	XIII.	(Stephens' θ'?) Written by order of the Emperor Michael Palæologus. Defective Matt. xiv. 15—xv. 30; xx. 14—xxi. 27: Mark xii. 3—xiii. 4.	?	19	?
39	Paris, Coisl. 23.	XII.	Cursorily collated by Wetstein and Scholz. Once at Mt. Athos. A copy of 34 (Wetst.) [derived from a common original. Burgon. Commentary on Mark claimed for Victor].	—	—	—
40	Paris, Coisl. 22.	XI.	C. c. Wetstein, Scholz. Commentary [Victor's on Mark]. From Constantinople, once at Mt. Athos. Ends at John xx. 25.	—	—	—
41	Paris, Coisl. 24.	XI.	C. c. Wetstein, Scholz. Contains Matt., Mark, with commentary. [This is a commentary, not a text. On St. Mark it is expressly claimed for Victor. Burgon.]	—	—	—
42	. . . .	—	Mill's *Med.* Possibly the same as K above.	—	—	—
43	Bibl. de l'Arsenal, Paris, 4.	XI.	Inspected by Simon and Scholz. Known as *San-Maglorianus.*	130	54	—
44	Brit. Mus., Addl. MS. 4949.	XI.	De Missy in Wetstein.	—	—	—
45	Bodleian, Baroc. 31.	XIV.	Mill's *Bodl.* 1. Inspected by Griesbach.	—	—	—
46	Bodleian, Baroc. 29.	XV.	Mill's *Bodl.* 2.	—	—	—
47	Bodleian, Misc. 9.	XV.	Mill's *Bodl.* 6. Ussher in Walton's Polyglott (*Bodl.* 1).	—	—	—

	Identification.	Date.	Collator. Remarks.	Paul.	Acts.	Apoc.
48	Bodleian, Misc. 1.	XII.	Mill's *Bodl.* 7. Scholia.	—	—	—
49	Bodleian, Roe. 1.	XI.	Mill's *Roe.* 1.	—	—	—
50	Bodleian, Laud. [Græc.] 33.	XI.	Mill's *Laud.* 1. Catena [that on Mark claimed for Cyril]. Defective Matt. i. 1—ix. 35; xii. 3—24; xxv. 20—31: Mark xiv. 40—xvi. 20: John v. 18—end of Gosp.	—	—	—
51	Bodleian, Laud. 31.	XIII.	Mill's *Laud.* 2. Inspected by Griesbach.	38	32	—
52	Bodleian, Laud. 3.	1286.	Mill's *Laud.* 5. Inspected by Griesbach.	—	—	—
53	Bodleian, Selden. 53 [28].	XIV.	Mill's *Seld.* 1.	—	—	—
54	Bodleian, Selden. 54 [29].	1338.	Mill's *Seld.* 2.	—	—	—
55	Bodleian, Selden. 5 [6].	XV.	Mill's *Seld.* 3.	—	—	—
56	Linc. Coll. Oxf., 18.	XV.	Ussher in Walton. Mill (*Lin.*). Inspected by Dobbin (with 61).	—	—	—
57	Magd. Coll. Oxf., 9.	XI.	Hammond in Walton. Mill's *Magd.* 1. Defective Mark i. 1—11.	41	35	—
58	New Coll. Oxf., 68.	XVI.	Ussher in Walton *Nov.* 1. Mill's *N.* 1. Dobbin (with 61).	—	—	—
59	Caius Coll. Camb., 403.	XII.	Scrivener. Ussher's *Gon.* in Walton. So also in Mill.	—	—	—
60	Camb. Univ. Lib. MS. Dd. 9. 69.	1297.	Mill's *M*(*ori*). 1. (The Apocalypse added at a later time.)	—	—	10
61	Trin. Coll. Dublin, G. 97.	XVI.	Ussher in Walton. Barrett in edn. of Cod. Z. Dobbin. Known as *Montfortianus.*	40	34	92
62	Camb. Univ. Lib. MS. Kk. 5. 35.	XV.	Walton's *Goog.*	—	—	—
63	Trin. Coll. Dublin, A. 1. 8.	X.	Mill's *Usser.* 1. Scrivener states that this ms. has been lately collated by Rev. G. Twycross.	—	—	—
64	*Not identified.*	?	Mill's *Usser.* 2 (and probably also Walton's *Eur.*).	—	—	—
65	Brit.Mus., Harl. 5776.	XIII.	Mill's *Cov.* 1.	—	—	—
66	*Not identified.*	?	Mill's *Gal.* Scholia. Once belonged to Thomas Gale.	—	—	—
67	Bodleian, Misc. 76.	XI.	Mill's *Hunt.* 2. Defective John vi. 64 to end of Gosp.	—	—	—
68	Linc. Coll. Oxf., 17.	XII.	Mill's *Wheel.* 1.	—	—	—
69	The Leicester MS.	XIV.	Tregelles and Scrivener. Cited as m Acts, Epp.; f, Apoc. (See Horne's Introd. vol. iv. ed. Treg., pp. 210, 211. Scriv.'s Codex Augiensis pp. xl—xlvii.)	37	31	14
70	Camb. Univ. Lib. MS. Ll. 2. 13.	XV.	Mill's *Bu*(*nckle*). Written by Hermonymus. (Not at Trin. Coll. as Sz., Tischdf.)	—	—	—
71	Lambeth, 528.	1160.	Scrivener's g (*above*). Mill's *Eph.*	—	—	—
72	Brit.Mus., Harl. 5647.	XI.	Wetstein. Catena. Various readings on margin *prima manu.*	—	—	—
73	Ch. Ch. Oxf., Wake 26.	XI.	Walker (in Wetstein).	—	—	—
74	Ch. Ch. Oxf., Wake 20.	XIII.	Walker (in Wetstein). Written by Theodore. Defective Matt. i. 1—14; v. 29—vi. 1.	—	—	—
75	Geneva, 19.	XI.	Cellerier (in Scholz).	—	—	—

	Identification.	Date.	Collator. Remarks.	Paul.	Acts	Apoc.
76	Vienna, Theol. 300, N.	XI.	(Lambec. 28.) G. à Mästricht (in Wetstein). Alter. Collated with Gospp. 218.	49	43	—
77	Vienna, Theol. 154, N.	XI.	(Lambec. 29: "Nessel 114" is probably a misprint in Scholz.) Treschow. Alter. Collated with Gospp. 218. Commentary [Victor's on Mark].	—	—	—
78	Supposed to be in Hungary. (Lib. of N. Jancovich de Vadass?)	XII.	Borner (in Küster's Mill). Additional readings in Scholz. Belonged to Carpzov.	—	—	—
79	Leyden, 74.	?	Inspected in John viii. Defective. Lat. version.	—	—	—
80	*Not identified.*	XI.	Bynæus (in Wetstein). Belonged to T. G. Græviùs, then to J. Van der Hagen.	—	—	—
(81)	. . . .	—	(Under this number certain mss. mentioned in a *Correctorium* of cent. XIII. have been cited.)			
(82)	. . . .	—	(Number used as equivalent to "found by L. Valla (*Annotationes* 1440) in one or more of the mss. consulted by him.")			
83	Munich, 518.	XI.	Bengel's *Augustanus* 1. Contains John vii. 53—viii. 11, with marks down the margin.]	—	—	—
84	Munich, 568.	XII.	Bengel's *Augustanus* 2. Contains only Matt., Mark. Defective Matt. i. 1—18; xiii. 10—27, 42—xiv. 3; xviii. 25—xix. 9; xxi. 33—xxii. 4: Mark vii. 13—end.	—	—	—
85	Munich, 569. (Munich = Public Library at Munich.)	XIII.	Bengel's *Augustanus* 3. Contains only the following passages: Matt. viii. 15—ix. 17; xvi. 12—xvii. 20; xxiv. 26—45; xxvi. 25—54: Mark vi. 13—ix. 45: Luke iii. 12—vi. 44: John ix. 11—xii. 5; xix. 6—24; xx. 23—xxi. 9.	—	—	—
86	Presburg.	XI.	Bengel's *Byzantinus*. Endlicher's complete collation given in Rosenmüller's Commentationes Theologicæ, vol. ii. part ii. pp. 85—166.	—	—	—
87	Trèves.	XII.	Contains John, with a catena. Edited at Antwerp by Corderius. (Wetstein's 87 is 250 of this and Scholz's list.)	—	—	—
88	*Not identified.*	?	Cited by Joachim Camerarius in his Annotationes in N. T.	—	—	—
89	Gottingen.	1006.	Bengel. Matthæi's 20.	—	—	—
90	*Not identified.*	XVI.	A copy of one of Theodore's mss. made by James Favre of Daventer.	14	47	—
91	*Not identified.*	X.	*Codex Perronianus.* Extracts in Mill.	—	—	—
92	*Not identified.* [Basle O. ii. 27.]	? [XIV. or XV.]	*Codex Fœschii* 1. Contains Mark, with Victor's commentary [followed by Scholia on Cath. Ep. from various Fathers].	—	49[5]	—

[[5] Burgon identifies ms. 92 with Acts (or rather Cath.) 47. Letter III. to the Rev. F. H. Scrivener.]

	Identification.	Date.	Collator. Remarks.	Paul.	Acts.	Apoc.
93	*Not identified.*	?	*Codex Gravii.* Once cited by Vossius. "Aut est idem Codex atque 63 aut ei simillimus" (Wetst.).	—	—	—
94	*Not identified.* [Basle O. ii. 23.]	? [XVI. or XVII.]	*Codex Fœschii* 2. Contains Mark, Luke, with a commentary [Victor's on Mark: Tit-bostr. on Luke].	—	—	—
95	Linc. Coll. Oxf., 16.	XII.	Mill's *Wheel(er)* 2. Contains Luke (from xi. 2), John (except 3 leaves). John v.—vii. re-collated for Scholz.	—	—	—
96	Bodleian, Misc. 8.	XV.	Ussher (in Walton) and Mill. Cited by them as *Trit.* because written by Abbot John Trithemius. Contains John.	—	—	—
97	*Not identified.*	1500.	A copy of John closely related to 96. Written by Nicholas, a monk of Hirsau. Readings in Wetstein. Scholz denies that it was ever at Giessen as Michaelis, &c. have stated.	—	—	—
98	Bodleian, Clarke 5.	XII.	Matt. vi. ix. x.: Mark v. vi.: Luke iv.—vi. collated by Scholz.	—	—	—
99	Leipsic.	XVI.	Matthæi's 18. Contains Matt. iv. 8—v. 27; vi. 2–xv. 30: Luke i. 1—13.	—	—	—
100	Pesth, Univ. Lib.	X.	Cited only once. Defective John xxi. 25.	—	—	—
101	*Not identified.*	XVI.	*Codex Uffenbachianus* 3. Contains John. Cited by Scholz at John vii. 53.	—	—	—
(102)	. . . .	. . .	Some ms. readings cited by Wetstein (Matt. xxiv.—Mark viii.) from the Margin of a Gk. Test. of Plantin's. The readings seem to have been derived from Cod. B. (So Rev. B. F. Westcott in Scriv. Introd.)	—	—	—
103	Paris, 196.	XI.	Readings in Curcellæus (edn. of Gk. Test.). Scholz ("cursim collatus"). [Theophylact on St. Matt. and St. Luke, written over an older ms. of the 8th or 9th century.]	—	—	—
104	*Not identified.*	X.	*Codex Vignerii.* Readings in Wetstein.	—	—	—
105	Bodleian, Misc. 136.	XII.	Cited by Wetstein on John viii. 1.	24	48	—
106	Earl of Winchilsea's Library.	X.	Jackson (in Wetstein).	—	—	—
107	Bodleian, Clarke 6.	XIV.	Readings from Matt. vi. ix. x.: Mark v. vi.: Luke iv.—vi.: John v. vi. in Scholz.	—	—	—
108	Vienna, Theol. 4, Kol. (Forlos. 5).	XI.	Alter, Birch, Scholz. Commentary [Victor's on Mark]. 2 vols. Belonged to Parrhasius.	—	—	—
109	Brit. Mus., Addl. MSS. 5115-6-7.	1326.	Inspected by Wetstein. Belonged to Meade and then to Askew.	75	22	—
(110)	. . . .	XVI.	A transcript (2 vols.) of the Complutensian edition, at Berlin, known as the *Codex Ravianus.*	—	—	—

	Identification.	Date.	Collator. Remarks.	Paul.	Acts.	Apoc.
111	Bodleian, Clarke 7.	XII.	Scholz (in same passages as 107). Defective John xx. 25—end.	—	—	—
112	Bodleian, Clarke 10.	XI.	Scholz (selected chapters).	—	—	—
113	Brit. Mus., Harl. 1810.	XI.	Griesbach (in Mark xvi.: Luke iii. 16—38; viii. 15—39; xi. 1—24: John v. 1—vi. 36; vii. 53—viii. 12).	—	—	—
114	Brit. Mus., Harl. 5540.	XIII.	Inspected by Griesbach. Defective Matt. xvii. 4—18; xxvi. 59—73; xxviii. 19—Mark i. 12.	—	—	—
115	Brit. Mus., Harl. 5559.	XII.	Inspected by Griesbach. Defective Matt. i. 1—viii. 10: Mark v. 23—36: Luke i. 78—ii. 10; vi. 4—15: John xi. 2—xxi 25.	—	—	
116	Brit. Mus., Harl. 5567.	XII.	Inspected by Griesbach.	—	—	—
117	Brit. Mus., Harl. 5731.	XIV.	Inspected by Griesbach. Defective Matt. i. 1—18. Fragments of a lectionary at end.	—	—	—
118	Bodleian, Misc. 13.	XIII.	Griesbach (in Symb. Crit. i. 202). Matt. i. 1—vi. 3: Luke xiii. 35—xiv. 20; xviii. 8—xix. 9: John xvi. 25—xxi. 25 supplied by a later hand.	—	—	—
119	Paris, 85.	XII.	Küster's *Par.* 5. Griesbach. [Formerly belonged to Taller of Rheims.]	—	—	—
120	Paris, 185 A [i. e. Supplément Grécque, 185].	XIII.	Stephens' ιδ'. Griesbach. Contains only Matt., Luke, John.	—	—	—
121	*Not identified.*	1284.	Griesbach. Once at St. Geneviève, Paris. Defective Matt. v. 21—viii. 24.	—	—	—
122	Leyden, Meermann's 116.	XII.	Dermout.	219	177	—
123	Vienna, Theol. 240, N.	XI.	Alter. Birch. (Lambec. 30.)	—	—	—
124	Vienna, Theol. 188, N.	XII.	Alter. Birch. Defective Luke xxiii. 31—xxiv. 28. Closely allied to 13, 69, and 346. (Lambec. 31.)	—	—	—
125	Vienna, Theol. 6, Kol.	X.	Alter. Birch. (Forlos. 16, so Scholz: but in Alter it is 16 in Kollar's Supplement; 6 in Auct. Forlos.)	—	—	—
126	Wolfenbüttel, xvi. 16.	XI.	Mentioned by Knittel. Consulted in some places by Tischendorf.	—	—	—
127	Vatican, 349.	XII.	Birch ("per omnia").	—	—	—
128	Vatican, 356.	XI.	Cited by Birch in Matt. v. 47 and John viii. 1.	—	—	—
129	Vatican, 358.	XII.	Birch (Luke i.—ix. and Matt. xxvii. 16, 17: Mark xvi. 9: John i. 28; xxi. 25). [Victor's commentary on Mark.]	—	—	—
130	Vatican, 359.	XIII.	Birch ("præter loca selecta ex Matt., Mar., Joh., integrum Lucæ Evangelium accurate contulimus"). Lat. version.	—	—	—
131	Vatican, 360.	XI.	Birch ("quatuor Evangelia accurate per omnia contuli").	77	70	66
132	Vatican, 361.	XI.	Birch ("Luc. i.—iv. accurate" and inspected in other places).	—	—	—

	Identification.	Date.	Collator. Remarks.	Paul.	Acts.	Apoc.
133	Vatican, 363.	XI.	Birch (Luke i.—x. and select places).	78	71	—
134	Vatican, 364.	XI.	Birch ("citatur Luc. i.—iv. et ad Joh. viii. 1").	—	—	—
135	Vatican, 365.	XI.	Birch ("Luc. i.—iii., accurate" and inspected in other places). The first 26 leaves supplied by a later hand.	—	—	—
136	Vatican, 665.	XIII.	Contains Matt. and Mark, with commentary. Inspected by Birch in select places of Matt.	—	—	—
137	Vatican, 756.	XII.	Cited in a few passages by Birch. With a marginal commentary [Victor's on Mark].	—	—	—
138	Vatican, 757.	XII.	Inspected by Birch. Commentary [Victor's on Mark] and scholia.	—	—	—
139	Vatican, 758.	XII.	Contains Luke and John, with commentary. Inspected by Birch.	—	—	—
140	Vatican, 1158.	XII.	Inspected by Scholz.	—	—	—
141	Vatican, 1160.	XIII.	Inspected by Scholz.	86	75	40
142	Vatican, 1210.	XI.	Inspected by Scholz.	87	76	—
143	Vatican, 1229.	XI.	Luke i.—vi. accurately collated by Birch. Commentary [Victor's on Mark].	—	—	—
144	Vatican, 1254.	XI.	Inspected by Birch and Scholz.	—	—	—
145	Vatican, 1548.	XIII.	Inspected by Birch and Scholz. Contains only Luke, John. Luke xvii.—xxi. written by a different hand from the rest. Defective Luke iv. 15—v. 36: John i. 1—26.	—	—	—
146	Vatican, Palat. 5.	XII.	Contains Matt., Mark, with marginal commentary. Inspected by Birch and Scholz.	—	—	—
147	Vatican, Palat. 89.	XI.	Inspected by Birch and Scholz.	—	—	—
148	Vatican, Palat. 136.	XII.	Inspected by Birch and Scholz. Scholia.	—	—	—
149	Vatican, Palat. 171.	XIV.	Inspected by Birch and Scholz.	88	77	25
150	Vatican, Palat. 189.	XII.	Inspected by Birch and Scholz.	—	—	—
151	Vatican, Palat. 220.	XI.	Inspected by Birch and Scholz. Scholia.	—	—	—
152	Vatican, Palat. 227.	XI.	Inspected by Birch and Scholz.	—	—	—
153	Vatican, Palat. 229.	XIII.	Scholz ("maxima pars").	—	—	—
154	Vatican, Alex. 28.	XIII.	Inspected by Birch and Scholz Thl.'s commentary.	—	—	—
155	Vatican, Alex. 79.	XIV.	Inspected by Birch and Scholz.	—	—	—
156	Vatican, Alex. 189.	XII.	Inspected by Birch and Scholz.	—	—	—
157	Vatican, Urb. 2.	XII.	Inspected by Birch and Scholz.	—	—	—
158	Vatican, Pio 53.	XI.	Inspected by Birch and Scholz.	—	—	—
159	Rome: Barberini, 8.	XI.	Inspected by Birch and Scholz.	—	—	—
160	Rome: Barberini, 9.	1123.	Inspected by Birch and Scholz.	—	—	—
161	Rome: Barberini, 10.	X.	Inspected by Birch and Scholz. Defective John xvi. 6—xxi. 25.	—	—	—
162	Rome: Barberini, 11.	1153.	Inspected by Birch and Scholz.	—	—	—
163	Rome: Barberini, 12.	XI.	Inspected by Birch and Scholz.	—	—	—
164	Rome: Barberini, 13.	1040.	Inspected by Birch and Scholz.	—	—	—
165	Rome: Barberini, 14.	1197.	Inspected by Birch and Scholz With the Vulgate Latin.	—	—	—
166	Rome: Barberini, 115.	XIII.	Inspected by Birch and Scholz. Contains Luke ix. 33—xxiv. 24, and John.	—	—	—

	Identification.	Date.	Collator. Remarks.	Paul.	Acts.	Apoc.
167	Rome: Barberini, 208.	XIV.	Inspected by Birch and Scholz.	—	—	—
168	Rome: Barberini, 211.	XIII.	Inspected by Birch and Scholz. Thl.'s commentary.	—	—	—
169	Rome: Vallicella, B. 133.	XII.	Inspected by Birch and Scholz.	—	—	—
170	Rome: Vallicella, C. 61.	XII.	Inspected by Birch and Scholz.	—	—	—
171	Rome: Vallicella, C. 73.	XIV.	Inspected by Birch and Scholz.	—	—	—
172	*Not identified.*	XII.	Vallicella, F. 90. Formerly contained the four Gospels.	—	—	—
173	Vatican, 1983.	XII.	Inspected by Birch (*Basilianus* 22) and Scholz. Defective John xiii. 1—xxi. 25.	—	—	—
174	Vatican, 2002.	1053.	Inspected by Birch (*Bas.* 41) and Scholz. Defective Matt. i. 1—ii. 1: John i. 1—27; viii. 47—xxi. 25.	—	—	—
175	Vatican, 2080.	XII.	Inspected by Birch (*Bas.* 119) and Scholz. Defective Matt. i. 1—iv. 17.	194	41	20
176	Vatican, 2113.	XIII.	Inspected by Birch (*Bas.* 152) and Scholz. Defective Matt. i. 1—x. 13: John ii. 1—xxi. 25.	—	—	—
177	Vatican, (?)	XI.	Inspected by Birch and Scholz. Defective John i. 1—29. (Formerly Monastery of St. Basil, 163.)	—	—	—
178	Rome: Angelica, A. 1. 5.	XI.	Inspected by Birch and Scholz. Defective John xxi. 17—end.	—	—	—
179	Rome: Angelica, A. 4. 11.	XII.	Inspected by Birch and Scholz. Some leaves supplied by a later hand.	—	—	—
180	Rome: Propaganda, 250.	XI.	Readings given by Zoega (Engelbreth in Birch, as *Borg.* 4 (2 Sz.)) and Scholz. Acts and Epistles added in 1274.	92	82	44
181	*Not identified.*	XI.	A ms. belonging to Francis Xavier, Cardinal de Zelada, inspected by Birch. Scholia.	—	—	—
182	Florence: Laurentian, vi. 11.	XII.	Inspected by Birch and Scholz [Victor on Mark].	—	—	—
183	Florence: Laur. vi. 14.	XII.	Inspected by Birch and Scholz.	—	—	—
184	Florence: Laur. vi. 15.	XIII.	Inspected by Birch and Scholz.	—	—	—
185	Florence: Laur. vi. 16.	XII.	Inspected by Birch and Scholz.	—	—	—
186	Florence: Laur. vi. 18.	XI.	Inspected by Birch and Scholz. [Marginal commentary. Victor's on St. Mark.]	—	—	—
187	Florence: Laur. vi. 23.	XII.	Inspected by Birch and Scholz.	—	—	—
188	Florence: Laur. vi. 25.	XI.	Inspected by Birch and Scholz.	—	—	—
189	Florence: Laur. vi. 27.	XII.	Inspected by Birch and Scholz. John defective at end [from xix. 38].	239	141	—
190	Florence: Laur. vi. 28.	1285.	Inspected by Birch and Scholz.	—	—	—

	Identification.	Date.	Collator. Remarks.	Paul.	Acts.	Apoc.
191	Florence: Laur. vi. 29.	XIII.	Inspected by Birch and Scholz.	—	—	—
192	Florence: Laur. vi. 30.	XIII.	Inspected by Birch and Scholz.	—	—	—
193	Florence: Laur. vi. 32.	XI.	Inspected by Birch and Scholz.	—	—	—
194	Florence: Laur. vi. 33.	XI.	Inspected by Birch and Scholz. [Marginal commentary. Victor's on St. Mark.]	—	—	—
195	Florence: Laur. vi. 34.	XI.	Inspected by Birch and Scholz. [Marginal commentary. Victor's on St. Mark.]	—	—	—
196	Florence: Laur. viii. 12.	XII.	Inspected by Birch and Scholz. Catena. [Was given by a son of Cosmo de' Medici to the Convent of St. Mark at Florence in 1473.]	—	—	—
197	Florence: Laur. viii. 14.	XI.	Contains, besides Ep. of James, only fragments of Matt. and Mark, with Chr.'s commentary [on Matt., and Victor's on Mark. Mutilated at end]. Inspected by Birch and Scholz.	—	90	—
198	Florence: Laur. 256 [Ædil. 221].	XIII.	Inspected by Birch and Scholz.	—	—	—
199	*Not identified.* [Florence: Laur. 99.]	XII.	Inspected by Birch. Formerly No. 5 [67] in Lib. of Monastery of St. Mary, Florence [to which it was left by Antonio Corbinelli in 1423]. Scholia. [Harmony at foot of page in Matt., Mark, and parts of Luke, John.]	—	—	—
200	*Not identified.* [Florence: Laur. 69.]	X.	Inspected by Birch. Formerly No. 6 [66] in Lib. of Monastery of St. Mary, Florence. [Scholia.]	—	—	—
201	Brit. Mus., Addl. MS. 11837.	1357.	Scrivener. Cited as m in Gospp., h in Epp., and b in Apoc.	104	91	b
202	*Not identified.*	XII.	Inspected by Birch. Formerly No. 705 in Lib. of Monastery of St. Mary, Florence.	—	—	—
203]	. . . .	. . .	A ms. in modern Greek. Formerly No. 707 in Lib. of St. Mary, Florence.	—	—	—
204	Bologna: Can. Reg. [S. Salvador], 640 [now Royal Libr. 2775].	XI. [XIII.?]	Inspected by Birch.	105[6]	92	—
205	St. Mark's Venice, 5 [86: 4].	XV.	Inspected by Birch. Written for Cardinal Bessarion. In Gospp. and Apoc. apparently copied from 209 [so Rink: Burgon thinks them both derived from a more ancient (uncial) MS. Contains O. T. also].	106	93	88
206	St. Mark's Venice, 6 [86: 4].	XV. [XVI.?]	Inspected by Birch. [Duplicate of 205.]	107	94	—

[[6] Burgon's memorandum implies that ms. 204 does not contain any portion of St. Paul's Epistles.]

	Identification.	Date.	Collator. Remarks.	Paul.	Acts.	Apoc.
207	St. Mark's Venice, 8 [86 : 7].	X. [XI. or XII.?]	Inspected by Birch. Defective at beginning.	—	—	—
208	St. Mark's Venice, 9 [86 : 1].	X. [XI. or XII.?]	Inspected by Birch.	—	—	—
209	St. Mark's Venice, 10 [86 : 1].	XV. [XI.?]	Inspected by Birch. [Apoc. in more modern hand.]	108	95	46
210	St. Mark's Venice, 27 [86 : 4].	X. [XI. or XII.?]	Mentioned by Birch. Catena [Victor on Mark].	—	—	—
211	St. Mark's Venice, 539 [86 : 5].	XII.	Inspected by Birch. Arabic version. Defective at beginning of Luke [to ii. 32] and of John [to iv. 2. John unfinished].	—	—	—
212	St. Mark's Venice, 540 [86 : 6].	XI.	Inspected by Birch. [Mutilated.]	—	—	—
213	St. Mark's Venice, 542 [86 : 1].	XI.	Inspected by Birch. [Mutilated. John xviii. 40—end in more modern hand.]	—	—	—
214	St. Mark's Venice, 543 [86 : 7].	XIV.	Inspected by Birch.	—	—	—
215	St. Mark's Venice, 544 [86 : 5].	XI.	Inspected by Birch. Commentary [Chrysostom on Matt., Cyr. (or Victor) on Mark, Tit-bostr. &c. on Luke, Chr. &c. on John]. Additional readings (e. g. from Matt. xxiv.: Mark iv.: Luke iv.: John v.) in Scholz. [Corresponds with mss. 20, 300. Once belonged to Maximus, Bp. of Cythera (?).]	—	—	—
216	[Not at] St. Mark's Venice, (?)	?	Mentioned by Birch, as brought to Venice [Birch does not say *to Venice*], from Corcyra. [One of the Canonici mss., but not in the Bodleian.]	—	—	—
217	St. Mark's Venice, [Gr. Class.] I. 3 [86 : 1].	XIII.	Readings in Scholz, e. g. Matt. vi.: Mark iv.: Luke iv.: John v. [From Padua.]	—	—	—
218	Vienna, Theol. 23, N.	XIII.	Edited by Alter (Lambec. 1).	57	65	33
219	Vienna, Theol. 321, N.	XIII.	Alter. Birch (Lambec. 32).	—	—	—
220	Vienna, Theol. 337, N.	XIV.	Alter. Birch (Lambec. 33).	—	—	—
221	Vienna, Theol. 117, N.	XI.	Inspected by Birch (Lambec. 38). Commentary defective Matt. i. 1—11 and elsewhere: John vii. viii. (appy.) See Scholz in loc. [Victor on Mark.]	—	—	—
222	Vienna, Theol. 180, N.	XIV.	Birch (Lambec. 39). Fragments with a commentary [Victor on Mark].	—	—	—
223	Vienna, Theol. 301, N.	XIV.	Birch (Lambec. 40). Contains fragments of Matt., Luke, John, with catena.	—	—	—
224	Vienna, Theol. 8, Kol.	?	Contains only Matt. (Forlos. 30.)	—	—	—
225	Vienna, Theol. 9, Kol.	1192.	Alter? (Forlos. 31.)	—	—	—
226	Escurial, χ. iv. 17.	XI.	Readings by Moldenhauer (in Birch, *Esc.* 2.)	228	108	—

	Identification.	Date.	Collator. Remarks.	Paul.	Acts.	Apoc.
227	Escurial, χ. iii. 15.	XIII.	Readings by Moldenhauer (in Birch, *Esc.* 5).	—	—	—
228	Escurial, χ. iv. 12.	XIV.	Readings by Moldenhauer (in Birch, *Esc.* 7).	229	109	—
229	Escurial, χ. iv. 21.	1140.	Readings by Moldenhauer (in Birch, *Esc.* 8). Defective Mark xvi. 15—20: John i. 1—11.	—	—	—
230	Escurial, φ. iii. 5.	1013.	Readings by Moldenhauer (in Birch, *Esc.* 9).	—	—	—
231	Escurial, φ. iii. 6.	XII.	Readings by Moldenhauer (in Birch, *Esc.* 10).	—	—	—
232	Escurial, φ. iii. 7.	XIII.	Readings by Moldenhauer (in Birch, *Esc.* 11).	—	—	—
233	Escurial, υ. ii. 8.	XI.	Readings by Moldenhauer (in Birch, *Esc.* 12). Catena.	—	—	—
234	Copenhagen, 1.	1278.	Hensler (in Birch).	72	57	—
235	Copenhagen, 2.	1314.	Hensler (in Birch).	—	—	—
236	Camb. Univ. Lib., MS. Mm. 6. 9.	XII.	Scrivener (v in Gospp.; o in Acts and Epp.).	61	61	—
237	Moscow: Synod, 42.	X.	Matthæi (d). [Victor on Mark.]	—	—	—
238	Moscow: Synod, 48.	XI.	Matthæi (e). Contains Matt. and Mark, with catena [Victor on Mark].	—	—	—
239	Moscow: Synod, 47.	XI.	Matthæi (g). Contains Mark xvi. 2—8: Luke: John i. 1—xxi. 23, with commentary and catena.	—	—	—
240	Moscow: Synod, 49.	XII.	Matthæi (i). With Euthym.'s commentary. Defective Mark vii. 12—34; xiv. 17—54: Luke xv 32—xvi. 8.	—	—	—
241	Dresden.	XI.	Matthæi (k). Belonged to Matthæi.	120	104	47
242	Moscow: Synod, 380.	XII.	Matthæi (l).	121	105	48
243	Moscow: Typogr., 13.	XIV.	Matthæi (m). Contains Matt., Luke, with Thl.'s commentary.	—	—	—
244	Moscow: Typogr., 1.	XII.	Matthæi (n). Euthym.'s commentary.	—	—	—
245	Moscow: Synod, 265.	1199.	Matthæi (o).	—	—	—
246	Moscow: Synod, 261.	XIV.	Matthæi (p). Defective Matt. xii. 41—xiii. 55: John xvii. 24—xviii. 20.	—	—	—
247	Moscow: Synod, 373.	XII.	Matthæi (q).	—	—	—
248	Moscow: Synod, 264.	1275.	Matthæi (r).	—	—	—
249	Moscow: Synod, 94.	XI.	Matthæi (s). Contains John, with catena.	—	—	—
(250)	. . . .	—	The cursive portion of Codex V above. Better cited as V[r].	—	—	—
251	Moscow: Tab. Imp.	XI.	Matthæi (x).	—	—	—
252	Dresden.	XI.	Matthæi (z). Belonged to Matthæi.	—	—	—
253	?	XI.	Matthæi (10). Once belonged to St. Michael's Monastery at Jerusalem and then to Abp. Nicephorus. [Contains Victor on Mark.]	—	—	—
254	?	XI.	Matthæi (11). Belonged to Matthæi, in 1482 to the Monastery of St. Athanasius. Contains Luke, John, with scholia.	—	—	—

	Identification.	Date.	Collator. Remarks.	Paul.	Acts.	Apoc.
(255)	(Moscow: Synod, 139.)	XIII.	Matthæi (12). More properly a ms. of Chr.'s commentary [and scholia from Victor on Mark?]. It contains only fragments of the Gospels.	—	—	—
256	Moscow: Typogr., 3.	IX.?	Matthæi (14). Scholia [from Victor] on Mark, Luke, with fragments of the text.	—	—	—
(257)	. . . .	—	= Frag. Mosq. (*above, p.* 116).	—	—	—
258	Dresden.	XIII.	Matthæi, 17.	—	—	—
259	Moscow: Synod, 45.	XI.	Matthæi (a). [Contains Victor on Mark.]	—	—	—
260	Paris, 51.	XII.	Scholz ("maxima pars").	—	—	—
261	Paris, 52.	XII.	Scholz (Matt. xi.—xiii.: Mark v.—vii.: Luke i.—v.: John v.—viii.). Matt. i. 1—xi. 1 supplied in cent. XIV. Defective Luke xxiv. 39—end of Gosp.	—	—	—
262	Paris, 53	X.	Scholz ("integre"). Various readings from Jerusalem mss. given by the original scribe. Text very like that of Cod. Λ.	—	—	—
263	Paris, 61.	XIII.	Scholz (Matt. viii.—xiv.: Mark i.—iv.: John ii.—v.). Additional readings given by Reiche; who states that it does not contain the Apocalypse ("Codicum insigniorum Par. asserv. Descriptio").	137	117	(54)
264	Paris, 65.	XIII.	Scholz (Matt. xviii.—xxiv.: Mark iii.—v.: John iv.—viii.). [Harmony at the foot of each page.]	—	—	—
265	Paris, 66.	X.	Scholz (Matt., the whole: Mark i.—v.: Luke xxii.—xxiv.: John v.—viii.).	—	—	—
266	Paris, 67.	X.	Scholz (Matt. i.—xi.: Mark ii.—v.: John v.—ix.).	—	—	—
267	Paris, 69.	X.	Scholz (Matt. ii.—x.: John vii. viii.). Defective Matt. i. 1—8: Mark i. 1—7: Luke i. 1—8: xxiv. 50—John i. 12.	—	—	—
268	Paris, 73.	XII.	Scholz (Matt. xxvi.: Mark i.—iv.: John iv.—viii.).	—	—	—
269	Paris, 74.	XI.	Scholz (Matt.: Mark i.—iv.).	—	—	—
270	Paris, 75.	XI.	Scholz ("maxima pars").	—	—	—
271	Paris, 75 A [Supplément Grecque 75].	XII.	Scholz ("maxima pars").	—	—	—
272	Paris, 76 [lost ever since 1848].	XI.	Scholz (Matt. vi.—xi.: Mark i.—iii.: John v.—viii.).	—	—	—
273	Paris, 79.	XII. & XIV.	Inspected by Scholz.	—	—	—
274	Paris, 79 A [Supplément Grecque 79].	X.	Inspected by Scholz. Defective Mark i. 1—17: John i. 1—20. (Mark vi. 21—54: John iii. 18—iv. 1; vii. 23—42; ix. 10—27; xviii. 12—29, supplied by a later hand.)	—	—	—
275	Paris, 80.	XI.	Scholz (Matt.: Mark i. ii.: John iii.—viii.).	—	—	—
276	Paris, 81.	XI.	Scholz (Matt.: Mark i.—vi.: Luke iv. xxii.: John v. viii.).	—	—	—

	Identification.	Date.	Collator. Remarks.	Paul.	Acts.	Apoc.
277	Paris, 81 A.	XI.	Scholz ("maxima pars").	—	—	—
278	Paris, 82.	XII.	Inspected by Scholz. Matt. xiii. 43—xvii. 5 supplied by a later hand.	—	—	—
279	Paris, 86.	XII.	Inspected by Scholz.	—	—	—
280	Paris, 87.	XII.	Scholz (Matt. vi.—xii.: Mark i.—v.: Luke iv. v.: John iv.—viii.). Defective Mark viii. 3—xv. 36.	—	—	—
281	Paris. 88.	XII.	Scholz (Matt. vii.—x.: Mark i.—v.: John vi.—viii.). Defective Matt. xxviii. 11—end of Gosp.: Luke i. 1—9.	—	—	—
282	Paris, 90.	1176.	Inspected by Scholz.	—	—	—
283	Paris, 92.	XIV.	Inspected by Scholz.	—	—	—
284	Paris, 93.	XIII.	Scholz ("maxima pars").	—	—	—
285	Paris, 95.	XIV.	Scholz ("maxima pars"). [Wetstein's 10, Küster's *Par.* 1. Formerly belonged to Taller of Rheims.]	—	—	—
286	Paris, 96.	1432.	Inspected by Scholz.	—	—	—
287	Paris, 98.	XV.	Inspected by Scholz. [Written "per quendam Georgium Hermonimum virum litteratum Græcum."]	—	—	—
288	Paris, 99.	XVI.	Inspected by Scholz. Contains only Luke.	—	—	—
289	Paris, 100 A.	1625.	Inspected by Scholz. (Entered twice in Scholz's list. It appears from the printed catalogue (Appendix p. 609) not to be an evangelisterium, and should therefore not be cited as ev-59.)	—	—	—
290	Paris, 108 A.	XIII.	Inspected by Scholz.	—	—	—
291	Paris, 113.	XII.	Inspected by Scholz.	—	—	—
292	Paris, 114.	XI.	Inspected by Scholz. Defective Matt. i. 1—vii. 14: John xix. 14—xxi. 25.	—	—	—
293	Paris, 117.	1373.	Scholz (Matt. v.—x.: Mark ii.—vi.: Luke ii.: John v.—viii.).	—	—	—
294	Paris, 118.	XIII.	Inspected by Scholz. Defective Matt. i. 18—xii. 25.	—	—	—
295	Paris, 120.	XIII.	Inspected by Scholz. Defective Matt. i. 1—11.	—	—	—
296	Paris, 123.	XVI.	Inspected by Scholz. Written by Angelus Vergetius.	—	—	—
297	Paris, 140 A [Supplément Grecque 140].	XII.	Inspected by Scholz.	—	—	—
298	Paris, 175 A [Supplément Grecque 175].	XII.	Scholz ("maxima pars").	—	—	—
299	Paris, 177.	XI.	Scholz ("cod. integer"). [Commentary. Victor's on St. Mark.]	—	—	—
300	Paris, 186.	XI.	Scholz ("cod. integer"). [Corresponds with mss. 20, 215.] Contains Matt., Mark, and Luke, with catena and Thl.'s commentary [Chr. on Matt. and John, Cyril or Victor on Mark, Tit-bostr. on Luke].	—	—	—
301	Paris, 187.	XI.	Scholz ("cod. integer"). With a catena [that on Mark claimed for Victor].	—	—	—

	Identification.	Date.	Collator. Remarks.	Paul.	Acts.	Apoc.
302	Paris, 193.	XVI.	Inspected by Scholz. Contains fragments of Matt. and Luke, with a commentary.	—	—	—
303	Paris, 194 A.	XII.	Contains John i.—iv., with Thl.'s commentary. Bound up with ev-62.	—	—	—
304	Paris, 194.	XIII.	Inspected by Scholz. Contains Matt. and Mark. With a catena.	—	—	—
305	Paris, 195.	XIII.	Inspected by Scholz. Contains Matt. and Mark, with a catena. [Nothing but the commentary of Euthymius Zigabenus.]	—	—	—
306	Paris, 197.	XII.	Contains Matt. and John, with Thl.'s commentary.	—	—	—
307	Paris, 199.	XI.	Contains Matt. and John, with a commentary. [Only Chrys.'s homilies on Matt. and John. Mutilated at end.]	—	—	—
308	Paris, 200.	XII.	Contains Matt. and John, with a commentary. Defective in some parts.	—	—	—
309	Paris, 201	XII.	Inspected by Scholz. Contains the four Gospels, with Chr.'s commentary on Matt. and John, Victor's on Mark [not properly a text of the Gospel; but parts of the text interwoven with the commentary], and Tit-bostr.'s on Luke.	—	—	—
310	Paris, 202.	XI.	Inspected by Scholz. Contains Matt., with a catena.	—	—	—
311	Paris, 203.	XII.	Inspected by Scholz. Contains Matt., with a catena.	—	—	—
312	Paris, 206.	1308.	Inspected by Scholz. Contains Mark, with Victor's commentary. [Only a commentary: nearly a duplicate of ms. 309.]	—	—	—
313	Paris, 208.	XIV.	Inspected by Scholz. Contains Luke, with a catena. Defective.	—	—	—
314	Paris, 209.	XII.	Inspected by Scholz. Contains John, with commentary. [Catena (not Cramer's).]	—	—	—
315	Paris, 210.	XIII.	Inspected by Scholz. Contains John, with commentary. Defective ch. xiv. 25—xv. 16; xxi. 22—25.	—	—	—
316	Paris, 211.	XII.	Inspected by Scholz. Contains Luke and John, with a commentary. Defective.	—	—	—
317	Paris, 212.	XII.	Inspected by Scholz. Contains John x. 9—xxi. 25, with a catena.	—	—	—
318	Paris, 213.	XIV.	Inspected by Scholz. Contains John vii. 1—xxi. 25, with a commentary.	—	—	—
319	Paris, 231.	XII.	Inspected by Scholz. Commentary. Defective.	—	—	—
320	Paris, 232.	XI.	Inspected by Scholz. Contains Luke, with a commentary.	—	—	—
(321)	. . . .	. . .	[Paris 303.] Entered twice in Scholz's list. An evangelisterium. (See Catalogue of Paris mss., p. 45.) Should be cited as ev-101.	—	—	—

	Identification.	Date.	Collator. Remarks.	Paul.	Acts	Apoc.
322	Paris, 315.	XV.	Inspected by Scholz. [Should be cited as ev-14.]	—	—	—
323	Paris, 118 A.	XVI.	Contains Matt. vi. vii.	—	-	—
324	Paris, 376.	XII.	Scholz. Bound up with ev-97.	—	—	—
(325)	. . . .	. . .	Paris, 377. Is an evangelisterium (ev-98) written in cent. XIII. over more ancient writing. Entered twice in Scholz's list.	—	—	—
(326)	. . . .	. .	Paris, 378 (here entered in Scholz's list). Contains only certain passages, with comments.	—	—	—
(327)	. . . .	. . .	[Paris 380.] Entered twice in Scholz's list. An evangelisterium. (See Catalogue of Paris mss., p. 53.) Should be cited as ev-99.	—	—	—
(328)	. . . .	. . .	[Paris 381] = ev-100.	—	—	—
329	Paris, Coisl. 19.	XI.	Inspected by Scholz. [Victor's commentary on Mark.]	—	—	—
330	Paris, Coisl. 196.	XI.	Inspected by Scholz. [Has disappeared.]	131	132	—
331	Paris, Coisl. 197.	XII.	Inspected by Scholz.	—	—	—
332	Turin, 20 (B. iv. 20) [C. ii. 4].	XI.	Inspected by Scholz. [Contains Victor on Mark.]	—	—	—
333	Turin, 4 (B. iv. 1) [B. i. 9].	XIII.	Inspected by Scholz. Contains Matt. and John, with catena.	—	—	—
334	Turin, 43 (B. v. 23) [B. iii. 8].	XIV.	Inspected by Scholz. Contains Matt. and Mark, with commentary.	—	—	—
335	Turin, 44 (B. v. 21) [B. iii. 2].	XVI.	Inspected by Scholz.	—	—	—
336	Turin, 101 (C. iv. 17) [B. ii. 17].	XVI.	Inspected by Scholz. Contains Luke, with a catena.	—	—	—
(337)	. . . .	. . .	Turin, 52 (B. v. 32) [B. iii. 25]. Contains only select places of Matt., with a commentary.	—	—	—
338	Turin, 335 (B. i. 3) [B. vii. 33].	XII.	Inspected by Scholz.	—	—	—
339	Turin, 302 (C. ii. 5) [B. v. 8].	XIII.	Inspected by Scholz.	170	135	83
340	Turin, 344 (B. i. 13) [B. vii. 16].	XI.	Inspected by Scholz.	—	—	—
341	Turin, 350 (B. i. 21) [B. vii. 14].	1296.	Inspected by Scholz.	—	—	—
342	Turin, 149 (B. ii. 3) [B. v. 24].	XIII.	Inspected by Scholz.	—	—	—
343	Milan: Ambrosian Lib., 13 [H. 13 sup.].	XII.	Scholz (Matt., John).	—	—	-
344	Milan: Ambr., 16 [G. 16 sup.].	XII.	Inspected by Scholz. Defective John xxi. 12—25. [1st page of Matt. and several of Luke rewritten by a later hand, and Luke xxiii. 45 to John xxi. 25 supplied on paper.]	—	—	—
345	Milan: Ambr., 17.	XI.	Inspected by Scholz. Defective Matt. i. 1—11.	—	-	—
346	Milan: Ambr., 23 [S. 23 sup.].	XII.	Scholz ("integer"). Defective John iii. 6 [26, Burgon]—vii. 52.	—	—	—
347	Milan: Ambr., 35.	XII.	Inspected by Scholz.	—	—	—
348	Milan: Ambr., B. 56.	1023.	Inspected by Scholz.	—	—	—

	Identification.	Date.	Collator. Remarks.	Paul.	Acts.	Apoc.
349	Milan: Ambr., 61 [F. 61 sup.]	1322.	Inspected by Scholz. ["Evangelia Corcyræ *empta* 1322" Burgon.]	—	—	—
350	Milan: Ambr., B. 62.	XI.	Inspected by Scholz. The 4 first leaves supplied in cent. XVI. Defective John xxi. 9—25.	—	—	—
351	Milan: Ambr., 70 [B. 70 sup.].	XI.	Inspected by Scholz.	—	—	—
352	Milan: Ambr., B. 93.	XII.	Inspected by Scholz. Defective Matt. i. 1—17: Mark i. 1—15; xvi. 13—end of Gosp.: Luke i. 1—7; xxiv. 43—end of Gosp.: John i. 1—10; xxi. 3—25.	—	—	—
353	Milan: Ambr., M. 93.	XIII.	Scholz ("maxima pars"). Defective John xxi. 24, 25. [Contains Victor on Mark.]	—	—	—
354	Venice, 29 [86: 6?].	XI.	Inspected by Scholz. Contains Thl.'s commentary on Matt. [to the end of ch. xxvii.].	—	—	—
355	Venice, 541 [86: 6].	XI. [?]	Inspected by Scholz.	—	—	—
(356)	. . . .	. . .	Ven. 545 (cent. XVI.). Contains catena from Tit-bostr. [and others] on Luke. "Raro textus Lucæ laudatur" (Scholz).	—	—	—
357	Venice, 28 [86: 5].	XI.	Inspected by Scholz. Contains Luke and John, with a catena.	—	—	—
358	Modena, 9 (II. A. 9).	XIV.	Inspected by Scholz.	—	—	—
359	Modena, 243 [242] (III. B. 16).	XIV.	Inspected by Scholz.	—	—	—
360	At Parma? [2319. II. viii. 169.]	XI.	De Rossi (1.) in Scholz.	—	—	—
361	At Parma? [1821. II. xi. 143.]	XIII.	De Rossi (2.) in Scholz. [Mutilated Luke viii. 14 to xi. 20.]	—	—	—
362	Florence: Laur. (dei Conventi), 176. Olim Mon. Abbatiæ (Badia) 2564[7].	XIII.	A ms. of Luke vi. 28 or 29—xii. 10, with Nicetas' catena. Described by Lami, A.D. 1738, as then at St. Mary's Monastery (apparently identical with Badia), Florence.	—	—	—
363	Florence: Laur., vi. 13.	XIII.	Inspected by Scholz.	180	144	—
364	Florence: Laur., vi. 24.	XIII.	Inspected by Scholz. [First page supplied on paper.]	—	—	—
365	Florence: Laur., vi. 36.	XIII.	Inspected by Scholz. [Does not exist.]	181	145	—
366	Florence: Laur. (dei Conventi), 171. Olim Mon. Abbatiæ 2607[7].	XII.	Contains Matt., with a catena. Defective at beginning [to Matt. ii. 16].	—	—	—
367	Florence: Laur. (2708?)[7] [53].	1332.	Inspected by Scholz. [Bought for St. Mary's Mon. in 1482. Contains Apoc.]	182	146	?
368	Florence: Riccardi, 84.	XV.	Inspected by Scholz. Contains John, Apoc., Epp., a lectionary (cited as lect-37), and Plato's Ep. to Dionys.	230	150	84

[7] For particulars relating to mss. 362, 366, I am indebted to Mr. P. E. Pusey, who believes that 367 was with these removed to the Laurentian Library from St. Mary's Monastery (= Badia), and that the No. 2708 refers to its old designation there. [This suggestion is independently confirmed by the Rev. J. W. Burgon, Letter VII. to Rev. F. H. Scrivener.]

	Identification.	Date.	Collator. Remarks.	Paul.	Acts.	Apoc.
369	Florence: Riccardi, 90.	XII.	Fragments of Mark (vi. 25—ix. 45; x. 17—xvi. 9), bound up with a Greek Grammar, &c.	—	—	—
370	*Not identified.* [Florence: Riccardi, 5.]	XIV.	Formerly Riccardi, K. I. 11. Described by Lami. With Thl.'s commentary. [Matt. vii. 13—John xvi. 29.]	—	—	—
371	Vatican, 1159.	X.	Inspected by Scholz.	—	—	—
372	Vatican, 1161.	XV.	Inspected by Scholz. Defective John iii. 1—end of Gosp.	—	—	—
373	Vatican, 1423.	XV.	Inspected by Scholz. Catena. Defective at end.	—	—	—
374	Vatican, 1445.	XII.	Inspected by Scholz. Commentary [Victor's on Mark].	—	—	—
375	Vatican, 1533.	XII.	Inspected by Scholz.	—	—	—
376	Vatican, 1539.	XI.	Inspected by Scholz.	—	—	—
377	Vatican, 1618.	XV.	Inspected by Scholz.	—	—	—
378	Vatican, 1658.	XIV.	A fragment of Matt., with Chr.'s com.: bound up with other matter.	—	—	—
379	Vatican, 1769.	XV.	Inspected by Scholz.	—	—	—
380	Vatican, 2139.	XV.	Inspected by Scholz.	—	—	—
381	Vatican, Pal. 20.	XIV.	Inspected by Scholz. Contains Luke, with a catena.	—	—	—
382	Vatican, 2070.	XIII.	Scholz ("maxima pars"). Defective. Leaves misplaced.	—	—	—
383	Three mss. at the Collegio Romano.	XVI.	Commentary. Inspected by Scholz.	—	—	—
384		XVI.		—	—	—
385		XVI.		—	—	—
386	Vatican, Ottob. 66.	XV.	Inspected by Scholz.	199	151	70
387	Vatican, Ottob. 204.	XII.	Inspected by Scholz.	—	—	—
388	Vatican, Ottob. 212.	XII.	Inspected by Scholz.	—	—	—
389	Vatican, Ottob. 297.	XI.	Inspected by Scholz.	—	—	—
390	Vatican, Ottob. 381.	1252.	Inspected by Scholz.	203	164	71
391	Vatican, Ottob. 432.	XI.	Inspected by Scholz. Matt. i. 1—8: Luke i. 1—80: John vii. 53—viii. 11 supplied in cent. XV.	—	—	—
392	Rome: Barberini, 225.	XII.	Inspected by Scholz. Thl.'s commentary. Bound up with Cod. Y.	—	—	—
393	Rome: Vallicella, E. 22.	XVI.	Inspected by Scholz.	185	167	—
394	Rome: Vallicella, F. 17.	1330.	Inspected by Scholz.	186	170	—
395	Rome: Casanat., R. V. 33.	XII.	Inspected by Scholz.	—	—	—
396	Rome: Ghigi, R. IV. 6.	XII.	Inspected by Scholz. Defective Matt. i. 1—xxiii. 37.	—	—	—
397	Rome: Vallicella, C. 4.	XV.	Inspected by Scholz. Contains John, with a catena.	—	—	—
(398)	. . . .	XIII.	Turin, 92 (C. iv. 6) [C. ii. 5]. Only contains select passages with a catena.	—	—	—
(399)	. . . .	XV.	Turin, 109 (C. iv. 29) [C. ii. 14]. Contains a commentary on the Gospels, "sed textus non semper adscriptus" (Scholz).	—	—	—
400	Berlin (Diez, 10).	XV.	Pappelbaum. Contains (of the Gospels) only Matt. xii. 39—xiii. 2.	220	181	—
401	Naples, I. C. 24.	XI.	Inspected by Scholz. Contains Matt.: Mark vi. 1—end of Gosp.: Luke: John i. 1—xii. 1.	—	—	—

	Identification.	Date.	Collator. Remarks.	Paul.	Acts.	Apoc.
402	Naples, I. C. 28.	XV.	Inspected by Scholz.	—	—	—
403	Naples, I. C. 29.	XII.	Inspected by Scholz. Contains Matt. xii. 23—xix. 12; xix. 28—end of Gosp.: Mark: Luke i. 1—v. 21; v. 36—end of Gosp.: John i. 1—xviii. 36.	—	—	—
404	. . . .	XI.	Abbatis Scotti Neapolitani. Inspected by Scholz.	—	—	—
405	Venice, I. 10 [86: 1].	XI.	(Formerly Nan. 3.) Inspected by Scholz. [Formerly belonged to the Monastery of St. Cosmas and St. Damian at Broussa.]	—	—	—
406	Venice, I. 11 [86: 6].	XI.	(Nan. 4.) Inspected by Scholz. Defective Mark iv. 41—v. 14: Luke iii. 16—iv. 4. [Mutilated at end.]	—	—	—
407	Venice, I. 12 [86: 6].	XI.	(Nan. 5.) Inspected by Scholz. Contains Luke v. 30—end of Gosp.: John i. 1—ix. [2].	—	—	—
408	Venice, I. 14 [86: 6].	XII.	(Nan. 7.) Inspected by Scholz. [The first leaf, Matt. i. 1—12, supplied. Formerly belonged to the Monastery of Chrysostom near the Jordan.]	—	—	—
409	Venice, I. 15 [86: 1].	XII.	(Nan. 8.) Inspected by Scholz.	—	—	—
410	Venice, I. 17 [86: 6].	XIV.	(Nan. 10.) Inspected by Scholz. [Written by Joasaph, a monk.]	—	—	—
411	Venice, (I. 18?) [86: 6.]	XIV. [XI.?]	(Nan. 11.) (Inspected by Scholz?)	—	—	—
412	Venice, I. 19 [86: 6].	1301.	(Nan. 12.) Inspected by Scholz. [Written by Theodorus of Hagios Petros in the Morea.]	—	—	—
413	Venice, I. 20 [86: 6].	1302.	(Nan. 13.) Inspected by Scholz. [Written by Theodosius: once belonged to the Convent of St. Catharine on Mount Sinai.]	—	—	—
414	Venice, I. 21 [86: 6].	XIV.	(Nan. 14.) Inspected by Scholz. [Written by Philip, a monk.]	—	—	—
415	Venice, I. 22 [86: 6].	1356.	(Nan. 15.) Inspected by Scholz.	—	—	—
416	Venice, I. 24 [86: 1].	XIV.	(Nan. 17.) Inspected by Scholz. Defective Matt. i. 1—xxv. 35 [xxvi. 18—xxvii. 16; xxviii. 36—Mark ii. 26]: John xviii. 7—end of Gosp.	—	—	—
417	Venice, I. 25 [86: 6].	XIV. [XII.?]	(Nan. 18.) Contains Matt., Mark, Luke. Defective at beginning and end [to Matt. v. 43, and from Luke vi. 9].	—	—	—
418	Venice, [I. 28 (86: 1).]	? [XV.]	(Nan. 21.) Contains Matt. and Mark [to xiii. 32].	—	—	—
419	*Not identified*. [Venice, I. 9 (86: 1).]	XI.[?]	Formerly at Venice, Mon. of St. Michael [de Muriano], 241. Described by Mittarelli. Defective John [viii. 44—xi. 32] xxi. 7—end [supplied by a modern hand].	—	—	—
420	Messana, I.	XIV.	Inspected by Münter.	—	—	—
421	Syracuse.	XII.	Inspected by Münter.	218	176	—
422	Munich, 210.	XI.	Inspected by Scholz. John written later than cent. XI.	—	—	—

	Identification.	Date.	Collator. Remarks.	Paul.	Acts.	Apoc.
423	Munich, 36 [τόμος α].	XV. [1556[8].]	Inspected by Scholz. Contains Matt., with a catena.	—	—	—
424	Munich, 83.	XV. [XVI.]	Inspected by Scholz. Contains Luke, with commentary.	—	—	—
425	Munich, 37 [τόμος β].	XV. [XVI.]	Inspected by Scholz. Contains John, with commentary.	—	—	—
426	Munich, 473.	XIV.	(Augsburg, 9.) Contains Luke vi. 17—xi. 26, with catena.	—	—	—
427	Munich, 465.	XIII.	(Augsburg, 10.) Inspected by Scholz. Contains Mark and Luke, with Thl.'s commentary.	—	—	—
428	Munich, 381.	XIII.	(Augsburg, 11.) Scholz ("magna pars"). Closely related to ms. 300[9].	—	—	—
429	Munich, 208.	X.[1]	Inspected by Scholz. Contains questions and answers on Matt., John, and Luke i. 1—ii. 39, with a catena.	—	—	—
430	Munich, 437.	XI.	Inspected by Scholz. Contains John [i.—viii.], with a catena.	—	—	—
431	Strasburg, Molsheimensis.	XII.	Arendt (in German Theological Quarterly for 1833).	238	180	—
432	Munich, 99.	XVI.	Inspected by Scholz. Contains Mark, with Victor's commentary.	—	—	—
433	Berlin.	XII.	Pappelbaum (in Scholz and Dermout). Contains Matt. i. 1—21; vi. 12—32; xxii. 25—Mark v. 29: Mark ix. 21—xiii. 12: Luke viii. 27—John ix. 21: John xx. 15—end of Gosp.	—	—	—
434	Vienna, Theol. 71, N.	XIV.	(Lambec. 42.) Inspected by Scholz. Contains Luke, with a catena.	—	—	—
435	Leyden, Gronovii 131.	?	Dermout, Griesbach. Defective Matt. i. 20—ii. 13; xxii. 4—9.	—	—	—
436[2]	*Not identified.*	?	Once Meermann's 117. Entered by a mistake a second time in Scholz as ev-153.	—	—	—
437	St. Petersburg, (?)	XI.	Mentioned by Matthæi.	—	—	—
438	Brit. Mus. 5111, 5112.	XI.	Inspected by Bloomfield.	—	—	—
439	Brit. Mus. 5107.	1159.	Inspected by Bloomfield.	—	—	—
(440)	*The same ms. as* 236 *above.*	—	. . . .	221	111	—
(441)	Camb. Univ. Lib., MS. Nn. 5. 27.	—	A folio copy of the Greek Bible printed at Basle, 1545. A few notes are written on the margin.	222	110	—
(442)	Camb. Univ. Lib., MS. Nn. 3. 20, 21.	—	A copy of the printed Greek Test., 8vo, London, 1728, interleaved and bound up in two volumes. Contains ms. notes by John Taylor.	223	152	—

[8 "The scribe of this Codex produced also the next three" (i. e. 424, 425, 432). Burgon.]

[9 This is denied by Burgon, who believes (but is not sure about St. Mark) that it is nothing else but Thl. on the four Gospels.]

[1 Burgon assigns it to the XIIth or XIIIth cent., the dated inscription (978) having been copied from an older ms.]

[2 Mr. Burgon has a ms. of the XIIIth cent. to which this number is assigned, but it is not the one which Montfaucon saw and described as stated in Scholz's list. Its text resembles that of Scr's l m n.]

	Identification.	Date.	Collator. Remarks.		Paul.	Acts.	Apoc.
443	Camb. Univ. Lib., MS. Nn. 2. 36.	XII.	. . . .		—	—	—
444	Brit. Mus., Harl. 5796.	XV.	Scholz (Mark v.).		240	153	—
445	Brit. Mus., Harl. 5736.	1506.	Scholz (Mark v.).		—	—	—
446	Brit. Mus., Harl. 5777.	XV.	Scholz (Mark v.). Defective Matt. i. 1—17: Mark i. 7—9: Luke i. 1—18: John i. 1—22.		—	—	—
447	Brit. Mus., Harl. 5784.	XV.	Mill's *Cov.* 5. Scholz (Mark v.).		—	—	—
448	Brit. Mus., Harl. 5790.	1478.	Scholz (Mark v.).		—	—	—
449	Brit. Mus., 4950, 4951.	XIII.	Scholz (Mark v.).		—	—	—
450	Seven mss. at the great Greek Monastery at Jerusalem.	1043.	1 — 1 Contains Matt., Mark, Luke, with an Arabic version. Coxe's 6 (Scriv.). *In Scholz's list.* (Only inspected by him.) 6 has a commentary. 7 is Coxe's 43. (See Scrivener.)		—	—	—
451		XII.	2		—	—	—
452		XIV.	3		—	—	—
453		XIV.	4		—	—	—
454		XIV.	5		—	—	—
455		XIV.	6		—	—	—
456		XIII.	7		—	—	—
457	Ten mss. at the Monastery of St. Saba, near Jerusalem.	XIII.	Inspected by Scholz, who distinguishes them by the annexed numbers.	2	234	186	—
458		1272.		3	—	—	—
459		XII.		7	—	—	—
460		XII.		8	—	—	—
461		?		9	—	—	—
462		XIV.		10	235	187	86
463		XIV.		11	—	—	—
464		XI.		12	—	—	—
465		XIII.		19	—	—	—
466		XIII.		20	237	189	89
467	Three mss. at the Monastery of St. John, Patmos.	XI.	Inspected by Scholz and Coxe.	2	—	—	—
468		XII.		6	—	—	—
469		XIV.		21	—	—	—

A few EVANGELISTERIA have been occasionally quoted, but as their evidence has been no where particularly examined in this edition it will be sufficient to refer to Scrivener's Introduction to N. T. Criticism, as containing the latest information with regard to them. ev-y has been very frequently cited: see above under Scrivener's Manuscripts[3].

SECTION II.

ANCIENT VERSIONS OF THE N. T. REFERRED TO IN THIS EDITION.

(*See more complete accounts of these by Tregelles in Horne, edn.* 10, *vol.* iv., *and Tischendorf in his Gk. Test., edn.* 7, *prolegg. p.* ccxxviii *ff.*)

The ancient Latin versions before Jerome are known to us by the following MSS. (Horne, edn. 10, pp. 237—243.)

lat-*a*, Codex Vercellensis, *fourth century.*

[[3] See also Burgon's letters to Scrivener, Letter XVIII. In Letter XVII. several mss. not hitherto enumerated are described.]

lat-*b*, Codex Veronensis, *fourth* or *fifth century.*
lat-*c*, Codex Colbertinus, *eleventh century.*
lat-*e*, Codex Palatinus Vindobonensis, *fourth* (or *fifth*) *century.*
lat-*f*, Codex Brixianus, about *sixth century.*
lat-ff_1, lat-ff_2, Codices Corbeienses (*very ancient*).
lat-g_1, lat-g_2, Codices Sangermanenses (*very ancient*).
lat-*h*, Codex Claromontanus (*very ancient*).
lat-*i*, Codex Vindobonensis, about *fifth century.*
lat-*k*, Codex Taurinensis [Bobbiensis], *fifth century.*
lat-*l*, Codex Rhedigerianus, about *seventh century.*
lat-*n*, Codex San-Gallensis, *fourth* or *fifth century.*
lat-*o*, Fragmentum San-Gallense, about *seventh century.*
lat-*p*, "Frag. San-Gallense Scottice scriptum sæc. vii. vel viii."
lat-*q*, Codex Monacensis, *sixth century.*
spec, the Latin readings contained in a MS. 'Speculum' at Rome. Published by Mai.

vulg, the Vulgate version (A.D. 383), since its completion by Jerome variously emended and edited : quoted from the authorized edition of the Church of Rome put forth by Clement VIII. in 1592, which differs in many respects from the equally authoritative edition of Sixtus V. in 1590. See Horne, pp. 243—257.

The following ancient MSS. of Jerome's Vulgate are cited when they differ from the Clementine edition.

am, Amiatinus, written about 541. Tischendorf has published it entire, and considers it the oldest and most valuable extant.
fuld, Fuldensis, about *sixth century.*
tol, Toletanus, at Toledo, written in gothic letters.
em, Monasterii S. Emerami, A.D. 870.
flor, Floriacensis.
forj, Forojuliensis.
foss, Fossatensis.
gat, S. Gatiani.
harl, Harleianus 1775, about *seventh century.*
ing, Ingoldstadiensis, about *seventh century.*
lux, Luxoviensis.
mm, Majoris monasterii, *tenth century?*
mt, Martini Turonensis, *eight century?*
per, Perusinus.
san, Fragmenta San-Gallensia.

latt, the Latin versions: an abbreviated way of writing 'vulg lat-*a b c*' &c.

Syr, the Peschito (or simple) Syriac version. Supposed to have been made as early as the *second century.* The text as edited is in a most unsatisfactory state.

syr, the later or Philoxenian version made at the instigation of Philoxenus, Bishop of Hierapolis in Phrygia A.D. 488—508. Revised, A.D. 616, by Thomas of Harkel [Heraclea] in Palestine [others say in Syria or Mesopotamia], to whom the readings on the margin (cited as 'syr-mg' or 'syr-mg-gr') are due[4].

syr-cu, the Syriac version discovered by Dr. Cureton amongst the Nitrian MSS. in the British Museum. Perhaps the earliest and most important of all the versions.

syr-jer, the Jerusalem Syriac Lectionary, made from an ancient and valuable Greek text, probably in the *fifth century*.

syrr = Syr syr (these two alone).

copt, the Coptic or Memphitic Egyptian version. *Fourth century?*

copt-wilk, Wilkins' edition of the Coptic version.

copt-schw, that of Schwartze.

copt-dz, Codex Diez, written about the *fourteenth century* (so Tregelles).

sah, the Thebaic or Sahidic Egyptian version. *Third century?*

sah-georgi, the Sahidic text of Codex T (John vi. 21—58, 68—viii. 23): see above § i.

sah-ming, Mingarel's edition of the Thebaic.

sah-mnt, Munter's ditto.

sah-woide, the MS. of the Thebaic published in Woide's appendix to the Codex Alexandrinus.

coptt—denotes that the Egyptian versions agree in supporting a given reading. The ordinary citations, repeated in this volume, cannot be thoroughly relied upon.

goth, the Gothic version. Made from the Greek by Ulphilas about the middle of the *fourth century*.

æth, the Æthiopic version. Assigned to the *fourth century*.

æth-rom, the edition given in the Roman polyglott.

æth-pl, Pell Platt's edition.

arm, the Armenian version. Made in the *fifth century*.

arm-usc, arm-zoh, the editions of Uscan and Zohrab respectively.

The Persian, Arabic, Georgian, Sclavonic, and Anglo-Saxon versions have not been cited, being all of them comparatively recent translations from the versions named above, and not from the original Greek.

[4] [On the subject of the Harclean text, see a pamphlet by G. H. Bernstein, Wratislav 1854.] A supplement to the Harclean text is cited in the *Pericope Adulteræ* as 'syr-uss,' from a MS. of Archbishop Ussher's [and another published by White from a Codex Barsalibæus, as syr-bars. On syr-w-ast, syr-w-ob, see above, p. 102 and note].

SECTION III.

ABBREVIATIONS USED IN CITING FATHERS, &c.[5]

(N.B.—The abbreviation is designated by the thick type. In the remainder of the word or sentence *Latin* writers are described in *italics.*)

Ambr*ose, Bp. of Milan,* A.D. 374—397

Ambr*osia***st***er,* i. e. *Hilary the Deacon,* fl. 384

Ammonius of Alexandria, 220

Amphilochius, Bp. of Iconium, 374

Anastasius of Sinai, fl. 560 to end of cent^{y}.

Andreas of Crete, 635

Antio**ch**us of Ptolemais, 614

Antony the Hermit, b. 251, d. 356

Archelaus of Mesopotamia, 278

Arnob*ius of Africa,* 306

Athanasius, Bp. of Alexandria, 326—373

Athenagoras of Athens, 177

Aug*ustine, Bp. of Hippo,* 395—430

Avit*us, Bp. of Vienne,* 490—523

Barnabas, cent^{y}. i. or ii.

Basil, Bp. of Cæsarea in Cappadocia, 370—379

Basil of **Sel**eucia, fl. 440

Bede, *the Venerable,* 731

Cæsarius of Constantinople, 368

Cæs*arius, Episc.* **Arel***atensis,* 502—544

Canons Apostolic, cent^{y}. iii.

Carpocrates, cent^{y}. ii.

Cassiod*orus,* b. 479, d. 575

Chrom*atius, Bp. of Aquileia,* 402

Chronicon Paschale Alexandrinum, cent^{y}. vii.

Chrysocephalus, cent^{y}. xiii.

Chrysol*ogus, Peter, Bp. of Ravenna,* 433—450

Chrysostom, Bp. of Constantinople, 397—407: **Chr-montf**, a MS. cited from Montfaucon; **Chr-wlf**, Wolfenbüttel MS. of Chr. written in cent^{y}. vi.; **Chr-Fd**, Field's edn. of the Hom. on Matt.[6]

Clement of Alexandria, fl. 194

[5] When a citation is made thus [Ambr], it means [that the citation has been added in this (seventh) edition]; when thus (Ambr), that there is nothing to indicate from which of the Evangelists the Father is quoting, or that he is quoting loosely or paraphrastically. '$\text{Ambr}_{\text{alic}}$,' '$\text{Ambr}_{\text{aliq}}$,' '$\text{Ambr}_{\text{sæpe}}$,' ['$\text{Ambr}_{\text{ubique}}$,'] '$\text{Ambr}_{\text{h. l.}}$,' '$\text{Ambr}_{\text{expr}}$,' '$\text{Ambr}_{\text{certe}}$'—mean respectively that the Father indicated quotes a particular reading *alicubi* or *aliquoties* (= sometimes), *often*, [*always*,] in his commentary *on the particular passage, expressly, certainly.* 'Ps-' prefixed to the name of a Father = Pseudo-.

[6] The following MSS. have been cited in St. Matthew's Gospel:—

A. Trin. Coll. Camb., B. 8. 4. *Cent.* xii. or xiii.
B. Emm. Coll. Camb., I. 1. 12, 13. *Cent.* xi.
C. Bodleian, Cromwell 19. *Cent.* xi.
D. Bodleian, Barocc. 198. *Cent.* xi.
E. Bodleian, Barocc. 233. *Cent.* xi.
F. British Museum, Arundel 543. *Cent.* xi.
G. Trin. Coll. Camb., B. 9. 12. *Cent.* xi.
H Paris, 687. *Cent.* xi.
K. Paris, 695. *Cent.* xi.

[OVER

Clement, Bp. of **Rome**, 91—101
Cosmas Indicopleustes, 535
Constitutions, Apostolic, cent[y]. iii.
Cypr*ian, Bp. of Carthage*, 248—258
Cyril, Bp. of Alexandria, 412—444
Cyril, Bp. of **Jer**usalem, 348—386
Damascenus, Johannes, 730
Dialogue against the Marcionites printed amongst the works of Origen.
[" **Dialogi de Trinitate**" variously ascribed to Ath. Thdrt. Max.]
Didymus, of Alexandria, 370
Diodorus, Bp. of Tarsus, 378—394
Dionysius, Bp. of Alexandria, 247—265
Dionysius **Areop**agita, cent[y]. v.
Ephrem Syrus, b. 299, d. 378
Epiphanius, Bp. in Cyprus, 368—403
Eucher*ius, Bp. of Lyons*, 434—454
Eulogius, Bp. of Alexandria, 581—608
Eusebius, Bp. of Cæsarea, 315—320: **Eus Canon,** his harmonizing tables
Eustathius, Bp. of Antioch, 323
Euthalius, Bp. of Sulci, 458
Euthymius Zigabenus, 1116
Evagrius Ponticus, 380
Fast*idius, Bp. in Britain*, 430
Faustin*us*, 383
Faust*us the Manichee, cited by Aug.*
Firm*icus, Julius F. Maturnus*, 345
Fulg*entius, Bp. in Africa*, 508—533
Gaud*entius, Bp. of Brescia*, 387
Gelasius of Cyzicum, fl. 476
Gennadius, Bp. of Constantinople, 458—471
Gild*as*, fl. 581
Glycas of Sicily, 1120
Greg*ory, Bp. of Rome*, 590—605
Haymo, *Bp. of Halberstadt*, 841—853
Heracleon the Gnostic, fl. cir. 125, cited in Orig.'s comm. on John
Hesychius of Jerusalem, cent[y]. vi.
Hil*ary, Bp. of Poictiers*, 354
Hippolytus, disciple of Irenæus, Bp. of Portus, 220
Homilies ascribed to **Clement**, cent[y]. iii.
Ignatius, Bp. of Antioch, d. 107
Irenæus, Bp. of Lyons, 178 (**Iren-int** as represented by his interpreter; **Iren-gr,** when his own words are preserved)
Isidore of Pelusium, 412
Jacobus, Bp. of **Nisib**is, cir. 320—340 [7]
Jer*ome*, fl. 378—420
Julian (*cited by Aug.*), *Pelagian Bp. in Italy*, 416
Justin Martyr, fl. 140—164
Juv*encus*, 330
Lact*antius*, 306
Leo, *Bp. of Rome*, 440—461
Leontius Scholasticus, 580
Lucif*er, Bp. of Cagliari*, 354—367
Macarius of Egypt, 301—391
Macedonius of Constantinople, 381
Marcellus, cited by Eus.
Marcion (130) Fragments in Epiph. (**Mcion-e**) and Tert. (**Mcion-t**)

L. Paris, 685. *Cent.* x.
M. Emm. Coll. Camb., I. 1. 14, 15. *Cent.* xi. or xii.
N. Middlehill, 436. *Cent.* xii.
P. Paris, 688. *Cent.* xi.
1. 3. 5. 8. α. β of the former part. } Matthæi's, chiefly
2. 6. 9. γ. η. ρ. of the latter part. } at Moscow.

[[7] The homilies attributed to Jac-nisib are really the work of Aphraates the Persian sage, edited by Dr. Wright. 4to, 1869.]

Marcosii, cited by Iren.
Max*imus* **Taur***inensis*, 430—466
Maximus **Conf**essor, fl. 630—662
Meletius, Bp. of Antioch, 381
Methodius, fl. 290—312
Michael Psellus of Constantinople, d. 1078
Nazianzenus, Gregory, fl. 370—389
Nestorius, Bp. of Constantinople, 428—431
Nonnus of Panopolis, cent^y^. v.
Novat*ian*, 251
Nyssa, Gregory, Bp. of, 371
Opt*atus*, fl. 364—375
Op*us Imperfectum in Matthæum*, cent^y^. xi.
Origen, b. 185, d. 254
Oros*ius*, 416
Orsiesius the Egyptian, 345
Pac*ianus, Bp. of Barcelona*, 370
Palladius, Bp. of Hellenopolis, 368—401
Pamphilus of Palestine, fl. 294
Paulin*us, Bp. of Aquileia*, 776—804
Pel*agii Ep. ad Demetr.* 417 ?
Peter, Bp. of Alexandria, 300—311
Philas*trius, Bp. of Brescia*, fl. 380
Phœb*adius, Bp. of Agen*, cir. 350—390
Photius, Bp. of Constantinople, 858—891
Polycarp, Bp. of Smyrna, d. 169
Porphyry, d. 304
"**Prædest***inatus*." *A work ascribed to Vincent of Lerins* (434)
Proclus, Bp. of Constantinople, 434
Procopius of Gaza, 520
"*De* **Promiss***ionibus dimid. temp.*" cent^y^. iv.
Prosp*er of Aquitaine*, 434
Protevangelium Jacobi, cent^y^. ii.
Prud*entius*, 406
Ptolemæus gnosticus apud Epiphanium
"**Quæst***iones ex Vet. et Nov. Testt.*" *Printed among the works of Aug.*
"*De* **Rebap***tismate*" *Among Cypr.'s works*
Recognitions, the Clementine, cent^y^. iii.
Ruf*inus of Aquileia*, 397
Salv*ianus*, 440
Sedul*ius*, 430
Serapion of Egypt, 345
Severianus, Bp. in Syria, 400
Severus of Antioch, cent^y^. vi.
"*De* **Sing***ularitate* **Cler***icorum*." *Among Cypr.'s works*
Socrates of Constantinople, 440
Sozomen of Constantinople, d. 450
Suidas the lexicographer, 980
Syncellus, George, of Constantinople, 792
Synodical **Ep**istle of Council held at **Ant**ioch against Paul of Samosata, 269
Synopsis ascribed to Athanasius
Tatian of Syria, 172
Tert*ullian*, 200
Thalassius, 640
Thaumaturgus, Gregory, Bp. of Neocæsarea, 243
Theodore of **Herac**lea, 394
Theodore, Bp. of **Mops**uestia, 399—428
Theodore of the **Stud**ium, 795—826
Theodoret, Bp. of Cyrus, 420—458
Theodotus the Gnostic. Extracts made by Clement of Alexandria
Theodotus of **Ancy**ra, 433
Theophanes Cerameus, 1040
Theophilus, Bp. of **Ant**ioch, 170—182

SECTION IV.

LIST, AND SPECIFICATION OF EDITIONS OF OTHER BOOKS QUOTED, REFERRED TO, OR MADE USE OF IN THIS COMMENTARY, VOL. I.

AMBROSE : cited throughout from the Benedictine pages in the Abbé Migne's Patrologia Latina, voll. xiv.—xvii.

ATHANASIUS: cited by Benedictine pages in Migne's Patrologia Græca, voll. xxv.—xxviii.

AUGUSTINE: cited throughout by the work and the section, *without pages*, from Migne's Patrologia Latina, voll. xxxii.—xlvii.

BECK, Umriss der Biblischen Seelenlehre, Stuttgart 1848.

BENGEL, Gnomon Novi Testamenti, vol. i. Tübingen 1836.

BERNHARDY, Wissenschaftliche Syntax der Griechischen Sprache, Berlin 1829.

BINGHAM, Origines Ecclesiasticæ, Works, 2 voll. fol. London 1726.

BLEEK, DR. F., Beiträge zur Evangelien-Kritik, Berlin 1846 ; Synoptische Erklärung der drei ersten Evangelien, Leipzig 1862.

BLOOMFIELD, DR., The Greek Testament, with English Notes, &c., 9th edn., London 1855.

CALVIN in N. T. Commentarii, ed. Tholuck, Berlin 1834.

CATENA AUREA, Commentary on the Gospels from the Fathers, collected by Thomas Aquinas, 4 voll. Oxford 1843.

CHRYSOSTOM, Homiliæ in Matthæum (vol. vii.), Hom. in Joannem (vol. viii.), and other works: cited throughout from the Benedictine pages in Migne's Patrologia Græca, voll. xlvii.—lxiv.

CLEMENT OF ALEXANDRIA: cited by Potter's pages in Migne's Patrologia Græca, voll. viii. ix.

CYPRIAN: cited by Migne's pages in his Patrologia Latina, vol. iv.

CYRIL OF ALEXANDRIA: cited by Aubert's pages in Migne's Patrologia Græca, voll. lxviii.—lxxvii.

CYRIL OF JERUSALEM: cited by Benedictine pages in Migne's Patrologia Græca, vol. xxxiii.

DAVIDSON, DR. S., Introduction to the New Testament, vol. i., The Four Gospels, London 1849.

DEVARIUS, De Gr. Ling. Particulis. Ed. Klotz, 2 voll. Lipsiæ 1835.

DE WETTE, DR. W. M. L., Kurzgefasstes Exegetisches Handbuch zum Neuen Testament, 3rd edn., Leipzig 1845 (Matt.—Mark, Luke, and John, 1846). Subsequent editions by Brückner, who has added much valuable matter of his own.

DIDYMUS: cited by Migne's pages in his Patrologia Græca, vol. xxxix.

DORNER, DR. J. A., Entwickelungs-Geschichte der Lehre von der Person Christi, Stuttgart 1845.

EBRARD, Wissenschaftliche Kritik der Evangelischen Geschichte, Frankfurt 1842; Das Evangelium Johannis und die Neueste Hypothese über seine Entstehung, Zürich 1845.

ELLICOTT, BP., Historical Lectures on the Life of our Lord, London 1860.

EPIPHANIUS: cited by Petavius's pages in Migne's Patrologia Græca, voll. xli.—xliii.

EUSEBIUS, Historia Ecclesiastica: cited by book and section, *without pages:* his other works cited by Valesius' &c. pages in Migne's Patrologia Græca, voll. xix.—xxiv.

EUTHYMIUS ZIGABENUS, Ἑρμηνεία εἰς τὰ Τέσσαρα Εὐαγγέλια, 2 voll. Athens 1842 (his works are in Migne's Patrologia Græca, voll. cxxviii.—cxxx.).

FRIEDLIEB, J. H., Archäologie der Leidensgeschichte unsers Herrn Jesu Christi, Bonn 1843.

GREGORY THE GREAT: cited by Benedictine pages in Migne's Patrologia Latina, voll. lxxv.—lxxix.

GRESWELL, DR. E., Harmonia Evangelica, 3rd edn. Oxford 1840; Prolegomena in Harm. Evang. ibid. 1840; Dissertations on a Harmony of the Gospels, 3 voll. ibid. 1830; Preliminary Dissertations, ibid. 1834; An Exposition of the Parables and other parts of the Gospels, 5 voll. ibid. 1834.

GRINFIELD, E. G., Novum Test. Græcum. Editio Hellenistica, 2 voll. London 1843; Scholia Hellenistica in Novum Testamentum, London 1848.

GROTIUS: cited from the Critici Sacri and Pole's Synopsis.

HARE, ARCHDEACON, The Mission of the Comforter, 2 voll. Cambridge 1846.

HARTUNG, Lehre von den Partikeln der Griechischen Sprache, 2 voll. Erlangen 1832.

HASE, DR. KARL, Das Leben Jesu, 2nd edn. Leipzig 1835.

HERVEY, LORD ARTHUR [Bp. of Bath and Wells], On the Genealogies of our Lord, Cambridge 1853.

HILARIUS: cited by Benedictine pages in Migne's Patrologia Latina, voll. ix. x.

HIPPOLYTUS: cited by Migne's pages in his Patrologia Græca, vol. x.

HORNE, THOMAS HARTWELL, Introduction to the Critical Study and Knowledge of the Holy Scriptures, 4 voll. 10th edn. London 1856. (See Tregelles, below.)

HUG, Einleitung in die Schriften des Neuen Testaments, 2 voll. 4th edn. Stuttgart u. Tübingen 1847.

IRENÆUS: cited by Benedictine pages in Migne's Patrologia Græca, vol. vii.

JEROME, Works: cited by Benedictine pages in Migne's Patrologia Latina, voll. xxii.—xxx.

JONES, JEREMIAH, On the Canon of the New Testament, 3 voll. Oxford 1827.

JOSEPHUS, ed. Richter, 6 voll. Leipzig 1826.

JUSTIN MARTYR, Works: cited by Benedictine pages in Migne's Patrologia Græca, vol. vi.

KÜHNER, Ausführliche Grammatik der Griechischen Sprache, 2 voll. Hanover 1834.

KUINOEL, Novi Test. Libri Historici Græce, cum Commentariis D. Christiani Theoph. Kuinoel, 3 voll. London 1835.

KYPKE, Observationes Sacræ, Wratislav 1755.

LACHMANN, Novum Test. Græce et Latine, vol. i. Berlin 1842.

LAMPE, Comm. Exeg. Analyticus in Evang. Johannis, 3 voll. 4to, Amsterdam 1726.

LARDNER, DR. NATHANAEL, Works, 11 voll. London 1788.

LEO THE GREAT, Works: cited by Ballerini's pages in Migne's Patrologia Latina, voll. liv.—lvi.

LIGHTFOOT, Horæ Hebraicæ in N. T. 2 voll. fol. Franequeræ 1618.

LÜCKE, DR., Commentar über das Evangelium des Johannes, 3rd edn. Bonn 1840.

LUTHARDT, Das Johanneische Evangelium nach seiner Eigenthümlichkeit geschildert u. erklärt, 2 voll. Nürnberg 1853.

F. M., Anonymous Notes on the Gospels and Acts, 2 voll. Pickering, London 1838.

MAI, Cardl. Angelo, Novum Testamentum (vol. v. of the whole work) ex antiquissimo codice Vaticano, Rome 1858. The second Roman edition, corrected by Vercellone, has been used throughout. See this edition characterized above, under B in the list of MSS.

MALDONATUS, Evangelia, 2 voll. 8vo, Mainz 1855.

MATTHIÆ, Greek Grammar. Translated by Rev. E. V. Blomfield. 2 voll. London 1829.

MEYER, DR. H. A. W., Kritisch-exegetischer Kommentar über das Neue Testament. From the 2nd edn. Göttingen 1844-52: St. Matthew, 4th edn. ibid. 1858; St. John from the 3rd edn. ibid. 1856.

MIDDLETON, BP., On the Greek Article, ed. Rose, Cambridge 1833.

MILL, PROFESSOR, The historical character of St. Luke's first chapter vindicated against some recent mythical interpreters, Cambridge 1841; The Evangelical Accounts of the Descent and Parentage of the Saviour vindicated, &c. ibid. 1842; The Accounts of our Lord's Brethren in the N. T. vindicated, &c. ibid. 1843.

MILMAN, DEAN, The History of Latin Christianity, 2nd edn. London 1857.

NEANDER, DR. AUGUST., Das Leben Jesu Christi, 4th edn. Hamburg 1845.

OLSHAUSEN, Biblischer Commentar, 3rd edn. Königsberg 1837.

ORIGEN, Works: cited by Benedictine pages in Migne's Patrologia Græca, voll. xi.—xvii.

PATRES APOSTOLICI: cited from Migne's Patrologia Græca, voll. i. ii. and v.

PHILO-JUDÆUS, Opera Omnia, 8 voll. ed. Richter, Leipzig 1828: cited by Mangey's pages.

PHRYNICI Eclogæ Nominum, &c. ed. Lobeck, Leipzig 1820.

ROBINSON, DR. EDWARD, Biblical Researches in Palestine, Mount Sinai, and Arabia Petræa, 3 voll. London 1841; A Harmony of the Four Gospels in Greek, with Explanatory Notes, Boston, U. S. 1845.

ROSENMÜLLER, Scholia in N. T. 6 voll. 5th edn. Nuremberg 1803.

ROUTH, DR. M., Reliquiæ Sacræ, Oxford 1846.

SCHLEIERMACHER, DR. F., Essay on the Gospel of Luke, English translation, London 1825; Predigten, 4 voll. Berlin 1843.

SCHOETTGEN, Horæ Heb. et Talmudicæ in N. T. 2 voll. 4to, Dresden and Leipzig 1733.

SCHOLZ, DR. M. A., Novum Test. Græce, 2 voll. Leipzig 1840-6.

SCHROEDER, Nova Janua Hebraica, 3 voll. Leipzig 1835.

SCRIVENER, Collation of about Twenty Manuscripts of the Holy Gospels, Cambridge 1853; Codex Augiensis, ibid. 1859; Introduction to New Testament Criticism, ibid. 1861; A Full Collation of the Codex Sinaiticus, Cambridge and London 1864 [2nd edn. 1867]; Bezæ Codex Cantabrigiensis, ibid. 1864.

SMITH, DR., A Biblical Dictionary, by various Writers, London 1861.

STANLEY, DEAN, Sermons and Essays on the Apostolic Age, Oxford 1847; Sinai and Palestine, London 1855.

STIER, DR. RUDOLF, Die Reden des Herrn Jesu, 6 voll. Barmen 1843-8: 2nd edn. ibid. 1852-4.

TERTULLIANUS: cited by Migne's pages in his Patrologia Latina, voll. i. ii.

THEODORE of MOPSUESTIA: cited by Migne's pages from his Patrologia Græca, vol. lxvi.

THEOPHYLACT, Comment. in IV. Evangelia, Act. &c.: cited usually from the works of others.

THOLUCK, DR. A., Philologisch-theologische Auslegung der Bergpredigt Christi nach Matthäus, 2nd edn. Hamburg 1835; Commentar zum Evangelium Johannis, 6th edn. ibid. 1844.

THOMSON, DR. W. M., The Land and the Book, &c. London 1860.

TISCHENDORF, DR. Æ. F. C., Novum Testamentum Gr. 2nd edn. Leipzig 1849; 7th do. ibid. 1859; 8th do., parts 1—3, ibid. 1865-7 [4—6, 1867-9]; Codex Ephremi Syri Rescriptus, ibid. 1843; Novum Testamentum Sinaiticum, ibid. 1863; Novum Testamentum Vaticanum, ibid. 1867.

TITTMANN, de Synonymis Novi Test., Lipsiæ 1829.

TREGELLES (DR. S. P.), An Account of the printed Text of the Gr. Test. London 1854; Greek Testament, parts i. ii. ibid. 1858, 1861; Introduction to the Holy Scriptures (Horne), vol. iv. (written by Tregelles), ibid. 1856.

TRENCH, ABP., Notes on the Parables, London 1841; Notes on the Miracles, 2nd edn. ibid. 1847; The Sermon on the Mount illustrated from the Writings of S. Augustine, ibid. 1844; Synonyms of the N. T. ibid. 1854.

VIGER de Idiotismis, ed. Hermann, 4th edn. Leipzig 1834.

WETSTEIN, Nov. Test. Græcum, Amsterdam 1751.

WIESELER, Chronologische Synopse der vier Evangelien, Hamburg 1843; Chronologie des Apostolischen Zeitalters bis zum Tode der Apostel Petrus und Paulus, Göttingen 1848.

WILLIAMS, REV. GEORGE, The Holy City; or, Historical and Topographical Notices of Jerusalem, London 1848. (1st edn.)

WINER, DR. G. B., Biblisches Realwörterbuch, 2 voll. 3rd edn. Leipzig 1847-8; Grammatik des Neutestamentlichen Sprachidioms, 6th edn. ibid. 1855 (English translation, Edinburgh 1859) [Moulton's edn. ibid. 1870].

WORDSWORTH, [BP.,] The New Testament in Greek—part i. London 1856; part ii. ibid. 1857; part iii. ibid. 1859: and subsequent editions.

The later classics, Strabo, Dionysius Halicarnasseus, Diodorus Siculus, Plutarch, Appian, Ælian, Ptolemy, Dio Cassius, Arrian, &c., are cited from the small Berlin editions of Tauchnitz.

READINGS OF THE CODEX VATICANUS.

Readings of the Codex Vaticanus (B) in the text of this volume ascertained by the Editor's personal inspection of the MS. at Rome, February, 1861; and, marked with an asterisk, by the Rev. E. C. Cure, April, 1862.

N.B. The original scribe's *corrections*, here noted as '*a prima manu*,' are described by Tischdf. as B². In consequence, my '*secunda manus*' = Tischdf.'s B³.

Matt. i. 4. *ναασσων* bis, not *-εων* as Btly.
9. *εζεκειαν* 1. m. 2. m. has not inked over the *ε*. (Sic: Tischdf.'s account is incorrect.)
23. *ημων* **ο** *θεος*, not om *ο* as Bch.
ii. 22. *αυτου ηρωδου*, not *αυτου* **του** *ηρ.* as Btly.
23. *ναζαρετ*, not *-εθ* as Btly.
iii. 14. *και* **συ** *ερχη*, not *και ερχη* as Mai. (So also Burgon.)
iv. 6. *και* **λεγει**, not *και* **ειπεν** as Blc.
13. *ναζαρα* 1. m., not *-ρατ* as Rl.
15.**γαλιλαια* (not *-ας*).
24.***απηλθεν** (not *ηλθεν*).
v. 16. *εργα* in marg. is 1. m., not 2. m. as Mai.
18. *αν* written over is 2. m.
20.**υμων η δικαιοσυνη*.
42. 1. m. has *δανισασθαι*, not *δανεισ-* as Mai.
vi. 4. *η σου η ελεημ.*, not *η σου ελεημ.* as Verc. (So also Burgon.)
34. 1. m. has *μεριμνησει αυτης*, not *εαυτης* as Mai.
vii. 9. *εστιν* is 1. m. in marg. as Verc.
18. *ου δυναται*, not **ει** *ου* as Btly.
24.**τουτους* is written in a very unusually small hand in marg.
viii. 29. *τι ημιν και* **σοι**, not **σε** as Blc.
ix. 5. *εγειραι*, not *-ρε*.
36. 1. m. *εριμμ*.
x. 14. *μη* (*μην* Tischdf.) *δεξηται* [also *ν*, Tischdf.] is in marg. 1. m.
21. *πατηρ τεκνον*, not **π. το** *τεκνον* as Btly.
28. **φοβηθητε**, not **-εισθε** as Btly.
32, 33. *εν* **τοις** *ουρ.* in both verses. (So also Burgon.)

Matt. x. 37. *και* to *αξιος* is in marg. 1. m.
xi. 18. Rl. notes on *δαιμονιον*, "ad marg., quasi *δαιμονια* scribere voluerit." This is very doubtful. The mark on marg. is not distinct enough to make it even probable.
xii. 48. *μου* (at end) is written over by both 1. m. and 2. m.
xiii. 17. *φηται και δικαιοι* is in marg. 1. m. (Sic: not as Tischdf.)
32. *κατασκηνοιν* is 1. m.
36. *λεγοντες* is not omitted as Blc.
39. **ο** *διαβ.*, not *διαβ.* as Btly.
xiv. 2. *δια τουτο* is in marg. 2. m.
3. *τη* (before *φυλακη*) is written over by 1. m.
7. *αιτησηται*, as Verc.
18. *ωδε* is not omitted.
30. *ισχυρον* in marg. is 1. m.
36. *αυτον* in marg. is 1. m. (B³ appy., Tischdf.)
xv. 39. *το πλοιον*, not *τον πλοιον* as printed in Verc.
xvi. 4. *επιζητει* is 1. m. in marg.
12.**αλλα απο*.
17. *οτι* is 1. m. in marg.
20. *επετειμησεν* in 1. m.; *διεστειλατο* in a writing more recent than 2. m. (that commonly used). Tischdf. states that the same was written in marg. by his B² or even by the original scribe.
24. 2. m. has corrected 1. m. to *ο ις*.
xviii. 14. *μου* **του** *εν ουρ.*, not *μου εν ουρ.* as Verc.

Matt. xviii. 15. αμαρτηση, not -σει as Blc.

19. συμ(or ν ?)φωνησωσιν, not -ουσιν as Btly.

22. αλλα εως.

xix. 12. 1. m. δυνομενος; 2. m. δυναμενος.

14. 1. m. αφεται.

17. εις is written over by 2. m.

xx. 5.*παλιν, omitting δε.

xxi. 4. πληρωθη, not πλερ- as Hug. This and the four following words are written *twice* by 1. m.

33. εξεδετε 1. m.

xxii. 6.*δουλους αυτου.

10. 1. m. ο νυμφων: ο γαμος is written as an alternative in marg. by 1. m., and inked over by 2. m.

31. υπο, not απο: the υ is dotted (ϋ).

xxiii. 37. αυτης (after νοσσια) is in marg. 1. m.

xxiv. 17. τα (not τι) εκ της οικ.

xxv. 10. 1. m. has ηκλεισθη.

40. The marginal writing supposed to be των αδελφων μου, or τουτων, was quite illegible to me.

42. 1st ουκ omitted: inserted over the line by 1. m.

xxvi. 3.*του λαου omitted 1. m., inserted 2. m.

4. και αποκτεινωσιν is in marg. both 1. m. and 2. m.

13. δε is written over by 1. m.

xxviii. 15. Rl. notes that τα (before αργυρια) is erased and has been reinserted. There is no τα at all. (Tischdf. says that it has been written over the line by his B^3.)

Mark i. 28.*αυτου ευθυς.

38.*εχομενα (not -ας).

42. εκαθερισθη is 1. m., not 2. m. as Verc.

ii. 3. αιρομενων is 1. m., but 1. m. has corrected it to -νον.

4. κραβαττον is 1. m., but 1. m. has erased the former τ.

9. Here, and in ver. 11, 1. m. has κραββαττον. (Sic in these three places, not as Tischdf.)

16.*As in Mai, edn. 1.

26.*εισηλθεν (no πως).

Mark iii. 17.*βοανηργες.

iv. 22. ινα (1st) is not omitted in cod.

v. 15. 1. m. probably λεγιωνα (so Mr. Cure: λεγεωνα Tischdf.).

29. εξηρανθη in cod.

vi. 5. 1. m. συγγενευσιν.

17. την γυναικα in marg. is 1. m.

37. δωσομεν, not δωσωμεν as Mai.

54. αυτων in marg. is 1. m.

vii. 9. και ελεγεν αυτοις is not omitted, as Btly.

15. τον is not omitted as Bch.

32. μογιλ. is 1. m.

viii. 14. επελαθεντο 1. m.

17. 1. m. συνιειτε; 2. m. συνιετε. (Tischdf. σῡειτε 1. m.)

19. οτε, not και οτε as Mai.

35.*την ψυχην αυτου (2nd time).

ix. 41. απολεση, not -σει as Btly.

42. ενα των, not ενα τουτων των as Bch.

x. 40. Cod. (2. m.) αλλ οις, not αλλοις.

46. 2nd και to ιερειχω are in marg. 1. m.

xi. 32. αλλα ειπωμεν is in cod.

xii. 4. εκεφαλιωσαν is in cod.

xiii. 13. Cod. has εις τελος.

25. πειπτοντες in cod., not εκπ.

xiv. 37. εισχυσας 1. m., but 1. m. (B^3 Tischdf.) has erased the ε.

xvi. 8. After εφοβουντο γαρ follows, as at end of other Gospels, the subscription, κατα μαρκον: but the remaining greater portion of the column, and the whole of the next to the end of the page, are left vacant. I found no other instances of this in the N. T.: the next book always beginning on the next column.

Luke ii. 5. εμνηστευμενη is 1. m., not 2. m. as in Mai, edn. 2: 2. m. has μεμν-.

14. In ευδοκιας, the C is left *very* pale: it certainly has been there.

25. συμεων is in cod., not σιμεων.

33. Cod. has μητηρ θαυμαζοντες, not μητηρ αυτου θ. as in Mai, edn. 1.

36. 2. m. has— αυτς
μετα του ανδρος ετη επτα.

38. αυτη τη ωρα, not τη αυτη ωρα as Btly.

Luke iii. 1. βασιλειας, alternative reading for ηγεμονιας, is in marg. 1. m. ορεινης, in marg. after ιτουραιας, is 1. m.
14. ποιησωμεν is in cod.
37. ιαρετ is 1. m., ισρεδ 2. m., not the converse as stated in Mai, edn. 2.
v. 7. επλησαν, not επλησθησαν as Blc.
vi. 17. ιουδαιας και ιερουσαλημ και της παραλιου, not ιουδαιας και της παραλιου as in Mai, edn. 2.
vii. 1. επειδη is in cod.
12.*αυτη ην.
41. χρεοφ. is in cod.
43. σιμων, not ο σιμων as Btly.
viii. 3. εκ is in cod., not απο as in Mai, edn. 1.
9. ειη is accentuated ἐι(not εἶ, as Tischdf.) ἥ.
12. ακουσαντες, not ακουοντες as Muralto.
16. τιθησιν, not επιτιθησιν as Muralto.
25. εστιν is in cod.
30. 2. m. has λεγεων, not λεγιων as stated in Mai, edn. 2: 1. m. perhaps had λεγαιων, or -ειων as in Mai and Tischdf.
40. εν δε τω, not εγενετο δε εν τω as Btly.
51. τινα, not τινας as Mai, edn. 1.
ix. 2. κηρυσσειν, not -σσεν as Mai, edn. 2.
10. υπεχωρησεν, not συνεχ. as Mai, edn. 1.
12. ηδη, not ηδε as Mai, edn. 1.
37. εγενετο δε τη, not εν τη as Mai, edn. 1.
59. κυριε is written over by 1. m. (B³ Tischdf.).
x. 1. δυο twice, not once only as Btly.
2. εκβαλη, not εκβαλλη as Btly.
15. του (before ουρ.) is added by 1. m. (B³ Tischdf.).
27. σου (after θεον) is written over by 1. m. (B³ Tischdf.).
31. κατεβαινεν τη, not εν τη as Mai, edn. 1.
34. επιβιβασας, not επιβασας as Mai, edn. 2.
36. των τριων, not τριων as Btly.

Luke x. 36. πλησιον δοκει σοι, not πλησιον σοι δ. σοι as Mai.
39. 1. m. has apparently μαριαμ η και, but there has been a long erasure, and all is in confusion. For κυριου, 1. m. perhaps had ιησου. (See digest in loc.)
xi. 2 ff. The Lord's prayer was carefully collated and found to be as Mai, edn. 2, omitting the obelized clauses.
25.*ελθον.
29. η γενεα αυτη γενεα πονηρα, not omitting the 2nd γενεα as in Mai, edn. 2.
40. ουκ is 1. m.
42. του θεου is written over by 1. m. αφιεναι is 2. m. (but παρειναι is restored: Tischdf.).
44. οι περιπ., not without οι as Btly.
xii. 20. αφρων, not αφρον as Mai, edn. 1.
25. πηχυν, not πηχυν ενα as Woide. (The Bentley collation itself is right.)
33. βαλλαντια, not βαλαντ. as Mai, edn. 1.
35. 1. m. οσφυαις, 2. m. οσφυεις (not as Tischdf. οσφυες).
xiii. 14. εν αις is written over by 1. m.
15. 1. m. has απαγων (B² ut vdtr., et B³ απαγαγων: Tischdf.).
27.*λεγων.
xiv. 10. 1. m. has κληθεις.
*1. m has αναπεσε.
12. γενηται ανταποδομα σοι, not αντ. σοι γεν. as Btly.
16. μεγα has ν written over by 2. m. (but corrected, Tischdf.).
27. The first ου is written over by 1. m. (B³ appy., Tischdf.).
xv. 29. αυτου is not omitted as Mai, edn. 1.
30. τον σιτευτον μοσχον is in cod.
xvi. 4. εκ is not omitted as in Mai, edn. 1.
9. 1. m. has εκλιπη; 2. m. has written over ε, between the λ and the ι.
xvii. 24. αστραπη αστραπτουσα, not αστραπη η αστρ. as in Mai, edn. 1.
35.*η μια.

Luke xviii. 9. εξουθενουντες, not **και** εξ. as Mai, edn. 1.

13.*στηθος εαυτου.

15. αυτων is written over by 1. m.

30. ος ουχι **μη**, not ος ουχι **ου** as in Mai, edn. 1.

xix. 8. ημισια is 1. m.: 2. m. has written ε over, between σ and ι.

22. "κρίνω, hoc acc." Btly. There is no accent at all in cod.

25. κυριε is written over by 1. m.

40. σιωπησουσιν, not -σωσιν as Mai.

44. λιθον επι λιθον εν σοι, not λιθον εν σοι επι λιθω as Woide. (The Bentley collation itself is right.)

xx. 20. λογου, not λογον as Btly.

αι
xxi. 34. In cod. it is κρεπαλη : 1. m. has written the α over the ε, and 2. m. has added the ι to it. (Sic: though Tischdf. seems to disapprove.)

xxii. 19. ποιειτε την εμην αναμν. 1. m.: εις is written over by 2. m.

αι
30. Cod. has καθησθε: all 1. m.

35, 36. βαλλαντ. both times.

37. και **γαρ** το, not και το as Btly.

και
39. αυτω οι μαθηται: all 1. m.

εισελθειν
40. μη εις πειρασμον: all 1. m.

42. γενεσθω is 2. m. (not γιν. as Tischdf.).

ο
xxiii. 6. ει ανθρωπος: all 1. m.

35. θεου ο εκλεκτος, not omitting ο as Mai, edn. 1.

38. **ο** βασιλ., not omitting ο as Mai, edn. 1.

53. **αυτον** not αυτο as Mai. (It stands αυτο‾ at the end of a line: just before, ver. 51 we have ιουδαιω‾ in the same position.)

xxiv. 15. Between συνζητειν and αυτους, και is written over, uncertain whether by 1. m. or 2. m.

17. ἐσταθησαν.

21. 1. m. has ηλπιζαμεν.

27.*περι εαυτ.

34. οτι οντως ηγερθη ο κς, not οτι ο κς οντως ηγερθη as Woide. (The Bentley collation itself is right.)

ν
John i. 13. The 2nd ν in εγενηθησαν is 2. m., not 1. m. as Verc.

14. The και between χαριτος and αληθειας is 2. m., not 1. m.

ν
15. ουτος ην ο ειπ. is in cod., the ν being written over by 2. m., and no sign of a horizontal line by 1. m.

18. μονογενης **θς** carefully substantiated.

50. απεκριθη αυτω, not omitting αυτω as Mai, edn. 1.

ii. 11. σημιων 1. m.; -ειων 2. m.

iii. 4. νεικοδ. hoc loco 1. m.

34. το πν. is in marg., 1. m. (So also Verc.)

iv. 5. συχαρ, not σιχαρ as Mai, edn. 1.

9. ουσης is not omitted as in Mai, edn. 1.

15. διερχομαι is in cod.

ως συν ως συν
40. ουν ηλθον (ουν ηλθον ουν, Tischdf.) is in cod.: all 1. m. (Tischdf. says that the first Ο was originally C, and was altered by the original scribe.)

42. ελεγον ουκετι, not ελεγον **οτι** ουκετι as Mai, edn. 1.

κοσμου, not κοσμ. **ο χριστος** as Mai, edn. 1.

52. αυτην is in cod.

v. 3—5. ξηρων· ην δε τις carefully substantiated.

6. τουτον, not αυτον as Btly.

10. και is not omitted as in Mai, edn. 1.

30. με is not omitted as Btly.

vi. 13. κρειθινων 1. m.

15. ερχεσθε is in cod.

ib. **ανε**χωρησεν, not εχωρ. as Btly., &c.

17. εληλυθει, not -θεν as Btly.

18. διεγειρ. is in cod.

71. εμε**λλ**εν, not εμελεν as Btly.

vii. 8. ο εμος καιρος is in cod.

10. τοτε is not omitted as Btly.

26. αληθως is in cod.

30. εληλυθει, not -θεν as Btly.

34. ελθειν εκει, not omitting εκει as Mai, edn. 1.

39. αγιον δεδομενον carefully substantiated.

John vii. 52—viii. 12. { φητης ουκ εγειρεται / παλιν ουν αυτοις ελαλει } without a break.

viii. 23. Cod. at end, *εκ του κοσμου τουτου*, not *εκ τουτου του κοσμου* as Mai, edn. 2.

24. *υμειν* is 1. m., not 2. m. as Mai.

45. *δε* is in cod.

56. 1. m. has *ειδη*: 2. m. has left the *ε* pale.

ix. 10. *ηνεωχθησαν* is in cod., not *εν-* as Mai, edn. 2.

11. **τον** *σιλ*. is in cod.

11.***και** *νιψαμενος*.

21.*om *αυτος* (before *ηλικιαν*).

x. 6. *ην* is in cod., not *η* as Mai, edn. 2.

26. **αλλα.**

xii. 6. *εμελεν*, not *εμε***λλ***εν* as Mai, edn. 2. There is no sign of reduplication.

40. *επωρωσεν* is 1. m.: 2. m. has written *π* and *κ* over.

xiii. 6. *τους*, not **μου** *τους* as Btly.

8. *απεκριθη* ις *αυτω*, not *απεκριθη αυτω* as Mai.

26. *αποκρινεται ουν* ις, not **ο** ις as Btly.

27. *ταχ***ει***ον* 1. m.

xiv. 3.***και** *ετοιμασω*.

10.**πιστευσεις* 1. m.

ib.*1. m. has *α εγω υμιν* corrected by the insertion of *λεγω* over the line (by B³ appy., Tischdf.).

John xiv. 14. **τουτο ποιησω*, omitting *εγω*.

xvii. 1. **ο** *υιος*, not *υιος* as Btly.

6. *ους εδωκας*, not *ους* **δεδ**. as Mai, edn. 1.

11. *ω δεδωκας* examined and substantiated.

ημεις (not *υμεις*).

15, 16. In cod. it is thus:

τους εκ του κο   *σμου αλλ ινα τηρη*
π νηρ   *σης αυτους*
νκ του εκ του κοσμου   *εκ του κοσμου.*

The *π* and *νηρ* written over the text, are 2. m. The marginal writing,

σμου αλλ ινα τηρη
σης αυτους
εκ του κοσμου

is 1. m. and 2. m. (not, as Tischdf., his B³ only. He has observed, what apparently escaped me, the whole being very difficult to discern, that the first *κο* was written *πο* and corrected, over, *κο*, as he says by B³. For my *νκ του*, he gives *νηρου*, which he also says B³ marked for omission).

xix. 23.**αρραφος*.

xx. 17. *τον πατερα πορευου δε*, not *τον πατ.* **μου** *πορ. δε* as Mai, edn. 1.

30. *σημεια εποιησεν*, not *σημεια* **α** *επ*. as Btly.

[ΕΥΑΓΓΕΛΙΟΝ]

ΚΑΤΑ ΜΑΘΘΑΙΟΝ.

BEKL MSUVΓ ΔΠℵ 1. 33

I. 1 [a] Βίβλος [b] γενέσεως Ἰησοῦ [c] χριστοῦ [d] υἱοῦ Δαυεὶδ

a Mark xii. 26. Luke iii. 4 al. Gen. ii. 4. v. 1.
b ver. 18. Luke i. 14. James i. 23. iii. 6 only. Gen. xxxvii. 2. Wisd. vii. 5.
c Lev. iv. 5, 16. 1 Kings xxiv. 7, 11. Ps. ii. 2. civ. 15. Dan. ix. 25 (26 LXX).
d ch. xii. 23. xxi. 9. xxii. 42 ‖.

TITLE. rec το κατα ματθ. αγιον(om αγ. elz) ευαγγ.: ευαγγ. κατα μαθθ. CEKMSUV [Γ]Δ 33, and D(head of pages) L(before the κεφάλαια): κατα μαθθ. B[1] ℵ(head of pages). [Π def.]

[*N.B.* lat-*b* is defective up to Βαβυλωνος ver 11.]

Title] [**εὐαγγέλιον**, in earlier Greek, signifies *a present made as a return for good news* (see Hom. Od. ξ. 152, 166, also 2 Kings iv. 10), or *a sacrifice offered in thanksgiving for the same* (Aristoph. Eq. 658); in later Greek, *the good news itself*, as in LXX (2 Kings xviii. 20, 22, 25, in all which the noun may be, either from reading or construction, -ία or -ιον), and N. T. passim, in the appropriated sense of **the good news of salvation by Christ Jesus.** Hence it came to be applied to the writings themselves which contain this good news, very early: so Justin M. Apol. i. 66, p. 83, οἱ ἀπόστολοι ἐν τοῖς γενομένοις ὑπ' αὐτῶν ἀπομνημονεύμασιν, ἃ καλεῖται **εὐαγγέλια.**] **κατὰ** M.] *as delivered by Matthew*—implies *authorship* or *editorship:* so Ὅμηρος **κατὰ** Ἀρίσταρχον. This use of the prep. denotes, generally, the *relation* of *things* to *persons*, cf. Thuc. vi. 16, ἐν τῷ κατ' αὐτοὺς βίῳ,—i. 54, τὰ κατὰ σφᾶς ναυάγια,—and see Bernhardy, Syntax, p. 241. It is not merely = a genitive—*of Matthew* (as τὸ εὐαγγ. **μου**, Rom. xvi. 25, al.), which would have been *used*, had it been meant. Nor does it signify, that the original teaching was Matthew's, and the present Gospel drawn up after that teaching. See Prolegg. to Matt. Eusebius, H. E. iii. 24, says, Ματθαῖος . . . . γραφῇ παραδοὺς **τὸ κατ' αὐτὸν εὐαγγέλιον.**

CHAP. I. 1—17. GENEALOGY OF JESUS CHRIST. **1. βίβλος γενέσεως**] Not always used of a pedigree only: see reff. Here however it appears that it refers exclusively to the genealogy, by Ἰησοῦ χριστοῦ being used in the enunciation, and the close being Ἰησοῦς ὁ λεγόμενος χριστός. Then ver. 17 forms a conclusion to it, and ver. 18 passes on to other matter. **Ἰησοῦ**] see on ver. 21. **χριστοῦ**] = מָשִׁיחַ, **anointed.** In reff. it is used of kings, priests, prophets, and of the promised Deliverer. Theophylact says, λέγεται ὁ κύριος, **χριστός**· καὶ **ὡς βασιλεύς**, ἐβασίλευσε γὰρ κατὰ τῆς ἁμαρτίας· καὶ **ὡς ἱερεύς**, προσήγαγε γὰρ ἑαυτὸν θῦμα ὑπὲρ ἡμῶν· ἐχρίσθη δὲ καὶ αὐτὸς κυρίως τῷ ἀληθινῷ ἐλαίῳ, τῷ ἁγίῳ πνεύματι. It is here used (see ver. 16) in that sense in which it became affixed to Ἰησοῦς as the name of our Lord. It does not once thus occur in the progress of the Evangelic *history;* only in the prefatory parts of the Gospels, here and vv. 16, 17, 18: Mark i. 1: John i. 17, and once in the mouth

e Gen. xxv. 20. υἱοῦ Ἀβραάμ. [2] [e] Ἀβραὰμ [e] ἐγέννησεν τὸν [e] Ἰσαάκ, Ἰσαὰκ
δὲ ἐγέννησεν τὸν Ἰακώβ, Ἰακὼβ δὲ ἐγέννησεν τὸν Ἰούδαν
καὶ τοὺς ἀδελφοὺς αὐτοῦ, [3] Ἰούδας δὲ ἐγέννησεν τὸν C και τους...
f ver. 16. Gal. iv. 4, 22, 23. Φαρὲς καὶ τὸν Ζαρὰ [f] ἐκ τῆς Θαμάρ, Φαρὲς δὲ ἐγέννησεν BCEKL MSUVΓ
τὸν Ἐσρώμ, Ἐσρὼμ δὲ ἐγέννησεν τὸν Ἀράμ, [4] Ἀρὰμ δὲ ΔΠℵ 1. 33
ἐγέννησεν τὸν Ἀμειναδάβ, Ἀμειναδὰβ δὲ ἐγέννησεν τὸν
Ναασσών, Ναασσὼν δὲ ἐγέννησεν τὸν Σαλμών, [5] Σαλμὼν
δὲ ἐγέννησεν τὸν Βοὲς [f] ἐκ τῆς Ῥαχάβ, Βοὲς δὲ ἐγέννησεν
τὸν Ἰωβὴδ [f] ἐκ τῆς Ῥούθ, Ἰωβὴδ δὲ ἐγέννησεν τὸν

CHAP. I. 2. *ισακ* (twice) ℵ[1](txt ℵ[2]: so ℵ elsewhere). om 1st *δε* ℵ[1] [lat-*c ff*$_1$ *g*$_1$] syr-cu.
3. *ζαρε* B. 4. *αμιναδαμ* (2nd) ℵ Scr's c h p q r s evv-150-z (P$_2$-y).
5. rec *βοοζ*, with L rel latt: *βοος* C 33: txt Bℵ lat-*k* coptt. om *εκ της ραχαβ* Δ[1] lat-*a*. rec *ωβηδ* (twice), with C[3]L rel (*οβηδ* E(1st time) L) æth-pl: txt BC[1]Δℵ (33) coptt æth-rom Epiph Jer.

of our Lord himself, John xvii. 3 (on Pilate's words, ch. xxvii. 17, 22, see note there); but passim in the Acts and Epistles. This may serve to shew that the evangelic memoirs themselves were of earlier date than their incorporation into our present Gospels. **υἱοῦ** both times refers to our Lord. בֶּן דָּוִד (Ben-David) was an especial title of the Messiah: see reff. That He should be *son of Abraham*, was too solemn a subject of prophecy to be omitted here, even though implied in the other. These words serve to shew the character of the Gospel, as written *for Jews*: *οὐδὲν γὰρ οὕτως ἀνέπαυε τοὺς ἐξ Ἰουδαίων πεπιστευκότας, ὡς τὸ μαθεῖν ὅτι ἐκ σπέρματος Ἀβραὰμ καὶ Δαυὶδ ἦν ὁ χριστός.* Euthymius. Luke, ch. iii. 23 ff., carries his genealogy further back. **2. καὶ τ. ἀδελφ.**] These additions probably indicate that Matt. did not take his genealogy from any family or public documents, but constructed it himself. Cf. also Grot., 'Obiter Matthæus Christum ut cognatum omnibus Israelitis commendat.' **3.**] These children of Judah were not born in marriage: see Gen. xxxviii. 16—30. Both the sons are named, probably as recalling the incident connected with their birth. The reason for the women (Thamar, Rahab, Ruth, and Bathsheba) being mentioned, has been variously assigned: by Wetst., *ut tacitæ Judæorum objectioni occurreretur*: by Fritzsche, *for the sake of minute accuracy*. It most probably is that given by Maldonatus: 'Prætermisit Evangelista quod ordinarium erat, quod autem singulare et dubium exposuit.' There may be something also in that suggested by Grotius: 'Mulieres in hoc sensu obiter paucæ nominantur, extraneo ortu aut criminibus nobiles, quarum historia ad vocationem idololatrarum et criminosorum per Christi evangelium proludit:' as also in De Wette's view, that they serve as types of the mother of our Lord, and are consequently named in the course of the genealogy, as she is at the end of it. **5. Ῥαχάβ**] "Rachab illam Hierichuntinam dici, vel articulus, **τῆς Ῥ.**, ejusque vis relativa docet." Bengel. It has been imagined, on chronological grounds, that this Rachab must be a different person from Rahab of Jericho. But those very grounds completely tally with their identity. For Naashon (father of Salmon), prince of Judah (1 Chron. ii. 10), offered his offering at the setting up of the tabernacle (Num. vii. 12) 39 years before the taking of Jericho. So that Salmon would be of mature age at or soon after that event; at which time Rahab was probably young, as her father and mother were living (Josh. vi. 23). Nor is it any objection that Achan, the fourth in descent from Judah by Zara, is contemporary with Salmon, the sixth of the other branch: since the generations in the line of Zara average 69 years, and those in the line of Phares 49, both within the limits of probability. The difficulty of the interval of 366 years between Rahab and David does not belong to this passage only, but equally to Ruth iv. 21, 22; and is by no means insuperable, especially when the extreme old age of Jesse, implied in 1 Sam. xvii. 12, is considered. I may add that, considering Rahab's father and mother were alive, the house would hardly be called *the house of Rahab* except on account of the character commonly assigned

Ἰεσσαί, 6 Ἰεσσαὶ δὲ ἐγέννησεν τὸν Δαυεὶδ τὸν βασιλέα.
Δαυεὶδ δὲ ἐγέννησεν τὸν Σολομῶνα [f] ἐκ [g] τῆς [g] τοῦ Οὐρίου, [g] see ch. x. 2, 3. Luke vi. 16. xxiv. 10. John xxi. 15.
7 Σολομῶν δὲ ἐγέννησεν τὸν Ῥοβοάμ, Ῥοβοὰμ δὲ ἐγέν-
νησεν τὸν Ἀβιά, Ἀβιὰ δὲ ἐγέννησεν τὸν Ἀσάφ, 8 Ἀσὰφ
δὲ ἐγέννησεν τὸν Ἰωσαφατ, Ἰωσαφὰτ δὲ ἐγέννησεν τὸν
Ἰωράμ, Ἰωρὰμ δὲ ἐγέννησεν τὸν Ὀζείαν, 9 Ὀζείας δὲ
ἐγέννησεν τὸν Ἰωάθαμ, Ἰωάθαμ δὲ ἐγέννησεν τὸν Ἄχαζ,
Ἄχαζ δὲ ἐγέννησεν τὸν Ἐζεκίαν, 10 Ἐζεκίας δὲ ἐγέννησεν
τὸν Μανασσῆ, Μανασσῆς δὲ ἐγέννησεν τὸν Ἀμώς, Ἀμὼς
δὲ ἐγέννησεν τὸν Ἰωσείαν, 11 Ἰωσείας δὲ ἐγέννησεν τὸν

6. rec aft δα. δε ins *ο βασιλευς*, with CL rel latt syr æth : om Bℵ [Scr's g p] forj lat-$g_{1.2}$ *k* Syr syr-cu coptt Aug Op. (*Possibly omitted to conform to the rest of the genealogy : so Meyer. But the words may have been inserted from the preceding.*) σαλομων ℵ[1] : σαλωμωνα ℵ[2] 33.

7. σαλωμων ℵ[2] (1. 33). αβιας (2nd) ℵ[1](*s* marked by ℵ[2] for erasure).

7, 8. rec (for ασαφ, twice) ασα (*conformed to* LXX), with L rel vulg lat-*a f* ff_1 syrr syr-cu : txt (*cf* D *in Luke*) BCℵ 1 lat-*c* $g_{1.2}$ *k* syr-mg coptt æth arm.

9. αχας (2nd) ℵ (so 1st ℵ-corr[1]).

10. μανασση (2nd) ℵ[2]. rec αμων (twice), with L rel vulg lat-*a f* syrr syr-cu : txt (*cf* D *in Luke and* A *in* LXX) BCM[Γ]Δ[Π]ℵ 1. 33 lat-*c* ff_1 $g_{1.2}$ coptt æth arm Epiph Op.

11. aft εγεννησεν ins (*to obviate the omission, see note ; cf* D *in Luke*) τον ιωακειμ. ιωακ. δε εγεννησεν MU (1) 33 syr(mss with ast, or without, or on marg) syr-jer Iren (*Joseph enim Joacim et Jechoniæ filius ostenditur, quemadmodum et Matthæus generationem ejus exponit*) : om BCℵ rel latt Syr syr-cu coptt Porph$_{certe}$ Eus(says of Jechonia and Joacim εἷς δὲ ἦν καὶ ὁ αὐτὸς διωνυμίᾳ χρώμενος) Hil$_{certe}$.

to her. **6. τῆς τοῦ Οὐ.**] This construction, which is not properly elliptical, but possessive (Grotius compares 'Hectoris Andromache,' Virg., — Meyer, *Luther's Katharina*, and Bernhardy, Syntax, p. 160, Διὸς Ἄρτεμις, — Ζηνὸς Ἀπόλλων Plut. de Pyth. or. p. 402,—Ἱππίου Ἀρχεδίκην Thuc. vi. 59, &c.), occurs in the Gospels to designate various relations: see reff. **8. Ἰωρὰμ . . . . . Ὀζείαν**] Three kings, viz., Ahaziah, Joash, Amaziah (1 Chron. iii. 11, 12), are here omitted (supplied in syr-cu, lat-*a*, D in Luke). Some (Spanheim, Lightf., Ebrard, &c.) think that they were erased on account of their connexion, by means of Athaliah, with the accursed house of Ahab. Simeon is omitted by Moses in blessing the tribes (Deut. xxxiii.): the descendants of Zebulun and Dan are passed over in 1 Chron., and none of the latter tribe are sealed in Rev. vii. But more probably such erasion, even if justifiable by that reason, was not made on account of it, but for convenience, in order to square the numbers of the different portions of the genealogies, as here. Compare as illustrating such omissions, 1 Chron. viii. 1 with Gen. xlvi. 21.
11. Ἰωσείας . . . . . Ἰεχον.] Eliakim, son of Josiah and father of Jechonias, is omitted; which was objected to the Christians by Porphyry. The reading which inserts Joacim (i. e. Eliakim) rests on hardly any foundation, and would make fifteen generations in the second tesseradecade. The solution of the difficulty by supposing the name to apply to both Eliakim and his son, and to mean the former in ver. 11 and the latter in ver. 12, is unsupported by example, and contrary to the usage of the genealogy. When we notice that the ἀδελφοί of Jechonias are his *uncles*, and find this way of speaking sanctioned by 2 Chron. xxxvi. 10, where Zedekiah, one of these, is called his brother, we are led to seek our solution in some recognized manner of speaking of these kings, by which Eliakim and his son were not accounted two distinct generations. If we compare 1 Chron. iii. 16 with 2 Kings xxiv. 17, we can hardly fail to see that there is some confusion in the records of Josiah's family. In the latter passage, where we have "his father's brother," the LXX render τὸν υἱὸν αὐτοῦ. Lord A. Hervey, in his careful work on the genealogies of our Lord, has suggested a reason for the difficulty: viz. that the text may originally have stood thus: Ἰωσείας δὲ ἐγέννησεν τὸν Ἰωακεὶμ καὶ

h ver. 17 bis only. 4 Kings xxiv. 16. 1 Chron. v. 22. Obad. 20. Nah. iii. 10. (-κίζειν, Acts vii. 4, 43.)
i constr., ch. iv. 15. x. 5. Gen. iii. 24. Jer. ii. 18. γῆς πατρῴας νόστος, Eur. Iph. T. 1073.
j vv. 3, &c. reff.
k ch. xxvii. 17, 22.
l ch. xxiii. 35. Luke xi. 51. 1 Kings xv. 7.
m vv. 11, 12 reff.

Ἰεχονίαν καὶ τοὺς ἀδελφοὺς αὐτοῦ, ἐπὶ τῆς [h] μετοικεσίας [i] Βαβυλῶνος. 12 μετὰ δὲ τὴν [h] μετοικεσίαν Βαβυλῶνος Ἰεχονίας γεννᾷ τὸν Σαλαθιήλ, Σαλαθιὴλ δὲ
γεννᾷ τὸν Ζοροβάβελ, 13 Ζοροβάβελ δὲ γεννᾷ τὸν
Ἀβιούδ, Ἀβιοὺδ δὲ ἐγέννησεν τὸν Ἐλιακείμ, Ἐλιακεὶμ
δὲ ἐγέννησεν τὸν Ἀζώρ, 14 Ἀζὼρ δὲ ἐγέννησεν τὸν
Σαδώκ, Σαδὼκ δὲ ἐγέννησεν τὸν Ἀχείμ, Ἀχεὶμ δὲ
ἐγέννησεν τὸν Ἐλιούδ, 15 Ἐλιοὺδ δὲ ἐγέννησεν τὸν
Ἐλεάζαρ, Ἐλεάζαρ δὲ ἐγέννησεν τὸν Μαθθάν, Μαθθὰν
δὲ ἐγέννησεν τὸν Ἰακώβ, 16 Ἰακὼβ δὲ ἐγέννησεν τὸν
Ἰωσὴφ τὸν ἄνδρα Μαρίας, [j] ἐξ ἧς ἐγεννήθη [k] Ἰησοῦς
ὁ [k] λεγόμενος [k] χριστός. 17 πᾶσαι οὖν αἱ γενεαὶ [l] ἀπὸ
Ἀβραὰμ [l] ἕως Δαυεὶδ γενεαὶ δεκατέσσαρες, καὶ [l] ἀπὸ
Δαυεὶδ [l] ἕως τῆς [m] μετοικεσίας Βαβυλῶνος γενεαὶ δεκατέσ-

P της μετ... BCEKL MPSUV ΓΔΠℵ 1. 33
Z ι ουν αι... BCEKL MPSUV ZΓΔΠℵ 1. 33

12. rec (for *γεννα,* twice in this ver and once in next) *εγεννησε*, with CLPℵ rel: txt B. *σελαθιηλ* (twice) B lat-*k*. (The vowel points of syr-cu are surely no evidence, yet Tischdf cites them.)
13. *αβιουτ* (twice) ℵ[1](txt ℵ[2](so *ελιουτ*, vv. 14, 15).)
14. *σαδωχ* (twice) ℵ[1][: *σαδακ* Γ Scr's p].
15. *ματθαν* (twice) ℵ [*cf* D *in Luke*].
16. for *τον ανδρα* to end of ver., *cui desponsata virgo maria peperit xpm ihm* D-lat, simly lat-*a b c* g_1 syr-cu arm [Gaud Op].

τοὺς ἀδελφοὺς αὐτοῦ, Ἰωακεὶμ δὲ ἐγέννησεν τὸν Ἰωαχεὶμ ἐπὶ τῆς μετοικεσίας Βαβυλῶνος, μετὰ δὲ τὴν μετ. Β. Ἰωαχεὶμ ἐγέννησεν τὸν Σαλαθιήλ, κ.τ.λ., and a copyist may have omitted the *Ἰωακ. δ. ἐγ. τὸν Ἰωαχ.* as an accidental repetition. This view may perhaps be imagined to derive some support from the digest: but it seems to me that the objection to it is, the present occurrence of *Ἰεχονίαν* and *-ας* in all our copies. This Lord A. Hervey does not satisfactorily account for in saying "the form *Ἰεχονίας* was doubtless substituted in St. Matthew's Gospel much later, to bring it into accordance with 1 Chron. iii." **ἐπὶ τῆς μετ.**] **at the time of the migration to Babylon** (on this usage of *ἐπί* with a gen., derived from its meaning of *local juxta-*, or *superimposition*, see Bernhardy, Syntax, p. 246):—and *μετὰ τὴν μετ.*, **after the migration.** For the construction, *μετ. Βαβ.*, see reff.

12. Ἰεχον. . . . . Σαλαθ.] So also the genealogy in 1 Chron. iii. 17. When, therefore, it is denounced (Jer. xxii. 30) that Jeconiah should be 'childless,' this word must be understood as explained by the rest of the verse, 'for no man of his seed shall prosper, sitting upon the throne of David and ruling any more in Judah.' The LXX render this word עֲרִירִי, *ἐκκήρυκτον*: but the Talmudical writers explain it according to our rendering. **Σαλαθ. . . . . . Ζοροβ.**] There is no difficulty here which does not also exist in the O. T. Zerubbabel is there usually called the son of Shealtiel (Salathiel). Ezra iii. 2, &c.: Neh. xii. 1: Hag. i. 1, &c. In 1 Chron. iii. 19, Zerubbabel is said to have been the son of Pedaiah, brother of Salathiel. Either this may have been a different Zerubbabel, or Salathiel may, according to the law, have raised up seed to his brother.

13. Ζοροβ. . . . . Ἀβιούδ] Abiud is not mentioned as a son of the Zerubbabel in 1 Chron. iii. Lord A. Hervey, p. 122 ff., has made it probable that Abiud is identical with the Hodaiah of 1 Chron. iii. 24, and the Juda of Luke iii. 26. Dr. Mill (p. 178, note) mentions this conjecture, but does not adopt it. The objection, that thus the first generation after Zerubbabel would be omitted, need not have much weight, after the omission of three generations in the last tesseradecade. I cannot but recommend to the student the perusal of Lord A. Hervey's work. Whether or not we may be inclined to adopt his conjectures on so intricate and uncertain a subject as the reconciling of the genealogies, too much praise cannot be given to the spirit of combined Christian reverence and enlightened critical courage in which it is treated throughout. On

σαρες, καὶ [l] ἀπὸ τῆς μετοικεσίας Βαβυλῶνος [l] ἕως τοῦ
χριστοῦ γενεαὶ δεκατέσσαρες.
18 Τοῦ δὲ Ἰησοῦ χριστοῦ ἡ [n] γένεσις οὕτως ἦν.
[o] μνηστευθείσης [[p] γὰρ] τῆς μητρὸς αὐτοῦ Μαρίας τῷ
Ἰωσήφ, [q] πρὶν ἢ [r] συνελθεῖν αὐτοὺς [s] εὑρέθη [t] ἐν [t] γαστρὶ

n ver. 1 reff. o Luke i. 27. ii. 5 only. Deut. xx. 7. xxii. 23. p see Acts xxiv. 5. 2 Cor. xi. 5. 2 Tim. ii. 7. q Mark xiv. 30. Acts ii. 20. Gen. xxix. 26. Exod. i. 19. Isa. vii. 15, 16. r = here only (see 1 Cor. vii. 5 v. r. & note). s = Luke xvii. 18. 1 Cor. iv. 2. Dan. v. 27 Theod. t ver. 23, from Isa. vii. 14 Aℵ. ch. xxiv. 19 ‖. Luke xxi. 23. 1 Thess. v. 3. Rev. xii. 2. Exod. xxi. 22. γ., = as above, Luke i. 31 (Tit. i. 12) only. 2 Kings xi. 5.

18. χρ. bef ιησ. B, *Chr autem Jesu* Orig-int(in Luc. Hom. 28, vol. iii. p. 965): om ιησ. D-lat latt syr-cu Petr $Iren_3$(. . *potuerat dicere Matth. "Jesu vero" &c sed . . ait "Christi autem" &c* Iren-int: but in Iren-gr(iii. 11. 8, p. 191, omitted in Grabe) for "*Christi autem*" we read του δε ιησ. χρ.) [Ps Ath] Thl-ms Aug Chrysol Vig Op: txt CLPZΔℵ rel syrr coptt æth arm Orig-gr(ubi supra) Eus [Did Epiph]. rec γεννησις (*prob corrn from verb so often used above*), with L rel: txt BCPSZΔℵ 1 syr Ath Eus $Dial\text{-}trin_{expr}$. (In schol ascribed to Orig and annexed to some mss, it is noticed that γενεσις and γεννησις differ in meaning and that ἀμφότερα ληπτὰ ἐν δσιότητι εἰς χριστόν.) om γαρ (*perhaps as difficult and superfluous*) BC^1Zℵ 1 latt syrr coptt arm Did Epiph Dial-trin [Chr-6-mss] Iren-int Aug: ins C^2LP rel D-lat Eus.

the comparison of this genealogy with that given in Luke, see notes, Luke iii. 23—38. **17. γενεαὶ δεκατέσσαρες**] If we carefully observe Matthew's arrangement, we shall have no difficulty in completing the three tesseradecades. For the first is from Abraham to David, of course inclusive. The second from David (again inclusive) to the *migration;* which gives no name, as before, to be included in both the second and third periods, but which is mentioned simultaneously with the begetting of Jechonias, leaving him for the third period. This last, then, takes in from Jechonias to Jesus Christ inclusive. So that the three stand thus, according to the words of this verse: (1) ἀπὸ Ἀβραὰμ ἕως Δαυίδ. (2) ἀπὸ Δαυὶδ ἕως τ. μετ. Βαβ., i.e. about the time when Josiah begat Jechonias. (3) ἀπὸ τ. μετ. Βαβ. (i.e. from Jechonias) ἕως τοῦ χριστοῦ. We may safely say, that the **πᾶσαι** *does not*, as Meyer, imply that Matthew intended to give the genealogy complete, and was not aware of the omissions. For why should this be so? May it not just as well be said, that having, for the convenience of his readers, reduced the genealogy to this form, he then says to them, "So then you have from Abraham to David, 14 generations, &c.?"

18—25. Circumstances of his Birth.

18. τοῦ δὲ Ἰησοῦ χριστοῦ] The combined name is emphatically put first as resuming the subject of ver. 1, and the **δέ** takes up the δέ which has connected all the previous members of the series, introducing a reason for this inversion ἐξ ἧς ἐγεννήθη, with which this last one had been brought in, ver. 16. **γένεσις**] The ordinary reading γέννησις seems to have been taken up from ver. 16, and the γάρ, which follows, appended to account for the exception in this last case to the direct sequence of ἐγέννησεν throughout the genealogy. **γένεσις** must be understood in a wide sense, as nearly identical in meaning with γέννησις; as "= '*origo*,' not merely '*birth*,'" Mey. It probably is chosen by the Holy Spirit to mark a slight distinction between the γέννησις of our Lord and that of ordinary men. See schol. in digest. **μνηστευθείσης**] The interval between betrothal and the consummation of marriage was sometimes considerable, during which the betrothed remained in her father's house, till the bridegroom came and fetched her. See Deut. xx. 7. **[γάρ]** here is explicative; '*quum videlicet . . .*' So Soph. Trach. 475, πᾶν σοι φράσω τἀληθὲς οὐδὲ κρύψομαι. ἔστιν γὰρ οὕτως ὥσπερ οὗτος ἐννέπει. Lysias, Eratosth. § 19, εἰς τοσαύτην . . . . αἰσχροκέρδειαν ἀφίκοντο, τῆς γὰρ πολεμάρχου γυναικὸς κ.τ.λ. See more examples in Hartung, Partikellehre, i. 469. We may perhaps with equal likelihood say that it is apologetic for the οὕτως: 'thus it took place; and an account of it is needed, *for* &c.' **πρὶν ἤ** is said to belong to the middle age of Attic. With an aor. following, it betokens the entire completion of the act indicated. See it treated in Hermann on Viger, p. 442; Klotz on Devarius, p. 726. **συνελθεῖν**] Here to be understood of living together in one house as man and wife; the deductio in domum mariti: see especially Kypke, Observationes Sacræ, p. 1 ff., who remarks well, that it answers to the word παραλαβεῖν, vv. 20, 24. Chrys. Hom. iv. 2, vol. vii. p. 49, opposes this view: οὐκ εἶπε πρὶν ἢ

u = ver. 20. John i. 13. Rom. ix. 10.
v ch. iii. 11 ‖ al. fr. Ps. l. 11. Isa. lxiii. 10, 11.
w = Mark vi. 20. Luke xx. 20. Job i. 1.

[t] ἔχουσα [u] ἐκ [v] πνεύματος [v] ἁγίου. 19 Ἰωσὴφ δὲ ὁ ἀνὴρ BCEKL MPSUV ZΓΔΠℵ 1. 33
αὐτῆς, [w] δίκαιος ὤν, καὶ μὴ θέλων αὐτὴν [x] * δειγματίσαι,
[y] ἐβουλήθη [z] λάθρα [a] ἀπολῦσαι αὐτήν. 20 ταῦτα δὲ αὐτοῦ
[b] ἐνθυμηθέντος ἰδοὺ [c] ἄγγελος κυρίου κατ' [d] ὄναρ ἐφάνη

x Col. ii. 15 only †. παραδ , Heb. vi. 6 only. Num. xxv. 4. Ezek. xxviii. 17. Polyb. xv. 32. 5 and al5. y 1 aor. pass., James i 18. iv. 4. 2 John 12 only. Exod. x. 27. z ch. ii. 7. John xi. 28. Acts xvi. 37 only. 1 Kings xviii. 22. a = ch. v. 31, 32 al.‡ Esdr. ix. 36. b ch. ix. 4 only. Josh. vi. 18. c ch. ii. 13, 19. xxviii. 2. Luke i. 11, 13. ii. 9 al. Exod. iii. 2 al. d ch. ii. 12, 13, 19, 22. ch. xxvii. 19 only †. see Gen. xx. 6.

19. * rec παραδειγματίσαι, with CLPℵ[1.3] rel syr-mg-gr: *traducere* latt: *præpalare* D-lat: *divulgare* lat-*k* Aug: *detegere* Vig: *lege in eam decerni* Hil: txt BZℵ[2] 1 Eus. (Eusebius' words are as follows: Εὖ γοῦν μοι εἰρῆσθαι δοκεῖ ὑπὸ τοῦ εὐαγγελιστοῦ καὶ τὸ μὴ θέλειν αὐτὴν δειγματίσαι· οὐ γὰρ ἔφησεν μὴ θέλειν αὐτὴν παραδειγματίσαι, ἀλλά, μὴ δειγματίσαι θέλων, πολλῆς οὔσης ἐν τούτοις διαφορᾶς· . . . . τὸ μὲν γὰρ παραδειγματίσαι τὴν ἐπὶ κακῷ πράξαντι πάντας φανέρωσίν τε καὶ διαβολὴν ὑποβάλλει νοεῖν· ὁ τοίνυν Ἰωσὴφ δίκαιος ὢν καὶ μὴ θέλων αὐτὴν δειγματίσαι τουτέστιν εἰς φανερὸν τοῖς πᾶσιν ἀγαγεῖν ἐβουλήθη λάθρα ἀπολῦσαι αὐτήν. These words taken from Eus. ad Steph. have been preserved in a scholium blunderingly given in Cramer's Catena: the above is plainly the true reading. The corresponding passage of the Latin translation will be found ed. Migne, vol. iv. p. 884.)

ἀχθῆναι αὐτὴν εἰς τὴν οἰκίαν τοῦ νυμφίου, καὶ γὰρ ἔνδον ἦν. ἔθος γὰρ τοῖς παλαιοῖς ὡς τὰ πολλὰ ἐν οἰκίᾳ τὰς μεμνηστευμένας ἔχειν, κ.τ.λ. But it seems most agreeable to the context. His following remark is doubtless a just one: καὶ τίνος ἕνεκεν οὐ πρὸ τῆς μνηστείας ἐκύησεν; ἵνα . . . συσκιασθῇ τὸ γινόμενον τέως, καὶ ἵνα πᾶσαν πονηρὰν διαφύγῃ ἡ παρθένος ὑπόνοιαν.

εὑρέθη] not merely for ἦν, as some have said, but in its proper meaning:—**she was discovered to be**, no matter by whom: ἐπὶ τῶν παραδόξων, καὶ παρ' ἐλπίδα πᾶσαν ἐκβαινόντων, καὶ οὐ προσδοκωμένων λέγεσθαι εἴωθε, Chrys. The words ἐκ πν. ἁγ. are the addition of the Evangelist declaring the matter of fact, and do not belong to the discovery.

ἐκ πν. ἁγ.] **by** (the agency of) **the Holy Ghost**. See reff. and those to ver. 20: and compare by all means Chrys.'s remarks, Hom. iv. 3, p. 50 f. The interpretation of πν. ἁγ. in this place must thus be sought: (1) Unquestionably **τὸ πν. τὸ ἅγ.** is used in the N. T. as signifying *the Holy Ghost*. Luke iii. 22: Acts i. 16: Eph. iv. 30. (2) But it is a well-known usage to omit the articles from such words under certain circumstances, e. g. when a preposition precedes, as εἰς λιμένα (Plato, Theæt. § 1), &c. We are therefore justified in interpreting ἐκ πν. ἁγ. according to this usage, and understanding τὸ πν. τὸ ἅγ. as the agent referred to. And (3) even independently of the above usage,—when a word or an expression came to bear a technical conventional meaning, it was also common to use it without the art. as if it were a proper name: e. g. θεός, νόμος, υἱὸς θεοῦ, &c.

19. ἀνήρ] so called, though they were as yet but betrothed: so in Gen. xxix. 21: Deut. xxii. 24. **δίκαιος**] **just**; καὶ μὴ θ. being, as the **μή** plainly shews, not the explanation of δίκαιος, but an additional particular. He was a strict observer of the law,—and (yet) not willing to expose her. The sense of '*kind*,' '*merciful*,' is inadmissible.

λάθρα] Not '*without any writing of divorcement*,' which would have been unlawful; but according to the form prescribed in Deut. xxiv. 1. The husband might either do this, or adopt the stronger course of bringing his wife (or betrothed, who had the same rights, Maimon. in Wetstein, and Philo de legg. spec. ad cap. 6 et 7 decal. § 12, vol. ii. p. 311, αἱ ὁμολογίαι γάμοις ἰσοδυναμοῦσι) to justice openly. The punishment in this case would have been death by stoning. Deut. xxii. 23. Maimonides (quoted by Buxtorf de divort.) says, "Femina ex quo desponsata est, licet nondum a viro cognita, est uxor viri, et si sponsus eam velit repudiare, oportet, ut id faciat libello repudii."

ἐβουλήθη] **intended,—was minded**: θέλω expresses the *mere wish*, βούλομαι the wish ripened into *intention*: see 1 Tim. v. 14, note, and Buttmann's Lexilogus, i. p. 26.

20.] **ἰδού** answers to the Hebrew הִנֵּה, and is frequently used by Matt. and Luke to introduce a new event or change of scene: not so often by Mark, and never with this view in John.

ἄγγελος κ.] The announcement was made to Mary openly, but to Joseph in a dream; for in Mary's case faith and concurrence of will were necessary,—the communication was of a higher kind,—and referred

D παρα-λαβειν... ...δε υιον P. BCDEK LMSUV ZΓΔΠℵ 1. 33

αὐτῷ λέγων Ἰωσὴφ υἱὸς Δαυείδ, μὴ φοβηθῇς [e] παραλαβεῖν
Μαριὰμ τὴν [f] γυναῖκά σου· τὸ γὰρ ἐν αὐτῇ γεννηθὲν
[g] ἐκ πνεύματός ἐστιν ἁγίου. 21 [h] τέξεται δὲ υἱόν, καὶ
[i] καλέσεις τὸ [i] ὄνομα αὐτοῦ Ἰησοῦν· αὐτὸς γὰρ [j] σώσει
τὸν λαὸν αὐτοῦ ἀπὸ τῶν ἁμαρτιῶν αὐτῶν. 22 τοῦτο δὲ

e = ver. 24 only. Cant. viii. 2.
f = Rev. xix. 7. xxi. 9. Deut. xxii. 24.
g = ver. 18. Acts v. 39. Rom. ii. 29.
h vv. 23 (from Isa. vii. 14), 25. ch. ii. 2. Luke i. 31, 57. ii. 6, 7, 11 al. Gen. xvii. 19. xli. 50.
i Luke i. 13, 31. ii. 21. Gen. as above (i). 1 Kings i. 20.
j = (but w. ἐκ) Ezek. xxxvi. 29.

20. μαριαν BL **1** coptt Eus Chr-β Cyr. αγιου bef εστιν DL [ev-y] latt Orig Iren-int$_2$: txt BCPZℵ rel Eus$_2$.
21. om 1st αυτου ℵ[1](? ins ℵ-corr[1]).

to a thing future; but here it is simply an advertisement for caution's sake of an event which had already happened, and is altogether a communication of an inferior order: see Gen. xx. 3. But see on the other hand the remarks at the close of the notes on ver. 21. **κατ' ὄναρ**] ὄναρ, simply, is the classical equivalent,—κατ' ὄναρ belonging to later writers, Strabo, Plutarch, &c. οὐ χρὴ κατ' ὄναρ λέγειν, ὥσπερ οὐδὲ καθ' ὕπαρ, ἀλλὰ ὄναρ καὶ ὕπαρ οἷον· ὄναρ εἶδον τὸν δεῖνα, Thom. Mag. See Lobeck on Phrynichus, p. 423. **υἱὸς Δαυείδ**] These words would recall Joseph's mind to the promised seed, the expectation of the families of the lineage of David, and at once stamp the message as the announcement of the birth of the Messiah. May it not likewise be said, that this appellation would come with more force, if Mary also were a *daughter* of David? The nom. for the vocative is frequent in the Gospels: generally with an article. See Luke viii. 54: ch. xi. 26, al., and particularly John xx. 28. **τὴν γυν. σου**] Not '*as thy wife*:' but in apposition with Μαριάμ, **Mary thy wife**: see ver. 24, which decides this, as Meyer, ed. 3, now acknowledges. The addition serves to remind Joseph of that relation which she already held by betrothal, and which he was now exhorted to recognize. See above on ver. 19. **τὸ γὰρ ἐν αὐ. γ.**] ἐν is here not instrumental, '*that which is conceived by her*,' but local, **that which is begotten in her.** The gender here is not to be pressed as involving any doctrinal consequence, but to be regarded as the usual way of speaking of the unborn fœtus: we have υἱόν first after τέξεται, ver. 21. See also John iii. 6: 1 John v. 4. **21. Ἰησοῦν**] The same name as Joshua, the former deliverer of Israel. It is written יְהוֹשֻׁעַ in the Law and Prophets, but יֵשׁוּעַ in the Hagiographa. Philo says, Ἰησοῦς ἑρμηνεύεται, σωτηρία κυρίου. De mut. nom. § 21, vol. i. p. 597. **αὐτός**] He, emphatically: **He alone**: best rendered, perhaps, '*it is He that*.' **τὸν λαὸν αὐτοῦ**] (not αὑτοῦ, any where, except when a special emphasis is intended: and there is none here, no distinction between *His* people, and the people of *any other*, being made). In the primary sense, *the Jews*, of whom alone Joseph could have understood the words: but in the larger sense, all who believe on Him: an explanation which the tenor of prophecy (cf. Gen. xxii. 18: Deut. xxxii. 21), and the subsequent admission of the Gentiles, warrant. Cf. a similar use of '**Israel**' by St. Peter, Acts v. 31. **ἀπὸ τῶν ἁμαρτιῶν**] It is remarkable that in this early part of the evangelic history, in the midst of pedigrees, and the disturbances of thrones by the supposed temporal King of the Jews, we have so clear an indication of the ***spiritual nature of the office of Christ.*** One circumstance of this kind outweighs a thousand cavils against the historical reality of the narration. If I mistake not, this announcement reaches further into the deliverance to be wrought by Jesus, than any thing mentioned by the Evangelist subsequently. It thus bears the internal impress of a message from God, treasured up and related in its original formal terms. Meyer understands the words of a political emancipation and prosperity of the Jewish people, and strangely enough refers to Luke i. 68 for confirmation of this idea; adding, however, that a religious and moral reformation was considered as intimately connected with such a change. **ἁμαρτία** is not put for the *punishment of sin*, but is the sin itself—**the practice of sin**, in its most pregnant sense. 'How suggestive it is,' remarks Bishop Ellicott, 'that while to the loftier spirit of Mary the name of Jesus is revealed with all the prophetic associations of more than David's glories—to Joseph, perchance the aged Joseph, who might have long seen and realized his own spiritual needs, and the needs of those around him, it is specially said, Thou shalt call his name Jesus: *for He shall save his people*

k see Mark iv. 22. Rom. xi. 11, 32. l = Gospp. passim. James ii. 23. 2 Chron. xxxvi. 21, 22. m ch. ii. 15 (17. iii. 3 v. r.). xxii. 31 only. n as above (m). ch. ii. 23 al. Mt. only. o Isa. vii. 14 (καλέσεις). p ver. 18 reff. q ver. 21 reff.

ὅλον γέγονεν [k] ἵνα [l] πληρωθῇ τὸ [mn] ῥηθὲν [m] ὑπὸ κυρίου
[n] διὰ τοῦ προφήτου λέγοντος 23 [o] Ἰδοὺ ἡ παρθένος [p] ἐν
[p] γαστρὶ [p] ἕξει καὶ [q] τέξεται [q] υἱόν, καὶ [q] καλέσουσιν τὸ
[q] ὄνομα αὐτοῦ Ἐμμανουήλ· ὅ ἐστιν [r] μεθερμηνευόμενον
Μεθ' ἡμῶν ὁ θεός. 24 ἐγερθεὶς δὲ ὁ Ἰωσὴφ ἀπὸ τοῦ
ὕπνου ἐποίησεν ὡς [s] προσέταξεν αὐτῷ ὁ ἄγγελος κυρίου,
καὶ [t] παρέλαβεν τὴν γυναῖκα αὐτοῦ. 25 καὶ οὐκ [u] ἐγί-

BCDEK LMSUV ZΓΔΠℵ 1. 33

r Mt., here only. Mark v. 41 al.† Prol. Sir. s ch. viii. 4 ||. (xxi. 6 v. r.) Acts x. 33, 48. xvii. 26 only. Gen. l. 2. t = ver. 20 only. Xen. Œc. vii 5. διελθούσης . . ἑπταετίας τ. Ῥαχήλαν παρέλαβεν, Jos. Antt. i. 19. 6. u = Luke i. 34 only. Gen. iv. 1, 25 al.

22. rec ins του bef κυριου, with L rel (Syr coptt?) Eus: om BCDZΔℵ 1. 33. aft δια ins ησαιου D: aft προφ. ℵ²-marg lat-*a b c f g*$_1$ syr-cu-jer syr arm Iren-int$_1$. (Similar insns are made by ℵ² lat-*a* and syr-mg in ch. ii. 5.)

23. καλεσεις (*as* LXX) D [ev-y] Eus$_1$ Epiph Vig: *vocabit* lat *f*¹ D-lat¹: *vocabitis* Cypr: *vocabitur* syr-cu Iren-int Orig-int. om αυτου ℵ¹(ins ℵ-corr¹). ενμανουηλ D.

24. rec διεγερθεις, with C³DL·rel, *exsurgens* latt: txt BC¹Zℵ 1 Epiph. om ο (bef ιωσ.) KZ[Γ]Δ[Π]ℵ Scr's k p w. aft παρελαβεν ins μαριαμ ℵ³ᵃ(but afterwards erased) [coptt Chr-5-mss(-αν)]. εαυτου Zℵ².

from their sins.' Historical Lectures on the Life of our Lord, p. 56. **22. τοῦτο δὲ ὅλον**] It is impossible to interpret ἵνα in any other sense than **in order that**. The words τοῦτο δὲ ὅ. γέγ. and the uniform usage of the N. T., in which ἵνα is never used except in this sense, forbid any other. Nor, if rightly viewed, does the passage require any other. Whatever may have been the partial fulfilment of the prophecy in the time of Ahaz, its reference to a different time, and a higher deliverance, is undeniable: and then, whatever causes contributed to bring about τοῦτο ὅλον, might be all summed up in the fulfilment of the divine purpose, of which that prophecy was the declaration. The accomplishment of a promise formally made is often alleged as the cause of an action extending wider than the promise, and purposed long before its utterance. And of course these remarks apply to every passage where ἵνα or ὅπως πληρωθῇ are used. Such a construction can have but one meaning. If such meaning involve us in difficulty regarding the prophecy itself, far better leave such difficulty, in so doubtful a matter as the interpretation of prophecy, unsolved, than create one in so simple a matter as the rendering of a phrase whose meaning no indifferent person could doubt. **πληρωθῇ**] The immediate and literal fulfilment of the prophecy seems to be related in Isa. viii. 1—4. Yet there the child was *not* called Emmanuel: but in ver. 8 that name is used as applying to one of far greater dignity. Again, Isa. ix. 6 seems to be a reference to this prophecy, as also Micah v. 3. **23. ἡ παρθένος**] Such is the rendering of the LXX. The Hebrew word is the more general term הָעַלְמָה, and is translated by Aquil., Symm., and Theodot. ἡ νεᾶνις. De Wette cites the LXX rendering as a proof that the prophecy was then understood of the Messiah. But is it not much more probable that Aquila and the others rendered it νεᾶνις to *avoid* this application? Can it be shewn that the birth of the Messiah from a παρθένος *was matter of previous expectation*? Certainly Pearson (on the Creed, art. iii.) fails to substantiate this. **καλέσουσιν**] This indefinite plural is surely not without meaning here. **Men shall call**—i. e. it shall be a name by which He shall be called—one of his appellations. The change of person from καλέσεις, which could not well have been cited here, seems to shew, both that the prophecy had a literal fulfilment at the time, and that it is here quoted in a form suited to its greater and final fulfilment. The Hebrew has קָרָאת, '*thou shalt call*' (fem.). **Ἐμμανουήλ**] = עִמָּנוּ אֵל, **God (is) with us.** In Isaiah, prophetic primarily of deliverance from the then impending war; but also of final and glorious deliverance by the manifestation of God in the flesh. **ὅ ἐστιν μεθ.**] This addition is by some used to shew that Matthew wrote his Gospel in Greek, not in Hebrew, in which it would not be likely to occur. On the other hand, it is said, it might have been inserted by the person who translated the Gospel into Greek. See Prolegomena, and John iv. 25. **24.**] **ἀπὸ τοῦ ὕπνου**, *from his sleep*—the

νωσκεν αὐτὴν [v] ἕως οὗ [q] ἔτεκεν * υἱόν *, καὶ [q] ἐκάλεσεν τὸ
[q] ὄνομα αὐτοῦ Ἰησοῦν.

II. 1 Τοῦ δὲ Ἰησοῦ γεννηθέντος ἐν Βηθλεὲμ τῆς Ἰουδαίας ἐν [w] ἡμέραις Ἡρώδου τοῦ βασιλέως, ἰδοὺ [x] μάγοι

v ch. xiii. 33. Gen. viii. 7. Ps. cxi. 8.
w Luke i. 5. iv. 25. xvii. 26, 28. Esth. i. 1.
x vv. 7, 16 bis. Acts xiii. 6, 8 only. Dan. ii. 2 (10 LXX. elsw. Theod. i. 20 al.) only.

25. *εγνω cognovit* D lat-*b c f ff*$_1$ *g*$_{1.2}$ Syr Hil. (lat-*a* def.) om *οὗ* B[1]. * rec ins τὸν bef *υιον* and adds αὐτῆς τὸν πρωτότοκον (*from Luke* ii. 7 ?), with CD[1] rel vulg lat-*f ff*$_1$ syrr æth arm: *filium suum unigenitum* lat-*g*$_2$: *τον υιον* copt: *τον υιον αυτης* sah: *τον υιον τον πρωτοτοκον* D-corr(and lat) L: om BZℵ 1. 33 lat-*a* (appy) *b c g*$_1$ *k* syr-cu Ambr$_2$ Hil Jer Greg.

Chap. II. 1. *ηρωδους* D. om 2nd *του* ℵ[2](ins ℵ[1·3]).

sleep which was on him when he had the dream. 25.] "'*non cognovit eam, donec.*' Non sequitur, ergo *post*: sufficit tamen confirmari virginitatem ad partum usque: de reliquo tempore lectori æquo relinquitur existimatio." Bengel. And with regard to the much-controverted sense of this verse we may observe, (1) That the primâ facie impression on the reader certainly is, that *οὐκ ἐγίνωσκεν* was confined to the period of time here mentioned. (2) That there is nothing in Scripture tending to remove this impression, either (*a*) by narration,—and the very use of the term, *ἀδελφοὶ κυρίου* (on which see note at ch. xiii. 55), without qualification, shews that the idea was not repulsive: or (*β*) by implication,—for every where in the N. T. marriage is spoken of in high and honourable terms; and the words of the angel to Joseph rather imply, than discountenance, such a supposition. (3) On the other hand, the words of this verse do not *require* it: the idiom being justified on the contrary hypothesis. See reff. On the whole it seems to me, that *no one would ever have thought of interpreting the verse any otherwise than in its primâ facie meaning, except to force it into accordance with a preconceived notion of the perpetual virginity of Mary.* It is characteristic, and historically instructive, that the great impugner of the view given above should be Jerome, the impugner of marriage itself: and that his opponents in its interpretation should have been branded as heretics by after-ages. See a brief notice of the controversy in Milman, Hist. of Latin Christianity, i. 72 ff. As to the *expression*, compare the remarkable parallel, Diog. Laert. iii. 1. 2, where he says of the father of Plato, *καθαρὰν γάμου φυλάξαι, ἕως τῆς ἀποκυήσεως*, with ib. 4 (said of Plato) *ἔσχε δ' ἀδελφοὺς Ἀδείμαντον κ. Γλαύκωνα κ. ἀδελφὴν Ποτώνην.*

ἐκάλεσεν] i. e. Joseph; see ver. 21.

Chap. II. 1—12.] Visit and Adoration of Magi from the East. 1. **Βηθ. τῆς Ἰουδ.**] There was another Bethlehem in the tribe of Zebulun, near the sea of Galilee, Josh. xix. 15. The name Bethlehem-Judah is used, Judg. xvii. 7, 8, 9: 1 Sam. xvii. 12. Another name for our Bethlehem was Ephrath, Gen. xxxv. 19; xlviii. 7; or Ephrata, Micah v. 2. It was six Roman miles to the south of Jerusalem, and was known as 'the city of David,' the origin of his family, Ruth i. 1, 19. **ἐν ἡμέραις Ἡρώδου**] Herod the Great, son of Antipater, an Idumean, by an Arabian mother, made king of Judæa on occasion of his having fled to Rome, being driven from his tetrarchy by the pretender Antigonus. (Jos. Antt. xiv. 14. 4.) This title was confirmed to him after the battle of Actium by Octavianus. He sought to strengthen his throne by a series of cruelties and slaughters, putting to death even his wife Mariamne, and his sons Alexander and Aristobulus. His cruelties, and his affectation of Gentile customs, gained for him a hatred among the Jews, which neither his magnificent rebuilding of the temple, nor his liberality in other public works, nor his provident care of the people during a severe famine, could mitigate. He died miserably, five days after he had put to death his son Antipater, in the seventieth year of his age, the thirty-eighth of his reign, and the 750th year of Rome. The events here related took place a short time before his death, but necessarily more than forty days; for he spent the last forty days of his life at Jericho and the baths of Callirrhoe, and therefore would not be found by the magi at Jerusalem. The history of Herod's reign is contained in Josephus, Antt. books xiv.—xvii. **μάγοι ἀπὸ ἀνατολῶν**] Magi from the East; (not *ἀπ. ἀνατ. παρεγ.*) The absence of

y ch. viii. 11 al. Gen. xxv. 6. Num. iii. 38. Job i. 3.
z Luke xi. 6 al. 3 Kings iii. 15.
a ch. i. 21 reff.
c ver. 9.

ἀπὸ [y] ἀνατολῶν [z] παρεγένοντο εἰς Ἱεροσόλυμα 2 λέγοντες
Ποῦ ἐστιν ὁ [a] τεχθεὶς βασιλεὺς τῶν Ἰουδαίων; εἴδομεν
γὰρ αὐτοῦ τὸν [b] ἀστέρα [c] ἐν τῇ ἀνατολῇ, καὶ ἤλθομεν

BCDEK LMSUV ΖΓΔΠℵ 1. 33

b vv. 7, 9, 10. ch. xxiv. 29 ‖ Mk. 1 Cor. xv. 41 3ce. Jude 13. Rev. i. 16 al13. Gen. i. 16.

the art. after *μάγοι* is no objection to this interpretation. In fact it could not have been here expressed, because the *concrete* noun *μάγοι* is not *distributed:* as neither could it in such an expression as ἄνθρωπος ἐν πνεύματι ἀκαθάρτῳ, Mark i. 23. In the case of an anarthrous *abstract* noun, the art. *may follow,* but may also be omitted, cf. χαρὰ ἐν πνεύματι ἁγίῳ, Rom. xiv. 17: the distinction being, that χ. ἡ ἐν πν. ἁγ. would specify, among various kinds of joy, *that one,* which is ἐν πν. ἁγ., whereas χ. ἐν πν. ἁγ. merely asserts the fact that the joy *is* ἐν πν. ἁγ., without suggesting any comparison with other kinds. De W. remarks, that if ἀπὸ ἀνατ. belonged to παρεγ., it would probably *follow* that verb, as ἐξ ὁδοῦ does, ref. Luke. I may add, that παραγίνομαι occurs with a preposition and a substantive twelve times in the N.T., and *in no case are they prefixed.* It would be useless to detail all the conjectures to which this history has given rise. From what has been written on the subject it would appear, (1) That ἀνατολαί may mean either *Arabia, Persia, Chaldæa,* or *Parthia, with the provinces adjacent.* See Judg. vi. 3: Isa. xli. 2; xlvi. 11: Num. xxiii. 7. Philo (leg. ad Caium 34, vol. ii. p. 584) speaks of ἔθνη τὰ ἑῷα καὶ ἡγεμόνες αὐτῶν Παρθυαῖοι. In all these countries there were magi, at least persons who in the wider sense of the word were now known by the name. The words in ver. 2 seem to point to some land not very near Judæa, as also the result of Herod's enquiry as to the date, shewn in ἀπὸ διετοῦς. (2) If we place together (α) the prophecy in Num. xxiv. 17, which could hardly be unknown to the Eastern astrologers,—and (β) the assertion of Suetonius (Vesp. c. 4), 'Percrebuerat Oriente toto *vetus et constans* opinio, esse in fatis, ut eo tempore Judæa profecti rerum potirentur,'—and Tacitus, v. 13, 'Pluribus persuasio inerat, antiquis sacerdotum literis contineri, eo ipso tempore fore ut valesceret Oriens, profectique Judæa rerum potirentur,'—and (γ) the prophecy, also likely to be known in the East, of the seventy weeks in Daniel, ix. 24;—we can, I think, be at no loss to understand how any remarkable celestial appearance at this time should have been interpreted as it was. (3) There is no ground for supposing the magi to have been *three* in number (as first, apparently, by Leo the Great, A.D. 450; "tribus igitur magis in regione Orientis stella novæ claritatis apparuit," Serm. xxxi. 1, vol. i. p. 112), or to have been *kings.* The *first* tradition appears to have arisen from the number of their gifts: the *second,* from the prophecy in Isa. lx. 3. (Tertullian seems to deduce it from the similar prophecy in Ps. lxxii. 10. "Reges Arabum et Saba munera afferent illi: nam et magos reges fere habuit Oriens." Adv. Jud. 9, vol. i. p. 619: adv. Marc. iii. 13, p. 339.) **2. αὐτοῦ τὸν ἀστέρα**] (Much has been said and written on the following note in no friendly spirit; but, for the most part, in entire misunderstanding of its drift and character. It seems to me that the preliminary question for us is, Have we here in the sacred text a miracle, or have we some natural appearance which God in His Providence used as a means of indicating to the magi the birth of His Son? Different minds may feel differently as to the answer to this question: but I submit that it is not for any man to charge another, who is as firm a believer in the facts related in the sacred text as he himself can be, with weakening that belief, because he feels an honest conviction that it is here relating, not a miracle but a natural appearance. It is, of course, the far *safer* way, as far as reputation is concerned, to introduce miraculous agency wherever possible: but the present Editor aims at truth, not popularity.) This expression of the magi, **we have seen his star,** *does not seem to point to any miraculous appearance,* but to something observed in the course of their watching the heavens. *We know the magi to have been devoted to astrology:* and on comparing the language of our text with this undoubted fact, I confess that it appears to me the most ingenuous way, fairly to take account of that fact in our exegesis, and *not to shelter ourselves from an apparent difficulty by the convenient but forced hypothesis of a miracle.* Wherever supernatural agency is asserted, or may be reasonably inferred, I shall ever be found foremost to insist on its recognition, and impugn every device of rationalism or semi-rationalism; but it does not therefore follow that I should consent to attempts, however

[d] προςκυνῆσαι αὐτῷ. 3 ἀκούσας δὲ ὁ βασιλεὺς Ἡρώ-

d w. dat., vv. 8, 11 al. fr. Mt. Mk. John iv. 21, 23. ix. 38. Acts vii. 43. 1 Cor. xiv. 25. Heb. i. 6, from Deut. xxxii. 43. Rev. iv. 10 al. Gen. xxiii. 7. 2 Kings xii. 20. Ps. xxviii. 2. see ch. iv. 10 reff.

3. rec ηρωδης bef ο βασιλευς (*to conform to ver* 1), with CL rel vulg lat-*a f ff*$_1$

well meant, *to introduce miraculous interference where it does not appear to be borne out by the narrative.* The principle on which this commentary is conducted, is that of *honestly endeavouring to ascertain the sense of the sacred text, without regard to any preconceived systems, and fearless of any possible consequences.* And if the scientific or historical researches of others seem to contribute to this, my readers will find them, as far as they have fallen within my observation, made use of for that purpose. Now we learn from astronomical calculations, that a remarkable conjunction of the planets of our system took place a short time before the birth of our Lord. (I may premise, that the whole of the statements in this note have been remarkably confirmed, except in the detail now corrected, "that an ordinary eye would regard them (the planets) as one star of surpassing brightness," by the Rev. C. Pritchard, in a paper read by him before the Royal Astronomical Society, containing his calculations of the times and nearnesses of the conjunctions, as verified by the Astronomer Royal at Greenwich. The exact days and hours have been inserted below from Mr. Pritchard's paper.) In the year of Rome 747, on the 20th of May (29th, Pritchard), there was a conjunction of Jupiter and Saturn in the 20th degree of the constellation Pisces, close to the first point of Aries, which was the part of the heavens noted in astrological science as that in which the signs denoted the greatest and most noble events. On the 27th of October (29th Sept., Pritchard), in the same year, another conjunction of the same planets took place, in the 16th degree of Pisces: and on the 12th of November (5th Dec., Pritchard), a third, in the 15th degree of the same sign. (Ideler, Handbuch der Chronologie, ii. 329, sqq., also Winer, Realwörterbuch, under 'Stern der Weisen,' which see.) Supposing the magi to have seen the *first* of these conjunctions, they saw it actually **in the East**; for on the 29th of May *it would rise* 3½ hours before sunrise (Pritchard). If they then took their journey, and arrived at Jerusalem in a little more than *five months* (the journey from Babylon took Ezra *four* months, see Ezra vii. 9), if they performed the route from Jerusalem to Bethlehem in the evening, as is implied, the *December conjunction,* in 15° of Pisces, would be before them *in the direction of Bethlehem.* ("1½ hour east of the meridian at sunset." Pritchard.) These circumstances would seem to form a remarkable coincidence with the history in our text. They are in no way inconsistent with the word ἀστέρα, which cannot surely (see below) be pressed to its mere literal sense of one single star, but understood in its wider astrological meaning: nor is this explanation of *the star directing them to Bethlehem* at all repugnant to the plain words of vv. 9, 10, importing its motion from S.E. towards S.W., the direction of Bethlehem. We may further observe, that *no part of the text respecting the star, asserts, or even implies, a miracle;* and that the very slight apparent inconsistencies with the above explanation are no more than the *report of the magi* themselves, and the *general belief of the age* would render unavoidable. If this *subservience of the superstitions of astrology to the Divine purposes* be objected to, we may answer with Wetstein, 'Superest igitur ut illos ex regulis artis suæ hoc habuisse existimemus: quæ licet certissime futilis, vana, atque fallax esset, casu tamen aliquando in verum incidere potuit. Admirabilis hinc elucet sapientia Dei, qui hominum erroribus et sceleribus usus Josephum per scelus fratrum in Ægyptum deduxit, regem Babelis per haruspicia et sortes Judæis immisit, (Ezech. xxi. 21, 22) et magos hic per astrologiam ad Christum direxit.'

It may be remarked that Abarbanel the Jew, who knew nothing of *this* conjunction, relates it (Maajne haschnah, cited by Münter in Ebrard, Wissensch. Kritik, p. 248) as a tradition, that no conjunction could be of mightier import than that of Jupiter and Saturn, which planets were in conjunction A.M. 2365, before the birth of Moses, in the sign of Pisces; and thence remarks that that sign was the most significant one for *the Jews.* From this consideration he concludes that the conjunction of these planets in that sign, in his own time (A.D. 1463), betokened the near approach of the birth of the Messiah. And as the Jews did not invent astrology, but learnt it from the Chaldæans, this idea, that a conjunction in Pisces betokened some great event in Judæa, must have prevailed among Chaldæan astrologers. (It is fair to notice the influence on the position maintained in

δης [e] ἐταράχθη, καὶ πᾶσα Ἱεροσόλυμα μετ᾽ αὐτοῦ, 4 καὶ
[f] συναγαγὼν πάντας τοὺς ἀρχιερεῖς καὶ [gh] γραμματεῖς τοῦ
[h] λαοῦ [i] ἐπυνθάνετο παρ᾽ αὐτῶν ποῦ ὁ χριστὸς [j] γεννᾶται.
5 οἱ δὲ εἶπον αὐτῷ Ἐν Βηθλεὲμ τῆς Ἰουδαίας. οὕτως
γὰρ [k] γέγραπται διὰ τοῦ προφήτου, 6 [l] Καὶ σὺ Βηθλεὲμ γῆ

BCDEK LMSUV ZΓΔΠℵ 1. 33

e = ch. xiv. 26. John xiv. 1, 27. Esth. iii. 15.
f = ch. xxii. 10 al. 1 Chron. xxiii. 2. Ps. xlix. 5.
g Mt. Mk. L., passim. John, never [exc. viii. 3?]. Acts iv. 5. vi. 12. xxiii. 9. 1 Cor. i. 20 only. Neh. viii. 1, &c.
h here only. 1 Macc. v. 42.
i Mt., here only. w. παρά, John iv. 52 only. Gen. xxv. 22.
j pres., ch. xxvii. 63. 1 Cor. xv. 35. 2 Pet. iii. 11.
k w. διά = Luke xviii. 31 only. see Acts xv. 23. 2 Cor. ii. 4.
l Micah v. 2.

syrr syr-cu sah(Treg) arm : txt BDZℵ 1 lat-*b c k* copt Eus. om πασα D : aft πασα ins η Z Eus.

4. om παρ᾽ αυτων D(*end of a page*) [Γ].

5. ειπαν Bℵ. om αυτω $ℵ^2$(ins $ℵ^{1 \cdot 3}$?).

this note of the fact which Mr. Pritchard seems to have substantiated, that the planets did not, during the year B.C. 7, approach each other so as to be mistaken by any eye for one star: indeed not "within double the apparent diameter of the moon." I submit, that even if this were so, the inference in the note remains as it was. The *conjunction of the two planets,* complete or incomplete, would be that which would bear astrological significance, not their looking like one star. The two bright planets seen in the east, —the two bright planets standing over Bethlehem,—these would on each occasion have arrested the attention of the magi; and this appearance would have been denominated by them ὁ ἀστὴρ αὐτοῦ. To object that it is ἀστήρ, not ἄστρον, is surely mere trifling: the appearance could not be called "ἄστρον, a constellation," as required by Bp. Wordsworth, who suggests the ingenious solution for all the difficulties of the narrative, that "the star, it is probable, was visible to the magi *alone.*") **ἐν τῇ ἀνατ.**] Not '*at its rising,*' in which case we should expect to find αὐτοῦ, if not here, certainly in ver. 9,—but **in the East,** i.e. either in the *Eastern country from which they came,* or in the *Eastern quarter of the heavens,* as above explained. In ver. 9, ἐν τ. ἀνατ. is opposed to ἐπάνω οὗ ἦν τὸ παιδίον.
προσκυνῆσαι] **To do homage to him,** in the Eastern fashion of prostration. 'Necesse est enim, si in conspectum veneris, venerari te Regem, quod illi προσκυνεῖν vocant.' Corn. Nep. Conon, 3. 3. **ἐταράχθη**] Josephus, Antt. xvii. 2. 4, represents these troubles as raised by the Pharisees, who prophesied a revolution. Ἡρώδῃ μὲν καταπαύσεως ἀρχῆς ὑπὸ Θεοῦ ἐψηφισμένης αὐτῷ τε καὶ γένει τῷ ἀπ᾽ αὐτοῦ. Herod, as a foreigner and usurper, feared one who was *born* King of the Jews: the people, worn away by seditions and slaughters, feared fresh tumults and wars. There may also be a trace of the popular notion that the times of the Messiah would be ushered in by great tribulations: so Schöttgen, ii. p. 512, from the book Sohar, "quo tempore Sol redemptionis ipsis illucescet, tribulatio post tribulationem et tenebræ post tenebras venient ipsis: dum vero in his versantur, illucescet ipsis Lux Dei S. B." **πᾶσα Ἱεροσόλυμα**] Here and apparently at ch. iii. 5, used as a feminine singular. Joseph. Bell. Jud. vi. 10. 1, uses ἑάλω Ἱεροσ. . . . . ἁλοῦσα . . . . , but none of these instances are decisive: an ellipsis of ἡ πόλις being possible.
4. **συναγαγών**] i.e. says Lightfoot, he *assembled the Sanhedrim.* For the Sanhedrim consisting of seventy-one members, and comprising Priests, Levites, and Israelites (Maimonides), under the term ἀρχιερεῖς are contained the two first of these, and under γραμ. τ. λαοῦ the third.
ἀρχ. are most likely the High Priest and those of his race,—any who had served the office,—and perhaps also the presidents of the twenty-four courses (1 Chron. xxiv. 6). **γρ.** consisted of the teachers and interpreters of the Divine law, the νομικοί and νομοδιδάσκαλοι of St. Luke. But the πρεσβύτεροι τοῦ λαοῦ are usually mentioned with these two classes as making up the Sanhedrim. See ch. xvi. 21; xxvi. 3, 59. Possibly on this occasion the ἀρχ. and γρ. only were summoned, the question being one of Scripture learning. "**ἀρχιερεῖς,**" says Bp. Wordsworth, "is a word suggestive of the confusion now introduced into the nomination to the office of High Priest, when the true High Priest came from heaven to 'purify the sons of Levi' (Mal. iii. 3)." Instead of one High Priest for life, there were many, made and unmade in rapid succession. As Spanheim says, Dub. Evan. ii. 37, "ἀρχιερωσύνη confusa, Christo exhibito. Summum sacerdotium pessime habitum, Herodis et Romanorum licentia." **γεννᾶται**] The present tense is often used indefinitely

Ἰούδα, [m] οὐδαμῶς [n] ἐλαχίστη εἶ ἐν τοῖς ἡγεμόσιν Ἰούδα.
ἐκ σοῦ γὰρ [o] ἐξελεύσεται [p] ἡγούμενος, ὅστις [q] ποιμανεῖ
τὸν λαόν μου τὸν Ἰσραήλ. 7 τότε Ἡρώδης [r] λάθρα
[s] καλέσας τοὺς [t] μάγους [u] ἠκρίβωσεν παρ' αὐτῶν τὸν χρόνον τοῦ φαινομένου ἀστέρος, 8 καὶ πέμψας αὐτοὺς εἰς
Βηθλεὲμ εἶπεν [v] Πορευθέντες [w] ἐξετάσατε [x] ἀκριβῶς περὶ
τοῦ παιδίου· [y] ἐπὰν δὲ εὕρητε, ἀπαγγείλατέ μοι, ὅπως
κἀγὼ [z] ἐλθὼν [a] προσκυνήσω αὐτῷ. 9 οἱ δὲ ἀκούσαντες
τοῦ βασιλέως ἐπορεύθησαν. καὶ ἰδοὺ ὁ ἀστὴρ ὃν εἶδον ἐν
τῇ ἀνατολῇ [b] προῆγεν αὐτοὺς ἕως [z] ἐλθὼν ἐστάθη ἐπάνω

...τον ισραηλ Z.
BCDEK LMSUV ΓΔΠℵ 1. 33

m here only +. n = ch. v. 19. xxv. 40, 45 al. 4 Kings xviii. 24. o Acts xv. 24. Heb. vii. 5. Gen. xvii. 6. p = Acts vii. 10. Gen. xlix. 10. Dan. ix. 25, 26 Theod. q = Rev. ii. 27 al. 2 Kings v. 2. r ch. i. 19 reff. s = ch. xx. 8. Gen. xli. 8. Judg. iv. 13. t ver. 1 reff. u here and ver. 16 only +. Isa. xlix. 16 Aq. v = 1 Pet. iii. 19. w ch. x. 11. John xxi. 12 only. Deut. xix. 18. Ps. x. 5, 6. x Luke i. 3. Acts xviii. 25, 26. xxiii. 15, 20. xxiv. 22. Eph. v. 15. 1 Thess. v. 2 only. Deut. as above (w). Wisd. xix. 18 only. Dan. vii. 19 Theod. y Luke xi. 22, 34 only. z ver. 23. ch. iv. 13. Eph. ii. 17 al. Gen. xxvii. 35. Prov. xxiii. 35. a ver. 2 reff. b = ch. xiv. 22 al. fr. + Wisd. xix. 11.

6. for *γη ιουδα*, *της ιουδαιας* D lat-*a c f* g_1 Syr. for *ουδαμως*, *μη non* D lat-*a b c f* g_1 Syr syr-cu coptt Tert Cypr Hil, *numquid* tol lat-ff_1. for *εκ σου*, *εξ ου* Cℵ: [*εξ σου* B¹:] *εκ ου* D. om *γαρ* ℵ¹(ins ℵ²). ins *μοι* bef *εξελευσεται* CK[Γ] arm Protev-2-mss Thdrt: om BDZ rel Just Eus. *ποιμενει* (sic) D.
7. *ηκρειβασεν* D(so ver 16).
8. aft *ειπεν* ins *αυτοις* D Syr syr-cu. rec *ακριβως* bef *εξετασατε* (*for emphasis?*), with C³L rel $Orig_2$: *ακρ.* aft *παιδιου* Syr syr-cu: txt BC¹Dℵ 1. 33 latt syr coptt Eus Aug. for *επαν*, *οταν* D. *επαγγ.* D¹(txt D²).
9. *τες* of *ακουσαντες* is added by D³. *προηγον* (but corrd) ℵ¹. rec (for *εσταθη*) *εστη*, with L rel Protev Eus_1: txt BCDℵ 1. 33 Orig Eus_1.

of subjects of prophecy, e. g. *ὁ ἐρχόμενος*, ch. xi. 3: Heb. x. 37; *ἔρχεται*, in an expression exactly parallel to this, John vii. 42. **6. καὶ σύ**] This is a free paraphrase of the prophecy in Micah v. 2. It must be remembered that though the words are the answer of the Sanhedrim to Herod, and not a citation of the prophet by the Evangelist, yet they are adopted by the latter as correct. Lightfoot renders the Hebrew, 'parvum est ut sis inter chiliadas,' and adds, that the Chaldee paraphrast, who may possibly have been present at this very council, renders the words 'intra pauxillum es ut præficiaris.' **γῆ Ἰούδα**] *γῆ* need not be supposed to be put for *πόλις*: the *district* may be intended, as described in ver. 16. **ἡγεμόσιν**] or *χιλιάσιν* (LXX). The tribes were divided into chiliads, and the names of the chiliads inscribed in the public records of their respective cities. In Judg. vi. 15 Gideon says *ἰδοὺ ἡ χιλιάς μου ἠσθένησεν ἐν Μανασσῇ*, on which R. Kimchi (cited by Lightfoot) annotates, "Some understand Alphi to mean 'my father,' as if it were Alluph, whose signification is 'prince or lord.'" And thus, it appears, did the Sanhedrim understand the word (which is the same) in Micah v. 2. The word באלפי, without points, may mean either בְּאַלְפֵי, *ἐν χιλιάσιν*, or בְּאַלֻּפֵי, *ἐν ἡγεμόσιν.* **ἐκ σοῦ γὰρ ἐξ.**] It has been remarked that the singular Latin expression, which occurs both in Tacitus and Suetonius (see the passages above in note on *μάγοι ἀπ. ἀν.*) '*Judæa profecti*,' may have been derived from these words of the LXX. **7. ἠκρίβωσεν**] **ascertained accurately.** **φαινομένου**] lit. **the time** (or, *duration*: perhaps as an element in his calculation of age) **of the star which appeared**: **φ.** being the part. pres., *referred back to the time when they saw the star*. The position of **φ.** between the art. and its subst. forbids such renderings as '*the time when the star appeared*.' **8. πορευθέντες . . . ἐλθών**] The pleonastic use of these words, common as a Hebraism in the N. T. (see reff.), is also idiomatic in English; and it may be remarked, that although not strictly needed in the sentences where they occur, their insertion always gives fulness and accuracy to the meaning. **9.**] On this see note on ver. 2. **ἐπάνω οὗ ἦν** (elliptic for *τόπου οὗ ἦν*) **τὸ π.** may mean, '*over that part of Bethlehem where the young child was*,' which they might have ascertained by enquiry. Or it may even mean, '*over the whole town of Bethlehem*.' If it is to be understood as standing *over the house*, and thus *indicating* to the magi the *position of the object of their search*,

οὗ ἦν τὸ παιδίον. 10 ἰδόντες δὲ τὸν ἀστέρα [c] ἐχάρησαν
[c] χαρὰν μεγάλην [d] σφόδρα· 11 καὶ ἐλθόντες εἰς τὴν οἰκίαν
εἶδον τὸ παιδίον μετὰ Μαρίας τῆς μητρὸς αὐτοῦ, καὶ
[e] πεσόντες [ae] προςεκύνησαν αὐτῷ καὶ [f] ἀνοίξαντες τοὺς
[fg] θησαυροὺς αὐτῶν [h] προςήνεγκαν αὐτῷ [h] δῶρα, [i] χρυσὸν
καὶ [ikl] λίβανον καὶ [lm] σμύρναν. 12 καὶ [n] χρηματισθέντες
κατ᾽ [o] ὄναρ μὴ [p] ἀνακάμψαι πρὸς Ἡρώδην, δι᾽ ἄλλης
ὁδοῦ [q] ἀνεχώρησαν εἰς τὴν χώραν αὐτῶν. 13 [q] ἀναχωρη-

BCDEK LMSUV ΓΔΠℵ 1. 33

c (1 Thess. iii. 9.) see John iii. 29. constr., Mark iv. 42. 1 Tim. i. 18. vi. 12 al. Deut. vii. 23. Judg. xi. 33.
d ch. xvii. 6, 23 al4. Mark xvi. 4. Luke xviii. 23. Acts vi. 7. Rev. xvi. 21 only. Deut. ix. 21.
e = ch. iv. 9 reff. 2 Kings i. 2.
f Deut. xxviii. 12. Jer. xxvii. (l.) 25.
g ch. vi. 19, 20, 21 al5. Mark x. 21. Luke vi 45 al3. (not John.) 2 Cor. iv. 7. Col. ii. 3. Heb. xi. 26 only. Josh. vi. 19.
h ch. v. 23, 24. viii. 4. Heb. v. 1. viii. 3, 4. Gen. xliii. 26. Psa. lxxi. 10.
i Isa. lx. 6.
k Rev. xviii. 13 only.
l Cant. iii. 6.
m John xix. 39 only. Ps. xliv. 8. (-νίζειν, Mark xv. 23.)
n = ver. 22 (w. κατ᾽ ὄναρ). Luke ii. 26. Acts x. 22. Heb. xi. 7. Jer. xxxvii. (xxx.) 2. ἐχρ. αὐτῷ κατὰ τ. ὕπνους ὁ Θ., Jos. Antt. xi. 8. 4.
o ch. i. 20 reff. and note. Mt. only.
p Luke x. 6. Acts xviii. 21. Heb. xi. 15 only. Judg. xi. 39 A. 3 Kings xii. 20.
q Mt., here 3ce. ver. 22 al6. Mark iii. 7. John vi. 15. Acts xxiii. 19. xxvi. 31 only. = Exod. ii. 15. Hosea xii. 12.

for *ου ην το παιδιον*, *του παιδιου* D lat-*b c* g_1.

10. *αστεραν* Cℵ¹(but *ν* erased).

11. rec (for *ειδον*) *ευρον* (*prob from ver* 8), with vulg lat-*b c* ff_1 g_1 Epiph Promiss Vig : txt BCDℵ rel Scr's-25-mss lat-*a f* [*k q*] syrr syr-cu coptt æth arm Orig Eus_2 Chr Thl Iren-int Juv Leo Op. *τον παιδα* D (so vv 13(twice), 14, 20, 21). *θηνσαυρους* Dℵ, simly forj lat-*a b f h k*. *ζμυρναν* D.

12. *εις την εαυτων χωραν* ℵ¹(txt ℵ²) 1.

the whole incident must be regarded as miraculous. But this is not necessarily implied, even if the words of the text be literally understood; and in a matter like astronomy, where popular language is so universally broad, and the Scriptures so generally use popular language, it is surely not the letter, but the spirit of the narrative with which we are concerned.

11. μετὰ Μαρίας] No stress must be laid on the omission of Joseph here. In the parallel account as regarded the shepherds, in Luke ii. 16, he is mentioned. I would rather regard the omission here as indicating a *simple matter of fact*, and contributing to shew the truthfulness of the narrative:—that Joseph *happened not to be present* at the time. If the meaning of *τὴν οἰκίαν* is to be pressed (as in a matter of detail I think it should), it will confirm the idea that Joseph and Mary, probably under the idea that the child was to be brought up at Bethlehem, *dwelt there some time* after the Nativity. Epiphanius supposes that Mary was at this time on a visit to her kindred at Bethlehem (possibly at a passover) as much as two years after our Lord's birth. (Hærr. xx. xxx. 29, li. 8, vol. i. pp. 48, 154, 430.) But if Mary had kindred at Bethlehem, how could she be so ill-provided with lodging, and have (as is implied in Luke ii. 7) sought accommodation at an inn? And the supposition of two years having elapsed, derived probably from the *διετοῦς* of ver. 16, will involve us in considerable difficulty. There seems to be no reason why the magi may not have come within the forty days before the Purification, which itself may have taken place in the interval between their departure and Herod's discovery that they had mocked him. No objection can be raised to this view from the *ἀπὸ διετοῦς* of ver. 16: see note there. The general idea is, that the Purification was *previous* to the visit of the magi. Being persuaded of the historic reality of these narratives of Matt. and Luke, we shall find no difficulty in also believing that, *were we acquainted with all the events as they happened, their reconcilement would be an easy matter*; whereas now the two independent accounts, from not being aware of, seem to exclude one another. This will often be the case in ordinary life; e. g. in the giving of evidence. And nothing can more satisfactorily shew the veracity and independence of the narrators, where their testimony to the main facts, as in the present case, is consentient. (I must caution the reader against the misunderstanding of these last remarks in Bishop Ellicott's Lectures on the Life of our Lord, p. 70, note 4; and indeed of my own views as regards apparently irreconcilable narrative in the Gospels, generally throughout his notes to that work.) **θησαυρούς]** *chests* or *bales*, in which the gifts were carried during their journey. The ancient Fathers were fond of tracing in the gifts symbolical meanings: *ὡς βασιλεῖ*

Z και την… BCDEK LMSUV ZΓΔΠℵ 1. 33

σάντων δὲ αὐτῶν, ἰδοὺ ἄγγελος κυρίου φαίνεται κατ'
[o] ὄναρ τῷ Ἰωσὴφ λέγων Ἐγερθεὶς [r] παράλαβε τὸ παιδίον
καὶ τὴν μητέρα αὐτοῦ, καὶ φεῦγε εἰς Αἴγυπτον, καὶ [s] ἴσθι
ἐκεῖ ἕως ἂν εἴπω σοί· μέλλει γὰρ Ἡρώδης [t] ζητεῖν τὸ
παιδίον [u] τοῦ ἀπολέσαι αὐτό. 14 ὁ δὲ ἐγερθεὶς [r] παρέλαβεν
τὸ παιδίον καὶ τὴν μητέρα αὐτοῦ νυκτὸς καὶ [q] ἀνεχώρησεν
εἰς Αἴγυπτον, 15 καὶ [s] ἦν ἐκεῖ ἕως τῆς [v] τελευτῆς Ἡρώδου·
ἵνα [w] πληρωθῇ τὸ [w] ῥηθὲν [w] ὑπὸ κυρίου [w] διὰ τοῦ προφήτου
λέγοντος [x] Ἐξ Αἰγύπτου ἐκάλεσα τὸν υἱόν μου. 16 τότε

r ch. xvii. 1 al. Gen. xxii. 3.
s = Gen. xxix. 14.
t = Rom. xi. 3, from 3 Kings xix. 10, 14. see John vii. 1, 19, &c.
u constr., ch. iii. 13 reff.
v here only. = Gen. xxvii. 2. Josh. i. 1. Xen. Cyr. viii. 7. 3 fin.
w ch. i. 22 reff.
x Hosea xi. 1.

13. transp *αναχωρ.* and *αυτων* D. for *αυτων*, *τον μαγον* (sic) C³, *των μαγων* Dʳ (Kipl. not Scr.). aft *αυτων* ins *εις την χωραν αυτων* B. *εφανη* B latt sah-ms arm Iren-int lat-ff: txt CDLZΔℵ rel.—*κατ οναρ* bef verb (*cf κατ οναρ εφανη, ch* i. 20) BCK[Π] 33 [Thl]: txt DLℵ rel vulg. *αυτον* D. *σοι* bef *ειπω* D 243.
14. *διεγερθεις* (here and in ver 21) D 33 (= *δε εγερθεις*?).
15. rec ins *του* bef *κυριου* (*as frequently*), with L rel: om BCDZ[Γ]Δ[Π]ℵ 1. 33.

τὸν χρυσόν, ὡς δὲ τεθνηξομένῳ τὴν σμύρναν, ὡς δὲ θεῷ τὸν λιβανωτόν. Origen, ag. Celsus, i. 60, vol. i. p. 375, and similarly Irenæus, iii. 9. 2, p. 184:—χρυσὸν αὐτῷ γεννηθέντι βασιλείας σύμβολον προσεκόμισαν οἱ μάγοι. (Clem. Alex. Pæd. ii. 8 (63), p. 206 P.) We cannot conclude from these gifts that the magi came from *Arabia*,—as they were common to all the East. Strabo says, xvi. p. 1129, Wetst., that the best frankincense comes from the borders of Persia.

13—23.] Flight into Egypt.

13. ἐγερθεὶς παρ.] **Arise and take with thee**; not, '*When thou hast arisen* (*in the morning*), *take*.' The command was immediate; and Joseph made no delay. He must be understood, on account of *νυκτός* below, as having arisen the same night and departed forthwith. The words *ἐγερθεὶς παρέλαβεν* are also used in vv. 20, 21, where *no haste* is necessarily implied. Egypt, as *near*, as *a Roman province and independent of Herod*, and *much inhabited by Jews*, was an easy and convenient refuge. **τοῦ ἀπολ.** is not a Hebraism, but pure Greek, implying *the purpose*. See Soph. Trach. 57, and Hermann's note. Bernhardy, Syntax, p. 357, notices that it is rarely found in earlier Greek writers, but more common as we advance to the middle and later Attic. A few instances occur in Xenophon, more in Demosthenes, and abundance in after-writers. See on the usage, Winer, edn. 6, § 44. 4. b. **15. ἐξ Αἰγύπτου**] This citation shews the almost universal application in the N. T. of the prophetic writings to the expected Messiah, as the general antitype of all the events of the typical dispensation. We shall have occasion to remark the same again and again in the course of the Gospels. It seems to have been a received axiom of interpretation (which has, by its adoption in the N. T., received the sanction of the Holy Spirit Himself, and now stands for our guidance), that the subject of all allusions, the represented in all parables and dark sayings, was He who was to come, or the circumstances attendant on His advent and reign. The words are written in Hosea *of the children of Israel*, and are rendered from the Hebrew. A similar expression with regard to Israel is found in Exod. iv. 22, 23. **ἵνα** must not be explained away; it never denotes the event or mere result, but always the *purpose*. **16.**] Josephus makes no mention of this slaughter; nor is it likely that he would have done. Probably no great number of children perished in so small a place as Bethlehem and its neighbourhood. The modern objections to this narrative may be answered best by remembering the monstrous character of this tyrant, of whom Josephus asserts (Antt. xvii. 6. 5), μέλαινα χολὴ αὐτὸν ᾕρει ἐπὶ πᾶσιν ἐξαγριαίνουσα. Herod had marked the way to his throne, and his reign itself, with blood; had murdered his wife and three sons (the last just about this time); and was likely enough, in blind fury, to have made no enquiries, but given the savage order at once.

Besides, there might have been a reason for not making enquiry, but rather taking the course he did, which was sure, as he thought, to answer the end, without divulging the purpose. The word λάθρα in ver. 7 seems to favour this view. Macrobius (Saturnalia, ii. 4) relates an anecdote of Augustus: 'Cum audisset inter pueros

Ἡρώδης ἰδὼν ὅτι [y] ἐνεπαίχθη ὑπὸ τῶν [z] μάγων, [a] ἐθυμώθη
λίαν, καὶ [b] ἀποστείλας [c] ἀνεῖλεν πάντας τοὺς παῖδας τοὺς
ἐν Βηθλεὲμ καὶ ἐν πᾶσιν τοῖς [d] ὁρίοις αὐτῆς, [e] ἀπὸ [f] διετοῦς καὶ [g] κατωτέρω, κατὰ τὸν χρόνον ὃν [h] ἠκρίβωσεν
παρὰ τῶν [z] μάγων. 17 τότε [i] ἐπληρώθη τὸ [i] ῥηθὲν [i] διὰ
Ἱερεμίου τοῦ προφήτου λέγοντος 18 [k] Φωνὴ ἐν Ῥαμᾶ
ἠκούσθη, [l] κλαυθμὸς καὶ [m] ὀδυρμὸς πολύς, Ῥαχὴλ
[n] κλαίουσα τὰ τέκνα αὐτῆς καὶ οὐκ ἤθελεν [o] παρακληθῆ-
ναι, ὅτι οὐκ [p] εἰσίν. 19 τελευτήσαντος δὲ τοῦ Ἡρώδου,
ἰδοὺ ἄγγελος κυρίου [q] φαίνεται κατ' [q] ὄναρ τῷ Ἰωσὴφ ἐν

BCDEK LMSUV ZΓΔΠℵ 1. 33

y = Luke xiv. 29. of our Lord's sufferings, ch. xx. 19 ‖ and xxvii. 29 &c. ‖ only. Gen. xxxix. 14, 17. Exod. x. 2.
z ver. 1 reff.
a here only. Gen. xxx. 2 al. fr.
b = Mark vi. 17. Gen. xli. 14.
c Mt., here only. Luke xxii. 2. xxiii. 32 and Acts ii. 23 al18. 2 Thess. ii. 8. Heb. x. 9 only. = Exod. xxi. 29 al.
d ch. iv. 13 al. Mt. Mk. only, exc. Acts xiii. 50. Exod. viii. 2. Num. xxxiv. 2, &c.
e = 1 Chron. xxvii. 23. 2 Chron. xxxi. 16.
f here only. 2 Macc. x 3 only. (-τία, Acts xxiv. 27. see also [e] above.)
g here only. (κάτω) 1 Chron. as above (e). (-τερος, Eph. iv. 9.) of time, Diod. Sic. i. 3 (κατωτέρω τῶν Μακεδονικῶν καιρῶν).
h ver. 7 reff.
i = ch. i. 22 reff.
k Jer. xxxviii. (xxxi.) 15.
l ch. xiii. 42, 50 al4. Mt. only, exc. Luke xiii. 28. Acts xx. 37. Gen. xlv. 2.
m 2 Cor. vii. 7 only. Jer. l. c. 2 Macc. xi. 6 only.
n w. acc., here only. Gen. xxxvii. 35. 1 Macc. ix. 20.
o = ch. v. 4. Luke xvi. 25 al. Gen. xxiv. 67.
p = Gen. xxxvii. 30. see Gen. xlii. 13.
q ch. i. 20 (reff.) and note. Mt. only.

16. διετειας D[1](txt D[2]): *bimatu* latt Lucif lat-ff. for κατωτερω, κατω D. om ον Z.

17. aft ρηθεν ins υπο κυριου D. rec (for δια) υπο, with L rel syr-mg-gr: txt BCDZℵ 33 latt Syr syr-txt æth arm Just Chr Jer. ηρεμιου D-gr[: ιηρ. D[2]Π[2]].

18. rec ins θρηνος και bef κλαυθμος (*from* LXX; *if any of the three had been omitted by mistake, it would not have been the first of them but the second or the third: the eye of the copyist passing on from* -ος και *to* -ος και *or from* -ος *to* -ος), with CDL rel syr-cu syr arm: om BZℵ 1 latt Syr syr-jer coptt æth Just Ambr Jer(remarking *nec juxta Heb. nec juxta* LXX) Hil Op. for οδυρμος, βρυγμος Z. ηθελησεν DZ latt Hil: txt BCL[ℵ] rel syr Just Hipp. (lat-*b* def.)

19. rec κατ οναρ bef φαινεται (*see on ver* 13), with CL rel syr: txt BDZℵ 1 sah, *apparuit in somnis* vulg lat-*a c f ff*$_1$, *apparuit angelus domini in somnis* am lat-*b* Syr.

quos in Syria Herodes rex Judæorum intra bimatum jussit interfici, filium quoque ejus occisum, ait, Melius est Herodis porcum esse (τὸν ὗν?) quam filium (τὸν υἱόν?).' But Macrobius wrote in the fifth century, and the words 'intra bimatum' look very like a quotation from our narrative. Besides, the anecdote shews great ignorance of the chronology of Herod's reign. Antipater, the last put to death of his sons, was of full age at his execution. See Ellicott's note, Lectures, p. 78. **ἐνεπαίχθη**] 'Loquitur Matth. ex sensu et opinione Herodis.' (Calvin.) **ἀπὸ διετοῦς**] i. e. παιδίου, not χρόνου. This expression must not be taken as any very certain indication of the time when the star did actually appear. The addition καὶ κατωτέρω implies that there was uncertainty in Herod's mind as to the age pointed out; and if so, why might not the jealous tyrant, although he had accurately ascertained the date of the star's appearing, have taken a range of time extending before as well as after it, the more surely to attain his point? **τοῖς ὁρίοις αὐτῆς** will betoken, as Meyer, the insulated houses, and hamlets, which belonged to the territory of Bethlehem. **17. τὸ ῥηθ. διὰ Ἱερ.**] Apparently, an accommodation of the prophecy in Jer. xxxi. 15, which was originally written of the Babylonish captivity. We must not draw any fanciful distinction between τότε ἐπληρώθη and ἵνα πληρωθῇ, but rather seek our explanation in the acknowledged system of prophetic interpretation among the Jews, still extant in their Rabbinical books, and now sanctioned to us by N. T. usage; at the same time remembering, for our caution, how little even now we understand of the full bearing of prophetic and typical words and acts. None of the expressions of this prophecy must be closely and literally pressed. The link of connexion seems to be *Rachel's sepulchre*, which (Gen. xxxv. 19: see also 1 Sam. x. 2) was '*in the way to Bethlehem*;' and from that circumstance, perhaps, the inhabitants of that place are called *her children*. We must also take into account the close relation between the tribes of Judah and Benjamin, which had long subsisted. Ramah was six miles to the *north* of Jerusalem, in the tribe of Benjamin (Jer. xl.

Αἰγύπτῳ 20 λέγων [r] Ἐγερθεὶς [s] παράλαβε τὸ παιδίον
καὶ τὴν μητέρα αὐτοῦ, καὶ πορεύου εἰς γῆν Ἰσραήλ·
τεθνήκασιν γὰρ οἱ [t] ζητοῦντες τὴν [t] ψυχὴν τοῦ παιδίου.
21 ὁ δὲ ἐγερθεὶς [s] παρέλαβεν τὸ παιδίον καὶ τὴν μητέρα
αὐτοῦ καὶ εἰςῆλθεν εἰς γῆν Ἰσραήλ. 22 ἀκούσας δὲ ὅτι
Ἀρχέλαος [u] βασιλεύει [ἐπὶ] τῆς Ἰουδαίας [v] ἀντὶ τοῦ
πατρὸς αὐτοῦ Ἡρώδου, ἐφοβήθη [w] ἐκεῖ [x] ἀπελθεῖν, [y] χρη-
ματισθεὶς δὲ [y] κατ' [y] ὄναρ [z] ἀνεχώρησεν εἰς τὰ [a] μέρη τῆς
Γαλιλαίας, 23 καὶ [b] ἐλθὼν [c] κατῴκησεν εἰς πόλιν λεγο-

...και την Z. BCDEK LMSUV ΓΔΠℵ 1. 33

r 1 Chron. xxii. 19.
s vv. 13, 14 reff.
t Rom. xi. 3 only. Exod. iv. 19.
u w. ἐπί and gen., Rev. v. 10 only. 2 Chron. xxii. 12. (accus., Luke i. 33 reff.) w. gen. only, 1 Kings xi. 12. pres., John i. 40 reff.
v = here only. 3 Kings iii. 7 al. fr. see John i. 16. Xen. Anab. i. 1. 4.
w = ch. xvii. 20. John xviii. 3 al. Deut. i. 37.
x = ch. xiv. 25 reff.
y ver. 12 (reff.) only.
z = vv. 12, 14 reff. 1 Kings xix. 10.
a = ch. xv. 21. xvi. 13 al. Neh. iii. 15.
b = ver. 8 reff.
c w. εἰς, ch. iv. 13. Acts vii. 4. 2 Chron. xix. 4 Ed-vat. [not B].

21. rec (for εισηλθεν) ηλθ., with DL rel latt syrr sah: txt BCℵ copt. for γην, την D(not D^r-lat).
22. om επι Bℵ 1. 13. 33 Scr's a c q ev-y arm Eus. rec ηρωδου bef του πατρος αυτου, with C^{3}DL rel vulg Eus: txt BC^{1}ℵ. (not αυτου του ηρ. in B, as Btly.)

1: "Er-Ram, marked by the village and green patch on its summit, the most conspicuous object from a distance in the approach to Jerusalem from the South, is certainly 'Ramah of Benjamin.'" Stanley, Sinai and Palestine, p. 213); so that neither must this part of the prophecy be strictly taken. **20. τεθνήκασιν γάρ**] The plural here is not merely idiomatic, nor, as Wordsw., "for lenity and forbearance, in speaking of the dead;" but perhaps a citation from Exod. iv. 19, where the same words are spoken to Moses (ζητεῖν τὴν ψυχήν = בִּקֵּשׁ נֶפֶשׁ): or, as Meyer, betokening, not the number, but the category. Cf. Soph. Œd. Col. 966. Herod the Great died of a dreadful disease at Jericho, in the seventieth year of his age, and the thirty-eighth of his reign, A.U.C. 750. Jos. B. J. i. 33. 8. **22. ἀκούσας δέ**] ARCHELAUS was the son of Herod by Malthace, a Samaritan woman: he was brought up at Rome (Jos. B. J. i. 31. 1); succeeded his father, but never had the title of king, only that of Ethnarch, with the government of Idumæa, Judæa, and Samaria, the rest of his father's dominions being divided between his brothers Philip and Antipas. (Jos. Antt. xvii. 11. 4.) But, (1) very likely the word βασιλεύω is here used in the wider meaning:—(2) Archelaus did, in the beginning of his reign, give out and regard himself as king: τὸ πλῆθος . . . εὐχαριστεῖ . . . τῆς πρὸς αὐτὸν θεραπείας ὡς πρὸς βέβαιον ἤδη βασιλέα (Jos. B. J. ii. 1. 1): (3) in ch. xiv. 9, Herod the Tetrarch is called ὁ βασιλεύς. In the ninth year of his government Archelaus was dethroned, οὐ μόνον Ἰουδαίοις, ἀλλὰ καὶ Σαμαρεῦσι χρησάμενος ὠμῶς, πρεσβευσαμένων ἑκατέρων κατ' αὐτοῦ πρὸς Καίσαρα, . . . φυγαδεύεται μὲν εἰς Βιένναν, πόλιν τῆς Γαλατίας . . . i. e. Vienne, in Gaul. (ibid. ii. 7. 3.) **ἀνεχώρησεν εἰς τ. μ. τ. Γαλ.**] This account gives rise to some difficulty as compared with St. Luke's history. It would certainly, on a first view, appear that this Evangelist was not aware that Nazareth had been before this the abode of Joseph and Mary. And it is no real objection to this, that he elsewhere calls Nazareth τὴν πατρίδα αὐτοῦ, ch. xiii. 54, 57. It is perhaps just possible that St. Matthew, writing for Jews, although well aware of the previous circumstances, may not have given them a place in his history, but made the birth at Bethlehem the prominent point, seeing that his account begins at the birth (ch. i. 18), and does not localize what took place before it, which is merely inserted as subservient to that great leading event. If this view be correct, all we could expect is, that his narrative would contain *nothing inconsistent* with the facts related in Luke; which we find to be the case. I should prefer, however, believing, as more consistent, *in foro conscientiæ*, with the fair interpretation of our text, that St. Matthew himself was not aware of the events related in Luke i. ii., and wrote under the impression that Bethlehem was the original dwelling-place of Joseph and Mary. Certainly, *had we only his Gospel*, this inference from it would universally be made. **ἀνεχώρησεν** must not be pressed (as Wordsw., al.) into the service of reconciling the two accounts by being rendered '*returned;*' for the same

d ch. i. 22 reff. e Mt., ch. ii. 1. ver. 13 only. Mark xiv. 43 only. John iii. 23 [viii. 2 rec.] only. 1 Cor. xvi. 3. 2 Tim. iv. 16. Heb. ix. 11 only, exc. Luke vii. 4, 20 al6. Acts v. 21, 22, 25 al18. = Josh. v. 14. 1 Macc. iv. 46.

μένην Ναζαρέτ· ὅπως [d] πληρωθῇ τὸ [d] ῥηθὲν διὰ τῶν προ- BCDEK LMSUV ΓΔΠℵ 1. 33
φητῶν, ὅτι Ναζωραῖος κληθήσεται.
III. 1 Ἐν δὲ ταῖς ἡμέραις ἐκείναις [e] παραγίνεται

23. for δια, υπο Cℵ2a.

Chap. III. **1.** om δε D-gr L rel tol lat-*b ff*$_1$ *g*$_1$ syr-cu(as often elsw) copt-ms arm Chr Thl Hil: ins BCU[Γ]ℵ 1 (33, e sil) vulg Dr-lat *a c f g*$_2$ syrr coptt.

word is used (ver. 14) of the journey to Egypt. **23. ὅπως πληρωθῇ**] These words refer to the *divine* purpose in the event, not to that of Joseph in bringing it about. **τὸ ῥηθὲν δ. τ. πρ.**] These words are no where verbatim to be found, nor is this asserted by the Evangelist; but that the sense of *the prophets* is such. In searching for such sense, the following hypotheses have been made—none of them satisfactory:—(1) Euthymius says, ποῖοι προφῆται τοῦτο εἶπον, μὴ ζητήσῃς· οὐχ εὑρήσεις γάρ· διότι πολλὰ τῶν προφητικῶν βιβλίων ἀπώλοντο, τὰ μὲν ἐν ταῖς αἰχμαλωσίαις, τὰ δὲ καὶ ἐξ ἀμελείας τῶν Ἑβραίων, τινὰ δὲ καὶ ἐκ κακουργίας. So also Chrys., Theophyl., Le Clerc, &c. But the expression διὰ τ. πρ. seems to have a wider bearing than is thus implied. (2) The general sense of the prophets is, that Christ should be a *despised person, as the inhabitants of Nazareth were* (John i. 47). So Michaelis, Paulus, Rosenm., Kuin., Olsh., &c. But surely this part of the Messiah's prophetic character is not general or prominent enough, in the absence of any direct verbal connexion with the word in our text, to found such an interpretation on: nor, on the other hand, does it appear that an inhabitant of Nazareth, as such, was despised; only that the obscurity of the town was, both by Nathanael and the Jews, contrasted with our Lord's claims. (3) The *Nazarites* of old were men holy and consecrated to God; e.g. Samson (Judg. xiii. 5), Samuel (1 Sam. i. 11), and to this the words are referred by Tert., Jerome, Erasm., Beza, Calvin, Grot., Wetst., al. But (α) our Lord did not (like John the Baptist) lead a life in accordance with the Nazarite vow, but drank wine, &c., and set himself in marked contrast with John in this very particular (ch. xi. 18, 19); and (β) the word for *Nazarite* is Ναζίρ (Judg. xiii. 5 B), or Ναζειραῖος (ib. and xvi. 18 A,—Lam. iv. 7), whereas this, denoting an *inhabitant of Nazareth,* is Ναζωραῖος always in the N. T., except in Mark (i. 24; x. 47; xiv. 67; xvi. 6), and Luke iv. 43 (xviii. 37; xxiv. 19 v. r.), where it is Ναζαρηνός. (4) There may be an allusion to נֵצֶר, a branch, by which name our Lord is called in Isa. xi. 1, and from which word it appears that the name Nazareth is probably derived. So '*eruditi Hebræi,*' in Jerome on Isa. xi. 1, and Pisc., Casaub., Fritz., De Wette, &c. But this word is only used in the place cited; and in by far the more precise prophecies of the Branch, Zech. iii. 8; vi. 12: Jer. xxiii. 5; xxxiii. 15, and Isa. iv. 2, the word צֶמַח is used. I leave it, therefore, as an unsolved difficulty.

Chap. III. **1—12.**] Preaching and baptism of John. Mark i. 1—8. Luke iii. 1—17. Here the *synoptic narrative* begins, its extent being the same as that specified by Peter in Acts i. 22, '*from the baptism of John unto that same day that He was taken up from us.*' For a critical comparison of the narratives in the various sections, see notes on St. Mark. In *this* Gospel, I have generally confined myself to the *subject matter.* **1. ἐν δὲ ταῖς ἡμ. ἐκ.**] The last matter mentioned was the dwelling at Nazareth: and though we must not take the connexion strictly as implying that *Joseph* dwelt there all the intermediate thirty years, the ἡμέραι ἐκεῖναι must be understood to mean that we take up the persons of the narrative where we left them; i.e. dwelling at Nazareth. See Exod. ii. 11, LXX. **παραγίνεται**] **Comes forward**—'makes his appearance.' Euthym. asks the question, πόθεν; and answers it, ἀπὸ τῆς ἐνδοτέρας ἐρήμου. But this can hardly be, owing to the ἐν τῇ ἐρήμῳ following. The verb is used absolutely. The title Ἰω. ὁ βαπτ. shews that St. Matthew was writing for those who well knew John the Baptist as an historical personage. Josephus, in mentioning him (Antt. xviii. 5. 2), calls him Ἰωάννης ὁ ἐπικαλούμενος βαπτιστής. John was strictly speaking a *prophet;* belonging to the legal dispensation; a rebuker of sin, and preacher of repentance. The expression in St. Luke, ἐγένετο ῥῆμα θεοῦ ἐπὶ Ἰωάννην, is the usual formula for the Divine commission of the Prophets (Jer. i. 1: Ezek. vi. 1; vii. 1, &c.).

Ἰωάννης ὁ βαπτιστής, [f] κηρύσσων ἐν τῇ [g] ἐρήμῳ τῆς
Ἰουδαίας, 2 λέγων [h] Μετανοεῖτε· [i] ἤγγικεν γὰρ ἡ βασι-
λεία τῶν οὐρανῶν. 3 [k] οὗτος γάρ ἐστιν ὁ [l] ῥηθεὶς διὰ
Ἡσαΐου τοῦ προφήτου λέγοντος Φωνὴ [m] βοῶντος ἐν τῇ

f = Gospp. (not John) & Epp. passim. Exod. xxxii. 5.
g ch. iv. 1. xi. 7 al. Exod. iii. 1. Judg. i. 16.
h ch. xi. 20 al. fr. in Gospp., exc. John. Epp., 2 Cor. xii. 21 only. Rev. ii. 5 bis al10. Isa. xlvi. 8. Jer. xviii. 8 al.
i = ch. iv. 17 ‖ Mk. xxi. 34. Lam. iv. 18. Ezek. xii. 23.
k Isa. xl. 3.
l = ch. xxiv. 15. see John i. 15.
m John i. 23 (from l. c.) reff.

2. rec ins και bef λεγων (*to conform to ch* iv. 17), with CDL rel latt syr arm: om Bא lat-g_2 coptt æth Hil.

3. rec (for δια) υπο, with L rel: txt BCDא 1. 13. 33 latt Syr sah æth arm.

And the effect of the Holy Spirit on John was more in accordance with the O. T. than the N. T. inspiration; more of a sudden overpowering influence, as in the Prophets, than a gentle indwelling manifested through the individual character, as in the Apostles and Evangelists. The baptism of John was of a deeper significance than that usual among the Jews in the case of proselytes, and formed an integral part of his divinely appointed office. It was emphatically the baptism of *repentance* (λουτρὸν μετανοίας, says Olshausen (cf. Luke iii. 3), but not λουτρὸν παλιγγενεσίας, Titus iii. 5). We find in Acts xviii. 24—26; xix. 1—7, accounts of persons who had received the baptism of John, who believed and (in Apollos's case) taught accurately the things (i. e. facts) concerning the Lord; but required instruction (in doctrine) and rebaptizing in the name of the Lord Jesus. Whether the baptism practised by the disciples before the Resurrection was of the same kind, and required this renewal, is uncertain. The fact of our Lord Himself having received baptism from John, is decisive against the identity of the two rites, as also against the idea (Olsh. i. 154, note) derived from Acts xix. 4, that John used the formula βαπτίζω σε εἰς τὸν ἐρχόμενον. His whole mission, as Olsh. well observes, was calculated, in accordance with the office of the law which gives the knowledge of sin (Rom. iii. 20), to bring men's minds into that state in which the Redeemer invites them (ch. xi. 28), as weary and heavy laden, to come to him. **ἐν τῇ ἐρήμῳ**] where also he had been brought up, Luke i. 80. This tract was not strictly a *desert*, but thinly peopled, and abounding in pastures for flocks. Josephus, B. J. iii. 10. 7, says, that the Jordan διατέμνει τὴν Γεννήσαρ μέσην, ἔπειτα πολλὴν ἀναμετρούμενος **ἐρημίαν** εἰς τὴν Ἀσφαλτῖτιν ἔξεισι λίμνην. See Judg. i. 16: 1 Kings ii. 34. This ἔρημος answers to πᾶσα περίχωρος τοῦ Ἰορδάνου in Luke iii. 3. See note on ch. iv. 1. **2. μετανοεῖτε**] Used by the Baptist in the O. T. sense of *turning to God as His people*, from the spiritual idolatry and typical adultery in which the faithless among the Jews were involved. This, of course, included personal amendment in individuals. See Luke iii. 10—14. Josephus describes John, Antt. xviii. 5. 2, as τοὺς Ἰουδαίους κελεύοντα ἀρετὴν ἐπασκοῦντας καὶ τῇ πρὸς ἀλλήλους δικαιοσύνῃ καὶ πρὸς τὸν θεὸν εὐσεβείᾳ χρωμένους βαπτισμῷ συνιέναι. **ἡ βασιλεία τῶν οὐρανῶν**] An expression peculiar in the N. T. to St. Matthew. The more usual one is ἡ βασ. τοῦ θεοῦ: but ἡ β. τῶν οὐρ. is common in the Rabbinical writers, who do not however, except in one or two places, mean by it *the reign of the Messiah*, but *the Jewish religion*—the *theocracy*. Still, from the use of it by St. Matthew here, and in ch. iv. 17; x. 7, we may conclude that it was used by the Jews, and understood, to mean *the advent of the Christ*, probably from the prophecy in Dan. ii. 44; vii. 13, 14, 27. It has been observed by recent critics, that wherever the term βασ. τ. οὐρ. (or its equivalent) is used in the N. T., it signifies, not the Church, nor the Christian religion, but strictly the *kingdom of the Messiah which is to be revealed hereafter.* I should doubt this being *exclusively* true. The state of Christian men *now* is undoubtedly a part of the bringing in of the kingdom of Christ, and, as such, is included in this term. See Mark xii. 34, and note on ch. v. 3. **3. οὗτος γάρ ἐστιν**] *Not the words of the Baptist*, meaning ἐγὼ γάρ εἰμι, as in John i. 23, but *of the Evangelist*; and ἐστιν is not for ἦν, but is the prophetic present, representing to us the place which the Baptist fills in the divine purposes. Of **γάρ**, Bengel says well, "Causa cur Johannes ita exoriri tum debuerit uti ver. 1, 2 describitur, quia sic prædictum erat." The words ἐν τῇ ἐρήμῳ belong in the Hebrew to ἑτοιμάσατε, but in the LXX and here to βοῶντος. The primary and literal application of this prophecy to *the*

[g] ἐρήμῳ, ἑτοιμάσατε τὴν ὁδὸν κυρίου, [n] εὐθείας ποιεῖτε τὰς
[o] τρίβους αὐτοῦ. 4 [p] αὐτὸς δὲ ὁ Ἰωάννης εἶχεν τὸ [q] ἔνδυμα
αὐτοῦ ἀπὸ τριχῶν [r] καμήλου καὶ [st] ζώνην [tu] δερματίνην περὶ
τὴν [v] ὀσφὺν αὐτοῦ· ἡ δὲ [w] τροφὴ ἦν αὐτοῦ [x] ἀκρίδες καὶ
[y] μέλι [z] ἄγριον. 5 τότε [a] ἐξεπορεύετο πρὸς αὐτὸν Ἱεροσόλυμα καὶ πᾶσα ἡ Ἰουδαία καὶ πᾶσα ἡ [b] περίχωρος τοῦ

BCDEK LMSUV ΓΔΠℵ 1. 33

n ‖ L. reff. o ‖ only. Gen. xlix. 17. 1 Kings vi 12. p Mark vi. 17. xii. 36, 37. 1 Thess. v. 23. q ch. vi. 25, 28 al4. Mt. only, exc. Luke xii. 23. Zeph. i. 8. r ch. xix. 24 reff. s ‖ Mk. ch. x. 9 ‖ Mk. Acts xxi. 11 bis. Rev. i. 13. xv. 6. t 4 Kings i. 8. u ‖ Mk. only. Gen. iii. 21. v ‖ Mk. Luke xii. 35. Acts ii. 30. Eph. vi. 14. Heb. vii. 5, 10. 1 Pet. i. 13 only. Gen. xxxv. 11. w ch. vi. 25 al. fr. Ps. cx. 5. x Mark i. 6. Rev. ix. 3, 7 only. Lev. xi. 22. y ‖ Mk. Rev. x. 9, 10 only. Judg. xiv. 8. z = Mark i. 6 (Jude 13) only. 4 Kings iv. 39. Polyb. xii. 3. 9 al. a = Rev. xvi. 14. see Deut. xxviii. 7. b ch. xiv. 35 al. (not John.) Gen. xiii. 10.

4. om ὁ D 13. 218 Chr-*a*. rec *αυτου* bef *ην*, with L rel latt: txt BCDℵ 1.

return from captivity is very doubtful. If it *ever had* such an application, we may safely say that its predictions were so imperfectly and sparingly fulfilled in that return, or any thing which followed it, that we are necessarily directed onward to its greater fulfilment—the announcement of the kingdom of Christ. Euthymius remarks, *ὁδὸν δὲ κυρίου καὶ τρίβους αὐτοῦ καλεῖ τὰς ψυχάς, ὧν ἐπιβαίνειν ἔμελλεν ὁ λόγος τοῦ εὐαγγελίου, ἃς καὶ προτρέπεται ἑτοιμάζειν, ἤγουν καθαίρειν, τῷ ἐργαλείῳ τῆς μετανοίας ἀνασπῶντας μὲν τὰς ἀκάνθας τῶν παθῶν, ἐκρίπτοντας δὲ τοὺς λίθους τῆς ἁμαρτίας, καὶ οὕτως εὐθείας καὶ ὁμαλὰς αὐτὰς ἀπεργάζεσθαι πρὸς ὑποδοχὴν αὐτοῦ.*

4. αὐτὸς δὲ ὁ Ἰω.] **αὐτός** recalls the reader from the prophetic testimony, to the person of John: **now John himself . . . .** As John was the Elias of prophecy, so we find in his outward attire a striking similarity to Elias, who was *ἀνὴρ δασύς, καὶ ζωνὴν δερματίνην περιεζωσμένος τὴν ὀσφὺν αὐτοῦ.* 4 Kings i. 8. The garment of camel's hair was not the camel's skin with the hair on, which would be too heavy to wear, but raiment woven of camel's hair, such as Josephus speaks of (B. J. i. 24. 3), *ἐσθῆτες ἐκ τριχῶν πεποιημέναι*, as a contrast to *ἐσθ. βασιλικαί*. From Zech. xiii. 4, it seems that such a dress was known as the prophetic garb: 'neither shall they (the prophets) wear a rough garment (*δέῤῥιν τριχίνην*, LXX, who, however, make it a garment of *penitence for having deceived*) to deceive.' **ἀκρίδες**] There is no difficulty here. The *ἀκρίς*, permitted to be eaten, ref. Levit., was used as food by the lower orders in Judæa, and mentioned by Strabo and Pliny as eaten by the Æthiopians, and by many other authors as articles of food. Jerome, adv. Jovinian. ii. 7, vol. ii. p. 334, says, "Apud Orientales et Libyæ populos quia per desertam et calidam eremi vastitatem locustarum nubes reperiuntur, locustis vesci moris est: hoc verum esse Joannes quoque Baptista probat." Shaw found locusts eaten by the Moors in Barbary. (Travels, p. 164.) Epiphanius, Hær. xxx. 13, vol. i. p. 138, quotes this from the Gospel according to the Ebionites as follows: *καὶ τὸ βρῶμα αὐτοῦ μέλι ἄγριον, οὗ ἡ γεῦσις ἦν τοῦ μάννα, ὡς ἔγκρις ἐν ἐλαίῳ*, and adds, *ἵνα δῆθεν μεταστρέψωσι τὸν τῆς ἀληθείας λόγον εἰς ψεῦδος, καὶ ἀντὶ ἀκρίδων ποιήσωσιν ἐγκρίδας ἐν μέλιτι.* **μέλι ἄγριον**] See 1 Sam. xiv. 25. Here, again, there is no need to suppose any thing else meant but honey made by wild bees; *τὸ ἐν ταῖς τῶν πετρῶν σχισμαῖς ὑπὸ τῶν μελισσῶν γεωργούμενον.* Euthym. Schulz (cited by Winer, Realw., and De Wette) found such honey in this very wilderness in our own time. See Psalm lxxxi. 16: Judg. xiv. 8: Deut. xxxii. 13. The passage usually cited from Diodorus Siculus (xix. 94) to shew that *μέλι ἄγριον* exuded from trees, does not necessarily imply it; *φύεται γὰρ παρ' αὐτοῖς τὸ πέπερι ἀπὸ τῶν δένδρων, καὶ μέλι πολὺ τὸ καλούμενον ἄγριον, ᾧ χρῶνται ποτῷ μεθ' ὕδατος.* Suidas certainly makes it a gum: *μ. ἄγ. ὅπερ ἀπὸ τῶν δένδρων ἐπισυναγόμενον, μάννα τοῖς πολλοῖς προσαγορεύεται.* And Meyer prefers this view, on account of the predicate *ἄγριον*, which, he says, is a terminus technicus, pointing out this particular kind of honey. But he does not give any authority for this assertion: and it seems just as likely that *ἄγριον* might be applied to it as made by wild bees.

5. τότε ἐξεπ.] The latter *καί* here has been supposed to mean '*especially*,' seeing that Judæa was part of the *περίχωρος*; as in the expression *ἄλλως τε καί*. But the former *καὶ πᾶσα* will hardly allow this. **καὶ πᾶσα ἡ περ.** means all the neighbourhood of Jordan not included in Jerusalem and Judæa before mentioned. Parts of Peræa, Samaria, Galilee, and Gaulonitis come under this denomination.

There need be no surprise at such mul-

Ἰορδάνου, 6 καὶ [c] ἐβαπτίζοντο ἐν τῷ Ἰορδάνῃ ποταμῷ
ὑπ' αὐτοῦ, [d] ἐξομολογούμενοι τὰς ἁμαρτίας αὐτῶν. 7 ἰδὼν
δὲ πολλοὺς τῶν Φαρισαίων καὶ Σαδδουκαίων ἐρχομένους

c vv. 11 bis, 13, &c. al. fr. 4 Kings v. 14.
d = || Mk. reff. ὁμολ. ἐφ' ἁμαρτ. Sir. iv. 26.

6. aft εβαπτιζοντο ins παντες (*from Mark* i. 5 ?) C² 33 Hil. rec om ποταμω (*see* || *Mark*), with C³DL rel latt Hil: ins BC¹MΔℵ **1. 13.** 33 Scr's **a** b d g q r v w² ev-z_{bis} ev-150 syrr syr-cu syr-jer coptt æth arm [$Orig_1$] Bas. (om εν τω ιορδανη ποταμω Chr, so Field and Matthæi's 6 mss.) om υπ' αυτου ℵ¹(ins ℵ^2a).

titudes going out to John. The nature of his announcement, coupled with the prevalent expectation of the time, was enough to produce this effect. See, as strictly consistent with this account, chap. xi. 7—15. **6 ἐβαπτίζοντο**] When *men* were admitted as proselytes, three rites were performed—*circumcision, baptism,* and *oblation;* when women, two—*baptism* and *oblation.* The baptism was administered in the day-time, by immersion of the whole person; and while standing in the water the proselyte was instructed in certain portions of the law. The whole families of proselytes, including infants, were baptized. It is most probable that John's baptism in outward form resembled that of proselytes. See above, on ver. 1. Some (De Wette, Winer, Paulus, Meyer) deny that the proselyte baptism was in use before the time of John: but the contrary has been generally supposed, and maintained (cf. Lightfoot, Schöttgen, Buxtorf, Wetstein, Bengel). Indeed the baptism or lustration of a proselyte on admission would follow as a matter of course, by analogy from the constant legal practice of lustration after all uncleannesses: and it is difficult to imagine a time when it would not be in use. Besides, it is highly improbable that the Jews should have borrowed the rite from the Christians, or the Jewish hierarchy from John. **ἐξομολογούμενοι τ. ἁμ. αὐ.**] From the form and expression this does not seem to have been merely 'shewing a contrite spirit,' 'confessing themselves sinners,' but *a particular and individual confession;* not, however, made privately to John, but before the people: see his exhortation to the various classes in Luke iii. 10—15: nor in every case, but in those which required it. Josephus uses the very same expression, Antt. viii. 4. 6. The present participle carries with it a certain logical force; "confessing, as they did,"—almost = "on condition of confessing." So Fritzsche, "si peccata sua confiterentur." **7. Φαρισ. καὶ Σαδδ.**] These two sects, according to Josephus, Antt. xiii. 5. 9, originated at the same period, under Jonathan the High Priest (B.C. 159—144). The Pharisees, deriving their name probably from פָּרַשׁ, 'he separated' (διὰ τὴν ἐθελοπερισσοθρησκείαν, Epiph. Hær. xvi. 1, vol. i. p. 34), took for their distinctive practice the strict observance of the law and all its requirements, written and oral. They had great power over the people, and are numbered by Josephus, as being, about the time of the death of Herod the Great, above 6000. (Antt. xvii. 2. 4.) We find in the Gospels the Pharisees the most constant opponents of our Lord, and His discourses frequently directed against them. The character of the sect as a whole was *hypocrisy;* the outside acknowledgment and honouring of God and his law, but inward and practical denial of Him: which rendered them the enemies of the simplicity and genuineness which characterized our Lord's teaching. Still among them were undoubtedly pious and worthy men, honourably distinguished from the mass of the sect; John iii. 1: Acts v. 34. The various points of their religious and moral belief will be treated of as they occur in the text of the Gospels. **Σαδδουκαίων**] Are *said* to have derived their name from one Sadok, about the time of Alexander the Great (B.C. 323): but more probably, as stated by Epiphanius, Hær. xiv. 1, vol. i. p. 31, ἐπονομάζουσιν ἑαυτοὺς Σαδδουκαίους δῆθεν ἀπὸ δικαιοσύνης τῆς ἐπικλήσεως ὁρμωμένης· σεδὲκ γὰρ (whence the adjectival form, צַדִּיק, see Gen. vi. 9; xviii. 25 al. fr.) ἑρμηνεύεται δικαιοσύνη. They *rejected all tradition,* but did not, as some have supposed, confine their canon of Scripture to the Pentateuch. The denial of a future state does not appear to have been an original tenet of Sadduceism, but to have sprung from its abuse. The particular side of religionism represented by the Sadducees was bare literal moral conformity, without any higher views or hopes. They thus escaped the dangers of tradition, but fell into deadness and worldliness, and a denial of spiritual influence. While our Lord was on earth, this state of mind was very prevalent among the educated classes

e ἐπὶ τὸ βάπτισμα [αὐτοῦ], εἶπεν αὐτοῖς fg Γεννήματα
fh ἐχιδνῶν, τίς i ὑπέδειξεν ὑμῖν φυγεῖν ἀπὸ τῆς j μελλούσης ...φυγειν D[1].
k ὀργῆς; 8 l ποιήσατε οὖν l καρπὸν m ἄξιον τῆς μετανοίας, BCEKL
9 καὶ μὴ n δόξητε λεγειν o ἐν p ἑαυτοῖς Πατέρα ἔχομεν τὸν MSUVΓ ΔΠℵ 1.
Ἀβραάμ· λέγω γὰρ ὑμῖν ὅτι δύναται ὁ θεὸς ἐκ τῶν λίθων 33
τούτων q ἐγεῖραι τέκνα τῷ Ἀβραάμ. 10 ἤδη δὲ ἡ r ἀξίνη
s πρὸς τὴν ῥίζαν τῶν δένδρων t κεῖται· πᾶν οὖν δένδρον μὴ

e = Luke xxiii. 48. f ‖ L. ch. xii. 34. xxiii. 33. g as above (f). (ch. xxvi. 29 ‖ Mk. L. Luke xii. 18.) 2 Cor. ix. 10 only. Josh. xv. 14 F compl. [not AB.] h as above (f). Acts xxviii. 3 only +. Isa. lix. 5 Aq. i ‖ L. Luke vi. 47. xii. 5. Acts ix. 16. xx. 35 only. 2 Chron. xv. 3. j = ‖ L. ch. xii. 32. 1 Tim. iv. 8. Heb. ii. 5. k see 1 Thess. i. 10. l Mt. L. fr. Rev. xxii. 2. Gen. i. 11, 12. see Isa. v. 4. διδόναι κ., ch. xiii. 8. Mark iv. 7, 8. φέρειν κ. in John, xii. 24. xv. 2, &c. m = Luke xxiii. 41. Acts xxvi. 20. 2 Macc. iv. 25. n (ἄρξησθε ‖ L.) 1 Cor. xi. 16. Phil. iii. 4. Susan. 5. o ch. ix. 3, 21 al. fr. Gen. xviii. 12. Esth. vi. 6. p 2nd pers., ch. xvi. 8. xxiii. 31 al. fr. q = ch. xi. 11. Acts xiii. 22. Judg. ii. 18. r ‖ L. only. Deut. xix. 5 al. s = Luke xxii. 56. t = John ii. 6. xix. 29. xxi. 9. Rev. iv. 2.

7. om *αυτου* Bℵ[1] sah $Orig_3$ Chr-β [Hil]: ins CDLℵ[2a] rel Scr's mss latt syr-cu syr copt.

8. rec **καρπους αξιους** (*perhaps as more appropriate, or from ‖ Luke*), with LU 33 lat-*a* g_2 Syr syr-cu Bas Chr Cyr Thl Euthym Ambr Aug_{alic} spec Op: txt BCD[r](and lat) ℵ rel vulg lat-*b c f* ff_1 syr coptt æth arm $Orig_{expr}$ Iren-int Hil. om 2nd *της* D[r].

10. rec aft *ηδη δε* ins *και* (*see ‖ Luke*), with L rel syr: om BCD[r](*ηδη δη*) MΔℵ 1 Scr's b[1] latt Syr syr-cu coptt æth arm Iren-gr Orig Bas Did Lucif. (lat-*a* def.)—om *η* also Δ.

throughout the Roman empire; and most of the Jews of rank and station were Sadducees. The two sects, mutually hostile, are found frequently in the Gospels united in opposition to our Lord (see ch. xvi. 1, 6, 11; xxii. 23, 34: also Acts iv. 1); the Pharisees representing hypocritical superstition; the Sadducees, carnal unbelief. **ἐρχομένους**] **as they came.** It would appear here as if these Pharisees and Sadducees came with others, and because others did, without any worthy motive, and they were probably deterred by his rebuke from undergoing baptism at his hands. We know, from Luke vii. 30, that the Pharisees in general '*were not baptized of him.*' **ἐπί** denotes the *moral direction of their purpose*, not merely *motion towards*: as in Μενέλαον στέλλειν ἐπὶ τὰν Ἑλέναν, Eur. Iph. Aul. 178,—and similar expressions; cf. Bernhardy, Syntax, p. 252 f., where many examples are given. Some interpret it in a hostile sense, 'to *oppose* his baptism,' as in ἑπτὰ ἐπὶ Θήβας: but this is manifestly inconsistent with the context. **τῆς μελλούσης ὀργῆς**] The reference of John's ministry to the prophecy concerning Elias, Mal. iii. 1; iv. 5 (Mark i. 2), would naturally suggest to men's minds 'the wrath to come' there also foretold. It was the general expectation of the Jews that troublous times would accompany the appearance of the Messiah. John is now speaking in the true character of a prophet, foretelling the wrath soon to be poured on the Jewish nation. **8.**] **οὖν** expresses an inference from their apparent intention of fleeing from the wrath to come: q. d., 'if you are really so minded,' . . . **9. μὴ δόξητε λ.**] Not pleonastic: but, **Do not fancy you may say**, &c. In Justin Martyr's dialogue with Trypho the Jew, § 140, p. 230, we read: *εἰσὶ δὲ λάκκοι συντετριμμένοι καὶ ὕδωρ μὴ συνέχοντες, οὓς ὤρυξαν ὑμῖν οἱ διδάσκαλοι ὑμῶν αὐτῶν . . . . . . καὶ πρὸς τούτοις ἑαυτοὺς καὶ ὑμᾶς βουκολοῦσιν, ὑπολαμβάνοντες ὅτι πάντως τοῖς ἀπὸ τῆς σπορᾶς τῆς κατὰ σάρκα τοῦ Ἀβραὰμ οὖσι, κἂν ἁμαρτωλοὶ ὦσι, καὶ ἄπιστοι, καὶ ἀπειθεῖς πρὸς τὸν θεόν, ἡ βασιλεία ἡ αἰώνιος δοθήσεται.* The expression *λέγειν ἐν ἑαυτοῖς*, as similar expressions in Scripture (e. g., Ps. ix. 6 (27), 11 (32); xiii. 1: Eccl. i. 16; ii. 15 al. fr.), is used to signify the act by which outward circumstances are turned into thoughts of the mind. See Beck, Biblische Seelenlehre, p. 83. **ἐκ τῶν λ. τ.**] The pebbles or shingle on the beach of the Jordan. He possibly referred to Isa. li. 1, 2. This also is prophetic, of the admission of the Gentile Church. See Rom. iv. 16: Gal. iii. 29. Or we may take the interpretation which Chrysostom prefers, also referring to Isa. li. 1, 2: *μὴ νομίζετε, φησίν, ὅτι ἐὰν ὑμεῖς ἀπόλησθε, ἄπαιδα ποιήσετε τὸν πατριάρχην. οὐκ ἔστι τοῦτο, οὐκ ἔστι. τῷ γὰρ θεῷ δυνατὸν καὶ ἀπὸ λίθων ἀνθρώπους αὐτῷ δοῦναι, καὶ εἰς συγγένειαν αὐτοῦ ἀγαγεῖν, ἐπεὶ καὶ ἐξ ἀρχῆς οὕτως ἐγένετο. τῷ γὰρ ἐκ λίθων ἀνθρώπους γενέσθαι ὅμοιον ἦν τὸ ἀπὸ τῆς μήτρας ἐκείνης τῆς σκληρᾶς προελθεῖν παιδίον.* **10.**] Of **ἤδη δέ**, Klotz says, Devar. p. 606, " Respondent Latinis particulis *jam vero*, et habent idoneum atque alacrem transitum ab una re ad aliam

[l] ποιοῦν [l] καρπὸν καλὸν [u] ἐκκόπτεται καὶ εἰς πῦρ βάλλεται. 11 ἐγὼ μὲν βαπτίζω ὑμᾶς ἐν ὕδατι [v] εἰς μετάνοιαν·
ὁ δὲ [w] ὀπίσω μου ἐρχόμενος [x] ἰσχυρότερός μου ἐστίν, οὗ
οὐκ εἰμὶ [y] ἱκανὸς τὰ [z] ὑποδήματα [a] βαστάσαι· αὐτὸς ὑμᾶς
βαπτίσει [b] ἐν πνεύματι ἁγίῳ καὶ πυρί. 12 [c] οὗ τὸ [d] πτύον
...II. ἐν τῇ χειρὶ [c] αὐτοῦ, καὶ [e] διακαθαριεῖ τὴν [f] ἅλωνα αὐτοῦ,

u Luke xiii. 7, 9. Rom. xi. 22, 24. Dan. iv. 11 (14 Theod-F.). v = ch. viii. 4. xxvi. 13 al. 1 Kings ix. 14. Wisd. xi. 23. w = ‖ Mk. John i. 15, 27, 30 only. Neh. xiii. 19. x ‖. Luke xi. 22. Num. xxii. 6 A compl. Ald. y = ‖ Mk. reff. z ‖. ch. x. 10 al. Gen. xiv. 23. a = Mark xiv. 13. Luke vii. 14 al. b = Mark ix. 50. Luke xxi. 34. John xiii. 35. Isa. iv. 4. c constr., Mark vii. 25. Acts xv. 17, from Amos ix. 12. Rev. iii. 8. vii. 2, 9. Gen. i. 11. Num. xi. 21. d ‖ L. only †. Theocr. vii. 156. Hom. Il. ν. 588. e ‖ L. only †. not found elsewhere. f ‖ L. only. Ruth iii. 2. Job xxxix. 12. Isa. xxv. 10 al.

11. aft μεν ins γαρ ℵ. υμας bef βαπτιζω (*to correspond with* υμ. βαπτισει *below, where there is no other reading*) Bℵ[1] 1. 33 am(with forj) lat-ff_1 g_2 Just Orig (Clem) Bas Chr Cyr $Cypr_1$ spec : υμ. εν υδ. β. ℵ[2] $Orig_2$. om και πυρι ESV Scr's a d f i k l m n o q r u v ev-z ev-150 (al fere 100 Tischdf) syr-jer Thl $Euthym_{expr}$ spec : ins (*from* ‖ *Luke?*) BCD[r](and lat) ℵ rel latt syrr syr-cu copt Just $Orig_3$ Eus (Iren-int) Cypr Hil.

. . . . . Transitum faciunt illæ particulæ, ut nos ad rem præsentem revocent:" Eurip. Med. 772: Rhes. 499: Herodot. vii. 35. The *presents*, **κεῖται, ἐκκόπτεται**, and **βάλλεται,** imply the law, or habit, which now and henceforward, in the kingdom of heaven, prevails: '*from this time it is so.*' **11. ἐν ὕδ.**] ἐν is not redundant, but signifies the *vehicle* of baptism, as in ἐν πν. ἁγ. κ. πυρί afterwards. **ἐρχόμενος**] The present participle is used of a certain and predetermined future event; "he that is to come." See on ch. ii. 4. **τὰ ὑποδ. βαστάσαι**] Lightfoot (from Maimonides) shews that it was the token of a slave having become his master's property, to *loose* his shoe, to *tie* the same, or to *carry* the necessary articles for him to the bath. The expressions therefore in all the Gospels amount to the same. **ἐν πν. ἁγ. κ. πυρί**] This was literally fulfilled at the day of Pentecost: but Origen and others refer the words to the baptism of the *righteous by the Holy Spirit*, and of *the wicked by fire.* I have no doubt that this (which I am surprised to see upheld by Neander, De Wette, and Meyer) is a mistake in the present case, though apparently (to the superficial reader) borne out by ver. 12. The *double* symbolic reference of fire, elsewhere found, e. g. Mark ix. 50, as purifying the good and consuming the evil, though *illustrated* by these verses, is hardly to be pressed into the interpretation of πυρί in this verse, the prophecy *here* being solely of that higher and more perfect baptism to which that of John was a mere introduction. To separate off πν. ἁγίῳ as belonging to one set of persons, and πυρί as belonging to another, when both are united in ὑμᾶς, is in the last degree harsh, besides introducing confusion into the whole. The members of comparison in this verse are *strictly parallel* to one another: the *baptism by water*, the end of which is μετάνοια, a mere transition state, a note of preparation,—and the *baptism by the Holy Ghost and fire*, the end of which is (ver. 12) *sanctification*, the entire aim and purpose of man's creation and renewal. So Chrys.: τῇ ἐπεξηγήσει τοῦ πυρὸς πάλιν τὸ σφοδρὸν καὶ ἀκάθεκτον τῆς χάριτος ἐνδεικνύμενος. Thus the *official superiority* of the Redeemer (which is all that our Evangelist here deals with) is fully brought out. The superiority of *nature* and *pre-existence* is reserved for the fuller and more dogmatic account in John i. **12. οὗ τὸ πτύον**] οὗ . . . αὐτοῦ, a very common redundancy. See reff. οὗ is not '*whose*,' which is implied in τό: it belongs (against Meyer) to χειρί, not to πτύον, and the sense is just as if it had stood, οὗ ἐν τῇ χειρὶ αὐτοῦ τὸ πτύον. In the Rabbinical work Midrash Tehillim, on Ps. ii., is found: 'Advenit trituratio, stramen projiciunt in ignem, paleam in ventum, sed triticum conservant in area: sic nationes mundi erunt sicut conflagratio furni: ast Israel conservabitur solus.' (Quoted by Lightfoot on John iii. 17.) **τὴν ἅλωνα**] *The contents of the barn-floor.* (De Wette, &c.) Thus in ref. Job, εἰσοίσει δέ σου (σοι F, not A) τὸν ἅλωνα. Or perhaps owing to διακαθ. (**shall cleanse from one end to the other**) the *floor itself*, which was an open hard-trodden space in the middle of the field. See "The Land and the Book," p. 538 ff., where there is an illustration. "Very little use is now made of the *fan*, but I have seen it employed to *purge the floor* of the refuse dust, which the owner throws

g ‖ L. ch. vi. 26. xiii. 30.
h = John iv. 36. Gen. xli. 35.
i as above (g). Luke xii. 18, 24 only. 1 Chron. xxviii. 11, 12. Ezek. xxviii. 13.
j ‖ L. only. Gen. xxiv. 25. Exod. v. 7, &c.

καὶ [gh] συνάξει τὸν σῖτον αὐτοῦ εἰς τὴν [gi] ἀποθήκην, τὸ δὲ
[j] ἄχυρον [k] κατακαύσει πυρὶ [l] ἀσβέστῳ.
13 Τότε [m] παραγίνεται ὁ Ἰησοῦς ἀπὸ τῆς Γαλιλαίας
ἐπὶ τὸν Ἰορδάνην πρὸς τὸν Ἰωάννην, [n] τοῦ βαπτισθῆναι
ὑπ' αὐτοῦ. 14 ὁ δὲ [Ἰωάννης] [o] διεκώλυεν αὐτὸν λέγων
Ἐγὼ [p] χρείαν [p] ἔχω ὑπὸ σοῦ βαπτισθῆναι, καὶ σὺ ἔρχῃ

P νεται ο... BCEKL MPSUV ΓΔℵ 1. 33

k ‖ L. ch. xiii. 30 (40 v. r.). Acts xix. 19. 1 Cor. iii. 15 al. Deut. vii. 5, 25. l ‖ L. Mark ix. 43 [45] only †. m ver. 1 reff. Isa. lvi. 1. n constr., ch. ii, 13. xxiv. 45. Acts xiii. 47. xxi. 12 al. fr. Ps. cxxxix. 4. o here only †. Judith xii. 7 only. p w. inf., ch. xiv. 16. John xiii. 10. 1 Thess. i. 8. iv. 9. v. 1. Dan. iii. 16.

12. om 3rd *αυτου* (*see ‖ Luke*) ELU 13 Scr's i v harl[1] lat-*a b ff*$_1$ *g*$_{1.2}$ syrr syr-cu arm Just Clem Cyr Iren-int Ambr Aug$_1$: ins BCD[r](and lat) ℵ rel vulg lat-*c f* coptt Hil spec. aft *αποθηκην* ins *αυτου* BELU Scr's v w[2] harl[1] lat-*b ff*$_1$ *g*$_1$ syrr syr-cu æth arm Cyr Ambr spec: om CD[r](and lat) ℵ rel vulg lat-*a c f* coptt Just Clem Iren-int Hil Aug. (*See ‖ Luke.*)

14. om *ιωαννης* Bℵ[1] sah Eus: *ιωαν.* after the verb in D-lat *a b c g*$_1$: txt C P(appy) ℵ-corr[1·2 or 2a] rel vulg lat-*f ff*$_1$ vss. (B does not om *συ*, as in Mai.)

away as useless." p. 540. **ἄχυρον**] Not only *the chaff*, but also *the straw:* see reff.: 'all that is not wheat.'

13—17.] Jesus Himself baptized by him. Mark i. 9—11. Luke iii. 21, 22. It does not appear exactly *when the baptism of our Lord took place.* If the comparative age of the Baptist is taken into account, we should suppose it to have been about six months after this latter began his ministry. But this is no sure guide. The *place* was *Bethany* (the older reading), *beyond Jordan;* John i. 28.

13. τοῦ βαπτ.] Why should our Lord, who was *without sin,* have come to *a baptism of repentance?* Because He was *made sin for us:* for which reason also He suffered the curse of the law. It became Him, being *in the likeness of sinful flesh,* to go through those appointed rites and purifications which belonged to that flesh. There is no more strangeness in His having been baptized by John, than in His keeping the Passovers. The one rite, as the other, belonged to *sinners*—and *among the transgressors He was numbered.* The prophetic words in Ps. xl. 12, spoken in the person of our Lord, indicate, in the midst of sinlessness, the most profound apprehension of the sins of that nature which He took upon him. I cannot suppose the baptism to have been sought by our Lord merely *to honour John* (Kuinöel), or as *knowing that it would be the occasion of a divine recognition* of his Messiahship (Paulus), and thus preordained by God (Meyer): but *bona fide,* as bearing the infirmities and carrying the sorrows of mankind, and thus beginning here the triple baptism of water, fire, and blood, two parts of which were now accomplished, and of the third of which He himself speaks, Luke xii. 50, and the beloved Apostle, 1 John v. 8, where *πνεῦμα* = *πῦρ.* His baptism, as it was our Lord's *closing* act of obedience under the Law, in His hitherto concealed life of legal submission, His *πληρῶσαι πασ. δικ.,* so was His *solemn inauguration and anointing for the higher official life of mediatorial satisfaction* which was now opening upon Him. See Rom. i. 3, 4. We must not forget that the *working out of perfect righteousness in our flesh* by the entire and spotless keeping of God's law (Deut. vi. 25), was, in the main, *accomplished during the thirty years previous to our Lord's official ministry.* **14. διεκώλυεν**] A much stronger word than *κωλύω,* implying the active and earnest preventing, with the gesture or hand, or voice, as here. The imperfect tense conveys, not that he *endeavoured* merely to hinder Him (see Hermann's note on Soph. Ajax, 1105), but *began* to hinder Him, **was hindering Him.** There is only an *apparent* inconsistency between the speech of John in this sense, and the assertion made by him in John i. 33, 'I knew him not.' Let us regard the matter in this light:—John begins his ministry by a commission from God, who also admonishes him, that He, whose Forerunner he was, would be in time revealed to him by a special sign. Jesus comes to be baptized by him. From the nature of his relationship to our Lord, he could not but know those events which had accompanied his birth, and his subsequent life of holy and unblameable purity and sanctity. My impression from the words of this verse certainly is, that he *regarded Him as the Messiah.* Still, his belief wanted that full and entire assurance which the occurrence of the pre- *

πρός με; 15 Ἀποκριθεὶς δὲ ὁ Ἰησοῦς εἶπεν πρὸς αὐτόν
[q] Ἄφες ἄρτι. οὕτως γὰρ [r] πρέπον ἐστὶν ἡμῖν [s] πληρῶσαι
[t] πᾶσαν [t] δικαιοσύνην. τότε [q] ἀφίησιν αὐτόν. 16 βαπτισθεὶς δὲ ὁ Ἰησοῦς ἀνέβη εὐθὺς ἀπὸ τοῦ ὕδατος. καὶ ἰδοὺ

q = ch. xxiii. 14 al. Sir. xxiii. 1.
r 1 Cor. xi. 13. Eph. v. 3. 1 Tim. ii. 10. Tit. ii. 1. Heb. ii. 10. vii. 26 only. Ps. xxxii. 1.
1 Macc. xii. 11.
s = Acts xiii. 25. Rom. viii. 4. Ps. xix. 4.
t Acts xiii. 10. 1 Kings xii. 7.

15. for *προς αυτον*, *αυτω* B 13. 124 evv-y-z latt copt Eus. **ημας** א[1](txt א[2.3a]) vulg.

16. rec (for *βαπτισθεις δε*) *και βαπτ.*, with C[3]D[r](and lat) P(Tischdf) rel Scr's mss lat-*a b c f* g_1 *h* syr-cu syr Hipp Chr Hil Vig: om Δ: txt BC[1]א 13 vulg lat-ff_1 *l* Syr coptt Op. *ευθυς* bef *ανεβη* (*see* ‖ *Mark*) BD[r]א 1 latt Syr syr-cu coptt æth Hipp

dicted sign gave him, which the word *ᾔδειν* implies, and which would justify him in announcing Him to his disciples as the Lamb of God. See the ancient opinions in Maldonatus's note. **15. ἀποκριθείς**] Bp. Wordsworth remarks, on this, the first occurrence of this very common form, that it is stigmatized by the grammarians as a solecism. The passage is in Phrynichus, Eclog. ed. Lobeck, p. 108,—*ἀποκριθῆναι διττὸν ἁμάρτημα. ἔδει γὰρ λέγειν ἀποκρίνασθαι, καὶ εἰδέναι ὅτι τὸ διαχωρισθῆναι σημαίνει, ὥσπερ οὖν καὶ τὸ ἐναντίον αὐτοῦ, τὸ συγκριθῆναι, εἰς ἓν καὶ ταὐτὸν ἐλθεῖν. εἰδὼς οὖν τοῦτο, ἐπὶ μὲν τὸ ἀποδοῦναι τὴν ἐπερώτησιν, ἀποκρίνεσθαι λέγε, ἐπὶ δὲ τοῦ διαχωρισθῆναι, τὸ ἀποκριθῆναι.* **ἄρτι**] The exact meaning is difficult. It cannot well be that which the E. V. at first sight gives, that something was to be done *now*, inconsistent with the actual and hereafter-to-be-manifested relation of the two persons. Rather —'*though what has been said* (ver. 14) *is true, yet the time is not come for that*:—**as yet**, *ἄρτι*, **now**, *are we in another relation* (viz. our Lord as the *fulfiller* of the law, John as a *minister* of it), *therefore suffer it.*' So Chrysostom: *οὐ διηνεκῶς ταῦτα ἔσται, ἀλλ' ὄψει με ἐν τούτοις οἷς ἐπιθυμεῖς· ἄρτι μέντοι ὑπόμεινον τοῦτο* (Hom. xii. 1, p. 161). 'This *ἄρτι* is spoken from the Lord's foreknowledge, that this relation of subjection to John was only temporary, and that hereafter their relative situations would be inverted.' Meyer. Stier remarks (Reden Jesu, vol. i. p. 14, edn. 2), that now was fulfilled the prophetic announcement of Ps. xl. 7, 8.

ἡμῖν] not for *μοί*, but for *μοὶ καὶ σοί*. I cannot help thinking that this word glances at the relationship and previous acknowledged destinations of the speakers. It has however a wider sense, as spoken by Him who is now first coming forth officially as the *Son of Man*, extending over *all those whose baptism plants them in his likeness*, Rom. vi. See Stier, ibid.

* **δικαιοσύνην**] **requirements of the law.** See ch. vi. 1, where the sense is general, as here. **16. βαπτισθείς**] On this account I would make the following remarks. (1) The appearance and voice seem to have been manifested to *our Lord and the Baptist only*. They may have been *alone* at the time: or, if not, we have an instance in Acts ix. 7, of such an appearance being confined to one person, while the others present were unconscious of it. We can hardly however, with some of the Fathers, say, that it was *πνευματικὴ θεωρία*,—or *ὀπτασία, οὐ φύσις τὸ φαινόμενον*, Theod. Mopsuest.,—or 'Aperiuntur cœli non reseratione elementorum, sed spiritualibus oculis, quibus et Ezechiel in principio voluminis sui apertos eos esse commemorat.' Jerome in loc. (2) The Holy Spirit descended not only in the *manner* of a dove, but *σωματικῷ εἴδει* (‖ Luke): which I cannot understand in any but the literal sense, as THE BODILY SHAPE OF A DOVE, seen by the Baptist. There can be no objection to this, the straightforward interpretation of the narrative, which does not equally apply to the Holy Spirit being *visible at all*, which John himself asserts Him to have been (John i. 32—34), even more expressly than is asserted here. Why the Creator Spirit may not have assumed an organized body bearing symbolical meaning, as well as any other material form, does not seem clear. This was the ancient, and is the *only honest* interpretation. All the modern explanations of the *ὡσεὶ περιστ.* as importing the *manner* of coming down, belong, as Meyer has rightly remarked, to the vain rationalistic attempt to reduce down that which is miraculous. The express assertion of Luke, and the fact that all four Evangelists have used the same expression, which they would not have done if it were a mere tertium comparationis, are surely a sufficient refutation of this rationalizing (and, I may add, blundering) interpretation. **εὐθύς** belongs to *ἀνέβη*, not to *βαπτ.*, nor to *ἀνεῴχθ.* It is the first member of the

u || L. Acts x. 11. Rev. xix. 11. Ezek. i. 1.
v omg articles, (ch. xii. 28 w. prep.) Rom. viii. 9, 14. 1 Cor. vii. 40 al. see Luke iv. 18.
w = ch. ix. 36. Ps. liv. 6.
x || Mk. L. ch. x. 16. xxi. 12 ||. Luke ii. 24, from Lev. xii. 8. John i. 32. ii. 14, 16 only.
y ||. ch. xvii. 5 ||. Acts x. 13, 15. 2 Pet. i 17, 18. 3 Kings xix. 13.

ᵘ ἀνεῴχθησαν αὐτῷ οἱ ᵘ οὐρανοί, καὶ εἶδεν [τὸ] ᵛ πνεῦμα
[τοῦ] ᵛ θεοῦ καταβαῖνον ʷ ὡσεὶ ˣ περιστερὰν [καὶ] ἐρχόμενον ἐπ' αὐτόν. 17 καὶ ἰδοὺ ʸ φωνὴ ἐκ τῶν οὐρανῶν λέ-

D καταβ... BCDEK LMPSU VΓΔℵ 1. 33

Chr Hil Vig Op: om ευθυς 33: txt CLP rel D-lat *h* syr arm spec. ηνεωχθησαν B Hipp. om αυτω (*as unnecessary, and not understood*) Bℵ[1](ins ℵ[2a]) tol syr-cu sah Iren-int-mss Hil_2 Vig. πνευμα θεου (omg το and του) Bℵ. aft καταβαινον ins εκ του ουρανου D gat(with mm) lat-*a b c* $g_{1.2}$ *h l* Hil. for ωσει, ως D Eus_1. om και (bef ερχομενον) Bℵ[1](ins ℵ[3a]) am(with forj harl[1] tol) lat-*a b c* g_2 *h* copt Iren-int Hil. for επ' (bef αυτον), εις D[1] Eus Ebionite-gosp: προς C[1]E[1]: txt BC[3]D[2]ℵ rel Iren-int. (P 33 def.)

conjunctive clause of which καὶ ἰδού is the second—as we say, **the moment that Jesus was gone up out of the water, behold.** (3) Two circumstances may be noticed respecting the manner of the descent of the Spirit: (α) it was, *as a dove:*—the Spirit as manifested in our Lord was *gentle* and *benign.* Lord Bacon (Meditationes Sacræ, cited in Trench on the Miracles, p. 37) remarks:—"Moses edidit miracula, et profligavit Ægyptios pestibus multis: Elias edidit, et occlusit cœlum ne plueret super terram: Elisæus edidit, et evocavit ursas de deserto quæ laniarent impuberes: Petrus Ananiam sacrilegum hypocritam morte, Paulus Elymam magum cæcitate percussit: sed nihil hujusmodi fecit Jesus. Descendit super eum Spiritus in forma columbæ, de quo dixit, Nescitis cujus Spiritus sitis. Spiritus Jesu, spiritus columbinus: fuerunt illi servi Dei tanquam boves Dei triturantes granum, et conculcantes paleam: sed Jesus agnus Dei sine ira et judiciis." On the *history* of this symbol for the Holy Spirit, see Lücke's Comm. on John, vol. i. 425. (β) This was not a sudden and temporary descent of the Spirit, but a *permanent* though special anointing of the Saviour for his holy office. It '*abode upon Him,*' John i. 32. And from this moment His ministry and mediatorial work (in the active official sense) begins. εὐθέως, the Spirit carries Him away to the wilderness: the day of His return thence (possibly; but see notes on John i. 29) John points Him out as the Lamb of God: then follows the calling of Andrew, Peter, Philip, and Nathanael, and the third day after is the first miracle at the marriage in Cana. But we must not imagine any *change* in the nature or person of our Lord to have taken place at his baptism. The anointing and crowning are but *signs* of the official assumption of the power which the king has by a right independent of, and higher than these. (4) The whole narrative is in remarkable parallelism with that of the Transfiguration. There we have our Lord supernaturally glorified in the presence of two great prophetic personages, Moses and Elias, who speak of His decease,—on the journey to which He forthwith sets out (ch. xvii. 22, compared with xix. 1); and accompanied by the same testimony of the voice from heaven, uttering the same words, with an addition accordant with the truth then symbolized. (5) In connexion with apocryphal additions, the following are not without interest: κατελθόντος τοῦ Ἰησοῦ ἐπὶ τὸ ὕδωρ, καὶ πῦρ ἀνήφθη ἐν τῷ Ἰορδάνῃ· καὶ ἀναδύντος αὐτοῦ ἀπὸ τοῦ ὕδατος κ.τ.λ. Justin Martyr, Dial. § 88, p. 185. The author of the tract 'de Rebaptismate,' among the works of Cyprian, blames the spurious book called 'Petri Prædicatio,' for relating, among other things, of Christ, "cum baptizaretur, iguem super aquam esse visum, quod in evangelio nullo est scriptum." (ch. ix.) The Ebionite gospel, according to Epiphanius, Hær. xxx. 13, vol. i. p. 138, added, after ἐν ᾧ εὐδόκησα,—ἐγὼ σήμερον γεγέννηκά σε. καὶ εὐθὺς περιέλαμψε τὸν τόπον φῶς μέγα. ὃν ἰδὼν ὁ Ἰωάννης λέγει αὐτῷ Σὺ τίς εἶ κύριε; καὶ πάλιν φωνὴ ἐξ οὐρανοῦ πρὸς αὐτόν· οὗτός ἐστιν ὁ υἱός μου ὁ ἀγαπητός, εἰς ὃν ηὐδόκησα. καὶ τότε ὁ Ἰωάν. προσπεσὼν αὐτῷ ἔλεγε Δέομαί σου κύριε, σύ με βάπτισον. ὁ δὲ ἐκώλυεν αὐτῷ λέγων Ἄφες, ὅτι οὕτως ἐστὶ πρέπον πληρωθῆναι πάντα. Jerome gives the following opening of the narrative from the gospel according to the Hebrews: "Ecce mater domini et fratres ejus dicebant ei Joannes baptista baptizat in remissionem peccatorum: eamus et baptizemur ab eo. Dixit autem eis Quid peccavi ut vadam et baptizer ab eo? nisi forte hoc ipsum quod dixi ignorantia est."

17.] **φων. λ.** does not require ἐγένετο or any word to be supplied, nor the participle to be understood as a past tense. **Lo, a voice from heaven, saying.**

γουσα Οὗτός ἐστιν ὁ υἱός μου ὁ [z] ἀγαπητός, ἐν ᾧ [a] εὐδόκησα.

IV. 1 Τότε Ἰησοῦς [b] ἀνήχθη εἰς τὴν ἔρημον ὑπὸ τοῦ
πνεύματος [c] πειρασθῆναι ὑπὸ τοῦ [d] διαβόλου. 2 καὶ [e] νη-

z ||. ch. xii. 18. xvii. 5 ||. 2 Pet. i. 17. Gen. xxii. 2. = μονογενήν, Aq.
a ||. 1 Cor. x. 5. 2 Cor. xii. 10. [2 Thess. ii. 12.] 2 Kings xxii. 20. Ps. cxlix. 4. cli. 5. Mal. ii. 17.
b Luke ii. 22 al. Gen. l. 4. 2 Macc. v. 9.
c 1 Cor. vii. 5. James i. 13. 3 Kings x. 1. Dan. i. 12.
d || L. al. fr. (not Mark.) 1 Chron. xxi. 1. Job i. 6. Wisd. ii. 24.
e ch. vi. 16 bis, 17, 18. ix. 14, 15 || Mk. L. Luke xviii. 12. Acts x. 30. xiii. 2, 3 only. not in John nor Epp. Judg. xx. 26 al. (-στις, ch. xv. 32. -στεύειν, Luke ii. 37.)

17. aft *λεγουσα* ins *προς αυτον* D lat-*a b* g_1 *h* [syr-cu]. for *ουτος εστιν*, *συ ει* D lat-*a* syr-cu Aug_1. *ηυδοκησα* CL[P]ℵ[1.3] Scr's b evv-x-y $Orig_2$ Eus_3.

Chap. IV. 1. for *τοτε ιησ. ανηχθη*, *αν. δε ο ιησ.* C[1](appy) L. rec ins *ο* bef *ιησ.*, with CDPℵ rel: om BUΔ. (33 def.) *υπο τ. πνευματος* bef *εις τ. ερημον* Kℵ [Syr syr-cu].

See similar constructions, Luke v. 12; xix. 20 al. fr. **εὐδόκησα**] not the usitative aorist, but declarative of the definite past *εὐδοκία* of the Father in Him, Eph. i. 4:—see above. On the solemn import, as regards us, of our Blessed Lord's baptism, cf. Athanas. Or. i., contra Arianos 47, vol. i. (ii. Migne) p. 355 f.: *εἰ δὲ ἡμῶν χάριν ἑαυτὸν ἁγιάζει* (John xvii. 18, 19), *καὶ τοῦτο ποιεῖ ὅτε γέγονεν ἄνθρωπος, εὔδηλον ὅτι καὶ ἡ εἰς αὐτὸν ἐν τῷ Ἰορδάνῃ τοῦ πνεύματος γενομένη κάθοδος, εἰς ἡμᾶς ἦν γενομένη διὰ τὸ φορεῖν αὐτὸν τὸ ἡμέτερον σῶμα. καὶ οὐκ ἐπὶ τῇ βελτιώσει τοῦ Λόγου γέγονεν, ἀλλ' εἰς ἡμῶν πάλιν ἁγιασμόν, ἵνα τοῦ χρίσματος αὐτοῦ μεταλάβωμεν . . . . τοῦ γὰρ κυρίου ὡς ἀνθρώπου λουομένου εἰς τὸν Ἰορδάνην, ἡμεῖς ἦμεν οἱ ἐν αὐτῷ καὶ παρ' αὐτοῦ λουόμενοι· καὶ δεχομένου δὲ αὐτοῦ το πνεῦμα, ἡμεῖς ἦμεν οἱ παρ' αὐτοῦ γενόμενοι τούτου δεικτικοί.* What follows is well worth reading, shewing the pre-eminence of our Lord's anointing over that of all others, Ps. xlv. 7: Isa. lxi. 1: Acts x. 38.

Chap. IV. 1—11.] Temptation of Jesus. Mark i. 12, 13. Luke iv. 1—13.

1. ἀνήχθη εἰς τ. ἔ.] The Spirit carried Him away, (see Acts viii. 39,) *αὐτὸν ἐκβάλλει*, Mark i. 12: compare Chrysostom's excellent remarks on this agency of the Holy Spirit, in the opening of his 13th homily, p. 167. Had St. Luke's *ἤγετο ἐν τῷ πν.* been our *only* account, we might have supposed what took place to have been done *in a vision:* but the expressions in the two other Evangelists, entirely preclude this. The *desert* here spoken of may either be the traditional place of the Temptation near Jericho (thence called *Quarantaria:* it is described in "The Land and the Book," p. 617, as a high and precipitous mountain, with its side facing the plain perpendicular, and apparently as high as the rock of Gibraltar, and with caverns midway below, hewn in the rock), or as scripture parallelism between Moses, Elias, and our Lord, leads one to think, the *Arabian desert of Sinai.* **πειρασθῆναι**] The express *purpose* of *ἀνήχθη.* No other rendering is even grammatical. Hence it is evident that our Lord at this time was not 'led up' of his own will and design, but as a part of the conflict with the Power of Darkness, He was *brought* to the Temptation. As He had been subject to his earthly parents at Nazareth, so now He is subject, in the outset of His official course, to his Heavenly Parent, and is by His will thus carried up to be tempted. In reverently considering the nature and end of this temptation, we may observe, (1) That the whole is *undoubtedly an objective historical narrative,* recording an actual conflict between our Redeemer and the Power of Evil. (2) That it is undetermined by the *letter* of the sacred text, whether the Tempter appeared *in a bodily shape,* or, *as a spirit,* was permitted to exert a certain power, as in ver. 5, and ver. 8, over the person of our Lord, even as the Holy Spirit did in ver. 1. If the latter were the case, the words spoken at the various stages of the temptation, were suggested by this Evil Power to the soul of our Redeemer. But (3) such an interpretation, while it cannot justly be accused of unreality by any who do not reject belief in the spiritual world, hardly meets the expressions of the text, *προσελθών* ver. 3, *ἐὰν πεσὼν προσκυνήσῃς μοι* ver. 9, and *ἀφίησιν αὐτόν* ver. 11. Nor do the two members of ver. 11 correspond to one another in this case, for the *ἄγγελοι* must have been visible and corporeal, as in the parallel case at Gethsemane, Luke xxii. 43.

διαβόλου] The *accuser,* or *adversary:* **Satan.** Not any *human* tempter or foe: no example can be adduced of a *man* being absolutely called **ὁ** *διάβ.* In John vi. 70, Judas is by our Lord called *διάβ.*,

στεύσας ἡμέρας τεσσεράκοντα καὶ νύκτας τεσσεράκοντα
[f] ὕστερον [g] ἐπείνασεν. 3 καὶ προσελθὼν ὁ [h] πειράζων
εἶπεν αὐτῷ Εἰ υἱὸς εἶ τοῦ θεοῦ, [i] εἰπὲ ἵνα οἱ λίθοι οὗτοι
[j] ἄρτοι [k] γένωνται. 4 ὁ δὲ ἀποκριθεὶς εἶπεν Γέγραπται
Οὐκ [l] ἐπ' ἄρτῳ μόνῳ [lm] ζήσεται ὁ ἄνθρωπος, ἀλλ' [n] ἐν

Z ο δε... BCDEK LMPSU VZΓΔℵ 1. 33

f = ch. xxi. 29, &c. John xiii. 36. Heb. xii. 11. Prov. v. 4.
g 1 Cor. iv. 11. xi. 21. Phil. iv. 12 al. Judg. viii. 4.
h pres. part., = 1 Thess. iii. 5 only.
i w. ἵνα, ‖ L. ch. xx. 21. Mark iii. 9. Luke x. 40. = Mark v. 43. Exod. xxxv. 1.
j plur., ch. xii. 4. xiv. 17 al. Exod. xvi. 29. xxix. 2.
k = John ii. 9. Rev. viii. 8. Exod. iv. 3.
l = ‖ L. only Gen. xxvii. 40. Deut. viii. 3.
m = ‖ L. 1 Cor. ix. 14 only. see John vi. 57.
n = John xvi. 30. 1 Cor. iv. 4.

2. *τεσσερακοντα* (2nd) bef *νυκτας* Dℵ.

3. *και προσηλθεν αυτω ο πειρ. και* D lat-*a b c*. rec ins *αυτω* bef *ο πειραζων*, with CDP rel lat-*a b c f* $g_{1,2}$ *h* syr-cu syr sah $\text{Just}_{\text{expr}}$: om Bℵ 1. 13. 33. 124 vulg lat-ff_1 *l* Syr copt æth arm [Chr].—rec om *αυτω* (aft *ειπεν*), with CP rel lat-*f* syr sah: ins BDℵ 1. 13. 33. 124 latt Syr syr-cu copt æth arm Chr. for *ειπε* (bef *ινα*), *ειπον* ℵ[2].

4. for *ο δε αποκρ.*, *αποκρ. δε ο ιησ.* D, simly *b c f* g_1 *l* syr-cu. rec om *ο* (bef *ανθρωπος*) (*omd by* KMS *and other mss in* ‖ *Luke, and also by some* LXX-*mss*), with KM[Γ] (S and Scr's mss, e sil) Eus: ins BCDPZℵ rel Scr's k. rec (for *εν*) *επι* (*to conform to* LXX *and to preceding*), with BPℵ rel Eus: txt CD 13. 59. 124. 243,

which is the generic substantive without the article; and in Esth. vii. 4 and viii. 1, Haman is called ὁ διάβολος, where the art. has no such meaning as would be here required. **2. νηστεύσας**] Not in the wider ecclesiastical sense of the word, but its strict meaning, of *abstaining from all food whatever; οὐκ ἔφαγεν οὐδὲν ἐν ταῖς ἡμέραις ἐκείναις*, Luke, ver. 2. Similarly Moses, Exod. xxxiv. 28, ἦν ἐναντίον κυρίου τεσσαράκοντα ἡμ. κ. τεσ. νύκ.· ἄρτον οὐκ ἔφαγε, καὶ ὕδωρ οὐκ ἔπιε, and Elias ἐπορεύθη ἐν ἰσχύϊ τῆς βρώσεως ἐκείνης τεσ. ἡ. καὶ τεσ. ν., 3 Kings xix. 8. **ὕστερον ἐπείν.**] Then probably *not during the time itself*. The period of the fast, as in the case of Moses, was spent in a spiritual ecstasy, during which the wants of the natural body were suspended.

3. καὶ προσελθών] From the words of both St. Mark and St. Luke, it appears that our Lord was tempted *also during the forty days*. Whether the words of St. Mark, ἦν μετὰ τῶν θηρίων, allude to *one kind* of temptation, is uncertain: see note on Mark i. 13. The word προσελθ. need not be understood of the *first* approach, but the first *recorded*—'at a certain time the tempter approaching, &c.' **ὁ πειράζων**, 'the tempter.' Here first we find the N. T. meaning of πειράζειν, *to solicit to sin*, which does not occur in the LXX, nor in the classics. The use of the pres. part. with the art., as denoting employ, or office, is very common. See, among other places, John iv. 36, 37, and ch. xiii. 3; xxvi. 46, 48. Cf. Winer, § 18. 3. **εἰ**] νομίζων ὑποκλέπτειν αὐτὸν τοῖς ἐγκωμίοις, Chrys. Or, as Euthymius, ᾤετο ὅτι παρακνισθήσεται τῷ λόγῳ, καθάπερ ὀνειδισθεὶς ἐπὶ τῷ μὴ εἶναι υἱὸς θεοῦ. At all events, there is no *doubt* expressed, as Wolf and Bengel think. **υἱὸς τοῦ θεοῦ**] In the N. T. are found *three combinations* of these two substantives and the article, and *all with one and the same meaning*, viz. The Son of God, in the highest and Messianic sense. (1) The expression in the text, of which our Lord says, John x. 36, ὃν ὁ Πατὴρ ἡγίασεν καὶ ἀπέστειλεν εἰς τὸν κόσμον ὑμεῖς λέγετε ὅτι βλασφημεῖς ὅτι εἶπον **Υἱὸς τοῦ θεοῦ** εἰμι; see also Matt. xxvii. 40. (2) ὁ υἱὸς τοῦ θ. In John ix. 35, we read, σὺ πιστεύεις εἰς **τὸν υἱὸν τοῦ θεοῦ**; . . . . . ὁ λαλῶν μετὰ σοῦ **ἐκεῖνός** ἐστιν. (3) υἱὸς θ. In Luke i. 35, τὸ γεννώμενον ἅγιον κληθήσεται **υἱὸς θεοῦ**. See also ch. xxvii. 54 (‖ Mk.), and notes there and on Luke xxiii. 47. **4.**] Our Lord does not give way to the temptation, so as to meet him with an open declaration, 'I am the Son of God:' thus indeed He might have asserted his Lordship over him, but not have been *his Conqueror for us*. The first word which He uses against him, reaches far deeper: '*Man* shall not live, &c.' "This, like the other text, is taken from the history of Israel's temptation in the wilderness: for Israel represents, in a foreshadowing type, the Son of Man, the servant of God for Righteousness, the one ἐρχόμενος, in whom alone that nature which in all men has degenerated into sin, πληροῖ πᾶσαν δικαιοσύνην. Adam stood not,—Israel according to the flesh stood not,—when the Lord their God tempted them: but rather, after Satan's likeness, tempted their God: but now the second Adam is come, the true Israel, by whose obedience the *way of life* is again made known and opened—'that man truly liveth on and in the eternal word of God.'" Stier's

παντὶ ῥήματι [o] ἐκπορευομένῳ διὰ στόματος θεοῦ. 5 τότε
[p] παραλαμβάνει αὐτὸν ὁ [d] διάβολος εἰς τὴν [q] ἁγίαν
[q] πόλιν, καὶ ἔστησεν αὐτὸν ἐπὶ τὸ [r] πτερύγιον τοῦ ἱεροῦ,
6 καὶ λέγει αὐτῷ Εἰ υἱὸς εἶ τοῦ θεοῦ, βάλε σεαυτὸν κάτω·
γέγραπται γὰρ ὅτι τοῖς ἀγγέλοις αὐτοῦ [s] ἐντελεῖται περὶ
σοῦ, καὶ [t] ἐπὶ χειρῶν ἀροῦσίν σε, μήποτε [u] προςκόψῃς
πρὸς λίθον τὸν πόδα σου. 7 Ἔφη αὐτῷ ὁ Ἰησοῦς
Πάλιν γέγραπται Οὐκ [v] ἐκπειράσεις κύριον τὸν θεόν σου.
8 πάλιν [p] παραλαμβάνει αὐτὸν ὁ [d] διάβολος εἰς [w] ὄρος

o = ch. xv. 11, &c. Num. xxxii. 24.
p = ch. ii. 13, &c. xvii. 1. Num. xxii. 41.
q ch. xxvii. 53. Rev. xi. 2. xxi. 2. xxii. 19 only. Isa. xlviii. 2. lii. 1. Dan. ix. 24 Theod.
r ‖ L. only. 1 Kings xv. 27.
s ch. xvii. 9 al. Gospp. only, exc. Acts i. 2. xiii. 47. Heb. ix. 20. xi. 22. Psa. xc. 11.
t = ch. xxiv. 17.
u trans., here and ‖ L. (from l. c.) only. intr., ch. vii. 27. John xi. 9, 10. Rom. ix. 32. xiv. 21. 1 Pet. ii. 8 only.
v ‖ L. Luke x. 25. [John viii. 4.] 1 Cor. x. 9 only. Deut. vi. 16 bis. Deut. viii. 16. Ps. lxxvii. 18 only. see Isa. vii. 12.
w (‖ L. v. r.) ch. xvii. 1 ‖ Mk. Rev. xxi. 10. Ezek. xl. 2.

in latt Hil. (Z lat-*b* def.) om εκπορευομενω δια στοματος D lat-*b* $g_{1.2}$ syr-jer (*so* ‖ *Luke*).

5. rec ιστησιν, with P rel: txt (*so also* ‖ *Luke*) BCDZℵ 1. 33 sah Eus.

6. for λεγει, ειπεν (‖ *Luke*) Zℵ[2] (txt ℵ[1·3a]) (vss ?). om του (bef θεου) D[1] (θ̄υ θ̄υ appy, Scriv: θεου Kipl). ins εντευθεν bef κατω (‖ *Luke*) C[1] syr-mg coptt arm. αιρουσιν D (but *tollent* D-lat: txt is the reading of ‖ Luke).

7. for ουκ εκπ., ου πειρασεις D.

Reden Jesu, vol. i. p. 16 (edn. 2). Observe also how our Lord resists Satan *in His humanity;* at once here numbering Himself with *men*, by adducing ὁ ἄνθρωπος as including His own case; and not only so, but thus speaking out the mystery of his humiliation, in which He had foregone his divine Power, of his own will. By '*every word* (or '*thing,*' for ῥῆμα is not expressed in the original) *that proceedeth out of the mouth of God,*' we must understand, *every arrangement of the divine will;* God, who ordinarily sustains by *bread*, can, if it please Him, sustain *by any other means*, as in the case alluded to. Compare John iv. 32, 34.

5. τότε παρ.] Power being most probably given to the tempter over the person of our Lord. In St. Luke, this temptation stands *third*. The real order is evidently that in the text; for otherwise our Lord's final answer, ver. 10, would not be in its place. It may be observed, that St. Luke makes no assertion as to succession, only introducing each temptation with καί: whereas τότε and πάλιν here seem to mark succession. Bishop Ellicott, for psychological reasons, which must be most untrustworthy when opposed to the express assertion of the sacred text (**τότε** ἀφίησιν αὐτόν), follows the order in St. Luke. For **ἁγ. πόλ.** see reff. **ἔστησεν**—by the same power by which he brought Him. **πτερύγιον**] Abundant instances have been produced to shew that πτέρον was applied to a *pointed roof* or *gable*. Now the LXX use πτέρυξ and πτερύγιον as synonymous with πτέρον; why may not the same be done in the N. T.? The general opinion, that our Lord was placed on *Herod's royal portico*, described in Jos. Antt. xv. 11. 5, is probably right; and the τό is in no way inconsistent with it. That portico overhung the ravine of Kedron from a dizzy height, ὡς, εἴ τις ἀπ' ἄκρου τοῦ ταύτης τέγους, ἄμφω συντιθεὶς τὰ βάθη, διοπτεύοι, σκοτοδινιᾶν, οὐκ ἐξικνουμένης τῆς ὄψεως εἰς ἀμέτρητον τὸν βυθόν. The argument that it was probably *on the other side, next the court,* is grounded on the perfectly gratuitous assumption, that an *exhibition to the people* was intended. There is no authority for this in the text; the temptation being one not of ambition, but of *presumption*. The inference from Eusebius, who, quoting Hegesippus, (Hist. ii. 23,) describes James the Just as set on and thrown from τὸ πτερύγιον τοῦ ναοῦ, among the people, is not decisive: for this term might embrace either side, as 'the cornice,' or 'the parapet' would.

6. γέγραπται] cited (nearly verbatim from the LXX, as almost all the texts in this narrative) as applying to all servants of God in general, and à fortiori to the Son of God: not as a prophecy of the Messiah.

7. πάλιν] not '*contra*,' which it never simply means, not even in Gal. v. 3: 1 John ii. 8: but '*rursus*' or '*iterum*,' as the versions rightly render it. The addition of a second Scripture *qualifies* and *interprets* the first; but *does not refute* it.

8. ὄρος ὑψ. λί.] The enquiry

ὑψηλὸν λίαν, καὶ δείκνυσιν αὐτῷ [x] πάσας τὰς [xy] βασιλείας
τοῦ [y] κόσμου καὶ τὴν [z] δόξαν αὐτῶν 9 καὶ εἶπεν αὐτῷ
Ταῦτά σοι πάντα δώσω, ἐὰν [a] πεσὼν [a] προσκυνήσῃς μοι.
10 τότε λέγει αὐτῷ ὁ Ἰησοῦς [b] Ὕπαγε [c] σατανᾶ· γέγραπται γάρ [d] Κύριον τὸν θεόν σου [e] προσκυνήσεις, καὶ
αὐτῷ μόνῳ [f] λατρεύσεις. 11 τότε [g] ἀφίησιν αὐτὸν ὁ
διάβολος, καὶ ἰδοὺ ἄγγελοι προσῆλθον καὶ [h] διηκόνουν
αὐτῷ.

BCDEK LMPSU VZΓΔℵ 1. 33

x Ezra i. 2. Dan. vii. 23 Theod., 27 LXX. y ‖ L. Rev. xi. 15. z = ch. vi. 29. Luke xii. 27. Dan. iv. 27 (30 Theod-F.). a = ch. ii. 11. xviii. 26. Acts x. 25. 1 Cor. xiv. 25. Rev. v. 14 al. Job i. 20. b N. T. intr., gospp. passim. elsw., James ii. 16. 1 John ii. 11. Rev. x. 8 al5. only. in LXX, transitive. Exod. xiv. 21 only. c ch. xii. 26 al. fr.† Sir. xxi. 27 only. d Deut. vi. 13. x. 20. e w. acc., here only in Mt. ‖ L. Luke xxiv. 52. John iv. (22,) 23, 24. Rev. ix. 20. xiii. 8, 12, 15. xiv. 9, 11. xx. 4 bis only. Gen. xxxvii. 7, 9. Judg. vii. 15 A. f ‖ L. Luke i. 74. ii. 37 only in Gospp. Acts vii. 7, 42 al. Exod. iii. 12. g = vv. 20, 22. John x. 12 al. fr. 2 Kings xv. 16. h = ‖ Mk. ch. xxv. 44. Mark xv. 41 †.

8. for δεικνυσιν, δικνυει(? υσι) ℵ, εδειξεν D (*from Luke* iv. 5).

9. rec (for ειπεν) λεγει, with P rel: txt BCDZℵ 33 latt Orig. rec ταυτα παντα σοι (*the simpler order*), with C3DP rel latt Iren-int: π. σ. τ. Orig1 Chr-3-5-8-a(and Field): π. τ. σ. Chr-1: txt BC1Zℵ 1. 33 am(with forj) lat-*l* Orig3 Chr-β.

10. aft υπαγε ins οπισω μου C2DZ rel harl1 lat-*b ff*1 *h l* (*a c g*1,2) syr-cu syr-with-ast æth arm Just Archel Petr Ath Chr Nest Damasc Thl Hil-ms Ambr Aug Vig Op: om BC1KP S(e sil) VΔℵ 1. 13. 124 vulg lat-*f k* [Syr] coptt Origexpr Petr Iren-int Tert Hil-ed Jerexpr Juv. (*There can, it appears to me, be no satisfactory reason assigned for the omission of these words, if originally in the text. On the other hand, if originally wanting, they were very likely to have been supplied from ch.* xvi. 23. *See also on* ‖ *Luke. Their omission is consequently more likely to be genuine than their insertion.*)

where and what this mountain was, is entirely nugatory, no data being furnished by the text. **δείκνυσιν αὐτ. π. τ. β.**] The additional words in Luke, ἐν στιγμῇ χρόνου, are valuable as pointing out to us clearly the supernatural character of this vision. If it be objected, that in that case there was no need for the ascent of the mountain,—I answer, that such natural accessories are made use of frequently in supernatural revelations: see especially Rev. xxi. 10. The attempts to restrict τοῦ κόσμου to *Palestine,* (which was, besides, God's peculiar portion and vineyard, as *distinguished from* the Gentile world,) or *the Roman* empire, are mere subterfuges: as is also the giving to δείκνυσιν the sense of 'points out the direction of.' The very passage of Polybius cited to support this view, completely refutes it, when taken entire. Hannibal, from the Alps, is directing the attention of his soldiers to the view of Italy; ἐνδεικνύμενος αὐτοῖς τὰ περὶ τὸν Πάδον πεδία (in sight) . . . . ἅμα δὲ καὶ τὸν τῆς Ῥώμης αὐτοῖς τόπον ὑποδεικνύων, where we may observe the distinction between the two compounds **ἐν-** and **ὑπο-**δείκνυμι: and further, that it is not **τὴν** Ῥ. but **τὸν** τῆς Ῥ. **τόπον** that he pointed out to them. Euthymius, however, interprets our verse thus, . . λέγων· ἐν τούτῳ μὲν τῷ μέρει κεῖται ἡ βασιλεία τῶν Ῥωμαίων, ἐν τούτῳ δὲ ἡ τῶν Περσῶν, ἐν ἐκείνῳ δὲ ἡ τῶν Ἀσσυρίων, καὶ τὰ ἑξῆς ὁμοίως· καὶ ὅτι ἡ μὲν ἔχει δόξαν ἐπὶ τοῖσδε τοῖς εἴδεσιν, ἡ δὲ ἐπὶ ταῖσδε, καὶ ἄλλη ἐπ' ἄλλοις, καὶ ἁπλῶς πάντα καταλέγει: and even Maldonatus approves it. In this last temptation the enemy reveals himself openly, as the ἄρχων τοῦ κόσμου τούτου, and as the father of lies; for though power is given him over this world and its sons, his assertion here is most untrue. **10.**] Our Lord at once repels him openly; not that He did not *know him before,*—but because he had *thus openly* tempted Him; but not even this of His own power or will; He adds, *for* it is written,—again, as Man, appealing to the Word of God. There does not appear to be sufficient ground for the distinction sometimes set up between the meanings of προσκυνεῖν with the dative and the same verb with the accusative. See, besides reff., Gen. xlix. 8: Exod. xi. 8.

From this time, our Lord is *known* by the devils, and casts them out by a word. Mark i. 24, 34; iii. 11; v. 7. **11. ἀφίησιν αὐτόν**] but *only for a season,* see ‖ Luke. The conflict, however often renewed in secret (of which we cannot speak), was certainly *again waged in Gethsemane*—αὕτη ὑμῶν ἐστιν ἡ ὥρα, καὶ ἡ ἐξουσία τοῦ σκότους. (Luke xxii. 53, compare John xiv. 30.) The expression in Luke x. 18, ἐθεώρουν τὸν σατανᾶν ὡς ἀστραπὴν ἐκ τοῦ οὐρανοῦ πεσόντα, must

12 Ἀκούσας δὲ ὅτι Ἰωάννης [i] παρεδόθη, [j] ἀνεχώρησεν
εἰς τὴν Γαλιλαίαν, 13 καὶ [k] καταλιπὼν τὴν Ναζαρᾶ
ἐλθὼν [l] κατῴκησεν [l] εἰς Καφαρναοὺμ τὴν [m] παραθα-
λασσίαν ἐν [n] ὁρίοις Ζαβουλὼν καὶ Νεφθαλείμ, 14 ἵνα

...καφαρναουμ Z. BCDEK LMPSU VΓΔℵ 1. 33

i = ‖ Mk. reff. ch. x. 19. j = ch. ii. 12. 2 Macc. v. 27. k = Heb. xi. 27. Josh. viii. 17. 4 Kings viii. 6 B. l ch. ii. 23 reff. m here only. 2 Chron. viii. 17 al. n ch. ii. 16 reff.

12. rec aft δε ins ο ιησους (*ver.* 12 *is the commencement of an ecclesiastical portion, and the name was therefore supplied, as so frequently is the case*), with C^2P rel latt syrr syr-cu arm Hil Gaud: om B C^1(appy) DZℵ 33 am(with forj) lat-*k* copt æth $Orig_3$ Eus_2 Aug. ιωαννης bef οτι $ℵ^1$(txt ℵ $corr^{1\cdot 2}$).

13. καταλειπων DELMZΔ 33: txt BCKPU[Γ]ℵ $Orig_3$. (Bch Matth are silent about S and V: *relinquens* D-lat Δ-lat; *relicta civitate* latt.) κατοικησεν D. παραθαλασσιον D [Cyr_1]: παρα θαλασσαν P$ℵ^1$(corrd to txt by origl scribe or $ℵ^2$).

be otherwise understood: see note there. **διηκόνουν**] viz. *with food*, as in the case of Elias, 1 Kings xix. 6, 7.

12—22.] Jesus begins his Ministry. Calling of Peter, Andrew, James, and John. Mark i. 14—20. Luke iv. 14, 15. Between the last verse and this is a considerable interval of time. After returning from the temptation (see note on John i. 28, end) our Lord was pointed out by John the Baptist, (ib. vv. 29—34,) and again on the morrow to two of his disciples, Andrew and (probably) John, who followed Him, and were (on the next day? see note, John i. 44) joined by Simon Peter (35—43): then on the morrow Philip and Nathanael were called (44—52); three days after was the marriage in Cana (ii. 1—11); then our Lord went down to Capernaum and remained not many days (12); then followed the Passover; the cleansing of the temple (13—22); the belief of many on Jesus (23—25); the discourse with Nicodemus (iii. 1—21); the baptizing by Jesus (i. e. his disciples) (22—24); the question about purifying, and testimony of the Baptist (25—36); the journey through Samaria into Galilee, and discourse with the woman of Samaria (iv. 1—42); the return to Cana and healing of the ruler's son in Capernaum (43—54); and the journey to Jerusalem related in John v. 1. After that chapter St. John breaks off the first part of his narrative, and between his v. 47 and vi. 1, comes in the synoptic narrative, Matt. iv. 12—xiv. 15: Mark i. 14—vi. 30: Luke iv. 14—ix. 10. This omission is in remarkable consistency with St. Matthew's account of his own calling in ch. ix. 9. Being employed in his business in the neighbourhood of Capernaum, he now first becomes personally acquainted with the words and actions of our Lord. From what circumstance the former miracle in Capernaum had not attracted his attention, we cannot, of course, definitely say; we can, however, easily conceive. Our Lord was not then *in* Capernaum; for the ruler sent to Him, and the cure was wrought by word at a distance. If Matthew's attention had not been called to Jesus before, he might naturally omit such a narrative, which John gives probably from personal knowledge. The *synoptic narrative generally* omits this whole section of our Lord's travels and ministry. Its sources of information, until the last visit to Jerusalem, seem to have been *exclusively Galilæan*, and *derived from persons who became attached to Him at a later period than any of the events recorded in that first portion of John's Gospel.* The objections to this view are, the narrative, in the three Gospels, of the baptism and temptation; but the former of these would be abundantly testified by John's disciples, many of whom became disciples of Jesus; and the latter could only have been derived from the mouth of our Lord Himself. **12. ἀνεχώρ.**] not '*returned*,' but **retired, withdrew**; see ch. ii. 22, and note. No notice is given *whence* this withdrawal took place. The narrative is evidently taken up after an interval, and without any intention that it should follow closely on ver. 11. Wieseler, Chron. Synops. pp. 162 ff., sees in this a proof that St. Matthew recognized a ministry in Judæa during the interval. I cannot quite think this, but certainly he does not *exclude* it. **13. καταλιπὼν τ. Ν.**] Not on account of the behaviour of the Nazarenes to Him after the preaching in the synagogue, Luke iv. 28, 29, as sometimes supposed; see notes, ib. ver. 31. **Καφαρναούμ**] This town, on the borders of the lake of Gennesaret, was central in situation, and in the most populous and frequented part of Galilee. It besides was the residence of four at least of the Apostles, Andrew and Peter, and James and John—and probably of Matthew. The town was named from a foun-

o ch. i. 22 reff. p Isa. ix. 1, 2. q ch. x. 5. Exod. xiii. 18. 1 Kings vi. 9. 3 Kings xviii. 43. r see Joel iii. 4. s = Luke i. 79. Isa. xlii. 7. t ch. x. 27. Luke xii. 3. elsw. John (i. 5 bis al6. 1 John i. 5. ii. 8, 9, 11 bis) only. Job xxviii. 3 only. u constr., Rev. ii. 7, 17. vi. 4.

BCDEK LMPSU VΓΔℵ 1. 33

[o] πληρωθῇ τὸ ῥηθὲν διὰ Ἡσαΐου τοῦ προφήτου λέγοντος
15 [p] Γῆ Ζαβουλὼν καὶ γῆ Νεφθαλείμ, [q] ὁδὸν θαλάσσης
πέραν τοῦ Ἰορδάνου, [r] Γαλιλαία τῶν ἐθνῶν, 16 ὁ λαὸς ὁ
[s] καθήμενος ἐν [t] σκοτίᾳ φῶς εἶδεν μέγα, καὶ [u] τοῖς [v] καθημένοις ἐν χώρᾳ καὶ [vw] σκιᾷ [vw] θανάτου φῶς [x] ἀνέτειλεν [u] αὐτοῖς. 17 [y] Ἀπὸ [y] τότε [z] ἤρξατο ὁ Ἰησοῦς [a] κηρύσσειν καὶ
λέγειν [b] Μετανοεῖτε· [b] ἤγγικεν γὰρ ἡ [b] βασιλεία τῶν [b] οὐρανῶν. 18 περιπατῶν δὲ [c] παρὰ τὴν θάλασσαν τῆς Γαλιλαίας π...

v Luke i. 79. Ps. cvi. 10. w Job xxviii. 3. Ps. xxii. 4. x intr., ch. xiii. 6 || Mk. Mark xvi. 2. Luke xii. 54. James i. 11. Ps. xcvi. 11. y ch. xvi. 21. xxvi. 16. Luke xvi. 16 only. Eccl. viii. 12 only. ἀπὸ τότε κ ἐκ τότε μὴ λέγε, ἀλλ' ἐξ ἐκείνου, Phryn. Lobeck. p. 461. z ch. xi. 7, 20 al. Gen. xi. 6. a = ch. iii. 1 reff. b ch. iii. 2 (reff. and note). c || Mk. ch. xiii. 1 al. 3 Kings iv. 29.

14. ins *του* bef *λεγοντος* D.

15. [om 2nd *γη* D Scr's g k s am.] *γαλιλαιας* (not B : see table) DL am(with forj, not fuld) lat-*a b c* f^1 ff_1 $g_{1.2}$ *h l* (but not *k*).

16. ins *τη* bef *σκοτ.* D. rec (for *σκοτια*) *σκοτει* (*simpler and more usual form : elsw, e.g. Luke* i. 79 : *Rom.* ii. 19, *σκοτει occurs without variation*), with C P(Tischdf) ℵ[1] rel (-*τι* CΔℵ[1]) Hipp $Orig_1$ Eus [Cyr_1] : txt BDℵ[2] (-*τεια* D, but -*τια* Bℵ[2]) $Orig_1$. rec *ειδ.* bef *φως* (*simpler order : see also* LXX), with DP rel vulg-ed Hipp $Orig_2$: txt BCℵ 1. 13. 33. 124 am(with forj) lat-*a b c f* ff_1 g_1 *h l* Orig Eus Chr Cyr. *ειδον* D lat-*a b c* g_1 *h*. om 1st *και* D lat-*b c* g_1 *h*. *οι καθημενοι* D, *qui sedebant* lat-*a b c* g_1 *h*. om 2nd *και* D[1](and lat), *in regione umbræ* vulg-ed(not am fuld) lat-*b* g_1 *h*.

17. aft *τοτε* ins *γαρ* D. om *ο* (bef *ιησ.*) D.

18. *και περιπατων* L, *autem Jesus ambulans* vulg (but *ambulans autem* am) : *περιπ.* (neither *δε* nor *και*) E[1] : *παραγων δε* D, *cum transiret* lat-*a b c f* g_1 *h* Eus spec. rec aft *περιπατων δε* ins *ο ιησους* (*beginning of an ecclesiastical portion*), with ELΔ vulg-ed lat-*a c h* arm spec ; *dominus noster* syr-cu : om BCDPℵ rel am(with forj harl

tain,—*πρὸς γὰρ τῇ τῶν ἀέρων εὐκρασίῃ καὶ πηγῇ διάρδεται γονιμωτάτῃ, Καφαρναοὺμ αὐτὴν οἱ ἐπιχώριοι καλοῦσι* (Joseph. B. J. iii. 10. 8),—כְּפַר נַחוּם, *vicus consolationis.* It is from this time called '*His own city,*' ch. ix. 1, see also ch. xvii. 24.

15.] This prophecy is spoken with direct reference to the days of the Messiah. It is here freely rendered from the Hebrew, without any regard to the LXX, which is wholly different. This, coming so immediately after a string of quotations literally from the LXX, seems to mark the beginning of a new portion of the Gospel, agreeably to what was said before. **ὁδὸν θαλάσσης**] the country round the coast of the lake. All the members of this sentence are in apposition with one another: thus **πέραν τοῦ Ἰορδ.** is not a description of the land before spoken of, which was not thus situated, but of a different tract. The later meaning of מֵעֵבֶר לַיַּרְדֵּן, as signifying the tract to the west of the Jordan, and which naturally sprung up during the captivity, is not to be thought of in Isaiah, who wrote before that event. See 1 Chron. xxvi. 30 in the Hebrew, where, however, the E. V. renders 'on *this side* Jordan westward.' Meyer [in edd. 1, 2; in edd. 3, 4, 5 he renders *ὁδ. θαλ.* '*seawards.*' See Moulton's Winer, p. 289, note 4] strangely makes *ὁδὸν θαλ.* the objective after *εἶδεν* understood, and construes '*the land of Zabulon and Nepthalim saw the way of the sea on the other side of the Jordan : Galilee of the Gentiles, &c. saw a great light :*' i. e. 'the light which went forth from Capernaum when Jesus dwelt there, is represented as sending its bright beams over the Galilæan sea, so that Zabulon and Nephthalim by this light could see the way leading along the other side of the sea.' **Γαλ. τ. ἐθν.**] *Galilee superior,* near to Tyre and Sidon, which was inhabited by a variety of nations.

17. **ἀπὸ τότε**] That is, *began His ministry in Galilee.* The account of Matthew, being that of an eye-witness, begins where his own experience began. It is not correct to suppose, as some of the German Commentators have done, (De Wette, Strauss,) that this preaching of repentance was *of a different character from the after-teaching of our Lord;* we recognize the same formula, though only partly cited, in ch. x. 7 : Luke x. 10. and find our Lord *still preaching repentance,* Luke xiii. 3, after repeated declarations of His Messiahship.

18. παρὰ τὴν θάλασσαν τῆς Γαλιλαίας] The lake of Gennesareth or Tibe-

εἶδεν δύο ἀδελφούς, Σίμωνα τὸν λεγόμενον Πέτρον καὶ
Ἀνδρέαν τὸν ἀδελφὸν αὐτοῦ, βάλλοντας [d] ἀμφίβληστρον
...εις P. BCDEK LMSUV ΓΔΠℵ 1. 33 εἰς τὴν θάλασσαν· ἦσαν γὰρ [e] ἁλιεῖς. 19 καὶ λέγει αὐτοῖς
[fg] Δεῦτε [fh] ὀπίσω μου, καὶ [i] ποιήσω ὑμᾶς [e] ἁλιεῖς ἀνθρώπων.
20 οἱ δὲ εὐθέως [j] ἀφέντες τὰ [k] δίκτυα ἠκολούθησαν αὐτῷ.
21 καὶ [l] προβὰς ἐκεῖθεν εἶδεν ἄλλους δύο ἀδελφούς, Ἰάκωβον τὸν τοῦ Ζεβεδαίου καὶ Ἰωάννην τὸν ἀδελφὸν αὐτοῦ,
ἐν τῷ πλοίῳ μετὰ Ζεβεδαίου τοῦ πατρὸς αὐτῶν [m] καταρτί-
...αυτους L. BCDEK MSUVΓ ΔΠℵ 1. 33 ζοντας τὰ [k] δίκτυα αὐτῶν, καὶ ἐκάλεσεν αὐτούς· 22 οἱ δὲ
εὐθέως [j] ἀφέντες τὸ πλοῖον καὶ τὸν πατέρα αὐτῶν ἠκο-
λούθησαν αὐτῷ.
23 Καὶ [n] περιῆγεν ἐν ὅλῃ τῇ Γαλιλαίᾳ, διδάσκων ἐν

d here (and Mark i. 16 v. r.) only. Ps. cxl. 10. Eccl. ix. 12. Hab. i. 15, 16, 17 only.
e ‖ Mk. bis. Luke v. 2 only. Job xl. 26 (31).
f ‖ Mk. only. 4 Kings vi. 19.
g ‖ Mk. ch. xi. 28. xxv. 34 al. Gen. xxxvii. 20.
h = ch. x. 38. xvi. 24. Luke xiv. 27. John xii. 19. Acts v. 37. 1 Tim. v. 15 al. 4 Kings vii. 15.
i = ch. v. 36 al. fr. Num. xxiv. 13.
j = ver. 11. k ‖ Mk. reff. l = ‖ Mk. (Luke i. 7, 18. ii. 36 of *time*) only. Xen. Ages. vi. 7.
m = ‖ Mk. Ezra vi. 12, 13, 16. met., Gal. vi. 1. 1 Thess. iii. 10 al. n ch. ix. 35. xxiii. 15. Mark vi. 6. Acts xiii. 11. w. ἐν, here only. trans., 1 Cor. ix. 5 only. Ezek. xxxvii. 2.

tol) lat-*b f ff*$_1$ *g*$_1$ *l* syrr copt æth Eus Chr Cyr Thl (simly in next ver, aft αυτοις C[2] lat-*a c h* Syr syr-cu æth Cyr spec ins ο ιησους). for λεγ., καλουμενον ℵ[2] Scr's h 27 [Eus]: επικαλουμ. E 457. αμφιβληστρος(but corrd) D[1].

19. aft υμας ins γενεσθαι (‖ *Mark*) Dℵ[2] 33 latt Syr syr-mg-ms æth [Cyr$_1$].

21. εαυτου ℵ-corr[1](appy: txt ℵ[1·2]). **22.** aft πλοιον ins αυτων ℵ[1](om ℵ[2]).

23. rec ολην την γαλιλαιαν (*adaptation to more usual construction*), omg εν (*homœotel*), with DLℵ[2] rel latt Eus Hil: txt BC(ℵ[1]) syrr [syr-cu] copt æth.—om ολη ℵ[1]. rec aft γαλ. ins ο ιησους (*supplementary* (*beg of pericope*) *as the variations shew*), with C[3] rel: aft περιηγεν, C[1]Dℵ 1. 33 latt syrr copt æth arm Eus Thl: om B 157 ev-20 lat-*k* syr-cu. aft διδασκων ins αυτους ℵ[1](ℵ[2] disapproving).

rias (John vi. 1), called in the O. T. "the sea of Chinnereth," Num. xxxiv. 11, or Chinneroth, Josh. xii. 3: the Γεννησαρῖτις λίμνη of Josephus, Antt. xviii. 2. 1: Strabo xvi. p. 755: Plin. v. 16: Ptol. v. 15. It is of an oval shape, about 13 geographical miles long, and 6 broad: and is traversed by the Jordan from N. to S. "Its most remarkable feature is its deep depression, being no less than 700 feet below the level of the ocean." See the interesting article by Mr. Porter in Smith's Biblical Dictionary. If we give any consideration to the circumstances here related, we cannot fail to see that the account in John is admirably calculated to complete the narrative. We have there furnished to us the reason why these two brethren were so ready to arise and follow One, whom, if we had this account only, we should infer they had never before seen. Add to this, that there is every probability that one of the other pair of brethren, John the son of Zebedee, is there described as having gone with Andrew to the dwelling of our Lord. It also tends to confirm the chronological view here taken, that Philip, the only one mentioned expressly by John as *having been called* by Jesus, is *not mentioned here as called:* and that Andrew, and the other disciple of John the Baptist, clearly were not *called* by Jesus in John i. 35—40, or the words παρ' αὐτῷ ἔμειναν τὴν ἡμέραν ἐκείνην, could not have been used: that these two *continued* disciples of the Baptist, is not probable; but that they were henceforth, but not invariably, attached to our Lord. I believe that the disciple whom Jesus loved was in His company during the whole of the events in John ii. iii. iv. and v., and on His return from Judæa with His disciples, John having for a time returned to his business, as our Lord was now resident in Capernaum, received, as here related, this more solemn and final call. We must remember, that the disciples would naturally have gone up to Jerusalem at the Passover, John ii. 23, *without a call from the Lord*, and by what they saw there would become more firmly attached to him. The circumstance related in John xxi., that even after they were assured of the Resurrection, the Apostles *returned to their occupation* as fishermen, gives additional probability to the usual explanation of the call in our text. **20. ἀφέντες κ.τ.λ.]** i. e. *from this time they were constant followers* of the Lord. But when He happened to be in the neighbourhood

o = gospp. (John vi. 59. xviii. 20 only) and Acts passim. see Gen. i. 9. Num. xvi. 24. Ps. lxi. 8.
p so Luke iv. 15. Acts viii. 5. xx. 2. 2 Cor. ii. 13. Gal. ii. 2 al.

ταῖς [o] συναγωγαῖς [p] αὐτῶν καὶ [q] κηρύσσων τὸ [r] εὐαγγέλιον
τῆς [rs] βασιλείας καὶ [t] θεραπεύων πᾶσαν [u] νόσον καὶ πᾶσαν
[v] μαλακίαν ἐν τῷ λαῷ. 24 καὶ [w] ἀπῆλθεν ἡ [x] ἀκοὴ αὐτοῦ
εἰς ὅλην τὴν Συρίαν· καὶ προςήνεγκαν αὐτῷ πάντας
τοὺς [y] κακῶς [y] ἔχοντας [z] ποικίλαις [u] νόσοις καὶ [a] βασάνοις

BCDEK MSUVΓ ΔΠℵ 1. 33

q w. accus., Mark i. 4, 14. Luke iii. 3. iv. 18 (from Isa. lxi. 1), 19 al. fr. Mt. Mk. L. P. only. (absol., 1 Pet. iii. 19. Rev. v. 2.) r ch. ix. 35. xxiv. 14 (Mark i. 14 v. r.) only. s see ch. viii. 12. xiii. 19. t = gospp. (John v. 10 only) and Acts passim. Rev. xiii. 3, 12 only ‡. Tobit xii. 3. Wisd. xvi. 12 al. u ch. viii. 17 al. Mt. Mk. L. (Acts xix. 12) only. Ps. cii. 3. v ch. ix. 35. x. 1 (both places w. νοσ.) only. Deut. vii. 15. Isa. xxxviii. 9. w = here only ‡. see ch. ix. 26. x = ch. xiv. 1. xxiv. 6 al. 2 Kings xiii. 30. y Mark vi. 55. Luke vii. 2 al. Ezek. xxxiv. 4. z Mark i. 34 ‖ L. only in Gospp. 2 Tim. iii. 6 al. a Luke xvi. 23, 28 only. 1 Kings vi. 3, 4, 8, 17. 2 Macc. ix. 5.

24. **εξηλθεν** (*Mark* i. 28) Cℵ 1. 33 syr-mg copt arm Orig : txt BD rel latt(*abiit*) Eus. αυτ. bef η ακ. D(but *opinio ejus* D-lat, with *a b c*) : om αυτ. Δ. for ολην, πασαν ℵ. βασανους ℵ[1] [om και βασ. E[1] v].

of their homes, they resumed their fishing, cf. Luke v. 1—11, which occurrence was, in my belief, different from, and later than the one related in our text. See notes there.

23—25.] He makes a Circuit of Galilee. (Mark i. 39. Luke iv. 44, ordinarily: but qu.? There is no necessity for believing this circuit of Galilee to be identical with those, even if we read Γαλιλαίας in the passage in Luke. Our Lord made *many such circuits*.)

23. **συναγωγαῖς**] These were the places of religious assembly among the Jews after the return from the captivity. Tradition, and the Targums, ascribe a very early origin to synagogues: and Deut. xxxi. 11, and Ps. lxxiv. 8, are cited as testimonies of it. But the former passage does not necessarily imply it: and it is doubtful whether that Psalm was not itself written after the captivity. They are generally supposed to have originated in Babylon, and thence to have been brought, at the return, into the mother land. See Neh. viii. 1—8. At the Christian era there were synagogues in every town, and in some larger towns several. See Acts ix. 2, 20. In Jerusalem, according to the Rabbinical writings, there were upwards of 450. (See Acts vi. 9, and note.) The people assembled in them on sabbath and festival days, and in later times also on the second and fifth days of each week, for public prayer and the hearing of portions of Scripture. τῶν ἱερέων δέ τις ὁ παρὼν ἢ τῶν γερόντων εἷς ἀναγινώσκει τοὺς ἱεροὺς νόμους αὐτοῖς καὶ καθ' ἕκαστον ἐξηγεῖται μέχρι σχεδὸν δείλης ὀψίας. Philo, Fragm. vol. ii. p. 630 (Euseb. Prep. Evang. viii. 7, vol. iii. p. 359). See Luke iv. 16: Acts xiii. 15. The officers of the synagogues were (1) the ἀρχισυναγωγός, Luke viii. 49; xiii. 14: Acts xviii. 8, 17, who had the care of public order, and the arrangement of the service; (2) the Elders, πρεσβύτεροι Luke vii. 3, ἀρχισυναγωγοί Mark v. 22: Acts xiii. 15, who seem to have formed a sort of council under the presidency of the **ἀρχισυναγωγός**; (3) the *legatus* or *angelus ecclesiæ*, who was the reader of prayers, and also secretary and messenger of the synagogues; (4) the ὑπηρέτης (Luke iv. 20), or chapel clerk, whose office was to prepare the books for reading, to sweep, open, and shut the synagogue. Besides these, there appear to have been alms-gatherers. The synagogue was fitted up with seats, of which the first row (πρωτοκαθεδρίαι) were an object of ambition with the scribes (ch. xxiii. 6). A pulpit for the reader, lamps, and a chest for keeping the sacred books, appear to complete the furniture of the ancient synagogue. Punishments, e. g. scourging, were inflicted in the synagogues. (See ch. x. 17; xxiii. 34: Luke ix. 49: Acts xxii. 19; xxvi. 11.) The catechizing also of children seems to have taken place there (Lightfoot, xi. 281), as also disputations on religious questions. Our Lord was allowed to read and teach in the synagogues, although of mean extraction according to the flesh, because of His miracles, and His supposed character as the professed leader and teacher of a religious sect. **αὐτῶν**] viz. of the Galilæans: the subject being taken up out of **Γαλιλαίᾳ** preceding. See reff., and Winer, § 22, 3. **κηρύσσων τὸ εὐαγ.**] For the exact meaning of these words, compare the declaration in the synagogue at Nazareth, Luke iv. 16—30. **24.** **Συρίαν**] Answering to ὅλην τὴν περίχωρον τῆς Γαλιλαίας, Mark i. 28. On **βάσανος**, see Lexx. Our word '*trial*' has undergone a change of meaning very similar. On the δαιμονιζόμενοι see note on ch. viii. 28. The σεληνιαζόμενοι were probably *epileptics*: see an instance in

[b] συνεχομένους, [c] δαιμονιζομένους καὶ [d] σεληνιαζομένους
καὶ [e] παραλυτικούς, καὶ [t] ἐθεράπευσεν αὐτούς. 25 καὶ
ἠκολούθησαν αὐτῷ ὄχλοι πολλοὶ ἀπὸ τῆς Γαλιλαίας
καὶ Δεκαπόλεως καὶ Ἱεροσολύμων καὶ Ἰουδαίας καὶ
πέραν τοῦ Ἰορδάνου.
V. 1 Ἰδὼν δὲ τοὺς ὄχλους [f] ἀνέβη εἰς [fg] τὸ ὄρος· καὶ

b = Luke iv. 38. viii. 37. Acts xxviii. 8 only. see Luke xii. 50. Jer. xxiii. 9. c ch. viii. 16, 28, 33 || Mk. al.† Ps. xc. 6 Aq. d ch. xvii. 15 only†. e ch. viii. 6. ix. 2, &c. || Mk. (Luke v. 24 v. r.) only†. f ch. xiv. 23. xv. 29. Mark iii. 13. Luke ix. 28. Exod. xix. 3. g as above (f). Luke vi. 12 al.

rec ins και bef δαιμονιζομενους, with C[3]Dℵ rel latt [syr-cu] : om BC[1] 13. 235 copt Eus. —om και δαιμ. MΔ.—δ. μο of δεμονιαζομενους(sic) is written over an erasure by ℵ-corr[1 or 2]. ins παντας bef εθεραπευσεν, omg αυτους, D lat-*a b c* g_1 *h* (syr-cu).

ch. xvii. 14 and ||. **25. Δεκαπόλεως**] A district principally east of the Jordan, so called from ten cities, some of the names of which are uncertain. Pliny (Nat. Hist. v. 18) says, "Jungitur ei lateri Syriæ Decapolitana regio, a numero oppidorum, in quo non omnes eadem observant. Plurimi tamen Damascum . . . . Philadelphiam, Raphanam, omnia in Arabiam recedentia; Scythopolin . . . Gadara . . . Hippon, Dion, Pellam . . . . Galasam, Canatham." Josephus appears not to include Damascus in Decapolis, for he calls Scythopolis μεγίστη τῆς Δεκαπόλεως (B. J. iii. 9. 7): and Cellarius thinks Cæsarea Philippi and Gergesa should be substituted for Damascus and Raphana. See Mark vii. 31. **πέραν τ. Ἰορδ.**] Peræa. The country east of the Jordan, between the rivers Jabbok and Arnon. See Jos. B. J. iii. 3. 3.

CHAPP. V. VI. VII.] THE SERMON ON THE MOUNT. In this form peculiar to Matthew. **1. ἰδὼν δέ**] Without attempting a solution of the many difficulties which beset the question of time, place, and arrangement of our Lord's Sermon on the Mount, I shall state the principal views of these subjects, and make some remarks upon them. One of the weightiest questions is, as to *the identity or otherwise of the Sermon with that given in Luke* vi. 20—49. There is (I) the view that they *are identical.* This is generally taken by ordinary readers of Scripture, from their similarity in many points. It is also taken by most of the modern German Commentators, who uniformly reject every attempt at harmonizing by supposing the same or similar words to have been twice uttered. This view is, however, beset by difficulties. For (α) the sermon in Luke is expressly said to have been delivered *after* the selection of the Apostles: whereas that in the text is as expressly, by continual consecutive notes of time extending to the call of Matthew, (before which the Apostles cannot have been chosen,) placed *before* that event. And it is wholly unlikely that St. Matthew, assuming him to be the author of our Gospel, would have made a discourse, which he must have heard immediately after his call as an Apostle, take place before that call. Then (β) *this* discourse was spoken on *a mountain,—that,* after descending from a mountain, in the *plain.* Possibly this may be got over, by rendering ἐπὶ τόπου πεδινοῦ "on a level place." See note on Luke, l. c.: and the citation from Stanley below. And again (γ), the two discourses are, though containing much common matter, *widely different.* Of 107 verses in Matt., Luke contains only *thirty:* his *four* beatitudes are balanced by as many *woes:* and in his text, parts of the sermon are introduced by sayings, which do not precede them in Matt. (e. g. Luke vi. 39 ff., 45 ff.), but which naturally connect with them. (II) St. Luke *epitomized* this discourse, leaving out whatever was unsuitable for his Gentile readers, e. g. ch. v. 17—38. But this is improbable: for Luke in several verses is *fuller* than Matthew, and the whole discourse, as related by him, is connected and consecutive. (III) The two discourses are *wholly distinct.* This view is maintained by Greswell, vol. ii. Dis. xi., and principally from the arguments above noticed. But it also is not without grave difficulties, especially if we suppose, as Gres. does, that Luke had the Gospel of Matthew before him (but on this see Prolegg. ch. i. § ii.). That two discourses wholly distinct should contain so much in common, seems unlikely and unnatural. It is hardly credible that two great public special occasions should be selected by the Lord near the commencement of His ministry, and two discourses delivered to the same audience, not *identical,* which might have been very probable, and impressive from that very circumstance,—nor consecutive, nor explanatory the one of the other, but only coinciding in fragments, and not even as two different reports at

h intr., ch. xiii. 48. xx. 21 al. fr. Ezek. xiv. 1. trans., 1 Cor. vi. 4.

[h] καθίσαντος αὐτοῦ προσῆλθον αὐτῷ οἱ [i] μαθηταὶ αὐτοῦ. BCDEK MSUVΓ ΔΠא 1. 33
2 καὶ [k] ἀνοίξας τὸ [k] στόμα αὐτοῦ ἐδίδασκεν αὐτοὺς λέγων

i Gospp. and Acts (only) passim †. (-τρια. Acts ix. 36. -τεύειν. ch. xiii. 52.) k = ch. xiii. 35, from Ps. lxxvii. 2. Acts viii. (32, from Isa. liii. 7) 35 al. Job iii. 1. see Eph. vi. 19

CHAP. V. 1. προσηλθαν B[1]א[1]. om αυτω B Orig.
2. εδιδαξεν *docuit* D.

the distance of some years might be expected to do. Add to this, that those parts of the discourses in which Luke and Matthew agree, occur in both in almost the same order, and that the beginning and conclusion of both are the same. (IV) St. Matthew *gives a general compendium of the sayings of our Lord during this part of His ministry*, of which St. Luke's discourse formed a *portion*, or perhaps was *another shorter compendium*. But the last stated objection applies with still greater force to this hypothesis, and renders it indeed quite untenable. Besides, it labours under the chronological difficulty in all its bearings. And to one who has observed throughout the close contextual connexion of the parts in this discourse, it will be quite incredible that they should be a mere collection of sayings, set down at hazard. See notes throughout. (V) The apparent discrepancies are sometimes reconciled by remembering, that *there is no fixed time mentioned in any Evangelist for the special ordination of the Apostles*, and that it is very doubtful whether they were at any set moment so ordained all together. Thus Matthew may have been a usual hearer of our Lord, and present with the whole of the Apostles, as related in Luke, though not yet formally summoned as related in Matt. ix. 9 ff. The introduction of the discourse in Luke by the words ἐγένετο δὲ ἐν ταῖς ἡμέραις ταύταις (which I maintain to be, on Luke vi. 12, not only *possibly*, but *expressly* indefinite, and to indicate that the event so introduced may have happened at any time during the current great period of our Lord's ministry, before, during, or after, those last narrated,) allows us great latitude in assigning Luke's discourse to any precise time. This, however, leaves the difficulties (above stated under I) in supposing the discourses identical, in force, except the chronological one. With regard to the many sayings of this sermon which occur, dispersed up and down, in Luke, see notes in their respective places, which will explain my view as to their connexion and original times of utterance, in each several instance. See also notes on Luke vi. 20—49. **τὸ ὄρος**] Either *some hill* near Capernaum well known by this name, and called by it in the reff. to Mark and Luke, (tradition, not earlier probably than the Crusades, which points out a hill between Capernaum and Tiberias as the Mount of Beatitudes, near the present Saphet, is in such a matter worthless as an authority. But the situation seems to modern travellers (see Stanley, 'Sinai and Palestine,' p. 368) "so strikingly to coincide with the intimations of the gospel narrative, as almost to force the inference that in this instance the eye of those who selected the spot was for once rightly guided. It is the only height seen in this direction from the shores of the lake of Gennesareth. The plain on which it stands is easily accessible from the lake, and from that plain to the summit is but a few minutes' walk. The platform at the top is evidently suitable for the collection of a multitude, and corresponds precisely to the 'level place' to which He would 'come down' as from one of its higher horns to address the people. Its situation is central both to the peasants of the Galilæan hills, and the fishermen of the Galilæan lake, between which it stands, and would therefore be a natural resort both to Jesus and His disciples when they retired for solitude from the shores of the sea, and also to the crowds who assembled 'from Galilee, from Decapolis, from Jerusalem, from Judæa, and from beyond Jordan.' None of the other mountains in the neighbourhood could answer equally well to this description, inasmuch as they are merged into the uniform barrier of hills round the lake: whereas this stands separate—'the mountain,' which alone could lay claim to a distinct name, with the exception of the one height of Tabor, which is too distant to answer the requirements,") or *the mountain district*, certainly imported by the word in ch. xiv. 23. See a full description of the locality in Tholuck, Bergpr., ed. 3, pp. 63 ff. **οἱ μαθηταί**] in the wider sense: including those of the Apostles already called, and all who had, either for a long or a short time, attached themselves to him as hearers. See John vi. 66.

2. ἀνοίξας τὸ στ. αὐ.] as in reff., a solemn introduction to some discourse or advice of importance. **αὐτούς**] i. e.

3 [l] Μακάριοι οἱ [m] πτωχοὶ τῷ [n] πνεύματι, ὅτι αὐτῶν ἐστιν
ἡ [o] βασιλεία τῶν [o] οὐρανῶν. 4 μακάριοι οἱ [p] πενθοῦντες,

l ch. xi. 6 al. fr. (not Mk.) Ps. xxxi. 1, 2 al.
m see ch. xi. 5 ‖. Rev. iii. 17. Isa. xxix. 19.
n = Mark viii. 12. John xi. 33 al. subj. dat., 1 Cor. vii. 34 al. Ps. xxxiii. 18.
o see note, ch. iii. 2.
p ch. ix. 15. 1 Cor. v. 2. Rev. xviii. 11, &c. Isa. lxi. 2.

3. om τω D[1](ins D[3]).
transp **vv. 4** and **5** D 33 vulg lat-*a c ff*$_1$ *g*$_{1.2}$ *h k l* syr-cu Clem Orig$_{expr}$ Eus-canon [Bas] Nyss Tert Hil$_2$ Jer Aug : txt BCℵ rel lat-*b f* syrr copt æth arm Orig$_1$ [Tert$_1$ (Tischdf)] Hil$_1$ Op.
4. aft πενθ. ins νυν ℵ[2] 33 copt.

τοὺς μαθητάς. The discourse (see vv. 13, 14, 20, 48; ch. vi. 9; vii. 6) was spoken directly to the disciples, but (see vii. 28, 29) also generally to the multitudes. It is a divine commentary on the words with which His own and the Baptist's preaching opened: μετανοεῖτε· ἤγγικεν γὰρ ἡ βασ. τ. οὐρανῶν. It divides itself into various great sections, which see below.

3—16.] The Description of the Lord's Disciples, their Blessedness, and Dignity. **3. οἱ πτ. τῷ πν.**] οὐκ εἶπεν, οἱ πτ. τοῖς χρήμασιν, ἀλλ', οἱ πτ. τῷ πνεύματι, τουτέστιν οἱ ταπεινοὶ τῇ προαιρέσει καὶ τῇ ψυχῇ. Euthym. τί ἐστιν "οἱ πτωχοὶ τῷ πνεύματι;" οἱ ταπεινοὶ καὶ συντετριμμένοι τὴν καρδίαν. Chrysostom, Hom. xv. in Matt. 1, vol. vii. p. 185. 'Ne quis putaret paupertatem, quæ nonnunquam necessitate portatur, a Domino prædicari, adjunxit, spiritu, ut humilitatem intelligeres, non penuriam. Beati pauperes spiritu, qui propter Spiritum Sanctum voluntate sunt pauperes' (Jerome in loc.). 'Pauperes spiritu, humiles et timentes Deum, id est, non habentes inflantem (or, inflatum) spiritum' (Augustine in loc.). Again: 'Pauper Dei in animo est, non in sæculo' (Aug. Enarr. in Ps. cxxxi. 26, vol. iv. pt. ii.). **τῷ πν.** is in opposition to τῇ σαρκί: so ἀπερίτμητοι τῇ καρδίᾳ, Acts vii. 51; ἁγία κ. τῷ σώματι κ. τῷ πνεύματι, 1 Cor. vii. 34. These words cannot be joined with μακάριοι (as Olearius, Wetst., Michaelis, Paulus): see ver. 8.

The meaning of *voluntary poverty*, as that of the religious orders, given by many Romish interpreters, is *out of the question*. It seems however to have been adopted by many of the Fathers. Basil (on Ps. xxxiii. 5, vol. i. p. 147) says, οὐκ ἀεὶ ἐπαινετὴ ἡ πτωχεία, ἀλλ' ἡ **ἐκ προαιρέσεως** κατὰ τὸν εὐαγγελικὸν σκοπὸν κατορθουμένη· πολλοὶ γὰρ πτωχοὶ μὲν τῇ περιουσίᾳ, πλεονεκτικώτατοι δὲ τῇ προαιρέσει τυγχάνουσιν. But the same father elsewhere explains the words, πτωχοὺς οὐ τοὺς κατὰ χρήματα ἐνδεεῖς λέγει, ἀλλὰ τοὺς **τῇ διανοίᾳ ἠλαττωμένους** (vol. i. p. 597). And Chrys. himself seems to waver: for next to the comment above cited, he says πνεῦμα γὰρ ἐνταῦθα τὴν ψυχὴν καὶ τὴν προαίρεσιν λέγει. He probably however means that the ψ. and προαίρ. are the *departments of our being in which* the πτωχεία takes place. See Clem. Alex., 'Quis dives salvus,' § 17, p. 934, P. As little can the *bare literal* sense of the words, which Julian scoffed at, be understood: viz. those who are *ill-furnished in mind*, and uneducated. See Rev. iii. 17. The idea (De Wette) is not improbable, that our Lord may have had a reference to the poor and subjugated Jewish people around him, once members of the theocracy, and now expectants of the Messiah's temporal kingdom; and, from their condition and hopes, taken occasion to preach to them the deeper spiritual truth. **αὐτῶν ἐστ. ἡ β. τ. οὐ.**] See Luke iv. 17—21: James ii. 5. The βασιλεία must here be understood in its widest sense: as the combination of all rights of Christian citizenship in this world, and eternal blessedness in the next, ch. vi. 33. But Tholuck well observes (Bergpredigt, p. 74 ff.), that all the senses of βασ. τ. θεοῦ (or οὐρ., or χριστοῦ) are only different sides of the same great idea —the *subjection of all things to God in Christ*. He cites from Origen (**περὶ** εὐχῆς, 25, vol. i. p. 239): τῇ οὖν ἐν ἡμῖν βασιλείᾳ τοῦ θεοῦ ἡ ἀκρότης ἀδιαλείπτως προκόπτουσιν ἐνστήσεται, ὅταν πληρωθῇ τὸ παρὰ τῷ ἀποστόλῳ εἰρημένον, ὅτι ὁ χριστός, πάντων αὐτῷ τ. ἐχθρῶν ὑποταγέντων, παραδώσει τ. βασιλείαν τῷ θεῷ κ. πατρί, ἵνα ᾖ ὁ θεὸς τὰ πάντα ἐν πᾶσι.

4. μακ. οἱ πενθ.] The spiritual qualification in the former verse must be carried on to this, and the mourning understood to mean not only that on account of sin, but *all such as happens to a man in the spiritual life*. All such mourners are blessed: for the Father of mercies and God of all consolation being their covenant God, His comfort shall overbear all their mourning, and taste the sweeter for it. In Luke ii. 25, the Messiah's coming is called ἡ παράκλησις τοῦ Ἰσραήλ.

This beatitude is by many editors (Lachmann, e. g.) placed after ver. 5. But the authority is by no means decisive, and I cannot see how the logical

ὅτι αὐτοὶ [q] παρακληθήσονται. 5 μακάριοι οἱ [r] πραεῖς, ὅτι BCDEK
αὐτοὶ [s] κληρονομήσουσιν τὴν γῆν. 6 μακάριοι οἱ [tu] πεινῶν- MSUVΓ
τες καὶ [tv] διψῶντες τὴν [w] δικαιοσύνην, ὅτι αὐτοὶ [x] χορτασ- ΔΠא 1.
θήσονται. 7 μακάριοι οἱ [y] ἐλεήμονες, ὅτι αὐτοὶ [z] ἐλεη- 33
θήσονται. 8 μακάριοι οἱ [a] καθαροὶ τῇ καρδίᾳ, ὅτι αὐτοὶ
τὸν [b] θεὸν [b] ὄψονται. 9 μακάριοι οἱ [c] εἰρηνοποιοί, ὅτι

q = ch. ii. 18 al. fr. Gen. xxiv. 67.
r ch. xi. 29. xxi. 5, from Zech. ix. 9. 1 Pet. iii. 4 only. Psa. xxxvi. 11.
s ch. xxv. 34. Heb. vi. 12 al. Gen. xv. 7. Ps. xxiv. 13.
t ch. xxv. 35, &c. John vi. 35. Rom. xii. 20, from Prov. xxv. 21. 1 Cor. iv. 11. Rev. vii. 16. Jer. xxxviii. (xxxi.) 25.
u = Luke i. 53 al.
v = John iv. 14. vii. 37. Rev. xxi. 6. xxii. 17. Isa. lv. 1. διψήσας τοὐμὸν αἷμα, Jos. B. J. i. 32. 2.
w = ver. 10.
x ch. xiv. 20 al. Ps. ciii. 13.
y Heb. ii. 17 only. Prov. xi. 17 al.
z Rom. xi. 30, 31. 1 Tim. i. 13, 16. 1 Pet. ii. 10. Ezek. vii. 9. Hos. ii. 25 (23) A.
a Ps. xxiii. 4. see 1 Tim. i. 5. Ps. l. 10. constr., ver. 3.
b see Heb. xii. 14. 1 John iii. 2. Rev. xxi. 4.
c here only †. Xen. Hell. vi. 3. 4. (-ποιεῖν, Col. i. 20. see James iii. 18.)

coherence of the sentences is improved by it. In placing these two beatitudes first, the Lord follows the order in Isa. lxi. 1, which He proclaimed in the synagogue at Nazareth, Luke iv. 18.

5. οἱ πραεῖς] A citation from Ps. xxxvii. 11. The usual dividers and allotters of the earth being mighty and proud conquerors, and the Messiah being expected as such a conqueror, this announcement, that the meek should inherit the earth, struck at the root of the temporal expectations of power and wealth in the Messiah's kingdom. This meekness is not mere outward lowliness of demeanour, but that true *πραΰτης* of Eph. iv. 2, whose active side (Stier) is *ἀγάπη*, and its passive side *μακροθυμία*. On the promise, compare Isa. lvii. 13—15; lx. 21: 1 Cor. iii. 22. That kingdom of God which begins in the hearts of the disciples of Christ, and is not **ἐκ** *τοῦ κόσμου τούτου*, shall work onwards till it shall become *actually a kingdom over this earth*, and its subjects shall *inherit the earth*: first in its millennial, and finally in its renewed and blessed state for ever.

6.] See Ps. cvii. 9; lxv. 4; xxii. 26: Isa. xli. 17. This *hunger and thirst* is the true sign of that new life on which those born of the Spirit (John iii. 3, 5) have entered; and it is after *δικαιοσ.*, i. e. *perfect conformity to the holy will of God.* This was *His* meat, John iv. 34. 'Illo cibo saturabuntur de quo ipse Dominus dicit, Meus cibus est ut faciam voluntatem Patris mei, quod est, justitia: et illa aqua, de qua quisquis biberit, ut Idem dicit, fiet in eo fons aquæ salientis in vitam æternam.' Aug. in loc. (vol. iii. pt. 2, Migne). But he elsewhere says (in Ev. Joh. Tract. 26. 1 (vol. iii. pt. 2)), after quoting this verse, 'Justitiam vero nobis esse Christum, Paulus Apostolus dicit. Ac per hoc qui esurit Hunc Panem, esuriat Justitiam: sed justitiam quæ de cœlo descendit, justitiam quam dat Deus, non quam sibi facit homo.' (Chrysostom confines himself to the moral explanation, as also Euthymius.) They shall be *satisfied—in the new heaven and new earth*, *ἐν οἷς* **δικαιοσύνη κατοικεῖ**, 2 Pet. iii. 13. Cf. the remarkable parallel, Ps. xvi. 15 (LXX), *ἐγὼ δὲ ἐν δικαιοσύνῃ ὀφθήσομαι τῷ προσώπῳ σου, χορτασθήσομαι ἐν τῷ ὀφθῆναι τὴν δόξαν σου.* This hunger and thirst after righteousness is admirably set forth in the three first petitions of the Lord's prayer,—'Hallowed be Thy name—Thy kingdom come—Thy will be done on earth, as it is in heaven.'

7. ἐλεήμονες] *οὐχὶ διὰ χρημάτων μόνον ἐστὶν ἐλεεῖν, ἀλλὰ καὶ λόγου· κἂν μηδὲν ἔχῃς, διὰ δακρύων. ποικίλος γὰρ ὁ τῆς ἐλεημοσύνης τρόπος, καὶ πλατεῖα αὕτη ἡ ἐντολή. ἐλεηθήσονται δέ, ἐνταῦθα μὲν παρὰ ἀνθρώπων· ἐκεῖ δὲ παρὰ τοῦ θεοῦ.* Euthymius, expanding Chrysostom. This beatitude comprises every degree of sympathy and mutual love and help; from that fulness of it which is shed abroad in those who have been forgiven much, and therefore love much, — down to those first beginnings of the new birth, even among those who know not the Lord, which are brought out in ch. xxv. 37—40, where see notes.

8. καθ. τῇ καρδίᾳ] See Ps. xxiv. 4, 6. It is no Levitical cleanness, nor mere moral purity, that is here meant: but that *inner purity*, which (Acts xv. 9) is brought about *τῇ πίστει*, has its fruit (1 Tim. i. 5) in *love*; which is, as in *καθαρὸν φῶς, καθαρὰ χαρά*, &c., opposed to all *διψυχία* (James i. 8), and all hypocrisy and outward colouring; so that the *καθ. τῇ κ.* are *οἱ ῥεραντισμένοι τὰς καρδίας ἀπὸ συνειδήσεως πονηρᾶς* (Heb. x. 22). 'Hoc est mundum cor, quod est simplex cor: et quemadmodum lumen hoc videri non potest nisi oculis mundis, ita nec Deus videtur nisi mundum sit illud quo videri potest.' (Aug. in loc.) But there is also allusion to the nearer vision of God attained by progressive sanctification, of which St. Paul speaks, 2 Cor. iii. 18,—begun indeed in this life, but not per-

[αὐτοὶ] [de] υἱοὶ [e] θεοῦ [df] κληθήσονται. 10 μακάριοι οἱ
[g] δεδιωγμένοι [h] ἕνεκεν [hi] δικαιοσύνης, ὅτι [k] αὐτῶν ἐστιν ἡ
[k] βασιλεία τῶν [k] οὐρανῶν. 11 μακάριοί ἐστε ὅταν [l] ὀνειδίσωσιν ὑμᾶς καὶ [g] διώξωσιν καὶ εἴπωσιν πᾶν πονηρὸν καθ'
ὑμῶν [m] ψευδόμενοι ἕνεκεν ἐμοῦ. 12 [n] χαίρετε καὶ [no] ἀγαλ-
λιᾶσθε, ὅτι ὁ [p] μισθὸς ὑμῶν πολὺς ἐν τοῖς οὐρανοῖς· οὕτως

d Hos. i. 10. e = Luke xx. 13. Rom. viii. 14, 19. Gal. iii. 16. (Gen. vi. 2.) f 1 John iii. 1. Isa. xlix. 6. g = Acts vii. 52. Gal. iv. 29 al. Ps. vii. 1. 2 Macc. v. 8. h Ps. xliv. 4. i = ver. 6. ch. vi. 1, 33. xxi. 32 al. k ver. 3. l = ch. xxvii. 44. 1 Pet. iv. 14. Ps. ci. 8. m Gospp., here only. = Rom. ix. 1. Heb. vi. 18 al. Isa. lix. 13. n 1 Pet. iv. 13. Rev. xix. 7. see John viii. 56. 1 Pet. i. 8. o Luke x. 21 al. Mt., here only: not in Mk. or Paul. Ps. ii. 11 al. p = ver. 46. ch. vi. 1, &c. John iv. 36 al. Jer. xxxviii. (xxxi.) 16.

9. om *αυτοι* CDא 13. 124 vulg-ed lat-*a b c* ff_1 *h l* Syr Hil Op: ins B **1**. 33 rel am (with gat) lat-*f k* syr-cu syr copt æth arm Orig-int $Cypr_2$.

10. *ενεκα* B. ins *της* bef *δικαιοσυνης* C. for *εστιν*, *εστε* (i. e. -*αι*) *erit* D. Clem(Strom. iv. 6(41) p. 582 P), after having quoted this verse as in text, says, ἤ ὥς τινες τῶν μετατιθέντων τὰ εὐαγγέλια, μακάριοι, φησίν, οἱ δεδ. ὑπὸ τῆς δικ., ὅτι αὐτοὶ ἔσονται τέλειοι, καὶ μακάριοι οἱ δεδιωγμένοι ἕνεκα ἐμοῦ, ὅτι ἕξουσι τόπον ὅπου οὐ διωχθήσονται.

11. transp *ονειδισ.* and *διωξ.* D lat-*h* syr-cu copt æth.—*ονειδισουσιν* D.—*διωξουσιν* DΔא. rec aft *πονηρον* ins *ρημα*, with C rel syrr Orig Constt Op: om BDא latt syr-jer copt æth [Cyr] Hil_2 Lucif. (lat-*a* def.) *καθ υμων* bef *παν πονηρον* (*for perspicuity*) D flor lat-*h k* syrr syr-cu Constt Tert Lucif spec. om *ψευδομενοι* (*probably as superfluous, its reference not being clearly understood, as its being placed after ενεκ. εμ. shews*) D flor lat-*b c* g_1 *h k* Orig Tert Hil_3 Lucif spec: ins aft *ενεκ. εμ.* lat-*f* Syr. for *εμου*, *δικαιοσυνης* D 47 lat-*a b c* g_1 Ambr Ambrst Hil_3.

12. *τω ουρανω* D lat-*a b h* Tert Hil_3 Lucif Op.

fected till the next, 1 Cor. xiii. 12. Read the magnificent conclusion of Augustine De Civit. Dei, xxii. 29 (vol. vii. Migne), in which he enters more deeply into the meaning of this verse. **9. εἰρηνοποιοί]** More than '*the peaceful*' ('pacifici,' Vulg.). It is doubtful whether the word ever has this meaning. Thus Euthymius, mostly after Chrysostom: οἱ μὴ μόνον αὐτοὶ μὴ στασιάζοντες, ἀλλὰ καὶ ἑτέρους στασιάζοντας συνάγοντες εἰς εἰρήνην· υἱοὶ δὲ θεοῦ κληθήσονται, ὡς μιμησάμενοι τὸν μονογενῆ υἱὸν αὐτοῦ· ᾧ γέγονεν ἔργον συναγαγεῖν τὰ διεστῶτα καὶ καταλλάξαι τὰ ἐκπεπολεμωμένα. But even thus we do not seem to reach the full meaning, which probably is, "*they that work peace;*" not confining the reference to the reconciliation of persons at variance: see note on James iii. 18: and, for the more special meaning, Xen. in reff. **κληθήσονται]** *implies* the reality, as in ver. 19; **shall** (not only be, but also) **be called**, i.e. recognized, in the highest sense, both generally, and by the Highest Himself, as such. Cf. Maldonatus: 'plus etiam quiddam mihi videtur *vocari* quam *esse* significare: nempe ita aliquid esse, ut appareat, ut omnium ore celebretur.' Let it ever be remembered, according to the order of these beatitudes, and the assertion of James iii. 17, that the wisdom from above is **πρῶτον** ἁγνή, **ἔπειτα** εἰρηνική, implying no compromise with evil. And it is in the working out of this ἁγνότης that Luke xii. 51 is especially true. **10.]** 'Martyres non facit pœna, sed causa. Nam si pœna martyres faceret, omnia metalla martyribus plena essent, omnes catenæ martyres traherent: omnes qui gladio feriuntur, coronarentur. Nemo ergo dicat, Quia patior justus sum. Quia ipse qui primo passus est, pro justitia passus est, ideo magnam exceptionem addidit. Beati qui persecutionem patiuntur *propter justitiam*.' (Aug. Enarr. in Ps. xxxiv. 13, vol. iv.) See 1 Pet. iii. 14; iv. 14, which probably refers to this verse. The repetition of the promise in ver. 3 is a close of the string of promises as it began. See the remarkable variation in the var. readd. **11.]** With the preceding verse the beatitudes end, in their general reference, and in this our Lord addresses *His disciples* particularly. The actions described in this verse are the expansion of δεδιωγμένοι in the last. **διώξωσιν**, however, still means **persecute**; its *legal* usage is unknown in the N. T. **ψευδόμενοι** does not belong to ἕνεκεν ἐμοῦ, as some recent Commentators have supposed (Tholuck, Meyer), but to εἴπωσιν. The pres. part., as usual, carries with it the logical condition. **12. ὁ μισθὸς ὑμ.]** A reward, not of debt, but of grace, as the parable in ch. xx. 1 ff. clearly

γὰρ [g] ἐδίωξαν τοὺς προφήτας [q] τοὺς πρὸ ὑμῶν. 13 Ὑμεῖς BCDEK MSUVΓ ΔΠℵ 1. 33
ἐστε τὸ [r] ἅλας τῆς γῆς· ἐὰν δὲ τὸ [r] ἅλας [s] μωρανθῇ, [t] ἐν
τίνι [u] ἁλισθήσεται; [v] εἰς οὐδὲν [w] ἰσχύει ἔτι, εἰ μὴ [x] βληθὲν

q Lev. xviii. 28. r Mark ix. 50 bis. Luke xiv. 34 bis. Col. iv. 6 only. Lev. ii. 13. s Luke xiv. 34. Rom. i. 22. 1 Cor. i. 20 only. 2 Kings xxiv. 10. t ch. vii. 6. u Mark ix. 49 bis only. Lev. ut supra. Ezek. xvi. 4 (Ezra iv. 14 compl.) only. v Acts xvii. 21. xix. 27. (2 Tim. ii. 14 v. r.) w = Gal. v. 6. James v. 16. x ch. xiii. 48. Luke xiv. 35. John xv. 6. 1 John iv. 18 al.

aft *υμων* ins *υπαρχοντων* D[1](-*τας* D[4]), simly *qui ante vos fuerunt* D-lat *a* Iren-int Hil Lucif: ins *οι πατερες αυτων* U lat-*b c*.

13. for 1st *αλας*, *αλα* D[1]ℵ[1](*s* is added by D[8]ℵ[3], but removed by the latter). for 2nd *αλας*, *αλα* [B[3](Tischdf)] ℵ. om *ετι* D mn lat-*a b* g_1 *h* Syr syr-cu Cypr Aug Jer. rec *βληθηναι εξω και καταπατεισθαι*, with D rel latt: txt BCℵ 1. 33 syr-ms Orig.

represents it. 'An expression,' as De Wette observes, 'taken from our earthly commerce, and applied to spiritual things;' in which however we must remember, that the principal reference is to God as the giver, and not to us as the deservers: see the parable above cited, where the *μισθός* is not what was *earned*, but what was *covenanted*. 'Deus est debitor noster non ex commisso, sed ex promisso.' Aug. (Tholuck.) These words, **ἐν τοῖς οὐρανοῖς**, must not be taken as having any bearing on the question as to the *future habitation* of the glorified saints. Their use in this and similar expressions is not *local*, but *spiritual*, indicating the blessed state when *ἡ βασιλεία τῶν οὐρανῶν* shall have fully come. The local question is to be decided by wholly different testimonies of Scripture;—by the general tenor of prophecy, and the analogies of the divine dealings: and all of these seem to point rather to this earth, purified and renewed, than to *the heavens* in any ordinary sense of the term, as the eternal habitation of the blessed. **ἐδίωξαν**] For instance, Jeremiah was scourged, Jer. xx. 2; Zechariah son of Jehoiada was stoned, 2 Chron. xxiv. 21; Isaiah, according to Jewish tradition, was sawn asunder by Manasseh. The reasoning implied in *γάρ* may be thus filled up: "and great will be *their* reward in heaven."

13.] The transition from the preceding verses is easy and natural, from the *δεδιωγμένοι ἕνεκεν δικαιοσύνης*, of which vv. 11, 12, were a sort of application, and the allusion to the ancient Prophets, to *ὑμεῖς ἐστε τὸ ἅλ. τ. γ.* Elisha *healed the unwholesome water* by means of *salt* (2 Kings ii. 20), and the ordinary use of salt for culinary purposes is to *prevent putrefaction*: so (see Gen. xviii. 23—33) are the righteous, the people of God, in this corrupt world. It hardly seems necessary to find instances of the *actual occurrence* of salt losing its savour, for this is merely hypothetical. Yet it is perhaps worth noticing, that Maundrell, in his travels, found salt in the Valley of Salt, near Gehul, which had the appearance, but not the taste, having lost it by exposure to the elements (see the citation below);—and that Schöttgen maintains that a kind of bitumen from the Dead Sea was called 'sal Sodomiticus,' and was used to sprinkle the sacrifices in the temple; which salt was used, when its savour was gone, to strew the temple pavement, that the priests might not slip. This, however, is but poorly made out by him, (Schöttgen, Hor. Hebr. in loc.) Dr. Thomson, 'The Land and the Book,' p. 381, mentions a case which came under his own observation: where a merchant of Sidon had stored up a quantity of salt in cottages with earthen floors, in consequence of which the salt was spoiled, and Dr. T. saw "large quantities of it literally thrown into the street, to be trodden under foot of men and beasts." He adds, "It is a well-known fact that the salt of this country, when in contact with the ground, or exposed to rain and sun, does become insipid and useless. From the manner in which it is gathered, much earth and other impurities are necessarily collected with it. Not a little of it is so impure that it cannot be used at all: and such salt soon effloresces and turns to dust—not to fruitful soil, however. It is not only good for nothing itself, but it actually destroys all fertility wherever it is thrown: and this is the reason why it is cast into the street." **τῆς γῆς**, *mankind and all creation*: but with a more *inward* reference, as to the working of the salt, than in *τοῦ κόσμου*, ver. 14, where the *light* is something *outwardly shewn*. **μωρανθῇ** = *ἄναλον γένηται*, Mark ix. 50. **ἁλισθήσεται**] i. e. the salt; not impersonal, as Luther has rendered it,—womit wird man salzen? '*wherewith shall salting be carried on?*' for *τὸ ἅλας* is the nom. to all three verbs, *μωρανθῇ*, *ἁλισθ.*, and *ἰσχύει*. The sense is: 'If you become

[x] ἔξω [y] καταπατεῖσθαι ὑπὸ τῶν ἀνθρώπων. 14 ὑμεῖς ἐστε
τὸ φῶς τοῦ κόσμου. οὐ [z] δύναται πόλις [z] κρυβῆναι
ἐπάνω ὄρους κειμένη, 15 οὐδὲ [ab] καίουσιν [ac] λύχνον καὶ
τιθέασιν αὐτὸν ὑπὸ [d] τὸν [e] μόδιον, ἀλλ᾽ ἐπὶ [d] τὴν [f] λυχνίαν,
καὶ [gh] λάμπει πᾶσιν τοῖς ἐν τῇ οἰκίᾳ. 16 [i] οὕτως [gk] λαμψάτω

L ουδε... ..καιουσι λυ. C. BDEKL MSUVΓ ΔΠℵ 1. 33

y ch. vii. 6. Luke viii. 5. xii. 1. Heb. x. 29 only. 2 Chron. xxv. 18. 1 Macc. iii. 51.
z 1 Tim. v. 25. Jer. xxix. (xlix.) 10.
a = Luke xii. 35. (John v. 35.) Exod. xxvii. 20. b = Rev. iv. 5. viii. 10. Isa. lxii. 1. c Luke viii. 16. xi. 33, &c. 2 Pet. i. 19 al. d art. = Mark iv. 38. John xxi. 8. e Mark iv. 21. Luke xi. 33 only †. f Mark iv. 21. Luke viii. 16. xi. 33. Heb. ix. 2. Rev. i. 12, &c. ii. 1, 5. xi. 4 only. Exod. xxv. 31. (in classical Greek, -ιον, see Phryn. Lobeck, p. 313 f.) g see below (k). otherwise, ch. xvii. 2. Luke xvii. 24. 2 Cor. iv. 6 only. Prov. iv. 18. h constr., here only. Wisd. v. 6 B (not Aℵ). i 1 Cor. ix. 24. k Acts xii. 7. 2 Cor. iv. 6. Isa. ix. 2.

untrue to your high calling, and spiritually effete and corrupted, there are no ordinary means by which you can be re-converted and brought back to your former state, inasmuch as you have no teachers and guides over you, but ought yourselves to be teachers and guides to others.' But we must not from this suppose that our Lord denies all repentance to those who have thus fallen: the scope of His saying must be taken into account, which is not to crush the fallen, but to quicken the sense of duty, and cause His disciples to walk worthily of their calling. (See Heb. vi. 4—6, and note on Mark ix. 49, 50.)

The *salt in the sacrifice* is the type of God's *covenant of sanctification*, whereby this earth shall be again hallowed for Him: His people are the *instruments*, in His hand, of this wholesome salting: all His servants in general, but the teachers and ministers of His covenant in particular. Chrysostom observes, *οἱ μὲν γὰρ ἄλλοι μυριάκις πίπτοντες δύνανται τυχεῖν συγγνώμης· ὁ δὲ διδάσκαλος ἐὰν τοῦτο πάθῃ, πάσης ἀπεστέρηται ἀπολογίας, καὶ τὴν ἐσχάτην δώσει τιμωρίαν* (Hom. xv. 7, p. 194). *ἀπὸ τότε ἔξω ῥίπτεται τοῦ διδασκαλικοῦ ἀξιώματος, καὶ καταπατεῖται, τουτέστι καταφρονεῖται.* Euthym. in loc. There does not appear to be any allusion to *ecclesiastical excommunication.*

14. τὸ φῶς τοῦ κόσ.] And yet only in a lower and derivative sense; Christ Himself being *τὸ φῶς τὸ ἀληθινόν, ὃ φωτίζει πάντα ἄνθρωπον, ἐρχόμενον εἰς τὸν κόσμον*, John i. 9; *τὸ φῶς τοῦ κόσμου*, viii. 12. His ministers are *λύχνοι*, John v. 35, and *φωστῆρες*, Phil. ii. 15, *receiving* their light, and only burning *for a time.* 'Johannes lumen illuminatum: Christus lumen illuminans.' Aug. Serm. ccclxxx. 7 (vol. v. pt. ii.). And here too, *φῶς* in this verse = *λύχνος* in ver. 15, where the comparison is resumed. So also Eph. v. 8: *ἦτε σκότος, νῦν δὲ φῶς* **ἐν κυρίῳ**—**light**, *as partaking of His Light:* for *πᾶν τὸ φανερούμενον* (see note, ib. ver. 13) *φῶς ἐστιν.* **οὐ δύναται . . . .**] Of course it is possible that our Lord may have had *some town* before Him thus situated, but *not Bethulia,* whose very existence is probably fabulous, being only mentioned in the apocryphal book of Judith. Recent travellers, as Drs. Stanley and Thomson ('Sinai and Palestine,' p. 429: 'The Land and the Book,' p. 273), have thought that, notwithstanding the fact shewn by Robinson, that the actual city of Safed was not in existence at this time, some ancient portion of it, at all events its fortress, which is 'as aged in appearance as the most celebrated ruins in the country' (Thomson), may have been before the eye of our Lord as He spoke. It is 'placed high on a bold spur of the Galilæan Anti-Lebanon,' and answers well to the description of a city 'lying on the mountain top.' 'The only other in view would be the village and fortress of Tabor, distinctly visible from the mount of Beatitudes, though not from the hills on the lake side. Either or both of these would suggest the illustration, which would be more striking from the fact, that this situation of cities on the tops of the hills is as rare in Galilee, as it is common in Judæa.' Stanley, ubi supra. But the CHURCH OF GOD, the *city on a hill* (Isa. ii. 2: Gal. iv. 26: see also Heb. xii. 22), in allusion to their present situation, on a mountain, is most probably the leading thought. **15. μόδιον**] A Latin word (the art. is by many supposed to express that the *μόδιος* is a vessel usually found in the house: but it is rather to be regarded as the sign of the *generic singular,* as in *κοινοῖ τὸν ἄνθρωπον*, ch. xv. 20)—called by the more general name *σκεῦος*, Luke viii. 16. **καίουσιν**, i. e. *men in general:* shewing, in the spiritual reference of the parable, that these lights of the world are '*lighted*' by Him for whose use they are. See above. **16. οὕτως**] i. e. *like a candle on a candlestick—like a city on a hill;* not *οὕτως, ὅπως*, 'so . . . . that,' as our English version seems rather to imply. By rendering *οὕτως* **in like manner**, the ambiguity will be avoided. See ref., and note there. The

l = ch. vi. 1 al. fr. m ch. xxvi. 10 ‖ Mk. John x. 32, 33. 1 Tim. iii. 1. v. 10, 25. vi. 18. Tit. ii. 7, 14. iii. 8, 14. Heb. x. 24. 1 Pet. ii. 12 only. n = N. T. passim. Ps. xxi. 23 al.

τὸ [k] φῶς ὑμῶν [l] ἔμπροσθεν τῶν ἀνθρώπων, ὅπως ἴδωσιν BDEKL MSUVΓ
ὑμῶν τὰ [m] καλὰ [m] ἔργα, καὶ [n] δοξάσωσιν τὸν [o] πατέρα ΔΠℵ 1. 33
ὑμῶν [o] τὸν ἐν τοῖς [o] οὐρανοῖς.
17 Μὴ νομίσητε ὅτι [p] ἦλθον [q] καταλῦσαι τὸν νόμον ἢ
τοὺς προφήτας· οὐκ [p] ἦλθον [q] καταλῦσαι, ἀλλὰ [r] πληρῶσαι. 18 [s] ἀμὴν γὰρ λέγω ὑμῖν, ἕως ἂν [t] παρέλθῃ ὁ οὐρα-

o = ver. 45. ch. vi. 1, 3, 9 al. fr. p constr., w. inf., ch. ii. 2. ix. 13 al. Gen. xlii. 5. Neh. vi. 10. q = Acts v. 38, 39. Rom. xiv. 20. Gal. ii. 18. 2 Macc. ii. 22. iv. 11. r = Luke xxii. 16. John xv. 11. 2 Cor. x. 6. (1 Macc. ii. 55.) s = Mt. Mk. passim. Luke iv. 24 al6. John (but always ἀμὴν ἀμήν,) i. 52 and passim ‡. = LXX γένοιτο. t = ch. xxiv. 34, 35 (bis) ‖. Luke xvi. 17. 2 Cor. v. 17. James i. 10. 2 Pet. iii. 10. Ps. cxlviii. 6.

16. [εργα in B is in marg, but *a prima manu*, not as Mai, *a secunda*.]

sense of this verse is as if it were ὅπως, ἰδόντες ὑμῶν τ. κ. ἔργ. δοξάσωσιν τ. π. ὑ. . . . . the *latter* verb, and not the former, carrying the purpose of the action. Thus the praise and glory of a well-lighted and brilliant feast would be given, not to the lights, but to the master of the house; and of a stately city on a hill, not to the buildings, but to those who built them. The whole of this division of our Lord's sermon is addressed to *all His followers*, not exclusively to the ministers of his word. All servants of Christ are the salt of the earth, the light of the world (Phil. ii. 15). And all that is here said applies to us all. But à fortiori does it apply, in its highest sense, to those who are, among Christians, selected to teach and be examples; who are as it were the towers and pinnacles of the city, not only not hid, but seen far and wide above the rest.

17—48.] *The* SECOND PART OF THE SERMON, *in which our Lord sets forth His relation, as a lawgiver, to the law of Moses, especially as currently interpreted according to the letter only.* **17.** **ἦλθον**] Observe how our Lord, through the whole sermon, sets forth Himself, in his proceeding forth from God, as *the true* ἐρχόμενος. **τὸν ν. ἢ τοὺς προφ.**] It is a question whether our Lord includes the *prophecies*, properly so called, in His meaning here. I think *not:* for no person professing himself to be the Messiah would be thought to *contradict the prophecies*, but *to fulfil them.* Neither, it appears, does He *here* allude to the *sacrificial* and *typical* parts of the law, but to the *moral* parts of both the law and the prophets; which indeed he proceeds to cite and particularize. If however we prefer to include both ceremonial and moral in this assertion, we may understand it in its more general sense, as applying, beyond the instances here given, to His typical fulfilment of the law, which could not as yet be unfolded. Thus Augustine: 'Hæc præcepta sunt morum; illa sacramenta sunt promissorum: hæc implentur per adjuvantem gratiam, illa per redditam veritatem, utraque per Christum, et illam semper gratiam donantem, nunc etiam revelantem, et hanc veritatem tunc promittentem, nunc exhibentem.' Contra Faust. xix. 18, vol. viii. Much unnecessary question has been raised (see Thol. Bergpred. edn. 3, p. 132 f.) respecting the ἤ, whether or not it can have the sense of καί. It is simply the *disjunctive* conjunction necessary in order to apply the καταλῦσαι to each severally, which would naturally be replaced by the *copulative*, where an *affirmative* assertion respecting the same two things is made. **πληρῶσαι** implies more than the *mere fulfilling:* see reff., where the word has the sense of **filling out** or expanding; i. e. here, giving a deeper and holier sense to—fulfilling in the *spirit*, which is nobler than the letter. Theophylact compares the ancient law to a *sketch*, which the painter οὐ καταλύει, ἀλλ' ἀναπληροῖ. . . . . . τοῦ νόμου γὰρ τὰ τέλη τῶν ἁμαρτημάτων κωλύοντος, ὁ χριστὸς καὶ τὰς ἀρχὰς ἐκώλυσεν. Euthym. in loc. ἐπεὶ ὁ χριστὸς οὔτε ἐξ ἱερατικῆς φυλῆς ἐτύγχανεν ὤν, καὶ ἅπερ ἔμελλεν εἰσηγεῖσθαι προσθήκη τις ἦν, οὐ μὴν ἐλαττοῦσα ἀλλ' ἐπιτείνουσα τὴν ἀρετήν· προειδὼς ἀμφότερα ταῦτα μέλλοντα αὐτοὺς ταράττειν, πρὶν ἢ τοὺς θαυμαστοὺς ἐκείνους ἐγγράψαι νόμους, ἐκβάλλει τὸ μέλλον αὐτῶν ὑφορμεῖν τῇ διανοίᾳ. τί δὲ ἦν τὸ ὑφορμοῦν καὶ ἀντικροῦον; ἐνόμιζον αὐτὸν ταῦτα λέγοντα ἐπ' ἀναιρέσει τῶν παλαιῶν νομίμων ποιεῖν. ταύτην τοίνυν ἰᾶται τὴν ὑπόνοιαν. Chrysost. Hom. xvi. 1, p. 203. See a history of the exegesis of the word in Thol. edn. 3, p. 135. The gnostic Marcion characteristically enough maintained that the Judaizing Christians had altered this verse, and that it originally stood,—τί δοκεῖτε, ὅτι ἦλθον πληρῶσαι τὸν νόμον ἢ τοὺς προφήτας; ἦλθον καταλῦσαι, ἀλλ'

νὸς καὶ ἡ γῆ, [u] ἰῶτα ἓν ἢ μία [v] κεραία οὐ μὴ [t] παρέλθῃ
ἀπὸ τοῦ νόμου, ἕως ἂν πάντα γένηται. 19 ὃς ἐὰν οὖν
[w] λύσῃ μίαν τῶν ἐντολῶν τούτων τῶν ἐλαχίστων καὶ
διδάξῃ οὕτως τοὺς ἀνθρώπους, ἐλάχιστος [x] κληθήσεται ἐν

u here only †.
v Luke xvi. 17 only †.
w = John v. 18. vii. 23. x. 35 only. see Eph. ii. 14. (not Esdr. ix. 46.)
x = ver. 9.

18. γενηται bef παντα D.
19. om εαν D¹ latt(exc D-lat *k*) latt-ff(exc Lucif): αν D³ 33 Scr's b g. λυσει (*itacism*) DL. om 2nd των D¹(ins D³ or ⁶) Δ. om ουτως D.

οὐ πληρῶσαι. **18. ἀμήν]** = ἀληθῶς in St. Luke, ix. 27; xii. 44; xxi. 3. See reff. The double **ἕως αν** renders the dependence of the members of the sentence rather difficult. The two expressions seem to be strictly parallel: *ἕως ἂν παρ. ὁ οὐρ. κ. ἡ γῆ*, and *ἕως ἂν πάντα γέν.* According to this view these latter words will mean, '*till the end of all things.*' But the other interpretation, '*till all* (that is written in the law) *shall have been fulfilled*' (as in the English version), is no doubt admissible, in which case the sense will stand thus:—**While heaven and earth last** (*ἕως ἂν ὁ κόσμος διαμένῃ*, Euthym.) **one jot or one tittle shall not pass away from the law without all being fulfilled.** Tholuck remarks on *παρέρχεσθαι*, "It denotes, as *παραδραμεῖν, παραφέρεσθαι, παράγειν*, 'to pass by,' 'to pass out of view' (see Wetst. in loc.): cf. Aristid. i. 216: *παρῆλθον ὥσπερ μῦθοι*, and the phrase *παρέρχεταί μέ τι*, 'something escapes my memory.' Cf. in the Heb., עָבַר, Ps. xxxvii. 36: Nah. i. 12: Job xxxiv. 20. Cf. the passing away of the heaven, ch. xxiv. 39: 2 Pet. iii. 10: Rev. xxi. 1;—*παράγεται*, 1 John ii. 17;—the intrans. *παράγει*, 1 Cor. vii. 31." **ἰῶτα** is the Hebrew (י) Jod, the smallest letter in the alphabet: **κεραῖαι** are the little turns of the strokes by which one letter differs from another similar to it. Origen on Ps. xxxiii. (cited by Wetstein) says—*τῶν στοιχείων παρ' Ἑβραίοις, λέγω δὲ τοῦ χὰφ καὶ τοῦ βὴθ* (כ and ב) *πολλὴν ὁμοιότητα σωζόντων, ὡς κατὰ μηδὲν ἀλλήλων διαλλάττειν ἢ βραχείᾳ κεραίᾳ μόνῃ.* The Rabbinical writings have many sayings similar in sentiment to this, but spoken of the *literal* written law. (See Lightfoot, Hor. Heb. in loc.) It is important to observe in *these days* how the Lord here *includes the O. T. and all its unfolding of the divine purposes regarding Himself, in His teaching* of the citizens of the kingdom of heaven. I say this, because it is always in *contempt and setting aside of the O. T.* that rationalism has begun. First, *its historical truth*—then its *theocratic dispensation* and the *types* and *prophecies* connected with it, are swept away; so that Christ came to fulfil nothing, and becomes only a teacher or a martyr: and thus the way is paved for a similar rejection of the N. T.;—beginning with the narratives of the birth and infancy, as theocratic myths—advancing to the denial of His miracles—then attacking the truthfulness of His own sayings which are grounded on the O. T. as a revelation from God—and so finally leaving us nothing in the Scriptures but, as a German writer of this school has expressed it, 'a mythology not so attractive as that of Greece.' That this is the course which unbelief *has run* in Germany, should be a pregnant warning to the decriers of the O. T. among ourselves. It should be a maxim for every expositor and every student, that Scripture is a *whole*, and stands or falls together. That this is now beginning to be deeply felt in Germany, we have cheering testimonies in the later editions of their best Commentators, and in the valuable work of Stier on the discourses of our Lord. (Since however these words were first written, we have had lamentable proof in England, that their warnings were not unneeded. The course of unbelief which induced the publication of the volume entitled "Essays and Reviews," was, in character and progress, exactly that above described: and owing to the injudicious treatment which multiplied tenfold the circulation of that otherwise contemptible work, its fallacies are now in the hands and mouths of thousands, who, from the low standard of intelligent Scriptural knowledge among us, will never have the means of answering them.)

19.] There is little difficulty in this verse, if we consider it in connexion with the verse preceding, to which it is bound by the *οὖν* and the *τούτων*, and with the following, to which the *γάρ* unites it. Bearing this in mind, we see (1) that **λύσῃ**, on account of what follows in ver. 20 and after, must be taken in the higher sense, as referring to the *spirit* and not the letter: **whosoever shall break** (have broken), in the sense presently to be laid down. (2) That **τῶν ἐντ. τούτ. τῶν ἐλ.** refers to *ἰῶτα ἓν ἢ μία κεραία* above, and

y ch. iii. 2 note.
z = Rom. v. 15. 2 Cor. i. 5 al. Eccl. iii. 19. 1 Macc. iii. 30.
a = vv. 6, 10. ch. vi. 1 al.
b constr., 1 John ii. 2. Rev. ix. 10. xiii. 11 (not John v. 36).

τῇ [y] βασιλείᾳ τῶν [y] οὐρανῶν· ὃς δ' ἂν ποιήσῃ καὶ διδάξῃ, BDEKL MSUVΓ
οὗτος μέγας [x] κληθήσεται ἐν τῇ [y] βασιλείᾳ τῶν [y] οὐρανῶν. ΔΠℵ 1. 33
20 λέγω γὰρ ὑμῖν ὅτι ἐὰν μὴ [z] περισσεύσῃ ὑμῶν ἡ [a] δικαιοσύνη πλεῖον τῶν [b] γραμματέων καὶ Φαρισαίων, οὐ μὴ

om last clause (*homœotel*) Dℵ[1](ins ℵ-corr[1]) lat-g_2.

20. om ver (*homœotel*) D. rec η δικαιοσυνη bef υμων, with S(e sil Bch) U 1. 33 $Clem_1$ Orig: txt Bℵ rel 13. 124 Just Constt $Clem_1$ Bas_3 Isid. πλεον ℵ[1] [237 Cyr_1 Bas_3 Chr-6-mss: πληονα L].

means one of those minute commands which seem as insignificant, in comparison with the greater, as the ἰῶτα and κεραία in comparison with great portions of writing. (3) That **ἐλάχιστος κληθ.** does not mean '*shall be excluded from,*' inasmuch as the question is not of *keeping or not keeping* the commandments of God in a legal sense, but of *appreciating, and causing others to appreciate,* the import and weight of even the most insignificant parts of God's revelation of Himself to man; and rather therefore applies to teachers than to Christians in general, though to them also through the λύσῃ and ποιήσῃ. (4) That *no deduction can be drawn from these words binding the Jewish law, or any part of it, as such, upon Christians.* That this is so, is plainly shewn by what follows, where our Lord proceeds to pour upon the letter of the law the fuller light of the spirit of the Gospel: thus lifting and expanding (not destroying) every jot and tittle of that precursory dispensation into its full meaning in the life and practice of the Christian; who, by the indwelling of the divine Teacher, God's Holy Spirit, is led into all truth and purity. (5) That *these words of our Lord are decisive against such persons,* whether ancient or modern, as *would set aside the Old Testament as without significance, or inconsistent with the New.* See the preceding note, and the Book of Common Prayer, Article vii.

ἐλάχιστος is in direct allusion to ἐλαχίστων; but it can hardly be said (De Wette, Tholuck) that, because there is no article, it means '*one of the least*' (ein geringster), for the article is often omitted after an appellative verb. **μέγας** rests on different grounds; being positive, and in its nature generic. See ch. xi. 11; xviii. 1—4. On **κληθήσεται**, see note on ver. 9. Observe the conditional aorists, λύσῃ, ποιήσῃ, διδάξῃ, combined with the indic. fut. κληθήσεται,—and thus necessitating the keeping the times distinct. The time indicated by κληθήσεται is one when the λῦσαι, ποιῆσαι, διδάξαι, shall be things of the past—belonging to a course of responsibility over and done with.

20.] An expansion of the idea contained in πληρῶσαι, ver. 17, and of the difference between λύσῃ, which the Scribes and Pharisees did by enforcing the letter to the neglect of the spirit—and ποιήσῃ καὶ διδάξῃ, in which particulars Christians were to exceed the Pharisees, the punctilious observers, and the Scribes, the traditional expounders of the law.

δικαιοσύνη, *purity of heart and life,* as set forth by example in the ποιοῦντες, and by precept in the **διδάσκοντες**. The whole of the rest of our Lord's sermon is a comment on, and illustration of, the assertion in this verse. **γραμματέων**] Persons devoted to the work of reading and expounding the law (Heb. סֹפֵר), whose office seems first to have become frequent after the return from Babylon. They generally appear in the N. T. in connexion with the Pharisees: but it appears from Acts xxiii. 9, that there were Scribes attached to the other sects also. In Matt. xxi. 15, they appear with the chief priests; but it is in the *temple,* where (see also Luke xx. 1) they acted as a sort of police. In the description of the assembling of the great Sanhedrim (Matt. xxvi. 3: Mark xiv. 53; xv. 1) we find it composed of ἀρχιερεῖς, πρεσβύτεροι, and γραμματεῖς; and in Luke xxii. 66, of ἀρχιερεῖς καὶ γραμματεῖς. The Scribes uniformly opposed themselves to our Lord; watching Him to find matter of accusation, Luke vi. 7; xi. 53, 54; perverting His sayings, Matt. ix. 3, and His actions, Luke v. 30; xv. 2; seeking to entangle Him by questions, Matt. xxii. 35 (see note there): Luke x. 25; xx. 21; and to embarrass Him, Matt. xii. 38. Their authority as expounders of the law is recognized by our Lord Himself, Matt. xxiii. 1, 2; their adherence to the oral traditionary exposition proved, Matt. xv. 1 ff.; the respect in which they were held by the people shewn, Luke xx. 46; their existence indicated not only in Jerusalem but also in Galilee, Luke v. 17,—and in Rome, Josephus, Antt.

εἰςέλθητε εἰς τὴν [y] βασιλείαν τῶν [y] οὐρανῶν. 21 Ἠκούσατε ὅτι [c] ἐῤῥήθη τοῖς [d] ἀρχαίοις [e] Οὐ φονεύσεις· ὃς δ' ἂν
φονεύσῃ, [f] ἔνοχος ἔσται τῇ [g] κρίσει. 22 ἐγὼ δὲ λέγω ὑμῖν,

c Rom. ix. 12. 26 (from Hos. i. 10). Jonah iii. 7. d = ver. 33. Luke ix. 8, 19. 2 Pet. ii. 5. 3 Kings iv. 30. Sir. xxxix. 1. constr. *by*, ch. vi. 1. Luke xxiii. 15. Gen. xxxi. 15, but ? *to*, Rom. ix. 12, 26. Gal. iii. 16. Rev. vi. 11. ix. 4. e Exod. xx. 15 (13). Deut. v. 17. f w. dat. of the judging power, here (4 times) only. (ἔν. ταῖς ἀραῖς, Demosth. p. 404. 4. Gen. xxvi. 11 Ed-vat. (B def.) Deut. xix. 10. see ch. xxvi. 66 reff.) g = here only.

xviii. 3. 5. They kept schools and auditories for teaching the youth, Luke ii. 46: Acts v. 34, compared with xxii. 3; are called by Josephus πατρίων ἐξηγηταὶ νόμων, Antt. xvii. 6. 2; σοφισταί, B. J. i. 33. 2. The construction πλεῖον τῶν γραμματέων καὶ τῶν Φαρισαίων elliptically for πλ. τῆς δικαιοσύνης τ. γρ. κ. τ. Φ., is illustrated in Kühner (Gram. ii. § 749) under the name of 'comparatio compendiaria,' by Hom. Il. φ. 191, κρείσσων δ' αὖτε Διὸς γενεὴ ποταμοῖο τέτυκται; Pindar, Olymp. i. init., μηδ' Ὀλυμπίας ἀγῶνα φέρτερον αὐδάσομεν, &c. Notice, that not only the *hypocrites* among the Scribes and Pharisees are here meant; but the declaration is, "Your righteousness must be of a *higher order* than any yet attained, or conceived, by Scribe or Pharisee." **οὐ μὴ εἰςέλ.**] A very usual formula (see ch. vii. 21; xviii. 3; xix. 17, 23, 24: John iii. 5 al.): implying exclusion from the blessings of the Christian state, and from the inheritance of eternal life. **21—48.**] *Six examples of the true* FULFILMENT *of the law by Jesus.* FIRST EXAMPLE. *The law of murder.* (For a very full discussion of the various points of Jewish and Christian law and morality occurring in this part of the sermon, consult throughout Tholuck's elaborate commentary, 3rd edn.)

21. ἠκούσατε] viz. by the reading of the law in the synagogues, and the exposition of the Scribes. **τοῖς ἀρχαίοις**] has been rendered, as in E. V., '*by* the ancients;' in which case, Moses and his traditional expounders are classed together; or, '*to* the ancients,'—which last interpretation seems to me to be certainly the right one. Both constructions are found (see reff.); but every instance of the former is either (as ch. vi. 1) resolvable into the latter, or ambiguous, and none can be produced with ἐῤῥήθη, whereas *all the latter* have *this very word*, which is never followed in the N. T. or LXX by any other substantive but that denoting the persons *to whom* the words are spoken. The omission of τοῖς ἀρχαίοις, vv. 27, 31, 38, 43, also favours the rendering *to*, which was the interpretation of the Greek fathers. Chrysostom expands it thus: τί οὖν αὐτός φησιν; ἠκούσατε ὅτι ἐῤῥέθη τοῖς ἀρχαίοις Οὐ φονεύσεις· καίτοι ὁ καὶ ἐκεῖνα δοὺς αὐτός ἐστιν· ἀλλὰ τέως ἀπροςώπως αὐτὰ τίθησιν. εἴτε γὰρ εἶπεν ὅτι ἠκούσατε ὅτι εἶπον τοῖς ἀρχαίοις, δυςπαράδεκτος ὁ λόγος ἐγίνετο, καὶ πᾶσιν ἂν προςέστη τοῖς ἀκούουσιν· εἴτε αὖ πάλιν εἰπὼν ὅτι ἠκούσατε ὅτι ἐῤῥέθη τοῖς ἀρχαίοις παρὰ τοῦ πατρός μου, ἐπήγαγεν Ἐγὼ δὲ λέγω, μείζων ἂν ἔδοξεν εἶναι ὁ αὐθαδιασμός, Hom. xvi. 5, p. 210. Meyer (ed. 2) has well observed that ἐῤῥήθη τοῖς ἀρχαίοις corresponds to λέγω δὲ ὑμῖν, and the ἐγώ to the understood subject of ἐῤῥ. He has not, however, apprehended the deeper truth which underlies the omission of the subject of ἐῤῥ., that it was the *same person* who said both. It will be noticed that our Lord does not here speak against the *abuse* of the law by tradition, but that every instance here given is either from *the law itself*, or *such traditional teaching as was in accordance with it* (e. g. the latter part of this verse is only a formal expansion of the former). The contrasts here are not between *the law misunderstood* and *the law rightly understood*, but between the *law and its ancient exposition*, which in their letter, and as given, were κενά,—and *the same as spiritualized*, πεπληρωμένα, *by Christ*: not between *two lawgivers*, Moses and Christ, but between οἱ ἀρχαῖοι and ὑμεῖς; between (the idea is Chrysostom's) the children, by the same husband, of the *bondwoman* and of the *freewoman*. The above remarks comprise a brief answer to the important but somewhat misapprehended question, whether our Lord impugned the Mosaic law itself, or only its inadequate interpretation by the Jewish teachers? See this treated at great length by Tholuck, Bergp. pp. 153—165, edn. 3. There is no inconsistency in the above view with the assertion in ver. 19: the just and holy and true law was necessarily restricted in meaning and degraded in position, until He came, whose office it was to fulfil and glorify it. **κρίσει**] viz. the courts in every city, ordered Deut. xvi. 18, and explained by Josephus Antt. iv. 8. 14 to consist of seven men, and to have the power of life and death. But τῇ κρίσει in the next verse (see note) is the court of judgment in the Messiah's

h ch. xviii. 34. xxii. 7. Luke xiv. 21. xv. 28. Eph. iv. 26. Rev. xi. 18. xii. 17. 3 Kings xi. 9. i = Col. ii. 18 (Rom. xiii. 4. 1 Cor. xv. 2. Gal. iii. 4. iv. 11) only. Prov. xxviii. 25 only. εἰκῇ κ. ἀλογίστως, Polyb. i. 52. 2. k = vv. 19, 21, 31. ch. xii. 32 al. fr. Exod. xxx. 33. l see notes. m ch. xxvi. 59 al. Prov. xxii. 10. 2 Macc. xiv. 5. n = Rom. v. 21. vi. 19. Rev. xiii. 3. o vv. 29, 30. ch. x. 38. xviii. 9. xxiii. 15, 33. Mark ix. 43, 45, 47. Luke xii. 5. James iii. 6 only †. (see note.) p ch. xviii. 9 || Mk. q constr., ch. xxiv. 15. Luke xvi. 8, 9. xviii. 6. Rom. i. 26 al.

ὅτι πᾶς ὁ [h] ὀργιζόμενος τῷ ἀδελφῷ αὐτοῦ [[i] εἰκῇ] [f] ἔνοχος
ἔσται τῇ [g] κρίσει· [k] ὃς δ' ἂν εἴπῃ τῷ ἀδελφῷ αὐτοῦ [l] ῥακά,
[f] ἔνοχος ἔσται τῷ [m] συνεδρίῳ· [k] ὃς δ' ἂν εἴπῃ [l] μωρέ,
[f] ἔνοχος ἔσται [n] εἰς τὴν [op] γέενναν τοῦ [pq] πυρός.
23 ἐὰν

BDEKL MSUVΓ ΔΠℵ 1. 33

22. om οτι ℵ². οργαζομενος D¹. om εικη BΔ²ℵ¹ 48. 198 vulg æth (Just) (Ptol) Orig_2 Ps-Bas $\text{Ps-Ath}_{\text{expr}}$ Niceph [Tert(appy)] Aug(expr, in his Retract. i. 19) Jer_3(expr: h. l. says it is not in most of the ancient mss, and pronounces it spurious) Juvenc Salv: ins DLΔ¹ℵ^{3b} 1. 33 rel mm lat-*a b c f ff*$_1$ *g*$_{1.2}$ *h l* syrr syr-cu syr-jer copt goth arm Eus Nyss Chr Cyr Isid Thdor-mops Thl Euthym Iren-int_2(once aft οργιζ.) Orig-int_1 Cypr Hil_2(once aft οργιζ.) spec Op_{expr} Lucif. (*I have not ventured wholly to exclude it, the authorities being so divided, and internal evidence being equally indecisive. Griesbach and Meyer hold it to have been* expunged *from motives of moral rigorism :—De Wette, to have been* inserted *to soften the apparent rigour of the precept. The latter seems to me the more probable.*) ραχα Dℵ¹(latt).

kingdom. **22.**] The sense is: 'There were among the Jews three well-known degrees of guilt, coming respectively under the cognizance of the local and the supreme courts; and after these is set the γέεννα τοῦ πυρός, the end of the malefactor, whose corpse, thrown out into the valley of Hinnom, was devoured by the worm or the flame. Similarly, in the spiritual kingdom of Christ, shall the sins even of thought and word be brought into judgment and punished, each according to its degree of guilt, but even the least of them before no less a tribunal than the judgment-seat of Christ.' The most important thing to keep in mind is, that there is no distinction of *kind* between these punishments, only of *degree*. In the thing compared, the κρίσις inflicted death by the sword, the συνέδριον death by stoning, and the disgrace of the γέεννα τοῦ πυρός followed as an intensification of the horrors of death; but the punishment is one and the same—*death*. So also in the subject of the similitude, *all the punishments are spiritual; all result in eternal death;* but with *various degrees* (the nature of which is as yet hidden from us), as the degrees of guilt have been. So that the distinction drawn by the Romanists between *venial* and mortal sins, finds not only no countenance, but direct confutation from this passage. The words here mentioned must not be superstitiously supposed to have any damning power in themselves (see below), but to represent *states of anger and hostility*, for which an awful account hereafter must be given. (On **εἰκῇ** (see var. readd.) Euthymius remarks: προσθεὶς δὲ τὸ εἰκῇ, οὐκ ἀνεῖλε παντάπασι τὴν ὀργήν, ἀλλὰ μόνην τὴν ἄκαιρον ἐξέβαλεν· ἡ γὰρ εὔκαιρος ὠφέλιμος. Grotius: 'Merito εἰκῇ additum. Neque enim iracundus est quisquis irasci solet, sed qui οἷς οὐ δεῖ, καὶ ἐφ' οἷς οὐ δεῖ, καὶ μᾶλλον ἢ δεῖ, ut Aristoteles loquitur.') On the sense, cf. 1 John iii. 15. **ῥακά**] רֵיקָא, empty; a term denoting contempt, and answering to ὦ ἄνθρωπε κενέ, James ii. 20. On the α representing the ◌ָ see Tholuck's note p. 172, edn. 3. **μωρέ**] Two interpretations have been given of this word. Either it is (1), as usually understood, a Greek word, '*Thou fool*,' and used by our Lord Himself of the Scribes and Pharisees, ch. xxiii. 17, 19,—and its equivalent ἀνόητοι of the disciples, Luke xxiv. 25; or (2) a Hebrew word, signifying '*rebel*,' and the very word for uttering which Moses and Aaron were debarred from entering the land of promise: . . . שִׁמְעוּ־נָא הַמֹּרִים: 'Hear now, ye rebels.' Num. xx. 10. "Others take the Greek word, according to the Hebrew usage of נָבָל, in the sense of ἄθεος. So Phavorinus: εἴρηται καὶ ἐπὶ τοῦ ἀθέου καὶ ἀπίστου." Thol. p. 174.

ἔνοχ. εἰς is perhaps a pregnant construction for ἔνοχος ὥστε βληθῆναι εἰς: but see reff. **τ. γέενναν τοῦ π.**] To the S.E. of Jerusalem was a deep and fertile valley, called גֵּי הִנֹּם, '*the vale of Hinnom*,' and rendered Γαίεννα, Josh. xviii. 16, LXX. In this valley (also called Tophet, Isa. xxx. 33: Jer. vii. 31) did the idolatrous Jews burn their children to Moloch, and Josiah (2 Kings xxiii. 10) therefore polluted it; and thenceforward it was the place for the casting out and burning all offal, and the corpses of criminals; and therefore its name, ἡ γέεννα τοῦ πυρός, was used to signify the place of everlasting punish-

οὖν [r] προςφέρῃς τὸ δῶρόν σου ἐπὶ τὸ θυσιαστήριον κἀκεῖ
μνησθῇς ὅτι ὁ ἀδελφός σου [s] ἔχει τὶ [s] κατὰ σοῦ, 24 [t] ἄφες
ἐκεῖ τὸ δῶρόν σου [u] ἔμπροσθεν τοῦ θυσιαστηρίου καὶ ὕπαγε
πρῶτον [v] διαλλάγηθι τῷ ἀδελφῷ σου, καὶ τότε ἐλθὼν
[r] πρόςφερε τὸ δῶρόν σου. 25 [w] ἴσθι [x] εὐνοῶν τῷ [y] ἀντιδίκῳ
σου ταχὺ [z] ἕως [z] ὅτου εἶ μετ᾽ αὐτοῦ [a] ἐν τῇ ὁδῷ· μήποτέ
σε [b] παραδῷ ὁ [y] ἀντίδικος τῷ κριτῇ καὶ ὁ κριτής σε
[b] παραδῷ τῷ [c] ὑπηρέτῃ, καὶ εἰς [de] φυλακὴν [e] βληθήσῃ.

r = ch. ii. 11. Mark i. 44 al. Lev. iv. 23.
s Mark xi. 25. Rev. ii. 4, 14, 20. Job xxxi. 35. see Col. iii. 13.
t = ch. iv. 11, 20, 22. xxiv. 2 al. fr.
u = Acts xviii. 17. ch. vii. 6. 2 Chron. v. 6.
v here only. 1 Kings xxix. 4.
w constr., Luke xix. 17. Sir. v. 10.
x here only†. (-νοία, Eph. vi. 7.)
y Luke xii. 58. xviii. 3. 1 Pet. v. 8 only. 1 Kings ii. 10.
z = here only. (1 Kings xxx. 4.)
a ch. xv. 32. xx. 17. Luke xxiv. 32. Gen. xlii. 38. xlv. 24.
b = Mark i. 14 reff.
c = ch. xxvi. 58 ‖ Mk. John vii. 32, &c. xviii. 3, &c. Acts v. 22, 26. Prov. xiv. 35.
d = N. T. passim. Gen. xlii. 17 al.
e ch. xviii. 30. Luke xxiii. 19. John iii. 24 al.

24. **καταλλαγηθι** D. προςφερεις D[1]. (*offers* am lat-*a b* : *offeres* D-lat.)

25. om εως D[1](ins D-corr[1]). for ει, η M. rec εν τη οδω bef μετ᾽ αυτου, with Δ rel vulg lat-*f ff*$_1$ *k* syr sah goth Clem [Carpoc(apud Epiph) Chr-montf]: txt BDLℵ 1. 33 lat-*a b c g*$_{1,2}$ *h* Syr syr-cu copt æth arm Arnob Ambr Op. om 2nd σε παραδω Bℵ 1. 13. 124-7[1] lat-*k* æth arm (Carpoc) Chr$_2$(xv. 3, p. 188, xx. 4, p. 264) (Hil Arnob). παραδωσει (1st) D[1](txt D-corr): (2nd) D. βληθησει (*itacism*) D[1](Scriv): βληθης D-corr: βληθεις L : *mittaris* latt.

ment. **23 f. οὖν**] an inference from the guilt and danger of all bitterness and hostility of mind towards another, declared in the preceding verse. Chrysostom remarks: καθάπερ σοφὸς ἰατρὸς οὐ μόνον τὰ προφυλακτικὰ τῶν νοσημάτων τίθησιν, ἀλλὰ καὶ τὰ διορθωτικά, οὕτω καὶ αὐτὸς ποιεῖ. τὸ μὲν γὰρ κωλύειν καλεῖν μωρόν, προφυλακτικόν ἐστι τῆς ἔχθρας· τὸ δὲ κελεύειν καταλλαγῆναι, τῶν μετὰ τὴν ἔχθραν γενομένων νοσημάτων ἀναιρετικόν. Hom. xvi. 10, p. 218. The whole of his comment on this verse is excellent. The **δῶρον** is any kind of gift—sacrificial or eucharistic. **ἔχει τὶ κατὰ σοῦ** is remarkable, as being purposely substituted for the converse. It is not *what complaints we have against others* that we are to consider at such a time, but *what they have against us;* not what ground *we have given* for complaint, but what complaints *they,* as matter of fact, *make* against us. See the other side dealt with, Mark xi. 25. Tholuck has shewn at length (p. 187, ff.) that the distinction attempted to be set up between διαλλάσσω as implying a *mutual,* and καταλλάσσω, a merely *one-sided* reconciliation, has no foundation in fact.. Our διαλλάγηθι is simply **become reconciled**—*thyself,* without being influenced by the status of the other towards thee. Remove the offence, and make friendly overtures to thy brother. **πρῶτον** belongs to ὕπαγε, not to διαλλάγηθι, (1) because ὕπ. πρῶτον is opposed to τότε ἐλθών, the *departure* to the *return,* not διαλλάγηθι to πρόςφερε; (2) by the analogy of the usage of such adverbs with imperatives. Compare ch. vii. 5 and the similar passage, Luke vi. 42: ch. vi. 33; xiii. 30: Mark vii. 27. No conclusion whatever can be drawn from this verse as to the admissibility of the term *altar* as applied to the Lord's Table under the Christian system. The whole language is Jewish, and can only be understood of Jewish rites. The *command,* of course, applies in full force as to reconciliation before the Christian offering of praise and thanksgiving in the Holy Communion; but further nothing can be inferred. **25.**] The whole of this verse is the earthly example of a spiritual duty which is understood, and runs parallel with it. The sense may be given: 'As in worldly affairs, it is prudent to make up a matter with an adversary before judgment is passed, which may deliver a man to a hard and rigorous imprisonment, so reconciliation with an offended brother in this life is absolutely necessary before his wrong cry against us to the Great Judge, and we be cast into eternal condemnation.' The **ἀντίδικος**, in its *abstract personification,* is the *offended law of God,* which will cry against us in that day for *all* wrongs done to others; but in its *concrete representation* it is the *offended brother,* who is to us that law, as long as he has its claim upon us. The **ὁδός**, in the interpretation, is the way in which all men walk, the ὁδὸς πάσης τῆς γῆς of 3 Kings ii. 2, the ὁδὸς ᾗ οὐκ ἐπαναστραφήσομαι of Job xvi. 22. In the civil process, it represents the attempt at arbitration or private arrange-

26 ἀμὴν λέγω σοι, οὐ μὴ ἐξέλθῃς ἐκεῖθεν ἕως ἂν [f] ἀποδῷς
τὸν ἔσχατον [g] κοδράντην. 27 Ἠκούσατε ὅτι ἐῤῥήθη [h] Οὐ
μοιχεύσεις. 28 ἐγὼ δὲ λέγω ὑμῖν ὅτι πᾶς ὁ βλέπων γυναῖκα [i] πρὸς τὸ [k] ἐπιθυμῆσαι αὐτὴν ἤδη [l] ἐμοίχευσεν αὐτὴν
[m] ἐν τῇ καρδίᾳ αὐτοῦ. 29 εἰ δὲ ὁ [n] ὀφθαλμός σου ὁ [n] δεξιὸς

G οφθ... BDEGK LMSUV ΓΔΠℵ 1. 33

f = ver. 33. ch. xviii. 25, &c. xxii. 21 ‖. Rom. xiii. 7. Deut. xxiii. 21.
g Mark xii. 42 only †.
h ch. xix. 18. Exod. xx. 14. Deut. v. 18.
i constr., ch. vi. 1 al. fr.
k w. acc., here only. Exod. xx. 17. Deut. v. 21. Soph. Œd. Tyr. 58. w. gen., Acts xx. 33 al. Exod. Deut. as above.
l constr., here bis only. (see ch. xix. 9 v. r. John viii. 4 rec. Lev. xx. 10.) Jer. v. 9.
m ch. xxiv. 48. 1 Cor. vii. 37. Deut. viii. 17.
n Zech. xi. 17 bis.

27. rec aft *ερρ.* ins *τοις αρχαιοις*, with LMΔ 33 vulg lat-*c* *ff*$_1$ *g*$_{1.2}$ *h* syr-cu syr-with-ast Eus$_4$ [Chr] Iren-int Cypr Hil : om BDℵ rel lat-*a b f k* Syr copt goth æth arm Orig Cyr Thl Euthym Hil spec.

28. rec (for 1st *αυτην*) *αυτης* (*grammatical corrn*), with Mℵ[?a] 1 Just Athen Orig$_1$ Eus : om ℵ[1] [Clem$_1$ Orig$_3$ Chr$_2$ Isid$_1$ Tert$_3$] : txt BD rel Thph-ant Clem Orig Constt Eus. *εαυτου* B.

ment before coming into court: see Thol. p. 192, 3rd edit. So Chrys.: *πρὸ μὲν γὰρ τῆς εἰσόδου σὺ κύριος εἶ τοῦ παντός· ἐὰν δὲ ἐπιβῇς ἐκείνων τῶν προθύρων, οὐδὲ σφόδρα σπουδάζων δυνήσῃ τὰ καθ' ἑαυτὸν ὡς βούλει διαθεῖναι.* Hom. xvi. 10, p. 219. **26.**] These words, which in the earthly example imply future liberation, because an earthly debt can be paid in most cases, so in the spiritual counterpart amount to a negation of it, because the debt can never be discharged. We have *ἕως ἀποδῷ τὸ ὀφειλόμενον* in ch. xviii. 30, where the payment was clearly impossible. **ὑπηρέτης** = *πράκτωρ* in Luke xii. 58, and is the officer of the court who saw the sentences executed. If we are called on to assign a meaning to *ὑπηρέτης* in the interpretation, it must represent the chief of those who in ch. xviii. 34, are hinted at by *βασανισταί*, viz. the great enemy, the minister of the divine wrath. **κοδράντην**, *quadrantem*, a Latin word (= *λεπτόν* in ‖ Luke), the fourth part of an *as*. See note on Luke, l. c.

27—30.] Second example. *The law of adultery.* **28. πᾶς ὁ βλέπων**] The precise meaning should in this verse be kept in mind, as the neglect of it may lead into error. Our Lord is speaking of the sin of *adultery*, and therefore, however the saying may undoubtedly apply by implication to cases where this sin is out of the question—e. g. to the impure beholding of an *un*married woman with a view to fornication (it being borne in mind that spiritually, and before God, all fornication *is* adultery, inasmuch as the unmarried person is bound in loyalty and chastity to *Him*. See Stier below)—yet the *direct* assertion in this verse must be understood as applying to the cases where *this* sin is in question. And, again, the *βλέπων πρὸς τὸ ἐπιθ.* must not be interpreted of the casual evil thought which is checked by holy watchfulness, but the gazing *with a view to feed that desire* (for so *πρὸς τό* with an inf. must mean). And again, *ἤδη ἐμ. αὐτ. ἐν τῇ κ. αὐτ.*, whatever it may undoubtedly *imply* respecting the guilt incurred in God's sight, does not *directly state* any thing; but, plainly understood, affirms that the man who can do this—viz. 'gaze with a view to feed unlawful desire'—has already in his heart passed the barrier of criminal intention; made up his mind, stifled his conscience; in thought, committed the deed. But perhaps there is justice in Stier's remark, Reden Jesu, i. 129 (edn. 2), that our Lord speaks here after the O. T. usage, in which, both in the seventh commandment and elsewhere, *adultery* also *includes fornication;* for marriage is the becoming one flesh,—and therefore every such union, except that after the manner and in the state appointed by God, is a violation and contempt of that holy ordinance.

29.] An admonition, arising out of the truth announced in the last verse, to *withstand the first springs and occasions of evil desire, even by the sacrifice of what is most useful and dear to us.* *ταῦτα προσέταξεν οὐ περὶ μελῶν διαλεγόμενος, ἄπαγε· οὐδαμοῦ γὰρ τῆς σαρκὸς τὰ ἐγκλήματα εἶναί φησιν, ἀλλὰ πανταχοῦ τῆς γνώμης τῆς πονηρᾶς ἡ κατηγορία. οὐ γὰρ ὁ ὀφθαλμός ἐστιν ὁ ὁρῶν, ἀλλ' ὁ νοῦς καὶ ὁ λογισμός.* Chrys. Hom. xvii. 3, p. 225: and to the same effect Euthymius, who adds *ἀλλ' ὀφθαλμὸν μὲν δεξιὸν καλεῖ τὸν δίκην ὀφθαλμοῦ στεργόμενον δεξιὸν φίλον· χεῖρα δὲ δεξιὰν τὸν δίκην χειρὸς χρησιμεύοντα δεξιὸν ὑπηρέτην, καὶ εἴτε ἄνδρες εἶεν εἴτε γυναῖκες. λέγει τοίνυν ὅτι ἐὰν οἱ τοιοῦτοι σκανδαλίζωσί σε πρὸς ἐμπάθειαν, μηδὲ τούτων φείσῃ· ἀλλ' ἔκκοψον αὐτοὺς τῆς πρός σε σχέσεως, καὶ ῥίψον πόῤῥω σου.* Philo Judæus reports that he had heard

[o] σκανδαλίζει σε, [p] ἔξελε αὐτὸν καὶ βάλε ἀπὸ σοῦ· [q] συμφέρει γάρ σοι [r] ἵνα ἀπόληται ἓν τῶν [s] μελῶν σου [t] καὶ μὴ
ὅλον τὸ σῶμά σου [u] βληθῇ εἰς [uv] γέενναν. 30 καὶ εἰ ἡ δεξιά
σου χεὶρ [o] σκανδαλίζει σε, [w] ἔκκοψον αὐτὴν καὶ βάλε ἀπὸ
σοῦ· [q] συμφέρει γάρ σοι ἵνα ἀπόληται ἓν τῶν [s] μελῶν
σου [t] καὶ μὴ ὅλον τὸ σῶμά σου εἰς [v] γέενναν [x] ἀπέλθῃ.
...δε Γ. ...αυτου G. 31 Ἐῤῥήθη δὲ [y] Ὃς ἂν [z] ἀπολύσῃ τὴν γυναῖκα αὐτοῦ,
δότω αὐτῇ [a] ἀποστάσιον. 32 ἐγὼ δὲ λέγω ὑμῖν ὅτι πᾶς
ὁ [z] ἀπολύων τὴν γυναῖκα αὐτοῦ [b] παρεκτὸς [c] λόγου

o ch. xvii. 27 al. fr.† Sir. ix. 5. xxiii. 8. xxxv. (xxxii.) 15 only. Prov. iv. 12 Aq.
p = ch. xviii. 9 only. (Acts vii. 10 al.) τῶν ὄψεων ἐξαιρεθεισῶν, Polyb. xii. 7. 5.
q w. ἵνα, ch. xviii. 6. John xi. 50. xvi. 7. w. inf., ch. xix. 10 reff.
r ch. x. 25. 1 Cor. iv. 3.
s gospp., here (bis) only. Paul, Rom. vi. 13 al. fr. James iii. 5, 6. iv. 1 only. Lev. i. 6 al.
t John xi. 50. Prov. viii. 10. Joel ii. 13.
u Mark ix. 45, 47 only. see ch. xviii. 9. Luke xii. 5.
v ver. 22 reff.
w ch. iii. 10. Rom. xi. 22, 24 al. Exod. xxi. 27. Jer. vi. 6.
x Mark ix. 43 only.
y Deut. xxiv. 3 (1).
z = ch. i. 19. xix. 3, &c. ||. Luke xvi. 18 bis ‡. Esdr. ix. 36. Jos. Antt. xv. 7. 10.
a ch. xix. 7 || only. Deut. xxiv. 3, 5 (1, 3). Isa. l. 1. Jer. iii. 8 only, but always w. βιβλίον.
b Acts xxvi. 29. 2 Cor. xi. 28 (ch. xix. 9 v. r.) only †. Deut. i. 36 Aq.
c = Acts x. 29. πρὸς τίνα λόγον ποιεῖται τοῦτο, Polyb. xl. 6. 5.

29. *ο δεξιος* bef *σου* D. *βληθησει* L : *απελθη eat* D lat-*a b c* g_1 *h* syr-cu copt.
30. om ver D (i. e. from *γεενναν* to *γεενναν*). for *και μη*, *η* ℵ[1](txt ℵ[2]). rec (for *εις γ. απελθη*) *βληθη εις γ.* (*from ver* 29), with ΓΔ rel lat-*f* syrr goth arm [Chr] : *βληθησει εις την γ.* L : txt Bℵ 1. 33 latt(including Δ-lat) syr-cu copt æth (Orig Ambr Aug Lucif).
31. om *δε* KΠℵ[1](ins ℵ[2.3]) Scr's a l m n p ev-H[1] Syr [syr-cu]. rec ins *οτι* bef *ος*, with Δ rel : om BDLℵ 1. 13. 33. 124 latt Chr Hil.
32. om *οτι* D lat-*a b* g_1 *h* Aug. rec (for *πας ο απολ.*) *ος αν απολυσῃ*, with D rel lat-*a b* g_1 *h k* syr-cu copt (Orig) : txt BKLMΔΠℵ 1. 33 Scr's u w evv-y-z-H-P vulg

ἀπὸ θεσπεσίων ἀνδρῶν an interpretation of Deut. xxv. 12, singularly agreeing with this verse: εἰκότως οὖν τὴν . . . χεῖρα. . . . ἀποκόπτειν διείρηται συμβολικῶς, οὐχ ὅπως ἀκρωτηριάζηται τὸ σῶμα στερόμενον ἀναγκαιοτάτου μέρους, ἀλλ' ὑπὲρ τοῦ πάντας τῆς ψυχῆς ἀθέους τέμνειν λογισμούς. De Spec. Legibus ad 6 et 7 decal. cap. § 32, vol. ii. p. 329. We may observe here, that our Lord grounds His precept of the most rigid and decisive *self-denial* on the considerations of the *truest self-interest*,—**συμφέρει σοι.** See ch. xviii. 8, 9, and notes. **ἵνα** belongs to *συμφ. σοι* (see John xvi. 7); and not (Meyer) to the foregoing, making *συμφ. γάρ σοι* parenthetical.

31, 32.] Third example. *The law of divorce.* See note on ch. xix. 7—9. Lightfoot, Hor. Hebr., gives a form of the *ἀποστάσιον*, which was a divorcement *a vinculo matrimonii*, and placed the woman absolutely in her own power, to marry whom she pleased, unless the husband inserted a special clause to bar this. In Deut. xxiv. 1, the allowable reason of divorce is 'some uncleanness.' This the disciples of Shammai interpreted only of adultery; those of Hillel of any thing which amounted to uncleanness in the eyes of the husband. 32.] **πορνείας** must be taken to mean sin, not only before marriage, but after it also, in a wider sense, as including *μοιχεία* likewise. In the similar places, Mark x. 11: Luke xvi. 18, this exception does not occur; see however our ch. xix. 9. Chrysostom explains the connexion of this verse with the former to be, ἵνα γὰρ μὴ ἀκούσας Ἔξελε τὸν ὀφθαλμόν, νομίσῃς καὶ περὶ γυναικὸς ταῦτα λέγεσθαι, εὐκαίρως ἐπήγαγε τὴν ἐπιδιόρθωσιν ταύτην, ἑνὶ τρόπῳ μόνῳ συγχωρῶν ἐκβάλλειν αὐτήν, ἑτέρῳ δὲ οὐδενί. Hom. xvii. 4, p. 228. The figurative senses of *πορνεία* cannot be admissible here, as the law is one having reference to a definite point in actual life; and this its aim and end restricts the meaning to that kind of *πορνεία* immediately applicable to the case. Otherwise this one strictly guarded exception would give indefinite and universal latitude. **ποιεῖ αὐτ. μοιχ.**] 'Per alias nuptias, quarum potestatem dat divortium.' Bengel. **καὶ ὃς ἐάν**] How far *the marriage of the innocent party after separation* (on account of *πορνεία*) *is forbidden* by this or the similar passage ch. xix. 9, is a weighty and difficult question. By the Roman Church such marriage is *strictly forbidden*, and the authority of Augustine much cited, who strongly upholds this view, but not without misgivings later in life. 'Scripsi duos libros de conjugiis adulterinis, ... cupiens solvere difficillimam quæstionem. Quod utrum enodatissime fecerim nescio;

d ch. xix. 9 bis ‖ only. Jer. ix. 2. Ezek. xvi. 32. (-χεύειν, see above [1].)
e Lev. xix. 12 (not LXX).

πορνείας ποιεῖ αὐτὴν [1] μοιχευθῆναι· καὶ ὃς ἐὰν [z] ἀπολελυμένην γαμήσῃ, [d] μοιχᾶται. 33 Πάλιν ἠκούσατε ὅτι ἐῤῥήθη
τοῖς ἀρχαίοις [e] Οὐκ [f] ἐπιορκήσεις, [gh] ἀποδώσεις δὲ τῷ

BDEKL MSUVΓ ΔΠℵ 1. 33

f here only †. Esdr. i. 48 (46). Wisd. xiv. 28 only. (-κος, 1 Tim. i. 10. -κία, Wisd. xiv. 25.) g = ch. xviii. 25, 26. Job xxii. 27. Sir. xviii. 22. h here only.

lat-*c f ff*$_1$ *g*$_2$ *l* syrr goth æth arm [spec]. rec μοιχ**ασθ**αι, with L rel Bas Chr$_1$: txt (*Griesbach supposes txt to be a corrn*, 'ut grammaticorum præceptis, qui μοιχευειν et μοιχασθαι de maritis, μοιχευεσθαι autem de uxoribus usurpari volunt, satisfieret,' *but see ref Ezek*) BDℵ 1. 13. 33. 124. 209 Thph-ant Orig$_2$ Chr$_{h.l}$ Thdrt. om και to μοιχαται (μοιχ. to μοιχ. ?) D 64 lat-*a b k* gr-and-lat-mss-mentd-by-Aug Tert. for εαν, αν K[1]ℵ[1](txt ℵ[2]) Scr's i. ο απολελυμενην γαμησας B (*see ch* xix. 9).

33. εφιορκησεις ℵ.

immo vero non me pervenisse ad hujus rei perfectionem sentio.' Retract. ii. 57, vol. i. On the other hand, the Protestant and Greek Churches *allow* such marriage. Certainly it would appear, from the literal meaning of our Lord's words (if ἀπολελ. be taken as perfectly general), that it *should not be allowed:* for if by such divorce the marriage be altogether dissolved, how can the *woman* be said μοιχᾶσθαι by a second marriage? or how will St. Paul's precept (1 Cor. vii. 11) find place, in which he says, ἐὰν δὲ καὶ χωρισθῇ, μενέτω ἄγαμος ἢ τῷ ἀνδρὶ καταλλαγήτω? for stating this as St. Paul does, prefaced by the words οὐκ ἐγώ, ἀλλ' ὁ κύριος, it must be understood, and has been taken, as *referring to this very verse,* or rather (see note in loc.) to ch. xix. 6 ff., and consequently can only suppose πορνεία as the cause. Besides which, the tenor of our Lord's teaching in other places (see above) seems to set before us the state of marriage as absolutely *indissoluble as such,* however he may sanction the expulsion *a mensâ et thoro* of an unfaithful wife. Those who defend the other view suppose the ἀπολελυμένην to mean, when *unlawfully* divorced, *not* for πορνεία: and certainly this is not improbable (see below). We may well leave a matter in doubt, of which Augustine could write thus: 'In ipsis divinis sententiis ita obscurum est utrum et iste, cui quidem sine dubio adulteram licet dimittere, adulter tamen habeatur si alteram duxerit, ut, quantum existimo, venialiter ibi quisque fallatur.' De Fide atq. Op. c. 19 (35), vol. vi. Meyer gives as a reason for believing ἀπολελ. to refer only to the *unlawfully divorced:* "ἀπολελ. is not qualified (cf. παρεκτὸς λόγου πορνείας), because the *punishment of death* was attached to adultery (Levit. xx. 10: Michaelis, Mos. Recht § 260 ff.), and consequently under the law the marrying a woman divorced for adultery could never happen." Stier says in a note to his 2nd edn.: "We hold it clear that ἀπολ. can only refer to the woman unlawfully divorced, and then there is no prohibition of the second marriage of one divorced on account of adultery; we see here nothing at all 'obscurum,' as Augustine in the passage cited by Alford." (I may remark, that **ἀπολελυμένην** is most naturally rendered, "*her, when divorced:*" not "*a divorced woman,*" as Wordsw. It is a secondary predicate, of which the subject is to be supplied out of αὐτήν above. Still less of course is it to be rendered "the divorced woman," τὴν ἀπολελυμένην. And thus understood, the saying concerning marriage after divorce applies only, *as far* as this passage is concerned, to *unlawful* divorce, not to that after πορνεία.)

33—37.] Fourth example. *The law of oaths.* 33, 34.] The exact meaning of these verses is to be ascertained by two considerations. (1) That the Jews held all those oaths *not to be binding,* in which *the sacred name of God did not directly occur:* as Philo states (De Special. Legg. ad 3, 4, 5 decal. cap. § 1, vol. ii. p. 271), προσλαβέτω τις, εἰ βούλοιτο, μὴ μὲν τὸ ἀνωτάτω καὶ πρεσβύτατον εὐθὺς αἴτιον, ἀλλὰ γῆν, ἥλιον, ἀστέρας, οὐρανόν, τὸν σύμπαντα κόσμον. And Lightfoot (Hor. Hebr. ad locum) cites from the Rabbinical books, 'Si quis jurat per cœlum, per terram, per solem, etc. . . . non est juramentum.' See note, ch. xxiii. 16. It therefore appears that a stress is to be laid on this technical distinction in the quotation made by our Lord; and we must understand as belonging to the quotation, 'but whatever thou shalt swear not to the Lord may be transgressed.' (2) Then our Lord passes so far beyond this rule, that He lays down (including in it the understanding that all oaths must be kept *if made,* for that they are all ultimately referable to swearing by God) the rule of the Christian community, which is *not to swear at all;* for that every such means

κυρίῳ τοὺς [hi] ὅρκους σου. 34 ἐγὼ δὲ λέγω ὑμῖν μὴ [k] ὀμό-
σαι [l] ὅλως, μήτε ἐν τῷ οὐρανῷ, ὅτι θρόνος ἐστὶν τοῦ θεοῦ,
35 μήτε ἐν τῇ γῇ, ὅτι [m] ὑποπόδιόν ἐστιν τῶν ποδῶν
αὐτοῦ, μήτε [n] εἰς Ἱεροσόλυμα, ὅτι πόλις ἐστὶν τοῦ [o] μεγάλου [o] βασιλέως, 36 μήτε ἐν τῇ κεφαλῇ σου [k] ὀμόσῃς,
ὅτι οὐ δύνασαι μίαν τρίχα λευκὴν ποιῆσαι ἢ [p] μέλαιναν.
37 * ἔσται δὲ ὁ λόγος ὑμῶν [q] ναὶ ναὶ [q] οὒ οὔ· τὸ δὲ [r] περισσὸν

i ch. xiv. 7, 9 || Mk. xxvi. 72. Luke i. 73. Acts ii. 30. Heb. vi. 16, 17. James v. 12 only. Num. xxx. 3. (-κίζειν, Mark v. 7. -κωμοσία, Heb. vii. 20.) k w. ἐν, ch. xxiii. 16, &c. Rev. x. 6. Ps. lxii. 11. Jer. v. 7. κατά, Heb. vi. 13. εἰς, ver. 35. acc., James v. 12. l 1 Cor. v. 1. vi. 7. xv. 29 only †. m Luke xx. 43 (|| v. r.), Acts ii. 35. vii. 49 and Heb. i. 13, from Ps. cix. 1. Heb. x. 13. James ii. 3 only. Isa. lxvi. 1. Ps. xcviii. 5. Lam. ii. 1. always w. ποδῶν (exc. 2 Chron. ix. 18 compl.). n = here only, see 1 Pet. iii. 12 and ref. (k) above. o = here only. Psa. xlvii. 2. Tobit xiii. 15. p = Rev. vi. 5, 12 (2 Cor. iii. 3. 2 John 12. 3 John 13) only. Lev. xiii. 37. Cant. i. 5. v. 11. Zech. vi. 2, 6 only. q 2 Cor. i. 17, 18, 19. James v. 12. r constr., here only = ver. 47. see Eph. iii. 20.

36. μηδε א[2](txt א[1.3]). τριχαν ELא[1](txt א[2]). rec η μελαιναν bef ποιησαι (*easier order*), with Δ rel syr goth: ποιειν(-ησαι D[2.4]) τρ. μι. λ. η μελ. D[1]: ποιησ. μελ. L: ποιησ. μ. τρικα λ. η μελ. 1: alii aliter: txt Bא 33. 124. 209 latt copt æth arm $Cypr_1$ Aug_1.

37. *rec ἔστω (*from James* v. 12, *or perhaps the imperatives following*), with DLא rel latt goth Just $hom\text{-}Cl_2$ $Clem_2$ Iren-int Tert $Cypr_2$: txt B 245 Eus.

of strengthening a man's simple affirmation arises out of the evil in human nature, is rendered requisite by the distrust that sin has induced, and is, therefore, out of the question among the just and true and pure of heart. See James v. 12, and note there, as explanatory why, in both cases, swearing by the name of God is not specified as forbidden. In the words, 'Swear not at all,' our Lord does not so much make a positive enactment by which all swearing is to individuals forbidden, e. g. on solemn occasions, and for the satisfaction of others, (for that would be a mere technical Pharisaism wholly at variance with the spirit of the Gospel, and inconsistent with the example of *God himself*, Heb. vi. 13—17; vii. 21; *of the Lord when on earth*, whose ἀμὴν ἀμὴν λέγω ὑμῖν was a solemn asseveration, and who at once respected the solemn adjuration of Caiaphas, ch. xxvi. 63, 64; of *His Apostles*, writing under the guidance of His Spirit, see Gal. i. 20: 2 Cor. i. 23: Rom. i. 9: Phil. i. 8, and especially 1 Cor. xv. 31; of *His holy angels*, Rev. x. 6,) as declare to us, that the *proper state* of Christians is, to *require no oaths*; that when τὸ πονηρόν is expelled from among them, every ναί and οὒ will be as decisive as an oath, every promise as binding as a vow. We observe (α) that these verses imply the unfitness of *vows* of every kind as rules of Christian action; (β) that the greatest regard ought to be had to the scruples of those, not only sects, but individuals, who object to taking an oath, and every facility given in a Christian state for their ultimate entire abolition. There is a very full account in Tholuck, Bergpredigt, pp. 258—75, of the history of opinions on this question. **34, 35.**] Compare ch. xxiii. 16—22. Archbp. Trench observes (Serm. on Mount, p. 55), 'Men had learned to think that, if only God's name were avoided, there was no irreverence in the frequent oaths by heaven, by the earth, by Jerusalem, by their own heads, and these brought in on the slightest need, or on no need at all; just as now-a-days the same lingering half-respect for the Holy Name will often cause men, who would not be wholly profane, to substitute for that name sounds that nearly resemble, but are not exactly it, or the name, it may be, of some heathen deity.' Observe that the predicates, θρόνος, ὑποπόδιον, πόλις, being placed for emphasis before the copulæ, are without articles: it would be ὅτι ἐστὶν ὁ θρόνος, &c. For the allusions see reff. Isa. and Ps. **34.**] **ὀμν. ἐν** is a Hebraism: the classical usage is with κατά and a gen., or simply with an acc.; see reff. **36. οὐ δύνασαι μίαν τρ. λ. π. ἢ μ.**] Thou hast no control over the appearance of grey hairs on thy head—thy head is not thine own;—thou swearest then by a creature of God, whose destinies and changes are in God's hand; so that *every oath is an appeal to God*. And, indeed, men generally regard it as such now, even unconsciously. **37. ναὶ ναὶ οὒ οὔ**] The similar place, ref. James, admirably illustrates this—ἤτω ὑμῶν τὸ ναὶ ναὶ καὶ τὸ οὒ οὔ—let these words only be used, and they in simplicity and unreservedness.

s - 1 John iii. 12.
t Exod. xxi. 24. Lev. xxiv. 20. Deut. xix. 21.
u Eph. vi. 13. James iv. 7 al. Num. x. 9.

τούτων [s] ἐκ τοῦ [s] πονηροῦ ἐστιν.
38 Ἠκούσατε ὅτι ἐῤῥήθη [t] Ὀφθαλμὸν ἀντὶ ὀφθαλμοῦ, καὶ ὀδόντα ἀντὶ ὀδόντος.
39 ἐγὼ δὲ λέγω ὑμῖν μὴ [u] ἀντιστῆναι τῷ [v] πονηρῷ· ἀλλ' ὅστις σε [w] ῥαπίζει εἰς τὴν δεξιὰν [x] σιαγόνα σου, στρέψον

G οςτις.. BDEGK LMSUV ΓΔΠℵ 1. 33

v = here only. see note and 1 Cor. v. 13. w ch. xxvi. 67 only. Hos. xi. 4. Esdr. iv. 30 only. (-ισμα, Mark xiv. 65.) x Luke vi. 29 only. Hos. xi. 4. Isa. l. 6.

38. om και D 13 lat-*a b c* $g_{1\cdot2}$ *l* Orig-int$_1$ Hil.

39. αντισταθηναι ℵ. rec ραπισει with D rel: txt Bℵ 33. rec (for εις) επι, with Dℵ^{3a} rel [Dial Bas$_1$] Eus: txt Bℵ^1 Scr's d r evv-y-H (Clem Orig) [Bas$_1$] Chr. (εις is the reading Luke vi. 29 of Dℵ^1, επι of the other mss.) om δεξιαν (*as in* ‖ *Luke*) D lat-mss-mentd-by-Aug (Dial Ephr Cypr) Hil Op. rec σου bef σιαγονα, with L rel [lat-*c* g_1 *k*] goth: om σου (*as* ‖ *Luke*) ℵ 1. 33 Scr's a l m n o^2 p v evv-y-P em lat-*a f h* Bas Chr Damasc Orig-int Op: txt BD Scr's b latt Eus.

ἐκ τοῦ πονηροῦ] See ref. The gender is ambiguous, as it may constructionally be in the Lord's prayer, ch. vi. 13, but see note there. It is quite immaterial to the *sense*, in which gender we understand it; for the evil of man's corrupt nature is in Scripture spoken of as the *work of ὁ πονηρός*, and is *itself τὸ πονηρόν*. See John viii. 44: 1 John iii. 8.

38—41.] Fifth example. *The law of retaliation.* **38.**] That is, *such was the public enactment of the Mosaic law*, and, as such, it implied a private spirit of retaliation which should seek such redress; for the example evidently refers to *private* as well as public retribution. Here again our Lord appears to speak of the *true status and perfection of a Christian community*,—not to forbid, in those mixed and but half-Christian states, which have ever divided so-called Christendom among them, the infliction of judicial penalties for crime. In fact Scripture speaks, Rom. xiii. 4, of *the minister of such infliction* as the *minister of God*. But as before, our Lord shews us the *condition to which* a Christian community should *tend*, and to further which every private Christian's own endeavours should be directed. It is quite beside the purpose for the world to say, that these precepts of our Lord are too highly pitched for humanity, and so to find an excuse for violating them. If we were disciples of His in the true sense, these precepts would, in their *spirit*, as indicative of frames of mind, be *strictly observed;* and, *as far* as we are His disciples, we shall *attain to such their observance*.

Here again, our Lord does not *contradict* the Mosaic law, but *expands* and *fulfils* it, declaring to us that the necessity for it would be altogether removed in the complete state of that kingdom which He came to establish. Against the notion that **ὀφθ. ἀντὶ ὀφθ.** κ.τ.λ. sanctioned all kinds of private revenge, Augustine remarks, 'Quandoquidem et illud antiquum ad reprimendas flammas odiorum, sævientiumque immoderatos animos refrænandos, ita præceptum est. Quis enim tantundem facile contentus est reponere vindictæ quantum accepit injuriæ? Nonne videmus homines leviter læsos moliri cædem, sitire sanguinem, vixque invenire in malis inimici unde satientur? . . . . . . Huic igitur immoderatæ et per hoc injustæ ultioni lex justum modum figens, pœnam talionis instituit: hoc est ut qualem quisque intulit injuriam, tale supplicium pendat. Proinde, "Oculum pro oculo, dentem pro dente," non fomes sed limes furoris est; non ut id quod sopitum erat inde accenderetur, sed ne id quod ardebat ultra extenderetur impositus.' Cont. Faust. xix. 25, vol. viii. See 1 Cor. vi. 1—6. The accusatives ὀφθαλμόν, ὀδόντα are perhaps in ref. Exod. governed by δώσει, which immediately precedes them. But it may be noticed, that in ref. Levit., where the construction would require nominatives, we have the saying, as a proverb, in the accusative form. In ref. Deut., the case is exactly as here. **39. μὴ ἀντιστῆναι**] Here again, we have our divine Lawgiver legislating, not in the bondage of the letter so as to stultify His disciples, and in many circumstances to turn the salt of the earth into a means of corrupting it,—but in the freedom of the spirit, laying down those great principles which ought to regulate the inner purposes and consequent actions of His followers. Taken *slavishly* and *literally*, neither did our Lord Himself conform to this precept (John xviii. 22, 23), nor his Apostles (Acts xxiii. 3). But *truly*, and in the *spirit*, our blessed Redeemer obeyed it; 'He gave his back to the smiters, and his cheeks to them that plucked off the hair, and hid not his face from shame and spitting' (Isa. l. 6): and his Apostles also, see 1 Cor. iv. 9—13.

τῷ πονηρῷ] **the evil man**; 'him who injures thee.' Or, perhaps, in the

αὐτῷ καὶ τὴν ἄλλην.
40 καὶ τῷ θέλοντί σοι [y] κριθῆναι
καὶ τὸν [z] χιτῶνά σου [a] λαβεῖν, [b] ἄφες αὐτῷ καὶ τὸ [z] ἱμάτιον.
41 καὶ ὅςτις σε [c] ἀγγαρεύσει [d] μίλιον ἕν, [e] ὕπαγε
μετ' αὐτοῦ δύο.
42 τῷ [f] αἰτοῦντί σε δός, καὶ τὸν
θέλοντα ἀπὸ σοῦ [g] δανείσασθαι μὴ [h] ἀποστραφῇς.

y = 1 Cor. vi. 1, 6. Gen. xxvi. 21. constr., here only. Job ix. 3 Bℵ.
z Luke vi. 29. John xix. 23. Acts ix. 39.
a = Rev. iii. 11. Gen. xxvii. 36.
b = & constr., here only. 1 Macc. x. 28, 32.
c ch. xxvii. 32. Mark xv. 21 only †.
d here only †.
e Luke xii. 58 ‡.
f absol. and constr., ch. vi. 8. vii. 11. Luke vi. 30. xi. 13.
g Luke vi. 34 bis, 35 only. Prov. xx. 4. Sir. xx. 15. (-στής, Luke vii. 41. -ον, ch. xviii. 27.)
h = 2 Tim. i. 15. Tit. i. 14. Heb. xii. 25. Wisd. xvi. 3. ἀπεστραμμένος ὁ Θ. τὰ ἅγια, Jos. B. J. ii. 19. 6.

40. for τω θελοντι, ο θελων *qui voluerit* D : τον θελοντα Δ. for αφες, αφησεις D [Bas$_1$]. for αυτω, τουτω ℵ[1](txt ℵ[2](?)[3a]). at end add σου ℵ 33 Scr's q r evv-z-P copt æth arm.

41. for σε, εαν Δ, σε εαν ℵ Scr's w(αν). αγγαρευει D : -ρευση EGKVΔℵ(ενγ., sic) 33 [Bas$_1$ Chr]. ins ετι αλλα bef δυο D lat-*a b c g*$_1$ Iren-int : *et alia duo* vulg lat-*h* : *alia duo* am(with forj) lat-*ff*$_1$ *l* syr-cu Iren$_1$-int [Aug].

42. for σε, σοι ℵ[1](txt ℵ[2]) ev-y. rec (for δος) διδου (*see Luke* vi. 30), with L rel : txt BDℵ 13. 124 Clem. τω θελοντι D 38 ev-12 latt. om απο σου D lat-*k* Clem Cypr Hil spec. δανισασθαι B[1]DΔℵ[: δανησ. L].

indefinite sense, as before, **evil**, generally, 'when thus directed against thee.' Only, the other possible meaning there, '*the evil one*,' is precluded here. ἀντίστητε τῷ διαβόλῳ: but not *this particular form* of his working (viz. malice directed against thyself) so as to revenge it on another. **40, 41.**] See note on ver. 39. **κριθῆναι** imports *legal contention only*, and is thus distinguished from the violence in ver. 39. (Meyer, against Tholuck (but not in edn. 3) and De Wette.) **λαβεῖν**, i. e. in pledge for a debt: see Exod. xxii. 26. **χιτῶνα**, the inner and less costly garment; **ἱμάτιον**, the outer and more valuable, used also by the poor as a coverlet by night (Exod. ubi supra). In Luke vi. 29 the order is inverted, and appears to be that in which the two garments would be taken from the body, that verse referring to abstraction by *violence*. See the apostolic comment on this precept, 1 Cor. vi. 7. **ἀγγαρεύσει**] Herod. viii. 98, after describing the Persian post-couriers, adds, τοῦτο τὸ δράμημα τῶν ἵππων καλέουσι Πέρσαι ἀγγαρήϊον. Æschylus, Agam. 285 (Dindorf), says of the beacons which brought the intelligence of the capture of Troy to Mycenæ, φρυκτὸς δὲ φρυκτὸν δεῦρ' ἀπ' ἀγγάρου πυρὸς ἔπεμπεν. 'The Jews particularly objected to the duty of furnishing posts for the Roman government; and Demetrius, wishing to conciliate the Jews, promised, among other things, κελεύω δὲ μηδὲ ἀγγαρεύεσθαι τὰ 'Ιουδαίων ὑποζύγια (Jos. Antt. xiii. 2. 3). Hence our Saviour represents this as a burden;—and in the same manner Epictetus says, ἂν δὲ ἀγγαρεία ᾖ καὶ στρατιώτης ἐπιλάβηται, ἄφες, μὴ ἀντίτεινε μηδὲ γόγγυζε.' Dr. Burton. The ἐπισταθμία, or billeting of the Roman soldiers and their horses on the Jews, was one kind of this ἀγγαρεία. **42.**] The proper understanding of the command in this verse may be arrived at from considering the way in which the Lord Himself, who declares, 'If ye shall ask any thing in my name, I will do it' (John xiv. 14), performs this promise to us. It would obviously be, not a promise of love, but a sentence of condemnation to us, understood in its bare literal sense; but our gracious Saviour, knowing what is good for us, so answers our prayers, that we never are sent empty away; not always, indeed, receiving *what* we ask,—but that which in the very disappointment we are constrained thankfully to confess is better than our wish. So, in his humble sphere, should the Christian giver act. To give every thing to every one—the sword to the madman, the alms to the impostor, the criminal request to the temptress—would be to act as the enemy of others and ourselves. Ours should be a higher and deeper charity, flowing from those inner springs of love, which are the sources of outward actions sometimes widely divergent; whence may arise both the timely concession, and the timely refusal. As Chrysostom observes on a former verse, μὴ τοίνυν ἁπλῶς τὰ πράγματα ἐξετάσωμεν, ἀλλὰ καὶ καιρὸν καὶ αἰτίαν καὶ γνώμην καὶ προσώπων διαφοράν, καὶ ὅσα ἂν αὐτοῖς ἕτερα συμβαίνῃ, πάντα μετὰ ἀκριβείας ζητῶμεν· οὐδὲ γάρ ἐστιν ἑτέρως ἐφίκεσθαι τῆς ἀληθείας. Hom. xvii. 6, p. 231. **δανείσασθαι**] Here, **to borrow**,—without *usury*, which was for-

43 Ἠκούσατε ὅτι ἐῤῥήθη Ἀγαπήσεις τὸν [i] πλησίον σου
καὶ μισήσεις τὸν ἐχθρόν σου. 44 ἐγὼ δὲ λέγω ὑμῖν, ...σου G.
ἀγαπᾶτε τοὺς ἐχθροὺς ὑμῶν καὶ [k] προσεύχεσθε [k] ὑπὲρ ..υμων V.
τῶν [l] διωκόντων ὑμᾶς, 45 ὅπως γένησθε υἱοὶ τοῦ [m] πατρὸς
ὑμῶν τοῦ [m] ἐν οὐρανοῖς, ὅτι τὸν ἥλιον αὐτοῦ [n] ἀνατέλλει Z ουρανοις...

i = here only. (see note and Lev. xix. 18. Deut. xv. 2, 3.)
k Eph. vi. 18, 19. Col. i. 9. 1 Kings xii. 19. Jer. xlix. 4 Ed-vat. (not ABℵ.)
l = ver. 10, &c. reff.
m ver. 16 reff.
n trans., here only. Gen. iii. 18. Isa. lxi. 11. Hom. Il. ε. 777. (see Ps. cxxxi. 17.) intr., ch. iv. 16 reff.

BDEKL MSUZΓ ΔΠℵ 1. 33

44. rec aft *υμων* ins *ευλογειτε τους καταρωμενους υμας*(D² : *υμειν* D¹) *καλως ποιειτε τους μισουντας υμας*, with DL rel(which however have *τοις μισουσιν*) lat-*c f h* syrr goth æth arm : om Bℵ 1. 11. 22. 58. 113. 209 lat-*k* syr-cu copt Thph-ant $Orig_5$ Eus Dial Iren-int $Tert_1$ $Cypr_3$ Hil_1 Ambr Jer Fulg. (*The insertion seems to have been made from Luke* vi. 27, 28. *Meyer and De Wette question this on account of the order of the clauses in Luke being different: but this inversion may easily have taken place by one or other of them being supplied in the margin, and both at last having found their way, irrespective of order, into the text. Their omission, if genuine, would be perfectly unaccountable. I therefore agree with Lachm, Tischdf, and Treg in expunging them here.*) The 1st clause is inserted alone (but qu? from Luke) by Athen Clem Eus_1 Thl : the 2nd, alone, by vulg lat-*a b* ff_1 g_1 *l* Epiph Phot Aug Juv Op. rec ins *επηρεαζοντων υμας και* bef *διωκοντων* (*επηρ. being the word answering to διωκ. in Luke* vi. 28 *was placed here in the margin: then insd in the text, the copula being added*), with (D)L rel latt syrr goth arm : om Bℵ 1. 11. 22. 24. 209 em lat-*k* syr-cu syr-jer copt æth Athen $Orig_5$($Orig_2$ has it, omg *κ. διωκ. υμ.* with goth) Dial Iren-int Cypr Aug Lucif.—om *υμας* D Eus.

bidden by the law, Exod. xxii. 25: Levit. xxv. 37: Deut. xxiii. 19, 20.

43—48.] Sixth example. *The law of love and hatred.* **43.**] The Jews called all Gentiles indiscriminately '*enemies.*' In the Pharisaic interpretation therefore of the maxim (the latter part of which, although a gloss of the Rabbis, is a true representation of the spirit of the law, which was enacted for the Jews as a theocratic people), it would include the 'odium humani generis' with which the Jews were so often charged. But our Lord's '*fulfilment*' of neighbourly love extends it to all mankind—not only foreign nations, but even those who are actively employed in cursing, reviling, and persecuting us; and the hating of enemies is, in His *fulfilment* of it, no longer an individual or national aversion, but a coming out and being separate from all that rebel against God. **45. ὅπως γένησθε**] Probably, as Wordsw., the signification "that ye may *become*" is not to be altogether lost sight of here. But the aor. somewhat modifies it, being literally "that ye may *have become,*" i. e. "may *be.*" See similar instances in ch. xviii. 3; xx. 26. **υἱοὶ τοῦ π.**] i. e. in being *like Him.* Of course there is allusion to our *state of υἱοί by covenant and adoption;* but the *likeness* is the point especially here brought out. So *μιμηταὶ τοῦ θεοῦ*, Eph. v. 1. The more we lift ourselves above the world's view of the duty and expediency of revenge and exclusive dealing, into the mind with which the 'righteous Judge, strong and patient, who is provoked every day,' yet does good to the unthankful and evil,—the more firmly shall we assure, and the more nobly illustrate, our place as sons in His family, as *εἰσελθόντες εἰς τὴν βασιλείαν τῶν οὐρανῶν.* Chrysostom beautifully observes, *καίτοιγε οὐδαμοῦ τὸ γενόμενον ἴσον, οὐ μόνον διὰ τὴν τῆς εὐεργεσίας ὑπερβολήν, ἀλλὰ καὶ διὰ τὴν τῆς ἀξίας ὑπεροχήν. σὺ μὲν γὰρ παρὰ τοῦ ὁμοδούλου καταφρονῇ, ἐκεῖνος δὲ παρὰ τοῦ δούλου καὶ μυρία εὐεργετηθέντος· καὶ σὺ μὲν ῥήματα χαρίζῃ εὐχόμενος ὑπὲρ αὐτοῦ, αὐτὸς δὲ πράγματα πολὺ μεγάλα καὶ θαυμαστά, τὸν ἥλιον ἀνάπτων καὶ τοὺς ἐτησίους ὄμβρους διδούς. ἀλλ' ὅμως καὶ οὕτω δίδωμι ἴσον εἶναι, ὡς ἄνθρωπον ἐγχωρεῖ εἶναι. μὴ τοίνυν μίσει τὸν ποιοῦντα κακῶς, τοιούτων ὄντα σοι πρόξενον ἀγαθῶν, καὶ εἰς τοσαύτην ἄγοντά σε τιμήν· μὴ καταρῶ τῷ ἐπηρεάζοντι· ἐπεὶ τὸν μὲν πόνον ὑπέστης, τοῦ δὲ καρποῦ ἀπεστερήθης· καὶ τὴν μὲν ζημίαν οἴσεις, τὸν δὲ μισθὸν ἀπολεῖς· ὅπερ ἐσχάτης ἐστὶν ἀνοίας, τὸ χαλεπώτερον ὑπομείναντας τὸ ἔλαττον τούτου μὴ φέρειν.* Hom. xviii. 4, p. 239. **ὅτι, because,** 'in that:' gives the particular in which the conformity implied by *υἱοί* consists. **τ. ἥλιον ἀνατ.**] Meyer quotes a sentiment of Seneca remarkably parallel: "Si deos imitaris, da et ingratis beneficia: nam et sceleratis sol oritur, et piratis patent maria."

46.] On *ἀγαπᾷν* and *φιλεῖν*, see Tittmann,

ἐπὶ πονηροὺς καὶ ἀγαθοὺς καὶ [o] βρέχει ἐπὶ δικαίους καὶ
ἀδίκους. 46 ἐὰν γὰρ ἀγαπήσητε τοὺς ἀγαπῶντας ὑμᾶς,
τίνα [p] μισθὸν ἔχετε; οὐχὶ καὶ οἱ [q] τελῶναι οὕτως
ποιοῦσιν; 47 καὶ ἐὰν [r] ἀσπάσησθε τοὺς ἀδελφοὺς ὑμῶν
μόνον, τί [s] περισσὸν ποιεῖτε; οὐχὶ καὶ οἱ [t] ἐθνικοὶ τὸ
αὐτὸ ποιοῦσιν; 48 ἔσεσθε οὖν ὑμεῖς [u] τέλειοι ὡς ὁ [v] πατὴρ

o Luke vii. 38, 44. xvii. 29. James v. 17 bis. Rev. xi 6 only. Gen. ii. 5. Ps. lxxvii. 27.
p — ver. 12. ch. vi. 1, &c. x. 41, 42. 1 Cor. iii. 8, 14. Eccl. iv. 9.
q ch. x. 3 al. Mt. L. only, exc. Mark ii. 15, 16 †. Polyb. xii. 13. 9. (-νεῖσθαι, 1 Macc. xiii. 29.)
r Luke i. 40. x. 4. Exod. xviii. 7.
s Rom. iii. 1. Prov. xiv. 23.
t ch. vi. 7. xviii. 17. 3 John 7 only †. (-ῶς, Gal. ii. 14.)
u ch. xix. 21. Col. i. 28. James iii. 2. Gen. vi. 9. Deut. xviii. 13 al.
v ch. vi. 14, 26, &c. xv. 13. xxiii. 9 only. see ch. xviii. 35.

45. om last clause (*homœotel*) ℵ[1](ins ℵ-corr[1]).

46. εξετε D 13. 124 latt(exc ff_1 g_1) Cypr Lucif Aug. om ουχι ℵ[1](ins ℵ[3a]) (syr-cu [Thph-ant]). rec (for ουτως) το αυτο (*see below ver* 47 *and Luke* vi. 33), with BLℵ rel: τουτο 1 latt: *hæc* lat-g_1 syrr goth arm: txt DZ 33 lat-*h* *k* syr-cu copt æth Cypr Lucif.

47. for αδελφους, φιλους (*probably a gloss*) L rel Scr's-mss lat-*f* *h* syr goth arm Bas Thl Lucif: txt BDZℵ 1 (Scr's u, e sil) latt Syr syr-cu copt æth Cypr. rec (for εθνικοι) τελωναι (*see preceding ver*), with L rel lat-*h* *k* Syr syr-ms goth arm: txt BDZℵ 1. 33 latt syr-cu syr-jer copt æth Constt Chr(appy, see Matthæi) Bas Cypr Lucif. rec (for το αυτο) ουτω, with (but ουτως) EKLSΔ[Π] lat-*h* syr-cu syr copt: txt BDMUZℵ 1. 33 latt(*hoc*) Syr goth æth arm Cypr Lucif. (*It being thus determined that* το αυτο *is the reading here, it seems to follow that ver* 46 *was altered to* το αυτο *to conform it to this, and consequently that* ουτως *must be read there.*)

48. rec ωσπερ (*corrn for elegance*), with D rel: txt BLZℵ Coisl-LXX-marg 1. 13. 33.

Syn. p. 54. He remarks, "Manifesta est ratio cur Dominus jusserit ἀγαπᾶν τοὺς ἐχθρούς, non autem φιλεῖν. Nam φιλεῖν, amare, pessimum quemque vir honestus non potest: sed poterit eum tamen ἀγαπᾶν, i. e. bene ei cupere et facere, quippe homo homini, cui etiam Deus benefaciat. Amor imperari non potest, sed dilectio: dilectio humanitatis est, amor eorum tantum, quibus eadem mens est, idem animus." See further in notes on John xi. 5. **τελῶναι**] This race of men, so frequently mentioned as the objects of hatred and contempt among the Jews, and coupled with sinners, were not properly the *publicans*, who were wealthy Romans, of the rank of knights, farming the revenues of the provinces; but their underlings, heathens or renegade Jews, who usually exacted with recklessness and cruelty. "The Talmud classes them with thieves and assassins, and regards their repentance as impossible." Wordsw. In interpreting these verses we must carefully give the persons spoken of their correlative value and meaning: ye, Christians, sons of God, the true theocracy, the βασιλ. τ. οὐρ.,—these τελῶναι or ἐθνικοί, men of this world, actuated by worldly motives,—'what thank have *ye* in being like *them?*' **47. ἀσπάσησθε**] Here, most probably in its literal sense. Jews did not salute Gentiles: Mohammedans do not salute Christians even now in the East. **48. ἔσεσθε**] Not altogether imperative in meaning, but including the imperative sense: such shall be the state, the aim of Christians. **τέλειοι**] **complete**, in your love of others; not one-sided, or exclusive, as these just mentioned, but all-embracing, and God-like = οἰκτίρμονες, Luke vi. 36. **ὑμεῖς** is emphatic. No countenance is given by this verse to the ancient Pelagian or the modern heresy of perfectibility in this life. Such a sense of the words would be utterly at variance with the whole of the discourse. See especially vv. 22, 29, 32, in which the imperfections and conflicts of the Christian are fully recognized. Nor, if we consider this verse as a solemn conclusion of the second part of the Sermon, does it any the more admit of this view, asserting as it does that likeness to God in inward purity, love, and holiness, must be the continual aim and end of the Christian in all the departments of his moral life. But how far from having attained this likeness we are, St. Paul shews us (Phil. iii. 12); and every Christian feels, just *in the proportion in which he has striven after it*. Augustine argues for the true sense of this and similar passages of Scripture against the Pelagians at length, De peccatorum meritis et remissione, lib. ii. ch. 12 (17—20), and De perfectione justitiæ hominis, ch. 8, 9, vol. x. οἱ μὲν ἀγαπῶντες τοὺς ἀγαπῶντας αὐτοὺς ἀτελεῖς εἰσιν εἰς ἀγάπην, οἱ δὲ τοὺς ἐχθρούς, τέλειοι. Euthym. On the sense see 1 Pet.

w as above (v). Luke ii. 13. Acts xxvi. 19 only †. Esdr. vi. 15. 2 Macc. vii. 34 AB (not ed vat.). ix. 10 only. Dan. iv. 23 Theod.
x ch. x. 17. Luke xxi. 34. Deut. xii. 23. 2 Chron. xxv. 16.

ὑμῶν ὁ [vw] οὐράνιος [u] τέλειός ἐστιν. VI. 1 [x] Προςέχετε BDEKL MSUZΓ ΔΠℵ 1. 33
[δὲ] τὴν [y] δικαιοσύνην ὑμῶν μὴ ποιεῖν ἔμπροσθεν τῶν
ἀνθρώπων πρὸς τὸ [z] θεαθῆναι [a] αὐτοῖς· [b] εἰ δὲ μήγε,
[c] μισθὸν οὐκ ἔχετε παρὰ τῷ [m] πατρὶ ὑμῶν τῷ [m] ἐν τοῖς
οὐρανοῖς. 2 ὅταν οὖν ποιῇς [d] ἐλεημοσύνην, μὴ [e] σαλπίσῃς

y = ch. v. 20. Acts x. 35. Heb. xi. 33. 1 John ii. 29. Tobit xii. 8 [9. xiv. 11 AB (not ℵ).]
z pass., ch. xxiii. 5. Mark xvi. 11 only ‡. (trans. ch. xi. 7.) a constr., ch. xxiii. 5, Luke xxiii. 15. xxiv. 35.
b ch. ix. 17 reff. c ch. v. 12 reff. d here 3ce, Luke xi. 41. xii. 33. Acts iii. 2, 3, 10. ix. 36. x. 2, 4, 31. xxiv. 17 only. Dan. iv. 24 (27). Tobit xii. 8. Sir. xiii. 3. e 1 Cor. xv. 52. Rev. viii. 6, &c. ix. 1, 13. x. 7. xi. 15 only. Judg. vi. 34. 1 Kings xiii. 3.

124. 225 ($Clem_3$ $Orig_3$) Eus [Ath] Chr-1-3(and Field) Damasc. rec (for ουρανιος) *εν τοις ουρανοις* (*see ver* 45), with E² rel lat-*b c* g_1 *h* Syr syr-cu $Clem_1$ Chr-txt Lucif, εν ουρανοις D¹ Chr-8-α: txt B D²(perhaps) E¹LUZℵ Coisl-LXX-marg 1. 13. 33. 124 vulg lat-*a f* ff_1 g_2 *l* syr æth arm $Clem_1$ $Orig_3$ [Bas] Ath Damasc Cypr.

CHAP. VI. 1. rec om δε, with BD rel latt syr-cu goth arm Hil: ins LZℵ 1. 33 lat-g_1 syrr copt æth Op (*probably the omn arose from the connexion with ch* v. *being overlooked, and its being supposed that an entirely new subject commenced here*). rec (for δικαιοσυνην) ελεημοσυνην (*a mistaken gloss, the general nature of this opening caution not being perceived*), with LZ rel lat-f_1 *k* syr-cu syr copt(appy) goth æth arm Chr: δοσειν(sic) ℵ-corr¹: txt BDℵ¹·² 1 latt Orig-int Hil Jer [Aug] $Isid_1$. om τοις Dℵ (ins ℵ³ᵃ) 1. 33 [Chr-2-mss].

2. **ποιησεις** ℵ¹(? there is an erasure after ποιης).

i. 15. Thol. quotes from Plato, Theæt. p. 176, διὸ καὶ πειρᾶσθαι χρὴ ἐνθένδε ἐκεῖσε φεύγειν ὅτι τάχιστα· φυγὴ δὲ ὁμοίωσις θεῷ κατὰ τὸ δυνατόν· ὁμοίωσις δὲ δίκαιον καὶ ὅσιον μετὰ φρονήσεως γενέσθαι.

CHAP. VI. 1—18.] *The* THIRD DIVISION OF THE SERMON, *in which the disciples of Christ are warned against hypocritical display of their good deeds, by the examples of abuses of the duties of almsgiving* (ver. 2), *praying* (ver. 5), *and fasting* (ver. 16). **1.**] The discourse of our Lord now passes *from actions to motives;* not that He has not spoken to the heart before, but then it was only by inference, now directly. **δικαιοσύνη**] not '*benevolence*,' or '*alms*,' as צְדָקָה in Rabbinical usage,—for this meaning is never found in the N. T., and in the apocryphal reff. a distinction is made, though the two are coupled closely together. Besides, here we have ἐλεημοσύνη treated of as a distinct head below. It is best then to render δικ., **righteousness**, as in ch. v. 20, as a general term including the three duties afterwards treated of. The words **πρὸς τὸ θεαθ.** clearly define the course of action objected to:—not the open benevolence of the Christian who lets his light shine that men may glorify God, but the ostentation of him whose *object* is the praise and glory coming from man. ἔστι γὰρ καὶ ἔμπροσθεν τῶν ἀνθρώπων ποιοῦντα, μὴ πρὸς τὸ θεαθῆναι ποιεῖν· καὶ μὴ ποιοῦντα ἔμπροσθεν πάλιν, πρὸς τὸ θεαθῆναι ποιεῖν. Chrysostom, Hom. xix. 1, p. 245. **εἰ δὲ μήγε** does not apply to προσέχετε, so as to mean, '*if ye do not take heed;*' but to μὴ ποιεῖν, and means, **if ye do.** That this is so, is clear from the reff. On the force of the **γε**, modifying the condition expressed in the εἰ, and concentrating it on the example given, see Klotz ad Devar., p. 527, and ante, p. 308.

2—4.] FIRST EXAMPLE. *Almsgiving.* **2. μὴ σαλπίσῃς**] A proverbial expression, not implying any such custom of the hypocrites of that day, but the habit of self-laudation, and display of good works in general. οὐχ ὅτι σάλπιγγας εἶχον ἐκεῖνοι, ἀλλὰ τὴν πολλὴν αὐτῶν ἐπιδεῖξαι βούλεται μανίαν τῇ λέξει τῆς μεταφορᾶς ταύτης, κωμῳδῶν ταύτῃ καὶ ἐκπομπεύων αὐτούς. Chrys. Hom. xix. 1, p. 245. Meyer remarks that the word σαλπίσῃς is *tuba canas*, not *tuba cani cures*, and must therefore refer to what the person *himself* does: but all verbs of action may surely refer to action *per alterum*, so that this does not decide the point. Many Commentators, among whom are Calvin and Bengel, think that the words are to be taken literally; and Euthym. mentions this view: φασὶ δέ τινες ὅτι ὑποκριταὶ τότε διὰ σάλπιγγος συνεκάλουν τοὺς δεομένους. But Lightfoot says, "Non inveni, quæsiverim licet multum serioque, vel minimum tubæ vestigium in præstandis eleemosynis." See his note, containing an account of the practices of the Jews in giving alms;—and many illustrative passages in Tholuck;

ἔμπροσθέν σου, ὥσπερ οἱ [f] ὑποκριταὶ ποιοῦσιν ἐν ταῖς
συναγωγαῖς καὶ ἐν ταῖς [g] ῥύμαις, ὅπως [h] δοξασθῶσιν ὑπὸ
τῶν ἀνθρώπων. [i] ἀμὴν λέγω ὑμῖν [j] ἀπέχουσιν τὸν [c] μισθὸν
αὐτῶν. 3 σοῦ δὲ ποιοῦντος [d] ἐλεημοσύνην μὴ [k] γνώτω
ἡ [l] ἀριστερά σου τί ποιεῖ ἡ δεξιά σου, 4 ὅπως ᾖ σου ἡ
[d] ἐλεημοσύνη ἐν τῷ [m] κρυπτῷ· καὶ ὁ πατήρ σου ὁ βλέπων
ἐν τῷ [m] κρυπτῷ [n] ἀποδώσει σοι. 5 καὶ ὅταν προσεύχησθε,
οὐκ ἔσεσθε ὡς οἱ [f] ὑποκριταί, ὅτι [o] φιλοῦσιν ἐν ταῖς συναγωγαῖς καὶ ἐν ταῖς [p] γωνίαις τῶν [q] πλατειῶν ἑστῶτες

X σου... BDEKL MSUXZ ΓΔΠℵ 1. 33

f ch. xxiii. 14, &c. Mt. Mk. (vii. 6 only) L. only. Job xxxiv. 30. xxxvi. 13 only. (-ισις, Gal. ii. 13. -ίνεσθαι, Luke xx. 20.) in its classical sense, Aristoph. Vesp. 1279. Xen. Mem. ii. 2. 9. g Luke xiv. 21. Acts ix. 11. xii. 10 only. Prov. xxxi. 23 ℵ. Isa. xv. 3. Tobit xiii. 18 AB (not ℵ). Sir. ix. 7 only. h = John viii. 54. Rev. xviii. 7. Lam. i. 8. see Heb. v. 5. i ch. v. 18 reff. j = Luke vi. 24. Phil. iv. 18. Gen. xliii. 23. ἀπέχετε, ἔφη, τὴν ἀπόκρισιν, Æsch. p. 34, 35. k imperat. aor., ch. xxiv. 18. Deut. xxxiii. 6 al. l in N. T. always w. δεξ., Luke xxiii. 33 reff. m Rom. ii. 29. Ps. cxxxviii. 15 Symm. n = 2 Tim. iv. 8. Isa. lxv. 7. see ch. xvi. 27. o = ch. xxiii. 6. Luke xx. 46. Isa. lvi. 10. p ch. xxi. 42 ||, Acts iv. 11, & 1 Pet. ii. 7 (from Ps. cxvii. 22). Acts xxvi. 26. Rev. vii. 1. xx. 8 only. Prov. vii. 12 al. q Luke xiv. 21 reff. Prov. vii. 12

αμην is repeated by ℵ[1](ℵ[3a] disapproving the second). aft υμιν ins οτι Z 6. 122. 299 Scr's q evv-44-7. 50-P lat-*h* coptt.

4. η ελ. σου η D: ἡ σου ελ. η Δ(but om ἡ) ℵ[1] 33: txt B[sic, not as Verc] LZℵ[2] rel **1** lat-*a b c* Cypr. rec (aft κρυπτω) ins αυτος, with D rel lat-*h* syrr: om BKLUZℵ **1**. 13. 33. 124. 209 Scr's a s u v evv-P-z latt syr-cu copt goth æth arm (Constt) Orig Chr Thl Cypr. rec at end ins εν τω φανερω, with L rel lat-*a b c f* g_1 *h* syrr goth æth arm Constt Chr Op (*see below ver* 6): om BDZℵ **1**. 33. 209 vulg lat-ff_1 *k* syr-cu copt Orig(but perhaps refers to ver. 6) Euthym Cypr Jer Aug(in Græcis non invenimus) Chrom. (Π?)

5. rec προσευχῃ and εσῃ (*to suit the singulars bef and aft*), with DLX rel syrr syr-cu: txt BZℵ[3a] **1**. 118 latt(and Δ-lat) syr-mg coptt goth æth arm-mss Orig Chr Ambr Aug (ℵ[1] appears to have written προσευχησθε εσεσθε, and to have altered this to προσευχῃ ουκ εσεσθε). rec ωσπερ (*common alteration to more usual word*), with L rel Orig: txt BDZℵ 33. aft φιλουσιν ins στηναι, and (for προσευχεσθαι)

among which may be mentioned Cic. ad diversos xvi. 21, 'te buccinatorem fore existimationis meæ.' For the classical senses of **ὑποκριτής**, see Lexx. The N.T. sense, connected with that of "actor," is unknown to classic Greek, and first found in the LXX. See reff. **ἔμπρ. σου**] According to the way in which the former verse is taken, these words are variously understood to apply to the trumpet being *held up before the mouth in blowing* (as Meyer), or to *another person going before* (Thol., al.). **συναγωγαῖς** can hardly bear any sense but **synagogues**, see ver. 5: and if so, the literal meaning of σαλπίσῃς cannot well be maintained. The synagogues, as afterwards the Christian churches, were the regular places for the collection of alms: see Tholuck and Vitringa de Synag. vet. iii. 1. 13. **ἀπέχουσιν**] **have in full,—exhaust**: not *have* their *due reward*: see reff. Plutarch in Solon (Wetst.) says, that he who marries for pleasure, and not for children, τὸν μισθὸν ἀπέχει. 3.] **σοῦ**, emphatic: see ch. v. 48. **μὴ γνώτω**] Another popular saying, not to be pressed so as to require a literal interpretation of it in the act of almsgiving, as De Wette and others have done, but implying simplicity, both of intention and act. Equally out of place are all attempts to explain the right and left hand symbolically, as was once the practice. The sound sense of Chrysostom preserves the right interpretation, where even Augustine strays into symbolism: πάλιν ἐνταῦθα οὐ χεῖρας αἰνίττεται, ἀλλ' ὑπερβολικῶς αὐτὸ τέθεικεν. εἰ γάρ οἷόν τέ ἐστι, φησί, σεαυτὸν ἀγνοῆσαι, περισπούδαστον ἔστω σοι τοῦτο, κἂν αὐτὰς δυνατὸν ᾖ τὰς διακονουμένας χεῖρας λαθεῖν. Hom. xix. 2, p. 246. **4. ὁ βλ. ἐν τῷ κρυπτῷ**] Not to be rendered as if it were τὰ (or σε) ἐν τῷ κρ., or εἰς τὸ κρυπτόν, but as the Eng. Vers., **seeth in secret**: as we say, **in the dark**; **ἐν** introducing the *element*, or *sphere, in which*.

5—15.] Second example. *Prayer*.

5. φιλοῦσιν] not so well *solent*, as *amant*: **they take pleasure, or love**: see reff. and Winer, § 54. 4. The meaning *solere* for φιλεῖν is undoubtedly found: see Tholuck here. **ἑστῶτες**] No stress must be laid on this word as implying ostentation; for it was the ordinary posture of prayer. See 1 Sam. i. 26.

r see ch. xxiii. 28.
s ch. xxiv. 26. Luke xii. 3, 24 only. Isa. xxvi. 20.
t here only +.
u ch. v. 47 reff.
v constr., Luke xiii. 2, 4. John v. 45. James iv. 5 al.
w constr., 1 Cor. iv. 4. viii. 11.
x here only. Prov. x. 19 only.

προσεύχεσθαι, ὅπως [r] φανῶσιν τοῖς ἀνθρώποις. [i] ἀμὴν
λέγω ὑμῖν, ἀπέχουσιν τὸν [c] μισθὸν αὐτῶν. 6 σὺ δὲ ὅταν
προσεύχῃ, εἴσελθε εἰς τὸ [s] ταμεῖόν σου καὶ κλείσας τὴν
θύραν σου πρόσευξαι τῷ πατρί σου τῷ ἐν τῷ [m] κρυπτῷ·
καὶ ὁ πατήρ σου ὁ βλέπων ἐν τῷ [m] κρυπτῷ, [n] ἀποδώσει
σοι. 7 προσευχόμενοι δὲ μὴ [t] βατταλογήσητε ὥσπερ οἱ
[u] ἐθνικοί· [v] δοκοῦσιν γὰρ ὅτι [w] ἐν τῇ [x] πολυλογίᾳ αὐτῶν

G τω πατρι... BDEGK LMSUX ZΓΔΠℵ 1. 33

και προσευχομενοι D lat-*a b c h*: txt BZℵ rel vulg lat-*f ff*$_1$ syr goth æth arm Orig. rec aft οπως ins αν, with E rel: om BDKLZΠ^{1}ℵ 1. 13. 33. 124 Scr's p u v w^1 ev-y sah Orig$_2$ Chr. rec aft υμιν ins οτι, with L rel lat-*f* Orig$_1$ [Bas]: om BD X(appy) Zℵ 1. 13. 33. 124 latt æth arm Orig$_1$ [Bas$_1$] Chr lat-ff.

6. προσευχης(but *s* erased) ℵ^1. om τω bef εν D 1. 13. 124. 232 latt arm. rec at end ins εν τω φανερω, with L rel lat-*a b c f h* syrr goth æth arm Euthym: om BDZℵ 1. 209 Scr's u vulg lat-*f ff*$_1$ *g*$_2$ *k* syr-cu syr-jer^1 coptt Orig$_2$ hom-Cl Eus$_2$ Hil Ambr Jer Aug.

7. (βατταλογ. so Bℵ: βλαττολογησηται (i. e. -ε) D^1, βλατταλ- D^4.) for εθνικοι, υποκριται B syr-cu (and, apparently, no other ms).

1 Kings viii. 22 is perhaps hardly a case in point, 2 Chron. vi. 13 being a more specific statement. The command in Mark (xi. 25) runs, ὅταν στήκετε προσευχόμενοι . . . . . See also Luke xviii. 11, 13. Indeed, of the two positions of prayer, considering the place, kneeling would have been the more singular and savouring of ostentation. The *synagogues* were *places of prayer;* so that, as Theophyl. (Thol.), οὐ βλάπτει ὁ τόπος, ἀλλὰ ὁ τρόπος καὶ ὁ σκοπός. **6. εἴσελθε** κ.τ.λ.] Both Chrysostom and Augustine caution us against taking this merely literally. τί οὖν; ἐν ἐκλησίᾳ, φησίν, οὐ δεῖ προσεύχεσθαι; καὶ σφόδρα μέν, ἀλλὰ μετὰ γνώμης τοιαύτης. πανταχοῦ γὰρ ὁ θεὸς τὸν σκοπὸν ζητεῖ τῶν γιγνομένων. ἐπεὶ κἂν εἰς τὸ ταμιεῖον εἰσέλθῃς, καὶ ἀποκλείσας, πρὸς ἐπίδειξιν αὐτὸ ἐργάσῃ, οὐδέν σοι τῶν θυρῶν ὄφελος. ὅρα γοῦν καὶ ἐνταῦθα πῶς ἀκριβῆ τὸν διορισμὸν τέθεικεν εἰπὼν "ὅπως φανῶσι τοῖς ἀνθρώποις." ὥστε κἂν τὰς θύρας ἀποκλείσῃς, τοῦτο πρὸ τῆς τῶν θυρῶν ἀποκλείσεως κατορθῶσαί σε βούλεται, καὶ τὰς τῆς διανοίας ἀποκλείειν θύρας. Hom. xix. 3, p. 247. 'Parum est intrare in cubicula, si ostium pateat importunis, per quod ostium ea quæ foris sunt improbe se immergunt, et interiora nostra appetunt.' De Serm. Dom. l. ii. c. 3 (11), vol. iii. Cf. Ps. iv. 4. **7. βατταλογήσητε**] a word probably without any further derivation than an imitation of the sounds uttered by stammerers, who repeat their words often without meaning (κατὰ μίμησιν τῆς φωνῆς, Hesych.). Suidas, Eustath., and others, supposed it derived from a certain stammering Battus, Herod. iv. 155. But the name of this Battus seems to have been given *from the circumstance;* παῖς ἰσχνόφωνος καὶ τραυλός, τῷ οὔνομα ἐτέθη Βάττος. We have βατταρίζω and its derivatives with the same signification; and Æschines called Demosthenes βάταλος (περὶ στ. p. 288. 17 Bekker). Hence the sense has generally been held to be, '*do not make unmeaning repetitions.*' But most of the Fathers (see the passages in Thol., and in Suicer sub voce) understand by βαττ., the praying περὶ τὰ ἀνωφελῆ τε καὶ μάταια (so Greg. Nyss.), or λέγειν τὰ διεφθαρμένα ἔργα, ἢ λόγους, ἢ νοήματα ταπεινὰ τυγχάνοντα (Orig.), or ὅταν τὰ μὴ προσήκοντα αἰτῶμεν παρὰ τῷ θεῷ δυναστείας κ. δόξας: &c. Taking the word in its largest meaning, that of *saying things irrelevant and senseless,* it may well include all these. **ἐθνικοί**] 'Prece qua fatigent virgines sanctæ minus audientem carmina Vestam?' Hor. Od. i. 2. 26. 'Nisi illos (Deos) tuo ex ingenio judicas, Ut nil credas intelligere nisi idem dictum est centies.' Ter. Heaut. v. 1. What is forbidden in this verse is not *much* praying, for our Lord Himself passed whole nights in prayer: not praying *in the same words,* for this He did in the very intensity of His agony at Gethsemane; but the making number and length a *point of observance,* and imagining that prayer will be heard, not because it is the genuine expression of the desire of faith, but because it is of such a length, has been such a number of times repeated. The repetitions of Paternosters and Ave Marias in the Romish Church, as *practised* by them, are *in direct violation* of this precept; the *number* of repetitions being *pre-*

[y] εἰςακουσθήσονται. 8 μὴ οὖν [z] ὁμοιωθῆτε αὐτοῖς· οἶδεν
γὰρ ὁ πατὴρ ὑμῶν ὧν [a] χρείαν [a] ἔχετε [b] πρὸ τοῦ ὑμᾶς
[c] αἰτῆσαι αὐτόν. 9 οὕτως οὖν προςεύχεσθε ὑμεῖς· [d] Πάτερ

y Luke i. 13. Acts x. 31. 1 Cor. xiv. 21. Heb. v. 7 only. Ps. iv. 1.
z ch. vii. 24, 26. xiii. 24 al. Isa. xl. 18, 25.
a ch. ix. 12 ‖. xxi. 3. 1 Cor. xii. 21 bis al. 2 Macc. ii. 15.
b constr., Luke ii. 21. xxii. 15. John i. 49. Gal. ii. 12 al. Gen. xlii. 10.
c absol. and constr., ch. v. 42 reff.
d ch. v. 16 reff.

8. aft *γαρ* ins *ο θεος* B ℵ(but erased) sah. for *αιτησαι αυτον*, *ανοιξε το στομα* D lat-*h*. (D-lat def vv 8—20.)

scribed, and the *efficacy of the performance made to depend on it*. But the repetition of the Lord's Prayer in the Liturgy of the Church of England is not a violation of it, nor that of the Kyrie Eleison, because it is not the number of these which is the object, but each has its *appropriate place* and *reason* in that which is pre-eminently a reasonable service. Our Lord was also denouncing a *Jewish* error. Lightfoot quotes from the Rabbinical writings, 'Omnis qui multiplicat orationem, auditur.' Hor. Hebr. in loc. Augustine puts admirably the distinction between much *praying* and much *speaking*: 'Absit ab oratione multa locutio; sed non desit multa precatio, si fervens perseverat intentio. Nam multum loqui, est in orando rem necessariam superfluis agere verbis; multum autem precari, est ad eum quem precamur diuturna et pia cordis excitatione pulsare. Nam plerumque hoc negotium plus gemitibus quam sermonibus agitur; plus fletu, quam affatu.' Ep. cxxx. 10 (20), vol. ii. And Chrysostom, in one of his finest strains of eloquence, comments on this verse: *μὴ τοίνυν τῷ σχήματι τοῦ σώματος, μηδὲ τῇ κραυγῇ τῆς φωνῆς, ἀλλὰ τῇ προθυμίᾳ τῆς γνώμης τὰς εὐχὰς ποιώμεθα· μηδὲ μετὰ ψόφου καὶ ἠχῆς καὶ πρὸς ἐπίδειξιν, ὡς καὶ τοὺς πλησίον ἐκκρούειν, ἀλλὰ μετὰ ἐπιεικείας πάσης καὶ τῆς κατὰ διάνοιαν συντριβῆς καὶ δακρύων τῶν ἔνδοθεν.* Hom. xix. 3, p. 248. Those who have the opportunity should by all means read the whole passage, which is too long for insertion in a note.

8. οἶδεν γάρ] *εἰ οἶδε, φησίν, ὧν χρείαν ἔχομεν, τίνος ἕνεκεν εὔχεσθαι δεῖ; οὐχ ἵνα διδάξῃς, ἀλλ' ἵνα ἐπικάμψῃς· ἵνα οἰκειωθῇς τῇ συνεχείᾳ τῆς ἐντεύξεως, ἵνα ταπεινωθῇς, ἵνα ἀναμνησθῇς τῶν ἁμαρτημάτων τῶν σῶν.* Chrys. Hom. xix. 4, p. 249. 'Ipsa orationis intentio cor nostrum serenat et purgat, capaciusque efficit ad accipienda divina munera, quæ spiritualiter nobis infunduntur.' August. de Serm. Dom. ii. 3 (14).

9—13.] THE LORD'S PRAYER. **9.**] There is very slender proof of what is often asserted, that our Lord took nearly the whole of this prayer from existing Jewish formulæ. Not that such a view of the matter would contain in it any thing irreverent or objectionable; for if pious Jews had framed such petitions, our Lord, who came *πληρῶσαι* every thing that was good under the Old Covenant, might in a higher sense and spiritual meaning, have recommended the same forms to His disciples. But such does not appear to have been the fact. Lightfoot produces only the most general common-place parallels for the petitions, from the Rabbinical books.

With regard to the prayer itself we may remark, 1. The whole passage, vv. 7—15, is digressive from the subject of the first part of this chapter, which is the discouragement of the performance of religious duties to be seen of men, and is resumed at ver. 16. Neander (Leben Jesu, p. 349, note) therefore supposes that this passage has found its way in here as a sort of accompaniment to the preceding verses, but is in reality the answer of our Lord to the request in Luke xi. 1, more fully detailed than by that Evangelist. But to this I cannot assent, believing our Lord's discourses as given by this Evangelist to be no collections of scattered sayings, but veritable reports of continuous utterances. That the request related in Luke should afterwards have been made, and similarly answered, is by no means improbable. (That he should have thus related it *with this Gospel before him*, is more than improbable.) 2. It has been questioned whether the prayer was regarded in the very earliest times as a set form delivered for liturgical use by our Lord. The variations in Luke have been regarded as fatal to the supposition of its being used liturgically at the time when these Gospels were written. But see notes on Luke xi. 1. It must be confessed, that we find very few traces of such use in early times. Thol. remarks, "It does not occur in the Acts, nor in any writers before the third century. In Justin Mart. we find, that the *προεστώς* prays 'according to his power' (Apol. i. 67, p. 83, *ὁ πρ. εὐχὰς ὁμοίως κ. εὐχαριστίας ὅση δύναμις αὐτῷ ἀναπέμπει*) . . . . . Cyprian and Tert. make the first mention of the

e = 1 Pet. iii. 15. Exod. xx. 8. Isa. xxix. 23. Sir. xxxiii. 4. f ch. xxvi. 42 || L. Acts xxi. 14 only. g Acts vii. 51. ὡς ἔδοξεν αὐτοῖς, καὶ ἐποίουν, Thucyd. viii. 1.

ἡμῶν ὁ [d] ἐν τοῖς οὐρανοῖς, [e] ἁγιασθήτω τὸ ὄνομά σου, BDEGK LMSUX
10 ἐλθέτω ἡ βασιλεία σου, [f] γενηθήτω τὸ [f] θέλημά σου [g] ὡς ΖΓΔΠℵ 1. 33

10. ελθατω DE²GΔℵ: txt BZ rel. om ως D¹(ins D-corr¹) lat-*a b c* Tert Aug₁.

prayer as an 'oratio legitima et ordinaria.'" An allusion to it has been supposed to exist in 2 Tim. iv. 18, where see note. 3. The view of some that our Lord gave this, selecting it out of forms known and in use, as a prayer *ad interim, till the effusion of the Spirit of prayer,* is inadmissible, as we have no traces of any such temporary purpose in our Saviour's discourses, and to suppose any such would amount to nothing less than to set them entirely aside. On the contrary, one work of the Holy Spirit on the disciples was, to *bring to their mind all things whatsoever He had said unto them,* the depth of such sayings only then first being revealed to them by Him who *took of the things of Christ and shewed them to them.* John xiv. 26. **οὕτως**] παραδίδωσι τύπον εὐχῆς, οὐχ ἵνα ταύτην μόνην τὴν εὐχὴν εὐχώμεθα, ἀλλ' ἵνα ταύτην ἔχοντες πηγὴν εὐχῆς ἐκ ταύτης ἀρυώμεθα τὰς ἐννοίας τῶν εὐχῶν. Euthym. Considering that other manners of praying have been spoken of above, the βατταλογία and the πολυλογία, the οὕτως, especially in its present position of primary emphasis, cannot well be otherwise understood than **thus**, i. e. '*in these words,*' as a *specimen* of the *Christian's* prayer (the **ὑμεῖς** holds the second place in emphasis), no less than its *pattern.* This, which would be the inference from the context here, is decided for us by Luke xi. 2, ὅταν προσεύχησθε, λέγετε. **Πάτερ ἡμῶν**] This was a form of address almost unknown to the Old Covenant: now and then hinted at, as reminding the children of their rebellion (Isa. i. 2: Mal. i. 6), or mentioned as a last resource of the orphan and desolate creature (Isa. lxiii. 16); but never brought out in its fulness, as indeed it could not be, till He was come by whom we have received the adoption of sons. 'Oratio fraterna est: non dicit, Pater meus, tanquam pro se tantum orans, sed Pater noster, omnes videlicet una oratione complectens, qui se in Christo fratres esse cognoscunt.' Aug. Serm. lxiv. 4 App. vol. v. pt. ii. ἀπὸ δὲ τούτου καὶ ἔχθραν ἀναιρεῖ, καὶ ἀπόνοιαν καταστέλλει, καὶ βασκανίαν ἐκβάλλει, καὶ τὴν μητέρα τῶν ἀγαθῶν ἁπάντων ἀγάπην εἰσάγει, καὶ τὴν ἀνωμαλίαν τῶν ἀνθρωπίνων ἐξορίζει πραγμάτων, καὶ πολλὴν δείκνυσι τῷ βασιλεῖ πρὸς τὸν πτωχὸν τὴν ὁμοτιμίαν, εἴ γε ἐν τοῖς μεγίστοις καὶ ἀναγκαιοτάτοις κοινωνοῦμεν ἅπαντες. Chrysost. Hom. xix. 4, p. 250. **ὁ ἐν τοῖς οὐρανοῖς**] These opening words of the Lord's Prayer set clearly before us the status of the Christian, as believing in, depending upon, praying to, a real *objective personal* God, lifted above himself; to approach whom he must lift up his heart, as the eye is lifted up from earth to heaven. This strikes at the root of all *pantheistic* error, which regards the spirit of man as identical with the Spirit of God, —and at the root of all *Deism*; testifying as it does our relation to and covenant dependence on our Heavenly Father. The *local heavens* are no further to be thought of here, than as Scripture, by a parallelism of things natural and spiritual deeply implanted in our race (compare Aristotle, περὶ οὐρ. i. 3, πάντες γὰρ ἄνθρωποι περὶ θεῶν ἔχουσιν ὑπόληψιν, καὶ πάντες τὸν ἀνωτάτω τῷ θείῳ τόπον ἀποδιδόασι καὶ βάρβαροι καὶ Ἕλληνες ὅσοιπερ εἶναι νομίζουσι θεούς, δηλονότι ὡς τῷ ἀθανάτῳ τὸ ἀθάνατον συνηρτημένον), universally speaks of *heaven* and *heavenly*, as applying to the habitation and perfections of the High and Holy One who inhabiteth Eternity. **ἁγιασθήτω τὸ ὄνομά σου**] De Wette observes: 'God's Name is not merely His appellation, which we speak with the mouth, but also and principally the idea which we attach to it,—His Being, as far as it is confessed, revealed, or known.' The 'Name of God' in Scripture is used to signify that revelation of Himself which He has made to men, which is all that we know of Him (ὄνομα τοίνυν ἐστὶ κεφαλαιώδης προσηγορία τῆς ἰδίας ποιότητος τοῦ ὀνομαζομένου παραστατική. Orig. (Thol.)): into the depths of His Being, as it is, no human soul can penetrate. See John xvii. 6: Rom. ix. 17. **ἁγιάζω** here is in the sense of **keep holy, sanctify in our hearts**, as in ref. 1 Pet. τὰ σεραφὶμ δοξάζοντα οὕτως ἔλεγον Ἅγιος ἅγιος ἅγιος, ὥστε τὸ ἁγιασθήτω τοῦτό ἐστι δοξασθήτω. Chrys. Hom. xix. 4, p. 250. **10. ἐλθέτω ἡ βασιλεία σου**] 'Ut in nobis veniat, optamus; ut in illo inveniamur, optamus.' Aug. Serm. lvi. c. 4 (5), vol. v. pt. i. **Thy kingdom** here is the fulness of the accomplishment of the kingdom of God, so often spoken of in prophetic Scripture; and by implication, all that process of events which lead to that accomplishment.

ἐν οὐρανῷ [g] καὶ ἐπὶ γῆς· 11 τὸν ἄρτον ἡμῶν τὸν [h] ἐπιού-

h Luke xi. 3 only †, and no where else. (see note.)

rec ins της bef γης, with D rel Scr's mss Orig$_1$ Eus Constt$_2$ [Max-conf] : om BZΔℵ 1 Clem Orig$_4$ Chr-3-8.

Meyer, in objecting to all ecclesiastical and spiritual meanings of 'Thy kingdom,' forgets that the one for which he contends exclusively, *the Messianic kingdom*, does in fact include or imply them all. **γενηθήτω τὸ θ. σου**] i. e. not, 'may our will be absorbed into thy will;' but may it be conformed to and subordinated to thine. The literal rendering is, **Let thy will be done, as in heaven, (so) also on earth.** These last words, **ὡς ἐν οὐρανῷ καὶ ἐπὶ γῆς**, *may* be regarded as applying to the whole of the three preceding petitions, as punctuated in the text. A slight objection may perhaps be found in the circumstance, that the kingdom of God cannot be said to have *come* in heaven, seeing that it has always been fully established there, and thus the accuracy of correspondence in the particulars will be marred. It is true, this may be escaped by understanding, May thy kingdom *come* on earth, so as to be as fully established, as it is already in heaven. So that I conceive we are at liberty to take the prayer either way. 11. **τὸν ἄρτ.** κ.τ.λ.] **ἡμῶν**—as '*created for us*,' 'provided for our use by Thee:' τὸν δι' ἡμᾶς γενόμενον, Euthym. The word **ἐπιούσιον** has been very variously explained. Origen says of it, πρῶτον δὲ τοῦτ' ἰστέον, ὅτι ἡ λέξις ἡ ἐπιούσιος παρ' οὐδενὶ τῶν Ἑλλήνων οὔτε τῶν σοφῶν ὠνόμασται, οὔτε ἐν τῇ τῶν ἰδιωτῶν συνηθείᾳ τέτριπται, ἀλλ' ἔοικε πεπλάσθαι ὑπὸ τῶν εὐαγγελιστῶν. The derivations and meanings given may be thus classified (after Tholuck). I. **ἐπί, εἶναι** : and that, either (1) from the *participle*, as παρουσία, μετουσία, περιουσία, or (2) from the *subst.* **οὐσία**. Against *both*, an objection is brought that thus it would be ἐπούσ., not ἐπιούσ.; but this is not decisive; we have ἔποπτος and ἐπίοπτος, ἐπιανδάνω, ἐπίουρα, &c. Against (2) it is alleged that adjectives from substantives in -α and -ια end in -αιος or -ώδης,—ὡραῖος, ἀγοραῖος, βίαιος, and from οὐσία not οὔσιος but οὐσιώδης : συνούσιος, περιούσιος, not being from οὐσία but from the fem. particip. But this is not always so: we have πολυγώνιος from γωνία, ὑπεξούσιος from ἐξουσία, and ἐνούσιος and ἐξούσιος from οὐσία:—while περιούσιος itself is derived by some from οὐσία. II. **ἐπί, ἰέναι** : and that, either (1) from the fem. part. ἡ ἐπιοῦσα, understanding ἡμέρα, or (2) from ὁ ἐπιών, understanding χρόνος. (1) has much apparently in its favour. In the N. T., LXX, and Josephus, ἡ παροῦσα, ἡ προσιοῦσα, and this expression itself are often found in this elliptic sense. Jerome found for this word, in the Gospel according to the Hebrews, "mahar (מָחָר) quod dicitur crastinus." (So also *crastinum* copt.) The objection brought against it (Salmas. Suicer), that, viz., from the analogy of δευτεραῖος, τριταῖος, ποσταῖος, &c. does not seem valid to disprove the existence of the more general possessive adj. in -ιος. But the great objection to this derivation is in the *sense*: which would then be in direct opposition to ver. 34. Nor does it answer this to say, that by making to-morrow's bread the subject of prayer we divest ourselves of anxiety respecting it; since our Lord's command is not to feel that anxiety at all. The same objection will apply to (2) ὁ ἐπιὼν χρόνος, or to giving (as Grot. al.) a wider sense to ἡ ἐπιοῦσα, as meaning *all future time*, according to the Hebr. usage of מָחָר. (Cf. *venturum* or *venientem* sah.) Nor will σήμερον bear the Hebraistic interpretation of 'from day to day,' יוֹם יוֹם. Add to this that independently of the discrepancy with ver. 34, Salmasius's objection to this sense, 'quid est ineptius, quam panem crastini diei (and we may say à fortiori 'omnis futuri temporis') nobis quotidie postulare?' seems to me unanswerable. Returning then to the derivation from εἶναι, which has in its favour the authority of the Greek fathers, especially of Origen, and of the Peschito (*indigentiæ nostræ*), Tholuck thinks it most probable that it is formed after the analogy of περιούσιος, from the substantive οὐσία. The substantive signifies not merely *existence* (as alleged in the 1st edn. of this work), but also *subsistence*, compare Luke xv. 12, where τὸ ἐπιβάλλον μέρος τῆς οὐσίας is a curious illustration of this word. And even were οὐσία *existence* only, it would still be open for us to take the meaning of the Greek fathers, ὁ ἐπὶ τῇ οὐσίᾳ ἡμῶν κ. συστάσει τῆς ζωῆς συμβαλλόμενος,—Theophylact: similarly Chr., Basil, Greg. Nyss., and Suidas, and the Etym. Mag. Thus ἐπιούσιος will be **required for our subsistence —proper for our sustenance**, after the analogy of ἐπίγαμος, 'fit for marriage,'

σιον δὸς ἡμῖν σήμερον, 12 καὶ ik ἄφες ἡμῖν τὰ kl ὀφειλή-
ματα ἡμῶν m ὡς m καὶ ἡμεῖς i ἀφήκαμεν τοῖς n ὀφειλέταις
ἡμῶν, 13 καὶ μὴ o εἰςενέγκῃς ἡμᾶς εἰς p πειρασμόν, ἀλλὰ

i = ch. xii. 31, 32. xviii. 27, &c. Isa. xxii. 14. k 1 Macc. xv. 8. l Rom. iv. 4 only. Deut. xxiv. 10 ‡. m cf. ch. xviii. 33. xx. 14. Rev. xviii. 6. n ch. xviii. 24. Luke xiii. 4. Rom. i. 14. viii. 12. xv. 27. Gal. v. 3 only †. o = Luke xi. 4 only. (Luke v. 18, 19 reff. Deut. xxviii. 38.) p Luke iv. 13. James i. 2, 12 al. Deut. iv. 34.

...σημερον X.

V και μη...

BDEGK LMSUV ZΓΔΠℵ 1. 33

12. rec αφιεμεν (*the present seems to be from Luke* xi. 4), with Gℵ^{3a} rel Scr's mss vulg(with am) lat-*b c f ff$_1$ g$_{1.2}$ h* syr-cu syr goth æth arm (Orig$_1$) Constt Cypr : αφιομεν DELΔ[Π^2] : txt BZℵ^1 1 harl^1(with forj fuld) Syr Orig$_2$ Nyss Ps-Ath. (33 lat-*a* def.)

ἐπιδόρπιος, 'proper for the banquet,' &c. So that ὁ ἄρτος ὁ ἐπιούσιος will be equivalent to St. James's τὰ ἐπιτήδεια τοῦ σώματος (ii. 16), and the expressions are rendered in Syr. by the same word. Thus only, σήμερον has its proper meaning. The τὸ καθ' ἡμέραν in Luke xi. 3 is different; see there. It yet remains to enquire how far the expression may be understood *spiritually*—of the Bread of Life. The answer is easy: viz. that we may safely thus understand it, provided we keep in the foreground its primary physical meaning, and view the other as involved by implication in that. To explain ἐπιούσιος (as Orig. Cyr.-jer.), ὁ ἐπὶ τὴν οὐσίαν τῆς ψυχῆς κατατασσόμενος, and understand the expression of the Eucharist *primarily*, or even of spiritual feeding on Christ, is to miss the plain reference of the petition to our daily physical wants. But not to recognize those spiritual senses, is equally to miss the great truth, that the ἡμεῖς whose bread is prayed for, are not *mere* animals, but composed of body, soul, and spirit, all of which want daily nourishment by Him from whom all blessings flow. See the whole subject treated in Tholuck (pp. 353—371): from whom much of this note is taken. Augustine well says (Serm. lviii. 4 (5), vol. v. pt. 1): 'Quicquid animæ nostræ et carni nostræ in hac vita necessarium est, quotidiano pane concluditur.' The Vulg. rendering, *supersubstantialem* (substituted for the old lat. *quotidianum*), tallies with a large class of patristic interpretations which understand the word to point exclusively to the spiritual food of the Word and Sacraments. **12. τὰ ὀφειλ.**] i. e. **sins**, short-comings, and therefore 'debts' = παραπτώματα, ver. 14. Augustine remarks (contra Epist. Parmeniani, l. ii. c. 10 (20), vol. ix.): 'Quod utique non de illis peccatis dicitur quæ in baptismi regeneratione dimissa sunt, sed de iis quæ quotidie de seculi amarissimis fructibus humanæ vitæ infirmitas contrahit.' **ὡς καί**] Not '*for* we also,' &c. (as in Luke, καὶ γὰρ αὐτοὶ ἀφ.) nor '*in the same measure as we* also,' &c. but **like as** (*quippe;* not exactly *nam*, cf. Klotz ad Devar. p. 766. Hartung, Partikellehre, i. p. 460) **we also**, &c.; implying similarity in the two actions, of kind, but no comparison of degree. See especially the first ref., where manifestly while the kind of act was the same, the degrees were widely different. 'Augustine uses the testimony of this prayer against all proud Pelagian notions of an absolutely sinless state in this life' (Trench); and answers the various excuses and evasions by which that sect escaped from the conclusion. **ἀφήκαμεν** here implies that (see ch. v. 23, 24) the act of forgiveness of others is *completed before we approach* the throne of grace. **13.**] The sentiment is not in any way inconsistent with the Christian's joy when he πειρασμοῖς περιπέσῃ ποικίλοις, James i. 2, but is a humble self-distrust and shrinking from such trial in the prospect. As Euthym. says: παιδεύει ἡμᾶς ὁ λόγος μὴ θαῤῥεῖν ἑαυτοῖς, μηδ' ἐπιπηδᾷν τοῖς πειρασμοῖς ὑπὸ θαῤῥότητος . . . . . μὴ ἐπαγομένων μὲν τῶν πειρασμῶν παραιτητέον αὐτούς· ἐπαγομένων δὲ ἀνδριστέον. The **leading into temptation** must be understood in its plain literal sense: see ποιήσει σὺν τῷ πειρασμῷ καὶ τὴν ἔκβασιν, 1 Cor. x. 13. There is no discrepancy with James i. 13, which speaks not of the providential bringing about of, but the actual solicitation of, the temptation. Some (e. g. Isid. Pelus. on ch. xxvi. 41, Thl. on Luke xxii. 46, Aug., Bengel, al.) have attempted to fix on εἰςενέγκῃς and εἰςελθεῖν εἰς πειρ. the meaning of *bringing into the power of*, and *entering into, so as to be overcome by*, temptation. But this surely the words will not bear. **ἀλλά** must not be taken as equivalent to εἰ δὲ μή, q. d. '*but if thou dost, deliver,*' &c., but is rather the opposition to the former clause, and forms in this sense, but one petition with it,—'*bring us not into conflict with evil, nay rather deliver* (rid) *us from it altogether.*' In another view, however, as expressing the deep desire of all Christian hearts to be delivered from *all evil* (for τοῦ πονηροῦ is here certainly neuter, though taken masculine by Chrys.,

...αφητε τοις Z.

q ῥῦσαι ἡμᾶς ἀπὸ τοῦ r πονηροῦ. 14 Ἐὰν γὰρ i ἀφῆτε
τοῖς ἀνθρώποις τὰ s παραπτώματα αὐτῶν, i ἀφήσει καὶ
ὑμῖν ὁ t πατὴρ ὑμῶν ὁ t οὐράνιος· 15 ἐὰν δὲ μὴ i ἀφῆτε

q w. ἀπό, (Luke xi. 4 v. r.) Rom. xv. 31. 1 Thess. i. 10. 2 Thess. iii. 2. 2 Tim. iv. 18 only. Ps. cxxxix. 1. (w. ἐκ, Luke i. 74.) r ch. v. 37. neut., Rom. xii. 9. 2 Thess. iii. 3 (?). 2 Tim. iv. 18. Isa. v. 20. (In John masc. cf. 1 John ii. 13. John xvii. 15.) s ch. xviii. 35. Mark xi. 25, 26. Rom. iv. 25. v. 15, &c. 2 Cor. v. 19 al. Ps. xviii. 12. Ezek. iii. 20. xviii. 26. t ch. v. 48 reff.

13. rec aft *πονηρου* ins *οτι σου εστιν η βασιλεια και η δυναμις, και η δοξα εις τους αιωνας αμην* (*interpolation from the liturgies, in interruption of the context: see notes*), with L rel (most cursives) lat-*f* g_1 syrr syr-cu(omg *κ. η δυν.*) syr-jer goth æth arm $Constt_1$ Isid Chr Thl Euthym (*see below*): *quoniam est tibi virtus in sæcula sæculorum* lat-*k*: *quod tuum est robur et potentia in ævum ævi* sah: *οτι σου εστιν η βασ. κ. η δυν. κ. η δοξ. του πατρος κ. τ. υιου κ. τ. αγ. πν.* $Constt_1$: *quoniam tuum est regnum et virtus et gloria* Op:——om BDZℵ 1. 17. 118-30. 209 latt copt; the greek fathers, even when they expound the prayer in detail, e. g. $Orig_{certe}$ Cyr-jer Max-conf Nyss(who ends his *expos.* thus: *χαριτι χριστου, οτι αυτου η δυν. κ. η δοξ. αμα τω πατρι κ. τω αγιω πν. νυν και ε. τ. αι. των αι. αμην*) Euthym(who accuses the Massaliani for despising *το παρα των θειων φωστηρων κ. της εκκλησιας καθηγητων προστεθεν ακροτελευτιον επιφωνημα*); the latin fathers, e. g. Tert Cypr Ambr Sedul Fulg Jer &c schol (addg *τοδε οτι . . εν τισιν ου κειται μεχρι του αμην*) schol on Luke(observes that in Luke the prayer ends with *πειρασμον*, but that Matt adds *αλλα . . πονηρου*); also complut, Erasm, Camerar, Grot, Mill, Bengel, Wetst, Griesb, Scholz, Lachm, Tischdf, Treg; (see more in Wetst.)—Some have the *αμην*, omg the doxology.

14. om *γαρ* D[1](ins D[2]) L Scr's p evv-z-p (*at beg of lection*). *υμιν* bef *και* D lat-*b c* [*f* g_1 *h k q*].

Thl., Erasm., Beza, al.; the introduction of the mention of 'the evil one' would seem here to be incongruous. Besides, compare the words of St. Paul, 2 Tim. iv. 18, which look very like a reminiscence of this prayer: see note there) these words form a seventh and most affecting petition, reaching far beyond the last. They are the expression of the yearning for redemption of the sons of God (Rom. viii. 23), and so are fitly placed at the end of the prayer, and as the sum and substance of the personal petitions. So Augustine very beautifully says (Ep. cxxx. c. 11 (21), vol. ii.): "Cum dicimus *libera nos a malo*, nos admonemus cogitare, nondum nos esse in eo bono, ubi nullum patiemur malum. Et hoc quidem ultimum quod in dominica oratione positum est, tam late patet, ut homo Christianus in qualibet tribulatione constitutus in hoc gemitus edat, in hoc lacrymas fundat, hinc exordiatur, in hoc immoretur, ad hoc terminet orationem."

The *doxology* must on every ground of sound criticism be omitted. Had it formed part of the original text, it is absolutely inconceivable that all the ancient authorities should with one consent have omitted it. They could have had no reason for doing so; whereas the habit of terminating liturgical prayers with ascriptions of praise would naturally suggest some such ending, and make its insertion almost certain in course of time. And just correspondent to this is the evidence in the var. readd. We find *absolutely no trace of it in early times*, in any family of MSS. or in any expositors. The Peschito *has* it, but whether it *always had*, is another question. Stier eloquently defends its insertion, but *solely on subjective grounds:* maintaining that the prayer is incomplete without it, and asserting the right of such "innere Kritik" to over-ride all evidence whatever. It is evident that thus we should have no fixed principles at all by which to determine the sacred text: for what seems to one critic appropriate and necessary, is in the view of another an incongruous addition. It is quite open for us to regard it with Euthymius as *τὸ παρὰ τῶν θείων φωστήρων κ. τ. ἐκκλησίας καθηγητῶν προστεθὲν ἀκροτελεύτιον ἐπιφώνημα*, and to retain it as such in our liturgies; but in dealing with the sacred text we must not allow any à priori considerations, of which we are such poor judges, to outweigh the almost unanimous testimony of antiquity. The inference to be drawn from the words of St. Paul, 2 Tim. iv. 18, is rather against than for the genuineness of the doxology. The fact that he there adds a doxology, different from that commonly read here, seems to testify to the practice, begun thus early, of concluding the Lord's prayer with a solemn ascription of glory to God. This eventually fell into one conventional form, and thus got inserted in the sacred text.

14, 15.] Our Lord returns (*γάρ*) to explain the only part of the prayer which *peculiarly* belonged to the

τοῖς ἀνθρώποις τὰ [s] παραπτώματα αὐτῶν, οὐδὲ ὁ πατὴρ
ὑμῶν [i] ἀφήσει τὰ [s] παραπτώματα ὑμῶν. 16 ὅταν δὲ [u] νησ-
τεύητε, μὴ γίνεσθε ὡς οἱ [v] ὑποκριταὶ [w] σκυθρωποί· [x] ἀφανίζουσιν γὰρ τὰ πρόσωπα αὐτῶν, ὅπως [y] φανῶσιν τοῖς
ἀνθρώποις [u] νηστεύοντες. [z] ἀμὴν λέγω ὑμῖν, [z] ἀπέχουσιν
τὸν [z] μισθὸν αὐτῶν. 17 σὺ δὲ [u] νηστεύων [a] ἄλειψαί σου
τὴν κεφαλὴν καὶ τὸ [b] πρόσωπόν σου [bc] νίψαι, 18 ὅπως μὴ
[y] φανῇς τοῖς ἀνθρώποις [u] νηστεύων, ἀλλὰ τῷ πατρί σου
τῷ ἐν τῷ [d] κρυφαίῳ· καὶ ὁ πατήρ σου ὁ βλέπων ἐν τῷ

Γ νησ-τευητε... BDEGK LMSUV ΓΔΠℵ 1. 33

u ch. iv. 2 reff. v vv. 2, 5 reff. w Luke xxiv. 17 only. Gen. xl. 7. Sir. xxv. 23 only. Dan. i. 10 Theod. x vv. 19, 20. Acts xiii. 41 (from Hab. i. 5). James iv. 14 only. Ezek. iv. 17. xii. 19. y ver. 5. ch. xxiii. 28. z ver. 2 (reff.). a Mark vi. 13. xvi. 1. Luke vii. 38, 46 bis. John xi. 2. xii. 3. James v. 14 only. 2 Kings xii. 20. b here only. Gen. xliii. 31. c ch. xv. 2 || Mk. 1 Tim. v. 10. elsw. John (ix. 7 reff.) only. d here (bis) only. Jer. xxiii. 24. (-φή, Eph. v. 12.)

15. om τα παραπτωματα αυτων (*as unnecessary, and to conform to preceding ver: see below*) Dℵ 1. 118. 209 lat-*a h k* Syr Max-conf Aug Leo: ins bef εαν μη αφητε τ. ανθρ. vulg lat-*c* ff_2 g_1 *l*: ins in both places L 13. 235 lat-g_2 syr-jer copt æth arm. for 1st υμων, υμιν ℵ 301. aft αφησει ins υμιν D latt syrr coptt arm.

16. at beg ins και ℵ[1](ℵ-corr[1 or 2] disapproving). rec ωσπερ, with L rel: txt BDΔℵ 1. om οι ℵ[1](ins ℵ[3a]). το προσωπον ℵ[1] lat-*k* Syr Aug. εαυτων B Scr's s. aft αμην ins γαρ ℵ[1](ℵ[3] disapproving) 235. rec ins οτι bef απεχουσιν, with L rel vulg lat-*c* ff_1 g_1: om BDℵ 1 lat-*a b f h* æth arm lat-ff spec.

17. αλειψον D 293. 433 ev-44.

18. for οπως, ινα D. νηστευων bef τοις ανθρωποις (*transposition for uniformity, overlooking the emphasis*) B lat *k*. rec εν τω κρυπτω (*both times: from vv* 4, 6), with L rel: txt B(D)ℵ 1.—om τω (twice) D[1](ins D[3]).—κρυφια (1st time) D[1](corrd by D-corr[1]). om 2nd σου Δℵ[1](ins ℵ[2a]).

new law of love, and enforces it by a solemn assurance. On the sense, cf. Mark xi. 25, and the remarkable parallel Sir. xxviii. 2: ἄφες ἀδίκημα τῷ πλησίον σου, κ. τότε δεηθέντος σου αἱ ἁμαρτίαι σου λυθήσονται. See Chrysostom's most eloquent appeal on this verse, Hom. xix. 7, p. 255, end.

16—18.] Third example. *Fasting.* Another department of the spiritual life, in which *reality in the sight of God*, and not appearance in the sight of man, must be our object. While these verses determine nothing as to the manner and extent of Christian fasting, they clearly recognize it as a solemn duty, ranking it with almsgiving and prayer; but requiring it, like them, (see ch. ix. 14—17,) to spring out of reality, not mere formal prescription.

16. ἀφανίζουσιν] "Chrys. διαφθείρουσι, ἀπολλύουσι: Homb., Hammond, *colorem auferre*, comparing Antiochus, Hom. 55 *de invidia*, τὸ πρόσωπον ἐξαφανίζει, *pallorem inducit*: Erasm., Fritzsche, *e conspectu tollere*: Elsner, Meyer, *to hide, cover up*, viz. in mourning costume. But in later Greek the meaning is *deformare*, to disfigure, (which the *exterminare* of the vulg. may also mean,) as is shewn in many examples cited by Le Clerc h. l., Valcknär on Phœniss. 373, Schäfer ad Dion. de comp. verb. p. 124. In Stobæus, Serm. lxxiv. 62, Nicostratus uses it of women who paint: πόῤῥω δ' ἂν εἴη καὶ τοῦ δεηθῆναι γυνὴ ὑγιαίνουσα καὶ ψιμυθίου καὶ ὑπ' ὀφθαλμῷ ὑπογραφῆς καὶ ἄλλου χρώματος ζωγραφοῦντος καὶ **ἀφανίζοντος τὰς ὄψεις** 'which be-paints and *disfigures* the faces.' The allusion is therefore not to *covering* the face, which could only be regarded as a sign of *mourning*, but to the squalor of the uncleansed face and hair of the head and beard, as the contrast of washing and anointing shews." Tholuck: and this certainly appears to be the right view, especially when we compare vv. 19, 20 below. But he seems too hastily to have assumed the meaning in the passage from Stobæus: for there the verb may just as well signify *covering, plastering over*, as disfiguring. The Etym. Mag. says ἀφανίσαι, οἱ παλαι οὐχὶ τὸ **μολῦναι** ὡς νῦν, ἀλλὰ τὸ τελέως ἀφανῆ ποιῆσαι. Suidas, on the other hand, ἀφανίσαι οὐ τὸ μολῦναι καὶ χρᾶναι δηλοῖ, ἀλλὰ τὸ ἀνελεῖν καὶ ἀφανὲς ποιῆσαι: but it is possible that he may be speaking of its *classical* sense, as suggested by Le Clerc, who does not however, as Tholuck asserts, *cite any examples* of the other meaning.

17.] i. e. '*appear as usual:*' 'seem to men the same as if thou wert not fasting.' It has been observed that this precept applies only to voluntary and private fasts, (such as are mentioned Luke xviii. 12,) not to public

...ουρανω D.

BEGKL MSUVΓ ΔΠℵ 1. 33

[d] κρυφαίῳ ἀποδώσει σοι. 19 Μὴ [ef] θησαυρίζετε ὑμῖν [eg] θησαυροὺς ἐπὶ τῆς γῆς, ὅπου [h] σὴς καὶ [i] βρῶσις [k] ἀφανίζει,
καὶ ὅπου κλέπται [l] διορύσσουσιν καὶ κλέπτουσιν· 20 [e] θησαυρίζετε δὲ ὑμῖν [eg] θησαυροὺς ἐν οὐρανῷ, ὅπου οὔτε [h] σὴς
οὔτε βρῶσις [k] ἀφανίζει, καὶ ὅπου κλέπται οὐ [l] διορύσσουσιν οὐδὲ κλέπτουσιν. 21 ὅπου γάρ ἐστιν ὁ [g] θησαυρός σου,
ἐκεῖ ἔσται καὶ ἡ καρδία σου. 22 ὁ [m] λύχνος τοῦ σώματός
ἐστιν ὁ ὀφθαλμός. ἐὰν οὖν ᾖ ὁ ὀφθαλμός σου [n] ἁπλοῦς,
ὅλον τὸ σῶμά σου [o] φωτεινὸν ἔσται· 23 ἐὰν δὲ ὁ ὀφθαλμός
σου [p] πονηρὸς ᾖ, ὅλον τὸ σῶμά σου [q] σκοτεινὸν ἔσται.
εἰ οὖν τὸ φῶς τὸ ἐν σοὶ σκότος ἐστίν, τὸ σκότος πόσον.

e here (bis) only. Micah vi. 10.
f Luke xii. 21. Rom. ii. 5. 1 Cor. xvi. 2. 2 Cor. xii. 14. James v. 3. 2 Pet. iii. 7 only. 4 Kings xx. 17.
g ch. ii. 11 al. 2 Chron. xxxvi. 18.
h Luke xii. 33 only. Isa. l. 9. li. 8.
i = here only (John iv. 32 reff.)‡.
k ver. 16 reff.
l ch. xxiv. 43. Luke xii. 39 only. Job xxiv. 16. Ezek. xii. 5, 7, 12 only. (-υγμα, Exod. xxii. 2.)
m ch. v. 15 reff.
n (=) Luke xi. 34 only. Prov. xi. 25 only. (-ῶς, James i. 5.)
o ch. xvii. 5. Luke xi. 34, 36 bis only †. Sir. xvii. 31. xxiii. 19 only.
p = ch. vii. 17, 18. Jer. xxiv. 2, &c. see Rev. xvi. 2.
q Luke xi. 34, 36 only. Prov. iv. 19 al.

rec aft *σοι* ins *εν τω φανερω* (*see on vv* 4, 6), with EΔ lat-*a b c* g_1 *h k* æth arm-mss: om BDℵ rel vulg lat-*f* ff_1 *l* syrr syr-cu syr-jer copt goth arm-zoh Thl Euthym Aug spec.

19. *θησαυρισεται* D-gr. *αφανιζουσιν* D[1] $Orig_1$. aft *κλεπται* ins *και* D[2].

20. *ους* (of *θησαυρους*) is written twice by D[1]. for *ουδε*, *και* ℵ 1. 21 latt(exc *c* ff_1 *k*) syr-cu (coptt) Cypr [Aug Chron].

21. rec (for *σου* both times) *υμων* (*see Luke* xii. 34), with L rel lat-*f* syrr [syr-cu] goth arm: txt Bℵ 1 latt syr-ms-mg coptt æth Mac Bas Ephr Tert $Cypr_2$ Aug. om *και* (aft *εσται*) B.

22. aft 1st *οφθαλμος* add *σου* B latt æth $Orig\text{-}int_2$ Hil. om *ουν* ℵ Scr's s [ev-z] vulg lat-*a* ff_1 syr-cu Hil Ambr. rec *ο οφθ. σου απ.* bef *η*, with L rel: txt Bℵ Scr's b.

23. *η* bef *ο οφθ. σου πον.* ℵ[1](txt ℵ[2]): om *η* 33.

and enjoined ones. But this distinction does not seem to be necessary; the one might afford just as much occasion for ostentation as the other.

19—34.] From cautions against the hypocrisy of formalists, the discourse naturally passes to the *entire dedication of the heart to God,* from which all duties of the Christian should be performed. In this section this is enjoined, 1. (vv. 19—24) with regard to earthly *treasures,* from the impossibility of serving God and Mammon: 2. (vv. 25—34) with regard to earthly *cares,* from the assurance that our Father careth for us. **19, 20.**] It is to be observed that the qualifying clauses, **ἐπὶ τῆς γῆς, ἐν οὐρανῷ,** belong in each case to the verb *θησαυρίζετε,* not to the noun *θησαυρούς.* **βρῶσις**] more general in meaning than *rust*—the '*wear and tear*' of time, which eats into and consumes the fairest possessions. The **θησαυρίζετε θησ. ἐν οὐρ.** would accumulate the *βαλλάντια μὴ παλαιούμενα, θησαυρὸν ἀνέκλειπτον* of Luke xii. 33, corresponding to the *μισθός* of ch. v. 12, and the *ἀποδώσει σοι* of vv. 4, 6, 18. Cf. 1 Tim. vi. 19: Tobit iv. 9. **διορύσσουσιν**] usually joined with *οἰκίαν,* as ch. xxiv. 43. **21.**] The connexion with the foregoing is plain enough to any but the shallowest reader. 'The heart is, where the treasure is.' But it might be replied, 'I will have a treasure on earth and a treasure in heaven also: a divided affection.' This is dealt with, and its impracticability shewn by a parable from nature.

22, 23. ὁ λύχνος] as lighting and guiding the body and its members: not as containing light in itself. Similarly the inner light, the conscience, lights the spirit and its faculties, but by light supernal to itself. **ἁπλοῦς, clear,** untroubled in vision, as the eye which presents a well-defined and single image to the brain. **πονηρός, perverse,** as the eye which dims and distorts the visual images. **φωτεινὸς . . σκοτεινός**: *in full light,* as an object in the bright sunshine; *in darkness,* as an object in the deep shade. The comparison is found in Aristotle, Topic. i. 14 (Wetst.), *ὡς ὄψις ἐν ὀφθαλμῷ, νοῦς ἐν ψυχῇ*: in Galen, and Philo de Mund. Opif. **εἰ οὖν** κ.τ.λ.] **If then the** LIGHT **which is in thee is darkness, how dark must the** DARKNESS **be!** i. e. 'if the *conscience,* the eye and *light* of the soul, be *darkened,* in *how much grosser* darkness will all the *passions and faculties* be, which are of themselves *naturally dark!*' The opposition is between **τὸ φῶς** and **τὸ σκότος.** This interpretation is borne out

v Luke xvi. 13 bis. Col. iii. 24. 1 Kings vii. 3.
s Luke vii. 41. xvi. 13 bis. xvii. 34, 35. xviii. 10. Acts xxiii. 6. 1 Cor. iv. 6 only.
t Rom. ix. 13, from Mal. i. 2, 3. Gen. xxix. 30, 31.

24 οὐδεὶς δύναται δυσὶν κυρίοις [r] δουλεύειν· ἢ γὰρ τὸν [s] ἕνα [t] μισήσει καὶ τὸν [s] ἕτερον [t] ἀγαπήσει, ἢ [s] ἑνὸς [u] ἀνθέξεται καὶ τοῦ [s] ἑτέρου [v] καταφρονήσει. οὐ δύνασθε θεῷ [r] δουλεύειν καὶ [w] μαμωνᾷ.
25 διὰ τοῦτο λέγω ὑμῖν, μὴ [x] μεριμνᾶτε τῇ [y] ψυχῇ ὑμῶν τί φάγητε καὶ τί πίητε, μηδὲ τῷ σώματι

BEGKL MSUVΓ ΔΠℵ 1. 33

u Luke xvi. 13. 1 Thess. v. 14. Tit. i. 9 only. Prov. iii. 18.
v ch. xviii. 10. Luke xvi. 13. Rom. ii. 4 al. Prov. xix. 16.
w Luke xvi. 9, 11, 12 only +.
x here &c., 6 times. ch. x. 19. Luke x. 41. xii. 11, &c. 1 Cor. vii. 32, &c. xii. 25. Phil. ii. 20. iv. 6 only. 2 Kings vii. 10. Ps. xxxvii. 18.
y = ch. x. 39. John xii. 25. Exod. xxi. 23.

24. for 1st η, ει ℵ.

25. for και, η (*perhaps from ver* 31) B 33. 118-24 gat(with lux) lat-*c f* g_1 *h* coptt arm Orig Ath Bas [Max-$conf_1$] spec.—om κ. τι πιητε (*perhaps by negligence*, -ητε to ητε,—*perhaps thinking of Luke* xii. 22: *the* και *sufficiently distinguishes it from the similar clause, ver* 31) ℵ 1. 22 vulg lat-*a b* ff_1 *k l* syr-cu æth $Clem_{appy}$ Bas_1 Epiph Chr

by the Vulgate: 'Ipsæ tenebræ quantæ erunt!' by Jerome: 'Si sensus, qui lumen est, animæ vitio caligatur, ipsa putas caligo quantis tenebris obvolvetur!' and by Chrysostom: *ὅταν γὰρ ὁ κυβερνήτης ὑποβρόχιος γένηται, καὶ ὁ λύχνος σβεσθῇ, καὶ ὁ ἡγεμὼν αἰχμάλωτος γένηται, ποία λοιπὸν ἔσται τοῖς ὑπηκόοις ἐλπίς;* Hom. xx. 3, p. 264, and Euthymius: *εἰ οὖν τὸ φῶς τὸ ἐν σοί, ὅ ἐστιν ὁ νοῦς, ὁ δωρηθεὶς εἰς τὸ φωτίζειν καὶ ὁδηγεῖν τὴν ψυχήν, σκότος ἐστί, τουτέστιν ἐσκότισται, λοιπὸν τὸ σκότος, τὸ ἀπὸ τῶν παθῶν, πόσον ἔσται, εἰς τὸ σκοτίζειν τὴν ψυχήν, σκοτισθέντος τοῦ ἀνατέλλοντος αὐτῇ φωτός.* Augustine (de Serm. Dom. ii. c. 13 (46), vol. iii.) renders it similarly, but understands *σκότος* to refer to a different thing: 'Si ipsa cordis intentio, qua facis quod facis, quæ tibi nota est, sordidatur appetitu rerum terrenarum . . . atque cæcatur: quanto magis ipsum factum, cujus incertus est exitus, sordidum et tenebrosum est!' So too the Syr. æth. versions; and Erasm.: "Si ratio excæcata id judicat imprimis esse expetendum, quod vel contemnendum, vel neglectui habendum, in quas tenebras totum hominem rapiet ambitio reliquæque animi perturbationes, quæ suapte natura caliginem habent!"—Bucer, Luther. Stier expands this well, Reden Jesu, i. 208, edn. 2, "As the body, of itself a dark mass, has its light from the eye, so we have here compared to it the sensuous, bestial life (ψυχικόν) of men, their appetites, desires, and aversions, which belong to the lower creature. This dark region—human nature under the gross dominion of the flesh—shall become spiritualized, enlightened, sanctified, by the spiritual light: but if *this light* be darkness, how great must then the darkness of the *sensuous life* be!" The usual modern interpretation makes *τὸ σκότος πόσον* a mere expression of the greatness of the darkness thereby occasioned, and thus loses the force of the sentence.

24.] And this division in man's being *cannot take place*—he is and must be *one*—light *or* dark—serving God *or* Mammon. **δουλεύειν**] Not merely '*serve*,' but in that closer sense in which he who serves is the δοῦλος of, i. e. belongs to, and obeys entirely. *ὁ Ἰὼβ πλούσιος ἦν· ἀλλ' οὐκ ἐδούλευε τῷ μαμωνᾷ, ἀλλ' εἶχεν αὐτὸς καὶ ἐκράτει, καὶ δεσπότης, οὐ δοῦλος ἦν.* Chrysost. Hom. xxi. 1, p. 269. See Rom. vi. 16, 17. **ἢ γὰρ . . . ἢ . . .** is not a repetition; but the suppositions are the reverse of one another: as Meyer expresses it, 'He will either hate A and love B, or cleave to A and despise B:' *ὁ εἷς* and *ὁ ἕτερος* keeping their individual reference in both members. **μισεῖν** and **ἀγαπᾷν** must be given their full meaning, or the depth of the saying is not reached: the sense 'minus diligo, posthabeo' (Bretschneider) for *μισεῖν* would not bring out the opposition and division of the nature of man by the attempt. **μαμωνᾷ**] Chaldee, מָמוֹנָא, (from אָמַן, confisus est,) riches. 'Congruit et Punicum nomen, nam lucrum Punice mammon dicitur.' August. in loc. Mammon does not appear to have been the name of any Syrian deity, as Schleusner asserts. Tholuck has shewn that the idea rests only on the testimony of Papias, an obscure grammarian of the eleventh century. Schl. refers to Tertullian, who, however, says nothing of the kind (see adv. Marc. iv. 33, vol. ii. pp. 439 ff., which must be the place meant, but not specified by Schl.).

25. διὰ τοῦτο] A direct inference from the foregoing verse: the plainer, since **μεριμνάω** (the root being *μερίζω*) is 'to be distracted,' 'to have the mind drawn two ways.' The E. V., '*Take no thought*,' does not express the sense, but gives rather an exaggeration of the command, and thus makes it unreal and nugatory. **Be not anxious**, would be far better. In Luke xii. 29 we have *μὴ μετ-*

ὑμῶν τί [z] ἐνδύσησθε. οὐχὶ ἡ [y] ψυχὴ [a] πλεῖόν ἐστιν τῆς
τροφῆς, καὶ τὸ σῶμα τοῦ [b] ἐνδύματος; 26 [c] ἐμβλέψατε εἰς
τὰ [de] πετεινὰ τοῦ [d] οὐρανοῦ, ὅτι οὐ [f] σπείρουσιν οὐδὲ [f] θερί-
ζουσιν οὐδὲ [g] συνάγουσιν εἰς [g] ἀποθήκας, καὶ ὁ [h] πατὴρ ὑμῶν
ὁ [h] οὐράνιος [i] τρέφει αὐτά· οὐχ ὑμεῖς [lm] μᾶλλον [mn] διαφέρετε
αὐτῶν; 27 τίς δὲ ἐξ ὑμῶν [x] μεριμνῶν δύναται [o] προσθεῖναι
ἐπὶ τὴν [p] ἡλικίαν αὐτοῦ [q] πῆχυν ἕνα; 28 καὶ περὶ [b] ἐνδύματος τί [x] μεριμνᾶτε; [r] καταμάθετε τὰ [s] κρίνα τοῦ ἀγροῦ,

z ch. xxii. 11. Mark i. 6. vi. 9. Acts xii. 21. Rom. xiii. 12. Rev. i. 13. Lev. vi. 10. Jer. x. 9.
a = ch. xii. 41, 42. Heb. xi. 4.
b ch. iii. 4 al. Mt. only, exc. Luke xii. 23. Zeph. i. 8.
c w. εἰς, Acts i. 11. Isa. v. 30. li. 1. dat., Mark x. 21 al.
d ch. viii. 20 || L. xiii. 32 ||. Luke viii. 5. Acts x. 12. xi. 6. Ps. xlix. 11. Ezek. xxxi. 6.
e as above (d). ch. xiii. 4 || Mk. Luke xii. 24. Rom. i. 23. James iii. 7.
f John iv. 37 reff. plu., ver. 28 reff.
g ch. iii. 12 reff.
h ch. v. 48 reff.
i ch. xxv. 37. Luke iv. 16. xii. 24. xxiii. 29. Acts xii. 20. James v. 5. Rev. xii. 6, 14 only. Gen. xlviii. 15.
l = Mark vii. 36.
m Luke xii. 24 only.
n = ch. x. 31. xii. 12. 2 Macc. xv. 13.
o Luke iii. 20. xii. 25. Tobit v. 15.
p = Luke xii. 26. (xix. 3 reff.) John ix. 21, 23. Heb. xi. 11. Job xxix. 18.
q John xxi. 8 reff.
r here only. = Job xxxv. 4. Gen. xxxiv. 1.
s Luke xii. 27 only. Hos. xiv. 6.

Euthal Damasc Hil Op Aug Jer(expr: he says it is added in some mss). om 2nd *υμων* א[1](ins א[2a]).

26. ins *τας* bef *αποθηκας* Lא? Scr's a p Ath.

εωρίζεσθε, where see note. **τῇ ψυχῇ** = *περὶ τῆς ψυχῆς*, dat. commodi. See ver. 28. **οὐχὶ ἡ ψ.**] *τοῦτο εἶπε δηλῶν ὅτι ὁ τὸ πλεῖον δοὺς ἡμῖν καὶ τὸ ἔλαττον δώσει. πλεῖον δὲ τὸ μεῖζον λέγει.* Euthymius.

26. τὰ πετ.] The two examples, of the birds and the lilies, are not parallel in their application. The first is an argument from the less to the greater; that our Heavenly Father, who feeds the birds, will much more feed us: the second, besides this application, which (ver. 30) it also contains, is a reproof of the vanity of anxiety about clothing, which, in all its pomp of gorgeous colours, is vouchsafed to the inferior creatures, but not attainable by, as being unworthy of, us. Notice, it is not said, *μὴ σπείρετε—μὴ θερίζετε—μὴ συνάγετε*;—the birds are not our example to follow in their habits, for God hath made us to differ from them—the doing all these things is part of our *πόσῳ μᾶλλον διαφέρετε*, (Luke xii. 24,) and increases the force of the *à fortiori;* but it is said, *μὴ μεριμνᾶτε—μὴ μετεωρίζεσθε. τί γοῦν ὠφελήσεις οὕτως ἐπιτεταμένως μεριμνῶν; κἂν γὰρ μυρία σπουδάσῃς, οὐ δώσεις ὑετὸν οὐδὲ ἥλιον οὐδὲ πνοὰς ἀνέμων, οἷς ὁ σπόρος καρπογονεῖ. ταῦτα γὰρ ὁ θεὸς μόνος δίδωσιν.* Euthymius. **ὁ πατὴρ ὑμῶν**, not *αὐτῶν*:—thus by every accessory word does our Lord wonderfully assert the truths and proprieties of creation, in which *we*, his sons, are His central work, and the rest *for us.* **τοῦ οὐρ.**, and afterwards **τοῦ ἀγροῦ**, as Thol. remarks, are not superfluous, but serve to set forth the wild and uncaring freedom of the birds and plants. I may add,—also to set forth their lower rank in the scale of creation, as *belonging to* the air and the field. Who could say of mankind, *οἱ ἄνθρωποι τοῦ κόσμου?* Thus the *à fortiori* is more plainly brought out. **27.**] These words do not relate to the *stature*, the adding a cubit to which (= a foot and a half) would be a very great addition, instead of a very small one, as is implied here, and expressed in Luke xii. 26, *εἰ οὖν* **οὐδὲ ἐλάχιστον** *δύνασθε, κ.τ.λ.*,—but to the *time of life* of each hearer; as Theophylact on Luke xii. 26, *ζωῆς μέτρα παρὰ μόνῳ τῷ θεῷ, καὶ οὐκ αὐτός τις ἕκαστος ἑαυτῷ ὁριστὴς τῆς ζωῆς.* So Hammond, Wolf, Rosenm., Kuinoel, Olsh., De Wette, Meyer, Stier, Tholuck, &c. &c.: and the *context* seems imperatively to require it: for the object of food and clothing is not to *enlarge the body*, but to prolong life. The application of measures of space to time is not uncommon. See Ps. xxxix. 5: Job ix. 25: 2 Tim. iv. 7. In Stobæus, xcviii. 13, we have cited from Mimnermus, *ἡμεῖς δ' οἷά τε φύλλα φύει πολυάνθεμος ὥρη | ἔαρος, ὅτ' αἶψ' αὐγῇ αὔξεται ἠελίου, | τοῖς ἴκελοι, πήχυιον ἐπὶ χρόνον ἄνθεσιν ἥβης | τερπόμεθα.* Alcæus (Athen. x. 7) says, *δάκτυλος ἁμέρα*: and Diog. Laert. viii. 16 (Thol.) *σπιθαμὴ τοῦ βίου.*

28.] **καταμάθετε**, implying more attention than *ἐμβλέψατε*: the birds fly by, and we can but look upon them: the flowers are ever with us, and we can watch their growth. These *lilies* have been supposed to be the crown imperial, (fritillaria imperialis, *κρίνον βασιλικόν*, Kaiserkrone,) which grows wild in Palestine, or the amaryllis lutea, (Sir J. E. Smith, cited by F. M.,) whose golden liliaceous flowers cover the autumnal fields of the Levant. Dr. Thomson, "The Land and the Book," p. 256, believes the Huleh lily to be

t - ch. xii. 4. Mark v. 16.
u intr., Luke i. 80 al3. John iii. 30. Acts vi. 7 al3. Eph. ii. 21. iv. 15. Col. ii. 19. 2 Pet. iii. 18. (ch. xiii. 32 reff.)
v ch. xi. 28. Luke v. 5 al. Ps. cxxvi. 1.
w plu., w. neut., ver. 26. Mark iii. 11. v. 13. John x. 8. xix. 31. Rev. i. 19. iii. 2 al. Winer, § 58. 3 a.
x Luke xii. 27 only. Exod. (only) xxxv. 25 al.

[t] πῶς [u] αὐξάνουσιν. οὐ [vw] κοπιοῦσιν οὐδὲ [wx] νήθουσιν·
29 λέγω δὲ ὑμῖν ὅτι [y] οὐδὲ Σολομῶν ἐν πάσῃ τῇ δόξῃ αὐτοῦ
[z] περιεβάλετο ὡς ἓν τούτων. 30 εἰ δὲ τὸν [a] χόρτον τοῦ ...τουτω Γ.
ἀγροῦ σήμερον ὄντα καὶ [b] αὔριον εἰς [c] κλίβανον βαλλόμε- BEGKL
νον ὁ θεὸς οὕτως [d] ἀμφιέννυσιν, οὐ πολλῷ μᾶλλον ὑμᾶς MSUVΔ ΠℵN 1. 33
[e] ὀλιγόπιστοι; 31 μὴ οὖν [f] μεριμνήσητε λέγοντες τί φάγωμεν ἢ τί πίωμεν ἢ τί [z] περιβαλώμεθα; 32 πάντα γὰρ ταῦτα
τὰ ἔθνη [g] ἐπιζητοῦσιν· οἶδεν γὰρ ὁ [h] πατὴρ ὑμῶν ὁ [h] οὐράνιος ὅτι [i] χρῄζετε τούτων ἁπάντων. 33 [j] ζητεῖτε δὲ
πρῶτον τὴν [k] βασιλείαν [τοῦ [k] θεοῦ] καὶ τὴν δικαιοσύνην

y = 1 Cor. v. 1. xiv. 21 al. z Acts xii. 8. Rev. iii. 5, 18 al. Esth. v. 1. a ch. xiii. 36. Mark iv. 28. 1 Pet. i. 24 (3ce, from Isa. xl. 6, 7). Gen. i. 5. b Luke xii. 28. xiii. 33, 34. Acts xxiii. 15. Isa. xxii. 13. c Luke xii. 28 only. Gen. xv. 17. d ch. xi. 8 ‖ (Luke xii. 28 v. r.) only. Job xxxi. 19. (-έζειν, Luke xii. 28. see Job as above.) e ch. viii. 26. xiv. 31. xvi. 8. Luke xii. 28 only †. f vv. 25, &c. g ch. xii. 39. xvi. 4. Rom. xi. 7. Phil. iv. 17 al. 1 Kings xx. 1. h ch. v. 48 reff. i Luke xii. 30 reff. j = Col. iii. 1. 1 Pet. iii. 11, from Ps. xxiii. 15. 1 Macc. ii. 29. k ch. xii. 28. xxi. 31, 43. Mark i. 15 al. fr.

28. rec αυξανει . . κοπια . . νηθει (*grammatical correction: or from Luke* xii. 27), with L rel: txt B(ℵ 1(κοπιωσιν)) 33. 118. 209 Ath Chr. (In ℵ the passage was rewritten by the origl scribe, but the space occupied is too great for the supposition that the singular was written at first.)

32. ταυτα γαρ παντα Δℵ 157 Scr's v ev-x. rec επιζητει (*grammatical correction*), with L rel: txt Bℵ 1. 13. 33. 124. 209. for γαρ, δε ℵ3a(but erased) 235 lat-*b c* g_1 Syr copt. ins ο θεος bef ο πατηρ ℵ1(ℵ3a disapproving). om ο ουρανιος ℵ 237 latt(exc *f h*) syr-cu copt Clem $Cypr_3$ Jer.

33. την δικαιοσυνην και την βασιλειαν αυτου (omg του θυ) B: την βασ. και την δικ. αυτου ℵ; simly Scr's v am lat-g_2 copt æth Eus.

meant: "it is very large, and the three inner petals meet above, and form a gorgeous canopy, such as art never approached, and king never sat under, even in his utmost glory. And when I met this incomparable flower, in all its loveliness, among the oak woods around the northern base of Tabor, and on the hills of Nazareth, where our Lord spent His youth, I felt assured that it was this to which He referred." Probably, however, the word here may be taken in a wider import, as signifying all wild flowers. **πῶς** is not interrogative, but relative: **how they grow.** **29.**] We here have the declaration of the Creator Himself concerning the relative glory and beauty of all human pomp, compared with the meanest of His own works. See 2 Chron. ix. 15—28. And the meaning hidden beneath the text should not escape the student. As the beauty of the flower is unfolded by the Divine Creator-Spirit from *within*, from the laws and capacities of its *own* individual life, so must all true adornment of man be unfolded *from within* by the same Almighty Spirit. See 1 Pet. iii. 3, 4. As nothing from without can defile a man, (ch. xv. 11,) so neither can any thing from without adorn him. Our Lord introduces with λέγω ὑμῖν His revelations of omniscience: see ch. xviii. 10, 19. **30. τὸν χόρτον**] The wild flowers which form part of the meadow-growth are counted as belonging to the grass, and are cut down with it. Cut grass, which soon withers from the heat, is still used in the East for firing. See "The Land and the Book," p. 341. The pres. part. denotes the *habit*. "**κλίβανος**, or Att. **κρίβ.**, a covered earthen vessel, a pan, wider at the bottom than at the top, wherein bread was baked by putting hot embers round it, which produced a more equable heat than in the regular oven (ἰπνός), Herod. ii. 92: Aristoph. Vesp. 1153." Wilkinson and Webster's note. **32. οἶδεν γάρ**] This 2nd γάρ brings in an *additional* reason: see Xen. Symp. iv. 55. **33. ζητεῖτε πρῶτον**] Not with any reference to seeking all these things *after* our religious duties, e. g. beginning with prayer days of avarice and worldly anxiety, but **make your great object**, as we say, **your first care.** **δικαιοσύνην**] Not here the *forensic righteousness of justification*, but the *spiritual purity* inculcated in this discourse. τὴν δικ. **αὐτοῦ** answers to ἡ τελειότης αὐτοῦ, spoken of in ch. v. 48, and is

αὐτοῦ, καὶ ταῦτα πάντα [l] προςτεθήσεται ὑμῖν. 34 μὴ οὖν
[f] μεριμνήσητε [m] εἰς [n] τὴν [n] αὔριον· [n] ἡ γὰρ [n] αὔριον [f] μεριμ-
νήσει αὐτῆς. [o] ἀρκετὸν τῇ ἡμέρᾳ ἡ [p] κακία αὐτῆς.

X μη κρινετε., BEGKL MSUVX ΔΠℵ 1. 33

VII. 1 ΜΗ [q] κρίνετε, ἵνα μὴ κριθῆτε· 2 ἐν ᾧ γὰρ
[r] κρίματι κρίνετε κριθήσεσθε, καὶ [s] ἐν ᾧ μέτρῳ [st] μετρεῖτε
[t] μετρηθήσεται ὑμῖν. 3 τί δὲ βλέπεις τὸ [u] κάρφος τὸ ἐν

l Luke xii. 31. xvii. 5. Tobit v. 15.
m Acts iv. 3. Prov. xxvii. 1.
n here bis. Acts iv. 3, 5. James iv. 14 only. Exod. viii. 23.
o ch. x. 25. 1 Pet. iv. 3 only +. Deut. xxv. 2 Aq. constr., Prov. xxx. 27.
p = and Gospp., here only. (Acts viii. 22 al.) Eccl. xii. 1. Amos iii. 6.
q = Rom. ii. 1, 3. James iv. 11, 12.
r 1 Tim. iii. 6. Deut. xxi. 22. Zech. viii. 16.
s here bis. Mark iv. 24 bis. 2 Cor. x. 12 only.
t as above (s). Luke vi. 38. Rev. xi. 1, 2. xxi. 15, 16, 17 only. Exod. xvi. 18.
u here &c. 3ce. Luke vi. 41, 42 (bis) only. Gen. viii. 11 only.

34. rec aft μεριμνησει ins τα, with E rel; τα περι Δ: om BGLSVℵ Scr's f k o u. rec (for 1st αυτης) εαυτης, with ℵ rel: txt B[1](see table) LΔ.

Chap. VII. **2.** rec **αντιμετρηθησεται** (*from Luke* vi. 38), with Scr's i p evv-P-X-Z vulg-ed lat-*c f ff*$_1$ *g*$_1$ *h l* Polyc Clem Orig$_{alic}$ lat-ff: txt Bℵ rel(and rel-scr) am(with forj fuld tol) lat-*a b* syrr syr-cu copt æth arm Clem[rom] Orig$_1$ Dial Thdrt Thl Euthym Hil.

another reference to the being as our Heavenly Father is. In the Christian life which has been since unfolded, the righteousness of justification is a *necessary condition* of likeness to God; but it is not the δικ. αὐτ. *here* meant. **ταῦτα πάντα, these things, all of them**—the emphasis being on the genus—all such things: **πάντα ταῦτα, all these things**—'*the whole of the things mentioned*'—the emphasis being on πάντα,—the fact that *all without exception* are included. See Winer, § 18. 4. **προςτεθ.**] There is a traditional saying of our Lord, αἰτεῖτε, τὰ μεγάλα, καὶ τὰ μικρὰ ὑμῖν προςτεθήσεται· καὶ αἰτεῖτε τὰ ἐπουράνια, καὶ τὰ ἐπίγεια προςτεθήσεται ὑμῖν. Fabric. Cod. Apocr. i. 329. (Meyer.) **34. ἡ γὰρ αὔρ.**] **for the morrow will care for it,** viz. for ἡ αὔριον mentioned above: i. e., *will bring care enough about its own matters:* implying,—'after all your endeavour to avoid worldly cares, you will find quite enough, and more of them when to-morrow comes, about to-morrow itself: do not then increase those of to-day by introducing them before their time.' A hint, as is the following κακία, that in this state of sin and infirmity the command of ver. 31 will never be completely observed. **ἀρκετὸν—κακία**: thus, οὐκ ἀγαθὸν πολυκοιρανίη, Il. β. 204. And the same construction frequently occurs, both in Greek and Latin authors.

Chap. VII. 1—12.] *Of our* conduct towards other men: *parenthetically illustrated,* vv. 7—11, *by the benignity and wisdom of God in his dealings with us.* The connexion with the last chapter is *immediately,* the word **κακία**, in which a glance is given by the Saviour at the misery and sinfulness of human life at its best;—and now precepts follow, teaching us how we are to live in such a world, and among others sinful like ourselves:—*mediately,* and more generally, the continuing caution against hypocrisy, in ourselves and in others. **1.**] This does not prohibit *all* judgment (see ver. 20, and 1 Cor. v. 12); but, as Augustine (de Serm. Dom. ii. c. 18 (59), vol. iii.) says, 'Hoc loco nihil aliud nobis præcipi existimo, nisi ut ea facta quæ dubium est quo animo fiant, in meliorem partem interpretemur.' **κρίνειν** has been taken for κατακρίνειν here (κρίσιν ἐνταῦθα τὴν κατάκρισιν νόησον. Euthym. So also Theophylact, Tholuck, Olshausen); and this seems necessary, at least in so far that κρίνειν should be taken as implying an *ill judgment.* For if the command were merely 'not to form authoritative judgments of others' (as given in edn. 1 of this work), the second member, ἵνα μὴ κριθῆτε, would not, in its right interpretation, as applying to *God's* judgment of *us,* correspond. And the μὴ καταδικάζετε, which follows in Luke vi. 37, is perhaps to be taken rather as an epexegesis of κρίνετε, than as a climax after it. **κριθῆτε**] i. e. '*by God,*' for so doing;—a parallel expression to ch. v. 7; vi. 15; not '*by others.*' The bare passive, without the agent expressed, and without καί to refer it back to the former member of the clause, is solemn and emphatic. See note on Luke vi. 38; xvi. 9; and xii. 20. The sense then is, 'that you have not to answer before God for your rash judgment and its consequences.' The same remarks apply to ver. 2. **2.**] **ἐν**, not instrumental, but of the sphere in which the act takes place, i. e. in this case, the *measure, according to which:* as in ref. 2 Cor., ἐν ἑαυτοῖς ἑαυτοὺς μετροῦντες. **3—5.**] Lightfoot produces instances of this proverbial saying among

τῷ ὀφθαλμῷ τοῦ ἀδελφοῦ σου, τὴν δὲ ἐν τῷ σῷ ὀφθαλμῷ
[v] δοκὸν οὐ [w] κατανοεῖς; 4 ἢ πῶς ἐρεῖς τῷ ἀδελφῷ σου
[x] Ἄφες [y] ἐκβάλω τὸ [u] κάρφος [y] ἀπὸ τοῦ ὀφθαλμοῦ σου, καὶ
ἰδοὺ ἡ [v] δοκὸς ἐν τῷ ὀφθαλμῷ σου; 5 [z] ὑποκριτά, ἔκβαλε
πρῶτον ἐκ τοῦ ὀφθαλμοῦ σου τὴν [v] δοκόν, καὶ τότε C δοκον
[a] διαβλέψεις ἐκβαλεῖν τὸ [u] κάρφος ἐκ τοῦ ὀφθαλμοῦ τοῦ και... BCEGK
ἀδελφοῦ σου. 6 μὴ δῶτε τὸ ἅγιον τοῖς [b] κυσίν, μηδὲ LMSUV ΧΔΠℵ 1.33
βάλητε τοὺς [c] μαργαρίτας ὑμῶν [d] ἔμπροσθεν τῶν χοίρων,
μήποτε [e] καταπατήσουσιν αὐτοὺς [f] ἐν τοῖς ποσὶν αὐτῶν καὶ

v N. T. as above (u). Gen. xix. 8 al. w Luke vi. 41. xii. 24, 27 al. Ps. xciii. 9. x ch. xxiii. 14. Judg. xvi. 26 B. constr., ch. xxvii. 49 ‖ Mk. y Mark xvi. 9 reff. z ch. vi. 2, 5 reff. a Mark viii. 25. Luke vi. 42 only †. see Plato, Phæd. § 81, init. b = Phil. iii. 2. Rev. xxii. 15 (Luke xvi. 21. 2 Pet. ii. 22, from Prov. xxvi. 11) only. Isa. lvi. 11. c ch. xiii. 45, 46. 1 Tim. ii. 9. Rev. xvii. 4. xviii. 12, 16. xxi. 21 only †. d Acts xviii. 17. 2 Cor. v. 10. 2 Chron. iii. 15. e ch. v. 13 reff. f = ch. v. 13.

3. ins *δοκον την* bef *εν τω σω οφθαλμω* (omg *δοκον* below) ℵ[1](txt ℵ[3a]) Chr-ms.
4. for *ερεις*, *λεγεις* ℵ[1](txt ℵ[2·3a]) latt(exc $ff_{1.2}$ $g_{1.2}$) Lucif. aft 1st *σου* ins *αδελφε* ℵ [Gild]. for *απο*, *εκ* (*see ver* 5) Bℵ 1. 13. 33. 124. 209 Scr's b lat-*a b c* Lucif.
5. rec *την δοκον* bef *εκ του οφθαλμου σου* (*see next clause and Luke* vi. 42), with L rel lat-*a b c* Iren-int Lucif: txt B C(appy) ℵ. **εκβαλλειν** Δℵ Damasc.
6. rec *καταπατησωσιν*, with ℵ rel Clem: txt BCLX 33.

the Jews. With them, however, it seems only to be used of a person retaliating rebuke. 'Dixit Rabbi Tarphon, Miror ego, an sit in hoc sæculo, qui recipere vult correptionem; quin si dicat quis alteri, Ejice stramen ex oculo tuo, responsurus ille est, Ejice trabem ex oculo tuo:'—whereas our Lord gives us a further application of it, viz. to the incapability of one involved in personal iniquity to form a right judgment on others, and the clearness given to the spiritual vision by conflict with and victory over evil. There is also no doubt here a lesson given us of the true relative magnitude which our own faults, and those of our brother, ought to hold in our estimation. What is a *κάρφος* to one looking on another, is to that other himself a *δοκός*: just the reverse of the ordinary estimate. **τὸ κάρ.** and **ἡ δοκ.**, not as referring to a known proverb, but because the mote and beam are in situ, **ἐν τῷ ὀφθαλμῷ.** **βλέπεις, beholdest,** from without, a voluntary act: **οὐ κατανοεῖς, apprehendest not,** from within, that which is already there, and ought to have excited attention before. The same distinction is observed in Luke. **4.**] **πῶς ἐρεῖς** = *πῶς δύνασαι λέγειν*, Luke; wie darfst du sagen, Luther.
5. ὑποκριτά] *ὑποκριτὴν τὸν τοιοῦτον ὠνόμασεν ὡς ἰατροῦ μὲν τάξιν ἁρπάζοντα, νοσοῦντος δὲ τόπον ἐπέχοντα· ἢ ὡς προφάσει μὲν διορθώσεως τὸ ἀλλότριον σφάλμα πολυπραγμονοῦντα, σκοπῷ δὲ κατακρίσεως τοῦτο ποιοῦντα.* Euthym.
διαβλ., as in E. V., **thou shalt see clearly,** with purified eye. The close is remarkable. *Before,* **βλέπειν** *τὸ κάρφος* was all—to stare at thy brother's faults, and as people do who stand and gaze at an object, attract others to gaze also:—but *now*, the object is a very different one—**ἐκβαλεῖν** *τὸ κάρφος*—to help thy brother to be rid of his fault, by doing him the best and most difficult office of Christian friendship. The *βλέπειν* was vain and idle; the *διαβλέπειν* is for a blessed end, viz. (ch. xviii. 15) *κερδῆσαι τὸν ἀδελφόν σου.*
6.] The connexion, see below. **τὸ ἅγιον**] Some have thought this a mistranslation of the Chaldee, קְדָשָׁא, an ear-ring, or amulet; but the connexion is not at all improved by it. Pearls bear a resemblance to peas or acorns, the food of swine, but earrings none whatever to the food of dogs. The similitude is derived from *τὸ ἅγιον*, or *τὰ ἅγια*, *the meat offered in sacrifice*, of which no unclean person was to eat (Levit. xxii. 6, 7, 10, 14 (where *τὸ ἅγ.* is used), 15, 16). Similarly in the ancient Christian Liturgies and Fathers, *τὰ ἅγια* are the consecrated elements in the Holy Communion. The fourteenth canon of the Council of Laodicæa orders *μὴ τὰ ἅγια . . . . . . εἰς ἑτέρας παροικίας διαπέμπεσθαι.* Again, Cyril of Jerus.: *μετὰ ταῦτα λέγει ὁ ἱερεύς Τὰ ἅγια τοῖς ἁγίοις. ἅγια, τὰ προκείμενα, ἐπιφοίτησιν δεξάμενα ἁγίου πνεύματος.* (See Suicer on the word.) Thus interpreted, the saying would be one full of meaning to the Jews. As Abp. Trench observes (Serm. Mount, p. 136), "It is not that the dogs would not eat it, for it would be welcome to them; but that it would be a profanation to give it to them, thus to make it a *σκύβαλον*, Exod. xxii. 31." The other part

στραφέντες [g] ῥήξωσιν ὑμᾶς. 7 αἰτεῖτε, καὶ δοθήσεται ὑμῖν·
ζητεῖτε, καὶ εὑρήσετε· [h] κρούετε, καὶ ἀνοιγήσεται ὑμῖν·
8 πᾶς γὰρ ὁ αἰτῶν λαμβάνει, καὶ ὁ ζητῶν εὑρίσκει, καὶ
τῷ [h] κρούοντι ἀνοιγήσεται. 9 [i] ἢ τίς [ἐστιν] ἐξ ὑμῶν
ἄνθρωπος [j] ὃν αἰτήσει ὁ υἱὸς αὐτοῦ ἄρτον, μὴ λίθον
[k] ἐπιδώσει αὐτῷ; 10 ἢ καὶ ἰχθὺν αἰτήσει, μὴ ὄφιν [k] ἐπιδώσει
αὐτῷ; 11 εἰ οὖν ὑμεῖς πονηροὶ ὄντες [l] οἴδατε [m] δόματα
ἀγαθὰ διδόναι τοῖς τέκνοις ὑμῶν, πόσῳ μᾶλλον ὁ [n] πατὴρ
ὑμῶν ὁ [n] ἐν τοῖς οὐρανοῖς δώσει ἀγαθὰ τοῖς [o] αἰτοῦσιν

g ch. ix. 17 ‖. Mark ix. 18 ‖ L. Gal. iv. 27 (from Isa. liv. 1) only.
h Luke xi. 9, 10. xii. 36. xiii. 25. Acts xii. 13, 16. Rev. iii. 20 only. Judg. xix. 22.
i = ch. xii. 29. Rom. iii. 29 al.
j constr., Mark vi. 22, 23. Luke xi. 11. John xi. 22. Josh. xv. 18.
k Luke iv. 17. xi. 11 (bis), 12. xxiv. 30, 42. Acts xv. 30. xxvii. 15 only. Amos iv. 1.
l = Luke xii. 56. Phil. iv. 12. 2 Pet. ii. 9. 3 Kings v. 6.
m Luke xi. 13. Eph. iv. 8 (from Ps. lxvii. 18). Phil. iv. 17 only. 2 Chron. xxi. 3.
n ch. v. 45 reff.
o absol. and constr., ch. v. 42 reff.

8. for *ανοιγησεται*, *ανοιγεται* B syrr syr-cu copt.

9. om *εστιν* L 13 Scr's f[1] i s v em lat-*a b c h* syrr syr-cu coptt (Lachm has printed *ἥ τις* . . . . but em lat-*b c h* have *τίς*): ins B(B[1] has put it in the marg) Cℵ(*-στιν* rewritten by ℵ[1]) rel vulg lat-*f ff*$_1$ *g*$_1$ æth arm Cypr Aug. rec aft *ον* adds *εαν* (*to help out the construction*), with Xℵ[2] rel vulg lat-*f ff*$_1$ *g*$_2$ *h* Cypr; *αν* K[1]LΔ: om BCℵ[1] 1. 13. 229 mm lat-*a b c g*$_1$ *h* coptt arm [Aug]. (for *ον*, *ος* M 243-5·7 Scr's v.) rec *αιτηση* (here and ver 10), with X rel: txt BCLΔℵ, *petit* mm lat-*a b c g*$_1$ *h* coptt. (*-σεις* C[1].)

10. rec om *η*, with X rel syrr æth: ins BCKMSΠℵ 1. 13. 33 latt syr-cu coptt Cypr Aug.—rec aft *και* ins *εαν*, with X rel latt syrr syr-cu æth Cypr Aug, *αν* K[1]L: om BCℵ 1. 33 [sah arm].—*η εαν* (omg *και*) latt syr-cu Cypr Aug. (*Both as above to simplify the construction, and after Luke* xi. 12.)

of the similitude is of a different character, and belongs entirely to the swine, who having cast to them pearls, something like their natural food, whose value is inappreciable by them, in fury trample them with their feet, and turning against the donor, rend him with their tusks. The connexion with the foregoing and following verses is this: "*Judge not,*" &c.; "*attempt not the correction of others, when you need it far more yourselves:*" still, "*be not such mere children, as not to distinguish the characters of those with whom you have to do. Give not that which is holy to dogs,*" &c. Then, as a humble hearer might be disposed to reply, '*If this last be a measure of the* divine *dealings, what bounties can I expect at God's hand?*' (This, to which Stier objects, R. Jesu, i. 233, edn. 2, I must still hold to be the immediate connexion, as shewn by the *knowing how to give good gifts,* and the instances adduced below.)—(ver. 7), '*Ask of God, and He will give to each of you: for this is His own will, that you shall obtain by asking* (ver. 8),—*good things, good for each in his place and degree* (vv. 10, 11), *not unwholesome or unfitting things.* Therefore (ver. 12) *do ye the same to others, as ye wish to be done, and as God does, to you: viz. give that which is good for each, to each, not judging uncharitably on the one hand, nor casting pearls before swine on the other.*'

7.] The three similitudes are all to be understood of *prayer*, and form a climax: ἀπὸ δὲ τοῦ κρούειν τὸ μετὰ σφοδρότητος προσιέναι καὶ μετὰ θερμῆς διανοίας ἐδήλωσε. Chrys. Hom. xxiii. 4, p. 289.

8.] The only *limitation* to this promise, which, under various forms, is several times repeated by our Lord, is furnished in vv. 9—11, and in James iv. 3, αἰτεῖτε καὶ οὐ λαμβάνετε· διότι **κακῶς** αἰτεῖσθε.

9.] There are two questions here, the first of which is broken off, after an anacoluthon. See ch. xii. 11. The similitude of ἄρτος and λίθος also appears in ch. iv. 3. Luke (xi. 12) adds the egg and the scorpion. **11. πονηροί**] i. e. in comparison with God. It is not necessary to suppose a rebuke conveyed here, but only a general declaration of the corruption and infirmity of man. Augustine remarks, in accordance with this view, that the persons now addressed are the same who had been taught to say '*Our Father*' just now. ταῦτα δὲ ἔλεγεν οὐ διαβάλλων τὴν ἀνθρωπίνην φύσιν οὐδὲ κακίζων τὸ γένος· ἀλλὰ πρὸς ἀντιδιαστολὴν τῆς ἀγαθότητος τῆς αὐτοῦ. Chrys. Hom. xxiii. 4, p. 290. Stier remarks, "This saying seems to me the strongest *dictum probans* for original sin in the whole of the Holy Scriptures." R. J. i. 236. **ἀγαθά**] principally, *His Holy Spirit*, Luke xi. 13.

[o] αὐτόν. 12 πάντα οὖν ὅσα ἂν θέλητε ἵνα [p] ποιῶσιν ὑμῖν BCEGK LMSUV XΔΠℵ 1. 33
οἱ ἄνθρωποι, οὕτως καὶ ὑμεῖς [p] ποιεῖτε αὐτοῖς· οὗτος γάρ
[q] ἐστιν ὁ νόμος καὶ οἱ προφῆται.
13 [r] Εἰςέλθατε διὰ τῆς [s] στενῆς πύλης· ὅτι [tu] πλατεῖα
ἡ πύλη καὶ [tv] εὐρύχωρος ἡ ὁδὸς ἡ [w] ἀπάγουσα εἰς τὴν
[x] ἀπώλειαν, καὶ πολλοί εἰσιν οἱ [r] εἰςερχόμενοι δι᾽ αὐτῆς·
14 ὅτι [s] στενὴ ἡ πύλη καὶ [y] τεθλιμμένη ἡ ὁδὸς ἡ [w] ἀπ-

p Luke i. 49. Gen. xx. 9.
q = ch. xii. 48. 1 Thess. iv. 3.
r ch. xix. 24. Luke xiii. 24. John x. 1, 2, 9.
s Luke xiii. 24 only. Prov. xxiii. 27.
t Isa. xxxiii. 21.
u here only. Neh. vii. 4. (-τεῖα, ch. vi. 5. -τύνειν, ch. xxiii. 5. -τος, Eph. iii. 18.)
v here only. Ps. ciii. 25.
w = here (bis) only. (1 Cor. xii. 2.) see Prov. vii. 27.
x John xvii. 12. Acts viii. 20 al. Jer. xxvi. (xlvi.) 21.
y Mark iii. 9 reff.‡

12. om *ουν* (*beginning of pericope*) Lℵ^1(ins ℵ^2) 73. 127^1 Scr's v evv-P-z vulg lat-*c* *ff*$_1$ *l* Syr arm. for *αν*, *εαν* Cℵ [evv-y-z$_1$]. **ποιουσιν** C^{1}L. om *ουτως* L(but has *ουτως* for *ουτος*, so X) 61. 243 Scr's ev-x vulg lat-*c* *ff*$_1$ *l* syr-cu Chr(so in the mss).
13. (*εισελθατε*, so BCLΔℵ. (33 def.)) om *η πυλη* ℵ^1(ins ℵ^2) forj lat-*a b c h k* Clem$_2$ Orig$_4$[and int$_1$] Eus Cypr Arnob Hil Lucif$_2$ Ambr Jer Gaud Juv spec. om *εισιν* ℵ^1(ins ℵ^2) sah. for *εισερχ.*, *πορευομενοι* ℵ^{3a}(appy: but obliterated and txt left) 1(Treg) [*εισπορ.* L].
14. for *οτι*, *τι* (*appears to have been at first a clerical error, then retained, as it was imagined it might mean* 'quam.' *See note*) B^{2}CLℵ$^{2 \text{ or } 3a}$ 1^1 rel latt syrr syr-cu goth æth arm-zoh Ephr Pallad Phot Thl Euthym Chrysoc Cypr Jer Aug Fulg: txt B^1(sic) Xℵ^1 1^2 copt sah-mnt arm-mss Orig Gaud$_1$ spec. add *δε* B sah. om *η πυλη* Scr's p lat-*a*(appy) *h k* Orig$_7$(ins$_1$) Hipp Clem hom-Cl Eus Cypr Ambr$_1$ Aug$_2$ Jer Gaud$_1$ Leo spec.

The same argument *à fortiori* is used by our Lord in the parable of the unjust judge, Luke xviii. 6, 7. **12.**] Trench (Serm. Mount, p. 143) has noticed Augustine's refutation of the sneer of infidels (such as Gibbon's against this precept), that some of our Lord's sayings have been before written by heathen authors. (See examples in Wetst. ad loc.) 'Dixit hoc Pythagoras, dixit hoc Plato .... Propterea si inventus fuerit aliquis eorum hoc dixisse quod dixit et Christus, gratulamur illi, non sequimur illum. Sed prior fuit ille quam Christus. Si quis vera loquitur, prior est quam ipsa Veritas! O homo, attende Christum, non quando ad te venerit, sed quando te fecerit.' Enarr. in Ps. cxl. 6, § 19, vol. iv. pt. ii. **ουν** is the inference indeed from the preceding eleven verses, but *immediately* from the *δώσει ἀγαθὰ τοῖς αἰτοῦσιν αὐτόν* just said,—and thus closes this section of the Sermon with a lesson similar to the last verse of ch. v., which is, indeed, the ground-tone of the whole Sermon—'Be ye like unto God.' **οὕτως**, viz., *after the pattern of* *ὅσα ἄν*: not = *ταῦτα*, because what might suit *us*, might not suit others. We are to think what we should like done to *us*, and then apply that rule to our dealings with others: viz., by doing to them what we have reason to suppose *they would like done to them.* This is a most important distinction, and one often overlooked in the interpretation of this golden maxim.

13—27.] THE CONCLUSION OF THE DISCOURSE:—*setting forth more strongly and personally the dangers of hypocrisy,* both in *being led aside by hypocritical teachers,* and in *our own inner life.* The *πύλη* stands at the end of the *ὁδός*, as in the remarkable parallel in the Table of Cebes, c. 16: *οὐκοῦν ὁρᾷς θύραν τινὰ μικράν, καὶ ὁδόν τινα πρὸ τῆς θύρας, ἥτις οὐ πολὺ ὀχλεῖται, ἀλλ᾽ ὀλίγοι πάνυ πορεύονται: . . . . αὕτη ἐστὶν ἡ ὁδὸς ἡ ἄγουσα πρὸς τὴν ἀληθινὴν παιδείαν.* **14.**] **ὅτι** gives a second reason, on which that in ver. 13 depends: **strive, &c., for broad is, &c., because narrow is, &c.** The *reason why* the way to destruction is so broad, is *because so few find their way into the narrow path of life.* This is not merely an arbitrary assignment of the *ὅτι*, but there is a deep meaning in it. The reason why so many perish is not that it is so ordained by God, who will have all to come to the knowledge of the truth,—but because so few will come to Christ, that they may have life; and the rest perish in their sins. See notes on ch. xxv. 41. The reading *τί* (adopted by Lachmann, Tregelles, Meyer, De Wette) will not bear the signification commonly assigned to it, '*How narrow is the gate?*' And the interrogative meaning (Meyer) is inconsistent with *ὀλίγοι εἰσίν*, which follows. **τεθλιμμένη, restricted,—crushed in,** in breadth: i. e. as Clem. Alex. Strom. v. 5 (31), p. 664 P, . . . *τὴν μὲν . . . στενὴν κ. τεθλιμμένην τὴν κατὰ τὰς ἐντολὰς κ. ἀπαγορεύσεις περιεσταλμένην, τὴν δὲ ἐναντίαν*

ἄγουσα εἰς τὴν ζωήν, καὶ ὀλίγοι εἰσὶν οἱ εὑρίσκοντες
αὐτήν. 15 [z] προσέχετε [δὲ] [z] ἀπὸ τῶν [a] ψευδοπροφητῶν,
[b] οἵτινες ἔρχονται πρὸς ὑμᾶς ἐν [c] ἐνδύμασιν προβάτων,
ἔσωθεν δέ εἰσιν [de] λύκοι [df] ἅρπαγες. 16 ἀπὸ τῶν [g] καρπῶν
αὐτῶν [h] ἐπιγνώσεσθε αὐτούς. [i] μήτι [k] συλλέγουσιν ἀπὸ
[l] ἀκανθῶν [m] σταφυλὰς ἢ ἀπὸ [n] τριβόλων [o] σῦκα; 17 οὕτω
πᾶν δένδρον [p] ἀγαθὸν [g] καρποὺς [r] καλοὺς [q] ποιεῖ· τὸ δὲ
[s] σαπρὸν δένδρον [g] καρποὺς [t] πονηροὺς [q] ποιεῖ. 18 οὐ
δύναται δένδρον [p] ἀγαθὸν [g] καρποὺς [t] πονηροὺς [g] ποιεῖν,
οὐδὲ δένδρον [s] σαπρὸν καρποὺς [r] καλοὺς [q] ποιεῖν. 19 πᾶν
δένδρον μὴ [q] ποιοῦν [g] καρπὸν [r] καλὸν [u] ἐκκόπτεται καὶ
εἰς πῦρ βάλλεται. 20 [v] ἄρα [v] γε ἀπὸ τῶν [g] καρπῶν αὐτῶν [h] ἐπιγνώσεσθε αὐτούς. 21 Οὐ πᾶς ὁ λέγων μοι Κύριε

Z σταφυλ.... BCEGK LMSUV XZΔΠℵ 1. 33

z ch. x. 17. xvi. 6, 11, 12. Luke xii. 1. xx. 46. Lev. xxii. 2. Sir. xvii. 14.
a = ch. xxiv. 11, 24 ‖ Mk. 1 John iv. 1. Jer. xxxiv. (xxvii.) 9.
b = ch. xvi. 28. xxi. 41. xxiii. 27. xxv. 1 al. Ps. lxiii. 3.
c ch. vi. 25, 28 reff.
d Gen. xlix. 27.
e ch. x. 16. Luke x. 3. John x. 12 bis. Acts xx. 29 only. Zeph. iii. 3.
f Luke xviii. 11 reff.
g ch. iii. 8 reff.
h Luke xxiv. 16, 31. Gen. xxxvii. 32.
i ch. xii. 23. xxvi. 22, 25 ‖ Mk. John iv. 29 al. Mal. iii. 8 Bℵ[1].
k ch. xiii. 28, &c. Luke vi. 44 only. Cant. vi. 1.
l ch. xiii. 7, &c. ‖ xxvii. 29. Luke vi. 44. John xix. 2. Heb. vi. 8 only. Gen. iii. 18.
m Luke vi. 44. Rev. xiv. 18 only. Gen. xl. 10, 11.
n Heb. vi. 8 only. Gen. iii. 18. Prov. xxii. 5. Hos. x. 8 (2 Kings xii. 31) only.
o Mark xi. 13. Luke vi. 44. James iii. 12 only. 4 Kings xx. 7. (-κῆ, ch. xxi. 9.)
p = Luke viii. 8. Exod. iii. 8.
q = ch. iii. 8, 10. Isa. v. 2, 4.
r = ch. iii. 10. xii. 33. xiii. 8, &c.
s ch. xii. 33 bis. xiii. 48. Luke vi. 43 bis. Eph. iv. 29 only †.
t = ch. vi. 23 reff.
u = ch. iii. 10 reff.
v = ch. xvii. 26. Acts xi. 18 (xvii. 27) only. Gen. xxvi. 9.

15. om δε Bℵ ev-y 435 latt(exc *f*) Syr syr-cu sah æth arm Just Ath Chr Hil Lucif Aug.

16. rec **σταφυλην**, with L rel æth arm Lucif [Aug_1]: txt Bℵ **1**. 118. 209 latt syrr syr-cu goth [Bas] Chr Tert Hil [Ambr Aug_1]. (Z 33 defective, C [1]coptt doubtful.)

17. καρπ. ποιει καλ. B: καλ. ποι. καρπ. Δ. (*Inversions for emphasis.*)

18. [B does not, as the Bentley collation alleges, ins ει before ου.] for 1st **ποιειν**, **ενεγκειν** B $Orig_2$ Dial (txt rewritten by ℵ[1]): for 2nd ποιειν, ενεγκειν ℵ[1](txt ℵ[2·3a]) $Orig_1$.

19. aft παν ins ουν (*from ch* iii. 10 *and* ‖ *Luke*) C[2]LZ 33 lat-*b c* g_1 *h* syr-cu sah; *enim* lat-*f* Iren-int, *autem* lat-g_2: om BC[1]ℵ rel vulg lat-*a* $ff_{1.2}$ *k* syrr copt goth æth arm Hipp Cypr Lucif.

20. for απο, εκ C latt Lucif Aug.

τὴν εἰς ἀπώλειαν φέρουσαν, πλατεῖαν κ. εὐρύχωρον, ἀκώλυτον ἡδοναῖς τε καὶ θυμῷ . . . . **15.**] The connexion (with δέ) is as Chrys. Hom. xxiii. 6, p. 292: καὶ γὰρ πρὸς τῷ στενὴν εἶναι, πολλοὶ καὶ οἱ ὑποσκελίζοντες τὴν ἐκεῖσε φέρουσάν εἰσιν ὁδόν:—*strive to enter, &c.*: *but* (**δέ**, not *accordingly*, as Webst. and Wilk.) *be not misled by persons who pretend to guide you into it, but will not do so in reality.* These **ψευδοπρ.**, directly, refer to the false prophets who were soon to arise, to deceive, if possible, even the very elect, ch. xxiv. 24; and, indirectly, to all such false teachers in all ages. In **ἐνδύμασι προβ.** there may be allusion to the prophetic dress, ch. iii. 4: but most probably it only means that, in order to deceive, they put on the garb and manners of the sheep themselves. **16.**] The **καρποί** are both their corrupt doctrines and their vicious practices, as contrasted with the outward shews of almsgiving, prayer, and fasting, their sheep's clothing to deceive. 'Quærimus fructus caritatis, invenimus spinas dissentionis.' Aug. Enarr. in Ps. cxlix. 1, § 2, vol. iv. pt. ii. See James iii. 12: ch. xii. 33, 34. **17. σαπρόν**] See also ch. xiii. 48. From these two verses, 17, 18, the Manichæans defended their heresy of the two natures, good and bad: but Augustine answers them that such cannot possibly be their meaning, as it is entirely contrary to the whole scope of the passage (see for example ver. 13), and adds, 'Mala ergo arbor fructus bonos facere non potest; sed ex mala fieri bona potest, ut bonos fructus ferat.' Cont. Adimant. c. 26, vol. viii. On the other hand, these verses were his weapon against the shallow Pelagian scheme, which would look at men's deeds apart from the living Root in man out of which they grew, and suppose that man's unaided will is capable of good. Trench, Serm. on the Mount, p. 150. See also Orig. in Matt. Comm. Series, § 116, vol. iii. p. 914. **ἐπιγν.**, more than simply γνώσεσθε: '*ye shall thoroughly know them*:' see 1 Cor. xiii. 12. **21.**] *The doom of the hypocritical false prophets*

w ch. xii. 50. xxi. 31. Mark iii. 35. (Luke xii. 47.) John iv. 34 al. Isa. xlviii. 14.
x = ch. xxiv. 36 ‖ Mk. Luke x. 12. xvii. 26. 2 Thess. i. 10. 2 Tim. i. 12, 18. iv. 8.
y (Mark ix. 38 v. r.) James v. 10. Lev. xix. 12.
z Jer. xxxiv. 14 (12) Bℵ. (xxvii. 15 F [so A] ἐπὶ τῷ ὀν.)

κύριε εἰςελεύσεται εἰς τὴν βασιλείαν τῶν οὐρανῶν, ἀλλ' ὁ
w ποιῶν τὸ w θέλημα τοῦ πατρός μου τοῦ ἐν τοῖς οὐρανοῖς.
22 πολλοὶ ἐροῦσίν μοι ἐν x ἐκείνῃ τῇ x ἡμέρᾳ Κύριε κύριε, οὐ
yz τῷ σῷ yz ὀνόματι z ἐπροφητεύσαμεν καὶ y τῷ σῷ y ὀνόματι
a δαιμόνια a ἐξεβάλομεν καὶ y τῷ σῷ y ὀνόματι b δυνάμεις
πολλὰς ἐποιήσαμεν; 23 καὶ τότε c ὁμολογήσω αὐτοῖς ὅτι
οὐδέποτε ἔγνων ὑμᾶς· d ἀποχωρεῖτε ἀπ' ἐμοῦ οἱ ef ἐργαζόμενοι τὴν fg ἀνομίαν. 24 h Πᾶς οὖν h ὅςτις ik ἀκούει i μου
τοὺς i λόγους τούτους καὶ k ποιεῖ αὐτούς, * l ὁμοιώσω * αὐ-

BCEGK LMSUV XZΔΠℵ 1. 33

a ch. ix. 33, 34. x. 8 al. fr. Mt. Mk. L. b = ch. xiii. 54, 58. Acts ii. 22. Gal. iii. 5 al.‡ c = John i. 20. Heb. xi. 13. 2 Macc. vi. 6. d Luke ix. 39. Acts xiii. 13 only. Jer. xxvi. (xlvi.) 5. 2 Macc. iv. 33 only. e = ch. xxvi. 10. James ii. 9 al. Ps. xiv. 2. xxvii. 3. f Ps. v. 6. vi. 8. xiii. 4 al. g ch. xiii. 41. 2 Cor. vi. 14 al. Exod. xxxiv. 9. h ch. x. 32. Acts iii. 23. Col. iii. 17. i constr. acc., ch. x. 14. xii. 19. xiii. 20, &c. ‖. gen. and acc., see note. k Ezek. xxxiii. 31, 32. l Mark iv. 30. Luke vii. 31 al. Lam. ii. 13.

21. **τα** *θεληματα* ℵ^1(txt ℵ^2). rec om *τοις*, with L rel Orig [Cyr$_1$ Bas Chr]: ins BCZℵ **1.** 33 Scr's a p Just Hipp [Cyr$_2$]. aft *ουρανοις* add *ουτος εισελευσεται εις την βασιλειαν των ουρανων* (*supplementary gloss*) C^2 33 latt syr-cu Cypr Hil Jer.

22. for *οὐ τῷ*, *ουτως* C. aft *δαιμ.* ins *πολλα* ℵ^1(ℵ^2 disapproving). *εξεβαλλομεν* Lℵ^1(txt ℵ^{3a}) 299 [Damasc$_1$].

24. om *τουτους* B(but has it in marg *a prima manu*) 242-3-7. 301 lat-*a* g_1 *k* syr-jer goth Cypr Hil Epiph spec. * ὁμοιωθήσεται (*cf ver* 26) BZℵ **1.** 33 mss-mentd-by-Euthym vulg(*assimilabitur*) lat-*ff*$_1$ g_1 *l* syr-mg sah æth arm Orig Epiph [Bas$_1$] Chr Cyr Cypr Ambr: *similis est* lat-*a b c*: *ομοιωσω αυτον* C rel lat-*f h k* syrr syr-cu

introduces the doom of all hypocrites, and brings on the solemn close of the whole, in which the hypocrite and the true disciple are parabolically compared.

Observe that here the Lord sets Himself forth as the Judge in the great day, and at the same time speaks not of *τὸ θέλ.* **μου**, but *τὸ θέλ.* **τοῦ πατρός μου**: an important and invaluable doctrinal landmark in this very opening of His ministry in the first Gospel. **οὐ πᾶς** is not here *'no one,'* as some (Elsner, Fritzsche) have interpreted it. That meaning would require *πᾶς . . . . . οὐκ εἰσελεύσεται.* The context must rule the meaning of such wide words as **λέγει.** Here it is evidently used of mere lip homage; but in *οὐδεὶς δύναται εἰπεῖν Κύριος Ἰησοῦς εἰ μὴ ἐν πνεύματι ἁγίῳ*, 1 Cor. xii. 3, the "*saying*" has the deeper meaning of a genuine heartfelt confession. To seek for discrepancies in passages of this kind implies a predisposition to find them: and is to treat Holy Scripture with less than that measure of candour which we give to the writings of one another. **22.**] **ἐν ἐκείνῃ τῇ ἡμέρᾳ** perhaps refers to ver. 19: or it may be the expression so common in the Prophets of *the great day of the Lord*: e. g. Isa. ii. 20; xxv. 9, al. fr. So the Jews called the great day of judgment "that day," see Schöttgen, Hor. i. p. 82. **τῷ σῷ ὀνόματι** perhaps = **ἐν τ. σ. ὀν.**, *jussu et auctoritate tua*, but better **by thy Name**, that name having, as Meyer, filled out our belief and been the object of our confession of faith. The dative in this case is *instrumental*, cf. Winer, § 31. 7. **ἐπροφητ. preached**, not necessarily foretold future events: 1 Cor. xii. 10, and note. On **δαιμ. ἐξ.** see note on ch. viii. 32. **23.**] As the words now stand, **ὅτι** is merely recitative, and cannot be (Meyer) '*because*,' belonging to *ἀποχωρ.* Such an arrangement would be unprecedented. Orig., Chrys., Cypr., &c., placed *ὅτι οὐδ. ἔγν. ὑμ.* *after* *ἀποχ.*, &c., in which case the meaning '*for, because*,' would be right. See Luke xiii. 25—27. **ὁμολογήσω** is here a remarkable word, as a statement of the simple truth of facts, as opposed to the false colouring and self-deceit of the hypocrites—'I will tell them the plain truth.' **οὐδέποτε ἔγ. ὑμ.**, i. e., in the sense in which it is said, John x. 14, *γινώσκω τὰ ἐμὰ καὶ γινώσκομαι ὑπὸ τῶν ἐμῶν.* Neither the preaching Christ, nor doing miracles in His Name, are infallible signs of being His genuine servants, but only the devotion of life to God's will which *this knowledge* brings about. **24.**] **πᾶς οὖν ὅςτις** is a pendent nominative, of which examples are found in the classics, especially in Plato: so *Περσέφαττα δέ, πολλοὶ μὲν καὶ τοῦτο φοβοῦνται τὸ ὄνομα.* Cratyl. p. 464 c. See also ib. p. 403 A: Gorg. p. 474 E. Kühner, Gramm. ii. § 508. Notice the **ὅςτις**

τὸν ἀνδρὶ [m] φρονίμῳ, [n] ὅστις [op] ᾠκοδόμησεν αὐτοῦ τὴν
οἰκίαν ἐπὶ τὴν [p] πέτραν. 25 καὶ [q] κατέβη ἡ [r] βροχὴ καὶ
ἦλθον οἱ [s] ποταμοὶ καὶ [tu] ἔπνευσαν οἱ [t] ἄνεμοι καὶ [v] προς-
έπεσαν τῇ οἰκίᾳ ἐκείνῃ, καὶ οὐκ ἔπεσεν· [w] τεθεμελίωτο γὰρ
ἐπὶ τὴν πέτραν. 26 καὶ πᾶς ὁ [ik] ἀκούων [i] μου τοὺς [ik] λόγους τούτους καὶ μὴ [k] ποιῶν αὐτοὺς [l] ὁμοιωθήσεται ἀνδρὶ
[x] μωρῷ, [n] ὅστις [o] ᾠκοδόμησεν αὐτοῦ τὴν οἰκίαν ἐπὶ τὴν
[y] ἄμμον. 27 καὶ [q] κατέβη ἡ [r] βροχὴ καὶ ἦλθον οἱ [s] ποταμοὶ καὶ [tu] ἔπνευσαν οἱ [t] ἄνεμοι καὶ [z] προσέκοψαν τῇ οἰκίᾳ
ἐκείνῃ, καὶ ἔπεσεν· καὶ ἦν ἡ [a] πτῶσις αὐτῆς μεγάλη.

..επνευσαν οι G.

Γ τουτους... BCEKL MSUVX ZΓΔΠℵ 1. 33

m ch. x. 16. xxiv. 45. xxv. 2, &c. Prov. xiv. 17.
n = ver. 15 reff.
o ch. xxi. 33. Luke iv. 29. vi. 48, 49 al. Jer. xxii. 13, 14.
p ch. xvi. 18.
q = Luke viii. 23. Rev. xvi. 21. Ps. lxxi. 6.
r here (bis) only. Ps. lxvii. 9. civ. 32 only. (βρέχειν, ch. v. 45.)
s = Luke vi. 48, 49. Sir. xl. 13.
t here bis. John vi. 18. Rev. vii. 1. Sir. xliii. 20.
u as above (t). Luke xii. 55. John iii. 8. Acts xxvii. 40 only. Ps. cxlvii. 18 (7).
v = here only (Mark iii. 11 reff.). προσπεσόντες συντεταγμένοι ἀσυντάκτοις, Diod. Sic. ii. 26.
w (Luke vi. 48 v. r.) Eph. iii. 18. Col. i. 23. Heb. i. 10. 1 Pet. v. 10 only. Josh. vi. 26.
x ch. v. 22. xxiii. 17, 19. xxv. 2, 38. 1 Cor. i. 25, 27 al4. Mt. Paul only. Isa. xxxii. 5, 6.
y Rom. ix. 27, from Isa. x. 22. Heb. xi. 12. Rev. xii. 18. xx. 8 only. Gen. xiii. 16.
z ch. iv. 6 reff. Isa. iii. 5.
a Luke ii. 34 only. Ezek. xxvi. 15.

copt goth Phot-in-schol Cypr Arnob Hil Lucif. (Aug has both.) οικοδομησεν C[1] (so also in ver 26). rec την οικιαν bef αυτου (*more usual order*), with L rel lat-*a b c* $Orig_1$ [Bas] Cypr Hil Lucif: txt BCZℵ 1. 33 [$Orig_2$].

25. ηλθαν B (but -θον ver 27). (προσεπεσαν, so BCEXZΔℵ[2](-σεν ℵ[1]) 1 syr-mg-gr Chr Cyr Damasc. Lachm reads προσέπαισαν, taking the ε of text as an itacism for αι—*offenderunt* lat-*a b*, *impegerunt* lat-*c* Cypr Lucif.)

26. rec την οικιαν bef αυτου (*as ver* 24), with C rel lat-*a b c* Orig [Bas_1] Cypr Lucif: txt BZℵ 1. ψαμμον ℵ[3a](? but corrd) 41 [Chr Thl].

27. ηλθαν ℵ. om και επνευσαν οι ανεμοι (*homœotel*) ℵ[1](ins ℵ-corr[1]). for προσεκοψαν, προσερρηξαν CM 1 Bas Chr: προσεκρουσαν 13. 243: προσεπεσον Scr's g p 63 syr-mg sah goth: *irruerunt* vulg: *offenderunt* lat-*a b*: *impegerunt* lat-*c* Cypr: *inliserunt* Lucif: txt BZℵ rel.

both times, not merely ὅς. ὅς identifies only: ὅστις classifies. **μου** may be **from me**, as in Acts i. 4 ref.: and the τούτους makes this perhaps more probable than the ordinary rendering "*these words of mine*." **τοὺς λόγους τούτους** seems to bind together the Sermon, and preclude, as indeed does the whole structure of the Sermon, the supposition that these last chapters are merely a collection of sayings uttered at different times. **ὁμοιώσω αὐτόν** (or, **ὁμοιωθήσεται**)] Meyer and Tholuck take this word to signify, not 'I will *compare him*,' but 'I will *make him like*,' viz. ἐν ἐκείνῃ τῇ ἡμέρᾳ, as in ch. vi. 8: Rom. ix. 29. But it is, perhaps, more in analogy with the usage of the Lord's discourses to understand it, **I will compare him**: so ὁμοιώσω, ch. xi. 16: Luke xiii. 18, and reff.

25.] This similitude must not be pressed to an allegorical or symbolical meaning in its details, e.g. so that the rain, floods, and winds should mean three distinct kinds of temptation: but the Rock, as signifying Him who spoke this, is of too frequent use in Scripture for us to overlook it here: cf. 2 Sam. xxii. 2 (Ps. xviii. 2), 32, 47; xxiii. 3: Ps. xxviii. 1: xxxi. 2, al. fr.; lxi. 2: Isa. xxvi. 4 (Heb.); xxxii. 2; xliv. 8 (Heb.): 1 Cor. x. 4, &c. He founds his house on a rock, who, hearing the words of Christ, brings his heart and life into accordance with His expressed will, and is thus by faith in union with Him, founded on Him. Whereas he who merely hears His words, but does them not, has never dug down to the rock, nor become united with it, nor has any stability in the hour of trial.

In **τὴν πέτραν . . τὴν ἄμμον,**—the articles are categorical, importing that these two were usually found in the country where the discourse was delivered;—in **ἡ βροχή, οἱ ποταμοί, οἱ ἄνεμοι,** the same, implying that such trials of the stability of a house were common. In the whole of the similitude, reference is probably made to the prophetic passage Isa. xxviii. 15—18. **τεθεμελίωτο**] The N. T. writers usually omit the augment in the pluperfect: so πεποιήκεισαν, Mark xv. 7; ἐκβεβλήκει, xvi. 9; μεμενήκεισαν, 1 John ii. 19, al. fr. This is also done occasionally by Herodotus, and by Attic prose writers, where euphony is served by it. See Herod. i. 122; iii 42; ix. 22: and Winer, § 12. 9. **27. μεγάλη**] All the greater, because such an one as here supposed is a *professed dis-*

b ch. xxii. 33. Mark i. 22. Luke ii. 48. Acts xiii. 12 al. Eccl. vii. 17. Wisd. xiii. 4. 2 Macc. vii. 12 only.
c = Mark i. 22 reff.
d constr., Luke i. 10, 20 al. Jer. xxxiii. (xxvi.) 20.

28 Καὶ ἐγένετο ὅτε ἐτέλεσεν ὁ Ἰησοῦς τοὺς λόγους τούτους, BCEKL
[b]ἐξεπλήσσοντο οἱ ὄχλοι [c]ἐπὶ τῇ διδαχῇ αὐτοῦ· 29 [d]ἦν MSUVX ZΓΔΠℵ
γὰρ διδάσκων αὐτοὺς ὡς [e]ἐξουσίαν [e]ἔχων, καὶ οὐχ ὡς 1. 33
οἱ γραμματεῖς αὐτῶν.
VIII. 1 Καταβάντι δὲ [f]αὐτῷ ἀπὸ τοῦ ὄρους ἠκολούθησαν [f]αὐτῷ ὄχλοι πολλοί· 2 καὶ ἰδοὺ [g]λεπρὸς προσ-

e ch. ix. 6 ||. Mark i. 22. Luke xii. 5. xix. 17. John x. 18 bis. xix. 10 bis, 11. Acts ix. 14 al. 1 Macc. x. 35.
f constr., vv. (5 v. r.) 23, 28. ch. ix. 27. xxi. 23. Mark v. 2 al.
g || Mk. ch. x. 8. xi. 5 || L. xxvi. 6 || Mk. Luke iv. 27. xvii. 12 only. Lev. xiv. 2, 3.

28. rec συνετελεσεν (*see Luke* iv. 13), with L rel, *consumm.* latt: txt BC Z(appy) Γℵ 1. 33 Orig Chr. εξεπληττοντο ℵ[1](txt ℵ[2]) Scr's b [Eus_2]. επι τη διδ. αυ. bef οι οχλοι ℵ[1](txt ℵ[2.3]).—om οι οχλ. sah.

29. rec om αυτων (*see Mark* i. 22), with C[1]L rel lat-*b* goth: ins BC[3]KΔΠ[1.3]ℵ 1. 33 vulg lat-*a c f* $g_{1.2}$ *h l* syrr syr-cu syr-jer coptt æth arm Eus_2 Aug. (Z def.) at end ins και οι φαρισαιοι C 33 latt syrr syr-cu arm-usc Eus_1 Hil.

Chap. VIII. 1. for καταβαντι δε αυτω, και καταβαντος αυτου Z lat-*a b c* g_1 *h* syr-cu æth Hil_2: καταβαντος δε αυτου BCℵ[2] 33 vulg lat-*f* ff_1 syrr coptt goth arm: txt ℵ[1] rel (of these V[1](but corrd[1]) Δ lat-*k* om αυτω.)

ciple—ἀκούων τοὺς λόγους—and therefore would have the further to fall in case of apostasy.

29. ἦν διδάσκων] The assertion is spread more widely, by this resolved imperfect, over His whole course of teaching. Chrysostom's comment is, οὐ γὰρ εἰς ἕτερον ἀναφέρων, ὡς ὁ προφήτης καὶ ὁ Μωυσῆς, ἔλεγεν ἅπερ ἔλεγεν ἀλλὰ πανταχοῦ ἑαυτὸν ἐνδεικνύμενος εἶναι τὸν τὸ κῦρος ἔχοντα. καὶ γὰρ νομοθετῶν συνεχῶς προσετέθει Ἐγὼ δὲ λέγω ὑμῖν, καὶ τῆς ἡμέρας ἀναμιμνήσκων ἐκείνης, ἑαυτὸν ἐδείκνυ τὸν δικάζοντα εἶναι. Hom. xxv. 1, p. 306.

VIII. **1—4.**] Healing of a leper. Mark i. 40—45. Luke v. 12—14. We have now (in this and the following chapter), as it were a *solemn procession of miracles,* confirming the authority with which our Lord had spoken. ἀπὸ τῆς διδασκαλίας ἐπὶ τὰ θαύματα μεταβαίνει. ἐπεὶ γὰρ ὡς ἐξουσίαν ἔχων ἐδίδασκεν, ἵνα μὴ νομισθῇ κομπάζειν καὶ ἀλαζονεύεσθαι, δείκνυσι τὴν ἐξουσίαν αὐτοῦ καὶ ἐν τοῖς ἔργοις, καὶ βεβαιοῖ τοὺς λόγους ἀπὸ τῶν πράξεων. Euthym. **2.**] This same miracle is related by St. Luke without any mark of definiteness, either as to time or place,—**καὶ ἐγένετο, ἐν τῷ εἶναι αὐτὸν ἐν μιᾷ τῶν πόλεων . . . .** In this instance there is, and can be, no doubt that the transactions are identical: and this may serve us as a key-note, by which the less obvious and more intricate harmonies of these two narrations may be arranged. The plain assertion of the account in the text requires that the leper should have met our Lord on His descent from the mountain, while great multitudes were following Him. The accounts in St. Luke and St. Mark require no such fixed date. This narrative therefore fixes the occurrence. I conceive it highly probable that St. Matthew was himself a hearer of the Sermon, and one of those who followed our Lord at this time. From St. Luke's account, the miracle was performed in, or rather, perhaps, in the neighbourhood of, some city: what city, does not appear. As the leper is in all three accounts related to have *come* to Jesus (καὶ ἰδού implying it in Luke), he may have been outside the city, and have run into it to our Lord. **λεπρός**] The limits of a note allow of only an abridgment of the most important particulars relating to this disease. Read Levit. xiii. xiv. for the Mosaic enactments respecting it, and its nature and symptoms. See also Exod. iv. 6: Num. xii. 10: 2 Kings v. 27; xv. 5: 2 Chron. xxvi. 19, 21. The whole ordinances relating to leprosy were symbolical and typical. The disease was *not contagious:* so that the view which makes them mere sanitary regulations is out of the question. The fact of its non-contagious nature has been abundantly proved by learned men, and is evident from the Scripture itself: for the priests had continually to be in close contact with lepers, even to handling and examining them. We find Naaman, a leper, commanding the armies of Syria (2 Kings v. 1); Gehazi, though a leper, is conversed with by the king of Israel (2 Kings viii. 4, 5); and in the examination of a leper by the priest, if a man was *entirely* covered with leprosy, he was to be pronounced clean (Levit. xiii. 12, 13). The leper was not shut out from

ελθὼν προςεκύνει αὐτῷ λέγων Κύριε, ἐὰν θέλῃς, δύνασαί
με [h] καθαρίσαι. 3 καὶ [i] ἐκτείνας τὴν χεῖρα ἥψατο αὐτοῦ
λέγων Θέλω, [h] καθαρίσθητι. καὶ εὐθέως [h] ἐκαθαρίσθη

h ‖. ch. x. 8 al. Lev. xiii. 17. xiv. 31 al.
i ‖. ch. xii. 13 bis ‖, 49. Acts iv. 30. in N. T. always w. χείρ, exc. Acts xxvii. 30. Gen. viii. 9.

2. rec ελθων (*the* 1*st syllable of* προσελθων *being omd, from* λεπρος *preceding. This is more prob than that the* -προς *of* λεπρος *shd be mistaken for a prep in comp with* ελθων), with C rel latt Syr syr-cu copt [Did_1] Hil: txt BEMΔℵ 1 syr sah goth æth arm Chr Cyr Damasc Thl. (Z defective.)

3. aft χειρα ins αυτου $ℵ^{1.3}$(om $ℵ^2$) 124 Syr syr-cu. rec aft αυτου ins ο ιησους (*supplied for clearness*), with C^2L rel lat-*b h* syr arm Hil, and before ηψατο vulg lat-*a c f* $g_{1.2}$ Syr syr-cu: om BC^1 Z(appy) ℵ 1. 33 am lat-ff_1 *k* coptt goth æth. om ευθεως $ℵ^1$(ins $ℵ^2$). [εκαθεριςθη B^1ELXΠ[1].]

the synagogue (Lightfoot, vol. i. p. 513), nor from the Christian churches (Suicer, Thesaurus Patrum, under λεπρός). Besides, the analogy of the other uncleannesses under the Mosaic law, e. g. having touched the dead, having an issue, which are joined with leprosy (Num. v. 2), shews that sanitary caution was not the motive of these ceremonial enactments, but a far deeper reason. This disease was specially selected, as being the most loathsome and incurable of all, to represent the effect of the defilement of sin upon the once pure and holy body of man. "Leprosy was, indeed, nothing short of a living death, a poisoning of the springs, a corrupting of all the humours, of life; a dissolution, little by little, of the whole body, so that one limb after another actually decayed and fell away." (Trench on the Miracles, p. 213.) See Num. xii. 12. The leper was the type of one dead in sin: the same emblems are used in his misery as those of mourning for the dead: the same means of cleansing as for uncleanness through connexion with death, and which were never used except on these two occasions. Compare Num. xix. 6, 13, 18, with Levit. xiv. 4—7. All this exclusion and mournful separation imported the perpetual exclusion of the abominable and polluted from the true city of God, as declared Rev. xxi. 27, *οὐ μὴ εἰςέλθῃ εἰς αὐτὴν πᾶν κοινὸν καὶ ποιῶν βδέλυγμα καὶ ψεῦδος.* And David, when after his deadly sin he utters his prayer of penitence, 'Purge me with hyssop, and I shall be clean,' Ps. li. 7, doubtless saw in his own utter spiritual uncleanness, that of which the ceremonial uncleanness that was purged with hyssop was the type. Thus in the above-cited instances we find leprosy inflicted as the punishment of rebellion, lying, and presumption. 'I put the plague of leprosy in an house' (Levit. xiv. 34), 'Remember what the Lord thy God did to Miriam' (Deut. xxiv. 9), and other passages, point out this plague as a peculiar infliction from God. "The Jews termed it 'the finger of God,' and emphatically 'the stroke.' They said that it attacked first a man's house; and if he did not turn, his clothing; and then, if he persisted in sin, himself. So too, they said, that a man's true repentance was the one condition of his leprosy leaving him." Trench, p. 216. The Jews, from the prophecy Isa. liii. 4, had a tradition that the Messiah should be a leper. **προςεκύνει**] *πεσὼν ἐπὶ πρόσωπον,* Luke v. 12 (*γονυπετῶν,* Mark i. 40). These differences of expression are important. See beginning of note on this verse. **κύριε**] Not here merely a title of respect, but an expression of faith in Jesus as the Messiah. "This is the *right* utterance of *κύριε,* which will never be made in vain." Stier. When Miriam was a leper, *ἐβόησε Μωυσῆς πρὸς κύριον, λέγων Ὁ θεός, δέομαί σου, ἴασαι αὐτήν,* Num. xii. 13. **3. ἥψατο αὐτοῦ**] He who just now expansively fulfilled the law by *word and commands,* now does the same by *act and deed:* the law had forbidden the touching of the leper, Levit. v. 3. It was an act which stood on the same ground as the healing on the Sabbath, of which we have so many instances. So likewise the prophets Elijah and Elisha touched the dead in the working of a miracle on them (1 Kings xvii. 21: 2 Kings iv. 34). The same almighty power which suspends natural laws, supersedes ceremonial laws. Here is a noble example illustrating His own precept so lately delivered, 'Give to him that asketh thee.' Again, we can hardly forbear to recognize, in His touching the leper, a deed symbolic of His taking on him, touching, laying hold of, our nature. Compare Luke xiv. 4, *καὶ ἐπιλαβόμενος ἰάσατο αὐτόν,* with Heb. ii. 16, *σπέρματος Ἀβραὰμ ἐπιλαμβάνεται.* **θέλω**] 'Echo prompta ad fidem leprosi maturam.' Bengel ad loc. **ἐκαθ. αὐτ. ἡ λέπ.**] Luke's words

j Mark i. 42. Luke v. 12, 13 only. Lev. xiii. 2, 3.
k ‖ Mk. ch. xviii. 10. Heb. viii. 5, from Exod. xxv. 40. Rev. xix. 10. xxii. 9.

BCEKL MSUVX ZΓΔΠℵ 1. 33

αὐτοῦ ἡ [j] λέπρα. 4 καὶ λέγει αὐτῷ ὁ Ἰησοῦς [k] Ὅρα μηδενὶ εἴπῃς, ἀλλὰ ὕπαγε σεαυτὸν δεῖξον τῷ ἱερεῖ, καὶ [l] προςένεγκον τὸ [l] δῶρον ὃ [m] προςέταξεν Μωυσῆς, [n] εἰς [n] μαρτύριον αὐτοῖς.

5 Εἰςελθόντος δὲ αὐτοῦ εἰς Καφαρναοὺμ προςῆλθεν

l = ch. ii. 11. v. 23 al. fr. Num. xxxi. 50. m ch. i. 24 reff. Lev. xiv. 3, 4, 10. Lev. x. 1. n ‖. ch. x. 18 ‖. xxiv. 14 ‖. Heb. iii. 5. James v. 3. Josh. xxiv. 27.

4. for λεγει, ειπεν ℵ[1](txt ℵ[3a]). rec προσενεγκε (‖) with Lℵ rel: txt BC. (*offer* vulg Cypr Hil, *offeres* lat-*c*, *offers* lat-*a b*.—Z def.)

5. rec εισελθοντι, with C[2] F(Wetst) L rel Chr Thl Hil Op: txt BC[1]Zℵ 1. 33 syr copt æth arm.—rec (for αυτου) τω ιησου, with C[2]L (lat-*c*) Syr: αυτω F(Wetst) rel: txt BC[1]EZℵ.—*cum autem introisset* vulg, simly lat-*a b c* &c syr-cu goth Hil.

(ver. 13), ἡ λέπρα ἀπῆλθεν ἀπ' αὐτοῦ, are more strictly correct in construction. See also Mark i. 42. A curious instance of the theological littleness which has been shewn in treating our Lord's great acts of Divine Love, is cited here by Bp. Wordsw. from Ambrose: "Dicit 'volo' propter Photinum (who said that our Lord was a mere man): imperat propter Arium (who denied His equality with the Father): tangit propter Manichæum (who said that Christ had not human flesh, but was only a phantom)." **4. ὅρα μηδενὶ εἴπῃς**] Either (1) these words were a moral admonition, having respect to the state of the man (διδάσκων τὸ ἀκόμπαστον καὶ ἀφιλότιμον, Chrysost.), for the injunction to silence was not our Lord's uniform practice (see Mark v. 19, ‖ Luke), and in this case they were of lasting obligation, that the cleansed leper was not to make his healing a matter of boast hereafter; or (2) they were a cautionary admonition, only binding till he should have shewn himself to the priest, in order to avoid delay in this necessary duty, or any hindrance which might, if the matter should first be blazed abroad, arise to his being pronounced clean, through the malice of the priests; or (3), which I believe to be the true view, our Lord almost uniformly repressed the fame of His miracles, for the reason given in ch. xii. 15—21, that, in accordance with prophetic truth, He might be known as the Messiah not by wonder-working power, but by the great result of his work upon earth: οὐκ ἐρίσει, οὐδὲ κραυγάσει, οὐδὲ ἀκούσει τις ἐν ταῖς πλατείαις τὴν φωνὴν αὐτοῦ . . . , ἕως ἂν ἐκβάλῃ εἰς νῖκος τὴν κρίσιν. Thus the Apostles always refer primarily to the Resurrection, and only incidentally, if at all, to the wonders and signs. (Acts ii. 22—24; iii. 13—16.) These latter were tokens of power common to our Lord and his followers; but in His great conflict, ending in His victory, He trod the wine-press alone. **σεαυτὸν δεῖξ. κ.τ.λ.**] Read Levit. xiv. 1—32. This command has been used in support of the theory of satisfaction by priestly confession and penance. But even then (Trench on the Miracles, p. 221) the advocates of it are constrained to acknowledge that Christ alone is the cleanser. 'Ut Dominus ostenderet, quod non sacerdotali judicio, sed largitate divinæ gratiæ peccato emundatur, leprosum tangendo mundavit, et postea sacerdoti sacrificium ex lege offerre præcepit.' (Gratian de Pœnitentia, Dist. 1, c. 34, p. 1529 Migne.) 'Dominus leprosum sanitati prius per se restituit, deinde ad sacerdotes misit quorum judicio ostenderetur mundatus . . . quia etsi aliquis apud Deum sit solutus, non tamen in facie Ecclesiæ solutus habetur, nisi per judicium sacerdotis. In solvendis ergo culpis vel retinendis ita operatur sacerdos evangelicus et judicat, sicut olim legalis in illis qui contaminati erant lepra quæ peccatum signat.' (Peter Lombard. Sent. iv. dist. 18. 6, p. 887 Migne.) It is satisfactory to observe this drawing of parallels between the Levitical and (popularly so called) Christian priesthood, thus completely shewing the fallacy and untenableness of the whole system; all those priests being types, not of future human priests, but of Him, who abideth a Priest for ever in an unchangeable priesthood, and in Whom not a class of Christians, but *all* Christians, are priests unto God. **μαρτύριον αὐτοῖς**] **A testimony** both *to*, and *against* **them**: the *dativus* both *commodi* and *incommodi*. The man disobeyed the injunction, so that our Lord could no more enter the city openly: see Mark i. 45.

5—13.] Healing of the centurion's servant. Luke vii. 1—10, where we have a more detailed account of the former part of this miracle. On the chronological arrangement, see Prolegomena. The centurion did not himself *come* to our Lord, but sent elders of the Jews to Him, who

αὐτῷ [o] ἑκατόνταρχος [p] παρακαλῶν αὐτὸν
6 καὶ λέγων Κύριε, ὁ [q] παῖς μου [r] βέβληται ἐν τῇ οἰκίᾳ [s] παραλυτικός, [t] δεινῶς [u] βασανιζόμενος.
7 λέγει αὐτῷ Ἐγὼ ἐλθὼν θεραπεύσω αὐτόν.
8 * καὶ ἀποκριθεὶς ὁ [o] ἑκατόνταρχος ἔφη Κύριε, οὐκ εἰμὶ [v] ἱκανὸς ἵνα μου ὑπὸ τὴν [w] στέγην εἰσέλθῃς· ἀλλὰ μόνον εἰπὲ [x] λόγῳ, καὶ ἰαθήσεται ὁ [q] παῖς μου.
9 καὶ γὰρ ἐγὼ ἄνθρωπός εἰμι [y] ὑπὸ [y] ἐξουσίαν, ἔχων ὑπ' ἐμαυτὸν στρατιώτας, καὶ λέγω τούτῳ Πορεύθητι, καὶ πορεύεται, καὶ ἄλλῳ Ἔρχου, καὶ ἔρχεται· καὶ τῷ

...δεινως βασαν Z.

G ερχεται...

o Mt. L. (Gosp. & Acts) only. Exod. xviii. 21, 25 al. fr. = κεντυρίων, Mark xv. 39, 44, 45. -χος, ch. xxvii. 54. Luke vii. 6 al. -χης, ver. 13 reff.
p ver. 31. ch. xviii. 29. 1 Kings xxii. 4.
q Mt. L. (Gosp. & Acts) only, exc. John iv. 51. = ch. xiv. 2. Luke xii. 45. Gen. ix. 27.
r = ver. 14. ch. ix. 2. Mark vii. 30 (see Luke xvi. 20)‡.
s ch. iv. 24 reff.†
t Luke xi. 53 only. Job x. 16. xix. 11. Wisd. xvii. 3. xviii. 17 BℵN only. (-νός, 2 Kings i. 9.)
u Mark vi. 48. 2 Pet. ii. 8. Rev. xii. 2 al. 1 Kings v. 3.
v = w. ἵνα, || L. only
h. iii. 11 reff.)
w || L. Mark ii. 4 only. Gen. viii. 13. xix. 8 A(not F). Esdr. vi. 4 only.
x dat., see cts ii. 40. Gal. vi. 11.
y || L. only. (2 Macc. iii. 6.)

6. om κυριε ℵ (ins ℵ²) syr-cu.

7. rec ins και bef λεγει, with CLℵ rel vulg lat-*a c f ff*₁ syr copt goth æth : om B ev-47 am lat-*b h k* Syr syr-cu sah arm. rec aft αυτω ins ο ιησους, with C rel latt : ακολουθι μοι ℵ¹ : om Bℵ^3a lat-*k* copt.

8. * ἀποκριθεὶς δὲ Bℵ¹ 33 sah : και αποκριθεις C(appy) ℵ^2·3 rel latt syr copt goth æth. for εφη, ειπεν Cℵ¹(txt ℵ²) 33. rec λογον, with Γ lat-*ff*₁ *g*₁ æth : txt (*which can hardly here be introduced from || Luke, as the authorities are so weighty*) BC [F(Wetst)] ℵ rel Scr's-mss vulg lat *b c f h* syrr syr-cu coptt goth arm Orig Chr Euthym Ambr Aug.

9. aft υπο εξουσιαν ins τασσομενος (*from || Luke*) Bℵ Scr's q vulg-ed lat-*a b c g*₁,₂ *h* Chr₂ Hil : om C rel am(with fuld forj) lat-*f ff*₁ syrr goth æth arm [Chr₂]. (υπο εξ. is joined to the follg in U mss-mentd-by-Chr lat-*f* goth Iren-int Hil.)

recommended him to His notice as loving their nation, and having built them a synagogue. Such variations, the concise account making a man *fecisse per se* what the fuller one relates him *fecisse per alterum*, are common in all written and oral narrations. In such cases the fuller account is, of course, the stricter one. Augustine, answering Faustus the Manichæan, who wished, on account of the words of our Lord in ver. 11, to set aside the whole, and used this variation for that purpose, makes the remark, so important in these days, 'Quid enim, nonne talibus locutionibus humana plena est consuetudo . . . . quid ergo, cum legimus, obliviscimur quemadmodum loqui soleamus? An Scriptura Dei aliter nobiscum fuerat, quam nostro more, locutura?' Contra Faustum, xxxiii. 7, vol. viii. On the non-identity of this miracle with that in John iv. 46 ff., see note there.

5. ἑκατόνταρχος] He was a *Gentile*, see ver. 10, but one who was deeply attached to the Jews and their religion; possibly, though this is uncertain, a proselyte of the gate (no such term as σεβόμενος, φοβούμενος τὸν θ. is used of him, as commonly of these proselytes, Acts x. 2 al.).

6. ὁ παῖς] From Luke we learn that it was δοῦλος, ὃς ἦν αὐτῷ ἔντιμος. The centurion, perhaps, had *but one* slave, see ver. 9. 'Lucas hoc modo dubitationem prævenit, quæ subire poterat lectorum animos; scimus enim non habitos fuisse servos eo in pretio, ut de ipsorum vita tum anxii essent domini, nisi qui singulari industria vel fide vel alia virtute sibi gratiam acquisierant. Significat ergo Lucas non vulgare fuisse sordidumque mancipium, sed fidelem et raris dotibus ornatum servum, qui eximia gratia apud dominum polleret: hinc tanta illius vitæ cura et tam studiosa commendatio.' (Calvin in loc.)

8.] The centurion heard that the Lord was coming, Luke vii. 6, and sent friends to Him with this second and still humbler message. He knew and felt himself, as a heathen, to be out of the fold of God, a stranger to the commonwealth of Israel; and therefore unworthy to receive under his roof the Redeemer of Israel.

9.] The meaning is, 'I know how to obey, being *myself* under authority: and in turn know how others obey, having soldiers under me:' inferring, 'if then I, in my subordinate station of command, am obeyed, how much more Thou, who art over all, and whom diseases serve as their Master!' That this is the right interpretation, is shewn by our Lord's special commendation of his faith,

δούλῳ μου Ποίησον τοῦτο, καὶ ποιεῖ. 10 ἀκούσας δὲ ὁ
Ἰησοῦς [z] ἐθαύμασεν καὶ εἶπεν τοῖς ἀκολουθοῦσιν [a] Ἀμὴν
λέγω ὑμῖν, παρ' οὐδενὶ τοσαύτην πίστιν ἐν τῷ Ἰσραὴλ
εὗρον. 11 λέγω δὲ ὑμῖν ὅτι πολλοὶ [b] ἀπὸ [bc] ἀνατολῶν καὶ
[cd] δυσμῶν ἥξουσιν καὶ [e] ἀνακλιθήσονται μετὰ Ἀβραὰμ
καὶ Ἰσαὰκ καὶ Ἰακὼβ ἐν τῇ βασιλείᾳ τῶν οὐρανῶν·
12 οἱ δὲ [fg] υἱοὶ τῆς [g] βασιλείας [h] ἐκβληθήσονται εἰς τὸ
[i] σκότος τὸ [k] ἐξώτερον· ἐκεῖ ἔσται ὁ [lm] κλαυθμὸς καὶ ὁ
[ln] βρυγμὸς τῶν ὀδόντων. 13 καὶ εἶπεν ὁ Ἰησοῦς τῷ
[o] ἑκατοντάρχῃ Ὕπαγε, ὡς ἐπίστευσας γενηθήτω σοι. καὶ
ἰάθη ὁ [p] παῖς [αὐτοῦ] ἐν τῇ ὥρᾳ ἐκείνῃ.

BCEGK LMSUV XΓΔΠℵ 1. 33

z ver. 27. ch. ix. 33 al. Isa. xli. 23.
a ch. v. 18 reff.
b ch. ii. 1 reff.
c ch. xxiv. 27. Luke xiii. 29. Rev. xxi. 13 only. 1 Chron. xii. 15. Isa. lix. 19.
d as above (c). Luke xii. 54 only.
e ch. xiv. 19 || Mk. L. Luke ii. 7. (vii. 36 v. r.) xii. 37. xiii. 29 only +. Judith xii. 15 (only?).
f = ch. ix. 15. Luke xx. 34, 36 reff.
g ch. xiii. 38 only.
h = ch. xxi. 39. xxii. 13. xxv. 30 al. Jer. xxii. 28.
i = 2 Pet. ii. 17. Jude 13. Job xviii. 17. Tobit xiv. 10. see below (k).
k ch. xxii. 13. xxv. 30 only (there also w. σκότος). 3 Kings vi. 29.
l ch. xiii. 42, 50. xxii. 13. xxiv. 51. xxv. 30. Luke xiii. 28 only.
m as above (l). ch. ii. 18, from Jer. xxxviii. (xxxi.) 15. Acts xx. 37 only. Gen. xlv. 2.
n (in N. T. always w. ὀδόντων) as above (l) only. Prov. xix. 12. Sir. li. 3 only. (βρύχειν, Acts vii. 54.)
o vv. 5, 8 reff. -χης, Acts x. 1, 22. xxiv. 23 al.
p ver. 6 reff.

10. aft ακολουθουσιν add αυτω C 33. 240-4-5-59 Scr's b latt syrr syr-cu coptt æth. rec ουδε εν τω ισρ. τοσ. πιστ. ευρ. (*adaptation from* || *Luke: Meyer holds the reading in txt to be an interpretation, both here and in Luke. But this can hardly be: and its occurrence* there (in very few vss) *is sufficiently accounted for by its being the genuine reading here*), with CLℵ rel lat-*f* syrr arm Orig [Chr $Damasc_1$] : txt B (1) gat lat-*a* g_1 *k* syr-cu syr-mg coptt æth Mcion Ambr Aug Op.—om εν τω ισρ. **1.**

12. for εκβληθ., εξελευσονται ℵ[1](appy: txt ℵ-corr[1]) Syr syr-cu $Cypr_1$(*exibunt*: txt_1) [$Aug_{sæpe}$], *ibunt* lat-*a b* Iren-int [$Aug_{sæpe}$].

13. rec ins και bef ως, with C rel vulg lat-*c f* ff_1 syr [goth æth arm] $Orig_2$ [Bas_1] Chr_1: om Bℵ lat-*a b* $g_{1.2}$ *h k l* Syr syr-cu coptt Chr_1 Iren-int. om αυτου Bℵ **1.** 33 latt syr-jer copt [Bas_1] : ins C rel syrr syr-cu sah goth æth arm Chr. απο της ωρας εκεινης CΔ 33 lat-*a b c* $g_{1.2}$ *h l* sah Bas_1 Chr_1 Bas-sel (*see ch* ix. 22; xv. 28; xvii. 18) : txt BLXℵ rel vulg lat-*f* ff_1 syrr syr-cu copt goth æth arm. at end ins (*from Luke* vii. 10) και υποτρεψας ο εκατονταρχος εις τον οικον αυτου εν αυτη τη ωρα ευρεν τον παιδα υγιαινοντα C E-with-ast MUXℵ(brackets inserted by ℵ[2] but removed) **1.** 33 lat-g_1 syr-jer syr æth. (aft παιδα ins αυτου M : al vary.)

ver. 10, 'volens ostendere Dominum quoque non per adventum tantum corporis, sed per angelorum ministeria posse implere quod vellet.' Jerome in loc. 'Potuisset Ratio excipere: "Servus et miles imperium libere audiunt: morbus non item." Sed hanc exceptionem concoquit sapientia fidelis, et ruditate militari pulchre elucens.' Bengel ad loc. 10, 11.] 'Amen, inquit, dico vobis, non inveni tantam fidem in Israel; propterea dico vobis quia multi ab Or. et Occ. . . . . &c. Quam late terram occupavit oleaster! Amara silva mundus hic fuit: sed propter humilitatem, propter "Non sum dignus ut sub tectum meum intres," multi ab Or. et Occ. venient. Et puta quia venient: quid de illis fiet? Si enim venient, jam præcisi sunt de silva: ubi inserendi sunt, ne arescant? Et recumbent, inquit, cum Abraham et Isaac et Jacob . . . . Ubi? In regno, inquit, cœlorum. Et quid erit de illis qui venerunt de stirpe Abrahæ? quid fiet de ruinis quibus arbor plena erat? quid nisi quia præcidentur, ut isti inserantur? Doce quia præcidentur: Filii autem regni ibunt in tenebras exteriores.' Aug. in Johan. tract. xvi. 6, vol. iii. pt. ii. Compare a remarkable contrast in the Rabbinical books illustrating Jewish pride: 'Dixit Deus S. B. Israelites: "In mundo futuro mensam ingentem vobis sternam, quod Gentiles videbunt et pudefient."' Schöttgen, i. p. 86. **ἐθαύμασεν**] to be accepted simply as a fact, as when Jesus rejoiced, wept, was sorrowful; not, as Aug. de Genes. cont. Manich. cited by Wordsw., to be rationalized away into a mere lesson to teach us what to admire. The mysteries of our Lord's humanity are too precious thus to be sacrificed to the timidity of theologians. **12. οἱ υἱοί**] the natural heirs, but disinherited by rebellion. **τὸ σκ. τὸ ἐξ. the darkness outside,** i. e. outside the lighted chamber of the feast, see ch. xxii. 13, and Eph. v. 7, 8. These verses are wanting in St. Luke, and occur when our Lord

14 Καὶ ἐλθὼν ὁ Ἰησοῦς εἰς τὴν οἰκίαν Πέτρου εἶδεν
τὴν [q] πενθερὰν αὐτοῦ [r] βεβλημένην καὶ [s] πυρέσσουσαν.
15 καὶ ἥψατο τῆς χειρὸς αὐτῆς, καὶ ἀφῆκεν αὐτὴν ὁ
[t] πυρετός, καὶ ἠγέρθη, καὶ [u] διηκόνει αὐτῷ. 16 [v] ὀψίας δὲ
γενομένης προσήνεγκαν αὐτῷ [w] δαιμονιζομένους πολλούς,
καὶ ἐξέβαλεν τὰ πνεύματα λόγῳ, καὶ πάντας τοὺς
[x] κακῶς [x] ἔχοντας ἐθεράπευσεν, 17 ὅπως πληρωθῇ τὸ
[y] ῥηθὲν διὰ Ἡσαΐου τοῦ προφήτου λέγοντος [z] Αὐτὸς τὰς
ἀσθενείας ἡμῶν [a] ἔλαβεν, καὶ τὰς νόσους [b] ἐβάστασεν.

q ||. ch. x. 35. Luke xii. 53 bis only. Ruth i. 14.
r ver. 6 reff.
s || Mk. only †.
t || (L. bis). John iv. 52. Acts xxviii. 8 only. Deut. xxviii. 22 only.
u ch. iv. 11 reff.
v ch. xiv. 15, 23 al. Mt. Mk. only, exc. John vi. 16. xx. 19 †. Judith xiii. 1 only.
w ch. iv. 24. vv. 28, 33 ||. John x. 21 †. Ps. xc. 6 Aq.
x || Mk. ch. iv. 24. ix. 12. xiv. 35 al. Ezek. xxxiv. 4.
y ch. i. 22 reff.
z Isa. liii. 4.
a = ch. x. 38. Lev. v. 1, 17. Ezek. xxxvi. 7.
b = ch. xx. 12. John xvi. 12. Rom. xv. 1. 4 Kings xviii. 14.

15. for ηγερθη και, εγερθεισα(appy) ℵ¹(txt ℵ²). rec (for αυτω) αυτοις (*from* || *Mark Luke*), with LM¹Δℵ² 1. 33 latt Syr syr-cu copt æth: txt BCℵ¹ rel Syr-ms syr goth arm Orig₁ Chr Thl Euthym.

repeated them on a wholly different occasion, ch. xiii. 28, 29. **ὁ κλ. κ. ὁ βρ.**] The articles here are not possessive, as Middleton supposes, for that would give a sense the most frigid possible, and would be a rendering inadmissible after ἔσται, which generalizes the assertion; they rather import the notoriety and eminence of the κλ. κ. βρ. 'Articulus insignis: in hac vita dolor nondum est dolor.' Bengel.

13. **ἰάθη**] Of what precise disease does not appear. In Luke ἤμελλεν τελευτᾶν—here he is παραλυτικός, δεινῶς βασανιζόμενος. But though these descriptions do not agree with the character of palsy among us, we read of a similar case in 1 Macc. ix. 55, 56: ἐν τῷ καιρῷ ἐκείνῳ ἐπλήγη Ἄλκιμος καὶ ἐνεποδίσθη τὰ ἔργα αὐτοῦ, καὶ ἀπεφράγη τὸ στόμα αὐτοῦ, καὶ παρελύθη, καὶ οὐκ ἐδύνατο ἔτι λαλῆσαι λόγον καὶ ἐντείλασθαι περὶ τοῦ οἴκου αὐτοῦ. καὶ ἀπέθανεν Ἄλκιμος ἐν τῷ καιρῷ ἐκείνῳ μετὰ βασάνου μεγάλης. The disease in the text may have been an attack of tetanus, which the ancient physicians included under paralysis, and which is more common in hot countries than with us. It could hardly have been apoplexy, which usually bereaves of sensation.

14—17.] Healing of Peter's wife's mother, and many others. Mark i. 29—34. Luke iv. 38—41. From the other Evangelists it appears, that our Lord had just healed a dæmoniac in the synagogue at Capernaum: for they both state, 'when they were come out of the synagogue, they entered into the house of Simon and Andrew, &c.' Both Mark and Luke are fuller in their accounts than the text. The expression (of the fever) **ἀφῆκεν αὐτήν** is common to the three, as is also the circumstance of her ministering *immediately* after: shewing that the fever left her, not, as it would have done if natural means had been used, weak and exhausted, but completely restored.

16.] *at sunset*, Mark ver. 32: Luke ver. 40. From St. Mark we learn that *the whole city was collected at the door;* from St. Luke, that *the dæmons cried out and said, 'Thou art Christ the Son of God.'* And from both, that *our Lord permitted them not to speak, for they knew Him.* They brought the sick in the evening, either because it was cool,—or because the day's work was over, and men could be found to carry them,—or perhaps because it was the sabbath (see Mark i. 21, 29, 32), which ended at sunset.

17.] This is a version of the prophecy differing from the LXX, which has οὗτος τὰς ἁμαρτίας ἡμῶν φέρει, καὶ περὶ ἡμῶν ὀδυνᾶται. The exact sense in which these words are quoted is matter of difficulty. Some understand **ἔλαβεν** and **ἐβάστασεν** as merely 'took away,' and 'healed.' But besides this being a very harsh interpretation of both words, it entirely destroys the force of αὐτός, and makes it expletive. Others suppose it to refer to the personal fatigue, (or even the spiritual exhaustion, (Olshausen,) which perhaps is hardly consistent with sound doctrine,) which our Lord felt by these cures being long protracted into the evening. But I believe the true relevancy of the prophecy is to be sought by regarding the miracles generally to have been, as we know so many of them were, lesser and typical outshewings of the great work of bearing the sin of the world, which He came to accom-

c ver. 28 al. Mt. Mk. only, exc. Luke viii. 22. Num. xxi. 13.
d ch. (ix. 18 v. r.) xix. 16. Mark ix. 17. Rev. viii. 13.
e ch. xxiv. 28. xxvi. 13 al. Ruth i. 16.
f = ch. x. 5. Rom. xv. 28. Isa. xxxvii. 37.
g || L. Luke xiii. 32 only. Judg. xv. 4.
h || L. only †.
i ch. vi. 26 reff.
j || L. only. Ezek. xxxvii. 27. (-νοῦν, ch. xiii. 32.)

18 Ἰδὼν δὲ ὁ Ἰησοῦς πολλοὺς ὄχλους περὶ αὐτὸν ἐκέ- BCEGK LMSUV ΧΓΔΠℵ 1. 33
λευσεν ἀπελθεῖν ᶜ εἰς τὸ ᶜ πέραν. 19 καὶ προσελθὼν ᵈ εἷς
γραμματεὺς εἶπεν αὐτῷ Διδάσκαλε, ἀκολουθήσω σοι
ᵉ ὅπου ἐὰν ᶠ ἀπέρχῃ. 20 καὶ λέγει αὐτῷ ὁ Ἰησοῦς Αἱ
ᵍ ἀλώπεκες ʰ φωλεοὺς ἔχουσιν, καὶ τὰ ⁱ πετεινὰ τοῦ ⁱ οὐρανοῦ ʲ κατασκηνώσεις, ὁ δὲ ᵏ υἱὸς τοῦ ᵏ ἀνθρώπου οὐκ
ˡ ἔχει ποῦ τὴν κεφαλὴν ᵐ κλίνῃ. 21 ⁿ ἕτερος δὲ τῶν
μαθητῶν αὐτοῦ εἶπεν αὐτῷ Κύριε, ᵒ ἐπίτρεψόν μοι πρῶτον
ἀπελθεῖν καὶ θάψαι τὸν πατέρα μου. 22 ὁ δὲ Ἰησοῦς

k Gospp. passim, and Acts vii. 56 only. Dan. vii. 13.
l || L. ch. xv. 32 || Mk. Luke xii. 4, 17. Josh. viii. 20.
m = || L. see John xix. 30. Luke xxiv. 5. (Luke ix. 12. xxiv. 29. Heb. xi. 34 only.)
n = ch. xi. 3. xii. 45 al. fr. Gen. viii. 10, 12 al.
o ch. xix. 8. Luke viii. 32 al. Esth. ix. 14.

18. *οχλον*, omg *πολλους*, B; simly *τους οχλους* ev-y, *οχλους* ℵ¹ copt; *οχλον πολυν* sah: *πολυν οχλον* 243 ev-x lat-g_1: *πολλους*, omg *οχλους*, ℵ³ᵃ(or txt) 106. (*Omission at first from similar endings, then variously explained and restored.*)

21. om *αυτου* Bℵ 33. 241-6 Scr's l lat-*a b c h* sah.

22. om *ιησ.* ℵ 33(appy) lat-*b c*.

plish; just as diseases themselves, on which those miracles operated, are all so many testimonies to the existence, and types of the effect, of sin. Moreover in these His deeds of mercy, He was 'touched with the feeling of our infirmities:' witness His tears at the grave of Lazarus, and His sighing over the deaf and dumb man, Mark vii. 34. The very act of compassion is (as the name imports) a *suffering with* its object; and if this be true between man and man, how much more strictly so in His case who had taken upon Him the whole burden of the sin of the world, with all its sad train of sorrow and suffering.

18—IX. 1.] Jesus crosses the lake. Incidents before embarking. He stills the storm. Healing of two dæmoniacs in the land of the Gadarenes. Mark iv. 35—v. 20. Luke ix. 57—60; viii. 22—39, on which passages compare the notes. **18.**] It is obviously the intention of St. Matthew to bind on the following incidents to the occurrence which he had just related.

19.] Both the following incidents are placed by St. Luke long after, during our Lord's last journey to Jerusalem. For it is quite impossible (with Greswell, Diss. iii. p. 155, sq.) in any common fairness of interpretation, to imagine that two such incidents should have twice happened, and both times have been related together. It is one of those cases where the attempts of the Harmonists do violence to every principle of sound historical criticism. Every such difficulty, instead of being a thing to be wiped out and buried up at all hazards (I am sorry to see, e. g., that Bp. Wordsw. takes no notice, either here or in St. Luke, of the recurrence of the two narratives), is a valuable index and guide to the humble searcher after truth, and is used by him as such (see Prolegomena, ch. i. § iv. 2 f.).

20. ὁ υἱὸς τοῦ ἀνθρώπου] "It is thought that this phrase was taken from Dan. vii. 13, to which passage our Saviour seems to allude in ch. xxvi. 64, and probably Stephen in Acts vii. 56. It appears from John xii. 34, that the Jews understood it to mean the Messiah: and from Luke xxii. 69, 70, that they considered *the Son of Man* to mean the same as *the Son of God*." Dr. Burton. It is the name by which the Lord ordinarily in one pregnant word designates Himself as the Messiah—the *Son of God manifested in the flesh of man*—the *second Adam*. And to it belong all those conditions, of humiliation, suffering, and exaltation, which it behoved the Son of Man to go through. **21.**] In St. Luke we find, that our Lord *previously commanded him* to follow Him. τοῦ κυρίου .... λέγοντος τῷ Φιλίππῳ, ἄφες τοὺς νεκ. κ.τ.λ. Clem. Alex. Strom. iii. 4 (25), p. 522 P. But if so, He had long ago ordered Philip to follow Him, taking St. Luke's order of the occurrence. A tradition of this nature was hardly likely to be wrong; so that perhaps the words **ἀκολούθει μοι** are to be taken (as in John xxi. 19, 22) as an admonition occasioned by some slackness or symptom of decadence on the part of the Apostle. The attempt to evade the strong words of our Lord's

λέγει αὐτῷ Ἀκολούθει μοι, καὶ ἄφες τοὺς νεκροὺς θάψαι
τοὺς ἑαυτῶν νεκρούς. 23 Καὶ [p] ἐμβάντι [q] αὐτῷ εἰς πλοῖον
ἠκολούθησαν [q] αὐτῷ οἱ μαθηταὶ αὐτοῦ. 24 καὶ ἰδοὺ
[r] σεισμὸς μέγας ἐγένετο ἐν τῇ θαλάσσῃ, ὥςτε τὸ πλοῖον
[s] καλύπτεσθαι ὑπὸ τῶν [t] κυμάτων· αὐτὸς δὲ ἐκάθευδεν.
25 καὶ προςελθόντες οἱ μαθηταὶ ἤγειραν αὐτὸν λέγοντες
Κύριε σῶσον, ἀπολλύμεθα. 26 καὶ λέγει αὐτοῖς Τί [u] δειλοί

...πλοιον G. BCEKL MSUVX ΓΔΠℵ 1. 33

p = ch. ix. 1. xiii. 2 al. so always in N. T. [exc. John v. 4 rec.]‡ (Nah. iii. 14.) 1 Macc. xv. 37. 2 Macc. xii. 3 only.
q constr., ver. 1 reff.
r = here only. (ch. xxiv. 7 al.) Jer. xxiii. 19. see Nah. i. 3.
s ch. x. 26. Luke viii. 16. xxiii. 30. 2 Cor. iv. 3 bis. James v. 20. 1 Pet. iv. 8 only. = Gen. vii. 19 Ed-vat. B def.). Exod. xv. 5.
t ‖ Mk. ch. xiv. 24. [Acts xxvii. 41.] Jude 13 only. Ps. cvi. 25, 29.
u ‖ Mk. Rev. xxi. 8 only. Judg. vii. 3. ix. 4 B. (-λία, 2 Tim. i. 7. -λιᾷν, John xiv. 27.)

rec (for λεγει) ειπεν, with L rel lat-g_1 spec: txt BCℵ 1. 33 latt Clem.

23. rec ins το bef πλοιον, with Lℵ[1.3] rel coptt: om BC V-marg ℵ[2] 1. 33 goth Orig.

24. for υπο, απο B[2][B[2.3], Tischdf].

25. aft προςελθοντες ins αυτω C[1](appy) vulg sah. om οι μαθηται (*see Luke* viii. 24) Bℵ 33(appy) am(with fuld em forj harl) lat-*a c* ff_1 *k l* coptt Jer. rec aft μαθηται ins αυτου, with C[1](appy) X 1 vulg lat-*b* g_1 syrr goth æth: om C[2]L rel lat-*h* arm Eus Thl. rec aft σωσον ins ημας (*supplementary*), with L rel vss Eus: om BCℵ 1.

command by supposing that **θάψαι τὸν πατέρα** means, '*to reside with my father till his death*' (Theophylact), is evidently futile, since **πρῶτον ἀπελθεῖν καὶ θάψαι** is plainly said of an *act waiting to be done;* and the reason of our Lord's rebuke was the peremptory and all-superseding nature of the command ἀκολούθει μοι. **22.** **νεκρούς**] *First* time, as Rev. iii. 1, *spiritually,*—second, *literally* dead. The two meanings are similarly used in one saying by our Lord in John xi. 25, 26. See Heb. vi. 1; ix. 14. ἐκώλυσεν αὐτόν, οὐ κωλύων τὸ τιμᾷν τοὺς γονεῖς, ἀλλὰ διδάσκων ὅτι χρὴ τὸν ἐφιέμενον τῶν οὐρανίων μὴ ὑποστρέφειν εἰς τὰ γήϊνα, μηδ' ἀπολιμπάνειν μὲν τὰ ζωηρά, παλινδρομεῖν δὲ εἰς τὰ νεκρωτικά, μηδὲ θεοῦ προτιμᾷν γονεῖς. ἐγίνωσκε γὰρ ὅτι θάψουσι τοῦτον ἄλλοι, καὶ οὐκ εἰκὸς τοῦτον ἀπολειφθῆναι τῶν ἀναγκαιοτέρων. οἶμαι δὲ ὅτι καὶ ἄπιστος ἦν ὁ τελευτήσας. Euthym. **23.**] This journey across the lake, with its incidents, is placed by St. Mark and St. Luke after the series of parables commencing with that of the sower, and recorded in ch. xiii. By Mark with a precise note of sequence: λέγει αὐτοῖς ἐν **ἐκείνῃ τῇ ἡμέρᾳ ὀψίας γενομένης**, Mark iv. 35. **24.**] **σεισμός**, usually of an earthquake, = λαῖλαψ, Mark and Luke,—a great commotion in the sea. **καλύπτεσθαι**] τὰ κύμ. ἐπέβαλλεν εἰς τὸ πλ. ὥςτε ἤδη γεμίζεσθαι τὸ πλοῖον, Mark iv. 37. συνεπληροῦντο, Luke viii. 23. By keeping to the strict imperfect sense we obviate all necessity for qualifying these words: (starker Ausdruck: die Wogen schlugen ins Schiff, De Wette) **was becoming covered,** &c. All lakes bordered by mountains, and indeed all hilly coasts, are liable to these sudden gusts of wind. **25.**] **κύριε σῶσον, ἀπολλ.** = διδάσκαλε, οὐ μέλει σοι ὅτι ἀπολλ.; Mark iv. 38 = ἐπιστάτα, ἐπιστάτα, ἀπολλ., Luke viii. 24. On these and such like variations, notice the following excellent and important remarks of Augustine (De Consensu Evv. ii. 24 (55), vol. vii.): 'Una eademque sententia est excitantium Dominum, volentiumque salvari; nec opus est quærere quid horum potius Christo dictum sit. Sive enim aliquid horum trium dixerint, sive alia verba quæ nullus Evangelistarum commemoravit, tantundem tamen valentia ad eandem sententiæ veritatem, quid ad rem interest?' We may well exclaim, 'O si sic omnia!' Much useless labour might have been spared, and men's minds led to the diligent enquiry into the real difficulties of the Gospels, instead of so many spending time in knitting cobwebs. But Augustine himself in the very next sentence, descends to the unsatisfactory ground of the Harmonists, when he adds, 'Quamquam et hoc fieri potuit, ut pluribus eum simul excitantibus, omnia hæc, aliud ab alio, dicerentur.' His mind however was not one to rest contented with such sophisms; and all his deeper and more earnest sayings are in the truer and freer spirit of the above extract. **26.**] The time of this rebuke in the text precedes, but in Mark and Luke follows, the stilling of the storm. See the last note. They were of *little* faith, in that they were afraid of perishing while they had on board the slumbering Saviour: they were not *faithless*, for they had recourse to that Saviour to help them. Therefore He acknow-

v ch. vi. 30. xiv. 31. xvi. 8. Luke xii. 28 only +.
w ||. Ps. cv. 9.
x || only +. Ps. cvi. 29 Symm.
y Mark xiii. 1 bis. Luke i. 29. vii. 39. 2 Pet. iii. 11. 1 John iii. 1.
z constr., ver. 1 reff.

ἔστε [v] ὀλιγόπιστοι; τότε ἐγερθεὶς [w] ἐπετίμησεν τοῖς ἀνέμοις
καὶ τῇ θαλάσσῃ, καὶ ἐγένετο [x] γαλήνη μεγάλη. 27 οἱ δὲ
ἄνθρωποι ἐθαύμασαν λέγοντες [y] Ποταπός ἐστιν οὗτος,
ὅτι καὶ οἱ ἄνεμοι καὶ ἡ θάλασσα αὐτῷ ὑπακούουσιν;
28 Καὶ * ἐλθόντι [z] * αὐτῷ [a] εἰς τὸ [a] πέραν εἰς τὴν χώραν
τῶν Γαδαρηνῶν, [b] ὑπήντησαν [z] αὐτῷ δύο [c] δαιμονιζό-

...λεγοντες Γ. BCEKL MSUVX ΔΠℵ 1. 33

a ver. 18 reff. 1 Kings xxvi. 13. b || L. (Mk. v. r.) ch. xxviii. 9 v. r. Luke xiv. 31. John iv. 31. xi. 20, 30. xii. 18. Acts xvi. 16 only +. Tobit vii. 1 (not ℵ) al. c ver. 16 reff.

26. τω ανεμω (||) ℵ^1(txt ℵ^2) 1. 13. 22. 124. 209 am lat-*a b* g_1 *h* syr sah Eus$_1$.

27. om 1st και (*as unnecessary*) C 34. 85 latt Syr coptt æth Hil Op. rec υπακουουσιν bef αυτω, with CL rel (vss) Hil: txt Bℵ 1. 33 Eus$_1$ Chr.

28. * ἐλθόντος αὐτοῦ BCℵ^2 1. 33: ελθοντων αυτων ℵ^1: ελθοντι αυτω L rel. rec (for γαδαρηνων) γεργεσηνων, with C^{3}Lℵ^{3a} rel copt goth æth arm: γεργεσαιων some mss in Epiph &c: γερασηνων D-lat mss-used-by-Orig(*see note*) latt(and Δ-lat) syr-mg[has also γεργεσ.] sah Nyss Ath Juv Hil Prud: txt BC^{1}M(Δℵ^1) "ολιγα"-in-Orig syrr Eus Epiph$_{expr}$. (33 syr-cu def.: the ver is passed over in Chr.)—γαραδ. Δ: γαζαρ. ℵ^1.

ledges the faith which they had; answers the prayer of faith, by working a perfect calm: but rebukes them for not having the stronger, firmer faith, to trust Him even when He seemed insensible to their danger. The symbolic application of this occurrence is too striking to have escaped general notice. The Saviour with the company of His disciples in the ship tossed on the waves, seemed a typical reproduction of the Ark bearing mankind on the flood, and a foreshadowing of the Church tossed by the tempests of this world, but having Him with her always. And the personal application is one of comfort, and strengthening of faith, in danger and doubt. **27. οἱ ἄνθρ.**] The men who were in the ship, besides our Lord and His disciples. **28.**] Among the difficulties attendant on this narrative, the situation and name of the place where the event happened are not the least. Origen's remarks are: ἡ περὶ τοὺς ὑπὸ τῶν δαιμονίων κατακρημνιζομένους καὶ ἐν τῇ θαλάσσῃ συμπνιγομένους χοίρους οἰκονομία ἀναγέγραπται γεγονέναι ἐν τῇ χώρᾳ τῶν Γερασηνῶν. Γέρασα δὲ τῆς Ἀραβίας ἐστὶ πόλις, οὔτε θάλασσαν οὔτε λίμνην πλησίον ἔχουσα. καὶ ούκ ἂν οὕτως προφανὲς ψεῦδος καὶ εὐέλεγκτον οἱ εὐαγγελισταὶ εἰρήκεσαν, ἄνδρες ἐπιμελῶς γινώσκοντες τὰ περὶ τὴν Ἰουδαίαν. ἐπεὶ δὲ ἐν ὀλίγοις εὕρομεν "εἰς τὴν χώραν τῶν Γαδαρηνῶν," καὶ πρὸς τοῦτο λεκτέον (lit. "we must speak also to (in reference to) this;" discuss this reading also. Dr. Bloomfield's conjecture, στικτέον, need only be considered by those who are not aware of this common expression). Γάδαρα γὰρ πόλις μέν ἐστι τῆς Ἰουδαίας, περὶ ἣν τὰ διαβόητα θερμὰ τυγχάνει, λίμνη δὲ κρημνοῖς παρακειμένη οὐδαμῶς ἐστιν ἐν αὐτῇ ἢ θάλασσα. Ἀλλὰ Γέργεσα, ἀφ' ἧς οἱ Γεργεσαιοι, πόλις ἀρχαία περὶ τὴν νῦν καλουμένην Τιβεριάδα λίμνην, περὶ ἣν κρημνὸς παρακείμενος τῇ λίμνῃ, ἀφ' οὗ δείκνυται τοὺς χοίρους ὑπὸ τῶν δαιμόνων καταβεβλῆσθαι. Comm. in Joan. tom. vi. § 24, vol. iv. p. 141. Notwithstanding this, it appears very doubtful whether there ever was a town named Gergesha near the lake. There were the Gergashites (Joseph. i. 6. 2) in former days, but their towns had been destroyed by the Israelites at their first irruption, and never, that we hear of, afterwards rebuilt (see Deut. vii. 1: Josh. xxiv. 11). Gerasa (now Dscherasch) lies much too far to the East. The town of Gadara, alluded to in the text, was (Joseph. B. J. iv. 7. 3) μητρόπολις τῆς Περαίας καρτερά, and (Euseb. Onomasticon) ἀντικρὺ Σκυθοπόλεως καὶ Τιβεριάδος πρὸς ἀνατολαῖς, ἐν τῷ ὄρει, οὗ πρὸς ταῖς ὑπουργίαις (Dr. Bloomfield in loc. conjectures ὑπωρείαις) τὰ τῶν θερμῶν ὑδάτων λουτρὰ παράκειται. It was on the river Hieromax ('Gaddara Hieromace præfluente,' Plin. v. 18), and sixty stadia from Tiberias (Joseph. Vit. § 65), πόλις Ἑλληνίς (Jos. Antt. xvii. 11. 4). It was destroyed in the civil wars of the Jews, and rebuilt by Pompeius (Jos. B. J. i. 7. 7), presented by Augustus to King Herod (Jos. Antt. xv. 7. 3), and after his death united to the province of Syria (Jos. B. J. ii. 6. 3). It was one of the ten cities of Decapolis. (Pliny, ibid.) Burckhardt and others believe that they have found its ruins at Omkeis, near the ridge of the chain which divides the valley of Jordan from that of the Sea of Tiberias. The territory of this city might

μενοι ἐκ τῶν [d] μνημείων ἐξερχόμενοι, [e] χαλεποὶ λίαν,
ὥςτε μὴ [f] ἰσχύειν τινὰ παρελθεῖν διὰ τῆς ὁδοῦ ἐκείνης.
29 καὶ ἰδοὺ ἔκραξαν λέγοντες [g] Τί ἡμῖν καὶ σοί, [h] υἱὲ τοῦ
[h] θεοῦ; ἦλθες ὧδε [i] πρὸ [i] καιροῦ [k] βασανίσαι ἡμᾶς; 30 ἦν
δὲ [l] μακρὰν ἀπ' αὐτῶν [m] ἀγέλη [n] χοίρων πολλῶν [o] βοσκο-
μένη· 31 οἱ δὲ [p] δαίμονες [q] παρεκάλουν αὐτὸν λέγοντες Εἰ
ἐκβάλλεις ἡμᾶς, ἀπόστειλον ἡμᾶς εἰς τὴν [m] ἀγέλην τῶν

d ch. xxvii. 52, 53 al. fr. Gen. xxiii. 6, 9.
e 2 Tim. iii. 1 only. Isa. xviii. 2 only. Wisd. iii. 19 al.
f = Mark v. 4. Luke vi. 48. Phil. iv. 13. Isa. lix. 1.
g Mark i. 24 || L. 2 Kings xvi. 10 al.
h ch. iv. 3 and note.
i 1 Cor. iv. 5 only. Sir. xxx. 24.
k = ||. Rev. ix. 5. xiv. 10. xx. 10 only. (ver. 6 al. 1 Kings v. 3.)
l Mark xii. 34. John xxi. 8 al. Isa. lvii. 19.
m here, &c. and || only. 1 Kings xxiv. 4.
n here, &c. and || only, exc. ch. vii. 6. Luke xv. 15, 16 †. Ps. lxxix. 14, Alius in Hexapl.
o here bis, and || only, exc. Luke xv. 15. John xxi. 15, 17. 3 Kings xii. 16.
p here (|| Mk., ver. 12, & Luke, ver. 29. Rev. xvi. 14. xviii. 2 v. r.) only †.
q ver. 5 reff.

29. rec aft *σοι* ins *ιησου* (*from* || *Mark Luke*), with C³X rel latt(and D-lat) syrr sah goth æth arm [Eus₂ Chr Promiss]: om BC¹Lℵ 1. 33 am(with forj harl¹ tol) lat-*ff*₁ *k l* copt Orig₁ Eus₅ Cypr Victorin spec. *ημας απολεσαι* (*ημας βασανισαι ημας* ℵ²) *προ καιρου* ℵ.

31. rec (for *αποστειλον*) *επιτρεψον ημας απελθειν* (*probably from* || *Luke, the alteration of Luke's* *εισελθειν* *to* *απελθ.* *being a trace of the original* *αποστειλον*. *The reason of the corrn may perhaps have been the connexion of* **αποστελλω** *with mission of a higher kind. If txt had been a corrn from* || *Mark,* *πεμψον* *and not* *αποστ.* *would have been adopted*), with CL rel lat-*f h* syrr goth arm: txt Bℵ 1. 33 latt(and D-lat) syr-mg-ms syr-jer coptt æth Cyr₁.

well extend to the shore of the lake. It may be observed, that there is nothing in any of the three accounts to imply that the city was close to the scene of the miracle, or the scene of the miracle close to the herd of swine, or the herd of swine, at the time of their possession, close to the lake. Indeed the expression *μακρὰν ἀπ' αὐτῶν*, ver. 30, implies the contrary with regard to the swine. It appears, from Burckhardt, that there are many tombs in the neighbourhood of the ruins of Gadara to this day, hewn in the rock, and thus capable of affording shelter. It may be well in fairness to observe, that *Γεργεσηνῶν* can hardly have arisen entirely from Origen's conjecture, as it pervades so many MSS. and ancient (it is true, not the *most* ancient) versions. We cannot say that a part of the territory of Gadara may not have been known to those who, like Matthew, were locally intimate with the shores of the lake, by this ancient and generally disused name. Still however, we are, I conceive, bound in a matter of this kind to follow the most ancient extant testimony. See further on || Mark, Luke. The excursus of Dr. Bloomfield, Gr. Test. edn. 9, vol. i. p. 890, though containing interesting matter confirming the fact of Gergesa having been a name actually used for a town near the lake, determines nothing as to the *reading* here, which must be settled purely on objective evidence. **δύο δαιμονιζόμενοι**] In Mark v. 2, and Luke viii. 27, but *one* is mentioned. All three Evangelists have some particulars peculiar to themselves; but Mark the most, and the most striking, as having evidently proceeded from an eye-witness. The *ὅτι πολλοί ἐσμεν* of Mark is worth noticing, in reference to the discrepancy of number in the two accounts, as perhaps connected with the mention of more than one by our Evangelist, who omits the circumstance connected with that speech. **χαλεποὶ λίαν**] See the terribly graphic account of Mark (v. 3–6). The dæmoniac was without clothes, which though related only by St. Luke (viii. 27), yet, with remarkable consistency, appears from St. Mark's narrative, where he is described as sitting, *clothed*, and in his right mind, at Jesus's feet, after his cure. **ὥςτε μὴ ἰσχ.**] Peculiar to this Gospel. **29. τί ἡμ. κ. σοί**] מַה־לָּנוּ וָלָךְ. See 2 Sam. xvi. 10; xix. 22. *πρὸ καιροῦ* is peculiar to this Gospel: *υἱὲ τοῦ θ.* common to all. **30. μακράν**] The Vulgate rendering, '*non longe*,' does not seem accordant with the other accounts, both of which imply distance: *ἦν δὲ ἐκεῖ πρὸς τῷ ὄρει*, Mark v. 11; *ἦν δὲ ἐκεῖ .... ἐν τῷ ὄρει*, Luke viii. 32. These, especially the first, would seem to imply that the swine were on the hills, and the scene of the miracle at some little distance, on the plain. **31. ἀπόστειλον ἡμ.**] St. Mark and St. Luke give, as the ground of this request, that they might not be sent *out of the land* = *into the abyss*, i. e. out of their permitted resi-

r .l. Acts vii. 57. xix. 29 only. 1 Kings xv. 19.

[n] χοίρων. 32 καὶ εἶπεν αὐτοῖς Ὑπάγετε. οἱ δὲ ἐξελθόντες
ἀπῆλθον εἰς * τὴν [m] ἀγέλην τῶν [n] * χοίρων· καὶ ἰδοὺ [r] ὥρμη-

BCEKL MSUVX ΔΠℵ 1. 33

32. aft αυτοις ins ο ῑς C lat-*b c* $g_{1.2}$ *h* Syr. απηλθαν B. * τοὺς χοίρους (*from* || *Mark Luke?*) BC[1]ℵ 1. 33 latt(and D-lat) Syr coptt æth Chr Cyr : την αγελην των χοιρων C[3]L rel lat-*f* ff_1 *h* syr goth arm.

dence on earth to βάσανος πρὸ καιροῦ in the ἄβυσσος. See note and reff. on Luke. **32.**] This remarkable narrative brings before us the whole question of DÆMONIACAL POSSESSIONS in the Gospels, which I shall treat here once for all, and refer to this note hereafter. I would then remark in general, (I. 1) that the Gospel narratives are *distinctly pledged to the historic truth of these occurrences.* Either they are true, or the Gospels are false. For they do not stand in the same, or a similar position, with the discrepancies in detail, so frequent between the Evangelists: but they form part of that general groundwork in which all agree. (2) Nor can it be said that they represent the *opinion of the time,* and use words in accordance with it. This might have been difficult to answer, but that they not only give such expressions as δαιμονιζόμενος, δαιμονισθείς (Mark v. 16: Luke viii. 36), and other like ones, but relate to us words *spoken by the Lord Jesus,* in which *the personality and presence of the dæmons is distinctly implied.* See especially Luke xi. 17—26. Now either our Lord spoke these words, or He did not. If He did not, then we must at once set aside the concurrent testimony of the Evangelists to a plain matter of fact; in other words establish a principle which will overthrow equally every fact related in the Gospels. If He did, it is wholly at variance with any Christian idea of the perfection of truthfulness in Him who was Truth itself, to suppose Him to have used such plain and solemn words repeatedly, before His disciples and the Jews, in encouragement of, and connivance at, a lying superstition. (3) After these remarks it will be unnecessary to refute that view of dæmoniacal possession which makes it *identical with mere bodily disease,*—as it is included above; but we may observe, that it is every where in the Gospels distinguished from disease, and in such a way as to shew that, at all events, the two were not in that day confounded. (See ch. ix. 32, 33, and compare Mark vii. 32.) (4) The question then arises, *Granted the plain historical truth of dæmoniacal possession,* WHAT WAS IT? This question, in the suspension, or withdrawal, of the gift of 'discerning of spirits' in the modern Church, is not easy to answer. But we may gather from the Gospel narratives some important ingredients for our description. The dæmoniac was one whose being was strangely interpenetrated ('*possessed*' is the most exact word that could be found) by one or more of those fallen spirits, who are constantly asserted in Scripture (under the name of δαίμονες, δαιμόνια, πνεύματα πονηρά, πνεύματα ἀκάθαρτα, their chief being ὁ διάβολος or σατανᾶς) to be the enemies and tempters of the souls of men. (See Acts v. 3: John xiii. 2 and passim.) He stood in a totally different position from the abandoned wicked man, who morally is given over to the devil. This latter would be a subject for punishment; but the dæmoniac for deepest compassion. There appears to have been in him a *double will* and *double consciousness*—sometimes the cruel spirit thinking and speaking in him, sometimes his poor crushed self crying out to the Saviour of men for mercy: a terrible advantage taken, and a personal realization, by the malignant powers of evil, of the fierce struggle between sense and conscience in the man of morally divided life. Hence it has been not improbably supposed, that some of these dæmoniacs may have arrived at their dreadful state through various progressive degrees of guilt and sensual abandonment. 'Lavish sin, and especially indulgence in sensual lusts, superinducing, as it would often, a weakness in the nervous system, which is the especial band between body and soul, may have laid open these unhappy ones to the fearful incursions of the powers of darkness.' (Trench on the Miracles, p. 160.) (5) The frequently urged objection, How comes it that this malady is not *now* among us? admits of an easy answer, even if the assumption be granted. The period of our Lord's being on earth was certainly more than any other in the history of the world under the dominion of evil. The foundations of man's moral being were broken up, and the 'hour and power of darkness' prevailing. Trench excellently remarks, 'It was exactly the crisis for such soul-maladies as these, in which the spiritual

σεν πᾶσα ἡ [m] ἀγέλη [τῶν [n] χοίρων] κατὰ τοῦ [s] κρημνοῦ εἰς τὴν θάλασσαν, καὶ ἀπέθανον ἐν τοῖς ὕδασιν.
33 οἱ δὲ [t] βόσκοντες ἔφυγον, καὶ ἀπελθόντες εἰς τὴν πόλιν [u] ἀπήγγει-

s || only. 2 Chron. xxv. 12 bis only.
t particip., ch. xiii. 3 reff.
u Luke xiii. 1 reff.

η αγελη bef πασα C[1] 21 syr: om πασα 17. 119 Scr's b. om 2nd των χοιρων (*see || Mark Luke*) BC[1]MΔℵ 1. 33 latt(and D-lat) syrr coptt goth æth arm Euthym: ins C[3]L rel Chr. απεθανεν C 262: -ναν ℵ[2].

and bodily should be thus strangely interlinked, and it is nothing wonderful that they should have abounded at that time; for the predominance of certain spiritual maladies at certain epochs of the world's history, which were specially fitted for their generation, with their gradual decline and disappearance in others less congenial to them, is a fact itself admitting no manner of question.' (pp. 162, 163.) Besides, as the same writer goes on to observe, there can be no doubt that the coming of the Son of God in the flesh, and the continual testimony of Jesus borne by the Church in her preaching and ordinances, have broken and kept down, in some measure, the grosser manifestations of the power of Satan. (See Luke x. 18.) But (6) the assumption contained in the objection above must not be thus unreservedly granted. We cannot tell in how many cases of insanity the malady may not even now be traced to direct dæmoniacal possession. And, finally, (7) the above view, which I am persuaded is the only one honestly consistent with any kind of belief in the truth of the Gospel narratives, will offend none but those who deny the existence of the world of spirits altogether, and who are continually striving to narrow the limits of our belief in that which is invisible; a view which at every step involves difficulties far more serious than those from which it attempts to escape. But (II.) a fresh difficulty is here found in the latter part of the narrative, in which the devils *enter into the swine*, and *their destruction follows*. (1) Of the *reason* of this permission, we surely are not competent judges. Of this however we are sure, that 'if this granting of the request of the evil spirits helped in any way the cure of the man, caused them to resign their hold on him more easily, mitigated the paroxysm of their going forth (see Mark ix. 26), this would have been motive enough. Or still more probably, it may have been necessary, for the permanent healing of the man, that he should have an outward evidence and testimony that the hellish powers which held him in bondage had quitted him.' (Trench, p. 172.) (2) The destruction of the swine is not for a moment to be thought of in the matter, as if that were an act repugnant to the merciful character of our Lord's miracles. It finds its parallel in the cursing of the fig-tree (ch. xxi. 18—22); and we may well think that, if God has appointed so many animals daily to be slaughtered for the sustenance of men's bodies, He may also be pleased to destroy animal life when He sees fit for the liberation or instruction of their souls. Besides, if the confessedly far greater evil of the possession of *men* by evil spirits, and all the misery thereupon attendant, was permitted in God's inscrutable purposes, surely much more this lesser one. Whether there may have been special reasons in this case, such as the contempt of the Mosaic law by the keepers of the swine, we have no means of judging: but it is at least possible. (3) The fact itself related raises a question in our minds, which, though we cannot wholly answer, we may yet approximate to the solution of. How can we imagine the bestial nature capable of the reception of dæmoniac influence? If what has been cited above be true, and the unchecked indulgence of sensual appetite afforded an inlet for the powers of evil to possess the human dæmoniac, then we have their influence joined to that part of man's nature which he has in common with the brutes that perish, the *animal and sensual soul* (ψυχή). We may thus conceive that the same animal and sensual soul in the brute may be receptive of similar dæmoniacal influence. But with this weighty difference: that whereas in man there is an individual, immortal spirit, to which alone belongs his personality and deliberative will and reason,—and there was ever in him, as we have seen, a struggle and a protest against this tyrant power; the oppressed soul, the real 'I,' calling out against the usurper—this would not be the case with the brute, in whom this personality and reflective consciousness is wanting. And the result in the text confirms our view; for as soon as the dæmons enter into the swine, their ferocity, having no self-conserving balance as in the case of man, impels them headlong to their own de-

λαν πάντα, καὶ [v] τὰ τῶν [w] δαιμονιζομένων. 34 καὶ ἰδοὺ
πᾶσα ἡ πόλις ἐξῆλθεν εἰς [x] * συνάντησιν * τῷ Ἰησοῦ· καὶ
ἰδόντες αὐτὸν [y] παρεκάλεσαν ὅπως μεταβῇ ἀπὸ τῶν
[z] ὁρίων αὐτῶν. IX. 1 καὶ [a] ἐμβὰς εἰς [[b] τὸ] πλοῖον F και εμβας...
[c] διεπέρασεν καὶ ἦλθεν εἰς τὴν [d] ἰδίαν πόλιν.
2 Καὶ ἰδοὺ προσέφερον αὐτῷ [e] παραλυτικὸν ἐπὶ [f] κλίνης
[g] βεβλημένον. καὶ ἰδὼν ὁ Ἰησοῦς τὴν πίστιν αὐτῶν εἶπεν D και ιδων... G αυτων ειπεν...

v ch. xvi. 23 ‖. xxi. 21. xxii. 21 ‖. Rom. viii. 5. 2 Pet. ii. 22.
w ver. 16 reff.
x here only. Gen. xviii. 2. Num. xx. 20 al.
y w. ὅπως, Acts xxv. 2 only. παρακαλεῖν τοὺς φίλους ὅπως διδάσκωσιν αὐτήν, Plut. Vit. Demetr. § 38.
z ch. ii. 16 reff. Num. xxi. 23.
a ch. viii. 23 reff.
b see ch. xiv. 22. Mark iv. 1 al.
c ch. xiv. 34 ‖ Mk. Mark v. 21. Luke xvi. 26. Acts xxi. 2 only. Deut. xxx. 13.
d = Luke ii. 3. John iv. 44. 1 Tim. iii. 4.
e ch. iv. 24 reff.
f Mark iv. 21 al. Deut. iii. 11.
g ch. viii. 6 reff.

BCDEF GKLMS UVXΔΠ ℵ 1. 33

34. * ὑπάντησιν Bℵ 1. 33: απαντησιν Scr's w ev-P: συναντησιν C rel [Cyr$_1$]. * τοῦ Cℵ 33 ev-y: τω BL rel. (for τω ιυ̅, αυτου ev-z.) for οπως, ινα B.

Chap. IX. 1. aft εμβας ins ο ις̅ C[3]F 76. 240-7-58[2] Scr's f k p v, aft πλοιον C[1] 244 Scr's b q r. om το BC[3]L V-marg Xℵ 1. 33 sah goth Orig$_1$ Chr[-β] : ins C[1] rel copt. 2. for προσεφερον, προσφερουσιν C.

struction. 34.] This request, which is related by all three Evangelists, was probably not from humility, but for fear the miraculous powers of our Lord should work them still more worldly loss. For the additional particulars of this miracle, see Mark v. 15, 16, 18—20: Luke viii. 35, and notes. IX. 1.] Certainly this verse should be the sequel of the history in the last chapter. It is not connected with the miracle following;—which is placed by St. Luke at a different time, but with the indefinite introduction of *ἐγένετο ἐν μιᾷ τῶν ἡμερῶν.* [**τὸ**] **πλοῖον**, not *the ship*, as applying to any particular ship previously used, or kept by our Lord and the disciples,—but simply generic,—and expressed idiomatically in English by **a ship**, as E. V. *τὰ πλοῖα*, '*ships*,' are the whole genus, in which embarkation might have been made: *τὸ πλοῖον*, the individual of that genus, in which embarkation *actually was made:* but no further defined by the article, than *as being* one of that genus, not as being any one previously mentioned ship, or one hired for that purpose. This import of the article has been denied by Middleton, and the generic rendering in this commentary consequently impugned by his followers. In reply, I may observe (1) that of the occurrence of the generic sense, there is no doubt, even on Middleton's own shewing. In ch. x. 36, *ἐχθροὶ τοῦ ἀνθρώπου, οἱ οἰκιακοὶ αὐτοῦ*, he recognizes in substance the generic sense, by rendering *τοῦ ἀνθρώπου*, '*every man*,' or '*men generally*,' though he calls the use 'hypothetic.' Compare also *ἐξῆλθεν ὁ σπείρων τοῦ σπείρειν*, ch. xiii. 3, where *ὁ σπ.* is merely in the singular what *οἱ σπείροντες* would be in the plural, viz. '*he that soweth*,' '*a sower*,' generic. See also ch. xv. 11: Luke xi. 24; ch. xix. 10: 1 Cor. vii. 3; ch. xxv. 32 (where in English also we might say, 'as the shepherd divideth the sheep from the goats'); also ch. x. 12, 27. (2) We may say, if we please, that *some πλοῖον* is *implied in ἐμβάς*, and that the article refers to such implication. But this in fact amounts to the generic sense. If I say, without any previous mention of a particular ship, 'When he had embarked in the ship;' I imply by the word 'embarked,' connexion with a genus, *ships:* by adding, 'in the ship,' I signify elliptically, 'in the ship in which he did embark;' but I no further identify the ship, than as belonging to the genus before implied. (3) The use of the English article in the expression, 'in the house' (= indoors), 'in the field,' &c. is a case in point: the articles here also being *generic*. **τὴν ἰδ. πόλ.**] Capernaum, where our Lord now dwelt; cf. ch. iv. 13.

2—8.] Healing of a paralytic at Capernaum. Mark ii. 1—12. Luke v. 17—26, in both of which the account is more particular. **2. τὴν πίστιν αὐτ.**] Namely, in letting him down through the roof, because the whole house and space round the door was full, Mark ii. 4. **αὐτῶν** must be supposed to include the sick man, who was at least a consenting party to the bold step which they took. These words are common to the three Evangelists, as also *ἀφέωνταί σου* (or *σοι*) *αἱ ἁμ.* Neander (Leben Jesu, pp. 431, 432) has some excellent remarks on this man's disease. Either it was the natural consequence of sinful indulgence, or by its means the feeling of sinfulness and guilt was more strongly aroused in him, and he recognized the misery of his disease as the punishment of his sins. At all events spiritual and bodily pain seem to have been connected and in-

τῷ [e] παραλυτικῷ [h] Θάρσει τέκνον, [ik] ἀφέωνταί σοῦ αἱ
[k] ἁμαρτίαι. 3 καὶ ἰδού τινὲς τῶν γραμματέων [m] εἶπον ἐν
[m] ἑαυτοῖς Οὗτος [n] βλασφημεῖ. 4 καὶ ἰδὼν ὁ Ἰησοῦς τὰς
[o] ἐνθυμήσεις αὐτῶν εἶπεν [p] Ἵνα τί [q] ἐνθυμεῖσθε πονηρὰ ἐν
ταῖς καρδίαις ὑμῶν; 5 τί γάρ ἐστιν [r] εὐκοπώτερον, εἰπεῖν
[ik] Ἀφέωνταί σου αἱ [k] ἁμαρτίαι, ἢ εἰπεῖν Ἔγειρε καὶ περιπάτει; 6 ἵνα δὲ εἰδῆτε ὅτι [s] ἐξουσίαν [s] ἔχει ὁ υἱὸς τοῦ

h ver. 22 (|| L. v. r.). Mark vi. 50. x. 49. John xvi. 31. Acts xxiii. 11 only. Gen. xxxv. 17. (·ῥρεῖν, 2 Cor. v. 6.)
i = ch. vi. 12 reff.
k ||. ch. xii. 31. Luke vii. 47—49. Lev. iv. 20.
m ch. xxi. 38. Luke vii. 39. xvi. 3. xviii. 4. (see Mark xii. 7. Luke xii. 45. ch. iii. 9.)
n = ch. xxvi. 65. John x. 36 al. 4 Kings xix. 4, 6, 22.
o ch. xii. 25. Acts xvii. 29. Heb. iv. 12 only †. Job xxi. 27 Symm.
p ch. xxvii. 46, from Ps. xxi. 1. Luke xiii. 7. Acts iv. 25. vii. 26. 1 Cor. x, 29 only. Gen. iv. 6.
q ch. i. 20 only. Josh. vii. 21. Wisd. iii. 14. Sir. xvii. 31.
r ||. ch. xix. 24 ||. Luke xvi. 17 only †. Sir. xxii. 15. 1 Macc. iii. 18 only.
s ch. vii. 29 reff.

αφιενται BNא Orig₁, *remittuntur* vulg lat-*f ff*₁ D-lat syrr goth æth Iren-int: *αφιονται* D Orig₁ Niceph. rec (for *σου αι αμαρτιαι*) *σοι αι αμ. σου*, with L rel latt(and D-lat) syrr copt goth arm Iren-int₁ Orig-int₁ Hil; *σου αι αμ. σου* M Niceph: *σοι αι αμ.*, without *σου*, DΔ² forj lat-*k* Orig₁ Did [Iren-int₁]: txt BCΔ¹א 1. 33 æth Orig₁. (*See || Mark Luke, where also the readings differ. The txt is best attested, most simple in meaning, and least simple in construction.*)

[**3.** *ειπαν* B.]

4. for *ιδων*, *ειδως* BE²MΠ¹ 1 fuld syrr sah goth arm Chr: txt CDא rel latt copt. aft *ειπεν* ins *αυτοις* D 13. 42. 61. 124 Scr's w evv-44-x lat-*c h* Syr sah arm. rec ins *υμεις* bef *ενθυμεισθε*, with L rel syr goth arm: om BCDא 1. 33 latt Syr(appy) sah æth Chr Cypr Hil.

5. om *γαρ* KMUΠ 209-48-53 Scr's f w latt æth goth arm. *αφιενται* Bא³ᵃ: *αφιονται* Dא¹. rec (for *σου*) *σοι*, with UΔΠ(S 1. 33, e sil) latt syrr coptt æth arm: txt BCDא rel goth Constt Chr. rec *εγειραι* (*itacism ?*), with B(sic) U: *εγειραν* Δ: txt CDא rel. om *και* א¹(ins א²).

6. *ο υιος του ανθρωπου* bef *εξουσιαν εχει* D 33 latt Hil.

terchanged within him, and the former to have received accession of strength from the presence of the latter. Schleiermacher (on St. Luke, p. 80) supposes the haste of these bearers to have originated in the prospect of our Lord's speedy departure thence; but, as Neander observes, we do not know enough of the paralytic's own state to be able to say whether there may not have been some cause for it in the man himself. **ἀφέωνται**] Winer remarks (§ 14. 3),—'The old grammarians themselves were divided about this word: some, as Eustathius, (Il. π. 590,) treat it as identical with ἀφῶνται, as in Homer ἀφέῃ for ἀφῇ: others, more correctly, take it for the preterite (= ἀφεῖνται), e. g. Herodian, the Etymologicon, and Suidas, with this difference however, that Suidas believes it to be a Doric, the author of the Etym. an Attic form; the former is certainly right, and this perfect-passive form is cognate with the perf.-act. ἀφέωκα.'

4. ἰδών] By the spiritual power indwelling in Him. See John ii. 24, 25. No other interpretation of such passages is admissible. St. Mark's expression, ἐπιγνοὺς τῷ πνεύματι αὐτοῦ, is more precise and conclusive. So we have ἐνεβριμήσατο τῷ πνεύματι, John xi. 33, synonymous with ἐμβριμώμενος ἐν ἑαυτῷ, ibid. ver. 33. **ἵνα τί**—supply γένηται: see Klotz on Devarius, pp. 631-2: so Plut. Apol. p. 26 c, ἵνα τί ταῦτα λέγεις; From **τί γὰρ . . . οἶκόν σου** is common (nearly verbatim) to the three Evangelists.

5. τί γάρ ἐστιν εὐκ.] "In our Lord's argument it must be carefully noted, that He does not ask, *which is easiest*, to *forgive sins*, or to *raise a sick man*—for it could not be affirmed that that of forgiving was easier than this of healing—but, which is easiest, to *claim this power* or *that, to say* Thy sins be forgiven thee, or *to say*, Arise and walk? That (i. e. the former) is easiest, and I will now prove my right to say it, by saying with effect and with an outward consequence setting its seal to my truth, the harder word, Arise and walk. By doing that which is capable of being put to the proof, I will vindicate my right and power to do that which in its very nature is incapable of being proved. By these visible tides of God's grace I will give you to know in what direction the great under-currents of His love are setting, and that both are obedient to My word. From this, which I will now do openly and before you all, you may conclude that it is 'no robbery' (Phil. ii. 6, but see note there) upon my part to claim also the power of forgiving men their

t = || (bis). ch. xiv. 12 || Mk. al. Jer. xvii. 27.
u ||. Luke ii. 20. vii. 16 al. (Ps. xxi. 23.)
v ch. x. 1 ||. xxi. 23 ||. xxviii. 18. Acts viii. 19 al.
w intr., || Mk. ver. 27. ch. xx. 30. Mark xv. 21. John [viii. 59 v. r.] ix. 1. 1 Cor. vii. 31 only. (mid., 1 John ii. 8, 17 only.) Ps. cxxviii. 8.

ἀνθρώπου ἐπὶ τῆς γῆς [ik] ἀφιέναι [k] ἁμαρτίας, τότε λέγει τῷ
[e] παραλυτικῷ Ἐγερθεὶς [t] ἆρόν σου τὴν [f] κλίνην, καὶ
ὕπαγε εἰς τὸν οἶκόν σου. 7 καὶ ἐγερθεὶς ἀπῆλθεν εἰς τὸν
οἶκον αὐτοῦ· 8 ἰδόντες δὲ οἱ ὄχλοι ἐφοβήθησαν καὶ
[u] ἐδόξασαν τὸν [u] θεὸν τὸν [v] δόντα [v] ἐξουσίαν τοιαύτην τοῖς
ἀνθρώποις.
9 Καὶ [w] παράγων ὁ Ἰησοῦς ἐκεῖθεν εἶδεν ἄνθρωπον

Γ ix. 6 (or 7).. BCDEF GKLMS UVXΓΔ Πℵ 1. 33

for εγερθεις, εγειρε BD latt syrr coptt æth Hil: txt Cℵ rel goth arm. add και D lat-*a* g_1 *h* *k* æth Hil. for υπαγε, πορευου ℵ[1](txt ℵ[3a]).

8. rec (for εφοβηθησαν) εθαυμασαν, with C rel syr arm Thdor-mops: txt BDℵ **1. 33** latt Syr coptt æth Aug Hil Juv. (*admirantes timuerunt* lat-*f* goth.—εθαυμ. και X-comm: om X-txt [Iren-int_1].)

9. εκειθεν bef ο ῑς D 124 latt copt Eus Thph-ant Thl Hil: om εκειθεν (*beg of peric*) Lℵ[1] Scr's g evv-P-Z: txt BCℵ' rel [syrr sah goth æth arm].

sins." Trench on the Miracles, p. 206.

6. ὁ υἱ. τ. ἀνθ.] The Messiah: an expression regarded by the Jews as equivalent to ὁ χριστὸς ὁ υἱὸς τοῦ θεοῦ, ch. xxvi. 63. See also John v. 27. "The Alexandrian Fathers, in their conflict with the Nestorians, made use of this passage in proof of the entire transference which there was of all the properties of Christ's divine nature to His human; so that whatever one had, was so far common, that it might also be predicated of the other. It is quite true that had not the two natures been indissolubly knit together in a single Person, no such language could have been used; yet I should rather suppose that 'Son of Man' being the standing title whereby the Lord was well pleased to designate Himself, bringing out by it that He was at once one with humanity, and the crown of humanity, He does not so use it that the title is every where to be pressed, but at times simply as equivalent to Messiah." Trench, p. 208.

ἐπὶ τῆς γῆς] Distinguished from ἐν τῷ οὐρανῷ, as in ch. xvi. 19; xviii. 18. Bengel finely remarks, "Cœlestem ortum hic sermo sapit." The Son of Man, as God manifest in man's flesh, has on man's earth that power, which in its fountain and essence belongs to God in heaven. And this not by delegation, but "because He (being God) is the Son of Man." John v. 27.

τότε λέγει] See a similar interchange of the persons in construction, Gen. iii. 22, 23.

τότε λέγει τῷ π. is not parenthetic, nor is **ἵνα δὲ εἰδῆτε** κ.τ.λ. an elliptic sentence; but the speech and narrative are intermixed. A simple construction would require either ἵνα δὲ **εἰδῆτε** . . . . ὧδε λέγω τῷ παρ. . ., or ἵνα δὲ εἰδῶσιν . . . . . **τότε λέγει** . . . We have, in the text, the first member of the former construction joined with the second of the latter.

8. τοῖς ἀνθρώποις] Not plur. for sing. '*to a man*,' nor '*for the benefit of men*;' but **to mankind.** They regarded this wonder-working as something by God granted to men —to mankind; and without supposing that *they* had before them the full meaning of their words, those words were true in the very highest sense. See John xvii. 8. In Mark they say, ὅτι οὕτως οὐδέποτε εἴδαμεν: in Luke, ὅτι εἴδομεν παράδοξα σήμερον.

9—17.] THE CALLING OF MATTHEW: THE FEAST CONSEQUENT ON IT: ENQUIRY OF JOHN'S DISCIPLES RESPECTING FASTING:—AND OUR LORD'S ANSWER. Mark ii. 13—22. Luke v. 27—39. Our Lord was going out to the sea to teach, Mark, ver. 13. All three Evangelists connect this calling with the preceding miracle, and the subsequent entertainment. The real difficulty of the narrative is the question as to the identity of Matthew in the text, and Levi in Mark and Luke. I shall state the arguments on both sides. (1) There can be no question that *the three narratives relate to the same event.* They are identical almost verbatim; inserted between narratives indisputably relating the same occurrences. (2) The almost *general consent* of all ages has supposed the *two persons the same.* On the other hand, (3) *our Gospel makes not the slightest allusion to the name of Levi,* either here, or in ch. x. 3, where we find Μαθθαῖος ὁ τελώνης among the Apostles, clearly identified with the subject of this narrative: whereas the *other two Evangelists,* having in this narrative spoken of Levi, in their enumerations of the Apostles (Mark iii. 18: Luke vi. 15), *mention Matthew without any note of identifica-*

καθήμενον ἐπὶ τὸ [x] τελώνιον, Μαθθαῖον λεγόμενον, καὶ
λέγει αὐτῷ Ἀκολούθει μοι· καὶ [y] ἀναστὰς [y] ἠκολούθησεν
αὐτῷ. 10 [z] καὶ ἐγένετο αὐτοῦ [a] ἀνακειμένου ἐν τῇ οἰκίᾳ,

x ‖ only +. y ‖. Num. xxii. 20. (3 Kings xix. 21.) z Luke v. 17 reff. a ch. xxii. 10, 11. Mark xiv. 18 al. + Esdr. iv. 10 only.

επι το τελ. bef καθημενον C 21 Chr Aug: ins εκει bef καθ. $\aleph^{3a}$(appy: but erased). om 2nd και $\aleph^{1}$(ins $\aleph^{2}$). for ηκολουθησεν, ηκολουθει D$\aleph$ 1. 209.

10. ανακειμενου bef αυτου (*see ‖ Mark*) C$\aleph^{3a}$ latt Eus: και ανακειμενων, omg εγενετο

tion with the Levi called on this occasion. This is almost inexplicable, on the supposition of his having borne both names. (4) *Early tradition separates the two persons.* Clement of Alexandria, (Stromata, iv. 9 (73), p. 595 P,) quoting from Heracleon the Gnostic, (ὁ τῆς Οὐαλεντίνου σχολῆς δοκιμώτατος κατὰ λέξιν,) mentions Ματθαῖος, Φίλιππος, Θωμᾶς, Λευΐς καὶ ἄλλοι πολλοί, as eminent men who had not suffered martyrdom from a public confession of the faith. (5) Again, Origen, (against Celsus, book i. § 62, vol. i. p. 376,) when Celsus has called the Apostles τελώνας καὶ ναύτας, after acknowledging Μαθθαῖος ὁ τελώνης adds, ἔστω δὲ καὶ ὁ Λεβὴς τελώνης ἀκολουθήσας τῷ Ἰησοῦ. ἀλλ' οὔτι γε τοῦ ἀριθμοῦ τῶν ἀποστόλων αὐτοῦ ἦν, εἰ μὴ κατά τινα τῶν ἀντιγράφων τοῦ κατὰ Μάρκον εὐαγγελίου. It is not quite clear from this, whether the copies of Mark substituted Levi's (?) name for Matthew's, or for some other: but most probably the latter. But Λεβὴς and Λευΐς are hardly more nearly allied than Λεβὴς and Λεββαῖος, with whom Levi has sometimes been supposed identical. Λεβὴν τὸν τελώνην may then have been the reading for Θαδδαῖον, Mark iii. 18, where we now find the reading Λεββαῖον in D lat-*a b* ff_2 *i.* (6) It certainly would hence appear, as if there were in ancient times an idea that the two names belonged to distinct persons. But in the very passages where it is mentioned, a confusion is evident, which prevents us from drawing any certain conclusion able to withstand the general testimony to the contrary, arising from the prima facie view of the Gospel narrative. (7) It is probable enough that St. Matthew, in his own Gospel, would *mention only his apostolic name,* seeing that St. Mark and St. Luke also give him this name, *when they speak of him as an Apostle.* (8) It is remarkable, as an indication that St. Matthew's frequently unprecise manner of narration did not proceed from want of information,—that in this case, when he of all men must have been best informed, his own account is the least precise of the three. (9) With regard to the narrative itself in the text, we may observe, that this solemn and peculiar call seems (see ch. iv. 19, 22) *hardly to belong to any but an Apostle;* and that, as in the case of Peter, it here also *implies a previous acquaintance and discipleship.*

9.] **λεγόμενον**, not preceded by any other appellation, must not be pressed to any closer signification than that his name was Matthew. See ch. ii. 23.

10.] We are told in Luke v. 29, that Levi *made him a great feast in his house;* and, similarly, Mark has ἐν τῇ οἰκ. αὐτοῦ. The narrative in our text is so closely identical with that in Mark, that it is impossible to suppose, with Greswell, that a different feast is intended. The arguments by which he supports his view are by no means weighty. From the words τῇ οἰκίᾳ, he infers that the house was not that of Matthew, but that in which our Lord usually dwelt, which he supposes to be intended in several other places. But surely the article might be used without any such significance, or designating any particular house,—as would be very likely if Matthew himself is here the narrator. (A similar mistake has been made in supposing τὸ πλοῖον, as in ver. 1, and elsewhere, to mean some one particular ship; whereas it is generic: see note there.) Again, Greswell presses to verbal accuracy the terms used in the accounts (e. g. συνανέκειντο and ἐλθόντες συνανέκειντο), and attempts to shew them to be inconsistent with one another. But surely the time is past for such dealing with the historic text of the Gospels; and, besides, he has overlooked a great inconsistency in his own explanation, viz., that of making in the second instance, according to him, Scribes and Pharisees present at the feast given by a Publican, and exclaiming against that which they themselves were doing. It was not *at,* but *after* the feast that the discourse in vv. 11—17 took place. And his whole inference, that δοχὴ μεγάλη must be the great meal in the day, and consequently in the evening, hangs on too slender a thread to need refutation. The real difficulty, insuperable to a Harmonist, is the connexion here of the raising of Jaeirus's daughter with this feast: on which see below, ver. 18. **καὶ ἐγέν. . . . .**

b ch. xxviii. 9 reff. c ch. v. 46 reff. d ‖ Mk. ch. xiv. 9. Mark vi. 22, 26. Luke vii. 49. xiv. 10 only †. 3 Macc. v. 39. e ch. vi. 8 al. fr. Prov. xviii. 2. f absol., ‖ Mk. Josh. xiv. 11 a. g Luke iv. 23 reff. h ch. viii. 16 reff. i = Mark ix. 10. Luke viii. 19. Acts x. 17 al. j ch. xii. 7, from Hosea vi. 7. k constr., as above (j).

zb καὶ b ἰδοὺ πολλοὶ c τελῶναι καὶ ἁμαρτωλοὶ ἐλθόντες BCDEF GKLMS UVXΓΔ ΠΝ 1. 33
d συνανέκειντο τῷ Ἰησοῦ καὶ τοῖς μαθηταῖς αὐτοῦ.
11 καὶ ἰδόντες οἱ Φαρισαῖοι *εἶπον τοῖς μαθηταῖς αὐτοῦ
Διὰ τί μετὰ τῶν c τελωνῶν καὶ ἁμαρτωλῶν ἐσθίει ὁ
διδάσκαλος ὑμῶν; 12 ὁ δὲ ἀκούσας εἶπεν Οὐ e χρείαν
e ἔχουσιν οἱ f ἰσχύοντες g ἰατροῦ, ἀλλ' οἱ h κακῶς h ἔχοντες.
13 πορευθέντες δὲ μάθετε τί i ἐστιν j Ἔλεος k θέλω καὶ οὐ
θυσίαν. οὐ γὰρ ἦλθον l καλέσαι m δικαίους, ἀλλὰ n ἁμαρτωλούς.
14 Τότε προσέρχονται αὐτῷ οἱ μαθηταὶ Ἰωάννου λέγοντες Διὰ τί ἡμεῖς καὶ οἱ Φαρισαῖοι o νηστεύομεν p πολλά,

ch. xxvii. 43. Heb. x. 5, 8, from Ps. xxxix. 6. Ps. l. 16 (18). l = ‖. 1 Cor vii. 17 al. see Num. xxiii. 11. m = ‖. Luke xv. 7. see ch. i. 19. n Luke xv. 2, 7, 10. Ps. iii. 7 al. o ch. iv. 2 reff. p = Mark i. 45. iii. 12. v. 10, 23, 38. 1 Cor. xvi. 5. James iii. 2. Job xxxv. 5.

αυτου, ℵ[1] Syr. om και bef ιδου Dℵ latt coptt æth [Jer]. αμαρτωλοι και τελωναι C 21 copt æth [Cyr_1]. om ελθοντες ℵ[1](ins ℵ[2]) 235-43 [lat-*a* sah]. for συνανεκ., συνεκειντο D[1], *simul discumbebant cum* D-lat, *recumbebant cum* lat-*a b c*: txt D[3].

11. ειδοντες δε D sah. *ἔλεγον (*cf* ‖ *Mark Luke*) BCLℵ 1. 33 latt Syr Cyr_1: ειπον D rel syr, *dixerunt* lat-*k*. αμαρτωλων και τελωνων D sah [Cyr_1] Aug_1. ο διδ. υμ. bef μ. τ. α. κ. τ. εσθ. D lat-*b c* g_1 *h* Aug: bef εσθ. C[1] 1 coptt.

12. rec aft ο δε ins ις (*from* ‖ *Mark Luke*), with C rel latt syrr copt: om BDℵ sah æth. (D-gr is deficient at this point, but it evidently read ο δε ακουσας, not αποκριθεις, as Wetst.) rec aft ειπεν ins αυτοις (*from* ‖ *Mark*), with C[3]L rel lat-*a f h* syrr copt goth arm: om BC[1]Xℵ vulg lat-*b c* ff_1 g_1 *l* D-lat sah æth Jer. (D-gr def.) ιατρων ℵ.

13. rec ελεον, with C[3]L rel [$Clem_2$ Bas_1]: txt BC[1]Dℵ 1. 33 $Clem_2$ hom-Cl. δικαιους bef καλεσαι C[1]. (αλλα, so BCDELMUXΓΔΠℵ.) rec aft αμαρτωλους ins εις μετανοιαν (*from* ‖ *Luke*), with C rel 33[1] lat-*c* $g_{1.2}$ coptt syr-mg ($Orig_1$) Chr Cyr Hil Vict-tun: om BDV[1]Γ[1]Δℵ 1[1]. 33-corr[1] vulg lat-*a b f* ff_1 *h l* syrr goth æth arm Clem-rom $Orig_1$ Bas_1 Ambr. Jer Aug_{expr}.

14. for πολλα, πυκνα (‖ *Luke*) ℵ-corr[1 or 2]: om (*see* ‖ *Mark*) Bℵ[1] 27 Scr's g: txt ℵ[3] rel vss.

καὶ ἰδ.] a Hebraism, see reff.; it occurs, but with the omission of ἰδού, in Mark's account. The not very usual word, συνανέκειντο, is also common to the two. St. Mark, with his usual precision, adds ἦσαν γὰρ πολλοὶ καὶ ἠκολούθησαν αὐτῷ: a clause answering to ἐλθόντες in our text. See last note. **11. ἰδόντες**] **having observed this**, see ver. 4. These Pharisees appear to have been the Pharisees *of the place:* Luke adds αὐτῶν: οἱ Φ. καὶ οἱ γραμ. αὐτῶν. The very circumstances related shew that this remonstrance cannot have taken place *at* the feast. The Pharisees say the words to the disciples: our Lord hears it. This denotes an occasion when our Lord and the disciples were present, but not surely intermixed with the ὄχλος τελωνῶν πολύς. **12. ἰσχύοντες . . . . κακῶς ἔχ.**] Both words, in the application of the saying, must be understood *subjectively* ('ironica concessio,' Calvin, Meyer): as referring to their respective opinions of themselves; as also δικαιους and ἁμαρτωλούς, ver. 13:—not as though the Pharisees were *objectively* either ἰσχύοντες or δίκαιοι, however much objective truth κακῶς ἔχοντες and ἁμαρτωλοί may have had as applied to the publicans and sinners. **13.**] **πορευθέντες μάθετε** answers to an expression frequent in the Talmud, צא ולמד. **ἔλεος θέλ.**] The whole of this discourse, with the exception of the citation, is almost verbatim in Mark, and (with ὑγιαίνοντες = ἰσχύοντες, ἐλήλυθα = ἦλθον, and the addition of εἰς μετάνοιαν) Luke also. **14.**] According to the detailed narrative of St. Mark (ii. 18) it was the disciples of John *and of the Pharisees* who asked this question. St. Luke continues the discourse as that of the former Pharisees and Scribes. This is one of those instances where the three accounts imply and confirm one another, and the hints incidentally dropped by one Evangelist form the prominent assertions of the other. The *fasting often* of the disciples of John

οἱ δὲ μαθηταί σου οὐ ° νηστεύουσιν; 15 καὶ εἶπεν αὐτοῖς ὁ
Ἰησοῦς Μὴ δύνανται οἱ [q] υἱοὶ τοῦ [r] νυμφῶνος [s] πενθεῖν
[t] ἐφ᾽ [t] ὅσον μετ᾽ αὐτῶν ἐστιν ὁ [u] νυμφίος; [v] ἐλεύσονται δὲ
[v] ἡμέραι ὅταν [w] ἀπαρθῇ ἀπ᾽ αὐτῶν ὁ [u] νυμφίος, καὶ τότε
° νηστεύσουσιν. 16 οὐδεὶς δὲ [x] ἐπιβάλλει [y] ἐπίβλημα [z] ῥά-

q = ch. viii. 12. xiii. 38. Luke xx. 34, 36 al. Ezra ii. 1. r ‖ only †. Tobit vi. 13, 16 only. s ch. v. 4 reff. t 2 Pet. i. 13. (1 Cor. vii. 39. Gal. iv. 1.) Xen. Cyr. v. 5. 8. u ‖. ch. xxv. 1. John ii. 9. iii. 29 (3ce). Rev. xviii. 23 only. Isa. lxii. 5. v ‖. Luke xvii. 22 al. Amos viii. 11. xi. 13. w ‖ only ‡. Gen. xii. 9. Exod. xii. 37. x = ‖ L. Mark xi. 7. elsw. chiefly with χείρ. Lev. xix. 19. y ‖ (L. bis) only. Isa. iii. 21 only. z ‖ Mk. only. Isa. lxiv. 6. Jer. xlv. (xxxviii.) 11 only.

15. for μη, μητι D, *numquid* latt. for νυμφωνος, νυμφιου D latt(*sponsi*) copt goth æth Arnob Aug. for πενθειν, νηστευειν (*from* ‖ *Mark Luke*) D 61[1] lat-*a b c f ff*$_1$ *g*$_1$ *h l* Syr syr-mg sah Chr Arnob Hil. om from νυμφιος to νυμφιος (*homœotel*) ℵ[1](ins ℵ-corr[1]). ins αι bef ημεραι D. for απαρθη, αρθη D 1 Scr's g. for νηστευσουσιν, νηστευουσιν D[1]X 75. 111 Scr's i w ev-y. at end add εν εκειναις ταις ημεραις (*from* ‖ *Mark Luke*) D 111 lat-*a b c g*$_1$ *h* syr-mg [Bas$_1$] Orig[-int$_1$].

must not be understood as done in mourning for their master's imprisonment, but as belonging to the asceticism which John, as a preacher of repentance, inculcated. On the fasts of the Pharisees, see Lightfoot in loc. **15.**] πενθεῖν = νηστεύειν Mark and Luke. The difference of these two words is curiously enough one of Greswell's arguments for the non-identity of the narratives. Even if there were any force in such an argument, we might fairly set against it that ἀπαρθῇ is common to all three Evangelists, and occurs no where else in the N. T. **ὁ νυμφίος**] This appellation of Himself had from our Lord peculiar appropriateness as addressed to the disciples of John. Their master had himself said (John iii. 29) ὁ ἔχων τὴν νύμφην, νυμφίος ἐστίν· ὁ δὲ φίλος τοῦ νυμφίου ὁ ἑστηκὼς καὶ ἀκούων αὐτοῦ, χαρᾷ χαίρει διὰ τὴν φωνὴν τοῦ νυμφίου. αὕτη οὖν ἡ χαρὰ ἡ ἐμὴ πεπλήρωται. Our Lord in calling Himself the Bridegroom, announces the fulfilment in Him of a whole cycle of O. T. prophecies and figures: very probably with *immediate* reference to Hosea ii., that prophet having been cited just before: but also to many other passages, in which the Bride is the Church of God, the Bridegroom the God of Israel. See especially Isa. liv. 5—10 Heb. and E. V. As Stier (Reden Jesu, i. 320, edn. 2) observes, the article here must not be considered as merely introduced on account of the parable, as usual elsewhere, but the parable itself to have sprung out of the emphatic name, ὁ νυμφίος. The υἱοὶ τοῦ νυμφῶνος are more than the mere guests at the wedding: they are the bridegroom's friends who go and fetch the bride. **ἐλεύσονται δὲ ἡμ.**] How sublime and peaceful is this early announcement by our Lord of the bitter passage before Him! Compare the words of our Christian poet: 'measuring with calm presage the infinite descent.' (Wizenmann mag dabei wohl fragen: ‚Welcher Mensch hat je so ruhig, so lieblich von einer solchen Höhe in eine solche Tiefe geschaut?' Stier, Reden Jesu, i. 322.)

ὅταν ἀπ.] **when the Bridegroom shall have been taken from them**: when His departure shall have taken place. **καὶ τότε ν.**] These words are not a declaration of a duty, or of an ordinance, as binding on the Church in the days of her Lord's absence: the whole spirit of what follows is against such a supposition: but they declare, in accordance with the parallel word πενθεῖν, that in those days they shall have *real occasion* for fasting; sorrow enough; see John xvi. 20:—a fast of God's own appointing in the solemn purpose of His will respecting them, not one of their own arbitrary laying on. This view is strikingly brought out in Luke, where the question is, Can ye ποιῆσαι νηστεύειν the children, &c., i. e. by your rites and ordinances? but, &c. and τότε νηστεύσουσιν: there is no constraint in this latter case: they shall (or better, they will) fast. And this furnishes us with an analogous rule for the fasting of the Christian life: that it should be the genuine offspring of inward and spiritual sorrow, of the sense of the absence of the Bridegroom in the soul,—not the forced and stated fasts of the old covenant, now passed away. It is an instructive circumstance that in the Reformed Churches, while those stated fasts which were retained at their first emergence from Popery are in practice universally disregarded even by their best and holiest sons,—nothing can be more affecting and genuine than the universal and solemn observance of any real occasion of fasting placed before them by God's Providence.

κους [a] ἀγνάφου ἐπὶ ἱματίῳ παλαιῷ· [b] αἴρει γὰρ τὸ [c] πλή- BCDEF
ρωμα αὐτοῦ ἀπὸ τοῦ ἱματίου, καὶ [d] χεῖρον [e] σχίσμα γίνεται. GKLMS
17 οὐδὲ [f] βάλλουσιν οἶνον νέον εἰς [g] ἀσκοὺς παλαιούς· UVXΓΔ
[h] εἰ δὲ μήγε, [i] ῥήγνυνται οἱ [g] ἀσκοί, καὶ ὁ οἶνος [k] ἐκχεῖται, Πℵ 1. 33
καὶ οἱ [g] ἀσκοὶ ἀπολοῦνται· ἀλλὰ [f] βάλλουσιν οἶνον νέον
εἰς [g] ἀσκοὺς καινούς, καὶ ἀμφότεροι [l] συντηροῦνται.

a ‖ Mk. only †. b absol., ‖ Mk. only. c = ‖ Mk. only ‡. d ‖ Mk. ch. xxvii. 64 al.† Wisd. xv. 18 only. e ‖ Mk. John vii. 43. ix. 16. x. 19. 1 Cor. i. 10. xi. 18. xii. 25 only †. f Mark vii. 33. John xviii. 11. Jer. xvii. 8. g here (4 times) and ‖ only. Josh. ix. 4, 13. Job xxxii. 19. h ‖ L. bis. (Mk. εἰ δὲ μή.) ch. vi. 1. Luke x. 6. xiii. 9. xiv. 32. 2 Cor. xi. 16 only. i ‖. Mark ix. 18 ‖ L. Gal. iv. 27 (from Isa. liv. 1) only. k (‖ Mk. v. r.) John ii. 15 al. Deut. xv. 23. l (‖ L. v. r.) Mark vi. 20. Luke ii. 19 only. Prov. xv. 4.

16. om *αυτου* ℵ[1](ins ℵ[2]).
17. for *μηγε*, *μη* (*see Mark* ii. 22) B 301. *ρησσει ο οινος ο νεος τους ασκους* D; so, but om *ο νεος*, lat-g_1 syr-jer Arnob. for *εκχειται κ. οι ασκ. απολ.*, *απολλυται κ. οι ασκ.* D lat-*k*.—for *απολουνται*, *απολλυνται* Bℵ 1 vulg lat-*f* syrr coptt goth. *οινον νεον εις ασκους* bef *βαλλουσιν* (*see* ‖ *Luke*) C 21 ev-36, simly lat-*a b c* Aug: *αλλ οινον νεον εις ασκ. καιν. βλητεον* ℵ: for *αλλα βαλλ.*, *βαλλ. δε* D. rec *αμφοτερα* (*corrn*), with lat-*h*(*utraque*) Euthym: txt BCDℵ rel Scr's mss.—(homœotel (*-ουνται* to *-ουνται*) *αλλα* to *συντηρουνται* S.) *τηρουνται servantur* D[1](txt D[3]) lat-*a c*.

It is also remarkable how uniformly a strict attention to artificial and prescribed fasts accompanies a hankering after the hybrid ceremonial system of Rome. Meyer remarks well that **τότε** refers to a definite point of time, not to the whole subsequent period. **16.**] Our Lord in these two parables contrasts the old and the new, the legal and evangelic dispensations, with regard to the point on which He was questioned. The idea of the *wedding* seems to run through them: the preparation of the robe, the pouring of the new wine, are connected by this as their leading idea to one another and to the preceding verses. The old system of prescribed fasts for fasting's sake must not be patched with the new and sound piece; the complete and beautiful whole of Gospel light and liberty must not be engrafted as a mere addition on the worn out system of ceremonies. For the πλήρωμα αὐτοῦ, the completeness of it, the new patch, by its weight and its strength pulls away the neighbouring weak and loose threads by which it holds to the old garment, and a worse rent is made. Stier notices the prophetic import of this parable: in how sad a degree the χεῖρον σχίσμα γίνεται has been fulfilled in the history of the Church, by the attempts to patch the new, the Evangelic state, upon the old worn out ceremonial system. 'Would,' he adds, 'that we could say in the interpretation, as in the parable, *No man doeth this!*' The robe must be *all new*, all consistent: old things, old types, old ceremonies, old burdens, sacrifices, priests, sabbaths, and holy days, all are passed away: behold all things are become new. **χεῖρον σχ. γίν.**] **a worse rent takes place**: not, as E. V., '*the rent is made worse*' (χ. γίν. τὸ σχ.,—or χ. τὸ σχ. γίν.), a worse rent, because the old, original rent was included within the circumference of the ἐπίβλημα, whereas this is outside it. **17.**] This parable is not a repetition of the previous one, but a stronger and more exact setting forth of the truth in hand. As is frequently our Lord's practice in His parables, He advances from the immediate subject to something more spiritual and higher, and takes occasion from answering a cavil, to preach the sublimest truths. The garment was something *outward*; this wine is *poured in*, is something *inward*, the spirit of the system. The former parable respected the outward freedom and simple truthfulness of the New Covenant; this regards its inner spirit, its pervading principle. And admirably does the parable describe the vanity of the attempt to keep the new wine in the ἀσκὸς παλαιός, the old ceremonial man, unrenewed in the spirit of his mind: **ῥήγνυνται οἱ ἀσκοί**: the new wine is something too living and strong for so weak a moral frame; it shatters the fair outside of ceremonial seeming; and **ὁ οἶνος ἐκχεῖται**, the spirit is lost, the man is neither a blameless Jew nor a faithful Christian; both are spoiled. And then the result: not merely the damaging, but the utter destruction of the vessel,—**οἱ ἀσκοὶ ἀπολοῦνται.** According to some expositors, the *new patch* and *new wine* denote the *fasting*; the *old garment* and *old bottles*, the *disciples*. ὃ δὲ λέγει, τοιοῦτόν ἐστιν· οὔπω γεγόνασιν ἰσχυροὶ οἱ μαθηταί, ἀλλ' ἔτι πολλῆς δέονται συγκαταβάσεως· οὔπω διὰ τοῦ πνεύματος ἀνεκαινίσθησαν. οὕτω δὲ δια-

18 Ταῦτα αὐτοῦ λαλοῦντος αὐτοῖς ἰδοὺ ἄρχων εἰςελθὼν [m] προςεκύνει αὐτῷ λέγων ὅτι Ἡ θυγάτηρ μου ἄρτι
...ἐπ' αυ. V. ἐτελεύτησεν· ἀλλὰ ἐλθὼν [n] ἐπίθες τὴν [n] χεῖρά σου ἐπ'
αὐτὴν καὶ [o] ζήσεται. 19 καὶ ἐγερθεὶς ὁ Ἰησοῦς * ἠκολούθει
αὐτῷ καὶ οἱ μαθηταὶ αὐτοῦ. 20 καὶ ἰδοὺ γυνὴ [p] αἱμοῤ-
...oπισθεν X. ῥοοῦσα δώδεκα ἔτη προςελθοῦσα ὄπισθεν ἥψατο τοῦ
BCDEF GKLMS UΓΔΠℵ 1. 33 [q] κρασπέδου τοῦ ἱματίου αὐτοῦ. 21 [r] ἔλεγεν γὰρ ἐν [r] ἑαυτῇ
Ἐὰν μόνον ἅψωμαι τοῦ ἱματίου αὐτοῦ, [s] σωθήσομαι.
22 ὁ δὲ Ἰησοῦς στραφεὶς καὶ ἰδὼν αὐτὴν εἶπεν [t] Θάρσει
θύγατερ, ἡ πίστις σου σέσωκέν σε. καὶ [s] ἐσώθη ἡ γυνὴ
ἀπὸ τῆς ὥρας ἐκείνης. 23 καὶ ἐλθὼν ὁ Ἰησοῦς εἰς τὴν

m ch. iv. 9 reff.
n constr., Mark (viii. 25 v. r.) xvi. 18. Acts ix. 17. Lev. i. 4 al. see ch. xix. 13, 15 reff.
o = John v. 25. Rev. ii. 8. xiii. 14. Ezek xxxvii. 3.
p here only. Lev. xv. 33 only.
q || L. ch. xiv. 36 ||. xxiii. 5 only. Num. xv. 38 bis, 39. Deut. xxii. 12. (Ezek. viii. 3 Ald. compl.) Zech. viii. 23 only.
r ch. iii. 9 reff. see Ps. xxxv. 1.
s = || Mk. Luke viii. 36. Acts iv. 9 al.
t ver. 2 reff.

18. rec (for εισελθων) ελθων: εις (i. e. εἷς) προσελθων Bℵ[2], *unus accessit et* latt syr goth æth arm: προσελθων ℵ[1] 13 & 157(Tischdf): τις προσηλθεν F: τις προσελθων C[3]GLU 13 Scr's b f g h s v evv-H-P-x-y sah(appy) Thl: τις ελθων Γ Scr's i l m n: εἷς ελθων και προσελθων Syr: τις εισελθων Scr's q r: txt CDEMXℵ[3a] 1 Scr's a p Chr Bas, εἷς ελθων KSVΔΠ 33 Scr's w.—add τω ιησου C[3]-marg FGLU Scr's b f[2] h s v evv-H-P. om οτι DMℵ 1. 33 latt Syr coptt æth arm Bas_1 Chr Hil: ins κυριε M vulg lat-*f* ff_1 *h* Hil.

19. * rec ἠκολούθησεν (*corrn to the usual historic tense, the force of the imperf being overlooked?*), with BL rel lat-*f k* syr coptt [Bas_1 Chr]: ηκολουθησαν EM Syr: ηκολουθει CDℵ 33 latt Hil.

21. om μονον ℵ[1](ins ℵ[2]) [lat-*a* g_1 *h*]: αψωμαι bef μονον D latt.

22. om ιησ. Dℵ[1](txt ℵ[2]), *qui autem* D-lat, *at ille* lat-*a b c*. rec **επιστραφεις** (*from || Mark*), with CL rel: *conversus* lat-*a b c*: εστη στραφεις *conversus stetit* D: txt Bℵ 13. 33 evv-P-x. θυγατηρ DGL: txt BCℵ rel $Orig_2$.

κειμένοις οὐ χρὴ βάρος ἐπιτιθέναι ἐπιταγμάτων. Chrysostom, Hom. in Matt. xxx. 4, p. 353. This view is stated and defended at some length by Neander, Leben Jesu, p. 346, note; but I own seems to me, as to De Wette, far-fetched. For how can fasting be called ἐπίβλημα ῥάκους ἀγνάφου, or how compared to new wine? And Neander himself, when he comes to explain the important addition in Luke (on which see Luke v. 39, and note), is obliged to change the meaning, and understand the new wine of the spirit of the Gospel. It was and is the custom in the East to carry their wine on a journey in *leather bottles*, generally of goats' skin, sometimes of asses' or camels' skin. (Winer, Realwörterbuch, 'Schlauch.')

18—26.] RAISING OF JAEIRUS'S DAUGHTER, AND HEALING OF A WOMAN WITH AN ISSUE OF BLOOD. Mark v. 21—43. Luke viii. 41—56. In Luke and Mark this miracle follows immediately after the casting out of the devils at Gadara, and our Lord's recrossing the lake to Capernaum; but without any precise note of time as here. He may well have been by the sea (as seems implied by Mark and Luke), when the foregoing conversation with the disciples of John and the Pharisees took place. The account in the text is the most concise of the three; both Mark and Luke, but especially the latter, giving many additional particulars. The miracle forms a very instructive point of comparison between the three Gospels.

18. ἄρχων] A *ruler of the synagogue*, named Jaeirus. In all except the connecting words, ταῦτα αὐτοῦ λαλοῦντος αὐτοῖς, and **εἰςελθ.**, which seems to imply that our Lord was still in Levi's house, the account in the text is summary, and deficient in particularity. I have therefore reserved full annotation for the account in Luke, which see throughout. **ἄρτι ἐτελεύτησεν**] She was *not dead*, but *dying*: at the last extremity. St. Matthew, omitting the message from the ruler's house (Mark v. 35: Luke viii. 49), gives the matter summarily in these words. **20.**] The **κράσπεδον**, see ref. Num., was the fringe or tassel which the Jews were commanded to wear on each corner of their outer garment, as a sign that they were to be holy unto God. The article, as in ch. xiv. 36, designates the particular tassel which was touched.

22.] The cure was effected on her touch-

οἰκίαν τοῦ ἄρχοντος καὶ ἰδὼν τοὺς [u] αὐλητὰς καὶ τὸν BCDEF GKLMS UΓΔΠℵ 1. 33
ὄχλον [v] θορυβούμενον
24 ἔλεγεν [w] Ἀναχωρεῖτε· οὐ γὰρ
ἀπέθανεν τὸ [x] κοράσιον, ἀλλὰ [y] καθεύδει. καὶ [z] κατεγέλων
αὐτοῦ.
25 ὅτε δὲ [a] ἐξεβλήθη ὁ ὄχλος, εἰσελθὼν [b] ἐκράτησεν τῆς [b] χειρὸς αὐτῆς, καὶ ἠγέρθη τὸ [x] κοράσιον.
26 καὶ [c] ἐξῆλθεν ἡ [d] φήμη αὕτη εἰς ὅλην τὴν γῆν ἐκείνην.
27 Καὶ [e] παράγοντι ἐκεῖθεν τῷ [f] Ἰησοῦ ἠκολούθησαν
[f] αὐτῷ δύο τυφλοὶ κράζοντες καὶ λέγοντες [g] Ἐλέησον ἡμᾶς
[h] υἱὸς Δαυείδ.
28 ἐλθόντι δὲ εἰς τὴν οἰκίαν προσῆλθον
αὐτῷ οἱ τυφλοί, καὶ λέγει αὐτοῖς ὁ Ἰησοῦς Πιστεύετε
ὅτι δύναμαι τοῦτο ποιῆσαι; λέγουσιν αὐτῷ Ναὶ κύριε.

u Rev. xviii. 22 only +. (-λος, 1 Cor. xiv. 7.)
v ‖ Mk. Acts xvii. 5. xx. 10 only. Judg. iii. 26.
w ch. ii. 12 reff.
x here & ‖ Mk. bis. ch. xiv. 11. Mark vi. 22, 28 bis only. 1 Kings ix. 11.
y = 1 Thess. v. 10 only. Dan. xii. 2.
z ‖ only. Prov. xvii. 5.
a = ‖ Mk. ch. xxi. 12.
b ‖. Mark i. 31. Gen. xix. 16. Isa. xlii. 6.
c = Mark i. 28. Rom. x. 18, from Ps. xviii. 4. 1 Thess. i. 8.
d Luke iv. 14 only. Prov. xvi. 2. (xv. 30.) 2 Macc. iv. 39 only.
e ver. 9 reff.
f constr., ch. viii. 1 reff.
g ch. xv. 22. xx. 30, 31 ‖ al. Ps. vi. 2.
h ch. i. 1 al. see note.

24. rec (for ελεγεν) λεγει (*from* ‖ *Mark*), with CL rel: txt BDℵ 1. 13. 33 vulg lat-*a b f ff*$_1$ *g*$_2$ coptt goth æth Chr, *dixit* lat-*c g*$_1$ *h*. rec adds αυτοις, with CL rel lat-*f g*$_1$ syrr goth arm: om BDℵ 1. 13. 33 latt coptt æth [Chr]. αυτον D¹(txt D⁴). add ειδοτες οτι απεθανεν (‖ *Luke*) ℵ¹(ℵ³ᵃ puts it in brackets) sah.

25. for εισελθ., ελθων D lat-*a b*. την χειρα D.

26. αυτης C¹ℵ 1. 33. 118-24 copt: αυτου C-corr¹ or ²[?] D Scr's g sah æth: txt B rel.

27. om αυτω BD ev-36¹ Chr-3-5-8-α(and Fd): ins CLℵ rel vss Chr-1-β-A. κραυγαζοντες ℵ. om και λεγοντες C¹(appy) L 124. 235 lat-*a k*. rec υιε (*gramml corrn*), with C²Dℵ rel: txt BGUΠ Ath Damasc. (C¹Δ uncert.)

28. for ελθοντι δε, και ερχεται D lat-*a b c g*$_1$ *h*: εισελθ. δε ℵ¹(txt ℵ³ᵃ). add αυτω Uℵ 22. 111. 235 Scr's f¹ o s ev-P. aft οικιαν ins και D lat-*a b c g*$_1$. [προσηλθαν B.] ins δυο bef τυφλοι Dℵ¹(ℵ³ᵃ disapproving) lat-*a b g*$_2$ *h* syr-jer. om ὁ ℵ¹(ins ℵ³ᵃ). aft δυν. ins υμιν ℵ¹·²(om ℵ-corr¹·³ᵃ), simly latt(not *b* D-lat) arm: ποιησαι bef τουτο C¹: του. δυν. ποι. B vulg.

ing our Lord's garment, Mark v. 27—29: Luke viii. 44. And our Lord enquired who touched Him (Mark, Luke), for He perceived that virtue had gone out of Him (Luke). She, knowing what had been done to her, came fearing and trembling, and told Him all. **24.**] No inference can be drawn from *these words* as to the fact of the maiden's actual death; for our Lord uses equivalent words respecting Lazarus (John xi. 11). And if it be answered that there He explains the sleep to *mean death*, we answer, that this explanation is only in consequence of the disciples misunderstanding his words. In both cases the words are most probably used *with reference to the speedy awakening which was to follow*, as Fritzsche (cited by Trench, Miracles, p. 183): 'Puellam ne pro mortua habetote, sed dormire existimatote, quippe in vitam mox rediturам.' Luke appends, after κατ. αὐτ.,—εἰδότες ὅτι ἀπέθανεν, in which words there is at least no recognition by the Evangelist of a mere apparent death.

25.] **ἐκρ. τῆς χ. αὐ.** is common to the three Evangelists. From Luke we learn that our Lord said ἡ παῖς, ἔγειρε: from Mark we have the words He actually uttered, ταλιθὰ κοῦμ: from both we learn that our Lord only took with him Peter, James, and John, and the father and mother of the maiden,—that she was twelve years old,—and that our Lord commanded that something should be given her to eat. She was an *only* daughter, Luke viii. 42.

27—31.] Healing of two blind men. *Peculiar to Matthew.* **27.**] **παρ. ἐκεῖθεν** is too vague to be taken as a fixed note of sequence; for ἐκεῖθεν may mean the house of Jaeirus, or the town itself, or even that part of the country,—as ver. 26 has generalized the locality, and implied some pause of time. **υἱὸς Δαυείδ**] εἰς τιμὴν αὐτοῦ τοῦτο κράζουσιν· ἐντιμοτάτη γὰρ παρ' Ἰουδαίοις ἦν ἡ τοιαύτη προσηγορία. Euthym. It is remarkable that, in all the three narratives of giving sight to the blind in this Gospel, the title **Son of David** appears. **28. τὴν οἰκίαν**] εἰκός, πιστοῦ τινος εἶναι τὴν οἰκίαν, εἰς ἣν κατήχθη. Euthym. Or, the house which our Lord inhabited at Capernaum (De Wette and others); but I conceive that ἡ οἰκία need not mean any particular house, merely, as we sometimes use the expression, *the house*, as opposed

29 τότε ἥψατο τῶν ὀφθαλμῶν αὐτῶν λέγων Κατὰ τὴν
πίστιν ὑμῶν [i] γενηθήτω ὑμῖν. 30 καὶ [k] ἠνεῴχθησαν αὐτῶν
οἱ [k] ὀφθαλμοί. καὶ [l] ἐνεβριμήθη αὐτοῖς ὁ Ἰησοῦς λέγων
[m] Ὁρᾶτε μηδεὶς γινωσκέτω. 31 οἱ δὲ ἐξελθόντες [n] διεφή-
μισαν αὐτὸν ἐν ὅλῃ τῇ γῇ ἐκείνῃ.
32 Αὐτῶν δὲ ἐξερχομένων ἰδοὺ προσήνεγκαν αὐτῷ [ἄν-
θρωπον] [o] κωφὸν [op] δαιμονιζόμενον. 33 καὶ [q] ἐκβληθέντος
τοῦ [q] δαιμονίου ἐλάλησεν ὁ κωφός· καὶ ἐθαύμασαν οἱ ὄχλοι
λέγοντες Οὐδέποτε ἐφάνη οὕτως ἐν τῷ Ἰσραήλ. 34 οἱ δὲ

i ch. viii. 13. xv. 28. xviii. 19. Luke i. 38.
k ch. xx. 33. John ix. 10, &c. Isa. xxxv. 5.
l Mark i. 43. xiv. 5. John xi. 33, 38 only †. Isa. xvii. 13 Symm.
m = ch. viii. 4 reff.
n ch. xxviii. 15. Mark i. 45 only †.
o ch. xii. 22. see Luke xi. 14. Mark ix. 25.
p ch. viii. 16 reff.
q ch. vii. 22 reff.

29. for οφθαλμων, ομματων D. for λεγων, και ειπεν D 1 lat-*h* Syr.
30. rec ανεωχ., with ℵ rel: ηνοιχθησαν C[1]: txt BD 33 [Chr-β]. οι οφθαλμοι bef αυτων D latt: om αυτων ℵ[1](txt ℵ[3a]). rec (for ενεβριμηθη) ενεβριμησατο, with B[2]CD rel: txt B[1]ℵ 1. 22. 118. om ο (bef ιησ.) D.
31. om ολη ℵ[1](ins ℵ[2]).
32. om ανθρωπον Bℵ 27. 99. 124 Syr coptt æth: ins CD rel.
33. rec aft λεγοντες ins οτι, with [V(Tischdf)] (Scr's l m n, e sil) lat-*a* arm: om BCDℵ rel vulg lat-*b c f* ff_1 $g_{1.2}$ *h* syrr copt goth æth Chr Thl. ουτως bef εφανη D 33 lat-*a b c* ff_1 $g_{1.2}$ *h* goth. om τω D[1](ins D[3]).

to *the open air:* see note on ver. 1. **τοῦτο ποιῆσαι**] i. e. the healing, implied in ἐλέησον ἡμᾶς. **υἱὸς Δ. . . . . κύριε**] See Ps. cx. 1, and ch. xxii. 45; also ch. xii. 23; xx. 30, 31. *Touching*, or *anointing* the eyes, was the ordinary method which our Lord took of impressing on the blind the action of the divine power which healed them. Ch. xx. 34: Mark viii. 25: John ix. 6. **29.**] In this miracle however we have this peculiar feature, that no direct word of power passes from our Lord, but a relative concession, making that which was done *a measure of the faith* of the blind men: and from the result the degree of their faith appears. Stier remarks (Reden Jesu, i. 383), "We may already notice, in the history of this first period of our Lord's ministry, that from having at first yielded immediately to the request for healing, He begins, by degrees, to prove and exercise the faith of the applicants." **30. ἐνεβριμήθη**] Suidas explains this word, μετὰ ἀπειλῆς ἐντέλλεσθαι, μετ' αὐστηρότητος ἐπιτιμᾶν. The purpose of our Lord's earnestness appears to have been twofold: (1) that He might not be so occupied and overpressed with applications as to have neither time nor strength for the preaching of the Gospel: (2) to prevent the already-excited people from taking some public measure of recognition, and thus arousing the malice of the Pharisees before His hour was come.

No doubt the two men were guilty of an act of disobedience in thus breaking the Lord's solemn injunction: for obedience is better than sacrifice; the humble observance of the word of the Lord, than the most laborious and wide-spread will-worship after man's own mind and invention. Trench (Miracles, p. 197) well remarks, that the fact of almost all the Romish interpreters having applauded this act, is "very characteristic, and rests on very deep differences."

32—34.] Healing of a dumb dæmoniac. *Peculiar to Matthew.* The word ἐξερχομένων, being a present participle, places this miracle in direct connexion with the foregoing. This narration has a singular affinity with that in ch. xii. 22, or still more with its parallel in Luke xi. 14. In both, the same expression of wonder follows; the same calumny of the Pharisees; only that in ch. xii. the dæmoniac is said (not in Luke xi.) to have been likewise blind. These circumstances, coupled with the immediate connexion of *this* miracle with the cure of the blind men, and the mention of 'the Son of David' in both, have led some to suppose that the account in ch. xii. is a repetition, or slightly differing version of the account in our text, intermingled also with the preceding healing of the blind. But the supposition seems unnecessary,—as, the habit of the Pharisees once being to ascribe our Lord's expulsion of devils to Beelzebub, the repetition of the remark would be natural:—and the other coincidences, though considerable, are not exact enough to warrant it. This was a dumbness *caused* by dæmoniacal posses-

Φαρισαῖοι ἔλεγον [r] Ἐν τῷ ἄρχοντι τῶν δαιμονίων [q] ἐκβάλλει τὰ [q] δαιμόνια.
35 Καὶ [s] περιῆγεν ὁ Ἰησοῦς τὰς πόλεις πάσας καὶ τὰς
κώμας, διδάσκων ἐν ταῖς συναγωγαῖς αὐτῶν καὶ [s] κηρύσσων τὸ [s] εὐαγγέλιον τῆς βασιλείας καὶ [s] θεραπεύων πᾶσαν
[s] νόσον καὶ πᾶσαν [s] μαλακίαν. 36 ἰδὼν δὲ τοὺς ὄχλους
[t] ἐσπλαγχνίσθη περὶ αὐτῶν, ὅτι ἦσαν [u] ἐσκυλμένοι καὶ
[v] ἐριμμένοι ὡσεὶ πρόβατα μὴ ἔχοντα ποιμένα. 37 τότε
λέγει τοῖς μαθηταῖς αὐτοῦ Ὁ μὲν [w] θερισμὸς πολύς, οἱ δὲ
[x] ἐργάται ὀλίγοι· 38 [y] δεήθητε οὖν τοῦ [z] κυρίου τοῦ [w] θερισμοῦ ὅπως [a] ἐκβάλῃ [x] ἐργάτας εἰς τὸν [w] θερισμὸν αὐτοῦ.

X -τι των... BCDEF GKLMS UXΓΔΠ ℵ 1. 33

r = Acts xvii. 31. 1 Cor. vi. 2.
s ch. iv. 23 reff.
t w. περί, here only. w. ἐπί, ch. xiv. 14. xv. 32 al.† 1 Kings xxiii. 21 Theod.(?). 2 Macc. vi. 8 only, but not =. see Prov. xvii. 5.
u Luke vii. 6. viii. 49 ‖ Mk. only †.
v = here only ‡. 1 Macc. xi. 4. 3 Macc. vii. 5.
w John iv. 35 reff. Jer. xxvii. (l.) 16.
x ch. x. 10. xx. 1, 2, 8. James v. 4 †. Wisd. xvii. 17 al.
y Matt., here only. w. ὅπως, Luke x. 2. Acts viii. 24.
z = ch. xx. 8. xxi. 40 ‖. Luke x. 2.
a Mark i. 12. Luke x. 2. John x. 4. 1 Macc. xii. 27. see Sir. xxx. (xxxvi.) 27.

34. om ver D lat-*a k* Juv Hil. om εν ℵ[1](ins ℵ[2]).
35. om 3rd και ℵ[1](ins ℵ[2]). rec at end ins εν τω λαω (*from ch* iv. 23), with C[3]Lℵ[1] rel gat(and tol) lat-*c* g_1 arm: ins further και πολλοι ηκολουθησαν αυτω L ℵ[1] (omg πολλοι) 76-7. 218 Scr's w[2] gat lat-*a b* g_1 *h*: om BC[1]DSΔℵ[2] 1[1]. 33 vulg lat-*f l* syrr coptt goth æth Chr Thl.
36. aft οχλους ins ο ιησους CM: pref, G lat-$g_{1.2}$ Syr syr-with-ast. rec for εσκυλμ., εκλελυμενοι (*explanatory gloss or mistake?*), with L ev-H: txt BCDℵ rel vss Constt Bas Chr Thl Euthym Hesych Hil Jer. rec ερριμμενοι, with B[2] rel: ρεριμμενοι D: ερρηγμενοι M 299: ερρημενοι X Scr's b i: ερημενοι L: txt B[1](sic in cod) C[D[r]]ℵ.—om και εριμ. Π 33. 258 ev-z [arm-usc]. ως [for ωσει] CDFLM 1. 33 [Bas_1 Chr]: txt Bℵ rel.
38. τον κυριον D[1](txt D[4]).

-sion: for the difference between this and the natural infirmity of a deaf and dumb man, see Mark vii. 31—37. **33. ἐφάνη οὕτως**] viz. the casting out of devils:—'*never was seen to be followed by such results as those now manifested.*' See above. οὕτως is not for τοῦτο or τοιοῦτό τι (De Wette, &c.); the passages cited as bearing out this meaning in the LXX do not apply, for in all of them οὕτως is so. 1 Kings xxiii. 17: Ps. xlvii. 8: Judg. xix. 30 A: Neh. viii. 17.

35—38.] Our Lord's compassion for the multitude. *Peculiar to Matthew.* In the same way as ch. iv. 23—25 introduces the Sermon on the Mount, so do these verses the calling and commissioning of the Twelve. These *general descriptions* of our Lord's going about and teaching at once *remove all exactness of date from the occurrence which follows*—as taking place at some time during the circuit and teaching just described. Both the Sermon on the Mount and this discourse are introduced and closed with these marks of indefiniteness as to time. This being the case, we must have recourse to the other Evangelists, by whose account it appears (as indeed may be implied in ch. x. 1), that the Apostles *had been called to their distinct office some time before this.* (See Mark iii. 16: Luke vi. 13.) After their calling, and selection, they probably remained with our Lord for some time before they were sent out upon their mission. **36. τοὺς ὄχλους**] Wherever He went, in all the cities.

ἐσκυλμένοι] '*Vexati*,'—**harassed,—plagued,**—viz. literally, with weariness in following Him; or spiritually, with the tyranny of the Scribes and Pharisees, their φορτία βαρέα, ch. xxiii. 4. **ἐριμμένοι**] '*Temere projecti*,' '*abjecti*,' '*neglecti*,' as sheep would be who had wandered from their pasture. The context shews that our Lord's compassion was excited by their being without competent spiritual leaders and teachers. **37.**] The *harvest* was primarily that of the Jewish people, the multitudes of whom before Him excited the Lord's compassion. ὅρα πάλιν τὸ ἀκενόδοξον. ἵνα μὴ ἅπαντας πρὸς ἑαυτὸν ἐπισύρηται, ἐκπέμπει τοὺς μαθητάς. οὐ διὰ δὲ τοῦτο μόνον, ἀλλ' ἵνα αὐτοὺς καὶ παιδεύσῃ, καθάπερ ἔν τινι παλαίστρᾳ τῇ Παλαιστίνῃ μελετήσαντας, οὕτω πρὸς τοὺς ἀγῶνας τῆς οἰκουμένης ἀποδύσασθαι. Chrysost. Hom. xxxii. 2, p. 367. **38.**] . . . τίνος οὖν ἕνεκεν ἔλεγε 'δεήθητε τοῦ κυρίου τοῦ θερισμοῦ, ἵνα ἐκβάλῃ ἐργάτας εἰς τὸν θερισμὸν αὐτοῦ,' καὶ οὐδένα αὐτοῖς προσέθηκεν; ὅτι καὶ

X. 1 Καὶ προςκαλεσάμενος τοὺς δώδεκα μαθητὰς
αὐτοῦ ἔδωκεν αὐτοῖς [b] ἐξουσίαν [c] πνευμάτων [cd] ἀκαθάρτων
ὥςτε ἐκβάλλειν αὐτά, καὶ [e] θεραπεύειν πᾶσαν [e] νόσον καὶ
πᾶσαν [e] μαλακίαν. 2 Τῶν δὲ δώδεκα [f] ἀποστόλων τὰ

V εδωκεν ... BCDEF GKLMS UVXΓΔ ΠΝ 1. 33

b w. gen. obj., John xvii. 2. Rom. ix. 21. 1 Cor. ix. 12. Sir. x. 4. xvii. 2.
c ch. xii. 43 al. fr. in Gospp. Acts v. 16. viii. 7. Rev. xvi. 13. xviii. 2. Zech. xiii. 2.
d in Gospp., of *spirits* only. Acts x. 14, 28. 1 Cor. vii. 14 (from Isa. lii. 11) al.
e ch. iv. 23 reff.
f = Matt., here only. Mark, vi. 30 only. Luke (Gosp. & Acts) and Paul, passim. 1 Pet. i. 1. 2 Pet. i. 1. iii. 2. Jude 17. Rev. xviii. 20. xxi. 14 only. for other senses, see John xiii. 16 reff.

CHAP. X. 1. εκβαλειν CD: txt BＮ rel. 2. om δε D[1]-gr(corrd 1. m.).

δώδεκα ὄντας πολλοὺς ἐποίησε λοιπόν, οὐχὶ τῷ ἀριθμῷ προςθείς, ἀλλὰ δύναμιν χαρισάμενος. εἶτα δεικνὺς ἡλίκον τὸ δῶρόν ἐστι, φησὶ 'δεήθητε τοῦ κυρίου τοῦ θερισμοῦ·' καὶ λανθανόντως ἑαυτὸν ἐμφαίνει τὸν τὸ κῦρος ἔχοντα. εἰπὼν γὰρ 'δεήθητε τοῦ κυρίου τοῦ θερισμοῦ,'—οὐδὲν δεηθέντων αὐτῶν, οὐδὲ εὐξαμένων, αὐτὸς αὐτοὺς εὐθὺς χειροτονεῖ, ἀναμιμνήσκων αὐτοὺς καὶ τῶν Ἰωάννου ῥημάτων, καὶ τῆς ἅλω, καὶ τοῦ λικμῶντος, καὶ τοῦ ἀχύρου, καὶ τοῦ σίτου. ὅθεν δῆλον ὅτι αὐτός ἐστιν ὁ γεωργός, αὐτὸς ὁ τοῦ θερισμοῦ κύριος, αὐτὸς ὁ τῶν προφητῶν δεσπότης. Chrysost. Hom. xxxii. 2, 3, p. 367.

* X. 1—XI. 1.] MISSION OF THE TWELVE APOSTLES. Mark vi. 7—13: Luke ix. 1—6,—for the *sending out* of the Apostles: Mark iii. 13—19: Luke vi. 13—16,—for their *names*. On the characteristic differences between this discourse and that delivered to the Seventy (Luke x. 1 ff.) see notes there. Notice, that this is not the *choosing*, but merely the *mission* of the twelve. The choosing had taken place some time before, but is not any where distinctly detailed by the Evangelists. 2.] We have in the N. T. *four* catalogues of the Apostles: the present one,—at Mark iii. 16,—Luke vi. 14,—Acts i. 13. All seem to follow one common outline, but fill it up very differently. The following table will shew the agreements and differences:—

<table>
<tr><th></th><th>Matthew x. 2.</th><th>Mark iii. 16.</th><th>Luke vi. 14.</th><th>Acts i. 13.</th></tr>
<tr><td>1</td><td colspan="4">Σίμων Πέτρος</td></tr>
<tr><td>2</td><td>Ἀνδρέας</td><td>Ἰάκωβος</td><td>Ἀνδρέας</td><td>Ἰωάννης</td></tr>
<tr><td>3</td><td>Ἰάκωβος</td><td>Ἰωάννης</td><td>Ἰάκωβος</td><td>Ἰάκωβος</td></tr>
<tr><td>4</td><td>Ἰωάννης</td><td>Ἀνδρέας</td><td>Ἰωάννης</td><td>Ἀνδρέας</td></tr>
<tr><td>5</td><td colspan="4">Φίλιππος</td></tr>
<tr><td>6</td><td colspan="3">Βαρθολομαῖος</td><td>Θωμᾶς</td></tr>
<tr><td>7</td><td>Θωμᾶς</td><td colspan="2">Ματθαῖος</td><td>Βαρθολομαῖος</td></tr>
<tr><td>8</td><td>Μαθθαῖος</td><td colspan="2">Θωμᾶς</td><td>Ματθαῖος</td></tr>
<tr><td>9</td><td colspan="4">Ἰάκωβος [ὁ τοῦ] Ἀλφαίου</td></tr>
<tr><td>10</td><td>Λεββαῖος</td><td>Θαδδαῖος</td><td>Σίμων ὁ καλ. ζηλωτής</td><td>Σίμων ὁ ζηλωτής</td></tr>
<tr><td>11</td><td colspan="2">Σίμων ὁ καναναῖος</td><td colspan="2">Ἰούδας Ἰακώβου</td></tr>
<tr><td>12</td><td>Ἰούδας ἰσκαριώτης</td><td colspan="2">Ἰούδας Ἰσκαριώθ</td><td>Vacant</td></tr>
</table>

From this it appears (1), that in all four *three classes* are enumerated, and that each class contains (assuming at present the identity of Λεββαῖος with Θαδδαῖος, and of Θαδδαῖος with Ἰούδας Ἰακώβου) the *same persons* in all four, but in different order, with the following exceptions:—that (2) *Peter, Philip, James the* (son?) *of Alphæus,* and *Judas Iscariot* hold the same places in all four. (3) That in the *first* class the two arrangements are (α), that of Matt. and Luke (Gospel),—*Peter* and *Andrew, brothers; James* and *John, brothers;*—i. e. according to their order of calling and connexion, and with reference to their being sent out in couples, Mark vi. 7: (β) Mark and Luke (Acts), —*Peter, James, John,* (the three principal,) and *Andrew;*—i. e. according to their personal pre-eminence. In the *second* class (γ), that of Matt., Mark, and Luke (Gospel), —*Philip* and *Bartholomew, Matthew* and *Thomas* (or, as given by Matthew himself, *Thomas* and *Matthew*),—i. e. in *couples:* (δ) Luke (Acts),—*Philip, Thomas, Barth., Matthew* (reason uncertain). In the *third* class (ε), Matt. and Mark,—*James, the* (son?) *of Alphæus* and (*Lebb.*) *Thaddæus, Simon the Cananæan* and *Judas Iscariot;* i. e. in *couples:* (ζ) Luke (Gosp. and Acts)

ὀνόματά ἐστιν ταῦτα· πρῶτος Σίμων ὁ λεγόμενος Πέτρος καὶ Ἀνδρέας ὁ ἀδελφὸς αὐτοῦ, Ἰάκωβος ὁ τοῦ Ζεβεδαίου καὶ Ἰωάννης ὁ ἀδελφὸς αὐτοῦ, 3 Φίλιππος καὶ Βαρθολο- BCDEF GKLMS UVXΓΔ ΠℵI. 33

ins και bef ιακωβος B ℵ(but erased) D-lat Syr syr-mg. om ο D[1](corrd 1. m.) F [ev-z_1].

James the (son?) *of Alphæus, Simon Zelotes, Judas* Ἰακώβου and *Judas Iscariot* (uncertain). (η) Thus in *all four*, the leaders of the three classes are *the same*, viz. *Peter*, *Philip*, and *James the* (son?) *of Alphæus;* and the *traitor* is always last. (4) It would appear then that the only difficulties are these two: the identity of Lebbæus with Thaddæus, and with Judas Ἰακώβου, and of Simon καναναῖος with Simon ὁ καλ. ζηλωτής. These will be discussed under the names.

πρῶτος] Not only as regards arrangement, or mere priority of calling, but as *primus inter pares*. This is clearly shewn from James and John and Andrew being set next, and Judas Iscariot the last, in all the catalogues. We find Simon Peter, not only in the lists of the Apostles, but also in their history, prominent on various occasions before the rest. Sometimes he *speaks in their name* (Matt. xix. 27: Luke xii. 41); sometimes *answers when all are addressed* (Matt. xvi. 16 ||); sometimes our Lord addresses him as *principal*, even among the three favoured ones (Matt. xxvi. 40: Luke xxii. 31); sometimes he is addressed by others as *representing the whole* (Matt. xvii. 24: Acts ii. 37). He appears as the *organ of the Apostles* after our Lord's ascension (Acts i. 15; ii. 14; iv. 8; v. 29): the first speech, and apparently that which decided the Council, is spoken by him, Acts xv. 7. All this accords well with the bold and energetic character of Peter, and originated in the unerring discernment and appointment of our Lord Himself, who saw in him a person adapted to take precedence of the rest in the founding of His Church, and shutting (Acts v. 3, 9) and opening (Acts ii. 14, 41; x. 5, 46) the doors of the kingdom of Heaven. That however no such idea was current among the Apostles as that he was destined to be the *Primate of the future Church* is as clear as the facts above mentioned. For (1) *no trace of such a pre-eminence is found in all the Epistles of the other Apostles;* but when he is mentioned, it is either, as 1 Cor. ix. 5, as one of the Apostles, one example among many, but in no wise the chief;—or as in Gal. ii. 7, 8, with a distinct account of a peculiar province of duty and preaching being allotted to him, viz. the apostleship of the circumcision, (see 1 Pet. i. 1,) as distinguished from Paul, to whom was given the apostleship of the uncircumcision:—or as in Gal. ii. 9, as one of the principal στύλοι, together with James and John;—or as in Gal. ii. 11, as subject to rebuke from Paul as from an equal. And (2) *wherever by our Lord Himself the future constitution of His Church is alluded to, or by the Apostles its actual constitution, no hint of any such primacy is given,* (see note on Matt. xvi. 18,) but the whole college of Apostles are spoken of as absolutely equal. Matt. xix. 27, 28; xx. 26, 28: Eph. ii. 20, and many other places. Again (3) *in the two Epistles which we have from his own hand, there is nothing for, but every thing against, such a supposition.* He exhorts the πρεσβύτεροι as being their συμπρεσβύτερος (1 Pet. v. 1): describes himself as τῆς μελλούσης ἀποκαλύπτεσθαι δόξης κοινωνός: addresses his second Epistle τοῖς ἰσότιμον ἡμῖν λαχοῦσιν πίστιν (2 Pet. i. 1): and makes not the slightest allusion to any pre-eminence over the other Apostles. So that πρῶτος here must be understood as signifying the prominence of Peter among the Apostles, as well as his early calling. (See John i. 42.)

ὁ λεγόμενος Πέτρος] Or Κηφᾶς, כֵּיפָא, so named by our Lord Himself (John as above) at His first meeting with him, and again more solemnly, and with a direct reference to the meaning of the name, Matt. xvi. 18. **Ἀνδρέας**] He, in conjunction with John (see note on John i. 37—41), was a disciple of the Baptist, and both of them followed our Lord, on their Master pointing Him out as the Lamb of God. They did not however from that time constantly accompany Him, but received a more solemn calling (see Matt. iv. 17—22: Luke v. 1—11)—in the narrative of which Peter is prominent, and so πρῶτος called as an Apostle, at least, of those four. **Ἰάκ. ὁ τ. Ζ. κ. Ἰωάν.**] Partners in the fishing trade with Peter and Andrew, Luke v. 10.

3. Φίλ. κ. Βαρθ.] Philip was called by our Lord the second day after the visit of Andrew and John, and the day after the naming of Peter. He was also of Bethsaida, the city of Andrew and Peter, James and John. Ἀνδρέας and Φίλιππος

μαῖος, Θωμᾶς καὶ Μαθθαῖος ὁ τελώνης, Ἰάκωβος ὁ τοῦ Ἀλφαίου καὶ Λεββαῖος, 4 Σίμων ὁ καναναῖος καὶ Ἰούδας

3. rec aft λεββαιος ins ο επικληθεις θαδδαιος, with C[2]L rel lat-*f* syrr æth arm (C[1] is uncert, but Tischdf thinks had more than λεβ. or θαδ.): for λεββ., θαδδαιος Bℵ(om και ℵ[1]) 17. 124 vulg lat-*c ff*$_1$ *g*$_2$ *l* coptt: θαδδ. ο επικλ. λεββ. 13. 346: *Judas zelotes* gat mm lat-*a b g*$_1$ *h* (add *et Thomas* lat-*a b*): txt D 122 mss-mentd-by-Aug lat-*k* Orig-int Hesych Ruf. (*Probably* ο επικλ. θαδδ. *found its way into the text from* || *Mark: then the substitution of* θαδδ. *was obvious.* λεββαιος *can hardly have been inserted, seeing that the name occurs no where else.*)

4. at beg ins και D lat-*h* [Syr]. rec (for καναναιος) κανανιτης, with ℵ rel sah [Chr]: txt BC D(χαν.) L 1. 33 latt copt Orig-int.

are Greek names. See John xii. 20—22.

Βαρθολομαῖος בַּר תַּלְמַי, son of Talmai or Tolomæus, has been generally supposed to be the same with Nathanael of Cana in Galilee; and with reason: for (1) the name Bartholomew is not his own name, but a patronymic:—(2) He follows next in order, as *Nathanael*, in John i. 46, to the Apostles just mentioned, with the same formula which had just been used of Philip's own call (ver. 44),—εὑρίσκει Φίλιππος τὸν Ναθ.:—(3) He is there, as here, and in Mark and Luke (Gospel), *in connexion with Philip* (that he was his *brother*, was conjectured by Dr. Donaldson; but rendered improbable by the fact that John in the case of Andrew a few verses above, expressly says εὑρίσκει τὸν ἀδελφὸν τὸν ἴδιον Σίμωνα, whereas in ver. 46 no such specification is found):—(4) In John xxi. 2, at the appearance of our Lord on the shore of the sea of Tiberias, Nathanael is mentioned as present, where seven Apostles (μαθηταί) are recounted.

Θωμᾶς κ. Μαθθ. ὁ τελ.] Thomas (תָּאֹם), in Greek Δίδυμος, John xi. 16; xx. 24; xxi. 2. Μαθθ. ὁ τελ. is clearly by this appellation identified with the Matthew of ch. ix. 9. We hear nothing of him, except in these two passages. Dr. Donaldson (Jashar. p. 10 f.) believed Matthew and Thomas to have been twin brothers. Eus., H. E. i. 13, preserves a tradition that Thomas's real name was Judas: Θωμᾶς, ὁ καὶ Ἰούδας.

Ἰάκ. ὁ τ. Ἀλφαίου] From John xix. 25, some infer (but see note there), that Mary the (wife?) of Κλωπᾶς was sister of Mary the mother of our Lord. From Mark xv. 40, that Mary was the mother of James τοῦ μικροῦ, which may be this James. Hence it would appear, if these two passages point to the same person, that Ἀλφαῖος = Κλωπᾶς. And indeed the two Greek names are but different ways of expressing the Hebrew name חַלְפַי. If this be so, then this James the Less *may possibly be* the ὁ ἀδελφὸς τοῦ κυρίου mentioned Gal. i. 19 apparently as an Apostle, and one of the ἀδελφοὶ αὐτοῦ mentioned Matt. xiii. 55 (where see note) (?). But on the difficulties attending this view, see note on John vii. 5.

Λεββαῖος] Much difficulty rests on this name, both from the various readings, and the questions arising from the other lists. The rec. reading appears to be a conjunction of the two ancient ones, Λεββαῖος and Θαδδαῖος: the latter of these having been introduced from Mark. (But it is noticeable, that in Mark D has Λεββαῖος.) Whichever of these is the true reading, the Apostle himself has generally been supposed to be identical with Ἰούδας Ἰακώβου in both Luke's catalogues, i. e. (see note there) Judas the brother (Dr. Donaldson supposed *son*: see note on Luke xxiv. 13) of James, and so son of Alphæus, and commonly supposed to be (?) one of the ἀδελφοὶ κυρίου named Matt. xiii. 55. In John xiv. 22 we have a 'Judas, not Iscariot,' among the Apostles: and the catholic epistle is written by a 'Judas brother of James.' What in this case the names Λεββαῖος and Θαδδαῖος are, is impossible to say. The common idea that they are cognate names, Λεβ. being from לֵב, heart, and Θαδ. from תַּד, breast, is disproved by De Wette, who observes that the latter signifies *mamma*, and not *pectus*. So that the whole rests on conjecture, which however does not contradict any known fact, and may be allowed as the only escape from the difficulty.

4. Σίμων ὁ καναν.] This is not a local name, but is derived from קַנְאָן (Hebr. קַנָּא) = ζηλωτής (Luke, Gosp. and Acts). We may therefore suppose that before his conversion he belonged to the sect of the Zealots, who after the example of Phinehas (Num. xxv. 7, 8) took justice into their own hands, and punished offenders against the law. This sect eventually brought upon Jerusalem its destruction. *

Ἰούδας ὁ ἰσκ.] Son of Simon (John vi. 71; (xii. 4 v. r.) xiii. 2, 26). Probably a native of Kerioth in Juda, Josh.

g of Judas, || Mk. ch. xxvi. 15, &c. ||. xxvii. 3, 4. John vi. 64, 71. xiii. 2, 11. xxi. 20.
h || Mk., al. fr. Josh. vi. 6.

ὁ ἰσκαριώτης ὁ καὶ [g] παραδοὺς αὐτόν. 5 τούτους τοὺς δώδεκα ἀπέστειλεν ὁ Ἰησοῦς [h] παραγγείλας αὐτοῖς λέγων Εἰς [i] ὁδὸν [j] ἐθνῶν μὴ [k] ἀπέλθητε, καὶ εἰς πόλιν Σαμαρειτῶν μὴ εἰςέλθητε, 6 πορεύεσθε δὲ μᾶλλον πρὸς τὰ [l] πρόβατα τὰ

BCDEF GKLMS UVXΓΔ Πℵ 1. 33

i ch. iv. 15. Jer. ii. 18. j Rom. iii. 29 al. Neh. v. 9. k = ch. viii. 19 reff. l ch. xv. 24. Luke xv. 4. Ps. cxviii. 176. Jer. xxvii. (l.) 6.

Steph om ο bef ισκ. (*with* || *Mark Luke*), with CLℵ² rel Orig: ins BDKMSΔΠℵ¹ 1. 33 [Chr].—ℵ¹ has ὁ bef ιουδας also. ισκαριωθ C [ev-H], *-oth* lat-*a b c ff*$_1$ *h*: σκαριωτης D am(with fuld) lat-*f k l* Syr arm: txt BLℵ rel vulg lat-g_1 syr coptt æth. παραδιδους FXΔ ℵ²(but corrd) evv-y-z: ος και παρεδωκεν L ev-H.

5. om τους δωδεκα C³ 27. 40. 234 evv-P-X-Z. aft αυτοις ins και D am(with fuld) lat-*a b c f* g_1 *h*. om λεγων and εθνων ℵ¹(ins ℵ²). σαμαριτανων D¹ latt Cypr.

6. for πορευεσθε, υπαγετε D. om δε D.

xv. 25, אִישׁ קְרִיּוֹת, a man of Kerioth, as Ἴστοβος, i.e. אִישׁ טוֹב, a man of Tob, Joseph. Antt. vii. 6. 1. That the name Ἰσκ. cannot be a surname, as Bp. Middleton supposes, the expression Ἰούδας Σίμωνος ἰσκαριώτης, used in all the above places of John, clearly proves. Dr. Donaldson assumed it as certain that the Simon last mentioned was the father of Judas Iscariot. But surely this is very uncertain, in the case of so common a name as Simon. **5. λέγων**] If we compare this verse with ch. xi. 1, there can be little doubt that this discourse of our Lord was *delivered at one time,* and that, the *first sending of the Twelve.* How often its solemn injunctions may have been repeated on similar occasions we cannot say: many of them reappear at the sending of the Seventy in Luke x. 2 ff. Its primary reference is to the *then Mission of the Apostles to prepare His way;* but it includes, in the germ, instructions prophetically delivered for the ministers and missionaries of the Gospel *to the end of time.* It may be divided into THREE GREAT PORTIONS, in each of which different departments of the subject are treated, but which follow in natural sequence on one another. In the FIRST of these (vv. 5—15), our Lord, taking up the position of the messengers whom He sends from the declaration with which the Baptist and He Himself began their ministry, ὅτι ἤγγικεν ἡ βασιλεία τῶν οὐρανῶν, gives them commands, *mostly literal and of present import, for their mission to the cities of Israel.* This portion concludes with a denunciation of judgment against that unbelief which should reject their preaching. The SECOND (vv. 16—23) refers to the general mission of the Apostles as *developing itself, after the Lord should be taken from them, in preaching to Jews and Gentiles* (vv. 17, 18), and subjecting them to persecutions (vv. 21, 22). This portion ends with the end of the apostolic period properly so called, ver. 23 referring primarily to the destruction of Jerusalem. In this portion there is a foreshadowing of what shall be the lot and duty of the teachers of the Gospel to the end, inasmuch as the 'coming of the Son of Man' is ever typical of His final coming to judgment. Still the direct reference is to the Apostles and their mission, and the other only by inference. The THIRD (vv. 24—42), the longest and weightiest portion, is spoken *directly* (with occasional reference only to the Apostles and their mission (ver. 40)) *of all disciples of the Lord,* — their position, — their encouragements, — their duties,—and finally concludes with the last great reward (ver. 42). In these first verses, 5, 6,—we have the *location;* in 7, 8, the *purpose;* in 9, 10, the *fitting out;* and in 11—14, the *manner of proceeding,*—of their mission: ver. 15 concluding with a prophetic denouncement, tending to impress them with a deep sense of the importance of the office entrusted to them. **Σαμαρειτῶν**] The Samaritans were the Gentile inhabitants of the country between Judæa and Galilee, consisting of heathens whom Shalmaneser king of Assyria brought from Babylon and other places. Their religion was a mixture of the worship of the true God with idolatry (2 Kings xvii. 24—41). The Jews had no dealings with them, John iv. 9. They appear to have been not so unready as the Jews to receive our Lord and His mission (John iv. 39—42: Luke ix. 51 ff., and notes);—but *this* prohibition rested on judicial reasons. See Acts xiii. 46. In Acts i. 8 the prohibition is expressly taken off: 'Ye shall be witnesses in Jerusalem, and in all Judæa, *and in Samaria,* and unto the uttermost part of the earth.' And in Acts viii. 1, 5, 8, we find the result. See ch. xv. 21—28. **6. τὰ**

[l] ἀπολωλότα [m] οἴκου Ἰσραήλ. 7 πορευόμενοι δὲ [n] κηρύσ-
σετε λέγοντες ὅτι [o] ἤγγικεν ἡ βασιλεία τῶν οὐρανῶν.
8 [p] ἀσθενοῦντας θεραπεύετε, [q] νεκροὺς [q] ἐγείρετε, [r] λεπροὺς
[r] καθαρίζετε, δαιμόνια ἐκβάλλετε. [s] δωρεὰν ἐλάβετε, [s] δωρεὰν δότε. 9 μὴ [t] κτήσησθε χρυσὸν μηδὲ [u] ἄργυρον μηδὲ
χαλκὸν [v] εἰς τὰς [w] ζώνας ὑμῶν, 10 μὴ [x] πήραν εἰς ὁδόν,
μηδὲ δύο [y] χιτῶνας, μηδὲ [z] ὑποδήματα, μηδὲ [a] ῥάβδον· ἄξιος
γὰρ ὁ [b] ἐργάτης τῆς [c] τροφῆς αὐτοῦ. 11 εἰς ἣν δ' ἂν πόλιν

P οτι ηγγικεν.. BCDEF GKLM PSUVX ΓΔΠℵ 1. 33

m ch. xv. 24. Acts ii. 36. vii. 42. Heb. viii. 8, 10. Ps. cxvii. 2. Ezek. xviii. 25, 29, 31 al.
n ch. iii. 1 al. fr. Exod. xxxii. 5.
o ch. iii. 2 reff. Ezek. vii. 7 al.
p = ch. xxv. 36. Mark vi. 56 al. see Judg. xvi. 7, &c.
q ch. xi. 5 ‖ L. Mark xii. 26. John v. 21. 1 Cor. xv. 15, &c.
r ch. viii. 2 reff.
s = Rom. iii. 24 al. (John xv. 25.) Isa. lii. 3.
t Luke xviii. 12. xxi. 19. Acts i. 18. viii. 20. xxii. 28. 1 Thess. iv. 4 only. Ezek. v. 1.
u Acts xvii. 29. 1 Cor. iii. 12. James v. 3. Rev. xviii. 12 only. Isa. lx. 9.
v = ‖ Mk.
w = ‖ Mk. (Mark i. 6 reff.) Xen. Anab. i. 4. 9.
x ‖ Mk. reff.
y John xix. 23 reff.
z ch. iii. 11 ‖. Luke xv. 22 al. Gen. xiv. 23.
a ‖. 1 Cor. iv. 21 al. Gen. xxxviii. 18.
b = ch. ix. 37, 38. xx. 1, &c. 1 Tim. v. 18. James v. 4 al.† Wisd. xvii. 17 al.
c ch. iii. 4. vi. 25 al. Ps. cx. 5.

7. om *οτι* B.

8. *θεραπευσατε, εγειρατε, καθαρισατε* D. rec *λεπρ. καθαρ.* bef *νεκρ. εγειρ.*, with (Scr's e j t, e sil) Syr-ed-Trem Cyr_3 : txt BC¹Dℵ¹ 1. 33 latt copt æth Chr_2 Cyr_1 Hil_1 : aft *εκβαλλετε* PΔ syr Chr_2 : om *νεκρ. εγ.* C³L rel lat-*f* Syr-mss sah æth-mss arm Eus_1 Ath Bas_1 Chr-comm Euthym Thl Juv Ambr Jer.—brackets have been put to *νεκρους εγειρετε* by ℵ-corr¹ or ² but erased: *νεκ.* is written by ℵ¹ over an erasure. for *εκβαλλ.*, *εκβαλετε* DF.

9. om *μηδε αργυρον* ℵ¹(ins ℵ², appy). 9, 10. *μητε* (5 times) DL Eus.

10. for *μη*, *μητε* D 245. 346 lat-*k* [Syr] coptt. *ραβδους* (*misunderstanding, see note*) CP rel lat-*a k* syr arm Chr Thl : txt BDℵ 1. 33 vulg lat-*b c f ff*$_1$ *g*$_1$ *h l* Δ-lat Syr syr-mss sah æth arm $Eus_{2(expr)}$ Hil. [copt doubtful.] rec aft *αυτου* ins *εστιν*, with P rel arm ; aft *αξιος γαρ*, D evv-H-y latt syr Iren-int Hil : om BCLℵ 1 lat-*h* coptt æth Thl.

11. *η πολις εις ην αν εισελθητε εις αυτην* D 28 sah.

πρόβ. τὰ ἀπολ.] See besides reff., ch. ix. 36 : John x. 16. **7.**] This announcement shews the *preparatory nature* of this first apostolic mission. Compare, shewing the difference of their ultimate message to the world, Col. i. 26—28. **8. δωρεὰν ἐλ., δωρεὰν δ.**] See Acts viii. 18—20. **9. μὴ κτήσησθε**] All the words following depend on this verb, and it is explained by the parallel expressions in Mark and Luke, *ἵνα μηδὲν αἴρωσιν* and *μηδὲν αἴρετε εἰς τὴν ὁδόν*. They were to make no preparations for the journey, but to take it in dependence on Him who sent them, just as they were. This forbidden provision would be of three kinds (1) *Money :* in Mark (vi. 8) *χαλκόν*, in Luke (ix. 3) *ἀργύριον* : here all the three current metals in order of value, connected by the *μηδέ* introducing a climax—no gold, nor yet silver, nor yet brass (so again in ver. 10)—in their *ζῶναι* (= *βαλάντια* Luke x. 4). (2) *Food :* here **πήρα** (*θήκη τῶν ἄρτων*, Suidas), in Mark *μὴ ἄρτον, μὴ πήραν* : similarly Luke. (3) Clothing—**μηδὲ δύο χιτ.** : so Mark and Luke—**μηδὲ ὑποδ.** ; in Mark expressed by *ὑποδεδεμένους σανδάλια* : explained in Luke x. 4, by *μὴ βαστάζετε ὑποδ.*, i. e. a *second* pair.—**μηδὲ ῥάβδον** = *εἰ μὴ ῥάβδ. μόνον* Mark, i. e., the former depending on *κτήσησθε*, the latter on *αἴρωσιν εἰς ὁδόν*, which has not quite the precision of the other. They were not to procure *expressly for this journey* even a staff: they were to take with them their usual staff only. The missing of this explanation has probably led to the reading *ῥάβδους* both here and in Luke. If it be genuine, it does not mean *δύο ῥάβδ.*; for who would ever think of taking a *spare* staff? but a *ῥάβδος* each. The whole of this prohibition was temporary only ; for their then journey, and no more. See Luke xxii. 35, 36. **10. ἄξιος γάρ**] This is a common truth of life—men give one who works for them his food and more ; here uttered however by our Lord in its highest sense, as applied to the workmen in His vineyard. See 1 Cor. ix. 13, 14 : 2 Cor. xi. 8 : 3 John 8. It is (as Stier remarks, vol. i. p. 352, ed. 2) a gross perversion and foolish bondage to the letter, to imagine that ministers of congregations, or even missionaries among the heathen, at this day are bound by the *literal* sense of our Lord's commands in this passage. But we must not therefore imagine that they are not bound by the *spirit* of them.

ἢ κώμην εἰςέλθητε, [d] ἐξετάσατε τίς ἐν αὐτῇ [e] ἄξιός ἐστιν,
κἀκεῖ μείνατε ἕως ἂν ἐξέλθητε. 12 εἰςερχόμενοι δὲ εἰς
τὴν οἰκίαν ἀσπάσασθε αὐτήν. 13 καὶ ἐὰν μὲν ᾖ ἡ οἰκία
[e] ἀξία, ἐλθέτω ἡ [f] εἰρήνη ὑμῶν ἐπ᾽ αὐτήν· ἐὰν δὲ μὴ
ᾖ [e] ἀξία, ἡ εἰρήνη ὑμῶν πρὸς ὑμᾶς [g] ἐπιστραφήτω.
14 καὶ [h] ὃς ἂν μὴ [i] δέξηται ὑμᾶς μηδὲ ἀκούσῃ τοὺς λόγους
ὑμῶν, ἐξερχόμενοι ἔξω τῆς οἰκίας ἢ τῆς πόλεως ἐκείνης

BCDEF GKLM PSUVX ΓΔΠℵ 1. 33

d ch. ii. 8. John xxi. 12 only. Deut. xix. 18.
e = ch. xxii. 8. Rev. iii. 4. xvi. 6.
f see John xiv. 27.
g = ch. xii. 44. 1 Pet. ii. 25. Ps. vii. 16. see Ps. xxxiv. 13.
h constr., 2 Cor. i. 20.
i = Luke ix. 53. x. 8, 10. Gal. iv. 14. Wisd. xix. 14. Xen. Anab. iv. 8. 23.

om η κωμην D 1. 28. 118. 209 lat-*a b* ff_1 *h* Aug_2 : ins aft εισελθητε L 124 sah. εν αυτη bef τις Kℵ Scr's p.

12. aft αυτην ins λεγοντες ειρηνη τω οικω τουτω (*from Luke* x. 5) DLℵ[1](ℵ[2][?][3] marked the insn with brackets but these have been erased) 1 Scr's d h p q r evv-H-y latt æth arm Thl Hil.

13. om και D : *si enim* D-lat. for 1st ᾖ, ην C[1]. for ελθετω, εστε *erit* D : εισελθετω SV 68 Thl. (-θατω CLℵ 33.) for εαν δε μη η αξ., ει δε μηγε D[1] : ει δε μηγε η D[2] : ει δε μη αξ. L.—for 2nd ᾖ, ην C. om η bef ειρ. D[1]. for προς, εφ Bℵ 243 Chr

14. rec εαν, with CP rel : txt BDKLℵ. rec om εξω (*not clearly necessary, and not in* ||), with CP rel arm : εκ L 237-45-7 [$Bas\text{-}mss_1$] : txt BDℵ 33 Scr's evv-H-y latt copt æth. om της οικ. η D arm[-zoh] : om η L. for της πολ., πολεως η κωμης ℵ. om εκεινης D 17. 119-20 vulg lat-*a c* ff_1 $g_{1.2}$ *h l*.

This literal first mission was but a foreshadowing of the spiritual subsequent sending out of the ministry over the world, which ought therefore *in spirit* every where to be conformed to these rules. **11. ἄξιος**] *Inclined to receive you and your message,—worthy that you should become his guest:* so ἄξιος is used with reference to the matter treated of in the context, see reff. Such persons in this case would be of the same kind as those spoken of Acts xiii. 48 as τεταγμένοι εἰς ζωὴν αἰώνιον. The precept in this verse is very much more fully set forth by Luke, x. 7 ff. **ἕως ἂν ἐξέλθητε**] **Until ye depart out** of the city.
12. τὴν οἰκίαν] Not *the* house of the ἄξιος, for this would be sure to be worthy; but *any house*, as is necessary from the subsequent ἐὰν ᾖ ἡ οἰκ. ἀξ., which on the other supposition (Meyer, &c.) would have been ascertained already. The full command as to their conduct, *from arriving to departing*, is given in ver. 11. Then, the subject being taken up again at their *arrival* in the city, the method of ἐξέτασις is prescribed to them in vv. 12, 13. When they enter into an house, (so, idiomatically, E. V.,) they are to salute it: and if on enquiry it prove worthy, then &c. See notes on ch. ix. 1, 28. **13. ἡ εἰρήνη ὑμ.**] The peace mentioned in the customary Eastern salutation שָׁלוֹם לָךְ. Luke has εἰρήνη τῷ οἴκῳ τούτῳ (x. 5). Compare with the spirit of vv. 10—13,—ch. vii. 6. Stier remarks (Reden Jesu, i. p. 355, ed. 2), that the spirit of these commands binds Christian ministers to all accustomed courtesies of manner in the countries and ages in which their mission may lie. So we find the Greek χαίρειν instead of the Jewish form of greeting, Acts xv. 23: James i. 1. And the same spirit forbids that repelling official pride by which so many ministers lose the affections of their people. And this is to be *without any respect to the worthiness or otherwise* of the inhabitants of the house. In the case of *unworthiness*, 'let your peace return (see Isa. xlv. 23) to you,' i. e. 'be as though you had never spoken it,' μηδὲν ἐνεργησάτω, ἀλλὰ ταύτην μεθ' ἑαυτῶν λαβόντες ἐξέλθετε. Euthym. **14.**] See Acts xiii. 51; xviii. 6. A solemn act which might have two meanings: (1) as Luke x. 11 expresses at more length,—'We take nothing of yours with us, we free ourselves from all contact and communion with you;' or (2),—which sense probably lies beneath both this and ver. 13, 'We free ourselves from all participation in your condemnation: will have nothing in common with those who have rejected God's message.' See 1 Kings ii. 5, where the *shoes on the feet* are mentioned as *partakers in the guilt of blood*. It was a custom of the Pharisees, when they entered Judæa from a Gentile land, to do this act, as renouncing all communion with Gentiles: those then who would not receive the apostolic message were to be treated as no longer

j ἐκτινάξατε τὸν k κονιορτὸν τῶν ποδῶν ὑμῶν. 15 l ἀμὴν
λέγω ὑμῖν, m ἀνεκτότερον ἔσται γῇ Σοδόμων καὶ Γομόῤῥας
ἐν n ἡμέρᾳ κρίσεως ἢ τῇ πόλει ἐκείνῃ. 16 Ἰδοὺ ἐγὼ
o ἀποστέλλω ὑμᾶς ὡς πρόβατα ἐν μέσῳ p λύκων· γίνεσθε
οὖν q φρόνιμοι ὡς οἱ q ὄφεις καὶ r ἀκέραιοι ὡς αἱ s περι-
στεραί. 17 t προσέχετε δὲ ἀπὸ τῶν ἀνθρώπων· u παραδώσουσιν γὰρ ὑμᾶς εἰς v συνέδρια, καὶ ἐν ταῖς συναγωγαῖς

j ‖ Mk. Acts xiii. 51. xviii. 6 only. Isa. lii. 2. Neh. v. 13. k ‖ L. Luke x. 11. Acts xiii. 51. xxii. 23 only. Exod. ix. 9. l ch. v. 18 reff. m (‖ Mk. v. r.) ch. xi. 22, 24. Luke x. 12, 14 only †. Thuc. ii. 35. n ch. xi. 22, 24. xii. 36. 2 Pet. ii. 9. iii. 7. Isa. xxxiv. 8. Prov. vi. 34. o ver. 5. ch. xi. 10 ‖. xxiii. 34. Rom. x. 15 al. Jer. xlii. (xxxv.) 15. p ch. vii. 15 reff. q Gen. iii. 1. r Rom. xvi. 19. Phil. ii. 15 only †. ἀκέραιος βίος, Jos. Antt. i. 2. 2. s ch. iii. 16 reff. t w. ἀπό, ch. vii. 15 al. Sir. xi. 33. u = ch. iv. 12 al. Jer. xlv. (xxxviii.) 20. v ch. v. 22 reff.

aft τ. κον. ins εκ (*supplied from misunderstanding*) Cℵ 33. 142-57 Syr arm.

15. aft και add γη Cℵ. rec γομορρων, with Bℵ rel latt [Bas_1] Hil : txt CDLMP 1 (one ρ DL) lat-ff_1 *h k* copt Chr. for εν, ενη D : εν τη D^8 : *in die* D-lat.

16. εις μεσον B. οφις B^1 : ο οφις $ℵ^1$(txt $ℵ^{3a}$) : ωσει οφεις L 236 Scr's r s evv-P(-y^1). for ακεραιοι, απλουστατοι D.

17. om δε D ev-z flor lat-*a c* g_1 $Orig_1$ spec. om υμας C^1. εις τας συναγωγας αυτων D-gr.

Israelites, but Gentiles. Thus the verse forms a kind of introduction to the next portion of the discourse, where the future mission to the Gentiles is treated of. The **ἢ τῆς πόλεως ἐκ.** brings in the alternative; "house, if it be a house that rejects you, city, if a whole city."

15.] The *first* ἀμὴν λέγ. ὑμ.; with which expression our Lord *closes each portion* of this discourse. **ἡμέρα κρίσεως,** the day of final judgment, = ἡμέρα ἐκείνη, Luke x. 12. The omission of the articles does not alter the definiteness of the meaning; as in the case also of υἱὸς θεοῦ. See note on ch. iv. 3. It must be noticed that this denunciatory part, as also the command to shake off the dust, applies *only to the people of Israel,* who had been long prepared for the message of the Gospel by the Law and the Prophets, and recently more particularly by John the Baptist; and in this sense it may still apply to the rejection of the Gospel by professing Christians: but as it was not then applicable to the Gentiles, so neither now can it be to the heathen who know not God.

16—23.] SECOND PART OF THE DISCOURSE. See above on ver. 5, for the subject of this portion. **16.**] **ἐγώ** is not without meaning. It takes up again the subject of their sending, and reminds them WHO sent them. (ἐγὼ ὁ πάντα δυνάμενος. Euthymius.) **ἀποστέλλω,** in direct connexion with their name ἀπόστολοι. **πρόβ. ἐν μ. λ.**] This comparison is used of the people of Israel in the midst of the Gentiles, in a Rabbinical work cited by Stier, p. 359: see also Sir. xiii. 17. Clem. Ep. ad Cor. ii. § 5, vol. i. p. 336, Migne, says: λέγει γὰρ ὁ κύριος Ἔσεσθε ὡς ἀρνία ἐν μέσῳ λύκων. ἀποκριθεὶς δὲ ὁ Πέτρος αὐτῷ λέγει Ἐὰν οὖν διασπαράξωσιν οἱ λύκοι τὰ ἀρνία; εἶπεν ὁ Ἰησοῦς τῷ Πέτρῳ Μὴ φοβείσθωσαν τὰ ἀρνία τοὺς λύκους μετὰ τὸ ἀποθανεῖν αὐτά, καὶ ὑμεῖς μὴ φοβεῖσθε τοὺς ἀποκτείνοντας ὑμᾶς καὶ μηδὲν ὑμῖν δυναμένους ποιεῖν· ἀλλὰ φοβεῖσθε τὸν μετὰ τὸ ἀποθανεῖν ὑμᾶς ἔχοντα ἐξουσίαν ψυχῆς κ. σώματος, τοῦ βαλεῖν εἰς γέενναν πυρός. **οἱ ὄφ. . . . αἱ περ.**] The articles are *generic,* as is also that before **ἀνθρ.** in the next verse, which has been mistaken, and supposed to have a distinct meaning. It is used on account of these two, οἱ ὄφ. . . . . αἱ περ. . . . . having just preceded. **ἀκέραιος,** ὁ μὴ κεκραμένος κακοῖς, ἀλλ' ἁπλοῦς καὶ ἀποίκιλος. Etym. Mag. (Meyer.)

17. προσέχετε] The wisdom of the serpent is needed for this part of their course; the simplicity of the dove for the μὴ μεριμνήσητε in ver. 19. The **δέ** turns from the internal character to behaviour in regard of outward circumstances. **συνέδρια**] See Acts iv. 6, 7; v. 40. They are the *courts of seven* (on which see Deut. xvi. 18), appointed in every city, to take cognizance of causes both civil and criminal, ch. v. 21: here perhaps put for any courts of assembly in general. **ἐν τ. συν. μαστιγ. ὑ.**] See Acts xxii. 19; xxvi. 11. Euseb. Hist. Eccl. v. 16, quoting a book against the Montanists, οὐδὲ μὴν οὐδὲ ἐν συναγωγαῖς Ἰουδαίων τῶν γυναικῶν τις ἐμαστιγώθη ποτέ, ἢ ἐλιθοβολήθη· οὐδαμόσε οὐδαμῶς. The scourging in the synagogues is supposed to have been inflicted by order of the Tribunal of Three, who judged in

αὐτῶν [w] μαστιγώσουσιν ὑμᾶς· 18 [x] καὶ ἐπὶ ἡγεμόνας [x] δὲ
καὶ βασιλεῖς ἀχθήσεσθε [y] ἕνεκεν ἐμοῦ, [z] εἰς [z] μαρτύριον
αὐτοῖς καὶ τοῖς ἔθνεσιν. 19 ὅταν δὲ [u] παραδιδῶσιν ὑμᾶς, ...δε παρα P. BCDEF
μὴ [a] μεριμνήσητε πῶς ἢ τί λαλήσητε· [b] δοθήσεται γὰρ GKLM
ὑμῖν ἐν ἐκείνῃ τῇ ὥρᾳ τί λαλήσητε· 20 οὐ γὰρ ὑμεῖς ἐστε SUVXΓ ΔΠℵ 1.
οἱ λαλοῦντες, ἀλλὰ τὸ [c] πνεῦμα τοῦ πατρὸς ὑμῶν τὸ 33
λαλοῦν ἐν ὑμῖν. 21 [d] παραδώσει δὲ ἀδελφὸς ἀδελφὸν [d] εἰς
[d] θάνατον, καὶ πατὴρ τέκνον· καὶ [e] ἐπαναστήσονται τέκνα
ἐπὶ γονεῖς καὶ [f] θανατώσουσιν αὐτούς. 22 καὶ ἔσεσθε
μισούμενοι ὑπὸ πάντων [g] διὰ τὸ [g] ὄνομά μου. ὁ δὲ [h] ὑπο-

w ch. xx. 19 ‖. xxiii. 34. John xix. 1. Heb. xii. 6 (from Prov. iii. 12) only. (-ίζειν, Acts xxii. 25.)
x John vi. 51. viii. 16, 17. xv. 27. Acts iii. 24.
y ch. v. 11. ver. 39. ch. xvi. 25 al.
z ch. viii. 4 reff.
a ch. vi. 25, &c. reff.
b = ch. xx. 23. Rev. vi. 4. vii. 2. xiii. 14 al. Gen. xxxi. 7.
c Ezek. xxxvi. 27.
d Mark xiii. 12. 2 Cor. iv. 11. Isa. liii. 12.
e Mark xiii. 12 only. Ps. iii. 1. Micah vii. 6. plur., ch. vi. 28 reff.
f Luke xxi. 16 al. 2 Chron. xxiii. 15.
g John xv. 21 reff.
h ch. xxiv. 13 ‖ Mk. Rom. xii. 12. Mal. iii. 2.

18. for *ηγ. δε κ. βασ.*, *ηγεμονων* D, *βασιλεων κ. ηγεμονων* Orig: *reges et præsides* (*potestates* Hil) lat-*a b c* Hil. om *δε* (D above) FGLXΔ Syr [Orig_1]: txt BCPℵ rel syr copt arm Orig_2 Petr. for *αχ.*, *σταθησεσθαι stabitis* D lat-*a b c* ff_1 g_1 *h* Iren-int_1 Orig-int_2 Cypr Hil spec.

19. *παραδωσιν* (*grammatical correction*) BE¹ℵ 1, *tradiderint* D-lat lat-*f* g_1 *k* Cypr: *παραδωσουσιν* (*corrn to sense*) D-gr GLX 33 latt(*tradent*) arm Ath most-lat-ff: *παραδωσωσιν* Orig Chr: txt C E-corr¹ rel. (P defective.) om *δοθησεται* (or -*ε*) to *λαλησητε* (or -*αι*) (*from similarity of endings*) DL flor harl¹ lat-*k* arm Orig_1 Cyr Thl Cypr_1 Op. for *ωρα*, *ημερα* C¹ syr-jer copt. rec [2nd time] *λαλησετε*, with KMSUΠ¹: txt BCℵ rel.

21. *αδελφος αδελφος*(sic) ℵ¹(txt ℵ³ ?). [B does not ins *το* bef *τεκνον*, as Btly.] *επαναστησεται* (*gramml corrn*) BΔ.

them. 18.] **καὶ . . . . δέ** implies, **yea and moreover**; assuming what has just been said and passing on to something more. The words are always separated, except in the Epic poets. See Viger, ed. Herm. p. 545 (note), 844: Hartung, Partikellehre, i. 181 f.: Klotz ad Devar. p. 645. **ἡγεμόνας**—Proconsuls, Proprætors, Procurators, as (Pontius Pilate,) Felix, Festus, Gallio, Sergius Paulus. **βασιλεῖς**, as (Herod,) Agrippa. The former verse was of *Jewish* persecution; this, of *Gentile*: the concluding words shew that the scope of both, in the divine purposes, as regarded the Apostles, was the same, viz. *εἰς μαρτ. αὐτ. κ. τ. ἔθν.* The **μαρτ.** is in both senses—a testimony *to*, and *against* them (see ch. viii. 4, note), and refers to both sets of persecutors: **αὐτοῖς**, to *them*, i. e. the Jews (not the *ἡγ. καὶ βασ.* for they are in most cases Gentiles themselves), **καὶ τοῖς ἔθν.** It was a testimony in the best sense *to* Sergius Paulus, Acts xiii. 7, but *against* Felix, Acts xxiv. 25; and this double power ever belongs to the word of God as preached—it is a *δίστομος ῥομφαία* (Rev. i. 16; ii. 12). 19.] **μὴ μεριμνήσητε**—**take not anxious** (or *distracting*) **thought.** A spiritual prohibition, answering to the literal one in vv. 9, 10. See Exod. iv. 12. **20. οὐ γὰρ ὑμ.** *κ.τ.λ.*] This shews the reference of the command to a *future* mission of the Apostles, see John xv. 26, 27. (1) It is to be observed that our Lord never in speaking to His disciples says *our* Father, but either *my* Father (ch. xviii. 10), or *your* Father (as here), or both conjoined (John xx. 17); never leaving it to be inferred that God is in the same sense His Father and our Father. (2) It is also to be observed that in the great work of God in the world, human individuality sinks down and vanishes, and God alone, His Christ, His Spirit, is the great worker, as here *οὐχ ὑμεῖς ἐστε . . . . ἀλλὰ τὸ πν. τοῦ π. ὑμ.* **21.**] Spoken perhaps of *official information* given against Christians, as there are no female relations mentioned. But the general idea is also included. **22. πάντων**] i. e. *all else but yourselves;* not, as De Wette so often interprets, 'a strong expression, intended to signify *many*, or *the majority of mankind*.' **ὁ δὲ ὑπομ.**] In order to understand these words it is necessary to enter into the character of our Lord's prophecies respecting His coming, as having an *immediate literal*, and a *distant foreshadowed* fulfilment. Throughout this discourse and the great prophecy in ch. xxiv.,

μείνας [i] εἰς τέλος, οὗτος σωθήσεται. 23 ὅταν δὲ [j] διώκωσιν
ὑμᾶς ἐν τῇ πόλει ταύτῃ, φεύγετε εἰς τὴν ἄλλην· [k] ἀμὴν
γὰρ λέγω ὑμῖν, οὐ μὴ [l] τελέσητε τὰς πόλεις Ἰσραὴλ ἕως
[m] ἔλθῃ [m] ὁ υἱὸς τοῦ ἀνθρώπου. 24 οὐκ ἔστιν μαθητὴς
[n] ὑπὲρ τὸν διδάσκαλον, οὐδὲ δοῦλος [n] ὑπὲρ τὸν κύριον

i ch. xxiv. 13. Luke xviii. 5. John xiii. 1. 1 Thess. ii. 6. Ps. lxxiii. 11.
j = ch. xxiii. 34. Acts xxvi. 11. 2 Kings xxi. 5.
k ver. 15.
l so Polyb. iii. 86. 9, διανύσας τὴν . . . χώραν. Diod. Sic. xi. 20, διανύσας τὸ Λιβυκὸν πέλαγος. see ch. xi. 1. Josh. iii. 17. iv. 1.
m ch. xxiv. 30, 44. xxv. 31. xxvi. 64 al.
n constr., Phil. ii. 9. 1 Kings xv. 22.

23. διωκουσιν DΔ. for αλλην, ετεραν Bℵ 1. 33 $Orig_5$ Petr [Ath_2 Cyr_1]. add καν εκ ταυτης διωκωσιν υμας, φευγετε εις την αλλην 1 $Orig_1$: καν εν τη ετερα διωκωσιν, παλιν φευγετε εις την αλλην Orig: εαν δε εν τη αλλη διωκουσιν υμας, φευγετε εις την αλλην D: καν εκ ταυτης εκδιωξουσιν ὑμας, φευγετε εις την ετεραν L lat-*a b* ff_1 $g_{1.2}$ *h* arm Ath_2 Thdrt $Tert_{appy}$ Juv Hil_{expr} Ambr Aug. (*The variations are fatal to the clause, shewing it to be an interpolation, caused by combining* αλλην *and* ετεραν. *Lachmann has edited, from his own invention,* κἂν ἐν τῇ ἑτέρᾳ διώκωσιν ὑμᾶς, φεύγετε εἰς τὴν ἄλλην.) om γαρ DM latt copt æth arm. aft υμιν ins οτι C. rec ins του bef ισραηλ, with Cℵ rel Orig: om BD. rec aft εως ins αν, with CD rel Orig: εως ου $ℵ^{3a}$: txt $BXℵ^1$.
24. aft διδασκ. ins αυτου FMℵ Scr's d h k q s evv-H-y syrr æth arm-mss.

we find the first apostolic period used as a type of the whole ages of the Church; and the vengeance on Jerusalem, which historically put an end to the old dispensation, and was in its place with reference to that order of things, the coming of the Son of Man, as a type of the final coming of the Lord. These two subjects accompany and interpenetrate one another in a manner wholly inexplicable to those who are unaccustomed to the wide import of Scripture prophecy, which speaks very generally not so much of *events themselves, points of time,*—as of *processions* of events, all ranging under one great description. Thus in the present case there is certainly direct reference to the destruction of Jerusalem; the τέλος directly spoken of is that event, and the σωθήσεται the preservation provided by the warning afterwards given in ch. xxiv. 15—18. And the next verse directly refers to the journeys of the Apostles over the actual cities of Israel, territorial, or where Jews were located. But as certainly do all these expressions look onwards to the great final coming of the Lord, the τέλος of all prophecy; as certainly the σωθήσεται here bears its full scripture meaning, of *everlasting salvation;* and the endurance to the end is the *finished course of the Christian;* and the precept in the next verse is to apply to the conduct of Christians of all ages with reference to persecution, and the announcement that hardly will the Gospel have been fully preached to all nations (or, to all the *Jewish nation,* i. e. *effectually*) when the Son of Man shall come. It is most important to keep in mind the *great prophetic parallels* which run through our Lord's discourses, and are sometimes separately, sometimes simultaneously, presented to us by Him. That the tracing out and applying such parallels should be called by such expositors as Meyer, 'lauter wortwidrige und nothgedrungene Ausflüchte' (Com. i. 211), is just as if a man should maintain that a language unknown to him had therefore no meaning.

24—42.] Third part of the discourse. See note on ver. 5. It treats of (I.) the *conflicts* (vv. 24—26), *duties* (vv. 26—28), and *encouragements* (vv. 28—32) of all Christ's disciples. (II.) The *certain issue of this fight in victory;* the *confession by Christ of those who confess Him,* set in strong light by the contrast of those who deny Him (vv. 32, 33); the *necessity of conflict to victory,* by the nature of Christ's mission (vv. 34—37), the *kind of self-devotion which he requires* (vv. 37—39): concluding with the *solemn assurance that no reception of His messengers for His sake, nor even the smallest labour of love for Him, shall pass without its final reward.* Thus we are carried on to the end of time and of the course of the Church.

24.] This proverb is used in different senses in Luke vi. 40 and John xiii. 16. The view *here* is, that disciples must *not expect a better lot* than their Master, but be well satisfied if they have no worse. The threefold relation of our Lord and His followers here brought out may thus be exemplified from Scripture: μαθητής and διδάσκαλος, Matt. v. 1; xxiii. 8: Luke vi. 20; δοῦλος and κύριος, John xiii. 13: Luke xii. 35—48: Rom. i. 1: 2 Pet. i. 1: Jude 1; οἰκοδεσπότης

αὐτοῦ. 25 ° ἀρκετὸν τῷ μαθητῇ ᵖ ἵνα γένηται ᵠ ὡς ὁ
διδάσκαλος αὐτοῦ, καὶ ὁ δοῦλος ᵠ ὡς ὁ κύριος αὐτοῦ. εἰ
τὸν ʳ οἰκοδεσπότην Βεελζεβοὺλ ˢ ἐπεκάλεσαν, πόσῳ μᾶλλον
τοὺς ᵗ οἰκιακοὺς αὐτοῦ; 26 μὴ οὖν φοβηθῆτε αὐτούς· οὐδὲν
γάρ ἐστιν ᵘ κεκαλυμμένον ὃ οὐκ ᵛ ἀποκαλυφθήσεται, καὶ
κρυπτὸν ὃ οὐ γνωσθήσεται. 27 ὃ λέγω ὑμῖν ἐν τῇ ʷ σκοτίᾳ
εἴπατε ἐν τῷ ˣ φωτί, καὶ ὃ ʸ εἰς τὸ οὖς ἀκούετε ᶻ κηρύξατε
ἐπὶ τῶν ᵃ δωμάτων. 28 καὶ μὴ ᵇ φοβήθητε ἀπὸ τῶν

BCDEF GKLM SUVXΓ ΔΠℵ 1. 33

o ch. vi. 34. 1 Pet. iv. 3 only †. Deut. xxv. 2 Aq.
p ch. xviii. 6. 1 Cor. iv. 3.
q = Isa. xxiv. 2.
r ch. xx. 1, 11 al.†
s = act., here only. 3 Kings vii. 1. pass., Acts i. 23. x. 5, 18 al.
t ver. 36 only †.
u ch. viii. 24 reff.
v = Luke ii. 35. xii. 2. Eph. iii. 5 al. Sir. i. 30.
w ch. iv. 6. Luke xii. 3. otherwise, John (i. 5 bis, al6. 1 John i. 5 al4.) only. Job xxviii. 3 only.
x = Luke xii. 3. Xen. Ages. ix. 1.
y Luke i. 44. Acts xi. 22. 1 Kings viii. 21.
z Prov. i. 21.
a ch. xxiv. 17 ‖ Mk. Luke v. 19. xii. 3. xvii. 31. Acts x. 9 only. 2 Kings xi. 2.
b w. ἀπό, Luke xii. 4 only. Lev. xxvi. 2. Deut. vii. 19. Jer. i. 17. Ezek. iii. 9.

25. τω δουλω L evv-36-y vulg lat-*b f ff*$_1$ *g*$_2$ syrr [Cyr$_1$]. τω οικοδεσποτη (*námml corrn*) B[1]. βεεζεβουλ Bℵ, βελζεβουλ DLX lat-*k* copt, *beelzebub* vulg lat-*c g*$_2$ Syr, *velzebul* lat-*b* : txt C rel lat-*a f ff*$_1$ *g*$_1$ *h* syr[and mg-gr] goth æth arm. rec εκαλεσαν (*corrn to more usual word, and avoidance of the unusual constr*), with 1 latt : καλουσιν D : εκαλεσαντο L : επεκαλεσαντο ℵ[1] : απεκαλεσαν U Chr Thdrt Thl : txt BCℵ[3a] rel Eus Ath$_1$ Cyr$_2$ Thl-ms. τοις οικιακοις (*see above*) B[1].
27. for κηρυξατε, κηρυσσεται D Orig$_1$ Eus$_2$: κηρυχθησετε(= αι) L.
28. for φοβηθητε, φοβεισθε Cℵ rel Just Ephr Eus$_1$ [Bas$_2$] Cyr$_1$ Thdrt : txt B(sic

and *οἰκιακοί*, Matt. xxvi. 26—29 ‖ : Luke xxiv. 30 : Matt. xxiv. 45 ff. ‖. **καὶ ὁ δοῦλος ὡς . .** is a broken construction; it would regularly be *καὶ τῷ δούλῳ, ἵνα κ.τ.λ.* **25. Βεελζεβούλ**] (Either בַּעַל זְבַל, 'lord of dung,'—or as in 2 Kings i. 2, בַּעַל זְבוּב, 'lord of flies,'—a god worshipped at Ekron by the Philistines; there is however another derivation more probable than either of these, upheld by Meyer (referring to Buxtorf, Lex. Talm. p. 333), from בַּעַל and זְבוּל, a house, by which it would exactly correspond to *οἰκοδεσπότης*)—A name by which the prince of the devils was called by the Jews, ch. xii. 24,—to which accusation, probably an usual one (see ch. ix. 34), and that in John viii. 48, our Lord probably refers. In those places they had not literally called *Him* Beelzebub, but He speaks of their mind and intention in those charges. They may however have literally done so on other unrecorded occasions. **26. μὴ οὖν**] The force of this is: 'Notwithstanding their treatment of Me your Master, Mine will be victory and triumph; therefore ye, My disciples, in your turn, need not fear.' Compare Rom. viii. 37. **οὐδὲν γάρ ἐστιν**] This solemn truth is again and again enounced by our Lord on different occasions, and with different references. See Luke viii. 17; xii. 2. The former part of the verse drew comfort and encouragement from the *past*: this from the *future*. 'All that is hidden must be revealed—(1) it is God's purpose in His Kingdom that the everlasting Gospel shall be freely preached, and this purpose ye serve. (2) Beware then of hypocrisy (see Luke xii. 2) through fear of men, for all such will be detected and exposed hereafter: and (3) fear them not, for, under whatever aspersions ye may labour from them, the day is coming which shall clear you and condemn them, if ye are fearlessly doing the work of Him that sent you' (ch. xiii. 43). *τίνος γὰρ ἕνεκεν ἀλγεῖτε; ὅτι γόητας ὑμᾶς καλοῦσι καὶ πλάνους; ἀναμείνατε μικρόν, καὶ σωτῆρας ὑμᾶς καὶ εὐεργέτας τῆς οἰκουμένης προσεροῦσιν ἅπαντες.* Chrys. Hom. xxxiv. 1, p. 390. **27.**] *An expansion of the duty of freeness and boldness of speech implied in the last verse.* The words may bear *two meanings*: either (1) that which Chrysostom gives, taking the expressions relatively, *ἐπειδὴ μόνοις αὐτοῖς διελέγετο καὶ ἐν μικρᾷ γωνίᾳ τῆς Παλαιστίνης, διὰ τοῦτο εἶπεν "ἐν τῇ σκοτίᾳ," καὶ "εἰς τὸ οὖς," πρὸς τὴν μετὰ ταῦτα παῤῥησίαν ἐσομένην*, Hom. xxxiv. 2, p. 390; or (2) as this part of the discourse relates to the *future* principally, the *secret speaking* may mean the communication which our Lord would hold with them hereafter by His Spirit, which they were to preach and proclaim. See Acts iv. 20. These senses do not exclude one another, and are possibly both implied. There is no need, with Lightfoot and others, to suppose any allusion to a custom in the synagogue, in the words **εἰς τὸ οὖς ἀκούετε.** They are a common expression derived from common life: we have it in a wider sense Acts xi.

[c] ἀποκτεννόντων τὸ σῶμα, τὴν δὲ ψυχὴν μὴ δυναμένων
ἀποκτεῖναι· φοβεῖσθε δὲ μᾶλλον τὸν δυνάμενον καὶ
[d] ψυχὴν καὶ σῶμα [d] ἀπολέσαι ἐν [e] γεέννῃ. 29 οὐχὶ

c (-νν-) Mark xii. 5. Luke xii. 4. 2 Cor. iii. 6. Rev. vi. 11.
d Sir. xx. 22.
e ch. v. 22, 29, 30. xiii. 15, 33. Luke xii. 5 al. see Josh. xviii. 16 Heb.

in cod, not as Btly) DS 1. 33 hom-Cl [Orig_1 Eus_1] Constt. rec αποκτεινοντων, with B Orig Eus_2 [Constt Cyr_1]: αποκτενοντων F(Wetst) GL rel Chr Cyr Thdrt Thl: txt CDUΓΔΠ[2]א 1. for αποκτειναι, σφαξαι D[1](txt D[4]). rec (for φοβεισθε) φοβηθητε, with DL rel: txt [B]Cא. ins την bef ψυχην and το bef σωμα F(Wetst) א[2] rel Thl: ins το (but not την) א[1] Scr's h: om BCDLXΠ 1. 33 Just Thdot Clem hom-Cl Constt Orig_3 [Bas Cyr]. εις γεενναν D latt Iren-int [Tert] Cypr Lucif.

22, and Gen. l. 4. **ἐπὶ τῶν δ.**] On the flat roofs of the houses. Thus we have in Josephus, ἀναβὰς ἐπὶ τὸ τέγος καὶ τῇ δεξιᾷ καταστείλας τὸν θόρυβον αὐτῶν . . . . ἔφη . . . B. J. ii. 21. 5.

28.] **φοβεῖσθαι ἀπό** is a Hebraism, יָרֵא מִן. The *present* indicates the *habit*. On the *latter part* of this verse much question has of late been raised, which never was, as far as I have been able to find, known to the older interpreters. Stier designates it as 'the only passage of Scripture whose words may equally apply to God and the enemy of souls.' He himself is strongly in favour of the *latter* interpretation, and defends it at much length; but I am *quite unable to assent to his opinion*. It seems to me *at variance with the connexion of the discourse*, and with the *universal tone of Scripture regarding Satan*. If such a phrase as φοβεῖσθαι τὸν διάβολον could be instanced as = φυλάξασθαι τὸν δ., or if it could be shewn that any where power is attributed to Satan analogous to that indicated by ὁ δυνάμενος καὶ ψ. κ. σ. ἀπολέσαι ἐν γ., I should then be open to the doubt whether he might not here be intended; but seeing that φοβεῖσθαι ἀπό indicating terror is changed into φοβεῖσθαι so usually followed by τὸν θεόν in a higher and holier sense (there is *no such contrast* in ver. 26, and therefore that verse cannot be cited as ruling the meaning of this), and that GOD ALONE is throughout the Scripture the *Almighty dispenser of life and death both temporal and eternal*, seeing also that Satan is ever represented as the *condemned* of God, not ὁ δυν. ἀπολ., I must hold by the general interpretation, and believe that both here and in Luke xii. 3—7 our Heavenly Father is intended as the right object of our fear. As to this being inconsistent with the character in which He is brought before us in the next verse, the very change of construction in φοβεῖσθαι would lead the mind on, out of the terror before spoken of, into that better kind of fear always indicated by that expression when applied to God, and so prepare the way for the next verse. Besides, this sense is excellently in keeping with ver. 29 in another way. 'Fear Him who is the only Dispenser of Death and Life: of *death*, as *here*; of *life*, as in the case of the sparrows for whom He cares.' 'Fear Him, above men: trust Him, in spite of men.' In preparing my 2nd edn., I carefully reconsidered the whole matter, and went over Stier's arguments with the connexion of the discourse before me, but found myself more than ever persuaded that it is quite impossible, for the above and every reason, to apply the words to the enemy of souls. The similar passage, James iv. 12, even in the absence of other considerations, would be decisive. Full as his Epistle is of our Lord's words from this Gospel, it is hardly to be doubted that in εἷς ἐστιν ὁ νομοθέτης καὶ κριτής, **ὁ δυνάμενος** σῶσαι καὶ **ἀπολέσαι**, he has this very verse before him. This Stier endeavours to escape, by saying that ἀπολέσαι *barely*, as the opposite to σῶσαι, is far from being = ψυχὴν ἀπολέσαι in a context like this. But as connected with νομοθέτης καὶ κριτής, what meaning can ἀπολέσαι bear, except that of *eternal destruction*? The strong things which he says, that his sense will only be doubted as long as men do not search into the depth of the context, &c. do not frighten me. The depth of this part of the discourse I take to be, the setting before Christ's messengers their Heavenly Father as the sole object of childlike trust and childlike fear—the former from His love,—the latter from His power,—His *power* to destroy, it is not said, *them*, but absolute, *body and soul*, in hell. Here is the true depth of the discourse: but if in the midst of this great subject, our Lord is to be conceived as turning aside, upholding as an object of fear the chief enemy, whose ministers and subordinates He is at the very moment commanding us *not to fear*, and speaking of *him* (which would indeed be an "ἅπαξ

f Luke xii. 6, 7 only. Eccl. xii. 4.
g Luke xii. 6 only †. gen. as Rev. vi. 6. 4 Kings vii. 1.
h Amos iii. 5.
i 1 Pet. iii. 1. iv. 9 only.
k Luke xii. 7. Rev. vii. 9 only. Ps. cxlvi. 4.
l ch. vi. 26 al. 2 Macc. xv. 13. 3 Macc. vi. 26.
m ch. vii. 24 reff.
n constr., Luke xii. 8 bis only. = John xii. 42. Rom. x. 9, 10.
o = ch. v. 16. xxvi. 70 al.

δύο [f] στρουθία [g] ἀσσαρίου πωλεῖται; καὶ ἓν ἐξ αὐτῶν BCDEF GKLM SUVXΓ ΔΠℵ 1. 33
οὐ [h] πεσεῖται ἐπὶ τὴν γῆν [i] ἄνευ τοῦ πατρὸς ὑμῶν. 30 ὑμῶν
δὲ καὶ αἱ τρίχες τῆς κεφαλῆς πᾶσαι [k] ἠριθμημέναι εἰσίν.
31 μὴ οὖν φοβεῖσθε· πολλῶν [f] στρουθίων [l] διαφέρετε ὑμεῖς.
32 [m] πᾶς οὖν [m] ὅςτις [n] ὁμολογησει ἐν ἐμοὶ [o] ἔμπροσθεν τῶν
ἀνθρώπων, [n] ὁμολογήσω κἀγὼ ἐν αὐτῷ [o] ἔμπροσθεν τοῦ
πατρός μου τοῦ ἐν τοῖς οὐρανοῖς. 33 ὅςτις δὲ [p] ἀρνή-
σηταί με [o] ἔμπροσθεν τῶν ἀνθρώπων, [p] ἀρνήσομαι κἀγὼ
αὐτὸν [o] ἔμπροσθεν τοῦ πατρός μου τοῦ ἐν τοῖς οὐρανοῖς.
34 μὴ [q] νομίσητε ὅτι ἦλθον [r] βαλεῖν εἰρήνην ἐπὶ τὴν
γῆν· οὐκ ἦλθον [r] βαλεῖν εἰρήνην ἀλλὰ [s] μάχαιραν.

p ch. xxvi. 70, 72 ||. Luke xii. 9 al. Gen. xviii. 15. Wisd. xii. 27. xvi. 16. xvii. 10 only.
q ch. xx. 10. Luke ii. 44. iii. 23. not Mark nor John. Acts vii. 25 al6. 1 Cor. vii. 26, 36. 1 Tim. vi. 5 only †. 2 Macc. iv. 32 al. Ps. xlix. 21 Symm.
r = John xx. 25. James iii. 3. Rev. xiv. 16, 19. Ezek. xxxiii. 24.
s Rom. viii. 35 al. Jer. ix. 16. xiv. 13.

29. ins *του* bef *ασσαριου* D¹ [Orig₁(om₁)]. **πωλουνται** D.
30. for *υμων δε*, *αλλα* D lat-*a b c ff₁ g₁ h* Clem Hil. aft *κεφαλης* ins *υμων* DL [Clem₁] (lat-*a b c g₁ h* Syr copt [goth] æth Iren-int Hil ?).
31. rec *φοβηθητε*, with C rel: txt BDLℵ 1. 33 Orig₁ Cyr.
32. for *εν αυτω*, *αυτον* D(L) latt Hil Did: om D-lat.—*αυτ.* bef *καγω* L. (lat-*a* def.) rec om *τοις*, with DLℵ rel Clem Orig₃ [Chr Cyr₁]: ins B[sic in cod] CKV 33(appy) Orig₁.
33. rec (for *δε*) *δ' αν*, with Dℵ rel Orig₂ [Chr Cyr₁]: txt B C(*δ'*) L. (33 def.) *αρνησεται* LX: *απαρνησηται* (*αν having been interpolated has been mistaken for απ*) C 1 Orig₂[-int₁]. (33 def.) rec *αυτον* bef *καγω*, with C rel syrr æth Orig₁: txt BDΔℵ 1. 33 latt (syr-cu) goth arm Orig₂ Chr Cyr Thdrt Hil. rec om *τοις*, with CDℵ rel Orig₂: ins BVX Orig₁ [Cyr].
34. *ειρηνην* bef *βαλειν* (1st time) ℵ [lat-*g₁ ff₂* Tert Hil].

λεγόμενον horrendum") as **ὁ δυνάμενος** *κ. ψ. κ. σῶ. ἀπολέσαι ἐν γεέννῃ*, to my mind all true and deep connexion is broken. It is remarkable how Stier, who so eloquently defends the insertion of **ὅτι σοῦ ἡ δύναμις** in the Lord's Prayer, can so interpret here. Reichel (whose works I have not seen) seems by a note in Stier, p. 380, to maintain the above view even more strongly than himself. Lange also, in the Leben Jesu, ii. 2, p. 721, maintained this view: but has now, Bibelwerk, i. p. 150, retracted it for reasons the same as those urged here. **29. στρουθία**] any small birds. **ἀσσαρίου**] This word, derived from *'as,'* was used in Greek and Hebrew (אִיסָר) to signify the meanest, most insignificant amount: see Buxtorf, Lex. Chald. sub voce.

καί, and yet: see examples in Hartung, Partikellehre, i. 147. 6. **πεσ. ἐπὶ τ. γ.**] which birds do when struck violently, or when frozen, wet, or starved = **die**, *ἓν ἐξ αὐτῶν οὐκ ἔστιν ἐπιλελησμένον ἐνώπιον τοῦ θεοῦ*, Luke xii. 6.

30.] See 1 Sam. xiv. 45: Luke xxi. 18: Acts xxvii. 34. The **ὑμῶν** is emphatic, corresponding to the *ὑμεῖς* at the end of ver. 31. But the emphatic **ὑμεῖς**, spoken directly to the Apostles, is generalized immediately by the **πᾶς οὖν** in ver. 32.

32. ὁμολ. ἐν ἐμοί] A Hebraistic or rather perhaps Syriac mode of expression (De Wette) for, 'shall make me the object of His acknowledgment among and before men.' The context shews plainly that it is a practical consistent confession which is meant, and also a practical and enduring denial. The Lord will not confess the confessing Judas, nor deny the denying Peter; the traitor who denied Him in act is denied: the Apostle who confessed Him even to death will be confessed. Cf. 2 Tim. ii. 12. We may observe that both in the Sermon on the Mount (ch. vii. 21—23) and here, *after mention of the Father*, our Lord describes *Himself* as the Judge and Arbiter of eternal life and death.

34.] In Luke xii. 51—53 this announcement, as here, is closely connected with the mention of our Lord's own sufferings (ver. 38). As He won His way to victory through the contradiction of sinners and strife, so must those who come after Him. The immediate reference is to the divisions in families owing to conversions to Christianity. Ver. 35 is quoted nearly literally from Micah vii. 6. When we read in Com-

35 ἦλθον γὰρ [t] διχάσαι [u] ἄνθρωπον κατὰ τοῦ πατρὸς
αὐτοῦ, καὶ θυγατέρα κατὰ τῆς μητρὸς αὐτῆς, καὶ [v] νύμφην κατὰ τῆς [w] πενθερᾶς αὐτῆς, 36 καὶ ἐχθροὶ τοῦ ἀνθρώπου οἱ [x] οἰκιακοὶ αὐτοῦ. 37 ὁ φιλῶν πατέρα ἢ μητέρα
[y] ὑπὲρ ἐμὲ οὐκ ἔστιν μου [z] ἄξιος, καὶ ὁ φιλῶν υἱὸν ἢ θυγατέρα [y] ὑπὲρ ἐμὲ οὐκ ἔστιν μου [z] ἄξιος, 38 καὶ ὃς οὐ
λαμβάνει τὸν σταυρὸν αὐτοῦ καὶ [a] ἀκολουθεῖ [a] ὀπίσω μου
οὐκ ἔστιν μου [z] ἄξιος. 39 ὁ [b] εὑρὼν τὴν [c] ψυχὴν αὐτοῦ
[d] ἀπολέσει αὐτήν· καὶ ὁ [d] ἀπολέσας τὴν [d] ψυχὴν αὐτοῦ
ἕνεκεν ἐμοῦ [b] εὑρήσει αὐτήν. 40 ὁ [e] δεχόμενος ὑμᾶς ἐμὲ
[e] δέχεται· καὶ ὁ ἐμὲ [e] δεχόμενος [e] δέχεται τὸν ἀποστεί-

t here only †. Deut. xiv. 6 Aq. in Append.
u Micah vii. 6.
v = Luke xii. 53 bis (John iii. 29. Rev. xviii. 23. xxi. 2, 9. xxii. 17) only. Gen. xxxviii. 11, 24.
w ch. viii. 14 ‖ Luke xii. 53 bis only. Ruth i. 14.
x ver. 25 only †.
y = Acts xxvi. 13. Philem. 16. 1 Kings xv. 22.
z w. gen., Acts xiii. 46. Rom. i. 32. Heb. xi. 38. Wisd. iii. 5.

a Mark viii. 34. 3 Kings xix. 20. see Num. xxxii. 11. 14. Prov. ii. 20.
b = ch. xi. 29. xvi. 25. Rev. xviii. 14. Prov. ii. 20.
c ch. vi. 25 reff. Gen. xii. 13.
d ch. xvi. 25 ‖ Mk. Luke xvii. 33. John xii. 25. Sir. xx. 22.
e = ver. 14 reff.

35. for ανθρωπον, υιον D (42.) 114[2] lat-*b c ff*$_1$ *g*$_1$ *h l* syr-cu Hil$_1$ Op.
37. om 2nd clause (*homœotel*) B[1](but in marg by same hand) D syr-ms [Orig$_1$(and int$_1$)] Eus(expr, as belonging to Matt) Cypr$_1$(ins$_2$).
39. om ο ευρων to και (*homœotel* ὁ to ὁ) ℵ[1](ins ℵ-corr[1]). for και ο, ο δε D Tert.
40. for και ο, ο δε ℵ[1](txt ℵ[3a]) : και ο εμε δεχομενος δεχεται is deficient in D-gr.

mentators, e. g. De Wette, that these divisions were not the purpose, but the inevitable results only, of the Lord's coming, we must remember that with God, *results* are all *purposed*. **36. τοῦ ἀνθρ.**] The article is generic, and is rightly rendered in the E. V. 'a man's foes,' &c. See on ch. ix. 1. **37.**] Compare Deut. xxxiii. 9, and Exod. xxxii. 26—29, to which passages this verse is a reference. Stier well remarks, that under the words *ἄξιός μου* there lies an exceeding great reward which counterbalances all the *seeming asperity* of this saying. **38.**] How strange must this prophetic announcement have seemed to the Apostles! It was no Jewish proverb (for crucifixion was not a Jewish punishment), no common saying, which our Lord here and so often utters. See ch. xvi. 24: Mark x. 21: Luke ix. 23. He does not here plainly mention *His* Cross; but leaves it to be understood, see ver. 25. This is one of those sayings of which John xii. 16 was eminently true. Neander (Leben Jesu, p. 546, note) quotes from Plutarch, de sera numinis vindicta, c. ix., *καὶ τῷ μὲν σώματι τῶν κολαζομένων ἕκαστος κακούργων ἐκφέρει τὸν αὑτοῦ σταυρόν* (meaning, as he explains it, a *guilty conscience*),—as a proof that our Lord used this saying without any conscious reference to His own Death. But he confesses that if the *ὑψοῦν* of John xii. 32 is to be understood as there interpreted (ver. 33), he should be ready to allow the allusion here also. Seeing then that we do thus understand it, his inference has no value for us. Besides which, the passage of Plutarch does not even prove the expression to have been proverbial. **39.**] **ψυχὴν . . . αὐτήν** refer to the *same thing*, but in somewhat different senses. The *first ψυχή* is the *life of this world*, which we here all count so dear to us; the *second*, implied in *αὐτήν*, the *real life of man* in a blessed eternity. **εὑρών** = *φιλῶν*, John xii. 25 = *σῶσαι θέλων*, Mark viii. 34. The past participles are used proleptically, with reference to that day when the loss and gain shall become apparent. But *εὑρών* and *ἀπολέσας* are again somewhat different in position: the first implying *earnest desire* to save, but not so the second any will or voluntary act to destroy. This is brought out by the *ἕνεκεν ἐμοῦ*, which gives the ruling providential arrangement whereby the *ἀπολέσας* is brought about. But besides the primary meaning of this saying as regards the laying down of life literally for Christ's sake, we cannot fail to recognize in it a far deeper sense, in which he who loses his life shall find it. In Luke ix. 23, the taking up of the cross is to be *καθ' ἡμέραν*: in ch. xvi. 24 ‖ Mark *ἀπαρνησάσθω ἑαυτόν* is joined with it. Thus we have the crucifying of the life of this world,—the death to sin spoken of Rom. vi. 4—11, and life unto God. And this life unto God is the real, true *ψυχὴ αὐτοῦ*, which the self-denier shall find, and preserve unto life eternal. See John xii. 25 and note. **40.**] Here in the conclusion of the discourse, the Lord recurs again to His

λαντά με. 41 ὁ [e] δεχόμενος προφήτην [f] εἰς [f] ὄνομα προ- Z -λαντα με...
φήτου [g] μισθὸν προφήτου λήμψεται· καὶ ὁ [e] δεχόμενος
δίκαιον [f] εἰς [f] ὄνομα δικαίου [g] μισθὸν δικαίου λήμψεται.
42 καὶ ὃς * ἐὰν [h] ποτίσῃ ἕνα τῶν [i] μικρῶν τούτων [k] ποτή- P και ος ...
ριον [l] ψυχροῦ μόνον [f] εἰς [f] ὄνομα μαθητοῦ, [m] ἀμὴν λέγω BCDEF
ὑμῖν, οὐ μὴ ἀπολέσῃ τὸν [g] μισθὸν αὐτοῦ. XI. 1 Καὶ GKLM PSUVX
ἐγένετο ὅτε [n] ἐτέλεσεν ὁ Ἰησοῦς [o] διατάσσων τοῖς δώδεκα ZΓΔΠℵ 1. 33
μαθηταῖς αὐτοῦ, [p] μετέβη [p] ἐκεῖθεν [q] τοῦ [q] διδάσκειν καὶ
κηρύσσειν ἐν ταῖς πόλεσιν αὐτῶν.
2 Ὁ δὲ Ἰωάννης ἀκούσας ἐν τῷ [r] δεσμωτηρίῳ τὰ

f ch. xviii. 20. (elsw. chiefly w. βαπτίζειν, ch. xxviii. 19. Acts viii. 16. xix. 5. 1 Cor. i. 13, 15. or πιστεύειν, John i. 12 al.)
g 1 Cor. ix. 17 al. Prov. xi. 21.
h ch. xxv. 35, &c. xxvii. 48. Mark ix. 44. Gen. xxi. 19. Exod. ii. 16.
i ch. xviii. 6, &c. Zech. xiii. 7.
k ch. xxvi. 27 ‖. Gen. xl. 11, 13, 21.
l Rev. iii. 15 bis, 16 only. Prov. xxv. 25. Sir. xliii. 20 only. ellips., here only. λοῦνται ψυχρῷ, Herod. ii. 37.
m vv. 15, 23.
n constr. w. particip., here only. see Josh. iii. 17. iv. 1.
o here only, exc. Luke (iii. 13 al3. Acts vii. 44 al4.) and Paul (1 Cor. vii. 17 al5.). Judg. v. 9. Dan. i. 5 Theod.
p ch. xii. 9. xv. 29. John vii. 3. Acts xviii. 7.
q constr., ch. iii. 13 reff.
r Acts v. 21, 23. xvi. 26 only. Gen. xxxix. 22 bis. xl. 3, 5 only.

41. om 2nd clause (*homœotel*) D.
42. * ἂν BD 33 : εαν CPZℵ rel. for μικρων, ελαχιστων D latt copt goth Cypr Hil Aug Op. aft ποτηριον ins υδατος D latt syr-cu copt goth æth arm Clem $Orig_2$ Hil. ψυχρουν MXZ 33 Scr's a b d s ev-y. om μονον D 6. 53-9 syr-cu copt goth Cypr. for απολεση τον μισθον, αποληται ο μισθος D lat-*a b c* g_1 *h* copt æth Cypr Aug_1. (lat-*a* defective.)

Apostles whom He was sending out. From ver. 32 has been connected with πᾶς ὅστις, and therefore general. **δέχεται,** see ver. 14; but it has here the wider sense of not only receiving to house and board,—but *receiving* in heart and life *the message* of which the Apostles were the bearers. On the sense of the verse, see John xx. 21, and on **τὸν ἀποστείλαντά με,** ἐγὼ ἀποστέλλω ὑμᾶς, ver. 16, and Heb. iii. 1. There is a difference between the representation of Christ by His messengers, which at most is only official, and even then broken by personal imperfection and infirmity (see Gal. ii. 11; iv. 13, 14),—and the perfect unbroken representation of the Eternal Father by His Blessed Son, John xiv. 9: Heb. i. 3. **41. μισθὸν προφήτου]** οἷον εἰκὸς τὸν προφήτην ἢ δίκαιον δεξάμενον λαβεῖν, ἢ οἷον ἐκεῖνος μέλλει λαμβάνειν. Chrysost. Hom. xxxv. 2, p. 401. **εἰς ὄνομα,** a Hebraism (לְשֵׁם): **because He is:** i. e. 'for the love of Christ, whose prophet he is.' The sense is, 'He who by receiving (see above) a prophet because he is a prophet, or a holy man because he is a holy man, recognizes, enters into, these states as appointed by Me, shall receive the blessedness of these states, shall derive all the spiritual benefits which these states bring with them, and share their everlasting reward.' **42. τῶν μικρῶν]** To whom this applies is not very clear. Hardly (De Wette) to the despised and meanly-esteemed for Christ's sake. I should rather imagine some *children* may have been *present:* for of such does our Lord generally use this term, see ch. xviii. 2—6. Though perhaps the expression may be meant of lower and less advanced converts, thus keeping up the gradation from προφήτης. This however hardly seems likely: for how could a disciple be in a downward gradation from δίκαιος? I may observe that Meyer denies the existence of the Rabbinical meaning of *disciples* commonly attributed to קְטַנִּים, little ones. In the passage from Bereschith Rabba quoted by Wetstein to support it, the word, he maintains, from the context, means *parvuli, children,* not *disciples.* **τὸν μισθ. αὐτ.]** **His** (i. e. the doer's) **reward:** not, 'the reward of *one of these little ones*,' as before μισθ. προφ., μισθ. δικαίου: —the article here makes the difference: and the expression is reflective.

XI. 1. **ἐκεῖθεν]** No fixed locality is assigned to the foregoing discourse. It was not delivered at Capernaum, but *on a journey,* see ch. ix. 35. **αὐτῶν** is also indeterminate, as in ch. iv. 23; ix. 35.

2—30.] Message of enquiry from the Baptist: our Lord's answer, and discourse thereon to the multitude. Luke vii. 18—35. There have been several different opinions as to the reason why this enquiry was made. I will state them, and append to them my own

ἔργα τοῦ [s] Χριστοῦ, πέμψας [t] διὰ τῶν μαθητῶν αὐτοῦ

s absol., of Jesus, Matt. here (and ch. i. 17) only. Mark ix. 41 only in Gospp. Epp. passim.
t 1 Pet. v. 12 (a). Rev. i. 1. 2 John 12. 3 John 13.

CHAP. XI. 2. for *χριστου*, *ιησου* D 61. 234. 421 Scr's q r evv-P-z syr-cu æth Orig Chr: *αυτου* syr-mg. rec (for *δια*) *δυο* (|| *Luke*), with C^3L rel vulg lat-ff_1 $g_{1.2}$ syr-mg copt æth Orig Chr Cyr: txt $BC^1DPZ\Delta\aleph$ 33 syrr goth arm, *discipulos* (for *δ. τ. μαθ.*) latt syr-cu Dial Hil Juv.

view. (1) It has been a very generally received idea that the question was asked *for the sake of the disciples themselves*, with the sanction of their master, and for the purpose of confronting them, who were doubtful and jealous of our Lord, with the testimony of His own mouth. This view is ably maintained by Chrysostom; τίνος οὖν ἕνεκεν ἔπεμψεν ἐρωτῶν; ἀπεπήδων τοῦ Ἰησοῦ οἱ Ἰωάννου μαθηταί· καὶ τοῦτο παντί που δῆλόν ἐστι· καὶ ζηλοτύπως ἀεὶ πρὸς αὐτὸν εἶχον. καὶ δῆλον ἐξ ὧν πρὸς τὸν διδάσκαλον ἔλεγον (John iii. 26), καὶ πάλιν (John iii. 25), καὶ αὐτῷ πάλιν προσελθόντες ἔλεγον (Matt. ix. 14),—οὔπω γὰρ ἦσαν εἰδότες τίς ἦν ὁ χριστός, ἀλλὰ τὸν μὲν Ἰησοῦν ἄνθρωπον ψιλὸν ὑποπτεύοντες, τὸν δὲ Ἰωάννην μείζονα ἢ κατὰ ἄνθρωπον, ἐδάκνοντο εὐδοκιμοῦντα τοῦτον ὁρῶντες, ἐκεῖνον δέ, καθὼς εἶπε, λοιπὸν λήγοντα. Hom. xxxvi. 2, 3, p. 408. And similarly Euthymius and Theophylact. This view is also adopted and eloquently defended by Stier, Reden Jesu, 2nd edn., i. p. 392 sq. The objections to this view are,—that the text evidently treats the question as coming from John himself; the answer is directed to John; and the following discourse is on the character and position of John. These are answered by Stier with a supposition that John *allowed the enquiry to be made* in his name; but surely our Saviour would not in this case have made the answer as we have it, which clearly implies that the object of the miracles done was *John's* satisfaction. (2) The other great section of opinions on the question is that which supposes doubt to have existed, for some reason or other, in the Baptist's own mind. This is upheld by Tertullian (cont. Marc. iv. 18, vol. ii. p. 402, ed. Migne, not iv. 5, as Bp. Wordsworth: nor is there any ambiguity in the main features of his view, as Bp. W. implies) and others, and advocated by De Wette, who thinks that the doubt was not perhaps respecting our Lord's *mission*, but His *way of manifesting Himself*, which did not agree with the theocratic views of the Baptist. This he considers to be confirmed by ver. 6. Olshausen (in loc.) and Neander (Leben Jesu, p. 92) suppose the ground of the doubt to have lain partly in the Messianic idea of the Baptist, partly in the weakening and bedimming effect of imprisonment on John's mind. Lightfoot carries this latter still further, and imagines that the doubt arose from dissatisfaction at not being liberated from prison by some miracle of our Lord. (Hor. Hebr. in loc.) This however is refuted by Schöttgen (Hor. Hebr. in loc.). The author of the Quæstiones et Resp. ad Orthodoxos among the works of Justin Martyr suggests, and Benson (Hulsean Lectures for 1820, p. 58 sqq.) takes up, the following solution: ἐπειδὴ διάφοροι φῆμαι περὶ ὧν ἐποιήσατο θαυμάτων ὁ Ἰησοῦς διέτρεχον, τῶν μὲν λεγόντων, Ἠλίας ἐστὶν ὁ ταῦτα ποιῶν· τῶν δέ, Ἱερεμίας· τῶν δέ, ἄλλος τις τῶν προφητῶν· ταύτας τὰς φήμας ἀκούων ὁ Ἰωάννης ἐν τῇ εἱρκτῇ πέμπει τοὺς μαθητὰς αὐτοῦ μαθεῖν εἰ ὁ τὰ σημεῖα ποιῶν αὐτός ἐστιν ὁ ὑπ' αὐτοῦ μαρτυρηθείς, ἢ ἕτερός τις ὁ παρὰ τῶν πολλῶν θρυλλούμενος. γνοὺς δὲ ὁ Ἰησοῦς τοῦ Ἰωάννου τὸν σκοπόν, ἐπὶ τῆς παρουσίας τῶν μαθητῶν Ἰωάννου ἐποίησε πολλὰ θαύματα, πείθων αὐτοὺς καὶ τὸν Ἰωάννην δι' αὐτῶν ὡς αὐτὸς εἴη ὁ πεποιηκὼς καὶ τὰ ἐπ' ὀνόματι ἑτέρων φημιζόμενα θαύματα, ὁ ὑπ' αὐτοῦ μαρτυρηθείς. Resp. 38, p. 456. (3) It appears to me that there are objections against each of the above suppositions, too weighty to allow either of them to be entertained. There can be little doubt on the one hand, that our Saviour's answer is directed to *John*, and not to the disciples, who are bonâ fide messengers and nothing more:—**πορευθέντες ἀπαγγείλατε Ἰωάννῃ** can, I think, bear no other interpretation: and again the words μακάριός ἐστιν ὃς ἐὰν μὴ σκανδαλισθῇ ἐν ἐμοί must equally apply to John in the first place, so that, *in some sense, he* had been offended at Christ. On the other hand, it is exceedingly difficult to suppose that there can have been in John's own mind any real doubt that our Lord was ὁ ἐρχόμενος, seeing that he himself had borne repeatedly such notable witness to Him, and that under special divine direction and manifestation (see ch. iii. 16, 17: John i. 26—37). The idea of his objective faith being shaken by his imprisonment is quite inconsistent not only with John's

3 εἶπεν αὐτῷ Σὺ εἶ ὁ [u] ἐρχόμενος, ἢ [v] ἕτερον [w] προςδοκῶ- BCDEF
μεν; 4 καὶ ἀποκριθεὶς ὁ Ἰησοῦς εἶπεν αὐτοῖς Πορευθέντες GKLM
ἀπαγγείλατε Ἰωάννῃ ἃ ἀκούετε καὶ βλέπετε. 5 τυφλοὶ PSUVX
[x] ἀναβλέπουσιν καὶ [y] χωλοὶ περιπατοῦσιν, [yz] λεπροὶ [yz] καθα- ΖΓΔΠℵ
ρίζονται καὶ [y] κωφοὶ ἀκούουσιν καὶ νεκροὶ [a] ἐγείρονται καὶ 1.33

u ‖ bis. John vi. 14, 27. Heb. x. 37, from Hab. ii. 3.
v ch. viii. 21. xii. 45 al.
w ‖ bis. 2 Pet. iii. 12, 13, 14. Ps. cxviii. 166. Lam. ii. 16 al.
x = ch. xx. 34. Acts ix. 12 al.‡ but see 1 Kings xiv. 27. Isa. xlii. 18. (-ψις, Luke iv. 19.)
y ch. xv. 30, 31 al.
z ch. viii. 2 reff.
a = N. T. passim. ch. x. 8 reff. Isa. xxvi. 19.

3. *ο εργαζομενος qui venis*, D[1](txt D[2]), *qui venturus es* latt Hil.
4. for *και αποκρ.*, *αποκρ. δε* D lat-*a b c* ff_1 g_1 *h*. ins *τω* bef *ιωαν.* ℵ[1](om ℵ[2]) 13.
5. om 1st *και* ΖΔ vulg lat-*c f* ff_1 $g_{1.2}$ *h* copt æth arm $Orig_2$: om *κ. χωλ. περιπ.* D 28. rec om *και* (bef *νεκροι*), with C rel vulg lat-*c f* ff_1 g_2 *h* copt æth $Orig_1$ Hil: ins BDLPZΔℵ 1 lat-*a b* g_1 syrr syr-cu goth arm Chr Bas-sel. (Π ?)

character, but with our Lord's discourse in this place, whose description of him seems almost framed to guard against such a supposition. The last hypothesis (that of the Pseudo-Justin) is hardly probable, in the form in which it is put. We can scarcely imagine that John can have doubted who this Person was, or have been confounded by the discordant rumours which reached him about His wonderful works. But that *one form* of this hypothesis is the right one, I am certainly disposed to believe, until some more convincing considerations shall induce me to alter my view. (4) The form to which I allude is this: John having heard all these reports, being himself fully convinced Who this Wonderworker was, was becoming impatient under the slow and unostentatious course of our Lord's self-manifestation, and desired to obtain from our Lord's own mouth a declaration which should set such rumours at rest, and (possibly) which might serve for a public profession of His Messiahship, from which hitherto He had seemed to shrink. He thus incurs a share of the same rebuke which the mother of our Lord received (John ii. 4); and the purport of the answer returned to him is, that the hour was not yet come for such an open declaration, but that there were sufficient proofs given by the works done, to render all inexcusable, who should be offended in Him. And the return message is so far from being a satisfaction designed for the *disciples*, that they are sent back like the messenger from Gabii to Sextus Tarquinius, with indeed a significant narrative to relate, but no direct answer; they were but the intermediate transmitters of the symbolic message, known to Him who sent it, and him who received it. It is a fact not to be neglected in connexion with this solution of the difficulty, that John is said to have heard of the works, not *τοῦ Ἰησοῦ*, but **τοῦ χριστοῦ**: the only place where that name, standing alone, is given to our Lord in this Gospel. So that it would seem as if the Evangelist had purposely avoided saying *τοῦ Ἰησοῦ*, to shew that the works were reported to John not as those of the Person whom he had known as Jesus, but of the Deliverer —the Christ; and that he was thus led to desire a distinct avowal of the identity of the two. I have before said that the opening part of the ensuing discourse seems to have been designed to prevent, in the minds of the multitude, any such unworthy estimations of John as those above cited. The message and the answer might well beget such suspicions, and could not from the nature of the case be explained to them in that deeper meaning which they really bore; but the character of John here given would effectually prevent them, after hearing it, from entertaining any such idea. **2. ἀκούσας**] From *his own disciples*, Luke vii. 18. The place of his imprisonment was Machærus. *ὁ μὲν ὑποψίᾳ τοῦ Ἡρώδου δέσμιος εἰς τὸν Μαχαιροῦντα πεμφθείς, ... (μεθόριον δέ ἐστι τῆς τε Ἀρέτα καὶ Ἡρώδου ἀρχῆς) . . . . ταύτῃ κτίννυται.* Jos. Antt. xviii. 5. 2. **4.**] *ἐν ἐκείνῃ τῇ ὥρᾳ ἐθεράπευσεν πολλοὺς ἀπὸ νόσων καὶ μαστίγων καὶ πνευμάτων πονηρῶν, καὶ τυφλοῖς πολλοῖς ἐχαρίσατο βλέπειν.* Luke, ver. 21. From *καὶ ἀποκριθεὶς . . . ἐν ἐμοί*, is nearly verbatim in the two Gospels. **5.**] The words **νεκροὶ ἐγ.** have raised some difficulty; but surely without reason. In Luke, the raising of the widow's son at Nain immediately precedes this message; and in this Gospel we have had the ruler's daughter raised. These miracles might be referred to by our Lord under the words *νεκ. ἐγ.*; for it is to be observed that He bade them tell John not only what things they saw, but what things they *had heard*, as in Luke. It must not be forgotten that the words here used by our Lord have an inner and spiritual sense,

[b] πτωχοὶ [bc] εὐαγγελίζονται, 6 καὶ [d] μακάριός ἐστιν ὃς ἐὰν
μὴ [e] σκανδαλισθῇ ἐν ἐμοί. 7 Τούτων δὲ πορευομένων
[f] ἤρξατο ὁ Ἰησοῦς λέγειν τοῖς ὄχλοις περὶ Ἰωάννου Τί
ἐξήλθατε εἰς τὴν ἔρημον [g] θεάσασθαι; [h] κάλαμον ὑπὸ
ἀνέμου [i] σαλευόμενον; 8 ἀλλὰ τί ἐξήλθατε ἰδεῖν; ἄνθρωπον ἐν [k] μαλακοῖς [l] ἠμφιεσμένον; ἰδοὺ οἱ τὰ [k] μαλακὰ

b ||. Luke iv. 18, from Isa. lxi. 1.
c constr. pass., ||. Heb. iv. 2, 6 only. (Luke xvi. 6 reff.) act., Rev. x. 7. (xiv. 6 v. r.)
d ch. v. 3 reff.
e w. ἐν, ch. xiii. 57. xxvi. 31, 33. Mark vi. 3 +. Sir. ix. 5. xxiii. 8. xxxv. (xxxii.) 15 only.
f ver. 20. ch. iv. 17. xii. 1 al. Gen. xi. 6.
g Luke xxiii. 55 reff.
h — ||. ch. xii. 20 (from Isa. xlii. 3). xxvii. 29, &c. Xen. Anab. i. 5. 1.
i ch. xxiv. 29 al. Ps. xvii. 7.
k = here (bis) and || L. (1 Cor. vi. 9) only ‡. Prov. xxv. 15. xxvi. 22 only. στολὰς μαλακότητι διαφόρους, Diod. Sic. v. 46.
l ch. vi. 30 reff.

6. for εαν, αν BD 1. 33.
7. om ο (bef ιησ.) D. (εξηλθατε, so BCDGLPZא, simly vv 8, 9.)
8. ανθρωπον bef ιδειν א[1](txt א[2]). om εν D[1](ins D[2]) א[3] latt Hil. rec aft μαλακοις ins ιματιοις (*from* || *Luke*), with CP rel gat lat-*b f h* syrr syr-cu copt goth æth arm: om BDZא vulg lat-*a c ff*$_1$ *g*$_{1.2}$ *k* Tert Hil Jer Aug Op. ημφιασμενον D.

as betokening the blessings and miracles of divine grace on the souls of men, of which His outward and visible miracles were symbolical. The words are mostly cited from Isa. xxxv. 5, where the same spiritual meaning is conveyed by them. They are quoted here, as the words of Isa. liii. are by the Evangelist in ch. viii. 17, as applicable to their partial external fulfilment, which however, like themselves, pointed onward to their greater spiritual completion. **εὐαγγελίζονται** is passive,—see reff. and 2 Kings xviii. 31 in the LXX. In ref. Luke it is also passive, but with the thing preached as its subject. Stier remarks the coupling of these miracles together, and observes that with νεκ. ἐγ. is united **πτωχοὶ εὐαγγελίζονται**, as being a thing hitherto unheard of and strange, and an especial fulfilment of Isa. lxi. 1. **6.**] See note on ver. 2.

7—30.] The discourse divides itself into TWO PARTS: (1) vv. 7—19, *the respective characters and mutual relations of John and Christ:* (2) vv. 20—30, *the condemnation of the unbelief of the time*—ending with *the gracious invitation to all the weary and heavy laden to come to Him, as truly* **ὁ ἐρχόμενος**. **7.**] The following verses set forth to the people the real character and position of John; identifying him who cried in the wilderness with him who now spoke from his prison, and assuring them that there was the same dignity of office and mission throughout. They are not spoken till after the departure of the disciples of John, probably because they were not meant for them or John to hear, but for the people, who on account of the question which they had heard might go away with a mistaken depreciation of John. ὁ πολὺς ὄχλος ἐκ τῆς ἐρωτήσεως τῶν Ἰωάννου μαθητῶν πολλὰ ἂν ἄτοπα ὑπενόησεν οὐκ εἰδὼς τὴν γνώμην μεθ' ἧς ἔπεμψε τοὺς μαθητάς. καὶ εἰκὸς ἦν διαλογίζεσθαι πρὸς ἑαυτοὺς καὶ λέγειν Ὁ τοσαῦτα μαρτυρήσας μετεπείσθη νῦν, καὶ ἀμφιβάλλει εἴτε οὗτος εἴτε ἕτερος εἴη ὁ ἐρχόμενος; ἆρα μὴ στασιάζων πρὸς τὸν Ἰησοῦν ταῦτα λέγει; ἆρα μὴ δειλότερος ὑπὸ τοῦ δεσμωτηρίου γενόμενος; ἆρα μὴ μάτην καὶ εἰκῇ τὰ πρότερα εἴρηκεν; ἐπεὶ οὖν πολλὰ τοιαῦτα εἰκὸς ἦν αὐτοὺς ὑποπτεύειν, ὅρα πῶς αὐτῶν διορθοῦται τὴν ἀσθένειαν, καὶ ταύτας ἀναιρεῖ τὰς ὑποψίας. Chrysostom, Hom. xxxvii. 1, p. 414. And our Lord, as usual, takes occasion, from reminding them of the impression made on them by John's preaching of repentance, to set forth to them deep truths regarding His own Kingdom and Office. **8. ἀλλά**] If it was not that, ...; so in Demosth. Coron. p. 233, τί γὰρ καὶ βουλόμενοι μετεπέμπεσθ' ἂν αὐτούς; ἐπὶ τὴν εἰρήνην; ἀλλ' ὑπῆρχεν ἅπασιν. **ἀλλ'** ἐπὶ τὸν πόλεμον: see Klotz, Devar. p. 5. **τί ἐξήλθατε**] The repetition of this question, and the order of the suggestive answers, are remarkable. The first sets before them the scene of their desert pilgrimage—the banks of Jordan with its reeds (as Dr. Burton quotes from Lucian Hermotim., κάλαμος ἐπ' ὄχθῃ παραποταμίῳ πεφυκὼς καὶ πρὸς πᾶν τὸ πνέον σαλευόμενος);—but no such trifles were the object of the journey: this suggestion is rejected without an answer. The second reminds them that it was a *man*—but not one in soft clothing, for such are not found in deserts. The third brings before them the real object of their pilgrimage in his holy office, and even amplifies that office itself. So that the great Forerunner is made to rise gradually and sublimely into his personality, and thus his preaching of repentance is revived in their minds. **ἐν μαλακοῖς**] Contrast this with the garb of John

[m] φοροῦντες ἐν τοῖς οἴκοις τῶν βασιλέων [εἰσίν]. 9 ἀλλὰ
τί ἐξήλθατε προφήτην ἰδεῖν; ναὶ λέγω ὑμῖν, καὶ [n] περισσότερον προφήτου. 10 οὗτος [γάρ] ἐστιν περὶ οὗ γέγραπται [o] Ἰδοὺ ἐγὼ ἀποστέλλω τὸν ἄγγελόν μου πρὸ
προσώπου σου, ὃς [p] κατασκευάσει τὴν ὁδόν σου ἔμπροσθέν
σου. 11 ἀμὴν λέγω ὑμῖν, οὐκ [q] ἐγήγερται ἐν [r] γεννητοῖς ...αμην P.
γυναικῶν μείζων Ἰωάννου τοῦ βαπτιστοῦ· ὁ δὲ [s] μικρό- BCDEF GKLM SUVXZ ΓΔΠℵ 1. 33

m John xix. 5. Rom. xiii. 4. 1 Cor. xv. 49 bis. James ii. 3 only. Prov. xvi. 23, 27. Sir. xi. 5. xl. 4 only.
n ch. v. 47 al. compar., ||. Mark vii. 36. xii. 40 || L. 1 Cor. xii. 23, 24 al.† Dan. iv. 33 (36) Theod. only.
o Mal. iii. 1.
p Mark i. 2 reff. Num. xxi. 27.
q = ch. xxiv. 11, 24 ||. Luke vii. 16. John vii. 52. Judg. ii. 16, 18.
r || only. Job xiv. 1. xv. 14.
s ||. ch. xiii. 32 || Mk. Luke ix. 48 only. Judg. vi. 15 B. 1 Kings ix. 21 A.

βασιλείων (or -ειῶν) EFGKSVXΠ[1]. om εισιν Bℵ[1](ins ℵ[3a]).

9. rec ιδειν bef προφητην (|| *Luke*), with CDPℵ[3] rel latt Orig Hil: txt B[Tischdf (N. T. Vat.) states that the letters προφ are written over an erasure and that ι is visible under π, the scribe having begun to write ιδειν] Zℵ[1] [Chr-comm].

10. om γαρ (|| *Luke*) BDZℵ lat-*b* g_1 *k* syr-cu æth Orig Ambr Op Quæst: ins CP rel vulg lat-*c f* ff_1 g_2 *h* syrr copt goth arm [Chr]. om εγω Z lat-*c* ff_1 g_2 copt Chr Ambr. for ος, και P lat-*a b c* syr copt Chr_2 $Ambr_1$ Jer.

11. ins τοις bef γεννητοις and των bef γυναικων D[1].

as described ch. iii. 4. Such an one, in soft raiment, might be the forerunner of a proud earthly prince, but not the preacher of repentance before a humble and suffering Saviour; might be found as the courtly flatterer in the palaces of kings, but not as the stern rebuker of tyrants, languishing in their fortress dungeons. **9. προφήτην**] We read, ch. xxi. 26, that 'all accounted John as a prophet.' **περισσότερον** is neuter (as always in N. T.), not masculine; as πλεῖον, ch. xii. 41, 42. E. V. rightly, **more than a prophet.**

John was more than a prophet, because he did not write of, but *saw* and *pointed out*, the object of his prophecy;—and because of his proximity to the Kingdom of God. He was moreover more than a prophet, because he himself was the subject as well as the vehicle of prophecy. But with deep humility, he applies to himself only that one, of two such prophetic passages, which describes him as *φωνὴ βοῶντος*, and omits the one which gives him the title of *ὁ ἄγγελός μου*, here cited by our Lord. **10. σου**] Our Lord here changes the person of the original prophecy, which is *μου*. And that He does so, making that which is said by Jehovah of Himself, to be addressed to the Messiah, is, if such were needed (compare also Luke i. 16, 17, and 76), no mean indication of His own eternal and co-equal Godhead. It is worthy of remark that all three Evangelists quote this prophecy *similarly changed*, although St. Mark has it in an entirely different place. The student should compare the passage in the LXX with the three citations,—h. l., Mark i. 2, and Luke vii. 27. Also, that the high dignity and honour which our Lord here predicates of the Baptist, has a further reference: He was thus great above all others, *because he was the forerunner of Christ*. How great then above all others and him, must HE be. **11. ἐγήγερται**] Not merely a word of course, but especially used of prophets and judges, see reff., and once of our Saviour Himself, Acts v. 30. **γεννητοῖς** is most likely masculine. See reff. **ὁ δὲ μικρότερος**] This has been variously rendered and understood. Chrysostom's interpretation is as follows:—"*ὁ δὲ μικρότερος, ἐν τῇ βασιλείᾳ τῶν οὐρανῶν μείζων αὐτοῦ ἐστι.*" *μικρότερος, κατὰ τὴν ἡλικίαν καὶ κατὰ τὴν τῶν πολλῶν δόξαν, καὶ γὰρ ἔλεγον αὐτὸν φάγον καὶ οἰνοπότην· καὶ "οὐχ οὗτός ἐστιν ὁ τοῦ τέκτονος υἱός;" καὶ πανταχοῦ αὐτὸν ἐξηυτέλιζον.* Hom. xxxvii. 2, p. 416. And a little afterwards:—*περὶ ἑαυτοῦ λέγων εἰκότως κρύπτει τὸ πρόσωπον διὰ τὴν ἔτι κρατοῦσαν ὑπόνοιαν καὶ τὸ μὴ δόξαι περὶ ἑαυτοῦ μέγα τι λέγειν· καὶ γὰρ πολλαχοῦ φαίνεται τοῦτο ποιῶν. τί δέ ἐστιν "ἐν τῇ βασιλείᾳ τῶν οὐρανῶν;" ἐν τοῖς πνευματικοῖς καὶ τοῖς κατὰ τὸν οὐρανὸν ἅπασι. καὶ τὸ εἰπεῖν δὲ "οὐκ ἐγήγερται ἐν γεννητοῖς γυναικῶν μείζων Ἰωάννου" ἀντιδιαστέλλοντος ἦν ἑαυτῷ τὸν Ἰωάννην, καὶ οὕτως ἑαυτὸν ὑπεξαιροῦντος. εἰ γὰρ καὶ γεννητὸς γυναικὸς ἦν αὐτός, ἀλλ' οὐχ οὕτως ὡς Ἰωάννης· οὐ γὰρ ψιλὸς ἄνθρωπος ἦν, οὐδὲ ὁμοίως ἀνθρώπῳ ἐτέχθη, ἀλλὰ ξένον τινὰ τρόπον καὶ παράδοξον*, ib. 2, 3, p. 417. So also Euthymius and Theophylact: but such an interpretation is surely adverse to the spirit of the whole discourse. We may certainly say that our Lord in such a passage as this would not designate Himself as *ὁ μικρότερος* compared with

τερος ἐν τῇ βασιλείᾳ τῶν οὐρανῶν μείζων ἐστὶν αὐτοῦ.
12 ἀπὸ δὲ τῶν ἡμερῶν Ἰωάννου τοῦ βαπτιστοῦ ἕως ἄρτι
ἡ βασιλεία τῶν οὐρανῶν ᵗ βιάζεται, καὶ ᵘ βιασταὶ ἁρπά-

t pass., here only. Sir. xxxiv. (xxxi.) 21. mid., Luke xvi. 16 only. Gen. xxxiii. 11. u here only +.

rec αυτου bef εστιν (|| *Luke*), with BD Z(appy) ℵ rel [Cyr_1]: txt C latt(exc lat-*b*).
12. om δε D[1](ins D corr[1]) copt Ambr. ins οι bef βιασται D Clem.

John, in any sense: nor again is it our Lord's practice to speak of Himself as one ἐν τῇ βασιλείᾳ τῶν οὐρανῶν, or of His own attributes as belonging to or dependent on that new order of things which this expression implies, and which was *in Him* rather than He in it. Besides, the bare use of the comparative ὁ μικρότερος, with its reference left to be inferred, is, unless I am mistaken, unprecedented. If this had been the meaning, we should surely have had αὐτοῦ after μικρότερος. Again, the analogy of such passages as Matt. v. 19; xviii. 1, would lead us to connect the preceding adjective μικρότερος with ἐν τῇ β. τ. οὐ., and not the following.

The other, the usual interpretation, I am convinced, is the right one: **but he that is least in the kingdom of heaven, is greater than he.** The comparative with the article is not put for the superlative, although in English we are obliged to render it so, but signifies *'he that is less than all the rest'* (Winer, § 35. 4); and here is generic, of *all the inferior* ones. There is very likely an allusion to Zech. xii. 8: "He that is feeble among them at that day shall be as David." Thus the parallelism is complete: *John*, not inferior to any born of women—but *these, even the least of them*, are born of *another birth* (John i. 12, 13; iii. 5). *John*, the nearest to the King and the Kingdom —*standing on the threshold*—but *never having himself entered; these*, ἐν τῇ βασιλείᾳ, subjects and citizens and indwellers of the realm, ὧν το πολίτευμα ἐν οὐρανοῖς. He, the *friend of the Bridegroom*; they, however weak and unworthy members, *His Body, and His Spouse.* Meyer, giving in substance the above interpretation, believes that αὐτοῦ, i. e. Ἰωάν. τοῦ β., is to be supplied after μικρότερος. This would be unobjectionable *in sense*, but is it, in usage? See reff., and remember that ἐν τ. βασ. . . . . is equivalent in *meaning* to **τῶν** ἐν τ. βασιλείᾳ. Maldonatus (cited by Meyer) quotes the logical axiom, 'minimum maximi est majus maximo minimi.' 12.] The sense of * this verse has been much disputed. (1) **βιάζεται** has been taken in a *middle sense*; *'forcibly introduces itself,' 'breaks in with violence,'* as in the similar passage Luke xvi. 16, πᾶς εἰς αὐτὴν βιάζεται. Certainly such a sense agrees better with εὐαγγελίζεται, which we find in Luke, than the passive explanation of βιάζεται: but it seems inconsistent with the latter half of the verse to say that *it breaks in by force*, and then that *others break by force into it.* (2) βιάζεται is taken *passively*; so πόλεις . . . τὰς βεβιασμένας, Xen. Hell. v. 2. 15 (Meyer;—which is however, like many of his citations, incorrect): *'suffereth violence,'* E. V. And thus the construction of the verse is consistent: 'and the violent take it by force.' Believing this latter interpretation to be right, we now come to the question, *in what sense are these words spoken?* Is βιάζεται in a good or a bad sense? Does it mean, *'is taken by force,'* and the following, *'and men violently press in for their share of it, as for plunder;'*—or does it mean, *'is violently resisted, and violent men* (viz. its opponents, the Scribes and Pharisees) *tear it to pieces?'* This latter meaning bears no sense as connected with the discourse before us. The subject is not the *resistance made* to the kingdom of heaven, but *the difference between a prophesied and a present* kingdom of heaven. The fifteenth verse closes this subject, and the complaints of the arbitrary prejudices of 'this generation' begin with ver. 16. We conclude then that these words imply **From the days of John the Baptist until now** (i. e. inclusively, from the beginning of his preaching), **the kingdom of heaven is pressed into, and violent persons**— eager, ardent multitudes—**seize on it.** Of the truth of this, notwithstanding our Lord's subsequent reproaches for unbelief, we have abundant proof from the multitudes who followed, and outwent Him, and thronged the doors where He was, and would (John vi. 15) take Him by force (the very word ἁρπάζω being used) to make Him a king. But our Lord does not mention this so much to commend the βιασταί, as to shew the undoubted fact *that* **ὁ ἐρχόμενος** *was come*:—that the kingdom of heaven, which before had been the subject of distant prophecy, a closed fortress, a treasure hid, was now *undoubtedly upon earth* (Luke xvii. 21 and note), laid open to the entrance of men, spread out that all might take. Thus this verse connects with ver. 28,

ζουσιν αὐτήν. 13 πάντες γὰρ οἱ [v] προφῆται καὶ ὁ νόμος BCDEF
[w] ἕως Ἰωάννου [v] ἐπροφήτευσαν· 14 καὶ εἰ θέλετε [x] δέξασθαι, GKLM SUVXZ
αὐτός ἐστιν Ἡλίας ὁ μέλλων ἔρχεσθαι. 15 ὁ ἔχων ὦτα ΓΔΠℵ 1. 33
ἀκουέτω. 16 τίνι δὲ [y] ὁμοιώσω τὴν γενεὰν ταύτην; ὁμοία
ἐστὶν παιδίοις καθημένοις [z] ἐν ταῖς ἀγοραῖς, ἃ [a] προσφω-

v 1 Pet. i. 10. Ezra v. 1. 3 Kings xxii. 12.
w ch. i. 17. Dan. ix. 25 Theod.
x Acts viii. 14. 1 Thess. i. 6. Deut. xxx. 1.
y ch. vii. 24 reff.
z ch. xxiii. 7 al. Cant. iii. 2.
a ||. Luke vi. 13. xiii. 12. xxiii. 20. Acts xxi. 40. xxii. 2 +. Esdr. ii. 21 (18). vi. 22. 2 Macc. xv. 15.

15. rec aft ωτα ins ακουειν (*from Mark* iv. 9, *Luke* viii. 8), with CZℵ rel latt &c Just Hipp Clem Orig: om BD lat-*k*.

16. rec παιδαριοις, with ev-y: txt BCDZℵ rel Clem Chr Thl. rec om ταις, with C rel: ins BZℵ ev-y copt.—rec εν αγοραις bef καθημενοις (|| *Luke*), with X rel Clem: aft καθ. BCDLMZΔℵ 33 latt syr copt Chr Thl.—τη αγορα (|| *Luke*) D latt Syr syr-cu æth arm Hil, αγορα Scr's a l s: εν αγορα καθ. εν τ. αγοραις 1. rec και προσφωνουσι (|| *Luke*), with L rel lat-*a b c f* g_1 *h* syrr syr-cu Hil: α προσφωνουσιν C: txt BDZℵ 1

δεῦτε πρός με πάντες, and with Luke xvi. 16, πᾶς εἰς αὐτὴν βιάζεται. Compare also with this throwing open of the kingdom of heaven for all to press into, the stern prohibition in Exod. xix. 12, 13, and the comment on it in Heb. xii. 18—24. **13, 14.**] The whole body of testimony as yet has been *prophetic*,—the Law and Prophets, from the first till Zacharias the priest and Simeon and Anna prophesied; and according to the declaration of prophecy itself, John, in the spirit and power of Elias, was the forerunner of the great subject of all prophecy. Neither this—nor the testimony of our Lord, ch. xvii. 12—is inconsistent with John's own denial that he was Elias, John i. 21. For (1) the question there was evidently asked as assuming a *re-appearance of the actual Elias upon earth:* and (2) our Lord cannot be understood in either of these passages as meaning that the prophecy of Mal. iv. 5 received its *full completion* in John. For as in other prophecies, so in this, we have a partial fulfilment both of the coming of the Lord and of His forerunner, while the great and complete fulfilment is yet future—at the great day of the Lord. Mal. iv. 1. **ὁ μέλλων ἔρχεσθαι** here may not be = ὃς ἔμελλεν ἔρχεσθαι (as Bengel, 'sermo est tanquam e prospectu testamenti veteris in novum'), but is perhaps *strictly future*, **who shall come.** Compare ch. xvii. 11, where the future is used. The **εἰ θέλετε δέξασθαι** must be taken as referring to the partial sense of the fulfilment implied: for it was (and is to this day) the belief of the Jews that Elias in person should come before the end.

15.] These words are generally used by our Lord when there is a further and deeper meaning in His words than is expressed: as here—'if John the Baptist is Elias, and Elias is the forerunner of the coming of the Lord, then know surely that the Lord is come.' **16. δέ**] Implying 'the men of this generation have ears, and hear not; will not receive this saying; are arbitrary, childish, and prejudiced, not knowing their own mind.' **τίνι ὁμοιώσω;**] See similar questions in Mark iv. 30: Luke xiii. 18, 20; and note on ch. vii. 24. **ὁμοία ἐστὶν παιδίοις**: as children in their games imitate the business and realities of life, so these in the great realities now before them shew all the waywardness of children. The similitude is to two bodies of children, the one inviting the other to play, first at the imitation of a wedding, secondly at that of a funeral;—to neither of which will the others respond. Stier remarks that the great condescension of the preaching of the Gospel is shewn forth in this parable, where the man sent from God, and the eternal Word Himself, are represented as children among children, speaking the language of their sports. Compare Heb. ii. 14. It must not be supposed that the two bodies of children are two divisions of the Jews, as some (e. g. Olsh.) have done: the children who *call* are the *Jews*, those *called to*, the *two Preachers;* both belonging, according to the flesh, to ἡ γενεὰ αὕτη,—but neither of them corresponding to the kind of *mourning* (in John's case) with which the Jews would have them mourn, or the kind of *joy* (in the Lord's case) with which the Jews would have them rejoice. The converse application, which is commonly made, is against the **ὁμοία** ἐστὶν **παιδίοις**, by which the first παιδία must be the *children of this generation;* and nothing can be more perplexed than to render ὁμοία ἐστίν '*may be illustrated by*,' and invert the persons in the parable. Besides which, this interpretation would lay the waywardness to the charge of the *Preachers*,

νοῦντα τοῖς [b] ἑταίροις [αὐτῶν] 17 λέγουσιν [c] Ηὐλήσαμεν
ὑμῖν, καὶ οὐκ [de] ὠρχήσασθε· [f] ἐθρηνήσαμεν, καὶ οὐκ
[eg] ἐκόψασθε. 18 ἦλθεν γὰρ Ἰωάννης μήτε [h] ἐσθίων μήτε
[h] πίνων, καὶ λέγουσιν [i] Δαιμόνιον [i] ἔχει. 19 ἦλθεν ὁ υἱὸς
τοῦ ἀνθρώπου [h] ἐσθίων καὶ [h] πίνων, καὶ λέγουσιν Ἰδοὺ [k] ἄνθρωπος [l] φάγος καὶ [m] οἰνοπότης, τελωνῶν φίλος καὶ ἁμαρτωλῶν. καὶ [n] ἐδικαιώθη ἡ σοφία [o] ἀπὸ τῶν * τέκνων αὐτῆς.
20 Τότε [p] ἤρξατο [q] ὀνειδίζειν τὰς πόλεις ἐν αἷς ἐγένοντο

...μητε πινων Z. BCDEF GKLM SUVXΓ ΔΠℵ 1. 33

b ch. xx. 13. xxii. 12. xxvi. 50 only. Mt. Cant. viii. 13.
c || L. 1 Cor. xiv. 7 only +. (-λήτης, ch. ix. 23.)
d || L. ch. xiv. 6 || Mk. only. 2 Kings vi. 16.
e Eccl. iii. 4.
f ||. Luke xxiii. 27. John xvi. 20 only. Joel i. 5.
g = ch. xxiv. 30. Luke viii. 52. xxiii. 27. Rev. i. 7. xviii. 9 (ch. xxi. 8 || Mk.) only. Gen. xxiii. 2. l. 10.
h ch. xxiv. 49. Mark ii. 16 al. 3 Kings i. 25.
i ||. Luke viii. 27. John vii. 20. viii. 48, 49, 52. x. 20.
k ch. xiii. 45, 52. xviii. 23. xx. 1. xxii. 2. Luke ii. 15 al. Gen. ix. 20.
l || only +.
m || only. Prov. xxiii. 20 only. (-τεῖν, Prov. xxxi. [see xxiv.] 3.)
n Luke vii. 29, 35. Rom. iii. 4, from Ps. l. 4(6). Sir. i. 21.
o = 1 Cor. i. 30. 2 Cor. vii. 13. James i. 13. Rev. xii. 6. ch. xvi. 21. Isa. xlv. 26.
p ver. 7.
q = (but w. acc. of thing) Mark xvi. 14. Wisd. ii. 12. (ch. v. 11 al. Ps. lxviii. 9.

vulg lat-*ff*$_1$ *g*$_2$ *l* syr-mg copt. (Π ?) ετεροις BCDZℵ rel, *aliis* lat-*g*$_2$ *k* D-lat goth; *invicem* or *ad invicem* lat-*a b c g*$_1$ copt; *ad alterutrum* lat-*f*: txt GUΠ²(SV, e sil) syrr syr-cu æth arm, *æqualibus* or *coæqualibus* vulg lat-*ff*$_1$ *g*$_2$.—om αυτων BD Z(appy) ℵ latt copt goth: ins C rel syrr syr-cu æth arm. (*The question of the reading here is confused by the constant habit of writing* αι *for* ε, *and vice versâ. Thus A, in Luke* viii. 3, *has* εταιραι for ετεραι: *D, in Matt* xxvi. 50, ετεραι for εταιρε, *&c &c. I believe* εταιροις αυτων *to have been the origl, then* ετεροις *to have been written by mistake,* αυτων *being retained at first, but afterwards expunged. Lachm has edited* τοῖς ἑταίροις, *Tischdf* τοῖς ἑτέροις, *both omg* αυτων.)

17. rec ins και bef λεγουσιν (*necessitated by* προσφωνουσιν *above*), with CL rel syrr syr-cu: om BD Z(appy) ℵ 1 vulg lat-*ff*$_1$ *l* copt. rec aft εθρηνησαμεν ins υμιν (|| *Luke*), with C(sic) rel lat-*a b h* syrr syr-cu æth arm: om BDZℵ 1 vulg lat-*c f ff*$_1$ *g*$_{1.2}$ *l* copt goth Clem [Chr$_1$] Aug.

19. φιλος bef τελωνων (|| *Luke*) Lℵ lat-*c f h* [copt] Clem [Aug]. * ἔργων (= τεχνων ?) B¹ℵ 124 mss-mentd-by-Jer syrr copt [æth] arm: τεκνων B²CD rel vulg lat-*a c f ff*$_1$ *g*$_{1.2}$ *h l* syr-cu syr-mg [goth].

20. aft ηρξατο ins ο ιησους CKLΠ 1 Scr's l m n q r s² lat-*g*$_1$ *h* syrr syr-cu æth Chr Jer (*beginning of an ecclesiastical lection*). γεγονεισαν D: *factæ sunt* latt.

not to that of the Jews. **18. μήτε ἐσθ. μήτε πίν.**] Luke vii. 33 fills up this expression by inserting ἄρτον and οἶνον. See ch. iii. 4. The neglect of John's preaching, and rejection of his message, is implied in several places of the Gospels (see ch. xxi. 23—27: John v. 35, πρὸς ὥραν): but hence only do we learn that they brought against him the same charge which they afterwards tried against our Lord. See John vii. 20; x. 20.

19. ἐσθίων καὶ πίνων] Alluding to our Lord's practice of frequenting entertainments and feasts, e. g. the marriage at Cana, the feast in Levi's house, &c. See also ch. ix. 14. **καί = and yet**; see John xvi. 32. **ἡ σοφία, the divine wisdom** which hath ordered these things. **ἐδικ. was justified**—the same tense as ἦλθεν both times—refers to the *event*, q. d., 'they were events in which wisdom was justified, &c.' The force of the aorist is not to be lost by giving a *present* meaning to either of the verbs. The meaning seems to be, that the waywardness above described was not universal, but that the τέκνα σοφίας (in allusion probably to the Book of Proverbs, which constantly uses similar expressions: see ch. ii. 1; iii. 1, 11, 21; iv. 1, &c.) were led to receive and justify (= clear of imputation) the Wisdom of God, who did these things. Cf. Luke vii. 29, where in this same narrative it is said, οἱ τελῶναι **ἐδικαίωσαν** τὸν θεόν, βαπτισθέντες τὸ βάπτισμα Ἰωάννου. The τέκνα σοφίας are opposed to the wayward παιδία above, the child*like* to the child*ish*; and thus this verse serves as an introduction to the saying in ver. 25. Chrysostom understands the verse differently: τουτέστιν, εἰ καὶ ὑμεῖς οὐκ ἐπείσθητε, ἀλλ' ἐμοὶ λοιπὸν ἐγκαλεῖν οὐκ ἔχετε. Thus ὑμεῖς = τὰ τέκνα τῆς σοφ., as being the people of the Lord; and ἡ σοφία is our Lord Himself. This seems far-fetched, and not so consistent with the context as the other interpretation. **ἀπό** (reff.), not exactly equivalent to ὑπό, but implying '*at the hands of*' the person whence the justification comes. **20—30.**] SECOND PART OF THE DISCOURSE. See on ver. 7.

αἱ πλεῖσται [r] δυνάμεις αὐτοῦ, ὅτι οὐ [s] μετενόησαν. BCDEF
21 Οὐαί σοι Χοραζείν· οὐαί σοι Βηθσαϊδάν· ὅτι εἰ ἐν GKLM SUVXΓ
Τύρῳ καὶ Σιδῶνι ἐγένοντο αἱ [r] δυνάμεις αἱ γενόμεναι ΔΠℵ 1. 33
ἐν ὑμῖν, [t] πάλαι ἂν ἐν [uv] σάκκῳ καὶ [uw] σποδῷ [s] μετενόησαν.
22 [x] πλὴν λέγω ὑμῖν, Τύρῳ καὶ Σιδῶνι [y] ἀνεκτότερον ἔσται ἐν [y] ἡμέρᾳ κρίσεως ἢ ὑμῖν. 23 καὶ σὺ Καφαρναούμ,
μὴ [z] ἕως οὐρανοῦ [a] ὑψωθήσῃ, [b] ἕως [bc] ᾅδου [d] καταβήσῃ· ὅτι

r = ch. vii. 22. xiii. 54, 58. xiv. 2 ‖ Mk. al.
s ch. iii. 2 reff.
t Mark xv. 44. Luke x. 13. 2 Cor. xii. 19. Heb. i. 1. 2 Pet. i. 9. Jude 4 only. Isa. xxxvii. 26 only.
u Luke x. 13. Isa. lviii. 5. Jon. iii. 6.
v as above (u). Rev. vi. 12. xi. 3 only. 3 Kings xxi. (xx,) 31, 32. Isa. xx. 2.
w as above (u). Heb. ix. 13 only. Sir. xl. 3.
x = ch. xviii. 7. xxvi. 39, 64. Sir. xxix. 8.
y ch. x. 15 reff.
z Luke x. 15. 2 Cor. xii. 2. Deut. iv. 11.
a ch. xxiii. 12 al. fr. Gen. xxiv. 35.
b Luke x. 15. Isa. lvii. 9.
c ch. xvi. 18. Luke x. 15. xvi. 23. Acts ii. 27 (from Ps. xv. 10), 31. (1 Cor. xv. 55 v. r.) Rev. i. 18 a 13.
d Rev. xii, 12. Ezek. xxxi. 15, 17.

for αι, α D[1](txt D-corr[1]). om αυτου D[1] lat-g_1 syr-cu.

21. for 2nd ουαι σοι, και D lat-*a b c* ff_1 g_1 *h* Hil. εγεγονεισαν D : εγενηθησαν 33. 157 ev-36. aft σποδω ins καθημενοι (*from Luke* x. 13) CUℵ 33 syr Orig Bas Gaud, -μεναι Δ 1.

23. rec (for μη) η, with B[2](but without aspirate) D[1] rel ms-in-Jer lat-*f* g_1 *h* syrr Chr : txt B[1]CD[2]ℵ 1[2] latt syr-cu copt æth arm Iren-int. rec ins του bef ουρανου, with C rel : om BDΔℵ Scr's k ev-y. rec υψωθεισα, with E[1]KMXΔΠ[1] 33 syr-mg-gr : υψωθησ' Scr's a : υψωθης E-corr[1] rel lat-*f h* syrr Chr : txt BCDLℵ 1 latt syr-cu copt æth arm Iren-int. ins η bef 2nd εως D[1]L (ἣ L, *aut* lat-*a b* D-lat). rec καταβιβασθηση (*cf Luke* x. 15), with Cℵ rel syrr syr-cu copt arm : txt BD latt goth

20. τότε ἤρξατο] This expression betokens a change of subject, but not of locality or time. The whole chapter stands in such close connexion, one part arising out of another (e.g. this out of ver. 16—19), and all pervaded by the same great undertone, which sounds forth in vv. 28—30, that it is quite impossible that this should be a collection of our Lord's sayings uttered at different times. I would rather regard the τότε ἤρξατο as a token of the report of an ear-witness, and as pointing to a pause or change of manner on the part of our Lord. See note on Luke x. 13. **ὅτι οὐ μετ.**] Connect this with the first subject of our Lord's preaching, ch. iv. 17. The reference is to some unrecorded miracles, of which we know (Luke iv. 23: John xxi. 25) that there were many. **21. Χοραζείν**] According to Jerome (cited by Winer, Realwörterbuch) *a town of Galilee, two* (according to Eusebius *twelve*, but most likely an error in the transcription) *miles from Capernaum.* It is no where mentioned except here and in the similar place of Luke. The etymology is uncertain. Some would read χώρα ζίν. **Βηθσαϊδάν**] Called πόλις John i. 45,—κώμη Mark viii. 23,—*in Galilee* John xii. 21;—*on the western bank of the lake of Gennesaret, near the middle, not far from Capernaum;* the birth-place of Simon Peter, Andrew, and Philip. Both this and Chorazin appear to be put as examples of the lesser towns in which our Lord had wrought His miracles (the κωμοπόλεις of Mark i. 38), as distinguished from Capernaum, the chief town (ver. 23) of the neighbourhood. **Τύρῳ κ. Σιδῶνι**] These wealthy cities, so often the subject of prophecy, had been chastised by God's judgment under Nebuchadnezzar and Alexander, but still existed (Acts xii. 20; xxi. 3, 7; xxvii. 3). **ἐν σάκ. κ. σποδῷ μετ.** is probably an allusion to Jonah iii. 6, or to general Eastern custom. **23.**] The sense has been variously interpreted. Some suppose it to allude to the *distinguished honour conferred on* Capernaum by our Lord's residence there. So Euthymius: ἡ Καπερναοὺμ ἔνδοξος γέγονε διὰ τὸ κατοικεῖν ἐν αὐτῇ τὸν χριστὸν καὶ τὰ πολλὰ τῶν θαυμάτων ἐν αὐτῇ τελέσαι. Others (as Grotius) to the *rich fisheries carried on at* Capernaum, by means of which the town was proud and prosperous. Jerome says, 'Ideo ad inferna descendes, quia contra prædicationem meam superbissime restitisti.' He also mentions the first interpretation. Others, as Stier (Reden Jesu, i. 491), refer the expression to the *lofty situation of* Capernaum, which however is very uncertain. The first interpretation appears to me the most probable, seeing that our Lord chose that place to be the principal scene of His ministry and residence, ἡ ἰδία πόλις ch. ix. 1. The very sites of these three places are now matter of dispute among travellers. See Robinson, vol. iii. pp. 283—300. Dr. Thomson, "The Land and the Book," p. 359, was sure he found Chorazin in the ruins bearing the name Kho-

εἰ ἐν Σοδόμοις ἐγενήθησαν αἱ [e] δυνάμεις αἱ γενόμεναι
ἐν σοί, ἔμεινεν ἂν [f] μέχρι [g] τῆς [fh] σήμερον.
24 [x] πλὴν λέγω
ὑμῖν ὅτι γῇ Σοδόμων [i] ἀνεκτότερον ἔσται ἐν [i] ἡμέρᾳ
x. ... η σοι κρίσεως ἢ σοί.
25 Ἐν ἐκείνῳ τῷ [k] καιρῷ [l] ἀποκριθεὶς
ὁ Ἰησοῦς εἶπεν [m] Ἐξομολογοῦμαί σοι, πάτερ [n] κύριε

e vv. 20, 21. f ch. xxviii. 15. g ch. vi. 34 al. Exod. xiii 4. h ch. xxvii. 8. Rom. xi. 8 al. Gen. iv. 14. xxi. 26 al. i ch. x. 15 reff. k ch. xii. 1. xiv. 1 al. fr. Deut. iii. 23 al. l = ch. xvii. 4 || Mk. xxvi. 63. Luke i. 60. Acts iii. 12. Rev. vii. 13 al. Deut. xxv. 9. m = Luke x. 21. Rom. xiv. 11. xv. 9. (ch. iii, 6 al.) 2 Kings xxii. 50. n Luke x. 21. Acts xvii. 24, Gen. xxiv, 7.

æth. rec **εγενοντο** (*from ver* 21), with L rel: txt BCDℵ 1. 157. for *σοι*, *υμιν* ℵ[1](appy). rec *εμειναν*, with D rel: *εμεινον* LXΔ: *εμενον* M ev-y: txt BCℵ 1. 33.—*σοι εμεινεν* is written over an erasure by ℵ-corr[1].

24. om *οτι* ℵ(insd appy by ℵ[2], but erased) 33 [Iren-int]. *γης* D Scr's c. *ανεκτ. εσται* bef *γη σοδ.* ℵ Iren-int. for *η*, *ην* D[1](so ver 22). for *σοι*, *υμιν* D M-marg forj lat-*a b c ff$_1$ g$_1$ h* arm Iren-int.

razy, lying in a side valley of the Wady Nashif, which runs down to the lake on the East of Tell Hûm (Capernaum). And this, in spite of Dr. Robinson's rejection of the identification. **ἐν Σοδόμοις**] The comparison between sinful Israel and Sodom is common in the O.T. See Deut. xxxii. 32: Isa. i. 10: Lam. iv. 6: Ezek. xvi. 46—57. **ἔμεινεν ἄν**] This declaration of the Lord of all events, opens to us an important truth, that the destruction of Sodom was brought about, not by a necessity in the divine purposes —still less by a connexion of natural causes—but by the iniquity of its inhabitants, who, had they turned and repented, might have averted their doom. The same is strikingly set before us in the history of Jonah's preaching at Nineveh. **24, and 22.**] These verses are connected with those respectively preceding them thus:—'If these mighty works had been done in Tyre and Sidon—in Sodom —they would have, &c.; but, since no such opportunity was afforded *them*, and *ye*, Bethsaida, Chorazin, and Capernaum, have had and rejected such, it shall be more tolerable, &c.' And as to the saying of our Lord, 'If more warnings had been given they would have repented,'—it is not for the infidel to say, 'Why then were not more given?'—because every act of God for the rescue of a sinner from his doom is purely and entirely of free and undeserved grace, and the proportion of such means of escape dealt out to men is ruled by the counsel of His will who is holy, just, and true, and willeth not the death of the sinner; but whose ways are past our finding out. We know enough when we know that all are inexcusable, having (see Rom. i. ii.) the witness of God in their consciences; and *our* only feeling should be overflowing thankfulness, when we find ourselves in possession of the light of the glorious Gospel, of which so many are deprived. That the reference here is to the *last great day* of judgment is evident, by the whole being spoken of in the future. Had our Lord been speaking of the *outward* judgment on the rebellious cities, the future might have been used of *them*, but could not of Sodom, which was already destroyed. This **ἀνεκτότερον ἔσται** is one of those mysterious hints at the future dealings of God, into which we can penetrate no further than the actual words of our Lord reveal, nor say to what difference exactly they point in the relative states of those who are compared. See also Luke xii. 47, 48. **25, 26.**] This is certainly a continuation of the foregoing discourse; and the **ἀποκριθείς**, which seems to have nothing to refer to, does in reality refer to the words which have immediately preceded. The **ἐν ἐκείνῳ τῷ κ.** is not *chronological*, but gives additional solemnity to what follows. There may have been a slight break in the discourse; the older interpreters, and Meyer, insert the return of the Apostles; but I do not see any necessity for it. The whole ascription of praise is an *answer*: an answer to the mysterious dispensations of God's Providence above recounted. With regard to the arrangement in Luke, see note on Luke x. 21. **ἐξομολογοῦμαι**] Not merely, '*I praise Thee*,' but '**I confess to Thee**,' '*I recognize the justice of Thy doings*;' viz. in the words **ναὶ ὁ πατήρ ὅτι κ.τ.λ.** Stier remarks that this is the *first public mention* by our Lord of His Father; the words in ch. x. 32, 33 having been addressed to the twelve (but see John ii. 16). We have two more instances of such a public address to His Father, John xi. 41; xii. 28; and again Luke xxiii. 34. It is to be observed that He does not address the Father as *His* Lord, but as Lord *of heaven and earth*;

o Luke x. 21. 1 Cor. i. 19, rom Isa. xxix. 14. Prov. xvi. 21. p as above (o). Acts xiii. 7 only. q 1 Cor. ii. 10. Phil. iii. 15. Sir. iv. 18. r = Luke x. 21. Rom. ii. 20. 1 Cor. iii. 1 al. Ps. xviii. 7. s constr., ch. xxvii. 29. Mark x. 47. Luke xii. 32. xviii. 11, 13. John xx. 28. Rev. vi. 10. Ps. v. 2. t = Luke x. 21. Eph. i. 5, 9. Phil. ii. 13. Ps. xviii. 14. u ch. xviii. 14. Luke x. 21. v = 1 Cor. xv. 24. w ch. vii. 16, 20. 1 Cor. xiii. 12. x absol., ch. xxviii. 19. Mark xiii. 32. Luke x. 22. John iii. 35, 36 al. y ch. iv. 19 reff. 4 Kings vi. 19. xxii. 13.

BCDEF GKLM SUVΓΔ ΠN 1. 33

τοῦ [n] οὐρανοῦ καὶ τῆς [n] γῆς, ὅτι ἔκρυψας ταῦτα ἀπὸ
[o] σοφῶν καὶ [op] συνετῶν, καὶ [q] ἀπεκάλυψας αὐτὰ [r] νηπίοις.
26 ναὶ [s] ὁ πατήρ, ὅτι οὕτως ἐγένετο [t] εὐδοκία [u] ἔμπροσθέν
σου. 27 πάντα μοι [v] παρεδόθη ὑπὸ τοῦ πατρός μου, καὶ
οὐδεὶς [w] ἐπιγινώσκει [x] τὸν υἱὸν εἰ μὴ [x] ὁ πατήρ· οὐδὲ [x] τὸν
[x] πατέρα τις [w] ἐπιγινώσκει εἰ μὴ [x] ὁ υἱὸς καὶ ᾧ ἐὰν βούληται [x] ὁ υἱὸς [q] ἀποκαλύψαι. 28 [y] Δεῦτε πρός με πάντες οἱ

25. rec **απεκρυψας** (*see Luke* x. 21), with C rel Marcos Orig: txt BDℵ hom-Cl.
26. ευδοκια bef εγενετο (*see Luke* x. 21) Bℵ 1. 33 lat-*k* copt Marcos: txt CD rel latt syrr syr-cu æth arm $Orig_{appy}$ [Chr] Hil.
27. om μου ℵ[1](ins ℵ[2], appy) Scr's g Just Hil. for 1st επιγιν., γινωσκει (*see Luke* x. 22) C Scr's g $Just_1$ $Clem_1$ [$Eus\text{-}mss_1$ Did_2] Chr: εγνω $Just_1$ Marcos Val hom-Cl [$Clem_{sæpe}$ $Orig_{sæpe}$ Syn-ep-Ant Eus_2 Did_1]. for εαν, αν D 33 $Just_3$ [Marcos hom-Cl] $Clem_4$(txt_1) $Orig_4$.

as *ὁ τὰ πάντα ἐνεργῶν κατὰ τὴν βουλὴν τοῦ θελήματος αὐτοῦ*, Eph. i. 11. **ἔκρυψας . . . . ἀπεκάλυψας**] **didst hide**, and **didst reveal** in the deeper and spiritual sense of the words; the time pointed at being that in the far past, when the divine decrees as to such hiding and revealing were purposed. See 1 Cor. ii. 9—12. **ταῦτα**, *these mysterious arrangements*, by which the sinner is condemned in his pride and unbelief, the humble and childlike saved, and God justified when He saves and condemns. These are 'revealed' to those who can in a simple and teachable spirit, as *νήπιοι*, obey the invitation in vv. 28—30, but 'hidden' from the wise and clever of this world, who attempt their solution by the inadequate instrumentality of the mere human understanding. See 1 Cor. i. 26—31. **27.**] In two other places only in the three first Gospels (besides the similar passage, Luke x. 22) does the expression *ὁ υἱός* occur: see reff. The spirit of this verse, and its form of expression, are quite those of the Gospel of John; and it serves to form a link of union between the three synoptic Gospels and the fourth, and to point to the vast and weighty mass of discourses of the Lord which are not related except by John. We may also observe another point of union:—*this very truth* (John iii. 35) had been part of the testimony *borne to Jesus by the Baptist*—and its repetition here, in a discourse of which the character and office of the Baptist is the suggestive groundwork, is a coincidence not surely without meaning. The verse itself is in the closest connexion with the preceding and following, and is best to be understood in that connexion: **πάντα μοι παρεδόθη** || *ἀπεκάλυψας αὐτά* in ver. 25 (on the tenses, see note above, ver. 25), only *ἀπεκάλυψας* could not be used of the Eternal Son, but *παρεδόθη*, for He is Himself the Revealer;—**οὐδεὶς ἐπιγ. τ. υἱὸν . . . .**, none but the Almighty Father has full entire possession of the mystery of the Person and Office of the Son: it is a depth hidden from all being but His, Whose Purposes are evolved in and by it:—**οὐδὲ τ. πατέρα . . . .** nor does any fully apprehend, in the depths of his being, the love and grace of the Father, except the Son, and he to whom the Son, by the Eternal Spirit, proceeding from the Father and the Son, will reveal Him. (Certainly *αὐτόν* must be understood after *ἀποκαλύψαι*, as in E. V.; some, e. g. Stier, take *ἀποκ.* absolutely, '*make His revelations.*' Luther supplies '*it.*') See Col. ii. 2. Some (from ver. 25) understand the Father as the Revealer here also; and undoubtedly He is so, but *mediately through the Son*. See John vi. 45, 46. Then in close connexion with the **ᾧ ἐὰν βούληται**, which by itself might seem to bring in an arbitrariness into the divine counsel, follows, by the eternal Son Himself, the *δεῦτε πρός με πάντες*, the wonderful and merciful generalization of the call to wisdom unto salvation. In Luke this verse is introduced by *καὶ στραφεὶς πρὸς τοὺς μαθητὰς εἶπεν*. The words however are of doubtful genuineness: see there. **28.**] This is the great and final answer to the question *σὺ εἶ ὁ ἐρχόμενος, ἢ ἕτερον προσδοκῶμεν; . . . .* **δεῦτε πρός με πάντες**. As before, we may observe the closest connexion between this and the preceding. As the Son is *the great Revealer*, and as the *ᾧ ἐὰν*

[z] κοπιῶντες καὶ [a] πεφορτισμένοι, κἀγὼ [b] ἀναπαύσω ὑμᾶς.
29 [c] ἄρατε τὸν [d] ζυγόν μου ἐφ' ὑμᾶς καὶ μάθετε ἀπ' ἐμοῦ,
ὅτι [e] πραΰς εἰμι καὶ [f] ταπεινὸς τῇ καρδίᾳ, καὶ [gh] εὑρήσετε
[gi] ἀνάπαυσιν ταῖς [h] ψυχαῖς ὑμῶν. 30 ὁ γὰρ [d] ζυγός μου
[k] χρηστὸς καὶ τὸ [l] φορτίον μου [m] ἐλαφρόν ἐστιν.
XII. 1 Ἐν ἐκείνῳ τῷ [n] καιρῷ ἐπορεύθη ὁ Ἰησοῦς
τοῖς [o] σάββασιν διὰ τῶν [p] σπορίμων· οἱ δὲ μαθηταὶ αὐτοῦ
[q] ἐπείνασαν, καὶ [r] ἤρξαντο [s] τίλλειν [t] στάχυας καὶ ἐσθίειν.

...ἐπορεύθη F. Note. F still appears in the digest, because many portions of it were collated by Wetstein, which are now wanting.

z = John iv. 6. Rev. ii. 3. 2 Kings xvii. 2. Jer. xvii. 16.
a Luke xi. 46 only. Ezek. xvi. 33 only.
b 1 Cor. xvi. 18. Rev. xiv. 13. 1 Chron. xxii. 9, 18. Isa. xiv. 3.
c ch. xvi. 24 al. Lam. iii. 27.
d = Acts xv. 10. Gal. v. 1. 1 Tim. vi. 1 (Rev. vi. 5) only. Jer. v. 5.
e ch. v. 5, xxi. 5, from Zech. ix. 9. 1 Pet. iii. 4 only. (-ός [see v. r.], 2 Macc. xv. 12 only.)
f Luke i. 52. Rom. xii. 16. 2 Cor. vii. 6. x. 1. James i. 9. iv. 6, and 1 Pet. v. 5 (from Prov. iii. 34) only. Ps. xxxiii. 18.
g ch. xii. 43 || L. Rev. xiv. 11 only. Isa. xxxiv. 14. Sir. vi. 28. li. 27.
h Jer. vi. 16.
i as above (g). Rev. iv. 8 only.
k = Luke (v. 39) vi. 35. Rom. ii. 4 (1 Cor. xv. 33. Eph. iv. 32). 1 Pet. ii. 3 (from Ps. xxxiii. 8) only.
l ch. xxiii. 4. Luke xi. 46 bis. Acts xxvii. 10. Gal. vi. 5 only. 2 Kings xix. 35.
m 2 Cor. iv. 17 only. Exod. xviii. 26. (-φρία, 2 Cor. i. 17.)
n ch. xi. 25 reff.
o dat. pl., vv. 5, 10, 11, 12. Mark i. 21 al. Mt. Mk. L. only †. Jos. Vit. § 54. (-βάτοις, Num. xxviii. 10 al.)
p || only. Gen. i. 29 bis. Lev. xi. 37 only.
q ch. iv. 2 reff.
r ch. xi. 7 reff.
s || only. Ezra ix. 3. Isa. xviii. 7 only.
t ||. Mark iv. 28 bis only. Gen. xli. 5, 6. Deut. xxiv. 1 (xxiii. 25).

28. aft πεφορτισμενοι ins εσται *estis* D^1 latt Iren-int $Cypr_2$ Hil_3.
29. om απ εμου $\aleph^1$(ins ℵ-$corr^1$). (πραυς, so $BC^1D\aleph$ Clem $Orig_2$ Ath-ms Bas [Cyr_1].)

Chap. XII. 1. om τοις D^1(ins D^3). σαββατοις B. ins του bef σταχυας D, τους U.—σταχυας bef τιλλειν D.

βούληται is by His grace extended to *all the weary*—all who feel their need—so He here *invites them to receive this revelation*, μάθετε ἀπ' ἐμοῦ. But the way to this heavenly wisdom is by quietness and confidence, rest unto the soul, the reception of the divine grace for the pardon of sin, and the breaking of the yoke of the corruption of our nature. No *mere man* could have spoken these words. They are parallel with the command in Isa. xlv. 22, which is spoken by Jehovah Himself. **κοπιῶντες καὶ πεφορτισμένοι**, the active and passive sides of human misery, the *labouring* and the *burdened*, are invited. Doubtless, outward and bodily misery is not shut out; but the promise, **ἀνάπαυσις ταῖς ψυχαῖς**, is only a spiritual promise. Our Lord does not promise to those who come to Him *freedom from* toil or burden, but *rest in the soul*, which shall make all yokes easy, and all burdens light. The main invitation however is to those burdened with the yoke of sin, and of the law, which was added because of sin. All who feel that burden are invited. 29.] **μάθετε ἀπ' ἐμοῦ**, both '*from My example*,' which however is the lower sense of the words, and '*from My teaching*,' from which alone the ἀνάπαυσις can flow; the ἀποκάλυψις of vv. 25 and 27. **εὑρήσετε ἀνάπ. τ. ψ. ὑμ.** quoted from Jer. vi. 16 Heb. Thus we have it revealed here, that the rest and joy of the Christian soul is, *to become like Christ*; to attain by His teaching this πραότης and ταπεινότης of His. Olshausen makes an excellent distinction between ταπεινὸς τῇ καρδίᾳ, an attribute of divine Love in the Saviour, and ταπεινὸς or πτωχὸς τῷ πνεύματι, ch. v. 3: Prov. xxix. 23, which can only be said of sinful man, knowing his unworthiness and need of help. **καρδία** is *only here* used of Christ. (Stier on John xiv. 1.) 30.] **χρηστός**, easy, 'not exacting;' answering to 'kind,' spoken of persons, Luke vi. 35. See 1 John v. 3. Owing to the conflict with evil ever incident to our corrupt nature even under grace, the ἀνάπαυσις which Christ gives is yet to be viewed as a yoke and a burden, seen on this its painful side, of conflict and sorrow: but it is a *light yoke*; the inner rest in the soul giving a peace which passeth understanding, and bearing it up against all. See 2 Cor. iv. 16.

XII. 1—8.] The disciples pluck ears of corn on the Sabbath. Our Lord's answer to the Pharisees thereon. Mark ii. 23—28. Luke vi. 1—5. In Mark and Luke this incident occurs after the discourse on fasting related Matt. ix. 14 sq.; but in the former without any definite mark of time: St. Mark has ἐγένετο παραπορεύεσθαι αὐτὸν ἐν τοῖς σάββασιν κ.τ.λ.: St. Luke ἐγέν. δὲ ἐν σαββάτῳ [δευτεροπρώτῳ] κ.τ.λ., on which see note there. The expression **ἐν ἐκείνῳ τῷ καιρῷ** is, I conceive, a more definite mark of connexion than we find in the other Gospels, but cannot here be fixed to the meaning which it clearly has in ch. xi. 25, where the context deter-

2 οἱ δὲ Φαρισαῖοι ἰδόντες εἶπαν αὐτῷ Ἰδοὺ οἱ μαθηταί BCDEG
σου ποιοῦσιν ὃ οὐκ ἔξεστιν ποιεῖν ἐν σαββάτῳ. 3 ὁ KLMSU
δὲ εἶπεν αὐτοῖς Οὐκ [u] ἀνέγνωτε τί ἐποίησεν Δαυεὶδ ὅτε VΓΔΠℵ 1. 33
[q] ἐπείνασεν καὶ οἱ μετ' αὐτοῦ; 4 [v] πῶς εἰσῆλθεν εἰς τὸν
οἶκον τοῦ θεοῦ καὶ τοὺς [w] ἄρτους τῆς [wx] προθέσεως * ἔφαγεν, [y] ὃ οὐκ [z] ἐξὸν ἦν αὐτῷ φαγεῖν οὐδὲ τοῖς μετ' αὐτοῦ,
[a] εἰ μὴ τοῖς ἱερεῦσιν μόνοις; 5 ἢ οὐκ [ub] ἀνέγνωτε ἐν τῷ
[b] νόμῳ ὅτι τοῖς [c] σάββασιν οἱ ἱερεῖς ἐν τῷ ἱερῷ τὸ [d] σάββατον [de] βεβηλοῦσιν καὶ [f] ἀναίτιοί εἰσιν; 6 λέγω δὲ ὑμῖν
ὅτι τοῦ ἱεροῦ μεῖζόν ἐστιν ὧδε. 7 εἰ δὲ ἐγνώκειτε [g] τί

u ch. xix. 4. xxi. 16, 42 al. Isa. xxix. 12.
v 1 Kings xxi. 6.
w ||. Heb. ix. 2 only. Exod. xl. 21 (23) al. see Exod. xxv. 30. 3 Kings vii. 48. Neh. x. 33.
x = as above (w) only. (Acts xi. 23 al.)
y constr., Rev. xxi. 8. (see Col. ii. 17.) Soph. Œd. Tyr. 542, τυραννίδα . . . ὃ πλήθει . . . ἁλίσκεται.
z Acts ii. 29. 2 Cor. xii. 4 only. Esth. iv. 2 (only ?). see ver. 2.
a Rev. ix. 4. xxi. 27. see Gal. ii. 16.
b Neh. viii. 8. see ch. xxi. 42. Mark xii. 26.
c ver. 1 reff.
d Neh. xiii. 17. Ezek. xxii. 8.
e Acts xxiv. 6 only. Ezek. xxii. 20. (-λος, 1 Tim. i. 9.)
f here (bis) only. Deut. xxi. 8 al. (in LXX, always w. αἷμα.)
g ch. ix. 13. Hosea vi. 7.

2. aft ιδοντες ins αυτους CDLΔ 33 lat-*a b c ff*$_1$ *g*$_1$ *h k* Syr syr-cu. (ειπαν, so BCℵ 33.)

3. rec aft επεινασεν ins αυτος (*from* || *Mark Luke*), with L Scr's i w² (a d h l m n q r s, e sil) lat-*a b c f ff*$_1$ *g*$_1$ *h* syr-mg arm [Chr]: om BCDℵ rel vulg syrr syr-cu copt æth Eus$_1$.

4. προσθεσεως D: προσεως C. * ἔφαγον Bℵ Scr's o: εφαγεν CD rel vss Eus$_1$ [Chr]. rec (for ὃ) οὓς (|| *Mark Luke*), with Cℵ rel vulg lat-*a c* &c Orig$_1$ [Eus$_1$ Chr]: [*os* V:] txt BD 13. 124 harl¹ lat-*b k*. ην εξον D: εξην Orig$_1$: εξεστιν (|| *Mark Luke*) C 33: txt Bℵ rel Eus.

5. ins εν bef τοις σαββασιν CD ev-z Cyr.

6. for δε, γαρ D lat-*k* syr-cu. rec μειζων (*from misunderstanding, see note*), with CLΔ latt: txt BDℵ rel lat-*ff*$_1$ copt Chr [Cyr$_1$] Thl, *plus* Iren-int.

mines it. We can merely say that it seems to have occurred about the same time as the last thing mentioned—in the same journey or season. The plucking the ears was allowed Deut. xxiii. 25, but in the Talmud expressly forbidden on the Sabbath. (Lightfoot in loc.) It was also (Levit. xxiii. 14, apparently, but this is by no means certain: see note on Luke) forbidden until the sheaf of first-fruits had been presented to God, which was done on the second day of the feast of unleavened bread at the Passover. This incident, on that supposition, must have occurred between that day and the harvest. It is generally supposed to have been on the first Sabbath after the Passover. For a fuller discussion of the time and place, see note on Luke as before. **3.**] It appears from 1 Sam. xxi. 6, that hot bread had been put in on the day of David's arrival; which therefore, Levit. xxiv. 8, was a sabbath. The example was thus doubly appropriate. Bengel maintains, on the commonly received interpretation of σάβ. δευτερόπρωτον Luke vi. 1, that 1 Sam. xxi. was the lesson for the day. But the Jewish calendar of lessons cannot be shewn to have existed in the form which we now have, in the time of the Gospel history. **4.**] **εἰ μή**, in the construction, is not for ἀλλά, but belongs to **οὐκ ἐξὸν ἦν**, and retains its proper meaning of **except**. **5.**] The priests were ordered to offer double offerings on the Sabbath (Num. xxviii. 9, 10), and to place fresh (*hot*, and therefore baked that day) shewbread. In performing these commands they must commit many of what the Pharisees would call profanations of the Sabbath. So that, as Stier (ii. 4), not only does the sacred *history* furnish examples of exception to the law of the Sabbath from *necessity*, but the *Law itself ordains* work to be done on the Sabbath as a *duty*. **6.**] **μεῖζον** seems the better supported reading, and sustains the parallel better: **a greater thing than the temple is here.** See John ii. 19. The inference is, 'If the priests in the temple and for the temple's sake, for its service and ritual, profane the Sabbath, as ye account profanation, and are blameless, how much more these disciples who have grown hungry in their appointed following of Him who is greater than the temple, the *true Temple of God on earth*, the Son of Man!' I cannot agree with Stier that the *neuter* would represent only "something greater, more weighty than the temple,—namely, merciful consideration of the hungry, or the like:" it seems to

ἐστιν Ἔλεος [h] θέλω καὶ οὐ θυσίαν, οὐκ ἂν [i] κατεδικάσατε
τοὺς [f] ἀναιτίους. 8 κύριος γάρ ἐστιν τοῦ σαββάτου ὁ
[k] υἱὸς τοῦ [k] ἀνθρώπου.
9 Καὶ [l] μεταβὰς [l] ἐκεῖθεν ἦλθεν εἰς τὴν συναγωγὴν
αὐτῶν. 10 καὶ ἰδοὺ ἄνθρωπος χεῖρα ἔχων [m] ξηράν· καὶ
ἐπηρώτησαν αὐτὸν λέγοντες [n] Εἰ ἔξεστιν τοῖς [c] σάββασιν
[o] θεραπεύειν; ἵνα [p] κατηγορήσωσιν αὐτοῦ. 11 ὁ δὲ εἶπεν
αὐτοῖς Τίς [q] ἐξ ὑμῶν ἄνθρωπος ὃς ἕξει πρόβατον ἕν, καὶ

X και μεταβας ... BCDEG KLMSU VXΓΔΠ ℵ 1. 33

h constr., as above (g). ch. xxvii. 43. Heb. x. 5, 8. Ps. l. 16.
i ver. 37. Luke vi. 37 (bis). James v. 6 only. Ps. xxxvi. 33. xciii. 21.
k ch. viii. 20 reff.
l ch. xi. 1 reff.
m = ‖ L. John v. 3 (ch. xxiii. 15. Luke xxiii. 31. Heb. xi. 29) only ‡. (Isa. lvi. 3.)
n ch. xix. 3. Luke xiii. 23. Acts i. 6. 1 Kings xxiv. 2, 11.
o ch. iv. 23 al. fr.
p John v. 45 al.+ 1 Macc. vii. 6, 25 al.
q ch. xxvi. 73 al. 4 Kings x. 25.

7. rec ελεον, with L rel $Orig_1$ [Chr] : txt BCDℵ 1. 33 $Orig_1$.
8. rec ins και bef του σαββατου (*from* ‖ *Mark Luke*), with [1. 33 vulg (see below)] lat-*f* syr : txt BCDℵ rel Scr's mss lat-*a b c* $ff_{1.2}$ $g_{1.2}$ *h* Syr syr-cu copt æth arm Orig Chr Thl Euthym Tert Cypr.—[ο υι. τ. α. bef και τ. σαβ. 1. 33 vulg.]
9. aft εκειθεν ins ο ιησους CEG Scr's q lat-*c* g_1 *h* Syr arm.
10. rec ins ην την bef χειρα (*from* ‖ *Luke*), with X rel lat-*b c* g_2 : ην εκει την DLMΔ 1. 33 lat-*a f* ff_2 g_1 *h* syrr arm : ην εκει ανθρ. την E : ην ανθρ. εκει την U : txt BCℵ vulg lat-*k l* syr-cu copt æth Chr. θεραπευσαι DLℵ. κατηγορησουσιν DX.
11. rec aft τις(τι D) ins εσται, with BC^2ℵ rel vulg lat-*c* g_2 syr : εστι D 33. 157 Scr's h ev-y lat-*f* arm-mss [Chr Vict-ed] : om C^1LX lat-*b* $ff_{1.2}$ g_1 *h* Syr syr-cu copt æth [Vict-2-mss]. (*The variation points out the supplementary character of the insertion.*) for εξ υμων, εν υμειν D. εχει D Scr's c lat-*b c f* g_1.

me, as above, to bear a more general and sublime sense than the masculine; see ver. 41, &c. **7.**] The law of this new Temple-service is the law of charity and love:—mercy and not sacrifice, see ch. ix. 13:—all for man's sake and man's good;—and if their hearts had been ready to receive our Lord, and to take on them this service, they would not have condemned the guiltless. **8.**] On the important verse preceding this in Mark ii. 27, see note there. The sense of it must here be supplied to complete the inference. Since the Sabbath was an ordinance instituted for the use and benefit of man,—the Son of Man, who has taken upon Him full and complete Manhood, the great representative and Head of humanity, has this institution under his own power. See this teaching of the Lord illustrated and expanded in apostolic practice and injunctions, Rom. xiv. 4, 5, 17: Col. ii. 16, 17.

9—14.] HEALING OF THE WITHERED HAND. Mark iii. 1—6. Luke vi. 6—11.

9. μεταβὰς ἐκεῖθεν] This change of place is believed by Greswell to have been a journey back to Galilee after the Passover. (Diss. viii. vol. ii.) It is true that no such change is implied in Mark and Luke; but the words here point to a journey undertaken, as in ch. xi. 1; xv. 29, the only other places in this Gospel where the expression occurs. In John vii. 3, the cognate expression μετάβηθι ἐντεῦθεν is used of a journey from Galilee to Judæa. So that certainly it is not implied here (as Meyer, al., suppose) that the incident took place on the *same day* as the previous one. We know from Luke vi. that it was on another (the next?) sabbath. **αὐτῶν**, not, of the Pharisees; but of the Jews generally, of the people of the place. **10.**] This narrative is found in Mark and Luke with considerable variation in details from our text, those two Evangelists agreeing however with one another. In both these accounts, they (*the Scribes and Pharisees*, Luke) were watching our Lord to see whether He would heal on the Sabbath:—and He (*knowing their thoughts*, Luke) ordered the man to stand forth in the midst, and asked *them* the question here given. The question about the animal does not occur in either of them, but in Luke xiv. 5, on a similar occasion. The additional particulars given are very interesting. By Luke,—it was the *right* hand; by Mark,—*our Lord looked round on them* μετ' ὀργῆς, συνλυπούμενος ἐπὶ τῇ πωρώσει τῆς καρδίας αὐτῶν:—and the *Herodians were joined with the Pharisees* in their counsel against Him. See notes on Luke.

ξηράν = ἐξηραμμένην Mark, **of which the use had been lost and the vital powers withered.** **11.**] The construction of this verse is involved:

ἐὰν [rs] ἐμπέσῃ τοῦτο τοῖς [c] σάββασιν εἰς [rt] βόθυνον, οὐχὶ
[u] κρατήσει αὐτὸ καὶ [v] ἐγερεῖ; 12 πόσῳ οὖν [w] διαφέρει
ἄνθρωπος προβάτου; [x] ὥςτε ἔξεστιν τοῖς [c] σάββασιν
[y] καλῶς [y] ποιεῖν. 13 τότε λέγει τῷ ἀνθρώπῳ [z] Ἔκτεινόν
σου τὴν [z] χεῖρα· καὶ ἐξέτεινεν, καὶ [a] ἀπεκατεστάθη [b] ὑγιὴς
ὡς ἡ ἄλλη. 14 οἱ δὲ Φαρισαῖοι [cd] συμβούλιον [c] ἔλαβον
κατ' αὐτοῦ ἐξελθόντες, ὅπως αὐτὸν [e] ἀπολέσωσιν. 15 ὁ δὲ
Ἰησοῦς γνοὺς [f] ἀνεχώρησεν ἐκεῖθεν· καὶ ἠκολούθησαν αὐτῷ
[ὄχλοι] πολλοί, καὶ ἐθεράπευσεν αὐτοὺς πάντας, 16 καὶ
[g] ἐπετίμησεν αὐτοῖς ἵνα μὴ [hi] φανερὸν αὐτὸν [i] ποιήσωσιν.
17 ἵνα πληρωθῇ τὸ [j] ῥηθὲν [j] διὰ Ἡσαΐου τοῦ προφήτου
λέγοντος 18 [k] Ἰδοὺ ὁ παῖς μου ὃν [l] ᾑρέτισα, ὁ ἀγαπητός

BCDEG KLMSU VXΓΔΠ ℵ 1. 33

r Luke vi. 39. Isa. xxiv. 18.
s as above (r). Luke x. 36. 1 Tim. iii. 6, 7. vi. 9. Heb. x. 31 only.
t as above (r). ch. xv. 14 only. 2 Kings xviii. 17.
u ch. xviii. 28. xxi. 46 al. Judg. xvi. 26 B. Cant. iii. 4.
v = here only.
w = ch. x. 31 reff.
x = ch. xix. 6 ‖. xxiii. 31 al. fr.
y Luke vi. 27. Acts x. 33 al. Zech. viii. 15.
z ch. viii. 3 reff.
a ‖. ch. xvii. 11 ‖. Mark viii. 25. Acts i. 6. Heb. xiii. 19 only. Lev. xiii. 16. Job v. 18. constr., Phil. iii. 21. 1 Thess. iii. 13. Winer, § 66. 3 *g*.
b ch. xv. 31. Mark v. 34. John v. [4 v. r.] 6, &c. vii. 23. Acts iv. 10. Tit. ii. 8 only. Isa. xxxviii. 21.
c only in Matt., ch. xxii. 15. xxvii. 1, 7. xxviii. 12. = σ. διδόναι, Mark iii. 6. = σ. ποιεῖν, Mark xv. 1.
d as above (c). Acts xxv. 12 only †. Prov. xv. 22 Theod.
e ch. ii. 13 al. Gen. xx. 4.
f ch. ii. 14 reff. 1 Kings xix. 10.
g ch. xvi. 20, 22 al. Mt. Mk. L. only, exc. 2 Tim. iv. 2. Jude 9. Gen. xxxvii. 10.
h = Mark vi. 14 reff.
i ‖ Mk. only. 2 Macc. xii. 41 only.
j ch. i. 22 reff.
k Isa. xlii. 1.
l here only. Num. xiv. 8. 1 Chron. xxix. 1. 1 Macc. ix. 30.

om εαν D lat-*b*. for εμπεσῃ, πεσῃ Γℵ[1](txt ℵ[2]) Scr's f[1] ev-y. om τουτο D lat-*a c f ff*$_1$ *g*$_1$ *h* Syr syr-cu æth. for κρατησει, κρατει D: κρατησας (omg και) ℵ lat-*ff*$_1$ *h*. εγειρει (*error*) CDGL syrr syr-cu: εγ. bef αυτο ℵ vulg lat-*c ff*$_{1.2}$ *h*: om αυτο U.

12. ins του bef προβατου D[1]. σαββατοις B.

13. rec την χειρα bef σου (*see* ‖ *Luke*), with CD rel [Chr]: txt BLℵ[1] 1. 33 Scr's c evv-H-y.—ℵ[3] wrote σου in both places, but erased the second. rec αποκατεσταθη (*gramml emendation*), with DK: απεκατεστη U[Π]: αποκατεστη 1: txt BC[2]ℵ rel. (C[1] illegible.) om ως η αλλη (*so* ‖) ℵ.

14. εξελθοντες δε bef οι φαρισαιοι BCℵ 1. 33 vulg lat-*c* copt æth Eus Chr: οι δε φ. εξ. L 13. 124-57 arm [Chr-1-3-5-8-β]: και εξελθ. οι φ. D lat-*a b g*$_1$ Syr (syr-cu): om εξελθ. Δ 77. 123. 225-45 ev-y(and other evv): txt X rel syr. (*Assimilations to* ‖ *Mark*, BC *retaining the* δε, D *altering to* και, *verbatim as in* ‖. *The rec would be perfectly unaccountable on the hyp of* εξ. δε *being genuine.*)

15. om οχλοι Bℵ latt æth Eus$_1$[ins$_1$]: πολλοι bef οχλοι X 4. 262.

16. for και, δε ους εθεραπευσεν D 1 lat-*a b c ff*$_1$ *h k*. for επιτιμ., επεπληξεν D Eus$_1$: επεπλησσεν 1. αυτους U[1]Δ 1 ev-y.

17. rec (for ινα) οπως, with L rel [Chr]: txt BCDℵ 1. 33 Orig Eus$_2$.

18. ins εις bef 1st ον D.

there is a double question, as in ch. vii. 9. Our Lord evidently asks this as being a thing allowed and done at the time when He spoke: but subsequently (perhaps, suggests Stier, on account of these words of Christ), it was forbidden in the Gemara; and it was only permitted to *lay planks for the beast to come out.* **13.**] Our Lord does no outward act: the healing is performed without even a word of command. The stretching forth the hand was to prove its soundness, which the divine power wrought in the act of stretching it forth. Thus his enemies were disappointed, having no legal ground against Him. **14.**] This is the first mention of counsel being taken by the Pharisees (*and Herodians*, Mark, as above) to put our Lord to death.

15—21.] *Peculiar in this form to Matthew.* See Mark iii. 7—12. Luke vi. 17—19. **15.**] **αὐτοὺς πάντας**: see similar expressions, ch. xix. 2: Luke vi. 19;—i. e. '*all who wanted healing.*' **16. ἐπετίμησεν**] see ch. viii. 4, and note. **17.**] On **ἵνα πληρωθῇ**, see note on ch. i. 22. Neither it nor ὅπως πλ. must be understood '*and thus was fulfilled,*' as Webster and Wilkinson: both are used only of the purpose, not of the result, here or any where. It is strange that any should be found, at this period of the progress of exegesis, to go back to a view which is both superficial and ungrammatical. The prophecy is partly from the LXX, partly an original translation. The LXX have Ἰακὼβ ὁ παῖς μου . . . Ἰσραὴλ ὁ ἐκλεκτός μου . . . . , but the Rabbis generally un-

μου [m] ὃν [m] εὐδόκησεν ἡ ψυχή μου. θήσω τὸ πνεῦμά μου
ἐπ' αὐτόν, καὶ κρίσιν τοῖς ἔθνεσιν [n] ἀπαγγελεῖ. 19 οὐκ
[o] ἐρίσει οὐδὲ [p] κραυγάσει, οὐδὲ ἀκούσει τις ἐν ταῖς [q] πλατείαις τὴν φωνὴν αὐτοῦ. 20 [r] κάλαμον [s] συντετριμμένον οὐ
[t] κατεάξει, καὶ [u] λίνον [v] τυφόμενον οὐ [w] σβέσει, ἕως ἂν
[x] ἐκβάλῃ εἰς [y] νῖκος τὴν [z] κρίσιν. 21 καὶ τῷ ὀνόματι
αὐτοῦ ἔθνη [a] ἐλπιοῦσιν.

22 Τότε προσηνέχθη αὐτῷ [bc] δαιμονιζόμενος τυφλὸς καὶ
[cd] κωφός· καὶ ἐθεράπευσεν αὐτόν, ὥστε τὸν [d] κωφὸν λαλεῖν
καὶ βλέπειν. 23 καὶ [e] ἐξίσταντο πάντες οἱ ὄχλοι καὶ
ἔλεγον [f] Μήτι οὗτός ἐστιν ὁ [g] υἱὸς Δαυείδ; 24 οἱ δὲ
Φαρισαῖοι ἀκούσαντες εἶπον Οὗτος οὐκ [h] ἐκβάλλει τὰ

m constr., Heb x. 6, 8. Lev. xxvi. 34, 41. Ps. l. 16. lxxxiv. 1.
n Heb. ii. 12. 1 John i. 2, 3. Gen. xiv. 13.
o here only. 1 Kings xii. 14.
p ch. xv. 22. John xi. 43 al4. Acts xxii. 23 only. Ezra iii. 13.
q Luke xiv. 21 reff.
r ch. xi. 7 reff.
s Mark v. 4. xiv. 3. Luke ix. 39. John xix. 36. Rom. xvi. 20. Rev. ii. 27 only. Gen. xix. 9. Isa. lxi. 1.
t John xix. 31, 32, 33 only. Deut. xxxiii. 11. 2 Kings xxii. 35. Jer. xxxi. (xlviii.) 25. Hab. iii. 12 only.
u Rev. xv. 6 only. Isa. xliii. 17.
v here only †.
w ch. xxv. 8. Mark ix. 44, 46, 48. Eph. vi. 16. 1 Thess. v. 9. Heb. xi. 34 only. Job xl. 7 (12). Isa. lxvi. 24.
x = ver. 35. ch. xiii. 52. John x. 4. Acts xvi. 37.
y 1 Cor. xv. 54 (w. εἰς), 55, 57 only. 2 Kings ii. 26. Job xxxvi. 7.
z = John v. 27, 30 al. fr.
a w. dat., here only. τῇ τύχῃ ἐλπίσας, Thuc. iii. 97.
b ch. viii. 16 reff.
c ch. ix. 32.
d ch. xi. 5.
e Matt., here only. Mark ii. 12 al3. Luke, Gosp. ii. 47 al2. Acts ii. 7, 12 al6. Paul, 2 Cor. v. 13 only. Gen. xliii. 33. Exod. xxiii. 27. Jer. iv. 9.
f ch. vii. 16 reff.
g ch. i. 1. ix. 27. xx. 30 al.
h ch. ix. 34.

rec ins εις bef 2nd ον (*see 2 Pet* i. 17), with C²Lℵ² rel Eus_2: εν ω (*see ch* iii. 17) C¹(appy) D 1. 33 latt copt Iren-int (Dial from Isa) Eus_1 Hil: txt Bℵ¹ 115. 244 lat-ff_1 Eus_2. απαγγελλει D-gr Eus.

19. for ακουσει, ακουει D-gr.

20. om καλαμον συντετριμμενον D¹(ins D⁶). κατιαξεις D¹: -εαξεν D⁶. ληνον B². ins μη bef ζβεσει(sic) D¹.

21. rec ins εν bef τω ονοματι, with D latt arm Eus_1 Iren-int Hil: om BCℵ rel Scr's mss Bas Chr Thl. (om ver, 33.) ελπιζουσιν D¹-gr.

22. προσηνεγκαν αυτ. δαιμονιζομενον τυφλον και κωφον B syrr syr-cu copt æth. for αυτον, αυτους ℵ¹(txt ℵ^3a). rec aft ωστε τον ins τυφλον και (*from above*), with C rel arm: aft τον κωφον ins και τυφλον LXΔ 1 evv-H-y Syr syr(appy): om BDℵ lat-ff_1 g_1 *k* syr-cu copt [æth]. rec ins και bef λαλειν (*for precision*), with Cℵ^3a rel syr arm: om BDℵ¹ 1. 33 Scr's l m n evv-H-y-z-36 latt Syr copt æth.

23. aft μητι ins οτι D¹-gr.

derstood it of the Messiah. **18. κρίσιν τ. ἔθν. ἀπ.**] **He shall announce judgment to the Gentiles**, viz. in his office as Messiah and Judge. In these words the majesty of his future glory is contrasted with the meekness about to be spoken of: q. d. 'And yet He shall not,' &c. **20. κάλαμ. συντ. κ.τ.λ.**] A proverbial expression for, 'He will not crush the contrite heart, nor extinguish the slightest spark of repentant feeling in the sinner.' The form κατεάξω for the *future* seems to have crept in from the aor., as a convenient distinction from κατάξω from κατάγω. See Winer, § 12. 2. [Moulton, p. 82, note 6, cites κατεάξω from Ps. xlvii. 8 Symm.] In ref. Hab. the regular future κατάξω is used. **ἕως ἂν ἐκβ.**] Until He shall have brought out the conflict, the cause, the judgment, unto victory,—caused it, i. e., to *issue in victory: ἐκβάλῃ, exire jusserit*, see reff.:—i. e. such shall be his behaviour and such his gracious tenderness, during the day of grace: while the conflict is yet going on,—the judgment not yet decided.

22—45.] Accusation of casting out devils by Beelzebub, and our Lord's discourse thereon. Demand of a sign from Him: His further discourse. Mark iii. 20—30. Luke xi. 14—36, where also see notes. This account is given by Luke later in our Lord's ministry, but without any fixed situation or time, and with less copiousness of detail. See also ch. ix. 32, and notes there. St. Mark (iii. 23—29) gives part of the discourse which follows, but without any determinate sequence, and omitting the miracle which led to it. **23. Μήτι**] This form of question is properly a doubtful denial, involving in fact a surmise in the affirmative. 'Surely this is not . . . . ?' **ὁ υἱὸς Δ.**] see ch. ix. 27, and note. **24. οἱ δὲ Φ. ἀκούσ.**]

[h] δαιμόνια εἰ μὴ ἐν τῷ Βεελζεβοὺλ [h] ἄρχοντι τῶν [h] δαιμονίων. 25 εἰδὼς δὲ τὰς [i] ἐνθυμήσεις αὐτῶν εἶπεν αὐτοῖς
Πᾶσα βασιλεία [k] μερισθεῖσα καθ' ἑαυτῆς [l] ἐρημοῦται· καὶ
πᾶσα πόλις ἢ οἰκία [k] μερισθεῖσα καθ' ἑαυτῆς οὐ σταθήσεται. 26 καὶ εἰ ὁ [m] σατανᾶς τὸν [m] σατανᾶν ἐκβάλλει, ἐφ'
ἑαυτὸν [k] ἐμερίσθη· πῶς οὖν σταθήσεται ἡ βασιλεία αὐτοῦ;
27 καὶ εἰ ἐγὼ [n] ἐν Βεελζεβοὺλ ἐκβάλλω τὰ δαιμόνια, οἱ
υἱοὶ ὑμῶν [n] ἐν τίνι ἐκβάλλουσιν; διὰ τοῦτο αὐτοὶ κριταὶ

BCDEG KLMSU VXΓΔΠ ℵ 1. 33

i ch. ix. 4. Acts xvii. 29. Heb. iv. 12 only +. Job xxi. 27 Symm.
k = ‖ Mk. 1 Cor. i. 13 (Mark vi. 41 al.) only. 3 Kings xvi. 21.
l ‖ L. Rev. xvii. 16. xviii. 16, 19 only. Jer. xxxiii. (xxvi.) 9.
m ch. iv. 10, and passim. Sir. xxi. 27 only. (see 3 Kings xi. 14.)
n ‖ L. Mark xvi. 17 al.

25. for *ειδως*, *ιδων* D ℵ²(but corrd) 13. 33. 86 lat-*ff*₁ *h k* syr-cu copt. rec aft *ειδως δε* ins *ο ιησους*, with C rel latt syrr æth arm Hil: om BDℵ lat-*k* syr-cu copt. *εφ εαυτην in se* (twice) D [Chr-3-5-8-α-β]: *καθ εαυτην* (1st) LX 1 [Ath₁], (twice) 33 Scr's i ev-H. for *σταθησεται*, *στησεται* D¹(txt D³) 13. 124.
26. for *και ει*, *ει δε και* D.
27. for *και ει*, *ει δε* D 1. 33 evv-H-y. rec (for *κρ. εσ. υμ.*) *υμων εσονται κριται*,

St. Mark states (iii. 22) that this accusation was brought by the *γραμματεῖς οἱ ἀπὸ Ἱεροσολύμων καταβάντες*. Luke (xi. 15), by *τινὲς ἐξ αὐτῶν*, i. e. *τῶν ὄχλων*. On the charge itself, Trench remarks, 'A rigid monotheistic religion like the Jewish, left but one way of escape from the authority of miracles, which once were acknowledged to be indeed such, and not mere collusions and sleights of hand. There remained nothing to say but that which we find in the N. T. the adversaries of our Lord continually did say, namely, that these works were works of hell.'

25.] The Pharisees said this covertly to some among the multitude; see Luke, vv. 15, 17. "There is at first sight a difficulty in the argument which our Saviour draws from the oneness of the kingdom of Satan: viz. that it seems the very idea of this kingdom, that it should *be this anarchy;* blind rage and hate not only against God, but each part of it warring against every other part. And this is most deeply true, that hell is as much in arms against itself as against Heaven: neither does our Lord deny that *in respect of itself* that kingdom is infinite contradiction and division: only He asserts that in relation to the *kingdom of goodness* it is at one: there is one life in it and one soul in relation to that. Just as a nation or kingdom may embrace within itself infinite parties, divisions, discords, jealousies, and heart-burnings: yet, if it is to subsist as a nation at all, it must not, *as regards other nations*, have lost its sense of unity; when it does so, of necessity it falls to pieces and perishes." Trench, Miracles, p. 58. We may observe (1) that our Lord here in the most solemn manner re-asserts and confirms the truths respecting the kingdom of evil which the Jews also held. The *βασιλεῖαι* are so set parallel with one another, that the denial of the reality of the one with its *ἄρχων*, or the supposing it founded merely in assent on the part of our Lord to Jewish notions, inevitably brings with it the same conclusions with regard to the other. They are both *real*, and so is the conflict between them. (2) That our Lord here appeals not to *an insulated case* of casting out of devils, in which answer might have been made, that the craft of Satan might sometimes put on the garb and arts of an adversary to himself, for his own purposes,—but to the *general and uniform tenor of all such acts* on his part, in which He was found as the continual Adversary of the kingdom of Satan. (3) That our Lord proceeds to shew that the axiom is true of all human societies, even to a family, the smallest of such. (4) That He does *not* state the same of an individual man, '*Every man divided against himself falleth,*' rests upon deeper grounds, which will be entered on in the notes on vv. 30, 31.

27.] The interpretation of this verse has been much disputed; viz. as to whether the casting out by the *υἱοὶ Φαρισαίων* (**scholars,—disciples**; see 2 Kings ii. 3 and passim) were real or pretended exorcisms. The occurrence mentioned Luke ix. 49 does not seem to apply; for there John says, *ἐπιστάτα, εἴδομέν τινα ἐπὶ τῷ ὀνόματί σου ἐκβάλλοντα δ.*, which hardly could have been the case with those here referred to. Nor again can the *περιερχόμενοι Ἰουδαῖοι ἐξορκισταί* of Acts xix. 13 be the same as these, inasmuch as they also named over the possessed *the name of the Lord Jesus:* or at all events it

ἔσονται ὑμῶν. 28 εἰ δὲ ⁿ ἐν πνεύματι θεοῦ ἐγὼ ἐκβάλλω o ‖ L. Rom. ix. 31.
τὰ δαιμόνια, ἄρα ° ἔφθασεν ἐφ' ὑμᾶς ἡ βασιλεία τοῦ θεοῦ. 2 Cor. x. 14. Phil. iii. 16.
29 ἢ πῶς δύναταί τις εἰσελθεῖν εἰς τὴν οἰκίαν τοῦ ᵖ ἰσχυροῦ 1 Thess. ii. 16. iv. 15 only. Eccl. viii.
καὶ τὰ ᑫ σκεύη αὐτοῦ ἁρπάσαι, ἐὰν μὴ πρῶτον δήσῃ 14. p = ‖. Rev.
τὸν ᵖ ἰσχυρόν; καὶ τότε τὴν οἰκίαν αὐτοῦ ʳ διαρπάσει. xix. 18. Josh. x. 2.
30 ὁ μὴ ὢν ˢ μετ' ἐμοῦ κατ' ἐμοῦ ἐστιν, καὶ ὁ μὴ ᵗ συνάγων q = ‖. 2 Tim. ii. 20, 21. Heb. ix. 21. Rev. xviii.

12 bis. Gen. xxvii. 3. Deut. i. 41. 1 Kings xiii. 20, 21. r ‖ Mk. (bis) only. Esth. iii. 13.
s ‖ L. Rev. xvii. 14. xix. 20. Josh. iii. 7. viii. 5. t ch. iii. 12. xiii. 30, 47 al. Gen. xli. 35.

with C rel arm: κρ. υμ. εσ. 1 vulg lat-*c* g_2 [Chr Ambrst Op]: υμ. κρ. εσ. L: txt BDא am(with forj) lat-*a b f* $ff_{1.2}$ g_1 *h l* Cyr. (*Cf Luke* xi. 19.)

28. rec εγω bef εν πνευματι θεου (*from ver 27, not perceiving the emphasis*), with (Scr's a g l m n q r, e sil) vulg lat-*f* Syr-ms syr-cu spec [Chr]: om εγω M 238-43-53 lat-*b c* g_1 syr Did $Ambr_1$ Op_1: txt BCDא rel lat-*a* $ff_{1.2}$ *h* Syr copt Ath Thl Victorin Hil.

29. rec (for αρπασαι) **διαρπασαι** (‖ *Mark*), with C²Dא rel latt Eus [Chr] Iren-int Hil: txt BC¹X 1 Val-in-Thdot. for **διαρπασει, διαρπασαι** Δ: **διαρπαση** DGKΠ¹א 13. 33. 124 am(with forj) arm Chr Euthym: txt BC rel latt Eus Iren-int.

can be no such invocation which is *here* referred to. In Josephus (Antt. viii. 2. 5) we read that Solomon τρόπους ἐξορκώσεων κατέλειπεν, οἷς ἐνδόμενα τὰ δαιμόνια ὡς μηκέτ' ἐπανελθεῖν ἐκδιώκουσι. καὶ αὕτη μέχρι νῦν παρ' ἡμῖν ἡ θεραπεία πλεῖστον ἰσχύει. It is highly necessary to institute this enquiry as to the reality of their exorcisms: for it would leave an unworthy impression on the reader, and one very open to the cavils of unbelief, were we to sanction the idea that our Lord would have solemnly compared with his own miracles, and drawn inferences from, a system of imposture, which on that supposition, these Pharisees *must have known* to be such. I infer then that the *υἱοὶ Φαρ. did really* cast out devils; and I think this view is confirmed by what the multitudes said in ch. ix. 33, where upon the dumb speaking after the devil was cast out they exclaimed οὐδέποτε ἐφάνη οὕτως ἐν τῷ Ἰσραήλ: meaning that this was a more complete healing than they had ever seen before. The difficulty has arisen mainly from forgetting that miracles, *as such*, are *no test of truth*, but have been permitted to, and prophesied of, false religions and teachers. See Exod. vii. 22; viii. 7: ch. xxiv. 24, &c.: Deut. xiii. 1—5. There is an important passage in Justin Martyr, Dial. with Trypho, § 85, p. 182, as follows:—κατὰ γὰρ τοῦ ὀνόματος αὐτοῦ τούτου τοῦ υἱοῦ τοῦ θεοῦ . . . πᾶν δαιμόνιον ἐξορκιζόμενον νικᾶται καὶ ὑποτάσσεται. ἐὰν δὲ κατὰ παντὸς ὀνόματος τῶν παρ' ὑμῖν γεγενημένων ἢ βασιλέων, ἢ δικαίων, ἢ προφητῶν, ἢ πατριαρχῶν ἐξορκίζητε ὑμεῖς, οὐχ ὑποταγήσεται οὐδὲν τῶν δαιμονίων. ἀλλ' εἰ ἄρα ἐξορκίζοι τις ὑμῶν κατὰ τοῦ θεοῦ Ἀβραὰμ καὶ θεοῦ Ἰσαὰκ καὶ θεοῦ Ἰακώβ, ἴσως ὑποταγήσεται. Irenæus (cited by Grotius) says that "hujus invocatione etiam ante adventum Domini nostri salvabantur homines a spiritibus nequissimis, et a dæmoniis universis," and adds, "Judæi usque nunc hac ipsa invocatione dæmonas fugant." Jer., Chrys., Hil., understand **υἱοὶ ὑμῶν** to mean the Apostles: ὅρα κἀνταῦθα τὴν ἐπιείκειαν· οὐ γὰρ εἶπεν Οἱ μαθηταί μου, οὐδὲ Οἱ ἀπόστολοι, ἀλλ' Οἱ υἱοὶ ὑμῶν . . . ὃ δὲ λέγει τοιοῦτόν ἐστιν· Οἱ ἀπόστολοι ἐν τίνι ἐκβάλλουσι; . . . . θέλων δεῖξαι ὅτι φθόνου ἦν τοῦ πρὸς αὐτὸν τὰ εἰρημένα μόνον . . . . Εἰ γὰρ ἐγὼ οὕτως ἐκβάλλω, πολλῷ μᾶλλον ἐκεῖνοι οἱ παρ' ἐμοῦ τὴν ἐξουσίαν λαβόντες. ἀλλ' ὅμως οὐδὲν τοιοῦτον εἰρήκατε αὐτοῖς. Chrys. Hom. xli. 2, p. 446. **κριταὶ ὑμῶν**] **your judges**, in the sense of *convicting you of partiality*. **28.**] **ἐν πνεύματι θ.** = **ἐν δακτύλῳ θ.**, Luke; see Exod. viii. 19. **ἔφθασεν**] emphatic in position: but merely, **has come upon you**: not in the more proper sense of φθάνω, 'is *already* upon you,' i. e. 'before you looked for it,'—as Stier and Wesley. It does not seem to occur in this latter sense in the N. T. But Fritzsche's dictum, ad Rom. ii. 356, "Alexandrinis scriptoribus φθάνειν nihil nisi *venire, pervenire, pertinere* valet," certainly is not right; for we have it indisputably in the sense of to *anticipate, prevent*, 1 Thess. iv. 15. **29.**] Luke has the word ἰσχυρότερος applied to the spoiler in this verse; a title given to our Lord by the Baptist, ch. iii. 11 ‖, and also in prophecy, Isa. xl. 10 (μετὰ ἰσχύος, LXX). See also Isa. liii. 12 (LXX); xlix. 24, 25. See note on Luke xi. 21 f., which is the fuller report of this parabolic saying. **30.**] These words have been variously understood.

u ‖ L. John x. 12. xvi. 32. 2 Cor. ix. 9 only. 2 Kings xxii. 15.
v ch. ix. 2 al. Isa. xxii. 14.
w = ch. vi. 12 reff.
x ch. xv. 19. xxvi. 65 al. Ezek. xxxv. 12. w. gen. obj., here only.

BCDEG KLMSU VXΓΔΠ ℵ 1. 33

μετ' ἐμοῦ [u] σκορπίζει. 31 διὰ τοῦτο λέγω ὑμῖν Πᾶσα
[v] ἁμαρτία καὶ βλασφημία [vw] ἀφεθήσεται [ὑμῖν] τοῖς ἀνθρώποις, ἡ δὲ τοῦ πνεύματος [x] βλασφημία οὐκ [w] ἀφεθήσεται
[τοῖς ἀνθρώποις]. 32 καὶ ὃς ἐὰν εἴπῃ λόγον κατὰ τοῦ
υἱοῦ τοῦ ἀνθρώπου, [w] ἀφεθήσεται αὐτῷ· ὃς δ' ἂν εἴπῃ κατὰ
τοῦ πνεύματος τοῦ ἁγίου, οὐκ [w] ἀφεθήσεται αὐτῷ οὔτε ἐν

30. at end add *με* ℵ 33 copt.

31. rec om 2nd *υμιν*, with CDℵ rel Orig Hil: ins B 1 Ath. om 2nd *τοις ανθρωποις* Bℵ 1. 22. 59. 142. 209 vulg lat-g_2 *k* copt æth arm Cyr-jer [Ath_1 Bas-ms_1] Hil Op.

32. rec (for *εαν*) *αν*, with D Scr's i (S 1. 33 h o s, e sil): txt BCℵ rel Orig. ins *ουκ* bef 1st *αφεθησ*. B[1](erased by same hand: *probably a mistake owing to ου of ανθρωπου*). om *του* (bef *αγιου*) D. for *ουκ αφεθησεται*, *ου μη αφεθη* B: *ου μη*

Chrysostom and Euthymius understand them to refer to the devil: Bengel, Schleiermacher, and Neander, to the Jewish exorcists named above. Grotius and others understand it as merely a general proverb, and the *ἐμοῦ* to mean '*any one*,' and here to apply to Satan, the sense being, '*If I do not promote Satan's kingdom, which I have proved that I do not, then I must be his adversary*.' But this is on all accounts improbable: see below on *συνάγων* and *σκορπίζει*. I believe Stier is right in regarding it as a saying setting forth to us generally the entire and complete disjunction of the two kingdoms, of Satan and God. There is and can be in the world *no middle party*: they who are not with Christ, who do not gather with Him,—are against Him and his work, and as far as in them lies are undoing it. See Rom. viii. 7. And thus the saying connects itself with the following verse:—this being the case, **διὰ τοῦτο** *λέγω ὑμῖν*,—the sin of an open belying of the present power of the Holy Spirit of God working in and for His Kingdom, assumes a character surpassingly awful. This saying is no way inconsistent with that in Mark ix. 40: Luke ix. 50. That is not a conversion of this, for the terms of the respective propositions are not the same. See note on Mark ix. 40. As usual, this saying of our Lord reached further than the mere occasion to which it referred, and spoke forcibly to those many half-persuaded hesitating persons who flattered themselves that they could strike out a line avoiding equally the persecution of men and the rejection of Christ. He informed them (and informs us also) of the impossibility of such an endeavour. In the **συνάγων** there is an allusion to the idea of gathering the harvest: see ch. xiii. 30: John xi. 52, and for **σκορπίζει**, John x. 12, in all which places the words exactly bear out their sense here. 31, 32.] **διὰ τοῦτο, because this is the case**: see last note. Notice again the **λέγω ὑμῖν**, used by our Lord when He makes some revelation of things hidden from the sons of men: see ch. vi. 29; xviii. 10, 19: and ver. 36 below. The distinction in these much-controverted verses seems to be, between (1) the sin and blasphemy which arises from culpable ignorance and sensual blindness, as that of the fool who said in his heart 'There is no God,'—of those who, e. g. Saul of Tarsus, opposed Jesus as not being the Christ; which persons, to whatever degree their sin may unhappily advance, are capable of enlightenment, repentance, and pardon:—and (2) the blasphemy of those who, acknowledging God, and seeing his present power working by His Holy Spirit, *openly oppose* themselves to it, as did, or as were very near doing (for our Lord does not actually imply that they *had* incurred this dreadful charge), these Pharisees. They may as yet have been under the veil of ignorance; but this their last proceeding, in the sight of Him who knows the hearts, approximated very near to, or perhaps reached, this awful degree of guilt. The principal misunderstanding of this passage has arisen from the prejudice which possesses men's minds owing to the use of the words, 'the *sin* against the Holy Ghost.' It is not a particular species of sin which is here condemned, but a definite act shewing a *state* of sin, and that state a wilful determined opposition to the present power of the Holy Spirit; and this as shewn by its fruit, *βλασφημία*. The declaration, in substance, often occurs in the N. T. See 1 John v. 16, and note on *ἁμαρτία* there: 2 Tim. iii. 8: Jude 4, 12, 13: Heb. x. 26—31; vi. 4—8. Euthymius expands the sense well and clearly: *ὃς μὲν ἂν ἁμάρτῃ κατὰ τῆς ἀνθρωπότητός μου, φησί, τουτέστιν, ὅστις ἂν εἴπῃ βλάσφημον λόγον κατ' αὐτῆς, ... ὁ*

[yz]τούτῳ τῷ [yz]αἰῶνι οὔτε ἐν τῷ [za]μέλλοντι. 33 ἢ [b]ποι-
ήσατε τὸ δένδρον [c]καλὸν καὶ τὸν [c]καρπὸν αὐτοῦ [c]καλόν,
ἢ ποιήσατε τὸ δένδρον [c]σαπρὸν καὶ τὸν [c]καρπὸν αὐτοῦ
[c]σαπρόν· [d]ἐκ γὰρ τοῦ καρποῦ τὸ δένδρον [d]γινώσκεται.
34 [e]γεννήματα [e]ἐχιδνῶν, πῶς δύνασθε ἀγαθὰ λαλεῖν
πονηροὶ ὄντες; [f]ἐκ γὰρ τοῦ [g]περισσεύματος τῆς καρδίας
τὸ στόμα [f]λαλεῖ. 35 ὁ ἀγαθὸς ἄνθρωπος ἐκ τοῦ ἀγαθοῦ

y Eph. i. 21.
z Luke xvi. 8 al. fr.
a = ch. iii. 7 reff.
b = ch. iii. 3. v. 36 al.
c ch. vii. 17, 18 (reff.).
d Luke vi. 44. 1 John iii. 24. iv. 6. see John i. 49.
e ch. iii. 7 (reff.).
f John iii. 31. viii. 44. xii. 49.
g || L. Mark viii. 8. 2 Cor. viii. 14 bis only. Eccl. ii. 15 (only ?).

αφεθησεται ℵ^1(txt ℵ^2(?)^3). for τουτω τω νυν (see 1 *Tim* vi. 17 : 2 *Tim* iv. 10 : *Tit* ii. 12) L rel Ath Bas Epiph Cyr Phot Thl : τω αι. τουτω ΚΧΔΠ Orig$_2$ Cyr-jer Did [Chr] : txt BCDℵ 1. 13. 33 Orig$_1$.

33. for 2nd καλον, αγαθον ℵ^1(corrd eadem manu).

34. τα of γεννηματα is added over the line by ℵ^1 [appy]. aft λαλει ins αγαθα D^1(and lat : om D^4-gr).

35. om 1st ο D^1(ins D^4) [Orig$_1$ (freely)].

τοιοῦτος συγγνωσθήσεται πάντως ὡς οὐκ ἐθελοκακήσας, ἀλλ' ἐν ἀγνοίᾳ τῆς ἀληθείας βλασφημήσας· ὁ δὲ βλέπων τὰς θεοπρεπεῖς μου ἐνεργείας, ἃς μόνος δύναται ποιεῖν ὁ θεός, καὶ τῷ Βεελζεβοὺλ ταύτας ἐπιγραφόμενος, ὡς καὶ ὑμεῖς νῦν, καὶ οὕτω βλασφημῶν κατὰ τοῦ πνεύματος τοῦ ἁγίου, ἤτοι κατὰ τῆς θεότητος (ταύτην γὰρ νῦν καλεῖ **πνεῦμα ἅγιον** (?)) οὗτος ὡς ἐθελοκακήσας προδήλως καὶ ἐν γνώσει καθυβρίσας τὸν θεὸν καὶ ἀναπολόγητα πλημμελήσας οὐ συγχωρηθήσεται.

No *sure* inference can be drawn from the words **οὔτε ἐν τῷ μέλλοντι**—with regard to forgiveness of sins in a future state. Olshausen remarks that a parallel on the other side is found in ch. x. 41, 42, where the *recognition* of divine power in those sent from God is accompanied with promise of eternal reward. He himself however understands the passage (as many others have done) to imply forgiveness on repentance *in the imperfect state of the dead* before the judgment, and considers it to be cognate with 1 Pet. iii. 18 ff. Augustine speaks very strongly, de Civ. Dei xxi. 24, vol. vii. : 'Neque enim de quibusdam veraciter diceretur, quod non eis remittatur neque in hoc sæculo neque in futuro, nisi essent quibus, etsi non in isto, tamen remittatur in futuro.' See, on the whole subject, note on 1 Pet. iii. 18 ff. In the almost entire silence of Scripture on any such doctrine, every principle of sound interpretation requires that we should hesitate to support it by two difficult passages, in neither of which does the plain construction of the words absolutely require it. The expressions αἰὼν οὗτος (= ὁ νῦν αἰών, Tit. ii. 12 : 2 Tim. iv. 10; καιρὸς οὗτος, Mark x. 30; αἰὼν τοῦ κόσμου τούτου, Eph. ii. 2; αἰὼν ἐνεστὼς πονηρός, Gal. i. 4) and αἰὼν μέλλων (= αἰὼν ὁ ἐρχόμενος, Mark x. 30; αἰὼν ἐκεῖνος, Luke xx. 35; αἰῶνες ἐπερχόμενοι, Eph. ii. 7) were common among the Jews, and generally signified respectively the time before and after the coming of the Messiah. In the N. T. these significations give place to—*the present life*, and *that to come :* the present mixed state of wheat and tares, and the future completion of Messiah's Kingdom after the great harvest. The expression κόσμος μέλλων is not found. αἰὼν μέλλων, &c., seem to differ from βασιλ. τ. οὐρανῶν or τ. θεοῦ, in never being spoken of, or as in, individuals, but as an age of time belonging to the universal Church.

33, 34.] **ποιήσατε**, not, as generally understood, = 'ponite,'—'*represent . . . . . as :*' for then the clause **ἐκ γὰρ κ.τ.λ.** loses its meaning : — but literally, **make.** The verse is a parable, not merely a similitude. 'There are but two ways open : either *make* the *tree and its fruit* both *good*, or both *bad : for* by the fruit the tree is known.' How *make*, the parable does not say : but let us remember, the Creator speaks, and sets forth a law of his own creation, with which our judgments must be in accord. This verse resumes again the leading argument, and sets forth the inconsistency of the Pharisees in representing Him as in league with evil, whose works were uniformly good. But the words have a double reference: to our Lord Himself, who could not be evil, seeing that His works were good; and (which leads on to the next verse) to the Pharisees, who could not speak good things, because their works were evil.

35—37.] The treasure spoken of is that inner storehouse of good and evil only

h ch. ii. 11 reff. Isa. xxxiii. 6.
i = ver. 20. ch. xiii. 52. Luke x. 35 al.
k ch. xx. 3, 6 reff.
l Luke xvi. 2. Acts xix. 40. 1 Pet. iv. 5. Dan. vi. 2 Theod.
m ch. x. 15 reff.
n Rom. ii. 13. iii. 20. Gal. ii. 16 al. Ps. l. 4. cxlii. 2.
o ver. 7 reff. Job xxxiv. 29.
p see ch. xi. 25 reff.
q = ch. xvi. 1, 4. John iv. 48. vi. 30 al. Isa. vii. 11, 14. Jer. x. 2.
r ch. xvi. 4 ‖ Mk. Rom. vii. 3 bis. James iv. 4. 2 Pet. ii. 14 only. Prov. xxx. (see xxiv.) 20. Ezek. xvi. 38. xxiii. 45 bis. Hos. iii. 1. Mal. iii. 5 only.
s ch. vi. 32 reff.

BCDEG KLMSU VXΓΔΠ ℵ 1. 33

[h] θησαυροῦ [i] ἐκβάλλει τὰ ἀγαθά, καὶ ὁ πονηρὸς ἄνθρωπος ἐκ τοῦ πονηροῦ θησαυροῦ [i] ἐκβάλλει πονηρά.
36 λέγω
δὲ ὑμῖν ὅτι πᾶν ῥῆμα [k] ἀργὸν ὃ λαλήσουσιν οἱ ἄνθρωποι,
[l] ἀποδώσουσιν περὶ αὐτοῦ [l] λόγον ἐν [m] ἡμέρᾳ κρίσεως.
37 ἐκ γὰρ τῶν λόγων σου [n] δικαιωθήσῃ, καὶ ἐκ τῶν λόγων
σου [o] καταδικασθήσῃ.
38 Τότε [p] ἀπεκρίθησαν αὐτῷ τινες
τῶν γραμματέων καὶ Φαρισαίων λέγοντες Διδάσκαλε
θέλομεν ἀπὸ σοῦ [q] σημεῖον ἰδεῖν.
39 ὁ δὲ ἀποκριθεὶς
εἶπεν αὐτοῖς Γενεὰ πονηρὰ καὶ [r] μοιχαλὶς [q] σημεῖον [s] ἐπιζητεῖ, καὶ [q] σημεῖον οὐ δοθήσεται αὐτῇ εἰ μὴ τὸ [q] σημεῖον

rec aft 1st *θησαυρου* ins *της καρδιας* (*gloss*), with lat-f_1 ff_2 Clem Orig$_1$, *της καρδιας αυτου* L 1. 33 ev-w² gat(with mm) syr-cu æth arm Clem Ath Bas Chr-8-α-E Orig-int$_1$ Gaud Fulg: om BCDℵ rel Scr's mss latt syrr copt Orig Dial Naz Nyss [Did] Chr(most mss) Thl Cypr Lucif Hil Ambrst. om *τα* (bef *αγαθα*) BD rel Did Chr-β Thl: ins CLUΔℵ 33 Scr's i (1 Scr's c d f k s, e sil) Orig [Chr]. aft 2nd *θησαυρου* ins *της καρδιας αυτου* L 33. 115-57 syr-cu arm Chr-1-3-8-α-β-A-E Tich Fulg. ins *τα* bef *πονηρα* LUΔ 13. 33. 157. 209 Scr's c d k s Chr-1-3-8-α-β.

36. rec aft *ο* ins *εαν*, with C rel; *αν* L Orig: om BDℵ, *quod* latt Iren-int Cypr. rec *λαλησωσιν*, with LXΔ rel latt Orig Iren-int Cypr: *λαλουσιν* D: txt BCℵ. *απο* (of *αποδωσ.*) was marked for erasure by ℵ², but the marks have been removed.

37. for *και*, *η* D-gr lat-*a c* g_1 Hil Paulin. om 2nd *σου* ℵ.

38. rec om *αυτω* (*possibly because an ecclesiastical lection began at απεκρ.*), with X rel: ins BCDLMℵ 13. 33 latt syr-cu syr copt æth arm Chr. om *και φαρισαιων* (*homœotel?*) B 59. 235 [Chr-comm]: *φ. κ. γρ.* K [Chr-txt-ms].

39. for *αυτη*, *σοι* D¹-gr(txt D¹).

seen by God and (partially) by ourselves. And on that account—because words, so lightly thought of by the world and the careless, spring from the inner fountains of good and ill, therefore they will form subjects of the judgment of the great day, when the whole life shall be unfolded and pronounced upon. See James iii. 2—12.

36.] **ῥῆμα ἀργόν** is nom. pendens, as ch. x. 14, 32. αἱρετώτερόν σοι ἔστω λίθον εἰκῇ βάλλειν, ἢ λόγον ἀργόν, Pythag. in Stobæus, xxxiv. 11. Wetst. **ἀργός** = ἀεργός, and is perhaps best taken here in its milder and negative sense, as not yet determined on till the judgment: so that our Lord's saying is a deduction "a minori," and if of every ῥῆμα ἀργόν, then how much more of every ῥῆμα πονηρόν!

37.] The **λόγος** being the περίσσευμα τῆς καρδίας, is a specimen of what is within; is the outward utterance of the *man*, and on this ground will form a subject of strict enquiry in the great day, being a considerable and weighty part of our works.

38.] St. Luke (xi. 15, 16) places the accusation of casting out devils by Beelzebub and this request together, and then the discourse follows. It seems that the first part of the discourse gave rise, as here related, to the request for a sign (from Heaven); but, as we might naturally expect, and as we learn from St. Luke, on the part of *different persons from those who made the accusation*. In consequence of our Lord declaring that his miracles were wrought by the Holy Ghost, they wish to see some decisive proof of this by a sign, not from Himself, but *from Heaven*. The account in ch. xvi. 1—4 manifestly relates to a different occurrence: see notes there. Cf. John vi. 30, 31; xii. 28.

39.] **μοιχαλίς** (see reff.), because they had been the peculiar people of the Lord, and so in departing from Him had broken the covenant of *marriage*, according to the similitude so common in the Prophets. The expression **σημεῖον οὐ δοθ. αὐτῇ** does not, as De Wette maintains, exclude our Lord's miracles from being σημεῖα: but is the direct answer to their request in the sense in which we know they used σημεῖον, 'a sign, not *wrought by Him, and so able to be suspected of magic art*, but one *from Heaven*.' Besides, even if this were not so, how can the refusing to work a miracle *to satisfy them*, affect the nature or signification of those wrought on

Ἰωνᾶ τοῦ προφήτου.
40 [t] ὥςπερ γὰρ ἦν Ἰωνᾶς ἐν τῇ [u] κοιλίᾳ τοῦ [v] κήτους τρεῖς ἡμέρας καὶ τρεῖς νύκτας, οὕτως ἔσται ὁ υἱὸς τοῦ ἀνθρώπου ἐν τῇ [w] καρδίᾳ τῆς γῆς τρεῖς ἡμέρας καὶ τρεῖς νύκτας.
41 ἄνδρες [x] Νινευεῖται [y] ἀναστήσονται [y] ἐν τῇ [y] κρίσει μετὰ τῆς γενεᾶς ταύτης καὶ [z] κατακρινοῦσιν αὐτήν, ὅτι [a] μετενόησαν [b] εἰς τὸ [c] κήρυγμα Ἰωνᾶ, καὶ ἰδοὺ πλεῖον Ἰωνᾶ ὧδε.
42 [d] βασίλισσα [e] νότου [f] ἐγερθήσεται ἐν τῇ κρίσει μετὰ τῆς γενεᾶς ταύτης καὶ [z] κατακρινεῖ αὐτήν, ὅτι ἦλθεν ἐκ τῶν [g] περάτων τῆς γῆς ἀκοῦσαι τὴν σοφίαν Σολομῶνος, καὶ ἰδοὺ πλεῖον Σολο-

t ch. xiii. 40. xxiv. 37, 38 al. Eccl. v. 15.
u ch. xv. 17 al. Jonah ii. 1.
v here only. Jon. l. c. Gen. i. 21.
w = here only. John ii. 4.
x Jonah iii. 5.
y ‖ L. Ps. i. 5.
z = ‖ L. Heb. xi. 7. Wisd. iv. 16.
a ch. iii. 2 reff.
b 2 Tim. ii. 26.
c ‖ L. Rom. xvi. 25. 1 Cor. i. 21. ii. 4. xv. 14. 2 Tim. iv. 17. Tit. i. 3 only. 2 Chron. xxx. 5. Prov. ix. 3. Jon. iii. 2. Esdr. ix. 3 only.
d ‖ L. Acts viii. 27. Rev. xviii. 7 only. 2 Chron. ix. 1.
e = ‖ L. Luke (xii. 55 reff.) xiii. 29. Rev. xxi. 13 only. Zech. vi. 6.
f 1 Cor. xv. 42, 43. Isa. xxvi. 19.
g ‖ L. Rom. x. 18 (Heb. vi. 16) only. Ps. xcvii. 3.

40. ωσπερι D   om ην D-gr Scr's c.   aft εσται ins και DEFL lat-*a b ff*$_1$ *g*$_1$ *h* syr-cu copt arm Ign Eus$_2$ Chr Cyr Thl Iren-int Orig-int Ambr.
42. ins του bef 1st σολομ. D(so Scr: D[1] Treg).

different occasions, and with a totally different view? And yet on ground like this it is (De Wette, vol. i. p. 147) that rationalistic systems are built. τί οὖν; οὐκ ἐποίησεν ἔκτοτε σημεῖον; ἐποίησεν, ἀλλ' οὐ δι' αὐτούς, πεπωρωμένοι γὰρ ἦσαν, ἀλλὰ διὰ τὴν τῶν ἄλλων ὠφέλειαν. Euthym. in loc. Notice **ἐπιζητεῖ**; not merely quærit, but requirit; misses, and demands as a sine quâ non. See Palm and Rost's Lex. sub voce. The *sign of Jonas* is the most remarkable foreshadowing in the O. T. of the resurrection of our Lord. It was of course impossible that His resurrection should be represented by an actual resurrection, as his birth was by births (Isaac, Samson, Samuel, Mahershalalhashbaz), and His death by deaths (Abel; the substitute for Isaac; Zechariah the prophet; the daily and occasional sacrifices); so that we find the events symbolic of his resurrection (Joseph's history; Isaac's sacrifice; Daniel's and Jonah's deliverance), representing it in a figure (Heb. xi. 19, ἐν παραβολῇ). In the case before us the figure was very remarkable, and easily to be recognized in the O. T. narrative. For Jonah himself calls the belly of the sea monster בֶּטֶן שְׁאוֹל (Jonah ii. 2), 'the belly of Hades,' = καρδίᾳ τῆς γῆς here. And observe, that the type is not of our Lord's *body being deposited in the tomb* of Joseph of Arimathea, for neither could that be called 'the heart of the earth,' nor could it be said that 'the Son of Man' was there during the time; but of our Lord's *personal descent into the place of departed souls*:—see Eph. iv. 9: 1 Pet. iii. 19, and note on Luke xxiii. 43. **40.**] If it be necessary to make good the three days and nights during which our Lord was in the heart of the earth, it must be done by having recourse to the Jewish method of computing time. In the Jerusalem Talmud (cited by Lightfoot) it is said "that a day and night together make up a עוֹנָה (a νυχθήμερον), and that any part of such a period is counted as the whole." See Gen. xl. 13, 20: 1 Sam. xxx. 12, 13: 2 Chron. x. 5, 12: Hosea vi. 2. **41.**] In this verse there is no reference to the *sign* of Jonas *spoken of above*, but to a different matter, another way in which he should be a sign to this generation. See Luke xi. 29 f., and note. (But the preaching of Jonas to the Ninevites was a sign after *his* resurrection: so shall the preaching of the Son of Man by His Spirit in His Apostles be after His resurrection. Stier.)

41, 42. πλεῖον Ἰωνᾶ ὧδε . . . πλεῖον Σολ. ὧδε] On the neuter, see above, ver. 6, note. **There is more than Jonas here.** No matter so worthy of arousing repentance had ever been revealed or preached as the Gospel: no matter so worthy of exciting the earnest attention of all. And the Lord *Himself*, the Announcer of this Gospel, is greater than all the sons of men: his *preaching*, greater than that of Jonah: his *wisdom*, than that of Solomon.

42. βασίλισσα νότου] Josephus, Antt. viii. 6. 5, calls her τὴν τῆς Αἰγύπτου καὶ τῆς Αἰθιοπίας τότε βασιλεύουσαν γυναῖκα, i. e. of Meroe (whose queens were usually called Candace. Plin. Hist. vi. 29). Abyssinian tradition agrees with this account, calls her Maqueda, and supposes her to have embraced the Jewish religion in Jerusalem. The Arabians on the other hand

h ch. x. 1 reff. i ‖ L. 2 Pet. ii. 17. Jude 12 only. Ps. lxii. 1. Jer. ii. 6. k Ruth iii. 1 B Sir. xxiv. 7. l ch. xi. 29 reff. m ch. xxiv. 18 ‖. Gen. xliv. 13 al. n (‖ L. v. r.) 1 Cor. vii. 5 only. Exod. v. 8, 17 bis. Ps. xlv. 10 only. τόπον σχολάζοντα, Plutarch. C. Gracchus, c. 12. o ‖. Luke xv. 8 only †. ‖ L. only

μῶνος ὧδε. 43 Ὅταν δὲ τὸ [h] ἀκάθαρτον [h] πνεῦμα ἐξέλθῃ
ἀπὸ τοῦ ἀνθρώπου, διέρχεται δι᾽ [i] ἀνύδρων τόπων [k] ζητοῦν
[kl] ἀνάπαυσιν, καὶ οὐχ [l] εὑρίσκει. 44 τότε λέγει Εἰς τὸν
οἶκόν μου [m] ἐπιστρέψω ὅθεν ἐξῆλθον· καὶ ἐλθὸν εὑρίσκει
[n] σχολάζοντα, [o] σεσαρωμένον καὶ [p] κεκοσμημένον. 45 τότε
πορεύεται καὶ [q] παραλαμβάνει μεθ᾽ ἑαυτοῦ ἑπτὰ ἕτερα
πνεύματα [r] πονηρότερα ἑαυτοῦ, καὶ εἰςελθόντα κατοικεῖ
ἐκεῖ, καὶ γίνεται [s] τὰ ἔσχατα τοῦ ἀνθρώπου ἐκείνου [t] χείρονα τῶν πρώτων. οὕτως ἔσται καὶ τῇ γενεᾷ ταύτῃ τῇ
πονηρᾷ.

Z οταν δε... F εξηλθον... BCDEF GKLMS UVXZ ΓΔΠℵ 1. 33

p ch. xxiii. 29 al. Ezek. xxiii. 41. q ch. xvii. 1 reff. r compar., s 2 Pet. ii. 20. Rev. ii. 19. Ps. lxxii. 17. t ch. ix. 16 reff.

44. rec επιστρεψω bef εις την οικιαν μου (*from Luke* xi. 24), with C rel latt syrr syr-cu arm Orig-int: txt BDZℵ 33 æth.—(υποστρεψω Z 1. 13. 124 Scr's g q r [Chr-ms].) ελθων DFGXΓ 13. 33. 157 syr [Chr-ms]: εξελθον U: ηλθον Δ: om ℵ[1]: txt BCℵ-corr[1] rel. (Z def.) aft ευρισκει ins τον οικον D. ins και bef σεσαρωμενον C[1] Z(appy) ℵ 235 Scr's i m s ev-36 lat-*a c h* syrr syr-cu Chr-β-8(and Fd's mss exc E F) Thl: om BD rel vulg lat-*b f* g_1 syr-mg-gr copt æth arm.

45. ετερα bef επτα Z 240-4 Scr's i lat-*b c* Chr. for 2nd εαυτου, αυτου DE[1] Scr's c evv-y-z. aft εσχατα ins αυτου D[1]. for χειρονα, χειρον D[1](txt D[2]).

also claim her, calling her Balkis (Koran, c. xxvii., cited by Winer), which latter view is probably nearer the truth, Sheba being a tract in Arabia Felix, near the shores of the Red Sea, near the present Aden (see Plin. vi. 23), abounding in spice and gold and precious stones. **43.**] **ὅταν**, not '*whenever*;' the indefinite conj. does not assert universality, but is hypothetical; **δέ** connects strictly with what has preceded. This important parable, in the similitude itself, sets forth to us an evil spirit driven out from a man, wandering in his misery and restlessness through desert places, the abodes and haunts of evil spirits (see Isa. xiii. 21, 22; xxxiv. 14), and at last determining on a return to his former victim, whom he finds so prepared for his purposes, that he associates with himself seven other fiends, by whom the wretched man being possessed, ends miserably. In its interpretation we may trace three distinct references, each full of weighty instruction. (1) The direct application of the parable is to *the Jewish people*, and the parallel runs thus:—The old dæmon of idolatry brought down on the Jews the Babylonish captivity, and was cast out by it. They did not after their return fall into it again, but rather endured persecution, as under Antiochus Epiphanes. The emptying, sweeping, and garnishing may be traced in the growth of Pharisaic hypocrisy and the Rabbinical schools between the return and the coming of our Lord. The re-possession by the one, and accession of seven other spirits more malicious (πονηρότερα) than the first, hardly needs explanation. The desperate infatuation of the Jews after our Lord's ascension, their bitter hostility to His Church, their miserable end as a people, are known to all. Chrysostom, who gives in the main this interpretation, notices their continued infatuation in his own day: and instances their joining in the impieties of Julian. (2) Strikingly parallel with this runs the history of the Christian Church. Not long after the Apostolic times, the golden calves of idolatry were set up by the Church of Rome. What the effect of the captivity was to the Jews, that of the Reformation has been to Christendom. The first evil spirit has been cast out. But by the growth of hypocrisy, secularity, and rationalism, the house has become empty, swept, and garnished: swept and garnished by the decencies of civilization and discoveries of secular knowledge, but empty of living and earnest faith. And he must read prophecy but ill, who does not see under all these seeming improvements the preparation for the final development of the man of sin, the great re-possession, when idolatry and the seven πνεύματα πονηρότερα shall bring the outward frame of so-called Christendom to a fearful end. (3) Another important fulfilment of the prophetic parable may be found in the histories of individuals. By religious education or impressions, the devil has been cast out

46 Ἔτι αὐτοῦ λαλοῦντος τοῖς ὄχλοις ἰδοὺ ἡ μήτηρ
καὶ οἱ ἀδελφοὶ αὐτοῦ εἱστήκεισαν ἔξω [u] ζητοῦντες αὐτῷ [u] Luke ix. 9. xiii. 24. John vii. 1, &c. Exod. ii. 15.
λαλῆσαι. 47 εἶπεν δέ τις αὐτῷ Ἰδοὺ ἡ μήτηρ σου καὶ
οἱ ἀδελφοί σου ἔξω ἑστήκασιν [u] ζητοῦντές σοι λαλῆσαι.
48 ὁ δὲ ἀποκριθεὶς εἶπεν τῷ λέγοντι αὐτῷ Τίς [v] ἐστιν [v] ch. xxvi. 26 ref.
ἡ μήτηρ μου, καὶ τίνες [v] εἰσὶν οἱ ἀδελφοί μου; 49 καὶ
[w] ἐκτείνας τὴν [w] χεῖρα αὐτοῦ ἐπὶ τοὺς μαθητὰς αὐτοῦ εἶπεν [w] ch. viii. 3 reff. Exod. xiv. 21.
Ἰδοὺ ἡ μήτηρ μου καὶ οἱ ἀδελφοί μου. 50 ὅστις γὰρ ἂν
[x] ποιῇ τὸ θέλημα τοῦ πατρός μου τοῦ ἐν οὐρανοῖς, αὐτός [x] ch. vii. 21 reff. Ps. cxlii. 10.
μου ἀδελφὸς καὶ ἀδελφὴ καὶ μήτηρ ἐστίν.

46. rec aft ετι ins δε, with C rel syr æth: λαλουντος δε αυτου DLZ Syr [Orig$_1$]: txt Bℵ 33 vulg lat-*c f* copt arm. om 2nd αυτου Z ℵ-corr(? but re-insd) 301: αυτου bef και οι αδελφοι vulg lat-*a b f ff*$_{1.2}$ *g*$_1$ *h* Orig Chr. λαλησαι bef αυτω DL 33. 80. 124 ev-36 latt syrr syr-cu Orig: om ζητ. αυτω λαλ. ℵ¹(txt ℵ-corr¹).

47. om ver (*homœotel*) BLΓℵ¹ lat-*ff*$_1$ *k* syr-cu. aft τις ins των μαθητων αυτου (omg αυτω) ℵ-corr¹. εστ. bef εξω D 33: om εξω **1**. εστηκεισαν D¹(-κασαν D²) Scr's w: om ℵ-corr¹ (vulg copt). λαλησαι bef σοι D lat-*b c f ff*$_2$ *g*$_1$ *h* syrr: for ζητ. σοι λαλ., ζητουσιν σε (‖ *Mark*) ℵ-corr¹ [vulg copt].

48. rec (for λεγοντι) ειποντι, with CΠ¹-corr rel: om τ. λ. X: txt BD Z(Treg, expr) Π¹(appy) ℵ 33 ev-36. for και, η D lat-*a ff*$_{1.2}$ *g*$_2$ *k* arm.

49. om 1st αυτου Dℵ¹(ins ℵ-corr¹) 235. 300 Scr's k vulg lat-*a b ff*$_1$ *g*$_1$ Orig [Aug].

50. om αν D 235. rec ποιηση (*from* ‖ *Mark*), with Bℵ rel latt; ποιησει KLZΓ 13 Scr's h i evv-y-z copt: ποιει (omg αν) *facit* D: txt CΔ.

of a man; but how often do the religious lives of men spend themselves in the sweeping and garnishing (see Luke xi. 39, 40), in formality and hypocrisy, till utter emptiness of real faith and spirituality has prepared them for that second fearful invasion of the Evil One, which is indeed worse than the first! (See Heb. vi. 4, 6: 2 Pet. ii. 20—22.)

46—50.] His Mother and Brethren seek to speak with Him. Mark iii. 31—35. Luke viii. 19—21. In Mark the incident is placed as here: in Luke, after the parable of the sower. **46.**] In Mark iii. 21 we are told that his relations *went out to lay hold on Him, for they said, He is beside Himself*: and that the reason of this was his continuous labour in teaching, which *had not left time so much as to eat*. There is nothing in this care for his bodily health (from whatever source the act may have arisen on the part of his *brethren*, see John vii. 5) inconsistent with the known state of his *mother's* mind (see Luke ii. 19, 51). They stood ἔξω, i. e. outside the throng of hearers around our Lord; or, perhaps, outside the house. He meets their message with a reproof, which at the same time conveys assurance to His humble hearers. He came for *all men*, and though He was born of a woman, He who is the second Adam, taking our entire humanity on Him, is not on that account more nearly united to her, than to all those who are united to Him by the Spirit; nor bound to regard the call of earthly relations so much as the welfare of those whom He came to teach and to save. It is to be noticed that our Lord, though He introduces the additional term ἀδελφή into his answer, does not (and indeed could not) introduce πατήρ, inasmuch as He never speaks of an earthly Father. See Luke ii. 49. All these characteristics of the mother of our Lord are deeply interesting, both in themselves, and as building up, when put together, the most decisive testimony against the fearful superstition which has assigned to her the place of a goddess in the Romish mythology. Great and inconceivable as the honour of that meek and holy woman was, we find her repeatedly (see John ii. 4) the object of rebuke from her divine Son, and hear Him here declaring, that the honour is one which the humblest believer in Him has in common with her.

Stier remarks (Reden Jesu, ii. 57 note), that the juxtaposition of *sister* and *mother* in the mouth of our Lord makes it probable that the *brethren* also were his actual brothers according to the flesh: see note on ch. xiii. 55.

y see note. Deut. xxxiii. 44.
z ch. iv. 18. Mark v. 21. Acts x. 6. Heb. xi. 12. 3 Kings iv. 29.
a = ch. xviii. 20. xxii. 34. xxvi. 3, 57. Acts iv. 5, &c. Neh. viii. 1.

BCDEF GKLMS UVXZ ΓΔΠℵ 1. 33

XIII. 1 Ἐν τῇ [y] ἡμέρᾳ ἐκείνῃ ἐξελθὼν ὁ Ἰησοῦς ἀπὸ
τῆς οἰκίας ἐκάθητο [z] παρὰ τὴν θάλασσαν· 2 καὶ [a] συνήχθησαν πρὸς αὐτὸν ὄχλοι πολλοί, ὥστε αὐτὸν εἰς
[b] πλοῖον [c] ἐμβάντα καθῆσθαι, καὶ πᾶς ὁ ὄχλος [d] ἐπὶ τὸν
[e] αἰγιαλὸν εἱστήκει. 3 καὶ ἐλάλησεν αὐτοῖς πολλὰ ἐν
[f] παραβολαῖς, λέγων Ἰδοὺ ἐξῆλθεν [g] ὁ [g] σπείρων [h] τοῦ

b ch. viii. 23. ix. 1 al. fr. c ch. viii. 23 reff. d constr., John i. 32, 33. Rev. vii. 15. e ver. 48. John xxi. 4. Acts xxi. 5. xxvii. 39, 40 only. Judg. v. 17 A. Sir. xxiv. 14 ABℵ[1] (not ℵ[3a] F) only. f vv. 10, &c. ch. xv. 15 al. fr. Mt. Mk. L. only, exc. Heb. ix. 9. xi. 19. 3 Kings iv. 32. g partic. = ch. iv. 3. viii. 33. Eph. iv. 28. 1 Thess. v. 24. iii. 5 al. h constr., ch. ii. 13. iii. 13 al. Ps. cxlix. 7, 9.

Chap. XIII. 1. rec aft εν ins δε, with CD rel lat-*f h* syrr copt: om BZℵ 33 latt æth arm Orig Hil. εξηλθεν, insg και bef εκαθητο, D lat-*a b e* $ff_{1.2}$ g_1 *h* Syr syr-cu Orig-int Hil. om απο της οικιας D lat-*a b e* $ff_{1.2}$ $g_{1.2}$ Hil.—for απο, εκ Zℵ 33 $Orig_1$ Chr: om απο B 1. 124 evv-H-36-49 $Orig_1$: txt C rel vulg lat-*c f h* $Orig\text{-}int_1$.

2. rec ins το bef πλοιον, with D rel copt arm: om BCLZℵ 1. 33. om εμβαντα L. εστηκει [for ειστ.] D[1](txt D[5]).

3. εν παραβολαις bef πολλα C 157. 241-52 Scr's l m n [$Orig_1$]: om πολλα LV 236-43 copt. om του D.

Chap. XIII. 1—52.] The seven parables. (The parallels, see under each.) 1, 2.] Mark iv. 1. **1. ἐν τῇ ἡμέρᾳ ἐκείνῃ**] These words may mean literally *in the same day*. But it is not absolutely necessary. The words certainly do bear that meaning in Mark iv. 35, and important consequences follow (see note there): but in Acts viii. 1 they are as evidently indefinite. The instances of their occurrence in John (xiv. 20; xvi. 23, 26) are not to the point, their use there being prophetical. **ἀπὸ τῆς οἰκ.** perhaps implies that the foregoing discourse was delivered *in a house*, as some have thought: but the article need not (any more than τό before πλοῖον, see notes on ch. ix. 1, 28) imply *any particular house*. **3. ἐν παραβολαῖς**] The senses of this word in the N. T. are various, and may be found in the lexicons. My present concern with it is to explain its meaning as applied to the "*parables*" of our Lord. (1) The *Parable* is not a *Fable*, inasmuch as the Fable is concerned only with the maxims of worldly prudence, whereas the Parable conveys spiritual truth. The *Fable* in its form rejects probability, and teaches through the *fancy*, introducing speaking animals, or even inanimate things; whereas the *Parable* adheres to probability, and teaches through the *imagination*, introducing only things which may possibly happen. ἔστι παραβολὴ λόγος ὡς περὶ γενομένου, μὴ γενομένου μὲν κατὰ τὸ ῥητόν, δυναμένου δὲ γίνεσθαι. Origen, cited by Trench on the Parables, p. 4. (2) Nor is the Parable a *Myth*: inasmuch as in Mythology the course of the story is set before us *as the truth*, and simple minds receive it as the truth, only the reflective mind penetrating to the distinction between the vehicle and the thing conveyed; whereas in the Parable these two stand distinct from one another to all minds, so that none but the very simplest would ever believe in the Parable as fact. (3) Nor is the Parable a *Proverb*: though παραβολή is used for *both* in the N. T. (Luke iv. 23; v. 36: Matt. xv. 14, 15), and παροιμία in John for a Parable (John x. 6; xvi. 25, 29). It is indeed more like a Proverb than either of the former; being an expanded Proverb, and a Proverb a concentrated Parable, or Fable, or result of human experience expressed without a figure. Hence it will be seen that the Proverb ranges far wider than the Parable, which is an expansion of only one particular case of a Proverb. Thus '*Physician heal thyself*' would, if expanded, make a parable; '*ne sus Minervam*,' a fable; '*honesty is the best policy*,' neither of these. (4) Nor is the Parable an *Allegory*: inasmuch as in the Allegory the imaginary persons and actions are placed in the very places and footsteps of the real ones, and stand there instead of them, declaring all the time by their names or actions who and what they are. Thus the Allegory is self-interpreting, and the persons in it are invested with the attributes of those represented; whereas in the Parable the courses of action related and understood run indeed parallel, but the persons are strictly confined to their own natural places and actions, which are, in their relation and succession, typical of higher things. (5) It may well hence be surmised what a Parable *is*. It is *a serious narration, within the limits of probability, of a course of action pointing to some moral or spiritual Truth* ('Collatio per narratiunculam

σπείρειν. 4 καὶ [i] ἐν τῷ σπείρειν αὐτόν, [k] ἃ μὲν ἔπεσεν
παρὰ τὴν ὁδόν, καὶ ἐλθόντα τὰ [l] πετεινὰ [m] κατέφαγεν αὐτά.
5 ἄλλα δὲ ἔπεσεν ἐπὶ τὰ [n] πετρώδη, ὅπου οὐκ εἶχεν γῆν
πολλήν, καὶ εὐθέως [o] ἐξανέτειλεν [p] διὰ τὸ μὴ ἔχειν βάθος
γῆς· 6 ἡλίου δὲ [q] ἀνατείλαντος [r] ἐκαυματίσθη καὶ [p] διὰ τὸ
μὴ ἔχειν ῥίζαν [s] ἐξηράνθη. 7 ἄλλα δὲ ἔπεσεν ἐπὶ τὰς

i constr., ver. 25. Acts xi. 15 al. fr. Isa. xxvii. 1.
k || Mk. see || L. (1 Cor. xii. 8.)
l ch. vi. 26 al. Deut. xiv. 19, 20 al.
m ||. Luke xv. 30. John ii. 17, from Ps. lxviii. 10. Rev. x. 9, 10. xii. 4. xx. 9 only. (εσθίειν, Luke xx. 47 reff.)
n || Mk. ver. 20 || Mk. only †.
o || Mk. only. (trans. in LXX.) Gen. ii. 9. Ps. cxlvi. 8 al.
p ch. xxiv. 12. Luke ix. 7. xix. 11 al. Judg. iii. 12.
q ch. iv. 16 reff.
r || Mk. Rev. xvi. 8, 9 only †.
s ch. xxi. 19, 20. James i. 11 al. Ps. cxxviii. 6.

σπειραι(*from* ||) DLMXℵ 1. 13. 33. 209-35 Just Orig$_2$ (Eus) Chr Thl.

4. om κ. εν τω σπειρειν (σπ. to σπ.) C. rec (for ελθοντα) ηλθεν, insg και bef κατεφαγεν (*from* || *Mark*), with Cℵ rel Orig: ηλθον και DLZ 33: txt B 13. 124 evv-H-y. aft πετεινα ins του ουρανου (*from* || *Luke*) E[1]KMΠ 13. 124 Scr's d p r w evv-H-y vulg lat-*b ff*$_1$ *h* syr-cu syr æth arm Orig.

5. for αλλα, α D Chr; *quædam* lat-*b c d.* ευθυς D 40. (transferred in L to next ver bef εκαυμ.) εξανετειλαν B. ins της bef γης (*prob error*) B. [Z def.]

6. του δε ηλιου D. εκαυματωθη B: -τισθησαν (and εξηρανθησαν) D: εκαυματισεν Δ[1]: txt CZℵ rel.

7. for επι, εις (|| *Mark*) D 13. 124. 346 lat-*a* Just Orig; *in spinis* lat-*b c* D-lat.

fictam, sed veri similem, serio illustrans rem sublimiorem.' Unger, de Parabolis Jesu (Meyer)); and derives its force from real analogies impressed by the Creator of all things on His creatures. The great Teacher by parables therefore is He who needed not that any should testify of man; for He knew what was in man, John ii. 25: moreover, He *made* man, and orders the course and character of human events. And this is the reason why none can, or dare, teach by parables, except Christ. We do not, as He did, see the inner springs out of which flow those laws of eternal truth and justice, which the Parable is framed to elucidate. *Our* parables would be in danger of perverting, instead of guiding aright. The Parable is especially adapted to different classes of hearers at once: it is understood by each according to his measure of understanding. See note on ver. 12. The seven parables related in this chapter cannot be regarded as a collection made by the Evangelist as relating to one subject, the Kingdom of Heaven and its development; they are clearly indicated by ver. 53 to have been all spoken on *one and the same occasion*, and form indeed a complete and glorious whole in their inner and deeper sense. The *first four* of these parables appear to have been spoken *to the multitude from the ship* (the interpretation of the parable of the sower being interposed); the *last three, to the disciples in the house.* From the expression ἤρξατο in || Mk. compared with the question of the disciples in ver. 10,—and with ver. 34,—it appears that this was the *first beginning of our Lord's teaching by parables,* expressly so delivered, and properly so called. And the natural sequence of things here agrees with, and confirms Matthew's arrangement against those who would place (as Ebrard) all this chapter before the Sermon on the Mount. He there spoke *without parables,* or mainly so; and continued to do so till the rejection and misunderstanding of his teaching led to His judicially adopting the course here indicated, χωρὶς παρ. οὐδὲν ἐλάλει αὐτοῖς. The other order would be inconceivable: that after such parabolic teaching, and such a reason assigned for it, the Lord should, that reason remaining in full force, have deserted his parabolic teaching, and opened out his meaning as plainly as in the Sermon on the Mount.

3—9.] THE SOWER. Mark iv. 2—9. Luke viii. 4—8. See note on the locality in vv. 51, 52. **3.**] For the explanation of the parable see on vv. 19—23. **ὁ σπ.,** *generic,* singular of οἱ σπείροντες — *a sower;* **he that soweth.** **4.**] **παρὰ τ. ὁδ., by** (by the side of, along the line of) **the path** through the field. Luke inserts καὶ κατεπατήθη, and after τὰ πετ., —τοῦ οὐρανοῦ. **5.**] **τὰ πετρώδη** (= τὴν πέτραν Luke), stony places where the native rock is but slightly covered with earth (which abound in Palestine), and where therefore the radiation from the face of the rock would cause the seed to spring up quickly, the shallow earth being heated by the sun of the day before. **6.**] **ῥίζαν** = ἰκμάδα Luke. If the one could have struck down, it would have found the other. **7.**] **ἐπὶ τ. ἀκ. =**

t ἀκάνθας, καὶ u ἀνέβησαν αἱ t ἄκανθαι καὶ v ἀπέπνιξαν
αὐτά. 8 ἄλλα δὲ ἔπεσεν ἐπὶ τὴν γῆν τὴν w καλήν, καὶ
x ἐδίδου x καρπὸν y ὃ μὲν ἑκατὸν y ὃ δὲ ἑξήκοντα y ὃ δὲ
τριάκοντα. 9 ὁ ἔχων ὦτα ἀκουέτω. 10 καὶ προσελθόντες
οἱ μαθηταὶ εἶπαν αὐτῷ Διὰ τί ἐν παραβολαῖς λαλεῖς αὐτοῖς; 11 ὁ δὲ ἀποκριθεὶς εἶπεν αὐτοῖς Ὅτι ὑμῖν z δέδοται
a γνῶναι τὰ ab μυστήρια τῆς βασιλείας τῶν οὐρανῶν, ...της βασιλ. Z.
ἐκείνοις δὲ οὐ z δέδοται. 12 ὅστις γὰρ ἔχει, δοθήσεται BCDEF GKLMS
αὐτῷ καὶ c περισσευθήσεται· ὅστις δὲ οὐκ ἔχει, καὶ ὃ ἔχει UVXΓΔ ΠℵN 1. 33

t ch. vii. 16 reff. Jer. iv. 3. u = ‖ Mk. (bis). Mark iv. 32. Isa. xxxii. 13. v ‖ L. Luke viii. 33 only †. Tobit iii. 8 (not ℵ) only. w = ‖ Mk. ch. xii. 33 al. Num. xiii. 20. x ‖ Mk. (bis). Zech. viii. 12. y ch. xxi. 35. xxii. 35. Rom. ix. 21. 2 Tim. ii. 20. οὓς μὲν . . . οὓς δέ, Polyb. i. 7. 3. see ver. 4 reff. z ‖. ch. xix. 11. 2 Tim. i. 18. Rev. iii. 21 al. Gen. xxxi. 7. Num. xxi. 23. a ‖ L. Wisd. ii. 22. see Eph. iii. 3. Col. ii. 2. b ‖ only in Gospp. = Rom. xi. 25. 1 Cor. xiii. 2. xv. 51. Dan. ii. 29 al. c pass., ch. xxv. 29 only ‡. trans., 2 Cor. iv. 5 al3. (Paul) ‡. intr., ch. xiv. 20. Luke xii. 15 al. fr.

for απεπν., επνιξαν Dℵ 13. 124. 346.

8. επεσαν C 33. [for επι, εις B¹(Tischdf): corrd eadem manu.] εδιδουν D.

9. rec aft ωτα ins ακουειν (*from* ‖), with CDZℵ³ᵃ rel: om BLℵ¹ lat-*e ff*$_1$ *k* Tert.

10. aft προσελθοντες ins αυτω C copt. aft μαθηται ins αυτου CX Scr's g q r lat-*a b c f g*$_1$ *h* D-lat Syr syr-cu syr-with-ast copt æth Eus Chr-6-8-η-ρ: om BDZℵ rel vulg lat-*e ff*$_1$ *g*$_2$ arm Orig. [ειπαν, so BLℵ 33.] αυτοις bef λαλεις ℵ¹(txt ℵ²) [Eus$_1$].

11. om αυτοις CZℵ lat-*ff*$_1$ copt æth Eus Chr-6-8-η-ρ.

εἰς τὰς ἀκ. Mark; = ἐν μέσῳ τῶν ἀκ. Luke. In places where were the roots of thorns, beds of thistles, or such like.

ἀνέβησαν . . . . καί = συμφυεῖσαι Luke; **ἀπέπν.** = συνέπν. Mark, who adds καὶ καρπὸν οὐκ ἔδωκεν. **8.**] **ἐδίδου** = φυὲν ἐποίησεν Luke. After καρ. Mark inserts ἀναβαίνοντα καὶ αὐξανόμενον. Luke gives only ἑκατονταπλασίονα. **9.**] is common to all three Evangelists (Mark and Luke insert ἀκούειν).

10—17.] Our Lord's reason for teaching in parables. Mark iv. 10—12. Luke viii. 9, 10, but much abridged.

10.] **οἱ μαθηταί** = οἱ περὶ αὐτὸν σὺν τοῖς δώδεκα Mark. This question took place during a pause in our Lord's teaching, not when He had entered the house, ver. 36. The question shews the *newness of this method of teaching to the disciples.* It is not mentioned in Mark: only the enquiry into the meaning of the parable just spoken: nor in Luke; but the answer implies it. **11.**] The Kingdom of Heaven, like other Kingdoms, has its secrets (**μυστήριον**,—see a definition by St. Paul in Rom. xvi. 25 f.,—viz. χρόνοις αἰωνίοις σεσιγημένον, φανερωθὲν δὲ νῦν) and inner counsels, which strangers must not know. These are only revealed to the humble diligent hearers, **ὑμῖν**: to those who were immediately around the Lord with the twelve; not **ἐκείνοις** = τοῖς λοιποῖς Luke, = ἐκείνοις τοῖς ἔξω Mark. (1 Cor. v. 12, 13.) **οὐ δέδοται** = ἐν παραβολαῖς Luke, and τὰ πάντα γίνεται Mark. **12.**] In this saying of the Lord is summed up the *double force*—the *revealing* and *concealing* properties of the parable. By it, he who *hath*,—he who not only hears with the ear, but understands with the heart, has more given to him; and it is for this main purpose undoubtedly that the Lord spoke parables: to be to His Church revelations of the truth and mysteries of His Kingdom. But His present purpose in speaking them, as further explained below, was the quality possessed by them, and declared in the latter part of this verse, of hiding their meaning from the hard-hearted and sensual. By them, he who *hath not*, in whom there is no spark of spiritual desire nor meetness to receive the engrafted word, has taken from him even that which he hath ("*seemeth to have*," Luke); even the poor confused notions of heavenly doctrine which a sensual and careless life allow him, are further bewildered and darkened by this simple teaching, into the depths of which he cannot penetrate so far as even to ascertain that they exist. No practical comment on the latter part of this saying can be more striking, than that which is furnished to our day by the study of the German rationalistic (and, I may add, some of our English harmonistic) Commentators; while at the same time we may rejoice to see the approximate fulfilment of the former in such commentaries as those of Olshausen, Neander, Stier, and Trench. In ch. xxv. 29, the fuller meaning of this saying, as applied not only to

ἀρθήσεται ἀπ' αὐτοῦ. 13 διὰ τοῦτο ἐν παραβολαῖς αὐτοῖς
λαλῶ, ὅτι βλέποντες οὐ βλέπουσιν καὶ ἀκούοντες οὐκ
ἀκούουσιν οὐδὲ συνιοῦσιν. 14 καὶ [d] ἀναπληροῦται αὐτοῖς
ἡ [e] προφητεία Ἠσαΐου ἡ λέγουσα [f] Ἀκοῇ ἀκούσετε καὶ οὐ
μὴ συνῆτε, καὶ βλέποντες βλέψετε καὶ οὐ μὴ ἴδητε.
15 [g] ἐπαχύνθη γὰρ ἡ καρδία τοῦ λαοῦ τούτου, καὶ τοῖς
ὠσὶν [h] βαρέως ἤκουσαν, καὶ τοὺς ὀφθαλμοὺς αὐτῶν [i] ἐκάμμυσαν, μήποτε ἴδωσιν τοῖς ὀφθαλμοῖς καὶ τοῖς ὠσὶν
ἀκούσωσιν καὶ τῇ καρδίᾳ συνῶσιν καὶ [k] ἐπιστρέψωσιν, καὶ
ἰάσομαι αὐτούς. 16 ὑμῶν δὲ μακάριοι οἱ [l] ὀφθαλμοὶ ὅτι

d Gospp., here only. Gal. vi. 2. Phil. ii. 30. 1 Thess. ii. 16. 1 Cor. xiv. 16. Gen. xxix. 28. (-ρωσις Esdr. i. 57.)
e = Gospp., here only. Epp. (Rom. xii. 6 al.), 2 Pet. i. 20, 21 only. Rev. i. 3 al5. 2 Chron. xxxii. 32.
f 1 Cor. xii. 17. Heb. v. 11 al. Isa. vi. 9.
g Acts xxviii. 27 (from l. c.) only. Deut. xxxii. 15.
h Acts as above (from l. c.) only. Gen. xxxi. 35. 2 Macc. xi. 1. xiv. 27 only.
i Acts as above only. Isa. l. c. xxix. 10. Lam. iii. 44 (45) only.
k absol., ‖ Mk. Luke xxii. 32. Acts iii. 19 al. Zech. v. 1. vi. 1.
l Luke x. 23. Gen. xlv. 12. Deut. xxix. 4.

13. for *αυτοις λαλω*, *λαλει αυτοις* D[1]-gr: *ελαλει αυτοις* D[2].—om *αυτοις* L lat-*c* Iren Cyr-jer: *λαλω* bef *αυτοις* **1**. 13. 33. 124 evv-H-y-36 vulg lat-*a b f* $ff_{1.2}$ $g_{1.2}$ D-lat Syr syr-cu arm Chr Iren-int Orig-int Tert. **ινα βλ. μη** *βλεπωσιν κ. ακ.* **μη** *ακουσοσιν* **κ. μη** *συνωσιν* **μη ποτε επιστρεψωσιν** (*from* ‖ *Mark*) D **1** (ev-H) lat-*b c* ff_2 g_1 *h* syr-cu Eus Cyr-jer Iren-int Tert. *συνωσιν* D ev-H: *συνιωσιν* B[2] **1**. 33 ev-z.
14. aft 1st *και* ins *τοτε* D **1** lat-*a b c* $ff_{1.2}$ g_1 *h* Eus. for *αναπληρουται*, *πληρωθησεται* D 17 Scr's s evv-H-y lat-*c* ff_1 g_1 *h k*: *πληρουται* **1** lat-*a* ff_2. rec ins *επ'* bef *αυτοις* (*explanatory*), with DM[1] (Scr's s (and ev-y ?), e sil) vulg lat-*b f* $ff_{1.2}$ *h k* Syr copt æth Eus Iren-int: om *αυτοις* lat-*a c* g_2 syr-cu: txt BCא rel Scr's mss am (with forj harl[1]) syr arm [Bas Chr-β]. ins *του* bef *ησαιου* D. for *η λεγουσα*, *λεγουσα πορευθητι και ειπε τω λαω τουτω* (*from* LXX) D lat-*a b c* $ff_{1.2}$ g_1 *h* Eus. *ακουσατε* B[1] [*-σητε* EFGMUVΓ]. *βλεψητε* EFGMUVΓא 33.
15. aft 1st *ωσιν* ins *αυτων* (*from* LXX) Cא lat-*b c* g_2 *h k* Syr syr-cu copt æth arm Iren-int. aft 2nd *ωσιν* ins *αυτων* א[2] Scr's i. om *ακουσωσιν* (*homœotel*) C. *συνιωσιν* CE[2]. *επιστρεψουσιν* EFGKVΠ. rec *ιασωμαι*, with E[2]KUXΔ[1] **1** latt [Chr-β]: txt BCDא rel [Chr].
16. om *οι* (aft *μακαριοι*) DM[1].

hearing, but to the whole spiritual life, is brought out by our Lord. **13.] ὅτι βλ. οὐ βλέπουσιν** κ.τ.λ. = (in Mark, Luke; similarly below) *ἵνα βλ. μὴ βλέπωσιν κ.τ.λ.* In the deeper view of the purpose of the parable, both of these run into one. Taking the saying of ver. 12 for our guide we have *ὅστις οὐκ ἔχει* = *ὅτι βλέπ. οὐ βλέπουσιν*,—and *καὶ ὃ ἔχει ἀρθ. ἀπ' αὐτοῦ* = *ἵνα βλ. μὴ βλέπωσιν*. The difficulties raised on these variations, and on the prophecy quoted in vv. 14, 15, have arisen entirely from not keeping this in view. **14, 15.]** This prophecy is quoted with a similar reference John xii. 40: Acts xxviii. 26, 27; see also Rom. xi. 8. **ἀναπληροῦται, is being fulfilled,** 'finds one of the stages of its fulfilment:' a partial one having taken place in the contemporaries of the prophet. The prophecy is cited verbatim from the LXX, which changes the imperative of the Hebrew ('Make the heart of this people fat,' &c., E. V.) into the indicative, as bearing the same meaning. **αὐτοῖς** is a dat. of relation, 'with regard to them:' see Kühner, Gramm. § 581.

ἐπαχύνθη, grew fat; from prosperity:—'torpens, omni sensu carens' (Simonis Lex. under שָׁמַן). **βαρέως ἤκουσαν, heard heavily,** *sluggishly and imperfectly*. **ἐκάμμυσαν, closed** (Heb. '*smeared over*') **their eyes.** All this have they done: all this is increased in them by their continuing to do it, and all lest they should (and so that they cannot) hear, see, understand, and be saved. **ἰάσομαι αὐτ.** = ἀφεθῇ αὐτοῖς Mark. This citation gives no countenance to the fatalist view of the passage, but rests the whole blame on the hard-heartedness and unreadiness of the hearers, which is of itself the cause why the very preaching of the word is a means of further darkening and condemning them (see 2 Cor. iv. 3, 4). On the fut. indic. after *μήποτε*, "verentis ne quid futurum sit, sed indicantis simul, putare se ita futurum esse ut veretur," see Winer, § 56. 2: Herm. ad Soph. Aj. 272. **16, 17.]** See ref. Prov. These verses occur again in a different connexion, and with the form of expression slightly varied, Luke x. 23, 24. It was a saying likely to be re-

BCDEF GKLMS UVXΓΔ ΠΝ 1. 33

[l] βλέπουσιν, καὶ τὰ [m] ὦτα [ὑμῶν] ὅτι [m] ἀκούουσιν.
17 ἀμὴν γὰρ λέγω ὑμῖν ὅτι πολλοὶ προφῆται καὶ δίκαιοι
ἐπεθύμησαν ἰδεῖν ἃ βλέπετε, καὶ οὐκ εἶδον, καὶ ἀκοῦσαι ἃ
ἀκούετε, καὶ οὐκ ἤκουσαν. 18 ὑμεῖς οὖν ἀκούσατε τὴν
παραβολὴν τοῦ σπείραντος. 19 [n] παντὸς ἀκούοντος τὸν
[o] λόγον τῆς [o] βασιλείας καὶ μὴ συνιέντος ἔρχεται ὁ [p] πονηρὸς καὶ [q] ἁρπάζει τὸ ἐσπαρμένον ἐν τῇ καρδίᾳ αὐτοῦ·

m Job xxix. 11. Prov. xx. 12.
n ch. xviii. 19. Acts x. 14. Exod. xx. 4. Lev. iv. 2.
o here only. see ch. iv. 23 reff.
p masc., ver. 38. (ch. v. 37?) John xvii. 15. Eph. vi. 16. 1 John ii. 13 al.
q = Acts viii. 39. αἰχμὴν παρά τινος ἁρπάσας, Xen. Cyr. iv. 6. 4.

om **τα** D ev-z. om 2nd *υμων* B 6. 75. 252 lat-*a b c ff$_2$ g$_1$* Chr-ρ Hil. rec **ακουει** (*gramml corrn*), with L rel: txt BCDMXℵ 1. 33 Orig Eus Chr-η-ρ-2-9(and Fd) Cyr$_3$ Damasc Constt.

17. om *γαρ* Xℵ Scr's a q r lat-*a b c f ff$_{1.2}$ g$_{1.2}$* æth arm Hil$_2$. om *και δικαιοι* B[1], insd in marg by B[1](sic: see table). *ηδυνηθησαν ειδειν* D. (*ειδαν* Bℵ 33.)

18. rec *σπειροντος* (*from ver* 3, *the parable having acquired that name, as with us,* "the parable of the sower:" *see below, on ver* 39), with CDℵ[3a] rel: txt BXℵ[1] 33 evv-H-4 syr Chr-β-η.

19. *συνιοντος* DF ev-z: *συνηωντος* L. for *εσπαρμενον*, *σπειρομενον* D. for *αυτου*, *αυτων* D-gr.

peated. There it is *μακάρ. οἱ ὀφθ. οἱ βλέποντες ἃ βλέπετε*: and for *δίκαιοι* we have *βασιλεῖς*. On the fact that prophets, &c. desired to see those things, see 2 Sam. xxiii. 5: Job xix. 23—27: also Exod. iv. 13, and Luke ii. 29—32.

18—23.] INTERPRETATION OF THE PARABLE OF THE SOWER. Mark iv. 10—20. Luke viii. 9—18. Both of them incorporate with the answer of our Lord to the request of the disciples, much of our last section. **18.**] **ἀκούσατε**, in the sense of the verse before—**hear the true meaning of**, '*hear in your hearts*.' With regard to the parable itself, we may remark that its great leading idea is that *μυστήριον τῆς βασιλείας*, according to which the grace of God, and the receptivity of it by man, work ever together in bringing forth fruit. The *seed* is one and the same every where and to all: but *seed does not spring up without earth, nor does earth bring forth without seed;* and the success or failure of the seed is the consequence of the adaptation to its reception, or otherwise, of the spot on which it falls. But of course, on the other hand, as the enquiry, 'Why is this ground rich, and that barren?' leads us up into the creative arrangements of God,—so a similar enquiry in the spiritual interpretation would lead us into the inscrutable and sovereign arrangements of Him who 'preventeth us that we may have a good will, and worketh with us when we have that will' (Art. X. of the Church of England). See, on the whole, my Sermons before the University of Cambridge, February, 1858.

19.] In Luke we have an important preliminary declaration, implied indeed here also: **ὁ σπόρος ἐστὶν ὁ λόγος τοῦ θεοῦ.** This *word* is in this parable especially meant of the word *preached*, though the word *written is not excluded:* nor the word *unwritten*—the providences and judgments, and even the creation, of God. (See Rom. x. 17, 18.) The similitude in this parable is alluded to in 1 Pet. i. 23: James i. 21. The sower is first the Son of Man (ver. 37), then His ministers and servants (1 Cor. iii. 6) to the end. He sows over all the field, unlikely as well as likely places; and commands His sowers to do the same, Mark xvi. 15. Some, Stier says, (Reden Jesu, ii. 76, ed. 2,) have objected to the parable a want of truthful correspondence to reality, because sowers do not thus waste their seed by scattering it where it is not likely to grow; but, as he rightly answers,—the simple idea of the parable must be borne in mind, and its limits not transgressed—'a sower went out *to sow*'—his SOWING—sowing over all places, is the idea of the parable. We see him only as a *sower*, not as an economist. The parable is not about *Him*, but about the *seed* and *what happens to it*. He is the fit representative *τοῦ διδόντος θεοῦ πᾶσιν ἁπλῶς καὶ μὴ ὀνειδίζοντος*, James i. 5. **παντὸς κ.τ.λ.**] an anacoluthon, to throw the emphasis on *παντὸς κ.τ.λ.*, for *ὁ πονηρὸς . . . κ. ἁρπάζει τὸ ἐσπ. ἐν τῇ καρδ. παντὸς κ.τ.λ.* **καὶ μὴ συνιέντος** is peculiar to Matthew, and very important; as in Mark and Luke this first class of hearers are without any certain index to denote them. The *reason* of *μὴ συνιέντος* is clearly set forth by the parable: the heart is hardened, trodden down; the

οὗτός ἐστιν ὁ παρὰ τὴν ὁδὸν σπαρείς. 20 ὁ δὲ ἐπὶ τὰ
[r] πετρώδη σπαρείς, οὗτός ἐστιν ὁ τὸν λόγον ἀκούων καὶ
εὐθὺς [s] μετὰ χαρᾶς λαμβάνων αὐτόν, 21 οὐκ ἔχει δὲ
[t] ῥίζαν ἐν ἑαυτῷ, ἀλλὰ [u] πρόσκαιρός ἐστιν, γενομένης δὲ
θλίψεως ἢ [v] διωγμοῦ διὰ τὸν λόγον εὐθὺς [w] σκανδαλίζεται.
22 ὁ δὲ εἰς τὰς [x] ἀκάνθας σπαρείς, οὗτός ἐστιν ὁ τὸν λόγον
ἀκούων, καὶ ἡ [y] μέριμνα τοῦ [z] αἰῶνος καὶ ἡ [a] ἀπάτη τοῦ
πλούτου [b] συνπνίγει τὸν λόγον, καὶ [c] ἄκαρπος γίνεται.

r ver. 5. s ||. ch. xxviii. 8. Luke xxiv. 52. Phil. i. 3 al. 1 Chron. xxix. 22. t Job xix. 28. u || Mk. 2 Cor. iv. 18. Heb. xi. 25 only †. v || Mk. Mark x. 30. Acts viii. 1. xiii. 50. Paul, Rom. viii. 35 al4. Prov. xi. 19. Lam. iii. 19. 2 Macc. xii. 23 only. w = ch. xi. 6 reff. x ver. 7. y ||. Luke xxi. 34. 2 Cor. xi. 28 (constr.). 1 Pet. v. 7 only. Sir. xxxiv. (xxx.) 1. z absol., || Mk. ver. 39 [40 v. r.] ch. xxiv. 3. xxviii. 20 only. a || Mk. Eph. iv. 22. Col. ii. 8. 2 Thess. ii. 10. Heb. iii. 13. 2 Pet. ii. 13 only †. Judith ix. 10, 13. xvi. 8 only. (-τᾶν, Eph. v. 6.) b || (Mk. bis). Luke viii. 42 only †. c || Mk. 1 Cor. xiv. 14. Eph. v. 11. Tit. iii. 14. 2 Pet. i. 8. Jude 12 only. Jer. ii. 6. Wisd. xv. 4 only.

21. om εν D¹-gr(ins D-corr¹). ευθεως D 33.

22. for σπαρεις, σπειρομενος D lat-*a c ff₂ g₁*. rec aft του αιωνος ins τουτου (*explanatory*), with C ℵ²(appy) rel vulg lat-*b c f ff₁* syrr syr-cu copt æth Orig: om BDℵ¹ Scr's f o¹ lat-*a ff₂ g₁ h k* arm. πλουτους D¹.

seed cannot penetrate. **ὁ πονηρὸς** = ὁ σατανᾶς (Mark, who also inserts εὐθύς), = ὁ διάβολος (Luke). The parable itself is here most satisfactory as to the *manner* in which the Evil One proceeds. By fowls of the air—passing thoughts and desires, which seem insignificant and even innocent—does Satan do his work, and rob the heart of the precious seed. Luke adds the purpose of Satan in taking away the word: ἵνα μὴ πιστεύσαντες σωθῶσιν. **ὁ . . . σπαρείς**: not '*he that received seed by the way side*,' but **he that was sown by the way side**. This is not a confusion of similitudes,—no 'primary and secondary interpretation' of σπόρος,—but the deep truth, both of nature and of grace. The seed sown springing up in the earth, *becomes the plant*, and bears the fruit, or fails of bearing it; it is therefore the representative, when sown, of the individuals of whom the discourse is. And though in this first case it does not spring up, yet the same form of speech is kept up: throughout they are οἱ σπαρέντες, as, when the question of bearing fruit comes, they must be. We are said to be ἀναγεγεννημένοι διὰ λόγου ζῶντος θεοῦ, 1 Pet. i. 23. It takes us up into itself, as the seed the earth, and we become a new plant, a καινὴ κτίσις: cf. also below, ver. 38, τὸ δὲ καλὸν σπέρμα, **οὗτοί εἰσιν** κ.τ.λ. **20, 21.**] In this *second* case, the surface of the mind and disposition is easily stirred, soon excited: but beneath lies a heart even harder than the trodden way. So the plant, springing up under the false heat of excitement, having no root struck down into the depths of the being, is, when the real heat from without arises which is intended to strengthen and forward the healthy-rooted plant, withered and destroyed. **πρόσκαιρός ἐστιν**, not only 'endureth for a while,' but also 'is the creature of circumstances,' changing as they change. Both ideas are included. **γενομ. . . . . σκανδ.** = ἐν καιρῷ πειρασμοῦ ἀφίστανται Luke, thus accommodating themselves to that καιρός. **22.**] In this *third* sort, *all as regards the soil is well;* the seed goes deep, the plant springs up; all is as in the next case, with but one exception, and that, *the bearing of fruit*—**ἄκαρπος γίνεται** = οὐ τελεσφοροῦσι Luke. And this because the seeds or roots of thorns are in, and are suffered to spring up in, the heart, and to overwhelm the plant. There is a divided will, a half-service (μέριμνα from μερίζω, see on ch. vi. 25) which ever ends in the prevalence of evil over good. This class is not confined to the *rich:* πλοῦτος in Scripture is not riches *absolutely*, as possessed, but riches *relatively*, as estimated by the desire and value for them. Mark adds καὶ αἱ περὶ τὰ λοιπὰ ἐπιθυμίαι, viz. the τὰ λοιπά which shall be added to us if we seek first the Kingdom of God and His righteousness. The identity of the *seeds sown* with the individuals of these classes, as maintained above, is strikingly shewn in Luke here: τὸ δὲ εἰς τὰς ἀκάνθας πεσόν, **οὗτοί εἰσιν** οἱ ἀκούσαντες κ.τ.λ. (viii. 14.) We may notice: (I) That there is in these three classes a PROGRESS, and that a *threefold* one:—(1) in TIME:—the first receives a hindrance *at the very outset:* the seed never springs up:—the second *after it has sprung up*, but *soon* after:—the third *when it has entered, sprung up, and come to maturity:* or *while it is so*

23 ὁ δὲ ἐπὶ τὴν καλὴν γῆν σπαρείς, οὗτός ἐστιν ὁ τὸν BCDEF
λόγον ἀκούων καὶ * συνιῶν· ὃς δὴ [d] καρποφορεῖ καὶ GKLMS
[e] ποιεῖ ὁ μὲν ἑκατὸν ὁ δὲ ἑξήκοντα ὁ δὲ τριάκοντα. UVXΓΔ
24 Ἄλλην παραβολὴν [f] παρέθηκεν αὐτοῖς λέγων [g] Ὡμοιώθη ΠℵN 1. 33
ἡ βασιλεία τῶν οὐρανῶν ἀνθρώπῳ σπείραντι καλὸν
σπέρμα ἐν τῷ ἀγρῷ αὐτοῦ. 25 [h] ἐν δὲ τῷ καθεύδειν τοὺς
ἀνθρώπους ἦλθεν αὐτοῦ ὁ ἐχθρὸς καὶ [i] ἐπέσπειρεν [k] ζιζάνια

d ‖. Mark iv. 28. Rom. vii. 4, 5. Col. i. 6, 10 only. Hab. iii. 17. Wisd. x. 7 only.
e ch. iii. 10 reff.
f ver. 31. Exod. xix. 7.
g ch. xi. 15. xviii. 23 al. = Cant. vii. 7. Isa. i. 9. Ezek. xxxi. 8.
h constr., ver. 4 al. fr.
i here only +.
k here, &c. (8 times) only +.

23. rec (for *την καλην γην*) *την γην την καλην* (*see* ‖ *Mark*), with D rel: txt BCLΔℵ 1. 33 Orig. *ακουων* bef *τον λογον* D latt Syr syr-cu. * *συνιείς* BDℵ Orig: *συνιων* C rel. (*συνειων* C, *συνιῶν* EMUXΓΠ, *συνιών* GL, *συνίῶν* K.) for *ος δη*, *τοτε* D lat-*a b c h*: *ος δε* Δ ev-y: *et* vulg lat-*f ff*$_1$ *g*$_{1.2}$ *k*^{2} *l* (and spec) Syr syr-cu æth arm.

24. [*παρεθηκε* is written over an erasure in B. *ομοιωθη* CFΔ ev-y Chr-ms.] rec *σπειροντι*, with CD rel lat-*h* syr-mg-ms Eus$_2$ [Chr]: txt BMX Δ-gr Πℵ 13. 33 latt syrr syr-cu copt æth schol-Orig Ambr. (*It is possible that -αντι might be an emendn to the sense: but far more probable that -οντι came from the foregoing parable: see on ver* 39.) *αγρω εαυτου* B: *ιδιω αγρω* D Eus$_2$.

25. rec (for *επεσπ.*) *εσπειρε* (*mistake?*), with CD-gr rel lat-*e* Iren-gr$_1$; *επεσπαρκεν* ℵ^1: txt Bℵ^2 1. 13. 157 latt arm Iren$_1$[and int$_1$] Clem Orig Nyss Naz Ambr Fulg Zeno

coming.—(2) in APPARENT DEGREE. The climax is *apparently* from *bad* to *better*;—the first *understand not*: the second *understand and feel*: the third *understand, feel, and practise.* But also (3) in REAL DEGREE, from *bad* to *worse*. Less awful is the state of those who *understand not* the word and *lose it immediately*, than that of those who *feel it, receive it with joy*, and in time of trial *fall away*: less awful again this last, than that of those who *understand, feel, and practise*, but are *fruitless and impure*. It has been noticed also that the first is more the fault of *careless inattentive* CHILDHOOD; the second of *ardent shallow* YOUTH; the third of *worldly self-seeking* AGE. (II) That these classes do *not* EXCLUDE *one another*. They are great general divisions, the outer circles of which fall into one another, as they very likely might in the field itself, in their different combinations. **23.**] Here also the *fourth* class must not be understood as a decided well-marked company, excluding all the rest. For the soil is *not good by nature*: the natural man receiveth not the things of the Spirit of God; but every predisposition to receive them is of God:—even the shallow soil covering the rock, even the thorny soil, received its power to take in and vivify the seed, from God. So that divine grace is the enabling, vivifying, cleansing power throughout: and these sown on the good land are no naturally good, amiable, or pure class, but those prepared by divine grace—receptive, by granted receptive power. The sowing is not necessarily the *first* that has ever taken place: the field has been and is continually resown, so that the *care of the husbandman* is presupposed. Again, no irresistible grace or absolute decree of God must be dreamt of here. God working not barely *upon*, but *with* man, is, as we said above, the *μυστήριον τῆς βασιλείας* here declared,—see Jer. iv. 3: Hosea x. 12: Gal. vi. 7. See note on Luke viii. 15. **ἑκατόν, ἑξήκοντα, τριάκοντα**, the different degrees of faithfulness and devotedness of life with which fruit is brought forth by different classes of persons. There is no point of comparison with the different classes in the parable of the *talents*: for he who had five talents yielded the *same* increase as he who had two. **συνιῶν**] So *συνιοῦσιν* ver. 13, and 2 Cor. x. 12 (rec.), and this word itself Rom. iii. 11, from *συνιέω*, i. q. *συνίημι*,—of which the inf. *συνιεῖν* is found in Theognis, 565. It should be accented *συνιῶν*, or *συνίων* (from *συνίω*), not *συνιών*, which would be from *σύνειμι*. See Winer, § 14. 3.

24—30.] SECOND PARABLE. THE TARES OF THE FIELD. *Peculiar to Matthew.* For the explanation of this parable see below, vv. 36—43. **24.**] **ὡμοιώθη . . ἀνθρώπῳ**, '*is like the whole circumstances about to be detailed; like the case of a man*,' &c. A similar form of construction is found in ch. xviii. 23, and in other parables in Matthew. **25.**] **τοὺς ἀνθ.** not, '*the men*' belonging to the owner of

[l]ἀνὰ [l]μέσον τοῦ σίτου καὶ ἀπῆλθεν. 26 ὅτε δὲ [m]ἐβλάστη-
σεν ὁ [n]χόρτος καὶ καρπὸν [e]ἐποίησεν, τότε ἐφάνη καὶ τὰ
[k]ζιζάνια. 27 προσελθόντες δὲ οἱ δοῦλοι τοῦ [o]οἰκοδεσπό-
του εἶπον αὐτῷ Κύριε, οὐχὶ καλὸν σπέρμα ἔσπειρας ἐν τῷ
σῷ ἀγρῷ; πόθεν οὖν ἔχει [k]ζιζάνια; 28 ὁ δὲ ἔφη αὐτοῖς
Ἐχθρὸς [p]ἄνθρωπος τοῦτο ἐποίησεν. οἱ δὲ αὐτῷ λέγουσιν Θέλεις οὖν ἀπελθόντες [q]συλλέξωμεν αὐτά; 29 ὁ δέ
φησιν Οὔ, [r]μήποτε [q]συλλέγοντες τὰ [k]ζιζάνια [s]ἐκριζώσητε
[t]ἅμα αὐτοῖς τὸν σῖτον. 30 ἄφετε [u]συναυξάνεσθαι ἀμφότερα
ἕως τοῦ [v]θερισμοῦ, καὶ ἐν καιρῷ τοῦ [v]θερισμοῦ ἐρῶ τοῖς
[w]θερισταῖς [q]Συλλέξατε πρῶτον τὰ [k]ζιζάνια καὶ δήσατε
αὐτὰ [x]δέσμας πρὸς τὸ [y]κατακαῦσαι αὐτά, τὸν δὲ σῖτον

l = Mark vii. 31. (1 Cor. vi. 5.) Rev. vii. 17 only. Isa. lvii. 5.
m intr., Mark iv. 27. Heb. ix. 4. Isa. xxvii. 6. trans., James v. 18 only. Gen. i. 11.
n = Mark iv. 28. Jer. ix. 22.
o ch. x. 25 reff.
p ch. xi. 19 reff.
q here, &c. (6 times). ch. vii. 16. Luke vi. 44 only. Lev. xix. 9.
r ch. xv. 32 al. Exod. xxxii. 12.
s ch. xv. 13. Luke xvii. 6. Jude 12 only. Jer. i. 10. Zeph. ii. 4.
t Gospp., ch. xx. 1 only. Acts xxiv. 26. xxvii. 40. Paul, Rom. iii. 12 (from Ps. xiii. 3) al5. only.
u here only +. 2 Macc. iv. 4 only.
v John iv. 35 (bis) reff.
w ver. 39 only +. Bel and Dr. 33 only.
x here only. Exod. xii. 22 only. constr., Luke ix. 14.
y ch. iii. 12 reff.

Chrysol. και (2nd) is written above the line by D[1].

26. om 2nd και D 13. 124. 264 lat-*a b c ff*$_2$ *g*$_1$ *h* syr-cu Chr-6-9-η-ρ(and Fd's mss exc H).

27. aft οικοδεσποτου ins εκεινου D. εσπειρες CD rel: εσπειραμεν M: txt BKLSUΓΔΠℵ 33 (1, e sil) [Chr]. rec ins τα bef ζιζανια, with LXℵ[1] syr-mg copt arm-mss: om BCDℵ[2] rel arm-zoh Chr. (33 def.)

28. rec aft οι δε ins δουλοι, with Cℵ rel vulg lat-*f ff*$_1$ syr (æth arm): om B 157 lat-*g*$_2$ copt.—λεγ. αυτω οι δουλοι θελεις D lat-*a b c e ff*$_2$ *g*$_1$ *k* (Syr syr-cu). rec (for αυτω λεγουσιν) ειπον αυτω, with L rel vulg lat-*f ff*$_1$ syr æth arm: λεγ. αυτω Dℵ: txt BC copt. om ουν D 252[1] latt(exc *f*) Syr arm Eulog Aug.

29. rec (for φησιν) εφη, with L rel lat-*a* syr-ed: λεγει αυτοις D 33 lat-*h k* Syr syr-cu æth arm: txt BCℵ vulg lat-*b c f ff*$_{1.2}$ *g*$_{1.2}$ syr-mg-ms. τον σιτον bef αμα αυτοις Scr's i: aft αμα ins συν Γ: αμα και τον σιτον συν αυτοις D 61. 99. 240-3-4 am syr-cu arm.

30. αμφοτερα bef συναυξανεσθαι D latt. rec (for εως) μεχρι, with C ℵ[2](appy) rel Chr-H-K: αχρι Lℵ[1·3](?) Chr-6-η-ρ(and Fd): txt BD Chr-2 Eulog. rec aft εν ins τω (*not required after a preposition*), with CELℵ[1·3](?) syr-cu copt: om BDℵ[2](appy) rel Epiph [Chr-ms]. om 1st αυτα D 24[1]. 125 lat-*e f h k* Epiph Aug. rec ins εις bef δεσμας, with BCℵ rel vulg lat-*ff*$_1$ syr copt æth arm-mss: om DLXΔ 1. 33 am(with em forj gat mm) lat-*a b c* [*e f*] *ff*$_2$ *g*$_{1.2}$ [*h k*] Syr syr-cu arm-zoh Orig Chr-mss(in Matthæi, but see Fd). om 2nd αυτα D 86 latt(not *f k*) arm Aug.

the field, but **men** generally: and the expression is used only to designate '*in the night time*,' not to charge the servants with any want of watchfulness. **ἐπέσπ.**] '*superseminavit*,' **sowed over the first seed. ζιζάνια**, apparently the *darnel*, or *bastard wheat* (lolium album), so often seen in our fields and by our hedgerows; if so, what follows will be explained, that the **tares** appeared when the wheat came into ear, having been previously not noticeable. It appears to be an Eastern word, expressed in the Talmud by זוּנִין. Our Lord was speaking of an act of malice practised in the East:—persons of revengeful disposition watch the ground of a neighbour being ploughed, and in the night following sow destructive weeds. (Roberts's Oriental Illustrations, p. 541, cited by Trench on the Parables, p. 68.) (The practice is not unknown even in England at present. Since the publication of the first edition of this commentary, a field belonging to the Editor, at Gaddesby in Leicestershire, was maliciously sown with charlock (sinapis arvensis) over the wheat. An action at law was brought by the tenant, and heavy damages obtained against the offender.) **29.**] Jerome in loc. says: 'Inter triticum et zizania quod nos appellamus lolium, quamdiu herba est, et nondum culmus venit ad spicam, grandis similitudo est, et in discernendo nulla aut perdifficilis distantia.' Jerome, it must be remembered, resided in Palestine. As regards the construction, ἅμα is not a prep. governing αὐτοῖς, but merely an

z ver. 24.
a ||. ch. xvii. 20. Luke xvii. 6 only.
b (=) as above (a). John xii. 24. 1 Cor. xv. 37 only ‡. Lam. iv. 5 only.)
c as above (a) only †.
d ch. xxvii. 24, 48. Num. iii. 6.
e ch. xi. 11 reff.
f pass., 1 Pet. ii. 2 (or mid., Mark iv. 8. 2 Cor. x. 5. Col. i. 6, 10) only. Exod. i. 7. trans., 1 Cor. iii. 6, 7. 2 Cor. ix. 10 only. intr., ch. vi. 28. Luke i. 80 al. fr., but never in LXX.
g || Mk. Luke xi. 42. Rom. xiv. 2 only. Gen. ix. 3. 3 Kings xx. (xxi.) 2. Ps. xxxvi. 2. Prov. xv. 17 only.
h ch. vi. 26 reff.
i ||. Acts ii. 26 only. Ps. ciii. 12.
k ||. ch. xxi. 8. xxiv. 32. Mark xiii. 28. Rom. xi. 16, &c. only. Ezek. xxxi. 7. Dan. iv. 9 (12) &c.

[y] συναγάγετε εἰς τὴν [y] ἀποθήκην μου. 31 Ἄλλην παρα- BCDEF
βολὴν [z] παρέθηκεν αὐτοῖς λέγων Ὁμοία ἐστὶν ἡ βασιλεία GKLMS UVXΓΔ
τῶν οὐρανῶν [ab] κόκκῳ [ac] σινάπεως, ὃν [d] λαβὼν ἄνθρωπος ΠА 1. 33
ἔσπειρεν ἐν τῷ ἀγρῷ αὐτοῦ. 32 ὃ [e] μικρότερον μέν ἐστιν
πάντων τῶν σπερμάτων· ὅταν δὲ [f] αὐξηθῇ, μεῖζον τῶν
[g] λαχάνων ἐστὶν καὶ γίνεται δένδρον, ὥςτε ἐλθεῖν τὰ
[h] πετεινὰ τοῦ [h] οὐρανοῦ καὶ [i] κατασκηνοῖν ἐν τοῖς [k] κλάδοις

for συναγαγετε, συναγετε BΓ 1: συνλεγεται (= -τε) D. αποθην (sic) D¹(corrd D²).
31. for παρεθηκεν, ελαλησεν D 1. 13. 124 lat-*a b c f ff*$_2$ *h* syr-cu (so also L, but παρεθ. substituted by original scribe).
32. om των (aft παντων) D¹(ins D⁷) 124. αυξηση D א³(appy, but corrd) 13. 124. 346. μειζων D-gr Scr's f s w evv-H-z$_1$ [Chr-ms]. ins παντων bef των λαχανων (*from* || *Mark*) KΠ (76-7 e sil) 157. 218 37-41-2 Scr's a d l m n o p q r s² w ev-z$_1$ latt syrr syr-cu æth Euthym Hil Ambr. rec κατασκηνουν (for -νοιν), with B²(sic) Cא rel: txt B¹(sic in cod) D.

adv. used for elucidation; see Klotz, Devar. p. 97. Still the construction here would hardly bear its omission.

31, 32.] THIRD PARABLE. THE GRAIN OF MUSTARD SEED. Mark iv. 30—34. Luke xiii. 18, 19. On the connexion of this parable with the two last, Chrysostom observes (Hom. in Matt. xlvi. 2, p. 483), ἐπειδὴ γὰρ εἶπεν ὅτι ἀπὸ τοῦ σπόρου τρία μέρη ἀπόλλυται, καὶ σώζεται ἕν, καὶ ἐν αὐτῷ πάλιν τῷ σωζομένῳ τοσαύτη γίνεται βλάβη, ἵνα μὴ λέγωσι 'καὶ τίνες καὶ πόσοι ἔσονται οἱ πιστοί;' καὶ τοῦτον ἐξαιρεῖ τὸν φόβον, διὰ τῆς παραβολῆς τοῦ σινάπεως ἐνάγων εἰς πίστιν αὐτοὺς καὶ δεικνὺς ὅτι πάντως ἐκταθήσεται τὸ πρᾶγμα. The comparison of kingdoms to *trees* was familiar to the Jews: see Dan. iv. 10—12, 20—22: Ezek. xxxi. 3—9; xvii. 22—24: Ps. lxxx. 8—11. **31.**] **ἐν τ. ἀγρῷ** = εἰς τ. κῆπ. Luke.

32. μικρότερον κ.τ.λ.] **less than all**, not for the superlative. The words are not to be pressed to their literal sense, as the mustard seed was a well-known Jewish type for any thing exceedingly small.

The mustard tree attains to a large size in Judæa. Lightfoot quotes (Hor. Hebr. in l.) Hieros. Peah. fol. 20. 2, 'Caulis erat sinapis in Sichin, e quo enati sunt rami tres; e quibus unus decerptus cooperuit tentoriolum figuli, produxitque tres cabos sinapis. Rabbi Simeon ben Chalaphta dixit, Caulis sinapis erat mihi in agro meo, in quam ego scandere solitus sum, ita ut scandere solent in ficum.'

This parable, like most others respecting the kingdom of God, has a *double reference—general* and *individual*. (1) In the *general* sense, the insignificant beginnings of the kingdom are set forth: the little babe cast in the manger at Bethlehem; the Man of sorrows with no place to lay His Head; the crucified One; or again the hundred and twenty names who were the seed of the Church after the Lord had ascended; then we have the Kingdom of God waxing onward and spreading its branches here and there, and different nations coming into it. "He must increase," said the great Forerunner. We must beware however of imagining that the *outward Church-form* is this Kingdom. It has rather *reversed* the parable, and is the worldly power waxed to a great tree and the Churches taking refuge under the shadow of it. It may be, where not corrupted by error and superstition, subservient to the growth of the heavenly plant: but is not itself that plant. It is at best no more than (to change the figure) the scaffolding to aid the building, not the building itself. (2) The *individual* application of the parable points to the small beginnings of divine grace; a word, a thought, a passing sentence, may prove to be the little seed which eventually fills and shadows the whole heart and being, and calls 'all thoughts, all passions, all delights' to come and shelter under it. Jerome has a comment on this parable (in loc.) too important to be passed over: 'Prædicatio Evangelii minima est omnibus disciplinis. Ad primam quippe doctrinam, fidem non habet veritatis, hominem Deum, Deum mortuum, et scandalum crucis prædicans. Confer hujuscemodi doctrinam dogmatibus Philosophorum et

αὐτοῦ. 33 Ἄλλην παραβολὴν ἐλάλησεν αὐτοῖς, Ὁμοία
ἐστὶν ἡ βασιλεία τῶν οὐρανῶν [l] ζύμῃ, ἣν [d] λαβοῦσα γυνὴ
[m] ἐνέκρυψεν εἰς [n] ἀλεύρου [o] σάτα τρία, ἕως οὗ [p] ἐζυμώθη

l ||. ch. xvi. 6 ||, 11, 12. Luke xii. 1. 1 Cor. v. 6, &c. (4 times). Gal. v. 9 only. Exod. xii. 15 al. fr.
m here (& || L. v. r.) only. Ezek iv. 12 vat. (-φία, ib. Gen. xviii. 6.) n || only. 3 Kings iv. 22.
o || only †. Gen xviii. 6 Aq and Sym (there also w. τρία). p ||. 1 Cor. v. 6. Gal. v. 9 only. Hos. vii. 4.

33. for ελαλησεν αυτοις, παρεθηκεν αυτοις C 243 : om D 76 lat-*k* syr-cu : txt Bא rel syrr.—add λεγων CLMUXא am lat-g_2 *h l* arm.

libris eorum, et splendori eloquentiæ, et compositioni sermonum, et videbis quanto minor sit cæteris seminibus sementis Evangelii. Sed illa cum creverit, nihil mordax, nihil vividum, nihil vitale demonstrat, sed totum flaccidum, marcidumque et mollitum ebullit in olera et in herbas quæ cito arescunt et corruunt. Hæc autem prædicatio quæ parva videbatur in principio, cum vel in anima credentis, vel in toto mundo sata fuerit, non exsurgit in olera, sed crescit in arborem.'

33.] FOURTH PARABLE. THE LEAVEN. Luke xiii. 20, 21. Difficulties have been raised as to the interpretation of this parable which do not seem to belong to it. It has been questioned whether **ζύμη** must not be taken in the sense in which it so often occurs in Scripture, as symbolic of *pollution* and *corruption*. See Exod. xii. 15, and other enactments of the kind, passim in the law; and ch. xvi. 6 : 1 Cor. v. 6, 7. And some few have taken it thus, and explained the parable of the *progress of corruption and deterioration* in the outward visible Church. But then, how is it said that the *Kingdom of Heaven is like* this leaven? For the construction is not the same as in ver. 24, where the similitude is to the *whole course of things related*, but answers to κόκκῳ σινάπεως, ὃν λαβὼν ἄνθ. : so ζύμῃ, ἣν λαβοῦσα γυνή. Again, if the progress of the Kingdom of Heaven be *towards corruption, till the whole is corrupted*, surely there is an end of all the blessings and healing influence of the Gospel on the world. It will be seen that such an interpretation cannot for a moment stand, on its *own* ground; but much less when we connect it with the parable preceding. The two are intimately related. *That* was of the *inherent self-developing power* of the Kingdom of Heaven as a seed containing in itself the principle of expansion; *this*, of the *power which it possesses of penetrating and assimilating a foreign mass*, till all be taken up into it. And the comparison is not only to the *power* but to the *effect* of leaven also, which has its *good* as well as its bad side, and for that good is used : viz. to make wholesome and fit for use that which would otherwise be heavy and insalubrious. Another striking point of comparison is in the fact that leaven, as used ordinarily, is a *piece of the leavened loaf* put amongst the new dough—(τὸ ζυμωθὲν ἅπαξ ζύμη γίνεται τῷ λοιπῷ πάλιν. Chrys. Hom. xlvi. 2, p. 484)—just as the Kingdom of Heaven is the renewal of humanity by the righteous Man Christ Jesus. The Parable, like the last, has its *general* and its *individual* application: (1) in the penetrating of the *whole mass of humanity*, by degrees, by the influence of the Spirit of God, so strikingly witnessed in the earlier ages by the dropping of heathen customs and worship :—in modern times more gradually and secretly advancing, but still to be plainly seen in the various abandonments of criminal and unholy practices (as e. g. in our own time of slavery and duelling, and the increasing abhorrence of war among Christian men), and without doubt in the end to be signally and universally manifested. But this effect again is not to be traced in the establishment or history of so-called Churches, but in the hidden advancement, without observation, of that deep leavening power which works irrespective of human forms and systems. (2) In the transforming power of the 'new leaven' on the whole being of individuals. "In fact the Parable does nothing less than set forth to us the mystery of regeneration, both in its first act, which can be but once, as the leaven is but once hidden; and also in the consequent (subsequent?) renewal by the Holy Spirit, which, as the ulterior working of the leaven, is continual and progressive." (Trench, p. 97.) Some have contended for this as the sole application of the parable; but not, I think, rightly. As to whether the **γυνή** has any especial meaning, (though I am more and more convinced that such considerations are not always to be passed by as nugatory,) it will hardly be of much consequence here to enquire, seeing that γυναῖκες σιτοποιοί would be every where a matter of course. **ἐγκρύπτω** has given rise to a technical word **ἐγκρυφίας**, signifying a *leavened cake* (which however, Passow, Lex. explains to be a cake *baked under hot ashes*, thus applying the ἐγκρύπτω differently : cf. ref. Ezek.). See

q ch. v. 2 reff. Psa. lxxvii. 2.
r here only. Ps. xviii. 2. (ἐξερ., Ps. cxviii. 171.)
s absol., here only. = Luke xi. 50 al. elsw. in N. T. w. κόσμου, exc. Heb. xi. 11 †. (2 Macc. ii. 29 only.)
t = Mark iv. 36 al. fr. Ps. civ. 20.
u ch. xv. 15 only. Job vi. 24. xii. 8 only.
v ver. 25, &c. only †.
w = N. T. passim ‡. Wisd. xi. 17 al.

ὅλον. 34 Ταῦτα πάντα ἐλάλησεν ὁ Ἰησοῦς ἐν παραβολαῖς τοῖς ὄχλοις, καὶ χωρὶς παραβολῆς οὐδὲν ἐλάλει
αὐτοῖς, 35 ὅπως πληρωθῇ τὸ ῥηθὲν διὰ τοῦ προφήτου
λέγοντος q Ἀνοίξω ἐν παραβολαῖς τὸ q στόμα μου, r ἐρεύ-
ξομαι κεκρυμμένα ἀπὸ s καταβολῆς.
36 Τότε t ἀφεὶς τοὺς ὄχλους ἦλθεν εις τὴν οἰκίαν. καὶ
προσῆλθον αὐτῷ οἱ μαθηταὶ αὐτοῦ λέγοντες u * Φράσον
ἡμῖν τὴν παραβολὴν τῶν v ζιζανίων τοῦ ἀγροῦ. 37 ὁ δὲ
ἀποκριθεὶς εἶπεν Ὁ σπείρων τὸ καλὸν σπέρμα ἔστιν ὁ υἱὸς
τοῦ ἀνθρώπου, 38 ὁ δὲ ἀγρὸς ἔστιν ὁ w κόσμος, τὸ δὲ

BCDEF GKLMS UVXΓΔ Πℵ 1. 33

34. rec (for *ουδεν*) *ουκ* (*from* ‖ *Mark*), with Dℵ[3a] rel latt Syr syr-cu copt(appy) æth $Orig_1$(and int_1) Eus_2 Tert: txt BCMΔℵ[1] lat-*f* syr arm Clem $Orig_1$ Chr_2. **ελαλησεν** (*from above*) Δℵ[1](txt ℵ[3a]).

35. ins *ησαιου* bef *προφητου* (*false gloss*) ℵ[1](om ℵ[2]) 1. 13. 33. 124. 253 [æth-ms] hom-Cl; also mss mentd by Eus, Jer, and Porph, and in catena on Psalms: Jer conjectures *ασαφ*. rec aft *καταβολης* ins *κοσμου* (*explanatory gloss: see also ch* xxv. 34), with CDℵ[1] rel latt [syrr copt] hom-Cl [Chr]: om B ℵ[2](but re-insd) 1 lat-*e k* syr-cu æth (Orig).

36. **εισηλθεν** ℵ Orig. rec aft *οικιαν* ins *ο ιησους* (*beginning of an ecclesiastical lection*), with C rel lat-*f h* syrr: aft *ηλθ.* Γ; *αυτου* 1. 118 evv-H-Y-13-14-18 $Orig_4$ Chr: om BDℵ latt syr-cu copt æth $Orig_2$. **προσηλθαν** B 33: -**θεν** ℵ[1](but corrd to txt).

* διασάφησον (*the verb occurs only here and in ch* xviii. 31) Bℵ[1] $Orig_1$, *enarra* lat-*a b* g_1 *h*: *φρασον* CDℵ[3a] rel $Orig_4$. (*dissere* vulg lat-*c f* ff_1 g_2 [*narra* lat-ff_2 *k*].)

37. rec aft *ειπεν* ins *αυτοις*, with C rel gat lat-*c f* g_2 *h* syrr syr-cu arm [Chr]: om BDℵ am(with em forj fuld) lat-*a b* $ff_{1.2}$ g_1 *k l* copt æth Orig(appy).

reff. **σάτον**, סְאָה (Aram. סָאתָא), = the third part of an ephah = *μόδιον καὶ ἥμισυ Ἰταλικόν*, Jos. Antt. ix. 4. 5. Three of these, an ephah, appears to have been the usual quantity prepared for a baking: see Gen. xviii. 6: Judg. vi. 19: 1 Sam. i. 24. This being the case, we need not perhaps seek for any symbolical interpretation: though Olsh.'s hint that the *body, soul,* and *spirit* may perhaps be here intended can hardly but occur to us, and Stier's, that "of the *three sons of Noah* was the whole earth overspread," is worth recording.

34, 35.] Conclusion of the parables spoken to the multitudes. Mark iv. 33, 34. **34. καὶ χωρ. π. οὐδ. ἐλ.**] *κατὰ τὸν καιρὸν ἐκεῖνον δηλαδή· πολλὰ γὰρ πολλάκις ἐλάλησεν αὐτοῖς δίχα παραβολῆς.* Euthym. **35. ὅπως πλ.**] in **order that** &c., not '*so that thus,*' or '*and in this way*' (?) as Webst. and Wilk.,—here, or any where else. See note on ch. i. 22. The *prophet*, according to the superscription of Psalm lxxviii., is Asaph, so called 2 Chron. xxix. 30, LXX. The former clause of the citation is identical with the LXX; the latter = *φθέγξομαι προβλήματα ἀπ' ἀρχῆς*, LXX. When we find De Wette, &c. maintaining that the Psalm *contains no parable*, and that consequently these words can only be cited *out of* their context, we must remember that such a view is wholly inconsistent with any deep insight into the meaning of the Scripture record: for the whole Psalm consists of a recounting of events which St. Paul assures us *τύποι ἡμῶν ἐγενήθησαν . . . . . τυπικῶς συνέβαινον ἐκείνοις, ἐγράφη δὲ πρὸς νουθεσίαν ἡμῶν.* 1 Cor. x. 6, 11.

36—43.] Interpretation of the parable of the tares of the field. *Peculiar to Matthew.* **38.**] This verse has been variously interpreted, notwithstanding that its statements are so plain. The consideration of it will lead us into that of the general nature and place of the parable itself. **The field is the world**; if understood of the Church, then the Church only as *commensurate with the world*, *πορευθέντες εἰς* **τὸν κόσμον ἅπαντα** *κηρύξατε τὸ εὐαγγέλιον πάσῃ τῇ κτίσει* (Mark xvi. 15); the Church *standing for* the world, not, the *world* for the *Church*. (This latter view, Stier says, Augustine upholds against the Donatists: but I cannot find it in his Ep. contra Donatistas (vol. ix.), where he several times plainly asserts the field to be

καλὸν σπέρμα, οὗτοί εἰσιν οἱ [xy] υἱοὶ τῆς [y] βασιλείας, τὰ δὲ
[v] ζιζάνια εἰσὶν οἱ [z] υἱοὶ τοῦ [za] πονηροῦ, 39 ὁ δὲ ἐχθρὸς ὁ
σπείρας αὐτὰ ἔστιν ὁ [b] διάβολος, ὁ δὲ [c] θερισμὸς [d] συντέ-

x = ch. ix. 15. Luke xx. 34, 36 reff. Ezek. xxx. 5. 1 Macc. iv. 2.
y ch. viii. 12 only.
z see Acts xiii. 10. a masc., ver. 19 reff. b ch. iv. 1 reff. Zech. iii. 1. c ver. 30.
d (in N. T. always w. αἰ.) ver. 49. ch. xxiv. 3. xxviii. 20. Heb. ix. 26 only. Deut. xi. 12. Dan. xii. 4, 13.

39. om *αυτα* D lat-ff_1. *εστιν* bef *ο σπειρας αυτα* B. (B does not om *ο* bef

commensurate with the world, and the Church to be the 'triticum inter zizania.') And the parable has, like the former ones, its various references to various counterworkings of the Evil One against the grace of God. Its two principal references are, (1) to *the whole history of the world* from beginning to end; the coming of sin into the world by the malice of the devil, the mixed state of mankind, notwithstanding the development of God's purposes by the dispensations of grace,—and the final separation of the good and evil at the end. The very declaration 'the harvest is the *end* of the world' suggests the original sowing as the *beginning* of it. Yet this sowing is not in the fact, as in the parable, *one only*, but repeated again and again. In the parable the Lord gathers as it were the whole human race into *one lifetime*, as they will be gathered in one harvest, and sets that forth as simultaneous, which has been scattered over the ages of time. But (2) as applying principally to the *βασ. τ. οὐρ.* which lay in the future and began with the Lord's incarnation, the parable sets forth to us *the universal sowing of* GOOD SEED *by the Gospel*: it sows *no bad* seed: all this is done by the enemy, and further we may not enquire. Soon, even as soon as Acts v. in the history of the Church, did the tares begin to appear; and in remarkable coincidence with the wheat bringing forth fruit (see Acts iv. 32—37). Again, see Acts xiii. 10, where Paul calls Elymas by the very name *υἱὸς διαβόλου*. And ever since, the same has been the case; throughout the whole world, where the Son of Man sows good seed, the Enemy sows tares. And *it is not the office*, however much it may be the desire, of the servants of the householder, the labourers in His field, to *collect* or *root up* these tares, to put them out of the world literally, or of the Church spiritually (save in some few exceptional cases, such as that in Acts v.); *this is reserved for another time and for other hands*,—for the *harvest*, the *end*; for the *reapers*, the *angels*. (3) It is also most important to notice that, as the Lord here gathers up ages into one season of seed time and harvest, so He also gathers up the various changes of human character and shiftings of human will into *two distinct classes*. We are not to suppose that the wheat can never become tares, or the tares wheat: this would be to contradict the purpose of Him who willeth not the death of a sinner, but rather that he should be converted and live; and this gracious purpose shines through the command *ἄφετε συναυξάνεσθαι ἀμφότερα*—let time be given (as above) for the *leaven to work*. As in the parable of the sower, the various classes were the *concentrations of various dispositions*, all of which are frequently found in one and the same individual, so here the line of demarcation between wheat and tares, so fixed and impassable *at last*, is, *during the probation time*, the time of *συναύξησις*, *not yet determined* by Him who *will have all to be saved, and to come to the knowledge of the truth*. In the very first example, that of our first parents, the good seed degenerated, but their restoration and renewal was implied in the promises made to them, and indeed in their very punishment itself; and we their progeny are by nature the children of wrath, till renewed by the same grace. The parable is delivered by the Lord as *knowing all things*, and *describing by the final result*; and gives no countenance whatever to predestinarian error. (4) The parable has an historical importance, having been much in the mouths and writings of the Donatists, who, maintaining that the Church is a perfectly holy congregation, denied the applicability of this Scripture to convict them of error, seeing that it is spoken not of the Church but of the world: missing the deeper truth which would have led them to see that, after all, the world *is the Church*, only overrun by these very tares. **τὸ δὲ καλὸν σπ., οὗτοί εἰσιν** strikingly sets forth again the identity of the seed, in its growth, with those who are the *plants*: see above on ver. 19. **οἱ υἱοὶ τ. βασ.**] not in the same sense as in ch. viii. 12,—SONS *there*, by covenant and external privilege: *here*,—by the effectual grace of adoption: the KINGDOM, *there*, in mere paradigm, on this imperfect earth: *here*, in its true accomplishment.

e ver. 30 only †. Bel and Dr. 33 only.
f ver. 28 reff.
g see ver. 22 reff.
h ch. xvi. 23. Rom. xiv. 13. 1 John ii. 10. Josh. xxiii. 13. Judg. ii. 3. Wisd. xiv. 11.
i 1 John iii. 4 only. Ps. xxxvi. 1.
j ch. vii. 23 reff.
k ver. 50 only. Dan. iii. 6, &c.
l as above (k). Rev. i. 15. ix. 2 only. Job xli. 11.
m ch. viii. 12 reff.
n here only. Ezek. xliii. 2. Dan. xii. 3 Theod.-A.
o see Luke xii. 32.
p ch. ii. 11 reff. Prov. ii. 4.
q = ch. xiv. 26. xviii. 7. Luke xxiv. 41. John xxi. 6. Acts xii. 14 al. 2 Chron. v. 6. Ps. cvi. 34.
r ch. xiv. 15 al. Gen. xli. 57. Deut. ii. 6. Isa. lv. 1.

λεια αἰῶνός ἐστιν, οἱ δὲ [e] θερισταὶ ἄγγελοί εἰσιν. 40 ὥσπερ
οὖν [f] συλλέγεται τὰ [v] ζιζάνια καὶ πυρὶ καίεται, οὕτως
ἔσται ἐν τῇ [d] συντελείᾳ τοῦ [g] αἰῶνος [τούτου]. 41 ἀποστε- P εν τῃ.
λεῖ ὁ υἱὸς τοῦ ἀνθρώπου τοὺς ἀγγέλους αὐτοῦ, καὶ [f] συλ- BCDEF GKLM
λέξουσιν ἐκ τῆς βασιλείας αὐτοῦ πάντα τὰ [h] σκάνδαλα καὶ PSUVX ΓΔΠℵ 1.
τοὺς [i] ποιοῦντας τὴν [ij] ἀνομίαν, 42 καὶ βαλοῦσιν αὐτοὺς 33
εἰς τὴν [kl] κάμινον τοῦ [k] πυρός· ἐκεῖ ἔσται ὁ [m] κλαυθμὸς
καὶ ὁ [m] βρυγμὸς τῶν ὀδόντων. 43 τότε οἱ δίκαιοι [n] ἐκλάμψουσιν ὡς ὁ ἥλιος ἐν τῇ [o] βασιλείᾳ τοῦ [o] πατρὸς
αὐτῶν. ὁ ἔχων ὦτα ἀκουέτω.
44 Ὁμοία ἐστὶν ἡ βασιλεία τῶν οὐρανῶν [p] θησαυρῷ
κεκρυμμένῳ ἐν τῷ ἀγρῷ, ὃν εὑρὼν ἄνθρωπος ἔκρυψεν·
καὶ [q] ἀπὸ τῆς χαρᾶς αὐτοῦ ὑπάγει καὶ πωλεῖ πάντα ὅσα
ἔχει, καὶ [r] ἀγοράζει τὸν ἀγρὸν ἐκεῖνον. 45 Πάλιν ὁμοία

διαβ. as Btly.) rec ins του bef αιωνος, with Cℵ[3a] rel copt ($Orig_1$): του αι. τουτου G: η συντ. του αι. Scr's g i s ev-y Chr (*corrns: the articles are omd before the verb*): txt BD ℵ-corr[1] 13. 33. 124 $Orig_1$. (homœotel in ℵ[1] δε θερισμ. to δε θεριστ.)

40. συνλεγονται D. rec **κατα**καιεται (*from ver* 30), with Bℵ 1 [Cyr_1], κατακαιονται D: txt C rel Chr Damasc. om τουτου (*to conform to ver* 39) BDΓℵ 1 latt syr-cu æth arm Cyr Iren-int Orig-int Hil Lucif Aug: ins CP rel lat-*f h* syrr copt [Chr].

41. om 1st αυτου Fℵ. **42.** βαλλουσιν D[1]X ℵ[1](but corrd) fuld lat-*e*.

43. for εκλαμ., λαμψουσιν D 124. 238 Orig. rec aft ωτα ins ακουειν, with CDPℵ[3a] rel vulg lat-*c f* $ff_{1.2}$ $g_{1.2}$ *h* [syrr syr-cu copt] Orig Hil: om Bℵ[1] am(with forj) lat-*a b e k* Hil-mss. (*cf ver* 9 *var read.*)

44. rec ins παλιν bef ομοια (*from vv* 45, 47), with CP rel lat-*f h* syrr arm Orig Hil: ομ. δε ℵ[2]: om BDℵ[1] latt syr-cu copt æth. om εν τω αγρω ℵ[1](ins ℵ-corr[1]): om τω D Scr's d h i l m n u evv-H-z Chr. for ανθρωπος, τις D. rec παντα οσα εχει bef πωλει (*see Mark* x. 21), with CP rel lat-*b* syr æth arm $Orig_1$: txt (B)Dℵ 1 latt Syr syr-cu copt $Orig_1$[-int].—om παντα B 38. 61. 113. 248 arm-mss $Orig_1$ (*see Mark* x. 21).

in the new heavens and earth wherein dwelleth righteousness: but in their state among the tares, waiting for the manifestation of the sons of God. **41. τὰ σκάνδ.**] generally understood of those men who give cause of offence, tempters and hinderers of others: Stier would rather understand it of *things*, as well as men, who are afterwards designated. On **ὁ κλ. κ. ὁ βρ.**, see note at ch. viii. 12. **43. ἐκλάμψουσιν**] **shall shine out** (their light here being enfeebled and obscured), as the sun from a cloud. **τοῦ πατρός**, answering to *οἱ υἱοί*, ver. 38. This sublime announcement is over and above the interpretation of the parable.

44.] Fifth parable. The hidden treasure. *Peculiar to Matthew.* This and the following parable are closely connected, and refer to two distinct classes of persons who become possessed of the treasure of the Gospel. Notice that these, as also the seventh and last, are spoken *not to the multitude but to the disciples.*

In this parable, a man, labouring perchance for another, or by accident in passing, finds a treasure which has been hidden in a field; from joy at having found it he goes, and selling all he has, buys the field, thus (by the Jewish law) becoming the possessor also of the treasure. Such hiding of treasure is common even now, and was much more common in the East (see Jer. xli. 8 (cf. Hitzig in loc.): Job iii. 21: Prov. ii. 4). This sets before us the case of a man who unexpectedly, without earnest seeking, finds, in some part of the outward Church, the treasure of true faith and hope and communion with God; and having found this, for joy of it he becomes possessor, not of the treasure without the field (for that the case supposes impossible) but of the field at all hazards, to secure the treasure which is in it: i. e. he possesses himself of the means of grace provided in that branch of the

ἐστὶν ἡ βασιλεία τῶν οὐρανῶν [s] ἀνθρώπῳ [t] ἐμπόρῳ ζητοῦντι [u] καλοὺς [v] μαργαρίτας· 46 εὑρὼν δὲ ἕνα [w] πολύ-
τιμον [v] μαργαρίτην, ἀπελθὼν [x] πέπρακεν πάντα ὅσα εἶχεν,
καὶ [r] ἠγόρασεν αὐτόν. 47 Πάλιν ὁμοία ἐστὶν ἡ βασιλεία
τῶν οὐρανῶν [y] σαγήνῃ βληθείσῃ εἰς τὴν θάλασσαν καὶ
ἐκ παντὸς [z] γένους [a] συναγαγούσῃ, 48 ἣν ὅτε ἐπληρώθη
[b] ἀναβιβάσαντες [αὐτὴν] ἐπὶ τὸν [c] αἰγιαλὸν [καὶ] [d] καθί-

s vv. 28, 52. ch. xx. 1. John ix. 16 b al. Gen. ix. 20 al.
t Rev. xviii. 3, 11, 15, 23 only. Gen. xxiii. 16.
u = Luke xxi. 5. Gen. ii. 12.
v ch. vii. 6 reff +
w John xii. 3 (: v. r.). 1 Pet. i. 7 only +.
x ch. xviii. 25. xxvi. 9 ||. Acts ii. 45. iv. 34. v. 4. Rom. vii. 14 only. Deut. xxi. 14 al. perf. as aor., Rev. v. 7. vii. 14. viii. 5. Winer, § 40. 4.
y here only. Isa. xix. 8 al.
z = Mark ix. 29 [: Mt.?]. 1 Cor. xii. 10, 28. xiv. 10 only. (Mark vii. 26 al.) Gen i. 11, &c.
a ch. iii. 12. xxv. 24 al. Hab. i. 15.
b here only. Gen. xxxvii. 28.
c ver. 2 reff.
d intr., ch. v. 1 al. 2 Kings vii. 1.

45. om *ανθρωπω* (*passed over as superfluous*) Bℵ[1](ins ℵ[2]) 50-9 Chr Ambr.

46. rec (for *ευρων δε*) *ος ευρων* (*simplification*), with CP rel lat-*f* syr copt [Chr Cyr_1]: txt BDLℵ 1. 33 latt Syr syr-cu æth arm Cyr_1 Cypr. om *ενα* (*as superfluous*) D 32 lat-*a b e* g_1 *h* syr-cu copt Cypr. for *πεπρακεν*, *επωλησεν* D. for *παντα οσα*, *α* D lat-*a c* ff_2 *h*.

48. for *ἣν ὅτε*, *οτε δε* D lat-*a b f* ff_2 g_1 *h* Ambr Aug. *ανεβιβασαν* (for *-σαντες*) D lat-*a b f* ff_2 g_1 *h*. rec om *αυτην*, with BCℵ rel vulg lat-*c* ff_1 æth arm [Cyr_2]: ins DPSΔ Scr's s lat-*a b e f* ff_2 g_1 *h* Syr syr-cu Ambr Aug. (*The Hellenistic constr has been altered*, (1) *by οτε δε* &c: (2) *by omg αυτην*.) rec ins *και*, with BDPℵ[1.3](?) rel lat-*b e f* ff_2 g_1 *h* syrr syr-cu copt æth arm; bef *επι* Cℵ[2] 1 vulg lat-*c* ff_1 g_2 Cyr Orig-int: om L 13. 124. 346 lat-*a*.

Church, where, to use a common expression, he has "gotten his good:" he makes that field his own. **45, 46.**] Sixth parable. The pearl of great price. In this parable our Lord sets before us, that although in ordinary cases of finding 'the truth as it is in Jesus,' the buying of the field is the necessary prelude to becoming duly and properly possessed of it; yet there are cases, and those of a nobler kind, where such condition is not necessary. We have here a *merchantman*,—one whose business it is,—*on the search* for goodly pearls; i.e. a man who intellectually and spiritually is a seeker of truth of the highest kind. "He whom this pursuit occupies, is a merchantman; i.e. one trained, as well as devoted, to business. The search is therefore determinate, discriminate, unremitting. This case then corresponds to such Christians only as from youth have been trained up in the way which they should go. In these alone can be the settled habits, the effectual self-direction, the convergence to one point of all the powers and tendencies of the soul, which are indicated by the illustration." (Knox's Remains, i. 460.) But as the same writer goes on to observe, even here there is *a discovery*, at a particular time. The person has been seeking, and finding, goodly pearls; what is true, honest, just, pure, lovely, and of good report: but at last he finds *one pearl* of great price—the efficacious principle of inward and spiritual life. We hear of no emotion, no great joy of heart, as before; but the same decision of conduct; he sells all and buys it. He chooses vital Christianity, at whatever cost, for his portion. But here is no *field*. The pearl is bought pure—by itself. It is found, not unexpectedly in the course of outward ordinances,—with which therefore it would become to the finder inseparably bound up,—but by diligent search, spiritual and immediate, in its highest and purest form. Trench instances (Parables, p. 100) Nathanael and the Samaritan woman as examples of the finders without seeking;—Augustine, as related in his Confessions (we might add St. Paul, see Phil. iii. 7), of the diligent seeker and finder. Compare with this parable Prov. ii. 3—9, and to see what kind of buying is *not* meant, Isa. lv. 1: ch. xxv. 9, 10. Also see Rev. iii. 18.

47—52.] Seventh parable. The draw-net. *Peculiar to Matthew.*

47.] **σαγήνη** is a drag, or **draw-net**, drawn over the bottom of the water, and permitting nothing to escape it. The leading idea of this parable is the ultimate separation of the holy and unholy in the Church, with a view to the selection of the former for the master's use. We may notice that the *fishermen* are kept out of view and never mentioned: the comparison not extending to them. A net is cast into the sea and gathers of every kind (of *fish*: not of *things*, as mud, weeds, &c., as Stier supposes); when this is full, it is

e vv. 28, 30, &c.
f here only. Deut. xxiv. 2 (xxiii. 24) al. (-γεῖον, ch. xxv. 4. 1 Kings ix. 7.)
g ch. vii. 17, 18 reff.
h vv. 39, 40 reff.
i ch. xxv. 32 bis. Acts xiii. 2 al. Lev. xx. 25.
k Acts xvii. 33. xxiii. 10. 1 Cor. v. 2. 2 Cor. vi. 17, from Isa. lii. 11. Col. ii. 14. 2 Thess. ii. 7 only. Jer. xxviii. (li.) 6.
l ver. 42 (reff.).
m Luke ii. 50. xxiv. 45 al. Neh. viii. 8. Hos. xiv. 10.

σαντες [e] συνέλεξαν τὰ καλὰ εἰς [f] ἄγγη, τὰ δὲ [g] σαπρὰ ἔξω
ἔβαλον. 49 οὕτως ἔσται ἐν τῇ [h] συντελείᾳ τοῦ αἰῶνος.
ἐξελεύσονται οἱ ἄγγελοι καὶ [i] ἀφοριοῦσιν τοὺς πονηροὺς
[k] ἐκ μέσου τῶν δικαίων, 50 [l] καὶ βαλοῦσιν αὐτοὺς εἰς τὴν
[l] κάμινον τοῦ [l] πυρός· ἐκεῖ ἔσται ὁ [l] κλαυθμὸς καὶ ὁ
[l] βρυγμὸς τῶν ὀδόντων. 51 [m] Συνήκατε ταῦτα πάντα; ...οδοντων P.
λέγουσιν αὐτῷ Ναί. 52 ὁ δὲ εἶπεν αὐτοῖς Διὰ τοῦτο πᾶς BCDEF GKLM SUVXΓ ΔΠℵ 1. 33

for καλα, καλλιστα D lat-a b ff$_2$ g$_1$ syr-cu arm Ambr Aug. rec (for αγγη) αγγεια, with Δ rel Orig$_1$: τα αγγια D: αγια L: αγγια C[3]PX: αγγειον 33: txt BC[1]M[2]ℵ 1. 124 Orig$_3$ Cyr [?] Isid. εβαλαν D: εβαλλον VΔℵ[1](txt ℵ[2], appy) Scr's q r.
49. for αιωνος, κοσμου D. **50.** βαλλουσιν D[1]-gr Xℵ: txt D-corr ℵ[2](appy).
51. rec (at beg) ins λεγει αυτοις ο ιησους, with C rel lat-f h syrr arm: *et dixit* lat-a: *dixit autem eis* lat-g$_2$: *Jesus ait illis discipulis suis* syr-cu: om BDℵ vulg lat-b c e ff$_{1.2}$ copt æth Orig. (Π ?) rec aft ναι ins (*for reverence sake?*) κυριε, with C rel lat-a b c e f g$_{1.2}$ h syrr copt arm [Chr] Orig-int: om BDℵ 1. 13. 124 vulg lat-ff$_{1.2}$ k syr-cu syr-jer copt æth-pl Orig [Ath$_1$] Eus Hil.
52. om ο δε D vulg lat-f ff$_2$ Syr syr-cu copt. aft ο δε ins ιησους CU syr-mg. for ειπεν, λεγει B[2]D latt.

drawn to shore, and the good collected into vessels, while the bad (the legally unclean, those out of season, those putrid or maimed) are cast away. This net is the *Church gathering from the sea* (a common Scripture similitude for nations: see Rev. xvii. 15: Isa. viii. 7: Ps. lxv. 7) *of the world, all kinds* (see Rev. vii. 9); and when it is full, it is drawn to the *bank* (the limit of the ocean, as the συντέλεια is the limit of the αἰών), and the *angels* (not the same as the fishers, as Olshausen maintains; for in the parable of the tares the *servants* and *reapers* are clearly distinguished) shall gather out the wicked from among the just, and cast them into everlasting punishment. It is plain that the comparison must not be strained beyond its limits, as our Lord shews us that the earthly here gives but a faint outline of the heavenly. Compare the mere ἔξω ἔβαλον of the one, with the fearful antitype of vv. 49, 50. On **ὁ** κλ. κ. **ὁ** βρ. see note on ch. viii. 12. **51, 52.**] SOLEMN CONCLUSION OF THE PARABLES. When our Lord asks, 'Have ye understood all these things?' and they answer, 'Yea, Lord,' the reply must be taken as spoken from their *then standing-point*, from which but little could be seen of that inner and deeper meaning which the Holy Spirit has since unfolded. And this circumstance explains the following parabolic remark of our Lord: that every γραμματεύς (*they*, in their study of the Lord's sayings, answering to the then γραμματεῖς in their study of the Law) who is μαθητευθείς, enrolled as a disciple and taught as such, is like an householder (the Great Householder being the Lord Himself, compare ch. xxiv. 45), who puts forth from his store new things and old; i.e. 'ye yourselves, scribes of the Kingdom of Heaven, instructed as ye shall fully be in the meaning of these sayings, are (shall be) like householders, from your own stores of knowledge respecting them hereafter bringing out, not only your present understanding of them, but ever new and deeper meanings.' And this is true of **πᾶς** γρ. κ.τ.λ. *Every* real spiritually-learned scribe of the Kingdom of Heaven is able, from the increasing stores of his genuine experimental knowledge of the word (not merely from books or learning, or the Bible itself, but ἐκ τοῦ θησ. **αὐτοῦ**), to bring forth things new and old. The **διὰ τοῦτο** is an expression of *consequence*, but not a strong one: answering nearly to our **Well, then.** This is perhaps the fittest place to make a few *general remarks* on this wonderful cycle of Parables. We observe, (1) How naturally they are evolved from the objects and associations surrounding our Lord at the time (see on this the very interesting section of Stanley, Sinai and Palestine, ch. xiii. § 2, p. 420 ff., "On the Parables"). He sat in a boat in the sea, teaching the people who were on the land. His eye wandered over the rich plain of Gennesareth (where πᾶν πεφυτεύκασιν οἱ νεμόμενοι, Jos. B. J. iii. 10. 8, and Robinson, iii. 290):—the field-paths, the stony places, the neglected spots choked with

[n] γραμματεὺς [o] μαθητευθεὶς τῇ βασιλείᾳ τῶν οὐρανῶν
ὅμοιός ἐστιν [p] ἀνθρώπῳ [q] οἰκοδεσπότῃ, ὅστις [r] ἐκβάλλει ἐκ
τοῦ θησαυροῦ αὐτοῦ καινὰ καὶ παλαιά.
53 Καὶ ἐγένετο ὅτε ἐτέλεσεν ὁ Ἰησοῦς τὰς παραβολὰς
ταύτας [s] μετῆρεν ἐκεῖθεν. 54 καὶ ἐλθὼν εἰς τὴν [t] πατρίδα
αὐτοῦ ἐδίδασκεν αὐτοὺς ἐν τῇ συναγωγῇ αὐτῶν, ὥστε
[u] ἐκπλήσσεσθαι αὐτοὺς καὶ λέγειν Πόθεν τούτῳ ἡ σοφία
αὕτη καὶ αἱ [v] δυνάμεις; 55 οὐχ οὗτός ἐστιν ὁ τοῦ [w] τέκ-

n ch. ii. 4 reff. Ezra vii. 6.
o ch. xxvii. 57 (intr.). xxviii. 19. Acts xiv. 21 only †.
p ver. 45 reff.
q ch. x. 25 reff.
r = ch. xii. 35 reff.
s ch. xix. 1 only. = Gen. xii. 8 Aq. trans. in LXX.
t here bis and ‖ Mk. Luke iv. 23, 24. John iv. 44. Heb. xi. 14 only. Jer. xxii. 10.
u ch. xi. 20, 21 reff. Wisd. xiii. 4.
v ch. vii. 22 reff.
w ‖ Mk. only. 4 Kings xxii. 6.

rec εις την βασιλειαν (*gloss, or perhaps the* εις *of the previous word repeated, and then the case changed*), with L Θ(which exists, but is almost illegible, from ver 46 to 55. This is the only reading quoted) Π-marg rel: εν τη βασιλεια (*corrn*) DM latt Chr [Cyr-p$_{alic}$] Iren-int Hil Ambr Aug: txt BCKΠℵ 1. 13. 33 lat-*e k* Syr copt æth arm Orig$_4$ Ath Cyr$_{10}$ Procop. ομοια (sic) ℵ[1].

54. αντιπατριδα (sic) ℵ[1]. rec εκπληττεσθαι, with KMΓ(S, e sil): txt BCDℵ rel Eus. (EFL εκπλησεσθαι.) ins πασα bef η σοφια D æth Eus$_2$.

wild vegetation (*οὔτε γὰρ αὐτή τι φυτὸν ἀρνεῖται διὰ τὴν πιότητα*, ib.), the plots of rich and deep soil, were all before him. The same imagery prevails in the parable of the tares of the field, and in that of the mustard seed; and the result of the tilling of the land is associated with the leaven in the lump. Then He quits the sea-shore and enters the house with the disciples. There the link to the former parable is the exposition of the tares of the field. From the working of the land for seed to finding a treasure in a field the transition is easy—from the finding without seeking to seeking earnestly and finding, easy again: from the seed to the buried treasure, from the treasure to the pearl,—the treasure of the deep,—again simple and natural. The pearl recalls the sea; the sea the fishermen with their net; the mixed throng lining the beach, the great day of separation on the further bank of Time. (2) The seven Parables compose in their inner depth of connexion, a great united whole, beginning with the first sowing of the Church, and ending with the consummation. We must not, as Stier well remarks, seek with Bengel, al., minutely to apportion the series prophetically, to various historical periods: those who have done so (see Trench, p. 142, edn. 4) have shewn caprice and inconsistency; and the *parable*, though in its manifold depths the light of prophecy sometimes glimmers, has for its main object to *teach*, not to foretell. More than a general outline, shewn by the prominence of those points to which the respective parables refer, in the successive periods of the Church, we can hardly expect to find. But as much we unquestionably do find. The apostolic age was (1) the greatest of all the seed times of the Church: then (2) sprang up the tares, heresies manifold, and the attempts to root them out, almost as pernicious as the heresies themselves: nay the so-called *Church Catholic* was for ages employed in rooting up the wheat also. Notwithstanding this (3) the little seed waxed onward—the kingdoms of the earth came gradually in —(4) the leaven was secretly penetrating and assimilating. Then is it, (5) during the period of dissensions, and sects, and denominations, that here and there by this man and that man the treasure shall be found: then is it, (6) during the increase of secular knowledge, and cultivation of the powers of the intellect, that merchantmen shall seek goodly pearls up and down the world, and many shall find, each for himself, the Pearl of Price. And thus we are carried on (7) through all the ages during which the great net has been gathering of every kind, to the solemn day of inspection and separation, which will conclude the present state.

53—58.] Teaching, and rejection, at Nazareth. Mark vi. 1—6. See Luke iv. 16—29 and notes. **53, 54.**] **τὴν πατ. αὐ.**, viz. Nazareth. Perhaps the proceedings of ch. viii. 18—ix. 34 are to be inserted between these two verses. In Mark iv. 35, the stilling of the storm and voyage to the Gadarenes are bound to the above parables by what appears a distinct note of sequence: *ἐν ἐκείνῃ τῇ ἡμέρᾳ ὀψίας γενομένης*: for we can hardly interpret *ὀψ. γεν.* on any other hypothesis than that *ἐν ἐκ. τ. ἡμ.* means '*on the same day.*' The teaching was on the Sabbath

τονος υἱός; οὐχ ἡ μήτηρ αὐτοῦ λέγεται Μαριάμ, καὶ οἱ ἀδελφοὶ αὐτοῦ Ἰάκωβος καὶ Ἰωσὴφ καὶ Σίμων καὶ Ἰούδας;

...αυτου F. BCDEG KLMSU VXΓΔΠ ℵ 1. 33

55. rec (for 2nd ουχ) ουχι, with D rel Eus_1 [Chr]: *nonne* lat-*a b*: txt BCMΔℵ 33 $Orig_3$ Eus_1. for μαριαμ, μαρια C 127 Scr's h evv-y-z_1 [latt (*as usually*) copt-ms] $Orig_1$(but txt_2) Eus [Chr-2-6-9-γ-η-ρ]. rec ιωσης, with KLΔΠ lat-*k* Syr syr-txt æth arm-zoh: ιωση S-marg 24. 118-57. 218 Scr's s: ιωαννης D ℵ[1](appy) rel Scr's b c f h k o evv-H-z $Orig_1$: *et johannes et joseph* gat mm: txt BC ℵ-corr[1] 1. 33 ev-y latt syr-cu syr-mg copt arm-ms $Orig_2$ Eus_1 Jer.

(Mark). **55. οἱ ἀδελφοὶ αὐτοῦ**] It is an enquiry of much interest and some difficulty, who these were. After long examination of the evidence on the subject, I believe that the truth will best be attained by disencumbering the mind in the first place of all *à priori considerations*, and *traditions* (which last are very inconsistent and uncertain), and fixing the attention on the *simple testimony of Scripture itself*. I will trace the ἀδελφοὶ αὐτοῦ or ἀδ. κυρίου through the various mentions of them in the N. T., and then state the result; placing at the end of the note the principal traditions on the subject, and the difficulties attending them. (I) The expression οἱ ἀδ. αὐτοῦ occurs *nine times* in the Gospels, and *once* in the Acts. Of these the *three first* are in the narratives of the coming of His mother and brethren to speak with Him, Matt. xii. 46: Mark iii. 31: Luke viii. 19: the *two next* are the present passage and its || in Mark vi. 3, where they are mentioned in connexion with His mother and sisters; the *four others* are in John ii. 12; vii. 3, 5, 10, in the *first* of which He and his mother and brethren and disciples are related to have gone down to Capernaum: and in the *three last* His brethren are introduced as urging Him to shew Himself to the world, and it is stated that they did not believe on Him. The *last* is in Acts i. 14, where we read that the Apostles 'continued in prayer and supplication with the women, and with Mary the mother of Jesus, *and with his brethren*.' In another place, 1 Cor. ix. 5, Paul mentions οἱ λοιποὶ ἀπόστολοι, καὶ **οἱ ἀδ. τ. κυρίου**, κ. Κηφᾶς. Such are all the places where the meaning is *undoubted*, that persons called, and being in some usual sense, *brethren of the Lord*, are mentioned. (Besides these the Lord Himself uses the words οἱ ἀδελφοί μου Matt. xxviii. 10: John xx. 17, but apparently with a wider meaning, including at least the eleven Apostles in the term, as He does in Matt. xii. 49 ||.) Now I would observe (α) that in all the mentions of them in the Gospels, except those in John vii., they are *in connexion with His mother*: the same being the case in Acts i. 14. (β) That it is no where asserted or implied that any of them were *of the number of the twelve*; but from John vii. 5, following upon vi. 70 (by μετὰ ταῦτα vii. 1), they are *excluded from that number*. John would certainly not have used the words οὐδὲ γὰρ οἱ ἀδ. αὐτ. ἐπίστ. εἰς αὐτόν, had *any of them* believed on Him at that time (see this substantiated in note ad loc.):—and again in Acts i. 14, by being mentioned after the Apostles have been enumerated by name, and after the mother of Jesus, they are indicated at that time also to have been *separate from the twelve*, although *then* certainly believing on Him. (γ) Their *names*, as stated here and in Mark vi. 3, were JACOB, JOSEPH (or JOSES), SIMON, and JUDAS, all of them among the commonest of Jewish names. Of JOSEPH (or JOSES;—certainly not the Joseph Barsabas Justus of Acts i. 23; see ib. ver. 21) and SIMON (not Simon Cananæus or Zelotes: see above) *we know from Scripture nothing*. Of the *two others* we have the following traces—(δ) JACOB (JAMES) appears in the apostolic narrative as ὁ ἀδελφὸς τοῦ κυρίου, Gal. i. 19: he is there called an *apostle*. This however determines nothing as to his having been among *the twelve* (which is a very different matter); for *Paul and Barnabas are called apostles*, Acts xiv. (4) 14, and Paul always calls himself such. See also Rom. xvi. 7: 1 Thess. ii. 7 compared with i. 1. That he is identical with the James of Gal. ii. 9, whom Paul mentions with Cephas and John as having given him and Barnabas the right hand of fellowship, fourteen years after the visit related ib. i. 19, does not appear for certain, but has been pretty generally assumed. (See this whole subject discussed in the prolegg. to the Epistle of James.) (ε) The JUDE who has left an epistle, and was brother of James, not only does not call himself an apostle, ver. 1 (as neither does James, nor indeed John himself, so that this cannot be urged), but in ver. 17 (see note there) seems to draw a distinction between himself and the Apostles. Whether this indicate that the James and Jude,

56 καὶ αἱ ἀδελφαὶ αὐτοῦ οὐχὶ πᾶσαι [x] πρὸς ἡμᾶς εἰσιν ;
Z -δαλιζοντο... πόθεν οὖν τούτῳ ταῦτα πάντα ; 57 καὶ [y] ἐσκανδαλίζοντο ἐν

x ℞ Mk. Mark ix. 19. John i. 1. 1 John i. 2.
y ch. xi. 6. ver. 21 al. fr.

56. παντα bef ταυτα D rel latt $Orig_1$ [Bas_1] : txt BCMUΓΠℵ **1.** 33 (S, e sil) Eus_1.

the authors of the Epistles, were two of these ἀδελφοὶ τ. κυρίου, is uncertain; but it may at least be mentioned in the course of our enquiry. I shall now state the result of that enquiry, which has been based on Scripture testimony *only*. (1) That there were *four persons known as οἱ ἀδ. αὐτοῦ or τ. κυρίου*, NOT OF THE NUMBER OF THE TWELVE. (2) That these persons are found in all places (with the above exception) where their names occur in the Gospels, *in immediate connexion with Mary, the mother of the Lord*. (It is a strange phænomenon in argument, that it should have been maintained by an orthodox writer, that my inference from this *proves too much*, because Joseph is here introduced as His father: as if a mistake of the Jews with regard to a supernatural fact, which they could not know, invalidated their cognizance of a natural fact which they knew full well.) (3) That not a word is any where dropped to prevent us from inferring that the ἀδελφοί and ἀδελφαὶ αὐτοῦ were His relations *in the same literal sense* as we know ἡ μήτηρ αὐτοῦ to have been; but that His own saying, where He distinguishes His relations according to the flesh from His disciples (ch. xii. 50 ||), seems to *sanction that inference*. (4) That nothing is said from which it can be inferred whether Joseph had been married before he appears in the Gospel history;—or again, whether these ἀδ. were, according to the flesh, older or younger than our Lord. (5) That the silence of the Scripture narrative leaves it free for Christians to believe these to have been *real* (younger) *brethren and sisters of our Lord, without incurring any imputation of unsoundness of belief as to His miraculous conception.* That such an imputation has been cast, is no credit to the logical correctness of those who have made it, who set down that, because this view *has been taken* by impugners of the great Truth just mentioned, *therefore*, it eventually leads, or may fairly be used, towards the denial of it (see Dr. Mill on the Brethren of our Lord, p. 224); for no attempt is made to shew its connexion with such a conclusion. The fact is, that the two matters, the *miraculous conception of the Lord Jesus* by the Holy Ghost, and *the subsequent virginity of His Mother, are* ESSENTIALLY AND ENTIRELY DISTINCT; see note on Matt. i. 25: see also, respecting a supposed difficulty attending this view, note on John xix. 27. (II) I will now state the principal *traditionary* views respecting the brethren of the Lord. (1) That they were *all sons of Alphæus* (or Clopas) *and Mary the sister of the mother of our Lord;* and so *cousins* of Jesus, and called agreeably to Jewish usage *His brothers.* This is the view taken in the remarkable fragment of Papias, quoted in Dr. Mill, p. 238, adopted by Jerome (cont. Helvidium 13, vol. ii. p. 219), and very generally received in ancient and modern times. But it seems to me that a comparison of the Scripture testimonies cited above will prove it untenable. One at least of the sons of this Alphæus was an apostle, *of the number of the twelve*, viz. Ἰάκωβος ὁ τοῦ Ἀλφαίου (see all the lists, on ch. x. 3); which (see above) would *exclude him from the number of the brethren of the Lord.* But even if *one* of the four could be thus detached (which, from John vii. 5, I cannot believe), it is generally assumed that Ἰούδας Ἰακώβου (see Luke's two lists as above) is Jude the *brother* of James; and if so, this would be *another* son of Alphæus, and another subtraction from the number who did not believe on Him. Again Matthew (see note on Matt. ix. 9), if identical with Levi (Mark ii. 14), was *another son of Alphæus:* which would make a fifth brother, and leave therefore, *out of five, three believing on Him at the time when it was said* οὐδὲ γὰρ οἱ ἀδ. . . . κ.τ.λ. This view besides labours under the difficulty arising from these brethren accompanying and being found in connexion with Mary the mother of our Lord, whereas throughout that time *their own mother was living.* The way in which the assertors of this view explain John vii. 5, is either by supposing that all the brethren are not *there* implied, or that all are not *here* mentioned; both suppositions, it seems to me, very unlikely (compare e. g. John's minute accuracy where an exception was to be made, ch. vi. 23, 24). (2) That they were *children of Joseph by a former marriage* (or even by a later one with Mary wife of Clopas, to raise up seed to his dead *brother*,—as Clopas is said to have been: but this needs no refutation). This view was taken by several early Fathers, e. g. Hilary, Epiphanius, and mentioned by Origen, who

z ‖ Mk. 1 Cor. iv. 10. xii. 23 only. Isa. liii. 3.
a ver. 54.
b ‖ Mk. Mark xvi. 14. Rom. iii 3. xi. 20. Heb. iii. 12, 19 al.† Wisd. xiv. 25 only.
c ch. xi. 25 reff.
d ‖ L. Luke iii. 19. Acts xiii. 1 only †. (-χεῖν, Luke iii. 1.)
e ch. iv. 24. xxiv. 6 al. 2 Kings xiii. 30. Isa. liii. 1.
f ch. viii. 6 reff. = παῖδες βασιλέως, Diod. Sic. xvii. 36.

BCDEG KLMSU VXZΓΔ Πℵ 1. 33

αὐτῷ. ὁ δὲ Ἰησοῦς εἶπεν αὐτοῖς Οὐκ ἔστιν προφήτης
[z] ἄτιμος εἰ μὴ ἐν τῇ [t] πατρίδι καὶ ἐν τῇ οἰκίᾳ αὐτοῦ.
58 καὶ οὐκ ἐποίησεν ἐκεῖ [a] δυνάμεις πολλὰς διὰ τὴν [b] ἀπιστίαν αὐτῶν.
XIV. 1 Ἐν ἐκείνῳ τῷ [c] καιρῷ ἤκουσεν Ἡρώδης ὁ
[d] τετράρχης τὴν [e] ἀκοὴν Ἰησοῦ, 2 καὶ εἶπεν τοῖς [f] παισὶν

57. om *ιησους* ℵ. for *ειπεν*, *λεγει* Z Orig$_1$. ins *ιδια* bef *πατριδι* CZℵ 13. 124 Scr's u lat-*ff*$_1$ Orig$_1$. rec aft *τη πατριδι* ins *αυτου*, with C rel vulg lat-*b c f ff*$_2$ *g*$_{1.2}$ *h* syrr syr-cu copt æth arm Orig$_2$: om BDZℵ 33 lat-*a k*.
58. *τας απιστειας* *incredulitates* D lat-*k*.

Chap. XIV. **1.** *ηκουσεν ηρωδης* bef *εν εκ. τω καιρω* ℵ[1](but corrd). aft *εν εκεινω* ins *δε* D 300 Syr syr-cu copt. *τετρααρχης* CZΔℵ.

(Winer, Realwörterbuch, i. p. 663) says respecting it, *οἱ ταῦτα λέγοντες τὸ ἀξίωμα τῆς Μαρίας ἐν παρθενίᾳ τηρεῖν μέχρι τέλους βούλονται.* This however, while *by no means impossible*, and in some respects agreeing with the *apparent* position of these brothers as older (according to the flesh) than the Lord (John vii. 3), has no countenance whatever in Scripture, either in their being called sons of any other woman, or in any distinct mention of Joseph as their father, which surely in this case would be required. (III) On the *à priori considerations* which have influenced opinions on this matter, see note on Matt. i. 25; and on the *traditional literature*, see the tract of Professor Mill on the Brethren of our Lord. See also Winer, Realwörterbuch, Art. *Jesus*, § 3. Greswell, Dissertations, vol. ii. Diss. iii. Blom, Disputatio Theologica de τ. ἀδ. τ. κ. Lug. Bat. 1839. Wieseler, Stud. und Kritiken, 1842, i. 96 ff. (these two last I have not seen); also, a letter on this my note, referred to above under I. 2, in the Journal of Sacred Literature for July, 1855. This letter is too much based on *à priori* considerations, but contains some valuable suggestions on this confessedly difficult question. Neander, Leben J. p. 48, brings out the importance of the view which I have above, under (I), endeavoured to justify, as shewing that the account of the miraculous conception is *not mythical*, in which case all would have been arranged to suit the views of virginity from which it had arisen,—but *strictly historical*, found as it is with no such arrangements or limitations. **58.] οὐκ ἐποίησεν** = *οὐκ ἠδύνατο ποιῆσαι*, Mark vi. 5, where see note. On the identity, or not, of this preaching at Nazareth with that related much earlier by Luke iv. 16 sq., see note there.

Chap. XIV. 1—12.] Herod hears of the fame of Jesus. Parenthetical account of the death of John the Baptist. Mark vi. 14—29. Luke ix. 7—9, who does not relate the death of John.

1.] This Herod was Herod Antipas, son of Herod the Great, *ἐκ Μαλθάκης τῆς Σαμαρεΐτιδος*, and own brother of Archelaus (Jos. B. J. i. 28. 4). The portion of the kingdom allotted to him by the second will of his father (in the first he was left as king) was the tetrarchy of Galilee and Peræa (Jos. Antt. xvii. 8. 1). He married the daughter of the Arabian king Aretas; but having during a visit to his half-brother Herod Philip (not the tetrarch of that name, but another son of Herod the Great, disinherited by his father) become enamoured of his wife Herodias, he prevailed on her to leave her husband, and live with him. (See below, on ver. 4.) This step, accompanied as it was with a stipulation of putting away the daughter of Aretas, involved him in a war with his father-in-law, which however did not break out till a year before the death of Tiberius (A.D. 37, U.C. 790; Jos. Antt. xviii. 5. 1—3), and in which he was totally defeated and his army destroyed by Aretas; a divine vengeance, according to the Jews, for the death of John the Baptist (Josephus, ibid.). He and Herodias afterwards went to Rome at the beginning of Caligula's reign, to complain of the assumption of the title of king by Agrippa his nephew, son of Aristobulus; but Caligula having heard the claims of both, banished Antipas and Herodias to Lyons in Gaul, whence he was afterwards removed to Spain, and there died: Jos. Antt. xviii. 7. 1, 2. The following events apparently took place at Machærus, a frontier fortress between Peræa and Arabia: see below on ver. 10.

τὴν ἀκοὴν Ἰησοῦ] It was the fame of the *preaching and miracles of the twelve*, on

αὐτοῦ Οὗτός ἐστιν Ἰωάννης ὁ βαπτιστής· αὐτὸς [g] ἠγέρθη
ἀπὸ τῶν [g] νεκρῶν, καὶ διὰ τοῦτο αἱ [h] δυνάμεις [i] ἐνεργοῦσιν
ἐν αὐτῷ. 3 ὁ γὰρ Ἡρώδης [j] κρατήσας τὸν Ἰωάννην
ἔδησεν αὐτὸν καὶ ἐν τῇ [k] φυλακῇ [l] ἀπέθετο διὰ Ἡρωδιάδα
τὴν γυναῖκα τοῦ ἀδελφοῦ αὐτοῦ. 4 ἔλεγεν γὰρ αὐτῷ
ὁ Ἰωάννης Οὐκ [m] ἔξεστίν σοι [n] ἔχειν αὐτήν. 5 καὶ θέλων

g w. ἀπό, ch. xxvii. 64. xxviii. 7.
h ‖ Mk. Mark v. 30 ‖ L. Luke vi. 19. 1 Cor. xii. 10, 28, 29.
i ‖ Mk. James v. 16. elsw. Paul (Rom. vii. 5 all5.) only. Isa. li. 4.
j ch. xii. 11. Ps. cxxxvi. 9.
k = ch. v. 25. xviii. 30 al. Gen. xlii. 17.
l = here only. Lev. xxiv. 12. Num. xv. 34. 2 Chron. xviii. 26. (Acts vii. 58 al.)
m ch. xii. 2, &c.
n = ‖ Mk. ch. xxii. 28. 1 Cor. v. 1. vii. 2, 29. Deut. xxviii. 30.

2. ins μητι *numquid* bef ουτος D gat mm lat-*b f* g_2 aft βαπτιστης ins ον εγω απεκεφαλισα (*from* ‖ *Mark*) D 5 gat tol lat-*a b* ff_1 g_2 *h*. for αυτος, ουτος C 1. 61 D-lat $Orig_1$-ms Chr. om δια τουτο B^1(ins B^2-marg). εναργουσιν D^1(txt D^8). om εν Z Scr's g s ev-z.

3. aft ηρωδης ins τοτε B 13. 124. om αυτον (*as unnecessary*) B$ℵ^1$(ins ℵ-$corr^1$) lat-ff_1 *h* $Orig_1$(ins_1). rec και εθετο εν φυλακη, with C rel vulg lat-*b c f* ff_2 g_1 syrr syr-cu copt arm : εν τη φυλακη (alone) D lat-*a*(appy) *e k* æth $Orig_1$: εν τη φυλ. και απεθετο $ℵ^{3a}$: "εν τη φυλακη . . . Z (sequ. ut vid. e spatio και εθετο s. fortasse και απεθετο)." Treg : txt B($ℵ^1$) (13. 124 ?) lat-ff_1 *h* : κ. απεθ. εν τη φ. 1 $Orig_1$: εν φ. και απεθετο 33 $Orig_1$. (*The original stumbling-block seems to have been the unusual word* απεθετο, *which was changed to* εθετο, *or as above, and transposed : then by erasures before and after* εν τ. φ., *disappeared, and was variously reinstated in the text.*) rec om τη (bef φυλακη) (*as unnecessary or misunderstood*), with $B^1C ℵ^1$ rel $Orig_1$: ins B^1(written over by origl scribe) DZ$ℵ^{3a}$ 1 copt $Orig_2$. rec ins φιλιππου bef του αδελφου (*from* ‖ *Mark, where none omit it*), with BCZℵ rel gat(and mm) lat-[*b*] *f* ff_2 g_2 *h* syrr syr-cu [æth arm] Orig [Chr] : om D vulg lat-*a c e* ff_1 g_1 *k* Aug.

4. ο ιωαννης bef αυτω BZ$ℵ^{3a}$: om αυτω $ℵ^1$ 26-8 : txt CD rel 1. 33 latt Orig.—om ὁ Dℵ Scr's b f evv-H^1-z.

their mission, of which Herod heard,—probably in conjunction with the works of Christ: see ‖ Mark. **2.**] **παῖς** = δοῦλος. **αὐτός**] emphatic; equivalent in English to "*it is he, that*" . . . In Luke ix. 7 it is said that Herod διηπόρει διὰ τὸ λέγεσθαι ὑπό τινων ὅτι Ἰωάνν. ἐγήγ. κ.τ.λ. There is no inconsistency in these accounts: the report originated with others: but if Herod διηπόρει concerning it, he, in the terrors of a guilty conscience, doubtless gave utterance to these words himself. There is no evidence that Herod was a Sadducee, or a disbeliever in the resurrection as then held by the Pharisees. See also note on Mark viii. 14. There is no allusion here to metempsychosis, but to the veritable bodily resurrection, and supposed greater power acquired by having passed through death. This is an incidental confirmation of John x. 41, where we read that John *wrought no miracle while living*. **4.**] The marriage was unlawful for these three reasons: (1) *The former husband of Herodias*, Philip, *was still living*. This is expressly asserted by Josephus, Antt. xviii. 5. 4, Ἡρωδιάς, ἐπὶ συγχύσει φρονήσασα τῶν πατρίων, Ἡρώδῃ γαμεῖται τοῦ ἀνδρὸς τῷ ὁμοπατρίῳ ἀδελφῷ, **διαστᾶσα ζῶντος**. (A reply to the attempt made by some to interpret these last words, '*having previously been divorced from him while living*,' is hardly needed, in the presence of the two unqualified synchronous participles, φρονήσασα and διαστᾶσα. Besides, the part. *is not* **ἀποστᾶσα**, *as erroneously quoted by the Bp. of Exeter* [Philpotts]: see his published speech of Feb. 25, 1851, note.) The same is surely implied by the whole narrative, and the word μετοικίσασθαι, Antt. xviii. 5. 1. (2) *The former wife of Antipas was still living*, and fled to her father Aretas on hearing of his intention to marry Herodias: Jos. ibid. (3) *Antipas and Herodias were already related to one another within the forbidden degrees of consanguinity*. For θυγάτηρ ἦν Ἀριστοβούλου, καὶ οὗτος ἀδελφὸς αὐτῶν (of Antipas and Philip), Jos. ib. See the Bp.'s note, and a reply to it in substance the same as the foregoing, in the Quarterly Journal of Sacred Lit. for Oct. 1852 and Jan. 1853. I may add that the remark of Josephus (Antt. xviii. 5. 4), that Salome's birth had taken place previously to the infidelity of Herodias, is not given, as understood by the Bp. (after Tertullian, adv. Marcion. iv. 34, vol. ii. p. 443), as the technical reason why her conduct was ἐπὶ συγχύσει τῶν πατρίων, but as a moral aggravation of her unnatural crime. It was unlawful by Levit. xviii. 16. **5.**] This verse is further expanded in Mark: ὁ γὰρ Ἡρ. ἐφοβεῖτο

o = ch. xxi. 26, 46. Phil. ii. 29. Philem. 17.
p ‖ only +. = ἡμέρα γενεσεως, Gen. xl. 20.
q ‖ Mk. ch. xi. 17 ‖ L. only. 2 Kings vi. 16, 20, 21.
r = Mark iii. 3 ‖ L. xiv. 60. John [viii. 4, 9] xx. 19, 26.
s ‖ Mk. only in Gospp. Acts vi. 5. elsw. Paul (Rom. viii. 8 al.) only. Esth. ii. 4, 9.

αὐτὸν ἀποκτεῖναι ἐφοβήθη τὸν ὄχλον, ὅτι ὡς προφήτην
αὐτὸν [o] εἶχον. 6 [p] γενεσίοις δὲ γενομένοις τοῦ Ἡρώδου
[q] ὠρχήσατο ἡ θυγάτηρ τῆς Ἡρωδιάδος ἐν τῷ [r] μέσῳ καὶ
[s] ἤρεσεν τῷ Ἡρώδῃ· 7 [t] ὅθεν [u] μεθ' [u] ὅρκου [v] ὡμολόγησεν
αὐτῇ δοῦναι ὃ ἂν αἰτήσηται. 8 ἡ δὲ [w] προβιβασθεῖσα
ὑπὸ τῆς μητρὸς αὐτῆς Δός μοι φησὶν ὧδε ἐπὶ [x] πίνακι
τὴν κεφαλὴν Ἰωάννου τοῦ βαπτιστοῦ. 9 καὶ [y] λυπηθεὶς
ὁ βασιλεύς, [z] διὰ τοὺς ὅρκους καὶ τοὺς [a] συνανακειμένους

Θ -πτισ-του και.. F και τους...

BCDEF GKLM SUVXZ ΓΔΘΠא 1. 33

t Acts xxvi. 19. Heb. ii. 17. iii. 1. vii. 25. viii. 3. ix. 18. xi. 19. 1 John ii. 18. Judith viii. 20.
u ch. xxvi. 72 only. Lev. v. 4 al. see Heb. vii. 20. ὅρκ., ch. v. 33 reff.
v = Acts vii. 17. Jer. li. (xliv.) 25. ἐδέοντο δὲ . . . . ὁ δὲ ὡμολόγει, Xen. Anab. vii. 4. 13.
w Acts xix. 33 only. Exod. xxxv. 34. Deut. vi. 7 only.
x ‖ (bis). Luke xi. 39 only +.
y ch. xvii. 23 al. fr. Dan. vi. 14.
z ‖ Mk. Josh. ix. 20.
a ch. ix. 10 reff.

5. for *οτι*, *επει* B[1].

6. rec *γενεσιων δε* **αγομενων** (*the gen was an emendn of the constr, and αγομ. a gloss on γεν.*), with X rel syr-mg: *-ιων δε γενομενων* CK Chr$_1$: *-ιοις δε αγομενοις* **1**: *die natalis* latt: txt BDLZא syrr syr-cu copt æth arm. for *της ηρωδιαδος*, *αυτου ηρωδιας* D-gr.

7. *μετα* א. for *ωμολ.*, *ωμοσεν* Z 13. 124. 346 ev-y Syr Chr. rec (for *αν*) *εαν*, with CZא rel: txt BD 33.

8. for *δος μοι φησιν*, *ειπεν δος μοι* D lat-*a b c f ff*$_2$ *h l* Syr syr-cu æth.—*ειπεν* was perhaps written by א[2] but erased. om *επι πινακι* D. om *την* D[1](ins D[2]).

9. rec **ελυπηθη** (*emendn of constr*), with CLא rel vulg lat-*b c f ff*$_{1.2}$ *g*$_1$ *h* syrr syr-cu copt æth arm: txt BD **1**. 13. 124 lat-*a*. (Z 33 def. Θ ?) rec aft *δια* ins *δε*, with CZ א rel vulg lat-[*c*] *f g*$_2$ syrr copt arm: om BDL[1] **1**. 13. 124 lat-*a b ff*$_{1.2}$ *g*$_1$ *h* æth. ins *δια* bef *τους συνανακειμενους* D lat-*a b c f ff*$_{1.2}$ *g*$_1$ *h* syr-cu æth.

τὸν Ἰωάν. εἰδὼς αὐτὸν ἄνδρα δίκαιον καὶ ἅγιον, καὶ συνετήρει αὐτόν, καὶ ἀκούσας αὐτοῦ πολλὰ ἐποίει, καὶ ἡδέως αὐτοῦ ἤκουεν. Josephus, not being aware of any other grounds for his imprisonment, alleges purely political ones: δείσας Ἡρώδης τὸ ἐπὶ τοσόνδε πιθανὸν αὐτοῦ τοῖς ἀνθρώποις μὴ ἐπὶ ἀποστάσει τινὶ φέροι . . . . πολὺ κρεῖττον ἡγεῖται, πρίν τι νεώτερον ἐξ αὐτοῦ γενέσθαι, προλαβὼν ἀναιρεῖν . . . . Antt. xviii. 5. 2. **εἶχον**] literally, '*possederunt* eum tanquam prophetam;' and thus Meyer maintains it must be rendered: but as our '*hold*,' so ἔχω comes to be applied to the *estimate formed* of a man or thing, which subjectively is our *possession* of him or it.

6. γενεσίοις] **the birthday.** This name was given in classical Greek to *an anniversary celebration of the memory of the dead.* So Herod., iv. 26, having described such a celebration among the Issedones, adds, παῖς δὲ πατρὶ τοῦτο ποιέει κατάπερ οἱ Ἕλληνες τὰ **γενέσια.** Phrynichus, Hesych., and Ammonius lay it down that γενέσια is *not to be used for* γενέθλια, a *birthday.* But the adj. was certainly so used in later Greek: e. g. ἄγοντες τ. γενέσιον ἡμέραν τ. παιδίου, Jos. Antt. xii. 4. 7 (in Dio Cassius xlvii. 18, lvi. 46, lxvii. 2, usually cited, the γενέσια, though bearing this meaning, are in each case in honour of a *dead* person). See Suicer, Thes. under γενέθλια, and Lobeck's note, Phryn. p. 103. Heins., Grot., al., hold that the word here means the feast of Herod's *accession:* but they give no proof that it ever had such a meaning. Among the seasons kept by the Gentiles, enumerated in the Rabbinical work Avoda Sara, we have גנוסיא של מלכים: see Lightfoot in loc. [On the dative "compare the examples quoted by Jelf, § 699." Moulton's Winer, p. 276, note 1.] A great feast was given to the nobility of Galilee, Mark vi. 21. The damsel's name was Salome (Jos. Antt. xviii. 5. 4), daughter of Herodias by her former husband Philip. She afterwards married her uncle Philip, tetrarch of Ituræa and Trachonitis: and he dying childless, she became the wife of her cousin Aristobulus, son of Herod king of Chalcis, by whom he had three sons, Herod, Agrippa, and Aristobulus. The dance was probably a pantomimic dance.

9.] **ὁ βασιλεύς** was a title which Herod never properly possessed. Subsequently to this event, Herodias prevailed on him to go to Rome to get the title, which had been granted to his nephew Agrippa. He was opposed by the emissaries of Agrippa, and was exiled to Lugdunum. See note on ver. 1, and Josephus there cited. Herod was grieved because he heard John gladly (Mark vi. 20), and from

ἐκέλευσεν δοθῆναι. 10 καὶ [b] πέμψας [c] ἀπεκεφάλισεν Ἰωάννην ἐν τῇ [d] φυλακῇ. 11 καὶ ἠνέχθη ἡ κεφαλὴ αὐτοῦ
ἐπὶ [x] πίνακι καὶ ἐδόθη τῷ [e] κορασίῳ· καὶ ἤνεγκεν τῇ μητρὶ
αὐτῆς. 12 καὶ προσελθόντες οἱ μαθηταὶ αὐτοῦ ἦραν τὸ
[f] * σῶμα καὶ ἔθαψαν αὐτόν, καὶ ἐλθόντες ἀπήγγειλαν τῷ
I_c ανεχωρησεν... Ἰησοῦ. 13 ἀκούσας δὲ ὁ Ἰησοῦς ἀνεχώρησεν ἐκεῖθεν ἐν
πλοίῳ εἰς ἔρημον τόπον [g] κατ' [g] ἰδίαν. καὶ ἀκούσαντες
οἱ ὄχλοι ἠκολούθησαν αὐτῷ [h] πεζῇ ἀπὸ τῶν πόλεων.
14 καὶ ἐξελθὼν εἶδεν πολὺν ὄχλον, καὶ [i] ἐσπλαγχνίσθη
ἐπ' αὐτοῖς καὶ ἐθεράπευσεν τοὺς [k] ἀῤῥώστους αὐτῶν.
15 ὀψίας δὲ γενομένης προσῆλθον αὐτῷ οἱ μαθηταὶ λέ-

b Acts xix. 31. see Gen. xxxii. 5. xxxviii. 25.
c || (Mk. bis) only. 1 Kings xxxi. 9 complut. Ps. cli. 7 only.
d = ver. 3.
e ch. ix. 24, 25 reff. Esth. ii. 9.
f = Luke xvii. 37. Heb. xiii. 11. 1 Kings xxxi. 10, 12.
g || Mk. L. ver. 23. ch. xvii. 1, 19 al. Mt. Mk. L. (Acts xxiii. 19) only, exc. Gal. ii. 2. 2 Macc. iv. 5 only.
h || Mk. only. 2 Kings xv. 17 vat. (only ?) (πεζεύειν, Acts xx. 13.)
i ch. ix. 36 reff.
k Mark vi. 5, 13. xvi. 18. 1 Cor. xi. 30 only. 3 Kings xiv. 5 A Ald. &c. (see xii. 24 sq. B.) Mal. i. 8. Sir. vii. 35 only. (-τεῖν, 2 Kings xii. 15. -τημα, Sir. x. 10. -τία, Ps. xl. 3.)

10. rec ins τον bef ιωαννην, with CD$א^{3a}$ rel: om BZΘ$א^1$ 1.
11. ins τω bef πινακι D (1. 13).
12. for προσελθ., ελθ. Z Orig. * πτῶμα (|| *Mark*) BCDLא 1. 13. 33. 124 Syr syr-cu copt: σωμα X rel syr. (Z def. Θ ?) add αυτου DL א(marked for erasure; but marks removed) 157 Scr's d i ev-y vulg lat-*f* $ff_{1.2}$ g_2 *h l* Syr syr-cu æth. rec (for αυτον) αυτο (|| *Mark*), with CD $א^2$(appy) rel vulg lat-*b c*: txt BΘ$א^1$ lat-*a* ff_1. (Z 33 def.)
13. rec (for ακουσας δε) και ακ. (*as more appropriate copula*), with C rel syr æth arm: txt BDLZא 1. 13. 33. 124. 209 lat-*f k* (Syr syr-cu copt) Orig Chr. om ο ιησους Θ Scr's e. πεζοι I_cLZא 157. 225-45 Scr's s ev-z vulg lat-*b c* &c syr-mg.
14. rec aft εξελθων ins ο ιησους, with CI_c rel lat-*f h* syrr Orig: aft ειδεν L evv-P-z lat-*a* (*beginning of an eccles lection*): om BDא 1. 33. 124 vulg lat-*b c* $ff_{1.2}$ g_1 syr-cu [copt æth arm]. (Θ ?) οχλον bef πολυν D 33. 435 latt Chr. rec επ' αυτους, with 33 (Scr's l p q r s, e sil): επ' αυτον I_c [$Orig_1$]: εν αυτοις L: περι αυτων D: txt BCא rel $Orig_1$. αρρωστουντας D.
15. προσηλθαν B 33. rec aft μαθηται ins αυτου, with CD rel lat-*a c* syrr syr-cu

policy did not wish to put him to death on so slight a cause. This is not inconsistent with his *wishing to put him to death:* his estimate of John was wavering and undecided, and he was annoyed at the decision being taken out of his hands by a demand, compliance with which would be irrevocable. **10.**] It appears from the damsel's expression δός μοι ὧδε and this verse, that the feast was held either at Machærus or at no great distance from it. Antipas had a palace near, τὰ πλησίον Ἰορδάνου βασίλεια κατὰ Βηθαράμαθον, B. J. ii. 4. 2; but he was not there *on account of the war with Aretas,*—see above.

13—21.] Feeding of the five thousand. Mark vi. 30—44. Luke ix. 10—17. John vi. 1—13, where also see notes.

13.] There is some difficulty here in conceiving how the narration is to proceed continuously. The death of the Baptist is evidently retrospectively and parenthetically inserted: and yet the retirement of our Lord in this verse seems to be the immediate consequence of his hearing of that occurrence. But this may well have been so: for (1) the disciples of John would be some days in bringing the news from Machærus to Capernaum, and the report mentioned in ver. 1 might reach Herod meantime; (2) the expression with which that report is introduced, ἐν ἐκείνῳ τῷ καιρῷ, extends it over a considerable space of time; and (3) the message which the disciples of John brought to our Lord might have included both particulars, the death of their Master, and the saying of Herod respecting Himself. He went across the lake (John vi. 1) into a desert place belonging to the city called Bethsaïda (Luke ix. 10). His retirement (Luke, ibid., and Mark vi. 30) was connected also with the return of the twelve from their mission: compare the full and affecting account of the whole transaction in Mark vi. 30—35. **14.**] ἐξελθών, from his place of retirement. **15.**] This ὀψία was the first evening, the decline of the day, about 3 p.m.; the ὀψία in ver. 23, after the miracle, was late in the night.

γοντες Ἔρημός ἐστιν ὁ τόπος, καὶ ἡ ὥρα ἤδη [l] παρῆλθεν·
[m] ἀπόλυσον [οὖν] τοὺς ὄχλους ἵνα ἀπελθόντες εἰς τὰς
κώμας [n] ἀγοράσωσιν ἑαυτοῖς [o] βρώματα. 16 ὁ δὲ Ἰησοῦς
εἶπεν αὐτοῖς Οὐ [p] χρείαν ἔχουσιν ἀπελθεῖν· [q] δότε αὐτοῖς
ὑμεῖς [q] φαγεῖν. 17 οἱ δὲ λέγουσιν αὐτῷ Οὐκ ἔχομεν ὧδε
εἰ μὴ πέντε ἄρτους καὶ δύο ἰχθύας. 18 ὁ δὲ εἶπεν Φέρετέ
μοι ὧδε αὐτούς. 19 καὶ κελεύσας τοὺς ὄχλους [r] ἀνακλι-
θῆναι ἐπὶ * τοὺς [s] χόρτους, λαβὼν τοὺς πέντε ἄρτους καὶ
τοὺς δύο ἰχθύας, [t] ἀναβλέψας εἰς τὸν οὐρανὸν [u] ηὐλόγησεν, καὶ [v] κλάσας ἔδωκεν τοῖς μαθηταῖς τοὺς ἄρτους, οἱ
δὲ μαθηταὶ τοῖς ὄχλοις. 20 καὶ ἔφαγον πάντες καὶ [w] ἐχορ-
τάσθησαν· καὶ ἦραν τὸ [x] περισσεῦον τῶν [y] κλασμάτων

P αγορασωσιν... BCDEF $G I_c$ KL MPSUV XZΓΔΘ Πℵ 1. 33

...και εκελευ Z.

T_c xiv. 19 (appy) ...

l = Acts xxvii. 9. Gen. xli. 53. Dan. ii. 9 Theod.
m || Mk. L. ch. xv. 23 al. Ps. xxxiii. tit.
n ch. xiii. 44 al. Gen. xlii. 7.
o Luke iii. 11. John iv. 34 al. Gen. xli. 35.
p w. inf., ch. iii. 14 reff.
q || Mk. L. ch. xxv. 35, 42. Mark v. 43 || L. John vi. 31 al. 2 Chron. xxviii. 15.
r ch. viii. 11 reff.
s ch. vi. 30 al. plu., here only.
t = || Mk. L. Mark vii. 34 al. Gen. xv. 5.
u ch. xxvi. 26. 1 Cor. x. 16 al. Gen. i. 22, 28. 1 Kings ix. 13.
v = ch. xxvi. 26 || al. Jer. xvi. 7.
w Phil. iv. 12. James ii. 16. Rev. xix. 21 al. Ps. xxxvi. 19. lviii. 15.
x || L. J. ch. v. 20. xv. 37 al. Tobit iv. 16 [ℵ def.].
y || (J. bis). ch. xv. 37 || Mk. Mark viii. 19, 20 only. Lev. ii. 6. Judg. ix. 53. 1 Kings xxx. 12. Ezek. xiii. 19.

copt æth $Orig_2$ [Chr] : om B Z[from the space] ℵ 33 lat-*b k* arm $Orig_2$. (I_c def.) παρηλθεν bef ηδη Z(appy) ℵ 1 $Orig_2$. rec om ουν (*as || Mark, or perhaps passed over from the -ον preceding*), with BDI_c rel vss Orig : ins CZℵ 1 syr-mg copt $Orig_2$. ins κυκλω bef κωμας (*from || Mark Luke*) C^1 33. 61. 108 Scr's w^2 ev-P^1 syr-mg syr-jer arm. χωρας Δ-gr $ℵ^1$(txt $ℵ^{3a}$).

16. om ιησους $Dℵ^1$(ins $ℵ^{3a}$) 61 lat-*k* Syr syr-cu copt æth arm. υμεις φαγειν bef αυτοις D.

17. for λεγουσιν, (. . .)ον (ειπον or ελεγον) Z, *dixerunt* lat-*f ff*$_1$ *g*$_1$. αρτους bef ει μη πεντε $ℵ^1$(txt $ℵ^{3a}$).

18. aft ειπεν ins αυτοις P. rec αυτους bef ωδε (*to bring* αυτους *nearer the verb*), with CP rel vulg lat-*f* syrr æth : om ωδε D 1 lat-*a b c ff*$_2$ *g*$_1$ *h* syr-cu copt : txt BZℵ 33. (I_c def.)

19. κελευσατε B^1 (*imperative as in || Luke John*) : εκελευσεν Z(appy) ℵ ev-y [$Orig_1$], *jussit* lat-*ff*$_1$. τον οχλον D-gr latt arm-zoh. * τοῦ χόρτου BC^1I_cℵ 1. 33 Scr's o latt Syr syr-cu syr-mg copt æth arm $Orig_4$: τον χορτους L : τον χορτον D 16. 61, *fœnum* latt (*corrns to escape the unusual plural and accus?*) : τους χορτους C^2P rel Scr's mss syr-txt [Chr]. rec ins και bef λαβων, with C^1I_c X(Treg) ℵ lat-*ff*$_1$ *h* copt arm : om BC^2(D)P rel latt syr Orig Thl.—for λαβων, ελαβεν D. [Θ ?]

20. om των κλασματων Θ lat-*a ff*$_1$ *g*$_1$.

ἡ ὥρα] the time of the day is now late, ἦν τῆς ὥρας μικρὸν πρὸ δύντος ἡλίου, Xen. Hell. vii. 2. 22. **16, 17.**] **δότε αὐτοῖς ὑμεῖς φ.**, which is common to the three first Evangelists, is considerably expanded in the more detailed account of John, vv. 3—7; it was *Andrew who spoke* in our ver. 17, and the five loaves and two fishes were *brought by a lad:* John vi. 8, 9. They were *barley loaves* and (*salt*) *fish;* ibid. And we have (perhaps, but see note there) the vast concourse accounted for in John by the fact that *the Passover was at hand*, and so they were collected on their journey to Jerusalem. See a very similar miracle in 2 Kings iv. 42—44; only then there were twenty barley loaves and an hundred men. See also Num. xi. 21, 22.

19. ηὐλόγησεν] Luke supplies αὐτούς, the loaves and fishes: John has for it εὐχαριστήσας. Both are one. The thanks to heaven *is* the blessing on the meat. ὁ Σωτὴρ πρῶτον ἀνέβλεψεν εἰς τὸν οὐρανὸν ταῖς ἀκτῖσι τῶν ὀφθαλμῶν αὐτοῦ οἱονεὶ καταβιβάζων δύναμιν ἐκεῖθεν τὴν ἀνακραθησομένην τοῖς ἄρτοις καὶ τοῖς ἰχθύσι μέλλουσι τρέφειν τοὺς πεντακισχιλίους, καὶ μετὰ τοῦτο ηὐλόγησε τ. π. ἄρτους κ. τ. δ. ἰχθ., τῷ λόγῳ κ. τῇ εὐλογίᾳ αὔξων κ. πληθύνων αὐτούς. Orig. in loc. This miracle was one of symbolic meaning for the twelve, who had just returned from their mission, as pointing to the δωρεὰν ἐλάβετε, δωρεὰν δότε of ch. x. 8 in a higher sense than they then could have understood it:—but see the sy[illegible]bolic import of the miracle treated in t[illegible]e notes to John vi.

Meyer well remarks that the *process* of the miracle is thus to be conceived:—th[illegible] Lord blessed, and gave the loaves and fi[illegible] to the disciples, *as they were;* and th[illegible] *during their distribution of them,*

δώδεκα [z] κοφίνους πλήρεις. 21 οἱ δὲ ἐσθίοντες ἦσαν ἄνδρες
[a] ὡσεὶ πεντακισχίλιοι [b] χωρὶς γυναικῶν καὶ παιδίων.
22 Καὶ εὐθέως [c] ἠνάγκασεν τοὺς μαθητὰς [d] ἐμβῆναι
εἰς τὸ πλοῖον καὶ [e] προάγειν αὐτὸν εἰς τὸ πέραν, ἕως οὗ
[f] ἀπολύσῃ τοὺς ὄχλους. 23 καὶ [f] ἀπολύσας τοὺς ὄχλους
[g] ἀνέβη εἰς τὸ [g] ὄρος [h] κατ' ἰδίαν προσεύξασθαι. [i] ὀψίας
δὲ [i] γενομένης μόνος ἦν ἐκεῖ. 24 τὸ δὲ πλοῖον ἤδη [k] μέσον
τῆς θαλάσσης ἦν [l] βασανιζόμενον ὑπὸ τῶν [m] κυμάτων, ἦν
γὰρ [n] ἐναντίος ὁ ἄνεμος. 25 τετάρτῃ δὲ [o] φυλακῇ τῆς νυκτὸς [p] ἀπῆλθεν πρὸς αὐτοὺς [q] περιπατῶν [q] ἐπὶ τὴν θάλασσαν.

...ανεβη I$_c$. BCDEF GKL MPST$_c$ UVXΓΔ ΘΠℵ 1. 33

z ||. ch. xvi. 9. || Mk. only. Judg. vi. 19 B. Ps. lxxx. 6 only.
a John ix. 14. Acts ii. 41 al. Judg. iii. 29.
b = ch. xv. 38. 2 Cor. xi. 28. (Heb. iv. 15.) Gen. xlvi. 26.
c ||. Luke xiv. 23. Acts xxvi. 11 al. Prov. vi. 7.
d ch. viii. 23 reff.
e = ch. xxi. 31 xxvi. 32. Mark x. 32 al.+ Wisd. xix. 11.
f = ver. 15.
g ch. v. 1 reff. h ver. 13. i ch. viii. 16. ver. 15 (see note there) al. fr. k constr., John i. 26. Num. xxxv. 5. μέσον Ἰωνίης, Herod. i. 170. l = || Mk. only. (2 Pet. ii. 8 al.) m ch. viii. 24 reff. n absol., Acts xxvii. 4 only. Ezek. xviii. 18, but not =. (see Mark xv. 39.) w. dat., || Mk. o = || Mk. ch. xxiv. 43. Luke ii. 8 (?). xii. 38 only. Exod. xiv. 24. p = ch. ii. 22. Rev. x. 9. Gen. xxiv. 56. Exod. iv. 19. q acc., here bis only. gen., ||. Job ix. 8.

21. for *ωσει*, *ως* DI$_c$Δ 1. 33: om Θ 241-7 latt(not *f*) Syr syr-cu copt Orig: txt BCPℵ rel [Chr]. transp *γυναικων* and *παιδιων* D 1 lat-*a b c* &c(not *f*) copt Orig$_2$ Ambr.

22. om *ευθεως* C[1]ℵ[1](ins ℵ[2]) lat-*ff*$_1$ syr-cu [Chr-γ]. rec aft *ηναγκασεν* ins *ο ιησους* (*beg of an eccl lection*), with C[3]L rel: bef *ηναγκ.* lat-*a b c ff*$_2$ *g*$_{1.2}$ *h*: om BC[1]DI$_c$PΔΘℵ 1. 33 Scr's c[1] k am(with em forj fuld tol) lat-*e f ff*$_1$ syrr syr-cu syr-jer copt æth arm Orig$_2$ Chr Arnob. [T$_c$?] rec aft *μαθητας* ins *αυτου* (|| *Mark*), with BEFKPXΠ lat-*a b c ff*$_{1\,2}$ *g*$_{1.2}$ *h* syrr syr-cu copt æth: om CDI$_c$ℵ rel vulg lat-*e f l* arm Orig$_{expr}$ Chr Euthym Arnob. (T$_c$?) om *το* (bef *πλοιον*) B 1. 33. 124 Scr's s arm Eus Chr-2-9-G-H: ins CDI$_c$Pℵ rel Orig$_7$. om *αυτον* (*see* || *Mark*) D 37. 49 ev-y$_1$ lat-*a b e ff*$_2$ *g*$_1$ *h* arm Arnob: *αυτους* I$_c$Θ ev-H[1].

23. om *απολυσας τους οχλους* ℵ[1](ins ℵ-corr[1]) ev-P[1].

24. om *ηδη* (*see* || *Mark*) D 253 ev-36 Scr's o[1] vulg lat-*a f ff*$_1$ *l* Syr syr-cu copt æth arm. *ην εις μεσον της θαλ. βασανιζ.* D lat-*e*: *σταδιους πολλους απο της γης απειχεν βασανιζ.* B 13. 124 Syr syr-cu (syr-jer copt) arm: txt CPℵ rel syr æth Orig [Chr] Hil (Θ?) for *ην γαρ*, *η γαρ* D[1].

25. *τεταρτης δε φυλακης* D. *ηλθεν* (*απηλθ. not being understood*) BC[2] P(Treg) T$_c$ℵ 1. 33 latt syrr syr-cu copt æth arm Orig$_1$ Eus$_2$ Bas Chr: *ερχεται* syr-mg: txt C[1](appy) D P(Tischdf) rel syr-txt. rec ins *ο ιησους* bef *προς αυτους*, with C[3]L rel lat-*a b c e f ff*$_2$ *g*$_2$ *h* Syr syr-cu arm Eus: om BC[1]DPST$_c$VΓΔ Θ(appy) ℵ 1. 33 vulg lat-*f ff*$_1$ *g*$_1$ *l* syr copt æth Orig Bas Chr Arnob. *περιπατων* bef *προς αυτους* D. rec *επι της θαλασσης*, with CD rel Eus$_2$: txt BPT$_c$ΔΘℵ 1 Orig$_1$.

the miraculous increase took place, so that they broke and distributed enough for all.

20. κοφίνους] in the construction, is in apposition with τὸ περισσεῦον. The *cophinus* was the usual accompaniment of the Jew: see Juv. Sat. iii. 14—'Judæis, quorum cophinus fœnumque supellex;' and Sat. vi. 542. Reland, whom Schöttgen (in loc.) follows, supposes that the basket was to carry their own meats on a journey, for fear of pollution by eating those of the Gentiles, and the hay to sleep on for the same reason. **21.**] **χωρὶς γυν. κ. παιδ.** is peculiar to Matt., although this might have been inferred from ἄνδρες being used in the other three Evangelists. See note on John vi. 10.

22—33.] Jesus walks on the sea. Mark vi. 45—52. (Luke omits this incident.) John vi. 16—21. The conviction of the people after the foregoing miracle was, that Jesus was the Messiah; and their disposition, to take Him by force, and make Him a king. See John vi. 14, 15. For this reason he constrained His disciples to leave Him, because they were but too anxious to second this wish of the multitude; and *their* dismissal was therefore an important step towards the other.

22. εἰς τὸ πέραν] Mark adds πρὸς Βηθσαϊδάν, John εἰς Καφαρναούμ: for the Bethsaïda, the city of Philip and Andrew and Peter, was distinct from Bethsaïda Julias, in whose neighbourhood the miracle took place,—and in the direction of Capernaum. **25.**] The *fourth watch* according to the *Roman* calculation, which was by this time common among the Jews (who themselves divided the night into three parts or watches). This would be,—near the vernal equinox which this was,—*between three and six in the morn-*

r = ch. ii. 3 al. Gen. xl. 6.
s ‖ Mk. only †. Wisd. xvii. 15 only.
t ch. xiii. 44 reff.
u John iv. 26. xviii. 5, 6, 8 al. Deut. xxxii. 39.
v = ch. xii. 38 al.
w = here only. Ezek. xxvii. 29.
x ch. xviii. 6 only. 2 Kings xx. 19 al.
y Matt., here only. Mark viii. 23. Luke ix. 47 al. Exod. iv. 4.
z ch. vi. 30. viii. 26. xvi. 8. Luke xii. 28 only †.
a = ch. xxvi. 8 ‖ Mk. Mark xv. 34 only. Wisd. iv. 17.
b ch. xxviii. 17 only †.
c = ‖ Mk. ch. xv. 39. John xxi. 11. Acts xxi. 6. Jon. i. 3 Ed-vat. (not ABℵ.)
d ‖ Mk. Mark iv. 39 only. Gen. viii. 1. Jon. i. 11, 12.
e w. dat., ch. ii. 2 reff.
f ch. iv. 3.

26 *καὶ ἰδόντες αὐτὸν οἱ μαθηταὶ* [q] *ἐπὶ τῆς θαλάσσης*
[q] *περιπατοῦντα* [r] *ἐταράχθησαν* λέγοντες ὅτι [s] *φάντασμά*
ἐστιν, καὶ [t] *ἀπὸ τοῦ φόβου ἔκραξαν.* 27 *εὐθέως δὲ ἐλά-*
λησεν αὐτοῖς [ὁ Ἰησοῦς] *λέγων* Θαρσεῖτε, [u] *ἐγώ* [u] *εἰμι,*
μὴ φοβεῖσθε. 28 [v] *ἀποκριθεὶς δὲ αὐτῷ ὁ* Πέτρος *εἶπεν*
Κύριε, *εἰ σὺ εἶ, κέλευσόν με ἐλθεῖν πρός σε ἐπὶ τὰ ὕδατα.*
29 *ὁ δὲ εἶπεν* Ἐλθέ. *καὶ* [w] *καταβὰς ἀπὸ τοῦ πλοίου* ..ειπεν ελ. Θ.
Πέτρος [q] *περιεπάτησεν* [q] *ἐπὶ τὰ ὕδατα ἐλθεῖν πρὸς τὸν* BCDEF GKLM
Ἰησοῦν. 30 *βλέπων δὲ τὸν ἄνεμον ἰσχυρὸν ἐφοβήθη, καὶ* PST_cU VXΓΔΠ
ἀρξάμενος [x] *καταποντίζεσθαι ἔκραξεν λέγων* Κύριε *σῶσόν* ℵ 1. 33
με. 31 *εὐθέως δὲ ὁ* Ἰησοῦς *ἐκτείνας τὴν χεῖρα* [y] *ἐπελά-*
βετο αὐτοῦ καὶ λέγει αὐτῷ [z] Ὀλιγόπιστε [a] *εἰς* [a] *τί* [b] *ἐδίσ-*
τασας; 32 *καὶ* [c] *ἀναβάντων αὐτῶν εἰς τὸ πλοῖον* [d] *ἐκό-*
πασεν ὁ ἄνεμος. 33 *οἱ δὲ ἐν τῷ πλοίῳ* [*ἐλθόντες*] [e] **προσ-**
εκύνησαν αὐτῷ λέγοντες Ἀληθῶς [f] *θεοῦ υιος εἶ.*

26. *οι* **δε** *μαθ.* bef *ιδοντες αυτον* (*from* ‖ *Mark*) BD ℵ-corr[1] 13. 61. 124 lat-*f*: *ιδοντες δε αυτον* (omg *οι μ.*) ℵ[1] lat-*a b e* $ff_{1.2}$ g_1 *h* [Eus_1]: *και ιδ. αυτ.* 1 vulg lat-*c* g_2 [Eus_1] Chr-γ Arnob Aug: txt CP rel syrr syr-cu copt æth. (T_c ?) *περιπ.* bef *επι τ. θαλ.* T_c 33 lat-g_1 syrr syr-cu Eus. rec *την θαλασσαν*, with P rel: txt $BCDT_c$ℵ 1. 33 Eus_2 Chr Thl.

27. *ευθυς* (*from* ‖ *Mark*) BDT_cℵ: txt C[P] rel Eus [Chr]. om *ο ιησ.* DT_cℵ 231 lat-ff_1 syr-cu copt Eus: ins bef *αυτοις* B ℵ-corr[1] 131: aft CP rel lat-*f* syr æth arm: *ο ιησ. ελ. αυτ.* latt Syr. *θαρρειτε* D.

28. om *αυτω* Δ 157. 209 Scr's c l m n w evv-H-y-z vulg lat-*a c* æth Euthym: *ο πετρος ειπεν* bef *αυτω* B 120. 240-4-5 lat-g_1 Syr copt: txt CD[P]ℵ rel lat-*b e f* $ff_{1.2}$ g_2 *h* syr arm Eus. (T_c ?)—om *ο* D. *ει συ ει* bef *κυριε* ℵ. for *με*, *μοι* CΔ Scr's s. rec *προς σε* bef *ελθειν*, with L[P] rel vulg-ed: txt BCDΔΘℵ 1. 33 am lat-*a b c* &c syrr syr-cu [copt] æth arm Eus. (T_c ?)

29. rec ins *ο* bef *πετρος*, with C[P] rel: om BDℵ Eus. (T_c ?) for *ελθειν*, *και ηλθεν* (*corrn from the less usual infinitive*) B (not C[1], if Tischdf has accurately edited it: there is not room) syr-cu arm Chr: *et veniens* æth: *ελθιν ηλθεν ουν* ℵ[1]: txt C[2](C[1] ?) D[P]ℵ[3a] rel latt(*ut veniret*) Orig. [T_c ?]

30. om *ισχυρον* B[1]-txt ℵ 33 copt: ins B[1]-marg rel &c. [T_c ?]

31. *ευθυς* ℵ. om *ο* D [om *ο ιησ.* E[1]].

32. rec **εμβαντων**, with CP rel: txt BDT_cℵ 13. 33. 124 Orig Cyr-jer.

33. om *ελθοντες* BC^2T_cℵ 1 lat-ff_1 copt æth Orig Did: txt DP rel latt syrr syr-cu arm. *υιος θεου ει* and add *συ* D lat-*a b*.

ing. **ἀπῆλθεν πρὸς αὐτ.**] a mixed construction for *ἀπῆλθεν ἀπὸ τοῦ ὄρους καὶ ἦλθεν πρὸς αὐτ.* The words **περιπατ. ἐπὶ τὴν θάλ.** (or **τῆς θαλάσσης**,—the gen. of the mere appearing on the spot, the accus. of motion,—*over the sea.* Webst. and Wilk. cite *ἐπὶ πολλὰ ἀλήθην* Od. ξ. 120,—*ἐπ' ἔννεα κεῖτο πέλεθρα* Od. λ. 577) are common to the three Evangelists, and can have no other meaning here, than that the Lord *walked bodily on the surface of the water.* The passages commonly cited to shew that *ἐπί* with a gen. can mean 'on the bank of,' are not applicable here, being all after verbs of *rest*, not of motion. 4 Kings ii. 7: Dan. viii. 2 Theod.: John xxi. 1. In ref. Job we read of the Almighty, *ὁ τανύσας τὸν οὐρανὸν μόνος καὶ περιπατῶν ὡς ἐπ' ἐδάφους ἐπὶ θαλάσσης.* Mark adds *καὶ ἤθελεν παρελθεῖν αὐτούς*: John, *καὶ ἐγγὺς τοῦ πλοίου γινόμενον.* See notes on John. **28.**] This narrative respecting Peter is peculiar to Matthew. It is in very strict accordance with his warm and confident character, and has been called almost a 'rehearsal' of his denial afterwards. It contains one of the most pointed and striking revelations which we have of *the nature and analogy of faith;* and a notable

34 Καὶ [g] διαπεράσαντες ἦλθον εἰς τὴν γῆν Γεννησαρετ.
35 καὶ [h] ἐπιγνόντες αὐτὸν οἱ ἄνδρες [i] τοῦ τόπου ἐκείνου
ἀπέστειλαν εἰς ὅλην τὴν [k] περίχωρον ἐκείνην, καὶ προσήνεγκαν αὐτῷ πάντας τοὺς [l] κακῶς [l] ἔχοντας, 36 καὶ
[m] παρεκάλουν αὐτὸν ἵνα μόνον [n] ἅψωνται τοῦ [o] κρασπέδου
τοῦ ἱματίου αὐτοῦ, καὶ ὅσοι [n] ἥψαντο [p] διεσώθησαν.
XV. 1 Τότε προσέρχονται τῷ Ἰησοῦ οἱ ἀπὸ Ἱεροσολύμων γραμματεῖς καὶ Φαρισαῖοι λέγοντες 2 Διὰ τί οἱ
μαθηταί σου [q] παραβαίνουσιν τὴν [r] παράδοσιν τῶν [s] πρεσβυτέρων; οὐ γὰρ [tu] νίπτονται τὰς [u] χεῖρας αὐτῶν ὅταν
ἄρτον ἐσθίωσιν. 3 ὁ δέ ἀποκριθεὶς εἶπεν αὐτοῖς [v] Διὰ τί

g ch. x. al.
h ch. vii. 16, 20. Luke xxiv. 16, 31. Gen. xxxvii. 32, 33.
i Gen. xxxviii. 21, 22.
k ch. iii. 5 al. 1 Chron. v. 16.
l ch. iv. 24. ix. 12 ‖ al. Ezek. xxxiv. 4.
m w. ἵνα, ‖ Mk. Mark v. 10, 18 ‖ L. 1 Cor. xvi. 12, 15 al.
n ch. ix. 20, 21 al. Hag. ii. 12, 13.
o ch. xxiii. 5 reff. Zech. viii. 23.
p Luke vii. 3. Acts xxiii. 24. xxvii. 43, 44. xxviii. 1, 4. 1 Pet. iii. 20 only. Jer. viii. 20.
q Acts i. 25 (2 John 9 v. r.) only. Isa. xxiv. 5 A. Sir. x. 19.
r here, &c. and ‖. 1 Cor. xi. 2. Gal. i. 14. Col. ii. 8. 2 Thess. ii. 15. iii. 6 only ‡. (Jer. xxxix. [xxxii.] 4. xli. [xxxiv.] 2 only.)
s = ‖. Heb. xi. 2 only.
t ch. vi. 17 reff.
u ‖ Mk. (John xiii. 9) only. Exod. xxx. 19.
v see Num. xiv. 41.

34. επι την γην γενν. (*as in ‖ Mark*) C[1] 13. 124-57 Chr-2-6-9-η-ρ: επι την γην εις γενν. (*combn of Matt and Mark*) BDT_cΔℵ 33 syr arm: alii aliter: txt P rel copt arm $Orig_3$ Chr(Fd).

35. om εκεινου ℵT_c. (No readings of T_c are given from this point to ch xv. 2.)

36. om αυτοι B[1](insd in marg *a prima manu* [by B[3], appy, Tischdf]) $Orig_1$ Chr. aft οσοι ins αν C Scr's m. for διεσωθ., εσωθησαν ℵ.

Chap. XV. 1. for προσερχ., προερχονται D[1]-gr(txt D[3]). for τω ιησου, προς αυτον D latt(exc *f*) æth Hil [Aug_1]: αυτω 1 Orig. om οι (*as in the way: that it should have been insd from ‖ Mark, as Meyer, is improb, seeing that the form of the sentence there is different*) BDℵ 1. 124[1]. 209 Scr's a c ev-y copt $Orig_2$: ins CP rel. transp γραμματεις and φαρισαιοι (*see ‖ Mark*) BDℵ 1. 13. 33. 124 lat-*e* Syr copt arm Orig: txt CP rel syr-cu syr æth Hil.

2. om αυτων (*as unnecessary: see also Mark* vii. 3) B[T_c]Δℵ 1. 229[1] lat-*f* g_1 arm $Orig_2$ [Cyr_1] Chr-γ-L.

3. om αυτοις D lat-*e* copt.

example of the power of the higher spiritual state of man over the inferior laws of matter, so often brought forward by our Lord. See ch. xvii. 20; xxi. 21.

32.] John (vi. 21) adds καὶ εὐθέως ἐγένετο τὸ πλοῖον ἐπὶ τῆς γῆς εἰς ἣν ὑπῆγον:—see note there. 33.] These persons were probably the crew of the ship, and distinct from the disciples. On **θεοῦ υἱός**, see note, ch. iv. 3. It is the first time that our Lord is called so by *men* in the three synoptic Gospels. See ch. iii. 17; iv. 3; viii. 29: and John i. 34, 50. This feeling of amazement and reverence pervaded *the disciples also*: see the strong expressions of Mark vi. 52. 34—36.] Mark vi. 53—56. *Gennesar* or *Gennesaret*, a district from which the lake was also occasionally so called, extended along its western shore. See Josephus's glowing description of the beauty and fertility of this plain, B. J. iii. 10. 7. At its northern end was Capernaum, near which our Lord landed, as would appear from John vi. 24, 25. 36. **παρεκάλ. . . . . ἵνα**] For a discussion of the construction of verbs of entreaty, &c. with ἵνα and ὅπως, see note, 1 Cor. xiv. 13. On **κρασπ.** see note on ch. ix. 20. **διεσ.** as E. V., **were made perfectly whole.**

Chap. XV. 1—20.] Discourse concerning eating with unwashed hands. Mark vii. 1—23. From Mark it appears that these Scribes and Pharisees had come *expressly* from Jerusalem *to watch our Lord*: most probably after that Passover which was nigh at the time of feeding the five thousand, John vi. 4.

2.] The Jews attached more importance to the traditionary exposition than to the Scripture text itself. They compared the written word to water; the traditionary exposition to the wine which must be mingled with it. The duty of washing before meat is not inculcated in the law, but only in the traditions of the Scribes. So rigidly did the Jews observe it, that Rabbi Akiba, being imprisoned, and having water scarcely sufficient to sustain life given him, preferred dying of thirst to eating without washing his hands. **πρεσβύτεροι** are not *the elders*, but the

w ch. iv. 6 || (from Ps. xc. 11). xix. 7 al. Gen. ii. 16.
x ||. ch. xix. 19 ||. Exod. xx. 12. = Prov. iii. 9.
y Exod. xxi. 16.
z || Mk. Mark ix. 39. Acts xix. 9 only. Prov. xx. 20. 1 Kings iii. 13.
a ||. Exod. l. c. see John xii. 33. Rev. ii. 23. Lev. xx. 9.

καὶ ὑμεῖς [q] παραβαίνετε τὴν ἐντολὴν τοῦ θεοῦ διὰ τὴν
[r] παράδοσιν ὑμῶν; 4 ὁ γὰρ θεὸς [w] ἐνετείλατο λέγων
[x] Τίμα τὸν πατέρα καὶ τὴν μητέρα, καὶ [y] Ὁ [z] κακολογῶν
πατέρα ἢ μητέρα [a] θανάτῳ [a] τελευτάτω· 5 ὑμεῖς δὲ λέγετε
Ὃς ἂν εἴπῃ τῷ πατρὶ ἢ τῇ μητρὶ [b] Δῶρον ὃ ἐὰν ἐξ ἐμοῦ
[c] ὠφεληθῇς· 6 [καὶ] οὐ μὴ τιμήσει τὸν πατέρα αὐτοῦ [ἢ
τὴν μητέρα αὐτοῦ]· καὶ [d] ἠκυρώσατε τὸν νόμον τοῦ θεοῦ
διὰ τὴν [q] παράδοσιν ὑμῶν. 7 ὑποκριταί, [e] καλῶς [f] ἐπροφήτευσεν περὶ ὑμῶν Ἡσαΐας λέγων 8 [g] Ὁ λαὸς οὗτος τοῖς

...την εν. P.
Θ λεγων τιμα...
BCDEF GKLMS T_cUVX ΓΔΘΠℵ 1. 33

b = ch. v. 23, 24 al. Lev. xxvii. 9. c ch. xvi. 26. Mark v. 26 al. Jer. ii. 11. vii. 8. d || Mk. Gal. iii. 17 only †. Esdr. vi. 32 only. (-ρος, Prov. i. 25. v. 7.) e = || Mk. Mark xii. 28, 32 al. Jer. i. 12. f ch. xi. 13 al. Jer. xx. 1. g Isa. xxix. 13.

om *και* ℵ[1](ins ℵ[2]) Iren-int$_2$.

4. for *ενετ. λεγ.*, *ειπεν* (*from* || *Mark*) BDT_cℵ[3a](appy: but corrd) **1. 124** latt Syr syr-cu syr-mg copt æth arm Ptol Orig Cyr Iren-int Jer: txt CΘℵ[1] rel lat-*f*. rec aft *τον πατερα* ins *σου* (|| *Mark*), with C[2] [E[1](certe *σ* scriptum erat. Tischdf)] KLMUΠ 33 am lat-*a b c f ff*$_2$ *g*$_1$ Syr syr-cu syr-with-ob copt arm ([Ptol] Orig$_1$): om BC[1]Dℵ rel vulg-ed(with forj harl[1]) lat-*e ff*$_1$ *g*$_2$ æth Orig$_1$ Chr$_1$ [Cyr$_1$] Iren-int Cypr Aug.

6. at beg ins *ουδεν εστιν* ℵ[1](ℵ-corr[1 or 3] disapproving). om *και* (*to simplify the construction*) BCDT_cℵ **1. 33** lat-*a b e ff*$_2$ *g*$_1$ syr-cu copt æth Orig Cyr$_2$: ins L rel vulg lat-*c f* syrr arm Jer Quæst. rec *τιμηση* (*to corresp with ειπη above*), with Lℵ rel Cyr$_1$: txt BCDE[2]T_cΔΘΠ[2]ℵ **1. 33** Orig Cyr$_1$ Aug Jer. om *η τ. μητ. αυτου* (*possibly from homœotel*) BDℵ lat-*a e* syr-cu [om *αυτου* T_c 33 Chr Cyr$_1$ Jer]. rec (for *τον νομον*) *την εντολην* (*from Mark* vii. 9), with LΘ rel vulg lat-*c f g*$_1$ syr-txt arm-mss Orig$_1$[and int$_1$] Cyr: *τον λογον* (*from Mark* vii. 13?) BD ℵ[3a](appy, but *νομον* restored) lat-*a b e ff*$_{1.2}$ Syr syr-cu syr-mg copt æth arm [Orig$_1$] Eus Iren-int Aug: txt CT_cℵ[1] 13. 124. 346 Ptol.

8. rec ins *εγγιζει μοι* bef *ο λαος ουτος* and adds *τω στοματι αυτων και* (*as* LXX-B),

ancients. See ref. Heb. **3. καὶ ὑμ.**] The *καί* implies that there was a *παράβασις* also on *their part*—acknowledging that on the part of the disciples. **τὴν ἐντ. τ. θ.**] A remarkable testimony from our Lord to the divine origin of the Mosaic law: not merely of the Decalogue, as such, for the second command quoted is not in the Decalogue, and it is to be observed that where the text has **ὁ θεὸς ἐνετείλατο**, Mark (vii. 10) has **Μωυσῆς εἶπεν.** **4.**] **θανάτῳ τελ.** is a Hebraism, מוֹת יוּמָת: see reff. LXX. **5.**] Lightfoot on this verse shews that the expression cited by our Lord did not always bind the utterer to consecrate his property to religious uses, but was by its mere utterance sufficient to absolve him from the duty of caring for his parents: see further on the word Corban in Mark vii. 11. The construction of this and the following ver. is: **But ye say, Whosoever shall say to his father or mother, That from which thou mightest have been benefited by me, is an offering** (consecrated to God; see above) . . . . (understand, **is free**). **[And] such an one will certainly not honour his father [or his mother].** So || Mark, *οὐκέτι ἀφίετε κ.τ.λ.*

The joining of [*καὶ*] *οὐ μὴ κ.τ.λ.* to the *ὃς ἄν* above, and making the aposiopesis after *μητ. αὐτοῦ*, is inconsistent with the usage of *οὐ μή*, which contains in itself an apodosis, being an elliptical construction for *οὐ δέος μή* or the like; see Hartung, Partikellehre, ii. p. 155 ff. The *future ind.* after *οὐ μή* makes the certainty more apparent: so *καὶ τοῦτο γὰρ εὖ εἰδέναι χρὴ ὅτι οὐ μὴ δυνήσεται Κῦρος εὑρεῖν* . . . . Xen. Cyr. viii. 1. 5. See more examples in Hartung, ib. Of course the apodosis is *our Lord's* saying, not that of the Pharisees. **8.**] The portion of Isaiah from which this citation is made (ch. xxiv.—xxxv.) sets forth, in alternate threatenings and promises, the punishment of the mere nominal Israel, and the salvation of the true Israel of God. And, as so often in the prophetic word, its threats and promises are for all times of the Church;—the particular event then foretold being but one fulfilment of those deeper and more general declarations of God, which shall be ever having their successive illustrations in His dealings with men. The prophecy is nearly according to the LXX, which compare. The citation in Mark is (if the spurious words in the rec. here be

..xv. 8 (appy)T_c

[h] χείλεσίν με τιμᾷ, ἡ δὲ καρδία αὐτῶν [i] πόῤῥω [j] ἀπέχει ἀπ'
ἐμοῦ. 9 [k] μάτην δὲ [l] σέβονταί με διδάσκοντες [m] διδασκαλίας [n] ἐντάλματα ἀνθρώπων. 10 καὶ προςκαλεσάμενος
τὸν ὄχλον εἶπεν αὐτοῖς Ἀκούετε καὶ συνίετε. 11 οὐ τὸ
[o] εἰςερχόμενον εἰς τὸ στόμα [p] κοινοῖ τὸν ἄνθρωπον, ἀλλὰ
τὸ [q] ἐκπορευόμενον ἐκ τοῦ στόματος τοῦτο [p] κοινοῖ τὸν
ἄνθρωπον. 12 τότε προςελθόντες οἱ μαθηταὶ λέγουσιν
αὐτῷ Οἶδας ὅτι οἱ Φαρισαῖοι ἀκούσαντες τὸν λόγον
[r] ἐσκανδαλίσθησαν; 13 ὁ δὲ ἀποκριθεὶς εἶπεν Πᾶσα [s] φυτεία
ἣν οὐκ [t] ἐφύτευσεν ὁ [u] πατήρ μου ὁ [u] οὐράνιος [v] ἐκριζωθή-
σεται. 14 [w] ἄφετε αὐτούς· [x] ὁδηγοί εἰσιν τυφλοὶ τυφλῶν·
τυφλὸς δὲ τυφλὸν ἐὰν [y] ὁδηγῇ, ἀμφότεροι εἰς [z] βόθυνον
πεσοῦνται. 15 ἀποκριθεὶς δὲ ὁ Πέτρος εἶπεν αὐτῷ

Z ο δε... BCDEF GKLMS UVXZΓ ΔΘΠℵ 1. 33

h || from l. c. Rom. iii. 13. 1 Cor. xiv. 21. Heb. xi. 12. xiii. 15. 1 Pet. iii. 10 only. Prov. vi. 2. Mal. ii. 6.
i || Mk. Luke xiv. 32. xxiv. 28 only. l. c. Job v. 4.
j = || from l. c. Luke vii. 6. xv. 20. xxiv. 13. Ezek. xi. 15.
k || only. 3 Kings xx. (xxi.) 20.
l constr., ||. Acts xvi. 14. xviii. 7, 13. xix. 27 (absol., Acts xiii. 43, 50. xvii. 4, 17) only. Josh. iv. 24.
m ||. elsw. Paul only, Eph. iv. 14 al. Prov. ii. 17.
n ||. Col. ii. 22 only. l. c. Job xxiii. 11 (12 Bℵ) only.
o = Acts xi. 8. Ezek. iv. 14.
p = here, &c. and ||. Heb. ix. 13. Acts xxi. 28 (x. 15. xi. 9) only †.
q = ch. iv. 4. Eph. iv. 29. Num. xxxii. 24.
r ch. xiii. 21 al. fr.
s here only. 4 Kings xix. 29. Ezek. xvii. 7. Mic. i. 6 only.
t ch. xxi. 33 ||. Luke xiii. 6. xvii. 6, 28. 1 Cor. iii. 6, &c. ix. 7 only. Gen. ii. 8 al.
u ch. v. 48 reff.
v ch. xiii. 29. Luke xvii. 6. Jude 12 only. Jer. i. 10.
w Mark xiv. 6. 4 Kings iv. 27.
x ch. xxiii. 16, 24. Acts i. 16. Rom. ii. 19 only. Ezra viii. 1 only. Wisd. vii. 15 al.
y Luke vi. 39. John xvi. 13. Acts viii. 31. Rev. vii. 17 only. Ps. xxiv. 5.
z ch. xii. 11. Luke vi. 39 only. Isa. xxiv. 18 al.

with C rel lat-*f* syr : om BDLT_cℵ 33. 124 latt Syr syr-cu copt æth arm Clem-rom Just Ptol Clem Orig(expr: *παρέθετο ῥητὸν ἀπὸ τοῦ Ἡσαΐου, ὅπερ αὐταῖς λέξεσιν οὕτως ἔχει, καὶ εἶπε κύριος Ἐγγίζει μοι ὁ λαὸς οὗτος ἐν τῷ στόματι αὐτῶν καὶ τὰ ἑξῆς· καὶ προείπομέν γε ὅτι οὐκ αὐταῖς λέξεσιν ἀνέγραψεν ὁ Ματθαῖος τὸ προφητικόν.* Comm in Matt, tom xi. 11, vol iii. p 492) [Eus_2] Bas Chr Cyr Tert Cypr Hil Ambr Ambrst Jer Gaud Juv. (*ο λαος ουτ. εγγ. μοι*(alone) 1.) for *απεχει*, *εστιν* D lat-*a b c* Clem, *est a me* Hil lat-ff(exc Tert Cypr).

11. aft *ου* ins *παν* D. for *εισερχ.*, *ερχομενον* B. aft *στομα* ins *τουτο* (*see below*) ℵ[1](ℵ[3a] disapproving). *κοινωνει* D[1](twice: txt D[4]?), *communicat* D-lat (and lat-*c* the second time) Tert Jer(verbum *communicat* proprie scripturarum est et publico sermone non teritur ("non teritur" is quoted "conteritur" by Tischdf)) Aug(and in vv 18, 20) : *coinquinat* most latt. for *τουτο*, *εκεινο* D.

12. rec aft *μαθηται* ins *αυτου* (|| *Mark*), with C rel vss: om BDℵ 13. 61. 124. rec (for *λεγουσιν*) *ειπον* (*change to historic tense*), with C rel latt syr æth [Chr], *ειπαν* ℵ: txt BD 1. 13. 33. 61. 124 lat-ff_1 Syr syr-cu arm.

14. for *αυτους*, *τους τυφλους* D. for *οδ. εισιν τυφλοι τυφλων*, *τυφλοι εισιν οδηγοι* BD : *οδ. εισι τυφλων* K : *οδ. εισιν τυφλοι* ℵ[1] : *τυφλοι εισιν οδ. τυφλων* L Z(appy) ℵ[3a](but former readg restored) 1. 33 vulg lat-*a c* syrr æth $Orig_2$ Bas_{oft} Cyr_7 Cypr Jer Gild (*all apparently emendns of the arrangement, or mistakes owing to the recurrence of τυφλοι τυφλων*) : txt C rel syr-cu. for *βοθυνον*, *βοθρον* D 1 Cyr : *εις βοθ.* is aft the verb in DLZ 1 æth. *εμπεσουνται* DF 99. 238-40-4-6-8-50-3-9 Scr's l m n o ev-y [Bas_1(and mss_1)] Chr Cyr.

15. *αυτω* bef *ειπεν* B.

cancelled) verbatim the same with that in the text. Stier however maintains (vol. ii. p. 142) that the words in question ought to be supplied in Mark, because *ἐγγίζει* is wanted to oppose to *πόῤῥω ἀπέχει*, and *στόματι* to connect with *στόμα* in ver. 11. **9.**] LXX, *ἐντάλματα ἀνθ. καὶ διδασκαλίας*. The two are here in apposition, as in E. V. **10.**] *ἐκείνους μὲν ἐπιστομίσας καὶ καταισχύνας ἀφῆκεν ὡς ἀνιάτους· τρέπει δὲ τὸν λόγον πρὸς τὸν ὄχλον ὡς ἀξιολογώτερον.* Euthym. **12.**] This took place after our Lord had entered the house and was apart from the multitude: see Mark ver. 17. **τὸν λόγον**] the saying addressed to the multitude in ver. 11. **13.**] The **plant** is the teaching of the Pharisees, altogether of human, and not of divine planting. That this is so, is clear by *ἄφετε αὐτούς* following, and by the analogy of our Lord's parabolic symbolism, in which *seed*, *plant*, &c., are compared to *doctrine*, which however in its growth becomes identified with, and impersonated by, its recipients and disseminators. See this illustrated in notes

[a] Φράσον ἡμῖν τὴν παραβολὴν [ταύτην]. 16 ὁ δὲ εἶπεν ..v.15 Θ.
[b] Ἀκμὴν καὶ ὑμεῖς [c] ἀσύνετοί ἐστε; 17 οὔπω νοεῖτε ὅτι πᾶν
τὸ [d] εἰςπορευόμενον εἰς τὸ [d] στόμα εἰς τὴν [e] κοιλίαν [f] χωρεῖ
καὶ εἰς [g] ἀφεδρῶνα ἐκβάλλεται; 18 τὰ δὲ [h] ἐκπορευόμενα
ἐκ τοῦ στόματος ἐκ τῆς καρδίας ἐξέρχεται, κἀκεῖνα
[h] κοινοῖ τὸν ἄνθρωπον. 19 ἐκ γὰρ τῆς καρδίας ἐξέρχονται [i] διαλογισμοὶ πονηροί, φόνοι, [k] μοιχεῖαι, [l] πορνεῖαι,
[m] κλοπαί, [n] ψευδομαρτυρίαι, [o] βλασφημίαι. 20 ταῦτά
ἐστιν τὰ [h] κοινοῦντα [p] τὸν ἄνθρωπον· τὸ δὲ [q] ἀνίπτοις
χερσὶν φαγεῖν οὐ [h] κοινοῖ [p] τὸν ἄνθρωπον. ...χερσιν F.
21 Καὶ ἐξελθὼν ἐκεῖθεν ὁ Ἰησοῦς [r] ἀνεχώρησεν εἰς τὰ BCDEG KLMSU
[s] μέρη Τύρου καὶ Σιδῶνος. 22 καὶ ἰδοὺ γυνὴ Χαναναία VXZΓΔ
ἀπὸ τῶν [t] ὁρίων ἐκείνων ἐξελθοῦσα [u] * ἐκραύγασεν λέγουσα ΠΝ 1. 33

a ch. xiii. 36 only. Job vi. 24. xii. 8 only.
b here only. ὁ ὄχλος ἀκμὴν διέβαινε, Xen. Anab. iv. 3. 26.
c ‖ Mk. Rom. i. 21, 31. x. 19 (from Deut. xxxii. 21) only. Wisd. i. 5.
d here only. see ver. 11.
e ‖. 1 Cor. vi. 13. Rev. x. 9, 10 al. 2 Kings xx. 10. 2 Chron. xxi. 15, 19.
f = & w. εἰς, 2 Pet. iii. 9 only ‡. (ch. xix. 11, 12 al. 2 Macc. xv. 37.)
g ‖ only +. (-δρος, Lev. xv. 10, 20.)
h ver. 11 reff.
i Luke ii. 35. ix. 47. 1 Cor. iii. 20. James ii. 4 al. Ps. lv. 5.
k ‖ Mk. [John viii. 3 and Gal. v. 19 rec.] only. Jer. xiii. 27. Hos. ii. 2. iv. 2. Wisd. xiv. 26 only.
l 1 Cor. vi. 13, 18, &c. Hos. ii. 2.
m ‖ only. Gen. xl. 15.
n ch. xxvi. 59 only +. (-ρεῖν, ch. xix. 18.)
o ch. xii. 31 al. fr. Ezek. xxxv. 12.
p art., ch. v. 15 reff.
q Mark vii. 2 (5 v. r.) only +. Hom. Il. ζ. 266.
r = ch. ii. 12, &c. reff.
s = ch. ii. 22. xvi. 13. Mark viii. 10 al. Neh. iii. 15.
t ch. ii. 16. xix. 1 al. Mt. Mk. only, exc. Acts xiii. 50. Josh. xv. 1.
u ch. xii. 19. John xi. 43 al4. Acts xxii. 23 only. Ezra iii. 13.

om ταυτην (*as not in Mark* vii. 17) BZℵ 1 copt Orig: ins CDΘ rel latt [syrr syr-cu æth arm, αυτην Δ], bef τ. παραβ. 13. 124.

16. rec ins ιησους bef ειπεν, with CL rel lat-*f* syr arm: om BDZℵ 33 latt Syr syr-cu copt æth.

17. for ουπω, ου (*see* ‖ *Mark*) BDZ 33 latt Syr syr-cu æth: txt Cℵ rel syr copt. for εισπορευομ., εισερχομενον B $Orig_1$[txt_1]. ins τον bef αφεδρωνα Γℵ [Chr].

18. om from εξερχεται to εξερχ. next ver (*homœotel*) ℵ[1](ins ℵ-corr[1]). for κακεινα, εκεινα D lat-*c* ff_1 copt. κοινωνει D[1][(and lat) Aug_1].

19. βλασφημεια D[1]-gr lat-*e* syr-cu syr æth.

20. εισιν τα κοινωνουντα, and κοινωνει D[1].

22. * ἔκραζεν (*more usual word*) BDℵ[3a] 1 lat-*c* ff_1 syr-cu copt arm: εκραξεν Zℵ vulg lat-*a e f* $g_{1.2}$ syr Orig Chr Hil: εκραυγαζεν M: εκραυγασεν C rel. rec aft εκρ. ins αυτω, with L rel lat-*f* ff_1 syr; οπισω αυτου D: aft λεγουσα ins αυτω vulg

on the parable of the sower, ch. xiii. 'φυτόν, naturâ: φυτεία, curâ.' Bengel. On this verse see John xv. 1, 2. **15.**] The saying in ver. 11, which is clearly the subject of the question, was not strictly a παραβολή, but a plain declaration; so that either Peter *took it* for a parable,—or παραβ. must be taken in its wider sense of 'an hard saying.' Stier thinks that their questioning as to the meaning of parables in ch. xiii. had habituated them to asking for explanations in this form. **16.**] The saying in ver. 11 was spoken for the multitude, who were exhorted ἀκούετε κ. συνίετε: much more then ought the disciples to have understood it. ἀκμήν = *adhuc* is a later Greek word: Phrynichus (p. 123, ed. Lobeck) says that Xenophon uses it once (ref.): but this is not in the sense of ἔτι, but ἄρτι, '*even now,*' '*in articulo;*' see Lobeck's note, where he gives more examples. **17.**] στόματι, δι' οὗ γίνεται θνητῶν μέν, ὡς ἔφη Πλάτων, εἴσοδος, ἔξοδος δὲ ἀφθάρτων. ἐπεισέρχεται μὲν γὰρ αὐτῷ σιτία καὶ ποτά, φθαρτοῦ σώματος φθαρταὶ τροφαί. λόγοι δὲ ἐξίασιν, ἀθανάτου ψυχῆς ἀθάνατοι νόμοι, δι' ὧν ὁ λογικὸς βίος κυβερνᾶται. Philo de Opif. Mundi, 40, vol. i. p. 29.

21—28.] The Canaanitish woman. Mark vii. 24—30: omitted by Luke. It is not quite clear whether our Lord actually passed the frontier into the land of the heathen, or merely was *on* the frontier. The usage of εἰς τὰ μέρη in Matthew favours the former supposition: see ch. ii. 22; xvi. 13; also for ὅρια, ch. ii. 16; iv. 13; viii. 34. Exod. xvi. 35, εἰς μέρος τῆς Φοινίκης, 'to the borders of Canaan,' has been quoted as supporting the other view; but the usage of our Evangelist himself seems to carry greater weight. And the question is not one of importance; for our Lord did not go to teach or to heal, but, as it would appear, to avoid the pre-

Ἐλέησόν με κύριε υἱὸς Δαυείδ· ἡ θυγάτηρ μου [v] κακῶς
[w] δαιμονίζεται. 23 ὁ δὲ οὐκ ἀπεκρίθη αὐτῇ [x] λόγον. καὶ
...οι μαθ. Z. προσελθόντες οἱ μαθηταὶ αὐτοῦ [y] ἠρώτουν αὐτὸν λέγοντες
[z] Ἀπόλυσον αὐτήν, ὅτι κράζει [a] ὄπισθεν ἡμῶν. 24 ὁ δὲ
ἀποκριθεὶς εἶπεν Οὐκ ἀπεστάλην εἰ μὴ [b] εἰς τὰ [c] πρόβατα
τὰ [c] ἀπολωλότα [c] οἴκου Ἰσραήλ. 25 ἡ δὲ ἐλθοῦσα [d] προσεκύνει αὐτῷ λέγουσα Κύριε [e] βοήθει μοι. 26 ὁ δὲ ἀποκριθεὶς εἶπεν [f] Οὐκ ἔξεστιν λαβεῖν τὸν ἄρτον τῶν τέκνων καὶ
[g] βαλεῖν τοῖς [h] κυναρίοις. 27 ἡ δὲ εἶπεν Ναὶ κύριε, καὶ

v = ch. xvii. 15. xxi. 41. (John xviii. 23. Acts xxiii. 5. James iv. 3.) elsw. w. ἔχειν, ch. iv. 24 al.
w ch. viii. 6 reff.
x 4 Kings xviii. 36. see ch. viii. 8. xxi. 24.
y = Phil. iv. 3. 1 Thess. iv. 12. 2 Thess. ii. 1. form, here only (Mark iv. 10 v. r.).
z = ch. xiv. 15 reff. a w. gen., Luke xxiii. 26 (ch. ix. 20 ‖. Rev. iv. 6. v. 1) only. Gen. xviii. 10.
b = Acts ix. 2. c ch. x. 6 (reff.). d ch. ii. 2 reff. Gen. xliii. 26. e Mark ix. 22, 24. Acts xvi. 9. xxi. 28. 2 Cor. vi. 2, from Isa. xlix. 8. Heb. ii. 18. Rev. xii. 16 only. Ps. lxix. 5. cxviii. 117. f ch. xii. 2 al. fr. g = ch. vii. 6. h here (bis) and ‖ only †.

lat-*c* g_1 : om BCZℵ 1 am lat-*a e* Syr syr-cu copt æth arm Orig [Chr-2]. rec (for υιος) υιε, with CZℵ rel lat-*a c d* Orig : .txt BD Bas.

23. om λογον Z. rec ηρωτων, with E²L rel, -τον E¹M : txt BCDXℵ.

24. aft προβατα ins ταυτα D.

25. προσεκυνησεν (*corrn to historical tense*) Cℵ³ rel vulg lat-*a f l* syrr syr-cu copt Chr Thl : txt BD M(-νη) ℵ¹ 1. 33 lat-*b c* $ff_{1.2}$ $g_{1.2}$ *k* arm Orig.

26. rec (for εξεστιν) εστι καλον (*from* ‖ *Mark*), with BCℵ rel vulg lat-*e f* g_2 *k* [syrr syr-cu] $Orig_1$ [Chr] : txt D(and perhaps no other ms) lat-*a b c* $ff_{1.2}$ g_1 *l* $Orig_2$ hom-Cl Bas-sel Hil_2 Ambr Ambrst Jer.

sent indignation of the Pharisees. Mark's account certainly implies that the woman was in the same place where our Lord was wishing to be hid, and could not. **22.**] **ἀπὸ τ. ὁρ. ἐκ. . .** does not belong to ἐξελθ., but means **of** or **from those parts.** **ἐξελθ.**] **coming out** (they were going by the way, see ver. 23) : i. e. from her house, or town, or village. The inhabitants of these parts are called Canaanites, Num. xiii. 29 : Judg. i. 30, 32, 33 ; and Phœnicians, Exod. vi. 15 (LXX) : Josh. v. 1 (LXX). Mark calls her Ἑλληνίς, i. e. a heathen by religion, and Σύρα Φοινίκισσα τῷ γένει : and describes her only as having come to our Lord *in the house.* But by the account in our text, she had been crying after the Lord and the disciples by the way previously ; and Mark's account must be understood to begin at our ver. 25. From Mark iii. 8, Luke vi. 17, we learn that the fame of our Lord had been spread in these parts, and multitudes from thence had come to Him for healing. It was not this woman's dwelling-place, but her *descent,* which placed the bar between her and our Lord's ministrations. The expression υἱὸς Δαυείδ shews her acquaintance with Jewish expressions and expectations ; but the whole narrative is against De Wette's supposition, that she may have been a proselyte of the gate. **23.**] The reason alleged by the disciples must be coupled with our Lord's unwillingness to be known, stated by Mark (vii. 24), and means, '*she will draw the attention of all upon us.*' The word **ἀπόλυσον** does not necessarily imply *granting* her request, nor the contrary ; but simply **dismiss her,** leaving the method to our Lord Himself. **24.**] See ch. x. 5. Such was the purpose of our Lord's personal ministry ; yet even this was occasionally broken by such incidents as this. The 'fountain sealed' sometimes broke its banks, in token of the rich flood of grace which should follow. See Rom. xv. 8. **25.**] **ἐλθοῦσα,** i. e. into the house where our Lord was. See Mark vii. 24. **26. κυναρίοις**] No *further* contempt is indicated by the *diminutive,* still less any allusion to the *daughter* of the woman : the word is commonly used of *tame* dogs, as diminutives frequently express familiarity. So in Xen. Cyr. viii. 4. 20, εἰ δὲ μεγάλην γαμεῖς, ἥν ποτε βούλῃ αὐτὴν ὀρθὴν φιλῆσαι, προσάλλεσθαί σε δεήσει ὡς **τὰ κυνάρια.** **27.**] The sense of **καὶ γάρ** is not given by '*yet*' in the E. V. The woman, in her humility, *accepts* the appellation which our Lord gives her, and *grounds her plea upon an inference from it.* Her words also have a reference to ἄφες πρῶτον χορτασθῆναι τὰ τέκνα, expressed by Mark vii. 27. The Vulgate has rightly, 'Etiam Domine : *nam et* catelli edunt.' **Yea, Lord : for even the dogs eat** : or, **for the dogs too eat** Our Lord in the use of the familiar diminutive, has expressed not the *unclean-*

γὰρ τὰ [h] κυνάρια [i] ἐσθίει ἀπὸ τῶν [k] ψιχίων τῶν [l] πιπτόν- BCDEG KLMSU VXΓΔΠ ℵ 1. 33
των ἀπὸ τῆς [l] τραπέζης τῶν κυρίων αὐτῶν. 28 τότε
ἀποκριθεὶς ὁ Ἰησοῦς εἶπεν αὐτῇ Ὦ γύναι, μεγάλη σου ἡ
πίστις· [m] γενηθήτω [m] σοι ὡς θέλεις. καὶ ἰάθη ἡ θυγάτηρ
αὐτῆς ἀπὸ τῆς ὥρας ἐκείνης.
29 Καὶ [n] μεταβὰς [n] ἐκεῖθεν ὁ Ἰησοῦς ἦλθεν παρὰ τὴν P μεταβας...
θάλασσαν τῆς Γαλιλαίας· καὶ [o] ἀναβὰς εἰς [o] τὸ ὄρος
ἐκάθητο ἐκεῖ. 30 καὶ προςῆλθον αὐτῷ ὄχλοι πολλοὶ
ἔχοντες μεθ' ἑαυτῶν [p] χωλούς, τυφλούς, [q] κωφούς, [r] κυλλοὺς καὶ ἑτέρους πολλούς· καὶ [s] ἔῤῥιψαν αὐτοὺς παρὰ H παρα...
τοὺς πόδας αὐτοῦ, καὶ ἐθεράπευσεν αὐτούς, 31 ὥςτε
τὸν ὄχλον θαυμάσαι βλέποντας [q] κωφοὺς λαλοῦντας, F οχλους θαυμασαι...
[r] κυλλοὺς ὑγιεῖς, καὶ [p] χωλοὺς περιπατοῦντας, καὶ τυφ-

i w. ἀπό, || only. Gen. iii. 1, 2, 5 (φαγεῖν). w. ἐκ, 1 Cor. ix. 7 al.
k || (Luke xvi. 21 v. r.) only †.
l Luke xvi. 21.
m ch. viii. 13. ix. 29. Luke i. 38.
n ch. xi. 1 reff.
o ch. v. 1 reff.
p ch. xi. 5 al. fr. Isa. xxxv. 6.
q ch. ix. 32 al. Hab. ii. 18.
r ch. xviii. 8 || Mk. only †.
s ch. ix. 36. xxvii. 5. Luke iv. 35. xvii. 2. Acts xxvii. 19, 29 only. = 2 Macc. iii. 15. (-πτεῖν. Acts xxii. 23.)

27. om γαρ (*as superfluous : see also in || Mark*) B lat-*e* Syr. εσθιουσιν D ev-y_1. for ψιχιων, ψειχων D. for κυριων, κυναριων D[1](not lat). [at end Syr syr-cu add *et vivunt.*]

28. om ο ιησ. D[Γ] fuld syr-cu. om ω D 259 forj.

30. χωλ. κυλλ. τυφλ. κωφ. B : χωλ. κωφ. τυφλ. κυλλ. CKΠ : χωλ. τυφλ. κυλλ. D 219 Scr's c lat-g_2 *l* : κωφ. χωλ. τυφλ. κυλλ. LMΔ am(with fuld) syr : χωλ. τυφ. κυλλ. κωφ. ℵ lat-*a b* ff_2 : κωφ. τυφλ. χωλ. κυλλ. 1(Tischdf) 33 ev-y vulg-ed æth $Orig_2$: [χωλ. κωφ. κυλ., omg τυφ. S :] al vary : txt P rel syr syr-cu copt arm. for παρα, υπο D lat-*b*.—om π. τ. C[1]. rec (for αυτου) του ιησου, with CP rel lat-*f* syrr æth : txt BDLℵ 33 latt syr-cu copt arm Chr Aug. aft [last] αυτους add παντας D lat-*b c* ff_2 g_1 : αυτοις C[1].

31. rec τους οχλους (*perhaps to conform to* οχλοι *above and* βλεποντας *below*), with BP rel : txt CDUΔℵ 1. 33 ev-y $Orig_1$ Chr-γ-H-K. βλεποντας bef θαυμασαι B : βλεποντα 33. 237 ev-H[1] Chr-γ. for λαλουντας, ακουοντας B 59. 115. 238 syr-mg æth : add και D 13. 157 syrr. om κυλλους υγιεις ℵ 1 ev-y latt syr-cu copt æth Jer(" ubi Latinus interpres transtulit *debiles*, in Græco scriptum est κυλλούς, quod non generale debilitatis sed unius infirmitatis est nomen, ut quomodo claudus dicitur qui uno claudicat pede, sic κυλλός appelletur, qui unam manum debilem habet. Nos proprietatem hujus verbi non habemus. Unde et in consequentibus *Evangelista cæterorum debilium exposuit sanitates, horum tacuit.* Quid enim sequitur ? 'Et curavit &c.' De κυλλοῖς tacuit, quia quid e contrario diceret non habebat." Comm in loc. Tischdf, ed 2, made Jer state "interpretem id præteriisse ;" in ed 8 (simly ed 7) he says " Hieron. de interprete latino *de* κυλλοῖς *tacuit quia quid*" &c : it will be seen from the full quotation given above that for "interp. lat." Tischdf ought to have written " evangelista," what Jer says of the interp. lat. having ref to κυλλούς ver 30). rec om και (bef χ.), with L rel latt arm : ins BCDMPΔℵ 1 lat-*f* syrr syr-cu

ness of the dog so much, as his *attachment to and dependence on the human family :* she lays hold on this favourable point and makes it her own, 'if we are dogs, then may we fare as such ;—be fed with the crumbs of Thy mercy.' She was, as it were, under the edge of the table—close on the confines of Israel's feast. Some say that the ψίχια are the pieces of bread on which the hands were wiped, εἰς ὃ τὰς χεῖρας ἀποματτόμενοι εἶτα κυσὶν ἔβαλλον (Eustathius, cited by Trench on Mir. p. 342) ; but the πιπτόντων looks more like accidental falling, and the ψίχια like minute crumbs. **28.**] In Mark, διὰ τοῦτον τὸν λόγον, ὕπαγε. The greatness of the woman's faith consisted in this, that in spite of all discouragements she continued her plea; and not only so, but accepting and laying to her account all adverse circumstances, she out of them made reasons for urging her request. St. Mark gives the additional circumstance, that on returning to her house she found the devil gone out, and her daughter lying on the bed.

29—39.] HEALING BY THE SEA OF GALILEE. *Peculiar to Matthew* (see Mark vii. 31—37). FEEDING OF THE FOUR THOUSAND. Mark viii. 1—10.

λοὺς βλέποντας, καὶ [t] ἐδόξασαν τὸν [u] θεὸν [u] Ἰσραήλ.
32 ὁ δὲ Ἰησοῦς προςκαλεσάμενος τοὺς μαθητὰς αὐτοῦ
εἶπεν [v] Σπλαγχνίζομαι ἐπὶ τὸν ὄχλον, ὅτι ἤδη [w] ἡμέραι
τρεῖς [x] προςμένουσίν μοι καὶ οὐκ [y] ἔχουσιν τί φάγωσιν.
καὶ [z] ἀπολῦσαι αὐτοὺς [a] νήστεις οὐ θέλω, μήποτε [b] ἐκ-

t = ch. v. 16. ix. 8 al. Ps. lxxxv. 9, 13.
u Luke i. 68. Isa. xxix. 23.
v ch. xiv. 14 reff.
w constr., || Mk. Luke ix. 28. Acts v. 7.
x | Mk. Acts xi. 23. xiii. 43. xviii. 18. 1 Tim. i. 3. v. 5 only. Judg. iii. 25 A. Wisd. iii. 9 only.
y ch. viii. 20 reff.
z = ver. 23.
a || only. Dan. vi. 18 LXX only.
b || Mk. Gal. vi. 9. Heb. xii. 3, 5 only. Judg. viii. 15. 1 Kings xiv. 28. 1 Macc. iii. 17.

copt æth. ins *τους* bef *τυφλους* D. *εδοξαζον* Lℵ 1. 33 Scr's d l m n p ev-y latt(not D-lat) syr-cu arm Orig Chr Thl.

32. om *αυτου* ℵ. for *ειπεν*, *λεγει* C: add *αυτοις* CKΠℵ-corr[1] copt. (*See Mark* viii. 1.) aft *οχλον* add *τουτον* DE[2] Scr's c lat-*b c f* copt Hil. om *ηδη* B 106. 301 lat-*l*: *ιδου* Syr copt. rec *ημερας* (*gramml emendation*), with E(Treg) ℵ Orig$_2$ [Chr]: txt BCDP rel [Bas$_1$].—*ημεραι γ εισιν και* D arm (*also an emendation, but testifying to ημεραι being the original*). for *μηποτε*, *μη* ℵ.

29.] **τὸ ὄρος** is the high land on the coast of the lake, not any particular mountain. From this account it is uncertain to which side of the lake our Lord came; from Mark vii. 31 we learn that it was to the eastern side, *ἀνὰ μέσον τῶν ὁρίων Δεκαπόλεως*. 30.] **κυλλοί** are persons *maimed in the hands*; see Jerome in var. readd. (But it is also used of the feet, *τί δεῦρο πόδα σὺ* **κυλλὸν** *ἀνὰ κύκλον κυκλεῖς*; Aristoph. Av. 1379.) The meaning need not be, that a *wanting member was supplied* to these persons; but that a debility, such as that arising from paralysis or wound, was healed. **ἔρριψαν**, not in neglect, but from haste and rivalry. 31.] Mark (vii. 32—37) gives an instance of **κωφοὺς λαλοῦντας**. **τὸν θ. Ἰσραήλ**] Perhaps this last word is added as an expression of the joy of the disciples themselves, who contrasted the fulness and abundance of the acts of mercy now before them with the instance which they had just seen of the difficulty with which the faith of a Gentile had prevailed to obtain help. 32.] The modern German interpreters assume the identity of this miracle with that narrated in ch. xiv. 14 ff. If this be so, then our Evangelists must have *forged* the speech attributed to our Lord in ch. xvi. 9, 10. But, as Ebrard justly remarks (Evangelienkritik, p. 532), every circumstance which could vary, does vary, in the two accounts. The situation in the wilderness, the kind of food at hand, the blessing and breaking, and distributing by means of the disciples, these are *common to the two accounts*, and were likely to be so: but *here* the matter is introduced by our Lord Himself with an expression of pity for the multitudes who had continued with Him three days: here also the provision is greater, the numbers are less than on the former occasion. But there is one small token of authenticity which marks these two accounts as referring to two distinct events, even had we not such direct testimony as that of ch. xvi. 9, 10. It is, that whereas the baskets in which the fragments were collected on the other occasion are called by all four Evangelists **κόφινοι**, those used for that purpose after this miracle are in both Matt. and Mark **σπυρίδες**. And when our Lord refers to the two miracles, *the same distinction is observed*; a particularity which could not have arisen except as pointing to a matter of fact, that, whatever the distinction be, which is uncertain, different kinds of baskets were used on the two occasions. Perhaps the strangest reason for supposing the two identical (given by De Wette, Schleiermacher, and others) is an imagined difficulty in the question of the disciples, *πόθεν ἡμῖν κ.τ.λ.*, so soon after the former miracle; as if the same slowness to believe and trust in divine power were not repeatedly found among men, and instanced in Scripture itself;—compare Exod. xvi. 13 with Num. xi. 21, 22; and read in Exod. xvii. 1—7 the murmurings of the Israelites immediately after their deliverance at the Red Sea. And even could we recognize this as a difficulty, it is not necessarily implied in the text. Our Lord puts the matter to them as a question, without the slightest intimation of His intention to supply the want supernaturally. They make answer in the same spirit, without venturing (as indeed it would have been most unbecoming in them to do, see John ii. 3, 4) to suggest the working of a miracle. De Wette's assumption that the usage of *κόφινοι* and *σπυρίδες* shews two different traditional sources used by the author, would make it necessary to suppose that the *forger* of ch. xvi. 9, 10 has been skilful enough to preserve this distinction; an

λυθῶσιν [c] ἐν τῇ ὁδῷ. 33 καὶ λέγουσιν αὐτῷ οἱ μαθηταὶ BCDEF
[d] Πόθεν ἡμῖν ἐν [e] ἐρημίᾳ ἄρτοι τοσοῦτοι [f] ὥστε [g] χορτάσαι GHKL MPSUV
ὄχλον τοσοῦτον; 34 καὶ λέγει αὐτοῖς ὁ Ἰησοῦς Πόσους ΧΓΔΠℵ 1. 33
ἄρτους ἔχετε; οἱ δὲ εἶπον Ἑπτά, καὶ ὀλίγα [h] ἰχθύδια.
35 καὶ ἐκέλευσεν τοῖς ὄχλοις [i] ἀναπεσεῖν ἐπὶ τὴν γῆν·
36 καὶ λαβὼν τοὺς ἑπτὰ ἄρτους καὶ τοὺς ἰχθύας [k] εὐχαριστήσας [l] ἔκλασεν καὶ ἔδωκεν τοῖς μαθηταῖς, οἱ δὲ μαθηταὶ
τοῖς ὄχλοις. 37 καὶ ἔφαγον πάντες καὶ [g] ἐχορτάσθησαν,
καὶ τὸ [m] περισσεῦον τῶν [m] κλασμάτων ἦραν ἑπτὰ [n] σπυρίδας πλήρεις. 38 οἱ δὲ ἐσθίοντες ἦσαν τετρακισχίλιοι ἄνδρες χωρὶς γυναικῶν καὶ παιδίων. 39 καὶ [o] ἀπολύσας ...απολυσας P.
τοὺς ὄχλους [p] ἀνέβη εἰς τὸ πλοῖον καὶ ἦλθεν εἰς τὰ [q] ὅρια
Μαγαδάν.

c Gen. xlii. 38.
d = ch. xiii. 27, 54 al. Num. xi. 13.
e || Mk. 2 Cor. xi. 26. Heb. xi. 38 only. Ezek. xxxv. 4.
f 1 Cor. xiii. 2. Num. viii. 11.
g ch. xiv. 20 al. Ps. cxxxi. 15.
h || only †.
i ||. Mark vi. 40 || John. John xxi. 20. Tobit ii. 1. Judith xii. 16.
k absol., ch. xxvi. 26, 27. 1 Thess. v. 18 †. Wisd. xviii. 2.
l ch. xiv. 19 reff.
m ch. xiv. 20 reff.
n ||. ch. xvi. 10 ||. Acts ix. 25 only †.
o ch. xiv. 15 reff.
p = ch. xiv. 32 || Mk. John xxi. 11. Acts xxi. 16. Jon. i. 3 Ed-vat. (not B).
q ver. 22 reff.

33. rec aft μαθηται ins αυτου (*from* || *Mark*), with CDP rel lat-*c f* syrr syr-cu æth: om Bℵ 1. 237 vulg lat-*a b e* $ff_{1.2}$ g_1 *l* copt arm. aft ποθεν ins ουν D 1 latt(not *f*) æth arm. for ερημια, ερημω τοπω (*ch* xiv. 13, 15: *Luke* ix. 12) C copt Orig.
34. ειπαν ℵ 33. aft ειπ. ins αυτω D-gr 106 syrr syr-cu.
35. for εκελευσεν, παραγγειλας (*see* || *Mark*) BDℵ 1. 13. 33. 124 copt Orig(expr, ἐνθάδε οὐ κελεύει, ἀλλὰ παραγγέλλει), *præcipit* latt, *cum jussisset* D-lat: txt CP rel arm Hil(*turbis jubetur discumbere*). τω οχλω (*as* || *Mark*) B D[-gr] ℵ 1. 13. 33. 124 vulg lat-*b c* $ff_{1.2}$ $g_{1.2}$ *l* syr æth arm Orig: τους οχλους CU[1] Scr's c Chr-2-6-9-η-ρ(and Fd): txt P U[1]-corr rel lat-*a e f k* [D-lat] Syr syr-cu copt Chr-κ-λ-μ Hil.
36. for και λαβων, ελαβεν (*grammatical emendation*) BDℵ 1. 13. 33. 124 copt: txt CP rel æth arm. ins δυο bef ιχθυας (*ch* xiv. 19) ℵ[1](ℵ[3a] disapproving). ins και bef ευχ. BDℵ 1 latt Syr syr-cu copt. ευχαριστησεν (omg εκλασεν) C[1](appy) (lat-*a*?). for εδωκεν, εδιδου (*from* || *Mark*) BDℵ 1. 13. 33. 124 Chr Thdor-mops: txt CP rel vss. rec aft μαθηταις ins αυτου (*from* || *Mark*), with CP rel vulg lat-*a b f* syrr syr-cu: om BDℵ 1. 13. 33. 124 em lat-*c* ff_1 g_2 copt arm Chr. rec τω οχλω (*from* || *Mark*), with CDP rel latt(*populo*) syr arm [Chr]: txt BKLMΠℵ 1. 13. 33. 124 lat-*e f* ff_1 Syr syr-cu copt.
37. rec ηραν bef το περ. των κλ. (*from* || *Mark*), with CPℵ rel lat-*f* ff_1 (syrr syr-cu) copt arm [Chr]: txt B D(written over an erasure) 1. 33 latt æth.
38. ins ως bef τετρακισχιλιοι (*from* || *Mark &c*) B ℵ(ωσι) 1. 13. 33. 124 lat-ff_1 syr æth arm.—ανδρες bef ωσι τετρ. ℵ. transp γυναικων and παιδιων Dℵ 1. 124 latt(not *f*) syr-cu copt æth Aug.
39. rec ενεβη (*emendation to more usual word*, || *Mark also having* εμβας), with Bℵ (S 1. 33, e sil); ενβαινει D: txt C rel (and 15 of Scr's mss) Chr. rec **μαγδαλα**, with L rel syr æth arm [Chr]: μαγδαλαν CM 33 copt: txt B D(της μαγ.) ℵ[1] syr-cu(-don) syr-jer, also μαγεδαν ℵ[3a] latt Jer Aug, and *magado* Syr. (*Txt appears to have been original, and the better known name* Magdala *to have been substituted: see note.*)

accuracy seldom found in interpolations of early Christian times. On **ἡμέρια τρεῖς** see reff. and Winer, § 62. 2, note.

37.] The **σπυρίς** (commonly derived from σπεῖρα, as being of woven work; or by some from πυρός, wheat, as being τὸ τῶν πυρῶν ἄγγος. Hesych.) was large enough to contain a man's body, as Paul was let down in one from the wall of Damascus, ref. Acts. Greswell (Diss. viii. pt. 4, vol. ii. p. 325) supposes that they may have been used to sleep in, during the stay in the desert.

39.] Of **Magadan** nothing is known. Lightfoot (Centurio Chorograph. Marco præmissa, p. 413) shews *Magdala* to have been only a sabbath-day's journey from Chamnath Gadara on the Jordan, and on the east side of the lake: but probably he is mistaken, for most travellers (see Winer, Realwörterbuch, in v.) place it about three miles from Tiberias, on the west side of the lake, where is now a village named Madschel. *Dalmanutha*, mentioned by Mark (viii. 10), seems to have been a village in the neighbourhood.

XVI. 1 Καὶ προσελθόντες οἱ Φαρισαῖοι καὶ Σαδδουκαῖοι [r] πειράζοντες ἐπηρώτησαν αὐτὸν [s] σημεῖον ἐκ τοῦ
οὐρανοῦ [t] ἐπιδεῖξαι αὐτοῖς. 2 ὁ δὲ ἀποκριθεὶς εἶπεν αὐτοῖς
[[u] Ὀψίας [u] γενομένης λέγετε [v] Εὐδία, [w] πυῤῥάζει γὰρ ὁ
οὐρανός· 3 καὶ πρωΐ Σήμερον [x] χειμών, [w] πυῤῥάζει γὰρ
[y] στυγνάζων ὁ οὐρανός· τὸ μὲν [z] πρόσωπον τοῦ οὐρανοῦ
[a] γινώσκετε [b] διακρίνειν, τὰ δὲ [c] σημεῖα τῶν [d] καιρῶν οὐ
δύνασθε;] 4 γενεὰ πονηρὰ καὶ [e] μοιχαλὶς σημεῖον [f] ἐπιζη-
τεῖ· καὶ σημεῖον οὐ δοθήσεται αὐτῇ, εἰ μὴ τὸ σημεῖον

r ch. iv. 1, 3 al. 3 Kings x. 1.
s ch. xii. 39 reff.
t ch. xxii. 19. xxiv. 1. Acts ix. 39 al. Sir. l. 21 al.
u ch. xiv. 15, 23 al. Judith xiii. 1 only.
v here only +. Sir. iii. 15 only.
w here (bis) only +. (-ρός, Rev. vi. 4. -ρίζειν, Lev. xiii. 19.)
x = Acts xxvii. 20 (ch. xxiv. 20 || Mk. John x. 22. 2 Tim. iv. 21) only. Job xxxvii. 6.
y Mark x. 22 only. Ezek. xxvii. 35. xxviii. 19 A. xxxii. 10 only. (-γνός, Wisd. xvii. 5.)
z Luke xii 56. James i. 11. Ps. ciii. 30.
a constr., see Neh. xiii. 24.
b = 1 Cor. xi. 29. (ch. xxi. 21 al.) Job xii. 11.
c = ch. xxiv. 3 reff.
d = Acts i. 7. 1 Thess. v. 1.
e ch. xii. 39 reff.
f ch. vi. 32 reff.

Chap. XVI. 1. om *οι* 1. 33. 124 ev-y Orig. ins *οι* bef *σαδ.* Δℵ[3a] Scr's o ev-H. *αυτον* bef *επηρωτησαν* D. *επηρωτων* ℵ[1] 1. 13 copt Orig : *ηρωτησαν* ℵ[3a], but former readg restored.

2. om *αυτοις* D ev-y lat-*a c* ff_1 g_1. om *οψιας* to end of ver 3 BV X-txt Γℵ mss-mentd-by-Jer syr-cu arm-zoh Orig(appy) : with asterisks in E: ins CD rel latt syrr copt æth Eus-canon Chr Thl Euthym Hil Juv. (*The omn has prob arisen from the similar passage, ch* xii. 38.)

3. for *ουρανος*, *αηρ* D-gr. rec ins *υποκριται* bef *το μεν* (*see Luke* xii. 56), with E rel lat-*b e f ff* g_1 Syr copt; *και* C[2] 33 : om C[1]DLΔ 1. 33 Scr's b ev-z vulg lat-*a c* ff_2 *l* syr æth arm Aug

4. om *και μοιχαλις* D lat-*a e* $ff_{1.2}$ g_1 Prosp. for *επιζητει*, *αιτει* B[1](sic, from inspection) : *ζητει* (and bef *σημιαν*(sic)) D[1]-gr, *quærit* latt : txt B[1][marg] Cℵ rel.

Chap. XVI. 1—4.] Request for a sign from heaven. Mark viii. 11—13, but much abridged. See also Luke xii. 54 and notes. **1. σημεῖον ἐκ τοῦ οὐρανοῦ**] see notes at ch. xii. 38. There is no ground for supposing that this narrative refers to the same event as that. What can be more natural than that the adversaries of our Lord should have met His miracles again and again with this demand of a sign *from heaven?* For in the Jewish superstition it was held that dæmons and false gods could give signs *on earth*, but only the true God signs *from heaven*. In the apocryphal Epistle of Jeremiah, ver. 67, we read of the gods of the heathen, σημεῖά τε ἐν ἔθνεσιν ἐν οὐρανῷ οὐ μὴ δείξωσιν . . . . And for such a notion they alleged the bread from heaven given by Moses (see John vi. 31), the staying of the sun by Joshua (Josh. x. 12), the thunder and rain by Samuel (1 Sam. xii. 17, compare Jer. xiv. 22), and Elijah (James v. 17, 18). And thus we find that immediately after the first miraculous feeding the same demand was made, John vi. 30, and answered by the declaration of our Lord that He was the true bread from heaven. And what more natural likewise, than that our Lord should have uniformly met the demand by the same answer,—the *sign of Jonas*, one so calculated to baffle his enemies and hereafter to fix the attention of His disciples? Here however that answer is accompanied by other rebukes sufficiently distinctive. It was now probably the evening (see Mark viii. 10, εὐθύς) and our Lord was looking on the glow in the west which suggested the remark in ver. 2. On the practice of the Jews to *demand a sign*, see 1 Cor. i. 22. **2.**] Mark viii. 12 adds καὶ ἀναστενάξας τῷ πνεύματι αὐτοῦ . . . , omitting however the sentences following. The Jews were much given to prognosticating the rains, &c. of the coming season in each year. See Lightf. who cites examples. **3.**] Polybius iv. 21. 1, speaks of the ἠθῶν αὐστηρίαν (of the Arcadians) ἥτις αὐτοῖς παρέπεται διὰ τὴν τοῦ περιέχοντος (ἀέρος) ψυχρότητα καὶ στυγνότητα. 'Si circa occidentem rubescunt nubes, serenitatem futuræ diei spondent; concavus oriens pluvias prædicit; idem ventos cum ante exorientem eum nubes rubescunt: quod si et nigræ rubentibus intervenerint (πυῤῥάζει στυγνάζων) et pluvias.' Plin. Hist. Nat. xviii. 35. **πρόσωπον**, because στυγνός and στυγνάζω are properly used of sadness and obscurity in the visage of man. **τῶν καιρῶν, of times**, generally. The Jews had been, and were, most blind to the signs of the times, at all the great crises of their history;—

ʼΙωνᾶ. καὶ καταλιπὼν αὐτοὺς ἀπῆλθεν. 5 Καὶ ἐλθόντες BCDEF
οἱ μαθηταὶ g εἰς τὸ g πέραν h ἐπελάθοντο ἄρτους λαβεῖν. GHKL MSUVX
6 ὁ δὲ ʼΙησοῦς εἶπεν αὐτοῖς ʽΟρᾶτε καὶ i προσέχετε ἀπὸ ΓΔΠℵ 1. 33
τῆς j ζύμης τῶν Φαρισαίων καὶ Σαδδουκαίων. 7 οἱ δὲ
k διελογίζοντο ἐν ἑαυτοῖς λέγοντες ʼΌτι ἄρτους οὐκ ἐλάβομεν. 8 γνοὺς δὲ ὁ ʼΙησοῦς εἶπεν Τί k διαλογίζεσθε ἐν
ἑαυτοῖς l ὀλιγόπιστοι, ὅτι ἄρτους οὐκ ἐλάβετε; 9 οὔπω
νοεῖτε οὐδὲ m μνημονεύετε τοὺς πέντε ἄρτους τῶν πεντα-
κισχιλίων, καὶ πόσους n κοφίνους ἐλάβετε, 10 οὐδὲ τοὺς
ἑπτὰ ἄρτους τῶν τετρακισχιλίων, καὶ πόσας o σπυρίδας
ἐλάβετε; 11 πῶς οὐ νοεῖτε ὅτι οὐ περὶ ἄρτων εἶπον ὑμῖν;

g ch. viii. 18, 28. xiv. 22 al. Mt. Mk. only, exc. Luke viii. 22. Judg. xi. 29.
h ‖. Luke xii. 6. Phil. iii. 14. Heb. vi. 10. xiii. 2, 16. James i. 24 only. Gen. xli. 30. Ps. cxviii. 16.
i w. ἀπό, ch. vii. 15 reff.
j ch. xiii. 33 ‖. Exod. xii. 15. met., ‖. vv. 11, 12. Luke xii. 1. 1 Cor. v. 6, &c. Gal. v. 9 only.
k ch. xxi. 25. Mark ii. 6, 8. Luke iii. 15 al. Ps. ix. 23 (2). 2 Macc. xii. 43.
l ch. xiv. 31 reff.
m constr., 1 Thess. ii. 9. 2 Tim. ii. 8. 1 Chron. xvi. 12. Exod. xiii. 3.
n ch. xiv. 20 reff.
o ‖. ch. xv. 34 ‖. Acts ix. 25 only †.

rec aft *ιωνα* ins *του προφητου* (*from ch* xii. 39), with C rel latt syrr syr-cu copt æth arm Orig: om BDLℵ am(with em forj fuld harl tol) lat-ff_1 g_1 *l* Hil.

5. *εις το περαν επελαθοντο* bef *οι μαθηται* D lat-*a b c e* $ff_{1.2}$ *g* syr-cu Hil.—om *οι μαθ.* Δ 301. rec aft *μαθηται* adds *αυτου*, with L rel latt syrr syr-cu copt æth Orig: om BCDℵ 209. 346 ev-y lat-*e* arm Hil. *λαβειν* bef *αρτους* (*see* ‖ *Mark*) BKΠ Scr's e w lat-*e*.

6. om *αυτοις* ℵ ev-y. **7.** for *οι δε*, *τοτε* D 4 lat-*a b c e* ff_2 g_1 Lucif.

8. rec aft *ειπεν* ins *αυτοις*, with C X(Treg) rel lat-*a* ff_1 Syr syr-cu copt: om BDKLMS X(Tischdf) ΔΠℵ 1. 33. 124[1] Scr's a e w[1] ev-y vulg lat-*c e f* g_2 *l* syr æth arm Orig Thl [Lucif]. for *ελαβετε*, *εχετε* (*from* ‖ *Mark*) BDℵ 13. 124 latt syr-ms-mg copt æth arm Lucif: txt C rel lat-*f* syrr syr-cu $Orig_1$ [Eus_1] Chr.

9. om *ουδε μνημονευετε* Xℵ[1](ins ·ℵ[3a]). aft *μνημονευετε* ins *οτε quando* DΔ. **τοις πεντακισχιλειοις** D(and so **τοις** *τετρ.* below), simly lat-*c f* ff_2 g_2.

11. rec **αρτου**, with D-gr rel latt Orig Lucif Ambr: txt BCKLMSΠℵ 1. 33 lat-*e f* D-lat syr-ms copt Chr. *υμιν* bef *ειπον* C 209-37-59: om *υμιν* D lat-*a b* ff_2 Lucif.

and also particularly to the times in which they were *then* living. The sceptre had departed from Judah, the lawgiver no longer came forth from between his feet, the prophetic weeks of Daniel were just at their end; yet they discerned none of these things. **4.**] See note on ch. xii. 39.

5—12.] Warning against the leaven of the Pharisees and Sadducees. Mark viii. 13—21. **5.**] This crossing of the lake was not the voyage to Magadan mentioned in ch. xv. 39, for after the dialogue with the Pharisees, Mark adds (viii. 13), *πάλιν ἐμβὰς ἀπῆλθεν εἰς τὸ πέραν.* **ἐπελάθ.**] not for a pluperfect: **After they had come to the other side, they forgot to take bread;** viz. *on their land journey further.* This is also to be understood in Mark (viii. 14), who states their having only one loaf in the ship, not to shew that they *had* forgotten to take bread before starting, but as a reason why they should have provided some on landing. **6. τῆς ζύμης**] see beginning of note on ch. xiii. 33. It is from the penetrating and diffusive power of leaven that the comparison, whether for good or bad, is derived. In Luke xii. 1, where the warning is given on a wholly different occasion, the leaven is explained to mean, *hypocrisy;* which is of all evil things the most penetrating and diffusive, and is the charge which our Lord most frequently brings against the Jewish sects. In Mark we read, *καὶ τῆς ζύμης ʽΗρώδου.* The Herodians were more a political than a religious sect, the dependants and supporters of the dynasty of Herod, for the most part Sadducees in religious sentiment. These, though directly opposed to the Pharisees, were yet united with them in their persecution of our Lord, see ch. xxii. 16: Mark iii. 6. And their leaven was the same,—*hypocrisy,*—however it might be disguised by external difference of sentiment. They were all unbelievers at heart. **7.**] **ἐν ἑαυτοῖς** = *πρὸς ἀλλήλους* Mark viii. 16. This is an important parallelism to which I may have occasion to refer again.

8—12.] Not only had they forgotten these miracles, but the weighty lesson given them in ch. xv. 16—20. The reproof is much fuller in Mark, where see note. On **κοφίνους** and **σπυρίδας**, see

ᵖ προσέχετε δὲ ἀπὸ τῆς ᵖ ζύμης τῶν Φαρισαίων καὶ Σαδ- p ver. 6.
δουκαίων. 12 τότε συνῆκαν ὅτι οὐκ εἶπεν ᵖ προσέχειν ἀπὸ
τῆς ᵖ ζύμης τῶν ἄρτων, ἀλλὰ ἀπὸ τῆς ᑫ διδαχῆς τῶν q ch. vii. 28. John vii. 16 al. Ps. lix. tit. only.
Φαρισαίων καὶ Σαδδουκαίων.
13 Ἐλθὼν δὲ ὁ Ἰησοῦς εἰς τὰ ʳ μέρη Καισαρείας τῆς r = ch. ii. 22. xv. 21. Mark viii. 10. Acts ii. 10. xix. 1. xx. 2. Exod. xvi. 35.
Φιλίππου ἠρώτα τοὺς μαθητὰς αὐτοῦ λέγων Τίνα λέγου-
σιν οἱ ἄνθρωποι εἶναι τὸν υἱὸν τοῦ ἀνθρώπου; 14 οἱ δὲ

rec (for προσεχετε δε) προσεχειν, with X rel syr-cu syr arm : προσεχετε D[1] 13. 124 latt (Syr) Lucif Ambr : προσεχειν προσεχετε δε C[2] 33. 237-52[1]. 346 Scr's a d i[2] p : προσεχειν αλλ' [M[2]] 3. 76. 238-43-7 evv-y-z Thl (*all emendations from misunderstanding txt*) : txt BC[1]Lℵ 1. 6. 148. 234[2] copt æth Orig.—[aft ζυμης ins δε X.]

12. rec (for των αρτων) του ἀρτου, with C rel lat-*c f*: om D 124[1] lat-*a b* ff_2 arm Lucif: των φαρισαιων και σαδδουκαιων ℵ lat-ff_1 syr-cu, των φαρ. 33: txt BLℵ[3a] 1 ev-y vulg lat-$g_{1,2}$ *l* syr-ms copt æth. (rec αλλ, with EF [SV, e sil]: om 33: txt B(see table) CDℵ rel.) διδασκαλιας ℵ[1](txt ℵ[3a]) 153 Chr. transp φαρ. and σαδ. B.

13. om αυτου D. rec ins με bef λεγουσιν (*from* || *Mark Luke. This is more apparent from the readings in* C *and* D), with L rel syrr syr-cu $Orig_2$ [Cyr_2-p] Hil Aug Leo: τινα λεγουσιν με κ.τ.λ. C: τινα με οι ανθ. λ. ειναι κ.τ.λ. D lat-*a b* g_2 Iren-int: txt B(ℵ) vulg lat-*c* syr-jer copt æth Iren-[int-]ms $Orig_{1 \text{ or } 2}$ $Ambr_1$.—οι ανθρωποι ειναι λεγ. ℵ[1]: οι αν. λεγ. ειν. ℵ[3a]. om τον D.

note, ch. xv. 36. This voyage brought them to Bethsaïda: i. e. Bethsaïda Julias, on the North-Eastern side of the lake: see Mark viii. 22, and the miracle there related.

13—20.] Confession of Peter. Mark viii. 27—30. Luke ix. 18—21. Here St. Luke rejoins the synoptic narrative, having left it at ch. xiv. 22. We here begin the *second great division* of our Saviour's ministry on earth, introductory to His sufferings and death. Up to this time we have had no distinct intimation, like that in ver. 21, of these events. This intimation is brought in by the solemn question and confession now before us. And as the former period of His ministry was begun by a declaration from the Father of His Sonship, so this also, on the Mount of Transfiguration. **13. Καισαρείας τῆς Φ.**] A town in Gaulonitis at the foot of Mount Libanus, not far from the source of the Jordan, a day's journey from Sidon, once called Laish (Judg. xviii. 7, 29) and afterwards Dan (ibid.), but in later times Paneas, or Panias, from the mountain Panium, under which it lay (Jos. Antt. xv. 10. 3. Φιλίππου Καισαρείας, ἣν Πανεάδα Φοίνικες προσαγορεύουσι, Euseb. H. E. vii. 17). The tetrarch Philip enlarged it and gave it the name of Cæsarea (Jos. Antt. xviii. 2. 1). In after times King Agrippa further enlarged it and called it Neronias in honour of the Emperor Nero (Jos. Antt. xx. 9. 4). This must not be confounded with the Cæsarea of the Acts, which was Cæsarea Stratonis, on the Mediterranean. See Acts x. 1, and note. The following enquiry took place ἐν τῇ ὁδῷ, Mark viii. 27. St. Luke gives it without note of place, but states it to have been asked on the disciples joining our Lord, who was praying alone, Luke ix. 18. **τίνα λέγουσιν**] **who do men say that the Son of Man is?** τὸν υἱὸν τοῦ ἀνθρ. being equivalent to με in the corresponding sentence below, ver. 15. Of those who read με in the text, some would render as if our Lord had said, '*Who say men that I am? the Son of Man?*' i. e. *the Messiah?* (Beza, Le Clerc, and others,) but this is inadmissible, for the answer would not then have been expressed as it is, but *affirmatively* or *negatively*. Equally inadmissible is Olshausen's rendering ἐμὲ τὸν υἱὸν τοῦ ἀνθ. (ὡς οἴδατε) ὄντα, 'Me, who am, as ye are aware, the Son of Man?' an expression, Olshausen says, by which the disciples would be led to the idea of the *Son of God*. But then this would destroy the simplicity of the following question, **But who say ye that I am?** because it would put into their mouths the answer intended to be given. The E. V. has beyond doubt the right rendering of *this reading*: and τὸν υἱ. τ. ἀνθ. is a pregnant expression, which we now know to imply the *Messiahship in the root of our human nature*, and which even then was taken by the Jews as = *the Son of God*, (see Luke xxii. 69, 70,) which would serve as a test of the faith of the disciples, according to their understanding of it. **οἱ ἄνθρωποι** (generic: = οἱ ὄχλοι in Luke), i. e. the σὰρξ κ. αἷμα of ver. 17, the *human opinion*.

14.] It is no contradiction to this verdict

s ch. i. 1 reff. t ch. xxvi. 63 (Acts xiv. 15. Rom. ix. 26 [from Hos. i. 10]. 2 Cor. iii. 3 al.). Ps. xli. 2. u 1 Cor. xv. 50. Gal. i. 16. Eph. vi. 12. Heb. ii. 14 only. Sir. xiv. 18. v = ch. xi. 25, 26 al. fr. Jer. xi. 20.

εἶπον Οἱ μὲν Ἰωάννην τὸν βαπτιστήν, ἄλλοι δὲ Ἡλίαν,
ἕτεροι δὲ Ἱερεμίαν ἢ ἕνα τῶν προφητῶν. 15 λέγει αὐτοῖς
Ὑμεῖς δὲ τίνα με λέγετε εἶναι; 16 ἀποκριθεὶς δὲ Σίμων
Πέτρος εἶπεν Σὺ εἶ ὁ [s] χριστὸς ὁ υἱὸς τοῦ [t] θεοῦ [t] τοῦ
[t] ζῶντος. 17 ἀποκριθεὶς δὲ ὁ Ἰησοῦς εἶπεν αὐτῷ Μακάριος εἶ Σίμων Βαριῶνα· ὅτι [u] σὰρξ καὶ [u] αἷμα οὐκ
[v] ἀπεκάλυψέν σοι, ἀλλ' ὁ πατήρ μου ὁ ἐν τοῖς οὐρανοῖς.

BCDEF GHKL MSUVX ΓΔΠℵ 1. 33

14. ειπαν BΠ[1] 33. om οι μεν (*see* || *Mark Luke*) D lat-*a b e ff*$_1$ *g*$_1$: αλλοι Δ. for αλλοι, οι B Eus Chr.

15. aft αυτοις ins ο ις C 33 vulg lat-*b c f g*$_1$ arm-zoh.

16. aft ειπεν ins αυτω D lat-*ff*$_1$ arm-usc. for του ζωντος, το(του D-corr[1]) *σωζοντος salvatoris* D[1](txt D[8]).

17. rec (for αποκρ. δε) και αποκρ., with C rel lat-*f ff*$_1$ syr : om syr-cu : txt BDℵ 1. 13. 33 vulg lat-*b c ff*$_2$ *g*$_{1.2}$ *l* copt Eus. om αυτω D am(with fuld). (om οτι B[1], but ins in marg B[1].) **αλλα** ℵ. om τοις (bef ουρ.) B ev-y Orig$_1$(ins$_2$).

that some called him *the Son of David* (ch. ix. 27; xii. 23; xv. 22); for either these were or were about to become His disciples, or are quoted as examples of rare faith, or as in ch. xii. 23, it was the passing doubt on the minds of the multitude, not their settled opinion. The same may be said of John vii. 26, 31; iv. 42. On our Lord's being taken for John the Baptist, see ch. xiv. 2, from which this would appear to be the opinion of *the Herodians.* **ἕνα τῶν προφ.** = ὅτι προφ. τις τῶν ἀρχαίων ἀνέστη, Luke ix. 19. It was not a metempsychosis, but a bodily resurrection which was believed. On Ἡλίαν, see note at ch. xi. 14. Jeremiah was accounted by the Jews the first in the prophetic canon (Lightfoot on Matt. xxvii. 9). **16.]** *τί οὖν τὸ στόμα τῶν ἀποστόλων ὁ Πέτρος, ὁ πανταχοῦ θερμός, ὁ τοῦ χοροῦ τῶν ἀποστόλων κορυφαῖος; πάντων ἐρωτηθέντων αὐτὸς ἀποκρίνεται,* Chrysost. Hom. liv. 1, p. 546. The confession is not made in the terms of the other answer: it is not 'we say' or 'I say,' but **Thou art.** It is the expression of an inward conviction wrought by God's Spirit. The excellence of this confession is, that it brings out both the human and the divine nature of the Lord: **ὁ χριστός** is the Messiah, the Son of David, the anointed King: **ὁ υἱὸς τοῦ θεοῦ τοῦ ζῶντος** is the Eternal Son, begotten of the Eternal Father, not 'Son of God' in any inferior figurative sense, not *one of* the sons of God, of angelic nature, but THE SON OF THE LIVING GOD, having in Him the Sonship and the divine nature *in a sense in which they could be in none else.* This was a view of the Person of Christ quite distinct from the Jewish Messianic idea, which appears to have been (Justin Mart. Dial. § 48, p. 144) that he should be a man born from men, but selected by God for the office on account of his eminent virtues. This distinction accounts for the solemn blessing pronounced in the next verse. **τοῦ ζῶντος** must not for a moment be taken here as it sometimes is used, (e. g. ref. Acts,) as merely distinguishing the true God from dead idols; it is here emphatic, and imparts force and precision to **υἱός.** That Peter, when he uttered the words, understood by them in detail all that we now understand, is not of course here asserted: but that they were his testimony to the true Humanity and true Divinity of the Lord, in that sense of deep truth and reliance, out of which springs the Christian life of the Church.

17.] **μακάριος,** as in ch. v. 4, &c., is a solemn expression of blessing, an inclusion of him to whom it is addressed in the kingdom of heaven, not a mere word of praise. And the reason of it is, the fact that the Father had revealed the Son to him (see ch. xi. 25—27); cf. Gal. i. 15, 16, in which passage the occurrence of *σαρκὶ καὶ αἵματι* seems to indicate a reference to this very saying of the Lord. The whole declaration of St. Paul in that chapter forms a remarkable parallel to the character and promise given to St. Peter in our text,—as establishing Paul's claim to be another such *πέτρα* or *στύλος* as Peter and the other great Apostles, because the Son had been revealed in him not of man nor by men, but by God Himself. The name **Simon Bar Jonas** is doubtless used as indicating his fleshly state and extraction, and forming the greater contrast to his spiritual state, name, and blessing, which follow. The same 'Simon son of Jonas' is uttered when he is reminded by the thrice repeated enquiry,

18 κἀγὼ δὲ σοὶ λέγω ὅτι σὺ εἶ Πέτρος, καὶ ἐπὶ ταύτῃ τῇ
πέτρᾳ οἰκοδομήσω μου τὴν [w] ἐκκλησίαν, καὶ [x] πύλαι
[xy] ᾅδου οὐ [z] κατισχύσουσιν αὐτῆς. 19 [καὶ] δώσω σοὶ τὰς

w Gospp., ch. xviii. 17 bis only. Acts, Epp. Rev., passim. Prov. v. 14. 1 Chron. xiii. 2.

x here only. Isa. xxxviii. 10. 3 Macc. v. 51. see Rev. i. 18. y ch. xi. 23 al. z Luke xxi. 36. xxiii. 23 only. Exod. xvii. 11. Jer. xv. 18. Wisd. vii. 30 Aℵ.

18. *ταυτην την πετραν* D Eus. *την εκκλησιαν* bef *μου* D latt Tert Cypr.
19. om *και* B[1]C[2]Dℵ **1.** 33 Syr syr-cu. *σοι* bef *δωσω* DL vulg lat-*b c* &c Chr

'Lovest thou me?' of his frailty, in his previous denial of his Lord. **18.**] The name **Πέτρος** (not now first given, but prophetically bestowed by our Lord on His first interview with Simon, John i. 43) or Κηφᾶς, signifying a rock, the termination being only altered to suit the masculine appellation, denotes the *personal position of this Apostle in the building of the Church of Christ*. He was the first of those *foundation-stones* (Rev. xxi. 14) on which the living temple of God was built: this building itself beginning on the day of Pentecost by the laying of *three thousand living stones* on this very foundation. That this is the simple and only interpretation of the words of our Lord the whole usage of the New Testament shews: in which not doctrines nor confessions, but *men*, are uniformly the pillars and stones of the spiritual building. See 1 Pet. ii. 4—6: 1 Tim. iii. 15 (where the pillar is not Timotheus, but the congregation of the faithful) and note: Gal. ii. 9: Eph. ii. 20: Rev. iii. 12. And it is on Peter, as by divine revelation making this confession, as thus under the influence of the Holy Ghost, as standing out before the Apostles in the strength of this faith, as himself founded on the one foundation, **Ἰησοῦς χριστός**, 1 Cor. iii. 11—that the Jewish portion of the Church was built, Acts ii.—v., and the Gentile, Acts x. xi. After this we hear little of him; but during this, the first building time, he is never lost sight of: see especially Acts i. 15; ii. 14, 37; iii. 12; iv. 8; v. 15, 29; ix. 34, 40; x. 25, 26. We may certainly exclaim with Bengel (Gnomon, p. 117), 'Tute hæc omnia dicuntur; nam quid hæc ad Romam?' Nothing can be further from any legitimate interpretation of this promise, than the idea of a perpetual primacy in the successors of Peter; the very notion of *succession* is precluded by the form of the comparison, which concerns the person, and *him only*, so far as it involves a *direct* promise. In its other and general sense, as applying to all those living stones (Peter's own expression for members of Christ's Church) of whom the Church should be built, it implies, as Origen (in Matt. tom. xii. 11, vol. iii. p. 525) excellently comments on it, *καὶ εἴ τις λέγει τοῦτο πρὸς αὐτόν, οὐ σαρκὸς καὶ αἵματος ἀποκαλυψάντων αὐτῷ, ἀλλὰ τοῦ ἐν τοῖς οὐρανοῖς πατρός, τεύξεται τῶν εἰρημένων, ὡς μὲν τὸ γράμμα τοῦ εὐαγγελίου λέγει, πρὸς ἐκεῖνον τὸν Πέτρον, ὡς δὲ τὸ πνεῦμα αὐτοῦ διδάσκει, πρὸς πάντα τὸν γενόμενον ὁποῖος ὁ Πέτρος ἐκεῖνος.* The application of the promise to St. Peter has been elaborately impugned by Wordsw., whose note see. His zeal to appropriate *πέτρα* to Christ has somewhat overshot itself. In arguing that the term can apply to none but God, he will find it difficult surely to deny all reference to a rock in the name Πέτρος. To me, it is equally difficult, nay impossible, to deny all reference, in *ἐπὶ ταύτῃ τῇ πέτρᾳ*, to the preceding *πέτρος*. Let us keep to the plain straightforward sense of Scripture, however that sense may have been misused by Rome. In this as in so many other cases we may well say, 'Non tali auxilio, nec defensoribus istis.' In the prefixing of **μου** to *τὴν ἐκκλησίαν*, there is no mystic sense, nor solecism, as Wordsw. fancies (nor even emphasis, which is never expressed by the abbreviated enclitic form *μου*, but always by *ἐμοῦ*): it is the very commonest arrangement. Cf. ch. vii. 24, *ὅστις ἀκούει μου τ. λόγους*: ib. 26; ch. viii. 8; xvii. 15: Mark xiv. 8: Luke vi. 47; xii. 18 al. freq. **ἐκκλησίαν**] This word occurs but in one place besides in the Gospels, ch. xviii. 17 bis, and there in the same sense as here, viz., **the congregation of the faithful**: only there it is one portion of that congregation, here the whole. **πύλαι ᾅδου**] The **gates of Hades** by a well-known oriental form of speech, = the *power of the kingdom of death*. The form is still preserved when the Turkish empire is known as 'the Ottoman Porte.' This promise received a remarkable literal fulfilment in the person of Peter in Acts xii. 6—18, see especially ver. 10. The meaning of the promise is, that over the Church so built upon him who was by the strength of that confession the Rock, no adverse power should ever prevail to extinguish it. **19.**] Another personal promise to

[a] κλεῖδας τῆς βασιλείας τῶν οὐρανῶν· καὶ ὃ ἂν [b] δήσῃς BCDEF
ἐπὶ τῆς γῆς ἔσται [b] δεδεμένον ἐν τοῖς οὐρανοῖς, καὶ ὃ ἐὰν GHKL MSUVX
[c] λύσῃς ἐπὶ τῆς γῆς ἔσται [c] λελυμένον ἐν τοῖς οὐρανοῖς. ΓΔΠℵ 1. 33
20 τότε [d] διεστείλατο τοῖς μαθηταῖς ἵνα μηδενὶ εἴπωσιν ὅτι
αὐτός ἐστιν ὁ χριστός. 21 [e] Ἀπὸ τότε ἤρξατο Ἰησοῦς
δεικνύειν τοῖς μαθηταῖς αὐτοῦ ὅτι δεῖ αὐτὸν εἰς Ἱεροσόλυμα [f] ἀπελθεῖν καὶ πολλὰ παθεῖν [g] ἀπὸ τῶν πρεσβυτέ-

a Luke xi. 52. Rev. i. 18. iii. 7. ix. 1. xx. 1 only. Judg. iii. 25. 1 Chron. ix. 27. Isa. xxii. 22 only.
b = ch. xviii. 18. Num. xxx. 2, &c. Heb.
c ch. xviii. 18. Isa. xl. 2. Sir. xxviii. 2.
d Mark v. 43. vii. 36 bis. viii. 15. ix. 9. Acts xv. 24. Heb. xii. 20 only. Ezek. iii. 18.
e ch. iv. 17. xxvi. 16. Luke xvi. 16 only. Eccl. vi i. 12 only.
f = ch. xiv. 25 reff.
g ch. xi. 19 reff.

Cypr. rec (for κλειδας) κλεις, with B^{r}(sic, from inspection [B^{3}, Tischdf]) CDℵ^{3a} rel Orig$_1$ Eus Chr Phot: txt B^{1}Lℵ^{1} Orig$_5$. rec (for αν) εαν, with Cℵ rel: txt BD 1 Orig. την γην ℵ^{1}(txt ℵ^{3a}). for εαν, αν D 1.

20. for διεστειλατο, επετιμησεν (*from* ‖ *Mark Luke*) B^{1}D mss-mentd-by-Orig syr-cu arm Hil, *comminatus est* D-lat: txt B^{r}(sic, from inspection [Tischdf ascribes a similar marginal corrn to his B^{2} or even to B^{1}]) CLXℵ rel 1. 33 syrr copt æth Orig$_4$. rec aft μαθηταις ins αυτου, with L rel latt syrr syr-cu copt æth Orig$_3$: om BCDℵ arm Orig$_3$ Hil. ουτος DU. rec ins ιησους bef ο χριστος, with Cℵ^{3a} rel vulg lat-*f g$_2$ l* D-lat syr copt æth: aft ο χρ., D-gr fuld lat-*c ff$_2$*: om BL X(Tischdf) ΓΔΠℵ^{1} 1 lat-*a b e ff$_1$ g$_1$* Syr syr-cu arm Orig$_4$ Chr Thl-ed Euthym Hil Ambr. (*Prob the insn of* ιησ. *was a mere mechanical mistake of an inattentive copyist.*)

21. rec ins ο bef ιησ., with CLℵ^{3b} rel Orig$_{oft}$: om BDℵ^{1}. (-ο *preceding might have caused either the omission or the insertion.*) aft ιησ. ins χριστος B^{1}ℵ^{1} copt: om B^{2}ℵ^{3b}: om ιησ. also ℵ^{3a} [Orig$_1$ Chr$_1$ Iren-int$_1$]. δεικνυναι B Orig$_1$. rec απελθειν bef εις ιεροσολυμα, with C rel vss: txt B D-gr ℵ 1. 33(appy) lat-*e* Orig$_6$ Iren-int Hil. for απο, υπο D.

Peter, remarkably fulfilled in his being *the first to admit both Jews and Gentiles into the Church*; thus using the power of the keys to open the door of salvation. As an instance of his shutting it also, witness his speech to Simon Magus,—οὐκ ἔστιν σοι μερὶς οὐδὲ κλῆρος ἐν τῷ λόγῳ τούτῳ, Acts viii. 21. Those who deny the reference of ver. 18 to St. Peter, will find it very difficult to persuade any unbiassed Greek scholar, that the καὶ δώσω σοί, with σοι thus lying unemphatically behind the verb, is not a continuation of a previous address, but a change of address altogether. **ὃ ἂν δήσῃς** κ.τ.λ.] This same promise is repeated in ch. xviii. 18, to *all the disciples generally*, and to *any two or three gathered together in Christ's name*. It was first however verified, and in a remarkable and prominent way, to Peter. Of the *binding*, the case of Ananias and Sapphira may serve as an eminent example: of the *loosing*, the ὃ ἔχω, τοῦτό σοι δίδωμι, to the lame man at the Beautiful gate of the Temple. But strictly considered, the binding and loosing belong to the *power of legislation* in the Church committed to the Apostles, in accordance with the Jewish way of using the words אסר and התיר for *prohibuit* and *licitum fecit*. They cannot relate to the *remission and retention of sins*, for (as Meyer observes) though **λύειν** ἁμαρτίας certainly appears (reff. LXX) to mean *to forgive sins*, **δέειν** ἁμαρτ. for *retaining* them would be altogether without example, and, I may add, would bear no meaning in the interpretation: it is *not the sin*, but the *sinner*, that is *bound*, ἔνοχος αἰωνίου ἁμαρτήματος (Mark iii. 29). Nor can the ancient custom of fastening doors by means of cord be alluded to; for the expressions, **ὃ** ἄν, **ὃ** ἐάν, clearly indicate *something bound* and *something loosed*, and not merely the power of the keys just conferred. The meaning in John xx. 23, though an expansion of this in one particular direction (see note there), is not to be confounded with this. **20.**] See note on ch. viii. 4.

21—28.] Our Lord announces His approaching Death and Resurrection. Rebuke of Peter. Mark viii. 31—ix. 1. Luke ix. 22—27. See note on ver. 13. Obscure intimations had before been given of our Lord's future sufferings, see ch. x. 38: John iii. 14, and of His resurrection, John ii. 19 (x. 17, 18?), but never yet plainly, as now. With Mark's usual precise note of circumstances, he adds, καὶ παῤῥησίᾳ τὸν λόγον ἐλάλει.

21.] On **δεῖ**, which is common to the three Evangelists, see Luke xxiv. 26: John iii. 14, and ch. xxvi. 54. **πολλὰ παθεῖν** = ἀποδοκιμασθῆναι in Mark and Luke. These πολλά were afterwards ex-

ρων καὶ ἀρχιερέων καὶ γραμματέων, καὶ ἀποκτανθῆναι,
καὶ τῇ τρίτῃ ἡμέρᾳ [h] ἐγερθῆναι. 22 καὶ [i] προςλαβόμενος
αὐτὸν ὁ Πέτρος λέγει αὐτῷ [k] ἐπιτιμῶν [l] Ἵλεώς σοι κύριε,
οὐ μὴ [m] ἔσται [m] σοι τοῦτο. 23 ὁ δὲ στραφεὶς εἶπεν τῷ
Πέτρῳ Ὕπαγε ὀπίσω μου, [n] σατανᾶ, [o] σκάνδαλον εἶ ἐμοῦ·

h ch. x. 8. xiv. 2 al. Isa. xxvi. 10.
i || Mk. Acts xvii. 5 al.
k = ch. xii. 16 reff.
l Heb. viii. 12 (from Jer. xxxviii. [xxxi.] 34) only. 1 Kings xiv. 45 A. 2 Kings xx. 20. xxiii. 17. 1 Chron. xi. 19. 1 Macc. ii. 21.
m Mark xi. 24. Luke ii. 10. xiv. 10. τί σφισιν ἔσται, Xen. Anab. i. 7. 8.
n ch. iv. 10 al.† Sir. xxi. 27 only. -τάν, 3 Kings xi. 14.
o ch. xiii. 41 al. fr. Ps. cxviii. 165.

for τη τριτη ημ., μετα τρεις ημερας D, *post tertium diem* lat-*a b c e ff*$_2$ *g*$_1$ copt.
for εγερθηναι, αναστηναι D (Just), *resurgere* latt Hil.

22. rec ηρξατο επιτιμαν αυτω λεγων (*from* || *Mark*), with Cא rel vulg lat-*e f g*$_2$ Orig$_1$ (for αυτω, αυτον H : ins και bef λεγων F) : ηρξ. αυτω επιτιμαν λεγ. 1 Orig$_1$: ηρξ. αυτω επιτιμαν κ. λεγειν D lat-*a b c ff*$_2$ *g*$_1$: *et dixit ei* syr-cu : txt B 346. (Tischdf refers to corrns Mark xiv. 69; x. 41: but against this is the fact that B has not corrected it in this instance in || Mark.) τουτο bef σοι D : om σοι lat-*a b* syr-cu Hil.

23. επιστραφεις (*from* || *Mark*) DKLΠ : txt BCא rel Orig$_2$. rec (for ει εμου) μου ει (*for perspicuity*), with L rel Orig$_6$ [Cyr$_2$-p] : ει εμοι D latt Marcell-in-Eus Jer :

plicitly mentioned, ch. xx. 18: Luke xviii. 31, 32. **πρεσβ. κ. ἀρχ. κ. γραμ.**] The various classes of members of the Sanhedrim: see note on ch. ii. 4. On the prophecy of the *resurrection*, some have objected that the disciples and friends of our Lord appear *not to have expected it* (see John xx. 2: Luke xxiv. 12). But we have it directly asserted (Mark ix. 10 and 32) that they *did not understand* the saying, and therefore were not likely to make it a ground of expectation. Certainly enough was known of such a prophecy to make the Jews set a watch over the grave (Matt. xxvii. 63), which of itself answers the objection. Meyer in loc. reasons about the state of the disciples after the crucifixion just as if they had not suffered any remarkable overthrow of their hopes and reliances, and maintains that they *must* have remembered this precise prophecy if it had been given by the Lord. But on the other hand we must remember how slow despondency is to take up hope, and how many of the Lord's sayings must have been completely veiled from their eyes, owing to their non-apprehension of His sufferings and triumph as a *whole*. He Himself reproaches them with this very slowness of belief after His resurrection. It is in the highest degree improbable that the precision should have been given to this prophecy *after the event*, as Meyer supposes: both from the character of the Gospel History in general (see Prolegomena), and because of the carefulness and precision in the words added by Mark; see above. **22.**] The same Peter, who but just now had made so noble and spiritual a confession, and received so high a blessing, now shews the weak and carnal side of his character, becomes a stumbling-block in the way of his Lord, and earns the very rebuff with which the Tempter before him had been dismissed. Nor is there any thing improbable in this, as Schleiermacher would have us believe (Translation of the Essay on St. Luke, p. 153); the expression of spiritual faith may, and frequently does, precede the betraying of carnal weakness; and never is this more probable than when the mind has just been uplifted, as Peter's was, by commendation and lofty promise. **προςλαβ. αὐτ.**] *by the dress* or *hand*, or perhaps ἀντὶ τοῦ παραλαβὼν κατ' ἰδίαν. Euthym. **ἵλεώς σοι**] Supply εἴη ὁ θεός. ἵλεως with a dative is practically equivalent to the Hebrew חָלִילָה לְּ, for which (see reff., especially 1 Chron. xi. 19 compared with the Heb.) the LXX have sometimes used it. **οὐ μὴ ἔσται**] I cannot think with Winer (§ 56. 3) that this means, 'absit, ne accidat;' it is an authoritative declaration, as it were, on Peter's part, **This shall not happen to Thee**, implying that he *knew better*, and could ensure his Divine Master against such an event. It is this spirit of confident rejection of God's revealed purpose which the Lord so sharply rebukes. On οὐ μή with the future, see note on ch. xv. 6: and consult Winer, as above. **23.**] As it was Peter's *spiritual discernment*, given from above, which made him a foundation-stone of the Church, so is it his *carnality*, proceeding from want of unity with the divine will, which makes him an adversary now. Compare ch. iv. 10, also Eph. vi. 12. **σκάνδαλον εἶ ἐμοῦ**] **Thou art my stumbling-block** (not merely *a* stumbling-block to me; the definite article is omitted before a noun thrust forward for emphasis, but in English it must be supplied), my πέτρα

p ∥ Mk. only in Gospp. Acts xxviii. 22. Rom. viii. 5 al. 1 Macc. x. 20.
q ch. viii. 33 reff.
r ch. iv. 19 reff. Num. xxxii. 11.
s ∥ Mk. (L. v. r.) only.
t as above (s). elsw. of Peter's denial (ch. xxvi. 34, &c. ∥) only, exc. Luke xii. 9. Isa. xxxi. 7 only.
u ∥. ch. x. 38. xxvii. 32 ∥ Mk. J. Mark x. 21.
v ∥ Mk. ch. x. 39. Luke xvii. 33. Sir. xx. 22.
w ch. xv. 5 reff. Prov. x. 2. xi. 4 A Ald.

ὅτι οὐ p φρονεῖς q τὰ τοῦ θεοῦ ἀλλὰ q τὰ τῶν ἀνθρώπων. BCDEF GHKL MSUVX ΓΔΠℵ 1. 33
24 τότε ὁ Ἰησοῦς εἶπεν τοῖς μαθηταῖς αὐτοῦ Εἴ τις θέλει
r ὀπίσω μου ἐλθεῖν, st ἀπαρνησάσθω s ἑαυτὸν καὶ ἀράτω
τὸν u σταυρὸν u αὐτοῦ καὶ ἀκολουθείτω μοι. 25 ὃς γὰρ
ἐὰν θέλῃ τὴν v ψυχὴν αὐτοῦ σῶσαι, v ἀπολέσει αὐτήν· ὃς
δ' ἂν v ἀπολέσῃ τὴν v ψυχὴν αὐτοῦ ἕνεκεν ἐμοῦ, εὑρήσει
αὐτήν. 26 τί γὰρ w ὠφεληθήσεται ἄνθρωπος, ἐὰν τὸν
x κόσμον x ὅλον y κερδήσῃ, τὴν δὲ z ψυχὴν αὐτοῦ za ζημιωθῇ; ἢ τί bc δώσει ἄνθρωπος cd ἀντάλλαγμα τῆς ψυχῆς
αὐτοῦ; 27 e μέλλει γὰρ ὁ υἱὸς τοῦ ἀνθρώπου ἔρχεσθαι
f ἐν τῇ δόξῃ τοῦ πατρὸς αὐτοῦ μετὰ τῶν ἀγγέλων αὐτοῦ·
καὶ τότε g ἀποδώσει ἑκάστῳ κατὰ τὴν h πρᾶξιν αὐτοῦ.

x ∥. ch. xxvi. 13. Rom. i. 8 al. 2 Macc. viii. 18. y ∥. ch. xxv. 17, &c. James iv. 13†. Job xxii. 3 Symm. z acc., ∥ Mk. Phil. iii. 8. Prov. xix. 19. a ∥ Mk. L. 1 Cor. iii. 15. 2 Cor. vii. 9. Phil. as above only. b = ch. xxvii. 10. Gen. xxv. 34. c 3 Kings xx. (xxi.) 2 A. Jer. xv. 13. d ∥ Mk. only. Sir. vi. 15. e = ch. ii. 13 al. Isa. xlviii. 6. Job iii. 8.
f ∥. ch. xxv. 31. Ps. ci. 16. g = ch. vi. 4, &c. Rom. ii. 6. 2 Tim. iv. 8, 14. Rev. xxii. 12. Prov. xxiv. 12.
h Luke xxiii. 51. Acts xix. 18. Rom. viii. 13. xii. 4. Col. iii. 9 only. 2 Chron. xii. 15. Sir. xxxii. (xxxv.) 19.

μοι ει V lat-*e f* copt Hil_3 Aug Ruf: *μου* Cℵ[3]: txt Bℵ[1]. αλλα(or αλλ' ἃ?) **του ανθρωπου** *sed quæ* (*sunt* D[7]) *hominis* D lat-ff_1 sah æth Aug_{aliq}.

24. om *ο* (bef *ιησ.*) B[1](Mai, expr [so also Tischdf N. T. Vat.]).

25. [*εαν*, so BCℵ.] for *απολεση*, *απολεσει* (*itacism?*) DHLΔ 33: txt BCℵ rel $Orig_2$.

26. rec *ωφελειται* (*from* ∥ *Luke: this is much more prob than with Meyer, to believe the fut to have been an emendation to suit δωσει below*), with CD rel latt arm Just [Ps-Ign] Clem Hil Lucif: txt BLℵ 1. 33 gat lat-*e f* syrr syr-cu coptt $Orig_3$ Chr_1 Cyr_{oft} Cypr. **οταν** ℵ[3a](but *εαν* restored). [*κερδ***αν***η* LΠ $Orig_1$:] *κερδη* D.

27. ins *αγιων* bef *αγγελων* D (∥ *Luke*), *τ. αγγ. τ. αγιων* C (∥ *Mark*). for *την πραξιν*, *τα εργα* ℵ[1](txt ℵ[3a]) F[1] 1 latt(incl D-lat, but not am gat-*e* g_2) syrr [syr-cu] coptt arm [Chr_1-2-6-9-η-ρ(txt_1) Cyr Avit].

σκανδάλου (in Peter's own remarkable words, 1 Pet. ii. 7, 8,—joined too with the very expression, *ὃν* **ἀπεδοκίμασαν** *οἱ οἰκοδομοῦντες*, which, as above noticed, occurs in this passage in Mark and Luke). Wordsw.'s note here, "our blessed Lord keeps up the metaphor of **πέτρος**, or a stone: thou who wert just now, by thy faith in confessing Me, *a lively stone*, art now by thy carnal weakness *a stumbling stone* to Christ," seems to shew that his strong repudiation of any allusion to **πέτρος** in the **πέτρα** of ver. 18 has not carried full conviction to its writer. Before this rebuke St. Mark inserts *καὶ ἰδὼν τοὺς μαθητὰς αὐτοῦ*, that the reproof might be before them all. **24.**] *προσκαλεσάμενος τὸν ὄχλον σὺν τοῖς μαθ. αὐτοῦ*, Mark viii. 34; *ἔλεγε δὲ πρὸς πάντας*, Luke ix. 23. This discourse is a solemn sequel to our Lord's announcement respecting Himself and the rebuke of Peter: teaching that not only He, but also His followers, must suffer and self-deny; that they all have a life to save, more precious than all else to them; and that the great day of account of that life's welfare should be ever before them. On this and the following verse, see ch. x. 38, 39. After **τὸν στ. αὐτοῦ**, Luke inserts *καθ' ἡμέραν*.

26.] There is apparently a reference to Psalm xlviii. (LXX) in this verse. Compare especially the latter part with ver. 8 of that Psalm. **τὴν ψ. ζημιωθῇ** = *ἑαυτὸν δὲ ἀπολέσας* Luke. Compare also 1 Pet. i. 18. In the latter part of the verse, *ἄνθρωπος* and *αὐτοῦ* refer to the same person:—*ἀντάλλαγμα* = *ἐξίλασμα*, *τὴν τιμὴν τῆς λυτρώσεως τῆς ψ. αὐτοῦ* Ps. xlviii. 7, 8. **What shall a man give to purchase back his life? ψυχή**, not *soul*, but life, in the higher sense.

27.] A further revelation of this important chapter respecting the Son of Man. He is to be JUDGE OF ALL—and, as in ch. xiii. 41, is to appear with *His* angels, and in the glory of His Father—the *δόξα ἣν δέδωκάς μοι*, John xvii. 22. Mark and Luke place here, not this declaration, but that of our ch. x. 33. Our Lord doubtless joined the two. Compare ch. xxiv. 30; xxv. 31. **γάρ** implies, "And it is

28 [i] ἀμὴν λέγω ὑμῖν, εἰσίν τινες τῶν ὧδε ἑστώτων, [k] οἵτινες
οὐ μὴ [lm] γεύσωνται [l] θανάτου ἕως ἂν ἴδωσιν τὸν [n] υἱὸν τοῦ
...αυτου X. [n] ἀνθρώπου [o] ἐρχόμενον ἐν τῇ [o] βασιλείᾳ αὐτοῦ.
XVII. 1 Καὶ μεθ' ἡμέρας ἓξ [p] παραλαμβάνει ὁ Ἰησοῦς

i ch. v. 18 reff. k ch. vii. 15 reff. l ||. John viii. 52. Heb. ii. 9. m ch. xxvii. 34 al. Job xx. 18. Ps. xxxiii. 8. Num. xxiii. 14. n ch. viii. 20 reff. o Luke xxiii. 42. p = ch. ii. 13, &c. iv. 5, 8 al.

28. ins *οτι* bef *εισιν* (*from* || *Mark*) BLℵ 33 lat-*b c e f ff*$_{1.2}$ *g*$_1$ syrr syr-cu sah [Epiph$_1$] Hil$_2$: om CD rel vulg lat-*a* Orig$_2$ [Chr(Fd and Mt's mss)]. rec *των ωδε εστηκοτων* (*see* || *Mark*), with KMΠ Thdot: *ωδε εστωτες* E rel 131. 218 ev-36 Scr's b f g h i k l m n o (syr) Thl, *των ωδε εστωτες* Scr's c r ev-H: txt BCDLSUℵ 1. 13. 33. 124 Scr's s ev-y latt Syr syr-cu syr-w-ast coptt æth arm Orig$_{expr}$ Ephr Epiph Chr Thdrt Damasc. for *βασιλεια, δοξη του πατρος* (*ver* 27) ℵ^{3a} 245 ev-y [Bas$_2$].

CHAP. XVII. 1. aft *και* ins *εγενετο* D lat-*a b c e ff*$_{1.2}$ *g*$_{1.2}$ Hil.

not without reason that I thus speak: a time will come when the truth of what I say will be shewn." **τὴν πρ.**] his **work**, considered as *a whole*. **28.**] * This declaration refers, in its full meaning, certainly *not to the transfiguration which follows*, for that could in no sense (except that of being a *foretaste*; cf. Peter's own allusion to it, 2 Pet. i. 17, where he evidently treats it as such) be named 'the Son of Man coming in His Kingdom,' and the expression, **τινὲς . . . οὐ μὴ γ. θ.**, indicates a distant event,—but *to the destruction of Jerusalem*, and the full manifestation of the Kingdom of Christ by the annihilation of the Jewish polity; which event, in this aspect as well as in all its terrible attendant details, was a *type* and *earnest* of the final coming of Christ. See John xxi. 22, and compare Deut. xxxii. 36 with Heb. x. 30. This dreadful destruction was indeed judgment beginning at the house of God. The interpretation of Meyer, &c., that our Lord referred to His *ultimate glorious* παρουσία, the time of which was hidden from Himself (see Mark xiii. 32: Acts i. 7), is self-contradictory on his own view of the Person of Christ. That our Lord, in His humanity in the flesh, *did not know* the day and the hour, we have from His own lips: but that *not knowing it*, He should have uttered a determinate and solemn prophecy of it, is utterly impossible. His **ἀμὴν λέγω ὑμῖν** always introduces His solemn and authoritative revelations of divine truth. The fact is, there is a reference back in this discourse to that in ch. x., and the *coming* here spoken of is the same as that in ver. 23 there. Stier well remarks that this cannot be the great and ultimate coming, on account of *οὐ μὴ γεύσ. θανάτου ἕως ἂν ἴδωσιν*, which implies that they *should taste* of death *after they had seen* it, and would therefore be inapplicable to the final coming (Reden Jesu, ii. 224). This is denied by Wordsw., who substitutes for the simple sense of *οὐ μὴ γεύσ. θαν.* the fanciful expositions, "shall not feel its bitterness," "shall not taste of the death of the *soul*," and then, thus interpreting, gives the prophecy the very opposite of its plain sense: "they will not taste of death till I come: *much less will they taste of it then*." It might be difficult to account for such a curious wresting of meaning, had he not added, "the signification of ἕως ἂν here may be compared to ἕως οὗ in Matt. i. 25." "Latet anguis in herba."

CHAP. XVII. **1—13.**] THE TRANSFIGURATION. Mark ix. 2—13. Luke ix. 28—36. This weighty event forms the solemn installation of our Lord to His sufferings and their result. Those three Apostles were chosen to witness it, who had before witnessed His power over death (Mark v. 37), and who afterwards were chosen to accompany Him in His agony (ch. xxvi. 37), and were (John xx. 2: Mark xvi. 7) in an especial sense witnesses of His resurrection. The Two who appeared to them were the representatives of the *law* and the *prophets*: both had been removed from this world in a mysterious manner:—the one without death,—the other by death indeed, but so that his body followed not the lot of the bodies of all; both, like the Greater One with whom they spoke, had endured that supernatural fast of forty days and nights: both had been on the holy mount in the visions of God. And now they came, endowed with glorified bodies before the rest of the dead, to hold converse with the Lord on that sublime event, which had been the great central subject of all their teaching, and solemnly to consign into His hands, once and for all, in a symbolical and glorious representation, their delegated and expiring power. And then follows the Divine Voice, as at the Bap-

q — ‖ Mk. Luke xxiv. 51 (Heb. vii. 27 al.) only. Neh. xii. 31.
r ch. iv. 8 reff. Isa. xl. 9.
s ch. xiv. 13 reff.
t ‖ Mk. Rom. xii. 2. 2 Cor. iii. 18 only +. Ps. xxxiii. tit. Symm.
u ch. v. 15, 16 reff.
v see Ps. ciii. 2.
w = ‖. Luke i. 11. xxii. 43 al. Exod. xxiv. 11.

BCDEF GHKL MSUVΓ ΔΠℵ 1. 33

τὸν Πέτρον καὶ Ἰάκωβον καὶ Ἰωάννην τὸν ἀδελφὸν
αὐτοῦ, καὶ [q] ἀναφέρει αὐτοὺς εἰς [r] ὄρος [r] ὑψηλὸν [s] κατ᾽
[s] ἰδίαν.
2 καὶ [t] μετεμορφώθη ἔμπροσθεν αὐτῶν, καὶ [u] ἔλαμψεν τὸ πρόσωπον αὐτοῦ ὡς ὁ ἥλιος, τὰ δὲ [v] ἱμάτια αὐτοῦ ἐγένετο λευκὰ ὡς τὸ [v] φῶς.
3 καὶ ἰδοὺ [w] ὤφθη

ins τον bef ιακωβον Dℵ 33 [Cyr_1], and bef ιω. D[1] 253 [Cyr_1]. αναγει D-gr 1 latt Orig. for κατ ιδιαν, λειαι *nimis* D [Eus_1].

2. μεταμορφωθεις ο ιησ., omg και below, D. for το φως, χιων D latt syr-cu æth arm-mss Dion Hil_3 Aug Juv.

3. rec **ωφθησαν** (*gramml corrn*), with C rel vulg-ed(with forj al) lat-*f* ff_1 : txt BDℵ

tism, commanding however here in addition the *sole hearing and obedience* of Him whose power and glory were thus testified. There can be no doubt of the *absolute historical reality* of this narration. It is united by definite marks of date with what goes before; and by intimate connexion with what follows. It cannot by any unfairness be severed from its context. Nor again is there any thing mentioned which casts a doubt on the *reality* of the appearances (see below, on ὅραμα, ver. 9). The persons mentioned *were seen by all—spoke*—and *were recognized.* The concurrence between the three Evangelists is exact in all the circumstances, and the fourth alludes, not obscurely, to the event, which it was not part of his purpose to relate; John i. 14. Another of the three spectators distinctly makes mention of the facts here related, 2 Pet. i. 16—18. (I cannot but add, having recently returned from the sight of the wonderful original at Rome, that the great last picture of Raffaelle is one of the best and noblest comments on this portion of the Gospel history. The events passing, at the same time, on, and under, the Mount of Transfiguration, are by the painter combined, to carry to the mind of the spectator the great central truth, There is none but Christ to console and to glorify our nature. It is a touching reflection, that this picture was left unfinished by the painter, and carried in his funeral procession. July, 1861.)

1.] μεθ᾽ ἡμέρας ἕξ = *μετὰ τοὺς λόγους τούτους ὡσεὶ ἡμ. ὀκτώ* Luke ix. 28. The one computation is inclusive, the other not; or perhaps, from the ὡσεί being inserted, the one is accurate, the other roughly stated. The time of the transfiguration was probably *night,* for the following reasons. (1) Luke informs us that the Lord had gone up to the mount *to pray;* which He usually did at night (Luke vi. 12; xxi. 37; xxii. 39: Matt. xiv. 23, 24 al.). (2) All the circumstances connected with the glorification and accompanying appearances would thus be more prominently seen. (3) The Apostles were *asleep,* and are described, Luke, ver. 32, as '*having kept awake through it*' (διαγρηγορήσαντες). (4) They *did not descend till the next day* (Luke, ver. 37), which would be almost inexplicable had the event happened by day, but a matter of course if by night. **ὄρος ὑψ.**] The situation of this mountain is uncertain. It was not, probably, Tabor, according to the legend; for on the top of Tabor then most likely stood a fortified town (De Wette, from Robinson). Nor is there any likelihood that it was Panium, near Cæsarea Philippi, for the six days would probably be spent in journeying; and they appear immediately after to have come to Capernaum. It was most likely one of the mountains bordering the lake. Luke speaks of it merely as τὸ ὄρος. Stanley, Sinai and Palestine, p. 399, contends for Hermon: as does, though doubtingly, Dr. Thomson, The Land and the Book, p. 231. Stanley thinks that our Lord would still be in the neighbourhood of Cæsarea Philippi: and that "it is impossible to look up from the plain to the towering peaks of Hermon, almost the only mountain which deserves the name in Palestine, and one of whose ancient titles ('the lofty peak') was derived from this very circumstance, and not be struck with its appropriateness to the scene .... High up on its southern slopes there must be many a point where the disciples could be taken 'apart by themselves.' Even the transient comparison of the celestial splendour with the snow, where alone it could be seen in Palestine, should not perhaps be wholly overlooked." **2.] μετεμορ.** = *ἐγένετο τὸ εἶδος τοῦ προσώπου αὐτοῦ ἕτερον* Luke. In what way, is not stated; but we may conclude from what follows, by being lighted with radiance both from

αὐτοῖς Μωυσῆς καὶ Ἡλίας μετ' αὐτοῦ [x] συλλαλοῦντες.
4 [y] ἀποκριθεὶς δὲ ὁ Πέτρος εἶπεν τῷ Ἰησοῦ Κύριε [z] καλόν
ἐστιν ἡμᾶς ὧδε εἶναι· εἰ θέλεις, ποιήσω ὧδε τρεῖς [a] σκηνάς,
σοὶ [b] μίαν καὶ Μωυσεῖ [b] μίαν καὶ Ἡλίᾳ [b] μίαν. 5 ἔτι
αὐτοῦ λαλοῦντος ἰδοὺ νεφέλη [c] φωτεινὴ [d] ἐπεσκίασεν αὐτούς, καὶ ἰδοὺ φωνὴ ἐκ τῆς νεφέλης λέγουσα Οὗτός ἐστιν
ὁ [e] υἱός μου ὁ [e] ἀγαπητός, ἐν ᾧ [f] εὐδόκησα· [g] ἀκούετε
αὐτοῦ. 6 καὶ ἀκούσαντες οἱ μαθηταὶ [h] ἔπεσαν ἐπὶ [h] πρόσωπον αὐτῶν καὶ [i] ἐφοβήθησαν [ik] σφόδρα. 7 καὶ προσελθὼν ὁ Ἰησοῦς [l] ἥψατο αὐτῶν καὶ εἶπεν Ἐγέρθητε καὶ [m] μὴ
φοβεῖσθε. 8 [n] ἐπάραντες δὲ τοὺς [n] ὀφθαλμοὺς αὐτῶν
οὐδένα εἶδον εἰ μὴ τὸν Ἰησοῦν μόνον. 9 καὶ [o] καταβαι-

x w. μετά, Acts xxv. 12. πρός, Luke iv. 36. dat., ‖. Luke xxii. 4 only. Exod. xxxiv. 35. Isa. vii. 6.
y = ch. xi. 25 reff.
z ch. xviii. 8, 9 ‖ Mk. xxvi. 24. Rom. xiv. 21. 1 Cor. vii. 8 al. Job x. 3. Sir. xiv. 3.
a ‖. Luke xvi. 9. Acts vii. 43, 44. xv. 16 (from Amos ix. 11) al.
b ch. xx. 12. 1 Kings x. 3.
c ch. vi. 22. Luke xi. 34, 36 bis only †. Sir. xvii. 31. xxiii. 19 only.
d ‖. Luke i. 35. Acts v. 15 only. Exod. xl. 29 (35).
e ch. iii. 17 ‖. 2 Pet. i. 17. Gen. xxii. 2.
f ch. iii. 17. xii. 18. Isa. lxii. 4. Hag. i. 8.
g Deut. xviii. 15, 19.
h ch. xxvi. 39. Luke v. 12. xvii. 16. 1 Cor. xiv. 25. Rev. xl. 16. Lev. ix. 24. Judg. xiii. 20.
i ch. xxvii. 54. Num. xxii. 3.
k ch. ii. 10 reff.
l Dan. viii. 18.
m ch. xxviii. 5, 10 al. Deut. i. 21.
n Luke vi. 20. xvi. 23. John iv. 35. vi. 5. xvi. 1 al. Gen. xiii. 10. 1 Chron. xxi. 16 al.
o (but w. ἀπό, ch. viii. 1.) Exod. xxxiv. 29 B (ἀπό A). ἐκ, elsw. of οὐρανός, ch. xxviii. 2 al.

33 am(with em fuld gat mm tol) lat-*a b c e* $g_{1.2}$ *l* Bede. συλλαλουντες bef μετ' αυτου Bא 1 lat-$ff_{1.2}$ Syr syr-cu coptt æth $Orig_2$ Chr Cyr.

4. rec ποιησωμεν (*from ‖ Luke*), with C[3]D rel vulg lat-*a c* &c syrr syr-cu coptt æth arm $Orig_2$: txt BC[1]א lat-*b* ff_1 g_1. σκηνας bef τρεις B lat-*e*. rec μιαν bef ηλια, with B rel arm : txt CDKLΔΠא 1. 33 latt syrr syr-cu æth [Bas_1 Chr].

5. επεσκιαζεν D[1](txt D[4]). rec αυτου bef ακουετε (*from ‖ Luke—as also it has been corrd in ‖ Mark*), with C rel latt [Chr] Tert Cypr Hil : txt BDא 1. 33 lat-ff_1 Hipp Orig Tert.

6. for και ακουσ., ακουσ. δε D sah. (επεσαν, so BCDא 33.)

7. κ. προσηλθεν ο ιησ. κ. αψαμενος αυτ. ειπ. Bא : κ. προσηλθεν ο ι. κ. ηψ. αυτ. κ. ειπ. D latt Syr syr-cu : txt C rel. for εγερθητε, εγειρεσθαι D.

8. aft αυτων ins ουκετι C[1]. for τον, αυτον B[1](א [but aft ιησ.]). μονον bef τον ιησουν D latt. add μεθ εαυτων (*from ‖ Mark*) C[2] 33.

without and from within. **λευκὰ ὡς τὸ φῶς** = λευκὸς ἐξαστράπτων Luke; = λευκὰ λίαν, οἷα γναφεὺς ἐπὶ τῆς γῆς οὐ δύναται οὕτως λευκᾶναι Mark.

3.] There need be no question concerning the *manner* of the recognition of Moses and Elias by the disciples: it may have been intuitive and immediate. We can certainly not answer with Olshausen, that it may have arisen from subsequent information derived from our Lord, for Peter's words in the next verse preclude this. Luke adds, οἱ ὀφθέντες ἐν δόξῃ ἔλεγον τὴν ἔξοδον αὐτοῦ ἣν ἔμελλεν πληροῦν ἐν Ἱερουσαλήμ. **4.**] Luke inserts, that the Apostles *had been asleep*, but wakened through this whole occurrence;—thereby distinguishing it from a mere vision of sleep; and that this speech was made ἐν τῷ διαχωρίζεσθαι αὐτοὺς ἀπ' αὐτοῦ. Both Mark and Luke add, that Peter *knew not what he said:* and Mark—ἔκφοβοι γὰρ ἐγένοντο. The speech was probably uttered with reference to the sad announcement recently made by our Lord, and to which his attention had been recalled by the converse of Moses and Elias.

A strange explanation of this verse is adopted by Meyer from Paulus, 'It is fortunate that we disciples are here: let us make,' &c. Surely the *words* καλόν ἐστιν ἡμᾶς ὧδε εἶναι will not bear this.

It is one of those remarkable coincidences of words which lead men on, in writing, to remembrances connected with those words, that in 2 Pet. i. 14, 15, σκήνωμα and ἔξοδος have just been mentioned before the allusion to this event: see note there. **κύριε** = ῥαββεί Mark, = ἐπιστάτα Luke. **5.**] **αὐτούς**, viz. our Lord, Moses, and Elias. Luke adds, ἐφοβήθησαν δὲ ἐν τῷ εἰσελθεῖν αὐτοὺς εἰς τὴν νεφέλην. That the Apostles did not enter the cloud, is shewn by the voice being heard **ἐκ τῆς νεφέλης**. The **ἀκούετε αὐτοῦ**, and disappearance of the two heavenly attendants, are symbolically connected,—as signifying that God, who had *

p here only, exc. Acts vii. 31 al10. Exod. iii. 3.
q w. ἐκ ν., (Mark vi. 14, 16 v. r.) Luke ix. 7. John ii. 22. xii. 1, &c. xxi. 14. Acts iii. 15. Rom. iv. 24 al. ἀπὸ ν., ch. xiv. 2.
r Mal. iv. 5.
s = ch. xvi. 21 al. Dan. ii. 28.
t pres., ch. xi. 3.
u ∥ Mk. ch. xii. 13 ∥. Mark viii. 25. Acts i. 6. Heb. xiii. 19 only. Mal. iv. 6. Jer. xvi. 15. (-στασις, Acts iii. 21.)
v ch. xiv. 35 al. 1 Kings xxvi. 17.
y ch. xiii. 23, 51 al.
a ch. iv. 24 only †.

νόντων αὐτῶν ἐκ τοῦ [o] ὄρους ἐνετείλατο αὐτοῖς ὁ Ἰησοῦς
λέγων Μηδενὶ εἴπητε τὸ [p] ὅραμα, ἕως οὗ ὁ υἱὸς τοῦ ἀνθρώπου ἐκ νεκρῶν [q] ἐγερθῇ. 10 καὶ ἐπηρώτησαν αὐτὸν οἱ
μαθηταὶ αὐτοῦ λέγοντες Τί οὖν οἱ γραμματεῖς λέγουσιν
ὅτι [r] Ἠλίαν [s] δεῖ ἐλθεῖν πρῶτον; 11 ὁ δὲ ἀποκριθεὶς εἶπεν
[αὐτοῖς] Ἠλίας μὲν [t] ἔρχεται καὶ [u] ἀποκαταστήσει πάντα·
12 λέγω δὲ ὑμῖν ὅτι Ἠλίας ἤδη ἦλθεν, καὶ οὐκ [v] ἐπέγνωσαν αὐτόν, ἀλλὰ ἐποίησαν [w] ἐν αὐτῷ ὅσα ἠθέλησαν· οὕτως
καὶ ὁ υἱὸς τοῦ ἀνθρώπου [x] μέλλει πάσχειν ὑπ' αὐτῶν.
13 τότε [y] συνῆκαν οἱ μαθηταὶ ὅτι περὶ Ἰωάννου τοῦ βαπτιστοῦ εἶπεν αὐτοῖς. 14 Καὶ ἐλθόντων πρὸς τὸν ὄχλον
προσῆλθεν αὐτῷ ἄνθρωπος [z] γονυπετῶν αὐτὸν καὶ λέγων
15 Κύριε ἐλέησόν μου τὸν υἱόν, ὅτι [a] σεληνιάζεται καὶ

Z του ορους...
BCDEF GHKL MSUVZ ΓΔΠℵ 1. 33
X και ελθοντων...

w Luke xxii. 37. xxiii. 31. 1 Cor. ix. 15. Gen. xxxiv. 7, but? x = ver. 22 al.
z ch. xxvii. 29. Mark [i. 40] x. 17 only †. γονυπετοῦσα, Polyb. xv. 29. 9.

9. καταβαινοντες, omg αυτων, D. rec (for εκ) απο, with K[1] Orig$_1$: txt BCD K[1]-corr(appy) ℵ rel Orig$_1$ Chr Thl Euthym. rec (for εγερθη) αναστη (*from* ∥ *Mark*), with CZℵ rel Orig$_2$ [Chr]: txt BD sah.

10. om αυτου LZℵ 1. 33 latt coptt arm Orig: ins BCD rel lat-*f* syrr syr-cu æth [Chr].

11. rec aft ο δε ins ιησους, with C rel lat-*f* æth: om BDLZℵ 1. 33 latt syrr coptt. om αυτοις BD 33 am lat-*a b c e ff*$_2$ coptt: ins bef ειπεν 1: txt CZℵ rel vulg-ed lat-*f g*$_1$ syrr syr-cu æth arm. ins οτι bef ηλιας ℵ. rec aft ερχεται ins πρωτον (*from* ∥ *Mark, and ver* 10), with CZ rel syrr æth: bef παντα L: om BDℵ 1. 33 latt syr-cu coptt arm Just Hil Aug. αποκαταστησαι, omg και, D lat-*a b c ff*$_2$ *g*$_1$ Syr syr-cu sah: και αποκαθιστησι L.

12. om ηδη Z(appy) Syr syr-cu. (αλλα, so CDKMΠ 33.) om εν DFUℵ lat-*a b c* &c syr-txt copt Just [Chr-γ]: om εν αυτω Δ. ουτως to υπ' αυτων is after ver 13 in D lat-*a b c* &c(not *f*).

14. for ελθοντων, ελθων (*from* ∥ *Mark*) D latt syr-cu syr-jer copt-ms Hil Aug. rec aft ελθ. ins αυτων, with C rel syrr copt æth arm Orig Chr: om (*perhaps from similarity of endings*) B(D)Zℵ 1 sah. rec (for αυτον) αυτω, with (E[1] ?)[M[1] ?] Orig$_2$: ενπροσθεν αυτου D latt syr: om αυτ. lat-*e f ff*$_1$ *l* Syr syr-cu arm Hil: txt BCZℵ (E[1]-corr ?) rel [Orig-ed$_1$] Thl.

15. om κυριε Zℵ. μου τον υιον μου B[1].

spoken in times past to the Fathers by the Prophets, henceforth would speak by His Son. Vv. 6, 7 are peculiar to Matthew.

9.] No unreality is implied in the word **ὅραμα**, for it = ἃ εἶδον in Mark, and . . . . ὧν ἑωράκασιν in Luke: see Num. xxiv. 3, 4. St. Luke, without mentioning the condition of time imposed on them, remarkably confirms it by saying, οὐδενὶ ἀπήγγειλαν ἐν ἐκείναις ταῖς ἡμέραις οὐδὲν . . .

10.] The occasion of this enquiry was, that they had just seen Elias withdrawn from their eyes, and were enjoined not to tell the vision. How (οὖν) should this be? If this was not the coming of Elias, *was he yet to come?* If it was, how was it so *secret* and so short? On ver. **12**, see note on ch. xi. 14. Our Lord speaks here plainly *in the future*, and uses the very word of the prophecy Mal. iv. 6. The *double* allusion is only the assertion that the Elias (in spirit and power) who foreran our Lord's first coming, was a partial fulfilment of the great prophecy which announces the *real Elias* (the words of Malachi will hardly bear any other than a personal meaning), who is to forerun His greater and second coming.

14–21.] Healing of a possessed lunatic. Mark ix. 14—29. Luke ix. 37—42. By much the fullest account of this miracle is contained in Mark, where see notes. It was *the next day:* see Luke ix. 37, and note on our ver. 1. Our Lord found the Scribes and the disciples dis-

[b] κακῶς [b] * πάσχει· πολλάκις γὰρ πίπτει εἰς τὸ πῦρ, καὶ
πολλάκις εἰς τὸ ὕδωρ. 16 καὶ προσήνεγκα αὐτὸν τοῖς
μαθηταῖς σου, καὶ οὐκ ἠδυνήθησαν αὐτὸν θεραπεῦσαι.
17 ἀποκριθεὶς δὲ ὁ Ἰησοῦς εἶπεν Ὦ [c] γενεὰ [d] ἄπιστος καὶ
[ce] διεστραμμένη, [f] ἕως πότε μεθ' ὑμῶν ἔσομαι; [f] ἕως πότε
...ωδε Z. [g] ἀνέξομαι ὑμῶν; φέρετέ μοι αὐτὸν ὧδε. 18 καὶ [h] ἐπετίμη-
BCDEF GHKL MSUVX σεν αὐτῷ ὁ Ἰησοῦς, καὶ [i] ἐξῆλθεν ἀπ' αὐτοῦ τὸ [i] δαιμό-
ΓΔΠℵ 1. 33 νιον, καὶ ἐθεραπεύθη ὁ παῖς ἀπὸ τῆς ὥρας ἐκείνης.
19 τότε προσελθόντες οἱ μαθηταὶ τῷ Ἰησοῦ [k] κατ' [k] ἰδίαν
εἶπον Διὰ τί ἡμεῖς οὐκ ἠδυνήθημεν [l] ἐκβαλεῖν αὐτό; 20 ὁ
δὲ λέγει αὐτοῖς Διὰ τὴν [m] * ὀλιγοπιστίαν ὑμῶν. ἀμὴν γὰρ
λέγω ὑμῖν, ἐὰν [n] ἔχητε [n] πίστιν ὡς [o] κόκκον [o] σινάπεως,
ἐρεῖτε τῷ ὄρει τούτῳ [p] Μετάβα [q] ἔνθεν [r] ἐκεῖ, καὶ [s] μεταβή-
σεται. καὶ οὐδὲν [t] ἀδυνατήσει ὑμῖν. [21 τοῦτο δὲ τὸ
[u] γένος οὐκ [v] ἐκπορεύεται εἰ μὴ [w] ἐν προσευχῇ καὶ [x] νηστείᾳ.]
I_d δε... 22 [y] Ἀναστρεφομένων δὲ αὐτῶν ἐν τῇ Γαλιλαίᾳ εἶπεν
αὐτοῖς ὁ Ἰησοῦς [z] Μέλλει ὁ υἱὸς τοῦ ἀνθρώπου [a] παρα-

b here only. Wisd. xviii. 19.
c ‖ L. Phil. ii. 15. Deut. xxxii. 5.
d = ‖. Rev. xxi. 8 al. Isa. xvii. 10.
e as above (c). Luke xxiii. 2. Acts xiii. 8, 10. xx. 3 only. Exod. v. 4.
f ‖ Mk. (bis) L. John x. 24. Rev. vi. 10 only. Ps. xciii. 3.
g ‖. 2 Cor. xi. 1, &c. Eph. iv. 2. Isa. xlvi. 4. Gen. xlv. 1.
h ch. xvi. 22 al. fr. Gen. xxxvii. 10.
i (‖ Mk.) Mark vii. 29, 30. Luke viii. 33, &c.
k ch. xiv. 13 reff.
l ch. vii. 22 al.
m here only †. (-στος, ch. vi. 30.) ἀπιστ., ch. xiii. 58. Mark xvi. 14. Rom. iv. 20 al.
n ch. xxi. 21. Mark iv. 40. Acts xiv. 9. 1 Cor. xiii. 2.
o ch. xiii. 31 reff.
p act., ch. viii. 34. John v. 24. xiii. 1. 1 John iii. 14 †. Wisd. vii. 27 al.
q Luke xvi. 26 only.
r = ch. ii. 22 al. Gen. xix. 20, 22 al.
s fut., here only.
t Luke i. 37 only. Gen. xviii. 14. Job xlii. 2.
u ch. xiii. 47 reff.
v = Acts xix. 12 only.
w = Luke xxi. 34. Acts xiii. 39 al.
x Luke ii. 37 reff.
y 2 Cor. i. 12. Eph. ii. 3. 1 Tim. iii. 11. 1 Pet. i. 17. 2 Pet. ii. 18. Josh. v. 5. Ezek. xix. 6. συστρ., Acts xxviii. 3.
z ver. 12. ch. xvi. 37.
a = ch. x. 17, &c. xx. 18, 19 al. fr. Ezek. xxiii. 28.

* ἔχει (*perhaps substitution of more usual expression, or perhaps emendation, κακ. πασχ. appearing pleonastic*) BL Z(appy) ℵ sah $Orig_1$ [Chr-2-mss]: πασχει CD rel vulg lat-*a c* &c. (*torquetur* lat-*b*.) for (2nd) πολλακις, ενιοτε D 1 lat-*a b c*(*aliquando*) arm $Orig_2$(ὅτι δὲ καὶ εἰς τὸ πῦρ σπανιώτερον) Aug: *sæpius* D-lat(1st *aliquotiens*).

16. ηδυνασθησαν B: ηδυναντο Z: txt CDℵ rel. θεραπευσαι bef αυτον D latt (not *e* ff_1).

17. for αποκρ. δε, ο δε αποκρ. (omg ο ιησ.) ℵ[1]: τοτε αποκρ. Zℵ[3a] ev-y_1 forj copt æth: *et respondens* lat-*a*: *respondens*(alone) am lat-*b* $ff_{1.2}$ g_1 *l* Syr syr-cu sah. aft ειπεν ins αυτοις ℵ. for απιστος, πονηρα Z ev-y_1. διεστρεμμενη Z. rec εσομαι bef μεθ' υμων, with L rel latt syrr æth [Chr] Hil: txt BCDZℵ 1. 33 lat-ff_1 Orig.

18. om ο παις ℵ.

20. rec aft ο δε ins ιησους, with C rel vulg lat-*b c e f* syrr: om BDℵ 33 am(with forj tol) lat-*a* $ff_{1.2}$ $g_{1.2}$ *n* syr-cu coptt æth arm. rec (for λεγει) ειπεν, with C rel vulg lat-*a f* g_3 arm: txt BDℵ 1. 13. 33. 124 am(with forj fuld) lat-*b c e* $ff_{1.2}$ g_1 *n*.
*rec ἀπιστίαν (*see reff*), with CD rel latt syrr arm-ms Chr: ολιγοπιστιαν Bℵ 1. 33 syr-cu coptt æth arm Orig Chr-γ_{expr} Hil. aft υμιν ins οτι C ev-27 coptt Orig. κοκκος D[1](txt D[2]): κοκο L. rec μεταβηθι εντευθεν (*see John* vii. 3), with C rel Eus; μεταβηθι ενθεν D $Orig_1$: txt Bℵ 1 $Orig_2$.

21. om ver Bℵ[1] 33 lat-*e* ff_1 syr-cu syr-jer copt-mss sah: ins CD ℵ[3b](but εκβαλλεται) rel latt syrr copt-ed æth-pl arm Orig Chr Thl Euthym Hil Ambr Aug Juv.

22. συστρεφομενων (*perhaps to prevent the word being understood of* return into *Gal: see below*) Bℵ 1, *conversantibus* vulg lat-*a b f* ff_2 $g_{1.2}$ D-lat Hil.—αυτων δε αναστρ. D-gr.

puting (Mark). **15.**] He was an *only* son, Luke ix. 38. The dæmon had deprived him of speech, Mark ix. 17. **17.**] Bengel remarks, "severo elencho discipuli accensentur turbæ." Compare the διὰ τὴν **ὀλιγοπιστίαν** ὑμῶν, ver. 20, which however does not make this so certain, linked as it is to ὦ γενεὰ **ἄπιστος**, as in the rec. text: see digest. **μεθ' ὑμῶν** = πρὸς ὑμᾶς Luke. **19.**] It was *in the house*, Mark ix. 28.

22, 23.] Our Lord's second an-

δίδοσθαι εἰς χεῖρας ἀνθρώπων, 23 καὶ ἀποκτενοῦσιν αὐτόν, BCDEF
καὶ τῇ τρίτῃ ἡμέρᾳ [b] ἐγερθήσεται. καὶ [c] ἐλυπήθησαν GHI$_d$K LMSUV
[d] σφόδρα. ΧΓΔΠℵ 1. 33
24 Ἐλθόντων δὲ αὐτῶν εἰς Καφαρναοὺμ προσῆλθον οἱ
τὰ [e] δίδραχμα [f] λαμβάνοντες τῷ Πέτρῳ καὶ εἶπαν Ὁ
[g] διδάσκαλος ὑμῶν οὐ [h] τελεῖ τὰ [e] δίδραχμα; 25 λέγει
Ναί. καὶ ἐλθόντα εἰς τὴν οἰκίαν [i] προέφθασεν αὐτὸν
ὁ Ἰησοῦς λέγων Τί σοὶ δοκεῖ, Σίμων; [j] οἱ βασιλεῖς τῆς
[j] γῆς [k] ἀπὸ τίνων [fk] λαμβάνουσιν [l] τέλη ἢ [m] κῆνσον; ἀπὸ
τῶν [n] υἱῶν αὐτῶν, ἢ ἀπὸ τῶν [o] ἀλλοτρίων; 26 λέγει αὐτῷ

b = ch. xxvi. 32. xxvii. 52 al. 4 Kings iv. 31.
c ch. xiv. 9. xviii. 31. xix. 22. 2 Cor. ii. 2, &c. vi. 10 al. Neh. v. 6.
d ver. 6.
e here (bis) only. Gen. xxiii. 15, 16 al. fr. for Heb. שֶׁקֶל.
f = ch. xxi. 34. Heb. vii. 8, 9. Exod. xxx. 16.
g ch. ix. 11. xii. 38 al. fr.† 2 Macc. i. 10 only.
h = Rom. xiii. 6 (ch. x. 23 al.) only ‡.
i here only. 1 Kings xx. 25. Ps. xvi. 13.
j Acts iv. 26, from Ps. ii. 2. Rev. vi. 15 al.
k 1 John ii. 27. iii. 22. 3 John 7 only. 4 Kings v. 20 Ed-vat. (παρά, AB.)
l = Rom. xiii. 7 (ch. x. 22 al. fr.) only. Num. xxxi. 28, &c. 1 Macc. x. 31.
m ch. xxii. 17 ∥ Mk., 19 only †. = φόρος, Luke xx. 22.
n see ch. viii. 12. xiii. 38.
o = John x. 5. Heb. xi. 34. Ps. xlviii. 10.

23. αποκτεινουσιν D-gr. for τη τριτη [τρι B[1], τη added by B[3], appy, Tischdf] ημερα, μετα τρεις ημερας D copt; *post tertiam diem* lat-*a b c n*, *post triduum* lat-*e*. for εγερθησεται, αναστησεται (*from* ∥ *Mark*) B 13. 124. 209 Scr's f Orig$_1$ Chr.
24. for ελθ. δε, και ελθ. D latt(not *f*) Syr syr-cu. τα διδραγματα (1st) D (*didragma* am(with forj fuld gat) lat-*ff*$_2$). και ειπαν bef τω πετρω D syr-jer. (ειπαν, so BDℵ[3a].) om 2nd τα Dℵ[1](ins ℵ[3a]).
25. rec (for ελθοντα) οτε εισηλθεν (*explanatory corrn*), with I$_d$ rel vulg lat-*c e f ff*$_1$ *g*$_{1.2}$ syrr coptt arm; οτε ηλθον C ev-27; οτε εισηλθον U 241-2-6[1]-7-51 syr-cu: ελθοντων αυτων 33: εισελθοντι D lat-*b*: εισελθοντων 13. 124. 346: εισελθοντα ℵ[1·3b](?): txt B ℵ[3a](?) 1 æth. τινος B (sah?) æth arm [Cyr-p(txt$_2$, Tischdf)].
26. for λεγει αυτω, ειποντος δε (*emendn of style—see below*) B 1 coptt æth-rom arm Orig Chr: ο δε εφη ℵ: txt D rel syrr syr-cu (æth-pl?), and (but see below) CL. (I$_d$ def.) rec aft αυτω ins ο πετρος, with C rel lat-*f* syr; πετρος H; σιμων Syr syr-cu:

NOUNCEMENT OF HIS DEATH AND RESURRECTION. Mark ix. 30—32. Luke ix. 43—45. This followed immediately after the miracle (Mark ix. 30);—our Lord went privately through Galilee; **ἐδίδασκεν γὰρ κ.τ.λ.**:—the imparting of this knowledge more accurately to His disciples, which He had begun to do in the last chapter, was the reason for His privacy. For more particulars, see Luke, ver. 45: Mark, ver. 32.

24—27.] DEMAND OF THE SACRED TRIBUTE, AND OUR LORD'S REPLY. *Peculiar to Matthew.* The narrative connects well with the whole chapter, the aim of the events narrated in which is, to set forth Jesus as the undoubted *Son* of God. **24. οἱ τὰ δίδρ. λαμβ.**] This **tribute**, hardly properly so called, was a sum paid annually by the Jews of twenty years old and upwards, *towards the temple* in Jerusalem. Exod. xxx. 13: 2 Kings xii. 4: 2 Chron. xxiv. 6, 9. The LXX reckon according to the Alexandrian *double drachma*, and have therefore, as in the first of the above places, ἥμισυ τοῦ διδράχμου: but Josephus and Philo reckon as here, and Aquila, Exod. xxxviii. 26, and an anonymous interpreter (see Hexapla), and apparently Jerome, Gen. xxiv. 22, translate בֶּקַע by δίδραχμ. Josephus (B. J. vii. 6. 6) says of Vespasian, φόρον δὲ τοῖς ὅπου δήποτ' οὖσιν Ἰουδαίοις ἐπέβαλε, δύο δραχμὰς ἕκαστον κελεύσας ἀνὰ πᾶν ἔτος εἰς τὸ καπετώλιον φέρειν, ὥσπερ πρότερον εἰς τὸν ἐν Ἱεροσολύμοις νεὼν συνετέλουν. See, for more particulars, Winer, RWB., art. *Sekel*.

It does not quite appear whether this payment was *compulsory* or not; the question here asked would look as if it were *voluntary*, and therefore *by some declined*.

Many Commentators both ancient and modern, and among them no less names than Clement Alex., Origen, Jerome, and Augustine, have entirely missed the meaning of this miracle, by interpreting the payment as a *civil* one, which it certainly was not. **οἱ τ. δ. λαμβ.** are not the *publicans*, but **they who received** *the* **didrachma**, i. e. one for each person. Peter answered in the affirmative, probably because he had known it paid before.

25, 26.] The whole force of this argument depends on the fact of the payment being a *divine* one. It rests on this: 'if the *sons* are *free*, then on *Me*, being the *Son of God*, has this tax no claim.' **κῆνσος**, money taken according to the

...αρα C. Z αρα... BDEFG HI_dKL MSUVX ZΓΔΠא 1. 33

Ἀπὸ τῶν [o] ἀλλοτρίων. ἔφη αὐτῷ ὁ Ἰησοῦς [p] Ἄρα [p] γε
[q] ἐλεύθεροί εἰσιν οἱ υἱοί. 27 ἵνα δὲ μὴ [r] σκανδαλίσωμεν
αὐτούς, πορευθεὶς εἰς θάλασσαν [s] βάλε [st] ἄγκιστρον, καὶ
τὸν [u] ἀναβάντα πρῶτον ἰχθὺν ἆρον· καὶ ἀνοίξας τὸ
στόμα αὐτοῦ εὑρήσεις [v] στατῆρα· ἐκεῖνον [w] λαβὼν δὸς
αὐτοῖς [x] ἀντὶ ἐμοῦ καὶ σοῦ. XVIII. 1 Ἐν ἐκείνῃ τῇ
ὥρᾳ προσῆλθον οἱ μαθηταὶ τῷ Ἰησοῦ λέγοντες Τίς ἄρα
[y] μείζων ἐστὶν ἐν τῇ βασιλείᾳ τῶν οὐρανῶν; 2 καὶ [z] προσκαλεσάμενος παιδίον ἔστησεν αὐτὸ [a] ἐν μέσῳ αὐτῶν

p ch. vii. 20 reff.
q = 1 Cor. vii. 39. ix. 1, 19. Rom. vii. 3. 1 Kings xvii. 25 A (B def.). 1 Macc. xv. 7.
r ch. xv. 12 reff.
s Isa. xix. 8.
t here only. 4 Kings xix. 28.
u = here only. Καρκῖνος ἀπὸ τ. θαλάσσης ἀναβάς, Æsop. Fab. 95.
v here only †. Exod. xxxviii. 24 Aq.
w ch. xiii. 31, 33 reff.
x = ch. v. 38, Gen. xxviii. 1. but ? rather ch. xx. 28.
y ch. xiii. 32 al.
z ch. x. 1 al.
a ch. x. 16. ver. 20 al. Ezek. xliii. 7.

om BDא 1 latt syr-jer coptt æth arm Cyr. (I_d def.) ins ειποντος δε αυτου απο των αλλοτριων bef εφη C 73[2] æth-rom(not pl): so but omg αυτου Lא.

27. σκανδαλιζωμεν LZא. rec ins την bef θαλασσαν (*art supplied, but not necessary aft a prepn: cf Middleton* vi. 1), with DEFGHSX [Chr]: om BI_dZא rel Did. αναβαινοντα E^2FGI_dSX Z(appy) ΓΔ Cyr_1: txt BDא rel Orig Chr [Bas Cyr-p]. aft ευρησεις ins εκει D lat-*a b o* g_1.

CHAP. XVIII. 1. aft εκεινη ins δε BM copt sah-ms. for ωρα, ημερα 1. 33 lat-*a b c* &c(not *f*) syr-cu arm Orig(κατὰ μέν τινα τῶν ἀντιγράφων ἐν ἐκ. τ. ὥρᾳ . . ., κατὰ δὲ ἄλλα, ἐν ἐκ. τ. ἡμέρᾳ,—and he leaves it undecided: Com in Matt tom xiii. 14, vol iii. p 588) Hil. μειζω D^1(txt D^2).

2. rec aft προσκαλεσαμενος ins ο ιησους, with DI_d rel vulg lat-*e f* g_1 syrr syr-cu sah arm Orig: pref, lat-*a b c* g_2: om $BFLV^1$א 1 copt æth Chr. (Z 33 def.) aft παιδιον ins ἐν D [lat-*e*] syr-cu.

reckoning of the census,—*a capitation tax:* a Latin word. **ἀλλοτρίων,** all who are not their children; those out of their family. **27.**] In this, which has been pronounced (even by Olshausen) the most difficult miracle in the Gospels, the deeper student of our Lord's life and actions will find no difficulty. Our Lord's words amount to this:—"that, notwithstanding this immunity, *we* (graciously including the Apostle in the earthly payment, and omitting the distinction between them, which was not now to be told to any), that we may not offend them, will pay what is required—and shall find it furnished by God's special providence for us." In the foreknowledge and power which this miracle implies, the Lord recalls Peter to that *great confession* (ch. xvi. 16), which his hasty answer to the collectors shews him to have again in part forgotten. Of course the miracle is to be understood in its literal historic sense. The *natural* interpretation (of Paulus and Storr), that the fish was to be sold for the money (and a wonderful price it would be for a fish caught with a hook), is refuted by the terms of the narrative,—and the *mythical* one, besides the utter inapplicability of all mythical interpretation to any part of the evangelic history,—by the absence of all possible occasion, and all possible significancy, of such a myth. The stater = *four drachmæ,*—the exact payment required. **ἀντί,** because the payment was a *redemption* paid for the *person,* Exod. xxx. 12—to this also refers the ἐλεύθεροι above. **ἐμοῦ κ. σοῦ**—not ἡμῶν,—as in John xx. 17:—because the footing on which it was given was *different.*

CHAP. XVIII. 1—35.] DISCOURSE RESPECTING THE GREATEST IN THE KINGDOM OF HEAVEN. Mark ix. 33—50. Luke ix. 46—50. **1.**] In Mark we learn that this discourse arose out of a dispute among the disciples *who should be the greatest.* It took place soon after the last incident. Peter had returned from his fishing: see ver. 21. The dispute had taken place before, on the way to Capernaum. It had probably been caused by the mention of the Kingdom of God as at hand in ch. xvi. 19, 28, and the preference given by the Lord to the Three. In Mark it is our Lord who *asks them what they were disputing about,* and they are silent. **ἄρα** need not necessarily refer to the incident last related. As De Wette remarks, it may equally well be understood as indicating the presence in the mind of the querist of something that had passed in the preceding dispute.

3 καὶ εἶπεν Ἀμὴν λέγω ὑμῖν, ἐὰν μὴ [b] στραφῆτε καὶ
γένησθε ὡς τὰ παιδία, οὐ μὴ εἰσέλθητε εἰς τὴν βασιλείαν
τῶν οὐρανῶν. 4 ὅστις οὖν [c] ταπεινώσει ἑαυτὸν ὡς τὸ
παιδίον τοῦτο, οὗτός ἐστιν ὁ [y] μείζων ἐν τῇ βασιλείᾳ τῶν
οὐρανῶν. 5 καὶ ὃς ἐὰν δέξηται ἓν παιδίον [d] τοιοῦτον
[ef] ἐπὶ τῷ [f] ὀνόματί μου, ἐμὲ δέχεται· 6 ὃς δ' ἂν [g] σκανδαλίσῃ ἕνα τῶν [h] μικρῶν τούτων τῶν [i] πιστευόντων εἰς ἐμέ,
[j] συμφέρει αὐτῷ [k] ἵνα [l] κρεμασθῇ [m] μύλος [n] ὀνικὸς εἰς τὸν
τράχηλον αὐτοῦ, καὶ [o] καταποντισθῇ ἐν τῷ [pq] πελάγει

...ου μη Id. BDEFG HKLMS UVXZΓ ΔΠℵ 1. 33

b John xii. 40. Acts vii. 39. 1 Kings x. 6.
c ch. xxiii. 12. Luke xiv. 11. xviii. 14. James iv. 10 al. Prov. xiii. 7.
d constr., see John vi. 9 reff.
e = ch. xix. 9.
f ch. xxiv. 5 reff. Deut. xxviii. 5.
g ch. v. 29, 30. xiii. 21. xvii. 27 al. fr.+ Sir. ix. 5 al.
h ch. x. 42. vv. 10, 14. Acts viii. 10 al. Zech. xiii. 7.
i w. εἰς, John ii. 12 reff.
j ch. v. 29, 30 reff.
k ch. x. 25. 1 Cor. iv. 3.
l w. εἰς, here only. ch. xxii. 40. Luke xxiii. 39. Acts v. 30. x. 39. xxviii. 4. Gal. iii. 13 (from Deut. xxi. 23) only. 1 Macc. i. 61.
m ‖ Mk. ch. xxiv. 41. (Luke xvii. 2 v. r.) Rev. xviii. (21 v. r.) 22 only. 2 Kings xi. 21.
n ‖ Mk. (L. v. r.) only +.
o ch. xiv. 30 only. Ps. lxviii. 15.
p Acts xxvii. 5 only +. 2 Macc. v. 21 only.
q here only +.

4. rec ταπεινωσῃ, with (Scr's p w, e sil) vulg lat-*a* *b* D-lat Clem: txt BDZℵ rel Scr's mss $Orig_1$ [Bas]. (33 def.) αυτον LΓΔ.

5. for εαν, αν DLZ $Orig_1$: txt Bℵ rel $Orig_2$ [Chr].—om latt Lucif: εαν μη Δ. rec παιδιον τοιουτον bef ἕν, with E rel: παιδ. ἕν τοι. Gℵ syr arm: om ἕν SXΔ lat-*e* Syr coptt Chr: txt BDLZ 1 latt [æth] $Orig_3$ Lucif.—τοιουτο B(Mai [and Tischdf]) KLMVZΓΔΠℵ 1 Orig [Chr_1-ms].

6. for μ. ονικος, μυλος (. .)υλικος (*see Luke* xvii. 2) Z: λιθος μυλικος L ev-y_2. rec επι (*more usual than* εις), with DU: περι (*from* ‖ *Mark and Luke* xvii. 2) BLZℵ 28. 157 Scr's p evv-y-tisch[1] $Orig_1$ Bas [Cyr_2] Bas-sel: txt G rel 1. 13. 22. 124-31. 209 Scr's mss(18 in number) latt(*in collo*) copt arm $Orig_1$ Chr.

2.] From Mark ix. 36 it appears that our Lord first placed the child in the midst, and then took it in His arms: possibly drawing a lesson for His disciples from its ready submission and trustfulness.

3.] **στραφῆτε** = *μετανοῆτε*: it also conveys the idea of *turning back* from the course previously begun, viz. that of ambitious rivalry. Without this they should not only not be pre-eminent in, but not even admitted into, the Christian state—the Kingdom of Heaven. **4.**] Not *ὡς τὸ παιδ. τ. ταπεινοῖ ἑαυτό*: 'iste parvulus non se *humilitat*, sed *humilis est*.' Valla (in Meyer). 'Quales pueri natura sunt, ab ambitu scilicet alieni, tales nos esse jubemur *τῇ προαιρέσει*.' Grotius.

5.] Having shewn the child as the pattern of humility, the Lord proceeds to shew the honour in which children are held in His heavenly kingdom; and not only actual, but *spiritual* children—for both are understood in the expression *ἓν παιδίον τοιοῦτον*. The **receiving in My name** is the serving (*ἔσται πάντων διάκονος* Mark ix. 35) with Christian love, and as belonging to Christ (see also ch. xxv. 40).

6.] Here St. Mark and St. Luke insert the saying of John respecting one casting out dæmons in Jesus' name, who followed not with the Apostles: which it appears gave rise to the remark in this verse. St. Luke however goes on no further with the discourse: St. Mark inserts also our ch. x. 42. The verbs **κρεμασθῇ, καταποντισθῇ**, may perhaps be understood in their strict tenses: it is better for him that a millstone *should have been* hanged, &c., and he drowned . . . . *before the day when he gives this offence*. But this is somewhat doubtful. The aorists more probably, as so often, denote an act complete in itself and accomplished at once: without any strict temporal reference. The punishment here mentioned, *drowning*, may have been practised in the sea of Galilee ('secundum ritum provinciæ ejus loquitur, quo majorum criminum ista apud veteres Judæos pœna fuerit, ut in profundum ligato saxo demergerentur.' Jerome in loc.). De Wette however denies this, saying that it was not a Jewish punishment; but it certainly was a Roman, for Suetonius mentions it as practised by Augustus on the rapacious attendants of Caius Cæsar (Aug. ch. lxvii.):—and a Macedonian (Diod. Sic. xvi. 35, *ὁ δὲ Φίλιππος τὸν μὲν Ὀνόμαρχον ἐκρέμασε, τοὺς δ' ἄλλους ὡς ἱεροσύλους* **κατεπόντισε**). Compare also Livy i. 51, where Turnus Herdonius ("novo genere leti," it is true) "dejectus ad caput aquæ Ferentinæ, crate superne injecta, saxisque congestis, mergitur." **ὀνικός**, as belonging to a mill turned by an ass, and therefore larger than the stones of a handmill. In the Digests, the '*mola jumentaria*' is distinguished from the

..θαλασ-σης Z.

τῆς [q] θαλάσσης. 7 [r] οὐαὶ τῷ κόσμῳ [s] ἀπὸ τῶν [t] σκαν-
δάλων· ἀνάγκη γὰρ ἐλθεῖν τὰ [t] σκάνδαλα, πλὴν οὐαὶ τῷ
ἀνθρώπῳ ἐκείνῳ δι' οὗ τὸ [t] σκάνδαλον ἔρχεται. 8 [u] εἰ
δὲ ἡ χείρ σου ἢ ὁ πούς σου [u] σκανδαλίζει σε, [u] ἔκκοψον
αὐτὸν καὶ βάλε ἀπὸ σοῦ· [v] καλόν σοι ἐστὶν εἰςελθεῖν εἰς
τὴν ζωὴν χωλὸν ἢ [w] κυλλόν, [x] ἢ δύο χεῖρας ἢ δύο πόδας
ἔχοντα βληθῆναι εἰς τὸ [y] πῦρ τὸ [y] αἰώνιον. 9 καὶ εἰ ὁ
ὀφθαλμός σου [u] σκανδαλίζει σε, [u] ἔξελε αὐτὸν καὶ βάλε
ἀπὸ σοῦ· [v] καλόν σοι ἐστὶν [z] μονόφθαλμον εἰς τὴν
ζωὴν εἰςελθεῖν [x] ἢ δύο ὀφθαλμοὺς ἔχοντα βληθῆναι εἰς
τὴν [u] γέενναν τοῦ πυρός. 10 ὁρᾶτε μὴ [a] καταφρονήσητε
ἑνὸς τῶν [b] μικρῶν τούτων· λέγω γὰρ ὑμῖν ὅτι οἱ

r ch. xi. 21 al. fr. Hos. ix. 12 al.
s = ch. xiii. 44 al. aft. οὐαί, here only.
t ch. xiii. 41 reff.
u see ch. v. 29, &c. reff.
v ch. xvii. 4 reff.
w ‖ Mk. ch. xv. 30, 31 only †.
x constr., ‖ Mk. (3ce). Luke xv. 7. xvii. 2. 1 Cor. xiv. 19. Gen. xxxviii. 26. Ps. cxvii. 8. Jon. iv. 3.
y ch. xxv. 41. Jude 7 only.
z ‖ Mk. only.
a ch. vi. 24. Luke xvi. 13. Rom. ii. 4 al. Prov. xiii. 13.
b ver. 6 reff.

7. rec ins εστιν bef ελθειν, with Dℵ rel latt syr-cu syr $Orig_2$ [Chr] Hil Lucif: om BL 1. 33 Syr sah æth Chr-2 [Cyr_1 Damasc-ms]. aft πλην ins δε D[1]. om εκεινω DFLℵ 1 am(with forj) lat-g_1 syrr syr-cu copt: ins B(Mai, expr [and Tischdf]) rel latt sah æth arm Dial [Bas] Hil Lucif.

8. for εκκοψον, εξελε ℵ[1](txt ℵ[3a]). rec αυτα, with X rel syr copt: txt BDLℵ 1 latt Syr syr-cu sah æth arm Hil Lucif. κυλλον η χωλον (*transposition to suit* χειρ *and* πους) Bℵ 157 Scr's f latt. transp χειρας and ποδας D lat-*a b c* Chr-L(-H-K-2).

9. for και ει, το αυτο ει και D. σκανδαλει (sic) B. om του πυρος D.

10. τουτων bef των μικρων DL vulg lat-*a b* ff_1 *m* Syr syr-cu (sah ?) $Orig_2$ Lucif:

'*mola manuaria;*' and in Cato, de re rustica, c. 10, we have 'molas asinarias duas, trusatiles unas.' **πελάγει**, i. e. the deep part, in the open sea. **7.**] See 1 Cor. xi. 19. Stier suggests that Judas, who took offence at the anointing in Bethany, may have been on other occasions the man by whom the offence came, and so this may have been said with special reference to him. Still its *general* import is undeniable and plain. See also Acts ii. 23. **8.**] The connexion is—'*Wilt thou avoid being the man on whom this woe is pronounced?—then cut off all occasion of offence in thyself first.*' The cautions following are used in a wider sense than in ch. v. 29, 30. In Mark, the '*foot*' is expanded into a separate iteration of the command. **καλὸν . . , ἤ . . .**, a mixture of the two constructions, καλὸν . . . . καὶ μὴ . . . , and κάλλιον . . . ἢ . . . See reff. **τὸ πῦρ τὸ αἰώνιον**, which here first occurs, is more fully in Mark τὸ πῦρ τὸ ἄσβεστον, ὅπου ὁ σκώληξ αὐτῶν οὐ τελευτᾷ καὶ τὸ πῦρ οὐ σβέννυται.

9.] **μονόφθαλμος**, in classical Greek, is '*born blind of one eye;*' here it is used for ἑτερόφθαλμος. See Herod. iii. 116.

10.] Hitherto our text has been parallel with that of Mark ix.; from this, Matthew stands alone. The warning against contempt of these little ones must not be taken as only implying 'maxima debetur puero reverentia' (Juv. xiv. 47), nor indeed as relating exclusively, or even principally, to children. We must remember with what the discourse began—a contention who should be greatest among them: and the **μικροί** are those who are the furthest from these 'greatest,' the humble and new-born babes of the spiritual kingdom. And **καταφρονήσητε** must be understood of that kind of contempt which ambition for superiority would induce for those who are by weakness or humility incapacitated for such a strife. There is no doubt that *children are included* in the word **μικροί**, as they are always classed with the humble and simple-minded, and their character held up for our imitation. The *little children* in the outward status of the Church are in fact the only disciples who are sure to be that in reality, which their Baptism has put upon them, and so exactly answer to the wider meaning here conveyed by the term: and those who would in after-life enter into the kingdom must turn back, and become as these little children—as they were when they had just received the new life in Baptism. The whole discourse is in deep and constant reference to the *covenant with infants*, which was to be made and ratified by an ordinance, in the Kingdom of Heaven, just as then.

On the reason assigned in the latter part

c = Acts xii. 15. Rev. i. 20, &c.
d Mark v. 5. Luke xxiv. 53. Acts ii. 25, from Ps. xv. 8 al.
e here only. see Acts xx. 25, 38. 1 Thess. iii. 10. 4 Kings xxv. 19. Jer. lii. 25.

[c] ἄγγελοι αὐτῶν ἐν τῷ οὐρανῷ [d] διὰ παντὸς [e] βλέπουσιν
τὸ [e] πρόσωπον τοῦ πατρός μου τοῦ ἐν οὐρανοῖς. [11 ἦλθεν γὰρ ὁ υἱὸς τοῦ ἀνθρώπου σῶσαι τὸ [f] ἀπολωλός.]
12 τί ὑμῖν δοκεῖ; ἐὰν [g] γένηταί τινι ἀνθρώπῳ ἑκατὸν πρόβατα, καὶ [h] πλανηθῇ ἓν ἐξ αὐτῶν, οὐχὶ [i] ἀφεὶς τὰ ἐννενηκονταεννέα [j] ἐπὶ τὰ ὄρη πορευθεὶς ζητεῖ τὸ [h] πλανώμενον;

I_d σωσαι ... BDEFG HI$_d$KL MSUVX ΓΔΠℵ 1. 33

f = ch. x. 6. xv. 24 al. Ps. cxviii. 176. Isa. xiii. 14. liii. 6. g Rom. vii. 3, 4. Lev. xxii. 12. Jer. iii. 1. Hos. iii. 3. h = Heb. v. 2. 1 Pet. ii. 25. i = ch. iv. 11, 20, 22. John x. 12 al. j ch. xiii. 2. xxiv. 2. xxvii. 45.

add *των πιστευοντων εις εμε* D lat-*b c ff*$_{1.2}$ *g*$_{1.2}$ syr-cu sah Hil. rec (for *εν τω ουρανω*) *εν ουρανοις* (*to conform to following*), with Dℵ rel latt syrr syr-cu copt æth arm Lucif; *εν τοις ουρανοις* H : txt B : *εν ουρανω* 33.—om altogether (*as superfluous, εν ουρ. occurring again below: but it is here solemn and characteristic, and could by no possibility have been interpolated*) 1. 13. 245 lat-*e ff* Syr-ed sah Clem$_2$ Orig$_4$ Bas Chr Thdrt Hil. (Γ is cited by Tischdf, ed 8, both for rec and for the omn.) ins *τοις* bef *ουρανοις* DV 33 Orig Eus.

11. om ver BL[1]ℵ 1[1]. 33 lat-*e ff*$_1$ syr-jer coptt æth-ms-iii Orig Eus-Canon [Hil] Jer Juv: ins DI$_d$ rel latt syrr syr-cu copt-ms æth arm Chr.—aft *ανθρ.* ins *ζητησαι και* G lat-*c* æth syr; *ζητησε σωσε* L[2]. (*That this verse has not been inserted from Luke* xix. 10 *appears*, 1*st, from the absence of any sufficient reason for insn;* 2*ndly, from the nearly unanimous omn of Luke's ζητησαι και wh wd have exactly suited the ζητει of ver* 12.)

12. aft *τι* ins *δε* D [Scr's q] lat-*a* syr-cu copt. for *αφεις*, *αφησει* BL 1 am lat-*a b c* &c æth arm: *αφιησιν* D vulg-ed lat-*ff*$_1$ coptt (*probably emendns of style to avoid the two participles*): txt I$_d$ℵ rel syrr syr-cu. aft *εννενηκον.* ins *προβατα* B 13 arm. om *επι τα ορη* ℵ[1](ins ℵ-corr[1]). ins *και* (*see above*) bef *πορευ.* BDL latt Syr syr-cu copt æth arm: om I$_d$ℵ rel syr sah. for *πορευθεις*, *πορευομενος* D.

of this verse (**λέγω γὰρ** *κ.τ.λ.*), there have been many opinions; some of which (e. g. that given by Webster and Wilkinson, '*ἄγγελοι*, their *spirits* after death:' a meaning which the word never bore,—see Suicer sub voce,—and one respecting which our Lord never could have spoken in the present tense, with *διὰ παντός*) have been broached merely to evade the plain sense of the words, which is—that *to individuals* (whether invariably, or under what circumstances of minor detail, we are not informed) *certain angels are allotted as their especial attendants and guardians.* We know elsewhere from the Scriptures, both of the Old and New Testament (Ps. xxxiv. 7; xci. 11: Heb. i. 14 al.), that the angels do *minister about the children of God:* and what should forbid that in this service, *a prescribed order* and *appointed duty* should regulate their ministrations? Nay, is it not analogically certain that such would be the case? But this saying of our Lord assures us that such *is* the case, and that those angels whose honour is high before God are entrusted with the charge of the humble and meek,—the children in age and the children in grace.

The phrase **λέγω γὰρ ὑμῖν**, or *λέγω ὑμῖν*, as in Luke xv. 7, 10, is an introduction to a revelation of some previously unknown fact in the spiritual world. Stier has some very beautiful remarks on the guardian angels, and on the present general neglect of the doctrine of angelic tutelage, which has been doubtless a reaction from the idolatrous angel-worship of the Church of Rome (see Acts xii. 15: Dan. xii. 1: in the former case we have an individual, in the latter a national, guardianship). **βλέπουσιν τὸ πρόσωπον** *κ.τ.λ.*, i. e. are in high honour before God; not perhaps *especially* so, but the meaning may be, 'for they have angelic guardians, who always,' &c. See Tobit xii. 15. [**11.** The angels are the servants and messengers of the Son of Man; and they therefore (*ἦλθ.* **γὰρ** *κ.τ.λ.*) are appointed to wait on these little ones whom He came to save: and who, in their utter helplessness, are especially examples of *τὸ ἀπολωλός*. 'Here,' remarks Stier (ii. 241), 'is Jacob's ladder planted before our eyes: beneath are the little ones;—then their angels;—then the Son of Man in heaven, in whom alone man is exalted above the angels, Who, as the Great Angel of the Covenant, cometh from the Presence and Bosom of the Father;—and above Him again (ver. 14) the Father Himself, and His good pleasure.'] **12, 13.**] See notes on Luke xv. 4—6, where the same parable is more expanded. Compare also Ezek. xxxiv. 6, 11, 12. **ἐπὶ τὰ ὄρη**

13 καὶ ἐὰν [k] γένηται εὑρεῖν αὐτό, ἀμὴν λέγω ὑμῖν ὅτι
[l] χαίρει ἐπ' αὐτῷ μᾶλλον ἢ ἐπὶ τοῖς ἐννενηκονταεννέα τοῖς
μὴ [g] πεπλανημένοις. 14 οὕτως οὐκ ἔστιν θέλημα [m] ἔμπροσθεν τοῦ πατρὸς ὑμῶν τοῦ ἐν οὐρανοῖς, ἵνα ἀπόληται
* εἷς τῶν [a] μικρῶν τούτων. 15 ἐὰν δὲ [n] ἁμαρτήσῃ [[n] εἰς σὲ]
69 σου καὶ... ὁ ἀδελφός σου, ὕπαγε [o] ἔλεγξον αὐτὸν [p] μεταξὺ σοῦ καὶ
αὐτοῦ μόνου· ἐάν σου ἀκούσῃ, [q] ἐκέρδησας τὸν ἀδελφόν
σου. 16 ἐὰν δὲ μὴ ἀκούσῃ, [r] παράλαβε μετὰ σοῦ ἔτι ἕνα
ἢ δύο, [s] ἵνα [t] ἐπὶ στόματος δύο μαρτύρων ἢ τριῶν [t] σταθῇ

k Acts xx. 16. Gal. vi. 14. Gen. xliv. 7, 17. 3 Kings xx. (xxi.) 3.
l w. ἐπί, Luke i. 14. Acts xv. 31. 1 Cor. xiii. 6 al. 4 Kings xx. 13.
m ch. xi. 26. Luke x. 21.
n = ver. 21. Luke xv. 18, 21. xvii. (3 v. r.) 4. 1 Cor. vi. 18. viii. 12. 1 Kings xxiv. 12. Xen. Hel. i. 7. 20.
o = Luke iii. 19. 1 Tim. v. 20. Gen. xxi. 25. Lev. xix. 17.
p ch. xxiii. 35. Acts xv. 9 al.† Wisd. iv. 10 al2.
q = 1 Cor. ix. 19. 1 Pet. iii. 1 †. Job xxii. 3 Symm.
r ch. xvii. 1 reff.
s Deut. xix. 15.
t Mark xiii. 9. Acts xxiv. 20. 2 Cor. xiii. 1, from l. c. A.

14. om εμπροσθεν ℵ syr-cu copt $Orig_1$. for υμων, μου (*to suit ver* 10, *and more usual*) $BFHI_d\Gamma$ 33 Syr-ms syr-txt coptt æth arm $Orig_3$: ημων (*also corrn from the unusual* υμων) D¹-gr harl¹ Chr-2-6-9-η-ρ-G : txt D²Lℵ rel latt Syr syr-mg syr-cu Chr(Fd) Aug. (B does not omit 2nd του, as Vercellone.) aft εν ins τοις D(E¹V¹, appy) 33 $Orig_2$. * ἕν (*perhaps gramml corrn*) BDLM²ℵ 33 harl¹ lat-*e*¹ : εἷς I_d rel latt $Orig_3$.

15. αμαρτη 33. 77 Orig Chr [Bas_4] Damasc : αμαρτησει (and ακουσει) L. (not B as Bartol.) om εις σε (*see note*) Bℵ 1. 22. 234¹ sah Orig [Bas_3 Cyr_1]. rec ins και bef ελεγξον, with I_d rel latt copt æth Hil Lucif : om BDℵ 1. 33 lat-$ff_{1.2}$ syrr syr-cu sah arm Orig Bas_1 Chr Cyr_1 Damasc Cypr Ambr. εκερδησες D.

16. aft μη ins σου (*from ver* 12) LΔ 33 latt(not forj) Syr syr-cu coptt æth [Bas_2 Cyr_1] $Orig\text{-}int_1$. for σου, σεαυτου ℵ[KLM] 1. 13. 33. 69. 77. 157. 346 Orig Bas Chr. ετι ενα η δυο bef μετα σου B lat-ff_1 copt. om μαρτυρων D 435 Aug_1 : ins bef δυο L : aft τριων ℵ 1 vulg lat-*e* ff_1 $g_{1.2}$ *h* Syr syr-cu coptt æth arm $Orig_3$ Tert Lucif. σταθησεται I_dMUΔ 33 lat-*e* ff_1 Orig.

belongs to ἀφείς, not to πορευθ. See var. read. The preposition of motion, ἐπί, gives the idea of the wandering and scattering of the flock over the mountains. If we join the words to πορευθείς, we give them an unmeaning emphasis, besides destroying the elegance of the sentence.

14.] This verse sets forth to us the *work of the Son as accomplishing the will of the Father*;—for it is unquestionably the Son who is the Good Shepherd, searching for the lost, ver. 11. For similar declarations see Ezek. xviii. 23; xxxiii. 11: 2 Pet. iii. 9. The inference from this verse is—'then whoever despises or scandalizes one of these little ones, acts in opposition to the will of your Father in Heaven.' Observe, when the dignity of the little ones was asserted, it was πατρός **μου**: now that a motive directly acting on the conscience of the Christian is urged, it is πατρὸς **ὑμῶν**.

15—20.] Of the method of proceeding with an offending brother: and of the power of the Christian assembly in such cases. **15.**] The connexion of this with the preceding is: Our Lord has been speaking of **σκάνδαλα**, which subject is the ground-tone of the whole discourse. One kind is, when *thou sinnest against another*, vv. 7—14. A second kind, when *thy brother sins against thee*. The remedy for the former must be, in each individual being cautious in his own person,—that of the latter, in the exercise of brotherly love, and if that fail, the authority of the congregation, vv. 15—17. Then follows an exposition of what that authority is, vv. 18—20.

On this verse see Levit. xix. 17, 18. This direction is only in case of *personal offence* against ourselves, and then the *injured person* is to *seek private explanation*, and that by *going to his injurer*, not waiting till *he* comes to apologize. The stop must be after μόνου, as ordinarily read, and not after αὐτοῦ, as proposed by Fritzsche and Olshausen, which construction would be contrary to the usage of the N. T. An attempt has apparently been made (see var. readd.) to render the passage applicable to *sin in general*, and so to give the Church power over sins upon earth. **ἐκέρδησας**, in the higher sense, reclaimed, gained for God, see reff.: and for thyself too: πρῶτον γὰρ ἐζημίου τοῦτον, διὰ τοῦ σκανδάλου ῥηγνύμενον ἀπὸ τῆς ἀδελφικῆς σου συν-

u Luke i. 37. ii. 15. Acts x. 37.
v = here (Mark v. 36) only. Esth. iii. 3, 8. iv. 14. Isa. lxv. 12 only.
w ch. xvii. 9.
x ch. xvi. 18 reff. 1 Macc. iii. 13.
y ch. v. 47. vi. 7. 3 John 7 only †. (-κῶς, Gal. ii. 14.)
z ch. v. 46 reff.
a ch. xvi. 19 reff.

πᾶν ᵘ ῥῆμα. 17 ἐὰν δὲ ᵛ παρακούσῃ αὐτῶν, ʷ εἰπὲ τῇ BDEFG
ˣ ἐκκλησίᾳ. ἐὰν δὲ καὶ τῆς ἐκκλησίας ᵛ παρακούσῃ, ἔστω HI_dKL MSUVX
σοὶ ὥσπερ ὁ ʸ ἐθνικὸς καὶ ὁ ᶻ τελώνης. 18 ἀμὴν λέγω ΓΔΠℵ 1. 33. 69
ὑμῖν, ὅσα ἂν ᵃ δήσητε ᵇ ἐπὶ τῆς γῆς ἔσται ᵃ δεδεμένα ᵇ ἐν
οὐρανῷ, καὶ ὅσα ἐὰν ᵃ λύσητε ᵇ ἐπὶ τῆς γῆς ἔσται ᵃ λελυ-
μένα ᵇ ἐν οὐρανῷ. 19 πάλιν ἀμὴν λέγω ὑμῖν ὅτι ἐὰν δύο
ᶜ συμφωνήσουσιν ἐξ ὑμῶν ἐπὶ τῆς γῆς περὶ ᵈ παντὸς πράγματος οὗ ἐὰν αἰτήσωνται, ᵉ γενήσεται αὐτοῖς ᶠ παρὰ τοῦ

b ch. vi. 10. xxviii. 18 al. c ch. xx. 2, 13. Luke v. 36. Acts v. 9. xv. 15 only. Gen. xiv. 3. 4 Kings xii. 8. Isa. vii. 2 only. (-νος, 1 Cor. vii. 5.) d = ch. xiii. 19 reff. e = ch. viii. 13 al. f ch. xxi. 42 ∥ Mk., from Ps. cxvii. 23. τὰ . . . . χωρία μοι ἔσεσθαι παρὰ σοῦ, Xen. Anab. vii. 2. 25.

17. ειπον Lℵ $Orig_1$. ins ως bef ο τελωνης D 301 lat-ff_1 syr syr-cu.

18. rec (for 1st αν) εαν, with I_dℵ rel $Orig_1$: txt BDKLΓΠ 69 [Bas_1]. om εσται δεδ. to της γης (*homœotel*) D^1. δεδεμενον $ℵ^1$(appy, but corrd eadem manu or by ℵ-$corr^1$). rec (twice) εν τω ουρ. (*insn of art as usual*), with X rel $Orig_1$: εν τοις ουρ. (twice) D(1st D^7) L 33 lat-*f* coptt : δεδ. εν τω ουρ. and λελ. εν τοις ουρ. M : δεδ. εν τοις ουρ. and λελ. εν ουρ. ℵ : txt B $Orig_1$. (I_d def.) for εαν, αν $D^7Lℵ^1$(txt $ℵ^{2\cdot3}$) Bas.

19. rec om αμην, with DLΓℵ 1 vulg lat-ff_2 *l* Syr copt arm Orig : for αμην, δε MΔ [æth Chr]: txt B I_d(appy) rel mm lat-*a b c f* $g_{1,2}$ *h n* syr-cu sah Bas. δυο bef εαν D-gr. rec συμφωνησωσιν, with B(sic, from inspection) rel $Orig_2$ [Bas_1 Chr]: txt $DEHI_dLV$Δℵ 33. rec om εξ, with I_d rel lat-*c* arm Orig : ins BDLℵ (69 vulg lat-*b c f* syrr syr-cu) æth $Orig_1$ Chr [Cypr].—rec υμων bef συμφ., with I_d rel Orig : txt BDLℵ. ins του bef πραγματος D^1. for εαν, αν D. αυτοις bef γενησεται ℵ.

ἀφείας. Euthym. **16. παρ. . ἔτι] Go again, and take . . .** The *first* attempt of brotherly love is to heal the wound, to remove the offence, *in secrecy*: to *cover* the sin: but if this cannot be done, the *next* step is, to take two or three, still, in case of an adjustment, *preventing publicity*; but in the other event, *providing sufficient legal witness*. See reff. and John viii. 17. **ῥῆμα**, not *thing*, but **word**, as always. Cf. St. Paul's apparent reference to these words of our Lord, 2 Cor. xiii. 1. **17. παρακούσῃ]** a stronger word than μὴ ἀκ., implying something of *obduracy*. **τῇ ἐκκλησίᾳ**, by what follows, certainly not 'the Jewish synagogue' (for how could vv. 18—20 be said in any sense *of it?*), but **the congregation** of Christians; i. e. in early times, such as in Acts iv. 32, the *one* congregation,—in after times, that congregation of which thou and he are members. That it cannot mean *the Church as represented by her rulers*, appears by vv. 19, 20,—where *any* collection of believers is gifted with the power of deciding in such cases. Nothing could be further from the spirit of our Lord's command than proceedings in what were oddly enough called 'ecclesiastical' courts. **ἔστω σοὶ κ.τ.λ.]** 'let him no longer be accounted as a brother, but as one of those without,' as the Jews accounted Gentiles and Publicans. Yet even then *not with hatred*, see 1 Cor. v. 11, and compare 2 Cor. ii. 6, 7, and 2 Thess. iii. 14, 15. The articles ὁ ἐθν., ὁ τελ., are *generic*; the expressions being the singulars of οἱ ἐθνικοί, οἱ τελῶναι. And thus the quality expressed by ἐθνικός and τελώνης, rather than the individual who may happen to bear these characters, is prominent in the sentence: the ἐθν. or the τελ., inasmuch and as far as he is ἐθν. or τελ. But this is not, as Words., the effect of the article only; the predicate ἐθνικός conveys plainly enough, that it is *as a heathen*, not as a man, that he is here introduced. **18.]** This verse reasserts in a wider and more general sense the grant made to Peter in ch. xvi. 19. It is here not only to him as the first stone, but to the whole building. See note there, and on John xx. 23, between which and our ch. xvi. 19 this is a middle point. **19. παντὸς πρ.]** '*every thing*:'—but the construction is an instance of attraction: πᾶν πρᾶγμα, the subject of the sentence, is thrown into government after the verb: the plain construction would be ὅτι πᾶν πρ., ἐὰν δύο ὑμ. συμφ. ἐπὶ τ. γ. περὶ αὐτοῦ, οὗ ἐὰν αἰτήσωνται, γενήσεται κ.τ.λ.: so that παντὸς πρ. amounts in English to **any thing**. This refers to that entire accordance of hearty faith, which could hardly have place except also in accordance with

...μου του I$_J$.

πατρός μου τοῦ ἐν οὐρανοῖς. 20 οὗ γάρ εἰσιν δύο ἢ τρεῖς
[g] συνηγμένοι [h] εἰς τὸ ἐμὸν ὄνομα, ἐκεῖ εἰμὶ ἐν [i] μέσῳ αὐτῶν.
21 Τότε προσελθὼν ὁ Πέτρος εἶπεν αὐτῷ Κύριε, [j] ποσάκις
[k] ἁμαρτήσει [k] εἰς ἐμὲ ὁ ἀδελφός μου καὶ ἀφήσω αὐτῷ; [l] ἕως
[m] ἑπτάκις; 22 λέγει αὐτῷ ὁ Ἰησοῦς Οὐ λέγω σοι [l] ἕως
[m] ἑπτάκις, ἀλλὰ [l] ἕως [n] ἑβδομηκοντάκις ἑπτά. 23 διὰ
τοῦτο [o] ὡμοιώθη ἡ βασιλεία τῶν οὐρανῶν [p] ἀνθρώπῳ
βασιλεῖ, ὃς ἠθέλησεν [q] συνᾶραι λόγον μετὰ τῶν δούλων
αὐτοῦ. 24 ἀρξαμένου δὲ αὐτοῦ [q] συναίρειν [r] προσήχθη
αὐτῷ εἷς [s] ὀφειλέτης μυρίων [t] ταλάντων. 25 μὴ [u] ἔχοντος

g ch. ii. 4. John xi. 52. Ps. ii. 2.
h ch. xxviii. 19 reff.
i ver. 2. Luke ii. 46. viii. 7.
j ch. xxiii. 37. Luke xiii. 34 only. 2 Chron. xviii. 15. Ps. lxxiv. 40. Sir. xx. 17 only.
k ver. 15.
l = Mark vi. 23 reff.
m Luke xvii. 4 (bis) only. Ps. cxviii. 164 al.
n here only. Gen. iv. 24 only.

o ch. xiii. 24, &c. p ch. xiii. 45, 52 reff. q ch xxv. 19 only‡. Exod. xxiii. 5 Ed-vat. (and Bl). (σ. λόγ. = συλλογίζεσθαι, Lev. xxv. 50.) r Luke ix. 41. Acts xvi. 20. xxvii. 27. 1 Pet. iii. 18 only. Gen. xlviii. 9. s ch. vi. 12. Luke xiii. 4. Rom. i. 14. viii. 12. xv. 27. Gal. v. 3 only †. t here and ch. xxv. 15, &c. only. Exod. xxv. 39 al. (-τιαῖος, Rev. xvi. 21.) u Luke vii. 42. xii. 4. xiv. 14. Eph. iv. 28. Heb. vi. 13.

20. **οπου** ℵ^2(appy: txt ℵ$^{1\cdot 3}$) Orig$_2$(txt$_2$) Eus$_{oft}$ Constt$_1$ Ath$_1$ Bas$_2$.—*ουκ εισιν γαρ*, and *παρ' οις ουκ ειμι* D^1(*ου γαρ εισιν* D^4, *non enim sunt* D-lat), simly lat-g_1. om *η* ℵ^1(ins ℵ^2).

21. rec *αυτω* bef *πετρος ειπεν*, with Lℵ^{3a} rel lat-*a* (*b c*) syr copt (sah) arm Chr Lucif$_2$: om *αυτω* ℵ Damasc: txt B D(om *ὁ*) Orig. *ο αδελφος μου* bef *εις εμε* B 69. 124. 346.

22. (*αλλα*, so BD.) **επτακις** D^1 lat-*a b c* Lucif.

24. rec *προσηνεχθη* (*more usual word, see ch* xii. 22; xix. 13, *and for προσηχθη, reff*), with Lℵ rel latt Orig$_2$ [Chr Damasc$_1$] Lucif: txt BD Orig$_2$. *εἷς* bef *αυτω* Bℵ^1 (txt ℵ^{3a}). for *μυρ.*, *πολλων* ℵ^1(txt ℵ^{3a}) coptt Orig$_7$[txt$_1$(and int$_1$)] Juv.

the divine will. It was apparently misunderstood by the Apostles James and John;—see St. Mark's account, ch. x. 35, in which they nearly repeat these words. Notice again the **ἀμὴν λέγω ὑμῖν**: see on ch. xvi. ult. **20.**] A generalization of the term **ἐκκλησία**, and the powers conferred on it, which renders it independent of particular forms of government or ceremonies, and establishes at once a canon against pseudo-catholicism in all its forms: cf. 1 Cor. i. 2. **ἐκεῖ εἰμί** must be understood of the presence of the Spirit and Power of Christ, see chap. xxviii. ult.

21—35.] Reply to Peter's question respecting the limit of forgiveness; and by occasion, the Parable of the forgiven but unforgiving servant. See Luke xvii. 3, 4. It is possible that Peter may have asked this question in virtue of the power of the keys before (ch. xvi. 19) entrusted to him, to direct him in the use of them: but it seems more likely, that it was asked as in the person of any individual: that Peter wished to follow the rules just laid down, but felt a difficulty as to the limit of his exercise of forgiveness.

The Rabbinical rule was, to forgive *three times and no more*; this they justified by Amos i. 3, &c.: Job xxxiii. 29, 30 LXX, and marg. E. V. The expression 'seven times' is found Prov. xxiv. 16, in connexion with sinning and being restored: see also Levit. xxvi. 18—28. In our Lord's answer we have most likely a reference to Gen. iv. 24. **Seventy times seven**, not '*seven and seventy times*,' is the rendering. οὐκ ἀριθμὸν τιθεὶς ἐνταῦθα, ἀλλὰ τὸ ἄπειρον καὶ διηνεκὲς καὶ ἀεί. Chrys. Hom. lxi. 1, p. 611. **23. διὰ τοῦτο**] 'because this is so,' because unlimited forgiveness is the law of the Kingdom of Heaven. The δοῦλοι here are not *slaves*, but ministers or stewards. By the πραθῆναι of ver. 25 they could not be slaves in the literal sense. But in Oriental language (see Herodotus passim) all the subjects of the king, even the great ministers of state, are called δοῦλοι. The individual example is one in *high trust*, or his debt could never have reached the enormous sum mentioned. See Isa. i. 18.

24.] Whether these are talents of silver or of gold, the debt represented is enormous, and far beyond any private man's power to discharge. 10,000 talents of silver is the sum at which Haman reckons the revenue derivable from the destruction of the whole Jewish people, Esth. iii. 9. Trench remarks (Parables, p. 124) that we can best appreciate the sum by comparing it with other sums mentioned in Scripture. In the construction of the tabernacle, twenty-nine talents of gold were used (Exod. xxxviii. 24): David pre-

δὲ αὐτοῦ [v] ἀποδοῦναι ἐκέλευσεν αὐτὸν ὁ κύριος [w] πραθῆναι, ...εκελευσεν αυ. X.
καὶ τὴν γυναῖκα [αὐτοῦ] καὶ τὰ τέκνα καὶ πάντα ὅσα [x] ἔχει,
καὶ [v] ἀποδοθῆναι. 26 [y] πεσὼν οὖν ὁ δοῦλος προσεκύνει BDEFG HKLMS
αὐτῷ λέγων [z] Μακροθύμησον ἐπ' ἐμοί, καὶ πάντα [v] ἀπο- UVΓΔΠ ℵ 1. 33.
δώσω [σοι]. 27 [a] σπλαγχνισθεὶς δὲ ὁ κύριος τοῦ δούλου 69
ἐκείνου [b] ἀπέλυσεν αὐτόν, καὶ τὸ [c] δάνειον [d] ἀφῆκεν αὐτῷ.
28 ἐξελθὼν δὲ ὁ δοῦλος ἐκεῖνος εὗρεν ἕνα τῶν [e] συνδούλων
αὐτοῦ ὃς ὤφειλεν αὐτῷ ἑκατὸν [f] δηνάρια, καὶ [g] κρατήσας
αὐτὸν [h] ἔπνιγεν λέγων Ἀπόδος εἴ τι ὀφείλεις. 29 [i] πεσὼν C μοι ει ...

v ch. v. 26 reff. Judg. xvii. 4. w ch. xiii. 46 reff. x pres., John i. 40 reff. y = ch. iv. 9 reff. 1 Kings xx. 41 al. z Luke xviii. 7. 1 Cor. xiii. 4. James v. 7 al. Prov. xix. 11. Sir. xviii. 11. xxxii. (xxxv.) 18. a ch. ix. 36 reff. b = ch. xxvii. 15, &c. John xix. 10, 12. Acts iv. 21, 23. Heb. xiii. 23 al. 1 Macc. x. 29. c here only. Deut. xv. 8. xxiv. 11 only (?). see ch. v. 42 reff. d ch. vi. 12 reff. e here, &c. (4 times). ch. xxiv. 49. Col. i. 7. iv. 7. Rev. vi. 11. xix. 10. xxii. 9 only. Ezra iv. 7, 9 al6. only. f ch. xx. 2 reff. g ch. xii. 11 reff. h = here only. (Mark v. 13. 1 Kings xvi. 14, 15 only.) i ver. 26.

25. rec aft κυριος ins αυτου (*to avoid misunderstanding*), with E rel vulg lat-*b c e f ff*$_{1.2}$ *h* syrr coptt æth arm [Damasc$_1$]: om BDLℵ 1 am(with em forj harl) lat-*a* g_2 Jer Lucif. aft γυν. om αυτου Bℵ 1 lat-*h*. for τεκνα, πε(i. e. αι)δια ℵ Chr. rec ειχε (*for conformity: but the pres in such cases is* idiomatic,—*see reff*), with Dℵ rel latt Lucif: txt B 1. 124 syrr syr-cu sah Orig$_{expr}$. for αποδοθ., αποθηναι D.

26. for ουν, δε D ev-y latt syr-txt sah (æth) arm Lucif. aft δουλος ins εκεινος (*from below*) DLΔℵ[3a] 33 latt syrr syr-cu copt æth Lucif: om Bℵ[1] rel sah arm [Damasc$_1$]. rec aft λεγων ins κυριε, with Lℵ rel lat-*f ff*$_2$ g_1 syrr coptt æth arm [Damasc$_1$]; aft επ. εμ., gat mm; aft μακρ., lat-*b*: om BD ev-y vulg lat-*a c e ff*$_1$ g_2 *h l* syr-cu Orig Lucif. (*The* omn *conforms to ver* 29, *but the* insn *to the spiritual interpretation.*) εμε DL. rec σοι bef αποδωσω, with Δ rel lat-*f* [Chr Damasc]: αποδ. σοι BLℵ 33. 69 vulg lat-*a c* g_1 *h* syrr syr-cu coptt æth arm Orig Lucif: αποδ. (omg σοι) D lat-*b e ff*$_{1.2}$ copt.

27. om εκεινου B 1. 124.

28. om εκεινος B [245] arm-zoh. δηναρια bef ρ̄ D. rec aft αποδος ins μοι (*supplementary and explanatory*), with C rel lat-*e f* syrr syr-cu arm [Chr]: om BDLΠ[1]ℵ 1. 33 ev-y latt coptt æth Orig$_2$ Damasc Lucif. rec (for ει τι) ο τι, with 69-marg latt(*quod*) æth arm Lucif: txt BCDℵ rel Scr's mss Orig$_2$ Chr Damasc Thl Euthym Thphn.

pared for the temple 3000 talents of gold, and the princes 5000 (1 Chron. xxix. 4—7): the Queen of Sheba presented to Solomon 120 talents (1 Kings x. 10): the King of Assyria laid on Hezekiah thirty talents of gold (2 Kings xviii. 14): and in the extreme impoverishment to which the land was brought at last, one talent of gold was laid on it, after the death of Josiah, by the King of Egypt (2 Chron. xxxvi. 3). **25. ἐκέλευσεν αὐτ. . . . . κ.τ.λ.]** See Exod. xxii. 3: Levit. xxv. 39, 47: 2 Kings iv. 1. The similitude is however rather from Oriental despotism: for the selling was under the Mosaic law softened by the liberation at the year of jubilee. The imprisonment also, and the tormentors, vv. 30, 34, favour this view, forming no part of the Jewish law. **ἀποδοθῆναι,** impersonal, as in E. V., **payment to be made. 26.]** Luther explains this as the voice of mistaken self-righteousness, which when bitten by sense of sin and terrified with the idea of punishment, runs hither and thither, seeking help, and imagines it can build up a righteousness before God without having yet any idea that God Himself will help the sinner. Trench remarks, "It seems simpler to see in the words nothing more than exclamations characteristic of the extreme fear and anguish of the moment, which made him ready to promise impossible things, even mountains of gold." p. 127. **28.]** Perhaps we must not lay stress on ἐξελθών, as indicating any wrong frame of mind already begun, as Theophylact does:—the sequel shews how completely he had 'gone out' from the presence of his Lord. At all events the word corresponds to the time when the trial of our principle takes place: when we 'go out' from the presence of God in prayer and spiritual exercises, into the world. We may observe, that *forgiveness of sin* does not imply *a change of heart or principle in the sinner.* The fellow-servant is probably not in the same station as himself, but none the less a fellow-servant. The insignificance of the sum is to shew us how trifling any offence against one another is in comparison to the vastness of our sin against God. Chrysostom finely remarks: ὁ δὲ οὐδὲ τὰ

οὖν ὁ [e] σύνδουλος αὐτοῦ [εἰς τοὺς πόδας αὐτοῦ] [k] παρεκάλει αὐτὸν λέγων [i] Μακροθύμησον ἐπ' * ἐμέ, καὶ ἀποδώσω
σοι. 30 ὁ δὲ οὐκ ἤθελεν, ἀλλὰ ἀπελθὼν ἔβαλεν αὐτὸν
εἰς [l] φυλακήν, [m] ἕως ἀποδῷ τὸ ὀφειλόμενον. 31 ἰδόντες οὖν
οἱ [e] σύνδουλοι αὐτοῦ τὰ γενόμενα [n] ἐλυπήθησαν [no] σφόδρα
καὶ ἐλθόντες [p] διεσάφησαν τῷ κυρίῳ ἑαυτῶν πάντα τὰ
γενόμενα. 32 τότε [q] προσκαλεσάμενος αὐτὸν ὁ κύριος
αὐτοῦ λέγει αὐτῷ Δοῦλε πονηρέ, πᾶσαν τὴν [r] ὀφειλὴν
ἐκείνην [s] ἀφῆκά σοι, ἐπεὶ [k] παρεκάλεσάς με· 33 οὐκ [t] ἔδει
καὶ σὲ [u] ἐλεῆσαι τὸν [e] σύνδουλόν σου ὡς κἀγώ σε [u] ἠλέησα;
34 καὶ [v] ὀργισθεὶς ὁ κύριος αὐτοῦ παρέδωκεν αὐτὸν τοῖς
[w] βασανισταῖς, ἕως οὗ ἀποδῷ πᾶν τὸ ὀφειλόμενον.

k ch. viii. 5. xxvi. 53. 1 Kings xxii. 4. Esth. vii. 7 Ald. compl.
l = ch. xiv. 3, 10 al. 3 Kings xxii. 27.
m Luke xv. 4. xvii. 8. (Ps. lxxi. 7 al.)
n ch. xvii. 23 (reff.).
o ch. ii. 10 reff.
p here and ch. xiii. 36 v. r. only. Deut. i. 5 only. 1 Macc. xii. 8 al.
q ver. 2.
r Rom. xiii. 7. 1 Cor. vii. 3 only †.
s ver. 27.
t ch. xxiii. 23. xxv. 27 al.
u ch. ix. 27. xv. 22 al. Ps. vi. 2. cxxii. 3.
v ch. v. 22 reff.
w here only †. (-ιστήριον, Jer. xx. 2 Symm.)

29. om εις τους ποδας αυτου BC¹DGLℵ 1 latt syr-cu sah Orig Lucif: ins C² Δ(sic) rel lat-*f* syrr arm. (*Meyer would omit it, as a* gloss on πεσων. *But then how comes it, that* no such gloss *was insd* above, *ver* 26? *There would be* two reasons *for* omg *the words,* (1) the desire to conform the ver to ver 26: (2) the homœoteleuton αυτου *to* αυτου:—*but none for insg them, which would not apply equally to ver* 26.)
* rec ἐμοί, with Bℵ rel: εμε CDL. (*All our* MSS *conform the two verses, except* possibly C, *which is deficient in ver* 26, *so that we have nothing to guide us.*)
for και, καγω D. rec aft και ins παντα (*to conform to ver* 26), with C²LΓΠℵ³ᵃ 1. 33 vulg lat-*c f ff*₁.₂ *g*₁.₂ Syr syr-mg coptt æth [Chr]: aft σοι, K: om BC¹Dℵ¹ rel lat-*a b e h* Syr-ms syr-cu syr-txt arm Damasc Thl Euthym Lucif. σοι bef αποδωσω C²ΓΠ 33. 69 Scr's e f p w ev-y lat-*f* Chr.
30. ηθελησεν D 69. 124 latt Damasc Lucif. for αλλα, και ℵ¹(txt ℵ³ᵃ). rec aft εως ins ου, with D rel: om BCLℵ arm. αποδη ℵ¹(txt ℵ³ᵃ). ins παν bef το οφειλομενον C 124. 245 tol lat-*g*₁ sah-mss Chr₁ [Damasc].
31. rec (for ουν) δε, with C ℵ³ᵃ(but ουν restored) rel latt syrr syr-cu coptt æth [Chr Damasc] Lucif: txt BDℵ¹ 33 lat-*e*. αυτου bef οι συνδουλοι B. for 1st γεν., γινομενα D(γειν.) L ℵ³ᵃ(but γεν. restored) latt Chr Euthym Lucif. for και, οι δε ℵ. rec (for εαυτων) αυτων, with DHL S(αὑτων) 1: txt BCℵ rel Orig₁.
32. om αυτω D 22 [64].
33. aft ουκ εδει ins ουν D latt(not forj *e*) syr-cu sah arm Aug. (καγω, so BDLℵ 33 Orig.)
34. om οὗ B arm Orig. om παν D (64) ev-y Chr(Fd: παν added only in mss-G-γ). rec aft οφειλομενον ins αυτω, with C ℵ(marks for erasure added, but removed) rel syrr coptt æth [Damasc]: om BD latt syr-cu arm Orig.

ῥήματα ᾐδέσθη δι' ὧν ἐσώθη· καὶ γὰρ αὐτὸς ταὐτὰ εἰπὼν ἀπηλλάγη τῶν μυρίων ταλάντων· καὶ οὐδὲ τὸν λιμένα ἐπέγνω δι' οὗ τὸ ναυάγιον διέφυγεν· οὐ τὸ σχῆμα τῆς ἱκετηρίας ἀνέμνησεν αὐτὸν τῆς τοῦ δεσπότου φιλανθρωπίας· ἀλλὰ πάντα ἐκεῖνα ὑπὸ τῆς πλεονεξίας καὶ τῆς ὠμότητος καὶ τῆς μνησικακίας ἐκβαλών, θηρίου παντὸς χαλεπώτερος ἦν, ἄγχων τὸν σύνδουλον. τί ποιεῖς, ἄνθρωπε; σεαυτὸν ἀπαιτῶν οὐκ αἰσθάνῃ, κατὰ σεαυτοῦ τὸ ξίφος ὠθῶν, καὶ τὴν ἀπόφασιν καὶ τὴν δωρεὰν ἀνακλούμενος; Hom. lxi. 4, p. 616. **ἔπνιγεν**] So 'obtorto collo ad prætorem trahor,' Plaut. Pœnul. iii. 5. 45. See other examples in Wetstein. The εἴ τι ὀφείλεις, which is beyond doubt the true reading, must be understood as a haughty expression of one ashamed to meet the mention of the paltry sum really owing, and by this very expression generalizing his unforgiving treatment to all who owed him aught. **31.**] The fellow-servants **ἐλυπήθησαν**, the lord **ὀργίζεται.** *Anger* is not *man's* proper mood towards sin, but *sorrow* (see Ps. cxix. 136), because all men are sinners. These fellow-servants are the *praying people of God*, who plead with Him against the oppression and tyranny in the world. **32.**] ὅτε μὲν μυρία τάλαντα ὤφειλεν, οὐκ ἐκάλεσε πονηρόν, οὐδὲ ὕβρισεν, ἀλλ' ἠλέησεν. Chrysost. Hom. lxi. 4, p. 616. **34. τοῖς βασανισταῖς**] not merely *the prison-keepers*, but

x here only. see ch. v. 48 reff.
y John iii. 12. 1 Cor. xv. 40 al. Ps. lxvii. 14. 2 Macc. iii. 39 only. Dan. iv. 23 Theod.-A. (οὐρ. BF.)
z ἀπό, = here only. Judg. xvi. 17, 18 A. usu. w. ἐκ, Mark xii. 30, 33.
a ch. xiii. 53 only. Gen. xii. 8 Aq. transit., 4 Kings xxv. 11 al.
b ch. ii. 16 reff. Josh. xix. 49.

35 οὕτως καὶ ὁ ˣ πατήρ μου ὁ [ˣʸ ἐπ]ουράνιος ποιήσει BCDEF GHKL
ὑμῖν, ἐὰν μὴ ˢ ἀφῆτε ἕκαστος τῷ ἀδελφῷ αὐτοῦ ᶻ ἀπὸ τῶν MSUVΓ ΔΠℵ 1.
ᶻ καρδιῶν ὑμῶν. 33. 69

XIX. 1 Καὶ ἐγένετο ὅτε ἐτέλεσεν ὁ Ἰησοῦς τοὺς
λόγους τούτους, ᵃ μετῆρεν ἀπὸ τῆς Γαλιλαίας καὶ ἦλθεν
εἰς τὰ ᵇ ὅρια τῆς Ἰουδαίας ᶜ πέραν τοῦ Ἰορδάνου. 2 καὶ
ἠκολούθησαν αὐτῷ ὄχλοι πολλοί, καὶ ᵈ ἐθεράπευσεν
αὐτοὺς ἐκεῖ. 3 καὶ προσῆλθον αὐτῷ Φαρισαῖοι ᵉ πειράζοντες αὐτὸν καὶ λέγοντες ᶠ Εἰ ἔξεστιν ᵍ ἀπολῦσαι τὴν
γυναῖκα αὐτοῦ κατὰ ʰ πᾶσαν ⁱ αἰτίαν; 4 ὁ δὲ ἀποκριθεὶς

c ch. iv. 15 al. Gen. l. 10. d ch. iv. 23, 24 reff. e ch. iv. 1, 3. xvi. 1. xxii. 18 35. 3 Kings x. 1. f ch. xii. 10 reff. g ch. v. 31, 32 reff. h = ch. xiii. 19. xviii. 19 al. i Luke viii. 47. Acts x. 21. 2 Tim. i. 6, 12 al. Gen. iv. 13. 2 Macc. xii. 40. Prov. xxviii. 17.

35. *ουρανιος* (*more usual phrase: see also ch* vi. 14) BC²DKLΠℵ 33 Orig₂ Damasc: *επουρανιος* C¹ rel Chr. *υμιν ποιησει* bef *ο πατ. μ. ο ουρ.* D lat-*a b c* (Orig₂) Lucif. rec at end adds *τα παραπτωματα αυτων* (*from ch* vi. 14, 15: *Mark* xi. 25, 26), with C rel lat-*f h* syrr sah-mnt arm [Chr Damasc]: om BDLℵ 1 latt syr-cu coptt æth Orig Lucif Ambr Jer Aug.

Chap. XIX. **1.** for *ετελεσεν*, *ελαλησεν* D lat-*a b c e ff*$_{1.2}$ *g*$_1$ Hil. *και ηλθεν* is repeated by ℵ, but marked for erasure.

3. rec ins *οι* bef *φαρισαιοι* (*so also in* ‖ *Mark: it was natural to supply the art*), with Dℵ rel sah Orig$_1$ Naz: txt BCLMΔΠ 1. 33 Scr's w evv-H-y copt [Damasc$_1$-ms]. for *λεγοντες*, *λεγουσιν* D¹(and lat: txt D³). rec aft *λεγ.* ins *αυτω*, with D rel lat-*c h* syr Op: om BCKLM¹ΓΠℵ 1 vulg lat-*a b* &c Syr syr-cu coptt æth arm Orig Naz Hil. rec aft *εξεστιν* ins *ανθρωπω* (*see ver* 5, *and also* ‖ *Mark*), with CDℵ⁵ rel latt syrr syr-cu coptt Orig$_2$ Naz [Damasc$_1$] Hil Op: om BLΓℵ¹ 125¹ Scr's f Aug.

the torturers. Remember he was to have been sold into slavery before, and now *his punishment is to be greater*. The condition following would amount in the case of the sum in the parable to *perpetual* imprisonment. So Chrysostom, τουτέστι διηνεκῶς· οὔτε γὰρ ἀποδώσει ποτέ. Hom. lxi. 4, p. 617. See note on ch. v. 26. There is a difficulty made, from the punishment of this debtor for *the very debt which had been forgiven*, and the question has been asked, 'utrum peccata semel dimissa redeant.' But it is the spiritual meaning which has here ruled the form of the parable. He who falls from a state of grace falls into a state of condemnation, and is overwhelmed with 'all that debt,' not of this or that actual sin formerly remitted, but of a *whole state* of enmity to God. Meyer (Comm. in loc.) well remarks, that the motive held up in this parable could only have full light cast on it by the great act of Atonement which the Lord was about to accomplish. We may see from that consideration, how properly it belongs to this last period of His ministry. **35. ὁ π. μου**] not ὑμῶν, as in the similar declaration in ch. vi. 14, 15. This is more solemn and denunciatory (οὐ γὰρ ἄξιον τοῦ τοιούτου πατέρα καλεῖσθαι τὸν Θεόν, τοῦ οὕτω πονηροῦ κ. μισανθρώπου. Chrys. Hom. lxi. 4, p. 617). ἐπουράνιος is not elsewhere used by our Evangelist.

Chap. XIX. 1—12.] Reply to the Pharisees' question concerning divorce. Mark x. 1—12. This appears to be the journey of our Lord into the region beyond Jordan, mentioned John x. 40. If so, a considerable interval has elapsed since the discourse in ch. xviii. **1.] τὰ ὅρια τῆς Ἰουδ. πέρ. τοῦ Ἰορδ.** form one continuous description. Bethany, where He went, was beyond Jordan, but on the confines of Judæa. See notes on Mark x. 1, and Luke ix. 51. **2.]** This agrees with what is said John x. 41, 42. For **ἐθεράπ.**, St. Mark has ἐδίδασκεν.
3.] This was a question of dispute between the rival Rabbinical schools of Hillel and Shammai; the former asserting the right of arbitrary divorce, from Deut. xxiv. 1, the other denying it except in case of adultery. It was also, says De Wette, a delicate question in the place where our Lord now was,—in the dominions of Herod Antipas. **κ. πᾶσαν αἰτ.**, as E. V., **for every cause**;—i. e. *is any charge which a man may choose to bring against his wife to justify him in divorcing*

Z οτι ο... εἶπεν Οὐκ ἀνέγνωτε ὅτι ὁ [k] ποιήσας [k] ἀπ' ἀρχῆς [lm] ἄρσεν
καὶ [ln] θῆλυ ἐποίησεν αὐτοὺς 5 καὶ εἶπεν [o] Ἕνεκα τούτου
Id πατερα... [p] καταλείψει ἄνθρωπος τὸν πατέρα καὶ τὴν μητέρα καὶ
[q] κολληθήσεται τῇ γυναικὶ αὐτοῦ, καὶ ἔσονται οἱ δύο [r] εἰς
N εισιν δυο... σάρκα μίαν; 6 ὥστε οὐκέτι εἰσὶν δύο, ἀλλὰ σὰρξ μία· ὃ
οὖν ὁ θεὸς [s] συνέζευξεν, ἄνθρωπος μὴ [t] χωριζέτω. 7 λέγουσιν αὐτῷ Τί οὖν [u] Μωυσῆς ἐνετείλατο δοῦναι [v] βιβλίον [p]

k see Isa. xlv. 21.
l ‖ Mk. Rom. i. 27. Gal. iii. 28 only. Gen. i. 27.
m as above (1). Luke ii. 23. Rev. xii. 5 only.
n as above (1). Rom. i. 26 only.
o Gen. ii. 24.
p Luke v. 28. x. 40. Eph. v. 31, from l. c. Gen. xliv. 22.
q Acts v. 13. ix. 26 al. Ruth ii. 8. 2 Kings xx. 2.
r ch. xxi. 42. Luke iii. 5. Rom. ii. 26. Gen. xv. 6.
s ‖ Mk. only. Ezek. i. 11, 23 A only.
t Rom. viii. 35, 39. 1 Cor. vii. 10, &c. Ezek. xlvi. 19. Lev. xiii. 46.
u Deut. xxiv. 3 (1).
v = ‖ (from l. c.) only. 4 Kings x. 1, &c.

4. rec aft ειπεν ins αυτοις, with C rel vulg lat-*b f* $g_{1.2}$ syrr syr-cu (arm) [Damasc] Op: om BDLℵ lat-*a c e* $ff_{1.2}$ *h* coptt æth Orig. for ποιησας, κτισας B 1. 22. 33. 124 coptt arm $Orig_2$ hom-Cl Meth Tit-bostr Ath: txt CDZℵ rel latt [$Constt_1$ Naz_1 Chr $Damasc_1$] Orig-int_1 [Aug]. θηλυν D^1.

5. rec ενεκεν, with CD rel Constt [Meth]: txt BLZℵ Orig. aft πατερα ins αυτου CEI_dΔ 1. 33 syrr syr-cu coptt æth arm-mss Constt Tit-bostr [Chr] $Damasc_1$ Orig-int_1 Op spec: om BDZℵ rel latt Thph Ath Orig-int_1. aft μητ. ins αυτου Γ 69 syrr syr-cu coptt æth Thph Ath Thl Orig-int_1[om_1] Op. rec προσκολληθησεται (*from* LXX), with CKLMZΓΔΠℵ [Tit-bostr Ath_1 Chr $Damasc_1$]: *adhærebit* lat-*b c*: txt BDI_d rel Orig(but κολλαται comm) Epiph. om οι Z.

6. μια bef σαρξ Dℵ latt. om ο (bef θεος) Z 6 [Cyr_1]. aft συνεζευξεν ins εις εν D lat-*a* e^2 $ff_{1.2}$ *h* Aug Chrom. αποχωριζετω D.

7. ins ο bef μωυσης D. aft ενετειλατο ins ημιν N.

her? So Jos. Antt. iv. 8. 23, γυναικὸς τῆς συνοικούσης βουλόμενος διαζευχθῆναι καθ' ἃς δηποτοῦν αἰτίας,—πολλαὶ δ' ἂν τοῖς ἀνθρώποις τοιαῦται γίνοιντο,—γράμμασι μὲν περὶ τοῦ μηδέποτε συνελθεῖν ἰσχυριζέσθω. **4—6.**] On these verses we may remark (1) that our Lord refers to the Mosaic account of the Creation as *the historical fact* of the first creation of man; and grounds his argument on the *literal* expressions of that narrative. (2) That He cites both from the first and second chapters of Genesis, and in immediate connexion; thus shewing them to be consecutive parts of a continuous narrative, which, from their different diction, and apparent repetition, they have sometimes been supposed not to be. (3) That He quotes as *spoken by the Creator* the words in Gen. ii. 24, which were actually said by Adam; they must therefore be understood as said in prophecy, *divino afflatu*, which indeed the terms made use of in them would require, since the relations alluded to by those terms did not yet exist. Augustin. de Nupt. ii. 4 (12), vol. x. pt. i., 'Deus utique per hominem dixit quod homo prophetando prædixit.' (4) That the force of the argument consists in the *previous unity* of male and female, not indeed organically, but by implication, in Adam. Thus it is said in Gen. i. 27, not ἄνδρα καὶ γυναῖκα ἐποίησεν αὐτούς, but ἄρσεν καὶ θῆλυ ἐπ. αὐ. **He made them** (man, as a race) **male** (not, *a* male) **and female**: but then the male and female were implicitly shut up in one; and therefore after the creation of woman from man, when one man and one woman were united in marriage they should be *one flesh*, ἕνεκεν τούτου, *because* woman was taken out of man. The answer then is, that *abstractedly*, from the nature of marriage, *it is indissoluble.* The words **οἱ δύο** are in the LXX and the Samaritan Pentateuch, but not in the Hebrew. **5. εἰς σάρκα μίαν**] εἶναι εἰς is not Greek, but a Hebraism, הָיָה לְ (Meyer). Stier remarks, that the essential bond of marriage consists *not in unity of spirit and soul*, by which indeed the marriage state should ever be hallowed and sweetened, but without which it still exists in all its binding power:—the wedded pair are ONE FLESH, i. e. ONE MAN *within the limits of their united life in the flesh*, for *this world:* beyond this limit, the marriage is broken by the *death of the flesh*. And herein alone lies the justification of a *second* marriage, which in no way breaks off the unity of love in spirit with the former partner, now deceased. Vol. ii. p. 267, edn. 2. **7—9.**] In this second question, the Pharisees imagine that they have overthrown our Lord's decision by a *permission* of the law, which they call a *command* (compare ἐνετείλατο, ver. 7, with ἐπέτρεψεν, ver. 8). But He answers them that this was done by Moses *on account of their hardness and sinfulness*, as a *lesser of evils*, and belonged to that dispensation

w ||. ch. v. 3 (reff.) only.
x ver. 3.
y ||. Mark xvi. 14 only. Deut. x. 16. Sir. xvi. 10 only. (-διος, Prov. xvii. 20. Ezek. iii. 7.)
z ch. v. 32. 1 Cor. vii. 2 al. Ezek. xvi. 15, &c.
a ch. v. 32 reff. (-χεύειν, ch. v. 28, 32 reff.)
b — here only. 1 Cor. vi. 12. x. 23.

BCDEF GHI$_d$K LMNS UVZΓΔ Πℵ 1. 33. 69

^w ἀποστασίου καὶ ^x ἀπολῦσαι αὐτήν; 8 λέγει αὐτοῖς Ὅτι
Μωυσῆς πρὸς τὴν ^y σκληροκαρδίαν ὑμῶν ἐπέτρεψεν ὑμῖν
^x ἀπολῦσαι τὰς γυναῖκας ὑμῶν· ἀπ' ἀρχῆς δὲ οὐ γέγονεν
οὕτως. 9 λέγω δὲ ὑμῖν, ὃς ἂν ^x ἀπολύσῃ τὴν γυναῖκα
αὐτοῦ μὴ ἐπὶ ^z πορνείᾳ καὶ γαμήσῃ ἄλλην, ^a * μοιχᾶται·
καὶ ὁ ^x ἀπολελυμένην γαμήσας ^a μοιχᾶται. 10 λέγουσιν
αὐτῷ οἱ μαθηταὶ [αὐτοῦ] Εἰ οὕτως ἐστὶν ἡ ^b αἰτία τοῦ
^c ἀνθρώπου μετὰ τῆς γυναικός, οὐ ^d συμφέρει γαμῆσαι.

c = 1 Cor. vii. 1. d w. inf., John xviii. 14. 2 Cor. xii. 1. Esth. iii. 8. absol.,

om *αυτην* (*see* || *Mark*) DLZℵ 1 vulg lat-*a e ff*$_1$ *g*$_{1.2}$ *h l* syr-jer sah-mnt æth arm Orig$_2$ Aug Op: ins BC I$_d$(appy) N rel lat-*f* syrr [Damasc] (*αυτας* coptt, *uxorem* gat mm lat-*b c ff*$_2$ syr-cu Iren-int Ambr).

8. ins *και* bef *λεγει* D^1-gr æth. aft *αυτοις* ins *ο ῑς* ℵ ev-z: pref M lat-*a b c*. *προς . . . υμιν* bef *μωυσης* D lat-*a b c* &c(not *g*$_2$). for *ου γεγονεν*, *ουκ εγενετο* D hom-Cl Chr.

9. rec ins *οτι* bef *ος* (*see ver* 8), with CI$_d$Nℵ rel vulg lat-*f ff*$_2$ *g*$_1$ syrr syr-cu coptt æth arm spec [Bas$_1$ Chr Damasc$_1$]: om BDZ lat-*a b c e ff*$_1$ *g*$_2$ *h* Aug Op. *εαν* CM. rec ins *ει* bef *μη* (*explanatory*), with 69^2 (Scr's u, e sil) [Bas$_1$].—*παρεκτος λογου πορνειας* (*from ch* v. 32) BD 1. 33. 69^1 mss-in-Aug lat-*a b c e ff*$_{1.2}$ *g*$_1$ *h* syr-cu coptt Orig$_3$ [Bas$_1$ Cyr$_2$-p] Chr Aug Op spec: (*πλὴν εἰ μὴ ἐπὶ λόγῳ πορν.* Clem:) txt CI$_d$NZℵ rel vulg lat-*g*$_2$ syrr æth arm Damasc Thl. om *κ. γαμ. αλλην* BN 1 lat-*ff*$_1$ copt (Clem Orig) Tert Aug$_2$ Op$_1$: ins CDI$_d$Z rel latt syrr syr-cu sah æth arm [Damasc$_1$] Aug$_1$ Op$_1$. *ποιεῖ αὐτὴν μοιχευθῆναι (*from ch* v. 32) BC^{1}N 1 lat-*ff*$_1$ syr-jer(appy) copt Orig$_2$ [Cyr$_2$-p] Aug$_2$: (*μοιχᾶται αὐτήν, τοῦτ' ἔστιν ἀναγκάζει μοιχευθῆναι* Clem:) *adulterium committit adversus eam* syr-cu: *adulterium facit* spec: *μοιχαται* C^{3}DI$_d$Zℵ rel latt syrr sah æth arm [Bas$_1$] Tert Aug$_1$ Op. om *κ. ο απολ. γαμ. μοιχ.* (*homœotel*) C^{3}DLSℵ 69 gat(with mm) lat-*a b e ff*$_{1.2}$ *g*$_1$ *h l* syr-cu copt-ms sah [Orig$_1$] Chr: ins BC^{1}I$_d$NZ rel vulg lat-*c f g*$_2$ syrr syr-jer copt æth arm [Bas$_1$ Damasc$_1$] (Tert).—for *γαμησας*, *γαμων* CI$_d$NΔΠ 1. 33.

10. om *αυτω* ℵ^1(ins ℵ^{3a}). om *αυτου* Bℵ lat-*e ff*$_1$ *g*$_1$ sah-ms [Damasc$_1$-ms]. om *ει* ℵ^1. for *ανθρωπου*, *ανδρος* (*corrn for precision*) D ev-y lat-*a b c ff*$_2$ *g*$_1$ *h* arm(appy) Ambr Op Ambrst: om lat-*ff*$_1$ Aug$_{oft}$.

which *παρεισῆλθεν*, Rom. v. 20; *τῶν παραβάσεων χάριν προσετέθη*, Gal. iii. 19. This He expresses by the *ὑμῶν, ὑμῖν, ὑμῶν*, as opposed to *ἄνθρωπος*, and to *ἀπ' ἀρχῆς*. Only that *πορνεία*, which *itself breaks marriage*, can be a ground for dissolving it. The question, whether demonstrated *approaches to πορνεία*, short of the act itself, are to be regarded as having the same power, must be dealt with cautiously, but at the same time with full remembrance that our Lord does not confine the guilt of such sins to the outward act only: see ch. v. 28. St. Mark gives this last verse (9) as spoken *to the disciples in the house*; and his minute accuracy in such matters of detail is well known. This enactment by our Lord is a formal repetition of what He had said before in the Sermon on the Mount, ch. v. 32. Notice, as on ch. v. 32, *ἀπολελυμένην* without the art., and thus logically confined to the case of her who has been divorced *μὴ ἐπὶ πορνείᾳ*. This not having been seen, expositors (e.g. of late Bp. Wordsworth) have fallen into the mistake of supposing that the dictum applies to the marrying a woman divorced *ἐπὶ πορνείᾳ*, which grammatically would require *τὴν ἀπολελυμένην*. The proper English way of rendering the word as it now stands, would be, **a woman thus divorced**, viz., *μὴ ἐπὶ πορνείᾳ*.

10.] **αἰτία**, not the *cause* of divorce just mentioned; nor, the *condition* of the man with his wife: but **the account to be given**, '*the original ground and principle*,' of the relationship of man and wife:—*ἐὰν τοιαύτη ἐστὶν ἡ αἰτία τῆς συζυγίας*, Euthym., who however mentions other renderings. The disciples apprehend that the trials and temptations of marriage would prove sources of sin and misery. This question and its answer are peculiar to Matthew. Meyer refers *αἰτία* back to the *αἰτία* in ver. 3, and understands it to mean *the only reason justifying divorce*; but the above interpretation seems to me preferable.

11 ὁ δὲ εἶπεν αὐτοῖς Οὐ πάντες [e] χωροῦσιν τὸν λόγον
τοῦτον, ἀλλ' οἷς [f] δέδοται. 12 εἰσὶν γὰρ [g] εὐνοῦχοι οἵτινες
[h] ἐκ κοιλίας μητρὸς ἐγεννήθησαν οὕτως, καί εἰσιν [g] εὐνοῦχοι οἵτινες [i] εὐνουχίσθησαν ὑπὸ τῶν ἀνθρώπων, καί
εἰσιν [g] εὐνοῦχοι οἵτινες [i] εὐνούχισαν ἑαυτοὺς διὰ τὴν
βασιλείαν τῶν οὐρανῶν. ὁ δυνάμενος [e] χωρεῖν [e] χω-
ρείτω.
13 Τότε προσηνέχθησαν αὐτῷ παιδία, ἵνα τὰς χεῖρας
[k] ἐπιθῇ αὐτοῖς καὶ προσεύξηται. οἱ δὲ μαθηταὶ [l] ἐπετί-
μησαν αὐτοῖς. 14 ὁ δὲ Ἰησοῦς εἶπεν [m] Ἄφετε τὰ παιδία
καὶ μὴ [n] κωλύετε αὐτὰ ἐλθεῖν πρός με· [o] τῶν γὰρ τοιούτων ἐστὶν ἡ βασιλεία τῶν οὐρανῶν. 15 καὶ [k] ἐπιθεὶς τὰς
χεῖρας αὐτοῖς ἐπορεύθη ἐκεῖθεν.
16 Καὶ ἰδοὺ [p] εἷς προσελθὼν αὐτῷ εἶπεν [q] Διδάσκαλε,

...οιτινες Z.
...προσηνε N.
[...xix. 13 Π?]
...κωλυετε I_d BCDEF GHKL MSUVΓ Δℵ 1. 33. 69

e = 2 Cor. vii. 2. (Gen. xiii. 6.)
f ch. xiii. 11 reff.
g here (3ce) and Acts viii. 27, &c. only. Isa. lvi. 3, 4. see Gen. xxxix. 1.
h Luke i. 15. Acts iii. 2. xiv. 8. Gal. i. 15. Job i. 21.
i here (bis) only †. Jos. Antt. x. 2. 2.
k constr., Mark v. 23. vi. 5 al. fr. Job xl. 27 B (w. ἐπί, Aℵ).
see ch. ix. 18 reff.
l ch. xii. 16 reff.
m = ch. iii. 15 al.
n = ||. Mark ix. 38, 39 || L. Luke xi. 52. xxiii. 2 al. Num. xi. 28.
o constr., 1 Cor. iii. 21. vi. 19.
p || Mk. see ch. viii. 19 reff.
q ch. xvii. 24 reff.

11. om τουτον B 1 ev-y lat-*e* æth $Orig_2$ $Cypr_2$: ins CDI_dNZℵ rel latt $Clem_1$ [$Damasc_1$] Orig-int Ambr Aug Philast. (om τον λογον τουτον Chr.)
12. om γαρ ℵ[1](ins ℵ[3a]). δυνομενος B[1](sic).
13. rec προσηνεχθη (*gramml corrn*), with I_d(appy) [Π] rel Orig-comm [Chr]: txt BCDLℵ 33 Orig-txt. επιθη bef τας χειρας D sah æth. επετιμων C latt Hil.
14. aft ειπεν ins αυτοις CDLMℵ vulg lat-*f* $g_{1.2}$ *l* Syr syr-cu syr-with ast copt æth Chr: om BI_d rel latt sah arm. κωλυσητε D 13. 69[2](-σετε 69[1]). εμε LΔℵ.
15. rec αυτοις bef τας χειρας, with C rel latt syr arm [Chr]: txt BDL Δ-corr[1] (ℵ) 69 Syr syr-cu coptt æth $Orig_2$.—επ' αυτους ℵ, επ αυτα Scr's q r.
16. τω καιρω εκεινω νεανισκος τις προσηλθεν τω ιυ γονυπετων αυτον και λεγων C[3], simly G[2] Scr's s[2] x evv-H-P-y-z. rec ειπεν bef αυτω (*to avoid ambiguity*), with C rel syrr syr-cu Orig [Bas_1]: λεγει αυτω D vulg: txt Bℵ 69 sah æth arm Hil.
rec aft διδασκαλε ins αγαθε (*from* || *Mark Luke*), with C rel vulg lat-*b c f* ff_2 $g_{1.2}$ *h* syrr syr-cu coptt arm [Bas_1 $Cyr\text{-}jer_1$ Chr] Iren-int Hil_1 Aug: om BDLℵ 1 lat-*a e* ff_1

11, 12.] **τὸν λόγον τοῦτον, this saying of yours,** viz. *οὐ συμφέρει γαμῆσαι*. The **γάρ** in ver. 12 shews that the sense is carried on: see ch. i. 18. Our Lord mentions the *three exceptions*, the *οἷς δέδοται οὐ γαμῆσαι*. 1. Those who from natural incapacity, or if not that, inaptitude, *have no tendencies* towards marriage: 2. Those who by actual physical deprivation, or compulsion from men, *are prevented* from marrying: 3. Those who in order to do the work of God more effectually (as e. g. Paul), *abstain* from marriage, see 1 Cor. vii. 26. The εὐνοῦχοι and εὐνουχίζω in the two first cases are to be taken both literally and figuratively: in the latter, figuratively only. It is to be observed that our Lord does not here utter a word from which any superiority can be attributed to the state of celibacy: the imperative in the last clause being not a command but a permission, as in Rev. xxii. 17. His estimate for us of the expediency of celibacy, as a general question, is to be gathered from the parable of the talents, where He visits with severe blame the burying of the talent for its safer custody. The remark is Neander's, and the more valuable, as he himself lived and died unmarried. See his Leben Jesu, edn. 4, p. 584. **12.**] **χωρεῖν,** as in E. V. and in ver. 11, **to receive it.**

13—15.] THE BRINGING OF CHILDREN TO JESUS. Mark x. 13—16. Luke xviii. 15—17. After the long divergence of ch. ix. 51—xviii. 14, Luke here again falls into the synoptic narrative. This incident is more fully related in Mark, where see notes. Our Evangelist gives *τὰς χ. ἐπιθ. αὐτ. κ. προσεύξ.* (see Gen. xlviii. 14: Acts vi. 6), where the other two have only '*that He should touch them.*' The connexion in which it stands here and in Mark seems to be natural, *immediately after the discourse on marriage*. Some further remarks of our Lord, possibly on the fruit of marriage, may have given rise to the circumstance.

16—30.] ANSWER TO THE ENQUIRY OF A RICH YOUNG MAN, AND DISCOURSE

r ‖. ver. 29 ‖. ch. xxv. 46. Luke x. 25 only in three first Gospp. John passim. Dan. xii. 2.
s ch. xviii. 8, 9 ‖ Mk.
t = ch. xxiii. 3. xxviii. 20. John viii. 51, &c. 1 John ii. 3, 4 al. Prov. iii. 21.
u 1 Cor. vii. 19. 1 John iii. 22, 24 al. Sir. xxxv. (xxxii.) 23.

τί ἀγαθὸν ποιήσω ἵνα σχῶ [r] ζωὴν [r] αἰώνιον; 17 ὁ δὲ BCDEF
εἶπεν αὐτῷ Τί με ἐρωτᾷς περὶ τοῦ ἀγαθοῦ; εἷς ἐστιν GHKL
ὁ ἀγαθός. εἰ δὲ θέλεις [s] εἰς τὴν [s] ζωὴν [s] εἰςελθεῖν, [t] τήρει MSUVΓ
τὰς [u] ἐντολάς. 18 λέγει αὐτῷ [v] Ποίας; ὁ δὲ Ἰησοῦς ΔℵI. 33. 69
εἶπεν [w] Τὸ οὐ φονεύσεις, οὐ μοιχεύσεις, οὐ κλέψεις, οὐ
[x] ψευδομαρτυρήσεις, 19 τίμα τὸν πατέρα καὶ τὴν μητέρα,
[y] καὶ ἀγαπήσεις τὸν πλησίον σου ὡς σεαυτόν. 20 λέγει
αὐτῷ ὁ [a] νεανίσκος Πάντα ταῦτα [b] ἐφύλαξα· τί ἔτι [c] ὑστε-

v ch. xxi. 22, &c. reff. w Exod. xx. 12—16. Deut. v. 16—20. x ‖ (and Rom. xiii. 9 v. r.) from l. c. Mark xiv. 56, 57 only. (-ρία, ch. xv. 19.) y Levit. xix. 18. a here bis. Mark xiv. 51 (bis v. r.). xvi. 5. Luke vii. 14. Acts ii. 17 (from Joel ii. 28). v. 10. 1 John ii. 13, 14 only. b act., ‖ L. Luke xi. 28. Acts vii. 53. xvi. 4. xxi. 24. Lev. xviii. 5. Eccl. xii. 13. c constr., 2 Cor. xi. 5. xii. 11. Ps. xxxviii. 4. (‖ Mk. Luke xv. 14. xxii. 35. Rom. iii. 23. 1 Cor. i. 7 al.)

æth Orig Hil$_1$. ποιησας, omg ινα, (‖ *Luke*) Lℵ 28. 33 [Bas$_1$ Chr Iren-int$_1$]. rec εχω (*more usual*), with C(now) rel [Bas$_1$ Cyr-jer$_1$ Chr]: κληρονομησω (Lℵ 33) syr-cu syr-mg copt (æth Iren-int) Orig$_1$-comm [Bas$_1$]: txt B C[1](perhaps) D Orig-txt. —ζ. αι. bef κληρ. Lℵ 33 æth Iren-int.

17. rec τι με λεγεις αγαθον (*from ‖ Mark Luke*), with C rel lat-*f* Syr syr-txt sah Just Chr Cyr$_1$ Euthym Thl Iren-int Hil$_3$ Op: τι με αγαθον Δ: om Γ: txt (om του D Orig$_1$) BDLℵ 1. 22. 251 latt syr-cu syr-mg syr-jer copt æth arm Orig$_4$(expr$_1$: *ὁ μὲν οὖν Ματθ. ὡς περὶ ἀγαθοῦ ἔργου ἐρωτηθέντος τοῦ σωτῆρος ἐν τῷ 'τί ἀγαθὸν ποιήσω;' ἀνέγραψεν· ὁ δὲ Μάρκος καὶ Λουκᾶς φασὶ τὸν σωτ. εἰρηκέναι 'τί με λέγεις ἀγαθόν; οὐδεὶς ἀγαθὸς εἰ μὴ εἷς ὁ θ.'*) Eus Cyr$_1$ Dion-areop Antch Novat Jer Aug Juv. rec ουδεις αγαθος ει μη εις (*also from ‖ Mark Luke*), with C rel lat-*f g$_1$* syrr sah æth Eus Chr Dion-areop [Antch] (Hil) Ambr Op spec: txt B[om εις B[1]: ins B[2.3], Tischdf N. T. Vat] DLℵ 1 latt syr-cu syr-jer copt arm Iren Orig$_2$ [Novat Jer]. (om ο D 1 Iren.) rec adds ο θεος, with CΔ rel(om ὁ U) vulg lat-*b c f ff$_2$ g$_1$ h l* syrr syr-cu coptt æth Eus Antch Novat (Hil): om BDLℵ 1. 22 lat-*a* syr-jer arm Orig$_2$. rec εισελθειν bef εις την ζωην, with Δ rel syrr syr-cu coptt [Chr]: εις τ. ζ. ελθειν D lat-*a b c e ff$_2$ g$_1$* Lucif Ambr: txt BCKLℵ 33 vulg lat-*f ff$_1$* æth Orig hom-Cl Iren-int Cypr Jer. rec τηρησον (*more usual tense*), with Cℵ rel Orig$_2$ [Chr]: txt BD hom-Cl.

18. ποιας φησιν (omg αυτω) Lℵ. for ειπεν, εφη B(but λεγει above) 13. om το DM ev-y. om ου μοιχ. ου κλεψ. ℵ[1](ins ℵ-corr[1]).

19. rec aft πατερα ins σου, with C[2] 33. 69 vulg lat-*a b f ff$_{1.2}$ h* syrr syr-cu coptt æth Aug: om BC[1]Dℵ rel am lat-*c e g$_{1.2}$* arm Orig$_2$ Iren-int Cypr Hil Aug Jer Ambr.

20. ταυτα bef παντα (*from ‖ Mark Luke*) BDHKM 1. 69 syrr syr-cu æth Orig$_1$ Hil Ambr Op: txt Cℵ rel latt Orig$_1$ Ath Cypr. rec εφυλαξαμην (*from ‖ Mark*), with C rel Orig [Chr]: txt BDLℵ 1. 22 Ath[-ms] Cypr. rec adds εκ νεοτητος μου (*from ‖ Mark*), with Cℵ[3b] rel latt syrr syr-cu coptt æth arm Orig Hil Op: εκ νεοτητος (*from ‖ Luke*) D: om BLℵ[1] 1 am(with em forj fuld harl) lat-*ff$_1$ g$_{1.2}$* Iren-int Cypr Ambr Jer Aug Juv Promiss Bede.

Thereupon. Mark x. 17—31. Luke xviii. 18—30. **16.**] From Luke ver. 18 we learn that he was *a ruler:* from Mark ver. 17, that he *ran* to our Lord. The spirit in which he came,—which does not however appear here so plainly as in the other Gospels, from the omission of ἀγαθέ, and the form of our Lord's answer,—seems to have been that of excessive admiration for Jesus as a man of eminent virtue, and of desire to know from Him by what work of exceeding merit he might win eternal life. This spirit He reproves, by replying that there is but One Good, and that the walking by His grace in the way of holiness is the path to life. On the question and answer, as they stand in the received text,—and on their doctrinal bearing, see notes to Mark. This passage furnishes one of the most instructive and palpable cases of the smoothing down of apparent discrepancies by correcting the Gospels out of one another and thus reducing them to conformity. **18.**] De Wette observes well, that our Lord gives this enumeration of the commandments to *bring out the self-righteous spirit* of the young man, which He before saw. He only mentions those of the second table, having in ver. 17, in His declaration respecting ἀγαθός, included those of the first. Mark has the addition of μὴ ἀποστερήσῃς, representing probably the tenth commandment. **19.**] **καὶ ἀγαπ.** κ.τ.λ. is peculiar to Matthew. **20.**] We may remark that this young man, though self-

Z πωλησον... | X ακουσας... | BCDEF GHKL MSUV XZΓΔℵ 1. 33. 69

ρῶ; 21 ἔφη αὐτῷ ὁ Ἰησοῦς Εἰ θέλεις [d] τέλειος εἶναι,
ὕπαγε πώλησόν σου τὰ [e] ὑπάρχοντα καὶ [f] δὸς τοῖς πτωχοῖς, καὶ ἕξεις [g] θησαυρὸν ἐν οὐρανοῖς, καὶ [h] δεῦρο ἀκολούθει μοι. 22 ἀκούσας δὲ ὁ [a] νεανίσκος τὸν λόγον
[τοῦτον] ἀπῆλθεν [i] λυπούμενος, [k] ἦν γὰρ ἔχων [l] κτήματα
πολλά. 23 ὁ δὲ Ἰησοῦς εἶπεν τοῖς μαθηταῖς αὐτοῦ Ἀμὴν
λέγω ὑμῖν ὅτι πλούσιος [m] δυςκόλως εἰςελεύσεται εἰς τὴν
βασιλείαν τῶν οὐρανῶν. 24 πάλιν δὲ λέγω ὑμῖν, [n] εὐκοπώτερόν ἐστιν [o] κάμηλον διὰ [p] τρυπήματος [q] ῥαφίδος
* εἰςελθεῖν, ἢ πλούσιον εἰς τὴν βασιλείαν * τῶν οὐρανῶν.
25 ἀκούσαντες δὲ οἱ μαθηταὶ [r] ἐξεπλήσσοντο [s] σφόδρα λέ-

d ch. v. 48 reff. e w. gen., ch. xxiv. 47. xxv. 14. Luke xi. 21 al5. 1 Cor. xiii. 3. Heb. x. 34. Prov. vi. 31. (dat., Luke viii. 3 al.) f ‖ Mk. ch. xxvi. 9 ‖. Luke xix. 8. Prov. xxviii. 27. g ch. ii. 11 reff. h = ‖. John xi. 43. Acts vii. 3 (from Gen. xii. 1 [so Ed-vat. (not A. B def.)]), 34 (Rom. i. 13). Rev. xvii. 1. xxi. 9 only. Judg. ix. 14. i ch. xvii. 23 reff. k constr., Mk. ii. 18. xiii. 25. Luke i. 10, 20, 21. v. 16, &c. Exod. iii. 1. l ‖ Mk. Acts ii. 45. v. 1 only. Prov. xxxi. 16. m ‖ only †. (-λος, Mark x. 24.) n ‖. ch. ix. 5 ‖. Luke xvi. 17 only †. 1 Macc. iii. 18. Sir. xxii. 15 only. o ‖. ch. iii. 4 ‖ Mk. xxiii. 24 only. LXX, passim. p here (‖ v. r.) only †. = τρυμαλιᾶς. ‖ Mk. τρήματος, ‖ L. (-πᾶν, Exod. xxi. 6.) q ‖ Mk. (L. v. r.) only †. (-φιδευτής, Exod. xxvii. 6.) r ch. vii. 28 reff. s ch. ii. 10 reff. Jon. iv. 9.

21. for εφη, λεγει (*to conform to ver* 20) B 69. 124 Cypr. for ειναι, γενεσθε(=-αι) ℵ[1](txt ℵ[3a]). rec om τοις (*as in* ‖ *Mark Luke*), with CZℵ rel [Clem$_2$] Orig$_5$ Bas Cyr-jer [Chr]: ins BD coptt. rec ουρανω (*from* ‖ *Mark*), with Zℵ rel latt copt arm Orig$_2$[and int$_2$ Ath Bas] Cypr$_2$: txt BCDΓ lat-*e* *g*$_1$ sah Cyr-jer Chr [Cyr$_1$] Isid Cypr$_1$ Hil Aug.

22. om δε D forj lat-*f* *h*. (D-corr[1] has υ above the line after ο, as if beginning ουν.) om τον λογον LZℵ Chr: ins BCD rel vulg lat-*ff*$_2$ *g*$_{1.2}$ syr copt arm Orig$_1$ Chr-L-(γ?). rec om τουτον, with CDZℵ rel: ins B lat-*a* *b* *c* *ff*$_1$ Syr syr-cu copt-ms sah. χρηματα B Chr(Fd's and Mt's mss exc L).

23. rec δυςκολως bef πλουσιος, with X rel lat-*e* *f*[1] *ff*$_2$ *h* syrr syr-cu arm Orig$_1$ [Damasc] Hil Aug: txt BCDLZℵ 1. 33. 69 latt æth Orig$_1$ [Chrom].

24. aft υμιν ins οτι CLM Z(appy) ℵ syrr syr-cu coptt æth. καμιλον (*itacism? but see notes*) 59. 61. 225-35 evv-x-31-32. τρυμαλιας (*from* ‖ *Mark*) CKMU Orig$_4$ Eus: τρηματος (*from* ‖ *Luke*) Bℵ[1] Orig-mss: txt DZℵ[3a] rel [Clem$_1$] Orig$_2$. * rec διελθεῖν (*as easier word; and see* ‖ *Mark*), with BDGXΓ (SV, e sil) latt syr-cu (appy) Orig$_1$ [Damasc$_1$] Hil [Arnob]: εισελθειν CZℵ rel syrr coptt æth(appy) arm Orig$_3$ Eus Chr Aug. * rec τοῦ θεοῦ (*perhaps from* ‖ *Mark Luke*), with BCDℵ rel syrr coptt æth arm Orig$_3$ [Damasc] Arnob: των ουρανων Z 1. 33. 157. 236 ev-48 latt syr-cu Clem Orig$_1$ Eus Chr Hil Ambr Jer Aug. rec at end of ver ins εισελθειν (*see* ‖ *Mark Luke*), with C rel syr [Damasc$_1$] Hil: aft πλουσιον, BD latt Syr coptt æth Orig$_1$: om LZℵ 1. 33. 61. 124-57. 235 lat-*ff*$_1$ *g*$_1$ syr-cu Orig$_3$ Eus Chr Arnob Aug.

25. om δε ℵ[1](ins ℵ-corr[1·3]). rec aft οι μαθηται ins αυτου, with C[3] rel lat-*ff*$_1$ syr-cu æth [Damasc] Op: BC[1]DKLZΔℵ 33. 69 latt syrr coptt arm Hil Aug. aft εξεπλ. add και εφοβηθησαν D mm lat-*a* *b* *c* *e* *ff*$_2$ *g*$_2$ syr-cu.

righteous, was *no hypocrite,* no Pharisee: he spoke earnestly, and really strove to keep, as he really believed he had kept, all God's commandments. Accordingly Mark adds, that Jesus looking upon him *loved him:* in spite of his error there was a nobleness and openness about him, contrasted with the hypocritical bearing of the Pharisees and Scribes. **21, 22.**] Our Lord takes him on his own shewing. As Mark and Luke add, "*One thing is wanting to thee.*" Supposing thy statement true, this topstone has yet to be laid on the fabric. But then it is to be noticed, that part of that one thing is **δεῦρο ἀκολούθει μοι** (ἄρας τὸν σταυρόν, Mark). Stier remarks, that this was a test of his observance of the *first commandment* of the first table: of breaking which he is by the result convicted. **ἦν γὰρ ἔχ. κτ. π.** is common to Mark, verbatim.

24.] No alteration to κάμιλον is necessary or admissible. That word, as signifying a *rope,* or *cable,* seems to have been invented to escape the fancied difficulty here; see Palm and Rost's or Liddell and Scott's Lex. sub voce, and for the scholia giving the interpretation, Tischendorf's note here. Lightfoot brings instances from the Talmud of similar proverbial expressions regarding an *elephant:* we have a case in ch. xxiii. 24, of a *camel* being

γοντες Τίς ἄρα δύναται σωθῆναι; 26 [t] ἐμβλέψας δὲ ὁ
Ἰησοῦς εἶπεν αὐτοῖς [u] Παρὰ ἀνθρώποις τοῦτο ἀδύνατόν
ἐστιν, [u] παρὰ δὲ θεῷ πάντα δυνατά. 27 τότε [v] ἀποκριθεὶς
ὁ Πέτρος εἶπεν αὐτῷ Ἰδοὺ ἡμεῖς [w] ἀφήκαμεν πάντα καὶ
ἠκολουθήσαμέν σοι· τί ἄρα [x] ἔσται ἡμῖν; 28 ὁ δὲ Ἰησοῦς
εἶπεν αὐτοῖς [y] Ἀμὴν λέγω ὑμῖν ὅτι ὑμεῖς οἱ ἀκολουθή-
σαντές μοι, ἐν τῇ [z] παλιγγενεσίᾳ ὅταν καθίσῃ ὁ υἱὸς τοῦ
ἀνθρώπου [a] ἐπὶ [b] θρόνου [b] δόξης αὐτοῦ, καθίσεσθε καὶ
ὑμεῖς [a] ἐπὶ δώδεκα θρόνους [c] κρίνοντες τὰς δώδεκα φυλὰς ...κρινοντες Z.
τοῦ Ἰσραήλ. 29 καὶ πᾶς ὅστις [w] ἀφῆκεν ἀδελφοὺς ἢ BCDEF
ἀδελφὰς ἢ πατέρα ἢ μητέρα ἢ τέκνα ἢ ἀγροὺς ἢ οἰκίας GHKL MSUV XΓΔℵ
[d] ἕνεκεν τοῦ [d] ὀνόματός μου, [e] πολλαπλασίονα λήμψεται 1. 33. 69

t ch. vi. 26. Mark x. 21 reff.
u ‖. (Luke i. 37.) Rom. ii. 13. Gen. xviii. 14.
v = ch. xi. 25 reff.
w = ch. iv. 11, 20, 22 al. fr. Exod. ix. 21.
x Luke i. 7. Acts vii. 5. Rom. ix. 9.
y ch. v. 18 reff.
z Tit. iii. 5 only †. π. τῆς πατρίδος, Jos. Antt. xi. 3. 9. Philo, passim.
a see Rev. iv. 2 and note.
b ch. xxv. 31. Isa. xxii. 23. see Heb. iv. 16. viii. 1.
c = Luke xxii. 30. 1 Cor. vi. 2, 3. Gen. xlix. 16 al. see Dan. vii. 22.
d Luke xxi. 12 only. see ch. x. 22.
e ‖ L. only †.

26. om *παρα ανθρωποις* (*homœotel*) ℵ^1(ins ℵ-corr^1). *α* of *αδυνατον* is added by D-corr^1. ins *τω* bef *θεω* DM [Damasc$_1$]. *δυνατα* bef *παντα* LZℵ copt. rec adds *εστι* (*from* ‖ *Mark Luke*), with C^{3}DEFGMV^2 latt Op: om BC^{1}Zℵ rel syrr arm Orig Chr [Damasc] Thl Paulin.

27. om *τοτε* C. (*αποκριθεις δε*, omg *τοτε* (*beg of pericope*), evv-H·P-y-z.) *ηκολουθηκαμεν* D^1(txt D^2).

28. for *αυτοις*, *αυτω* D 53 ev-H^1. *καθησεσθε* (*itacism, hardly a var reading*) BD^{2}GLMUXΔℵ 69^1 Orig$_4$(txt$_1$): *καθεσθησεσθε* Z 1. 435 Did. for *υμεις*, *αυτοι* DLZℵ 1. 124 Orig$_2$ Ambr$_2$ Gaud. *δεκα δυο* D (1st time). om *τας* D^1(ins D^2).

29. rec (for *οστις*) *ος* (*see* ‖ *Mark Luke*), with X rel vulg lat-*a b f ff*$_2$ *g*$_1$ Hil: txt BCDE^{1}KLΔℵ 1. 33. 69 lat-*c e ff*$_1$ *g*$_2$ *h* Orig$_2$ Bas Chr Cyr [Damasc$_1$] Thl Iren-int. rec aft *αφηκεν* ins *οικιας η*, omg *η οικιας* below (‖ *Mark Luke*), with BC^{3}D rel lat-*e* syrr syr-cu sah [Bas$_1$ Damasc$_1$] (*οικιαν η* K 33 latt [arm Hil]): txt C^{1}Lℵ-corr^1 1 (forj) syr-jer copt (æth Iren-int) Orig$_2$ [Chr Cyr$_1$].—ℵ^1 omits *η οικ.* altogether. om *η πατερα* D lat-*b ff*$_{1.2}$ syr-cu Hil Paulin spec. rec ins *η γυναικα* bef *η τεκνα* (*from* ‖ *Luke*), with Cℵ rel vulg lat-*c g*$_2$ *h* syrr syr-cu coptt arm [Chr Bas Cyr$_1$ Damasc$_1$] Ambr$_1$ Promiss: om BD 1 lat-*a b e ff*$_{1.2}$ *n* syr-jer Orig(expr: *οὐ συγκατηρίθμηται δὲ τούτοις γυνή*) Iren-int Hil Ambr$_1$ Paulin. *ενεκα* Dℵ [Cyr$_1$]. *του εμου ονοματος* Bℵ 124. rec (for *πολλαπλασιονα*) *εκατονταπλασιονα* (*from* ‖ *Mark*), with CD^{2}ℵ rel copt Clem(appy): *εκατονταπλασιον* D^1, *centuplum* latt Iren-int Hil: txt BL sah syr-jer Orig$_4$(expr$_1$, addg *ἢ ὡς ὁ Μάρκος φησὶν ἑκατονταπλασίονα*) Eus Cyr.

put for any thing very large: and we must remember that the object here was to set forth the greatest human impossibility, and to magnify divine grace, which could accomplish *even that*. **25.**] **τίς**, not *τίς πλούσιος*, which would have been a far shallower and narrower enquiry, but a general question—**what man?** Besides the usual reason given for this question, ‘*since all are striving to be rich*,’ we must remember that the disciples yet looked for a temporal Kingdom, and therefore would naturally be dismayed at hearing that it was so difficult for any rich man to enter it. **26. ἐμβλέψας**] Probably to give force to and impress what was about to be said, especially as it was a saying reaching into the spiritual doctrines of the Gospel, which they could not yet apprehend. **τοῦτο**, salvation in general, and even of those least likely to be saved. **παρά** in both cases, as in E. V., **with**, ‘in the estimation of,’ ‘penes:’ a subjective force of the preposition derived from its local meaning of close juxtaposition, in which sense we have it only once in the N. T., John xix. 25.

27.] The disciples, or rather Peter speaking for them, recur to the *ἕξεις θησ. ἐν οὐρ.* said to the young man, and enquire what *their* reward shall be, who have done all that was required of them. He does not ask respecting *salvation*, but *some pre-eminent reward*, as is manifest by the answer. The ‘all’ which the Apostles had left, was not in every case contemptible. The sons of Zebedee had hired servants (Mark i. 20), and Levi (Matthew?) could make a great feast in his house. But whatever it was, it *was their all*.

28—30.] We may admire the *simple truthfulness* of this answer of our Lord. He

καὶ [f] ζωὴν [f] αἰώνιον [g] κληρονομήσει. 30 πολλοὶ δὲ ἔσονται
πρῶτοι [h] ἔσχατοι, καὶ ἔσχατοι πρῶτοι. XX. 1 ὁμοία
γάρ ἐστιν ἡ βασιλεία τῶν οὐρανῶν [hi] ἀνθρώπῳ [hk] οἰκοδεσ-

f ver. 16.
g ch. v. 5. xxv. 34. Prov. iii. 35.
h ch. xiii. 52.
i ch. xiii. 45. Gen. ix. 20.
k ch. x. 25. xiii. 27 al.†

30. εσχατοι πρωτοι κ. πρωτ. εσχ. L‎א æth-rom. ins οι bef 2nd εσχατοι CM 22. 69 Scr's c p.

Chap. XX. 1. for ομ. γαρ εστ., ειπεν ο ις την παραβολην ταυτην ομνυοθει C^3 and evangelistaria.

does not hide from them their reward: but tells them prophetically, that in the new world, the accomplishment of that regeneration which He came to bring in (see Acts iii. 21: Rev. xxi. 5: Matt. xxvi. 29), when He should sit (καθίσῃ in the *active*) on His throne of glory (ἐπ. θρόνου τ. δ. αὐ., the gen. expressing the simple fact of His session on His throne), then they also should sit (καθίσεσθε in the *middle*) on twelve thrones (ἐπ. δώ. θρόνους, the accus. expressing motion towards, as prescribed for them by another: "shall be promoted to, and take your seats upon . . .") judging (see ref. 1 Cor.) the twelve tribes of Israel (see Rev. xx. 4; xxi. 12, 14:—one throne, Judas's, another took, Acts i. 20). At the same time he informs them, ver. 29, that this reward should *not* in its most blessed particulars be *theirs alone*, but that of *every one who should deny himself for Him* (see 2 Tim. iv. 8): and (ver. 30) cautions them, referring perhaps especially to Judas, but with a view to all, as appears by the following parable, that *many first should be last*, and *last first*. On ver. 29, Stier remarks that the family relations are mentioned by St. Matthew in the order in which *they would be left*. On the other points requiring notice, see note on Mark x. 29, 30. Meyer's rendering of ver. 30, joining πρῶτοι with ἔσονται, and thus making ἔσχατοι the subject and πρῶτοι the predicate of the first clause and vice versâ in the second, is not so good as the ordinary one: for whereas the πρῶτοι in the first clause, if it belonged to πολλοί, would naturally lose its article, ἔσχατοι, if it belonged to πολλοί, being divided from it by the predicate πρῶτοι, would take its article as the subject; πολλοὶ δὲ ἔσονται πρῶτοι οἱ ἔσχατοι: and the same of πρῶτοι in the second clause: καὶ ἔσχατοι οἱ πρῶτοι, ch. xx. 16, by which Meyer defends his rendering, does not necessitate it, containing the same propositions stated in different order.

Chap. XX. 1—16.] Parable of the labourers in the vineyard. *Peculiar to Matthew.* In interpreting this difficult parable, we must first carefully observe its occasion and connexion. It is bound by the γάρ to the conclusion of chap. xix., and arose out of the question of Peter in ver. 27, τί ἄρα ἔσται ἡμῖν; (1) Its 'punctum saliens' is, that the Kingdom of God is of *grace*, not of debt; that *they who were called first, and have laboured longest, have no more claim upon God than those who were called last:* but that *to all, His covenant promise shall be fulfilled in its integrity.* (2) Its *primary application* is to the *Apostles*, who had asked the question. They were not to be of such a spirit, as to imagine, with the murmurers in ver. 11, that they should have something supereminent (because they were called first, and had laboured longest) above those who *in their own time* were to be afterward called (see 1 Cor. xv. 8—11). (3) Its *secondary applications* are to all those to whom such a comparison, of *first and last called*, will apply:—*nationally*, to the Jews, who were first called, and with a *definite covenant*, and the Heathens who came in afterwards, and on a covenant, though *really made* (see Jer. xxxi. 33: Zech. viii. 8: Heb. viii. 10), yet *not so open and prominent;*—*individually*, to those whose call has been in early life, and who have spent their days in God's active service, and those who have been summoned later; and to various other classes and persons between whom comparison, not only of *time*, but of advantages, talents, or any other distinguishing characteristic, can be made: that none of the first of these can boast themselves over the others, nor look for higher place and greater reward, inasmuch as there is but one "gift" of God according to the covenant of grace. And the "first" of these are to see that they do not by pride and self-righteousness become the "last," or worse—be rejected, as nationally were the Jews; for among the many that are called, there are few chosen —many who will fail of the reward in the end. (4) In subordination to this leading idea and warning of the parable must the circumstances brought before us be in-

l = ch. vii. 24, 26 al. fr.
m ch. xiii. 29 reff. Neh. vii. 3. 1 Macc. iv. 6.
n ver. 7 only. Judg. xviii. 4 al.
o ch. x. 10 reff.

πότῃ, [l] ὅςτις ἐξῆλθεν [m] ἅμα πρωῒ [n] μισθώσασθαι [o] ἐργάτας
εἰς τὸν [p] ἀμπελῶνα αὐτοῦ. 2 [q] συμφωνήσας δὲ μετὰ τῶν
[o] ἐργατῶν [r] ἐκ [s] δηναρίου [t] τὴν ἡμέραν ἀπέστειλεν αὐτοὺς
εἰς τὸν [p] ἀμπελῶνα αὐτοῦ. 3 καὶ ἐξελθὼν [u] περὶ τρίτην

Π xx. 3.. BCDEF GHKL MSUV ΧΓΔΠℵ 1. 33. 69

p here, &c. ch. xxi. 28, &c. ||. Luke xiii. 6. 1 Cor. ix. 7 only. Isa. v. 1, &c. q ch. xviii. 19 reff.
r ch. xxvii. 7. Acts i. 18. 1 Cor. vii. 5. xiii. 9. 2 Cor. viii. 13. s ch. xviii. 28. xxii. 19 || al. Gospp. only, exc. Rev. vi. 6 bis †. t John iii. 34. u here (vv. 3, 5, [6,] 9) ch. xxvii. 46. Acts x. 3, 9 only.

2. for συμφ. δε, και συμφ. Δ[1](but corrd) rel lat-*e* syr-cu Chr: om δε F[1]: txt BCDLSℵ 1. 33. 69 latt syrr coptt Cyr.

3. **διεξελθων** D. rec aft περι ins την, with V(e sil) Δ: om B C(prob) Dℵ rel Orig$_2$ Cyr Thl. (C has a space for 3 letters, occasioned appy by τρι having been twice

terpreted. The *day* and its *hours* are not any fixed time, such as the duration of the world, or our Lord's life on earth, or the life of man, exclusively: but *the natural period of earthly work* as applied to the various meanings of which the parable is capable. The *various times of hiring* are not to be pressed as each having an exclusive meaning in each interpretation: they serve to spread the calling over the various periods, and to shew that it is again and again made. They are the *quarters* of the natural day, when the aliquot parts of the day's wages could be earned, and therefore labourers would be waiting. The *last* of these is inserted for a special purpose, and belongs more expressly to the instruction of the parable. (5) The **μισθος** bears an important part in the interpretation. I cannot with Stier (whose comment on this parable I think much inferior to his usual remarks) suppose it to mean "the promise of this life" attached to godliness. His anxiety to escape from the danger of *eternal life being matter of wages*, has here misled him. But there is no such danger in the interpretation of the parable which I believe to be the true one. The μισθός is the *promise of the covenant*, uniformly represented by our Lord and His Apostles as a *'reward,'* Matt. v. 12: Luke vi. 35; xiv. 14: John iv. 36: 1 Cor. iii. 14: 2 John 8: Heb. x. 35; xi. 6 al., *reckoned indeed of free grace;* but still, forensically considered, answering to, and represented by, 'wages,' as claimed under God's covenant with man in Christ. (The freeness and sovereignty of God's gift of grace is pointedly set before us in ver. 14, **θέλω δὲ** τοὐ. τ. ἐσχ. δοῦναι ....) This μισθός I believe then to be *eternal life*, or, in other words, GOD HIMSELF (John xvii. 3). And this, rightly understood, will keep us from the error of supposing, that the parable involves a declaration that all who are saved will be in an absolute equality. This gift is, and will be, to each man, as he is prepared to receive it. To the envious and murmurers, it will be as the fruit that turned to ashes in the mouth; by their own unchristian spirit they will "lose the things that they have wrought" (2 John 8), and their reward will be null: in other words, they will, as the spiritual verity necessitates, *not enter into that life to which they were called.* God's covenant is fulfilled to them —they have received their denarius—but, from the essential nature of the μισθός, are disqualified from enjoying its use: for as Gregory the Great remarks (Hom. 19 in Evv., p. 1512) 'cœlorum regnum nullus murmurans accipit: nullus qui accipit murmurare poterit.' To those who have known and loved God, it will be, to each as he has advanced in the spiritual life, joy unspeakable and full of glory. (In the 2nd edn. of the Reden Jesu (p. 299, note), Stier has even more emphatically declared himself in favour of his former view, and that with reference to my note; wenn auch Alford mir widerspricht und meine Exegese hier "much inferior to his usual remarks" nennt, so muß ich erwarten, ob vielleicht die zweite Auflage mit ihren genaueren Beziehungen ihn besser überzeugt. But after carefully weighing the whole, I am quite unable to accede to his view; indeed I feel more repugnance to it than ever. The "promise of the life that now is" seems to me wholly beneath the dignity of the parable, and in his explanation he appears painfully to feel it so. The text above quoted, 2 John 8, seems to me to furnish the key to the parable, and to have been written with reference to it: and there no one surely could interpret μισθός otherwise than of the μισθὸς ἐν τοῖς οὐρανοῖς of our ch. v.) 1. **ἅμα πρωΐ**] see Jer. xxxv. 14, and other places. **ἐργάτας**] in the primary meanings of the parable, 'apostles, prophets, ministers:' distinct from the *vines* in the vineyard. But inasmuch as every workman is himself subject to the treatment of the husbandman (see John xv. 1, 2), and every man in the Kingdom of God is in some sense or other a worker on the rest, the distinction is not to be pressed—the parable ranges over both comparisons. **ἀμπελῶνα**]

[u] ὥραν· εἶδεν ἄλλους ἑστῶτας ἐν τῇ ἀγορᾷ [v] ἀργούς,
4 καὶ ἐκείνοις εἶπεν Ὑπάγετε καὶ ὑμεῖς εἰς τὸν ἀμπελῶνα,
καὶ ὃ ἐὰν ᾖ [w] δίκαιον δώσω ὑμῖν. οἱ δὲ ἀπῆλθον. 5 πάλιν δὲ ἐξελθὼν [u] περὶ ἕκτην καὶ ἐνάτην [u] ὥραν ἐποίησεν
[x] ὡςαύτως. 6 [u] περὶ δὲ τὴν ἑνδεκάτην ἐξελθὼν εὗρεν
N αυτοις τι... ἄλλους ἑστῶτας, καὶ λέγει αὐτοῖς Τί ὧδε ἑστήκατε [y] ὅλην
τὴν [y] ἡμέραν [v] ἀργοί; 7 λέγουσιν αὐτῷ Ὅτι οὐδεὶς ἡμᾶς
[z] ἐμισθώσατο. λέγει αὐτοῖς Ὑπάγετε καὶ ὑμεῖς εἰς τὸν
Z λωνα μου... ἀμπελῶνα. 8 [a] ὀψίας δὲ [a] γενομένης λέγει ὁ [b] κύριος τοῦ
ἀμπελῶνος τῷ [c] ἐπιτρόπῳ αὐτοῦ Κάλεσον τοὺς [d] ἐργάτας

BCDEF GHKL MNSU VXZΓΔ ΠＮ 1. 33. 69

v ch. xii. 36. 1 Tim. v. 13 bis. Tit. i. 12. James ii. 20. 2 Pet. i. 8 only. Wisd. xv. 15. (-γεῖν, 2 Pet. ii. 3.)
w Phil. i. 7. Col. iv. 1. 2 Pet. i. 13. Prov. xxix. 26.
x ch. xxi. 30, 36. Mark xii. 21 al. Ezek. xlii. 5.
y Rom. viii. 36 (from Ps. xliii. 22). x. 21 (from Isa. lxv. 2) only. Ps. xxiv. 5.
z ver. 1.
a ch. viii. 16 reff.
b = ch. ix. 38 reff. Exod. xxi. 28, 3. Gal. iv. 2 only †. 2 Macc. xi. 1. xiii. 2. xiv. 2 only.
c Luke viii.
d ver. 1.

written.) ωρ. bef τρ. DΔ latt(not *e*). for ειδεν, ευρεν D 245 lat-*a b c ff*$_2$ *h* Juv: txt Bא rel vulg lat-*e f ff*$_1$ *g*$_{1.2}$ Orig. (ιδεν CKVX.)

4. rec (for και εκ.) κακ., with CDKLSΠ Chr Cyr: txt Bא rel. aft αμπελωνα ins μου CΠא 33. 69 Scr's w vulg-ed(not am forj) lat-*a f ff*$_{1.2}$ *h* sah æth arm Chr-K-L [Cyr$_1$] Greg Op. for εαν, αν DL 1 Orig$_1$ Chr-2-6-9-η-ρ [Cyr$_1$].

5. rec om δε, with B(see table) rel mm lat-*a b c e ff*$_1$ *h n* copt: ins CDLא 33 vulg lat-*ff*$_2$ *g*$_{1.2}$ *l* Syr syr-with-ast sah æth arm Cyr Op. ωραν bef εκτ. και εν. D[ενν.] lat-*f* Arnob Op.

6. rec aft ενδεκατην ins ωραν, with C rel lat-*c e f* syrr syr-cu coptt arm Hil: om BDLא latt sah[-mnt] æth Orig$_2$ Cyr Op. for εξελθων, εξηλθεν א[1](corrd א[1] or -corr[1]): εξηλθεν και D latt. rec aft εστωτας ins αργους, with C[1] rel lat-*f h* syrr arm: om BC[2]DLא 33 latt syr-cu(sic) coptt æth Orig$_2$ Cyr$_1$ Arnob.

7. om ημας א[1](ins א-corr[1]). aft αμπελωνα ins μου C[3]DZΠ vulg-ed(with forj) lat-*a b* &c sah æth Chr Cyr$_2$ Op: om BC[1]Lא rel am lat-*c ff*$_1$ syrr syr-cu copt arm Orig Chr-G-L-H-2-γ Arnob. rec at end adds και ο εαν η δικαιον ληψεσθε (*from ver* 4), with CN rel lat-*f h* syrr copt-ed arm [Chr]: simly with δωσω υμιν for ληψ. tol syr-cu syr-jer æth Op: om BDLZא 1 latt copt-mss sah Orig$_2$ Cyr$_2$ Hil Arnob Jer Juv.

not the Jewish church *only*, as Greswell, Parables, iv. 355 ff., maintains. The Jewish Church was God's vineyard especially and typically; *His Church in all ages* is His *true* vineyard, see John xv. 1. Our language admits of the idiom **εἰς τὸν ἀμ. αὐ.** being exactly rendered—**into his vineyard**, E. V. **2.**] **ἐκ** seems to point, as commonly in other references, at the source or foundation of the *συμφωνία*: see reff. This view is more probable than that which supposes *μισθώσασθαι* understood. Meyer remarks that the accus. **τὴν ἡμέραν** must not be regarded as one of time, which would not suit with *συμφων.* to which it belongs, but as one of secondary reference. The *denarius a day* was the pay of a Roman soldier in Tiberius' time, a few years before this parable was uttered (see Tacitus, Annal. i. 17). Polybius, ii. 15. 6 (but in illustrating the exceeding fertility and cheapness of the country), mentions that the charge for a day's entertainment in the inns in Cisalpine Gaul was half an as, $= \frac{1}{20}$th of the denarius. This we may therefore regard as liberal pay for the day's work.

3, 4.] The *third hour*, = at the equinox, our 9 a.m., and in summer 8, was the πλήθουσα ἀγορά, or ἀγορᾶς πληθώρα—when the market was fullest. "The market-place of the world is contrasted with the vineyard of the Kingdom of God: the greatest man of business in worldly things is a mere idle gazer, if he has not yet entered on the true work which alone is worth any thing or gains any reward." Stier, ii. p. 307. No positive stipulation is made with these second, but they are to depend on the justice of the householder. They might expect $\frac{3}{4}$ths of a denarius. From the same dialogue being implied at the sixth and ninth hour (*ἐποίησεν ὡσαύτως*) the ὃ ἐὰν ᾖ δίκαιον is probably in each case the corresponding part of the denarius, at least *in their expectation*; so that *it cannot be said that no covenant was made.* **8.**] By the Mosaic law (Deut. xxiv. 15) the wages of an hired servant were to be paid him *before night*. This was at the twelfth hour, or sunset: see ver. 12. I do not think the **ἐπίτροπος** must be pressed as having a spiritual meaning. If it has, it represents

καὶ ἀπόδος [αὐτοῖς] τὸν [e] μισθὸν [f] ἀρξάμενος [fg] ἀπὸ τῶν
ἐσχάτων [g] ἕως τῶν πρώτων. 9 καὶ ἐλθόντες οἱ [u] περὶ τὴν
ἑνδεκάτην [u] ὥραν ἔλαβον [h] ἀνὰ [s] δηνάριον. 10 καὶ ἐλθόντες οἱ πρῶτοι [i] ἐνόμισαν ὅτι πλεῖον λήμψονται· καὶ
ἔλαβον [[k] τὸ] [h] ἀνὰ δηνάριον καὶ αὐτοί. 11 λαβόντες δὲ
[l] ἐγόγγυζον κατὰ τοῦ [m] οἰκοδεσπότου 12 λέγοντες [ὅτι]
οὗτοι οἱ ἔσχατοι μίαν ὥραν [n] ἐποίησαν, καὶ [o] ἴσους ἡμῖν
αὐτοὺς ἐποίησας τοῖς [p] βαστάσασιν τὸ [q] βάρος τῆς ἡμέρας
καὶ τὸν [r] καύσωνα. 13 ὁ δὲ ἀποκριθεὶς εἶπεν ἑνὶ αὐτῶν
[s] Ἑταῖρε, οὐκ ἀδικῶ σε· οὐχὶ [t] δηναρίου [t] συνεφώνησάς
μοι; 14 ἆρον τὸ σὸν καὶ ὕπαγε· θέλω δὲ τούτῳ τῷ ἐσ-
χάτῳ δοῦναι ὡς καὶ σοί. 15 [ἢ] οὐκ ἔξεστίν μοι ὃ θέλω
ποιῆσαι ἐν τοῖς ἐμοῖς; ἢ ὁ [u] ὀφθαλμός σου [u] πονηρός ἐστιν,

Frag. Sin. πρωτων..

...εμοις Frag. Sin. BCDEF GHKL MNSU VXZΓΔ Πℵ 1. 33. 69

e = Luke x. 7. Acts i. 18 al. esp. 2 John 8, and ch. v. 12. vi. 1, &c.
f Luke xxiii. 5. xxiv. 27, 47 [John viii. 9]. Acts i. 22. viii. 35. x. 37. 1 Pet. iv. 17. Gen. xliv. 12.
g ch. i. 17 al. Gen. xix. 11.
h Luke ix. [3,] 14 (‘| Mk. v. r.). x. 1. John ii. 6. Rev. iv. 8. xxi. 21 only.
i ch. x. 34 reff.
k Mark ix. 23 reff.
l Luke v. 30. John vi. 41, 43, 61. vii. 32. 1 Cor. x. 10 bis, only. Exod. xvi. 7 A [διαγογγ. B]. Judg. i. 14.
m ch. x. 25 al.†
n = Rev. xiii. 5. Ruth ii. 19. 4 Kings xii. 11; or Acts xv. 33. 2 Cor. xi. 25. James iv. 13. Prov. xiii. 23.
o Mark xiv. 56, 59. Luke vi. 34. John v. 18. Acts xi. 17. Phil. ii. 6. Rev. xxi. 16 only. Ezek. xl. 5.
p ch. viii. 17 reff. Gal. vi. 2.
q Acts xv. 28. 2 Cor. iv. 17. Gal. vi. 2. 1 Thess. ii. 6. Rev. ii. 24 only. 2 Macc. ix. 10. Sir. xiii. 2.
r Luke xii. 55. James i. 11 only. Gen. xxxi. 40 A [B def.]. Isa. xlix. 10.
s ch. xi. 17 reff.
t ver. 2 reff.
u ch. vi. 23. Mark vii. 22. Sir. xiv. 8, 10. xxxiv. (xxxi.) 13. see Deut. xv. 9.

8. om αυτοις CLZℵ Orig$_3$: ins BDN rel vss [Chr].
9. for και ελθ., ελθ. δε B syr-cu sah : ελθ. ουν D 33. 69. 124. 346 latt : txt CZℵ rel syrr copt æth.
10. rec (for και ελθ.) ελθ. δε, with Zℵ rel syr copt : ελθ. δε και N Scr's d vulg lat-*a c* &c arm : txt BCD 33. 69 lat-*e* Syr syr-cu æth Chr. rec πλειονα (*corrn to plur, to indicate* 'most in number'), with C³LXℵ rel : πλειω D : txt BC¹NZ 1. 69 latt Orig$_1$ (πλεον Orig$_1$). for και ελαβον, ελαβον δε D latt. rec και αυτοι bef [το] α. δην. (*transposition for emphasis*), with CDN rel latt syr-cu syr coptt : txt BLZℵ 33 Syr æth arm. rec om το (*perhaps as superfluous*, or *not understood*), with BD rel [Chr] : ins CLNZℵ 33.
11. εγογγυσαν D 243 lat-*a b c* &c Syr syr-cu.
12. om οτι (*perhaps as superfluous, or from similarity to* ουτοι) BC²Dℵ 1 latt syrr syr-cu æth [Orig$_1$] Chr Arnob : ins C¹(appy) NZ rel coptt arm Orig$_1$. (33 def.) om οι C¹. (so H¹ but corrd by origl scribe.) αυτους bef ημιν (*perhaps to bring* ισους αυτους *together*) DLZℵ 69 latt Syr syr-cu coptt æth Jer : txt BCN rel lat-*c* (syr) arm Orig$_1$ [Chr].
13. αυτων ενι ειπεν B : ενι αυτων ειπεν Dℵ 124 latt(*a* def) arm Orig$_1$ [Chr-2]. (for ενι, μοναδι Δ.) συνεφωνησα σοι LZ 33 coptt æth Orig$_1$ [Nyss$_1$] Antch.
14. for θ. δε, θ. εγω B æth : θ. δε και E latt Orig$_1$: ει θελω syr-cu arm. τω εσχατω bef τουτω D Chr-γ.
15. om 1st η (*see below*) BDLZ syr-cu arm : ins CNℵ rel latt syrr coptt æth [Chr]. for εξεστιν, εστιν D¹-gr(txt Dʳ). rec ποιησαι bef ο θελω (*to avoid ambiguity*), with CN rel lat-*b ff$_2$ g$_2$* (syr-cu) syr coptt (arm) : txt BDLZℵ 33. 69 vulg lat-*a c e ff$_1$ g$_1$ h l* Syr æth Chr. Steph (for 2nd η) ει, with B²HS 1. 69 Chr Did : txt B¹CDNZℵ rel [Nyss$_1$]. (33 def.) (*I think with De W, against Meyer and Tischdf* (ed 7 [ed 8 has η]), *that* η *both times is genuine, and its omn the first time, and alteration to* ει *the second, have been on account of its apparent irrelevancy.*)

Christ (see Heb. iii. 6, and ch. xi. 27). **ἀρξάμενος** is not merely expletive, but definite, as in Luke xxiii. 5. **9.**] After **ὥραν** supply ἀπεσταλμένοι εἰς τὸν ἀμπελῶνα. **10.**] The precedent cited by Greswell for this method of payment, from Josephus, Antt. xx. 9. 7, does not apply. It is there said that in the rebuilding of the temple, εἰ μίαν τις ὥραν τῆς ἡμέρας ἐργάσαιτο, τὸν μισθὸν ὑπὲρ ταύτης εὐθέως ἐλάμβανεν : the ταύτης referring to the μίαν ὥραν, not to τῆς ἡμ., and the fact related being that if any one worked only one hour in the day, he was immediately paid *for that hour*. Indeed the manifest effect of such a *rule* as Greswell supposes, would have been to stop the building, not to hasten it, for if a man could get his day's pay for an hour's work, why work more? **12.**] Some take **ἐποίησαν**, as in Acts xv. 33, to mean "*have tarried*,"—but the sense in the former reff. seems the best. **13, 14.**] **ἑταῖρε**, at first sight a friendly word

ὅτι ἐγὼ ἀγαθός εἰμι; 16 οὕτως ἔσονται οἱ ἔσχατοι πρῶτοι,
καὶ οἱ πρῶτοι ἔσχατοι[· πολλοὶ γάρ εἰσιν [vw] κλητοί, ὀλίγοι
δὲ [vx] ἐκλεκτοί].
17 Καὶ [y] ἀναβαίνων ὁ Ἰησοῦς εἰς Ἱεροσόλυμα [z] παρέλαβεν τοὺς δώδεκα μαθητὰς [a] κατ' [a] ἰδίαν καὶ [b] ἐν τῇ ὁδῷ
εἶπεν αὐτοῖς 18 [c] Ἰδοὺ [y] ἀναβαίνομεν εἰς Ἱεροσόλυμα, καὶ
...ανθρω-που F. ὁ υἱὸς τοῦ ἀνθρώπου παραδοθήσεται τοῖς ἀρχιερεῦσιν καὶ
γραμματεῦσιν, καὶ [d] κατακρινοῦσιν αὐτὸν θανάτῳ, 19 καὶ
παραδώσουσιν αὐτὸν τοῖς ἔθνεσιν εἰς τὸ [e] ἐμπαῖξαι καὶ
[f] μαστιγῶσαι καὶ [g] σταυρῶσαι, καὶ τῇ τρίτῃ ἡμέρᾳ [h] ἐγερθήσεται. 20 Τότε προσῆλθεν αὐτῷ ἡ μήτηρ τῶν υἱῶν

v ch. xxii. 14. Rev. xvii. 14.
w as above (v). Rom. i. 1, 6, 7. viii. 28. 1 Cor. i. [1,] 2, 24. Jude 1 only. 2 Kings xv. 9.
x as above (v). ch. xxiv. 22, &c. || Mk. Luke xviii. 7. Rom. viii. 33. Prov. xvii. 3. Isa. xxviii. 16.
y ||. Luke ii. 42. xix. 32. John ii. 13. Acts xi. 2 al. Ezra ii. 1.
z ch. xvii. 1 al. Num. xxii. 41.
a ch. xiv. 13 reff.
b ch. v. 25 reff. c ch. x. 16. xi. 10, from Mal. iii. 1. d ch. xii. 41, 42 || L. xxvii. 3 al. Esth. ii. 1. Wisd. iv. 16. Sus. 41 & 48 Theod., 53 only. dat., || Mk. 2 Pet. ii. 6. e ch. ii. 16. xxvii. 29, 31, 41 al. Mt. Mk. L. Exod. x. 2. Ps. ciii. 26. f ch. x. 17 reff. Jer. v. 3. g ch. xxiii. 34. xxvi. 2. xxvii. 22, &c. ||. Acts ii. 36 al. Esth. vii. 9 only. h = ch. xvii. 9 reff.

16. om πολλ. to εκλεκτοι BLZℵ coptt æth-mss: ins CDN rel latt(*a* def) syrr syr-cu æth-ed arm Orig Chr (Barnab Clem hom-Cl Iren-int). (*The words were prob omitted as appy inappropriate here, or even from homœotel: it is hardly possible, as Tischdf in* 1849, *that they should have been* inserted from ch xxii. 14, *as they are there in a wholly different connexion.* [Tischdf still omits the clause in ed 8.])

17. μελλων δε αναβαινειν (||*Mark Luke*) B 1 Syr (copt) sah Orig$_2$(txt$_1$). [om ὁ B.] om μαθητας (||*Mark Luke*) DLZℵ 1 syr-cu copt æth-rom arm Orig$_4$: ins BCN rel latt syrr sah æth-pl [Chr].—add αυτου Γ ev-y lat-*a c e g*$_1$ Syr. rec εν τη οδω bef και, with CDN rel lat-*a* (*c*) *e f h* syrr syr-cu æth Orig$_1$ [Chr]: om εν τ. οδ. vulg lat-*b ff*$_{1.2}$ *g*$_{1.2}$ *l* Hil: txt BLZℵ 1. 33. 69 ev-z coptt arm Orig$_2$.

18. om θανατω B æth: εις θανατον ℵ.

19. om last και ℵ[1](ins ℵ[1] or -corr[1]). rec (for εγερθησεται) αναστησεται (*from* || *Mark Luke*), with BC[2]D rel Orig$_1$ [Bas-sel$_1$]: txt C[1]LNZℵ Orig$_1$ Chr$_1$ [Cyr$_1$].

merely, assumes a more solemn aspect when we recollect that it is used in ch. xxii. 12 to the guest who had not the wedding garment; and in ch. xxvi. 50 by our Lord to Judas. **ὕπαγε** hardly denotes (as Stier in his 1st edn.) expulsion and separation from the householder and his employment: it is here only a word of course, commanding him to do what a paid labourer naturally should do.

15. ὀφθ. πον.] here **envious**: so רַע is used Prov. xxviii. 22. **16.**] The last were first, as *equal to the first;* first, *in order of payment;* first, *as superior to the first* (no others being brought into comparison), in that their reward was *more* in proportion to their work, and *not marred* by a murmuring spirit. The first were last in these same respects.

The last words of the verse belong not so much to the parable, as to the first clause, and are placed to account for its being as there described; for, while multitudes are called into the vineyard, many, by murmuring and otherwise disgracing their calling, will nullify it, and so, although first by profession and standing, will not be of the number of the elect: although called, will not be chosen. In ch. xxiii. 14 the reference is different.

17—19.] Mark x. 32—34. Luke xviii. 31—34. Fuller declaration of His sufferings and death—revealing His *being delivered to the Gentiles*—and (but in Matthew only) *His crucifixion.* See the note on the more detailed account in Mark.

20—28.] Ambitious request of the mother of the sons of Zebedee; our Lord's reply. Mark x. 35—45. Not related by Luke. This request seems to have arisen from the promise made to the twelve in ch. xix. 28. In Mark's account, the *two brethren themselves* make the request. But the *narration* in the text is the more detailed and exact; and the two immediately coincide, by our Lord *addressing His answer* to the two Apostles (ver. 22). The difference is no greater than is perpetually to be found in narrations of the same fact, persons being often related to have done *per se* what, accurately speaking, they did *per alterum.* The mother's name was *Salome;*—she had followed our Lord from Galilee,—and afterwards witnessed the crucifixion, see Mark xv. 40. Probably the two brethren had directed this request *through*

Ζεβεδαίου μετὰ τῶν υἱῶν αὐτῆς [i] προςκυνοῦσα καὶ
[k] αἰτοῦσά τι * ἀπ' αὐτοῦ· 21 ὁ δὲ εἶπεν αὐτῇ Τί θέλεις;
λέγει αὐτῷ [l] Εἰπὲ ἵνα καθίσωσιν οὗτοι οἱ δύο υἱοί μου
[m] εἷς [n] ἐκ [n] δεξιῶν σου καὶ [m] εἷς [o] ἐξ [op] εὐωνύμων σου ἐν τῇ
βασιλείᾳ σου. 22 ἀποκριθεὶς δὲ ὁ Ἰησοῦς εἶπεν Οὐκ
οἴδατε τί αἰτεῖσθε. δύνασθε πιεῖν τὸ [q] ποτήριον ὃ ἐγὼ
μέλλω πίνειν; λέγουσιν αὐτῷ Δυνάμεθα. 23 λέγει αὐτοῖς
Τὸ μὲν [q] ποτήριόν μου πίεσθε, τὸ δὲ καθίσαι [n] ἐκ δεξιῶν

...σου απο. N. BCDEG HKLM SUVXZ ΓΔΠℵ 1. 33. 69

i ch. ix. 18. xv. 25 al. Gen. xxxiii. 6, 7.
k w. ἀπό, Luke xii. 20 only. w. παρά, John iv. 9. Acts iii. 2. ix. 2. James i. 5. 1 John v. 15 only. Isa. vii. 11 al.
l w. ἵνα, ch. iv. 3. Mark iii. 9. Luke x. 40. = Exod. xxxv. 1.
m ch. xvii. 4. Lev. xii. 8.
n ch. xxii. 44 || (also Acts ii. 34. Heb. i. 13, from Ps. cix. 1). xxvi. 64 al. fr.
o always in N. T. w. ἐκ δεξ. (|| v. r.). ch. xxv. 33, &c. xxvii. 38 || Mk. (L. v. r.). Exod. xiv. 22, 29.
p as above (o). Acts xxi. 3. Rev. x. 2 (w. δεξ.) only.
q = ||. ch. xxvi. 39 reff.

20. * rec παρ' (*more usual expression. See reff*), with CNZℵ rel [Bas-sel$_1$ Damasc$_1$]: απ' BD.

21. η δε λεγει αυτω MN lat-*b n*: η δε ειπεν B lat-*e* sah [Damasc$_1$] Op$_1$: txt CDNZℵ rel. om ουτοι (*as superfluous*) C 56-8 lat-*a e n* coptt Bas[-sel$_3$] Isid. (Z def.) om 1st σου (*see* ||) Bℵ [Damasc$_1$-ms]. rec om 2nd σου, with D (1. 33, e sil) vulg lat-*b c e ff*$_{1.2}$ arm spec: ins BCNZℵ rel harl(with tol) lat-*a f g*$_{1.2}$ *h l n* syrr syr-cu coptt æth Bas-sel Isid [Damasc] Thl Op.

22. αιτειτε D[1](corrd D[1] or -corr[1]). το ποτηριον bef πιειν D[Γ] æth. for πινειν, πιειν B Scr's p s ev-z [Bas-sel$_1$]: πίειν (i. e. appy πινειν) G. rec aft πινειν adds και το βαπτισμα ο εγω βαπτιζομαι βαπτισθηναι (*from* || *Mark*), with C rel lat-*f h* syrr arm Chr [Bas-sel$_1$] Thl Op$_1$ (but for και, η C[E]FGHKM[U]VX[ΓΔΠ lat-*f h* syrr arm]): om BDLZℵ 1 latt syr-cu copt æth Orig$_{expr}$ Epiph$_2$ [Damasc$_1$-ms] Hil Ambr Jer Juv Op$_1$. om αυτω D am syr-cu æth.

23. rec ins και bef λεγει, with C rel syr copt æth Op$_1$: om BD Z(appy) ℵ 1 latt Syr syr-cu sah arm [Damasc$_1$] Ambr. aft αυτοις ins ο ιησους DΔ 69 lat-*a b c e ff*$_{1.2}$ *g*$_2$ *h* syr-cu copt arm Ambr spec. rec aft πιεσθε adds κ. το βαπτισμα ο εγω βαπτιζομαι βαπτισθησεσθε (*from* || *Mark*), with C rel lat-*f h* syrr arm Chr [Bas-sel$_1$] Thl Op:

their mother, because they remembered the rebuke which had followed their former contention about precedence.

21.] The *places close to the throne* were those of *honour*, as in Josephus, speaking of Saul (Antt. vi. 11. 9), τοῦ μὲν παιδὸς Ἰωνάθου ἐκ δεξιῶν, Ἀβενήρου δὲ τοῦ ἀρχιστρατήγου ἐκ τῶν ἑτέρων . . . In the Rabbinical work Midrasch Tehillim, cited by Wetstein,—God, it is said, will seat the King Messiah at His right hand, and Abraham at his left. *One of these brethren*, John, the beloved disciple, had his usual place close to the Lord, John xiii. 23: *the other* was among the chosen Three (this request hardly can imply in their minds any idea of the rejection of Peter from his peculiar post of honour by the rebuke in ch. xvi. 23, for since then had happened the occurrences in ch. xvii. 1—8, and especially ib. vv. 24—27). *Both* were called Boanerges, or the sons of thunder, Mark iii. 17. They thought the kingdom of God was *immediately to appear*, Luke xix. 11.

22.] One at least of these brethren saw *the Lord on His Cross—on His right and left hand the crucified thieves.* Bitter indeed must the remembrance of this ambitious prayer have been at that moment! Luther remarks, 'The flesh ever seeks to be glorified, before it is crucified: exalted, before it is abased.' The '*cup*' is a frequent Scripture image for joy or sorrow: see Ps. xxiii. 5; cxvi. 13: Isa. li. 22: Matt. xxvi. 42. *It* here seems to signify more the *inner* and spiritual bitterness, resembling the agony of the Lord Himself,—and the *baptism*, which is an important addition in Mark, more the *outer* accession of persecution and trial,—through which we must pass to the Kingdom of God. On the latter image see Ps. xlii. 7; lxix. 2; cxxiv. 4. Stier rightly observes that this answer of our Lord contains in it *the kernel of the doctrine of the Sacraments* in the Christian Church: see Rom. vi. 1—7: 1 Cor. xii. 13, and note on Luke xii. 50. Some explain their answer as if they understood the Lord to speak of *drinking out of the royal cup*, and *washing in the royal ewer*: but the words **δύνασθε** πιεῖν, and **δυνάμεθα**, indicating a *difficulty*, preclude this.

23.] The *one* of these brethren was the *first of the Apostles to drink the cup of suffering, and be baptized with the baptism of blood*, Acts xii. 1, 2; the *other had the longest experience among them of a life of trouble and persecution.*

μου καὶ [o] ἐξ [p] εὐωνύμων, οὐκ ἔστιν ἐμὸν τοῦτο δοῦναι [r] ἀλλ'
οἷς [s] ἡτοίμασται ὑπὸ τοῦ πατρός μου. 24 * ἀκούσαντες δὲ
οἱ δέκα [t] ἠγανάκτησαν [u] περὶ τῶν δύο ἀδελφῶν. 25 ὁ δὲ
Ἰησοῦς προσκαλεσάμενος αὐτοὺς εἶπεν Οἴδατε ὅτι οἱ
ἄρχοντες τῶν ἐθνῶν [v] κατακυριεύουσιν αὐτῶν, καὶ οἱ
μεγάλοι [w] κατεξουσιάζουσιν αὐτῶν. 26 [x] οὐχ οὕτως ἔσται
ἐν ὑμῖν· ἀλλ' ὃς ἐὰν θέλῃ * ὑμῶν [y] μέγας γενέσθαι, ἔσται
ὑμῶν [z] διάκονος. 27 καὶ ὃς ἂν θέλῃ ἐν ὑμῖν εἶναι πρῶτος,
ἔστω ὑμῶν δοῦλος· 28 ὥςπερ ὁ υἱὸς τοῦ ἀνθρώπου οὐκ
ἦλθεν [a] διακονηθῆναι, ἀλλὰ [a] διακονῆσαι καὶ [b] δοῦναι τὴν
[c] ψυχὴν αὐτοῦ [d] λύτρον ἀντὶ [e] πολλῶν. 29 Καὶ ἐκπορευ-

r = Mark iv. 22. ix. 8. cf. ch. xvii. 8.
s = ||. ch. xxv. 34, 41. 1 Cor. ii. 9 al. Gen. xxiv. 14. Isa. xxx. 33.
t ||. ch. xxi. 15. xxvi. 8, 11. Mark x. 14. xiv. 4. Luke xiii. 14 only †. Wisd. v. 22. (-τησις, 2 Cor. vii. 11.)
u Mark xii. 14. Luke ii. 18. Gen. xii. 17. Exod. viii. 12.
v ||. Acts xix. 6. 1 Pet. v. 3 only. Gen. i. 28.
w || only †. x Gen. xxxiv. 7. Ps. i. 4. y 4 Kings v. 1. z ||. Rom. xiii. 4 al. Esth. i. 10. ii. 2. vi. 3 BℵA only. a ch. xxv. 44. Acts xix. 22. Rom. xv. 25 al.† b = Gal. i. 4. 1 Tim. ii. 6. Tit. ii. 14. see Exod. xxi. 23. Sir. xxix. 15. c = ch. vi. 25 al. Josh. ii. 14. d || only. Exod. xxi. 30. Lev. xix. 20. xxv. 51. Isa. xlv. 13. (ἀντίλυτρ., 1 Tim. ii. 6.) e Rom. viii. 29. Heb. ii. 10. ix. 28.

om BDLZℵ 1 latt syr-cu coptt æth [Epiph Damasc$_1$] Ambr Jer Juv. for και, η BL 1. 33 latt(not am *ff*$_1$ *g*$_1$) sah Orig$_1$. rec aft ευωνυμων ins μου, with X rel lat-*c* *g*$_2$ *h l* syrr syr-cu coptt æth arm [Bas-sel] : om BCDKLMSZΠ^{1}ℵ 1. 33. 69 vulg lat-*a b e f ff*$_{1.2}$ *g*$_1$ *n* Orig Chr [Epiph$_1$ Damasc$_1$-ms] Thl Ambr Jer Op. rec om τουτο (|| *Mark*), with BZℵ rel latt Orig : ins CDΔ 33 syr coptt Chr [and before ουκ U syr-cu : aft δουναι Π^1 ev-w].

24. * rec καὶ ἀκούσαντες (*from* || *Mark*), with BCDℵ^1 rel latt syr-cu syr æth arm : ακουσαντες δε LZℵ^{3a} 33. 69 forj Syr coptt Orig$_1$. for ηγ., ηρξαντο αγανακτειν (|| *Mark*) ℵ Scr's d.

25. aft ειπεν ins αυτοις D lat-*e* Syr syr-cu coptt æth. κατακυριευσουσιν B 124.

26. rec aft ουτως ins δε (*from* || *Mark*), with CMXΓ (33, e sil) lat-*ff*$_2$ syrr syr-cu copt æth Orig-int$_1$: om BDZℵ rel latt sah arm Thl Jer. εστιν (*from* || *Mark, where it is better attested*) BDZ sah Chr-H-K-M-γ spec : txt Cℵ rel latt copt æth arm Chr [Damasc$_1$-ms] Orig-int. for εαν, αν BD. * rec ἐν ὑμῖν (*from* || *Mark ?*), with B(but aft μεγ.) C(aft γεν.) Dℵ rel latt syrr syr-cu coptt æth arm : υμων LZ. rec εστω, with HLMSℵ^{3a} vulg lat-*f ff*$_1$ *g*$_{1.2}$ *l* æth arm Chr Jer : txt BCDZℵ^1 rel lat-*a b c e ff*$_2$ *h* coptt Orig Did Thl spec.

27. (αν, so BDZℵ : om Π^1.) for εν υμ. ειν., ειναι υμων B : υμων ειναι X. εσται (*from* || *Mark*) CDKLMUZΔΠ^{1}ℵ 1. 33. 69 latt coptt Did [Damasc$_1$-ms] Thl Orig-int : txt B rel Orig Jer.

28. aft πολλων ins υμεις δε ζητειτε εκ μεικρου αυξησαι και εκ μειζονος ελαττον ειναι εισερχομενοι δε και παρακληθεντες δειπνησαι μη ανακλεινεσθαι εις τους εξεχοντας τοπους μη ποτε ενδοξοτερος σου επελθη και προσελθων ο δειπνοκλητωρ ειπη σοι ετι κατω χωρει και καταισχυνθηση εαν δε αναπεσης εις τον ηττονα τοπον και επελθη σου ηττων ερει σοι ο δειπνοκλητωρ συναγε ετι ανω και εσται σοι τουτο χρησιμον D ; simly em lat-*a b c e ff*$_{1.2}$ *g*$_2$ *h n* syr-cu syr-ms Hil Leo(appy) Juv spec. (For the variations, see Lachm, Scholz, Tischdf, or Treg.)

The last clause of the verse may be understood as in the E. V., 'is not mine to give, *but it shall be given to them* for whom it is prepared of my Father ;' so Meyer, al. ; or, taking **ἀλλά** as = εἰ μή (see reff.), 'is not mine to give, *except* to those for whom,' &c. So Chrys. &c., Grot. al. If however we understand after ἀλλά 'it shall be given *by Me*,' we may say with Bengel, 'res eodem recidit, sive oppositione, sive exceptione.' **25.**] The two clauses, . . . **κατακυρ. αὐτῶν** and . . . **κατεξ. αὐτῶν**, are parallel, and αὐτῶν in both cases refers to τῶν ἐθνῶν. Grotius and others would take the second αὐτῶν to refer to οἱ ἄρχοντες, but wrongly. Observe the **κατα** in composition in both verbs, signifying subjugation and oppression. **26 – 28.**] **μέγας . . . . πρῶτος**, i. e. in the *next life*, let him be διάκ. and δοῦλος *here*. Thus also the **ἦλθεν**, ver. 28, applies to the coming of the Son of man *in the flesh only*. **λύτρον ἀντὶ πολ.** is a plain declaration of the sacrificial and vicarious nature of the death of our Lord. The principal usages of λύτρον are the following :—(1) a payment as equivalent for a life destroyed, Exod. xxi. 30 ; (2) the price

ομένων αὐτῶν ἀπὸ Ἱεριχὼ ἠκολούθησεν αὐτῷ ὄχλος N μενων αυτων... BCDEG HKLM NSUVX ΖΓΔΠℵ 1. 33. 69

29. ηκολουθησαν αυτω οχλοι πολλοι D (Scr's p) fuld lat-c *e* ff_1 g_2 syr coptt Chr(Fd and mss) [Bas-sel].—om αυτω ℵ^1(ins ℵ-corr^1(appy)^3).

of redemption of a slave, Levit. xxv. 51 al.; (3) 'propitiation for,' as in Prov. xiii. 8, where Aquila, Symmachus, and Theodotion have ἐξίλασμα. **λύτρον ἀντὶ πολλῶν** here = ἀντίλυτρον ὑπὲρ πάντων 1 Tim. ii. 6. No stress is to be laid on this word πολλῶν as not being πάντων here; it is placed in opposition to the *one* life which is given—the *one* for *many*—and not with any distinction from πάντων. (I may observe once for all, that in the usage of these two words, as applied to our redemption by Christ, πάντων is the OBJECTIVE, πολλῶν the SUBJECTIVE designation of those for whom Christ died. He *died for all,* objectively; subjectively, the great multitude whom no man could number, πολλοί, will be the saved by Him in the end.) 'As the Son of man came to give His life for many and to serve many, so ye, being many, should be to each one the object of service and self-denial.' Hofmann, Schriftbeweis, ii. 1, p. 197, argues for ἀντὶ πολλῶν being taken with δοῦναι, not with λύτρον. But Meyer well remarks, 1) that the sense of ἀντί will not be altered by this, and 2) that this sense is clearly marked by λύτρον to be that of *substitution*, not, as Hofm., that of compensation merely.

29—34.] HEALING OF TWO BLIND MEN ON HIS DEPARTURE FROM JERICHO. Mark x. 46—52. Luke xviii. 35—43; xix. 1, with however some remarkable differences. In the much more detailed account of St. Mark, we have but one blind man, mentioned by name as Bartimæus; St. Luke also relates it of only one, and besides says that it was ἐν τῷ ἐγγίζειν αὐτὸν εἰς Ἱεριχώ. The only fair account of such differences is, that they existed in the sources from which each Evangelist took his narrative. This later one is easily explained, from the circumstance having happened close to Jericho—in two accounts, just on leaving it—in the third, on approaching to it: but he must be indeed a slave to the *letter*, who would stumble at such discrepancies, and not rather see in them the corroborating coincidence of testimonies to the fact itself (see Olshausen, Comment. i. 752). Yet Mr. Greswell (as Theophylact, Neander,—and Ebrard, Evangelien-kritik, p. 572) strangely supposes our Lord to have healed *one blind man* (as in Luke) *on entering Jericho*, and *another* (Bartimæus, as in Mark) *on leaving it,*—and Matthew to have, 'with his characteristic brevity in relating miracles,' *combined both these in one.* But then what becomes of Matthew's assertion, **ἐκπορευομένων αὐτῶν ἀπὸ Ἱερ.**? Can we possibly imagine, that the Evangelist, having *both facts* before him, could combine them and preface them with what he *must know to be false?* It is just thus that the Harmonists utterly destroy the credibility of the Scripture narrative. Accumulate upon this the absurd improbabilities involved in two men, under the same circumstances, addressing our Lord in the same words at so very short an interval,—and we may be thankful that biblical criticism is at length being emancipated from 'forcing narratives into accordance.' See notes on Mark: and a more curious and more recent example of harmonistic ingenuity, in Wordsw.'s note here. It is highly instructive to us, that a Commentator, with the marks of sequence in time given by ἐν τῷ ἐγγίζειν αὐτὸν εἰς Ἱερ. and ἐκπορευομένων αὐτῶν ἀπὸ Ἱερ., should fly for a solution to the Rabbinical canon, "non est prius aut posterius in Scriptura." JERICHO, 150 stadia (= 18 rom. miles) N.E. of Jerusalem (Jos. B. J. iv. 8. 3), and 60 (= 7.2 rom. miles) W. from the Jordan (Jos. ibid.), in the tribe of Benjamin (Josh. xviii. 21), near the borders of Ephraim (Josh. xvi. 7). The environs were like an oasis surrounded by high and barren limestone mountains, —well watered and fertile, rich in palm-trees (Deut. xxxiv. 3: Judg. i. 16; iii. 13), roses (Sir. xxiv. 14), and balsam (Jos. Antt. iv. 6. 1 al.). After its destruction by Joshua, its rebuilding was prohibited under a curse (Josh. vi. 26), which was incurred by Hiel the Bethelite in the days of Ahab (1 Kings xvi. 34): i. e. he *fortified* it, for it was an inhabited city before (see Judg. iii. 13: 2 Sam. x. 5). We find it the seat of a school of the prophets, 2 Kings ii. 4 ff. After the captivity we read of it Ezra ii. 34: Neh. vii. 36: and in 1 Macc. ix. 50 we read that Jonathan strengthened its fortifications. It was much embellished by Herod the Great, who had a palace there (Jos. Antt. xvi. 5. 2 al.), and at this time was one of the principal cities of Palestine, and the residence of an ἀρχιτελώνης on account of the balsam trade (Luke xix. 1). At present there is on or near the site only a misera-

πολύς. 30 καὶ ἰδοὺ δύο τυφλοὶ καθήμενοι [f] παρὰ τὴν
ὁδὸν ἀκούσαντες ὅτι Ἰησοῦς [g] παράγει ἔκραξαν λέγοντες
Κύριε [h] ἐλέησον ἡμᾶς υἱὸς Δαυείδ. 31 ὁ δὲ ὄχλος
[i] ἐπετίμησεν αὐτοῖς ἵνα [k] σιωπήσωσιν. οἱ δὲ [l] μεῖζον
ἔκραξαν λέγοντες Κύριε [h] ἐλέησον ἡμᾶς υἱὸς Δαυείδ.
32 καὶ στὰς ὁ Ἰησοῦς [m] ἐφώνησεν αὐτοὺς καὶ εἶπεν Τί
[n] θέλετε [ἵνα] ποιήσω ὑμῖν; 33 λέγουσιν αὐτῷ Κύριε, ἵνα
[o] ἀνοιγῶσιν οἱ ὀφθαλμοὶ ἡμῶν. 34 [p] σπλαγχνισθεὶς δὲ
ὁ Ἰησοῦς ἥψατο τῶν [q] ὀμμάτων αὐτῶν, καὶ εὐθέως
[r] ἀνέβλεψαν καὶ ἠκολούθησαν αὐτῷ. XXI. 1 Καὶ

f ch. xiii. 4 al. g ch. ix. 9 reff. pres., John i. 40 reff. h ch. ix. 27 reff. i ch. xvi. 22. w. ἵνα, ch. xii. 16 reff. k ‖ Mk. (L. v. r.) ch. xxvi. 63. Mark iii. 4 al4. Luke i. 20. xix. 40. Acts xviii. 9 only. Neh. viii. 11. l constr., here only. μεγ., = ch. xxiv. 31 al. m = ch. xxvii. 47 ‖ Mk. Mark ix. 35. John i. 49. ii. 9 al.‡ Tobit v. 8 (not ℵ). n w. ἵνα, ch. vii. 12. Mark vi. 25. John xvii. 24 al. without, . ch. xiii. 28. xxvii. 17, 21 al. o ch. ix. 30 reff. p ch. ix. 36 reff. Mt. Mk. L. only †. q Mark viii. 23 only. Prov. vi. 4 al3. Wisd. xv. 15 only. r ch. xi. 5 reff.

30. ηκουσαν and aft παραγ. ins και D vulg lat-*e*. rec ελεησον ημας bef κυριε, with CN rel lat-*f* ff_2 syrr Orig$_3$ [Damasc$_1$] Op: om κυριε Dℵ 69 lat-*b c e* ff_1 *h n* syr-cu arm: txt BLZ vulg lat-$g_{1.2}$ *l* syr-jer coptt æth. ins ιησου bef υι. LNℵ 69 lat-*c e h n* syr-jer copt arm Ambr. υιε CDEFLNΠ¹ℵ 1. 33. 69 Orig$_2$ Eus Chr Damasc Thl: txt BZ rel Orig$_2$.

31. οι δε οχλοι επετιμησαν N syr-cu(sic) (lat-ff_1 Syr, Tischdf). σιωπησουσιν LNΔ. for μειζον, πολλω μαλλον (‖) ℵ[: πλεον U]. rec εκραζον (*see* ‖ *Mark Luke*), with CN rel latt syr: εκραυγεζον 69: txt BDLZΠ¹ℵ Syr syr-cu coptt. rec ελεησον ημας bef κυριε, with CN rel lat-*f* ff_2 syr-cu syr: txt BDLZℵ 69 latt(*a* def) Syr coptt æth arm. υιε CDLNℵ(υυ ℵ¹) 33: txt BZ rel.

32. rec om ινα (*to conform to* ‖ *Mark Luke, where* θελ. ποι. *is undoubted*), with BCDNℵ¹ rel lat-*a b e n* Syr æth arm: ins LZℵ^{3a} 106. 238 vulg lat-*c f* $ff_{1.2}$ $g_{1.2}$ *h* syr-cu syr sah Orig$_2$.

33. rec ανοιχθωσιν (*more usual tense*), with CN rel: txt BDLZℵ 33. 69¹ Orig$_2$ Chr. rec ημων bef οι οφθαλμοι, with CN rel [Bas-sel]: txt BDLZℵ(υμων ℵ¹) 33 latt Orig.

34. rec (for ομματων) οφθαλμων (*more usual word*), with CNℵ rel Orig$_1$ [Bas-sel$_1$ Damasc$_1$]: txt BDLZ 69 Orig$_1$. αυτων bef των ομμ. B: αυτου ℵ¹(txt ℵ-corr ¹ ᵒʳ ²). rec aft ανεβλεψαν ins αυτων οι οφθαλμοι (*from ch* ix. 30?), with CN rel (Syr) syr-txt: om BDLZℵ 1. 33 latt syr-cu syr-mg syr-jer coptt æth arm Bas-sel [Damasc$_1$-ms] Op.

ble village, Richa or Ericha. Winer, RWB. **30, 31.**] The multitude appear to have silenced them, lest they should be wearisome and annoying to our Lord; not because they called Him the Son of David,—for the multitudes could have no reason for repressing this cry, seeing that they themselves (being probably for the most part the same persons who entered Jerusalem with Jesus) raised it very soon after: see ch. xxi. 9. I have before noticed (on ch. ix. 27) the singular occurrence of these words, 'Son of David,' in the three narratives of healing the blind in this Gospel. **32.**] ἐφώνησεν = εἶπεν Φωνήσατε Mark, = ἐκέλευσεν ἀχθῆναι Luke. **34.**] ἥψ. τῶν ὀμμ., not mentioned in the other Gospels. In both we have the addition of the Lord's saying, ἡ πίστις σου σέσωκέν σε. The question preceding was to elicit their faith.

CHAP. XXI. 1—17.] TRIUMPHAL ENTRY INTO JERUSALEM: CLEANSING OF THE TEMPLE. Mark xi. 1—11, 15. Luke xix. 29—44. John xii. 12—36. This occurrence is related by all four Evangelists, with however some differences, doubtless easily accounted for, if we knew accurately the real detail of the circumstances in chronological order. In John (xii. 1),—our Lord came six days before the Passover to Bethany, where the anointing (of Matt. xxvi. 6—13) took place: and on the morrow, the triumphal entry into Jerusalem was made. According to Mark xi. 11,—on the day of the triumphal entry He only entered the city, went to the temple, and *looked about on all things*,—and then, when now it was late in the evening, returned to Bethany, and *on the morrow* the cleansing of the temple took place. The account in Luke, which is the fullest and most graphic of the four, agrees chronologically with that in the text. I would venture to suggest, that the supposition of the triumphal entry in Mark being related

ὅτε [s] ἤγγισαν εἰς Ἱεροσόλυμα καὶ ἦλθον εἰς Βηθφαγῆ εἰς τὸ [t] ὄρος τῶν [t] ἐλαιῶν, τότε ὁ Ἰησοῦς
ἀπέστειλεν δύο μαθητὰς 2 λέγων αὐτοῖς Πορεύεσθε εἰς
τὴν [u] κώμην τὴν [v] * ἀπέναντι ὑμῶν, καὶ εὐθέως εὑρήσετε
ὄνον δεδεμένην, καὶ [w] πῶλον μετ' αὐτῆς· λύσαντες ἄγετέ
μοι. 3 καὶ ἐάν τις ὑμῖν εἴπῃ τι, ἐρεῖτε ὅτι ὁ [x] κύριος
αὐτῶν [y] χρείαν ἔχει· εὐθέως δὲ ἀποστελεῖ αὐτούς.
4 τοῦτο δὲ γέγονεν [z] ἵνα πληρωθῇ τὸ [z] ῥηθὲν [z] διὰ τοῦ

BCDEG HKLM NSUVX ΖΓΔΠℵ 1. 33. 69

s || Mk. Luke xviii. 35, 40. xix. 29, &c. Ezra iv. 2.
t || Mk. ch. xxiv. 3 al. Mt. Mk. L. only (exc. John viii. 1 rec.). see || L. Luke xxi. 37. Acts i. 12. Zech. xiv. 4.
u || Mk. L. ch. ix. 35 al. Num. xxxii. 42.
v = ch. xxvii. (24) 61 (Acts iii. 16. xvii. 7. Rom. iii. 18) only. Gen. xxiii. 19.
w here, &c. (3ce) and || (Mk. L. 4 times, J. once) only. Gen. xxxii. 15.
x = || Mk. L. Mark v. 19. xiii. 20.
y ch. vi. 8 reff.
z ch. i. 22 (reff.).

Chap. XXI. 1. (Z def.) ηλθεν C^3EUV-marg Δℵ[1](txt ℵ[3a]) lat-*e g* gat Syr syr-cu syr-jer Orig Chr (of these all but EUΔℵ[1] have ηγγισεν also). [βηθσφαγη $B^2FKM^2N^1$UXΓΠ latt syrr syr-cu syr-jer Orig Chr, βηδφ. Z coptt.] aft βηθ. ins και βηθανιαν (*from* || *Mark Luke*) C^2 33. 69 syr-jer. rec (for 3rd εις) προς (*from* || *Mark Luke*), with DNℵ rel vulg lat-*f* $g_{1,2}$ $Orig_2$ Chr: txt BC^2 33 lat-*b c e* ff_1 *h n* $Orig_1$. (C^1Z *a* def.) om ο (bef ιησ.) BDEHV Scr's k o w[1] Orig. απεστειλεν bef ο ιησ. N Scr's p.

2. rec (for πορευεσθε) πορευθητε, with CN rel: txt BDLZℵ 33. 69 $Orig_1$ Eus_1 Chr. *κατέναντι (*from* || *Mark Luke*) BCDLZℵ 33. 69 $Orig_1$ Eus_1 Chr: απεναντι N rel Orig-ed_1 Eus_2. ευθυς LZℵ: om lat-*a b c* ff_1 *h n* syr-cu copt Chr Orig-int. rec αγαγετε (*from* || *Luke*), with CNZℵ rel Orig Eus_3 [Chr]: txt BD 56-8.

3. αν D. aft τι ins ποιειτε D 157 æth Orig Eus_2. for αυτων, αυτου ℵ. εχει bef χρειαν D^1(corrd *eadem manu* or by D-corr[1]). for ευθ. δε, και ευθ. D 33 latt Syr syr-cu: txt BCNℵ rel syr sah $Orig_3$.—ευθυς BLℵ $Orig_2$: txt CDN rel $Orig_4$ [Chr]. (Z def.) αποστελλει (*from* || *Mark, where it is better attested*) CNZ rel lat-*h* D-lat syrr syr-cu arm-zoh Chr Thl: αποστέλει M: αποστέλη H(Tischdf): txt B D-gr ℵ 69 latt(*a* def) coptt æth arm-mss $Orig_5$ [Op].

4. rec aft δε ins ολον (*from similar passages in ch* i. 22; xxvi. 56), with BC^3N rel vulg lat-g_2 syrr sah arm Chr-γ-L Op: om C^1D[L]Zℵ am(with fuld forj) lat-*a b c* &c syr-cu copt æth Orig Chr Hil Jer. [aft ρηθεν ins δια του πληρωθη το ρηθεν B^1 (marked for erasure *eadem manu*).] for δια, υπο LZ 69 Scr's p.

a day too soon, will bring all into unison. If this be so, our Lord's first entry into Jerusalem was *private*: probably the journey was interrupted by a short stay at Bethany, so that He did not enter the city with the multitudes. That this was the fact, seems implied in Mark xi. 11. Then it was that, περιβλεψάμενος πάντα, He noticed the abuse in the temple, which next day He corrected. Then in the evening He went back with the twelve to Bethany, and the supper there, and anointing, took place. Meantime the Jews (John xii. 9) knew that He was at Bethany; and many went there that evening to see Him and Lazarus. (Query, had not Lazarus followed Him to Ephraim?) Then on the morrow multitudes came out to meet Him, and the triumphal entry took place, the weeping over the city (Luke xix. 41), and the cleansing of the temple. The cursing of the fig-tree occurred early that morning, as He was leaving Bethany with the twelve, and before the multitude met Him or the asses were sent for. (On Matthew's narrative of this event see below on ver. 18.) According to this view, our narrative omits the supper at Bethany, and the anointing (in its right place), and passes to the events of the next day. On the day of the week when this entry happened, see note on John xii. 1. **Βηθφαγῆ** = בֵּית פַּגֵּא, *the house of figs*: a considerable suburb, nearer to Jerusalem than Bethany, and sometimes reckoned part of the city. No trace of it now remains: see 'The Land and the Book,' p. 697.

2, 3.] τὴν κ. τ. ἀπ., * i. e. Bethphage. Mark and Luke mention the πῶλος only, adding "*whereon never yet man sat*" (see note on Mark): John ὀνάριον. Justin Martyr (Apolog. i. 32, p. 63) connects this verse with the prophecy in Gen. xlix. 11, δεσμεύων πρὸς ἄμπελον τὸν πῶλον αὐτοῦ, καὶ τῇ ἕλικι τὸν πῶλον τῆς ὄνου αὐτοῦ. **ὁ κύριος,** here, 'the LORD,' **Jehovah** (see reff.): most probably a general intimation to the owners, that they were wanted *for the service of God*. I cannot see how this interpretation errs against decorum, as Stier (ii. 332, edn. 2) asserts. The meanest animals might be wanted for the ser-

προφήτου λέγοντος 5 [a]Εἴπατε τῇ θυγατρὶ Σιὼν Ἰδοὺ ὁ
βασιλεύς σου ἔρχεταί σοι [b]πραῢς [c]ἐπιβεβηκὼς ἐπὶ ὄνον
καὶ ἐπὶ [a]πῶλον [d]υἱὸν [e]ὑποζυγίου. 6 πορευθέντες δὲ οἱ
μαθηταὶ καὶ ποιήσαντες καθὼς [f]συνέταξεν αὐτοῖς ὁ
Ἰησοῦς, 7 ἤγαγον τὴν ὄνον καὶ τὸν πῶλον, καὶ [g]ἐπέθηκαν
ἐπ' αὐτῶν τὰ ἱμάτια, καὶ [h]ἐπέκαθισεν [i]ἐπάνω αὐτῶν. 8 ὁ
δὲ [k]πλεῖστος ὄχλος [l]ἔστρωσαν ἑαυτῶν τὰ ἱμάτια ἐν τῇ
ὁδῷ. ἄλλοι δὲ [m]ἔκοπτον [n]κλάδους ἀπὸ τῶν δένδρων

F ονον και...

a Isa. lxii. 11. Zech. ix. 9.
b ch. v. 5 reff.
c = here only. (see Luke x. 34. xix. 35.) Gen. xxiv. 61. Num. xxii. 22. 2 Kings xix. 26.
d = Ps. xxviii. 1.
e 2 Pet. ii. 16 only. Exod. iv. 20.
f ch. xxvi. 19 reff.
g ch. xxiii. 4 al. Gen. xxi. 14. constr., ἐπί & gen., ch. xxvii. 29. (Luke viii. 16 v. r.) 1 Kings vi. 18. 3 Kings xviii. 23.
h here only. Gen. xxxi. 34. Lev. xv. 20. trans., 3 Kings i. 38, 44.
i ch. xxviii. 2. Luke iv. 39. Rev. vi. 8. xx. 3 al. Gen. vii. 18.
k = ch. xi. 20 (1 Cor. xiv. 27) only. Isa. ix. 3 al. (in LXX always w. gen., exc. Isa. vii. 22.)
l ||. Mark xiv. 15 || L. Acts ix. 34 only. Esth. iv. 3. Job xvii. 13. Prov. xv. 19.
m = || Mk. only. Num. xiii. 24. see ch. xi. 17 reff.
n ch. xiii. 32 reff.

5. rec aft πραυς ins και (*corrn to* LXX), with BCNZℵ rel am(with forj) lat-*c f* $g_{1.2}$ $Orig_3$ [Chr] : om D 61 vulg lat-*a b e* $ff_{1.2}$ *h* æth arm Cypr Hil Jer Op. rec om 2nd επι (*as superfluous, and not in* LXX), with CD rel latt copt arm Orig : ins BLNℵ 1 Syr syr-cu syr-w-ast sah æth. (Z lat-*a* def.) om υιον LZ ℵ-corr[1 or 2](appy, but restored) am[1] lat-*e* $Orig_2$(see below) : for υι. υποζ., νεον 1 Orig(μὴ αὐταῖς λέξεσιν ὁ ματθ. κ. ὁ ἰωάν. ἐξέθεντο τὸ προφητικόν· . . . . ὁ ματθ. . . . . ἀντὶ τοῦ καὶ ἐπιβεβηκὼς ἐπὶ ὄν. κ. πῶλ. υἱὸν ὑποζυγίου καὶ πῶλον νέον ἢ ὡς ἔν τισι πῶλον ὑποζυγίου). υποζυγιον D[1.r](txt D-corr[1]) lat-*b c* ff_2 g_1 *h* sah-mnt Hil.

6. for και ποιησαντες, εποιησαν D 61. 243 latt sah. rec προςεταξεν (*more usual word, substituted in error*), with LNZℵ rel $Orig_3$ Eus : txt BCD 33.

7. ins και bef ηγαγον D ℵ-corr[1](but erased) 243 latt Syr syr-cu sah. rec (for επ') επανω, with CN rel : txt BDLZℵ 33. 69 $Orig_2$. for αυτων, αυτον D lat-*a b e f* $ff_{1.2}$ g_2 Orig-ms : αυτω (*so rec in* || *Mark*) 33. 69 : *super pullum* Syr syr-jer[2] : om επ' αυτων syr-cu. rec aft ιματια ins αυτων, with CNZ ℵ-corr[1] rel vulg lat-*a c f* g_1 syrr syr-cu syr-jer coptt æth arm-ms $Orig_1$: om BDℵ[1] gat lat-*b e* $ff_{1.2}$ g_2 arm. elz επεκαθισαν (*from* επεβιβασαν τον ιησ. *in* || *Luke. This is more prob than that* -σεν *should have come from* εκαθισεν *in* || *Mark John*), with (L) ℵ[3a](εκαθισαν ℵ[1]) 218 vulg lat-$g_{1.2}$ copt (εκαθησαν 225, επεκαθησαν L 16. 57. 61) : εκαθητο D : om κ. επ. επανω αυτ. EG 1 Scr's c[r] s : επ( ) Z : txt BC rel syr sah arm Just $Orig_3$ Arnob (-σεν Scr's mss) : επεκαθησεν H Scr's b f k v evv-P-x-y, εκαθισεν NΠ Thl Euthym, εκαθησεν K, *et equitavit Jesus* Syr syr-cu æth, *sedebat* lat-*a b c e* $ff_{1.2}$ D-lat, *sedit* lat-*f h*. for 2nd αυτων, αυτου D ev-27 lat-*b c e f* $ff_{1.2}$ g_2 *h* Syr syr-jer : αυτον ℵ[3a] : επ' αυτω ℵ[1] : om vulg lat-g_2 *l* Op.

8. for εαυτων, αυτων DLΔ 69 : txt BCNZℵ rel $Orig_3$. for απο, εκ N.

vice of the Lord Jehovah. And after all, what difference is there as to *decorum*, if we understand with him ὁ κύρ. to signify "the King Messiah"? The two disciples were perhaps Peter and John : compare Mark xiv. 13 and Luke xxii. 8.

4.] A formula of our Evangelist's (see ch. i. 22), spoken with reference to the *divine counsels*, but *not to the intention of the doers* of the act; for this application of prophecy is in John xii. 16 distinctly said not to have occurred to the *disciples* at the time, but after Jesus was glorified.

6, 7.] In Mark, εὗρον πῶλον δεδεμένον πρὸς θύραν ἔξω ἐπὶ τοῦ ἀμφόδου. Our Lord sat on the *foal* (Mark, Luke), and the mother accompanied, apparently after the manner of a sumpter, as prophets so riding would be usually accompanied (but not of course doing the work of a sumpter). In the last **αὐτῶν**, probably the *animals*, not the garments, are to be understood. Thus we say, 'the postilion rode on the horses.' Meyer objects to this interpretation, that no such latitude of expression is found in ver. 5. But I cannot see how this affects the matter. Even if we take ἐπάνω αὐτῶν of the garments, the former ἐπ' αὐτῶν will require similar latitude of interpretation. That this riding and entry were *intentional* on the part of our Lord, is clear: and also that He did not thereby mean to give any countenance to the temporal ideas of His Messiahship, but solemnly to fulfil the Scriptures respecting Him, and to prepare the way for his sufferings, by a public avowal of His mission. The typical meaning also is not to be overlooked. In all probability the evening visit to the temple was on the very day when the Paschal Lamb was to be taken up—i. e. set apart for the sacrifice.

8, 9.] Which was a royal honour : see 2 Kings ix. 13.

o = ch. xiv. 22 reff.
p ‖ Mk. bis, J. ver. 15 only +.
q ‖. ch. xxiii. 39. Luke i. 64 al. Judg. v. 2. Psa. cxvii. 26.
r ‖ Mk. L. Luke ii. 14 only. Job xvi. 20. (see Isa. lvii. 15. Mark v. 7 reff.)
s = ch. xxviii. 4. (xxvii. 51. Heb. xii. 26, from Hag. ii. 6. Rev. vi. 13 only.) Ezek. xxxi. 16.
t Luke xvii. 28. Rev. xiii. 17. Isa. xxiv. 2.
u = ‖ Mk. Luke xix. 23. John ii. 15 only ‡. v ‖ Mk. John ii. 15 only +. w ‖ Mk. only. Judg. vii. 13 A. x ‖ Mk. ch. xxiii. 2 only. Ps. i. 1. y ch. iii. 16 reff.

...εν Z. BCDEF GHKL MNSUV ΧΓΔΠℵ 1. 33. 69

καὶ [1] ἐστρώννυον ἐν τῇ ὁδῷ. 9 οἱ δὲ ὄχλοι οἱ [o] προάγοντες αὐτὸν καὶ οἱ ἀκολουθοῦντες ἔκραζον λέγοντες
[p] Ὡσαννὰ τῷ υἱῷ Δαυείδ, [q] εὐλογημένος ὁ ἐρχόμενος ἐν
ὀνόματι κυρίου, [p] ὡσαννὰ [r] ἐν τοῖς [r] ὑψίστοις. 10 καὶ εἰσ-
ελθόντος αὐτοῦ εἰς Ἱεροσόλυμα [s] ἐσείσθη πᾶσα ἡ πόλις
λέγουσα Τίς ἐστιν οὗτος; 11 οἱ δὲ ὄχλοι ἔλεγον Οὗτός
ἐστιν ὁ προφήτης Ἰησοῦς ὁ ἀπὸ Ναζαρὲθ τῆς Γαλιλαίας.
12 καὶ εἰςῆλθεν Ἰησοῦς εἰς τὸ ἱερὸν τοῦ θεοῦ, καὶ ἐξέβαλεν
πάντας τοὺς [t] πωλοῦντας καὶ [t] ἀγοράζοντας ἐν τῷ ἱερῷ,
καὶ τὰς [u] τραπέζας τῶν [v] κολλυβιστῶν [w] κατέστρεψεν καὶ
τὰς [x] καθέδρας τῶν πωλούντων τὰς [y] περιστεράς, 13 καὶ

εστρωσαν [for εστρωνν.] Dℵ[1](txt ℵ[3a]) lat-*c e ff*$_2$ copt Orig$_1$.

9. rec om αυτον (‖ *Mark*), with N rel latt arm Hil Op: ins BCDLℵ 1. 33. 69 lat-*ff*$_1$ syrr syr-cu coptt æth Orig$_1$ Eus. εκραζαν D, εκραξαν L.

10. for εισελθ., ελθοντος ℵ[1](txt ℵ[3a]) 237-8 Scr's b.

11. for οχλοι, πολλοι D (1) lat-*a b c e ff*$_1$ *h.* for ελεγον, ειπον D lat-*a b c e.* aft ελεγον ins οτι N. rec ιησ. bef ο προφ. (*more obvious arrangement*), with CN rel vulg lat-*b c* &c syrr syr-cu æth Orig$_2$ [Chr]: txt BDℵ 157 coptt arm Orig$_1$ Eus. om ο (bef απο) DΔ.

12. rec ins ο bef ιησ., with DN ℵ-corr(but erased) rel Orig$_1$: om BCEHMVXΔℵ[1] Orig$_2$. om του θεου (*as superfluous and not in* ‖) BLℵ 33 lat-*b* coptt æth arm Orig$_2$ [Meth$_1$] Chr Hil: ins CDN rel vulg lat-*a c* &c syrr syr-cu Orig$_3$ [Bas$_1$] Op.

ὁ πλεῖστος ὄχλος, the greater part of the multitude. Meyer refers to Plato, Rep. iii. p. 397 D; Thuc. vii. 78, in both which the same expression occurs; and Xen. Anab. iii. 2. 36, ὁ πολὺς ὄχλος. **κλ. ἀπ. τ. δένδ.** = τὰ βάϊα τῶν φοινίκων John, = στιβάδας Mark: see 1 Macc. xiii. 51: 2 Macc. x. 7. **ὡσαννά**] from Psalm cxviii. 25, הוֹשִׁיעָה נָּא, σῶσον δή LXX; a formula originally of supplication, but conventionally of gratulation, so that it is followed by a dative, and by **ἐν τοῖς ὑψ.**, meaning, 'may it be also ratified in heaven!' see 1 Kings i. 36: Luke ii. 14, where however it is an *assertion*, not a wish. This is far better than Grotius's interpretation, 'idem valere quod *summè; ut si Latinè dicas terque quaterque.*' **ἐν ὀν. κυρ.** is to be joined with ὁ ἐρχ., not with εὐλογ., and forms a title of the Messiah. Luke adds βασιλεύς, John καὶ ὁ βασ. τοῦ Ἰσρ. **12.**] Compare the notes on John ii. 13—18. The cleansing related in our text is *totally distinct* from that related there. It is impossible to suppose that St. Matthew and St. John, or any one but moderately acquainted with the events which he undertook to relate, should have made such a gross error in chronology, as must be laid to the charge of one or other of them, if these two occurrences were *the same.* I rather view the omission of the first in the synoptic accounts as in remarkable consistency with what we otherwise gather from the three Gospels—that their narrative is *exclusively Galilæan* [with one exception, Luke iv. 44 in our text] *until this last journey to Jerusalem*, and consequently the first cleansing is passed over by them (see Prolegomena, circa init.). On the difference from Mark, see note on ver. 1. Both comings of Jehovah to His temple were partial fulfilments of Mal. iii. 1—3,—which shall not receive its final accomplishment till His great and decisive visit at the latter day. The **ἱερόν** here spoken of was the *court of the Gentiles.*

We have no traces of this *market* in the O. T. It appears to have first arisen after the captivity, when many would come from foreign lands to Jerusalem. This would also account for the *money-changers*, as it was unlawful (from Exod. xxx. 13) to bring foreign money for the offering of atonement. κόλλυβος λέγεται τὸ λεπτὸν νόμισμα παρ' Ἕλλησιν, ὃ Ῥωμαῖοι νοῦμμον (nummum) ὀνομάζουσι, Theophylact.

τὰς περιστ.] The poor were allowed to offer these instead of the lambs for a trespass-offering, Levit. v. 7; also for the purification of women, Levit. xii. 8: Luke ii. 24. **13.**] Stier remarks that the verse quoted from Jeremiah is in con-

λέγει αὐτοῖς [z] Γέγραπται [a] Ὁ οἶκός μου [b] οἶκος [b] προσευχῆς κληθήσεται· ὑμεῖς δὲ αὐτὸν ποιεῖτε [c] σπήλαιον
...λη-στων X. [d] λῃστῶν. 14 καὶ προσῆλθον αὐτῷ [e] τυφλοὶ καὶ [e] χωλοὶ
ἐν τῷ ἱερῷ, καὶ ἐθεράπευσεν αὐτούς. 15 ἰδόντες δὲ οἱ
ἀρχιερεῖς καὶ οἱ γραμματεῖς τὰ [f] θαυμάσια ἃ ἐποίησεν, καὶ
τοὺς παῖδας τοὺς κράζοντας ἐν τῷ ἱερῷ καὶ λέγοντας
[g] Ὡσαννὰ τῷ υἱῷ Δαυείδ, [h] ἠγανάκτησαν 16 καὶ εἶπαν
αὐτῷ Ἀκούεις τί οὗτοι λέγουσιν; ὁ δὲ Ἰησοῦς λέγει
αὐτοῖς Ναί· οὐδέποτε ἀνέγνωτε [i] ὅτι ἐκ στόματος [k] νηπίων
καὶ [l] θηλαζόντων [m] κατηρτίσω [n] αἶνον; 17 καὶ καταλιπὼν
αὐτοὺς ἐξῆλθεν ἔξω τῆς πόλεως εἰς Βηθανίαν καὶ [o] ηὐλίσθη
ἐκεῖ. 18 [p] πρωΐας δὲ [q] ἐπαναγαγὼν εις τὴν πόλιν [r] ἐπεί-

z ch. iv. 4, &c. Esth. x. 2.
a Isa. lvi. 7. Jer. vii. 11.
b ‖ (from l. c. Isa.) only. Isa. lx. 7.
c ‖ (from l. c. Jer.) John xi. 38. Heb. xi. 38. Rev. vi. 15 only. Gen. xix. 30 al.
d ‖. ch. xxvi. 55 ‖ Mk. L. xxvii. 38 ‖ Mk., 44 al. Ezek. xxii. 9.
e Lev. xxi. 18.
f here only. Deut. xxxiv. 12. Ps. lxxvi. 14. cvi. 24.
g ver. 9.
h ch. xx. 24 reff.
i Psa. viii. 2.
k = 1 Cor. xiii. 11 (5 times) al. (ch. xi. 25 reff.)
l of the child, Luke xi. 27. Job iii. 12. of the mother, ch. xxiv. 19 ‖ (Luke xxiii. 29 v. r.) only. Gen. xxi. 7.
m = Rom. ix. 22. Heb. x. 5 (from Ps. xxxix. 6). xi. 3.
n Luke xviii. 43 only. Ezra iii. 11.
o Luke xxi. 37 only. Judg. xix. 6, &c.
p ch. xxvii. 1 reff. constr., here only. Eccl. x. 16 Ald.
q Luke v. 3, 4 only †. Sir. xvii. 26. xxvi' 28. 2 Macc. ix. 21. xii. 4 only.
r ch. iv. 2 reff.

13. om ο (bef οικ.) D[1](ins D[8]). rec εποιησατε (*from* ‖ *Luke*), with CDN rel latt sah arm [Bas] Iren-int Hil: πεποιηκατε (*from* ‖ *Mark*) 1 Just $Orig_2$: txt BLℵ 124 copt æth $Orig_2$ Eus.—bef αυτον N 28 latt Iren-int Hil.

14. προσελθοντες ℵ[1](but corrd). transp τυφλοι and χωλοι (*see Luke* xiv. 13) CN rel syr sah Chr Thl: txt BDLℵ 1. 33. 69 [latt] Syr copt æth arm [$Orig_2$].

15. rec om 2nd τους (*from misunderstanding?*), with C rel $Orig_1$ [$Meth_1$]: ins BDLNℵ.

16. (ειπαν, so BDLℵ.) for αυτοις, αυτω D[1]-gr(txt D[2.4]). om οτι Dℵ 45 lat-*b e ff*$_{1.2}$ *h* æth [$Meth_1$] Chr Iren-int Hil.

17. καταλειπων (*itacism?*) CD rel: txt BE[2]GHNΓΠℵ 1. 69 (SV, e sil) Scr's b ev-x $Orig_2$. (33 def.) om εξω της πολεως ℵ[1](ins ℵ-corr[1]) 28. [βηθανια (for -αν) B[1].] ηυλισθησαν and om εκει C[1].

18. for πρωιας, πρωι BDℵ[1] ev-x: txt CNℵ[3a] rel [Chr]. rec (for επαναγαγων) επαναγων, with B[2]CNℵ[3a] rel vulg lat-*f g*$_{1.2}$ syrr copt æth arm $Orig_1$: παραγων *transiens* D lat-*a b c ff*$_{1.2}$ *h* syr-cu Hil: txt B[1]Lℵ[1].

nexion with the charge of *murder*, and the *shedding of innocent blood* (see Jer. vii. 6). Luther translates σπ. λῃστ., Mördergrube. On the intention of this act of our Lord, see notes on John ii. 15. It was a purely Messianic act; see Mal. iii. 1—3. **15, 16.**] The circumstance that *the children were crying* 'Hosanna to the Son of David' *in the temple*, seems to me to fix this event, as above, *on the day of the triumphal entry*.

Psalm viii. is frequently cited in the N. T. of Christ: see 1 Cor. xv. 27: Heb. ii. 6: Eph. i. 22. In understanding such citations as this, and that in ver. 4, we must bear in mind the important truth, that the external fulfilment of a prophecy is often itself only a type and representation of that inner and deeper sense of the prophecy which belongs to the spiritual dealings of God. Those who can, should by all means consult Stier's admirable remarks on this truth, vol. ii. p. 340 f. edn. 2. **17.**] If this is to be literally understood of the *village* (and not of a district round it, including part of the Mount of Olives; see Luke xxi. 37), this will be the *second night spent at Bethany*. I would rather of the two understand it *literally*, and that the spending the nights *on the Mount of Olives* did not begin till the *next night* (Tuesday).

18—22.] The curse of the barren fig-tree. Mark xi. 12—14, 20—26, where see notes. St. Luke omits the incident.

The cursing of the fig-tree *had in fact taken place on the day before*, and the withering of it was *now noticed*. St. Mark separates the two accounts, which are here given together. We must remember that this miracle was *wholly typical and parabolical*. The fig-tree was the Jewish people—full of the leaves of an useless profession, but without fruit:—and further, all hypocrites of every kind, in every age. It is true, as De Wette observes, that no trace of a parabolic meaning appears in the narrative (and yet, strangely enough, he himself a few lines after, denying the truth of the miracle, accounts

νασεν, 19 καὶ ἰδὼν συκῆν [s] μίαν ἐπὶ τῆς ὁδοῦ ἦλθεν ἐπ'
αὐτήν, καὶ οὐδὲν εὗρεν ἐν αὐτῇ εἰ μὴ [t] φύλλα μόνον· καὶ
λέγει αὐτῇ [Οὐ] μηκέτι ἐκ σοῦ καρπὸς γένηται [u] εἰς τὸν
αἰῶνα. καὶ [v] ἐξηράνθη [w] παραχρῆμα ἡ συκῆ. 20 καὶ
ἰδόντες οἱ μαθηταὶ ἐθαύμασαν λέγοντες [x] Πῶς [w] παραχρῆμα
[v] ἐξηράνθη ἡ συκῆ; 21 ἀποκριθεὶς δὲ ὁ Ἰησοῦς εἶπεν αὐτοῖς
[y] Ἀμὴν λέγω ὑμῖν, ἐὰν [z] ἔχητε [z] πίστιν καὶ μὴ [a] διακριθῆτε,
οὐ μόνον [b] τὸ τῆς συκῆς ποιήσετε, ἀλλὰ κἂν τῷ ὄρει
τούτῳ εἴπητε Ἄρθητι καὶ βλήθητι εἰς τὴν θάλασσαν, γενή-
σεται· 22 καὶ πάντα ὅσα ἂν αἰτήσητε ἐν τῇ [c] προσευχῇ
πιστεύοντες λήμψεσθε.

23 Καὶ [d] * ἐλθόντι αὐτῷ εἰς τὸ ἱερὸν προσῆλθον [d] αὐτῷ
διδάσκοντι οἱ ἀρχιερεῖς καὶ οἱ [e] πρεσβύτεροι τοῦ [e] λαοῦ
λέγοντες [f] Ἐν [g] ποίᾳ ἐξουσίᾳ ταῦτα ποιεῖς, καὶ τίς σοι
ἔδωκεν τὴν ἐξουσίαν ταύτην; 24 ἀποκριθεὶς δὲ ὁ Ἰησοῦς

s ch. v. 18, 41. ver. 24 al. fr.
t ‖ Mk. bis. ch. xxiv. 32 ‖ Mk. Rev. xxii. 2 only.
u Mark iii. 29. John viii. 35. Deut. xv. 17.
v = ‖. ch. xiii. 6 ‖. John xv. 6. James i. 11. Rev. xiv. 15. (Mark iii. 1. v. 29 al.) Ps. ci. 4, 11.
w here bis. elsw. Luke (Gosp., i. 64 al9. Acts iii. 7 al5.) only. Num. vi. 9. Isa. xxx. 13.
x = Mark x. 23, 24 ‖ L. Luke xii. 50. John xi. 36. Wisd. v. 5.
y ch. v. 18 reff.
z ch. xvii. 20 reff.
a = ‖. Acts x. 20. Rom. iv. 20. xiv. 23. James i. 6 bis ‡. (Jer. xv. 10.)
b ch. viii. 33 reff.
c = Dan. ix. 21.
d constr., ch. viii. 1 reff.
e ch. xxvi. 3 al. Mt. only. (see Luke xxii. 66.) Num. xi. 16. xxii. 36 al. 2 Kings xv. 2. 3 Kings xiii. 12.
f = Luke i. 17. iv. 14. Acts iv. 7.
g = ch. xix. 18.

..επειvασεν και ℵ.
..γενηται Γ.
BCDEF GHKL MSUV ΔΠℵ 1. 33. 69
Θ_c xxi. 22 (appy) ...
Z αυτω διδασκοντι...

19. om ευρεν ℵ[1] (ins ℵ-corr[1], appy). rec om ου (*as superfluous*), with CDℵ rel Orig$_4$ [Meth] Petr : ins BL. for εκ σου, εξ ου D-gr Scr's b. γενοιτο ℵ Orig$_3$.
21. for καν, και (insg εαν bef τουτω) D (Scr's c).
22. (αν, so BHUΘ_cℵ (1. 33, e sil) Orig$_1$: om D.)
23. * ἐλθόντος αὐτοῦ (*corrn of Hellenistic idiom, see ch* viii. 1, &c) BCDLℵ 1. 33. 69 Orig$_2$: ελθοντι αυτω Θ_c rel (εισελθ. K). for και (bef τις), η C lat-ff_1 g_2.
24. om δε LZ latt copt.

for the narrative by supposing it to have *arisen out of a parable* spoken by our Lord); but neither does there in that of the driving out the buyers and sellers from the temple, and in those of many other actions which we know to have been symbolic. **19.**] **μίαν**, 'unam illo loco:' a solitary fig-tree. **ἐπὶ τ. ὁδ.**] "**by the road-side**: so Herod. vii. 6, αἱ ἐπὶ Λήμνου ἐπικείμεναι νῆσοι: Demosth. p. 300. 16, ἡ ἐπὶ τοῦ ποταμοῦ μάχη. It was the practice to plant fig-trees by the road-side, because it was thought that the dust, by absorbing the exuding sap, was conducive to the production of the fruit. Plin. N. H. xv. 19." Meyer. [But "M. *now* translates '*over the road*,' adding that we may either suppose that the tree simply projected over the road, or that it was planted on an elevation by the road-side, or that the road here passed through a ravine." Moulton's Winer, p. 468, note 4.] **21, 22.**] This assurance has occurred before in ch. xvii. 20. That truest and *highest faith*, which implies a mind and will perfectly in unison with that of God, can, even in its least degree, have been in Him only who spoke these words. And by it, and its elevating power over the functions and laws of inferior natures, were His most notable miracles wrought. It is observable, that such a state of mind entirely precludes the idea of an *arbitrary* exercise of power—none such can therefore be intended in our Lord's assertion—but we must understand,—"if expedient." Though we cannot reach this faith in its fulness, yet every approach to it (ver. 21) shall be endued with some of its wonderful power,—in obtaining requests from God. See the remarkable and important addition in Mark xi. 25, 26.

23—32.] Mark xi. 27—33. Luke xx. 1—8. Our Lord's authority questioned. His reply. Now commences that series of parables, and discourses of our Lord with His enemies, in which He developes more completely than ever before His hostility to their hypocrisy and iniquity:—and so they are stirred up to compass His death. **23. οἱ ἀρχ. κ. οἱ πρεσ. τ. λ.**] Mark and Luke add γραμματεῖς, and so make up the members of the Sanhedrim. It was an *official message*, sent with a view to make our Saviour declare Himself to be a prophet sent from God—in which case the San-

εἶπεν αὐτοῖς Ἐρωτήσω ὑμᾶς κἀγὼ [h] λόγον ἕνα, ὃν ἐὰν
...xxi. 24 (appy)$Θ_c$ BCDEF GHKL MSUVZ ΔΠא 1. 33. 69 εἴπητέ μοι, κἀγὼ ὑμῖν ἐρῶ [f] ἐν [g] ποίᾳ ἐξουσίᾳ ταῦτα
ποιῶ. 25 τὸ [i] βάπτισμα τὸ Ἰωάννου πόθεν ἦν; ἐξ οὐρα-
νοῦ ἢ ἐξ ἀνθρώπων; οἱ δὲ [k] διελογίζοντο [l] παρ᾽ ἑαυτοῖς
λέγοντες Ἐὰν εἴπωμεν ἐξ οὐρανοῦ, ἐρεῖ ἡμῖν Διὰ τί οὖν
οὐκ ἐπιστεύσατε αὐτῷ; 26 ἐὰν δὲ εἴπωμεν ἐξ ἀνθρώπων,
φοβούμεθα τὸν ὄχλον· πάντες γὰρ ὡς προφήτην [m] ἔχουσιν τὸν Ἰωάννην. 27 καὶ ἀποκριθέντες τῷ Ἰησοῦ εἶπον
Οὐκ οἴδαμεν. ἔφη αὐτοῖς καὶ αὐτὸς Οὐδὲ ἐγὼ λέγω
Χ τι δε... ὑμῖν [f] ἐν [g] ποίᾳ ἐξουσίᾳ ταῦτα ποιῶ. 28 τί δὲ ὑμῖν δοκεῖ;
ἄνθρωπος εἶχεν τέκνα δύο. καὶ προσελθὼν τῷ πρώτῳ
εἶπεν Τέκνον ὕπαγε σήμερον [n] ἐργάζου ἐν τῷ ἀμπελῶνι.
29 ὁ δὲ ἀποκριθεὶς εἶπεν [o] Οὐ θέλω· ὕστερον δὲ [p] μετα-

h ‖. 2 Kings iii. 13. see ch. xxvii. 14. Acts xxviii. 25.
i ch. iii. 7 al.†
k ch. xvi. 7, 8 reff. Ps. ix. 22. (2.)
l = Luke i. 30. ii. 52. 1 Pet. ii. 20.
m ch. xiv. 5 reff.
n Luke xiii. 14. Acts xviii. 3. 1 Cor. iv. 12. Gen. ii. 15. iii. 23. Jer. xxxiv. (xxvii.) 11.
o ch. xv. 32. xviii. 30. xxii. 3 al. Gen. xxxvii. 35. xxxix. 8.
p here bis. ch. xxvii. 3. 2 Cor. vii. 8. Heb. vii. 21 (from Ps. cix. 4) only. Prov. xxv. 8.

επερωτησω D Scr's p q r. και εγω א(twice). ενα bef λογον (‖ *Mark*) CDF latt Orig Ambr Aug Op. om ον D[1] (lat-*c e* ff_1 *h* D-lat: ins D[4]-gr).

25. rec om το (bef ιωαννου), with D rel [Cyr$_1$]: ins BCZא 33 Orig$_1$. for ην, η א[1](txt א[3a]). for παρ᾽, εν (*more usual; see ch* xvi. 7, 8) BLM[2]Z 33 latt Syr syr-cu [Chr Ps-Ath$_1$] Cyr: txt CDא rel syr. om ουν DL 237-44-5-8-58 Scr's a v ev-z, lat-*a b e* ff_2 Syr Orig.

26. rec εχουσιν τον ιωαννην bef ως προφητην (*overlooking the emphasis*), with D rel latt syr copt arm: txt BCLZא 33 Syr syr-cu æth Cyr Aug.

27. ειπαν Dא. for και αυτος, ο ιησους א lat-(*a*) *e* ff_1 *h* Syr syr-cu, simly *c* ff_2.

28. aft ανθρωπος ins τις CEMUΔ 1. 33. 69 latt syrr syr-cu arm Orig$_1$ Eus Cyr Ps-Ath Hil Op: om BDZא rel am(with forj gat harl[1]) lat-g_2 æth Orig$_2$ [Chr]. δυο bef τεκνα B 142. 299 latt Hil. om και LZא[1](ins א[3a]) lat-*e* ff_1 copt Orig Ps-Ath.
for εν τω αμπελωνι, εις τον αμπελωνα D forj lat-*a b c e f* g_1 *h* Chr Ps-Ath [Damasc]. rec aft αμπ. ins μου, with BC[2]Z rel vulg lat-*c* $g_{1.2}$ *l* Orig-comm$_1$ [Eus$_2$] Cyr$_1$ [Ps-Ath$_1$] Op: om C[1]DKLMΔΠ[1]א 1. 33 lat-*a b e f* $ff_{1.2}$ *h* syrr syr-cu syr-jer copt(Treg) æth arm Orig-txt Bas Chr [Damasc$_1$].

29. for ου θελ. υ. δ. μ., εγω κυριε και ουκ (*see note*) B 238 syr-jer copt æth Isid Ps-Ath Damasc: υπαγω κυριε κ. ουκ (13?) 69. 124 tol[2] arm. om δε Hא[1](ins א[3a]) lat-*b e* g_2 *h* Orig$_1$.

hedrim had power to take cognizance of His proceedings, as of a professed Teacher. Thus the Sanhedrim sent a deputation to John on his appearing as a Teacher, John i. 19. The question was *the result of a combination to destroy Jesus*, Luke xix. 47, 48. They do not now ask, as in John ii. 18, τί σημεῖον δεικνύεις ἡμῖν ὅτι ταῦτα ποιεῖς; for they had had many signs which are now included in their ταῦτα. The second question, **καὶ τίς** κ.τ.λ., is an expansion of ποίᾳ. **25.**] **τὸ βάπτ.**, meaning thereby *the whole office and teaching*, of which the *baptism* was the central point and seal. If they had recognized the heavenly mission of John, they must have also acknowledged the authority by which Jesus did these things, for John expressly declared that he was sent to testify of him, and bore witness to having seen the Holy Spirit descend and rest upon Him. John i. 33, 34. **ἐπιστ. αὐτῷ**] believe him, 'give credit to his words:' 'for those words were testimonies to me.' **26.**] These 'blind leaders of the blind' had so far made an insincere concession to the people's persuasion as to allow John to pass for a prophet—but they shrunk from the reproof which was sure to follow their acknowledging it now. This consultation among themselves is related almost verbatim by the three Evangelists. The intelligence of it may have been originally derived from Nicodemus or Joseph of Arimathea. The οὐδὲ ἐγὼ λέγω of our Lord is an answer, not to their outward words οὐκ οἴδαμεν, but to their inward thoughts, οὐ θέλομεν λέγειν. **28.**] **τί δὲ ὑ. δ.**: a formula of connexion—but doubtless here intended to help the questioners to the true answer of their difficulty about John's baptism. The following parable (peculiar to Matthew) refers, under the image of the two sons, to two classes of persons, both summoned by the great

q = ch. xiv. 25 reff.
r Acts ix. 10. 1 Kings iii. 4, 8.
s ch. vii. 21 reff.
t ch. xiv. 22. xxvi. 32. xxviii. 7 †. Wisd. xix. 11.
u 2 Pet. ii. 2. Job xxiv. 13. Prov. xxi. 16. see Luke i. 79. Acts xvi. 17. 2 Pet. ii. 2.
v = ch. v. 6, 10. vi. 1, 33 al.
w ver. 25. Deut. ix. 23.
x = Luke iv. 10. xxii. 31 al. fr.

μεληθεὶς [q] ἀπῆλθεν. 30 προςελθὼν δὲ τῷ ἑτέρῳ εἶπεν
ὡςαύτως. ὁ δὲ ἀποκριθεὶς εἶπεν [r] Ἐγὼ κύριε· καὶ οὐκ ...ειπεν Z.
ἀπῆλθεν. 31 τίς ἐκ τῶν δύο [s] ἐποίησεν τὸ [s] θέλημα τοῦ BCDEF
πατρός; λέγουσιν Ὁ πρῶτος. λέγει αὐτοῖς ὁ Ἰησοῦς GHKL MSUVX
Ἀμὴν λέγω ὑμῖν ὅτι οἱ τελῶναι καὶ αἱ πόρναι [t] προάγου- ΔΠℵ 1. 33. 69
σιν ὑμᾶς εἰς τὴν βασιλείαν τοῦ θεοῦ. 32 ἦλθεν γὰρ
Ἰωάννης πρὸς ὑμᾶς ἐν [u] ὁδῷ [uv] δικαιοσύνης, καὶ οὐκ
[w] ἐπιστεύσατε αὐτῷ, οἱ δὲ τελῶναι καὶ αἱ πόρναι ἐπίστευσαν
αὐτῷ, ὑμεῖς δὲ ἰδόντες οὐ[δὲ] [p] μετεμελήθητε ὕστερον [x] τοῦ
πιστεῦσαι αὐτῷ.

aft *απηλθεν* add *εις τον αμπελωνα* D lat-*a b c* syr-cu syr-jer arm.

30. rec (for *προςελθ. δε*) *και προςελθ.*, with C rel lat-*h* syrr [Eus_1] Chr; *και* (alone) syr-cu æth: txt BDLZℵ 1. 33. 69 latt syr-jer copt arm Cyr Op. rec (for *ετερω*) *δευτερω* (*as following πρωτω*), with BC²LMSVZℵ³ᵃ 1. 33 copt $Orig_1$ Chr: txt C¹Dℵ¹ rel latt syrr syr-cu æth arm $Orig_1$ Eus $Ps\text{-}Ath_2$ Cyr Damasc. om *ο δε αποκρ. ειπεν* ℵ¹(ins ℵ³ᵃ). for *εγω κυριε και ουκ*, *ου θελω υστερον μεταμεληθεις* B 13. 69. 124. 238 tol² syr-jer copt æth-2-mss arm [$Ps\text{-}Ath_1$]. aft *κυριε* ins *υπαγω* D.

31. *το θελ. τ. πατρος* bef *εποιησεν* D. rec aft *λεγουσιν* ins *αυτω*, with C rel latt syrr syr-cu Eus: om BDLℵ 33. 69 fuld(with forj tol) lat-g_1 *l* copt æth arm Chr(so mss and Fd). for *πρωτος*, *υστερος* B syr-jer copt æth-2-mss arm; *novissimus* am(with forj fuld harl¹ tol) lat-*a b e* $ff_{1,2}$ g_1 *h l* Aug: *dicunt voluntati juniorem obedisse* Hil: *εσχατος* D(*αισχ.*) 69. 238 Hipp Ps-Ath Damasc: txt CLℵ rel vulg-ed(with gat mm) lat-*c f* g_2 syrr syr-cu æth-ed [$Hipp_1$(in Niceph)] Eus Chr Jer_{expr}. om *οτι* ℵ¹(ins ℵ³ᵃ) ev-y.

32. rec *προς υμας* bef *ιωαννης*, with D rel latt syrr syr-cu copt: om *προς υμας* arm-zoh: txt BCLℵ 33 lat-*c* æth Orig Chr. rec *ου* (*the force of ουδε not being seen*), with Cℵ rel $Orig_2$ Chr: om D lat-*e*: *ουδε* B 1. 33. 69 vulg lat-*a b* &c syrr syr-cu copt æth Hil Op.

Father to "work in His vineyard" (see ch. xx. 1); *both Jews* and of His family. The *first* answer the summons by a direct and open refusal—these are the *open sinners*, the publicans and harlots, who disobey God to His face. But afterwards, when better thoughts are suggested, they repent, and go. The *second* class (no stress is to be laid on the *order* of calling—the parable merely mentions that the call was made **ὡςαύτως**—it is the mistaken desire to set the chronology right which has given rise to such confusion in the readings) receive the summons with a respectful assent (not unaccompanied with a self-exaltation and contrast to the other, implied in the emphatic **ἐγώ**)—having however no intention of obeying (there is no mention of a *change of mind* in this case): but go not. These are *the Scribes and Pharisees*, with their shew of legal obedience, who "said, and did not" (ch. xxiii. 3). It will of course admit of wider applications—to Jews and Heathens, or any similar pair of classes who may thus be compared. **31.**] In connexion with the reading *ὁ ὕστερος*, which Tregelles has adopted *without the preceding transposition*, it may be mentioned, that some (not Origen, that I can find) have understood it to mean, *ὁ ὕστερον μεταμεληθείς*. **προάγουσιν**, either the declarative present – **go before you**, in the matter of God's arrangements,—or the assertive present, of the mere matter of fact, **are going before you.** I prefer this latter on account of the explanation following:—'go before,'—*not entirely without hope* for you, that you may *follow*, but *not necessarily implying* your following. The door of mercy was not yet shut for them: see John xii. 35: Luke xxiii. 34. *προάγ.* answers to *ὕπαγε κ. ἐργ.* in the parable. The idea of 'shewing the way' by being their example, is also included. There were publicans among the disciples, and probably repentant harlots among the women who followed the Lord. **32.**] **ὁδῷ δικ.**, not only in the **way of God's commandments**, so often spoken of, but in the very path of ascetic purity which you so much approve; yet perhaps it were better to let the simpler sense here be the predominant one, and take *δικαιοσύνης* for 'repentance,' as Noah is called *δικ. κήρυξ* (2 Pet. ii. 5) in similar circumstances. **μετεμελ. ὕστ.** are words repeated from the parable (ver. 29), and serving to fasten the application on

33 Ἄλλην παραβολὴν ἀκούσατε. [y] Ἄνθρωπος ἦν
[z] οἰκοδεσπότης ὅστις [a] ἐφύτευσεν [b] ἀμπελῶνα· καὶ [b] φραγ-
μὸν αὐτῷ περιέθηκεν καὶ [c] ὤρυξεν ἐν αὐτῷ [d] ληνὸν καὶ
ᾠκοδόμησεν [e] πύργον, καὶ [f] ἐξέδετο αὐτὸν [g] γεωργοῖς, καὶ
[h] ἀπεδήμησεν. 34 ὅτε δὲ [i] ἤγγισεν ὁ [ik] καιρὸς τῶν καρπῶν,
[l] ἀπέστειλεν τοὺς δούλους αὐτοῦ [l] πρὸς τοὺς [g] γεωργοὺς
[m] λαβεῖν τοὺς καρποὺς αὐτοῦ· 35 καὶ [n] λαβόντες οἱ
[g] γεωργοὶ τοὺς δούλους αὐτοῦ [o] ὃν μὲν [p] ἔδειραν [o] ὃν δὲ
ἀπέκτειναν [o] ὃν δὲ [q] ἐλιθοβόλησαν. 36 πάλιν ἀπέστειλεν
ἄλλους δούλους πλείονας τῶν πρώτων· καὶ ἐποίησαν
Z υστε-ρον... αὐτοῖς ὡσαύτως. 37 ὕστερον δὲ [l] ἀπέστειλεν [l] πρὸς αὐτοὺς
τὸν υἱὸν αὐτοῦ λέγων [r] Ἐντραπήσονται τὸν υἱόν μου.
38 οἱ δὲ γεωργοὶ ἰδόντες τὸν υἱὸν εἶπον ἐν ἑαυτοῖς Οὗτός

y ch. xiii. 45. xxi. 33.
z ch. xx. 1, 11 al.+
a ch. xv. 13 reff. Deut. xx. 6.
b ‖ Mk. Luke xiv. 3. Eph. ii. 14 only. Num. xxii. 24. Ps. cxxix. 12.
c ‖ Mk. ch. xxv. 18 only. Isa. v. 2.
d Rev. xiv. 19, 20 bis. xix. 15 only. Deut. xvi. 13. Prov. iii. 10.
e ‖ Mk. Luke xiii. 4. xiv. 28 only. Gen. xi. 4.
f ‖. ver. 41 only. Exod. ii. 21. Sir. vii. 25. 1 Macc. x. 58.
g here, &c. ‖. John xv. 1. 2 Tim. ii. 6. James v. 7 only. Jer. xiv. 4. (-γιον, 1 Cor. iii. 9. -γεῖσθαι, Heb. vi. 7.)
h ‖. ch. xxv. 14, 15. Luke xv. 13 only +. (-μος, Mark xiii. 34.)
i Luke xxi. 8. Lam. iv. 18.
k Ps. i. 3.
l ch. xxiii. 34, 37. Jer. xxv. 4.
m = ch. xvii. 24 reff.
n = ‖ Mk. ver. 39. John xix. 1 al. 2 Kings x. 4.
o ch. xiii. 8 reff.
p ‖. Mark xiii. 9. Luke xii. 47, 48. Acts v. 40 al. 2 Chron. xxix. 34 A (ἐκδ., B) only.
q (‖ Mk. v. r.) ch. xxiii. 37. Luke xiii. 34. (John viii. 5 rec.) Acts vii. 58, 59. xiv. 5. Heb. xii. 20 (from Exod. xix. 13) only. Exod. viii. 26 al.
r mid. trans., ‖. Luke xviii. 2, 4. Heb. xii. 9. Exod. x. 3. Job xxxii. 21. absol., 2 Thess. iii. 14. Tit. ii. 8. Ps. xxxiv. 26. act., 1 Cor. iv. 14 only.

33. rec aft *ανθρωπος* ins *τις*, with C³X rel lat-*e f h* Syr syr-cu arm Eus [Chr Cyr₁] (Iren-int) spec: om BC¹DKLSVΔΠא 1. 33 latt(*a* def) syr copt æth Orig₂ [Chr-2] Thl Lucif Hil. om *εν* (*homœotel*) Vא¹(ins א³ᵃ) 69. 243-51. (*εξεδετο*, so B¹([but *τε*) see table) C¹Lא¹(-*ο*- א³ᵃ).]
36. at beg ins *και* א¹(א³ᵃ disapproving) Syr: *παλιν ουν* D.
37. for *προς αυτους*, *αυτοις* D ev-z₁ lat-*a b c ff₂ h* Iren-int Lucif Arnob Ambr.

the hearers. **τοῦ πισ., that ye might believe on Him**: see reff.

33—46.] Parable of the vineyard let out to husbandmen. Mark xii. 1—12. Luke xx. 9—19. This parable is in intimate connexion with Isa. v. 1 ff., and was certainly intended by our Lord as an express application of that passage to the Jews of His time. Both Mark and Luke open it with an ἤρξατο λέγειν . . . , as a fresh beginning, by our Lord, of a series of parables. Luke adds, that it was spoken πρὸς τὸν λαόν. Its subject is, of course, *the continued rejection of God's prophets by the people of Israel, till at last they rejected and killed His only Son.* The **οἰκοδεσπότης ἐφύτευσεν ἀμπελῶνα**: i. e. '*selected it out* of all His world, and *fenced it in,* and *dug a receptacle for the juice* (in the rock or ground, to keep it cool, into which it flowed from the press above, through a grated opening), *and built a tower* (of recreation—or observation to watch the crops).' This exactly coincides with the state of the Jewish nation, under covenant with God as His people. All these expressions are in Isaiah v. The *letting out to husbandmen* was probably that kind of letting where the tenant pays his rent *in kind,* although the καρποί *may* be understood of money. God began about 430 years after the Exodus to send His prophets to the people of Israel, and continued even till John the Baptist; but all was in vain; they "persecuted the prophets," casting them out, and putting them to death. (See Neh. ix. 26: Matt. xxiii. 31, 37: Heb. xi. 36—38.) The *different sendings* must not be pressed; they probably imply the *fulness and sufficiency of warnings given,* and set forth the longsuffering of the householder; and the increasing rebellion of the husbandmen is shewn by their increasing ill-treatment of the messengers. Meyer understands αὐτοῦ after καρπούς, ver. 34, to mean *His* fruits; i. e. in *money*.

37.] See Luke ver. 13: Mark ver. 6. Our Lord sets forth His heavenly Father in human wise deliberating, τί ποιήσω; (Luke) and ἴσως ἐντρ., to signify His gracious adoption, for man's sake, of every means which may turn sinners to repentance. The difference here is fully made between the Son and all the other messengers; see Mark; ἔτι ἕνα υἱὸν εἶχεν ἀγαπητόν . . .: and, as Stier remarks, this is the real and direct answer to the question in ver. 23. The Son appears here, not in his character of Redeemer, but in that of a preacher—a messenger demanding the fruits of the vineyard. (See ch.

s ‖. Rom. viii. 17. Gal. iv. 1 al. Judg. xviii. 7 B. 2 Kings xiv. 7.
t ‖. Mk. (L. v. r.) ch. iv. 19. xi. 28 al. Gen. xxxvii. 20.
u ‖. Luke xii. 13. Acts vii. 5. Heb. xi. 8 al. Num. xxvii. 9 al.
v ver. 35 reff.
w ‖. John ix. 34, 35. Acts vii. 58 al. Lev. xiv. 40.
x = ch. xx. 8. Mark xiii. 35 al. Exod. xxi. 28.

ἐστιν ὁ [s] κληρονόμος· [t] δεῦτε ἀποκτείνωμεν αὐτὸν καὶ BCDEF
σχῶμεν τὴν [u] κληρονομίαν αὐτοῦ. 39 καὶ [v] λαβόντες GHKL MSUVX
αὐτὸν [w] ἐξέβαλον [w] ἔξω τοῦ ἀμπελῶνος καὶ ἀπέκτειναν. ΖΔΠℵ 1. 33. 69
40 ὅταν οὖν ἔλθῃ ὁ [x] κύριος τοῦ ἀμπελῶνος, τί ποιήσει
τοῖς γεωργοῖς ἐκείνοις; 41 λέγουσιν αὐτῷ [y] Κακοὺς [y] κακῶς ἀπολέσει αὐτούς, καὶ τὸν ἀμπελῶνα [z] ἐκδώσεται ἄλλοις γεωργοῖς, οἵτινες [a] ἀποδώσουσιν αὐτῷ τοὺς [a] καρποὺς
ἐν τοῖς καιροῖς αὐτῶν. 42 λέγει αὐτοῖς ὁ Ἰησοῦς Οὐδέποτε ἀνέγνωτε ἐν ταῖς [b] γραφαῖς [c] Λίθον ὃν [d] ἀπεδοκίμασαν

y see Wisd. vi. 6. z ver. 33 reff. a Heb. xii. 11. Rev. xxii. 2. Lev. xxvi. 4. see Ps. i. 3. b = John v. 39 reff. c ‖. Acts iv. 11. 1 Pet. ii. 6. Psa. cxvii. 22. constr., 1 Cor. x. 16. d ‖. Luke ix. 22 ‖ Mk. xvii. 25. Heb. xii. 17. 1 Pet. ii. 4, 7 only. Jer. vi. 30.

38. rec **κατασχωμεν** (*gloss*), with C rel Eus [Chr]: txt BDLZℵ 1. 33 latt(*habebimus*) arm Orig [Cyr-p] Iren-int Lucif.

39. *απ. κ. εξεβαλαν ε. τ. αμπ.* (*see* ‖ *Mark*) D mm lat-*a b c e ff*$_2$ *h* Lucif Juv.—*εβαλον* ℵ [: *εξεβαλλον* Z].

41. rec *εκδοσεται*, with 69 (Scr's a b ev-z, e sil): txt BDFSVℵ rel Orig Eus: *εκδωσει* C Cyr. (Z def.)

iv. 17.) **38. οὗτός ἐστιν**] So Nicodemus, John iii. 2, **οἴδαμεν** *ὅτι ἀπὸ θ. ἐλήλυθας διδάσκαλος*, even at the beginning of His ministry; how much more then after three years spent in His divine working. The latent consciousness that Jesus *was the Messiah*, expressed in the prophecy of Caiaphas (John xi. 49—52; cf. the *σὺ εἶπας* of our ch. xxvi. 64), added no doubt to the guilt of the Jewish rulers in rejecting and crucifying Him, however this consciousness may have been accompanied with *ἄγνοια* of one kind or other in all of them,—see Acts iii. 17 and note. **ὁ κληρον.**] This the Son is in virtue of *His human nature:* see Heb. i. 1, 2. **δεῦ. ἀποκτ. αὐτ.**] The very words of the LXX, ref. Gen., where Joseph's brethren express a similar resolution: and no doubt used by the Lord in reference to that history, so deeply typical of His rejection and exaltation. This resolution had actually been taken, see John xi. 53: and that immediately after the manifestation of His power as the Son of God (*πάτερ, εὐχαριστῶ σοι κ.τ.λ.* John xi. 41), in the raising of Lazarus, and also immediately (*οὖν*) after Caiaphas's prophecy. **καὶ σχ.**] see John xi. 48. As far as this, the parable is History: from this point, Prophecy. **39.**] This is partly to be understood of our Lord being given up to the heathen to be judged; but also literally, as related by all three Evangelists. See also John xix. 17, and Heb. xiii. 11, 12. In Mark the order is different, *ἀπέκτειναν κ. ἐξέβ. ἔξω.*

40, 41.] See Isa. v. 5. All means had been tried, and nothing but judgment was now left. Mark and Luke omit the important words *λέγουσιν αὐτῷ*, though Luke has given us the key to them, in telling us that the parable was spoken in the hearing of the *people*, who seem to have made the answer. Perhaps however the Pharisees (as suggested by Trench, Parables, in loco) may have made this answer, having *missed*, or (as Olshausen thinks, Biblisch. Comm. i. p. 793, and Stier, R. J. ii. 363) *pretended* to miss, *the sense of the parable;* but from the strong *κακοὺς κακῶς*, I incline to the former view. Whichever said it, it was a self-condemnation, similar to that in ch. xxvii. 25: the *last form*, as Nitzsch finely remarks (cited by Stier, ib.), of the divine warnings to men, 'when they themselves speak of the deeds which they are about to do, and pronounce judgment upon them.' So striking, even up to the last moment, is the mysterious union of human free-will with divine foresight (see Acts ii. 23: Gen. i. 20), that after all other warnings frustrated, the conscience of the sinner himself interposes to save him from his sin. The expression *κακοὺς κακῶς ἀπολ.* is one of the purest Greek:—*ἀπό σ' ὀλῶ κακὸν κακῶς*, Aristoph. Plut. 65, and indeed passim in the best writers. **οἵτινες**] **of a kind, who:** *οἵ* would identify, **οἵτινες** classifies. They do not specify *who*, but only *of what sort*, the new tenants will be. The clause is peculiar to Matthew. We may observe that our Lord here makes **ὅταν ἔλθῃ ὁ κύριος** *coincide with the destruction of Jerusalem*, which is incontestably the overthrow of the wicked husbandmen. This passage forms therefore an important key to our Lord's prophecies, and a decisive justification for those who, like myself, firmly hold that

οἱ οἰκοδομοῦντες, οὗτος ἐγενήθη [e] εἰς κεφαλὴν [f] γωνίας·
παρὰ κυρίου ἐγένετο [g] αὕτη, καὶ ἔστιν [h] θαυμαστὴ [i] ἐν ὀφθαλμοῖς ἡμῶν ; 43 διὰ τοῦτο λέγω ὑμῖν ὅτι ἀρθήσεται ἀφ'
ὑμῶν ἡ βασιλεία τοῦ θεοῦ, καὶ δοθήσεται ἔθνει [k] ποιοῦντι
τοὺς [k] καρποὺς αὐτῆς. 44 καὶ ὁ πεσὼν ἐπὶ τὸν λίθον
τοῦτον [l] συνθλασθήσεται· ἐφ' ὃν δ' ἂν πέσῃ, [m] λικμήσει
αὐτόν. 45 καὶ ἀκούσαντες οἱ ἀρχιερεῖς καὶ οἱ Φαρισαῖοι
τὰς παραβολὰς αὐτοῦ ἔγνωσαν ὅτι περὶ αὐτῶν [n] λέγει·
46 καὶ ζητοῦντες αὐτὸν [o] κρατῆσαι ἐφοβήθησαν τοὺς ὄχλους, [p] ἐπεὶ [q] εἰς προφήτην αὐτὸν [r] εἶχον.

XXII. 1 Καὶ [s] ἀποκριθεὶς ὁ Ἰησοῦς πάλιν εἶπεν

...οι αρχιερ. Z.

e = ch. xix. 5 reff.
f ||. ch. vi. 5 reff.
g fem., || Mk. 1 Kings iv. 8. Ps. xxvi. 4.
h || Mk. reff.
i || Mk. 1 Kings xxvi. 21, 24. 1 Macc. i. 12 al.
k ch. iii. 8 reff.
l || L. only. Ps. lvii. 6. Mic. iii. 3.
m || L. only. Job xxvii. 21. Dan. ii. 44 Theod.
n pres., John i. 40 reff.
o = ch. xii. 11. xiv. 3. xviii. 28. xxii. 6 al. fr. Ps. lv. tit.
p = ch. xxvii. 6. Luke i. 34 al. fr.
q = Acts vii. 5, 21. xiii. 22. 4 Kings iv. 1. Isa. xlix. 6.
r = ch. xiv. 5 reff.
s = ch. xi. 25 reff.

42. κυριω ℵ[1](txt ℵ[3a]). υμων D[1](and lat: txt D[2]) **1**. 69. 251 Scr's l.
43. om οτι [B[1](Tischdf N. T. Vat)] ℵ 243 evv-H-y. αυτου ℵ[1](txt ℵ[3a]) $Orig_1$.
44. om ver D 33 lat-*a*(appy) *b e* $ff_{1.2}$ Orig Iren-int Lucif (*and Tischdf, as introduced from || Luke; but the words* are not the same, *and it wd not have been insd* here *but* aft ver 42. *Its omn may be accounted for, as Meyer, by* the copyist passing from **αυτης** to **αυτον**).
45. for και ακουσ., ακουσ. δε LZℵ 33 syr-cu copt.
46. for τους οχλους, τον οχλον Cℵ[1](txt ℵ[3a]) lat-*b* Syr syr-cu copt. rec επειδη, with C rel: txt BDLℵ **1**. 33 $Orig_3$. rec (for εις) ως (*from ver* 26), with CD rel latt syrr syr-cu copt arm: txt BLℵ **1**. 22 $Orig_6$.

the coming of the Lord is in many places to be identified, primarily, with that overthrow. **42.**] A citation from *the same Psalm of triumph from which the multitudes had taken their Hosannas.* This verse is quoted with the same signification in Acts iv. 11: 1 Pet. ii. 6, 7, where also the cognate passage Isa. xxviii. 16 is quoted, as in Rom. ix. 33. The words here are those of the LXX. **αὕτη . . . θαυμαστὴ** . . . are feminine by a Hebraism, in which idiom the fem. is used as the neuter, there being no neuter. Meyer takes it as agreeing with κεφ. γωνίας, but surely with the examples in the reff. before us, it is simpler and better to understand the construction as above.

The **οἰκοδομοῦντες** answer to the *husbandmen*, and the addition is made in this changed similitude to shew them that *though they might reject and kill the Son, yet He will be victorious in the end.* **εἰς κεφ. γων.**] The *corner-stone* binds together both walls of the building; so Christ unites Jews and Gentiles in Himself. See the comparison beautifully followed into detail, Eph. ii. 20—22.

On **θαυμαστὴ ἐν ὀφθ. ἡμ.**, cf. Acts iv. 13, 14. **43.**] Our Lord here *returns to the parable,* and more plainly than ever before announces to them their rejection by God. The ἀμπελών is now ἡ βασ. τ. θ. The **ἔθνος** here spoken of is not the Gentiles in general, but *the Church of the truly faithful,*—the **ἔθνος ἅγιον, λαὸς εἰς περιποίησιν** of 1 Pet. ii. 9: see Acts xv. 14. **44.**] A reference to Isa. viii. 14, 15, and Dan. ii. 44, and *a plain identification of the stone there mentioned with that in* Ps. cxviii. The stone is *the whole kingdom and power of the Messiah summed up in Himself.* **ὁ πεσὼν . . . .** he that *takes offence,* that *makes it a stone of stumbling,* **shall be broken**: see Luke ii. 34: but **on whomsoever,** as its enemy, *it shall come in vengeance,* as prophesied in Daniel, **λικμήσει αὐτόν, it shall dash him in pieces.** Meyer maintains that the meaning of λικμ. is not this, but literally *'shall winnow him,'* throw him off as chaff (see ref. Job). But the confusion in the parable thus occasioned is quite unnecessary. The result of winnowing is complete separation and dashing away of the worthless part: and it is surely far better to understand this *result* as the work of the falling of the stone, than to apply the words to a part of the operation for which the *falling of a stone* is so singularly unsuited.

45, 46.] All three Evangelists have this addition. St. Mark besides says καὶ ἀφέντες αὐτὸν ἀπῆλθον, answering to our ch. xxii. 22. Supposing Mark's insertion of these words to be in the right place, we have the following parable spoken *to the people and disciples*: see below.

CHAP. XXII. 1—14.] PARABLE OF THE

ἐν παραβολαῖς αὐτοῖς λέγων [2] [t] Ὡμοιώθη ἡ βασιλεία τῶν
οὐρανῶν [u] ἀνθρώπῳ βασιλεῖ ὅςτις [v] ἐποίησεν [w] γάμους τῷ
υἱῷ αὐτοῦ, [3] καὶ [x] ἀπέστειλεν τοὺς δούλους αὐτοῦ [y] καλέσαι
τοὺς [z] κεκλημένους εἰς τοὺς [w] γάμους, καὶ [a] οὐκ ἤθελον
ἐλθεῖν. [4] πάλιν ἀπέστειλεν ἄλλους δούλους λέγων
Εἴπατε τοῖς [z] κεκλημένοις Ἰδοὺ τὸ [b] ἄριστόν μου ἡτοίμακα,
οἱ [c] ταῦροί μου καὶ τὰ [d] σιτιστὰ [e] τεθυμένα, καὶ πάντα
ἕτοιμα· δεῦτε εἰς τοὺς [w] γάμους. [5] οἱ δὲ [f] ἀμελήσαντες

C defective in vv. 2, 3. BCDEF GHKL MSUVX ΔΠℵ 1. 33. 69

t ch. vii. 24 reff. u = ch. xiii. 45 reff. v = ch. xxvi. 18. Mark vi. 21. Luke v. 29. xiv. 13, 16. Gen. xxix. 22. Tobit viii. 19 AB (not ℵ). w plur. here, &c. ch. xxv. 10. Luke xii. 36. xiv. 8 only. Esth. ii. 18. see note. x Prov. ix. 3. y see ch. ix. 13. z = Luke xiv. 7, &c. 1 Cor. x. 27. Esth. v. 12. a ch. xxi. 29 reff. b Luke xi. 38. xiv. 12 (15 v. r.) only. 2 Kings xxiv. 15. 3 Kings iv. 22 complut. Tobit xii. 13. Sus. 13 Theod. Bel & Dr. 34, 37 only. c Acts xiv. 13. Heb. ix. 13. x. 4 only. Gen. xxxii. 15. d here only †. Ps. xxi. 13 Symm. σιτιστοὺς ἄρνας ἑκατόν, Jos. Antt. viii. 2. 4. (-τευτός, Luke xv. 23, &c.) e = Luke xv. 23, 27, 30. John x. 10. Acts x. 13. xi. 7. 1 Kings xxv. 11. xxviii. 24. 3 Kings xix. 21. (see Mark xiv. 12.) f 1 Tim. iv. 14. Heb. ii. 3. viii. 9 (2 Pet. i. 12 v. r.) only. Jer. iv. 17. xxxviii. (xxxi.) 32. Wisd. iii. 10. 2 Macc. iv. 14 only.

Chap. XXII. **1.** rec *αυτοις* bef *εν παραβολαις*, with C rel syr-cu syr arm: om *αυτοις* Syr æth [Chr]: txt BDLℵ 1. 33. 69 vulg lat-g_2 Orig.—om *ειπεν αυτοις* E.—om *εν* ℵ[1](ins ℵ-corr[1·3]).

4. rec *ητοιμασα* (*change to more usual historical tense*), with C[3]X rel Orig [Chr Cyr_1 $Damasc_1$]: *ετοιμον* ev-y: txt BC[1]DLℵ 1. 33.

Marriage of the King's Son. *Peculiar to Matthew.* A parable resembling this in several particulars occurs in Luke xiv. 15—24, yet we must not hastily set it down as the same. Many circumstances are entirely different: the locality and occasion of delivery different, and in both cases stated with precision. And the difference in the style of the parables is correspondent to the two periods of their utterance. That in Luke is delivered earlier in our Lord's ministry, when the enmity of the Pharisees had yet not fully manifested itself: the refusal of the guests is more courteous, their only penalty, *exclusion;*—here they *maltreat the servants,* and are *utterly destroyed.* This binds the parable in close connexion with that of the wicked husbandmen in the last chapter, and with this period of our Lord's course. **2.**] The *householder* of the former parable is the King here, who *ποιεῖ γάμους* for his Son. **γάμοι** are not always necessarily 'a marriage,' but any great celebration, as accession to the throne, or coming of age, &c. See Esth. i. 5, LXX. Meyer (in loc.) denies this, but does not refer to the passage of Esther just cited, which to my mind is decisive. Esth. ix. 22 is not satisfactorily explained on his interpretation, viz. that the LXX translate freely and exegetically,—but is another instance in point. Here however the notion of a marriage is *certainly included;* and the interpretation is, *the great marriage supper* (Rev. xix. 9) *of the Son of God:* i. e. His full and complete union to His Bride the Church in glory: which would be to the guests the ultimate result of accepting the invitation. See Eph. v. 25—27. The difficulty, of the *totality of the guests* in this case constituting *the Bride,* may be lessened by regarding the ceremony as an enthronization, in which the people are regarded as being espoused to their prince. On the whole imagery, cf. Ps. xlv. **3.**] These **δοῦλοι** are not the Prophets, not the same as the servants in ch. xxi. 34, as generally interpreted:—the parable takes up its ground nearly from the conclusion of that former, and is altogether a *New Testament parable.* The office of these *δοῦλοι* ("*κλήτορες, δειπνοκλήτορες,* vocatores, invitatores," Webst. and Wilk.) was *καλέσαι τοὺς κεκλημένους,* to *summon* those who had been invited, as was customary (see Esth. v. 8 and vi. 14); these being *the Jewish people,* who had been before, by their prophets and covenant, invited. These first *δοῦλοι* are then *the first messengers of the Gospel,*—John the Baptist, the Twelve, and the Seventy,—who preached, saying 'The Kingdom of heaven is at hand.' And even our Lord Himself must in some sort be here included, inasmuch as He *μορφὴν δούλου ἔλαβεν,* and preached this same truth, with however the weighty addition of **δεῦτε πρός με.**

4.] We now come to a different period of the Evangelic announcement. Now, all is ready: *the sacrifice,* or the meat for the feast, *is slain.* We can hardly help connecting this with the declarations of our Lord in John vi. 51—59, and supposing that this second invitation is the preaching of the Apostles and Evangelists *after the great sacrifice was offered.*

ἀπῆλθον, [g] * ὃς μὲν εἰς τὸν ἴδιον ἀγρόν, [g] ὃς δὲ ἐπὶ τὴν
[h] ἐμπορίαν αὐτοῦ. 6 οἱ δὲ λοιποὶ [i] κρατήσαντες τοὺς
δούλους αὐτοῦ [k] ὕβρισαν καὶ ἀπέκτειναν. 7 ὁ δὲ βασιλεὺς
[l] ὠργίσθη, καὶ πέμψας τὰ [m] στρατεύματα αὐτοῦ ἀπώλεσεν
τοὺς [n] φονεῖς ἐκείνους, καὶ τὴν πόλιν αὐτῶν [o] ἐνέπρησεν.
8 τότε λέγει τοῖς δούλοις αὐτοῦ Ὁ μὲν γάμος ἕτοιμός
ἐστιν, οἱ δὲ [p] κεκλημένοι οὐκ ἦσαν [q] ἄξιοι. 9 πορεύεσθε
οὖν ἐπὶ τὰς [r] διεξόδους τῶν ὁδῶν, καὶ ὅσους ἐὰν εὕρητε
[p] καλέσατε εἰς τοὺς [s] γάμους. 10 καὶ ἐξελθόντες οἱ δοῦλοι
ἐκεῖνοι εἰς τὰς ὁδοὺς [t] συνήγαγον πάντας ὅσους εὗρον,

g ch. xiii. 8 reff.
h here only. Isa. xlv. 14. Ezek. xxvii. 15.
i ch. xxi. 46 reff.
k Luke xi. 45. xviii. 32. Acts xiv. 5. 1 Thess. ii. 2 only. 2 Kings xix. 43.
l ch. v. 22 reff.
m Luke xxiii. 11. Acts xxiii. 10, 27. Rev. ix. 16. xix. 14, 19 bis only +. 2 Macc. v. 24 al.
n Acts iii. 14. vii. 52. xxviii. 4. 1 Pet. iv. 15. Rev. xxi. 8. xxii. 15 only +. Wisd. xii. 5 only. (-νευτής, 4 Kings ix. 31.)
o here only. Josh. viii. 19. Judg. xv. 6 B.
p ver. 3 reff.
q = ch. x. 11 reff.
r here only. Ps. i. 3. cxviii. 136.
s vv. 2 &c. reff.
t ch. xiii. 2 reff.

5. rec *ο μεν* and *ο δε*, with C²X rel Chr: *οι μεν* and *οι δε* D lat-*b c e* ff_2 *h* Iren-int Lucif: * ὃ μέν and *ος δε* C¹ℵ: *ος μεν* and *ος δε* BL 1. 69 Orig$_2$. (33 def, but has *ος δε*.) rec (for *επι*) *εις* (*mechanical repetition of former*), with L rel Chr-H [Damasc$_1$] Iren-int Op: txt BCDℵ 33. 69 latt Orig$_2$ Chr Lucif. *αυτων* D lat-*b c* ff_2 *h* Iren-int Lucif.

6. om *αυτου* L Orig$_1$ Eus Iren-int-4-mss: ins B(see table) ℵ rel &c.

7. rec (for *ο δε*) *ακουσας δε ο*, with 33(appy) Syr: *ο δε βασ. ακ.* 13. 69. 124. 346 vulg lat-ff_1 $g_{1.2}$ *h* copt arm Eus Chr Iren-int: *και ακουσας ο βασ. εκεινος* C rel lat-*f* syr Damasc: *εκεινος ο βασ. ακουσας* D, *ille autem* &c lat-*a b c e* ff_2 Lucif: txt BLℵ 1. 22. 118. 209 lat-*l* syr-cu copt-ms sah æth [Cyr$_1$]. (*It appears from the variety of position, as if ακουσας had been a supplementary gloss, because the king was* not present, *and εκεινος insd after ch* xviii. 28, or *ver* 10.) for *τα στρατευματα*, *το στρατευμα* D 1. 118. 209-38 lat-*a b c* &c syr-cu copt Orig [Eus$_2$ Lucif].

9. rec (for *εαν*) *αν*, with DGKLSΠ Orig$_2$ [Chr Bas$_1$]: txt BCℵ rel Orig$_1$.

10. for *εκεινοι*, *αυτου* D 49 latt(not *f*) Iren-int: om arm Chr Lucif. for *οσους*, *ους* [B¹(Tischdf, expr)] Dℵ Scr's c v vulg lat-*f* g_1. [*ευραν* D.]

That *thus* the slaying of the Lord is not the *doing of the invited*, but is mentioned as *done for the Feast*, is no real difficulty. Both sides of the truth may be included in the parable, as they are in Acts ii. 23, and indeed wherever it is set forth. The discourse of Peter in that chapter is the best commentary on πάντα ἕτοιμα· δεῦτε εἰς τοὺς γ. Meyer well remarks that 'ἄριστον is not = δεῖπνον, but is the meal at noon with which the course of marriage festivities *began*.' This will give even greater precision to the meaning of the parable as applying to these preparatory foretastes of the great feast, which the Church of God now enjoys. As the former parable had an O. T. foundation, so this: viz. Prov. ix. 1 ff. **5, 6.**] Two classes are here represented: the *irreligious* and careless *people* (notice τὸν **ἴδιον** ἀγρόν, bringing out the selfish spirit), and the *rulers*, who *persecuted and slew God's messengers*. Stephen,—James the brother of John, James the Just, and doubtless other of the Apostles of whose end we have no certain account, perished by the hands or instigation of the Jews: they persecuted Paul all through his life, and most probably brought him to his death at last: and the guilt of the death of the Lord abode upon them (ch. xxvii. 25). They repeatedly insulted and scourged the Apostles (see Acts iv. 3; v. 18, 40). **7.**] The occurrence of this verse before the opening of the Feast to the Gentiles has perplexed some interpreters: but it is strictly exact: for although the Gospel was preached to the Gentiles forty years before the destruction of Jerusalem, yet the final rejection of the Jews and the *substitution of the Gentiles* did not take place till that event. **τὰ στρατ. αὐτοῦ**] The *Roman* armies; a similar expression for the unconscious instruments of God's anger is used Isa. x. 5; xiii. 5: Jer. xxv. 9: Joel ii. 25. **τὴν πόλιν αὐ.**] no longer *His*, but *their* city. Compare ὁ οἶκος **ὑμῶν** ch. xxiii. 38. This is a startling introduction of the *interpretation into the parable;* we knew not before that they had *a city*. **8—10.**] On **οὐκ ἄξιοι** see Acts xiii. 46. ἦσαν, as Bengel,—"*præteritum* indignos eo magis *prætermittit*." **διέξοδοι** are the places of resort at the meetings of streets, the squares, or con-

u ch. v. 45. v ch. ix. 10. xxvi. 20. Luke xxii. 27 al.† Esdr. iv. 10 only. w Luke xxiii. 55 reff. x ch. vi. 25. xxvii. 31 al. Zeph. i. 8. Isa. lxi. 10. Zech. iii. 5. y ch. iii. 4. vi. 25, 28. xxviii. 3. Matt. only, exc. Luke xii. 23. 4 Kings x. 22. ix. 21 al. Ruth ii. 14. xxv. 4 [only]). 1 Pet. ii. 15 only.

[u] πονηρούς τε καὶ [u] ἀγαθούς· καὶ ἐπλήσθη ὁ γάμος [v] ἀνα- BCDEF GHKL MSUVX ΔΠℵ 1. 33. 69
κειμένων. 11 εἰςελθὼν δὲ ὁ βασιλεὺς [w] θεάσασθαι τοὺς
[v] ἀνακειμένους εἶδεν ἐκεῖ ἄνθρωπον οὐκ [x] ἐνδεδυμένον [y] ἔνδυμα
γάμου. 12 καὶ λέγει αὐτῷ [z] Ἑταῖρε, πῶς εἰςῆλθες [a] ὧδε μὴ
ἔχων [y] ἔνδυμα γάμου; ὁ δὲ [b] ἐφιμώθη. 13 τότε ὁ βασιλεὺς εἶπεν τοῖς διακόνοις Δήσαντες αὐτοῦ πόδας καὶ χεῖρας [c] ἐκβάλετε αὐτὸν εἰς τὸ [c] σκότος τὸ [c] ἐξώτερον· ἐκεῖ

z ch. xi. 17 reff. a = ch. viii. 29. xiv. 18. Mark xi. 3. Acts b ver. 34. Mark i. 25 ||. iv. 39. 1 Tim. v. 18 (& 1 Cor. ix. 9 v. r., from Deut. c ch. viii. 12 reff.

for *γαμος*, *νυμφων* B¹Lℵ: txt B¹-marg(sic, from personal inspection; B² has retouched it) CD rel Orig₃ [Chr] (*ο αγαμος* C). ins *των* bef *ανακειμενων* D 69.

11. om *εκει* ℵ¹(ins ℵ³ᵃ) Chr. for *ουκ*, *μη* C³D.

12. for *εισηλθ.*, *ηλθες* D lat-*b c* &c syr-cu Iren-int Lucif Aug Ambr₁. for *ο*, *ος* D.

13. rec *ειπεν* bef *ο βασιλευς*, with CD rel vss Iren-int Lucif: txt BLℵ 33. 69 lat-*h*. rec bef *εκβαλετε* ins *αρατε αυτον και* (*see below*), with C rel lat-*f ff*₁ syr: om BLℵ 1. 69 am(with fuld) lat-*g*₁.₂ *l* Syr coptt æth arm Orig₇ Chr Cyr_appy [Eus] Hil₁ Aug Op.—*αρατε αυτον ποδων κ. χειρων κ. βαλετε* D lat-*a b c e ff*₂ *h* syr-cu Iren-int Hil₁ Lucif Donat: *tollite eum ligatis pedibus et manibus et mittite eum* lat-*ff*₁ Ambrst Jer Vict-tun. (The *origin of the variations seems to have been, the difficulty presented by a person* bound hand and foot *being* cast out,—*without some expression implying his being* taken up by the hands of others. *This has* perhaps *led to the insertion in rec and the change of the sentence in* D.) for *εκβ.*, *βαλετε* DH 69. 240-4-8, *mittite* latt. rec om *αυτον* (*see above*), with C rel lat-*b f*: ins BDLℵ 1 latt syrr syr-cu coptt æth arm Orig₂ Eus Iren-int Lucif.

fluences of ways. De Wette and Meyer are wrong in saying that they are not in the city, 'for that was destroyed:' it is not *the city of the murderers, but that in which the feast is supposed to be held*, which is spoken of: not Jerusalem, but God's world. **πονηρ. τε κ. ἀγαθ.**] Both the open sinners and the morally good together. See ch. xiii. 47, where the net collects ἐκ παντὸς γένους. Stier remarks that we might expect, from ch. xxi. 31, to find the guest who by and by is expelled, *among the* **ἀγαθοί**. **ὁ γάμος** is here **the feast**, not *the place where it was held*. Here, so to speak, the *first act* of the parable closes; and here is the situation of the Church at this day;—collected out of all the earth, and containing both bad and good. **ἐπλήσθη**, as Meyer well remarks, is emphatic.

11, 12.] This second part of the parable is in direct reference to the word of prophecy, Zeph. i. 7, 8: cf. especially ver. 8, καὶ ἔσται ἐν ἡμέρᾳ θυσίας κυρίου καὶ ἐκδικήσω . . . ἐπὶ πάντας τοὺς ἐνδεδυμένους ἐνδύματα ἀλλότρια. The coming of the King to see his guests is the final and separating Judgment of the Church, see ch. xxv. 19,—when that distinction shall be made, which God's ministers have no power nor right to make in admissions into the visible Church. Yet as Trench remarks (Parables, p. 207), this coming of the King is not *exclusively* the final one, but every trying and sifting judgment adumbrates it in some measure.

With regard to the **ἔνδυμα γάμου**, we must not, I think, make too much of the usually cited Oriental custom of presenting the guests with such garments at feasts. For (1) it is not distinctly proved that such a custom existed; the passages usually quoted (Gen. xlv. 22: Judg. xiv. 12: 2 Kings v. 22) are nothing to the purpose; 2 Kings x. 22 shews that the worshippers of Baal were provided with vestments, and *at a feast*: and at the present day those who are admitted to the presence of Royalty in the East are clothed with a *caftan*: but all this does not make good the assumption: and (2) even granting it, it is not to be pressed, as being manifestly not the punctum saliens of this part of the parable. The guest was bound to provide himself with this proper habit, out of respect to the feast and its Author: *how* this was to be provided, does not *here* appear, but does *elsewhere*. The garment is *the imputed and inherent righteousness of the Lord Jesus*, put on *symbolically* in Baptism (Gal. iii. 27), and *really* by a true and living faith (ib. ver. 26),—without which none can appear before God in His Kingdom of Glory;—Heb. xii. 14: Phil. iii. 7, 8: Eph. iv. 24: Col. iii. 10; Rom. xiii. 14:—which truth could not be put forward *here*, but at its subsequent mani-

ἔσται ὁ [c] κλαυθμὸς καὶ ὁ [c] βρυγμος τῶν ὀδόντων.
14 [d] πολλοὶ γάρ εἰσιν [d] κλητοί, ὀλίγοι δὲ [d] ἐκλεκτοί.
15 Τότε πορευθέντες οἱ Φαρισαῖοι [e] συμβούλιον [e] ἔλαβον
ὅπως αὐτὸν [f] παγιδεύσωσιν ἐν λόγῳ. 16 καὶ ἀποστέλλουσιν αὐτῷ τοὺς μαθητὰς αὐτῶν μετὰ τῶν Ἡρωδιανῶν
Z αληθης... λέγοντες [g] Διδάσκαλε, οἴδαμεν ὅτι [h] ἀληθὴς εἶ, καὶ τὴν
[i] ὁδὸν τοῦ [i] θεοῦ [k] ἐν ἀληθείᾳ διδάσκεις, καὶ οὐ [l] μέλει σοι
περὶ οὐδενός, οὐ γὰρ [m] βλέπεις εἰς [n] πρόσωπον ἀνθρώπων.
17 εἰπὲ οὖν ἡμῖν τί σοι δοκεῖ; ἔξεστιν δοῦναι [o] κῆνσον
Καίσαρι ἢ οὔ; 18 γνοὺς δὲ ὁ Ἰησοῦς τὴν [p] πονηρίαν
αὐτῶν εἶπεν Τί με [q] πειράζετε ὑποκριταί; 19 [r] ἐπιδείξατέ
μοι τὸ [s] νόμισμα τοῦ [o] κήνσου. οἱ δὲ προςήνεγκαν αὐτῷ

d ch. xx. 16 reff.
e ch. xii. 14 reff.
f here only. 1 Kings xxviii. 9. Eccl. ix. 12 only. Prov. vi. 2 Symm.
g ch. ix. 11 reff.
h so John iii 33. 2 Cor. vi. 8 al.
i ||. (Acts xviii. 26 v. r.) see Acts xiii. 10 al.
k 2 Cor. vii. 14. 1 John iii. 18. 2 John 1. 3 John 1. 2 Chron. xix. 9.
l w. περί, || Mk. John x. 13. xii. 6. (1 Cor. ix. 9 v. r.) 1 Pet. v. 7 only. Wisd. xii. 13. 1 Macc. xiv. 43 only. (Mark iv. 38 reff.)
m || Mk. 2 Cor. x. 7.
n 2 Cor. x. 7. 1 Thess. ii. 17. Jude 16. Lev. xix. 15. Deut. x. 17. 1 Kings xvi. 7.
o || Mk. ch. xvii. 25 only +.
p Mark vii. 22. Luke xi. 39. Acts iii. 26. Rom. i. 29. 1 Cor. v. 8. Eph. vi. 12 only. Ps. cxl. 4.
q ch. iv. 1 al. Exod. xvii. 2.
r ch. xvi. 1 reff.
s here only Ezra viii. 36. Neh. vii. 71 Ed-vat.[ℵ3] (not ABℵ1). 1 Macc. xv. 6 only.

15. om ελαβον ℵ[1](ins ℵ[3a]). aft ελαβον ins κατ' αυτου C[2]-marg Δ **1.** 33 copt arm Orig: κατα του ιησου C[3]M 258. for οπως, πως D lat-*f* syrr syr-cu. [οπ. αυ. παγ. is written over an erasure by B[1].] om εν λογω ℵ[1](ins ℵ[3a]) Cyr.
16. for αυτω, προς αυτον D lat-*a c f.* **λεγοντας** BLℵ: txt CD rel [Damasc$_1$-ms]. **επ'** D Eus$_1$[(txt$_1$) Cyr$_1$]. **αληθειας** (but *s* written above the line) D.
17. **ειπον** LZ 33.—om ειπε ουν ημιν D lat-*a b e ff*$_{1.2}$ [Cyr$_1$].

festation threw its great light over this and other such similitudes and expressions. This guest imagines *his own garment* will be as acceptable, and therefore neglects to provide himself. See 1 John v. 10: Isa. lxiv. 6; lxi. 10: Rev. xix. 8. **ἑταῖρε**] see note on ch. xx. 13: and, as a curiosity of exegetical application, Wordsw.'s note here. **13, 14.**] The **διάκονοι** are not the same as the δοῦλοι above, but *the angels,* see ch. xiii. 41, 49. The 'binding of his feet and hands' has been interpreted of his being now *in the night, in which no man can* work; but I doubt whether this be not too fanciful. Rather should we say, with Meyer, that it is to render his escape from the outer darkness impossible. On **τὸ σκ. τὸ ἐξ.** see reff. In ver. 14 our Lord shews us that this guest, thus single in the parable, is, alas, to be the representative of a numerous class in the visible Church, who, although sitting down as guests before His coming, have not on the ἔνδυμα γάμου.

15—22.] Reply concerning the lawfulness of tribute to Cæsar. Mark xii. 13—17. Luke xx. 20—26. On the *Herodians,* see above, ch. xvi. 6. By the union of these two hostile parties they perhaps thought that the ἐγκάθετοι (Luke), who were to feign themselves honest men, Luke xx. 20, would be more likely *to deceive our Lord.* For this also is their *flattery* here designed. 'The devil never lies so foully, as when he speaks the truth.' Meyer compares that other οἴδαμεν ὅτι, John iii. 2. The application may have been as if to settle a dispute which had sprung up between the Pharisees, the strong theocratic repudiators of Roman rule, and the Herodians, the hangers-on of a dynasty created by Cæsar. In case the answer were *negative,* these last would be witnesses against Him to the governor (Luke xx. 20); as indeed they became, with false testimony, when they could not get true, Luke xxiii. 2; in case it were *affirmative,* He would be compromised with the Roman conquerors, and could not be the people's deliverer, their expected Messias; which would furnish them with a pretext for stirring up the multitudes against Him (see Deut. xvii. 15). **17.**] **κῆνσος** = φόρος, Luke xx. 22; = ἐπικεφάλαιον: a poll-tax, which had been levied since Judæa became a province of Rome. **18—22.**] Our Lord not only detects their plot, but answers their question; and in answering it, teaches them each a deep lesson.
The **νόμισμα κήνσου** was a denarius. It was a saying of the Rabbis, quoted by Lightfoot and Wetstein, that 'wherever any king's money is current, there that king is lord.' The Lord's answer convicts them, by the matter of fact that this money was current among them, of

t ch. xx. 2 reff. u || only in Gospp. Rom. i. 23. Heb. x. 1 al. Gen. v. 1. v ||. Mark xv. 26 :|| L. only +. w Rom. xiii. 7 al. Deut. xxiii. 21. x ch. xi. 17 reff. y = Gospp., here &c. ||. Luke (ii. 34.) xiv. 14. John v. 29 bis. xi. 24, 25 only. Acts i. 22 al. Lam. iii. 63. Zeph. iii. 8. 2 Macc. vii. 14. xii. 43 only. z Deut. xxv. 5. a = Gen. xxxviii. 8 Ed-vat. (B def. γαμβ. A.) b here only. Gen. xxxiv. 9 al. but not =.

[t] δηνάριον. 20 καὶ λέγει αὐτοῖς Τίνος ἡ [u] εἰκὼν αὕτη καὶ
ἡ [v] ἐπιγραφή; 21 λέγουσιν [αὐτῷ] Καίσαρος. τότε λέγει ...επιγραφη C.
αὐτοῖς [w] Ἀπόδοτε οὖν [x] τὰ Καίσαρος Καίσαρι· καὶ [x] τὰ
τοῦ θεοῦ τῷ θεῷ. 22 καὶ ἀκούσαντες ἐθαύμασαν, καὶ
ἀφέντες αὐτὸν ἀπῆλθαν. ...απηλθον X.
23 Ἐν ἐκείνῃ τῇ ἡμέρᾳ προσῆλθον αὐτῷ Σαδδουκαῖοι BDEFG
λέγοντες μὴ εἶναι [y] ἀνάστασιν. καὶ ἐπηρώτησαν αὐτὸν HKLM SUVZΔ
24 λέγοντες Διδάσκαλε, Μωυσῆς εἶπεν [z] Ἐάν τις ἀποθάνῃ ΠΝ 1. 33. 69
μὴ ἔχων τέκνα, [ab] ἐπιγαμβρεύσει ὁ ἀδελφὸς αὐτοῦ τὴν

20. for 1st και, ο δε C : om D [69, Wtst] lat-*b e* $ff_{1.2}$ $g_{1.2}$ *h* (sah). aft αυτοις add ο ῑς DLZ 33. 69 latt Syr syr-cu copt æth arm-mss Op_1. κ. η επιγρ. bef αυτη LZ.
21. om αυτω Bℵ lat-g_2 Syr arm [Promiss]. om ουν D 157 Scr's k lat-*a b c e* ff_1 syr-cu copt æth arm ($Orig_2$[ins_1] Did) Chr Tert Ambr. ins τω bef καισαρι DKΔ[Π] Scr's e Just $Orig_2$ [Bas_1 $Damasc_1$-ms].
22. (απηλθαν, so BD.)
23. at beg ins και ℵ[1](ℵ[3a] disapproving). om αυτω ℵ[1](ins ℵ[3a]). rec ins οι bef λεγοντες, with Lℵ[3a] rel syr coptt arm, *qui dicunt* latt : om BDMSZ [Δ(*hom* λεγ. to λεγ. next ver)] Π[1]ℵ[1] 1. 33 æth $Orig_3$ [$Meth_1$ $Epiph_1$] Thl.—*et dicentes ei* Syr syr-cu. (*Both variations arose appy from termn* -καιοι *of preceding word.*)
24. ins ινα bef επιγαμβρευσει D Z(appy) latt(*a* def) copt : [και 13(Tischdf) 69 :] om

subjection to (Tiberius) Cæsar, and recognition of that subjection: **Pay therefore,** He says, **that which is Cæsar's to Cæsar, and** (not perhaps without reference to the Herodians, but with much deeper reference) **that which is God's, to God.** These weighty words, so much misunderstood, bind together, instead of separating, the political and religious duties of the followers of Christ. See Jer. xxvii. 4—18: Rom. xiii. 1 : 1 Pet. ii. 13, 14 : John xix. 11. The second clause comprehends the first, and gives its true foundation : q. d. 'this obedience to Cæsar is but an application of the general principle of obedience to God, of Whom is all power.' The latter clause thus reaches infinitely deeper than the former : just as our Lord in Luke x. 41, 42 declares a truth reaching far beyond the occasion of the meal. *Man is the coinage*, and *bears the image*, of God (Gen. i. 27) : and this image *is not lost by the fall* (Gen. ix. 6 : Acts xvii. 29 : James iii. 9. See also notes on Luke xv. 8, 9 : and compare Tertull. contr. Marc. iv. 38, vol. ii. p. 453, "Quæ erunt Dei? quæ similia sunt denario Cæsaris, imago scilicet et similitudo ejus. Hominem igitur reddi jubet Creatori, in cujus imagine et similitudine et nomine et materia expressus est"). We owe then *ourselves* to God : and this solemn duty is implied, of giving ourselves to Him, with all that we have and are. The answer also *gives them the real reason why they were now under subjection to Cæsar* : viz. *because they had fallen from their allegiance to God.* 'The question was as if an adulterer were to ask, whether it were lawful for him to pay the penalty of his adultery.' (Claudius, cited by Stier ii. 388.) They had again and again rejected their theocratic inheritance;—they refused it in the wilderness;—they would not have God to reign over them, but a king;—therefore were they subjected to foreigners (see 2 Chron. xii. 8).

23—33.] Reply to the Sadducees respecting the resurrection. Mark xii. 18—27. Luke xx. 27—40. From Acts xxiii. 8, the Sadducees denied resurrection, angel, and *spirit;* consequently the *immortality of the soul, as well as the resurrection of the body.* This should be borne in mind, as our Lord's answer is directed against both errors. It is a mistake into which many Commentators (including Wordsw. on the authority of Jerome) have fallen, to suppose that the Sadducees recognized only the Pentateuch: they acknowledged *the prophets also*, and rejected tradition only (see this abundantly proved by Winer, Realwörterbuch, Sadducäer). **23. λέγ.**] In Luke, οἱ ἀντιλέγ. = οἵτινες λέγουσιν Mark. Here, the art. being absent, we must understand that they came, saying that there was no resurrection : i. e. either, in pursuance of their well-known denial of that doctrine,—or, which is more probable, actually saying, maintaining it against our Lord : viz., in

γυναῖκα αὐτοῦ, καὶ [ac] ἀναστήσει [ad] σπέρμα τῷ ἀδελφῷ αὐτοῦ. 25 ἦσαν δὲ [e] παρ' ἡμῖν ἑπτὰ ἀδελφοί· καὶ ὁ πρῶτος
γήμας ἐτελεύτησεν, καὶ μὴ ἔχων [d] σπέρμα [f] ἀφῆκεν τὴν
γυναῖκα αὐτοῦ τῷ ἀδελφῷ αὐτοῦ. 26 ὁμοίως καὶ ὁ δεύτερος καὶ ὁ τρίτος, [g] ἕως τῶν ἑπτά. 27 [h] ὕστερον δὲ πάντων
ἀπέθανεν ἡ γυνή. 28 ἐν τῇ [y] ἀναστάσει οὖν τίνος τῶν
ἑπτὰ ἔσται γυνή; πάντες γὰρ [i] ἔσχον αὐτήν. 29 ἀποκριθεὶς δὲ ὁ Ἰησοῦς εἶπεν αὐτοῖς [k] Πλανᾶσθε μὴ εἰδότες τὰς
[l] γραφὰς μηδὲ τὴν δύναμιν τοῦ θεοῦ. 30 ἐν γὰρ τῇ
[y] ἀναστάσει οὔτε γαμοῦσιν οὔτε [m] γαμίζονται, ἀλλ' ὡς
ἄγγελοι [θεοῦ] ἐν τῷ οὐρανῷ εἰσιν. 31 περὶ δὲ τῆς
[yn] ἀναστάσεως τῶν [n] νεκρῶν οὐκ ἀνέγνωτε τὸ [o] ῥηθὲν ὑμῖν

Γ και ο πρωτος.. . πρωτος Z. Θ_b is cited for γαμησας, but not again till του θεου ver. 30.

c = Acts iii. 22, 26.
d = ||. Gen. iv. 25.
e John xvii. 5. Rev. ii. 13. Prov. ii. 1.
f = John xiv. 18. Ps. xvi. 14.
g Mark vi. 23 al.
h ch. iv. 2 reff. constr., || L. only. Jer. xxxvi. (xxix.) 2.
i = ch. xiv. 4 reff.
k = 2 Tim. iii. 13. 1 Cor. vi. 9. xv. 33. Gal. vi. 7. Isa. xliv. 8.
l John v. 39 reff.
m || Mk. Luke xvii. 27 [1 Cor. vii. 38 bis] only †. see || L.
n (ἀν. ἐκ ν., Luke xx. 35 reff.) Acts xvii. 32. xxiii. 6. xxiv. 15, 21. 1 Cor. xv. 12, &c.
o ch. i. 22 reff.

Bℵ rel syrr syr-cu sah æth arm Orig. om την γυν. αυτου D.

25. om δε D. rec (for γημας) γαμησας, with DΘ_b rel: txt BLℵ 1. 33 Orig.

27. rec ins και bef η γυνη (*see* ||), with D[Θ_b ?] rel vss: om BLUΔΠ[1]ℵ 1 lat-*e* syr-cu æth.

28. rec ουν bef αναστ., with E[Θ_b ?] rel: txt BDLℵ 1. 69 vulg lat-*b c e f ff*$_{1.2}$ *g*$_1$ *h l*. εσται bef των επτα D vulg lat-*c ff*$_{1.2}$ *g*$_1$ *h*. [om τ. επ. lat-*b e* syr-cu.]

29. for αποκ. δε, και αποκ. ℵ: om δε lat-*b e h* Syr syr-cu.

30. rec εκγαμιζονται, with E rel syr-mg-gr Orig$_1$: εγγαμισκονται 69: *nubentur* vulg lat-*e f ff*$_1$ *g*$_1$: *uxores ducunt* lat-*b c ff*$_2$: txt BDLℵ 1 (Clem) Orig$_2$ Ath [Cyr$_1$-p] Isid Thdrt: γαμισκονται 33 Orig$_2$ [Meth$_2$ Epiph$_2$ Chr]. rec aft αγγελοι ins του, with ΔΘ_b rel vulg lat-*ff*$_1$ *g*$_1$ syrr copt æth Orig-int$_2$: om Lℵ 33. 69 Scr's s evv-H-z [Chr]: om θεου also (*see* || *Mark*) BDE[1] 1 harl[1] lat-*a b c e f ff*$_2$ *h* syr-cu sah arm Orig$_5$ Ambr Aug. rec om τω bef ουρανω, with D Θ_b(appy) rel [Meth Epiph Chr]: ins BLℵ 1. 33. 69 coptt Orig$_3$.

shape and manner following. **24. ἀναστ. σπέρ.**] The first-born son of a leviratical marriage was reckoned and registered as the son of the deceased brother, Michaelis, Mos. R. ii. 98 (Meyer). **28.**] **γυνή** is the predicate. **29, 30.**] **τὰς γρ. μ. τ. δ. τ. θ.**, not = τὴν δ. τ. θ. τὴν ἐν ταῖς γρ.,—but to be rendered literally; **ye do not understand the Scriptures**, which imply the resurrection (ver. 31), **nor the power of God**, before which all these obstacles vanish (ver. 30). See Acts xxvi. 8: Rom. iv. 17; viii. 11: 1 Cor. vi. 14. **γαμοῦσιν**, of males; **γαμίζ.**, of females. Our Lord also asserts here against them the *existence of angels*, and reveals to us the similarity of our glorified state to their present one. Not ἐν τῷ οὐρ. εἰσιν, ὡς ἄγ. [θεοῦ], but εἰσιν, ὡς ἄγ. [θεοῦ] ἐν τῷ οὐ. (see note on Luke xx. 35, and 1 Cor. xv. 44);—the *risen* are *not in heaven*, but *on earth*. Wetstein quotes the *Rabbinical* decision of a similar question—'Mulier illa quæ duobus nupsit in hoc mundo, priori restituitur in mundo futuro.' **31—33.**] Our Lord does not cite the strong testimonies of the Prophets, as Isa. xxvi. 19: Ezek. xxxvii. 1—14: Dan. xii. 2, but says, as in Luke (xx. 37), '*even Moses* has shewn,' &c., leaving those other witnesses to be supplied. The books of Moses were the great and ultimate appeal for all doctrine: and thus the assertion of the Resurrection comes from the very source whence their difficulty had been constructed. On the passage itself, and our Lord's interpretation of it, much has been written. Certain it is that our Lord brings out in this answer a depth of meaning in the words, which without it we could not discover. Meyer, in reply to Strauss and Hase, finely says, "Our Lord here testifies of the conscious intent of God in speaking the words. God uttered them, He tells us, to Moses, in the consciousness of the still enduring existence of his peculiar relation to Abraham, Isaac, and Jacob." The groundwork of His argument seems to me to be this:—the words 'I am thy God' imply a *covenant; there is another side* to them: "Thou art Mine" follows upon "I am thine." When God therefore declares that He *is the God* of Abraham, Isaac, and Jacob, He declares *their continuance*, as the other parties in this

p Exod. iii. 6, 15, 16.
q ch. vii. 28 reff.
r ver. 12 reff.
s ch. xiii. 2 reff.
t Acts iv. 26 (from Ps. ii. 2) only. 2 Kings x. 15. Neh. vi. 2.
u as above (t). Luke xvii. 15. Acts i. 15. ii. 1, 44. (iii. 1.) 1 Cor. vii. 5. xi. 20. xiv. 23 only.
v ch. xxvii. 48. Mark ix. 17. Luke xvii. 15. xxii. 50 al. Gen. iii. 22.
w Matt., here only. Luke vii. 30 al5. Tit. iii. 9, 13 only +.
x ch. iv. 1, 3. ver. 18.
y = ch. xxi. 23 reff.

[o] ὑπὸ τοῦ θεοῦ λέγοντος 32 [p] Ἐγώ εἰμι ὁ θεὸς Ἀβραὰμ καὶ
ὁ θεὸς Ἰσαὰκ καὶ ὁ θεὸς Ἰακώβ; οὐκ ἔστιν ὁ θεὸς [θεὸς]
νεκρῶν, ἀλλὰ ζώντων. 33 καὶ ἀκούσαντες οἱ ὄχλοι
[q] ἐξεπλήσσοντο ἐπὶ τῇ [q] διδαχῇ αὐτοῦ. 34 Οἱ δὲ Φαρισαῖοι
ἀκούσαντες ὅτι [r] ἐφίμωσεν τοὺς Σαδδουκαίους, [st] συνήχθησαν [tu] ἐπὶ τὸ [tu] αὐτό, 35 καὶ ἐπηρώτησεν [v] εἷς ἐξ αὐτῶν
[w] νομικὸς [x] πειράζων αὐτὸν καὶ λέγων 36 Διδάσκαλε,
[y] ποία [z] ἐντολὴ μεγάλη ἐν τῷ νόμῳ; 37 ὁ δὲ ἔφη αὐτῷ
[a] Ἀγαπήσεις κύριον τὸν θεόν σου [b] ἐν ὅλῃ [τῇ] καρδίᾳ σου Z κυριον τον...
καὶ [b] ἐν ὅλῃ τῇ ψυχῇ σου καὶ [b] ἐν ὅλῃ τῇ [c] διανοίᾳ σου. BDEFG HKLM
38 αὕτη ἐστὶν ἡ μεγάλη καὶ πρώτη [z] ἐντολή. 39 δευτέρα SUVZΓ
δὲ ὁμοία αὐτῇ [d] Ἀγαπήσεις τὸν πλησίον σου ὡς σεαυτόν. ΔΘ$_b$Πℵ 1. 33. 69
40 ἐν ταύταις ταῖς δυσὶν ἐντολαῖς ὅλος ὁ νόμος [e] κρέμαται
καὶ οἱ προφῆται.

z ch. v. 19 al. Lev. iv. 13. a Deut. vi. 5. b John iv. 23, 24. (ἐξ, ǁ and Luke x. 27, from l. c.) c ǁ and Luke x. 27, from l. c. B. Luke i. 51. Eph. ii. 3 al. Exod. ix. 21. d Levit. xix. 18. e = and w. ἐν, here only. w. ἐκ, Judith viii. 24. (elsw. lit. w. εἰς, ch. xviii. 6. [ἐπὶ & acc., and περί, ib. v. r.] gen., Acts v. 30. x. 39. Gal. iii. 13, from Deut. xxi. 23. ἐκ, Acts xxviii. 4. ἐν, Ezek. xvii. 10. absol., Luke xxiii. 39.) Plato, Legg. viii. p. 831, ἐξ ὧν κρεμαμένη πᾶσα ψυχὴ πολίτου.

32. om 2nd and 3rd ὁ ℵ Orig. om 4th ὁ DHℵ. om 5th θεος (*see* ǁ *Mark Luke*) BDLΔℵ 1. 33 latt Syr syr-cu coptt Orig$_2$[and int$_1$] Eus Chr Damasc Iren-int Tert Hil$_3$ Aug: ins E Θ$_b$(appy) rel syr (æth) arm Orig$_3$ Chr(but om (not ms-γ) preceding ο θεος).

34. for επι το αυτο, επ αυτον D lat-*b c e ff*$_2$ syr-cu æth Hil.

35. om και λεγων (*see* ǁ *Mark*) BLℵ 33 vulg lat-*e ff*$_1$ *g*$_{1.2}$ *l* Syr coptt æth Orig-int: ins DΘ$_b$ rel lat-*b c f ff*$_2$ *h* syr syr-cu [(arm) Chr]. (lat-*a* def.)

36. εν τω νομω bef μεγαλη D 122.

37. rec aft ο δε ins ιησους (*see* ǁ *Mark*), with Θ$_b$ rel syrr æth arm: aft αυτω (omg ο δε) D latt syr-cu: txt BLℵ 33 coptt Orig-int. rec (for εφη) ειπεν, with 69(e sil): txt BDℵ rel Scr's mss Bas Thl. om 1st τη Bℵ[1] rel Clem: ins DKLMSZΠℵ[3a]. om 2nd τη B rel Thl: ins DKLMSZΠℵ Clem. aft 3rd σου ins και εν ολη τη ισχυι σου (ǁ *Mark*) Θ$_b$ 69 Syr syr-jer copt-dz æth.

38. rec πρωτη και μεγαλη (*because* πρωτη *is the* leading predicate,—*cf* δευτ. *below. So also Meyer, and in part De W*), with Θ$_b$ rel lat-*f* syr arm [Bas] Op: η πρ. κ. μεγ. Δ: txt B D-gr(om η) L(η πρω.) Zℵ 1. 33. 69 latt Syr syr-cu syr-jer coptt æth Orig-int$_2$ Hil Aug.

39. om δε Bℵ[1](ins ℵ[3a]). ομοιως, omg αυτη, B. ταυτη D Cypr Hil Zeno Oros Op: αυτης Δ Chr Bas. (αὔτη EFGHKMUVΓΠ Bas: dative Γ 1. 33. 69 vss.) for σεαυτ., εαυτον H[1]VΘ$_b$ 1. 69. 237-8. 243-5-8. 251-8 Scr's b? c e o q r s w evv-x-z [Bas$_1$].

40. om ολος ℵ[1] Syr syr-cu coptt: ins ℵ[3a] Aug$_{expr}$. rec και οι προφ. κρεμανται (*gramml corrn*), with Θ$_b$ rel syr coptt arm Clem Orig$_1$[and int$_1$ Bas$_1$] Zeno: txt BDLZℵ 33 latt Syr syr-cu æth [Bas$_1$ Jac-nisch$_1$] Orig-int$_4$ Tert Hil Cypr.

covenant. It is an assertion which *could not be made of an annihilated being of the past.* And notice also (with Bengel), that Abraham's (&c.) *body,* having had upon it *the seal of the covenant,* is included in this. Stier (after Lavater) remarks that this is a weighty testimony against the so-called 'sleep of the soul' in the intermediate state. Compare πάντες γὰρ αὐτῷ ζῶσιν Luke xx. 38, and ζῶσι τῷ θεῷ 4 Macc. vii. 19; [xvi. 25,] spoken of the Patriarchs Abraham, Isaac, and Jacob. Thus the burden of the Law, 'I am the Lord thy God,' contains in it the seed of immortality and the hope of the resurrection.

34—40.] Reply concerning the great commandment. Mark xii. 28—34. In the more detailed account of Mark (Luke has a similar incident in another place, x. 25), this question does not appear as that of one *maliciously* tempting our Lord: and his seems to me the view to be taken,—as there could not be any evil consequences to our Lord, whichever way He had answered the question. See the notes there. **34.] ἐπὶ τὸ αὐτό is**

41 [f] Συνηγμένων δὲ τῶν Φαρισαίων ἐπηρώτησεν αὐτοὺς
ὁ Ἰησοῦς 42 λέγων Τί ὑμῖν δοκεῖ περὶ τοῦ χριστοῦ; τίνος
υἱός ἐστιν; λέγουσιν αὐτῷ Τοῦ Δαυείδ. 43 λέγει αὐτοῖς
Πῶς οὖν Δαυεὶδ ἐν [g] πνεύματι καλεῖ αὐτὸν κύριον, λέγων
44 [h] Εἶπεν Κύριος τῷ κυρίῳ μου Κάθου [i] ἐκ [i] δεξιῶν μου,
ἕως ἂν θῶ τοὺς ἐχθρούς σου [k] ὑποκάτω τῶν ποδῶν σου.
45 εἰ οὖν Δαυεὶδ καλεῖ αὐτὸν κύριον, πῶς υἱὸς αὐτοῦ
ἐστιν; 46 καὶ οὐδεὶς ἐδύνατο ἀποκριθῆναι αὐτῷ [l] λόγον,
οὐδὲ [m] ἐτόλμησέν τις ἀπ' ἐκείνης τῆς ἡμέρας ἐπερωτῆσαι
αὐτὸν οὐκέτι.

XXIII. 1 Τότε ὁ Ἰησοῦς [n] ἐλάλησεν τοῖς ὄχλοις καὶ

f ver. 34.
g = || Mk. see Luke ii. 27. iv. 1. Rev. i. 10 al.
h Psa. cix. 1.
i ch. xx. 21 al. fr.
k || Mk. Mark vi. 11. vii. 28. Luke viii. 16. John i. 51. Heb. ii. 8, from Ps. viii. 6. Rev. v. 3 al3. Ezek. xxiv. 5.
l ch. xv. 22. Isa. xxxvi. 21.
m Matt., here only. ||. Mark xv. 43. John xxi. 12. Acts v. 13 al. Esth. vii. 5.
n ch. xiii. 3. xiv. 27. xxviii. 18. John viii. 12. Gen. xlii. 22. Lev. iv. 1, 2.

42. om 2nd *του* ℵ.

43. aft *αυτοις* ins *ο ῑς* LZ 1. 33 lat-*f* *ff*$_1$ copt æth arm Dial Orig-int Ambr. [Θ$_b$?] rec *κυριον αυτον καλει* (*transposition for emphasis*), with E rel lat-*e* arm Dial Orig-int: *καλ. κυρ. αυτον* LZℵ: txt B[but B[1] repeats *αυτον*] D 33 latt Syr syr-cu coptt Did [Cyr$_1$] Hil Aug. (Θ$_b$?)

44. rec ins *ο* bef *κυριος* (*from* LXX), with LΘ$_b$ rel coptt Dial [Did$_1$(Epiph$_1$)]: om BDZℵ. rec (for *υποκατω*) *υποποδιον* (*from* LXX), with Δ(sic) Θ$_b$ rel vulg lat-*a c* &c æth arm [Cyr$_1$] Orig-int Hil: *υποποδιον υποκατω* syr: txt BDGL U(Treg) ZΓℵ 69 lat-*b e h* Syr syr-cu coptt Aug.

45. ins *εν πνευματι* bef *καλει* DKMΔΠ 69 fuld lat-*a b c f ff*$_2$ *g*$_2$ *h l* syr-with-ast syr-jer copt Dial Eus [Nyss$_1$ Thdrt$_1$] Hil Cypr Ambr.

46. *ηδυνατο* B[2] 1 [Cyr$_1$]: txt B[1]Θ$_b$ℵ rel. rec *αυτω* bef *αποκριθηναι* with Θ$_b$ rel vulg-ed(with gat) lat-*e f ff*$_{1.2}$ Orig-int$_1$ Ambr: txt BDKLZΔΠℵ 33. 69 am(with forj fuld tol) lat-*a b c g*$_{1.2}$ *h l* syrr syr-cu [Cyr$_1$] Orig-int$_1$ Op. for *ημερας*, *ωρας* D E[1](appy) 1 lat-*a* syr-cu syr-ms-mg [Cyr$_1$] Orig-int Op.

Chap. XXIII. 1. om *ο* BV. *ελαλησεν* bef *ο ιησ.* D 69 evv-H-P syr-cu æth Orig-int.

local; not of *their purpose.* **35. νομικός**] These were Mosaic jurists, whose special province was the interpretation of the Law. *γραμματεύς* is a wider term, including them. **πειράζων**] see above.

36. ποία ἐντ. μεγ.] Not, '*which is the great commandment,*'—but **which** (*what kind of a*) **commandment is great in the law?** In Mark, otherwise. **37. κύρ. τ. θ. σου**] Not, '*The LORD as thy God,*' —but **the LORD thy God.** **40. ὁ ν. κ. οἱ πρ.**] in the sense of ch. v. 17; vii. 12—all the details of God's ancient revelation of His will, by whomsoever made.

41—46.] The Pharisees baffled by a question respecting Christ and David. Mark xii. 35—37. Luke xx. 41—44. (See also Acts ii. 34.) Our Lord now questions his adversaries (according to Matt.:—in Mark and Luke He asks the question not *to,* but *concerning* the Scribes or interpreters of the law), and again convicts them of ignorance of the Scriptures. From the universally recognized title of the Messiah as the Son of David, which by His question He elicits from them, He takes occasion to shew them, who understood this title in a mere worldly political sense, the difficulty arising from David's own reverence for this his Son: the solution lying in the incarnate Godhead of the Christ, of which they were ignorant. **43. ἐν πνεύμ.**] **by the inspiration of the Holy Spirit:** = *ἐν πν. ἁγίῳ* Mark. This is a weighty declaration by our Lord of the inspiration of the prophetic Scriptures. The expression was a Rabbinical one: see Schöttgen in loc. Mark (ver. 37) adds to this "the common people heard him gladly." Here then end the endeavours of His adversaries to entrap Him by questions: they now betake themselves to other means. 'Nova dehinc quasi scena se pandit.' Bengel.

Chap. XXIII. 1—39.] Denunciation of the Scribes and Pharisees. *Peculiar to Matthew.* **1.**] Much of the matter of this discourse is to be found in Luke xi. and xiii. On its appearance there, see the notes on those passages. There can, I think, be no doubt that it was delivered, as our Evangelist here relates it, all at one time, and in those the last days of our Lord's ministry. On the notion entertained by some recent critics, of St. Matthew having arranged the scattered

τοῖς μαθηταῖς αὐτοῦ [2] [n] λέγων Ἐπὶ τῆς Μωυσέως [o] καθέδρας [p] ἐκάθισαν οἱ γραμματεῖς καὶ οἱ Φαρισαῖοι· [3] πάντα
οὖν ὅσα ἂν [q] εἴπωσιν ὑμῖν ποιήσατε καὶ [r] τηρεῖτε· κατὰ δὲ
τὰ ἔργα αὐτῶν μὴ ποιεῖτε· λέγουσιν γὰρ καὶ οὐ ποιοῦσιν.
4 [s] δεσμεύουσιν δὲ [t] φορτία [u] βαρέα *καὶ ἐπιτιθέασιν ἐπὶ τοὺς
[v] ὤμους τῶν ἀνθρώπων, αὐτοὶ δὲ τῷ [w] δακτύλῳ αὐτῶν οὐ

...λεγουσιν Z. BDEFG HKLM SUVΓΔ Θ_bΠℵ 1. 33. 69

o ch. xxi. 12 ‖ only. 1 Kings xx. 18. Ps. cvi. 32.
p intr., ch. v. 1 reff.
q = Mark v. 43 al. Exod. xxxv. 1.
r ch. xix. 17 reff.
s Acts xxii. 4 only. Gen. xxxvii. 7. Job xxvi. 8.
t ch. xi. 30 reff.
u ver. 23. Acts xx. 29. xxv. 7. 2 Cor. x. 10. 1 John v. 3 only. Ps. xxxvii. 4.
v Luke xv. 5 only. Judg. xvi. 3 al.
w Mark vii. 33. Luke xi. 20, 46. xvi. 24. John [viii. 6] xx. 25, 27 only. Lev. iv. 6.

2. *καθεδρας* bef *μωυσεως* D 69. 238 latt Orig hom-Cl Iren-int Hil$_4$.

3. *παντα ουν* is repeated by D[1]. for *αν*, *εαν* ZΘ_bℵ rel: txt BDΓ (FKS, e sil) Eus [Ephr-1-ms Chr Damasc$_1$]. om *υμιν* D-gr copt Aug. rec aft *υμιν* ins *τηρειν* (*gloss, as* *ποιειν* *shews*), with Θ_b rel lat-f_1(appy) syrr: *ποιειν* Γ Chr Damasc Phot [Ephr] Orig-int: om BDLZℵ 1 latt syr-cu coptt æth arm Eus Iren-int Orig-int$_2$ Hil Ambr Aug Op Gild. rec *τηρειτε κ. ποιειτε* (*ποιησατε* *being first altered to* *ποιειτε* *for conformity, then transposed for logical accuracy: so Meyer*), with Θ_b rel latt(*a* def) syrr syr-cu Iren-int Hil: *ποιειτε* (alone) Γ Scr's f[1] Chr [Damasc$_1$] Orig-int$_2$ Hil$_1$ Aug$_{oft}$: *τηρει κ. ποιειτε* F: *ποιειτε κ. τηρειτε* D 1. 209 Eus$_1$ Damasc$_1$: *ποιησατε* (alone: *homœotel*) ℵ[1]: txt BLZℵ[3a] fuld(with forj) syr-jer coptt æth arm Eus$_1$ Damasc$_1$ Hil$_1$.

4. rec (for 1st *δε*) *γαρ* (*as more suitable*), with D[1] rel vulg lat-*e f h* Chr [Damasc$_1$] Iren-int Hil: om D-corr Γ 238 arm: txt BLMΔΠℵ 1. 33 am(with tol) lat-*a b c* $ff_{1.2}$ $g_{1.2}$ *l* syrr syr-cu coptt Thl Ambr Aug Jer Op. (Θ_b?) aft *φορτια* ins *μεγαλα* ℵ.
*rec aft *βαρεα* ins καὶ δυςβάστακτα (*from Luke* xi. 46?), with BD(αδυςβ. D[1]) Θ_b rel vulg lat-*c f* ff_1 $g_{1.2}$ *l* syr sah æth arm [Chr Damasc$_1$]: om Lℵ 1. 209 lat-*a b e* ff_2 *h* Syr syr-cu copt Iren-int Hil Ambr. rec (for *αυτοι δε τω*) *τω δε*, with Θ_b rel latt syr arm [Chr Damasc$_1$]: txt BDLℵ 33 Syr syr-cu coptt æth Iren-int Ambr Jer Op$_1$.

sayings of the Lord into longer discourses, see Prolegomena to Matthew. A trace of this discourse is found in Mark xii. 38—40: Luke xx. 45—47. In the latter place it is spoken *to* the disciples, *in hearing of* the crowd: which (see ver. 8 ff.) is the exact account of the matter. It bears many resemblances to the Sermon on the Mount, and may be regarded as the solemn close, as that was the opening, of the Lord's public teaching. It divides itself naturally into three parts: (1) introductory description of the Scribes and Pharisees, and contrast to Christ's disciples (vv. 1—12): (2) solemn denunciations of their hypocrisy (vv. 14—33): (3) conclusion, and mournful farewell to the temple and Jerusalem. **2.**] **Moses' seat** is the office of judge and lawgiver of the people: see Exod. ii. 13—25: Deut. xvii. 9—13. Our Lord says, 'In so far as the Pharisees and Scribes enforce the law and precepts of Moses, obey them: but imitate not their conduct.' **ἐκάθισαν** must not be pressed too strongly, as conveying blame,—'*have seated themselves;*'—it is merely stated here as a *matter of fact*. Vv. 8, 10 however apply to their *leadership* as well as their faults; and declare that *among Christians* there are to be *none sitting on the seat of Christ*. **3. πάντα οὖν ὅσα ἄν**] The *οὖν* here is very significant:—*because* they sit on Moses' seat: and this clears the meaning, and shews it to be, 'all things which they, as successors of Moses, out of his law, command you to observe, do;' there being a distinction between their lawful teaching as expounders of the law, and their frivolous traditions superadded thereto, and blamed below. **ποιήσατε**, do, as occasion arises. **τηρεῖτε**, observe, having respect to them as a constant rule of conduct. The *present* binds on the habitual practice to the mere momentary act of the *aorist*. **4.**] The warning was, *imitate* them not—for they do not themselves what they enjoin on others. And this verse must be strictly connected with ver. 3. The **φορτία** then are not, as so often misinterpreted (even by Olshausen, i. 834), *human traditions* and observances, but the *severity of the law*, which they enforce on others, but do not observe (see Rom. ii. 21—23): answering to the *βαρύτερα τοῦ νόμου* of ver. 23. The irksomeness and unbearableness of these rites did not belong to the Law *in itself*, as rightly explained, but were created by the rigour and ritualism of these men, who followed the letter and lost the spirit: 'omnem operam impendebant (says Grotius) ritibus urgendis et ampliandis.' **τῷ δακ. αὐτῶν**, not *αὑτῶν*: the emphasis is not on the pronoun, but on the **δακτύλῳ**. As a general rule, when the pron. is simply re-

θέλουσιν [x] κινῆσαι αὐτά. 5 πάντα δὲ τὰ ἔργα αὐτῶν
ποιοῦσιν [y] πρὸς τὸ [z] θεαθῆναι τοῖς ἀνθρώποις. [a] πλα-
τύνουσιν * γὰρ τὰ [b] φυλακτήρια αὐτῶν, καὶ [c] μεγαλύνουσιν
τὰ [d] κράσπεδα, 6 [e] φιλοῦσιν δὲ τὴν [f] πρωτοκλισίαν ἐν τοῖς
δείπνοις, καὶ τὰς [g] πρωτοκαθεδρίας ἐν ταῖς συναγωγαῖς,
7 καὶ τοὺς [h] ἀσπασμοὺς ἐν ταῖς ἀγοραῖς, καὶ [i] καλεῖσθαι
ὑπὸ τῶν ἀνθρώπων [k] ῥαββὶ [ῥαββί]. 8 ὑμεῖς δὲ μὴ
κληθῆτε [k] ῥαββί· εἷς γάρ ἐστιν ὑμῶν ὁ διδάσκαλος,
πάντες δὲ ὑμεῖς ἀδελφοί ἐστε. 9 καὶ [l] πατέρα μὴ καλέσητε

x ch. xxvii. 39 || Mk. Acts xvii. 28. xxi. 30. xxiv. 5. Rev. ii. 5. vi. 14 only. Job xvi. 5.
y ch. vi. 1 al. Jer. xxxiv. (xxvii.) 10. xli. (xxxiv.) 10.
z ch. vi. 1 reff.
a 2 Cor. vi. 11, 13 only. Isa. liv. 2. Jer. xxviii. (li.) 58.
b here only †.
c Luke i. 46, 58. Acts v. 13. x. 46. xix. 17. 2 Cor. x. 15. Phil. i. 20 only. = 1 Kings ii. 21. Dan. iv. 8 (11) Theod.
d ch. ix. 20 || L. xiv. 36 || only. Num. xv. 38 al.
e = || L. ch. vi. 5.
f ||. Luke (xi. 43 v. r.) xiv. 7, 8 only †.
g ||. Luke xi. 43 only †.
h ||. Luke i. 29, 41, 44. 1 Cor. xvi. 22. Col. iv. 18. 2 Thess. iii. 17 only †.
i constr., ch. vi. 5. Isa. lvi. 10.
k ch. xxvi. 25, 49. Mark ix. 5. xi. 21. xiv. 45 (bis). not in Luke. John i. 39, 50 al6. only †. (-βουνί, Mark x. 51.)
l = 4 Kings ii. 12. vi. 21.

5. * rec δέ, with Θ_b rel syr-cu [Bas$_1$]: om arm: γαρ BDLℵ X-comm **1. 33. 69** latt syrr coptt Chr [Bas$_1$] Damasc [Orig-int$_1$]. rec aft κρασπεδα ins των ιματιων αυτων (*interpolation from such places as ch* ix. 20; xiv. 36), with Θ_b rel gat(with mm) lat-*f ff$_2$ h* syrr syr-cu copt arm Chr Orig-int Op$_1$; των ιματιων LΔ: om BDℵ X-comm **1** latt Op$_1$.

6. rec (for δε) τε (*corrn as more suitable copula; but Matt never uses it*), with Θ_b [Π^2] rel [Bas$_1$ Damasc$_1$]: om Γ arm Cypr: txt BDKLM^{2}ΔΠ^{1}ℵ **1. 69** latt syr coptt Hil. τας πρωτοκλισιας L(Treg, expr) ℵ^{3a} **1. 33** vulg lat-*a c f ff$_1$ g$_{1.2}$ h* D-lat syrr syr-cu copt æth arm Bas [Damasc$_1$] Hil Op: τ. πρωτοκλησιαν ΓΘ_b rel: txt BDEKM SUΠℵ^1 lat-*b e ff$_2$* Cypr.

7. om 2nd ραββι BLΔΘ_b^{2} ℵ-corr^1 **1.** 33(appy) latt Syr coptt æth Chr [Bas$_1$-ms Damasc$_1$] Cypr Op. (*The omn was easy, and the fact of the reduplication not occurring below, seems to testify to its genuineness here.*)—homœotel ραββι to ραββι next ver ℵ^1.

8. rec (for διδασκαλος) καθηγητης (*mechanical altern from below, ver* 10), with DLΘ_bℵ^1 rel [Nyss$_1$ Bas$_1$ Damasc$_1$]: txt BU ℵ^{3a}(but καθ. restored) 33 lat-*a b c* Syr syr-jer copt [Clem$_1$] Orig$_1$ Eus$_1$ Chr. rec adds ο χριστος, with E^1 rel syr-cu syr-with-ast [Damasc$_1$]; χριστος HU: om BDE^{2}L Θ_b(appy) Πℵ **1.** 33(appy) latt Syr syr-ms syr-jer coptt æth arm [Orig$_1$] Bas Chr Thl Cypr.

flexive, the smooth breathing should always be printed. **5—7.**] But whatever they *do* perform, has but one motive. **φυλακ.**, Heb. Totaphoth, or subsequently and more generally, Tephillin (see Gesen. Thes. Hebr., and Buxtorf, Lex. Rabbin.), were strips of parchment with certain passages of Scripture, viz. Exod. xiii. 11—16 and 1—10: Deut. xi. 13—21; vi. 4—9, written on them, and worn on the forehead between the eyes, on the left side next the heart, and on the left arm. The name in the text was given because they were considered as charms. They appear not to have been worn till after the captivity; and are still in use among the Rabbinical Jews. Their use appears to have arisen from a superstitious interpretation of Exod. xiii. 9: Deut. vi. 8, 9. See Jos. Antt. iv. 8. 13. The fringes were commanded to be worn for a memorial, Num. xv. 38. See note on ch. ix. 20.

6, 7.] See Mark xii. 38, 39: Luke xx. 46, 47. On **πρωτ. ἐν τοῖς δεῖπ.** see Luke xiv. 7. **8—10.**] The prohibition is against loving, and in any religious matter, using such titles, signifying dominion over the faith of others. It must be understood in the spirit and not in the letter. Paul calls Timotheus his '*son*' in the faith, 1 Tim. i. 2, and exhorts the Corinthians (1 Cor. xi. 1) to be followers of him as he of Christ. To understand and follow such commands in the slavery of the letter, is to fall into the very Pharisaism against which our Lord is uttering the caution. See (e. g.) Barnes's note here. **ῥαββί** = רַבִּי, my master: an expression used, and reduplicated as here, by *scholars to their masters*, who were never called by their own name by their scholars. So the Lord says, John xiii. 13, ὑμεῖς φωνεῖτέ με Ὁ διδάσκαλος κ. ὁ κύριος, καὶ καλῶς λέγετε, εἰμὶ γάρ. * See Schöttgen, Hor. Heb. ii. 900. The Teacher is probably not *Christ*, as supplied here in the rec., but the Holy Spirit (see John xiv. 26: Jer. xxxi. 33, 34: Ezek. xxxvi. 26, 27), only *not here named*, because this promise was only given in private *to the disciples*. If this be so, we have God, in His Triunity, here declared to us as the only Father, Master, and Teacher of Christians; their πατήρ, καθηγητής (= ὁδηγὸς

m ch. v. 48 reff. n here bis (ver. 8 v. r.) only †. occ. in Plut., Dion. Hal., Diog. Laert. v. Lexx. and cf. Ezek. xlv. 8. o ch. xiii. 32 al. p ch. xx. 26 al. fr. Gospp. (not Luke) & Paul. Esth. i. 10. ii. 2. vi. 3 Bℵ only. q Luke xiv. 11 bis. xviii. 14 bis. 2 Cor. xi. 7. James iv. 10. 1 Pet. v. 6. Ps. lxxvii. 15. r as above (q). ch. xi. 23 al. Deut. xvii. 20. 2 Chron. xxvi. 16. s as above (q). ch. xviii. 4. Luke iii. 5, from Isa. xl. 4. 2 Cor. xii. 21. Phil. ii. 8. iv. 12 only. Isa. x. 33. t = Isa. xlv. 1. u = ch. iii. 15. Sir. xxiii. 1. v = ch. iv. 23 reff. w Heb. xi. 29. Gen. i. 10. Jon. i. 9.

ὑμῶν ἐπὶ τῆς γῆς· εἷς γάρ ἐστιν ὁ [m] πατὴρ ὑμῶν ὁ BDEFG HKLM
[m] οὐράνιος. 10 μηδὲ κληθῆτε [n] καθηγηταί, ὅτι [n] καθηγητὴς SUVΓΔ
ὑμῶν ἐστὶν εἷς ὁ χριστός. 11 ὁ δὲ [o] μείζων ὑμῶν ἔσται Θ_bΠℵ 1. 33. 69
ὑμῶν [p] διάκονος. 12 ὅςτις δὲ [qr] ὑψώσει ἑαυτὸν [qs] ταπεινωθήσεται, καὶ ὅςτις [qr] ταπεινώσει ἑαυτὸν [qs] ὑψωθήσεται.
14 οὐαὶ δὲ ὑμῖν γραμματεῖς καὶ Φαρισαῖοι ὑποκριταί, ὅτι ...xxiii. 14(appy)
κλείετε τὴν βασιλείαν τῶν οὐρανῶν [t] ἔμπροσθεν τῶν ἀν- Θ_b.
θρώπων· ὑμεῖς γὰρ οὐκ εἰςέρχεσθε, οὐδὲ τοὺς εἰςερχομέ- Z υμεις γαρ...
νους [u] ἀφίετε εἰςελθεῖν. 15 οὐαὶ ὑμῖν γραμματεῖς καὶ Φα- BDEFG HKLM
ρισαῖοι ὑποκριταί, ὅτι [v] περιάγετε τὴν [w] θάλασσαν καὶ τὴν SUVZΓ ΔΠℵ 1. 33. 69

9. for 1st *υμων*, *υμιν* D(*υμειν*) latt Syr [copt(Tischdf)] sah arm Clem Cypr Aug Opt Op. *υμων* bef *ο πατηρ* BUℵ 33. rec (for *ουρανιος*) *εν τοις ουρανοις* (*to suit επι της γης*), with Θ_b rel latt Clem Orig [Nyss$_1$ Bas$_1$ Cyr$_1$] Tert; *εν ουρανοις* DΔ 1 ev-y$_1$ [Damasc$_1$]: txt BLℵ 33. 69 æth arm [Bas$_1$ Cyr$_1$].

10. rec *εις γαρ υμων εστιν ο καθηγητης* (*corrn of order from ver* 8), with E(Θ_bΔℵ) rel lat-*f* syrr copt(appy) æth [Bas$_1$]: (*εστ.* bef *υμ.* ΔΘ_bℵ [Nyss$_1$]: om *ο* (bef *καθ.*) U: om *υμ.* K[Π[1]] 243-5-53-9 Scr's e g w: *υμ.* aft *καθ.* 69:) txt B(D)GL (1) 33 lat-(*a b*) *c* $ff_{1.2}$ $g_{1.2}$ *h l* Ambr Op. (D-gr vulg &c *εἷς* bef *εστιν*: 1 om *εστιν εις*: lat-*a e* D-lat [syr-cu] arm [Hil] om *εἷς*.)

11. om *δε* D latt Hil Op. om 2nd *υμων* ℵ.

[**13.** rec ins *ουαι υμιν γρ. κ. φαρ. υποκρ., οτι κατεσθιετε τας οικιας των χηρων, κ. προφασει μακρα προσευχομενοι· δια τουτο ληψεσθε περισσοτερον κριμα* (*from Mark* xii. 40: *Luke* xx. 47: *this is further shewn by οτι κατεσθιετε being conformed to the other vv here, and προφ. μ. προσευχομενοι being carelessly left as in Mark*)—Steph, bef ver 14, with Θ_bΠ rel lat-*f* syrr copt æth Chr Damasc Op—elz, aft ver 14, with 69 vulg lat-*b c* ff_2 *h* syr-cu Hil (*for numerous other varns see Lachm and Scholz*): om BDL Z(appy) ℵ 1. 33 am(with em forj fuld gat harl mm) lat-*a e* ff_1 $g_{1.2}$ copt-mss sah-mnt arm Orig(calls ver 15 *δεύτερον ταλανισμόν*)[and int$_1$(appy)] Eus-canon(appy) Jer.]

14. Steph om *δε*, with ℵ[1] rel lat-*f h* syrr syr-cu copt-ms æth arm Eus [Cyr$_1$] Orig-int Hil: ins BDL ℵ-corr[1] 1 latt copt.

τυφλῶν Rom. ii. 19), and *διδάσκαλος*—the only One, in all these relations, on whom they can rest or depend. They are all *brethren:* all substantially equal—*none by office or precedence nearer to God than another; none standing between his brother and God.* 'And the duty of all Christian teachers is to bring their hearers to the confession of the Samaritans in John iv. 42: *οὐκέτι διὰ τὴν σὴν λαλιὰν πιστεύομεν· αὐτοὶ γὰρ ἀκηκόαμεν, καὶ οἴδαμεν ὅτι οὗτός ἐστιν ἀληθῶς ὁ σωτὴρ τοῦ κόσμου.*' (Olshausen, Christus der einige Meister, p. 10, cited by Stier, ii. 444.)

πατέρα μὴ κ. ὑμ., name not any Father of you on earth: no '*Abba*' or '*Papa*' (see the account of the funeral of John Wesley, Coke and More's Life, p. 441, and the opening of the Author's dedication of the book). **11.**] It may serve to shew us how little the letter of a precept has to do with its true observance, if we reflect that he who of all the Heads of sects has most notably violated this whole command, and caused others to do so, calls himself '*servus servorum Dei.*'

12.] This often-repeated saying points here not only to the universal character of God's dealings, but to the speedy humiliation of the lofty Pharisees; and as such finds a most striking parallel in Ezek. xxi. 26, 27. **14.**] In Luke xi. 52 it is added *ἤρατε τὴν κλεῖδα τῆς γνώσεως*—the Key being, not the Key *of*, i. e. *admitting to,* Knowledge, but *the Knowledge itself*, the true simple interpretation of Scripture which would have admitted them, and caused them to admit others, into the Kingdom of Heaven by the recognition of Him of whom the Scriptures testify; whereas now by their perverse interpretations they had shut out both themselves and others from it. See a notable instance of this latter in John ix. 24. They shut the door as it were in men's faces who were entering. On the interpolated ver. 13, see notes in Mark (xii. 40). **15.**] And with all this be-

[wx] ξηρὰν ποιῆσαι ἕνα [y] προσήλυτον, καὶ ὅταν γένηται,
ποιεῖτε αὐτὸν [z] υἱὸν [a] γεέννης [b] διπλότερον ὑμῶν. 16 οὐαὶ
ὑμῖν [c] ὁδηγοὶ τυφλοὶ οἱ λέγοντες Ὃς ἂν [d] ὀμόσῃ ἐν τῷ
ναῷ, [e] οὐδέν ἐστιν· ὃς δ' ἂν [d] ὀμόσῃ ἐν τῷ χρυσῷ τοῦ
ναοῦ, [f] ὀφείλει. 17 μωροὶ καὶ τυφλοί, [g] τίς γὰρ μείζων
C η ο ναος... ἐστίν, ὁ χρυσός, ἢ ὁ ναὸς ὁ [h] ἁγιάσας τὸν χρυσόν; 18 καὶ
Ὃς ἂν [d] ὀμόσῃ ἐν τῷ [i] θυσιαστηρίῳ, [e] οὐδέν ἐστιν· ὃς δ'
ἂν [d] ὀμόσῃ ἐν τῷ δώρῳ τῷ ἐπάνω αὐτοῦ, ὀφείλει. 19 τυφλοί, [g] τί γὰρ μεῖζον, τὸ δῶρον, ἢ τὸ [i] θυσιαστήριον τὸ
[h] ἁγιάζον τὸ δῶρον; 20 ὁ οὖν [d] ὀμόσας ἐν τῷ [i] θυσιαστηρίῳ [d] ὀμνύει ἐν αὐτῷ καὶ ἐν πᾶσιν τοῖς ἐπάνω αὐτοῦ·
21 καὶ ὁ [d] ὀμόσας ἐν τῷ ναῷ [d] ὀμνύει ἐν αὐτῷ καὶ ἐν τῷ
[j] κατοικήσαντι αὐτόν· 22 καὶ ὁ [d] ὀμόσας ἐν τῷ οὐρανῷ

x ch. xii. 10 reff. = as above(w). Sir. xxxvii. 3 al.
y Acts ii. 10. vi. 5. xiii. 43 only. Exod. xii. 48, 49. Lev. xvii. 8 al.
z ch. viii. 12. 1 Kings xx. 31.
a ch. v. 22 reff.
b 1 Tim. v. 17. Rev. xviii. 6 bis only. Isa. xl. 2. comp., here only †.
c ch. xv. 14 reff.
d ch. v. 34 reff. w. ἐν, 1 Kings xx. 42.
e = John viii. 54. 1 Cor. vii. 19. xiii. 2. 2 Cor. xii. 11.
f absol., here only. Isa. xxiv. 2. see Luke xi. 4.
g = πότερος, ch. xxi. 31, xxvii. 17, 21. Luke vii. 42. Phil. i. 22. τίς κτῆσις (of two) δικαία ἐστί; Xen. Cyr. i. 3. 17.
h John x. 36. xvii. 17, 19 al. Gen. ii. 3. xxix. 37 al. fr.
i ver. 35. ch. v. 23, 24. Luke i. 11. xi. 51. 1 Cor. ix. 13 al. Gen. viii. 20. xii. 7, 8.
j constr., Luke xiii. 4. Acts i. 19. ii. 9, 14 al5. Rev. (xii. 12 v. r.) xvii. 2 only. Ps. cxxxiv. 21 al. fr.

15. ινα ποιησητε D latt.
16. aft *οδηγ.* ins *οι* ℵ(but erased). om *οι* D¹(ins D³ ?).
17. *τι γαρ μειζον* Z latt.—*μειζω* D. rec **αγιαζων** (*as more simple, and used in ver* 19), with CLΠ rel latt: txt BDZℵ.
18. rec (for 1st *αν*) **εαν**, with E rel: txt BCDFKLΠℵ 33. 69. (Z def.) (vv. 18—27 lat-*b* def.)
19. rec ins *μωροι και* bef *τυφλοι* (*from ver* 17: *no reason could be assigned for its omission, if genuine*), with BC rel lat-*c f* Syr syr[w-ast(appy)] copt sah-mnt arm Orig-int: om DLZℵ 1 vulg lat-*a e ff*$_{1.2}$ *g*$_{1.2}$ *h l* syr-cu copt-mss æth. *μειζω* D.
20. for *επανω*, *επ'* Z(appy).
21. rec *κατοικουντι*, with BHℵ 69 (S 1, e sil) latt syr æth arm: txt CDZ rel Damasc.

trayal of your trust as *οἱ διδάσκαλοι τοῦ Ἰσραήλ* (John iii. 10), *as if all your work at home were done*, ye **περιάγ. τ. θ. κ.τ.λ.** This was their work of supererogation—not commanded them, nor in the spirit of their law. The Lord speaks not here of those pious Godfearing men, who were found dwelling among the Jews, favouring and often attending their worship—but of the *proselytes of righteousness*, so called, who by persuasion of the Pharisees, took on them the *whole Jewish law and its observances*. These were rare—and it was to the credit of our nature that they were. For what could such a proselyte, made by such teachers, become? A disciple of hypocrisy merely—neither a sincere heathen nor a sincere Jew—doubly the child of hell—condemned by the religion which he had left—condemned again by that which he had taken. The expression *διπλότερον ὑμῶν* occurs in the same connexion, and probably in allusion to this passage, in Justin Martyr, Tryph. § 122, p. 215, *οἱ δὲ προσήλυτοι οὐ μόνον οὐ πιστεύουσιν, ἀλλὰ διπλότερον ὑμῶν βλασφημοῦσιν εἰς τὸ ὄνομα αὐτοῦ.*

16—22.] The Lord *forbade all swearing* to His own disciples, ch. v. 34; and by the very same reasoning—because every oath is really and eventually an oath by God—shews these Pharisees the validity and solemnity of every oath. "This subterfuge became notorious at Rome, 'Ecce negas, jurasque mihi per templa Tonantis; Non credo: jura, verpe, per Anchialum,' = am chai aloh (as God liveth). Martial xi. 94" (F. M.). The gold here is probably not the ornamental gold, but the Corban—the sacred treasure. (This Meyer doubts, because the question here is not of *vows*. But in the absence of any examples of an oath *by the gold of the temple*, it is just as likely as the other interpretation.) They were **fools and blind**, not to know and see, that *no inanimate thing can witness an oath*, but that all these things are called in to do so because of *sanctity* belonging to them, of which *God is the primary source*—the *order* likewise of the *things hallowed*, being, in their foolish estimate of them, *reversed*: for, the *gold* must be less than the *temple which hallows it*, and the *gift*

[d] ὀμνύει ἐν τῷ [k] θρόνῳ τοῦ θεοῦ, καὶ ἐν τῷ [l] καθημένῳ
ἐπάνω αὐτοῦ. 23 οὐαὶ ὑμῖν γραμματεῖς καὶ Φαρισαῖοι
ὑποκριταί, ὅτι [m] ἀποδεκατοῦτε τὸ [n] ἡδύοσμον καὶ τὸ [o] ἄνη-
θον καὶ τὸ [p] κύμινον, καὶ [q] ἀφήκατε τὰ [r] βαρύτερα τοῦ
νόμου, τὴν [s] κρίσιν καὶ τὸ ἔλεος καὶ τὴν [t] πίστιν· ταῦτα
δὲ ἔδει ποιῆσαι, κἀκεῖνα μὴ [q] ἀφεῖναι. 24 [u] ὁδηγοὶ τυφλοί,
[v] διυλίζοντες τὸν [w] κώνωπα, τὴν δὲ [x] κάμηλον [y] καταπί-
νοντες. 25 οὐαὶ ὑμῖν γραμματεῖς καὶ Φαρισαῖοι ὑποκριταί,
ὅτι [z] καθαρίζετε τὸ ἔξωθεν τοῦ ποτηρίου καὶ τῆς [a] παροψί-
δος, [b] ἔσωθεν δὲ [bc] γέμουσιν ἐξ [d] ἁρπαγῆς καὶ [e] ἀκρασίας.

...γραμματεῖς Z. BCDEF GHKL MSUVΓ ΔΠℵ 1. 33. 69

k = ch. v. 34. Acts vii. 49, from Isa. lxvi. 1. Heb. i. 8. viii. 1. xii. 2 al.
l w. ἐπάνω, ch. xxviii. 2. Rev. vi. 8 only. see ch. xxi. 7.
m Luke xi. 42. xviii. 12. Heb. vii. 5 only. Gen. xxviii. 22. Deut. xiv. 22.
n Luke xi. 42 only †.
o here only †.
p here only. Isa. xxviii. 25, 27 bis only.
q = Mark vii. 8 reff.
r = 2 Cor. x. 10. Acts xxv. 7. (ver. 4 reff.)
s Isa. i. 17.
t = Rom. iii. 3. Tit. ii. 10. Prov. xii. 22.
u ver. 16.
v here only. Amos vi. 6 only.
w here only †. (-πιον, Judith x. 21.)
x ch. xix. 24 reff.
y 1 Cor. xv. 24, from Isa. xxv. 8. 2 Cor. ii. 7. v. 4. Heb. xi. 29. 1 Pet. v. 8. Rev. xii. 16 only. Num. xvi. 32.
z Mark vii. 19 al. fr.
a here (and ver. 26 v. r.) only †.
b ver. 27. Rev. iv. 8.
c w. ἐξ, here only. see Rev. viii. 5. w. gen. ver. 27 reff.
d Luke xi. 39. Heb. x. 34 only. Isa. iii. 14.
e 1 Cor. vii. 5 only †. (-τής, 2 Tim. iii. 3.)

23. αφηκετε B[1]. rec τον ελεον, with C rel(το M) [Epiph$_1$ Damasc$_1$]: txt BDLℵ 33 Chr Epiph Cyr. rec om δε, with Dℵ rel vulg lat-*c f ff*$_{1.2}$ *g*$_{1.2}$ arm [Bas$_1$ Chr$_3$] Lucif: ins BCKLMΔΠ 33 lat-*a h* D-lat syrr syr-cu copt æth Chr-η Orig-int. rec αφιεναι, with CD rel: txt BLℵ.

24. rec aft τυφλοι ins οι, with C(οι διυλιζονται C[1]) D-corr[1 or 4] ℵ[1](marked for erasure but restored) rel syrr syr-cu [Bas$_1$]: om BD[1]L. for την, τον D.

25. εξω [for εξωθεν] D X-comm Clem Chr-γ(and Fd's mss exc κ). om εξ (*as unnecessary*) CD X-comm latt copt arm Chr [Orig-int]: ins Bℵ rel. for ακρασιας, αδικιας (*gloss on unusual word, as is shewn by the varns below*) C rel lat-*f* Syr [syr-ms Bas-ms$_1$] Chr Thl Euthym Op Promiss: ακρ. κ. αδικ. syr-w-ob: ακαθαρσιας vulg lat-*ff*$_1$ *g*$_{1.2}$ *l* coptt Clem: πλεονεξιας M Chr-M[1] [Damasc$_1$]: αδικ. κ. πλεον. æth: πονηριας 243: txt BDLΔΠℵ 1. 33. 69 lat-*a c ff*$_2$ *h* syr arm [Bas$_2$].

than the *altar*—not as if this were of any real consequence, except to shew their folly—for, vv. 20—22, *every oath* is really an *oath by God*. But these men were servants only of the temple (ὁ οἶκος ὑμῶν, ver. 38) and the altar, and had forgotten God. **ὀφείλει, is bound** (see Exod. xxix. 37). **κατοικήσαντι** (not κατοικοῦντι) is remarkable: God did *not then* dwell in the Temple, nor had He done so since the Captivity. (This *may* perhaps be so: but grammatically it is hardly probable. Rather should I say now, with Meyer, that the aor. refers to the one definite act by which God took possession of the temple as His dwelling-place on its dedication by Solomon; without any allusion to present circumstances.)

23, 24.] It was doubtful, whether Levit. xxvii. 30 applied to every smallest garden herb: but the Pharisees, in their over-rigidity in externals, stretched it to this, letting go the heavier, more difficult, and more important (see ver. 4) matters of the Law. In the threefold enumeration, our Lord refers to Micah vi. 8 (see also Hosea xii. 6)—where *to do justly, to love mercy, and to walk humbly with God*, are described as being better than all offerings. **ταῦτα,** these last, are the great points on which your exertions should have (ἔδει, *oportebat*) been spent—and then, if for the sake of these they be observed, the others should not be neglected. Stier gives an instance of this, in (*Scripture*) *philology*, which if it be applied in subjection to a worthy appreciation of the *sense and spirit of the Writer*, may profitably descend to the minutest details: but if the philologian begin and end with his 'micrology,' he incurs the μωρὲ καὶ τυφλέ of the Pharisees (ii. 515, edn. 1). **διυλίζοντες τ. κ.**] The *straining the gnat* is not a mere proverbial saying. The Jews (as do now the Buddhists in Ceylon and Hindostan) strained their wine, &c., carefully, that they might not violate Levit. xi. 20, 23, 41, 42 (and, it might be added, Levit. xvii. 10—14). The "strain *at* a gnat" in our present auth. vers. for "strain *out* a gnat" of the earlier English vss., seems not to have been a mistake, as sometimes supposed, but a deliberate alteration, meaning, "strain (out the wine) at (the occurrence of) a gnat." **τόν** and **τήν** indicate reference to a proverb or fable. The camel is not only *opposed*, as *of immense size*, but is also joined with the other, as being equally unclean. **25—28.**] This woe

26 Φαρισαῖε τυφλέ, [z] καθάρισον πρῶτον τὸ [f] ἐντὸς τοῦ
ποτηρίου, ἵνα γένηται καὶ [g] τὸ [g] ἐκτὸς αὐτοῦ καθαρόν.
27 οὐαὶ ὑμῖν γραμματεῖς καὶ Φαρισαῖοι ὑποκριταί, ὅτι
[h] παρομοιάζετε [i] τάφοις [k] κεκονιαμένοις, [l] οἵτινες ἔξωθεν
μὲν φαίνονται [m] ὡραῖοι, [n] ἔσωθεν δὲ [no] γέμουσιν [p] ὀστέων
νεκρῶν καὶ πάσης [q] ἀκαθαρσίας. 28 οὕτως καὶ ὑμεῖς
ἔξωθεν μὲν [r] φαίνεσθε τοῖς ἀνθρώποις [r] δίκαιοι, ἔσωθεν δέ
ἐστε [s] μεστοὶ [t] ὑποκρίσεως καὶ [u] ἀνομίας. 29 οὐαὶ ὑμῖν
γραμματεῖς καὶ Φαρισαῖοι ὑποκριταί, ὅτι [v] οἰκοδομεῖτε
τοὺς [i] τάφους τῶν προφητῶν καὶ [w] κοσμεῖτε τὰ [x] μνημεῖα
τῶν δικαίων, 30 καὶ λέγετε Εἰ [y] ἤμεθα ἐν ταῖς ἡμέραις τῶν
πατέρων ἡμῶν, οὐκ ἂν [y] ἤμεθα αὐτῶν [z] κοινωνοὶ ἐν τῷ
[a] αἵματι τῶν προφητῶν. 31 ὥςτε [b] μαρτυρεῖτε [c] ἑαυτοῖς
ὅτι υἱοί ἐστε τῶν [d] φονευσάντων τοὺς προφήτας· 32 καὶ

X ακαθαρσιας ...

f = here (Luke xvii. 21) only. Ps. cii. 10.
g here only +.
h here only +. (-μοιος, Mark vii. 8, 13.)
i Matt. only (ch. xxvii. 61, &c. xxviii. 1), exc. Rom. iii. 13, from Ps. v. 9. (-φή, ch. xxvii. 7 only.)
k Acts xxiii. 3 only. Deut. xxvii. 2, 4. Prov. xxi. 9 only.
l = ch. vii. 15 reff.
m Acts iii. 2, 10. Rom. x. 15 only. 3 Kings i. 6.
n ver. 25. Rev. iv. 8.
o w. gen., Luke xi. 39. Rom. iii. 14, from Ps. x. 28 (7). Rev. iv. 6, 8. v. 8 al3. Gen. xxxvii. 25. acc., Rev. xvii. 3, 4.
p Luke xxiv. 39 reff.
q Gospp., here only. elsw. Paul only, Rom. i. 24 al. fr. Lev. v. 3 al.
r Prov. xxi. 2.
s John xix. 29 (bis) reff.
t Mark xii. 15. Luke xii. 1. Gal. ii. 13. 1 Tim. iv. 2. (James v. 12 v. r.) 1 Pet. ii. 1 only +. 2 Macc. vi. 25 only.
u ch. vii. 23. 2 Cor. vi. 14. Heb. i. 9 (from Ps. xliv. 7 Bℵ). viii. 12 al. Gen. xix. 15.
v ch. vii. 24, 26 al. fr. 1 Macc. xiii. 27.
w ch. xii. 44 ‖ L. 1 Pet. iii. 5 al. Ezek. xxiii. 41.
x ch. viii. 28 al. fr. Gen. xxiii. 6, 9.
y here bis. Acts xxvii. 7. Eph. ii. 3.
z Gospp., Luke v. 10 only. 1 Cor. x. 18, 20. Heb. x. 33 al. Isa. i. 23.
a = ch. xxvii. 6, &c. Acts xx. 28. Ezek. xxii. 4. xxiv. 6, 8. Sir. viii. 16.
b constr., Luke iv. 22. John iii. 26, 28. v. 33. Gal. iv. 15 al. Gen. xliii. 3 Ed-vat. (B def.)
c 2nd pers., ch. iii. 9 reff.
d ver. 35. ch. v. 21. xix. 18 ‖ and Rom. xiii. 9, from Exod. xx. 15 (13), or Deut. v. 17. James ii. 11. iv. 2. v. 6 only.

26. rec aft ποτηριου add και της παροψιδος (*repetition from ver* 25), with BCℵ rel vulg lat-*c* [syrr æth arm Bas_2 Chr_1 $Damasc_1$] Orig-int: om D 1. 209 lat-*a e* Clem Chr_1 Iren-int. for εκτος, εξωθεν D Clem : εντος ℵ¹(txt ℵ3a). rec αυτων (*to suit the insn of* κ. της παροψ. *above*), with [B²]Cℵ rel syrr copt arm [Bas_1] : om X-comm vulg lat-*c* D-lat Clem Chr Iren-int Orig-int : txt B¹DE¹ 1. 69 lat-*a e* æth hom-Cl [Bas_1 $Damasc_1$].

27. [for παρομ.] ομοιαζετε (*see varr readd in Matt* xxvi. 73 : *Mark* xiv. 70) B 1. for οιτ. εξ. μ. φ. ωρ., &c., εξωθεν ο ταφος φαινεται ωραιος εσ. δ. γεμει D Clem [Cyr_1] Iren-int.—om οιτινες ℵ¹(ins ℵ3a).

28. rec μεστοι bef εστε (*for euphony*), with X rel latt [Bas_1 $Damasc_1$ Orig-int] Iren-int Lucif: txt BCDLℵ 33. 69.

30. rec (for ημεθα) ημεν (twice), with KM¹SUΠ 1 Orig Chr : txt BCDℵ rel Orig-ms Cyr. rec κοινωνοι bef αυτων, with Cℵ rel latt Orig [Cyr Chr_2] : txt BD 1. 69 Chr_1.

is founded not on a literally, but a typically denoted practice of the Pharisees. Our Lord, in the ever-deepening denunciation of His discourse, has now arrived at the delineation of their *whole* character and practices by a parabolic similitude. **γέμουσιν ἐξ**] not, '*are filled by*' (Dr. Burton), but, **are full of**: מָלֵא מִן in Hebrew. The straining out of the gnat is a cleansing pertaining to the ἔξωθεν, as compared with the *inner composition of the wine itself*, of which the cup is full: see Rev. xviii. 3. **ἵνα γέν.**] The exterior is not in reality pure when the interior is foul: it is not 'a clean cup,' unless both exterior and interior be clean : 'alias enim illa mundities externa non est munditles.' Bengel. Observe, the emphasis is on γένηται: "that its exterior also may not appear to be, but really *become*, pure." **τάφ. κεκον.**] The Jews used once a year (on the fifteenth of the month Adar) to *whitewash the spots where graves were*, that persons might not be liable to uncleanness by passing over them (see Num. xix. 16). This goes to the root of the mischief at once: 'your heart is not a temple of the living God, but a grave of pestilent corruption: not a heaven, but a hell. And your religion is but the whitewash—hardly skin-deep.'

29—33.] The guilt resting on these present Pharisees, from being the last in a progressive series of generations of such hypocrites and persecutors, forms the matter of the last Woe. The burden of this hypocrisy is, that they, being one with their fathers, treading in their steps, but vainly disavowing their deeds, were, by the very act of building the sepulchres of the prophets, joined with their prophet-persecuting acts, convicting themselves of con-

ὑμεῖς ᵉ πληρώσατε τὸ ᶠ μέτρον τῶν πατέρων ὑμῶν. BCDEF GHKL
33 ᵍ ὄφεις ʰ γεννήματα ʰ ἐχιδνῶν, πῶς φύγητε ἀπὸ τῆς MSUVX
ⁱ κρίσεως τῆς ᵏ γεέννης; 34 διὰ τοῦτο ἰδοὺ ἐγὼ ˡ ἀπο- ΓΔΠℵ 1. 33. 69
στέλλω ˡ πρὸς ὑμᾶς προφήτας καὶ σοφοὺς καὶ ᵐ γραμματεῖς·
ⁿ ἐξ αὐτῶν ἀποκτενεῖτε καὶ σταυρώσετε, καὶ ⁿ ἐξ αὐτῶν
ᵒ μαστιγώσετε ἐν ταῖς συναγωγαῖς ὑμῶν καὶ ᵖ διώξετε
ἀπὸ πόλεως εἰς πόλιν, 35 ὅπως ᵠ ἔλθῃ ἐφ' ὑμᾶς πᾶν ʳ αἷμα

e = Mark i. 15. Phil. iv. 19. Dan. viii. 23. see Gen. xv. 16.
f ch. vii. 2. Mark iv. 24. Luke vi. 38 bis. Rom. xii. 3. Eph. iv. 7 al. Deut. xxv. 14.
g ch. vii. 10. x. 16 al. Ps. cxxxix. 3. = here only.
h ch. iii. 7 (reff.).
i = John v. 24, 29. Heb. x. 27. 2 Pet. ii. 4 al. Isa. liii. 8.
k ch. v. 22 reff.
l ch. xxi. 34. Jer. xxv. 4.
m = ch. xiii. 52 reff.
n Luke xi. 49. xxi. 16. 2 John 4 al. 3 Kings x. 22 B.
o ch. x. 17 reff.
p = Acts xxvi. 11. 1 Macc. v. 22.
q John xviii. 4. Rev. iii. 10. Deut. xxviii. 15.
r = ver. 30. Gen. ix. 5, 6. iv. 10.

32. πληρωσετε B^1 lat-*e*: επληρωσατε DH 244-53 Scr's c s evv-y-z_1 (*both corrns, the imperative not being understood*): txt B^2Cℵ rel Orig Eus [Cyr_3 Chr Aug].
33. φυγεται(= -τε) DH X-txt 69. 243-58 evv-x_1-z_1.
34. om εγω D 33. 251 $Orig_1$ Chr Phot Iren-int_2 $Lucif_2$. αποστελω D-gr 33. 238-43-58 Scr's c k evv-x_1-z_1 copt $Orig_1$ Chr[also txt(Tischdf)]: txt BCℵ rel latt syrr æth arm Orig [Did_1] Iren-int_2 Lucif. om προς υμας D ev-y. rec ins και bef 1st εξ αυτων, with CD rel latt syr-w-ob copt æth arm-mss $Orig_1$ [Did_1 Chr] Iren-int Lucif: om BMΔΠℵ 1. 33. 69 am(with fuld $harl^1$) lat-*e* Syr arm $Orig_1$. αποκτεινειτε D. om κ. εξ αυτ. μαστ. εν τ. συν. υμ. D lat-*a* Iren-int Lucif.—εξ αυτ. bef και $ℵ^1$(txt $ℵ^{3a}$).
35. aft οπως ins αν C^2 M-marg $ℵ^{3a}$ 33. 69. om παν $ℵ^1$(ins $ℵ^{3a}$) 69.

tinuity with their fathers' wickedness. See, as clearly setting forth this view, Luke xi. 47, 48. '(Sit licet divus, dummodo non vivus). Instead of the penitent confession, "We have sinned, we and our fathers," this last and worst generation in vain protests against their participation in their fathers' guilt, which they are meanwhile developing to the utmost, and filling up its measure (Acts vii. 52).' Stier (ii. 453). Again notice the emphasis, which is now markedly on υἱοί; thus bringing out that relation in all its fulness and consequences.

πληρώσατε, imper., **fill ye also** (as well as they) **the measure** (of iniquity) **of your fathers.** Ver. 33 repeats almost verbatim the first denunciation of the Baptist—in this, the last discourse of the Lord: thus denoting the unchanged state of these men, on whom the whole preaching of repentance had now been expended. One weighty difference however there is: then it was, **τίς ὑπέδειξεν** ὑμῖν φυγεῖν; the wonder was, *how they bethought themselves* of escaping—now, **πῶς φύγητε; how shall ye escape?** On **ὄφεις**, see Rev. xii. 9. **34.**] From the similar place in the former discourse (Luke xi. 49, see notes there) it would appear that the **διὰ τοῦτο** refers to the *whole* last denunciation: 'quæ cum ita sint'—'since ye are bent upon filling up the iniquities of your fathers, in God's inscrutable purposes ye shall *go on* rejecting His messengers.' Notice the difference between ἡ σοφία τοῦ θ. in Luke xi. 49, and **ἐγώ**, with its emphasis here. These words are no where *written* in Scripture, nor is it necessary to suppose that to be our Lord's meaning. He speaks this as Head of His Church, of those whom He was about to send: see Acts xiii. 1: 1 Cor. xii. 8: Eph. iii. 5. He cannot, as some (Olsh.) think, include *Himself* among those whom He sends—the Jews may have *crucified* many Christian teachers before the destruction of Jerusalem. And see Euseb. H. E. iii. 32, where he relates from Hegesippus the crucifixion of Symeon son of Clopas, in the reign of Trajan. The καί takes out the σταυρώσετε, the special, from the ἀποκτενεῖτε, the general; with, of course, somewhat of emphasis. The **προφῆται** were the *Apostles*, who, in relation to the Jews, were such—the **σοφοί**, Stephen and such like, men full of the Holy Ghost—the **γραμματεῖς**, Apollos, Paul (who indeed was all of these together), and such. On **μαστ. ἐν τ. συν. κ.τ.λ.** see Acts v. 40; xxii. 19; xxvi. 11. **35.**] **ὅπως**, not '*in such a way that*' (?), as Webst. and Wilk.: but strictly 'in order that.'

αἷμα δίκ. or ἀθῷον is a common expression in the O. T. See 4 Kings xxi. 16; xxiv. 4: Jer. xxxiii. (xxvi.) 15; and more especially Lam. iv. 13, which perhaps our Lord referred to in speaking this.

πᾶν αἷ.] Thus in Babylon, Rev. xviii. 24, is found *the blood of all that were slain upon the earth.* Every such signal judgment is the judgment for a series of long-crying crimes—and these judgments do not exhaust God's anger, Isa. ix. 12, 17, 21.

The *murder of Abel* was the *first* in the strife between unrighteousness and holiness, and as these Jews represent, in their

δίκαιον [s] ἐκχυννόμενον ἐπὶ τῆς γῆς, ἀπὸ τοῦ αἵματος
Ἄβελ τοῦ δικαίου ἕως τοῦ αἵματος Ζαχαρίου υἱοῦ Βαραχίου, ὃν [t] ἐφονεύσατε [u] μεταξὺ τοῦ ναοῦ καὶ τοῦ [v] θυσιαστηρίου. 36 [w] ἀμὴν λέγω ὑμῖν [ὅτι] [x] ἥξει πάντα ταῦτα
ἐπὶ τὴν γενεὰν ταύτην. 37 Ἱερουσαλὴμ Ἱερουσαλὴμ ἡ
ἀποκτείνουσα τοὺς προφήτας καὶ [y] λιθοβολοῦσα τοὺς
[1] ἀπεσταλμένους [1] πρὸς [z] αὐτήν, [a] ποσάκις ἠθέλησα [b] ἐπι-

s ch. xxvi. 28 || Mk. L. Luke xi. 50. Acts xxii. 20. Gen. ix. 6.
t ver. 31 reff.
u = ||. Luke xi. 51. Acts xii. 6 +. (Wisd. xvi. 19 al2.)
v vv. 18, &c. reff.
w ch. v. 18 reff.
x w. ἐπί, Luke xix. 43. Rev. iii. 3 bis. Jer. ii. 3. ἥκει ἐπ' ἐκείνους αἰτία, Demosth. p. 624.
y ch. xxi. 35 reff.
z = Luke i. 45 (?). xiii. 34. Rev. xviii. 24. Isa. xxii. 16 Heb.
a ch. xviii. 21. Luke xiii. 34 only. 2 Chron. xviii. 15. Ps. lxxvii. 40. Sir. xx. 17 only.
b ch. xxiv. 31 || Mk. Mark i. 33. Luke xii. 1. xiii. 34. xvii. 37 only. 2 Chron. xx. 26.

rec *εκχυνομενον* [for *-νν-*], with B³L rel Orig: txt B¹CDGUΔΠℵ 1. 33. om 1st *του* DL 33 ev-y Eus₂. om 2nd *του* D 33. om *υιου βαραχιου* ℵ¹ evv-6-13 Eus (but Iren Orig have it): "In Evangelio quo utuntur Nazareni, pro filio Barachiæ, *filium Joiadæ* reperimus scriptum" (Jer in loc).

36. rec om *οτι* (*see Luke* xi. 51), with BDLℵ 1 latt æth arm Iren-int Lucif: ins C rel lat-*f* syrr Orig Chr Thl. rec *ταυτα* bef *παντα*, with C D-gr LMS X-comm ℵ latt copt Orig [Chr₂] Lucif: txt B rel Iren-int.

37. *τ. προφ.* bef *αποκτ.* ℵ¹(omg *η*: txt ℵ³ᵃ·ᵇ) [Orig]. *αποκτεννουσα* CGKΠ² ℵ¹·³ᵃ·ᵇ Thdrt-ms: *-ενουσα* Δ 33. 69 Thl: txt BD rel Clem Orig₄ Eus [Bas₁ Cyr-p Thdrt]. for *αυτην*, *σε* D arm. (*ad te missi sunt* latt Iren-int Orig-int₃ Cypr Hil.)

conduct both in former times and now, the murderer of the first, they must bear the vengeance of the whole in God's day of wrath. Who **Zacharias son of Barachias** is has been much disputed. We may conclude with certainty that it cannot be (as Aug. and Greswell suppose) a *future* Zacharias, mentioned by Josephus, B. J. iv. 5. 4, as son of Baruch, and slain in the temple just before the destruction of Jerusalem—for our Lord evidently speaks of an event *past*, and never *prophesies* in this manner elsewhere. Origen has preserved a tradition (in Matt. Comm. Series, 24, vol. iii. p. 846), that *Zacharias father of John the Baptist* was slain by them in the temple; but in the absence of all other authority, this must be suspected as having arisen from the difficulty of the allusion here. Most likely (see Lightfoot in loc., and note on Luke xi. 49) it is *Zacharias the son of Jehoiada*, who was killed there, 2 Chron. xxiv. 21, and of whose blood the Jews had a saying, that it never was washed away till the temple was burnt at the captivity. **υἱοῦ Βαραχίου** does not occur in Luke xi. 51, and perhaps was not uttered by the Lord Himself, but may have been inserted by mistake, as *Zacharias the prophet* was son of Barachiah, see Zech. i. 1: a circumstance suppressed by Bp. Wordsworth in his elaborate account of the mystical reason of the patronymic being used here, as "signifying Son of the Blessed, which was a name of Christ Himself." See his note. **μετ. τ. ν. κ. τ. θ.**] He was killed in the *priests' court*, where the altar of burnt-offerings was. On ver. 36, see note on ch. xxiv. 34. It is no objection to the interpretation there maintained, that the *whole period* of the Jewish course of crime is not filled up by it: the *death of Abel* can by no explanation be brought within its limits or responsibility; and our Lord's saying reaches far deeper than a mere announcement of their responsibility for what *they themselves had done.* The Jews stood in the *central point of God's dealings with men;* and as they were the chosen for the election of grace, so, rejecting God and His messengers, they became, in an especial and awful manner, vessels of wrath. Our Lord mentions *this last murder*, not as being the *last* even before His own day, but *because it was connected specially with the cry of the dying man,* 'The Lord look upon it *and require it.*' Compare Gen. iv. 10. This death of Zacharias *was the last* in the *arrangement of the Hebrew Canon* of the O. T., though *chronologically* that of Urijah, Jer. xxvi. 23, was later.

37.] These words were before spoken by our Lord, Luke xiii. 34: see notes there. On the construction of *αὐτήν*, see reff. **Ἱερουσαλήμ**, which is *Luke's* more usual form, does not occur elsewhere in Matt. This is to be accounted for by these verses being a solemn utterance of our Lord, and the sound yet dwelling on the mind of the narrator; and not by supposing the verses to be spurious and inserted out of Luke, as Wieseler has done, Chronolog. Synops. p. 322. His assertion that ver. 39 has no sense here, is implicitly refuted below.

συναγαγεῖν τὰ τέκνα σου [c] ὃν [c] τρόπον [d] ὄρνις [b] ἐπισυν-
άγει τὰ [e] νοσσία αὐτῆς [f] ὑπὸ τὰς [fg] πτέρυγας, καὶ οὐκ
ἠθελήσατε. 38 ἰδοὺ [h] ἀφίεται ὑμῖν ὁ [i] οἶκος ὑμῶν [i] ἔρημος.
39 λέγω γὰρ ὑμῖν Οὐ μή με ἴδητε [j] ἀπ' ἄρτι, ἕως ἂν εἴπητε
[k] Εὐλογημένος ὁ ἐρχόμενος ἐν ὀνόματι κυρίου.
XXIV. 1 Καὶ ἐξελθὼν ὁ Ἰησοῦς ἀπὸ τοῦ ἱεροῦ
ἐπορεύετο· καὶ προσῆλθον οἱ μαθηταὶ αὐτοῦ [l] ἐπιδεῖξαι
αὐτῷ τὰς [m] οἰκοδομὰς τοῦ ἱεροῦ. 2 ὁ δὲ ἀποκριθεὶς εἶπεν
αὐτοῖς Οὐ βλέπετε ταῦτα πάντα; ἀμὴν λέγω ὑμῖν, οὐ μὴ
[n] ἀφεθῇ ὧδε [o] λίθος ἐπὶ λίθον, ὃς οὐ [p] καταλυθήσεται.

c Luke xiii. 34. Acts i. 11. vii. 28 (from Exod. ii. 14). 2 Tim. iii. 8 only. Isa. xiv. 20, 24. xxxviii. 19. (καθ' ὃν τρ., Acts xv. 11. see Jude 7.)
d Luke xiii. 34 only. 3 Kings iv. 23 AB (not Ed-vat.) only. (-νεον, Rev. xviii. 2.)
e here only. Ps. lxxxiii. 3 only. (-σός, Luke ii. 24. -σία, Luke xiii. 34.)
f Luke xiii. 34 only. Ps. xc. 4 (xvi. 8) al. g Luke as above. Rev. iv. 8. ix. 9. xii. 14 only. h = ch. xxiv. 2 reff. i Hag. i. 9. see Isa. lxiv. 10, 11. j ch. xxvi. 29, 64. John (i. 52 v. r.) xiii. 19. xiv. 7. Rev. xiv. 13 only. k ch. xxi. 9 reff. Psa. cxvii. 26. l ch. xvi. 1 reff. m = ‖ Mk. (bis). 1 Cor. iii. 9. 2 Cor. v. 1. Eph. ii. 21. 1 Chron. xxix 1 A. Ezek. xl. 2. met., Paul only, Rom. xiv. 19 al.
n ‖. ch. iv. 11, 20. xxiii. 38. Luke xiii. 8. Judg. ii. 23. iii. 1. Ps. xvi. 14. o Hag. ii. 16. p = ‖. ch. xxvi. 61. Acts vi. 14. 2 Cor. v. 1. Gal. ii. 18. Ezra v. 12.

...καταλυθησεται X. BCDEF GHKL MSUVΓ ΔΠℵ 1. 33. 69

επισυναγειν ℵ[1]. rec επισυναγει bef ορνις, with C rel [Cyr$_1$]: txt BDKLℵ 1. 33. 69 latt copt Clem Orig$_5$[and int$_3$] Eus$_3$ [Cæs] Bas Cyr$_3$ Thdrt Hil. rec εαυτης (*see Luke* xiii. 34), with Cℵ[3a] rel Orig$_3$ [Cæs$_1$ Bas$_2$ Cyr$_2$ Chr Thdrt: om B[1]-txt Clem$_1$ Orig$_2$ Eus$_4$ Cypr]: txt B[1]-marg(see table) DMΔℵ[1] 33 latt Clem Eus$_2$ [Cyr$_2$ Thdrt-ms] Iren-int Hil. aft πτερυγας ins αυτης XΔ evv-x$_1$-z fuld(with gat mm) lat-*a b c* &c syrr [syr-jer] copt æth Clem Orig$_1$[and int$_1$] Cypr Hil: om BCDLℵ rel vulg-ed(with am forj &c) lat-*ff*$_1$ arm Orig$_5$ Eus$_4$ [Cyr$_4$ Thdrt$_1$] Iren-int$_2$.

38. ημων D[1]-gr(perhaps). om ερημος (*corrn to Luke* xiii. 35: *see there*) BL lat-*ff*$_2$ copt-ms Orig-ms.

39. aft υμ. ins οτι (*from* ‖ *Luke*) D 1. 69 lat-*a b c f ff*$_2$ *h* syrr arm Orig-int. for κυριου, θεου D.

Chap. XXIV. **1.** rec επορ. bef απ. τ. ιερ. (*corrn to avoid* **εξελθ. απο**, *see* B *below*), with C rel: εκ τ. ιερ. επορ. B: txt DLΔℵ 1. 33. 69 latt syrr syr-jer copt æth arm Chr Orig-int Hil Op.

2. rec (for αποκριθεις) ιησους, with C rel lat-*f* syr (αποκρ. *seeming inappropr*): txt BDLℵ 1. 33. 69 latt syr-jer copt æth arm Chr: om H lat-*l* Syr. om [1st] ου (*see* ‖ *Mark*) DLX 33 latt coptt æth arm Thl Orig-int$_1$ Ambr Op: ins BCℵ rel syrr Chr Orig-int$_1$. rec παντα bef ταυτα, with DEFGKSΔ lat-*e* syr: om παντα ℵ[1](appy): txt BC ℵ-corr[1] rel latt Syr copt arm Chr Thl Orig-int$_2$ Ambr. aft υμιν ins οτι D [syr]. rec aft ος ου ins μη, with GKUΠ (1. 33, e sil): om BCDℵ rel Chr Mac Thl.

ποσάκις ἠθ. must be understood of all the messages of repentance and mercy sent by the prophets, for our Lord's words embrace the whole time comprised in the historic survey of ver. 35, as well as His own ministry. On the similitude, see Deut. xxxii. 11: Ps. xvii. 8; xxxvi. 7; lvii. 1; lxi. 4: Isa. xxxi. 5: Mal. iv. 2, and compare ch. xxiv. 28. **οὐκ ἠθ.**] see Isa. xxviii. 12; xxx. 15. The tears of our Lord over the perverseness of Jerusalem are witnesses of *the freedom of man's will to resist the grace of God.*

38, 39.] This is our Lord's last and solemn departure from the temple—the *true* μεταβαίνωμεν ἐντεῦθεν ('motus excedentium Deorum.' Tacitus). **οἶκος ὑμῶν**] no more *God's*, but **your house**—said primarily of the temple,—then of Jerusalem,—and then of the whole land in which ye dwell. **οὐ μή με ἴδητε**] He did not shew Himself to all the people after His resurrection, but only to chosen witnesses, Acts x. 41. **ἕως ἂν εἴπ.**] until that day, the subject of all prophecy, when your repentant people shall turn with true and loyal Hosannas and blessings to greet 'Him whom they have pierced:' see Deut. iv. 30, 31: Hosea iii. 4, 5: Zech. xii. 10; xiv. 8—11. Stier well remarks, 'He who reads not this in the prophets, reads not yet the prophets aright.'

Chap. XXIV. 1—51.] Prophecy of His coming, and of the times of the end. Mark xiii. 1—37. Luke xxi. 5—36. Matt. omits the incident of the widow's mite, Mark xii. 41—44. Luke xxi. 1—4.

1, 2.] St. Mark expresses their remarks on the buildings; see note there:—they were probably occasioned by ver. 38 of the last chapter. Josephus writes, B. J. vii. 1. 1, κελεύει Καῖσαρ ἤδη τήν τε πόλιν ἅπασαν καὶ τὸν νεὼν κατασκάπτειν . . . . τὸν δ' ἄλλον ἅπαντα τῆς πόλεως περί-

3 καθημένου δὲ αὐτοῦ ἐπὶ τοῦ [q] ὄρους τῶν [q] ἐλαιῶν προσῆλθον αὐτῷ οἱ μαθηταὶ [r] κατ' [r] ἰδίαν λέγοντες Εἰπὲ ἡμῖν
πότε ταῦτα ἔσται, καὶ τί τὸ [s] σημεῖον τῆς σῆς [t] παρουσίας
καὶ [u] συντελείας τοῦ αἰῶνος. 4 καὶ ἀποκριθεὶς ὁ Ἰησοῦς
εἶπεν αὐτοῖς [v] Βλέπετε μή τις ὑμᾶς [w] πλανήσῃ. 5 πολλοὶ

q ch. xxi. 1 reff. r ch. xiv. 13 reff. s = ch. xvi. 3. ver. 30. Luke ii. 12. (2 Cor. xii. 12.) Exod. iii. 12. 4 Kings xx. 8, 9. t = vv. 27, 37, 39 (only in Gospp.). 1 Cor. xv. 23. 1 Thess. ii. 19 al3. 2 Thess. ii. 1, 8, 9. James v. 7, 8. 2 Pet. i. 16 al2. 1 John ii. 28 +. (2 Macc. viii. 12. xv. 21 only.) u ch. xiii. 39 reff. v = ||. 1 Cor. viii. 9. Gal. v. 15. Col. ii. 8 al. w here & || Mk. (bis). vv. 11, 24. 2 Tim. iii. 13 al. Mic. iii. 5.

3. aft ελαιων ins κατεναντι του ιερου (*from* || *Mark*) C. aft μαθηται ins αυτου CUΓΔΠ Syr copt æth Orig-int : om BDLℵ rel latt(*c* ?) syr arm [Chr]. [καθ Bℵ.] της παρ. σου D. rec ins της bef συντελειας, with D rel [Chr] : om BCLℵ 1. 33 Cyr-jer.

βολον οὕτως ἐξωμάλισαν οἱ κατασκαπτοντες, ὡς μηδὲ πώποτ' οἰκισθῆναι πίστιν ἂν ἔτι παρασχεῖν τοῖς προσελθοῦσιν. There is no difficulty in οὐ here used interrogatively. See a similar case John vi. 70. Meyer has abandoned his former view that we should read οὗ, "where ye see, &c.," and takes the common interpretation. He notices some curious renderings in his note: "Do not look (so wonderingly) on . . . . (μὴ βλ.)," Paulus; "Do ye not wonder at . . . ?" Chrys. al., and De W.: "Ye see not *all* this . . ." viz. not the desolation that shall come. Grulich, de loci Matt. xxiv. 1, 2, interp. Torg. 1839: "Ye do not see: all this, I say to you, shall not . . . ." Bornemann. **3.**] From Mark we learn, that it was *Peter and James and John and Andrew* who asked this question. With regard to the question itself, we must, I think, be careful not to press the clauses of it too much, so as to make them bear separate meanings corresponding to the arrangements of our Lord's discourse. As expressed in the other Evangelists, the question was concerning the time, and the sign, of *these things* happening, viz. the overthrow of the temple and desolation of Judæa, with which, in the then idea of the Apostles, our Lord's coming and the end of the world were connected. Against this mistake He warns them, vv. 6, 14,—Luke ver. 24,—and also in the two first parables in our ch. xxv. For the understanding of this necessarily difficult prophetic discourse, it must be borne in mind that the whole is spoken in the pregnant language of prophecy, in which various fulfilments are involved. (1) The view of the Jewish Church and its fortunes as *representing the Christian Church and its history,* is one key to the interpretation of this chapter. *Two parallel interpretations* run through the former part as far as ver. 28; the destruction of Jerusalem and the final judgment being both enwrapped in the words, but the former, in this part of the chapter, predominating. Even in this part, however, we cannot tell how applicable the warnings given may be to the events of the last times, in which apparently Jerusalem is again to play so distinguished a part. *From ver.* 28, the lesser subject begins to be swallowed up by the greater, and our Lord's *second coming* to be the predominant theme, with however certain hints thrown back as it were at the event which was immediately in question: till, in the latter part of the chapter and the whole of the next, the *second advent,* and, at last, the *final judgment* ensuing on it, are the subjects. (2) Another weighty matter for the understanding of this prophecy is, that (see Mark xiii. 32) any obscurity or concealment concerning the *time* of the Lord's second coming, must be attributed to the right cause, which we know from His own mouth to be, that the divine Speaker Himself, in His humiliation, *did not know the day nor the hour.* All that He had heard of the Father, He made known unto His disciples (John xv. 15): but that which the Father kept in His own power (Acts i. 7), He did not in His abased humanity know. He told them the *attendant circumstances* of His coming; He gave them enough to guard them from error in supposing the day to be close at hand, and from carelessness in not expecting it as near. (Regarding Scripture prophecy as I do as a *whole,* and the same great process of events to be denoted by it all, it will be but waste labour to be continually at issue, in the notes of this and the succeeding chapter, with Meyer and others, who hold that the *Gospel prophecies* are inconsistent in their eschatology with *those after the Ascension,* and those again with *the chiliastic ones of the Apocalypse.* How untenable this view is, I hope the following notes will shew; but to be continually meeting it, is the office of polemic, not of exegetic theology.) **4, 5.**] Our Lord does not answer the πότε but by **admo-**

γὰρ ἐλεύσονται [x] ἐπὶ τῷ [x] ὀνόματί μου λέγοντες Ἐγώ εἰμι
ὁ χριστός, καὶ πολλοὺς [w] πλανήσουσιν. 6 [y] μελλήσετε δὲ
ἀκούειν πολέμους καὶ [z] ἀκοὰς πολέμων. ὁρᾶτε, μὴ [a] θρο-
εῖσθε· [b] δεῖ γὰρ [πάντα] [b] γενέσθαι, ἀλλ' οὔπω ἐστὶν τὸ
[c] τέλος. 7 [d] ἐγερθήσεται γὰρ ἔθνος ἐπὶ ἔθνος καὶ βασιλεία
ἐπὶ βασιλείαν, καὶ ἔσονται λιμοὶ καὶ σεισμοὶ [e] κατὰ τόπους.

BCDEF GHKL MSUVΓ ΔΠℵ 1. 33. 69

x Mark ix. 39 || L. Acts iv. 17, 18. v. 28, 40. Jer. xxiii. 25. y ch. xvi. 27. Acts xxiv. 15. Rom. viii. 13 al. Jer. xxxvi. (xxix.) 10. fut., 2 Pet. i. 12 only. z || Mk. ch. iv. 24 al. Isa. lii. 7. a = || Mk. 2 Thess. ii. 2 only. Cant. v. 4 only. b ||. ch. xxvi. 54. Rev. i. 1. iv. 1. xxii. 6. Dan. ii. 28. c = ver. 14 reff. d Isa. xix. 2. e ||. Acts xxii. 19. xiv. 23. ii. 46. v. 42 al. συνίστασθαι κατὰ τόπους, Philo de Mund. Opif. 20, vol. i. p. 14.

5. aft λεγοντες ins οτι C^1 evv-H_1-y lat-*f* syrr arm Orig-int.

6. μελλετε D Scr's p $Orig_1$ Chr-2. om παντα BDLℵ 1. 33 lat-g_2 coptt æth Ps-Ath Orig-int : ταυτα latt syr-jer Cypr : (παντα *appearing too* general, *it was either omd after* || *Mark, or changed to* ταυτα *after* || *Luke*) txt C rel lat-*f* syrr Chr.

7. for επι, επ' CKLΠℵ 1 ev-y. rec aft λιμοι ins και λοιμοι (*from* || *Luke, as also the varns shew*), with C rel lat-*h* syrr syr-mg-gr copt æth arm [Chr Ps-Ath] Orig-int : pref λοιμοι και, L 33 vulg lat-*c f* ff_1 $g_{1.2}$ *l* Oros : transp σεισμ. and λιμ. ℵ : txt BDE^1 lat-*a b e* ff_2 Cypr Hil Arnob.

nitions not to be deceived. See a question similarly answered, Luke xiii. 23, 24.

πολλ. γάρ] This was the first danger awaiting them: not of being drawn away from Christ, but of *imagining that these persons were Himself.* Of such persons, before the destruction of Jerusalem, we have no distinct record; doubtless there were such: but (see above) I believe the prophecy and warning to have a further reference to the latter times in which its complete fulfilment must be looked for. The persons usually cited as fulfilling this (Theudas, Simon Magus, Barchochab, &c.) are all too early or too late, and not correspondent to the condition, **ἐπὶ τῷ ὀνόμ. μου**, 'with My name as the *ground* of their pretences.' See Greswell on the Parables, v. 380 note. Luke gives an addition (ver. 8) to the speech of the false Christs, καὶ ὁ καιρὸς ἤγγικεν.

6—8.] **πόλεμοι** and **ἀκοαὶ πολέμων** there certainly *were* during this period; but the prophecy must be interpreted rather of those of which the *Hebrew Christians would be most likely to hear* as a cause of terror. Such undoubtedly were the *three threats of war against the Jews* by Caligula, Claudius, and Nero; of the first of which Josephus says, Antt. xix. 1. 2, ἔθνει τε τῷ ἡμετέρῳ οὐδὲ εἰς ὀλίγον ἐξεγεγόνει μὴ οὐκ ἀπολωλέναι, μὴ ταχείας αὐτῷ (Γαίῳ) τελευτῆς παραγενομένης. Luke couples with πολ., ἀκαταστασίας,—and to this **ἔθνος ἐπὶ ἔθνος** seems also to point. There were serious disturbances,—(1) at Alexandria, which gave rise to the complaint against and deposition of Flaccus, and Philo's work against him (A.D. 38), in which the Jews as a nation were the especial objects of persecution; (2) at Seleucia about the same time (Jos. Antt. xviii. 9. 8, 9), in which more than 50,000 Jews were killed; (3) at Jamnia, a city on the coast of Judæa near Joppa (Philo, legat. ad Caium, § 30, vol. ii. p. 575 f.). Many other such national tumults are recorded by Josephus. See especially B. J. ii. 17. 10; 18. 1—8, in the former of which places, he calls the sedition προοίμιον ἁλώσεως, and says that ἕκαστος τῶν μετρίων ἐτετάρακτο: and adds, δεινὴ δὲ ὅλην τὴν Συρίαν ἐπέσχε ταραχή, καὶ πᾶσα πόλις εἰς δύο διῄρητο στρατόπεδα. **λιμός**, and λοιμός, which is coupled to it in || Luke, are usual companions: a proverb says, μετὰ λιμὸν λοιμός. With regard to the *first*, Greswell (Parr. vol. v. p. 261 note) shews that the famine prophesied of in the Acts (xi. 28) happened in the ninth of Claudius, A.D. 49. It was great at Rome,—and therefore probably Egypt and Africa, on which the Romans depended so much for supplies, were themselves much affected by it. Suetonius (Claud. 18) speaks of *assiduæ sterilitates;* and Tacitus (Ann. xii. 43) of 'frugum egestas, et orta ex eo fames,' about the same time. There was a famine in Judæa in the reign of Claudius (the true date of which however Mr. Greswell believes (Diss. vol. ii. p. 5) to be the third of Nero), mentioned by Josephus, Antt. iii. 15. 3. And as to λοιμοί, though their occurrence might, as above, be inferred from the other, we have distinct accounts of a pestilence at Rome (A.D. 65) in Suetonius, Nero 39, and Tacitus, Ann. xvi. 13, which in a single autumn carried off 30,000 persons at Rome. But such matters as these are not often related by historians, unless of more than usual severity.

σεισμοί] The principal *earthquakes* occurring between this prophecy and the

8 πάντα δὲ ταῦτα ἀρχὴ [f] ὠδίνων. 9 τότε [g] παραδώσουσιν
ὑμᾶς εἰς [h] θλῖψιν καὶ ἀποκτενοῦσιν ὑμᾶς, καὶ ἔσεσθε
[i] μισούμενοι ὑπὸ πάντων τῶν ἐθνῶν [j] διὰ τὸ [j] ὄνομά μου.
10 καὶ τότε [k] σκανδαλισθήσονται πολλοὶ καὶ ἀλλήλους
[l] παραδώσουσιν καὶ μισήσουσιν ἀλλήλους. 11 καὶ πολλοὶ
[m] ψευδοπροφῆται [n] ἐγερθήσονται καὶ [o] πλανήσουσιν πολ-

...αλλη-λους C.

f ‖ Mk. Acts ii. 24. 1 Thess. v. 3 only. Exod. xv. 14. Job xxi. 17. Isa. xxi. 3. g = and w. εἰς, ch. x. 20 al. fr. Mt. Mk. L. (Gosp. & Acts) & P. Isa. xxxiv. 2. h ch. xiii. 21 ‖ Mk. Rev. vii. 14 al. fr. Ps. xix. 1. i ‖. ch. x. 22. Ezek. xxxvi. 3. constr., ch. vii. 29 reff. j John xv. 21 reff. k ch. v. 29, 30 reff. xiii. 21 al. l ch. x. 4 al. fr. m ch. vii. 15 al. Jer. vi. 13. Zech. xiii. 2. n ver. 7. o vv. 4, 5.

8. **οδυνων** D¹(txt D²).

9. *αποκτεινουσιν* D-gr. om *παντων* ℵ¹(ins ℵ³ᵃ). elz om *των* (*homœotel*), with D¹ (Scr's c, e sil): om *των εθνων* (‖ *Luke*) C 1. 32. 237-40-4-7-59 lat-*l* Chr Ps-Ath Orig-int: txt BD³Lℵ rel vss [Orig-int₁]. [at end add v 13 (retaining it at its own place) C M-marg Γ.]

10. for *και μισ. αλλ.*, *εις θλιψιν* ℵ Arnob.

11. *εξεγερθησονται* D. *πολλους* bef *πλανησουσιν* Lℵ 33.

destruction of Jerusalem were, (1) a great earthquake in Crete, A.D. 46 or 47 [Philostr. Vita Apollonii iv. 34]; (2) one at Rome on the day when Nero assumed the toga virilis, A.D. 51 [Zonaras xi. 10, p. 565]; (3) one at Apamæa in Phrygia, mentioned by Tacitus (Ann. xii. 58), A.D. 53; (4) one at Laodicea in Phrygia (Tacitus, Ann. xiv. 27), A.D. 60; (5) one in Campania (Tacitus, Ann. xv. 22). Seneca, Ep. 91, § 9, in the year A.D. 58, writes: 'Quoties Asiæ, quoties Achaiæ urbes uno tremore ceciderunt! quot oppida in Syria, quot in Macedonia devorata sunt! Cyprum quoties vastavit hæc clades! quoties in se Paphus corruit; frequenter nobis nuntiati sunt totarum urbium interitus.' The prophecy, mentioning *κατὰ τόπους* (place for place,—i. e. here and there, each in its particular locality; as we say, "up and down"), does not seem to imply that the earthquakes should be in Judæa or Jerusalem. We have an account of one in Jerusalem, in Josephus, B. J. iv. 4. 5, which Mr. Greswell [Parr. v. 259 note] places about Nov. A.D. 67. On the additions in Luke xxi. 11, see notes there; and on this whole passage see the prophecies in 2 Chron. xv. 5—7, and Jer. li. 45, 46. **ἀρχὴ ὠδίνων**] in reference to the *παλιγγενεσία* (ch. xix. 28), which is to precede the *συντέλεια τοῦ αἰῶνος*. So Paul in Rom. viii. 22, *πᾶσα ἡ κτίσις . . . . συνωδίνει ἄχρι τοῦ νῦν*. The death-throes of the Jewish state precede the 'regeneration' of the universal Christian Church, as the death-throes of this world the new heavens and new earth. **9—13.**] **τότε, at this time,—during this period,** not 'after these things have happened.' De Wette presses this latter meaning, that he may find a contradiction to Luke, ver. 12, *πρὸ δὲ τούτων πάντων* . . . . These words serve only definitely to fix the time of the indefinite *τότε*, here and in ver. 10. The *τότε* in ver. 14 is, from the construction of the sentence, more definite. For **ἀποκτ. ὑμ.** Luke has *θανατώσουσιν* **ἐξ ὑμῶν**, viz. the Apostles. This sign was early given. *James the brother of John* was put to death, A.D. 44: *Peter and Paul* (traditionally, Euseb. H. E. ii. 25) and *James the Lord's brother*, before the destruction of Jerusalem: and possibly others. **ἔσεσθε μισ.**] see Acts xxviii. 22, *ἡ αἵρεσις αὕτη . . . . πανταχοῦ ἀντιλέγεται*: also Tacitus, Ann. xv. 44, where Nero, for the conflagration of Rome, persecutes 'Christianos, genus hominum ob flagitia invisos:' also see 1 Pet. ii. 12; iii. 16; iv. 14—16. In chap. x. 22, from which these verses are repeated, we have only *ὑπὸ πάντων*—here *τῶν ἐθνῶν* is added, giving particularity to the prophecy. **10.**] See 2 Tim. iv. 16, and the repeated warnings against apostasy in the Epistle to the Hebrews. The persons spoken of in this verse are *Christians.* 'Primo conrepti qui fatebantur, deinde *indicio eorum* multitudo ingens.' Tac. Ann. xv. 44. On **μισ. ἀλλ.**, compare the deadly hatred borne to Paul and his work by the Judaizers. In the Apocryphal works called the Clementines, which follow teaching similar to that of the factions adverse to Paul in the Corinthian Church, he is hinted at under the name *ὁ ἐχθρὸς ἄνθρωπος* (Ep. Pet. to James 2, and Recognitions, i. 70, cited by Stanley, Essays on Apostolic Age, p. 377). These Judaizing teachers, among others, are meant by the *ψευδοπροφῆται*, as also that plentiful crop of heretical teachers which sprang up every where with the good seed of the Gospel when first sown. See especially Acts xx. 30: Gal. i. 7—9: Rom. xvi. 17, 18: Col. ii. 17—end: 1 Tim. i. 6, 7, 20; vi. 3—5, 20, 21: 2 Tim. ii. 18; iii. 6—8:

λούς.
12 καὶ διὰ τὸ [p] πληθυνθῆναι τὴν [q] ἀνομίαν [r] ψυγήσεται ἡ ἀγάπη [s] τῶν πολλῶν·
13 ὁ δὲ [t] ὑπομείνας [t] εἰς τέλος, οὗτος σωθήσεται.
14 καὶ [u] κηρυχθήσεται τοῦτο τὸ [v] εὐαγγέλιον τῆς [v] βασιλείας ἐν ὅλῃ τῇ [w] οἰκουμένῃ, [x] εἰς [x] μαρτύριον πᾶσιν τοῖς ἔθνεσιν. καὶ τότε ἥξει τὸ [y] τέλος.
15 Ὅταν οὖν ἴδητε τὸ [z] βδέλυγμα τῆς [a] ἐρημώσεως, τὸ

Z λυγμα της... BDEFG HKLM SUVZΓ ΔΠℵ 1. 33. 69

p Gospp., here only. Acts vi. 1, 7 al. = 1 Pet. i. 2. 2 Pet. i. 2. Jude 2. Ps. cxviii. 69.
q ch. xxiii. 28 reff.
r here only. act. (but not =), Num. xi. 32. 2 Kings xvii. 19. Jer. vi. 7 bis. viii. 2 only.
s Rom. v. 15. xii. 5. 1 Cor. x 17. 2 Cor. ii. 17.
t ch. x. 22 (reff.).
u = || Mk. ch. xxvi. 13 || Mk. Luke xxiv. 47 al. see Joel iii. 9.
v ch. iv. 23. ix. 35 (Mark i. 14 v. r.) only.
w Matt., here only. not Mk. nor John. Paul, Rom. x. 18 (from Ps. xviii. 4) only. Heb. i. 6. ii. 5. Luke ii. 1 al2. Acts xi. 28 al7. Rev. iii. 10. xii. 9. xvi. 14. Isa. x. 23.
x ch. viii. 4 reff.
y ver. 6. 1 Pet. iv. 7. 1 Cor. xv. 24. Dan. xi. 13 Theod.
z || Mk. Luke xvi. 15 only, besides Rev. xvii. 4, 5. xxi. 27. Deut. xxix. 17 al. fr. Dan. ix. 27. xii. 11.
a || Mk. Luke xxi. 20 only. Jer. xxxii. (xxv.) 18.

12. *πληθυναι* D Chr-2.
14. *το ευαγγελιον* bef *τουτο* D Scr's k Orig[not int_1] Eus Chr Cypr: om *τουτο* (|| *Mark*) Γ 53. 242-7-59 Scr's b e f^2 lat-*a* arm [$Ps\text{-}Ath_1$]. *εις ολην την οικουμενην* ℵ.
15. for *ουν*, *δε* Lℵ3a Syr copt (æth) Eus Bas Chr Iren-int.

2 Pet. ii. (and Jude): 1 John ii. 18, 22, 23, 26; iv. 1, 3: 2 John 7; ψευδαπόστολοι, 2 Cor. xi. 13. Even De Wette, who attempts to deny the historical fulfilment of the former signs (ver. 7) confesses that this was historically fulfilled (Exeget. Handbuch in loc.). **12.**] It is against this **ἀνομία** especially that James, in his Epistle, and Jude, in more than the outward sense *the brother of James,* were called on to protest,—the mixture of heathen licentiousness with the profession of Christianity. But perhaps we ought to have regard to the *past tense* of πληθυνθῆναι, and interpret, '*because* the iniquity is filled up,' on account of the horrible state of morality (parallel to that described by Thucydides, iii. 82—84, as prevailing in Greece, which had destroyed all mutual confidence), the love and mutual trust of the generality of Christians shall grow cold. **τῶν πολλῶν,**—thus we have ch. xxv. 5, ἐνύσταξαν **πᾶσαι** καὶ ἐκάθευδον. Even the Church itself is leavened by the distrust of the evil days. See 2 Thess. ii. 3. **13.**] The *primary* meaning of this seems to be, that whosoever remained faithful till the destruction of Jerusalem, should be preserved from it. No Christian, that we know of, perished in the siege or after it: see below. But it has *ulterior* meanings, according to which τέλος will signify, to an individual, the *day of his death* (see Rev. ii. 10),—his martyrdom, as in the case of some of those here addressed,—to the Church, *endurance in the faith to the end of all things.* See Luke, xxi. 19, and note.

14.] We here again have the *pregnant* meaning of prophecy. The Gospel had been preached through the whole 'orbis terrarum,' and every nation had received **its testimony**, before the destruction of Jerusalem: see Col. i. 6, 23: 2 Tim. iv. 17. This was necessary not only as regarded the Gentiles, but to give to God's people the Jews, who were scattered among all these nations, *the opportunity of receiving or rejecting the preaching of Christ.* But in the wider sense, the words imply that the Gospel shall be preached in *all the world, literally taken,* before the great and final end come. The *apostasy of the latter days,* and the *universal dispersion of missions,* are the two great signs of the end drawing near. **15.**] **βδέλυγ. τ. ἐρημ.**] The LXX rendering and that of Theod. (B omits τῆς) of שִׁקּוּץ שֹׁמֵם, Dan. xii. 11. The similar expression in ch. xi. 31, is rendered in the same manner by the LXX, but by Theod. βδέλ. ἠφανισμένον, and in ch. ix. 27, LXX and Theod. τὸ βδέλ. τῶν ἐρημώσεων. To what *exactly* the words in Daniel apply, is not clear. Like other prophecies, it is probable that they are pregnant with several interpretations, and are not yet entirely fulfilled. They were interpreted of *Antiochus Epiphanes* by the Alexandrine Jews; thus 1 Macc. i. 54 we read ᾠκοδόμησαν βδέλυγμα ἐρημώσεως ἐπὶ τὸ θυσιαστήριον. Josephus refers the prophecy to the *desolation by the Romans:* Antt. x. 11. 7, Δανιῆλος καὶ περὶ τῆς τῶν Ῥωμαίων ἡγεμονίας ἀνέγραψε, καὶ ὅτι ὑπ' αὐτῶν ἐρημωθήσεται. The principal Commentators have supposed, that the *eagles of the Roman legions* are meant, which were βδέλυγμα, inasmuch as they were *idols worshipped by the soldiers.* These, they say, stood in *the holy place,* or *a* holy place, when the Roman armies encamped round Jerusalem under Cestius Gallus first, A.D. 66, then under Vespasian, A.D. 68, then lastly under Titus, A.D. 70. Of these the *first* is generally taken as the sign meant. Josephus

[b] ῥηθὲν διὰ Δανιὴλ τοῦ προφήτου, [c] ἑστὸς ἐν [d] τόπῳ [d] ἁγίῳ (ὁ ἀναγινώσκων [e] νοείτω), 16 τότε οἱ ἐν τῇ Ἰουδαίᾳ φευ-

b w. διά, ch. i. 22 reff. = ch. iii. 3. c neut. form, (|| Mk. v. r.) Rev. xiv. 1. d Acts vi. 13. xxi. 28. Lev. x. 13. Ps. lxvii. 5. Isa. lx. 13. e = || Mk. Rom. i. 20. 2 Tim. ii. 7. Prov. i. 2, 6.

δανιηλου D[1](txt D-corr[1]). elz (for εστος) εστως, with B[r]D[1]EKMSUΓ 1. 69 Hipp Eus [Chr]: txt B[1]D[8]ℵ rel Cyr-jer [Ath$_1$]. (Z def.)

relates, B. J. ii. 20. 1, that after Cestius was defeated, πολλοὶ τῶν ἐπιφανῶν Ἰουδαίων, ὥσπερ βαπτιζομένης νέως, ἀνενήχοντο τῆς πόλεως. But, without denying that this *time* was that of the sign being given, I believe that all such interpretations of its meaning are wholly inapplicable. The error has mainly arisen from supposing that the parallel warning of Luke (ver. 20, ὅταν δὲ ἴδητε **κυκλουμένην ὑπὸ στρατοπέδων** Ἱερ. τότε γνῶτε ὅτι ἤγγικεν ἡ ἐρήμωσις αὐτῆς) is identical in meaning with our text and that of Mark. The two first Evangelists, writing for Jews, or *as* Jews, give the *inner* or *domestic* sign of the approaching calamity: which was to be seen *in the temple,* and was to be the *abomination* (always used of something caused by the Jews themselves, see 2 Kings xxi. 2—15: Ezek. v. 11; vii. 8, 9; viii. 6—16) which should *cause the desolation,*—the last drop in the cup of iniquity. Luke, writing for Gentiles, gives the *outward state of things* corresponding to this inward sign. That the *Roman eagles cannot be meant,* is apparent: for the sign would thus be *no sign,* the Roman eagles having been seen on holy ground *for many years past,* and at the very moment when these words were uttered. Also τόπος ἅγιος must mean *the temple:* see reff. Now in searching for some event which may have given such alarm to the Christians, Josephus's unconscious admission (B. J. iv. 6. 3) is important: ἦν γὰρ δή τις παλαιὸς λόγος ἀνδρῶν, ἔνθα τότε τὴν πόλιν ἁλώσεσθαι, καὶ καταφλεγήσεσθαι τὰ ἅγια νόμῳ πολέμου, στάσις ἐὰν κατασκήψῃ, καὶ χεῖρες οἰκεῖαι προμιάνωσι τὸ τοῦ θεοῦ τέμενος· οἷς οὐκ ἀπιστήσαντες οἱ ζηλωταὶ διακόνους ἑαυτοὺς ἐπέδοσαν. The party of the Zelots, as we learn from ib. ch. 3. 6, 7, had taken possession of the temple,—τὸν νεὼν τοῦ θ. **φρούριον αὐτοῖς** ποιοῦνται, καὶ καταφυγὴ καὶ τυραννεῖον αὐτοῖς ἦν **τὸ ἅγιον.** In the next section (8) he tells us that they chose one Phannius as their high-priest, an ignorant and profane fellow, brought out of the field,—ὥσπερ ἐπὶ σκηνῆς ἀλλοτρίῳ κατεκόσμουν προσωπείῳ, τήν τε ἐσθῆτα περιτιθέντες ἱεράν, καὶ τὸ τί δεῖ ποιεῖν ἐπὶ καιροῦ διδάσκοντες,—χλεύη δ' ἦν ἐκείνοις καὶ παιδιὰ τὸ τηλικοῦτον ἀσέβημα,—τοῖς δὲ ἄλλοις ἱερεῦσιν ἐπιθεωμένοις πόῤῥωθεν παιζόμενον τὸν νόμον δακρύειν ἐπῄει, καὶ κατέστενον τὴν τῶν ἱερῶν τιμῶν κατάλυσιν. I own that the above-cited passages strongly incline me to think that if not this very impiety, some similar one, about or a little before this time, was the sign spoken of by the Lord. In its place in Josephus, this very event *seems* to stand a little too late for our purpose (A.D. 67, a year after the investment by Cestius): but the narrative occurs in a description of the atrocities of the Zelots, and *without any fixed date,* and they had been in possession of the temple from the very first. So that this or some similar abomination may have about this time filled up the cup of iniquity and given the sign to the Christians to depart. Whatever it was, it was a *definite, well-marked event,* for the flight was to be immediate, *on one day* (μηδὲ σαββάτῳ), and universal from all parts of Judæa. Putting then St. Luke's expression and the text together, I think that some *internal desecration of the holy place by the Zelots* coincided with the approach of Cestius, and thus, both from without and within, the Christians were warned to escape. See Luke xxi. 20: also Bp. Wordsw.'s note here, which however introduces much mystical and irrelevant matter, though coming to what I regard as the right conclusion. **ὁ ἀναγ. νοείτω**] This I believe to have been an ecclesiastical note, which, like the doxology in ch. vi. 13, has found its way into the text. If the two first Gospels were published before the destruction of Jerusalem, such an admonition would be very intelligible. The words *may* be part of our Lord's discourse directing attention to the prophecy of Daniel (see 2 Tim. ii. 7: Dan. xii. 10); but this is not likely, especially as *the reference to Daniel* does not occur in Mark, where these words are also found. They *cannot* well be the words of the *Evangelist,* inserted to bespeak attention, as this in the three first Gospels is wholly without example. **16—18.**] The Christian Jews are said (Euseb. H. E. iii. 5) to have fled to *Pella,* a town described by Josephus (B. J. iii. 3. 3) as the northernmost boundary of Peræa. Eusebius says they were directed thither by a certain prophetic intimation (τινὰ χρησμόν), which however

γέτωσαν ἐπὶ τὰ ὄρη, 17 ὁ ἐπὶ τοῦ [f] δώματος μὴ κατα- BDEFG HKLM SUVZΓ ΔΠא 1. 33. 69
βαινέτω ἆραι τὰ ἐκ τῆς οἰκίας αὐτοῦ, 18 καὶ ὁ ἐν τῷ
ἀγρῷ μὴ [g] ἐπιστρεψάτω ὀπίσω ἆραι * τὰ ἱμάτια αὐτοῦ.
19 [h] οὐαὶ δὲ ταῖς ἐν [i] γαστρὶ [i] ἐχούσαις, καὶ ταῖς [k] θηλαζούσαις ἐν ἐκείναις ταῖς ἡμέραις. 20 προσεύχεσθε δὲ ἵνα
μὴ γένηται ἡ [l] φυγὴ ὑμῶν [m] χειμῶνος μηδὲ σαββάτῳ·
21 ἔσται γὰρ τότε [n] θλῖψις μεγάλη, οἵα οὐ γέγονεν [o] ἀπ᾽
ἀρχῆς [p] κόσμου ἕως τοῦ νῦν, οὐδ᾽ οὐ μὴ γένηται. 22 καὶ
εἰ μὴ [q] ἐκολοβώθησαν αἱ ἡμέραι ἐκεῖναι, οὐκ ἂν ἐσώθη

f ch. x. 27 reff. g ‖ Mk. ch. xii. 44. Luke xvii. 3 al. Ezek. vii. 13. imperat. aor., ‖ Mk. ch. vi. 3. Deut. xxxiii. 6 al. h ch. xxiii. 13, &c. Luke vi. 24, 25 al. i ch. i. 18 reff. k = ‖ [Luke xxiii. 29 v. r.] only. (ch. xxi. 16. Luke xi. 27 only.) Gen. xxi. 7. l ‖ Mk. only. Isa. lii. 12. m = ‖ Mk. John x. 22. 2 Tim. iv. 21 (ch. xvi. 3. Acts xxvii. 20) only. Cant. ii. 11. n ver. 9 reff. Dan. xii. 1. 1 Macc. ix. 27. o ch. xix. 4, 8 ‖. 1 John i. 1 al. fr. Eccl. iii. 11. p = 2 Macc. vii. 23 al.‡ art. om., ch. xiii. 35. 1 Cor. iii. 22. 2 Cor. v. 19. Gal. vi. 14. q here & ‖ Mk. bis only. 2 Kings iv. 12 only. see Lev. xxi. 18. xxii. 23.

16. for *επι*, *εις* (*from* ‖ *Mark Luke*) BDΔ 1 vulg lat-*f ff*$_1$ *g*$_{1.2}$ arm Hipp Eus Ath Cyr-jer Chr Isid Socr Iren-int [Orig-int$_1$ Cypr Aug$_1$].

17. aft *ο* ins *δε* D 33 lat-*e* [Isid$_1$]. (*et qui in* latt syrr æth Iren-int Cypr.) *καταβατω* (*from* ‖ *Mark*) BDLZא 33 Orig Chr [Cæs$_1$ Isid$_1$]. rec (for *τα*) *τι* (*from* ‖ *Mark*), with DE[1] 1. 33 latt æth arm Hipp [Cæs$_2$ Isid$_1$] Iren-int Orig-int Cypr: *το* א[1](txt א[3a]). om *αυτου* D lat-*a b ff*$_2$ Iren-int Cypr Hil.

18. * τὸ ἱμάτιον (*corrn from* ‖ *Mark, where there is no variety*) BDKLZΠא 1. 33. 69 latt Syr coptt æth Hipp [Cæs$_2$] Isid [Orig-int$_1$] Cypr Hil Aug Arnob Op: txt E rel lat-*f* syr arm [Ath$_1$ Chr].

19. *θηλαζομεναις lactantibus* D.

20. rec ins *εν* bef *σαββατω*, with EFGH (Z perhaps) arm [Chr]: om Bא rel latt Orig Eus Thdrt Thl Cypr Hil.—*σαββατου* DLM Thdrt-ms.

21. for *ου γεγονεν*, *ουκ εγενετο* D X-comm א Eus Chr. om *του* D. for *ουδ ου*, *ουδε* DU X-comm Δ copt Eus Chr$_1$ Thdrt. *γενοιτο fiet* D[1](txt D[8]) lat-*a b c* Iren-int Cypr.

cannot be *this*; as Pella is not *on the mountains*, but beyond them (but in order to reach it would not they have to fly exactly **ἐπὶ** τὰ ὄρη—over, along, across them? See note on ch. xviii. 12):—Epiphanius (de mensuris et pond. § 15, vol. ii. p. 171) that they προεχρηματίσθησαν ὑπὸ ἀγγέλου. **17.**] A person might run on the flat-roofed houses in Jerusalem from one part of the city to another, and to the city gates. Perhaps however this is not meant, but that he should descend by the outer stairs instead of the inner, which would lose time. **19, 20.**] It will be most important that so sudden a flight should not be encumbered, by *personal* hindrances (**τ. ἐν γ. ἐχ.**), or by hindrances of *accompaniment* (**τ. θηλ.**), see 1 Cor. vii. 26; and that those things which are *out of our power to arrange*, should be propitious,—weather, and freedom from legal prohibition. The words **μηδὲ σαβ.** are peculiar to Matthew, and shew the strong Jewish tint which caused *him alone* to preserve such portions of our Lord's sayings. That they were not said as any *sanction* of observance of the Jewish Sabbath, is most certain: but merely as referring to the *positive impediments* which might meet them on that day, the shutting of the gates of cities, &c., and their own scruples about travelling further than the ordinary Sabbath-day's journey (about a mile English); for the Jewish Christians adhered to the law and customary observances till the destruction of Jerusalem. **21, 22.**] In ver. 19 there is probably also an allusion to the horrors of the siege, which is here taken up by the **γάρ**. See Deut. xxviii. 49—57, which was literally fulfilled in the case of Mary of Peræa, related by Josephus, B. J. vi. 3. 4.

Our Lord still has in view the prophecy of Daniel (ch. xii. 1), and this citation clearly shews the *intermediate* fulfilment, by the destruction of Jerusalem, of that which is yet future in its *final* fulfilment: for Daniel is speaking of the end of all things. Then only will these words be accomplished in their full sense: although Josephus (but he only in a figure of rhetoric) has expressed himself in nearly the same language (B. J. procem. § 4): τὰ γοῦν πάντων ἀπ᾽ αἰῶνος ἀτυχήματα πρὸς τὰ Ἰουδαίων ἡττᾶσθαί μοι δοκεῖ κατὰ σύγκρισιν. **22.**] If God had not in his mercy shortened (by His decree, to which the aor. refers) those days (ἡμέρας ἐκδικήσεως, Luke xxi. 22), *the whole nation* (in the ultimate fulfilment, *all*

[r] πᾶσα σάρξ· διὰ δὲ τοὺς [s] ἐκλεκτοὺς [q] κολοβωθήσονται
X τοτε ... αἱ ἡμέραι ἐκεῖναι. 23 τότε ἐάν τις ὑμῖν εἴπῃ Ἰδοὺ ὧδε ὁ
χριστὸς ἢ ὧδε, μὴ πιστεύσητε. 24 [t] ἐγερθήσονται γὰρ
[u] ψευδόχριστοι καὶ [t] ψευδοπροφῆται, καὶ [v] δώσουσιν [w] σημεῖα
μεγάλα καὶ [wx] τέρατα, ὥςτε [y] πλανῆσαι εἰ δυνατὸν καὶ
...υμιν Z BDEFG HKLM SUVXΓ ΔΠℵ 1. 33. 69 τοὺς [s] ἐκλεκτούς. 25 ἰδοὺ [z] προείρηκα ὑμῖν. 26 ἐὰν οὖν
εἴπωσιν ὑμῖν Ἰδοὺ ἐν τῇ ἐρήμῳ ἐστίν, μὴ ἐξέλθητε· Ἰδοὺ
ἐν τοῖς [a] ταμείοις, μὴ πιστεύσητε. 27 ὥσπερ γὰρ ἡ [b] ἀστραπὴ ἐξέρχεται [c] ἀπὸ [d] ἀνατολῶν καὶ φαίνεται ἕως [d] δυσμῶν, οὕτως ἔσται ἡ [e] παρουσία τοῦ υἱοῦ τοῦ ἀνθρώπου.

r = ||. Luke i. 37. John iii. 15, 16. Acts x. 14 al. Exod. xv. 26. Gen. vi. 12 al.
s here & || Mk. bis. ver. 31 || Mk. Luke xviii. 7. Col. iii. 12. 2 Tim. ii. 10. Tit. i. 1. 1 Pet. ii. 9. Isa. lxv. 23. Wisd. iii. 9.
t ver. 11.
u here (|| Mk. v. r.) only †.
v = Acts ii. 19. Deut. xiii. 1. 3 Kings xiii. 3, 5.
w || Mk. John iv. 48. Acts ii. 19 (from Joel l. c.), 22, 43 al6. Rom. xv. 19. 2 Cor. xii. 12. 2 Thess. ii. 9. Heb. ii. 4. Deut. xiii. 1, 2 al.
x in N. T. always w. σημ., as above (w) only. Exod. xv. 11.
y vv. 5, 6.
z Rom. ix. 29. 2 Cor. xiii. 2. 2 Pet. iii. 2. Jude 17 al.† 2 Macc. ii. 32 al.
a ch. vi. 6. Luke xii. 3, 24 only. Isa. xxvi. 20.
b = ch. xxviii. 3. Luke x. 18 (xi. 36). xvii. 24 only, exc. Rev. iv. 5 al3. Zech. ix. 14. Ep. Jer. 61.
c ch. ii. 1 reff.
d ch. viii. 11 reff.
e ver. 3 reff.

22. εκολοβωθησαν ℵ[1](txt ℵ[3a]).
23. for η ωδε, η εκει D ev-16 vulg lat-*f ff*$_1$ *g*$_2$ (*a b c e g*$_1$ *h*) copt arm [(Cyr-jer$_1$) Ps-Ath] Thdrt Jer Aug. πιστευετε [for -σητε] B[1] (|| *Mark*) : -ευητε B[2] [Orig$_1$-mss].
24. δωσωσιν Z. om μεγαλα ℵ [|| *Mark*]. πλανηθηναι Dℵ vulg lat-*b ff*$_2$ *g*$_{1,2}$ [Orig-int$_1$] Cypr [Jer Ambr] : πλανασθαι LZ 1. 33 Orig [Cyr-jer$_1$ Ath$_1$-mss] : txt B rel.
26. om ουν ℵ[1](ins ℵ[3b]) [Orig-int$_1$ Archel$_1$].
27. for φαινεται, φαινει DG 1. 118. rec aft εσται ins και, with MΔ (69, e sil) vulg lat-*b c e*·*f ff*$_2$*g*$_{1,2}$ syr æth Hipp [Cyr-jer] Chr Damasc Cypr : om BDℵ rel harl lat-*a ff*$_1$ *h* Syr coptt arm Orig [Dial] Hil.

flesh) would have perished: but for the sake of the chosen ones,—the believing,—or those who should believe,—or perhaps the preservation of the chosen race whom God hath not cast off, Rom. xi. 1,—they shall be shortened. It appears that besides *the cutting short in the Divine counsels,* which must be hidden from us, various causes combined to shorten the siege. (1) Herod Agrippa had begun strengthening the walls of Jerusalem in a way which if finished would have rendered them πάσης ἀνθρωπίνης κρείττονα βίας, but was stopped by orders from Claudius, A.D. 42 or 43, Jos. Antt. xix. 7. 2. (2) The Jews, being divided into factions among themselves, had totally neglected any preparations to stand a siege. (3) The magazines of corn and provision were burnt just before the arrival of Titus; the words of Josephus are remarkable on this, κατακαῆναι δὲ πλὴν ὀλίγου πάντα τὸν σῖτον, ὃς ἂν αὐτοῖς οὐκ ἐπ' ὀλίγα διήρκεσεν ἔτη πολιορκουμένοις, B. J. v. 1. 5. (4) Titus arrived suddenly, and the Jews voluntarily abandoned parts of the fortification (B. J. vi. 8. 4). (5) Titus himself confessed, (B. J. vi. 9. 1,) σὺν θεῷ γ' ἐπολεμήσαμεν, καὶ θεὸς ἦν ὁ τῶνδε τῶν ἐρυμάτων Ἰουδαίους καθελών, ἐπεὶ χεῖρές τε ἀνθρώπων ἢ μηχαναὶ τί πρὸς τούτους τοὺς πύργους δύνανται; (The foregoing particulars are from Mr. Greswell, Par. v. 343 ff. note.) Some such providential shortening of the great days of tribulation, and hastening of God's glorious Kingdom, is here promised for *the latter times*. **23—26.**] These verses have but a faint reference (though an unmistakable one) to the time of the siege (Jos., B. J. ii. 13. 4, says, πλάνοι γὰρ ἄνθρωποι καὶ ἀπατεῶνες προσχήματι θειασμοῦ νεωτερισμοὺς καὶ μεταβολὰς πραγματευόμενοι, δαιμονᾶν τὸ πλῆθος ἀνέπειθον . . . . .): their *principal reference* is to the *latter days*. In their first meaning, they would tend to correct the idea of the Christians that the Lord's coming was to be simultaneous with the destruction of Jerusalem: and to guard them against the impostors who led people out into the wilderness (see Acts xxi. 38), or invited them to consult them privately, with the promise of deliverance. In their main view, they will preserve the Church firm in her waiting for Christ, through even the awful troubles of the latter days, unmoved by enthusiasm or superstition, but seeing and looking for Him who is invisible. On the *signs and wonders,* see 2 Thess. ii. 9—12: Deut. xiii. 1—3.

27, 28.] The coming of the Lord in the end, even as that in the type was, shall be *a plain unmistakable fact*, understood of all;—and like that also, *sudden* and *all-pervading*. But here again the full meaning of the words is only to be found in the

28 ὅπου ἐὰν ᾖ τὸ [f] πτῶμα, ἐκεῖ [g] συναχθήσονται οἱ [h] ἀετοί.
29 εὐθέως δὲ μετὰ τὴν θλῖψιν τῶν ἡμερῶν ἐκείνων ὁ [ik] ἥλιος
[il] σκοτισθήσεται, καὶ ἡ [km] σελήνη οὐ δώσει τὸ [n] φέγγος

BDEFG HKLM SUVXΓ ΔΠℵ 1. 33. 69

f Mark vi. 29 (|| Mt. v. r.) xv. 45. Rev. xi. 8, 9 bis only. Judg. xiv. 8. g ch. xiii. 2 reff. h Luke xvii. 37. Rev. iv. 7. viii. 13. xii. 14 only. Prov. xiii. 17. i || Mk. Luke xxiii. 45. Rev. ix. 2. Eccl. xii. 2. k ||. (Acts ii. 20.) 1 Cor. xv. 41. Rev. vi. 12, 13. viii. 12 (xxi. 23) only. Joel iii. 15. l as above (i). Rom. i. 21. xi. 10, from Ps. lxviii. 23 (Eph. iv. 18 v. r. only. m as above (k), and Rev. xii. 1 only. Isa. xiii. 10. n || Mk. (Luke xi. 33 v. r.) only. Ezek. i. 4, &c.

28. for *οπου*, *που* (but corrd) ℵ[1]. rec aft *οπου* ins *γαρ*, with E rel lat-*c ff*$_2$ syr arm [Hipp(Tischdf) Chr] Orig-int$_1$; *δε* Syr [Ps-Ath$_1$] (*both addns for connexion*): om BDLℵ 1. 33 coptt æth Hipp [Iren-int$_1$] Orig-int$_1$ Cypr Hil. for *εαν*, *αι* D Hipp [Ps-Ath$_1$] Chr. *σωμα* ℵ[1](txt ℵ[3a]), *corpus* latt(exc D-lat) Hil.

final fulfilment of them. The lightning, lighting both ends of heaven at once, seen of all beneath it, can only find its full similitude in His Personal coming, Whom *every eye shall see*, Rev. i. 7. **28.**] The stress is on **ὅπου ἐάν** and **ἐκεῖ**, pointing out the *universality*. In the similar discourse, Luke xvii. 37, before this saying, the disciples ask, 'Where, Lord?' The answer is,—first, *at Jerusalem:* where the corrupting body lies, thither shall the vultures (literally) gather themselves together, coming as they do from far on the scent of prey. Secondly, in its final fulfilment,—*over the whole world;*—for that is the *πτῶμα* now, and the *ἀετοί* the angels of vengeance. See Deut. xxviii. 49, which is probably here referred to; also Hosea viii. 1: Hab. i. 8. The interpretation (Theophylact, Euthym., Calvin, Bp. Wordsw., &c.) which makes the *πτῶμα* *our Lord*, and the *ἀετοί the elect*, is quite beside the purpose. The mystical defence of it may be seen in Wordsw.'s notes. Neither is any allusion (Lightfoot, Ham., Wetstein, Wolf, &c.) to the *Roman eagles* to be for a moment thought of. The *ἀετοί* are the *vultures* (vultur percnopterus, Linn.), usually reckoned by the ancients as belonging to the eagle kind, Plin. Nat. Hist. ix. 3. **29. εὐθέως**] All the difficulty which this word has been supposed to involve has arisen from confounding the *partial* fulfilment of the prophecy with its *ultimate* one. The important insertion in Luke (xxi. 23, 24) shews us that the *θλῖψις* includes *ὀργὴ τῷ λαῷ τούτῳ*, which is yet being inflicted: and the treading down of Jerusalem by the Gentiles, still going on (see note there): and immediately after *that tribulation* which shall happen *when the cup of Gentile iniquity is full*, and *when the Gospel shall have been preached in all the world* for a witness, *and rejected by the Gentiles*, (*πληρωθῶσιν καιροὶ ἐθνῶν*,) shall the coming of the Lord Himself happen. On the indefiniteness of this assigned period in the prophecy, see note on ver. 3. (The expression in Mark is equally indicative of a considerable interval; *ἐν ἐκείναις ταῖς ἡμέραις μετὰ τὴν θλῖψιν ἐκείνην*.) The fact of His coming and its attendant circumstances being known to Him, but the exact time unknown, He speaks *without regard to the interval*, which would be employed in His waiting till all things are put under His feet: see Rev. i. 1; xxii. 6—20. In what follows, *from this verse*, the Lord speaks mainly and directly of *His great second coming*. Traces there are (as e. g. in the literal meaning of ver. 34) of slight and indirect allusions to the destruction of Jerusalem;—as there were in the former part to the great events of which that is a foreshadowing:—but no direct mention. The contents of the rest of the chapter may be set forth as follows: (ver. 29) *signs which shall immediately precede* (ver. 30) *the coming of the Lord to judgment, and* (ver. 31) *to bring salvation to His elect. The certainty of the event, and its intimate connexion with its premonitory signs* (vv. 32, 33); *the endurance* (ver. 34) *of the Jewish people till the end—even till Heaven and Earth* (ver. 35) *pass away. But* (ver. 36) *of the day and hour none knoweth. Its suddenness* (vv. 37—39) *and decisiveness* (vv. 40, 41),—*and exhortation* (vv. 42—44) *to be ready for it. A parable setting forth the blessedness of the watching, and misery of the neglectful servant* (vv. 45—end), and forming a point of transition to the parables in the next chapter. **ὁ ἥλιος σκοτ.**] The darkening of the material lights of this world is used in prophecy as a type of the occurrence of trouble and danger in the fabric of human societies, Isa. v. 30; xiii. 10; xxxiv. 4: Jer. iv. 28: Ezek. xxxii. 7, 8: Amos viii. 9, 10: Micah iii. 6. But the type is not only in the *words* of the prophecy, but also in the events themselves. Such prophecies are to be understood *literally*, and indeed without such understanding would lose their truth and significance. The physical signs shall happen (see Joel ii. 31: Hag. ii. 6, 21, compared with Heb. xii.

αὐτῆς, καὶ οἱ [ko] ἀστέρες [p] πεσοῦνται ἀπὸ τοῦ [p] οὐρανοῦ,
καὶ αἱ [q] δυνάμεις τῶν οὐρανῶν [r] σαλευθήσονται. 30 καὶ
τότε φανήσεται τὸ [s] σημεῖον τοῦ [t] υἱοῦ τοῦ [t] ἀνθρώπου ἐν
οὐρανῷ, καὶ τότε [u] κόψονται πᾶσαι αἱ [v] φυλαὶ τῆς γῆς,
καὶ ὄψονται τὸν [t] υἱὸν τοῦ [t] ἀνθρώπου [w] ἐρχόμενον ἐπὶ
τῶν [w] νεφελῶν τοῦ οὐρανοῦ [x] μετὰ δυνάμεως καὶ δόξης
πολλῆς. 31 καὶ ἀποστελεῖ τοὺς ἀγγέλους αὐτοῦ μετὰ

o as above (k). ch. ii. 2, &c. Jude 13 al.
p (but w. ἐκ) Luke x. 18. Rev. viii. 10. ix. 1.
q = ‖. Rom. viii. 38. 1 Pet. iii. 22. Isa. xxxiv. 4. Dan. viii. 10 Theod.
r ch. xi. 7. Luke vi. 48. Acts iv. 31. xvi. 26 al. Ps. xvii. 7.
s ver. 3 reff.
t ch. viii. 20 reff.
u ch. xi. 17 reff. Zech. xii. 12.
v = (ch. xix. 28 al.) Rev. i. 7. v. 9. vii. 9. xi. 9. xiii. 7. xiv. 6 only. Ezek. xx. 32.
w ‖. ch. xxvi. 64 ‖ Mk. Rev. i. 7. Dan. vii. 13.
x = Dan. vii. 13. Isa. xxxiii. 17. Acts xxvi. 12.

29. for *απο*, *εκ* Dℵ Scr's b ev-y_1 Eus [Cyr-jer_1 Bas_1].
30. rec ins *τω* bef *ουρανω*, with E rel [Eus_1 Cyr-jer_1 Ps-Ath_1] Chr Thdrt Damasc: om BLℵ Cypr.—*του εν ουρανοις* D. *κοψ.* bef *τοτε* D 1. 69. 124. 209 lat-*a*: om *τοτε* ℵ[1](txt ℵ[3a]) 237-8 ev-y_1 [lat-*e* Cypr]. *πολλης* bef *κ. δοξης* D 115 latt(not *f*) Cypr Ambr Jer Aug.

26, 27) as accompaniments and intensifications of the awful state of things which the description typifies. The *Sun* of this world and the church (Mal. iv. 2: Luke i. 78: John i. 9: Eph. v. 14: 2 Pet. i. 19) is the Lord Jesus—the Light is the Knowledge of Him. The moon—human knowledge and science, of which it is said (Ps. xxxvi. 9), 'In thy light shall we see light:' reflected from, and drinking the beams of, the Light of Christ. The stars —see Dan. viii. 10—are the leaders and teachers of the Church. The Knowledge of God shall be obscured—the Truth nigh put out—worldly wisdom darkened—the Church system demolished, and her teachers cast down. And all this in the midst of the fearful signs here (and in Luke, vv. 25, 26, more at large) recounted: not *setting aside*, but *accompanying*, their *literal fulfilment*. **αἱ δυν. τ. οὐρ.**] not *the stars*, just mentioned;—nor *the angels*, spoken of by and by, ver. 31: but most probably the greater heavenly bodies, which rule the day and night, Gen. i. 16, and are there also distinguished from the ἀστέρες,—the λαμπροὶ δυνασταί of Æsch. Agam. init. See notes on 2 Pet. iii. 10—12, where the stars seem to be *included* in τὰ στοιχεῖα. Typically, the influences which rule human society, which make the political weather fair or foul, bright or dark; and encourage the fruits of peace, or inflict the blight and desolation of war. **30.**] This **τότε**, so emphatically placed and repeated, is a *definite declaration of time*,—not a mere sign of sequence or coincidence, as e. g. in ver. 23:—when these things shall have been somewhile filling men's hearts with fear,—THEN shall, &c. It is quite uncertain what the σημεῖον shall be:—plainly, not *the Son of Man Himself*, as some explain it (even Bengel, generally so valuable in his explanations, says 'Ipse erit signum sui,' and quotes Luke ii. 12 as confirming this view; but there the swaddling clothes and the manger were the 'sign,' not the *child*), nor *any outward marks on his body*, as his wounds; for both these would confuse what the prophecy keeps distinct—the seeing of the *sign* of the Son of Man, and all tribes of the earth mourning, and afterwards seeing *the Son of Man Himself*. This is manifestly *some sign in the Heavens*, by which all shall know that the Son of Man is at hand. The *Star of the Wise Men* naturally occurs to our thoughts—but a *star* would not be a sign which all might read. On the whole I think no sign completely answers the conditions but that of *the Cross*:—and accordingly we find the Fathers mostly thus explaining the passage. But as our Lord Himself does not answer the question, **τί** τὸ σημεῖον τῆς σῆς παρουσίας; we may safely leave the matter. I mention, just to shew how sensible expositors can be misled by a false interpretation of the whole, Wetstein's strange paraphrase of τὸ σημεῖον τ. υ. τ. ἀνθ.,—'fumus Hierosolymorum incensorum, qui interdiu solem, nocte vero lunam et stellas obscurat.' **πᾶσαι αἱ φ. τ. γ.**] see Zech. xii. 10—14, where the mourning is confined to the families of Israel:—here, it is universal: see reff. Rev.; also vi. 15—17. This coming of the Son of Man is not that spoken of ch. xxv. 31, but that in 1 Thess. iv. 16, 17, and Rev. xix. 11 ff.,—His coming *at the commencement of the millennial reign to establish His Kingdom*: see Dan. vii. 13, 14. **δύναμις** is the *power of this Kingdom*, not, the host of heaven. **31.**] In 1 Thess., as above, the voice of the Archangel and the trump of God are distinguished from one another, which seems to favour the reading which inserts

y σάλπιγγος z φωνῆς μεγάλης, καὶ a ἐπισυνάξουσιν τοὺς BDEFG
b ἐκλεκτοὺς αὐτοῦ ἐκ c τῶν τεσσάρων ἀνέμων ἀπ᾽ d ἄκρων HKLM SUVXΓ
οὐρανῶν ἕως d ἄκρων αὐτῶν. 32 ἀπὸ δὲ τῆς e συκῆς ΔΠℵ 1. 33. 69
μάθετε τὴν παραβολήν. ὅταν ἤδη ὁ f κλάδος αὐτῆς
γένηται g ἁπαλὸς καὶ τὰ h φύλλα i ἐκφυῇ, γινώσκετε ὅτι
ἐγγὺς τὸ j θέρος· 33 οὕτως καὶ ὑμεῖς ὅταν ἴδητε πάντα
ταῦτα, γινώσκετε ὅτι ἐγγύς ἐστιν k ἐπὶ k θύραις. 34 l ἀμὴν
λέγω ὑμῖν, οὐ μὴ m παρέλθῃ ἡ γενεὰ αὕτη ἕως ἂν πάντα

y 1 Cor. xv. 52. 1 Thess. iv. 16. Heb. xii. 19 al. 2 Kings vi. 15. Isa. xxvii. 13. z = 1 Cor. xiv. 7, 8 al. 2 Kings vi. 15. a || Mk. ch. xxiii. 37. Mark i. 33. Luke xii. 1. xiii. 34. xvii. 37 only. 2 Chron. xx. 26. Isa. lii. 12. (-αγωγή, 2 Thess. ii. 1.) b ver. 22 reff. c || Mk. Rev. vii. 1. Zech. ii. 6. d = here & || Mk. bis (Luke xvi. 24. Heb. xi. 21) only. Deut. xxx. 4. Neh. i. 9. Jer. xii. 12. e ||. ch. xxi. 19, &c. ||. Luke xiii. 6, 7. John i. 49, 51. James iii. 12. Rev. vi. 13 only. Isa. xxxiv. 4. f ch. xiii. 32 reff. g || Mk. only. Gen. xviii. 7 al. Lev. ii. 14 Aq. Symm. h ch. xxi. 19 reff. i || Mk. only †. Ps. ciii. 14 Symm. j || only. Gen. viii. 22. k || Mk. Acts v. 9. Prov. ix. 14. Cant. vii. 13. l ch. v. 18 reff. m ||. ch. v. 18. 2 Cor. v. 17. Ps. lxxxix. 5. Jer. viii. 20.

31. om φωνης (*as unnecessary*) LΔℵ 1 ev-y lat-*e* Syr syr-ms copt arm [Eus$_1$] Cyr-jer Chr Thdrt Orig-int Cypr Hil: μετα φωνης σαλπ. μεγαλης syr(but φωνης with ast) syr-jer æth: μ. σαλπ. και φωνης μεγαλης D latt [Damasc$_1$] Hil Jer Aug: txt B rel sah. συναξει [for επισ.] ℵ^1(txt ℵ^{3a}) 253 Hipp Hil. απο DX Scr's o. aft εως ins των B 1. 33. 69. aft αυτων ins Luke xxi. 21 (but αναβλεψατε for ανακυψ.) D lat-*b c h*.

32. om τα ℵ^1(but corrd) ev-y. εκφυῇ EFGHKMVΓΠ latt(*nata*) æth &c Aug: εκφύη B^{r}UX 1. 33. 69 D-lat lat-*ff*$_1$ arm, *producit* Orig-int$_1$, *miserit* Orig-int$_1$. [γινωσκεται (*itacism?*) B^2 D-gr Γ.] ins εστιν bef τ. θ. D Scr's p q^1 latt Orig-int: aft θερ. 33.

33. ταυτα bef παντα DHKUV^{1}ℵ 1. 33. 69 latt Syr copt arm Chr [Orig-int$_1$]: txt B rel lat-*e* syr.

34. aft υμιν ins οτι (*from || Mark Luke*) BDFL 1. 33. 69 latt syrr [Ps-Ath$_1$] Orig-int. om αν ℵ. ταυτα bef παντα DHL 69 lat-*a e ff*$_2$ *g*$_{1.2}$ *h l* Syr copt arm Chr [Orig-int$_1$]: om ταυτα Scr's a p u evv-H$_1$^{1}-y forj harl^2 lat-*b f ff*$_1$ Bas Ps-Ath Chr Orig-int$_1$ Op.

καί here. This *is not the great Trumpet of the general Resurrection* (ref. 1 Cor.), except in so far as that may be spoken of as including also the first resurrection: see on this verse the remarkable opening of Ps. l., which is itself a prophecy of these same times. **32, 33, 34.**] **τὴν παρ.**, not as E. V., '*a parable*,' but **the** (not, *its*: the fig-tree may teach many lessons besides this; cf. reff. Matt. Luke) **parable**,—the natural phænomenon which may serve as a key to the meaning. This coming of the Lord shall be as sure a sign that the Kingdom of Heaven is nigh, as the putting forth of the tender leaves of the fig-tree is a sign that summer is nigh. Observe πάντα ταῦτα, every one of these things,—this coming of the Son of Man *included*, which will introduce the millennial Kingdom. As regards the parable,—there is a reference to the *withered fig-tree which the Lord cursed*: and as that, in its judicial unfruitfulness, emblematized the Jewish people, so here the putting forth of the fig-tree from its state of winter dryness, symbolizes the *future reviviscence* of that race, which the Lord (ver. 34) declares shall not pass away till all be fulfilled. That this is the true meaning of that verse, must appear when we recollect that it forms the conclusion of this parable, and is itself joined by παρέλθῃ to the verse following. We cannot, in seeking for its ultimate fulfilment, *go back* to the taking of Jerusalem and make the words apply to it.

As this is one of the points on which the rationalizing interpreters (De Wette, &c.) lay most stress to shew that the prophecy has *failed*, it may be well to shew that **γενεά** has in Hellenistic Greek the meaning of *a race or family of people.* See Jer. viii. 3 LXX; compare ch. xxiii. 36 with ib. ver. 35, ἐφονεύσατε . . . but *this generation* did not slay Zacharias—so that the *whole people* are addressed: see also ch. xii. 45, in which the meaning absolutely requires this sense (see note there): see also Luke xvii. 25: Matt. xvii. 17: Luke xvi. 8 (where γενεά is predicated both of the υἱοὶ τοῦ αἰῶνος τούτου and the υἱοὶ τοῦ φωτός): Acts ii. 40: Phil. ii. 15. In all these places γενεά is = γένος, or nearly so; having it is true a more pregnant meaning, implying that the character of one generation *stamps itself upon the race*, as here in this verse also.

This meaning of γενεά is fully conceded by Dorner; 'omnes reor concessuros, vocem γ. si eam vertas *ætas*, multas easque

ταῦτα γένηται. 35 ὁ οὐρανὸς καὶ ἡ γῆ παρελεύσεται, οἱ
..παρελθωσιν X. δέ λόγοι μου οὐ μὴ παρέλθωσιν. 36 περὶ δὲ τῆς ἡμέρας
ἐκείνης καὶ ὥρας οὐδεὶς οἶδεν, οὐδὲ οἱ ἄγγελοι τῶν οὐρα- n = ch. ii. 1 reff. o ver. 3.
I_c ωςπερ νῶν, εἰ μὴ ὁ πατήρ [μου] μόνος. 37 ὥςπερ δὲ αἱ [n] ἡμέραι p ver. 30. ch. viii. 20 reff.
... BDEFG τοῦ Νῶε, οὕτως ἔσται ἡ [o] παρουσία τοῦ [p] υἱοῦ τοῦ [p] ἀν- q Luke xvii. 27. 2 Pet. ii. 5 only. Gen. vi. 17. vii. 6, &c.
HI$_c$KL MSUVΓ θρώπου. 38 ὡς γὰρ ἦσαν ἐν ταῖς [n] ἡμέραις τοῦ [q] κατα-
ΔΠℵ 1. 33. 69

35. om ver ℵ[1]. rec παρελευσονται (*from* ‖ *Mark Luke*), with Eℵ[3a] rel latt Orig$_2$ [Cyr-jer$_1$ Bas$_2$] Tert Hil$_{oft}$ Ambr: txt BDL 33 lat-*e* Iren Orig-ms Nyss [Eus$_2$] Mac Chr [Bas$_1$] Cyr$_{oft}$ Hesych Hil$_1$ Aug.

36. rec ins της bef ωρας (‖ *Mark*), with (S **1**. 33, e sil) syr-mg[-gr] Bas Chr [Damasc$_1$] Thl: om BDℵ rel Eus Chr-γ Cyr.—om κ. ωρ. L 258 Bas-mss. aft ουρανων ins ουδε ο υιος (*from* ‖ *Mark*) BDℵ[1] forj lat-*a b c f ff*$_1$ *h* syr-jer æth arm Chr Iren-int Orig-int Ambr$_{expr}$ Aug [Op]: *fil. hominis* lat-*e* Hil-mss: om EL ℵ[3a](appy, but restored) rel vulg lat-$g_{1.2}$ syrr copt: most lat-mss and gr-mss, as alleged by Jer ("In quibusdam Latinis codicibus additum est *neque filius;* quum in Græcis, et maxime Adamantii et Pierii exemplaribus, hoc non habeatur adscriptum"); ancient gr-mss mentd by Ambr; mss mentd by Paulin; [Bas$_1$ Did$_1$ Ps-Ath$_1$ Damasc$_1$ Euthym$_1$ Phœbad$_1$ Ambr$_1$ Paulin$_1$;] scholl vett; and at the council of Nicæa, as reported in Ath, it was alleged that these words were in Mark only. om μου (*see* ‖ *Mark*) BDL ΔΠ[1]ℵ **1**. 33. 69 latt syrr syr-jer coptt æth arm Bas [Did$_1$ Cyr$_1$] Ps-Ath Chr Damasc [Iren-int$_1$ Orig-int$_1$] Ambr Aug Op: ins E rel lat-*f*.

37. for δε, γαρ (*on account of* δε *having just preceded. This is more prob than that* δε *should have been on account of* γαρ *following. The change would be made on the second, not on the first occurrence of the word*) BDI$_c$ lat-*e* syr-mg copt Did Orig-int$_1$ spec Op: txt Lℵ rel latt syrr æth arm Clem Orig$_1$. rec aft εσται ins και (*from Luke* xvii. 26), with D rel vulg lat-*a b e f ff*$_2$ $g_{1.2}$ syr æth Orig-int Op: om B I$_c$(Treg) LUΓℵ harl[1] lat-*c ff*$_1$ *h* D-lat Syr copt arm Clem Orig Did. om του υιου (*homœotel*) ℵ[1](ins ℵ[3a]).

38. rec ωσπερ (*see ver* 27), with D rel [Did$_1$ Chr]: txt B I$_c$(Treg) Lℵ 33 Orig. rec aft ημεραις ins ταις προ, with I$_c$ℵ rel vulg lat-$g_{1.2}$ copt arm Orig-int; εκειναις προ D 253; εκειναις ταις προ B Scr's c lat-*b c f ff*$_2$ *h* syr (æth) spec: om L lat-*a e ff*$_1$ Orig$_2$. (*The reading in txt seems to have been the origl one, and to have presented a difficulty which was solved by insg* προ, ταις προ, *or* εκειναις; *and then the readgs were variously*

plane insuperabiles ciere difficultates, contextum vero et orationis progressum flagitare significationem *gentis*, nempe Judæorum.' (Stier, ii. 502.) The continued use of **παρέρχομαι** in vv. 34, 35, should have saved the Commentators from the blunder of imagining that the then living generation was meant, seeing that the prophecy is by the next verse carried on to the end of all things: and that, as matter of fact, the Apostles and ancient Christians *did continue to expect the Lord's coming, after that generation had past away.* But, as Stier well remarks, "there are men foolish enough now to say, heaven and earth will never pass away, but the words of Christ pass away in course of time —; of this, however, we wait the proof." ii. 505. **πάντα ταῦτα**] *all* the signs hitherto recounted—so that both these words, and **ὑμεῖς**, have their *partial*, and their *full* meanings. **ἐγγύς ἐστιν**] viz. τὸ τέλος. On ver. 35 see Ps. cxix. 89: Isa. xl. 8; li. 6: Ps. cii. 26. **36.**] **ἡμ. ἐκ.**, viz. of heaven and earth passing away; or, perhaps referring to ver. 30 ff. **ἡμ. κ. ὥρ.**, the exact time—as we say, 'the hour and minute.' The very important addition to this verse in Mark, and in some ancient MSS. here (but see digest), **οὐδὲ ὁ υἱός**, is indeed included in εἰ μὴ ὁ πατήρ [μου] μόνος, but could hardly have been inferred from it, had it not been expressly stated: ch. xx. 23. All attempts to soften or explain away this weighty truth must be resisted; it will not do to say with some Commentators, 'nescit ea *nobis*,' which, however well meant, is a mere evasion:—in the course of humiliation undertaken by the Son, in which He increased in wisdom (Luke ii. 52), learned obedience (Heb. v. 8), uttered desires in prayer (Luke vi. 12, &c.),—*this matter was hidden from Him:* and as I have already remarked, this is carefully to be borne in mind, in explaining the prophecy before us. **37—39.**] This comparison also occurs in Luke xvii. 26, 27, with the addition of 'the days of Lot' to it: see also 2 Pet. ii. 4—10; iii. 5, 6. It is important to notice the confirmation, by His mouth who is Truth itself, of the

r here only, exc. John vi. 54, &c. xiii. 18 †.
s here [1 Cor. vii. 38] only (exc. ch. xxii. 30 & Luke xvii. 27. xx. 34, 35 v. r.) †.
t Luke i. 20. xvii. 27. Acts i. 2.
u Luke xvii. 27. Heb. ix. 4. xi. 7. 1 Pet. iii. 20. Rev. xi. 19 only. Gen. vi. 14, &c.
v = Ruth iii. 4.
w = Luke xxiii. 18. Acts xxi. 36. Isa. lvii. 1. 1 Macc. v. 2.
x ch. xvii. 1. xx. 17. Num. xxii. 41. = John xiv. 3.

κλυσμοῦ [r] τρώγοντες καὶ πίνοντες, γαμοῦντες καὶ [s] ἐκγαμί- BDEFG
ζοντες, [t] ἄχρι [t] ἧς [t] ἡμέρας εἰςῆλθεν Νῶε εἰς τὴν [u] κιβωτόν, HI KL MSUVΓ
39 καὶ οὐκ [v] ἔγνωσαν ἕως ἦλθεν ὁ [q] κατακλυσμὸς καὶ ΔΠℵ 1. 33. 69
[w] ἦρεν ἅπαντας, οὕτως ἔσται ἡ [o] παρουσία τοῦ [p] υἱοῦ τοῦ
[p] ἀνθρώπου. 40 τότε δύο ἔσονται ἐν τῷ ἀγρῷ· εἷς [x] παραλαμβάνεται, καὶ εἷς [y] ἀφίεται. 41 δύο [z] ἀλήθουσαι ἐν
τῷ [a] μύλῳ· μία [x] παραλαμβάνεται, καὶ μία [y] ἀφίεται.
42 [b] γρηγορεῖτε οὖν, ὅτι οὐκ οἴδατε [c] ποίᾳ ἡμέρᾳ ὁ κύριος
ὑμῶν [d] ἔρχεται. 43 ἐκεῖνο δὲ γινώσκετε, ὅτι εἰ ᾔδει ὁ
[e] οἰκοδεσπότης [c] ποίᾳ [f] φυλακῇ ὁ κλέπτης ἔρχεται, [b] ἐγρη-
γόρησεν ἂν καὶ οὐκ ἂν [g] εἴασεν [h] διορυγῆναι τὴν οἰκίαν
αὐτοῦ. 44 διὰ τοῦτο καὶ ὑμεῖς [i] γίνεσθε ἕτοιμοι. ὅτι ᾗ

y = ch. xiii. 36 al. z Luke xvii. 35 only. Num. xi. 8. Judg. xvi. 21. Eccl. xii. 3, 4 only. a ch. xviii. 6 reff. b ‖ Mk. ch. xxv. 13. xxvi. 38, &c. ‖ Mk. Luke xii. 37, 39. 1 Cor. xvi. 13 al. 1 Macc. xii. 27. Jer. i. 12. c = ch. xxi. 23, &c. reff. d pres., ch. xi. 3 reff. e ch. xx. 1, 11 al. † f = ch. xiv. 25 reff. Ps. lxxxix. 4. g = Luke iv. 41. Acts xxviii. 4 al. Luke only, exc. here & 1 Cor. x. 13. (Rev. ii. 20 v. r.) Job ix. 18. h ch. vi. 19, 20 reff. i Luke xii. 40. 1 Cor. x. 7, 32. xi. 1 al. Exod. xix. 15.

combined, as in B *and* D.) ins και bef γαμουντες DLℵ[3a] lat-*a b* Syr spec [Op]. for εκγαμ., γαμισκοντες B; γαμιζοντες Dℵ 33 Chr-2-6-9-η-ρ-M: txt I_c rel [Did] Chr-Fd's-mss. for ης, της D[1]: της ημ. ης D[4]: om ης 69.

39. παντας D I_c(perhaps) Scr's v ev-y Did. rec aft εσται ins και (*see ver* 36; vi. 39: *Luke* xvii. 26), with I_cℵ rel vulg lat-*c e f* syr arm [Did_1] Orig-int spec: om BD lat-*a b* ff_1 g_2 Syr copt æth.

40. εσονται bef δυο (*Luke* xvii. 34) Bℵ[1](txt ℵ[3a]) Scr's p forj lat-*h*. rec ins ο bef εις (twice), with E rel [$Cæs_1$]: ins ο bef 2nd εις Δ Chr-2: txt B[D] I_c(def at 2nd) L 1. 33 (syrr, appy) Chr_4.

41. rec μυλωνι (*gloss on* μυλω), with DHM [$Cæs_1$ Chr]: txt B I_c(appy) ℵ rel Orig. at end ins (*from Luke* xvii. 34) δυο επι κλεινης μειας εις παραλαμβανεται κ. εις αφιεται D 69, simly vulg-sixt lat-*a b c f h* æth Orig-int Hil Juv.

42. rec (for ημερα) ωρα (*see ver* 44), with L rel latt Syr copt arm Ath Chr Orig-int Op: txt BDI_cΔℵ 1. 33. 69 lat-*f* ff_2 syr syr-jer (æth) [Cyr_1] Ath-2-mss Iren-int Hil.

43. om αν D 33 [Chr-2-6-9-η-ρ]. διορυχθηναι D I_c(perhaps) Lℵ 1. 33. εαυτου I_c 33.

historic reality of the flood of Noah. The security here spoken of is in no wise inconsistent with the anguish and fear prophesied, Luke xxi. 25, 26. They *say*, there is peace, and occupy themselves as if there were: but fear is at their hearts;—'surgit amari aliquid, quod in ipsis floribus angit.' The expression **πίνοντες** may serve to shew that it is a mistake to imagine that we have in Gen. ix. 20 the account of the *first* wine and its effects. On the addition in Luke xxi. 34—36, see notes there. **40, 41.**] From this point (or perhaps even from ver. 37, as historic resemblance is itself parabolic) the discourse begins to assume a parabolic form, and gradually passes into a series of formal parables in the next chapter. These verses set forth that, as in the times of Noah, men and women shall be employed in their ordinary work: see Exod. xi. 5 (LXX), Isa. xlvii. 2. They also shew us that the elect of God will *to the last be mingled in companionship and partnership with the children of this world* (see Mark i. 19, 20). We may notice, that these verses do not refer to the same as vv. 16—18. *Then* it is a question of *voluntary flight; now* of *being taken* (by the angels, ver. 31: the *present* graphically sets the incident before us; or perhaps describes the *rule* of proceeding. See on the sense of **παραλαμβ.** especially ref. John), *or left.* Nor again do they refer to the great judgment of ch. xxv. 31, for then (ver. 32) *all* shall be summoned:—but they refer to the millennial dispensation, and the gathering of the elect to the Lord *then.* The "women grinding at the mill" has been abundantly illustrated by travellers, as even now seen in the East. See especially 'The Land and the Book,' pp. 526, 7. **ἐν**, either because the pair of stones is the element in which the act of grinding takes place,—or, more probably, because that which is ground is *within*, between the stones. **42—44.**] Our Lord here resumes the tone of direct

οὐ δοκεῖτε ὥρᾳ ὁ υἱὸς τοῦ ἀνθρώπου ἔρχεται. 45 τίς ἄρα
ἐστὶν ὁ πιστὸς δοῦλος καὶ [k] φρόνιμος, ὃν [l] κατέστησεν ὁ
C εαυτον ... κύριος ἐπὶ τῆς [m] οἰκετείας αὐτοῦ, τοῦ [n] δοῦναι αὐτοῖς τὴν
[n] τροφὴν [o] ἐν καιρῷ; 46 [p] μακάριος ὁ δοῦλος ἐκεῖνος ὃν
ἐλθὼν ὁ κύριος αὐτοῦ εὑρήσει οὕτως ποιοῦντα. 47 ἀμὴν
λέγω ὑμῖν ὅτι [q] ἐπὶ πᾶσιν τοῖς [r] ὑπάρχουσιν αὐτοῦ [q] καταστήσει αὐτόν. 48 ἐὰν δὲ [s] εἴπῃ ὁ κακὸς δοῦλος ἐκεῖνος
[s] ἐν τῇ [t] καρδίᾳ αὐτοῦ [u] Χρονίζει μου ὁ κύριος ἐλθεῖν,

k ch. vii. 24 reff. l ch. xxv. 21, 23. Luke xii. 14, 42. Acts vi. 3 al. Gen. xxxix. 4. Dan. ii. 48. m here only †. Job i. 3 Symm. (-της, Luke xvi. 13.) n Ps. ciii. 27. o Luke xii. 42. xx. 10. 1 Pet. v. 6. Ps. i. 3. p ch. v. 2, &c. q dat., Luke xii. 44 only. Gen. xli. 41 Ed-vat. (B def.) οἱ ἐπὶ ταῖς μηχαναῖς, Xen. Cyr. vi. 3. 28. acc., ch. xxv. 21. Ps. viii. 6. gen., ver. 45. r = ch. xix. 21 reff. s Luke xii. 45. Rom. x. 6. Eccl. ii. 1 t = Mark ii. 6, 8. u ch. xxv. 5. Luke i. 21. xii. 45. Heb. x. 37 (from Hab. ii. 3) only. Gen xxxiv. 19. Deut. xxiii. 21. Judg. v. 28.

44. rec ωρα bef ου δοκειτε (*for perspicuity ?*), with E rel lat-*e f* g_1 syrr æth arm [Chr Orig-int_1]: txt BDI_cℵ vulg copt [Ath_2].

45. for αρα, γαρ D ev-y Orig-int Op. καταστησει (|| *Luke*) Mℵ [copt Chr_2]. rec aft κυριος ins αυτου (*for perspicuity*), with E rel vulg lat-*b c f* $ff_{1.2}$ g_1 *l* syrr copt æth arm Bas[?] Chr Orig-int Op: om BDI_cLℵ 1. 33 forj lat-*a e* g_2 *h* Orig [Bas_1] Iren-int Hil Ambr Hesych spec. rec (for οικετειας) θεραπειας (*from Luke* xii. 42, οικετ. *no where else occurring*), with D rel: οικιας ℵ 69 æth Ephr Bas Chr: txt BI_cLΔΠ[1] 33. εαυτον C. om του D [Ephr Chr]. rec (for δουναι) διδοναι (*from* || *Luke*), with E rel [Ephr]: txt $BCDI_c$LUΔℵ 1. 33. 69 Bas Chr.

46. rec ποιουντα bef ουτως (*from* || *Luke*) with E rel lat-*f* syrr arm Bas_2 Orig-int: txt $BCDI_c$Lℵ 1. 33. 69 latt æth [Ephr] Iren-int Hil Ambr.

48. om εκεινος Γℵ[1](ins ℵ[3a]) 56-8. 243 Scr's d ev-y Ephr Chr Iren-int Aug. εαυτου ℵ. rec ο κυριος bef μου (|| *Luke*), with E rel latt hom-Cl Bas Chr [$Damasc_1$]: txt $BCDI_c$Lℵ 33 Orig [Ephr]. om ελθειν (*as unnecessary, see ch* xxv. 5) Bℵ 33 coptt [Ephr] Iren-int.

exhortation with which He commenced. To the secure and careless He will come as a thief in the night: to His own, as their Lord. See Obad. 5: Rev. iii. 3; xvi. 15: 1 Thess. v. 1—10, where the idea is expanded at length. Compare ver. 7 there with our ver. 49, and on the distinction between those who are of the day, and those who are of the night, see notes there. **45—47.**] Our Lord had given this parabolic exhortation before, Luke xii. 42—46. Many of these His last sayings in public are solemn repetitions of, and references to, things already said by Him. That this was the case in the present instance, is almost demonstrable, from the implicit allusion in Luke xii. 36, to the *return from the wedding*, which is here expanded into the parable of ch. xxv. 1 ff. How much more natural that our Lord should have preserved in his parabolic discourses the same leading ideas, and again and again gathered his precepts round them,—than that the Evangelists should have thrown into utter and inconsistent confusion, words which would have been treasured up so carefully by them that heard them;—to say nothing of the promised help of the Spirit to bring to mind all that He had said to them. **τίς ἄρα ἐστ.**] a question asked *that each one may put it to himself*,—and to signify the high honour of such an one. **πιστ. κ. φρ.**] Prudence in a servant can be only the *consequence of faithfulness to his master*. This verse is especially addressed to the Apostles and ministers of Christ. The **δοῦναι τὴν τροφήν** (= τὸ σιτομέτριον Luke xii. 42) answers to ἐργάτην ἀνεπαίσχυντον, ὀρθοτομοῦντα τὸν λόγον τῆς ἀληθ. in 2 Tim. ii. 15. On ver. 47, compare ch. xxv. 21: 1 Tim. iii. 13: Rev. ii. 26; iii. 21, which last two passages answer to the promise here, that *each* faithful servant shall be over *all* his master's goods. That promotion shall not be like earthly promotion, wherein the eminence of one excludes that of another,—but rather like the diffusion of love, in which, the more each has, the more there is for all. **48—51.**] The question is not here asked again, τίς ἐστιν κ.τ.λ., but the transition made from the good to the bad servant, or even the good to the bad mind of the same servant, by the epithet **κακός**. On this graphic use of the demonstrative pronoun, see Kühner, Gramm. ii. 325. **χρονίζει**] then manifestly, a *long delay is in the mind of the Lord*: see above on ver. 29. Notice that *this servant also* is *one set over the household—one who says* ὁ κύριός **μου**—and began well—but now **ἄρξηται τύπ.**, &c.—

49 καὶ [v] ἄρξηται τύπτειν τοὺς [w] συνδούλους αὐτοῦ, ἐσθίῃ
δὲ καὶ πίνῃ μετὰ τῶν [x] μεθυόντων, 50 ἥξει ὁ κύριος τοῦ
δούλου ἐκείνου ἐν [y] ἡμέρᾳ ᾗ οὐ [yz] προσδοκᾷ καὶ ἐν ὥρᾳ ᾗ
οὐ [a] γινώσκει, 51 καὶ [b] διχοτομήσει αὐτόν, καὶ τὸ [cd] μέρος
αὐτοῦ μετὰ τῶν ὑποκριτῶν [d] θήσει· ἐκεῖ ἔσται ὁ [e] κλαυθμὸς
καὶ ὁ [e] βρυγμὸς τῶν [e] ὀδόντων. XXV. 1 Τότε [f] ὁμοιωθήσεται ἡ βασιλεία τῶν οὐρανῶν δέκα [g] παρθένοις, [h] αἵτινες
λαβοῦσαι τὰς [i] λαμπάδας ἑαυτῶν ἐξῆλθον εἰς [k] ὑπάντησιν

BCDEF GHI$_c$K LMSÛV ΓΔΠℵ 1. 33. 69

X τοτε... ..εαυτων I$_c$. Z των εξηλθον ... BCDEF GHKL MSUVX ZΓΔΠℵ 1. 33. 69

v ch. iv. 17 al. Gen. xviii. 27. w ch. xviii. 28, &c. reff. x John ii. 10 reff. 3 Kings xvi. 9. y Lam. ii. 16. z Luke iii. 15. Acts xvii. 33. a ver. 39. b Luke xii. 46 only. Exod. xxix. 17 only. c - John xiii. 8. Rev. xx. 6. xxi. 8. xxii. 19. d Luke xii. 46 only. see Ps. xlix. 18. e ch. viii. 12 reff. f ch. xiii. 24. xviii. 23 al. g vv. 7, 11. ch. i. 23, from Isa. vii. 14. Luke i. 27 bis. Acts xxi. 9. 1 Cor. vii. 25, &c. 2 Cor. xi. 2. Rev. xiv. 4 only. h ch. vii. 15 reff. i here, &c. and John xviii. 3. Acts xx. 8. Rev. iv. 5. viii. 10 only. Gen. xv. 17. k ὑπάντ., John xii. 13 only. Judg. xi. 34 B only (?). ἀπ., ver. 6, Acts xxviii. 15. 1 Thess. iv. 17 only. 1 Kings ix. 14, &c. always w. εἰς in N. T. & LXX. (not Apocr., 2 Macc. xii. 30 al.)

49. rec om αυτου (*see* || *Luke*), with E rel hom-Cl: ins BCDI$_c$L 1. 33. 69 latt syrr coptt æth arm Bas-old-mss Chr [Damasc$_1$] Thl Euthym Orig-int Hil Op, εαυτου ℵ. rec εσθιειν δε κ. πινειν (|| *Luke*), with G(πινην) Π[1] lat-*a* [Ephr Damasc$_1$]: txt BCDI$_c$ℵ rel vulg-*b c* &c syrr copt æth arm Bas Chr Thl Euthym Op. (εσθιει, πινει FHK[Γ] 69: εσθιη, πινει M 33.) for δε, τε (|| *Luke*) C 1. 33. 245 Scr's a i m n Syr æth [Ephr] Bas.
51. θησει bef μετα τ. υποκρ. D latt(*a* def) Hil.

Chap. XXV. 1. rec αυτων, with CI$_c$ℵ rel Orig Bas [Meth$_1$ Chr Damasc$_1$]: txt BDL (*see note*). rec απαντησιν (*from ver* 6), with DL rel [Bas Chr]: txt BCℵ 1 Meth.

falls away from his truth and faithfulness;—the sign of which is that he begins (lit. shall have begun) to κατακυριεύειν τῶν κλήρων 1 Pet. v. 3, and to revel with the children of the world. In consequence, though he have not lost his *belief* (ὁ κύρ. μου), he shall be *placed with* those who believed not, the hypocrites.
51.] διχ. refers to the punishment of cutting, or sawing asunder: see Dan. ii. 5; iii. 29: Sus. ver. 59; see also Heb. iv. 12; xi. 37. The expression here is perhaps not without a symbolical reference to that dreadful *sundering of the conscience and practice* which shall be the reflective torment of the condemned:—and by the mingling and confounding of which only is the anomalous life of the wilful sinner made in this world tolerable.

Chap. XXV. 1—13.] Parable of the Virgins. *Peculiar to Matthew.*
1. τότε] *at the period spoken of at the end of the last chapter*, viz. the coming of the Lord to His personal reign—not His final coming to judgment. **δέκα παρθ.**] The subject of this parable is not, as of the last, the distinction between the faithful and unfaithful servants; no *outward* distinction here exists—all are virgins—all companions of the bride—all furnished with brightly-burning lamps—all, up to a certain time, fully ready to meet the Bridegroom—the difference consists in *some having made a provision* for feeding the lamps in case of delay, and *the others none*—and the moral of the parable is *the blessedness of endurance unto the end.* 'In eo vertitur summa parabolæ, quod non satis est ad officium *semel* accinctos fuisse et paratos, nisi ad finem usque duremus.' Calvin. There is no question here of apostasy, or unfaithfulness—but of the *want of provision* to keep the light bright against the coming of the bridegroom however delayed.
Ten was a favourite number with the Jews—*ten* men formed a congregation in a synagogue. In a passage from Rabbi Salomo, cited by Wetstein, he mentions ten lamps or torches as the usual number in marriage processions: see also Luke xix. 13. **εἰς ὑπ. τ. ν.**] It would appear that these virgins had left their own homes, and were waiting somewhere for the bridegroom to come,—probably at the house of the bride; for the object of the marriage procession was to *fetch the bride to the bridegroom's house.* Meyer however supposes that in this case the wedding was to be *held* in the bride's house, on account of the thing signified—the coming of the Lord to his Church;—but it is better to take the ordinary custom, and interpret accordingly, where we can. In both the wedding parables (see ch. xxii.) the *bride* does not appear—for she, being the Church, is in fact the aggregate of the guests in the one case, and of the companions in the other. We may perhaps say that she is here, in the strict interpretation, the Jewish Church, and these ten virgins Gentile congregations accompanying her. The reading καὶ τῆς

τοῦ [l] νυμφίου. 2 πέντε δὲ ἐξ αὐτῶν ἦσαν [m] μωραί, καὶ
πέντε [n] φρόνιμοι. 3 αἱ γὰρ [m] μωραὶ λαβοῦσαι τὰς
[l] λαμπάδας αὐτῶν οὐκ ἔλαβον μεθ᾽ ἑαυτῶν [o] ἔλαιον· 4 αἱ
δὲ [n] φρόνιμοι ἔλαβον [o] ἔλαιον ἐν τοῖς [p] ἀγγείοις μετὰ τῶν
[l] λαμπάδων αὐτῶν. 5 [q] χρονίζοντος δὲ τοῦ [l] νυμφίου
[r] ἐνύσταξαν πᾶσαι καὶ ἐκάθευδον. 6 [s] μέσης δὲ [s] νυκτὸς

l ch. ix. 15 reff. m ch. vii. 26 reff. n ch. vii. 24 reff. o Mark vi. 13 reff. Num. iv. 9. p here (& ch. xiii. 41 v. r.) only. Jer. xlvii. (xl.) 10 al. q ch. xxiv. 48 reff.

r 2 Pet. ii. 3 only. Ps. cxviii. 28 AB2ℵ(not F. B[1] def.). cxx. 3, 4. s here only. 3 Kings iii. 20. see Mark xiii. 35.

(Z doubtful.) aft νυμφιου add και της νυμφης (*prob a clumsy interpolation: see note*) DX[1] 1[1] latt Syr syr-w-ast(with a margl note, "*sponsa* non in omnibus exemplaribus invenitur nominatim in Alexandrino") arm Orig-int Hil Arnob Tich Op: om BCZℵ rel coptt æth Meth Bas Chr [Damasc$_1$ Orig-int-com] Aug.

2. [vv. 2—16 lat-*a* def.] ins αι bef 1st πεντε Z. rec ησαν bef εξ αυτων, with X rel Bas Chr-H: om εξ αυτων Chr-2(and ed-Fd): txt BCDLZΔ[1]ℵ 1 [vulg] lat-*b c* &c arm Bas Chr-6-9-η-ρ Orig-int. rec transp μωραι and φρονιμοι (*more natural order. It has hardly, as Mey and De W, been altered to txt to suit ver* 3) with X rel lat-*f* syrr Bas Chr Thl: txt BCDLZℵ 1. 33 latt syr-jer copt æth arm Orig-int. Steph ins αι bef 2nd πεντε (*error from the last letters of* και?), with E rel Bas$_2$ [Chr] Thl: om BCD K(Tischdf) LZΠℵ 1. 33 [Bas$_1$].

3. rec (for αι γαρ) αιτινες (*mechanical repetition from ver* 1, αιτινες λαβουσαι κ.τ.λ.?), with X rel Bas Chr: αι δε Z (1) latt æth: αι ουν D lat-*ff*$_2$: και αι Syr syr-ms: αι syr arm: txt BCLℵ 33 copt. (γαρ *not being understood,* δε, ουν, και *were substituted; or as rec: this seems to me far more likely than that* αι γαρ *should have been substituted for* αιτινες, *as Mey and De W think.*) rec (for αυτων) εαυτων, with Z(appy) (S 1, e sil): om Lℵ vulg lat-*ff*$_{1.2}$ *g*$_{1.2}$ *l* arm: txt BCD rel Bas. aft ελαιον ins εν τοις αγγειοις αυτων D Scr's q[1] ev-y$_1$ Arnob.

4. rec aft αγγειοις ins αυτων, with C rel latt syr copt æth [Bas$_1$ Chr Aug]: om B D-gr LZℵ 1 forj lat-*h* Syr arm Arnob. om 2nd αυτων CZ vulg lat-*f ff*$_2$ *g*$_{1.2}$ *h* Aug: εαυτων Bℵ.

νύμφης is probably an interpolation, such as are of frequent occurrence in D and its cognates. This **ἐξῆλθον** is *not their final going out* in ver. 6, for only half of them did so,—but *their leaving their own homes:* cf. λαβοῦσαι—ἔλαβον, &c. vv. 3, 4. The interpretation is—these are souls come out from the world into the Church, and there waiting for the coming of the Lord—not hypocrites, but *faithful souls, bearing their lamps* (τ. λ. ἑαυτῶν, cf. 1 Thess. iv. 4)—the inner spiritual life fed with the oil of God's Spirit (see Zech. iv. 2—12: Acts x. 38: Heb. i. 9). All views of this parable which represent the foolish virgins as having only a *dead faith,* only the lamp without the light, the body without the spirit, &c., are *quite beside the purpose;*—the lamps (see ver. 8) were *all burning* at first, and for a certain time. Whether the *equal partition* of wise and foolish have any deep meaning we cannot say; it *may* be so. **3, 4.**] These were not torches, nor wicks fastened on staves, as some have supposed, but properly *lamps:* and the oil vessels (which is most important to the parable) were *separate from* the lamps. The lamps being the hearts lit with the flame of heavenly love and patience, supplied with the oil of the Spirit,—now comes in the difference between the wise and foolish:—the one *made no provision for the supply* of this—the others *did.* How so? The wise ones *gave all diligence to make their calling and election sure* (2 Pet. i. 10 and 5—8), making their bodies, souls, and spirits (their *vessels,* 2 Cor. iv. 7) a means of supplying spiritual food for the light within, by seeking, in the appointed means of grace, more and more of God's Holy Spirit. The others *did not this*—but trusting that the light, once burning, would ever burn, made no provision for the strengthening of the inner man by watchfulness and prayer. **5—7. χρονίζ.**] compare ch. xxiv. 48. But the thought of the foolish virgins is very different from that of the wicked servant: his—'there will be plenty of time, my Lord tarrieth;'—theirs, 'surely He will soon be here, there is no need of a store of oil.' This may serve to shew how altogether diverse is the ground of the two parables. **ἐν. πᾶσ. κ. ἐκ.**] I believe no more is meant here than that all, being weak by nature, gave way to drowsiness: as indeed the wakefulness of the holiest Christian, compared with what it should be, is a sort of slumber:—but, the while, how much difference was there between them! **ἐνύστ.**] *dormitabant:* we have Aristoph. Vesp. 12, ὕπνος νυστακ-

[t] κραυγὴ γέγονεν Ἰδοὺ ὁ [l] νυμφίος, ἐξέρχεσθε [u] εἰς [u] ἀπάντησιν. 7 τότε ἠγέρθησαν πᾶσαι αἱ [u] παρθένοι ἐκεῖναι καὶ
[v] ἐκόσμησαν τὰς [i] λαμπάδας ἑαυτῶν. 8 αἱ δὲ [m] μωραὶ ταῖς
[n] φρονίμοις εἶπαν Δότε ἡμῖν ἐκ τοῦ [o] ἐλαίου ὑμῶν, ὅτι αἱ
λαμπάδες ἡμῶν [w] σβέννυνται. 9 ἀπεκρίθησαν δὲ αἱ φρόνιμοι λέγουσαι [x] Μήποτε οὐ μὴ [y] ἀρκέσῃ ἡμῖν καὶ ὑμῖν.
πορεύεσθε μᾶλλον πρὸς τοὺς πωλοῦντας, καὶ ἀγοράσατε
[z] ἑαυταῖς. 10 ἀπερχομένων δὲ αὐτῶν ἀγοράσαι ἦλθεν ὁ
νυμφίος· καὶ αἱ [a] ἕτοιμοι εἰσῆλθον μετ' αὐτοῦ εἰς τοὺς
[b] γάμους, καὶ ἐκλείσθη ἡ θύρα. 11 ὕστερον δὲ ἔρχονται

A ἐξερχεσθε... ABCDE FGHKL MSUVX ZΓΔΠℵ 1. 33. 69

Θ_h xxv. 9(appy) ...

t Luke i. 42. Acts xxiii. 9. Eph. iv. 31. Heb. v. 7. Rev. xiv. 18. xxi. 4 only. 1 Kings iv. 6.
u see ver. 1 reff.
v = here only. (ch. xxiii. 29 al.) Ezek. xxiii. 41. τράπεζαν κοσμεῖν, Xen. Cyr. viii. 2. 6.
w ch. xii. 20 reff. Job xviii. 5, 6. Prov. xiii. 9.
x Gen. xxiv. 5, 39.
y = John vi. 7. xiv. 8. 2 Cor. xii. 9. (Luke iii. 14 reff.) Num. xi. 22.
z 2nd pers., ch. iii. 9 reff.
a 2 term., here only. see 2 Cor. ix. 5. 1 Pet. i. 5.
b plu., ch. xxii. 2, &c. reff.

6. for *γεγονεν*, *εγενετο* B. rec aft *νυμφιος* ins *ερχεται*, with C[3]X rel latt syrr æth arm [$Meth_1$ Ephr] Bas Chr Orig-int Op: om BC[1]DLZℵ coptt $Meth_1$ Ephr Cyr. for *εξερχεσθε*, *εξερχεται* D[1](txt D[1]-corr). *συναντησιν* C. rec aft *απαντησιν* ins *αυτου*, with AD rel [$Meth_1$ Ephr Bas Chr]; *αυτω* C latt: om Bℵ [$Meth_1$] Cyr. (Z 33 def.)

7. om *εκειναι* D ev-22 (Syr ?) arm. rec (for *εαυτων*) *αυτων*, with CD rel [Bas_2]: txt ABLZℵ. (33 def.)

8. [*ειπαν*, so BCL 33.] aft *ημιν* ins *ελαιον* A. for *ημων*, *υμων* C[1]LUΠ[1].

9. for *λεγουσαι*, *ειπον* Θ_h. rec (for *ου μη*) *ουκ*, with ALZℵ 33. 69 [Bas_1]: txt BCDΘ_h rel Ephr Bas_1. *αρκεσει* D[1]-corr 33 Scr's s evv-H_1-P_1-y_1. *υμιν και ημιν* ℵ 247 Bas_1. rec aft *πορευεσθε* ins *δε*, with CZΘ_h rel lat-ff_2 syrr copt-wilk [Bas_2]: om ABDEGHSVΓΔℵ latt copt-schw æth arm Orig-int_2 Aug Op.

10. for *απ. δε αυτ.*, *εως υπαγουσιν cum vadunt* D [om *αυτων* Θ_h^1]. *ετοιμαι* A ev-y_1. *ηκλεισθη* B[1].

τής: and Plato, Rep. p. 405 c, speaks of a *νυστάζων δικαστής*. Wordsw., after Hilary, understands this verse of sleep in death. But, not to mention that this will not fit the machinery of the parable (see below on ver. 8), it would assume (**πᾶσαι**) that none of the faithful would be living on earth when the Lord comes. **κραυγὴ γ.**] see Isa. lxii. 5—7: and the porter's duty, Mark xiii. 34. This warning cry is *before* the coming: see ver. 10. **γέγονεν,** not, *was*, but to be rendered *present*, graphically setting the reality before us: **there ariseth a cry.** **πᾶσαι**] *All* now seem alike—all wanted their lamps trimmed—but for the neglectful, there is not wherewith! It is not enough to *have burnt*, but to *be burning*, when He comes. Raise the wick as they will, what avails it if the oil is spent? **ἐκόσμησαν**] "by pouring on fresh oil, and removing the fungi about the wick: for the latter purpose a sharp-pointed wire was attached to the lamp, which is still seen in the bronze lamps found in sepulchres. Virgil's Moretum, 'Et producit acu stupas humore carentes.'" Webst. and Wilk.

8, 9.] **σβ., are going out,**—not as E. V., and even recently Bp. Wordsw. to support his interpretation of ver. 5,—'*are gone out*:' and there is deep truth in this: the lamps of the foolish virgins are *not extinguished altogether*. **μήπ. οὐ μὴ ἀρ.**] see Ps. xlix. 7: Rom. xiv. 12. No man can have more of this provision than will supply his own wants. **πορεύεσθε**] This is not said in mockery, as some (Luther, Calv.) suppose: but in earnest. **οἱ πωλοῦντες** are the ordinary dispensers of the means of grace—*ultimately* of course God Himself, who alone can give his Spirit. The counsel was good, and well followed—but the time was past. (Observe that those who sell are a *particular class* of persons—no mean argument for a *set and appointed ministry*—and moreover for a *paid* ministry. If they *sell*, they *receive* for the thing sold: cf. our Lord's saying, Luke x. 7. This *selling* bears no analogy with the crime of Simon Magus in Acts viii.: cf. our Lord's other saying, Matt. x. 8.)

10—12.] We are *not told that they could not buy*—that the shops were shut—but simply that it was *too late—for that time.* For it is *not the final coming of the Lord to judgment, when the day of grace will be past*, that is spoken of,—except in so far as it is hinted at in the background, and in the individual application of the parable (virtually, not actually) coincides, to each man, with the day of his death. *This feast* is the *marriage supper* of Rev.

...ανοιξον η Z. ABCDE FGHKL MSUVX ΓΔΘ_hΠℵ 1. 33. 69

καὶ αἱ λοιπαὶ παρθένοι λέγουσαι Κύριε κύριε ἄνοιξον
ἡμῖν. 12 ὁ δὲ ἀποκριθεὶς εἶπεν Ἀμὴν λέγω ὑμῖν, [c] οὐκ
οἶδα ὑμᾶς. 13 Γρηγορεῖτε οὖν, ὅτι οὐκ οἴδατε τὴν ἡμέραν
οὐδὲ τὴν ὥραν. 14 ὥςπερ γὰρ ἄνθρωπος [d] ἀποδημῶν
ἐκάλεσεν τοὺς ἰδίους δούλους καὶ [e] παρέδωκεν αὐτοῖς τὰ
[f] ὑπάρχοντα αὐτοῦ, 15 καὶ [g] ᾧ μὲν ἔδωκεν πέντε [h] τάλαντα,
[g] ᾧ δὲ δύο, [g] ᾧ δὲ ἕν, ἑκάστῳ [i] κατὰ τὴν ἰδίαν [i] δύναμιν,
καὶ [d] ἀπεδήμησεν εὐθέως. 16 πορευθεὶς δὲ ὁ τὰ πέντε
[h] τάλαντα λαβὼν [k] ἠργάσατο [l] ἐν αὐτοῖς καὶ [m] ἐποίησεν
ἄλλα πέντε [[h] τάλαντα]. 17 ὡςαύτως καὶ ὁ τὰ δύο

..xxv. 16 (appy)Θ_h

c see ch. vii. 23.
d ch. xxi. 33 ‖. Luke xv. 13 only †.
e = Luke iv. 6. Acts xxvii. 1 al.
f ch. xix. 21 reff. Eccl. v. 18.
g ch. xiii. 8 reff.
h here, &c. and ch. xviii. 24 only. 2 Kings xii. 30.
i 2 Cor. viii. 3. 1 Chron. xxix. 2.
k absol., Acts xviii. 3. Rom. iv. 4 al. Sir. x. 27.
l = ch. v. 13. Rom. xvi. 16. James iii. 9. Rev. ii. 16.
m = ch. iii. 10. Luke xix. 18. Deut. viii. 18.

11. for *ερχονται*, *ηλθον* D lat-*c f* syr copt Orig-int Op. om *και* DHZ forj lat-*b c f h* copt æth Aug: ins ABCΘ_hℵ rel vulg lat-$ff_{1.2}$ $g_{1.2}$ syrr arm Bas Orig-int Aug Op.
13. rec aft *ωραν* ins *εν η ο υιος του ανθρωπου ερχεται* (*gloss*), with C^3E rel syr-jer-mg: om ABC^1DLXΔ$\Theta_h$$Π^1$ℵ 1^1. 33 latt syrr syr-jer coptt æth arm Eus(appy) Ath Bas Chr Orig-int Hil Aug.
14. om *γαρ* D arm Orig. aft *ανθρωπος* ins *τις* C^3FM Scr's f k^2 v evv-H_1-P_2-y_1-z_1 arm [Orig-int_1]. for *αυτου*, *αυτων* A.
15. for ἕν, *ενα* D. for *ιδ. δυν.*, *δυναμιν αυτου* D.
16. *ευθεως πορευθεις*, omg *δε*, B[Tischdf Nov. T. Vat. proleg p. xxxiii describes B as omg the 2nd *και* in ver 15; it is inserted in his transcript of the MS in loco] $ℵ^1$(txt $ℵ^{3a}$) lat-*b* ff_1 g_1: *ευθεως δε πορ.* 1. 243 lat-*c f* ff_2 *h* syr-jer Op: *πορ. δε ευθεως* arm. (*ηργασατο*, so B^1DL$ℵ^1$ 69.) for *εποιησεν*, *εκερδησεν* (*prob from vv* 17, 22) A^rBCDL$ℵ^{3a.b}$ 1. 33. 69 [latt Syr syr-mg æth arm Orig-int_1]: txt $A^1$$\Theta_h$$ℵ^1$ rel [Bas_1]. om 2nd *ταλαντα* (*as unnecessary: it is hardly possible it should have been* inserted) BL 1. 33 latt(not *f*) Syr syr-jer coptt arm Op.
17. for *ωσαυτως*, *ομοιως* D.—A adds *δε*. om *και* C^1L$ℵ^1$(ins $ℵ^{3a}$) 33 am(with em forj $fuld^2$ tol) lat-*b* g_2 [Orig-int_1]. aft *δυο* ins *ταλαντα λαβων* D lat-*c* æth-rom; *λαβων* vulg lat-*a b* &c copt Orig-int.

xix. 7—9 (see also ib. xxi. 2); *after which* these improvident ones gone to buy their oil shall be *judged in common with the rest of the dead*, ibid. xx. 12, 13. Observe here, **οὐκ οἶδα ὑμ.** is very different, as the whole circumstances are different, from *οὐδέποτε ἔγνων ὑμ.* in ch. vii. 23, where the *ἀποχωρεῖτε ἀπ' ἐμοῦ* binds it to the *πορεύεσθε ἀπ' ἐμοῦ* in our ver. 41, and to the time of the *final judgment*, spoken of in that parable. (See the note at the end of the chapter.)

14—30.] Parable of the talents. *Peculiar to Matthew.* The similar parable contained in Luke xix. 11—27 is altogether distinct, and uttered on a different occasion: see notes there. 14. **ὥςπ. γ.**] The ellipsis is rightly supplied in the E. V., **For the Kingdom of Heaven is as a man,** &c. We have this parable and the preceding one alluded to in very few words by Mark, xiii. 34—36. In it we have the *active* side of the Christian life, and *its* danger, set before us, as in the last the contemplative side. There, the foolish virgins failed *from thinking their part too easy*—here the wicked servant fails *from thinking his too hard.* The parable is still concerned with *Christians* (**τοὺς ἰδίους δούλους**), and *not the world at large.* We must remember the relation of master and slave, in order to understand his delivering to them his property, and punishing them for not fructifying with it. 15.] In Luke each *receives the same*, but the *profit made by each* is *different*: see notes there. Here, in fact, they *did each receive the same*, for they received *according to their ability*—their character and powers. There is no Pelagianism in this, for each man's powers are themselves the gift of God. 16—18.] The increase gained by each of the two faithful servants was *the full amount of their talents*:—of each will be required as much as has been given. "**εἰργάσατο** is the technical term, common in the classics, and especially in Demosthenes: see Reiske's index. **ἐν** is instrumental." Meyer. **ἐποίησεν** is not a Latinism (*conficere pecuniam*), but answers to *ποιεῖν καρπὸν* ch. iii. 10. The *third servant here* is not to be confounded with the *wicked servant* in ch. xxiv. 48. This one is *not actively an ill-doer*, but a *hider* of the money entrusted to him—one who brings

n ch. xvi. 26 reff. o ch. xxi. 33. Mark xii. 1 only. Gen. xxi. 30. p ch. xviii. 23, 24 (reff.) only. q = Luke iii. 20. xvi. 26 al. r = here bis only. (Mark xiv. 7. Acts xv. 29. Eph. vi. 3, from Exod. xx. 12. see Luke xix. 17.) s = here bis only. see Luke x. 19 al. t see ch. xxiv. 45, 47 reff. u Heb. iii. 11 &c., from Ps. xciv. 11. v John xv. 11. xvi. 20. 2 Cor. i. 24. Heb. xii. 2.

ABCDE FGHKL MSUVX ΓΔΠℵ 1. 33. 69

[n] ἐκέρδησεν [καὶ αὐτὸς] ἄλλα δύο. 18 ὁ δὲ τὸ ἓν λαβὼν
ἀπελθὼν [o] ὤρυξεν * γῆν καὶ ἔκρυψεν τὸ ἀργύριον τοῦ
κυρίου αὐτοῦ. 19 μετὰ δὲ πολὺν χρόνον ἔρχεται ὁ κύριος
τῶν δούλων ἐκείνων καὶ [p] συναίρει λόγον μετ' αὐτῶν.
20 καὶ προσελθὼν ὁ τὰ πέντε [h] τάλαντα λαβὼν προσήνεγ-
κεν ἄλλα πέντε [h] τάλαντα λέγων Κύριε, πέντε [h] τάλαντά
μοι [e] παρέδωκας, ἴδε ἄλλα πέντε τάλαντα [n] ἐκέρδησα [q] ἐπ'
αὐτοῖς. 21 ἔφη αὐτῷ ὁ κύριος αὐτοῦ [r] Εὖ δοῦλε ἀγαθὲ
καὶ πιστέ, [s] ἐπὶ ὀλίγα ἦς πιστός, ἐπὶ [t] πολλῶν σε [t] κατα-
στήσω· [u] εἴσελθε εἰς τὴν [v] χαρὰν τοῦ κυρίου σου. 22 προσ-

om και αυτος (*as unnecessary aft ωσαυτως*) BC¹Lℵ 33 latt [Syr] coptt æth arm Bas Orig-int Op: ins AC³ (D bef εκερδ.) X rel lat-*h* syr.

18. aft ἓν ins ταλαντον A [ev-P_1] lat-*a b c* &c. om απελθων D 5. 36. 59 lat-*a b c* &c(not *f h*). *rec ἐν τῇ γῇ, with AC³D rel am syrr: την γην C¹: γην BLℵ 33 lat-ff_1 æth arm. (*The decision here is difficult.* ΞΕΝΕΝΤΗΓΗ *was likely enough to be mistaken, one* ΕΝ *being passed over, for* ΞΕΝΤΗ̄ΓΗ̄, *and then the* ΤΗ̄ *omitted: and on the other hand,* ΞΕΝΓΗ̄ *was just as likely to be mistaken for* ΞΕΝΕΝΓΗ, and then the ΤΗ inserted.) rec απεκρυψε, with X rel: txt ABCDLℵ 33.

19. rec χρονον bef πολυν, with A rel syrr: txt BCDGLℵ 1. 33. 69 latt. copt arm Orig Op. rec μετ αυτων bef λογον, with A rel lat-ff_1 syrr Orig: txt BCDLℵ 1. 33 latt [copt æth arm].

20. for και προσελθ., προσελθ. δε A copt. om 1st ταλαντα ℵ, 2nd Δ ev-y_1 lat-*h* Syr æth, 4th C¹L latt Syr æth. επεκερδησα D, *superlucratus sum* latt arm Orig-int. om επ αυτοις (*as difficult and appy superfluous; the readings of* D &c *above, and* E &c *below, have also been attempts to correct it*) BDLℵ 33 latt copt æth arm [Orig-int-txt Ambr]: ins AC rel syrr [Orig-int-com], εν αυτοις (*from ver* 16) EG 238-47.

21. rec aft εφη ins δε, with A rel syr copt: om BCDEKLΓℵ (MU, Tischdf) 33 latt Syr arm Orig-int. ευγε (*see Luke* xix. 17) A¹(appy) latt [$Orig_1$(appy, and int_5) Bas_1] Iren-int Lucif. for 1st επι, επι (i. e. επει) επ' D latt arm [$Orig\text{-}int_2$]: *quia in* (οτι εν) D-lat Iren Lucif.

no profit: see on ver. 24. **19—23.** **μετὰ πολὺν χρόνον**] Here again, as well as in the χρονίζ. of ver. 5 and ch. xxiv. 48, we have an intimation that the interval would be *no short one.* This proceeding *is not,* strictly speaking, *the last judgment,* but still *the same as that in the former parable; the beginning of judgment at the house of God*—the judgment of the *millennial advent.* This, to the servants of Christ (τοὺς ἰδίους δούλους, ver. 14), is *their* final judgment—but not that of the rest of the world. We may observe that this great *account* differs from the coming of the bridegroom, inasmuch as this is altogether concerned with a course of action *past*—that with a present state of preparation. This holds, in the individual application, of *the account after the resurrection:* that, at the utmost (and not in the direct sense of the parable even so much), of being ready for his summons at death. **20.**] The faithful servant does not take the praise to himself —μοι παρέδωκας is his confession—and ἐπ' αὐτοῖς the enabling cause of his gain;—'without Me, ye can do nothing,' John xv. 5. This is plainer in Luke (xix. 16), ἡ μνᾶ σου δέκα προσηργάσατο μνᾶς. See 1 Cor. xv. 10;—and on the joy and alacrity of these faithful servants in the day of reckoning, 1 Thess. ii. 19: 2 Cor. i. 14: Phil. iv. 1. **21.**] In Luke = ὅτι ἐν ἐλαχίστῳ πιστὸς ἐγένου, ἴσθι ἐξουσίαν ἔχων ἐπάνω δέκα πόλεων—where see note. (I cannot imagine with Meyer that εὖ is to be taken with ἐπὶ ὀλίγα ἦς π., or that it will not bear the sense of 'Well done!' Although εὖγε is the more usual word, we have (see Passow) in later Greek such expressions as μαλ' εὖ, which is as near as possible to that meaning.) The **χαρά** here is not a *feast,* as sometimes interpreted, but that **joy** spoken of Heb. xii. 2, and Isa. liii. 11—that joy of the Lord arising from the completion of his work and labour of love, of which the first Sabbatical rest of the Creator was typical—

ελθὼν δὲ καὶ ὁ τὰ δύο τάλαντα εἶπεν Κύριε, δύο τάλαντά
μοι [w] παρέδωκας, ἴδε ἄλλα δύο τάλαντα [p] ἐκέρδησα [q] ἐπ᾽
αὐτοῖς. 23 ἔφη αὐτῷ ὁ κύριος αὐτοῦ [r] Εὖ δοῦλε ἀγαθὲ
καὶ πιστέ, [s] ἐπὶ ὀλίγα ἧς πιστός, ἐπὶ πολλῶν σε [t] κατα-
στήσω· [u] εἴςελθε εἰς τὴν [v] χαρὰν τοῦ κυρίου σου. 24 προςελθὼν δὲ καὶ ὁ τὸ ἓν τάλαντον εἰληφὼς εἶπεν Κύριε,
ἔγνων σε ὅτι [x] σκληρὸς εἶ ἄνθρωπος, [y] θερίζων ὅπου οὐκ
ἔσπειρας, καὶ [z] συνάγων ὅθεν οὐ [a] διεσκόρπισας· 25 καὶ
φοβηθείς, ἀπελθὼν ἔκρυψα τὸ τάλαντόν σου ἐν τῇ γῇ.
ἴδε ἔχεις [b] τὸ σόν. 26 ἀποκριθεὶς δὲ ὁ κύριος αὐτοῦ
εἶπεν αὐτῷ Πονηρὲ δοῦλε καὶ [c] ὀκνηρέ, ᾔδεις ὅτι [y] θερίζω
ὅπου οὐκ ἔσπειρα, καὶ [z] συνάγω ὅθεν οὐ [a] διεσκόρπισα;
27 ἔδει σε οὖν [d] βαλεῖν τὸ ἀργύριόν μου τοῖς [e] τραπεζίταις,

w ver. 14.
x = here only. (John vi. 60 reff.) 1 Kings xxv. 3. Isa. xix. 4.
y ch. vi. 26. John iv. 36, &c. al. Jer. xii. 13.
z = ch. vi. 26. xiii. 47. John vi. 13. Gen. xli. 35.
a ch. xxvi. 31 ‖ Mk. (from Zech. xiii. 7 A [ℵ^{3a. b}].) Luke i. 51. xv. 13. xvi. 1. John xi. 52. Acts v. 37 only. Ezek. x. 2.
b ch. xx. 14.
c = Rom. xii. 11 (Phil. iii. 1) only. Prov. vi. 6, 9.
d = ch. xxvii. 6. Mark xii. 41, &c. ‖ L.
e here only †. ὁ Σκιπίων συνέταξε τῷ τραπεζίτῃ, Polyb. xxxii. 13. 6. Jos. Antt. xii. 2. 3. (see ch. xxi. 12.)

22. om δε Bℵ[1](ins ℵ[3a]). rec aft ταλαντα ins λαβων, with Dℵ rel vulg lat-*b c* [copt æth arm Orig-int$_1$]; ειληφως 157. 243 : om ABCLΠ 1. 33. 69 syrr. (a space is left in Rettig's edn of Δ.) om κυριε ℵ. παρεδωκες D. for ιδε, ιδου D (and ver 25). επεκερδησα D lat-*f*. om επ αυτοις BDLℵ 33 latt copt æth arm [Orig-int$_1$] : ins AC rel syrr.
23. ευγε and επει επ, as before, ver 21. πιστος bef ης B lat-*h*. (om ης lat-*c*.)
24. om 1st και D 1 lat-*a b c* $g_{1\ or\ 2}$ Lucif. for ἕν, ενα D[1]. om σε D 46 latt arm [Chr$_2$] Orig-int Hil Op. for σκλ. ει ανθ., ανθρωπος αυστηρος ει (*Luke* xix. 21) ℵ lat-*b*. for οθεν, οπου D 56 latt.
25. απηλθον και D 252[1](appy) latt æth [Orig-int$_1$].
26. δουλε bef πονηρε A latt Syr copt hom-Cl Chr-ed(not Fd) Damasc Orig-int$_1$ Hil Lucif Ambr Jer Op.
27. rec ουν bef σε, with AD rel latt copt Orig-int Op: txt BCLℵ 33 ev-y$_1$ syr. τα αργυρια (*corrn*) Bℵ[1](txt ℵ[3a]).

Gen. i. 31; ii. 2,—and of which his faithful ones shall in the end partake: see Heb. iv. 3—11: Rev. iii. 21. Notice the identity of the praise and portion of him who had been faithful in less, with those of the *first*. The words are, as has been well observed, "not, 'good and successful servant,' but 'good and faithful servant:'" and faithfulness does not depend on *amount*. **24, 25.**] This sets forth the excuse which men are perpetually making of human infirmity and inability to keep God's commands, when they never apply to that grace which may enable them to do so—an excuse, as here, self-convicting and false at heart. **θερίζ. ὅπ. οὐκ ἔσπ.**] The connexion of thought in this our Lord's *last* parable, with His *first* (ch. xiii. 3—9), is remarkable. He looks for fruit where He has sown—*this is truth:* but not beyond the power of the soil by Him enabled—*this is man's lie*, to encourage himself in idleness. **φοβ.**] see Gen. iii. 10. But that pretended fear, and this insolent speech, are *inconsistent*, and betray the falsehood of his answer. **ἔχεις τὸ σόν**] This is also false—it was not τὸ σόν—for there was *his lord's time*,—and *his own labour, which was his lord's—to be accounted for.* **26, 27.**] Luke prefixes ἐκ τοῦ στόματός σου κρινῶ σε,—viz. 'because, knowing the relation between us, that of absolute power on my part over thee, —if thou hadst really thought me such an hard master, **ἔδει σε κ.τ.λ.**, in order to avoid utter ruin. But this was *not* thy real thought—thou wert πονηρὸς κ. ὀκνηρός.' The **ᾔδεις**, &c. is not concessive, but hypothetical;—God is *not really* such a Master. **τοῖς τραπ.**] in Luke (xix. 23) ἐπὶ τράπεζαν. τραπεζίτης is interpreted κολλυβιστής (see ch. xxi. 12) by Hesychius. There was a saying very current among the early Fathers, γίνεσθε δόκιμοι τραπεζῖται, which some of them seem to attribute to the Lord, some to one of the Apostles. It is supposed by some to be taken from this place, and it is just possible it may have been: but it more likely was traditional, or from some apocryphal gospel. Suicer, Thes.,

f — Heb. xi. 19. Gen. xxxviii. 20.
g Luke xix. 23 only. Ezek. xviii. 13 al.
h pass., ch. xiii. 12 (reff.) only.
i Luke xvii. 10 only. 2 Kings vi. 22. Ep. Jer. 17 (15) B only. (-ειοῦσθαι, Rom. iii. 12.)
k ch. viii. 12 reff.
l ch. viii. 20 reff.
m ch. xvi. 27 || al. Ps. ci. 16.

καὶ ἐλθὼν ἐγὼ [f] ἐκομισάμην ἂν τὸ ἐμὸν σὺν [g] τόκῳ.
28 ἄρατε οὖν ἀπ᾽ αὐτοῦ τὸ τάλαντον, καὶ δότε τῷ ἔχοντι
τὰ δέκα τάλαντα. 29 τῷ γὰρ ἔχοντι παντὶ δοθήσεται καὶ
[h] περισσευθήσεται· τοῦ δὲ μὴ ἔχοντος, καὶ ὃ ἔχει ἀρθήσεται ἀπ᾽ αὐτοῦ. 30 καὶ τὸν [i] ἀχρεῖον δοῦλον ἐκβάλετε εἰς ...εκβαλεται C.
τὸ [k] σκότος τὸ [k] ἐξώτερον· ἐκεῖ ἔσται ὁ [k] κλαυθμὸς καὶ ὁ
[k] βρυγμὸς τῶν ὀδόντων. ...οδοντων X.
31 Ὅταν δὲ ἔλθῃ ὁ [l] υἱὸς τοῦ [l] ἀνθρώπου ἐν τῇ [m] δόξῃ

ABDEF GHKL MSUV ΓΔΠℵ 1. 33. 69

εγω bef ελθων A [ev-i] lat-*ff*$_1$ *g*$_2$ *h* Clem(εγω ανελθ.) Orig Cyr Chr(καγω) [Cassiod].
28. for δεκα, πεντε D.
29. om παντι D ev-H$_1$ Syr Chr. περισσευσεται D. rec απο δε του μη (*from Luke* xix. 26), with AC rel syr Orig$_2$ Chr [Damasc$_1$] : txt BDLℵ 1. 33 latt Syr. for εχει, δοκει εχειν (*from Luke* viii. 18) LΔ 33. 69 vulg lat-*f* *g*$_{1.2}$ *l* syr Orig$_3$ Chr-K-L Thl-edd Tert Ambr Jer Philast Op.
30. rec εκβαλλετε, with FG^2(om ver G^1) H 69 : βαλετε εξω D 51 lat-*a b c e ff*$_{1.2}$ *g*$_2$: txt ABCℵ rel Chr Thl Euthym-mss.

under the word, discusses the question, and inclines to think that it was a way of expressing the general moral of the two parables in Matt. and Luke. But, in the *interpretation*, who are these τραπεζῖται? The explanation (Olsh., and adopted by Trench, Parables, p. 247) of their being those *stronger characters* who may lead the more timid to the useful employment of gifts which they have not energy to use, is objectionable, (1) as not answering to the *character addressed*—he was not timid, but false and slothful;—and (2) nor to the *facts of the case:* for it is impossible to employ the grace given to one through *another's* means, without working one's self. I rather take it to mean, 'If thou hadst really been afraid, &c., slothful as thou art, thou mightest at least, without trouble to thyself, have provided that I should have not been defrauded of the interest of my money—but now thou art both slothful and wicked, in having done me this injustice.' Observe there would have been no praise due to the servant—but **τὸ ἐμόν** would not have lost its **τόκος**. The *machinery of religious and charitable societies in our day* is very much in the place of the τραπεζῖται. Let the subscribers to them take heed that they be not in the degraded case of this servant, even if his excuse had been genuine.

28—31.] This command is answered in Luke xix. 25, by a remonstrance from those addressed, which the Master overrules by stating the great law of his Kingdom. In ch. xiii. 12 we have explained this as applied to the system of *teaching by parables.* Here it is predicated of the whole Christian life. It is the case even in nature: a limb used is strengthened; disused, becomes weak. The transference of the talent is not a matter of justice between man and man, but is done in illustration of this law, and in virtue of that sovereign power by which God does what He will with his own: see Rom. xi. 29, and note there. In **τὸ σκ. τὸ ἐξ.** there is again an allusion to the marriage supper of the Lamb, from which the useless servant being excluded, gnashes his teeth with remorse without: see ch. xxii. 13.

31—46.] THE FINAL JUDGMENT OF ALL NATIONS. *Peculiar to Matthew.* In the two former parables we have seen the difference between, and judgment of, *Christians*—in their inward readiness for their Lord, and their outward diligence in profiting by his gifts. And *both these had reference to that first resurrection and millennial Kingdom,* the reality of which is proved by the passages of Scripture cited in the notes above, and during which *all Christians* shall be judged. We now come to the great and universal judgment at the end of this period, also prophesied of distinctly in order in Rev. xx. 11—15—in which *all the dead,* small and great, shall stand before God. This last great judgment answers to the judgment on Jerusalem, *after* the Christians had escaped from it: to the gathering of the eagles (ministers of vengeance) to the carcase. Notice the precision of the words in ver. 31, **ὅταν δὲ ἔλθῃ**—the **ὅταν** setting forth the indefiniteness of the time—the **δέ** the distinction from the two parables foregoing; and **τότε**, to mark a precise time when all this shall take place—a *day* of judgment. Compare for the better understanding of the distinction,

I$_c$ ωσπερ ... ...εκ δεξιων αυτου H. ABDEF GI$_c$KL MSUVΓ ΔΠℵ 1. 33. 69

αὐτοῦ, καὶ πάντες οἱ ἄγγελοι μετ' αὐτοῦ, τότε [n] καθίσει
ἐπὶ [o] θρόνου [o] δόξης αὐτοῦ, 32 καὶ [p] συναχθήσονται ἔμπροσθεν αὐτοῦ πάντα τὰ ἔθνη, καὶ [q] ἀφοριεῖ αὐτοὺς ἀπ' ἀλλήλων, ὥςπερ ὁ ποιμὴν [q] ἀφορίζει τὰ πρόβατα ἀπὸ τῶν
[r] ἐρίφων, 33 καὶ στήσει τὰ μὲν πρόβατα ἐκ [s] δεξιῶν αὐτοῦ,
τὰ δὲ [t] ἐρίφια ἐξ [s] εὐωνύμων. 34 τότε ἐρεῖ ὁ βασιλεὺς
τοῖς ἐκ [s] δεξιῶν αὐτοῦ [u] Δεῦτε οἱ [v] εὐλογημένοι [w] τοῦ
πατρός μου, [x] κληρονομήσατε τὴν [y] ἡτοιμασμένην ὑμῖν
βασιλείαν ἀπὸ [z] καταβολῆς [z] κόσμου. 35 [a] ἐπείνασα γὰρ
καὶ [b] ἐδώκατέ μοι [b] φαγεῖν, [a] ἐδίψησα καὶ [c] ἐποτίσατέ με,

n = ch. xix. 28. xxiii. 2. Ps. ix. 4. see Isa. vi. 1.
o ch. xix. 28. Isa. xxii. 23. see Heb. iv. 16. viii. 1.
p ch. xiii. 2 reff. plur., ch. vi. 28 reff.
q ch. xiii. 49 reff. Lev. xiv. 12.
r Luke xv. 29 only. Gen. xxvii. 9 al. (-φιον, ver. 33.)
s ch. xx. 21, 23 reff.
t here only †. (-φος, ver. 32.)
u ch. iv. 19. xi. 28. xxii. 4 al. Gen. xxxvii. 20. v Luke i. 28, 42. (see Gen. xxiv. 31 Ed-vat. [B def.]) Isa. lxi. 9. w gen., John vi. 45. Philem. 1. Winer, § 30. 2. x ch. v. 5. xix. 29. Luke x. 25. xviii. 18. 1 Cor. vi. 9, 10. xv. 50 al. Gen. xv. 7. Isa. xlix. 8. y = ch. xx. 23 reff.
z w. ἀπό, Luke xi. 50. Heb. iv. 3. ix. 26. Rev. xiii. 8. xvii. 8. πρό, John xviii. 24 al. see ch. xiii. 35 reff
a ch. v. 6 reff. b ch. xiv. 16 reff. c ch. x. 42 ||. Rom. xii. 20 (from Prov. xxv. 21) al. Judg. iv. 19

31. rec ins *αγιοι* bef *αγγελοι* (*usual epithet: insd from Mark* viii. 38, *or Luke* ix. 26), with A rel lat-*f* syrr Chr: om BDLΠ[1]ℵ 1. 33 latt syr-jer copt æth arm Orig Eus [Cyr-jer$_1$ Did$_1$] Ath Chr-K-L(and wlf-ms) Cyr Max-conf Cypr Hil Ambr Aug Op.
32. rec *συναχθησεται* (*gramml corrn*), with A rel Eus$_1$ [Bas-sel$_1$ Thdrt$_1$]: txt BDGKLUΠℵ 33. 69 [Hipp$_1$] Eus$_1$ Thdrt. for *αφοριει*, *αφορισει* LΔℵ[1](txt ℵ[3]) 1 Scr's c Cyr$_1$ Thdrt$_2$. for *απ'*, *απο* D. *εριφιων* B.
33. om *μεν* D lat-*a b c e f ff$_1$ h* Syr syr-ms æth arm. om *αυτου* A ℵ(ins aft *ευων*.) [Cyr$_1$] Bas-sel Orig-int [Cypr$_1$] Avit.

and connexion, of these 'two comings' of the Lord, 1 Thess. iv. 16, 17, and 2 Thess. i. 7—10. This description is not a parable, though there are in it parabolic passages, e. g. ὥςπερ ὁ ποιμ. κ.τ.λ.: and for that very reason, that which is illustrated by those likenesses is *not itself parabolic*. It will heighten our estimation of the wonderful sublimity of this description, when we recollect that it was spoken by the Lord *only three days before His sufferings*. **ἐν τῇ δόξ. αὐτ.**] This expression, repeated again at the end of the verse, is quite distinct from μετὰ δυνάμ. κ. δόξ. πολλῆς ch. xxiv. 30: see Rev. xx. 11. This *His glory* is that also of all his saints, with whom He shall be accompanied: see Jude, ver. 14. In this his coming *they are with the angels*, and *as* the angels: see Rev. xix. 14 (compare ver. 8): Zech. xiv. 5. **32.**] The expression **πάντα τὰ ἔθνη** implies **all the nations of the world**, as distinguished from the ἐκλεκτοί *already gathered to Him*, just as the Gentiles were by that name distinguished from his chosen people the Jews. Among these are "the other sheep which He has, not of this fold," John x. 16. **ἀφοριεῖ** κ.τ.λ.] see Ezek. xxxiv. 17. The **sheep** are those referred to in Rom. ii. 7, 10; the **goats** in ib. vv. 8, 9, where this same *judgment according to works* is spoken of. **34.**] The King—here for the first and only time does the Lord give Himself this name: see Rev. xix. 16: Rom. xiv. 9.
δεῦτε κ.τ.λ.] Whatever of good these persons had done, was all *from Him* from whom cometh every good gift—and *the fruit of his Spirit*. And this Spirit is only purchased for man by the work of the Son, in whom the Father is well pleased: and to whom all judgment is committed. And thus *they are the blessed of the Father*, and those for whom this kingdom is prepared. It is not to the purpose to say that those **εὐλογημ.....** must be the elect of God in the *stricter sense* (οἱ ἐκλεκτοί)—and that, because the Kingdom has been prepared for them from the foundation of the world. For evidently this would, in the divine omniscience, be true of every single man who shall come to salvation, whether belonging to those who shall be found worthy to share the first resurrection or not. The Scripture assures us of *two resurrections:* the *first*, of *the dead in Christ*, to meet Him and reign with Him, and hold (1 Cor. vi. 2) judgment over the world; the *second*, of *all the dead*, to be judged according to their works. And to what purpose would be a judgment, if *all were to be condemned?* And if *any* escape condemnation, to them might the words of this verse be used: so that this objection to the interpretation does not apply. *Election to life* is the universal doctrine of Scripture; but *not the reprobation of the wicked:* see below, on ver. 41. On

[d] ξένος [e] ἤμην καὶ [f] συνηγάγετέ με, 36 γυμνὸς καὶ [g] περι- ABDEF
εβάλετέ με, [h] ἠσθένησα καὶ [i] ἐπεσκέψασθέ με, ἐν [j] φυλακῇ GI_cKL MSUVΓ
[e] ἤμην καὶ ἤλθατε πρός με. 37 τότε ἀποκριθήσονται αὐτῷ ΔΠℵ 1. 33. 69
οἱ δίκαιοι λέγοντες Κύριε, πότε σὲ εἴδομεν [a] πεινῶντα καὶ
[k] ἐθρέψαμεν, ἢ [a] διψῶντα καὶ [c] ἐποτίσαμεν; 38 πότε δέ σε
εἴδομεν [d] ξένον καὶ [f] συνηγάγομεν, ἢ γυμνὸν καὶ [g] περιεβά-
λομεν; 39 πότε δέ σε εἴδομεν [h] ἀσθενοῦντα ἢ ἐν [j] φυλακῇ
καὶ ἤλθομεν πρός σε; 40 καὶ ἀποκριθεὶς ὁ βασιλεὺς ἐρεῖ
αὐτοῖς [l] Ἀμὴν λέγω ὑμῖν, [m] ἐφ' [m] ὅσον [n] ἐποιήσατε ἑνὶ τούτων τῶν [o] ἀδελφῶν μου τῶν [p] ἐλαχίστων, ἐμοὶ [n] ἐποιήσατε.
41 τότε ἐρεῖ καὶ τοῖς [q] ἐξ εὐωνύμων [r] Πορεύεσθε ἀπ' ἐμοῦ οἱ
[s] κατηραμένοι εἰς τὸ [t] πῦρ τὸ [t] αἰώνιον τὸ [u] ἡτοιμασμένον $Θ_h$ xxv. 41(appy) ...

d = here (4 times) and ch. xxvii. 7. Acts xvii. 21. Eph. ii. 19. Heb. xi. 13. 3 John 5 only. Ruth ii. 10.
e ch. xxiii. 30 bis. Mark xiv. 49 al.
f = here only. Deut. xxii. 2. Judg. xix. 18. 2 Kings xi. 27.
g ch. vi. 29, 31. Luke xxiii. 11 al. Isa. lviii. 7. Ezek. xviii. 7.
h = ch. x. 8 reff.
i Luke i. 68, 78. vii. 16. Acts vii. 23. xv. 36. James i. 27 al. Exod. iv. 31. Sir. vii. 35.
j = ch. v. 25. xiv. 3, 10 || Mk. al. Gen. xl. 3 al.
k ch. vi. 26 reff.
l ch. v. 18 reff.
m = Rom. xi. 13 only.
n ch. xx. 32.
o ch. xii. 48, &c. ||. xxviii. 10. Heb. ii. 11.
p = ch. ii. 6 reff. 1 Cor. xv. 9. Wisd. vi. 6.
q ver. 33.
r Luke iv. 42. Acts v. 41. Gen. viii. 3.
s (ch. v. 44 v. r.) Mark xi. 1. Luke vi. 28. Rom. xii. 14. James iii. 9 only. Num. xxiv. 9.
t ch. xviii. 8. Jude 7 only.
u ver. 34.

36. rec ηλθετε, with KMSUVΓΠ 1: txt ABDℵ rel [Chr-wlf-ms]. (I_c doubtful.) εμε ℵ.

37. ειδαμεν B^1I_c.

38. ειδομεν bef σε D Clem: ειδαμεν I_c(but ειδομεν ver 69). for η, και D.

39. for ποτε δε, η ποτε D latt copt Clem Orig-int [om δε $Π^1$ lat-*ff* sah arm: also Π sah Cypr in ver 38]. rec (for ασθενουντα) ασθενη (*from ver* 44), with AI_cℵ rel latt: ασθενην Δ ev-P_1: txt BD 237-59 Clem $Cypr_1$. for η, και I_c Cypr. ηλθαμεν D [ev-P_1].

40. ερει αυτοις bef ο β. D: om ο βασ. lat-*a*. om των αδελφων μου (*see ver* 45) B^1 lat-$ff_{1.2}$ $Clem_2$ [Hil_1] Ambr Aug Gaud Chrom. (Either αυτων or των αδελφων μου is written in marg of B, but it is now illegible. From inspection. [Tischdf Nov. Test. Vat. gives without remark των αδελφων μου as the margl reading.])

41. for πορευεσθε, υπαγετε ℵ Hipp. om οι BLℵ 33 [Cyr_1]. (I_c def.) for το ητοιμασμενον, ο ητοιμασεν ο πατηρ μου D 1. 22 lat-*a b c* ff_1 g_1 *h* Just Clem Hipp Iren-int_4 [$Cypr_1$] Aug_1 Juv Gaud Ruf Leo Salv Paulin Promiss. (Orig Tert Hil have both.)

ἀπὸ καταβολῆς κόσμου, see John xvii. 24: 1 Pet. i. 20. **35.**] **συνηγάγετε**, sc. εἰς οἶκον, or εἰς ὑμᾶς,—a meaning confined to the LXX and N. T.—received me with hospitality—**took me in**; the idea is, 'numbered me among your own circle.' **37—40.**] The answer of these δίκαιοι appears to me to shew plainly (as Olshausen and Stier interpret it) that they are *not* to be understood as being the covenanted servants of Christ. Such an answer it would be impossible for *them* to make, who had done all distinctly *with reference to Christ*, and for his sake, and with his declaration of ch. x. 40—42 before them. Such a supposition would remove all reality, as indeed it has generally done, from our Lord's description. See the remarkable difference in the answer of the faithful servants, vv. 20, 22. *The saints* are *already in his glory*—judging the world with Him (1 Cor. vi. 2)—accounted as parts of, representatives of, Himself (ver. 40)—in this judgment *they* are **not** the judged (John v. 24: 1 Cor. xi. 31). But *these* who *are* the judged, *know not* that all their deeds of love have been done *to and for Christ*—they are overwhelmed with the sight of the grace which has been working in and for them, and the glory which is now their blessed portion. And notice, that it is not the *works, as such,* but the *love* which prompted them—that love which *was their faith,*—which felt its way, though in darkness, to Him who is Love,—which is commended. **τῶν ἀδελφ.**] Not necessarily the saints with Him in glory—though primarily those—but also any of the great family of man. Many of those here judged may never have had opportunity of doing these things to the saints of Christ properly so called. In this is fulfilled the covenant of God to Abraham, ἐνευλογηθήσονται **ἐν τῷ σπέρματί σου πάντα τὰ ἔθνη τῆς γῆς**. Gen. xxii. 18. **41—43.**] It is very important to observe the distinction between the blessing, ver. 34, and the curse here. 'Blessed—*of my Father*:'—but not

τῷ [v] διαβόλῳ καὶ τοῖς [w] ἀγγέλοις [w] αὐτοῦ. 42 [a] ἐπείνασα v ch. iv. 1 reff. w Rev. xii. 7, 9.
γὰρ καὶ οὐκ [b] ἐδώκατέ μοι [b] φαγεῖν, [a] ἐδίψησα καὶ οὐκ —p see above, vv. 35—40.
[c] ἐποτίσατέ με, 43 [d] ξένος [e] ἤμην καὶ οὐ [f] συνηγάγετέ με,
γυμνὸς καὶ οὐ [g] περιεβάλετέ με, [x] ἀσθενὴς καὶ ἐν [j] φυλακῇ x = Luke x. 9. Acts v. 15, 16.
καὶ οὐκ [i] ἐπεσκέψασθέ με. 44 τότε ἀποκριθήσονται καὶ
αὐτοὶ λέγοντες Κύριε, πότε σὲ εἴδομεν [a] πεινῶντα ἢ
[a] διψῶντα ἢ [d] ξένον ἢ γυμνὸν ἢ ἀσθενῆ ἢ ἐν [j] φυλακῇ καὶ
..xv. 44 (appy)Θ_h οὐ [y] διηκονήσαμέν σοι; 45 τότε ἀποκριθήσεται αὐτοῖς λέ- y ch. iv. 11 ‖ Mk. Mark xv. 41 al. †
γων Ἀμὴν λέγω ὑμῖν, [m] ἐφ' [m] ὅσον οὐκ [n] ἐποιήσατε ἑνὶ
...ουδε I_c τούτων τῶν [p] ἐλαχίστων, οὐδὲ ἐμοὶ [n] ἐποιήσατε. 46 καὶ z 1 John iv. 18 only. Ezek. xliii. 11 al. (-άζειν, Acts iv. 21.)
ABDEF GKLMS UVΓΔΠ ℵ 1. 33. 69 ἀπελεύσονται οὗτοι εἰς [z] κόλασιν [a] αἰώνιον, οἱ δὲ δίκαιοι εἰς
[a] ζωὴν [a] αἰώνιον. a ch. xix. 16 reff. 4 Macc. xv. 2.

XXVI. 1 Καὶ ἐγένετο ὅτε ἐτέλεσεν ὁ Ἰησοῦς πάντας

42. the 1st ουκ is inserted over the line by B¹. ins και bef εδιψησα B¹L Syr æth.
43. om γυμν. και ου περιεβ. με (*homœotel*) ℵ¹(ins(exc με)ℵ^3a).
44. rec aft αποκριθησονται ins αυτω, with (Scr's o, e sil) vulg-ed lat-*f* *ff*$_2$ *h*: om ABDΘ_h(ℵ) rel Scr's mss am lat-*a b c* syrr coptt goth æth arm Constt Thl Cypr$_3$ Op.—ℵ¹ has αυτωοι (the ω is marked for erasure prima manu), omg και which is supplied by ℵ^3a. ουκ ηδιηκονησαμεν (sic) ℵ.

'cursed of my Father,' because all man's salvation *is of God*—all his condemnation *from himself*. 'The Kingdom, *prepared for you*;' but 'the fire, which has been prepared for *the devil and his angels*' (notice **τὸ** πῦρ **τὸ** αἰών. **τὸ** ἡτοιμ. . . . . greater definiteness could not be given: that particular fire, that eternal fire, created for a special purpose)—not, for *you*: because *there is election to life*—but there is *no reprobation to death*:—a *book of Life*—but *no book of Death*; no hell *for* man—because the blood of Jesus hath purchased life *for all*: but they who will *serve the devil, must share with him in the end*. The *repetition* of all these particulars shews how exact even for every individual the judgment will be. Stier excellently remarks, that the *curse* shews the *termination of the High Priesthood of Christ*, in which office He only intercedes and blesses. Henceforth He is King and Lord—his enemies being now for ever put under his feet. **44, 45.**] See note on ver. 37. The sublimity of this description surpasses all imagination—Christ, as the Son of Man, the Shepherd, the King, the Judge—as the centre and end of all human love, bringing out and rewarding his latent grace in those who have lived in love—everlastingly punishing those who have quenched it in an unloving and selfish life—and in the accomplishment of his mediatorial office, causing, even from out of the iniquities of a rebellious world, his sovereign mercy to rejoice against judgment. **46.**] See John v. 28, 29; and as taking up the prophetic history at this point, Rev. xxi. 1—8. Observe, the *same epithet* is used for κόλασις and ζωή—which are here *contraries*—for the ζωή here spoken of is not bare *existence*, which would have *annihilation* for its opposite; but *blessedness* and *reward*, to which *punishment* and *misery* are antagonist terms. I thought it proper to state in the 3rd edition, that I did not feel by any means that full confidence which I once did, in the exegesis, quoad prophetical interpretation, given of the three portions of this chap. xxv. But I had no other system to substitute: and some of the points here dwelt on seemed to me as weighty as ever. I very much questioned whether the thorough study of Scripture prophecy would not make me more and more distrustful of all human systematizing, and less willing to hazard strong assertion on any portion of the subject. At the same time, the coincidence of these portions with the process of the great last things in Rev. xx. and xxi. is never to be overlooked, and should be our guide to their explanation, however distrustful we may be of its certainty. Those who set this coincidence aside, and interpret each portion by itself, without connexion with the rest, are clearly wrong.

CHAP. XXVI. 1, 2.] FINAL ANNOUNCEMENT OF HIS SUFFERINGS, NOW CLOSE AT HAND. (Mark xiv. 1. Luke xxii. 1.) The

τοὺς λόγους τούτους, εἶπεν τοῖς μαθηταῖς αὐτοῦ 2 Οἴδατε
ὅτι μετὰ δύο ἡμέρας τὸ [b] πάσχα γίνεται, καὶ ὁ υἱὸς τοῦ
ἀνθρώπου [c] παραδίδοται εἰς τὸ σταυρωθῆναι. 3 τότε
[d] συνήχθησαν οἱ ἀρχιερεῖς καὶ οἱ πρεσβύτεροι τοῦ λαοῦ
εἰς τὴν [e] αὐλὴν τοῦ ἀρχιερέως τοῦ λεγομένου Καϊάφα,
4 καὶ [f] συνεβουλεύσαντο ἵνα τὸν Ἰησοῦν δόλῳ [g] κρατήσω-
σιν καὶ ἀποκτείνωσιν. 5 ἔλεγον δὲ [h] Μὴ ἐν τῇ ἑορτῇ, ἵνα
μὴ [i] θόρυβος γένηται ἐν τῷ λαῷ.
6 Τοῦ δὲ Ἰησοῦ γενομένου ἐν Βηθανίᾳ ἐν οἰκίᾳ Σίμωνος

Θ_e xxvi. 3(appy). ...

H εις την αυλην... ABDEF GHKL MSUVΓ $\Delta\Theta_e\Pi$ℵ 1. 33. 69

b here, &c. and ||. John ii. 13, 23 al8. Acts xii. 4. 1 Cor. v. 7. Heb. xi. 28. 4 Kings xxiii. 22.
c ch. xxvii. 2, &c. || Mk. al. Isa. liii. 6, 12.
d = ch. xiii. 2 reff.
e vv. 58, 69 ||. Mark xv. 16. John x. 1, 16. Rev. xi. 2 only. Ps. xxviii. 2. Esdr. ix. 1. 2 Macc. xiii. 15.
f John xi. 53. xviii. 14. Acts ix. 23. Rev. iii. 18 only. Exod. xviii. 19.
g ch. xxi. 46 reff. 2 Kings vi. 6.
h = || Mk. John xiii. 9. Ps. cxiii. 9 (cxiv. 1).
i || Mk. ch. xxvii. 24. Mark v. 38. Acts xx. 1. xxi. 34. xxiv. 18 only. Ezek. vii. 7, 11. (-βεῖν, ch. ix. 23.)

CHAP. XXVI. 1. om *αυτου* D.

2. om *οιδατε* D.

3. rec aft *αρχιερεις* ins *και οι γραμματεις* (*from* || *Mark Luke*), with E rel gat lat-*c f* g_2 syrr arm Chr; *και γραμ.* SΔ: om ABDLΘ_eℵ 1. 33(appy) vulg lat-*a b* $ff_{1,2}$ g_1 *l* coptt æth Orig-int-comm Aug. om *του λαου* B[1](in marg B[2] [B[2·3], Tischdf]).

4. *συνεβουλευοντο* D Chr-6-9-γ-η-ρ-K-M. rec *κρατησωσιν* bef *δολω*, with coptt: txt ABDℵ rel Scr's mss latt syrr æth arm Chr Thl Orig-int. (Θ_e?) om *κ. αποκτ.* B[1](inserts it in marg: from inspection).

public office of our Lord as a *Teacher* having been now fulfilled, His *priestly office* begins to be entered upon. He had not completed *all* his discourses, for He delivered, after this, those contained in John xiv.—xvii.—but *not in public;* only to the inner circle of his disciples. From this point commences THE NARRATIVE OF HIS PASSION. **2. μετὰ δύο ἡμ.**] This gives no certainty as to the time when the words were said: we do not know whether the current day was included or otherwise. But thus much of importance we learn from them: that the delivery of our Lord to be crucified, and the taking place of the Passover, *strictly coincided.* The solemn mention of them in this connexion is equivalent to a declaration from Himself, if it were needed, of the identity, both of time and meaning, of the two sacrifices; and serves as the fixed point in the difficult chronological arrangement of the history of the Passion. The latter clause, **καὶ ὁ υἱὸς** *κ.τ.λ.* depends on *οἴδατε* as well as the former. Our Lord had doubtless before joined these two events together in his announcements to his disciples. To separate this clause from the former, 'and then' &c. seems to me to do violence to the construction. It would require *καὶ τότε.*

3—5.] CONSPIRACY OF THE JEWISH AUTHORITIES. Mark xiv. 1. Luke xxii. 2. This assembling has no connexion with what has just been related, but follows rather on the end of ch. xxiii. *ὁ λεγόμενος* K. is in Jos. Antt. xviii. 2. 2, *Ἰώσηπος ὁ καὶ Καϊάφας.* Valerius Gratus, Procurator of Judæa, had appointed him instead of Simon ben Kamith. He continued through the procuratorship of Pontius Pilate, and was displaced by the proconsul Vitellius, A.D. 37. See note on Luke iii. 2, and chronological table in Prolegg. to Acts, Vol. II. **τοῦ λεγ.** does not mean 'surnamed,' but (see ver. 14) implies that *some name* is to follow, which is more than, or different from, the real one of the person. **μὴ ἐν τ. ἑ.**] This expression must be taken as meaning the whole period of the feast—the seven days. On the *feast-day,* i. e. the day on which the Passover was sacrificed (E. V.), they could not lay hold of and slay any one, as it was a day of sabbatical obligation (Exod. xii. 16). See note on ver. 17.

6—13.] THE ANOINTING AT BETHANY. Mark xiv. 3—9. John xii. 1—8. On Luke vii. 36—50, see note there. This history of the anointing of our Lord is here inserted *out of its place.* It occurred *six days before the Passover,* John xii. 1. It perhaps can hardly be said that in its position *here,* it accounts in any degree for the subsequent application of Judas to the Sanhedrim (vv. 14—16), since his name is not even mentioned in it: but I can hardly doubt that it originally was placed where it here stands by those who were aware of its connexion with that application. The paragraphs in the beginning of this chapter come in regular sequence, thus: Jesus announces his approaching Passion: the chief priests, &c. meet and

τοῦ [j] λεπροῦ 7 προςῆλθεν αὐτῷ γυνὴ [k] ἀλάβαστρον [l] μύρου ἔχουσα [m] βαρυτίμου, καὶ [n] κατέχεεν ἐπὶ τὴν κεφαλὴν
..xxvi. 7 (appy)Θ_e αὐτοῦ [o] ἀνακειμένου. 8 ἰδόντες δὲ οἱ μαθηταὶ [p] ἠγανάκτησαν λέγοντες [q] Εἰς τί ἡ [r] ἀπώλεια αὕτη; 9 ἐδύνατο γὰρ
τοῦτο [s] πραθῆναι [t] πολλοῦ καὶ [u] δοθῆναι [u] πτωχοῖς. 10 γνοὺς
δὲ ὁ Ἰησοῦς εἶπεν αὐτοῖς Τί [v] κόπους [v] παρέχετε τῇ

j ch. viii. 2 reff. k || (Mk. bis) only. 4 Kings xxi. 13 only Herod. iii. 20. l here, &c. and ||. Luke vii. 37, &c. xxiii. 56. John xi. 2. Rev. xviii. 13 only. Ps. cxxxii. 2. m here only +. n || Mk. only. Gen. xxxix. 21. Job xli. 14. Ps. lxxxviii. 45 only. o ch. ix. 10. xxii. 11 al.+ Esdr. iv. 10 only. p ch. xx. 24 reff. q = ch. xiv. 31 reff. r || Mk. John xvii. 12. Lev. vi. 3, 4. s ch. xiii. 46 reff. t gen., ch. x. 29 reff. u ch. xix. 21 reff. v || Mk. Luke xviii. 5. Gal. vi. 17. Sir. xxix. 4 Aℵ.

6. λεπρωσου D.

7. εχουσα bef αλαβαστρον μυρου (*from* || *Mark*) BDLΘ_eℵ 33. 69 latt syrr coptt æth arm [Chr-wlf-ms] Orig-int: txt A rel [Bas_1] Chr. for βαρυτιμου, πολυτιμου (*from* || *John*) ADLMΠℵ 33 Syr syr-mg coptt(appy) Chr-wlf-ms: txt BΘ_e rel syr [Bas_1] Chr. της κεφαλης (*from* || *Mark*) BDMΘ_eℵ 1. 69 [Chr-2-9-γ-η-ρ-wlf-ms]: txt A rel [Bas_1]. aft ανακειμενου ins αυτου D-gr mm lat-*a b c f ff*$_2$ *h* Orig-int Ambr.

8. rec aft μαθηται ins αυτου, with A rel lat-*c f* syrr æth [Bas_1] Chr Orig-int: om BDLΘ_eℵ 33. 69 vulg lat-*a b* &c coptt arm.

9. (εδυνατο, so B[1]KLΔΘ_eΠℵ.) rec aft τουτο ins το μυρον (*see* || *John Mark*), with E-corr rel lat-*c* Orig Chr: om ABDE[1]LΔΘ_eΠℵ 1[1] vulg lat-*a b* &c syrr coptt æth arm Bas Bas-sel Orig-int Hil Ambr. ins τοις bef πτωχοις AD rel Chr: om B F(e sil) G(Treg, expr) LMUΘ_s ℵ 1. 33. 69 Orig [Bas_1 $Amphil_1$] Chr-G-K(-6, e sil).

10. om ὁ D.

plot His capture, but *not during* the feast: *but when Jesus was in Bethany*, &c. occasion was given for an offer to be made to them, which led to its being effected, after all, during the feast. On the rebuke given to Judas at this time having led to his putting into effect his intention of betraying our Lord, see note on John xii. 4. The trace of what I believe to have been the original reason of the anointing being inserted in this place, is still further lost in Mark, who instead of τοῦ δὲ Ἰησ. γενομένου . . . . has καὶ ὄντος αὐτοῦ . . . . just as if the narrative were continued, and at the end instead of our τότε πορευθεὶς . . . . has καὶ ὁ Ἰούδας . . . . as if there were no connexion between the two. It certainly cannot be said of St. Matthew (De Wette, Neander, Stier) that he relates the anointing as *taking place two days before the Passover:* of St. Mark it *may* be said.

It may be observed that St. Luke relates nothing of our Lord's visits to Bethany. **6. Σίμωνος τοῦ λ.]** Not at this time a leper, or he could not be at his house receiving guests. It is at least *possible*, that he may have been healed by our Lord. Who he was, is wholly uncertain. From Martha serving (John xii. 2), it would appear as if she were at home in the house (Luke x. 38 sqq.); and that Lazarus was one τῶν ἀνακειμένων need not necessarily imply that he was a *guest* properly so called. He had been probably (see John xii. 9) absent with Jesus at Ephraim, and on this account and naturally for other reasons would be an object of interest, and one of the ἀνακείμενοι. **7. ἀλάβαστρον]** ἄγγος μύρου μὴ ἔχον λαβάς, λίθινος, ἢ λίθινος μυροθήκη. Suidas. See Herod. iii. 20. It was the usual cruse or pot for ointment, with a long narrow neck, and sealed at the top. It was thought (Plin. xiii. 3) that the ointment kept best in these cruses. On the nature of the ointment, see note on νάρδου πιστικῆς, Mark xiv. 3. **τὴν κεφ. αὐτ.]** His *feet*, according to John xii. 3. See Luke vii. 38, and note there. **ἀνακειμένου** is not to be taken with **αὐτοῦ**, but is a separate gen. absol. by itself; **on His head while He was reclining at table.** See on this construction, Kühner, Gr. Gr. ii. p. 368, where many examples are given.

8. οἱ μαθηταί] *Judas alone* is mentioned, John xii. 4. It may have been that some were found ready to second his remark, but that John, from his peculiar position at the table,—if, as is probable, the same as in John xiii. 23,—may not have observed it. If so, the independent origin of the two accounts is even more strikingly shewn.

ἀπώλεια] Bengel remarks, 'Immo tu, Juda, perditionis es (ὁ υἱὸς τῆς ἀπωλείας, John xvii. 12).' **9. πολλοῦ]** 300 denarii (John),—even more than that (Mark). On the singular relation which these three accounts bear to one another, see notes on Mark. **δοθῆναι**, viz. the πολύ for which the ointment might have been sold: the subject being supplied out of the preceding sentence. So Herod. ix. 8, τὸν ἰσθμὸν

γυναικί; [wx] ἔργον γὰρ [w] καλὸν [xy] εἰργάσατο [y] εἰς ἐμέ. ABDEF
11 [z] πάντοτε γὰρ τοὺς πτωχοὺς ἔχετε μεθ' [a] ἑαυτῶν, ἐμὲ δὲ GHKL MSUVΓ
οὐ [z] πάντοτε ἔχετε. 12 [b] βαλοῦσα γὰρ αὕτη τὸ [1] μύρον τοῦτο ΔΠℵ 1. 33. 69
ἐπὶ τοῦ σώματός μου, πρὸς τὸ [c] ἐνταφιάσαι με ἐποίησεν.
13 ἀμὴν λέγω ὑμῖν, ὅπου ἐὰν [d] κηρυχθῇ τὸ εὐαγγέλιον
τοῦτο ἐν [e] ὅλῳ τῷ [e] κόσμῳ, [f] λαληθήσεται καὶ ὃ ἐποίησεν
αὕτη εἰς [g] μνημόσυνον αὐτῆς.
14 Τότε πορευθεὶς εἷς [h] τῶν [h] δώδεκα ὁ λεγόμενος Ἰούδας

w ch. v. 16 reff. x || Mk. John vi. 28. ix. 4. Acts xiii. 14, from Hab. i. 5. 1 Cor. xvi. 10. y 3 John 5. Prov. iii. 30 Aℵ[3a]. z Matt., here (bis) only. Mark || bis only. Luke xv. 31. xviii. 1. John vi. 34 al. fr. Wisd. xix. 18. see Deut. xv. 11.
a = ch. iii. 9 reff. b = ch. xxvii. 6. λοῦτρά τ' ἐπὶ χροὸς βάλε, Eur. Orest. 297. c (-ασμός, || Mk. J.) John xix. 40 only. Gen. l. 2 bis only. d ch. iii. 1. iv. 23 reff. e || Mk. ch. xvi. 26 ||. 1 John ii. 2. v. 19 only. 2 Macc. viii. 18. f = || Mk. Acts ii. 11. Ruth iv. 1 Ed-vat(not B). g || Mk. Acts x. 4 only. Exod. xii. 14. xvii. 14. Mal. iii. 16. Sir. x. 17. l. 16. h vv. 20, 47 al. see 2 Kings xxiii. 15, 19.

om γαρ ℵ[3a](? ins ℵ[3b] ?) 1 am fuld lat-*a b c ff*$_1$ *g*$_{1.2}$ Syr copt-dz sah æth arm Orig-int. ηργασατο B[1](Tischdf [N. T. Vat.]) Dℵ[1](txt ℵ[3a]) ev-x.
13. aft αμην add δε B(written over the line by B[1]) Δ arm. for εαν, αν DL 69 Orig.

ἐτείχεον καί σφι ἦν πρὸς τέλεϊ, sc. τὸ τεῖχος. See other examples in Kühner, Gr. Gr. ii. pp. 36, 7. **10. ἔργ. γὰρ καλ. εἰργ.**] Stier remarks that this is a stronger expression than ἔργ. ἀγαθὸν ἐποίησεν would have been. See ch. v. 16. It was not only 'a good work,' but a noble act of love, which should be spoken of in all the churches to the end of time. On ver. 11, see notes on Mark, where it is more fully expressed. **12.**] I can hardly think that our Lord would have said this, unless there had been in Mary's mind a distinct reference to His burial, in doing the act. All the company surely knew well that His death, and that by crucifixion, was near at hand: can we suppose one who so closely observed His words as Mary, not to have been possessed with the thought of that which was about to happen? The προέλαβεν μυρίσαι μου τὸ σῶμα of Mark (xiv. 8), and the ἵνα εἰς τὴν ἡμ. τοῦ ἐνταφ. μου τηρήσῃ αὐτό of John (xii. 7), point even more strongly to *her intention*. **13.**] The only case in which our Lord has made such a promise. We cannot but be struck with the majesty of this prophetic announcement; introduced with the peculiar and weighty **ἀμὴν λέγω ὑμῖν**,—conveying, by implication, the whole mystery of the **εὐαγγέλιον** which should go forth from His Death as its source,—looking forward to the end of time, when it shall have been preached in the whole world,—and specifying the fact that this deed should be recorded wherever it is preached. We may notice (1) that this announcement is a distinct prophetic recognition by our Lord of the existence of *written records*, in which the deed should be related; for in no other conceivable way could the universality of mention be brought about: (2) that we have here (if indeed we needed it) a convincing argument against that view of our three first Gospels which supposes them to have been compiled from an original document: for if there had been such a document, it must have contained this narrative, and no one using such a Gospel could have failed to insert this narrative, accompanied by such a promise, in his own work; which St. Luke has failed to do: (3) that the same consideration is equally decisive against Luke having used, or even seen, our present Gospels of Matthew and Mark. (See the English translation of Schleiermacher's Essay on Luke, p. 121.) (4) As regards the practical use of the announcement, we see that though the honourable mention of a noble deed is thereby recognized by our Lord as a legitimate source of joy to us, yet by the very nature of the case all regard to such mention as a *motive* is excluded. The motive was *Love alone*.

14—16.] Compact of Judas with the Chief Priests to betray Him. Mark xiv. 10, 11. Luke xxii. 3—6. (See also ἤδη, John xiii. 2.) *When* this took place, does not appear. In all probability, immediately after the conclusion of our Lord's discourses, and therefore coincidently with the meeting of the Sanhedrim in ver. 3. As these verses bring before us the first overt act of Judas's treachery, I will give here what appears to me the true estimate of his character and motives. In the main, my view agrees with that given by Neander, in his Leben Jesu, p. 688. I believe that Judas at first became attached to our Lord with much the same view as the other

Ἰσκαριώτης πρὸς τοὺς ἀρχιερεῖς
15 εἶπεν Τί θέλετέ μοι δοῦναι [i] κἀγὼ ὑμῖν παραδώσω αὐτόν; οἱ δὲ [j] ἔστησαν αὐτῷ τριάκοντα [k] ἀργύρια·
16 καὶ [l] ἀπὸ τότε ἐζήτει [m] εὐκαιρίαν ἵνα αὐτὸν παραδῷ.
17 Τῇ δὲ πρώτῃ τῶν [n] ἀζύμων προςῆλθον οἱ μαθηταὶ τῷ

i = ch. xi. 28. xxi. 24. John xx. 15. 2 Cor. vi. 17. James ii. 18.
j = here only? 2 Kings xiv. 26, but? Zech. xi. 12. see Acts vii. 60. (i. 23. vi. 6.)
k plur., ch. xxvii. 3, &c. xxviii. 12, 15. see Acts xix. 19.
l ch. iv. 17 reff.
m ‖ L. (-ρως, ‖ Mk.) only. Ps. ix. 9, 21. (x. 1.) cxliv. 15. Sir. xxviii. 24. 1 Macc. xi. 42 only. (-ρος, Mark vi. 21.)
n ‖. Mark xiv. 1 ‖ L. Acts xii. 3. xx. 6. 1 Cor. v. 7, 8 only. Lev. ii. 4, &c.

15. ins *και* bef *ειπεν* D(having *πορευθεις* above) latt(*abiit* above) Syr æth Orig-int$_1$. add *αυτοις* D latt Syr copt æth Eus Orig-int$_2$. for *τι*, *ι*(= *ει*) ℵ[1](but corrd). *και εγω* DE[2]FGHMUVΓΔℵ 1 [Constt$_1$ Chr$_1$]. *οις δε* D[1]. for *αυτω*, *αυτων* A. *αργυρα* [for -*ρια*] A: *στατηρας* D lat-*a b* Eus Orig-int(txt Orig).
16. aft *παραδω* ins *αυτοις* D-gr lat-*b c h* syr-jer copt arm Eus Orig-int.

Apostles. He appears to have been a man with a practical talent for this world's business, which gave occasion to his being appointed the Treasurer, or Bursar, of the company (John xii. 6; xiii. 29). But the self-seeking, sensuous element, which his character had in common with that of the other Apostles, was deeper rooted in him; and the spirit and love of Christ gained no such influence over him as over the others, who were more disposed to the reception of divine things. In proportion as he found our Lord's progress disappoint his greedy anticipations, did his attachment to Him give place to coldness and aversion. The exhibition of miracles alone could not keep him faithful, when once the deeper appreciation of the Lord's Divine Person failed. We find by implication a remarkable example of this in John vi. 60—66, 70, 71, where the denunciation of the one unfaithful among the twelve seems to point to the (then) state of his mind, as already beginning to be scandalized at Christ. Add to this, that latterly the increasing clearness of the Lord's announcements of his approaching passion and death, while they gradually opened the eyes of the other Apostles to some terrible event to come, without shaking their attachment to Him, was calculated to involve in more bitter disappointment and disgust one so disposed to Him as Judas was. The actually exciting causes of the deed of treachery at this particular time may have been many. The reproof administered at Bethany (on the Saturday evening probably),—disappointment at seeing the triumphal entry followed, not by the adhesion, but by the more bitter enmity of the Jewish authorities,—the denunciations of our Lord in ch. xxii. xxiii. rendering the breach irreparable,—and perhaps his last announcement in ver. 2, making it certain that his death would soon take place, and sharpening the eagerness of the traitor to profit by it:—all these may have influenced him to apply to the chief priests as he did. With regard to *his motive* in general, I cannot think that he had any design but that of *sordid gain, to be achieved by the darkest treachery.* See further on this the note on ch. xxvii. 3. **15.**] **ἔστησαν** may be either **weighed out**, or **appointed.** That the money was *paid* to Judas (ch. xxvii. 3) is no decisive argument for the former meaning; for it may have been paid on the delivery of Jesus to the Sanhedrim. The *συνέθεντο* of Luke and *ἐπηγγείλαντο* of Mark would lead us to prefer the other. **τριάκοντα ἀργύρια**] thirty shekels, = the price of the life of a servant, Exod. xxi. 32. Between three and four pounds of our money. St. Matthew is the only Evangelist who mentions the sum. De Wette and others have supposed that the mention of thirty pieces of silver with the verb *ἔστησαν*, has arisen from the prophecy of Zechariah (ref.), which St. Matthew clearly has in view. The others have simply *ἀργύριον*. It is just possible that the thirty pieces may have been merely *earnest-money:* but a difficulty attends the supposition; if so, Judas would have been entitled to the *whole* on our Lord being delivered up to the Sanhedrim (for this was all he undertook to do); whereas we find (ch. xxvii. 3) that, after our Lord's condemnation, Judas brought only the thirty pieces back, and nothing more. See note there.

17—19.] Preparation for celebrating the Passover. Mark xiv. 12—16. Luke xxii. 7—13. The whole narrative which follows is extremely difficult to arrange and account for chronologically. Our Evangelist is the least circumstantial, and, as will I think appear, the least exact in detail of the three. St. Mark partially fills up the outline;—but the account of St. Luke is the most detailed, and I believe the most exact. It is to be noticed *

o constr., ch. xx. 32 reff.
p = ch. xxii. 4 al. Gen. xliii. 16.

Ἰησοῦ λέγοντες Ποῦ ᵒ θέλεις ᵖ ἑτοιμάσωμέν σοι φαγεῖν τὸ

ABDEF GHKL MSUVΓ ΔΠℵ 1. 33. 69

17. rec aft λεγοντες ins αυτω (|| *Mark*), with A rel lat-*f* Syr æth Orig-int: om BDK LΔΠℵ 1. 33. 69 latt syr coptt arm Hil. ετοιμασομεν DKU 1. 69 Orig Chr-mss.

that the narrative which St. Paul gives, 1 Cor. xi. 23—25, of the institution of the Lord's Supper, and which he states he '*received from the Lord*,' coincides almost verbatim with that given by Luke. But while we say this, it must not be forgotten that over all three narratives extends the great difficulty of explaining **ἡ πρώτη τῶν ἀζ.** (Matt., Mark), or **ἡ ἡμ. τ. ἀζ.** (Luke), and of reconciling the impression undeniably conveyed by them, that the Lord and his disciples *ate the usual Passover*, with the narrative of St. John, which not only does not sanction, but I believe absolutely excludes such a supposition. I shall give in as short a compass as I can, the various solutions which have been attempted, and the objections to them; fairly confessing that none of them satisfy me, and that at present I have none of my own. I will first state the *grounds of the difficulty itself*. The day alluded to in all four histories as that of the supper, which is unquestionably one and identical, is Thursday, the 13th of Nisan. Now the day of the Passover being slain and eaten was the 14th of Nisan (Exod. xii. 6, 18: Levit. xxiii. 5: Num. ix. 3; xxviii. 16: Ezek. xlv. 21), *between the evenings* (בֵּין הָעַרְבַּיִם), which was interpreted by the generality of the Jews to mean the interval between the first westering of the sun (3 p.m.) and his setting,—but by the Karaites and Samaritans that between sunset and darkness:—in either case, however, *the day* was the same. The feast of unleavened bread began at *the very time of eating the Passover* (Exod. xii. 18), so that the *first day of the feast of unleavened bread was the* 15*th* (Num. xxviii. 17). All this agrees with the narrative of John, where (xiii. 1) the last supper takes place **πρὸ τῆς ἑορ. τοῦ πάσχα**—where the disciples think (ib. ver. 29) that Judas had been directed to buy the things ὧν χρείαν εἶχον εἰς τὴν ἑορτήν—where the Jews (xviii. 28) would not enter into the prætorium, lest they should be defiled, ἀλλ' ἵνα φάγωσιν τὸ πάσχα (see note on John xviii. 28)—where at the exhibition of our Lord by Pilate (on the Friday at noon) it was (xix. 14) παρασκευὴ τοῦ πάσχα—and where it could be said (xix. 31) ἦν γὰρ μεγάλη ἡ ἡμέρα ἐκείνου τοῦ σαββάτου,—being as it was a *double Sabbath*,—the coincidence of the first day of unleavened bread, which was sabbatically hallowed (Exod. xii. 16), with an actual sabbath. But as plainly it *does not agree* with the view of the three other Evangelists, who not only relate the meal on the evening of the 13th of Nisan to have been *a* Passover, but manifestly regard it as the *ordinary legal time* of eating it. τῇ πρ. ἡμ. τ. ἀζ., ὅτε τὸ πάσχα **ἔθυον** (Mark xiv. 12), ᾗ **ἔδει θύεσθαι** τὸ πάσχα (Luke xxii. 7), and in our Gospel by implication, in the use of τὸ πάσχα, &c., without any qualifying remark. The solutions which have been proposed are the following: (1) that the Passover which our Lord and his disciples ate, was not the ordinary, but an *anticipatory* one, seeing that He himself was about to be sacrificed as the true Passover at the legal time. To this it may be objected that such an anticipation would have been wholly unprecedented and irregular, in a matter most strictly laid down by the law: and that in the three Gospels there is no allusion to it, but rather every thing (see above) to render it improbable. (2) That our Lord and his disciples ate the Passover, but at the time observed by *a certain portion of the Jews*, while He himself was sacrificed at the time *generally* observed. This solution is objectionable, as wanting any historical testimony whereon to ground it, being in fact a pure assumption. Besides, it is clearly inconsistent with Mark xiv. 12: Luke xxii. 7, cited above. A similar objection lies against (3) the notion that *our Lord* ate the Passover at the strictly legal, *the Jews* at an inaccurate and illegal time. (4) Our Lord ate only a πάσχα **μνημονευτικόν**, such as the Jews now celebrate, and not a πάσχα **θύσιμον** (Grotius). But this is refuted by the absence of any mention of a π. μνημ. *before the destruction of Jerusalem;* besides its inconsistency with the above-cited passages. (5) Our Lord *did not eat the Passover at all*. But this is manifestly not a *solution* of the difficulty, but a setting aside of one of the differing accounts: for the three Gospels manifestly give the impression that He *did* eat it. (6) The solution offered by Chrys., on our ver. 58 (Hom. lxxxiv. 2, p. 800), is at least ingenious. The Council, he says, did not eat their Passover at the proper time, but ἐν ἑτέρᾳ

[q]πάσχα; 18 ὁ δὲ εἶπεν Ὑπάγετε εἰς τὴν πόλιν πρὸς τὸν

q ver. 2 reff. Exod. xii. 11. Ezra vi. 21. — φασέκ, 2 Chron. xxx. 18.

ἡμέρᾳ ἔφαγον, καὶ τὸν νόμον ἔλυσαν, διὰ τὴν ἐπιθυμίαν τὴν περὶ τὴν σφαγὴν ταύτην . . . . εἵλοντο καὶ τὸ πάσχα ἀφεῖναι, ὑπὲρ τοῦ τὴν φονικὴν αὐτῶν ἐμπλῆσαι ἐπιθυμίαν. This had been suggested before in a scholium of Eusebius: see Wordsw.'s note on John xviii. 28, in which it is adopted. But St. John's habit of noticing and explaining all such exceptional circumstances, makes it very improbable. (I may state, as some solutions have been sent me by correspondents, that I have seen nothing besides the above, which justifies any extended notice.) I will conclude this note by offering a few hints which, though not pointing to any particular solution, ought I think to enter into the consideration of the question. (*a*) That, on the evening of the 13th (i. e. the beginning of the 14th) of Nisan, the Lord *ate a meal with his disciples*, at which the announcement that one of them should betray Him was made: after which He went into the Garden of Gethsemane, and was betrayed (Matt., Mark, Luke, John):—(β) That, *in some sense or other*, this meal *was regarded as the eating of the Passover* (Matt., Mark, Luke). (The same may be inferred even from John; for some of the disciples must have gone into the prætorium, and have heard the conversation between our Lord and Pilate (John xviii. 33—38): and as they were equally bound with the other Jews to eat the Passover, would equally with them have been incapacitated from so doing by having incurred defilement, *had they not eaten theirs previously*. It would appear too, from Joseph of Arimathea *going to Pilate* during the παρασκευή (Mark xv. 42, 43), that *he also had eaten his passover*.) (γ) That it was *not the ordinary passover of the Jews*: for (Exod. xii. 22) when that was eaten, none might go out of the house until morning; whereas not only did Judas go out during the meal (John xiii. 29), but our Lord and the disciples went out when the meal was finished. Also when Judas went out, it was understood that he was gone to *buy*, which could not have been the case, had it been the night of eating the passover, which in all years was sabbatically hallowed. (δ) John, who omits all mention of the Paschal nature of this meal, also omits all mention of the distribution of the symbolic bread and wine. The latter act was, strictly speaking, anticipatory: the Body was not yet broken, nor the Blood shed (but see note on ver. 26 ad fin.). Is it possible that the words in Luke xxii. 15, 16 may have been meant by our Lord as an express declaration of the anticipatory nature of that passover meal likewise? May they mean, 'I have been most anxious to eat this Paschal meal with you to-night (before I suffer), for I shall not eat it to-morrow,—I shall not eat of it any more with you?' May a hint to the same effect be intended in ὁ **καιρός μου** ἐγγύς ἐστιν (ver. 18), as accounting for the time of making ready—may the present tense ποιῶ itself have the same reference? I may remark that the whole of the narrative of John, as compared with the others, satisfies me that *he can never have seen their accounts*. It is inconceivable, that one writing for the purpose avowed in John xx. 31, could have found the three accounts as we have them, and have made no more allusion to the discrepancy than the faint (and to all appearance undesigned) ones in ib. ch. xii. 1; xiii. 1, 29; xviii. 28. **17. τῇ πρ. τ. ἀζ.**] If this night had been the ordinary time of sacrificing the Passover, the day preceding would not indeed have been strictly the first day of unleavened bread; but there is reason to suppose that it was accounted so. The putting away leaven from the houses was part of the work of the day, and the eating of the unleavened bread actually commenced in the evening. Thus Josephus, Antt. ii. 15. 1, ἑορτὴν ἄγομεν ἐφ' ἡμέρας **ὀκτώ**, τὴν τῶν ἀζύμων λεγομένην,—including this day in the feast. **ποῦ θέλεις**] The 'making ready' would include the following particulars: the preparation of the guest-chamber itself (which however in this case was already done, see Mark xiv. 15 and note);—the lamb already kept up from the 10th (Exod. xii. 3) had to be slain in the fore-court of the temple (2 Chron. xxxv. 5: see also Jos. B. J. vi. 9. 3);—the unleavened bread, bitter herbs, &c., prepared;—and the room arranged. This report does not represent the whole that passed: it was *the Lord who sent* the two disciples; and *in reply* this enquiry was made (Luke). **18.**] The person spoken of was unknown even by name, as appears from Mark and Luke, where he is to be found by the *turning in of a man with a pitcher of water*. The

[r] δεῖνα, καὶ εἴπατε αὐτῷ Ὁ [s] διδάσκαλος λέγει Ὁ [t] καιρός ABDEF
μου [u] ἐγγύς ἐστιν, πρὸς σὲ [v] ποιῶ τὸ [qv] πάσχα μετὰ τῶν GHKL MSUVΓ
μαθητῶν μου. 19 καὶ ἐποίησαν οἱ μαθηταὶ ὡς [w] συνέταξεν ΔΠℵ 1. 33. 69
αὐτοῖς ὁ Ἰησοῦς, καὶ [p] ἡτοίμασαν τὸ [q] πάσχα. 20 [x] ὀψίας
δὲ [x] γενομένης [y] ἀνέκειτο μετὰ τῶν δώδεκα. 21 καὶ ἐσθιόντων αὐτῶν εἶπεν Ἀμὴν λέγω ὑμῖν ὅτι [z] εἷς ἐξ ὑμῶν παρα- Z εξ
δώσει με. 22 καὶ [a] λυπούμενοι σφόδρα ἤρξαντο λέγειν υμων...
αὐτῷ [b] εἷς [b] ἕκαστος [c] Μήτι ἐγώ εἰμι, κύριε; 23 ὁ δὲ ἀπο- C εις
κριθεὶς εἶπεν Ὁ [d] ἐμβάψας μετ' ἐμοῦ τὴν χεῖρα ἐν τῷ [e] τρυ- εκαστος ...

r here only †. 1 Kings xxi. 2 Aq. Sym. (?) Theod. s ch. ix. 11 reff. t ch. xxi. 41. Luke i. 20. John vii. 6, 8. 2 Tim. iv. 6 al. 1 Kings iv. 20. u = ch. xxiv. 32 al. fr. Joel i. 15. see Lam. iv. 18. v Heb. xi. 28. (see Acts xviii. 21 v. r.) Deut. xvi. 1 al. w ch. xxi. 6. xxvii. 10 only. Gen. xxvi. 11. Diod. Sic. i. 70. Polyb. iii. 50. 7. x ch. viii. 16 reff. y = ch. xxii. 10, 11 reff. z ‖ Mk. John vi. 71. vii. 50 al. Gen. xlii. 16. a ch. xvii. 23 reff. b Luke iv. 40. xvi. 5. Acts ii. 6. Col. iv. 6 al. c ch. vii. 16 reff. d ‖ Mk. (John xiii. 26 v. r. bis) only †. e ‖ only. Num. vii. 13, 19, &c. Sir. xxxiv. (xxxi.) 14.

ABCDE FGHKL MSUVZ ΓΔΠℵ 1. 33. 69

18. om ο διδασκαλος λεγει A Mich-const. ποιησω D Orig-int.
20. aft δωδεκα ins μαθητων ALMΔΠℵ 33 am lat-*f* *ff*$_1$ *g*$_1$ syr syr-jer copt arm Chr$_1$ [μαθ. αυτου vulg lat-*a b c h* (Syr) æth (Orig-int$_1$) Chr$_1$].
21. for ειπεν, λεγει ℵ.
22. for αυτω εις εκαστος, αυτω εκαστος αυτων A rel: αυτω εις εκ. αυτων M syr: εις εκ. αυτων D 69 copt: txt BCLZℵ 33 sah.
23. ενβαπτομενος D. rec εν τω τρυβλιω bef την χειρα, with C rel Chr: την χ. μετ εμου εις το τρυβλιον D(τρυβαλιον) coptt Clem: txt ABLZℵ 33 latt æth Orig.

Lord spoke not from any previous arrangement, as some have thought, but in virtue of His knowledge, and command of circumstances. Compare the command ch. xxi. 2 sq., and that in ch. xvii. 27. In the words **πρὸς τὸν δεῖνα** here must be involved the additional circumstance mentioned by Mark and Luke, but perhaps unknown to our narrator: see note on Luke xxii. 10, where the fullest account is found. The words **ὁ διδάσκ.**, common to the three accounts, do not imply that the man was *a disciple of our Lord*. It was the common practice during the feast for persons to receive strangers into their houses gratuitously, for the purpose of eating the Passover: and in this description of Himself in addressing a stranger, our Lord has a deep meaning, as (perhaps, but see note) in *ὁ κύριος* in ch. xxi. 3. 'Our Master and thine says.' It is His form of 'pressing' for the service of the King of this earth, the things that are therein.

ὁ καιρός μου is not 'the *time of the feast*,' but **my time**, i. e. for suffering: see John vii. 8 al. freq. There is no reason for supposing from this expression that *ὁ δεῖνα* was aware of its meaning. The bearers of the message were; and the words, to the receiver of it, bore with them a weighty subjective reason, which, with such a title as *ὁ διδάσκαλος* prefixed, he was bound to respect. For these words we are indebted to St. Matthew's narrative.

20—25.] Jesus, celebrating the Passover, announces His betrayer. Mark xiv. 17—21. John xiii. 21 ff. Our Lord and the twelve were a full Paschal company; *ten* persons was the ordinary and minimum number. Here come in (1) *the expression of our Lord's desire to eat this Passover before His suffering*, Luke xxii. 15, 16; (2) *the division of this first cup*, ib. vv. 17, 18; (3) *the washing of the disciples' feet*, John xiii. 1—20 (? see note, John xiii. 22). I mention these, not that I have any desire to reduce the four accounts to a harmonized narrative, for that I believe to be impossible, and the attempt wholly unprofitable; but because they are *additional* circumstances, placed by their narrators at this period of the feast. I shall similarly notice all such additional matter, but without any idea of harmonizing the apparent discrepancies of the four (as appears to me) entirely distinct and independent reports. **21.**] This announcement is common to Matt., Mark, and John. In the part of the events of the supper *which relates to Judas*, St. Luke *is deficient*, giving no further report of them than vv. 21—23. The whole minute detail is given by St. John, who bore a considerable part in it. **22.**] In the accounts of Luke and John, this enquiry is made *πρὸς ἑαυτούς* or *εἰς ἀλλήλους*. The real enquiry *from the Lord was made by John himself, owing to a sign from Peter*. This part of John's narrative stands in the highest position for accuracy of detail, and the facts related in it are evidently the ground of the other

βλίῳ, οὗτός με παραδώσει. 24 ὁ μὲν υἱὸς τοῦ ἀνθρώπου
[f] ὑπάγει [g] καθὼς γέγραπται περὶ αὐτοῦ· οὐαὶ δὲ τῷ ἀνθρώπῳ ἐκείνῳ δι' οὗ ὁ υἱὸς τοῦ ἀνθρώπου παραδίδοται·
[h] καλὸν ἦν αὐτῷ [i] εἰ οὐκ ἐγεννήθη ὁ ἄνθρωπος ἐκεῖνος.
25 [k] ἀποκριθεὶς δὲ Ἰούδας ὁ παραδιδοὺς αὐτὸν εἶπεν [c] Μήτι
ἐγώ εἰμι, [l] ῥαββί; λέγει αὐτῷ [m] Σὺ [m] εἶπας. 26 ἐσθιόν-

f = here and ‖ Mk. only in Greek (?). see John xiii. 3, &c. xiv. 4, 5, 28. xvi. 5, &c. Gen. xv. 2. Josh. xxiii. 14. 3 Kings ii. 2. Ps. xxxviii. 13. Wisd. iv. 2. = οἴχομαι, Xen. Anab. iii. 1. 22. g ch. xxi. 6. xxviii. 6 only in Matt. N. T. passim. Num. xxvi. 54. Dan. ix. 13 Theod. h = ch. xvii. 4 reff. i = ‖ Mk. Mark ix. 42. Luke xii. 49. 2 Cor. xi. 15. 1 Kings xxiv. 7. k = ch. xi. 25 reff. l ch. xxiii. 7, 8 reff. m ver. 64 only. see ch. xxvii. 11.

24. aft μεν ins ουν DZ 253 Scr's p Chr-G-6·9··η-ρ. εαυτου A. aft παραδιδ. add δια τουτο D lat-*a*(appy). for ει, η AΔ. εγενηθη A.
25. ins ο bef ιουδας D 237-43. aft αυτω ins ο ιησους ℵ Scr's v lat-*a b c f* ff_2 *h* Orig-int_1.

accounts. **23.**] These first words represent the *answer of our Lord to John's question* (John xiii. 26). The latter (ver. 24) *were not said now*, but (Luke, vv. 21, 22) *formed part of the previous announcement in our ver.* 21. **25.**] I cannot understand these words (which are peculiar to our Gospel) otherwise than as an imperfect report of what really happened, viz. that the Lord *dipped the sop, and gave it to Judas*, thereby answering the general doubt, in which the traitor had impudently presumed to feign a share. If the question **μήτι ἐγώ εἰμι**; before, represented ἔβλεπον εἰς ἀλλήλους ἀπορούμενοι, and was our author's impression of what was in reality not a *spoken* but a *signified* question,—why now also should not this question and answer represent that Judas took part in that ἀπορία, and was, *not by word of mouth, but by a decisive sign*, of which our author was not aware, declared to be the traitor? *Both* cannot have happened;—for (John xiii. 28) *no one knew* (not even John, see note there) *why Judas went out;* whereas if he had been openly (and it is out of the question to suppose a *private* communication between our Lord and him) declared to be the traitor, reason enough would have been furnished for his immediately leaving the chamber. (Still, consult the note on Luke, vv. 24—30, where I have left room for modifying this view.) I am aware that this explanation will give offence to those who believe that every part of each account may be tessellated into one consistent and complete whole. Stier (Reden Jesu, vi. 46) handles the above supposition very roughly, and speaks of its upholders in no measured terms. Valuable as are the researches of this Commentator into the inner sense of the Lord's words, and ready as I am to acknowledge continual obligation to him, I cannot but think that in the whole interpretation of this part of the Gospel-history, he and his school have fallen into the error of a too minute and letter-serving exposition. In their anxiety to retain *every portion* of *every account* in its strict literal sense, they are obliged to commit many inconsistencies. A striking instance of this is also furnished in Mr. Birks's Horæ Evangelicæ, p. 411: where in treating of this difficulty he says, "If we suppose St. Matthew to express the *substantial meaning* of our Lord's reply, *rather than its precise words*, the two accounts are easily reconciled. The question of Judas might concur with St. John's private enquiry, and *the same sign which revealed the traitor to the beloved disciple, would be an affirmative reply to himself, equivalent to the words in the Gospel*—'Thou hast said.'" Very true, and nearly what I have maintained above: but the literal harmonizers seem to be quite blind to the fact, that this principle of interpretation, which *they use when it suits them*, is the very one against which they so vehemently protest when others use it, and for the use of which they call them such hard names. On **σὺ εἶπας**, see below, ver. 64, note.

26—29.] Institution of the Lord's Supper. Mark xiv. 22—25. Luke xxii. 19, 20. 1 Cor. xi. 23—25. We may remark on this important part of our narrative, (1) That it was demonstrably our Lord's intention to *found an ordinance* for those who should believe on Him; (2) that this ordinance had some *analogy with that which He and the Apostles were then celebrating*. The *first* of these assertions depends on the express word of the Apostle Paul; who in giving directions for the due celebration of the rite of the Lord's Supper, states in relation to it that he had *received from the Lord* the account of its institution, which he then gives. He who

των δὲ αὐτῶν λαβὼν ὁ Ἰησοῦς [τὸν] ἄρτον καὶ [n] εὐλογήσας
[o] ἔκλασεν καὶ ἐδίδου τοῖς μαθηταῖς καὶ εἶπεν [p] Λάβετε

ABCDE FGHKL MSUVZ ΓΔΠℵ 1. 33. 69

n ch. xiv. 19. Luke xxiv. 30. 1 Cor. xiv. 16. 1 Kings ix. 13.
o ch. xiv. 19 reff.
p Gen. iii. 6.

26. *αυτων δε εσθ.* D 69 lat-*a b c ff*$_2$ *g*$_{1.2}$(?) *h* syrr. *ο ιησ.* bef *λαβ.* D: om *ο ιησ.* Δ. om *τον* (*as in* ‖ *Mark Luke Paul*) BCDGLZℵ 1. 33 Chr-2-γ(and Fd) Thl: ins A rel [Bas$_1$] Chr-L(6-9-η-ρ, e sil). for *ευλογησας*, *ευχαριστησας* (*from* ‖ *Luke Paul*) A rel syr-txt Bas Chr Tit-bostr Thl Euthym [Orig-int$_1$]: txt BCDGLZℵ 33 latt Syr syr-mg coptt æth arm. for *εδιδου*, *δους* and om *και* (*appy corrn to the foregoing constructions. Had the rec been a corrn from* ‖ *Mark Luke it would have been εδωκεν, not εδιδου*) BDLZ ℵ-corr^1(?)^3 1. 33. 69 copt: txt AC ℵ^1(but om *και*) rel syrr æth arm [Bas$_1$].

can set this aside, must set aside with it all apostolic testimony whatever. The *second* is shewn by the fact, that what now took place was *during the celebration of the Passover:* that the same Paul states that *Christ our Passover is sacrificed for us;* thus identifying the body broken, and blood shed, of which the bread and wine here are symbolic, with the Paschal feast. (3) That the *key to the right understanding of what took place* must be found in *our Lord's discourse after the feeding of the five thousand* in John vi., since He *there*, and *there only*, besides this place, *speaks of His flesh and blood in the connexion found here.* (4) *It is impossible to assign to this event its precise place in the meal.* St. Luke inserts it *before* the announcement of the treason of Judas: St. Matt. and St. Mark *after* it. It is doubtful whether the accounts found in the Talmud and elsewhere of the ceremonies in the Paschal feast (see Lightfoot ad loc., De Wette) are to be depended on:—they are exceedingly complicated. Thus much seems clear,—that our Lord blessed and passed round *two cups*, one before, the other after the supper,—and that He distributed the unleavened cake during the meal. More than this is conjecture. The dipping of the hand in the dish, and dipping and giving the sop, may also possibly correspond to parts of the Jewish ceremonial.

26.] **While they were eating,** *during the meal,*—as distinguished from the distribution of the cup, which was *after* it. No especial stress must be laid on the article before *ἄρτον*, if read; it would be *the bread which lay before Him:* see below. The bread would be *unleavened*, as the day was *ἡ πρώτη τῶν ἀζύμων* (see Exod. xii. 8). **εὐλογήσας** and **εὐχαριστήσας** amount to the same in practice. The looking up to heaven and giving thanks was a virtual 'blessing' of the meal or the bread. **εὐλογ.** must be construed transitively (1 Cor. x. 16). **ἄρτον** is governed by all four verbs, *λαβών, εὐλογήσας, ἔκλασεν, ἐδίδου* (see also Luke ix. 16, and the reff. to the text here). It was customary in the Paschal meal for the Master, in breaking the bread, to *give thanks* for the fruit of the earth. But our Lord did more than this: "Non pro veteri tantum creatione, sed et pro nova, cujus ergo in hunc orbem venerat, preces fudit, gratiasque Deo egit pro redemtione humani generis quasi jam peracta." Grotius. From this *giving of thanks for* and *blessing* the offering, the Holy Communion has been from the earliest times also called *εὐχαριστία*, viz. by Justin Martyr, Cyril of Jerusalem, Origen, Clem. Alex., Chrysostom, &c. The passages may be seen in Suicer's Thesaurus, under the word. **ἔκλασεν**] It was a round cake of unleavened bread, which the Lord broke and divided: signifying thereby both the breaking of his body on the Cross, and the participation in the benefits of his death by all His. Hence the act of communion was known by the name *ἡ κλάσις τοῦ ἄρτου*, Acts ii. 42. See 1 Cor. x. 16, also Isa. lviii. 7: Lam. iv. 4. **ἐδίδου**, imperf. He gave to each, distributed. **λάβετε φάγετε**] Our Gospel alone has both words. *φάγετε* is spurious in Mark: both words, in 1 Cor. xi. 24. Here, they are undoubted: and seem to shew us (see note on Luke, ver. 17) that the Lord *did not Himself partake of the bread or wine.* It is thought by some however that He *did:* e. g. Chrysostom, Hom. lxxxii. 1, p. 783, *τὸ ἑαυτοῦ αἷμα αὐτὸς ἔπιεν.* But the analogy of the whole, as well as these words, and *πίετε ἐξ αὐτοῦ πάντες* below, lead us to a different conclusion. *Our Lord's* non-participation is however *no rule for the administrator of the rite* in after times. Although in one sense he *represents Christ*, blessing, breaking, and distributing; in another, he is *one of the disciples*, examining himself, confessing, partaking. Throughout all Church ministrations this double capacity must be borne in mind. Olshausen (ii. 449) maintains the opposite view, and holds that

[p] φάγετε, τοῦτό [q] ἐστιν τὸ σῶμά μου. 27 καὶ [r] λαβὼν

q = ch. xiii. 37. John xv. 1. 1 Cor. x. 4. Gen. xli. 26, 27. Exod. xii. 11. Ezek. xxxvii. 11.
r ‖ Mk. Jer. xxxii. (xxv.) 15.

the ministrant cannot unite in himself the two characters. But setting the inner verity of the matter for a moment aside, how, if so, should an *unassisted* minister *ever* communicate? **τοῦτό ἐστιν τὸ σῶμά μου**] *τοῦτο*, **this**, which I now offer to you, this *bread*. The form of expression is important, not being *οὗτος ὁ ἄρτος*, or *οὗτος ὁ οἶνος*, but *τοῦτο*, in both cases, or *τοῦτο τὸ ποτήριον*, not the bread or wine itself, but the *thing* in each case; —*precluding all idea of a substantial change.* **ἐστιν**] On this much controverted word *itself* no stress is to be laid. In the original tongue in which our Lord spoke, *it would not be expressed*: and as it now stands, it is merely the *logical copula* between the subject, *this*, and the predicate, *my Body*. The connexion of these two will require deeper consideration. First we may observe, as above of the subject, so here of the predicate, that it is not *ἡ σάρξ μου* (although that very expression is didactically used in its general sense in John vi. 51, as applying to the bread), but *τὸ σῶμά μου*. The *body* is made up of flesh and blood; and although analogically the bread may represent one and the wine the other, the assertion here is not to be analogically taken merely: *τοῦτο, this* which I give you, (is) *τὸ σῶμά μου*. Under *this* is the mystery of my Body: the assertion has a *literal*, and has also a *spiritual* or *symbolic* meaning. And it is the *literal* meaning which gives to the spiritual and *symbolic* meaning its fitness and fulness. In the *literal* meaning then, *this* (is) *my Body*, we have BREAD, 'the staff of life,' identified with THE BODY OF THE LORD: not *that particular* ἄρτος with *that particular* σάρξ which at that moment constituted the Body before them, nor *any* particular ἄρτος with the *present Body of the Lord in heaven*: but **τοῦτο**, *the food of man*, with **τὸ σῶμά μου**. This is strikingly set forth in John vi. 51, *καὶ* **ὁ ἄρτος δὲ ὃν ἐγὼ δώσω ἡ σάρξ μου** *ἐστὶν ὑπὲρ* **τῆς τοῦ κόσμου ζωῆς**. Now the mystery of the Lord's Body is, that *in and by it is all created being upheld*: *τὰ πάντα ἐν αὐτῷ συνέστηκεν*, Col. i. 17; *ἐν αὐτῷ ζωὴ ἦν*, John i. 4. And thus *generally*, and *in the widest sense*, is the Body of the Lord *the sustenance and upholding of all living*. Our very bodies are *dependent upon his*, and unless by his Body standing pure and accepted before the Father, *could not exist nor be nourished.* So that to all living things, in this largest sense, *τὸ ζῆν, χριστός*. And all our nourishment and means of upholding are Christ. In this sense *his Body is the Life of the world.* Thus the fitness of the symbol for the thing now to be signified is shewn, not merely by analogy, but by the deep verities of Redemption. And this general and lower sense, underlying, as it does, all the spiritual and higher senses in John vi., brings us to the *symbolic* meaning which the Lord now first and expressly attaches to this sacramental bread. Rising into the higher region of spiritual things,—*in and by the same Body of the Lord*, standing before the Father in accepted righteousness, is all *spiritual being upheld*, but by the *inward and spiritual process of feeding upon Him by faith*: of making that Body our own, causing it to pass into and nourish our souls, even as the substance of the bread passes into and nourishes our bodies. Of this *feeding upon Christ in the spirit* by faith, is the sacramental bread the *symbol* to us. When the faithful in the Lord's Supper press with their teeth that sustenance, which is, even to the animal life of their bodies, *the Body of Christ*, whereby alone all animated being is upheld,—*they feed in their souls on that Body of righteousness and acceptance, by partaking of which alone the body and soul are nourished unto everlasting life.* And as, in the more general and natural sense, all that nourishes the body is the Body of Christ given for *all*,—so to *them*, in the *inner spiritual sense*, is the sacramental bread symbolic of that Body given for *them*,—their standing in which, in the adoption of sons, is witnessed by the sending abroad of the Spirit in their hearts. This last leads us to the important addition in Luke and 1 Cor. (but omitted here and in Mark) *τὸ ὑπὲρ ὑμῶν* (*διδόμενον*, Luke,—omitted in 1 Cor.),—*τοῦτο ποιεῖτε εἰς τὴν ἐμὴν ἀνάμνησιν*. On these words we may remark (1) that the participle is *present*: and, rendered with reference to the time when it was spoken, would be **which is being given.** The Passion had already begun; in fact the whole life on earth was this giving and breaking, consummated by His death: (2) that the *commemorative* part of the rite here enjoined strictly depends upon the *symbolic* meaning, and that, for its fitness, upon the *literal* meaning. The commemoration is

[r] ποτήριον καὶ [s] εὐχαριστήσας ἔδωκεν αὐτοῖς λέγων [t] Πίετε ἐξ αὐτοῦ πάντες· 28 τοῦτο γάρ [q] ἐστιν τὸ [u] αἷμά μου τῆς

ABCDE FGHKL MSUVZ ΓΔΠℵ 1. 33. 69

s ch. xv. 36 reff.
t w. ἐκ (here bis) || Mk. 1 Cor. x. 4. xi. 28. Rev. xiv. 10. xviii. 3. Gen. ix. 21. w. ἀπό, Luke xxii. 18.
u Heb. ix. 20 (from Exod. xxiv. 8). x. 29.

27. rec ins το bef ποτηριον (*from || Luke Paul*), with ACD rel Chr: om BEFGLZ Δℵ 1. 33. om 2nd και CLZΔ 1. 33 arm: ins ABDℵ rel Chr Orig-int. om παντες D-gr(‘*nunc*, ubi deficit membrana’) lat-*b*.

28. om γαρ C^3(perhaps) 1. 240-3-4 lat-*a c* Syr æth sah Chr Iren-int. rec ins το bef της (*gramml emendn*), with AC rel syr [Chr]: om BDLZℵ 33 Syr copt [Cyr_1].

of Him, in so far as He has come down into Time, and enacted the great acts of Redemption on this our world,—and shewn himself to us as living and speaking *Man*, an object of our personal love and affectionate remembrance:—but the other and higher parts of the Sacrament have regard to the *results* of those same acts of Redemption, as they are *eternized* in the counsels of the Father,—as the Lamb is slain *from the foundation of the world* (Rev. xiii. 8). **27.] ἔδωκεν**, aor. He gave, not to each, but once for all: in remarkable coincidence with Luke xxii. 17, λάβετε τοῦτο κ. διαμερίσατε ἑαυτοῖς. This was *after the meal was ended*: ὡσαύτως καὶ τὸ ποτήριον μετὰ τὸ δειπνῆσαι. (Luke and 1 Cor.) As remarked above, it is quite uncertain whether our Lord followed minutely the Jewish practices, and we cannot therefore say whether the cup was one of wine and water mixed. It hardly follows from the expression of ver. 29, ἐκ τούτου τοῦ γεν. τ. ἀμπ., that it was of unmixed wine. The word **ὡσαύτως** (in Luke and 1 Cor.) contains our λαβὼν καὶ εὐχαρ. ἔδωκ. **πίετε ἐξ αὐτοῦ πάντες]** Peculiar to Matthew, preserved however in substance by Mark's καὶ ἔπιον ἐξ αὐτοῦ πάντες. The **πάντες** is remarkable, especially with reference to the practice of the Church of Rome, which forbids the cup to the laity. Calvin remarks: "Cur de pane simpliciter dixit ut ederent; de calice, ut *omnes* biberent? Ac si Satanæ calliditati ex destinato occurrere voluisset." (Cited in Stier, vi. 115.) It is on all accounts probable, and this command confirms the probability, that Judas *was present*, and *partook of both parts* of this first communion. The expressions are such throughout as to lead us to suppose that the same persons, οἱ δώδεκα, were present. On the circumstance mentioned John xiii. 30, which has mainly contributed to the other opinion, see note there. **28. τοῦτο γάρ ἐστιν τὸ αἷμά μου τῆς [καινῆς] διαθ.]** So Mark also, omitting γάρ and καινῆς. In Luke and 1 Cor. there is an important verbal difference. τοῦτο τὸ ποτήριον ἡ καινὴ διαθ. [ἐστὶν] ἐν τῷ ἐμῷ αἵματι. But if we consider the matter closely, the *real* difference is but trifling, if any. Let us recur to the Paschal rite. The lamb (χριστὸς τὸ πάσχα ἡμῶν) being killed, the blood (τὸ αἷμα τῆς διαθήκης, Exod. xxiv. 8) is sprinkled on the doorposts, and is a sign to the destroying angel to spare the house. The *blood of the covenant* is the blood of the lamb. So also in the new covenant. The blood of the Lamb of God, slain for us, being not only, as in the former case, sprinkled on, but actually *partaken spiritually and assimilated by*, the faithful soul, is the *blood of the new covenant*; and the sacramental cup, is, signifies, sets forth (καταγγέλλει, 1 Cor. xi. 26), this covenant *in His blood*, i. e. consisting in a participation in His blood. With this explanation let us recur to the words in our text. First it will be observed that there is not here that absolute assertion which τοῦτό ἐστιν τὸ σῶμά μου conveyed. It is not τοῦτό ἐστιν τὸ αἷμά μου absolutely. Wine, *in general*, does not represent by itself the effects (on the creation) of the blood of Christ; it, like every other nourishment of the body, is nourishment to us *by and in Him*, forasmuch as in Him all things consist: but there is no peculiar propriety whereby it is to us his Blood alone. But it is *made so by a covenant office* which it holds in his own declaration. Without shedding of blood was no remission of sins under the old covenant: and *blood* was, throughout, the covenant sign of forgiveness and acceptance. (See ref. Heb., where the Author, substituting τοῦτο for ἰδού in the LXX of Exod. xxiv. 8, seems to be alluding to this very formula.) Now all this blood of sacrifice finds its true reality and fulfilment in the blood of Christ, shed for the remission of sins. This is the very promise of the new covenant, see Heb. viii. 8—13, as distinguished from the old: the ἄφεσις ἁμαρτιῶν, once for all,—whereas the old had *continual* offerings, which could not do this, Heb. x. 3, 4. And of this ἄφεσις, the result of the outpouring of the blood of Christ,—*first and most generally* in bringing all creation into

[ᵛ καινῆς] ᵘᵛ διαθήκης τὸ περὶ πολλῶν ʷ ἐκχυννόμενον εις
ˣ ἄφεσιν ἁμαρτιῶν. 29 λέγω δὲ ὑμῖν οὐ μὴ ᵗ πίω ʸ ἀπ'
ἄρτι ἐκ τούτου τοῦ ᶻ γενήματος τῆς ᵃ ἀμπέλου, ᵇ ἕως τῆς
ᵇ ἡμέρας ἐκείνης ὅταν αὐτὸ πίνω μεθ' ὑμῶν καινὸν ἐν
τῇ ᶜ βασιλείᾳ τοῦ ᶜ πατρός ᶜ μου. 30 καὶ ᵈ ὑμνήσαντες

...μεθ' υμων Z.

v ‖ (Mk. v. r.). 2 Cor. iii. 6. Heb. viii. 8 (from Jer. xxxviii. [xxxi.] 31). ix. 15.
w ‖. ch. xxiii. 35 al. Gen. ix. 6.
x Luke i. 77. iii. 3. xxiv. 47 al. Matt., here only. see Ps. xxiv. 18. Isa. xxii. 14.
y ch. xxiii. 39 reff.
z = ‖. Luke xii. 18. (ch. iii. 7 al.) Exod. xxiii. 10. Isa. xxxii. 12. Hab. iii. 17. τὰ γ. τῶν ἀγρῶν Deut. xxxii. 13. see Polyb. i. 71. 1.
a ‖ Mk. L. John xv. 1, 4, 5. James iii. 12. Rev. xiv. 18, 19 only. Isa. v. 2.
b ‖ Mk. Luke i. 80. Judg. i. 21.
c here only. see ch. xiii. 43.
d abs., ‖ Mark only. (w. acc., Acts xvi. 25. Heb. ii. 12 [from Ps. xxi. 22] only.) Ps. lxiv. 14. Neh. xii. 24 A B(? not Ed-vat.) ℵ.

om καινης BLZℵ 33 [Cyr_1] : ins ACD rel latt syrr copt æth arm Iren-int Orig-int Cypr. (*See* ‖ *Luke Paul.*) for περι, υπερ D Orig (Chr) [Cyr_1]. (εκχυννομενον, so $AB^1CDLZ\Delta\Pi^1$ℵ 1. 33 Orig Chr.)

29. rec aft υμιν ins οτι (*from* ‖ *Mark*), with AC rel gat(with mm) lat-*f ff*$_2$ *g*$_2$ syrr copt [$Epiph_1$ $Orig\text{-}int_1$] : om BDZℵ 1. 33. 69 latt æth arm [$Clem_1$] Orig(appy) [Eus_1 $Epiph_1$] Chr Cyr Iren-int Cypr. om του CL ℵ[1](ins ℵ[3a]). rec γεννηματος, with GK (S 33. 69, e sil) Clem : txt ABCDℵ rel. (Z def.) for πινω, πιω D 25 Clem Orig Eus_2 [$Epiph_2$] Chr Cyr-schol. καινον bef μεθ' υμων CLZ 1. 33 æth Eus Epiph Chr Cyr.

reconciliation with the Father (see Col. i. 20),—*secondly and individually*, in the application by faith of that blood to the believing soul,—do the faithful in the Lord's Supper partake. **τὸ περὶ πολλῶν** (Luke, ὑμῶν) **ἐκχ.**] On the present participle, see above. The situation of the words in Luke is remarkable; for τὸ ποτήριον is the subject of the sentence, and ἡ κ. διαθήκη the predicate. See note there. **πολλῶν**] see note, ch. xx. 28. Cf. also Heb. ix. 28. **εἰς ἄφεσιν ἁμαρτιῶν**] Peculiar to Matthew: see above. The connexion is not πίετε . . . . εἰς ἄφεσιν ἁμ. In the Sacrament, not the forgiveness of sins itself, but the refreshing and confirming *assurance of that state of forgiveness* is conveyed. The disciples (with one exception) were clean *before the institution :* John xiii. 10, 11. St. Paul, in 1 Cor. xi. 25, repeats the τοῦτο ποιεῖτε ὁσάκις ἂν πίνητε εἰς τὴν ἐμὴν ἀνάμνησιν. On the words ὁσάκις ἂν πίνητε, see note there. In concluding this note I will observe that it is not the office of a Commentator to enter the arena of controversy respecting *transubstantiation*, further than by his exegesis his opinions are made apparent. It will be seen how entirely opposed to such a dogma is the view above given of the Sacrament. Once introduce it, and it *utterly destroys both the verity of Christ's Body*, and *the sacramental nature of the ordinance.* That it has done so, is proved (if further need be) by the *mutilation of the Sacrament*, and disobedience to the divine command, in the Church of Rome. See further notices of this in notes on 1 Cor. x. 16, and on John vi.

29.] This declaration I believe to be distinct from that in Luke xxii. 18. That was spoken over the first cup—this over one of the following. In addition to what has been said on Luke, we may observe, (1) that our Lord *still* calls the sacramental cup τὸ γέν. τῆς ἀμπ., although by Himself pronounced to be his blood : (2) that these words *carry on the meaning and continuance* of this eucharistic ordinance, even into the new heavens and new earth. As Thiersch excellently says, in his Lectures on Catholicism and Protestantism, ii. 276 (cited by Stier, vi. 160), "The Lord's Supper points not only to the past, but to the future also. It has not only a commemorative, but also a prophetic meaning. In it we have not only to shew forth the Lord's death, *until He come*, but we have also *to think of the time when He shall come* to celebrate his holy Supper with His own, new, in his Kingdom of Glory. Every celebration of the Lord's Supper is a foretaste and prophetic anticipation of the *great Marriage Supper* which is prepared for the Church at the second appearing of Christ. This import of the Sacrament is declared in the words of the Lord, οὐ μὴ πίω ἀπ' ἄρτι κ.τ.λ. These words ought never to be omitted in any liturgical form of administering the Communion."

30—35.] Declaration that all should forsake Him. Confidence of Peter. Mark xiv. 26—31. See Luke xxii. 31—38: John xiii. 36—38. Here, accurately speaking perhaps between ὑμνήσαντες and ἐξῆλθον, come in the discourses and prayer of our Lord in John xiv. xv. xvi. xvii., spoken (see note on John xiv. 31) without change of place, in the supper-chamber. **30.**] The **ὕμνος** was in all probability the last part of the Hallel, or

ἐξῆλθον εἰς τὸ [e] ὄρος τῶν [e] ἐλαιῶν.
31 τότε λέγει αὐτοῖς
ὁ Ἰησοῦς Πάντες ὑμεῖς [f] σκανδαλισθήσεσθε ἐν ἐμοὶ ἐν τῇ
νυκτὶ ταύτῃ· γέγραπται γὰρ [g] Πατάξω τὸν ποιμένα, καὶ
[h] διασκορπισθήσονται τὰ πρόβατα τῆς [i] ποίμνης.
32 [k] μετὰ
δὲ τὸ [l] ἐγερθῆναί με [m] προάξω ὑμᾶς εἰς τὴν Γαλιλαίαν.
33 ἀποκριθεὶς δὲ ὁ Πέτρος εἶπεν αὐτῷ Εἰ πάντες [f] σκανδαλισθήσονται ἐν σοί, ἐγὼ οὐδέποτε [f] σκανδαλισθήσομαι.
34 ἔφη αὐτῷ ὁ Ἰησοῦς [n] Ἀμὴν λέγω σοι ὅτι ἐν ταύτῃ τῇ

I_c νυκτι ταυτη... ABCDE FGHI$_c$ KLMSU VΓΔΠℵ 1. 33. 69

e ch. xxi. 1 reff.
f ch. xi. 6 || L. xxii. 57 || Mk. Rom. xiv. 21. Sir. xxiii. 8.
g || Mk., from Zech. xiii. 7.
h ver. 51 || L. bis. Acts vii. 24. xii. 7, 23. Rev. xi. 6. xix. 15 only. Exod. ii. 12. Gen. viii. 21.
h ch. xxv. 24, 26 reff. plur., ch. vi. 28 reff.
i Luke ii. 8. John x. 16. 1 Cor. ix. 7 bis only. Gen. xxxii. 16 bis. Zech. l. c. Aℵ3 only.
k || Mk. Mark i. 14. xvi. 19. Luke xii. 5. xxii. 20. Acts i. 3 al. 1 Chron. ii. 24.
l = ch. xvii. 23 reff.
m ch. xiv. 22. xxi. 31 †. Wisd. xix. 11.
n ch. v. 18 reff.

31. rec διασκορπισθησεται (*gramml corrn*), with D rel Orig Eus Chr: txt ABCGH[1] I_cLMℵ 33. 69 Orig$_1$.

33. rec aft ει ins και (*from* || *Mark*), with FKΠℵ[3a] vulg syrr æth arm Orig$_2$[(and int$_1$) Bas$_1$] Chr Hil: om ABCD ℵ[1](omits ει also) rel lat-*a b c ff*$_2$ coptt Orig-int.
aft εγω ins δε C[3]EFGHKMUΓ 69 lat-*h* coptt æth arm [Bas$_1$].

34. om εν D fuld lat-*a b c h* Chr(so Fd).

great Hallel, which consisted of Psalms cxv.—cxviii.; the former part (Ps. cxiii. cxiv.) having been sung during the meal. It is unlikely that this took place *after* the solemn prayer in John xvii. **ἐξῆλθ.**] Luke (ver. 39) adds κατὰ τὸ ἔθος—namely, of every evening since his return to Jerusalem. **31.**] **πάντες** (emphatic) **ὑμεῖς** seems to be used as distinguishing those present from the one, who had gone out. **σκανδ.**] see note on ch. xi. 6. The word is here used in a pregnant meaning, including what followed,—desertion, and, in one case, denial.

γέγραπται γάρ] This is a very important citation, and has been much misunderstood; *how much*, may appear from Grotius's remark: "Tantum abest ut Zachariæ verbis directe Christum putem respici, ut multo magis credam agi inibi de aliquo *non bono* pastore," &c. But, on the contrary, if we examine Zech. xi. xii. xiii., we must I think come to the conclusion that the shepherd spoken of xi. 7—14, who is *rejected* and *sold*, who is said to have been *pierced* (xii. 10), is also spoken of in ch. xiii. 7. Stier (Reden Jesu, vi. 176 ff.) has gone at length into the meaning of the whole prophecy, and especially that of the word עֲמִיתִי, 'my fellow,' and shewn that the reference can be to *no other than the Messiah*. The citation agrees verbatim with the LXX-A, except that πάταξον is changed into πατάξω—God who *commands the striking*, into God who *Himself strikes*. **32.**] In this announcement our Lord seems to have in mind the remainder of the verse in Zechariah: "and I will turn (הֲשִׁיב, reducere manum, i. e. impiis sublatis curam agere, &c. Schröder) mine hand upon the little ones." As this could not be *cited* in any intelligible connexion with present circumstances, our Lord gives the announcement of its fulfilment, in a promise to *precede* them (προάγ., a pastoral office, see John x. 4) into Galilee, whither they should naturally return after the feast was over: see ch. xxviii. 7, 10, 16. Schleiermacher thinks it "extremely improbable that Jesus, if He foresaw so exactly the days of His resurrection, and therefore could not but know that He should see his disciples again more than once in Jerusalem, should here have said that He would lead them into Galilee" (English Translation, p. 298). I confess that I see no improbability in the case; but the three references to this promise just quoted make it surely in the highest degree improbable that it should have been *subsequently foisted in.* We do not find such elaborate attempts to preserve the appearance of consistency in our Gospels. The reader who sees in it the reference to prophecy, will form a very different opinion. **33.**] Nothing can bear a greater impress of exactitude than this reply. Peter had been before warned (see note on Luke, vv. 31—34); and still remaining in the same spirit of self-confident attachment, now that he is included among the πάντες, not specially addressed, —breaks out into this asseveration, which carries completely with it the testimony that it was *not the first.* Men do not bring themselves out so strongly (εἰ πάντες, οὐκ ἐγώ: and not only so, but, οὐδέποτε, as opposed to ἐν τῇ νυκτὶ ταύτῃ) unless their fidelity has been previously attainted.

34.] The very words *in their order*

νυκτὶ πρὶν [o] ἀλέκτορα [p] φωνῆσαι, τρὶς [q] ἀπαρνήσῃ με.
35 λέγει αὐτῷ ὁ Πέτρος [r] Κἂν δέῃ με σὺν σοὶ ἀποθανεῖν,
οὐ μή σε [q] ἀπαρνήσομαι. ὁμοίως καὶ πάντες οἱ μαθηταὶ
εἶπον. 36 Τότε ἔρχεται μετ᾽ αὐτῶν ὁ Ἰησοῦς εἰς [s] χωρίον

o here, &c. || only. Prov. xxx. 31 only.
p = here, &c. || only. Jer. xvii. 11. || Mk. L. ch. xvi. 24 ||. Luke xii. 9 (John xiii. 28 v. r.) only. Isa. xxxi. 7 only.
q here bis, ver. 72 &
r Mark xvi. 18. John viii. 14. x. 38 al. see Esth. iv. 16.
s || Mk. John iv. 5. Acts i. 18, 19. iv. 34. v. 3, 8. xxviii. 7 only. 1 Chron. xxvii. 27 bis. 2 Macc. xi. 5. xii. 7 only.

απαρνηση με bef *τρις* A coptt.—*απαρνησει* B(but -*ση* below) C Scr's c f i ev-y.—*με* bef *απαρν.* ℵ[1](txt ℵ[3a]) 33 latt Orig-int Hil.

35. om *ὁ* D. *απαρνησωμαι* AEGKUVΠ 69 Thl. aft *ομοιως* ins *δε* A rel syr-ms coptt æth Chr Thl: om BCD I_c(appy) LSℵ 33 latt syrr arm Orig-int.

36. *ο ιησ.* bef *μετ αυτ.* D latt arm.

are, I doubt not, reported by St. Mark—ἀμὴν λ. σοι ὅτι σήμερον ταύτῃ τῇ νυκτὶ πρὶν ἢ δὶς ἀλέκτορα φωνῆσαι τ. με ἀπ. The contrast to Peter's boast, and the climax, is in these words the strongest; and the inference also comes out most clearly, that they likewise were not now said for the first time. The *first* cock-crowing is at midnight; but inasmuch as *few hear it,*—when the word is used *generally,* we mean the *second* crowing, early in the morning, before dawn. If this view be taken, the ἀλέκτ. φων. and δὶς ἀλ. φ. amount to the same—only the latter is the *more precise* expression. It is most likely that Peter understood this expression as only a *mark of time,* and therefore received it, as when it was spoken before, as merely an expression of distrust on the Lord's part; it was this solemn and circumstantial repetition of it which afterwards struck upon his mind when the sign itself was literally fulfilled. A question has been raised whether *cocks were usually kept* or even allowed in Jerusalem. No such bird is mentioned in the O. T., and the Mischna states that the inhabitants of Jerusalem, and the priests every where, kept no fowls, because they scratched up unclean worms. But the Talmud is here not consistent with itself: and Lightfoot brings forward a story which proves it. And there might be many kept by the resident Romans, over whom the Jews had no power. We must not overlook the spiritual parabolic import of this warning. Peter stands here as a representative of all disciples who deny or forget Christ—and the watchful bird that cries in the night is that warning voice which 'speaketh once, yea twice,' to call them to repentance: see Rom. xiii. 11, 12.

35.] This **ἂν δέῃ** again appears to have the precision of a repeated asseveration. Mark has the stronger expression ἐκ περισσοῦ ἔλεγεν, which even more clearly indicates that the συναποθανεῖν was not now first said. The rest said it, but not so earnestly perhaps;—at all events, Peter's confidence cast theirs into the shade.

36—46.] Our Lord's agony at Gethsemane. Mark xiv. 32—42. Luke xxii. 39—46. John xviii. 1. The account of the temptation, and of the agony in Gethsemane is peculiar to the three first Evangelists. But it does not therefore follow that there is, in their narratives, any inconsistency with St. John's setting forth of the Person of Christ. For it must be remembered, that, as we find in *their* accounts frequent manifestations of the *divine nature,* and indications of *future glory,* about, and during this conflict,—so in St. John's account, which brings out more the divine side of our Lord's working and speaking, we find frequent allusions to his *human weakness* and *distress of spirit.* For examples of the first, see vv. 13, 24, 29, 32, 53, and || in Mark and Luke; and Luke xxii. 30, 32, 37, 43; of the latter, John xii. 27; xiii. 21; xiv. 30; xvi. 32. The right understanding of the whole important narration must be acquired by bearing in mind the *reality of the manhood of our Lord, in all its abasement and weakness:* —by following out in Him the analogy which pervades the characteristics of human suffering—the strength of the resolved spirit, and calm of the resigned will, continually broken in upon by the inward giving way of human feebleness, and limited power of endurance. But as in us, so in the Lord, these seasons of dread and conflict stir not the ruling *will,* alter not the firm resolve. This is most manifest in His *first* prayer—εἰ δυνατόν ἐστιν—'if consistent with that work which I have covenanted to do.' Here is the reserve of the *will* to suffer—*it is never stirred* (see below). The conflict however of the Lord differs from ours in this,—that in *us,* the ruling *will* itself is *but* a phase of our *human* will, and may be and is often carried away by the excess

t = ch. xiii. 48. xxiii. 2. Gen. xxii. 5.
u = Acts xviii. 19. xxi. 4 (xv. 34 v. r.) only. 2 Kings xx. 4.
v ch. xvii. 1 al. fr. Num. xxii. 41.

λεγόμενον Γεθσημανεῖ, καὶ λέγει τοῖς μαθηταῖς [t] Καθίσατε [u] αὐτοῦ, ἕως οὗ ἀπελθὼν ἐκεῖ προσεύξωμαι.
37 καὶ [v] παραλαβὼν τὸν Πέτρον καὶ τοὺς δύο υἱοὺς Ζεβεδαίου, ἤρξατο [w] λυπεῖσθαι καὶ [x] ἀδημονεῖν.
38 τότε λέγει αὐτοῖς

ABCDE FGHI$_c$ KLMSU̅ VΓΔΠℵ 1. 33. 69

w ch. xiv. 9. xvii. 23 al. 2 Kings xix. 2. x || Mk. Phil. ii. 26 only †. Job xviii. 20 Aq.

(γεθσημανει, so ABC [D(γεθσαμ.)] FI$_c$KS 1. 69, -νι LUΓΠℵ.) aft *μαθηταις* ins *αυτου* (*from* || *Mark*) ACDℵ 1 latt syrr copt æth Hil: [*αυτοις* 69 arm:] om B I$_c$(appy) rel sah Chr. om *αυτου* C¹ℵ. for *οὗ, αν* DKLM[r][Γ]Δ 1. 69 Chr-txt: *οὗ αν* A: om CM¹ℵ 33 Chr-comm Thl. rec *προσευξ.* bef *εκει* (*to avoid ambiguity*), with ACI$_c$ rel syr: om *εκει* (|| *Mark*) 244 Syr arm Chr-comm: txt BDLℵ 33. 69 latt coptt æth Orig-int Hil. *προσευξομαι* DFHΓ Chr-2-6-γ-G-H-K.

38. aft *αυτοις* ins *ο ις* C³ rel lat-*a f h* syr Thl: om ABC¹DI$_c$Lℵ 1. 33(Treg, expr). 69 vss Chr.

of depression and suffering; whereas in *Him* it was the *divine Personality* in which the *higher Will of the covenant purpose was eternally fixed*,—struggling with the flesh now overwhelmed with an horrible dread, and striving to escape away (see the whole of Ps. lv.). Besides that, by that uplifting into a superhuman circle of *Knowledge*, with which the indwelling of the Godhead endowed his humanity, his flesh, with all its capacities and apprehensions, was brought *at once* into immediate and simultaneous contact with every circumstance of horror and pain that awaited Him (John xviii. 4), which is never the case with us. Not only are the objects of dread *gradually* unveiled to our minds, but *hope* (ἐλπὶς κινδύνῳ παραμύθιον οὖσα, Thuc. v. 103) is ever suggesting that things may not be so bad as our fears represent them.

Then we must not forget, that as the *flesh* gave way under dread of suffering, so the *human ψυχή* was troubled with all the attendant circumstances of that suffering—betrayal, desertion, shame (see Ps. lv. again, vv. 12—14, 20, 21; xxxviii. 11, 12; lxxxviii. al.). Nor again must we pass over the last and deepest mystery of the Passion—the consideration, that upon the holy and innocent Lamb of God rested the burden of *all* human sin—that to Him, death, as the punishment of *sin*, bore a dark and dreadful meaning, inconceivable by any of us, whose inner will is tainted by the *love* of Sin. See on this part of the Redeemer's agony, Ps. xl. 12; xxxviii. 1—10 al. See also as a comment on the whole, Heb. v. 7—10, and notes there. The three accounts do not differ in any important particulars. Luke merely gives a general summary of the Lord's prayers and his sayings to the disciples, but inserts (see below) two details not found in the others. Mark's account and Matthew's are very nearly related, and have evidently sprung from the same source. **36.**] Mark alone, besides our account, mentions the name of the place—Luke merely calls it *ὁ τόπος*, in allusion to *κατὰ τὸ ἔθος* before. John informs us that it was *a garden*. The name is גַּת שְׁמָנֵא or שְׁמָנֵי, '*an oil press.*' It was at the foot of the Mount of Olives, in the valley of the Kedron, the other side of the brook from the city (John xviii. 1). **καθίσ.**] not strictly and literally '*sit*,' but = *μείνατε* ver. 38, **stay here.** **προσεύξωμαι**] Such is the name which our Lord gives to that which was coming upon Him, in speaking to the Eight who were not to witness it. *All conflict of the holy soul* is *prayer*: all its struggles are continued communion with God. In Gen. xxii. 5, when Abraham's faith was to be put to so sore a trial, he says, 'I and the lad will *go yonder and worship*.' Our Lord (almost on the same spot) unites in Himself, as the priest and victim, as Stier strikingly remarks, Abraham's Faith and Isaac's Patience.

ἐκεῖ] probably some spot deeper in the garden's shade. At this time the gorge of the Kedron would be partly in the moonlight, partly shaded by the rocks and buildings of the opposite side. It may have been from the moonlight into the shade that our Lord retired to pray.

37.] These three—Peter, the foremost in attachment, and profession of it—the two sons of Zebedee, who were to drink of the cup that He drank of—He takes with Him, not only nor principally as *witnesses* of his trial—this indeed, in the full sense, they were not—but as a *consolation* to Him in that dreadful hour—to 'watch with Him.' In this too they failed—yet from his returning to them between his times of prayer, it is manifest that, in the abasement of his humanity, He regarded

[y] Περίλυπός ἐστιν ἡ ψυχή μου [z] ἕως θανάτου· μείνατε
ὧδε καὶ [a] γρηγορεῖτε μετ᾽ ἐμοῦ. 39 καὶ [b] προελθὼν μικρὸν
[c] ἔπεσεν ἐπὶ [c] πρόσωπον αὐτοῦ προσευχόμενος καὶ λέγων
Πάτερ μου, εἰ δυνατόν ἐστιν, [d] παρελθάτω ἀπ᾽ ἐμοῦ τὸ

y || Mk. Mark vi. 26. Luke xviii. 23, 24 only. Ps. xli. 5, 11. xlii. 5. Esdr. viii. 71, 72 (69, 70) only. z = Mark vi. 23. Luke xxii. 51. Jon. iv. 9. a ch. xxiv. 42, 43 reff. b || Mk. Mark vi. 33. Luke i. 17. xxii. 47. Acts xii. 10. xx. 5, 13. 2 Cor. ix. 5 only. Gen. xxxiii. 3 Ed-vat.(B def.). c ch. xvii. 6 reff. 2 Chron. vii. 3. Num. xvi. 22. d = || Mk. only.

39. προσελθων (*prob error*) ACDI$_c$ℵ rel syr [Chr-mss]: txt BMΠ[1] vss Orig-int Hil lat-ff. om μου LΔ **1**. 218 am lat-*a* Just Iren-gr Val Orig$_9$ Dial$_3$ Eus$_6$ Ath Naz Bas Did Chr [Bas-sel$_4$] Cypr$_2$ Hil$_2$ Aug: ins (*possibly to conform to ver* 42, *where no MS omits it: but see also Luke* xxii. 42) ABCDℵ rel vss(but fluctuate between *mi pater, pater mi, pater meus*) Hil$_3$ Ambr [Aug$_1$]. (παρελθατω, so ACDEFGLΔℵ 33.)

them as some comfort to Him. 'In magnis tentationibus juvat solitudo, sed tamen ut in propinquo sint amici.' Bengel. **ἤρξατο**—not merely idiomatic here—**He began**, *as He had never done before.* **λυπεῖσθαι** = ἐκθαμβεῖσθαι Mark. 'Dicit incursum objecti horribilis.' Bengel (see below on ver. 38). **ἀδημονεῖν** = λίαν λυπεῖσθαι, ἀπορεῖν, Suidas; τὸ βαρυθυμεῖν νοεῖται, Euthym.; ἀγωνιᾷν, Hesychius; ἀδήμων, ὁ ἐξ ἅδου, ὅ ἐστι κόρου τινὸς ἢ λύπης, ἀναπεπτωκώς. ἀδημονεῖν, τὸ ἀλύειν καὶ ἀμηχανεῖν, Eustathius. **38.**] Our Lord's whole inmost life must have been one of *continued trouble of spirit*—He was a *man of sorrows*, and *acquainted with grief*—but there was an *extremity of anguish* now, reaching even to the *utmost limit of endurance*, so that it seemed that *more* would be *death itself*. The expression is said to be *proverbial* (see ref. Jonah): but we must remember that though with *us men*, who see from below, proverbs are merely bold guesses at truth,—with *Him*, who sees from above, they are *the truth itself*, in its very purest form. So that although when used *by a man*, a proverbial expression is not to be pressed to literal exactitude,—when used *by our Lord*, it is, just *because* it is a proverb, to be searched into and dwelt on all the more. The expression **ἡ ψυχή μου**, in this sense, spoken by our Lord, is only found besides in John xii. 27. It is the *human soul*, the seat of the affections and passions, which is troubled with the anguish of the body; and it is distinguished from the πνεῦμα, the *higher spiritual being*. Our Lord's soul was crushed down even to death by the weight of that anguish which lay upon Him—and that *literally*—so that He (as regards his humanity) *would have died*, had not strength (*bodily* strength, upholding his human frame) been ministered from on high by an angel (see note on Luke xxii. 43).

γρηγορεῖτε μετ' ἐμοῦ] not προσεύχεσθε μετ' ἐμοῦ, for in that work the Mediator must be *alone;* but (see above) *watch* with Me—just (if we may compare *our* weakness with His) as we derive comfort in the midst of a terrible storm, from knowing that some are awake and with us, even though their presence is no real safeguard. **39.**] **προελθὼν μικρόν** (Matt., Mark) = ἀπεσπάσθη ἀπ' αὐτῶν ὡσεὶ λίθου βολήν Luke, who in this description is the more precise. ἀπεσπ., I cannot help thinking, implies something more than *mere removal* from them—something of the *reluctance* of parting. The distance would be very small, not above forty or fifty yards. Hence the disciples might well catch the leading words of our Lord's prayers, before drowsiness overpowered them. Luke has however only θεὶς τὰ γόνατα, which is not so full as our account. **προσευχ.**] Stier finely remarks: 'This was in truth a different prayer from that which went before, which John has recorded.' But still in the same spirit, uttered by the same Son of God and Redeemer of men. The *glorifying* (John xvii. 1) begins with suffering, as the previous words, ἐλήλυθεν ἡ ὥρα, might lead us to expect. The 'power over all flesh' shews itself first as power of the conflicting and victorious spirit over *his own flesh*, by virtue of which He is 'one of us.' Mark expresses the *substance* of the prayer, and *interprets* ποτήριον by ὥρα. Luke's report differs only in verbal expression from Matthew's. In the address, we have here and in Luke **Πάτερ**—in Mark ἀββᾶ ὁ πατήρ. In all, and in the prayer itself, there is the deepest feeling and apprehension in the Redeemer's soul of *his Sonship and the unity of the Father*—the most entire and holy submission to His Will. We must not for a moment think of the Father's *wrath* abiding on Him as the cause of his suffering. Here is

e = ||. ch. xx. 22, 23 ||. John xviii. 11. Rev. xiv. 10. xvi. 19. xviii. 6. Isa. li. 17. Ezek. xxiii. 33.
f = ch. xi. 22. xviii. 7 al.
g = Mark iv. 40. vii. 18. John xviii. 22. 1 Cor. vi. 5. Gal. iii. 3.
h ch. viii. 28 reff.
i ||. ch. vi. 13. 1 Tim. vi. 9. James i. 2, 12. Deut. iv. 34.

[e] ποτήριον τοῦτο. [f] πλὴν οὐχ ὡς ἐγὼ θέλω, ἀλλ' ὡς σύ.
40 καὶ ἔρχεται πρὸς τοὺς μαθητὰς καὶ εὑρίσκει αὐτοὺς
καθεύδοντας, καὶ λέγει τῷ Πέτρῳ [g] Οὕτως οὐκ [h] ἰσχύσατε
μίαν ὥραν [a] γρηγορῆσαι μετ' ἐμοῦ; 41 [a] γρηγορεῖτε καὶ
προσεύχεσθε ἵνα μὴ εἰσέλθητε εἰς [i] πειρασμόν. τὸ μὲν

ABCDE FGHI KLMSU VΓΔΠℵ 1. 33. 69

at end add Luke xxii. 43, 44 C^3-mg 69 evv-H-P.

40. aft *μαθητας* ins *αυτου* D[*αυτους* was originally written under *τους μα*] latt(not am g_2) Syr copt æth Orig-int Hil. *ισχυσας* (*corrn, from τω π. above*) A gat lat-ff_2 g_2 syr-mg arm-mss Chr-comm Juv.

no fear of wrath,—but, in the depth of his human anguish, the very tenderness of filial love. The variation in Mark and Luke in the substance of the prayer, though slight, is worthy of remark. **εἰ δυνατόν ἐστιν** = *πάντα δυνατά σοι*, = *εἰ βούλει*. All these three find their union in one and the same inward feeling. That in the text expresses, 'If, within the limits of Thy holy Will, this may be;'—that in Mark, 'All things are (absolutely) possible to Thee—Thou *canst* therefore—but not what I will, but what Thou *wilt*:'—that in Luke, 'If it be Thy *Will* to remove, &c. (Thou canst): but not my will, but Thine be done.' The *very words used* by our Lord, the Holy Spirit has not seen fit to give us—shewing us, even in this solemn instance, the comparative indifference of the *letter*, when we have the inner *spirit*. That our Lord should have uttered *all three* forms of the prayer, is not for a moment to be thought of; and such a view could only spring out of the most petty and unworthy appreciation of the purpose of Scripture narrative. **παρελθάτω**] as we should say of a threatening cloud, 'It has *gone over*.' But what is the *ποτήριον* or *ὥρα*, of which our Lord here prays that it may *pass by?* Certainly, not the mere present feebleness and prostration of the bodily frame: not any mere section of his sufferings—but *the whole*—the betrayal, the trial, the mocking, the scourging, the cross, the grave, and all besides which our thoughts cannot reach. Of this all, his soul, in humble subjection to the higher Will, which was absolutely united and harmonious with the Will of the Father, prays that if possible it may pass over. And this prayer *was heard*—see Heb. v. 7—*ἀπὸ τῆς εὐλαβείας*—on account of His pious resignation to the Father's will, or *on the ground of* it, so that it prevailed—He was strengthened from Heaven. He did indeed drink the cup to the dregs—but He was *enabled* to do it, and this *ἐνίσχυσις* was the answer to his prayer. **πλὴν οὐχ . . . . .**] The Monothelite heresy, which held *but one will* in the Lord Jesus, is here plainly convicted of error. The distinction is clear, and marked by our Lord Himself. In His *human soul*, He willed to be freed from the dreadful things before Him—but this human will was overruled by the *inner and divine purpose*—the Will at unity with the Father's Will. **40.**] Mark agrees, except in relating the beginning of the address in the *singular*—no doubt accurately—for it was Peter (Simon, der hier kein Petrus war. Stier), who had *pledged himself to go with Him to prison and death.* **οὕτως**] see reff., '*adeo*:'—it implies their *utter inability*, as shewn by their present state of slumber. **Are ye so entirely unable, &c.** **μίαν ὥραν** need not imply that our Lord had been absent *a whole hour*:—if it is to be taken in any close meaning, it would be that the *whole trial would last* about that time. But most likely it is in allusion to the *time* of our Lord's *trial*, so often called by that name. **41.**] Luke gives this command at the beginning and end of the whole; but his account is manifestly only a compendium, and not to be pressed chronologically. The command has respect to the immediate trial which was about to try them, and (for **γρηγ.** is a word of *habit*, not merely, as *ἐγείρω* Eph. v. 15, or *ἐκνήφω* 1 Cor. xv. 34, one of immediate import) also to the *general duty of all disciples in all time.* **εἰσελθεῖν εἰς π.** is not to *come into* temptation merely, to be *tempted*: this lies not in our own power to avoid, and its happening is rather joy than sorrow to us—see James i. 2, where the word is *περιπέσητε*—but it implies an **entering into temptation** with the *will*, and *entertaining* of the temptation. Grotius compares *ἐμπίπτειν εἰς πειρασμόν* 1 Tim. vi. 9. 'Plenius Hebræi dicunt, intrare in manum tenta-

[k]πνεῦμα [l]πρόθυμον, ἡ δὲ [k]σὰρξ ἀσθενής. 42 πάλιν [m]ἐκ
[m]δευτέρου ἀπελθὼν προσηύξατο λέγων Πάτερ μου, [n]εἰ
[n]οὐ δύναται τοῦτο [d]παρελθεῖν ἐὰν μὴ αὐτὸ πίω, [o]γενη-
θήτω τὸ [o]θέλημά σου. 43 καὶ ἐλθὼν πάλιν εὗρεν αὐτοὺς
καθεύδοντας, ἦσαν γὰρ αὐτῶν οἱ ὀφθαλμοὶ [p]βεβαρημένοι.
44 καὶ [q]ἀφεὶς αὐτοὺς πάλιν ἀπελθὼν προσηύξατο τὸν
αὐτὸν λόγον εἰπών. 45 τότε ἔρχεται πρὸς τοὺς μαθητὰς
καὶ λέγει αὐτοῖς Καθεύδετε [r]λοιπὸν καὶ [s]ἀναπαύεσθε·

...τοτε ερχεται I_c

k so || Mk. 2 Cor. vii. 1.
l || Mk. Rom. i. 15 only. 1 Chron. xxviii. 21.
m Mark xiv. 72. John ix. 24. Acts x. 15. xi. 9. Heb. ix. 28. Josh. v. 2.
n Rom. viii. 9. 1 Cor. vii. 9.
o || L. ch. vi. 10. Acts xxi. 14 only.
p (|| Mk. v. r.) Luke ix. 32. xxi. 34. 2 Cor. i. 8. v. 4. 1 Tim. v. 16 only †. Isa. i. 4 Aq., &c.
q = ch. iv. 11 reff.
r || Mk. reff.
s || Mk. Mark vi. 31. Deut. xxxiii. 20. Dan. xii. 13.

42. aft προσηυξ. ins ο ῑς L ℵ-corr[1 or 2](but erased) 1. 69 arm. om λεγων B lat-g_1. rec aft τουτο ins το ποτηριον (*from ver* 39, *as the varr shew*), with E rel vulg lat-*a c* Syr copt arm Hil_1 : pref D 69 lat-*l* Hil_1 : bef εαν Δ[1] : om ABCI_cL Δ-corr Π[1]ℵ 1. 33 lat-*b* ff_2 syr sah æth $Orig_2$ Eus_4 Chr Ambr. rec aft παρελθειν ins απ εμου (*from ver* 39), with ACI_c rel lat-*f* ff_2 syr arm Chr Orig-int Hil_1 Leo : om BDLℵ 1. 33(appy). 69 latt Syr coptt æth $Orig_2$ Eus_3 Hil_2 Ambr.

43. rec ευρισκει (*from ver* 40), with E rel : txt ABCDI_cKLΔΠℵ 1. 33. 69. ευρ. αυτους bef παλιν A rel lat-*a* syr : txt BCDI_cLΓℵ 1. 33 vulg lat-*b c* &c Syr syr-mg coptt æth arm.

44. rec απελθων bef παλιν, with E rel lat-*f* Syr æth : aft προσηυξ. AK(Γ ?)ΔΠ 238 Scr's e g p w syr (arm) : bef αυτους sah : om U-txt 1. 69 forj lat-*a* : txt BCDI_cLℵ 33 ev-y vulg lat-*b c* &c copt. (παλιν *seems to have been omd on account of the insn of* εκ τριτου *below, and then variously insd.*) rec aft προσηυξατο ins εκ τριτου (*to correspond with ver* 42), with BCI_cℵ[3a](aft τον αυτον ℵ[1]) rel vss ; τριτου E[1] : om ADKΠ 1 lat-*a b*. at end ins παλιν BLℵ lat-*a* copt.

45. rec aft μαθ. ins αυτου, with D rel latt Syr copt æth Ath Orig-int : om ABCKL MΔΠℵ 1. 33(appy). 69 syr sah arm. rec ins το bef λοιπον (*so also in* || *Mark*),

tionis, hoc est, in ejus potestatem atque dominium, ita ut ab ea subjugemur atque absorbeamur' (Witsius, Exerc. in Orat. Dom. p. 196, cited by Stier, vi. 237). **τὸ μὲν πν.**] I cannot doubt that this is said by our Lord in its most general meaning, and that *He Himself is included* in it. At that moment He was giving as high and pre-eminent an example of its truth, as the disciples were affording a low and ignoble one. He, in the willingness of the spirit—yielding Himself to the Father's Will to suffer and die, but weighed down by the weakness of the flesh: they, having professed, and really *having*, a willing spirit to suffer with Him, but, even in the one hour's watching, overcome by the burden of drowsiness. Observe it is here **πνεῦμα**, not ψυχή; and compare ver. 38 and note. To enter further into the depths of this assertion of our Lord would carry us beyond the limits of annotation: but see Stier's remarks, vi. 237—242. **42.**] Mark merely says of this second prayer, τὸν αὐτὸν λόγον εἰπών. Luke gives it as ἐκτενέστερον προσηύχετο—and relates in addition, that His sweat was like the fall of drops of blood on the ground: see notes on Luke xxii. 44. (At what precise time the angel appeared to Him is uncertain: I should be inclined to think, *after the first prayer*, before He came to his disciples.) The words are not exactly the same: "the Lord knew that the Father always heard Him (John xi. 42); and therefore He understands the continuance of His trial as the answer to His last words, **as Thou wilt.**" Stier. Here therefore the prayer is, **If it be not possible . . . . thy will be done.** It is spoken in the fulness of self-resignation. 'Jam addita *bibendi* mentione, propius ad bibendum se confert.' Bengel. **43.**] Mark adds, and it is a note of accuracy, καὶ οὐκ ᾔδεισαν τί ἀποκριθῶσιν αὐτῷ. **44.**] **τὸν αὐτόν**, viz. as the last. This third prayer is merely *indicated* in Mark, by ἔρχεται τὸ τρίτον, on our Lord's *return*. **45, 46.**] The clause **καθεύδετε λ. κ. ἀναπ.** has been variously understood. To take it interrogatively does not improve the sense, and makes an unnatural break in the sentence, which proceeds indicatively afterwards. It seems to me that there can be but two ways of interpreting it—and both with an imperative construction. (1) Either it was said *bona fide*,—'Since ye are not able to watch with Me, now ye may sleep on—for my hour is come, and I am

t = ch. iii. 2 reff.
u = John iv. 35. vii. 33. Jer. xxxi. (xlviii.) 12.
v ch. xvii. 22 reff. Job xvi. 12. Ps. cv. 41.
w = Mark i. 38. John xi. 7, 15, 16. xiv. 13.
x = ch. xxi. 1 reff.

ἰδοὺ [t] ἤγγικεν ἡ ὥρα, [u] καὶ ὁ υἱὸς τοῦ ἀνθρώπου [v] παρα- ABCDE FGHKL MSUVΓ ΔΠℵ 1. 33. 69
δίδοται εἰς χεῖρας ἁμαρτωλῶν. 46 ἐγείρεσθε [w] ἄγωμεν,
ἰδοὺ [x] ἤγγικεν ὁ [y] παραδιδούς με. 47 καὶ [z] ἔτι αὐτοῦ
[z] λαλοῦντος ἰδοὺ Ἰούδας εἷς τῶν δώδεκα ἦλθεν, καὶ μετ᾽
αὐτοῦ ὄχλος πολὺς [a] μετὰ μαχαιρῶν καὶ [b] ξύλων, ἀπὸ
τῶν ἀρχιερέων καὶ [c] πρεσβυτέρων τοῦ [c] λαοῦ. 48 ὁ δὲ

y pres. part., ch. iv. 3. xiii. 3. 1 Thess. iii. 5 al. z || Mk. L. Luke xxii. 60. Gen. xxix. 9. Job i. 16, 17, 18. a = ch. xxiv. 30. Acts xiii. 17. xxvi. 12. b = here, bis, & || only. ξύλῳ παισθέντα, Herodian vii. 7. c ch. xxi. 23 reff.

with ADℵ rel Ath: om BCL Chr. (33 def.) aft ιδου ins γαρ BE 238 Scr's p sah arm Ath: aft ηγγ. 1.
46. παραδιδων ℵ[1] (txt ℵ[3a]). 47. for και ετι, ετι δε D.

about to be taken from you'—which sense however is precluded by the ἐγείρεσθε ἄγωμεν below: or (2) it was said with an understanding of '*if you can*' as Bengel; 'si me excitantem non auditis, brevi aderunt alii qui vos excitent. Interea dormite, si vacat.' (Only let us beware of the so-called "deeper sense," suggested by Wordsw. here, "Now you may hope for sleep and rest (? cf. Mark xiii. 37: 1 Thess. v. 6, 7), for I am about to die.")

ἰδοὺ ἤγγ. = ἀπέχει· ἦλθεν Mark. The ἀπέχει implies, '*It is enough*'—enough of reproof to them for drowsiness—enough of exhortations to watch and pray—that was now coming which would cut all this short. This *first* ἰδού is hardly to be taken literally of the *appearance* of Judas and his band; it merely announces the approach of *the hour*, of which the Lord had so often spoken: but at the utterance of the *second*, it seems that they were *in sight*, and that may be taken literally. This expression, παραδ. εἰς χεῖρας **ἁμαρτωλῶν**, should be noticed, as an echo of the Redeemer's anguish—it was the contact with *sin*,—and death, the wages of *sin*,—which all through His trial pressed heavily on His soul.

47—56.] Betrayal and apprehension of Jesus. Mark xiv. 43—52. Luke xxii. 47—53. John xviii. 2—11. Mark's account has evidently been derived from the same source originally as Matthew's, but both had gained some important additions before they were finally committed to writing. Luke's is, as before, an abridged narrative, but abounding with new circumstances not related by the others. John's account is at first sight very dissimilar from either: see text above cited, and notes there. It may suffice now to say, that all which John, vv. 4—9, relates, must have happened *on the first approach of the band*—and is connected with our ἐγείρεσθε ἄγωμεν. Some particulars also must have happened, which are omitted by *all*: viz. the rejoining of the eight Apostles (*not* alluded to in Luke ver. 46, as Greswell supposes), and the preparing *them* for what was about to take place. On the other hand, John gives a hint that something had been passing *in* the garden, by his word ἐξῆλθεν, ver. 4. The two first Evangelists were evidently unaware of any such matter as that related by John, for they (Matt. ver. 49: Mark ver. 45) introduce *the Kiss* by an εὐθέως. **47.**] Judas is specified as εἷς τῶν δώδεκα, probably because the appellation, as connected with this part of his history, had become the usual one—thus we have in Luke ὁ λεγόμενος Ἰούδ. εἷς τῶν δώδεκα—fuller still. To the *reader*, this specification is not without meaning, though that meaning may not have been intended. **ὄχλος πολύς**] consisting of (1) a detachment of the Roman cohort which was quartered in the tower of Antonia during the feast in case of an uproar, called ἡ σπεῖρα, John vv. 3, 12. (2) The ὑπηρέται of the council, the same as the στρατηγοὶ τοῦ ἱεροῦ, Luke ver. 52. (3) Servants and others deputed from the high-priest to assist, see our ver. 51. (4) Possibly, if the words are to be taken exactly (Luke ver. 52), some of the chief priests and elders themselves, forward in zeal and enmity. There is nothing improbable in this (as Meyer, Schleiermacher, &c. maintain), seeing that we have these persons mixing among the multitude and stirring them up to demand the crucifixion of Jesus afterwards. **ξύλων**] not *clubs*—but **staves**,—or any tumultuary weapons. The intention of the chief priests evidently was to produce an impression to the effect that a seditious plot was to be crushed, and resistance might be expected. John mentions also *lanterns* and *torches*—to search perhaps in the dark parts of the garden, most of which would by this time be in the shade. **48.**] The

[y] παραδιδοὺς αὐτὸν ἔδωκεν αὐτοῖς [d] σημεῖον λέγων Ὃν
ἐὰν [e] φιλήσω αὐτός ἐστιν, [f] κρατήσατε αὐτόν. 49 καὶ
εὐθέως προςελθὼν τῷ Ἰησοῦ εἶπεν [g] Χαῖρε [h] ῥαββί, καὶ
[i] κατεφίλησεν αὐτόν. 50 ὁ δὲ Ἰησοῦς εἶπεν αὐτῷ
[k] Ἑταῖρε, ἐφ᾽ [l] ὃ [m] πάρει. . . Τότε προςελθόντες [n] ἐπέβαλον τὰς χεῖρας ἐπὶ τὸν Ἰησοῦν καὶ [f] ἐκράτησαν
αὐτόν. 51 καὶ ἰδοὺ [o] εἷς τῶν μετὰ Ἰησοῦ [p] ἐκτείνας

d τὸ σημεῖον τοῦ πυρός, Thucyd. iv. 111. see ch. xii. 38.
e = || Mk. Luke xxii. 47 only. Gen. xxvii. 26, 27. (-λημα, Luke vii. 45.)
f ch. xxi. 46 reff.
g ch. xxvii. 29 || Mk. J. xxviii. 9. Luke i. 28. see Acts xv. 23 al.
h ch. xxiii. 7, 8 reff.
i || Mk. Luke vii. 38, 45. xv. 20. Acts xx. 37 only. Gen. xxxi. 55. Sir. xxix. 5.
k ch. xi. 17 reff.
l acc., Mark xv. 24. Luke xxiii. 28. 1 Cor. vii. 36. James v. 14.
m John xi. 28. Acts x. 21 al. Num. xxii. 20.
n || Mk. Luke xx. 19. xxi. 12. John vii. 30 (44 v. r.). Gen. xxii. 12.
o constr., ver. 47 ||. Luke v. 17. viii. 22 al.
p ch. viii. 3 reff. Gen. xxii. 10.

48. rec αν (*from || Mark, where but few read* εαν), with BCDLU (S, e sil) $Orig_1$ [Chr]: txt Aℵ rel $Orig_1$ Eus [Chr-γ].
49. aft ειπεν ins αυτω C copt æth Eus.
50. om ιησ. ℵ ev-z: ειπεν δε αυτω ο ιησ. D, simly latt æth Lucif. εφ᾽ ο παρει bef εταιρε D lat-*a c f* Syr Lucif. rec ἐφ᾽ ᾧ, with UΓ 1. 33 Eus Chr: txt ABCDℵ rel Epiph.
51. for μετα ιησ., μετ᾽ αυτου B.

common rendering of **ἔδωκεν** as a plusq. perf. is unnecessary and unwarranted: the aorist is simply *historical*,—**gave them a sign**;—*when* is not stated. On Mark's addition, καὶ ἀπαγάγετε ἀσφαλῶς, see notes there. **49. εὐθέως**] see above on ver. 47. The *purpose* of the kiss, supposing it to have taken place *after* John vv. 4—8, (and it is surely out of the question to suppose it to have taken place before, contrary to the plain meaning of John ver. 4,) has been doubted. Yet I think on a review of what had happened, it is very intelligible—not perhaps as some have supposed, to shew that Jesus could be approached with safety—but at all events as the *sign agreed on* with the Roman soldiers, who probably did not personally know Him, and who besides would have had their orders from the city, to take Him whom Judas should kiss. Thus the kiss would be necessary in the course of their military duty, as their authorization, —notwithstanding the previous declaration by Jesus of Himself. **κατεφ.** is hardly as in my earlier editions, another word for ἐφίλ. It may well have its common and proper meaning, 'Kissed him eagerly,' with ostentation, as a studied and prearranged sign. See Ellicott, Lectures on the Life of our Lord, p. 331 note: and comp. Xenophon, Mem. ii. 6. 33, cited by Meyer, ὡς τοὺς καλοὺς φιλήσοντός μου, τοὺς δ᾽ ἀγαθοὺς καταφιλήσαντος.

50.] In Luke we have Ἰούδα, φιλήματι τὸν υἱὸν τ. ἀνθ. παραδίδως,—which sense is involved in the text also: that variation shewing perhaps that one of the accounts is not from an eye-witness.

ἑταῖρε] see ch. xxii. 12 and note. ὁ ἑταῖρος οὐ πάντως φίλος. καὶ ἑταῖροι, οἱ ἐν συνηθείᾳ καὶ ἐν συνεργίᾳ πολὺν χρόνον γεγονότες. Ammonius. **ἐφ᾽ ὃ πάρει** can hardly be a question. No such use of the simple relative ὅς has ever been adduced: "pronomen ὅς pro interrogativo τίς usurpari, falsa est Hoogeveeni opinio, ad Viger. v. 14, alienissimo Demosthenis loco (p. 779) abutentis." Lobeck on Phryn. p. 57 note. It therefore must be either an exclamation, as Fritzsche, "ad qualem rem perpetrandam ades!" which would be equally alien from the usage of ὅς, exclamations of this sort in Greek being expressed in an interrogative form:—or an aposiopesis, as Euthym., δι᾽ ὃ παραγέγονας, ἤγουν τὸ κατὰ σκοπὸν πράττε, τοῦ προσχήματος ἀφιέμενος. And to this I should incline. "Friend, there needs not this shew of attachment: I know thine errand,—hoc age." But the command itself is suppressed. See Meyer's note, who also takes this view. On any understanding of the words, it is an appeal to the conscience and heart of Judas, in which sense (see above) it agrees with the words spoken in Luke:—see note there. The fact that at this period our Lord was laid hold of and secured (by hand—not yet *bound*) by the band, is important, as interpreting Luke's account further on. **51.**] The **εἷς** (or εἷς τις of Luke) was *Peter*;—John ver. 10. Why he was not mentioned, is idle to enquire: one supposition only must be avoided—that there is any *purpose* in the omission. It is absurd to suppose that the mention of his name in a book

q = here (Luke xxii. 41. Acts xx. 30. xxi. 1) only ‡. (Josh. viii. 6 al.) see 1 Kings xvii. 51 (29) A. Ezek. xxvi. 15. r ver. 31 reff. Exod. xxi. 12. s = ‖ Mk. L. 1 Kings xvii. 51. v. 4. t ‖ L. (Mk. J. v. r.) only. Deut. xv. 17. 1 Kings ix. 15. 25 b. 2 Chron. v. 7. 19, 32 al. 1 Kings xxii. 4. xxiii. 13, 21. see Jon. iv. 11.

τὴν [p] χεῖρα [q] ἀπέσπασεν τὴν μάχαιραν αὐτοῦ καὶ ABCDE
[r] πατάξας τὸν δοῦλον τοῦ ἀρχιερέως [s] ἀφεῖλεν αὐτοῦ FGHKL
τὸ [t] ὠτίον. 52 τότε λέγει αὐτῷ ὁ Ἰησοῦς [u] Ἀπόστρεψον MSUVΓ
τὴν μάχαιράν σου εἰς τὸν [v] τόπον αὐτῆς· πάντες γὰρ οἱ ΔΠℵ 1.
λαβόντες μάχαιραν [w] ἐν μαχαίρῃ ἀπολοῦνται. 53 ἢ δο- 33. 69
κεῖς ὅτι οὐ δύναμαι ἄρτι [x] παρακαλέσαι τὸν πατέρα μου,
καὶ [y] παραστήσει μοι [z] πλείω δώδεκα [a] λεγεῶνας ἀγγέλων ;

u = here (ch. xxvii. 3 v. r.) only. (ch. v. 42 al.) Exod. xxiii. 4. v = Acts i. 25 b. w Heb. xi. 37. Rev. vi. 8 al. 4 Kings xix. 37. x ch. viii. 5. xviii. 19, 32 al. y Acts xxiii. 24, 33. 2 Cor. iv. 14 al. 2 Macc. vi. 35. z Acts xxiii. 13, 21. a Mark v. 9 ‖ L., 15 only †.

επαταξεν and ins *και* bef *αφειλεν* D lat-*a b c* &c syrr Lucif.

52. rec *σου* bef *την μαχαιραν*, with AC rel sah : om *σου* (*see* ‖ *John*) KUΠ 33 Syr copt Chr : txt BDLℵ 1. 69 latt Orig Bas Cyr. rec *μαχαιρα* (for -*ρη*), with B²D rel $Orig_1$: txt AB¹CLℵ 33. for *απολουνται*, *αποθανουνται* FHKMSUVΓΔ 69 syrr æth Orig-ms Bas [Chr-com] Euthym Thl [Aug].

53. for *δοκεις*, *δοκει σοι* C¹(appy) 1 Scr's p syr-mg Orig. [*δυνομαι* B¹.] *αρτι* aft *παραστ. μοι* BL[ℵ] 33 vulg lat-ff_1 g_1 Syr coptt arm Cyr Jer.—aft *μοι* ins *ωδε* ℵ¹(ℵ³ᵃ disapproving) copt. rec (for *πλειω*) *πλειους*, with ACℵ³ᵃ rel Orig Bas Chr : txt BDℵ¹. rec ins *η* bef *δωδεκα* (*for perspicuity*), with AC rel Orig Bas [Chr] : om BDLℵ. *λεγεωνων αγγελων* (*gramml corrn after πλει.* : *in AC carelessly left in after the insn of η*) ACL(ℵ¹ ?) 33 (Tischdf inverts the readings of ACL and KΔ, but appy in error) : *λεγεωνων αγγελους* (*misunderstanding*) KΔΠ¹ ℵ-corr¹ : txt BDℵ³ᵃ rel [Orig Bas Chr]. (*λεγειωνης* D¹, *λεγειονας* D⁴ : *λεγι-* B¹Lℵ¹[-*γαι-* ℵ³ᵃ] : -*ονων* A : *duodecim milia legiones* lat-*b c f* ff_2 g_1 *h* Hil Leo.)

current only among Christians, many years after the fact, could lead to his apprehension, which did not take place *at the time*, although he was recognized as the striker in the palace of the High-priest, John ver. 26. The real reason of the non-apprehension was, that the servant was *healed* by the Lord. This is the first opposition to 'Thy will be done.' Luke expresses it, that they *saw what would happen*—and asked, 'Lord, shall we smite with the sword?' Then, while the other (for there were but two swords in the company) was waiting for the reply, the rash Peter, in the very spirit of ch. xvi. 22, smote with the sword—the weapon of the flesh:—an outbreak of the natural man no less noticeable than that more-noticed one which followed before morning. All four Evangelists agree in this account. Luke and John are most exact—the latter giving the name of the slave,—Malchus. The aim was a deadly one, and Peter narrowly escaped being one *ὅστις ἐν τῇ στάσει φόνον πεποιήκει.* From Luke, ver. 51, we learn that our Lord said *ἐᾶτε ἕως τούτου* (on the meaning of which see note there), touched the ear and healed it. **ὠτίον**] "Plerisque corporis partibus vulgaris dialectus formam deminutivam tribuit, *τὰ ῥινία*, Aristot. Physiogn. iii. 57, *τὸ ὀμμάτιον* iii. 46, *στηθίδιον*, *χελύνιον*, *σαρκίον* (corpus)." Lobeck on Phryn. p. 211, note. **52. τὴν μάχ. σου**] '*tuum gladium* : alienissimum a mea causa.' Bengel. **τὸν τόπον αὐτῆς** = *τὴν θήκην* John. The sheath is *the place for the Christian's sword*—'gladius extra vaginam non est in loco suo, nisi ubi subservit iræ divinæ,' Bengel : see note on Luke xxii. 36. Our Lord does not say '*Cast away* thy sword;' only in His willing self-sacrifice, and in that kingdom which is to be evolved from his work of redemption, is the sword altogether out of place. **πάντες γὰρ κ.τ.λ.**] Peculiar to Matthew. There is no allusion, as Grotius and some of the ancients thought, to the Jews perishing by the Roman sword ('crudeles istos et sanguinarios, etiam te quiescente, gravissimas Deo daturos pœnas suo sanguine,' Grot., Euthym.) : for the very persons who were now taking Him *were Romans*. The saying is *general*—and the stress is on **λαβόντες**—it was this that Peter was doing—'taking up the sword'—of his own will; taking that vengeance which belongs to God, into his own hand. **ἐν μαχαίρῃ ἀπολ.** is a command; not merely a future, but an *imperative* future; a repetition by the Lord in this solemn moment of Gen. ix. 6. This should be thought of by those well-meaning but shallow persons, who seek to abolish the punishment of death in Chris-

54 πῶς οὖν [b] πληρωθῶσιν αἱ [c] γραφαὶ ὅτι οὕτως [d] δεῖ
γενέσθαι; 55 ἐν ἐκείνῃ τῇ ὥρᾳ εἶπεν ὁ Ἰησοῦς τοῖς ὄχλοις
Ὡς ἐπὶ [e] λῃστὴν ἐξήλθατε [f] μετὰ [f] μαχαιρῶν καὶ [f] ξύλων
[g] συλλαβεῖν με. [h] καθ' ἡμέραν ἐν τῷ ἱερῷ [i] ἐκαθεζόμην
διδάσκων καὶ οὐκ [j] ἐκρατήσατέ με. 56 τοῦτο δὲ ὅλον
γέγονεν ἵνα [b] πληρωθῶσιν αἱ [c] γραφαὶ τῶν προφητῶν.
τότε οἱ μαθηταὶ πάντες [k] ἀφέντες αὐτὸν ἔφυγον. 57 οἱ

b ch. i. 22. Luke iv. 21 al. fr. 3 Kings ii. 27.
c plur., John v. 39 reff.
d = ch. xxiv. 6 reff.
e ch. xxi. 13 reff.
f ver. 47.
g = ||. Acts i. 16. xii. 3 al. Josh. viii. 23. see Luke v. 9.
h || Mk. L. Luke ix. 23. xvi. 19. Acts ii. 46, 47 al. Num. iv. 16.
i Luke ii. 46. John iv. 6. xi. 20. xx. 12. Acts vi. 15. xx. 9 only. Lev. xii. 5. Job xxxix. 27. Ezek. xxvi. 16 only.
j vv. 48, 50.
k = ver. 44.

54. πληρωθησονται D. εδει C 1 Orig-ed.

55. ο ιησ. bef ειπεν D lat-*a*. rec εξηλθετε, with HKMSUVΓΠ Petr Eus [Cyr_2-p]: ηλθατε D: txt ABCℵ rel. rec aft καθ ημεραν ins προς υμας (*from* || *Mark*), with CD rel latt syrr arm Eus Orig-int: aft εκαθεζ. A æth: om BLℵ 33 coptt Chr Cyr_2 [Orig-int-com]. rec εν τω ιερω aft διδασκων, with A rel vulg lat-*f* ff_1 g_1 syr: aft εκαθ. C D(εκαθημην) K lat-*a b c* ff_2 g_2 *h* (æth) arm-mss Eus Thl Orig-int: txt BLℵ (1.) 33 Syr (coptt) arm [Cyr-p] $Orig\text{-}int_1$.—om διδασκ. 1.

56. aft μαθηται ins αυτου B gat(with mm) lat-*a h n* sah æth Chr. [B¹ repeats εφυγον to κρατησαντες next ver.]

tian states. John adds the words τὸ ποτήριον ὃ δέδωκέν μοι ὁ πατήρ, οὐ μὴ πίω αὐτό; on which see notes there.

53, 54 are peculiar to Matthew. **53.**] The Majesty of our Lord, and His Patience are both shewn here. **πλείω δώδ.** is a strictly Attic idiom, the neuter πλεῖον or πλείω, and the unchanged construction omitting the ἤ. So Plato, Legg. vi. p. 759, ἔτη μὴ ἔλαττον ἑξήκοντα γεγονώς: Paus. x. 57. 295, οἱ ἄνθρωποι πλέον ἡμίσεις ἁλιεῖς εἰσι. See the matter discussed, and more examples given, in Phryn. Lobeck, p. 410. **δώδεκα**—not perhaps so much from the number of the Apostles, who were now οἱ ἕνδεκα, but from that of the *then* company, viz. the Lord and the eleven. **λεγεῶνας**—because they were Roman soldiers who were taking Him. The complement of the legion was about 6000 men. The power, implied in **δοκεῖς ὅτι οὐ δύναμαι,** shews the entire and continued free self-resignation of the Lord throughout—and carries on the same truth as He expressed John x. 18. **54. οὖν**] not, '*but;*'—**How then**—considering that this is so, that I voluntarily abstain from invoking such heavenly aid,—**shall the Scriptures be fulfilled, that thus it must be,** if thou in thy rashness usest the help of fleshly weapons? **55.**] Mark begins this with an ἀποκριθείς—it was an answer to their *actions,* not to their words. Luke, here minutely accurate, informs us that it was *to the chief priests and* στρατηγοὺς τοῦ ἱεροῦ *and elders,* that our Lord said this. It is strange that the exact agreement of this classification with μεθ' ὑμῶν ἐν τῷ ἱερῷ did not prevent Schleiermacher from casting a doubt on the truth of the circumstance (English Translation, p. 302).

In his submission to be reckoned among the transgressors, our Lord yet protests against any suspicion that He could *act* as such. There seems to be no necessity for putting an interrogation after **συλλαβεῖν με.** **καθ' ἡμέραν**—during the week past, and perhaps at other similar times. **ἐκαθεζόμην** (Matt. only) to indicate complete quiet and freedom from attack. **ἐκαθεζόμην διδάσκων** is the greatest possible contrast to λῃστής. **56.**] It is doubted whether these words are a continuation of our Lord's speech, or a remark inserted by Matthew. The use of τοῦτο δὲ ὅλον γέγονεν in this Gospel would lead us to the latter conclusion: but when we reflect that thus our Lord's speech would lose all its completeness, and that Mark gives in different words the speech going on to this same purport, we must I think decide for the other view. Besides, if the remark were Matthew's, we should expect some particular citation, as is elsewhere his practice: see ch. i. 22; xxi. 4. Mark gives it elliptically, ἀλλ' ἵνα πληρωθῶσιν αἱ γραφαί. The Passion and Death of Christ were especially ἡ τῶν γραφῶν πλήρωσις. In this they all found their central point. Compare his dying word on the Cross,—τετέλεσται,—with this his assertion. On the addition in Luke, see note there. There is an admirable sermon of Schleiermacher (vol. ii. of the Berlin ed. of 1843, p. 104) on vv. 55, 56. **τότε οἱ μαθ.**] Some of them did

δὲ [j] κρατήσαντες τὸν Ἰησοῦν ἀπήγαγον πρὸς Καϊάφαν
τὸν ἀρχιερέα, ὅπου οἱ γραμματεῖς καὶ οἱ πρεσβύτεροι
[l] συνήχθησαν. 58 ὁ δὲ Πέτρος ἠκολούθει αὐτῷ [m] ἀπὸ
[mn] μακρόθεν [o] ἕως τῆς [p] αὐλῆς τοῦ ἀρχιερέως, καὶ εἰςελθὼν ἔσω ἐκάθητο μετὰ τῶν ὑπηρετῶν ἰδεῖν τὸ τέλος.
59 οἱ δὲ ἀρχιερεῖς καὶ τὸ [q] συνέδριον ὅλον ἐζήτουν [r] ψευδομαρτυρίαν κατὰ τοῦ Ἰησοῦ, ὅπως αὐτὸν [s] * θανατώσουσιν, 60 καὶ οὐχ [t] εὗρον καὶ πολλῶν προςελθόντων

l = ch. xiii. 2 reff. Ps. ii. 2. m = ‖ Mk. ch. xxvii. 55 ‖. Mark v. 6. (viii. 3.) xi. 13. Luke xvi. 23. Rev. xviii. 10, 15, 17 only. Ps. cxxxvii. 6. n as above (m). Luke xviii. 13. xxii. 54 only. Gen. xxi. 16. Prov. xxv. 25. o ch. xi. 23 reff. 1 Macc. xiv. 10 b. p ver. 3. (-ρεῖν, ch. xix. 18.) q ch. v. 22. John xi. 47 al. Prov. xxii. 10. r ch. xv. 19 only +. s ch. x. 21. Luke xxi. 16. Rom. viii. 26, from Ps. xliii. 22. 2 Cor. vi. 9 al. t ch. xii. 43.

N τεροι συνηχθησαν...

Θ_f xxvi. 59 (appy) ...

ABCDE FGHKL MNSUV ΓΔΘ_fΠℵ 1. 33. 69

57. απηγον [for -γαγον] C. **58.** om απο CFLΔΠ[1]ℵ 1. 33 arm.

59. rec aft αρχιερεις (ο δ. αρχιερευς coptt $Orig_1$: *princeps vero* lat-*a*) ins και οι πρεσβυτεροι (*from* ‖ *Luke*), with ACNΘ_f rel lat-*f* syrr æth Orig-int: om BDLℵ 69 latt coptt arm $Orig_2$ Eus Cyr Aug. ολον bef το συνεδριον (*from* ‖ *Mark*) N 243-53 latt Orig-int. θανατωσ. bef αυτον (*from* ‖ *Mark*) A rel arm $Orig_2$ Eus: txt BC D-gr LN[Θ_f] 1. 33. 69 latt [Cyr_1] Orig-int. *rec θανατώσωσι (*gramml corrn*), with B (C^1 perhaps) KMSUVΓΠ[2]ℵ: txt AC[1 or 2]N rel Orig.

60. om 2nd και (*see next page*) BC[1]LN[1]ℵ 1 vulg lat-*a* *b* ff_1 $g_{1.2}$ *l* *n* coptt arm $Orig_2$ Cyr: ins AC[2]Θ_f rel lat-*f* ff_2 *h* syrr æth Orig-int: το εξης και D.—rec πολλ. ψευδ. προσελθ., with CN rel latt arm (ελθοντων K 69): προσελθ. πολλ. ψευδ. 1 coptt: πολλοι προσηλθον ψευδομαρτυρες D: txt ABLΘ_fℵ 33 $Orig_2$ [Cyr_1].—rec ins ουχ ευρον bef

not flee far. Peter and John went after Him to the palace of the High-priest: John, ver. 15. On the additional circumstance in Mark, ver. 51, see note there. Chrys.'s remark is worth noting: ὅτε μὲν γὰρ κατεσχέθη, ἔμενον· ὅτε δὲ ἐφθέγξατο ταῦτα πρὸς τοὺς ὄχλους, ἔφυγον· εἶδον γὰρ λοιπόν, ὅτι οὐκ ἔτι διαφυγεῖν ἔνι, ἑκόντος ἑαυτὸν παραδόντος αὐτοῖς καὶ λέγοντος κατὰ τὰς γραφὰς τοῦτο γίνεσθαι.

57—68.] Hearing before Caiaphas. Mark xiv. 53—65. (Luke xxii. 54, 63—65.) John xviii. 24. Previous to this took place a hearing *before* Annas, the *real* High-priest (see note on Luke iii. 2), to whom the Jews took Jesus first;—who enquired of Him about his disciples and his teaching (John, vv. 19—23), and then (ver. 24) sent Him bound to Caiaphas. Only John, *who followed*, relates this first hearing. See notes on John, vv. 12—24, where this view is maintained. It may be sufficient here just to indicate the essential differences between *that* hearing and *this*. On that occasion no witnesses were required, for it was merely a private unofficial audience. Then the High-priest questioned and our Lord replied: whereas now, under false witness and reproach, He (as before Herod) is silent.

57. Καϊάφαν τὸν ἀρχ.] He was ἀρχιερεὺς τοῦ ἐνιαυτοῦ ἐκείνου, Annas having been deposed, and since then the High-priests having been frequently changed by the Roman governors. **ὅπου οἱ γρ.**] Probably they had assembled by a preconcerted design, expecting their prisoner. This was *a* meeting of the Sanhedrim, but not the regular assembly, which condemned him and handed Him over to Pilate. That took place *in the morning*, Luke xxii. 66—71 (where see note).

58.] "**ἀπὸ μακρόθεν** is a well-known pleonasm. μακρόθεν itself is a late Greek word. See Lob. on Phryn. p. 93." Meyer.

We have not here the more complete detail of John xviii. 15—19. The **αὐλή** is one and the same great building, in which both Annas and Caiaphas lived. This is evident from a comparison of the narratives of Peter's denial: see below. The circumstance of a fire being lighted and the servants sitting round it, mentioned by the other three Evangelists, is here omitted. **59. ψευδομ.**] ὡς μὲν ἐκείνοις ἐδόκει, μαρτυρίαν, ὡς δὲ τῇ ἀληθείᾳ, ψευδομαρτυρίαν. Euthym. But is this quite implied? Is it not the intention of the Evangelist to represent that they *sought false witness*, not that they would not take true if they could get it, but that *they knew it was not to be had?*

This hearing is altogether omitted in Luke, and only the indignities following related, vv. 63—65. **60.**] **οὐχ εὗρον**, i. e. sufficient for the purpose, or perhaps, consistent with itself. See note

[u] ψευδομαρτύρων. [v] ὕστερον δὲ προςελθόντες δύο 61 εἶπον
Οὗτος ἔφη Δύναμαι [w] καταλῦσαι τὸν ναὸν τοῦ θεοῦ καὶ
[x] διὰ τριῶν ἡμερῶν οἰκοδομῆσαι. 62 καὶ ἀναστὰς ὁ ἀρχιερεὺς εἶπεν αὐτῷ Οὐδὲν ἀποκρίνῃ [y] τί οὗτοί σου [z] κατα-
Z μαρτυρουσιν... μαρτυροῦσιν ; 63 ὁ δὲ Ἰησοῦς [a] ἐσιώπα. καὶ [b] ἀποκριθεὶς
ὁ ἀρχιερεὺς εἶπεν αὐτῷ [c] Ἐξορκίζω σε [d] κατὰ τοῦ [e] θεοῦ
τοῦ [e] ζῶντος ἵνα ἡμῖν εἴπῃς [f] εἰ σὺ εἶ ὁ χριστὸς ὁ υἱὸς
τοῦ θεοῦ. 64 λέγει αὐτῷ ὁ Ἰησοῦς [g] Σὺ εἶπας. [h] πλὴν

u 1 Cor. xv. 15 only †. see above (r) and Prov. xix. 5, 9.
v ch. iv. 2 reff.
w John ii. 19. ch. xxiv. 2. xxvii. 40 al. Ezra v. 12.
x || Mk. Mark ii. 1. Acts xxiv. 17. Deut. xv. 1. see ch. xxvii. 40.
y || Mk. see Acts xi. 17, and Mark xv. 24.
z || Mk. ch. xxvii. 13 (|| Mk. v. r.) only. Job xv. 6.
a Matt., ch. xx. 31 (reff.) only.
b = ch. xi. 25 reff.
c here only. Gen. xxiv. 3. Judg. xvii. 2 A only. (ὁρκ., Mark v. 7 reff.)
d 2 Chron. xxxvi. 13. Judith i. 12.
e ch. xvi. 16 reff.
f ch. xii. 10 reff.
g ver. 25 only.
h ver. 39 al. Sir, xlv. 22.

υστερον, with AC^{2} N^{2}(but om *και ουχ ευρον* above) Θ$_{f}$ rel syr Orig-int; *και ουχ ευρον το εξης et non invenerunt rei sequentia* D, *quicquam in eo* lat-*ff*$_{2}$, *in eum quicquam* lat-*h*, *exitum rei* lat-*a*, *culpam* lat-*f*: om BC^{1}LNא 1 vulg lat-*b ff*$_{1}$ *g*$_{1\cdot 2}$ *l* Syr syr-jer coptt arm Orig Cyr. (*The account, I believe, with Mey and Rinck, to be this: txt was the original, and the 2nd* και *was not understood: thence the 2nd* ουχ ευρον *was supplied. The readg of D &c is very curious. A note was made in the marg, that* το εξης, i. e. "the order of the words," *was*, πολ. προςηλθ. ψ. κ. ουχ ευρον. *Hence* το εξης *was taken into the text, repeated with the second* ουχ ευρον, *and interpreted as above in the old latin vss.*) for *προσελθοντες*, *ηλθον* D latt. rec aft *δυο* ins *ψευδομαρτυρες*, with A^{2}CDΘ$_{f}$ rel latt syr arm Orig$_{1}$(and int$_{1}$); *τινες ψ.* N Scr's j: *μαρτυρες* A^{1}(appy): om BLא 1 Syr syr-jer coptt æth Orig$_{1}$.

61. ins *και* bef *ειπον* D latt Syr æth. *ειπαν* א. for *ουτ. εφ.*, *τουτον ηκουσαμεν λεγοντα* (*see* || *Mark*) D(*τουτου ηκ. λεγοντος* D^{4}) lat-*h*: *ηκ. τ. λ.* lat-*b c f ff*$_{2}$. rec at end adds *αυτον* (*from John* ii. 19), with ADN rel vulg lat-*a f ff*$_{1\cdot 2}$ *g*$_{1\cdot 2}$ syrr Orig-int; bef *οικ.*, CLΘ$_{f}$א 33 lat-*b h* Orig$_{1}$: om B 1. 69 æth arm Orig$_{2}$.

62. om *αυτω* to *αυτω* next ver (*homœotel*) א^{1}(ins א-corr$^{1 \text{ or } 2}$(but erased)^{3}) ev-x$_{1}$. *σοι* A^{1} Scr's d ev-z$_{1}$.

63. om *αποκριθεις* (*to suit the former clause*) BGLZא^{3} 1. 33. 69 vulg lat-*ff*$_{1}$ *g*$_{1\cdot 2}$ *l* copt æth Orig [Cyr$_{1}$]: ins AC(D)NΘ$_{f}$ rel lat-*a b c f ff*$_{2}$ *h* syrr sah arm.—for *και αποκρ.*, *αποκρ. ουν* D. for *εξορκ.*, *ορκιζω* DL 69 Cyr$_{1}$[txt$_{1}$]. om 2nd *ει* Θ$_{f}$ 126(Tischdf) [Orig$_{1}$]. at end ins *του ζωντος* C^{1}NΔ[Θ$_{f}$] Scr's j ev-y$_{1}$ lat-*ff*$_{2}$ syr coptt Chr.

on ἴσαι, Mark ver. 56. **61.**] See ch. xxvii. 40: the *false witness* consisted in *giving that sense to His words*, which it appears by ch. xxvii. 63 they *knew they did not bear*. There is perhaps a trace, in the *different reports* of Matt. and Mark, of the *discrepancy between the witnesses*. There is considerable difference between τὸν ναὸν τοῦ θ. . . . οἰκοδομῆσαι, and τὸν ν. τοῦτον τὸν χειροποίητον . . . . ἄλλον ἀχειροποίητον. The instance likewise of his zeal *for the honour of the temple* which had so lately occurred, might tend to perplex the evidence produced to the contrary. **62.**] **Dost thou not answer what it is which these testify against thee?** i. e. wilt Thou give no explanation of the words alleged to have been used by Thee? Our Lord was silent; for in answering He must have opened to them the meaning of these his words, which was not the work of this His hour, nor fitting for that audience.
It is not easy to say whether this sentence ought to be taken as one question or two. Meyer, in his former editions, maintained the latter, on the ground that ἀποκρίνῃ would require πρός after it. But he has now discovered in his fourth edition that ἀποκρίνεσθαι may be constructed with an accusative simply, and that τί may be equivalent to ὅτι. So that there is no serious objection remaining to the usual way of construction. **63.**] See Levit. v. 1. **ἐξορκίζω σε**, 'I put thee under an oath,' the form of which follows. The junction of **ὁ υἱὸς τ. θ.** with **χριστός** must not be pressed beyond the meaning which Caiaphas probably assigned to it—viz. the title given to the Messiah from the purport of the prophecies respecting Him. It is however a very different thing when our Lord by his answer *affirms this*, and invests the words with their fullest meaning and dignity. **64.**] By **σὺ εἶπας**, more may perhaps be implied than by Mark's ἐγώ εἰμι: *that* is a simple assertion: *this* may refer to the convictions

i ch. xxiii. 39 reff. j ch. xxii. 44 ||. Acts ii. 34 and Heb. i. 13, from Ps. cix. 1. k = || only. so δόξης, 2 Pet. i. 17. l ch. xxiv. 30 reff. m || Mk. Luke v. 6. viii. 29. Acts xiv. 14 only. Lev. xxi. 10. Josh. vii. 6. n abs., ch. ix. 3. John x. 36. 4 Kings xix. 6. o ch. vi. 8 reff. Wisd. xiii. 16. p = ch. xii. 31. Ezek. xxxv. 12.

λέγω ὑμῖν, [i] ἀπ' ἄρτι ὄψεσθε τὸν υἱὸν τοῦ ἀνθρώπου
[j] καθήμενον ἐκ δεξιῶν τῆς [k] δυνάμεως καὶ [l] ἐρχόμενον
ἐπὶ τῶν [l] νεφελῶν τοῦ οὐρανοῦ. 65 τότε ὁ ἀρχιερεὺς ...αρχιε- ρευς
[m] διέρρηξεν τὰ ἱμάτια αὐτοῦ λέγων [n] Ἐβλασφήμησεν· τί διερ. N.
ἔτι [o] χρείαν [o] ἔχομεν μαρτύρων; ἴδε νῦν ἠκούσατε τὴν ABCDE FGHKL MSUVZ
[p] βλασφημίαν. 66 τί ὑμῖν δοκεῖ; οἱ δὲ ἀποκριθέντες ΓΔΘ$_f$Πℵ 1. 33. 69
εἶπον [q] Ἔνοχος θανάτου ἐστίν. 67 τότε [r] ἐνέπτυσαν εἰς
τὸ πρόσωπον αὐτοῦ, καὶ [s] ἐκολάφισαν αὐτόν, οἱ δὲ [t] ἐράπισαν 68 λέγοντες [u] Προφήτευσον ἡμῖν χριστέ, τίς ἐστιν ὁ
[v] παίσας σε; 69 Ὁ δὲ Πέτρος ἐκάθητο ἔξω ἐν τῇ [w] αὐλῇ, X ο δε πετρος...
καὶ προσῆλθεν αὐτῷ [x] μία [y] παιδίσκη λέγουσα Καὶ σὺ

q w. gen., || Mk. Mark iii. 29. 1 Cor. xi. 27. Heb. ii. 15. James ii. 10 (ch. v. 21, 22, 3ce) only. Gen. xxvi. 11 A. 2 Macc. xiii. 6. r || Mk. ch. xxvii. 30 || Mk. Mark x. 34 || L. Num. xii. 14. Deut. xxv. 9 only. (-υσμα, Isa. l. 6.) s || Mk. 1 Pet. ii. 20. 1 Cor. iv. 11. 2 Cor. xii. 7 only †. t ch. v. 39 only. Hos. xi. 4. Esdr. iv. 30 only. (-ισμα, John xviii. 22.) u = || Mk. L. only ‡. see 4 Kings vi. 12. v || L. Mark xiv. 47 || J. Rev. ix. 5 only. Num. xxii. 28. w ver. 3 reff. x ch. viii. 19. Mark xii. 42. [John vi. 9.] Gen. xxii. 13. Dan. viii. 3. y ||. Luke xii. 45 al. Gen. xx. 17 al.

64. aft *υμιν* ins *οτι* D Syr.

65. om *ὁ* ℵ[1](ins ℵ[2]) Scr's n. for *λεγων*, *και λεγει* ℵ[1](txt ℵ[3a]) Syr. rec aft *λεγων* ins *οτι*, with AC[1] rel: *ιδε* ℵ[1] Syr æth: om BC[2]DLZΘ$_f$ℵ[3a] 33 latt syr arm Orig Chr Cyr. *μαρτυριων* ℵ. rec aft *βλασφημιαν* ins *αυτου* (*as some also in || Mark*), with ACΘ$_f$ rel gat(with mm) lat-*b f* ff_2 g_2 syrr goth æth arm Orig: om BDLZℵ vulg lat-*a c* ff_1 g_1 *h l* coptt Chr.—*της βλασφημιας* Θ$_f$ Chr.

66. for *αποκριθεντες*, *απεκριθησαν παντες και* D gat lat-*a b c h*. *ειπαν* ℵ[1] (txt ℵ[3a]) 33.

67. for *οι δε*, *αλλοι δε* D sah goth. (rec *ερραπ*., with E rel: txt ABCDLZΓΔΘ$_f$ℵ.) add *αυτον* DG 1 lat-*a b c f* ff_1 g_1 syrr [Orig-int$_1$].

69. rec *εξω* bef *εκαθητο*, with AC rel syr goth: aft *αυλη* Chr: [*εκαθητο* aft *αυλη* Δ[1]:] txt BDLZΘ$_f$ℵ 1. 33 latt Syr syr-jer coptt æth arm Orig-int.

and *admissions* of Caiaphas (see John xi. 49). But this is somewhat doubtful. The expression is only used here and in ver. 25: and there does not appear to be any reference in it as said to Judas, to any previous admission of his. **πλήν**] **but**—i. e. '*there shall be a sign of the truth of what I say, over and above this confession of Mine.*' **ἀπ' ἄρτι**] The glorification of Christ is by Himself said to *begin with his betrayal*, see John xiii. 31: **from this time**—from the accomplishment of this trial now proceeding. In what follows, the whole process of the triumph of the Lord Jesus even till its end is contained. The **ὄψεσθε** is to the council, the representatives of the chosen people, so soon to be judged by Him to whom all judgment is committed—the **τῆς δυνάμεως** in contrast to his present weakness—**καθήμενον**—even as they now sat to judge Him; and the **ἐρχ. ἐπὶ τ. ν. τ. οὐρ.** (see Dan. vii. 13) looks onward to the awful time of the end, when every eye shall see Him. **65.**] In Levit. xxi. 10 (see also Levit. x. 6) the High-priest is ordered *not to rend his clothes*; but that appears to apply only to *mourning for the dead*. In 1 Macc. xi. 71, and in Josephus, B. J. ii. 15. 4, we have instances of High-priests rending their clothes. On rending the clothes at hearing blasphemy, see 2 Kings xviii. 37. **66.**] This was not a formal condemnation, but only a previous vote or expression of opinion. *That* took place *in the morning*, see ch. xxvii. 1, and especially Luke xxii. 66—71.

67.] Luke gives these indignities, and in the same place as here, adding, what indeed might have been suspected, that it was not the members of the Sanhedrim, but *the men who held Jesus in custody*, who inflicted them on Him. **κολαφίζω** is *to strike with the fist*; **ῥαπίζω**, generally, *to strike a flat blow with the back of the hand*—but also, and probably here, since another set of persons are described as doing it, *to strike with a staff*.

69—75.] Our Lord is thrice denied by Peter. Mark xiv. 66—72. Luke xxii. 56—62. John xviii. 17, 18, 25—27. This narrative furnishes one of the clearest instances of the *entire independency of the four Gospels of one another*. In it, they all differ, and, supposing the denial to have taken place

[z] ἦσθα μετὰ Ἰησοῦ τοῦ Γαλιλαίου. 70 ὁ δὲ [a] ἠρνήσατο

z ‖ Mk. only. Gen. xl. 13 al.
a = ‖. Luke viii. 45. John i. 20 al. fr. Gen. xviii. 15.

for γαλιλαιου, ναζωραιου C 238-52[1] Syr.

thrice, and *only thrice*, cannot be literally harmonized. The following table may serve to shew what the agreements are, and what the differences:—

	MATTHEW.	MARK.	LUKE.	JOHN.
1st denial.	Sitting in the hall without, is charged by a maid servant with having been with Jesus the Galilæan. 'I know not what thou sayest.'	Warming himself in the hall below,—&c. as Matt. —goes out into the vestibule—the cock crows. 'I know not, neither understand what thou sayest.'	Sitting πρὸς τὸ φῶς is recognized by the maid and charged — replies, 'Woman, I know Him not.'	Is recognized by the porteress on being introduced by the other disciple. 'Art not thou also one of this man's disciples?' He saith, 'I am not.'
2nd denial.	He has gone out into the porch—*another* maid sees him. 'This man also was with Jesus of Naz.' He denies with an oath, 'I do not know the man.'	The same maid (possibly: but see note, p. 284, col. 1, line 34) sees him again, and says, 'This man is of them.' He denies again.	Another (but a *male* servant) says: 'Thou also art of them.' Peter said, 'Man, I am not.'	Is standing and warming himself. They said to him, 'Art not thou also of His disciples?' He denied, and said, 'I am not.'
3rd denial.	After a little while, the standers-by say, 'Surely thou art of them; for thy dialect betrayeth thee.' He began to curse and to swear: 'I know not the man.'	As Matt. 'Surely thou art of them: for thou art also a Galilæan.'	After about an hour, another persisted saying, 'Truly this man was with Him, for he is a Galilæan.' Peter said, 'Man, I know not what thou sayest.'	One of the slaves of the High-priest, his kinsman whose ear Peter cut off, says, 'Did I not see thee in the garden with Him?' Peter then denied again.
	Immediately the cock crew, and Peter remembered, &c.—and going out he wept bitterly.	A second time the cock crew, and Peter remembered, &c. — and ἐπιβαλὼν he wept.	Immediately while he was yet speaking the cock crew, and the Lord turned and looked on Peter, and Peter remembered, &c.—and going out he wept bitterly.	Immediately the cock crew.

On this table I would make the following remarks:—that *generally*,—(1) supposing the four accounts to be *entirely independent of one another*,—we are *not bound to require accordance*, nor would there in all probability be any such accordance, *in the recognitions of Peter by different persons*. These may have been *many* on *each occasion* of denial, and independent narrators may have fixed on different ones among them. (2) *No reader* who is not slavishly bound to the inspiration of the *letter*, *will require that the actual words spoken by Peter should in each case be identically reported.* See the admirable remarks of Aug. cited on ch. viii. 25: and remember, that the *substantive fact of a denial* remains the same, whether οὐκ οἶδα τί λέγεις, οὐκ οἶδα αὐτόν, or οὐκ εἰμί are reported to have been Peter's answer. (3) I do not see that we are obliged to limit the narrative to *three*

b = ch. v. 16. vi. 1 al. fr. Isa. xlv. 1.
c = ‖ Mk. Mark x. 38. Luke ix. 33 al.

[b] ἔμπροσθεν πάντων λέγων Οὐκ [c] οἶδα τί λέγεις. 71 ἐξελ-

...xxvi. 70(appy) Θ_f ABCDE FGHKL MSUVX ZΓΔΠℵ 1. 33. 69

70. ins αυτων bef παντων (*appy an explany addn, as it is omd by so many and weighty* MSS. *Otherwise the omn might seem to be from homœotel*) AC[1] rel goth(appy) Chr: om BC²DEGLZΘ_fℵ latt [syrr copt] sah [Orig-int$_2$].—αυτων for παντ. K [Π] 243-8 Scr's e g w ev-y_1 Thl.   aft λεγεις ins ουδε επισταμαι (*see* ‖ *Mark*) D Δ-gr[ουτε] Θ_f 1. 209 mm lat-*a b n* syr-jer Cypr.

sentences from Peter's mouth, each expressing a denial, *and no more.* On *three occasions* during the night *he was recognized,*—on *three occasions he was a denier* of his Lord: such a statement may well embrace *reiterated expressions of recognition,* and *reiterated* and *importunate denials,* on *each* occasion. And these remarks being taken into account, I premise that all difficulty is removed from the synopsis above given: the only resulting inferences being, (a) *that the narratives are genuine truthful accounts of facts underlying them all:* and (b) *that they are, and must be, absolutely and entirely independent of one another.* For (1) the four accounts of the FIRST denial are remarkably coincident. In *all four,* Peter was in the outer hall, where the fire was made (see on ver. 69): *a maid servant* (Matt., Mark, Luke),—*the maid servant who kept the door* (John) taxed him (in *differing words in each,* the comparison of which is very instructive) with being a disciple of Jesus: in all four he denies, again in differing words. I should be disposed to think this first recognition to have been *but one,* and the variations to be owing to the independence of the reports. (2) In the narratives of the SECOND denial, our first preliminary remark is well exemplified. The same maid (Mark possibly: but not necessarily—perhaps, only the παιδίσκη in the προαύλιον)—another *maid* (Matt.), *another* (*male*) *servant* (Luke), the *standers-by generally* (John), charged him: again, in differing words. It seems he had retreated from the fire as if going to depart altogether (see note, ver. 69), and so attracted the attention both of the group at the fire and of the porteress. It would appear to me that for some reason, John was not so precisely informed of the details of this as of the other denials. The "*going out*" (Matt., Mark) is a superadded detail, of which the "*standing and warming himself*" (John) does not seem to be possessed. (3) On the THIRD occasion, *the standers-by recognize him as a Galilæan* (*simply,* Mark (txt.), Luke: *by his dialect,* Matt., an interesting additional particular),—and *a kinsman of Malchus* crowns the charge by *identifying* him in a way which might have proved most perilous, had not Peter immediately withdrawn. This third time again, his denials are differently reported:—but here, which is most interesting, we have in Matt. and Mark's "*he began to curse and to swear*" a very plain intimation, that he spoke *not one sentence only,* but *a succession of vehement denials.* It will be seen, that the main fallacy which pervaded the note in my first edition, was that of requiring the *recognitions,* and the *recognizers,* in each case, to have been *identical in the four.* Had they been thus identical, in a case of this kind, the four accounts *must have sprung from a common source,* or have been *corrected to one another:* whereas their present varieties and coincidences are most valuable as indications of *truthful independence.* What I wish to impress on the minds of my readers is, that in narratives which have sprung from such truthful independent accounts, they must be prepared sometimes (as e. g. in the details of the day of the Resurrection) for discrepancies which, *at our distance, we cannot satisfactorily arrange:* now and then we may, as in *this* instance, be able to do so with something like verisimilitude:—in some cases, *not at all.* But whether we can thus arrange them or not, being thoroughly persuaded of the holy truthfulness of the Evangelists, and of the divine guidance under which they wrote, our faith is in no way shaken by such discrepancies. We value them rather, as testimonies to independence: and are sure, that if for one moment we could be put in *complete possession of all the details as they happened,* each account would find its justification, and the reasons of all the variations would appear. And this I firmly believe will one day be the case. (See the narrative of Peter's denials ably treated in an article on my former note, in the "Christian Observer" for Feb. 1853.) **69.**] "An oriental house is usually built round a quadrangular interior court; into which there is a passage (sometimes arched) through the front part of the house, closed next the street by a heavy folding gate, with a small wicket for single persons, kept by a porter. In the text, the interior court, often paved

θόντα δὲ αὐτὸν εἰς τὸν [d] πυλῶνα εἶδεν αὐτὸν ἄλλη, καὶ
λέγει αὐτοῖς ἐκεῖ Καὶ οὗτος ἦν μετὰ Ἰησοῦ τοῦ Ναζωραίου. 72 καὶ πάλιν [a] ἠρνήσατο [e] μετὰ [e] ὅρκου [f] ὅτι οὐκ
οἶδα τὸν ἄνθρωπον. 73 μετὰ [g] μικρὸν δὲ προσελθόντες οἱ
ἑστῶτες εἶπον τῷ Πέτρῳ [h] Ἀληθῶς καὶ σὺ [i] ἐξ αὐτῶν εἶ,
καὶ γὰρ ἡ [k] λαλιά σου [l] δῆλόν σε ποιεῖ. 74 τότε ἤρξατο
[m] καταθεματίζειν καὶ ὀμνύειν ὅτι οὐκ οἶδα τὸν ἄνθρωπον.
καὶ εὐθέως [n] ἀλέκτωρ [n] ἐφώνησεν. 75 καὶ [o] ἐμνήσθη ὁ
Πέτρος τοῦ ῥήματος Ἰησοῦ εἰρηκότος ὅτι πρὶν [n] ἀλέκτορα
[n] φωνῆσαι τρὶς [n] ἀπαρνήσῃ με· καὶ ἐξελθὼν ἔξω [pq] ἔκλαυσεν
[qr] πικρῶς. XXVII. 1 [s] Πρωΐας δὲ γενομένης [t] συμβούλιον [t] ἔλαβον πάντες οἱ ἀρχιερεῖς καὶ οἱ [u] πρεσβύτεροι
τοῦ [u] λαοῦ κατὰ τοῦ Ἰησοῦ, ὥςτε [v] θανατῶσαι αὐτόν,
2 καὶ δήσαντες αὐτὸν ἀπήγαγον καὶ [w] παρέδωκαν Ποντίῳ
Πιλάτῳ τῷ [x] ἡγεμόνι.

...αυτοις εκει Z. ABCDE FGHKL MSUVX ΓΔΠℵ 1. 33. 69

...θανατωσαι αυτον D.

d Luke xvi. 20. Acts x. 17 al[4]. Rev. xxi. 12, &c. (10 times.) xxii. 14 only. Judg. xviii. 16 A. 3 Kings xiv. 27.
e ch. xiv. 7 (reff.) only.
f ch. ix. 18. Mark i. 37 al. 3 Kings i. 30.
g = || Mk. John xiii. 33. xiv. 19. xvi. 16, &c. Heb. x. 37. Isa. xxvi. 20.
h | Mk. ch. xiv. 33. xxvii. 54 || Mk. Jer. xxxv. (xxviii.) 6.
i Acts xxi. 8. 2 Tim. iii. 6. Obad. 11.
k (|| Mk. v. r.) John iv. 42. viii. 43 only. Job xxiii. 1. Cant. iv. 3.
l 1 Cor. xv. 27. Gal. iii. 11 only. Num. xxvii. 21.

m here only †. Iren. Hær. i. 13. 4; 16. 3. n ver. 34 reff. o w. gen., Luke i. 54, 72. xxiii. 42. xxiv. 8. Acts xi. 16 al. Gen. ix. 15. p Matt., ch. ii. 18 only. Mark v. 38, 39. Luke vi. 21, 25 al. Gen. l. 1. q || L. Isa. xxii. 4. xxxiii. 7. r || L. only. Jer. xxvii. (l.) 21. 2 Macc. vii. 30 only. s || J. ch. xxi. 18. John xxi. 4 only. 2 Kings xxiii. 4. Lam. iii. 23. t ch. xii. 14 reff. u ch. xxi. 23 reff. v ch. xxvi. 59 al. 2 Kings viii. 2. w see Luke xx. 20. x = vv. 11, &c. Luke xx. 20. Acts xxiii. 24, &c. xxiv. 1, 10. xxvi. 30. Πιλ. ὁ τῆς Ἰουδαίας ἡγεμών, Jos. Antt. xviii. 3. 1.

71. **εξελθοντος** δε **αυτου** (*corrn of the Hellenistic idiom, as also is the omn of αυτον*) D ev-17 vulg coptt: om αυτον BLZℵ 33 lat-*a*: txt AC rel lat-*b* arm. aft αλλη ins παιδισκη D latt [arm Orig-int]. rec (for αυτοις) τοις (*for perspicuity*), with BDE[2]GKSΠ[1]ℵ vss Thl: txt ACZ rel. om [last] και (*as unnecessary*) BDℵ sah.

72. (**μετα**, so ABCKLΔΠ[1]ℵ 33.) for οτι, λεγων D lat-*b c ff*$_2$: om ℵ.

73. om και συ D 1: om και lat-*b c h l* [Orig-int]. aft γαρ ins γαλιλαιος ει και (*from || Mark*) C[1] syr-w-ast. for δηλ. σ. ποι., ομοιαζει (*see on || Mark*) D lat-*a b c ff*$_2$ *h*. [om last clause L.]

74. rec καταναθεματιζειν: txt ABCDℵ rel 2(Delitzsch) Scr's mss Chr Thl. ευθυς BL.

75. rec ins του bef ιησ., with C[2]KLMSUVΠ[1] 1. 33. 69 Chr [Bas$_1$ Damasc$_1$]: om ABC[1]Dℵ rel Chr-L. rec aft ειρηκοτος ins αυτω (*see also || Mark*), with AC rel lat-*b f* syrr copt æth [Bas$_1$ Damasc$_1$] Orig-int: om BDLℵ 33 [vulg] lat-*c ff*$_{1.2}$ *g*$_{1.2}$ *h l* sah arm Chr. om οτι D latt æth. aft πριν ins η A 238 Bas.

Chap. XXVII. **1.** for ελαβον, εποιησαν D gat lat-*a c f* arm. **ινα θανατωσουσιν** D.

2. rec aft παρεδωκαν ins αυτον, with AC[3] rel Syr syr-w-ob [coptt goth]: om BC[1]KLℵ 33 ev-y latt arm Orig. om ποντιω (*see || Mark Luke*) BLℵ 33 Syr coptt Orig Petr.

or flagged, and open to the sky, is the *αὐλή* where the attendants made a fire; and the passage beneath the front of the house from the street to this court, is the *προαύλιον* or *πυλών*. The place where Jesus stood before the High-priest may have been an open room or place of audience on the ground-floor, in the rear or on one side of the court; such rooms, open in front, being customary." Robinson, Notes to Harmony, p. 225. **70.**] **οὐκ οἶδα τί λέγεις** is an indirect form of denial, conveying in it absolute ignorance of the circumstances alluded to. **73. ἡ λαλιά**] Wetstein (ad loc.) gives many examples of various provincial dialects of Hebrew. The Galilæans could not pronounce properly the gutturals, confounding א, ע, and ח; and they used ח for ש. **74.**] **καταθεματ.** is a corrupted form, belonging probably to the class of vulgarisms. *κατάθεμα* occurs Rev. xxii. 3. 'Nunc gubernaculum animæ plane amisit,' says Bengel. **75.**] **ἔξω**—viz. from the *πυλών* where the second and third denial had taken place: the motive being, *ἵνα μὴ κατηγορηθῇ διὰ τῶν δακρύων*, as Chrys.

Chap. XXVII. 1, 2.] Jesus is led away to Pilate. Mark xv. 1. Luke xxii. 66 (who probably combines with this

3 Τότε ἰδὼν Ἰούδας ὁ [y] παραδιδοὺς αὐτὸν ὅτι [z] κατ- ABCEF
εκρίθη, [a] μεταμεληθεὶς [b] ἔστρεψεν τὰ τριάκοντα [c] ἀργύρια GHKL
τοῖς ἀρχιερεῦσιν καὶ πρεσβυτέροις 4 λέγων Ἥμαρτον MSUVX
παραδοὺς [de] αἷμα [ef] ἀθῷον. οἱ δὲ εἶπον [g] Τί [g] πρὸς ἡμᾶς; ΓΔΠℵ 1.
σὺ [h] ὄψῃ. 5 καὶ ῥίψας τὰ [c] ἀργύρια ἐν τῷ ναῷ [i] ἀνεχώ- 33. 69
ρησεν καὶ ἀπελθὼν [k] ἀπήγξατο. 6 οἱ δὲ ἀρχιερεῖς λαβόντες τὰ [c] ἀργύρια εἶπον Οὐκ ἔξεστιν [l] βαλεῖν αὐτὰ εἰς τὸν
[m] κορβανᾶν, ἐπεὶ [n] τιμὴ αἵματός ἐστιν. 7 [o] συμβούλιον δὲ
[o] λαβόντες ἠγόρασαν [p] ἐξ αὐτῶν τὸν ἀγρὸν τοῦ [q] κεραμέως, [r] εἰς [s] ταφὴν τοῖς [t] ξένοις. 8 διὸ [u] ἐκλήθη ὁ ἀγρὸς

y ch. xxvi. 46, 48. z ch. xx. 18 reff. a ch. xxi. 29, 32 reff. 1 Macc. xi. 10. b = here only. Isa. xxxviii. 8. see Acts xiii. 46. c ch. xxvi. 15 reff. d = vv. 24, 25 al. e here only. 1 Kings xix. 5. Ps. xciii. 21 al. fr. f ver. 24 only. g John xxi. 22, 23. h = ver. 24. Acts xviii. 15. 3 Kings xii. 16 Heb. i ch. ii. 12, 13, 14 reff. k here only. 2 Kings xvii. 23. Tobit iii. 10 only. l = ch. xxvi. 12. Mark xii. 41. m here only †. τὸν ἱερὸν θησαυρὸν καλεῖται δὲ κορβανᾶς, Jos. Bell. ii. 9. 4. (-βᾶν, Mark vii. 11.) n = ver. 9. Acts iv. 34. v. 2, 3. xix. 19. 1 Cor. vi. 20. vii. 23 al. Num. xx. 19. Isa. lv. 1. o ch. xii. 14 reff. p Luke xvi. 9. Acts i. 18. Ep. Jer. 25. q here bis. Rom. ix. 21 only. Isa. xxix. 16. Jer. xviii. 2. (-μικός, Rev. ii. 27.) r = ch. xxvi. 28 al. fr. s here only. Deut. xxxiv. 6 B. Isa. liii. 9. t ch. xxv. 35, &c. reff. u Judg. ii. 5 A. xv. 19 al.

3. παραδους (*corrn, the betrayal having passed*) BL 33 latt syr coptt Orig-int. for μεταμελ., μετεμεληθη και ℵ^1(txt ℵ^{3a}). rec **απεστρεψε** (*corrn for precision*), with AC rel Eus Chr: *rettulit* latt Lucif: txt BLℵ ev-y D-lat(*misit*) Orig$_2$. rec ins τοις bef πρεσβυτεροις, with A rel Chr: om BCLℵ 33 Orig$_3$ Eus$_2$.

4. for αθωον, δικαιον (*explany from ch* xxiii. 35) B-marg L latt(and D-lat) syr-jer coptt arm Orig$_3$ Cypr$_{expr}$ Lucif Ambr Leo Promiss: txt ABCℵ rel syrr syr-mg-gr goth Orig$_2$ Eus [Cyr-jer$_1$] Chr. rec οψει (*more usual form*), with EUΓ 1. 69^1(appy) Orig$_1$ Eus Chr(so Fd): txt ABCℵ rel syr-mg-gr Orig$_1$ Cyr-jer Chr-wlf-ms.

5. ins τριακοντα bef αργ. ℵ(λ) 122 Chr-wlf-ms. εις τον ναον BLℵ 33. 69 goth æth Orig$_1$(txt$_1$) Eus Chr. απεχωρ. C.

6. (ειπαν BL 33 Eus.) κορβαν B^1 lat-*f g q* æth, *corbam a d h*.

morning meeting of the Sanhedrim some things that took place at their earlier assembly), xxiii. 1. John xviii. 28. The object of this taking counsel, was **ὥστε θ. αὐ.**—to condemn Him formally to death, and *devise the best means* for the accomplishment of the sentence. **2. Ποντ. Πιλ. τ. ἡγ.**] See note on Luke iii. 1;—and on the reason of their taking Him to Pilate, on John xviii. 31. Pilate ordinarily resided at Cæsarea, but during the feast, in Jerusalem.

3—10.] Remorse and suicide of Judas. *Peculiar to Matthew.* This incident does not throw much light on the motives of Judas. One thing we learn for certain—that our Lord's being condemned, which he inferred from His being handed over to the Roman governor, *worked in him remorse*, and that *suicide was the consequence.* Whether this condemnation was *expected* by him or not, does not here appear; nor have we any means of ascertaining, except from the former sayings of our Lord respecting him. I cannot (see note on ch. xxvi. 14) believe that his intent was other than sordid gain to be achieved by the darkest treachery. To suppose that the condemnation *took him by surprise*, seems to me to be inconsistent with the spirit of his own confession, ver. 4. There **παραδοὺς αἷμα ἀθῷον** expresses his *act*—his *accomplished purpose.* The bitter feeling in him now is expressed by ἥμαρτον, of which he is vividly and dreadfully conscious, now that the result has been attained. **3.**] Observe it was **τὰ τρ. ἀργ.** which he brought back—clearly *the price* of the Lord's betrayal,—not *earnest-money* merely;—for by this time, nay when he delivered his Prisoner at the house of Annas, he would have in that case received the *rest.* Observe also **ὁ παραδιδοὺς αὐτόν**, *His betrayer,* the part. pres. being used as a designation, as in ὁ πειράζων, "*the Tempter,*" ch. iv. 3. **5. ἐν τῷ ναῷ**] in the *holy place*, where the priests only might enter. We must conceive him as speaking to them without, and throwing the money into the ναός. **ἀπήγξατο**] **hanged, or strangled himself.** On the account given Acts i. 18, see note there. Another account of the end of Judas was current, which I have cited there.

6.] They said this probably by analogy from Deut. xxiii. 18. **τιμ. αἵμ., the price given for** shedding of blood, the wages of a murderer. **7. τὸν ἀγρ. τ. κερ.**] the field of some well-known pot-

ἐκεῖνος ἀγρὸς αἵματος [v] ἕως [w] τῆς [vw] σήμερον. 9 [x] τότε
[x] ἐπληρώθη τὸ [y] ῥηθὲν διὰ Ἱερεμίου τοῦ προφήτου λέγοντος [z] Καὶ ἔλαβον τὰ τριάκοντα ἀργύρια, τὴν [a] τιμὴν τοῦ
[b] τετιμημένου ὃν [b] ἐτιμήσαντο [c] ἀπὸ υἱῶν Ἰσραήλ, 10 καὶ
[d] ἔδωκαν αὐτὰ [r] εἰς τὸν ἀγρὸν τοῦ [q] κεραμέως, [e] καθὰ
[f] συνέταξέν μοι κύριος.
11 Ὁ δὲ Ἰησοῦς ἐστάθη [g] ἔμπροσθεν τοῦ [h] ἡγεμόνος·
καὶ ἐπηρώτησεν αὐτὸν ὁ [h] ἡγεμὼν λέγων Σὺ εἶ ὁ [i] βασιλεὺς τῶν [hi] Ἰουδαίων; ὁ δὲ Ἰησοῦς ἔφη αὐτῷ [k] Σὺ λέγεις.
12 καὶ [l] ἐν τῷ [m] κατηγορεῖσθαι αὐτὸν ὑπὸ τῶν ἀρχιερέων
καὶ [τῶν] πρεσβυτέρων οὐδὲν ἀπεκρίνατο. 13 τότε λέγει
αὐτῷ ὁ Πιλάτος Οὐκ ἀκούεις πόσα σοῦ [n] καταμαρτυροῦ-
σιν; 14 καὶ οὐκ ἀπεκρίθη αὐτῷ πρὸς [o] οὐδὲ [op] ἓν [p] ῥῆμα,

...ιουδαιων C.

D ουδεν απεκρινετο... ...ουδεν α X.

ABDEF GHKL MSUV ΓΔΠℵ 1. 33. 69

v Rom. xi. 8. 2 Cor. iii. 15. 1 Kings xxix. 6. Sir. xlvii. 7.
w w. ἡμ., ch. xxviii. 15. Acts xx. 26. 2 Cor. iii. 14. Gen. xix. 37, 38. without ἡμέρα, ch. xi. 23. Acts xix. 40 only. 1 Kings xxx. 25.
x ch. ii. 17 only
y ch. i. 22 reff.
z Zech. xi. 13.
a ver. 6 reff.
b = here bis only. Lev. xxvii. 8.
c ver. 21. Luke vi. 13. Heb. vii. 2. Exod. xvii. 5.
d = ch. xvi. 26 ||. Gen. xxv. 34.
e here only. Gen. vii. 9. Exod. xii. 35.
f ch. xxvi. 19 reff.
g ch. xxvi. 70 reff.
h ver. 2.
i here, &c. and ||. ch. ii. 2.
k = || only. Luke xxii. 70. see ch. xxvi. 25, 64.
l constr., ch. xiii. 4, 25 al. fr.
m pass., Acts xxii. 30. xxv. 16 only +. 2 Macc. x. 13. act., ch. xii. 10 al. fr.+ 1 Macc. vii. 6, 25 al.
n (|| Mk. v. r.) ch. xxvi. 62 || Mk. only. Job xv. 6.
o John i. 3. Acts iv. 32. Rom. iii. 10 (1 Cor. vi. 5 v. r.). 2 Kings xiii. 30.
p Acts xxviii. 25. see ch. xxi. 24.

9. for τοτε, και ℵ[1](txt ℵ[3a]); *et tunc* am. om ιερεμιου 33. 157 lat-*a b* Syr mss-mentd-by-Aug: ζαχαριου 22 syr-mg: *esaiam* lat-*l* (*but Orig Eus Aug Jer testify to the word, and found it in old* MSS. *Orig and Eus suspect* ζαχ. *to be the right reading, but only as a conjecture.* ιερ. *is in all* MSS *vss and fathers not above mentd*).—(ιηρ. AC[1]Π[2].)

10. εδωκεν A[1](appy): εδωκα ℵ ev-H(?) syrr [syr-jer].

11. rec (for εσταθη) εστη, with A rel latt Orig Chr: txt BCLℵ 1. 33 Orig-ms. ο (bef ηγεμων) is written above the line in ℵ. om αυτω Lℵ 33 Scr's s D-lat-*a* syr-jer coptt arm [Chr-2-6-9-γ-η-ρ-wlf-ms].

12. om των (bef πρεσβυτερων) B[1]LXΓℵ 1. 69 Orig$_2$ Chr. (33 def.) απεκρεινετο D lat-*b ff$_2$ h* syr-jer Orig$_1$[and int$_1$].

13. for ποσα, τοσα D[1] [οσα B[1]]. καταμ. bef σου D[1](txt D[6]).

14. om προς ουδε D gat(with tol) lat-*a b c* &c sah (arm).

ter—purchased at so small a price probably from having been rendered useless for tillage by excavations for clay: see note on Acts i. 19. **τοῖς ξ.**] not for Gentiles, but for *stranger Jews* who came up to the feasts. **8.**] **ἀγρ. αἵμ.,**—חֲקֵל דְּמָא. See Acts i. 19. **ἕως τῆς σήμ.**] This expression shews that a considerable time had elapsed since the event, before Matthew's Gospel was published. **9.**] The citation is not from Jeremiah (see ref.), and is probably quoted from memory and unprecisely; we have similar instances in two places in the apology of Stephen, Acts vii. 4, 16,—and in Mark ii. 26. Various means of evading this have been resorted to, which are not worth recounting. Jer. xviii. 1, 2, or perhaps Jer. xxxii. 6—12, may have given rise to it: or it may have arisen from a Jewish idea (see Wordsw. h. l.), "Zechariam habuisse spiritum Jeremiæ." The quotation here is very different from the LXX, which see,—and not much more like the Hebrew. I put it to any faithful Christian to say, whether of the two presents the greater obstacle to his faith, the solution given above, or that in Wordsw.'s note, that the name of one prophet is here substituted for that of another, to teach us not to regard the prophets as the *authors* of their prophecies, but to trace them to divine Inspiration.

11—14.] He is examined by Pilate. Mark xv. 2—5. Luke xxiii. 2—5. John xviii. 29—38. Our narrative of the hearing before Pilate is the least circumstantial of the four—having however two remarkable additional particulars, vv. 19 and 24. John is the fullest in giving the words of our Lord. Compare the notes there.

11.] Before this Pilate had come out and demanded the cause of his being delivered up; the Jews not entering the Prætorium.

The primary accusation against Him seems to have been that He ἔλεγεν ἑαυτὸν χριστὸν βασιλέα εἶναι. This is presupposed in the enquiry of this verse. **σὺ λέγεις** is not to be rendered as a *doubtful answer*—much less with Theophylact,

q ‖ Mk. [L.] Luke ii. 41. r Mark x. 1. Luke iv. 16. Acts xvii. 2 only. Num. xxiv. 1. Sir. xxxvii. 14 only. s ch. xviii. 27 reff. Acts iii. 13. t ‖ Mk. only in Gospp. Acts xvi. 25, 27. Eph. iii. 1. 2 Tim. i. 8 al. Eccl. iv. 14. u Rom. xvi. 7 only. Esth. v. 4. 3 Macc. vi. 1. ἐπίσημος ἦν ἡ φιλαργυρία, Polyb. xviii. 38. 1. οἱ διὰ πλῆθος ἀδικημάτων ἐ., Jos. Antt. v. 7. 1. v = ch. xiii. 2 reff. w ch. ii. 17. x Phil. i. 15.

ὥςτε θαυμάζειν τὸν [h] ἡγεμόνα λίαν.
15 [q] κατὰ δὲ ἑορτὴν [r] εἰώθει ὁ [h] ἡγεμὼν [s] ἀπολύειν ἕνα τῷ ὄχλῳ [t] δέσμιον ὃν ἤθελον.
16 εἶχον δὲ τότε [t] δέσμιον [u] ἐπίσημον λεγόμενον Βαραββᾶν.
17 [v] συνηγμένων οὖν αὐτῶν εἶπεν αὐτοῖς ὁ Πιλάτος Τίνα θέλετε [s] ἀπολύσω ὑμῖν; Βαραββᾶν, ἢ [w] Ἰησοῦν τὸν [w] λεγόμενον [w] χριστόν;
18 ᾔδει γὰρ ὅτι [x] διὰ

ABDEF GHKL MSUV ΓΔΠא 1. 33. 69

15. ins *την* bef *εορτην* D. *δεσμιον* bef *τω οχλω* D ev-36 syr copt: *τω οχλω* bef *ενα δεσμιον* M 69. 237-43-7 Scr's a c d e m p evv-H_1-P_2-X-Z_2 latt syr-jer Orig-int: *τω οχ. δ.* bef *ενα* 33 arm. for *ηθελον*, *παρητουντο* (‖ *Mark*) א[1](txt א[3a]).

16. ins *τον* bef *λεγομενον* D. ins *ιησουν* bef *βαραββαν* (here and in ver 17) 1[1] syr-jer arm; 'de hoc nomine in hoc loco tacent Orig ipse et Orig-int' (Treg on ver 16): Orig quotes ver 17 without the addn, but the interpreter of a lost passage makes him say '*In multis exemplaribus non continetur quod Barabbas etiam Jesus dicebatur, et forsitan recte, ut ne nomen Jesu conveniat alicui iniquorum;*' a marginal schol in S and 20 others, ascribed to Anastasius or Chr, states παλαιοῖς πάνυ ἀντιγράφοις ἐντυχὼν εὗρον καὶ αὐτὸν τὸν Βαραββᾶν Ἰησοῦν λεγόμενον· οὕτως γοῦν εἶχεν ἡ τοῦ Πιλάτου πεῦξις ἐκεῖ, "τίνα θέλετε τῶν δύο ἀπολύσω ὑμῖν, Ἰησοῦν τὸν Βαραββᾶν ἢ Ἰησοῦν τὸν λεγόμενον χριστόν;" (*But if so, how could ver 20 have been expressed as it is*—ἵνα αἰτήσωνται τὸν Βαραββᾶν, τὸν δὲ Ἰησοῦν ἀπολέσωσιν (*see Lachm pref* p. xxxvii)? *Mey and Fritzsche defend the insn, thinking* *ιησουν* *to have been erased from reverence.* Tischdf, *who insd it in former edns, now* [edd 7, 8] *rejects it, and thinks it arose from Jer's account of the* ‖ *reading in the gosp accdg to the Hebrews, or as Treg* (*see below*). *I believe the true account to be, that some ignorant scribe, unwilling to concede to Barabbas the epithet* ἐπίσημον, *wrote in the marg* ἰησοῦν, *and it thence found its way into the text in ver* 16: *and, when once supposed to be a prefix to Barabbas, in ver* 17 *also. On ver* 17 *Treg remarks* 'Hæc lectio orta fuisse videtur e litteris posterioribus vocis ὑμῖν casu bis scriptis.')

17. for *ουν*, *δε* D 69 Scr's c lat-*a b c f* ff_2 g_1 *h* (Syr) goth (æth) om arm. *υμιν* bef *απολυσω* D lat-*c*. ins *τον* bef *βαραββαν* B Orig: ins *ιησουν τον*, 1[1] syr-jer arm Orig-int.

as meaning, '*Thou sayest it, not I:*' but as a *strong affirmative*. See above on ch. xxvi. 64. **12—14.**] This part of the narrative occurs only in Mark besides, but is explained by Luke, ver. 5. The charges were, of *exciting the people* from Galilee to Jerusalem. On the mention of Galilee, Pilate *sent Him to Herod*, Luke, vv. 6—12.

15—26.] Barabbas preferred to Him. He is delivered to be crucified. Mark xv. 6—15. Luke xxiii. 17—25. John xviii. 39, 40. In the substance of this account the Four are in remarkable agreement. John gives merely a compendium, uniting in one these three attempts of Pilate to liberate Jesus, and omitting the statement of the fact of Barabbas being liberated, and Jesus delivered to them. **15. κατὰ ἑορτήν**] **feast by feast**; i. e. at every feast. This distributive force of κατά is found both in local and temporal connexions: e.g. κατ' οἶκον, house by house, κατ' ἄνδρα, man by man, καθ' ἡμέραν, day by day. See Bernhardy, Syntax, p. 240 f. We have no other historic mention of this practice. Livy (v. 13) says of the feast of the Lectisternium, 'vinctis quoque dempta in eos dies vincula.' **16.**] The subject of εἶχον, as of ἤθελον above, is the ὄχλος. He was one of them, so they *had* him. The name Barabbas, בַּר אַבָּא, 'son of his father,' was not an uncommon one. The plays on this name Barabbas (e. g. τὸν υἱὸν τοῦ πατρὸς αὐτῶν, τοῦ διαβόλου, ἐξῃτήσαντο . . . . Theophylact, see also Olshausen in loc. vol. ii. p. 507) are utterly unworthy of serious exegesis. It does not appear why this man was ἐπίσημος. The murderers in the insurrection in which he was involved were *many* (Mark, ver. 7). **17.**] In John's narrative, the suggestion of liberating Barabbas seems to come from the Jews themselves; but not necessarily so: he may only be giving, as before, a general report of what passed. The **συνηγμ. οὖν αὐτ.** seems to imply that a great crowd had collected outside the Prætorium while the trial was going on. It is pos-

[x] φθόνον παρέδωκαν αὐτόν. 19 καθημένου δὲ αὐτοῦ ἐπὶ
τοῦ [y] βήματος ἀπέστειλεν πρὸς αὐτὸν ἡ γυνὴ αὐτοῦ
λέγουσα Μηδὲν [z] σοὶ καὶ τῷ δικαίῳ ἐκείνῳ· πολλὰ γὰρ
ἔπαθον σήμερον [a] κατ᾽ [a] ὄναρ δι᾽ αὐτόν. 20 οἱ δὲ ἀρχιερεῖς
καὶ οἱ πρεσβύτεροι ἔπεισαν τοὺς ὄχλους ἵνα [b] αἰτήσωνται
τὸν Βαραββᾶν, τὸν δὲ Ἰησοῦν [c] ἀπολέσωσιν. 21 ἀποκριθεὶς δὲ ὁ [d] ἡγεμὼν εἶπεν αὐτοῖς [e] Τίνα θέλετε [f] ἀπὸ τῶν
δύο [g] ἀπολύσω ὑμῖν; οἱ δὲ εἶπον Βαραββᾶν. 22 λέγει
αὐτοῖς ὁ Πιλάτος Τί οὖν [g] ποιήσω [w] Ἰησοῦν τὸν [w] λεγόμενον [w] χριστόν; λέγουσιν πάντες [h] Σταυρωθήτω.
23 ὁ δὲ ἔφη, Τί γὰρ [i] κακὸν ἐποίησεν; οἱ δὲ [k] περισσῶς
ἔκραζον λέγοντες [h] Σταυρωθήτω. 24 ἰδὼν δὲ ὁ Πιλάτος
ὅτι οὐδὲν [l] ὠφελεῖ, ἀλλὰ μᾶλλον [m] θόρυβος γίνεται,

y = John xix. 13. Acts (vii. 5) xii. 21. xviii. 12, 16, 17. xxv. 6, 10, 17. Rom. xiv. 10. 2 Cor. v. 10 only. 2 Macc. xiii. 26.
z ch. viii. 29. Josh. xxii. 24. 2 Kings xvi. 10.
a ch. i. 20. ii. 12, 13, 19, 22 only +.
b ‖ Mk. L. ver. 58. ch. xiv. 7. Acts iii. 14 al.
c = ch. ii. 13. John x. 10 al. Esth. iii. 9.
d ver. 2.
e = ch. xxiii. 17, 19 reff.
f ver. 9.
g = ‖ Mk. only.
h ch. xx. 19 reff.
i ‖ Mk. L. Acts xxiii. 9. Rom. iii. 8 al. Gen. xxvi. 29.
k ‖ Mk. Mark x. 26. Acts xxvi. 11 only. Ps. xxx. 23. Isa. lvi. 12 F(not ABℵ). 2 Macc. viii. 27.
l John vi. 63. xii. 19. Heb. xiii. 9 al. Sir. xxxi. (xxxiv.) 23.
m ch. xxvi. 5 reff.

21. ins *τον* bef *βαραββαν* BLℵ 1. 33.
22. *ποιησωμεν* D-gr lat-*a b c* ff_2 *h* Orig-int. rec aft *λεγουσιν* ins *αυτω*, with L rel lat-*f* æth: om ABDKΔΠ[1]ℵ 1. 33. 69 latt syrr syr-jer coptt arm Orig-int Aug.
23. rec aft *ο δε* ins *ηγεμων* (*from ver* 21), with A rel syr: txt Bℵ 33. 69 syr-jer sah arm Chr.—*λεγει αυτοις ο ηγεμων* DL 1 latt copt æth. *εκραξαν* D-gr Syr.

sible that the addition *τὸν λεγόμενον χριστόν*, which Pilate could hardly have heard from the Jews, may have been familiar to him by his wife's mention of Jesus. See below. **18.**] The whole narrative presupposes what this verse and the next distinctly assert, that *Pilate was before acquainted with the acts and character of Jesus.* **19.**] The **βῆμα** was in a place called in Hebrew Gabbatha, the Pavement—John xix. 13—where however Pilate is not related to have gone thither, till *after* the scourging and mocking of the soldiers. But he may have sat there when he came out in some of his previous interviews with the Jews. **ἡ γυνὴ αὐτ.**] It had become the custom in Augustus's time for the governors of provinces to take their wives with them abroad; Cæcina attempted to pass a law forbidding it (Tacit. Ann. iii. 33 ff.), but was vehemently opposed (by Drusus among others) and put down. We know nothing more of this woman than is here related. Tradition gives her the name of Procla or Claudia Procula. In the Gospel of Nicodemus, c. 2, we read that Pilate called the Jews and said to them, *οἴδατε ὅτι ἡ γυνή μου θεοσεβὴς ἐστιν, καὶ μᾶλλον ἰουδαΐζει σὺν ὑμῖν. λέγουσιν αὐτῷ Ναί, οἴδαμεν.* On the question raised by the words *καθημένου δὲ αὐτοῦ ἐπὶ τοῦ βήματος* as to the place which this incident holds in the trial, see Tischendorf, Pilati circa Christum judicio, &c., pp. 13 ff. **ὁ δίκαιος ἐκεῖνος** is a term which shews that she knew the character for purity and sanctity which Jesus had. In the Gospel of Nicodemus, the Jews are made to reply, *μὴ οὐκ εἴπαμέν σοι ὅτι γόης ἐστίν; ἰδοὺ ὀνειροπόλημα ἔπεμψε πρὸς τὴν γυναῖκά σου.* **20.**] So Mark also. Luke and John merely give, that they all cried out, &c. The exciting of the crowd seems to have taken place while Pilate was receiving the message from his wife. **ἵνα** conveys a mixture of the purport with the purpose of the *ἔπεισαν*. See note on 1 Cor. xiv. 13. **21. ἀποκρ.**] not necessarily to the incitements of the Sanhedrists which he overheard (Meyer), but rather to the state of confusion and indecision which prevailed. **22.**] They chose crucifixion as the ordinary Roman punishment for sedition, and because of their hate to Jesus. The double accusative after verbs of doing and saying of or to any one is the common construction. See Kühner, Gr. ii. p. 225. Cf. Xen. Cyr. iii. 2. 15, *οὐδεπώποτε ἐπαύοντο πολλὰ κακὰ ἡμᾶς ποιοῦντες.* **23.**] **γάρ** implies a sort of concession—a placing one's self in the situation of the person addressed, and then requiring a reason for his decision: and is generally found in this connexion, *τί γάρ*, in the utterance of impassioned feeling. See Hartung, Partikellehre, i. 479. **24.**]

λαβὼν ὕδωρ [n] ἀπενίψατο τὰς χεῖρας [o] * ἀπέναντι τοῦ ὄχλου
λέγων [p] Ἀθῷός εἰμι [q] ἀπὸ τοῦ αἵματος τούτου· ὑμεῖς
[r] ὄψεσθε. 25 καὶ ἀποκριθεὶς πᾶς ὁ λαὸς εἶπεν Τὸ αἷμα
αὐτοῦ [s] ἐφ' ἡμᾶς καὶ [s] ἐπὶ τὰ τέκνα ἡμῶν. 26 τότε ἀπέλυσεν αὐτοῖς τὸν Βαραββᾶν, τὸν δὲ Ἰησοῦν [t] φραγελλώ-
σας παρέδωκεν ἵνα σταυρωθῇ.
27 Τότε οἱ στρατιῶται τοῦ ἡγεμόνος [u] παραλαβόντες
τὸν Ἰησοῦν εἰς το [v] πραιτώριον συνήγαγον ἐπ' αὐτὸν
ὅλην τὴν [w] σπεῖραν· 28 καὶ [x] ἐκδύσαντες αὐτὸν [y] χλαμύδα
[z] κοκκίνην [a] περιέθηκαν αὐτῷ, 29 καὶ [b] πλέξαντες στέφανον
ἐξ [c] ἀκανθῶν [d] ἐπέθηκαν ἐπὶ τῆς κεφαλῆς αὐτοῦ καὶ

N τον δε ιησουν... ABDEF GHKL MNSU VΓΔΠℵ 1. 33. 69

n here only. Prov. xxx. 12, 20. 3 Kings xxii. 38 only.
o ch. xxi. 2 reff. Deut. xxvi. 10 Ed-vat. (B omits).
p ver. 4 only. 2 Kings iii. 28, there also w. ἀπό.
q = Acts xx. 26. Gen. xxiv. 8.
r = ver. 4 reff.
s Acts v. 28. 3 Kings ii. (iii.) 37. Jer. xxxiii. (xxvi.) 15.
t || Mk. only +. (-λλιον, John ii. 15.)
u ch. xvii. 1 reff.
v || Mk. John xviii. 28 bis, 33. xix. 9. Acts xxiii. 35. Phil. i. 13 only +.
w || Mk. John xviii. 3, 12. Acts x. 1. xxi. 31. xxvii. 1 only +. Judith xiv. 11. 2 Macc. viii. 23. xii. 20, 22 only. τοῦτο δὲ καλεῖται τὸ σύνταγμα τῶν πεζῶν παρὰ Ῥωμαίοις κοόρτις, Polyb. xi. 23. 1.
x ver. 31 || Mk. Luke x. 30. 2 Cor. v. 4 only. Gen. xxxvii. 23.
y ver. 31 only +. 2 Macc. xii. 35 only.
z Heb. ix. 19. Rev. xvii. 3, 4. Exod. xxv. 4 al.
a || Mk. ver. 48 || Mk. J. ch. xxi. 33 || Mk. 1 Cor. xii. 23 only. Ruth iii. 3.
b || (there also w. στέφ.) only. Isa. xxviii. 5. Exod. xxviii. 14 only.
c ch. vii. 16 reff. Ps. cxvii. 12.
d constr. ἐπί & gen., ch. xxi. 7 reff.

24. * κατέναντι BD: απεναντι Aℵ rel [Chr]. aft ειμι ins εγω D, simly lat-*a b c*. rec ins του δικαιου bef τουτου (*see ch* xxiii. 35, *and ver* 4 *var read*), with Lℵ rel vulg lat-*c ff*$_1$ syr [Constt$_1$ Cyr-jer$_1$ Cyr$_1$]; aft τουτου AΔ lat-*f h* Syr syr-jer coptt æth arm: om BD mm lat-*a b* Chr Orig-int$_3$. aft υμεις ins δε ℵ^1(om ℵ^{3a}).
26. φλαγελλ. D^1(txt D-corr^1). aft παρεδωκεν ins αυτοις DFLN ℵ^{3a}(but erased) 1 vulg lat-*a c* &c syr-jer æth [Aug$_1$]. for σταυρωθη, σταυρωσωσιν αυτον D gat lat-*a b c ff*$_2$ *h* syr-jer æth.
27. συνηγαγεν D-gr.
28. ενδυσαντες (*from* || *Mark, cf the varns below*) BDℵ^{3a}(txt ℵ$^{1\cdot3b}$) lat-*a b c ff*$_2$ Orig-int. aft αυτον ins ιματιον πορφυρουν και (|| *Mark*) D lat-*a* (*b*) *c f ff*$_2$ *h* Juv Hil; τα ιματια αυτου 33. 238 ev-P$_1$ syr-mg: om ABNℵ rel vulg lat-*ff*$_1$ *g*$_2$ vss Eus. rec περιεθ. αυτ. bef χλ. κοκκ. (*to avoid confusion in* εκδ. αυτ. χλ. κοκκ.), with AN rel syrr æth arm: txt BDLℵ 69 latt syr-jer coptt Eus Chr-wlf-ms Orig-int.
29. περιεθηκαν B Chr-6(and ed Fd): εθηκαν KNΔΠ 1. 69 lat-*a b c*: txt ADℵ rel Eus Chr. rec επι την κεφαλην, with ADN rel Chr: τη κεφαλη H 33: txt BLℵ 69

Peculiar to Matt. **οὐδὲν ὠφελεῖ**] rightly rendered in E. V. **that he prevailed nothing**—not 'that *it* prevailed nothing.' The *washing of the hands*, to betoken innocence from blood-guiltiness, is prescribed Deut. xxi. 6–9, and Pilate uses it here as intelligible to the Jews. The Greeks would have used the gen. after **ἀθῷος** without **ἀπό**: so ἀθῷος πληγῶν, Aristoph. Nub. 1413. See Kühner, Gram. ii. p. 164. **25.**] **αἷμα** λέγουσι τὴν τοῦ αἵματος καταδίκην, Euthym.: but more probably with a much wider reference—as the *adherence of blood to the hands of a murderer* is an idea not bearing any necessary reference to *punishment*, only to *guilt*. **26.**] **φραγελ.** is a late word, adopted from the Latin. The custom of scourging before execution was general among the Romans. After the scourging, John xix. 1—16, Pilate made a last attempt to liberate Jesus—which answers to παιδεύσας ἀπολύσω, Luke, ver. 16. **παρέδωκεν**] to the Roman soldiers, whose office the execution would be.

27—30.] Jesus mocked by the soldiers. Mark xv. 16—19. (Omitted in Luke.) John xix. 1—3. The assertion παρέδωκεν ἵνα σταυρωθῇ in ver. 26 is not strictly correct *there*. Before that, the contents of this passage come in, and the last attempt of Pilate to liberate Him. **27. εἰς τὸ πραιτ.**] The residence of the Roman governor was *the former palace of Herod*, in the upper city (see Winer, Realwörterbuch, 'Richthaus'). **ὅλ. τ. σπ.**] The **σπεῖρα** is the **cohort**—the *tenth part of a legion*. The word **ὅλ.** is not to be pressed. **ἐπ' αὐτόν**] **to Him**—*to make sport with Him*. This happened in the guard-room of the cohort: and the narrative of it we may well believe may have come from the centurion or others (see ver. 54), who were afterwards deeply impressed at the crucifixion. **28.**] Possibly the mantle in which he had been sent back from Herod

e κάλαμον ἐν τῇ δεξιᾷ αὐτοῦ, καὶ f γονυπετήσαντες
ἔμπροσθεν αὐτοῦ g ἐνέπαιζον αὐτῷ λέγοντες Χαῖρε h * ὁ
i βασιλεὺς τῶν i Ἰουδαίων. 30 καὶ k ἐμπτύσαντες εἰς αὐτὸν
ἔλαβον τὸν e κάλαμον καὶ l ἔτυπτον εἰς τὴν κεφαλὴν
αὐτοῦ. 31 καὶ ὅτε g ἐνέπαιξαν αὐτῷ, m ἐξέδυσαν αὐτὸν τὴν
m χλαμύδα, καὶ n ἐνέδυσαν αὐτὸν τὰ ἱμάτια αὐτοῦ, καὶ
o ἀπήγαγον αὐτὸν εἰς τὸ σταυρῶσαι. 32 ἐξερχόμενοι δὲ
εὗρον ἄνθρωπον Κυρηναῖον, ὀνόματι Σίμωνα· τοῦτον
p ἠγγάρευσαν ἵνα q ἄρῃ τὸν r σταυρὸν αὐτοῦ. 33 Καὶ
ἐλθόντες εἰς τόπον λεγόμενον Γολγοθᾶ, ὅ ἐστιν s κρανίου

e ch. xi. 7 reff.
f w. dat., ch. xvii. 14. w. acc., Mark (i. 40) x. 17 only +.
g ch. ii. 16. Mark x. 34 al. Gen. xxxix. 17.
h voc. constr., Mark ix. 25. Luke viii. 54. xviii. 11 al.
i ver. 11.
k ch. xxvi. 67 reff.
l w. εἰς, here [and Luke xviii. 13] only. Prov. xxvi. 22. w. ἐπί, Luke vi. 29.
m ver. 28 (reff.).
n ch. vi. 25 reff.
o = ver. 2. ch. xxvi. 57. Ep. Jer. 18. abs., Acts xii. 19. Num. xi. 12. Lam. iii. 27.
p ‖ Mk. ch. v. 41 only +.
q ch. ix. 6 reff.
r ch. xvi. 24 reff.
s ‖ only. Judg. ix. 53. 4 Kings ix. 35 only.

Eus Chr-wlf-ms. rec **επι** *την δεξιαν* (*mechanical repetition of* επι την κεφαλην), with E rel lat-*b f ff*$_2$ *h* syr-txt : txt ABD L(επη δεξ.) Nא 1. 33. 69 vulg lat-*a c ff*$_1$ *g*$_{1.2}$ Syr syr-mg syr-jer coptt æth arm Chr-2-γ-G-M(and wlf-ms) Orig-int [Aug,]. ενεπαιξαν (*corrn to historical tense*) BDLΓא 33. for λεγοντες, δεροντες A.
* βασιλεῦ BD Δ(sic) Π 1 : ο βασιλευς Aא rel.

31. εκδυσαντες Lא 33. om 2nd και א 33 copt-dz sah. om και (bef απηγ.) D[1](and lat[1] : ins D[2]) sah.

32. aft κυρην. ins εις απαντησιν αυτου D gat(with harl ing lux mm) lat-*a b c ff*$_2$ *g*$_2$ *h* ; ερχομενον απ αγρου 33.

33. **τον** τοπον **τον** B. om λεγομενον א[1](ins א[3a]). rec ος (*corrn to agree with* τοπος), with A(sic) E[2]SVΔΠ : txt BDNא rel latt coptt [Ps-]Ath.

—see note on Luke, ver. 11: or perhaps one of the ordinary soldiers' cloaks.

29.] It does not appear whether the purpose of the crown was *to wound*, or simply *for mockery*—and equally uncertain is it, of what kind of thorns it was composed. The *acanthus* itself, with its large succulent leaves, is singularly unfit for such a purpose: as is the plant with very long sharp thorns commonly known as *spina Christi*, being a *brittle* acacia (robinia),—and the very length of the thorns, which would meet in the middle if it were bent into a wreath, precluding it. Some *flexile* shrub or plant must be understood—possibly some variety of the cactus or prickly pear. 'Hasselquist, a Swedish naturalist, supposes a very common plant, *naba* or *nubka* of the Arabs, with many small and sharp spines; soft, round, and pliant branches; leaves much resembling ivy, of a very deep green, as if in designed mockery of a victor's wreath,' Travels, 288. 1766 (cited by F. M). **κάλ.**, for a sceptre. **ὁ βασ.**, nominative with art. for vocative, a Hebraism, see reff. **30.**] Observe the aor. **ἔλαβον** of the one act of taking the reed, but the imperfects **ἐνέπαιζον** and **ἔτυπτον** of the continued and repeated acts of mocking and striking. Here follows the *exhibition of Jesus* by Pilate, and his last attempt to release him, John xix. 4—16.

31—34.] He is led to crucifixion. Mark xv. 20—23. Luke xxiii. 26—33. John xix. 16, 17. The four accounts are still essentially and remarkably distinct. Matthew's and Mark's are *from the same source*, but varied in expression, and in detail; Luke's and John's stand *each alone*; Luke's being the fullest, and giving us the deeply interesting address to the daughters of Jerusalem. **31.**] Peculiar to Matt. and Mark. **ἀπήγ.** = ἐξάγουσιν Mark. Executions usually took place *without* the camp, see Num. xv. 35, or city, 1 Kings xxi. 13: Acts vii. 58: Heb. xiii. 11—13. Grotius brings examples to shew that the same was the custom of the Romans. **32.**] Previously, Jesus had *borne his own cross*: John, ver. 17. So Plutarch, de sera numinis vindicta, ἕκαστος τῶν κακούργων ἐκφέρει τὸν αὐτοῦ σταυρόν, c. ix. We have no data to ascertain any further particulars about this Simon of Cyrene. The only assumption which we are perhaps justified in making, is that he was afterwards known in the Church as a convert: see note on Mark, ver. 21. He was *coming from the country*, Mark, ibid.; Luke, ver. 26. Meyer suggests, to account for the selection of one out of the multitude present, that possibly he was a slave: the indignity of the service to be rendered preventing their taking any other person. On **ἀγγαρεύω** see note at ch. v. 41. **33.**]

t John iv. 7, 10. Rev. xvi. 6.
u ver. 48 ‖ (John 3ce) only. Psa. lxviii. 21. Num. vi. 3 bis. Ruth ii. 14. Prov. xxv. 20 only.

τόπος λεγόμενος, 34 ᵗ ἔδωκαν αὐτῷ ᵗ πιεῖν ᵘ ὄξος μετὰ
ᵛ χολῆς ʷ μεμιγμένον· καὶ ˣ γευσάμενος οὐκ ἠθέλησεν πιεῖν. ...και γευ N. ABDEF GHKL MSUVΓ ΔΠℵ 1. 33. 69
35 Σταυρώσαντες δὲ αὐτὸν ʸ διεμερίσαντο τὰ ἱμάτια αὐτοῦ
ᶻ βαλόντες ᶻ κλῆρον. 36 καὶ καθήμενοι ᵃ ἐτήρουν αὐτὸν

v = here (Acts viii. 23) only. Jer. viii. 14. ix. 15.
w w. μετά, Luke xiii. 1 (Rev. viii. 7. xv. 2) only. Prov. xx. 22 compl. (not in ABℵ) (4 Kings xviii. 23 al.)
x John ii. 9 al. Job xii. 11.
y ‖ (J. from Ps. xxi. 18). Luke xi. 17, 18. xii. 52, 53. xxii. 17. Acts ii. 3, 45 only.
z ‖ only. Joel iii. 3. Obad. 11. Jon. i. 7.
a ver. 54. Acts xii. 5, 6 al. Prov. xxiii. 26.

rec λεγομ. bef κρ. τοπος (*for perspicuity*), with AN[1] rel syr: om λεγ. D ℵ[3a](appy, but marks of erasure removed) latt coptt arm [Aug$_1$] Promiss: μεθερμηνευομενος κρ. τοπ. (‖ *Mark*) M Syr æth: κρ. τοπ. ερμην. N[2]: txt BL[ℵ[1]] 1. 33 lat-*ff*$_1$ [Ps-]Ath.

34. ins και bef εδωκαν D latt(not *f*) Syr Orig-int. πειν (twice) Dℵ[1](txt ℵ[3a]) [om 1st L copt arm-mss]. for οξος, οινον (*from* ‖ *Mark*) BDKLΠ[1]ℵ 1. 33. 69 vulg lat-*a b ff*$_{1.2}$ *g*$_{1.2}$ *l* syr-mg syr-jer(twice) coptt æth arm [Ps-]Ath Damasc Hil Juv: txt AN rel lat-*c f h* syrr syr-jer[2](once) Chr Orig-int Tert. rec ηθελε (*more usual*), with A ℵ[3a](but txt restored) rel [Ps-Ath Chr-2-mss Damasc$_1$]: txt BDE[2]Lℵ[1] 1. 33. 69 latt syrr Chr Sev Orig-int.

35. rec βαλλοντες (*from* ‖ *Mark*), with B rel [Ps-Ath$_1$]: txt ADΠ[1]ℵ 1 Eus [Ps-Ath-2-mss]. rec aft κληρον ins ινα πληρωθη το ρηθεν υπο του προφητου, Διεμερισαντο τα ιματια μου εαυτοις, και επι τον ιματισμον μου εβαλον κληρον (*see note*), with Δ(but δια τ. προφ. and αυτοις) 1. 69(but δια τ. π. and κληρους) latt syr-txt arm Eus [Ps-]Ath: om ABDℵ rel vulg-sixt(with em forj fuld ing tol[1]) lat-*f ff*$_{1.2}$ *g*$_1$ *l* Syr syr-mg("hæc periodia prophetæ non inventa est in duobus (tribus) exemplaribus Græcis neque in illo (ipso) antiquo syriaco") coptt æth Tit-bostr Chr Thl Euthym Orig-int Juv Hil Aug.

Γολγοθᾶ, in Chaldee גָּלְגָּלְתָּא, in Hebrew גֻּלְגֹּלֶת, a skull: the name is by Jerome, and generally, explained from its being the usual place of executions and *abounding with skulls*—not however *unburied*, which was not allowed. This last consideration raises an objection to the explanation,—and as the name does not import κρανίων τόπος, but κρανίου τ. or simply **κρανίον** (Luke), many, among whom are Reland, Paulus, Lücke, De Wette, Meyer, &c., understand it as applying to the *shape* of the hill or rock. But neither does this seem satisfactory, as we have no analogy to guide us (Meyer's justification of the name from κράνιον, or κρανεῖον, a wood near Corinth, does not apply: for that is so called from κράνον, the *cornel tree*—De Wette), and no such hill or rock is known to have existed. As regards the *situation*, we await some evidence which may decide between the conflicting claims of the commonly-received site of Calvary and the Holy Sepulchre, and that upheld by Mr. Ferguson, who holds that the Dome of the Rock, usually known as the Mosque of Omar, is in reality the spot of our Lord's entombment. See his Article "Jerusalem" in Dr. Smith's Biblical Dictionary: and on the other side, Williams's Holy City, and Stanley's Sinai and Palestine, edn. 3, p. 459 ff. **34.**] It was customary to give a stupefying drink to criminals on their way to execution: of which our Lord would not partake, having shewn by tasting it, that he was aware of its purpose. In Mark's account it is ἐσμυρνισμένος οἶνος—and though οἶνος and ὄξος might mean the same, ἐσμυρνισμένος and μετὰ χολ. μεμιγ. cannot. We may observe here (and if the remark be applied with caution and reverence, it is a most useful one), how Matt. often adopts in his narrative *the very words of prophecy*, where one or more of the other Evangelists give the matter of fact detail: see above on ch. xxvi. 15, and compare with this verse, Ps. lxix. 21.

35—38.] He is crucified. Mark xv. 24—28. Luke xxiii. 32—34, 38. John xix. 18—24. The four accounts are distinct from one another, and independent of any one source in common. **35. σταυρώσαντες**] The cross was an upright pale or beam, intersected by a transverse one at right angles, generally in the shape of a **T**. In this case, from the 'title' being placed *over the Head*, the upright beam probably projected above the horizontal one, as usually represented ┼. To this cross the criminal, being stripped of his clothes, was fixed by nails driven through the hands and (not always, nor perhaps generally, though certainly not seldom—see note at Luke xxiv. 39) through the feet, separate or united. The body was not *supported by* the nails, but by a piece of wood which passed between the legs—ἐφ' ᾧ ἐποχοῦνται

ἐκεῖ. 37 καὶ ἐπέθηκαν ἐπάνω τῆς κεφαλῆς αὐτοῦ τὴν
[b] αἰτίαν αὐτοῦ γεγραμμένην Οὗτός ἐστιν Ἰησοῦς ὁ [i] βασιλεὺς τῶν [i] Ἰουδαίων. 38 Τότε σταυροῦνται σὺν αὐτῷ δύο
[c] λῃσταί, [d] εἷς ἐκ [d] δεξιῶν καὶ [d] εἷς ἐξ [d] εὐωνύμων. 39 οἱ
δὲ [e] παραπορευόμενοι [f] ἐβλασφήμουν αὐτὸν [gh] κινοῦντες
τὰς [h] κεφαλὰς αὐτῶν 40 καὶ λέγοντες Ὁ [i] καταλύων τὸν
ναὸν καὶ ἐν τρισὶν ἡμέραις οἰκοδομῶν, σῶσον σεαυτόν, εἰ
[k] υἱὸς εἶ τοῦ [k] θεοῦ, κατάβηθι ἀπὸ τοῦ σταυροῦ.
41 [l] ὁμοίως [[l] δὲ] [l] καὶ οἱ ἀρχιερεῖς [m] ἐμπαίζοντες μετὰ τῶν

b = ‖ Mk. Acts xxv. 18, 27. Gen. iv. 23.
c ch. xxi. 13 reff.
d ch. xx. 21 (reff.). 2 Chron. iii. 17.
e ‖ Mk. Mark ii. 23. ix. 20. xi. 20 only. Deut. ii. 4.
f = Tit. iii. 2. James ii. 7. (1 Cor. xiv. 13 v. r.) 4 Kings xix. 6, 22.
g ch. xxiii. 4 reff.
h ‖ Mk. only. Ps. xxi. 8. see Ps. xliii. 14.
i ch. xxvi. 61. Acts vi. 14 al. Ezra v. 12.
k see ch. iv. 3, 6 and note.
l (‖ Mk. v. r.) Luke v. 10. x. 32. 1 Cor. vii. 3, 4. James ii. 25 only.
m vv. 29, 31.

39. την κεφαλην D copt-ms.

40. aft λεγ. ins ουα DMΔ latt(not am lat-*f* *ff*$_1$ *g*$_1$) syr syr-mg-gr syr-jer arm Eus$_2$ Orig-int$_2$ Ambr Jer Cassiod. υιος θεου ει B latt Orig-int$_2$. ins και bef καταβ. (*taking* ει &c *with* σωσον σεαυτ.) ADℵ[1](ℵ[3a] disapproving) lat-*a b c h* Syr syr-jer Chr-wlf-ms Cyr.

41. om δε και ALΠ[1]ℵ Scr's g forj lat-*b* [copt-wlk-dz]: om δε BK **1. 33. 69** vulg lat-*a c f ff*$_2$ *h* D-lat Syr copt[-schw] arm Eus Orig-int. for πρεσβ., φαρισαιων D (64) ev-z$_1$ gat lat-*a b c ff*$_2$ *g*$_{1.2}$(Treg) *h* Eus Cassiod: πρεσβ. και φαρισαιων Δ rel lat-*f* syrr Thl Orig-int: πρεσβ. κ. γραμ. ℵ 238 Eus: om και πρ. Γ evv-P$_1$[1]-x$_1$: txt ABL **1. 33. 69** vulg lat-*ff*$_1$ [syr-ms] coptt æth.

οἱ σταυρούμενοι, Justin Mart. dial. c. Tryph. § 91, p. 188. On the rest of the verse, see notes on John. The words omitted in the text are clearly interpolated from John, ver. 24, with just the phrase τὸ ῥηθὲν ὑπὸ (or διὰ) τοῦ προφήτου assimilated to Matthew's usual form of citation. **36. ἐτήρουν**] This was usual, to prevent the friends taking crucified persons down. There were *four* soldiers, John, ver. 23; a centurion and three others. **37.**] **ἐπέθ.** is not to be taken as a plusq. perf. — Matthew finishes relating what the soldiers did, and then goes back to the course of the narrative. 'The soldiers' need not even be the nominative case to ἐπέθ. The 'title' appears to have been *written by Pilate* (see John, ver. 19) and sent to be affixed on the cross. It is not known whether the affixing of this title was customary. In Dio Cassius (cited by Meyer, but incorrectly), we read of such a title being hung round the neck of a criminal on his way to execution. So also Suet. Domit. 10,—"canibus objecit, cum hoc titulo, 'Impie locutus parmularius:'" and Caligula 32, — "præcedente titulo, qui caussam pœnæ indicaret." On the difference in the four Gospels as to the *words of the inscription itself* it is hardly worth while to comment, except to remark, that the advocates for the verbal and literal exactness of each Gospel may here find an *undoubted* example of the absurdity of their view, which may serve to guide them in less plain and obvious cases. (See this further noticed in the Prolegg. ch. i. § vi. 18.) *A title was written, containing certain words;* not *four titles, all different,* but *one,* differing probably from all of these four, but certainly from three of them. Let us bear this in mind when the narratives of words spoken, or events, differ in a similar manner. Respecting the title, see further on John, vv. 20–22. **38.**] **τότε**, after the crucifixion of Jesus was accomplished. These thieves were led out with Jesus, and crucified, perhaps by the same soldiers, or perhaps as Meyer says, inferring this from the καθήμενοι ἐτήρουν αὐτὸν ἐκεῖ, ver. 36, by another band.

39—44.] He is mocked on the cross. Mark xv. 29—32. Luke xxiii. 35—37; 39–43. Our narrative and that of Mark are from a common source. Luke's is wholly distinct. The whole of these indignities are omitted by John. **39. οἱ παραπ.**] These words say nothing as to its being a *working-day,* or as to the situation of the spot. A matter of so much public interest would be sure to attract a crowd, among whom we find, ver. 41, the chief priests, scribes, and elders. These passers-by were the multitude going in and out of the city, some coming to see, others returning. **κιν. τ. κεφ.**] see Ps. xxii. 7. The first reproach refers to ch. xxvi. 61; the second to ibid., ver. 64. **40. ὁ καταλύων**] Notice the characterizing present partici-

γραμματέων καὶ πρεσβυτέρων ἔλεγον 42 Ἄλλους ἔσωσεν,
ἑαυτὸν οὐ δύναται σῶσαι. βασιλεὺς Ἰσραήλ ἐστιν·
καταβάτω νῦν ἀπὸ τοῦ σταυροῦ, καὶ πιστεύσομεν αὐτῷ.
43 [n] πέποιθεν ἐπὶ τὸν θεόν· [o] ῥυσάσθω νῦν αὐτὸν εἰ [p] θέλει
αὐτόν. εἶπεν γὰρ ὅτι [k] θεοῦ εἰμι [k] υἱός. 44 [q] τὸ δ' αὐτὸ
καὶ οἱ λῃσταὶ οἱ [r] συνσταυρωθέντες σὺν αὐτῷ [s] ὠνείδιζον
αὐτόν. 45 ἀπὸ δὲ ἕκτης ὥρας σκότος ἐγένετο ἐπὶ πᾶσαν
τὴν γῆν [t] ἕως [t] ὥρας ἐνάτης. 46 [u] περὶ δὲ τὴν ἐνάτην

Θ_f xxvii. 44 (appy) ... ABDEF GHKL MSUVΓ $\Delta\Theta_f\Pi$א 1. 33. 69

n w. ἐπί and acc., = here (2 Cor. ii. 3. 2 Thess. iii. 4. εἰς, Gal. v. 10) only. Ps. cxxiv. 1. dat., Heb. ii. 13, from Isa. viii. 17.
o 2 Pet. ii. 7. Rom. xi. 26. Ps. cxxxix. 1. Psa. xxi. 8.
p ch. ix. 13 & xii. 7, from Hos. vi. 7. Heb. x. 5, 8, from Ps. xxxix. 6. with acc. of person, Ps. xvii. 19. xl. 11.
q = Phil. ii. 18.
r || Mk. John xix. 32. Rom. vi. 6. Gal. ii. 20 only †.
s = || Mk. ch. v. 11 reff.
t || Mk. L. 2 Kings xxiv. 15.
u ch. xx. 3, 5, (6,) 9. Acts x. 3, 9.

for ελεγον, λεγοντες D-gr am lat-$g_{1.2}$ syr coptt æth.

42. rec ins ει bef βασιλευς (*from ver* 40, *as also in* D &c *bef* πεποιθεν *below*), with A rel latt syrr copt æth arm Eus [Ps-Ath$_1$] Orig-int : om BDLא 33 sah. πιστευομεν A 244-58 [Scr's c] latt Orig-int : πιστευσωμεν EFHLMΓΔא 33. 69. for αυτω, επ' αυτον BLא 33 Cyr : επ' αυτω Δ rel syrr Thl(*corrns to express* 'believe on him') : txt AD 1. 69 latt goth arm Eus [Ps-Ath$_1$] Orig-int.

43. om to 2nd αυτον Γ. ins ει bef πεποιθεν D 1. 118. 209 lat-*a b h l* coptt (æth) arm Eus$_1$[om$_1$]. for τον θεον, τω θεω B Eus$_1$[txt$_1$]. om νυν AHΠ[1] 69 lat-ff_2 copt Eus$_1$[ins$_1$]. om 1st αυτον BLא 33 vulg Orig-int [Aug$_1$].

44. [δε D.] for αυτο, αυτοι D[1]. σταυρωθεντες [for συνσ.] DL. rec om συν, with A rel : ins BDLא, μετ' αυτου Θ_f. rec (for αυτον) αυτω (*emendn of constr*), with Scr's c(e sil) : txt ABDא rel Scr's mss goth Antch Thl. (Θ_f ?)

45. for επι πασαν, εφ' ολην א-corr[1] 245 [Chr-wlf-ms] : om επι πασαν την γην א[1] 248 lat-*l* [Lact$_1$]. ενατης bef ωρ. D.

ple, as ὁ πειράζων, ch. iv. 3: **thou puller down of . . . .** **42.**] Luke gives, more exactly, the second reproach in this verse as *proceeding from the soldiers.*

43.] See Ps. xxii. 7, 8. This is not according to the LXX, which has ἤλπισεν ἐπὶ κύριον· ῥυσάσθω αὐτόν, σωσάτω αὐτόν, ὅτι θέλει αὐτόν. This is omitted by Mark and Luke. θέλειν τινά for *amare aliquem,* occurs in reff. Ps. We have θέλειν with an accus. of the *thing* in reff. and Ezek. xviii. 23, 32 al.: and followed by ἐν with a person, 1 Kings xviii. 22: 1 Chron. xxviii. 4 (not Col. ii. 18; see note there), al. **44.**] Neither Matt. nor Mark is in possession of the more particular account given by Luke, vv. 39—43, where see notes. For the other incident which happened at this time, see John, vv. 25—27, and notes.

45—50.] Supernatural darkness. Last words, and death of Jesus. Mark xv. 33—37. Luke xxiii. 44—46. John xix. 28—30. The three accounts are here and there very closely allied; Matthew and Mark almost verbally. Luke only, however, contains the *words which the Lord uttered before he expired,*—omits the incident which takes up our vv. 46—49, and inserts *here* the rending of the veil. John is *entirely distinct.*

45.] According to Mark, ver. 25, it was the *third hour* when they crucified Him. If so, He had been on the cross three hours, which *in April* would answer to about the same space of time in our day—i. e. from 9—12 A.M. On the difficulty presented by John's declaration ch. xix. 14, see notes there and on Mark. **σκότος**] This was *no eclipse of the sun,* for it was *full moon* at the time—nor any partial obscuration of the sun such as sometimes takes place before an earthquake—for it is clear that no *earthquake in the ordinary sense of the word* is here intended. Those whose belief leads them to reflect WHO was then suffering, will have no difficulty in accounting for these signs of sympathy in Nature, nor in seeing their applicability. The consent, in the same words, of all three Evangelists, must silence all question as to the universal belief of this darkness as a *fact;* and the early Fathers (Julius Africanus, in Routh, Reliq. Sacr. ii. p. 297 f.: Tertull. Apol. c. 21, vol. i. p. 401: Origen c. Cels. ii. 33, vol. i. p. 414: Euseb. in Chronicon. Cf. Wordsw. h. l.) appeal to profane testimony for its truth. The omission of it in John's Gospel is of no more weight than the numerous other instances of such omission. See Amos viii. 9, 10. **ἐπὶ πᾶσαν τὴν γῆν**] Whether these words are to be taken in all their strictness is doubtful. Of course, the *whole globe* cannot be meant—as it would be night *naturally* over *half of it.* The question is, are we to understand *that part of*

[u] ὥραν [v] ἀνεβόησεν ὁ Ἰησοῦς φωνῇ μεγάλῃ λέγων Ἠλὶ
ἠλὶ λεμὰ σαβαχθανί; τοῦτ᾽ ἔστιν [w] Θεέ μου θεέ μου,
C τινες… [x] ἵνα τί με [y] ἐγκατέλιπες; 47 τινὲς δὲ τῶν ἐκεῖ ἑστώτων
ἀκούσαντες ἔλεγον ὅτι Ἠλίαν [z] φωνεῖ οὗτος. 48 καὶ
εὐθέως δραμὼν [a] εἷς ἐξ αὐτῶν καὶ λαβὼν [b] σπόγγον πλήσας [c] τε [d] ὄξους καὶ [e] περιθεὶς [f] καλάμῳ [g] ἐπότιζεν αὐτόν.
49 οἱ δὲ λοιποὶ ἔλεγον [h] Ἄφες ἴδωμεν εἰ ἔρχεται Ἠλίας

v Luke ix. 38 (Mark xv. 8 v. r.) only. Num. xx. 16. Isa. xxxvi. 13 B. Ezek. xi. 13.
w Psa. xxi. 1.
x ch. ix. 4 reff.
y = || Mk. Acts ii. 27 (from Ps. xv. 10), 31. 2 Cor. iv. 9. 2 Tim. iv. 10, 16. Heb. xiii. 5 al. Wisd. x. 13.
z = ch. xx. 32 reff.
a ch. x. 20. xx. 32 reff.
b || Mk. J. only †.
c (|| only in Mk.) ch. xxii. 10. (xxiii. 6 v. r.) xxviii. 12 only in Matt.
d ver. 34 reff.
e ver. 28 reff. Lev. viii. 13 al.
f ch. xi. 7 reff.
g ch. x. 42. xxv. 35, &c. Gen. xxi. 19.
h = and constr. || Mk. ch. vii. 4.

46. εβοησεν (|| *Mark*) BL 33. 69 Eus. om ὁ D. ελωι B(-ει) ℵ 33 harl copt: αηλι L. rec λαμα, with D 1 gat mm lat-*a b h* æth arm Eus_2 [$Orig\text{-}int_1$]: *lamma* vulg lat *c* g_2: λιμα AKUΓΔ$Θ_f$Π 69 lat-*f* syr goth Eus Chr-wlf-ms: λειμα EFGHMSV Scr's b f i o evv-H-P_1-x: txt BLℵ 33 am(with forj harl) lat-ff_1 g_1 Eus. ζαφθανει D lat-*h*: σαβακτ. B. εγκατελειπες AEFGHKMΔ$Θ_f$$Π^1$ 33.
47. εστηκοτων (*see* || *Mark*) BCLℵ 33. om οτι DLℵ 33 latt(not *f*) Syr æth arm.
48. om εξ αυτων ℵ. om τε D. οξου [for -ους] D 69.
49. for ελεγ., ειπαν B; ειπον D 69; simly lat-*a b c* ff_2 g_2.

it over which there was day? I believe we *are*; but see no strong objection to any limitation, provided *the fact itself*, as happening at Jerusalem, is *distinctly recognized*. This last is *matter of testimony*, and the three Evangelists are *pledged to its truth*: the present words cannot stand on the same ground, not being matter of testimony properly so called. **46.**] See Ps. xxii. 1. The words **λεμὰ σαβαχθανί** are Chaldee, and not Hebrew. Our Lord spoke them in the ordinary dialect, not in that of the sacred text itself. The weightiest question is, *In what sense did He use them?* His inner consciousness of union with God must have been complete and indestructible—but, like His higher and holy Will, liable to be obscured by human weakness and pain, which at this time was at its very highest. We must however take care not to ascribe *all* his suffering to *bodily pain*, however cruel: his *soul was in immediate contact with and prospect of death*—the wages of *sin*, which He had *taken on Him*, but *never committed*—and the conflict at Gethsemane was renewed. 'He himself,' as the Berlenberg Bible remarks (Stier, vi. 442), 'becomes the expositor of the darkness, and shews what it imports.' In the words however, '*My God*'—there speaks the same union with the Divine Will, and abiding in the everlasting covenant purpose, as in those, 'Not my will, but thine.' These are the only words on the Cross related by Matt. and Mark—and they are related by none besides. The form **θεέ** is very seldom used,—only in Judg. xvi. 28 B, Ezra ix. 6. The LXX here has the usual vocative ὁ θεός: as also Mark. **47.**] This was not said by the *Roman soldiers*, who could know nothing of Elias; nor was it a *misunderstanding* of the Jewish spectators, who must have well understood the import of ἠλί: nor again was it said in any apprehension, from the supernatural darkness, that Elias *might really come* (Olsh.); but it was replied in *intended mockery*, as **οὗτος**,—'this one among the three,'—clearly indicates.

This is one of the cases where those who advocate an original Hebrew Gospel of Matthew are obliged to suppose that the Greek translator has *retained the original words*, in order to make the reason of the reply clear. **48.**] This was on account of the words 'I thirst,' uttered by our Lord: see John, ver. 28. Mark's account is somewhat different; there *the same person* gives the vinegar and utters the scoff which follows. This is quite intelligible—contempt mingled with pity would doubtless find a type among the bystanders. There is no need for assuming that the *soldiers offering vinegar* in Luke, ver. 36, is the same incident as this. Since then, the bodily state of the Redeemer had greatly changed; and what was then offered in mockery, might well be now asked for in the agony of death, and received when presented. I would not however absolutely deny that Luke *may* be giving a less precise detail; and may represent this incident by his ver. 36. The **ὄξος** is the *posca*, sour wine, or vinegar and water, the ordinary drink of the Roman soldiers. On the other particulars, see notes on John. **49.**] If we take our account as the strictly precise

σώσων αὐτόν. 50 ὁ δὲ Ἰησοῦς πάλιν [i] κράξας φωνῇ
μεγάλῃ [k] ἀφῆκεν τὸ πνεῦμα. 51 καὶ ἰδοὺ τὸ [l] καταπέτασμα τοῦ ναοῦ [m] ἐσχίσθη [n] ἀπὸ [n] ἄνωθεν [o] ἕως [o] κάτω

ABCDE FGHKL MSUVΓ ΔΘfΠא 1. 33. 69

i Mark i. 26. v. 7. Acts vii. 60. Rev. vi. 10 al. Ps. cxli. 1.
k = here only. Gen. xxxv. 18. see || Mk. Gen. xlv. 2.
l || Mk. L. Heb. vi. 19, ix. 3. x. 20 only. Exod. xxvi. 31, &c.
m || Mk. L. Mark i. 10 al. Isa. xlviii. 21. Zech. xiv. 4.
n || Mk.
o || Mk. Ezek. i. 27.

σωσαι א[1](txt א[3a]) 47. 56-8. 69. 70 ev-y lat-*f* g_2 syrr goth: και σωσει D 1 lat-*a b c* ff_2 *h l* Orig-int. at end ins αλλος δε λαβων λογχην ενυξεν αυτου την πλευραν, και εξηλθεν υδωρ κ. αιμα (*from John* xix. 34: *see note*) BCL U(κ. ευθεως and αιμ. κ. υδ.) Γא gat(with mm) æth mss-mtd-by-Sev schol(thus given by Tischdf, ὅτι εἰς τὸ καθ' ἱστορίαν εὐαγγέλιον Διοδώρου(?) καὶ Τατιανοῦ(?) καὶ ἄλλων διαφόρων ἁγ. πατέρων τοῦτο πρόσκειται, τοῦτο λέγει καὶ ὁ Χρυσόστομος. ὅταν οὖν ὁ Ματθ. πρὸ τελευτῆς αὐτοῦ σφαζόμενον ὑπὸ τοῦ στρατιώτου τῇ λόγχῃ εἰς τὴν πλευρὰν ἐδήλωσεν, εἶθ' οὕτως νυχθέντα τελευτῆσαι, ὁ δέ γε Ἰω. τοῦτον ἔφη λόγχῃ νυχθῆναι μετὰ τὸ τελειωθῆναι, οὐ μάχης τὸ εἰρημένον· ἀμφότεροι γὰρ τὸ ἀληθὲς ἐμήνυσαν κ. τ. λ.) Chr(but adds τί γένοιτ' ἂν τούτων παρανομώτερον, τί δὲ θηριωδέστερον· οἳ μέχρι τοσούτου τὴν ἑαυτῶν μανίαν ἐξέτειναν καὶ εἰς νεκρὸν σῶμα λοιπὸν ὑβρίζοντες): syr-jer has this portion of Matt twice among the lections of which it consists, one time omg, and the other insg, the doubtful words: Orig favours the omn when he says ἤδη δ' αὐτοῦ ἀποθανόντος εἷς τῶν στρατιωτῶν λόγχῃ κ.τ.λ.

51. rec εις δυο bef απ. αν. εως κατω (*see* || *Mark*), with A(D)Θ_fא rel latt syrr [goth arm Cyr_2] Orig-int Promiss: txt BC[1]L 33 copt [æth].—om εις δυο (C[2] ?) $Orig_2$ Eus_2.—aft εις δυο ins μερη D latt Orig-int. απ' BCΘ_f: επ' 69: om απο Lא Orig [Cyr_1(txt_1)].

one, the *rest*—in mockery—*call upon this person* to desist, and wait for Elias to come to save Him: if that of Mark, *the giver of the drink calls upon the rest* (also in mockery) to let this suffice or to let *him* (the giver) alone, and wait, &c. The former seems more probable. It is remarkable that the words undeniably interpolated from John should have found their place here *before the death of Jesus*, and can only be attributed to carelessness, there being no other place here for the insertion of the indignity but this, and the interpolator not observing that in John it is related as inflicted *after death*.

50.] It has been doubted whether the τετέλεσται of John (ver. 30) and πάτερ, εἰς χ. σου παρατίθεμαι τ. πν. μου of Luke (ver. 46) are to be *identified with this crying out*, or to be taken as *distinct from it*. But a nearer examination of the case will set the doubt at rest. The παρέδωκεν of John (ib.) *implies the speech in Luke*; which accordingly was that uttered in this φωνὴ μεγάλη. The τετέλεσται was said before: see notes on John.

51–56.] SIGNS FOLLOWING HIS DEATH. Mark xv. 38—41. Luke xxiii. 47—49. The three narratives are essentially distinct. That of Luke is more general—giving only the *sense* of the centurion's words—twice using the indefinite πάντες—and not specifying the women. The whole is omitted by John. **51.**] The **ἰδού** gives solemnity. This was the *inner veil*, screening off the holy of holies from the holy place, Exod. xxvi. 33: Heb. ix. 2, 3. This circumstance has given rise to much incredulous comment, and that even from men like Schleiermacher. A right and deep view of the O. T. symbolism is required to furnish the key to it; and for this we look in vain among those who *set aside that symbolism entirely*. That was now accomplished, which was the one and great antitype of all those sacrifices offered in the holy place, *in order to gain*, as on the great day of atonement (for that day may be taken as the representation of their intent), *entrance into the holiest place,—the typical presence of God*. What those sacrifices (ceremonially) procured for the Jews (the type of God's universal Church) through their High-priest, was now (really) procured for all men by the sacrifice of Him, who was at once the victim and the High-priest. When Schleiermacher and De Wette assert that no use is made of this event in the Epistle to the Hebrews, they surely cannot have remembered, or not have deeply considered, Heb. x. 19—21. Besides, suppose it *had* been referred to plainly and by name—what would then have been said? Clearly, that *this* mention was *a later insertion, to justify that reference*. And *almost* this latter, Strauss, *recognizing the allusion in Heb.*, actually does. Schleiermacher also asks, *how could the event be known*, seeing none but priests could have witnessed it, and they would not be likely to betray it? To say nothing of the *almost certain spread of the rumour*, has he forgotten that (Acts vi. 7) "a *great company of the priests* were obedient unto the faith?" Neander, who

[p] εἰς δύο, καὶ ἡ γῆ [q] ἐσείσθη, καὶ αἱ πέτραι [m] ἐσχίσθησαν,
52 καὶ τὰ [r] μνημεῖα ἀνεῴχθησαν, καὶ πολλὰ σώματα τῶν
[s] κεκοιμημένων [t] ἁγίων ἠγέρθησαν 53 καὶ ἐξελθόντες ἐκ τῶν

p || Mk. Eph. ii. 15. Rev. xvi. 19. Judg. ix. 43. q = (ch. xxi. 10. xxviii. 4.) Heb. xii. 26, from Hag. ii. 7. Rev. vi. 13 only. Joel iii. 16. r ch. viii. 28. Isa. xxvi. 19. s Acts vii. 60. xiii. 36. 1 Cor. vii. 39. xi. 30. xv. 6, &c. al. Isa. xiv. 8, 18. t = Gospp., here only. Acts ix. 13, 32, 41. xxvi. 10 only. Epp. passim.

52. om 1st clause (*homœotel*) $\aleph^1$ 238. for μνημεια, μνηματα A. ανεωχθη AΠ[1] Scr's a g p w: ηνεωχθη C[1] $Orig_1$ (*gramml corrns*): ηνεωχθησαν $C^3L\Theta_f$ **1. 33.** [Cyr_1]: txt BD$\aleph^{3a}$ rel $Orig_1$ [Eus_1 Cyr_1]. rec ηγερθη (*gramml corrn; not as Meyer, the origl, and altered to suit the context: see above*), with $AC\Theta_f$ rel [Cyr_1]: txt BDGL$\aleph$ **1. 33.** 69 $Orig_2$ Eus.

gives this last consideration its weight (but only as a possibility, that *some* priests may have become converts, and apparently without reference to the above fact), has an unworthy and shuffling note (L. J. p. 757), ending by quoting two testimonies, one apocryphal, the other Rabbinical, from which he concludes that '*some* matter of fact lies at the foundation' of this (according to him) *mythical adjunct.* **ἡ γῆ ἐσείσθη**] Not an ordinary earthquake, but connected with the two next clauses, and finding in them its explanation and justification. **αἱ πέτραι ἐσχίσθησαν**] It would not be right altogether to reject the testimonies of travellers to the fact of extraordinary rents and fissures in the rocks near the spot. Of course those who know no other proof of the historical truth of the event, will not be likely to take this as one; but to us, who are firmly convinced of it, every such trace, provided it be soberly and honestly ascertained, is full of interest. **52. καὶ τὰ μν. . . . .** to end of ver. **53.**] The first clause, as following on an earthquake which splits the rocks, is by the modern Commentators received as genuine, and thrown into the same probability as the earthquake itself: but the following ones meet with no mercy at their hands. Ein mythisch apokryphischer Ansatz is Meyer's description of them—and as he cannot find any *critical* ground for this, the *Greek Editor of Matthew* has the blame of *having added them.* I believe on the contrary that these latter clauses contain *the occasion of the former ones.* The whole transaction was *supernatural* and *symbolic:* no other interpretation of it will satisfy even ordinary common sense. Was the earthquake a *mere coincidence!* This not even those assert, who deny all symbolism in the matter. Was it a mere *sign of divine wrath* at what was done—a mere *prodigy*, like those at the death of Cæsar? Surely no Christian believer can think this. Then *what was it?* What but the *opening of the tombs*—the symbolic declaration '*mors janua vitæ,*'—that *the death* which had happened had broken the bands of death for ever? These following clauses (which have no mythical nor apocryphal character—ἐνεφανίσθησαν **πολλοῖς**, and no more, is not the way of any but authentic history: see the Gospel of Nicodemus, ch. xvii. ff. in Jones's Canon of the N. T. vol. ii. p. 255) require only this explanation to be fully understood. The graves were opened *at the moment of the death* of the Lord; but inasmuch as He is the first-fruits from the dead—*the* Resurrection and the Life—the bodies of the saints in them *did not arise till He rose,* and having appeared to many after his resurrection,—possibly during the forty days,—went up with Him into his glory. (Cf. on this Corn.-a-Lap., h. l.: who maintains that this was so, for five reasons: 1) "quia hoc decebat Christum, ut fructum mortis et resurrectionis suæ statim ostenderet in beata hac Sanctorum resurrectione: 2) quia animæ horum jam erant beatæ, ac proinde par erat eas non uniri corporibus nisi gloriosis et immortalibus: 3) quia exigua fuisset earum felicitas, ac longe major miseria, quod mox rursum deberent mori: 4) quia congruebat, ut hi Sancti Christum resurgentem et scandentem in cœlum, ejusque triumphum sua resurrectione decorarent: 5) quia convenit ut Christus in cœlo habeat Beatos quorum aspectu et collocutione externa se pascat humanitas, ne alioqui solitaria sit, expersque humanæ consolationis." On this side, he claims Orig. (in Matt. Comm. series, vol. iii. p. 928; but wrongly, for Origen gives the whole a spiritual sense, more suo), Jerome, Bede, Thos. Aquinas, Anselm, Clem. Alex. (Strom. vi. 47, p. 764 P.), Euseb. (Dem. Evang. iv. 12, vol. iv. p. 284), Epiph. (Hær. lxxv. p. 911), al. On the other side are Thl., Euthym., Aug. (Ep. 164 (99) ad Evod. 3 (2) vol. ii.), al. Augustine is moved chiefly by the fact that David's body appears from Acts ii. 29, 34, to have been still in his tomb after the Ascension.) Moses and Elias, who were before in glory, were not *from the dead,* properly speaking: see note on ch. xvii. 1.

u here only. Judg. vii. 19 A. Ps. cxxxviii. 2. Esdr. v. 62 (59) only.
v ch. iv. 5 reff.
w pass., Heb. ix. 24 only †. Wisd. i. 2. xvii. 4 only. act., John xiv. 21, 22 reff.
x ver. 36.
y ch. xxiv. 7 al.
z ch. xvii. 6. Num. xxii. 3
a ch. xxvi. 73 reff.
b ch. xiv. 33.
c vv. 40, 43.
d ch. xxvi. 58 reff.
e = ch. vii. 15. xxv. 1 al. fr.
f ch. xx. 28 reff.

[r] μνημείων μετὰ τὴν [u] ἔγερσιν αὐτοῦ εἰςῆλθον εἰς τὴν
[v] ἁγίαν [v] πόλιν καὶ [w] ἐνεφανίσθησαν πολλοῖς. 54 ὁ δὲ
ἑκατόνταρχος καὶ οἱ μετ' αὐτοῦ [x] τηροῦντες τὸν Ἰησοῦν,
ἰδόντες τὸν [y] σεισμὸν καὶ τὰ γινόμενα, [z] ἐφοβήθησαν
[z] σφόδρα λέγοντες [ab] Ἀληθῶς [bc] υἱὸς [c] θεοῦ ἦν οὗτος.
55 ἦσαν δὲ ἐκεῖ γυναῖκες πολλαὶ [d] ἀπὸ [d] μακρόθεν θεωροῦσαι, [e] αἵτινες ἠκολούθησαν τῷ Ἰησοῦ ἀπὸ τῆς Γαλιλαίας [f] διακονοῦσαι αὐτῷ· 56 ἐν αἷς ἦν Μαρία ἡ Μαγδαληνή, καὶ Μαρία ἡ τοῦ Ἰακώβου καὶ Ἰωσῆ μήτηρ, καὶ ἡ ...xxvii. 56(appy)
μήτηρ τῶν υἱῶν Ζεβεδαίου.

Θ_f ABCDE FGHKL MSUVΓ ΔΠℵ 1. 33. 69

53. ηλθον D latt(not *f*).—om εισηλθ. and 2nd και ℵ. εφανησαν D¹: ενεφανεισαν D³.

54. εκατονταρχης Dℵ [Orig₁]. rec γενομενα (*corrn to sense, and* ‖ *Luke*), with ACΘ_fℵ rel Orig₁: txt BD 33 latt Orig₁ Orig-int₂. rec θεου bef υιος (*see ch* xiv. 33), with ACΘ_fℵ^{3a} rel am(with forj fuld gat ing) lat-*a c f ff*₁.₂ *g*₁.₂ D-lat goth Orig₂: υιος ην του θεου (*see* ‖ *Mark*) ℵ¹: txt B D-gr vulg lat-*b h l* Syr Orig-int Hil₁ Aug [Jer₁]. for ην, εστιν C lat-*f g*₁ goth Aug₁[txt₁] Vigil.

55. for εκει, και (‖ *Mark*) D 56 Chr-wlf-ms: κακει ℵ: εκει και FKLΠ syr-mg. om απο ΑΚΔΠ Scr's c e ev-w Chr. αγιλειλαιας D-gr.

56. om μαρια η μαγδ. και ℵ¹(ins ℵ^{3a}). om η (bef μαγδ.) D¹(ins D²): μαριαμ η μαγδ. C[C¹ pref και] LΔ 1 syr. και μαριαμ CΔ Syr. ιωσηφ D¹Lℵ 69² ev-x latt(*a* def) syr-mg copt æth Eus₁[txt₁] Orig-int: ιωσητος D³.—και η μαρ. η ιωσ. και η μαρια η των υιων ℵ¹: κ. η ιωσ. μηρ κ. η μητηρ των υ. ℵ^{3a}.

The explanation (Fritzsche) of **μετὰ τὴν ἔγερσιν αὐτοῦ** as '*after He had raised them,*' is simply ridiculous. The words belong to the *whole sentence*, not merely to εἰςῆλθον. **ἠγέρθησαν** is the *result*—not the *immediate accompaniment*, of the opening of the tombs. It is to prevent this being supposed, that the qualification μετ. τ. ἔ. αὐ. is added. **54.**] **τὸν σεισμὸν καὶ τὰ γιν.** = ὅτι οὕτως ἐξέπνευσεν Mark. Does the latter of these look as if compiled from the former? The circumstances of our vv. 51—53, except the rending of the veil, are not in the possession of Mark, of the minute accuracy of whose account I have no doubt. *His* report is that of *one man*—and that man, more than probably, a *convert*. Matthew's is of *many*, and represents their general impression. Luke's is also *general*. **τὰ γινόμενα** points to the crying out, as indeed does the οὕτως in Mark:—but see notes there. **υἱὸς θεοῦ ἦν**—which the Centurion had heard that *He gave Himself out for*, John xix. 7, and our ver. 43. It cannot be doubtful, I think, that he used these words *in the Jewish sense*—and with some idea of that which they implied. When Meyer says that he must have used them in a heathen sense, meaning a *hero or demigod*, we must first be shewn that υἱὸς θεοῦ was *ever so used*. I believe Luke's to be a different report: see notes there.

55, 56.] **ἠκολ.**, the historic aorist in a relative clause, see Acts i. 2: John xi. 30 al. fr.: and Winer, § 40. 5, end: where the true account of the idiom is given; viz. that in such clauses, the Greek merely states the event as a past one, where we commonly use the pluperfect. **ἡ Μαγδ., from Magdala**: see note on ch. xv. 39. She is not to be confounded with Mary who anointed our Lord, John xii. 1, nor with the woman who did the same, Luke vii. 36: see Luke viii. 2. **Μαρ. ἡ τ. Ἰακ.**] The wife of Alphæus or Clopas, John xix. 25: see note on ch. xiii. 55. **Ἰακ.**] Mark adds τοῦ μικροῦ, to distinguish him from the brother of our Lord (probably not from the son of Zebedee, see Prolegg. to Epistle of James, § i. 8). **μήτ. τ. υἱ. Ζ.** = Σαλώμη Mark. Both *omit Mary the mother of Jesus*:—but we must remember, that if we are to take the group as described at this moment, *she was not present*, having been, as I believe (see note on John, ver. 27), led away by the beloved Apostle immediately on the speaking of the words, 'Behold thy mother.' And if this view be objected to, yet she could not be named here, nor in Mark, except separately from these three—for she could

57 [g] Ὀψίας δὲ γενομένης ἦλθεν ἄνθρωπος πλούσιος ἀπὸ
Ἀριμαθαίας [h] τοὔνομα Ἰωσήφ, ὃς καὶ αὐτὸς [i] ἐμαθήτευσεν
τῷ Ἰησοῦ· 58 οὗτος προσελθὼν τῷ Πιλάτῳ [k] ᾐτήσατο τὸ
[l] σῶμα τοῦ Ἰησοῦ. τότε ὁ Πιλάτος ἐκέλευσεν [m] ἀποδοθῆναι τὸ [l] σῶμα. 59 καὶ λαβὼν τὸ [l] σῶμα ὁ Ἰωσὴφ
[n] ἐνετύλιξεν αὐτὸ ἐν [o] σινδόνι καθαρᾷ 60 καὶ ἔθηκεν αὐτὸ
ἐν τῷ καινῷ αὐτοῦ [p] μνημείῳ ὃ [q] ἐλατόμησεν ἐν τῇ πέτρᾳ,
καὶ [r] προςκυλίσας λίθον μέγαν τῇ [s] θύρᾳ τοῦ [s] μνημείου

g ch. viii. 16. Mark i. 32 al. Judith xiii. 1 only.
h here only.
i intr., here only. trans., ch. xxviii. 19. Acts xiv. 21. pass., ch. xiii. 52 only †.
k ver. 20.
l = ch. xiv. 12 reff.
m = here only. Exod. v. 18. see Acts iv. 33.
n ‖ L. John xx. 7 only †.
o ‖ Mk. bis. L. Mark xiv. 51, 52 only. Judg. xiv. 12, 13 A. Prov. xxxi. 24 only.
p vv. 52, 53.
q ‖ Mk. only. Isa. xxii. 16. li. 1.
r ‖ Mk. only †.
s ‖ Mk. Mark xvi. 3 only.

57. om δε A[1]. το ονομα D. εμαθητευθη (*gramml corrn*) CDℵ 1 (33 syrr, appy).

58. προςηλθεν . . και D latt [Orig-int$_1$]. at end om το σωμα (*for elegance, as it is thrice repeated*) BLℵ 1. 33 syr-jer: αυτο (*for same reason*) copt.

59. **παραλαβων** D. ιωσ. bef το σωμα D lat-*a*(addg *jesu*) Syr. om ο DL. rec om εν (‖ *Mark Luke*), with ACℵ rel lat-g_1 Hil: ins BD ev-x latt copt [Orig-int Aug]. (33 def.)

60. om αυτο Lℵ 69 arm. ins επι bef τη θυρα A 242-3, *ad osteum* lat-*a b c* &c. (*osteo* D-lat.)

not well have been one of the διακονοῦσαι αὐτῷ. There must have been also *another group*, of His *disciples*, within sight;—e. g. Thomas, who said, 'Except I see in his hands the print of the nails,' &c., and generally those to whom He afterwards shewed his hands and feet as a proof of his identity.

57—61.] Joseph of Arimathæa begs, and buries the body of Jesus. Mark xv. 42—47. Luke xxiii. 50—56. John xix. 38—42. The four accounts, agreeing in substance, are remarkably distinct and independent, as will appear by a close comparison of them. **57.**] *Before sunset*, at which time the Sabbath, and that an high day, began: see Deut. xxi. 23. The *Roman custom* was for the bodies to remain on the crosses till devoured by birds of prey:—'non pasces in cruce corvos.' Hor. Epist. i. 16. 48. On the other hand, Josephus, B. J. iv. 5. 2, says, Ἰουδαίων περὶ τὰς ταφὰς πρόνοιαν ποιουμένων ὥστε καὶ τοὺς ἐκ καταδίκης . . . . ἀνασταυρωμένους πρὸ δύντος ἡλίου καθελεῖν καὶ θάπτειν. **ἦλθεν**] probably *to the Prætorium*. Meyer supposes, *to the place of execution;* which is also possible, and seems supported by the ἦλθεν οὖν καὶ ἦρεν John ver. 38, and ἦλθεν δὲ καὶ . . . . ib. ver. 39, which certainly was *to Golgotha*. **πλούσιος**] He was also a *counsellor*, i. e. one of the Sanhedrim: see Mark, ver. 43: Luke, ver. 51. **Ἀριμαθαίας**] Opinions are divided as to whether this was Rama in Benjamin (see ch. ii. 18.), or Rama (Ramathaim) in Ephraim, the birth-place of Samuel. The form of the name is more like *the latter*.

58.] The repetition of **τὸ σῶμα** is remarkable, and indicates a common origin, in this verse, with Mark, who after ἐδωρήσατο expresses τὸ πτῶμα on account of the expression of Pilate's surprise, and the change of subject between.

59.] John (ver. 39) mentions *the arrival of Nicodemus* with an hundred pound weight of myrrh and aloes, in which also the Body was wrapped. The Three are not in possession of this—nor Matthew and John of the subsequent design of the women to embalm It. What wonder if, at such a time, one party of disciples should not have been aware of the doings of another? It is possible that the women, who certainly *knew what had been done* with the Body (see ver. 61), may have intended to bestow on it more elaborate care, as whatever was done this night was *hurried*,—see John, vv. 41, 42.

60.] Matt. alone relates that it was Joseph's *own* tomb. John, that it was *in a garden*, and *in the place where He was crucified*. All, except Mark, notice the *newness* of the tomb. John does not mention that it *belonged to Joseph*—but the expression ἐν ᾧ οὐδέπω οὐδεὶς ἐτέθη looks as if he knew more than he has thought it necessary to state. His reason for the Body being laid there is, that *it was near*, and the Preparation rendered haste necessary. But then we may well ask, How should the body of an executed person be laid in a new tomb, without the consent of the owner being first obtained? And who so likely to provide a tomb, as he whose pious care for the Body was so eminent? All

ἀπῆλθεν. 61 ἦν δὲ ἐκεῖ Μαρία ἡ Μαγδαληνὴ καὶ ἡ ἄλλη ABCDE FGHKL
Μαρία καθήμεναι [t] ἀπέναντι τοῦ [u] τάφου. 62 Τῇ δὲ MSUVΓ
[v] ἐπαύριον, [w] ἥτις ἐστὶν μετὰ τὴν [x] παρασκευήν, [y] συν- ΔΠℵ 1. 33. 69
ήχθησαν οἱ ἀρχιερεῖς καὶ οἱ Φαρισαῖοι πρὸς Πιλάτον
63 λέγοντες Κύριε, ἐμνήσθημεν ὅτι ἐκεῖνος ὁ [z] πλάνος
εἶπεν ἔτι ζῶν Μετὰ τρεῖς ἡμέρας [a] ἐγείρομαι. 64 κέλευσον
οὖν [b] ἀσφαλισθῆναι τὸν [u] τάφον [c] ἕως τῆς τριτης ἡμέρας,
[d] μήποτε ἐλθόντες οἱ μαθηταὶ αὐτοῦ [e] κλέψωσιν αὐτὸν

t = ch. xxi. 2 (reff.) only.
u ch. xxiii. 27, 29 reff.
v Mark xi. 12. John i. 29 al4. Acts x. 9 al9. only. Gen. xix. 34.
w Luke ii. 4, 10 al.
x (=) Mark xv. 42. Luke xxiii. 54. John xix. 14, 31, 42 only ‡. (Exod. xxxv. 24 Ed-vat. [κατασκ. AB]. xxxix. 23 (43) A [αποσκ. B]. 2 Macc. xv. 21 only.)
y ch. xxii. 34. xxvi. 3 al. fr.
z 2 Cor. vi. 8. 1 Tim. iv. 1. 2 John 7 bis only. Job xix. 4. Jer. xxiii. 32 only.
a pres., ch. xvii. 11. xxvi. 2. John xiv. 3. xxi. 23. Gal. iii. 8. 2 Pet. iii. 11.
b here (3ce) and Acts xvi. 24 only. Isa. xli. 10. Wisd. xiii. 15.
c ver. 45.
d ch. v. 25. vii. 6 al. Sir. xlii. 9, 10, 11.
e ch. xxviii. 13. Tobit i. 18.

61. μαριαμ η μαγδ. BCLΔℵ 1.—om η D^1(ins D^2). om 2nd η AD. κατεναντι D.
63. ο πλανος bef εκεινος B^2C^2 E^1(perhaps) G 33. 69 latt(*a* def) copt arm Chr_1 Did [$Aug_1(txt_1)$] Promiss. aft ζων ins οτι D Scr's k syrr arm Chr Orig-int.
64. om 1st της DL 251-3 ev-z Chr-ϐ-ρ. ημερας bef τρ. D latt [$Orig\text{-}int_1$]. om αυτου Bℵ. rec aft αυτου ins νυκτος, with C^3FGLMUΓ 69 arm: aft κλ. αυτον S 3 Scr's h i Syr æth: om ABC^1Dℵ rel latt syr copt goth Chr Damasc Orig-int (Thl Euthym appy). κλεψουσιν ℵ.

that we can determine respecting the sepulchre from the data here furnished is, (1) That it was not a *natural* cave, but an *artificial excavation* in the rock. (2) That it was not cut *downwards*, after the manner of a grave with us, but *horizontally, or nearly so,* into the face of the rock—this I conceive to be implied in προσκυλίσας λίθ. μέγ. τῇ θύρᾳ τοῦ μν., as also by the use of παρακύπτω John xx. 5, 11, and εἰσῆλθεν, ib. 5, 6. (3) That it was *in the spot* where the crucifixion took place. Cyr-jer. speaks of τὸ μνῆμα τὸ πλησίον, ὅπου ἐτέθη, κ. ὁ ἐπιτεθεὶς τῇ θύρᾳ λίθος, ὁ μέχρι σήμερον παρὰ τῷ μνημείῳ κείμενος. Catech. xiii. 39, p. 202. On ἐλατόμησεν, the aor. in a relative clause, see above, ver. 55 note.

61.] Luke mentions more generally *the women who came with Him from Galilee;* and specifies that they *prepared spices and ointments,* and rested the sabbath-day according to the commandment.

62—66.] THE JEWISH AUTHORITIES OBTAIN FROM PILATE A GUARD FOR THE SEPULCHRE. *Peculiar to Matthew.*

62. τῇ ἐπ.] not on that night, but on the next day. A difficulty has been found in its being called the day μετὰ τὴν παρασκευήν, considering that it was *itself the sabbath,* and the *greatest sabbath in the year.* But I believe the expression to be carefully and purposely used. The chief priests, &c. did not go to Pilate on the sabbath,—but *in the evening, after the termination of the sabbath.* Had the Evangelist said ἥτις ἐστὶ τὸ σάββατον, the incongruity would at once appear of such an application being made on the sabbath—and he therefore designates the day as the first after that, which, as the day of the Lord's death, the παρασκευή, was uppermost in his mind. The narrative following has been much impugned, and its historical accuracy very generally given up by even the best of the German Commentators (Olshausen, Meyer; also De Wette, Hase, and others). The chief difficulties found in it seem to be: (1) How should the chief priests, &c. *know of His having said,* 'in three days I will rise again,' when the saying was hid even from His own disciples? The answer to this is easy. The *meaning* of the saying may have been, and was, hid from the disciples; but the *fact of its having been said* could be no secret. Not to lay any stress on John ii. 19, we have the direct prophecy of Matt. xii. 40—and besides this, there would be a rumour current, through the intercourse of the Apostles with others, that He had been in the habit of so saying. As to the *understanding of* the words, we must remember that *hatred is keener sighted than love;*—that the *raising of Lazarus* would shew, *what sort of a thing rising from the dead was to be;*—and that the fulfilment of the Lord's announcement of his *crucifixion* would naturally lead them to look further, to *what more* he had announced. (2) How should the women, who were solicitous about the *removal* of the stone, not have been still more so about its being sealed, and a guard set? The answer to this has been given above—*they were not aware of the*

καὶ εἴπωσιν τῷ λαῷ [f] Ἠγέρθη ἀπὸ τῶν [f] νεκρῶν, καὶ
ἔσται ἡ [g] ἐσχάτη [h] πλάνη [i] χείρων τῆς [g] πρώτης. 65 ἔφη
αὐτοῖς ὁ Πιλάτος Ἔχετε [k] κουστωδίαν· ὑπάγετε [b] ἀσφα-
λίσασθε ὡς οἴδατε. 66 οἱ δὲ πορευθέντες [b] ἠσφαλίσαντο
τὸν [l] τάφον [m] σφραγίσαντες τὸν λίθον [n] μετὰ τῆς [k] κουστωδίας.

XXVIII. 1 [o] Ὀψὲ δὲ [p] σαββάτων, τῇ [q] ἐπιφωσκούσῃ

f w. ἀπό, ch. xiv. 2. xxviii. 7.
g ch. xii. 45 ‖ L. 2 Pet. ii. 20. 2 Kings xiii. 15.
h here only in Gospp. 1 Thess. ii. 3 al. Prov. xiv. 8.
i N. T. as above (g) al. Wisd. xv. 18 only.
k here bis and ch. xxviii. 11 only †.
l ch. xxiii. 27 reff.
m Rev. xx. 3. 2 Cor. i. 22. 4 Kings xxii. 4.
n = Luke xvii. 15. Acts v. 26. xiii. 17.
o Mark xi. 19. xiii. 35 only. Exod. xxx. 8.
p plur., ch. xii. 1. Luke iv. 16. Acts xiii. 14. xvi. 13 al. Exod. xxxi. 15 al.
q Luke xxiii. 54 only. Job xli. 9 (10) A (ἐπιφαυσκ. B א) only. ἅμ' ἡμέρῃ διαφωσκ., Herod. iii. 86.

for ειπ., ερουσιν *dicent* D. χειρον א 69: χειρω DL.

65. rec aft εφη ins δε, with ACDM[1]UΔΠא (SV, e sil) syr-w-ast Orig-int: om B rel 33. 69 latt Syr copt goth arm. εχεται, υπαγεται D, ασφαλισασθαι [C]D[א]. for κουστωδιαν, φυλακας *custodes* D[1] lat-*a b c f ff*$_2$ *g*$_1$ arm-usc. for ως, εως L.

66. ησφαλισαν D[1](txt D[3]). for της κουστωδιας, τ(.)ν φυλακ(.)ν D', *custodibus* latt arm. [goth def.]

circumstance, because the guard was not set till the evening before. There would be no need of the application before the *approach of the third day*—it is only made for a watch **ἕως τῆς τρίτης ἡμέρας**, ver. 64—and it is not probable that the circumstance would transpire that night—certainly it seems not to have done so. (3) That Gamaliel was of the council, and if such a thing as this, and its sequel ch. xxviii. 11—15, had really happened, he need not have expressed himself doubtfully, Acts v. 39, but would have been certain that this was from God. But, first, it does not necessarily follow that *every member* of the Sanhedrim was present and applied to Pilate, or even had they done so, that all bore a part in the act of ch. xxviii. 12. One who, like Joseph, had not consented to their deed before—and we may safely say that there were others such—would naturally withdraw himself from further proceedings against the person of Jesus. On Gamaliel and his character, see note on Acts, l. c. (4) Had this been so, the three other Evangelists would not have passed over so important a testimony to the Resurrection. But surely we cannot argue in this way—for thus every important fact narrated by *one Evangelist alone* must be rejected—e. g. (which stands in much the same relation) the *satisfaction of Thomas*,—and other such narrations. *Till we know much more about the circumstances under which, and the scope with which, each Gospel was compiled, all à priori arguments of this kind are good for nothing.*

65.] **ἔχετε**—either 1), indicative, **Ye have**:—but then the question arises, *What guard* had they? and if they had one, why go to Pilate? Perhaps we must understand some detachment placed at their disposal during the feast—but there does not seem to be any record of such a practice. That the guards *were under the Sanhedrim* is plain from ch. xxviii. 11, where they make their report ('ut mos militiæ, factum esse quod imperasset,' Tacitus, Ann. i. 6), *not to Pilate*, but *to the chief priests*:—or 2), as De Wette and Meyer take it, imperative; which doubtless it may be, see 2 Tim. i. 13 and note: and the sense here on that hypothesis would be, **Take a body of men for a guard.** And *to* this latter I now rather incline, on account of the order of the words, in which ἔχετε seems to have an emphasis hardly satisfied on the other view. **ὡς οἴδατε**] **as you know how:—in the best manner you can.** There is no irony in the words, as has been supposed. **66.**] **μετά** belongs to ἠσφαλ., and implies the *means whereby*, as in reff. So Thucyd. viii. 73,—Ὑπέρβολον . . . . ἀποκτείνουσι μετὰ Χαρμίνου ἑνὸς τῶν στρατηγῶν,—iii. 66, οὐ μετὰ τοῦ πλήθους ὑμῶν εἰσελθόντες,—v. 82, ἡ κατὰ θάλασσαν μετὰ τῶν Ἀθηναίων ἐπαγωγὴ τῶν ἐπιτηδείων. Duker, on the first of these, remarks, 'μετά τινος fieri dicuntur, quæ alicujus voluntate, auxilio, et consilio fiunt.' The sealing was by means of a cord or string passing across the stone at the mouth of the sepulchre, and fastened at either end to the rock by sealing-clay.

Chap. XXVIII. **1—10.**] Jesus having risen from the dead, appears to the women. Mark xvi. 1—8. Luke xxiv. 1—12. John xx. 1—10. The independence and distinctness of the four narratives in this part have never been questioned, and indeed herein lie its principal

r ‖. John xx. 19. Acts xx. 7. 1 Cor. xvi. 2.
s = as above (r). Gen. i. 5. Ezra iii. 6. Ezek. xxxii. 1.
t ch. xxvii. 55 al. Ps. lxiii. 9.
u ch. xxvii. 54 al. Ezek. xxxviii. 19.

εἰς [rs] μίαν [r] σαββάτων, ἦλθεν Μαρία ἡ Μαγδαληνὴ καὶ ἡ
ἄλλη Μαρία [t] θεωρῆσαι τὸν τάφον.
2 καὶ ἰδοὺ [u] σεισμὸς
ἐγένετο μέγας· ἄγγελος γὰρ κυρίου καταβὰς ἐξ οὐρανοῦ
προσελθὼν [v] ἀπεκύλισεν τὸν λίθον καὶ ἐκάθητο [w] ἐπάνω
αὐτοῦ.
3 ἦν δὲ ἡ [x] ἰδέα αὐτοῦ ὡς [y] ἀστραπὴ καὶ τὸ [za] ἔνδυμα αὐτοῦ [a] λευκὸν ὡς [a] χιών.
4 [bc] ἀπὸ δὲ τοῦ φόβου

ABCDE FGHKL MSUVΓ ΔΠℵ 1. 33. 69

v ‖ Mk. (bis v. r.) L. only. Gen. xxix. 3, 8, 10. Judith xiii. 9 only. w ch. xxi. 7 al. x here only. Gen. v. 3. Dan. i. 13 Theod. y ch. xxiv. 27 reff. Dan. x. 6. z ch. xxii. 11, 12 reff. a Dan. vii. 9 Theod. b ch. xiii. 44. xviii. 7 al. Ps. lxxv. 6. c Ezek. xxxi. 16.

CHAP. XXVIII. 1. *μαριαμ* (1st) CLΔℵ. om 1st *η* D^1(ins D^2). om 2nd *η* A.
2. for *εξ*, *απ'* D. ins *και* bef *προσελθων* BCLℵ 33 latt Syr copt æth Orig Dion Chr. rec aft *λιθον* add *απο της θυρας*, with AC rel lat-*f h* Syr arm : *απ. τ. θ. του μνημειου* E^2(appy) FLM^2UΓ 1. 33 syr copt Eus_1 Chr : om BDℵ latt Dion (Hil).
3. om *ην δε η ιδ. αυτου* (*homœotel*) $ℵ^1$. (*ειδεα* A B[*ειδε* B^1(Tischdf N. T. Vat.)] CDEHM ℵ-corr^1.) rec *ωσει χ.*, with A rel Dion [Chr] : *ως η* (? = *ωσει*) $ℵ^{3a}$ 69 : txt BDK$Π^1ℵ^1$ 1.

difficulties. With regard to them, I refer to what I have said in the Prolegomena, that *supposing us to be acquainted with every thing said and done, in its order and exactness, we should doubtless be able to reconcile, or account for, the present forms of the narratives;* but not having this key to the harmonizing of them, all attempts to do so in minute particulars must be full of arbitrary assumptions, and carry no certainty with them. And I may remark, that *of all harmonies,* those of *the incidents of these chapters* are to me the *most unsatisfactory.* Giving their compilers all credit for the best intentions, I confess they seem to me to *weaken* instead of strengthening the evidence, which now rests (speaking merely *objectively*) on the unexceptionable testimony of three independent narrators, and of one, who besides was an eye-witness of much that happened. If we are to compare the four, and ask which is to be taken as most nearly reporting the *exact* words and incidents, on this there can I think be no doubt. On internal as well as external ground, *that of John* takes the *highest place:* but not, of course, to the exclusion of those parts of the narrative which he *does not touch.* The *improbability* that the Evangelists had seen one another's accounts, becomes, in *this part* of their Gospels, an *impossibility.* Here and there we discern traces of a common narration as the ground of their reports, as e. g. Matt. vv. 5—8: Mark vv. 5—8, but even these are very few.

As I have abandoned all idea of harmonizing throughout, I will beg the student to compare carefully the notes on the other Gospels. **1. ὀψὲ δὲ σαβ.**] not, '*at the end of the week.*' The words *σαββάτων* and *μίαν σαββ.* are opposed, both being *days.* **At the end of the Sabbath.** There is some little difficulty here, because the end of the sabbath (and of the week) was at *sunset the night before.* It is hardly to be supposed that St. Matthew means the *evening* of the sabbath, though *ἐπέφωσκε* is used of the day beginning at sunset (Luke xxiii. 54, and note). It is best to interpret a doubtful expression in unison with the other testimonies, and to suppose that here both the *day* and the *breaking of the day* are taken in their *natural,* not their *Jewish* sense. **μίαν σαβ.** is a Hebraism; the Rabbinical writings use אחד, שני, שלישי, &c., affixing בשבת to each, for Sunday, Monday, Tuesday, &c. **Μαρ. ἡ Μ. κ. ἡ ἄλ. Μ.**] In Mark, *Salome also.* John speaks of *Mary Magdalene alone.* See notes there. **θεωρ. τ. τ.**] It was to *anoint* the Body, for which purposes they had bought, since the end of the Sabbath, ointments and spices, Mark. In Mark it is *after the rising of the sun;* in John, *while yet dark;* in Luke, *at dim dawn:* the two last agree with our text.

2.] This must not be taken as pluperfect, which would be altogether inconsistent with the text. **καὶ ἰδοὺ . . ἐγένετο** must mean that the women were *witnesses of the earthquake,* and *that which happened.* **σεισμός** was not *properly* an earthquake, but was the sudden opening of the tomb by the descending Angel, as the **γάρ** shews. The rolling away was not done naturally, but by a shock, which = *σεισμός.* It must not be supposed that the Resurrection of our Lord took place *at this time,* as sometimes imagined, and represented in paintings. It *had taken place before;*—**ἠγέρθη** *κ.τ.λ.* are the words of the Angel. It was not *for Him,* to whom (see John xx. 19, 26) the

αὐτοῦ [c] ἐσείσθησαν οἱ [d] τηροῦντες καὶ ἐγενήθησαν [e] ὡς
[e] νεκροί. 5 [f] ἀποκριθεὶς δὲ ὁ ἄγγελος εἶπεν ταῖς γυναιξὶν
Μὴ φοβεῖσθε ὑμεῖς· οἶδα γὰρ ὅτι Ἰησοῦν τὸν ἐσταυρωμένον ζητεῖτε. 6 οὐκ ἔστιν ὧδε· ἠγέρθη γὰρ [g] καθὼς
εἶπεν. [h] δεῦτε ἴδετε τὸν τόπον ὅπου ἔκειτο [ὁ [i] κύριος].
7 καὶ ταχὺ πορευθεῖσαι εἴπατε τοῖς μαθηταῖς αὐτοῦ ὅτι
[j] ἠγέρθη ἀπὸ τῶν [j] νεκρῶν, καὶ ἰδοὺ [k] προάγει ὑμᾶς εἰς
τὴν Γαλιλαίαν· ἐκεῖ αὐτὸν ὄψεσθε. ἰδοὺ εἶπον ὑμῖν.
8 καὶ ἀπελθοῦσαι ταχὺ ἀπὸ τοῦ [l] μνημείου [m] μετὰ φόβου
καὶ χαρᾶς μεγάλης ἔδραμον [n] ἀπαγγεῖλαι τοῖς μαθηταῖς

d ch. xxvii. 36, 54.
e Ps. cxlii. 3.
f = ch. xi. 25 reff.
g ch. xxvi. 24 reff.
h ch. xxi. 38 reff.
i = Matt., here only.
j w. ἀπό, ch. xiv. 2. xxvii. 64.
k ch. xiv. 22 reff.
l ch. xxvii. 52, 53, 60 al. fr.
m Mark iii. 5 al. fr. 1 Chron. xxix. 22.
n ch. ii. 8 al. fr.

4. rec εγενοντο (*more usual*), with A (C^2 ?) rel Dion Eus: txt BCDLא 33. rec ωσει, with C rel [Dion] Eus: txt ABDLΔא 1.
5. om δε C(appy). om ταις γυναιξιν $א^1$(ins א-$corr^{1.3}$). φοβηθητε $א^1$(txt $א^{3a}$).
6. om ο κυριος Bא 33 lat-*e* copt æth arm Chr Orig-int: ins ACD rel latt syrr Chr-H-L-M-wlf.
7. om απο των νεκρων D vulg lat-*a b e* ff_1 g_1 *h l* arm Cyr-jer Orig-int Ambr Aug. om 1st ιδου D lat-*a b c* ff_2 *h* Cyr-jer $Chrysol_1$ Orig-int. ειπα $א^1$(txt $א^{3a}$).
8. rec εξελθουσαι (*from* ‖ *Mark*), with AD rel: txt BCLא 33. 69 lat-*e* Syr copt.

stone was *no hindrance*, but *for the women and His disciples*, that it was rolled away.

3. ἡ ἰδέα] not his *form*, but **his appearance**; not in *shape* (as some would explain it away), but in brightness.

4.] **αὐτοῦ**, objective, **of him**, the angel; as John vii. 13: Heb. ii. 15.

5.] In Mark, *a young man in a white robe was sitting in the tomb on the right hand*: in Luke *two men in shining raiment* (see Acts i. 10) *appeared* (ἐπέστησαν) *to them*. John relates, that Mary Magdalene looked into the tomb and saw (but this must have been afterwards) two angels in white sitting one at the head, the other at the feet where the Body had lain. All attempts to *deny* the angelic appearances, or *ascribe them to later tradition*, are dishonest and absurd. That related in John is as definite as either of the others, and he certainly had it from Mary Magdalene herself. **ὑμεῖς** is emphatic, addressed to the women.

6.] **καθὼς εἶπεν** is further expanded in Luke, vv. 6, 7. See ch. xvi. 21; xvii. 23. **ὁ κύριος** (see ref.) is emphatic;—'gloriosa appellatio,' Bengel.

7.] This appearance in Galilee had been foretold before his death, see ch. xxvi. 32. It is to be observed that Matthew records *only this one* appearance to the Apostles, and in Galilee. It appears strange that this should be the entire testimony of Matthew: for it seems hardly likely that he would omit those important appearances in Jerusalem when the Apostles were assembled, John xx. 19, 26, or that one which was closed by the Ascension. But perhaps it may be in accord with his evident design of giving the general form and summary of each series of events, rather than their characteristic details. See below on ver. 20. **ὅτι** is recitative. The **προάγει** here is not to be understood as implying the *journeying* on the part of our Lord himself. It is cited from His own words, ch. xxvi. 32, and there, as here, merely implies that *He would be there when they arrived*. It has a reference to the collecting of the flock which had been scattered by the smiting of the Shepherd: see John x. 4. **ἐκεῖ αὐτὸν ὄψεσθε** is determined, by κἀκεῖ με ὄψονται below, to be *part of the message to the disciples*: not spoken to the women directly, but certainly indirectly including them. The idea of their being *merely* messengers to the Apostles, without bearing any share in the promise, is against the spirit of the context: see further in note on ver. 17. **ἰδοὺ εἶπον ὑμῖν** is to give solemnity to the command. These words are peculiar to Matthew, and are a mark of accuracy.

8.] μετὰ φόβου, ἐφ' οἷς εἶδον παραδόξοις· μετὰ χαρᾶς δέ, ἐφ' οἷς ἤκουσαν εὐαγγελίοις. Euthym.

9.] Neither Mark nor Luke recounts, or seems to have been aware of, this appearance. Mark even says οὐδενὶ οὐδὲν εἶπον· ἐφοβοῦντο γάρ. But (see above) it does not therefore follow that the narratives are inconsistent. Mark's account (see note there) is evidently broken off suddenly; and Luke's (see also note there) appears to have been derived from one of those who went to Emmaus,

αὐτοῦ. 9 ° καὶ ° ἰδοὺ Ἰησοῦς p * ἀπήντησεν αὐταῖς λέγων
q Χαίρετε. αἱ δὲ προσελθοῦσαι r ἐκράτησεν αὐτοῦ τοὺς
πόδας καὶ s προσεκύνησαν αὐτῷ. 10 τότε λέγει αὐταῖς ὁ
Ἰησοῦς Μὴ φοβεῖσθε· ὑπάγετε n ἀπαγγείλατε τοῖς
t ἀδελφοῖς μου ἵνα ἀπέλθωσιν εἰς τὴν Γαλιλαίαν, κἀκεῖ με
ὄψονται.

11 Πορευομένων δὲ αὐτῶν ἰδού τινες τῆς u κουστωδίας
ἐλθόντες εἰς τὴν πόλιν n ἀπήγγειλαν τοῖς ἀρχιερεῦσιν
ἅπαντα τὰ γενόμενα. 12 καὶ v συναχθέντες μετὰ τῶν
πρεσβυτέρων w συμβούλιόν x τε w λαβόντες y ἀργύρια

ABCDE FGHKL MSUVΓ ΔΠℵ 1. 33. 69

o al26. in Matt.: usually at beg. of sent. freq. aft. gen. absol.: aft. ὡς, never in Matt. (see Luke xxiv. 4. Acts [i. 10.] x. 17.) Gen. xxiv. 15.
p Matt., here only. Mark v. 2. xiv. 13. Luke (xiv. 31 v. r.) xvii. 12. (John iv. 51. Acts xvi. 16 v. r.) only. 3 Kings ii. 34. ὑπ., ch. viii. 28 reff.
q = ch. xxvi. 49. xxvii. 29. Luke i. 28 al.
r ch. xii. 11.
s dat., ch. ii. 2 reff.
t = ch. xxv. 40 reff.
u ch. xxvii. 65, 66 only +.
v = ch. xxii. 34 al.
w ch. xii. 14 reff.
x ch. xxvii. 48 reff.
y ch. xxvi. 15 al.

9. rec at beg ins *ως δε επορευοντο απαγγειλαι τοις μαθηταις αυτου*, with AC rel lat-*f* syr æth ; *ως δε επορευοντο*, omg *και*, 14 lect-53 ; *ως δε επορευοντο απαγγειλαι* 235 : om BDℵ 33. 69 ev-y latt Syr syr-jer copt arm Orig [Eus_1 Cyr-jer and Cyr(Tischdr)] Jer Aug. (*At first sight, it would appear as if the clause had been omd from* homœotel. *But on more examination, I am disposed to question this.* (1) *The testimonies for its omn are not* (*perhaps with the exception of* ℵ) *those* MSS *&c which* most frequently fall into this error. (2) *The idiom, ως επορ., is* foreign to the usage of Matt, *who always uses a gen abs in this case.* (3) *The two minor* varns *are just what we should expect as* shorter and neater glosses, *but* not as corrns *of a genuine clause: esp the striking out of the και bef ιδου to substitute the other introductory clause. After all, it is difficult to decide, the homœotel being so very obvious ; but on more careful thought I determine, with Mill, Bengel, Gersdorff, Schulz, Rinck, Lachm, Tischdf, Treg, Mey, and De Wette, against the clause. It is defended by Griesb, Fritzsche, Scholz, and Bornemann.*) rec ins *ο* bef *ιησ.*, with DLΓ (S, e sil) 1. 33. 69 Orig Eus [$Cyr\text{-}jer_1$ Chr-ed] : om ABCℵ rel Chr-wlf-ms [Cyr_1] Thl. * *ὑπήντησεν* BCΠℵ[1] 1 Orig Chr-wlf-ms Cyr_1: *απηντησεν* ADℵ[3a] rel Eus [$Cyr\text{-}jer_1$] Chr. *τους ποδας* bef *αυτου* D latt [Chr-wlf-ms].

10. om *μου* ℵ[1](ins ℵ[3a]). for *απελθ.*, *ελθωσιν* ℵ[1](txt ℵ[3a]) latt. om *την* D[1](ins D[3]). *οψεσθαι videbitis* D lat-*e h*.

11. *ανηγγειλαν* Dℵ Orig [Chr]. *παντα* A Orig.

12. om *τε* D ev-y latt. for *λαβοντες*, *εποιησαν* ℵ[1], *εποιησαν και λαβοντες* ℵ-corr[1.3b] : txt ℵ[3a]. *αργυριον ικανον* D latt Syr arm.

who had evidently but an imperfect knowledge of what happened before they left the city. This being taken into account, we may fairly require that the judgment should be suspended in lack of further means of solving the difficulty. **ἐκρ. τ. π.**] partly in fear and as suppliants, for the Lord says *μὴ φοβεῖσθε*,—but shewing also the *χαρά* with which that fear was mixed (ver. 8),—joy at having recovered Him whom they loved. **προσεκ. αὐτ.**] 'Jesum ante passionem alii potius alieniores adorarunt quam discipuli.' Bengel. **10. τοῖς ἀδελφ.**] so also to Mary Magdalene, John xx. 17. The repetition of this injunction by the Lord has been thought to indicate that this is a portion of another narrative inwoven here, and may possibly belong to the same incident as that in ver. 7. But all probability is against this : the passages are distinctly consecutive, and moreover both are in the well-known style of Matthew (e. g. *καὶ ἰδού* in both). There is perhaps more probability that this may be the same appearance as that in John xx. 11—18, on account of *μή μου ἅπτου* there and *τοὺς ἀδελφ. μου*,—but in our present imperfect state of information, this must remain a *mere* probability.

11—15.] The Jewish authorities bribe the guards to give a false account of the resurrection. *Peculiar to Matthew.* **11. πορ. δ. αὐ**] **While they were going.** **12.**] **συναχθέντες**, i. e. **οἱ ἀρχιερεῖς**, a change of the subject of the sentence as in Luke xix. 4 al. This was a meeting of the Sanhedrim, but surely hardly an *official* and *open* one; does not the form of the narrative rather imply that it was a secret compact between those (the majority) who were bitterly hostile to Jesus? The cir-

[z] ἱκανὰ ἔδωκαν τοῖς στρατιώταις 13 λέγοντες Εἴπατε ὅτι
οἱ μαθηταὶ αὐτοῦ νυκτὸς ἐλθόντες [a] ἔκλεψαν αὐτὸν ἡμῶν
[b] κοιμωμένων. 14 καὶ ἐὰν [c] ἀκουσθῇ τοῦτο [d] ἐπὶ τοῦ
ἡγεμόνος, ἡμεῖς πείσομεν αὐτὸν καὶ ὑμᾶς [e] ἀμερίμνους
ποιήσομεν. 15 οἱ δὲ λαβόντες τὰ [y] ἀργύρια ἐποίησαν ὡς
ἐδιδάχθησαν. καὶ [f] διεφημίσθη ὁ λόγος οὗτος παρὰ Ἰουδαίοις μέχρι τῆς [g] σήμερον ἡμέρας.
16 Οἱ δὲ ἕνδεκα μαθηταὶ ἐπορεύθησαν εἰς τὴν Γαλιλαίαν,
εἰς τὸ ὄρος οὗ ἐτάξατο αὐτοῖς ὁ Ἰησοῦς. 17 καὶ ἰδόντες
αὐτὸν [h] προσεκύνησαν, οἱ δὲ [i] ἐδίστασαν. 18 καὶ προς-

..ποιησομεν C.

...και ιδοντες L.

ABDEF GHKM SUVΓΔ ΠℵI. 33. 69

z = Matt., here (ch. iii. 11 ||. viii. 8) only. Mark x. 46. (xv. 15.) Luke vii.[11,] 12 al. John never. Hab. ii. 13. 1 Macc. xiii. 49.
a ch. xxvii. 64. Tobit i. 18.
b = Luke xxii. 45. John xi. (11?) 12. Acts xii. 6. (ch. xxvii. 52 al.) only. Prov. iv. 16.
c pass., Mark ii. 1 reff.
d Acts xxiv. 19. xxv. 9. xxvi. 2. 1 Tim. v. 19.
e 1 Cor. vii. 32 only †. Wisd. vi. 15. vii. 23 only.
f ch. ix. 31 Mark i. 45 only †.
g ch. xi. 23. with ἡμ., Matt., here only. Acts xx. 26. Rom. xi. 8. 2 Cor. iii. 14. 1 Kings xxix. 6 al. fr.
h ver. 9.
i ch. xiv. 31 only †. διστάζοντος δὲ Θησέως περὶ τῆς διαβολῆς, Diod. Sic. iv. 62.

13. οτι bef ειπατε ℵ: om οτι 33.
14. αν D¹(txt D-corr¹) L. for επι, υπο (*corrn as more simple*) BD latt. om αυτον Bℵ 33 lat-*e* æth Orig$_1$. ποιησωμεν E¹FGHMℵ 33. 69: of these E¹GH 69 have πεισωμεν also [and UΓ].
15. om τα B(see table [Tischdf N. T. Vat. gives τα αργ. B³; but the note in Dean Alford's collation is "no τα at all"]) ℵ¹(ins ℵ³). **καθως** ℵ³ᵃ. for διεφ., εφημισθη Δℵ 33. 69 Orig$_2$. aft παρα ins τοις D. for μεχρι, εως Dℵ¹(txt ℵ³ᵃ) Orig$_1$(txt$_1$) Chr[txt wlf-ms]. rec om ημερας (*as unusual with Matt: see ch* xi. 23; xxvii. 8), with Aℵ rel lat-*e* Orig$_2$: ins BDL latt Syr Chr.
16. om ο D.
17. rec aft προσεκ. ins αυτω, with A rel syrr [copt]; αυτον Γ 3. 237-45-58-9 Scr's c cvv-p-x-y: om BDℵ 33 latt Eus Chr Aug.

cumstance that Joseph had taken no part in their counsel before, leads us to think that others may have withdrawn themselves from the meeting, e.g. Gamaliel, who could hardly have consented to such a measure as this. **14.**] Not only '*come to the ears of the governor*,' but **be borne witness of before the governor,** come before him officially: i.e. 'if a stir be made, and you be in trouble about it:' see reff. [**πείσομεν**, viz. by a bribe of money, see Trench on the A. V. p. 72.] **15.**] Justin Martyr, Dial. c. Tryph. § 108, p. 202, says, *καὶ οὐ μόνον οὐ μετενοήσατε μαθόντες αὐτὸν ἀναστάντα ἐκ νεκρῶν, ἀλλὰ ἄνδρας χειροτονήσαντες ἐκλεκτούς, εἰς πᾶσαν τὴν οἰκουμένην ἐπέμψατε κηρύσσοντες ὅτι αἵρεσίς τις ἄθεος καὶ ἄνομος ἐγήγερται ἀπὸ Ἰησοῦ τινος Γαλιλαίου πλάνου* (see ch. xxvii. 63) *ὃν σταυρωσάντων ὑμῶν οἱ μαθηταὶ αὐτοῦ κλέψαντες κ.τ.λ.* **ὁ λόγος οὗτος**—**this account of the matter.** Eisenmenger (Entdecktes Judenthum, cited by Meyer and De Wette) gives an expansion of this lie of the Jews from the book called Toldoth Jeschu.

16—20.] Appearance of the Lord on a mountain in Galilee. This journey into Galilee was *after the termination of the feast*, allowing *two first days of the week*, on which the Lord appeared to the assembled Apostles (John xx. 19, 26), to elapse. It illustrates the imperfect and fragmentary nature of the materials out of which our narrative is built, that the appointment of this mountain as a place of assembly for the eleven *has not been mentioned*, although **τὸ ὄρος οὗ** seems to imply that it has. Stier well remarks (Reden Jesu, vii. 209) that in this verse Matthew gives a hint of *some interviews having taken place previously to this* in Galilee. And it is important to bear this in mind, as suggesting, if not the solution, at least the *ground* of solution, of the difficulties of this passage. Ver. 17 seems to present an instance of this imperfect and fragmentary narrative. The impression given by it is that the majority *of the eleven* worshipped Him, but some doubted (not, *whether they should worship Him;* which is absurd and not implied in the word. On **οἱ δέ**, cf. ch. xxvi. 67. *ᾤχοντο εἰς Δεκέλειαν, οἱ δ' ἐς Μέγαρα*, Xen. Hell. i. 2. 14: see also Anab. i. 5. 13). This however would hardly be possible, *after the two appearances at Jerusalem* in John xx. We are therefore obliged to conclude that *others were present.* Whether these others were the '500 brethren at once' of whom Paul speaks 1 Cor. xv. 6, or some other disciples, does not ap-

ελθὼν ὁ Ἰησοῦς [k] ἐλάλησεν αὐτοῖς [k] λέγων [i] Ἐδόθη μοι
πᾶσα [l] ἐξουσία [m] ἐν οὐρανῷ καὶ [m] ἐπὶ τῆς γῆς. 19 πορευθέντες [n] μαθητεύσατε πάντα [o] τὰ ἔθνη, [p] βαπτιζοντες αὐτοὺς

k ch. xxiii. 1 reff Gen. xvii. 3.
l ch. ix. 8. x. 1. xxi. 23 ||. John i. 12 al. Dan. vii. 14.
m ch. vi. 10. xvi. 19. xviii. 18. iv. 17. Num. xiv. 15.
n ch. xiii. 52. Acts xiv. 21 (intr., ch. xxvii. 57) only†.
o Gal. iii. 8. 1 Tim.
p Acts viii. 16. xix. 5. Rom. vi. 3. 1 Cor. i. 13. x. 2. Gal. iii. 27.

. ελαλησεν αυτοις G.
ABDEF HKMS UVΓΔΠ ℵ 1. 33. 69

18. om *αυτοις* ℵ[1](ins ℵ[3a]). *ουρανοις* D [Bas_1]. rec om *της* (*to conform with εν ουρ.*), with Aℵ rel $Orig_2$ [$Ps\text{-}Ath_1$ Bas_3] Chr Cyr_2: ins BD copt Eus Chr-wlf-ms [Cyr_1].

19. *πορευεσθε* D(-*αι*) lat-*e* $Orig_1$ Tert Cypr. rec aft *πορ.* ins *ουν*, with BΔΠ 1. 33 ev-y vulg lat-*c e f* $ff_{1.2}$ g_1 syrr copt æth arm $Cypr_4$ Zeno: *νυν* D lat-*a b h n* Hil_3 Victorin: om Aℵ rel Orig [$Hipp_1$ $Constt_2$] Eus_{oft} Ath_{oft} Bas Amphil [$Nyss_2$ $Epiph_2$] Chr Cyr[$_3$-p] Thl Iren-int Tert Lucif Ambr Aug. *βαπτισαντες* (*corrn for ecclesiastical propriety?*) BD: txt Aℵ rel Hipp [$Constt_2$] Eus Ath Amphil [Bas] Chr Cyr_2.

pear. Olshausen and Stier suppose, from the previous announcement of this meeting, and the repetition of that announcement by the angel, and by our Lord, that it probably included *all the disciples* of Jesus; at least, all who would from the nature of the case be brought together. **18. προσελθ.**] * They appear to have first seen Him at a distance, probably on the top of the mountain. This whole introduction, **προσελθ. ἐλάλ. αὐτ. λέγ.**, forbids us to suppose that the following words are a mere compendium of what was said on various occasions. Like the opening of ch. v., it carries with it a direct assertion that what follows was spoken *then, and there.* **ἐδόθη μοι** κ.τ.λ.] The words are a reference to ref. Dan. (LXX), which compare. *Given,*—by the Father, in the fulfilment of the Eternal Covenant, in the Unity of the Holy Spirit. *Now first* is this covenant, in its fulness, proclaimed upon earth. The Resurrection was its last seal—the Ascension was the *taking possession* of the Inheritance. But the Inheritance is already won; and the Heir is only remaining on earth for a temporary purpose—the assuring His joint-heirs of the verity of his possession. 'All power in heaven and earth;' see Eph. i. 20—23: Col. ii. 10: Heb. i. 6: Rom. xiv. 9: Phil. ii. 9—11: 1 Pet. iii. 22.

19.] *οὖν* (in rec.) is probably a gloss, but an excellent one. It is the glorification of the Son by the Father through the Spirit, which is the foundation of the Church of Christ in all the world. And when we baptize into the Name (i. e. into the fulness of the consequence of the objective covenant, and the subjective confession) of Father, Son, and Holy Ghost, it is *this* which forms the ground and cause of our power to do so—that this flesh of man, of which God hath made *πάντα τὰ ἔθνη*, is *glorified in the Person of our Redeemer,* through whom we all have access by one Spirit to the Father. **πορ. μαθ.**] Demonstrably, this was not understood as spoken to the Apostles *only,* but to all the brethren. Thus we read, **πάντες** *διεσπάρησαν . . . πλὴν τῶν ἀποστόλων* (Acts viii. 2): **οἱ** *μὲν οὖν* **διασπαρέντες διῆλθον εὐαγγελιζόμενοι** *τὸν λόγον* (ibid. ver. 4). There is peculiar meaning in **μαθητεύσατε.** All *power* is given me—go therefore and . . . subdue? Not so: the purpose of the Lord is to bring men to the *knowledge of the truth*—to work on and in their hearts, and lift them up to be partakers of the divine Nature. And therefore it is not 'subdue,' but **make disciples of** (see below). **πάντα τὰ ἔθνη** again is closely connected with *πᾶσα ἐξουσία ἐπὶ τῆς γῆς.* **πάντα τὰ ἔθνη**] **all nations,** including the Jews. It is absurd to imagine that in these words of the Lord there is implied a *rejection of the Jews,* in direct variance with his commands elsewhere, and also with the world-wide signification of *ἐπὶ τῆς γῆς* above. Besides, the (temporary) rejection of the Jews consists in this, that they are *numbered among πάντα τὰ ἔθνη,* and not a peculiar people any longer: and are become, in the providence of God, the subjects of that preaching, of which by original title they ought to have been the promulgators. We find the first preachers of the gospel, so far from excepting the Jews, uniformly bearing their testimony to them *first.* With regard to the difficulty which has been raised on these words,—that if they had been thus spoken by the Lord, the Apostles would never have had any doubt about the admission of the Gentiles into the Church,—I would answer, with Ebrard, Stier, De Wette, Meyer, and others, 'that the Apostles *never had any doubt whatever* about *admitting* Gentiles,—only whether they should not be *circumcised* first.' In this command, the prohibition of ch. x. 5 is for ever removed. **βαπτίζοντες**] Both these present participles are the conditioning components of the imperative aor. preceding. The *μαθητεύειν* consists

[p] εἰς τὸ ὄνομα τοῦ πατρὸς καὶ τοῦ υἱοῦ καὶ τοῦ ἁγίου
πνεύματος, 20 διδάσκοντες αὐτοὺς [q] τηρεῖν πάντα ὅσα
[r] ἐνετειλάμην ὑμῖν· καὶ ἰδοὺ ἐγὼ [s] μεθ' ὑμῶν εἰμι [t] πάσας
τὰς ἡμέρας [u] ἕως τῆς [v] συντελείας τοῦ αἰῶνος.

q ch. xix. 17 reff.
r ch. xvii. 9. xix. 7 al. Gen. ii. 16.
s ch. i. 23. John iii. 2. Deut. i. 42 al.
t Gen. viii. 22.
u ch. xxvi. 29. xxvii. 45, 64 al.
v ch. xiii. 39, 40 reff.

ΚΑΤΑ ΜΑΘΘΑΙΟΝ.

om του (bef υιου) D.

20. ειμι bef μεθ υμ. Dℵ Orig$_2$(txt$_8$). rec at end adds αμην, with A[2] rel am(with forj gat) lat-*a b c f* syrr copt-ms æth: om A[1](appy) BDℵ 1. 33 vulg lat-*e ff*$_{1.2}$ *g*$_{1.2}$ *h n* copt arm [Orig Eus Ath] Chr Cyr Thl.

Subscription. κατα μαθθαιον B: ευαγγελιον κατα ματθαιον AEH(K)UVΔΠ: ευ. κατα μαθθαιον ετελεσθη αρχεται ευ. κατα ιωαννην D, simly lat-*b e f*; and so, but *marcum* for ιωαν., forj &c: FMℵ lat-*a* have no subscr: K(aft enumerating the number of στίχοι &c) Scr's e g k p s v ev-w το κατα ματθ. (ins αγιον al) ευ. εξεδοθη (εγραφη al) υπ αυτου εν ιεροσολυμοις(εν παλαιστινη al syrr, εν ανατολη al, and add εβραιστι or τη εβραιδι διαλεκτω: om εν ιεροσ. ev-w) μετα χρονους η της του χριστου (add του θεου ημων al) αναληψεως (add ηρμηνευθη δε υπο ιακωβου αδελφου του κυριου, or υπο ιωαννου al).

of two parts—the *initiatory*, admissory *rite*, and the *subsequent teaching*. It is much to be regretted that the rendering of μαθ. '*teach*,' has in our Bibles clouded the meaning of these important words. It will be observed that in our Lord's words, as in the Church, the process of ordinary discipleship is *from baptism to instruction*—i. e. is, *admission in infancy to the covenant*, and *growing up into* τηρεῖν πάντα κ.τ.λ.—the *exception* being, what circumstances rendered so frequent in the early Church, *instruction before baptism*, in the case of *adults*. On this we may also remark, that baptism as known to the Jews included, just as it does in the Acts (ch. xvi. 15, 33) *whole households—wives and children*. As regards the command itself, no unprejudiced reader can doubt that it regards the *outward rite* of Baptism, so well known in this Gospel as having been practised by John, and received by the Lord Himself. And thus it was immediately, and has been ever since, understood by the Church. As regards all attempts to explain away this sense, we may say—even setting aside the testimony furnished by the Acts of the Apostles,—that it is in the highest degree improbable that our Lord should have given, at a time when He was summing up the duties of his Church in such weighty words, a command couched in figurative or ambiguous language—one which He must have known would be interpreted by his disciples, now long accustomed to the rite and its name, otherwise than He intended it. **εἰς τὸ ὄν. . . .**] Reference is apparently made to the Baptism of the Lord Himself, where the whole Three Persons of the Godhead were in manifestation.

Not τὰ ὀνόματα—but **τὸ ὄνομα**—setting forth the Unity of the Godhead.

It is unfortunate again here that our English Bibles do not give us the force of this εἰς. It should have been **into**, (as in Gal. iii. 27 al.,) both here and in 1 Cor. x. 2, and wherever the expression with εἰς is used. It imports, not only a *subjective recognition* hereafter by the child of the truth implied in τὸ ὄνομα κ.τ.λ., but an *objective admission* into the covenant of Redemption—*a putting on of Christ*. Baptism is the *contract of espousal* (Eph. v. 26) between Christ and his Church. Our word '*in*' being retained both here and in our formula of Baptism, it should always be remembered that *the Sacramental declaration is contained in this word;* that it answers (as Stier has well observed, vii. 268) to the τοῦτό ἐστιν in the other Sacrament. On the difference between the *baptism of John*, and *Christian baptism*, see notes on ch. iii. 11: Acts xviii. 25; xix. 1–5. **20.**] Even in the case of the adult, this teaching must, *in greater part*, follow his baptism; though as we have seen (on ver. 19), in *his* exceptional case, *some of it* must *go before*. For this teaching is nothing less than the building up of the whole man into the obedience of Christ. In these words, inasmuch as the then living disciples *could not teach all nations*, does the Lord *found the office of Preachers* in his Church, with all that belongs to it,—the duties of the *minister*, the *schoolteacher*, the *scripture reader*. This '*teach-*

ing' is not merely the *κήρυγμα* of the gospel—not mere proclamation of the good news—but the whole catechetical office of the Church upon and in the baptized.

καὶ ἰδοὺ . . . .] These words imply and set forth the *Ascension*, the manner of which is not related by our Evangelist.

ἐγώ, I, in the fullest sense: not the *Divine Presence*, as *distinguished from the Humanity* of Christ. His Humanity is with us likewise. The vine lives in the branches. Stier remarks (vii. 277) the contrast between this '*I am with you*,' and the view of Nicodemus (John iii. 2) 'no man can do these miracles—except *God be with him*.' **μεθ' ὑμ.**] mainly, *by the promise of the Father* (Luke xxiv. 49) *which he has poured out on His Church*. But the presence of the Spirit is the effect of the presence of Christ—and the presence of Christ is part of the *ἐδόθη* above—the effect of the well-pleasing of the Father. So that the mystery of His name Ἐμμανουήλ (with which, as Stier remarks, this Gospel begins and ends) is fulfilled—God is *with us*. And **πάσας τὰς ἡμέρας**—**all the** (*appointed*) **days**—for they are numbered by the Father, though by none but Him. **ἕως τῆς συντ. τ. αἰ.**] that time of which they had heard in so many parables, and about which they had asked, ch. xxiv. 3—the completion of the *state of time*. After that, He will be no more properly speaking *with us*, but we *with Him* (John xvii. 24) where He is. To understand *μεθ' ὑμῶν* only of the Apostles and their (?) successors, is to destroy the whole force of these most weighty words. Descending even into literal exactness, we may see that *διδάσκοντες αὐτοὺς τηρεῖν πάντα ὅσα ἐνετειλάμην ὑμῖν*, makes *αὐτούς* into *ὑμεῖς*, as soon as they are *μεμαθητευμένοι*. The command is to the Universal Church—to be performed, in the nature of things, by her *ministers* and *teachers*, the manner of appointing which is not here prescribed, but to be learnt in the unfoldings of Providence recorded in the Acts of the Apostles, who by His special ordinance were the founders and first builders of that Church—but whose office, *on that very account, precluded the idea of succession or renewal*. That Matthew does not record the fact or manner of *the Ascension*, is not to be used as a ground for any presumptions regarding the authenticity of the records of it which we possess. The narrative here is *suddenly brought to a termination*; that in John ends with an express declaration of its incompleteness. What reasons there may have been for the omission, either subjective, in the mind of the author of the Gospel, or objective, in the fragmentary character of the apostolic reports which are here put together, it is wholly out of our power, in this age of the world, to determine. As before remarked, the *fact itself* is here and elsewhere in this Gospel (see ch. xxii. 44; xxiv. 30; xxv. 14, 31; xxvi. 64) clearly *implied*.

ΕΥΑΓΓΕΛΙΟΝ

ΚΑΤΑ ΜΑΡΚΟΝ.

I. 1 [a] Ἀρχὴ τοῦ εὐαγγελίου Ἰησοῦ χριστοῦ [b] υἱοῦ [b] θεοῦ. a Phil. iv. 1 Hos. i. 2.
2 Ὡς [c] γέγραπται [d] ἐν τῷ Ἡσαΐᾳ τῷ προφήτῃ [e] Ἰδοὺ b see Matt. iv. 3 and note.

c N. T. passim. 2 Chron. xxxii. 32. d = Rom ix. 25. (xi. 2.) Heb. iv. 7. e Mal. iii. 1.

P ως γεγραπται... ABDEF HKLM PSUVΓ ΔΠℵ 1. 33. 69

Title. rec το κατα μαρκον αγιον ευαγγελιον, with Scr's i l m n p s v: εκ του κατα μαρκον ευαγγελιου 69 [-λιον Scr]: κατα μαρκον B(so Verc Tischdf Treg) Fℵ: txt AD rel.

Chap. I. 1. om υιου θεου $ℵ^1$ 28. 255 Iren-gr-int(but om ιησ. χρ. also) $Orig_3$ Bas Jer_3 Victorin. (insd by ℵ-corr[1] $Iren_{2\ expr\ 1}$ Ambr Jer_1.)—rec ins του bef θεου, with A rel [Cyr_1]: om BDL ℵ-corr[1] Sevrn.

2. **καθως** BKLΔΠ[1]ℵ **1.** 33 $Orig_3$ Bas Tit [Serap] Sevrn: txt ADP rel Iren-gr $Orig_1$ [$Epiph_1$]. rec (for τω ησαια τω προφητη) τοις προφηταις (*corrn, the cit being from Mal and Isa*), with AP rel syr-txt æth arm-zoh Chr[?] Phot [Thl] $Iren\text{-}int_2$: txt BDLΔℵ **1.** 33 latt Syr syr-mg syr-jer copt goth arm-mss $Iren\text{-}gr\text{-}int_1$ Orig(ὁ Μάρκος δύο προφητείας ἐν διαφόροις εἰρημένας τόποις ὑπὸ δύο προφητῶν εἰς ἓν συνάγων πεποίηκε· καθὼς γέγραπται ἐν τῷ Ἡσαΐᾳ τῷ προφήτῃ κ.τ.λ.) Serap Porph Eus Epiph Bas Tit-bostr Vict Sevrn Jer('nomen Isaiæ putamus additum Scriptorum vitio') Aug.—om 1st τω D

N.B. Throughout Mark, the parallel places in Matthew are to be consulted. Where the agreement is verbal, or nearly so, no notes are here appended, except grammatical and philological ones.

* Chap. I. 1—8.] The preaching and baptism of John. Matt. iii. 1—12. Luke iii. 1—17. The object of Mark being to relate *the official life and ministry* of our Lord, he begins with His *baptism*; and as a necessary introduction to it, with *the preaching of John the Baptist*. His account of John's baptism has many phrases in common with both Matt. and Luke; but from the additional prophecy quoted in ver. 2, is certainly *independent* and *distinct* (see Prolegomena to the Gospp. ch. i. § ii.). **1. ἀρχὴ** κ.τ.λ.] This is probably a title to what follows, as Matt. i. 1, and not connected with ver. 4, as Fritzsche and Lachm., nor with ver. 2, as Meyer. It is simpler and gives more majesty to the exordium, to put a period at the end of ver. 1, and make the citation from the Prophet a new and confirmatory title. **Ἰησ. χρ.**] of, as its author, or its subject, as the context may determine. "If the genit. after εὐαγγ. is *not* a person, it is always that of the *object*, as εὐαγγ. τῆς βασιλείας, τῆς σωτηρίας, κ.τ.λ. (Matt. iv. 23: Eph. i. 13; vi. 15 al.). If θεοῦ follows, the genit. is one of the *subject* (ch. i. 15: Rom. i. 1, 15, 16, al.), as also when μου follows (Rom. ii. 16; xvi. 25: 1 Thess. i. 5, al.). But if χριστοῦ follows (Rom. i. 9; xv. 19: 1 Cor. ix. 12, al.), it may be either genit. of the *subject* (*auctoris*) or of the *object*: and only the context can determine. Here it decides for the latter (vv. 2—8). Render therefore, **the glad tidings concerning Jesus Christ.**" Meyer. **2, 3.**] This again

ἀποστέλλω τὸν ἄγγελόν μου πρὸ προσώπου σου, ὃς ABDEF
f κατασκευάσει τὴν ὁδόν σου· 3 g Φωνὴ βοῶντος ἐν τῇ HKLM PSUVΓ
ἐρήμῳ Ἑτοιμάσατε τὴν ὁδὸν κυρίου, h εὐθείας ποιεῖτε τὰς ΔΠℵ 1. 33. 69
i τρίβους αὐτοῦ. 4 j Ἐγένετο Ἰωάννης ὁ βαπτίζων ἐν τῇ
ἐρήμῳ jk κηρύσσων l βάπτισμα lm μετανοίας εἰς n ἄφεσιν
ἁμαρτιῶν. 5 καὶ o ἐξεπορεύετο πρὸς αὐτὸν πᾶσα ἡ
Ἰουδαία χώρα καὶ οἱ Ἱεροσολυμῖται πάντες, καὶ ἐβαπτίζοντο ὑπ' αὐτοῦ ἐν τῷ Ἰορδάνῃ ποταμῷ p ἐξομολογούμενοι τὰς ἁμαρτίας αὐτῶν. 6 καὶ q ἦν ὁ Ἰωάννης
r ἐνδεδυμένος τρίχας καμήλου καὶ s ζώνην s δερματίνην
περὶ τὴν s ὀσφὺν αὐτοῦ, καὶ t ἔσθων u ἀκρίδας καὶ u μέλι
u ἄγριον. 7 καὶ v ἐκήρυσσεν λέγων Ἔρχεται ὁ w ἰσχυρό-

f Matt. xi. 10 ‖ L. Luke i. 17. Heb. iii. 3, 4 bis. ix. 2, 6. xi. 7. 1 Pet. iii. 20 only. Wisd. vii. 27.
g Isa. xl. 3.
h ‖ L. reff.
i ‖ only. Ps. xxvi. 11.
j constr., ch. ix. 3, 7. 2 Cor. vi. 14. Col. i. 18. Heb. v. 12. Rev. iii. 2. xvi. 10. Mic. ii. 1. see ver. 39. Luke i. 10, 20.
k Matt. iv. 23 reff.
l ‖ L. Acts xiii. 24. xix. 4 only.
m Matt. iii. 8, 11 al. (not John.) Prov. xiv. 15. Wisd. xi. 23. xii. 10, 19. Sir. xliv. 16 only.
n Matt. xxvi. 28 reff. Deut. xv. 3.
o ‖ Mt. L. al. fr.
p = ‖ Mt. Acts xix. 18. James v. 16 ‡.
q Luke i. 10, 20 al. fr. Jer. xxxiii. (xxvi.) 20. see ver. 4.
r Matt. vi. 25 reff.
s ‖ Mt. reff. 4 Kings i. 8.
t -θω, Luke xxii. 30 reff. Lev. xvii. 10 al.
u ‖ Mt. reff.
v = Matt. iii. 1. iv. 17. vv. 38, 39, 45 al. fr. Exod. xxxii. 5.
w ‖ Mt. reff.

1. 63 (255) Iren-gr Orig$_2$ [Tit$_1$ Bas$_1$ Serap$_1$ Epiph$_3$]. rec ins εγω bef αποστελλω (*perhaps from Matt* xi. 10, *where* Z *only omits it. It is insd in l. c. of* LXX *by* A *al*), with APℵ rel vulg syr goth æth arm Orig$_5$ Eus Phot Jer$_2$: om BD am(with em fuld gat ing mm mt taur tol) lat-*a b c i* Orig[?] Sevrn Iren-int Ambr Jer$_1$ Aug Vigil-taps Bede. αποστελω ℵ [Orig$_1$]. rec at end adds εμπροσθεν σου (*from Matt* xi. 10: *Luke* vii. 27), with A rel vulg lat-*f ff*$_{1.2}$ *g*$_{1.2}$ syr copt-wilk goth arm Orig$_3$ Eus Sevrn Phot Tert Jer$_1$: om BDKLPΠ^{1}ℵ am(with em fuld ing mt taur tol) lat-*a b c l* Syr syr-jer copt-schw æth Orig$_{3\ expr\ 1}$ Iren-int Vict Jer$_2$ Aug.

3. for αυτου, του θεου υμων (*from* LXX) D 34-marg, *dei nostri* mt lat-*a b c f ff*$_2$ *g*$_2$ goth syr-ms-mg (Iren-int).

4. at beg ins και ℵ^1(ℵ^{3a} disapproving). rec om ο, with A(D)P rel: ins BLΔℵ 33 copt.—εν τ. ερ. bef βαπτ. D 28 latt(not *f*) Syr. rec ins και bef κηρυσσων, with ADℵ rel vss: om B 33. (P def.) (*The account of the varns seems to be the ignorance of the transcribers that* ιω. ο βαπτιζων *is, with Mark,* John the Baptist,—*see* ch vi. 14, *where* D al *have corrd to* βαπτιστης : *thence* βαπτιζων *became joined with* εγενετο, *and* και *insd.*)

5. εξεπορευοντο (*corrn to suit* ιεροσολυμιται &c) EFHLSV Γ(Tischdf) harl^1(with taur) lat-*b ff*$_1$ *g*$_1$ copt-2-mss goth Thl. om οι D Scr's c. rec και εβαπτιζοντο bef παντες, with AP rel syr goth (æth): om και ℵ^1 69 lat-*a*, om παντες 69 lat-*f*: txt BDLΔℵ^{3a} 33 vulg lat-*b l* copt arm Orig$_2$ Eus. (παντες *was omd, as not in* ‖ *Matt, and seeming to assert too much : then re insd from marg with* εβαπτ.) rec εν τω ιορδ. ποταμω bef υπ' αυτου (*from* ‖ *Matt*), with ADP rel syr goth: txt BLℵ 33 vulg lat-*b c f ff*$_{1.2}$ *g*$_{1.2}$ *l* arm Orig$_2$ Eus.—om τω D^1(ins D^3).—om ποταμω D mt lat-*a b c ff*$_{1.2}$ *g*$_1$ Orig$_1$.

6. rec (for και ην) ην δε (*from Matt* iii. 4), with A D[-gr] P rel mt lat-*a c f ff*$_2$ syrr copt-schw goth æth arm Thl: txt BLℵ 33 vulg lat-*b ff*$_1$ *g*$_{1.2}$ D-lat copt-wilk. rec om ο, with ADHSΔΠ 33: ins BLℵ rel Thl. for τριχας, δερρην D-gr lat-*a*. om και ζ. to αυτου D lat-*a b ff*$_2$. rec εσθιων, with ADP ℵ^{3a}(appy) rel: txt BL^{1}Δℵ^1 33.

7, 8. και ελεγεν αυτοις εγω μεν υμας βαπτιζω εν υδατι ερχεται δε οπισω μου ο

stands independently, not ἐγέν. Ἰωάν. (ὁ) βαπτ. . . . . ὡς γέγρ. The citation here is from *two Prophets*, Isa. and Mal.: see reff. The fact will not fail to be observed by the careful and honest student of the Gospels. Had the citation from Isaiah stood first, it would have been of no note, as Meyer observes. Consult notes on Matt. xi. 10; iii. 3. **4.**] See on Matt. iii. 1. **βάπτ. μετ.**, the baptism *symbolic of* ("gen. of the characteristic quality," Meyer) *repentance and forgiveness*—of the death unto sin, and new birth unto righteousness. The *former* of these only comes properly into the notion of John's baptism, which did not confer the Holy Spirit, ver.

τερός μου ὀπίσω μου [x] οὗ οὐκ εἰμὶ [y] ἱκανὸς [z] κύψας λῦσαι
τὸν [a] ἱμάντα τῶν ὑποδημάτων [x] αὐτοῦ. 8 ἐγὼ ἐβάπτισα
ὑμᾶς ὕδατι, αὐτὸς δὲ βαπτίσει ὑμᾶς πνεύματι ἁγίῳ.
9 καὶ ἐγένετο ἐν [b] ἐκείναις ταῖς ἡμέραις, ἦλθεν Ἰησοῦς ἀπὸ
Ναζαρὲτ τῆς Γαλιλαίας, καὶ ἐβαπτίσθη [c] εἰς τὸν Ἰορδάνην
ὑπὸ Ἰωάννου. 10 καὶ εὐθὺς ἀναβαίνων ἐκ τοῦ ὕδατος
εἶδεν [d] σχιζομένους τοὺς οὐρανούς, καὶ τὸ πνεῦμα ὡς
[e] περιστερὰν [f] καταβαῖνον εἰς αὐτόν· 11 καὶ [g] φωνὴ ἐγένετο
ἐκ τῶν οὐρανῶν Σὺ εἶ ὁ υἱός μου ὁ [h] ἀγαπητός· ἐν σοὶ

..αγαπητος εν P.

x constr., Matt. iii. 12 reff.
y — & constr., (Matt. viii. 8 ‖ L.) 1 Cor. xv. 9. 2 Cor. (ii. 16.) iii. 5. 2 Tim. ii. 2. (Exod. iv. 10. Joel ii. 11.)
z here [and John viii. 6 (8 v. r.)] only. Exod. iv. 31 al.
a ‖ L. J. Acts xxii. 25 only. Job xxix. 10. Isa. v. 18, 27. Sir. xxx. (xxxiii.) 26 only.
b ch. viii. 1. xiii. 17 ‖ Mt., 24. Luke v. 35. ix. 36 al. Judg. xvii. 6.
c = John ix. 7.
d = here only. see ch. xv. 38 ‖.
e ‖ Mt. reff.
f ‖. Matt. vii. 25. John i. 32 al. fr. Isa. lxiii. 14.
g Luke ix. 35 reff.
h ‖. Matt. xii. 18. xvii. 5 ‖. 2 Pet. i. 17. Gen. xxii. 2. = μονογενής, Aq.

ισχυροτερος μου οὗ ουκ ειμι ικανος λυσαι τον ιμαντα των υποδηματων αυτου και αυτος υμας βαπτισει εν πνευματι αγιω D lat-(*a*) *ff*$_2$ &c (*see Luke* iii. 16). ισχυρος A ev-x. om 2nd μου B (al ? 102 = B ?) Orig$_1$: om οπισω μου Δ ev-P lat-*ff*$_2$.

8. rec aft εγω ins μεν (*from* ‖ *Matt Luke*), with A(D)P rel mt lat-*a f ff*$_2$ syr goth æth : om BLℵ 33. 69 vulg lat-*b c ff*$_1$ *g*$_{1.2}$ Syr copt arm Orig [Aug$_1$]. rec ins εν bef υδατι (*from* ‖ *Matt, where* none *omit it*), with ADP rel gat(with mm mt) lat-*a c* &c [copt] : om BHΔℵ 33 vulg Orig(addg μόνος Ματθαῖος τούτῳ προσέθηκε τὸ εἰς μετάνοιαν) Aug. om 2nd υμας ℵ[1](ins ℵ[3a]) lat-*b* : υμας bef βαπτισει D 69 lat-*a ff*$_2$. rec ins εν bef πν. αγ. (*from* ‖ *Matt*), with ADPℵ rel gat(with mm mt) copt Orig : om BL vulg lat-*b* Aug[-txt]. at end add και πυρι (*from* ‖ *Matt Luke*) P 47. 54-6-8. 259 Scr's v syr-w-ast.

9. om 1st και B Scr's c. ταις ημεραις bef εκειναις DΔ Scr's c lat-*b f ff*$_{1.2}$ *g*$_1$. ins ο bef ιησ. DMΓΔ 69 Scr's c d e i l m n r s w[2] evv-H-P-x-y-z. rec υπο ιω. bef εις τ. ιορδ., with AP rel vulg lat-*c f* syr goth æth arm : txt BDLℵ (1) 33. 69 am(with fuld ing tol) lat-*a b ff*$_{1.2}$ *g*$_{1.2}$ Syr copt Orig. εις την ιορδ. D[1](txt D-corr[1]).

10. rec ευθεως, with AP rel : om D lat-*a b* æth : txt BLΔℵ 33. rec (for εκ) απο (*from* ‖ *Matt*), with AP rel : txt BDLℵ 33. 69 latt goth æth(appy) arm. for σχιζ., ηνυγμενους (= ηνοιγ.) D, *apertos* lat-*b*, *aperiri* lat-*c*, *adaperiri* lat-*a*. rec ωσει (*from* ‖ *Matt*), with MP (1. 33. 69, e sil) : txt ABDℵ rel (syr-mg-gr). καταβαινων D[1]. add και μενον (*from John* i. 33) ℵ (10) 33. 86. 106 Scr's g vulg lat-*b ff*$_{1.2}$ *g*$_{1.2}$ *l* copt-wilk æth Ambr. (Δ has a space left.) rec (for εις) επ' (*from* ‖), with APℵ rel lat-*f g*$_1$: txt BD 13. 69. 124 lat-*a* (*b*) *l*.

11. om εγενετο D ℵ[1](ins ℵ[3a]) mt lat-*ff*$_2$. rec (for σοι) ω (*from* ‖ *Matt*), with A rel lat-*b f g*$_1$ D-lat syr-mg copt-wilk arm-mss : txt B D[-gr] LΔℵ 1. 33. 69 vulg lat-*a c ff*$_2$ *g*$_2$ *l* Syr syr-txt copt-schw goth æth arm-zoh. (P def.)

8. **7. κύψας λῦσαι . . . .]** The expression is common to Mark, Luke, and John (i. 27). It amounts to the same as *bearing the shoes*—for he who did the last would necessarily be also employed in loosing and taking off the sandal. But the variety is itself indicative of the independence of Matt. and Mark of one another. John used the two expressions at different times, and our witnesses have reported both. **κύψας** is added by Mark, who, as we shall find, is more minute in circumstantial detail than the other Evangelists. **8.]** Matt. and Luke add καὶ πυρί.

9—11.] Jesus is baptized by him. Matt. iii. 13—17. Luke iii. 21, 22. **ἀπὸ Ναζ.** is contained here only. The words with which this account is introduced, express indefiniteness as to time. It was (Luke iii. 21) *after all the people were baptized* : see note there. The commencement of this Gospel has no marks of an eye-witness : it is the *compendium of generally current accounts*.

10.] εὐθύς, or **-θέως**, is a favourite connecting word with Mark. St. Mark has here taken the oral account verbatim, and applied it to Jesus, '*He saw*,' &c.—and αὐτόν must mean *Himself* : otherwise we must understand **ὁ Ἰωάν.** before **εἶδεν**, and take **ἀναβ.** as *pendent*, which is very improbable. The construction of the sentence is a remarkable testimony of the independence of Mark and Matt. even when parts of the narrative agree verbatim. See note on Matt. iii. 16. **σχιζ.**, peculiar to Mark ; and more de-

[i] εὐδόκησα. 12 καὶ εὐθὺς τὸ πνεῦμα αὐτὸν [k] ἐκβάλλει εἰς
τὴν ἔρημον. 13 καὶ ἦν ἐν τῇ ἐρήμῳ ἡμέρας τεσσεράκοντα
[l] πειραζόμενος ὑπὸ τοῦ σατανᾶ, καὶ ἦν μετὰ τῶν θηρίων,
καὶ οἱ ἄγγελοι [m] διηκόνουν αὐτῷ. G και οι αγγ....
14 Καὶ μετὰ τὸ [n] παραδοθῆναι τὸν Ἰωάννην, ἦλθεν ὁ ABDEF GHKL
Ἰησοῦς εἰς τὴν Γαλιλαίαν κηρύσσων τὸ [o] εὐαγγέλιον τοῦ MSUVΓ ΔΠℵ 1.
[o] θεοῦ 15 λέγων ὅτι [p] πεπλήρωται ὁ [p] καιρὸς καὶ [q] ἤγγικεν 33. 69
ἡ [r] βασιλεία τοῦ [r] θεοῦ· [s] μετανοεῖτε καὶ [t] πιστεύετε ἐν τῷ

i ||. Matt. xvii. 5. 1 Cor. x. 5. 2 Cor. xii. 10. [2 Thess. ii. 12.] Heb. x. 38, from Hab. ii. 4. 2 Kings xxii. 20. Mal. ii. 17.
k = Matt. ix. 38. John x. 4. 1 Macc. xii. 27.
l || and N. T. passim.
m ch. xv. 41 al. fr.†
n = Acts viii. 3. xvi. 4. 2 Pet. ii. 4. Ps. lxxxvii. 8. constr., Ezek. xliv. 26 al. fr.
o Rom. i. 1. xv. 16. 2 Cor. xi. 7. 1 Thess. ii. 2, 8, 9. 1 Pet. iv. 17 (Acts xx. 24. 1 Tim. i. 11) only. εὐ. τῆς βασ., Matt. iv. 23. ix. 35. xxiv. 14 only.
p Luke xxi. 24. see Lam. iv. 18.
q = || Mt. al. fr. Ezek. vii. 7, 12.
r Matt. [vi. 33] xii. 28 al2. ch. iv. 11, 26. 30 and freq. in Mk., Luke, Acts & Paul. John iii. 3, 5. Rev. xii. 10.
s Matt. iii. 2 reff.
t w. ἐν, John iii. 15 only. Ps. lxxvii. 22. Jer. xii. 6.

12. ευθεως ADE¹K M-marg Π¹ **1** : txt Bℵ rel. aft πνευμα ins το αγιον D. εκβαλλει bef αυτον DΔ 33. 69 latt.

13. rec ins εκει bef εν τη ερημω (*marg corrn for* εν τ. ερ. (*as appears by* εν τ. ερ. *being omd by* KΠ¹ &c) *aftds admd with it into the txt*), with Δ rel syrr (arm) : om ABDLℵ 33 latt copt goth æth Orig [Eus_1] : om εν τη ε. [also] KΠ¹ **1.** 69. 124. 209-53 Scr's e w¹ lat-*a* arm. τεσσερακοντα bef ημερας BLℵ 33 vulg lat-(*e*) ff_1 g_1 *l* copt [æth] Orig Eus. add κ. τεσσερακ. νυκτας L(M) 13. 33 Scr's c v ev-w² vulg lat-(*c*) ff_1 g_1 *l* (syr-mg) copt æth Orig Eus. ins και bef πειραζομενος D latt. om οι AM 33. 238 Scr's c d evv-H-y-z.

14. rec (for και μετα) μετα δε (|| *Matt*), with ALℵ rel vulg lat-*f* ff_1 g_2 syrr [copt-dz] goth æth arm Orig Eus : *sed postquam* lat-*b* g_1 D-lat : txt B[B¹ oms τα of μετα] D-gr lat-*a* (*c*) copt. om τον AEFG¹HSUVΓ Eus-ed. om ο AEFHKM(S ?)U V²[om ο ιησ. V¹] ΓΠ Eus. rec aft ευαγγελιον ins της βασιλειας (*from Matt* iv. 23), with AD rel vulg lat-*a* *f* $ff_{1.2}$ $g_{1.2}$ Syr syr-ms æth : om BLℵ **1.** 33. 69 mt lat-*b* *c* ff_2 syr-ed copt goth(Treg) arm $Orig_2$.

15. rec ins και bef λεγων, with BKLMΔΠ **1.** 33. 69 vulg lat-*a* *b* &c syrr copt : om AD rel lat-*f* ff_2 g_1 goth.—om και λεγων ℵ¹(ins ℵ-corr¹, appy) mt lat-*c* Orig. πεπληρωνται οι καιροι D mt lat-*a* *b* *c* ff_2 g_1.

scriptive than ἀνεῴχθησαν, Matt. Luke.

11.] σὺ εἶ, Mark, Luke; οὗτός ἐσ., Matt.—ἐν ᾧ εὐδ., Matt.; ἐν σοὶ εὐδ., Mark and Luke. I mention these things to shew how extremely improbable it is that Mark had either Matt. or Luke before him. Such arbitrary alteration of documents could never have been the practice of any one seriously intent on an important work.

12, 13.] Temptation of Jesus. Matt. iv. 1—11. Luke iv. 1—13. **12, 13.**] **ἐκβάλλω** = ἀνάγω Matt., = ἄγω Luke. It is a more forcible word than either of these to express the mighty and cogent impulse of the Spirit. **σατανᾶ** = **διαβ.** Matt., Luke: see note, Matt. iv. 1.

It seems to have been permitted to the evil one to tempt our Lord *during the whole of the* 40 *days*, and of this we have here, as in Luke, an implied assertion. The additional intensity of temptation at the *end* of that period, is expressed in Matt. by the tempter *coming to* Him—becoming visible and audible. Perhaps the *being with the beasts* may point to one form of temptation, viz. that of *terror*, which was practised on Him:—but of the *inward trials* who may speak? **οἱ ἄγγ.**, as **τῶν** θηρ. generic. There is nothing here to *contradict* the fast spoken of in Matt. and Luke, as De W. maintains. Our Evangelist perhaps implies it in the last words of ver. 13. It is remarkable that those Commentators who are fondest of maintaining that Mark constructed his narrative out of those of Matt. and Luke (De W., Meyer) are also most keen in pointing out what they call irreconcileable differences between him and them. No apportionment of these details to the various successive parts of the temptation is given by our Evangelist. They are simply stated to have happened, compendiously.

14, 15.] Jesus begins His ministry. Matt. iv. 12—17. Luke iv. 14, 15. **14.**] See note on Matt. iv. 12. **παραδ.** seems to have been the usual and well-known term for the imprisonment of John. **τὸ εὐαγ. τ. θ.**] See reff., and note on ver. 1. **15. πεπλ. ὁ καιρ.**] See Gal. iv. 4. "The end of the old covenant is at hand; . . . . the Son is born, grown

εὐαγγελίῳ. 16 καὶ παράγων παρὰ τὴν θάλασσαν τῆς
Γαλιλαίας εἶδεν Σίμωνα καὶ Ἀνδρέαν τὸν ἀδελφὸν Σίμωνος [u] ἀμφιβάλλοντας ἐν τῇ θαλάσσῃ, ἦσαν γὰρ [v] ἁλεεῖς.
17 καὶ εἶπεν αὐτοῖς ὁ Ἰησοῦς [w] Δεῦτε [t] ὀπίσω μου καὶ
ποιήσω ὑμᾶς γενέσθαι [v] ἁλεεῖς ἀνθρώπων. 18 καὶ εὐθέως
[x] ἀφέντες τὰ [y] δίκτυα [αὐτῶν] ἠκολούθησαν αὐτῷ. 19 καὶ
[z] προβὰς ὀλίγον εἶδεν Ἰάκωβον τὸν τοῦ Ζεβεδαίου καὶ
Ἰωάννην τὸν ἀδελφὸν αὐτοῦ, καὶ αὐτοὺς ἐν τῷ πλοίῳ
[a] καταρτίζοντας τὰ [y] δίκτυα. 20 καὶ εὐθὺς ἐκάλεσεν
αὐτούς· καὶ [x] ἀφέντες τὸν πατέρα αὐτῶν Ζεβεδαῖον ἐν τῷ
πλοίῳ μετὰ τῶν [b] μισθωτῶν [c] ἀπῆλθον [c] ὀπίσω αὐτοῦ.

C υμας γενεσθαι ...

u here only. Hab. i. 17 only.
v ‖ Mt. bis. Luke v. 2 only. Jer. xvi. 16. (-εύειν, John xxi. 3.)
w ‖ Mt. only. 4 Kings vi. 19.
x = Matt. iv. 11 al. fr.
y ‖ Mt. bis. Luke v. 2, 4, 5, 6. John xxi. 6, 8, 11 bis only.
z = ‖ Mt. (Luke i. 7, 18. ii. 36) only.
a ‖ Mt. Gal. vi. 1 al. Ezra iv. 12, 13, 16.
b John x. 12, 13 bis only. Exod. xii. 45. = μίσθιος, Luke xv. 17, 19.
c John xii. 19.

16. rec (for και παραγων) περιπατων δε (*from* ‖ *Matt*), with A rel (Syr) syr-txt : txt BDLℵ 33. 69 latt (syr-mg) copt goth arm. ins τον bef σιμωνα D 28. 69. 124. 346. rec (for σιμωνος) αυτου (*from* ‖ *Matt*), with DGΓ 33 latt Syr æth : αυτου του σιμωνος (*combination of readings*) E^{1}FHKSUVΠ syr goth : txt BLMℵ lat-*a* copt arm, του σ. AE^{2}Δ 1. 69. rec (for αμφιβαλλ.) βαλλοντας (*from* ‖ *Matt*), with E^{2}MΓΠ^2 1 arm : txt A(-τες) BDℵ rel. rec adds αμφιβληστρον (*from* ‖ *Matt*), with A rel lat-*b* ff_2 syr copt goth ; -τρα vss, -τρα bef βαλλοντας 1. 237-59 Scr's a ; τα δικτυα D 13. 28. 69. 124 vulg lat-*a c f* ff_1 $g_{1.2}$ *l* Syr arm : om BLℵ 33 æth (appy). rec αλιεις, with ℵ rel : αλειεις D (L doubtful) : txt AB^{1}Δ (so in ver 17, where Cℵ have -εεις also).

18. ευθυς Lℵ 33. om αυτων BCLℵ 13. 33. 69 vulg lat-ff_1 g_2 copt arm : ins A rel lat-*f* g_1 syrr goth æth.—for τα δικτυα, παντα D lat-*a b c* ff_2. ηκολουθουν B.

19. προςβας D^1. rec aft προβας ins εκειθεν (*from* ‖ *Matt*), with ACℵ rel vulg lat-*c f* ff_1 $g_{1.2}$ syr goth æth arm : aft ολιγον 33 : om BDL 1 lat-*a b* ff_2 g_1 Syr copt. om ολιγον ℵ^1(ins bef εκειθεν ℵ^{3a}) 56-7-8 Thl. aft δικτυα ins αυτων (*from* ‖ *Matt*) C^{2}KMΓΠ^1 1 Syr syr-w-ast copt[?] æth.

20. rec ευθεως, with ACD rel : txt BLℵ 13. 33 : om 124. 433 lat-*b* æth : ins bef αφεντες Δ (69) lat-*c* ff_2 Syr arm. for απ. οπ. αυτ., ηκολουθησαν αυτω (‖ *Matt*) D latt copt-wilk æth.

up, anointed (in his baptism), tempted, gone forth, the testimony of his witness is given, and now He witnesses Himself; now begins that last speaking of God, *by His Son* (Heb. i. 1), which henceforth shall be proclaimed in all the world till the end comes." Stier, R. J. i. 57.

καὶ πιστ.] These words are in Mark only. They furnish us an interesting characteristic of the difference between the preaching *of John*, which was that of repentance—and *of our Lord*, which was repentance *and faith*. It is not *in Himself as the Saviour* that this faith is *yet* preached : this He did not proclaim till much later in his ministry : but in *the fulfilment of the time and approach of the kingdom of God.* **ἐν** is not *instrumental* (as Fritzsche), '*by means of* the Gospel:' but **in the Gospel**, which, in its completion, sets forth Jesus Christ as the object of faith. "The object of the faith is conceived as that on which the faith lays hold." Meyer.

16—20.] Calling of Peter, Andrew, James, and John. Matt. iv. 18—22. Almost verbatim as Matt. The variations are curious : after Σίμωνα, Mark omits τὸν λεγ. Πέτρ. :—although the name was prophetically given by our Lord before this, in John i. 43, it perhaps was not *actually* given, till the twelve became a distinct body, see ch. iii. 16. Matt. has εἰς τὴν θ., for our ἐν τ. θ., an inconceivable variation if one copied the other, as is also ἀμφιβάλλ. for βάλλ. ἀμφίβληστρον. The παράγων παρά, and the ἀμφιβ. ἐν τ. θαλ. are noticed by Meyer as belonging to the graphic delineation which this Evangelist loves. **17.**] **γενέσθαι** is here inserted before **ἁλεεῖς** for minute accuracy. **19.**] μετὰ Ζ. τ. πατρ. αὐτ. (Matt.) is omitted here, and Z. inserted below, where Matt. has simply τ. πατ. **καὶ αὐτούς, these also**, as well as the former pair of brothers. It belongs only to ἐν τῷ πλοίῳ, not to the following clause. **20.**] **μετὰ τῶν μισθ.** is in-

ABCDE FGHKL MSUVΓ ΔΠℵ 1. 33. 69

21 Καὶ εἰςπορεύονται εἰς Καφαρναούμ. καὶ εὐθέως [d] τοῖς
σάββασιν * ἐδίδασκεν [e] εἰς τὴν συναγωγήν. 22 καὶ [f] ἐξεπλήσσοντο [g] ἐπὶ τῇ διδαχῇ αὐτοῦ, ἦν γὰρ διδάσκων
αὐτοὺς ὡς [h] ἐξουσίαν ἔχων καὶ οὐχ ὡς οἱ γραμματεῖς.
23 καὶ εὐθὺς ἦν ἐν τῇ συναγωγῇ αὐτῶν ἄνθρωπος [i] ἐν
[i] πνεύματι [i] ἀκαθάρτῳ, καὶ [j] ἀνέκραξεν 24 λέγων [k] Τί ἡμῖν
καὶ * σοὶ Ἰησοῦ Ναζαρηνέ; ἦλθες ἀπολέσαι ἡμᾶς; οἶδά
σε τίς εἶ, ὁ [l] ἅγιος τοῦ [l] θεοῦ. 25 καὶ [m] ἐπετίμησεν αὐτῷ

d plur., Matt. xii. 1, &c. ch. ii. 24. iii. 2, 4 al. fr.
e constr., ver. 39 al.
f constr., Matt. vii. 28. xxii. 33. ch. xi. 18. Luke iv. 32. ix. 43. Acts xiii. 12.
g = ch. iii. 5. x. 22, 24 al. Exod. xviii. 9.
h Matt. vii. 29 reff.
i ch. v. 2. cf. Luke i. 17 bis. Isa. liii. 3, 4.
j ‖ L. ch. vi. 49. Luke viii. 28. xxiii. 18 only. Judg. vii. 20.
k ‖ L. Matt. viii. 29. 2 Kings xvi. 10 al.
l ‖. John vi. 69 only. see Acts iii. 14. 1 John ii. 20.
m Matt. xvi. 22. Jude 9. Zech. iii. 3.

21. εισεπορευοντο D-gr 33. ευθυς Lℵ 1. 33 Orig₁. ins εν bef τοις σαββασιν CG. *rec εἰςελθὼν εἰς τὴν συναγωγὴν ἐδίδασκεν, with ABD rel latt syr goth æth arm: εδιδ. εισελθ. εις τ. συν. al: ελθων ε. τ. σ. εδ. al: εις τ. συν. αυτων εδιδασκ. Δ ev-Π: εδιδασκ. (εν) τοις σαββ. εις τ. συν. C Syr copt: εδιδασκεν εις την συναγωγην (C)Lℵ Orig₂. (*The varns seem to shew that the construction gave offence and was supplied by* εισελθ. *or* ελθ.)—εδιδαξεν ℵ¹(txt ℵ³ᵃ). add αυτους D latt syr-w-ast goth æth arm.

22. om 2nd και D¹(ins D²) lat-*b c e*. aft γραμματεις ins αυτων (*from Matt* vii. 29) CMΔ 33 lat-*c f g₂* syrr æth.

23. rec om ευθυς (*as inappropriate*), with ACD rel latt syrr goth æth arm: ins BLℵ 1. 33. 131. 209 copt Orig. εν τη συν. αυ. bef ην C Orig. om αυτων DL 72 lat-*b c e ff₂ g₁* copt-wilk. ενεκραξεν D.

24. rec ins εα bef τι (*from* ‖ *Luke. It was not correctly stated by Tischdf* (ed 7) *that nearly the same* MSS *omit it in Luke as here: e.g.,* B *has it there*), with ACℵ³ᵃ rel syr goth arm Orig Eus₂ [Cyr₁]: om BDℵ¹ latt Syr copt æth Aug. *σύ (*confusion of vowels?*) ABΓΔ Scr's e ev-z: σοι CDℵ rel. ημας bef απολεσαι C Vict. οιδαμεν L Δ-gr ℵ copt æth arm Orig Eus Cyr-jer Bas Chr Thdor-mops Cyr Iren-int Tert [Hil₂] Aug Paulin: txt ABCD rel latt syrr goth.

serted for particularity, and perhaps to *soften* the leaving their father alone. It gives us a view of the station of life of Zebedee and his sons; they were not *poor* fishermen, but had *hired servants*. Matt. has ἠκολούθησ. αὐτ. Now may we not venture to say that both these accounts came *from Peter* originally? Matthew's an earlier one, taught (or given in writing perhaps) without any definite idea of making it part of a larger work; but this carefully corrected and rendered accurate, even to the omitting the name *Peter*, which though generally known, and therefore mentioned in the *oral* account, was perhaps not yet formally given, and was therefore omitted in the *historical*.

21—28.] HEALING OF A DÆMONIAC IN THE SYNAGOGUE AT CAPERNAUM. Luke iv. 31—37. **21.**] Not *immediately* after the preceding. The *calling of the Apostles*, the *Sermon on the Mount*, the *healing of the leper*, and *of the centurion's servant*, precede the following miracle. **22.**] A formula occurring entire at the end of the Sermon on the Mount, Matt. vii. 28, and the first clause of it,—and, in substance, the second also,—in the corresponding place to this in Luke iv. 32.

23—28.] This account occurs in Luke iv. 33—37, nearly verbatim: for the variations, see there. It is very important for our Lord's official life, as shewing that He rejected and forbade all testimony to his Person, *except that which He came on earth to give*. The dæmons *knew Him*, but *were silenced*. (See Matt. viii. 29: ch. v. 7.) It is of course utterly impossible to understand such a testimony as that of the *sick person*, still less of the *fever* or *disease*. **23. ἄνθ. ἐν πν.**] The use of the prep. in this connexion is unusual: see reff. I think the best account of it is, that it falls under a large class of usages of ἐν, expressing the *element in which* the man lived and moved, as possessed and interpenetrated by the evil spirit,—as in the common expressions ἐν κυρίῳ, ἐν χριστῷ, cf. 2 Cor. xii. 2, and Acts xvii. 28. **24. Ναζ.**] We may observe that this epithet often occurs under strong contrast to His Majesty and glory; as here, and ch. xvi. 6, and Acts ii. 22—24; xxii. 8; and, we may add, John xix. 19. **ἡμᾶς**, generic: "communem inter se causam habent dæmonia," Bengel.

ὁ Ἰησοῦς λέγων [n] Φιμώθητι καὶ ἔξελθε ἐξ αὐτοῦ. 26 καὶ
[o] σπαράξαν αὐτὸν τὸ πνεῦμα τὸ ἀκάθαρτον καὶ φωνῆσαν
φωνῇ μεγάλῃ ἐξῆλθεν ἐξ αὐτοῦ. 27 καὶ [p] ἐθαμβήθησαν
ἅπαντες, ὥςτε [q] συνζητεῖν πρὸς [r] ἑαυτοὺς λέγοντας Τί
ἐστιν τοῦτο; διδαχὴ καινὴ [s] κατ' ἐξουσίαν· καὶ τοῖς πνεύμασιν τοῖς ἀκαθάρτοις [t] ἐπιτάσσει, καὶ ὑπακούουσιν αὐτῷ.
28 καὶ ἐξῆλθεν ἡ [u] ἀκοὴ αὐτοῦ εὐθὺς [v] πανταχοῦ εἰς ὅλην
τὴν [w] περίχωρον τῆς Γαλιλαίας. 29 Καὶ εὐθὺς ἐκ τῆς
συναγωγῆς ἐξελθόντες ἦλθον εἰς τὴν οἰκίαν Σίμωνος καὶ
Ἀνδρέου μετὰ Ἰακώβου καὶ Ἰωάννου. 30 ἡ δὲ [x] πενθερὰ
Σίμωνος [y] κατέκειτο [z] πυρέσσουσα, καὶ εὐθὺς λέγουσιν

n Matt. xxii. 12 reff.
o ch. ix. 20 || L., 26 only. 2 Kings xxii. 8. Jer. iv. 19 only.
p ch. x. 24, 32 only. 2 Kings xxii. 8. 1 Macc. vi. 8.
q w. πρός, ch. ix. (14 v. r.) 16. Luke xxii. 23. Acts ix. 29. dat., ch. viii. 11 al.+
r = ch. x. 26 reff.
s = Acts xix. 20. Rom. vii. 13. Eph. iv. 16.
t || L. ch. ix. 25. Luke viii. 25. Gen. xlix. 33.
u — Matt. iv. 24 reff. 3 Kings ii. 28.
v ch. xvi. 20. Luke ix. 6. Acts xvii. 30. xxiv. 3. xxviii. 22. 1 Cor. iv. 17 only. Isa. xlii. 23.
w Matt. iii. 5 || L. xiv. 35 al. Deut. iii. 13, 14
x ||. Matt. x. 35. Luke xii. 53 bis only. Ruth i. 14.
y ch. ii. 4. John v. 3, 6. Acts xxviii. 8. Prov. vi. 9.
z || Mt. only+.

25. om ο ιησ. D 142[1] lat-*b* g_1. om λεγων A[1](possibly) ℵ[1]. (λεγων φιμωθητι is written (*prima manu?*) over an erasure in A: λεγων is inserted in ℵ by corr[1].) for εξ, απ' HL 33. 237-8-48 Scr's c s v 8-pe lat-*f* ff_2 $g_{1.2}$ *l* Damasc Orig-int. for αυτου, του ανθρωπου D 8-pe latt(not *f*). at end add πνευμα ακαθαρτον D (8-pe) gat mm lat-*b c e* ff_2 $g_{1.2}$ goth æth.

26. κ. εξηλθ. το πν. το ακ. σπαραξας αυτον κ. κραξας φ. μ. εξηλθ. απ αυτου D, simly lat-*e* ff_2. om το πνευμα B (al? 102 = B?). rec (for φωνησαν) κραξαν (*more usual word*), with AC(D) rel: txt BLℵ 33 Orig [Damasc$_1$-ms]. for εξ, απ' (*from* || *Luke*) CDMΔ 33 latt Damasc: txt ABℵ rel goth arm Orig.

27. εθαμβησαν D Orig. rec (for απαντες) παντες (|| *Luke*), with ACD rel: txt BLUℵ 157. 433 Orig. om προς Bℵ (al? 102 = B?). rec (for εαυτ.) αυτους, with BGLSℵ: txt ACD rel. λεγοντες (*from* || *Luke*) ACE[1]MΔ[2] 33: txt BDℵ rel. (Π?) rec (for διδαχη καινη κατ' εξουσιαν) τις η διδαχη η καινη αυτη οτι κατ' εξουσιαν, with C rel (latt) syrr goth: τις η καινη αυτη διδ. οτι A: alii aliter: τις η διδαχη εκεινη η καινη αυτη η εξουσια οτι D, omg τι εστιν τουτο, as also do gat (and mm mt) lat-*b c e* $ff_{1.2}$ g_2: txt BLℵ 1[aft καινη ins αυτη] 33. 131. 209. (*Txt seems to have been origl, and to have been variously conformed to* || *Luke.*) for πνευμασιν D[1] wrote πνευνα with a mark of abbreviation; the α was afterwards erased.

28. rec (for και εξηλθ.) εξηλθ. δε, with A rel lat-*f* syr goth arm: txt BCDLMΔℵ 33 evv-Π-y-z latt Syr copt æth. om ευθυς ℵ[1] 1. 28. 31-3. 59[1]. 131 Scr's e v lat-*b c e* ff_2 g_1 copt-wilk[and -dz] æth arm: ins A B(see table) CDℵ[3a] rel vulg lat-*f* ff_1 g_2 syrr copt-schw goth. rec om πανταχου (*see* || *Luke*), with ADℵ[1] rel vulg lat-*c f* $ff_{1.2}$ $g_{1.2}$ syrr goth arm: ins BC (Lℵ[3a], -χη) 69 lat-*b e* copt. for της γαλιλαιας, της ιουδαιας ℵ[1](txt ℵ[3a]): του ιορδανου 28: εκεινην Scr's s[1].

29. rec ευθεως, with AC rel: om D lat-*c e* ff_2 g_1 Syr æth: txt BLΔℵ 1. 33. [69.] εξελθων δε εκ τ. σ. ηλθεν D lat-(*b c*) *e*. εξελθων ηλθεν (*from* || *Matt Luke*) B(D) 1. 69 gat(with mm) (lat-*b c e f* ff_2 g_1) syr-ms-mg æth arm Thl Euthym: *egrediens . . . venerunt* mt(with tol) lat-ff_1 *l* Syr-ms: txt ACℵ rel vulg Syr syr-txt copt goth.

30. κατεκ. δε η π. σιμ. D latt(exc *f*). rec ευθεως, with AC rel: om 1 lat-*b c* ff_2 g_1 Syr æth: txt BDLℵ 33. 69.

26. σπαράξ.] having convulsed him, see reff. Luke adds, that he did not *injure* him at all. **27.**] **πρὸς ἑαυτούς** is not, each man within himself, but amounts to πρὸς ἀλλήλους, see reff. Meyer well remarks, that the reason of the reflexive pronoun being used, is probably to be found in the narrative representing what was said *among themselves*, not to Jesus and his disciples. We may either take καινή with κατ' ἐξουσίαν, '*new in respect of power*,' as Meyer: or regard καινή and κατ' ἐξουσίαν as two separate predicates of διδαχή. The latter view is preferable as more borne out by the adverbial use of κατά with nouns signifying *power* in the reff. Render then **a teaching new and powerful.** **28.**] This miracle, which St. Mark and St. Luke relate first of all, is not stated by them to have been *the first*. Cf. John ii. 11.

29—34.] Healing of Simon's mother-in-law. Matt. viii. 14—17. Luke iv. 38—41. The three accounts, perhaps

αὐτῷ περὶ αὐτῆς. 31 καὶ προσελθὼν ἤγειρεν αὐτὴν
a κρατήσας τῆς χειρός, καὶ ἀφῆκεν αὐτὴν ὁ b πυρετὸς
εὐθέως, καὶ c διηκόνει αὐτοῖς. 32 d ὀψίας δὲ de γενομένης, ...διηκονει αυτοις H.
ὅτε f * ἔδυσεν ὁ ἥλιος, ἔφερον πρὸς αὐτὸν πάντας τοὺς ABCDE
g κακῶς g ἔχοντας καὶ τοὺς g δαιμονιζομένους, 33 καὶ ἦν FGKL MSUVΓ
ὅλη ἡ πόλις h ἐπισυνηγμένη πρὸς τὴν θύραν. 34 καὶ ΔΠℵ 1. 33. 69
ἐθεράπευσεν πολλοὺς g κακῶς g ἔχοντας i ποικίλαις νόσοις,
καὶ δαιμόνια πολλὰ ἐξέβαλεν, καὶ οὐκ j ἤφιεν λαλεῖν τὰ Θ_f i. 34
δαιμόνια ὅτι ᾔδεισαν αὐτόν. 35 καὶ πρωῒ k ἔννυχα λίαν (appy)...
ἀναστὰς ἐξῆλθεν καὶ ἀπῆλθεν εἰς ἔρημον τόπον, κἀκεῖ
l προσηύχετο. 36 καὶ m * κατεδίωξαν αὐτὸν Σίμων καὶ οἱ

a gen., ch. v. 41 ‖. (ix. 27.) Heb. iv. 14. vi. 18 only. Gen. xix. 16.
b = ‖ (L. bis). John iv. 52. Acts xxviii. 8 only. Deut. xxviii. 22 only.
c Matt. iv. 11 reff.
d ‖ Mt. al. fr. Mt. Mk. only. exc. John vi. 16 (xx. 19). Judith xiii. 1.
e = ch. xv. 33 al. Exod. x. 13.
f ‖ L. only. Gen. xxvii. 11 al. ἔδυσ., (but not —) Exod. xv. 10 only.
g ‖ Mt. reff.
h ch. xiii. 27 ‖ Mt. Matt. xxiii. 37. Luke xii. 1. xiii. 34. xvii. 37 only. 2 Chron. xx. 26.
i = Matt. iv. 24. 2 Tim. iii. 6 al.‡
j ἤφ., ch. xi. 16 only. = Matt. iii. 15. xxiii. 14 al. Ps. civ. 14.
k here only †. 3 Macc. v. 5.
l abs., Matt. vi. 5 and passim.
m here only. Josh. ii. 16, 22. Ps. xxii. 6.

31. εκτεινας την χειρα κρατησας ηγ. αυτην D lat-(*b*) *f*. rec aft χειρα ins αυτης (*from* ‖ *Matt*), with AC rel latt [syrr copt &c]: om B(D)Lℵ lat-*b*. om ευθεως (‖ *Matt Luke*) BCLℵ **1**. 33. 131. 209 lat-*e* copt arm: ins bef αφηκ. D vulg lat-*c f* ff_2 $g_{1.2}$ Syr: bef διηκ. 253: bef ο πυρ. lat-*b*: txt A rel syr goth æth.

32. for οψ. γεν. οτε, *cum autem* (*perhaps the origl txt, and* οψ. γεν. *insd from* ‖ *Matt*) lat-*b*. * rec ἔδυ, with ACℵ rel: εδυσεν BD. εφεροσαν D. aft εχοντας ins νοσοις ποικιλαις (*from* ‖ *Luke*) D lat-*b c e* ff_2 g_1.

33. om from και **ver 32** as far as 2nd και **ver 34** ℵ^1. rec η πολ. ολ. επισ. ην, with A rel lat-*c f* (ff_2 $g_{1.2}$) syrr copt-wilk goth æth arm: txt BCDLℵ^{3a} 33 (ev-y) vulg lat-*b e l* copt-schw. (om ην UΓ.) aft θυραν ins αυτου D lat-*c* (ff_2 g_1, appy).

34. for ver, κ. εθεραπευσεν αυτους κ. τους δαιμονια εχοντας εξεβ. αυτα απ αυτων κ. ουκ ηφιεν αυτα λαλ. οτι ηιδεισαν αυτον. κ. εθεραπευσεν πολ. κακ. εχ. ποικ. νοσοις κ. δαιμ. πολλα εξεβαλεν D, simly κ. εθερ. to απ' αυτων lat-ff_2 g_1. om ποικιλαις νοσοις L (and appy the prototype of ℵ: see above). εξεβαλλεν ℵ Scr's b c v vulg lat-*a f* $ff_{1.2}$ $g_{1.2}$. τα δαιμονια bef λαλειν B (al? 102 = B?): αυτα λαλειν D latt (not *f*). aft αυτον ins χριστον ειναι (*from* ‖ *Luke*) BL **1**. 124-31. 209 Scr's l m n q^1 evv-H-w^2-y; τον χρ. ειν. GMℵ^{3a} 33(appy) 69 Scr's c r; ηδ. τον χρ. αυτ. ειν. C lat-ff_1 g_1 *l*: txt ADΘ_fℵ^1 rel latt Syr goth Vict.

35. rec εννυχον, with A rel Orig: txt BCDLΘ_fℵ **1**. 33. 131. 209 evv-H-y. om αναστας D-gr 226 lat-*a c*. om και απηλθεν B 28. 56. 2-pe lat-*b c e* ff_2 g_1 Syr copt-wilk[and -dz]. aft εις ins τον D. προσευξετο *orabat* D.

36. * κατεδίωξεν BMUℵ 28. 237-52-9 ev-y vulg lat-ff_1 g_2 [copt]: κατεδιωξαν ACDΘ_f rel [syrr]. rec ins ο bef σιμων, with ACΘ_f rel; ο τε KΠ **1**. 50. 68-9. 124. 209 Scr's d e p w; τοτε D^1(and lat, but at first τε only): om BLℵ 33. om οι B^1.

from a common source (but see notes on Luke), are all identical in substance, but very diverse in detail and words.

31.] **ἀφῆκεν αὐτήν**, of the *fever*, is common to all, and **διηκόνει αὐτοῖς**, but *no more*. The same may be said of vv. 32—34:—the words **καὶ ἦν ὅλ. ἡ πόλ. ἐπ. . . . θύραν** are added in our text, shewing the accurate detail of an eye-witness, as also does the minute specification of the house, and of the two accompanying, in ver. 29. Observe the distinction between the *sick* and the *dæmoniacs*: cf. ch. iii. 15. Observe also πολλούς, πολλά, in connexion with the statement that the sun had set. There was not time for *all*. Meyer, who notices this, says also that in some the conditions of healing may have been wanting. But we do not find this obstacle existing on other occasions: cf. Matt. iv. 24; xii. 15; xiv. 14: Acts v. 16. On the not permitting the dæmons to speak, see note above, vv. 23—28. I should be disposed to ascribe the account to Peter. Simon, Andrew, James, and John occur together again, ch. xiii. 3.

35—38.] Jesus, being sought out in His retirement, preaches and heals throughout Galilee. Luke iv. 42, 43, where see note. Our Lord's present purpose was, not to remain in any one place, but to make the circuit of Galilee; not to work miracles, but to preach. **35.**] **ἔννυχα**, acc. plur. neut.

μετ αὐτοῦ, 37 καὶ εὗρον αὐτὸν καὶ λέγουσιν αὐτῷ ὅτι
πάντες ζητοῦσίν σε. 38 καὶ λέγει αὐτοῖς [n] Ἄγωμεν
[o] ἀλλαχοῦ εἰς τὰς [p] ἐχομένας [q] κωμοπόλεις, ἵνα κἀκεῖ
κηρύξω· [r] εἰς τοῦτο γὰρ [s] ἐξῆλθον. 39 καὶ ἦν κηρύσσων
[t] εἰς τὰς συναγωγὰς αὐτῶν [u] εἰς ὅλην τὴν Γαλιλαίαν, καὶ
τὰ δαιμόνια ἐκβάλλων.

40 Καὶ ἔρχεται πρὸς αὐτὸν [v] λεπρὸς [w] παρακαλῶν αὐτὸν
[καὶ [x] γονυπετῶν αὐτὸν] [καὶ] λέγων αὐτῷ ὅτι ἐὰν
θέλῃς δύνασαί με [y] καθαρίσαι. 41 ὁ δὲ Ἰησοῦς [z] σπλαγχνισθείς, [y] ἐκτείνας τὴν χεῖρα αὐτοῦ ἥψατο καὶ λέγει
αὐτῷ Θέλω, καθαρίσθητι. 42 καὶ εἰπόντος αὐτοῦ εὐθὺς

...καθαρισθητι F.

n = Matt. xxvi. 46. John xi. 7, 15, 16. xiv. 31.
o here only †. (-χόθεν, John x. 1. -χῇ, Wisd. xviii. 18.)
p = Luke xiii. 33. Acts xiii. 44. xx. 15. xxi. 26 only. 2 Macc. xii. 39.
q here only †. τὸ ἴλιον κωμ. τὶς ἦν, Strabo xiii. p. 837.
r John xviii. 37 reff.
s = John viii. 42. xvi. 28. Isa. xi. 1.
t constr., ver. 21. ch. iv. 15. John viii. 26 al.
u ch. xiii. 9, 16. Acts vii. 4 al.
v || Mt. reff.
w = Matt. xviii. 29 al. Esth. vii. 7 Ald. compl.
x acc., ch. x. 17. dat., Matt. xvii. 14. absol., Matt. xxvii. 29 only †.
y || Mt. reff.
z Matt. ix. 36 al[4]. ch. vi. 34. viii. 2. ix. 22. Luke vii. 13 al[2]. Mt. Mk. L. only †.

37. rec **ευροντες**, omg 2nd και, with ACΘ$_f$ rel lat-*a f ff*$_2$ *g*$_{1.2}$ D-lat copt goth arm : aft 1st και ins οτε and om 2nd και D-gr vulg syrr : txt BLℵ lat-*e* copt-ms æth. σε bef ζητουσιν (*for emphasis: see Wordsw's note*) AΘ$_f$ rel lat-*a f* goth Vict : txt BCDLΔℵ 1. 33 vulg lat-(*b c*) *e ff*$_{1.2}$ *g*$_{1.2}$ arm.

38. [αυτοι (for -οις) B[1].] αγομεν ℵ. rec om αλλαχου (*as superfl, and not in || Luke*), with AC[3]DΘ$_f$ rel latt syrr goth : ins BC[1]Lℵ 33 copt (æth arm). for εχομενας, εγγυς D : εχομενα B(see table). κωμας κ. εις τας πολεις D, simly latt Syr goth. ins και bef εξ. C. rec **εξεληλυθα**, with AD rel : εληλυθα Δ Θ$_f$(ελεληλ.) 28. 69. 124. 346 Scr's d g l m n p q r w[2] evv-P-z latt Syr syr-mg goth arm : txt BCLℵ 33 syr.

39. for ην, ηλθεν BLℵ copt æth : txt ACDΘ$_f$ rel latt syrr goth arm. κηρυσσιν ℵ[1](txt ℵ[3a]). rec εν ταις συναγωγαις, with E rel : txt ABCDKLΔΘ$_f$Πℵ 1. 69.

40. for παρακαλων, ερωτων D. om και γονυπετων αυτον (*perhaps homœotel : not insd from || Matt Luke, the expression is different*) BDGΓ lat-*a b c ff*$_2$ *g*$_1$: ins bef κ. παρακ. Syr : txt ACΘ$_f$(Lℵ) rel vulg lat-*e f ff*$_1$ *g*$_2$ syr copt goth æth (arm).—om αυτον Lℵ 1. 209 Scr's g arm. (The preceding αυτον is omd by 69 ev-y.) om και (bef λεγ.) Bℵ[1] 69[1] lat-*e* copt-mss : ins ACDΘ$_f$ℵ[3a] rel. om αυτω DΓ am(with em fuld ing tol) arm. om οτι D 28 vulg lat-*b ff*$_1$ *g*$_2$ *l* Syr : for οτι, κυριε (|| *Matt Luke*) CL mm(with mt) lat-*c e ff*$_2$ *g*$_1$ copt æth arm : ins κυριε bef οτι B : bef δυνασαι Θ$_f$: txt A 33. 69(sic) rel lat-*a* syr goth. θελεις D Π[1](appy). for δυνασαι, δυνη B.

41. for ο δε ιησ. σπλ., και σπλ. Bℵ (al? 102 = B?) lat-*e* copt-wilk[and -dz] : και οργισθεις (και *is from || Matt Luke*) D lat-*a ff*$_2$: σπλ. δε ο ιησ. L [æth] : txt ACΘ$_f$ rel vulg lat-*c f ff*$_1$ *g*$_2$ *l* syrr copt-ms goth [arm]. rec ηψατο bef αυτου (*from || Matt Luke, to avoid ambiguity*), with ACΘ$_f$ rel vulg lat-*a e f* (*ff*$_2$ *g*$_{1.2}$) goth arm : αυτ. ηψ. αυτ. D : txt BLℵ. om αυτω ℵ 1 lat-*b c ff*$_1$ Syr.

42. om ειποντος αυτου (|| *Matt Luke*) BDLℵ 69 lat-*a b c e ff*$_2$ *g*$_1$ Syr copt : ins ACΘ$_f$ rel vulg lat-*f g*$_2$ syr goth æth arm. rec ευθεως, with ACDΘ$_f$ rel : txt BLℵ 33.

of ἔννυχος, as in the sing. σήμερον, αὔριον, νέον, &c., a form not so used in the classics. We have however πάννυχα, Soph. Ajax, 911. **ἐξῆλθ.** from the house of Peter and Andrew, ver. 29.

36. οἱ μετ' αὐτ.] Andrew, John, and James, ibid. **38.**] **ἐξῆλθ.** = ἀπεστάλην, Luke: not '*undertook this journey*:' He had *not yet begun any journey*, and it cannot apply to ἐξῆλθεν above, for that was not to any city, nor to preach. The word has its more solemn sense, as in reff. John, though of course not understood *then* by the hearers. To deny this, as Meyer, is certainly not safe. **39.**] See on Matt. iv. 23: also on Luke iv. 44. **κηρ. εἰς**] not for ἐν, but as ἐς τὸν δῆμον λέγειν, Thuc. v. 45, and similar expressions: see reff.

40—45.] Cleansing of a leper. Matt. viii. 2—4. Luke v. 12—14. The account here is the fullest, and evidently an original one, from an eye-witness. St. Luke mentions (ver. 15) the spreading of the fame of Jesus, without assigning the cause as in our ver. 45. See note on Matt. **41.**] **σπλαγχνισθείς** gives the reason of ἐκτείνας: **Jesus being moved with compassion stretched out his hand and touched him.** This is characteristic of St. Mark.

ἀπῆλθεν ἀπ' αὐτοῦ ἡ [y] λέπρα, καὶ [y] ἐκαθερίσθη. 43 καὶ
[a] ἐμβριμησάμενος αὐτῷ εὐθὺς [b] ἐξέβαλεν αὐτὸν 44 καὶ
λέγει αὐτῷ [c] Ὅρα μηδενὶ μηδὲν εἴπῃς, ἀλλὰ ὕπαγε σεαυτὸν
δεῖξον τῷ ἱερεῖ, καὶ [y] προςένεγκε περὶ τοῦ [d] καθαρισμοῦ
σοῦ ἃ [e] προςέταξεν Μωυσῆς, [y] εἰς [y] μαρτύριον αὐτοῖς.
45 ὁ δὲ ἐξελθὼν ἤρξατο [f] κηρύσσειν [g] πολλὰ καὶ [h] διαφημί-
ζειν τὸν [i] λόγον, ὥςτε μηκέτι αὐτὸν δύνασθαι [j] φανερῶς
εἰς πόλιν εἰςελθεῖν· ἀλλὰ ἔξω [k] ἐπ' ἐρήμοις τόποις ἦν, καὶ
ἤρχοντο πρὸς αὐτὸν [l] πάντοθεν.
II. 1 Καὶ εἰςελθὼν πάλιν εἰς Καφαρναοὺμ [m] δι' ἡμερῶν
[n] ἠκούσθη ὅτι [o] εἰς οἶκόν [p] ἐστιν, 2 καὶ εὐθέως [q] συνήχθη-

ABCDE GKLMS UVΓΔ Θ_fΠℵ 1. 33. 69

a Matt. ix. 30. ch. xiv. 5. John xi. 33, 38 only +. Isa. xvii. 13 Symm.
b see ver. 12 reff.
c || Mt. Matt. xviii. 10. Heb. viii. 5, from Exod. xxv. 40. Rev. xix. 10. xxii. 9.
d || L. Luke ii. 22. John ii. 6. iii. 25. Heb. i. 3. 2 Pet. i. 9 only. Lev. xv. 13.
e Matt. i. 24 reff. Levit. xiv. 2, 30.
f = ch. v. 20 || L.
g Matt. ix. 14 reff.
h Matt. ix. 31. xxviii. 15 only +.
i = Matt. xxviii. 15. John xxi. 23. Exod. xviii. 19.
j John vii. 10. Acts x. 3 only +.
k = ch. xiii. 29 ||. John v. 2.
l Luke xix. 43. Heb. ix. 4 only. Jer. xx. 9. Sir. li. 7. Sus. 22 only.
m ch. xiv. 58 || Mt. Acts xxiv. 17. Gal. ii. 1. Deut. ix. 11.
n pass., Matt. xxviii. 14. John ix. 32. Acts xi. 22. 1 Cor. v. 1. 2 Chron. xxvi. 15.
o ch. i. 39.
p pres., John i. 40 reff.
q Matt. xxii. 34 al.

η λεπρα bef απ' αυτου ΑΚΘ_fΠ Scr's a d e w syr: η λεπρα bef απηλθεν απ' αυτου (|| *Matt*) C copt goth: απηλθεν η λεπρα αυτου Δ 235: txt BDLℵ rel latt Syr copt-ms arm. (εκαθερισθη, so A B[1](sic: see table) CGLΔΘ_fΠ[1], but καθαρ. in ver 41.)

43. ενβρισαμενος D 69. rec ευθεως, with ACΘ_f rel: txt BDLℵ 33.—εξεβ. αυτον bef ευθ. AKΠ Scr's e w arm: om ευθ. Syr æth.

44. om μηδεν (*see || Matt Luke*) ADLΔℵ 33. 69 latt Syr copt æth Vict Thl: ins BCΘ_f rel syr goth arm. rec αλλ', with MΓ (SV **1**. 33, e sil): txt ABCDΘ_fℵ rel. δειξον bef σεαυτον D latt. σαυτον ℵ. προσενεγκαι (*itacism?*) CLΘ_f. for ἅ, καθως (|| *Luke*) C[1] æth: καθ' ἅ 33.

45. om πολλα D latt. om 1st αυτον D Scr's k: δυνασθαι bef αυτον ℵ 75. 245 92. εις πολιν bef φανερως CLℵ 28. 33. 124 copt: εισελθειν bef εις πολιν D vulg ed Syr: txt ABΘ_f rel am(with fuld) syr goth arm. (αλλα, so ACDMΔ.) rec (for επ') εν (*from || Luke*), with ACDΘ_f rel: txt BLΔℵ 28. 124. om ην B (al ?): om ην και lat-*b e*. rec πανταχοθεν, with EGUVΓ: txt ABCDΘ_fℵ rel.

Chap. II. **1.** rec παλιν εισηλθεν, with vulg lat-*b f* $ff_{1.2}$ $g_{1.2}$ D-lat: εισηλθε(ν) παλιν ACΘ_f rel (most mss, appy) lat-*e* syr goth Thl: εισηλθεν ο ιησ. παλιν FGΓ 236 Scr's f i s Syr: εισηλθε (only) S lat-*c*: txt B D[-gr] Lℵ 33 lat-*a* copt æth arm.—rec ins και bef ηκ. (*to suit the corrn above*), with ACDΘ_f rel vulg lat-*b e* g_1 syrr goth: om BLℵ 33 lat-*a c f* copt [æth] arm. (*The difficulty of a nom for* ηκουσθη *has occasioned the corrn to* εισελθ. και.) εν οικω (*corrn*) BDLℵ 33 latt copt: txt ACΘ_f rel lat-g_1.

2. om ευθεως BLℵ 33 vulg lat-*b* g_2 *l* Syr copt æth arm Aug Bede.

43.] **ἐξέβαλεν** need not necessarily imply that the healing was *in a house* (Meyer); it might have been *in a city*, as in Luke. **44.]** **σεαυτόν**, being prefixed to the verb, has an emphasis: trouble not thyself with talking to others, but go complete *thine own* case by getting thyself formally declared pure. **45.]** **ἤρξατο**, he lost no time in doing it. **τὸν λόγον**] not, '*what Jesus had said to him*,' but **the account**, of his healing. ἤρχοντο tells us more than ἦλθον would have done. Our Lord did not wish to put a stop to the multitudes seeking Him, but only to avoid that kind of concourse which would have beset Him in the *towns:* the seeking to Him for teaching and healing *still went on* and that from all parts.

Chap. II. 1—12.] Healing of a paralytic at Capernaum. Matt. ix. 2—8, where see notes. Luke v. 17—26. The three are evidently independent accounts; Mark's, as usual, the most precise in details; e. g. "*borne of four;*" Luke's also bearing marks of an eye-witness (see ver. 19, end); Matthew's apparently at second hand. **1.]** **δι' ἡμερῶν**, after an interval of some days: see reff. **εἰς οἶκον**, *in doors;* as εἰς ἀγρόν, *to the country*, ch. xvi. 12: = εἰς τὸν οἶκον, εἰς τὸν ἀγρόν,—the practice of omitting the art. after a preposition being universal, and apparently regulated by no assignable rule. See examples in Middleton, ch. vi. § 1, which however in later Greek are by no means

σαν πολλοί, ὥςτε μηκέτι [r] χωρεῖν μηδὲ τὰ [s] πρὸς τὴν
θύραν· καὶ [t] ἐλάλει αὐτοῖς τὸν [tu] λόγον. 3 καὶ ἔρχονται
φέροντες πρὸς αὐτὸν [v] παραλυτικὸν [w] αἰρόμενον ὑπὸ τεσσάρων. 4 καὶ μὴ δυνάμενοι [x] προςεγγίσαι αὐτῷ διὰ τὸν
H και ἐξορυξ-αντες... ὄχλον [y] ἀπεστέγασαν τὴν [z] στέγην ὅπου ἦν, καὶ [a] ἐξορύξ-
αντες [b] χαλῶσιν τὸν [c] κράβαττον ὅπου ὁ [v] παραλυτικὸς
[d] κατέκειτο. 5 ἰδὼν δὲ ὁ Ἰησοῦς τὴν πίστιν αὐτῶν λέγει
τῷ [v] παραλυτικῷ Τέκνον, [ef] ἀφέωνταί σου αἱ [f] ἁμαρτίαι.
6 ἦσαν δέ τινες τῶν γραμματέων ἐκεῖ καθημένοι καὶ
[g] διαλογιζόμενοι [h] ἐν ταῖς καρδίαις αὐτῶν 7 Τί οὗτος οὕτως
λαλεῖ; [i] βλασφημεῖ· τίς δύναται [ef] ἀφιέναι [f] ἁμαρτίας εἰ
F και ευθυς... μὴ [k] εἷς ὁ θεός; 8 καὶ εὐθὺς [l] ἐπιγνοὺς ὁ Ἰησοῦς τῷ

r = John ii. 6. xxi. 25. Gen. xiii. 6.
s ch. xi. 4. Acts iii. 2.
t = ch. iv. 33. Acts iv. 29, 31. viii. 25 al. (see ch. viii. 32.)
u = Luke i. 2 reff.
v Matt. iv. 24 reff.
w = Matt. iv. 6. Num. xi. 12.
x here only. Gen. xxxiii. 6, 7 al.
y here only +.
z Matt. viii. 8 || L. only. Gen. viii. 13. xix. 8 A (not F) Ald. Esdr. vi. 4 only.
a Gal. iv. 15 only. Judg. xvi. 21 A. 1 Kings xi. 2. Prov. xxix. 22 only.
b Luke v. 4, 5. Acts ix. 25. xxvii. 17, 30. 2 Cor. xi. 13 only. Jer. xlv. (xxxviii.) 6 al.
c vv. 9, 11, 12. ch. vi. 55. John v. 8, &c. Acts v. 15. ix. 33 only +.
d ch. i. 30 reff.
e Matt. vi. 12 al. Ps. xxiv. 18.
f || Mt. reff.
g Matt. xvi. 7, 8 reff.
h Matt. xxiv. 48 al. Deut. viii. 17. Ps. iv. 4.
i = || Mt. reff.
k ch. x. 18.
l Matt. xiv. 35 reff.

for αυτοις, προς αυτους D lat-*b c ff*$_2$. om τον D.

3. rec πρ. αυ. παραλυτικον bef φεροντες, with AC$^3\Theta_f$ rel goth æth: πρ. αυτ. φερ. παρ. C^{1}DG **1**. 69. 124-31. 209 latt syrr arm: txt BLℵ 33 am [with fuld ing mt tol] lat-*g*$_1$ *l*.

4. for προσεγγισαι, προσενεγκαι BLℵ (33) vulg lat-*f l* Δ-lat syr copt æth: txt ACDΘ_f rel lat-*a* (*b*) *c e ff*$_2$ *g*$_{1.2}$ Syr goth arm. αυτω bef προσεγγ. K^{2}Π Scr's w: om αυτω DK^1 [copt-wilk-dz] arm-mss. for δια τον οχλον, απο του οχλου D vulg lat-*b c* &c. aft ην ins ο ιησους DΔ mt lat-*a c* &c Syr goth æth arm. om εξορυξαντες D latt Syr æth. rec (for 2nd οπου) εφ ω (*see var read* || *Luke ver* 25), with ACΘ_f rel lat-*b c* &c syrr copt goth æth arm (εφ ο Γ Scr's c ev-y): εφ ου 13. 33. 69: txt BDLℵ lat-*a g*$_1$. for ο π. κατεκειτο, ην ο π. κατακειμενος D lat-*g*$_2$.

5. for ιδων δε, και ιδων (*from* || *Matt Luke*) BCLℵ 33. 69 lat-*e* copt æth: txt ADΘ_f rel latt syrr goth arm. ins θαρσει bef τεκνον C. aft τεκνον ins μου ℵ^1 [copt]. αφιενται B 33 vulg lat-*a c e g*$_1$ syrr goth: αφιονται Δ: αφεονται G 69: txt ACDΘ_fℵ rel lat-*b f*. rec (for σου αι αμαρτιαι) σοι αι αμ. σου (*from* || *Luke*), with AC^3 rel vulg lat-*a c f* D-lat syrr æth arm Orig-int: σοι αι αμ. C$^1\Theta_f$ am(with em fuld ing mt) lat-*b e ff*$_{1.2}$: σου αι αμ. σου M^1 245: txt B D[-gr] GLΔℵ **1**. 33. 69.

6. at end ins λεγοντες D lat-*a b* &c (copt-mss) æth.

7. for τι, οτι B Scr's p. rec (for λαλει; βλασφημει) λαλει βλασφημιας (*from* || *Luke*), with AC rel lat-*e* syrr copt goth æth arm: txt BDLℵ latt copt-ms. (Θ_f?) ins τας bef αμαρτιας D^1. om εἰς D-gr.

8. rec ευθεως, with ACΘ_f rel: txt BLℵ 33: om D 28. 64. 2-pe lat-*a b c ff*$_2$ *g*$_1$ Syr æth arm. ο ιησ. bef επιγν. ℵ: om ο ιησ. K^1 ev-y.

limited to the class of nouns there mentioned, but are found with nouns of all classes of meaning. The **εἰς** combines motion with the construction,—'that he had gone home, and was there.' **2.**] In this verse we have again the peculiar minute depicting of Mark. Wordsw. believes "these minute notices . . . to be recorded by the Evangelist with a studied design, lest it should be supposed that, because he incorporates so much which is in St. Matthew's Gospel, he was only a copyist: and in order to shew that he did so because he knew from ocular testimony that St. Matthew's narrative was adequate and accurate." I mention this, to shew to what shifts the advocates of the theory of the "interdependence" of the Evangelists are now reduced. **μηκέτι . . . μηδέ**] **so that not even the parts towards the door** (much less the house) **would any longer hold them** (they once sufficed to hold them). **ἐλάλει**, in the strict imperfect sense: **He was speaking to them the word**, when that which is about to be related happened. **3, 4.**] It would appear that Jesus was speaking to the crowd from the upper story of the house, they being assembled in the court, or perhaps (but less probably) in the street. Those who bore the paralytic ascended the stairs which led direct from the street to the flat roof of the house, and let him down through the tiles (**διὰ τῶν κεραμῶν**, Luke).

[m] πνεύματι αὐτοῦ ὅτι οὕτως [αὐτοὶ] [g] διαλογίζονται [n] ἐν
ἑαυτοῖς, λέγει αὐτοῖς Τί ταῦτα [g] διαλογίζεσθε ἐν ταῖς
[h] καρδίαις ὑμῶν; 9 τί ἐστιν [o] εὐκοπώτερον, εἰπεῖν τῷ Frag. Sang. ii.
[v] παραλυτικῷ [ef] Ἀφέωνταί σου αἱ [f] ἁμαρτίαι, ἢ εἰπεῖν 9 (appy)
Ἐγείρου ἆρον τὸν [p] κράβαττόν σου καὶ περιπάτει; 10 ἵνα ... ABCDE
δὲ εἰδῆτε ὅτι [q] ἐξουσίαν [q] ἔχει ὁ [r] υἱὸς τοῦ [r] ἀνθρώπου FGHKL MSUVΓ
[ef] ἀφιέναι ἐπὶ τῆς γῆς [f] ἁμαρτίας, λέγει τῷ [v] παραλυτικῷ ΔΘ$_f$Πℵ Frag. Sang.
11 Σοὶ λέγω, ἔγειρε ἆρον τὸν [p] κράβαττόν σου καὶ 1. 33. 69
ὕπαγε εἰς τὸν οἶκόν σου. 12 καὶ ἠγέρθη καὶ εὐθὺς ἄρας
τὸν [p] κράβαττον ἐξῆλθεν [s] ἐναντίον πάντων· ὥστε [t] ἐξίσ- ...ii. 12
τασθαι πάντας καὶ [u] δοξάζειν τὸν θεὸν ὅτι [v] οὕτως οὐδέ- (appy)Θ$_f$
ποτε εἴδαμεν.

13 Καὶ ἐξῆλθεν πάλιν παρὰ τὴν θάλασσαν, καὶ πᾶς ὁ

m = ch. viii. 12. Luke i. 80. John xi. 33. Acts xix. 21. Isa. xxix. 24.
n Matt. ix. 3 reff.
o ch. x. 25 reff.
p ver. 4 reff.
q Matt. vii. 29 reff.
r Matt. viii. 20 reff.
s = Luke xx. 26. Acts vii. 20. viii. 32, from Isa. liii. 7. Gen. vii. 1 al.
t Matt. xii. 23 reff.
u Mark, here only. ‖ Mt. al. fr. Exod. xv. 2. Ps. xc. 15.
v Matt. ix. 33.

om *αυτου* D 258 lat-*a b c e* ff_2 copt-wilk. om *ουτως* B [102 = B?] lat-*a b c e* ff_2 g_1. rec om *αυτοι* (*as superfluous*), with BDGLℵ 1 latt Syr copt æth arm: ins ACΘ$_f$ rel syr goth Thl. rec (for λεγει) ειπεν (*from* ‖ *Matt Luke*), with ACDΘ$_f$ rel lat-*a b c* ff_2 g_1: txt BLℵ 33 vulg lat-*e f* g_2. om *αυτοις* B [102 = B?] lat-ff_2.

9. παραλυτω [for -τικω] D. αφιενται Bℵ 28. 2-pe vulg lat-*a c e f* g_1 syrr goth: txt ACDΘ$_f$ rel lat-*b*. the 2 sayings are transposed in D lat-*a*. rec (for *σου αι αμ.*) *σοι α. αμ.*, with ACDΓΔΘ$_f$ (S, e sil) vulg lat-*c* Eus: *σοι αι αμ. σου* vss: txt Bℵ rel. rec εγειραι, with UΔΘ$_f$ [Frag-sang], εγειρε ACDℵ rel: txt BL. (*Mey contends that* εγειρε *is every where to be written, the active form not being understood, and altered to* -ραι *or* -ρου. *But* -ραι *is hardly to be clearly reasoned about, on account of the itacism: and* -ρου *is read neither in ver* 11 *nor in* ‖.) rec ins *και* bef *αρον* (*from* ‖ *Matt Luke*), with ABΘ$_f$ℵ Frag-sang rel am lat-*a* g_1 D-lat syr [copt-ms] goth æth: om C D[-gr] L 1. 33 vulg-ed(with fuld) lat-*f l* Syr copt arm. rec *σου* bef *τ. κρ.* (*Matt, ver* 6), with Δ Frag-sang 33 rel: txt ABCDKLMΠ^{1}ℵ 1. 69 vulg lat-*a f* g_1 *l* Eus. for περιπατει, υπαγε (D)LΔℵ Frag-sang lat-*a* ff_2 g_2 goth(appy). add *εις τ. οικον σου* D 33 lat-*a* ff_2 arm.

10. *ιδητε* (*itacism?*) ACL. *επι της γης* bef *αφιεναι* (*from* ‖ *Matt Luke*) CDHLMΔΘ$_f$ℵ Frag-sang 33 latt Syr copt goth arm: *αμαρτιας* bef *επι της γης* B 142-57 æth: txt A rel syr.

11. εγειρε bef *σοι λεγω* ℵ: om *σοι λεγω* ev-y. rec εγειραι, with LUΔ Frag-sang: εγειρον K: txt ABCDΘ$_f$ℵ rel. rec ins *και* bef *αρον* (‖ *Luke*), with AΘ$_f$ Frag-sang rel lat-*c* g_2 D-lat syr (goth) æth: om BC D[-gr] LΓℵ 33 vulg lat-*a b e f* $ff_{1.2}$ g_1 *l* Syr copt arm Ephr Ath Ambr Aug.

12. rec *ευθ.* bef *και*, with AC^{3}Θ$_f$ Frag-sang rel syrr goth æth: *ευθ.* bef *ηγερθη* D evv-47-60 (vulg) lat-(*a f*) g_1 *l* copt-schw: txt BC^{1}Lℵ 33 copt-ms arm.—ευθεως ACDΘ$_f$ Frag-sang rel: txt BLℵ. [aft *κραβ.*] ins *αυτου* HL 33 lat-*c* Syr copt æth. for εναντιον, εμπροσθεν BLℵ, ενωπιον Θ$_f$ 33 Scr's c. for *παντας*, *παντες* A. rec aft *θεον* ins *λεγοντας* (*supplemy: cf var in* D), with ACΘ$_f$ℵ Frag-sang rel: *και λεγειν* D: om B lat-*b*. rec *ουδεποτε* bef *ουτως* (*for perspicuity?*), with ACΘ$_f$ Frag-sang rel vulg lat-*a c* f^1 ff_2 syr: txt BDLℵ lat-(*b*) *e* arm. rec *ειδομεν*, with ABΘ$_f$ℵ^{3a} Frag-sang rel: *εφανη εν τω ισραηλ* ℵ^1: txt CD.

13. εξηλθον, ℵ^1(txt ℵ^{3a}). om *παλιν* D-gr copt-ms Aug. for *παρα*, *εις* ℵ^1(txt ℵ^{3a}), *επι* 69. om *ο* D^1(ins D-corr^1).

See the extract from Dr. Robinson, describing the Jewish house, in note on Matt. xxvi. 69. **7. οὗτος οὕτως**] The first word depreciates: the second exaggerates. **8.**] The knowledge was *immediate* and *supernatural*, as is most carefully and precisely here signified.

11. σοὶ λ.] The stress is on *σοί*. The words are *precisely those used*, as so often in Mark,—and denote the turning to the paralytic and addressing him. There may have been something in his state, which required the emphatic address.

13—22.] The calling of Levi. Feast at his house: question concerning fasting. Matt. ix. 9—17. Luke

ὄχλος ἤρχετο πρὸς αὐτόν, καὶ ἐδίδασκεν αὐτούς. 14 καὶ
[w] παράγων εἶδεν Λευεὶν τὸν τοῦ Ἀλφαίου καθήμενον ἐπὶ w || Mt. reff.
τὸ [x] τελώνιον, καὶ λέγει αὐτῷ Ἀκολούθει μοι. καὶ x || only +.
[y] ἀναστὰς ἠκολούθησεν αὐτῷ. 15 [z] καὶ γίνεται ἐν τῷ y ||. Num. xxii. 20. (3 Kings xix. 21.)
[a] κατακεῖσθαι αὐτὸν ἐν τῇ οἰκίᾳ αὐτοῦ [z] καὶ πολλοὶ z || Mt. reff.
[b] τελῶναι καὶ ἁμαρτωλοὶ [c] συνανέκειντο τῷ Ἰησοῦ καὶ τοῖς a || Luke. ch. xiv. 3. 1 Cor. viii. 10.
μαθηταῖς αὐτοῦ· ἦσαν γὰρ πολλοὶ καὶ ἠκολούθουν αὐτῷ. b Mark, here 3ce only. Matt. v. 46 reff.
16 καὶ οἱ γραμματεῖς καὶ οἱ Φαρισαῖοι ἰδόντες αὐτὸν
...ii. 16 (appy) Frag. Sang. ἐσθίοντα μετὰ τῶν ἁμαρτωλῶν καὶ [b] τελωνῶν ἔλεγον τοῖς c || Mt. reff.
μαθηταῖς αὐτοῦ ὅτι μετὰ τῶν [b] τελωνῶν καὶ ἁμαρτωλῶν
ἐσθίει καὶ πίνει. 17 καὶ ἀκούσας ὁ Ἰησοῦς λέγει αὐτοῖς Οὐ

for αυτον, αυτους ℵ^1(txt ℵ^{3a}).

14. for λευειν [so BE^{1}LMℵ^{3a}](λευει ℵ^1), ιακωβον D 13. 69. 124 lat-*a b c e ff*$_{1.2}$ *g*$_1$ mss-mtd-by-Orig. ηκολουθει C^1 1.

15. rec (for γινεται) εγενετο (*from* || *Matt*), with ACD rel : txt BLℵ 33. om εν τω BLℵ 33. 69 : ins AC Frag-sang rel vulg lat-*f ff*$_1$ *g*$_{1.2}$.—κατακειμενων αυτων (|| *Matt*) D lat-*a b c e ff*$_2$. om 2nd και D 1. 28. 238-58 Scr's s latt Syr. ins ελθοντες bef συνανεκειντο (*from* || *Matt*) AC^1 : om BC^{3}Dℵ rel vss. aft 2nd πολλοι ins οι D latt. rec ηκολουθησαν, with ACD rel lat-*a b c e f* [*q*] syrr : txt BLΔℵ Frag-sang vulg lat-*ff*$_1$ *g*$_{1.2}$.

16. om 1st οι L(Δ)ℵ 33. for και οι φαρισαιοι, των φαρισαιων (*possibly from thus understanding* || *Luke*) BLΔℵ [Frag-sang(appy)] 33 lat-*b* copt-ms. ins και bef ιδοντες LΔℵ 33 copt æth : κ. ειδαν D lat-*b* (and κ. ελεγον below D). for αυτον εσθιοντα, οτι εσθιει (*see note*) B 33. 2-pe lat-*b d ff*$_2$ Syr : οτι ησθιεν DLℵ vulg lat-*c* (*ff*$_1$ *g*$_1$) syr æth : txt AC Frag-sang rel lat-*a f* [*q*] goth.—μετα των αμαρτ. κ. τελ. (1st) bef εσθιοντα A. rec transp 1st αμαρτ. and τελ. (|| *Matt*), with ACL^{2}ℵ Frag-sang rel vulg lat-*f ff*$_2$ syrr copt goth arm : txt BDL^1 33 am lat-*a b c ff*$_1$ *g*$_1$ [*q*] copt-ms æth.—aft 3rd και ins των B^1(above the line) D 33.—om αμ. κ. (|| *Luke*) 69 syr-jer. ins και bef ελεγον D. rec ins τι bef οτι (*to make it interrogative, as in* || *Matt Luke : see var in* D. *The* τι *cannot be omd from homœotel, as that would apply to the* οτι *only; nor is* τι *omd in any* MSS *in Luke* ii. 49 : *Acts* v. 4, 9, *where* τι οτι *occurs*), with AC rel : δια τι (|| *Matt Luke*) Dℵ latt : txt BL 33. transp 2nd τελ. and αμαρτ. D lat-*a* æth : txt A B(see table) Cℵ rel vss.—aft 4th και ins των BD.—om κ. αμ. U. om και πινει (*not expressed above, nor in* || *Matt*) BDℵ lat-*a b e ff*$_2$: ins ACLΔ rel vulg lat-*c f* [*ff*$_1$ *g*$_1$ *q*] syrr (copt) goth (æth) arm-mss. (G syr-jer arm-zoh have plur, *as* || *Luke*). add ο διδασκαλος υμων (|| *Matt*) LΔℵ 69 vulg lat-*f ff*$_1$ *g*$_1$ *l* copt-ed Aug : ins bef εσθιει C (lat-*c*) æth.

17. om αυτοις D 1. 209 lat-*a b c ff*$_2$ *g*$_1$ [*q*]. ins οτι bef ου BΔ.

v. 27—39. I have discussed the question of the identity of Matthew and Levi in the notes on Matt. The three accounts are in matter nearly identical, and in diction so minutely and unaccountably varied, as to declare here, as elsewhere, their independence of one another, except in having had some common source from which they have more or less deflected. (These remarks do not apply to the diversity of the names Matthew and Levi, which must be accounted for on other grounds. See, as throughout the passage, the notes on Matt.)

13. πάλιν] See ch. i. 16. On **τὸν τοῦ Ἀλφαίου** see notes, Matt. xiii. 55; and x. 1 ff. **15.]** The entertainment was certainly in *Levi's* house, not as Meyer, al., in *that of our Lord*, which last is a pure fiction, and is not any where designated in the Gospel accounts. Certainly the **καλέσαι**, ver. 17, gives no countenance to the view. Our Lord, and those following Him as disciples, were ordinarily entertained where He was invited, which will account for ἠκολούθουν αὐτῷ:—and the change of subject in the two, αὐτόν and αὐτοῦ, is no uncommon thing: see a similar change in Luke xix. 3, where to be consistent Meyer ought to understand ὅτι τῇ ἡλ. μικ. ἦν of our Lord. To help out his interpretation he strangely enough makes καλέσαι, ver. 17, mean '*to invite*.' **ἦσαν γὰρ . . . αὐτῷ**, peculiar to Mark. **16.] ἰδόντες αὐτ. ἐσθ., having observed Him eating**; but not to be literally pressed. The question was *after*

d Matt. vi. 8 al. fr. Sir. xv. 12.
e abs., || Mt. Josh. xiv. 11 a.
f Luke iv. 23 reff.
g Matt. viii. 16 reff.
h ||. Matt. ii. 2. v. 17 al. Neh. vi. 10.
i constr., see note.
k here 6 times. Matt. iv. 2 reff.
l Matt. vii. 3, 22 (3ce). xiii. 27. John iv. 42 al. Ps. lxxxviii. 11.
m Matt. viii. 12. Luke xx. 34, 36 reff.
n || only +. Tobit vi. 13, 16 only.
o (= ἐφ' ὅσον Matt.) || L. John v. 7.

[d] χρείαν [d] ἔχουσιν οἱ [e] ἰσχύοντες [f] ἰατροῦ, ἀλλ' οἱ [g] κακῶς ABCDE FGHK
[g] ἔχοντες. οὐκ [h] ἦλθον καλέσαι δικαίους, ἀλλὰ ἁμαρτω- LMSUV ΓΔΠℵ 1.
λούς. 18 Καὶ [i] ἦσαν οἱ μαθηταὶ Ἰωάννου καὶ οἱ Φαρισαῖοι 33. 69
[ik] νηστεύοντες, καὶ ἔρχονται καὶ λέγουσιν αὐτῷ Διὰ τί οἱ
μαθηταὶ Ἰωάννου καὶ οἱ μαθηταὶ τῶν Φαρισαίων [k] νηστεύουσιν, οἱ δὲ [l] σοὶ μαθηταὶ οὐ [k] νηστεύουσιν; 19 καὶ εἶπεν
αὐτοῖς ὁ Ἰησοῦς Μὴ δύνανται οἱ [m] υἱοὶ τοῦ [n] νυμφῶνος
[o] ἐν ᾧ ὁ [p] νυμφίος μετ' αὐτῶν ἐστιν [k] νηστεύειν; [q] ὅσον
[q] χρόνον ἔχουσιν τὸν [p] νυμφίον μετ' αὐτῶν, οὐ δύνανται
[k] νηστεύειν· 20 [r] ἐλεύσονται δὲ ἡμέραι ὅταν [s] ἀπαρθῇ ἀπ'
αὐτῶν ὁ [p] νυμφίος, καὶ τότε [k] νηστεύσουσιν ἐν ἐκείνῃ τῇ
ἡμέρᾳ. 21 οὐδεὶς [t] ἐπίβλημα [u] ῥάκους [v] ἀγνάφου [w] ἐπι-
ράπτει ἐπὶ ἱμάτιον παλαιόν· εἰ δὲ μή, αἴρει ἀπ' αὐτοῦ τὸ

p here 3ce. ||. Matt. xxv. 1, &c. (4 times). John ii. 9. iii. 29 (3ce). Rev. xviii. 23 only. Jer. vii. 34. xl. (xxxiii.) 11.
q here only. = ἐφ' ὅσ. χρ. Paul, Rom. vii. 1. 1 Cor. vii. 39. Gal. iv. 1. (see ch. ix. 21.) Josh. iv. 14.
r || Mt. reff.
s || only ‡. Gen. xii. 9. Exod. xii. 37.
t || (L. bis) only. Isa. iii. 21 only.
u || Mt. only. Isa. lxiv. 6. Jer. xlv. (xxxviii.) 11 only.
v || Mt. only +.
w here only +. ῥαπ. ἐπί, Job xvi. 16.

αλλα B(Tischdf [N. T. Vat.]). for *ουκ*, *ου γαρ* CL ev-y vulg lat-*c f ff$_2$ g$_2$* copt-ed. rec at end adds *εις μετανοιαν* (*from || Luke, whence it has also been insd in || Matt*), with C rel lat-*a c ff$_1$ g$_1$*: om ABDKLΔΠℵ 1[1] vulg lat-*b e f ff$_2$ g$_1$ i l* syrr copt goth æth arm Aug.

18. rec (for *οι φαρισαιοι*) *οι των φαρισαιων* (*to suit what follows*), with L rel lat-*a ff$_1$ g$_1$ l* Syr (syr-mg) æth: txt ABCDKMΠℵ 69 vulg lat-*b c e f ff$_2$ g$_2$ i* [*q*] syr-txt copt goth arm Aug. rec om 3rd *μαθηται* (|| *Luke*), with C[2]D rel vulg lat-(*b*) *c ff$_1$ g$_1$* Syr syr-txt copt-schw [om *οι* also Δ]: txt BC[1]Lℵ 33 lat-*e* syr-mg æth.—om *κ. οι μ. τ. φ.* A. om last *μαθηται* B 127: for *σοι μαθ.*, *μαθηται σου* E[1]ℵ, *σου μαθηται* Δ.

19. om *ο ιησ.* D 28 lat-*b i* [*q*]. om *οσον* to *νηστευειν* (*homœotel*) DU **1**. 33 lat-*a b e ff$_2$ g$_1$ i* Syr æth. rec *μεθ' εαυτων* bef *εχουσι τον νυμφιον*, with A rel lat-*f ff$_1$ g$_2$* syr copt-schw goth arm: alii aliter: txt BC(L)ℵ lat-*c* copt-wilk.—rec *μεθ' εαυτων*, with AL rel: txt BCℵ 124. 2-pe.

20. for *απαρθη*, *αρθη* C 13. 28. 69. 124. 346. *νηστευουσιν* (for *-σουσιν*) D[1]-gr FUΠ goth. rec **εκειναις ταις** *ημεραις* (|| *Luke*), with E rel latt copt: txt ABC DKLΔΠ[1]ℵ **1**. 33. 69 am lat-*ff$_2$ i l* [*q*] syrr goth æth arm.

21. rec ins *και* bef *ουδεις*, with E rel æth: *ουδεις δε* (|| *Matt*) DGM lat-*a c* (*g$_2$*) syr-mg: txt ABCKLSΔℵ **1**. 33. 69 vulg lat-*b e f i* [*q*] syrr copt goth arm. *αγναφους* EFGLΔ: txt ABCDℵ rel. rec *επιρραπτει*, with B[2]KMSUΓ 33: *επισυνραπτει* D: txt AB[1]Cℵ rel. rec *ιματιω παλαιω* (*from || Matt?*), with A rel: txt BCDLℵ 33. rec (for *απ' αυτου το πληρωμα*) *το πληρωμα αυτου*, with C rel Syr

the feast, at which, being in the house of a Publican, they *were not present.*

18. καὶ ἦσαν κ.τ.λ.] Mark here gives a notice for the information of his readers, as in ch. vii. 3, which places shew that his Gospel was not written for the use of Jews. It appears from this account, which is here the more circumstantial, that the Pharisees and disciples of John asked the question in *the third person*, as *of others*. In Matt. it is *the disciples of John*, and they join ἡμεῖς καὶ οἱ Φαρ. In Luke, it is the *Pharisees and Scribes*, and they ask as here. Mey. understands it, that the disciples of John and the Pharisees were *at that particular time keeping a fast*, and that this gave occasion to the question. The verb subst. with the part. *may* mean this, and Mark himself apparently uses it so, ch. x. 32, and xiv. 4: but much more frequently it describes a practice or state, e. g. ἦν γὰρ ἔχων κτήματα πολλά, Matt. xix. 22,—οἱ ἀστ. ἔσονται ἐκ τ. οὐρ. πίπτοντες, ch. xiii. 25. See also ch. i. 6, 22, 39. I cannot think that the fact of their being *at that time keeping a fast* would be thus expressed: it certainly would be *further specified.* **19. ὅσον . . . νηστεύειν]** This repetition, *contained neither in Matt. nor Luke*, is inconsistent with the design of an abridger; and sufficiently shews the primary authority of this report, as also the **ἐν ἐκείνῃ τῇ ἡμ.** ver. 20. St. Mark especially loves these solemn repetitions:

[x] πλήρωμα τὸ καινὸν [y] τοῦ παλαιοῦ, καὶ χεῖρον [z] σχίσμα
γίνεται. 22 καὶ οὐδεὶς [a] βάλλει οἶνον νέον εἰς [b] ἀσκοὺς
παλαιούς· εἰ δὲ μή, [c] ῥήξει ὁ οἶνος τοὺς [b] ἀσκούς, καὶ ὁ
οἶνος ἀπόλλυται καὶ οἱ [b] ἀσκοί.
23 Καὶ [d] ἐγένετο αὐτὸν ἐν [e] τοῖς [e] σάββασιν [f] παραπορεύεσθαι διὰ τῶν [g] σπορίμων, καὶ οἱ μαθηταὶ αὐτοῦ [h] ἤρξαντο
[i] ὁδὸν [i] ποιεῖν [k] τίλλοντες τοὺς [l] στάχυας. 24 καὶ οἱ

...εγενετο F.

x = || Mt. only ‡. y constr., here only. z || Mt. John vii. 43. ix. 16. x. 19. 1 Cor. i. 10. xi. 18. xii. 25 only +. (-μή, Isa. ii. 21.) a = ch. vii. 33. John xviii. 11. Ps. cxxv. 6 Ed-vat. (B def.) ℵ[3a].

b here (3ce) & ||. (4 times) only. Josh. ix. 4, 13. c || Mt. reff. d constr., Matt. xviii. 13. Luke. iii. 21. principally Luke and Acts. e || Mt. reff. f ch. ix. 30 (w. διά, as also Deut. ii. 4). xi. 20. xv. 29. Mark only, exc. Matt. xxvii. 39. Exod. ii. 5. g || only. Gen. i. 29 bis. Lev. xi. 37 only. h ch. vi. 7 reff. i here only. see note. k || only. Ezra ix. 3. Isa. xviii. 7 only. l ||. ch. iv. 28 bis only. Deut. xxiv. 1 (xxiii. 25).

æth (arm): το πλ. αφ εαυτου B: το πληρ. απ αυτου L ℵ(omg το) 1. 131. 209. 435 goth: το πληρωμα, insg απο bef του παλαιου, D 13. 28. 69. 124 vulg lat-*a b e f* [$ff_2 g_2$ *i q*]: txt AKΔΠ[1] 33 lat-*l* syr. (*I adopt the reading of txt, with Mey, and Tischdf ed 2, as the least conformed to || Matt, from which come the* απο του παλαιου *of* D *&c, the* αιρει το πληρ. *of* B *and* C, *and the* το πλ. αυτου *of* C.) χειρων D.

22. for μη, μηγε (|| *Matt Luke*) CLM[2]. rec ρησσει (*see || Matt, from which rec goes on to borrow*), with A rel em(with fuld ing) lat-*c e* ff_2 syr copt goth æth arm: txt BCDLℵ 33 vulg lat-*b* ff_1 g_1 [*i q*]. rec aft οινος ins ο νεος (*from || Matt*), with AC[2] rel gat lat-*e f* syr goth æth: om BC[1]DLℵ 69 vulg lat-*c* $ff_{1.2}$ g_1 *i l* [*q*] Syr copt arm. rec (for απολλυται) εκχειται (*from || Matt*), with ACLℵ rel vulg lat-*c f* ff_1 g_1 [*q*] syr goth æth arm: om D lat-*a b e* ff_2 *i*: txt B copt. rec aft οι ασκοι ins απολουνται (*from || Luke*), with ACDℵ rel latt syr goth æth arm: om BL copt. rec further adds αλλα οινον νεον εις ασκους καινους βλητεον (*from || Luke*), with AC ℵ-corr[1] rel vulg lat-*c e f* g_1 [*q*] vss, also (omg βλητεον) Bℵ[1]: om D lat-*a b* ff_2 *i*.

23. aft εγενετο ins παλιν D (13 ?) vulg lat-*a* $ff_{1.2}$ $g_{1.2}$ *i l* [*q*]: pref (13 ?) 69. 124. om εν (|| *Matt*) CLΔ 1. 13. 131. 244-59 Scr's a e i v evv-H-P-X. rec παραπορευεσθαι bef αυτον εν τοις σαββασιν, with A rel (Syr) syr copt goth (æth): τοις σαβ. παρα(or δια-)πορευεσθαι αυτον CL 33: αυτον παραπ. εν τοις σαβ. U 69. 124: παραπ. αυτον δια των σπορ. εν τοις σαβ. KΠ 265 Scr's w: txt (BDΔ)ℵ (latt). διαπορευεσθαι (*from || Luke*) BCD latt arm: πορευεσθαι (*from || Matt*) 13. 69. 124: txt Aℵ rel. rec ηρξαντο bef οι μαθηται αυτου, with A rel syr goth: txt BCDLℵ 33. 69 latt copt æth arm.—om αυτου D-gr 435 lat-ff_2 arm. for οδον ποιειν, οδοποιειν BGH: om (|| *Matt*) D lat-*b c e* ff_2 g_1 *i*: οδοιπορουντες 13. 69. 124. 346: txt ACℵ rel. for τιλλοντες, τιλλειν D 346.

24. for και οι, οι δε (|| *Matt*) D latt.

cf. ch. ix. 42 ff. It is strange to see such a Commentator as De Wette calling the ἐν ἐκείνῃ τῇ ἡμ. a proof of *carelessness.* It is a touching way, as Meyer well observes, of expressing 'in that *atra dies.*'

21.] Render, **the filling-up takes away from it, the new from the old, and a worse rent takes place.** See note on || Matt. The addition here of **τὸ καινόν** confirms the view taken of the parable there.

23—28.] The disciples pluck ears of corn on the Sabbath. Matt. xii. 1—8. Luke vi. 1—5. The same may be said of the three accounts as in the last case, with continually fresh evidence of their entire independence of *one another.*

23. παραπ. διά] He passed by or **journeyed** (so our Evangelist uses the word, see reff.) **through,** &c. **ὁδὸν ποιεῖν τίλ.** is matter of detail and minute depiction. The interpretation of this narrative given by Meyer, which I still believe to be an entirely mistaken one, I cannot pass over so slightly as I did in my first edition. He urges the strict classical sense of ὁδὸν ποιεῖν, '*to make a way,*' *viam munire,* or *sternere,* and insists on the sense conveyed by our narrative being, as distinguished from those in || Matt., Luke, that the disciples *made a way for themselves through the wheat field by plucking the ears of corn,* further maintaining, that there is no allusion *here* to their having eaten the grains of wheat, as in || Matt. Luke. But (1) the foundation on which all this is built is insecure. For ὁδὸν ποιεῖν in the LXX does undoubtedly mean '*to make one's journey,*' representing the Heb. עָשָׂה דֶרֶךְ, in Judg. xvii. 8 (examples are also quoted in the lexx. from Xenophon (the romancer)'s Ephesiaca and from Polyænus). And (2) as to no allusion being made to

Φαρισαῖοι ἔλεγον αὐτῷ Ἴδε τί ποιοῦσιν [e] τοῖς [e] σάββασιν ABCDE
ὃ οὐκ ἔξεστιν. 25 καὶ [m] αὐτὸς ἔλεγεν αὐτοῖς Οὐδέποτε GHKL MSUV
ἀνέγνωτε τί ἐποίησεν Δαυεὶδ ὅτε [n] χρείαν [n] ἔσχεν καὶ ΓΔΠℵ 1. 33. 69
ἐπείνασεν αὐτὸς καὶ οἱ μετ' αὐτοῦ; 26 [πῶς] εἰςῆλθεν εἰς
τὸν οἶκον τοῦ θεοῦ [o] ἐπὶ Ἀβιάθαρ ἀρχιερέως, καὶ τοὺς
[p] ἄρτους τῆς [p] προθέσεως ἔφαγεν, οὓς οὐκ ἔξεστιν φαγεῖν
εἰ μὴ τοῖς ἱερεῦσιν, καὶ ἔδωκεν καὶ τοῖς σὺν αὐτῷ οὖσιν;

m ch. vi. 45. viii. 29.
n abs., Acts ii. 45. iv. 35. Eph. iv. 28. 1 John iii. 17.
o = Luke iii. 2. iv. 26. Acts xi. 28.
p || Mt. reff.

om αυτω D lat-*e i*. aft ποιουσιν ins οι μαθηται σου (*see* || *Matt*) DM 1. 13. 28. 69. 124-31. 346 Scr's c gat lat-*a b* (*c*) *f ff*$_{1.2}$ (*g*$_{1.2}$) *i l* syr-jer goth æth: om ABCℵ rel vulg lat-*e* syrr copt arm. rec ins εν bef τοις σαββασι, with L rel: om ABCDKM ΔΠℵ 1. 69 latt. ο ουκ εξ. bef τοις σαβ. A. aft εξεστιν add αυτοις D lat-*a b c ff*$_2$ *g*$_1$.

25. for αυτος, αποκριθεις (|| *Luke*) D lat-*a*; om αυτος (|| *Matt*) BCLℵ 33. 69 vulg lat-*b f ff*$_2$ *g*$_1$ *i l* [*q*] copt: txt A rel lat-*c e* syr. for ελεγεν, λεγει CLℵ 33. 69 vulg lat-*b f g*$_1$ [*q* D-lat] copt: ειπεν D[-gr] lat-*a c e ff*$_2$ Syr: txt AB rel syr copt-ms. aft αυτου ins οντες (|| *Luke*) D; ησαν Δ latt.

26. om πως (*possibly insd from* || *Matt, where there is no varn*) BD: ins ACℵ rel. (B has not ηλθεν as Btly: see table.) om του (bef θεου) C[1]. om επι αβιαθαρ αρχιερεως (*perhaps to conform to* || *Matt Luke, perhaps owing to the difficulty*) D 271 lat-*a b e ff*$_2$ *i*: transposed in Scr's c. rec ins του bef αρχιερεως (*vain attempt to escape the difficulty: see note*), with AC(Δ)Π 1. 33. 69 copt: om Bℵ rel goth. ιερεως Δ lat-*f* goth. προςθεσεως D. εδωκεν τοις μετ' αυτου ουσιν ους ουκ εξεστιν φαγειν ει μη τοις ιερευσιν D lat-*a b* (*c*) *e g*$_1$ *i* arm. [for ους, ος B[1](Tischdf).] for τοις ιερευσιν, τους ιερεις (|| *Luke*) Bℵ: τοις ιερεις L: txt ACD rel. aft ιερ. ins μονοις (|| *Matt*) Δ 33 lat-*b c e f ff*$_1$ *g*$_{1.2}$ *l* copt-wilk goth æth arm: pref 13. 69. 124.

their having eaten the corn, how otherwise could the χρείαν ἔχειν have been common to the disciples and to David? Could it be said that any *necessity* compelled them to clear the path by pulling up the overhanging stalks of corn? How otherwise could the remarkable addition in our narrative, ver. 27, at all bear upon the case? Fritzsche's rendering, 'cœperunt viam exprimere spicas evellendo,' which he explains, 'to mark the way by plucking ears, and strewing them in it,' is still worse. The classical sense of ὁδὸν ποιεῖν must evidently not be pressed: it here = ὁδὸν ποιεῖσθαι. **25. αὐτός**] Himself, taking up the cause of his disciples and not leaving their defence to themselves. **26. ἐπὶ Ἀβ. ἀρχ.] during the high-priesthood of Abiathar.** But in 1 Sam. xxi., from which this account is taken, *Ahimelech, not Abiathar*, is the high-priest. There is however considerable confusion in the names about this part of the history: *Ahimelech himself is called Ahiah*, 1 Sam. xiv. 3; and whereas (1 Sam. xxii. 20) Ahimelech *has a son Abiathar*, in 2 Sam. viii. 17, Ahimelech *is the son of Abiathar*, and in 1 Chron. xviii. 16, *Abimelech*. Amidst this variation, we can hardly undertake to explain the difficulty in the text. The insertion of the art. before ἀρχ. has been apparently done to give the words the sense 'In the time of Abiathar the High-priest,' so that the difficulty might be avoided by understanding the event to have happened in the time of (but not necessarily during the high-priesthood of) Abiathar (who was afterwards) the High-priest. But supposing the reading to be so, what author would in an ordinary narrative think of designating an event thus? Who for instance would speak of the defeat of the Philistines at Ephesdammim, where Goliath fell, as happening ἐπὶ Δαυεὶδ τοῦ βασιλέως? Who would ever understand ἐπὶ Ἐλισσαίου τοῦ προφήτου, 'in the time of Elisæus the prophet,' as importing, in matter of fact, any other period than that of the *prophetic course* of Elisha? (The ἐγέννησεν Δαυεὶδ τὸν βασιλέα of Matt. i. 6 is not a case in point.) Yet this is the way in which the difficulties of the Gospels have been attempted to be healed over. (See Middleton on the article, in loc.) With the restoration of the true reading, even this resource fails. (I am sorry to see that Bp. Wordsw. writes, "ἐπὶ Ἀβιάθαρ ἀρχιερέως intimates indeed that it was in the days of Abiathar, but it rather suggests that he was *not* the High-priest then:" comparing ἐπὶ ἀρχιερέως Ἄννα, Luke iii. 2. But surely Bp. W. must know, that such a rendering is ungrammatical: that ἀρχ-

27 καὶ ἔλεγεν αὐτοῖς Τὸ σάββατον διὰ τὸν ἄνθρωπον
ἐγένετο, καὶ οὐχ ὁ ἄνθρωπος διὰ τὸ σάββατον. 28 [q] ὥςτε
κύριός ἐστιν ὁ υἱὸς τοῦ ἀνθρώπου καὶ τοῦ σαββάτου.
III. 1 Καὶ εἰςῆλθεν πάλιν εἰς συναγωγήν· καὶ ἦν ἐκεῖ
ἄνθρωπος [r] ἐξηραμμένην ἔχων τὴν χεῖρα· 2 καὶ [s] παρ-
ετήρουν αὐτὸν εἰ τοῖς σάββασιν θεραπεύσει αὐτόν, ἵνα
κατηγορήσωσιν αὐτοῦ. 3 καὶ λέγει τῷ ἀνθρώπῳ τῷ
τὴν χεῖρα ἔχοντι [t] ξηρὰν Ἔγειρε εἰς τὸ [u] μέσον. 4 καὶ
λέγει αὐτοῖς Ἔξεστιν τοῖς σάββασιν [v] ἀγαθοποιῆσαι ἢ
[w] κακοποιῆσαι, [x] ψυχὴν [y] σῶσαι ἢ ἀποκτεῖναι; οἱ δὲ [z] ἐσιώπων. 5 καὶ [a] περιβλεψάμενος αὐτοὺς [b] μετ᾽ ὀργῆς [c] συν-

q = Matt. xii. 12 al. fr.
r = ch. ix. 18 only. (Matt xiii. 6 al.) 3 Kings xiii. 4.
s ‖ L. Luke xiv. 1. xx. 20. Acts ix. 24 (Gal. iv. 10) only. Ps. xxxvi. 12. Dan. vi. 11 Theod. (= τηρ., LXX.)
t = John v. 3 reff.
u absol., = Matt. xiv. 6 reff.
v Luke vi. 9, 33, 35 (Acts xiv. 17 v. r.). 1 Pet. ii. 15, 20. iii. 6, 17. 3 John 11 only. Num. x. 32. Judg. xvii. 13 A.
w = ‖ Luke (1 Pet. iii. 17. 3 John 11) only. Gen. xxxi. 29. (-ποιός, 1 Pet. ii. 12.)
x = Matt. ii. 20. vi. 25 al. fr.
y see Matt. xvi. 25 reff.
z Matt. xx. 31 reff.
a ‖ L. elsw. Mark only, ver. 24. ch. v. 32. ix. 8. x. 23. xi. 11. Exod. ii. 12.
b = Eph. vi. 7. 1 Tim. ii. 9. 1 Pet. iii. 15 al.
c here only. Ps. lxviii. 20. Isa. li. 19 only (?).

27. for και ελεγεν αυτοις, λεγω δε υμιν D lat-*a b c e* ff_2 g_1 *i*. om το σαββ. δια to ωστε ver. 28 D lat-*a c e* ff_2 *i*. rec om 2nd και, with AC^3 rel lat-*b f* goth arm: ins BC^1LΔℵ 33 vulg lat-ff_1 $g_{1.2}$ *l* Syr syr-w-ob copt æth.

Chap. III. **1.** rec aft εις ins την (‖ *Matt Luke, where there is no varn*), with ACD rel: om Bℵ 7-pe. εκει bef ην A: txt BCDℵ rel. for εξηραμμενην, ξηραν (‖ *Matt*) D.

2. παρετηρουντο (*from* ‖ *Luke, where it is more strongly attested*) AC^1DΔ 1: txt BC^3Lℵ rel. ins εν bef τοις σαββασιν CDHMℵ ev-y copt: om AB rel latt goth. for θεραπευσει, θεραπευει Δℵ 271. om 2nd αυτον D latt goth æth: ins bef θερ. KΠ Scr's d. κατηγορησουσιν (*confusion of vowels?*) CD. for αυτου, αυτον D^1(txt D^2).

3. rec (for την χειρα εχοντι ξηραν) τ. εξηραμμενην εχοντι την χειρα (*see above*), with A rel Syr goth (arm): εχ. τ. χ. εξηραμ. D 28 latt: τ. ξηρ. χ. εχ. C^1Δℵ: ξηρ. εχ. τ. χ. 33. 435: txt BL. rec εγειραι, with UΓ: txt ABCDℵ rel. for εις το μεσον, και στηθι εν μεσω D (lat-*c f* æth).

4. for λεγει αυτοις, ειπεν προς αυτους (*see* ‖ *Luke*) D lat-*a b c f* g_1 [*q*]. ins εν bef τοις σαββασιν ADE 69 copt goth: om BCℵ rel latt. ins τι bef αγαθ. D lat-*b e* g_1. αγαθον ποιησαι Dℵ. aft σωσαι ins μαλλον D 28. 124. for αποκτειναι, απολεσαι $LΔ^1$ 1. 124-31. 209-37-51-2^2-9 latt Syr goth arm Vict.

ιερέως without the article must be simply predicatory, whether it precedes or follows the proper name; "when Abiathar was High-priest,"—and cannot be titular. The expression in 1 Macc. xiii. 42, which he quotes as similar, is not a case in point, as any reader may judge: ἐπὶ Σίμωνος ἀρχιερέως μεγάλου κ. στρατηγοῦ καὶ ἡγουμένου τῶν Ἰουδαίων: the epithet μεγάλου makes all the difference.) **27.**] **τὸ σάβ. . . . διὰ τὸ σ.** is peculiar to Mark, and highly important. The Sabbath was an ordinance *for man;* for man's rest, both actually and typically, as setting forth the rest which remains for God's people (Heb. iv. 9). But He who is now speaking has taken on Himself *Manhood,* the whole nature of Man; and is *rightful lord* over creation *as granted to man,* and *of all that is made for man,* and therefore *of the Sabbath.* The whole dispensation of *time* is created for *man,* for *Christ as He is man,* and is *in his absolute power.* There is a remarkable parallel, in more than the mere mode of expression, in 2 Macc. v. 19: οὐ διὰ τὸν τόπον τὸ ἔθνος, ἀλλὰ διὰ τὸ ἔθνος τὸν τόπον ὁ κύριος ἐξελέξατο.

28. καί] as well as of His other domains or elements of lordship and power.

Chap. III. 1—6.] Healing of the withered hand. Matt. xii. 9—14. Luke vi. 6—11. On Matthew's narrative, see notes on Luke. The two other accounts are cognate, though each has some particulars of its own. **1. πάλιν**] See ch. i. 21, = ἐν ἑτέρῳ σαβ., Luke. The synagogue was at Capernaum. **2.**] Luke only adds that it was *the Scribes and Pharisees* who watched Him. **4. αὐτοῖς**] Luke adds ἐπερωτῶ ὑμᾶς εἰ ἔξεστιν: as his account is the most detailed, I refer to the notes there. **ἀποκτ.** does not belong to ψυχήν: **to save life or to kill?** **5.**] **συνλ. . . . αὐτῶν,** peculiar to Mark.

d Eph. iv. 18. e as above (d). Rom. xi. 25 only +. (-ροῦν, ch. vi. 52. Job xvii. 7 B.) f Matt. viii. 3 reff. g || Mt. reff. h here only. (=σ. ποιεῖν, ch. xv. 1,—σ. λαμβάνειν, Matt. xii. 14 reff.) i Matt. ii. 13, 14 reff. k Mark, here bis only. = Luke i. 10. ii. 13. John v. 3 al. Deut. xxvi. 5. 2 Chron. xiii. 8.

P επι τη ... F και εξετεινεν ... ABCDE FGHKL MPSUV ΓΔΠℵ 1. 33. 69

λυπούμενος ἐπὶ τῇ [de] πωρώσει τῆς [d] καρδίας αὐτῶν, λέγει
τῷ ἀνθρώπῳ [f] Ἔκτεινον τὴν [f] χεῖρα. καὶ [f] ἐξέτεινεν, καὶ
[g] ἀπεκατεστάθη ἡ χεὶρ αὐτοῦ. 6 καὶ ἐξελθόντες οἱ Φαρισαῖοι εὐθὺς μετὰ τῶν Ἡρωδιανῶν [h] συμβούλιον [h] ἐδίδουν
κατ' αὐτοῦ, ὅπως αὐτὸν ἀπολέσωσιν.
7 Καὶ ὁ Ἰησοῦς μετὰ τῶν μαθητῶν αὐτοῦ [i] ἀνεχώρησεν
πρὸς τὴν θάλασσαν, καὶ πολὺ [k] πλῆθος ἀπὸ τῆς Γαλιλαίας
ἠκολούθησεν, καὶ ἀπὸ τῆς Ἰουδαίας 8 καὶ ἀπὸ Ἱεροσολύμων καὶ ἀπὸ τῆς Ἰδουμαίας καὶ πέραν τοῦ Ἰορδάνου, καὶ
[οἱ] περὶ Τύρον καὶ Σιδῶνα, [k] πλῆθος πολύ, ἀκούοντες
ὅσα [l] * ποιεῖ, ἦλθον πρὸς αὐτόν. 9 καὶ [m] εἶπεν τοῖς μαθη-

l pres., John i. 40 reff. m w. ἵνα, Matt. iv. 3 reff.

5. for πωρωσει, νεκρωσει D lat-*c ff$_2$ i*. rec aft χειρα ins σου (*from* || *Luke*), with ACDPℵ 1(sic) rel: om BEMSUVΓ. (33 def.) rec αποκατεσταθη, with DΠ[1] 1: . π . κατεστη C: txt ABPℵ rel. aft αυτου ins ευθεως D lat-*ff$_2$* (*g$_{1.2}$*) *i*. rec at end adds υγιης ως η αλλη (*from* || *Matt*), with C[3]L rel; ως η αλλη 131 lat-*a b c g$_2$* syr-jer copt-ms: om ABC[1]DKPΔΠℵ 1. 33 vulg lat-*e f ff$_2$ g$_1$ i* syrr copt goth æth arm Chrysol Bede.

6. for και εξ., εξελθοντες δε D vulg lat-*b c ff g$_{1.2}$*. rec ευθεως, with AP rel: txt BCΔℵ 33.—om DL mt lat-*b c ff$_2$ g$_{1.2}$ i* æth. rec (for εδιδουν) εποιουν, with AP rel vulg lat-*b c* &c copt-wilk[and -dz(or -ησαν)] goth arm: εποιησαν CΔℵ Thl: ποιουντες D-gr *exierunt facientes* lat-*a* (*the varns tend to shew that* εποιουν, *see ch* xv. 1, *was substd for the unusual* εδιδουν): txt BL 69 (syrr ?) copt-schw.

7. for και ο, ο δε D latt(not am *g$_2$*). rec ανεχωρησε bef μετα των μαθητων αυτου, with AP rel lat-*b c e f* syr goth: txt BCDLΔℵ 1. 33. 69 vulg lat-*a ff$_{1.2}$ g$_{1.2}$ i* Syr copt arm. for προς, εις DHP 53. 131. 209-38-45-53-8-9 Scr's s evv-y-z Thl: παρα 13. 69. 124: txt ABC rel. for πολυ πληθος, πολυς οχλος D vulg lat-*a*. rec ηκολουθησαν, with Cℵ rel lat-*ff$_1$* copt-schw goth (æth arm, appy): om D 28. 124 lat-*a b c e ff$_2$ i* [copt-dz]: txt ABGK[2]LMPSΓΠ 1. 131. 209 vulg lat-*f g$_{1.2}$* [copt-wilk] Vict. rec aft ηκολουθ. adds αυτω, with AP rel vulg lat-*f ff$_1$ g$_2$* syrr goth æth arm: αυτον Δ: om BCDLℵ 124 lat-*a b c e ff$_2$ i* copt. και απο τ. ιουδαιας bef ηκολουθ. CΔℵ 238 vulg lat-*f g$_{1.2}$ l* copt-ms. om 2nd απο D 124 latt copt-wilk.

8. om 2nd απο D-gr 237-52-9. 433 Scr's a copt-wilk.—om και απο της ιδουμ. ℵ[1](ins ℵ[3a]) 118. 258 Scr's c lat-*e ff$_2$* arm. ins οι bef περαν D-gr lat-*f*. om 4th και ℵ[1](ins ℵ[3a]). om οι (*to conform to the other clauses ?*) BCLΔℵ lat-*b c e f ff$_2$ g$_2$ i* D-lat Syr æth: ins A D[-gr] P rel vulg lat-*a g$_1$* syr copt goth arm. ins οι περι bef σιδωνα D-gr. rec ακουσαντες, with AC D-gr P rel syrr arm: txt BΔℵ 1. 69 vulg lat-*b c e f* D-lat copt goth æth. for οσα, α CD 28. 6-pe vulg lat-*a g$_1$ i* copt: txt ABPℵ rel lat-*b c e f* syrr goth æth arm. * rec ἐποίει, with ACDPℵ rel: ποιει BL. ηλθαν D: ηλθεν U.

συνλ. probably implies *sympathy with* their (spiritually) miserable state of hard-heartedness: but see note on Rom. vii. 22. On **πώρωσις**, see note, Eph. iv. 18, and Fritzsche on Rom. xi. 7.

6. **Ἡρωδιανῶν**] See notes on Matt. xvi. 6, and xxii. 16. Why the Pharisees and Herodians should *now* combine, is not apparent. There must have been some reason of which we are not aware, which united these opposite sects in enmity against our Lord. **συμβ. ἐδίδουν**, as also ἐποίουν, ch. xv. 1, is an expression peculiar to Mark.

7—12.] A GENERAL SUMMARY OF OUR LORD'S HEALING AND CASTING OUT DEVILS BY THE SEA OF GALILEE. *Peculiar* in this shape *to Mark;* but probably answering to Matt. xii. 15—21. Luke vi. 17—19. The description of the multitudes, and places whence they came, sets before us, more graphically than any where else in the Gospels, the composition of the audiences to which the Lord spoke, and whom He healed. The repetition of **πλῆθος πολύ** (ver. 8) is the report of one who *saw* the numbers from Tyre and Sidon coming and going. **9.**] Meyer explains the construction **εἶπεν ἵνα**, by that which was said being regarded as the purpose of its

ταῖς αὐτοῦ ἵνα [n] πλοιάριον [o] προςκαρτερῇ αὐτῷ διὰ τὸν
ὄχλον, ἵνα μὴ [p] θλίβωσιν αὐτόν. 10 πολλοὺς γὰρ ἐθεράπευσεν, ὥστε [q] ἐπιπίπτειν αὐτῷ ἵνα αὐτοῦ ἅψωνται ὅσοι
εἶχον [r] μάστιγας· 11 καὶ τὰ [s] πνεύματα τὰ [s] ἀκάθαρτα,
[t] ὅταν αὐτὸν [u] ἐθεώρουν, [v] προςέπιπτον αὐτῷ καὶ ἔκραζον
λέγοντα ὅτι σὺ εἶ ὁ [w] υἱὸς τοῦ [w] θεοῦ, 12 καὶ [x] πολλὰ
[y] ἐπετίμα αὐτοῖς ἵνα μὴ αὐτὸν [za] φανερὸν [a] * ποιῶσιν.
13 καὶ [b] ἀναβαίνει εἰς [b] τὸ ὄρος, καὶ προςκαλεῖται οὓς
ἤθελεν αὐτός, καὶ [c] ἀπῆλθον πρὸς αὐτόν. 14 καὶ [d] ἐποίησεν δώδεκα ἵνα ὦσιν μετ' αὐτοῦ, καὶ ἵνα ἀποστέλλῃ
αὐτοὺς κηρύσσειν 15 καὶ [e] ἔχειν [e] ἐξουσίαν ἐκβάλλειν τὰ

n (ch. iv. 36 v. r.) Luke v. 2. John vi. 22, 23, 24. xxi. 8 only †.
o = Acts viii. 13. x. 7 ‡. Susan. 6. (Acts i. 14. Col. iv. 2 al. Num. xiii. 21 only.)
p = here only ‡. (Matt. vii. 14. 2 Cor. i. 6 al. Ps. cxviii. 157.)
q = here only. see Luke xv. 20. Gen. xlv. 14.
r = ch. v. 29, 34. Luke vii. 21 (Acts xxii 24. Heb. xi. 36) only. Ps. xxxi. 10. 2 Macc. ix. 11.
s Matt. x. 1 reff.
t w. ind., see note. Exod. xvii. 11.
u plur., Matt. vi. 28 reff.
v Matt. vii. 25. ch. v. 33. vii. 28. Luke v. 8. viii. 28, 47. Acts xvi. 29 only. Ps. xciv. 6.
w see Matt. iv. 3 note.
x Matt. ix. 14 reff.
y || Mt. reff.
z = ch. vi. 14 al. fr.
a || Mt. only.
b Matt. v. 1 reff.
c = Matt. xiv. 25 reff.
d = Acts ii. 36. Rev. i. 6. see Heb. iii. 2 and note. 1 Kings xii. 6.
e ch. ii. 10. Matt. vii. 29 reff.

9. πλοιαρια B. at end add πολλοι D lat-*a i*; οι οχλοι 13. 28. 69. 124 (lat-ff_2).
10. εθεραπευεν (for -σεν) KΠ Scr's e w latt Syr [copt]. ins εν bef αυτω D latt. ins και bef οσοι A 28 lat-*f* Syr copt goth.
11. om τα (twice) D 13. 69. 124. aft οταν ins ουν D-gr. rec εθεωρει (*gramml corrn*), with AP rel (-ρη FH): txt BCDGLΔא 33. 69. rec προσεπιπτεν, with EHSUV: txt A B(-πταν) CDא rel Thl. (P def.) rec εκραζε, with EHMSUV: txt ABCDא rel Thl. (P def.) λεγοντες DKא 69^2: txt ABC rel. om οτι D latt(exc *f*) Syr copt æth. ins ο χριστος bef ο υιος CMP syr-w-ast; ο θεος (omg follg ο but retaining υιος τ. θεου) 69: om ABDא rel vss.
12. φανερον bef αυτον AP rel Thl: txt BCDΔא 1. 33. 69. * rec ποιήσωσιν (*from Matt* xii. 16? D^2 *reads* ποιωσιν *there as here*), with AB^{1}CPא rel: ποιωσιν B^{2}DK LΠ^1 13. 69. 124. at end add οτι ηδεισαν τον χριστον αυτον ειναι (*from Luke* iv. 41) C Scr's w^2 lat-*a*; *quoniam sciebant eum* lat-*b* (ff_2) $g_{1.2}$ [*q*].
13. for αναβαινει, ανεβη P 1. for 3rd και, οι δε CΔא. απηλθεν A^{1}L: ηλθον D Scr's s, *venerunt* latt Syr æth Aug.
14. aft δωδεκα ins ους και αποστολους ωνομασεν (*from* || *Luke*) B C^1(appy) Δא 69 syr-mg copt æth: om AC^{2}DP rel latt syrr goth arm. ινα ωσιν bef δωδεκα D vulg lat-*a c i l* Aug: ινα ωσ. μ. αν. bef δωδ. Δ. om 2nd ινα B ev-48. aft κηρυσσειν ins το ευαγγελιον D am(with mt) lat-*a b e f* $ff_{1.2}$ g_1 *i* [*q*].
15. for εχειν, εδωκεν αυτοις D vulg lat-*b c f* ff_2 g_1 *l* æth. rec aft εξουσιαν ins θεραπευειν τας νοσους και (*see Matt* x. 1: *Luke* ix. 1; *and cf ch* vi. 7), with AC^{2}D P(appy) rel latt syrr goth (æth) arm: om B C^1(appy) LΔא copt.

being said. **10.**] Luke vi. 19.

11. ὅταν . . . ἐθεώρουν] See ref. The indic. is sometimes found with ὅταν in the N. T., see Rev. iv. 9, but generally amidst variety of readings: Matt. x. 19: Mark xi. 25: Luke xiii. 28: Rom. ii. 14. Meyer thus accounts for it—that in later Greek the ἄν became completely attached to the ὅτε, and the **whenever** was treated as merely an expression of time—so that in German it would not be wenn sie Ihn irgend sahen, but wenn irgend sie Ihn sahen.

The unclean spirits are here spoken of in the person of those possessed by them, and the two fused together: for as it was impossible that *any but the spirits* could have *known* that He was the Son of God, so it was the material body of the possessed which fell down before Him, and *their* voice which uttered the cry: see note on Matt. viii. 32. The notion of the semi-rationalists, that the sick *identified themselves* with the dæmons (Meyer), is at once refuted by the universal agreement of the testimony given on such occasions, *that Jesus was the Son of God*.

13—19.] The Appointment of the Twelve, and its Purposes. Matt. x. 1—4. Luke vi. 12—16. See Luke, where we learn that He went up *overnight to pray*, and called His disciples to Him when it was day,—and notes on Matt. On **τὸ ὄρος** see Matt. v. 1. **14. ἐποίησεν**] **nominated,—set apart**: see reff. We have here the most distinct intimation of any, of the *reason* of this appointment.

f - = here bis only. 4 Kings xxiv. 17.
g see ch. ii. 19 al.
h || Mt. reff.
i = ch. ii. 2. Eph. v. 3.
k = here only (see ch. v. 26. John xvii. 7). 1 Macc. ii. 15, 17. xiii. 52.
l Matt. xxi. 46 reff.

δαιμόνια· 16 * καὶ [f] ἐπέθηκεν ὄνομα τῷ Σίμωνι Πέτρον.
17 καὶ Ἰάκωβον τὸν τοῦ Ζεβεδαίου, καὶ Ἰωάννην τὸν
ἀδελφὸν τοῦ Ἰακώβου, καὶ [f] ἐπέθηκεν αὐτοῖς ὀνόματα
Βοανηργές, ὅ ἐστιν [g] υἱοὶ βροντῆς· 18 καὶ Ἀνδρέαν, καὶ
Φίλιππον, καὶ Βαρθολομαῖον, καὶ Μαθθαῖον, καὶ Θωμᾶν,
καὶ Ἰάκωβον τὸν τοῦ Ἀλφαίου, καὶ Θαδδαῖον, καὶ Σίμωνα τὸν καναναῖον, 19 καὶ Ἰούδαν Ἰσκαριώθ, ὃς καὶ
[h] παρέδωκεν αὐτόν.
Καὶ ἔρχονται εἰς οἶκον, 20 καὶ συνερχεται πάλιν ὁ
ὄχλος, ὥστε μὴ δύνασθαι αὐτοὺς [i] μηδὲ ἄρτον φαγεῖν.
21 καὶ ἀκούσαντες [k] οἱ παρ' αὐτοῦ ἐξῆλθον [l] κρατῆσαι

...του ιακω. P. ABCDE FGHKL MSUV ΓΔΠℵ 1. 33. 69

16. * at beg ins *καὶ ἐποίησεν τοὺς δώδεκα* B C¹(appy) Δℵ æth-ms; *πρωτον σιμωνα* (*from Matt* x. 2) 13. 69. 124. 346: om AC²DP rel latt syrr copt goth æth-ed arm. rec *τω σιμωνι* bef *ονομα*, with A D(omg *τω*) P rel vulg lat-*a b* &c syrr goth: om *ονομα* 33. 157: txt BCLΔℵ evv-y-36-49 lat-*c e* copt [arm] Vict.
17. *τον* bef *ιακωβον* D. ins *τον* bef *ιωαννην* D. for *του ιακ.*, *αυτου* G 28. 69. 244 lat-$g_{1.2}$: *αυτου ιακ.* AF Scr's c e: om *του* CKSΔ 1. 13. 131. 237-8-57-8 Scr's d f g o v: txt BDPℵ rel. *εαυτοις* D. for *ονοματα*, *ονομα* B D-gr 225 Syr.
18. for *θαδδαιον*, *λεββαιον* D lat-*a b* ff_2 *i* [*q*]: mss-mtd-by-Orig had *λεβης τελωνης* here or ch. ii. 14. (*τελωνην* is added aft *μαθθαιον* (*from* || *Matt*) in 13. 61-9. 124 syr-mg arm.) rec *καναvιτην*, with A rel syr goth arm: txt BCDLΔℵ 33 latt Syr copt æth.
19. *ιουδας* D lat-*b c*. rec *ισκαριωτην*, with A rel vulg syr copt goth: *σκαριωθ* D lat-*b* $ff_{1.2}$ $g_{1.2}$ *l* [*q*], *scariotha* lat-*c* Syr: txt BCLΔℵ 33 tol. *ερχεται* BΓℵ¹ lat-*b* copt-wilk-dz [Vict]: *εισερχονται* D[-gr copt-schw]; *introivit* lat-*e* ff_2 *i*: txt CLℵ³ᵃ rel vulg lat-*f* ff_1 g_1 [*q*] D-lat [syrr goth].
20. rec om *ο* (bef *οχλος*), with CL¹ℵ¹ rel: ins ABD L(as corrd by origl scribe) Δℵ³ᵃ. om *αυτους* D goth. rec *μητε*, with CDℵ rel: txt ABKLUΔΠ¹ 33. *αρτους* D-gr.
21. *και οτε ηκουσαν περι αυτου οι γραμματεις κ. οι λοιποι εξηλθον* D lat-*a b c* &c

16. καὶ ἐπ. . . . .] for Σίμωνα, ᾧ ἐπ. . . .
On the list of the Apostles, see note at Matt. x. 2. The name, according to Mark, seems to be *now first given*. This, at all events, does not look like *the testimony of Peter*: but perhaps the words are not to be so accurately pressed. **17.**] **Βοανηργές** = בְּנֵי רֶגֶשׁ,—*Sheva* being expressed by *οα* in Aramaic (Meyer, from Lightf.),—perhaps on account of their *vehement and zealous disposition*, of which we see marks Luke ix. 54: Mark ix. 38; x. 37: see also 2 John 10; but this is uncertain. **ὀνόματα**, since *both* bore the name, and the Hebrew word is plural.

There is an interesting notice of the catalogues of the Apostles, and the questions arising out of them, in the Lectures of Bleek on the three Gospels, published since his death by Holzmann, Leipzig, 1862.

20—35.] Charges against Jesus,—of madness by his relations,—of dæmoniacal possession by the Scribes. His replies. Matt. xii. 22—37, 46—50. Luke xi. 14—26; viii. 19—21. Our Lord *had just cast out a deaf and dumb spirit* (see notes on Matt.) in the open air (Matt., ver. 23), and now they retire into the house. The omission of this, wholly inexplicable if Mark had had either Matt. or Luke before him, belongs to the fragmentary character of his Gospel. The common accounts of the compilation of this Gospel are most capricious and absurd. In one place, Mark omits a discourse—'*because it was not his purpose to relate discourses*;'—in another he gives a discourse, omitting the occasion which led to it, as here. The *real fact being*, that the sources of Mark's Gospel are generally of *the highest order*, and *most direct*, but the *amount of things contained* very scanty and discontinuous: see Prolegg. ch. iii. § viii. **20. πάλιν**] resumed from ch. ii. 2. **ὥστε μὴ δ.**] shewing that one of the *αὐτοί* is the narrator. **21.**] Peculiar to Mark.
οἱ παρ' αὐτοῦ = **his relations**, beyond a doubt—for the sense is resumed in ver. 31: see reff. **ἐξῆλθ.** (perhaps *from Nazareth*,—or, answering to John

αὐτόν, ἔλεγον γὰρ ὅτι [m] ἐξέστη. 22 καὶ οἱ γραμματεῖς οἱ
ἀπὸ Ἱεροσολύμων καταβάντες ἔλεγον ὅτι Βεελζεβοὺλ
[n] ἔχει, καὶ ὅτι [o] ἐν τῷ ἄρχοντι τῶν δαιμονίων [p] ἐκβάλλει
τὰ [p] δαιμόνια. 23 καὶ προςκαλεσάμενος αὐτοὺς [q] ἐν [q] παραβολαῖς ἔλεγεν αὐτοῖς Πῶς δύναται [r] σατανᾶς [r] σατανᾶν
ἐκβάλλειν; 24 καὶ ἐὰν βασιλεία [s] ἐφ' ἑαυτὴν [t] μερισθῇ,
οὐ δύναται σταθῆναι ἡ βασιλεία ἐκείνη· 25 καὶ ἐὰν οἰκία
[s] ἐφ' ἑαυτὴν [t] μερισθῇ, οὐ δυνήσεται ἡ οἰκία ἐκείνη στῆναι·
26 καὶ εἰ ὁ [r] σατανᾶς [u] ἀνέστη ἐφ' ἑαυτὸν καὶ [t] μεμέρισται,
οὐ δύναται στῆναι, ἀλλὰ τέλος ἔχει. 27 ἀλλ' οὐ δύναται οὐδεὶς * τὰ [v] σκεύη τοῦ ἰσχυροῦ εἰςελθὼν εἰς τὴν οἰκίαν
αὐτοῦ [w] διαρπάσαι, ἐὰν μὴ πρῶτον τὸν ἰσχυρὸν δήσῃ, καὶ
τότε τὴν οἰκίαν αὐτοῦ [w] διαρπάσει. 28 [x] ἀμὴν λέγω ὑμῖν

m = 2 Cor. v. 13 only. Job xii. 17 (?). (Matt. xii. 23 reff.) ἐξεστηκότα τῶν φρενῶν, Jos. Antt. x. 7. 3.
n = ver. 30. Matt. xi. 18 al.
o ch. ix. 29. xvi. 17 al.
p Matt. vii. 22 reff.
q ch. iv. 11. Matt. xiii. 3, 10 al. Ps. lxxvii. 2.
r Matt. iv. 10 al. fr.† Sir. xxi. 27 only.
s = ‖ L. Matt. x. 21. Acts xiii. 50. ἀγέλην συστᾶσαν ἐπὶ τοὺς νομέας κ.τ.λ., Xen. Cyr. i. 1. 2.
t ‖ Mt. reff.
u = Acts v. 36, 37 al. Gen. iv. 8.
v = ‖ Mt. reff. Deut. i. 41.
w here (bis) and ‖ Mt. only. Gen. xxxiv. 27, 29.
x Matt. v. 18 reff.

(not *l*) goth. [εξεσταται 13. 69 :] εξεσταται(εξεσται D-corr) αυτους *exsentiat eos* D[1], lat-*a b ff*$_2$ *i*.

23. om αυτοις D 33 lat-*b*.—aft ελεγεν ins ο κυριος ιησους D lat-*a ff*$_2$ *g*$_{1.2}$ *i* (æth) : aft αυτοις ins ο ῑς U lat-*b c* (Syr). εκβαλειν D 69.

25. rec (for δυνησεται) δυναται (*from ver* 24), with AD rel vulg lat-*b c e f ff*$_2$ [*q*] : txt BCLΔℵ em(with fuld ing tol) lat-*a g*$_1$ *i*. rec σταθηναι (*from ver* 24), with ACℵ rel : εσταναι D : txt BKLΠ.—rec στ. bef η οικια εκεινη (*cf ver* 24), with A rel lat-*a* (*b*) syr copt goth (æth arm) : txt BCDLΔℵ vulg lat-*c f ff*$_2$ *g*$_1$ [*i q*] Syr.

26. for ει, εαν D. for ανεστ. εφ ε. κ. μεμ., σαταναν εκβαλλει μεμερισται(-θαι D[1]) εφ εαυτον (*see* ‖ *Matt*) D lat-*a b* (*c*) *g*$_1$ *i* [*q*]. for και μεμερισται, εμερισθη και C[1] (appy) Δℵ[1] (latt), και εμερ. και ℵ[3a] : και εμερισθη BL. (*See var readd*, 1 *Cor* vii. 33, 34, *which may have exercised some influence in producing confusion here.*) rec σταθηναι, with AD rel : txt BCLℵ.—add η βασιλεια αυτου D lat-*a b g*$_1$ *i* [*q*]. ins το bef τελος D.

27. rec om αλλ' (*as superfl*), with AD rel latt syrr goth : for αλλ', και C[2](appy) G æth : txt B C[1](appy) LΔℵ 1. 33. 69 syr-mg copt arm. ουδεις bef δυναται and om ου (*simplification*) AD rel latt syrr goth arm : txt BCΔℵ copt. * εἰς τ. οἰκ. τ. ἰσχ. εἰςελθ. τὰ σκ. αὐτοῦ διαρπ. (*perhaps transposn for perspicuity*) BCLΔ 33 (Syr copt) æth : so, but εισελθ. bef εις τ. οικ. ℵ : om εισελ. ε. τ. οικ. αυτ. G : τα σκ. τ. ισχ. εισελθ. ε. τ. οικ. αυ. διαρπ. A(D) rel (latt) syr goth arm.—om αυτου D latt. for διαρπασει, διαρπαση (*confusion of vowels or conformation to δηση*) AEFGKUVΓ[Π] 33 : διαρπαζει D : txt BCℵ rel.

ii. 12, *from Capernaum*), **set out**: see ch. v. 14. They heard of his being so beset by crowds: see vv. 7—11. **ἔλεγον**] i. e. His relations—not *τινές*. **ἐξέστη**] **He is mad**: thus E. V.; and the sense requires it. They had doubtless heard of the accusation of his *having a dæmon*: which we must suppose not to have first begun after this, but to have been going on throughout this course of miracles. The understanding this that *his disciples* went out to repress *the crowd*, for they said, '*It is mad*,' is as contrary to Greek as to sense. It would require at least *αὐτούς* and *ἐξέστησαν*, or *τὸν ὄχλον* for *αὐτόν*, and would even then give no intelligible meaning. **22.**] **οἱ γρ. οἱ ἀπὸ Ἱερ. . . . .**, peculiar to Mark: see note on Matt. ver. 24. Here Matt. has *οἱ Φαρισ.*—Luke *τινὲς ἐξ αὐτῶν*, i. e. *τῶν ὄχλ.* **ὅτι Β. ἔχει**] This addition is most important. If He was *possessed by* Beelzebub, the *prince of the dæmons*, He would thus have authority over the inferior evil spirits. **23.**] **προςκαλ. αὐτούς** is not inconsistent (De Wette) with His *being in an house*—He *called them to Him*, they having been far off. We must remember the *large courts* in the oriental houses. **ἐν παρ.**] namely, *a kingdom*, &c., *a house*, &c., *the strong man*, &c. **σατανᾶς σατ.**] The *external unity* of Satan and his kingdom is strikingly declared by this simple way

y Matt. vi. 12 reff.
z (ch. iv. 12 v. r.) Rom. iii. 25. 1 Cor. vi. 18 only. Hos. x. 8.
a || Mt. Matt. xxvi. 65. Ezek. xxxv. 12. Dan. iii. 29 Theod.
b w. εἰς, Luke xii. 10 only. Dan. iii. 29 LXX. Bel and Dr. 9.
c = Heb. ix. 22. x. 18.
d w. gen., Matt. xxvi. 66 reff.
e Matt. x. 1 reff.
f ver. 22.
g ch. xi. 25. otherwise, Paul only, Rom. xiv. 4. 1 Cor. xvi. 13. Gal. v. 1 al[1]. Exod. xiv. 13 A.
h = Matt. xxvi. 26 reff.

ABCDE FGHKL MSUV ΓΔΠℵ 1. 33. 69

ὅτι πάντα [y] ἀφεθήσεται τοῖς υἱοῖς τῶν ἀνθρώπων τὰ
[z] ἁμαρτήματα, καὶ αἱ [a] βλασφημίαι ὅσα ἐὰν βλασφημήσω-
σιν. 29 ὃς δ' ἂν [b] βλασφημήσῃ εἰς τὸ πνεῦμα τὸ ἅγιον,
οὐκ ἔχει [c] ἄφεσιν εἰς τὸν αἰῶνα, ἀλλὰ [d] ἔνοχός ἐστιν
αἰωνίου [z] ἁμαρτήματος· 30 ὅτι ἔλεγον [e] Πνεῦμα [e] ἀκάθαρτον [f] ἔχει. 31 καὶ ἔρχονται * οἱ ἀδελφοὶ αὐτοῦ καὶ ἡ
μήτηρ αὐτοῦ, καὶ ἔξω [g] στήκοντες ἀπέστειλαν πρὸς αὐτὸν
καλοῦντες αὐτόν. 32 καὶ ἐκάθητο περὶ αὐτὸν ὄχλος. καὶ
λέγουσιν αὐτῷ Ἰδοὺ ἡ μήτηρ σου καὶ οἱ ἀδελφοί σου [καὶ
αἱ ἀδελφαί σου] ἔξω ζητοῦσίν σε. 33 καὶ ἀποκριθεὶς αὐτοῖς λέγει Τίς [h] ἐστιν ἡ μήτηρ μου ἢ οἱ ἀδελφοί; 34 καὶ

28. rec *τα αμ. τ. υιοις τ. ανθρωπων* (*simplification*), with M^1 rel (lat-*f* Syr) syr goth; so, omg *τ. αμ.*, F; *τοις ανθρ. τα αμ.* Δ: txt ABCDLM^2ℵ 1. 33 ev-y vulg lat-*a b* g_1 *l* [*i q*] copt arm. rec om *αι* (*error, owing to και preceding*), with D rel: txt ABCEFGHLΔℵ 1. 33. 69 copt. rec *οσας* (*gramml corrn*), with AC rel: txt B DE^1GHΔ$Π^1$ℵ 69. rec (for *εαν*) *αν*, with ADℵ rel: txt BCFLΔ 33 ev-y.

29. for *ος δ' αν*, *ος αν δε τις* D. om 1st *εις* D-gr vulg lat-*a b* goth arm. om *εις τον αιωνα* D 1. 22-8. 209. 2-pe lat-*a b e* ff_2 g_1 [*q*] Ath$_1$ Cypr$_2$. (*αλλα*, so ADLΔℵ.) for *ενοχος*, *ενος* D^1(but corrd). *εσται* DLΔℵ 33 vulg lat-*a c e* ff_2 g_1 æth arm Cypr$_1$. rec (for *αμαρτηματος*) *κρισεως*, with A rel tol lat-*f* syrr æth: *κολασεως* 61. 184 (*both corrns for the unusual exprn in txt*): *αμαρτιας* C^1(appy) D 69 Ath Ps-Ath: txt BLΔℵ 33 latt copt goth arm Cypr$_2$ Aug.

30. *εχειν* D 77. 235 lat-*a b c e* ff_2 g_1: *αυτον εχει* C æth.

31. rec (for *και ερχ.*) *ερχ. ουν*, with A rel syr: txt BCDGLΔℵ 1. 69 latt Syr copt goth æth. *ερχεται* DGℵ lat-*a b e* ff_2 g_1: txt ABC rel vss [Aug$_1$]. rec *οι αδ. κ. η μ. αυ.*, with E rel: * ἡ μήτηρ αὐτοῦ καὶ οἱ ἀδελφοὶ αὐτοῦ (*as* ||) BCDGLΔℵ (1) 33 (latt) Syr copt goth æth: *οι αδ. αυ. κ. η μ. αυ.* AKMΠ.—rec om 1st *αυτου*, with EFHSUVΓ (1) 69 (vulg) syr: ins ABCℵ rel Syr copt goth (æth). rec (for *στηκοντες*) *εστωτες*, with AD rel: *εστηκοτες* $C^{2\text{ or }3}$ GL 1: *σταντες* ℵ: txt BC^1Δ. rec (for *καλουντες*), *φωνουντες*, with D rel: *ζητουντες* A: om Δ(but a space is left) lat-*a*: txt BCL[ℵ] 1. 69.

32. rec *οχλος* bef *περι αυτον* (*simplification?*), with E rel æth: txt ABCKLMΔ[Π] ℵ$(^1)^3$ 1. 33. 69 vulg lat-*b c* (*e*) *f* $ff_{1.2}$ $g_{1.2}$ [*q* D-lat] syrr goth.—for *περι*, *προς* $ℵ^1$: for *περι αυτον οχλος*, *προς τον οχλον* D[-gr]. rec (for *και λεγουσιν*) *ειπον δε* (*from* || *Matt*), with A rel syr goth (arm): txt BCDLΔℵ 69 vulg lat-*b f* $ff_{1.2}$ $g_{1.2}$ *l* [*q*] Syr syr-ms-mg copt æth. rec om *και αι αδελφαι σου* (*neglect, or as not mentd in* || *nor in vv* 31, 34?), with BCGKLΔΠℵ 1. 33 [69] vulg lat-*e* ff_1 $g_{1.2}$ Syr copt æth arm: ins AD rel lat-*a b c f* ff_2 *l* [*q*] syr-mg goth.

33. rec *απεκριθη αυτ. λεγων*, with AD rel lat-(*a*) *b f* goth arm: [*απεκ. α. κ. λεγει* 1. 69:] txt B(C)LΔℵ vulg (lat-*c e*) syr copt.—*λεγει* bef *αυτοις* C. for *ἤ*, *και* (*see* || *Matt and ver* 34) BCGLUVΔℵ 1 vulg lat-*a b* g_1 *l* syrr copt: txt AD rel lat-*c e f* ff_2 goth æth arm. om *οι* (bef *αδελφοι*) D. rec aft *αδελφοι* ins *μου* (*from ver* 34 *and* || *Matt*), with ACℵ rel (vss): txt B D-gr arm.

34. om *και* B.

of putting the question: see note on Matt. The expression must not be taken as meaning, Can one devil cast out another? The *σατανᾶς* and *σατανᾶν* are the same person: cf. ver. 26. **26.**] **ἀλλὰ τέλ. ἔχει**, peculiar to Mark. **28.**] The putting of **πάντα** first, and separating it from its noun by the intervening words, gives it a prominent emphasis.

29. αἰωνίου ἁμαρτήματος] Beza explains *αἰωνίου* by '*nunquam delendi.*' It is to the critical treatment of the sacred text that we owe the restoration of such important and deep-reaching expressions as this. It finds its parallel in *ἀποθανεῖσθε ἐν ταῖς ἁμαρτίαις ὑμῶν*, John viii. 24. Kuinoel's idea, quoted and adopted by Wordsw., that *ἁμάρτημα* means in the LXX *the punishment of sin*, seems to be entirely unfounded. And as to its being "a Novatian error to assert that sin is *αἰώνιον*" (Wordsw.), it is at all events a

...κυκλω Γ. [i] περιβλεψάμενος [k] κύκλῳ τοὺς περὶ αὐτὸν καθημένους
λέγει Ἴδε ἡ μήτηρ μου καὶ οἱ ἀδελφοί μου. 35 ὃς ἂν
[l] ποιήσῃ τὰ [lm] θελήματα τοῦ θεοῦ, οὗτος ἀδελφός μου καὶ
ἀδελφὴ καὶ μήτηρ ἐστίν.

IV. 1 Καὶ πάλιν ἤρξατο διδάσκειν [n] παρὰ τὴν θάλασ-
σαν· καὶ [o] συνάγεται πρὸς αὐτὸν ὄχλος πλεῖστος, [p] ὥστε
αὐτὸν [q] ἐμβάντα εἰς [r] τὸ πλοῖον καθῆσθαι [s] ἐν τῇ θαλάσσῃ·
καὶ πᾶς ὁ ὄχλος [t] πρὸς τὴν θάλασσαν ἐπὶ τῆς γῆς ἦσαν.
2 καὶ ἐδίδασκεν αὐτοὺς [u] ἐν παραβολαῖς πολλά, καὶ
ἔλεγεν αὐτοῖς ἐν τῇ διδαχῇ αὐτοῦ 3 Ἀκούετε. ἰδοὺ ἐξῆλθεν ὁ [v] σπείρων σπεῖραι. 4 καὶ ἐγένετο ἐν τῷ σπείρειν,

i ver. 5 reff.
k ch. vi. 6 || L., 36. Rom. xv. 19. Rev. iv. 6. v. 11. vii. 11 only. 1 Kings xxvi. 5. Isa. xlix. 18.
l Matt. vii. 21 reff.
m plur., Acts xiii. 22. Eph. ii. 3 (both w. ποιεῖν) only. see 3 Kings v. 8.
n Matt. iv. 18 al. fr. 3 Kings iv. 29.
o Matt. xxii. 34 al. fr. Neh. viii. 1.
p = ch. iii. 10 al.
q Matt. viii. 23 reff.
r Matt. xiv. 22. ch. vi. 32 al.
s = Rev. xviii. 19.
t = Luke xxii. 56.
u ch. iii. 23 reff.
v part., = ||. Matt. iv. 3. Eph. iv. 28 al.

τους περι αυτον bef κυκλω (*being first omd, it was aft insd in the most likely place: see below*) BCLΔℵ copt: τους κυκλω, omg περι αυτον, D lat-*b*; τ. κυκ. π. αυ. 1. 13. 69. 124. 209: om altogether 61 lat-*a e* (Syr æth?): txt A rel syr goth arm. for λεγει, ειπεν DG 69 lat-*a c ff*$_2$. ιδου (*from* || *Matt*) ADGKMΔ[Π] 1. 33. 69: txt BCℵ rel.

35. rec aft ος ins γαρ (*from* || *Matt*), with ACDℵ rel vulg lat-*f ff*$_1$ *g*$_1$ [*q*] vss: om B lat-*a b c e* copt Aug. rec (for τα θεληματα) το θελημα (*from* || *Matt*), with ACDℵ rel: txt B. μου bef αδελφος D lat-*b e g*$_1$ [*q* Aug]. rec aft αδελφη ins μου, with C rel vulg lat-*a ff*$_1$ *g*$_2$ syrr copt æth: om ABDLΔℵ 1. 33. 69 lat-*b c e f ff*$_2$ *g*$_1$ [*q*] goth arm Ambr [Aug].

Chap. IV. **1.** ηρξατο bef παλιν D (209) lat-*a b c e g*$_1$ [*q*] æth Orig-int$_1$. for παρα, προς D. rec (for συναγεται) συνηχθη, with D rel latt syr-ms [Orig-int]: συνηχθησαν (*from* || *Matt*) A 235 Scr's h syrr (goth æth arm with nomin pl): συνερχεται 1. 209: txt BCLΔℵ 69. for οχλος, ο λαος D. rec (for πλειστος) πολυς (*from* || *Matt*), with AD rel: txt BCLΔℵ. εις το πλοιον bef εμβαντα (*from* || *Matt*) BCDLUΔℵ 33 latt arm Thl: txt A rel syr copt goth æth Orig-int. om το (*see on* || *Matt*) CKLMΠℵ 1. 33. 131. 209 [goth]: ins A B(above the line) D rel copt. for εν τη θ., περαν της θ. *circa mare* D (lat-*a*). for προς τ. θ., εις την θ. Δ: παρα την θ. 1. 118. 209: περαν της θαλασσης *circa mare* D lat-*a l* [*q*]: *in litore* lat-*b c e f ff*$_2$ *g*$_1$. om επι της γ. D lat-*a b c e f ff*$_2$ *g*$_1$. rec (for ησαν) ην (*gramml corrn*), with A D[-gr] rel vulg lat-*a b ff*$_1$ *g*$_2$ [*q*] syr Orig-int: txt BCLΔℵ 33 evv-H-y D-lat.

2. πολλαις D.—πολλα bef εν παραβ. ℵ.

3. ακουσατε C 15. 269. 417. 2-pe. rec ins του bef σπειραι (*from* || *Matt*), with ACℵ^{3a} rel Eus: om Bℵ^1.—om σπειραι also D [copt-ms].

4. om εγενετο DF vulg lat-*b c* &c Syr æth. σπειραι D.

legitimate inference from οὐκ ἔχει ἄφεσιν εἰς τὸν αἰῶνα. If a sin remains unremitted for ever, what is it but eternal?

Ver. 30 explains the ground and meaning of this awful denunciation of the Lord. **31.**] **ἔξω στ. ἀπ. . . .**, one of Mark's precise details. **32.**] **καὶ ἐκ. . . .**, another such. **34.**] Matt. here has some remarkable and graphic details also: ἐκτείνας τὴν χεῖρα αὐτ. ἐπὶ τ. μαθητὰς αὐτ. . . . . . Both accounts were from eye-witnesses, *the one* noticing the outstretched hand; *the other*, the look cast round. Deeply interesting are such particulars, the more so, as shewing the way in which the records arose, and their united strength, derived from their independence and variety.

Chap. IV. **1—9.**] Parable of the sower. No fixed mark of date. Matt. xiii. 1—9. Luke viii. 4—8. There is the same intermixture of absolute verbal identity and considerable divergence, as we have so often noticed: which is wholly inexplicable on the ordinary suppositions. In this case the vehicles of the parable in Matt. and Mark (see Matt. vv. 1—3: Mark, vv. 1, 2) bear a strong, almost verbal, resemblance. *Such a parable* would be carefully treasured in all the Churches as a subject of catechetical instruction: and, in general, in proportion to the popular nature of the discourse, is the resemblance stronger in the reports of it. **1. πάλιν**] See ch. iii. 7. The **ἤρξατο** is coincident with the gathering together of the crowd.

w ‖ Mt. reff. x ‖. Matt. vi. 26. Deut. xiv. 19, 20 al. y ‖ Mt. reff. z ver. 16 ‖ Mt. only +. a ‖ Mt. only. (LXX., trans. only.) Gen. ii. 9. Ps. cxlvi. 8. b Matt. xxiv. 12. ch. v. 4. Luke ii. 4. Acts xviii. 2, 3 al. Judg. iii. 12. c intr., Matt. iv. 16 reff. d ‖ Mt. Rev. xvi. 8, 9 only +. e = Matt. xxi. 19, 20 reff. f Matt. vii. 16 reff. Jer. iv. 3. g = ‖ Mt. ver. 32. Isa. xxxii. 13. h ver. 19 ‖. Luke viii. 42 only +. i ‖ Mt. only. (ἀποδ. κ., Heb. xii. 11. Rev. xxii. 2.) Zech. viii. 12. k ‖ Mt. Num. xiii. 20. l Matt. xiii. 32 reff. m ver. 20. ch. ix. 5 ‖. 1 Kings x. 3. n ‖ L. ver. 23. Luke xiv. 35. Deut. xxix. 4. (Isa. l. 4.) o Luke ix. 18 only. Ps. iv. 8. p Luke xxii. 49. (John xi. 19 v. r.) Acts xiii. 13 al. Ezek. xxxviii. 6.

ABCDE FGHKL MSUV ΔΠℵ 1. 33. 69

[w] ὃ μὲν ἔπεσεν παρὰ τὴν ὁδόν, καὶ ἦλθεν τὰ [x] πετεινὰ καὶ
[y] κατέφαγεν αὐτό. 5 καὶ [w] ἄλλο ἔπεσεν ἐπὶ τὸ [z] πετρῶδες
καὶ ὅπου οὐκ εἶχεν γῆν πολλήν, καὶ εὐθὺς [a] ἐξανέτειλεν
[b] διὰ τὸ μὴ ἔχειν βάθος γῆς· 6 καὶ ὅτε [c] ἀνέτειλεν ὁ
ἥλιος, [d] ἐκαυματίσθη καὶ [b] διὰ τὸ μὴ ἔχειν ῥίζαν [e] ἐξηράνθη.
7 καὶ [w] ἄλλο ἔπεσεν εἰς τὰς [f] ἀκάνθας, καὶ [g] ἀνέβησαν αἱ
[f] ἄκανθαι καὶ [h] συνέπνιξαν αὐτό, καὶ [i] καρπὸν οὐκ [i] ἔδωκεν.
8 καὶ ἄλλα ἔπεσεν εἰς τὴν γῆν τὴν [k] καλήν, καὶ [i] ἐδίδου
[i] καρπὸν [g] ἀναβαίνοντα καὶ [l] αὐξανόμενον, καὶ ἔφερεν [m] εἷς
τριάκοντα καὶ [m] εἷς ἑξήκοντα καὶ [m] εἷς ἑκατόν. 9 καὶ
ἔλεγεν Ὃς ἔχει [n] ὦτα [n] ἀκούειν, ἀκουέτω. 10 καὶ ὅτε
ἐγένετο [o] καταμόνας, ἠρώτων αὐτὸν [p] οἱ [p] περὶ αὐτὸν σὺν

ηλθαν D: ηλθον HKΔ 33 Scr's p ev-y. rec aft πετεινα ins του ουρανου (*from* ‖ *Luke*), with DGM vulg-ed[with gat] lat-*a ff*$_1$ *g*$_2$ [*q*]: om ABCℵ rel am(with em fuld ing tol) lat-*b c e f ff*$_2$ *g*$_1$ *l* syrr copt goth æth arm Bede. κατεφαγαν D.

5. rec (for και αλ.) αλ. δε (*from* ‖ *Matt*), with A rel vulg lat-*c f* [*ff*$_{1.2}$ *g*$_{1.2}$ *i q*] syrr goth arm: αλ. (alone) M[1] lat-*b*: txt BCDLM[2]Δ 33 lat-*a* copt æth.—αλλα D-gr 13. 33. 69 lat-*e*.—επεσαν D. τα πετρωδη (*from* ‖ *Matt*) D ℵ[1](txt ℵ[3a]) 1. 33 vulg lat-*b c e f l* [*g*$_1$ *q*]. rec om και (‖ *Matt*), with AC[ℵ] rel vss: ins BD lat-*a*(appy) *b c e ff*$_2$ *i* [*q*]. for οπου, οτι D lat-*b c e ff*$_2$ *g*$_2$ *i*. rec ευθεως, with A rel: txt BCDLΔℵ. (33 def.) εξανεστειλεν D[1]. ins της bef γης B (*so also in* ‖ *Matt*): την γην D.

6. rec (for και οτε ανετειλεν ο ηλιος) ηλιου δε ανατειλαντος (*from* ‖ *Matt*), with A rel lat-*a f* syrr goth æth arm: txt BCDLΔℵ vulg lat-*ff*$_2$ *i l* [*q*] copt. εκαυματισθησαν B D-gr lat-*a e*. (*See* D, *ver* 5: *so also in* ‖ *Matt.*) εξηρανθησαν D-gr lat-*e*.

7. αλλος ℵ[1](txt ℵ[3a]): αλλα 33. for εις, επι CDM[2] 33 Scr's a c ev-z lat-*b*(*supra*) copt-mss.

8. rec αλλο (*appy conformation to the preceding. This is more prob, as* αλλο επεσεν *occurs twice before, than that* (*Mey*) *it should have been corrd to the plur to accord with* εἷς—εἷς—εἷς *below, or to suit* ‖ *Matt*), with AD ℵ[3a](but txt restored) rel latt syrr goth æth arm: txt BCLℵ[1] 33 lat-*e* copt. for εις, επι (‖ *Matt*) C 1 syrr. [εδιδοσαν C.] rec αυξανοντα (*corrn, the intrans form being* (*see reff*) *more common in N. T.*), with C(Treg expr) rel: txt ADLΔ, αυξανομενα Bℵ. εφερον Cℵ: φερει D 124: *adferet* lat-*b* D-lat. rec ἕν (thrice), with S(e sil) 69 latt(with Δ-lat) Syr(appy): εν AC[2]D: ἐν E rel syr æth: εις 1st time, εν twice BL: txt C[1]Δℵ.

9. rec aft ελεγεν ins αυτοις, with M[2]-marg S(e sil) 3-pe: om ABCDℵ rel latt syrr copt goth æth arm Thl. rec ο εχων (*from* ‖ *Matt Luke*), with AC[2]ℵ[3a] rel: txt BC[1]DΔℵ[1]. add κ. ο συνιων συνιετω D lat-*a b ff*$_2$ *g*$_{1.2}$ *i* syr-mg.

10. rec [for και οτε] οτε δε, with A rel syrr æth arm: txt BCDLΔℵ latt copt goth. rec ηρωτησαν (*more usual historic sense*), with E rel vulg lat-*c f ff*$_2$ syrr: επηρωτησαν 13. 69. 124. 346: επηρωτων (‖ *Luke*) D: txt ABCLΔℵ 33 lat-*a b* Orig-int. (-τουν Cℵ.) for οι περι αυτ. συν τ. δ., οι μαθηται αυτου (‖ *Luke*) D 28. 69. 124 lat-*a b c ff*$_2$ *g*$_1$ *i* [*q*] Orig-int$_1$: om οι περι αυ. L 359.

2.] Out from among the πολλά, the great mass of His teaching, one parable is selected, which He spoke during it—**ἐν τῇ διδ. αὐτοῦ.** **3. ἀκούετε**] This solemn prefatory word is peculiar to Mark. **4—8.**] Matt. and Mark agree nearly verbally. In ver. 7 Mark adds **καὶ καρπὸν οὐκ ἔδωκεν**, and in ver. 8, **ἀναβαίνοντα κ. αὐξανόμενον.** On this latter, Meyer remarks, that the two present partt. are predicates of καρπόν, which therefore must not be understood here of the fruit properly so called, the corns of wheat in the ears, but of the haulm, the first fruit of the successful seed. The corns first come in after ἔφερεν.

10—12.] Reason for speaking in parables. Matt. xiii. 10—17. Luke viii.

τοῖς δώδεκα τὰς [q] παραβολάς. 11 καὶ ἔλεγεν αὐτοῖς
Ὑμῖν τὸ [r] μυστήριον [s] δέδοται τῆς βασιλείας τοῦ θεοῦ·
ἐκείνοις δὲ [t] τοῖς [t] ἔξω ἐν παραβολαῖς τὰ πάντα γίνεται,
12 ἵνα βλέποντες βλέπωσιν καὶ μὴ ἴδωσιν, καὶ ἀκούοντες
ἀκούωσιν καὶ μὴ συνιῶσιν, μήποτε [u] ἐπιστρέψωσιν, καὶ
[v] ἀφεθῇ αὐτοῖς. 13 καὶ λέγει αὐτοῖς Οὐκ [w] οἴδατε τὴν
παραβολὴν ταύτην; καὶ πῶς πάσας τὰς [q] παραβολὰς
[x] γνώσεσθε; 14 ὁ [y] σπείρων τὸν λόγον σπείρει. 15 οὗτοι
δέ εἰσιν οἱ παρὰ τὴν ὁδόν, ὅπου σπείρεται ὁ λόγος, καὶ
ὅταν ἀκούσωσιν, εὐθὺς ἔρχεται ὁ σατανᾶς καὶ [z] αἴρει τὸν
λόγον τὸν ἐσπαρμένον [a] εἰς αὐτούς. 16 καὶ οὗτοί εἰσιν

q Matt. xiii. 53.
r ‖ only in Gospp. Rom. xi. 25. 1 Cor. xiii. 2. xv. 51. Wisd. ii 22. vi. 22(24).
s ‖ Mt. reff.
t 1 Cor. v. 12, 13. Col. iv. 5. 1 Thess. iv. 12. see Acts xxvi. 11. (τοῖς ἐκτός, Sir. prol.)
u ‖ Mt., from Isa. vi. 10. Luke xvii. 4 al. Ps. l. 13 (15).
v ch. iii. 28 al.
w = here only.
x = Luke xviii. 34. John iii. 10. Job ix. 11. Rom. viii. 18.
y pres. part., ver. 3 reff.
z = ver. 25 ‖. ch. ii. 21 ‖.
a = ch. i. 39 reff.

rec την παραβολην (‖ *Luke*), with A rel vulg-ed(with fuld) Syr copt-ms goth æth arm : τις η παρ. αυτη (*from* ‖ *Luke*) D 13. 28. 69. 124 lat-*a b c f* ff_2 g_1 *i l* [*q*] Orig-int$_1$: txt BCLΔא am(with gat ing mm mt) lat-g_2 copt.

11. λεγει D lat-*a b f* [g_1 *i q*]. rec aft δεδ. ins γνωναι (*from* ‖ *Matt Luke*), with C²D rel lat-*a c* &c : om ABC¹KLΠא lat-ff_1 copt. rec δεδ. (γν.) bef το μυστ., with AD rel syrr copt-ms goth æth (arm) : txt B C¹(appy) Lא lat-ff_1. εξωθεν B. om τα DKΠא. for γιν., λεγεται D 64. 124 lat-*a b c* ff_2 g_1 *i* [*q*].

12. ins μη bef βλεπωσιν (‖ *Luke*) E¹FGHΔ Orig$_2$. ακουσωσιν CM 69 : ακουουσιν Π¹. for συνιωσιν, συνωσιν D¹L 1. αφεθησεται (*see fut, Matt* xiii. 15 *and Isa* vi. 10) AK[Π] Orig$_1$: αφεθησομαι D¹(and lat) lat-ff_2 g_1 *i* [*q*] æth(Treg) : αφησω D². rec at end adds τα αμαρτηματα, with AD rel syrr goth æth : τα αμ. αυτων Δ syr-w-ast æth(*peccatum illorum*) : τα παραπτωματα 53. 237-59 Thl (*all supplemy glosses*) : om BCLא 1. 209 lat-*b i* copt arm Orig$_2$.

14. for σπειρει, σπερει א.

15. for οπου, οις D 69² lat-ff_2 g_1 (Syr). for και, οι B. [ακουωσιν (for -σωσιν) D¹G.] rec ευθεως, with AD rel : om 1. 118 arm : txt BCLΔא 33. 69 ev-y. for αιρει, αφερει D : αρπαζει (‖ *Matt*) CΔא : *auferet* lat-*c* D-lat. rec (for εις αυτ.) εν ταις καρδιαις αυτων (*from* ‖ *Matt*), with D rel latt Syr syr-txt copt-ms-corr goth [arm] : απο τ. καρδιας αυτων (*from* ‖ *Luke*) A lat-*l* æth : εν αυτοις (*corrn of txt*) CLΔא lat-*c* copt syr-mg : txt B 1. 13. 28. 69. 118. 209.

9, 10. **10.**] **οἱ π. αὐτ. σὺν τ. δώδ.** = οἱ μαθ. αὐτοῦ Luke. **11.**] **τὸ μυστήριον** = τὰ μυστήρια Matt. and Luke. **τοῖς ἔξω** added here (= τοῖς λοιποῖς, Luke) means *the multitudes*—those out of the circle of his followers. In the Epistles, *all who are not Christians*,—the corresponding meaning for those days,—are designated by it. **τὰ πάντα γίνεται**] **the whole matter is transacted.** Herod. ix. 46, ἡμῖν οἱ λόγοι γεγόνασι. **12.**] We must keep the **ἵνα** strictly to its telic meaning—**in order that.** When God transacts a matter, it is idle to say that the result is not the purpose. He doeth all things after the counsel of His own will. Matt., as usual, quotes a prophecy; Mark hardly ever—except at the beginning of his Gospel; Luke, very seldom. **ἀφ. αὐτ.** = ἰάσομαι αὐτούς Matt., **it should be forgiven them**; i. e. '*forgiveness should be extended to them*.' no need to supply any thing, as the gloss of the rec. does: the expression is impersonal.

13—20.] Explanation of the parable of the sower. In **τὴν παρ. ταύτην**, the general question which had been asked ver. 10 (**τὰς παραβολάς**), is tacitly assumed to have had special reference to the one which has been given at length. Or we may understand, that the question of ver. 10 took the form which is given in ‖ Matt.: διὰ τί ἐν παραβολαῖς λαλεῖς αὐτοῖς; in which case the τάς must be generic: **asked Him concerning parables**; or **His parables.** The three explanations (see Matt. xiii. 18—23 : Luke viii. 9—15) are very nearly related to one another, with however differences enough to make the common hypotheses quite untenable. Matt. and Mark agree nearly verbatim, Matt. however writing throughout in the singular (ὁ σπαρεὶς κ.τ.λ.). Mark has some additions, e. g. **ὁ σπείρων τὸν λόγον σπ.**, ver. 14,—after ἡ ἀπ. τοῦ πλ., ver. 19, **καὶ αἱ π. τὰ λ. ἐπιθ.** :—and some variations, e. g. **σατανᾶς** for Matt.'s ὁ πονηρός,

b ver. 5. c ‖ Mt. reff. d ‖. Job xix. 28. e ‖ Mt. 2 Cor. iv. 18. Heb. xi. 25 only †. f ‖ Mt. reff. g = Matt. xi. 6 reff. h ver. 7. i ‖ Mt. reff. k = ch. vii. 15, 18 ‖ Mt., 19. l ‖ ver. 7. Luke viii. 42 only †. m ‖ Mt. reff. n Matt. vii. 15 reff. o Acts xv. 4. xvi. 21. xxii. 18. 1 Tim. v. 19. Heb. xii. 6 (from Prov. iii. 12) only. Exod. xxiii. 1. p ‖ Mt. reff. q ver. 8. r Matt. vii. 16 reff. xxvi. 22. s Matt. v. 15 reff.

ABCDE FGHKL MSUV ΔΠℵ 1. 33. 69

ὁμοίως οἱ ἐπὶ τὰ [b] πετρώδη σπειρόμενοι, οἳ ὅταν ἀκούσωσιν τὸν λόγον, εὐθὺς [c] μετὰ χαρᾶς λαμβάνουσιν αὐτόν,
17 καὶ οὐκ ἔχουσιν [d] ῥίζαν ἐν ἑαυτοῖς, ἀλλὰ [e] πρόσκαιροί
εἰσιν, εἶτα γενομένης θλίψεως ἢ [f] διωγμοῦ διὰ τὸν λόγον
εὐθὺς [g] σκανδαλίζονται. 18 καὶ ἄλλοι εἰσὶν οἱ εἰς τὰς
[h] ἀκάνθας σπειρόμενοι· οὗτοί εἰσιν οἱ τὸν λόγον ἀκούσαντες, 19 καὶ αἱ [i] μέριμναι τοῦ [i] αἰῶνος καὶ ἡ [i] ἀπάτη τοῦ
πλούτου καὶ αἱ περὶ τὰ λοιπὰ ἐπιθυμίαι [k] εἰσπορευόμεναι
[l] συνπνίγουσιν τὸν λόγον, καὶ [m] ἄκαρπος γίνεται. 20 καὶ
ἐκεῖνοί εἰσιν οἱ ἐπὶ τὴν γῆν τὴν καλὴν σπαρέντες, [n] οἵτινες
ἀκούουσιν τὸν λόγον καὶ [o] παραδέχονται, καὶ [p] καρποφοροῦσιν [q] ἓν τριάκοντα καὶ [q] ἓν ἑξήκοντα καὶ [q] ἓν ἑκατόν.
21 καὶ ἔλεγεν αὐτοῖς ὅτι [r] μήτι ἔρχεται ὁ [s] λύχνος ἵνα

16. om *ομοιως* D **1**. 13. 28. 69. 118-31. 209 lat-*a b c* ff_2 g_1 *i* [*q*] Syr arm Orig: *ομ.* bef *εισιν* CLΔℵ 33 copt(appy) æth. om 2nd *οι* B^1. rec *ευθεως*, with A rel Orig: om D 259 lat-*c* ff_2 *i* [*q*] copt-wilk: txt BCLΔℵ 33.

17. for *η*, *και* D vulg lat-*c f* $ff_{1.2}$ g_1 *l* [*i q*]. rec *ευθεως*, with AD rel Orig: txt BC LΔℵ 33. *σκανδαλισθησονται* D.

18. rec (for *αλλοι*) *ουτοι* (*from* ‖ *Luke*), with AC^2 rel lat-*f* syrr goth æth: om *α. ει.* **1**. 69 arm: txt BC^{1}DLΔℵ latt copt. for *εις*, *επι* CΔℵ [copt]. om *ουτοι εισιν* (*confusion from reading ουτοι εισιν at beg of ver*) AC^2 rel lat-*f* [*q*] æth Thl: ins BC^{1}DLΔℵ **1**. 69 latt Syr copt arm. rec *ακουοντες* (*from* ‖), with A rel latt syr goth æth arm: txt BCDLΔℵ 69 Syr copt.—*ακ.* bef *τον λογον* ℵ copt.

19. for *αιω.*, *βιου* D Scr's c goth, *victus* D-lat, *-ti* lat-*c*, *vitæ* lat-*b*. rec aft *αιων.* ins *τουτου* (*gloss*), with A rel lat-*f* syrr copt goth æth: om BCDLΔℵ **1** Scr's c latt arm. *κ. απαται του κοσμου* D arm. aft *πλουτου* ins *συνπνιγει τον λογον* ℵ^1(omg *συνπν. τ. λογ.* below: ℵ-corr^1 reads both). om *κ. αι π. τα λ. επιθ.* D **1** lat-*a b c* ff_2 *i* [*q*] arm. for *περι*, *παρα* ℵ^1(txt ℵ^{3a}). *ακαρποι γινονται* D 124 lat-*b c e* ff_2 g_1 *i* [*q*] copt-ms(appy).

20. rec (for *εκεινοι*) *ουτοι* (*from* ‖ *Luke*), with AD rel latt syr copt goth æth arm Orig$_1$: txt BCLΔℵ Syr. *τ. καλην γην* Cℵ (124?): om *την καλην* 237. om 2nd *εν* B C^1(appy) Scr's w: om 3rd *εν* B 406 Scr's d.—*εν* (thrice) ADΔℵ, (twice) C: *ἐν* (thrice) E rel syrr, (1st time) L: *ἕν* (thrice) S(e sil) latt copt goth (æth) arm:—see ver. 8 (*I cannot consent with Tischdf to edit εἰs in ver 8 and ἐν here. The mistake was so obvious, that the sense should be mainly regarded: and all the more because* ‖ *Luke has καρποφοροῦσιν ἐν.* No ms here reads *εις*).

21. rec om *οτι* (*as superfl*), with ACDℵ rel: ins BL. rec *ο λυχ.* bef *ερχ.*, with A rel goth arm: txt BC(D)LΔℵ **1**. 33 ev-y vulg lat-(*b c e* ff_2 g_1 *i*) *l* syrr copt.—for *ερχ.*, *απτεται* D lat-*c e* (*f*) ff_2 g_1 *i* copt-wilk æth.

and Luke's ὁ διάβ. Such matters are *not trifling*, because they shew the *gradual deflection of verbal expression* in different versions of the *same report*,—nor is the *general agreement* of Luke's, which seems to be from a different hearer. **16. ὁμοίως**] after the same analogy:—carrying on a like principle of interpretation. **20.**] Notice the concluding words of the interpretation exactly reproducing those of the parable, ver. 8, as characteristic. It is remarkable that the same is found in Matt., but in another form and order: one taking the climax, the other the anticlimax. In Luke, the two are varied. **21—25.**] Luke viii. 16—18; and for ver. 25, Matt. xiii. 12. The rest is mostly contained in other parts of Matt. (v. 15; x. 26; vii. 2), where see notes. Here it is spoken with reference to teaching by parables:—that they might take care to gain from them all the instruction which they were capable of giving:—not hiding them under a blunted understanding, nor, when they did understand them, neglecting the teaching of them to others.

21.] **ἔρχεσθαι** is also used in the classics of things without life: cf. Hom. Il. τ. 191, ὄφρα κε δῶρα | ἐκ κλισίης ἔλθωσι . . . and see Rost and Palm, Lex.

ὑπὸ [t] τὸν [u] μόδιον τεθῇ ἢ ὑπὸ [t] τὴν [v] κλίνην, οὐχ ἵνα ἐπὶ
τὴν [w] λυχνίαν τεθῇ; 22 οὐ γάρ ἐστίν [τι] κρυπτὸν ἐὰν μὴ
[ἵνα] φανερωθῇ· οὐδὲ ἐγένετο [x] ἀπόκρυφον, ἀλλ' ἵνα ἔλθῃ
εἰς φανερόν. 23 εἴτις ἔχει [y] ὦτα [y] ἀκούειν, ἀκουέτω.
Θ_b iv. 24 (appy)... 24 καὶ ἔλεγεν αὐτοῖς [z] Βλέπετε τί ἀκούετε. ἐν ᾧ μέτρῳ
[a] μετρεῖτε [a] μετρηθήσεται ὑμῖν, καὶ [b] προστεθήσεται ὑμῖν.
25 ὃς γὰρ ἔχει δοθήσεται αὐτῷ, καὶ ὃς οὐκ ἔχει, καὶ ὃ
ἔχει [c] ἀρθήσεται ἀπ' αὐτοῦ. 26 Καὶ ἔλεγεν Οὕτως ἐστὶν
ἡ βασιλεία τοῦ θεοῦ ὡς ἄνθρωπος [d] βάλῃ τὸν [e] σπόρον

t — Matt. ix. 1. x. 36. xiii. 3 al. fr.
u Matt. v. 15. Luke xi. 33 only †.
v ch. vii. 4 reff.
w Matt. v. 15 reff.
x ‖ L. Col. ii. 3 only. Isa. iv. 6. Dan. ii. 22 Theod.
y ver. 9.
z Eph. v. 15. Col. ii. 8. Heb. iii. 12 al.
a Matt. vii. 2 reff.
b = Matt. vi. 33. Luke xii. 31. xvii. 5. Tobit v. 15.
c = ver. 15.
d Luke xiii. 19 reff.
e Luke viii. 5, 11. 2 Cor. ix. 10 only. Deut. xi. 10.

τεθηναι (1st time, omg previous ινα) ℵ[1](txt ℵ[3a]). ins και bef ουχι ινα D. for επι, υπο B[1]ℵ 33. 69: txt A [B[2·3](Tischdf)] CD rel. rec λ. επιτεθη (*corrn as more appropr: so also in* ‖ *Luke*), with AK rel: txt BCDLΔℵ 33. 69.

22. om τι (*aft* ‖ *Luke*) BDHKMUΠ[1] 1. 69 lat-*b e ff₂ g₂ i* [*q*] copt(appy) æth: ins ACℵ rel vulg lat-*c f ff₁ g₁* syrr[?] goth arm. rec ο εαν μη, with E rel; ος αν μη U: εαν μη ινα B(sic, not as Bch) Δℵ: αλλ ινα D lat-*b ff₂ i* [*q*]: *quod non* vulg lat-*c f* goth: ει μη ινα 1. 69: εαν μη ACKLΠ 33. rec εις φανερον bef ελθη (*from* ‖ *Luke*), with A rel vulg lat-*b c* &c syr arm: φανερωθη (*gloss*) B Syr æth: txt CDLΔℵ ev-y copt.

24. for τι, τα D-gr. om και προστ. υμιν DG ev-y gat lat-*b e g₁*. rec at end adds τοις ακουουσιν, with AGΘ_b rel [lat-*q*] syrr; *credentibus* lat-*f* goth: om BCDLΔℵ latt copt æth arm. (*The whole passage is in considerable uncertainty:* τοις ακουουσιν *appears to have been a gloss insd to explain the connexion of the saying with* βλ. τι ακουετε; *but on the other hand* προστεθησεται, *omd here in* D al, *appears as a gloss on* δοθησεται *below. It seems as if the origl txt did not contain the clause* κ. προστ. υμιν. *At all events,* τοις ακουουσιν *cannot stand.*)

25. rec ins αν bef εχ. (*from* ‖ *Luke*), with ADΘ_b rel; εαν M: om BCLΔℵ (69).—rec εχη, with A rel: txt BCDE[1]FHKLΔΘ_bℵ 69. for δοθ., προστεθησεται D.

26. aft ελεγεν ins οτι C[1](appy). rec aft ως ins εαν, with AΘ_b rel [latt goth]; αν C: οταν 1. 53. 237-59: om B D-gr LΔℵ 33. 69 tol lat-*e* copt. το σπορον C[1].—σπ. βαλη D.

22.] **ἀλλά** here is almost equivalent to *εἰ μή*. Hartung, Partikel. ii. 43, cites Eur. Hippol. 633, *ῥᾷστον δ' ὅτῳ τὸ μηδὲν ἀλλ' ἀνωφελὴς | εὐηθίᾳ κατ' οἶκον ἵδρυται γυνή· | σοφὴν δὲ μισῶ.* We may add Xen. Mem. iii. 13. 6, *ἤρετο αὐτόν, εἰ καὶ φορτίον ἔφερε; μὰ Δί' οὐκ ἔγωγ', ἔφη, ἀλλὰ τὸ ἱμάτιον.* See Klotz, Devar. p. 7.

24.] **προστ. ὑμῖν** (see var. readd.), more shall be added, i. e. more *knowledge*: so Euthym.: *ἐν ᾧ μέτρῳ μετρεῖτε τὴν προσοχήν, ἐν τῷ αὐτῷ μετρηθήσεται ὑμῖν ἡ γνῶσις, τουτέστιν, ὅσην εἰσφέρετε προσοχήν, τοσαύτη παρασχεθήσεται ὑμῖν γνῶσις, καὶ οὐ μόνον ἐν τῷ αὐτῷ μέτρῳ, ἀλλὰ καὶ πλέον. ὃς ἂν ἔχῃ προσοχήν, δωθήσεται αὐτῷ γνῶσις, κ. ὃς οὐκ ἔχει, καὶ ὃ ἔχει σπέρμα γνώσεως ἀρθήσεται ἀπ' αὐτοῦ. καθάπερ γὰρ ἡ σπουδὴ αὔξει τὸ τοιοῦτον, οὕτω καὶ ἡ ῥαθυμία διαφθείρει. ἐν τῷ κατὰ Ματθαῖον δὲ τρόπον ἕτερον ἐῤῥήθησαν ταῦτα, καὶ κατ' ἄλλην ἔννοιαν.*

26—29.] PARABLE OF THE SEED GROWING WE KNOW NOT HOW. *Peculiar to Mark.* By Commentators of the Straussian school it is strangely supposed to be the same as the parable of the tares, *with the tares left out.* If so, a wonderful and most instructive parable has arisen out of the fragments of the other, in which the idea is *a totally different one.* It is, the *growth* of the once-deposited seed by the combination of its own development with the genial power of the earth, all of course under the creative hand of God,—but independent of human care and anxiety during this time of growth. **26.]** Observe **ἔλεγεν**, without *αὐτοῖς*—implying that He is now proceeding with his teaching to the *people*: cf. ver. 33. **ἄνθρωπος]** Some difficulty has been felt about the interpretation of this *man*, as to whether it is *Christ* or *his ministers.* The former certainly seems to be excluded by the **καθεύδῃ**, and **ὡς οὐκ οἶδεν αὐτός**, ver. 27; and perhaps the latter by **ἀποστ. τὸ δρ.**, ver. 29. But I believe the parable to be one taken simply from human things,—the sower being quite in the background, and the whole stress being on the SEED—its power and its development. The *man* then is just

ἐπὶ τῆς γῆς, 27 καὶ καθεύδῃ καὶ ἐγείρηται [f] νύκτα καὶ
[f] ἡμέραν, καὶ ὁ [e] σπόρος [g] βλαστᾷ καὶ [h] μηκύνηται ὡς οὐκ ...iv. 27 (appy) Θ_b
οἶδεν αὐτός. 28 [i] αὐτομάτη ἡ γῆ [j] καρποφορεῖ πρῶτον
[k] χόρτον εἶτα [l] στάχυν, εἶτα πλήρης σῖτος ἐν τῷ [l] στάχυϊ.
29 ὅταν δὲ [m] παραδοῖ ὁ καρπός, εὐθὺς [n] ἀποστέλλει τὸ Θ_b iv. 29 (appy)...
[o] δρέπανον, ὅτι [p] παρέστηκεν ὁ [q] θερισμός. 30 Καὶ ἔλεγεν ABCDE FGHKL MSUV
Πῶς [r] ὁμοιώσωμεν τὴν βασιλείαν τοῦ θεοῦ; ἢ ἐν τίνι ΔΘ$_b$Πℵ 1. 33. 69

f acc., Luke ii. 37. Acts xxvi. 7. 2 Thess. iii. 8 only. Gen. viii. 22. gen., ch. v. 5 reff. g (-άω, here only.) = Matt. xiii. 26. Heb. ix. 4 (James v. 18 trans.) only. 2 Kings xxiii. 5 al. h here only. Isa. vi. 12 Ald. xliv. 14. Ezek. xii. 25, 28 only. i Acts xii. 10 only. Lev. xxv. 5, 11. 4 Kings xix. 29. Wisd. xvii. 6 only. j ver. 20. k = Matt. xiii. 26. Jer. ix. 22. l ch. ii. 23 ‖ only. Gen. xli. 5—7. m = here only. (1 Pet. ii. 23.) Isa. xlvii. 3. -δοῖ, ch. xiv. 10, 11. see 1 Cor. xv. 24. n = here only. (Joel iii. 13.) o here only, exc. Rev. xiv. 14—19. Deut. xvi. 9. Joel l. c. p = here only. Joel l. c. see Exod. ix. 31. q Matt. xiii. 30 bis, 39. John iv. 35 bis, al. Gen. viii. 22. r Matt. vii. 24, 26. xiii. 24 al. Cant. i. 9.

27. εγειρεται EFGHLMℵ 69: εγερθη D: txt ABCΘ_b rel. rec **βλαστανη**, with AC[2]Θ_bℵ rel (-νει EFH 33): txt BC[1]DLΔ. μηκυνεται (*corrn, fancying that* βλαστᾷ *was* indic) DH: txt A B(Tischdf [N. T. Vat.]) ℵ rel.

28. rec aft αυτομ. ins γαρ, with Δ rel latt (Syr) syr-ms copt-ms goth: ins οτι bef αυτομ. D arm: om ABCLℵ syr copt æth Orig. aft πρωτον ins μεν Δ. ειτεν B[1](twice) [L(-τε . . -τεν) Δ(twice)] ℵ(2nd). σταχυας D-gr: om ειτα σταχυν ℵ[1](ins ℵ[3a]). rec πληρη σιτον (*gramml corrn, to put it in apposn with the precedg accusatives*), with AC[2]ℵ rel: πληρης σιτον C[1](appy): πληρες σιτος B: (latt uncertain:) πληρης ο σιτος D: txt (BC[1]D) copt.

29. και οταν D vulg lat-*a c f ff*$_1$ *g*$_{1.2}$. rec παραδω (*corrn to more usual form*), with ACΘ_bℵ[3a] rel: txt BDΔℵ[1]. rec ευθεως, with ADΘ_b rel: txt BCLℵ.

30. aft ελεγεν ins αυτοις ℵ-corr[1] 69. rec (for πως) τινι (*from* ‖ *Luke*), with AD rel vulg lat-*a*(appy) *c f ff*$_2$ *i* syrr copt goth æth arm Orig: txt BCLΔℵ 33. 69 ev-y lat-*b e* syr-mg. ομοιωσομεν C 1 latt [Orig-ms]: ομοιωσω (‖ *Luke*) K 69 Thl [arm-ms]. rec (for τινι) ποια, with AC[2]DΘ_b rel Syr syr-txt goth arm: txt B

the *farmer* or husbandman, hardly admitting an *interpretation*, but necessary to the machinery of the parable. Observe, that in this case it is not τὸν σπόρον **αὐτοῦ** as in Luke viii. 5,—and the agent is only hinted at in the most general way, e. g. ἀποστ. τ. δρέπ., without a nom. case expressed. If a meaning must be assigned, the best is "human agency" in general. (It will be seen from this note, that I regard the exposition given in my first edition as a mistaken one.) **βάλῃ, shall have cast**—past tense, whereas **καθεύδῃ** and **ἐγ.** are *present.* The construction seems to be, **The Kingdom of God is thus, that a man shall have cast**, i. e. *shall be as though he have cast:* but it is not easy, and, as far as I know, unexampled. It looks like a combination of ὡς ἄνθρ. βαλών, and ὡς ἐὰν ἄνθρ. βάλῃ. **27. καθ. κ. ἐγ.**] i. e. *employs himself otherwise—goes about his ordinary occupations.* The seed sown in the heart is in its growth dependent on other causes than mere human anxiety and watchfulness:—on a mysterious power implanted by God in the seed and the soil combined, the working of which is hidden from human eye. Beware of the mistake of Erasmus, who takes ὁ σπόρος as the subject of all the verbs in this verse. **28.**] No trouble of ours can accelerate the growth, or shorten the stages through which each seed must pass. It is the mistake of modern Methodism, for instance, to be always working at the seed, *taking it up to see whether it is growing,* instead of leaving it to God's own good time, and meanwhile diligently doing God's work elsewhere: see Stier, iii. p. 12. Wesley, to favour his system, strangely explains **καθεύδῃ καὶ ἐγ. νύκτ. κ. ἡμ.** *exactly contrary* to the meaning of the parable—"that is, has it continually in his thoughts." **εἶτα πλήρης σῖτος**] **then** (there is) **full corn in the ear**: if as D, **then the corn** (is) **full in the ear.** **29. παραδοῖ**] **offers itself**: see reff. and Winer, Gr. Gr. § 38. 1 [also Moulton's edn. p. 738, note 1]. **ἀποστέλλει**] **he puts in**—i. e. the husbandman, see above. See Joel iii. 13, to which this verse is a reference:—also Rev. xiv. 14, 15, and 1 Pet. i. 23—25.

30—34.] Parable of the grain of mustard seed. Matt. xiii. 31—35. Luke xiii. 18, 19. **30.**] This Rabbinical method of questioning before beginning a discourse is also found in Luke, ver. 18,—without however the condescending *plural,* which embraces the disciples, in their work of preaching and teaching,—and indeed gives all teachers an example, to what they may liken the Kingdom of God.

αὐτὴν παραβολῇ [s] θῶμεν; 31 ὡς [t] κόκκον [t] σινάπεως, ὃς
ὅταν σπαρῇ ἐπὶ τῆς γῆς, [u] μικρότερον ὂν πάντων τῶν
σπερμάτων τῶν ἐπὶ τῆς γῆς· 32 καὶ ὅταν σπαρῇ, [v] ἀναβαίνει καὶ γίνεται μείζων πάντων τῶν [w] λαχάνων, καὶ
[x] ποιεῖ [y] κλάδους μεγάλους, ὥστε δύνασθαι ὑπὸ τὴν [z] σκιὰν
αὐτοῦ τὰ [ab] πετεινὰ τοῦ [ab] οὐρανοῦ [bc] κατασκηνοῦν. 33 Καὶ
τοιαύταις παραβολαῖς πολλαῖς [d] ἐλάλει αὐτοῖς τὸν [d] λόγον
[e] καθὼς ἠδύναντο [f] ἀκούειν· 34 χωρὶς δὲ παραβολῆς οὐκ
ἐλάλει αὐτοῖς· [g] κατ' [g] ἰδίαν δὲ τοῖς ἰδίοις μαθηταῖς [h] ἐπ-
έλυεν πάντα.
...iv. 35 (appy) Θ_b. 35 Καὶ λέγει αὐτοῖς ἐν ἐκείνῃ τῇ ἡμέρᾳ [i] ὀψίας [i] γενο-

s = here only. t ‖ Mt. reff. u Matt. xi. 11 reff. v ver. 7. w ‖ Mt. Luke xi. 42. Rom. xiv. 2 only. Gen. ix. 3. x = Matt. iii. 8 reff. y ‖ Mt. reff. z Matt. iv. 16, from Isa. ix. 2. Luke i. 79. Acts v. 15. Col. ii. 17. Heb. viii. 5. x. 1 only. Ps. lxxix. 10. a Matt. vi. 26 reff. b Ps. ciii. 12. (Dan. iv. 18.) c Acts ii. 26 only. Job xviii. 15. d = ch. ii. 2 reff. e Acts ii. 4. xi. 29. Num. xxvi. 54. f = 1 Cor. xiv. 2. Gen. xi. 7. xlii. 23. g Matt. xiv. 13 reff. h = here (Acts xix. 39) only. Gen. xli. 12 F (not A. B def.) only. Hos. iii. 4 Theodot. (-λυσις, 2 Pet. i. 20.) i ch. i. 32 ‖ al. Mt. Mk. only, exc. John vi. 16 (xx. 19) †. Judith xiii. 1 only.

C[1](appy) LΔא 1. 69 ev-y latt syr-mg copt æth Orig. rec παραβολη παραβαλωμεν αυτην, with AC[2]DΘ_b rel (latt) Syr (syr-txt goth) arm: txt B C[1](appy) LΔא lat-*b e* syr-mg(also παραθωμεν) copt Orig_1; παρ. θωμεν αυ. παραβαλομεν αυτην 69. (*It is here somewhat difficult to decide between the two, both* ἅπαξ λεγόμενα, *π. παραβαλωμεν,* and *π. θωμεν. But the latter seems to merit the preference. For* (1) *it is the* less obvious exprn, *and it is hardly possible that it should have been substd for the other:* (2) *it has* the harsher order of words on its side, *making the other appear as if it came in with the more elegant arrangement:* (3) *it has* the most ancient testimony: (4) *we have already a trace of the love of such corrns as* παραβολη παραβαλωμεν, in αμφιβαλλοντας αμφιβληστρον, also in A &c, in ch i. 16.)

31. for ως, ομοια εστιν D (lat-*c*) copt. rec κοκκω (*the dat has almost certainly come from ‖ Matt Luke. At all events* D *is no evidence here, as it takes ‖ Matt Luke verbatim*), with BDΠ[1]א: κοκως Δ[but *s* marked for erasure]: txt ACLΘ_b rel Hesych Thl. for ος οταν, ο οτι αν D[1](txt D[S]): om ος (insg ο bef μικρ.) א[1](txt א[3]). την γην DL. rec μικροτερος (*gramml corrn to suit* ος), with ACD[3]Θ_b rel: txt BD[1]LM Δ[μακρ. Δ-gr] א 33. (homœotel in 69.) rec μ. παντων τ. σπ. εστ. τ. ε. τ. γ., with Θ_b rel; so, omg τ. ε. τ. γ., C: μ. εστιν π. τ. σπ. α εισιν ε. τ. γ. D(ins μεν aft μ. D[3], but erased) vulg lat-*a c f* ff_2 g_1 *l*; μ. εστιν π. τ. σπ. τ. ε. τ. γ. M-marg: μ. π. τ. σπ. των επ. τ. γ. εστιν A: (*all more or less from ‖ Matt, on account of the difficult constr, as is also shewn by the various posns of* εστιν: ον *being omd by homœotel:*) txt B L(ων, *corrn*) Δא (*minor cum sit* lat-*e*).

32. om κ. οτ. σπ. αναβ. D lat-(*b e*) *i*. rec π. των λ. bef μειζ., with A rel goth: txt BCDL M-marg Δא 1. 33 latt syrr [copt] æth arm. (Θ_b?) μειζον (*corrn: see also ‖ Matt*) ABCELVא 33. (Θ_b?) κατασκηνοιν B.

33. om πολλαις (*homœotel*) LΔ 1. 33 lat-*b c e* Syr copt-wilk æth: ins bef παρ. D vulg lat-ff_2 g_1 [*i q*] *l* goth: txt ABC[2]Θ_bא rel syr [arm]. (C[1] is lost.) om αυτοις D lat-ff_2 g_1 *i*. εδυναντο ADΘ_b rel: txt BCUΔא 33 (FS 1, e sil).

34. και χωρις (‖ *Matt*) B Syr copt. rec for ιδ. μαθ., μαθηταις αυτου (*more usual exprn*), with ADΘ_b rel vulg lat-*b c e f*: txt BCLΔא. απελυεν Θ_b Scr's w. for παντα, αυτας D lat-*e* ff_2 *i* [*q*].

θῶμεν, as ἐτίθει, of Hephæstus, Il. σ. 541, &c.,—'sollers nunc hominem ponere, nunc deum,' Hor. Od. iv. 8. 8,—see also de Art. Poet. 34. **31.**] The *repetition of expressions verbatim* in discourses is peculiar to Mark: so **ἐπὶ τῆς γῆς** here, and **οὐ δύν. σταθῆναι** ch. iii. 24, 25, 26: and see a very solemn instance, ch. ix. 44—48. **32.**] **καὶ ποιεῖ κλ. μεγ.** is also peculiar. See notes on Matt. **33. καθὼς ἠδ. ἀκ.] according to their capacity of receiving**:—see note on Matt. xiii. 12. **34. κατ' ἰδίαν δὲ . . .**] We have *three* such instances—the *sower*, the *tares*, Matt. xiii. 36 ff., and the *saying concerning defilement*, Matt. xv. 15 ff. To these we may add the *two parables in John*,—ch. x. 1—18, which however was *publicly* explained,—and ch. xv. 1—12;—and perhaps Luke xvi. 9; xviii. 6—8.

35—41.] THE STILLING OF THE STORM. Matt. viii. 18, 23—27. Luke viii. 22—25. Mark's words bind this occurrence by a precise date to the preceding. It took

j — ‖ L. Luke ii. 15 al. 3 Kings xviii. 5.
k Matt. viii. 18 reff.
l = Matt. xiii. 36 al. Ps. civ. 20.
m Matt. xvii. 1 al. Num. xxii. 41.
n John vi. 51 reff.
o ‖ L. 2 Pet. ii. 17 only. Jer. xxxii. (xxv.) 32.
p ‖ Mt. reff.
q = here only. (cf. παραδοῖ, ver. 29.) see ch. xiv. 72.
r ch. xv. 36. Luke xiv. 23. xv. 16. John ii. 7 al. Gen. xlv. 17.
s Acts xxvii. 29, 41 only +.
t ver. 21 reff.
u here only. Ezek. xiii. 18, 20. Esdr. iii. 8 only.

ABCDE FGHKL MSUV ΔΠℵ 1. 33. 69

μένης [j] Διέλθωμεν εἰς [k] τὸ [k] πέραν. 36 καὶ [l] ἀφέντες τὸν
ὄχλον [m] παραλαμβάνουσιν αὐτὸν ὡς ἦν ἐν τῳ πλοίῳ,
[n] καὶ ἄλλα [[n] δὲ] πλοῖα ἦν μετ᾽ αὐτοῦ. 37 καὶ γίνεται
[o] λαῖλαψ μεγάλη ἀνέμου, καὶ τὰ [p] κύματα [q] ἐπέβαλλεν εἰς
τὸ πλοῖον, ὥςτε ἤδη [r] γεμίζεσθαι τὸ πλοῖον. 38 καὶ ἦν
αὐτὸς ἐν τῇ [s] πρύμνῃ ἐπὶ [t] τὸ [u] προσκεφάλαιον καθεύδων.
καὶ ἐγείρουσιν αὐτὸν καὶ λέγουσιν αὐτῷ Διδάσκαλε, οὐ
[v] μέλει σοι ὅτι ἀπολλύμεθα ; 39 καὶ [w] διεγερθεὶς [x] ἐπετίμησεν τῷ ἀνέμῳ καὶ εἶπεν τῇ θαλάσσῃ Σιώπα, [y] πεφίμωσο.
καὶ [z] ἐκόπασεν ὁ ἄνεμος, καὶ ἐγένετο [a] γαλήνη μεγάλη.
40 καὶ εἶπεν αὐτοῖς Τί [b] δειλοί ἐστε οὕτως ; [c] πῶς οὐκ
[d] ἔχετε [d] πίστιν ; 41 καὶ [e] ἐφοβήθησαν φόβον μέγαν, καὶ
ἔλεγον πρὸς ἀλλήλους Τίς ἄρα οὗτός ἐστιν, ὅτι καὶ ὁ
ἄνεμος καὶ ἡ θάλασσα ὑπακούει αὐτῷ ;

v w. ὅτι, Luke x. 40 only. (Matt. xxii. 16. Acts xviii. 17. 1 Cor. vii. 21. Job xxii. 3. Tobit x. 5 [not ℵ].) w (ver. 38. Matt. i. 24 v. r.) Luke viii. 24. John vi. 18. 2 Pet. i. 18. iii. 1 only +. 2 Macc. vii. 21. xv. 10 only. x ‖. Ps. cv. 9. y Matt. xxii. 12 reff. z ch. vi. 51 ‖ Mt. only. Gen. viii. 1. Jon. i. 11, 12. Num. xvi. 48. a ‖ only +. Ps. cvi. 29 Symm. b ‖ Mt. Rev. xxi. 18 only. Judg. vii. 3. ix. 4 B. (-λια, 2 Tim. i. 7. -λιᾶν, John xiv. 27.) c = Matt. xvi. 11. Luke xii. 56. d Matt. xxi. 12 reff. e Luke ii. 9. Jon. i. 10. (iv. 1.) constr., Matt. ii. 10 reff.

36. *κ. αφιουσι τ. οχλ. και* D 69 lat-*c* [&c] Syr. for *τ. οχλ.*, *αυτον* A. for *αλλα* to *αυτου*, *τα αλλα τα οντα μετ αυτου πλοια* 1 (arm) : *αλλα δε πλοια πολλα* (*αλλαι δε πλοιαι πολλαι* D[1]) *ησαν μετ αυτου* D lat-*ff*$_2$. om *δε* (*not understood*) BC[1]LΔℵ vulg lat-*b c f ff*$_{1.2}$ *g*$_{1.2}$ *i* Syr copt arm. rec **πλοιαρια** (*see John* vi. 23), with L rel : txt ABCDKMΔΠℵ 1. 33. 69. om *ην* L 1 copt-ms-wilk æth arm : *ησαν* DΔℵ.
37. *εγενετο* D vulg lat-*b c* [&c syrr copt goth] arm. *μεγαλου* C 252[2]-8 Scr's c [lat-*e*] : *μεγας* ℵ[1](txt ℵ[3a]). rec *αν.* bef *μεγ.* (*transpn : λ. αν. being in* ‖ *Luke*), with A(C) rel lat-(*e*) *f* syr goth : txt BDLΔℵ([1])[3a] 1. 69 vulg lat-*b c* [&c] Syr æth arm. rec *τα δε* (*to avoid repetn*), with A rel syr arm : txt BCDLΔℵ 1. 69 latt Syr copt goth æth. *επεβαλεν* EFLMΠ[1]ℵ : *εβαλεν* D. rec *αυτο ηδη γεμ.* (*corrn for elegance*), with A rel syrr goth arm : om *ηδη* vulg lat-*b c* &c æth : for *γεμ.*, *βυθιζεσθαι* G 1. 33 ev-y : txt BCDLΔ ℵ-corr[1](*and apparently the more ancient* MS *from which* ℵ*'s text sprung : for* ℵ[1] *omits from πλοιον to πλοιον*) syr-mg copt æth.
38. *αυτος* bef *ην* (*corrn to usual order*) BCLΔℵ : txt ADΠ rel. rec (for *εν*) *επι*, with Π rel : txt ABCDLΔℵ 1. 69 latt. om *το* D 1.—*προσκεφαλαιου* D 131. rec **διεγειρουσιν** (*from* ‖ *Luke*), with AB[2]C[2] rel : *διεγειραντες* (omg 3rd *και*) D 28. 2-pe lat-*b c f ff*$_2$ *i* [*q*] : *εγειραντες* (omg *κ.*) 13. 69. 124. 346 : txt B[1] C[1](appy) ΔΠ[1]ℵ.
39. *εγερθεις* D 69. *κ. τη θαλ. κ. ειπεν* D 1 lat-*b* (*c*) *e ff*$_2$ *i* arm. for *πεφ.*, *και φιμωθητι* D am copt.
40. for *ειπεν*, *λεγει* ℵ[3a], *ait* latt ; *ελεγεν* L. for *ουτως πως ουκ*, *ουπω* BDLΔℵ latt copt æth : *ουτως* bef *δειλ.* 1. 69 arm (*τι δ. εστε ; being read as in* ‖ *Matt, the corrn, or mistake, was obvious, and the varns followed*) : txt AC rel.
41. *εστιν* bef *ουτος* D 251 vulg lat-*c* [&c] arm. *οι ανεμοι* DEℵ[3a](but txt restored) 1. 33 lat-*b c ff*$_2$ *g*$_1$ *i* [*q*] Syr copt æth [Vict$_1$].—transp *οι αν.* and *η θ.* D lat-*a b* (*c*) *ff*$_2$. rec **υπακουουσιν** *αυτω* (*from* ‖ *Luke*), with A rel : *υπακουουσιν* (only) D-gr : *αυτω υπακουει* (*order as in* ‖ *Matt*) CΔℵ[1] 1. 69 Vict : txt BLℵ[3a.b].

place *in the evening of the day on which the parables were delivered :* and our account is so rich in additional particulars, as to take the highest rank among the three as to *precision*. **36.**] **ὡς ἦν**—without any preparation—**as he was,** E.V. Cf. Jos. B. J. i. 17. 7, *αὐτὸς ὡς ἦν ἔτι θερμὸς ἐκ τῶν ὅπλων λουσόμενος ᾔει στρατιωτικώτερον.* **ἄλ. δὲ πλ.**] These were probably some of the multitudes following, who seem to have been separated from them in the gale. **καὶ . . δέ, moreover.** See Hartung, Partikell. i. 182. **37.**] **λαῖλ. ἀν.** is also in Luke, whose account is in the main so differently worded. **ἐπέβαλλεν**] not *ὁ λαῖλαψ ἐπέβαλλεν τὰ κύμ.*—but **τὰ κ. ἐπέβαλλεν,** —intransitive : see reff. **38. τὸ προσκ.**] the cushion or seat at the stern, used by our Lord as a pillow. Pollux,

V. 1 Καὶ ἦλθον εἰς [f] τὸ [f] πέραν τῆς θαλάσσης εις τὴν
χώραν τῶν Γεργεσηνῶν. 2 καὶ ἐξελθόντι [g] αὐτῷ ἐκ τοῦ
πλοίου εὐθὺς [h] ἀπήντησεν [g] αὐτῷ ἐκ τῶν [i] μνημείων ἄνθρωπος [k] ἐν [kl] πνεύματι [kl] ἀκαθάρτῳ, 3 ὃς τὴν [m] κατοίκη-
σιν εἶχεν ἐν τοῖς [n] μνήμασιν, καὶ οὐδὲ [o] ἁλύσει οὐκέτι
οὐδεὶς ἐδυνατο αὐτὸν δῆσαι, 4 διὰ τὸ αὐτὸν πολλάκις
[p] πέδαις καὶ [o] ἁλύσεσιν δεδέσθαι καὶ [q] διεσπᾶσθαι ὑπ᾽ αὐτοῦ
τὰς [o] ἁλύσεις καὶ τὰς [p] πέδας [r] συντετρίφθαι, καὶ οὐδεὶς
[s] ἴσχυεν αὐτὸν [t] δαμάσαι, 5 καὶ [u] διὰ παντὸς [v] νυκτὸς καὶ

f ch. iv. 35 al. Matt. viii. 18 reff.
g Matt. viii. 1 reff.
h Matt. xxviii. 9 reff.
i || Mt. Matt. xxvii. 52, 53 al. Gen. xxiii. 6, 9.
k = ch. i. 23 only. see Matt. xii. 27, 28.
l Matt. x. 1 reff.
m here only. Gen. x. 30 al. (-κία, Acts xvii. 26.)
n here (bis) || L. Luke xxiii. 53. xxiv. 1. Acts ii. 29. vii. 16. Rev. xi. 9 only. Isa. lxv. 4.
o here (3ce) || L. Acts xii. 6, 7. xxi. 33. xxviii. 20. Eph. vi. 20. 2 Tim. i. 16. Rev. xx. 1 only. 2 Chron. iii. 16 compl. Wisd. xvii. 17 only.
p here (bis) || L. only. Ps. civ. 18 al.
q Acts xxiii. 10 only. Jer. ii. 20.
r Matt. xii. 20 reff.
s Matt. viii. 28 reff.
t James iii. 7, 8 only. Dan. ii. 40 (bis Theod.) only.
u Matt. xviii. 10 reff.
v gen., Luke xviii. 7. Acts ix. 24. 1 Thess. ii. 9. iii. 10. Rev. iv. 8 al. Isa. xxxiv. 10. acc., ch. iv. 27 reff.

CHAP. V. 1. ηλθεν CGLMΔ 69 syrr[not syr-mg] copt arm. for της θαλ., και D-gr: om 69 lat-ff_2 [*i q*] D-lat æth. rec (for γεργεσηνων) γαδαρηνων, with AC rel syrr goth: γερασηνων BDℵ[1] latt (Orig) (Nyss?): txt (*see proleg ch* vi) LU Δ-gr ℵ[3a] 1. 33 ev-y syr-mg copt æth arm Epiph(εἶτα πάλιν ἐλθὼν εἰς τὰ μέρη τῶν Γεργεσηνῶν, ὡς ὁ Μάρκος λέγει· ἢ ἐν τοῖς ὁρίοις τῶν Γεργεσηνῶν, ὡς ὁ Λουκᾶς φησι· ἢ Γαδαρηνῶν, ὡς ὁ Ματθαῖος· ἢ Γεργεσαίων, ὡς ἀντίγραφά τινα ἔχει) Thl(τὰ ἀκριβέστερα τῶν ἀντιγράφων εἰς τ. χώρ. τῶν Γεργεσηνῶν ἔχει).

2. εξελθοντος αυτου BCLΔℵ 1. 33. 69 ev-y lat-*b f* syrr copt æth: -αντων αυτων D lat-*c e f* ff_2 (*The attempts to mend the Hellenistic constr have been universal; so that the considn of the || places hardly comes in*): txt A rel am(with mt em al). rec ευθεως, with AD rel: om B lat-*b c e* ff_2 *i* Syr arm: txt CLΔℵ. υπηντησεν (*from || Matt Luke*) BCDGLΔℵ 1. 69 Damasc: txt A rel. ανθρωπος bef εκ των μνημ. D lat-(*b*) *c e f i* [*q*] goth arm.

3. ειχεν bef την κατοικησιν D-gr 2-pe lat-*a* (*b*) *c e* ff_2 goth. rec μνημειοις, with DH (1, e sil) 69-txt: txt ABCLΔΠℵ 69-corr rel. rec ουτε, with A rel: txt BC DLΔℵ 33. rec αλυσεσιν (*corrn to suit the follg*), with AC[2]Dℵ rel vulg lat-*b f* $ff_{1.2}$ g_1 *i* [*l q*] syrr copt goth æth arm: txt BC[1]L 33 lat-*c e*. rec om ουκετι (*on acct of the recurrence of negatives, as is also shewn by the readg* ετι), with AC[2] rel lat-*i* [*q*] syrr copt goth æth: ins BC[1]DLΔℵ 69 latt: ουδεις ετι 1. 118-31 (arm). rec ηδυν., with B[2]C[2]F S(e sil) 1: txt AB C[1]Dℵ rel.—ετολμα M. αυτ. bef εδυν. D am(with fuld ing tol) lat-*i*.

4. om το ℵ[1]: for το αυτον, τουτον ℵ[3a]. οτι πολλακις αυτον δεδεμενον πεδαις και αλυσεσιν εν αις εδησαν διεσπακεναι και τας πεδας συντετριφεναι και μηδενα αυτον ισχυιν(-χυν D[1]) δαμασαι D lat-*l*: simly lat-ff_2 *i* [*l q*]: δια το αυτον πολλας πεδας κ. αλυσεις αις εδησαν αυτον διεσπακεναι κ. συντετριφεναι κ. ουδεις ισχυσεν αυτον δαμασαι 1: *quoniam compedes etiam frangebat ac conterebat* (only) æth. rec αυτον bef ισχ., with D rel lat-(*b*) *e i*: txt ABCKLMUΔΠℵ 1. 33. 69 latt. for δαμασαι, δησαι A: om ℵ[1](ins ℵ[3a]).

5. for και δια π. νυκτ., νυκτος δε D lat-*b c e* ff_2 *i* [*q*].

Onom. (cited by Kuin., h. l.), proves from Cratinus that the word is put for the cushion used by rowers. **39. σιώπα, πεφ.**] These remarkable words are given only here. On the variations in the accounts, see on Matt. ver. 25. **41.**] The **ἄρα** expresses the inference from the event which they had witnessed: **Who then is this?**

CHAP. V. 1—20.] HEALING OF A DÆMONIAC AT GERGESA. Matt. viii. 28—34. Luke viii. 26—39. The accounts of Mark and Luke are strictly cognate, and bear traces of having been originally given by two eye-witnesses, or perhaps even by one and the same, and having passed through others who had learnt one or two minute additional particulars. Matt.'s account is evidently not from an eye-witness. Some of the most striking circumstances are there omitted. See throughout notes on Matt., *wherever the narrative is in common*. **3. οὐδὲ ἁλύσει**] **not even with a chain.** **4.**] The **διὰ τό** gives the reason, not why *he could not* be bound, but why *the conclusion was come to* that he could not. The πέδαι are shackles for the feet, the ἁλύσεις chains in general,

w here only. 2 Chron. xxxiv. 7.
x Matt. xxvi. 58 reff.
y Matt. iv. 10 reff.
z ||. 2 Kings xvi. 10 al.
a = || L. Luke i. 32, 35, 76. vi. 35. Acts vii. 48. xvi. 17. Heb. vii. 1 only. (Matt. xxi. 9 reff.) Ps. xc. 1 al. fr.
b (and constr.) Acts xix. 13 only. (2 Chron. xxxvi. 13. Neh. xiii. 25 BN.) ἐνορκ., 1 Thess. v. 27. Neh., as above A. ἐξορκ., Matt. xxvi. 63.
c || Mt. reff.
d Matt. x. 1 reff.
e || L. ver. 15. Matt. xxvi. 53 only †.
f = Matt. viii. 5, 31 al. 1 Kings xxii. 4. w. ἵνα, Matt. xiv. 36 reff.
g Matt. ix. 14 reff.
h = Luke xix. 37. John xviii. 16. xx. 11, 12. Rev. i. 13. Josh. ix. 1.
i || Mt. (reff.)

[v] ἡμέρας ἐν τοῖς [n] μνήμασιν καὶ ἐν τοῖς ὄρεσιν ἦν κράζων ABCDE
καὶ [w] κατακόπτων ἑαυτὸν λίθοις. 6 καὶ ἰδὼν τὸν Ἰησοῦν FGHKL MSUV
[x] ἀπὸ [x] μακρόθεν ἔδραμεν καὶ [y] προσεκύνησεν αὐτόν, 7 καὶ ΔΠא 1. 33, 69
κράξας φωνῇ μεγάλῃ λέγει [z] Τί ἐμοὶ καὶ σοὶ Ἰησοῦ υἱὲ
τοῦ θεοῦ τοῦ [a] ὑψίστου; [b] ὁρκίζω σε τὸν θεὸν μή με
[c] βασανίσῃς. 8 ἔλεγεν γὰρ αὐτῷ Ἔξελθε τὸ [d] πνεῦμα τὸ
[d] ἀκάθαρτον ἐκ τοῦ ἀνθρώπου. 9 καὶ ἐπηρώτα αὐτὸν Τί
ὄνομά σοι; καὶ λέγει αὐτῷ [e] Λεγιὼν ὄνομά μοι, ὅτι
πολλοί ἐσμεν. 10 καὶ [f] παρεκάλει αὐτὸν [g] πολλὰ ἵνα μὴ
αὐτοὺς ἀποστείλῃ ἔξω τῆς χώρας. 11 ἦν δὲ ἐκεῖ [h] πρὸς
τῷ ὄρει [i] ἀγέλη [i] χοίρων μεγάλη [i] βοσκομένη· 12 καὶ [f] παρ-

rec transp μν. and ορ., with D rel lat-(*b*) *e i* [*q*]: txt ABCKLMUΔΠא 1. 33. 69 vulg lat-*f* ff_2 *l* syrr copt goth æth arm. μνημειοις D 1. 69. κραζον D: κραυγαζων 69. 124. 346.

6. rec ιδων δε (*from* || *Luke*), with AD rel vulg lat-*b e f* $ff_{1.2}$ $g_{1.2}$ [*i l q*] syrr goth æth arm: txt BCLΔא 1. 69 copt. om απο AKLMΠ goth [$Damasc_1$]. rec αυτω, with Dא rel [$Damasc_1$-ms]: txt ABCLΔ [$Damasc_1$-ed].

7. rec (for λεγει) ειπε (*from* || *Luke*), with D rel vulg lat-*b c e f* [*i q*] copt goth: txt ABCKLMΔא 1. 33 am(with em) syr arm [$Damasc_1$], λεγον Π. for υψ., ζωντος (*Matt* xvi. 16) A syr-mg.

8. for ελεγεν γαρ, και ελεγεν א: om γαρ A[1](appy) G. aft αυτω ins ο ιησους D fuld lat-ff_2. το πν. το ακ. bef εξελθε A. for εκ, απο A 33 vulg lat-*c f l* [*i q*].

9. επηρωτησεν (|| *Luke*) A em lat-*a c e* ff_2 *i* [*q*] Syr [$Damasc_1$]. rec σοι bef ονομα (*from* || *Luke*), with D rel latt $Orig\text{-}int_1$: txt ABCKLMΔ Π-txt א 1. 33. 69 syr goth [arm] Damasc.—add εστιν (|| *Luke*) D latt (copt) Orig-int. rec (for λεγ. αυτ.) απεκριθη λεγων, with E rel: απεκ. (only) D 253 lat-*a b e f i* [*q*]: txt ABCKLMΔ Π-txt א 1. 69 vulg lat-g_2 *l* syrr copt goth æth (arm) Damasc. (33 def.) rec λεγεων (*from* || *Luke*), with AB[2] rel goth Orig, λεγαιων א[3a]: txt B[1]CDLΔא[1] latt syrr copt. aft μοι ins εστιν B 69 vulg lat-*f* g_2 *i l*; so, but in different order, lat-*b c* g_1 copt (*the varns help to shew* εστιν *to be supplemy*): om A(sic) CLΔא rel lat-*a e* vss Orig [$Damasc_1$].—εστιν μοι ονομα λεγιων D [lat-*q*].

10. παρεκαλουν AΔ 1 vulg-sixt lat-*c* ff_2 $g_{1.2}$ arm Damasc. for αυτους αποστ., αυτα αποστ. (*corrn to* παρεκαλει) BCΔ; *se expelleret* vulg lat-$g_{1.2}$ *l* [*i q* D-lat]: αυτον αποστ. Lא 258 lat-*b e*: αποστ. αυτους AM fuld lat-*c f* ff_2 *i* syr (copt) goth arm: αποστ. αυτον KΠ 229-48-53 Scr's o w ev-z Syr æth.

11. rec προς τα ορη: om 1. 33(appy): txt ABCD(א) rel Scr's-mss vss Thl Euthym (ορι was appy supplied by א-corr[1]). αγ. χ. μ. β. bef πρ. τ. ορ. (*see* || *Luke*) AK(M)U Π-txt syr copt goth æth. om μεγ. DLU ev-y lat-*b e* ff_2 *i* goth: ins aft βοσκ. M arm. βοσκομενων (*see also* || *Luke*) ALΔא[3a] lat-*b* [*q*] D-lat.

without specifying for what part of the body. **6.**] **ἀπὸ μακ. ἔδρ.**, peculiar to Mark. **7.**] **ὁρκ. σε τ. θ.** = δέομαί σου Luke. **8.**] Mark generally uses the direct address in the second person: see ver. 12. **ἔλεγεν**] *not imperf. for pluperf., either here or any where else*; for **He was saying to him**, &c. **9.**] **ὅτι πολλοί ἐσ.** has perhaps given rise to the report of *two* dæmoniacs in Matt. I cannot see in the above supposition any thing which should invalidate the testimony of the Evangelists. Rather are all such tracings of discrepancies to their source, most interesting and valuable. Nor can I consent for a moment to accept here the very lame solution (repeated by Bp. Wordsw.), which supposes *one of the dæmoniacs not to be mentioned* by Mark and Luke: in other words, that the *least circumstantial* account is in possession of an additional particular which gives a new aspect to the *whole*: for the *plural*, used here and in Luke of the *many dæmons in one man*, is there used of the *two men*, and their separate dæmons. On **λεγιών** see note, Luke, ver. 30. **10.**] **ἀποστ. ἔξω τ. χ.** = ἐπιτάξῃ αὐτ. εἰς τ. ἄβυσσον

εκάλεσαν αὐτὸν λέγοντες Πέμψον ἡμᾶς εἰς τοὺς [i] χοίρους,
ἵνα εἰς αὐτοὺς εἰςέλθωμεν. 13 καὶ [k] ἐπέτρεψεν αὐτοῖς
[εὐθέως ὁ Ἰησοῦς]. καὶ ἐξελθόντα τὰ [d] πνεύματα τὰ
[d] ἀκάθαρτα [l] εἰςῆλθον εἰς τοὺς [i] χοίρους, καὶ [m] ὥρμησεν ἡ
[i] ἀγέλη κατὰ τοῦ [n] κρημνοῦ εἰς τὴν θάλασσαν ὡς δισχίλιοι,
καὶ [o] ἐπνίγοντο ἐν τῇ θαλάσσῃ. 14 καὶ οἱ [i] βόσκοντες
αὐτοὺς ἔφυγον καὶ ἀπήγγειλαν εἰς τὴν πόλιν καὶ εἰς
τοὺς ἀγρούς. καὶ ἦλθον ἰδεῖν τί [p] ἐστιν τὸ γεγονός.
15 καὶ ἔρχονται πρὸς τὸν Ἰησοῦν, καὶ [q] θεωροῦσιν τὸν
[r] δαιμονιζόμενον καθήμενον [s] ἱματισμένον καὶ [t] σωφρονοῦντα, τὸν [u] ἐσχηκότα τὸν [v] λεγιῶνα, καὶ ἐφοβήθησαν.
16 καὶ [w] διηγήσαντο αὐτοῖς οἱ ἰδόντες πῶς [x] ἐγένετο [x] τῷ
[r] δαιμονιζομένῳ, καὶ περὶ τῶν [i] χοίρων. 17 καὶ ἤρξαντο
[y] παρακαλεῖν αὐτὸν ἀπελθεῖν ἀπὸ τῶν [z] ὁρίων αὐτῶν.
18 καὶ [a] ἐμβαίνοντος αὐτοῦ εἰς τὸ πλοῖον [b] παρεκάλει

k Matt. viii. 21. John xix. 38. Acts xxi. 40 al. Esth. ix. 14.
l plur., Matt. vi. 28 reff.
m = '. Acts vii. 57. xix. 29 only. 1 Kings xv. 19.
n || only. 2 Chron. xxv. 12 bis only.
o Matt. xviii. 28 only. 1 Kings xvi. 14, 15 only.
p pres., John i. 40 reff.
q ch. iii. 11. Luke xxiii. 48. John ix. 8 al. Ps. lxiii. 9.
r Matt. viii. 16 reff.
s || L. only +.
t = || L. 2 Cor. v. 13 (Rom. xii. 3. Tit. ii. 6. 1 Pet. iv. 7) only +.
u = ch. iii. 22, 30. ix. 17. Matt. xi. 18 al.
v ver. 9 reff.
w ch. ix. 9. Luke viii. 39. ix. 10. Acts viii. 33 (from Isa. liii. 8). ix. 27. xii. 17. Heb. xi. 32 only. Ps. ix. 1. (-γησις, Luke i. 1.)
x Matt. ix. 29 reff.
y w. inf., Luke viii. 41. Acts viii. 31. ix. 38 al. 2 Macc. iv. 34.
z Matt. ii. 16 reff.
a Matt. viii. 23 reff. 1 Macc. xv. 37.
b vv. 10, 12.

12. παρεκαλουν ADKM Π-txt vulg lat-*b e f ff*$_2$ *g*$_{1.2}$ Syr copt(ms ctra) [Damasc$_1$]. rec aft αυτον ins παντες οι δαιμονες (*gloss appy, cf the varr*), with A rel syr goth arm : οι δαιμονες (*from* || *Matt*) KM Π-txt Syr, *spiritus illi* lat-*b*, *spiritus* vulg, *dæmones* lat-*c* : τα δαιμονια (*Luke* viii. 33) D : *universa dæmonia* lat-*a* : *multum* æth : om BCLΔℵ 1. 69 copt. λεγοντας L : ειποντα D : om 69. απελθωμεν D-gr.

13. κ. ευθεως κυριος ιησ. επεμψεν αυτους εις τ. χοιρους D lat-*ff*$_2$, simly *a c*.—for επετρ., επεμψεν DH. om ευθεως (*as* || *Luke : it is characteristic of Mark*) BCLΔℵ 1 lat-*b e* Syr copt æth arm : ins A(D) rel vulg lat-*f* syr. om ο ιησ. (*as* || *Luke*) BCELΔℵ 1 lat-*b e* Syr copt arm : ins A (D, see above) rel vulg lat-*f g*$_1$ syr goth æth [Damasc$_1$]. for τα πν. τ. ακαθ., τ. ακαθ. πν. 33 : om τα ακαθαρτα A[1]F Scr's l. εισηλθεν B 252. 435 Scr's a. rec ins ησαν δε bef ως δισχ. (*supplemy*), with AC[2] rel lat-*a f g*$_2$ *i* goth (arm) : ησαν γαρ 58[1]. 225 Scr's h syr : om BC[1]DLΔℵ 1 vulg lat-*b c e ff*$_2$ *g*$_1$ [*q*] Syr copt.

14. rec (for και οι) οι δε (*from* || *Matt : see also* || *Luke*), with D rel vulg lat-*b c f ff*$_2$ *g*$_{1.2}$ [*i l q*] arm : txt ABCLMΔℵ 1. 33. 69 lat-*a e* syrr copt goth æth. rec (for αυτους) τους χοιρους, with A rel syr goth arm : txt BCDLΔℵ 69 latt Syr copt (æth).—(αυτος D[1] : txt D[2].) rec ανηγγ., with Δ rel : txt ABCDKLMΠ ℵ(-λον) 1. 33 ev-y. (απηγ. *is too strongly supported by* MSS *to be regarded as introduced from* ||.) rec εξηλθον (*from* || *Matt Luke*), with CDℵ[1] rel vulg lat-*b c e f* [*ff*$_2$ *i l*] Syr æth arm : txt ABKLMUΠ[1]ℵ[3a] 33 ev-y syr copt goth. om εστιν A[1](appy) : om τι εστιν H [*as* || *Luke*].

15. ηρχοντο ℵ[1](txt ℵ-corr[1](appy)[3a]), *venerunt* gat(with mm) lat-*b c f*. ins αυτον bef τ. δαιμ. D lat-*b* (*c*). rec ins και bef ιματισμενον, with AC rel [lat-*q*] syr goth (æth) : om BDL(MΔ)[ℵ] 1. 33. 69 latt copt arm.—(om καθημενον Δ : om ιμ. M[1] ev-z.) om τ. εσχ. τ. λεγ. D latt(not mt) æth. rec λεγεωνα, with A(B[2] ?)C rel : λεγαιωνα ℵ[3a] : txt B[1](from inspection : Tischdf [N. T. Vat., not ed 8] gives λεγεωνα) LΔℵ[1].

16. διηγ. δε (*from* || *Luke*) DEFHUV Π-marg lat-*b c ff*$_2$ *i* [*q*]. ins αυτω bef τω δ. D.

17. for ηρξαντο παρακαλειν, παρεκαλουν D 225. 2-pe [lat-*a*(appy)]. for απελθειν, ινα απελθη D latt.

18. rec εμβαντος (*to accord with* || ; *but in error*), with E rel : txt ABCDKLMΔΠℵ 1. 33 latt goth. for παρεκαλει, ηρξατο παρακαλειν D vulg lat-(*c*) *f ff*$_2$ *g*$_{1.2}$ *i l*.

ἀπελθεῖν Luke : see on Matt. ver. 30. 13.] **ὡς δισχ., to the number of two thousand** :—peculiar to Mark, who gives us usually accurate details of this kind : see ch. vi. 37,—where however John (vi. 7) also mentions the sum. 15, 16.] Omitted by Matt., as also vv. 18—20. The whole of this is full of minute and

αὐτὸν ὁ [r] δαιμονισθεὶς [b] ἵνα μετ' αὐτοῦ ᾖ. 19 καὶ οὐκ
[c] ἀφῆκεν αὐτόν, ἀλλὰ λέγει αὐτῷ Ὕπαγε εἰς τὸν οἶκόν
σου πρὸς τοὺς σούς, καὶ ἀπάγγειλον αὐτοῖς ὅσα ὁ κύριός
σοι [d] πεποίηκεν καὶ [e] ἠλέησέν σε. 20 καὶ ἀπῆλθεν καὶ
ἤρξατο κηρύσσειν ἐν τῇ Δεκαπόλει ὅσα [d] ἐποίησεν αὐτῷ
ὁ Ἰησοῦς, καὶ πάντες ἐθαύμαζον.
21 Καὶ [f] διαπεράσαντος τοῦ Ἰησοῦ ἐν τῷ πλοίῳ πάλιν
[g] εἰς τὸ [g] πέραν [h] συνήχθη ὄχλος πολὺς ἐπ' αὐτόν· καὶ ἦν
παρὰ τὴν θάλασσαν. 22 καὶ ἔρχεται εἷς τῶν [i] ἀρχισυναγώγων ὀνόματι Ἰάειρος, καὶ ἰδὼν αὐτὸν [k] πίπτει [k] πρὸς
τοὺς [k] πόδας αὐτοῦ, 23 καὶ [l] παρακαλεῖ αὐτὸν [l] πολλά,
λέγων ὅτι τὸ [m] θυγάτριόν μου [n] ἐσχάτως [o] ἔχει· [p] ἵνα

ABCDE FGHKL MSUV ΔΠℵ 1. 33. 69

c = Matt. iii. 15. xxiii. 14 al. Sir. xxiii. 1.
d Matt. vii. 12. Luke i. 49 al. Gen. xx. 9.
e Matt. ix. 27 reff.
f Matt. ix. 1. xiv. 34. ch. vi. 53. Luke xvi. 26. Acts xxi. 2 only. Deut. xxx. 13.
g Matt. viii. 18 reff.
h Matt. xiii. 2 reff. xxii. 34 al.
i vv. 35 ‖ L., 36, 38. Luke xiii. 14. Acts xiii. 15. xviii. 8, 17 only †.
k John xi. 32. Acts v. 10. Rev. i. 17. (Exod. iv. 25.) παρά, Luke viii. 41. ἐπί, Acts x. 25.
l ver. 10.
m ch. vii. 25 only †. Athen. xiii. p. 581 c.
n here only †.
o Matt. iv. 24. x.v. 35. ch. xvi. 18. Acts xvii. 11. xxi. 13 al. Gen. xliii. 27.
p Eph. v. 33. see ch. xii. 19.

rec ᾖ bef μετ' αυτου, with D rel vulg lat-*b c f* [*i l q*] copt æth: txt ABCKLMU[Δ] Π-txt ℵ 1. 33 lat-*e* syrr goth arm.—(for ᾖ, ην (retaining ινα) B¹Δ.)

19. rec (for και) ο δε ιησους, with D rel lat-*b c e* $ff_{1.2}$ g_1 *i* [*q*] æth arm: [και ο ιησ. 69 gat:] txt ABCKLMΔΠℵ 1. 33 vulg lat-*f l* syrr copt goth. for αλλα λεγει, και ειπεν D. rec αναγγ., with A rel: διαγγ. D 1. 69: txt BCΔℵ. rec σοι bef ο κυριος (*from* ‖ *Luke*), with A rel latt Syr goth (æth) arm: aft πεποιηκεν ℵ syr(Tischdf) copt(Tischdf): σοι ο θεος D 238: txt BCΔ am lat-ff_2 copt(Treg). rec εποιησεν (*from* ‖ *Luke, to suit* ηλεησεν), with DK 1: txt ABCℵ rel Thdor-heracl Sev. ins οτι bef ηλεησεν D lat-*b* (*c*) ff_1 g_2 *i l* Syr.

20. [aft εν ins ολη C(appy, Tischdf).] for οσα (so Δ-corr), α CΔ¹.

21. om εν τω πλοιω (‖ *Luke*) D 1 lat-*a b c e* $ff_{1.2}$ *i* [*q*] arm.—om τω B 447. εις το περαν bef παλιν Dℵ lat-*a b e* $ff_{1.2}$ g_1 *i* [*q*] syrr. for επ', προς D 69 latt. om και ην D lat-*b c e f* $ff_{1.2}$ *i* [*q*] æth.

22. rec aft και ins ιδου (*from* ‖ *Matt Luke*), with AC rel lat-*c f l* syr goth arm: om BDLΔℵ vulg lat-*a b e* ff_2 $g_{1.2}$ [*i q*] Syr copt æth. for εις, τις D latt(not *b*). om ονομ. ιαειρ. D lat-*a e* ff_2 *i*. for κ. ιδ. αυτ. π., κ. προσεπεσεν D (lat-*e*).

23. rec κ. παρεκαλει (*from* ‖ *Luke*), with B rel vulg lat-*c f* copt [goth] arm: παρακαλων D lat-*a b e* ff_2 *i* [*q*]: txt ACLℵ 33 (lat-$g_{1.2}$?). om πολλα D 38. 235 Scr's lat-*b c* ff_2 *i* [*q*]. ins και bef λεγων D lat-*a b* ff_2 *i* [*q*]. om οτι D 13. 69 lat-*a c e* Syr.

interesting detail. **18.**] Euthym. and Theophyl. suppose that he feared a fresh incursion of the evil spirits. **19.**] There was perhaps *some reason* why this man should be sent to proclaim God's mercy to his friends. His example may in former times have been prejudicial to them:—see note on Matt. ver. 32 (I. 4). **20.**] *Gadara* (see on Matt. viii. 28) was one of the cities of Decapolis (see also on Matt. iv. 25): ὁ μὲν χριστὸς μετριοφρονῶν, τῷ πατρὶ τὸ ἔργον ἀνέθηκεν· ὁ δὲ θεραπευθεὶς εὐγνωμονῶν, τῷ χριστῷ τοῦτο ἀνετίθει. Euthym. He commands the man to tell this, for He was little known in Peræa where it happened, and so would have no consequences to fear, as in Galilee, &c.

21—43.] Raising of Jaeirus's daughter, and healing of a woman with an issue of blood. Matt. ix. 18—26. Luke viii. 41—56. The same remarks apply to these three accounts as to the last. Matt. is even more concise than there, but more like an eye-witness in his narration (see notes on Matt. and Luke);—Mark the fullest of the three. **21.**] **συνήχθ.** . . . . = ἀπεδέξατο αὐτ. ὁ ὄχλ. Luke. **23.**] Notice the affectionate diminutive **θυγάτριον**, peculiar to Mark. **ἐσχ. ἔχει** = ἄρτι ἐτελεύτησεν Matt. It is branded as an idiom of lower Greek by Phrynichus: ἐσχάτως ἔχει ἐπὶ τοῦ μοχθηρῶς ἔχει καὶ σφαλερῶς τάττουσιν οἱ σύρφακες, ed. Lobeck, p. 389, where see Lobeck's note. Before **ἵνα** understand πάρειμι, or αἰτῶ σε: or as Meyer suggests, connect it with the fact just announced: 'this tidings I bring, in order that,' &c. To do this *without any* filling up, 'My daughter is, &c., in order that,' &c., is far-fetched, and savours too much of the *sentimental*. Or, it has been suggested that ἵνα might, by a mixture of construc-

ἐλθων [q] ἐπιθῇς τὰς [q] χεῖρας αὐτῇ ἵνα σωθῇ καὶ ζήσῃ.
24 καὶ ἀπῆλθεν μετ' αὐτοῦ, καὶ ἠκολούθει αὐτῷ ὄχλος
πολὺς καὶ [r] συνέθλιβον αὐτόν. 25 καὶ γυνή [τις] οὖσα [s] ἐν
[t] ῥύσει αἵματος ἔτη δώδεκα, 26 καὶ πολλὰ παθοῦσα ὑπὸ
πολλῶν [u] ἰατρῶν καὶ [v] δαπανήσασα τὰ [w] παρ' αὐτῆς πάντα,
καὶ μηδὲν [x] ὠφεληθεῖσα ἀλλὰ μᾶλλον [y] εἰς τὸ [y] χεῖρον
ἐλθοῦσα, 27 ἀκούσασα [τὰ] περὶ τοῦ Ἰησοῦ, ἐλθοῦσα ἐν τῷ
ὄχλῳ [z] ὄπισθεν, ἥψατο τοῦ ἱματίου αὐτοῦ· 28 ἔλεγεν γὰρ
ὅτι ἐὰν ἅψωμαι [a] κἂν τῶν ἱματίων αὐτοῦ, [b] σωθήσομαι.
29 καὶ εὐθὺς [c] ἐξηράνθη ἡ [d] πηγὴ τοῦ αἵματος αὐτῆς, καὶ
ἔγνω τῷ σώματι ὅτι [e] ἴαται ἀπὸ τῆς [f] μάστιγος. 30 καὶ
εὐθὺς ὁ Ἰησοῦς [g] ἐπιγνοὺς ἐν ἑαυτῷ τὴν ἐξ αὐτοῦ [h] δύναμιν
ἐξελθοῦσαν, ἐπιστραφεὶς ἐν τῷ ὄχλῳ ἔλεγεν Τίς μου
ἥψατο τῶν ἱματίων; 31 καὶ ἔλεγον αὐτῷ οἱ μαθηταὶ αὐτοῦ
Βλέπεις τὸν ὄχλον [i] συνθλίβοντά σε, καὶ λέγεις Τίς μου
ἥψατο; 32 καὶ [k] περιεβλέπετο ἰδεῖν τὴν τοῦτο ποιήσασαν.
33 ἡ δὲ γυνὴ φοβηθεῖσα καὶ [l] τρέμουσα, εἰδυῖα ὃ [m] γέγονεν

q Matt. xix. 13, 15 reff.
r ver. 31 only. Sir. xxxiv. (xxxi.) 14 only.
s = ‖ L. reff.
t ‖ L. bis only. Lev. xv. 25. (there also w. αἵμ.)
u Luke iv. 23 reff.
v Luke xv. 14. Acts xxi. 24. 2 Cor. xii. 15. James iv. 3 only +. 1 Macc. xiv. 32 al.
w ch. iii. 21. Luke x. 7. Phil. iv. 18.
x pass., Matt. xv. 5. xvi. 26 ‖ L. al. Jer. ii. 11.
y here only. (Matt. ix. 16 reff.) see 2 Tim. iii. 13.
z Matt. xv. 23 reff.
a ch. vi. 56. Acts v. 15. 2 Cor. xi. 16.
b = ‖. ch. vi. 56. Acts iv. 9 al.
c ch. iii. 1. iv. 6 ‖ al. = Ps. cv. 9. Isa. xix. 5.
d = here only. (John iv. 6 al.) = ῥύσις, ‖ L.
e pres., John i. 40 reff.
f ch. iii. 10 reff.
g Matt. xiv. 35 reff.
h Matt. xiv. 2 reff.
i ver. 24 only.
k ch. iii. 5 reff.
l ‖ L. 2 Pet. ii. 10 only. Isa. lxvi. 2, 5.
m Matt. ix. 29 reff. ver. 16.

for ινα ελθων επιθ., ελθε αψαι D vulg lat-*c e f* $g_{1.2}$ *i l* Syr æth.—rec (for τ. χ. αυτη) αυτη τας χ., with E rel syr goth arm: αυτω τας χ. AK: txt BCL(Δ)א 1 vulg lat-*a f* [æth]. —ελθε αψαι αυτης εκ των χειρων σου D lat-*b i* [*q*]:—aft χειρας ins σου Δ lat-*c* Syr copt æth. rec (for 2nd ινα) οπως (*to avoid repetition: it is most improb that the transcribers shd take into acct that* οπως *is only once used by* Mark (ch iii. 6), *and so alter it to* ινα, *as Meyer supposes*), with A rel: txt BCDLΔא 69. rec ζησεται (*from* ‖ *Matt*), with A rel lat-*c e* arm: txt BCDLΔא 69 vulg lat-*a b f* ff_2 [$g_{1.2}$ *i q*] copt goth.

24. for απηλθεν, υπηγεν D 124. ηκολουθησεν CL M-marg.

25. om τις (*as superfl and not in* ‖: *no reason could be given for its* insn) ABCLΔא 1. 33 vulg lat-*b c e* ff_2 [*i*] syr copt æth: ins D rel lat-*a f* Syr goth arm. δωδ. bef ετη (*from* ‖ *Matt*) BCLΔא 1. 33. 69 [copt]: txt AD rel latt syrr goth.

26. for 1st και, ἡ D lat-*b c f* ff_2 *i* (Syr). rec τα παρ' εαυτης, with CKΔΠא: τα εαυτης D 1 latt: txt AB rel. for εις, επι D. om ελθουσα D-gr.

27. rec om τα, with AC²Dא³ rel latt syrr copt goth æth arm: ins B C¹(appy) Δא¹. transp εν τω οχλω to end of ver D 2-pe [lat-*a i*]. for οπισθεν, οπιθεν א¹(txt א-corr¹·³) ev-P. ins και bef ηψατο D¹ latt Syr syr-w-ob.

28. for ελεγεν γαρ, λεγουσα D lat-*b c* ff_2 *i* [*q*] æth. add εν εαυτη (‖ *Matt*) DKΠ 1. 33 lat-*a c* ff_2 *i* [*q*] arm. rec καν των ιμ. αυ. bef αψ. (omg εαν), with A(D) rel: εαν μονον αψ. του ιμ. αυτ. (‖ *Matt*) 33: txt B(καν 'superadditur') CLΔ(א). του ιματιου Dא 33 latt [copt]. εαυτου D.

29. (ευθυς, so BCLΔא 33: also in ver 30.) om της (bef μαστ.) C.

30. κ. ευθ. επιγ. και ο ῑς την δυν. (add την D⁵) εξελθ. απ αυτου κ. επιστραφεις εν τω οχ. ειπεν D.—επιγ. bef ο ιησ. DL lat-*a* ff_2 copt æth.—om εν εαυτω D lat-*b c e* ff_2 *i* [*q*] æth. ηψ. των ιμ. bef μου D latt(not *e*).

31. οι δε μ. αυτ. λεγουσιν αυτω D 2-pe lat-(*a*) *e* g_1 *i* [*q*].

33. aft τρεμ. ins δι ο πεποιηκει λαθρα D 50. 124. 2-pe lat-*a* ff_2 *i* arm: και א¹(om

tions, depend on the foregoing παρεκάλει. **24.**] Matt. adds, καὶ οἱ μαθηταὶ αὐτ. **27.**] **ἀκούσασα** is subordinated to **ἐλθοῦσα** as giving a reason for it: 'owing to having heard . . . . came.' **28.**] **ἔλεγεν γάρ** perhaps need not to be pressed to mean that she actually *said* it to some one—ἐν ἑαυτῇ may be understood. At the same time, the *imperfect* looks very like the minute accuracy of one reporting what had been an habitual saying of the poor woman in her distress. **29.**] On these particulars see notes on Luke. **ἔγνω τῷ σώμ.**, elliptic—**knew** *by feeling* **in her**

ABCDE FGHKL MSUV ΔΠℵ 1. 33. 69

[m] αὐτῇ, ἦλθεν καὶ [n] προσέπεσεν αὐτῷ καὶ εἶπεν αὐτῷ πᾶσαν
τὴν [o] ἀλήθειαν. 34 ὁ δὲ εἶπεν αὐτῇ Θυγάτηρ, ἡ πίστις
σου σέσωκέν σε· ὕπαγε [p] εἰς εἰρήνην, καὶ ἴσθι [q] ὑγιὴς
ἀπὸ τῆς [r] μάστιγός σου. 35 ἔτι αὐτοῦ λαλοῦντος ἔρχονται
ἀπὸ τοῦ [s] ἀρχισυναγώγου λέγοντες ὅτι ἡ θυγάτηρ σου
ἀπέθανεν· τί ἔτι [t] σκύλλεις τὸν διδάσκαλον; 36 ὁ δὲ
Ἰησοῦς [εὐθέως] [u] παρακούσας τὸν λόγον λαλούμενον λέγει τῷ [s] ἀρχισυναγώγῳ Μὴ φόβου, μόνον [v] πίστευε. 37 καὶ
οὐκ [w] ἀφῆκεν οὐδένα μετ' αὐτοῦ [x] συνακολουθῆσαι εἰ μὴ τὸν
Πέτρον καὶ Ἰάκωβον καὶ Ἰωάννην τὸν ἀδελφὸν Ἰακώβου.
38 καὶ ἔρχονται εἰς τὸν οἶκον τοῦ [s] ἀρχισυναγώγου, καὶ
[y] θεωρεῖ [z] θόρυβον [a] καὶ [b] κλαίοντας καὶ [c] ἀλαλάζοντας
[d] πολλά. 39 καὶ εἰσελθὼν λέγει αὐτοῖς Τί [e] θορυβεῖσθε
καὶ [b] κλαίετε; τὸ παιδίον οὐκ ἀπέθανεν, ἀλλὰ καθεύδει.
40 καὶ [f] κατεγέλων αὐτοῦ. ὁ δὲ ἐκβαλὼν πάντας [g] παραλαμβάνει τὸν πατέρα τοῦ παιδίου καὶ τὴν μητέρα καὶ

n ch. iii. 11 reff.
o = John xvi. 7. 2 Cor. xii. 6 al. 2 Chron. xviii. 15.
p || L. Luke vii. 50. 1 Kings i. 17. 2 Kings xv. 9.
q Matt. xii. 13 reff.
r ver. 29.
s ver. 22 reff.
t || L. Matt. ix. 36. Luke vii. 6. viii. 49 only †.
u = here only. (Matt. xviii. 17 bis only. Isa. lxv. 12.) Aristoph. Ran. 750. Plato, Euthyd. p. 300 D.
v abs., ch. xv. 32. xvi. 16, 17. Matt. xxi. 22 al.
w = Matt. xxiii. 14. ch. i. 34. x. 14 al. Gen. xx. 6.
x ch. xiv. 51. Luke xxiii. 49 only. Num. xxxii. 11 Ald. (συνεπακ. AB.) 2 Macc. ii. 4 only.
y ver. 15.
z Matt. xxvi. 5 reff.
a = ch. i. 5. Matt. xxiii. 34 al.
b Matt. xxvi. 75 reff.
c 1 Cor. xiii. 1 only. = Jer. iv. 8.
d Matt. ix. 14 reff.
e || Mt. Acts xvii. 5. xx. 10 only. Judg. iii. 26.
f || only. 2 Chron. xxx. 10.
g Matt. xvii. 1 ||. xviii. 16 al. fr. Num. xxii. 41.

ℵ-corr[1](?)[3]). rec ins επ' bef αυτη (*various preposns were insd to shew that* αυτη *was not the nom case*), with A rel goth: εν αυτη F(Wetst) Δ vulg lat-*c f* g_1 æth: επ αυτην 13. 69. 124: txt BCDLℵ lat-*a* Syr copt, εαυτη ev-y. for προσεπ. αυτω, προσεκυνησεν αυτον C 6-pe.

34. aft ο δε ins ιησους CD M-marg **1**. 69 lat-*a b c* &c syr-w-ast arm. αυτω A. rec θυγατερ (|| *Matt*), with A C[2][C[1] uncert] ℵ rel: txt BD Scr's e. (θαρσει θυγατερ (|| *Matt*) C[2] 67-8 ev-P.)

35. aft λεγοντες ins αυτω D 33 lat-*b i*.

36. om ευθεως BDLΔℵ 1 vulg lat-*b c* &c Syr copt æth arm: ins AC rel (lat-*a*) syr goth. rec ακουσας (*from* || *Luke, the unusual* παρακ. *not being understood*), with ACDΠ ℵ[3](but txt restored) rel: txt BLΔℵ[1] lat-*e*. τ. λ. τον λαλ. B: τουτον τον λογον D.

37. ουδεενα D[-gr]. rec (for μετ' αυτου) αυτω, with A(D) rel latt syr: txt BCLΔℵ lat-*e* Syr goth.—for μετ' αυ. συνακ., παρακολουθησαι αυτω D (1).—for συνακ., ακολουθησαι AKΠ[1] 33 am lat-*a b c f* g_1 *i* syrr. rec om τον (|| *Luke*), with AD rel: ins BCΔℵ. for ιακωβου, αυτου DGΔ 1 lat-*a* syr-txt.

38. rec ερχεται (*to conform to follg* θεωρει), with L rel lat-*a c f* ff_2 syr goth æth arm: txt ABCDFΔℵ **1**. 33 vulg lat-*b e* $g_{1.2}$ (*i*) *l* [*q*] Syr copt. την οικιαν D 2-pe. εθεωρει D[-gr]. rec (aft θορυβον) om και (*as irrelevant, it being thought that the* θορ. was *the* κλ. *and* αλαλ., *as in* D *distinctly*), with (D) rel lat-*a b c e f* ff_2 *i* copt: ins ABCLMUΔΠℵ **1**. 33. 69 vulg lat-g_1 *l* syrr goth æth arm.—θορ. κλαιοντων κ. αλαλαζοντων D-gr lat-*a*: *turbam flentem ac lamentantem* lat-*b* (*c*) [*f i q*] D-lat.

39. ins τι bef κλαιετε D lat-*b f* ff_2 [*i q*].

40. for 1st και, οι δε D lat-*a b c* &c [not *f*]. for ο δε, αυτος δε (*from* || *Luke*) BCDLΔℵ 33 latt copt goth(appy): ο δε ιησους M **1** Syr syr-w-ast: txt A rel syr-txt æth(appy) arm. rec απαντας (with S Scr's l u, e sil): τους οχλους εξω D lat-*b c e*: txt ABCℵ rel. κ. τ. μητερα bef τ. παιδιου D latt.

body. **32.**] Peculiar to Mark, and indicative of an eye-witness. **34.**] **καὶ ἴσθι . . . . . σου**, peculiar to Mark, and inexplicable, except because the Lord *really spoke the words*, as a solemn ratification of the healing which she had as it were surreptitiously obtained: see note on Luke, ver. 48. **36.**] **But Jesus having [straightway] overheard the message being spoken**: a mark of accuracy which is lost in the rec. text. **38.**] The **καί** after θόρυβον takes out one particular from the general description before given: see reff. **40.**] How capricious, ac-

τοὺς μετ' αὐτοῦ, καὶ εἰσπορεύεται ὅπου ἦν τὸ παιδίον.
41 καὶ [h] κρατήσας τῆς χειρὸς τοῦ παιδίου λέγει αὐτῇ
Ταλιθὰ κοῦμ, ὅ ἐστιν [i] μεθερμηνευόμενον Τὸ [j] κοράσιον, σοὶ
λέγω, ἔγειρε. 42 καὶ εὐθὺς ἀνέστη τὸ [j] κοράσιον καὶ περι-
επάτει· ἦν γὰρ [k] ἐτῶν δώδεκα. καὶ [lm] ἐξέστησαν εὐθὺς
[mn] ἐκστάσει μεγάλῃ. 43 καὶ [o] διεστείλατο αὐτοῖς [p] πολλὰ
ἵνα μηδεὶς [q] γνοῖ τοῦτο, καὶ [r] εἶπεν [s] δοθῆναι αὐτῇ [s] φαγεῖν.
VI. 1 Καὶ ἐξῆλθεν ἐκεῖθεν καὶ ἔρχεται εἰς τὴν [t] πατρίδα αὐτοῦ, καὶ ἀκολουθοῦσιν αὐτῷ οἱ μαθηταὶ αὐτοῦ.
2 καὶ γενομένου σαββάτου ἤρξατο ἐν τῇ συναγωγῇ διδά-

h gen., || Mt. L. ch. i. 31. ix. 27. Heb. iv. 14. vi. 18 only. Gen. xix. 16.
i Matt. i. 23. ch. xv. 22, 34. John i. 39, 42. Acts iv. 36. xiii. 8 only†. Sir. prol.
j || Mt. Matt. xiv. 11. ch. vi. 22, 28 bis. 1 Kings ix. 11.
k Luke ii. 37, 42. iii. 23. viii. 42. Acts iv. 22. Exod. vii. 7. Esdr. i. 43 (41).
l Matt. xii. 23 reff. ch. vi. 51 al.
m Gen. xxvii. 33. Ezek. xxvi. 16.
n ch. xvi. 8 reff.
o Matt. xvi. 20 reff.
p Matt. ix. 14 reff.
q form, ch. ix. 30. see ch. iv. 29. xiv. 10. John xiii. 2· also Moulton's note on Winer, p. 360, 2.
r = Matt. xvi. 11, 12. ch. viii. 7. x. 49. Luke ix. 54. xii. 13. Exod. xxxv. 1.
s Matt. xiv. 16 reff.
t || Mt. reff. Jer. xxvi. (xlvi.) 16.

aft αυτου ins οντας D latt. εισεπορευετο D 2-pe lat-*a b c* &c. for οπου, ου A. rec at end adds ανακειμενον, with AC rel syrr goth arm: κειμενον 31. 57^2. 253, *jacens* vulg lat-*c f* g_2 *l* [*q*]: κατακειμενον 1. 28 Thl: κατακλιμενον 13. 69: καταβεβλημενον 57^1: om BDLΔℵ 33 lat-*a b e* ff_2 *i* copt [æth].

41. την χειρα D 435. aft αυτη add ραββι D. ταβιτα D, ταλιτα Δ. rec κουμι, with D rel vulg lat-*b c f* syrr(and syr-mg-gr) copt æth arm, κουμει A 69 [goth]: om lat-*a* g_2: txt BCLMℵ 1. 33 lat-ff_2 Suid Thl. rec εγειραι (*itacism ?*), with U Scr's i (a d h l m n q r s, e sil) ev-z: txt ABCDℵ rel.

42. (ευθυς, so BLΔℵ 33.) for γαρ, δε D latt. add ωσει CΔℵ 124: ως 1. 33 arm. rec om 2nd ευθυς, with AD rel vss: ins BCLΔℵ 33 copt æth. add παντες D lat-*c f* ff_2 g_2 *i* [*q*].

43. om πολλα D Scr's e lat-*b c* &c. rec γνω, with Cℵ rel: txt ABDL. for δοθηναι, δουναι D-gr lat-(*e*) $g_{1.2}$.

Chap. VI. **1.** rec (for ερχεται) ηλθεν (*after* || *Matt*), with A rel [syr-txt] goth arm-mss Orig: καπηλθεν (for και απηλθ. or κ. ηλθ. ?) D: *abiit* vulg lat-*b c f* ff_2 $g_{1.2}$ *l* D-lat: txt BCLΔℵ syr-mg.

2. for γεν. σαβ., ημερα σαββατων D lat-ff_2 *i*. διδασκειν bef εν τ. συναγωγη (*corrn to the usual order,—see ch* ii. 23; x. 28,—*and to that in* || *Matt*) BCDLΔℵ 33 syrr

cording to modern criticism, must this Evangelist have been, who compiled his narrative out of Matt. and Luke, adding minute particulars—in leaving out here εἰδότες ὅτι ἀπέθανεν (Luke), *a detail so essential*, if Mark had really been what he is represented. Can testimony be stronger to the untenableness of such a view, and the independence of his narration? And yet such abound in every chapter.

41.] ταλ. κοῦμ (or **κοῦμι**) =טְלִיתָא קוּמִי. **σοὶ λέγω** is *added in the translation*. The accuracy of Mark's reports,—not, as has been strangely suggested (see Webst. and Wilk. p. 174), the wish to indicate that our Lord did not use mystic magical language on such occasions,—often gives occasion to the insertion of the *actual Syriac and Aramaic words* spoken by the Lord: see ch. vii. 11, 34; xiv. 36. **Talitha**, in the ordinary dialect of the people, is a word of endearment addressed to a young maiden: = κοράσιον. So that the words are equivalent to **Rise, my child**. On the nom. with the article standing as a vocative, see Winer, § 29. 2. Bernhardy, Syntax, p. 67, remarks that the idiom had originally something harsh in it, being used only in emphatically imperative addresses. This however it lost, as the present use and that in || Luke and Luke xii. 32 sufficiently shew. **42.] καὶ περιεπ.**, peculiar to Mark. The whole account is probably derived from the testimony of Peter, who was present. The **ἦν γὰρ ἐτῶν δώδεκα** is added, as Bengel, to shew that she "rediit ad statum ætati congruentem." Ver. 43 betokens an eye-witness, who relates what passed *within*. Matt. says nothing of this, but tells what took place *without*, viz. the spreading abroad of the report. Notice in the last words, that her *further* recovery of strength is left to natural causes.

Chap. VI. 1—6.] Rejection of Jesus by his countrymen at Nazareth. Matt. xiii. 54—58, where see notes.

1.] ἐξῆλθ. ἐκεῖθ., not, *from the house of Jaeirus*, by the expression τὴν πατρίδα

u Matt. vii. 28 reff. v || Mt. Matt. xv. 33. Luke i. 43. Num. xi. 13. w = Luke xxiv. 17. x = Matt. xi. 20, 21 reff. y Acts ii. 23. v. 12. xix. 26 al. Gen. xxxix. 23. z || Mt. only. 2 Kings v. 11 al. a = || Mt. Matt. xxvi. 55. ch. ix. 19. John i. 1. 1 John i. 2. b Matt. xxvi. 31, 33 reff. c Matt. xii. 24 al. fr.

σκειν, καὶ [οἱ] πολλοὶ ἀκούοντες [u] ἐξεπλήσσοντο λέγοντες ABCDE FGHKL MSUV ΔΠℵ 1. 33. 69
[v] Πόθεν τούτῳ ταῦτα, καὶ [w] τίς ἡ σοφία ἡ δοθεῖσα τούτῳ,
καὶ [x] δυνάμεις τοιαῦται [y] διὰ τῶν [y] χειρῶν αὐτοῦ γίνονται;
3 οὐχ οὗτός ἐστιν ὁ [z] τέκτων, ὁ υἱὸς τῆς Μαρίας, καὶ
ἀδελφὸς Ἰακώβου καὶ Ἰωσῆτος καὶ Ἰούδα καὶ Σίμωνος;
καὶ οὐκ εἰσὶν αἱ ἀδελφαὶ αὐτοῦ ὧδε [a] πρὸς ἡμᾶς; καὶ
[b] ἐσκανδαλίζοντο ἐν αὐτῷ. 4 καὶ ἔλεγεν αὐτοῖς ὁ Ἰησοῦς
ὅτι [c] οὐκ ἔστιν προφήτης [d] ἄτιμος [c] εἰ μὴ ἐν τῇ [e] πατρίδι
αὐτοῦ καὶ [f] ἐν τοῖς [g] συγγενέσιν αὐτοῦ καὶ ἐν τῇ οἰκίᾳ
αὐτοῦ. 5 καὶ οὐκ [h] ἐδύνατο ἐκεῖ ποιῆσαι οὐδεμίαν [x] δύναμιν,

d || Mt. 1 Cor. iv. 10. xii. 23 only. Isa. liii. 3. e ver. 1. f = Matt. xi. 11 al. g Luke i. 36 (-νις, v. r.), 58. ii. 44. xiv. 12. xxi. 16. John xviii. 26. Acts x. 24. Rom. ix. 3. xvi. 7, 11, 21. Lev. xxv. 45. h 1 Cor. x. 21. xii. 3. Gen. xix. 22.

copt (æth) arm: txt A rel latt(not *f ff*$_1$) goth. rec om οι, with ACDℵ rel: ins BL 69. ακουσαντες D-gr FHLΔ[Π] 13. 69. 124. 236 evv-H-y lat-*a* (syrr). aft εξεπλησσοντο ins επι τη διδαχη αυτου D 2-pe 247 (not ev-y, as Tischdf) latt syr arm. aft ταυτα ins παντα C^2(απαντα C^1) ℵ vulg lat-*f g*$_{1.2}$ æth: pref παντα Δ. rec (for 2nd τουτω) αυτω (*corrn for elegance*), with AD rel latt: txt BCLΔℵ copt. rec ins οτι bef και (*for connexion*), with U(Treg, but omg και) lat-(*b*) *f ff*$_2$ *i* syrr(Treg) goth arm: ινα C^{1}DKΠ: om ABC^{2}ℵ rel vulg lat-*a c e* copt æth Thl. ins αι bef δυναμεις BΔℵ 33: om ACD rel. ins αι bef τοιαυται Δℵ^{3a}. aft τοιαυται ins αι LΔℵ^{3a} vulg lat-*c* (copt) æth. for γινονται, γινομεναι (*corrn to better the constrn, and to conform it to || Matt*) BLΔℵ 33 copt: γινωνται (cf ινα above) DKΠ arm-zoh: txt AC rel syrr goth æth.

3. for ο τεκτων, ο του τεκτονος υιος και 33. 69 ev-y gat(with mm tol) lat-*a b c i* æth arm Orig: ο του τεκτονος ο υιος και 13: om syr-jer. (*All are attempts to get rid of the fact implied. Orig says of Celsus: οὐ βλέπων ὅτι οὐδαμοῦ τῶν ἐν ταῖς ἐκκλησίαις φερομένων εὐαγγελίων τέκτων αὐτὸς ὁ Ἰησοῦς ἀναγέγραπται.*) rec om της, with AD rel: ins BCLΔℵ ev-y. rec (for και αδελφος) αδελφος δε, with A rel syr goth: αδελφος (alone) latt arm: txt BCΔ lat-*e* Syr copt æth, και ο αδελφος DLℵ. (33 def.) rec (for ιωσητος) ιωση, with AC rel syrr goth arm: ιωσηφ ℵ 121 vulg lat-*b e f g*$_{1.2}$ [*q*] æth: txt BDLΔ 33. 69 lat-*a* copt. (om ιω. κ. lat-*c ff*$_2$ *i*.) for και ουκ, ουχι και D lat-*a c f*: ου Δ: *nonne* lat-*b g*$_2$ Δ-lat: *nonne et* vulg lat-*g*$_1$. αι αδ. α. ω. π. ημας bef εισιν D vulg lat-*a f* [*g*$_1$ *i q*].

4. rec (for και ελεγ.) ελεγ. δε (*from || Matt*), with A rel lat-*c* syr goth æth arm: txt BCDLΔℵ 33 vulg lat-*a b e f i l* [*q*] Syr copt. ins ιδια bef πατριδι ALℵ^{3a}, simly 69. εαυτου L ℵ^1(txt ℵ^{3a}) 69. om τοις συγγ. αυτου και εν ℵ^1 lat-*c e*. for τοις, ταις D^1(txt D-corr^1) E^1(appy). συγγενευσιν B^1[sic, from inspection] D-corr^1 EFGHLUVΔ 1. 33. 69. rec (aft συγγ.) om αυτου, with AC^2 D[-gr] ℵ-corr^1 rel lat-*a* (*ff*$_2$) goth arm: ins BC^{1}KL M-marg [latt] syrr copt æth, εαυτου Δ. (33 def.)

5. (εδυνατο, so AB^{1}CKLMΠ Scr's a f p o w ev-y Orig$_1$.) rec ουδ. δυν. bef ποι., with A rel syr goth: ουδ. ποι. δυν. D ev-y lat-*a* Orig: txt BCLΔℵ 1 (Syr) copt (æth).

αὐτ. in the corresponding clause. I may go out of my own house *into a neighbour's*, but I do not say, I go *out of my own house* into Lincolnshire: the two members of such a sentence must *correspond*:—I go *out of Leicestershire* into Lincolnshire—so, as corresponding to τ. πατρίδ. αὐτ., ἐκεῖθεν must mean *from that city*, i. e. Capernaum. This against Meyer, who tries on this misinterpretation to ground a difference between Matt. and Mark.

2.] Before **δυνάμεις** we must understand another πόθεν, to make the construction complete.

3. ὁ τέκτων] This expression does not seem to be used at random, but to signify that the Lord had *actually worked* at the trade of his reputed father. Justin Martyr, Dial. § 88, p. 186, says ταῦτα γὰρ τὰ τεκτονικὰ ἔργα εἰργάζετο ἐν ἀνθρώποις ὤν, ἄροτρα καὶ ζυγά. Cf. the conflicting but apparently careless assertion of Orig. in the var. readd. See also the anecdote told by Theodoret, H. E. iii. c. 18, p. 940.

5. οὐκ ἐδύνατο] The *want of ability* spoken of is not *absolute*, but *relative*: οὐχ ὅτι αὐτὸς ἀσθενὴς ἦν, ἀλλ' ὅτι ἐκεῖνοι ἄπιστοι ἦσαν. Thl. The same voice, which

εἰ μὴ ὀλίγοις [i] ἀῤῥώστοις [j] ἐπιθεὶς τὰς [j] χεῖρας ἐθεράπευσεν. 6 καὶ ἐθαύμαζεν διὰ τὴν [k] ἀπιστίαν αὐτῶν.
Καὶ [l] περιῆγεν τὰς κώμας [m] κύκλῳ διδάσκων. 7 καὶ
προςκαλεῖται τοὺς δώδεκα, καὶ [n] ἤρξατο αὐτοὺς ἀποστέλ-
λειν [o] δύο [o] δύο, καὶ ἐδίδου αὐτοῖς [p] ἐξουσίαν τῶν [q] πνευμάτων
τῶν [r] ἀκαθάρτων, 8 καὶ [s] παρήγγειλεν αὐτοῖς ἵνα μηδὲν
[s] αἴρωσιν εἰς ὁδὸν εἰ μὴ ῥάβδον μόνον, μὴ ἄρτον μὴ
[t] πήραν μὴ εἰς τὴν [u] ζώνην [v] χαλκόν, 9 ἀλλὰ [w] ὑποδεδεμένους [x] σανδάλια, καὶ μὴ [y] ἐνδύσησθε δύο [z] χιτῶνας. 10 καὶ
ἔλεγεν αὐτοῖς Ὅπου ἐὰν εἰςέλθητε εἰς οἰκίαν, ἐκεῖ μένετε
ἕως ἂν ἐξέλθητε ἐκεῖθεν. 11 καὶ ὃς ἂν τόπος μὴ δέξηται

i Matt. xiv. 14 reff.
j Matt. xix. 13, 15 reff.
k ‖ Mt. reff.
l Matt. iv. 23 reff.
m ch. iii. 34 reff. Gen. xxxv. 5.
n ch. ii. 23 ‖ Mt. vv. 2, 32. Gen. xi. 6 al.
o here only. Gen. vi. 20. vii. 2, 3 al. (see vv. 39, 40.)
p constr., Matt. x. 1 reff. Ps. cxxxv. 8, 9.
q Matt. x. 1 reff.
r w. ἵνα, 2 Thess. iii. 12.
s = Matt. iv. 6. Luke xxii. 36. Gen. xliv. 1.
t ‖. Luke x. 4. xxii. 35, 36 only. 4 Kings iv. 42 compl. Judith x. 5. xiii. 10, 15 only.
u = ‖ Mt. (ch. i. 6 reff.)
v = ch. xii. 41 reff.
w Acts xii. 8. Eph. vi. 15 only. 2 Chron. xxviii. 15. Ezek. xvi. 10 AB(not Ed-vat.) only. (-δημα, ch. i. 7.)
x Acts xii. 8 only. Isa. xx. 2. Judith x. 4. xvi. 9 only.
y Matt. vi. 25 reff.
z John xix. 23 reff.

6. εθαυμα**σ**εν B E[1](appy) ℵ. for απιστιαν, πιστιν D-gr.

7. προςκαλε**σαμενος** D 1 lat-*a b c* [ff_2 *i q*] Gaud. aft δωδεκα ins μαθητας D lat-*b* ff_2 g_2 *i* [*q*]. for και to αποστελλειν, απεστειλεν αυτους D lat-*a b c e* ff_2 [*i*] æth Gaud. for δυο δυο, ανα β′ *per binos* D: *binos* latt. for και εδιδου, δους D 2-pe lat-[*c*] *e* ff_2 *i*. om εξουσιαν to αυτοις next ver (*homœotel*) ℵ[1](ins ℵ-corr[1·3]). om των (twice) CΔ 33. 69.

8. for αιρωσιν, αρωσιν CLΔℵ 69. for μη, μητε (thrice) D. rec transp αρτον and πηραν (*from* ‖ *Luke*), with AD rel latt syrr goth arm [Gaud]: txt BCLΔℵ 33 copt æth.

9. (αλλ**α**, so ABCDLUℵ.) elz ενδυσ**α**σθ**αι** (*for the construction, itacism confusing the word*), with B[2]SΠ[1] vulg lat-*e* (*b c* ff_2 $g_{1.2}$ *i* [*l q*]) syrr æth: ενδεδυσθαι L evv-H-z_2: ενδυσασθε B[1] 33: txt ℵ rel lat-*a* copt goth arm Gaud, ενδυσησθαι AC(Tischdf) DΔℵ.

10. for ελεγεν, λεγει A Scr's b lat-*b* [*q*]. οποι C[1]. for εαν, αν ADLΔ. om εις οικιαν D lat-*a* ff_2 *i*.

11. rec (for ος αν τοπος μη δεξηται) οσοι αν μη δεξωνται (*from* ‖ *Luke*), with AC[2]D rel latt syrr goth arm Orig-int (but εαν AC[2]DHKΠ 33): ος αν μη δεξηται (*see* ‖ *Matt*) C[1](appy) 1. 118. 209: txt BL Δ-gr ℵ 13. 28. 69. 124 syr-mg copt æth.

could still the tempests, could any where and under any circumstances have commanded diseases to obey; but in most cases of human infirmity, it was our Lord's practice to require *faith* in the recipient of aid: and that being wanting, the help *could not* be given. However, from what follows, we find that *in a few instances* it *did* exist, and the help was given accordingly. **6. ἐθαύμαζεν**] This need not surprise us, nor be construed otherwise than as a literal description of the Lord's mind: in the mystery of his humanity, as He was compassed by human infirmity,—grew in wisdom,—learned obedience,—knew not the day nor the hour (ch. xiii. 32),—so He might *wonder* at the unbelief of His countrymen. Observe, owing to the **διά** with an accus., that their unbelief is not here said to be the *object*, but the *cause*, of the Lord's wonder. **καὶ περιῆγεν**] See Matt. ix. 35.

7—13.] The sending forth of the Twelve. Matt. x. 1—15. Luke ix. 1—5. See also Matt. ix. 36—38, as the introduction to this mission. The variations in the three accounts are very trifling, as we might expect in so solemn a discourse delivered to all the twelve. See the notes to Matt.;—and respecting the subsequent difference between Matt. (ver. 16 ff.) and Luke,—those on Luke x. **7.**] **δύο δύο** (see reff.) is a Hebraism: see Winer, § 37. 3. The Greek expression would be *κατά*, or *ἀνὰ δύο*, as in ‖ Luke. Winer observes that the Syriac version always renders this latter expression by doubling the cardinal number. These *couples* are pointed out in Matt.'s list of the Apostles—*not however in Mark's*, which again shews the total absence of *connecting design* in this Gospel, such as is often assumed. **8.**] Striking instances occur in these verses, of the independence of the three reports in their present form. μηδὲ ῥάβδον Matt. = εἰ μὴ ῥ. μόνον Mark = μήτε ῥάβδον (-ους v. r.) Luke. See notes on Matt., also in the next clause. **9. ὑποδεδεμένους**]

ὑμᾶς μηδὲ [a] ἀκούσωσιν ὑμῶν, ἐκπορευόμενοι ἐκεῖθεν [bc] ἐκ- ABCDE
τινάξατε τὸν [bd] χοῦν τὸν [e] ὑποκάτω τῶν ποδῶν ὑμῶν [f] εἰς FGHKL MSUV
[f] μαρτύριον αὐτοῖς. 12 καὶ ἐξελθόντες ἐκήρυξαν [g] ἵνα μετα- ΔΠℵ 1. 33. 69
νοῶσιν, 13 καὶ δαιμόνια πολλὰ ἐξέβαλλον, καὶ [hi] ἤλειφον
[hk] ἐλαίῳ πολλοὺς [l] ἀῤῥώστους καὶ ἐθεράπευον. 14 καὶ ἤκουσεν ὁ βασιλεὺς Ἡρώδης· [m] φανερὸν γὰρ [m] ἐγένετο τὸ
ὄνομα αὐτοῦ. καὶ ἔλεγεν ὅτι Ἰωάννης ὁ [n] βαπτίζων [o] ἐκ
[o] νεκρῶν [o] ἀνέστη, καὶ διὰ τοῦτο [p] ἐνεργοῦσιν αἱ [p] δυνάμεις
ἐν αὐτῷ· 15 ἄλλοι δὲ ἔλεγον ὅτι Ἡλίας ἐστίν· ἄλλοι δὲ
ἔλεγον ὅτι προφήτης ὡς εἷς τῶν προφητῶν. 16 ἀκούσας

a constr., Gal. i. 23. Xen. ii. 4. 24.
b Isa. lii. 2.
c ‖ Mt. Acts xiii. 51. xviii. 6 only. Neh. v. 13.
d Rev. xviii. 19 only. Isa. xlviii. 19.
e Matt. xxii. 24 reff. 2 Kings xxii. 10.
f Matt. viii. 4 reff. Gen. xxi. 30.
g = ver. 8 al. fr. see note.
h Luke vii. 46. James v. 14. 2 Kings xiv. 2.
i Matt. vi. 17 reff.
k as above (h). Matt. xxv. 3, 4, 8. Luke x. 34. xvi. 6. Heb. i. 9 (from Ps. xliv. 7). Rev. vi. 6. xviii. 13 only.
l ver. 5.
m Acts vii. 13. 1 Cor. iii. 13. Phil. i. 13 al. 1 Macc. xv. 9.
n = ch. i. 4.
o (Matt. xvii. 9, v. r.) ch. ix. 9, 10. xii. 25. Luke xvi. 31. xxiv. 46. John xx. 9. Acts x. 41 al.
p = ‖ Mt. reff.

om τον υποκατω (‖ *Matt*) D 33 vulg lat-*a b* &c æth arm. rec at end adds αμην λεγω υμιν ανεκτοτερον εσται σοδομοις η γομορροις εν ημερα κρισεως η τη πολει εκεινη (*from* ‖ *Matt: prob, as Meyer,* from memory, ‖ *Matt having* (as 33 here) γη σοδομων κ. γομορρας), with A rel lat-*a f* g_2 [*q*] syrr copt-schw[-wilk] goth æth: om BCDLΔℵ vulg lat-*b c* ff_2 g_1 *i l* arm.

12. rec (for εκηρυξαν) εκηρυσσον (*corrd to* εξεβαλλον *below*), with A rel latt syr[-txt]: εκηρυσσεν F: txt BCDLΔℵ Syr syr-mg goth. add αυτοις ℵ[1](ℵ-corr[1] appy disapproving). rec μετανοησωσι (*amml corrn*), with ACℵ rel: txt BDL.

13. εξεβαλον CDMΔ 33. for ηλειφον, αλειψαντες, omg 3rd και, D lat-*b c* ff_2 *i* [*q*].

14. ηρωδης bef ο βασιλευς (*see* ‖ *Matt Luke*) C[3]DF 2-pe ev-y am(with fuld ing tol harl) lat-*a b c f i* [*q*] Syr æth. ελεγον B 6. 271 lat-*a b* ff_2 Aug_1, ελεγοσαν D. for βαπτιζων, βαπτιστης DS 33. 69 latt arm. rec (for ανεστη) ηγερθη (‖ *Matt*), with C rel: εγηγερται (‖ *Luke*), BDLΔℵ 33: txt AK Π-txt 28. 72 Scr's e o w Thl.—verb bef εκ νεκρων (‖ *Luke, cf also* ‖ *Matt*) BCDLΔℵ 33 latt Syr copt æth arm: txt A rel syr goth. αι δυναμεις bef ενεργουσιν (‖ *Matt*) KΔΠ[1] 33 vulg (not am) lat-*a* (*c* ff_2 *i* [*q*]) syrr.

15. rec om 1st δε, with M(Treg expr) U (FV, e sil) Syr arm: ins ABCDℵ rel latt syr copt goth. (homœotel 1st to 2nd οτι G 33.) om 2nd ελεγον ℵ 1. 28 lat-*a b c* ff_2 Syr arm. om προφητης ως D lat-*b c* ff_2 *i*. rec aft προφητης ins εστιν, with AC[2] rel vulg lat-*a f* g_1 [*q*] syrr copt goth æth arm: om BC[1]LΔℵ 1. 33 Orig. rec ins ἤ bef ως, with Δ 1 syr arm: om ABCℵ rel vulg lat-*f* g_1 *l* [*q*] Syr copt goth æth Orig Vict Thl.

Scil. πορεύεσθαι, or some equivalent infinitive. We have another change of construction in **ἐνδύσησθε.** These breaks serve to give the narrative a more lively form. **12.**] It is impossible to restrict the **ἵνα** after **ἐκήρυξαν** entirely to the telic meaning, as Meyer, who is a purist on this point, attempts to do. There is certainly the mingling of the purport and the purpose, so often found in this particle after verbs implying declaration or request. See this treated of in note, 1 Cor. xiv. 13. **13. ἤλειφον ἐλαίῳ**] This oil was not used *medicinally*, but as *a vehicle of healing power committed to them;*—a symbol of a deeper thing than the oil itself could accomplish. That such anointing has nothing in common with the extreme unction of Romanists, see proved in note on James v. 14. See for instances of such symbolic use of external applications, 2 Kings v. 14: Mark viii. 23: John ix. 6, &c.

14—29.] Herod hears of it. By occasion, the death of John the Baptist is related. Matt. xiv. 1—12. Luke ix. 7—9. (The account of John's death is not in Luke.) Our account is, as usual, the fullest of details. See notes on Matt. **14.**] Herod was not *king* properly, but only *tetrarch:*—see as above. He heard most probably of the *preaching of the twelve.* **15.**] (He is) **a prophet like one of the prophets;**—i. e. in *their* meaning, 'He is not *The Prophet* for whom all are waiting, but only *some* prophet like those who have gone before.' Where did our Evangelist get this remarkable expression, in his *supposed compilation from Matt. and Luke?*

δὲ ὁ Ἡρώδης ἔλεγεν [q] Ὃν ἐγὼ [r] ἀπεκεφάλισα Ἰωάννην,
οὗτος ἠγέρθη. 17 Αὐτὸς γὰρ ὁ Ἡρώδης ἀποστείλας
[s] ἐκράτησεν τὸν Ἰωάννην καὶ ἔδησεν αὐτὸν ἐν φυλακῇ διὰ
Ἡρωδιάδα τὴν γυναῖκα Φιλίππου τοῦ ἀδελφοῦ αὐτοῦ, ὅτι
αὐτὴν ἐγάμησεν. 18 ἔλεγεν γὰρ ὁ Ἰωάννης τῷ Ἡρώδῃ ὅτι
οὐκ ἔξεστίν σοι [t] ἔχειν τὴν γυναῖκα τοῦ ἀδελφοῦ σου. 19 ἡ
δὲ Ἡρωδιὰς [u] ἐνεῖχεν αὐτῷ, καὶ ἤθελεν αὐτὸν ἀποκτεῖναι,
καὶ οὐκ ἠδύνατο. 20 ὁ γὰρ Ἡρώδης ἐφοβεῖτο τὸν
Ἰωάννην, εἰδὼς αὐτὸν ἄνδρα δίκαιον καὶ ἅγιον, καὶ
[v] συνετήρει αὐτόν, καὶ ἀκούσας αὐτοῦ πολλὰ * ἐποίει, καὶ
[w] ἡδέως αὐτοῦ ἤκουεν. 21 καὶ γενομένης ἡμέρας [x] εὐκαίρου
Γ οτε ηρωδης.. ὅτε Ἡρώδης τοῖς [y] γενεσίοις αὐτοῦ δεῖπνον ἐποίησεν τοῖς

q constr., Matt. xxi. 42 ||, from Ps. cxvii. 22. 1 Cor. x. 16 al.
r || Mt. ver. 28 only. 1 Kings xxxi. 9 complut. Ps. cli. 7 only.
s Matt. xxi. 4 reff.
t || Mt. reff.
u = Luke xi. 53 (Gal. v. 1) only. Gen. xlix. 23 (Ezek. xiv. 4) only.
v = Matt. ix. 17 [|| L. v. r.] (Luke ii. 19) only. Job xxvii. 18 compl. F (not A).
w ch. xii. 37. 2 Cor. xi. 19 only. Prov. ix. 17. 2 Macc. vi. 30. (-διστα, 2 Cor xii. 9, 15.)
x Heb. iv. 16 only. Ps. ciii. 27. 2 Macc. xiv. 29 xv. 20 only. (-ρως, ch xiv. 11.)
y || only †.

16. om ο CDK¹UV 13. 28. 131. 346. 2-pe Scr's c f¹ m p q r s w¹ evv-x-y-z [copt]. rec (for ελεγεν) ειπεν (|| *Matt Luke*), with AD rel lat-*a c ff*$_2$ syrr: txt BCLΔℵ 33 lat-*f* copt. rec ins οτι bef ον (*to conform to preceding*), with AC rel copt goth: om BDLℵ 1. 33 latt syrr æth arm Orig. for ιωαννην ουτος, ουτος ιωαννης ℵ¹,-corr¹ (txt ℵ^{3a}): om ιωαννην D. rec aft ουτος ins εστιν αυτος (*from* || *Matt*), with AC rel (lat-*a b i* [*q*]) syr goth (æth) arm: αυτος (only) ℵ corr¹: om BDLΔℵ$^{1.3}$ (33) 69 vulg lat-*c ff*$_2$ *g*$_{1.2}$ (Syr) copt. rec aft ηγερθη ins εκ νεκρων (*see ver* 14), with A rel lat-*b c f ff*$_2$ [*q*] D-lat syrr goth æth arm; pref D[-gr] 13. 69. 124 vulg lat-*a g*$_{1.2}$ *i*; απο των νεκρων (|| *Matt*) C 237-53-9 Scr's c Orig$_1$: om BLΔℵ 33 syr-jer copt.

17. for αυτος γαρ ο, ο γαρ L ℵ^{3a}(but txt restored) copt goth(Tischdf): for γαρ, δε A lat-*g*$_2$: om ο D 69 ev-y. εν φυλακη bef και εδησεν αυτον A: και εβαλεν αυτον εις την φυλακην 28(Schulz) Syr-ed: for εν φυλακη, και εβαλεν εις φυλακην D 13. 69. 124 lat-*a b f ff*$_2$ *i* Syr-ms arm. rec ins τη bef φυλακη, with 1(e sil): om ABCℵ rel goth. (την γυναικα is omd in txt but insd on marg B¹.) εγαμησεν bef αυτην D latt.

18. om ο D Scr's p ev-y. om οτι D 28. 131. 245 ev-x vulg lat-*c f ff*$_2$ *g*$_1$ [*i*] æth. for σοι, σε D[-gr] lat-*a*. for την, αυτην (but αυ obliterated) D.

19. for ηθελεν, εζητει C¹ lat-*a b c i* [*q*] D-lat. αποκτειναι bef αυτον DU vulg lat-*a c i* [*q*]. αυτον απολεσαι C¹. εδυνατο AKΔΠ.

20. aft αγιον ins ειναι D lat-(*c*) *g*$_2$ *i*. om 2nd και B. * ἠπόρει BLℵ copt: εποιει ACD rel [latt] syrr goth æth arm. (om εποιει και Δ.)

21. aft γενομενης ins δε D¹ lat-(*a*) *b c* copt-ms. om οτε D lat-*a b* [*f q*]. for γενεσιοις, γενεχλιοις D¹(γενεθλιοις D-corr¹). rec (for εποιησεν) εποιει (*prob corrn to sense*, 'was making.' *Mey thinks it a mere mechanical repetn from ver* 20),

16.] On this repeated declaration of Herod, with its remarkable attraction of construction, De Wette strangely observes, 'Mark here combines the text of Luke with that of Matt.' "**ἐγώ** has the emphasis given by his guilty conscience." Meyer. The principal additional particulars in the following account of John's imprisonment and execution are,—ver. 19, that it was *Herodias* who persecuted John (on **ἐνεῖχεν** see reff. and note Luke xi. 53), whereas Herod knew his worth and holiness, and listened to him with pleasure, and even complied in many things with his injunctions:—that the maiden went and *asked counsel of her mother* before making the request:—and that a σπεκουλάτωρ, one of the body-guard (see note on ver. 27 below), was sent to behead John.

18.] **ἔλεγεν**—more than once: it was the burden of John's exhortations to him.

20. **συνετ.**] **preserved him**; not, '*esteemed him highly*:'—kept him in safety that he should not be killed by Herodias. The reading ἠπόρει is remarkable, and perhaps has some connexion with the διηπόρει of Luke ix. 7. The imperfects imply time, and habit. Whether Herod heard him only at such times as he happened to be at Machærus, or took him also to his residence at Tiberias, is, as Meyer remarks, uncertain.

21.]

z Rev. vi. 15. xviii. 23 only. Jon. iii. 7 al.
a John xviii. 12. Rev. vi. 15. xix. 18 only, exc. Acts xxi.—xxv. passim. 1 Chron. xiii. 1.
b = Luke xix. 47. Acts xiii. 50. xxv. 2.
c ‖ Mt. Matt. xi. 17 ‖ L. only. 2 Kings vi. 16.
d ‖ Mt. reff.
e Matt. ix. 10 reff.
f ch. v. 41, 42 reff.
g constr., Matt. vii. 9 reff.
h = Matt. xviii. 21, 22. xxvi. 38. Luke xxii. 51. Esth. v. 3.
i Luke i. 39. Exod. xii. 11.
j as above (i). Rom. xii. 8, 11. 2 Cor. vii. 11, 12. viii. 7, 8, 16. Heb. vi. 11. 2 Pet. i. 5. Jude 3 only.
k w. ἵνα, & subj., Matt. vii. 12. ch. x. 35. John xvii. 24.
l Acts x. 33. xi. 11. xxi. 32. xxiii. 30. Phil. ii. 23 only.
m ver. 28 and ‖. Luke xi. 39 only †.
n ch. xiv. 34 ‖ Mt. Luke xviii. 23, 24 only. Ps. xli. 5, 11. xlii. 5. Esdr. viii. 71, 72 (69, 70) only.
o Matt. ix. 10 reff.
p = here only. (ch. vii 9 al.) Ps. xiv. 4.

ABCDE FGHKL MSUV ΓΔΠℵ 1. 33. 69

z μεγιστᾶσιν αὐτοῦ καὶ τοῖς a χιλιάρχοις καὶ τοῖς b πρώτοις
τῆς Γαλιλαίας, 22 καὶ εἰςελθούσης τῆς θυγατρὸς αὐτῆς
τῆς Ἡρωδιάδος καὶ c ὀρχησαμένης, d ἤρεσεν τῷ Ἡρώδῃ
καὶ τοῖς e συνανακειμένοις, ὁ δὲ βασιλεὺς εἶπεν τῷ
f κορασίῳ g Αἴτησόν με ὃ ἐὰν θέλῃς, καὶ δώσω σοί.
23 καὶ ὤμοσεν αὐτῇ ὅτι ὃ ἐάν με αἰτήσῃς δώσω σοί,
h ἕως ἡμίσους τῆς βασιλείας μου. 24 καὶ ἐξελθοῦσα
εἶπεν τῇ μητρὶ αὐτῆς Τί αἰτήσωμαι; ἡ δὲ εἶπεν Τὴν
κεφαλὴν Ἰωάννου τοῦ βαπτίζοντος. 25 καὶ εἰςελθοῦσα
εὐθὺς i μετὰ ij σπουδῆς πρὸς τὸν βασιλέα ᾐτήσατο λέγουσα
k Θέλω ἵνα l ἐξ αὐτῆς δῷς μοι ἐπὶ m πίνακι τὴν κεφαλὴν
Ἰωάννου τοῦ βαπτιστοῦ. 26 καὶ n περίλυπος γενόμενος
ὁ βασιλεύς, διὰ τοὺς ὅρκους καὶ τοὺς o ἀνακειμένους οὐκ
ἠθέλησεν p ἀθετῆσαι αὐτην. 27 καὶ εὐθὺς ἀποστείλας ὁ

with A rel syrr: txt BCDLΔℵ 69 latt. om [2nd] αυτου D 1 vulg lat-*a b f* [*q*].

22. for εισελθ., ελθουσης ℵ[1](txt ℵ[3a]). for κ. εισελθ., εισελθ. δε D-gr 28 (vulg lat-*a c*). for αυτης της, αυτου BDLΔℵ: om αυτης (*see* ‖ *Matt*) 1. 118. 209 lat-*b c f* Syr copt goth æth arm. rec (for ηρεσεν) και αρεσασης (*to help the construction*), with AC[3]D rel vulg lat-*a b f g*$_2$ [*i q*] (syrr) goth (æth): txt BC[1]L(Δ)ℵ 33 lat-*c ff*$_2$ copt arm. rec ειπεν ο βασ., omg δε (*part of preceding corrn*), with C[3]D rel lat-*a b ff*$_2$ syr goth arm: ειπεν δε ο β. A lat-*c ff*$_2$ copt [(Syr æth)]: txt BC[1]LΔℵ 33. αιτησαι ℵ. om εαν DΔ 1 lat-*a b c f*. θελεις DHL 1: εθελης Δ. και δωσω σοι bef ο εαν θελ. KΠ[1] ev-w.

23. om αυτη L: aft αυτη ins πολλα D 28. 2-pe lat-*a* (*b* ?) *ff*$_2$ arm. for οτι ο εαν, ο τι εαν BΔ: ει τι αν D-gr. αιτησης bef με AKΠ[1] goth arm: om με HLℵ 69 vulg lat-*b c l* [*q*] copt. for εως ημισους, και το ημισυ D latt.

24. rec (for και) η δε (*from* ‖ *Matt*), with ACD rel lat-*a b f ff*$_2$ syrr goth: txt BLΔℵ 33 copt æth. rec αιτησομαι, with E rel: txt ABCDGLΔℵ 33. rec (for βαπτιζοντος) βαπτιστου (*corrn to more usual word; but see ch* i. 4, *and ver* 14), with ACD 33(Treg expr) rel [latt]: txt BLΔℵ syr goth.

25. for εισελθ., ελθουσα ℵ[1](txt ℵ[3a]) Scr's s. (ευθυς, so BCΔℵ 33: om DL 1 lat-*a b c i l* [*q*] copt.) om μετα σπουδης D lat-*a b c* [*i q*]. βασ. ειπεν δος μοι επι πινακι ωδε D (*see* ‖ *Matt*).—for ητησ. λεγ., ειπεν DΔ 1 lat-*a* (*b*) *ff*$_2$ *i* [*q*] (Syr) arm. —rec μοι δως εξαυτης, with A rel (syr) arm: txt BC[1]LΔℵ vulg lat-*a b i* Syr copt æth. for βαπτιστου, βαπτιζοντος L goth.

26. om 1st και D-gr. aft βασιλευς ins ως ηκουσεν D lat-*c ff*$_2$ *g*$_2$ *i*. ins δια bef 2nd τους D vulg lat-*a b* &c goth. rec **συνανακειμενους** (*from ver* 42 *and* ‖ *Matt*), with AC[2]Dℵ rel: txt B C[1](appy) LΔ Syr. rec αυτην bef αθετησαι, with AD rel vss: txt BCLΔℵ.

27. for και, αλλα D 2-pe vulg lat-*a c f ff*$_2$ *g*$_1$ [*i*] *l* Syr. (ευθυς, so BCLΔℵ: om vulg lat-*c ff*$_2$ *g*$_1$ *i l*.) ο βασ. bef αποστ. KΠ Scr's d ev-w: om ο βασ. D 1 Scr's a

εὐκαίρ., not, a *festal* day, as Hammond and others interpret it, for this use of εὔκαιρος hardly seems to be justified—but, a **convenient** day (see ver. 31 and Acts xxiv. 25,—and cf. Soph. Œd. Col. 32) for the purposes of Herodias: which shews that the dance, &c. *had been all previously contrived by her.* **μεγιστᾶνες**, a Macedonian word, which came into use at the Alexandrine conquest. See Lobeck on Phrynichus, p. 197. He adduces the nom. form μεγιστᾶνος from Anna Comnena, xi. 324 c. **23.**] The contracted **ἡμίσους** belongs to later Greek, as does also **ἀθετέω**, ver. 26. Webst. and Wilk. quote a parallel from Cic. de Senectute, c. xii.: "Flaminius, cum esset consul in Gallia, exoratus in convivio a scorto est, ut securi feriret aliquem eorum, qui in vinculis essent, damnati rei capitalis."

βασιλεὺς [q] σπεκουλάτορα [r] ἐπέταξεν ἐνέγκαι τὴν κεφαλὴν
αὐτοῦ. 28 καὶ ἀπελθὼν [s] ἀπεκεφάλισεν αὐτὸν ἐν τῇ φυλακῇ
καὶ ἤνεγκεν τὴν κεφαλὴν αὐτοῦ ἐπὶ [t] πίνακι, καὶ ἔδωκεν
αὐτὴν τῷ [u] κορασίῳ, καὶ τὸ [u] κοράσιον ἔδωκεν αὐτὴν
τῇ μητρὶ αὐτῆς. 29 καὶ ἀκούσαντες οἱ μαθηταὶ αὐτοῦ
ἦλθαν καὶ [v] ἦραν τὸ [w] πτῶμα αὐτοῦ καὶ ἔθηκαν αὐτὸ ἐν
μνημείῳ.

30 Καὶ [x] συνάγονται οἱ ἀπόστολοι πρὸς τὸν Ἰησοῦν,
καὶ ἀπήγγειλαν αὐτῷ πάντα ὅσα ἐποίησαν καὶ ὅσα
ἐδίδαξαν. 31 καὶ λέγει αὐτοῖς [y] Δεῦτε ὑμεῖς αὐτοὶ [z] κατ᾽
[z] ἰδίαν εἰς ἔρημον τόπον, καὶ [a] ἀναπαύσασθε [b] ὀλίγον.
ἦσαν γὰρ οἱ ἐρχόμενοι καὶ οἱ ὑπάγοντες πολλοί, καὶ

q here only †.
r constr., without dat., here only. Tobit iii. 6. see ver. 39.
s ver. 16.
t ver. 25.
u ver. 22.
v || Mt. 1 Macc. ix. 19.
w || Mt. v. r. Matt. xxiv. 28. ch. xv. 45. Rev. xi. 8, 9 bis only. Judg. xiv. 8.
x Matt. xiii. 2 reff.
y Matt. iv. 19 reff.
z Matt. xvii. 1, 19 al. 2 Macc. iv. 5 only.
a ch. xiv. 41 || Mt. Luke xii. 19. Dan. xii. 13.
b James iv. 14. 1 Pet. i. 6. v. 10. Rev. xvii. 10. Prov. xxiv. 33.

latt. rec ενεχθηναι (*so || Matt*, δοθηναι), with AD rel latt syrr : txt BCΔ(ℵ ?).—homœotel in ℵ 33 -νεγκε(sic [ℵ]) την κεφ. αυτου to ηνεγκε την κεφ. αυτου next ver. at end ins επι πινακι CΔ vulg lat-*c* g_1. [ℵ 33 ? not 1, appy.]

28. rec (for και) ο δε (*corrn for elegance*), with AD rel syr goth arm : txt BCLΔ 1 ev-y lat-*a c* ff_2 *i* Syr copt-schw (æth). om αυτου D lat-*a*. om 1st αυτην LΔ 1 lat-*b c* Syr arm [Thl]. for 2nd εδωκεν, ηνεγκεν C 33 copt-ms. om 2nd αυτην D 33 vulg lat-*a c* ff_2 *i* Syr æth arm.

29. ακ. δε D 6-pe copt-wilk. (ηλθαν, so BL 33.) for αυτο, αυτον ℵ 346(Sz). Steph ins τω bef μνημειω, with D (1, e sil) : om ABCℵ rel.

30. rec aft παντα ins και (*appy to correspond to* και οσα *below*), with A rel syr goth : om BCDELVΔℵ 1. 33 latt Syr copt æth arm Aug. om 2nd οσα C^1 $ℵ^1$(ins $ℵ^{3a}$) 1 latt.

31. rec (for λεγει) ειπεν, with AD rel lat-*a* syr : txt BCLΔℵ 33 vss. aft αυτοις ins ο ῑς D 69 lat-*a b c* &c arm. for υμεις αυτοι κατ᾽ ιδιαν, υπαγωμεν D lat-*a c* ff_2 *i* æth. for εις, επ $LΔℵ^{3a}$. rec αναπαυεσθε, with DLℵ rel : txt ABCMΔ 69. om οι (bef υπαγοντες) C^1(perhaps) KM.

27.] **σπεκουλάτωρ** is supposed by some to represent *spiculator*, and to mean δορύφορος, as Suidas: by others, *speculator*, κατάσκοπος, as Philoxenus, in Gloss., one of the body-guard, which is the meaning taken by Meyer here. The Commentators refer to Seneca de Ira, i. 16, "Centurio supplicio præpositus condere gladium speculatorem jubet:" de Benef. iii. 25, "Speculatoribus occurrit, nihil se deprecari quo minus imperata peragerent dixit, et deinde cervicem porrexit:" Julius Firmicus, viii. 26, calls those "speculatores, qui nudato gladio hominum amputant cervices." See Suet. Claud. 25: and a list of the sources of information in Schleusner, sub voce.

30—44.] Feeding of the five thousand. Matt. xiv. 13—21. Luke ix. 10—17. John vi. 1—13. This is one of the very few points of comparison between the *four Gospels* during the ministry of our Lord. And here again I believe Mark's report to be an original one, and of the *very highest* authority. Professor Bleek (Beiträge zur Evangelienkritik, p. 200) believes that Mark has *used the Gospel of John*,—on account of the 200 denarii in our ver. 37 and John ver. 7;—and that he generally compiles his narrative from Matt. and Luke (ibid. p. 72—75), which has been elsewhere shewed to be utterly untenable. I believe Mark's to be an *original full account;* Matt.'s a compendium of *this same account*, but drawn up independently of Mark's:—Luke's a compendium of *another account:*—John's an *independent narrative of his own as an eye-witness.*

30.] Mentioned by Luke, *not* by Matt. **31—34.**] One of the most affecting descriptions in the Gospels, and in this form peculiar to Mark. Matt. has a brief compendium of it. Every word and clause is full of the rich recollections of one who saw, and felt the whole. Are we mistaken in tracing the warm heart of him who said, 'I will go with thee to prison and to death?' **31.**] **ὑμεῖς αὐτοί**—not others; 'you alone.'

οὐδὲ φαγεῖν ᶜ εὐκαίρουν. 32 καὶ ἀπῆλθον εἰς ἔρημον
τόπον τῷ πλοίῳ ᶻ κατ' ᶻ ἰδίαν. 33 καὶ εἶδον αὐτοὺς ὑπ-
άγοντας καὶ * ἔγνωσαν πολλοί, καὶ ᵈ πεζῇ ἀπὸ πασῶν
τῶν πόλεων ᵉ συνέδραμον ἐκεῖ καὶ ᶠ προῆλθον αὐτούς.
34 καὶ ἐξελθὼν εἶδεν πολὺν ὄχλον, καὶ ᵍ ἐσπλαγχνίσθη
ἐπ' αὐτούς, ὅτι ἦσαν ὡς ʰ πρόβατα ʰ μὴ ἔχοντα ʰ ποιμένα,
καὶ ἤρξατο διδάσκειν αὐτοὺς πολλά. 35 καὶ ἤδη ⁱ ὥρας
ⁱ πολλῆς γενομένης προσελθόντες αὐτῷ οἱ μαθηταὶ αὐτοῦ
ἔλεγον ὅτι ἔρημός ἐστιν ὁ τόπος, καὶ ἤδη ⁱ ὥρα ⁱ πολλή·
36 ᵏ ἀπόλυσον αὐτούς, ἵνα ἀπελθόντες εἰς τοὺς ˡ κύκλῳ
ἀγροὺς καὶ κώμας ἀγοράσωσιν ἑαυτοῖς τί φάγωσιν.

...ηυκαιρουν C. ABDEF GHKL MSUVΓ ΔΠℵ 1. 33. 69

c Acts xvii. 21. 1 Cor. xvi. 12 only +. constr., here only.
d ‖ Matt. only. 2 Kings xv. 17 B only (?).
e = Acts iii. 11 (1 Pet. iv. 4) only ‡. Judith vi. 16 al.
f constr., Luke xxii. 47 only ‡. (ch. xiv. 35 al.)
g ‖ Mt. Matt. xv. 32. ch. i. 14 al.+
h Matt. ix. 36. see Num. xxvii. 17. 3 Kings xxii. 17.
i here bis only. (= ὀψία, ‖ Mt.) ἐμάχοντο ἤδη πολλῆς ὥρας, Dion. Hal. ii. 54.
k = ‖ Mt. reff.
l ch. iii. 34 reff.

for ευκαιρουν, *ευκαιρος*(so D^1, -*ρως* D^2) ειχον D. (ευκ., so ABEFGHLVΓΔℵ.)

32. και αναβαντες εις το πλοιον απηλθ. εις D vulg lat-*a c* &c. εν τω πλ. εις ερ. τ. (*see Matt* xiv. 13) BLΔ (ℵ 33) 69 copt arm (om εν 33, om τω ℵ).

33. ειδαν D. rec aft υπαγοντας ins οι οχλοι (*from* ‖ *Matt Luke*), with 69: om ABDℵ rel latt (Syr) syr copt æth arm. *rec ἐπέγνωσαν, with AB^2Lℵ rel: εγνωσαν B^1D 1. rec adds αυτον, with Γ rel; αυτους AKLMUΔΠℵ 33 lat-*f* syrr copt æth: om BD 1 latt arm. for πασων των, παντων (sic) D. rec at end ins και συνηλθον προς αυτον, with E rel lat-*f* syr: om BLΔℵ 1 ev-y vulg lat-*c l* Syr copt arm Euthym. (*The follg acct of the many varns, mostly after Meyer, is perhaps the right one.* προηλθον αυτους *was origl* (so Lachm Tischdf-1849-66 Treg Mey): then for προ-, προσηλθον αυτους L 31. 258 ev-y,—προσηλθ. αυτοις Δ Scr's s,—προσηλθ. αυτω 69,—προσηλθ. αυτοι Γ,—προσηλθεν αυτους 346(Sz),—προσηλθεν αυτος 427(Sz), &c: —then συνηλθον αυτου D lat-*b*,—συνεδραμον προς αυτον A,—συνεισηλθον προς αυτους 69,—συνηλθον αυτω 28(Sz),—συνηλθον προς αυτον, as rec,—*and these either single or combined with* προηλθον αυτους.)

34. for ειδεν, και ειδων D lat-(*a b c* ff_2) *i* [*q*]. rec adds ο ιησους, with Δ rel lat-ff_2 syr: pref AUΠ lat-*c f* (*i*) Syr æth: aft οχλον D 253 vulg lat-*a b l* [*q*]: om BLℵ 1. 33. 69 lat-g_1 copt arm. οχλον bef πολυν ℵ [33] Scr's p vulg-ed lat-*a f*. om και (bef εσπλ.) D lat-*a b c* ff_2 *i*. rec επ' αυτοις (*from* ‖ *Matt*), with A rel lat-*a c* ff_2: txt BDFℵ vulg lat-*b f i* [*l q*]. om ως προβατα $ℵ^1$(ins $ℵ^{3a}$). αυτους bef διδασκειν AKΓΠ vulg(not am) lat-ff_2.

35. ηδη δε D-gr 2-pe lat-*a*. γινομενης Dℵ. οι μαθηται bef αυτω, omg αυτου (so also 1. 69 lat-*c* arm), A: transp αυτω, insg aft verb, DKΠ lat-*b* g_2 [*q*]: om αυτω $ℵ^1$ vulg lat-*a* æth arm: txt B$ℵ^{3a}$ rel syrr. rec (for ελεγον) λεγουσιν, with AD rel (Syr) syr: txt BLΔℵ 33 copt. om ο and και D^1(ins D^2).

36. for κυκλω, εγγιστα D latt. for κωμ., εις τας κωμ. ινα D. rec aft εαυτοις ins αρτους, with A rel: βρωματα ℵ, *cibos* vulg lat-*b c f l*: om BDLΔ lat-*a* ff_2 *i* copt arm. rec (for τι φαγ.) τι γαρ φαγωσιν ουκ εχουσιν, with A rel lat-(*b*) *f* syrr æth arm: τι φαγειν D: txt BLΔℵ vulg lat-*a c* ff_2 g_2 *i l* copt. (αρτους *was a gloss from ver* 37: *then* τι φαγ. *was filled up from ch* viii. 2 *or Matt* xv. 32.)

33.] **πεζῃ**, not '*a-foot*,' but **by land**: and so most usually: e. g. Herod. vii. 110,—τουτέων οἱ μὲν παρὰ θάλ. κατοικημένοι ἐν **νηυσὶ** εἵποντο· οἱ δὲ αὐτέων τὴν μεσόγαιαν οἰκέοντες . . . **πεζῇ** . . . εἵποντο.

34. ἐξελθών] **having disembarked**, most probably. Meyer would render it, '*having come forth from his solitude*,' in Matt.,—and '*having disembarked*' here: but I very much doubt the former. There is nothing in Matt. to imply that He had *reached his place of solitude before* the multitudes came up. John indeed, vv. 3—7, *seems* to imply this; but He may very well have mounted the hill or cliff from the sea before He saw the multitudes, and this would be *on his disembarkation*. To shew how arbitrary is the assumption of Mark having combined Matt and Luke,—see how easily the same might be said of *Luke himself*, with regard to *Matt.* and *Mark* here:—ἐθεράπευσεν τοὺς ἀρρώστους αὐτῶν, Matt.:—ἤρξατο διδάσκειν αὐτ. πολ., Mark;—ἐλάλει αὐτοῖς περὶ τ. βασ. τ. θ., κ. τοὺς χρείαν ἔχ. θεραπείας ἰᾶτο, Luke: = Matt.

37 ὁ δὲ ἀποκριθεὶς εἶπεν αὐτοῖς [m] Δότε αὐτοῖς ὑμεῖς [m] φαγεῖν. καὶ λέγουσιν αὐτῷ Ἀπελθόντες ἀγοράσωμεν [n] δηναρίων διακοσίων ἄρτους, καὶ [m] δώσομεν αὐτοῖς [m] φαγεῖν;
38 ὁ δὲ λέγει αὐτοῖς Πόσους [o] ἄρτους ἔχετε; ὑπάγετε ἴδετε.
καὶ [p] γνόντες λέγουσιν Πέντε, καὶ δύο ἰχθύας.
39 καὶ [q] ἐπέταξεν αὐτοῖς [r] ἀνακλῖναι πάντας [st] συμπόσια [st] συμπόσια ἐπὶ τῷ [uv] χλωρῷ [uw] χόρτῳ.
40 καὶ [x] ἀνέπεσαν [ty] πρασιαὶ [ty] πρασιαί, [z] κατὰ ἑκατὸν καὶ [z] κατὰ πεντήκοντα.
41 καὶ [a] λαβὼν τοὺς πέντε ἄρτους καὶ τοὺς δύο ἰχθύας
[b] ἀναβλέψας εἰς τὸν οὐρανὸν [c] εὐλόγησεν, καὶ [d] κατέκλασεν τοὺς ἄρτους καὶ ἐδίδου τοῖς μαθηταῖς, ἵνα [e] παρατιθῶ-

m || Mt. reff.
n gen. aft. ἀγορ., here only, see Matt. xxvi. 9. ch. xiv. 5 ||. John xii. 5.
o = ||. ch. viii. 5 ||. Luke xi. 5 al. 1 Kings xxi. 3.
p abs., 1 Cor. xiii. 9.
q constr. dat. & inf., Luke viii. 31. Acts xxiii. 2. Esth. i. 8. see ver. 27. ch. i. 27.
r constr., || L. Luke ii. 7. (Matt. viii. 11 reff.)
s here bis only. Esth. vii. 7.
t constr., ver. 7. Gen. vii. 2, 3. Exod. viii. 14. Ezek. xiv. 4.
u Rev. viii. 7. Gen. i. 30 al.
v as above (u). Rev. vi. 8. ix. 4 only. Exod. x. 15.
w || Mt. J Matt. vi. 30 al.
x Matt. xv. 35 reff.
y here bis only †. Sir. xxiv. 31 only.
z = 1 Cor. xiv. 27. John xxi. 25.
a ||. ch. viii. 6 al. Gen. xxi. 14.
b = || Mt. reff.
c ch. viii. 7. xiv. 22 || Mt. L. 1 Cor. x. 16. Gen. i. 22, 28.
d || L. only. Ezek. xix. 12 only.
e || L. ch. viii. 6 bis, 7. Luke x. 8. Acts xvi. 34. 1 Cor. x. 27 al. Gen. xliii. 31, 32.

37. for ο δε, και D latt æth. om 1st αυτοις AL 1. 33: add ο ῑς D lat-*a* (*c*) *i*. rec διακ. bef δην. (*see* || *John*), with DMΓ vulg lat-*c* ff_2 g_2 Syr æth arm: txt ABא rel am(with fuld ing tol) lat-*a b f* g_1 *i* [*q*] syr. rec δωμεν (*corrn to* αγορασωμεν, *from misunderstanding the constr: see below*), with E rel: δωσωμεν Dא 33. 69: txt A B(sic, from inspection) LΔ latt.

38. for ο δε, και D vulg lat-*a f* g_2 [*i q*] æth. aft αυτοις ins ο ῑς D lat-*b* [*q*]. εχετε bef αρτους BLΔ æth. rec ins και bef ιδετε, with A rel vulg lat-*a f* ff_2 [*i q*] syr: om BDLא 1. 33 lat-*b c* Syr copt æth arm-zoh. for γνοντες, ελθοντες א[1](txt א[3a]). aft λεγουσιν ins αυτω (*see* || *Matt*) AD M-marg 69 tol lat-*a b f* ff_2 *i l* Syr æth arm. aft πεντε ins αρτους (|| *Matt*) D 2-pe gat(with mm) lat-*a c f* ff_2 *i* [*q*] Syr copt.

39. for αυτοις, ο ῑς D: αυτοις ο ῑς mt lat-*a b f* g_2 D-lat. ανακλιθηναι (*corrn to* || *Matt, the* active *not being understood*) B[1]Gא 1. 69 $Orig_1$. for συμπ. συμπ., κατα την συμποσιαν *secundum contubernia* D vulg lat-*b c* &c: om lat-*a*: om 2nd συμπ. L 69[1] Scr's c[2] f[2] n[2] p.

40. (ανεπεσαν, so BEFGHMVΔא 1.) om 2nd πρασιαι LΔא; om both lat-*a*. rec for κατα (twice), ανα (*from* || *Luke*), with A rel: txt BDא copt(retaining the gr words κατα ρ' κατα ν').

41. om τους (bef πεντε) D. for κατεκλασεν, κλασας (omg και, which is insd by א[3a]) א[1] (38) ev-y: εκλασεν L. ins πεντε bef 2nd αρτους D lat-*b c*. rec aft μαθηταις ins αυτου, with A D-gr rel [latt] syrr æth: om BLΔא (33) lat-g_2 D-lat copt arm. rec (for παρατιθ.) παραθωσιν (|| *Luke*), with ADא[3] rel: txt BLM[1]ΔΠ[1]א[1].

† Mark. **35.**] See notes on John vi. 3—7, and Matt. xiv. 15—17. The *Passover was near*, which would account for the multitude being on the move.

37.] This verse is to me rather a decisive proof that (see above) Mark had *not seen* John's account; for how could he, having done so, and with his love for accurate detail, have so generalized the particular account of Philip's question? That generalization was *in the account which he used*, and the circumstance was more exactly related by John, as also the following one concerning Andrew. **δώσομεν**] I prefer placing the interrogation at the end of the sentence, as simpler and less harsh than the arrangement of Lachm. (interrog. aft. ἄρτους, full stop at end) or Tischdf. (comma, full stop). The two verbs will then be rendered **must we go and buy, &c. . . . , and shall we** (thus) **give them to eat?**

40.] **πρασιαί** (ref. Sir.) λέγονται τὰ ἐν τοῖς κήποις διάφορα κόμματα, ἐν οἷς φυτεύονται διάφορα πολλάκις λάχανα. Theophylact. Similarly Suidas, who adds καὶ πράσιον λάχανον, viz. hore-hound: but the derivation is more probably from πράσον, a leek. The word occurs in Hom. Od. η. 127, ἔνθα δὲ κοσμηταὶ πρασιαὶ παρὰ νείατον ὄρχον | παντοῖαι πεφύασιν, where the Schol., αἱ λαχανεῖαι ἢ αἱ τῶν φυτειῶν τετράγωνοι σχέσεις, ὡς τὰ πλινθία. The distributive repetitions of these words are Hebraisms: see reff., and note on ver. 7.

41.] **κατέκλασεν** and **ἐμέρισεν**,

σιν αὐτοῖς, καὶ τοὺς δύο ἰχθύας [f] ἐμέρισεν πᾶσιν. 42 καὶ
ἔφαγον πάντες καὶ [g] ἐχορτάσθησαν· 43 καὶ ἦραν [h] κλάσματα δώδεκα [i] κοφίνων [k] πληρώματα, καὶ ἀπὸ τῶν
ἰχθύων. 44 καὶ ἦσαν οἱ φαγόντες τοὺς ἄρτους πεντακισχίλιοι ἄνδρες. 45 Καὶ εὐθὺς [l] ἠνάγκασεν τοὺς μαθητὰς
αὐτοῦ [m] ἐμβῆναι εἰς τὸ πλοῖον καὶ [n] προάγειν εἰς τὸ πέραν
πρὸς Βηθσαϊδάν, ἕως αὐτὸς [o] ἀπολύει τὸν ὄχλον.
46 καὶ [p] ἀποταξάμενος αὐτοῖς ἀπῆλθεν εἰς τὸ ὄρος προς-
εύξασθαι. 47 καὶ ὀψίας γενομένης ἦν τὸ πλοῖον ἐν
μέσῳ τῆς θαλάσσης, καὶ αὐτὸς μόνος ἐπὶ τῆς γῆς.
48 καὶ ἰδὼν αὐτοὺς [q] βασανιζομένους ἐν τῷ [r] ἐλαύνειν,
ἦν γὰρ ὁ ἄνεμος [s] ἐναντίος αὐτοῖς, περὶ τετάρτην [t] φυλακὴν τῆς νυκτὸς ἔρχεται πρὸς αὐτοὺς [u] περιπατῶν [u] ἐπὶ

X οψιας
ÄBDEF GHKL MSUVX ΓΔΠℵ 1. 33. 69

f = Rom. xii. 3. 1 Cor. vii. 17. 2 Cor. x. 13. Heb. vii. 2. Josh. xiii. 7.
g Matt. v. 6. ch. vii. 27 al. Ps. ciii. 13.
h ||. ch. viii. 8 || Mt., 19, 20 only. Ezek. xiii. 19 al.
i ||. ch. viii. 19 || Mt. only. Judg. vi. 19 B. Ps. lxxx. 5 only.
k ch. viii. 20 reff.
l || Mt. reff.
m Matt. viii. 23 reff.
n Matt. xiv. 22 reff.
o ver. 36.
p (=) Luke ix. 61. xiv. 33. Acts xviii. 18, 21. 2 Cor. ii. 13 only ‡. (Eccl. ii. 20. Jer. xx. 2. 1 Macc. xi. 3 only.)
q = || Mt. only. (2 Pet. ii. 8 al.)
r = || J. (Luke viii. 29. James iii. 4. 2 Pet. ii. 17) only. 3 Kings ix. 27. Isa. xxxiii. 21.
s = || Mt. Acts xxvii. 4. (ch. xv. 39. Acts xxvi. 9. xxviii. 17. 1 Thess. ii. 15. Tit. ii. 8 only. Prov. xiv. 7.)
t = || Mt. reff.
u ||. Job ix. 8.

for *αυτοις, κατεναντι αυτων* D: *ante eos* vulg lat-*a b* &c.

43. rec *κλασματων*, with ADℵ rel: om **1**: txt BLΔ. rec *κοφινους*, with AD rel: txt Bℵ 13. 69. 124. 209. 346. rec (for *πληρωματα*) *πληρεις* (|| *Matt*), with AD rel: txt BLΔℵ **1**. 69.

44. om *τους αρτους* D ℵ[1.3](ℵ[3a] wrote *το* but expunged it) **1** vulg lat-*a b l* arm Thl. rec ins *ωσει* bef *πεντακισχιλιοι* (*from* || *Matt*), with (**1** Scr's s, e sil) arm; *ως* ℵ 20: om ABD rel Scr's-mss latt syrr copt æth.

45. (*ευθυς*, so BLΔℵ. (33 def.)) aft *ευθ.* ins *εξεγερθεις* D lat-*a b c ff*$_2$ *g*$_2$ *i* [*q*]. om *αυτου* Orig(expr: *παρὰ τῷ Μάρκῳ . . ἁπλῶς τοὺς μαθητάς*). om *το* (bef *πλοιον*) ℵ **1**. 33. 253. aft *προαγ.*(*προσαγ.* D[1]) ins *αυτον* D **1**. 69 latt Syr copt æth arm Orig. for *εως αυτος, αυτος δε* D-gr 2-pe lat-*b*: *εως αυτους* L: *εως ιδειν αυτον* Δ. rec *απολυση* (*from* || *Matt*), with A rel, *απολυσει* E[1]KΓ 69: txt BDLΔℵ **1**.

47. aft *ην* ins *παλαι jam* D[-gr] **1**. 251 lat-*a b g*$_2$ *i*. *εν μεση τη θαλασση* D 2-pe. aft *μονος* ins *ην* AU 131: aft *γης* M 271 copt(Treg).

48. rec (for *ιδων*) *ειδεν* (*corrn for elegance, on account of the parenthetic clause ην γαρ . . . αυτοις*), with E rel, *ιδεν* AKMVXΠ[1]: txt BDLΔℵ vulg lat-*a b f ff*$_2$ [*q*] copt. *βασ. και ελαυνοντας* D, *remigantes et laborantes* lat-*a b c ff*$_2$ [*i q*]; simly 2-pe. *εναντιος* bef *ο ανεμος* Aℵ **1**. rec ins *και* bef *περι* (*to suit ειδεν above*), with ADX rel vulg lat-(*c i*) *f ff*$_2$ [*q*] syrr æth arm: om BLΔℵ lat-*a* (*b*). for *προς αυτους, ο ις*

aorists, each express the one act by which He broke up the bread, and divided the fishes: **ἐδίδου**, imperf., that He gave the bread, *bit by bit*, to His disciples to distribute: with the fish there was no need of this bit by bit giving—one assignment sufficed. See Bp. Wordsw.'s note. The dividing of the *fishes*, and (ver. 43) the taking up fragments from the *fishes*, are both peculiar to and characteristic of Mark: but it would have been most inconsistent with his precision to have omitted *χωρὶς γυν. κ. παιδ.* in ver. 44, had he had it before him.

45—52.] Jesus walks on the sea. Matt. xiv. 22—33. John vi. 16—21. Omitted in Luke. Matt. and Mark very nearly related as far as ver. 47. John's account altogether original, and differing materially in details: see notes there, and on Matt. **45.**] **τὸ πλ.**, the ship in which they had come. **Βηθσαϊδάν**] This certainly seems (against Lightfoot, Wieseler, Thomson (The Land and the Book), al.: see Bp. Ellicott's note, Lectures on Life of our Lord, p. 207) to have been the city of Peter and Andrew, James and John,—on the west side of the lake—and in the same direction as Capernaum, mentioned by John, ver. 17. The miracle just related took place near the other Bethsaïda (*Julias*),—Luke ix. 10. The pres. **ἀπολύει** is a change to the oratio directa, not unusual in Greek. So Herod. iii. 84, *οἱ δὲ λοιποὶ τῶν ἑπτὰ ἐβουλεύοντο ὡς βασιλέα δικαιότατα στήσονται.* See Kühner, Gram. ii. p. 594: Bernhardy, Syntax, p. 389, and numerous examples in both.

46.] **ἀποταξάμ.** in this sense belongs to later Greek: Phrynichus says,

τῆς θαλάσσης. καὶ ἤθελεν παρελθεῖν αὐτούς· 49 οἱ
δὲ ἰδόντες αὐτὸν [u] περιπατοῦντα [u] ἐπὶ τῆς θαλάσσης
[v] ἔδοξαν [w] φάντασμα εἶναι, καὶ [x] ἀνέκραξαν· 50 πάντες
γὰρ αὐτὸν εἶδον, καὶ [y] ἐταράχθησαν. καὶ εὐθὺς ἐλάλησεν
μετ' αὐτῶν, καὶ λέγει αὐτοῖς Θαρσεῖτε, ἐγώ εἰμι, μὴ
φοβεῖσθε. 51 καὶ [z] ἀνέβη πρὸς αὐτοὺς εἰς τὸ πλοῖον, καὶ
[a] ἐκόπασεν ὁ ἄνεμος· καὶ λίαν [b] ἐκ περισσοῦ ἐν ἑαυτοῖς
[c] ἐξίσταντο. 52 οὐ γὰρ [d] συνῆκαν ἐπὶ τοῖς ἄρτοις· ἦν
γὰρ αὐτῶν ἡ καρδία [e] πεπωρωμένη.
N vi. 53 (appy)... 53 Καὶ [f] διαπεράσαντες ἦλθον ἐπὶ τὴν γῆν Γεννησαρὲτ
καὶ [g] προσωρμίσθησαν. 54 καὶ ἐξελθόντων αὐτῶν ἐκ τοῦ
πλοίου εὐθὺς [h] ἐπιγνόντες αὐτὸν 55 [i] περιδραμόντες ὅλην

v = Luke viii. 18 al. fr.
w ‖ Mt. only †. Wisd. xvii. 15 only.
x ch. i. 23 reff. 1 Kings iv. 5.
y Mark, here only. Matt. ii. 3 reff.
z ‖ Mt. reff.
a ch. iv. 39 reff.
b here only. Dan. iii. 22. (ὑπερεκπ., Eph. iii. 20. 1 Thess. iii. 10.)
c Matt. xii. 23 reff.
d constr., here only. with εἰς, Ps. xxvii. 5. ἐν, Neh. viii. 12. ἐπί with acc., Ps. xl. 1.
e ch. viii. 17. John xii. 40. Rom. xi. 7. 2 Cor. iii. 14 only. Job xvii. 7 B only. (-ρωσις, ch. iii. 5.)
f Matt. ix. 1 reff. Isa. xxiii. 2.
g here only †.
h ‖ Mt. reff.
i here only. Jer. v. 1. Amos viii. 12 only.

D lat-*a ff*$_2$ *i* : πρ. αυτ. ο ις 61 lat-*f g*$_2$ Syr. ηθελησεν D.

49. επι τ. θ. bef περιπ. (*from ‖ Matt*) BLΔא 33. for φαντ. ειναι, οτι φαντασμα εστιν (‖ *Matt*) BLΔא 33.

50. om γαρ αυτον ειδον D 2-pe lat-*a b c ff*$_2$ *i* [*q*]. (ειδαν Bא.) for 2nd και, ο δε BLΔא 33 copt : txt ADX rel latt syrr æth arm. (ευθυς, so BLΔא : om D 33 lat-*c i*.) for μετ' αυτων, προς αυτους D 33 lat-*a b ff*$_2$ *i* : αυτοις 2-pe. for και λεγει αυτοις, λεγων D.

51. εις το πλοιον bef προς αυτους D 2-pe ev-49 lat-*a*(appy) *c i* [*q*] copt. om λιαν D-gr 1 lat-*b*. om εκ περισσου BLΔא lat-*a*(appy) Syr copt(appy) æth : περισσως D lat-*b* : εκπερισσως 1. rec adds και εθαυμαζον, with AD rel lat-(*a*) *b f* [*q*] syrr æth arm : om BLΔא 1 vulg lat-*c i l* copt.

52. for ην γαρ, αλλ' ην (*corrn for elegance, and to sense*) BL M-marg SΔא 33 syr-mg copt : txt AD rel vulg lat-*a c* &c syrr æth arm. rec η καρδια bef αυτων, with DLΔ 1. 69 latt : txt ABא rel.

53. aft διαπερασαντες ins εκειθεν D 45 lat-(*a*) *b c ff*$_2$ (*i*) [*q*]. επι τ. γην ηλθον εις γενν. BL (Δ, but om ηλθον) א 33 : ηλθ. εις γην γενν. 69 : ηλθ. εις τ. γ. γενν. X 247 Scr's c h (*cf ‖ Matt and var readd; there the same corrn has been attempted by* BDΔא) : txt ADN rel latt syrr copt æth. (γεννησαρετ, so AB^{2}LMΓΔ 33 : γεννησαρ D.) προσωρμηθησαν א^1 Scr's i : om και προσωρμισθησαν D 1 lat-*a b c ff*$_2$ *i* [*q*] Syr arm. add εκει N.

54. om αυτων B^1-txt(ins B^1-marg). (ευθυς, so BLΔא 69.) for επιγνοντες, επεγνωσαν D 2-pe latt syrr copt æth. at end add οι ανδρες του τοπου εκεινου (*from ‖ Matt*) AGΔ 1. 33 (69) lat-(*c*) *g*$_2$ Syr arm.

55. περιεδραμον and ins και bef ηρξ. BLΔא 33. 69 Syr copt æth : περιδραμοντες δε

ed. Lob. p. 24, ἀποτάσσομαί σοι, ἔκφυλον πάνυ. χρὴ γὰρ λέγειν, ἀσπάζομαί σε. See Lobeck's note. **48.**] **κ. ἤθ. παρ. αὐτ.**, peculiar to Mark. "A silent note of Inspiration. He was about to pass by them. He intended so to do. But what man could say this? Who knoweth the mind of Christ but the Spirit of God? Compare 1 Cor. ii. 11." Wordsw. But it may be doubted whether this is either a safe or a sober comment. ἤθελεν has here but a faint subjective reference, and is more nearly the "would have passed by them" of the E. V. See on Luke xxiv. 28, for the meaning. Lange, Leben Jesu, ii. p. 788 note, well remarks, that this ἤθελεν παρελθεῖν, and the ἤθελον οὖν of John vi. 21, mutually explain one another. **50.**] **πάντες . . . ἐταράχθ.**, peculiar to Mark. After this follows the history respecting Peter, which might naturally be omitted here if this Gospel were drawn up under his *inspection*—but this is at least doubtful in any general sense.

52.] Peculiar to Mark. **οὐ γὰρ συν.**] They did not, from the miracle which they had seen, infer the power of the Lord over nature. **ἐπί**, hardly as Kuinoel, al., *post*, but rather denoting, as usual, close superposition of the preceding on the following: there was no intelligent comprehension *founded on* the miracle of the loaves.

53—56.] Matt. xiv. 34—36. The two

k ch. ii. 4 reff. l Matt. iv. 24. ix. 12 ‖ al. Ezek. xxxiv. 4. m 2 Cor. iv. 10. Eph. iv. 14 (Heb. xiii. 9. Jude 12 v. r.) only. Prov. x. 24. Eccl. vii. 8. 2 Macc. vii. 27 only. o constr., Acts ii. 45. 1 Cor. xii. 2. p Matt. xi. 16. xxiii. 7 ‖. q w. ἵνα, ‖ Mt. reff. r ch. v. 28. Acts v. 15. 2 Cor. xi. 16. s ‖ Mt. Matt. ix. 20 ‖ L. xxiii. 5 only. Num. xv. 38. Zech. viii. 23.

ABDEF GHKL MNSUV XΓΔΠℵ 1. 33. 69

τὴν χώραν ἐκείνην ἤρξαντο ἐπὶ τοῖς [k] κραβάττοις
τοὺς [l] κακῶς ἔχοντας [m] περιφέρειν ὅπου ἤκουον ὅτι ἐκεῖ
ἐστιν. 56 καὶ ὅπου [o] ἂν εἰςεπορεύετο εἰς κώμας ἢ εἰς πόλεις ἢ εἰς ἀγρούς, ἐν ταῖς [p] ἀγοραῖς ἐτίθεσαν τοὺς ἀσθενοῦντας, καὶ [q] παρεκάλουν αὐτὸν ἵνα [r] κἂν τοῦ [s] κρασπέ-
δόυ τοῦ ἱματίου αὐτοῦ ἅψωνται, καὶ ὅσοι [o] ἂν ἥπτοντο
αὐτοῦ [t] ἐσώζοντο.
VII. 1 Καὶ [u] συνάγονται πρὸς αὐτὸν οἱ Φαρισαῖοι
καί τινες τῶν γραμματέων ἐλθόντες ἀπὸ Ἱεροσολύμων.
2 καὶ ἰδόντες τινὰς τῶν μαθητῶν αὐτοῦ [v] κοιναῖς χερσίν,
τουτέστιν [w] ἀνίπτοις, ἐσθίοντας [x] τοὺς ἄρτους· 3 οἱ γὰρ

t ch. v. 28 reff. u = Matt. xiii. 2 reff. v = ver. 5. Acts x. 14, 28. xi. 8. Rom. xiv. 14 (3ce). Heb. x. 29. Rev. xxi. 27 only ‡. 1 Macc. i. 62. w Matt. xv. 20 (ver. 5 v. r.) only †. x art., see 2 Thess. iii. 12.

D lat *a*. rec (for χωραν) περιχωρον (*from* ‖ *Matt*), with ADN rel lat-*b* [*q*] syr arm: txt BLΔℵ 33 vulg lat-*a c* &c Syr copt-gr goth (æth). for επι, εν ℵ[1] latt [not *a*]. om τοις D 1. 69: τοις is written twice by ℵ[1] but the 2nd marked for erasure by ℵ[3a]. for περιφερειν, φερειν DM 1 Scr's c copt goth.—φερειν παντας τ. κ. εχ. περιεφερον γαρ αυτους οπου αν ηκουσαν τον ιησ. ειναι D Scr's c, simly lat-*a b* ff_2 *i* æth. ηκουσθη (*see ch* ii. 1) ℵ. om εκει (*as superfluous*) B(D)LΔℵ (latt) Syr goth æth: ins AN rel syr copt arm.

56. for οπου, που D. εαν XΓΔℵ 33 Scr's h k s ev-z. εισεπορευοντο ALM: εισπορευονται Δ. rec om 2nd and 3rd εις, with AN rel copt, om 3rd F: ins BD LΔℵ 33 (vulg) lat-*c* syr goth arm.—εις αγρ. η εις τας πολεις D. aft αγρους ins η ℵ. for αγοραις, πλατειαις D 2-pe vulg lat-*b c f* ff_2 $g_{1.2}$ *l* [*i q*] syrr copt goth. (*in foro et in platæis* lat-*a*.) rec ετιθουν (*corrn to conform to* παρεκαλουν *below*), with ADN rel: txt BLΔℵ. αψονται HKN Scr's evv-H-y. om αν (bef ηπτ.) (*see* ‖ *Matt*) DΔℵ 1. 33. for ηπτοντο, ηψαντο (*from* ‖ *Matt*) B D-gr LΔℵ 1. 33. 69 lat-*a* ff_2: txt AN rel vulg lat-*b c f* [*i q*] D-lat syrr. for [2nd] αυτου, αυτον D: om Δ lat-*a b* ff_2 *i* [*q*]. διεσωζοντο N 1. 69: διεσωθησαν Δ.

Chap. VII. **1.** ins οι bef ελθοντες N, *qui venerunt* lat-*a b f*.

2. for ιδοντες, ειδοτες D-gr. τινες ℵ[1]. ins ειπον οτι bef κοιν. Δ.—εσθιουσιν, insg οτι bef κοιν. (*emendn of constrn*), BL(Δ)ℵ 33 Syr copt: txt ADN rel lat-*a* goth, *manducare* vulg lat-*b c f* ff_2 [*i q*]. rec om τους (*see* ‖ *Matt*), with A rel: αρτον ℵ 240-4-58 Scr's e [lat-*b c* ff_2 D-lat Syr]: txt B D[-gr] LNΔ 33. 69. rec at end ins εμεμψαντο, with FKMNUΠ 1 (S, e sil) vulg lat-*a c f* ff_2 g_2 *l* syrr arm; κατεγνωσαν D; εμεμψατο F[1] 33 (*supplemy, to complete sense, as varns shew*): om ABℵ rel lat-*b* copt goth æth.

accounts much alike, but Mark's the richer in detail: e. g. **καὶ προσωρμίσθησαν** ver. 53, **καὶ ὅπου . . . . ἀσθενοῦντας** ver. 56. **53.**] **ἐπί** denotes the direction of their course, **προσωρμ.** the fact of their *arrival*: we can hardly make the distinction in English, but must render ἐπί, **to**: '*towards*,' or '*off*' would not indicate enough. But '*into*' (E. V.) indicates too much. **55.**] **περιφ.** implies that they occasionally had wrong information of His being in a place, and had to carry the sick about, following the rumour of his presence. **ὅπ. ηκ. ὅτι ἐκ. ἐστιν**, *to the places*, **where they heard He was (there)**. —ὅπου . . . . ἐκεῖ does not signify merely *ubi* (as Grot., Wetst., &c.) by a Hebraism; there is in fact here no unusual construction at all: ὅπου stands by itself, and ἐκεῖ ἐστιν is the matter introduced by the ὅτι recitantis. **56.**] In **ὅπου ἂν εἰςεπορεύετο . . . ὅσοι ἂν ἥπτοντο**, the ἄν belongs not so much to the verbs, which are certain and definite, as to the indefinites ὅπου and ὅσοι, rendering them more indefinite, and spreading the assertion over every several occasion of the occurrence. See remarks on this in Klotz, Devar. ii. p. 145 f.: and cf. reff. and Lucian, Dial. mort. ix. 2, μακάριος ἦν αὐτῶν ὅντινα ἂν καὶ μόνον προσέβλεψα.

Chap. VII. 1—23.] Discourse concerning eating with unwashed hands. Matt. xv. 1—20. The two reports differ rather more than usual in their additions to what is common, and are not

Frag. Cant. και... ...πρεσβυτερων Frag. Cant. ...vii. 4 (appy) Ν.

Φαρισαῖοι καὶ πάντες οἱ Ἰουδαῖοι, ἐὰν μὴ [y] πυγμῇ
[z] νίψωνται τὰς [z] χεῖρας, οὐκ ἐσθίουσιν, [ab] κρατοῦντες τὴν
[ac] παράδοσιν τῶν πρεσβυτέρων· 4 καὶ [d] ἀπ' ἀγορᾶς ἐὰν
μὴ [e] βαπτίσωνται, οὐκ ἐσθίουσιν· καὶ ἄλλα πολλά ἐστιν
ἃ [f] παρέλαβον [b] κρατεῖν, [g] βαπτισμοὺς ποτηρίων καὶ
[h] ξεστῶν καὶ [i] χαλκίων καὶ [k] κλινῶν· 5 καὶ ἐπερωτῶσιν
αὐτὸν οἱ Φαρισαῖοι καὶ οἱ γραμματεῖς Διὰ τί οὐ [l] περιπατοῦσιν οἱ μαθηταί σου κατὰ τὴν [c] παράδοσιν τῶν
[m] πρεσβυτέρων, ἀλλὰ [n] κοιναῖς χερσὶν ἐσθίουσιν [n] τὸν

y here only. Exod. xxi. 18. Isa. lviii. 4 only. z ‖ Mt. reff. a 2 Thess. ii. 15 b = Rev. ii. 13, 14, 15, 25. (w. gen., Heb. iv. 14. vi. 18.) c = ‖ Mt. Gal. i. 14 al. ‡ Jer. xxxix. (xxxii.) 4. xli. (xxxiv.) 2 only. d constr., see note and ver. 28. e = Luke xi. 38 only. 4 Kings v. 14. f = 1 Cor. xi. 23. xv. 1, 3. Gal. i. 9, 12. g [ver. 8.] Col. ii. 12. Heb. vi. 2. ix. 10 only +. h here [& ver. 8] only +. ὁ δὲ βάδος δύναται χωρῆσαι ξέστας ἑβδ. δύο, Jos. Antt. viii. 2. 9. i here only +. (-εῖον, 2 Chron. xxxv. 13. Job xli. 22. Esdr. i. 12 only.) k Matt. ix. 2 | L. 6. ch. iv. 21 ‖ L. ver. 30 al. Deut. iii. 11. l = Acts xxi. 21. Rom. viii. 4 al. 4 Kings xx. 3. m = ‖ Mt. Heb. xi. 2 only. n ver. 2 (reff.).

3. πυγμην 59 syr-mg-gr: πυκμη *primo* D: πυκνα ℵ: om Δ. (*momento* lat-*a*, *subinde* lat-*b*, *pugillo* lat-*c ff*$_2$ *i* [*q*], *prius crebro* lat-*g*$_2$, *crebro* vulg lat-*f g*$_1$ *l* copt goth æth(Treg), '*diligenter* Syr syr'(Treg), '*sedulo* syrr, *intense* æth'(Tischdf).) νιψονται EN ev-y. εσθιωσιν ΓΝ. aft εσθ. add αρτον (‖ *Matt*) D Frag-cant(appy) Scr's g lat-*a b ff*$_2$ *i* æth arm; τον αρτον M^2 ev-z, *panem suum* lat-*c*. παραδοσιαν D^1(but -σιν at first).

4. (απ', so ABDLΔΠ.) aft αγορας ins οταν ελθωσιν D vulg-sixt(with tol) lat-*a b* (*c*) *f ff*$_2$ *i l* [*q*] arm, δε οταν εισελθωσιν Scr's c. βαπτισονται KNX, ραντισωνται Bℵ Scr's g Euthym. for α παρελαβον, απερ ελαβον B. for κρατειν, αυτοις τηρειν D: *tradita sunt illis servare* vulg lat-*c f l* [*ff*$_2$ *g*$_2$ *i q*]. om και κλινων (*homœotel?*) BLΔℵ copt.

5. rec (for και) επειτα (*corrn for connexn*), with A rel lat-*f* syr goth arm: Δ has both: txt BDLℵ **1.** 33 latt Syr copt (æth). aft γραμματεις ins λεγοντες D Δ[om κ. οι γρ.] 69 lat-*a* (*c*) *ff*$_2$ *g*$_2$ *i*. rec οι μαθ. σου bef ου περιπατουσιν (*from* ‖ *Matt*), with AD rel latt syrr goth arm: txt BLΔℵ 33 copt æth. rec (for κοιναις) ανιπτοις (*gloss*), with Aℵ^{3a} rel lat-*b c f ff*$_2$ syrr goth (æth): *immundis* lat-*a*: txt BDℵ^1 **1.** 33 vulg lat-*g*$_2$ *i* [*q*] copt arm.—κοιναις χερσιν ανιπτοις 13. 69. 124. 346. ins ταις bef χερσιν D 28. om τον ΚΠ ev-w.

so frequently in verbal agreement where the matter is the same. **2. ἴδ. τιν. τ. μαθ.**] See ch. ii. 16. A mark of particularity. **τουτέστιν ἀνίπ.** is supposed by some to be a gloss, explaining **κοιναῖς**: but the explanation seems necessary to what follows, especially for Gentile readers. **3. πυγμῇ**] This word has perplexed all the Commentators. Of the various renderings which have been given of it, two are excluded by their not being grammatical—(1) that which makes it mean '*up to the elbow*' (Euthym. and Thl.); '*including the hand as far as the wrist*,' Lightf.: (2) '*having clenched the hand*,' '*facto pugno*' (Grot. and others).

The two meanings between which our choice lies are, (3) '*frequently*' (as E. V. 'oft,' and Vulg. 'crebro'), taking πυγμῇ = πυκνῇ = πυκνῶς, which however is not very probable: or (4), to which I most incline, and which Kuinoel gives, '*sedulo*,' '*fortiter*,' **diligently**; **πυγμή**, he observes, meaning 'the fist,' answers in the LXX to the word אֶגְרֹף, see reff. But this same word אֶגְרֹף is used to signify *strength* and *fortitude*, and *strong men* are called in the Rabbinical writings בעלי אגרופין, 'lords of fists.' And the Syr. interpreter renders it by the same word as he does ἐπιμελῶς, Luke xv. 8. **4. ἀπ' ἀγ.**] i.e. (as indeed some MSS. insert: see var. readd.) ὅταν ἔλθωσιν. Winer, § 66. 2 note, takes ἀπ' ἀγορᾶς with ἐσθίωσιν, justifying it by Arrian, Epict. iii. 19. 5, φαγεῖν ἐκ βαλανείου. **βαπτ.** is variously understood,—of *themselves*, or the *meats bought*. It certainly refers to *themselves*; as it would not be any unusual practice to wash things bought in the market:—but probably not to washing their *whole bodies*: see below. **ξεστ.**, not from ξέω, to polish, but a corruption of *sextarius*. See the passage of Josephus cited in the reff.

χαλκ., *brazen vessels*; earthen ones, when unclean, were to be *broken*, Levit. xv. 12. These **βαπτισμοί**, as applied to **κλινῶν** (meaning probably here *couches* (triclinia) *used at meals*), were certainly *not immersions*, but sprinklings or affusions of water. On the whole subject, see Lightfoot ad loc. **5.**] The construc-

ἄρτον; 6 ὁ δὲ εἶπεν αὐτοῖς [ὅτι] [o] καλῶς ἐπροφήτευσεν
Ἠσαΐας περὶ ὑμῶν τῶν [p] ὑποκριτῶν, ὡς γέγραπται
[q] Οὗτος ὁ λαὸς τοῖς [r] χείλεσίν με τιμᾷ, ἡ δὲ καρδία Frag.
αὐτῶν [s] πόῤῥω [t] ἀπέχει ἀπ' ἐμοῦ. 7 [u] μάτην δὲ [v] σέβονταί Cant. ρρω...
με, διδάσκοντες [w] διδασκαλίας [x] ἐντάλματα ἀνθρώπων.
8 [y] ἀφέντες τὴν ἐντολὴν τοῦ θεοῦ [z] κρατεῖτε τὴν [za] παράδοσιν τῶν [a] ἀνθρώπων[, [b] βαπτισμους [b] ξεστῶν καὶ ποτη- ...ποτη-
ρίων, καὶ ἄλλα [c] παρόμοια τοιαῦτα πολλὰ ποιεῖτε]. 9 καὶ ριων Frag.
ἔλεγεν αὐτοῖς [d] Καλῶς [e] ἀθετεῖτε τὴν ἐντολὴν τοῦ θεοῦ, Cant. ABDEF
ἵνα τὴν [z] παράδοσιν ὑμῶν [f] τηρήσητε. 10 Μωυσῆς γὰρ GHKL MSUVX
εἶπεν [g] Τίμα τὸν πατέρα σου καὶ τὴν μητέρα σου, καὶ Ὁ ΓΔΠℵ 1. 33. 69
[h] κακολογῶν πατέρα ἢ μητέρα [i] θανάτῳ [i] τελευτάτω·
11 ὑμεῖς δὲ λέγετε Ἐὰν εἴπῃ ἄνθρωπος τῷ πατρὶ ἢ τῇ
μητρὶ [k] Κορβᾶν, ὅ ἐστιν δῶρον, ὃ ἐὰν ἐξ ἐμοῦ [l] ὠφεληθῇς,

o = ‖ Mt. reff. p Mark, here only. Matt. vi. 2, 5 reff. q Isa. xxix. 13. r ‖ Mt. reff. s ‖ Mt. Luke xiv. 32. xxiv. 28 only. l. c. Job vii. 1. t ‖ Mt. reff. u ‖ Mt. only. 3 Kings xx. (xxi.) 20. v constr., ‖ Mt. reff. w ‖. elsw. Paul only. Eph. iv. 14 al. Prov. ii. 17. x ‖ Mt. Col. ii. 22 only. l. c. Job xxiii. 11 (12 Bℵ) only. = Matt. xxiii. 23. Rom. i. 17. Rev. ii. 4. Judg. ix. 9, &c. A. z ver. 3 reff. a Col. ii. 8. b ver. 4 reff. c ver. 13 only †. d = 2 Cor. xi. 4. e = 1 Cor. i. 19. Gal. ii. 21. iii. 15. Heb. x. 28. Ps. lxxxviii. 34. f Matt. xix. 17 reff. g Exod. xx. 12. h ‖ Mt. ch. ix. 39. Acts xix. 9 only. Exod. xxi. 16. Prov. xx. 20. 1 Kings iii. 13. i ‖ Mt. reff. k here only †. (-ανᾶς, Matt. xxvii. 6.) l ‖ Mt. reff.

6. rec ins αποκριθεις bef ειπεν (*from* ‖ *Matt*), with AD rel latt syr goth arm: om BLΔℵ 33 Syr copt æth. om οτι (*see ver* 9) BLΔℵ 33 latt Syr copt æth: ins AD rel lat-*b*(Tischdf) syr goth arm. περι υμων bef ησαιας A 28 (Scr's a) lat-g_2 Syr copt (æth). om των D. for ως γεγραπται, ως ειπεν 1 arm: και ειπεν D lat-*i*, *qui dixit* lat-*a b*; *dicens* lat-*c* [ff_2]. add οτι BLℵ Syr. ο λαος bef ουτος (*see* ‖ *Matt*) BD vulg lat-*b c f* g_1 *i l* Syr: om ουτος lat-*a* ff_2: txt Aℵ rel syr copt goth æth arm Clem-rom. for τιμα, αγαπα D-gr lat-*a b c*: *honorant me et amant me* æth. for απεχει απ', αφεστηκεν αφ' D: απεστιν απ' L 2-pe Clem-rom: απεστη απ' Δ: *est a* latt: *abest a* fuld(with em ing mt) lat-$g_{1.2}$.

8. homœotel in Frag-cant, αφεντες to ανθρωπων. rec aft αφεντες ins γαρ, with A rel vulg lat-*f l* syrr goth: om BDLΔ[1]ℵ lat-*a b c* ff_2 *i* [*q*] copt æth arm. for εντ., τολην D[1](txt D[3]), βουλην Δ. om βαπτισμους to ποιειτε BLΔℵ 1 copt arm: ins (AD) Frag-cant rel (vulg) lat-*f l* syrr goth [æth] arm-usc.—the 2 clauses of the ver are transposed in D lat-*a b c* ff_2 *i* [*q*].—βαπτισμου and om αλλα A.—ποιειτε bef πολλα FKΠ vulg: παρομοια α ποιειται τοιαυτα πολλα D lat-*a* ff_2 *i*. (*On the whole, the evidence* for *the clause preponderates. There could be* no reason *for* inserting *it from vv* 4, 13,—*and were it thus insd, we should have it exprd as it is in those vv. Besides,* ανθρωπων *is the termination of the sentence in* ‖ *Matt, and was also the* end of a lection: *and this was very likely to exclude the clause. The varns are no more than might be accounted for by a desire to bring it better into the context.*)

9. (B does not om κ. ελεγ. αυτ. as Btly. From inspection.) for τηρησητε, τηρητε B ev-15: στησητε D-gr 1 Syr goth(appy) arm, *statuatis* lat-*a b c f* ff_2 *i* [*q*] Cypr Jer Zeno, *tradatis* D-lat. (*Griesb approves* στησητε, *and Fritz Tischdf*(ed 1: not edd 7, 8) *adopt it: but it seems to have been substd* as a more appropr word: *Mey refers to Rom* iii. 31: *Heb* x. 9.)

10. om 2nd σου D 69 arm. τελευτειτω D.

11. for 1st εαν, ος αν A 33[omg ανθρ.]. aft πατρι ins αυτου D Scr's q[1] r lat-*a c* ff_2 g_2 *i* [*q*] Syr copt goth æth Avit. (aft μητρι ins αυτου K Scr's d i o w Syr copt æth.) ο αν D: om ο Δ 69. μου [for εξ εμου] D[1](corrd 1. m. (D[5], Scr), *ex me* lat).

tion is an anacoluthon,—begun with καὶ ἰδόντες, ver. 2, which *subject* being lost sight of in the long parenthesis, is here renewed with καὶ ἐπερ. κ.τ.λ. **8.**] Not contained in Matt., but important, as setting forth their *depreciating* of God's command in comparison with human tradition, before their absolute *violation* of that command in vv. 10, 11. **9.**] **καλῶς** — ironical: see ref. **10.**] **Μωυσ. γὰρ εἶπ.** = ὁ γὰρ **θεὸς** ἐνετείλατο Matt. **11.**] **κορβᾶν** = קָרְבָּן, an offering without a sacrifice. οἱ **κορβᾶν** αὐτοὺς ὀνομάσαντες τῷ θεῷ,—**δῶρον** δὲ

12 [καὶ] οὐκέτι [m] ἀφίετε αὐτὸν οὐδὲν [n] ποιῆσαι τῷ πατρὶ ἢ
τῇ μητρί, 13 [o] ἀκυροῦντες τὸν λόγον τοῦ θεοῦ τῇ [z] παραδόσει ὑμῶν [p] ᾗ [q] παρεδώκατε. καὶ [r] παρόμοια τοιαῦτα
πολλὰ ποιεῖτε. 14 καὶ προσκαλεσάμενος πάλιν τὸν ὄχλον
ἔλεγεν αὐτοῖς Ἀκούσατέ μου πάντες καὶ σύνετε. 15 οὐδέν
ἐστιν ἔξωθεν τοῦ ἀνθρώπου εἰσπορευόμενον εἰς αὐτὸν ὃ
δύναται αὐτὸν [s] κοινῶσαι· ἀλλὰ τὰ ἐκ τοῦ ἀνθρώπου ἐκπορευόμενα, ἐκεῖνά ἐστιν τὰ [s] κοινοῦντα τὸν ἄνθρωπον.
[16 εἴτις ἔχει ὦτα ἀκούειν, ἀκουέτω.] 17 καὶ ὅτε εἰσῆλθεν
εἰς οἶκον [t] ἀπὸ τοῦ ὄχλου, [u] ἐπηρώτων αὐτὸν οἱ μαθηταὶ
αὐτοῦ τὴν παραβολήν. 18 καὶ λέγει αὐτοῖς [v] Οὕτως καὶ
ὑμεῖς [w] ἀσύνετοί ἐστε; οὐ [x] νοεῖτε ὅτι πᾶν τὸ ἔξωθεν εἰσπορευόμενον εἰς τὸν ἄνθρωπον οὐ δύναται αὐτὸν [s] κοινῶσαι,
19 ὅτι οὐκ εἰσπορεύεται αὐτοῦ εἰς τὴν καρδίαν ἀλλ' εἰς τὴν
[y] κοιλίαν· καὶ εἰς τὸν [z] ἀφεδρῶνα ἐκπορεύεται καθαρίζων

m = ch. v. 37 reff. n Matt. vii. 12. Luke i. 49. Gen. xx. 9. o || Mt. Gal. iii. 17 only +. Esdr. vi. 32 only. (-ρος, Prov. i. 25. v. 7.) p attr., Matt. xxiv. 50. ch. xiii. 19. Luke ii. 20. iii. 29. ix. 43. John xv. 20. Acts i. 1 al. fr. Gen. xxii. 2. Winer, § 24. 1. q Luke i. 2 reff. r here [& ver. 8] only +. s || Mt. reff. t = Luke xxiv. 31. Acts i. 9, 11, 22. u constr., ch. xi. 29. Luke xx. 40. Num. xxvii. 21. see John xviii. 21. v Matt. xxvi. 40 reff. w ||. Rom. i. 21. 2 Kings xii. 19. 31. x. 19 (from Deut. xxxii. 21) only. Wisd. i. 5. x || Mt. Matt. xvi. 9, 11 al. y 1 Cor. vi. 13. Rev. x. 9, 10. 2 Kings xx. 10. z || only +. (-δρος, Lev. xv. 19, 20.)

12. om και (*to ease the construction, see on || Matt*) BDΔℵ 1. 69 lat-*a b c ff₂ i* [*q*] copt æth: for και, οτι L. for ουκετι, ουκ εν D-gr ('confusis τι cum ν?' Tischdf). om τω π. η τ. μητ. Δ. rec aft πατρι ins αυτου (*from || Matt*), with A rel vulg lat-*f ff₂ g₂ l* syrr copt goth æth: om BDLΓℵ 69 lat-*a b c i* [*q*] arm Avit. rec aft μητρι ins αυτου, with A rel syrr copt goth æth: om BDLℵ 1. 69 latt arm Avit.

13. aft υμων add τη μωρα D lat-*a b c ff₂ g₂ i n* [*q*] syr-mg. πολλα bef τοιαυτα ℵ[M¹ 1. 69]. for τοιαυτα, τα αυτα D¹-gr: ται τα αυτα (sic) D⁵: ταυτα ev-z

14. rec (for παλιν) παντα (παλιν *was not understood,—*παντα *seemed to suit* παντες *below*), with A rel lat-*f* syrr goth arm: απαντα ev-y: om 235-8 lat-*c*: txt BDLΔℵ vulg lat-(*a*) *b ff₂ g₁.₂ i l n* [*q*] syr-mg copt æth. for ελεγεν, λεγει B 59. rec ακουετε (*from || Matt*), with Aℵ rel: txt BDHL. om μου παντες (|| *Matt*) Δℵ: om παντες L copt. rec συνιετε (*from || Matt*), with Aℵ rel: συνιτε D: txt BHLΔ.

15. for ουδεν, ουδ D¹(txt D³). for εις, επ ℵ¹. for ο δυν. αυ. κοινωσαι, το κοινουν αυτον (|| *Matt*) B [Aug]: κοινωσαι bef αυτον LΔℵ. rec (for τα εκ τ. ανθρ. εκπορ.) τα εκπορ. απ αυτου (*the transcriber's eye passed from* εκ *to* εκπορευομενα, *then* απ αυ. *was supplied*), with A rel syrr arm Aug: txt BDLΔℵ 33 latt copt (goth æth). om εκεινα (*as superfluous*) BLΔℵ copt-wilk[(omg also rest of ver)-schw-dz]. (B does not om τον, as Bch. From inspection.)

16. om ver BLΔ¹ℵ copt. (*The omn is easily accounted for from its not occurring in || Matt: the insn, at the end of a lection, was also very obvious.*)

17. εισηλθον Uℵ 131 copt-wilk Vict. ins τον bef οικον Δℵ: την οικιαν D. rec περι της παραβολης, with A rel vss: txt BDLΔℵ 33 latt.

18. [for ου] ουπω (|| *Matt*) LUΔℵ 1 Scr's c g evv-H-y lat-*f* syr-mg. om εις τον ανθρωπον ℵ. for δυναται αυτον κοινωσαι, κοινοι τον ανον ℵ.

19. ου γαρ εισερχεται εις τ. καρ. αυ. αλλ εις τ. κοι. κ. εις τον οχετον εξερχεται D.—for οτι ουκ, ου γαρ D lat-*a b i n* [*q*].—εις την καρδιαν bef αυτου DΔ latt. for εκπορ., εκβαλλεται ℵ Scr's c. rec καθαριζον (*corrn, see note*), with KMUΓΠ 33 (V, e sil): -ζει D-gr goth, *et purgat* lat-*i*: txt ABℵ rel Scr's f p ev-y Orig Thaum.

τοῦτο σημαίνει κατὰ Ἑλλήνων γλῶτταν—Jos. Antt. iv. 4. 4. **12.**] See note on Matt. ver. 5. **13.**] **καὶ παρ.**, a repetition from ver. 8;—common in Mark. **14.**] Both Matt. and Mark notice that our Lord called the multitude to Him, when He uttered this speech. It was especially this, said in the hearing of both the Pharisees and them, that gave offence to the former. **17. εἰς οἶκον**] Not necessarily into *a* house, so that any inference can (Meyer) be drawn from it, —but *within doors*: see note on ch. ii. 1. **ἐπ. . . . οἱ μαθ.** = ἀποκρ. ὁ Πέτρος εἶπ. Matt. **19. καθαρίζων**] The masc. part. applies to ἀφεδρῶνα, by a construc-

a Mark, here only. Matt. xiv. 15. Luke iii. 11. ix. 13. John iv. 34. Rom. xiv. 15 bis, 20. 1 Cor. iii. 2 al. Gen. xli. 35.
b = ||. Luke ii. 35. ix. 47 al. Ps. lv. 5.
c ||. Acts xv. 20, 29. 1 Cor. vi. 13, 18 al. Hos. ii. 2.
d || only. Gen. xl. 15.
e | (reff.) only.
f Luke xii. 15. 2 Cor. ix. 5. Col. iii. 5. 2 Pet. ii. 3, 14 al. Jer. xxii. 17. Ezek. xxii. 27.

πάντα τὰ [a] βρώματα. 20 ἔλεγεν δὲ ὅτι τὸ ἐκ τοῦ ἀνθρώπου ἐκπορευόμενον, ἐκεῖνο [s] κοινοῖ τὸν ἄνθρωπον.
21 ἔσωθεν γὰρ ἐκ τῆς καρδίας τῶν ἀνθρώπων οἱ [b] διαλο- N vii. 21 (appy)...
γισμοὶ οἱ κακοὶ ἐκπορεύονται, [c] πορνεῖαι, [d] κλοπαί, φόνοι, ABDEF
[e] μοιχεῖαι, 22 [f] πλεονεξίαι, [g] πονηρίαι, δόλος, [h] ἀσέλγεια, GHKL MNSUV
[l] ὀφθαλμὸς [i] πονηρός, [k] βλασφημία, [l] ὑπερηφανία, [m] ἀφρο- ΧΓΔΠℵ 1. 33. 69
σύνη. 23 πάντα ταῦτα τὰ πονηρὰ ἔσωθεν ἐκπορεύεται καὶ
[n] κοινοῖ τὸν ἄνθρωπον.
24 Ἐκεῖθεν δὲ [o] ἀναστὰς ἀπῆλθεν εἰς τὰ [p] * μεθόρια
Τύρου. καὶ εἰςελθὼν εἰς οἰκίαν, οὐδένα ἤθελεν γνῶναι,

g Matt. xxii. 18 reff. Isa. i. 16. h Rom. xiii. 13. 2 Cor. xii. 21. Gal. v. 19. 1 Pet. iv. 3 al.† Wisd. xiv. 26 only. i Matt. vi. 23. xx. 15. Sir. xxxiv. 13. see Deut. xv. 9. k Matt. xii. 31. Eph. iv. 31 al. Ezek. xxxv. 12. l here only. Deut. xvii. 12 al. (-νος, Luke i. 51.) m 2 Cor. xi. 1, 17, 21 only. Job iv. 6. n vv. 15, &c. o = ch. x. 1. Luke i. 39. iv. 38. xv. 18, 20. Exod. xxiv. 13. p here only †. Ezek. xlvii. 8 Symm. ἐν μ. τῆς Ἀρμενίας καὶ Καππαδοκίας, Jos. B. J. vii. 1. 3.

20. ελεγον D-gr F. εκεινα D latt.
21. om 2nd οι D[1](ins D[3]). rec μοιχ. πορν. φον. κλοπ., with AN rel vulg lat-*f ff*$_2$ syr : μ. π. κ. φ. 1. 33 Syr arm : μ. κλ. π. φ. lat-*a b c i* [*q*] D-lat : πορνεια κλεμματα μ. φονος D(but *fornicationes homicidia* D-lat) : txt BLΔℵ copt æth.
22. πλεονεξια D em(with fuld) lat-*a b* (*c*) *f ff*$_2$ *g*$_2$ *i* [*q*] Syr. δολ. bef πον. D. πονηρια D lat-*a b c f ff*$_2$ *i* Syr æth. βλασφημιαι D-gr 238-53 Scr's h s ev-y lat-*b c g*$_2$ copt-wilk[-dz] goth. υπερηφανιαι D-gr 238 Scr's s lat-*b*.
23. for και, κακεινα ℵ. [κοινον(but corrd) B[1](Tischdf N. T. Vat.)]
24. rec και εκειθ. αναστ. (*from* || *Matt*), with AN rel vulg syr[-txt] goth arm : *et* &c but om εκειθ. lat-*a b c i* : κ. αναστ. εκειθ. D lat-*f ff*$_2$ *g*$_1$: κακειθεν δε αναστ. 33 copt : txt BLΔℵ syr-mg. * ὅρια(*more usual*) BDLΔℵ 1. 69 Orig$_2$: μεθορια AN rel. rec aft τυρου adds και σιδωνος (*from* || *Matt : there can be no possible reason given why it shd have been* omitted, *had it formed part of the origl txt : see also on ver* 31), with ABNℵ rel vulg lat-*c f g*$_{1,2}$ [*q*] vss : om DLΔ lat-*a b ff*$_2$ *i n* Orig$_2$. rec ins την bef οικιαν, with D Orig$_1$: om ABℵ rel Thl. ηθελησεν Δℵ 69 Scr's c ev-y vulg lat-*a b d f ff*$_2$ [Orig$_1$].

tion of which there are examples, in which the grammatical *object* of the sentence is regarded as the logical *subject*, e. g. λόγοι δ' ἐν ἀλλήλοισιν ἐῤῥόθουν κακοί, φύλαξ ἐλέγχων φύλακα, Soph. Ant. 259. See Kühner, Gramm. ii. § 678. 1. There need not be any difficulty in this additional clause: what is stated is *physically* true. The ἀφεδρών is that which, by the removal of the part carried off, purifies the meat; the portion available for nourishment being in its passage converted into chyle, and the remainder (the κάθαρμα) being cast out. **21, 22.**] The **καρδία** is the laboratory and the fountain-head of all that is good and bad in the inner life of man: see Beck, biblische Seelenlehre, § 21: Delitzsch, biblische Psychologie, ed. 2, § 12, pp. 248 ff. Matt.'s catalogue follows the order of the second table of the decalogue. Mark's more copious one varies the order, and replaces ψευδομαρτυρίαι by πλ., πον., δόλ., ἀσέλ., ὀφθ. πον., and βλασφ. by βλασφ., ὑπερη., ἀφροσ. Compare Rom. i. 29: Eph. iv. 19: Wisd. xiv. 25, 26. **ἀφροσύνη**, the opposite to **σωφροσύνη**, *unreasoning folly*: not in speaking only, but in thought, leading to words and acts.

24—30.] THE SYROPHŒNICIAN WOMAN. Matt. xv. 21—28. Omitted by Luke. A striking instance of the independence of the two narrations. Mark, who is much more copious in particulars, *omits* a considerable and important part of the history: this would be most arbitrarily and indeed inexcusably done, if the common account of his having *combined and epitomized Matt. and Luke* is to be taken. Our Lord's retirement was *to avoid the Pharisees:* see notes on Matt. throughout. **24.**] **ἐκεῖθεν** is not, *from the land of Gennesaret* (Meyer), —for ch. vi. 55, 56, has completely removed definiteness from the locality;— but refers to the (unspecified) place of the last discourse. **μεθόρια**] The place must have been the *neighbourhood of Tyre.* The word is used in Xen. Cyr. i. 4. 16, ἐν τοῖς μεθορίοις τοῖς τε αὐτῶν καὶ

καὶ οὐκ ἠδυνήθη [q] λαθεῖν· 25 ἀλλ᾽ εὐθὺς ἀκούσασα γυνὴ
περὶ αὐτοῦ, [r] ἧς εἶχεν τὸ [s] θυγάτριον [r] αὐτῆς [t] πνεῦμα
[t] ἀκάθαρτον, ἐλθοῦσα [uv] προςέπεσεν [v] πρὸς τοὺς [v] πόδας
αὐτοῦ· 26 ἡ δὲ γυνὴ ἦν Ἑλληνίς, Σύρα Φοινίκισσα τῷ
[w] γένει, καὶ [x] ἠρώτα αὐτὸν ἵνα τὸ δαιμόνιον ἐκβάλῃ ἐκ τῆς
θυγατρὸς αὐτῆς. 27 καὶ ἔλεγεν αὐτῇ [y] Ἄφες πρῶτον
[z] χορτασθῆναι τὰ τέκνα· οὐ γάρ ἐστιν καλὸν λαβεῖν τὸν
ἄρτον τῶν τέκνων καὶ τοῖς [a] κυναρίοις βαλεῖν. 28 ἡ δὲ
ἀπεκρίθη καὶ λέγει αὐτῷ Ναὶ κύριε, καὶ γὰρ τὰ [a] κυνάρια
[bc] ὑποκάτω τῆς [b] τραπέζης ἐσθίουσιν ἀπὸ τῶν [d] ψιχίων
τῶν παιδίων. 29 καὶ εἶπεν αὐτῇ Διὰ τοῦτον τὸν λόγον
Frag. Cant. ὕπαγε· ἐξελήλυθεν ἐκ τῆς θυγατρός σου τὸ δαιμόνιον.
δαιμονιον... 30 καὶ ἀπελθοῦσα εἰς τὸν οἶκον αὐτῆς εὗρεν τὸ παιδίον
[e] βεβλημένον ἐπὶ τὴν [f] κλίνην καὶ τὸ δαιμόνιον ἐξεληλυθός.

q Luke viii. 47. Acts xxvi. 26. Heb. xiii. 2. 2 Pet. iii. 5, 8 only. Job xxiv. 1. Wisd. x. 8.
r constr., Matt. iii. 12 reff.
s ch. v. 23 only +.
t ch. i. 23. v. 2 al. Matt. x. 1 reff.
u ch. v. 33 reff.
v here only. Exod. iv. 25. Esth. viii. 3. see ch. v. 22 reff.
w = Acts iv. 36. xviii. 2, 24 al. Jer. xxxviii. (xxxi.) 1.
x = Luke vii. 36 reff.
y ch. v. 37 reff.
z Matt. v. 6. ch. vi. 42 ||. viii. 4, 8 || al. Ps. xvi. 15.
a here (bis) and || Mt. only +.
b Judg. i. 7.
c Matt. xxii. 44 reff. Exod. xx. 4.
d | (Luke xvi. 21 v. r.) only +.
e = Matt. viii. 6 reff.
f ver. 4 reff.

ηδυνασθη Bℵ : εδυνηθη KΔ[Π] Scr's o p ev-y : txt ADN rel. (33 def.) λαλειν ℵ[1].

25. αλλα ℵ. rec ακουσασα γαρ γυνη, with AN rel lat-(*a* g_2) *n* syr[-txt] : γυνη δε ευθεως (D[1] adds ως) ακουσασα D latt : (*both attempts to better the constrn : cf also the varns :*) ευθυς γαρ ακουσασα γ. τις Syr : ακ. γυνη arm : ακ. δε γ. 248 : ακ. γαρ η γυν. M 69 : txt BLΔℵ 33 lat-*f* syr-mg copt goth. om αυτης DΔ[ℵ] 1. 69 arm. εισελθουσα LΔℵ vulg lat-*b c* &c D-lat. ins και bef προσεπεσεν D[1]Δ lat-*a f* [ff_2 $g_{1.2}$ *i*(appy) *q*].

26. rec ην δε η γ., with AN rel am lat-*f* $g_{1.2}$ *i* syr goth arm : txt BDLΔℵ 1. 33 lat-*a* Syr copt. rec συροφοινισσα, with vulg lat-*b c f* ff_2 $g_{1.2}$ *l* D-lat : συρα φοινισσα U lat-*a :* φοινισσα D[-gr] lat-*i :* συροφοινικισσα AKL S[1]-marg V-marg ΔΠℵ [1] goth æth Bas : txt BN rel Syr syr(appy) copt arm('appy' Treg).—(συρ. and φοιν. are disjoined in EFGHMSVX[Γ].) rec εκβαλλη, with FH K[1](Tischdf) M (69) : txt ABD G(Treg, expr) Nℵ rel. for εκ, απο D[-gr] 115 lat-*c* ff_2 ; *de* vulg lat-*a b f* $g_{1.2}$ *l* D-lat : om L 1. 69 Scr's g [lat-*q*].

27. rec (for και ελεγεν) ο δε ιησ. ειπεν (*see* || *Matt*), with AN rel (lat-*f*) syr goth (æth) arm : και λεγει D[-gr] lat-*a* g_1 : *et dixit* D-lat : txt BLΔℵ 33 copt. rec καλον bef εστιν, with AN rel goth arm : txt BDLΔℵ 1 latt syrr. (33 def.) rec βαλειν bef τοις κυναριοις (*from* || *Matt*), with ADN rel : txt Bℵ 1.

28. for και λεγει αυτω, αυτω λεγουσα D lat-*a f i n* [*q*] : λεγουσα (omg αυτω) 1. 69 (lat-g_1 arm). om ναι D 69 lat-*b c* ff_2 *i* arm. om γαρ (*corrn : so also in* || *Matt*) BHΔℵ 33. 69 Syr copt æth arm : αλλα και D lat-*b c* ff_2 *i*. εσθ. bef υποκ. (so ℵ-corr[1], αποκ. ℵ[1], who for κ at first wrote τ) της τραπ. ℵ. (*It would appear that the scribe omitted* υποκατω της τραπ., *and was writing* απο των ψιχ. *when he perceived his error and partially corrected it.*) rec εσθιει (*from* || *Matt, where only* D *reads* εσθιουσιν), with AN rel : txt BDLΔℵ 1. 33. 69.

29. aft αυτη ins ο ις N. υπαγε bef δια (*corrn to avoid ambiguity*) D 1 lat-*a b c f g i n* Syr. om τον D. rec τα δαιμ. bef εκ τ. θ. σου (*simpler arrangement*), with ADN rel vulg lat-*a c f* g_2 *i* syrr copt-schw goth æth arm : txt BLΔℵ copt-wilk.

30. om τον (bef οικον) DL. εαυτης ℵ 33 : om D 1 lat-*b* ff_2 *i* [*n q*]. rec το δαιμ. εξ. κ. την θυγατερα βεβλ. επι της κλινης, with AN rel lat-(*a*) *n* syr goth arm : txt BD[but την θυγατερα] (LΔ)ℵ Frag-cant (1. 33) vulg lat-(*b c f*) ff_2 g_2 *i l* Syr syr-jer copt æth. (*Mey defends rec, on the ground that the transcriber passed from* και *aft* εξελ. *to* και *in ver* 31, *and then the omd clause was insd in what appeared the fitting place. But we may answer, that if this were so, we should have in some ms or vs the supposed omn : whereas it does not occur in any.*)

τοῖς Μήδων, in a sense approaching that in our text: the repetition of the τοῖς assigning μεθόρια to *both* countries.
οὐδ. ἠθ. γν.] Not (Fritz.), '*wished to know no man*,' but **would have no man know it.**
25.] The woman (**Ἑλληνίς, a Gentile**) *had been following Him and His disciples before*, Matt.
26.] **Σύρα**

31 Καὶ πάλιν ἐξελθὼν ἐκ τῶν [g] ὁρίων Τύρου ἦλθεν διὰ
Σιδῶνος εἰς τὴν θάλασσαν τῆς Γαλιλαίας, [h] ἀνὰ [h] μέσον
τῶν [g] ὁρίων Δεκαπόλεως. 32 καὶ φέρουσιν αὐτῷ [i] κωφὸν
[k] μογιλάλον, καὶ [l] παρακαλοῦσιν αὐτὸν ἵνα [m] ἐπιθῇ
αὐτῷ τὴν χεῖρα. 33 καὶ [n] ἀπολαβόμενος αὐτὸν [o] ἀπὸ
τοῦ ὄχλου [p] κατ' [p] ἰδίαν [q] ἔβαλεν τοὺς [r] δακτύλους αὐτοῦ
εἰς τὰ ὦτα αὐτοῦ καὶ [s] πτύσας ἥψατο τῆς γλώσσης
αὐτοῦ, 34 καὶ [t] ἀναβλέψας [t] εἰς τὸν οὐρανὸν [u] ἐστέναξεν,
καὶ λέγει αὐτῷ Ἐφφαθά, ὅ ἐστιν [v] διανοίχθητι. 35 καὶ

ABDEF GHKL MNSUV ΧΓΔΠℵ Frag. Cant. 1. 33. 69

g Matt. ii. 16 reff.
h Matt. xiii. 25. 1 Cor. vi. 5. Rev. vii. 17 only. Ezek. xlvii. 16.
i Matt. ix. 32, 33. xi. 5 || L. xv. 31. ch. ix. 25 al. Mt. Mk. L. Exod. iv. 11.
k here only. Isa. xxxv. 6 only. Exod. iv. 11 Aq. Symm. Theod.
l = Matt. xiv. 36 reff.
m Matt. xix. 13 15 reff.
n = here only‡. (Luke vi. 34 al. Num. xxxiv. 14.) 2 Macc. iv. 46. vi. 21 (viii. 6) only.
o ver. 17.
p Matt. xiv. 13 reff.
q = John xx. 25 bis, 27. James iii. 3 al.
r Matt. xxiii. 4 reff.
s ch. viii. 23. John ix. 6 only. Num. xii. 14. Sir. xxviii. 12 only.
t = Matt. xiv. 19 reff.
u Gospp., here only. Rom. viii. 23. 2 Cor. v. 2, 4. Heb. xiii. 17. James v. 9 only. Isa. xix. 8.
v Mark, here (bis v. r.) only. elsw. Luke (xxiv. 31 reff.) only.

31. for εκ, απο Frag-cant. rec (for ηλθεν δια σιδ.) και σιδωνος ηλθε (*alteration to avoid the unlikelihood of the long detour by Sidon: see note, and cf ver* 24), with AN Frag-cant rel [lat-*q*] syrr goth arm : txt BDLΔℵ 33 latt syr-jer copt æth. rec (for εις) προς, with AN rel : txt BDLΔℵ Frag-cant **1**. 33. 69. ins της bef δεκαπολεως D Frag-cant.

32. aft κωφον ins και BDΔℵ Frag-cant latt æth arm-zoh Synop Vict. παρεκαλουν Frag-cant 33 vulg Syr. for την χειρα, τας χειρας NΔℵ[1] Frag-cant 33 lat-*a*. (τας illegible in Frag-cant.)

33. **επιλαβομενος** E[1]Γ Frag-cant : λαβομενος Δ. κατ ιδιαν bef απο τ. οχλ. ℵ copt. πτυσας bef εβαλεν D lat-*a b c i* [*q*] : πτυσας bef εις τα ωτα 69.—**ελαβεν** ℵ[1].—for εβαλεν τους δακτυλους αυτου, επτυσεν εις τους δακτυλους αυτου και εβαλεν, omg πτυσας, Frag-cant.—om 1st αυτου Lℵ lat-*c* [*i*]. for 2nd αυτου, του κωφου Frag-cant. for 3rd αυτου, του μογγιλαλου Frag-cant.

34. **ανεστεναξεν** D Frag-cant 69 : εστεναξε B. εφφεθα D-gr(*effecta* D-lat) ℵ[3a] (but corrd) vulg(with am) lat-*c* [*f i l q*].

35. rec aft 1st και ins ευθεως (*prob supplied here, as being so common in Mark, and in narratives of miracles : it is hardly ever* omd by the MSS which here om it), with AN Frag-cant-marg rel vulg lat-*c f* syrr goth æth arm : bef ελυθη LΔℵ : om BD Frag-

Φ., because there were also Λιβυφοίνικες, Carthaginians. **27.**] **ἄφες πρῶτον** ....] This important addition in Mark sets forth the whole ground on which the present refusal rested. The Jews were *first* to have the Gospel offered to them, for their acceptance or rejection; it was *not yet time* for the Gentiles. **28.** **καὶ γὰρ** ....] See on Matt. **30.**] These particulars are added here. **βεβλ. ἐπὶ τ. κλ.**—which the torments occasioned by the evil spirit would not allow her to be before :—κειμένην ἐν εἰρήνῃ, Euthym.

31—37.] Healing of a deaf and dumb person. *Peculiar to Mark.* A miracle which serves a most important purpose; that of clearly distinguishing between the cases of the *possessed* and the *merely diseased* or *deformed*. This man was what we call 'deaf and dumb;' the union of which maladies is often brought about by the inability of him who never has heard sounds to utter them plainly :—or, as here apparently, by some accompanying physical infirmity of the organs of speech. **31.**] He went first northward (perhaps for the same reason, of privacy, as before) through Sidon, then crossed the Jordan, and so approached the lake on its E. side. On *Decapolis*, see Matt. iv. 25. We have the same journey related Matt. xv. 29; and κωφοὺς λαλοῦντας mentioned among the miracles, for which the people glorified the God of Israel. **33.** **ἀπολ. αὐτ.**] No reason that we know can be assigned why our Lord should *take aside* this man, and the blind man, ch. viii. 23; but how many might there be which we do not know,—such as some peculiarity in the *man himself*, or the *persons around*, which influenced His determination. It is remarkable that the *same medium* of conveying the miraculous cure is used also in ch. viii. 23. By the symbolic use of external means, our Lord signified the healing virtue for afflicted human kind, which resides in and proceeds from Him incarnate in our flesh. He uses either his own touch,—something from Himself,—or the cleansing element to which He so often

ἠνοίγησαν αὐτοῦ αἱ [w] ἀκοαί, καὶ ἐλύθη ὁ [x] δεσμὸς τῆς
γλώσσης αὐτοῦ, καὶ ἐλάλει [y] ὀρθῶς. 36 καὶ [z] διεστείλατο αὐτοῖς ἵνα μηδενὶ [a] λεγωσιν· ὅσον δὲ αὐτοῖς [z] διεστέλλετο, αὐτοὶ μᾶλλον [b] περισσότερον ἐκήρυσσον. 37 καὶ
[c] ὑπερπερισσῶς [d] ἐξεπλήσσοντο λέγοντες Καλῶς πάντα
πεποίηκεν, καὶ τοὺς κωφοὺς [e] ποιεῖ ἀκούειν καὶ [f] ἀλάλους
λαλεῖν.

VIII. 1 Ἐν ἐκείναις ταῖς ἡμέραις πάλιν πολλοῦ ὄχλου ὄντος καὶ μὴ ἐχόντων τί φάγωσιν, προσκαλεσάμενος
τοὺς μαθητὰς αὐτοῦ λέγει αὐτοῖς 2 [g] Σπλαγχνίζομαι ἐπὶ
τὸν ὄχλον, ὅτι ἤδη [h] ἡμέραι τρεῖς [i] προςμένουσιν, καὶ οὐκ

w plur., = Luke vii. 1. Acts xvii. 20. Heb. v. 11. 2 Macc. xv. 39.
x Luke xiii. 16. Phil. i. 13 al. Job xxxix. 5.
y = here (Luke vii. 43. x. 28. xx. 21) only. 1 Kings xvi. 17.
z Matt. xvi. 20 reff.
a ch. viii. 30.
b 2 Cor. x. 8. Heb. vi. 17. μᾶλ. with comp., Phil. i. 23. 2 Cor. vii. 13.
c here only †. (-σσεύειν, Rom. v. 20. ὑπερεκπ., 1 Thess. v. 13.)
d Matt. vii. 28 reff.
e = ch. i. 17. Acts iii. 12.
f ch. ix. 17, 25 only. Ps. xxx. 18. xxxvii. 13 only.
g ch. i. 41 al.†
h constr., || Mt. Luke ix. 28. Acts v. 7.
i || Mt. reff.

cant 33 lat-*a b ff*$_2$ *i* [*q*] copt. rec διηνοιχθησαν (*from ver* 34), with AN Frag-cant rel: *ηνοιχθησαν* L: txt BDΔℵ 1. *αι ακ.* bef *αυτου* D, *aures ejus* latt. ins *του μογγιλαλου* bef *ελυθη* Frag-cant. om 2nd *αυτου* Frag-cant(appy).

36. aft *μηδενι* ins *μηδεν* D 28. 2-pe. rec (for *λεγωσιν*) *ειπωσιν* (*very common in similar passages: cf ch* viii. 30: *Matt* viii. 4; xvi. 20; xvii. 9: *ch* i. 44 &c), with ADN rel: txt BLΔℵ Frag-cant 33. om *οσον* to *διεστ.* D lat-*b c ff*$_2$ *i.* rec ins *αυτος* bef 2nd *αυτοις* (*prob combination of two readings? the omn of αυτοι below in rec makes it suspicious*), with N rel syrr goth æth arm; aft 33: om ABLXΔℵ Frag-cant 1 vulg lat-*a f g*$_2$ *l* copt. ins *οι δε* bef *αυτοι* D[1](and lat). rec om *αυτοι* (*see above*), with A rel vulg lat-*a g*$_2$ syr æth: ins BDLNΔℵ Frag-cant [33] lat-*f* Syr copt [goth] arm. *περισσοτερως* D Frag-cant(appy).

37. for *υπερπερισσως*, *παντες* Frag-cant: *υπερεκπερισσως* DU 1. for *πεποιηκεν*, *ποιει* Frag-cant. add *ως* B copt(appy). om *και* (bef *τ. κωφ.*) Frag-cant. rec ins *τους* bef *αλαλους* (*corrn to correspond with τους κωφους*), with ADN Frag-cant rel: om BLΔℵ 33.

Chap. VIII. 1. aft *εκειναις* ins *δε* D 28 lat-*a b c f ff*$_2$ *i* [*q*] Syr goth (æth). rec for *παλιν πολλου*, *παμπολλου* (*παντολλου for παλιν π.* (?) (*see* X *below*), *then altered to παμπολλ.—παμπολυς, though not elsw found in N. T., is a very common gr word* (*see lexx and the index to Plato*), *and might easily occur to a transcriber*), with A Frag-cant rel [lat-*q*] syrr: *παντολου* X: txt BDGLMNΔℵ 1. 33. 69 latt copt goth æth arm. for *οντος*, *συναχθεντος* Frag-cant(appy). aft *εχοντων* ins *αυτων* D 2-pe. rec aft *προσκαλεσαμενος* ins *ο ιησους* (*beg of lection*), with X rel lat-*f*: om ABDKLMNΔΠℵ Frag-cant 1 [33] latt syrr copt goth æth arm. om *αυτου* DLNΔℵ Frag-cant 1. 28. 209 latt(exc em *g*$_2$) syr copt(Tischdf) goth.

2. for *τον οχλον*, *το νοχλου τουτου* D.—add *τουτον* L al lat-(*b c*) *i* [*q*] Syr; *turbæ huic* lat-*a*. rec *ημερας*, with Δ 1. 69: *ημεραις* (and *τρισιν*) B: txt A[D]Nℵ Frag-cant rel. for *προσμενουσιν*, *εισιν απο ποτε ωδε εισιν* D lat-*a b i.* rec aft *προσμ.* ins *μοι* (*from* || *Matt, where none om it*), with ANℵ Frag-cant rel vulg lat-*g*$_1$ *l* syrr copt-

compares his word. **34.**] He looked to heaven *in prayer*: see John xi. 41, 42. He sighed, as Chrysostom (or Pseudo-Chrys.) in Cramer's Catena, h. l., says, *τὴν τοῦ ἀνθρώπου φύσιν ἐλεῶν, ἐς ποίαν ταπείνωσιν ἤγαγεν αὐτὴν ὅ τε μισόκαλος διάβολος, καὶ ἡ τῶν πρωτοπλάστων ἀπροσεξία*: see John xi. 36—38. **ἐφφαθά** = אֶתְפַּתַּח (Syr.-chald.), imperative Hithp. from פְּתַח, *aperuit*: the word used in Isa. xxxv. 5, "*Then shall the ears of the deaf be unstopped, ... and the tongue of the dumb sing.*" **35.**] **ὁ δεσμός**—the hindrance, whatever it was, which prevented him from speaking *ὀρθῶς* before.

36.] See ch. i. 45. **37. καλῶς πάν. πεπ. . . . .**] So *πάντα ὅσα ἐποίησεν καλὰ λίαν*, Gen. i. 31. This work was properly and worthily compared with that first one of creation—it was the same Beneficence which prompted, and the same Power that wrought it.

Chap. VIII. 1—10.] Feeding of the four thousand. Matt. xv. 32—39. The accounts agree almost verbatim. Mark adds *καί τινες αὐτῶν ἀπὸ μακ. εἰσ.* ver. 3,

k ‖ only +. Dan. vi. 18 LXX only.
l ‖ Mt. reff.
m Matt. xxvi. 58 reff.
n ch. vi. 42 reff.
o ch. xi. 4. John xxi. 1 al.
p ‖ Mt. reff.
q Luke v. 14. viii. 29, 56 al. Josh. vi. 6.
r ‖ Mt. reff.
s absol., ‖ Mt. reff.
t ‖. Matt. xxvi. 26 al. Jer. xvi. 7.
u ch. vi. 41 reff. Gen. xviii. 8.
v ‖ only +.
w ch. vi. 41 reff.
x Matt. xii. 34 reff.
y Matt. xiv. 20 reff.
z ‖. ver. 20 ‖. Acts ix. 25 only +.
a Matt. xiv. 15 reff.

ἔχουσιν τί φάγωσιν. 3 καὶ ἐὰν ἀπολύσω αὐτοὺς [k] νήστεις
εἰς οἶκον αὐτῶν, [l] ἐκλυθήσονται ἐν τῇ ὁδῷ· καί τινες
αὐτῶν [m] ἀπὸ [m] μακρόθεν εἰσίν. 4 καὶ ἀπεκρίθησαν αὐτῷ
οἱ μαθηταὶ αὐτοῦ ὅτι πόθεν τούτους δυνήσεταί τις ὧδε
[n] χορτάσαι ἄρτων [o] ἐπ' [p] ἐρημίας; 5 καὶ ἠρώτα αὐτοὺς
Πόσους ἔχετε ἄρτους; Οἱ δὲ εἶπαν Ἑπτά. 6 καὶ
[q] παραγγέλλει τῷ ὄχλῳ [r] ἀναπεσεῖν ἐπὶ τῆς γῆς. καὶ
λαβὼν τοὺς ἑπτὰ ἄρτους [s] εὐχαριστήσας [t] ἔκλασεν, καὶ
ἐδίδου τοῖς μαθηταῖς αὐτοῦ ἵνα [u] παρατιθῶσιν, καὶ [u] παρ-
έθηκαν τῷ ὄχλῳ. 7 καὶ εἶχαν [v] ἰχθύδια ὀλίγα· καὶ
[w] εὐλογήσας αὐτὰ [u] παρέθηκεν. 8 * ἔφαγον * δὲ καὶ [n] ἐχορτάσθησαν, καὶ ἦραν [x] περισσεύματα [y] κλασμάτων ἑπτὰ
[z] σπυρίδας. 9 ἦσαν δὲ ὡς τετρακισχίλιοι. καὶ [a] ἀπέλυσεν

C -που επτα... ABCDE FGHKL MNSUV XΓΔΠℵ Frag. Cant. 1. 33. 69

edd goth æth arm : om B(D) copt-mss. εχωσιν LNXΔ Frag-cant 33 ev-y.

3. for εαν απ. αυ., απολυσαι αυτους D 2-pe lat-*a b i* [*ff*$_2$ *q*], *si illos remiserimus ire* lat-*c*. for 1st αυτων, ου θελω (*see* ‖ *Matt*) D (lat-*b*). μη εκλυθωσιν D. rec (for και τινες) τινες γαρ, with AN Frag-cant rel vulg lat-*f* [*l*] syr goth æth arm : οτι και τινες D : *quoniam quidam* lat-*a* (*b*) *c* (*i*) : txt BLΔℵ 1. 33 [lat-*q*] (Syr) copt. aft τινες ins εξ D Scr's d k q[1] r lat-*c f ff*$_2$ *g*$_2$ *i l* [*q*] syrr. rec om απο, with AN Frag-cant rel : ins BDLΔℵ 1. 33. 69 latt syrr. elz (for εισιν) ηκουσι (*prob corrn as more appropr : so also* ηκασιν. *It is hardly possible, as Mey supposes, that the pres* ηκουσι *gave offence, and was altered to* ηκασιν *and* εισιν. *Cf Matt* viii. 11 : *Luke* xiii. 29), with Frag-cant rel : Steph ηκασιν, with ADNℵ 1. 33. 69 (SV, e sil) latt syrr goth æth arm : txt BLΔ copt.

4. om αυτω ℵ lat-*ff*$_2$. rec om οτι (*as harsh, and needless, and not in* ‖ *Matt*), with ADN Frag-cant rel : ins BLΔ.—for οτι, και ειπαν ℵ. om ωδε DH 69 vulg-ms lat-*b c ff*$_2$ *i* [*q*] goth : ins ABNℵ rel vulg, aft χορτασαι Frag-cant, aft δυνησ. 1 lat-*f*. επ' ερημιαις AKΔΠ[1].

5. rec επηρωτα (*by far the commoner word in Matt and Mark*), with ADN Frag-cant rel : επηρωτησεν M vulg lat-*b f ff*$_2$ *g*$_{1.2}$ [*i l q*] Syr : txt BLΔℵ. αρτους bef εχετε Dℵ 33 latt syrr copt æth : om αρτους X. (ειπαν, so BNΔℵ.)

6. rec παρηγγειλε (*see* ‖ *Matt*), with ACN Frag-cant rel vss('quæ sæpe præsentem per præt. exprimunt.' Treg) : txt BDLΔℵ (copt ?). ins και bef ευχαριστησας CDSV lat-*a f g*$_1$ Syr goth æth : om ABNℵ Frag-cant rel vulg lat-*b c ff*$_2$ [*i l q*] syr copt arm. rec (for παρατιθ.) παραθωσι, with ADN Frag-cant rel : txt BCLMΔℵ 33. 69.

7. (ειχαν, so BDΔℵ.) for ευλογ., ευχαριστησας D [lat-*q*]. rec om αυτα, with (D)E rel [lat-*q*]: ins bef ευλογ. MN Frag-cant 1. 69 latt (syrr) arm, ταυτα ευλογ. AFKΠ: txt BCLΔℵ copt æth. rec (for παρεθηκεν) ειπε παραθειναι και αυτα, with M[1] rel syr goth; and, but παραθηναι, EFHK S(Tischdf) Γ, παρατεθηναι A Scr's c evv-z-18-19 : ειπ. παρ. αυτα Syr : ειπ. παραθειναι (*see Luke* ix. 16) N Frag-cant(-θηναι) 1 latt arm : ειπ. παρατιθεναι M[2] : ειπ. αυ. παραθειναι V : ειπ. κ. αυτα παραθετε C(ταυτ.) 33 æth : ειπ. κ. ταυ. παρατιθεναι BLΔ ℵ-corr[1] copt : και αυτους εκελευσεν παρατειθεναι D : txt ℵ[1]. add αυτοις N copt : τω οχλω M[2].

8. * καὶ ἔφαγον (*see Matt* xiv. 20 ; xv. 27, *and ch* vi. 42) BCDLΔℵ 1. 33 latt Syr copt æth : εφαγον δε AN Frag-cant rel syr goth. add παντες ℵ ; aft εχορτ. KMΠ 33 Scr's c d o w. ins τα bef περισσευματα Cℵ copt : το περισσευμα των D (*quod superaverat* latt). [σπυρ. bef επτα DL lat-*b q*.]

9. rec aft ησαν δε ins οι φαγοντες (*from ch* vi. 44 : *see also* ‖ *Matt*), with ACDN Frag-cant 69(sic) rel latt syrr goth : om BLΔℵ 33 copt. ωσει M ev-z : om ℵ ev-y copt.

and again omits χωρὶς γυναικ. κ. παιδ. Matt. ver. 38. 7.] We have a curious instance here of correction and confusion in the principal MSS. 10.] Matt. mentions *Magadan*, ver. 39. Dalmanutha was probably a village in the neighbour-

αὐτούς, 10 καὶ εὐθὺς [b] ἐμβὰς εἰς τὸ πλοῖον μετὰ τῶν
μαθητῶν αὐτοῦ ἦλθεν εἰς τὰ [c] μέρη Δαλμανουθά. 11 καὶ
ἐξῆλθον οἱ Φαρισαῖοι καὶ ἤρξαντο [d] συνζητεῖν αὐτῷ, ζητοῦντες παρ' αὐτοῦ [e] σημεῖον ἀπὸ τοῦ οὐρανοῦ, [f] πειράζοντες
αὐτόν. 12 καὶ [g] ἀναστενάξας τῷ [h] πνεύματι αὐτοῦ λέγει
Τί ἡ γενεὰ αὕτη ζητεῖ σημεῖον; [i] ἀμὴν λέγω [ὑμῖν], [k] εἰ
δοθήσεται τῇ γενεᾷ ταύτῃ σημεῖον. 13 καὶ [l] ἀφεὶς αὐτοὺς
πάλιν [m] ἐμβὰς ἀπῆλθεν εἰς [n] τὸ [n] πέραν· 14 καὶ [o] ἐπελάθοντο λαβεῖν ἄρτους, καὶ εἰ μὴ ἕνα ἄρτον οὐκ εἶχον μεθ'
ἑαυτῶν ἐν τῷ πλοίῳ. 15 καὶ [p] διεστέλλετο αὐτοῖς λέγων
[q] Ὁρᾶτε, [r] βλέπετε [s] ἀπὸ τῆς [t] ζύμης τῶν Φαρισαίων καὶ

b Matt. viii. 23 reff. see ver. 13.
c — Matt. ii. 22 al. fr. Exod. xvi. 35.
d w. dat., ch. ix. 14. xii. 28. Acts vi. 9 al. †
e Matt. xii. 30, 39 al.
f Matt. xix. 3 reff. ch. x. 2 al.
g here only. Lam. i. 4. Sir. xxv. 18. Sus. 22. 2 Macc. vi. 30 only.
h ch. ii. 8 reff.
i Matt. v. 18 reff.
k Heb. iii. 11 and iv. 3, 5, from Ps. xciv. 11. Gen. xiv. 23. Num. xiv. 30 al.
l = Matt. iv. 11 al.
m absol. = here only. Eur. Troad. 455.
n ‖ Mt. reff.
o ‖ Mt. Phil. iii. 14. James i. 24 al. Gen. xli. 30. Ps. cxviii. 16.
p Matt. xvi. 20 reff.
q Matt. viii. 4 reff.
r ch. xiii. 5 ‖, 9. Heb. xii. 25 al.
s ch. xii. 38. Matt. vii. 15. Luke xii. 1.
t Matt. xiii. 33 reff.

10. εμβας bef ευθ. AKMNUΠ Frag-cant **1.** 69 syrr goth. (ευθυς, so BCLΔℵ **1.** 69: om D lat-*b c* ff_2 *i.*) aft εμβας ins αυτος B: και αυτος ανεβη D (2-pe) lat-*b i.* ins και bef ηλθεν D 2-pe. aft ηλθεν ins ο ιησους L ℵ[1](om ℵ[3a·b]) copt. for μερη, ορια D lat-*c f* arm usc. δαλμανουνθα B: μελεγαδα D[1]: μαγαιδα D-corr[1]: μαγδαλα or -λαν 1. 69 vss: txt ACNℵ Frag-cant rel syr-mg-gr vulg lat-*f* $g_{1.2}$ [*l q*] syrr copt æth (arm).

11. εξηλθοσαν D. ins συν bef αυτω D-gr latt. ins το bef σημ. D. aft σημ. ins ιδειν ℵ lat-*c*.

12. εαυτου AL: om DM[1]Γ **1** vulg lat-*b* g_2 *i l.* rec (for ζητει σημ.) σημ. επιζητει (*from* ‖ *Matt*), with AN Frag-cant rel vulg lat-*f* $g_{1.2}$ syr goth arm $Orig_1$: txt BCD LΔℵ **1.** 33 am(with fuld ing tol) lat-*a b c i l* Syr copt æth. om υμιν BL: ins ACDNℵ Frag-cant rel vss Orig.

13. for αφεις, καταλιπων (‖ *Matt*) N. for αυτους, αυτου A. rec εμβας bef παλιν, with AN Frag-cant rel vulg lat-*f* ff_2 $g_{1.2}$ syr goth: txt BCDLΔℵ 33. 69 lat-*a i* [*q*] copt-ms æth arm. rec adds εις το πλοιον, with DHKNUΓΠ Frag-cant **1.** 69 vss, so (omg το) A rel: om BCLΔℵ am(with tol) lat-ff_2 g_1.

14. απελαθεντο B[1]. aft επελαθ. add οι μαθηται D 76-7. 218-52 Scr's s[1] lat-*c*; οι μαθηται αυτου (‖ *Matt*) U Frag-cant 13. 28. 69. 124-31. 238-41-5-6-7 Scr's l m n q r. om και and ουκ D lat-*a* g_2 (*c* ff_2 *i q*) arm.

15. om ορατε D **1** tol lat-*a* [*q*] arm. ins και bef βλεπετε C Frag-cant 69 vulg lat-*c f l* copt-schw æth.

hood,—see note on Matt., and The Land and the Book, p. 393;—a striking instance of the independence of Mark: called by the Harmonists "an addition to St. Matthew's narrative, to shew his independent knowledge of the fact." Wordsw. What very anomalous writers the Evangelists must have been!

11—13.] Request of a sign from heaven. Matt. xvi. 1—4, who gives the account more at length: without however the graphic and affecting **ἀναστ. τῷ πν. αὐ.** ver. 12. 12.] **εἰ δοθ.**, a Hebrew form of strong abjuration: see reff., and Winer, § 55 end.

14—21.] Warning against the leaven of the Pharisees and of Herod. Matt. xvi. 5—12. Our account is fuller and more circumstantial,—relating *that they had but one loaf* in the ship, ver. 14; inserting the *additional reproofs*, ver. 18, and the reference to the two miracles of feeding more at length, vv. 19—21. Mark however omits the *conclusion* in Matt.,—that *they then understood that He spake to them of the doctrine, &c.* Possibly this was a conclusion drawn in the mind of the narrator, not altogether identical with that to be drawn from our account here—for the *leaven of Herod* could not be *doctrine* (**καὶ τ. ζ. Ἡρ.**, ver. 15—Mark only), but must be understood of the irreligious lives and fawning worldly practices of the hangers-on of the court of Herod. 14.] **ἐπελ.** is *not pluperfect*: see on Matt. ver. 5. The subject to the verb is the disciples, unexpressed: see next verse. 15.] **ὁρᾶτε** is merely *take heed*, and does not belong to **ἀπό**. **βλέπ. ἀπό** is not *'turn your eyes away from'* (Tittm. and Kuin. in Meyer), but as in reff. The ζύμη Ἡρώδου here

τῆς [t] ζύμης Ἡρώδου. 16 καὶ [u] διελογίζοντο πρὸς ἀλλήλους ὅτι ἄρτους οὐκ [v] ἔχουσιν. 17 καὶ γνοὺς λέγει
αὐτοῖς Τί [u] διαλογίζεσθε ὅτι ἄρτους οὐκ ἔχετε; οὔπω
νοεῖτε οὐδὲ συνίετε; [w] πεπωρωμένην ἔχετε τὴν καρδίαν
ὑμῶν; 18 ὀφθαλμοὺς ἔχοντες οὐ βλέπετε, καὶ ὦτα ἔχοντες
οὐκ ἀκούετε; καὶ οὐ μνημονεύετε, 19 ὅτε τοὺς πέντε ἄρτους
[x] ἔκλασα [y] εἰς τοὺς πεντακισχιλίους, πόσους [z] κοφίνους
[z] κλασμάτων πλήρεις ἤρατε; λέγουσιν αὐτῷ Δώδεκα.
20 ὅτε [δὲ] τοὺς ἑπτὰ [y] εἰς τοὺς τετρακισχιλίους, πόσων
[a] σπυρίδων [b] πληρώματα [z] κλασμάτων ἤρατε; καὶ λέγουσιν
αὐτῷ Ἑπτά. 21 καὶ ἔλεγεν αὐτοῖς * Οὔπω συνίετε;
22 Καὶ ἔρχονται εἰς Βηθσαϊδάν. καὶ φέρουσιν αὐτῷ

u ‖ Mt. reff.
v pres., John i. 40 reff.
w ch. vi. 52. John xii. 40. Rom. xi. 7. 2 Cor. iii. 14 only. Job xvii. 7 B only.
x ver. 6.
y = Matt. xxvi. 10. Luke ix. 13.
z Matt. xiv. 20 (reff.).
a ver. 8 reff.
b ch. vi. 43. Rom. xv. 29. 1 Cor. x. 26, from Ps. xxiii. 1. Eph. iv. 13. Eccl. iv. 6.

...αρτους Frag. Cant. ABCDE FGHKL MNSUV XΓΔΠℵ 1. 33. 69

16. for διελ., ελογιζοντο N. rec aft αλληλους ins λεγοντες (*to mend constrn: from ‖ Matt*), with ACN Frag-cant rel vulg lat-*f* $g_{1.2}$ syrr copt goth æth arm: om BDℵ 1 lat-*a b c* ff_2 *i* [*q*]. rec (for εχουσιν) εχομεν (*cf ‖ Matt, and above*), with ACNℵ rel vulg lat-*f* g_1 syrr goth æth arm: ειχαν (*corrn of tense*) D lat-*a b* ff_2 g_2 *i* [*q*]: txt B 1 lat-*c* copt.

17. rec aft γνους ins ο ιησους (*from ‖ Matt*), with ACDNℵ^{1} rel am(with fuld [ing tol]) lat-*a c f* g_2 [*q* syrr goth]: aft αυτοις, L Scr's c vulg lat-*b* ff_2: om BΔ^{1}ℵ^{3a} lat-*i* copt. aft διαλογιζεσθε ins εν ταις καρδιαις υμων DU lat-*a b c* ff_2 g_2 [*i q*] syr-w-ast æth arm; εν εαυτοις (‖ *Matt*) M 69; ολιγοπιστοι, in addition, (‖ *Matt*) 69 syr-w-ast(noting on marg "εν τ. καρδ. υμ. ολιγοπ. non inventum est in 2 exx. græcis neque in antiquo syr.") arm. [συνειτε B^{1}(Tischdf): but see table.] rec ins ετι bef πεπωρ. (*prob from the last syll of* συνιετε,—*the sense seeming also to justify it*), with A rel vulg lat-*f* g_2 *l* [*q*] syrr, *sic* lat-*b c* ff_2 *i* D-lat, οτι 106 goth: om BC D-gr LNΔℵ 1. 33 lat-*a* copt æth arm. πεπηρωμενη (ω over η)(sic) εστιν η καρδ. D, *obtusum est cor* lat-*a* (*b c* ff_2 *i*) [*q*] æth.

18. om 1st και ℵ^{1}(ins ℵ-corr^{1}) copt-dz. for και ου μνημ., ουδε μνημ. D 2-pe latt; ουπω νοειτε N.

19. aft αρτους ins τους D-gr; ους 69 lat-*b c* ff_2 *i k* D-lat copt. ins και bef ποσους (‖ *Matt*) CDMΔℵ [1] 33 am(with em fuld ing) lat-*f* $g_{1.2}$ *l* æth arm. rec πληρ. bef κλ., with AN rel lat-*f* syr goth: ηρ. bef πλ. D[-gr]: om πλ. 69. 237-59 Scr's h^{1} lat-*a* [*b*] *c* ff_2 *i k* [*q*] D-lat: txt BCLΔℵ 1. 33 ev-y vulg lat-$g_{1.2}$ *l* Syr (copt).

20. om δε BL 2-pe: ins ACD rel lat-*a f* ff_2 *i* [*q*] syr goth æth arm.—for δε, και Δℵ vulg lat-$g_{1.2}$: add και CN lat-*f*: και οτε (omg δε) lat-*c* Syr. aft επτα ins αρτους CM^{2}ℵ 13. 69. 124. 346 ev-z vulg lat-*c f* g_2 *l* [*q*] goth æth arm. ποσας σπυριδας, omg πληρωματα, D(σφυρ.) 49. 2-pe vulg lat-*a c* ff_2 $g_{1.2}$ *i* [*q*] arm. rec (for και λεγουσιν) οι δε ειπον, with ADN rel lat-*b c i* [*q*] syr goth arm: txt BCLℵ vulg lat-g_2 copt æth, so (omg και) Δ lat-g_1 *k l* Syr. rec om αυτω, with ADNℵ rel lat-*a b c f* ff_2 *i k* [*q*] syrr goth arm: ins BCLΔ vulg lat-$g_{1.2}$ *l* copt æth.

21. for ελεγεν, λεγει DFKΠ lat-*a b c f* ff_2 $g_{1.2}$ *i k* [*q*] Syr [ειπεν 1 goth]. (N ?) * rec πῶς οὐ, with B rel lat-*b* [*q*] D-lat copt (æth): πως ουπω (*combination*) A D-gr MNUX 33 vulg lat-*a c* ff_2 $g_{1.2}$ *i l* syrr goth Thl: πως ουν ο πω 69 lat-*f* arm: ου πως K: ουπω CLΔΠℵ [1] Scr's e ev-y. for συνιετε, νοειτε (*from ‖ Matt*) BD^{2}: συννοειτε *intellexistis* D^{1} lat-*b*.

22. rec ερχεται (*corrn, see ch* v. 38), with ANℵ^{1} rel syrr: txt BCDLΔℵ^{3a} 33. 69 vulg lat-g_1 *k* (*a b c f* ff_2 [g_2 *q*]) copt (goth æth) arm. for βηθσαιδαν, βηθανιαν D lat-*a f* ff_2 *i l* [*q*] goth.

seems to answer to the ζ. Σαδδουκαίων in Matt. But we must not infer from this that Herod was a Sadducee. He certainly was a bad and irreligious man, which would be quite enough ground for such a caution. We have a specimen of the morals of his court in the history of John the Baptist's martyrdom. In the *last* **οὔπω**, ver. 21, Meyer sees a *new* climax, and refers the *not yet* to the moment even after the reminiscence of vv. 18—20. It may doubtless be so, and the idea would well accord with the graphic precision of St. Mark.

22—26.] Healing of a blind man at Bethsaida. *Peculiar to Mark.* This

τυφλόν, καὶ [c] παρακαλοῦσιν αὐτὸν ἵνα αὐτοῦ ἅψηται.
23 καὶ [d] ἐπιλαβόμενος τῆς χειρὸς τοῦ τυφλοῦ [e] ἐξήνεγκεν
αὐτὸν ἔξω τῆς κώμης, καὶ [f] πτύσας εἰς τὰ [g] ὄμματα αὐτοῦ,
[h] ἐπιθεὶς τὰς χεῖρας αὐτῷ [i] ἐπηρώτα αὐτὸν εἴ τι βλέπεις.
24 καὶ [k] ἀναβλέψας ἔλεγεν Βλέπω τοὺς ἀνθρώπους, ὅτι
ὡς δένδρα ὁρῶ περιπατοῦντας. 25 εἶτα πάλιν ἔθηκεν τὰς
χεῖρας ἐπὶ τοὺς ὀφθαλμοὺς αὐτοῦ· καὶ [l] διέβλεψεν· καὶ

c Matt. xiv. 36 reff.
d Acts xxiii. 19 al. Zech. xiv. 13.
e = here only. (Luke xv. 22 reff.)
f ch. vii. 33 reff.
g Matt. xx. 34 (reff.) only.
h Matt. xix. 13, 15 reff.
i vv. 5, 27, 29.
k Matt. xiv. 19 reff.
l Matt. vii. 5. Luke vi. 42 only †.

23. λαβομενος την χειρα D. rec (for εξηνεγκεν) εξηγαγεν (*substitution of appy more appropr word*), with ADN rel vulg lat-*f* vss : txt BCLΔℵ 33. for αυτω, αυτου AKΔ vulg lat-*f l* Syr copt goth. επηρωτησεν N. rec (for βλεπεις) βλεπει, with A D[1]-corr(appy) Nℵ rel latt syrr goth arm : txt BC D[1]-gr Δ copt æth.

24. for ελεγεν, λεγει DN 69 vulg lat-*a b f* $g_{1.2}$ [*i l q*] : ειπεν C ℵ[1](txt ℵ[3a]) Scr's u lat-*c* ff_2 *k* Syr. elz-1633 ως δενδρα περιπ., omg οτι and ορω, with C[2]D M-marg 1 latt syrr copt æth arm : txt ABC[1]Nℵ rel goth.

25. for ειτα, και D lat-*b c* ff_2 *i k* [*q*] æth : om Syr arm. rec επεθηκε (*corrn aft ver* 23), with ACNℵ rel vulg lat-*b c f* ff_2 *i k* D-lat : επειθεις D-gr lat-*a* : txt BL. aft χειρας ins αυτου N lat-*c* syrr copt. rec (for διεβλεψεν) εποιησεν αυτον αναβλεψαι, with AN rel lat-*a f* [*q*] syr goth ; so, addg κ. διεβλεψεν, 69 : ηρξατο αναβλεψαι D vulg lat-*b c* ff_2 *i l* : ενεβλεψεν C[2] : txt BC[1]LΔℵ 1 lat-*k* copt æth. (*The acct seems to be this :* διεβλεψεν *was not understood. Hence the corrn of* D—then *that of* A *rec, to make* our Lord *the* subject, *as before, and to give* αναβλ. *the same meaning as before, ver* 24. *The readg of* C[2], ενεβλεψεν, *is a mechanical corrn to the word occurring just after. The question of the origl txt is not without some difficulty, but the above seems to me more prob than that a corrector shd have changed to a new subject and dropped* εποιησεν αυτον. *Lachm edits as rec : Tischdf and Treg, as in txt.*)—om κ.

appears to have been Bethsaïda Julias, on the N.E. side of the lake. Compare ver. 13 : and see on this Bethsaïda, Jos. Antt. xviii. 4. 6 : B. J. iii. 10. 7 : Plin. Nat. Hist. v. 15. Wieseler, Chron. Synops. p. 273 f. See however against the idea that there were two Bethsaïdas, The Land and the Book, pp. 373 f. 23.] The leading of this blind man out of the town appears as if it had been from *some local reason.* In ver. 26 we find him forbidden expressly to enter into or tell it *in the town,* and with a repetition of **κώμη**, which looks as if the place had been somehow unworthy of such a work being done there. (This is a serious objection against Meyer's reason, that the *use of spittle* in both miracles occasioned the same privacy here and in ch. vii. 33.) Or we may perhaps find the reason in our Lord's *immediate departure* to such a distance (ver. 27) ; and say, that He did not wish multitudes to gather about and follow Him. **πτύσας . . . ἐπιθεὶς . . .**] See above on ch. vii. 33. We cannot say what may have induced our Lord to perform this miracle *at twice*—certainly not the reason assigned by Dr. Burton, "that a blind man would not, on suddenly recovering his sight, know one object from another, because he had never seen them before," and so would require a double miracle ;—a second to open the eyes of *his mind also,* to comprehend what he saw. This assumes the man to have been *born* blind, which he was not, from ver. 24 ; for how should he know *how trees appeared ?* and besides, the case of the man born blind in John ix. required no such double healing. These things were *in the Lord's power,* and He ordered them as He pleased from present circumstances, or for our instruction. 24.] **I see men, because I see them walking as it were trees ;** i. e. not distinct in individual peculiarity, but as trees in the hedge-row flit by the traveller. It is a minute mark of truth, that he describes the appearance of persons as he doubtless had often had occasion to do during the failing of sight which had ended in his blindness. By no possibility can the words convey, as Wordsw., three different stages of returning vision : "I see men. I see them standing still, and dimly, as trees. I see them walking." For thus the **ὅτι** is altogether passed over, and περιπατοῦντας taken out of its government, and most unnaturally made into a sentence by itself. 25.] The distinction in the text here adopted, between διέβλεψεν and ἐνέβλεπεν, would be **he saw clearly** (the work of that instant), **and was thoroughly restored, and** (thenceforward) **saw all things plainly.** But

m Matt. xii. 13 reff.
n w. acc., here only. Isa. v. 12. = Acts xxii. 11.
o here only +. (-γής, Job xxxvii. 21. -γησις, Ps. xvii. 12. -γημα, Lev. xiii. 23.) τηλαυγέστερον ὁρᾷν, Diod. Sic. i. 50.
p Matt. xi. 7 al.
q Matt. i. 1 reff.
r = Matt. xii. 16 reff. xx. 31.

ABCDE FGHKL MNSUV ΧΓΔΠℵ 1. 33. 69

ᵐ ἀπεκατέστη καὶ ⁿ ἐνέβλεπεν ᵒ τηλαυγῶς ἅπαντα. 26 καὶ
ἀπέστειλεν αὐτὸν εἰς οἶκον αὐτοῦ λέγων Μηδὲ εἰς τὴν
κώμην εἰςέλθῃς, μηδὲ εἴπῃς τινὶ ἐν τῇ κώμῃ.
27 Καὶ ᵖ ἐξῆλθεν ὁ Ἰησοῦς καὶ οἱ μαθηταὶ αὐτοῦ εἰς τὰς
κώμας Καισαρείας τῆς Φιλίππου. καὶ ἐν τῇ ὁδῷ ἐπηρώτα
τοὺς μαθητὰς αὐτοῦ λέγων αὐτοῖς Τίνα με λέγουσιν οἱ
ἄνθρωποι εἶναι; 28 οἱ δὲ εἶπαν αὐτῷ λέγοντες ὅτι Ἰωάννην τὸν βαπτιστήν, καὶ ἄλλοι Ἡλίαν, ἄλλοι δὲ ὅτι εἷς
τῶν προφητῶν. 29 καὶ αὐτὸς ἐπηρώτα αὐτοὺς Ὑμεῖς δὲ
τίνα με λέγετε εἶναι; ἀποκριθεὶς ὁ Πέτρος λέγει αὐτῷ Σὺ
εἶ ὁ ᵠ χριστός. 30 καὶ ʳ ἐπετίμησεν αὐτοῖς ἵνα μηδενὶ λέ-

διεβ. Syr. rec (for απεκατεστη) αποκατεσταθη, with DUΠ¹ 1: απεκατεσταθη AN rel: txt CLΔℵ, αποκατεστη B. rec ενεβλεψεν (*to correspond with the other aorists*), with ACN rel syr copt: ωστε αναβλεψαι D vulg lat-*b c ff₂ i l*: ανεβλεψεν FM¹ Thl: εβλεψεν ℵ¹: txt BLℵ³ᵃ 69, ανεβλεπε Δ. δηλαυγως C(L)Δ ℵ¹(txt ℵ³ᵃ): δηλως 33. rec απαντας (*corrn to suit ανθρωπους above*), with AC² M(Treg, expr) N rel goth: om 33 lat-*c k*: txt BC¹ D(παντα) LΔℵ 1. 69 [vulg lat-*a b f ff₂ i l q*] syrr copt æth arm.

26. εις οικ. bef αυτον ℵ¹. rec ins τον bef οικον, with GMUXΔℵ³ᵃ 1. 69 copt: om ABCDNℵ¹ rel goth. for λεγων, κ. λεγει αυτω D. aft λεγων ins υπαγε εις τον οικον σου και (*see ch* ii. 11: *Matt* ix. 6) D 13. 28. 61-9. 124. 346. 2-pe vulg lat-*a b f ff₂ g₁.₂ l*.—om μηδε εις την κωμην εισελθης D lat-*c k*: for μηδε, εαν 13. 28. 61-9. 346. 2-pe vulg lat-*a b f ff₂ g₁.₂ l* syr-mg arm. for 1st μηδε, μη ℵ¹. om μηδε ειπ. τιν. ε. τ. κωμη BLℵ 1¹. 209 copt.—for μηδε ειπης τινι, μηδενι ειπης D syr-mg arm, *nemini dixeris* vulg lat-*b f ff₂ g₁.₂ l*: μηδενι ειπης μηδε 13. 69: μηδενι μηδεν ειπης μηδε 28. 61. 346.—for εν τη κωμη, εις την κωμην (*confusing the two clauses*) D: om vulg lat-*b f ff₁ g₁.₂ l*. (*The stumbling-block was, that if he* did not enter into the town, *he* could not tell it to any one in the town. Hence B *&c om the 2nd clause: D &c alter the 1st: others insert a saving clause,* 'if thou shouldest enter &c.:' *txt is the reading of* ACN rel syrr goth æth, *rec, Lachm, Tischdf* 1857 (ed 8 follows BLℵ), *Treg.*)

27. for τας κωμας καισαρειας, καισαριαν D lat-*a b ff₂ i* [*q*]. om 2nd αυτου A arm. om αυτοις DLΔ 33 tol lat-*a b k* [*q*] arm: in ℵ it was marked for erasure, but the marks removed. ειναι bef οι ανθρ. D vulg lat-*a* (*c*) *f ff₂* [*q* Tert Ambr].

28. rec (for ειπαν) απεκριθησαν (*see* || *Luke*), with AD rel latt syr goth arm: txt BCLΔℵ lat-*k* Syr copt [æth]. rec om αυτω λεγοντες (*see* || *Matt Luke*), with AN rel syrr goth: om λεγοντες C² 33 æth: ins BC¹DLΔℵ 69 latt copt. rec om 1st οτι, with AC²DNℵ³ᵃ rel latt syr goth: οι μεν (|| *Matt*) C¹Δ 69: txt Bℵ¹ Syr. for και αλλ., αλλοι δε (|| *Matt*) DN 69 lat-*a f k* [*q*] copt-dz: αλλοι VΔ vulg lat-*b c*: txt ABCℵ rel lat-*ff₂ i*. rec (for οτι εἷς) ενα (*to suit ιωαννην and ηλιαν*), with AC³N rel lat-*k* syrr goth arm: ως ενα D latt: txt BC¹Lℵ copt.

29. for και αυτος, αυτος δε (|| *Luke*) D lat-*a c ff₂*: om (|| *Matt*) 1 lat-*k* æth arm. rec (for επηρωτα αυτους) λεγει αυτοις (*from* || *Matt*), with AC³N rel vulg lat-*b* (*f* syrr) goth æth arm: txt BC¹DLΔℵ lat-*a c ff₂* [*q*] copt. rec aft αποκριθεις ins δε (*from* || *Matt Luke*), with CDℵ rel lat-*f ff₂* goth syr: pref και AN 33 lat-*a b i* (*k*) [*q*] æth: om BL vulg syrr copt Eus. at end add ο υιος του θεου Lℵ, add further του ζωντος 69 Syr syr-jer (|| *Matt*).

the text is in much uncertainty.

26.] See above in this note,—and var. readd. The first and second **μηδέ** both carry a separate climax with them: he was not even to *go* into the village, no, nor so much as tell it to *any who dwelt in the village.*

27—30.] Confession of Peter. Matt. xvi. 13—20. Luke ix. 18—21. With the exception of the introduction in Luke, which describes the Lord to have been *alone praying, and joined by his disciples,* —and the omission of the praise of and promise to Peter by both Mark and Luke, the three are in exact accordance. On this latter omission no stress must there-

γωσιν περὶ αὐτοῦ. 31 Καὶ ἤρξατο διδάσκειν αὐτοὺς ὅτι
δεῖ τὸν [s] υἱὸν τοῦ [s] ἀνθρώπου πολλὰ παθεῖν καὶ [t] ἀποδοκιμασθῆναι ὑπὸ τῶν πρεσβυτέρων καὶ τῶν ἀρχιερέων καὶ
τῶν γραμματέων καὶ ἀποκτανθῆναι, καὶ μετὰ τρεῖς ἡμέρας
[u] ἀναστῆναι· 32 καὶ [v] παῤῥησίᾳ τὸν λόγον ἐλάλει. καὶ
[w] προςλαβόμενος ὁ Πέτρος αὐτὸν ἤρξατο [x] ἐπιτιμᾶν αὐτῷ.
..viii. 33 (appy) N. 33 ὁ δὲ [y] ἐπιστραφεὶς καὶ ἰδὼν τοὺς μαθητὰς αὐτοῦ [x] ἐπετίμησεν Πέτρῳ καὶ λέγει Ὕπαγε ὀπίσω μου σατανᾶ, ὅτι οὐ
[z] φρονεῖς [a] τὰ τοῦ θεοῦ, ἀλλὰ [a] τὰ τῶν ἀνθρώπων. 34 καὶ
προςκαλεσάμενος τὸν ὄχλον σὺν τοῖς μαθηταῖς αὐτοῦ
εἶπεν αὐτοῖς Ὅςτις θέλει [b] ὀπίσω μου [b] ἀκολουθεῖν,
[c] ἀπαρνησάσθω ἑαυτὸν καὶ ἀράτω τὸν [d] σταυρὸν [d] αὐτοῦ
καὶ ἀκολουθείτω μοι. 35 ὃς γὰρ ἐὰν θέλῃ τὴν [e] ψυχὴν
αὐτοῦ σῶσαι, [e] ἀπολέσει αὐτήν· ὃς δ' ἂν [e] ἀπολέσει τὴν
[e] ψυχὴν αὐτοῦ ἕνεκεν ἐμοῦ καὶ τοῦ εὐαγγελίου, σώσει

s Matt. viii. 20 reff.
t Matt. xxi. 42 reff.
u Matt. xii. 41. xx. 19. ch. xvi. 9 al. Isa. xxvi. 19.
v John vii. 13, 26. x. 24 al.
w ‖ Mt. Acts xviii. 26. Rom. xiv. 1, 3 al. 2 Macc. viii. 1.
x = ‖ Mt. Matt. xvii. 18. xix. 3. ch. i. 25 al. Zech. iii. 3.
y ch. v. 30. John xxi. 20 1 Kings x. 9.
z = ‖ Mt. Rom. viii. 5. xii. 16 bis. Phil. iii. 19. Col. iii. 2. 1 Macc. x. 20.
a Matt. viii. 33. reff.
b Matt. x. 38. 3 Kings xix. 20. see Num. xxxii. 11.
c ‖ Mt. and of Peter's denial only, exc. Luke xii. 9. Isa. xxxi. 7 only.
d ‖ Mt. reff.
e ‖ Mt. reff. see Prov. i. 19.

30. for λεγωσιν, ειπωσιν (*from* ‖ *Matt*) CDG.
31. rec (for υπο) απο (*from* ‖ *Matt Luke*), with A rel: txt BCDGKLΠℵ 33. (N?) ins απο bef των αρχ. D [vulg] lat-*a b f k* [*l*] Syr. rec om των (bef αρχ.) (‖ *Matt Luke*), with AN rel: ins BCDEHM [S(Tischdf)] UVXℵ goth. rec om των (bef γραμ.), with AGKNXΔ[Π] 1. 33. 69 goth: ins BCD [S(Tischdf)] ℵ rel.
32. ελαλει bef τον λογ. N. rec αυτον bef ο πετρος (‖ *Matt*), with ACℵ rel vulg lat-*f k* copt goth arm: om αυτον D: txt BL lat-*a*. (N?)
33. aft ο δε ins ιησ. AKΠ lat-*f* syr. rec ins τω bef πετρω (‖ *Matt*), with AC rel: om BDLℵ. rec (for κ. λεγει) λεγων, with AD rel latt syr goth arm: txt BCLΔℵ lat-ff_2 *k* Syr copt æth. om 2nd τα D-gr 225.
34. om αυτοις DXΔ lat-*a b c* ff_2 *i k*. for οστις, ει τις (*from* ‖ *Matt Luke*) BC[1]DLΔℵ 1. 33. 69 latt syr-mg arm $Orig_1$[int_1] $Synop_1$: txt AC[2] rel syrr copt goth æth. rec (for ακολουθειν) ελθειν (*from* ‖ *Matt*), with ABC[2]KLΓΠℵ lat-*c* g_1 *k* syrr copt arm Orig-int_1 [$Synop_1$]: ελθειν κ. ακολουθειν Δ: txt C[1]D rel vulg lat-(*a b* ff_2) *f i n* [*q*] goth æth $Orig_1$. for απαρν., αρνησασθω D. for 2nd αυτου, εαυτου ℵ.
35. rec (for εαν) αν, with AD rel $Orig_1$: txt BCKMΔΠℵ 1. 33. for 1st ψ. αυτου, εαυτου ψ. B Orig: ψ. εαυ. D-corr[1]. om ος δ' αν απ. τ. ψ. αυ. D[1] lat-*k* æth. rec (for 2nd απολεσει) απολεση (*corrn, and from* ‖ *Matt Luke*), with A rel $Orig_1$: txt BC D-corr ΓΔℵ. for 2nd ψυχην αυτου, εαυτου ψυχην C[3] rel: txt A B(sic cod: see table) C[1]LΔℵ [1. 33].—αυτην D-corr Γ lat-*i*[1]. om εμου και D lat-*a b i* (*k*) *n* æth arm $Orig_1$. rec ins ουτος bef σωσει (*from* ‖ *Luke*), with C[2] M-marg rel: txt AB C[1](appy) DKLM[1]XΔΠℵ 1. 33 latt syrr copt goth æth arm $Orig_1$ Dial.

fore be laid as to the character of *Mark's Gospel*, as has been done. (Thl. in l.—cited by De W.)

31—IX. 1.] Announcement of His approaching death and resurrection. Rebuke of Peter. Matt. xvi. 21—28. Luke ix. 22—27. Luke omits the rebuke of Peter. Mark adds, ver. 32, παῤῥησίᾳ τ. λ. ἐλάλει: and, in the rebuke of Peter, that the Lord said the words ἰδὼν τοὺς μαθητὰς αὐτοῦ. In vv. 34, 35, the agreement is close, except that Luke adds καθ' ἡμέραν, aft. τὸν στ. αὐτοῦ, and Mark καὶ τοῦ εὐαγγ. aft. ἐμοῦ, ver. 35 (it is perhaps worthy of remark that St. Mark writes ἀκολουθεῖν in ver. 34: possibly from the information of him, to whom it was said, τί πρός σε; σύ μοι ἀκολούθει, John xxi. 22); and informs us, in ver. 34, that our Lord said these words, *having called the multitude with his disciples*. This Meyer calls *a contradiction to Matt. and Luke*,—and thinks it arose from a misunderstanding of Luke's πάντας. Far rather should I say that our account represents every detail to the life, and that the πρὸς πάντας contains *traces of it*. What wonder that a crowd should here, as every

αὐτήν. 36 τί γὰρ [f] ὠφελεῖ [[g] τὸν] ἄνθρωπον [h] κερδῆσαι
τὸν κόσμον ὅλον καὶ [i] ζημιωθῆναι τὴν ψυχὴν αὐτοῦ; 37 τί
γὰρ [[k] δώσει ἄνθρωπος] [l] ἀντάλλαγμα τῆς ψυχῆς αὐτοῦ;
38 ὃς γὰρ ἐὰν [m] ἐπαισχυνθῇ με καὶ τοὺς ἐμοὺς λόγους ἐν
τῇ γενεᾷ ταύτῃ τῇ [n] μοιχαλίδι καὶ [o] ἁμαρτωλῷ, καὶ ὁ
υἱὸς τοῦ ἀνθρώπου [m] ἐπαισχυνθήσεται αὐτόν, ὅταν ἔλθῃ
[p] ἐν τῇ δόξῃ τοῦ πατρὸς αὐτοῦ μετὰ τῶν [q] ἀγγέλων τῶν
[q] ἁγίων. IX. 1 καὶ ἔλεγεν αὐτοῖς Ἀμὴν λέγω ὑμῖν ὅτι
εἰσίν τινες ὧδε τῶν ἑστηκότων, [r] οἵτινες οὐ μὴ [s] γεύσωνται
θανάτου ἕως ἂν ἴδωσιν τὴν βασιλείαν τοῦ θεοῦ ἐληλυθυῖαν
[t] ἐν δυνάμει.
2 Καὶ μετὰ ἡμέρας ἓξ [u] παραλαμβάνει ὁ Ἰησοῦς τὸν
Πέτρον καὶ τὸν Ἰάκωβον καὶ Ἰωάννην καὶ [v] ἀναφέρει
αὐτοὺς εἰς [w] ὄρος [w] ὑψηλὸν [x] κατ' [x] ἰδίαν μόνους, καὶ [y] μετεμορφώθη [z] ἔμπροσθεν αὐτῶν. 3 καὶ τὰ ἱμάτια αὐτοῦ

N ix. 1 (appy)... ABCDE FGHK LMNSU VXΓΔΠ ℵ 1. 33. 69. Frag. Cant. μβανει.. ...εμπροσ. Frag. Cant.

f Matt. xv. 5 reff. Prov. x. 2.
g art., = Matt. xv. 11 al.
h ||. Matt. xxv. 17, &c. James iv. 13+. Job xxii. 3 Symm.
i = constr., || Mt. reff. Herod. vii. 39.
k || Mt. Matt. xxvii. 10. Gen. xxv. 34.
l || Mt. only. Jer. xv. 13 only.
m || L. bis. Rom. i. 16. 2 Tim. i. 8, 12. Heb. ii. 11 al. Job xxxiv. 19 Bℵ. Isa. i. 29 A ℵ[1·3b] only.
n Matt. xii. 39 reff.
o adj. (Luke v. 8. xix. 7?). Rom. vii. 13. Isa. i. 4.
p ||. Matt. xxv. 31 al. Ps. ci. 16.
q || L. Acts x. 22. Rev. xiv. 10.
r Matt. xiii. 15 reff.
s ||. Heb. ii. 9 (there also w. θαν.). Job xx. 18. Ps. xxxiii. 8.
t Rom. i. 4. Col. i. 29. see Matt. xxiv. 30.
u ||. Matt. ii. 13, &c. iv. 5, 8 al. Num. xxii. 41.
v || Mt. reff. (= ἀναβιβάζω, Num. xxii. 41.)
w Matt. iv. 8 reff.
x Matt. xiv. 13 reff.
y || Mt. Rom. xii. 2. 2 Cor. iii. 18 only +. Ps. xxxiii. tit. Symm.
z = Matt. v. 16. vi. 1 al.

36. rec ωφελησει (*from || Matt; not txt from || Luke*), with ACD rel vulg lat-*b c f ff₂ k* syr Orig₁: ωφεληθησεται 33: txt B(L)ℵ lat-*a* [*n*] Syr arm. rec om τον, with BKUℵ[3a] (SV, e sil) goth: ins AC[1]D Orig₁.—ανθρωπος (|| *Matt Luke*) C[3]EFGHL MXΓΔℵ[1] 1. 33. 69 Petr. rec (for κερδησαι and ζημιωθηναι) εαν κερδηση and ζημιωθη (*from || Matt*), with AC rel latt Orig: κερδησας (*see || Luke*) ζημιωθηναι L: txt Bℵ.—τ. κ. ολ. bef κερδ. C 33 Syr Petr₁.

37. rec (for τι γαρ) η τι (*from || Matt*), with ACD[2] rel latt syrr goth æth: η τι γαρ D[1]-gr: txt BLΔℵ copt arm Orig₁. om δωσει ανθρωπος Δ: ins A(B)CDL(ℵ) rel latt Orig₁. (*Prob the origl txt was* τί γὰρ ἀντάλλαγμα τῆς ψυχῆς αὐτοῦ; *as Tischdf edited* (ed 7: in ed 8 he follows ℵ[1]), δώσει ἄνθρ. *being from || Matt. But the single codex Sangallensis is hardly warrant enough for this.*)—δοι Bℵ[1], δω Lℵ[3a]. ins ο bef ανθρ. B. εαυτου B: αυτω C.

38. rec (for εαν) αν (*see || Luke*), with GHKUΠ 69 (S 1. 33, e sil) Clem₁: om A vulg lat-*f*: ος δ αν D: txt BCℵ rel. επαισχυνθησεται εμε D.—for με, μεν A[1].

Chap. IX. **1.** rec των bef ωδε (*see || Matt Luke*), with ACD[2]Nℵ rel vulg lat-*f* syr goth arm: των εστηκοτων bef ωδε 1 Syr copt Orig₁: om ωδε lat-*b i*: txt BD[1] lat-*a ff₂* (appy) æth. for εστηκοτων, εστωτων (||) ℵ 33. aft εστ. ins μετ' εμου D lat-*a b* (*ff₂*) [*n q*]. γευσονται E[1]HKLNX 69 ev-y Orig₁.

2. (μετα, so B C(appy) DLΔℵ.) ο ιησ. bef παρ. A. om 2nd τον ΧΓΔ Frag-cant. rec ins τον bef ιωαννην, with CDKLUXΠℵ 1. 33. 69: om ABN Frag-cant rel. αναγει [for αναφ.] D Frag-cant 2-pe. aft υψηλον ins λιαν ℵ (52). μεταμορφουται Frag-cant: τατεμορφωθη (sic) D.

where else, have collected about Him and the disciples? **37.**] If (see var. readd.) the words in brackets be omitted, the sense will be, **For what can be an equivalent for his life?** **38.**] Mark and Luke here agree: and Matt., ver. 27, bears traces of this verse, having apparently abridged it in transcribing his report, not to repeat what he had before said, in ch. x. 33. On **μοιχαλίδι**, see Matt. xii. 39, and observe the addition ἐν τῇ γ. ταύ. τῇ μ. καὶ ἁμ. as belonging to the precision and graphic character of our Evangelist's narrative.

Ch. IX. **1.**] See on || Matt.

ὧδε τῶν ἑστ.] **there are some here of the standers-by.** Remember, our Lord was speaking *to the multitude with his disciples.*

2—13.] The Transfiguration. Matt. xvii. 1—13. Luke ix. 28—36. Here again, while Matt. and Mark's accounts seem to have *one and the same source*, they have deflected from it, and additional particulars have found their way into our text. Luke's account is from a *different source.*

[a] ἐγένοντο [b] στίλβοντα, λευκὰ λίαν, οἷα [c] γναφεὺς [d] ἐπὶ
τῆς γῆς οὐ δύναται οὕτως [e] λευκᾶναι. 4 καὶ [f] ὤφθη
αὐτοῖς Ἡλίας σὺν Μωυσῇ, καὶ ἦσαν [g] συλλαλοῦντες τῷ
Ἰησοῦ. 5 καὶ [h] ἀποκριθεὶς ὁ Πέτρος λέγει τῷ Ἰησοῦ
Ῥαββεί, [i] καλόν ἐστιν ἡμᾶς ὧδε εἶναι, καὶ ποιήσωμεν
τρεῖς σκηνάς, σοὶ [k] μίαν καὶ Μωυσῇ [k] μίαν καὶ Ἡλίᾳ
μίαν. 6 οὐ γὰρ ᾔδει τί ἀποκριθῇ, [l] ἔκφοβοι γὰρ ἐγένοντο. 7 καὶ [am] ἐγένετο νεφέλη [n] ἐπισκιάζουσα αὐτοῖς, καὶ
Frag. Cant. [o] ἦλθεν [o] φωνὴ ἐκ τῆς νεφέλης Οὗτός ἐστιν ὁ υἱός μου
μου... ὁ [p] ἀγαπητός, [q] ἀκούετε αὐτοῦ. 8 καὶ [r] ἐξάπινα [s] περι-
βλεψάμενοι οὐκέτι οὐδένα εἶδον, ἀλλὰ τὸν Ἰησοῦν μόνον
...και κα Frag. Cant. μεθ᾽ ἑαυτῶν. 9 καταβαινόντων δὲ αὐτῶν ἀπὸ τοῦ ὄρους

a constr., w. part., ch. i. 4 reff. plur., Matt. vi. 48 reff. b here only. Ezek. xl. 3 al. c here only. 4 Kings xviii. 17. Isa. vii. 3. xxxvi. 2 only. d Matt. vi. 10. Rev. v. 3 al. e Rev. vii. 14 only. Ps. l. 7 (9) al. f ||. Luke i. 11. 1 Cor. xv. 5—8 al. Exod. iii. 2, 16. g w. dat., || L. Luke xxii. 4. Exod. xxxiv. 35. Isa. vii. 6. w. μετά, || Mt. Acts xxv. 12. w. πρός, Luke iv. 36 only. h red., Matt. xi. 25 reff. i || Mt. reff. k 1 Kings x. 3. l Heb. xii. 21 only. Deut. ix. 19. 1 Macc. xiii. 2 Aℵ only. (-βεῖν, 2 Cor. x. 9.) m || L. n ||. Luke i. 35. Acts v. 15 only. Exod. xl. 35. o = John xii. 28. p || Mt. al. Gen. xxii. 2. q Deut. xviii. 15, 19. r here only. Num. vi. 9 al. s absol., ch. v. 32. x. 23. 3 Kings xxi. (xx.) 40. w. acc., ch. iii. 5 (reff.).

3. rec εγενετο (*amml altern : cf || Matt*), with BCℵ rel: txt ADGKLNVXΓΠ 1. 33. 69 (γινονται Orig) Thl. rec aft λιαν ins ως χιων (*reminiscence of Matt* xxviii. 3), with A D-gr N rel latt syrr copt goth, ωσει χ. KΠ: om BCLΔℵ 1 lat-*k* D-lat copt-ms sah æth arm. ως ου δυναται τις λευκαναι επι της γης D (lat-*b i*) Syr[: om X lat-*a n*]. rec om ουτως, with A(D) rel (latt) Syr goth : ins BCL N[aft. λευκ.] Δℵ 33. 69 lat-(*ff*$_2$) *k* coptt æth arm(appy) Orig. (*Mey calls it* 'an irrelevant gloss;' *but it is in fact an Hellenistic idiom, akin to* ὃς . . αὐτός.)

4. for ησαν συλλαλουντες, ησαν λαλουντες ℵ Scr's c [vulg lat-*b ff*$_2$ *g*$_{1.2}$ *i l* D-lat]: συνελαλουν (*see || Luke*) D[-gr] 1 lat-*a n* [*q*]. (συλλαλουν K.)

5. for λεγει, ειπεν D 2-pe lat-*a* (*b*) [*n*] Syr : ελεγεν 1. 69. for τω ιησ., αυτω N. for και ποιησωμεν, θελεις ποιησω D lat-*b i* : θελεις ποιησωμεν 69, *si vis faciamus* lat-*a c*. [add ωδε (*see || Matt*) C lat-*c ff*$_2$.] rec σκηνας bef τρεις (*|| Luke : so* B *in || Matt*), with ADN rel lat-*f* [*q*] syr goth arm : txt BCLΔℵ 33 latt Syr æth.

6. rec (for αποκριθη) λαλησῃ, with C[3]U[1] Chr, λαλησει ADN 69(sic) rel syrr [latt sah æth]: txt BC[1]LΔℵ 1. 33 lat-*k* copt (απεκριθη ℵ Orig$_2$). (*Peter's words not being strictly an* answer, *some omd* αποκρ. *above,—others, tolerating it as idiomatic, were offended at this* αποκριθη, *which expressed the same so much more plainly. Hence it was altered to* λαλησει *or* λαλησῃ, *from* ετι αυτου λαλουντος *in || Matt.*) rec (for εκφ. γ. εγ.) ησαν γαρ εκφ. (*corrn to avoid* εγενοντο και εγενετο), with AN rel vulg lat-*f* syrr goth : txt BCDLΔℵ 33 copt sah(appy) Chr$_1$.

7. for και εγεν., εγεν. δε N ev-z. for ηλθεν, εγενετο (*from || Luke*) BCLΔ(ℵ) Syr syr-mg copt arm. εκ της νεφ. bef φωνη ℵ. rec aft νεφελης ins λεγουσα (*from || Matt Luke*), with ADL 1. 33. 69 latt Syr syr-w-ast sah æth arm zoh; λεγων Δ: om BCNℵ rel lat-*k* copt goth arm-mss. aft ο αγαπητος ins εν ω ευδοκησα (Δ) ℵ-corr[1] : ον εξελεξαμην Frag-cant. rec αυτου bef ακουετε (*from || Luke : so also rec in || Matt*), with AN rel lat-*b f* [*q*] syrr goth : txt BCDLℵ Frag-cant 1. 33 vulg lat-*a c ff*$_2$ *g*$_1$ *k l* coptt.—om ακ. αυτου Δ.

8. for εξαπινα, ευθεως D Frag-cant 69 vulg lat-*a g*$_{1.2}$. for αλλα, ει μη (*from || Matt*) BDNℵ Frag-cant 33 latt copt goth æth : txt AC rel sah arm. om τον Frag-cant. μεθ(μετα B) εαυτων bef αλλα τον ιησ. μονον B 33 lat-*c f* : om μ. εαυτων Frag-cant lat-*a ff*$_2$ *k l*.

9. for καταβ. δε, και καταβ. (*from || Matt*) BCDLNΔℵ Frag-cant 33 latt Syr copt æth : txt A rel lat-*f* syr goth arm. for απο, εκ (*from || Matt*) BD 33 : txt ACNℵ

If we might conjecture, Peter has furnished the accounts in Matt. and Mark :— this latter being *retouched*,—perhaps by himself : while that of Luke may have had another origin. The additional particulars in our text are,—the very graphic and noble description in ver. 3, **στίλβ. . . . . λευκᾶναι**, and **οὐ γὰρ ᾔδει τί ἀποκρ. . . . . ἔκφοβοι.** Mark omits ἐν ᾧ εὐδόκησα, Matt. ver. 5. **2.**] The omission of an art. before **Ἰωάννην** serves to bind together the pair of brothers. **3.**] **ἐγένοντο** is

[t] διεστείλατο αὐτοῖς ἵνα μηδενὶ ἃ εἶδον [u] διηγήσωνται, εἰ
μὴ ὅταν ὁ υἱὸς τοῦ ἀνθρώπου [v] ἐκ νεκρῶν [v] ἀναστῇ.
10 καὶ τὸν λόγον [w] ἐκράτησαν πρὸς ἑαυτούς, [x] συνζητοῦντες τί [y] ἐστιν [z] τὸ [v] ἐκ νεκρῶν [v] ἀναστῆναι. 11 καὶ [a] ἐπηρώτων αὐτὸν λέγοντες [b] Ὅτι λέγουσιν οἱ γραμματεῖς ὅτι
Ἠλίαν [c] δεῖ ἐλθεῖν πρῶτον; 12 ὁ δὲ ἔφη αὐτοῖς Ἠλίας
μὲν ἐλθὼν πρῶτον [d] ἀποκαθιστάνει πάντα· καὶ πῶς γέγραπται [e] ἐπὶ τὸν υἱὸν τοῦ ἀνθρώπου, ἵνα πολλὰ πάθῃ
καὶ [f] * ἐξουδενηθῇ; 13 ἀλλὰ λέγω ὑμῖν ὅτι καὶ Ἠλίας
ἐλήλυθεν, καὶ [g] ἐποίησαν αὐτῷ ὅσα ἤθελον, καθὼς γέ-

ABCDE FGHK LMNSU VXΓΔΠ ℵ 1. 33. 69

t Matt. xvi. 20 reff.
u ch. v. 16 reff.
v ch. vi. 14 reff.
w = here only. Dan. v. 12 Theod.
x = ch. xii. 28. Luke xxiv. 15 al.+
y = Matt. ix. 13 reff.
z = ver. 23 reff.
a ch. viii. 27 al. fr.
b = (see note) ver. 28 only. 1 Chron. xvii. 6.
c = Matt. xxiv. 6 reff.
d || Mt. reff.
e = Rom. iv. 9. 1 Tim. i. 18. Heb. vii. 13.
f (-δ) here (2 Cor. x. 10 v. r.) only. Cant. viii. 1 & 7 A. (-θ-) Luke xviii. 9 al. -νοῦν, here v. r. only. Judg. ix. 38 al. (δένωσις, Ps. cxviii. 22.)
g Matt. vii. 12. xx. 32. Gen. xx. 9.

rel. διεστελλετο C 1. rec διηγ. bef α ειδον (*for elegance*), with A rel lat-*c f ff*$_2$ syrr &c: txt BCDLΔℵ 1 (69[εξηγ.]) vulg lat-*a b g*$_{1,2}$ *i k l n* [*q*].—ειδοσαν D.—διηγησονται HKNX Scr's c s u. om ει μη ℵ[1](ins ℵ-corr[1]).

10. for το εκ ν. αναστ., οταν εκ νεκρων αναστη D 1. 69 latt (Syr) syr.

11. επηρωτησαν A 1. 33. 69 lat-*a g*$_1$ [*q*]. οι γρ. bef λεγουσιν D lat-*a* copt. ins οι φαρισαιοι και bef οι γρ. Lℵ vulg lat-*c g*$_1$. om οτι D-gr 1 lat-*b ff*$_2$ *i k* [*q*]. πρωτον bef ελθειν D lat-*a b c f g*$_1$ *i k* [*q*].

12. rec (for εφη) αποκριθεις ειπεν (*from* || *Matt*), with ADN rel latt syr goth æth arm: txt BCLΔℵ Syr copt. ins ει bef ηλιας D. om μεν (D)L 1 latt Syr syr-mg æth arm. (*So Tischdf edits,* μεν *occurring in* || *Matt: but it was likely to be cancelled here as having no* δε *to correspond: and* D *is hardly to be cited, as it reads* ει ηλιας.) rec αποκαθιστα, with NX rel: αποκαταστησει C latt syr-mg (appy) copt æth arm: αποκαταστανει D-gr ℵ[1]: αποκατιστανει B[1]: txt AB[2]LΔℵ[3a] 1. 33 lat-*k* goth. for και πως, καθως (*prob borrowed from* καθως γεγρ. *below*) AKMΔΠ syr-mg: πως ουν arm. *rec ἐξουδενωθῇ, with ACℵ rel: -νηθη BDLN. (εξουθ. LNℵ 69.)

13. om οτι ℵ[1]. om 1st και (|| *Matt*) M[1]NUΓ 1. 69 lat-*a k l* copt [(goth)] æth arm. for εληλυθεν, ηδη ηλθεν (|| *Matt*) C [gat] 1 lat-*f i* [(goth)], ηδη εληλ. N Scr's w[2]-marg. ins εν bef αυτω (|| *Matt*) KLΠℵ[3a] Syr syr-mg. rec ηθελησαν (|| *Matt*), with AC[2]Δ latt: txt B C[1](appy) D-gr Lℵ. (N? [om αυ. οσα ηθ. X.])

of itself a graphic touch, bringing out the glistening of each separate portion of His clothing. **8. οὐδένα**] **none of those who appeared, but** (sondern, '*nay, on the contrary*') **Jesus alone.** 9—13.] Two remarkable additions occur in our text;—ver. 10, which indicates *apostolic authority*, and that of *one of the Three*;—and **καὶ . . . . ἐξουδ.** in ver. 12. **10. τ. λ. ἐκράτ.**] Not, '*they kept the command*:'—for **συνζητ.** explains it to mean **kept secret the saying,** as in ref. Dan. **τί ἐστιν τὸ ἐκ ν. ἀν.** does not refer to the *Resurrection generally*, for it was an article of Jewish belief, and connected with the times of the Messiah;—but to *His Resurrection as connected with His Death; the whole* was enigmatical to them. 11.] The **ὅτι** may be merely recitantis, '*they asked him, saying* (*that*) *the Scribes say, that Elias must first come*:' leaving **ἐπηρώτων** to find its application in the difficulty thus suggested by them. But it is better to take it in the unusual sense (undoubted there) of ver. 28 [see Moulton on Winer, p. 208, note 4]: see further on in this note. 12.] Meyer and others place the interrogation after **τοῦ ἀνθρώπου**, and regard **ἵνα πολ. . . .** as its answer. But not to mention that such a sentence would be without example in our Lord's discourses, the sense given by it is meagre in the extreme. As it stands in the text, it forms a counter-question to that of the Apostles in ver. 11. *They asked*, **How say the Scribes that Elias must first come?** Our Lord answers it by telling them that it is even so; and returns the question by another: **And how is it (also) written of the Son of Man, that He, &c.?** then comes the conclusion in ver. 13 with **ἀλλὰ λέγω ὑμῖν,** stating that Elias *has come*, and leaving it therefore to be inferred that the sufferings of the Son of Man were close at hand. Notice how the **γέγρ. ἐπ' αὐτόν**

γραπται [e] ἐπ᾽ αὐτόν. 14 Καὶ ἐλθὼν πρὸς τοὺς μαθητὰς
εἶδεν ὄχλον πολὺν περὶ αὐτοὺς καὶ γραμματεῖς [h] συνζη-
τοῦντας αὐτοῖς. 15 καὶ εὐθὺς πᾶς ὁ ὄχλος ἰδόντες αὐτὸν
[i] ἐξεθαμβήθησαν, καὶ [k] προστρέχοντες [l] ἠσπάζοντο αὐτόν.
16 καὶ [m] ἐπηρώτησεν αὐτοὺς Τί [n] συνζητεῖτε πρὸς αὐτούς;
17 καὶ ἀπεκρίθη αὐτῷ [o] εἷς ἐκ τοῦ ὄχλου [p] Διδάσκαλε,
ἤνεγκα τὸν υἱόν μου πρός σε [q] ἔχοντα πνεῦμα [r] ἄλαλον.
18 καὶ ὅπου ἐὰν αὐτὸν [s] καταλάβῃ, [t] ῥήσσει αὐτόν, καὶ
[u] ἀφρίζει καὶ [v] τρίζει τοὺς ὀδόντας καὶ [w] ξηραίνεται· καὶ

I_c ιδεν οχλον...

h w. dat., ch. viii. 11 reff. w. πρός, ch. i. 27 reff. see ver. 10 reff.
i ch. xiv. 33. xvi. 5, 6 only †. Sir. xxx. 9 only.
k ch. x. 17. Acts viii. 30 only. Gen. xviii. 2.
l Luke i. 40 al. 1 Macc. vii. 29, 33.
m ver. 11.
n ver. 10, 14.
o Matt. xxii. 35 reff.
p Matt. xvii. 24 reff.
q ch. v. 15 reff.
r ver. 25 (there also w. πν.). ch. vii. 37 only. Ps. xxx. 18. xxxvii. 13 only.
s = here only. (John i. 5. Rom. ix. 30 al.)
t Matt. vii. 6 reff.
u ver. 20 only †. (-ρος, ‖ L.)
v here only †. (τρισμός, Ps. lxv. 11 Aq.)
w = ch. iii. 1. Ps. ci. 4, 11.

14. ελθοντες and ειδον BLΔℵ lat-*k* arm. (-δαν B[1].) for περι, προς D 28 lat-*a b c ff₂ i k*. ins τους bef γραμματεις DI_c 69 arm. for αυτοις, προς αυτους (*see ver* 16) BCI_cLΔℵ[3a] 1 latt goth: πρ. εαυτους Gℵ'.

15. (ευθυς, so BCLΔℵ 1. 69.) om ο (bef οχλος) D. rec ιδων αυτ. εξεθαμβηθη (*corrn to agree with* οχλος), with AN rel vulg lat-*f* $g_{1.2}$ *k* [*l q*] syr-txt: txt BC(D) I_cLΔℵ 1. 33. 69 ev-y lat-*a* (*b c* ff_2) *i* Syr syr-mg copt-schw goth æth arm.—for αυτον, τον ιησουν D vulg lat-*b c* ff_2.—for εξεθ., εθαμβηθησαν D. προτρεχοντες AC: προσχαιροντες *gaudentes* D lat-*c* ff_2 *i k*.

16. rec (for 1st αυτους) τους γραμματεις (*explan derived from ver* 14), with ACN rel lat-*a* syrr goth: txt BDLΔℵ 1 vulg lat-*b c f* ff_2 $g_{1.2}$ *i k* [*l q*] copt æth arm. (I_c def.) for 2nd αυτους, εαυτους AGMΓ ℵ-corr[1](but ε erased) 33 [copt ?]: εν υμειν *inter vos* D latt.

17. rec αποκριθεις and aft οχλου ins ειπε, with AC I_c(appy) N rel vulg lat-*f* syrr goth (æth) arm: txt BDLΔℵ 33 lat-*a b c i k* copt. rec om αυτω, with AN rel vulg lat-*f* syrr goth arm: ins BCDLΔℵ 33 lat-*a b c i k* [*q*] copt (æth), and (aft ειπε) I_c 1. 69 (αυτοις).

18. rec αν, with CDI_cN rel: om ℵ[1] 1: txt ABKΔΠℵ[3a]. ρασσει *applontat* D. om 2nd αυτον Dℵ lat-*k*. (om 1st αυτ. Δ.) rec aft τ. οδοντ. ins αυτου, with AC[3]I_cN rel lat-*b f* syrr copt goth æth arm: om BC[1]DLΔℵ 1. 33. 69 vulg lat-*a c i k l* [*q*].

binds both together. Just as the first coming of the Son of Man is to suffer and to die, so has the first coming of Elias been as it was written of him; but there is a future coming of Elias **ἀποκαθιστάνειν πάντα**, and of the Son of Man in glory. See further in notes on Matt. The first **καί** in ver. 13 is **also**, binding what is said of Elias to that which has been said of the Son of Man: the second **καί** is simply **and**. [On the various forms of **ἔξου.** see Moulton on Winer, p. 113, note 2.]

14—29.] Healing of a possessed lunatic. Matt. xvii. 14—21. Luke ix. 37—42. The account of Mark is by far the most copious: and here, which is very rarely the case in the official life of our Lord, the three accounts appear to have been *originally different and independent*. The descent from the mountain was on the *day following* the transfiguration, Luke ver. 37. **14.**] The Scribes were probably boasting over the disciples, and reasoning from *their* inability to *that of their Master also*. As Stier remarks, there is hardly such another contrast to be found in the Gospel as this, between the open heaven and the sons of glory on the mount, and the valley of tears with its terrible forms of misery and pain and unbelief. I have already in the notes to Matt. spoken of the noble use made of this contrast in the last and grandest picture of the greatest of painters—the Transfiguration of Raffaelle. **15.**] The Lord's countenance probably retained traces of the glory on the mount; so strong a word as **ἐξεθαμβήθησαν** would hardly have been used merely of their surprise at His sudden approach: see Exod. xxxiv. 29, 30. *That* brightness, however, *terrified* the people: this *attracts* them: see 2 Cor. iii. 7—18. **16.**] **αὐτούς** (1st), **them**, i. e. '*the multitude*,' regarding the Scribes as *a part of the* ὄχλος. *One of the multitude* answers. **17. πρός σε**] i. e. *intended* to do so, not being aware of His absence. From Luke, ver. 38, we learn that this was his *only* son. **ἄλαλον**, *causing* deafness and dumbness, and fits of epilepsy: see Luke xi. 14. **18. ξηρ.**] **wastes** or **pines away**, as E. V., or perhaps **becomes dry or stiff.** **ἵνα** combines the pur-

[x] εἶπα τοῖς μαθηταῖς σου ἵνα αὐτὸ ἐκβάλωσιν, καὶ οὐκ
[y] ἴσχυσαν. 19 ὁ δὲ ἀποκριθεὶς αὐτοῖς λέγει Ὦ γενεὰ
[z] ἄπιστος, [a] ἕως [a] πότε [b] πρὸς ὑμᾶς ἔσομαι; [a] ἕως [a] πότε
[c] ἀνέξομαι ὑμῶν; φέρετε αὐτὸν πρός με. 20 καὶ ἤνεγκαν
αὐτὸν πρὸς αὐτόν. καὶ [d] ἰδὼν αὐτὸν τὸ πνεῦμα εὐθὺς
[e] ἐσπάραξεν αὐτόν, καὶ πεσὼν ἐπὶ τῆς γῆς [f] ἐκυλίετο
[g] ἀφρίζων. 21 καὶ ἐπηρώτησεν τὸν πατέρα αὐτοῦ Πόσος
χρόνος ἐστὶν [h] ὡς τοῦτο [i] γέγονεν αὐτῷ; ὁ δὲ εἶπεν
Ἐκ [k] παιδιόθεν· 22 καὶ πολλάκις καὶ εἰς πῦρ αὐτὸν
ἔβαλεν καὶ εἰς ὕδατα ἵνα ἀπολέσῃ αὐτόν· ἀλλ' εἴ τι
[l] δύνῃ, [m] βοήθησον ἡμῖν [n] σπλαγχνισθεὶς ἐφ' ἡμᾶς. 23 ὁ
δὲ Ἰησοῦς εἶπεν αὐτῷ [o] τὸ εἰ δύνῃ [πιστεῦσαι], πάντα

...εφ ημας I_c. ABCDE FGHKL MNSU VXΓΔΠ ℵ 1. 33. 69

x = here only. see Matt. iv. 3 reff.
y abs., Luke xiii. 24. Phil. iv. 13.
z = ||. John xx. 27. Isa. xvii. 10.
a || (Mt. bis). John x. 24. Rev. vi. 10 only. Ps. xciii. 3.
b = || L. (= μεθ' ὑμῶν, Mt.) ch. vi. 3 reff.
c ||. 2 Cor. xi. 1, 19. Isa. xlvi. 4.
d constr., Rev. iv. 1, 8. xi. 15. xix. 14. Winer, § 59. 4.
e || L. ch. i. 26. ver. 26 only. 2 Kings xxii. 8.
f here only. Josh. x. 18. (-ισμός, 2 Pet. ii. 22.)
g ver. 18 only †.
h = Luke xii. 58 reff.
i ch. v. 16. John v. 14. Acts vii. 40, from Exod. xxxii. 1.
k here only †.
l constr., Luke xii. 26. 2 Cor. xiii. 8.
m Matt. xv. 25.
n Matt. xv. 32. ch. i. 41 al. †.
o Luke i. 62. ix. 46, or xxii. 37. Acts xxii. 30. Rom. viii. 26.

(ειπα, so BFLℵ 1. (I_c def.)) aft ισχ. ins εκβαλειν αυτο D lat-*a b* arm.

19. for ο δε, και D 1. 69 lat-*a b c f i k* [*q*] æth. rec αυτω (*corrn, the answer being considered as addressed to the last speaker. This is far more likely than that* -τω *should have been corrd to* -τοις *to suit the* follg words. *A transcriber would regard not so much the* sense follg, *as the* fact precedg), with C^3 N[aft λεγει] rel lat-g_1 [*q*] Syr syr-mg: om C^1 69 lat-*k*: txt ABDLΔ$Π^1$ℵ 1. 33 vss. (I_c def.) απιστε D. εμε ℵ.

20. om πρ. αυτ. D latt. rec ευθεως το πν. (*to disconnect* το πν. *from* ιδων), with AI_cN rel vulg lat-g_1 goth: om ευθ. D lat-*a b* ff_2 *i* [*q*]: txt BCLΔℵ 33 lat-*c f* g_2 *k* syrr copt (æth) arm. συνεσπαραξεν (*from* || *Luke*) BCLΔℵ 33: εταραξεν (*a testimony for* εσπ., *not* συνεσπ.) D-gr, *conturbavit* latt: txt AI_cN rel.

21. for ως, εως B: αφ ου N: εξ ου C^1L(Δ)$ℵ^{3a}$ 33: *ex quo* latt syrr copt æth arm: txt AC^3D$ℵ^1$ rel goth. [I_c def.] rec om εκ (*as redundant*), with A rel arm(appy): ins BC(D)GI_cLNΔℵ 1. 33.—εκ παιδος D 2-pe Chr.—παιδοθεν EI_cN 1, παιδωθεν X.

22. rec αυτον bef κ. εις πυρ (*for perspicuity*), with AC^3(D)N rel vulg lat-*b c f i* (*k* [*l q*]) goth (æth): αυτ. εβ. aft υδατα I_c 2-pe: om αυτον K: txt BC^1LΔℵ.—om 2nd και DI_c 1. 69 vulg lat-*a b i k l* [*q*] Syr. ins το bef πυρ AEFGKMVΓ$Π^2$ Thl. κ. εις υδ. βαλλει D [lat-*b i q*]. αυτ. bef απολ. DI_c 1 vulg lat-*b c* $g_{1.2}$ [*i l q*]. αλλα Dℵ. for ει τι, ετι A. rec δυνασαι (*commoner form*), with ACN rel: txt BDI_cLΔℵ 1. (So next ver, exc that L$ℵ^{3a}$ there have rec, and N txt.) aft ημιν ins κυριε DG lat-*a b* g_2 *i* [*q*] arm: aft δυνη I_c.

23. om το DKNUΠ 69. om πιστευσαι BC^1LΔℵ 1 lat-k^1 copt æth arm: ins AC^3D rel latt syrr goth Chr_1. (*The true reading is very doubtful. Either* πιστεῦσαι *has been* omd *because it was supposed that our Lord was merely repeating the* εἰ δύνῃ *of the father, or it has been* inserted *by those who did not see that this was intended. The best* MSS *being divided, I have thought it best to leave* πιστεῦσαι *in brackets. See note.*)

pose of the **εἶπα** with the purport: see note on 1 Cor. xiv. 13. **19. γενεά**] not addressed to *the man*, as unbelieving, —nor to the disciples,—but *generally*, to the race and generation among whom the Lord's ministry was fulfilled. The additional words καὶ διεστραμμένη (Matt. Luke) are probably from Deut. xxxii. 5: see further ib. ver. 20, where ἄπιστος is also expressed by υἱοὶ οἷς οὐκ ἔστι πίστις ἐν αὐτοῖς. The question is not asked in a spirit of longing to be gone from them, but of holy impatience of their hardness of heart and unbelief. In this the father, disciples, Scribes, and multitude are equally involved. **20.**] **ἰδών** is out of strict concord with **πνεῦμα**, but has regard to its personal signification: see also ver. 26 below. This construction is often found in the Apocalypse (reff.). "The kingdom of Satan, in small and great, is ever stirred into a fiercer activity by the coming near of the kingdom of Christ. Satan has great wrath, when his time is short." (Trench, Mir. 365.) Vv. **21**—**27** are peculiar to Mark. **21.**] The Lord takes occasion to enquire thus of the father, to bring in the trial of his faith. **22.**] See Matt. ver. 15. **εἴ τι δύνῃ**] This bespeaks, if *any* faith, at most but a very

δυνατὰ τῷ πιστεύοντι. 24 εὐθὺς κράξας ὁ πατὴρ τοῦ
παιδίου ἔλεγεν Πιστεύω· [m] βοήθει μου τῇ [p] ἀπιστίᾳ.
25 ἰδὼν δὲ ὁ Ἰησοῦς ὅτι [q] ἐπισυντρέχει ὄχλος, [r] ἐπετίμησεν
τῷ [s] πνεύματι τῷ [s] ἀκαθάρτῳ λέγων αὐτῷ [t] Τὸ [u] ἄλαλον
καὶ [v] κωφὸν πνεῦμα, ἐγὼ [w] ἐπιτάσσω σοί, ἔξελθε ἐξ αὐτοῦ,
καὶ μηκέτι εἰςέλθῃς εἰς αὐτόν. 26 καὶ κράξας καὶ πολλὰ
[x] σπαράξας ἐξῆλθεν, καὶ ἐγένετο [y] ὡςεὶ νεκρός, ὥςτε

p Matt. xiii. 58 reff.
q here only †. pres., John i. 40 reff.
r ch. i. 25 reff. viii. 32, 33 al.
s Matt. x. 1 reff.
t constr., Matt. xi. 26 reff.
u ver. 17. ch. vii. 37 only. Ps. xxx. 18. xxxvii. 13 only.
v ch. vii. 32 reff.
w ch. i. 27 reff.
x ver. 20 reff.
y Matt. iii. 16. Ps. xxxvii. 13.

24. rec **και** ευθεως, with AC^3DN rel lat-*a b* &c: και (alone) C^1ℵ[1] fuld æth: txt BLΔℵ lat-*c* copt. rec aft του παιδιου ins μετα δακρυων, with A^2C^3DN rel latt (Syr) syr (goth): om A^1BC^1LΔℵ lat-*k* copt æth arm. for ελεγεν, λεγει D: ειπεν 69. rec aft πιστ. ins κυριε, with C^2N rel latt copt-wilk arm-usc: om ABC^1DLℵ am lat-g_1 *i k l* syrr copt-schw goth æth arm-zoh Chr. τη απιστια bef μου D latt [not *i q*].

25. for ιδων δε ο, και οτε ειδεν D latt(not *f*). ins ο bef οχλος ALM(S ?)XΔΠℵ 33. 69 arm. for λεγων, ειπων D-gr. rec το πν. το αλ. κ. κωφ., with AC^3N rel (Syr) syr goth æth: txt BC^1DLΔℵ 1. 33 latt copt arm. om εγω ℵ[1] 33 gat: aft εγω ins a 2nd εγω B^1. rec σοι bef επιτ., with ADN rel am(with fuld ing tol) lat-*a b c f i* goth arm [Did_1]: txt BCLΔℵ 33 vulg lat-ff_2 *k* syrr copt æth. for εξ, απ C^1Δ latt(with D-lat): txt ABC^3 D-gr Nℵ rel goth.

26. rec κραξαν and σπαραξαν (*gramml corrns*), with AC^3N rel: κραξας . . σπαραξαν Δ: txt BC^1DLℵ. rec aft σπ. ins αυτον, with AC^3N ℵ[1](marked for erasure, but the marks erased) rel vulg lat-*a c f* g_1 *k* [*l q*] syrr copt goth æth arm: om BC^1DLΔ lat-*b* ff_2 *i*. aft εξηλθ. ins απ' αυτου D latt[not *q*]; επ αυτω Δ-gr. for ωσει, ως D.

ignorant and weak one. **ἡμᾶς**] The wretched father counts his child's misery his own: thus the Syrophœnician woman, Matt. xv. 25, βοήθει **μοι**. **23.**] In **τὸ εἰ δ.** [**πισ.**], the **τό** involves the sense in some difficulty. The most probable rendering is to make it designatory of the whole sentence, **Jesus said to him the saying, "If thou canst believe, all things are,"** &c.: a saying which doubtless He often uttered on similar occasions. Kuinoel quotes a similar construction from Polyænus, iii. 9. 11, Ἰφικράτης ὑπολαβὼν ἔφη τὸ τίς ἂν ἤλπισε τοῦτο ἔσεσθαι. Some (e.g. Tischdf.) omitting the πιστεῦσαι would set an interrogation after δύνῃ, and suppose our Lord to be citing the father's words: *"didst thou say, 'if thou canst?'—all things are,"* &c. Others, as Dr. Burton, suppose it to mean τὸ 'εἰ δύνῃ' πίστευσαι (imperative):—'Believe what you have expressed by your εἴ τι δύνῃ, &c.' But both these renderings involve methods of construction and expression not usual in the Gospels. The εἰ δύνῃ is a manifest reference to the εἴ τι δύνῃ before, and meant to convey a reproof, as the father's answer testifies. The sentence, also, unless I am mistaken, is meant to convey an intimation that the healing was not to be *an answer* to the εἴ τι δύνῃ, so that *the Lord's power* was to be challenged and proved,—but an answer to *faith*, which (of course by laying hold on Him who πάντα δύναται) *can do all things*. **24.**] Nothing can be more touching and *living* than this whole most masterly and wonderful narrative. The poor father is drawn out into a sense of the unworthiness of his distrust, and "the little spark of faith which is kindled in his soul reveals to him the abysmal deeps of unbelief which are there." (Trench, p. 367.) "Thus," remarks Olshausen (B. Comm. i. 534), "does the Redeemer shew himself to the father as a μαιευτὴς πίστεως first, before He heals his son. In the struggle of his anxiety, the strength of Faith is *born*, by the aid of Christ, in the soul empty of it before." There is strong analogy in the Lord's treatment of the father here, for the *sponsorial engagement* in infant baptism. The *child* is by its infirmity *incapacitated;* it is therefore *the father's faith* which is tested, and when that is proved, the child is healed. The fact is, that the analogy rests far deeper: viz. on the 'inclusion' of 'the old man' in Adam and the 'new man' in Christ: see Rom. v. 12—21. It may be well to remind the reader that there is nothing "more pathetic and expressive" (Wordsw.) in μου τῇ ἀπιστίᾳ than in τ. ἀπ. μου: see on Matt. xvi. 18.

25.] This took place at a distance from the crowd, among those who had run forward to meet our Lord, ver. 15. **ἐγὼ ἐπ. σοί**] The personal pronoun

z constr., here and Acts iii. 7 only. see 1 Kings xv. 27.
a = ch. i. 31. Acts iii. 7. Dan. x. 10.
b rep., Matt. viii. 1 reff. see ch. vii. 25.
c Matt. xiv. 13 reff.
d = ver. 11 only.
e = Matt. xiii. 47 reff.
f = Matt. xii. 24, 27, 28. Acts iv. 9, 12.
g [|| Mt.] Matt. xxi. 22 al. 2 Kings vii. 27.
h Luke ii. 37 reff.
i ch. ii. 23 reff.
j ch. v. 43 reff.
k Matt. xxiv. 9 reff. Ezek. xxiii. 28.
l ch. viii. 31 reff.
m Gospp., || L. only. = Acts xiii. 27. Rom. x. 3 al. Wisd. xv. 11.

τοὺς πολλοὺς λέγειν ὅτι ἀπέθανεν. 27 ὁ δὲ Ἰησοῦς
[z] κρατήσας αὐτὸν τῆς χειρὸς [a] ἤγειρεν αὐτόν, καὶ ἀνέστη.
28 Καὶ εἰσελθόντα [b] αὐτὸν εἰς οἶκον οἱ μαθηταὶ αὐτοῦ
[c] κατ' [c] ἰδίαν ἐπηρώτων [b] αὐτὸν [d] Ὅτι ἡμεῖς οὐκ ἠδυνήθημεν ἐκβαλεῖν αὐτό; 29 καὶ εἶπεν αὐτοῖς Τοῦτο τὸ
[e] γένος [f] ἐν οὐδενὶ δύναται ἐξελθεῖν εἰ μὴ ἐν [g] προσευχῇ
[καὶ [h] νηστείᾳ].
30 Κἀκεῖθεν ἐξελθόντες [i] παρεπορεύοντο διὰ τῆς Γαλιλαίας, καὶ οὐκ ἤθελεν ἵνα τὶς [j] γνοῖ. 31 ἐδίδασκεν γὰρ
τοὺς μαθητὰς αὐτοῦ καὶ ἔλεγεν αὐτοῖς ὅτι ὁ υἱὸς τοῦ
ἀνθρώπου [k] παραδίδοται εἰς χεῖρας ἀνθρώπων, καὶ ἀπο- ...αποκτενουσιν 33.
κτενοῦσιν αὐτόν, καὶ ἀποκτανθεὶς μετὰ τρεῖς ἡμέρας [l] ἀνα- ABCDE
στήσεται. 32 οἱ δὲ [m] ἠγνόουν τὸ ῥῆμα, καὶ ἐφοβοῦντο FGHKL MNSU
αὐτὸν ἐπερωτῆσαι. VXΓΔΠ ℵ 1. 69
33 Καὶ ἦλθον εἰς Καφαρναούμ, καὶ ἐν τῇ οἰκίᾳ γενόμενος

rec om τους (*as unnecessary*), with CDN rel goth: ins ABLΔℵ 33. for λεγειν, λεγοντας D-gr.

27. for αυτον της χειρος, της χειρος αυτου (*corrn to more usual constr,—see Matt* ix. 35: *ch* i. 31; v. 41: *Luke* viii. 54) BDLΔℵ 1. 69 ev-y latt copt arm: txt AC[3]N rel goth.—add αυτου C[1] syrr æth.

28. εισελθοντος αυτου (*corrn of Hellenistic constr as often elsewhere*) BCDLΔℵ 1. 69 syrr: txt A N[ελθ.] rel goth arm. ins τον bef οικ. AM copt-wilk. rec επηρ. αυτ. bef κατ ιδ., with AC[3]N rel (lat-*c*) syrr copt goth æth: txt BC[1]DLΔℵ 1. 33. (69) vulg lat-*a b* &c arm.—ηρωτων D 1. for οτι, δια τι (οτι *not being understood*) ADKΠ 33 Syr: οτι δια τι U 238: txt BCNℵ rel.

29. for εν ουδ., ου C[1]. om και νηστεια B ℵ[1](ins ℵ[3b]) lat-*k*. (*So Tischdf has edited: referring to* 1 *Cor* vii. 5, *where see note. In* || *Matt the whole sentence is doubtful, but none who insert it omit* these words.)

30. rec και εκειθεν, with ACN rel: txt BDLΔℵ. for παρεπ., επορευοντο (*more usual*) B[1] D-gr lat-*a c f* goth æth. rec γνω, with AN rel: txt BCDLℵ.

31. om αυτοις B lat-*k*. om ο D[1](ins D-corr[1]). for ανθρωπων, ανθρωπου D-gr. και αποκτεινουσιν D-gr. om αποκτανθεις D ev-y lat-*a c* g_1 *k* copt. rec τη τριτη ημερα (*from* || *Matt: Mey thinks* μετ. τρ. ημ. *a conformation to ch* viii. 31, *because there is* there *no corrn to the* || *Matt Luke. But such corrns were not so systematic as to warrant such an inference*), with AC[3]N rel vulg lat-*f* g_1 *l* syrr goth æth arm: txt BC[1]DLΔℵ lat-(*a*) *b c i* (*k*) syr-mg copt.

33. rec ηλθεν (*to suit* γενομενος *following*), with ACN rel lat-*f* [*q*] syr (copt) goth (æth) arm: ηλθοσαν D: txt Bℵ 1 latt Syr. γεναμενος N.

is emphatic, as opposed to the want of power on the part of the disciples. This is the only place where we have such a charge as **μηκέτι εἰσέλθ. εἰς αὐ.**,—shewing the excessive malignity and tenacity of this kind (see ver. 29) of spirit. This is also shewn by ver. 26. **27.**] See ch. v. 41; also Matt. xvii. 6, 8: Rev. i. 17: Dan. x. 9, 10. **29.**] The answer is given more at length in Matt. ver. 20, and the Lord there distinctly includes the *disciples* in the γενεὰ ἄπιστος, by telling them διὰ τὴν ἀπιστίαν **ὑμῶν**. The assurance also occurs there, which was repeated Matt. xxi. 21, where see notes.

τοῦτο τὸ γένος] That there are *kinds*, more and less malicious, of evil spirits, we find from Matt. xii. 45—and the pertinacity and cruelty of this one shewed him to belong to the worst kind. The Lord's saying here (if the doubtful words are to stand) is rather for their *after* guidance, than their present; for *they could not fast while He was with them*, ch. ii. 19.

30—32.] Second announcement of His death and resurrection. Matt. xvii. 22, 23. Luke ix. 43—45, where see notes, as this account is included in the two others.

33—50.] Discourse respecting the

ἐπηρώτα αὐτοὺς Τί ἐν τῇ ὁδῷ [n] διελογίζεσθε; [34] οἱ δὲ
[o] ἐσιώπων, [p] πρὸς ἀλλήλους γὰρ [pq] διελέχθησαν ἐν τῇ ὁδῷ
τίς [r] μείζων. [35] καὶ [s] καθίσας [t] ἐφώνησεν τοὺς δώδεκα
καὶ λέγει αὐτοῖς Εἴ τις θέλει πρῶτος εἶναι, ἔσται πάντων
ἔσχατος καὶ πάντων [u] διάκονος. [36] καὶ λαβὼν παιδίον
ἔστησεν αὐτὸ ἐν μέσῳ αὐτῶν, καὶ [v] ἐναγκαλισάμενος αὐτὸ
εἶπεν αὐτοῖς [37] Ὃς ἂν ἓν τῶν τοιούτων παιδίων δέξηται
[w] ἐπὶ τῷ ὀνόματί μου, ἐμὲ δέχεται· καὶ ὃς ἂν ἐμὲ δέχηται,
οὐκ ἐμὲ δέχεται, ἀλλὰ τὸν ἀποστείλαντά με. [38] ἔφη
αὐτῷ ὁ Ἰωάννης λέγων Διδάσκαλε εἴδομέν τινα [x] ἐν τῷ
ὀνόματί σου ἐκβάλλοντα δαιμόνια, ὃς οὐκ ἀκολουθεῖ

n Matt. xvi. 7 reff.
o Matt. xx. 31 reff.
p Acts xvii. 17 (also w. dat.). xxiv. 12. Exod. vi. 27.
q Gospp. here only. Acts xvii. 2 al9. Heb. xii. 5. Jude 9 only.
r ‖. Matt. xxiii. 11 al.
s Matt. v. 1 reff.
t = Matt. xx. 32 reff.
u Matt. xxiii. 11 reff.
v ch. x. 16 only. Prov. vi. 10. xxiv. 33 only.
w = Matt. xix. 9. Acts iv. 21. see ver. 39.
x ver. 29.

rec aft οδω ins *προς εαυτους*, with AN rel lat-*f* syr goth æth; aft διελογ. **1.** 69 Syr (arm): om BCDL Δ(sic) ℵ latt copt.

34. εσιωπουν CN. διελεγχθησαν ℵ. om εν τη οδω (*as superfluous*) ADΔ lat-*a b f i* [*l q*] goth: ins BCNℵ rel vulg lat-*c* $ff_2 g_1$ *k* syrr copt æth arm Orig$_1$. aft μειζων ins εστιν ℵ Orig: γενηται αυτων D 2-pe æth, simly latt syr copt [æth].

35. for 1st και, τοτε D lat-*b* [ff_2 *i*]. om και λεγ. to διακονος (‖ *Matt Luke*) D lat-*k*.

36. ins το bef παιδ. D. for 1st αυτο, αυτον DΔ. αναγκαλισ. C, ανακλισ. D^1(txt D^3), αναγκαλεσ. L, εναγκαλησ. X, εκαλισ. Δ.

37. rec (for 1st αν) εαν, with NX rel Orig$_3$: txt ABCDLΔℵ **1.** 69. om ἕν DXΓ ev-y Syr æth arm: εκ 69, *ex* lat-*b c* ff_2 *i* (*unum ex* vulg lat-(*a*) *f* g_1 [*l*]). των π. τουτων CΔℵ. for επι, εν D 69. rec (for 2nd αν) εαν, with ACN rel: om ℵ: txt BDLΔ. rec δεξηται (*to conform to* δεξ. *above, and* ‖ *Luke*), with ACDN rel vulg lat-*b* ff_2: δεχεται ℵ Scr's c: txt BL 69 lat-*a c f* $g_{1.2}$ [*q*].

38. rec (for εφη) απεκριθη δε (*conformation to* ‖ *Luke, as also appears by the varns*), with AN rel lat-*c f* ff_2 goth (æth) arm: απεκριθη D-gr vulg lat-*b i k l* syr: αποκριθεις δε εφη C: και αποκριθεις 69: txt BLΔℵ Syr copt. om ο (*see* ‖ *Luke*) ADN rel: ins BCLMXΔℵ. om λεγων B(C)Δℵ lat-*k* Syr copt: και ειπεν D-gr lat-*c* ff_2: ειπεν 69 lat-*a* D-lat. ειδαμεν DN. Steph om εν, with A rel Thl: επι (*from* ‖ *Luke and ver* 39) U ev-z: txt BCDLNΔℵ **1.** 69 latt. om ος ουκ ακ. ημ. (*to conform to* ‖ *Luke*) BCLΔℵ lat-*f* Syr copt æth: ins A(D)N rel latt syr (goth

GREATEST AMONG THEM. Matt. xviii. 1—9. Luke ix. 46—50. Here again the three accounts are *independent*, and differ in some particulars unimportant in themselves, but very instructive for a right comparison of the three Gospels. First take Luke's account.—*The disciples had been disputing;—our Lord knowing the strife of their hearts, took a child*, &c.—Then compare Mark—*our Lord asked them, on coming into a house, what had been the subject of their dispute;—they were silent from shame;—He sat down, delivered his sentence to the twelve,—and then took the child*, &c.—Lastly turn to Matt. There, *the disciples themselves referred the question to our Lord, and He took the child*, &c. Who can forbear seeing in these narratives the unfettered and independent testimony of three witnesses, consistent with one another in the highest form and spirit of truthfulness, but differing in the mere letter? Mark's account is again the richest and fullest, and we can hardly doubt that if the *literal exact detail* of fact is in question, we have it here. **33.**] Between the coming to Capernaum, and this discourse, happened the *demand of the tribute money*, Matt. xvii. 24—27. **34.**] There is no real difference in the matter in question here (and in Luke), and in Matt. The kingdom of heaven was looked on as about soon to appear: and their relative rank *now* would be assumed as their relative rank *then*. The difference in the *expression* of this is a mark of independence and authority. **35.**] See Matt. xx. 26, and note. **36. ἐναγκ. αὐτό**] This particular we learn from Mark. **37.**] See Matt. x. 40. **38.**] Only found besides in Luke, vv. 49, 50. Notice the *repetition* of **οὐκ ἀκολ. ἡμ.** as characteristic of Mark. The connexion of this remark with what goes before, is: 'If the receiving any one, even a little child, *in thy Name*, be receiving Thee; were we doing right when we forbade one who

ἡμῖν· καὶ [y] ἐκωλύομεν αὐτὸν ὅτι οὐκ ἀκολουθεῖ ἡμῖν. ABCDE FGHKL MNSU VXΓΔΠ ℵ 1. 69
39 ὁ δὲ Ἰησοῦς εἶπεν Μὴ [y] κωλύετε αὐτόν. οὐδεὶς γάρ
ἐστιν ὃς ποιήσει [z] δύναμιν [a] ἐπὶ τῷ ὀνόματί μου καὶ
δυνήσεται [b] ταχὺ [c] κακολογῆσαί με. 40 ὃς γὰρ οὐκ ἔστιν
καθ' ἡμῶν, ὑπὲρ ἡμῶν ἐστιν. 41 ὃς γὰρ ἂν [d] ποτίσῃ ὑμᾶς
ποτήριον ὕδατος [e] ἐν [f] ὀνόματι ὅτι [g] χριστοῦ ἐστέ, [h] ἀμὴν
λέγω ὑμῖν ὅτι οὐ μὴ ἀπολέσῃ τὸν [i] μισθὸν αὐτοῦ. 42 καὶ

y = ch. x. 14 ‖. Luke xi. 52. Acts xi. 17. Num. xi. 28. z = Matt. xi. 20 reff. a = Matt. xxiv. 5. Acts ii. 38. b = here only. (Matt. xxviii. 7, 8 al.) c ch. vii. 10 ‖ Mt. (from Exod. xxi. 16.) Acts xix. 9 only. d Matt. xxv. 35, &c. xxvii. 48 al. Gen. xxi. 19. Exod. ii. 16. e ἐν ὀν. ὅτι here only. ἐν τῷ ὀν., ver. 38 al. fr. f = 1 Pet. iv. 16. Rev. iii. 1. g gen., Rom. xiv. 8. 1 Cor. i. 12. iii. 21, 22, 23. 2 Tim. ii. 19. h Matt. v. 18 reff. i Matt. x. 41, 42 reff.

arm).—μεθ' ημων (*as* ‖ *Luke*) D lat-*a k*. rec εκωλυσαμεν (*from* ‖ *Luke*), with ACN rel latt &c : B D-gr LΔℵ 1. om οτι ουκ ακ. ημιν (*as superf; but Mark often thus repeats. Certainly had the clause been adopted from* ‖ *Luke, we should have read* μεθ' ημων *instead of* ημιν,—*which now only* L *has*) DX 1. 69 latt arm : ins ABC(L)Nℵ rel lat-*f* Syr syr-w-ast copt goth æth.—for ημιν, μεθ ημων L Scr's q r. ηκολουθει BΔℵ.

39. for ιησ., αποκριθεις D 2-pe lat-*a b ff₂ i k*: om **1. 69** arm. om αυτον (*see* ‖ *Luke*) D 115 lat-*a b i k*.

40. Steph υμων (both times: *prob from* ‖ *Luke, but the inference is hardly a safe one, as* AXΔ[ℵ[1]] *there read* ημων *the 2nd time*), with ADN rel latt syrr goth æth Vict Opt : txt BCΔℵ 1. 69 lat-*k* copt syr-mg arm.—υμ. υπερ ημ. UX : ημ. υπερ υμ. L.

41. εαν ℵ. rec ins τω bef ονοματι, with DHMΔ 69 arm : om ABCNℵ rel. rec adds μου, with C³Dℵ¹ rel latt syr-mg copt goth æth : om ABC¹KLNΠ¹ℵ³ᵃ 1 syrr arm. for χριστου, εμου ℵ¹. rec om 2nd οτι, with AC³N rel vulg lat-*a c f i* æth arm : ins BC¹DLΔℵ gat lat-*b ff₂ g₂ k l [q]* syrr copt goth. απολεσει (*itacism?*) DE : txt A B(sic : not as Btly) CNℵ rel.

used thy Name, but did not follow us?' "Observent hoc," says Bengel, "*qui charismata alligant successioni canonicæ.*" This man actually did what the very Apostles themselves were specially appointed to do : and our Lord, so far from prohibiting, encourages him: see Num. xi. 26—29. **39.**] See 1 Cor. xii. 3. The very success of the miracle will awe him, and prevent him from soon or lightly speaking evil of me. We must beware of supposing that the application of this saying is to be confined to the *working of a miracle*—ver. 40 shews that it is general—a weighty maxim of Christian toleration and charity, and caution to men how they presume to limit the work of the Spirit of God to any sect, or succession, or outward form of Church : cf. Phil. i. 16—18. See the way in which the nearly opposite inference is extracted from the words, in the very curious note of Bp. Wordsw. here. **40.**] This saying is not inconsistent with that in Matt. xii. 30. They do not refer to the same thing. This is said of *outward conformity*—that, of *inward unity of purpose*—two widely different things. On that saying, see note there. On this, we may say—all those who, notwithstanding outward differences of communion and government, *believe in and preach* Jesus Christ, without bitterly and uncharitably opposing each other, are hereby declared to be *helpers forward of each other's work*. O that all Christians would remember this! Stier (Red. J. iii. 24) strongly deprecates the reading ἡμῶν—ἡμῶν; "The us in the mouth of our Lord here confuses and destroys nearly the whole purport of his weighty saying. For this is the very fault of the disciples, that they laid down outward and visible communion with *them* as the decisive criterion of communion with the Lord : and this very fault the Lord rebukes with his repudiatory ὑμῶν." Still, there is a propriety, a tempering the rebuke with a gracious reminiscence of their unity with Him, and something exceedingly suiting the χριστοῦ ἐστέ below, in ἡμῶν—ἡμῶν. In the divided state of the critical evidence, the reading must be ever doubtful. **41.**] This verse does not take up the discourse from ver. 37, as some think, but is immediately connected with ver. 40 :—'Even the *smallest* service done in my Name shall not be unrewarded—much more should not so great an one as casting out of devils be prohibited.'

ἐν ὀνόματι ὅτι signifies **by reason that, but** not without an allusion to τ. ὄνομά μου, which furnishes the reason. **χριστ. ἐστέ**] The only place in the Gospels where this expression is used. Paul has it : see reff. and Rom. viii 9 : 1 Cor. iii. 4.

ὃς ἂν [k] σκανδαλίσῃ ἕνα τῶν [l] μικρῶν [τούτων] τῶν
[m] πίστιν ἐχόντων, [n] καλόν ἐστιν αὐτῷ [o] μᾶλλον [p] εἰ
[q] περίκειται [r] μυλὸς [r] ὀνικὸς περὶ τὸν [s] τράχηλον αὐτοῦ καὶ
βέβληται εἰς τὴν θάλασσαν. 43 καὶ ἐὰν [k] σκανδαλίζῃ σε
ἡ χείρ σου, [t] ἀπόκοψον αὐτήν· [n] καλόν ἐστίν σε [u] κυλλὸν
εἰςελθεῖν εἰς τὴν ζωήν, [v] ἢ τὰς δύο χεῖρας ἔχοντα [w] ἀπελθεῖν εἰς τὴν [x] γέενναν εἰς τὸ πῦρ τὸ [y] ἄσβεστον, 44 ὅπου
ὁ [z] σκώληξ αὐτῶν οὐ τελευτᾷ καὶ τὸ πῦρ οὐ [a] σβέννυται.
45 καὶ ἐὰν ὁ πούς σου [k] σκανδαλίζῃ σε, [t] ἀπόκοψον αὐτόν·
[n] καλόν ἐστίν σε εἰςελθεῖν εἰς τὴν ζωὴν [b] χωλόν, [v] ἢ τοὺς
δύο πόδας ἔχοντα βληθῆναι εἰς τὴν [x] γέενναν [εἰς τὸ πῦρ
τὸ [y] ἄσβεστον], 46 ὅπου ὁ [z] σκώληξ αὐτῶν οὐ τελευτᾷ καὶ
τὸ πῦρ οὐ [a] σβέννυται. 47 καὶ ἐὰν ὁ ὀφθαλμός σου

k Matt. v. 29, 30 reff.
l Matt. x. 42. xviii. 6, 10. Acts viii. 10 al. Zech. xiii. 7.
m Matt. xvii. 20. xxi. 21. ch. iv. 40. xi. 22 al.
n = ver. 5 reff.
o w. posit., Acts xx. 15. 1 Cor. ix. 15. (xii. 22.) Gal. iv. 27 (from Isa. liv. 1) only.
p = Matt. xxvi. 24 reff.
q Luke xvii. 2. Acts xxviii. 20. Heb. v. 2. xii. 1 only +.
r Mt. reff.
s || Mt. Luke xv. 20. xvii. 2. Acts xv. 10. xx. 37. Rom. xvi. 4 only. Gen. xlv. 14.
t here bis. John xviii. 10, 26. Acts xxvii. 32. Gal. v. 12 only. Deut. xxv. 12.
u || Mt. Matt. xv. 30, 31 only +.
v constr., || Mt. reff.
w Matt. xxv. 46.
x Matt. v. 30 reff.
y Matt. iii. 12 || L. only +.
z here (3ce) only. Deut. xxviii. 39. Isa. xvi. 24.
a Matt. xii. 20 reff.
b Matt. xi. 5. xv. 30, 31 al. Deut. xv. 21.

42. εαν AC rel: txt BDLNא (V, e sil) **1**. 69. σκανδαλιζη D-gr. rec om τουτων, with C¹(appy, Treg) X rel lat-*f* arm: ins (*from* || *Matt?*) ABC²DLM²NΔא **1** lat-(*b*) *c i* [*q*] (*ff*₂ *l* Syr) syr copt goth æth. rec πιστευοντων εις εμε (*from* || *Matt*), with ABC²NX rel vss: πιστευοντων (alone) Δא lat-*b ff*₂ *i k*¹ copt-mss: txt C¹(see Tischdf's Codex Ephr Appendix) D lat-*a*. (*πιστινεχοντων was very likely to pass into πιστευοντων, especially as producing conformity to* || *Matt. I have therefore edited it, as did Tischdf ed* 7.) αυτω bef εστιν A. (om αυτω U æth.) περιεκειτο D. rec λιθος μυλικος (*from Luke* xvii. 3, *where it is best attested: see there*), with AN rel syr copt(appy): μυλωνικος λιθος 69. 258 Thl: *mola* D-lat: txt BC D[-gr] LΔא **1** latt Syr goth æth arm. for περι, επι D 251. εις τ. θ. εβληθη D latt.

43. σκανδαλιση (*repeated from last ver*) BLΔא vulg lat-*a f ff*₂ *k*; -σει H. rec (for εστιν σε) σοι εστι (*from* || *Matt*), with AN rel goth: εστιν σοι D vulg lat-*b c f ff*₂ [*i k*] *l* syrr æth arm: txt BCLΔא 69 lat-*a*. rec εις τ. ζω. bef εισελθ. (*from* || *Matt, ver* 9), with NX rel syr goth (arm): txt ABCDLΔא latt Syr copt æth. om τας D [ev-z]. for απελθ., βληθηναι D gat lat-*a f* (*ff*₂?) *k*: εισελθειν א¹(txt א³ᵃ). for εις το πυρ το ασβεστον, του πυρος F: om LΔ א³ᵃ(?) 240-4 Syr: for εις, οπου εστιν D lat-*b c ff*₂ *i k*. (In א marks for erasure have been added and afterwards erased.)

44 and **46**. om BCLΔא **1** lat-*k* copt arm. (*The whole history of the omns is to be found in* || *Matt. No such addns as vv* 44, 46 *occurrg* there, *they were omd* here, *as also was, in mss* 92. 218-55, *ver* 45, *which does not occur there: but, the* || *passage* ending at ver 47, ver 48 was not subjected to the same erasion. *Tischdf*, after Mey, *has here been misled by the correctors, and has erased vv* 44, 46: *not so Lachm. Treg inserts the verses in brackets.*)

45. καν D. σκανδαλιζει (*itacism?*) Xא Scr's c: -λισει L. aft καλ. ins γαρ ΑΚΠ lat-*c*. rec εστι σοι (|| *Matt*), with M¹NUΓ vulg lat-*a c f ff*₂ *k* D-lat syrr æth: σοι εστιν D-gr M²S lat-*b* goth arm(appy): txt ABCא rel. εις την ζωην bef εισελθειν FΓא Scr's b f (g): χωλ. bef εισελθ. εις τ. ζ. D latt arm. aft ζ. ins αιωνιον D latt(not *f ff*₂ *k*) arm. ins κυλλον η bef χωλον א. εις την γεενναν bef βληθηναι א. om 2nd την M¹NX. om εις το πυρ το ασβεστον BCLΔא **1** lat-*b k* Syr copt arm-zoh (so also LΔ Syr in ver 43): ins ADN rel lat-*f* goth æth arm-usc[: του πυρος F lat-*c g*₂].

47. κ. ο οφθ. σου ει (omg εαν) D.

42.] See Matt. xviii. 6. **43—48.**] These solemn repetitions of former declarations (see Matt. v. 29; xviii. 8, 9) are by no means to be regarded as arbitrary insertions by this or that Evangelist, but as the truth of what was uttered by our Lord: see Prolegomena. Vv. **44, 46, 48** are only in Mark; they are cited from Isaiah (see reff.), where the prophecy is of the *carcases of those who have transgressed against the Lord.* This triple repetition gives sublimity, and leaves no

c Matt. vii. 4, 5. d || Mt. only +. e here bis and Matt. v. 13 only. Levit. ii. 13. Ezek. xvi. 4 (Ezra iv. 14 compl.) only. f here bis only. Levit. ii. 13. Ezek. xvi. 4. g Matt. v. 13 reff. h here only +. Ezek. xiii. 10 & xxii. 28 Aq. i || Mt. Matt. xxvi. 52. Heb. xi. 37 a. j Luke xiv. 34. Col. iv. 6 only +. Cant. viii. 2 Symm. k = Matt. iii. 9 reff. l Rom. xii. 18. 2 Cor. xiii. 11. 1 Thess. v. 13 only. 3 Kings xxii. 45. Job v. 24. Sir. vi. 6.

[k] σκανδαλίζῃ σε, [c] ἔκβαλε αὐτόν· [n] καλόν σε ἐστὶν [d] μον- ABCDE
όφθαλμον εἰςελθεῖν εἰς τὴν βασιλείαν τοῦ θεοῦ, [v] ἢ δύο FGHKL MNSU
ὀφθαλμοὺς ἔχοντα βληθῆναι εἰς τὴν [x] γέενναν, 48 ὅπου ὁ VXΓΔΠ ℵ 1. 69
[z] σκώληξ αὐτῶν οὐ τελευτᾷ καὶ τὸ πῦρ οὐ [a] σβέννυται.
49 πᾶς γὰρ πυρὶ [e] ἁλισθήσεται, καὶ πᾶσα θυσία [f] ἁλὶ
[e] ἁλισθήσεται. 50 καλὸν τὸ [g] ἅλας· ἐὰν δὲ τὸ [g] ἅλας
[h] ἄναλον γένηται, [i] ἐν τίνι αὐτὸ [j] ἀρτύσετε; ἔχετε ἐν
[k] ἑαυτοῖς [f] ἅλα, καὶ [l] εἰρηνεύετε ἐν ἀλλήλοις.

σκανδαλιζει (*itacism ?*) DX. rec (for σε εστιν) σοι εστι (*from* || *Matt*), with AC D-gr N rel copt goth : εστ. σοι M[1] latt syrr æth (arm) : εστιν σε LΔ : txt Bℵ. om εισελθειν ℵ[1](which also has ζω, at the end of a page, and, at the top of the next, σιλιαν : txt ℵ[3a]) : ins aft ε. τ. β. τ. θ. A. for βλ., απελθειν D 1 lat-*c i*. om την (*see Matt* v. 29, 33) BL. rec aft εις την γ. ins του πυρος (*from* || *Matt*), with ACN rel vulg lat-*f* (g_2) *i l* syrr goth æth : om BDLΔℵ 1 lat-*a b c* ff_2 *k* copt arm.—[for τ. γ., το πυρ το ασβεστον F.]

49. om πας γ. π. αλισθ. και (i. e. πας to πασ.) D 64-5[1] tol lat-*a b c* ff_2 *i*. ins εν bef πυρι Cℵ. for και πασα, πασα γαρ (*corrn from txt in consequence of the omn : see above*) D tol lat-*b c* ff_2 *i* : om κ. π. θυσ. αλι αλισθησεται (*homœotel* αλισθησεται to αλισθησεται) BLΔℵ 1 (lat-*k*) copt-mss arm-zoh : om αλι (*also homœotel*) 238-48-53-9 ev-z em(with gat harl ing mt tol) lat-*a c* g_2 æth.

50. for 1st αλας, αλα LΔ. for 2nd αλας, αλα LΔℵ[1]. γενησεται D. αρτυσεται (*which however may be no real difference,* αι *being written for* ε : *but* may be *from Matt* v. 13) AC D[-gr] HLN : -σηται Δ : -σητε 69 : αρτυθησεται K 1 Scr's e ev-z lat-*f* [gat D-lat] Syr copt (goth æth) arm : txt BXℵ rel latt syr. rec (for αλα) αλας (*from above*), with A[2]CNℵ[3a] rel : txt A[1]BDLΔℵ[1].—pref το U. ειρηνευσατε V.

doubt of the discourse having been *verbatim* thus uttered. See note on Matt. v. 22. **49.**] In order to understand this difficult verse, it will be necessary first to examine its connexion and composition. (1) What is **γάρ**? It connects it with the solemn assertions in vv. 43—48, **καλόν ἐστίν σε** . . . and furnishes a *reason why* it is better for us to cut off and cast away, &c. **πᾶς** then is **every one,** absolutely: referring back both to the **σε,** and the **αὐτῶν** above—**πᾶσα θυσία** is (not *opposed* to (Meyer), but) *parallel with* **πᾶς,** and **καί** equivalent to **just as.** (2) This being stated, let us now enquire into *the symbolic terms* used. Fire is the *refiner's fire* of Mal. iii. 2, to which indeed there seems to be a reference; the fire of Matt. iii. 11 and Acts ii. 3; of Ezek. xxviii. 14 (see my Hulsean Lectures for 1841, pp. 9—12). Fire is *the symbol of the divine purity and presence :*—our God is a *consuming fire,* not only to his foes, but to his people: but in *them,* the fire shall only burn up what is impure and requires purifying out, 1 Cor. iii. 13: 1 Pet. i. 7; iv. 12, 17. This very fire shall be to them as *a preserving salt.* The salt of the covenant of God (ref. Levit.) was to be mixed with *every sacrifice;* and it is with fire that *all men are to be salted.* This fire is the divine purity and judgment *in the covenant,* whose promise is, 'I will dwell among them.' And in and among this purifying fire shall the people of God ever walk and rejoice everlastingly. Rev. xxi. 23. This is the right understanding of Isa. xxxiii. 14, 15, 'Who among us shall dwell with the devouring fire? &c. He that walketh in righteousness,' &c. And thus the connexion with the preceding verses is,—'it is better for thee to cut off,' &c.—'for it is *part of the salting of thee, the living sacrifice* (Rom. xii. 1), that every offence and scandal must be burnt out of thee before thou canst enter into life.' **50.**] The connexion of this (elsewhere said in other references, Matt. v. 13: Luke xiv. 34) is now plain. If this fire which is to purify and act as a preserving salt to you, have, from the nullity and vapidity of the grace of the covenant in you, *no such power,*—it can only *consume*—the salt has lost its savour—the covenant is void—you will be cast out, as it is elsewhere added, and the fire will be no longer the fire of *purification,* but of *wrath eternal.* I will just add that the interpretation of the sacrifice as the *condemned*—and the fire and salt as *eternal fire,*—except in the case of the salt having lost its savour, is

X. 1 Καὶ ἐκεῖθεν [m] ἀναστὰς ἔρχεται εἰς τὰ [n] ὅρια τῆς
Ἰουδαίας καὶ πέραν τοῦ Ἰορδάνου. καὶ [o] συνπορεύονται
πάλιν ὄχλοι πρὸς αὐτόν, καὶ ὡς [p] εἰώθει πάλιν ἐδίδασκεν
αὐτούς. 2 καὶ προσελθόντες Φαρισαῖοι [q] ἐπηρώτων αὐτὸν
[r] εἰ ἔξεστιν ἀνδρὶ γυναῖκα [s] ἀπολῦσαι, [t] πειράζοντες αὐτόν.
3 ὁ δὲ ἀποκριθεὶς εἶπεν αὐτοῖς Τί ὑμῖν [u] ἐνετείλατο
Μωυσῆς; 4 οἱ δὲ εἶπαν [v] Ἐπέτρεψεν Μωυσῆς [w] βιβλίον
[x] ἀποστασίου γράψαι, καὶ [s] ἀπολῦσαι. 5 ὁ δὲ Ἰησοῦς
εἶπεν αὐτοῖς [y] Πρὸς τὴν [z] σκληροκαρδίαν ὑμῶν ἔγραψεν
ὑμῖν τὴν ἐντολὴν ταύτην· 6 ἀπὸ δὲ ἀρχῆς [a] κτίσεως [b] ἄρσεν
καὶ [b] θῆλυ ἐποίησεν αὐτοὺς [ὁ θεός]. 7 ἕνεκεν τούτου

m ch. vii. 24 reff. n Matt. ii. 16 reff. o = here (Luke vii. 11. xiv. 25. xxiv. 15) only. Job i. 4. p Matt. xxvii. 15 reff. q ch. ix. 11 al. fr. r = ch. xv. 44. Luke vi. 7, 9. xxiii. 6. Jer. xxxvii. (xxx.) 6. s Matt. v. 31, 32 reff. t ch. viii. 11 al. 2 Chron. ix. 1. u John xv. 14, 17 al. Deut. xxix. 1. v ||. Matt. viii. 21, 31. Esth. ix. 14. w ||, from Deut. xxiv. 3 (1). 4 Kings x. 1, &c. x ||. Matt. v. 31 (reff.) only. y = Acts iii. 18. Heb. ix. 13. z || Mt. ch. xvi. 14 only. Deut. x. 16. Sir. xvi. 10 only. a = ch. xiii. 19. Rom. i. 20. 2 Pet. iii. 4. art. om., Matt. xix. 12 al. b || Mt. reff.

Chap. X. 1. rec κακειθ., with ALN (U, e sil) rel: txt BCDEΔℵ 1. 69. for ερχεται, ηλθεν N. rec (for και περαν) δια του περαν, with AN rel syr: περαν (|| *Matt*) C[2]DGΔ 1. 69 ev-y latt Syr goth arm(appy): txt BC[1]Lℵ copt (æth). (*It would at first sight appear as if* δια του *being the origl, was erased or* και *insd for conformity to* || *Matt: so De W., but Mey justly observes that this does not account for the* και *satisfactorily, which is therefore prob origl, and the* δια του *an explany corrn.*) συνερχεται παλιν ο οχλος D 2 pe arm: συμπορευεται ο οχλος (1) 69 lat-*b c* ff_2 *i* (Syr). ως ειωθ. bef και D lat-*b* ff_2 *i*.

2. rec ins οι bef φαρ., with CNVXℵ 1: om AB rel copt goth.—om προσελθ. φαρ. D lat-*a b k*. rec επηρωτησαν, with AN rel syr: επηρουν C: ηρωτων Δ: txt BDLMℵ latt.

3. for ενετ., ετειλατο D[1](txt D[3]) 28.

4. (ειπαν, so BCDℵ.) rec μω. bef επετρ. (*see* || *Matt*, vv 7, 8), with AN rel vulg lat-*f* g_2 syrr goth arm: μω. ενετειλατο 1 Scr's c copt: txt BCDLΔℵ ev-y. for γραψαι, δουναι (|| *Matt*) 61 lat-*b*, δουναι γραψαι (*combination*) *dare scriptam* D lat-*c* ff_2. at end add αυτην N.

5. rec (for ο δε) και αποκριθεις ο, with ADN rel (vulg lat-*a b* ff_1 *k*[*l q*]) *f* (Syr) syr goth (æth) arm: txt BCLΔℵ (lat-*c*) copt. om αυτοις D 235-52[1]. for εγρ., επετρεψεν N ev-z. add μωυσης D lat-(*b*) *c* (*f*) g_2 *k* Syr-ms. om υμιν D 13. 28. 69. 124 Scr's v lat-*b c* g_2 *k* arm-zoh.

6. om κτισεως D 255 ev-36 lat-*b* ff_2 Syr. θηλυν D[1]. om αυτους D 28. 219 fuld lat-*b f* ff_2 *k* copt goth æth. om ο θεος BCLΔℵ lat-*c* ff_2 copt: ins ADN rel vulg lat-*a b f* g_1 *k* [*l q*] syrr goth æth arm. (*The fact that* || *Matt ver* 4 ends αρσ. κ. θηλ. εποιησεν αυτους, *furnishes strong presumption that* ο θεος *has been* struck out here. *But as the words* may be a gloss, *I have bracketed them, as Lachm also has done: Tischdf and Treg omit them.*)

7. ins και ειπεν bef ενεκ. (*from* || *Matt, ver* 5) DN 69 Scr's e fuld(with gat harl mt)

contrary to the whole symbolism of Scripture, and to the exhortation with which this verse ends: 'Have this grace of God—this Spirit of adoption—this pledge of the covenant, in yourselves;—and,' with reference to the strife out of which the discourse sprung,—'have peace with one another.'

Chap. X. 1—12.] Reply to the Pharisees' question concerning divorce. Matt. xix. 1—12. **1. καὶ πέραν**] Our Lord retired, after His discourses to the Jews in John x. and before the raising of Lazarus, to Bethany (John i. 28; x. 40) beyond Jordan, and thence made his last journey to Jerusalem; so that in the strictest sense of the words He did come **into the borders of Judæa and beyond Jordan.** Matt. has πέραν τ. Ἰορ. without the copula. See Luke xvii. 11. Here a large portion of the sayings and doings of Jesus is omitted: cf. Matt. xviii. 10; xix. 3: Luke ix. 51—xviii. 15: John vii. 1 ff. **2—9.**] See notes on Matt., with whose account ours is nearly identical. Compare however our vv. 3, 4, 5 with Matt. vv. 7, 8, 9, and we have testimony to the *independence* of the two reports—for such an arbitrary alteration of arrangement is inconceivable. **4.**] **ἐπέτρεψεν** is emphatic. Moses gave an express permissory injunction. **7.**] Our Lord makes

[c] καταλείψει ἄνθρωπος τὸν πατέρα αὐτοῦ καὶ τὴν μητέρα ABCDE FGHKL MNSU VXΓΔΠ ℵ 1. 69
καὶ [d] προσκολληθήσεται πρὸς τὴν γυναῖκα αὐτοῦ,
8 καὶ ἔσονται οἱ δύο [e] εἰς σάρκα μίαν. ὥστε οὐκέτι εἰσὶν δύο,
ἀλλὰ μία σάρξ. 9 ὃ οὖν ὁ θεὸς [f] συνέζευξεν, ἄνθρωπος
μὴ [g] χωριζέτω. 10 καὶ [h] εἰς τὴν οἰκίαν πάλιν οἱ μαθηταὶ
[αὐτοῦ] περὶ τούτου ἐπηρώτων αὐτόν. 11 καὶ λέγει
αὐτοῖς Ὃς ἂν ἀπολύσῃ τὴν γυναῖκα αὐτοῦ καὶ γαμήσῃ
ἄλλην, [i] μοιχᾶται [k] ἐπ' αὐτήν· 12 καὶ ἐὰν αὐτὴ ἀπολύσασα
τὸν ἄνδρα αὐτῆς γαμήσῃ ἄλλον, [i] μοιχᾶται.
13 Καὶ προσέφερον αὐτῷ παιδία, ἵνα [l] ἅψηται αὐτῶν·

c ‖ Mt., from Gen. ii. 24. Matt. xvi. 4 al. Isa. xvii. 10 Bℵ.
d (‖ Mt. Acts v. 36 v. r.) Eph. v. 31 only. Gen. as above. Job xli. 8.
e ‖. Luke iii. 5. Rom. ii. 26. Gen. xv. 6.
f ‖ Mt. only. Ezek. i. 11, 23 A only.
g ‖ Mt. only in Gospp. Rom. viii. 35, 39 al. Lev. xiii. 46. Ezek. xlvi. 19.
h ch. xiii. 9 b.
i ‖ Mt. bis. Matt. v. 32 only. Jer. v. 7.
k = ch. ix. 12, 13. Luke ix. 5. 2 Cor. i. 23.
l = ‖ L. Matt. viii. 3, 15. ch. viii. 22 al.

lat-*b c ff*$_2$ *g*$_{1.2}$ [*q*]. ανθρωπων ℵ. om 1st αυτου DM[1]N. aft μητ. ins εαυτου D, αυτου Mℵ, simly lat-*a b c* [*f ff*$_2$] Syr copt goth æth. om και προσκολλ. to end (*homœotel: και to και*) Bℵ ev-48 goth. for προς την γυναικα, τη γυναικι (*corrn to* ‖ *Matt and* LXX-A), ACLNΔ 1 gat(with mt tol) lat-*a c f g*$_2$ Jer: txt (*as* LXX-Ed-vat [B def]) D rel vulg lat-*b ff*$_2$.

8. σαρξ bef μια (‖ *Matt*) ACFKM[2]UΓΠℵ 1. 69 copt arm: txt BDN rel latt syrr goth æth.

9. om ουν D-gr lat-*ff*$_2$ *k* syr (Clem). om ο AG Clem. for συνεζ., εζευξεν D-gr ev-z am lat-*c f*.

10. rec (for εις την οικ.) εν τη οικια, with ACN rel vulg lat-(*a*) *f g*$_2$ *k* [*l q*] copt goth æth arm: txt BDLΔℵ ev-y lat-*b*. (om lat-*c*.) om αυτου BCLΔℵ ev-y lat-*a* (*c*) *k* copt arm: ins ADN rel vulg lat-*b f g*$_2$ [*l q*] syrr goth æth. (*The omn was prob made for elegance: αυτου—τουτου—αυτον coming close together.*) rec (for τουτου) του αυτου, with D rel vulg lat-*b g*$_2$ [*q*] syr goth, αυτου Π Scr's s: τουτων ℵ: txt ABCLMNXΓΔ 1 lat-*a c f ff*$_2$ (*k*) Syr copt æth.—om π. τ. K 67 ev-z harl[1]. add λογου D lat-*c f ff*$_2$ *g*$_2$ *k*. rec επηρωτησαν, with ADN rel latt syrr copt goth: txt B C(-τουν) LΔℵ.

11. rec εαν, with AN rel (add ανηρ 1. 69 lat-*a* arm): txt BCDLΔℵ. αλλην bef γαμηση D vulg lat-*b c f* [*l q*].

12. rec (for αυτη) γυνη (*more general and perpicuous*), with ADN rel vulg lat-*f g*$_1$ syrr goth: txt BCLΔℵ [copt] æth. rec απολυση τ. ανδ. αυ. και (*to conform to ver* 11), with AN rel vulg lat-*f g*$_1$ syrr goth: -σασα . . . και Δ: εξελθη απο του ανδρος και D (69) lat-*a b* (*c*) *ff*$_2$ *g*$_2$ arm: txt B(C)Lℵ.—for αυτης, αυτου C. rec γαμηθη αλλω, with AC[2]N rel (arm): txt BC[1](D)L(Δ)ℵ 1. 69 syr copt goth (æth).—αλ. bef γαμ. D.—αλλην Δ.

13. αυτων bef αψηται (*from* ‖ *Luke*) BCLΔℵ ev-y [lat-*f*].

Adam's saying His own: in Matt. it is attributed to ὁ ποιήσας ἀπ' ἀρχῆς. The parallel is most instructive. **10—12.**] In Matt. this saying forms part of the discourse *with the Jews*. Here again Mark furnishes us with the *exact circumstantial* account of the matter. On the addition, Matt. vv. 10—12, see notes there. We may notice, that Mark omits Matt.'s κατὰ πᾶσαν αἰτίαν in ver. 2,—and his μὴ ἐπὶ πορνείᾳ in ver. 11; as also does Luke (xvi. 18). The one omission seems to involve the other. The report here gives the enquiry without this particular exception. As a general rule, Mark, so accurate in circumstantial details, is less exact than Matt. in preserving the order and connexion of the discourses. **12.**] This verse corresponds to ὁ ἀπολελυμένην γαμήσας μοιχᾶται in Matt. ver. 9—but it is *expressed* as if the *woman* were the active party, and put away her husband, which was allowed by Greek and Roman law (see 1 Cor. vii. 13), but not by Jewish (see Deut. xxiv. 1: Jos. Antt. xv. 7. 10). This alteration in the verbal expression may have originated in the source whence Mark's report was drawn. On μοιχᾶται, Grotius remarks, 'Mulier, cum domina sui non sit, si, marito relicto, ad aliud matrimonium se conferat, omnino adulterium committit, non interpretatione aliqua, aut per consequentiam, sed *directe*: ideo non debuit hic addi, ἐπ' αὐτόν.'

13—16.] The bringing of children to Jesus. Matt. xix. 13—15. Luke xviii. 15—17. The three are nearly identical:—from Matt., we have the additional reason καὶ προσεύξηται, and from Mark, ἐναγκαλ. αὐτά. **13. παιδία**] Not only *children*,

οἱ δὲ μαθηταὶ [m] ἐπετίμων τοῖς προσφέρουσιν. 14 ἰδὼν
δὲ ὁ Ἰησοῦς [n] ἠγανάκτησεν καὶ εἶπεν αὐτοῖς [o] Ἄφετε τὰ
παιδία ἔρχεσθαι πρός με, μὴ [p] κωλύετε αὐτά· τῶν γὰρ
τοιούτων ἐστὶν ἡ βασιλεία τοῦ θεοῦ. 15 [q] ἀμὴν λέγω
ὑμῖν, ὃς ἂν μὴ [r] δέξηται τὴν βασιλείαν τοῦ θεοῦ ὡς
παιδίον, οὐ μὴ εἰσέλθῃ εἰς αὐτήν. 16 καὶ [s] ἐναγκα-
...τιθεις L. λισάμενος αὐτά, [t] κατευλόγει [u] τιθεὶς τὰς χεῖρας ἐπ'
αὐτά.
17 Καὶ ἐκπορευομένου αὐτοῦ εἰς ὁδὸν [v] προσδραμὼν

m — ch. viii. 32, 33 reff. n abs., Matt. xxi. 15 (reff.). o ch. v. 37 reff. p ch. ix. 38 reff. q Matt. v. 18 reff. r = Acts vii. 38. 2 Cor. vi. 1. s ch. ix. 36 only. Prov. vi. 10. xxiv. 33 only. t here only †. Tobit xi. 1 (x. 13), 17 (not ℵ) only. u constr., 2 Cor. iii. 13. Rev. i. 17. 3 Kings ii. 24. v ch. ix. 15. Acts viii. 30 only. Gen. xxxiii. 4.

aft *μαθ.* ins *αυτου* D 406. 2-pe lat-*a c f* syrr goth æth. **επετιμησαν αυτοις** [omg *προσφ.*] (*from* || *Matt*) BCLΔℵ lat-*c k* copt.

14. παιδαρια D[1]. rec ins *και* bef *μη* (*from* || *Matt Luke*), with ACDLM[2]ℵ 1 latt syrr goth æth arm [Bas$_1$] : om BN rel copt.

15. rec εαν, with AN rel : txt BCDLΔℵ 1. *εις αυτην εισελευσεται* D-gr.

16. for *εναγκ.*, *προσκαλεσαμενος* D lat-*b c f ff$_2$* [*q*]. rec *τιθ. τ. χ. επ αυτα ηυλογει αυτα* (*avoiding the unusual κατευ. and conforming the order to* || *Matt*), with (AN) Γ (rel) vulg lat-*f g$_1$* goth arm : *ετιθει τ. χ. επ αυ. και ευλογει αυτα* D lat-*b c ff$_2$ k* syrr : txt BC(L)Δℵ (ev-y) syr-ms copt æth Vict.—rec ηυλογει, with Γ : *ευλογει* AD rel : *ευλογη* K[1] : *ευλογησεν* FGK[2] : *κατηυλογει* L N(-γι) ev-y : txt BCΔℵ.

17. for *προσδρ. εἷς*, *ιδου τις πλουσιος προσδρ.* (*it seems likely, as Mey, that the title of the section has somehow been mixed with the txt : for, from ver 22, πλουσιος could hardly be exprd here*) AK M(omg *τις*) Π 69 syr-mg arm : txt BCDℵ rel vulg lat-*a b*

but as in Luke, **infants** (*βρέφη*): and our Lord was not to *teach* them, but only to touch, and pray over them. This simple, seemingly superstitious application of *οἱ προσφέροντες* (perhaps not the mothers only) the disciples, interrupted in their converse on high and important subjects, despise and reprove. **14.**] We can hardly read our Lord's solemn saying, without seeing that it reaches further than the mere then present occasion. It might one day become a question whether the new Christian covenant of repentance and faith could take in the unconscious infant, as the old covenant did :—whether when Jesus was no longer on earth, little children might be brought to Him, dedicated to his service, and made partakers of his blessing? Nay, in the pride of the human intellect, this question was sure one day to be raised: and our Lord furnishes the Church, by anticipation, with an answer to it for all ages. Not only may the little infants be brought to Him, —but in order for us who are mature to come to Him, we must cast away all that wherein our maturity has caused us to differ from them, and *become* LIKE THEM. Not only is Infant Baptism *justified*, but it is (abstractedly considered;—not as to *preparation* for it, which from the nature of the case is precluded) the NORMAL PATTERN OF ALL BAPTISM; none can enter God's kingdom, except *as an infant*. In adult baptism, the *exceptional case* (see above), we strive to secure that state of simplicity and childlikeness, which in the infant we have ready and undoubted to our hands. **16.**] **κατευλόγει**, like all such compounds, is more forcible and complete than the simple verb would have been. It may be rendered **He fervently blessed them.**

17—31.] ANSWER TO AN ENQUIRER RESPECTING ETERNAL LIFE, AND DISCOURSE THEREUPON. Matt. xix. 16—30. Luke xviii. 18—30. On the different form of our Lord's answer in Matt., see notes there. As it here stands, so far from giving any countenance to Socinian error, it is a pointed rebuke of the very view of Christ which they who deny His Divinity entertain. He was no 'good Master,' to be singled out from men on account of His pre-eminence over his kind in virtue and wisdom: God sent us no such Christ as this, nor may any of the sons of men be thus called *good*. He was *one with Him* who only is good, the Son of the Father, come not to teach us merely, but to beget us anew by the divine power which dwells in Him. The low view then, which this applicant takes of Him and his office, He at once rebukes and annuls, as He had done before in the case of Nicodemus: see John iii. 1 ff. and notes.

w ‖ Mt. see Matt. viii. 19 reff. x acc., here [and ch. i. 40] only. (Mt. xvii. 14. xxvii. 29 only†.) y ‖ Mt. reff. z Matt. xxv. 34 reff. Num. xxvi. 55. a ‖ L. ch. xii. 37. xv. 12. Luke xx. 37. John xv. 15. b Exod. xx. 12—16. Deut. v. 16—20. c ‖ Mt. reff. d 1 Cor. vi. 7, 8. vii. 5. 1 Tim. vi. 5. James v. 4. Mal. iii. 5. e mid., = here only. Lev. xviii. 5. = act., ‖ Mt. reff.

ABCDE FGHK MNSU VXΓΔΠ ℵ 1. 69

[w] εἷς καὶ [x] γονυπετήσας αὐτὸν ἐπηρώτα αὐτὸν Διδάσκαλε
ἀγαθέ, τί ποιήσω ἵνα [y] ζωὴν [y] αἰώνιον [z] κληρονομήσω;
18 ὁ δὲ Ἰησοῦς εἶπεν αὐτῷ Τί με [a] λέγεις ἀγαθόν; οὐδεὶς
ἀγαθὸς εἰ μὴ εἷς ὁ θεός. 19 τὰς ἐντολὰς οἶδας, [b] Μὴ
μοιχεύσῃς, μὴ φονεύσῃς, μὴ κλέψῃς, μὴ [c] ψευδομαρτυρήσῃς, μὴ [d] ἀποστερήσῃς, τίμα τὸν πατέρα σου καὶ τὴν
μητέρα. 20 ὁ δὲ ἀποκριθεὶς ἔφη αὐτῷ Διδάσκαλε, ταῦτα
πάντα [e] ἐφυλαξάμην [f] ἐκ [fg] νεότητός μου. 21 ὁ δὲ Ἰησοῦς
[h] ἐμβλέψας αὐτῷ ἠγάπησεν αὐτόν, καὶ εἶπεν αὐτῷ Ἕν σε
[i] ὑστερεῖ· ὕπαγε, ὅσα ἔχεις πώλησον καὶ δὸς πτωχοῖς,
καὶ ἕξεις [k] θησαυρὸν ἐν οὐρανῷ· καὶ [l] δεῦρο ἀκολούθει
μοι [m] ἄρας τὸν [m] σταυρόν. 22 ὁ δὲ [n] στυγνάσας [o] ἐπὶ τῷ

f ‖ (Mt. v. r.) L. Acts xxvi. 4. Gen. viii. 21. Ps. lxxxvii. 15. g as above (f). 1 Tim. iv. 12 only. h w. dat., ver. 27. ch. xiv. 67. Luke xx. 17. xxii. 61. John i. 36, 43. 2 Macc. xii. 45. i constr., here only. (‖ Mt. reff.) Neh. ix. 21. k Matt. ii. 11 reff. l ‖ Mt. reff. m ch. viii. 34 ‖ Mt. n = here (Matt. xvi. 3) only Ezek. xxvii. 35. xxviii. 19 A. xxxii. 10 only. o = ch. i. 22 reff.

f ff$_2$ Syr copt goth æth. γονυπετων D 69. aft αυτον ins λεγων (‖ *Luke*) D 69 lat-*a b f g*$_2$ *k l* [*q*] Syr goth arm Clem. (Tischdf does not cite any readings from N in vv. 17, 18.)

18. for εἷς ὁ, μονος εις D txt (*see on* ‖ *Matt*) ABCℵ rel [Clem] Orig$_{expr}$.

19. μ. φον. bef μ. μοιχ. (*corrn to order of commandments and to* ‖ *Matt*) BCΔ ℵ-corr[1] lat-*c* copt; aft μ. κλεψ. Syr: om μη μοιχευσης ℵ[1].—for μ. φον., μ. πορνευσης D-gr Γ(aft κλεψ.) lat-*k*. om μη αποστερησης B-txt(ins B-marg) ΚΔΠ 1 Scr's e [arm]. om σου D [lat-*q*] Clem. aft μητ. ins σου (‖ *Luke*) CFNℵ[1] lat-*a b c f* Syr copt goth æth.

20. [for ο δε, και C am lat-*b g*$_1$.] om αποκριθεις (‖ *Luke*) BΔℵ [copt]. rec (for εφη) ειπεν (‖ *Luke*), with ADN rel: txt BCΔℵ. παντα bef τ. D fuld(with ing) lat-*b k* [*q*] copt Clem Orig$_1$. εφυλαξα (*more strongly attested in* ‖ *Matt Luke*) AD Clem Orig. at end add τι ετι υστερω (‖ *Matt*) KMNΠ 69 [lat-*a c*] syr-w-ast arm.

21. om ιησ. AKΓΠ. for αυτον, αυτω C. aft 2nd αυτω ins ετι ℵ 245-8: ει θελεις τελειος ειναι (‖ *Matt*) KMNΠ 69 syr-w-ast [copt-wilk æth] arm. rec (for σε) σοι (*from* ‖ *Luke*), with ADN rel Clem Orig$_1$: txt BCMΔΠ[1]ℵ ev-y. rec ins τοις bef πτωχοις, with CDℵ (1, e sil) copt: om ABN rel goth arm Clem. om αρας τον σταυρον (*see* ‖ *Matt Luke*) BCDΔℵ vulg lat-*b c f ff*$_2$ *g*$_{1.2}$ *k l* copt-schw Clem (Hil Ambr Aug): ins bef δευρο G 1. 69 lat-*a* Syr æth arm Iren$_1$: txt AN rel syr copt-wilk goth.

22. εστυγνασεν *contristatus* D lat-*a b c*. ins τουτω bef τω λογω D 69 lat-*a b* [*c*]

The dilemma, as regards the Socinians, has been well put (see Stier ii. 283, note): —*either*, "There is none good, but God: Christ is good: therefore Christ IS GOD;" —*or*, "There is none good, but God: Christ is not God: therefore Christ IS NOT GOOD." With regard to other points, the variations in the narratives are trifling, but instructive—εἰ δὲ θέλ. εἰς τ. ζ. εἰσ. τήρ. τ. ἐντ. λέγει αὐτῷ, Ποίας; ὁ δὲ Ἰησ. εἶπεν Τό. (Matt.) = τὰς ἐντολὰς οἶδας (Mark and Luke) without any break in the discourse. Similarly, in Matt., the young (Matt.) ruler (Luke) asks, ver. 20, τί ἔτι ὑστερῶ; but in Mark and Luke, Jesus says to him (and here with the remarkable addition of **ἐμβλ. αὐτ. ἠγ. αὐτ.**), **ἕν σε ὑστερεῖ** (or σοι λείπει). Such notices as these shew the point at which, not short of which nor beyond which, we may expect the Evangelists to be in accord; viz. in that *inner truthfulness of faithful report* which reflects to us the teaching of the Lord, but does not depend on slavish literal exactitude; which latter if we require, we overthrow their testimony, and most effectually do the work of our adversaries. **17.**] **εἰς ὁδόν**, out of the house, ver. 10, to continue His journey, ver. 32. The *running* and the *kneeling* are both found in the graphic St. Mark only. **19.**] Mark here takes exactly the commandments of the second table,—**μὴ ἀποστ.** standing for the tenth. Matt. adds their summary (ἀγαπ. τ. πλησίον σου ὡς σεαυτ.), omitting (with Luke) μὴ ἀποστ., perhaps on account of **μὴ κλ.** having gone before. **21.**] Notice the graphic details again, of *looking on him* and *loving him*. **ἄρας τὸν στ.** is

λόγῳ ἀπῆλθεν [p] λυπούμενος, [q] ἦν γὰρ ἔχων [q] κτήματα
πολλά. 23 καὶ [r] περιβλεψάμενος ὁ Ἰησοῦς λέγει τοῖς
μαθηταῖς αὐτοῦ [s] Πῶς [t] δυςκόλως οἱ τὰ χρήματα ἔχοντες
εἰς τὴν βασιλείαν τοῦ θεοῦ εἰςελεύσονται. 24 οἱ δὲ μαθηταὶ [u] ἐθαμβοῦντο [o] ἐπὶ τοῖς λόγοις αὐτοῦ. ὁ δὲ Ἰησοῦς
πάλιν ἀποκριθεὶς λέγει αὐτοῖς [v] Τέκνα, [s] πῶς [w] δύςκολόν
ἐστιν τοὺς [x] πεποιθότας ἐπὶ χρήμασιν εἰς τὴν βασιλείαν
τοῦ θεοῦ εἰςελθεῖν. 25 [y] εὐκοπώτερόν ἐστιν [z] κάμηλον διὰ
τῆς [a] τρυμαλιᾶς τῆς [b] ῥαφίδος διελθεῖν ἢ πλούσιον εἰς τὴν
βασιλείαν τοῦ θεοῦ εἰςελθεῖν. 26 οἱ δὲ [c] περισσῶς [d] ἐξεπλήσσοντο, λέγοντες πρὸς [e] ἑαυτοὺς Καὶ τίς δύναται
σωθῆναι; 27 [f] ἐμβλέψας αὐτοῖς ὁ Ἰησοῦς λέγει [g] Παρὰ
ἀνθρώποις ἀδύνατον, ἀλλ' οὐ [g] παρὰ θεῷ· πάντα γὰρ
δυνατά ἐστιν [g] παρὰ τῷ θεῷ. 28 [h] ἤρξατο λέγειν ὁ

p Matt. xvii. 23 reff.
q ‖ Mt. (reff.)
r abs., ch. v. 32 ix. 8 (reff.) only.
s = Matt. xxi. 20 reff.
t ‖ only †.
u ch. i. 27. ver. 32 only. 2 Kings xxii. 5.
v ch. ii. 5.
w here only. Jer. xxix. 8 (xlix. 9) only.
x = Luke xi. 22. xviii. 9. 2 Cor. i. 9. Heb. ii. 13, from Isa. viii. 17. Ps. ii. 12.
y ‖. ch. ii. 9 ‖. Luke xv. 17 only †. Sir. xxii. 15. 1 Macc. iii. 18 only.
z ‖ Mt. reff.
a here only. Judg. vi. 2 B. Jer. xiii. 4.
b ‖ Mt. (L. v. r.) only †.
c Matt. xxvii. 23 reff.
d Matt. vii. 28 reff.
e = ch. i. 27. xi. 31. xii. 7. xvi. 3 al.
f ver. 21 reff.
g ‖. (Luke i. 37.) Gen. xviii. 14.
h ver. 32. ch. vi. 7, 32. Matt. xxvi. 22 al.

ff$_2$ *k* [*q*] Syr. ins και bef απηλθεν D lat-*b c ff*$_2$. for κτηματα πολλα, πολλα χρηματα D lat-(*a*) [*b*] *ff*$_2$.

23. for λεγει, ελεγεν Cℵ[1] : ειπεν Δ Scr's g ev-z. om τα C. at end (omg ver 25) adds ταχειον καμηλος δια τρυμαλιδος ραφιδος διελευσεται η πλουσιος εις τ. βασιλειαν τ. θεου D, simly lat-*a b ff*$_2$.

24. aft μαθ. ins αυτου DΔ 1 lat-*a b c f ff*$_2$ *k* [*q*]. om ιησ. παλιν A. τεκνια AN 1 Clem, *filioli* latt[not *q*] : om EGKΠ 253-9 Scr's f² i v w [lat-*c k*]. om τους to χρημασιν (*homœotel, passing from* εστιν *to* χρημασιν) BΔℵ lat-*k* copt-ms. rec ins τοις bef χρ., with D 69 (1, e sil) : om ACNX rel goth arm Clem.

25. om ver D lat-*a b ff*$_2$. (*See on ver* 23.) aft ευκ. ins δε A; γαρ Scr's m n q². om της (twice) (*see* ‖ *Matt Luke*) ACKMNUΔΠℵ 1. 69 goth : om 1st FΓ : om 2nd G [copt]. for τρυμαλιας, τρηματος ℵ[1]. Steph (for διελθειν) εισελθειν (*see* ‖ *Matt Luke*), with ANℵ rel lat-*a k* syr-mg goth Clem : txt BCKΠ 1 (69) vulg lat-*b c f ff*$_2$ *g*$_{1.2}$ [*l q*] syrr copt æth arm.

26. for εαυτους, αυτον BCΔℵ copt : πρ. αλληλους M[1] arm.

27. rec aft εμβλεψας ins δε (‖ *Matt*), with AC²DN rel lat-*k* Syr (syr) æth arm; pref *et* vulg lat-*b c* &c : om B C[1](appy) Δℵ 1 copt goth. for λεγει, ειπεν Γℵ[1] [Clem], *dixit* lat-*a k q*. ins τουτο bef αδυνατον (*from* ‖ *Matt*) C²DN 69 lat-*b* (*c*) *g*$_2$ Syr arm. for αλλ' ου to δυν. εστιν, εστιν παρα δε τω θεω δυνατον D lat-(*a b c f*) *ff*$_2$ æth (Clem). rec ins τω bef θεω, with ADΠ (K, e sil) : om BCNℵ rel Clem Vict-ms Thl. om εστιν (*see* ‖ *Matt*) BCℵ 28. 124 evv-H-y. om τω (bef 2nd θεω) B 124 Scr's i.

28. rec ins και bef ηρξατο, with D latt syrr æth : add δε KNΠ lat-*f* copt-wilk-dz

added here. **22.**] **ἦν γὰρ ἔχων**—so also Matt. **23—31.**] Here our ver. 24 is a most important addition; the rest is much alike in the three. In that verse we have all misunderstanding of our Lord's saying removed, and "the proverb," as Wesley well observes (Stier ii. p. 290), "shifted to this ground: 'It is easier for a camel, &c. than for a rich man *to cast off his trust* in his riches.'" Yet the power of divine grace can and does accomplish even this. **24.**] **τέκνα** is remarkable and a trace of exactitude: see John xxi. 5:—so also **περιβλ.** ver. 23. **26.**] This reiterated expression of dismay, *after the explanation* in ver. 24, need not surprise us. The disciples were quite as well aware as we must be, if we deal truly with ourselves, that **οἱ τὰ χρήματα ἔχοντες** and **οἱ πεποιθότες ἐπὶ χρήμασιν** are too nearly commensurate, for the mind to be relieved of much of its dread at the solemn saying which preceded. Of the **καί** at the beginning of a question, Kühner remarks, on Xen. Mem. p. 117 (in Meyer) "cum vi auctiva ita ponitur, ut is qui interrogat cum admiratione quadam alterius orationem excipere, ex eaque conclusionem ducere significetur qua alterius sententia confutetur." **28.**] Here is an in-

Πέτρος αὐτῷ Ἰδοὺ ἡμεῖς [i] ἀφήκαμεν πάντα, καὶ ἠκολου-
θήκαμέν σοι. 29 ἔφη ὁ Ἰησοῦς Ἀμὴν λέγω ὑμῖν, οὐδείς
ἐστιν ὃς [i] ἀφῆκεν οἰκίαν ἢ ἀδελφοὺς ἢ ἀδελφὰς ἢ μητέρα
ἢ πατέρα ἢ τέκνα ἢ ἀγροὺς ἕνεκεν ἐμοῦ καὶ ἕνεκεν τοῦ
[k] εὐαγγελίου, 30 [l] ἐὰν μὴ λάβῃ [m] ἑκατονταπλασίονα νῦν
ἐν τῷ [n] καιρῷ τούτῳ, οἰκιας καὶ ἀδελφοὺς καὶ ἀδελφὰς
καὶ μητέρας καὶ τέκνα καὶ ἀγροὺς μετὰ [o] διωγμῶν, καὶ ἐν
τῷ [pq] αἰῶνι τῷ [q] ἐρχομένῳ [r] ζωὴν [r] αἰώνιον. 31 πολλοὶ δὲ
ἔσονται πρῶτοι ἔσχατοι, καὶ οἱ ἔσχατοι πρῶτοι.
32 Ἦσαν δὲ ἐν τῇ ὁδῷ [s] ἀναβαίνοντες εἰς Ἱεροσόλυμα,

i = Matt. iv. 11, 20, 22 al.
k = Matt. iv. 23. ch. viii. 35 al.
l Matt. xxvi. 42. ch. iv. 22.
m (|| Mt. v. r.) Luke viii. 8 only. 2 Kings xxiv. 3 only.
n = || L. Rom. iii. 26. viii. 18. Eph. ii. 12.
o Matt. xiii. 21 reff.
p Matt. xii. 32. Luke xx. 35. Eph. i. 21.
q || L. see Eph. ii. 7.
r ver. 18.
s || Mt. reff.

ABCDE FGHK MNSUV ΧΓΔΠא 1. 69

L τω ερχομενω..

goth, ουν 406 ev-y: om ABCא rel am copt[-schw and ms] arm Clem. rec ο πετρος bef λεγειν, with ADN rel lat-*a b c f ff*$_2$ *g*$_1$ *k* [*q*] syrr goth æth arm Clem: txt BCΔא (copt).—om ο D. rec ηκολουθησαμεν (*from* || *Matt, where only* D[1] *has* -καμεν, *and* || *Luke, where none have it*), with ANא rel Clem: txt BCD. at end add τι αρα εσται ημιν (|| *Matt*) א gat lat-*b*.

29. rec (for εφη ο ιησ.) αποκριθεις δε ο ιησ. ειπεν, with KΠ[1·3] lat-*c ff*$_2$ *k q* Clem$_2$: αποκ. δε ο ιησ. D: αποκ. δε ειπεν Γ: κ. αποκ. ο ιησ. ειπ. CEFGHN 1. 69 syr æth: αποκ. ο ιησ. ειπ. AΠ[2] rel vulg lat-*a b* Syr goth arm: txt BΔ(א) copt.—aft εφη ins αυτω א. aft υμιν add οτι A Scr's c. om οικιαν D lat-*b*. rec η πατ. bef η μητ. (*more natural order, so* || *Matt*), with ANא rel vulg lat-*b* syrr æth arm [Orig-int$_1$]: om η πατ. D harl[1] lat-*a ff*$_2$ *k*: txt BCΔ am lat-*c f q* copt goth. rec ins η γυναικα bef η τεκ. (*from* || *Luke, where none omit it: the omn can hardly be expld, as Mey, by conformation to ver* 30), with ACNX rel lat-*f q* syrr goth æth: om BDΔא 1 latt copt arm Clem$_2$ Orig$_{expr}$. om ενεκεν εμου και א[1]: for και, η D 1 arm Orig-int. rec om 2nd ενεκεν, with A B-txt S[1] lat-*c k*: ins B-marg C D(-κα) Nא rel vulg lat-*a b f ff*$_2$ *l* syrr copt goth æth arm Clem$_2$ Orig-int.

30. for εαν, ος αν D latt syr goth æth. **απο**λαβη (|| *Luke*) א 1 (Clem). om νυν D-gr 255. 406 lat-*a k q*. aft τουτω ins ος δε αφηκεν D lat-*a b ff*$_2$. om οικιας to διωγμων א[1] (ins א-corr[1·3]) lat-*c k*. οικιαν D lat-*a b ff*$_2$. κ. αδελφας bef κ. αδελφους D lat-*b ff*$_2$. aft αδελφας ins και πατερας N: κ. πατερα KMXΠא[3a]: om ABCD א-corr[1] rel. κ. μητερα (*the plur not being understood*) ACDKMXΠא[3a] 1 lat-*a b f ff*$_2$ *l* syr goth (æth) arm-mss: txt BN rel vulg Syr copt arm-zoh. διωγμ**ου** D-gr Syr æth: om και αγρους μετα διωγμων א-corr[1] ins א[3a]). om και D lat-*b ff*$_2$. αιωνι**αν** B. at end ins λημψεται D lat-*a b c ff*$_2$ *k*.

31. om οι (|| *Matt*) ADKLMVΔΠא 1 [copt] goth.

stance of a saying of Peter's reported, without any distinction indicating that he had a share in the report. See note on Matt. for the promise here made to the Apostles. **29, 30.**] Here our report is most important. To it and Luke we owe **νῦν ἐν τῷ καιρῷ τούτῳ**, without which the promise might be understood of a *future life only*:—and to it alone we owe *the particularizing of the returns* made, and the words **μετὰ διωγμῶν**, which light up the whole passage, and shew that it is the inheritance of the earth *in the higher sense* by the meek which is spoken of;—see 1 Cor. iii. 21, 22. Observe *mothers*—nature gives us only one—but love, many (see Rom. xvi. 13). We do not read, *fathers*, perhaps because of our high and absorbing relation to our Father in heaven, cf. Matt. xxiii. 9. On **καὶ τοῦ εὐαγγελίου**, Bp. Wordsw. observes, "See above, viii. 35, where this phrase (not found in the other Evangelists, see Matt. xvi. 25: Luke ix. 24) is inserted by St. Mark. Perhaps it made a greater impression upon *his* mind, because he had formerly shrunk from suffering ἕνεκεν τ. εὐαγγελίου. (See Acts xiii. 13; xv. 38.) St. Mark also alone here inserts our Lord's words, μετὰ διωγμῶν, perhaps from a recollection that he had been once affrighted by persecution from doing the work of the Gospel: and desiring to prepare others to encounter trials which for a time had mastered himself." Here follows in Matt. the parable of the Labourers in the vineyard, ch. xx. 1—16.

32—34.] Fuller declaration of

καὶ ἦν [t] προάγων αὐτοὺς ὁ Ἰησοῦς, καὶ [u] ἐθαμβοῦντο καὶ
ἀκολουθοῦντες ἐφοβοῦντο. καὶ [v] παραλαβὼν πάλιν τοὺς
δώδεκα [w] ἤρξατο αὐτοῖς λέγειν τὰ μέλλοντα αὐτῷ [x] συμ-
βαίνειν, 33 ὅτι ἰδοὺ [s] ἀναβαίνομεν εἰς Ἱεροσόλυμα, καὶ ὁ
[y] υἱὸς τοῦ [y] ἀνθρώπου [z] παραδοθήσεται τοῖς ἀρχιερεῦσιν
καὶ τοῖς γραμματεῦσιν, καὶ [a] κατακρινοῦσιν αὐτὸν θανάτῳ,
καὶ παραδώσουσιν αὐτὸν τοῖς ἔθνεσιν, 34 καὶ [b] ἐμπαίξουσιν
αὐτῷ καὶ [c] ἐμπτύσουσιν αὐτῷ καὶ [d] μαστιγώσουσιν αὐτόν,
καὶ ἀποκτενοῦσιν αὐτόν, καὶ μετὰ τρεῖς ἡμέρας [e] ἀναστήσεται. 35 Καὶ [f] προσπορεύονται αὐτῷ Ἰάκωβος καὶ
Ἰωάννης υἱοὶ Ζεβεδαίου λέγοντες αὐτῷ Διδάσκαλε, [g] θέλομεν ἵνα ὃ ἐὰν αἰτήσωμέν σε ποιήσῃς ἡμῖν. 36 ὁ δὲ εἶπεν

t Matt. xiv. 22 reff. constr., ver. 22.
u ver. 24.
v ch. ix. 2 reff.
w ver. 28.
x Luke xxiv. 14. Acts iii. 10. xx. 19. xxi. 35. 1 Cor. x. 11. 1 Pet. iv. 12. 2 Pet. ii. 22 only. Gen. xlii. 4.
y Matt. viii. 20 reff.
z ||. Matt. xvii. 22. Ezek. xxiii. 28.
a and constr., || Mt. reff.
b Matt. xxvii. 29, 31, 41 al. Exod. x. 2. Ps. ciii. 26.
c w. dat., ch. xiv. 65. xv. 19. w. εἰς, Matt. xxvi. 67. xxvii. 30. Num. xii. 14. pass., Luke xviii. 32 only.
d Matt. x. 17 reff. Jer. v. 3.
e ch. viii. 31 reff.
f here only. Exod. xxiv. 14 al.
g ch. vi. 25 reff.

32. προsαγων D, but *præcedens* D-lat. om και ακολ. εφοβ. DK lat-*a b*. for 3rd και, οι δε B C¹(appy) LΔℵ 1 (lat-*c k*) copt: και οι C² æth: txt AN rel vulg lat-*f* (*ff*₂) [*g*₁,₂ *l q*] syrr goth.

33. om 2nd τοις (|| *Matt*) CDN rel goth: ins ABLMΔℵ³ᵃ 1 (69, e sil) copt. [Tischdf gives M for the omn, H for the insn].—om και τοις γραμ. ℵ¹ 259. θανατου D¹(txt D²).

34. rec transp εμπτυσουσιν and μαστιγωσουσιν, with AN rel syrr goth [arm]: om κ. μαστ. αυτ. D 47 lat *ff*₂ *g*₂: om κ. εμπτυσ. αυτ. 28 [lat-*k*]: om both 258: txt BCLΔℵ latt syr-jer copt æth. (*The sentence fell into confusion by the various errors of omission, and was variously restored.*)—εμπτυουσιν ℵ¹, -υξουσιν D¹(txt D²).—om αυτον (aft μαστ.) N. om κ. αποκτ. αυτον A²D lat-*g*₂: om αυτον BLΔℵ 1 lat-*b c* arm. rec (for μετα τρεις ημερας) τη τριτη ημερα (*conformation to || Matt Luke*), with AN rel vulg lat-*f g*₂ syrr goth æth arm Orig₁ (om τη A¹): txt BCDLΔℵ lat-(*a*) *b* (*c*) *ff*₂ *i k* syr-mg copt.

35. παραπορευονται ℵ¹: προπορ. SΔ Scr's c ev-H¹. rec ins οι bef υιοι, with Dℵ rel Orig; οι δυο BC copt: om AKMNUXΠ¹ goth. for λεγοντες, και λεγουσιν D 406. 2-pe lat-*a* Syr Orig. rec om 2nd αυτω (*as superfl, and to avoid repetn*), with AN rel vulg lat-*b c f k* [*i q*] syr goth: ins BCDLΔℵ lat-*a* Syr copt æth arm Orig. homœotel in ℵ¹ ινα to ινα ver 37 (ins ℵ³ᵃ). om ινα D-gr 118. 245-58 lat-*i*. ο τι αν C¹: ο αν D 69. for αιτησωμεν, ερωτησωμεν D 1. 2-pe: αιτησομεν Aℵ³ᵃ. rec om σε, with X rel vulg lat-*c i k q* Syr: ins ABCLΔℵ³ᵃ 69 lat-*a ff*₂ syr copt æth arm, and bef the verb DKNΠ 1 lat-*b f* goth.

36. for ειπεν, λεγει D-gr.

HIS SUFFERINGS AND DEATH. Matt. xx. 17—19. Luke xviii. 31—34. (The remarkable particulars of ver. 32 are only found here.) This was (see Matt. xvi. 21; xvii. 22) the *third* declaration of His sufferings which the Lord had made to the disciples, and it was His *going before them,* accompanied most probably by something remarkable in his gait and manner —a boldness and determination perhaps, an eagerness, denoted in Luke xii. 50, which struck them with astonishment and fear. See an interesting note here in Wordsw. Observe, that ἦσαν and ἀναβαίνοντες must not be taken together. "They were in the way, as they went up to Jerusalem." **32.**] **ἤρξατο,** anew: He again opened this subject. **33.**] The circumstances of the passion are brought out in all three Evangelists with great particularity. The 'delivery to the Gentiles' is common to them all. **34.**] **ἐμπτ.** Mark and Luke:—σταυρῶσαι, *Matt. only,* which is remarkable, as being the first intimation, in plain terms, of the death He should die. The ἆρας τὸν στ., so often alluded to, might have had now for them a deep meaning—but see Luke ver. 34. After **τοῖς ἔθν.** the subject of the verbs (**ἐμπ., μαστ.** &c.) is τὰ ἔθνη.

35—45.] AMBITIOUS REQUEST OF THE SONS OF ZEBEDEE: OUR LORD'S REPLY. Matt. xx. 20—28, where see notes throughout, and especially on the difference in our

h ‖ Mt. Matt. xxii. 44 ‖ (al., from Ps. cix. 1). xxvii. 38. Luke i. 11. 3 Kings xxii. 19.
i Luke xxiii. 33 (reff.) only.
k intr., Matt. v. 1 reff. xxiii. 2.
l = Matt. xxvi. 39 reff.
m = (‖ Mt. v. r.) Luke xii. 50 only †. acc., Luke xii. 47 reff.
n (‖ Mt. v. r.) Luke xii. 50. Isa. xxi. 4.
o ‖ Mt. reff.
p constr. ellipt., Rom. vi. 21. Luke v. 25. xvii. 1.
q ‖ Mt. reff.
r vv. 28, 32.
s ‖ Mt. reff.
t = ‖ Mt. Luke ii. 18. 2 Cor. x. 8.
u Gal. ii. 6 a, 9. Sus. 5.
v Rom. xv. 12 (from Isa. xi. 10) only. Gen. xlv. 26.
w ‖ Mt. Acts xix. 16. 1 Pet. v. 3 only. Gen. i. 28. ix. 1.
x ‖ Mt. Heb. viii. 11, from Jer. xxxviii. (xxxi.) 34. Rev. xix. 5, 18.
y ‖ only †.

ABCDE FGHKL MNSUV ΧΓΔΠℵ 1. 69

αὐτοῖς Τί θέλετε ποιῆσαί με ὑμῖν; 37 οἱ δὲ εἶπαν αὐτῷ
Δὸς ἡμῖν ἵνα εἷς σου [h] ἐκ [h] δεξιῶν καὶ εἷς [i] ἐξ [i] ἀριστερῶν
[k] καθίσωμεν ἐν τῇ δόξῃ σου. 38 ὁ δὲ Ἰησοῦς εἶπεν αὐτοῖς
Οὐκ οἴδατε τί αἰτεῖσθε. δύνασθε πιεῖν τὸ [l] ποτήριον
ὃ ἐγὼ πίνω, ἢ τὸ [m] βάπτισμα ὃ ἐγὼ [n] βαπτίζομαι
βαπτισθῆναι; 39 οἱ δὲ εἶπαν αὐτῷ Δυνάμεθα. ὁ δὲ
Ἰησοῦς εἶπεν αὐτοῖς Τὸ [l] ποτήριον ὃ ἐγὼ πίνω πίεσθε,
καὶ τὸ [m] βάπτισμα ὃ ἐγὼ βαπτίζομαι [n] βαπτισθήσεσθε·
40 τὸ δὲ [k] καθίσαι [h] ἐκ [h] δεξιῶν μου ἢ ἐξ [o] εὐωνύμων οὐκ
ἔστιν ἐμὸν δοῦναι, ἀλλ' [p] οἷς [q] ἡτοίμασται. 41 καὶ
ἀκούσαντες οἱ δέκα [r] ἤρξαντο [s] ἀγανακτεῖν [t] περὶ Ἰακώβου
καὶ Ἰωάννου. 42 καὶ προσκαλεσάμενος αὐτοὺς ὁ Ἰησοῦς
λέγει αὐτοῖς Οἴδατε ὅτι οἱ [u] δοκοῦντες [v] ἄρχειν τῶν
ἐθνῶν [w] κατακυριεύουσιν αὐτῶν, καὶ οἱ [x] μεγάλοι αὐτῶν
[y] κατεξουσιάζουσιν αὐτῶν. 43 οὐχ οὕτως δέ ἐστιν ἐν

με bef *ποιησαι* L ℵ^{3b}(appy) : *με ποιησω* Bℵ^{3a} ; *ποιησω*, omg *τι θελ. με*, D; *ποιησω*, omg *με*, C 1. 69 : *πυιησομαι* Scr's c ev-y : *ινα ποιησω*, omg *με*, 251 : *ποιησαι*, omg *με*, Δ : txt ANX rel goth. (*The varns arose from Matt* xx. 32, *and our ver* 51.)

37. for *οι δε*, *και* D vulg lat-*b k*. (*ειπαν*, so BC^{1}DLΔ.) rec *εκ δεξ.* bef *σου* (‖ *Matt*), with AC^{3}DN rel : txt BC^{1}LΔℵ. rec (for *αριστερων*) *ευωνυμων* (‖ *Matt*), with ACDNℵ rel : txt BLΔ. rec adds *σου* (‖ *Matt*), with ACN rel vulg lat-*a* syrr copt goth æth : ins *σου* bef *εξ* Lℵ : om BDΔ 1 lat-*b c f ff*$_2$ *g*$_{1.2}$ *i k* [*q* arm].

38. aft *ιησ.* ins *αποκριθεις* D 1. 69 lat-*a b ff*$_2$ *i k q*. *πειν* D. rec (for *η*) *και* (*from ver* 39), with AC^3 rel syrr goth æth : txt BC^{1}DLNΔℵ 1. 69 latt syr-mg copt arm Orig$_2$.

39. (*ειπαν*, so BDLΔℵ.) om *αυτω* D 1 lat-*a b c k* [*ff*$_2$ *i q*]. *δυνομεθα* B^1. rec ins *μεν* bef *ποτηριον* (*from* ‖ *Matt*), with AC^{3}DN rel latt syr goth æth : om BC^{1}LΔℵ em(with gat) Syr copt arm.

40. rec (for *η*) *και* (‖ *Matt*), with ACN rel lat-*k* syrr æth arm : txt BDLΔℵ latt copt goth. rec aft *ευων.* ins *μου* (*to conform to δεξ. μου* : *so also in* ‖ *Matt*), with (Scr's l m n q r, e sil) Syr æth : om ABCDNℵ rel latt syr copt goth arm Thl Euthym. *ητοιμαθαι* (sic) D^1(txt D^2) : *ητοιμασθαι* 69. at end add *υπο του πατρος μου* (‖ *Matt*) ℵ^1(marked for erasure, but the marks removed) 1. 251 lat-*a* syr-mg.

41. om 1st *και* D-gr 64. ins *λοιποι* bef *δεκα* D lat-*a b c ff*$_2$ *i q* syr-jer copt-dz. for *ηρξ. αγ.*, *ηγανακτησαν* (*from* ‖ *Matt*) A 1 gat lat-*g*$_2$ *q*. ins *και* bef *περι* ℵ. ins *του* bef *ιακ.* D. for *ιακ. κ. ιω.*, *των δυο αδελφων* A (*from* ‖ *Matt*).

42. rec *ο δε ιησ. προσκ. αυτ.* (*from* ‖ *Matt*), with AN rel vulg lat-*f g*$_{1.2}$ *l q* syr goth arm : txt BCDLΔ(ℵ) lat-*a* (*b c ff*$_2$ *i*) *k* Syr copt æth.—om *ὁ* ℵ^1. *κατακυριευσουσιν* D[pref *και* D^1(and lat)] Scr's c s ev-y. for *μεγαλοι*, *βασιλεις* ℵ, *principes* vulg lat-*b f ff*$_2$ *g*$_2$ *i l*. om 2nd *αυτων* Nℵ 1 Scr's g.

43. om *δε* (‖ *Matt*) D 229 vulg lat-*a b f ff*$_2$ *i* [*q*]. rec *εσται* (*from* ‖ *Matt*), with

ver. 35. The two accounts of the discourse are almost verbatim the same, and that they came from one source is very apparent. Even here, however, slight deviations occur, which are unaccountable, if the one had actually before him the writing of the other. Besides, we have the whole additional particular of the baptism, with which He was to be baptized: see note on Matt. **38.**] Observe the present tenses, **πίνω** and **βαπτίζομαι.** The Lord had already the cup of His suffering at His lips: was already, so to speak, sprinkled with the first drops of spray of His baptism of blood [or they may be merely official, '*that I am to drink of and to be baptized with*']. **42.**] **οἱ δοκοῦντες ἄρχειν**, those who are reputed

...x. 43 (appy)N

ὑμῖν· ἀλλ' ὃς ἐὰν θέλῃ γενέσθαι [x] μέγας ἐν ὑμῖν, ἔσται
ὑμῶν [z] διάκονος· 44 καὶ ὃς ἐὰν θέλῃ ὑμῶν γενέσθαι
πρῶτος, ἔσται πάντων δοῦλος. 45 καὶ γὰρ ὁ υἱὸς τοῦ
ἀνθρώπου οὐκ ἦλθεν [a] διακονηθῆναι, ἀλλὰ [a] διακονῆσαι,
καὶ δοῦναι τὴν [b] ψυχὴν αὐτοῦ [c] λύτρον ἀντὶ πολλῶν.
46 Καὶ ἔρχονται εἰς Ἱεριχώ. καὶ ἐκπορευομένου αὐτοῦ
ἀπὸ Ἱεριχὼ καὶ τῶν μαθητῶν αὐτοῦ καὶ ὄχλου [d] ἱκανοῦ,
ὁ υἱὸς Τιμαίου Βαρτίμαιος τυφλὸς [e] προσαίτης ἐκάθητο
παρὰ τὴν ὁδόν. 47 καὶ ἀκούσας ὅτι Ἰησοῦς ὁ Ναζαρηνός [f] ἐστιν, [g] ἤρξατο κράζειν καὶ λέγειν [h] Ὁ υἱὸς Δαυεὶδ
Ἰησοῦ, ἐλέησόν με. 48 καὶ [i] ἐπετίμων αὐτῷ πολλοὶ ἵνα
[j] σιωπήσῃ· ὁ δὲ πολλῷ μᾶλλον ἔκραζεν Υἱὲ Δαυεὶδ ἐλέησόν με. 49 καὶ [k] στὰς ὁ Ἰησοῦς εἶπεν [j] Φωνήσατε αὐτόν.
καὶ [j] φωνοῦσιν τὸν τυφλὸν λέγοντες αὐτῷ Θάρσει, ἔγειρε,
[j] φωνεῖ σε. 50 ὁ δὲ [l] ἀποβαλὼν τὸ ἱμάτιον αὐτοῦ [m] ἀνα-

z Matt. xxiii. 11 reff.
a ‖ Mt. ch. i. 13 ‖ Mt., 31 ‖. Matt. xxv. 44 al.+
b = Matt. vi. 25. John x. 25 al. Josh. ii. 14.
c ‖ (reff.) only.
d = Matt. xxviii. 12 reff.
e John ix. 8 only +.
f pres., John i. 40 reff.
g vv. 28, 32, 41.
h nom., Matt. xi. 26 reff.
i w. ἵνα, Matt. xii. 16 reff.
j ‖ Mt. reff.
k = ‖ Mt. Matt. ii. 9. Acts viii. 38.
l Heb. x. 35 only. Prov. xxviii. 24 BΝ. Isa. i. 30. Jer. lii. 2 compl.
m here only. 1 Kings xxv. 9

AC³N rel lat-*q* syrr copt goth arm: txt BC¹DLΔℵ latt. for εαν, αν BDLΔℵ [33, Tischdf] 69. μεγ. εν υμ. ειναι D, *in vobis major esse* lat-*a b* (*c*).—μεγ. bef γεν. (‖ *Matt*) BC¹LΔℵ 1. 69 lat-*f ff*$_2$: txt AC³ rel syr copt goth. for εσται, εστω CXΔℵ 69. rec διακονος bef υμων, with 241(e sil): txt ABCDℵ rel Scr's-mss latt syrr goth arm.

44. rec (for εαν) αν, with BDΔℵ: txt AC rel. εν υμ. ειναι πρωτος (*from* ‖ *Matt*) BC¹L(Δ)ℵ vulg lat-*b*: υμων ειναι πρω. D: txt AC³ rel syrr goth æth arm. for παντων, υμων D 40. 2-pe lat-*a g*$_2$ æth.

46. ερχεται (*corrn to* ‖ *Luke*) D 61. 258 lat-*a b ff*$_2$ *g*$_2$ *i* Orig$_2$ [κ. ερχ. εις ιερ. is supplied in B-marg]. for απο ιερ., εκειθεν D 2-pe lat-*a b f ff*$_2$ *i q* goth Orig$_2$. for [3rd] και, μετα D lat-*a b* (*c*) *f ff*$_2$ *i* (*k*) *l* goth arm. rec om ο, with A rel goth: ins BCDLSΔℵ 1. 69 Orig. rec ins ο bef τυφλος (*the art has been transposed for elegance*), with AC rel: om BDLΔℵ ev-y copt goth Orig. ins και bef προσαιτης ℵ. rec εκαθ. π. τ. οδον προσαιτων (*order of* ‖ *Luke*), with AC² rel latt syrr goth æth; om προσαιτ. C¹; εκαθ. π. τ. οδον επαιτων (*from* ‖ *Luke*) D 2-pe Orig$_2$: txt BLΔℵ lat-*k* copt arm.

47. rec ναζωραιος (*from* ‖ *Luke*), with ACℵ rel goth: txt BLΔ 1 latt Orig$_1$, ναζορηνος D¹(-ωρηνος D²) lat-*l*¹ *q*². εστιν bef ο ναζ. B. for ο υιος, υιε (*from* ‖ *Luke*) BCLM²Δℵ: υιος, omg ο, DK 69 Orig: txt A rel.

48. επιτιμων A. αυτον B[αυτοι B¹] ev-y. εκραξεν D-gr am [Orig$_1$]. υιος DF Orig: ο υιος 1. 118 syr-mg.

49. rec ειπεν αυτον φωνηθηναι (*conformation to* ‖ *Luke, as appears by* εκελευσεν. *This is more prob than that the* oratio directa *should have been substd on acct of* ειπεν: *no such change was made in ch* v. 43), with AD rel syrr goth æth [Orig$_1$]; εκελευσεν αυτ. φωνηθηναι Scr's c ev-48 latt: txt BCLΔℵ ev-y lat-*k* syr-mg copt. οι δε λεγουσιν τω τυφ. D 2-pe lat-*a b ff*$_2$ *i q*. rec εγειραι, with U S(e sil) Orig: εγειρου 1. 69: txt ABCDℵ rel.

50. rec (for αναπηδησας) αναστας, with AC rel syrr æth arm: om Γ: txt BDLM²Δℵ latt syr-mg copt goth Orig$_2$.

to rule,—who have the title of rulers, not = 'those who *rule*,' which *God alone* does.

46—52.] Healing of blind Bartimæus on departure from Jericho. Matt. xx. 29—34. Luke xviii. 35—43. On the three accounts referring to one and the same miracle, see on Matt. I will only add here, that a similar difference of number between Matt. and Mark is found in the miracle in the neighbourhood of Gergesa, ch. v. 2. **46.**] Βαρτ. patronymic. בַּר טִמַּאי:—so *Bar*tholomew, ch. iii. 18, *Bar*jesus, Acts xiii. 6. **48.**] See on Matt. vv. 30, 31. **50.**] ἀποβαλών, κ.τ.λ.,—signs of an eye-witness, which make us again believe, that *here* we have the *literally exact* account of what took place.

n constr., ‖ L. ch. xv. 12. Matt. xxvii. 17.
o ch. vii. 12 reff.
p John xx. 16 only +.
q = Matt. xi. 5 reff.
r Matt. ix. 21 reff.
s ‖ Mt. L. Luke xxiv. 28 al. Ezra iv. 2.
t ‖ Mt. reff.
u (= ἀπεναντι, Mt.) ‖ L. ch. xii. 41. Matt. xxvii. 24 v. r. 2 Chron. vi. 12.
v ‖ only. Zech. ix. 9.
w intr., Matt. xxiii. 2. ch. x. 37, 40 ‖ al.
x = Luke xv. 23. Gen. xlvii. 16.

ABCDE FGHK LMSUV XΓΔΠℵ 1. 69

πηδήσας ἦλθεν πρὸς τὸν Ἰησοῦν.
51 καὶ ἀποκριθεὶς αὐτῷ ὁ Ἰησοῦς εἶπεν Τί ⁿθέλεις ᵒποιήσω σοί; ὁ δὲ τυφλὸς εἶπεν αὐτῷ ᵖῬαββουνί, ἵνα ᵠἀναβλέψω.
52 ὁ δὲ Ἰησοῦς εἶπεν αὐτῷ Ὕπαγε, ἡ πίστις σου ʳσέσωκέν σε. καὶ εὐθὺς ᵠἀνέβλεψεν, καὶ ἠκολούθει αὐτῷ ἐν τῇ ὁδῷ.

XI. 1 Καὶ ὅτε ˢἐγγίζουσιν εἰς Ἱεροσόλυμα, εἰς Βηθφαγὴ καὶ Βηθανίαν πρὸς τὸ ᵗὄρος τῶν ᵗἐλαιῶν, ἀποστέλλει δύο τῶν μαθητῶν αὐτοῦ,
2 καὶ λέγει αὐτοῖς Ὑπάγετε εἰς τὴν κώμην τὴν ᵘκατέναντι ὑμῶν, καὶ εὐθὺς εἰσπορευόμενοι εἰς αὐτὴν εὑρήσετε ᵛπῶλον δεδεμένον, ἐφ᾽ ὃν οὐδεὶς ἀνθρώπων ʷκεκάθικεν· λύσατε αὐτὸν καὶ ˣφέρετε.
3 καὶ ἐάν τις ὑμῖν εἴπῃ Τί ποιεῖτε τοῦτο;

for τον ιησ., αυτον D ev-y_1 latt(not em *f q*).

51. rec λεγει αυτω ο ιησ., with A rel lat-*a f* (Syr) goth: ο ιησ. λεγ. αυτω KΠ[1] 237-52-3-9 Scr's e o w vulg lat-*k* syr: txt BCDLΔℵ tol lat-g_2 *i q* copt (æth) arm. σοι bef θελ. ποιησω (*from* ‖ *Luke*) BCKLΔΠ[1]ℵ vulg lat-*i*: θελ. ποιησαι σοι Γ: txt ADX rel lat-*a b f* copt goth æth. for ραββουνι, κυριε ραββει D lat-*a b* ff_2 *i*.

52. for ο δε, και ο (*from* ‖ *Luke*) BLΔ ℵ[3a](but txt restored) lat-*q* Syr copt [æth]. (ευθυς, so BLΔℵ.) rec τω ιησου (*corrn on account of* αυτω *preceding*), with X rel syr goth $Orig_1$: txt ABCDLM[2]Δℵ 1. 69 latt syr-mg copt æth arm $Orig_1$.

Chap. XI. **1.** for εγγιζουσιν, ηγγιζεν D ev-z em lat-*b c f* ff_2 g_1 *i k l* [*q*] Syr copt æth, -σαν (‖ *Matt*) M 69 ev-y. (ιεροσολυμα, so BCDLΔℵ 1. 69.) aft ιερ. ins και AD lat-*a b c*.—om βηθφαγη και D latt $Orig_{expr}$(ἴδωμεν δὲ περὶ τῆς Βηθφαγὴ μὲν κατὰ Ματθαῖον, Βηθανίας δὲ κατὰ τὸν Μάρκον, Βηθφαγὴ δὲ καὶ Βηθανίας κατὰ τὸν Λουκᾶν) and so Lachm and Tischdf.—βηδφαγη and βηθανια (sic) B[1].—ins εις bef βηθανιαν C(D)ℵ (lat-*k*) æth arm. for των (bef ελαιων), το B. for αποστελλει, επεμψεν C (*Wetst and Lachm are in error*): απεστειλεν (‖ *Matt Luke*) FH 1 lat-*a b c f* g_2 k^3 Syr copt goth æth arm-mss.

2. for και λεγει, λεγων (‖ *Matt*) 1. 69 lat-*a* sah: κ. ειπεν D-gr. om την κατεναντι υμων ℵ[1](ins ℵ[3b]). (ευθυς, so BLΔℵ Orig.) om εις αυτην (‖ *Luke*) D lat-*a b c* ff_2 *i q* sah[appy]. aft ουδεις ins ουπω BLΔ vulg lat-*b f* ff_2 *i l q* $Orig_3$; aft ανθρωπων Cℵ 69 (Syr) copt-schw sah; aft εφ ον K[Π] (syr) goth: ουδεις πωποτε ανθρ. (‖ *Luke*) A: txt D rel em lat-*a* (*c*) $g_{1.2}$ *k* copt-wilk (æth) arm $Orig_1$. ('not yet' *was manifestly interpolated, as naturally occurring, and found in* ‖ *Luke.*) εκαθισεν (*from* ‖ *Luke*) BCLΔℵ $Orig_3$. rec λυσαντες αυτ. αγαγετε (*from* ‖ *Luke*) A (D-gr) rel goth: λυσαντες αυτ. κ. φερετε L: txt BCΔℵ latt syrr coptt æth arm Orig.—και αγ. D.

3. for εαν, αν D. for ποιειτε τουτο, λυετε τον πωλον (‖ *Luke ver* 33) D 69 lat-*a b f* ff_2 *i* arm $Orig_1$.

51.] **Ῥαββουνί** = רַבּוֹנִי, **Master,** or **My Master**, see ref. John. It was said (Drus. in Meyer) to be a more respectful form than ῥαββί. 52.] In Matt. only, Jesus *touches* him. The account here and in Luke seems to correspond better with the wonderful strength of his faith. Our Lord healed *by a word* in such cases, see Matt. viii. 10—13: ch. vii. 29, and other places. Luke adds, δοξάζων τὸν θεόν,—and that *all the people seeing him gave glory to God*: see also Luke xix. 37.

Chap. XI. 1—11.] Triumphal entry into Jerusalem. Matt. xxi. 1—17. Luke xix. 29—44. John xii. 12—36. On the general sequence of events of this and the following day, see note on Matt. ver. 1. 1, 2.] As far as εὑρήσετε, the agreement in Matt., Mark, and Luke is nearly verbal; after that Mark and Luke only mention the *foal*, and add, **on which never man sat.** Compare with this Luke xxiii. 53. Our Lord's birth, triumph, and burial were to be, in this, alike. 'A later tradition, sprung from the *sacred destination* of the beast (for beasts never yet

εἴπατε Ὁ κύριος αὐτοῦ [y] χρείαν [y] ἔχει, καὶ εὐθὺς αὐτὸν
ἀποστέλλει ὧδε. 4 καὶ ἀπῆλθον καὶ εὗρον [v] πῶλον
δεδεμένον [z] πρὸς θύραν ἔξω ἐπὶ τοῦ [a] ἀμφόδου, καὶ
λύουσιν αὐτόν. 5 καί τινες τῶν ἐκεῖ ἑστηκότων ἔλεγον
αὐτοῖς Τί [b] ποιεῖτε λύοντες τὸν [v] πῶλον; 6 οἱ δὲ εἶπον
...αυτοις καθως F. αὐτοῖς καθὼς εἶπεν ὁ Ἰησοῦς, καὶ [c] ἀφῆκαν αὐτούς.
N xi. 7 (appy)... 7 καὶ [x] φέρουσιν τὸν [v] πῶλον πρὸς τὸν Ἰησοῦν, καὶ
[d] ἐπιβάλλουσιν αὐτῷ τὰ ἱμάτια αὐτῶν, καὶ ἐκάθισεν [e] ἐπ'
αὐτόν. 8 καὶ πολλοὶ τὰ ἱμάτια αὐτῶν [f] ἔστρωσαν εἰς τὴν

y Matt. vi. 8 reff.
z = ch. ii. 2. xiv. 54 ‖ L.
a here only. Jer. xvii. 27. xxx. (xlix.) 27 only.
b John xi. 47. Acts xxi. 13. 1 Cor. xv. 29.
c = Matt. iii. 15 al.
d Luke v. 36 ‖ Mt. 1 Cor. vii. 35. Lev. xix. 19.
e w. acc. ‖ J. Matt. xix. 28. Rev. xx. 4. Gen. xlviii. 2.
f ‖ Mt. reff.

ins και bef ειπατε C^1(perhaps) [lat-*ff*$_2$]. rec aft ειπατε ins οτι (‖ *Luke*), with ACDℵ rel vulg lat-*f* [*l q* syrr sah goth] Orig$_2$: om BΔ lat-*a b c i k* æth. (ευθυς, so BCDLΔℵ Orig$_1$.) rec αποστελει (‖ *Matt*), with GUΠ 1 vulg lat-*a f ff*$_2$ *g*$_2$ *i k l q* D-lat Δ-lat coptt arm Orig$_4$: txt ABC D[-gr] ℵ rel em lat-*b c g*$_1$ syrr goth. aft αποστ. ins παλιν (*see note*) BDLΔℵ Orig$_2$: aft αυτον C^1(appy): om AC^2 rel latt syrr coptt goth æth arm Orig$_1$.—αποστ. παλιν αυτον B. (om αυτον Δ: αποστ. bef αυτον U.)

4. rec (for και απηλθ.) απηλθ. δε (*from* ‖ *Luke*), with AC rel syr sah goth: κ. απελθοντες (omg και aft) D vulg lat-(*a*) *b f l* [*i q*] copt Orig$_1$: απηλθον ουν και 1. 69: txt BLΔℵ lat-(*c*) *k* (Syr) æth Orig$_1$. rec ins τον bef πωλον, with CΔℵ sah arm Orig$_1$: om ABD rel copt goth Orig$_2$. rec ins την bef θυραν, with ACDℵ rel Orig$_1$: om BLΔ coptt goth arm Orig$_2$.

6. om αυτοις D lat-*b c ff*$_2$ *i k*. rec (for ειπεν) ενετειλατο, with A rel vulg lat-*a f* D-lat syrr goth: ειρηκει D[-gr] lat-*b c ff*$_2$ *i* [*q*] (*both corrns to avoid the recurrence of* ειπ., D also to *plusq-perf for sense*): txt BCLΔℵ 1 (lat-*k*?) coptt æth arm Orig$_1$.—add αυτοις DM 1. 69 latt Syr coptt goth æth.

7. rec (for φερουσιν) ηγαγον (*from* ‖ *Luke*), with AD rel latt syrr coptt goth æth arm-mss: αγουσιν Cℵ^1 1. 69 arm-usc-zoh: txt BLΔℵ^{3a} Orig$_1$; *ducere* lat-*a b ff*$_2$ *i*. rec (for επιβαλλουσιν) επεβαλον (*to suit* ηγαγον), with A rel lat-(*a*) *c f g*$_2$ *k* [*q*] syrr (sah?) goth æth arm-mss: txt BCDLΔℵ 1 vulg lat-*b ff*$_2$ *i l* copt arm-usc-zoh Orig$_1$. εαυτων Bℵ^{3a}; αυτου D-gr 256: om 1. 28 lat-*b ff*$_2$ *i k q* arm: αυτων τα ιματ. αυτω ℵ^1. καθιζει D-gr 1: εκαθισαν ℵ^1: -θησαν Scr's b^1 ev-y. rec επ' αυτω (*mechanical repetn from* επιβ. αυτω *above*), with AN rel: txt BCDLΔℵ.

8. rec (for και πολ.) πολ. δε (*from* ‖ *Matt Luke*), with ADN rel latt syrr sah goth arm: txt BCLΔℵ lat-*k q* copt æth. εαυτων B: αυτου K: om L. εστρωννυον D 1, *sternebant* lat-*a b c ff i k* Syr. εν τη οδω AKMNΠ 69^1 vulg lat-*a c f k l q* arm.

worked were used for sacred purposes, Num. xix. 2: Deut. xxi. 3: 1 Sam. vi. 7).' Meyer. But does it never strike such annotators, that this very usage would lead not only to the *narrative being so constructed*, but to the *command itself having been so given?* **3. ὁ κύρ. . . . . ὧδε**] The pres. ἀποστέλλει, is used of future things whose occurrence is undoubted; see Matt. xvii. 11; xi. 3 al.: but the words are somewhat ambiguous. From the ancient interpolation of πάλιν, it seems that they were understood *all to belong to ὁ κύριος—'the Lord hath need of it, and will immediately send it* [*back*].' Lachm., by printing the words without a stop, evidently adopts this rendering: and Origen, tom. xvi. in Matt. § 16, vol. iii. p. 741, favours it. But verisimilitude seems to me to be against it: and the final clause in ver. 6, καὶ ἀφῆκαν αὐτούς, appears to correspond with this. So that I would understand it as in E. V.: and **straightway he** (the speaker or owner) **will send it hither.** **4.**] The report of one of those sent: qu. Peter? **ἀμφοδ.** (a road leading round a place) is probably **the street**: see reff. Wordsw. interprets it, *'the back way, which led round the house.'* But there does not appear to be any reason for supposing the ἀμφι- to refer to the *house*, rather than to the whole block, or neighbourhood, of houses, round about which the street led. [Archbp. Trench, on the A. V. p. 116, would render it "*a way round*," "*a crooked lane*."] **8, 9.**] On the interesting addition in Luke vv. 37—40, see

g here only †. Ezek. xlvi. 23 Aq.
h = ‖ only. Num. xiii. 24 al. see Matt. xi. 17 reff.
i ‖ Mt. Matt. xiv. 22.
k ‖ Mt. reff.
l Psa. cxvii. 26.
m ‖. Matt. xxiii. 39.
n ‖ Mt. reff.
o ch. iii. 5 reff.
p adj. (but ?), here only †. see ch. iv. 35 reff.
q Matt. xxvii. 62. John i. 29, 35 al. Num. xi. 32.

ὁδόν, ἄλλοι δὲ [g] στιβάδας [h] κόψαντες ἐκ τῶν ἀγρῶν,
9 καὶ οἱ [i] προάγοντες καὶ οἱ ἀκολουθοῦντες ἔκραζον
[k] Ὡσαννά, [l] εὐλογημένος ὁ ἐρχόμενος [m] ἐν ὀνόματι κυρίου,
10 εὐλογημένη ἡ ἐρχομένη βασιλεία τοῦ πατρὸς ἡμῶν
Δαυείδ, Ὡσαννὰ [n] ἐν τοῖς [n] ὑψίστοις. 11 καὶ εἰςῆλθεν εἰς
Ἱεροσόλυμα εἰς τὸ ἱερόν· καὶ [o] περιβλεψάμενος πάντα,
[p] ὀψίας ἤδη οὔσης τῆς ὥρας ἐξῆλθεν εἰς Βηθανίαν μετὰ 33 Βηθ... ABCDE GHKL MNSUV ΧΓΔΠℵ
τῶν δώδεκα.
12 Καὶ τῇ [q] ἐπαύριον ἐξελθόντων αὐτῶν ἀπὸ Βηθανίας 1. 33. 69

rec στοιβαδας, with AC rel syr-mg-gr(Treg, -mss Tischdf) Orig$_1$: στυβ. N Scr's k ev-y syr-mg-gr(Tischdf) : στειβ. EG : εστιβ. D : txt BHKLMUΔΠℵ 69 Orig$_1$. rec εκοπτον εκ των δενδρων (*from* ‖ *Matt*), with ADN rel latt Syr syr(αγρ. marg) goth arm : εκοπτ. εκ τ. αγρ. C copt-schw[-dz] sah ; *cædebant ramos arborum ex agris* copt-wilk : txt BLΔℵ Orig$_1$. rec adds (*from* ‖ *Matt*) και εστρωννυον εις την οδον, with A D(omg εις) rel latt syrr copt goth arm (Orig) ; κ. ε. εν τ. οδω KMNΠ : om BCLΔℵ sah æth.

9. προςαγοντες D-gr. rec aft εκραζον ins λεγοντες (*from* ‖ *Matt*), with ADN rel vulg lat-*a b f g*$_1$ [*i l q*] syrr goth æth arm : om BCLΔℵ lat-*c ff*$_2$ *k* coptt Orig$_1$. om ωσαννα D lat-*b ff*$_2$.

10. ins και bef ευλογημ. AD[1]KMΠ Syr æth. rec aft βασιλ. repeats εν ονοματι κυριου, with AN rel lat-*q* syr goth æth Jer Euthym$_{expr}$: om BCDLUΔℵ 1. 69 ev-y latt Syr copt arm Orig$_2$.

11. εισελθων D lat-*a b c f ff*$_2$ *g*$_2$ *i*. rec aft ιεροσ. ins ο ιησους (*beg of a lection*), with AN rel lat-*q* syr goth ; bef εις ιεροσ., lat-*c f* Syr æth arm : om BCDLΔℵ 1 vulg lat-*a b ff*$_2$ *g*$_2$ *i k l* copt Orig$_1$. rec ins και bef εις το ιερον, with ADN rel lat-*q* syr goth arm : om BCLMΔℵ 69 latt Syr copt æth Orig$_1$. om και (bef περιβ.) D lat-*a b c f ff*$_2$ *i*. for οψιας, οψε CLΔℵ Orig$_1$: οψονης 2-pe. om της ωρας B : om της D 245. 2-pe : της ημερας 28. 69. aft δωδ. ins μαθητων D evv-H-y-z lat-*a b c f g*$_2$ *i* [*q*].

12. for εξελθ. αυτων, εξελθοντα D-gr(ον εξελθ. D[1]) : εξελθοντα αυτον Γ ; *cum exisset* mt lat-*b c ff*$_2$ [*q*] Syr.

notes there. **στιβ.** = βαΐα τ. φοινίκων John ver. 13 : but this word, by its derivation from στείβω, signifies not merely branches, but branches cut for the purpose of being littered to walk on : and thus *implies* ἐστρώννυον εἰς τ. ὁδόν, which has been unskilfully supplied. Bp. Wordsw. complains of the introduction of τῶν ἀγρῶν into the text, adding "other instances, unhappily far too numerous, might be cited, where corrupt glosses and barbarisms have been recently received as improvements into the Sacred Text." Surely a Commentator of Bp. W.'s learning and piety should know better than to write thus. He well knows, that it is not *as improvements*, that any such changes have been introduced as those to which he alludes, but simply and humbly in deference to the carefully weighed evidence of the best and oldest authorities, combined with that furnished by the existing phænomena of interpolation and adaptation of parallel places. The charge of attempting to "improve the Sacred Text" recoils on those, who in the face of such evidence, with such questions as "What writer would say, they cut branches off the fields?", shelter their own rationalizing subjectivities under received readings which have been themselves glosses and "improvements" on the Sacred Text. 10.] **εὐλ. . . . Δαυείδ**, peculiar to Mark, clearly setting forth the idea of the people that the Messianic Kingdom, the restoration of the *throne of David*, was come. See the additional particular of the weeping over the city, Luke vv. 41—44, and notes.

11.] See Matt. ver. 12, and notes on ver. 1 : also on John ii. 13—18. I am by no means certain that the solution proposed in the notes on Matt. is the right one, but I cannot suggest a better. When Mark, as here, relates an occurrence throughout, with such signs of an eyewitness as in ver. 4, it is *very difficult to suppose that he has transposed any thing* ; whereas Matt. certainly does not

[r] ἐπείνασεν. 13 καὶ ἰδὼν [s] συκῆν [t] ἀπὸ [t] μακρόθεν ἔχουσαν
[u] φύλλα, ἦλθεν [vw] εἰ [w] ἄρα τὶ εὑρήσει ἐν αὐτῇ, καὶ ἐλθὼν
[x] ἐπ' αὐτὴν οὐδὲν εὗρεν [y] εἰ μὴ [u] φύλλα· ὁ γὰρ [z] καιρὸς
οὐκ ἦν [a] σύκων. 14 καὶ [b] ἀποκριθεὶς εἶπεν αὐτῇ Μηκέτι
[c] εἰς τὸν αἰῶνα ἐκ σοῦ μηδεὶς καρπὸν φάγοι. καὶ ἤκουον
οἱ μαθηταὶ αὐτοῦ. 15 καὶ ἔρχονται εἰς Ἱεροσόλυμα. καὶ
εἰςελθὼν εἰς τὸ ἱερὸν [d] ἤρξατο [e] ἐκβάλλειν τοὺς πωλοῦντας καὶ τοὺς ἀγοράζοντας ἐν τῷ ἱερῷ, καὶ τὰς [f] τραπέζας
τῶν [g] κολλυβιστῶν καὶ τὰς [h] καθέδρας τῶν πωλούντων
τὰς [i] περιστερὰς [k] κατέστρεψεν, 16 καὶ οὐκ [l] ἤφιεν [m] ἵνα
τὶς [n] διενέγκῃ [o] σκεῦος διὰ τοῦ ἱεροῦ. 17 καὶ ἐδίδασκεν

r Matt. iv. 2 reff.
s Matt. xxiv. 32 reff.
t Matt. xxvi. 58 reff. Ps. cxxxvii. 6.
u ‖ Mt. reff.
v ellips., Acts viii. 22. Rom. i. 10. = Acts x. 18. xix. 2.
w Acts vii. 1. xvii. 27 only. Ps. lvii. 1.
x ‖. ch. vi. 53. Acts viii. 36.
y = Matt. xi. 27. xii. 4 al.
z = Matt. xiii. 30. xxi. 34, 41. Ps. i. 3.
a Matt. vii. 16. Luke vi. 44. James iii. 12 only. 4 Kings xx. 7.
b = Matt. xi. 25 reff. &c. Matt. xxvi. 22.
c ‖ Mt. John viii. 35, 51, 52 al. Deut. xv. 17.
d ch. x. 28, 32, John ii. 15 only ‡.
e ‖. Matt. ix. 25 al.
f = ‖. Luke xix. 23.
g ‖. John ii. 15 only †.
h ‖ Mt. Matt. xxiii. 2 only. Ps. i. 1.
i Matt. iii. 16 reff.
k ‖ Mt. only. Judg. vii. 13 A.
l ἤφ. ch. i. 34 only. = Matt. iii. 15 al. Ps. civ. 14.
m (see note) = ver. 28. Matt. iv. 3 al. fr.
n = here only †. Esdr. v. 55 (53).
o Luke viii. 16. 2 Tim ii. 20 al. Exod. iii. 22.

om επεινασεν ℵ[1] (ins ℵ-corr[1], appy).

13. *απο μακροθεν* bef *συκην* D Scr's c vulg lat-*a b f ff*$_2$ *g*$_{1.2}$ [*i l q*] Orig$_1$. aft *συκην* ins *μιαν* (‖ *Matt*) KMΠℵ ev-w Syr : pref Scr's c d p. rec om *απο*, with X rel goth arm : ins ABCDLMNΔℵ **1**. 33. 69 latt syrr æth Orig$_1$. for *ει αρα τι ευρ.*, *ειδειν εαν τι εστιν* D gat lat-*b c ff*$_2$ *i k* : *ως ευρησων τι* 2-pe lat-*a f q* Orig$_2$.—rec *ευρησει* bef *τι*, with X rel syrr goth arm : txt ABCKLNUΔΠ[1]ℵ **1**. 33 vulg lat-*g*$_1$. om *ελθων επ αυτην* D lat-*b c ff*$_2$ *i k* : om *επ αυτην* lat-*a g*$_1$ Syr. *μηδεν ευρων* D-gr(omg *και*, ver 14) 2-pe lat-*q* Orig : *ουδεν ουχ ευρεν* L. aft 2nd *φυλλα* ins *μονον* C[2]N 33. 69 lat-*b c q* æth Orig. rec *ου γαρ ην καιρος* (*see note*), with AC[2]N rel latt syr goth æth arm, so (but insg *ο* bef *καιρος*) D Orig$_2$: txt BC[1]LΔℵ Syr copt.

14. om *και* D 2-pe lat-*a q* Orig. rec aft *αποκριθεις* ins *ο ιησ.*, with X rel : om ABCDKLMNΔΠ[1]ℵ **1**. 33. 69 latt syrr copt goth æth arm Orig$_1$. rec *εκ σου* bef *εις τ. αι.*, with AN rel syr copt : txt BCDLΔℵ **1** latt Syr goth æth arm Orig$_2$. elz *ουδεις* : om Δ : txt ABCDNℵ rel Orig$_2$ Thl. *φαγη* DU **1**. 69 Orig$_2$.

15. for *ερχονται*, *ηρχοντο* C : *εισελθων* D-gr : *venit* lat-*b i* copt-dz æth.—for *εισελθων*, *οτε ην* D. rec aft *εισελθ.* ins *ο ιησους* (‖ *Matt*), with AN rel lat-*f q* syrr : om BCDLΔℵ **1**. 33 latt copt goth(Treg) æth arm Orig$_3$. for *εις τ. ιερ.*, *εν τω ιερω in templum* D. aft *εκβαλλειν* ins *και* A ; *εκειθεν* D lat-*b*. rec om *τους* (bef *αγοραζοντας*) (‖ *Matt*), with D rel Orig$_2$: ins ABCKLMNUΠℵ. for *τω ιερω*, *αυτω* A. aft *κολλ.* ins *εξεχεεν* (*see John* ii. 15) N 69 arm. *κατεστρεψεν* bef *κ. τ. καθεδρας των πωλ. τ. περιστερας* (‖ *Matt*) ℵ[1] Orig : om *κατεστρ.* D-gr lat-*c k*.

speak here so exactly, having transposed the anointing in Bethany: see notes on Matt. xxvi. 2, 6.

12—26.] The barren fig-tree. The cleansing of the Temple. Matt. xxi. 12—22. Our account here bears strong marks of being that of a beholder and hearer : e. g. **ἐξελθ. αὐ. ἀπὸ Βηθ.,—μακρόθεν,—ἔχουσαν φύλλα,—καὶ ἤκουον οἱ μαθ. αὐτ.** The times and order of the events are here more exact than in Matt., who places the withering of the tree *immediately after* the word spoken by our Lord.

13.] **εἰ ἄρα**, *si forte*, si, rebus ita comparatis : see Klotz ad Devar. ii. p. 178.

ὁ γὰρ κ. οὐκ ἦν σ.] The ellipsis may be supplied,—for the season was not (one) of figs,—or, for the season was not (that) of figs, i. e. *not yet the season for figs*. The latter suits the context best. The tree was *precocious*, in being clothed with leaves : and if it had had on it *winter figs*, which remain on from the autumn, and ripen early the next season, they would have been *ripe at this time*. But there were none—it was a *barren tree*. On the *import* of this miracle, see notes on Matt.

15—19.] Matt. xxi. 12, 13, where see notes: also Luke xix. 45—48.

16. οὐκ ἤφιεν ἵνα] "Observa, ἵνα et ὄφρα a recentioribus poëtis frequentari post verba jubendi." Herm. ad Viger., p. 849. See note on 1 Cor. xiv. 13. This was the *court of the Gentiles*, which was used as a thoroughfare; which desecration our Lord forbade. **σκεῦος** is

p Isa. lvi. 7. Jer. vii. 11. Isa. lx. 7. q ||. John xi. 38. Heb. xi. 38. Rev. vi. 15 only. Gen. xix. 30 al. r || Mt. reff. s constr., ch. xiv. 1, 11. Luke xii. 29. 1 Pet. v. 8. Isa. xl. 20. see Luke xxii. 2. t Matt. vii. 28 reff. u ch. i. 22 reff. Luke i. 29. Acts xiii. 12 al. v ch. xiii. 35. Matt. xxviii. 1 only. Exod. xxx. 8. w ch. ii. 23 reff. x Matt. [xvi. 3] xx. 1. ch. i. 35. xiii. 35. xv. 1. xvi. 2, 9. John xviii. 28. xx. 1. Acts xxviii. 23 only. Exod. xvi. 7. y ver. 13. z = || Mt. reff. a here only. Job xxxi. 12. b ch. xiv. 72. 1 Cor. iv. 17. 2 Cor. vii. 15. 2 Tim. i. 6. Heb. x. 32 only. Gen. viii. 1 Ed-vat. [B def.] (-μνησις, Luke xxii. 19.) c Matt. xxv. 41 reff. d Matt. xxi. 21 reff. e constr., Acts iii. 16 a. Rom. iii. 22. Gal. ii. 16, 20. iii. 22. James ii. 1 al. f = ||. Acts x. 20. Rom. iv. 20. James i. 6 ‡.

καὶ ἔλεγεν Οὐ γέγραπται ὅτι ὁ οἶκός μου [p] οἶκος ABCDE GHKL MNSUV ΧΓΔΠℵ 1. 33. 69
προσευχῆς κληθήσεται πᾶσιν τοῖς ἔθνεσιν ; ὑμεῖς δὲ πε-
ποιήκατε αὐτὸν [q] σπήλαιον [r] λῃστῶν. 18 καὶ ἤκουσαν οἱ
ἀρχιερεῖς καὶ οἱ γραμματεῖς καὶ [s] ἐζήτουν πῶς αὐτὸν
ἀπολέσωσιν· ἐφοβοῦντο γὰρ αὐτόν, πᾶς γὰρ ὁ ὄχλος
[t] ἐξεπλήσσετο [u] ἐπὶ τῇ διδαχῇ αὐτοῦ. 19 καὶ ὅτε [v] ὀψὲ
ἐγένετο, ἐξεπορεύετο ἔξω τῆς πόλεως. 20 καὶ [w] παραπορευόμενοι [x] πρωῒ εἶδον τὴν [y] συκῆν [z] ἐξηραμμένην [a] ἐκ
[a] ῥιζῶν. 21 καὶ [b] ἀναμνησθεὶς ὁ Πέτρος λέγει αὐτῷ
Ῥαββεὶ ἴδε ἡ [y] συκῆ ἣν [c] κατηράσω [z] ἐξήρανται. 22 καὶ
ἀποκριθεὶς ὁ Ἰησοῦς λέγει αὐτοῖς [d] Ἔχετε [de] πίστιν [e] θεοῦ.
23 ἀμὴν λέγω ὑμῖν ὅτι ὃς ἂν εἴπῃ τῷ ὄρει τούτῳ Ἄρθητι
καὶ βλήθητι εἰς τὴν θάλασσαν, καὶ μὴ [f] διακριθῇ ἐν τῇ

17. rec (for κ. ελεγ.) λεγων, with ADN rel latt syr goth arm : txt BCLΔℵ 69 lat-*k* (Syr) copt æth Orig$_1$. rec aft ελεγεν ins αυτοις (|| *Matt*), with ACDℵ rel [latt syr goth] Orig$_1$: om B 28 lat-*b* g_1 arm. om ου D 1 lat-*b c i k* copt arm. om οτι CD 69 lat-*a c* ff_2 *i k q* æth arm-mss : ins ABℵ rel vulg lat-*f* g_1 Orig. rec (for πεποιηκατε) εποιησατε (*from* || *Luke*), with ACDNℵ rel : txt BLΔ Orig. αυτον εποι. AMΠ[1] 1. 33 lat-*a*.—αυτην D (txt D-corr[1]).

18. rec transp αρχ. and γρ., with X rel syr goth : txt ABCDKLΔΠℵ 1. 33 latt Syr copt æth arm Orig$_1$. (N ?) om και (bef εζητ.) D latt(not *k*). rec απολεσουσιν, with KM[1]Δ (S, e sil) : txt ABCDN Γ(Tischdf) ℵ rel Orig. om αυτον AKΠ lat-*c* ff_2. rec (for πας γαρ) οτι πας (*to avoid the recurrence of* γαρ), with ADN rel latt syrr goth(Treg) arm Orig : txt BCΔℵ 1. 69 copt. εξεπλησσοντο MΔℵ Scr's d e vulg-mss lat-*c* copt-wilk.

19. οταν (*to suit* || *Matt, and to signify that* every evening *this took place : which however the context forbids*, only one such exit being here spoken of) BCKLΔΠ[1]ℵ 33 : txt ADN rel. εγινετο (*emendn with same intention as above, to represent it as a* daily act ?) AE[2]GHV[2]X 69. εξεπορευοντο (*corrn to suit the next ver ?*) ABKM[1]ΔΠ lat-*c* D-lat Syr syr-mg arm. for εξω, εκ D lat-*b c f k*.

20. παρεπορευετο and ins και bef ειδον ℵ[1]. rec πρωι bef παραπορευομενοι (*to conform to* οψε εγεν., *ver* 19 ?), with AN rel vulg lat-*f* ff_2 [*i*] syrr goth arm : txt BCD LΔℵ 1. 33 ev-y lat-*b i q* copt æth.—ins το bef πρωι D.

21. for ιδε, ιδου D Scr's s Orig$_1$. εξηρανθη DLNΔ 1. 33 Orig : εξηραται X 69 Thl.

22. rec (not Mill) om ο (bef ιησ.) : ins ABCDℵ rel. ins ει bef εχετε Dℵ 33[1]. 69 lat-*a b i* arm. ins του bef θεου D.

23. rec aft αμην ins γαρ (*for connexion*), with AC rel lat-*q* Syr-ms syr-w-ast copt goth æth : om BDNℵ 1 latt Syr arm. om οτι Dℵ 33 em(with tol) lat-g_2 *k* goth æth arm. εαν A 1. διακριθης D-gr[1] : *hæsitaveritis* lat-*c*. (but -*rit* D-lat.)

any vessel,—e. g. a pail or basket,—used for common life. **17.**] **πᾶσιν τοῖς ἔθν.**, omitted in Matt. and Luke, but contained in the prophecy :—'mentioned by Mark as writing for Gentile Christians.' —Meyer, but qu. ? **18.**] **πᾶς ὁ ὄχλ. . . .**] This remark, given by Mark and Luke, is omitted by Matt.: probably because he has given us so much of the **διδαχή** itself. **19.**] See note on Matt. ver. 17. On the Sunday and Monday evenings, our Lord appears to have gone *to Bethany*. **20—26.**] The answers are very similar to those in Matt., but with one important addition here, viz. vv. 25, 26 : see Matt. vi. 14, and 1 Tim. ii. 8. The connexion here seems to be, 'Though you should aim at strength of faith,—yet *your faith* should not work in all respects as you have seen me do, in judicial anger

καρδίᾳ αὐτοῦ, ἀλλὰ πιστεύῃ ὅτι ὃ λαλεῖ [g] γίνεται, ἔσται
αὐτῷ [ὃ ἐὰν εἴπῃ]. 24 διὰ τοῦτο λέγω ὑμῖν, πάντα ὅσα
[h] προσεύχεσθε καὶ [h] αἰτεῖσθε, πιστεύετε ὅτι ἐλάβετε, καὶ
ἔσται ὑμῖν. 25 καὶ ὅταν [i] στήκετε προσευχόμενοι, [j] ἀφίετε
εἴ τι [k] ἔχετε κατά τινος, ἵνα καὶ ὁ [l] πατὴρ ὑμῶν ὁ ἐν τοῖς
[l] οὐρανοῖς [j] ἀφῇ ὑμῖν τὰ [m] παραπτώματα ὑμῶν. 26 εἰ δὲ
F o εν... ὑμεῖς οὐκ [j] ἀφίετε, οὐδὲ ὁ [l] πατὴρ ὑμῶν ὁ ἐν [l] οὐρανοῖς
[j] ἀφήσει τὰ [m] παραπτώματα ὑμῶν.
27 Καὶ ἔρχονται πάλιν εἰς Ἱεροσόλυμα. καὶ ἐν τῷ
ἱερῷ περιπατοῦντος αὐτοῦ ἔρχονται πρὸς αὐτὸν οἱ ἀρχιερεῖς καὶ οἱ γραμματεῖς καὶ οἱ πρεσβύτεροι 28 καὶ ἔλεγον
αὐτῷ [n] Ἐν [o] ποίᾳ ἐξουσίᾳ ταῦτα ποιεῖς, ἢ τίς σοι τὴν

g = Matt. vi. 10. Gen. i. 3 al. fr.
h Col. i. 9.
i ch. iii. 31 reff.
j = Matt. vi. 12 reff.
k Matt. v. 23. Rev. ii. 4, 14, 20. Job xxxi. 35. see Col. iii. 13.
l Matt. v. 16 reff.
m Matt. vi. 14, 15 reff.
n ||. Luke i. 17. iv. 14. Acts iv. 7.
o = Matt. xix. 18. xxii. 36 al. 2 Kings xv. 2. 3 Kings xiii. 12.

rec πιστευση (*corrn to* διακριθῃ), with ACD rel, πιστευσι ΧΓ: -σητε 69: txt BLא, πιστευει Δ ev-y$_2$. rec α λεγει (*the plur to suit* αρθ. και βληθ.: λεγει, *as a commoner word*), with AC rel: txt BLNΔא 33.—for οτι to end, το μελλον ο αν ειπη γενησεται αυτω D, simly latt. om ο εαν ειπη BCLΔא 1[1] vulg lat-*f g*$_1$ *i l* copt æth: ins A(D)N 1[2] rel lat-*a b* (*c*) *ff*$_2$ *k q* syrr goth arm. (*The omn may be easily accounted for,* ο λαλει *having preceded; or even from* εσται υμιν *follg: see also* || *Matt: not so the insn: for if* εσται αυτω *required a subject to be supplied, why not* εσται υμιν *below?*)

24. rec aft οσα ins αν (*from* || *Matt*), with A rel arm: εαν ΚΝΠ 253 Scr's e w: om BCDLΔא goth. rec προσευχομενοι and om και (*to make* οσα *governed by* αιτεισθε *as in* || *Matt*), with AN rel vulg lat-*b f g*$_{1.2}$ [*i*] syr goth arm: txt BCDLΔא lat-*a c ff*$_2$ *k* Syr copt æth Cypr$_1$. rec (for ελαβετε) λαμβανετε, with AN rel syrr goth arm: ληψεσθε D 1 latt æth Cypr: txt BCLΔא copt. (*The aor not being understood was altered to the pres or fut: cf Orig.*)

25. rec στηκητε (*gramml emendn*), with B rel (Orig), στηκειτε E: εστηκηται Δ: στητε א: txt ACDHM[2]VX 1. 33. 69, εστηκετε L: *stabitis* latt. (N?) for αφιετε, αφετε C[1]. ins ων bef εν τ. ουρ. D (latt) Cypr$_3$. αφησει D ev-y. om 2nd υμων D Cypr$_1$(ins$_2$).

26. om ver (*homœotel*) BLSΔא lat-*g*$_2$ *k l* copt æth(-rom and ms *m*) arm-zoh Thl: ins ACDN rel latt syrr goth æth-pl(from ms *a*) arm-usc [Cypr$_2$]. (*I cannot agree with Tischdf Treg, in supposing our ver 26 to be interpolated from Matt* vi. 15. *For it varies from that ver in a manner quite unaccountable, if it is copied from it.*) rec ins τοις bef ουρανοις, with A rel: om CDKMΠ[1] 1.—[εν ουρανω N.]—om ο εν ουρ. 33 ev-y. aft αφησει ins υμιν (*so also in Matt* vi. 15) D 33. 69 latt syrr goth Cypr$_2$.

27. ερχεται DX lat-*b c ff*$_2$ *i* (*k*) [*q*] æth. aft πρεσβυτεροι ins του λαου (|| *Matt*) D.

28. rec (for ελεγον) λεγουσιν (*corrn to* ερχονται *above*), with ADN rel vulg lat-*i k* [*l q*] syrr arm: txt BCLΔא 1 lat-*a b c f* copt goth æth. rec (for η) και (*see* || *Matt*), with AN rel latt syrr goth æth arm: txt BLΔא 124 Scr's c ev-y syr-mg copt. (C uncertain).—om η τις to ποιης D 238-58 lat-*k*: om ινα τ. ποιης 2-pe lat-*a b ff*$_2$ *i* arm.

condemning the unfruitful and evil; but you must *forgive.*' **24.**] **ἐλάβετε** is aor., because the reception spoken of is the determination in the divine counsels coincident with the request—believe that when you asked, you received, and the fulfilment shall come, **ἔσται.** **25.**] On the matter cf. Matt. vi. 14 f. See also ib. v. 23 f., where the converse to this is treated of. In **ὅταν στήκετε**, the **ἄν** connects, not with the verb, but with the **ὅτε**, giving indefiniteness to the occasion, not to the act. See Klotz, Devar. p. 470, 475. He gives an example from Lycurgus contra Leocratem, p. 162 (§ 107), ὅταν ἐν τοῖς ὅπλοις ἐκστρατευόμενοί εἰσι.

26.] In **εἰ . . . . οὐκ**, the negative must be closely joined to the verb; the verb, not the conditional particle, carrying the negative: q. d. "*if ye refuse to forgive.*"

27—33.] THE AUTHORITY OF JESUS QUESTIONED. HIS REPLY. Matt. xxi. 23—32. Luke xx. 1—8. Our account and that of Matt. are very close in agreement. Luke's has (cf. ver. 6, ὁ λ. ἅπας κατ. ἡμ.) few and unimportant additions: see notes on Matt. **28.**] **ταῦτα** need not necessarily refer to the cleansing of the temple,

p = ver. 16 reff.
q ‖ Mt. reff.
r Matt. xvii. 7, 8 reff.
s ch. x. 26 reff.
t change of constr., Luke v. 14. Acts i. 4. xxiii. 22, 23, 24.
u Matt. xiv. 5 reff.
v Luke xxiii. 47. 1 Tim. v. 3, 5 al. Num. xxii. 37 only.

ABCDE FGHK LMNSU VXΓΔΠ ℵ 1. 33. 69

ἐξουσίαν ταυτην ἔδωκεν ᵖ ἵνα ταῦτα ποιῇς; 29 ὁ δὲ Ἰησοῦς εἶπεν αὐτοῖς Ἐπερωτήσω ὑμᾶς ἕνα ᑫ λόγον καὶ ἀποκρίθητέ μοι, καὶ ἐρῶ ὑμῖν ⁿ ἐν ᵒ ποίᾳ ἐξουσίᾳ ταῦτα ποιῶ.
30 τὸ βάπτισμα τὸ Ἰωάννου ἐξ οὐρανοῦ ἦν ἢ ἐξ ἀνθρώπων; ἀποκρίθητέ μοι. 31 καὶ ʳ διελογίζοντο ˢ πρὸς
ἑαυτοὺς λέγοντες Ἐὰν εἴπωμεν Ἐξ οὐρανοῦ, ἐρεῖ Διὰ τί
οὐκ ἐπιστεύσατε αὐτῷ; 32 ἀλλὰ εἴπωμεν Ἐξ ἀνθρώπων;
ᵗ ἐφοβοῦντο τὸν λαόν· ἅπαντες γὰρ ᵘ εἶχον τὸν Ἰωάννην
ᵛ ὄντως ὅτι προφήτης ἦν. 33 καὶ ἀποκριθέντες τῷ Ἰησοῦ
λέγουσιν Οὐκ οἴδαμεν. καὶ ὁ Ἰησοῦς λέγει αὐτοῖς Οὐδὲ
ἐγὼ λέγω ὑμῖν ⁿ ἐν ᵒ ποίᾳ ἐξουσίᾳ ταῦτα ποιῶ.

XII. 1 Καὶ ἤρξατο αὐτοῖς ἐν παραβολαῖς λαλεῖν.

εδωκ. bef τ. εξ. ταυτην (*from* ‖ *Matt*) BCLM²Δℵ (1) 33 latt[not *i q*] Syr copt. ποιεις HKLNUXΓ ev-y.

29. rec aft ιησ. ins αποκριθεις (*from* ‖ *Matt Luke*), with ADN rel latt syr goth arm: om BCLΔℵ 33 lat-g_1 *i k* Syr copt æth. rec aft υμας ins καγω, with DGMNΓℵ: και εγω EFHSUVX 69 [*et ego* latt]: καγω υμας AKΠ lat-g_2 k^3 goth [æth]: txt B C(perhaps) LΔ lat-k^1 copt. om 1st και D 28 lat-*a b c f* g_1 *i k* [*q*] (Syr) copt arm. καγω υμιν ερω LΔ ℵ³ᵃ(but υμιν erased) 33: και εγω λεγω υμιν D: εγω is expressed in lat-*c* Syr copt æth arm.

30. rec om 2nd το (‖ *Luke*), with NX rel: ins ABCDLΔℵ 33. aft ιωαννου ins ποθεν ην (‖ *Matt*) Cℵ 33 lat-*k* Syr sah æth. ουρανων *cælo* D. om ην CLℵ 33.

31. for και, οι δε N (latt). rec ελογιζοντο (*prob* ΔΙ *was lost in* ΑΙ *preceding: the* MSS *are too many and important to suppose* διελ. *taken from* ‖ *Matt*), with AN rel: προσελογ. ℵ: txt BCDGKLMΔ[Π] ℵ³ᵃ(but προσελ. restored) 1. 33. 69. aft λεγοντες ins τι ειπωμεν D 69 lat-*a* ff_2 *i k.* for ερει, λεγει D-gr lat-*b*. aft ερει ins ημιν (‖ *Matt*) D⁴(υμ. D¹-gr) M 1. 69 em(with gat mt tol) lat-*a b c f* ff_2 *i* k^3 [*q*] D-lat Syr sah æth arm. rec aft δια τι ins ουν (*from* ‖ *Matt, where only* DL al *omit it*), with BC² D-gr Nℵ rel vulg lat-*f* g_1 syr sah: om AC¹LMXΔ tol lat-*a b c* ff_2 *i k* [*q*] Syr[*et cur*] copt goth æth.

32. (αλλα, so A B(sic cod) CLΔℵ 33: om D.) rec ins εαν bef ειπωμεν (*supplied from not understanding txt*), with D 69 vulg lat-*a b c* [*f* ff_2] g_2 *q* (Syr) syr æth arm: om ABCNℵ rel lat-*k* coptt goth. φοβουμεν D¹: -μεθα (‖ *Matt*) D-corr¹ [N] 69 latt(not am em ing) coptt æth arm. for λαον, οχλον (‖ *Matt*) BCNℵ 33 syr-mg: txt AD rel vss(appy). for απαντες, παντες (‖ *Matt*) CDNℵ¹ 1. 33: txt ABℵ³ᵃ rel. for ειχον, ηδεισαν D 2-pe lat-*a b c f* ff_2 *i k* [*q*] arm. rec οτι bef οντως (*corrn to supposed sense*), with A rel syrr copt goth: οτι αληθως D vulg lat-*a f q*: om οντως Nℵ¹ 1 ev-y lat-*c k* æth arm: txt BCLℵ³ᵃ 69.—τον ιω. οντως ως προφητην Δ(N) sah.

33. rec λεγουσιν bef τω ιησου, with AD rel vulg lat-*b c* [*f*] *i k* syrr goth arm: txt BCLNΔℵ 33. 69 mt lat-*a* ff_2 copt. rec aft ιησους ins αποκριθεις (*prob mechanical repetn from above*), with X rel; bef ιησ. A D(omg και) KMΠ 1. 69 vulg lat-*b* ff_2 $g_{1.2}$ *i* [*l*] *q* syr goth æth: om BCLNΓΔℵ 33 lat-*a c f k* Syr coptt arm. for αυτοις, αυτω D-gr. εις ποιαν εξουσιαν D¹(txt D-corr¹ and lat).

CHAP. XII. 1. rec (for λαλειν) λεγειν (*from* ‖ *Luke*), with AC D-gr (N) rel lat-*k* syr[-txt] goth; λεγων Γ 126(Tischdf): txt BGLΔℵ 1. 69 latt Syr syr-mg coptt. (lat-*a* def.)—λεγειν bef αυτ. εν παρ. N.

as Meyer; but seems from ‖ Luke, to extend over our Lord's whole course of teaching and putting himself forward in public. **ἵνα ταῦτα ποιῇς** is not a periphrasis of the infinitive, but contains the *purpose* of τὴν ἐξ. τ. ἔδ. 29.] In **ἐπερωτήσω**, the preposition does not signify *in addition*, as Fritz., but merely indicates the *direction* of the question. 32.] The ἐάν being omitted as spurious, a note of interrogation must be set after **ἀνθρ.**—a question which is answered *by the Evan-*

[w] Ἀμπελῶνα [x] ἐφύτευσεν [y] ἄνθρωπος, καὶ [z] περιέθηκεν
[a] φραγμόν, καὶ [b] ὤρυξεν [c] ὑπολήνιον, καὶ ᾠκοδόμησεν
[d] πύργον, καὶ [e] ἐξέδετο αὐτὸν [f] γεωργοῖς, καὶ [g] ἀπεδήμησεν.
2 καὶ ἀπέστειλεν πρὸς τοὺς [f] γεωργοὺς τῷ [h] καιρῷ δοῦλον,
ἵνα παρὰ τῶν [f] γεωργῶν λάβῃ [i] ἀπὸ τῶν καρπῶν τοῦ
[w] ἀμπελῶνος· 3 καὶ λαβόντες αὐτὸν [k] ἔδειραν καὶ ἀπέστειλαν [l] κενόν. 4 καὶ πάλιν ἀπέστειλεν πρὸς αὐτοὺς ἄλλον
δοῦλον· κἀκεῖνον [m] ἐκεφαλαίωσαν καὶ [n] ἠτίμασαν. 5 καὶ
ἄλλον ἀπέστειλεν· κἀκεῖνον ἀπέκτειναν, καὶ πολλοὺς
ἄλλους, [o] οὓς μὲν [k] δέροντες, [o] οὓς δὲ [p] ἀποκτέννοντες.
6 ἔτι ἕνα εἶχεν υἱὸν [q] ἀγαπητόν· ἀπέστειλεν αὐτὸν ἔσχατον
πρὸς αὐτοὺς λέγων ὅτι [r] ἐντραπήσονται τὸν υἱόν μου.

w Matt. xx. 1, &c. al. Deut. xx. 6.
x Matt xv. 13 reff.
y = Matt. xxi. 28 al.
z Matt. xxvii. 28 reff.
a || Mt. Luke xiv. 23. Eph. ii. 14 only. Ps. cxxix. 12.
b || Mt. Matt. xxv. 18 only. Isa. v. 2.
c here only. Isa. xvi. 10. = προλήνιον, Isa. v. 2.
d || Mt. reff.
e || (Mt. bis) only. Exod. ii. 21. Sir. vii. 25.
f || Mt. reff.
g ||. Matt. xxv. 14, 15. Luke xv. 13 only †.
h Ps. i. 3. Lam. iv. 18. i Matt. xv. 27 al. ἐκ, Rev. xviii. 4. k || Mt. reff. l || L. bis. Luke i. 53. Gen. xxxi. 42. Deut. xvi. 16. m here only †. Sir. xxxv. (xxxii.) 8 only. n || L. John viii. 49. Acts v. 41. Rom. i. 24. ii. 23. James ii. 6 only. Ezek. xxviii. 24, 26 al. o Matt. xiii. 8 reff.
p (-νν-) Matt. x. 28 reff. q = Matt. iii. 17 reff. r || Mt. reff.

ανθρ. bef εφυτ. (*see* || *Luke*) BCΔℵ 33 copt æth, ανθρ. εποιησεν L: ανθ. (τις) εφυτ. αμπ. N(omg τις) 13. 69 lat-*c* Syr sah Orig$_1$: txt AD rel vulg lat-*a b f ff$_2$ g$_2$ i k* [*l q*] syr goth arm. ins αυτω bef φραγ. C²N 2-pe syr-w-ob sah arm Orig$_1$. (εξεδετο, so AB¹CKLℵ.) ins τοις bef γεωργ. D.

2. δουλον bef τω καιρω KNΠ Scr's d e w Syr. λαβοι ℵ¹. rec του καρπου (*see* || *Luke*), with A(D-[gr]) rel latt syr coptt goth æth arm: om Γ: txt BCLNΔℵ 33 lat-*f k* D-lat Syr. ινα απο τ. καρπου τ. αμπ. δωσουσιν αυτω (|| *Luke*) D lat-*a b c* &c(not $g_{1.2}$) (Syr) æth.

3. rec (for και) οι δε (*see* || *Luke*), with ACN rel syrr sah goth æth arm: txt BDLΔℵ 33 ev-y lat-*a b ff$_2$ i k q* copt. aft κενον ins προς αυτον D lat-*a b ff$_2$*.

4. om δουλον ℵ¹. και εκεινον DΔ. rec ins λιθοβολησαντες bef εκεφ. (*from* || *Matt*), with ACN rel syrr goth æth: om BDLΔℵ 1. 33 latt coptt arm. εκεφαλιωσαν BLℵ. rec (for ητιμασαν) απεστειλαν ητιμωμενον (*conformed to ver* 3), with ACN rel syrr goth [æth] arm: txt B D(-μηταν) Lℵ 33 latt coptt, ητωμασαν Δ.

5. rec aft και ins παλιν, with AN rel vulg lat-*f* [*l*] *q* syrr goth arm: om BCDLΔℵ 33 lat-*a b c ff$_2$ i k* coptt æth. aft απεστειλεν ins δουλον D lat-*a b* (*ff$_2$*) *i q*. rec (for οὓς) τους (twice), with ACN rel: txt B D(1st time) LΔℵ 1. 33.—αλλους δε D.—τον μεν δ. τους δε X¹(Treg). rec αποκτεινοντες (with Scr's g u, e sil): -κτενοντες NX rel, -κτιννουντες L, -κτιννυντες ℵ³ᵃ, -κταινοντες M S(Tischdf), -κτιναντες Δ, -κτεννυντες B: txt ACDEUVΓℵ¹.

6. rec aft ετι ins ουν, with ACDN rel vulg lat-[*l*] *q* syr: om BLΔℵ 1. 33. 69 lat-*b i* copt æth arm. rec (for ειχεν υιον) υιον εχων (*as more elegant*), with NX rel goth arm; εχων υιον AC¹D vulg lat-(*a*) *b ff$_2$* [*l*] (sah): txt BC²LΔℵ 33 syrr (æth). rec aft αγαπητον ins αυτου (*see* || *Luke*), with AN rel (lat-*c*) syr goth: om BCDLΔℵ vulg lat-*a b ff$_2$* [*i l q*] Syr coptt arm. rec ins και bef αυτον, with ACN rel syr goth: [om αυτον 1 copt:] txt BLX²Δℵ (lat-*a*) Syr æth (arm).—κακεινον απεστ. D vulg lat-*ff$_2$ i* [*l*]. rec προς αυτους bef εσχατον (*rearrangement consequent on inserting* και), with AN rel vulg syrr sah goth æth arm: om πρ. αυτ. D lat-*a ff$_2$ i k* [*q*]: txt BCLΔℵ 33. 69 copt. om οτι (|| *Matt*) LNΔ 1. 33 lat-*a b c* (Syr) sah. τ. υι. μ. bef εντρ. D lat-*a b i q*.

gelist, 'quoniam haud facile quisquam sibi aperte timorem adscribere consuevit.' Rinck. in Meyer.

Chap. XII. 1—12.] Parable of the vineyard let out to husbandmen. This parable is, for the most part, identical with that in Matt. xxi. 33—46, and Luke xx. 9—19. The *number*, and *treatment* of the servants sent, is enlarged on here;—and in ver. 4 there occurs the singular word **κεφαλαιόω**, which appears to be used by a solœcism for κεφαλίζω, '*to wound in the head.*' Some have rendered it, '*they made short work with him,*' which is the more usual sense of the word, but not probable here; for they *did not kill* him, but disgracefully used him. I must not allow any oppor-

7 ἐκεῖνοι δὲ οἱ [f] γεωργοὶ πρὸς [s] ἑαυτοὺς εἶπαν ὅτι οὗτός ABCDE
ἐστιν ὁ [t] κληρονόμος· [u] δεῦτε ἀποκτείνωμεν αὐτόν, καὶ FGHK LMNSU
ἡμῶν ἔσται ἡ [v] κληρονομία. 8 καὶ λαβόντες ἀπέκτειναν VXΓΔΠ ℵ 1. 33.
αὐτόν, καὶ ἐξέβαλον αὐτὸν ἔξω τοῦ [w] ἀμπελῶνος. 9 τί 69
ποιήσει ὁ [x] κύριος τοῦ [w] ἀμπελῶνος; ἐλεύσεται καὶ ἀπολέσει τοὺς [f] γεωργούς, καὶ δώσει τὸν [w] ἀμπελῶνα ἄλλοις.
10 οὐδὲ τὴν γραφὴν ταύτην ἀνέγνωτε; Λίθον ὃν [y] ἀπεδοκίμασαν οἱ οἰκοδομοῦντες, οὗτος ἐγενήθη [z] εἰς κεφαλὴν
γωνίας. 11 [a] παρὰ κυρίου ἐγένετο [b] αὕτη, καὶ ἔστιν [c] θαυμαστὴ [d] ἐν ὀφθαλμοῖς ἡμῶν. 12 καὶ [e] ἐζήτουν αὐτὸν
[f] κρατῆσαι, καὶ ἐφοβήθησαν τὸν ὄχλον· ἔγνωσαν γὰρ ὅτι
[g] πρὸς αὐτοὺς τὴν παραβολὴν εἶπεν. καὶ ἀφέντες αὐτὸν
ἀπῆλθον, 13 καὶ ἀποστέλλουσιν πρὸς αὐτόν τινὰς τῶν
Φαρισαίων καὶ τῶν Ἡρωδιανῶν, ἵνα αὐτὸν [h] ἀγρεύσωσιν
[i] λόγῳ. 14 καὶ ἐλθόντες λέγουσιν αὐτῷ Διδάσκαλε, οἴδαμεν ὅτι ἀληθὴς εἶ καὶ οὐ [k] μέλει σοι περὶ οὐδενός, οὐ γὰρ
[l] βλέπεις εἰς πρόσωπον ἀνθρώπων, ἀλλ' [m] ἐπ' ἀληθείας
τὴν [n] ὁδὸν τοῦ θεοῦ διδάσκεις. ἔξεστιν [o] κῆνσον Καίσαρι

s ch. x. 26 reff.
t ‖ Mt. reff.
u ‖ Mt. (Lk. v. r.) Matt. iv. 19. xi. 28 al. Gen. xxxvii. 20.
v ‖ Mt. reff.
w ver. 1.
x = Matt. ix. 38 reff.
y ‖ Mt. reff. Psa. cxvii. 22.
z Matt. xix. 5 reff.
a Luke ii. 1. John xvii. 7 al.
b fem., ‖ Mt. 1 Kings iv. 8. Ps. xxvi. 4.
c ‖ Mt., from l.c. John ix. 30. 1 Pet. ii. 9. Rev. xv. 1, 3 only. Exod. xxxiv. 10.
d ‖ Mt. 1 Macc. i. 12.
e ‖ Mt. Luke v. 18 al.
f ‖ Mt. reff.
g = Acts xxiii. 30 b.
h here only. Prov. v. 22. vi. 25, 26.
i = ‖. Acts xiv. 12. 2 Cor. x. 10. Col. iv. 6.
k ‖ Mt. reff.
l ‖ Mt. 2 Cor. x. 7.
m ‖ L. Luke iv. 25. Acts iv. 27. x. 34 al. Isa. xxxvii. 18.
n ‖. (Acts xviii. 26 v. r.) see Acts xiii. 10. Ps. cxviii. 15 al.
o ‖ Mt. bis. Matt. xvii. 25 only †.

7. for εκεινοι δε οι, οι δε D vulg lat-*a b* &c sah æth arm. aft γεωργ. ins ιδοντες N. rec ειπ. bef πρ. εαυ., with ADN rel latt syrr coptt goth: txt BCL Δ(αυτ.) ℵ 1. 33 (69 ev-y). (ειπαν, so BCDLΔℵ.) om οτι (‖ *Matt Luke*) D 1 latt sah æth.

8. rec 1st αυτον bef απεκτειναν, with ADN rel vulg lat-*ff*$_2$ copt goth arm: txt BCLΔℵ ev-y lat-*i k q* sah. [εξεβαλαν B.] rec om 2nd αυτον (*as superfl*), with ℵ rel vulg lat-*b k* [*l*] arm: ins ABCDMNΓΠ lat-*a c ff*$_2$ *q* syrr copt goth æth.

9. rec aft τι ins ουν (*from* ‖ *Matt*), with ACDNℵ rel latt [syrr &c]: om BL lat-*g*$_2$ copt. aft γεωργους ins τουτους (‖ *Luke*) C[2] 33 ev-y syrr; εκεινους GN 1 lat-*c* æth.

12. τ. παρ. bef πρ. αυτ. A sah. απηλθαν D.

13. om πρ. αυτ. D lat-*a c i k q*. for αγρευσωσιν, παγιδευσωσιν (‖ *Matt*) D 2-pe.

14. rec (for και) οι δε (*to indicate the change of subject*), with AN rel syrr goth arm: txt BCDLΔℵ 33 lat-*c ff*$_2$ *i k* (*a b* [*q*]) coptt æth. for ελθ. λεγ. αυτ., επηρωτων αυτον οι φαρισαιοι D: ελθοντες ηρξαντο ερωταν αυτον εν δολω λεγοντες G 1. 69. αλλα DLΔ. ins ειπη ουν ημιν ει bef εξεστιν (‖ *Matt*) (C)D gat lat-*a b c ff*$_2$ *i* [*q*] syr-w-ast; ειπον ουν ημιν MN tol lat-*g*$_2$ arm.—ειπον C[1]: om ει C[2].

tunity to pass of directing attention to the *sort* of difference, in similarity, between these three reports,—and observing that no origin of that difference is imaginable, except the *gradual deflection of accounts from a common, or a parallel, source.* See notes on Matt. throughout. **9.**] **ἐλεύσεται κ.τ.λ.** is not the answer of the Pharisees, or of the people, as the corresponding sentence in ‖ Matt. (see note there), but, here and in ‖ Luke, a continuation of our Lord's discourse. After ver. 11 comes in Matt. vv. 43—45. **12.**] Meyer makes **ὁ ὄχλος** (and ὁ λαός in ‖ Luke) the subject to **ἔγνωσαν**, but I think quite unnecessarily. The *fear of the people* is increased by the consciousness on the part of the rulers that He had spoken the parable against *them*: they are as men *convicted before the people.*

13—17.] Reply concerning the lawfulness of tribute to Cæsar. Matt. xxii. 15—22. Luke xx. 20—26. The parable of the wedding-garment, Matt. xxii. 1—14, is omitted. The only matters requiring additional remark in these verses are,—**13.**] **λόγῳ** is the instrument wherewith they would ἀγρεύειν: the verb being one taken from the chase. They wished to lay hold on him by some saying of His. **14.**] **ἐπ' ἀληθ., truly,—indeed,—**

[p] δοῦναι ἢ οὔ; δῶμεν ἢ μὴ δῶμεν; 15 ὁ δὲ εἰδὼς αὐτῶν
τὴν [q] ὑπόκρισιν εἶπεν αὐτοῖς Τί με [r] πειράζετε; φέρετέ μοι
[s] δηνάριον ἵνα ἴδω. 16 οἱ δὲ ἤνεγκαν. καὶ λέγει αὐτοῖς
Τίνος ἡ [t] εἰκὼν αὕτη καὶ ἡ [u] ἐπιγραφή; Οἱ δὲ εἶπαν αὐτῷ
Καίσαρος. 17 ὁ δὲ Ἰησοῦς εἶπεν [v] Τὰ Καίσαρος [w] ἀπόδοτε
Καίσαρι, καὶ [v] τὰ τοῦ θεοῦ τῷ θεῷ. καὶ [x] ἐθαύμαζον [x] ἐπ'
αὐτῷ. 18 Καὶ ἔρχονται Σαδδουκαῖοι πρὸς αὐτόν, [y] οἵτινες
λέγουσιν [z] ἀνάστασιν μὴ εἶναι, καὶ ἐπηρώτων αὐτὸν λέγοντες 19 Διδάσκαλε, [a] Μωυσῆς ἔγραψεν ἡμῖν ὅτι ἐάν τινος
...xii. 19 (appy) N. ἀδελφὸς ἀποθάνῃ καὶ [b] καταλίπῃ γυναῖκα καὶ μὴ [c] ἀφῇ
τέκνον, [d] ἵνα [e] λάβῃ ὁ ἀδελφὸς αὐτοῦ τὴν γυναῖκα καὶ
[f] ἐξαναστήσῃ [g] σπέρμα τῷ ἀδελφῷ αὐτοῦ. 20 ἑπτὰ ἀδελφοὶ

p = ||. Luke xxiii. 2.
q Matt. xxiii. 28 reff. Heb. vii. 4.
r Matt. iv. 1 and passim.
s Matt. xx. 2 reff.
t || Mt. reff.
u || ch. xv. 26 || L. only †.
v Matt. xi. 17 reff.
w = Rom. xiii. 7. Deut. xxiii. 12.
x || L. Luke iv. 22. ix. 43. Acts iii. 12. Isa. xiv. 16.
y = Matt. vii. 15 reff.
z || Mt. reff.
a Deut. xxv. 5.
b = || L. Prov. xx. 7.
c = Matt. xxiv. 2. Ps. xvi. 14.
d = ch. xi. 16 reff. xiii. 34. xv. 5 || only. Gen. xix. 32, 34.
e || L. Gen. iv. 19. Hos. i. 2, 3.
f = || L. (aor. intr., Acts
g = ||. Gen. iv. 25.

δουναι bef κηνσ. καισ. (|| *Matt*) BC (D, see below) LΔℵ 33 latt syr coptt æth: txt AN rel.—ημας δουναι επικαιφαλαιον καισ. D. om δωμ. η μη δ. D lat-*a b c* ff_2 g_1 *i l* æth: om η μη δ. 225 vulg lat-g_2 goth arm-mss.

15. aft ο δε ins ιησους DG **1**. 69 lat-(*a*) *b c* (ff_2) *i* [*q*] goth (æth) arm. ειδων *videns* Dℵ[1] 69 lat-*b c* ff_2 *i q* goth, ιδως Nℵ[3a]. aft πειραζετε ins υποκριται FGN **1**. 33. 69 syr-w-ast arm. aft δηναρ. ins ωδε ℵ[1].

16. om 2nd οι δε (|| *Matt*) AD vulg lat-*a b i* [*l q*]. (ειπαν, so BC D-gr L X(Treg) Δℵ: λεγουσιν (|| *Matt*) A vulg lat-*b i* [*l*] *q* D-lat.)

17. rec (for ο δε) και αποκριθεις, with AN rel syr goth arm: αποκρ. δε ο D vulg lat-*a b* [*i q*]: txt BCLΔℵ 33 (lat-*c* Syr) sah (æth). rec aft ειπ. ins αυτοις (|| *Matt*), with ACNℵ rel [vss]: om BD. rec αποδοτε bef τα καισαρος (*from* || *Matt Luke*), with A(D)N rel [(latt syr)] sah goth æth arm: txt BCLΔℵ (Syr) copt.—ins του bef καισαρος and τω bef καισαρι D. rec εθαυμασαν (|| *Matt*), with ACN rel lat-*k* syr sah goth: εθαυμαζοντο D[1]: εξεθαυμαζον Bℵ: txt D-corr LΔ latt Syr copt. επ' αυτον D 28.

18. πρ. αυτ. bef σαδ. D 28. 106 vulg lat-*b* [*i l q*]. rec επηρωτησαν (|| *Matt Luke*), with AN rel lat-*c* syr goth sah: txt B C(-τουν) DLΔℵ 33 vulg lat-*a b* ff_2 $g_{1.2}$ *k* Syr copt.

19. ημιν bef εγραψεν D vulg lat-*b* ff_2 *i* [*l*]. om οτι D-gr(*ut* D-lat) 69 sah. καταλιψει C: -ψη ℵ: εχη D 28 lat-*a b c* [ff_2 *i q*] *k*. rec τεκνα (|| *Matt*), with ACDℵ[1] rel vulg lat-*b i q* syrr sah goth æth: txt BLΔ ℵ[3a](but -να restored) **1** lat-*a c* ff_2 *k* copt arm. rec τεκν. bef μη αφη, with AD rel latt syrr copt goth arm: txt BCLΔℵ 33 sah (æth). rec aft γυναικα ins αυτου (*from* || *Matt*), with AD rel latt syrr sah goth æth arm: om BCLΔℵ **1** lat-*k* copt. εξαναστησει (*itacism?*) ACH 69, αναστησει Γ.

20. elz aft επτα ins ουν (*from* || *Luke*), with C[2](D) vulg lat-*c* æth arm; δε (*from* || *Matt*) 106(Sz) lat-*a* syr coptt: om ABC[1]ℵ rel lat-*k* Syr goth.—ησαν ουν παρ ημειν ζ αδελφοι D lat-*a b i* [*q*]: παρ ημιν also ℵ-corr[1](marked for erasure by ℵ[3]) 69 Scr's e lat-*c* syr-mg copt [arm].

see reff. and ver. 32. **δῶμεν ἢ μὴ δ.;** the originality of the report is shewn by these words. They wish to drive our Lord to an absolute affirmation or negation.

15.] **δηνάρ.**, Mark and Luke, = τὸ νόμισ. τοῦ κήνσ., Matt. 17.] **ἐθαύμαζον**, imperfect, is graphic. This was going on, when the next incident began.

18—27.] Reply to the Sadducees concerning the Resurrection. Matt. xxii. 23—33. Luke xx. 27—40. The three reports are very much alike in matter, and now and then coincide almost verbally (Matt. ver. 27, Luke ver. 32. Mark ver. 23 end, Luke ver. 33). The chief additions are found in Luke, vv. 34—36, where see notes, and on Matt. throughout.

19. **ἔγραψεν . . . . ἵνα**] This is one of the cases where purpose and purport are mingled in the ἵνα. See on 1 Cor. xiv. 13. It is better to take it so than with Meyer to suppose ἵνα dependent on *volo* under-

ἦσαν. καὶ ὁ πρῶτος [e] ἔλαβεν γυναῖκα καὶ ἀποθνήσκων
οὐκ [c] ἀφῆκεν [g] σπέρμα. 21 καὶ ὁ δεύτερος [e] ἔλαβεν αὐτὴν
καὶ ἀπέθανεν μὴ [b] καταλιπὼν σπέρμα, καὶ ὁ τρίτος ὡσαύτως, 22 καὶ οἱ ἑπτὰ οὐκ [c] ἀφῆκαν σπέρμα. ἔσχατον
πάντων καὶ ἡ γυνὴ ἀπέθανεν. 23 ἐν τῇ [z] ἀναστάσει ὅταν
ἀναστῶσιν, τίνος αὐτῶν ἔσται γυνή; οἱ γὰρ ἑπτὰ [h] ἔσχον
αὐτὴν γυναῖκα. 24 ἔφη αὐτοῖς ὁ Ἰησοῦς Οὐ διὰ τοῦτο
[i] πλανᾶσθε μὴ εἰδότες τὰς [k] γραφὰς μηδὲ την δύναμιν τοῦ
θεοῦ; 25 ὅταν γὰρ [l] ἐκ νεκρῶν [l] ἀναστῶσιν, οὔτε γαμοῦσιν
οὔτε [m] γαμίζονται, ἀλλ' εἰσὶν ὡς ἄγγελοι οἱ ἐν τοῖς οὐρανοῖς. 26 περὶ δὲ τῶν νεκρῶν ὅτι ἐγείρονται, οὐκ ἀνέγνωτε
ἐν τῇ βίβλῳ Μωυσέως [n] ἐπὶ τοῦ [o] βάτου, πῶς εἶπεν αὐτῷ
ὁ θεὸς λέγων [p] Ἐγὼ ὁ θεὸς Ἀβραὰμ καὶ θεὸς Ἰσαὰκ καὶ

ABCDE FGHK LMSUV XΓΔΠℵ 1. 33. 69

h = Matt. xiv. 4 reff.
i = ∥ Mt. reff.
k John v. 39 reff.
l ch. vi. 14 reff.
m ∥ Mt. Luke xvii. 27. 1 Cor. vii. 38 (?) only +.
n = (see note) ∥ L. only. see Acts xxiv. 20.
o ∥ L. Luke vi. 44. Acts vii. 30, 35 only. Exod. iii. 2—4. Deut. xxxiii. 16. Job xxxi. 40 only.
p Exod. iii. 2.

for *πρωτος*, *εις* ℵ^1(txt ℵ-corr$^{1.3}$). for *αποθνησκων*, *απεθανεν και* D 1 latt syr-txt sah.

21. rec (for *μη καταλιπων*) *και ουδε αυτος αφηκε* (*to conform to ver* 20: *cf the varns*), with A rel vulg lat-*a* (*b ff*$_2$) $g_{1.2}$ syrr arm; *κ. ουδε αυ. ουκ αφηκεν* D[-gr] ev-z; *κ. ουδ. ουτος αφ.* X lat-*a* D-lat goth: om lat-*k*: txt BCL[ℵ] 33 lat-*c* coptt (æth). om *κ. ο τρ. ωσαυτως* D lat-*ff*$_2$ *i*.

22. om 1st *και* X lat-*a i*. rec aft *και* ins *ελαβον αυτην*, with E M-marg Δ-marg rel (lat-*a i* Syr) æth; *ελαβ. αυ. ωσαυτως και*, A (vulg) lat-*l* syr goth: *ωσαυτ. ελ. αυ.* D: om BCLM^{1}Δ^{1}ℵ 33. 69 lat-*c k* coptt arm. rec ins *και* bef *ουκ αφηκ.*, with DM^1 rel vulg lat-*a c i l* syrr sah goth æth: om BCLΔℵ 33 lat-(*b* ?) *k* copt arm. (*Txt was evidently the origl, and has been variously emended from the context; this agst Mey and De W.*) *αφηκεν* ℵ^1 Scr's c w. om *εσχ. παντων* D. rec *εσχατη* (*corrn to suit γυνη, not the neut from* ∥), with A rel vulg lat-$g_{1.2}$ [*l*] syr goth arm: txt BCGHKLΔΠℵ 1. 33. 69 Syr copt æth. rec *απεθανε* bef *κ. η γυνη* (*from* ∥ *Matt*). with A rel vulg lat-$g_{1.2}$ [*l*] *q* syrr copt goth æth arm: txt BCDLΔℵ 1. 33. 69 ev-y lat-*a b ff*$_2$ *i k* (sah).

23. rec aft *τη* ins *ουν* (*from* ∥ *Matt Luke*), with AC^{2}KMΠ (33, e sil) Syr syr-w-ast æth arm: aft *αναστ.* DG 1 lat-*a ff*$_2$ *l*: om BC^{1}ℵ rel lat-*k q* goth. om *οταν αναστωσιν* (*as superfl and not in* ∥: *a* gloss *on εν τη αναστασει would be out of the question, and the pleonasm is in Mark's manner*) BCDLΔℵ 33 (lat-*b c k*) Syr coptt æth. (ins bef *εν τη αν.* 13. 69. 346.) ins *η* bef *γυνη* AD^1.

24. rec (for *εφη αυτ. ο ιησ.*) *αποκριθεις ο ιησ. ειπεν αυτ.* (*from* ∥ *Matt*: *cf* D *&c*), with A rel vulg lat-*b c ff*$_2$ [*i l q*] syr goth æth arm Orig_1; so, but *αποκ. δε*, D 1. 69 lat-*a*: txt BCLΔℵ 33 Syr copt. for *ειδ.*, *γινωσκοντες* D Orig. aft *θεου* ins *οιδατε* D.

25. *αναστησουσιν resurrexerint* D^1(txt D^2). om *ουτε γαμουσιν* (*homœotel*) ℵ^1 (ins ℵ-corr^1). for 1st and 2nd *ουτε*, *ου* and *ουδε* D. rec *γαμισκονται*, with XΠ rel Orig; *εκγαμισκονται* AFH: *γαμιζουσιν* D 2-pe: txt BCGLUΔℵ 1 Damasc. ins *οι* bef *αγγελοι* B Orig_1. om *οι* (*absorbed by last letters of αγγελοι*: *see also* ∥ *Matt*) CDFKLMUΔΠℵ 1. 33. 69 latt syr copt æth: ins AB rel Syr sah goth arm Orig.

26. rec (for *του*) *της* (*from* ∥ *Luke*), with D M(Treg, expr) 33(e sil) Orig_3: txt ABCℵ rel. rec (for *πως*) *ως* (*from* ∥ *Luke*), with AD rel Orig_1: txt BCLUΔℵ. om 2nd *ο* D Orig_2[ins_1]. rec ins *ο* bef 3rd and 4th *θεος* (*see* ∥ *Matt*), with ACℵ rel Orig_1: om BD Orig_2.

stood. **23.**] **ὅταν ἀναστῶσιν**, here not, '*when men* (the dead) *shall rise*,' but **when they** (the wife and seven brothers) **shall rise**: see on ver. 25.

24.] **διὰ τοῦτο** refers to the following participle **μὴ εἰδότες**: **for this reason . . . . because ye know not.** **25.**] The **ὅταν . . . . ἀναστῶσιν** here is general, not as in ver. 23: see note there. **26.**] **ἐπὶ τοῦ βάτου** (so also (τῆς) Luke);—either, '*in the chapter* containing the history of God appearing in the bush,' or, '*when he was at* the bush.' The former is the more probable, on account of the construction of the verse in our text. In Luke, if we had his account alone, the other rendering

θεὸς Ἰακώβ; 27 οὐκ ἔστιν θεὸς νεκρῶν, ἀλλὰ ζώντων· q Matt. xvi. 14. xviii. 24 al.
πολὺ ⁱ πλανᾶσθε. 28 Καὶ προςελθὼν q εἷς τῶν γραμ- r ch. ix. 10 reff.
ματέων ἀκούσας αὐτῶν r συνζητούντων, εἰδὼς ὅτι s καλῶς s = Matt. xv. 7 reff.
ἀπεκρίθη αὐτοῖς ἐπηρώτησεν αὐτὸν t Ποία ἐστὶν u ἐντολὴ t = Matt. xxi. 23 reff. u Matt. v. 19 al. Lev. iv. 13.
πρώτη v πάντων; 29 ἀπεκρίθη ὁ Ἰησοῦς ὅτι πρώτη ἐστὶν v neut., 1 Cor. xv. 8.
...ει[ς] εστιν C. Ἄκουε Ἰσραήλ, κύριος ὁ θεὸς ἡμῶν κύριος εἷς ἐστιν,
30 καὶ ἀγαπήσεις κύριον τὸν θεόν σου w ἐξ ὅλης τῆς καρ- w Eph. vi. 6. Col. iii. 23. Deut. vi. 5.
δίας σου, καὶ ἐξ ὅλης τῆς ψυχῆς σου, καὶ ἐξ ὅλης τῆς

27. rec ins ο bef θεος (*see* || *Matt*), with ACℵ rel $Orig_1$: txt BDKLM² X(e sil) ΔΠ $Orig_3$. rec ins θεος bef ζωντων, with EGHM¹SVΓ lat-*q* syr æth: om ABCDℵ rel latt Syr coptt goth arm $Orig_4$. rec aft ζωντων ins υμεις ουν (*for connexion and emphasis*), with AD rel vulg lat-*a b* ff_2 $g_{1.2}$ syrr sah æth arm; υμεις δε G 1 lat-*c* goth: om BCLΔℵ lat-*k* copt.

28. for αυτων, αυτω D¹(txt D-corr¹ ?). aft συνζητουντων ins και D 28 vulg lat-*b* ff_2 Syr. for ειδως, ιδων CDLℵ¹ 1. 69 latt syrr goth æth arm. rec αυτοις bef απεκρ. (*see* || *Matt*), with AD rel latt goth arm: txt BCLUΔ[ℵ] 1. 33. 69 syrr coptt æth. aft αυτον ins λεγων διδασκαλε D lat-*b c* ff_2 g_2 *i k q*. rec πρωτη π. bef εντολη, with A rel vulg lat-g_1: εντολη πρωτη D: txt BCLUΔℵ 33 syrr copt æth. rec (for παντων) πασων, with M¹ (Scr's l m n, e sil): om D 1. 69 lat-*a b c* ff_2 *i k q* arm: txt ABCℵ rel vulg lat-g_1.

29. rec ο δε ιησ. bef απεκριθη, addg αυτω, with AC rel vulg syr goth [Aug]: αποκριθεις δε ο ιησ. ειπεν αυτω D lat-*b* ff_2 (sah æth): txt BLΔℵ 33 copt. om οτι D 1 lat-*a b c* ff_2 *k* Syr arm [$Marcell_1$ Aug]. rec aft πρωτη ins πασων των εντολων (with Scr's l m n, e sil); παντων των εντ. E rel Scr's-mss Syr; παντων εντολη AKM²UΠ 33; πασων εντολη M¹: παντων εντολη εστιν αυτη C lat-ff_2: παντων X arm: ins παντων bef πρωτ. D 91 lat-*a b i*: txt BLΔℵ copt. rec om 1st εστιν, with AD rel Marcell: ins B(C)LΔℵ 69 vulg lat-*c* ff_2 coptt æth.

30. om της (3 times) B: om της (bef καρδ.) D¹(insd above the line) X. om κ. εξ ολ. τ. ψυ. σου KΠ¹ 248-53 Scr's c e v w¹ lat-*k* Marcell-ms. om κ. εξ ολ. τ. διαν. σου DH lat-*c* ff_2 g_1 *k* syr-jer arm [Marcell] $Cypr_3$: ins aft καρδ. σ. A.

might be admissible, 'Moses testified, at the bush:' but this will not answer in our text.

28—34.] Reply concerning the great commandment. Matt. xxii. 34—40, but with differing circumstances. There the question appears as that of one among the Pharisees' adherents, who puts this question, πειράζων αὐτόν,—and in consequence of the Pharisees coming up to the strife, after He had discomfited the Sadducees. I should be disposed to take Mark's as the strictly accurate account, seeing that there is nothing in the question which indicates enmity, and our Lord's answer, ver. 34, plainly precludes it. The man, from hearing them disputing, came up, and formed one of the band who gathered together for the purpose of tempting Him. Mark's report, which here is wholly unconnected in origin with Matt.'s, is that of some one who had taken accurate note of the circumstances and character of the man: Matt.'s is more general, not entering, as this, into individual motives, but classing the question broadly among the various "temptations" of our Lord at this time. **28.**] The motive, as shewn by the subordination of ἀκούσας to προσελθών, and of εἰδώς to ἐπηρώτησεν, seems to have been, *admiration of our Lord's wise answer*, and a desire to be instructed further by Him. **ἐντ. πρώτη πάντ.**] This was one of the μάχαι νομικαί (Titus iii. 9),—*which was the greatest commandment*. The Scribes had many frivolous enumerations and classifications of the commands of the law. **πάντων**, not πασῶν: **πρώτη-πάντων** is treated almost as *one word*, so that **πάντων** does not belong to ἐντ. understood, but, q. d. 'first-of-all of the commandments.' **29 f.**] Mark cites the passage entire,—Matt. only the command itself:—compare the LXX. In this citation the Vat. reading διανοίας and the Alex. καρδίας are *combined*: and ἰσχύος = δυνάμεως. "Thou shalt love the Lord with spirit, soul, and body:" with the inner spirit, and the outer life. This is *faith working by love*: for κ. ὁ θ. ἡμῶν is the language of *faith*. **30.**] ἰσχύς is the inner spiritual strength of the heart: see Beck's useful little manual, Die bib-

k ||. Luke i. 51. Eph. iv. 18 al. Deut. xxix. 18.
y Levit. xix. 18.
z ver. 28.
a ver. 14.
b = Gospp. here [John viii. 10 rec.] only. Acts viii. 1. xv. 28. xxvii. 22 only. Deut. iv. 35.
c Luke ii. 47. 1 Cor. i. 19 (from Isa. xxix. 14). Eph. iii. 4. Col. i. 9. ii. 2. 2 Tim. ii. 7 only. Prov. ii. 2.
d Matt. vi. 25. xii. 41, 42. Heb. xi. 4.

ABDEF GHKL MSUV ΧΓΔΠℵ 1. 33. 69

[x] διανοίας σου, καὶ ἐξ ὅλης τῆς ἰσχύος σου. 31 δευτέρα
αὕτη [y] Ἀγαπήσεις τὸν πλησίον σου ὡς σεαυτόν. μείζων
τούτων ἄλλη ἐντολὴ οὐκ ἔστιν. 32 καὶ εἶπεν αὐτῷ ὁ
γραμματεὺς [z] Καλῶς, διδάσκαλε· [a] ἐπ᾽ ἀληθείας εἶπας ὅτι
εἷς ἐστιν, καὶ οὐκ ἔστιν ἄλλος [b] πλὴν αὐτοῦ. 33 καὶ τὸ
ἀγαπᾶν αὐτὸν [w] ἐξ ὅλης τῆς καρδίας, καὶ ἐξ ὅλης τῆς
[c] συνέσεως, καὶ ἐξ ὅλης τῆς ψυχῆς, καὶ ἐξ ὅλης τῆς
ἰσχύος, καὶ τὸ ἀγαπᾶν τὸν πλησίον ὡς ἑαυτόν, [d] πλεῖόν
ἐστιν πάντων τῶν [e] ὁλοκαυτωμάτων καὶ θυσιῶν. 34 καὶ
ὁ Ἰησοῦς ἰδὼν αὐτὸν ὅτι [f] νουνεχῶς ἀπεκρίθη, εἶπεν αὐτῷ
Οὐ [g] μακρὰν εἶ ἀπὸ τῆς βασιλείας τοῦ θεοῦ. καὶ οὐδεὶς

only †. e Heb. x. 6, 8 (from Ps. xxxix. 6) only. Exod. x. 25. 1 Kings xv. 22. f here
g Matt. viii. 30. Acts xvii. 27 al. Josh. ix. 22.

rec at end ins *αυτη πρωτη εντολη* (*see* || *Matt*), with AD rel (vulg) lat-*b c i* (*k*) syrr goth æth [arm] $Cypr_3$ Hil : *αυ. πρ. παντων εντ.* KUΠ 33 Scr's d p w : om BELΔℵ (lat-*a*) coptt.
31. rec ins *και* bef *δευτερα*, addg *ομοια* (*see* || *Matt*), with A rel lat-*c q* syrr goth æth arm Marcell $Cypr_3$: *δευτ. δε ομ. ταυτη* D (Scr's f ev-x) : txt BL Δ(*η δευτ.*) ℵ coptt. add *εστιν* ℵ. aft *μειζων* ins *δε* Lℵ lat-*b i* Hil. *αλλη* bef *εντολη* D lat-*c* : om *εντ.* U 13.
32. om 1st *και* B Syr coptt. *ειπ.* bef *διδασκ.* D lat-*a b c i* [*q*] Hil. *ειπες* DEFHLVXΔΠ²ℵ¹. rec aft 1st *εστιν* ins *θεος*, with EFH vulg-ed lat-*a b c* ff_2 *i* syr-w-ast coptt arm Hil ; *ο θεος* DG 69 Marcell : om ABℵ rel am(with em fuld ing prag &c) lat-*l* Syr goth æth. om *αλλος* D lat-*a* $Marcell_1$.
33. om 1st *της* BUX. aft *καρδιας* ins *σου* Lℵ copt. for *συνεσεως*, *δυναμεως* D 2-pe lat-*a i q* : *ισχυος* 1. 33. om 3rd *και* to *ψυχης* BLΔℵ 1. 33 lat-*a* copt arm Marcell (*omd from homœotel. As Mey remarks, if it were an insn from ver* 30, *it would prob be placed aft καρδιας, as it stands there*). aft *ψυχ.* ins *αυτου* D-gr (*tua* D-lat). om 4th *και* to *ισχυος* D 33 [Hil]. om *της* (bef *ισχυος*) ℵ ev-P. aft *πλησ.* ins *σου* Δ ℵ¹(ℵ³ᵃ disapproving). **σεαυτον** ADL S[and U](Tischdf) ΓΔ²ℵ lat-*k*. for *πλειον*, *περισσοτερον* BLΔℵ 33 sah(appy). rec ins *των* bef *θυσιων*, with LMΔℵ 1. 33. 69 : om ABD rel.
34. om *αυτον* DLΔℵ 1. 33 vulg lat-*b c* ff_2 *i k l* syr æth arm [Chr] Hil. om *ει* L ℵ¹(ins ℵ-corr¹(appy)³ᵇ) : *απο τ. βασ.* bef *ει* Δℵ³ᵃ.

lische Seelenlehre, p. 110. **31.**] Our Lord adds this second, as an application or bringing home of the first. The first is the *Sun*, so to speak, of the spiritual life :—this the *lesser light*, which reflects the shining of that other. It is *like* to it, inasmuch as both are *laws of love:* both deduced from the great and highest love: both dependent on 'I am the Lord thy God,' Levit. xix. 18. Stier sets forth beautifully the strong contrast between the *requirements of these two commands*, and the *then state of the Jewish Church:* see John vii. 19. **32, 33.**] The Scribe shews that he had entered into the true spirit of our Lord's answer; and replies in admiration at its wisdom. Observe **συνέσεως** corresponding to *διανοίας*: and see Beck, p. 60. **ὁλοκ. κ. θ.**, the things to which the outward literal observers paid all their attention. **34.**] **νουνεχῶς**—Attice *νουνεχόντως*, opposed to ἀφρόνως, Isocr. v. 7 (Meyer). **οὐ μακρὰν . . .**] This man had hold of that principle in which Law and Gospel are one: he stood as it were *at the door* of the Kingdom of God. He only wanted (but the want was indeed a serious one) repentance and faith to be *within it.* The Lord shews us here that even outside His flock, those who can answer *νουνεχῶς*—who have knowledge of the *spirit* of the great command of Law and Gospel, are *nearer* to being of his flock, than the *formalists* :—but then, as Bengel adds, 'Si non procul es, intra : alias *præstiterit, procul fuisse.*' **καὶ οὐδεὶς . . . .**] This is apparently out of its place here, as it is *after the question which now follows*, that Matt. relates this discomfiture of his adversaries. We must not however conclude too hastily, especially where the minute accuracy of Mark is at stake. The question just asked *was the last put to our*

οὐκέτι [h] ἐτόλμα αὐτὸν ἐπερωτῆσαι. 35 Καὶ ἀποκριθεὶς ὁ
T_d xii. 35 (appy)... Ἰησοῦς ἔλεγεν διδάσκων ἐν τῷ ἱερῷ Πῶς λέγουσιν οἱ
γραμματεῖς ὅτι ὁ [i] χριστὸς [j] υἱὸς [j] Δαυείδ ἐστιν; 36 αὐτὸς
Δαυεὶδ εἶπεν [k] ἐν τῷ [k] πνεύματι τῷ ἁγίῳ [l] Εἶπεν Κύριος
τῷ κυρίῳ μου Κάθισον [m] ἐκ δεξιῶν μου ἕως ἂν θῶ τοὺς
ἐχθρούς σου [n] ὑποκάτω τῶν ποδῶν σου. 37 αὐτὸς Δαυεὶδ
...xii. 37 (appy) T_d. [o] λέγει αὐτὸν κύριον, καὶ [p] πόθεν αὐτοῦ ἐστιν υἱός; καὶ ὁ
[q] πολὺς ὄχλος ἤκουεν αὐτοῦ [r] ἡδέως. 38 καὶ ἐν τῇ διδαχῇ
αὐτοῦ ἔλεγεν [s] Βλέπετε [t] ἀπὸ τῶν γραμματέων τῶν θελόντων ἐν [u] στολαῖς περιπατεῖν, καὶ [v] ἀσπασμοὺς ἐν ταῖς
ἀγοραῖς 39 καὶ [w] πρωτοκαθεδρίας ἐν ταῖς συναγωγαῖς καὶ

h || Mt. reff.
i Matt. xi. 25 reff.
j Matt. i. 1.
k = || Mt. see Luke ii. 27. Rev. i. 10.
l Psa. cix. 1.
m Matt. xx. 21, 23 reff.
n || Mt. reff.
o ch. x. 18 reff.
p = Matt. xiii. 27, 54, 56. xv. 33. Luke i. 43.
q = here only.
r ch. vi. 20. 2 Cor. xi. 19 only. Prov. iii. 24. (ἥδιστα, 2 Cor. xii. 9, 15.)
s ch. viii. 15 reff.
t Matt. vii. 15. Luke xii. 1 al.
u ||. ch. xvi. 5. Luke xv. 22. Rev. vi. 11. vii. 9, 13 bis, 14. xxii. 14 only. Jon. iii. 6.
v Matt. xxiii. 7 reff.
w ||. Luke xi. 43 only †.

om ουκετι D-gr ev-z tol coptt: ετολμα bef ουκετι 69 lat-*a*. επερ. bef αυτον א[1] ev-x lat-*c*.

35. om ελεγεν and aft ιερω ins ειπεν D lat-*b* (*c*) *q*. rec εστιν bef δαυειδ, with A rel [latt syrr goth]: txt BDLM[2]T_dUΔא 1. 33. 69 lat-*k* copt.

36. rec aft αυτος ins γαρ, with A rel vulg lat-*b* *i* [*q*] syrr goth æth Hil: om BLT_dΔא 69 lat-*a* *k* copt: και ουτος (*see* || *Luke*), D(*et ipse* D-lat) arm. om εν B. om τω (twice) A rel: (1st T_d:) ins BDLUΔא 33 arm. (*See* || *Matt, where* πν. *is anarthrous.*) for 2nd ειπεν, λεγει A D-gr rel(F def) lat-*k* *q* goth: txt BLM[2]T_d UXΓΔא 1. 33. 69 latt syrr coptt æth arm Hil. (*It appears to have been read sometimes* λεγει *in the Psalm: Justin, according to Tischdf, has cited it so twice:*—D *reads* λεγει *in* || *Luke, so that the readg is by no means certain.*) rec ins ο bef κυρ. (*corrn to* LXX), with AT_dא rel: om BD. rec (for καθισον) καθου (LXX *and* || *Matt Luke*), with ADT_dא rel: txt B. for αν θω, θησω D-corr[1](θωσω D[1]). εκχθους (sic) D(but κ marked for erasure). rec (for υποκατω) υποποδιον (LXX), with Aא rel latt syrr goth æth arm Hil: txt B D-gr T_d coptt.

37. rec aft αυτος ins ουν (*for connexn, from* ||), with A rel vulg (lat-*b*) Syr syr-w-ast æth: om BDLT_dΔא lat-*a* (*c*) *i* *k* *q* coptt Hil. for ποθεν, πως M[1]א[1] 1. 33. 69. 238 lat-*b* sah æth arm. rec υιος bef αυτου εστιν (|| *Matt*), with Aא rel lat-*b* syrr coptt (æth): εστι υι. αυτ. D vulg lat-*a* *c* *ff*$_2$ [*i* *q*] arm Hil: εστ. αυτ. υι. Δ 238 (lat-*k*): txt BLT_d. om ο Dא 2-pe. ηκουσεν [M and T(Tischdf)] א [vulg (goth)]. ηδ. αυτ. ηκ. D[pref και] (vulg) lat-*b* *ff*$_2$ *i* *q*.

38. rec aft ελεγεν ins αυτοις, placing them bef εν τ. δ. αυτου, with A rel vulg lat-*q* syr sah goth (æth): ο δε διδασκων αμα ελ. αυτ. D-gr lat-*a* *b* *i*: txt BLΔא lat-*e* *k* copt. (order as txt but adds αυτοις 33 Syr.) for των θελοντων, και των τελωνων D-gr. (*et qui volunt* D-lat.) aft αγορ. ins ποιεισθαι *facitis* D.

Lord, and therefore the notice of its *being the last* comes in fitly here. The enquiry which follows did more than silence their *questioning:* it silenced their *answering too:* both which things Matt. combines as the result of this day, in his ver. 46. **ἐπερωτῆσαι,** not, 'to ask him any *more* questions:' see on ch. xi. 29.

35—37.] The Pharisees baffled by a question concerning Christ and David. Matt. xxii. 41—46. Luke xx. 41—44. The reports are apparently independent of any common original, and hardly agree verbally in the citation from the LXX. See notes on Matt. 35.] The whole controversy in the temple is regarded as *one:* hence the new point raised by our Lord is introduced as a *rejoinder,* with **ἀποκριθείς.** 36.] Observe **ἐν τῷ πνεύματι τῷ ἁγίῳ** (ἐν πν., Matt.) = **ἐν βίβλῳ ψαλμῶν** Luke: a coincidence not to be passed over. 37.] **πόθεν,** *from whence shall we seek an explanation for what follows:* see reff. **κ. ὁ πολ. ὄχ. ἤκ. αὐτ. ἡδ.** is peculiar to Mark.

38—40.] Denunciation of the Scribes. Luke xx. 45—47. These verses, nearly verbatim the same in the two Evangelists, and derived from a common report, are an abridgment of the discourse which occupies the greater part of Matt. xxiii.—with the additions of **θελ. ἐν στολ. περιπ.,** and **οἱ κατέσθ. . . . . κρῖμα** (see || Matt., text, and var. readd.). The words **ἐν τῇ διδ. αὐτ.** seem to imply that Mark *understood it as a compendium.* **ἀσπασμούς** and the following accusatives

ˣ πρωτοκλισίας ἐν τοῖς δείπνοις, 40 οἱ ʸ κατέσθοντες τὰς οἰκίας τῶν χηρῶν, καὶ ᶻ προφάσει μακρὰ προσευχόμενοι· οὗτοι λήμψονται ᵃ περισσότερον κρίμα. 41 Καὶ καθίσας ᵇ κατέναντι τοῦ ᶜ γαζοφυλακίου ἐθεώρει πῶς ὁ ὄχλος ᵈ βάλλει ᵉ χαλκὸν εἰς τὸ ᶜ γαζοφυλάκιον. καὶ πολλοὶ πλούσιοι ἔβαλλον πολλά, 42 καὶ ἐλθοῦσα ᶠ μία χήρα πτωχὴ ἔβαλεν ᵍ λεπτὰ δύο ὅ ἐστιν ʰ κοδράντης. 43 καὶ προσκαλεσάμενος τοὺς μαθητὰς αὐτοῦ λέγει αὐτοῖς Ἀμὴν λέγω ὑμῖν ὅτι ἡ χήρα αὕτη ἡ πτωχὴ πλεῖον πάντων βέβληκεν τῶν βαλλόντων εἰς τὸ ᶜ γαζοφυλάκιον. 44 πάντες γὰρ ἐκ τοῦ ⁱ περισσεύοντος αὐτοῖς ἔβαλον, αὕτη δὲ ἐκ τῆς

ABDEF GHKL MSUV ΧΓΔΠℵ 1. 33 69

x ‖ L. Luke (xi. 43 v. r.) xiv. 7, 8 only +. y ‖ L. reff. constr., Rev. i. 4, 5. ii. 18. x. 2 al. Exod. v. 14. xvii. 6. z ‖ L. John xv. 22. Acts xxvii. 30. Phil. i. 18. 1 Thess. ii. 5 only. Hos. x. 4. a ‖ L. (Mt. v. r.) Luke xii. 4. 1 Cor. xii. 23 al.+ Dan. iv. 33 (36) Theod. b ch. xi. 2 ‖ L. (Mt. v. r.) xiii. 3. Zech. xiv. 4. c here, &c. (3ce) and Luke xxi. 1. John viii. 20 only. Neh. x. 37. 2 Macc. v. 18 al. d = ‖. Matt. xxvii. 6. John xii. 6. e = ch. vi. 8 ‖ Mt. (1 Cor. xiii. 1. Rev. xviii. 12) only. f Matt. viii. 19 reff. g ‖ L. Luke xii. 59 only +. (-πτός, Gen. xli. 4.) h Matt. v. 26 only +. i ‖ L. Matt. xiv. 20. L. xv. 37. 1 Kings ii. 36.

40. rec κατεσθιοντες, with Aℵ rel: κατεσθιουσιν D 1 latt: txt B. om τας and των D 229. aft χηρ. add και ορφανων D 69 lat-*a b c e ff*$_2$ *g*$_2$ *i* [*q*] syr-jer.—om [follg] και D latt Syr.

41. om καθισας, insg κατεζομενος ο ιησ. aft γαζοφυλακιου, D. rec aft καθ. ins ο ιησους, with A (D, see above) rel vulg lat-*b c ff*$_2$ *g*$_2$ *i* [*q*] Syr æth arm Orig$_1$: om BLΔℵ lat-*a k* copt. απεναντι BU 33 [Damasc$_1$]. for εθ., θεωρει ℵ¹ [Orig$_1$]. om βαλλει χαλκ. to πολ. πλ. D. ins τον bef χαλκον ℵ [1. 69]. εξεβαλλον ℵ¹.

42. for και ελθ., ελθ. δε D 2-pe latt copt-2-mss sah Orig. for μια, αμα D-gr¹ (txt D-corr¹[appy] and lat). ins γυνη bef χηρα ℵ. om πτωχη D 2-pe lat-*a b c ff*$_2$ *i k q* arm.

43. for λεγει, ειπεν (*see* ‖ *Luke*) ABDKLMUΔΠℵ 33 lat-*a k* syrr coptt æth Orig$_1$ Damasc$_1$: txt X rel vulg lat-*b c* [*i q*] arm(appy). η πτωχη bef αυτη D ev-y lat-*a b ff*$_2$ *g*$_2$ *i q* Orig$_2$. πλεον ℵ [Damasc$_1$-ed]. for βεβληκεν, εβαλεν (*from* ‖ *Luke*) ABDLΔℵ³ᵃ 33 Orig$_2$ [Damasc$_1$], εβαλλεν ℵ¹: txt X rel. rec (for βαλλ.) βαλοντων, with FH [Damasc$_1$]: om 1 lat-*a b c ff*$_2$ *g*$_2$ *i* [*q*] arm-usc: txt ABD rel Orig$_2$.

44. aft γαρ ins ουτοι D 1. 33 sah.

are governed by **θελόντων.** **οἱ κατέσθοντες** may either be dependent on the preceding by a broken construction, or may be the beginning of a new sentence of exclamation, as Meyer takes it. The former is to me the more probable, and I have punctuated accordingly. It is a change of construction not without example in the classics: Herod. i. 51, Λακεδαιμονίων φαμένων εἶναι ἀνάθεμα, οὐκ ὀρθῶς λέγοντες. See also reff. The art. points them out graphically. They *devoured widows' houses*, by attaching them to themselves, and so persuading them to minister to them of their substance. A trace of this practice (but there out of gratitude and love) on the part of the Jewish women, is found in Luke viii. 2, 3. What words can better describe the corrupt practices of the so-called priesthood of Rome, than these of our Lord? The **πρόφασις** was, to make their sanctity appear to these women, and so win their favour. **περισσότερον**—because ye have joined thieving with hypocrisy.

41—44.] THE WIDOW'S MITES. Luke xxi. 1—4: probably from a common origin. **41. τοῦ γαζ.**] This is usually understood of *thirteen chests*, which stood in the court of the women, into which were thrown contributions for the temple, or the tribute (of Matt. xvii. 24). But it is hardly likely that *they* would be called **τὸ** γαζ., and we hear of a building by this name in Jos. Antt. xix. 6. 1. Lücke, on John viii. 20, believes *some part of the court of the women* to be intended, perhaps a chamber in connexion with these chests. Our Lord had at this time *taken his leave of the temple*, and was going out of it—between Matt. xxiii. end, and xxiv. **42.**] **λεπτά** = פרוטות the smallest Jewish coin: see Lightfoot. Mark adds **ὅ ἐστιν κοδ.** for his Roman readers: —the λεπτόν = $\frac{1}{8}$ of an as. **λεπτ. δύο**, Bengel remarks, are noticed: she

[j] ὑστερήσεως αὐτῆς πάντα ὅσα εἶχεν ἔβαλεν, ὅλον τὸν
[k] βίον αὐτῆς.

XIII. 1 Καὶ ἐκπορευομένου αὐτοῦ ἐκ τοῦ ἱεροῦ λέγει
αὐτῷ [l] εἷς [ἐκ] τῶν μαθητῶν αὐτοῦ Διδάσκαλε ἴδε [m] ποταποὶ
λίθοι καὶ [m] ποταπαὶ [n] οἰκοδομαί. 2 καὶ ὁ Ἰησοῦς εἶπεν
αὐτῷ Βλέπεις ταύτας τὰς μεγάλας [n] οἰκοδομάς; οὐ μὴ
[o] ἀφεθῇ λίθος ἐπὶ λίθῳ ὃς οὐ μὴ [p] καταλυθῇ. 3 καὶ
καθημένου αὐτοῦ [q] εἰς τὸ [r] ὄρος τῶν [r] ἐλαιῶν [s] κατέναντι
τοῦ ἱεροῦ, ἐπηρώτα αὐτὸν [t] κατ' [t] ἰδίαν Πέτρος καὶ Ἰάκωβος καὶ Ἰωάννης καὶ Ἀνδρέας 4 Εἰπὸν ἡμῖν πότε ταῦτα
ἔσται, καὶ τί τὸ [u] σημεῖον ὅταν μέλλῃ ταῦτα [v] συντελεῖσθαι
πάντα; 5 ὁ δὲ Ἰησοῦς [w] ἤρξατο λέγειν αὐτοῖς [x] Βλέπετε

j (-ημα, ‖ L.) Phil. iv. 11 only +. k — ‖. Luke viii. 43. xv. 12. Prov. xxxi. (see xxix.) 14 BN[1] F(not AN[3a]). l Matt. xxii. 35 reff. m Matt. viii. 27 reff. n = ‖ Mt. reff o ‖. Judg. ii. 23. p = ‖ Mt. reff. q = ver. 9. John xx. 7. Acts vii. 4. 2 Thess. ii. 4. r Matt. xxi. 1 reff. s ch. xii. 41 reff. t Matt. xiv. 13 reff. u Matt. xii. 38. Luke ii. 12. 1 Kings x. 7. v (Matt. vii. 28 v. r.) Luke iv. 2, 13. Acts xxi. 27. Rom. ix. 28 (from Isa. x. 23). Heb. viii. 8 only. Lam. ii. 17. Jer. xvi. 4. w Matt. iv. 17. xi. 7, 20. xvi. 21. xxvi. 22. x ‖ Mt. reff.

Chap. XIII. 1. rec om 2nd εκ (*as unnecessary*), with BLℵ rel: ins ADFXΔ 1. 69 latt coptt. διδασκαλε is marked for erasure by ℵ-corr[1.3]: om Scr's c. ποδαπ. (twice) D[1](txt D[4]). aft οικοδομαι ins του ιερου (‖ *Matt*) D gat(with mt tol) lat-*b c ff₂ g₂ k l q*.

2. rec aft ιησ. ins αποκριθεις (*see* ‖ *Matt*), with E rel lat-*q* æth arm; bef ο ιησ. A(D)KΔΠ 1. 69 lat-(*c*) *ff₂ k* syr: om BLℵ 33 lat-*e* Syr coptt.—και αποκρ. ειπεν αυτοις ο ιησ. D. βλεπετε (‖ *Matt*) D M-marg lat-*a b c e ff₂ g₂ i k* [*q*]. ins αμην λεγω υμειν οτι bef ου μη αφεθη D (1) lat-(*a*) *b c e ff₂ g₂ k l* arm; αμην λεγω σοι G 69. aft αφεθ. ins ωδε (*from* ‖ *Matt*) BDGLM[2]UΔℵ 1. 33 lat-*a b g₂ q* Syr syr-w-ast (coptt æth) arm: om A rel vulg lat-*ff₂ i*. for λιθω, λιθον (‖ *Matt*) BGLMUXΓΔΠℵ 1. 33. 69: txt AD rel (*see* ‖ *Luke, where* LXℵ[3a] *&c have* λιθον). om μη Lℵ[1]. καταλυθησεται, ℵ[1] 69. at end ins και δια τριων ημερων αλλος αναστησεται ανευ χειρων D lat-*a b* (*c*) *e* (*ff₂ g₂*) *i k n* Cypr.

3. rec επηρωτων, with AD rel latt (Syr) syr[-txt] (copt-schw æth) arm: txt BLℵ 33. 69 syr-mg copt-wilk.—(επερ. AEFGH, επιρ. Δ.) ins ο bef πετρος Dℵ 2-pe.

4. rec ειπε (‖ *Matt*), with A rel: txt BDLℵ 1. 33. 69. μελλει DEMXΓΔ 33. 69 ev-y. rec παντα bef ταυτα συντελεισθαι, with D rel lat-*a n*: ταυτα παντα συντ. AGHKMΓΠ 1. 33. 69 [lat-*q*] syrr copt: om παντα Δ ev-y lat-(*c*?) *k*: ταυτα μελλ. συντ. παντα L: txt Bℵ (æth).

5. rec aft ιησ. ins αποκριθεις (*from* ‖ *Matt*), with A rel syr: και αποκρ. ο ιησ. (‖ *Matt*) DG 69 vulg lat-*b* (*c*) [*i q*] æth: txt BLℵ 33 Syr coptt arm. rec αυτοις bef ηρξ. λεγ., with A rel syr: ειπεν αυτοις D 237 Scr's u lat-*a k n* arm: ηρ. αυτ. λεγ. M[2](Tischdf) Δ 69: txt BL M-marg(Treg) Uℵ 33 vulg lat-*b* (*c*) *ff₂ i l* [*q*] Syr coptt æth.

might have kept back *one*. **43.] πλεῖον**—more, *in God's reckoning*;—more, for *her own stewardship* of the goods entrusted to her care. "Non quantum detur, sed quantum resideat, expenditur." Ambr. in Bp. Wordsw.

Chap. XIII.] Jesus prophesies of His coming, and of the times of the end. Matt. xxiv. Luke xxi. 5—36. The accounts are apparently distinct, and each contains some fragments which have escaped the others. On the *matter* of the prophecy, I have fully commented in Matt., where see notes: also those on Luke.

1. ποταποὶ λίθοι] Josephus, B. J. v. 5. 2, 3, says, πέτραι δὲ τεσσαράκοντα πήχεις τὸ μέγεθος ἦσαν τοῦ δομήματος. And again, vi. 4. 1, ἓξ ἡμέραις ἀδιαλείπτως ἡ στεῤῥοτάτη πασῶν ἑλέπολις τύπτουσα τὸν τοῖχον οὐδὲν ἤνυσεν· ἀλλὰ καὶ ταύτης καὶ τῶν ἄλλων τὸ μέγεθος καὶ ἡ ἁρμονία τῶν λίθων ἦν ἀμείνων. See also Antt. xv. 11. 3. **3.] Πέτ. κ. Ἰάκ.** ...... = οἱ μαθηταὶ Matt., = τινές Luke. **4.] ταῦτα π.** implies that they viewed the destruction of the temple as part of a great series of events, which had now by frequent prophecy become familiar to them. '*All these things about which thou so often speakest.*' **5.] ἤρξατο λέγειν**—with this *begins* our Lord's full explanation on the matter. See reff.

μή τις ὑμᾶς [x]πλανήσῃ· 6 πολλοὶ ἐλεύσονται [y]ἐπὶ τῷ ABDEF
ὀνόματί μου, λέγοντες ὅτι [z]ἐγώ εἰμι, καὶ πολλοὺς πλανή- GHKL MSUV
σουσιν. 7 ὅταν δὲ [a]ἀκούσητε πολέμους καὶ [b]ἀκοὰς πολέ- ΧΓΔΠℵ 1. 33. 69
μων, μὴ [c]θροεῖσθε· [d]δεῖ [d]γενέσθαι, ἀλλ᾽ οὔπω τὸ τέλος.
8 [e]ἐγερθήσεται γὰρ ἔθνος ἐπ᾽ ἔθνος καὶ βασιλεία ἐπὶ
βασιλείαν, ἔσονται σεισμοὶ [f]κατὰ τόπους, ἔσονται λιμοὶ
[καὶ [g]ταραχαί]. 9 ἀρχαὶ [h]ὠδίνων ταῦτα. [i]βλέπετε δὲ
ὑμεῖς [i]ἑαυτούς· [j]παραδώσουσιν ὑμᾶς εἰς [k]συνέδρια, καὶ
[l]εἰς συναγωγὰς [m]δαρήσεσθε, καὶ [n]ἐπὶ ἡγεμόνων καὶ
βασιλέων [o]σταθήσεσθε [p]ἕνεκεν ἐμοῦ, εἰς [q]μαρτύριον
αὐτοῖς, 10 καὶ εἰς πάντα τὰ ἔθνη πρῶτον δεῖ κηρυχθῆναι
τὸ εὐαγγέλιον. 11 καὶ ὅταν [r]ἄγωσιν ὑμᾶς παραδιδόντες,
μὴ [s]προμεριμνᾶτε τί λαλήσητε, [μηδὲ [t]μελετᾶτε,] ἀλλ᾽ ὃ

y = ‖. ch. ix. 39. Luke xxiv. 47. z John iv. 26 reff. Zeph. ii. 15 (iii. 1). a = ‖. Matt. xi. 2. Acts xxiii. 16. 3 Kings x. 1. b ‖ Mt. Matt. iv. 24. 2 Kings xiii. 30. c ‖ Mt. 2 Thess. ii. 2 only. Cant. v. 4 only. d = ‖ Mt. reff. e = ‖ Mt. Isa. xix. 2. f ‖. Acts xxii. 19. ii. 46. v. 22. xiv. 23. g here (John v. 4 v. r.) only. Ezek. xxx. 4, 9 al. h ‖ Mt. Acts ii. 44. 1 Thess. v. 3 only. Exod. xv. 14. Job xxi. 17. Isa. xxi. 3. i 2 John 8. j = Matt. x. 17. xxvii. 18. k Matt. xxvi. 59. John xi. 47 al. Prov. xxii. 10. l ver. 3 reff. m Matt. xxi. 35 reff. n = Acts xxiv. 20. xxv. 10, 26 al. o Matt. xxvii. 11. p ch. x. 29. Matt. x. 18 al. q Matt. viii. 4 reff. Zeph. iii. 8. r Matt. x. 18. Acts vi. 12 al. s here only †. t (προμελ., ‖ L.) Acts iv. 25. 1 Tim. iv. 15 only. Prov. viii. 7.

πλανησει DHΓ.

6. rec aft πολλοι ins γαρ (‖ *Matt Luke*), with AD rel latt syrr coptt arm : om BLℵ lat-*i* æth. om οτι D 33 lat-*b c k* sah.

7. ακουσετε 69 : ακουητε B : txt ADℵ rel. aft πολεμων ins ορατε ℵ[1](marked for erasure, but the marks removed). for θροεισθε, θορυβεισθαι D[-gr] 57 [lat-*a n*]. rec aft δει ins γαρ (‖ *Matt Luke*), with ADℵ[3b] rel latt syrr æth arm : om Bℵ[1] coptt.

8. rec επι, with AD rel : txt BKLΔ[2]Π[1]ℵ 1. 69. om βασιλεια επι (*homœotel*) ℵ[1]. rec ins και bef 1st εσονται, with A rel vss : om BDLℵ coptt. om κατα τοπ. εσονται λιμοι (*homœotel* -μοι . . . -μοι) ℵ[1](ins ℵ[3b]). rec ins και bef 2nd εσονται (‖ *Matt*), with AD rel [vss] : om BLℵ[3b] copt arm. om 2nd εσονται D latt arm. om και ταραχαι (*as not occurring in* ‖ : *or perhaps because confounded with* αρχ. *follg : no possible reason can be given for the interpoln of the clause*) BDLℵ latt copt æth : ins A rel lat-*q* syrr sah arm [Orig-int_1].

9. αρχη (*from* ‖ *Matt, where there is no var*) BD E[1](perhaps) KLS[1]UΔΠ[1]ℵ 33 vulg lat-*a b* ff_2 g_2 *k* [g_1 *i n q*] syrr coptt æth arm : txt A rel. om βλεπετε δε υμεις εαυτους D 1 lat-*a* ff_2 *i n* arm : om εαυτους ℵ[1](ins ℵ[3b]) lat-*k* : αυτους Δ. rec aft παραδωσουσιν ins γαρ, with Aℵ rel vulg lat-*c* ff_2[(Sabat) *q*] syrr sah : ειτα υμας αυτους παραδωσουσιν D lat-*a* ff_2[Blanch] *i k n* : και παραδ. υμας 1 : txt BL copt æth arm. aft ηγεμονων ins δε (*see Matt* x. 18) AKΓΠ[1]. ενεκα B.

10. om τα D[1](ins D[2]). rec δει bef πρωτον, with A rel lat-*i*(appy) *q* syr copt (appy) : txt BDℵ vulg lat-*a* (*c* ff_2 g_2 *k*) *l n* ([sah] arm).—aft πρωτον ins λαον ℵ(but marked for erasure). aft ευαγ. ins εν πασιν τοις εθνεσιν D tol lat-ff_2 g_2 *i*.

11. rec οταν δε (*corrn from Matt* x. 19), with A rel lat-ff_2 *q* syrr sah æth arm Orig : txt BDLℵ 33 vulg lat-*a c k l* [*i n*] copt. rec **αγαγωσιν**, with EFHΓ (SV, e sil) : txt ABDℵ rel Orig. om μηδε μελετατε BDLℵ 1. 33. 69 vulg lat-*a c* ff_2 *i k l* coptt æth : ins A rel lat-*a n* syrr (arm).

8. ἔσονται . . . ἔσονται] By these repetitions majesty is given to the discourse. **9.**] **ἀρχαί** is put forward for emphasis—the *mere* beginnings. **ὑμεῖς** likewise has the emphasis—let *your* care be . . . **εἰς συναγ.**, a pregnant construction—'*ye shall be taken into the synagogues and beaten there.*' So also in ver. 16. Bp. Wordsw. explains the εἰς, "Ye will be exposed before the eyes of congregations in synagogues, for their pleasure:" and ἐν συν. would mean, "in the buildings, without any reference to the people in them." But how will this apply to ὁ εἰς τὸν ἀγρὸν ὤν, ver. 16? Meyer, with Lachmann al., would punctuate after συναγωγάς, and take δαρήσεσθε by itself. This is most improbable, especially when we remember that the synagogues were the places where the scourging was inflicted (see Acts xxii. 19), not to mention the objection to taking the verb thus by itself, which seems to me (against Meyer) alien from the character of the discourse. **11.**] Mark has vv. 10, 11 peculiar to himself. Luke (vv. 14, 15) has

...υμιν 33. ἐὰν [u] δοθῇ ὑμῖν ἐν ἐκείνῃ τῇ ὥρᾳ, τοῦτο λαλεῖτε· οὐ γάρ
ἐστε ὑμεῖς οἱ λαλοῦντες, ἀλλὰ τὸ πνεῦμα τὸ ἅγιον.
12 καὶ [v] παραδώσει ἀδελφὸς ἀδελφὸν [v] εἰς [v] θάνατον, καὶ
πατὴρ τέκνον· καὶ [w] ἐπαναστήσονται τέκνα ἐπὶ γονεῖς καὶ
[x] θανατώσουσιν αὐτούς, 13 καὶ ἔσεσθε μισούμενοι ὑπὸ
πάντων [y] διὰ τὸ [y] ὄνομά μου. ὁ δὲ ὑπομείνας εἰς τέλος,
οὗτος σωθήσεται. 14 Ὅταν δὲ ἴδητε τὸ [z] βδέλυγμα τῆς
[a] ἐρημώσεως ἑστηκότα ὅπου οὐ δεῖ· ὁ ἀναγινώσκων [b] νοείτω·
τότε οἱ ἐν τῇ Ἰουδαίᾳ φευγέτωσαν εἰς τὰ ὄρη, 15 ὁ δὲ
ἐπὶ τοῦ [c] δώματος μὴ [d] καταβάτω εἰς τὴν οἰκίαν μηδὲ
εἰςελθέτω τι ἆραι ἐκ τῆς οἰκίας αὐτοῦ· 16 καὶ ὁ [e] εἰς τὸν
ἀγρὸν ὢν μὴ [f] ἐπιστρεψάτω εἰς [g] τὰ ὀπίσω ἆραι τὸ ἱμάτιον
αὐτοῦ. 17 [h] οὐαὶ δὲ ταῖς [i] ἐν [i] γαστρὶ [i] ἐχούσαις καὶ ταῖς
[j] θηλαζούσαις ἐν ἐκείναις ταῖς ἡμέραις. 18 προσεύχεσθε
C γορ αι δὲ ἵνα μὴ γένηται [k] χειμῶνος. 19 ἔσονται γὰρ αἱ ἡμέραι
... ἐκεῖναι [l] θλῖψις, [m] οἵα οὐ γέγονεν [m] τοιαύτη ἀπ᾽ ἀρχῆς
[n] κτίσεως ἧς [o] ἔκτισεν ὁ θεὸς [p] ἕως τοῦ [p] νῦν, καὶ οὐ μὴ

u = Matt. x. 19 reff.
v Matt. x. 21. 2 Cor. iv. 11. Isa. liii. 12.
w Matt. x. 21 only. Deut. xix. 11. xxii. 26.
x Matt. x. 21. xxvi. 59. 2 Cor. vi. 9. 1 Pet. iii. 18. 2 Kings viii. 3.
y John xv. 21 reff.
z ‖ Mt. Luke xvi. 15. Rev. xvii. 4, 5. xxi. 27 only. Deut. xxix. 17 al.
a ‖ Mt. Luke xxi. 20 only. Jer. xxxii. (xxv.) 18. Dan. ix. 27. xii. 11.
b ‖ Mt. reff.
c Matt. x. 27 reff.
d imper. aor., ‖ Mt. Matt. vi. 3. Deut. xxxiii. 6.
e (ver. 3). Matt. ii. 23. Luke ix. 61 al.
f ‖ Mt. reff.
g Luke ix. 62. xvii. 31. John vi. 66 al.
h Matt. xxiii. 13, &c. Luke vi. 24, &c. xi. 42, &c.
i Matt. i. 18 reff.
j = ‖ [Luke xxiii. 29 v. r.] (Matt. xxi. 6. Luke xi. 27) only. Gen. xxi. 7.
k ‖ Mt. reff.
l constr., Rom. xiii. 3.
m pleon., here (1 Cor. xv. 48 bis. 2 Cor. x. 11. Sir. xlix. 14) only. see ch. vii. 25. Rev. vii. 2 al. fr.
n = ch. x. 6 reff.
o Paul, Rom. i. 25 al9. Rev. iv. 11 bis. x. 6. Deut. iv. 32.
p ‖ Mt. only. Gen. xviii. 12. ἄχρι τ. ν., Rom. viii. 22. Phil. i. 5.

for εαν, αν AD. for τουτο, αυτο D lat-*c*: εκεινο 28. 69 Orig.

12. rec παραδωσει δε (*from Matt* x. 21), with A rel vulg lat-ff_2 [*i q*] syrr æth $Orig_1$: txt BDLℵ lat-*a c k n* coptt. επαναστησεται (*gramml corrn*) B.

14. rec aft ερημωσεως ins το ρηθεν υπο δανιηλ του προφητου (*from* ‖ *Matt*), with A rel lat-*c k* n^2 syrr æth; so, but δια for υπο, 1 ev-y: om BDLℵ vulg lat-*a* ff_2 $g_{1.2}$ *i* n^1 *q* coptt arm Aug_{1expr} Vict Thl_{appy}. Steph εστος, with A rel: elz εστως, with KMUXΓΠ²: (*both from* ‖ *Matt*:) εστηκος D: στηκον 1. 69: txt BLℵ. aft νοειτω ins τι αναγινωσκει D lat-*a* g_2 *i n*.

15. om δε (*see* ‖ *Matt*) BFH lat-*c* coptt Orig: και ο (*see* ‖ *Luke*) D vulg lat-*a* ff_2 *k* [*i n q*] Syr æth: txt Aℵ rel syr arm. om εις την οικιαν (*see* ‖ *Matt*) BLℵ lat-*c k* Syr coptt: ins AD rel vulg lat-*a* ff_2 g_1 [*i l n q*] syr æth arm Orig. εισελθατω ADLΔℵ. rec αραι bef τι (*see* ‖ *Matt*), with ADℵ rel: txt BKLΠ¹.

16. om ων (*see* ‖ *Matt, and ver* 15) BDLΔℵ 1 lat-ff_2 *q* copt. επιστρεψετω D¹ (txt D²). om εις τα (‖ *Matt*) Dℵ vulg lat-(*a*) *c* ff_2 g_1 *k*.

17. om δε D[-gr]. θηλαζομεναις D: ενθηλαζουσαις L.

18. και προσευχεσθε D lat-*a i n*. rec aft γενηται ins η φυγη υμων (*from* ‖ *Matt*), with Aℵ^{3b} rel gat lat-g_2 *k* syrr sah goth æth: om B(DL)ℵ¹ vulg arm.—χειμωνος γενωνται D lat-*c l* [Aug_1]: μη χειμωνος γενηται ταυτα L lat-*a n* [*q*].

19. θλιψεις ADΔ ev-y. οιαι ουκ εγενοντο τοιαυται, and γενωνται D (ev-y) latt (arm). for ης, ην (*corrn*) BC¹Lℵ.—om ης εκτ. ο θ. D lat-*a c* ff_2 *i k n* arm. for και ου, ουδε D: ουδ ου FG 1. 69.

something very like them—Matt. nothing: but they occur Matt. x. 19, where see note. Meyer remarks that **μελετᾶτε** is the regular technical word for premeditating a discourse—in contrast to extempore speaking. Observe the emphasis on **ἐστε**—it *is* not you *at all*, but another.

12.] = καὶ ἀλλήλους παραδώσουσιν καὶ μισήσουσιν ἀλλήλους Matt. 13. **ὑπομείνας**] Scil. in the confession implied by διὰ τὸ ὄνομά μου preceding. 14. **ὅπου οὐ δεῖ**] See note on Matt. ver. 15. This is a less definite description of the place than we find there. In connexion with the reading ἑστηκότα in the text, the Oxf. Catena explains τὸ βδέλ. τῆς ἐρημ. by τὸν ἀνδριάντα τοῦ τότε τὴν πόλιν ἑλόντος. 18.] Matt. adds μηδὲ ἐν σαββάτῳ. Mark wrote mostly for Gentile readers, and thus perhaps was not likely

γένηται. 20 καὶ εἰ μὴ κύριος [q]ἐκολόβωσεν τὰς ἡμέρας,
οὐκ ἂν ἐσώθη [r]πᾶσα σάρξ· ἀλλὰ διὰ τοὺς [s]ἐκλεκτοὺς
οὓς ἐξελέξατο [q]ἐκολόβωσεν τὰς ἡμέρας. 21 καὶ τότε ἐάν
τις ὑμῖν εἴπῃ Ἴδε ὧδε ὁ χριστός, ἴδε ἐκεῖ, μὴ πιστεύετε.
22 [t]ἐγερθήσονται γὰρ [u]ψευδοπροφῆται καὶ ποιήσουσιν
[v]σημεῖα καὶ [v]τέρατα πρὸς τὸ [w]ἀποπλανᾶν εἰ δυνατὸν
τοὺς [s]ἐκλεκτούς. 23 ὑμεῖς δὲ [x]βλέπετε· [y]προείρηκα ὑμῖν
πάντα. 24 ἀλλὰ ἐν ἐκείναις ταῖς ἡμέραις μετὰ τὴν
[z]θλῖψιν ἐκείνην ὁ [a]ἥλιος [a]σκοτισθήσεται, καὶ ἡ [a]σελήνη
οὐ δώσει τὸ [a]φέγγος αὐτῆς, 25 καὶ οἱ [a]ἀστέρες [b]ἔσονται
ἐκ τοῦ οὐρανοῦ πίπτοντες, καὶ αἱ [c]δυνάμεις αἱ ἐν τοῖς
οὐρανοῖς [d]σαλευθήσονται. 26 καὶ τότε ὄψονται τὸν [e]υἱὸν
τοῦ [e]ἀνθρώπου [f]ἐρχόμενον ἐν [f]νεφέλαις [g]μετὰ δυνάμεως
πολλῆς καὶ δόξης. 27 καὶ τότε ἀποστελεῖ τοὺς ἀγγέλους

q here & || Mt. bis only. 2 Kings iv. 12 only. see Lev. xxi. 18. xxii. 23.
r = || Mt. reff.
s here & || Mt. bis. ver. 27 || Mt. Luke xviii. 7. Col. iii. 12. 2 Tim. ii. 10. Tit. i. 1. 1 Pet. ii. 9. Isa. lxv. 23. Wisd. iii. 9.
t = Matt. xi. 11 reff.
u || Mt. Matt. vii. 15 al. Jer. vi. 13. Zech. xiii. 2.
v || Mt. reff.
w 1 Tim. vi. 10 only. Prov. vii. 21.
x abs., = ver. 33 only.
y || Mt. reff.
z ver. 19.
a || Mt. reff.
b constr., Matt. xix. 22 reff.
c || Mt. reff.
d Matt. xi. 7. Luke vi. 48. Ps. xvii. 7. 12. Isa. xxxiii. 17. Dan. vii. 13.
e Matt. viii. 20 reff.
f || Mt. reff.
g Acts xxvi.

Frag. Neap. xiii. 21 (appy)... ABCDE FGHKL MSUV XΓΔΠℵ Frag. Neap. 1. 69

20. εκολ. bef κυριος (ει μη εκολοβωθησαν *being the arrangemt in* || *Matt*, κυριος *was transpd to suit it*) BLℵ vulg lat-*b* (*c ff*$_2$) $g_{1.2}$ [*i*] *k* æth. aft ημ. ins εκεινας EFGMΔ 1. 69 mt(with tol) lat-*c* $g_{1.2}$ Syr coptt æth arm Op Promiss. δια τους εκλεκτους αυτου D lat-*a b ff*$_2$ *i q* arm.

21. for εαν, αν DL. rec (for 1st ιδε) ιδου (*see* || *Matt*), with ACD rel: txt BLℵ. rec aft χριστος ins η (*interpoln for connexn, as the varr shew: see also Matt*), with ACD rel lat-*a b c ff*$_2$ g_2 *i* syr copt goth æth arm; και B prag Syr sah: om LUℵ 69 vulg lat-*k l* Cyr-jer [Vict$_1$] Promiss. rec (for 2nd ιδε) ιδου, with A Frag-neap rel: om C [copt]: txt BDLℵ. rec πιστευσητε (*from* || *Matt*), with X rel: txt ABCDEFHLVΔℵ 69 Vict Thl.

22. for γαρ, δε Cℵ. rec aft γαρ ins ψευδοχριστοι και (*from* || *Matt*), with ABCℵ rel [vss]: om D 124 lat-*i k*. rec (for ποιησουσιν) δωσουσι (*from* || *Matt, where there is no var*), with ABCℵ rel vulg lat-*b c ff*$_2$ *k* [syrr copt &c]: txt D 69 lat-*a* Vict$_1$. rec ins και bef τους εκλ. (*from* || *Matt*), with AC rel vss (Orig): om B D-gr ℵ.

23. rec ins ιδου bef προειρηκα (*from* || *Matt*), with ACDℵ rel vulg lat-*b* (*c*) *ff*$_2$ *k* syrr goth arm Cypr: txt BL lat-*a* copt æth. απαντα AKMUΠ.

24. (αλλα, so BCDΔℵ.) (*N.B.* lat-*b* is def from εκεινην to end of Mark.)

25. rec του ουρ. bef εσονται, omg εκ, with L Frag-neap rel vulg lat-*i* syr[-txt] goth: οι εκ του ουρ. εσ. D lat-*c ff*$_2$ *q* [syr-mg arm]: txt ABCUΠ^{1}ℵ 69 lat-*a* (*e* $g_{1.2}$) Syr [copt æth] Aug Promiss. rec εκπιπτοντες, with A rel vulg [lat-*q*] Promiss: txt BCDLΠ^{1}ℵ lat-*a c* [*e ff*$_2$ g_1 *i k*]. (*Txt appears to have been origl. If it had been corrd after* || *Matt*, απο, *not* εκ, *would have been adopted.*) for αι εν τ. ουρ., των ουρανων DK lat-*a c ff*$_2$ g_1 *i* (Syr) copt æth arm-mss Aug Promiss.

26. επι των νεφελων D. κ. δοξ. bef πολλ. (*see* || *Matt*) AMΔΠ 69 syr æth arm.

27. rec aft αγγελους ins αυτου (*from* || *Matt*), with ACℵ rel vulg lat-*c* [g_1] syrr coptt goth æth arm Orig-int$_1$: om BDL lat-*a e ff*$_2$ *i k q* copt-ms.

to report this. **19, 20.**] **κτίσεως ἧς ἔκτισεν . . . .** and **ἐκλεκτοὺς οὓς ἐξελέξατο**, peculiarities of Mark's style—for greater solemnity. [John xvii. 26: v. 16, cited strangely by Mr. Elliott to disprove this, are no cases in point. In both those, the expression is necessary to the sense: here, and usually in St. Mark, it is merely idiomatic.] Meyer remarks that the first **ι** in θλιψις, being long by nature, and not by position only, ought to be circumflexed. **24.**] **ἀλλά** is to be noticed. It is more than the simple '*but*:' and is best rendered by **nevertheless**: qu. d., though I have forewarned you of all things, yet some of those shall be so terrible as to astound even the best prepared among you. **ἐν ἐκ. τ. ἡμ. μετὰ τ. θλ. ἐκ.**—then *those days* come *after* that tribulation: see note on Matt. ver. 29.

25.] **ἔσονται π.** (= πεσοῦνται Matt.), Mark's usage. Our Evangelist

καὶ [h] ἐπισυνάξει τοὺς ἐκλεκτοὺς ἐκ τῶν [i] τεσσάρων ἀνέμων,
ἀπ' [k] ἄκρου γῆς ἕως [k] ἄκρου οὐρανοῦ. 28 Ἀπὸ δὲ τῆς
[l] συκῆς μάθετε τὴν παραβολήν. ὅταν αὐτῆς ἤδη ὁ [m] κλάδος [n] ἁπαλὸς γένηται καὶ [o] ἐκφυῇ τὰ [p] φύλλα, γινώσκεται
ὅτι ἐγγὺς τὸ [q] θέρος ἐστίν· 29 οὕτως καὶ ὑμεῖς, ὅταν
ταῦτα ἴδητε γινόμενα, γινώσκετε ὅτι ἐγγύς ἐστιν [r] ἐπὶ
θύραις. 30 [s] ἀμὴν λέγω ὑμῖν ὅτι οὐ μὴ [t] παρέλθῃ ἡ γενεὰ
αὕτη μέχρις οὗ ταῦτα πάντα γένηται. 31 ὁ οὐρανὸς
καὶ ἡ γῆ [t] παρελεύσονται, οἱ δὲ λόγοι μου οὐ [t] παρελεύσονται. 32 περὶ δὲ τῆς ἡμέρας ἐκείνης ἢ τῆς ὥρας
οὐδεὶς οἶδεν, οὐδὲ ἄγγελος ἐν οὐρανῷ, οὐδ' ὁ υἱός, εἰ μὴ ὁ

h || Mt. ch. i. 33. Matt. xxiii. 37. Luke xii. 1. xiii. 34. xvii. 37 only. 2 Chron. xx. 26. Isa. lii. 12.
i || Mt. Rev. vii. 1. Zech. ii. 6
k = here & || Mt. bis (Luke xvi. 24. Heb. xi. 21) only. Deut. xxx. 4. Neh. i. 9. Jer. xii. 12.
l || Mt. reff.
m Matt. xiii. 32 reff.
n || Mt. only. Gen. xviii. 7. Lev. ii. 14 Aq. Symm.
o || Mt. only †. Ps. ciii. 14 Symm.
p Matt. xxi. 19 reff.
q || only. Gen. viii. 22. Prov. ix. 14. Cant. vii. 13. Jer. viii. 20.
r || Mt. Acts v. 9.
s Matt. v. 18 reff.
t = Matt. v. 18. 2 Cor. v. 17. Ps. lxxxix. 5.

rec aft εκλεκτους ins αυτου (*from* || *Matt*), with ABCℵ rel vulg lat-*c* g_2 syrr coptt goth æth arm: om DL 1 lat-*a e* ff_2 *i k* Orig-int$_1$. (Frag-neap?) ακρων γ. D-gr lat-*a* æth: επ' ακρου V. ακρων ουρ. 1 æth.

28. ηδη ο κλαδ. bef αυτης (*from* || *Matt*) ABCDLΠℵ 69 vulg lat-*a c* ff_2 g_2 *k l* ([copt] arm). rec εκφύη, with F[S]UΓ 69 lat-*a k* syr copt goth æth: εκφυῆ E²GHKMVΠ Frag-neap vulg lat-*c* ff_2 g_2 *l* [*i q*] Syr sah. aft φυλλα ins εν αυτη D 28. 2-pe lat-*q* arm. rec γινωσκετε (*prob from* || *Matt*), with B¹Cℵ rel latt syrr coptt goth arm: txt AB² D-gr LΔ copt-ms æth. [aft οτι ins ηδη D.]

29. ιδητε bef ταυτα (*see* || *Matt*) ABCLUΠ¹ℵ 1. 69 vulg lat-*k l* syrr coptt goth: ιδητε παντα ταυτα D lat-(*c* ff_2 *q*) *i*. γινωσκεται ADLΔ.

30. for μεχρις, εως D 1. 69: μεχρι ℵ. for ου, οτου B; αν 1. 69: om ℵ. rec παντα bef ταυτα (|| *Matt*), with A D-gr rel vulg lat-ff_2 k^2 *q* arm: txt BCLΔℵ 69 D-lat syrr coptt.

31. παρελευσεται [1st] (|| *Matt*) A(C?) rel lat-*a k*: txt B (C¹ prob) DKUΓΠℵ 1. 69 vulg lat-*c* ff_2 g_1 [*i q*] arm. rec aft ου ins μη (*from* || *Matt, where there is no var*), with ACD⁴ℵ rel: om BD¹. rec (for 2nd παρελευσονται) παρελθωσι, with ACD rel: txt BLℵ ev-y.

32. rec (for η) και (*from* || *Matt*), with DFS¹ℵ 1. 69 lat-*a* g_1 *i k* Syr coptt æth arm (Ath$_1$ Iren-int): txt ABC rel vulg lat-*c* ff_2 syr (Ath$_1$ Bas Naz Cyr). om της (bef ωρ.) (|| *Matt*) A rel arm-zoh Ps-Ath Bas Thl: ins BCDKLMUΔΠℵ 1 arm. rec (for αγγελος εν ουρ.) οι αγγελοι οι εν ουρ., with AC rel [syr sah]: οι αγγ. εν τω ουρ. D Scr's r s: οι αγγ. εν ουρ. K¹Lℵ Frag-neap: οι αγγ. των ουρανων (|| *Matt*) U lat-*a* g_1 Syr æth: txt B, *neque angelus neque virtus* Aug. (*The clause seems to have been variously adapted to* || *Matt.*)

omits the mourning of the tribes of the earth, and the seeing the sign of the Son of Man. **27.**] **ἀπ' ἀκροῦ γῆς,** from the extremity of the visible plane of the earth, shall the collecting begin: and shall proceed ἕως ἀκροῦ οὐρανοῦ, to the point where the sky touches that plane on the other side. **28.**] **αὐτῆς,** emphatic, when *her* branch . . . . conveying an *a fortiori* in the application. If in so humble an example as the fig-tree you discern the nearness of a season, much rather should you in these sure and awful signs discern the approach of the end. **30. ἡ γενεὰ αὕτη**] See on Matt. ver. 34. Meyer, who is strongly for the literal and exact γενεά, states in a note that γενεά never *absolutely means* 'nation,' but that it may by the context acquire this *sense accidentally* from its meaning as *race*, '*progenies.*' This is exactly what is here wanted. Never were a nation so completely one **γενεά**, in all accuracy of meaning, as the Jewish people. **32.**] This is one of those things which the Father hath *put in his own power*, Acts i. 7, and with which *the Son*, in his mediatorial office, is not acquainted: see on Matt. We must not deal unfaithfully with a plain and solemn assertion of our Lord (and what can be more so than οὐδὲ ὁ υἱός, in which by the οὐδέ He is *not below* but *above* the angels?) by such evasions as "He does not know it so as to reveal it to us," Wordsw. ("non ita sciebat ut tunc discipulis indicaret." Aug.

πατήρ. 33 [u] βλέπετε, [v] ἀγρυπνεῖτε· οὐκ οἴδατε γὰρ πότε
ὁ καιρός [w] ἐστιν. 34 ὡς ἄνθρωπος [x] ἀπόδημος [y] ἀφεὶς
τὴν οἰκίαν αὐτοῦ καὶ [z] δοὺς τοῖς δούλοις αὐτοῦ τὴν [a] ἐξουσίαν, ἑκάστῳ τὸ ἔργον αὐτοῦ, καὶ τῷ [b] θυρωρῷ ἐνετείλατο
ἵνα [c] γρηγορῇ. 35 [c] γρηγορεῖτε οὖν· οὐκ οἴδατε γὰρ πότε
ὁ κύριος τῆς οἰκίας [w] ἔρχεται, ἢ [d] ὀψὲ ἢ [e] μεσονυκτίου ἢ
[f] ἀλεκτοροφωνίας ἢ [g] πρωΐ· 36 μὴ ἐλθὼν [h] ἐξαίφνης εὕρῃ
ὑμᾶς καθεύδοντας. 37 ὃ δὲ ὑμῖν λέγω, πᾶσιν λέγω,
[c] γρηγορεῖτε.

XIV. 1 Ἦν δὲ τὸ [i] πάσχα καὶ τὰ [k] ἄζυμα μετὰ δύο
ἡμέρας, καὶ [l] ἐζήτουν οἱ ἀρχιερεῖς καὶ οἱ γραμματεῖς πῶς

ABCDE FGHK LMSUV ΧΓΔΠℵ Frag. Neap. 1. 69

u abs., = ver. 23 only. v Luke xxi. 34. Eph. vi. 18. Heb. xiii. 17 only. Prov. viii. 34 al. (-πνία, 2 Cor. xi. 27.) w pres., Matt. xxvi. 2. John xiv. 3. x here only †. (-μεῖν, ch. xii. 1.) y = Matt. iv. 11 reff. z = Matt. xvi. 19. xxv. 15. Isa. xxii. 22. a = here only. b John x. 3. xviii. 16, 17 only. 4 Kings vii. 11. c Matt. xxiv. 42 reff. d Matt. xxviii. 1. ch. xi. 19 only. Gen. xxiv. 11. Isa. v. 11. e Luke xi. 5. Acts xvi. 25. xx. 7 only. Judg. xvi. 3. f here only †. (see Matt. xxvi. 34 reff.) g ch. xi. 20 reff. Gen. xxxii. 24. h Luke ii. 13. ix. 39. Acts ix. 3. xxii. 6 only. Prov. xxiv. 22. i ‖ Mt. reff. k ‖ L. ver. 12 ‖. Acts xii. 3. xx. 6. 1 Cor. v. 7, 8 only. Exod. xxiii. 15. l ch. xi. 18 reff.

33. aft βλεπετε ins ουν D lat-*c* ff_2 g_2 *i q*. rec aft αγρυπνειτε ins και προσευχεσθε (*usual addition: see Matt* xxvi. 41), with ACℵ rel vulg lat-*f* ff_2 [*i q*] syrr coptt æth arm: om BD tol[1] lat-*a c*. om εστιν D-gr lat-*a c*.
34. αποδημων DX 1. for αυτου (aft οικ. and δουλ.), εαυτου B. rec ins και bef εκαστω, with AC[2] rel lat-*i* syrr sah arm: om BC[1]DLℵ latt copt æth. θυρουρω D[1](txt D[2]).
35. rec om 1st ἤ, with AD rel latt syrr arm $Orig_1$[and int_1]: ins BCLΔℵ lat-*k* syr-mg coptt æth. rec μεσονυκτιου (*gramml corrn, to suit* αλεκτ.), with AD rel: -τιω Scr's c $Orig_1$: txt BCLΔℵ. (μεσαν. B[1].)
36. εξελθων D-gr Γ.
37. rec (for ὅ) ἅ, with A rel lat-*q* syr [Bas_1]: εγω δε D lat-*a*: txt BCKLXΔΠ[1]ℵ vulg lat-*c f k l* Syr (copt) sah arm. 1st λεγω bef υμιν DU 1 lat-*a* æth. om πασιν λεγω (*homœotel*) DE lat-*a* ff_2 *i*.

Chap. XIV. 1. om κ. τα αζ. D lat-*a* (ff_2?) *i*.

de Trin. xii. 3 (it should be i. 12 (23), vol. viii.)). Of such a sense there is not a hint in the context: nay, it is altogether alien from it. The account given by the orthodox Lutherans, as represented by Meyer, that our Lord knew this κατὰ κτῆσιν, but not κατὰ χρῆσιν, is right enough if at the same time it is carefully remembered, that it was this κτῆσις of which He emptied Himself when He became man for us, and which it belongs to the very essence of His mediatorial kingdom to hold in subjection to the Father. **33—37.**] Peculiar to Mark, and containing the condensed matter of Matt. vv. 43—47, and perhaps an allusion to the parable of the talents in Matt. xxv.

The **θυρωρ.** is the **door-porter**, whose office it would be to look out for approaching travellers,—answering especially to the ministers of the word, who are (Ezek. xxxiii.) *watchmen* to God's church.
The construction of ver. 34 is remarkable; the participial clauses being in subordination to ἀφείς, and constituting part of the householder's arrangements of departure, and the direct tense being assumed at ἐνετείλατο, as signifying what took place at his very going out of the door, where the porter would be stationed: as if it had been ἀφεὶς τ. οἰκ. αὐτοῦ (καί, &c.) ἐνετείλατο κ.τ.λ.

Chap. XIV. 1, 2.] Conspiracy of the Jewish authorities against Jesus. Matt. xxvi. 1—5. Luke xxii. 1, 2. The account of the events preceding the passion in our Gospel takes a middle rank between those of Matt. and Luke. It contains very few words which are not to be found in one or other of them; but at the same time the variations from both are so frequent and irregular, as in my opinion wholly to preclude the idea that Mark had ever seen either. The minute analysis of any passage in the three will, I think, convince an unprejudiced examiner of this.

On the chronological difficulties which beset this part of the Gospel history, see note on Matt. xxvi. 17. **1.**] **τὸ πάσχα καὶ τὰ ἄζ.**, classed together, because the time of eating the Passover was actually the commencement of the feast of unleavened bread. The announcement by our Lord of his approaching death (Matt. xxvi.

αὐτὸν [m] ἐν δολῳ [n] κρατήσαντες ἀποκτείνωσιν· 2 ἔλεγον
γὰρ [o] Μὴ ἐν τῇ ἑορτῇ, [p] μήποτε [p] ἔσται [q] θόρυβος τοῦ
λαοῦ. 3 Καὶ ὄντος αὐτοῦ ἐν Βηθανίᾳ ἐν τῇ οἰκίᾳ Σίμωνος τοῦ [r] λεπροῦ, [s] κατακειμένου αὐτοῦ ἦλθεν γυνὴ ἔχουσα
[t] ἀλάβαστρον [u] μύρου [v] νάρδου [w] πιστικῆς [x] πολυτελοῦς,

m = Luke xxi. 34. 11. 1 Thess. iii. 5. n Matt. xxi. 46 reff. o = || Mt. John xiii. 9. Ps. cxiii. 9 (cxv. 1). p constr., Col. ii. 8. Heb. iii. 12. see Gal. iv. 11. 1 Thess. iii. 5. q || Mt. reff. r Matt. viii. 3 reff. s = ch. ii. 15 reff. t || Mt. Luke vii. 37 only. 4 Kings xxi. 13 only (but masc.). Herod. iii. 20. u || Mt. reff. v || J. only. Cant. i. 12. iv. 13, 14 only. w || J. only †. x 1 Tim. ii. 9. 1 Pet. iii. 4 only. Prov. i. 13.

om *εν δολω* D-gr vulg-ms lat-*a i*: *εν λογω* U: om *εν* Δ **1.** 69 vulg lat-*ff*$_2$ *l*. aft *κρατησαντες* ins *και* D[1]Δ.

2. rec (for *γαρ*) *δε* (*from* || *Matt*), with AC[2] rel vulg-ed syr[-txt] sah æth arm: txt BC[1]DLℵ am lat-*a c f ff*$_2$ *i k l* syr-mg copt. *μηποτε εν τη εορτ. εσται θορ.* D lat-(*a*) *ff*$_2$ [*i q*]. rec *θορυβος* bef *εσται* (*see* || *Matt*), with A rel lat-*a f i* D-lat syr copt: *θορυβου οντος* Δ: *θορ. γενηται* (|| *Matt*) M 258-9 vulg arm: txt BC D-gr Lℵ lat-*k* Syr sah[appy].

3. for *αυτου, του ιησου* (|| *Matt*) D lat-*c f ff*$_2$ *g*$_2$ *i* [*q*] copt-dz sah. om *τη* ℵ[1] 251-3-9 Scr's d k o q[1] r s ev-P. om *ναρδ. πιστ. πολ.* D-gr: om *μυρ.* D-lat: om *ναρδ.* lat-*g*$_1$. *πολυτιμου* (|| *John*) AG M-marg **1.** 69.

2) is omitted by Mark and Luke. **2.**] **μήποτε ἔσται** indicates a certain expectation of that which is deprecated. See Winer, § 56. 2. b. Notice also **ἔσται**, not *γενήσεται*: "ne, quod suspicamur, tumultus futurus sit," h. e. "*erit* alioquin (neque enim oriendi notio inculcatur), ut suspicamur, tumultus." C. F. Fritzsche, in Fritzschiorum Opuscula, p. 285.

3—9.] The anointing at Bethany. Matt. xxvi. 6—13. John xii. 1—8. (On Luke vii. 36—50, see note there.) The whole narrative has remarkable points of similarity with that of John,—and is used by Professor Bleek (Beiträge zur Evangelienkritik, p. 83) as one of the indications that Mark *had knowledge of and used* the Gospel of John. My own view, as explained in the general Prolegomena, leads me to a different conclusion. I have already remarked (note on Matt. xxvi. 3), that while Matt. seems to have preserved trace of the parenthetic nature of this narrative, by his **τοῦ δὲ Ἰ. γενομένου** (ver. 6), and **τότε πορευθείς** (ver. 14),—such trace altogether fails in our account. It proceeds *as if continuous*. **3.** **νάρδου πιστικῆς**] It seems impossible to assign any certain, or even probable meaning, to **πιστικῆς** (a word found here and in John's narrative only). The Vulg. and the lat. mss. *c ff*$_2$ *q* render it "*spicati*." The ancient Commentators give us nothing but conjecture. Euthymius and Theophylact interpret it "*genuine*:" *καταπεπιστευμένην εἰς καθαρότητα*, Euth.; *ἄδολον καὶ μετὰ πίστεως κατασκευασθεῖσαν*, Theophyl.; '*veram et absque dolo*,' Jerome. Augustine supposes it to refer to some *place* from which the nard came. Origen's comment on the passage is lost. The expression no where occurs in the classics, nor in Clement of Alex., who gives a long account (Pædagog. ii. 8, pp. 76—79 P) of *ointments*. The word can therefore hardly signify *any particular kind of ointment* technically so called. The modern interpretations of the word are principally of two kinds: the first, agreeing with Euth. and Theophyl., '*genuine*,' '*unadulterated*;' which sense however of the word does not any where else occur. It is used transitively for *πειστικός*, '*persuasive*,' by Aristotle (Rhet. i. 2), and in some later writers for *πιστός*, as *ὁ πιστικώτατος τῶν θεραπόντων*, Cedrenus, Annal., cited by Lücke on John xii. 3. Euseb. also uses the word (Demonstr. Evang. ix. vol. iv. p. 684, ed. Migne), but in the sense of '*pertaining to the faith*,' as his Latin translator renders it, or, as Lücke thinks, perhaps '*potable*,' as a derivative of *πιστός* (from *πίνω*). This brings us to the second modern interpretation, which makes *πιστικός* '*liquid*,' '*potable*,' and derives it as above. There certainly was *a kind of ointment which they drank*; for Athenæus (xv. 39, p. 689) quotes from Hicesius, *τῶν μύρων ἃ μέν ἐστι χρίματα, ἃ δ' ἀλείμματα. καὶ ῥόδινον μὲν* **πρὸς πότον ἐπιτήδειον,** *ἔτι δὲ μύρσινον, μήλινον· τοῦτο δέ ἐστι καὶ εὐστόμαχον καὶ ληθαργικοῖς χρήσιμον . . . καὶ ἡ στακτὴ δ'* **ἐπιτήδειος πρὸς πότον,** *ἔτι δὲ* **νάρδος.** The only objection to this interpretation is, that the word is no where found—which however is not so decisive as in the last case, for, as *πιστικός* from *πιστός*, 'faithful,' so there might be *πιστικός* from *πιστός*, 'potable'—and from being a term confined to dealers in ointments, it might have escaped notice elsewhere. Lücke

y Matt. xii. 20 reff. Jer. ii. 13.
z ‖ Mt. (ἐπί w. acc.) only. Gen. xxxix. 21. Job xli. 14. Ps. lxxxviii. 45 only.
a Matt. xx. 24 reff.
b ch. x. 26 reff.
c = Matt. xiv. 31.
d ‖ Mt. Lev. vi. 3, 4.
e Matt. xiii. 46 reff.
f = 1 Cor. xv. 6 only. Exod. xxx. 14 al. elsw. of place, Luke iv. 39 al.

ABCDE FGHK LMSUV ΧΓΔΠℵ Frag. Neap. 1. 69

[y] συντρίψασα τὴν [t] ἀλάβαστρον [z] κατέχεεν αὐτοῦ τῆς κεφαλῆς. 4 ἦσαν δέ τινες [a] ἀγανακτοῦντες πρὸς [b] ἑαυτοὺς
[c] Εἰς τί ἡ [d] ἀπώλεια αὕτη τοῦ [u] μύρου γέγονεν; 5 ἠδύνατο
γὰρ τοῦτο τὸ [u] μύρον [e] πραθῆναι [f] ἐπάνω [g] δηναρίων τριακοσίων καὶ [h] δοθῆναι τοῖς [h] πτωχοῖς. καὶ [i] ἐνεβριμῶντο
αὐτῇ. 6 ὁ δὲ Ἰησοῦς εἶπεν [j] Ἄφετε αὐτήν· τί αὐτῇ [k] κόπους [k] παρέχετε; [l] καλὸν [lm] ἔργον [m] εἰργάσατο [n] ἐν ἐμοί.
7 πάντοτε γὰρ τοὺς πτωχοὺς ἔχετε μεθ' [o] ἑαυτῶν, καὶ
ὅταν θέλητε δύνασθε αὐτοῖς [ab] εὖ [bc] ποιῆσαι, ἐμὲ δὲ οὐ
πάντοτε ἔχετε. 8 ὃ [d] ἔσχεν ἐποίησεν, [e] προέλαβεν [f] μυρί-

g Matt. xx. 2 reff. h Matt. xix. 21 reff. i Matt. ix. 30. ch. i. 43. John xi. 33, 38 only †. Isa. xvii. 13 Symm. (-μημα, Lam. ii. 6.) j = Matt. xv. 14. 4 Kings iv 27. k ‖ Mt. Luke xviii. 5. Gal. vi. 17. Sir. xxix. 4 Aℵ. l Matt. v. 16 reff. m ‖ Mt. reff. n Matt. xvii. 12 reff. o 2nd pers., Matt. iii. 9 reff. a Matt. xxv. 21, 23 reff. b Josh. xxiv. 20. c dat., Matt. vii. 12. Luke i. 25, 49. Gen. xx. 9. d see John xiv. 30. e 1 Cor. xi. 21. Gal. vi. 1 only †., Wisd. xvii. 17 only. constr., ch. vii. 4 al. f here only †. (-ισμός, Judith xvi. 8.)

rec ins και bef συντριψασα, with ACD rel [vss]: om BLℵ copt. for συντριψασα, θραυσασα D: *aperiens* lat-*a* Syr æth: txt ABCℵ rel. rec (for την αλαβ.) το αλαβ., with (GM **1**, e sil) 69: τον αλ. ADℵ[1] rel: txt BCLΔℵ[3a]. rec ins κατα bef της κεφ., with A rel syrr arm; επι D ev-20 latt coptt: om BCLΔℵ **1**. της κεφαλης bef αυτου D vulg lat-*a c f ff*$_2$ *i* [*q*] arm.

4. οι δε μαθηται αυτου διεπονουντο D 2-pe lat-*a ff*$_2$ *i* (arm). for εαυτ., αυτους ℵ[1]. rec aft εαυτους ins και λεγοντες. with AC[2] rel vulg lat-(*a c*) *f* (*ff*$_2$) *k* syr (copt); και ελεγον D 2-pe Syr æth arm: om BC[1]Lℵ lat-*i* copt-ms. om γεγονεν (‖ *Matt*) D 64 lat-*a ff*$_2$ *i*.

5. (Tischdf gives no readings of Frag-neap from ηδυνατο ver 5 to εν εμοι ver 6.) om γαρ D lat-*k* æth arm. om τουτο ℵ. rec om το μυρον (*see* ‖ *Matt*), with E rel lat-*c k* Syr copt: ins ABCDKLUΔΠℵ **1** vulg lat-*a* (*f*) *g*$_1$ *i l* [*q*] syr sah goth æth arm Ambr.—πραθ. το μ. τουτου D 69 lat-*f l* [*q*]. rec τριακ. bef δην. (‖ *John*), with AB rel vulg lat-*f g*$_2$ syrr coptt goth æth arm Ambr: txt C(D)Lℵ lat-*a c ff*$_2$ *g*$_1$ *i k q*. ενεβριμουντο C[1](appy) ℵ Scr's c. ins εν bef αυτη D[1].

6. aft ειπεν ins αυτοις D 2-pe lat-*a c f ff*$_2$ *g*$_2$ *i k* [*q*] coptt arm. aft καλον ins γαρ (‖ *Matt*) Gℵ 69 lat-*c* syr-w-ast copt-dz (goth) arm. ηργασατο B[1]Dℵ[1] 69. rec (for εν εμοι) εις εμε (‖ *Matt*): txt ABCDℵ Frag-neap rel Scr's-mss syr(appy) Thl.

7. μεθ υμων D 91. 299. rec αυτους (*gramml corrn*), with Aℵ[3a] rel: εαυτους K: om ℵ[1]: txt BCDLUΓΔ **1**. 69. (Frag-neap?) add παντοτε BLℵ[3a] copt.

8. rec ειχεν, with **1**. 69: txt ABCD rel latt (coptt) goth arm Vict Thl. rec ins αυτη bef εποιησεν (*see* ‖ *Matt*), with ACD rel vulg lat-*c f ff*$_2$ *k* [*i q*]; aft Δ: om BLℵ **1**. 69 lat-*a* copt.

(from whom the substance of this note is derived) seems to incline to Augustine's conjecture (see above): but then surely the name would be *more common*, as 'balm of Gilead,' &c. The uncertainty being so great, the best rendering would be to leave the word *untranslated*, as Jer. Taylor does in his "Life of Christ" (sect. 15): 'Nard Pistick.' Bp. Wordsw. sees in the word the mystical sense, that "offerings to Christ should be . . . the fruits of a lively and loving πίστις, or faith, in Him." **συντρ. τὴν ἀλάβ.** can hardly mean only having broken the resin with which the cork was sealed. In ch. v. 4: John xix. 36: Rev. ii. 27, the word is used of *breaking*, properly so called: and I see no objection to supposing that the ἀλάβαστρον was crushed in the hand, and the ointment thus poured over His head. The feet would then (John xii. 3) be anointed with what remained on the hands of Mary, or in the broken vase (see note on Luke vii. 38). **4, 5. τινες**] See notes on Matt. The **δην. τριακοσ.** is common to our narrative and that of John. **ἐπάνω** does not govern **τρ. δην.**: the genitive is one of *price*. **6.**] **ἄφετε αὐτ.**, also common to John, but as *addressed to Judas*. **7.**] The agreement verbatim here of Matt. and John, whereas our narrative inserts the additional clause καὶ ὅταν θέλητε δύνασθε αὐτοὺς εὖ ποιῆσαι, is decisive against the

σαι μου τὸ σῶμα [g] εἰς τὸν [h] ἐνταφιασμόν. 9 ἀμὴν δὲ
λέγω ὑμῖν, ὅπου ἐὰν κηρυχθῇ τὸ εὐαγγέλιον [i] εἰς [k] ὅλον
τὸν [k] κόσμον, καὶ ὃ ἐποίησεν αὕτη λαληθήσεται εἰς
[l] μνημόσυνον αὐτῆς.
10 Καὶ Ἰούδας Ἰσκαριώθ, ὁ εἷς τῶν δώδεκα, ἀπῆλθεν
πρὸς τοὺς ἀρχιερεῖς, ἵνα αὐτὸν [m] παραδοῖ αὐτοῖς. 11 οἱ
δὲ ἀκούσαντες ἐχάρησαν καὶ [o] ἐπηγγείλαντο αὐτῷ ἀργύριον [o] δοῦναι· καὶ [p] ἐζήτει πῶς αὐτὸν [q] εὐκαίρως
[m] παραδοῖ.
12 Καὶ τῇ πρώτῃ ἡμέρᾳ τῶν [r] ἀζύμων, ὅτε τὸ [rs] πάσχα

g = Luke ix. 13 reff.
h ‖ J. (-άζειν, ‖ Mt.) only +.
i = ch. i. 39 al.
k ‖ Mt. reff.
l = Mt. Acts x. 4 only. Exod. xii. 14. Mal. iii. 16 al.
m Matt. xvii. 22 al. -δοῖ, ch. iv. 29. see ch. v. 43 reff.
o = Acts vii. 5.
p ver. 1.
q (-ρία, ‖ Mt. L.) 2 Tim. iv. 2 only +. Sir. xviii. 22 only. (-ρος, ch. vi. 21.)
r ver. 1 (reff.).
s ‖ L. 1 Cor. v. 7 only. Exod. xii. 21.

το σωμα bef *μου* (*see* ‖ *Matt*) BDLM²ℵ vulg lat-*a c f*.

9. rec om *δε* (‖ *Matt*), with ACFHMUX vss : ins BD Γ(Tischdf) ℵ rel lat-*a*. rec (for *εαν*) *αν*, with DL¹ : txt ABCℵ rel. rec aft *ευαγγελιον* ins *τουτο* (*from* ‖ *Matt*), with AC rel vulg lat-(*c f*) $g_{1.2}$ [*q*] Syr coptt goth æth arm : txt BDLℵ 69 lat-*a* ff_2 *i k*.

10. rec ins *ο* bef *ιουδας*, with X rel : om ABCDELM Γ(Tischdf) ΔΠℵ 1. 69 $Orig_1$ Eus_1. (Frag-neap ?) rec ins *ο* bef *ισκ.*, with AC²ℵ³ᵃ rel copt Eus_1 : om BC¹Dℵ¹ 69 Orig. rec *ισκαριωτης*, with AC² rel vulg [Orig Eus] : *σκαριωτης* D lat-*k* : txt B(C¹ ?)Lℵ lat-*a* ff_2 *i*. om *ο εις τ. δ.* A : *εις εκ τ. δ.* D. rec om *ο* (bef *εἷς*), with (D)ℵ¹ rel Orig Eus : ins B C¹(appy) LMℵ³ᵃ copt. rec *παραδ.* bef *αυτον* (‖ *Matt*), with A(D) rel latt coptt goth arm $Orig_1$ [Eus_1] : txt BCLΔℵ (Frag-neap) 69 lat-*f k q* Eus_1. rec *παραδω* (‖ *Matt*), with Aℵ rel Eus : txt B(C ?), *προδοι* D lat-*c*. *αυτοις* bef *παραδω* Frag-neap : om *αυτοις* D 28. 91. 299. 2-pe lat-*a c* ff_2 *i k* Orig [Eus_1].

11. (Tischdf gives no readings of Frag-neap in this ver.) for *οι δε*, *και* A. om *ακουσαντες* D lat-*a c* ff_2 *i k* (Eus_1). *απηγγιλαντο* ℵ¹. *αργυρια* (*corrn*) AKUΓΠ¹ syr Eus_1. rec *ευκαιρως* bef *αυτον*, with D rel lat-*q* goth arm : txt ABC LMΔℵ latt Eus_1. rec *παραδω*, with Aℵ rel : txt B(C ?)D.

idea that Mark compiled his account from the other two. In these words there appears to be a reproach conveyed to Judas, and perhaps an allusion to the *office of giving to the poor* being *his*. **8.**] We have here again a striking addition peculiar to Mark—**ὃ ἔσχεν ἐποίησεν**—**she did what she could**: a similar praise to that given to the poor widow, ch. xii. 44—*πάντα ὅσα εἶχεν ἔβαλεν*. We have also the expression **προέλαβεν μυρίσαι**, shewing, as I have observed on Matt., that the act was one of *prospective* love, grounded on the deepest apprehension of the reality of our Lord's announcement of His approaching death. **9.**] See notes on Matt. ver. 13.

10, 11.] Compact of Judas with the chief priests to betray Him. Matt. xxvi. 14—16. Luke xxii. 3—6. The only matters requiring notice are,—the elliptical **ἀκούσαντες**,—'*hearing the proposal,*'—and **ἐπηγγείλαντο**, implying, as does *συνέθεντο* in Luke, that the money was *not paid now*, either as full wages or as earnest-money,—but *promised;* and paid (most probably) when the Lord was brought before the Sanhedrim, which was what Judas undertook to do. The *ὁ* before *εἷς* is untranslatable in English: '*that* one of the twelve' is too strongly demonstrative: and yet *ὁ* is demonstrative, and expresses much.

12—16.] Preparation for celebrating the Passover. Matt. xxvi. 17—19. Luke xxii. 7—13. Our account contains little that is peculiar. **12.**] **ὅτε τὸ π. ἔθυον**, like Luke's expression **ᾗ ἔδει** *θύεσθαι τὸ π.*, denotes the *ordinary day*, when they (i. e. the Jews) sacrificed the Passover;—for that the Lord ate His Passover on that day, and at the usual time, is the *impression conveyed by the testimony of the three Evangelists:* see notes on Matt. ver. 17, and Luke ver. 7.

We may notice that if this Gospel, as traditionally reported, was drawn up under the superintendence of Peter, we could hardly have failed to have the *names of the two disciples* given;—nor again would our narrator have missed (and the omission is an important one) the fact that *the Lord first gave the command*, to go and prepare the Passover—which *Luke*

[st] ἔθυον, λέγουσιν αὐτῷ οἱ μαθηταὶ αὐτοῦ Ποῦ θέλεις
[u] ἀπελθόντες ἑτοιμάσωμεν ἵνα [v] φάγῃς τὸ [v] πάσχα; 13 καὶ
ἀποστέλλει δύο τῶν μαθητῶν αὐτοῦ, καὶ λέγει αὐτοῖς P αυτοις ...
Ὑπάγετε εἰς τὴν πόλιν, καὶ [w] ἀπαντήσει ὑμῖν ἄνθρωπος ABCDE
[x] κεράμιον ὕδατος βαστάζων· ἀκολουθήσατε αὐτῷ, 14 καὶ FGHKL MPSUV ΧΓΔΠℵ
ὅπου ἂν εἰσέλθῃ εἴπατε τῷ [y] οἰκοδεσπότῃ ὅτι ὁ [z] διδάσκα- Frag. Neap.
λος λέγει Ποῦ ἐστιν τὸ [a] κατάλυμά μου, ὅπου τὸ [v] πάσχα 1. 69
μετὰ τῶν μαθητῶν μου [v] φάγω; 15 καὶ αὐτὸς ὑμῖν δείξει
[b] ἀνάγαιον μέγα [c] ἐστρωμένον ἕτοιμον· καὶ ἐκεῖ [d] ἑτοιμάσατε
ἡμῖν. 16 καὶ ἐξῆλθον οἱ μαθηταὶ αὐτοῦ καὶ ἦλθον εἰς τὴν
πόλιν, καὶ εὗρον καθὼς εἶπεν αὐτοῖς, καὶ ἡτοίμασαν τὸ
πάσχα. 17 καὶ [e] ὀψίας [e] γενομένης ἔρχεται μετὰ τῶν
δώδεκα· 18 καὶ [f] ἀνακειμένων αὐτῶν καὶ ἐσθιόντων ὁ
Ἰησοῦς εἶπεν Ἀμὴν λέγω ὑμῖν ὅτι εἷς ἐξ ὑμῶν παραδώσει
με, ὁ ἐσθίων μετ' ἐμοῦ. 19 [g] ἤρξαντο [h] λυπεῖσθαι, καὶ ...εμου G.

t = as above (s). 1 Cor. x. 20 only. Gen. xxxi. 54.
u = Matt. viii. 19 reff.
v here (bis) & ‖ (L. 3ce). John xviii. 28 only. Ezra vi. 21.
w Matt. xxviii. 9 reff.
x ‖ L. only. Isa. v. 10. Jer. xlii. (xxxv.) 5 only.
y Matt. xx. 1, 11 al.+
z = ‖ John xi. 28.
a ‖ L. Luke ii. 7 only. 1 Kings ix. 22.
b ‖ L. only +.
c = ‖ L. Acts ix. 34 (Matt. xxi. 8 reff.) only. Ezek. xxiii. 41.
d abs., ‖ L. Luke ix. 52. Gen. xliii. 16.
e ch. iv. 35 reff.
f Matt. ix. 10 reff.
g ‖ Mt. al.
h Matt. xvii. 23 reff.

12. om *αυτου* D latt arm. aft *ετοιμασωμεν* ins *σοι* (‖ *Matt*) DΔ vulg lat-*c f* g_1 *k* [*i q*] Syr Orig-int.

13. aft *δυο* ins *εκ* D latt Orig-int$_1$. for *κ. λεγει αυτ.*, *λεγων* D 2-pe lat-*a* ff_2 *i q* [sah Orig-int$_1$]. *υπαγε* D[1]-gr(txt D[2]).

14. rec *εαν*, with CPℵ rel: txt ABDΔΠ. (Frag-neap?) rec om 1st *μου* (‖ *Luke*), with AP rel lat-*c* ff_2 *i k* syrr copt goth æth arm-zoh Orig-int$_1$: ins BCDLΔℵ 1. 69 vulg lat-*a f l q* syr-mg sah arm-usc Orig-int$_1$. *φαγομαι* D(which also transp *το πασχα* to end of ver) 1. 69: *φαγωμαι* G 28.

15. rec *ανωγεον*, with Γ 1: *ανωγαιον* B[2]MSUX syr-mg-gr: *αναγεον* Δ 69: txt AB[1] CD P(Tischdf) ℵ rel. aft *αν.* ins *οικον* D-gr. *εστρωμενον* bef *μεγα* D Orig-int$_1$. om *ετοιμον* (*see* ‖ *Luke*) AM[1]Δ vulg lat-*a l* arm Thl [syr has it w-ast].
rec om *και* (*see* ‖ *Luke*), with AP rel lat-*a c* ff_2 *i k* [*q*] syrr copt-ms sah arm Orig$_1$: ins BC(D)L(ℵ) vulg lat-*a f l* Syr copt goth æth, *κακει* Dℵ.

16. om *αυτου* BLΔℵ 1 coptt. om *και ηλθον* ℵ[1]. for *ευρον*, *εποιησαν* (‖ *Matt*) D lat-*a c* ff_2 *i* (*k*) *q* arm-ms.

17. *οψιας δε* (‖ *Matt*) D vulg lat-*c f* ff_2 $g_{1.2}$ *l* [*q*] sah-woide. *γενομενους* ℵ[1].

18. rec *ειπεν* bef *ο ιησ.*, with A rel syrr copt arm: *λεγει ο ιησ.* D 2-pe: txt BCLℵ. for *ο εσθ.*, *των εσθιοντων* (*corrn*) B (coptt).

19. rec ins *οι δε* bef *ηρξαντο*, with AD rel latt syrr sah-woide arm: *και* C sah-ming æth: om BLℵ copt Orig$_1$. (P def.)

only relates. It becomes a duty to warn students of the sacred word against fanciful interpretations. A respected Commentator of our own day explains the pitcher of water, which led the way to the room where the last Supper was celebrated, to mean "the baptismal grace" which we have "in earthen vessels," which "leads on to other graces, even to the Communion of Christ's Body and Blood." **15.**] In the midst of a verbal accordance with Luke we have here inserted **ἕτοιμον**, indicating that the guest-chamber was *already prepared* for the celebration of the Passover, as would indeed be probable at this time in Jerusalem. The disciples had therefore only to get ready *the Passover itself*.

17—21.] Jesus, celebrating the Passover, announces His betrayal by one of the twelve. Matt. xxvi. 20—25. Luke xxii. 14 (21—23). John xiii. 21 ff. The account of Luke (ver. 16) supplies *the important saying of our Lord respecting the fulfilment of the two parts of the Passover feast*—see notes there. After our ver. 17, comes in *the washing of the disciples' feet by the Lord*, as related in John xiii. 1—20. **18.**] The words **ὁ ἐσθίων μετ' ἐμοῦ** are peculiar to Mark, and, as we have seen before, bear a relation to John's account, where our Lord had just before cited *ὁ τρώγων κ.τ.λ.*, ver. 18. They do not *designate* any particular

λέγειν αὐτῷ [i] εἷς κατὰ εἷς [k] Μή τι ἐγώ; καὶ ἄλλος, [k] Μή
τι ἐγώ; 20 ὁ δὲ εἶπεν αὐτοῖς Εἷς ἐκ τῶν δώδεκα ὁ [l] ἐμβαπ-
τόμενος μετ' ἐμοῦ εἰς τὸ [m] τρυβλίον. 21 ὅτι ὁ μὲν [n] υἱὸς
τοῦ [n] ἀνθρώπου [o] ὑπάγει [p] καθὼς γέγραπται περὶ αὐτοῦ,
[q] οὐαὶ δὲ τῷ ἀνθρώπῳ ἐκείνῳ δι' οὗ ὁ [n] υἱὸς τοῦ [n] ἀνθρώπου παραδίδοται· [r] καλὸν αὐτῷ εἰ οὐκ ἐγεννήθη ὁ ἄνθρωπος ἐκεῖνος. 22 Καὶ ἐσθιόντων αὐτῶν λαβὼν ἄρτον,
[s] εὐλογήσας ἔκλασεν καὶ ἔδωκεν αὐτοῖς καὶ εἶπεν Λάβετε·
τοῦτό [t] ἐστιν τὸ σῶμά μου. 23 καὶ λαβὼν ποτήριον
[u] εὐχαριστήσας ἔδωκεν αὐτοῖς, καὶ [v] ἔπιον ἐξ αὐτοῦ πάντες.
24 καὶ εἶπεν αὐτοῖς Τοῦτό [t] ἐστιν τὸ [w] αἷμά μου τῆς [w] διαθήκης, τὸ [x] ἐκχυννόμενον ὑπὲρ πολλῶν. 25 ἀμὴν λέγω
ὑμῖν ὅτι οὐκέτι οὐ μὴ [v] πίω ἐκ τοῦ [y] γενήματος τῆς [y] ἀμ-

...εκχυννομενον P. N xiv.25 (appy)...

i [John viii. 9.] Rev. iv. 8 only. (Rom. xii. 5. 3 Macc. v. 34.)
k Matt. vii. 16 reff.
l ‖ Mt. (John xiii. 26 v. r. bis) only +.
m ‖ Mt. only. Num. vii. 13, 19, &c. Sir. xxxiv. (xxxi.) 14.
n Matt. viii. 20 reff.
o see ‖ Mt. reff.
p ‖ Mt. reff.
q Matt. xxiii. 14, &c.
r Matt. xvii. 4 reff.
s Matt. xiv. 19. Luke xxiv. 30. 1 Kings ix. 13.
t = Matt. xiii. 37. John xv. 1. 1 Cor. x. 4. Gen. xli. 26, 27. Exod. xii. 11. Ezek. xxxvii. 11.
u Matt. xv. 36 reff.
v w. ἐκ, ‖ Mt. reff.
w ‖ Mt. reff.
x Matt. xxiii. 35 reff.
y ‖ Mt. reff.

rec εις καθ' εις, with ADP rel: εις εκαστος C: txt BLΔℵ. aft 1st εγω add ειμι ραββι (*see* ‖ *Matt*) A: ειμι 69 [gat lat-g_2 copt] sah[-woide]. om και αλλος μη τι εγω (*prob from homœotel: or because the structure of the sentence seems not to admit the words aft* εις κατα εις. *Their* insertion *would be unaccountable*) BCLPΔℵ vulg lat-g_2 *l* syrr coptt æth arm: ins AD rel lat-*a f* ff_2 *i* (*k*) *q* syr-mg $Orig_1$.

20. rec ins αποκριθεις bef ειπεν αυτοις (‖ *Matt*), with AP rel lat-*k* syr æth arm: txt BCDLℵ latt Syr coptt. for ειπεν, λεγει D 2-pe latt. om εκ BCLℵ [coptt]. aft εμου ins την χειρα (‖ *Matt*) A vulg-ed(not am em harl[1] mg prag tol) lat-*a c* (*f*) ff_2 *q* coptt. εις το εντρυβλιον (or ἓν τρυβλιον) BC[1] (εν *was perhaps written in marg, from* ‖ *Matt, and then adopted ignorantly*): εν τω τρυβλιω (‖ *Matt*) 63 sah: εις το τρυβαλιον D[1].

21. rec om οτι (‖ *Matt: so also in* ‖ *Luke*), with ACDP rel lat-*a f* arm: ins BLℵ coptt. for υπαγει, παραδιδοται D lat-*a c i*. for γεγραπται, εστιν γεγραμμενον D. om ο υι. τ. ανθρ. D lat-*a*. rec aft καλον ins ην (‖ *Matt*), with ACDPℵ rel vulg lat-*a f* g_1 syrr copt æth arm: om BL prag lat-*c* (ff_2?) *i l q* sah. η ουκ εγενηθη (*cf* A *in* ‖ *Matt*) ALΔ: ει ουκ εγενηθη 69. 247 Scr's s.

22. rec aft λαβων ins ο ιησους (‖ *Matt*), with ACPℵ[1.3] rel vulg lat-*c f* [*q*] syrr copt æth arm: om BD ℵ-corr[1] lat-*a* ff_2 *i k* sah. ·εκλασεν bef ευλογ. ℵ. ευλογησεν και D 50 lat-*a* (*k*) Syr æth. rec aft λαβετε ins φαγετε (‖ *Matt*), with X rel lat-ff_2: om ABCDKLM[1]PU Δ(om λαβ. also Δ-gr) Πℵ 1 latt syrr coptt æth arm. τουτεστιν D(so ver 24).

23. rec ins το bef ποτηριον (‖ *Luke Paul*), with AP rel: om BCDLXΔℵ Frag-neap 1 arm. εδωκ. αυτ. bef ευχ. P.

24. om αυτοις B. rec ins το bef της (*somml emendn*), with AD[1]P rel lat-*i*: om BCD[2]ELVXℵ Frag-neap latt. rec ins καινης bef διαθηκης (*see* ‖ *Luke Paul*), with AP rel latt syrr sah-woide æth arm: om BCDLℵ lat-*k* copt sah-ming. rec περι πολλων εκχυν. (‖ *Matt*), with AP rel: υπερ π. εκχ. DΔ 69: txt BCLℵ. rec εκχυνομενον, with B[2] Frag-neap rel: txt AB[1]CDLPUΔΠ[1]ℵ.

25. om ουκετι CDLℵ em(with gat) lat-(*a f*) *c k* copt æth. προσθω πειν D 2-pe lat-*a f* arm. (rec γεννημ. with DKNΓ: txt ABCℵ rel.)

person, but give pathos to tne contrast which follows. **19.**] **εἷς κατά** (or καθ') **εἷς**, a later Greek phrase in which the preposition serves merely as an adverb of distribution, is treated by Winer, § 37. 3. The **ἄλλος** following is used as if not εἷς κατὰ εἷς but only εἷς had been used. Meyer remarks that such broken construction is suitable to the *graphic* tendency of our Evangelist. **20.**] This description of the traitor here again does not seem to *designate one* especially, nor to describe an action at that moment proceeding, but, as before, pathetically to describe the near relation of the betrayer to the Betrayed. Now however the relation pointed out is still closer than before —it is that of one dipping in the same dish—one of those nearest and most trusted.

z || Mt. Acts i. 22. Judg. i. 21.
a abs., || Mt. (reff.) only.
b Matt. xxi. 1 reff.
c = || Mt. reff.
d || Mt. reff. Zech. xiii. 7.
e Matt. xxv. 24, 26 reff. Zech. l. c. A [ℵ$^{3a \cdot b}$]. plur., Matt. vi. 28 reff.
f ch. i. 14. xvi. 19. Acts vii. 4 al. 1 Chron. ii. 24.
g Matt. xvii. 23 reff.
h Matt. xiv. 22 reff.
i ver. 72. Luke xviii. 12. Phil. iv. 16. 1 Thess. iv. 15. Jude 12 only. 3 Kings xi. 9.
j here, &c. || only. Prov. xxx. 31 only.
k here, &c. || only. Jer. xvii. 11.
l here, &c. ||. ch. viii. 34 ||. Luke xii. 9. (John xiii. 38 v. r.) only. Isa. xxxi. 7 only.
m here only. (see ch. vi. 51. Dan. iii. 22 Theod. Eph. iii. 20. 1 Thess. iii. 10. v. 13.)
n = Matt. xvi. 21 al.
o 2 Cor. vii. 3. 2 Tim. ii. 11 only †. Sir. xix. 9 only.

πέλου [z] ἕως τῆς [z] ἡμέρας ἐκείνης ὅταν αὐτὸ πίνω καινὸν ἐν   G ημερας
τῇ βασιλείᾳ τοῦ θεοῦ. 26 Καὶ [a] ὑμνήσαντες ἐξῆλθον εἰς   ABCDE FGHKL MNSUV XΓΔΠℵ Frag. Neap. 1. 69
τὸ [b] ὄρος τῶν [b] ἐλαιῶν. 27 καὶ λέγει αὐτοῖς ὁ Ἰησοῦς ὅτι
πάντες [c] σκανδαλισθήσεσθε, ὅτι γέγραπται [d] Πατάξω τὸν
ποιμένα, καὶ τὰ πρόβατα [e] διασκορπισθήσονται. 28 ἀλλὰ
[f] μετὰ τὸ [g] ἐγερθῆναί με [h] προάξω ὑμᾶς εἰς τὴν Γαλιλαίαν.
29 ὁ δὲ Πέτρος ἔφη αὐτῷ Εἰ καὶ πάντες [c] σκανδαλισθήσονται, ἀλλ᾽ οὐκ ἐγώ. 30 καὶ λέγει αὐτῷ ὁ Ἰησοῦς
Ἀμὴν λέγω σοι ὅτι σὺ σήμερον ταύτῃ τῇ νυκτὶ πρὶν ἢ
[i] δὶς [j] ἀλέκτορα [k] φωνῆσαι τρίς με [l] ἀπαρνήσῃ. 31 ὁ δὲ [m] ἐκπερισσῶς ἐλάλει Ἐάν με [n] δέῃ [o] συναποθανεῖν σοι, οὐ μή

27. for 1st και, τοτε D lat-*c* ff_2. aft παντες ins υμεις (|| *Matt*) D 69 gat lat-*a c* ff_2 g_2 *i k l* [*q*] (syrr) sah. rec aft σκανδαλισθησεσθε ins εν εμοι εν τη νυκτι ταυτη (*from* || *Matt*), with AC^{2}EFKMNUΠ$^{1 \cdot 3}$ vulg lat-*c* g_2 syrr sah æth arm: ins only εν εμοι G 28 lat-*a f i k* copt-wilk: om BC^{1}Dℵ rel am(with prag) lat-ff_2 copt-mss-schw. for οτι γεγρ., γεγραπται γαρ N [lat-*k*]: ιδου γεγρ. Δ. rec διασκορπισθησεται, with Frag-neap rel: txt ABCDFGKLNΔℵ. rec διασκ. bef τα προβ., with AN rel latt syrr copt æth: txt BCDLℵ 69 lat-*i k q* sah arm.

28. for αλλα, και C.

29. for εφη, λεγει D vulg lat-*a f* g_1 *i*; αποκριθεις λεγει 1. 69 (lat-*c k*) sah-woide. rec και bef ει (ει π. *after* || *Matt*), with AN rel syr copt: και εαν D: txt BCGLℵ 1. 69 arm. σκανδαλισθωσιν D 2-pe vulg lat-*c* ff_2 g_1 *i k* [*q*]. at end ins (|| *Matt*) ου σκανδαλισθησομαι D lat-ff_2 g_1 [*q* æth]. (D-corr om ου.)

30. rec om συ (|| *Matt*), with CDΔℵ lat-*a f* ff_2 *i q*: ins ABLN rel vulg lat-*c k* syrr coptt æth arm Thl Euthym. om σημερον (|| *Matt*) DS lat-*a f* ff_2 *i q* arm. rec εν τη νυκτι ταυτη (*from* || *Matt*), with AN rel vulg lat-*c* g_1: τη νυκτι ταυτη 1. 69: om S: txt BCDLℵ lat-*a f* ff_2 *i k* [*q*]. om η (|| *Matt Luke John*) Dℵ 69. om δις (|| *Matt Luke John*) C^{1}Dℵ tol^1(with prag) lat-*a c* ff_2 *i k* æth arm: ins aft αλεκτ. 69(τρις 69^1) Scr's c vulg: aft φων. C^2 coptt. rec απαρνηση bef με (|| *Matt*), with AN rel: om με L 69 lat-k^1: txt BCDΔ ℵ(σει) latt.

31. aft ο δε ins πετρος (|| *Matt*) ACGMNSU 1. 69 syr æth arm. rec (for εκπερισσως) εκ περισσου, with A rel: εκ περισιας Δ: περισσως L 69: txt BCDℵ. (N doubtful.) rec (for ελαλει) ελεγεν, with ACN rel syrr coptt: txt BDLℵ vulg lat-*c f* ff_2 *k* [*i q*] sah-ming. rec adds μαλλον (*gloss on* εκπερισ.), with A rel (lat-*c* ff_2 *k*) syr (æth); and, bef εκ περ. or περισσως, 1. 69: om BCDLℵ vulg lat-*a f* [*i q*] Syr coptt. δεη bef με (|| *Matt*) ABD^{2}LNℵ^{3a} Frag-neap 1. 69 latt Syr: txt C rel arm, εαν μη δεη D^1; εαν με η (sic) ℵ^1.

22—25.] Institution of the Lord's Supper. Matt. xxvi. 26—29. Luke xxii. 19, 20. 1 Cor. xi. 23—25. See notes on Matt.

26—31.] Declaration that all should forsake Him. Confidence of Peter. Matt. xxvi. 30—35. (See Luke xxii. 31—34, and notes there.) Our account is almost verbatim the same as that in Matt., where see notes. The few differences are there commented on.

29.] **εἰ καὶ πάντες**—**if even all**: *καὶ εἰ πάντες*—'*even if all.*' The *καί* before *εἰ* intensifies the whole hypothesis: the *και* after *εἰ* intensifies only that word which it introduces in the hypothesis. See Klotz on Devar. p. 519 f.: where however the account is not quite as clear as might be desired. **ἀλλά** has here its full adversative exceptional force—**notwithstanding**: cf. Il. θ. 153, 154, εἴπερ γάρ σ᾽ Ἕκτωρ γε κακὸν καὶ ἀνάλκιδα φήσει, **ἀλλ᾽** οὐ πείσονται Τρῶες καὶ Δαρδανίωνες: and Klotz on Devar. p. 93. 30.] Notice the climax: **σήμερον**, but not only this—**ταύτῃ τῇ νυκτί**, the part of it now present: nor only so, but **πρὶν ἢ δὶς ἀλέκτορα φωνῆσαι**, before a cock crow twice, i. e. long before the night is over. 31.] **ἐκπερισσῶς ἐλάλει**, went on

σε [1] ἀπαρνήσομαι. ὡσαύτως δὲ καὶ πάντες ἔλεγον.
32 Καὶ ἔρχονται εἰς [p] χωρίον οὗ τὸ ὄνομα Γεθσημανεῖ· καὶ
λέγει τοῖς μαθηταῖς αὐτοῦ Καθίσατε ὧδε [q] ἕως προσεύξωμαι. 33 καὶ [r] παραλαμβάνει τὸν Πέτρον καὶ Ἰάκωβον
καὶ Ἰωάννην μετ' αὐτοῦ, καὶ [s] ἤρξατο [t] ἐκθαμβεῖσθαι καὶ
[u] ἀδημονεῖν, 34 καὶ λέγει αὐτοῖς [v] Περίλυπός ἐστιν ἡ ψυχή
μου [w] ἕως θανάτου· μείνατε ὧδε καὶ [x] γρηγορεῖτε. 35 καὶ
[y] προελθὼν μικρὸν ἔπιπτεν ἐπὶ τῆς γῆς, καὶ [z] προσηύχετο
ἵνα εἰ δυνατόν ἐστιν [a] παρέλθῃ ἀπ' αὐτοῦ ἡ ὥρα, 36 καὶ
ἔλεγεν [b] Ἀββᾶ [b] ὁ πατήρ, πάντα δυνατά σοι· [c] παρένεγκε
τὸ [d] ποτήριον τοῦτο ἀπ' ἐμοῦ· ἀλλ' οὐ τί ἐγὼ θέλω,
ἀλλὰ τί σύ. 37 καὶ ἔρχεται καὶ εὑρίσκει αὐτοὺς καθεύδοντας, καὶ λέγει τῷ Πέτρῳ Σίμων, καθεύδεις; οὐκ
[e] ἴσχυσας μίαν ὥραν [f] γρηγορῆσαι; 38 [f] γρηγορεῖτε καὶ

p ‖ Mt. reff.
q constr., Luke xv. 4. Rev. vi. 11.
r ch. ix. 2 reff.
s ver. 19.
t ch. ix. 15. xvi. 5, 6 only +. Sir. xxx. 9 only.
u ‖ Mt. Phil. ii. 26 only. Job xviii. 20 Aq.
v ‖ Mt. ch. vi. 26. Luke xviii. 23, 24 only. Ps. xli. 5, 11.
w = ‖ Mt. reff.
x Matt. xxiv. 42 reff.
y ‖ Mt. reff.
z w. ἵνα, 1 Cor. xiv. 13.
a = Mt. only (see Matt. xxiv. 34, 35).
b Rom. viii. 15. Gal. iv. 6 only.
c = ‖ L. (Heb. xiii. 9. Jude 12) only. Ezra x. 7 (1 Kings xxi. 13) only.
d = ‖ Mt. reff.
e = Matt. viii. 28 reff.
f Matt. xxiv. 42 reff.

απαρνησωμαι EFGKMSUVXΓΠ²א. for ωsαυτωs, ομοιωs (‖ *Matt*) א¹. om και D[-gr].

32. for ου το, ῳ C 282. γετσημανει B : γησαμ. D : γεσσημ. EFGHX. om αυτου A lat-*k*¹. for τ. μ. αυτ., αυτοιs D lat-*a*. ωδε in B "superadditur" (Mai). aft εωs ins απελθων (*see* ‖ *Matt*) MN æth : αν απελθων U. προs-ευξομαι DHXΓ.

33. om τον א¹ Scr's g. rec ins τον bef ιακωβον, with ABKLΠ¹, of which ABKΠ¹ have also τον bef ιωανν. : alii aliter : om CDא rel Thl. rec μεθ' εαυτου, with AN rel : txt BCDא 69. ακηδεμονειν D¹(txt D-corr¹).

34. for και, τοτε D 69 lat-*a* arm.

35. προsελθων (*error*) AC D-gr rel lat-*ff*₂ syrr : txt BFKMNΠ¹·³א vss. rec (for επιπτεν) επεσεν (‖ *Matt*), with ACDN rel : txt BLא copt. add επι προsωπον (‖ *Matt*) DG 1. 69 [gat] lat-*a c f ff*₂ *g*₁.₂ *i k q* arm. ει δυν. εστιν bef ινα DG 1. 69 lat-*a k q* : om ινα א ; om εστιν א¹. παρελθιν א. at end add αυτη D lat-(*c ff*₂) *f i k*.

36. δυν. παντ. σοι D lat-*a i* copt : alii aliter. add εισιν D vulg lat-*ff*₂ [*f i q*]. παρcνεγκαι ACKΠ¹א Frag-neap. rec απ' εμου bef τουτο, with EFHSVΓ Frag-neap : τουτο το ποτ. απ' εμου DN 1 lat-*a* Orig₁ Hil : απ εμ. το π. τουτο KM[Π] prag lat-*c* syrr æth : txt ABCא rel vulg lat-*f ff*₂ *l* copt arm Orig₂. ins πλην bef αλλ (*see* ‖) N. for ου τι, ουχ ο D : ουχ ωs (‖ *Matt*) 13. 69. 346. 2-pe. for τι (bef συ), ο D 70 ; ωs (‖ *Matt*) 13. 69. 346. 2-pe : om Δ : ο τι G 1 : ει τι CU. aft συ add θελειs D lat-*a* (*c*) [*f ff*₂ *g*₂ *q* coptt æth arm].

37. om 3rd και A. om τω A. ισχυσατε (‖ *Matt*) D 1. 69 lat-*ff*₂ *k*.

repeating superabundantly: the **ἐλάλει** giving Peter's continued and excessive iteration, the **ἔλεγον** following expressing merely the one, or, at all events, less frequent saying of the same by the rest. The reading ἔλεγεν has apparently been a correction, λαλεῖν signifying to *speak* and not to *say*, and its peculiar fitness here being missed. **οὐ μή** with fut. indic. makes the certainty of the assertion doubly sure. The E. V. attempts to represent this by adding "*in any wise.*" We sometimes give the same effect by substituting the objective future for the subjective, "I never shall deny thee."

32—42.] Our Lord's agony at Gethsemane. Matt. xxvi. 36—46. Luke xxii. 39—46 (see John xviii. 1). The same remarks apply here also. 33.] Notice the graphic ἐκθαμβεῖσθαι, and see note on ch. ix. 15. St. Matt. has λυπεῖσθαι. 36.] **ἀββᾶ** = אַבָּא, an Aramaic form, and after Mark's manner inserted, as 'Ephphatha,' ch. vii. 34,—'Talitha cum,' ch. v. 41. **ὁ πατήρ** is not the interpretation of **ἀββᾶ**, but came to be attached to it *in one phrase*, as a form of address: see reff. Meyer rightly supplies the ellipsis after **ἀλλ'**: **nevertheless**, *the question is not* . . . : not οὐ

προσεύχεσθε, ἵνα μὴ ἔλθητε εἰς [g] πειρασμόν. τὸ μὲν ABCDE FGHKL
[h] πνεῦμα [i] πρόθυμον, ἡ δὲ [h] σὰρξ ἀσθενής. 39 καὶ πάλιν MNSUV
ἀπελθὼν προσηύξατο τὸν αὐτὸν λόγον εἰπών. 40 καὶ ΧΓΔΠℵ Frag.
πάλιν ἐλθὼν εὗρεν αὐτοὺς καθεύδοντας· ἦσαν γὰρ οἱ Neap. 1. 69
ὀφθαλμοὶ αὐτῶν [k] καταβαρυνόμενοι, καὶ οὐκ ᾔδεισαν τί
ἀποκριθῶσιν αὐτῷ. 41 καὶ ἔρχεται τὸ [l] τρίτον καὶ λέγει
αὐτοῖς Καθεύδετε [m] λοιπὸν καὶ [n] ἀναπαύεσθε· [o] ἀπέχει,
ἦλθεν ἡ ὥρα· ἰδοὺ [p] παραδίδοται ὁ υἱὸς τοῦ ἀνθρώπου εἰς
τὰς χεῖρας τῶν ἁμαρτωλῶν. 42 ἐγείρεσθε, [q] ἄγωμεν·
ἰδοὺ ὁ [r] παραδιδούς με ἤγγικεν. 43 Καὶ εὐθὺς ἔτι αὐτοῦ
λαλοῦντος [s] παραγίνεται ὁ Ἰούδας ὁ Ἰσκαριώτης, [t] εἷς
[ὢν] τῶν [t] δώδεκα, καὶ μετ' αὐτοῦ ὄχλος [u] μετὰ μαχαιρῶν
καὶ [v] ξύλων, παρὰ τῶν ἀρχιερέων καὶ τῶν γραμματέων
καὶ τῶν πρεσβυτέρων. 44 δεδώκει δὲ ὁ [r] παραδιδοὺς αὐτὸν

g Matt. vi. 13. 1 Tim. vi. 9. Deut. iv. 34.
h || Mt. 2 Cor. vii. 1.
i || Mt. Rom. i. 15 only. 1 Chron. xxviii. 21.
k here only. 2 Kings xiii. 25. (-ρεῖν, 2 Cor. xii. 16.)
l see John xxi. 14 reff.
m || Mt. 2 Cor. xiii. 11. 2 Tim. iv. 8. τὸ λ., Phil. iv. 8 al.
n || Mt. ch. vi. 31. Deut. xxxiii. 20. Dan. xii. 13.
o = here only, but? see Matt. vi. 2. cf. Num. xvi. 3.
p vv. 10, 11. Matt. xvii. 22 al. Ezek. xxiii. 28.
q = || Mt. ch. i. 38. John xi. 7, 15, 16. xiv. 13. only. (Matt. iii. 1 reff.)
r || Mt. reff.
s constr., w. παρά, here only.
t ver. 10.
u Matt. xxiv. 30. Acts xiii. 17. xxvi. 12.
v = here bis & || only. Herodian vii. 7.

38. om ινα D. rec εισελθητε (*from* || *Matt*), with ACDNℵ[3a] rel vss: txt Bℵ[1] 346 lat-*q* copt Cypr Fulg Paulin (*q* copt Cypr have ελθ. also, *from this place*, in || Matt).

39. om τον αυτον λογον ειπων D lat-*a c ff*$_2$ *k*.

40. rec υποστρεψας ευρ. αυτ. παλιν, with AC rel, and, but καθευδοντας bef παλιν, NX: om παλιν D lat-*a c ff*$_2$ *k q*: alii aliter: txt BLℵ copt. (*Txt being origl, and in Mark's manner,* παλιν *was transpd, and then* ελθων *expld and superseded by* υποστρ., *a word never used by Mark So Mey.*) αυτ. bef οι οφθ. (|| *Matt*) BCLΔℵ. rec (for καταβαρυνομενοι) βεβαρημενοι (*from* || *Matt*), with C rel: βαρυνομενοι M: καταβεβαρημενοι ℵ[1]: καταβαρουμενοι D 238-53: txt ABKLNUΔΠ[1]ℵ[3a] 1. 69. rec αυτω bef αποκριθωσιν, with N Frag-neap rel lat-*f k*: txt ABCDLU[2]ℵ latt syrr copt arm.

41. rec ins το bef λοιπον (*as also in* || *Matt*), with BGHKMNUV[1] Γ(Tischdf) ΔΠℵ 1. 69: txt ACD rel. (Frag-neap?) aft απεχει ins το τελος D 69 lat-*a c f ff*$_2$ syrr arm. for ηλθεν, και D. om τας AFKNUΠ Frag-neap 1. 69.

42. ηγγ. ο παραδιδων με D, and ηγγ. bef ο παρ. με [8-pe Scr's c] lat-*a c f ff*$_2$ *q* Syr coptt æth: ηγγισεν Cℵ.

43. (ευθυς, so BCLΔℵ: om D 1. 69 latt(not *f*) Syr arm.) rec om 1st ὁ (|| *Matt Luke*), with CDNℵ rel Orig$_1$: ins AB. rec om ο ισκαριωτης (|| *Matt Luke*), with BCNℵ rel am-txt coptt goth: ins A(D)KMUΠ Frag-neap latt am[2]-marg syrr arm Orig Thl.—om ο D Orig. om ων (*see* || *Matt Luke*) ABCDKLNSUΠℵ Frag-neap latt Syr coptt goth æth arm Orig Vict Thl: ins X rel syr. rec aft οχλος ins πολυς (*from* || *Matt*), with ACDN rel vulg lat-*c k* Orig: om BLℵ 69 prag lat-*a f ff*$_2$ *q* syrr coptt goth arm. for παρα, απο (|| *Matt*) B. ins απο bef των γραμματεων D am lat-*f*. om των (bef γραμ.) ACKMNΔ 1. 69. om των (bef πρεσβ.) AU ℵ[1](ins ℵ-corr[1]) 1. 69 [Orig$_1$].

44. for δεδωκει, εδωκεν D-gr lat-*a c k*.

γινέσθω, which would not come into construction with τί . . . τί. **39.] τὸν αὐτὸν λόγον**, not verbatim, but in substance: see || Matt. **41. ἀπέχει]** Scil. your γρηγορεῖν μετ' ἐμοῦ. The Lord had no need of it any more, now that the hour had come: not, as Bengel, Kuinoel, al., 'Satis somnorum est:' this, as Meyer observes, is refuted by the καθεύδετε λοιπόν. This meaning of ἀπέχει, *sufficit*, is found in very few and late, but those quite sufficient examples. Meyer mentions Pseud.-Anacreon, Od. xxviii. 33, **ἀπέχει**, βλέπω γὰρ αὐτήν: and Cyril on Hag. ii. 9, ἐμὸν φησὶ τὸ ἀργύριον καὶ ἐμὸν τὸ χρυσίον· τουτέστιν **ἀπέχει**, καὶ πεπλήρωμαι, καὶ δεδέημαι τῶν τοιούτων οὐδενός.

43—52.] Betrayal and apprehension of Jesus. Matt. xxvi. 47—56. Luke xxii. 47—53. **44.]** On the plu-

w σύσσημον αὐτοῖς λέγων Ὃν ἂν x φιλήσω αὐτός ἐστιν·
y κρατήσατε αὐτὸν καὶ z ἀπάγετε a ἀσφαλῶς. 45 καὶ
ἐλθὼν εὐθὺς προσελθὼν αὐτῷ λέγει Ῥαββεί, [ῥαββεί,]
καὶ b κατεφίλησεν αὐτόν· 46 οἱ δὲ bc ἐπέβαλον τὰς χεῖρας
αὐτῷ καὶ y ἐκράτησαν αὐτόν. 47 εἷς δὲ * τῶν d παρεστηκότων e σπασάμενος τὴν μάχαιραν f ἔπαισεν τὸν δοῦλον
τοῦ ἀρχιερέως καὶ g ἀφεῖλεν αὐτοῦ τὸ h ὠτάριον. 48 καὶ
i ἀποκριθεὶς ὁ Ἰησοῦς εἶπεν αὐτοῖς Ὡς ἐπὶ j λῃστὴν
ἐξήλθατε u μετὰ μαχαιρῶν καὶ v ξύλων k συλλαβεῖν με.
49 l καθ' ἡμέραν m ἤμην m πρὸς ὑμᾶς ἐν τῷ ἱερῷ διδάσκων,
καὶ οὐκ y ἐκρατήσατέ με. ἀλλ' n ἵνα πληρωθῶσιν αἱ γραφαί. 50 καὶ o ἀφέντες αὐτὸν ἔφυγον πάντες. 51 καὶ p εἷς

P συλλαβειν ...

w here only. Judg. xx. 38, & 40 B. Isa. v. 26. xlix. 22. lxii. 10 only. x || Mt. reff. y || Mt. Matt. xxi. 46 reff. z = Matt. xxvi. 57. xxvii. 2. a = Acts (ii. 36) xvi. 23 only. Tobit vi. 4. b || Mt. reff. c constr., Acts iv. 3 only. Isa. xix. 16. d vv. 69, 70. ch. xv. 35, 39. John xviii. 22 al. Sir. li. 3. e Acts xvi. 27 only. Num. xxii. 23, 31. f = || J. (Matt. xxvi. 68 || L. Rev. ix. 5) only. Num. xxii. 28. g || Mt. L. 1 Kings xvii. 51. h || J. only †. i red., Matt. xi. 25 reff. j Matt. xxi. 13 reff. k = || Mt. reff. l || Mt. reff. m Matt. xiii. 56. John i. 1. 1 Thess. iii. 4. n ellips., John i. 8. ix. 3. xiii. 18. o = Matt. iv. 11 al. p Luke xxii. 50. John xi. 49.

for *συσσημον*, *σημειον* D Scr's s : *συνσ.* ΔΝ. om *αυτοις* D 2-pe prag lat-*a c ff*$_2$ *k* [*q*]. *ον εαν* LN : *ο εαν* Δ. rec **απαγαγετε**, with ACN rel : *αγαγετε* F Scr's k o s ev-y : txt BDLℵ 69. add *αυτον* DN 13. 157. 2-pe ev-y lat-*a g*$_1$ Syr syr-w-ob coptt æth.

45. om *ελθων* D 1 lat-*a c ff*$_2$ *k* [*q*] Syr arm. (*ευθυς*, so BCLΔℵ : om D 251. 2-pe lat-*a c ff*$_2$ *k q*.) add *και* ℵ[1]. *λεγει* bef *αυτω* DFΓ lat-*a c ff*$_2$ (*k*) [*q*] Syr arm : *αυτω λεγει αυτω* EGHSV Frag-neap 1 : *τω ιησ. λεγ. αυτ.* N. (*ραββει*, so ABCDEHXℵ.) om 2nd *ραββει* (*see* || *Matt*) BC[1]DLMΔℵ am(with em fuld ing prag) lat-*f ff*$_2$ *g*$_{1.2}$ *k* [*q*] copt æth : *χαιρε ραββει* (|| *Matt*) C[2] 1. 69 ev-y latt syr-mg sah.

46. *επεβαλαν* Bℵ. rec *επεβ. επ αυτον τας χ. αυτων*, with X rel; and, omg *αυτων*, M[1]S vulg lat-*c f* syrr goth arm : *επεβ. τ. χ. αυτων επ αυτον* AKΠ coptt : *επεβ. τ. χ. αυτων* (*this reading seems to point at txt as origl*) C Δ(-*τον*) ℵ[1] : *επεβ. αυτω τ. χ. αυτων* N : txt BDLℵ[3a] 1. 69.

47. *rec aft *εις δε* ins *τις* (*from* || *Luke*), with BCN rel vulg lat-*a* syr goth arm : for *εις δε, και τις* D : *και εις τις* 1 lat-*c* [*ff*$_2$] *k q* : txt ALMℵ lat-*f* Syr coptt æth. om *των παρεστηκ.* D lat-*a*. om *την* D 1 evv-H-y. aft *μαχαιραν* ins *και* ℵ[1]. (*επαισεν* is itacised into *επεσεν* in CDHLΓΔΠ[1]ℵ.) rec (for *ωταριον*) *ωτιον* (|| *Matt*), with ACN rel : txt BDℵ 1 syr-mg.

48. for *και αποκ. ο*, *ο δε* D lat-*a ff*$_2$ *q*. om *ως* D. (*εξηλθατε*, so ABCDE GHLNXΔℵ 69 ev-y.)

49. *διδ.* bef *εν τω ιερ.* P Scr's c e lat-*f q* D-lat Syr copt æth arm. *εκρατει* B. at end add *των προφητων* (|| *Matt*) N 69 Scr's c syr-w-ast [sah] arm.

50. for *και*, *τοτε οι μαθηται* (|| *Matt*) N 69 Scr's c vulg lat-*c g*$_{1.2}$ *l* (Syr) syr sah (æth) arm. rec *παντες* bef *εφυγον* (|| *Matt*), with ADP rel latt syr (sah æth) arm : om *παντες* N Scr's s [Syr] : txt BCLΔℵ copt goth.

perfect without the augment, see Winer, § 12. 9. **σύσσημον** is a word belonging to later Greek. We have in Diod. Sic. xx. 42, ἦρε τὸ συγκείμενον πρὸς μάχην **σύσσημον**, ἀσπίδα κεχρυσωμένην. See other examples in Kypke. **ἀπάγετε ἀσφαλῶς**] It does not quite appear whether **ἀσφαλῶς** is to be subjectively taken, '*with confidence;*' or objectively, '*safely.*' Some suppose that it has an ironical meaning—q. d. 'He will know how to rescue himself—take care that you keep Him safe.' This of course depends upon the view taken of the whole character and purpose of Judas, on which see notes at Matt. xxvi. 14 and xxvii. 3. **45.**] **ῥαββεί** appears to have been the usual form in which Judas addressed our Lord—see Matt. xxvi. 25. But we must not conclude from this with Bengel, that he never seems to have called Him *Lord:* see Matt. vii. 21, 22. **51.**] It is impossible to determine, and therefore idle to enquire, *who this was.* Epiphanius, Hær. lxxviii. 13, vol. i. (ii., Migne) p. 1045, in recounting the traditional austerities of James the brother of the Lord, says, ὃς χιτώνιον δεύτερον οὐκ ἐνεδύσατο ὃς τριβωνίῳ ἐκέ-

q Matt. xix. 20, 22 reff.
r ch. v. 37 reff.
s Matt. vi. 29, 31 reff. ch. xvi. 5.
t here bis. ch. xv. 46 (bis) ‖ Mt. L. only. Judg. xiv. 12, 13 A. Prov. xxxi. 24 only.
u = Rev. xvii. 16. Job xxxi. 19.
v ‖ Mt. reff.
w see ch. xv. 38 ‖. Luke xxiii. 5. John ii. 7. 2 Chron. xxvi. 8.
x Matt. vii. 29 reff.
y Acts xxvi. 30 only. Exod. xxiii. 32 33 Ald.

τις [q] νεανίσκος [r] συνηκολούθει αὐτῷ [s] περιβεβλημένος ABCDE FGHKL
[t] σινδόνα ἐπὶ [u] γυμνοῦ· καὶ κρατοῦσιν αὐτόν, 52 ὁ δὲ κατα- MNPS UVXΓΔ
λιπὼν τὴν [t] σινδόνα γυμνὸς ἔφυγεν ἀπ' αὐτῶν. 53 Καὶ ΠΝ
ἀπήγαγον τὸν Ἰησοῦν πρὸς τὸν ἀρχιερέα, καὶ συνέρχον- Frag. Neap.
ται αὐτῷ πάντες οἱ ἀρχιερεῖς καὶ οἱ πρεσβύτεροι καὶ οἱ 1. 69
γραμματεῖς. 54 καὶ ὁ Πέτρος [v] ἀπὸ [v] μακρόθεν ἠκολούθησεν αὐτῷ [w] ἕως ἔσω· εἰς τὴν αὐλὴν τοῦ ἀρχιερέως, καὶ
[x] ἦν [y] συγκαθήμενος μετὰ τῶν ὑπηρετῶν καὶ [z] θερμαινό- ...μετα F.
μενος [a] πρὸς τὸ [b] φῶς. 55 οἱ δὲ ἀρχιερεῖς καὶ ὅλον τὸ
[c] συνέδριον [d] ἐζήτουν κατὰ τοῦ Ἰησοῦ μαρτυρίαν [e] εἰς τὸ

z ver. 67. John xviii. 18 bis, 25. James ii. 16 only. Hag. i. 6.
a = ch. xi. 4. Luke xxii. 56.
b = Luke xxii. 56 only. see Isa. l. 11. 1 Macc. xii. 29.
c Matt. v. 22. Acts v. 41 al. Prov. xxii. 10.
d = Matt. xii. 43. Luke xiii. 6, 7. Ruth iii. 2 B.
e Matt. xxvi. 2. Acts iii. 19. Rom. i. 11 al. fr.

51. *κ. νεαν. τις* (*corrn to more usual exprn*) BCLℵ lat-*a* Syr copt æth arm: *ν. δε τις* D vulg lat-*c f* (*ff*$_2$) *k l* [*q*] sah: txt ANP rel syr goth. rec (for *συνηκ.*) *ηκολουθει* (*corrn to more usual word, as in ch* v. 37), with D 1 latt Syr arm: *ηκολουθησεν* ANP rel syr goth Thl: *συνηκολουθησεν* Δ: txt BCLℵ. (Frag-neap?) for *αυτω*, *αυτους* D. rec at end ins *οι νεανισκοι* (*prob arising from the words τον νεανισκον in marg, as a gloss on αυτον. This is further shewn by οι νεαν. εκρατησαν αυτ. standing in some cursives, and οι ν. κρατουσιν αυτ. in another*), with AC²NP rel lat-*q* syr goth æth arm: om BC¹DLΔℵ latt Syr copt Thl.

52. *καταλειπων* (*itacism?*) DKPX Frag-neap. om *απ' αυτων* (*as superfl, no subject to κρατουσιν having been mentd*) BCLℵ lat-*c k* Syr coptt æth: ins ADNP rel vulg lat-*a f* syr goth arm. (Frag-neap?)

53. aft *αρχ.* ins *καιαφαν* AKMΠ 69 (Syr) syr sah-woide arm (Orig$_1$). om *αυτω* DLΔℵ 69 latt æth Orig: *προς αυτον* C Syr. (Frag-neap?) [om *παντες* C lat-*ff*$_2$.] om 2nd and 3rd *οι* D Orig$_1$. transp *πρεσβ.* and *γρ.* ADKΠ latt Syr æth arm Orig$_1$.

54. om *εσω* D Scr's d (c ev-y) 1 am(with gat) lat-*a ff*$_2$ *g*$_1$ *k l.* for *συγκαθ.*, *καθημενος* D. om *και* (bef *θερμ.*) D lat-*a c* [*k q*] sah. elz om *το*, with Scr's q¹ r(e sil): ins ABCDNℵ rel. [om *π. το φ.* 1.] (Tischdf has not cited any readings of Frag-neap in vv. 54, 56—59.)

55. for *μαρτυριαν*, *ψευδομαρτυριαν* A S¹(Tischdf) 259 Scr's e lat-*k* coptt. [for

χρητο λίνῳ μονωτάτῳ, καθάπερ ἐν εὐαγγελίῳ φησὶν· Ἔφυγεν ὁ νεανίας καὶ ἀφῆκε τὴν σινδόνα ἣν ἦν περιβεβλημένος. Chrys. al. supposed it to have been St. John: alii aliter. It seems to have been some attached disciple of the Lord (probably well known to the readers of Mark), who had gone to rest, and had been aroused by the intelligence. The *disciples* were not laid hold of:—this person perhaps was throwing some obstacle in the way of the removal of Jesus: or he may have been laid hold of merely in wantonness, from his unusual garb. **γυμνοῦ** does not require *σώματος* to be supplied, but *γυμνόν* is a neuter substantive: see on this usage generally Kühner, Gramm. ii. p. 118.

53—65.] Hearing before Caiaphas. Matt. xxvi. 57—68. (Luke xxii. 54, 63—65.) John xviii. 24. See throughout notes on Matt. **53. ἀρχιερέα**] *Caiaphas, de facto*, and in the view of our narrator;—so Matt. and Luke: but Jesus was *first* taken before *Annas*, who was *de jure* the high-priest: see John xviii. 12—23. It is not easy to interpret **συνέρχονται αὐτῷ.** Meyer, relying on the fact that the dative after *συνέρχεσθαι* is always one of companionship, maintains that *αὐτῷ* refers to our Lord—'*there come with him.*' And so Winer, ed. 6, § 31. 5 ad fin. But surely this is very precarious. For 1) St. Mark uses this verb once only besides here, and then absolutely. And there could be no difficulty in taking it thus here and applying *αὐτῷ* to the High-priest as a dative of *direction.* And 2) could it be said of one whom they *ἀπήγαγον*, that he *ἔρχεται* to the High-priest? I venture therefore to prefer the usual construction of the words, '*there come together to him.*' The E. V. has '*with him were assembled;*' and so Winer in former editions of his Grammar. **54.**] The usage of **φῶς** for *a fire* is found in Xen. Cyr. vii. 5. 27, *οἱ δ' ἐπὶ τοὺς φύλακας*

f θανατῶσαι αὐτόν, καὶ οὐχ ηὕρισκον. 56 πολλοὶ γὰρ
g ἐψευδομαρτύρουν κατ' αὐτοῦ, καὶ h ἴσαι αἱ μαρτυρίαι οὐκ
ἦσαν. 57 καί τινες i ἀναστάντες g ἐψευδομαρτύρουν κατ'
αὐτοῦ λέγοντες 58 ὅτι ἡμεῖς ἠκούσαμεν αὐτοῦ λέγοντος
ὅτι ἐγὼ k καταλύσω τὸν ναὸν τοῦτον τὸν l χειροποίητον,
καὶ m διὰ τριῶν ἡμερῶν ἄλλον n ἀχειροποίητον οἰκοδομήσω. 59 καὶ οὐδὲ οὕτως h ἴση ἦν ἡ μαρτυρία αὐτῶν.
60 καὶ i ἀναστὰς ὁ ἀρχιερεὺς o εἰς μέσον ἐπηρώτησεν τὸν
Ἰησοῦν λέγων Οὐκ ἀποκρίνῃ οὐδὲν p τί οὗτοί σου q κατα-
μαρτυροῦσιν; 61 ὁ δὲ r ἐσιώπα καὶ οὐδεν ἀπεκρίνατο.
πάλιν ὁ ἀρχιερεὺς ἐπηρώτα αὐτὸν καὶ λέγει αὐτῷ Σὺ
εἶ ὁ χριστὸς ὁ υἱὸς τοῦ s εὐλογητοῦ; 62 ὁ δὲ Ἰησοῦς
εἶπεν t Ἐγώ εἰμι· καὶ ὄψεσθε τὸν u υἱὸν τοῦ u ἀνθρώπου
v ἐκ δεξιῶν καθήμενον τῆς w δυνάμεως καὶ x ἐρχόμενον

I_c οικο-δομησω ...

33 τι...

...επη-ρωτα P.

f Matt. x. 21. xxvii. 1 al. 2 Chron. xxiii. 15.
g Matt. xix. 18 || (& Rom. xiii. 9 v. r.) only, from Exod. xx. 16. Deut. v. 20.
h = here bis only? (Matt. xx. 12 reff.)
i Acts i. 15. vi. 9. 2 Chron. xx. 5.
k || Mt. Matt. xxiv. 2. xxvii. 40. John ii. 19. Ezra v. 12.
l Acts vii. 48. xvii. 24. Eph. ii. 11. Heb. ix. 11, 24 only. Isa. ii. 18.
m || Mt. ch. ii. 1. Acts xxiv. 17. Gal. ii. 1. Deut. ix. 11.
n 2 Cor. v. 1. Col. ii. 11 only †.
o ch. iii. 3 || L. John xx. 19, 26.
p || Mt.
q || Mt. Matt. xxvii. 13. (ch. xv. 4 v. r.) only. Job xv. 6.
r Matt. xx. 31 reff.
s (see note) Luke i. 68. Rom. i. 25. ix. 5. 2 Cor. i. 3. xi. 31. Eph. i. 3. 1 Pet. i. 3 only. Gen. ix. 26.
t ch. xiii. 6 reff.
u Matt. viii. 20 reff.
v Matt. xx. 21, 23 reff.
w = || only. so δόξης, 2 Pet. i. 17.
x Matt. xxiv. 30 reff.

εις το θ] ιναθανατωσουσιν D 2-pe(-σωσ-) latt. (ηυρισκ., so BD F(Wetst) LP(Δ) 1.)

56. aft εψευδ. ins ελεγον D^1-gr(και ελεγ. D^2)

57. for και τινες, και αλλοι D lat-*a* *ff*$_2$ *k* *q* Orig-int$_1$; αλλοι δε 69. 2-pe lat-*c*. for κατ' αυτ. λεγ., και ελεγον κατ' αυτ. D; latt vary.

58. for ημεις to λεγοντος, ειπεν (*cf* || *Matt*) ℵ lat *c* *k*. καταλυω [for -σω] $AΠ^1$ 2 vulg-mss goth Orig-int$_1$. om τουτον D-gr goth. αλλον αχειρ. bef τρ. ημ. N. for αχειρ. οικοδ., αναστησω αχειρ. D lat-*a* (*c*) *ff*$_2$ *k*.

59. ην bef ιση DL 1 latt.

60. rec ins το bef μεσον, with D (M 1, e sil) copt: om $ABCI_c$Nℵ rel Orig Thl. αποκρινει HI_c ev-y. for τι, ο τι B.

61. ος δε $B^{2\cdot3}$(Tischdf, = B-corr$^{1\cdot2}$): εκεινος δε D vulg lat-*c* *ff*$_2$ *k* *l* [Orig$_2$]: ο δε ιησ. Aℵ 251 Syr [(æth)]. for εσιωπα, εσειγα D. ουκ απεκρ. ουδεν (*conformation to foregoing question*) BCLℵ 33 copt (sah goth) æth [Orig$_1$]: ουδεν απεκριθη D. aft παλιν ins ουν I_c [lat-*k*]: και παλιν 1. 69 [Syr]. for παλιν to αυτω, και λεγει αυτω ο αρχ. D lat-(*ff*$_2$ *k*) [*q*]: al vary, addg εκ δευτερου &c (*see Scholz*). επερωτα A: επηρωτησεν F(Wetst) I_c Orig$_1$. ins τ. θεου bef τ. ευλογ. AKΠ vulg-ed lat-*ff*$_2$ arm-zoh Euthym [Clem-int$_1$]: for ευλογ., θεου ℵ^1(txt ℵ$^{3a\cdot b}$).

62. aft ιησ. ins αποκριθεις DG 1. 69 lat-*a* *ff*$_2$ (*k*) *q* sah (arm) Orig$_1$ Clem-int$_1$. for ειπεν, λεγει D 2-pe Orig. add αυτω DG 1. 69 Scr's c ev-y latt syrr copt-[wilk-] mss æth arm Orig. rec καθ. bef εκ δεξ. (|| *Matt*), with AI_c X(Treg) 1. 33 vulg-ed lat-*c* *f* *ff*$_2$ *k* syrr coptt (æth) arm Orig: txt BCDNℵ rel am(with em fuld ing mt prag tol) lat-(*a*) *l* *q* goth Orig$_1$[and int$_1$] Clem-int. om της (bef δυν.] D^1(ins D^4). om κ. ερχ. D-gr.

ταχθέντες ἐπεισπίπτουσιν αὐτοῖς πίνουσι πρὸς φῶς πολύ. **56.**] **ἴσαι**—consistent with one another. It was necessary that two witnesses should agree. Deut. xvii. 6. (ἴσος should not be accentuated as in Homer, ἶσος, but as in later writers, ἴσος.) **57.**] **τινες,**—*two*: see Matt. **58.**] **ἡμεῖς** and **ἐγώ** are emphatic. Some have imagined (De Wette, Meyer) that they find in these words **χειροπ.** and **ἀχειρ.** traces of later Christian tradition, and an allusion to Heb. ix. 11: Acts vii. 48; but such conjectures are at best very unsafe, and the words are quite as likely to have been uttered by the Lord as they here stand. The allusion is probably to Dan. ii. 34. **59.**] Perhaps the inconsistency of these testimonies may be traced in the different reports here and in Matt. **οὕτως,**—'*in asserting this*'—i. e. they varied in the terms in which it was expressed. **60.**] On the most probable punctuation and construction, see note on Matt. ver. 62. **61.**] **τοῦ εὐλ.**, Heb. הַבָּרוּךְ, the ordinary Name for God. "This is the only

[y] μετὰ τῶν [x] νεφελῶν τοῦ οὐρανοῦ. 63 ὁ δὲ ἀρχιερεὺς
[z] διαῤῥήξας τοὺς [a] χιτῶνας αὐτοῦ λέγει Τί ἔτι [b] χρείαν
[b] ἔχομεν μαρτύρων; 64 ἠκούσατε τῆς [c] βλασφημίας. τί
ὑμῖν [d] φαίνεται; οἱ δὲ πάντες [e] κατέκριναν αὐτὸν [f] ἔνοχον
εἶναι θανάτου. 65 καὶ ἤρξαντό τινες [g] ἐμπτύειν αὐτῷ
καὶ [h] περικαλύπτειν αὐτοῦ τὸ πρόσωπον καὶ [i] κολαφίζειν
αὐτόν, καὶ λέγειν αὐτῷ [k] Προφήτευσον· καὶ οἱ ὑπηρέται
[l] ῥαπίσμασιν αὐτὸν [m] ἔλαβον. 66 Καὶ ὄντος τοῦ Πέτρου
κάτω ἐν τῇ [n] αὐλῇ ἔρχεται μία τῶν [o] παιδισκῶν τοῦ
ἀρχιερέως. 67 καὶ ἰδοῦσα τὸν Πέτρον [p] θερμαινόμενον,
[q] ἐμβλέψασα αὐτῷ λέγει Καὶ σὺ μετὰ τοῦ Ναζαρηνοῦ
[r] ἦσθα τοῦ Ἰησοῦ. 68 ὁ δὲ ἠρνήσατο λέγων Οὔτε οἶδα,

ABCDE GHI$_c$K LMNSU VXΓΔ Πℵ Frag. Neap. 1. 33. 69

..xiv. 66 (appy) Frag. Neap.

y ver. 43 ||. z || Mt. Luke v. 7. viii. 29. Acts xiv. 14 only. Lev. xxi. 10. Josh. vii. 6. a John xix. 23 (bis) reff. pl., = here (ch. vi. 9 al.) only. 2 Macc. iv. 38. b Matt. vi. 8 reff. Wisd. xiii. 16. c = Matt. xii. 31. Ezek. xxxv. 12. d = here only. e Matt. xx. 18 reff. f || Mt. reff. g || Mt. ch. x. 34 || L. xv. 19 || Mt. only. Num. xii. 14. Deut. xxv. 9 only. h || L. Heb. ix. 4 only. Exod. xxviii. 20. 3 Kings vii. 42. viii. 7 only. i || Mt. 1 Pet. iii. 20. 1 Cor. iv. 11. 2 Cor. xii. 7 +. k = || Mt. L. only. l John xviii. 22. xix. 3 only. Isa. l. 6 only. (-φίζειν, Matt. v. 39.) m = (appy) here only. n Matt. xxvi. 3 reff. o ||. Luke xii. 45. Acts xii. 13. Gen. xii. 16. xx. 17. p ver. 54 reff. q ch. x. 21 reff. r || Mt. only. Gen. xl. 13 al.

63. διαρηξας B[1]N. ins και bef λεγει D lat-*c ff*$_2$ *k* [*q*].

64. at beg ins ιδε νυν (|| *Matt*) ℵ. aft ηκ. ins παντες GN **1** Scr's c sah-woide arm. την βλασψημιαν (|| *Matt*) ADG **1.** 69. add αυτου DGI$_c$N gat(with mt) lat-*q* goth æth; του στοματος αυτου 69 (Syr) syr-mg sah-woide arm. for φαινεται, δοκει (|| *Matt*) DN ev-H sah. παντες δε D lat-*c k*: και παντες **1.** 69 lat-*a f ff*$_2$ *q*. αυτω D[1](txt D[4]). rec ειναι bef ενοχον, with AN rel latt coptt arm: om ειναι D lat-*ff*$_2$: txt BCLΔℵ 33 lat-*l q* goth. (I$_c$ def.)

65. for 1st αυτω, τω προσωπω αυτου (|| *Matt*) D lat-*a f* Syr coptt goth arm. om κ. περικ. αυτ. το προσωπον (|| *Matt*) D lat-*a f*. rec το προσωπον bef αυτου (|| *Matt*), with AI$_c$N rel vulg lat-*c ff*$_2$ *k* [*l q*]: txt BCLUΔℵ 33. εκολαφιζον αυτον κ. ελεγον D lat-*c k* goth. om 2nd αυτω I$_c$ **1.** 69 Syr arm. aft προφ. ins ημιν χριστε τις εστιν ο παισας σε (*see* ||) I$_c$UX(Δ) 33 (69) gat syr coptt æth arm: ημιν F(Wetst) Scr's g [lat-*c f k*]: νυν G **1.** om οι υπηρ. D. rec (for ελαβον) εβαλλον (*see note*), with H: εβαλον EMUX Frag-neap 33: ελαμβανον D(bef αυτ.) G **1.** 69 syr copt: txt ABCI$_c$Nℵ rel.

66. rec εν τ. αυλ. bef κατω, with AN rel vulg lat-*f* (*g*$_1$) *k* [*l*] syr goth [Aug$_1$]: om κατω DI$_c$ 69 lat-*a c ff*$_2$ *q* coptt Eus$_1$: txt BCLU[2]Xℵ 33 Syr æth arm. aft ερχ. ins προς αυτον D lat-*a c f ff*$_2$ (*k*) *q* Eus$_1$. for των παιδισκων, παιδισκη (|| *Matt*) Cℵ.

67. λεγει bef αυτω D lat-*c ff*$_2$ *q*. om 2nd και D-gr. rec μετα του ναζ. ιησ. ησθα, with AN rel: μετα τ. ιησ. τ. ναζ. ησθα (|| *Matt*) D(ναζορ.) Δ [latt] syr goth æth arm Eus: ησθα μετα ιησ. του ναζ. 33 coptt: μετα του[. . . . . .] I$_c$: μετα τ. ιησ. ησθα τ. ναζ. ℵ Syr: txt BCL. (τ. ιησ. *was omd as superfl: then variously reinsd.*) ης **1.** 69 Eus.

68. rec (for ουτε, twice) ουκ (|| *Matt Luke*) and ουδε, with AN rel lat-*a*: ουκ and ουτε CEGHSVΔ: [. . .] ουκ επιστ. τι I$_c$: txt BDLℵ 2-pe vulg lat-*c f* Eus.

place in the N. T. where the well-known Sanctus Benediccus of the Rabbis is thus absolutely given." Meyer. **62.**] The ἀπ' ἄρτι of Matt., and ἀπο τοῦ νῦν of Luke, are here omitted. **63.**] **χιτῶνας**—not his *priestly robe*, which was worn only in the temple, and when officiating: see on Matt. ver. 65. The plural, τοὺς χιτ., perhaps is due to the wearing of two inner garments by persons of note: see Winer, Realw. art. "Kleidung," i. p. 662.

65.] **ἤρξαντο**—when the sentence was pronounced. The **τινες** appear to be members of the Sanhedrim: the *servants* follow. **προφήτ.**] Matt. and Luke explain this: 'Prophesy, *who smote thee?*'

The reading **ἔλαβον** is harsh in sense, but the coincidence of ἐλάμβανον in DG al. seems to stamp it with genuineness. The meaning must be '*took Him in hand with*,' '*treated Him with*.' Meyer understands it, took Him into custody, with . . . , for the further carrying out of the sentence against Him. But the unemphatic position of the verb seems to preclude this.

66—72.] Our Lord is thrice denied by Peter. Matt. xxvi. 69—75. Luke

οὔτε ἐπίσταμαι σὺ τί λέγεις. καὶ ἐξῆλθεν ἔξω εἰς τὸ
[s] προαύλιον, καὶ [t] ἀλέκτωρ [t] ἐφώνησεν. 69 καὶ ἡ [o] παιδίσκη
ἰδοῦσα αὐτὸν [u] ἤρξατο λέγειν τοῖς [v] παρεστῶσιν ὅτι
οὗτος [w] ἐξ αὐτῶν ἐστιν· 70 ὁ δὲ πάλιν ἠρνεῖτο. καὶ
[x] μετὰ [xy] μικρὸν πάλιν οἱ [v] παρεστῶτες ἔλεγον τῷ Πέτρῳ
Ἀληθῶς [w] ἐξ αὐτῶν εἶ· καὶ γὰρ Γαλιλαῖος εἶ. 71 ὁ δὲ
[u] ἤρξατο [z] ἀναθεματίζειν καὶ ὀμνύναι ὅτι οὐκ οἶδα τὸν
ἄνθρωπον τοῦτον ὃν [a] λέγετε. 72 καὶ [b] ἐκ δευτέρου [t] ἀλέκτωρ [t] ἐφώνησεν. καὶ [c] ἀνεμνήσθη ὁ Πέτρος τὸ ῥῆμα ὡς
εἶπεν αὐτῷ ὁ Ἰησοῦς ὅτι πρὶν [t] ἀλέκτορα [t] δὶς [t] φωνῆσαι,
τρίς με [t] ἀπαρνήσῃ. καὶ [d] ἐπιβαλὼν [e] ἔκλαιεν.

...εξ αυτων I_c

s here only +.
t ver. 30 reff.
u Matt. xxvi. 22 al. fr.
v ver. 47 reff.
w = Acts xxi. 8. 2 Tim. iii. 6 al. Obad. 11.
x ‖ Mt. only.
y = John xiii. 33. xiv. 19. xvi. 16, &c. Heb. x. 37. Isa. xxvi. 20.
z Acts xxiii. 12, 14, 21 only ‡. see Num. xviii. 14.
a = John vi. 71.
b Matt. xxvi. 42 reff.
c ch. xi. 21 reff.
d see note.
e ‖ Mt. reff.

rec τι bef συ (συ omd, *as in* D, *from* ‖ *Matt, then reinsd*), with AI_c rel coptt goth arm Eus: om συ D latt: txt BCLNUΔℵ 1. 33. 2-pe. om 1st και D-gr. εις την προσαυλην D. om κ. αλ. εφων. (*to suit* ‖ *Matt*) BLℵ lat-*c* copt: ins ACDI_cN rel vulg lat-*a f ff*$_2$ *k* [*l q*] syrr sah-ming goth æth arm Eus.

69. rec aft αυτον ins παλιν (*interpoln, as is shewn by the varn of position*), with AI_cN rel (lat-*a c*) syr goth: aft ηρξατο CLΔℵ; bef ιδουσα D(π. δε ειδουσα αυτ. η παιδ.) 2-pe vulg (lat-*k* Syr): om BM coptt æth.—aft παιδ. ins (*by transpn from below*) ο δε παλιν ηρνησατο D. for ηρξ. λεγ., ειπεν B. rec παρεστηκοσιν, with ADN rel: txt BCI_cKLΔΠ[1]ℵ Eus. aft οτι ins και D 69 lat-*a c ff*$_2$ Syr æth arm. αυτος D.

70. om ο δε παλ. ηρν. D(*but see above, ver* 69): ηρνησατο F(Wetst) GMNXΔ 1. 69 latt syr coptt goth Eus. om 1st και ℵ copt-dz. παρεστηκοτες D: περιεστωτες G 1. om τω πετρω D lat-*a*. rec at end ins και η λαλια σου ομοιαζει, with AN rel lat-*q* syrr goth arm; λ. σ. δηλον σε ποιει æth; η λαλια σου δηλον σε ομοιαζει (sic) 33: om BCDLℵ 1 latt coptt Eus$_1$ Aug$_1$. (*The insn seems to be from* ‖ *Matt, where* D *reads* ομοιαζει: *homœotel is hardly sufficient to account for the omn.*)

71. rec ομνυειν (‖ *Matt*), with ACNℵ rel Eus: λεγειν D lat-(*a*) *q*: txt BEHLSUVXΓ. om τουτον D-gr KN goth[appy]: om τουτον ον λεγετε (*as not in* ‖ *Matt*) ℵ.

72. aft και ins ευθυς BLℵ latt Syr æth arm: ευθεως (*from* ‖ *Matt*) DG 69 [Eus$_1$]: om ACN rel syr coptt goth. om εκ δευτερου Lℵ lat-*c*. rec (for το ρημα ως) του ρηματος ου, with M 69: το ρ. ο DN rel latt syr-mg: txt ABCLΔℵ 33 coptt goth. om αυτω D-gr. om οτι to απαρνηση D 142[1] lat-*a*. rec φωνησαι bef δις, with AC[2]LN rel vulg lat-*g*$_2$ (Syr) syr goth: om δις (C[1]?)Dℵ lat-*c ff*$_2$ *g*$_1$ *l* [*q*] æth: txt B(C[1]?) lat-*k* coptt. rec απαρν. με bef τρις (*order of* ‖ *Luke*), with AN rel syr goth arm: txt BCLΔℵ vulg lat-*c ff*$_2$ *k* [*l q*] (Syr) coptt æth [Aug$_1$]. κ. ηρξατο κλαιειν D latt syrr sah goth arm: εκλαυσεν ℵ[1] [C copt].

xxii. 56—62. John xviii. 17, 18, 25—27. See the comparative table, and notes, on Matt. **66.**] **κάτω**, because the house was built round the αὐλή, and the rooms looked down into it. See note on Matt. xxvi. 69. **68.**] **οὔτε οἶδα**, scil. αὐτόν: an union of two separate answers, which form the 1st and 2nd in Matt. The οὔτε . . . οὔτε simply connect: the repetition being that of urgent denial. **τὸ προαύλ.** = τὸν πυλῶνα Matt. The omission of the words **καὶ ἀλ. ἐφ.** appears to be an attempt to harmonize the accounts.

69.] **ἡ παιδίσκη**—in Matt. ἄλλη, in Luke ἕτερος. Meyer does not appear to be justified in asserting that this is necessarily the same maid as before: it might be only *the maid* in waiting in the προαύλιον: see note on Matt. **70.**] **μετὰ μικρόν** = διαστάσης ὡσεὶ ὥρας μιᾶς, Luke. **καὶ γάρ**, for, in addition to all that has been hitherto said . . . .

72. ἐπιβαλών] No entirely satisfactory meaning has yet been given for this word. 1) Hammond and Palairet supply τοὺς ὀφθαλμοὺς τῷ Ἰησοῦ—but besides this being most fanciful, *the fact was not so*: see Luke ver. 61. 2) The vulgate, Syr., Euth., Thl.[2], Luth., Kuin., take ἐπιβαλὼν ἔκλαιεν for ἐπέβαλεν κλαίειν, '*he began to weep.*' But granting that this is a later meaning of the word (Kuin. cites ἐπέβαλε τερετίζειν, cantillare cœpit, Diog. Laërt. vi. 2. 4, and Suid. has ἐπέβαλεν· ἤρξατο), yet this participial construction will not bear that interpretation. Acts

XV. 1 Καὶ εὐθὺς [f ἐπὶ τὸ] g πρωῒ h συμβούλιον h ποιήσαντες οἱ ἀρχιερεῖς μετὰ τῶν πρεσβυτέρων καὶ γραμματέων, καὶ ὅλον τὸ i συνέδριον, δήσαντες τὸν Ἰησοῦν k ἀπ-
ήνεγκαν καὶ l παρέδωκαν Πιλάτῳ. 2 καὶ ἐπηρώτησεν ..πιλατω L.
αὐτὸν ὁ Πιλάτος Σὺ εἶ ὁ m βασιλεὺς τῶν m Ἰουδαίων; ὁ ABCDE GHKM
δὲ ἀποκριθεὶς αὐτῷ λέγει n Σὺ λέγεις. 3 καὶ o κατ- NSUVX ΓΔΠℵ 1.
ηγόρουν αὐτοῦ οἱ ἀρχιερεῖς πολλά. 4 ὁ δὲ Πιλάτος πάλιν 33. 69
ἐπηρώτα αὐτὸν λέγων Οὐκ ἀποκρίνῃ οὐδέν; ἴδε πόσα σου
o κατηγοροῦσιν. 5 ὁ δὲ Ἰησοῦς οὐκέτι οὐδὲν ἀπεκρίθη,
ὥστε θαυμάζειν τὸν Πιλάτον. 6 p Κατὰ δὲ ἑορτὴν

f Luke x. 35. Acts iii. 1. iv. 5. Esth. v. 8 F (not A [appy]). g ch. ix. 20 reff. h here only. =σ. διδόναι, ch. iii. 6. σ. λαμβάνειν, Matt. xii. 14 (reff.). i ch. xiv. 55 reff. k Luke xvi. 22. Acts xix. 12. 1 Cor. xvi. 3. Rev. xvii. 3. xxi. 10 only. Ps. xliv. 14, 15. l — Matt. v. 25 al. m here, &c. ||. Matt. ii. 2. n || only. see Matt. xxvi. 25, 64. o Matt. xii. 10 reff. p || Mt. [L.] Luke ii. 41.

Chap. XV. 1. (ευθυς, so BCLΔℵ: om lat-*a c* sah æth.) om επι το (*as unnecessary: no reason could be given for its insertion*) BCDLℵ vulg lat-*a ff*$_2$ *k l* coptt Orig$_1$: ins AN rel (goth) arm. for ποιησ., ετοιμασαντες CLℵ: εποιησαν and ins και bef δησ. D (ev-z$_1$) lat-*a c ff*$_2$ *k* [*q*] syrr sah æth Orig$_1$. for απηνεγκαν, απηγαγον (|| *Matt*) CDGN 1 latt syrr goth æth Orig. rec ins τω bef πιλατω, with AN rel: om BCDLΔℵ 1 Orig.

2. for ο δε, και D lat-*a* æth. rec (for αυτω λεγει) ειπεν αυτω (|| *John*), with AN rel D-lat syrr goth æth: [λεγει αυτω V 1:] txt B C(αυτω(. . .)) Dℵ copt arm.

3. κατηγορουσιν D-gr. at end add αυτος δε ουδεν απεκρινατο (*see Matt* xxvii. 12: *Luke* xxiii. 9) NUΔ [33] 69 lat-*a c* syr sah-ming æth arm Orig.

4. επηρ. αυτον bef παλιν CD lat-*k q* sah-ming æth: om παλιν U 238. rec επηρωτησεν (*corrn to above, ver* 2), with ACDNℵ rel: txt BU 33. 69 lat-*a k* syr-mg. om λεγων ℵ^1 1(Tischdf) lat-*a* sah. (ουδεν is on marg in B.) ιδοι (i. e. (?) ιδου) Δ. rec (for κατηγορουσιν) καταμαρτυρουσιν (*from* || *Matt*), with AN rel syrr sah goth arm: txt BCDℵ 1 latt copt æth Orig-int$_1$.

6. ins την bef εορτην D.

xi. 4, which Kuin. cites to support it, has quite another meaning—see note there. 3) Grot., Le Clerc, al. render it '*addens flevit*'—i. e. he continued weeping (so ἐπιβαλὼν ἐρωτᾶν Theophr. Char. 8. ἐπιβαλών φησι Diod. Sic. p. 345 B);—but then his *beginning* to weep would have been noticed before. Grot. wants to give it the sense of '*præterea*.' 4) Beza, Raphel, Bretschn., Wahl, al. say, '*quum se foras projecisset*;' but although ἐπιβάλλειν τινί or ἐπί τι may mean '*to rush upon*' (see 1 Macc. iv. 2), it cannot stand *alone* in this meaning. The chief support of this sense is the ἐξελθὼν ἔξω of Matt. and Luke: but this cannot decide the matter. 5) Thl. al. supply τὸ ἱμάτιον τῇ κεφαλῇ, '*casting or drawing his mantle over his head*;' but this, without any precedent for such an ellipsis, although it suits the sense very well, appears fanciful. 6) Wetst. al. take it for '*attendere*,' and some supply τῇ ἀλεκτοροφωνίᾳ, others τῷ ῥήματι: Wetst. and Kypke have however shewn that the word is used *absolutely* in this sense, in Polyb. and other late writers. One example given by Kypke is much to the point: 'ἀεὶ μὲν γινώσκει, ἄλλως δὲ καὶ ἄλλως ἐπιβάλλει, καὶ μᾶλλόν ἐστιν ὅτε καὶ ἧττον, semper quidem cognoscit, sed diversis modis res animadvertit, imo magis interdum et minus:' Hierocl. in carm. Pythag. p. 14. The above list is taken mainly from De Wette (Exeg. Handb. p. 247), who while preferring this last sense, yet thinks that it was before expressed in ἀνεμνήσθη. But ἐπιβαλών contains more than ἀνεμν.: *that* was the *bare momentary remembrance*—the ῥῆμα *occurred* to him;—*this* is the *thinking*, or, as we sometimes say, **casting it over**; going back step by step through the sad history. This sense, though not wholly satisfactory, appears to me the best. In **ἔκλαιεν**, Bp. Wordsw. well points out the imperf. "wept, and continued weeping: something more than ἔκλαυσε."

Chap. XV. 1—5.] Jesus is led away to Pilate, and examined by him. Matt. xxvii. 1, 2, 11—14. Luke xxiii. 1—5. John xviii. 28—38. Our account is very nearly related to that in Matt.: see notes there. The **ὅλον τὸ σ.** is a touch of accuracy. From ch. xiv. 53 we know that πάντες were assembled. Lightfoot quotes from Maimonides Sanhedr. 3 b.,

q ἀπέλυεν αὐτοῖς ἕνα r δέσμιον, s ὅνπερ ᾐτοῦντο. 7 ἦν δὲ
ὁ λεγόμενος Βαραββᾶς μετὰ τῶν t στασιαστῶν δεδεμένος,
u οἵτινες ἐν τῇ v στάσει w φόνον w πεποιήκεισαν. 8 καὶ
x ἀναβὰς ὁ ὄχλος ἤρξατο αἰτεῖσθαι y καθὼς ἀεὶ ἐποίει
αὐτοῖς. 9 ὁ δὲ Πιλάτος ἀπεκρίθη αὐτοῖς λέγων z Θέλετε
q ἀπολύσω ὑμῖν τὸν m βασιλέα τῶν m Ἰουδαίων; 10 ἐγίνωσκεν γὰρ ὅτι διὰ a φθόνον b παραδεδώκεισαν αὐτὸν οἱ
ἀρχιερεῖς. 11 οἱ δὲ ἀρχιερεῖς c ἀνέσεισαν τὸν ὄχλον ἵνα
μᾶλλον τὸν Βαραββᾶν q ἀπολύσῃ αὐτοῖς. 12 ὁ δὲ Πιλάτος πάλιν ἀποκριθεὶς ἔλεγεν αὐτοῖς Τί οὖν z θέλετε
P ιου-δαιων... d ποιήσω ὃν e λέγετε τὸν m βασιλέα τῶν m Ἰουδαίων;

q Matt. xviii. 27 reff. Acts iii. 13.
r ‖ Mt. Acts xvi. 25, 27. Eph. iii. 1 al. Eccl. iv. 14.
s here only.
t here only †. (-άζειν, 2 Macc. iv. 30.) συστ., Jos. Antt. xiv. 2. 1.
u = Matt. vii. 15 reff. Luke ii. 4. Deut. v. 26.
v ‖ L. bis. Acts xix. 40. Prov. xvii. 14.
w here only. see Rom. i. 32.
x see Acts xxi. 31. Rev. xx. 9.
y ellips., 2 Cor. iii. 13.
z constr., Matt. xx. 32 reff.
a ‖ Mt. only in Gospp., Rom. i. 29 al.† Wisd. vi. 23 (25). 1 Macc. viii. 16 only.
b ver. 1.
c Luke xxiii. 5 only †. Job ii. 3 Aq.
d = ‖ Mt. only.
e ch. x. 18 reff.

ον παρητουντο AB[1]א[1]: ον αν ητ. DG 69.

7. rec **συστασιαστων** (*to include Barabbas among the seditious, as is exprd in* ‖ *Luke? On the other hand* ΣΥ *may easily have been absorbed in the follg* ΣΤ. *The* unusual word *would hardly have occasd a corrn, as Mey and De W., for though the* word *may be unusual, the* analogy which it follows *is common enough*), with AN rel: txt BCDKא 1. 69 sah. πεπ. bef φον. D 2-pe vulg lat-c k [ff_2 l] sah. aft φον. ins τινα א. επεποιηκεισαν C[1](perhaps) F(Wetst): πεποιηκασαν Γ.

8. rec (for αναβας) αναβοησας (*corrn aft* ‖ *Luke*, ανεκραγον δε &c: *see note*), with ACNא[3b] rel syrr (arm): *ascendit et clamavit* æth: txt BDא[1] latt coptt goth. ins ολος bef ο οχλος (*see* παμπληθει, ‖ *Luke*) D lat-a (k) goth. aft αιτεισθαι ins αυτον D mt lat-k. om αει BΔא coptt(Tischdf).

9. **αποκριθεις λεγει αυτ.** D 2-pe lat-a ff_2. om υμιν D lat-ff_2.

10. **επεγεινωσκεν** AKΠ: ηδει (‖ *Matt*) D 1. 69: εγνωκει א[1]. for παραδεδ., παρεδωκεισαν AEGNVXΔ: παρεδωκαν D-gr HS 1. 69 lat-a c ff_2 sah. om οι αρχιερεις (‖ *Matt*) B 1 (lat-k) copt.

11. for ανεσεισαν, επεισαν *suaserunt* (‖ *Matt*) D lat-a: ανεπεισαν *persuaserunt* Γ 238 [ev-]48 Scr's f k^2 lat-c ff_2 k, simly sah arm. τω οχλω D[1]-gr(txt D[4]?). om 2nd τον D.

12. rec αποκριθεις bef παλιν, with AN rel (lat-a) arm: om παλιν DΓ prag lat-ff_2 k copt: om π. α. Syr: txt BCא 33 vulg lat-(c) $g_{1.2}$ l syr (sah) goth æth [Aug_1]. rec for ελεγεν) ειπεν (‖ *Matt*), with ADN rel lat-(a) k Syr goth: λεγει Γ vulg lat-ff_2: txt BCא syr. om θελετε (‖ *Matt*) BCΔא 1. 33. 69 coptt: ins ADN rel latt syrr goth æth arm. om ον B: om ον λεγετε AD 1. 69 latt sah arm: ins CNא rel syrr copt goth æth. rec om τον, with N rel goth: βασιλει D[1]: τω βασ. D[2]: txt ABCΔא 1. 69 arm.

"Synedrium septuaginta unius seniorum non necesse habet ut sedeant omnes, .. cum vero necesse est ut congregentur omnes, congregentur omnes."

6—15.] Barabbas preferred to Him. He is delivered to be crucified. Matt. xxvii. 15—26. Luke xxiii. 17—25. John xviii. 39, 40. Our account is nearly cognate to, but distinct from that of Matt., where see notes. The principal points of distinction will be noticed. 6.] **ἀπέλυεν**—'imperfectum ubi *solere* notat, non nisi de re ad certum tempus restricta dicitur,' Herm. ad Viger. p. 745. 7.] The circumstance that Barabbas was *one of a set* of murderers, shewn by the **τῶν** στασ. and the **οἵτινες**, is peculiar to our narrative, and shews that it is not compiled from Matt. and Luke. 8.] This is also peculiar to Mark—in Matt. it is Pilate who *first offers them* the choice—in Luke they cry out, but it is αἶρε τοῦτον κ.τ.λ. ver. 18. **αἰτεῖσθαι καθώς**—i. e. αὐτοῖς ποιεῖν, καθώς. **ἀναβάς** probably implies the *rising of the crowd* in excitement—or perhaps their *coming up towards the palace*, as συνηγμένων in Matt. 9.] Here our account differs from Matt. and agrees with John ver. 39. 10.] **ἐγίνωσκεν**, imperf. **He was aware, He perceived,** His apprehension of it was concurrent with the action going on. 12.] **ὃν λέγετε τ. βασιλ. τ. Ἰουδ.** = Ἰησοῦν τὸν λεγόμενον χριστόν Matt.

13 οἱ δὲ πάλιν ἔκραξαν Σταύρωσον αὐτόν. 14 ὁ δὲ Πιλάτος ἔλεγεν αὐτοῖς Τί γὰρ ἐποίησεν κακόν; οἱ δὲ [f]περισ-
σῶς ἔκραξαν Σταύρωσον αὐτόν. 15 ὁ δὲ Πιλάτος βουλόμενος τῷ ὄχλῳ τὸ [g]ἱκανὸν [g]ποιῆσαι, ἀπέλυσεν αὐτοῖς
τὸν Βαραββᾶν, καὶ [h]παρέδωκεν τὸν Ἰησοῦν [i]φραγελλώ-
σας ἵνα σταυρωθῇ. 16 Οἱ δὲ στρατιῶται ἀπήγαγον αὐτὸν
ἔσω τῆς [k]αὐλῆς, [l]ὅ ἐστιν [m]πραιτώριον, καὶ [n]συγκαλοῦσιν
ὅλην τὴν [o]σπεῖραν, 17 καὶ [p]ἐνδιδύσκουσιν αὐτὸν [q]πορφύ-
ραν, καὶ [r]περιτιθέασιν αὐτῷ [s]πλέξαντες [t]ἀκάνθινον στέφανον,
18 καὶ ἤρξαντο ἀσπάζεσθαι αὐτὸν Χαῖρε [u]ὁ βασιλεὺς τῶν
Ἰουδαίων. 19 καὶ ἔτυπτον αὐτοῦ τὴν κεφαλὴν [v]καλάμῳ καὶ
[w]ἐνέπτυον αὐτῷ καὶ [x]τιθέντες τὰ [xy]γόνατα προσεκύνουν
αὐτῷ. 20 καὶ ὅτε [z]ἐνέπαιξαν αὐτῷ, [a]ἐξέδυσαν αὐτὸν τὴν
[q]πορφύραν καὶ [b]ἐνέδυσαν αὐτὸν τὰ ἱμάτια τὰ ἴδια, καὶ

F και παρεδωκεν... ABCDE FGHK MNPS UVXΓΔ Πℵ 1. 33. 69

L και εξαγουσιν...

f ‖ Mt. reff. g here only. h ‖ Mt. L. Matt. xvii. 22. Ezek. xxiii. 28. i ‖ Mt. only †. (-λλιον, John ii. 15.) k Matt. xxvi. 3 reff. l attr., Gal. iii. 16. Eph. i. 14. 1 Tim. iii. 15 al. Winer, § 24. 3. m ‖ Mt. reff. n Luke xv. 6 reff. o ‖ Mt. reff. p (-διδύσκ.) Luke viii. 27. xvi. 19 only. 2 Kings i. 24. (see Mt. vi. 25 reff.) q (ροῦς, ‖ J. reff.) here bis. Luke xvi. 19. Rev. (xvii. 4 v. r.) xviii. 12 only. Exod. xxvi. 1. r ‖ Mt. ver. 36 ‖ Mt. ch. xii. 1 ‖ Mt. 1 Cor. xi. 23 only. Ruth iii. 3. s ‖ only. Exod. xxviii. 14. Isa. xxviii. 5 only. t John xix. 5 only. Isa. xxxiv. 13 Bℵ only. u voc., Luke xii. 32 reff. v Matt. xi. 7 reff. Ps. xliv. 1. w ch. xiv. 65 reff. (-υσμα, Isa. l. 6.) x Luke xxii. 41. Acts vii. 60 al3.† y as above (x). Luke v. 8. Rom. xiv. 11 (from Isa. xlv. 24 al.). z ch. x. 34 al. Exod. x. 2. a Matt. xxvii. 28, 31. Luke x. 30. 2 Cor. v. 4 only. Gen. xxxvii. 23. b Matt. vi. 25 reff. see ver. 17.

13. *εκρ.* bef *παλιν* D. ins *λεγοντες* bef *σταυρωσον* ADKMΠ gat lat-*a c ff*$_2$ sah-woide æth; *ανασειομενοι υπο των αρχιερεων και ελεγον* G 69 syr-mg, and, omg *κ. ελεγ.*, arm.
14. for *ελεγ.*, *λεγει* N. om *αυτοις* ℵ[1]. rec *κακον* bef *εποιησεν* (‖ *Matt*), with ADNℵ rel vss: txt BCΔ. rec *περισσοτερως*, with ENPUXΓ Π-marg (SV, e sil): txt ABCDℵ rel sah. (*Txt is so very strongly attested, that it can hardly in this case be regarded as from ‖ Matt. περισσοτερως is very common in St. Paul, and hence may have been substd here.*) *εκραζον* (*prob from ‖ Matt*) ADGKMPΠ[1] 1. 69 latt Syr arm. add *λεγοντες* ℵ 2-pe lat-*c*.
15. *βουλομενος ποιησαι το ικανον τω οχλω* Cℵ Syr coptt: om D lat-*ff*$_2$ *k*: for *ποιησαι*, *ποιειν* B. *παρεδ. δε* B copt.—*τον δε ιησ. φλαγ. παρεδ.* D(*φραγ.* D-corr[1]) sah. (lat-*a* (as also *b*, see ch xiii. 8) def from this point to the end of Mark: a supplement by a later hand begins at xvi. 7.)
16. *εσω εις την αυλην* (*see ch* xiv. 54) DP 1. 69 fuld(with em ing gat mt prag) lat-*g*$_2$ copt arm: *εις την αυλην* C[3]M vulg lat-*c ff*$_2$ *l*. *καλουσιν* D-gr.
17. rec (for *ενδιδυσκουσιν*) *ενδυουσιν* (*more common word*), with AN rel: txt BC D(*ενδυδισκ.*) FΔℵ 1. 69. *επιτιθεασιν* D vulg lat-*c ff*$_2$ *k* [*l*]. om *πλεξαντες* D.
18. aft *αυτον* ins *και λεγειν* (*cf* ‖ *Matt*) C[2]NUℵ 33 arm: *λεγοντες* M Scr's s[2] lat-*c*. rec (for *ο βασιλευς*) *βασιλευ* (*corrn*), with BD(*which have it also in* ‖ *Matt*) MPSVXℵ: txt ACN rel.
19. *αυτον καλαμω εις τ. κεφ.* (‖ *Matt*) D 2-pe lat-*c ff*$_2$ *k* (sah). *την κεφ.* bef *αυτου* C Scr's d e k p q r s vulg. *ενεπτυσαν* C[1](appy). om last clause (*homœotel*) D 253 ev-32 lat-*k*.
20. om *ενεπαιξαν αυτω* D. for *τα ιμ. τα ιδια*, *τα ιμ. αυτου* (*from* ‖ *Matt*) BCΔ: *τα ιδια ιμ. αυτου* ℵ [Scr's c]: om *τα ιδ.* D ev-z$_1$.

Neither of these expressions can well have been copied from the other. **13.**] **πάλιν** only refers to ἔκραξαν: cf. ver. 8, where this is implied in ἤρξαντο αἰτεῖσθαι:—they had not cried out *this* before. **15.**] **τὸ ἱκ. ποι., to satisfy.** Wetst. gives examples of the expression from Polyb., Diog. Laërt., and Appian.

16—19.] Jesus mocked by the soldiers. Matt. xxvii. 27—30 (omitted in Luke). John xix. 1—3. See notes on Matt. **16.**] **αὐλῆς**, the court or guard-room, but *open*—see note on Matt. xxvi. 69. **17.**] We have here a curious instance of a word used in two accounts in the same part of the narrative, but applied to different things, in **περιτιθέασιν**, here said of the *crown of thorns*, in Matt. of the *robe* (see Prolegg. ch. i. § iii., iv.). **πορφύρα** is vaguely used, to signify

[c] ἐξάγουσιν αὐτὸν ἵνα σταυρώσουσιν αὐτόν. 21 καὶ [d] ἀγ-
γαρεύουσιν [e] παράγοντά τινα Σίμωνα Κυρηναῖον ἐρχόμενον ἀπ' ἀγροῦ, τὸν πατέρα Ἀλεξάνδρου καὶ Ῥούφου,
ἵνα ἄρῃ τὸν σταυρὸν αὐτοῦ. 22 καὶ φέρουσιν αὐτὸν ἐπὶ
Γολγοθᾶν τόπον, ὅ ἐστιν [f] μεθερμηνευόμενον [g] κρανίου
τόπος. 23 καὶ ἐδίδουν αὐτῷ [h] ἐσμυρνισμένον οἶνον· ὁ δὲ
οὐκ ἔλαβεν. 24 καὶ σταυροῦσιν αὐτὸν καὶ [i] διαμερίζονται
τὰ ἱμάτια αὐτοῦ, [k] βάλλοντες [k] κλῆρον [l] ἐπ' αὐτὰ [m] τίς τί
ἄρῃ. 25 ἦν δὲ ὥρα τρίτη [n] καὶ ἐσταύρωσαν αὐτόν. 26 καὶ

...xv. 22 (appy) N.

c Luke xxiv. 50. John x. 3 al. Num. xv. 36.
d || Mt. Matt. v. 41 only †.
e Matt. ix. 9 reff.
f ch. v. 41 reff.
g || (Mt. reff.) only.
h here only †. (-ρνα, Matt. ii. 11.)
i || Mt. reff Psa. xxi. 18.
k || only. Joel iii. 3. Obad. 11. Jon. i. 7.
l constr., John xix. 24, from Ps. xxi. 18. 1 Cor. vii. 36. James v. 14.
m constr., Acts xi. 17. see Matt. xxvi. 62.
n = Luke xix. 43. Jer. xxxi. (xxxviii.) 12.

for εξαγ., αγουσιν A prag, *duxerunt* lat-*c ff*$_2$ [D-lat]. rec σταυρωσωσιν (*gramml corrn*), with Bℵ rel: txt ACDLNPΔ 33. om last αυτον Dℵ 1 lat-*ff*$_2$ *k*.

21. εγγαρ. B[1]ℵ[1]. τον σιμ. παραγοντα τον κυρηνεον D (lat-*ff*$_2$): om παραγοντα N. απο DNX 1.

22. for φερουσιν, αγουσιν D 69 vulg lat-*c ff*$_2$ *l* sah goth. ins τον bef γολγ. BC²FLNΔℵ 33. 69. τοπον bef γολγ. D: om τοπον ℵ[1] lat-*c*. (γολγοθαν, so B(Tischdf) FGKLMNSUVΓΔℵ.) μεθερμηνευομενος ABN: txt CDPℵ rel.

23. rec aft αυτω ins πιειν (*from* || *Matt*), with A D(πειν) P rel vulg lat-*c ff*$_2$ *k* [*l*] syrr sah goth æth [Aug$_1$]: om BC[1]LΔℵ lat-*n* copt arm. for ο δε, και D 1 vulg lat-*c ff*$_2$ *k* [*l n* Aug$_1$]: ος δε B Γ[1](appy) ℵ 33.

24. rec κ. σταυρωσαντες αυτ. δι. (*rearrangemt of constrn from* || *Matt*), with AC D-gr Pℵ rel vulg lat-*g*$_{1,2}$ *l n* (syrr, appy) goth: txt B lat-*c ff*$_2$ *k* coptt æth arm, and, omg 2nd και, L D-lat. rec (for διαμεριζονται) διεμεριζον: διαμεριζον ev-y$_1$: εκαθηντο διαμεριζοντες Scr's d: διεμεριζοντο 69 Scr's a c h: txt ABCDPℵ rel Scr's-mss. εαυτου ℵ[1](but corrd). om τις τι αρη D 157 ev-z$_1$ lat-*ff*$_2$ *k n*.

25. τριτη bef ωρα AC[1]KΠ[1]. for εσταυρωσαν, εφυλασσον D lat-*ff*$_2$ *k n*.

different shades of red, and is especially convertible with *crimson* = κοκκίνη Matt.

20—23.] HE IS LED TO CRUCIFIXION. Matt. xxvii. 31—34. Luke xxiii. 26—33. John xix. 16, 17. See notes on these.

21. Ἀλεξάνδρου κ. Ῥούφου] It is quite uncertain whether Alexander be identical with either of the persons of that name mentioned Acts xix. 33: 1 Tim. i. 20: 2 Tim. iv. 14, or whether those, or any two of them represent one and the same person. There is a Rufus saluted Rom. xvi. 13. The words **ἐρχόμ. ἀπ' ἀγρ.** determine nothing as to its being a working day or otherwise, any more than οἱ παραπορευόμενοι, Matt. ver. 39: nothing is said as to the *distance* from whence he came.

22.] **Γολγοθᾶν** must be regarded as accusative from Γολγοθᾶς, the name being Græcised. The construction is varied in the interpretation. **23.]** **ἐσμ. οἶν.** = ὄξος μετὰ χολῆς μεμ. Matt., which see. **ἐδίδουν**, they were giving, i. e. '*they offered.*'

24—28.] HE IS CRUCIFIED. Matt. xxvii. 35—38. Luke xxiii. 33, 34, 38. John xix. 18—24. **25. ὥρα τρίτη]** This date is in agreement with the subsequent account, ver. 33, and its || in Matt. and Luke, but, as now standing unexplained, *inconsistent with John*, xix. 14, where it is said to have been about the *sixth hour* at the time of the exhibition of our Lord by Pilate. I own I see no satisfactory way of reconciling these accounts, unless there has been (see note on John) some very early erratum in our copies, or unless it can be shewn *from other grounds than the difficulty before us*, that John's *reckoning of time* differs from that employed in the other Evangelists. The difficulty is of a kind in no way affecting the authenticity of the narrative, nor the truthfulness of each Evangelist; but requires some solution to the furnishing of which *we are not competent*. It is preposterous to imagine that two *such accounts as these* of the proceedings of *so eventful a day* should differ by *three whole hours* in their apportionment of its occurrences. So that it may fairly be *presumed*, that *some different method of calculation* has given rise to the present discrepancy. Meanwhile the chronology of *our text*,—as being carried on through the day, and as allowing time both for the trial, and the events of the crucifixion,—is that

ἦν ἡ [o] ἐπιγραφὴ τῆς [p] αἰτίας αὐτοῦ [q] ἐπιγεγραμμένη Ὁ ABCDE
[r] βασιλεὺς τῶν [r] Ἰουδαίων. 27 καὶ σὺν αὐτῷ σταυροῦσιν FGHKL MPSUV
δύο [s] λῃστάς, [t] ἕνα [t] ἐκ δεξιῶν καὶ [t] ἕνα [t] ἐξ εὐωνύμων ΧΓΔΠℵ 1. 33. 69
αὐτοῦ. 29 καὶ οἱ [u] παραπορευόμενοι [v] ἐβλασφήμουν αὐτόν,
[w] κινοῦντες τὰς [w] κεφαλὰς αὐτῶν καὶ λέγοντες [x] Οὐὰ ὁ
[y] καταλύων τὸν ναὸν καὶ οἰκοδομῶν τρισὶν ἡμέραις,
30 σῶσον σεαυτὸν καταβὰς ἀπὸ τοῦ σταυροῦ. 31 ὁμοίως
καὶ οἱ ἀρχιερεῖς [z] ἐμπαίζοντες πρὸς ἀλλήλους μετὰ τῶν
γραμματέων ἔλεγον Ἄλλους ἔσωσεν, ἑαυτὸν οὐ δύναται
σῶσαι, 32 ὁ χριστὸς ὁ βασιλεὺς τοῦ Ἰσραήλ. καταβάτω
νῦν ἀπὸ τοῦ σταυροῦ, ἵνα ἴδωμεν καὶ [a] πιστεύσωμεν. καὶ
οἱ [b] συνεσταυρωμένοι αὐτῷ [c] ὠνείδιζον αὐτόν. 33 καὶ [d] γενομένης ὥρας ἕκτης σκότος ἐγένετο ἐφ' ὅλην τὴν γῆν,
[e] ἕως [e] ὥρας ἐνάτης. 34 καὶ τῇ ἐνάτῃ ὥρᾳ ἐβόησεν ὁ

o ‖ L. Matt. xxii. 20 | only +.
p ‖ Mt. Acts xxv. 18, 27. Gen. iv. 13.
q (‖ L. v. r.) Acts xvii. 23. Heb. viii. 10 & x. 16, from Jer. xxxviii. (xxxi.) 33 A. Rev. xxi. 12 only. Prov. vii. 3.
r vv. 2, 9, 12, 18.
s Matt. xxi. 13 reff.
t Matt. xx. 21 (reff.).
u ch. ii. 23 reff.
v = (1 Cor. xiv. 13 v. r.) Tit. iii. 2. James ii. 7. 4 Kings xix. 6, 22.
w ‖ Mt. only. Ps. xxi. 8. see Ps. xliii. 14.
x here only.
y ch. xiv. 58 reff.
z ver. 20. Luke xviii. 32 al. Exod. x. 2.
a abs., ch. xvi. 16 al. fr.
b | Mt. John xix. 32. Rom. vi. 6. Gal. ii. 20 only +.
c = Matt. v. 11 reff.
d ver. 42. ch. vi. 21. Luke vi. 13 al.
e ‖ Mt. L. 2 Kings xxiv. 15.

26. for *και ην η*, *ην δε* D lat-*k* (sah); *η δε* D-corr. ins *ουτος εστιν* bef *ο βασ.* D (syr) goth; *ουτος* at end 33.

27. *σταυρουνται β' λησται* (*from* ‖ *Matt*) D¹-gr: *εσταυρωσαν* (‖ *Luke John*) B lat-*c ff*₂ *k* [*n*] D-lat goth. om *αυτου* C³D 1. 2-pe 71 lat-*c ff*₂ *k* [*n*].

[**28.** rec ins *και επληρωθη η γραφη η λεγουσα και μετα ανομων ελογισθη* (*see Luke* xxii. 37, *from which place prob it was noted in the margin here, and thence has come into the txt. Mark very rarely adduces prophetic testimony.* For *η γρ. η λεγουσα*, *see John* xix. 24), with L M-w-ast P Δ-w-ob rel vulg lat-*c ff*₂ *g*₁ syrr copt goth æth arm (Orig): om ABCDXℵ lat-*k* sah Eus-canon$_{appy}$.]

29. for *παραπορευομενοι*, *παραγοντες* D-gr Eus. om *αυτων* D 59 lat-*k n*. om *ουα* L¹ Δ-gr ℵ³ᵃ(appy: but re-insd) lat-*k* D-lat. rec *τρισιν ημεραις* bef *οικοδομων* (‖ *Matt*), with ACPℵ rel vulg lat-*ff*₂ [*l*] syr goth æth arm Eus₁: txt BDL lat-*c k n* Syr coptt. rec ins *εν* bef *τρισιν ημεραις* (‖ *Matt*), with B C(sic, Tischdf) ℵ rel vulg lat-*ff*₂ [*l m*] D-lat Eus₁: om A D-gr PV lat-*c k* sah.

30. rec (for *καταβας*) *και καταβα*, with AC rel lat-*c ff*₂ D-lat syrr sah(omg *κ.*) goth æth arm; *κ. καταβηθι* P 1 Eus₁: txt B D-gr LΔℵ vulg lat-*k* [*l*] *n* copt.

31. om *ομοιως* D 238 lat-*c ff*₂ *k n*. rec ins *δε* bef *και*, with C³M² 33 sah: om ABC¹(D)ℵ rel vulg lat-(*c ff*₂ *k*) *l* (Syr) syr copt goth arm Eus₁ Thl. for *προς*, *εις* D Eus₁.

32. om *του* (*see* ‖ *Matt*) BDKLΔΠℵ 1. 69: ins ACP rel coptt Eus₁. aft *πιστευσωμεν* ins *αυτω* C³DFGHM¹P V(as corrd by origl scribe) ΓΠ² 1. 69 fuld(with gat) lat-*c ff*₂ *k l n* Syr sah æth arm Eus; *επ. αυτω* Scr's q ev-y₁, *εις αυτον* evv-49₁-z, *αυτον* ev-49₁: om ABC¹ℵ rel [vulg](with am em prag ing) lat-*g*₁.₂ syr copt goth. aft *συνεστ.* ins *συν* (*from* ‖ *Matt*) BLℵ. om *αυτω* D-gr.

33. rec (for *και γεν.*) *γεν. δε* (‖ *Matt*), with ACP rel æth arm Eus₁ Orig-int₁: txt BDGLMSΔℵ 1. 33. 69 vulg lat-*c ff*₂ [*k l n*] Syr copt goth. *εφ ολης της γης* D Eus.

34. rec *τη ωρα τη εννατη* (*prob conformation to last verse*), with AC rel vulg lat-*ff*₂ [*l n*] D-lat syr copt arm: txt B D-gr FLℵ 1. 69 lat-*c* Syr goth æth Eus₁. for *εβοησεν*, *εφωνησεν* D. om *ο ιησ.* D lat-*k*.

which will I believe be generally concurred in. All the other solutions (so called) of the difficulty are not worth relating.

29—32.] He is mocked on the cross. Matt. xxvii. 39—44. Luke xxiii. 35—37, 39—43. (John xix. 25—27.) Our narrative, derived from a common source with that of Matt., omits the scriptural allusion, 'He trusted in God,' &c. Matt. ver. 43. **29.**] **οὐά**, an expression of *reproach*:—sometimes one of admiration and respect, as in Dio Cassius, lxiii. 20, where the Romans shout after Nero, on his triumphal entry after his victories in the Grecian games, *ὀλυμπιονίκα, οὐά, πυθιονίκα, οὐὰ αὔγουστε, αὔγουστε.*

32. κ. οἱ συνεστ.] See notes on Luke.

33—37.] Supernatural darkness.

Ἰησοῦς φωνῇ μεγάλῃ Ἐλωΐ ἐλωΐ λαμᾶ σαβαχθανί; ὅ
ἐστιν [f] μεθερμηνευόμενον [g] Ὁ θεός μου ὁ θεός μου, [h] εἰς τί
[i] ἐγκατέλιπές με; 35 καί τινες τῶν [k] παρεστηκότων ἀκούσαντες ἔλεγον Ἴδε Ἡλίαν [l] φωνεῖ. 36 δραμὼν δέ τις
[m] γεμίσας [n] σπόγγον [o] ὄξους [p] περιθεὶς [q] καλάμῳ [r] ἐπότιζεν
αὐτὸν λέγων [s] Ἄφετε ἴδωμεν εἰ ἔρχεται Ἡλίας [t] καθελεῖν
...εξ-επνευσεν P. αὐτόν. 37 ὁ δὲ Ἰησοῦς [u] ἀφεὶς φωνὴν μεγάλην [v] ἐξέπνευσεν. 38 καὶ τὸ [w] καταπέτασμα τοῦ ναοῦ [x] ἐσχίσθη [y] εἰς
...κεντυριων F. δύο [z] ἀπ' ἄνωθεν [z] ἕως [z] κάτω. 39 ἰδὼν δὲ ὁ [a] κεντυρίων
ὁ [k] παρεστηκὼς [b] ἐξ [b] ἐναντίας αὐτοῦ ὅτι οὕτως [v] ἐξέπνευσεν, εἶπεν [cd] Ἀληθῶς οὗτος ὁ ἄνθρωπος [d] υἱὸς ἦν θεοῦ.
40 Ἦσαν δὲ καὶ γυναῖκες [e] ἀπὸ [e] μακρόθεν θεωροῦσαι, ἐν

f ch. v. 41 reff. g Psa. xxi. 1. h = Matt. xiv. 31 reff. i = || Mt. 2 Cor. iv. 9. 2 Tim. iv. 10, 16. Heb. xiii. 5. Wisd. x. 13. k ch. xiv. 47 reff. l = Matt. xx. 32 reff. m ch. iv. 37 reff. n || Mt. J. only †. o Matt. xxvii. 34 reff. p ver. 17. q ver. 19. r Matt. x. 42. xxv. 35, &c. 1 Cor. iii. 2, &c. Gen. xxi. 19. s = & constr., Mt. Matt. vii. 4. t ver. 46 || L. Acts xiii. 29. Josh. viii. 29. u Gen. xlv. 2. v here (bis) & || L. only †. w || Mt. L. Heb. vi. 19. ix. 3. x. 20 only. Exod. xxvi. 31, &c. x || Mt. L. ch. i. 10 al. Isa. xlviii. 21. Zech. xiv. 4. y || Mt. reff. z see Ezek. i. 27. a here and vv. 44, 45 only †. b Tit. ii. 8 only. 4 Kings ii. 7. εναντ., ch. vi. 48 reff. c Matt. xxvi. 73 reff. d = Matt. xiv. 33. e Matt. xxvi. 58 reff.

rec aft μεγαλη ins λεγων (*from* || *Matt*), with ACP rel vulg lat-*c* [*l*] Syr goth (æth) arm: om BDLℵ lat-*ff*$_2$ *k* [*n*] copt. ηλει ηλει D 2-pe 131 lat-*c i k n* Syr arm Eus$_1$. (the aspirate with mss of vulg.) rec λαμμα, with (Scr's i v, e sil) vulg-ed: λιμα AP rel goth: λεμα CLΔℵ lat-*c g*$_2$ *l* (Syr, copt): txt BD 1 am(with gat) lat-*ff*$_2$ *g*$_1$ *n* arm Eus. σαβακτανει ℵ^1: σιβακθανει A goth: ζαβαφθ. B, ζαφθ. D. om 1st μου AEFGKPΓΔΠ 1. 69 Eus. om 2nd ο θεος μου B Iren-gr [Tert$_1$]. rec με bef εγκατελιπες (*from* || *Matt*), with AC rel lat-*k n* [D-lat] goth: txt B (D[-gr]) Lℵ vulg lat-*ff*$_2$ copt Iren-gr Eus.—for εγκατ., ωνιδισας D-gr.

35. παρεστωτων DUℵ 33: εστηκοτων B: εκει εστηκ. (|| *Matt*) A: txt C P(Tischdf) rel. (παρεσ(. . .) X.) om ακουσαντες C. rec ιδου, with AP rel: οτι ιδου ΚΠ 76 Scr's a d o p w evv-H-z$_1$: οτι (|| *Matt*) C 2-pe arm: om D gat(with tol) lat-*c k* Syr: txt BFLUΔℵ 1. 33. 69. (X def.) aft φωνει ins ουτος (|| *Matt*) D lat-*c ff*$_2$.

36. for δρ. δε, και δραμων D 1. 2-pe lat-*c ff*$_2$ [*k n*] (æth).—κ. δρ. πλησας σπ. οξ. επιθεις κ. D(om επ. κ. D-lat, simly 2-pe): κ. δραμοντες εγεμισαν σπ. οξ. κ. περιθεντες κ. εποτιζον αυτ. λεγοντες 13. 69. 124. 346. rec (for τις) εἷς (*see* || *Matt*), with ACDP rel vulg lat-*c ff*$_2$ goth: txt BLΔℵ æth. rec ins και bef γεμισας, with ACDP Δ(sic) ℵ rel vulg [lat-*k l n*(appy)] Syr goth æth arm: om BL lat-*c ff*$_2$ syr copt. rec aft περιθεις ins τε (*see* || *Matt, where* τε *follows* πλησας), with ACP rel vulg syrr æth arm: om BDLℵ 1. 33. 69 copt goth. αφες (|| *Matt*) DVℵ 1. 69 lat-*c i* [*k n*(appy)] (goth) arm-zoh.

38. aft δυο ins μερη D lat-*c* [*ff*$_2$ *i k n*]. (απ', so BDL X(appy) 69.)

39. for εξ εν. αυτ., εκει D 2-pe lat-*i*[sic, Tischdf] *n q* Orig-int$_1$. rec aft ουτως ins κραξας (*explany gloss on* ουτως), with AC rel vulg lat-*c ff*$_2$ [*n q* Aug$_1$]: om BLℵ copt.—ουτως αυτον κραξαντα και εξεπνευσεν *sic eum exclamasse et exspirasse* D. om ειπεν D. rec ο ανθρωπος bef ουτος (|| *Luke*), with AC rel am(with fuld ing frag tol) syr arm [Aug$_1$]: txt BDLΔℵ 33 [vulg] em lat-*c ff*$_2$ *k n q* Syr copt goth æth Orig-int. θεου bef ην (|| *Matt*) BLΓΔℵ vulg lat-[*l*] *n* (copt?) æth [Aug$_1$]; bef υιος D 2-pe lat-[*i*] *k q*. (X def.)

40. aft δε ins εκει (|| *Matt*) C.

Last words, and death of Jesus. Matt. xxvii. 45—50. Luke xxiii. 44—46. John xix. 28—30. Our account is nearly verbally the same with Matt. **34.**] **ἐλωΐ**, the Syro-chaldaic form, answering to ἠλί in Matt. Meyer argues that the words in Matt. must have been those actually spoken by our Lord, owing to the taunt, that He *called for Elias*. **36.**] On the difference in Matt., see notes there.

38—41.] Signs following his death. Matt. xxvii. 51—56. Luke xxiii. 45, 47—49. Omitted by John. See notes on Matt. **39.**] **ὁ παρεστ. ἐξ ἐναντ. αὐτ.**, a minute mark of accuracy, so common in Mark. **οὕτως**—οὕτω δεσποτικῶς, Thl. There was something in the manner of this last cry so unusual and superhuman, that the Centurion (see on Matt.) was convinced that He must have been *that*

f here only.
g Matt. xx. 28 reff.
h Acts xiii. 31 only. 2 Chron. xviii. 2.
i ch. iv. 35 reff.
k = || J. Matt. xviii. 32. Luke i. 34 al. see note.
l Matt. xxvii. 62 reff.
m here only †. Judith viii. 6 only.
n = Acts xiii. 50. xvii. 12. 1 Cor. vii. 35 (xii. 24) only. Prov. xi. 25 (only ?).
o || L. only. Job iii. 14. xii. 17 only. xxii. 46 reff. 2 Macc. iv. 2.
p = Luke ii. 25, 38. xii. 36. Acts xxiii. 21 al. Ps. liv. 8.
q Matt.
r ver. 6. Matt. xiv. 7.

αἷς [ἦν] καὶ Μαρία ἡ Μαγδαληνὴ καὶ Μαρία ἡ [f] Ἰακώβου
τοῦ [f] μικροῦ καὶ Ἰωσῆτος μήτηρ καὶ Σαλώμη, 41 αἳ καὶ
ὅτε ἦν ἐν τῇ Γαλιλαίᾳ ἠκολούθουν αὐτῷ καὶ [g] διηκόνουν
αὐτῷ, καὶ ἄλλαι πολλαὶ αἱ [h] συναναβᾶσαι αὐτῷ εἰς
Ἱεροσόλυμα.

42 Καὶ ἤδη [i] ὀψίας [i] γενομένης, [k] ἐπεὶ ἦν [l] παρασκευή, ὅ
ἐστιν [m] προσάββατον, 43 ἐλθὼν Ἰωσὴφ ὁ ἀπὸ Ἀριμαθαίας,
[n] εὐσχήμων [o] βουλευτής, ὃς καὶ αὐτὸς ἦν [p] προσδεχόμενος
τὴν βασιλείαν τοῦ θεοῦ, [q] τολμήσας εἰςῆλθεν πρὸς Πιλάτον καὶ [r] ᾐτήσατο τὸ σῶμα τοῦ Ἰησοῦ. 44 ὁ δὲ Πιλάτος

ABCDE GHKL MSUV XΓΔΠℵ 1. 33. 69

...του ιησου H.

om ην BLℵ am(with tol prag): ins (*so* || *Matt*) ACD rel. om 2nd και C^2DGUΓ 1. 33. 69 vulg [lat-*c ff*$_2$ *k n q*] syr copt goth arm. (X def.) μαριαμ (1st) BC 1. om 1st η D. om 2nd η DF^1(Wetst) L 33. 69 arm. rec ins του bef ιακωβου, with A rel: om BCD F^1(Wetst) KLUΔ$Π^1$ℵ [1. 69]. rec (for ιωσητος) ιωση (|| *Matt*), with ACℵ^1 rel syrr goth arm: *joseph* vulg lat-*c ff*$_2$ *g*$_{1.2}$ *l q* D-lat æth Aug: ιωσηβτος $Δ^1$: ιωσηπος 1: txt B D[-gr] Lℵ^{3a} 33. 69 lat-*k n* copt Jer. (X def.)—ins η bef ιωσ. B.

41. om αι ACLΔ vulg lat-*l* goth [Aug_1]. om 1st και Bℵ 33 lat-*c ff*$_2$ *k q* D-lat Syr copt æth arm. ηκολουθησαν D[-gr]. om και διηκ. αυτω (*homœotel*) CDΔ lat-*n*. for αλλαι, ετεραι A.

42. επειδη A. προς σαββατον AB^2EGLSUVΓ$Π^2$: πριν σαββατον D: *ante sabbatum* vulg lat-*ff*$_2$ [*l n q* D-lat] syrr copt arm(appy): *primus sabbatorum* goth: *tempore initii sabbati* æth: txt B^1Cℵ rel. (X def.)

43. rec (for ελθων) ηλθεν, with D rel vulg lat-*c ff*$_2$ [*k l n q*] syrr æth: txt ABC KLMUΓΔΠℵ 1. 33. 69 copt goth arm Thdrt. om ο D Scr's c r ev-z_1. om ος ℵ^1. ην bef και αυτος D 2-pe lat-*c ff*$_2$ *k n q*. for εισηλθεν, ηλθεν D. ins τον bef πιλατον (*see* || *Matt*) BLΔℵ 33. for σωμα, πτωμα D-gr æth.

Person, whom He was accused as having declared Himself to be. Observe the Latin **κεντυρίων** = ἑκατόνταρχος in || Matt. Luke. **40, 41.**] **τοῦ μικροῦ**—either in age, or in stature, so distinguished, hardly, at the time of this Gospel being written, from James the son of Zebedee, but more probably from James the brother of the Lord, the bishop of Jerusalem: see Prolegg. to Ep. of James, § i. 8. This Mary is the wife of Alphæus or Clopas: see John xix. 25. **Σαλώμη** = ἡ μήτηρ τῶν υἱῶν Ζεβεδαίου, Matt.: our Evangelist mentions that they had accompanied Him to Jerusalem;—and we may observe a curious variation of the wording, in ἠκολούθουν αὐτῷ **ὅτε ἦν ἐν τῇ Γ.**, and ἠκολούθησαν τῷ **Ἰ. ἀπὸ τῆς Γ.**—the *former* rendering necessary the additional clause, **αἱ συναναβᾶσαι** κ.τ.λ.

42—47.] Joseph of Arimathæa begs, and buries, the body of Jesus. Matt. xxvii. 57—61. Luke xxiii. 50—56. John xix. 38—42. For all notes on the substance of the common narrative, see Matt. **42. παρασκ., ὅ ἐστι προσάβ.**] The Friday afternoon (ἡ παρασκ., "the name by which Friday is now generally known in Asia and Greece." Wordsw.) before *sunset,* at which time the Sabbath would begin, and the taking down, &c. *would be unlawful.* The three Evangelists do not imply that this παρασκ. had any thing *especial* in it, as John does, ver. 31. It is very remarkable, that **ἐπεί** occurs only here in this Gospel, but is found in the corresponding clause of John, ver. 31, shewing perhaps in this place a *community of source* in two accounts otherwise so essentially distinct. **43.**] **ἐλθών,** or ἦλθεν, is common to Matt., Mark, and John, but in different connexion—see on Matt. **εὐσχήμων**—probably in its later sense of **noble,** 'honourable,' i. e. in *station.* But Meyer supposes it rather to refer to something noble in the character or appearance of Joseph. **βουλευτής,** a member of the Sanhedrim: see Luke ver. 51. **προσδ. τ. β. τ. θ.,** common to Mark and Luke. **τολμήσας εἰς.,** characteristic of Mark's narrative. On the change of mind produced in Joseph and in Nicodemus by the crucifixion, see note, John xix. 39. **44.**] There is no

ἐθαύμασεν [s] εἰ ἤδη τέθνηκεν· καὶ προςκαλεσάμενος τὸν
[t] κεντυρίωνα ἐπηρώτησεν αὐτὸν [u] εἰ [v] πάλαι ἀπέθανεν·
45 καὶ [w] γνοὺς ἀπὸ τοῦ [t] κεντυρίωνος, [x] ἐδωρήσατο τὸ
[y] πτῶμα τῷ Ἰωσήφ. 46 καὶ ἀγοράσας [z] σινδόνα, [a] καθελὼν αὐτὸν [b] ἐνείλησεν τῇ [z] σινδόνι. καὶ [c] κατέθηκεν
αὐτὸν ἐν * μνημείῳ ὃ ἦν [d] λελατομημένον ἐκ πέτρας, καὶ
[e] προςεκύλισεν λίθον ἐπὶ τὴν [f] θύραν τοῦ [f] μνημείου. 47 ἡ
δὲ Μαρία ἡ Μαγδαληνὴ καὶ Μαρία ἡ Ἰωσῆτος ἐθεώρουν
ποῦ τεθεῖται.

s constr., 1 John iii. 13. see Sir. xxvi. 11.
t here bis & ver. 39 only†.
u ch. x. 2 reff.
v = 2 Cor. xii. 19 (Matt. xi. 21 reff.) only.
w = ch. v. 43. Acts ix. 24.
x 2 Pet. i. 3, 4 only. Gen. xxx. 20.
y Matt. xxiv. 28. ch. vi. 29 (|| Mt. v. r.). Rev. xi 8, 9 only. Judg. xiv. 8.
z ch. xiv. 51 reff.
a ver. 36 reff. b here only. 1 Kings xxi. 9 only. c = here (Acts xxiv. 27. xxv. 9) only.
d || Mt. only. Isa. xxii. 16. li. 1. e || Mt. only †. f || Mt. ch. xvi. 3 only.

44. εθαυμαζεν Dℵ vulg lat-*c* [*ff*₂ *k* *l* *q* Aug₁]. for παλαι, ηδη (*repetn of* ηδη *above*) BD vulg lat-*c* *ff*₂ *l* syr-jer copt goth æth arm Thl. for τεθν., ειτεθνηκει (sic) D-gr. for απεθανεν, τεθνηκει D 6-pe.

45. for απο, παρα D 1. rec σωμα (*repetn of above: or as Mey, as a worthier word*), with AC rel vulg lat-*c* D-lat copt [Thdrt₁]: txt B D-gr Lℵ. add αυτου D lat-*q* Syr. for ιωσηφ, ιωση B.

46. for και, ο δε ιωσ. D 2-pe vulg lat-*c* *l* Syr syr-mg syr-jer arm [Aug₁]. rec ins και bef καθελων, with AC rel vulg syrr goth æth arm [Thdrt₁]: om BDLℵ lat-*n* copt. for καθελων, λαβων D. ins εν bef τη σινδ. 1 lat-*ff*₂: εις την σινδονα D. for κατεθηκεν, εθηκεν (*from* || *Matt Luke John*) BC²DLℵ 1. 33. 69: καθηκεν A: κατεθηκαν K: κατεθεικεν Γ: txt C¹ rel [Thdrt₁.—hom. in Δ αυτον to αυτον.] for 2nd αυτον, αυτο AM goth [Thdrt₁]. ins τω bef μνημ. D. * μνήματι (|| *Luke*) Bℵ: μνημειω (|| *Matt*) ACD rel. εκ της π. D 1: εν τη π. 69. for προsεκυλισεν, προsκυλισας D 1. aft λιθον ins μεγαν ℵ. at end ins (*see* || *Matt*) και απηλθεν D; απηλθεν G 1.

47. homœotel in ℵ¹ μαρια η μαγδ. to μαρια η μαγδ. next ver. om η (bef μαγδ.) D. rec om 3rd η, with DL rel: ins ABCGΔℵ³ᵃ 1. 33. (X def.) rec (for ιωσητος) ιωση, with C rel syrr goth: ιωσηφ A 258 vulg lat-*l* æth: ιακωβου D lat-*ff*₂ *n* *q*: ιακωβου κ. ιωσητος μητηρ 69 syr-jer arm: *jacobi et joseph* lat-*c*: txt BLΔℵ³ᵃ 1 lat-*k* copt. (*The next ver has given rise to much of the confusion.*) εθεασαντο *notaverunt* D lat-*c* *ff*₂ *q*. τον τοπον οπου (*see ch* xvi. 7) D lat-*c* *ff*₂ *q* arm. rec τιθεται (*corrn to more usual*), with E rel: τε. θυτα (sic) Δ: txt ABCDΠℵ³ᵃ 33. 69 vulg lat-*c* *ff*₂ arm, τεθηται L Scr's c. [X def.]

inconsistency, or but a very trifling one, with the order in John, ver. 31, *to break their legs and take them down.* The circumstances related there *had taken place,* but no *report of them had been made* to Pilate. And the Body of the Lord had not been taken down, for some reason which does not appear, but which we can easily guess;—if Joseph had declared to the soldiers his intention of begging the Body, nay, had immediately gone (perhaps with them) to Pilate for that purpose,—and **τολμήσας εἰςῆλθ.** looks like a sudden and unannounced application,—they would have left the Body for him to take down.

ἐθαύμασεν εἰ ἤδη τέθνηκεν—he wondered at the fact thus announced to him of His death having already taken place. See Kühner, Gram. ii. p. 481, and the examples there adduced, which make this clear, e. g. Demosth. p. 24. 23,—θαυμάζω, εἰ Λακεδαιμονίοις μὲν πότε . . . ἀντῄρατε, νυνὶ δ' ὀκνεῖτε . . . **45. ἐδωρήσατο**] The passage cited (Meyer, De Wette) from Cicero (in Verrem, v. 45) to shew that it was customary to give money on such occasions, is not to the point; 'mortis celeritatem pretio redimere cogebantur parentes' is not said of the body *after death,* but of a fee given to the officer, 'ne diu crucietur.' **46. ἀγορ.**] Therefore it was *not the first day of unleavened bread,* which was one of *sabbatical sanctity;* as indeed the whole of this narrative shews, but such expressions as this more strikingly. **καθαιρεῖν** is the technical word for taking down bodies from the cross. See the examples in Kypke from Philo and Josephus. So is κατατιθέναι for placing bodies in the tomb: cf. ibid. **ἐν μνημ.**] It is not said, but *implied,* both here and in Luke and John, that the tomb was *his own*—for how should he place the Body there other-

XVI. 1 Καὶ [g] διαγενομένου τοῦ σαββάτου Μαρία ἡ
Μαγδαληνὴ καὶ Μαρία ἡ τοῦ Ἰακώβου καὶ Σαλώμη
ἠγόρασαν [h] ἀρώματα, ἵνα ἐλθοῦσαι [i] ἀλείψωσιν αὐτόν.
2 καὶ [j] λίαν πρωῒ τῆς [k] μιᾶς [k] σαββάτων ἔρχονται ἐπὶ τὸ
μνημεῖον [l] ἀνατείλαντος τοῦ ἡλίου. 3 καὶ ἔλεγον πρὸς
[m] ἑαυτὰς Τίς [n] ἀποκυλίσει ἡμῖν τὸν λίθον ἐκ τῆς [o] θύρας
τοῦ [o] μνημείου; 4 καὶ [p] ἀναβλέψασαι θεωροῦσιν ὅτι
[q] ἀνακεκύλισται ὁ λίθος· ἦν γὰρ μέγας σφόδρα. 5 καὶ

ABCDE GKLM SUVXΓ ΔΠℵ 1. 33. 69

g Acts xxv. 13. xxvii. 9 only †. 2 Macc. xi. 26 only, but not =.
h ‖ L. bis. John xix. 40 only. 4 Kings xx. 13.
i Matt. vi. 17 reff.
j w. adv., ch. i. 35.
k ‖ Mt. reff.
l intr., Matt. iv. 16 reff.
m ch. x. 26 reff.
n ‖ Mt. L. only. Gen. xxix. 3, 8, 10. Judith xiii. 9 only.
o ch. xv. 46.
p = Matt. xiv. 19 reff.
q here only †. Sir. xxxvii. 3 Ald. (ἐνεκύλ. ABℵ) only

Chap. XVI. 1. for διαγ. to σαλωμη, πορευθεισαι merely D lat-*n*: lat-*q* has the passage twice, once as D, the other time as txt: διαγ. τ. σαβ. πορευθεισαι lat-*k*: aft ηγ. ins πορ. syr-jer arm. (πορ. is simly insd elsw.) om του (bef σαββ.) C^{2} 33. ins η bef 1st μαρια B^{1}(Tischdf) Lℵ^{3a}. om 2nd η EL 1. 69. om του (bef ιακ.) ℵ^{1} rel: ins ABKLΔΠℵ^{3a} 33. om ελθουσαι D lat-*c* ff_2 [*k n q*]. αυτον bef αλειψωσιν D lat-*c* ff_2 *k n* q_1.

2. ερχονται πρωι μιας σαββατου D: om λιαν also lat-*c k n* Syr arm: τη μια των σ. LΔℵ 33 copt Eus$_1$: της μιας των σ. K: μια των σ. B 1: txt AC rel Dion. μνημα ℵ^{1}[C^{1}]. ανατελλοντος D lat-*c n q* Tich$_{expr}$ Aug.

3. εαυτους D lat-*c*. ημιν bef αποκ. D 2-pe lat-*c* ff_2 *k n q*. (αποκαλυψει D^{1}, but corrd eadem manu.) for εκ, απο CD 69 vulg lat-*c* ff_2 *l* goth Eus$_1$ [Ps-]Nyss$_1$ Sev$_1$.

4. ην γαρ μεγ. σφ. κ. ερχονται κ. ευρισκουσιν αποκεκυλισμενον τον λ. D 2-pe lat-*c* ff_2 *n* Eus: simly syr-jer.—rec **αποκεκυλισται** (*repetn from above: see also ‖ Luke*), with AC rel [Ps-Nyss]: txt BL.—ανακεκυλισμενον τον λ. (omg οτι) ℵ, *revolutum* vulg lat-*k l q*.

wise? The *newness* of the tomb is not mentioned here, but by the other three Evangelists. **47.**] **Μ. ἡ Ἰωσῆτος**—understand, *mother*: see ver. 40. That she is so called here, and **Μαρία ἡ τοῦ Ἰακώβου** in the next verse, points to a *difference of origin* in the two accounts here, of the *Crucifixion* and *Resurrection*.

The mother of the Lord had in all probability previously departed: see notes on Matt. xxvii. 56 and John xix. 27.

Luke generalizes, and says, *the women who came with Him from Galilee*.

Some have understood by **Μ. Ἰωσῆτος** or Ἰωσῆ or Ἰωσήφ, the *wife* or *daughter* of Joseph of Arimathæa—some, the *mother of the Lord*: but both unnecessarily, and without proof. The perf. **τεθεῖται** is to shew that they came up after the burial had taken place; the pres. (**τίθεται**, rec.) would imply that they were present at the entombment. So Meyer.

Chap. XVI. **1—8.**] The women, coming to the sepulchre, are apprised of His resurrection. Matt. xxviii. 1—10. Luke xxiv. 1—12. John xx. 1—10. On the general difficulties of this portion of the Gospels, and my view respecting them, see notes on Matt. **1. διαγ. τ. σαβ.**] It was strictly *when the Sabbath was ended*, i.e. at sunset, that they bought the spices. Luke xxiii. 55, places it on the evening *before* the Sabbath; a slight but valuable discrepancy, as shewing the independence of the accounts. To suppose *two parties* of women (Greswell) or to take ἠγόρασαν as *pluperfect* (Beza, Grotius, &c.) is equally arbitrary and unwarranted. **ἀλείψ.**] This had not been done as yet. Nicodemus (John xix. 40) had only wrapped the Body hurriedly in the spices with the linen clothes. **2. ἀνατείλαντος τ. ἡλ.**] This does not agree with Matt., τῇ ἐπιφωσκ. εἰς μίαν σαβ.;—Luke, ὄρθρου βαθέος: or John, σκοτίας ἔτι οὔσης:—nor indeed with λίαν πρωΐ of our narrative itself. If the sun was up, it would be between 6 and 7 o'clock; which in the East especially, where even public business was transacted *very early*, could not be so called. The reading of D, ἀνατέλλοντος, would not help us much, as it was evidently *some time before sunrise*. Even Greswell virtually acknowledges a difficulty here. **3, 4.**] It had been rolled away by an angel, Matt. **ἦν γὰρ μέγ. σφ.** is stated as a reason why *they could see that it was rolled away on looking up*, possibly at some distance. This explanation is according to Mark's manner of describing minute circumstantial incidents; but to refer this clause back as the *reason why* they questioned

ἐλθοῦσαι εἰς τὸ μνημεῖον εἶδον [r] νεανίσκον καθήμενον [s] ἐν
τοῖς [s] δεξιοῖς, [t] περιβεβλημένον [u] στολὴν λευκήν· καὶ
[v] ἐξεθαμβήθησαν. 6 ὁ δὲ λέγει αὐταῖς Μὴ [v] ἐκθαμβεῖσθε·
Ἰησοῦν ζητεῖτε τὸν Ναζαρηνὸν τὸν ἐσταυρωμένον·
X. ...ηγερ. [w] ἠγέρθη, οὐκ ἔστιν ὧδε· ἴδε ὁ τόπος ὅπου ἔθηκαν αὐτόν.
7 ἀλλὰ ὑπάγετε εἴπατε τοῖς μαθηταῖς αὐτοῦ καὶ τῷ Πέτρῳ
ὅτι [x] προάγει ὑμᾶς εἰς τὴν Γαλιλαίαν· ἐκεῖ αὐτὸν ὄψεσθε,
καθὼς εἶπεν ὑμῖν. 8 καὶ ἐξελθοῦσαι ἔφυγον ἀπὸ τοῦ
X τρομος... μνημείου· [y] εἶχεν δὲ αὐτὰς [z] τρόμος καὶ [a] ἔκστασις, καὶ
οὐδενὶ οὐδὲν εἶπον, ἐφοβοῦντο γάρ.

[ΕΥΑΓΓΕΛΙΟΝ] ΚΑΤΑ ΜΑΡΚΟΝ.

r Matt. xix. 20, 22 reff.
s here only. see Eph. i. 20 al.
t Matt. vii. 29, 31 reff. ch. xiv. 51 al.
u ch. xii. 38 reff.
v here bis & ch. ix. 15. xiv. 33 only +. Sir. xxx. 9 only.
w || Mt. L. Acts v. 30 al. fr.
x = Matt. xiv. 22 reff.
y = here only. Job xviii. 20.
z 1 Cor. ii. 3. 2 Cor. vii. 15. Eph. vi. 5. Phil. ii. 12 only. Exod. xv. 15.
a ch. v. 42. Luke v. 26. Acts iii. 10. x. 10. xi. 5. xxii. 17 only. Deut. xxviii. 28.

5. rec εισελθουσαι (*from* || *Luke*), with ACDℵ rel: txt B 127. νεανισκον bef ειδον D 2-pe. for εξεθαμβηθησαν, εθανβησαν D.

6. for ο δε, και D lat-*c ff*$_2$ *n*. αυτοις D-gr. add ο αγγελος D lat-*ff*$_2$. for εκθ., φοβεισθε D Eus$_1$. ins τον bef ιησ. D. om τον ναζ. D ℵ[1](ins ℵ-corr[1]). for ιδε ο τοπος, ειδετε εκει (add τον D[3]) τοπον αυτου D, simly 2-pe lat-*c ff*$_2$ *n q*.

7. (αλλα, so AB[1]CDGKLΔΠℵ 33.) ins και bef ειπατε C[1](appy) D 33 prag(with mt) lat-*k* goth. ιδου, προαγω . . . . εκει με . . . . ειρηκα υμιν D.

8. rec aft εξελθ. ins ταχυ (*from* || *Matt*), with E: om ABCDℵ rel vulg lat-*a*^{2} *c ff*$_2$ [*k l n q*] syrr syr-jer copt goth æth arm Thl. for δε, γαρ BDℵ vulg lat-*a*^{2} *c ff*$_2$ *k l* [*n q*] Syr copt æth arm: txt AC rel syr goth. (X def.) for τρομος, φοβος D [Π[1](appy)]. ειπαν D.

Subscription (aft εφοβ. γαρ). κατα μαρκον B: ευαγγ. κατα μαρκ. ℵ arm-old-mss.

The supplementary passage appears to have been added by another hand in very early times. The external testimonies (I.) for and (II.) against it are as follows.

I. (1) It is contained in ACD rel vulg lat-*a*^{2} *c ff*$_2$ *g*$_{1.2}$ *l n q* Syr syr-cu(recommences at τ. πιστ. ver. 17) syr[-txt] syr-jer copt goth æth arm-recent-mss.

(2) It is cited by Iren (iii. 10. 6, p. 188 (gr in Cramer's addenda): *In fine autem*

who should remove the stone, is not only harsh, but inconsistent with the usage of this Gospel. **5.**] In Matt.,—an *angel*, sitting on the stone which he had rolled away. Here he is described *as he appeared*, and we are left to infer *what* he was. In Luke,—*two angels* ἐπέστησαν αὐταῖς in the tomb. The incident to which these accounts point, must be distinct from that related John xx. 11, which was *after Mary Magdalene returned from the city*. It is not worth while to detail the attempts which have been made to reconcile these various reports of the incident: they present curious examples of the ingenuity, and (probably unconscious) disingenuousness, of the Harmonists. I may mention that Greswell supposes the angels in Matt. and Mark to be distinct, and accounts for the **ἐξεθαμβήθησαν** in our text thus: 'After seeing one angel *without* already, they were probably less prepared than before to see another so soon after *within*' (Dissert. vol. iii. p. 187).

6.] From the δεῦτε of Matt. I should be inclined to think that his is the strictly accurate account. This word implies that the angel accompanied the women into the tomb; and if so, an imperfect narrative like that in the text might easily describe his whole appearance as taking place within. **7.**] **ἀλλά** breaks off the discourse and turns to a new matter—**But now rather** do ye . . . **καὶ τῷ Π.**] It is hardly perhaps likely that the *denial of Peter* was the ground of this message, though it is difficult not to connect the two in the mind. The mention of him here is probably merely official—as the 'primus inter pares.' We cannot say that others of the Apostles may not have denied their Master besides Peter.
It must not be concluded from this that we have a trace of Peter's hand in the narrative. **8.**] The idea of our narrative here is, that the women *fled* in terror from the sepulchre, and *did not deliver the message at the time*,—for they

b here only. (elsw. μία, ver. 2 al.) see Gen. viii. 5.

[9 Ἀναστὰς δὲ πρωῒ b πρώτῃ σαββάτου ἐφάνη πρῶτον ACDEG KLMS UVXΓΔ Π 1. 33. 69

evangelii ait Marcus: Et quidem dominus Jesus, postquam locutus est eis, receptus est in caelos, et sedet ad dexteram Dei), Hipp, Celsus(perhaps), Synops, Cæs, Jac-nisib, Cyr-jer, Damasc, Phot, Thl, Ambr, Aug, Greg, Cassian. Nestorius (in Cyril, vi. 46) quotes ver. 20.

II. (1) It is omd in Bℵ arm-old-mss. After the subscription in B the remaining greater portion of the column and the whole of the next to the end of the page are left vacant. There is no other instance of this in the whole N. T. portion of the MS, the next book in every other instance beginning on the next column. Some of the old mss of arm add it, but with the subscr above and a separate title ευαγγ. κ. μαρκ.

(2) L thus proceeds [so also lat-*k* æth-mss-mg]: φέρεταί που ταῦτα + πάντα δὲ τὰ παρηγγελμένα τοῖς περὶ τὸν πέτρον συντόμως ἐξήγγειλαν· μετὰ δὲ ταῦτα καὶ αὐτὸς ὁ ἰησοῦς, ἀπὸ ἀνατολῆς [ἀνατολῶν 274] καὶ ἄχρι δύσεως ἐξαπέστειλεν δι' αὐτῶν τὸ ἱερὸν καὶ ἄφθαρτον κήρυγμα τῆς αἰωνίου σωτηρίας + [so far syr-mg and 274 agree] ἔστι δὲ καὶ ταῦτα φερόμενα μετὰ τὸ ἐφοβοῦντο γάρ + ἀναστὰς δέ &c. 22 has it thus: ἐφοβοῦντο γάρ + τέλος· then *in red*, ἔν τισι τῶν ἀντιγράφων ἕως ὧδε πληροῦται ὁ εὐαγγελιστής· ἐν πολλοῖς δὲ καὶ ταῦτα φέρεται· ἀναστὰς δέ &c. 20. [215.] 300 have [but, appy, after ver 15], ἐντεῦθεν ἕως τοῦ τέλους ἔν τισι τῶν ἀντιγράφων οὐ κεῖται· ἐν δὲ τοῖς ἀρχαίοις πάντα ἀπαράλειπτα κεῖται. 23. 34-9. 41 have this scholion of Severus of Antioch: ἐν μὲν οὖν τοῖς ἀκριβεστέροις ἀντιγράφοις τὸ κατὰ μάρκον εὐαγγέλιον μέχρι τοῦ ἐφοβοῦντο γὰρ ἔχει τὸ τέλος. ἐν δέ τισι πρόσκειται καὶ ταῦτα· ἀναστὰς δὲ πρωῒ πρώτῃ σαββάτου ἐφάνη πρῶτον μαρίᾳ τῇ μαγδαληνῇ ἀφ' ἧς ἐκβεβλήκει ἑπτὰ δαιμόνια· τοῦτο δὲ ἐναντιῶσίν τινα δοκεῖ ἔχειν πρὸς τὰ ἔμπροσθεν εἰρημένα. 24 has, παρὰ πλείστοις ἀντιγράφοις οὐ κεῖνται ἐν τῷ παρόντι εὐαγγελίῳ ὡς νόθα νομίσαντες αὐτὰ εἶναι· ἀλλ' ἡμεῖς ἐξ ἀκριβῶν ἀντιγράφων ἐν πλείστοις εὑρόντες αὐτὰ καὶ κατὰ τὸ παλαιστιναῖον εὐαγγέλιον μάρκου ὡς ἔχει ἡ ἀλήθεια συντεθείκαμεν καὶ τὴν ἐν αὐτῷ ἐπιφερομένην δεσποτικὴν ἀνάστασιν μετὰ τὸ ἐφοβ. γάρ. Similar scholia are given in 36-7-8. 40. 108-29-37-8-43-81-6-95-9. 210-21-2. 374. In 1. 206-9, we have, ἔν τισι μὲν τῶν ἀντιγράφων ἕως ὧδε πληροῦται ὁ εὐαγγελιστής, ἕως οὗ καὶ εὐσέβιος ὁ παμφίλου ἐκανόνισεν· ἐν ἄλλοις δὲ ταῦτα φέρεται· ἀναστὰς δέ &c.

(3) In ALUΓΔ al_m, am fuld ing², the numbers of Eus and Ammon are not attached beyond ver. 8. In many mss the passage is insd with an asterisk.

(4) Clem-rom, Just, Clem-alex take no notice of it. Eus states that it is *wanted in many mss*: ἐν τούτῳ (ἐφοβ. γάρ) σχεδὸν ἐν ἅπασι τοῖς ἀντιγράφοις τοῦ κατὰ μάρκον εὐαγγελίου περιγέγραπται τὸ τέλος, and he calls these τὰ ἀκριβῆ τῶν ἀντιγράφων—Ad Marin. Quæst. 1, vol. iv. See the whole quoted in Davidson's Introd. i. 164. Sev, Vict, Greg-nyss(or Hesych of Jerus), Jer(ad Hedib. 3, vol. i. p. 825, *omnes Graeciae libros paene hoc capitulum in fine non habere*), Euthym say that it is wanting in the *greater number*, or, in the *more accurate*.

III. It would thus appear that while the passage was appended as early as the time of Irenæus, *it was still absent from the majority of codices* as late as Jerome's day. The legitimate inference is that *it was placed as a completion of the Gospel soon after the apostolic period*,—the Gospel itself having been, for some reason unknown to us, left incomplete. The most probable supposition is, that *the last leaf of the original Gospel was torn away*.

IV. The attempt to account for its absence by the hypothesis that it was *erased by reason of its inconsistency with the accounts in the other Gospels*, is *quite futile*. We have no instances of erasure of portions of the Gospels for any such reason: nor do the fathers who *mention the inconsistency* (Greg-nyss, Vict, Sev, Jer), allege such erasure to have been made: nor, had it been made, *need it have included the whole passage*. The inconsistency itself is a valuable testimony to the antiquity of the fragment, as having been composed from *independent testimony*, and *not from the other Gospels*.

V. The *internal evidence*, which is discussed in the notes, will be found to preponderate vastly *against the authorship of Mark*.

9. σαββατων KΠ 1. for εφανη πρωτον, εφανερωσεν πρωτοις D-gr.

were afraid. All attempts to reconcile this with the other Gospels are futile. It is a manifest evidence that our narrative is here suddenly broken off, and (perhaps?) that no more information about the women was in the possession of its

Μαρίᾳ τῇ Μαγδαληνῇ, [c] ἀφ' ἧς [c] ἐκβεβλήκει ἑπτὰ δαιμόνια.
10 ἐκείνη πορευθεῖσα ἀπήγγειλεν τοῖς μετ' αὐτοῦ γενομένοις, [d] πενθοῦσιν καὶ [d] κλαίουσιν. 11 κἀκεῖνοι ἀκούσαντες ὅτι ζῇ καὶ [e] ἐθεάθη ὑπ' αὐτῆς [f] ἠπίστησαν. 12 μετὰ
δὲ ταῦτα δυσὶν ἐξ αὐτῶν περιπατοῦσιν [g] ἐφανερώθη ἐν
ἑτέρᾳ [h] μορφῇ, πορευομένοις εἰς ἀγρόν. 13 κἀκεῖνοι
[i] ἀπελθόντες ἀπήγγειλαν τοῖς λοιποῖς· οὐδὲ ἐκείνοις
[j] ἐπίστευσαν. 14 [k] ὕστερον [l] ἀνακειμένοις αὐτοῖς τοῖς

c Matt. vii. 4. Acts xiii. 50 only. 2 Chron. xi. 6.
d Luke vi. 25. James iv. 9. Rev. xviii. 11, 15, 19. Neh. i. 4.
e pass., Matt. vi. 1. xxiii. 5 only‡. w. ὑπό, here only. (trans., ver. 14 al. fr.)
f ver. 16. Luke xxiv. 11, 41. Acts xxviii. 24. Rom. iii. 3. 2 Tim. ii. 13 only †. Wisd. x. 7 al.
g constr., John xxi. 1 reff.
h Phil. ii. 6, 7 only. Isa. xliv. 13.
i = Matt. xxv. 25 al.
j = John v. 46. Acts viii. 12. Gen. xv. 6.
k = Matt. iv. 2 reff.
l Mk., here (ch. v. 40 v. r.) only. = Matt. xxii. 10, 11 reff.

om τη D. for αφ', παρ' C[1]DL 33: txt AC[3] rel Eus$_2$.

10. aft εκεινη ins δε C[1] lat-*c ff*$_2$ [g_2 *l*] *q* arm. for πορευθ., απελθουσα ΚΠ Scr's o w. ins αυτοις bef τοις D.

11. εκεινοι δε C[1] D[2](appy) copt: *at illi* lat-*c ff*$_2$ *q*: εκεινοι LU. for ηπιστησαν, και ουκ επιστευσαν αυτω D[1](αυτη D-corr[1]).

12. ins και bef μετα δε D[1].

14. aft υστερον ins δε AD 1 lat-*c* g_1 *n o q* Syr syr-w-ast copt (æth).

author. The subsequent verses are quite disconnected from this; and contain the substance of their writer's information respecting the other appearances of the Lord.

[9—20.] Appearances of Jesus after his Resurrection: his Ascension. An addition to the narrative of a compendious and supplementary character, bearing traces of *another hand* from that which has shaped the diction and construction of the rest of the Gospel. The reasons for and against this inference will be found in the var. readd. and the course of this note, and a general statement of them at the end of it. **9.**] **πρώτῃ σαββάτου** = *μία σαββάτων* ver. 2, and is remarkable as occurring so soon after it (see Luke xviii. 12). **ἀφ' ἧς ἐκβ. . . . .**] This notice, coming so late, *after the mention of Mary Magdalene in ver.* 1, is remarkable. The instances quoted by De Wette to shew that the unexpected introduction of notices contained in the other Gospels is in Mark's manner, do not seem to me to apply here. This verse agrees with John xx. 1 ff. but is unconnected with the former narrative in this chapter. **10.**] **ἐκεῖνος** is *no where found used absolutely* by Mark,—but *always emphatically* (see ch. iv. 11; vii. 15, 20; xiv. 21); whereas here and ver. 11 it is absolutely used (not in vv. 13 b and 20, where it is emphatical). **πορευθ.**] This word, *never used by Mark*, is *three times contained in this passage* (vv. 12, 15). **τοῖς μετ' αὐτοῦ γεν.**, though found in the Acts (xx. 18), *never occurs in the Gospels:* nor does the word *μαθηταί* in this passage. **11.**] See John xx. 18: Luke xxiv. 11. **ἐθεάθη ὑπ' αὐτῆς** is a construction only found here in N. T., and *θεάομαι* (which occurs again ver. 14) is not used by Mark. **ἀπιστέω** is only used in ver. 16 and Luke xxiv. 11, 41, throughout the Gospels. **12.**] **μετὰ ταῦτα** is *not found in Mark*, though many opportunities occurred for using it. This verse epitomizes the events on the journey to Emmaus, Luke xxiv. 13—35. **περιπατοῦσιν ἐφανερώθη**, though in *general* accord with Luke's narrative, is not accurate in detail. It was not *as they walked*, but *as they sat at meat* that He was manifested to them. **ἐν ἑτέρᾳ μορφῇ**—a slight difference from Luke xxiv. 15, 16, which relates as the reason why they did not know Him, that *their eyes were holden*, his being *in his usual form* being declared by *αὐτὸς ὁ Ἰησοῦς*: but see notes there. **13.**] **κἀκεῖνοι**—as Mary Magdalene had done before. **τοῖς λοιποῖς**] Supply *τοῖς μετ' αὐτοῦ γενομένοις.* **οὐδὲ ἐκείνοις ἐπίστευσαν**—not consistent with Luke xxiv. 33, 34. Here again the Harmonists have used every kind of distortion of the plain meaning of words to reconcile the two accounts; assuming that some believed and some doubted, that they first doubted and then believed; or, according to Bengel, first believed and then doubted. **14.**] The following narrative, evidently intended by its author to represent what took place *at one and the same time*, joins together in one at least *four* appearances of the Lord: (1) that related in this verse and Luke xxiv. 36—49; (2) that on the mountain in Galilee (Matt. xxviii. 16—20),

m constr., here only. Wisd. ii. 12. acc. pers., Matt. xi. 20 al.
n Matt. xiii. 58 reff.
o ch. x. 5. Matt. xix. 8 only. Deut. x. 16. Sir. xvi. 10 only. (-διος, Ezek. iii. 7.)
p Mark, ver. 11 only. Luke xxiii. 55 reff.
q ver. 6 al. fr.

ἕνδεκα [g] ἐφανερώθη, καὶ [m] ὠνείδισεν τὴν [n] ἀπιστίαν αὐτῶν
καὶ [o] σκληροκαρδίαν, ὅτι τοῖς [p] θεασαμένοις αὐτὸν [q] ἐγηγερ-
μένον οὐκ [j] ἐπίστευσαν. 15 καὶ εἶπεν αὐτοῖς Πορευθέντες εἰς τὸν [r] κόσμον [r] ἅπαντα κηρύξατε τὸ εὐαγγέλιον
πάσῃ τῇ [s] κτίσει. 16 ὁ [t] πιστεύσας καὶ βαπτισθεὶς
σωθήσεται, ὁ δὲ [u] ἀπιστήσας [v] κατακριθήσεται. 17 [w] σημεῖα δὲ τοῖς πιστεύσασιν ταῦτα [x] παρακολουθήσει· [y] ἐν τῷ

H σκληροκαρδιαν... ...το ευαγγελιον D. ACEGH KLMSU VXΓΔΠ 1. 33. 69

r here only. see Col. i. 6. s = Rom. viii. 9, 22. Judith xvi. 14.
t abs., ch. xv. 32. Acts ii. 44. xix. 2 al. u ver. 11 reff. & note. v = 1 Cor. xi. 32.
w Matt. xii. 38 reff. x — here only †. (Luke i. 3 reff.) 2 Macc. viii. 11. y of Christ, Mark, here only. Matt. never. Luke x. 17 only. John, Acts, Epp. freq.

aft εγηγερμενον ins εκ νεκρων AC[1]XΔ 1. 33. 69 syr arm: om C[3]D rel vulg lat-*c* *ff*$_2$ Syr copt æth.

15. for αυτοις, προς αυτους D. om απαντα D-gr 225 gat copt. ins και bef κηρυξατε D lat-*c* [*q*] syr-w-ob (copt) æth [Ambr]. (Jer cont Pelag says that some mss, principally Greek, add *et illi satisfaciebant dicentes: Seculum istud iniquitatis et incredulitatis substantia*(*sub satana* ms$_1$) *est, quæ non sinit per immundos spiritus veram Dei apprehendi virtutem. Idcirco jam nunc revela justitiam tuam.*)

17. παρακολουθησει bef ταυτα AC[2] 33: ακολ. τ. C[1]L.

when the words in ver. 15 were spoken; (3) some unrecorded appearance when the rest of these words (vv. 16—18) were spoken,—unless we consider the whole to have been said on the mountain in Galilee; and (4) the appearance which terminated with the Ascension. The latter part of this ver. 14 appears to be an epitome of what our Lord said to them on several occasions—see Luke xxiv. 25, 38: John xx. 27: Matt. xxviii. 17.

15.] **τὸν κόσμον ἅπαντα** = πάντα τὰ ἔθνη, Matt. xxviii. 19: see note there. **κηρύσσειν τὸ εὐαγγέλιον**, without the addition of τῆς βασιλείας (Matt.) or τοῦ θεοῦ (Mark i. 14 only, Luke), is in *Mark's manner* (see ch. xiii. 10; xiv. 9). It only once occurs in Matt., viz. xxvi. 13. **πάσῃ τῇ κτ.**] Not to *men* only, although men only can hear the *preaching* of the Gospel; *all creation* is redeemed by Christ —see Col. i. 15, 23: Rom. viii. 19—23. 'Hominibus, primario, ver. 16, reliquis creaturis, secundario. Sicut maledictio, ita benedictio patet. Creatio per Filium, fundamentum redemtionis et regni.' Bengel in loc. **κτίσις** appears never in the N. T. to be used of *mankind alone*. Bengel's 'reliquis creaturis secundario' may be illustrated in the blessings which Christianity confers on the inferior creatures and the face of the earth by bringing civilization in its wake. By these words *the missionary office is bound upon the Church through all ages, till every part of the earth shall have been evangelized.* **16.**] These past participles must be noticed, as carrying on the thought to a time *beyond the work of the preacher:* when **σωθ.** and **κατακρ.** shall take place; and reserving the division of mankind into these two classes, till that day. On **βαπτ.** see note on Matt. xxviii. 19. There is no καὶ μὴ βαπτ. in the second clause here. Unbelief—by which is meant the rejection of the gospel in heart and life, not weakness or doubt as in ver. 14—shall condemn a man, whether *baptized or unbaptized.* And, conversely, it follows that our Lord does not set forth here the *absolute*, but only the *general* necessity of Baptism to salvation; as the Church of England also teaches. But that general necessity extends to all to whom Baptism is *accessible;* and it was well said 'Non privatio Baptismi, sed contemtus, damnat.'

These words cannot be taken, as those in Matt. xxviii. 19, 20, as setting forth the *order* in which faith and baptism must always come; *belief* and *disbelief* are in this verse the great leading subjects, and **πιστεύσας** must on that account stand first. On **ὁ πιστ. σωθ.** compare Acts xvi. 31. This is a solemn declaration of the doctrine of 'salvation by faith,' from the Lord Himself; but such a faith as is expanded, Matt. xxviii. 20, into διδάσκοντες αὐτοὺς **τηρεῖν πάντα ὅσα ἐνετειλάμην ὑμῖν**: which is its *proper fruits.* **κατακρ.**, 'will be *condemned;*' i. e. in the most solemn sense: for the *sin of unbelief:*—for those are now spoken of who *hear* the gospel preached, and *reject* it. **17.**] This promise is *generally* made, without limitation to the first ages of the Church. *Should occasion arise for its fulfilment,*

[y] *ὀνόματί μου δαιμόνια ἐκβαλοῦσιν,* [za] *γλώσσαις* [a] *λαλή-* z = Gospp., here only. (ch. vii. 33, 35. Luke i. 64. xvi. 24.)
σουσιν [b] *καιναῖς,* 18 [c] *ὄφεις* [d] *ἀροῦσιν· κἂν* [e] *θανάσιμόν τι* a Acts ii. 4. x. 46 al. fr.
πίωσιν, οὐ μὴ αὐτοὺς [f] *βλάψῃ· ἐπὶ* [g] *ἀῤῥώστους* [h] *χεῖρας* b = here only. see ch. i. 27. Acts xvii. 19.
[h] *ἐπιθήσουσιν, καὶ* [i] *καλῶς* [i] *ἕξουσιν.* 19 *Ὁ μὲν οὖν κύριος* = ἑτέραις, Acts ii. 4.
..xvi. 19 (appy)Π. *μετὰ τὸ λαλῆσαι αὐτοῖς* [j] *ἀνελήμφθη εἰς τὸν οὐρανὸν καὶ* c Luke x. 19.
[k] *ἐκάθισεν* [l] *ἐκ δεξιῶν τοῦ θεοῦ.* 20 *ἐκεῖνοι δὲ* [m] *ἐξελθόντες* d = ch. vi. 29. John viii.

59. 1 Macc. ix. 19. e here only. f Luke iv. 35 (reff.) only. g Matt. xiv. 14 reff. h and constr., Matt. ix. 18 reff. i here only. see John iv. 52. j = Acts i. 2, 11, 22. x. 16. 1 Tim. iii. 16. 4 Kings ii. 10. (-λημψις, Luke ix. 51.) k intr., Matt. v. 1 reff. l Matt xx. 21, 23 reff. m = Luke ix. 6. 1 John iv. 1.

om *καιναις* C[1]L Δ-gr copt arm.

18. ins *και εν ταις χερσιν* bef *οφεις* CLM[2]X Δ-gr **1.** 33 syr-cu syr-w-ast copt arm: om A rel vulg lat-*c* Syr æth Hipp$_1$. for *ου μη, ουδεν* C[1]. rec **βλαψει,** with Scr's i: txt AC rel Scr's-mss.

19. om *ουν* C[1]L arm. aft *κυριος* ins *ιησους* C[1]KLΔ **1.** 33 vulg-ed [with em fuld] lat-*c ff*$_2$ *o* syrr syr-cu copt æth arm Iren-int: om AC[3] rel am lat-*g*$_1$ Iren-gr.—for *κυρ., ιησ.* H. for **εκ δεξιων, εν δεξια** CΔ.

there can be no doubt that it will be made good in our own or any other time. But we must remember that *σημεῖα* are not needed where Christianity is *professed:* nor by missionaries who are backed by the influence of powerful Christian nations. There are credible testimonies of miraculous powers having been exercised in the Church considerably after the Apostles' time. **δαιμ. ἐκβ.**] The Lord Himself has declared how weighty a sign this was, Matt. xii. 28. For fulfilments of the promise, see Acts v. 16; viii. 7; xvi. 18. **γλώσ. λ. καιν.**] See 1 Cor. xiv. 22: Acts ii. 4 al. On the gift of tongues, see notes at those places. **18. ὄφ. ἀρ.**] See Acts xxviii. 3—5. **κἂν θαν. . . . . βλάψῃ**] We have no instance of this given in the Acts: but later, there are several stories which, if to be relied on, furnish examples of its fulfilment. Eusebius, H. E. iii. 39, says, . . . *ἕτερον παράδοξον περὶ Ἰοῦστον τὸν ἐπικληθέντα Βαρσαβᾶν γεγονός, ὡς δηλητήριον φάρμακον ἐμπιόντος καὶ μηδὲν ἀηδὲς διὰ τὴν τοῦ κυρίου χάριν ὑπομείναντος.* **ἐπὶ ἀῤῥ.**] *χεῖρας ἐπιθ. ἐπί τινα* is in *Mark's manner:* see ch. viii. 25; x. 16. There is no mention of the anointing with oil here, as in James v. 14. **19, 20.**] The **μὲν οὖν** is not to be taken here as if there were no **δέ** following:—the *μέν* answers to the *δέ* as in Luke iii. 18, 19—and the *οὖν* is the connecting link with what went before.

μὲν οὖν, ὁ κύριος, and *ὁ κύριος Ἰησοῦς,* are alike *foreign to the diction of Mark,* in speaking of the Lord: we have *ὁ κύριος* in the message (common to all three Gospels) ch. xi. 3—but that manifestly is no example. **μετὰ τὸ λαλ.** can only in fairness mean, '*when He had spoken these words.*' All endeavours of the Harmonists to include in them *οὐ μόνον τοὺς λόγους τούτους, ἀλλὰ πάντας ὅσους ἐλάλησε* (Euthym.) will have no weight with an honest reader, who looks to the *evident sense of his author alone,* and disregards other considerations. That other words *were* spoken, we know; but that *this author intended us to infer that,* surely is not deducible from the text, and is too often allowed in such cases to creep fallaciously in as an inference. We never shall read or comment on Scripture with full profit, till all such subterfuges are abandoned, and the gospel evidence treated in the clear light of intelligent and honest faith. We have an example of this last in Theophylact's exposition, *ταῦτα δὲ λαλήσας.* **ἀνελ.**] I should hardly say that the author of this fragment necessarily implies an ascension *from the place* where they were then assembled. The whole of these two verses is of a compendious character, and as **ἐκάθ. ἐκ δ. τ. θ.** must be understood as setting forth a fact not comprehended in the cycle of their observation, but certain in the belief of all Christians, so **ἀνελήμφ.** may very well speak of the *fact* as happening, not necessarily then and there, but (see remarks above) *after these words were spoken;* provided always that these words are recognized as *the last* in the view and information of our Evangelist. I say this not with any harmonistic view, but because the words themselves seem to require it. (See on the Ascension, notes on Luke xxiv. 51 ff.) **20.**] **ἐξελθόντες**—not, from the chamber where they were assembled (Meyer)—which would not answer to *ἐκήρυξαν πανταχοῦ,* but would require some immediate action of that

n ch. i. 28 reff. o Rom. viii. 28. 1 Cor. xvi. 16. 2 Cor. vi. 1. James ii. 22 only +. Esdr. vii. 2. 1 Macc. xii. 1 only. (-γος, Rom. iii. 6.) p = Luke i. 2 reff. q here only in Gospp. Rom. xv. 8. 1 Cor. i. 6, 8. 2 Cor. i. 21. Col. ii. 7. Heb. ii. 3. xiii. 9 only. Ps. xl. 12. cxviii. 28 only. r 1 Tim. v. 10, 24. 1 Pet. ii. 21 only. Job xxxi. 7.

ἐκήρυξαν [n] πανταχοῦ, τοῦ κυρίου [o] συνεργοῦντος καὶ τὸν [p] λόγον [q] βεβαιοῦντος διὰ τῶν [r] ἐπακολουθούντων σημείων.

ACEGH KLMSU VXΓΔ 1. 33. 69

ΕΥΑΓΓΕΛΙΟΝ ΚΑΤΑ ΜΑΡΚΟΝ.]

20. Steph adds *αμην*, with C[1] rel am(with gat prag) lat-*c o* copt æth : om AC[2] 1 33 vulg-ed(with ing) lat-*a*[2] *q* syrr syr-cu arm.

Subscription : *ευαγγελιον κατα μαρκον* ACEHLUΓΔ : Treg edits *κατα μαρκον* here on no ms authority, but only by the analogy of B in ver 8. MSXΠ[r] have no subscr : GKS have *το κατα μαρκον* (add *αγιον* G) *ευαγγελιον εξεδοθη*(*δωθη* G) *μετα χρονους ί*(*δεκα* K, *ιβ′* al) *της του χριστου*(*κυριου* G al) *αναληψεως* : al aft numbering the vv &c, add : *εγραφη ρωμαιστι εν ρωμη*(so Syr) or *εν αιγυπτω . . . . . υπηγορευθη υπο πετρου, επεδοθη μαρκω τω ευαγγελιστη, κ. εκηρυχθη εν αλεξανδρεια κ. παση τη περιχωρω αυτης.*

very day to correspond to it (see Matt. xii. 14);—but used in the more solemn sense of Rom. x. 18 (cited from Ps. xviii. 4 LXX), εἰς πᾶσαν τὴν γῆν ἐξῆλθεν ὁ φθόγγος αὐτῶν : see reff. **πανταχοῦ**] No inference can be drawn from this word as to the date of the fragment. In Acts ix. 32 Peter is said διερχόμενον διὰ πάντων κατελθεῖν . . . :—the expression being only *a general one*, indicating their performance, in their time and degree, of our Lord's words, **εἰς τὸν κόσμον ἅπαντα.** **τοῦ κυρ.**] the Lord, i. e. Jesus: see Matt. xxviii. 20 : Heb. ii. 3, 4, which last passage some have absurdly supposed to have been seen and used by our Evangelist. **ἐπακολ.** and **παρακολ.** (ver. 17) are *both foreign to the diction of Mark* often as he uses the simple verb.

A few concluding remarks may be added respecting vv. 9—20. (1) For the external evidence, see var. readd. As to its *genuineness as a work of the Evangelist Mark*, (2) internal evidence is, I think, very weighty *against Mark's being the author*. No less than *twenty-one words and expressions occur in it* (and some of them several times), which are *never elsewhere used* by Mark,—whose adherence to his own peculiar phrases is remarkable. (3) The inference therefore seems to me to be, that *it is an authentic fragment, placed as a completion of the Gospel in very early times* : by whom written, must of course remain wholly uncertain ; but coming to us with very weighty sanction, and having strong claims on our reception and reverence.]

[ΕΥΑΓΓΕΛΙΟΝ]

ΚΑΤΑ ΛΟΥΚΑΝ.

ABDE FKLM PRSUV ΧΓΔΛΞ Πℵ 1. 33. 69

I. 1 [a] Ἐπειδήπερ πολλοὶ [b] ἐπεχείρησαν [c] ἀνατάξασθαι

a here only †. Plato, Protag. p. 357 A.
b Acts ix. 29 xix. 13 only. Esth. ix. 25.
c here only. Eccl. ii. 20 Ald. (ἀποτ. ABℵ.)

TITLE: elz το κατα λ. ευαγγελιον: Steph το κατα λ. αγιον ευαγγελιον: λουκας $Λ^2$: om $Λ^1$: εκ του κ. λ. αγιου ευαγγελιου 69 al: κατα λουκαν BFℵ: ευαγ. κατα λ. ACDΞ rel.

CHAP. I. **1—4.**] PREFACE TO THEOPHILUS. The peculiar style of this preface,—which is purer Greek than the contents of the Gospel, and also more laboured and formal,—may be accounted for, partly because it is the composition of the Evangelist himself, and not translated from Hebrew sources like the rest, and partly because prefaces, especially when also dedicatory, are usually in a rounded and artificial style. **1. ἐπειδήπερ**] This compound, of rare occurrence, is in keeping with the rhetorical style of the preface. See Hartung, Partikellehre, i. p. 342. Valcknaer quotes from Ulpian a similar exordium: ἐπειδήπερ περὶ τούτου πολλοὶ ἐπεχείρησαν ἀπολογήσασθαι. **πολλοί**] Much depends on the meaning of this word, as guiding, or modifying, our opinion on the relation and sources of our Gospel histories. (1) That *the writers of our present Gospels exclusively* cannot be meant, is evident; since, even *supposing Luke to have seen all three Gospels*, one (that of John) was wholly, and another (that of Matthew) was in greater part, the production of an *eye-witness and minister of the word*,—which would leave only *one* for the **πολλοί**. (2) Apocryphal Gospels *exclusively* cannot be meant: for they would not be '*narrations concerning matters fully believed among us*,' nor '*delivered by eye-witnesses and ministers of the word*,' a great part of their contents being *excluded* by this very author from his *own* διήγησις. (3) A combination of these two *may* be intended—e. g. of the latter sort, *the Gospel according to the Hebrews*,—of the former, *that according to Mark*, but then also how shall we make out the **πολλοί**? Our present apocryphal Gospels arose far later than any likely date which can be assigned to Luke's Gospel: see Prolegomena to Luke, § iv. (4) I believe the only probable interpretation of the words to be, that many persons, in charge of Churches, or otherwise induced, drew up, here and there, statements (*narratives*, διηγ.) of the *testimony of eye-witnesses* and ὑπηρ. τ. λ. (see below), so far as they themselves had been able to collect them. (I do *not* believe that either the Gospel of Matt. or that of Mark *are to be reckoned* among these; or if they are, that Luke had seen or used them.) That such narratives should not have come down to us, is no matter of surprise: for (1) they would be absorbed by the more complete and sanctioned accounts of our present Evangelists; and (2) Church tradition has preserved very few fragments of authentic information of the apostolic age. It is probable that in almost every Church where an eye-witness

[d] διήγησιν περὶ τῶν [e] πεπληροφορημένων ἐν ἡμῖν πραγμάτων, 2 καθὼς [f] παρέδοσαν ἡμῖν οἱ [g] ἀπ' ἀρχῆς [h] αὐτόπται
καὶ [i] ὑπηρέται γενόμενοι τοῦ [k] λόγου, 3 [l] ἔδοξεν κἀμοὶ

d here only. Heb. ii. 6. Sir. ix. 15. 2 Macc. ii. 32. (-γεῖσθαι, ch. viii. 39.) e Rom. iv. 21. xiv. 5. Col. iv. 12. 2 Tim. iv. 5, 17 only. Eccl. viii. 11 only. (-φορία, Col. ii. 2.) f = Mark vii. 13. 1 Cor. xi. 2. Acts vi. 14. xvi. 4. 2 Pet. ii. 21. g Matt. xix. 4, 8. John xv. 27. Acts xxvi. 4 al. Isa. xlviii. 16. h here only †. i = Acts xiii. 5. xxvi. 16. 1 Cor. iv. 1. Wisd. vi. 4. k = ch. viii. 12, 13, 15. Mark xvi. 20. Acts vi. 4 al. l constr., dat. & inf., Acts xv. 22, 25, 28 (34 v. r.) only. L. = Esth. i. 19 al.

C και υπηρεται... ABCDE FKLM PRSUV ΧΓΔΛΞ Π א 1 33. 69

2. καθα D. παρεδωσαν AX Scr's b e l^1 m^1 evv-P-X-y-z : παρεδωκαν ΚΠ Scr's o w^1 [Ps-Ath_1]. γενομενου C.

preached, his testimony would be taken down, and framed into some *διήγησις*, more or less complete, of the life and sayings of the Lord. **ἐπεχείρησαν**] **have undertaken**; or, as E. V., **taken in hand.** This does not necessarily imply the *insufficiency* of such *διηγήσεις*, as Orig., Ambr., Theophyl., &c. have imagined. Nor is any such failure implied (as Bp. Wordsw.) in Acts xix. 13, where the *aorist* also is used. The failure then was not in the *ὀνομάζειν*, but in the issue. In Acts ix. 29, the failure is conveyed by the *imperfect* tense, not necessarily by the verb itself. The fact of that failure is indeed implied in Luke's description of his own work—but that, more because *it possessed completeness* (whereas they were fragmentary) than from any difference in kind. **ἀνατάξασθαι**] **to draw up—to arrange. διηγ.**] **a setting forth:** and so if in relation to *things past*, **a narration—history.** The word is clearly explained in Plato, Rep. iii. p. 392: *ἆρ' οὐ πάντα ὅσα ὑπὸ μυθολόγων ἢ ποιητῶν λέγεται, διήγησις οὖσα τυγχάνει ἢ γεγονότων ἢ ὄντων ἢ μελλόντων; Τί γάρ, ἔφη, ἄλλο; Ἆρα οὖν οὐχὶ ἤτοι ἁπλῇ διηγήσει ἢ διὰ μιμήσεως γιγνομένῃ ἢ δι' ἀμφοτέρων περαίνουσιν;* **πεπληρ.**, * according to some, *'fulfilled.'* De Wette supports this by the meaning of **πληρόω** Acts xix. 21; xii. 25, which is beside the purpose. The more likely rendering is that of E. V., **certainly believed.** (Meyer would render it, 'which have *found their completion* among *us,*' i. e. 'us of the apostolic times;' meaning *'Theophilus and himself,'* &c. This, I think, gives too emphatic a sense to **ἐν ἡμῖν**, which can only mean as ordinarily, *'among us,'* unless accompanied with some qualifying expression. His objection to the ordinary explanation,—that the participle ought, according to it, to be subjective to the *πράγματα*, surely is of no force.) See reff. and note on 2 Tim. iv. 5, 17. The use of the cognate noun *πληροφορία* supports this view: see 1 Thess. i. 5: Heb. vi. 11. There does not appear to be any reference to the filling of the sails of a ship, as Bp. Wordsw. The word with its cognates occurs only in a figurative sense, derived from "filling full" without any special reference. **ἡμῖν**] **among us Christians**, i. e. you and me, and all members of the Church of Christ—so also the *ἡμῖν* in ver. 2. **2. καθὼς παρ.**] The Apostles, &c., delivered these matters *orally* to the Churches in their teaching (see below on **κατηχ.**) and others drew up accounts from that catechetical instruction. It appears from this, that Luke *was not aware of any* **διήγησις** *drawn up by an eye-witness or* **ὑπ. τ. λ.** *Their* account of these matters was a *παράδοσις, from which* the *διηγήσεις* were drawn up. *He cannot therefore have seen* (or, having seen, not recognized as such, which is highly improbable) *the Gospel of Matthew.* Compare 1 John i. 1—3. **ἀπ' ἀρχῆς**—not, *'from the very beginning,'* i. e. the birth of the Lord, &c., but from the *official beginning:* see Acts i. 21 f. It differs from **ἄνωθεν** below. **αὐτ. κ. ὑπηρ. τοῦ λ.**] **αὐτ.** most probably stands alone: but it may well be taken with *τ. λ.* (see below.) **ὑπηρ.**,—see reff.,—**ministering servants**—but in connexion with *ἀπ' ἀρχῆς*. The fanciful idea of "remiges in navi, sc. ecclesia," cited by Wordsw. from Valckn., is out of the question. *ὑπηρέτης* had long lost trace of its original derivation, in its more common meaning; and it would be abhorrent from good taste to suppose St. Luke to have used it with so pedantic an allusion. **τ. λόγου**—not, *'the Λόγος'* (i. e. Christ: so Orig., Athanasius, Cyril, Euthym.), which would be altogether alien from Luke's usage (see on Heb. iv. 12. Bleek, in his posthumous "Erklärung der drei ersten Evv.," Leipz. 1862, also objects to the personal sense as too precise and definite for the rhetorical generalities of St. Luke in this passage)—nor *'the matter,'* so that *ὑπ. τ. λ.* would signify those who by their labours contributed to bring the matter about, 'qui ipsi interfuerunt rebus, tanquam pars aliqua'—for this is alien from Luke's usage of *ὑπηρ.*—see Acts xxvi. 16; but, **the word,**—'the *word preached:*'—so that *ὑπηρέτης τ. λόγ.* = *διάκονος τ. λόγ.* Acts vi. 4. **3. ἔδοξεν**

m παρηκολουθηκότι n ἄνωθεν πᾶσιν o ἀκριβῶς p καθεξῆς
H θεοφιλε... σοὶ γράψαι, q κράτιστε Θεόφιλε, 4 ἵνα r ἐπιγνῷς περὶ s ὧν
t κατηχήθης λόγων τὴν u ἀσφάλειαν.
5 Ἐγένετο ἐν ταῖς ἡμέραις Ἡρώδου [τοῦ] βασιλέως
τῆς Ἰουδαίας ἱερεύς τις ὀνόματι Ζαχαρίας, ἐξ v ἐφημερίας
Ἀβιά· καὶ γυνὴ αὐτῷ ἐκ τῶν θυγατέρων Ἀαρών, καὶ τὸ

m = 1 Tim. iv. 6. 2 Tim. iii. 10 (Mark xvi. 17) only +. 2 Macc. (viii. 11) ix. 27 only.
n = Acts xxvi. 5 (Matt. xxvii. 51 ‖ Mk. John iii. 3 al.) only.
o Matt. ii. 8 reff.
p ch. viii. 1. Acts iii. 24. xi. 4. xviii. 24 only +. L.
q Acts xxiii. 26. xxiv. 3. xxvi. 25 only. L. 2 Macc. iv. 12.
r ch. xxiii. 7. 1 Cor. xiii. 12. Jer. v. 5.
s constr., Matt. vii. 2. ch. xii. 40. Rom. iv. 17 al. Winer, § 24. 2. b.
t Acts xviii. 25. xxi. 21, 25. Rom. ii. 8. 1 Cor. xiv. 19. Gal. vi. 6 only +.
u = here (Acts v. 23. 1 Thess. v. 3) only ‡. (Prov. viii. 14 al.) (-λής, Acts xxi. 34. -λῶς, Acts ii. 36.)
v ver. 8 only. 2 Chron. xiii. 10. 1 CHRON. xxiv. 10. (-ρος, James ii. 15.)

4. επιγνοις ℵ[1]. for ων, των D[1].
5. om του BLRΞℵ : ins ACDP rel [Epiph$_1$ Cyr$_1$. (H def.)]. rec ins η bef γυνη, with APR rel : om BCDXΞℵ 1. 33 [Epiph$_1$ Cyr$_1$]. (H def.) rec αυτου, with AC[3]PR rel vulg-ed(with gat tol) lat-*b e f g$_2$* syrr copt goth [Epiph$_1$ Cyr$_1$] Ambr : αυτο (sic) X : txt BC[1]DLΞℵ 1. 33 am(with bodl em forj fuld ing mt) lat-*c ff$_2$ g$_1$ l q* Jer Aug$_1$. om το A.

κἀμοί] Luke by this classes himself with these *πολλοί*, and shews that he intended no disparagement nor blame to them, and was going to construct his own history from similar sources. The *παρηκ. ἄν. πᾶσιν ἀκρ.* which follows, implies however a conscious superiority of his own qualification for the work. There is here no *expressed claim* to inspiration, but at the same time no *disclaimer* of it. (The addition *et spiritui sancto*, after *κἀμοί*, which is found in 3 lat. mss. and in goth., makes the following clause an absurdity.) **παρηκ.**] **having traced down** (by research), and so become accurately acquainted with. The word is used in just this sense by Demosth., *περὶ τ. στ.*, p. 285 : *ἐκεῖνος ὁ καιρὸς καὶ ἡ ἡμέρα ἐκείνη οὐ μόνον εὔνουν καὶ πλούσιον ἄνδρα ἐκάλει, ἀλλὰ καὶ* **παρηκολουθηκότα** *τοῖς πράγμασιν ἐξ ἀρχῆς, καὶ συλλελογισμένον ὀρθῶς τίνος ἕνεκα ταῦτ' ἔπραττεν ὁ Φίλ., καὶ τί βουλόμενος.* **ἄνωθεν**] **from the beginning** —i. e. as in ver. 5 ;—as distinguished from those who only wrote of the *official* life of the Lord, or only fragments perhaps of that. **καθεξῆς, consecutively**: see reff. By this word we must not understand Luke to lay claim to any *especial chronological accuracy* in *writing* ;—which indeed is not found in his Gospel. He *traced* the events in order as they happened: but he may have *arranged* them as other considerations led him. The word is of later usage, e. g. by Plutarch, Ælian, &c. The classics have *ἐφεξῆς*. **κράτ. Θεόφ.**] It is wholly unknown who this person was. The name was a very common one. The conjectures about him are endless, and entirely without value. It appears that he was a person of dignity (see reff. on *κράτιστ.*), and a convert to Christianity. The idea of the name being not a proper, but a *feigned one*, designating 'those who loved God' (found as early as Epiphanius, Hær. ii. 51, p. 429, *εἴτουν τινὶ Θεοφίλῳ τότε γράφων τοῦτο ἔλεγεν, ἢ παντὶ ἀνθρώπῳ θεὸν ἀγαπῶντι* : and adopted again recently by Bp. Wordsworth), is far-fetched and improbable. **4.**] **ἐπιγνῷς**—here in its stricter sense, of acquiring *additional*, more accurate knowledge—see reff. **κατηχ.**] Theophilus had then been orally instructed in the narratives which form the subject of this Gospel : and Luke's intention in writing it is, that he might have a *more accurate knowledge of these histories.* **κατηχήθης** — literally, **catechized**, '*catechetically taught.*' Bleek, h. l., reminds us that this is not St. Luke's own usage of the verb : cf. Acts xxi. 21, 24, where it simply signifies hearing by report. But we may answer that in Acts xviii. 25, where the same construction occurs, this is the most likely sense. **λόγων** is not to be *rendered* 'things :' *neither it, nor ῥῆμα, nor* דָּבָר, *ever has this meaning*, as is commonly but erroneously supposed. In all the commonly-cited examples of this, '*things expressed in words*' are meant : here, **the histories,—accounts.** (See Prolegg. to the Gospels, i. 3.)

5—25.] ANNOUNCEMENT BY GABRIEL OF THE BIRTH OF JOHN. *Peculiar to Luke.* The style now totally alters and becomes Hebraistic, signifying that the following is translated or compiled from an Aramaic oral narration, or perhaps (from the very distinct character of these two first chapters) *document.* **5.**] **ἐξ ἐφ. Ἀβ.**, which was the *eighth* of the *four and twenty courses* of the priests (see ref. 1 Chron.). These courses kept their names

w Matt. i. 19 reff. x Mark ii. 12. (ver. 8 v. r.) ch. xx. 26. xxiv. 19. Acts vii. 10. viii. 32 (from Isa. liii. 7) only. y = Acts ix. 31. 1 Pet. iv. 3. 2 Pet. ii. 10 al. 1 Kings viii. 5. z Gen. xxvi. 5. Num. xxvi. 13. Deut. iv. 40. vi. 1 al. a Rom. i. 32. ii. 26. v. 16, 18. viii. 4. Heb. ix. 1, 10. Rev. xv. 4. xix. 8 only. Deut. xxx. 16 al.

ὄνομα αὐτῆς Ἐλισάβετ. 6 ἦσαν δὲ [w] δίκαιοι ἀμφότεροι
[x] ἐναντίον τοῦ θεοῦ, [y] πορευόμενοι ἐν πάσαις ταῖς [z] ἐντο- ..πασαις ται H.
λαῖς καὶ [za] δικαιώμασιν τοῦ κυρίου [b] ἄμεμπτοι. 7 καὶ ABCDE
οὐκ ἦν αὐτοῖς τέκνον, [c] καθότι ἦν ἡ Ἐλισάβετ [d] στεῖρα, FKLM PRSUV
καὶ ἀμφότεροι [e] προβεβηκότες ἐν ταῖς ἡμεραῖς αὐτῶν XΓΔΛ ΞΠℵ
ἦσαν. 8 ἐγένετο δὲ ἐν τῷ [f] ἱερατεύειν αὐτὸν ἐν τῇ [g] τάξει 1. 33. 69
τῆς [h] ἐφημερίας αὐτοῦ [i] ἔναντι τοῦ θεοῦ, 9 [k] κατὰ τὸ [kl] ἔθος
τῆς [m] ἱερατείας [n] ἔλαχεν τοῦ [o] θυμιᾶσαι εἰςελθὼν εἰς τὸν ...θυμιασαι F.
ναὸν τοῦ κυρίου. 10 καὶ πᾶν τὸ πλῆθος ἦν τοῦ λαοῦ ...κυριου Ξ.

b Phil. ii. 15. iii. 6. 1 Thess. iii. 13. Heb. viii. 7 only. Gen. xvii. 1. (-τως, 1 Thess. ii. 10.) constr., ch. xxi. 34. Acts xii. 10. c ch. xix. 9. Acts ii. 24, 45 al2. L. Lev. xxv. 16 bis only. d ver. 36. ch. xxiii. 29. Gal. iv. 27 (from Isa. liv. 1) only. Gen. xi. 30. e = ver. 18. ch. ii. 36 (Matt. iv. 21 ‖ Mk.) only. Gen. xviii. 11. Josh. xxiii. 1. f here only. Exod. xxviii. 1, 3, 4 al. fr. (-τεία, ver. 9. -τευμα, 1 Pet. ii. 5, 9.) g Heb. v. 6, 10; vi. 20 and vii. (11 bis) 17 (21 v. r.) from Ps. cix. 4. h ver. 5 (reff.) only. i Acts viii. 21 only. Gen. xix. 13 Ed-vat. [B def.] Num. xxxii. 13. k ch. ii. 42. xxii. 39 only. (2 Macc. xi. 25.) l as above (k). Acts vi. 14 al6. L. only, exc. John xix. 40. Heb. x. 25 †. Wisd. xiv. 16. 1 Macc. x. 89. 2 Macc. xiii. 4 only. m Heb. vii. 5 only. Exod. xxix. 9 al. n John xix. 24. Acts i. 17. 2 Pet. i. 1 only. 1 Kings xiv. 47 (w. τοῦ & inf.). Wisd. viii. 19 only. o here only. Exod. xxx. 7, 8 al. fr. (-αμα, vv. 10, 11. -ατήριον, Heb. ix. 4.)

6. rec (for εναντιον) ενωπιον, with AC³DPRΞ rel: txt BC¹Xℵ Cyr₂.
7. rec η ελισ. bef ην, with ACPR rel syrr copt arm: txt BDLXΔΞℵ 33. 69 latt goth [æth].—om η (bef ελ.) B 69. 258 ev-y. (F lat-*a* def.) ησαν bef προβ. εν τ. ημ. αυτ. D lat-*e*.
8. εναντιον (*corrn*) ACFMXΔΠℵ 69 Chr: ενωπιον K: txt BDPR rel.
9. το θυμ. (sic) C. for κυριου, θεου C¹ D-gr.
10. rec του λαου bef ην (*corrn of arrangemt, which is in the manner of Luke, both in Gosp and Acts*), with AC³DKΠ 1. 69 vulg-ed(with em gat) lat-*e f g₂* syr copt æth arm: ηνπερ λαου 33: txt BC³PRℵ rel am(with forj fuld ing) lat-*q* goth.

and order, though not their descent, after the captivity. The courses, though called ἐφημερίαι, were of a *week's* duration each: ἀπὸ σαββάτου ἐπὶ σάββατον, Jos. Antt. vii. 14. 7. Meyer observes that if any use is to be made of this note of time to fix the date, our reckoning must be made *backward* from the destruction of the temple, not *forward* from the restoration of the courses by Judas Maccabæus, because it is not certain *what course then began* the new order of things; whereas we have a fixed note for the destruction of the temple, that it was on the 9th of Ab, and the course in waiting was that of Jehoiarib. Comm. ii. p. 194. With the reading κ. γυνὴ αὐτῷ, we must render, **and he had a wife from among . . . .**

Ἐλισ.] The LXX rendering, Exod. vi. 23, of אֱלִישֶׁבַע, the wife of Aaron: signifying, *Deus juramentum.* John was thus of priestly descent by both parents. Cf. Jos. Vit. i. init., ἐμοὶ δὲ γένος ἐστὶν οὐκ ἄσημον, ἀλλ' ἐξ ἱερέων ἄνωθεν καταβεβηκός. ὥσπερ δὴ παρ' ἑκάστους ἄλλη τίς ἐστιν εὐγενείας ὑπόθεσις, οὕτως παρ' ἡμῖν ἡ τῆς ἱερωσύνης μετουσία τεκμήριόν ἐστι γένους λαμπρότητος. **6.**] **πορ. ἐν**, a Hebraism, as also **προβ. ἐν τ. ἡμέραις**, ver. 7, and **ἐγένετο ἐν τῷ ἱερ. . . . . ἔλαχεν**, vv. 8, 9. This last is a construction frequent in Luke. In the phrase **ἐντολαῖς κ. δικαιώμασιν** (see reff.), we must not press any difference between the terms. δικαίωμα, as Bleek remarks, is used of an ordinance of God, laying down what is δίκαιον for men. **7.**] **προβαίνειν** is only found in the classics in this sense with τήν or κατὰ τὴν ἡλικίαν, or τῇ ἡλικίᾳ.

9, 10. τοῦ θυμιᾶσαι (not θυμιάσαι)] This was the *most honourable office* which was allotted among the priests each day, and the same person could not serve it more than once. On the manner of casting the lots, see Lightfoot in loc.

τοῦ θ. εἰςελθών = to go in and to burn incense. The gen. **τοῦ** is in government after the verb ἔλαχεν: see Winer, § 44. 4. *a.* This verb commonly governs an accusative, but now and then a genitive: see Kühner, § 521: and cf. Il. ω. 76.

τὸν ναόν] **the holy place:** see Heb. ix. 1—6, and Exod. xxx. 7. An account of John Hyrcanus the high-priest having a vision at the time of offering incense occurs Jos. Antt. xiii. 10. 3: φασὶ γὰρ ὅτι κατ' ἐκείνην τὴν ἡμέραν καθ' ἣν οἱ παῖδες αὐτοῦ τῷ Κυζικηνῷ συνέβαλον, αὐτὸς ἐν τῷ ναῷ θυμιῶν μόνος, ὢν ὁ ἀρχιερεύς, ἀκούσειε φωνῆς ὡς οἱ παῖδες αὐτοῦ νενικήκασιν ἀρτίως τὸν Ἀντίοχον. καὶ τοῦτο προελθὼν ἐκ τοῦ ναοῦ παντὶ τῷ πλήθει

προσευχόμενον ἔξω τῇ ὥρᾳ τοῦ [p] θυμιάματος. 11 ὤφθη
δὲ αὐτῷ ἄγγελος κυρίου ἑστὼς [q] ἐκ δεξιῶν τοῦ [r] θυσιαστηρίου τοῦ [p] θυμιάματος. 12 καὶ [s] ἐταράχθη Ζαχαρίας
ἰδών, καὶ [t] φόβος [tu] ἐπέπεσεν ἐπ' αὐτόν. 13 εἶπεν δὲ πρὸς
αὐτὸν ὁ ἄγγελος Μὴ φοβοῦ Ζαχαρία, [v] διότι [wx] εἰσηκούσθη
ἡ [xy] δέησίς σου, καὶ ἡ γυνή σου Ἐλισάβετ [z] γεννήσει υἱόν
σοι, καὶ καλέσεις τὸ ὄνομα αὐτοῦ Ἰωάννην. 14 καὶ ἔσται
χαρά σοι καὶ [a] ἀγαλλίασις, καὶ πολλοὶ ἐπὶ τῇ [b] γενέσει
αὐτοῦ [c] χαρήσονται. 15 ἔσται γὰρ μέγας [d] ἐνώπιον τοῦ
κυρίου, καὶ [e] οἶνον καὶ [ef] σίκερα οὐ μὴ πίῃ, καὶ [g] πνεύματος
ἁγίου [gh] πλησθήσεται [i] ἔτι ἐκ [k] κοιλίας [k] μητρὸς αὐτοῦ,

H [α]υτον ο... ζαχαρια ..P. G γεννησει... ...ονομα R.

p here bis. Rev. v. 8. viii. 3, 4. xviii. 13 only. Exod. xxx. 1.
q Matt. xx. 21, 23 reff.
r Matt. xxiii. 18, &c. reff.
s = Matt. ii. 3. xiv. 26. Gen. xlv. 3.
t Acts (x. 10 v. r.) xix. 17. Rev. xi. 11. Exod. xv. 16. Josh. ii. 9.
u Acts viii. 16. Rom. xv. 3. Gen. xv. 12.
v ch. ii. 7. xxi. 28 only in Gospp. Acts xvii. 31 al. Epp. passim. Isa. xii. 2.
w = Matt. vi. 7. Acts x. 31. 1 Cor. xiv. 21. Heb. v. 7 only. Ps. iv. 1, 3.
x Ps. lx. 1 al. fr. LXX.
y ch. ii. 37 reff.
z = ver. 57 reff.
a ver. 44. Acts ii. 46. Heb. i. 9, from Ps. xliv. 7. Jude 24 only. LXX, Ps. only, xxix. 5 al.
b Matt. i. 1 reff.
c w. ἐπί, Matt. xviii. 13 reff. see ver. 47.
d Gospp., Luke only, exc. John xx. 30. Acts iv. 19. Rom. iii. 20. 1 John iii. 22 al. 1 Kings iii. 18.
e Lev. x. 9. Num. vi. 3. Judg. xiii. 4 A al.
f here only. Num. xxviii. 7.
g vv. 41, 67. Acts ii. 4. iv. 8, 31. ix. 17. xiii. 9. see Eph. v. 18.
h Luke only, exc. Matt. xxii. 40. xxvii. 48. John xix. 29. Ps. cxxv. 2.
i = here only.
k Matt. xix. 12. Acts iii. 2. xiv. 8. Gal. i. 15. Ps. xxi. 10. lxx. 6.

13. *και ειπεν* D mt lat-*b c e ff*$_2$ Syr. (lat-*a* def.) *ζαχαριας* R[1] lat-*ff*$_2$ *g*$_2$. for *διοτι*, *οτι* C[1]Δ. *ελισαβεδ* D(so vv 24, 41 bis). om *σοι* D-gr **1** sah Orig-int$_1$: ins bef *υιον* (Δ) latt syrr copt æth arm Thl.—*γεννη σοι υιον* (sic) Δ.
14. *σοι* bef *χαρα* D goth arm [Orig-int$_1$]. rec *γεννησει*, with GXΓ **1**. 33 (69, e sil): txt ABCDℵ rel Cyr$_1$.
15. om *του* ACL Γ(appy) ℵ **1**. 33 Cyr$_1$: ins BD rel.

φανερὸν ἐποίησε· καὶ συνέβη οὕτως γενέσθαι. Here also we have the people outside (in the courts of the men and women):—their prayers were offered *while the incense was burnt*, as the *smoke was symbolical* of the ascent of prayer, Rev. viii. 3, 4. It appears, from the allotment having been just mentioned, to have been the *morning* incense burning. So Meyer. Theophylact and others understand the whole as describing the entry into the Holy of holies on the great day of Atonement, Levit. xvi. But this is manifestly an error: for it would necessitate Zacharias having been high-priest, which he never was; and in this case there would have been no casting of lots. **11.**] The *altar of incense*, Exod. xxx. 1, must not be confounded with the *large altar of burnt-offering: that* stood *outside the holy place*, in the court of the priests. It was during the sacrifice on the great altar that the daily burning of the incense took place: one of the two priests, whose lot it was to offer incense, brought fire from off the altar of burnt-offering to the altar of incense, and then left the other priest there alone,—who, on a signal from the priest presiding at the sacrifice, kindled the incense: see Exod. xl. 5, 26. This is no *vision*, but an actual *angelic appearance*. The right is the *favourable side:* see Matt. xxv. 33. "We must understand the right as regarded the officiating priest, who stood with his face to the altar. It would thus be on the N. side of the holy place, where the table of shew-bread stood, whereas on the S. side was the golden candlestick." Bleek. **13.**] He had then *prayed for a son*—but as appears below, long since—for he now had ceased to look for an answer to his prayer. Many Commentators (Aug., Thl., Euth., Grot., &c.) have thought his prayer was for the salvation of Israel by the appearance of the Messiah: but the former view appears more probable.

Ἰωάννην = יְהוֹחָנָן, Ἰωανάν LXX, 1 Chron. iii. 24;—Ἰωνά, 4 Kings xxv. 23;—Ἰωάνης, 2 Chron. xxviii. 12;— = 'God is favourable.' **15.**] **ἐνώπ. τ. κ.**, signifying the spiritual nature of his office and influence. The priests were similarly prohibited to drink strong drink; and the Nazarites even more rigidly: see reff. **σίκ.** = שֵׁכָר (from שָׁכַר, 'inebriatus est'),—'any strong liquor not made from grapes.' [Wiclif renders "*He schal not drynke wyne ne sidir.*"]

πν. ἁγ. πλ. is a *contrast to*, and a reason for, the not drinking wine nor strong drink: compare Eph. v. 18. Olshausen and Meyer think that (comparing ver. 44) the meaning is, the Holy Spirit should in some wonderful manner act on the child even *before* his birth. But (see reff.) this is not necessary,

16 καὶ πολλοὺς τῶν υἱῶν Ἰσραὴλ [l] ἐπιστρέψει ἐπὶ κύριον ABCDE
τὸν θεὸν αὐτῶν. 17 καὶ [m] αὐτὸς [n] προελεύσεται [o] ἐνώπιον GHKL MSUV
αὐτοῦ ἐν [pq] πνεύματι καὶ [pr] δυνάμει Ἡλίου, [ls] ἐπιστρέψαι ΧΓΔΛ ΠΝ
[s] καρδίας [s] πατέρων ἐπὶ [s] τέκνα, καὶ [t] ἀπειθεῖς [u] ἐν [v] φρο- 1. 33. 69
νήσει δικαίων, [w] ἑτοιμάσαι κυρίῳ λαὸν [x] κατεσκευασμένον.
18 καὶ εἶπεν Ζαχαρίας πρὸς τὸν ἄγγελον [yz] Κατὰ [z] τί
[z] γνώσομαι τοῦτο; ἐγὼ γάρ εἰμι [a] πρεσβύτης, καὶ ἡ γυνή
μου [b] προβεβηκυῖα ἐν ταῖς ἡμέραις αὐτῆς. 19 καὶ ἀπο- Ξ και
κριθεὶς ὁ ἄγγελος εἶπεν αὐτῷ Ἐγώ εἰμι Γαβριὴλ ὁ αποκριθεις...

l trans., James v. 19, 20. Josh. xx. 4 A. intr., Acts xv. 19 al. m = Col. i. 17. n = ch. xxii. 47, but w. acc. (Matt. xxvi. 39 reff.) Gen. xxxiii. 3 Ed-vat., 14 (not Al. B def.). o = ch. iv. 7. Acts ii. 25, from Ps. xv. 8. (ver. 15 reff.) p Acts x. 38. 1 Cor. ii. 4. 1 Thess. i. 5. q = Acts vi. 10. 4 Kings ii. 9, 15. r = Eph. iii. 16. Col. i. 11. s Mal. iv. 6. see Sir. xlviii. 10. 3 Kings xviii. 37. t Acts xxvi. 19. Rom. i. 30. 2 Tim. iii. 2. Tit. i. 16. iii. 3 only. Deut. xxi. 18. u constr., see John iii. 35 reff. v Eph. i. 8 only. 3 Kings iii. 28. w ch. iii. 4 ‖ (from Isa. xl. 3). xii. 47 al. 2 Chron. xxvii. 6. x Mark i. 2 reff. y Eph. vi. 6. Philem. 14. κατ᾽ αὐτὸ τοῦτο μόνον, Aristoph. Vesp. 1062. z Gen. xv. 8. a Tit. ii. 2. Philem. 9 only. 1 Kings iv. 18. b ver. 7.

17. προσελευσεται (*cf* προσελθων, *Mark* xiv. 34) B[1](Tischdf) CLV: πορευσεται F(Wetst). ηλεια B[1]א, ἥλια L. ins τω bef κυριω AKΠ.
18. for τ. αγγ., αυτον C[1](appy).

—nay, would it not rather be in this case **ἐν** κοιλίᾳ . . . .? The **ἐκ** seems to fix the prior limit of the indwelling of the Spirit, *at his birth*. Meyer grounds his view on the meaning of **ἔτι** as distinguished from ἤδη, and takes the construction as embracing both particulars—he shall be so *in*, and shall become so *from* . . . So likewise Bleek, and Hoffmann, Weiss. und Erfüll. ii. 250 f. **16.**] The work of John was one of preparation and turning men's hearts towards God. For full notes on his office, see on Matt. xi. It may suffice here to repeat, that it was a *concentration of the spirit of the law*, whose office it was to *convince of sin*: and that he eminently represented the law and the prophets in their work of preparing the way for Christ. **17.**] **ἐνώπ. αὐτοῦ**—i.e. κυρίου τοῦ θ. αὐτῶν, manifest in the flesh. De Wette denies this interpretation, as contrary to all analogy: and yet himself explains the expression by saying that what the Messiah does, is in Scripture *ascribed to God as its doer* (similarly Meyer). But *why?* because Messiah is God with us. This expression is besides used (see Zech. xiv. 5) in places where the undoubted and sole reference is to the Messiah. See Bleek's note, in which he decides for this view, as against that which refers αὐτοῦ *directly* to the Messiah as the Son of God. **ἐν πν. κ. δυν.**] As a type, a partial fulfilment, of the personal coming of Elias in the latter days (see note on Matt. xi. 13, 14). Bleek remarks that it was not in the wonder-working agency of Elias that John was like him, for "John did no miracle,"—but in the power of his uttered persuasion.

ἐπιστρ. . . . .] The first member only of the sentence corresponds with Malachi, and that not verbatim. The angel gives the *exposition* of the second member,—καὶ καρδίαν ἀνθρώπου πρὸς τὸν πλησίον αὐτοῦ,—for of course that must be understood in the better sense, of the good prevailing, and the bad becoming like them.

ἀπειθής, as in reff., not *unbelieving*, but **disobedient**. On the verb ἀπειθεῖν, see note, Heb. iii. 18, and on ἀπείθεια, note, Eph. ii. 2. **ἐν** is elliptic for εἰς τὸ εἶναι ἐν . . . see reff. Augustine, De Civ. Dei, xx. 29, vol. vii.—'est sensus, ut etiam *filii sic intelligant legem*, id est, Judæi, *quemadmodum patres eam intellexerunt*, id est Prophetæ, in quibus erat et ipse Moyses:' so also Kuinoel, but erroneously, for both articles would be expressed,—τῶν πατέρων ἐπὶ τὰ τέκνα. **18.**] The birth of John, involving *human generation*, but *prophetically announced*, and *supernatural*, answers to the birth of Isaac in the O. T. But Abraham's faith was a strong contrast to the unbelief of Zacharias: see Rom. iv. 19. De Wette, without noticing the above remark (which is Olshausen's), says, "the same doubt, which Abraham also entertained in a similar case;" so that we have here, as often elsewhere, in the interpretation of Scripture (Gen. xv. 6, 8; xvii. 17; xviii. 12), De Wette versus Paul (Rom. as above):—the fact being, that the case Gen. xv. 8 was not similar. **πρεσβύτης**] The *Levites* (see Num. iv. 3; viii. 24, 25) became superannuated at the age of *fifty*: but it appears, by extracts from the Rabbinical writings given by Lightfoot, that this was not the case with the priests.

19.] **Γαβριήλ** = גַּבְרִיאֵל, Man of God: see Dan. viii. 16; ix. 21, also Tobit xii. 15.

[c] παρεστηκὼς ἐνώπιον τοῦ θεοῦ, καὶ [d] ἀπεστάλην [e] λαλῆσαι
πρός σε καὶ [f] εὐαγγελίσασθαί σοι ταῦτα. 20 καὶ ἰδοὺ ἔσῃ
[g] σιωπῶν καὶ μὴ δυνάμενος λαλῆσαι [h] ἄχρι ἧς ἡμέρας
γένηται ταῦτα, [i] ἀνθ' ὧν οὐκ [k] ἐπίστευσας τοῖς λόγοις
μου, [l] οἵτινες [m] πληρωθήσονται [n] εἰς τὸν καιρὸν αὐτῶν.
21 καὶ ἦν ὁ λαὸς [o] προςδοκῶν τὸν Ζαχαρίαν, καὶ [p] ἐθαύμαζον [q] ἐν τῷ [r] χρονίζειν αὐτὸν ἐν τῷ ναῷ. 22 ἐξελθὼν δὲ οὐκ ἐδύνατο λαλῆσαι αὐτοῖς. καὶ ἐπέγνωσαν
ὅτι [s] ὀπτασίαν ἑώρακεν ἐν τῷ ναῷ· καὶ αὐτὸς ἦν [t] δια-
νεύων αὐτοῖς, καὶ [u] διέμενεν [v] κωφός. 23 καὶ ἐγένετο ὡς
[w] ἐπλήσθησαν αἱ ἡμέραι τῆς [x] λειτουργίας αὐτοῦ, ἀπῆλθεν

Frag. Sang. νος λαλησαι...

c Mark xiv. 47 reff. = Exod. xxiv. 13. 3 Kings x. 8. d ver. 26. Heb. i. 14. Rev. v. 6. xxii. 6. Isa. vi. 6. Dan. x. 11. e w. πρός, ver. 55. ch. ii. 18, 20. Acts iii. 22. iv. 1 al. L. only, exc. 1 Thess. ii. 2. Heb. v. 5. xi. 18. Deut. xviii. 17 B. Dan. (Theod.) as above. f ch. ii. 10. Rom. x. 15, from Isa. lii. 7. 1 Kings xxxi. 9. g constr., Matt. xxiv. 9. vii. 29 reff. h Matt. xxiv. 38 reff. i ch. xii. 3. xix. 44. Acts xii. 23. 2 Thess. ii. 10 only. Gen. xxii. 18. Deut. viii. 20. k John ii. 22. v. 47 bis. xii. 38, from Isa. liii. 1. l = Matt. vii. 15 reff. m Matt. i. 22 reff. n constr., Acts xiii. 42. John xx. 7. o = & constr., ch. vii. 19, 20. Acts x. 24. (Luke only, exc. Matt. xi. 3. xxiv. 50. 2 Pet. iii. 12, 13, 14.) Ps. cxviii. 166. p w. ἐν, here only. Sir. xi. 21. q John v. 35. Rom. ii. 23 al. r Matt. xxiv. 48 reff. Exod. xxxii. 1. s ch. xxiv. 23. Acts xxvi. 19. 2 Cor. xii. 1 only. L.P.‡ (Mal. iii. 2. Sir. xliii. 2, 18) only. = Dan. ix. 23 al. Theod. t here only. Ps. xxxiv. 19. Sir. xxvii. 22. u ch. xxii. 28. Gal. ii. 5. Heb. i. 11, from Ps. ci. 26. 2 Pet. iii. 4 only. v Mark vii. 32 reff. w ver. 57 reff. x 2 Cor. ix. 12. Phil. ii. 17, 30. Heb. viii. 6. ix. 21 only. L.P.H. Num. viii. 22.

19. παρεστως D.
20. αχρις ημ. ης *usque in diem quo* D latt. πλησθησονται DΞ Orig$_1$.
21. for προsδοκων, προsδεχομενος D. for 1st εν, επι D. εν τω ναω bef αυτον BLΞ.
22. rec ηδυνατο, with B^{2}CDΞ 33(Treg, expr) rel: txt AB^{1}KΠℵ. [εορακεν B^1(Tischdf) EGHMVX.] διεμεινεν D-gr ev-P latt syrr copt æth.
23. ins τοτε bef απηλθεν D.

The *names* of the angels, say the Rabbis, came up with Israel from Babylon. We first read of both Michael and Gabriel in the book of Daniel. But we are not therefore to suppose that they were borrowed from any heathen system, as Strauss and the rationalists have done; the fact being, that the persons and order of the angels were known long before, and their *names* formed matter of subsequent revelation to Daniel: see Professor Mill's Vindication of Luke, i., § 4, and note A; also Josh. v. 13—16. **ὁ παρεστ. ἐν. τ. θ.**, one of the chief angels near the throne of God. They are called *seven* in Tobit (ibid.): see Dr. Mill's Tract, as above.

20.] We must not consider this dumbness *solely* as a punishment; it was also a *sign*, as Zacharias had required. It is impossible for us to say what the degree of unbelief in Zacharias was, and therefore we can be no judges as to his being deserving of the punishment (against Strauss and the rationalists). **κ. μ. δυν. λαλ.**] This is not a *repetition*, but an *explanation of the ground and reason*, of σιωπῶν.

ἄχρι ἧς ἡμέρας γέν. ταῦτα] ποία; ἡ γέννησις δηλαδή, καὶ ἡ κλῆσις τοῦ ὀνόματος. Euthym. **ἀνθ' ὧν** is not a Hebraism, but good Greek: see Passow, and Matthiæ, § 480. **οἵτινες** not merely identifies, but classifies: "being, as they are, of that kind which...."

21.] It was customary for the priest at the time of prayer not to remain long in the holy place, for fear the people who were without might imagine that any vengeance had been inflicted on him for some informality;—as he was considered the *representative of the people.* The words **ἐθαύμαζον ἐν** are best taken together, **wondered at**, as in ref. Sir. They *may* also be taken separately, taking ἐν as '*during*:' and so Meyer: but this is not so probable. **22.**] They knew, by some excitement, visible in his manner. It was not his office to *pronounce the benediction*, but that of the other incensing priest; so that his 'not being able to speak,' must mean, *in answer to the enquiries* which his unusual appearance prompted. This answer he gave by a sign: and the question was also by signs; for (see ver. 62) he was *deaf*, as well as dumb, which indeed is the strict meaning of **κωφός**—οὔτε λαλῶν, οὔτ' ἀκούων, Hesych. **23. ὡς ἐπλήσ.**] The week during which his course was on duty. Mr. Greswell, by much elaborate calculation, has made it probable, but only as one out of several alternatives, that this week was Tisri 18—25, = September 30—October 7, of the *sixth year before the Christian era* (Prolegg. p. 85 sqq.). A deaf and

εἰς τὸν οἶκον αὐτοῦ. 24 μετὰ δὲ ταύτας τὰς ἡμέρας ...αυτου Ξ.
[y] συνέλαβεν Ἐλισάβετ ἡ γυνὴ αὐτοῦ, καὶ [z] περιέκρυβεν ABCDE
ἑαυτὴν μῆνας πέντε λέγουσα 25 ὅτι οὕτως μοι [a] πεποίηκεν GHKL MSUV
[ὁ] κύριος ἐν [b] ἡμέραις [c] αἷς [d] ἐπεῖδεν [e] ἀφελεῖν [τὸ] [ef] ὄνει- ΧΓΔΛ ΠΝ
δός μου [g] ἐν ἀνθρώποις. 26 Ἐν δὲ τῷ μηνὶ τῷ ἕκτῳ Frag. Sang.
[h] ἀπεστάλη ὁ ἄγγελος Γαβριὴλ ἀπὸ τοῦ θεοῦ εἰς πόλιν 1. 33. 69
τῆς Γαλιλαίας ᾗ ὄνομα Ναζαρέτ, 27 πρὸς παρθένον
[i] μεμνηστευμένην ἀνδρὶ ᾧ ὄνομα Ἰωσήφ, ἐξ οἴκου Δαυείδ· Ξ [αν]δ-
καὶ τὸ ὄνομα τῆς παρθένου Μαριάμ. 28 καὶ εἰσελθὼν πρὸς ρι...
αὐτὴν εἶπεν [k] Χαῖρε [l] κεχαριτωμένη· ὁ [m] κύριος [m] μετὰ ..ειπενΞ.

y = vv. 31, 36. ch. ii. 21. (v. 9 al.) James i. 5 (but metaph.) only. Gen. iv. 1, 17 al.
z here only †.
a Matt. xxi. 36, 40.
b so Rev. x. 7.
c constr., Acts xiii. 2, 39. Winer, edn. 6, § 50. 7.
d Acts iv. 29 only. = Exod. ii. 25 B. 2 Macc. viii. 2.
e Gen. xxx. 23.
f here only. Isa. xxv. 8 al.
g Matt. xi. 11.
h ver. 19.
i ch. ii. 5. Matt. i. 18 only. Deut. xxii. 23, 25.
k Matt. xxvi. 49 reff.
l Eph. i. 6 only †. Sir. (ix. 8 Grabe) xviii. 17 only. Ps. xvii. 25 Symm.
m Judg. vi. 12.

24. for *μετα δε, και μετα* D. *τας ημ. ταυ.* DE 69 copt.
25. om *ο* CDLℵ 33 : ins AB rel. *εφειδεν* DΔ Frag-sang : *εφιδεν* X 69 Scr's c : *επιδεν* C : txt Bℵ rel. om *το* B^1DLℵ 1 : ins AB^2C rel.
26. *εν δε τω εκτω μηνι* D-gr. rec **υπο**, with ACD rel syr(appy) arm [$Thaum_1$] Eus [$Chron_1$] : txt BLℵ Frag-sang **1.** 69 Syr goth $Cyr\text{-}jer_1$. for *της γαλ., γαλιλαιαν* D : *της ιουδαιας* $ℵ^1$. om *η ον. ναζ.* D 255-9.
27. *εμνηστ.* A[B^1]$Lℵ^{1\cdot3b}$(?) : *μεμνησμενην* D: txt $B^2Cℵ^{3a}$ rel. aft *οικου* ins *και πατριας* (*see ch* ii. 4) C F(Wetst) Lℵ **1** $Thaum_1$ Eus_1 Chr_1 $Chron_1$.
28. *ελθων* A^1(but corrd by origl scribe). rec aft *εισελθων* ins *ο αγγελος*, with ACD rel latt syr goth [æth $Chron_1$ Aug_1]; aft *αυτην* F(Wetst) Δℵ 69 lat-*f* ff_2 *h l q*

dumb person, we thus see, was not precluded from some of the sacerdotal ministrations. **24, 25.] περιέκρυβεν**—either, *to avoid defilement:* see Judg. xiii. 13, 14,—to *hide her pregnancy* from her neighbours till it was certain and apparent,—or, from the precaution which the first months of pregnancy require. Kuinoel suggests, that the reason may have been, that she might devote herself more uninterruptedly to exercises of devotion and thankfulness, and that this is expressed by the words following. If so, **ὅτι** must mean '*because,*' as indeed is the usage of these first chapters,—see below on ver. 45; but it seems here to be only the usual particle by which a speech is introduced: see Gen. xxix. 33. And indeed **λέγουσα** really carries the reason of her hiding herself—"seeing that she said (within herself). . . . ." **ἐπεῖδεν]** There is no ellipsis of *ἐμέ* or *ἐπ' ἐμέ*, nor is the meaning, 'hath looked *upon me;*' but *ἐπ'* is to be taken with the infinitive following—**hath condescended to remove:** so *ἐφοράω*, Herod. i. 124: cf. *ἐπεσκέψατο λαβεῖν*, Acts xv. 14. **[τὸ] ὄνειδος**—of barrenness: see ref.

26—38.] Announcement by the same Angel of the birth of Christ. **26.] τῷ ἕκτῳ**—referring to the *πέντε* in ver. 24. **Ναζαρέτ]** In this particular the information of our Evangelist appears to be fuller than that of Matthew, who seems not to be aware of any residence at Nazareth previous to the birth of our Lord: but see note on Matt. ii. 22. **27.] ἐξ οἴκου Δ** *refers to Joseph* in this place, who (see Matt. i.) was of the direct lineage of David. That *Mary was so*, is no where *expressed* in the Gospels, but seems to be implied in ver. 32, and has been the general belief of Christians. The Son of David was to be the fruit of *his body* (Ps. cxxxii. 11); which He would not be, unless His virgin mother was of the house of David. See notes on the genealogy in ch. iii. (Still we must remember the absolute oneness in the marriage relation, which might occasion that Mary herself should be reckoned as being in very deed that which her husband was. Perhaps this has been hardly enough taken into account. Edn. 5, 1862.) **28.] κεχαριτωμ.**, not '*gratiâ plena,*' as the Vulg.;—for, though *χαριτόω* is not found in classical writers, the analogy of all verbs in *-όω* must rule it to mean, the passing on of the action implied in the radical substantive to the object of the verb—the '*conferring of grace or favour, upon.*' And this is its meaning in the only other place (see reff.) where it occurs in the N. T. Thl. explains it as corresponding to *εὗρες χάριν παρὰ τῷ θεῷ*, ver. 30:—*τοῦτο γάρ ἐστιν τὸ κεχαριτῶσθαι, τὸ εὑρεῖν χάριν παρὰ τῷ θεῷ.* **ὁ κύρ. μετὰ σοῦ]** i. e. *ἐστίν:* see

σοῦ. 29 ἡ δὲ [n] ἐπὶ τῷ λόγῳ [o] διεταράχθη, καὶ [p] διελογίζετο [q] ποταπὸς [r] εἴη ὁ [s] ἀσπασμὸς οὗτος. 30 καὶ εἶπεν ὁ
ἄγγελος αὐτῇ Μὴ φοβοῦ Μαριάμ· [tu] εὗρες γὰρ [t] χάριν
[v] παρὰ τῷ θεῷ. 31 καὶ ἰδοὺ [w] συλλήμψῃ [x] ἐν [x] γαστρί,
καὶ [y] τέξῃ υἱόν, καὶ [y] καλέσεις τὸ [y] ὄνομα αὐτοῦ Ἰησοῦν.
32 οὗτος ἔσται μέγας καὶ [z] υἱὸς [z] ὑψίστου [a] κληθήσεται, καὶ
δώσει αὐτῷ [b] κύριος ὁ [b] θεὸς τὸν θρόνον Δαυεὶδ τοῦ πατρὸς
αὐτοῦ, 33 καὶ βασιλεύσει ἐπὶ τὸν οἶκον Ἰακὼβ εἰς τοὺς
[c] αἰῶνας, καὶ τῆς βασιλείας αὐτοῦ οὐκ ἔσται τέλος.
34 εἶπεν δὲ Μαριὰμ πρὸς τὸν ἄγγελον Πῶς ἔσται τοῦτο,
[d] ἐπεὶ ἄνδρα οὐ [e] γινώσκω; 35 καὶ ἀποκριθεὶς ὁ ἄγγελος
εἶπεν αὐτῇ [f] Πνεῦμα ἅγιον [fg] ἐπελεύσεται ἐπὶ σέ, καὶ
[h] δύναμις [i] ὑψίστου [j] ἐπισκιάσει σοι, [k] διὸ καὶ τὸ [l] γεννώμε-

Ξ μη φοβου... | ...υιος υ Frag. Sang. | ...αυτου Ξ. | ABCDE GHKL MSUV XΓΔΛ ΠΝ 1. 33. 69

n ver. 47 reff. o here only. Hos. xi. 8 compl. only. p Matt. xvi. 7, 8 reff. q Matt. viii. 27. Mark xiii. 1. ch. vii. 39. 1 John iii. 1. 2 Pet. iii. 11 only †. r opt., ch. iii. 15. viii. 9. s ch. xx. 46 reff t Acts vii. 46. Heb. iv. 16. Exod. xxxiii. 16. u = as above (t). 2 Tim. i. 18. v ch. xviii. 27. Eph. vi. 9. James i. 17. w ver. 24. x Matt. i. 18 reff y Matt. i. 21. z Mark v. 7 (reff.). ch. (vi. 35.) viii. 28 only. a = Matt. v. 9, 19. b absol., Rev. i. 8. iv. 8. xxii. 5 al. c pl., Rom. i. 25. ix. 5. xi. 36 al. d Mark xv. 42. John xiii. 29. e = here (Matt. i. 25) only. Gen. (iv. 1, 25.) xix. 8. Num. xxxi. 17. Judg. xi. 39. f Acts i. 8. g ch. i. 35. xi. 22. xxi. 26 [35 v. r.]. Acts i. 8 al3. Luke only, exc. Eph. ii. 7. James v. 1. 1 Kings xi. 7. h = Mark xii. 24. i Mark v. 7 reff. j w. dat., Mark ix. 7. Acts v. 15. Ps. xc. 4. acc., ch. ix. 34 || Mt. only. k Acts x. 29. Rom. i. 24. Phil. ii. 9. l Matt. i. 20. Ps. ii. 7.

Syr arm-usc: om BLΞ 1 copt arm-zoh. rec aft *σου* adds *ευλογημενη συ εν γυναιξιν* (*from ver* 42), with ACD rel latt syrr goth [æth] Eus$_1$ Tert$_1$: om BLℵ Frag-sang(appy, Tischdf) 1 syr-jer coptt arm [Chron$_1$] Damasc$_2$ Promiss.

29. rec aft *η δε* ins *ιδουσα*, and *διεταραχθη* bef *επι τω λογω αυτου*, with A rel: *η δε ιδ. διετ.* (omg rest) C[1]: for *ιδουσα*, *cum audisset* vulg(not fuld) Chron: txt B D(*εταραχ.*) LXℵ 1 coptt arm [Chron$_1$] Damasc. (*Mey supposes the origl mistake was, passing from* *δε* to *διε* (*cf* D), *and thus arose the glosses and transposns, and reinsns of* *επι τω λογ.*) aft *διελογιζετο* ins *εν εαυτη* D 28 arm: *εν εαυτη λεγουσα* F(Wetst) X 33 syr-mg. *ποδαπος*(*ποτ.* D[3]) *αν ειη* D.

30. *αυτη* bef *ο αγγελος* D 69 Scr's q r lat-*b f* [*ff*$_2$ *g*$_1$ *q*] syrr æth. (lat-*a* def.) for *αυτη*, *πρ. αυτην* C 28. 46 ev-P lat-*e* goth Chron$_1$ Cypr$_1$ Ambr$_1$. *μαρια* D(so vv 39, 46, 56) latt Iren-int.

34. *και ειπεν* D lat-*a*. *μαρια* C[1](appy) D'(txt D[3]) lat-*c*. aft *εσται* ins *μοι* B[r]-marg C[3] F(Wetst) MX 1. 33. 69 syr coptt æth arm Thaum$_2$ Cyr-jer$_1$ Chr [Ps-Ath$_2$ Cyr$_1$ Epiph$_1$ Chron$_1$ Damasc$_1$].

35. *διοτι* A[1](appy). aft *γεννωμενον* ins *εκ σου* (*prob a particularizing addition,—see Matt* i. 16: *Gal* iv. 4: *so Mey*) C[1] 1. 33 vulg-ed(with gat per) lat-*a c e* Syr æth arm Protev-5-mss [Val(in Hipp)] Dial$_{expr}$ Thaum$_2$ Ath$_{expr}$ Epiph$_1$ Ephr [Amphil$_1$] Chr Thdrt Damasc$_1$ Iren-int [Tert$_1$] Cypr Hil Gaud Jer: om ABC[3]Dℵ rel am lat-*b f ff*$_2$ *g*$_2$ *l* syr syr-jer copt goth arm-mss Protev-6-mss Dion Petr Eus$_1$ [Cyr-jer$_1$ Cyr$_2$] Orig-int$_1$ Tert$_1$.

ref. **32. Δαυεὶδ τοῦ π. αὐτ.**] This announcement makes it almost certain (but see note above) that *Mary also* was of the house of David. No astonishment is expressed by her at this part of the statement, and yet, from the nature of her question, it is clear that *she did not explain it by supposing Joseph to be the destined father of her child.* See 2 Sam. vii. 13: Ps. lxxxix. 3, 4: Isa. ix. 7: Jer. xxxiii. 15. **34, 35.**] This question differs from that raised by Zacharias above. It is merely an enquiry after the *manner in which* so wonderful a thing should take place; not, *how shall I know this?*—it *takes for granted that it shall be*, and only asks, *How?* **πνεῦμα ἅγ.**] **the Holy Spirit**—the creative Spirit of God, of whom it is said, Gen. i. 2, that He ἐπεφέρετο ἐπάνω τοῦ ὕδατος. But as the world was not created *by the Holy Ghost*, but *by the Son*, so also the Lord was not begotten *by the Holy Ghost*, but *by the Father*: and that, *before the worlds.* "No more is here to be attributed to the Spirit, than what is necessary to cause the Virgin to perform the actions of a mother. . . . . As Christ was made of the substance of the Virgin, so He *was not made of the substance of the Holy Ghost*, Whose essence *cannot at all be made.* And because the Holy Ghost did not beget Him by any

νον ἅγιον κληθήσεται [m] υἱὸς [m] θεοῦ. 36 καὶ ἰδοὺ Ἐλισάβετ
ἡ [n] συγγενής σου καὶ αὐτὴ [o] * συνειληφυῖα υἱὸν ἐν [p] γήρει
αὐτῆς, καὶ οὗτος μὴν ἕκτος ἐστὶν αὐτῇ τῇ καλουμένῃ
[q] στείρᾳ, 37 ὅτι οὐκ [r] ἀδυνατήσει παρὰ τοῦ θεοῦ πᾶν [s] ῥῆμα.
38 εἶπεν δὲ Μαριὰμ Ἰδοὺ ἡ [t] δούλη κυρίου· [u] γένοιτό μοι
κατὰ τὸ ῥῆμά σου. καὶ ἀπῆλθεν ἀπ' αὐτῆς ὁ ἄγγελος.
39 [v] Ἀναστᾶσα δὲ Μαριὰμ ἐν ταῖς ἡμέραις ταύταις ἐπορεύθη

Ξ και ιδου... ...αδυνατησει Χ. ABCDE GHKL MSUVΓ ΔΛΞΠℵ 1. 33. 69

m Matt. xxvii. 43, 54. n Mark vi. 4 reff. o ver. 24 reff. p here only. Gen. xxi. 2, 7. q ver. 7 reff. r Matt. xvii. 20 only. Job xlii. 2. GEN. xviii. 14. s = Matt. iv. 4 (from Deut. viii. 3). xviii. 16 al. t ver. 48. Acts ii. 18 (from Joel ii. 29) only. u Mark ix. 21. John v. 14. Acts vii. 40 (from Exod. xxxii. 1). Gal. vi. 14. Gen. xliv. 17. v = Mark vii. 24 reff.

36. ελισαβεθ D(so ver 40) 69^1. συγγενις A B^1(Tischdf) C^{3}DEGHLΔΞℵ 69 syr-mg-gr. * συνείληφεν BLΞℵ latt copt : συνειληφυια ACD rel syrr [Cæs$_1$ Chron$_1$]. rec γηρα, with S(e sil)[not so Tischdf] : txt ABCDΞℵ rel [Chron$_1$]. ins ο bef μην A.
37. οτι ουκ αδυνατησει is repeated by B^1. παν ρ. bef π. τ. θ. D æth. rec τω θεω, with ACℵ^{3a} rel, θεω 1 : txt BDLΞℵ^1.
38. και ειπεν D lat-a. μαρια C^{1}D. for απηλθεν, απεστη *recessit* D.
39. for αναστ. δε, και αναστασα AK[Π]. επορευετο ℵ.

communication of His essence, therefore He is not the Father of Him, though He were conceived by Him." (Pearson on the Creed, p. 165, 166.) **ἐπισκιάσει**] The figure is perhaps from a bird (as Grotius: see ref. Ps.), or from a *cloud:* see the other reff. **ἅγιον**] Some take this for the predicate of **τὸ γενν.**, 'shall be called holy, the Son of God.' But it is more simple to take it as E. V., **that holy thing**, &c., making **τὸ γενν. ἅγ.** the subject, and **υἱ. θ.** the predicate. On the latter expression, see note on Matt. iv. 3.

36. **συγγενής**] On the *συγγενίς* in the var. readd., we may remark, that these fem. terminations of common adjectives belong to later Greek. *συγγενίς, ἐσχάτως βάρβαρον*, Pollux iii. 50. It is found in Plutarch, Quæst. Rom. (vi. 314), &c. See Lobeck on Phrynichus, p. 452†. Cf. *μοιχαλίς*, Matt. xii. 39 reff. *What relation*, no where appears in Scripture: and traditions are not worth recounting. But we must take the word in the narrower sense, not in the wider reference of Rom. ix. 3. Elisabeth was *of the tribe of Levi:* but this need not hinder connexion by marriage with other tribes. Aaron himself married into Judah, Exod. vi. 23. We find in Judg. xvii. 7 a young man of the family of Judah who was a Levite. Philo de Monarch. ii. 11 (vol. ii. p. 229), says, *προσέταξε τῷ μὲν ἀρχιερεῖ μνᾶσθαι μὴ μόνον γυναῖκα παρθένον, ἀλλὰ καὶ ἱέρειαν ἐξ ἱερέων . . . ἐπετράπη δὲ τοῖς ἄλλοις καὶ μὴ ἱερέων γαμεῖν θυγατέρας.* **37.**] The future, in Hebrew, expresses that which does not belong to any fixed time, but shall ever be so. **ῥῆμα**] See reff., and above on ver. 4. This place, and its original, Gen. xviii. 14, which are sometimes quoted to shew that *ῥῆμα* may mean simply "a *thing*," are in fact most decisive against any such supposition. For the declaration amounts to this, "Hath the Lord spoken and can He not do it?" **38.**] Her own faithful and humble assent is here given to the divine announcement which had been made to her. I believe that her conception of the Lord is to be dated *from the utterance of these words.* So Euthym.: *ἀπ' αὐτῆς — ἤδη συλλαβούσης ἅμα τῷ λόγῳ αὐτοῦ.* Similarly Iren., Tert., Ath., Maldonat., Grot. Lightfoot, holding a different opinion, says, *Agnosco quidem, communiter obtinuisse, quod Virgo in urbe Nazareta conceperit, idque eodem instante quo Angelus eam alloquebatur.* She was no unconscious vessel of the divine will, but (see ver. 45) in humility and faith, a fellow-worker with the purpose of the Father; and therefore *her own unity with that purpose* was *required*, and is here recorded.

39—56.] VISITATION OF ELISABETH BY MARY. **39.**] The situation of Elisabeth was not before this known to Mary; and on the intelligence of it from the angel, she arose and went to congratulate her kinswoman. But before this the events related in Matt. i. 18—25 had happened. Mary being betrothed to Joseph, had no communications with him, except through the *pronubæ;* who, on the first indications of her pregnancy, represented it to him. This would not take longer time than the expression **ἐν ταῖς ἡμ. ταύ.** might include—possibly three or four weeks. Then happened Matt. i. 19, 20; and immediately Joseph took her home. As a betrothed virgin she could

εἰς τὴν [w] ὀρεινὴν [x] μετὰ [x] σπουδῆς εἰς πόλιν Ἰούδα, 40 καὶ
εἰσῆλθεν εἰς τὸν οἶκον Ζαχαρίου καὶ ἠσπάσατο τὴν
Ἐλισάβετ. 41 καὶ ἐγένετο ὡς ἤκουσεν τὸν [y] ἀσπασμὸν
τῆς Μαρίας ἡ Ἐλισάβετ, [z] ἐσκίρτησεν τὸ [a] βρέφος ἐν τῇ
κοιλίᾳ αὐτῆς, καὶ [b] ἐπλήσθη [b] πνεύματος ἁγίου ἡ Ἐλισάβετ
42 καὶ [c] ἀνεφώνησεν [d] κραυγῇ μεγάλῃ καὶ εἶπεν [e] Εὐλογημένη σὺ [e] ἐν γυναιξίν, καὶ [f] εὐλογημένος ὁ [g] καρπὸς τῆς
[f] κοιλίας σου. 43 καὶ [h] πόθεν μοι τοῦτο [i] ἵνα ἔλθῃ ἡ
μήτηρ τοῦ κυρίου μου πρός με; 44 ἰδοὺ γὰρ ὡς [k] ἐγένετο
ἡ [l] φωνὴ τοῦ [m] ἀσπασμοῦ σου εἰς τὰ ὦτά μου, [z] ἐσκίρτησεν
ἐν [n] ἀγαλλιάσει τὸ [a] βρέφος ἐν τῇ κοιλίᾳ μου. 45 καὶ
μακαρία ἡ πιστεύσασα, ὅτι ἔσται [o] τελείωσις τοῖς λελαλη-

F [ασ-πα]σμον ...

w ver. 65 only. Gen. xiv. 10. Josh. xi. 21.
x Mark vi. 25 reff.
y ver. 29.
z here bis. ch. vi. 23 only. Gen. xxv. 22.
a = here bis only. (ch. ii. 12, 16. xviii. 15. Acts viii. 19. Luke only, exc. 2 Tim. iii. 15. 1 Pet. ii. 2 +. Sir. xix. 11. 1 Macc. i. 61. 2 Macc. vi. 10 only.)
b ver. 15 reff.
c here only. 1 Chron. xv. 28.
d Matt. xxv. 6 reff.
e Judg. v. 24.
f Deut. xxviii. 4.
g = Acts ii. 30. Gen. xxx. 2.
h = Matt. xiii. 27 ‖. xv. 33. Num. xi. 13.
i John xv. 8 reff.
k = ch. iii. 2. Jer. i. 4.
l = Heb. xii. 19. Sir. xliii. 17.
m vv. 29, 41.
n ver. 14 reff.
o Heb. vii. 11 only. Jer. ii. 2.

41. rec *η ελισ.* bef *τ. ασπ. της μαρ.*, with AC³ rel syrr copt goth æth [$Chron_1$]: txt BC¹DLΞℵ 1. 69 latt arm $Orig_1$[int_1 $Thaum_1$ Cyr_1] $Cypr_1$ $Ambr_1$. aft *εσκιρτ.* ins *εν αγαλλιασει* (*from ver* 44) ℵ¹ [2-pe]: *εσκ. εν τ. κοιλ. της ελ. το βρ. αυτης* D.
42. for *ανεφ.*, *ανεβοησεν* CFℵ 33. 69. rec (for *κραυγη*) *φωνη* (*more usual*), with ACDℵ rel syrr $Orig_1$[int_1 Cyr_1]: txt BLΞ $Orig_2$.
43. *εμε* Bℵ¹.
44. *το βρεφος* bef *εν αγαλλιασει* (*το βρ. next the verb as in ver* 41) AC³ rel lat-*e* syr copt goth $Orig_1$[int_1] Chron: om *εν αγ.* 33: txt BC¹DLΞℵ 1. 69 (F, e sil) vulg lat-*b c f ff₂ g₁* [*l q*] arm $Orig_2$-int_2.
45. om *και* C¹(appy).

not travel; but now immediately, and perhaps for the very reason of the circumstances under which Joseph had taken her home, she visits Elisabeth,—remaining with her about three months, ver. 56. So that we have, five months, during which Elisabeth hid herself, + the sixth month, during which takes place the Annunciation, the discovery of Mary's pregnancy, her taking home by Joseph, + three months visit of Mary = nine months, nearly her full time: see ver. 57.
πόλιν Ἰούδα may possibly mean "*the city of Juttah*," which (Josh. xxi. 16) was given, together with Hebron (in the hill country of Judæa: ib. ver. 11), and other neighbouring cities, to the children of Aaron the priest. But it may also mean '*a city of Judah;*' and this is perhaps more likely, as no place of residence is mentioned for Zacharias in ver. 23,—and one would hardly be introduced so abruptly here. See for Ἰούδα thus used, Matt. ii. 6: Josh. xxi. 11. It is *not Jerusalem;* for that would hardly have been described as in the hill country; and from vv. 23, 65, the Evangelist clearly indicates some other place than Jerusalem as the residence of the parents of John.

41.] The salutation uttered by Elisabeth is clearly implied to have been *an inspiration of the Holy Spirit.* No intimation had been made to her of the situation of Mary. The movement of the babe in her womb (possibly for the first time: *vel nunc primum, vel saltem vehementius, quam pro more,* Lightf.) was part of the effect of the same spiritual influence. The *known* mysterious effects of sympathy in such cases, at least lead us to believe that there may be corresponding effects where the causes are of a kind *beyond our common experience.*
τ. ἀσπασμ., not '*the salutation of Mary* (the Annunciation),' but **Mary's salutation**: the former construction is not according to Luke's usage. **42.**] **εὐλογ.** has a double meaning: that of *blessed,—from above*—blessed among women, i. e. *beyond* other women; and *praised,—from below*—i. e. called blessed *by* women. The former is the best rendering here: and then **ἐν γ.** will be the Hebrew superlative, as in Jer. xxix. (xlix.) 15, and Cant. i. 8.

43.] The word **κυρίου**, as applied to the unborn babe, can no otherwise be explained than as uttered in the spirit of prophecy, and expressing *the divine nature* of our Lord: see especially Ps. cx. 1, from which Bleek thinks the expression is adopted. **45.**] Either (as E. V., Vulg., Erasm., Beza, Meyer) **blessed is**

p Acts xxii. 30. q Matt. xxiii. 5 reff. = Acts v. 13. x. 46. 2 Kings vii. 26. Psa. xxxiii. 3. r act., Rev. xix. 7 only †. = mid., Matt. v. 12. Acts ii. 26 al. Psa. xii. 5. xxxiv. 9. Isa. lxi. 10. s ver. 29. Matt. xxii. 33. 2 Cor. vii. 13. 1 Tim. vi. 17. Philem. 7 al. t 1 Tim. i. 1. ii. 3. Tit. i. 3. ii. 10. iii. 4. Jude 25 only. Ps. lxiv. 5. see 1 Tim. iv. 10.

μένοις αὐτῇ [p] παρὰ κυρίου.
46 καὶ εἶπεν Μαριὰμ [q] Μεγα-
λύνει ἡ ψυχή μου τὸν κύριον,
47 καὶ [r] ἠγαλλίασεν τὸ
πνεῦμά μου [s] ἐπὶ τῷ [t] θεῷ τῷ [t] σωτῆρί μου,
48 ὅτι [uv] ἐπ-
έβλεψεν ἐπὶ τὴν [uw] ταπείνωσιν τῆς [u] δούλης αὐτοῦ. ἰδοὺ
γὰρ ἀπὸ τοῦ νῦν [x] μακαριοῦσίν με [y] πᾶσαι αἱ γενεαί,
49 ὅτι [z] ἐποίησέν μοι [a] * μεγαλεῖα ὁ [b] δυνατός· καὶ [c] ἅγιον
τὸ [c] ὄνομα αὐτοῦ,
50 καὶ τὸ [d] ἔλεος αὐτοῦ [e] εἰς γενεὰς καὶ
γενεὰς τοῖς [d] φοβουμένοις αὐτόν.
51 [f] ἐποιησεν [f] κράτος
ἐν [g] βραχίονι αὐτοῦ, [h] διεσκόρπισεν [i] ὑπερηφάνους [kl] διανοίᾳ [l] καρδίας αὐτῶν.
52 [m] καθεῖλεν [n] δυνάστας ἀπὸ θρό-

ABCDE FGHKL MSUVΓ ΔΛΞΠℵ 1. 33. 69 Cod. Guelph., Bodl.; Verona, and Zurich Psalters; and Cod. Sang. 17 contain vv. 46—55.

u 1 Kings i. 11. see Psa. xxx. 7. v ch. ix. 38. James ii. 3 only. Ps. xxiv. 16. w Acts viii. 33 (from Isa. liii. 8). Phil. iii. 21. James i. 10 only. Ps. cxxxv. 23. x James v. 11 only. Gen. xxx. 13. y Eph. iii. 21. z Matt. vii. 12. Mark v. 19 al. Gen. xx. 9. a Acts ii. 11 only. 1 Chron. xvii. 19. Psa. lxx. 19 only. Sir. xvii. 8 al. b absol. of God, here only. see Rom. ix. 22. c Psa. cx. 9. d Ps. cii. 17. e plur. here only †. sing., Ps. xlviii. 11 al. f here only. see Ps. cxvii. 16. g John xii. 38 (from Isa. liii. 1). Acts xiii. 17 only. Deut. v. 15. h Matt. xxvi. 31. John xi. 52. Psa. lxxxviii. 10. i Rom. i. 30. 2 Tim. iii. 2. James iv. 6 & 1 Pet. v. 5 (from Prov. iii. 34) only. Ps. cxviii. 21. k = Col. i. 21. (Matt. xxii. 37 reff.) l 1 Chron. xxix. 18. m Mark xv. 36, 46. Acts xix. 27. 2 Cor. x. 5 al. Sir. x. 14. n Acts viii. 27. 1 Tim. vi. 15 only. Prov. xxxi. 4.

47. for επι, εν D. (*in deo* latt Iren[-int$_1$ Orig-int$_1$]: *super deo* lat-*e*.)
48. aft επεβλεψεν ins κυριος D.
49. * μεγάλα BD[1]Lℵ[1] latt: μεγαλια CD[2]E[1]KU[1]ΓΞ[Π[1]]ℵ[3a] Guelph Ver Turic: μεγαλεια A rel. ins ο θεος bef ο δυνατος D. for ονομα, ελεος ℵ[1].
50. rec εις γενεας γενεων (*corrn arising from the formula* "in sæcula sæculorum;" *so Mey*), with AC[2]D[2] rel lat-*a b c* syr goth (æth) Chron$_1$ [Orig-int$_1$]: εις γενεαν γενεων D[1]: εις γενεαν κ. γενεαν FMℵ Guelph Bodl Ver Turic Sang 1. 69 lat-*f ff$_2$ g$_1$ l q* Isid [Cyr$_1$-p] Thl Euthym: απο γενεας εις γενεαν A(in the Magnif insd at the end of the Psalms) 2-pe sah: *a progenie in progenies* vulg arm: txt BC[1]LΞ am(with em forj fuld ing mt tol vat) Syr copt Aug$_1$.
51. διανοιας EFH ℵ[3a](but corrd) Guelph Ver.

she that believed, for, &c., or **blessed is she that believed that there shall be,** &c. The last is maintained by Bengel and De Wette, and supported by Acts xxvii. 25. But I own it seems to me very improbable here; the sense and the period would both suffer;—and the usage of these first chapters is to *render a reason* by ὅτι: see vv. 37, 48, 49, 68. De Wette and Bleek urge against it, that we should thus look for σοί and not αὐτῇ. But surely the preceding ἡ πιστεύσασα, rendering the sentence axiomatic, would prepare the way for the demonstrative pronoun of the third person, on either view of ὅτι. I much prefer the former rendering, as agreeable likewise to the analogy of Scripture, where *faith, in the recipient* of the divine purposes, is so often represented as a *co-ordinate cause* of the fulfilment of those purposes. Lightf. well suggests, that there may have been present to the mind of Elisabeth the *unbelief of her husband,* as contrasted with Mary's faith. **46—55.**] Compare throughout the song of Hannah, 1 Sam. ii. 1—10. As connected with the defence of the hymns contained in these two chapters, we may observe, *taking the very lowest ground,* that there is nothing improbable, as matter of fact, in holy persons, full of the thoughts which permeate the O. T. prophecies, breaking out into such songs of praise as these, which are grounded on and almost expressed in the words of Scripture (see Dr. Mill, Historical character of Luke i. vindicated, p. 40 ff.). The Christian believer however will take a *higher view than this,* and attribute to the mother of our Lord, that same inspiration of the Holy Spirit which filled Elisabeth (ver. 41) and Zacharias (ver. 67). **46, 47.**] **ψυχὴ — πνεῦμα,** the *whole inner being:* see on 1 Thess. v. 23. **σωτῆρι**—not merely '*Deliverer from degradation, as a daughter of David*'—but, in a higher sense, **author of that salvation which God's people expected** [among whom the Holy Virgin **reckons** herself. Only sinners need a Saviour]. **48.**] Bleek remarks, that the ἐπιβλέψαι ἐπὶ τὸν υἱόν μου of Luke ix. 38, is ἐλέησόν μου τὸν υἱόν in Matt. xvii. 15. **ταπείν.**] **low condition,** not *humility;* the noun is an *objective* one. **51—**

νων καὶ [op] ὕψωσεν [pq] ταπεινούς, 53 [r] πεινῶντας [rs] ἐνέπλησεν
[r] ἀγαθῶν καὶ [t] πλουτοῦντας [uv] ἐξαπέστειλεν [v] κενούς.
54 [w] ἀντελάβετο Ἰσραὴλ παιδὸς αὐτοῦ, [x] μνησθῆναι
[x] ἐλέους, 55 καθὼς ἐλάλησεν πρὸς τοὺς πατέρας ἡμῶν,
[x] τῷ Ἀβραὰμ καὶ τῷ σπέρματι αὐτοῦ εἰς τὸν αἰῶνα.
56 ἔμεινεν δὲ Μαριὰμ σὺν αὐτῇ ὡσεὶ μῆνας τρεῖς, καὶ
[y] ὑπέστρεψεν εἰς τὸν οἶκον αὐτῆς. 57 Τῇ δὲ Ἐλισάβετ
[z] ἐπλήσθη ὁ χρόνος τοῦ [a] τεκεῖν αὐτήν, καὶ [b] ἐγέννησεν
υἱόν. 58 καὶ ἤκουσαν οἱ [c] περίοικοι καὶ οἱ [d] συγγενεῖς
αὐτῆς ὅτι [e] ἐμεγάλυνεν κύριος τὸ ἔλεος αὐτοῦ μετ᾽ αὐτῆς,
καὶ [f] συνέχαιρον αὐτῇ. 59 καὶ ἐγένετο ἐν τῇ ἡμέρᾳ τῇ
ὀγδόῃ [g] ἦλθον περιτεμεῖν τὸ παιδίον, καὶ ἐκάλουν αὐτὸ
[h] ἐπὶ τῷ ὀνόματι τοῦ πατρὸς αὐτοῦ Ζαχαρίαν. 60 καὶ
[i] ἀποκριθεῖσα ἡ μήτηρ αὐτοῦ εἶπεν Οὐχί, ἀλλὰ κληθήσεται
Ἰωάννης. 61 καὶ εἶπον πρὸς αὐτὴν ὅτι οὐδείς ἐστιν ἐκ
τῆς [k] συγγενείας σου ὃς καλεῖται τῷ ὀνόματι τούτῳ.
62 [l] ἐνένευον δὲ τῷ πατρὶ αὐτοῦ [m] τὸ τί ἂν θέλοι καλεῖσθαι

o Matt. xi. 23. Sir. xv. 5.
p Ezek. xxi. 26.
q Matt. xi. 29 reff.
r Psa. cvi. 9. (Jer. xxxviii. [xxxi.] 25.)
s ch. vi. 25. John vi. 25. Acts xiv. 17. Rom. xv. 24 only.
t ch. xii. 21. 1 Cor. iv. 8 al. Prov. xxviii. 22.
u ch. xx. 10, 11. xxiv. 49. Acts vii. 12 al6. Gal. iv. 4, 6 only. L.P. 1 Kings vi. 3 al.
v ch. xx. 10, 11. Job xxii. 9.
w Acts xx. 35. 1 Tim. vi. 2 only. Isa. xli. 9. (-λημψις, 1 Cor. xii. 28.)
x 2 Chron. vi. 42. Psa. xcvii. 3.
y ch. ii. 20 reff.
z = ver. 23. ch. ii. 6, 21, 22. see Gen. xxv. 24.
a Matt. i. 21 reff.
b = ver. 13. ch. xxiii 29. John xvi. 21. Gal iv. 24.
c here only. Gen. xix. 29. Deut. i. 7. (-κεῖν, ver. 65.)
d Mark vi. 4 reff.
e Matt. xxiii. 5. = Gen. xix. 19.
f ch. xv. 6, 9. 1 Cor. xii. 26. xiii. 6. Phil. ii. 17, 18 only. Gen. xxi. 6 only.
g Matt. ii. 2. Gen. xlii. 5.
h Rom. v. 14. Ezra ii. 61. Neh. vii. 63.
i = Matt. xi. 25 reff.
k Acts vii. 3 (from Gen. xii. 1), 14 only. Exod. xii. 21.
l here only. Prov. vi. 13. x. 10 only.
m red., see Mark ix. 23.

52. om *και* Ver.
55. *εως αιωνος* A(at end of Psalter) CFMS Guelph Bodl Ver Turic Sang **1.** 69 goth Thaum$_1$: *in saecula* lat-*b c*. at end ins *αμην* Ver.
56. *ως* [for *ωσει*] BLΞℵ 1: om D 69 lat-*a b e ff*$_2$ *g*$_1$ *l q* copt-wilk sah Orig-int$_1$ Ambr$_1$.
58. om 2nd *οι* D. om *αυτης* L.
59. om *εν* DL 33 lat-*e* [Chron$_1$]. rec *τη ογδ. ημ.*, with A rel lat-*a*(appy): txt BCDLΞℵ 33. 69 vulg lat-*b c* arm Chron$_1$. *ηλθαν* D[1].
60. aft *κληθησεται* ins *το ονομα αυτου* C[1]D copt-wilk.
61. *ειπαν* DLΔΞℵ 1 Chron$_1$. rec *εν τη συγγενεια*, with C[2]D rel latt [syrr] goth arm: txt ABC[1]LΔΛΞ[Π]ℵ 33 copt æth Chron$_1$. *το ονομα τουτο nomen hoc* D.
62. *ο τι ο αν θελοι qui vult* D, *quem vellet* latt.—for *το*, *ο* Ξ.

55.] These aorists express, not the habit of the past, but the consequences involved for the future in that which the Lord had done to her. **51.**] The dative **διανοίᾳ** apparently expresses the realm in which the *ὑπερηφανία* is shewn. Bleek quotes from Symmachus, Ps. lxxv. 6, *ὑπερήφανοι τῇ καρδίᾳ*: but it is *τὴν καρδίαν*: the LXX however in the same place has *ἀσύνετοι τῇ καρδίᾳ*. Ver. **55** is not rendered in the E. V. according to the construction; from Ps. xcvii. 3 it will be seen that **μνησθῆναι ἐλέους τῷ Ἀβ.** are to be joined together, and therefore *καθὼς . . . . . ἡμῶν* will be parenthetical. See Micah vii. 20.

57—79.] Birth and naming of John the Baptist. **59.**] **ἐκάλουν—they were calling**—wished to call: see Matt. iii. 14 for this use of the imperfect. The names of children were given at circumcision, because, at the institution of that rite, the names of Abram and Sarai were changed to Abraham and Sarah,—Gen. xvii. 5, 15. **60.**] There is no reason for supposing, with Theophyl., Euthym., Meyer, that *Elisabeth* had had the name supernaturally intimated to her. She must necessarily have learnt it, in the course of communication by writing, from her husband. **62.**] The natural inference (see on ver. 22) from this verse is, that Zacharias was *deaf as well as dumb;* nor do I think Kuinoel, De Wette, Meyer, Olshausen, Bengel, Bleek, and Bp. Wordsworth have succeeded in invalidating this inference. There could have been no reason for *beckoning*, had Zacharias been able to hear articulate words. Bengel's reason, adopted by Bp. W., "commodius est muto innuentes videre quam loquentes audire," is surely too far-fetched.

αὐτό. 63 καὶ [n] αἰτήσας [o] πινακίδιον ἔγραψεν [p] λέγων
Ἰωάννης ἐστὶν [τὸ] ὄνομα αὐτοῦ. καὶ ἐθαύμασαν πάντες.
64 [q] ἀνεῴχθη δὲ τὸ στόμα αὐτοῦ [r] παραχρῆμα καὶ ἡ
γλῶσσα αὐτοῦ, καὶ ἐλάλει [s] εὐλογῶν τὸν θεόν. 65 καὶ
[t] ἐγένετο [u] ἐπὶ πάντας φόβος τοὺς [v] περιοικοῦντας αὐτούς,
καὶ ἐν ὅλῃ τῇ [w] ὀρεινῇ τῆς Ἰουδαίας [x] διελαλεῖτο πάντα
τὰ ῥήματα ταῦτα, 66 καὶ [y] ἔθεντο πάντες οἱ ἀκούσαντες ἐν
τῇ καρδίᾳ αὐτῶν λέγοντες [z] Τί ἄρα τὸ παιδίον τοῦτο
ἔσται; καὶ γὰρ [a] χεὶρ κυρίου ἦν μετ' αὐτοῦ. 67 καὶ
Ζαχαρίας ὁ πατὴρ αὐτοῦ ἐπλήσθη πνεύματος ἁγίου καὶ
ἐπροφήτευσεν λέγων 68 [b] Εὐλογητὸς κύριος ὁ [c] θεὸς τοῦ
[c] Ἰσραήλ, ὅτι [d] ἐπεσκέψατο καὶ [e] ἐποίησεν [f] λύτρωσιν τῷ

ABCDE FGHKL MSUV ΓΔΛΞ Πℵ 1. 33. 69 Frag. Sang.

και ελαλει...

...εσται Ξ.

Cod. Guelph., Bodl., and Zurich Psalters, and Cod. Sang. contain vv. 68—79.

n = Acts xvi. 29. 1 Cor. i. 22. Judg. v. 25. o here only +. Ezek. ix. 2 Symm. p (ch. iii. 4 v. r.) 2 Kings xi. 15. 4 Kings x. 1, 6. q = Num. xxii. 28. constr., 1 Cor. iii. 2. r ch. iv. 39 al8. Acts iii. 7 al5. Luke only, exc. Matt. xxi. 19, 20. Num. vi. 9. s ch. ii. 28. xxiv. 53. Judg. v. 2, 9. t ch. iv. 36. Acts v. 5, 11. Gen. xxxv. 5. u Acts iv. 33. v here only +. (-κος, ver. 58.) w ver. 39 only. Gen. xiv. 10. x ch. vi. 11 only +. Ps. lxxvii. 3 Symm. y ch. ix. 44. xxi. 14. Acts v. 4. xix. 21. 1 Kings xxi. 12. Hag. ii. 19. z John xxi. 21. Gen. xxxvii. 20. a Acts xi. 21. xiii. 11. 1 Kings xxii. 17. 2 Kings xiv. 19. b Mark xiv. 61 reff. Psa. xl. 13. lxxi. 18. cv. 48. c Matt. xv. 31. Isa. xxix. 23. d ver. 78. ch. vii. 16. Heb. ii. 6, from Ps. viii. 5. Exod. iv. 31. e = Acts xv. 3. Job xl. 15 (20). f ch. ii. 38. Heb. ix. 12 only. Ps. cx. 9. cxxix. 7. (-τροῦν, ch. xxiv. 21 reff. Psa. lxxvi. 14.)

rec (for αυτο) αυτον, with AC rel latt $Chron_1$: txt BDFGℵ 33. 69.

63. πινακιδα C^1(appy) D. om λεγων D lat-*e*. εσται CU 1 syr-mg $Orig_1$: txt ABDℵ rel vss $Orig_1$-int_2 [$Chron_1$]. om το (bef ονομα) B^1LΞ $Orig_2$: ins AB^2CDℵ rel [$Chron_1$]. aft αυτου add και παραχρημα ελυθη η γλωσσα αυτου, omg παραχρ. κ. η γλ. αυτ. in next ver, D lat-*a b* g_1.

64. om 2nd αυτου C^1 Scr's c lat-*e q*.

65. for και εγεν., εγεν. δε AK[Π]$ℵ^1$. for επι π. φοβ., φοβ. μεγας επι παντ. D 2-pe lat-*b c*. αυτον D goth. for διελαλειτο παντα, δια (sic) $ℵ^1$(txt ℵ-$corr^1$).

66. ακουοντες C D-gr copt-dz goth arm : txt ABℵ rel. ταις καρδιαις DLΞ lat-*e* arm : txt ABCℵ rel vss [$Chron_1$]. εαυτων B. rec om γαρ (*as superfl or perhaps from* χειρ *follg*), with $AC^{2 \text{ or } 3}$ rel syrr : ins BC^1DLℵ latt syr-mg copt goth æth. om ην D 59 lat-*l q* [arm] : ins bef χειρ 1. 131(Sz).

67. for επροφητευσεν λεγων, ειπεν D. (επροφ., so $AB^1CLℵ^1$ 1. 33.)

63.] **πινακίδ.** (= πινάκιον, Aristoph. Vesp. 167), a tablet smeared with wax, on which they wrote with a style. On **λέγων**, a Hebraism, as applied to *writing*, see reff. and Jos. Antt. xi. 4. 7,—Δαρεῖος ἀντιγράφει τῷ Σισίνῃ . . . . τάδε λέγων. **ἐθαύμ. πάντες**] This also confirms the view that Zacharias was deaf. There would be nothing wonderful in his *acceding to his wife's suggestion*, if he had *known it:* the *coincidence*, apparently without this knowledge, was the matter of wonder. 64.] For now first had the angel's words, καλέσεις τὸ ὄν. αὐτ. Ἰωάννην, ver. 13, received their fulfilment. 65.] For the construction **περιοικ. αὐτούς**, see Herod. v. 78: Xen. Anab. v. 6. 16. **ῥήματα, words**; not '*things*,' see above on vv. 4, 37. All this *tale* became matter of λαλιά throughout, &c. 66.] **λέγοντες** carries a slightly logical force with it;—almost = '*for they said.*' **ἄρα** refers back to the circumstances which have happened—**What then shall**, &c.: see ch. viii. 25: Acts xii. 18. **καὶ γὰρ χεὶρ κ. . . . .**, a remark inserted by the Evangelist himself, not a further saying of the speakers in the verse before, as Kuinoel and others maintain. The γάρ refers back to the question just asked, q. d., 'And they might well enquire thus, for' &c. **68—79.**] This Hymn of thanksgiving appears to have been uttered at the time of the circumcision of the child (in which case the matters related in vv. 65, 66 are parenthetical and anticipatory)—and, as the Magnificat, under the immediate influence of inspiration of the Holy Ghost. It is entirely *Hebrew* in its cast and idioms, and might be rendered in that language almost word for word. It serves, besides its own immediate interest to every Christian, to shew to us the *exact religious view* under which John was educated by his father. "It may be well for the student to read the beginning of this and the following chapter in Hebrew, in which they have been published in translations of the N. T. and in the Book of Common Prayer rendered into that language." Wordsw.

68.] After **ἐπεσκέψατο** (for Hebraistic

R κερας ... λαῷ αὐτοῦ, 69 καὶ [gh] ἤγειρεν [hi] κέρας σωτηρίας ἡμῖν ἐν
οἴκῳ [j] Δαυεὶδ [j] παιδὸς αὐτοῦ, 70 καθὼς ἐλάλησεν [k] διὰ
στόματος τῶν [l] ἁγίων [m] ἀπ᾿ αἰῶνος [l] προφητῶν αὐτοῦ,
71 σωτηρίαν ἐξ ἐχθρῶν ἡμῶν καὶ ἐκ [n] χειρὸς πάντων τῶν
μισούντων ἡμᾶς, 72 [o] ποιῆσαι ἔλεος [o] μετὰ τῶν πατέρων
ἡμῶν καὶ [p] μνησθῆναι [p] διαθήκης ἁγίας αὐτοῦ, 73 [q] ὅρκον
ὃν [q] ὤμοσεν πρὸς Ἀβραὰμ τὸν πατέρα ἡμῶν, 74 [r] τοῦ
δοῦναι ἡμῖν [s] ἀφόβως ἐκ χειρὸς ἐχθρῶν [t] ῥυσθέντας
[u] λατρεύειν αὐτῷ 75 ἐν [vw] ὁσιότητι καὶ [v] δικαιοσύνῃ
[x] ἐνώπιον αὐτοῦ πάσας τὰς ἡμέρας ἡμῶν. 76 [y] καὶ σὺ
[y] δέ, παιδίον, προφήτης [z] ὑψίστου κληθήσῃ· [a] προπορεύσῃ

g = ch. iii. 8. Acts xiii. 22. Judg. ii. 18.
h see Ps. cxxxi. 17. Ezek. xxix. 21.
i = here (Rev. v. 6 al.?) only. 2 Kings xxii. 3. Psa. xvii. 2.
j Acts iv. 25. 1 Chron. xvii. 4 AN, 24.
k Acts i. 16. iii. 18, 21. iv. 25. 2 Chron. xxxvi. 21.
l Acts iii. 21. 2 Pet. iii. 2.
m = Acts iii. 21. xv. 18. Gen. vi. 4. εκ τ. αἰ., John ix. 32.
n Acts xii. 11. xxiv. 7. Exod. xviii. 16. Psa. cv. 10.
o ch. x. 37. Acts xiv. 27. xv. 4. Gen. xxiv. 12. Tobit xii. 6.
p Exod. ii. 24. Psa. cv. 45.
q Gen. xxvi. 3.
r Matt. iii. 13 reff. Jer. xi. 5.
s 1 Cor. xvi. 10. Phil. i. 14. Jude 12 only. Prov. i. 33. Wisd. xvii. 4 BN (-βος, AC) only.
t Rom. vii. 24. 2 Cor. i. 10. Ps. xxx. 15.
u ch. ii. 37. iv. 8 ‖ Mt., from Deut. vi. 3. Acts vii. 7, 42 al. Exod. iii. 12 al.
v Wisd. ix. 3.
w Eph. iv. 24 only. Deut. ix. 5.
x ver. 17 reff.
y Matt. x. 18 reff.
z = vv. 32, 35. ch. vi. 35.
a Acts vii. 40 (from Exod. xxxii. 1) only. Deut. xxxi. 3.

69. rec ins τω bef οικω, with AR rel $Chron_1$: om BCDLMא Guelph Sang 1. 33. 69 Eus_2 Cyr_1. rec ins του bef παιδος, with ACR rel Eus_2 [$Chron_1$]: om BDLא [Cyr_1].
70. om των D. rec ins των bef απ αιωνος, with ACDR rel : om BLΔא Frag-sang 33. 69 $Orig_1$ Eus_2.—προφ. αυτ. των απ αιωνος D, simly lat-*a b c* &c Iren[-int_1]. αυτου bef προφητων א Eus.
71. for εξ, εκ χειρος (omg εκ χ. follg) D. **72.** om και D.
74. rec ins των bef εχθρων, with ACR rel [Cyr_1] Chron; παντων των K : om BDLא 1. 33. 69 $Orig_1$. rec aft εχθρων ins ημων, with ACDR rel latt $Orig_1$ [Cyr_1] $Chron_1$: om BLא Frag-sang 1 (33 ?) 69 lat-*e* Iren[-int_1 Orig-int_2]. (*The words have been conformed to ver* 71.)
75. πασαις ταις ημεραις BL vulg lat-*b c* &c. rec bef ημων ins της ζωης, with E(G ?)HMSΓΛ Bodl Sang arm $Orig_1$ [Cyr_1] $Chron_1$: om A(here and at end of Psalter) BCDRא rel latt syrr copt goth æth Iren-int_1 Orig-int_1 Jer.
76. rec om δε, with A rel latt syrr goth æth arm $Orig_1$[int_1] $Chron_1$ Iren-int_1 : ins

sense of which see reff.) must be understood, as an object, τὸν λαὸν αὐτοῦ, contained in the following dative. **69.**] **κέρας**—a metaphor from horned beasts, who are weak and defenceless without, but formidable with their horns: see reff.; and cf. Hor. Od. iii. 21. 18, 'addis cornua pauperi.' There does not seem to be any allusion (Selden, &c.) to the *horns of the altar*—the mere notion of a *refuge* is never connected with the Messiah's Kingdom. **70.**] Meyer cites τοὺς ἀπ᾿ αἰῶνος ῥήτορας, Longin. 34. **72. ποιῆσαι . . . .**] For a similar use of the infinitive, see ver. 54. We may take it here either as of the purpose, "*to perform . . .*," which is recommended by the ὅρκον ὃν κ.τ.λ., below,—or with Euthym., Bleek, al., as epexegetic, and equivalent to ἐν τῷ ποιῆσαι, or in English to a participial clause, 'performing,' &c. **73.**] **ὅρκον ὃν . . . .** for ὅρκου, ὃν . . . .: see Gen. xxii. 16—18. Calvin, al., suppose the construction to be κατὰ τὸν ὅρκον ὃν . . . .; Grotius makes the words dependent on ἐλάλησεν above, as also the infin. ποιῆσαι: Bleek thinks that the accusative is directly governed by μνησθῆναι, as well as the preceding genitive. "The Holy Spirit, speaking by Zacharias, seems to refer here to the providential dispensation signified in the names of the Baptist and his parents. The Baptist, by his name *John*, spake of the ἔλεος or grace of God: *Zacharias* (from זָכַר, *recordatus fuit*, and יָהּ, *Jah, Jehovah*) signifies θεὸς ἐμνήσθη, and *Elisabeth* (from אֵל, *El, Deus*, and שָׁבַע, *sheba, juravit*) is connected with the ὅρκος θεοῦ." Wordsw. This seems probable in the case before us: but the student must be reminded that it is ground to be very cautiously trodden, and where a morbid or pedantic fancy will be constantly going astray. **74, 75.**] The attempts to remove the Jewish worship by Antiochus Epiphanes and by the Romans, had been most calamitous to the people. This **ἐν ὁσι. κ. δικαιοσ.** sufficiently refutes the idea of some, that the whole subject of this song is the temporal theocratic greatness of the Messiah. **76.**] It is not

γὰρ πρὸ προσώπου κυρίου [b] ἑτοιμάσαι [b] ὁδοὺς αὐτοῦ,
77 [r] τοῦ δοῦναι γνῶσιν σωτηρίας τῷ λαῷ αὐτοῦ [c] ἐν
[d] ἀφέσει ἁμαρτιῶν αὐτῶν 78 διὰ [e] σπλάγχνα ἐλέους θεοῦ
ἡμῶν, ἐν οἷς [f] ἐπεσκέψατο ἡμᾶς [g] ἀνατολὴ ἐξ [h] ὕψους
79 [i] ἐπιφᾶναι τοῖς ἐν [k] σκότει καὶ [kl] σκιᾷ [k] θανάτου [k] καθημένοις, τοῦ [m] κατευθῦναι τοὺς πόδας ἡμῶν εἰς [n] ὁδὸν
[n] εἰρήνης. 80 Τὸ δὲ παιδίον [o] ηὔξανεν καὶ [p] ἐκραταιοῦτο
πνεύματι, καὶ ἦν ἐν ταῖς ἐρήμοις ἕως ἡμέρας [q] ἀναδείξεως
αὐτοῦ πρὸς τὸν Ἰσραήλ.

Ξ του δουναι ... ...τους Frag. Sang. ABCDE FGHK LMRSU VΓΔΛΞ ΠℵI. 33. 69

b ch. iii. 4 ‖ (from Isa. xl. 3). Rev. xvi. 12. c = 1 Cor. iv. 4. Eph. i. 3. d Mark i. 4. Acts ii. 38. Col. i. 14 al. Deut. xv. 3. e Col. iii. 12 al. Prov. xii. 10. f ver. 68. g Jer. xxiii. 5. Zech. iii. 9. vi. 12. = here only. h = ch. xxiv. 49. Eph. (iii. 18) iv. 8 (James i. 9. Rev. xxi. 16) only. Ps. xvii. 16. i = Acts xxvii. 20 (Tit. ii. 11. iii. 4) only L.P. Deut. xxxiii. 2. k Matt. iv. 16, from Isa. ix. 2. l Mark iv. 32 reff. m 1 Thess. iii. 11. 2 Thess. iii. 5 only. Ps. xxxix. 2. n Rom. iii. 17, from Isa. lix. 8 only. see Matt. xxi. 32. Acts xvi. 17. o Matt. xiii. 32. p ch. ii. 40. 1 Cor. xii. 13. Eph. iii. 16 only. Ps. xxx. 24. q here only †. Sir. xliii. 6 only. (-δεικνύναι, ch. x. 1. 2 Macc. ix. 23. x. 11.)

A(at end of Psalter) BCDLRℵ 33 copt. for *προ προσωπου*, *ενωπιον* Bℵ $Orig_1$[int_1].
77. for *αυτων*, *ημων* A(here and at end of Psalter) CMU R(Treg, expr) Guelph Bodl Turic 1 sah: txt BDℵ rel vulg syrr copt-schw goth [æth $Chron_1$] $Iren\text{-}int_1$.
78. **επισκεψεται** Bℵ[1] goth arm-zoh, **επεσκεψαιται** L: *visitabit* copt: *inviset* Syr.
79. aft **επιφαναι** ins *φως* D. **80.** **ηυξανετο** D[1].

necessary to interpret **κυρίου** of the Messiah: it may be said of God, whose people (ver. 77) Israel was. But the believing Christian will find it far more natural thus to apply it, especially in connexion with Matt. i. 21. **77.**] **ἐν ἀφέσει**, *in remission*, the element in which the former blessing was to be conferred. The *remission of sin* is the first opening for the *γνῶσις σωτηρίας*: see ch. iii. 7.

78.] **ἀνατολή** is (see reff.) the LXX rendering for צֶמַח a *branch* or *sprout*—and thus, '*that which springs up or rises*,' as *Light*:—which, from the clauses following, seems to be the meaning here.

ἐξ ὕψ. may be taken with **ἀνατ.**, as in E. V.:—or perhaps with the verb **ἐπιφᾶναι.** But however taken, the expression is not quite easy to understand. The word had come apparently to be a name for the Messiah: thus in ref. Zech. ἰδοὺ ἀνήρ, Ἀνατολὴ ὄνομα αὐτῷ: and then figures arising from the meaning of the word itself, became mixed with that which was said of Him. The day-spring does not come ἐξ ὕψους, but from beneath the horizon; but the Messiah *does*. Again the ἐπιφᾶναι κ.τ.λ. of the next verse belongs to the day-spring, and only figuratively to the Messiah. See Bleek's long note. **79.**] See reff. Care must be taken on the one hand not to degrade the expressions of this song of praise into mere anticipations of temporal prosperity, nor, on the other, to find in it (except in so far as they are involved in the inner and deeper sense of the words, unknown save to the Spirit who prompted them) the minute doctrinal distinctions of the writings of St. Paul. It is the expression of the aspirations and hopes of a pious Jew, waiting for the salvation of the Lord, finding that salvation brought near, and uttering his thankfulness in Old Testament language, with which he was familiar, and at the same time under prophetic influence of the Holy Spirit. That such a song should be *inconsistent* with dogmatic truth, is *impossible*: that it should unfold it minutely, is in the highest degree *improbable*. **80.**] A very similar conclusion to those in ch. ii. 40, 52, and denoting probably the termination of that record or document of the birth of the Baptist, which the Evangelist has hitherto been translating, or perhaps transcribing already translated. That this first chapter is such a separate document, appears from its very distinct style. Whether it had been preserved in the holy family, or how otherwise obtained by Luke, no trace now appears. It has a certain relation to, and at the same time is distinguished from, the narration of the next chapter. The Old Testament spirit is stronger here, and the very phraseology more in unison with Hebrew usage.

ταῖς ἐρ.] The ὀρεινή of Judæa was very near this wilderness, and from the character of John's official life afterwards, it is probable that in youth he would be given to solitude and abstemiousness. It cannot be supposed that the *Essenes*, dwelling in those parts, had any, or only the most general kind of influence over him, as their views were wholly different from his. **ἀναδ.**, opening of his official life: see note on ch. x. 1.

II. [1] Ἐγένετο δὲ [r] ἐν ταῖς ἡμέραις ἐκείναις, [s] ἐξῆλθεν
[t] δόγμα [u] παρὰ Καίσαρος Αὐγούστου [v] ἀπογράφεσθαι
πᾶσαν τὴν [w] οἰκουμένην. [2] αὕτη [x] ἀπογραφὴ πρώτη

r Exod. ii. 11. s = Matt. xv. 18, 19. Mark i. 28. ch. vi. 19. 1 Cor. xiv. 36. Dan. ii. 13 Theod.

t Acts xvi. 4. xvii. 7. Eph. ii. 15. Col. ii. 14 (Heb. xi. 23 v. r.) only. Dan. vi. 12. u ch. vi. 19. Lev. ix. 24. x. 2. v here 3ce and Heb. xii. 23 only. Judg. viii. 14 A. Prov. xxii. 20 only. 3 Macc. iv. 14. w Matt. xxiv. 14 reff. Ps. ix. 8. x Acts v. 37 only. 2 Macc. ii. 1 only.

CHAP. II. 1. om δε ΑΞ. αγουστου C[1]Δℵ. ins του bef απογραφεσθαι LΞ 33.

2. rec aft αυτη ins η, with ACRΞℵ[3a] rel coptt Eus_2 [$Chron_1$]: om BD ℵ-corr[1](appy)

CHAP. II. 1—20.] BIRTH OF CHRIST. ITS ANNOUNCEMENT, AND CELEBRATION BY THE HOSTS OF HEAVEN. 1, 2.] * We go back again now to the birth of John, or shortly after it. In annotating on these verses, I will first state the difficulty in which they appear to be involved,—then the remarkable way in which a solution has been found. The assertion in these verses is this—*that a decree went forth*, &c., *and that this enrolment first took place when Cyrenius* (Quirinus, see below) *was governor of Syria*. It would then appear, either that *this very enrolment took place under Quirinus*,—or that *the first* did so, and this was subsequent to it. Now *both of these senses* formerly seemed to be *inadmissible*. For Quirinus was not known to have been governor of Syria till the year 758 U.C., after the banishment of Archelaus, and the addition of his territory to the province of Syria. τῆς δὲ Ἀρχ. χώρας ὑποτελοῦς προσνεμηθείσης τῇ Σύρων, πέμπεται Κυρήνιος ὑπὸ Καίσαρος, ἀνὴρ ὑπατικός, ἀποτιμησόμενος τὰ ἐν Συρίᾳ, καὶ τὸν Ἀρχελάου ἀποδωσόμενος οἶκον. Jos. Antt. xvii. 13. 5. And the birth of our Lord occurred *at least eight years before this*, previous to Herod's death, and when *Sentius Saturninus was governor of Syria*. But in a Commentatio of A. W. Zumpt of Berlin (the nephew of the distinguished grammarian of that name), *De Syria Romanorum provincia ab Cæsare Augusto ad T. Vespasianum*, he makes it highly probable that Quirinus was TWICE governor of Syria. The substance of his researches is as follows:—In 9 B.C. Sentius Saturninus succeeded M. Titius in the province of Syria, and governed it three years. He was succeeded by T. Quintilius Varus (Jos. Antt. xvii. 5. 2), who, as it appears, remained governor up to the end of 4 B.C. Thenceforward we lose sight of him till he is appointed to the command in Germany, in which he lost his life in A.D. 7. We also lose sight of the governors of Syria till the appointment of P. Sulpicius Quirinus, in A.D. 6. Now from the maxim acted on by Augustus (Dio Cass. lii. 23), that none should hold an imperial province for less than three or more than five years, Varus cannot have been governor of Syria during the twelve years from B.C. 6 to A.D. 6. Who then were the missing governors? One of them has been found, L. Volusius Saturninus, whose name occurs as "legatus Syriae" on a coin of Antioch, A.D. 4 or 5. But his proconsulate will not fill the whole time, and one or two governors must be supplied between Varus, ending 4 B.C., and Volusius, 4 or 5 A.D. Just in that interval falls the census, of which it is said in the text, that it πρώτη ἐγένετο ἡγεμονεύοντος τῆς Συρίας Κυρηνίου. Could Quirinus have been governor at any such time? From Jan. to Aug. B.C. 12 he was consul. Soon after that he triumphed over the Homonadenses ("mox expugnatis per Ciliciam Homonadensium castellis insignia triumphi adeptus," Tac. Ann. iii. 48). Now Zumpt applies the exhaustive process to the provinces which could by any possibility have been under Quirinus at this time, and eliminates from the enquiry Asia,—Pontus and Bithynia,—and Galatia. Cilicia only remains. But at this time, as he shews, that province had been reduced by successive diminutions, had been separated (Dio Cass. liv. 4) from Cyprus, and, as is shewn by the history of the misconduct of Piso soon afterwards, who was charged with having, as ex-governor of Syria, attempted "repetere provinciam armis" (Tac. Ann. iii. 12), because he had attacked Celenderis, a fort in Cilicia (ib. ii. 78—80), attached to the province of Syria. This Zumpt also confirms by the accounts in Tacitus (Ann. vi. 41; xii. 55) of the Clitæ, a seditious tribe of Cilicia Aspera, who on two occasions were repressed by troops sent by the governors of Syria. Quirinus then appears to have been governor of Syria at some time during this interval. But at *what time*? We find him in the East (Tac. Ann. iii. 48), as "datus rector C. Cæsari Armeniam obtinenti;" and this cannot

y ch. iii. 1 only †. z John vii. 8, &c. Neh. vii. 6. a ver. 11 only. 2 Kings v. 9 al., but not of Bethlehem. b ch. ix. 30 reff. c Acts iii. 25. Eph. iii. 15. Num. i. 18.

ἐγένετο [y] ἡγεμονεύοντος τῆς Συρίας Κυρηνίου. 3 καὶ
ἐπορεύοντο πάντες [v] ἀπογράφεσθαι, ἕκαστος εἰς τὴν ἰδίαν
πόλιν. 4 [z] ἀνέβη δὲ καὶ Ἰωσὴφ ἀπὸ τῆς Γαλιλαίας ἐκ
πόλεως Ναζαρὲτ εἰς τὴν Ἰουδαίαν εἰς [a] πόλιν [a] Δαυεὶδ
[b] ἥτις καλεῖται Βηθλεέμ, διὰ τὸ εἶναι αὐτὸν ἐξ οἴκου
καὶ [c] πατριᾶς Δαυείδ, 5 [v] ἀπογράψασθαι σὺν Μαριὰμ

...γαλιλαιας R. ABCDE FGHKL MSUV ΓΔΛΞΠ ℵ 1. 33. 69

Eus$_1$, *αυτην απογραφην* ℵ^1. *εγενετο* bef *απογραφη πρωτη* D Orig-int$_1$.—*εγενετο* bef *πρωτη* ℵ^1. *κυρεινου* B latt Syr sah, *κηρυνιου* A.

3. *εκαστος απογραφεσθαι*, omg *παντες*, ℵ^1. for *ιδιαν*, *εαυτου* (*explany, cf* D *below*) BDLΞℵ^3 Eus$_1$: *εαυτων* ℵ^1 : txt ACR rel syr-mg-gr [Chr Chron$_1$]. for *πολιν*, *πατριδα* D : *χωραν* C^1 gat.

4. for *την ιουδ.*, *γην ιουδα* D lat-(*a*) *e*. ins *την* bef *πολιν* ℵ^1. transp *δια* to 2nd *δαυειδ* to end of ver 5 D.

5. *απογραφεσθαι* (*see ver* 3) ADℵ^1 33 Chr$_1$ Thl : *-ψεσθαι* Δ : txt BCΞℵ^{3a} rel Just$_1$ Eus$_2$ [Cyr-jer$_1$ Chron$_1$]. *μαρια* D Eus

have been during his well-known governorship of Syria, which began in A.D. 6; for Caius Cæsar died in A.D. 4. Zumpt, by arguments too long to be reproduced here, but very striking and satisfactory, fixes the time of his first governorship at from B.C. 4 to B.C. 1, when he was succeeded by M. Lollius. It is true this does not quite remove our difficulty. But it brings it within such narrow limits, that any slight error in calculation, or even the latitude allowed by the words *πρώτη ἐγένετο* might well cover it. I may mention it as remarkable, that Justin Martyr three times distinctly asserts that *our Lord was born under Quirinus*, and *appeals to the register then made*, as if from it the fact might, if necessary, be confirmed: Apol. i. 34, p. 65; 46, p. 71: Dial. 78, p. 175. We conclude then, that an *ἀπογραφή* or enrolment of names with a view to ascertain the population of the empire, *was commanded and put in force at this time*, unaccompanied (probably) by any payment of money. Mr. Greswell (vol. i. p. 511) cites a passage of Suidas—*ὅτι Αὔγουστος Καῖσαρ, δόξαν αὐτῷ, πάντας τοὺς οἰκήτορας Ῥωμαίων* (?) *κατὰ πρόσωπον ἀριθμεῖ, βουλόμενος γνῶναι πόσον ἐστὶ πλῆθος*: and has made it probable that, notwithstanding a difficulty in the numbers, this was a census *of the empire*, and not of the city. We know (see Tacitus, Ann. i. 11: Sueton. Aug. 28, 101: Dio liii. 30; lvi. 33) that Augustus drew up a *rationarium* or *breviarium totius imperii*, which took many years to arrange and complete, and of which the enrolment of the inhabitants of the provinces would naturally form a part. Of the data for this compilation, the enrolment in our text might be one. That Judæa *was not a Roman province at this time*, is no objection to our text; for the breviarium of Augustus contained the 'regna' of the Roman empire, as well as the 'provincias.'

For a statement of the case and its difficulties as they stood before Zumpt's discovery, see Wieseler, Chronol. Synops. i. 73—122; and a good summary and criticism of the various hypotheses in Winer's Realwörterbuch, edn. 3, art. Quirinus: and a new and curious hypothesis in Bp. Wordsw. h. l., who inclines to reject the above solution. In Dio Cassius, where we might expect to find information, this portion of the reign of Augustus is apparently defective. **Κυρην.**] P. Sulpicius *Quirinus* (not *Quirinius*, for *Κυρήνιος* is the Greek form of Quirinus, Meyer ii. 222: see Sueton. Tib. 49: Tacit. Ann. iii. 48, where however Beck reads Quirinius). **3—5.**] There is a mixture here of Roman and Jewish customs, which is not at all improbable, considering the circumstances. In the Roman census, men, women, and children were all obliged to go and be enrolled. Dion. Hal. iv. 15, *ἅπαντας ἐκέλευσε* (*ὁ Τύλλιος*) *τοὺς δμοπάγους κατὰ κεφαλὴν ὡρισμένον νόμισμά τι συνεισφέρειν, ἕτερον μέν τι τοὺς ἄνδρας, ἕτερον δέ τι τὰς γυναῖκας, ἄλλο δέ τι τοὺς ἀνήβους*. But then this census was made at their *dwelling-place*, not at that of their *extraction*. The latter practice springs from the Jewish genealogical habits, and its adoption in this case *speaks strongly for the accuracy of the chronology*. If this enrolment was by order of Augustus, and for the whole empire, it of course would be made so as to include *all*, after the Roman manner: but inasmuch as it was made *under the Jewish king Herod*, it was done *after the Jewish manner*, in taking this

...εμνη-στευμενη C.

τῇ [d] ἐμνηστευμένῃ αὐτῷ οὔσῃ [e] ἐγκύῳ. 6 Ἐγένετο δὲ
[f] ἐν τῷ εἶναι αὐτοὺς ἐκεῖ, [g] ἐπλήσθησαν αἱ [h] ἡμέραι
[h] τοῦ [hi] τεκεῖν αὐτήν· 7 καὶ [i] ἔτεκεν τὸν υἱὸν αὐτῆς τὸν
[k] πρωτότοκον, καὶ [l] ἐσπαργάνωσεν αὐτὸν καὶ [m] ἀνέκλινεν
αὐτὸν ἐν [n] φάτνῃ· [o] διότι οὐκ ἦν αὐτοῖς [p] τόπος ἐν τῷ
[q] καταλύματι. 8 Καὶ ποιμένες ἦσαν ἐν τῇ χώρᾳ τῇ αὐτῇ
[r] ἀγραυλοῦντες καὶ [s] φυλάσσοντες [s] φυλακὰς [t] τῆς [t] νυκτὸς

d ch. i. 27. Matt. i. 18 only. Deut. xxii. 23, 25.
e here only †. Sir. xlii. 10 only. Jer. xxxviii. (xxxi.) 8 alius in Hexapla.
f ch. i. 8, 21. 1 Kings xvi. 23.
g ch. i. 57 reff.
h Gen. xxv. 24.
i Matt. i. 21 reff.
k Rom. viii. 29. Col. i. 15, 18. Heb. i. 6. xi. 28. xii. 23. Rev. i. 5 only. Gen. iv. 4. (-κια, Heb. xii. 16.)
l ver. 12 only. Job xxxviii. 9. Ezek. xvi. 4 only.
m act., ch. ix. 15 || Mk. xii. 37. (Matt. viii. 11 reff.)
n vv. 12, 16. ch. xiii. 15 only. Job xxxix. 9.
o ch. i. 13 reff.
p = ch. xiv. 9, 22. Gen. xxiv. 23, 25. 1 Macc. ix. 45.
q ch. xxii. 11 || Mk. Exod. iv. 24.
r here only †.
s Num. iii. 28. Ezek. xliv. 8.
t Xen. Anab. v. 7. 14.

rec μεμνηστευμενη, with $B^2C^2D^{10}$ $\aleph^{3a}$(but txt restored) rel Eus_1 : txt $AB^1C^1D^1L\Xi\aleph^1$. rec aft αυτω ins γυναικι, with A C^2(appy) rel latt syr goth æth Eus_1 (Cyr-jer ?) Chr_2 [$Chron_1$] : om B C^1(appy) DLΞℵ 1 per lat-*e f* q^2 Syr coptt arm Eus_1.

6. for εγενετο to επλησθησαν, ως δε παρεγεινοντο ετελεσθησαν D.

7. for 1st εν, επι $\aleph^1$(but corrd eadem manu, so ver 12). rec ins τη bef φατνη, with Δ rel Eus_1 [$Amphil_1$] Cyr_1 Chr_2 [$Chron_1$] : om ABDLΞℵ goth arm Protev $Just_1$ Eus-2-mss.

8. for και ποιμ., ποιμ. δε D lat-*a b e f* ff_2 g_1 [*l q*] (Syr). χαρα D^1(txt $D^{2.4}$). ταυτη [for τη αυ.] D^1(txt D^{10}) Scr's c. ins τας bef φυλακας D 131. 242. om της νυκτος Ξ.

account of each *at his own place of extraction.* Mary being apparently *herself sprung from the lineage of David* (see ch. i. 32), might on this account go to Bethlehem, being, as some suppose, an inheritress; but this does not seem to be the Evangelist's meaning, but that, after the Roman manner, she *accompanied her husband.* No stress must be laid on **ἐμνηστ.**, as if she were *only* the *betrothed* wife of Joseph at this time;—she had been taken to his house before this: the history in our text happening during the time indicated by Matt. i. 25.

7.] Now that **πρωτότοκον** has disappeared from the text of St. Matthew [i. 25], it must be here remarked, that although the term may undoubtedly be used of an only child, such use is necessarily always connected with the expectation of others to follow, and can no longer have place when the whole course of events is before the writer and no others *have followed.* The combination of this consideration with the fact that brethren of our Lord are brought forward in this Gospel in close connexion with His mother, makes it as certain as any implied fact can be, that those brethren were the children of Mary herself.

Ancient tradition states the birthplace of our Lord to have been a *cave:* thus Justin Martyr, Dial. 78, p. 175, ἐπειδὴ Ἰωσὴφ οὐκ εἶχεν ἐν τῇ κώμῃ ἐκείνῃ ποῦ καταλῦσαι, ἐν **σπηλαίῳ τινὶ** σύνεγγυς τῆς κώμης κατέλυσε· καὶ τότε, ὄντων αὐτῶν ἐκεῖ, ἐτετόκει ἡ Μαρία τὸν χριστόν, καὶ ἐν φάτνῃ αὐτὸν ἐτεθείκει. And Origen, against Celsus, i. 51, p. 367: ἀκολούθως τῇ ἐν τῷ εὐαγγελίῳ περὶ τῆς γενέσεως αὐτοῦ ἱστορίᾳ δείκνυται **τὸ ἐν Βηθλεὲμ σπήλαιον** ἔνθα ἐγεννήθη, καὶ ἡ ἐν τῷ σπηλαίῳ φάτνη ἔνθα ἐσπαργανώθη. Similarly Eusebius, Athanasius, and others. This tradition is nowise inconsistent with our text—for caves are used in most rocky countries as stables. Bleek has noticed that Justin Martyr refers to a prophecy in Isa. xxxiii. 16 (οὗτος οἰκήσει ἐν ὑψηλῷ σπηλαίῳ πέτρας ἰσχυρᾶς, LXX), and is disposed to think with Calov., al., that the tradition may have arisen from this. But is not the converse much more likely?

καταλύματι, a public inn, or place of reception for travellers; not '*a room* in a private house,' for then the expression would be, 'They found no κατάλυμα.' Of what sort this inn was, does not appear. It probably differs from πανδοχεῖον, ch. x. 34, in not being kept by an host, πανδοχεύς: see note there.

8.] Mr. Greswell has made it highly probable (Diss. x. vol. i.) that our Lord was born on the evening of (i. e. which *began*) the 5th of April, the 10th of the Jewish Nisan: on which same day of April, and the 14th of Nisan, He suffered thirty-three years after. Before this time there would be abundance of grass in the pastures—the spring rains being over: but much after it, and till after the autumnal equinox again, the pastures would be comparatively bare: see note on John vi. 10.

ἀγρ.] **spending the night in the open field.** **φυλ. φυλακὰς τ. ν.,**

u = ver. 40. ch. v. 27. xii. 14. Rev. vii. 15.
v Matt. xxvi. 31 reff.
w ch. xxiv. 4. Acts iv. 1. xii. 7. L. only, exc. 1 Thess. v. 3. 2 Tim. iv. 2, 6.
x = ch. ix. 31. Lev. ix. 6, 23. Num. xiv. 10. xvi. 42.
y Acts xxvi. 13 only †.
z Mark iv. 41. Jon. i. 10 al. constr., Matt. ii. 10 reff.
a ch. i. 19 reff.
b John xi. 50. xviii. 14.
c Matt. i. 21 reff.

[u] ἐπὶ τὴν [v] ποίμνην αὐτῶν. 9 καὶ [ἰδοὺ] ἄγγελος κυρίου
[w] ἐπέστη αὐτοῖς καὶ [x] δόξα κυρίου [y] περιέλαμψεν αὐτούς, P ἐπέ-στη...
καὶ [z] ἐφοβήθησαν [z] φόβον μέγαν. 10 καὶ εἶπεν αὐτοῖς ABDEF
ὁ ἄγγελος Μὴ φοβεῖσθε· ἰδοὺ γὰρ [a] εὐαγγελίζομαι ὑμῖν GHKL MPSUV
χαρὰν μεγάλην, ἥτις ἔσται παντὶ τῷ [b] λαῷ, 11 ὅτι [c] ἐτέχθη ΓΔΛΞΠ ℵ 1. 33. 69
ὑμῖν σήμερον σωτήρ, ὅς ἐστιν χριστὸς κύριος, ἐν [d] πόλει
[d] Δαυείδ. 12 καὶ τοῦτο ὑμῖν τὸ [e] σημεῖον· εὑρήσετε
[f] βρέφος [g] ἐσπαργανωμένον καὶ κείμενον ἐν [g] φάτνῃ.
13 καὶ [h] ἐξαίφνης ἐγένετο σὺν τῷ ἀγγέλῳ [i] πλῆθος
[kl] στρατιᾶς [m] οὐρανίου [ln] αἰνούντων τὸν θεὸν καὶ λεγόν- ...στρατιας F.
των 14 [o] Δόξα [op] ἐν ὑψίστοις θεῷ, καὶ ἐπὶ γῆς εἰρήνη, ἐν
ἀνθρώποις [q] εὐδοκίας. 15 καὶ ἐγένετο ὡς ἀπῆλθον ἀπ᾽

d ver. 4. e = 2 Cor. xii. 12. 2 Thess. iii. 17. 4 Kings xix. 19. f ch. i. 41, 44 reff.
g ver. 7 (reff.). h Mark xiii. 36 reff. i = ch. v. 6. John xxi. 6. Acts xxviii. 3. Ps. cxlvi. 4.
k Acts vii. 42 only. 3 Kings xxii. 19. l constr., ch. xix. 37. Rev. xix. 14. m Matt. v. 48 reff. fem., Acts xxvi. 19. so 1 Tim. ii. 9. Rev. iv. 3. Winer, § 11. 1. n ver. 20. ch. xix. 37. [xxiv. 53.] Acts ii. 47. iii. 8, 9. Luke only, exc. Rom. xv. 11, from Ps. cxvi. 1. Rev. xix. 5. o ch. xix. 38 (see Ps. lxx. 19).
p Matt. xxi. 9 reff. q Eph. i. 5, 9. Phil. i. 15. ii. 13. 2 Thess. i. 11. Ps. v. 12. l. 18 (20). lxviii. 13.

9. om *ιδου* BLΞℵ lat-*e* g_1 syr-jer sah goth æth arm Eus_1: ins AD rel latt syrr copt [$Chron_1$]. for 2nd *κυριου*, *θεου* Ξℵ[3a] vulg lat-*c e* syr-mg Eus_1: om D 209 lat-*b ff*$_2$ *l* ($Orig_1$). *επελαμψεν αυτοις* ℵ[1]. for *φοβον μεγαν*, *σφοδρα* B.

10. om *γαρ* P. *εστιν* ℵ[1]. aft *εσται* ins *και* D.

12. *ημιν* ℵ[1]. om *το* BΞ: ins ADPℵ rel Eus_1. aft *σημειον* ins *εστω* D. rec om *και* (bef *κειμενον*), with A rel lat-*a* copt-ms: ins BLPSΞ ℵ-corr[1] 1. 33 vulg lat-*b c f* $g_{1.2}$ *l* [*q*] syrr copt-2-mss goth æth arm Eus_1 [Orig-int_2].—om *κειμενον* also D ℵ[1](ins ℵ-corr[1]) 68. rec ins *τη* bef *φατνη*, with F[2] (K, e sil): om ABDPΞ[ℵ] rel goth Eus_1. (33 def.)

13. *ουρανου* B[1][txt B[2.3], Tischdf] D[1](txt D[2]). *αιτουντων* D[1][-gr](txt D[3]).

14. rec *ευδοκια*, with A(in the "Gloria in excelsis" insd at the end of the Psalms) B[2]PΞ ℵ-corr rel Psalt-Turic syrr copt æth arm $Orig_3$ $Thaum_1$ $Constt_1$ Eus_2 $Epiph_1$ Bas_1 Naz Chr_1 Cyr_1 [Thdot-$ancy_1$ $Procl_1$?] Thdrt Thl: txt AB[1]Dℵ[1] goth Cyr-jer_1 Iren-int_1 Orig-int_3 lat-ff, *bonæ voluntatis* latt, *consolationis* D-lat.

either, **keeping watch by night**, or, **keeping the watches of the night.** The former seems most probable: and so Meyer and Bleek: see ref. Xen., and add Alexis in Athen. xv. 58, p. 700—ὁ πρῶτος εὑρὼν μετὰ λυχνούχου περιπατεῖν Τῆς νυκτός, ἦν τις κηδεμὼν τῶν δακτύλων. **9.**] **δόξα—the brightness of God's presence**—the *Shechinah* (see reff.) which also accompanied His angels when they appeared to men. It is agreeable at least to the analogy of the divine dealings, to suppose with Olshausen, that these shepherds, like Symeon, were *waiting for the consolation of Israel.* **10, 11.**] **παντὶ τῷ λ.**, not (E. V.) to all people, here: but to all THE **people**,—the Jewish people. To them was the first message of joy, before the bursting in of the Gentiles—just as here the one angel gives the prefatory announcement, before the multitude of the heavenly host burst in with their proclamation of 'peace on earth.' **σωτήρ**] **a Saviour**, as E. V.,—the name being particularized afterwards. **χρ. κύρ.**] This is the only place where these words come together. In ch. xxiii. 2 we have χρ. βασιλέα, and in Acts ii. 36 κύριον καὶ χρ. (In Col. iii. 24 we have, in a somewhat different meaning (said to servants), τῷ κυρίῳ χριστῷ δουλεύετε.) And I see no way of understanding this **κύριος**, but as corresponding to the Hebrew JEHOVAH. **12.**] Olshausen hazards a conjecture that the stable or cave may possibly have *belonged to* these shepherds. But I think the words **ἕως Β.**, ver. 15, do not look as if Bethlehem were their *home*. It seems clear that *the spot* was somehow known to them by the angel's description. **βρέφος**—not '*the* child;'—the angel in giving the sign, generalizes the term—they were to know the truth of his words, by finding **a child** wrapped in swaddling clothes, lying in a manger. **14.**] The disputes about this short song of praise are (with one exception, see below) so much solemn trifling. As to whether ἐστιν or ἔστω should be supplied, the same question might be raised of every proclamation

αὐτῶν εἰς τὸν οὐρανὸν οἱ ἄγγελοι [ʳ καὶ οἱ ˢ ἄνθρωποι]
οἱ ποιμένες εἶπον πρὸς ἀλλήλους ᵗ Διέλθωμεν ᵘ δὴ ἕως
Βηθλεὲμ καὶ ἴδωμεν τὸ ᵛ ῥῆμα τοῦτο τὸ ʷ γεγονὸς ὃ ὁ
R [σαν]-τες και... κύριος ˣ ἐγνώρισεν ἡμῖν. 16 καὶ ἦλθαν ʸ σπεύσαντες καὶ
ᶻ ἀνεῦρον τήν τε Μαριὰμ καὶ τὸν Ἰωσήφ, καὶ τὸ ᵃ βρέφος
κείμενον ἐν τῇ ᵃ φάτνῃ. 17 ἰδόντες δὲ ˣ ἐγνώρισαν περὶ
τοῦ ᵛ ῥήματος τοῦ λαληθέντος αὐτοῖς περὶ τοῦ παιδίου
τούτου. 18 καὶ πάντες οἱ ἀκούσαντες ᵇ ἐθαύμασαν περὶ
X η δε... τῶν λαληθέντων ὑπὸ τῶν ποιμένων πρὸς αὐτούς. 19 ἡ δὲ
Μαρία πάντα ᶜ συνετήρει τὰ ῥήματα ταῦτα ᵈ συμβάλ-

r red., ver. 21 reff.
s red., Matt. xiii. 45. xviii. 23. xx. 1. Gen. ix. 20.
t ch. viii. 22 reff.
u = Acts xiii. 2. xv. 36. 1 Cor. vi. 20. Gen. xviii. 4.
v = ch. i. 65. vv. 19, 51. Gen. xv. 1.
w = ch. iii. 2 reff.
x Acts ii. 28, from Ps. xv. 11. Rom. xvi. 26. Ezek. xliv. 23.
y Luke only (ch. xix. 5, 6. Acts xx. 16. xxii. 18), exc. 2 Pet. iii. 12. 1 Kings iv. 14, 16.
z Acts xxi. 4 only †.
a ver. 12.
b w. περί, here only. see Mark xii. 17.
c Matt. ix. 17. Mark vi. 20 (|| L. v. r.) only. Ezek. xviii. 19.
d ch. xiv. 31. Acts iv. 15. xvii. 18. xviii. 20. xx. 14 only. L. 2 Chron. xxv. 19.

15. οι αγγ. bef απ' αυτ. D (æth); bef ε. τ. ουρ. 33. 69 vulg lat-*f* g_1 syrr arm Orig-int_1, *discessit ab illis angelus in cœlum* lat-*b c e* ff_2 *l q*. om και οι ανθρωποι BLΞℵ 1 latt(not *q*) Syr coptt arm Eus_1 Orig-int Aug_1: ins ADP rel syr goth æth. om οι (bef ποιμενες) ℵ¹(ins ℵ-corr¹). ειπαν LΞ: ελαλουν Bℵ 2-pe, *loquebantur ad invicem* vulg lat-*a b* &c(not *c e q*). aft αλληλους ins λεγοντες ℵ. aft εως ins εις P ev-y forj [lat-*q*]. ειδομεν P, ιδομεν M. γεγονως D¹(txt D² or ⁴).
16. rec ηλθον, with AB²DPℵ rel Eus: txt B¹LΞ. σπευδοντες D 61: πιστευσαντες Ξ. ανευραν B¹ ℵ-corr¹(appy): ευραν LΞℵ³ᵃ; ευρον D 1. 69 Eus_1: txt AB²ℵ¹ rel. om τε D latt syrr copt Eus_1.
17. om δε Ξ. rec διεγνωρισαν, with APR rel: txt BDLΞℵ Eus_1. om τουτου DΛ 1 lat-*a e f* Syr copt æth arm.
18. ακουοντες D Scr's c. εθαυμαζον D-gr 241. 2-pe.
19. (μαρια, so BDRℵ¹ copt-2-mss Eus.) συνετηρει bef παντα DX Scr's a latt syrr æth: txt ABPRℵ rel Eus. om ταυτα B 77 Scr's a.

which was ever uttered. *The sense of both these is included.* It is both **There is,** and **Let there be, glory,** &c. The song in the rec. is in *three clauses,* forming a Hebrew parallelism, in which the third clause is subordinate to and an amplification of the second, and so is without a copula to it. **εὐδοκία** (see reff.) is that *good pleasure of God in Christ* by which He reconciles the world to Himself in Him (2 Cor. v. 19). And this it is, whether **εὐδοκία** or **εὐδοκίας** be read. The interpretation of the latter reading by the vulg. and R.-Cath. interpreters generally, as "bonæ voluntatis," "peace on earth for those that like it," is untenable in Greek as well as in theology. The only passage which seems in any degree to justify it is Phil. i. 15, τινὲς . . . . δι' εὐδοκίαν τὸν χριστὸν κηρύσσουσιν, where however we have nothing like the harsh usage which must be assumed here, of the subjective gen. with the absolute sense of the noun. The only admissible rendering is, '*Among men of God's good pleasure,*' i. e. among the elect people of God: cf. for the gen. Acts ix. 15: Col. i. 13. And so Bleek renders: und auf Erden Friede unter den Menschen des Wohlgefallens, nämlich, des göttlichen Wohlgefallens. A curious connexion of εὐδοκίας with εἰρήνη is found in the passage of Origen-int. by which the gen. is supported:—"Pax enim quam non dat Dominus super terram non est pax bonæ voluntatis." This might perhaps be admissible as matter of mere construction, especially as St. Luke loves to separate genitives from their nouns in construction by an intervening word or words: but it would be difficult to justify it exegetically. As regards the reading, the evidence is materially affected by the fact that B reads **εὐδοκίας** *a prima manu,* as I have myself ascertained at Rome: and that ℵ reads the same. I have therefore now edited the genitive without any marks of doubt. 1862. **15.**] If the bracketed words be retained, it will be better to understand them as applying to **the shepherds** merely, than (with De Wette and Meyer) to suppose **οἱ ἄνθ.** to be used *as distinctive of the shepherds from the angels.* Such distinctions are not usual, whereas the redundant **ἄνθρ.** is: see reff. οἱ ποιμένες specifies what οἱ ἄνθρ. stated generally: **the men, viz. the shepherds.** **19.**] **συνετ.,** *in her memory.* **ῥήμ.** may have its literal

λουσα ἐν τῇ καρδίᾳ αὐτῆς. 20 καὶ [e] ὑπέστρεψαν οἱ ποιμένες δοξάζοντες καὶ [f] αἰνοῦντες τὸν θεὸν [g] ἐπὶ πᾶσιν [h] οἷς
ἤκουσαν καὶ εἶδον καθὼς ἐλαλήθη πρὸς αὐτούς.

21 Καὶ ὅτε [i] ἐπλήσθησαν ἡμέραι ὀκτὼ [k] τοῦ περιτεμεῖν
αὐτόν, [l] καὶ [m] ἐκλήθη τὸ [m] ὄνομα αὐτοῦ Ἰησοῦς, τὸ κληθὲν
ὑπὸ τοῦ ἀγγέλου πρὸ τοῦ [n] συλλημφθῆναι αὐτὸν ἐν τῇ
[o] κοιλίᾳ.

22 Καὶ ὅτε [i] ἐπλήσθησαν αἱ ἡμέραι τοῦ [p] καθαρισμοῦ
αὐτῶν κατὰ τὸν νόμον Μωσέως, [q] ἀνήγαγον αὐτὸν εἰς
Ἱεροσόλυμα [r] παραστῆσαι τῷ κυρίῳ, 23 καθὼς γέγραπται
ἐν νόμῳ κυρίου ὅτι πᾶν [s] ἄρσεν [t] διανοῖγον [u] μήτραν

...αυτης Ξ. ...αυτους P. Ξ και οτε ... ABDEG HKLM RSUVX ΓΔΛΞΠ ℵ 1. 33. 69 ...μωυσεως Ξ.

e vv. 39, 43, 45. ch. i. 56. viii. 37, 40 al. Gen. xiv. 17.
f ver. 13 reff.
g = ch. ix. 43. Acts iv. 21. 1 Cor. i. 4 al.
h attr., Matt. xxiv. 50. ch. iii. 19. ix. 43 al. Jer. xv. 14.
i ch. i. 57 reff.
k ch. ii. 6 al. fr.
l red., Matt. ix. 10. ch. vii. 12. Acts i. 10. x. 17.
m Matt. i. 21 reff.
n ch. i. 24 reff.
o ch. i. 15 reff.
p Mark i. 44 reff. 1 Chron. xxiii. 28.
q ch. iv. 5 al. Acts vii. 41 al. Luke only, exc. Matt. iv. 1. Rom. x. 7. Heb. xiii. 20. Gen. i. 24.
r = Rom. vi. 13. Ps. v. 3.
s Matt. xix. 4 reff.
t ch. xxiv. 31, 32 reff. Exod. xiii. 2.
u Rom. iv. 19 only. Num. iii. 12.

εαυτης R ℵ[1](or corr[1]) 33.

20. rec επεστρεψαν: txt ABDPRℵ rel Scr's-mss Thl.

21. for επλησθησαν, συνετελεσθησαν D: επληρωθησαν 33. ins αι bef ημ. D 33. 69 syr-mg Eus$_1$ [Amphil$_1$]. ins αι bef οκτω D syr-mg. rec (for 1st αυτον) το παιδιον (*see ver* 59), with DEGHMV em(with gat) lat-*e* g_2 Syr Eus: αυτο το παιδ. Γ: txt ABRΞℵ rel am(with fuld forj ing mt per) (æth) syr copt goth arm Orig-int$_1$. om 2nd και D 69 latt(not *e q*) copt-2-mss [Orig-int$_1$]. for εκληθη, ωνομασθη *nominatum est* D. for κληθεν, λεχθεν ℵ[1]. αυτην ℵ[1](txt ℵ corr[1·3a]). for τη κοιλια, κοιλια μητρος D.

22. επληρωθησαν ℵ[3a] [Cyr-jer$_1$]. om του B[1]. elz αυτης, with 76 [Ps-Ath]: om 435 evv-H-P-X-y-z copt-2-mss Amphil$_1$ Iren-int$_1$: αυτου D 254 latt arm-usc [Chron$_1$]: txt ABRℵ rel lat-*q* syrr copt-schw sah[-mnt] goth arm-zoh æth [Cyr-jer$_1$] Cyr$_{expr}$ Orig-int$_{expr}$. παραστησεται ℵ[1]. om τω D.

23. ins τω bef νομω D F(Wetst) [Cyr-jer$_1$]. διανοιγων ℵ[1] Scr's e i w evv-P-y.

sense, **words**: viz. those spoken by the shepherds:—or its Hebraistic, as above, ver. 15, which is more probable—**all these things now spoken of.** **συμβ.**, **revolving them**—comparing one with another.

21.] His circumcision. The second **καί** must not be rendered '*also.*' It is simply redundant, as in reff. The Lord was made like unto His brethren (Heb. ii. 17; iv. 15) in all weakness and bodily infirmity, from which legal uncleanness arose. The body which He took on Him, though not a body of sin, was mortal, subject to the consequence of sin,—in the likeness of sinful flesh: but incorruptible by the indwelling of the Godhead (1 Pet. iii. 18). In the fulfilment therefore of His great work of redemption He became subject to legal rites and purifications—not that they were absolutely *necessary* for *Him*, but were included in those things which were πρέποντα for Him in His humiliation and 'making perfect:' and in His lifting up of that human nature, *for which* all these things were *absolutely necessary* (Gen. xvii. 14), into the Godhead.

22—38.] The purification in the Temple. Symeon and Anna recognize and prophesy of Him. **22.**] See Levit. xii. 1—8, where however *the child* is not, as here, expressly included in the purification. (It is hardly possible that *Joseph* should be implied in the **αὐτῶν**, as Euthym., Meyer, interpret it.) The reading αὐτοῦ is remarkable, and hardly likely to have been a correction. αὐτῆς, adopted by the E. V., is almost without authority (see var. readd.), and is a manifest correction. Bengel denies that either the Lord or His mother wanted purification; and mentions that some render αὐτῶν '*of the Jews,*' but does not approve of it (John ii. 6 is certainly no case in point). See the last note, on the necessity of purification for *both.* **23.**] God had taken *the tribe of Levi instead of the first-born that openeth the womb*, Num. iii. 12, and required only the excess in number of the first-born over the Levites to be redeemed (ib. vv. 44—51). This arrangement appears afterwards to have been superseded by a general command to redeem *all the first-born* at five shekels of the sanctuary (Num. xviii. 15, 16).

ἅγιον τῷ κυρίῳ κληθήσεται, 24 καὶ [v] τοῦ δοῦναι θυσίαν
κατὰ τὸ [w] εἰρημένον ἐν νόμῳ κυρίου, [x] ζεῦγος [y] τρυγόνων
ἢ δύο [z] νοσσοὺς [a] περιστερῶν. 25 Καὶ ἰδοὺ ἦν ἄνθρωπος
ἐν Ἱερουσαλὴμ ᾧ ὄνομα Συμεών, καὶ ὁ ἄνθρωπος οὗτος
δίκαιος καὶ [b] εὐλαβής, [c] προσδεχόμενος [d] παράκλησιν τοῦ
Ἰσραήλ. καὶ πνεῦμα ἦν ἅγιον [e] ἐπ' αὐτόν, 26 καὶ ἦν
αὐτῷ [f] κεχρηματισμένον ὑπὸ τοῦ πνεύματος τοῦ ἁγίου μὴ
[gh] ἰδεῖν [g] θάνατον [i] πρὶν ἢ [i] ἴδῃ τὸν [j] χριστὸν [j] κυρίου.
27 καὶ ἦλθεν [k] ἐν τῷ πνεύματι εἰς τὸ ἱερόν, καὶ [l] ἐν τῷ
εἰσαγαγεῖν τοὺς γονεῖς τὸ παιδίον Ἰησοῦν, [m] τοῦ ποιῆσαι
αὐτοὺς κατὰ τὸ [n] εἰθισμένον τοῦ νόμου [o] περὶ αὐτοῦ,
28 [p] καὶ αὐτὸς [q] ἐδέξατο αὐτὸ εἰς τὰς [r] ἀγκάλας [αὐτοῦ], καὶ
εὐλόγησεν τὸν θεὸν καὶ εἶπεν 29 Νῦν [s] ἀπολύεις τὸν δοῦλόν σου, [t] δέσποτα, κατὰ τὸ ῥῆμά σου [u] ἐν εἰρήνῃ, 30 ὅτι

...του ποι- [ησαι] R.

The Bodleian and Zurich Psalters and Cod. Sang. 17 contain vv. 29—32.

v ch. i. 74 al. w = ch. iv. 12. Acts xiii. 40 al. x ch. xiv. 19 only. Lev. v. 11. y here only. Gen. xv. 9. Levit. xii. 6, 8. z here only. Prov. xxx. 17. (-σία, ch. xiii. 34.) a Matt. iii. 16 reff. b Acts ii. 5. viii. 2. xxii. 12 only. L. Lev. xv. 31. Mic. vii. 2 AB2 only. (-βῶς, 2 Macc. vi. 11. -βεια, Heb. v. 7. -βεῖσθαι, Heb. xi. 7.) c Mark xv. 43 reff. d = 2 Cor. i. 3, &c. (Heb. vi. 18 al. L.P.H.) Nah. iii. 7. e = ver. 40. John i. 32, 33. 2 Chron. xv. 1. f = Matt. ii. 12 reff. g Heb. xi. 5. see John viii. 51. Ps. lxxxviii. 48. h = Acts ii. 27, from Ps. xv. 10. i constr., here only. see Acts xxv. 16. j Psa. ii. 2. k Matt. xxii. 43. ch. iv. 1. Col. i. 8. l Matt. xiii. 4, 25. ch. i. 8 al. fr. m ch. i. 74 al. n here only †. Sir. xxiii. 9 only. (-ισμός, 3 Kings xviii. 28.) o ch. xix. 37. John x. 33. Acts xv. 2. p red., ver. 21 reff. q ch. xvi. 6. xxii. 17. r here only. 3 Kings iii. 20. Prov. v. 20 only. s Matt. xiv. 15 al. Num. xx. 29. Tobit iii. 13. t of God, Acts iv. 24. 2 Pet. ii. 1. Jude 4. Rev. vi. 10 only. 2 Macc. xv. 22. u Acts xvi. 36. 1 Cor. vii. 15. xvi. 11 al. 2 Kings iii. 21, 23.

om τω (bef κυριω) D.

24. ins τω bef νομω BDLℵ : om AR rel Coisl-oct-marg [Ps-Ath$_1$]. rec νεοσσους, with ADR rel [Ps-]Ath$_1$: txt BEGHSVΛℵ Coisl-oct-marg.

25. om ιδου D Syr goth æth. ανθρωπος bef ην Bℵ vulg lat-*b f l* : om ην F(Wetst) 1. aft ονομα ins αυτου ℵ[1]. (B has συμεων as Mai, not σιμ. as Btly. See table at end of prolegomena.) ευσεβης KΓℵ[1] syr-mg(appy) arm. rec αγιον bef ην, with D Scr's v (b f, e sil) (latt syrr) goth arm Cyr-jer$_1$ [Did$_1$]: om ην 1 æth : txt ABRℵ rel.

26. κεχρηματισμενος δε ην D lat-*b c ff$_2$ g$_1$* [*l q*]. for πριν η, πριν 69 Scr's c : πριν αν B F(Wetst) : πριν η αν RX 33 : πριν ηνα L : εως αν ℵ[1] 259 [Did$_1$].

27. εισαγειν A 69(Scr) Scr's d ev-z [Ps-Ath$_1$]. om ιησουν ℵ[1]. for ειθισμενον, εθος D, *consuetudinem* vulg.

28. aft αυτος ins δε ℵ[1](om ℵ-corr[1]). om αυτου BLℵ lat-*a b l* Iren-gr$_1$ [Orig$_1$] Cyr-jer$_1$ Did$_1$. ηυλογησεν DΓ Cyr-jer$_1$.

29. απολλυεις ℵ[1].

24.] The offering (ref. Levit.) was, *a lamb for a burnt-offering, and a pigeon for a sin-offering*: but if the parties were too poor to bring a lamb, then *two pigeons*. But as Bleek remarks, we are not hereby justified in assuming *extreme poverty* to have been the condition of our Lord's family. This no where appears from the gospel history. **25.**] It appears that this Symeon might have been Symeon the son of Hillel,—and father of Gamaliel, mentioned in Acts v. 34 ff. But we have no means of ascertaining this. It is no objection to it that he is here merely ἄνθρωπος, seeing that Gamaliel himself is only φαρισαῖός τις in Acts v. 34. **παράκλ.**] See Acts xxviii. 20. It was a common form of adjuration among the Jews, 'Ita videam consolationem, si' &c., referring to Isa. xl. 1. On the general expectation of deliverance at this time, see on Matt. ii. 1 ff. **26.**] Of the nature of this intimation, nothing is said. Symeon was the subject of an especial indwelling and leading of the Holy Ghost, analogous to that higher form of the spiritual life expressed in the earliest days by *walking with God*—and according to which God's saints have often been directed and informed in an extraordinary manner by His Holy Spirit. In the power of this intimation, and in the spirit of prophecy consequent on it, he came into the Temple on this occasion. **28.**] **καί** here again is not *also*, but simply the introduction to the apodosis. **29.**] **ἀπολύεις**, not τοῦ ζῆν, or ἐκ τῆς γῆς,—but as being τὸν δοῦλόν σου, he thinks of his death as the termination of, and so dismissal from, *his servitude*. Meyer. Bleek thinks that there is no such allusion, but that the word is used absolutely, as in Gen. xv. 2: Num.

v ch. iii. 6. Acts xxviii. 28. Eph. vi. 17 (Tit. ii. 11) only. Ps. xcvii. 2. cxviii. 166. Isa. lx. 6.
w = Matt. xx 23 reff.
x Acts iii. 3. xxv. 16. 2 Cor. x. 1. 2 Chron. xiii. 7, 8.
y = Acts xiii. 47, from Isa. xlix. 6. 1 Kings xv. 11.
z = subj., here only ‡. (Rom. ii. 5 al.)
a constr., ch. iv.

εἶδον οἱ ὀφθαλμοί μου τὸ [v] σωτήριόν σου 31 ὃ [w] ἡτοίμασας
[x] κατὰ πρόσωπον πάντων τῶν λαῶν· 32 φῶς [y] εἰς [z] ἀποκάλυψιν ἐθνῶν καὶ δόξαν λαοῦ σου Ἰσραήλ. 33 καὶ [a] ἦν
ὁ πατὴρ αὐτοῦ καὶ ἡ μήτηρ [ab] θαυμάζοντες [b] ἐπὶ τοῖς
λαλουμένοις περὶ αὐτοῦ. 34 καὶ εὐλόγησεν αὐτοὺς Συμεών, καὶ εἶπεν πρὸς Μαριὰμ τὴν μητέρα αὐτοῦ Ἰδοὺ
οὗτος [c] κεῖται [c] εἰς [d] πτῶσιν καὶ [e] ἀνάστασιν πολλῶν ἐν τῷ
Ἰσραήλ, καὶ [c] εἰς [f] σημεῖον [g] ἀντιλεγόμενον· 35 [h] καὶ σοῦ
[h] δὲ αὐτῆς τὴν ψυχὴν [i] διελεύσεται [j] ῥομφαία· [k] ὅπως [k] ἂν
[l] ἀποκαλυφθῶσιν [m] ἐκ πολλῶν καρδιῶν [n] διαλογισμοί.

Ξ θαυμαζοντες ... ABDEG HKLM SUVXΓ ΔΛΞΠℵ 1. 33. 69.

31, 44. Mark xiv. 54 al. Ezra iv. 4, 24. b Mark xii. 17 reff. Lev. xxvi. 32. c Phil. i. 16 (17). 1 Thess. iii. 3. d Matt. vii. 27 only. Isa xvii. 1. li. 17. e = here only. (Matt. xxii. 23, &c. reff.) Lam. iii. 63. Zeph. iii. 8. f = ch. xi. 30. Josh. iv. 6. g Acts xiii. 45. xxviii. 19, 22. Rom. x. 21 al. L.P., exc. John xix. 12. Hos. iv. 4. h Matt. x. 18. ch. i. 76. 2 Macc. v. 15 Ed-vat.(not AB). i Mark x. 25. see Job xx. 25. j Rev. i. 16. ii. 12, 16. vi. 8. xix. 15, 21 only. Ps. xxi. 20. k Acts iii. 19. xv. 17 (from Amos ix. 12 A). Rom. iii. 4 (from Ps. l. 4 [6]) only. l Matt. xi. 25, 27 al. Exod. xx. 26. m = ch. xvii. 24. n Matt. xv. 19. ch. v. 22. Rom. i. 21. Ps. cxxxviii 20.

31. **παντος του λαου** Psalt-Turic. **32.** om εθνων D.

33. rec (for ο πατηρ αυτου) ιωσηφ, with A(ο ιωσ.) Δ rel lat-*a b c e f ff*$_2$ *g*$_1$ *l q* Syr goth Phot Thl Hil : txt BDLℵ 1 vulg lat-*g*$_2$ syr-ms-mg coptt [æth] arm Orig-int(*quæ igitur causa exstitit ut eum qui pater non fuit patrem esse memoraret?*) Cyr-jer Jer-agst-Helvid Aug$_1$. (*Mey contends, that if* ιωσηφ *had been substd for* ο πατ. αυτου *here, it would have been also in ver* 48. *But this has no force: for the words in ver* 48 *are spoken by Mary, who could not with any propriety be made to say* ιωσηφ. *No prob reason can be assigned for* ο πατηρ αυτου *being substd for* ιωσηφ, *whereas the converse corrn was certain to be made.*) rec aft μητηρ ins αυτου (*in conformity with the above substn*), with Aℵ[1] rel lat-*a b c e f ff*$_2$ *g*$_1$ *l* [*q*] syrr coptt goth [æth] arm Cyr-jer Hil$_1$: om B(sic : see table) D ℵ-corr[1] 1. 33 vulg lat-*g*$_2$ Orig-int$_3$ [Aug$_1$].

34. ins εις bef αναστασιν D vulg-ed (not am fuld &c) [lat-*c ff*$_2$ *g*$_1$ *l*] Orig-int$_2$. om 2nd εις ℵ[1].

35. om δε BLΞ vulg lat-*b f ff*$_2$ *g*$_{1.2}$ *l* [*q*] copt æth arm Orig[-int$_3$] : ins ADℵ rel lat-*a* (*c*) *e* syrr [goth] Orig$_1$ [Bas$_2$ Amphil$_1$ Cyr$_1$ Ps-Ath$_1$ Chron$_1$]. om αν DΞ. **ανακαλυφθωσιν** D. om εκ D gat lat-*a b c ff*$_2$ *g*$_{1.2}$ Syr æth arm-mss Hil Ambr Paulin Aug$_1$. at end ins πονηροι ℵ[1].

xx. 29. **32.**] See Isa. xlix. 6. The general term of the last verse (πάντ. τ. λαῶν) is here divided into two, the Gentiles, and Israel. It is doubtful, whether **δόξαν** is to be taken as co-ordinate with φῶς (so Bengel, Meyer, De W., al.), or with ἀποκάλυψιν. The former seems more probable; and so E. V. **33. ὁ πατ. αὐτοῦ**] In ver. 48 we have Joseph again called by this name. *Our Lord Himself would not speak of him thus*, see ver. 49; but in the simplicity of the narrative we may read οἱ γονεῖς αὐτοῦ and such expressions, without any danger of forgetting the momentous history of the Conception and Nativity.

34.] **κεῖται εἰς, is appointed for**—see reff.: not (Meyer) '*lies here, in my arms.*' **πτῶσιν,** as a stone of stumbling and rock of offence (Isa. viii. 14: Rom. ix. 33), at which they should fall through unbelief. **ἀνάστ., rising up**—in the sense of ch. i. 52—*by faith and holiness;* or, the **πτῶσις** and **ἀνάστ.** may refer to *the same persons;* as it is said by our Lord, 'He that humbleth himself shall be exalted.' I prefer this last interpretation, as cohering best with the next verse: see note on it. **35.**] This prophecy I do not believe to have its chief reference to the *deep sorrows* of the mother of our Lord *on beholding His sufferings* (Euthym., al.), much less to her *future death by martyrdom* (Epiphan., Lightf.); least of all to the Crucifixion, which by shedding the blood of her Son, would also pierce her heart and drain it of its life-blood and make it childless, as Bp. Wordsw. referring to Bede, Aug., who however (cf. Aug. Ep. ad Paulinum cxlix. 33, vol. ii., and Bede, in Luc. Expos. i. vol. iii. p. 346; Homil. lib. i. 15, vol. v. p. 81) say nothing of the kind, but simply refer the saying to her grief at beholding the Passion: and to Origen, who (in Luc. Hom. xvii. vol. iii. p. 952) gives a totally different interpretation, "pertransibit infidelitatis gladius, et ambiguitatis mucrone ferieris, et cogitationes tuæ te in diversa lacerabunt, cum videris illum quem Filium Dei

36 Καὶ ἦν Ἄννα [o] προφῆτις, θυγάτηρ Φανουήλ, ἐκ
φυλῆς Ἀσήρ, αὕτη [p] προβεβηκυῖα ἐν ἡμέραις πολλαῖς,
ζήσασα ἔτη μετὰ ἀνδρὸς ἑπτὰ ἀπὸ τῆς [q] παρθενείας αὐτῆς,
37 καὶ αὐτὴ χήρα ἕως [r] ἐτῶν ὀγδοηκοντατεσσάρων, ἣ
οὐκ [s] ἀφίστατο τοῦ ἱεροῦ, [t] νηστείαις καὶ [u] δεήσεσιν
[v] λατρεύουσα [w] νύκτα καὶ [w] ἡμέραν. 38 καὶ αὐτῇ τῇ ὥρᾳ
[x] ἐπιστᾶσα [y] ἀνθωμολογεῖτο τῷ θεῷ καὶ ἐλάλει περὶ
αὐτοῦ πᾶσιν τοῖς [z] προσδεχομένοις [a] λύτρωσιν [ἐν] Ἱερουσαλήμ.
39 Καὶ ὡς ἐτέλεσαν ἅπαντα τὰ κατὰ τὸν νόμον κυρίου,

o Rev. ii. 20 only. 4 Kings xxii. 14. p ch. i. 7 reff. q here only. Jer. iii. 4. r Mark v. 42 reff. s = ch. iv. 13. Acts xii. 10. xix. 9 al. Num. xvi. 27. constr., 1 Tim. iv. 1 only. t (Matt. xvii. 21 | Mk.) Acts xiv. 23. xxvii. 9. (1 Cor. vii. 5 v. r.) 2 Cor. vi. 5. xi. 27 only. 2 Kings xii. 16. Dan. ix. 3. Tobit xii. 8 (not ℵ). u ch. i. 13. v. 33 al. fr. Ps. xvi. 1 al. v abs., Acts xxvi. 7. Heb. ix. 9. x. 2. w Matt. iv. 27 reff. x = (Luke only.) ch. x. 40 al. Acts xxii. 13 al. (elsw., 1 Thess. v. 3. 2 Tim. iv. 2, 6 only.) y here only. Ps. lxxviii. 13. Esdr. viii. 91 (88). Sir. xx. 2 only. z ver. 25. a ch. i. 68 (reff.). Heb. ix. 12 only.

36. om ην D lat-*b* Syr. ins και bef αυτη D ℵ[3a](but erased) 254 (Syr). for ζησασα, χηρευσασα (appy) ℵ[1](corrd to txt eadem manu or by ℵ-corr[1]). ετη επτα μετα ανδρος ADK[Π] lat-*ff*$_2$ Syr Iren-gr: μετα ανδρος ετη επτα B[1]GLXΔΞℵ 33. 69 vulg lat-*a e f g*$_{1.2}$ [*q*] syr copt goth [æth Amphil$_1$ Ps-Ath$_1$] Ambr$_1$: (*both rearrangemts for perspicuity: it is characteristic of Luke to insert clauses between words in concord*:) txt E rel lat-*b c* [*l*] arm.—μετα του ανδρος αυτης ετη επτα B[2](sic: see table at end of prolegomena). rec παρθενιας, with ℵ rel: txt ABDEMXΔΞ.

37. rec αὕτη, with G[Π] (Scr's e f h l n o r w evv-x-y, e sil): txt EHKMUΓΛ. rec (for εως) ως, with X ℵ-corr rel syrr arm [Ps-Ath$_1$]: om D lat-*a b c e l q* goth æth Ambr$_1$: txt ABLΞℵ[1] 33 vulg lat-*f ff*$_2$ *g*$_{1.2}$ Δ-lat coptt Aug$_1$. for ογδ., εβδομηκοντατεσσαρων ℵ[1]. rec aft αφιστατο ins απο, with A rel latt goth [Amphil$_1$ Ps-Ath$_1$]: εκ ℵ[1]: om B D-gr F(Wetst) LΞ ℵ-corr(but εκ replaced) copt Constt$_1$. for ιερου, ναου D. νηστιας ℵ[1](txt ℵ-corr[1](appy)[3]). δεησιν (appy) ℵ[1](txt ℵ-corr[1]). ημερα AΓ.

38. rec και αὕτη αὐτῇ (*arising prob from* αυτη *without accents being taken for the nom, and then* αὐτῇ *being insd to complete the sense*), with E rel latt syrr goth arm [Amphil$_1$ Ps-Ath$_1$]: txt A B(sic in cod) DLXΔΞ[Π[1]]ℵ 33 copt æth Thl. rec (for θεω) κυριω, with A rel vulg lat-*b c e f ff*$_2$ syrr goth æth arm [Constt$_1$ Amphil$_1$ Ps-Ath$_1$]: txt BDLX[1]Ξℵ lat-*a* syr-mg copt. om εν BΞℵ 1 am(with em forj fuld ing mt tol) lat-*a b c e f ff*$_2$ *g*$_2$ *l q* Syr coptt goth æth arm Iren-int$_1$ Aug$_1$: ins AD rel gat syr [Amphil$_1$ Ps-Ath$_1$].

39. ετελεσεν [H]ℵ[1]. παντα B F(Wetst) LXΞℵ: txt AD rel. om τα

audieras . . . crucifigi &c." None of these interpretations satisfy us: for the words stand in a totally different connexion, and one far worthier of the honour of that holy woman, and of the spiritual character of Symeon's prophecy: that prophecy is, of the struggle of many in Israel through repentance to faith in this Saviour; among which number even *His mother herself was to be included.* The sharp pangs of sorrow for sin must pierce her heart *also* (cf. esp. Acts ii. 37); and the general end follows; *that the reasonings out of many hearts may be revealed;* that they who receive the Lord Jesus may be manifest, and they who reject Him: see John ix. 39. Similarly Bleek: finding moreover in the traces of her connexion with our Lord in the Evangelic history the piercing and dividing of her soul, and in the last notice of her in Acts i., the triumph of her faith after the Ascension.

37. νηστ. καὶ δεήσ.] Not merely in the ordinary hours of prayer, at nine, and three, or the ordinary fasts on Monday and Thursday, but in an ascetic-devotional method of life. **νύκτα** is put first, because fasts were reckoned from one evening to another. Meyer. Is it not rather because the greater solemnity and emphasis rests on the religious exercise by night?

38.] The **ἀνθωμολ.** has been understood (by Erasm., Calv., Calov., al.) to refer to *Symeon's also* having praised God: but Winer, Meyer, and Bleek more accurately regard the prep. as pointing to the retributive nature of the offering of praise. It was possibly at the hour of prayer; as she spoke of Him to numbers, who would at such a time be flocking to the temple.

39, 40.] Return to Nazareth.

39.] Certainly the obvious inference from this verse is, that Joseph and Mary re-

b ver. 20 reff.
c Mark iv. 8 reff.
d 1 Cor. xvi. 13. ch. i. 80. Eph. iii. 16 only. Ps. xxx. 24.
e Acts ii. 28 (from Ps. xv. 11). xiii. 52. Rom. xv. 13, 14. 2 Tim. i. 4. constr., Rom. i. 29. 2 Cor. vii. 4 only. 2 Macc. vii. 21.
f = ver. 52. ch. i. 30. Acts vii. 46. Eph. i. 6. Prov. iii. 4.
g here only.
h Mark v. 42 reff.
i = Matt. xx. 17, 18 reff. 1 Kings ii. 19. Zech. xiv. 16.
k ch. i. 9 reff.

[b] ὑπέστρεψαν εἰς τὴν Γαλιλαίαν εἰς πόλιν ἑαυτῶν Ναζα- ...ναζαρεθ Ξ.
ρέθ. 40 τὸ δὲ παιδίον [c] ηὔξανεν καὶ [d] ἐκραταιοῦτο [e] πλη- ABDEG HKLM SUVXΓ ΔΛΠℵ 1. 33. 69
ρούμενον σοφίᾳ, καὶ [f] χάρις θεοῦ ἦν ἐπ᾽ αὐτό.
41 Καὶ ἐπορεύοντο οἱ γονεῖς αὐτοῦ [g] κατ᾽ [g] ἔτος εἰς
Ἱερουσαλὴμ τῇ ἑορτῇ τοῦ πάσχα. 42 καὶ ὅτε ἐγένετο
[h] ἐτῶν δώδεκα, [i] ἀναβαινόντων αὐτῶν [k] κατὰ τὸ [k] ἔθος τῆς C λυμα κατα...

DLΔ[Π¹]ℵ 1. 69 arm. επεστρεψαν BΞ : επεστρεψεν ℵ¹ : txt ADℵ³ᵃ rel. om την ℵ¹. rec ins την bef πολιν, with AD²Ξℵ³ᵃ rel : om BD¹ℵ¹ 1. rec αυτων, with D³HΛ : txt ABD [S(Tischdf)] Γ(Treg, expr) Ξℵ rel. at end add καθως ερεθη δια του προφητου οτι ναζωραιος κληθησεται D lat-*a*.

40. aft παιδιον add ιησους D [Cæs$_1$]. transp εκραταιουτο and ηυξ. D lat-*b c e*.—ηυξανετο D¹. rec aft εκραταιουτο adds πνευματι (*from ch* i. 80), with A rel lat-*f q* syrr goth æth [Cæs$_1$] : om BDLℵ latt [syr-jer] coptt arm Cyr$_1$ Orig-int$_2$. rec σοφιας (*more usual, cf Acts* ii. 28 ; v. 28 al), with AD ℵ¹(but *s* erased) rel Cyr$_1$: txt BL 33. εν αυτω D vulg [lat-*f ff*$_2$ *g*$_{1.2}$] Aug$_1$: επ αυτω KUX 69 evv-x-y-z : επ αυτον M.

41. for και επορ., επορευοντο δε και D. κατα D. εθος ℵ¹(txt ℵ-corr¹). ins εν bef τη εορτη D latt(not *a*).

42. for ετων, αυτω ετη DL lat-*a b l q* arm Ambr$_1$: txt ABℵ rel vulg lat-*c e f ff*$_2$ *g*$_1$ Orig-int$_1$ [Aug$_1$]. ins και bef αναβ. ℵ¹. rec αναβαντων (*corrn to sense, and to* τελειωσ. *below*), with Δ rel : txt ABKLX[Π]ℵ 33 vulg lat-*f q*.—ανεβησαν οι γονεις αυτου εχοντες αυτον D [lat-*e*]. rec adds εις ιεροσολυμα (*explany gloss, carelessly insd without observing that* -σαλημ *and not* -σολυμα *is the form here used*), with AC rel latt syr goth æth arm : om BDLℵ Syr coptt.

turned from Jerusalem to Nazareth direct. But it is only an *inference,* and not the assertion of the text. This part of the gospel history is one where the Harmonists, by their arbitrary reconcilements of the two Evangelistic accounts, have given great advantage to the enemies of the faith. *As the two accounts now stand,* it is wholly impossible to suggest any satisfactory method of *uniting them;* every one who has attempted it has, in some part or other of his hypothesis, violated probability and common sense. But, on the other hand, it is equally impossible definitely to say that they *could not* be reconciled by *a thorough knowledge of the facts themselves;* and such an assertion, whenever made, shews great ignorance of the origin and course of oral narration. How many things will a relator say, being unaware of certain important circumstances outside his narrative, which *seem to preclude* those circumstances? How often will points of time be apparently brought close together in such a narration,—between which, events most weighty to the history have occurred? The *only* inference from these two accounts, which *is inevitable,* is, that they are *wholly independent* of one another. If Luke had seen the Gospel of Matthew, or vice versa, then the variations are *utterly inexplicable;* and the greatest absurdities of all are involved in the writings of those who *assume this,* and *then proceed to harmonize.* Of the dwelling at Nazareth before the Nativity, of the circumstances which brought Joseph and Mary to Bethlehem, of the Presentation in the temple, Matthew's account knows nothing; of the visit of the Magi, the murder of the Innocents, the flight to Egypt, Luke's is unaware. In all the main circumstances of the Conception and Nativity *they agree, or are easily and naturally reconciled* (see further in note on John vii. 42).

40.] ηὔξανεν—*in body.* **ἐκρ.,** *in spirit:* πνεύματι is a correct gloss. "The body advances in stature, and the soul in wisdom . . . the divine nature revealed its own wisdom in proportion to the measure of the bodily growth." Cyril. Oxf. transl. p. 30. **πληρ., becoming filled:** see ver. 52 and note there.

41—52.] Visit to the Temple at the Passover. The history of this incident serves for an example of the wisdom wherewith the Child was filled. Bleek. "The Evang. next shews that what he has said is true." Cyril. ib.

41.] See Exod. xxiii. 14—17. *Women,* according to the maxims of the school of Hillel, were bound to go up once in the year—to the Passover. **τῇ ἑορτῇ] at, or in the feast;** not '*to* the feast;' nor, '*on account of* the feast.' **42.]**

ἑορτῆς, 43 καὶ [l] τελειωσάντων τὰς ἡμέρας, ἐν τῷ [b] ὑποστρέφειν αὐτοὺς [m] ὑπέμεινεν [Ἰησοῦς] [n] ὁ παῖς ἐν Ἱερουσαλήμ, καὶ οὐκ ἔγνωσαν οἱ γονεῖς αὐτοῦ. 44 [o] νομίσαντες
δὲ αὐτὸν εἶναι ἐν τῇ [p] συνοδίᾳ ἦλθον ἡμέρας [q] ὁδόν, καὶ
[r] ἀνεζήτουν αὐτὸν ἐν τοῖς [s] συγγενέσιν καὶ τοῖς [t] γνωστοῖς·
45 καὶ μὴ εὑρόντες [b] ὑπέστρεψαν εἰς Ἱερουσαλὴμ [r] ἀναζητοῦντες αὐτόν. 46 καὶ [u] ἐγένετο μετὰ ἡμέρας τρεῖς εὗρον
αὐτὸν ἐν τῷ ἱερῷ [v] καθεζόμενον ἐν μέσῳ τῶν [w] διδασκάλων,
καὶ ἀκούοντα αὐτῶν καὶ [x] ἐπερωτῶντα αὐτούς. 47 [y] ἐξίσταντο δὲ πάντες οἱ ἀκούοντες αὐτοῦ [z] ἐπὶ τῇ [a] συνέσει
καὶ ταῖς [b] ἀποκρίσεσιν αὐτοῦ. 48 καὶ ἰδόντες αὐτὸν [c] ἐξ-

l = Acts xx. 24. m = Acts xvii. 14 only. (Matt. x. 22 al.) Num. xxii. 19. Jos. Antt. vi. 5. 2. n 1 Kings iii. 1. 1 Macc. v. 63. o Matt. x. 34 reff. p here only. Neh. vii. 5 bis, 64 only. q = Acts i. 12. Exod. iii. 18. r here (bis) and Acts xi. 25 only. Job iii. 4. x. 6. 2 Macc. xiii. 21 only. s Mark vi. 4 reff. t = ch. xxiii. 49 (Acts i. 19 al.) L. only, exc. John xviii. 15, 16. (Rom. i. 19.) Ps. lxxxvii. 8. u vv. 1, 6. Gen. iv. 3. v Matt. xxvi. 55 reff. w = John iii. 10. Rom. ii. 20 +. (2 Macc. i. 10 only.) x ch. iii. 10, 14. Matt. xii. 10. 1 Cor. xiv. 35. y = Matt. xii. 23 reff. ch. viii. 56. Exod. xix. 18. z Mark i. 22 reff. Jer. ii. 12. a Mark xii. 33 reff. Deut. iv. 6. b ch. xx. 26. John i. 22. xix. 9 only. Job xxxv. 3. c Matt. vii. 28 reff.

aft της εορτης ins των αζυμων DX lat-*a c e*.

43. τελεσαντων D 6-pe. απεμεινεν DX 1. 33 Cyr$_1$. om ιησους ℵ^1[V] : ο παις bef ιησ. D [vulg] lat-*c f* [*ff*$_2$ *g*$_1$ *l*] copt æth [Aug$_1$]. rec (for εγνωσαν οι γονεις) εγνω ιωσηφ κ. η μητηρ (*prob to avoid repetn of* οι γ. αυτ. *aft ver* 41 : *hardly for theological reasons, for* οι γ. αυτ. *in ver* 41 *is altered in some old lat mss only*), with AC(Δ) rel lat-*b c f g*$_1$ [*ff*$_2$ *l q*] syrr goth æth : txt BDLℵ 1. 33 vulg lat-*a e* syr-mg syr-jer coptt arm [Aug$_1$].—(εγνωσαν Δ ev-48 lat-*f ff*$_2$ *g*$_1$ goth.)

44. for νομ. δε, και νομ. D. rec εν τη συνοδια bef ειναι, with AC rel syr (goth) : txt BDLℵ 1. 33 latt (copt æth). οδον bef ημερας D latt syrr. συγγενευσιν B^1(Tischdf [N. T. Vat.], expr) LXΔΛ 1. 33. 69. rec ins εν bef τοις γνωστοις, with C^{3}D rel lat-*f* arm : om ABC^{1}KL^{2}MSℵ^{3a} 33. 69 (latt).—om και τ. γν. ℵ^1[L^1].

45. ευρισκοντες D. rec aft ευρ. ins αυτον, with AC^3 rel lat-*a b f q* syrr coptt goth : om BC^{1}DLℵ 1. 33 vulg lat-*c e ff*$_2$ *g*$_{1.2}$ *l* æth arm. rec (for αναζητ.) ζητουντες, with Aℵ^1 rel : txt BCDLℵ^3 1. 33. 69, *requirentes* vulg lat-*c*.

46. rec μεθ', with ACD rel : txt BLℵ 1. 33. καθ. bef εν τω ιερω D 254.—καθημενον D 1 : om G. om και (bef ακουοντα) D 240-4 Scr's g latt [coptt] arm.

47. om οι ακουοντες αυτου B [Orig-int$_1$].

At the age of twelve, a boy was called by the Jews בֶּן־הַתּוֹרָה, '*son of the law,*' and first incurred legal obligation. At that time, then, commences the *second step* (see note on ver. 52) of the life of the Lord, the time when the τὰ πρέποντα for Him began; his course of blameless legal obedience (see note on ver. 21) in his own person and by his own will. Now first (ver. 49) appear those higher consciousnesses to have found expression, which unfolded within Him, till the full time of his public ministry arrived. It cannot be inferred from this narrative, that it was the first time the holy Child had accompanied them to the Passover. **43.**] **τὰς ἡμ.**, *seven days*, Exod. xii. 15, 17. **44.**] **συνοδ.**, the company forming the *caravan*, or band of travellers;—all who came from the same district travelling together for security and company. **ἦλθ. . . . ἀνεζ.**] The interpretation that '*they went a day's journey, seeking him,*' is simply absurd: for they would have turned back sooner: a few minutes might have sufficed for the search. It was *not till they laid up for the night* that they missed him, as at that time (φέρεις μητέρι παῖδα) they would naturally expect his return to their own tent. Olshausen remarks, that being accustomed to his thoughtfulness and obedience, they were free from anxiety, till they discovered He really was not in the company. **45.**] **ἀναζητοῦντες αὐτόν**—as they went back, all the way. **46.**] Some (Grot., Kuin.) interpret the *three days*, of their *one* day's journey *out*, *one back*, and *one in Jerusalem*: but they were more likely *three days spent in search in Jerusalem* (De Wette); or, at all events, reckoned from their discovery of His not being with them (Meyer). **ἐν τῷ ἱερῷ**] In one of the *rooms attached to the temple*, where the Rabbis taught their schools. A tradition mentioned by Lightfoot, that till the death of Gamaliel the scholars *stood* in these schools, appears to be false, as Kuinoel has shewn. No stress must be laid on **ἐν μέσῳ**; it is only among

d Matt. xxi. 36. 2 Kings xii. 31.
e ch. xvi. 24, 25. Acts xx. 38 only. Isa. xl. 29.
f Acts v. 4, 9. 2 Kings xix. 25.
g Gen. xli. 51. Esth. vii. 9.
h Matt. xiii. 51. Ps. xci. 6.

επλάγησαν, καὶ εἶπεν πρὸς αὐτὸν ἡ μήτηρ αὐτοῦ Τέκνον,
τί [d] ἐποίησας ἡμῖν οὕτως; ἰδοὺ ὁ πατήρ σου κἀγὼ [e] ὀδυνώμενοι ἐζητοῦμέν σε. 49 καὶ εἶπεν πρὸς αὐτοὺς [f] Τί ὅτι
ἐζητεῖτέ με; οὐκ ᾔδειτε ὅτι ἐν [g] τοῖς τοῦ πατρός μου δεῖ
εἶναί με; 50 καὶ αὐτοὶ οὐ [h] συνῆκαν τὸ ῥῆμα ὃ ἐλάλησεν

ABCDE GHKL MSUVX ΓΔΛΠ א 1. 33. 69

48. (syr-cu contains Luke ii. 48—iii. 16.) rec *προς αυτον η μητηρ αυτου* bef *ειπεν*, with A rel: txt BCDLXא 1 lat-(*a*) *e f* Syr goth æth arm Cyr$_1$. *και εγω* C[1]L 1. 33. 69 [Cyr$_1$]. aft *οδυνωμενοι* add *και λυπουμενοι* D gat lat-*a e ff$_2$ g$_1$ l q* syr-cu Ambrst Quæst. *ζητουμεν* Bא[1] 6-pe.

49. *ζητειτε* [Δ-gr] א[1] [syr-cu copt]. **οιδατε** D lat-*a b c e f ff$_2$ l q* syr-cu Iren-gr$_1$[int$_1$ Cyr$_1$] Thdrt$_1$ Orig-int$_1$ Tert$_1$: txt ABCא rel vulg lat-*g$_1$* [Did$_1$ Cyr-jer$_1$ Epiph$_1$ Thdrt$_1$ Phot$_1$] Orig-int$_2$. *με* bef *ειναι* D 1. 69 latt Iren$_1$ Did Cyr[-jer] Epiph$_2$ [Thdrt$_1$] Orig-int$_3$ Tert$_1$.

50. for *και αυτοι*, *αυτοι δε* D lat-*e* Syr syr-cu copt Orig-int$_1$.

Nor must it be supposed from **ἐπερωτ.** that our Lord was acting the part of a *master*. It was the custom in the Jewish schools for the *scholars to ask questions of their teachers;* and a great part of the Rabbinical books consists of the answers of the Rabbis to such questions.

48—50.] The salient point of this narrative appears to lie in **ὁ πατήρ σου** contrasted with **τοῦ πατρός μου**. This was the first time that those wonderful words of self-consciousness had been heard from the holy Child—when He began to be "a son of the law," He first calls HIM His Father, Who gave Him the work to do on earth, of perfectly keeping that Law. *Every word of these verses is of the first importance to modern combatants for sound doctrine.* Let the adversaries answer us,—why should his *mother* here have spoken and not Joseph, unless there were some more than usual reason for her being put forward rather than his reputed father? Again, let the mythical school of Strauss give us a reason, why an incident altogether (*in their view*) so derogatory to the character of the subject of it, should have been inserted, if the myths arose out of *an exaggerated estimate of the dignity of that character?* **ὁ πατ. σου**] Then up to this time Joseph had been so called by the holy Child Himself: but from this time, *never.* Such words are not chance; had Mary said *ἡμεῖς*, the strong contrast with what follows could not have been brought out. **τί ὅτι ἐζ.;**] **τί, ὅτι . . .** what (reason) is there, that . . .: see reff. This is no *reproachful* question. It is asked in all the simplicity and boldness of holy childhood . . . 'did ye not know?' . . . it appeared as if that conviction, the expression of which now first breaks forth from HIM, must have been a matter known to them before.

δεῖ] This is that *δεῖ* so often used by our Lord of His *appointed and undertaken course.* Analogous to this first utterance of His conviction, is the dawn, amongst *ourselves*, of the *principle of duty* in the youthful and well-trained spirit about this same age,—this 'earing time' of human progress: see below on ver. 52. **ἐν τοῖς τοῦ π.**] Primarily, **in the** *house* **of my Father** (so in Sir. xlii. 10, *ἐν τοῖς πατρικοῖς αὐτῆς*: Theocr. ii. 76, *τὰ Λύκωνος*: Demosth. p. 1071, *τὰ τοῦ ἀποθανόντος*: see Lobeck on Phryn. p. 100); but we must not exclude the wider sense, which embraces *all places and employments of my Father's* (cf. *ἐν τούτοις ἴσθι*, 1 Tim. iv. 15). The best rendering would perhaps be,—**among my Father's matters.** The employment in which he was found, *learning the word of God*, would naturally be one of these. **αὐτ. οὐ συν.**] Both Joseph and His mother knew *in some sense, Who* He was: but were not prepared to hear *so direct an appeal* to God as His Father: understood not the deeper sense of these wonderful words. Still (ver. 51) they appear to have awakened in the mind of His mother a remembrance of *κληθήσεται υἱὸς θεοῦ*, ch. i. 35. And probably, as Stier remarks (i. 5), the unfolding of His childhood had been so gradual and natural, that even they had not been forcibly reminded by any strong individual notes, of that which He was, and which now shewed itself.

It is a remarkable instance of the blindness of the rationalistic Commentators to the richness and depth of Scripture narrative, that Meyer holds this *οὐ συνῆκαν* to be altogether inconceivable as coming after the angelic announcement to Mary. Can he suppose that she *συνῆκεν* that announcement itself? De Wette has given the right interpretation, sie ver-

αὐτοῖς. 51 καὶ [i] κατέβη μετʼ αὐτῶν καὶ ἦλθεν εἰς Ναζαρέθ,
καὶ ἦν [k] ὑποτασσόμενος αὐτοῖς. καὶ ἡ μήτηρ αὐτοῦ [l] δι-
ετήρει πάντα τὰ [m] ῥήματα [ταῦτα] ἐν τῇ καρδίᾳ αὐτῆς.
52 καὶ Ἰησοῦς [n] προέκοπτεν σοφίᾳ καὶ [o] ἡλικίᾳ καὶ [p] χάριτι
[q] παρὰ θεῷ καὶ ἀνθρώποις.
III. 1 Ἐν ἔτει δὲ πεντεκαιδεκάτῳ τῆς [r] ἡγεμονίας Τιβε-

i = ch. x. 30, 31. John iv. 47. Gen. xi. 10.
k ch. x. 17, 20. Rom. viii. 7, 20 al. 1 Chron. xxix. 24. 2 Macc. ix. 12.
l = here (Acts xv. 29) only. Gen. xxxvii. 11.
m = ch. i. 37 al.
n Rom. xiii. 12. Gal. i. 14. 2 Tim. ii. 16. iii. 9 only. L.P.+. Ps. xliv. 5 alius in Hex. (-πή, Phil. i. 12. Sir. li. 17.)
o Matt. vi. 27 reff. ch. xix. 3 reff.
p = ver. 40. Prov. iii. 4.
q ch. i. 30. 1 Pet. ii. 20.
r here only. Gen. xxxvi. 30. Sir. vii. 4.

51. om και ηλθεν C[1]D F(Wetst) copt: ins ABC[2]א rel latt syrr syr-cu [goth arm] Orig-int$_1$. for και η, η δε C[3]DEGHM 69 lat-*e* Syr syr-cu copt Eus$_1$ Orig-int$_1$: txt ABC[1]א rel latt syr goth arm. τα ρηματα bef παντα ADK[Π] : om τα ρηματα S.—απαντα AK[Π]. om ταυτα [B]DMא[1] lat-*a e* Syr-ed arm. (*Mey thinks that τα ρ. fell out through homœotel, and was variously restored.*)—add συμβαλουσα X, συμβαλλουσα א[3a] Scr's g [Eus$_1$]. εαυτης א[3a].

52. ins ο bef ιησ. א[1][Λ] Scr's c [Orig$_2$]. προεκοπται D, -τει M(Tischdf). ins τη bef σοφια B ; εν τη Lא [copt] Orig$_1$. transp σοφια and ηλικια DL lat-*a b c e l q* Syr (syr-cu syr-jer) copt Orig$_1$[int$_2$] Epiph$_1$ Amphil$_1$ Nyss$_2$ Cyr Thdrt$_2$. for παρα θεω, θεου א[1]. ins παρα bef ανθρωποις D.

Chap. III. 1. for ηγεμονιας (so B-txt), βασιλειας B[1]-marg. (See table at end of

ſtanden nicht den tiefern Sinn, and refers to chap. xviii. 34: so also Olsh., Ebrard. **51.**] The high consciousness which had manifested itself in ver. 49 did not interfere with His self-humiliation, nor render Him independent of his parents. This voluntary subjection probably shewed itself in working at his reputed father's trade: see Mark vi. 2 and note. From this time we have *no more mention of Joseph* (ch. iv. 22 is not to the point): the next we hear is of *His mother and brethren* (John ii. 12): whence it is inferred that, between this time and the commencement of our Lord's public life, *Joseph died.* **καὶ ἡ μήτ.**] These words tend to confirm the common belief that these opening chapters, or at least *this* narrative, may have been derived from the testimony of *the mother of the Lord herself.* She *kept* them, as in wonderful coincidence with the remarkable circumstances of His birth, and its announcement, and His presentation in the temple, and the offerings of the Magi; but in what way, or by what one great revelation all these things were to be gathered in one, did not yet appear, but was doubtless manifested to her afterwards: see Acts i. 14; ii. 1. **52.**] **ἡλικ.**, probably not only '*stature*' (as in ch. xix. 3), but **age** (ref. Matt.), which comprehends the other: so that **σοφ. κ. ἡλ.** would be **wisdom, as well as age.**

During these eighteen mysterious years we may, by the light of what is here revealed, view the holy Child advancing onward to that fulness of wisdom and divine approval which was indicated at His Baptism, by ἐν σοὶ εὐδόκησα. We are apt to forget, that it was *during this time* that *much of the great work of the second Adam was done.* The growing up through infancy, childhood, youth, manhood, from grace to grace, holiness to holiness, in subjection, self-denial, and love, *without one polluting touch of sin,*—this it was which, consummated by the three years of active ministry, by the Passion, and by the Cross, constituted "*the obedience of one man,*" by which many were made righteous. We must fully appreciate the words of this verse, in order to think rightly of Christ. He had emptied Himself of His glory: His infancy and childhood were no *mere pretence,* but the Divine personality was in Him carried through these states of weakness and inexperience, and gathered round itself the ordinary accessions and experiences of the sons of men. All the time, the consciousness of his mission on earth was ripening; 'the things heard of the Father' (John xv. 15) were continually imparted to Him; the Spirit, which was not given by measure to Him, was abiding more and more upon Him; till the day when He was fully ripe for his official manifestation,—that He might be offered to his own, to receive or reject Him,—and then the Spirit led Him up to commence his conflict with the enemy. As yet, He was in favour with man also: the world had not yet begun to hate Him; but we cannot tell how soon this feeling towards Him was changed, for He alleges (John vii. 7), "Me the world hateth,

s ch. ii. 2 only†. ρίου Καίσαρος, [s] ἡγεμονεύοντος Ποντίου Πιλάτου τῆς ABCDE GHKL
t here (3ce) only †. (-χής, ver. 19.) Ἰουδαίας, καὶ [t] τετραρχοῦντος τῆς Γαλιλαίας Ἡρώδου, MsUVX ΓΔΛΠ
Φιλίππου δὲ τοῦ ἀδελφοῦ αὐτοῦ [t] τετραρχοῦντος τῆς ℵ 1. 33. 69
Ἰτουραίας καὶ Τραχωνίτιδος χώρας, καὶ Λυσανίου τῆς
u Mark ii. 26. ch. iv. 27. Acts xi. 28. Ἀβιληνῆς [t] τετραρχοῦντος,
2 [u] ἐπὶ ἀρχιερέως Ἄννα

prolegg.) for ηγεμονευοντος, επιτροπευοντος D Eus_2 $Chron_1$, *procurante* latt. om της ιουδ. ℵ[1]. om κ. τετρ. τ. γαλ. D-gr. τετραaρχουντος (thrice) Cℵ [copt]. ηρωδου bef της γαλιλαιας AK[Π]. τετραρχ. τ. ιτουρ. is written twice in D-gr: from ιτουρ. to λυσανιου is written over an erasure by ℵ-corr[1], ℵ[3a] correcting τετραχωνιτιδος(sic) to και τραχ. aft ιτουραιας ins ορεινης B[1]-marg. (See table of readings.) αβιλλιανης D[1] (254) [lat-*a b e* ff_2].

2. rec επ': txt ABCDℵ rel Scr's-mss Eus_2 [$Thdrt_1$ $Chron_1$]. rec αρχιερεων, with Scr's r vulg lat-*a c* &c copt goth [Thdrt-ed] $Chron_1$ [$Orig\text{-}int_1$]: txt ABCDℵ rel lat-*b e* Eus_2 Thdrt[-ms].

because I testify of it that its deeds are evil;" and we can hardly conceive such testimony, in the years of gathering vigour and zeal, long withheld. The incident of ch. iv. 28, 29 can scarcely have arisen *only* from the anger of the moment.

CHAP. III. 1—22.] PREACHING AND BAPTISM OF JOHN. DIVINE TESTIMONY TO JESUS AT HIS BAPTISM. Matt. iii. 1—17. Mark i. 4—11. 1.] These dates are consistent with the **ἀκριβῶς παρακολουθεῖν** which Luke predicates of himself, ch. i. 3. In Matt. iii. 1 we have the same events indicated as to time by only *ἐν ταῖς ἡμ. ἐκείναις.* The fifteenth year of the *sole principate* of Tiberius began Aug. 19, U.C. 781, and reckoning backwards thirty years from that time (see ver. 23), we should have the birth of our Lord in U.C. 751 or about then; for **ὡσεὶ** *τριάκ.* will admit of some latitude. But Herod the Great died in the beginning of the year 750, and our Lord's birth must be fixed *some months at least before* the death of Herod. If then it be placed in 749, He would have been at least thirty-two at the time of His baptism, seeing that it took place some time after the beginning of John's ministry. This difficulty has led to the supposition that this fifteenth year is not to be dated from the *sole* but from the *associated* principate of Tiberius, which commenced most probably at the end of U.C. 764. According to this, the fifteenth of Tiberius will begin at the end of U.C. 779—and our Lord's birth would be U.C. 749 or 50: which will agree with the death of Herod. This latter explanation has usually been adopted. Our present æra was fixed by Dionysius Exiguus, in the sixth century, and places the birth of our Lord in 754 U.C. It may be doubted, however, whether in all these reckonings more accuracy has not been sought than the Gospel narrative warrants any expectation of our finding. The **ὡσεὶ ἐτῶν τρ.** is a wide expression, and might cover any age from thirty (see note on ver. 23) to thirty-two or thirty-three. See on Matt. ii. 2, where it appears probable from astronomical considerations, that our Lord was born as early as U.C. 747. Mr. Greswell has devoted several Dissertations to this enquiry: see his vol. i. p. 189 ff. **ἡγεμ. Π. Πιλ.**] Pilate was only *Procurator* of Judæa: the words cognate to *ἡγεμών* being used promiscuously of the leading officers of the Roman government. PONTIUS PILATE was the sixth procurator from the deposition of Archelaus, and came to Judæa about U.C. 779. He held the province ten years, and was sent to Rome to answer for his conduct by Vitellius, prefect of Syria, U.C. 789, the year of the death of Tiberius. See chronological table in Prolegg. Vol. II. **Ἡρώδου**] See note on Matt. xiv. 1. HEROD ANTIPAS became tetrarch of Galilee after the death of his father Herod, U.C. 750, and continued till he was deposed in 792. **Φιλίππου**] Son of Herod the Great by Cleopatra, a woman of Jerusalem, Jos. Antt. xvii. 1. 3. He was brought up at Rome, and after his father's death in U.C. 750 was made tetrarch of Batanæa, Gaulonitis, Trachonitis, Panias, Auranitis (Batanæa + Auranitis = Ituræa), and continued till his death in U.C. 786 or 787. He built Cæsarea Philippi. He was by far the best of Herod's sons, and ruled his portion mildly and well. He must not be confounded with *his half-brother Philip*, whose wife Herodias Herod Antipas seduced. This latter was disinherited by his father, and lived in privacy. See note on Matt. xiv. 1. **Λυσαν. τ. Ἀβ. τετρ.**] ABILENE, the district round Abila, a town eighteen miles north of Damascus, now, according to Pococke, Nebi Abel. It must not be confounded with Abila in Decapolis.

F εγε-νετο... καὶ Καϊάφα, [v] ἐγένετο ῥῆμα θεοῦ ἐπὶ Ἰωάννην τὸν
Ζαχαρίου υἱὸν ἐν τῇ ἐρήμῳ, 3 καὶ ἦλθεν εἰς πᾶσαν
[w] περίχωρον τοῦ Ἰορδάνου [x] κηρύσσων [y] βάπτισμα [yz] μετανοίας εἰς [a] ἄφεσιν ἁμαρτιῶν, 4 ὡς γέγραπται ἐν [b] βίβλῳ
...λογων E. λόγων Ἡσαΐου τοῦ προφήτου [c] Φωνὴ βοῶντος ἐν τῇ
ἐρήμῳ [d] Ἑτοιμάσατε τὴν [d] ὁδὸν κυρίου, [e] εὐθείας ποιεῖτε
τὰς [f] τρίβους αὐτοῦ. 5 πᾶσα [g] φάραγξ [h] πληρωθήσεται
Ξ και παν... καὶ πᾶν ὄρος καὶ [i] βουνὸς [k] ταπεινωθήσεται, καὶ [l] ἔσται τὰ
[m] σκολιὰ [l] εἰς [e] εὐθείας καὶ αἱ [n] τραχεῖαι [l] εἰς ὁδοὺς

v John x. 35. Acts vii. 31. x. 37 al. Gen. xv. 1, 4. Jer. i. 4.
w ‖ Mt. Matt. xiv. 35 al. Gen. xiii. 10.
x ‖ Mt. Mk., al. passim. Exod. xxxii. 5.
y ‖ Mk. Acts xiii. 24. xix. 4 only.
z ‖ Mk. reff. ch. v. 32. constr., John v. 29.
a ‖ Mk. Matt. xvi. 28. Deut. xv. 3.
b Matt. i. 1. Mark xii. 26.
c Isa. xl. 3, 4.
d ‖. ch. i. 76. Rev. xvi. 12.
e here (bis) & ‖ (from l. c.). Acts viii. 21. ix. 11. xiii. 10. 2 Pet. ii. 15 only.
f ‖ only. Gen. xlix. 17.
g here only. l. c. Josh. xv. 7.
h Matt. xiii. 48. Baruch v. 7.
i ch. xxiii. 30 only. Exod. xvii. 9, 10.
k 2 Cor. xii. 21. Phil. ii. 8. Prov. xiii. 7.
l Matt. xix. 5 ‖ Mk. 1 Cor. vi. 16 al. Gen. ii. 7.
m Acts ii. 40. Phil. ii. 15. 1 Pet. ii. 18. Deut. xxxii. 5.
n Acts xxvii. 29 only. l. c. Jer. ii. 25.

(καϊφα CD latt(so elsewhere) [Orig-int]: txt ABℵ rel am(with fuld) lat-*q* copt Eus [Thdrt Chron].) rec ins του bef ζαχαριου, with G 1(e sil) 69 Eus_1: om ABCDℵ rel $Clem_1$ $Orig_1$ $Chron_1$.

3. rec aft πασαν ins την, with CDℵ rel copt Eus_1 [$Chron_1$]: om ABL $Orig_3$.

4. for ως, καθως C Eus_1. βιβλιω B. rec aft προφητου ins λεγοντος (*from Matt* iii. 3), with AC rel lat-*f q* syrr goth æth [$Chron_1$]: om BDLΔℵ 1 latt syr-cu copt arm $Orig_1$ Eus_1. ins του bef κυριου A 243-8-58. for αυτου, υμων D-gr.

5. φαραξ AHL[1] [S(Tischdf)] X ev-y. rec ευθειαν (*corrn to* LXX), with ACℵ rel lat-*e f q* [D-lat] Syr syr-cu goth (æth) Iren-int-mss [$Chron_1$]: txt B D[-gr] Ξ latt $Orig_2$(expr: ἀντὶ ἑνικοῦ Εἰς εὐθεῖαν, . . . πληθυντικὸν Εὐθείας)[int_2] Iren-int-mss Leo_1. τροχιαι ℵ[1].

Josephus, Antt. xix. 5. 1, mentions it as among the districts which Claudius gave to king Agrippa I. under the name of Ἄβιλα ἡ Λυσανίου, and in B. J. ii. 11. 5, as ἑτέρα βασιλεία ἡ Λυσανίου καλουμένη. In Antt. xx. 7. 1, he has Ἀβίλᾳ. Λυσανίᾳ δὲ αὕτη ἐγεγόνει τετραρχία: cf. also Ptolem. v. 15, Ἄβιλα ἐπικληθεῖσα Λυσανίου (making it, however, one of the cities of Decapolis). This Lysanias however was son of Ptolemy, the son of Minnæus (B. J. i. 13. 1), and was killed by Antony, at Cleopatra's instigation (B.C. 34). The Lysanias here mentioned may be some descendant of the other, since we find him here *only ruling Abilene*, whereas the other is called by Dio (xlix. 32), king of Ituræa. Now at his death we learn that the οἶκος τοῦ Λυσ. was farmed by one Zenodorus (Antt. xv. 10. 1), whom (ib. § 3) Augustus deprived of his ἐπαρχία, and at his death, which immediately followed, gave the principal of his districts, Trachonitis, Auranitis (Antt. xvii. 11. 4), &c., to Herod, B.C. 23. Among these *Abilene is not named*, and it therefore is possible that it may have been *granted to a descendant of the former possessor*. The silence of Josephus is no reason against this supposition, as he does not minutely relate the fortunes of districts which do not lie in the path of his history. The appellation of Ἄβιλα ἡ Λυσανίου again in the time of Claudius, after this appellation has disappeared so long, looks as if there had been another Λυσανίας between. See Wieseler, i. 175 ff. Meyer, Comm. in loc. Bleek, Synoptische Erkl. in loc. **2.**] Annas (= Ananus, Jos. Antt. xviii. 2. 2) the high-priest, was deposed by Valerius Gratus (U.C. 779), and after several changes, Joseph or Caiaphas (Joseph. as above), his son-in-law (John xviii. 13), was made high-priest. It would appear from this verse (and the use of the singular, -εως, renders the inference more stringent. Cf. also St. Luke's own phrase, Acts iv. 6) that Annas, as *ex-high-priest*, and possibly retaining in the view of the Jews the *legitimate high-priesthood*, was *counted still as having the office*: he certainly (John xviii. 13) *exercised the power*,—and had influence enough to procure the actual high-priesthood for *five of his sons*, after his own deposition, Jos. Antt. xx. 9. 1. A substitute, or deputy to the high-priest (called by the Talmudists סְגַן כֹּהֲנַיָּא), appears to have been usual,—see 2 Kings xxv. 18; and Annas would thus be able to evade the Roman appointment and keep the authority. **ῥῆμα θ.**] See John i. 33. **3—6.**] Matt. iii. 1. Mark i. 4, where see note on βάπ. μετ. Vv. 5, 6 are peculiar to Luke. They are nearly verbatim from the LXX Alex., not F, who for ὁδοὺς λείας has πεδία. After

o here only. Gen. xxvii. 11. Prov. ii. 20.
p ch. ii. 30 reff.
q ‖ Mt. (reff.)
r Matt. xxvi. 22. Mark v. 17. vi. 7 al. Gen. xviii. 27.
s ‖ Mt. (reff.)
t ‖ Mt. only. Jer. xxvi. (xlvi.) 22.
u ‖ Mt. (reff.)
v Rom. i. 11. xii. 8. Eph. iv. 28. 1 Thess. ii. 8 only. Job xxxi. 17.
w = 1 Cor. xi. 22. Neh. viii. 10 (?).
x Matt. xiv. 15 reff.
y = Heb. i. 4. iii. 3. ix. 23 al.
z 1 Cor. vii. 17. Tit. i. 5. L.P. exc. Matt. xi. 1. Judg. v. 9.
a = ch. xix. 23 only. Dan. xi. 20 Theod.(?) 1 Macc. x. 35 (?).
b 1 Cor. ix. 7. 2 Cor. x. 3. 1 Tim. i. 18. 2 Tim. ii. 4. James iv. 1. 1 Pet. ii. 11 only. Isa. xxix. 7.

o λείας, 6 καὶ ὄψεται πᾶσα σὰρξ τὸ p σωτήριον τοῦ θεοῦ.
7 ἔλεγεν οὖν τοῖς ἐκπορευομένοις ὄχλοις βαπτισθῆναι ὑπ'
αὐτοῦ q Γεννήματα q ἐχιδνῶν, τίς q ὑπέδειξεν ὑμῖν φυγεῖν
ἀπὸ τῆς q μελλούσης ὀργῆς; 8 q ποιήσατε οὖν q καρποὺς
q ἀξίους τῆς z μετανοίας· καὶ μὴ r ἄρξησθε λέγειν s ἐν ...μετανοιας Ξ.
s ἑαυτοῖς Πατέρα ἔχομεν τὸν Ἀβραάμ· λέγω γὰρ ὑμῖν ὅτι ABCDF
δύναται ὁ θεὸς ἐκ τῶν λίθων τούτων t ἐγεῖραι τέκνα τῷ GHKL MSUVX
Ἀβραάμ. 9 ἤδη δὲ καὶ ἡ t ἀξίνη u πρὸς τὴν ῥίζαν τῶν ΓΔΛΠ ℵ 1. 33.
δένδρων u κεῖται· πᾶν οὖν δένδρον μὴ u ποιοῦν u καρ- 69
πὸν καλὸν u ἐκκόπτεται καὶ εἰς πῦρ βάλλεται. 10 καὶ
ἐπηρώτων αὐτὸν οἱ ὄχλοι λέγοντες Τί οὖν ποιήσωμεν;
11 ἀποκριθεὶς δὲ ἔλεγεν αὐτοῖς Ὁ ἔχων δύο χιτῶνας
v μεταδότω τῷ w μὴ w ἔχοντι, καὶ ὁ ἔχων x βρώματα ὁμοίως Ξ και ο εχων...
ποιείτω. 12 ἦλθον δὲ καὶ τελῶναι βαπτισθῆναι, καὶ
εἶπον πρὸς αὐτὸν Διδάσκαλε, τί ποιήσωμεν; 13 ὁ δὲ
εἶπεν πρὸς αὐτοὺς Μηδὲν πλέον y παρὰ τὸ z διατεταγμένον ὑμῖν a πράσσετε. 14 ἐπηρώτων δὲ αὐτὸν καὶ
b στρατευόμενοι λέγοντες Τί ποιήσωμεν καὶ ἡμεῖς; καὶ

6. for *θεου*, *κυριου* D æth.

7. *ελεγον* ℵ¹. for *ουν*, *δε* D 1. 69 ev-z lat-*e f* copt-dz goth. for *υπ'*, *ενωπιον* D lat-*b e l q*. *υμιν* bef *υπεδειξεν* DΛ.

8. *αξιους* bef *καρπους* B $Orig_1$: *καρπον αξιον* (‖ *Matt*) D 106 lat-*e* syr[-txt] copt goth æth (Did). for *εν εαυτοις*, *αυτοις* D¹-gr(*ενε* is added above the line) æth(Treg) : *εν αυτοις* L : om latt(not *f q*) syr-cu arm $Orig_1(txt_2)$ [$Ambr_1$] : add *οτι* L 33 Syr syr-cu syr-w-ast arm $Orig_2(om_1)$.

9. om 1st *και* D lat-*b* [*e q*] Syr syr-cu copt goth arm Did Orig-int, *jam enim* vulg [lat-*f* g_1 *l*], *jam quid enim* lat-*a*. *καρπους καλους* D Syr syr-cu.—om *καλον* am(with forj per) lat-*a* ff_2 $Orig_2$(*τὸ μὲν γὰρ μὴ ἔχον καρπὸν οὐδὲ καλὸν ἔχει καρπόν*) Iren-int_1-mss.

10. *επηρωτησαν* D 244, *interrogaverunt* lat-*b c e* ff_2 [*l*] *q* (*interrogabant* vulg). om *ουν* D ev-z lat-*b c e* [*l*] *q* copt-dz. rec *ποιησομεν*, with GKU **1** latt Orig-int_1 : txt ABCDℵ rel goth æth. add *ινα σωθωμεν* (*cf Acts* xvi. 30) D, *ut vivamus* gat lat-*b* g_1 *q* syr-cu.

11. rec (for *ελεγεν*) *λεγει*, with AC² D[-gr] rel : txt BC¹LXℵ 1. 33. 69 vulg lat-*c f*

12. aft *τελωναι* ins *ομοιως* D lat-*a*. aft *βαπτισθηναι* ins *υπ' αυτου* CKX[Π] syr-w-ob copt-dz-marg [Orig-int_2]. *ειπαν* C¹D. rec *ποιησομεν*, with GU **1** latt : txt ABCDℵ rel goth æth. add *ινα σωθωμεν* D.

13. for *προς αυτους*, *αυτοις* D mt lat-*a e f* [*l*] *q* : om *ειπον προς αυτους* ℵ¹. *μηθεν* AΔ $Constt_1$. *πλειον* C. add *πρασσετε* D mt lat-*a b c* [*e* ff_2 g_1 *l q* (syr-cu) æth]. for *πρασσετε*, *πρασσειν* D Syr : om lat-*a b c* [*e* ff_2 g_1 *l q*] syr-cu æth.

14. *επηρωτησαν* CD lat-*b c* ff_2 g_1 [*l*] *q* (goth ?). om *δε* C fuld. om *αυτον* D lat-*c*. rec *και ημεις* bef *τι ποι.*, with AC³ rel lat-*a* syr copt goth æth arm : om *και ημεις* D ev-7 : txt BC¹LΞℵ 1. 69 vulg lat-*b c e f l* [ff_2 g_1 *q*] Syr syr-cu.—rec *ποιησομεν*, with AGKU **1** latt : txt B(sic : see table) CDΞℵ rel goth æth. add *ινα σωθωμεν* D. for 3rd *και*, *ο δε* D lat-*e*.

this there is omitted *καὶ ὀφθήσεται ἡ δόξα κυρίου*, and then *καὶ ὄψ. . . . κ.τ.λ.* as LXX. **7—9.**] Matt. vv. 7—10. John's speech is verbatim as Matt., except that *καρπ. ἀξ.* is singular, and *δόξητε* Matt. = *ἄρξησθε* Luke. This indicates a common origin of this portion, which however is still thus slightly deflected; and let it be borne in mind that the slighter the deflection, the more striking the independence of the Evangelists. **μὴ ἄρξησθε λ.**] 'Omnem excusationis etiam *conatum* præcidit.' Bengel. **10—14.**] *Peculiar to Luke.* **10.**] Olshausen re-

εἶπεν αὐτοῖς Μηδένα [c] διασείσητε μηδὲ [d] συκοφαντήσητε,
καὶ [e] ἀρκεῖσθε τοῖς [f] ὀψωνίοις ὑμῶν. 15 [g] προςδοκῶντος δὲ τοῦ λαοῦ, καὶ [h] διαλογιζομένων πάντων ἐν ταῖς
E του... καρδίαις αὐτῶν περὶ τοῦ Ἰωάννου [i] μήποτε αὐτὸς εἴη ὁ
χριστός, 16 ἀπεκρίνατο ὁ Ἰωάννης ἅπασιν λέγων Ἐγὼ
μὲν ὕδατι βαπτίζω ὑμᾶς· ἔρχεται δὲ ὁ [k] ἰσχυρότερός
μου, [l] οὗ οὐκ εἰμὶ [m] ἱκανὸς λῦσαι τὸν [n] ἱμάντα τῶν [o] ὑποδημάτων [l] αὐτοῦ· αὐτὸς ὑμᾶς βαπτίσει [o] ἐν πνεύματι ἁγίῳ
καὶ πυρί. 17 [l] οὗ τὸ [p] πτύον ἐν τῇ χειρὶ [l] αὐτοῦ, καὶ
[q] διακαθαριεῖ τὴν [r] ἅλωνα αὐτοῦ, καὶ [r] συνάξει τὸν σῖτον
εἰς τὴν [r] ἀποθήκην αὐτοῦ, τὸ δὲ [r] ἄχυρον [r] κατακαύσει
πυρὶ [r] ἀσβέστῳ. 18 πολλὰ μὲν οὖν καὶ ἕτερα [s] παρακαλῶν [t] εὐηγγελίζετο τὸν λαόν. 19 ὁ δὲ Ἡρώδης ὁ

c here only. Job iv. 14 B. 3 Macc. vii. 21 (only ?).
d ch. xix. 8 only. Lev. xix. 11. Job xxxv. 9. Ps. cxviii. 122.
e = 1 Tim. vi. 8. Heb. xiii. 5. 3 John 10, but w. ἐπί (Matt. xxv. 9 reff.) ‡. 2 Macc. v. 15.
f 1 Cor. ix. 7. Rom. vi. 23. 2 Cor. xi. 8 only +. Esdr. iv. 56. 1 Macc. iii. 28. xiv. 32 only.
g ch. i. 21 reff.
h Matt. xvi. 7, 8 reff.
i see 2 Tim. ii. 25 and note.
k ||. ch. xi. 22. Num. xxii. 6
A compl. Ald.
l red., Matt. iii. 12 reff.
m = & constr., || Mk. reff.
n || Mk. reff.
o || Mt. reff.
pq || Mt. (reff.) only +.
r || Mt. reff.
s = Acts ii. 40 al.
t constr., Acts viii. 25. xiv. 21. xvi. 10 al.

rec (for αυτοις) προς αυτους (*from ver* 13), with AC³ℵ rel goth : txt BC¹DLΞ 1. 33 latt. for μηδε, μηδενα ℵ¹[H Syr syr-cu] : μηδεν ev-y.

15. εαυτων ℵ-corr¹. om του (bef ιωαννου) DΞ 1. 69 Eus₁.

16. for απ. ο ιω. απα. λεγ., απ. λεγ. πασιν ο ιω. Bℵ¹ lat-*e* Orig : απ. ο ιω. λεγ. πασ. K¹(απασιν K²) : απ. πασ. λεγ. ο ιω. Lℵ³ᵃ : επιγνους τα νοηματα αυτων ειπεν D : om ο F 69 Scr's g : for απασιν, αυτοις Scr's c Syr : πασιν Ξ : om Γ. εγω υμ. βαπτ. εν υδατι (*see* || *Matt*) D 1. 69 lat-*e* [Ambr₁]. add εις μετανοιαν (|| *Matt*) CD mt lat-*a b c* &c(not *f g₂ l*) syr-mg [Ambr₁]. (Contra, μόνος ματθαῖος . . . προςτέθεικε τὸ εἰς μετάνοιαν Orig.) ο δε ερχομενος ισχυροτερος μου εστιν (|| *Matt*) D lat-*l*. εμου C. του υποδηματος D syr copt Clem₁. om αυτου D lat-*a b ff₂ l* [*q*] arm Eus₁. om αυτος ℵ¹(ins ℵ-corr¹·³ᵇ(appy)).

17. for και διακαθαριει, διακαθαραι B ℵ¹(txt ℵ-corr¹) copt arm, *ad purgandum* lat-*a*, *emundare* Iren-int₁. for συναξει, συναγαγειν B ℵ¹(txt ℵ³ᵃ, -ξαι ℵ-corr¹) lat-*e* arm. —τον μεν σιτον bef συναξει D. ins μεν bef σιτον DEGΛ 69. om την and 3rd αυτου D copt-wilk Orig-int₁ : αυτου is marked for erasure in ℵ, but restored. for κατακαυσει, κατασβεσει ℵ¹(txt ℵ-corr¹).

18. for παρακαλων, παραινων D. ευηγγελιζε ℵ¹(txt ℵ-corr¹).

fers to the answer to a similar question under the N. T. dispensation, Acts ii. 37. See also Acts xvi. 30; xxii. 10. Deeds of justice and charity are the very first fruits of repentance: see Micah vi. 8. **12.** **τελῶναι**] See on Matt. v. 46. **13.**] **πράσσετε**, **exact**: see examples in Wetst. **14.**] **στρατευόμενοι**—properly, **men on march**: see Lexx.: but this need not be pressed, only that they were soldiers, serving in an army. Who these were, we have no means of determining. Certainly not soldiers of the army which Herod Antipas sent against Aretas, his father-in-law: see notes on Matt. xiv. 1 ff. **διασείειν** prim., *to shake violently*. So Plato, τὰς ἶνας εἰς ἀταξίαν διέσεισε, Tim. p. 85: also met., *to confound*, διασείσειν τὰ Ἀθηναίων φρονήματα ὥστε μηδίσαι, Herod. vi. 109. The meaning here, to **oppress** or **vex**, corresponding to the Lat. *concutere*, seems to be confined to ecclesiastical use. Macarius, Hom. xliii. p. 139, ed. Migne, has it in this sense: ὥσπερ εἰσὶν οἱ τελῶναι καθεζόμενοι εἰς τὰς στενὰς ὁδούς, καὶ κατέχοντες τοὺς παριόντας καὶ διασείοντες. **συκοφ.**] The way in which *soldiers* would be likely to act the part of informers, would be by laying vexatious charges of disaffection against persons. In assigning a derivation for this verb, notice Liddell and Scott's remark (after Passow): "The literal signif. is not found in any ancient writer, and is perhaps altogether an invention." **15—17.**] Ver. 15 peculiar to Luke, but = John i. 19—25. **προςδοκῶντος**, not **lingering about** (Bretschneider), but **being in expectation**, —i.e. that John would declare himself (Meyer). **16, 17.**] Matt. iii. 11, 12: Mark i. 7, 8: John i. 26, 27. The four accounts are cognate, but vary in expression and arrangement: ver. 17 is verbatim (except that **αὐτοῦ** is after **σῖτον** and **ἀποθήκην** in Matt.) as Matthew. **18—20.**] Luke only: con-

u ch. ix. 7 || Mt. Acts xiii. 1 only †. (-χεῖν, ver. 1.) v = Matt. xviii. 15. 1 Tim. v. 20. Gen. xxi. 25. w attr., ch. ii. 20. x Sir. iii. 27. see ch. xx. 11, 12 reff. y ch. xvi. 26 reff. z Acts xxvi. 10 only. Jer. xxxix. (xxxii.) 3. Wisd. xvii. 2, 16 (Judg. v. 27 ?) only. a Matt. xxv. 36, &c. reff. b w. aor., see note. ch. ii. 27. Ezek. ix. 8.

[u] τετράρχης [v] ἐλεγχόμενος ὑπ᾽ αὐτοῦ περὶ Ἡρωδιάδος
τῆς γυναικὸς τοῦ ἀδελφοῦ αὐτοῦ, καὶ περὶ πάντων [w] ὧν
ἐποίησεν πονηρῶν ὁ Ἡρώδης, 20 [x] προσέθηκεν καὶ τοῦτο
[y] ἐπὶ πᾶσιν, [καὶ] [z] κατέκλεισεν τὸν Ἰωάννην ἐν [a] φυλακῇ. ...φυλακῃ Ξ.
21 Ἐγένετο δὲ [b] ἐν τῷ βαπτισθῆναι ἅπαντα τὸν λαὸν ...λαον CF.
καὶ Ἰησοῦ βαπτισθέντος καὶ προσευχομένου [c] ἀνεῳχθῆ- ABDEG
ναι τὸν [c] οὐρανόν, 22 καὶ καταβῆναι τὸ πνεῦμα τὸ ἅγιον HKLM SUVXΓ
[d] σωματικῷ εἴδει ὡς [e] περιστερὰν ἐπ᾽ αὐτόν, καὶ [e] φωνὴν ΔΛΠℵ 1. 33. 69
ἐξ οὐρανοῦ [f] γενέσθαι Σὺ εἶ ὁ υἱός μου ὁ [g] ἀγαπητός,
[h] ἐν σοὶ [i] εὐδόκησα.
23 Καὶ αὐτὸς ἦν Ἰησοῦς ὡσεὶ [j] ἐτῶν τριάκοντα [k] ἀρχό-

c || Mt. reff. d 1 Tim. iv. 8 only †. 4 Macc. i. 32. (-κῶς, Col. ii. 9.) e || Mt. (reff.) f ver. 2 reff. g || Mt. reff. h = (Col. ii. 18 ?) 1 Kings xviii. 22. 2 Kings xv. 26. 3 Kings x. 9. 2 Chron. ix. 8. Ps. cxlvi. 10. i Matt. xvii. 5. 1 Cor. x. 5. 2 Kings xxii. 20. Mal. ii. 17. j Mark v. 42 reff. k see Acts xi. 4. Gen. xliv. 12.

19. rec aft γυναικος ins φιλιππου (*from Mark* vi. 17), with ACKX 33 syrr copt æth arm-mss: om BDΞℵ rel latt goth arm[-ed] Lucif$_1$. om και ℵ[1]. for ων εποι. πον., των πον. ων εποι. ℵ[1](txt ℵ[3]).

20. om 2nd και BDΞℵ[1] lat-*b e* Eus$_1$: ins ACℵ[3a] rel [latt syrr syr-jer goth] Lucif$_1$. ενεκλισε D; *inclusit* latt. rec ins τη bef φυλ., with AC rel: om BDKLMΛΞ[Π]ℵ 1 goth arm Eus$_1$.

21. for απ., παντα ℵ ev-49. και (2nd) is repeated in D[1]. ανοιχθηναι D.

22. rec ωσει, with A rel Eus$_1$: txt BDLℵ 33 Orig$_1$. for επ᾽, εις D latt[not *f*]. for εξ, εκ του D: απ᾽ Λ. rec aft γενεσθαι ins λεγουσαν (*see || Matt*), with A rel lat-*f ff*$_2$ *g*$_2$ *q* syrr goth æth arm: om BDLℵ latt copt Ambr$_1$. for συ to ευδοκησα, υιος μου ει συ εγω σημερον γεγεννηκα σε D lat-*a b c ff*$_2$[1] *l* Just$_2$ (Clem$_1$ Meth$_1$?) Lact Juv Hil$_3$ Faust Aug$_1$(who however says that the older gr-mss had it not). (ευδοκησα, so B F(Wetst) KMUΛ[Π]ℵ 1. 33. 69 Eus$_1$.)

23. for και αυτος ην, ην δε D Clem$_1$ Hipp$_1$ Ath$_1$ Epiph$_4$, *Jesus autem erat* copt Iren-int$_1$. rec ins ο bef ιησους, with A rel [Chron$_1$]: om BDLUXℵ 33. for ωσει, ως D 69. 258[2] Scr's e [Hipp$_1$ Epiph$_1$]. αρχ. ωσει ετ. τριακ. BLXℵ 1. 33 (69) vulg

taining the corroboration of the account in Mark vi. 20 of John's boldness in rebuking Herod, with this slight variation, that whereas in Mark Herod heard him gladly, and did many things in consequence, here the rebuke for general profligacy seems to have contributed to his imprisonment. These accounts however, though perfectly distinct, are by no means inconsistent. The same rebukes which stung Herod's conscience and aided the desire to imprison John, might work on that conscience, and cause the wish to hear more from the man of God. Vv. 19, 20 are *in anticipation* of what follows; which is in Luke's manner: see ch. i. 80.

21, 22.] Matt. iii. 13—17: Mark i. 9—11. Luke's account is much more concise than usual, and wholly independent of the others; see note on Mark i. 10: we have here however three additional particulars —1. that *all the people had been baptized before* the Lord's baptism: 2. that He *was praying* at the time of the descent of the Spirit: 3. that the Spirit appeared *in a bodily form*. On (1) we may remark that this is necessarily the meaning of ἐν τῷ βαπ.—for Luke when he means 'during,' &c. invariably uses the *present*; see for the past tense with ἐν τῷ reff. and ch. xiv. 1; xix. 15; xxiv. 30—for the present, ch. v. 1; viii. 5, &c., and for a comparison of the two, ch. viii. 40 and 42. On (3), see note at Matt. iii. 16, § 2.

23—38.] GENEALOGY OF OUR LORD. *Peculiar to Luke.* **23.] Jesus was about thirty years old when He began (His ministry)**; not, 'began to be about,' &c., which is ungrammatical. ἀρχόμενος τῆς εἰς τὸν λαὸν ἀναδείξεως αὐτοῦ, ἤτοι τῆς διδασκαλίας, Euthym., so also Orig., Bengel, Kuin., De Wette, Meyer, Wieseler: see also Acts i. 1. This **ὡσεὶ τρ.** admits of considerable latitude, but only in one direction; viz. *over* thirty years. He could not well be under, seeing that this was the appointed age for the commencement of public service of God by the Levites: see Num. iv. 3, 23, 43, 47.

If no other proof were in existence of the *total independence of the present Gospels of Matthew and Luke*, their *genealogies*

μενος, ὢν υἱὸς ὡς [1] ἐνομίζετο Ἰωσήφ, τοῦ Ἡλεί, 24 τοῦ [1] Matt. x. 34 reff.
Ματθάτ, τοῦ Λευεί, τοῦ Μελχεί, τοῦ Ἰανναί, τοῦ Ἰωσήφ,
25 τοῦ Ματταθίου, τοῦ Ἀμώς, τοῦ Ναούμ, τοῦ Ἐσλεί,
τοῦ Ναγγαί, 26 τοῦ Μαάθ, τοῦ Ματταθίου, τοῦ Σεμεείν

lat-*b c* $g_{1.2}$ *l q* [Hipp$_1$] Orig$_1$[int$_1$] Eus$_1$ Ath$_2$ Ambr$_1$ Vict Quæst. rec *ως ενομιζετο* bef *υιος*, with A(D) rel vulg (lat-*f*) syr copt æth arm: txt BLℵ 1 (lat-*a*) Orig$_1$ Eus$_3$ Ath$_1$ Epiph$_4$.—aft *ενομιζετο* ins *ειναι* D lat-(*b*) *c e* ff_2 g_1 *l*.

23 to 31. for *του ηλει* to *δαυειδ*, *του ιακωβ του μαθθαν του ελεαζαρ του ελιουδ του ιαχειν του σαδωκ του αζωρ του ελιακειμ του αβιουδ του ζοροβαβελ του σαλαθιηλ του ιεχονιου του ιωακειμ του ελιακειμ του ιωσεια του αμως του μανασση του εζεκεια του αχας του ιωαθαν του οζεια του αμασιου του ιωας του οχοζιου του ιωραμ του ιωσαφαδ του ασαφ του αβιουδ του ροβοαμ του σολομων του δαυειδ* (*see* || *Matt*) D.

24. *μαθθαθ* ℵ(but originally *μαθεαθ*) [em ing. for *λευει*, *ηλειει* B[1](but corrd, Tischdf)]. rec *ιαννα*, with A rel [syr] arm [Chron$_1$]: *αννα* X: *ιανναν* H: *ιωαννα* E[1]Λ ev-y: *ιωανναν* Γ: *ιωανναι* 1: txt BLΔℵ 33. 69 am lat-*b* ff_2 *l* Syr copt goth [æth].

25. *μαθθαθιου* B[1](*ματθ.* B[2]) ev-49: *ματθαιου* G: *ματθιου* HV 33 lat-ff_2 Syr arm: *ματαθιου* X 243-58.

26. rec *σεμει*, with KUΔ[Π] 69 vulg lat-*c f* ff_2 $g_{1.2}$ syrr æth arm: *σεμεει* A rel: txt

would furnish what I conceive to be an undeniable one. Is it possible that either of these Evangelists could have set down his genealogy *with that of the other before him?* Would no remark have been made on their many and (on *such a supposition*) unaccountable variations? It is quite beside the purpose of the present commentary to attempt to reconcile the two. It has never yet been accomplished; and every endeavour to do it has violated either ingenuousness or common sense. I shall, as in similar cases, only indicate the landmarks which may serve to guide us to all that is possible for us to discover concerning them. (1) The two genealogies are *both the line of Joseph*, and *not of Mary*. Whether Mary were an heiress or not, Luke's words here preclude the idea of the genealogy being *hers;* for the descent of the Lord is transferred putatively to Joseph by the **ὡς ἐνομίζετο**, before the genealogy begins; and it would be unnatural to suppose that the reckoning, which began with the real mother, would, after such transference, pass back through *her* to *her* father again, as it must do, if the genealogy be *hers*. The attempts of many, and recently of Wieseler, to make it appear that the genealogy is that of Mary, reading υἱὸς (ὡς ἐνομ. τοῦ Ἰωσὴφ) τοῦ Ἡλί, '*the son* (*as supposed of Joseph, but in reality*) *of Heli, &c.*' are, as Meyer (Comm. in loc.) has shewn, quite unsuccessful: see Dr. Mill's vindication of the Genealogies, p. 180 ff. for the history of this opinion. (2) Luke appears to have taken this genealogy entire from some authority before him, in which the expression υἱὸς θεοῦ as applied to Christ, was made good by tracing it up as here, through a regular ascent of progenitors till we come to Adam, who was, but here again inexactly, the son of God. This seems much more probable than that Luke should for his gentile readers have gone up to the origin of the human race instead of to Abraham. I cannot imagine any such purpose *definitely present* in the mind of the Evangelist. This view is confirmed by the entirely insulated situation of the genealogy here, between ver. 23 and ch. iv. 1. (3) The points of divergence between the genealogies are,—in Matt. the father of Joseph is Jacob—in Luke, Heli; this gives rise to different lists (except two common names, Zorobabel and Salathiel) up to David, where the accounts coincide again, and remain nearly identical up to Abraham, where Matt. ceases. (4) Here, as elsewhere, I believe that the accounts might be reconciled, or at all events good reason might be assigned for their differing, if we were in possession of data on which to proceed; but here as elsewhere, *we are not*. For who shall reproduce the endless combinations of elements of confusion, which might creep into a genealogy of this kind? Matthew's, we know, is squared so as to form three tesseradecads, *by the omission of several generations;* how can we tell that some similar step unknown to us may not have been taken with the one before us? It was common among the Jews for the same man to bear different names; how do we know how often this may occur among the immediate progenitors of Joseph? The levirate marriage (of a brother with a brother's wife to raise up seed, which then might be accounted to either husband) was common; how do we know how often this may have contributed to produce variations in the terms of a genealogy? With all

τοῦ Ἰωσήχ, τοῦ Ἰωδά, 27 τοῦ Ἰωανάν, τοῦ Ῥησά, τοῦ ABDEG HKLM SUVXΓ ΔΛΠℵ 1. 33. 69
Ζοροβάβελ, τοῦ Σαλαθιήλ, τοῦ Νηρεί, 28 τοῦ Μελχεί, τοῦ
Ἀδδεί, τοῦ Κωσάμ, τοῦ Ἐλμαδάμ, τοῦ Ἤρ, 29 τοῦ Ἰησοῦ,
τοῦ Ἐλιέζερ, τοῦ Ἰωρείμ, τοῦ Μαθθάτ, τοῦ Λευεί, 30 τοῦ
Συμεών, τοῦ Ἰούδα, τοῦ Ἰωσήφ, τοῦ Ἰωνάμ, τοῦ Ἐλια-
κείμ, 31 τοῦ Μελεᾶ, τοῦ Μεννᾶ, τοῦ Ματταθά, τοῦ
Ναθάν, τοῦ Δαυείδ, 32 τοῦ Ἰεσσαί, τοῦ Ἰωβήδ, τοῦ Βοός,
τοῦ Σαλμών, τοῦ Ναασσών, 33 τοῦ Ἀμειναδάβ, τοῦ Ἀδμείν,
τοῦ Ἀρνεί, τοῦ Ἐσρώμ, τοῦ Φαρές, τοῦ Ἰούδα, 34 τοῦ
Ἰακώβ, τοῦ Ἰσαάκ, τοῦ Ἀβραάμ, τοῦ Θάρα, τοῦ Ναχώρ,
35 τοῦ Σερούχ, τοῦ Ῥαγαῦ, τοῦ Φάλεκ, τοῦ Ἔβερ, τοῦ
Σαλά, 36 τοῦ Καϊνάμ, τοῦ Ἀρφαξάδ, τοῦ Σήμ, τοῦ Νῶε,

BLℵ lat-*b e* goth, σεμειν copt. rec ιωσηφ, with A rel vulg lat-*a f q* syrr [copt-ms] goth æth: txt BLΓℵ 1. 33. 69 am lat-*b* (*c*) *e* (*ff*$_2$) *g*$_{1.2}$ copt arm. rec ιουδα, with A rel latt syrr copt æth arm: ιωαδα 1: *iuda aut ioda* Δ-lat: txt BL X(ιωδ) Γℵ 33. 69 am(with em forj harl ing mt) lat-*g*$_1$ copt-dz goth.

27. rec ιωαννα, with KM[Π] vulg lat-*a c e f* (*ff*$_2$) *g*$_{1.2}$ goth: ιωναν Uℵ^1 æth (arm): ιαναν H (251-9): ιωανναν L[S]VXΓ 1 copt: txt AB ℵ-corr$^{1.3}$ rel syrr. ζορομβαβελ ΑΛ.

28. κωσα ℵ^1 lat-*b* (*e*) [*q*]. rec ελμωδαμ, with A rel lat-*f q* syr æth, *ermodam* goth: ελμωδαν Γ lat-*g*$_2$: txt BLℵ 33 (latt) copt.

29. rec (for ιησου) ιωση, with A rel lat-*q* syrr, *iosez* goth: ιωσηχ X: ιησω Γ 1: txt BLℵ 33. 69 latt copt arm. ελιαζερ ℵ^1. rec ματθατ, with B^2 rel: ματθαν Γ 1 lat-*q* syr: ματταθιου X: ματταθ AK[Π] 33: ματτθ (sic) L: μαθατ E: μαθθααθ ℵ^1: μαθθαθ ℵ^{3a}: txt B^1 346.

30. rec ιωναν, with A rel syr[-txt] copt: ιωνα Scr's h evv-49-H-y-z latt: ιωαναν ΕΔΛ[Π]: ιωανναν K 240-5-50-9: txt BΓℵ 1 lat-*c e g*$_1$ Syr syr-mg copt-dz arm.

31. rec (for μεννα) μαϊναν, with E rel lat-*f* syr goth æth [Chron$_1$]: om A 49. 51: μεναν Γ 1 lat-*q*: μενναν vulg-mss copt-2-mss: *enam* lat-*a e*, *enan* lat-*b*, *cenam* lat-*ff*$_2$: txt BLXℵ 33 vulg lat-*c g*$_{1.2}$ copt-schw arm. [μετταθα B(Mai Tischdf).] ναθαμ Bℵ^1 lat-*c e*.

32. rec (for ιωβηδ) ωβηδ, with E rel vulg lat-*f* [D-lat] (syrr?) goth [Chron$_1$], *obeth* lat-*a b e ff*$_2$ *g*$_1$ [*l q*]: ωβηλ D-gr: ιωβηλ Bℵ^1: txt A F(Wetst) LMUX[Γ]Δℵ^{3a} 33. 69 lat-*c* copt æth. rec βοοζ, with E rel vulg lat-*c f ff*$_2$ *g*$_1$ [*q*] goth [Chron$_1$]: βαλλς (but one λ marked) ℵ^1: *boes* copt: txt ABDLM^{1}X[Π]ℵ^{3a} 33. 69 lat-*a b e* arm. for σαλμων, σαλα Bℵ^1 æth.

33. for του αμειναδαβ, του αδαμ ℵ^1 om B. rec (for αδμειν του αρνει) αραμ, with ADEGHU[Π] 33 vulg lat-*a c f ff*$_2$ *g*$_{1.2}$ [*l q*] Syr goth: αραμ του ιωραμ F(Wetst) KMSVΔΛ syr(but mss vary): αραμ τ. ωριν æth: αραμ του αλμει του αρνει 1: txt BL(XΓ)ℵ syr-mg copt (but αδμιν ℵ, αθμη X, αλμειν Γ), αδμιν του αρηι(sic) 69. εσρων B ev-y tol lat-*b* Syr, ασρωμ *asron* D. om του φαρες A.

34. θαρρα Xℵ^{3a} 1. 33. 69 evv-H-y-z syr [copt-wilk Chron$_1$].

35. rec σαρουχ, with Scr's a b vulg-ed: txt ABℵ rel Scr's-mss am(with em forj fuld ing tol) lat-*a c f ff*$_2$ *g*$_{1.2}$ *l* copt goth arm [Chron$_1$], σερουκ D lat-*b*. φαλεγ AEGH KMSUΓΛ[Π] 1. 69 vulg-ed goth Chron: *phalech* lat-*a f g*$_1$ copt-wilk.

36. rec καιναν, with A rel latt copt (goth?) [Chron$_1$]: txt BLℵ 1. 33 æth, and A(twice) in Gen x. 24.—om του κα. D.

these elements of confusion, it is quite as presumptuous to pronounce the genealogies discrepant, as it is over-curious and uncritical to attempt to reconcile them. It may suffice us that they are inserted in the Gospels as authentic documents, and both of them merely to clear the Davidical descent of the putative father of the Lord. HIS OWN *real* Davidical descent *does not depend on either of them*, but must be *solely derived through his mother*. See much interesting investigation of the various solutions and traditions, in Dr. Mill's tract referred to above; and in Lord A. Hervey's work on the Genealogies of our Lord. **27. τ. Σαλαθ., τ. Νηρεί]** In Matt. i. 12, Ἰεχονίας γεννᾷ τ. Σαλαθ. **31. Ναθάν]** See 2 Sam. v. 14:

τοῦ Λάμεχ, 37 τοῦ Μαθουσάλα, τοῦ Ἐνώχ, τοῦ Ἰαρέδ,
τοῦ Μαλελεήλ, τοῦ Καϊνάν, 38 τοῦ Ἐνώς, τοῦ Σήθ, τοῦ
Ἀδάμ, τοῦ θεοῦ.

IV. 1 Ἰησοῦς δὲ [a] πλήρης πνεύματος ἁγίου [b] ὑπέστρεψεν ἀπὸ τοῦ Ἰορδάνου, καὶ [c] ἤγετο [d] ἐν τῷ πνεύματι ἐν τῇ
ἐρήμῳ 2 ἡμέρας τεσσεράκοντα [e] πειραζόμενος ὑπὸ τοῦ [f] διαβόλου. καὶ οὐκ ἔφαγεν οὐδὲν ἐν ταῖς ἡμέραις ἐκείναις,
καὶ [g] συντελεσθεισῶν αὐτῶν ἐπείνασεν. 3 εἶπεν δὲ αὐτῷ
ὁ [f] διάβολος Εἰ υἱὸς εἶ τοῦ θεοῦ, [h] εἰπὲ τῷ λίθῳ τούτῳ
[h] ἵνα [i] γένηται ἄρτος. 4 καὶ ἀπεκρίθη πρὸς αὐτὸν ὁ Ἰησοῦς

...θεου X. Ξ[Frag. Neap. (appy)] ιησους ... ...διαβολου Ξ ABDEG HKLM SUVΓΔ ΛΠℵ Frag. Neap. 1. 33. 69

a ch. v. 12. John i. 14. Acts vi. 3, 5, 8. Job x. 15.
b ch. ii. 20 reff.
c = John i. 43 al.
d ch. ii. 27. Rev. i. 10. iv. 2.
e ||. 1 Cor. vii. 5. James i. 13. Wisd. ii. 24.
f || Mt. 1 Chron. xxi. 1. Job i. 6. Wisd. ii. 24.
g ver. 13. Mark xiii. 4. Acts xxi. 27. Rom. ix. 28 (from Isa. x. 23). Heb. viii. 8 only. Job i. 5.
h constr., || Mt. reff.
i = John ii. 9 reff.

λαμεκ D-gr [MX].
37. [μαθθουσαλα B[1].] ιαρετ B[1](sic cod: see table) ℵ [lat-*a l q*]: ιαρεθ AK lat-*b c* g_1. μελελεηλ A Λ(Treg, expr) ℵ[1] [69(Tischdf)] copt-ms. καιναμ Lℵ lat-ff_2 copt-dz.
38. for σηθ, σημ A lat-*l*.

CHAP. IV. **1.** rec πνευματος αγιου bef πληρης, with A rel lat-*e* goth arm [Thdrt$_1$]: txt BDE F(Wetst) KLΞ[Π]ℵ 1. 33 latt syrr [æth Bas$_1$ Orig-int$_2$]. om υπεστρεψεν ℵ[1](ins ℵ-corr[1]). aft ηγετο ins το (sic) ℵ. rec εις την ερημον, with AΞ rel vulg-ed(with am forj) lat-*c e f* g_2 *l* [ff_2 copt Eus$_1$ Bas$_1$ Thdrt$_1$]: txt BDLℵ fuld(with em harl mt) lat-*a b* g_1 *q* sah.
2. for διαβολου, σατανα D 243 lat-*e*. ℵ[1] repeats ουδεν, marked for erasure by ℵ-corr[1][: for ουδεν, ουδε επιεν A Frag-neap 69 arm]. rec ins υστερον bef επεινασεν (*from* || *Matt*), with A rel lat-*f* ff_2 [*q*] syrr copt-dz[2] goth [Cyr$_1$]: om BDLℵ latt coptt æth arm.
3. rec (for ειπεν δε) και ειπεν (|| *Matt*), with A rel lat-*e q* syrr goth æth arm Thdrt$_1$: txt BDLℵ 1. 33 latt copt Ambr$_1$. for τω λιθω to αρτος, ινα οι λιθοι ουτοι αρτοι γενωνται (|| *Matt*) D ev-31 tol.
4. for και απεκρ., απεκρ. δε 69: κ. αποκριθεις D. rec (for προς αυτον ο ιησους) ιησους προς αυτον λεγων, with A rel syr sah goth arm (ο ιησ. M 1): ο ιησ. ειπεν D: ιησ. λεγων 69: πρ. αυτ. ο ιησ. λεγων Δ lat-*c e f* g_2 (*et dixit* lat-*a b* ff_2 g_1 *q*): txt BLℵ

Chron. iii. 5: Zech. xii. 12. **36. Καϊνάμ]** This name does not exist in our present Hebrew text, but in the LXX, Gen. x. 24; xi. 12, 13, and furnishes a curious instance of one of two things—either (1) the corruption of our present Hebrew text in these chronological passages; or (2) the incorrectness of the LXX, and notwithstanding that, the high reputation which it had obtained in so short a time. Lightfoot holds the latter alternative: but I own I think the former more probable. See on the whole question of the appearance of this second Cainam(n) among the ancestors of our Lord, Lord A. Hervey's work above cited, ch. viii., in which, with much research and acuteness, he has endeavoured to shew that the name was probably interpolated here, and got from hence into the LXX. Certainly it appears not to have existed in the earliest copies of that version.

CHAP. IV. 1—13.] TEMPTATION OF JESUS. Matt. iv. 1—11. Mark i. 12, 13.

Ver. **1** is peculiar to Luke, and very important. Our Lord was now full of the Holy Ghost, and in that fulness He is led up to combat with the enemy. He has arrived at the fulness of the stature of perfect man, outwardly and spiritually. And as when His Church was inaugurated by the descent of the Spirit in His fulness, so now, the first and fittest weapon for the combat is "the sword of the Spirit, which is the word of God." The discourse of Peter in Acts ii., like our Lord's replies here, is grounded in the testimony of the Scripture. The accounts of Matt. and Luke (Mark's is principally a compendium) are distinct: see notes on Matt. and Mark. **2.]** The literal rendering of the present text will be: **Jesus . . . . was led by** (*in, in the power of*, the ἐν of instrumentality by the conditioning element) **the Spirit in the wilderness, being tempted** (the pres. part. carries a slight ratiocinative force, as usual) **during forty days by the devil.** So that St. Luke, as also St. Mark, implies that the temptation continued *the whole forty days*.

οὐκ ἔφ. οὐδ. testifies to the strictness in which the term 'fasted' must be taken.

Γέγραπται ὅτι οὐκ ᵏἐπ' ἄρτῳ μόνῳ ᵏζήσεται ὁ ἄνθρωπος.
5 καὶ ˡἀναγαγὼν αὐτὸν ἔδειξεν αὐτῷ πάσας τὰς βασιλείας τῆς ᵐοἰκουμένης ἐν ⁿστιγμῇ χρόνου. 6 καὶ εἶπεν
αὐτῷ ὁ ᶠδιάβολος Σοὶ δώσω τὴν ᵒἐξουσίαν ταύτην ἅπασαν καὶ τὴν δόξαν αὐτῶν, ὅτι ἐμοὶ ᵖπαραδέδοται, καὶ ᾧ
ἂν θέλω δίδωμι αὐτήν· 7 σὺ οὖν ἐὰν ᵠπροσκυνήσῃς
ᵠἐνώπιον ἐμοῦ, ʳἔσται σου πᾶσα. 8 καὶ ἀποκριθεὶς αὐτῷ
εἶπεν [ὁ] Ἰησοῦς Γέγραπται ˢΠροσκυνήσεις κύριον τὸν
θεόν σου, καὶ αὐτῷ μόνῳ ˢλατρεύσεις. 9 ἤγαγεν δὲ
αὐτὸν εἰς Ἱερουσαλὴμ καὶ ἔστησεν ἐπὶ τὸ ᵗπτερύγιον
τοῦ ἱεροῦ, καὶ εἶπεν αὐτῷ Εἰ υἱὸς εἶ τοῦ θεοῦ, βάλε
σεαυτὸν ἐντεῦθεν κάτω· 10 γέγραπται γὰρ ὅτι τοῖς

k ‖ Mt. only. Gen. xx ii. 40. Deut. viii. 3.
l abs., = here only. see ch. ii. 22 reff.
m Matt. xxiv. 14 reff.
n here only. Isa. xxix. 5. 2 Macc. ix. 11 only.
o = Matt. xxviii. 18. Rev. xiii. 4. Dan. vii. 4.
p = Matt. xi. 27. Acts xxviii. 16. Deut. i. 8.
q Rev. iii. 9. xv. 4. Ps. lxxxv. 9. Isa. lxvi. 23.
r Matt. v. 3. xix. 14.
s ‖ Mt. (reff.)
t ‖ Mt. only. 1 Kings xv. 27. Dan. ix. 27 Theod. A B-marg. (not Ed-vat.)

Ξ και ειπεν...
F [απο]-κριθεις...
ABDEF GHKL MSUVΓ ΔΛΞΠℵ Frag. Neap. 1. 33. 69

33 vulg coptt. om *οτι* (*as* ‖ *Matt*) D 69. rec at end adds *αλλ' επι παντι ρηματι θεου*, with A rel; *αλλ' εν π. ρ. θ.* D latt; *αλλ' επι π. ρ. εκπορευομενω δια στοματος θεου* 118-57. 209 Scr's g r evv-H-z copt-wilk æth Thl: (*from* ‖ *Matt: the rec and the readg in* D *merely supplying the* sense, *the other* verbatim. *The* omission *would be unaccountable:*) om BLℵ copt-schw sah.

5. rec aft *αυτον* ins *ο διαβολος* (*from* ‖ *Matt*), with A rel vulg lat-*b c f* syrr goth æth [Hil_1]; *ο σατανας* syr-ms: om BDLℵ 1 lat-*a e* coptt arm [Cyr_1]. rec adds further *εις ορος υψηλον* (*from* ‖ *Matt. It is no objection* (Mey) *that rec does not add λιαν. The insn was made* carelessly from memory, *as above, as well as accurately, in* D), with A ℵ-corr¹ rel vulg lat-*c* [*f* ff_2 *q*] syrr goth; *ε. ο. υψ. λιαν* D 69 lat-*a* Δ-lat: om BLℵ¹ am(with em forj fuld harl mt tol) lat-*b* $g_{1.2}$ coptt [Cyr_1]. for *της οικουμενης, του κοσμου* (‖ *Matt*) D 5. 245 lat-*f* $Orig\text{-}comm_1$.

6. for *αυτω, προς αυτον* D lat-*a b c* [*e q*] Hil_1. for *απασ., πασαν* ℵ. for *αυτων, τουτων* D[-gr]. rec *εαν*, with Aℵ rel [Cyr_1]: txt BD. (33 def.) for *διδωμι, δωσω* ℵ¹.

7. aft *προσκυν.* ins *μοι* ℵ¹. rec (for *εμου*) *μου*, with Aℵ³ᵃ rel [Cyr_1]: txt BDE F(Wetst) HVΓΔΛΞℵ¹ 1 [Frag-neap]. rec *παντα*, *omnia* latt arm [Cyr_1]: txt AB D-gr Ξℵ rel Scr's-mss Thl.

8. *ειπ. αυτ. ο ιησ.* AKM¹[Π] lat-*a b c q*: *ο ιησ. ειπ. αυτ.* FL M-marg(in red) Ξℵ 1. 13. 33. 69 vulg [lat-*f* ff_2 $g_{1.2}$] Syr copt: *αυτω ο ιησ.* DΛ syr goth [arm]: txt B(omg *δ*) rel. rec aft *ιησ.* ins *υπαγε οπισω μου σατανα* (*see* ‖ *Matt and Matt* xvi. 23), with A rel lat-*b e q* syr copt-wilk [æth-ms] Thl: om BDLΞℵ 1. 33 vulg lat-*a c f* ff_2 $g_{1.2}$ (*l*?) Syr copt-schw sah goth æth arm Orig(speaking of ‖ Matt wholly rejects *οπ. μου*). rec aft *γεγραπται* ins *γαρ* (*from* ‖ *Matt*), with UΔΛ [Frag-neap] lat-*b q*: om ABDΞℵ rel vulg lat-*a c e f* ff_2 $g_{1.2}$ *l* syrr coptt goth æth arm Orig. *κυρ. τ. θ. σ.* bef *προσκ.* (*see* ‖ *Matt*) BDFLΛΞℵ 1. 33. 69 latt syrr copt goth æth $Orig_1$[int_1 Cyr_1] $Cypr_1$: txt A rel (lat-*a*) sah arm.

9. rec (for *ηγ. δε*) *και ηγ.*, with AD rel: txt BLΞℵ syr-mg coptt $Orig\text{-}int_1$. rec aft *εστησεν* ins *αυτον* (*see* ‖ *Matt*), with AD rel [vss]: om BLΞℵ lat-*e* [arm-ed] Orig-int_1. rec ins *ο* bef *υιος*, with Scr's b o: om ABDΞℵ rel Scr's-mss. for 2nd *του, τουτου* D¹.

10. om *γαρ* ℵ¹(ins ℵ-corr¹(appy)·³ᵃ).

3.] **τῷ λ. τ.**, pointing to some particular stone—**command that it become a loaf.** **4.**] The citation is given in full by Matt. **5.**] There can be little doubt that the order in Matt., in which this temptation is placed *last*, is to be adhered to in our expositions of the Temptation. No definite notes of succession are given in our text, but they *are* by Matt.: see notes there. Schleiermacher and Bleek suppose that the inversion has been made as suiting better the requirements of probability: it seeming more natural that our Lord should be first taken to the mountain and then to Jerusalem, than the converse. **6.**] Satan is set forth to us in Scripture as *the prince*, or *god of this world*,—by our Lord Himself, John xii. 31; xiv. 30; xvi. 11:—by Paul, 2 Cor. iv. 4 (Eph. vi. 12). On the *signification* of this temptation, see notes on Matt. **8.**] With the words ὕπ. ὀπ. μ. σ. (rec.) here, Luke could hardly have left the record as it stands: being the

ἀγγέλοις αὐτοῦ [u] ἐντελεῖται περὶ σοῦ τοῦ [v] διαφυλάξαι σε,
11 καὶ ὅτι [w] ἐπὶ χειρῶν [w] ἀροῦσίν σε, μήποτε [x] προςκόψῃς
πρὸς λίθον τὸν πόδα σου. 12 καὶ ἀποκριθεὶς εἶπεν αὐτῷ
ὁ Ἰησοῦς ὅτι [y] εἴρηται Οὐκ [z] ἐκπειράσεις κύριον τὸν θεόν
σου. 13 καὶ [a] συντελέσας παντα [b] πειρασμὸν ὁ διάβολος
[c] ἀπέστη ἀπ᾽ αὐτοῦ [d] ἄχρι καιροῦ.
14 Καὶ [e] ὑπέστρεψεν ὁ Ἰησοῦς ἐν τῇ [f] δυνάμει τοῦ πνεύματος εἰς τὴν Γαλιλαίαν, καὶ [g] φήμη ἐξῆλθεν [h] καθ᾽ ὅλης

u ‖ Mt. reff. Psa. xc. 11.
v here only. Gen. xxviii. 15, 20. Prov. ii. 8.
w w. gen., ‖ Mt. (from l. c.) only. Isa. lx. 4.
x ‖ Mt. reff.
y = ch. ii. 24 reff.
z ‖ Mt. reff. Deut. vi. 16.
a ver. 2 reff. 2 Chron. xxx. 22.
b ch. xi. 4. xxii. 28, 40, 46. 1 Pet. iv. 12 al. Deut. iv. 34.
c ch. ii. 37. Acts v. 38. 2 Cor. xii. 8. 1 Kings xvi. 23.
d Acts xiii. 11 Rom. i. 13. 2 Macc. xiv. 15.
e ch. ii. 20 reff.
f Acts i. 8. Rom. xv. 13, 19.
g Matt. ix. 26 only. Prov. xvi. 2 (xv. 30). 2 Macc. iv. 39 only.
h = ch. xxiii. 5. Acts ix. 31, 42. x. 37.

11. om *οτι* DEFGHSUVΓΔΛ lat-*a b l* Syr sah æth [Orig-int$_4$] Eus : ins ABℵ rel vulg lat-*c e f ff$_2$ g$_{1.2}$* syr copt goth Orig$_1$.

12. *ο ιησ.* bef *ειπ. αυ.* DΞ 33 vulg lat-*c f ff$_2$* (Syr) syr copt. om *οτι* D ℵ-corr[1] (but restored) latt(not *a*) Syr arm. for *ειρηται, γεγραπται* D Scr's c lat-*a b c e f ff$_2$ g$_1$ l* [*q* Orig-int$_1$] : om 243 ev-y.

13. *αχρι χρονου ad tempus* D lat-*b c*, *usque in tempore* lat-*a*.

first direct recognition by our Lord of His foe, after which, and in obedience to which command, he departs from Him.

10.] **τοῦ διαφ. σε** is wanting in Matt. The LXX following the Hebrew adds *ἐν πάσαις ταῖς ὁδοῖς σου.* **13. ἄχρι καιρ.**] See on Matt., ver. 11, and note on ch. xxii. 53.

14—32.] Circuit of Galilee. Teaching, and rejection, at Nazareth. *Peculiar to Luke* in this form : but see Matt. iv. 12—25; xiii. 53—58 ‖ Mark, and note below. **14.**] **ἐν τῇ δ. τ. πν., in the power** of that full anointing **of the Spirit** for His holy office, which He had received at His baptism: and also implying that this power was used by Him in doing mighty works. Here the chronological order of Luke's history begins to be confused, and the first evident marks occur of indefiniteness in arrangement, which I believe characterizes this Gospel. And in observing this, I would once for all premise, (1) that I have no bias for finding such chronological inaccuracy, and have only done so where no fair and honest means will solve the difficulty; (2) that where internal evidence appears to me to decide this to be the case, I have taken the only way open to a Commentator who would act uprightly by the Scriptures, and fairly acknowledged and met the difficulty; (3) that so far from considering the testimony of the Evangelists to be weakened by such inaccuracies, I am convinced that it becomes only so much the stronger (see Prolegomena to the Gospels). These remarks have been occasioned by the relation of this account, vv. 14—30, to the Gospels of Matthew and John. Our verses 14 and 15 embrace the narrative of Matthew in ch. iv. 12—25. But after that comes an event which belongs to a later period of our Lord's ministry. A fair comparison of our vv. 16—24 with Matt. xiii. 53—58 and Mark vi. 1—6, entered on without bias, and conducted solely from the narratives themselves, surely can hardly fail to convince us of their identity. (1) That *two such visits should have happened,* is of itself *not impossible ;* though (with the sole exception of Jerusalem for obvious reasons) our Lord did not ordinarily revisit the places where He had been rejected as in our vv. 28, 29. (2) That He should have been thus treated at His first visit, and then *marvelled at their unbelief* on His second, is *utterly impossible.* (Stier, in the 2nd ed. of his Reden Jesu, says, with reference to the above position of mine, "To this we give a very simple answer: It was at their persistence in unbelief, after their first emotion and confusion, after His continued teaching and working of miracles, that He wondered." But it may fairly be rejoined, is there any sign of this in the narratives of Matt. and Mark? Is it not a forcing of their spirit to suit a preconceived notion?) (3) That the same question should have been asked on both occasions, and answered by our Lord with the same proverbial expression, is in the highest degree improbable. (4) Besides, this narrative itself bears *internal* marks of belonging to a later period. The **ὅσα ἠκούσ. γεν. εἰς τὴν Καφαρν.** must refer to *more than one* miracle done there: indeed the whole form of the sentence points to the plain fact, that our Lord had been residing long in Capernaum. Compare too its introduction here without any notification, with its description as **πόλιν τῆς Γαλ.** in ver. 31, and the separateness

τῆς [i] περιχώρου περὶ αὐτοῦ. 15 καὶ αὐτὸς ἐδίδασκεν ἐν
ταῖς συναγωγαῖς [k] αὐτῶν, [l] δοξαζόμενος ὑπὸ πάντων.
16 καὶ ἦλθεν εἰς Ναζαρᾶ οὗ ἦν [m] τεθραμμένος, καὶ εἰςῆλθεν
[n] κατὰ τὸ [no] εἰωθὸς αὐτῷ ἐν τῇ [p] ἡμέρᾳ τῶν [p] σαββάτων
εἰς τὴν συναγωγήν, καὶ [q] ἀνέστη [r] ἀναγνῶναι. 17 καὶ
[s] ἐπεδόθη αὐτῷ βιβλίον τοῦ προφήτου Ἡσαΐου· καὶ
[t] ἀναπτύξας τὸ βιβλίον εὗρεν τὸν [u] τόπον οὗ ἦν γεγραμμένον 18 [v] Πνεῦμα κυρίου ἐπ᾽ ἐμέ, [w] οὗ [w] εἵνεκεν [x] ἔχρισέν

ABDEF GHKL MSUVΓ ΔΛΞΠℵ Frag. Neap. 1. 33. 69

i Matt. iii. 5. xiv. 35 al. Deut. iii. 14.
k Matt. iv. 23 reff.
l Matt. vi. 2 reff.
m = here only (Matt. vi. 26 reff.)‡. 1 Macc. iii. 33.
n Acts xvii. 2 only. Num. xxiv. 1 only.
o Matt. xxvii. 15 reff.
p Acts xiii. 14. xvi. 13 only. Exod. xx. 8. see ch. xiii. 14, 16. xiv. 5 (John xix. 31).
q Matt. ix. 9. xxvi. 62. ver. 29. 2 Chron. xx. 5.
r = Acts xiii. 27. xv. 21 al. Neh. viii. 8.
s Matt. vii. 9, 10 reff.
t here only. 4 Kings xix. 14.
u = here only. Xen. Mem. ii. 1. 20.
v Acts viii. 39. [see Matt. iii. 16 reff.] Isa. lxi. 1.
w here only. l. c. Hom. Il. α. 11, and passim in classics.
x Acts iv. 27. x. 38. 1 Cor. i. 21. Heb. i. 9 (from Ps. xliv. 7) only.

14. for περιχωρου, χωρας ℵ [*regionem* latt(not *a e*)].
15. om αυτος A 11-pe lat-*e*. om αυτων D lat-*a b l*.
16. ελθων δε D lat-*e*. rec ins την bef ναζαρα, with A rel Eus_1 : om BDLΔΛΞℵ 1 $Orig_1$ [Cyr_1]. (On the form of the proper name, see prolegomena.) οπου D 69. ανατεθραμμενος FLΞℵ 1. 33. 69 Eus_1 Cyr_2. om τεθραμμενος και εισηλθεν D -gr(ins D[8]). om αυτω D lat-*a c* copt-dz.
17. rec ησαιου bef του προφητου, with A rel vulg lat-*c e f ff₂ g₁*[*₂ l* syrr syr-jer] copt goth [æth arm] : ο προφητης ησαιας (omg βιβλ.) D : txt BLΞℵ 33. 69 am(with forj fuld ing per) lat-*a b q* Orig-int_1. for αναπτυξας, ανοιξας (*explany*) ABLΞ 33 syrr copt æth arm Jer : txt D[3]ℵ rel latt syr-jer goth Eus_1 Orig-int_1, απτυξας D[1]. om το βιβλιον D evv. om τον LΞℵ 33.
18. (εινεκεν, so every uncial MS.)

of the two pieces will be apparent: see further remarks in the notes below. Here however is omitted an important cycle of our Lord's sayings and doings, both in Galilee and Jerusalem; viz. that contained in John i. 29—iv. 54 included. This will be shewn by comparing Matt. iv. 12, where it is stated that our Lord's return to Galilee was *after the casting of John into prison,* with John iii. 24, where, on occasion of the Lord and the disciples baptizing in Judæa, it is said, *John was not yet cast into prison:* see note on Matt. iv. 12. **φήμη**] The report, namely, of His miracles in Capernaum, wrought **ἐν τῇ δυν. τ. πν.**, and possibly of what He had done and taught at Jerusalem at the feast. **15.**] Olshausen well remarks (Bibl. Comm. i. 190), that this verse, containing a general undefined notice of our Lord's synagogue-teaching, quite takes from what follows any chronological character. Indeed we find throughout the early part of this Gospel the same fragmentary stamp. Compare ἐν τοῖς σάββασιν, ver. 31—ἐν τῷ ἐπικεῖσθαι, ch. v. 1—ἐν τῷ εἶναι αὐτ. ἐν μιᾷ τ. πόλ., ch. v. 12—ἐν μιᾷ τ. ἡμερῶν, ch. v. 17; viii. 22—ἐν ἑτέρῳ σαβ., ch. vi. 6—ἐν ταῖς ἡμ. ταύτ., ch. vi. 12, &c. &c. **16.**] **οὗ ἦν τεθραμμένος** = ἐν τῇ πατρίδι σου, ver. 23: see John iv. 44 and note. **κατὰ τὸ εἰωθός** refers to the *whole* of what He did—it is not merely that He had been in the habit of *attending* the synagogues, but of *teaching* in them: see ver. 15. It was apparently the first time He had ever so taught in the synagogue at Nazareth. **ἀνέστη ἀναγν.**] The *rising up* was probably to shew His wish to *explain* the Scripture; for so ἀναγν. imports. Ezra is called an ἀναγνώστης τοῦ θείου νόμου, Jos. Antt. xi. 5. 1. The ordinary way was, for the ruler of the synagogue to call upon persons of any learning or note to read and explain. That the demand of the Lord was so readily complied with, is sufficiently accounted for by vv. 14, 15. See reff. **17.**] It is doubtful whether the Rabbinical cycle of Sabbath readings, or lessons from the law and prophets, were as yet in use: but some regular plan was adopted; and according to that plan, after the reading of the law, which always preceded, the portion from the prophets came to be read (see Acts xiii. 15), which, for that sabbath, fell in the prophet Isaiah. The roll containing that book (probably, that alone) was given to the Lord. But it does not appear that He read any part of the lesson for the day; but when He had unrolled the scroll, **found** (the fortuitous, i. e. *providential,* finding is the most likely interpretation, not the searching for and finding) the passage which follows.

No inference can be drawn as to the *time of the year* from this narrative; partly on account of the uncertainty above mentioned, and partly because it is not

..iv. 19 (appy) Frag. Neap.

με [yz] ευαγγελίσασθαι [z] πτωχοῖς, ἀπέσταλκέν με 19 [a] κηρύξαι
[b] αἰχμαλώτοις [c] ἄφεσιν καὶ τυφλοῖς [d] ἀνάβλεψιν, [e] ἀποστεῖλαι [f] τεθραυσμένους [g] ἐν [h] ἀφέσει, [i] κηρύξαι [k] ἐνιαυτὸν
κυρίου [l] δεκτόν. 20 καὶ [m] πτύξας τὸ βιβλίον, [n] ἀπο-
δοὺς τῷ [o] ὑπηρέτῃ [p] ἐκάθισεν· καὶ πάντων οἱ ὀφθαλμοὶ
ἐν τῇ συναγωγῇ ἦσαν [q] ἀτενίζοντες αὐτῷ. 21 ἤρξατο δὲ
λέγειν πρὸς αὐτοὺς ὅτι σήμερον πεπλήρωται ἡ [r] γραφὴ
αὕτη ἐν τοῖς [s] ὠσὶν ὑμῶν. 22 καὶ πάντες [t] ἐμαρτύρουν
αὐτῷ, καὶ [u] ἐθαύμαζον [u] ἐπὶ τοῖς λόγοις τῆς [v] χάριτος
τοῖς [w] ἐκπορευομένοις ἐκ τοῦ στόματος αὐτοῦ, καὶ ἔλεγον

...εκαθισεν Ξ. X ηρξατο...

y ch. i. 19 reff. w. dat. only, Rom. i. 15. Gal. i. 8. iv. 13.
z see ch. vii. 22 ‖ Mt.
a = ch. xxiv. 47.
b here only. Isa. lii. 2.
c = here only. Lev. xxv. 10.
d here only. Isa l. c. only.
e Mark viii. 26. Isa. lviii. 6.
f here only. Exod. xv. 6. Deut. xxviii. 33.
g ch. i. 77 reff.
h = here only. l. c.
i = ch. iii. 3 reff. k John xi. 49, 51 al. Lev. xxv. 10. l ver. 24. Acts x. 35. 2 Cor. vi. 2, from Isa. xlix. 8. Phil. iv. 18 only. m here only +. πτ. τὰς ἐπιστολάς, Jos. Antt. x. 1. 4. n = ch. ix. 42. o Matt. v. 25 reff. p intr., Matt. v. 1 reff. q Luke only, exc. 2 Cor. iii. 7, 13. dat., ch. xxii. 56. Acts iii. 12 al. Job vii. 8 A. r Mark xii. 10. John xix. 24, &c. Acts i. 16. s ch. i. 44. Acts xi. 22. Neh. xiii. 1 al. t = Matt. xxiii. 31 reff. u Mark xii. 17 reff. v = Eph. iv. 29. Col. iv. 6. Ps. xliv. 2. Prov. x. 32. w Matt. xv. 11, &c. Eph iv. 29. Num. xxxii. 24.

rec ευαγγελιζεσθαι (with **1. 33**, e sil): txt ABDΞℵ rel Scr's-mss $Orig_2$ Petr Eus_6 Ath_1 Cyr_1 Thdrt Suid. (-σασθαι *might be from* LXX *: but on the other hand the change to* -ζεσθαι *was obvious, and the ms authority is overwhelming.*) for απεσταλκεν με, απεσταλμαι D[1]-gr(txt D[3]). rec adds ιασασθαι τους συντετριμμενους την καρδιαν (*from* LXX), with A rel vulg-ed(with em gat) lat-*f* syrr goth Iren-int Hil: om BDLΞℵ 33. 69 am(with forj harl ing mt per tol) copt æth $Orig_2[int_1]$ Petr Eus_7 Ath_1 Tit-bostr Cyr_1 Aug.

19. τεθραυματισμενους D[1], τεθραυμενους D-corr.

20. rec εν τη συναγωγη bef οι οφθαλμοι, with D rel vulg lat-*a* syrr arm; εν τη συναγωγη ησαν bef οι οφθαλμοι AK[Π] lat-*b* copt goth: txt BFLℵ 33 lat(-*c*) *q* (æth) Eus_2.

21. om οτι D arm (Orig).

quite clear whether the roll contained only Isaiah, or other books also. **18—20.**] The quotation agrees mainly with the LXX:—the words **ἀποστεῖλαι τεθρ. ἐν ἀφέσει** are inserted from the LXX of Isa. lviii. 6. The meaning of this prophetic citation may be better seen, when we remember that it stands in the middle of the third great division of the book of Isaiah (ch. xlix.—lxvi.), that, viz. which comprises the prophecies of the Person, office, sufferings, triumph, and Church of the Messiah;—and thus by implication announces the *fulfilment of all that went before*, in Him who then addressed them. **18. πνεῦμα κ.**] See Isa. xi. 2; xlii. 1. **οὗ εἵν.**] because, = יַעַן. **αἰχμ. ἄφ.**] See ch. xiii. 12, 16. **τυφλ. ἀν.**] See John ix. 39. The Hebrew words thus rendered by the LXX, לַאֲסוּרִים פְּקַח־קוֹחַ, signify, '*to those who are bound, the opening of prison:*' so that we have here the LXX and literal rendering both included, and the latter expressed in the LXX words of Isa. lviii. 6. **19. ἐνιαυτ. κυρ. δεκ.**] See Levit. xxv. 8—17, where in ver. 10 we find that liberty was proclaimed to all in the land in the year of jubilee (in the prophecy, **κηρύξαι**=καλέσαι LXX). No countenance is given by this expression to the extraordinary inference from it of some of the Fathers (Clement of Alex., Origen), that the Lord's public ministry lasted *only a year, and something over.* Compare John ii. 13; vi. 4; xiii. 1. **20. ἐκάθισεν**] It was the custom in the synagogues to *stand* while reading the law, and *sit down* to explain it. Our Lord on other occasions taught *sitting*, e. g. Matt. v. 1: Mark iv. 1; xiii. 3. The **ὑπηρέτης** was the חַזָּן whose duty it was to keep the sacred books. **21.**] **ἤρξ. δὲ λέγειν**—implying that the following words are merely the substance of a more expanded discourse, which our Lord uttered to that effect: see another occasion in Matt. xi. 4, 5, where the same truth was declared by a series of gracious acts of mercy. **ἡ γρ. κ.τ.λ.**] Not '*this Scripture which is in your ears*'—as the Syriac (Etheridge's translation, p. 407); which would be ἡ γρ. αὕτη ἡ ἐν τ. ὠ., and even then an unusual form of construction: but, **is fulfilled in your hearing**, by My proclaiming it, and My course of ministry. **22.**] **ἐμαρτ. αὐ.**, **bore witness to him (that it was so).** The **λόγοι τ. χ.** must be the discourse of which ver. 21 is a compendium. **ἔλεγ.**] i. e. πάντες, not τινές. While acknowledging the truth of what He said, and the power with which He said it,

Οὐχὶ υἱός ἐστιν Ἰωσὴφ οὗτος; 23 καὶ εἶπεν πρὸς ABDEF GHKL
αὐτοὺς [x] Πάντως ἐρεῖτέ μοι τὴν παραβολὴν ταύτην, MSUVX ΓΔΛΠℵ
[y] Ἰατρὲ θεράπευσον σεαυτόν· ὅσα [z] ἠκούσαμεν [z] γενόμενα 1. 33. 69
[a] εἰς τὴν Καφαρναούμ, ποίησον καὶ ὧδε ἐν τῇ [b] πατρίδι
σου. 24 [c] εἶπεν δὲ [d] Ἀμὴν λέγω ὑμῖν ὅτι οὐδεὶς προφήτης
[e] δεκτός ἐστιν ἐν τῇ [b] πατρίδι αὐτοῦ. 25 [f] ἐπ᾽ ἀληθείας δὲ
λέγω ὑμῖν, πολλαὶ [g] χῆραι ἦσαν ἐν ταῖς ἡμέραις Ἡλίου
ἐν τῷ Ἰσραήλ, ὅτε [h] ἐκλείσθη ὁ [h] οὐρανὸς [[i] ἐπὶ] ἔτη τρία C επι ετη...
καὶ μῆνας ἕξ, ὡς ἐγένετο λιμὸς μέγας ἐπὶ πᾶσαν τὴν γῆν·
26 καὶ πρὸς οὐδεμίαν αὐτῶν ἐπέμφθη Ἡλίας, εἰ μὴ εἰς
Σάρεπτα τῆς Σιδωνίας πρὸς γυναῖκα [g] χήραν. 27 καὶ

x Acts xxi. 22. Rom. iii. 9 al. L.P.+ Tobit xiv. 8 (not ℵ). 2 Macc. iii. 13 only.
y ch. v. 31 ‖. viii. 43 ‖. Col. iv. 14 only. Jer. viii. 22.
z constr., Acts vii. 12. xxiv. 10. ch. viii. 46.
a = ver. 44. Mark i. 39 al.
b Matt. xiii. 54, 57 reff.
c ch. vi. 39. xii. 16. xiii. 20. xv. 11.
d Matt. v. 18 reff.
e ver. 19 reff.
f = ch. xxii. 59. (Mark xii. 14 reff.) Job ix. 2.
g Mark xii. 40, 42, 43 al. 3 Kings xvii. 9, 10.
h = Rev. xi. 6. see Sir. xlviii. 3.
i Acts xiii. 31. Heb. xi. 30 al.

22. rec *ουχ ουτ. εστ. ο υι. ιωσ.*, with A rel vulg lat-*b c f ff*$_2$ *g*$_1$ [*q*] syrr copt goth æth arm: *ουχι υι. ιωσ. εστ. ουτ.* D [lat-*a e* Cyr$_1$]: txt BLℵ 69 lat-*a e* Cyr$_2$, but *ουχ ο υι.* 69 [Cyr$_1$].
23. *γεινομενα* D. rec (for *εις την*) *εν τη* (*corrn to sense*), with X rel copt; *εν* AKΛ[Π] Epiph$_1$; *εις* DL 69: txt Bℵ. (*The art is retained, as unusual with a proper name aft a preposition, and as attested both by* Bℵ *and by the* MSS *which read εν τη.*)
24. *αμην* is repeated in D 300(Sz). *υμιν* bef *λεγω* AE[G]HVΓ Λ(Treg, expr) syr goth. *εαυτου* Dℵ.
25. om *δε* DK latt(not *f*) æth. ins *οτι* bef *πολλαι* LX [Λ(Tischdf)] ℵ 1. 33. 69^2 ev-y lat-*e f l* syrr goth arm [Bas$_1$] Orig-int. om *επι* BD vulg lat-*b c e f* Syr [syr-jer] copt Orig-int$_1$: ins ACℵ rel lat-*a* syr goth [Bas$_1$]. for *μηνας*, *μηνα* D.
26. rec *σιδωνος* (*more usual*), with E rel syrr(Treg) [Bas$_1$]: *σιδωνας* L am lat-*e*: txt ABCXΓℵ 1. 69 latt copt goth æth Orig$_1$[int$_1$], *σιδονιας* DV^r.

they wondered, and were jealous of Him, as being the son of Joseph—asking *πόθεν τούτῳ ταῦτα*: see Mark vi. 2—4. Between this verse and the next, the *ἐσκανδαλίζοντο ἐν αὐτῷ* is implied, for that is in a tone of reproof. **23. θερ. σ.**] Not, '*raise thyself from thy obscure station*,' but, **exert thy powers of healing in thine own country**, as presently interpreted; the Physician being represented as an inhabitant of Nazareth, and *σεαυτόν* including His own citizens in it. Stier remarks, that the reproach was *repeated under the Cross*. *Then*, with a strictly individual application. On the miracles previously wrought in Capernaum, see note on ver. 14. That in John iv. 47—53 was one such. **εἰς τὴν Κ.**] Whether we read *ἐν* or *εἰς*, the preposition is equally *local* in its signification, **in Capernaum**, not '*in the case of Capernaum*,' or '*to Capernaum*.' **24.**] See John iv. 44 and note. **εἶπεν δέ**] A formula usual with Luke—see reff.; and indicating, if I mistake not, the passing to a different source of information, or at least a break in the record, if from the same source.

25.] Our Lord brings forward instances where the two greatest prophets in Israel were *not directed to act in accordance with the proverb*, 'Physician heal thyself:' but their miraculous powers exerted on those who were strangers to God's inheritance. **ἔτη τρ. κ. μ. ἕξ**] So also in James v. 17;—but in 1 Kings xviii. 1 we find that it was *in the third year* that the Lord commanded Elijah to shew himself to Ahab, for He would send rain on the earth. But it does not appear from what time this third year is reckoned,—or at what time of the year, with reference to the usual former and latter rains, the drought caused by Elias's prayer began (it apparently had begun some time before the prophet was sent to be miraculously sustained, as this very fact implies failure of the ordinary means of sustenance); and thus, without forming any further hypothesis, we have latitude enough given for the three and a half years, which seems to have been the exact time. This period is one often recurring in Jewish record and in prophecy: see Dan. vii. 25; xii. 7: Rev. xi. 2, 3; xii. 6, 14; xiii. 5. Lightfoot (ii. 123) produces more instances from the Rabbinical writers. "The period of *three years and a half*, = 42 months or 1260 days, had an ominous sound in the ears of an Israelite, being the time of this famine, and of the duration of the desolation of the temple under Antiochus." Wordsw.

26.] Sarepta, now Sŭrafend, see Robinson,

πολλοὶ [k] λεπροὶ ἦσαν ἐν τῷ Ἰσραὴλ [l] ἐπὶ Ἐλισαίου τοῦ
προφήτου· καὶ οὐδεὶς αὐτῶν ἐκαθαρίσθη, εἰ μὴ Ναιμὰν
ὁ Σύρος. 28 καὶ [m] ἐπλήσθησαν πάντες θυμοῦ ἐν τῇ συναγωγῇ ἀκούοντες ταῦτα, 29 καὶ ἀναστάντες [n] ἐξέβαλον
αὐτὸν ἔξω τῆς πόλεως, καὶ ἤγαγον αὐτὸν ἕως [o] ὀφρύος
τοῦ ὄρους ἐφ' οὗ ἡ πόλις ᾠκοδόμητο αὐτῶν, [p] ὥστε
[q] κατακρημνίσαι αὐτόν. 30 αὐτὸς δὲ διελθὼν διὰ μέσου
αὐτῶν ἐπορεύετο, 31 καὶ κατῆλθεν εἰς Καφαρναοὺμ πόλιν
τῆς Γαλιλαίας· καὶ [r] ἦν διδάσκων αὐτοὺς ἐν τοῖς [s] σάββασιν. 32 καὶ [t] ἐξεπλήσσοντο ἐπὶ τῇ διδαχῇ αὐτοῦ, ὅτι

Ξ και εξεπλησσοντο...

k Matt. viii. 2 reff. (λεπροῦσθαι, 4 Kings v. 1.)
l = ch. iii. 2 reff.
m ch. v. 26. Acts iii. 10. Dan. iii. 19.
n Matt. xxi. 39 reff.
o here only ‡. Lev. xiv. 9 only.
p ch. ix. 52 reff.
q here only. 2 Chron. xxv. 12. 2 Macc. xii. 15. xiv. 43 only.
r Matt. xix. 22 reff.
s Matt. xii. 1 reff.
t Matt. vii. 28 reff

27. rec επι ελισ. τ. πρ. bef εν τω ισρ. (*order of ver* 25), with A rel syr goth : txt BCDLXℵ 1. 33. 69 latt Syr [syr-jer] copt æth arm. (ελισαιου (one σ), so ABDGLUVΔℵ.) (**ναιμαν**, so ABCKL[Π]ℵ 1. 69, -μας D.)

28. for και, οι δε D lat-*e*. ακου**σα**ντες D-gr 1 lat-*e* Syr.

29. om 1st αυτον ℵ[1]. rec ins της bef οφρυος, with D[1] arm, του D[2] 69 : om ABCℵ rel Orig$_1$. rec αυτων bef ωκοδ., with AC rel vulg lat-*b f ff$_2$* [*g$_{1.2}$ l q*] : txt BDLℵ 33. 69 lat-*a c e*. (οικοδομηται D.) rec (for ωστε) εις το (*explany*), with AC rel : txt BDLℵ 1. 33. 69 copt Orig$_1$.

31. aft γαλιλαιας ins την παραθαλασσιον εν οριοις ζαβουλων κ. νεφθαλειμ (*Matt* iv. 13) D.

iii. 413,—a large village, inland, halfway between Tyre and Sidon :—the ancient city seems to have been on the coast.

27.] Stier remarks that these two examples have a close parallelism with those of the Syro-Phœnician woman (Mark vii. 26) and the ruler's son at Capernaum (John iv. 46).

28—30.] The same sort of rage possessed the Jews, Acts xxii. 22, on a similar truth being announced to them. This whole occurrence, whenever it happened in our Lord's ministry, was but a foreshadowing of His treatment afterwards from the whole nation of the Jews—a foretaste of εἰς τὰ ἴδια ἦλθεν, καὶ οἱ ἴδιοι αὐτὸν οὐ παρέλαβον (John i. 11). The expression of St. Paul, Rom. xi. 25, πώρωσις ἀπὸ μέρους τῷ Ἰσραὴλ γέγονεν, has been regarded as corresponding with the judicial infliction on these Nazarenes, by means of which our Lord passed out from among them. But see my note, and Ellicott's, on Eph. iv. 18, from which it appears that πώρωσις cannot mean *blindness* at all. The modern Nazareth is at a distance of about two English miles from what is called the Mount of Precipitation; nor is it built literally on the *brow* of that mount or hill. But (1) neither does the narrative preclude a considerable distance having been traversed, during which they had our Lord in their custody, and were hurrying with Him to the edge of the ravine; nor (2) is it at all necessary to suppose the city built on the ὀφρύς, but only on the mountain, or range of hills, of which the ὀφρύς forms a part—which it is : see Robinson, iii. 187. Our Lord's passing through the midst of them is *evidently miraculous :* the circumstances were different from those in John viii. 59, where the expression is ἐκρύβη καὶ ἐξῆλθεν ἐκ τ. ἱεροῦ: see note there. Here, the Nazarenes had Him actually *in their custody*. **31 f.**] Mark i. 21, 22. The view maintained with regard to the foregoing occurrence in the preceding notes, of course precludes the notion that it was the *reason of our Lord's change of habitation to Capernaum*. In fact that change, as remarked on ver. 14, had been made *some time before :* and it is hardly possible that such an expression as ἦλθ. εἰς τὴν Ν. οὗ ἦν τεθραμμένος should be used, if He still resided there. The words **πόλιν τῆς Γ.** come in unnaturally after the mention of Καφαρν. in ver. 23, and evidently shew that *this* was originally intended to be the first mention of the place. What may have been the reason of the change of abode is quite uncertain. It seems to have included the whole family, except the sisters, who may have been married at Nazareth,—see note on John ii. 12, and Matt. iv. 13.

κατῆλθ., κατέβη John ii. 12, because Nazareth lay high, and Capernaum on the sea of Galilee. The expression καὶ οὐχ ὡς οἱ γραμματεῖς (Mark) is not added by Luke : see Matt. vii. 29.

u see ver. 36.
v Matt. xi. 18 reff.
w Matt. x. 1 reff. w. δαιμ., here only.
x || Mk. Mark vi. 19. ch. viii. 28. xxiii. 18 only. Judg. vii. 20.
y here (|| Mk. v. r.) only.
z Matt. viii. 29. 2 Kings xvi. 10 al.
a || Mk. John vi. 69 only. see Acts iii. 14. 1 John ii. 20.
b Matt. xii. 16 reff.
c Matt. xxii. 12 reff.
d see var. readd.
e Matt. xv. 30 reff.
f Mark xvi. 8 only †. Tobit xii. 2 al.
g ch. i. 65 reff.
h ch. v. 9. Acts iii. 10 only. Ezek. vii. 18.

[u] ἐν [u] ἐξουσίᾳ ἦν ὁ λόγος αὐτοῦ. 33 καὶ ἐν τῇ συναγωγῇ
ἦν ἄνθρωπος [v] ἔχων πνεῦμα δαιμονίου [w] ἀκαθάρτου, καὶ
[x] ἀνέκραξεν φωνῇ μεγάλῃ 34 [y] Ἔα, [z] τί ἡμῖν καὶ σοί, Q εα τι.. ABCDE
Ἰησοῦ Ναζαρηνέ; ἦλθες ἀπολέσαι ἡμᾶς· οἶδά σε τίς εἶ, FGHKL MQSUV
ὁ [a] ἅγιος [a] τοῦ θεοῦ. 35 καὶ [b] ἐπετίμησεν αὐτῷ ὁ Ἰησοῦς XΓΔΛΞ ΠℵΙ.
λέγων [c] Φιμώθητι καὶ [d] ἔξελθε [d] ἀπ' αὐτοῦ. καὶ [e] ῥῖψαν 33. 69
αὐτὸν τὸ δαιμόνιον εἰς τὸ μέσον ἐξῆλθεν ἀπ' αὐτοῦ μηδὲν
[f] βλάψαν αὐτόν. 36 καὶ [g] ἐγένετο [h] θάμβος ἐπὶ πάντας,
καὶ [i] συνελάλουν πρὸς ἀλλήλους λέγοντες [k] Τίς ὁ λόγος
οὗτος, ὅτι [l] ἐν [l] ἐξουσίᾳ καὶ [l] δυνάμει [m] ἐπιτάσσει τοῖς
ἀκαθάρτοις πνεύμασιν, καὶ ἐξέρχονται; 37 καὶ [n] ἐξεπορεύετο [o] ἦχος περὶ αὐτοῦ εἰς πάντα τόπον τῆς [p] περιχώρου.
38 Ἀναστὰς δὲ ἀπὸ τῆς συναγωγῆς εἰσῆλθεν εἰς τὴν
οἰκίαν Σίμωνος. [q] πενθερὰ δὲ τοῦ Σίμωνος ἦν [r] συνεχομένη
[s] πυρετῷ μεγάλῳ· καὶ [t] ἠρώτησαν αὐτὸν [t] περὶ αὐτῆς. R [ηρ]-ωτησαν ...

i constr., here only. (Matt. xvii. 3. Acts xxv. 12.) k 2 Kings i. 4. l = here only. see ch. v. 32. m || Mk. ch. viii. 25. Gen. xlix. 33. n = here only. o = here (Acts ii. 2. Heb. xii. 19) only ‡. p Matt. iii. 5. xiv. 35. ver. 14 al. Deut. iii. 13, 14. q || Mt. Mk. Matt. x. 35 ||. ch. xii. 53 bis only. Ruth i. 14. r = Matt. iv. 24. ch. viii. 37. Acts xxviii. 8. Job xxxi. 23. s here (bis) & ||. John iv. 52. Acts xxviii. 8 only. Deut. xxviii. 22 only. t John xvi. 26 reff.

33. ηv δε εν τη συν. D lat-*e*. δαιμονιον ακαθαρτον D vulg lat-*a b* (*c*) *e f ff*$_2$ *g*$_1$ (om πνευμα latt).

34. rec pref λεγων (|| *Mark*), with ACD rel latt [syrr syr-jer] goth arm Ath$_1$: om BLV[1]Ξℵ copt Orig$_1$. om εα (|| *Mark*) D 33 lat-*a b c e f ff*$_2$ [*l q*] syr-jer copt æth Tert$_1$. ναζορηναι D[1](-ζωρ- D[2]). ημας ωδε απολεσαι D 68.

35. rec (for απ) εξ (*from* || *Mark*), with ACQ rel: txt BDLVΞℵ 1. 69 latt Orig$_1$. (*Luke writes* ἀπό *after verbs compd with* ἐξ: *cf ver* 41; *ch* v. 8; viii. 2, 29, 38, 46; ix. 5; xi. 24; xvii. 29: *Mark* εξ, *cf Mark* i. 25, 26; vii. 29; ix. 25.) ρειψας D[1](txt D[2]). om το (bef μεσον) DEFGHKSUVΓΔΛ[Π] Orig. aft μεσον ins ανακραυγασαν τε D. βλαψας D[1].

36. aft θαμβος ins μεγας D 253 gat(with per) lat-*b g*$_1$ copt. for εξερχονται, υπακουουσιν αυτω ℵ-corr[1](on an erasure: txt ℵ[1.3a]).

37. for εξεπ. ηχ., εξηλθεν η ακοη (|| *Mark*) D (lat-*e*).

38. rec (for απο) εκ (*from* || *Mark*), with A rel goth: txt BCDLQΞℵ 1. 33. 69 Orig$_1$ (*a* D-lat: *de* latt). aft συναγωγης ins ο ιησους AM[Π]. ηλθεν D[Π] 248-51-3-4. aft οικ. ins του ℵ. aft 1st σιμωνος ins και ανδραιου (|| *Mark*) D lat-*b c ff*$_2$ *g*$_1$ *l* Ambr$_1$. rec η πενθ. δε, with 1(Treg, expr): η δε πενθ. C 251: txt ABDQΞℵ rel. (homœotel in [X[1]Λ[1]] 33.) κατεχομενη D, *detinebatur* lat-*a*.

33—37.] Healing of a dæmoniac in the synagogue at Capernaum. Mark i. 23—28, where see notes. The two accounts are very closely cognate—being the same narrative, only slightly deflected; not more, certainly, than might have arisen from oral repetition by *two* persons, at some interval of time, of what they had received *in the same words*. 33.] **πν.** is the *influence*, **δαιμ.** the *personality*, of the possessing dæmon. "Both St. Mark and St. Luke, writing for Gentiles, add the epithet ἀκάθαρτον to δαιμόνιον, which St. Matthew, writing to Jews (for whom it was not necessary), *never* does." Wordsw. The real fact is, that St. Mark uses the word δαιμόνιον thirteen times, and *never* adds the epithet ἀκάθαρτον to it (his word here is πνεῦμα only); St. Luke, eighteen times, and only adds it *this once*. So much for the accuracy of the data, on which inferences of this kind are founded. The true account of the use of ἀκάθαρτον here seems to be, that this evil spirit was of a kind, in its effects on its victim, especially answering to the epithet. 35.] **μηδ. βλάψ. αὐτ.** is here only. Mark's **σπαράξαν** may mean *'having convulsed him'*—and our text, *'without doing him bodily injury.'*

38—41.] Healing of Simon's wife's mother, and many others. Matt. viii. 14—17. Mark i. 29—34. Our ac-

39 καὶ [u] ἐπιστὰς [v] ἐπάνω αὐτῆς [w] ἐπετίμησεν τῷ [s] πυρετῷ,
καὶ [x] ἀφῆκεν αὐτήν· [y] παραχρῆμα δὲ ἀναστᾶσα διηκόνει
αὐτοῖς. 40 [z] δύνοντος δὲ τοῦ ἡλίου πάντες ὅσοι εἶχον
ἀσθενοῦντας [a] νόσοις [b] ποικίλαις ἤγαγον αὐτοὺς πρὸς
αὐτόν· ὁ δὲ [c] ἑνὶ [c] ἑκάστῳ αὐτῶν τὰς χεῖρας ἐπιτιθεὶς
ἐθεράπευεν αὐτούς. 41 ἐξήρχετο δὲ καὶ δαιμόνια ἀπὸ
πολλῶν, [d] * κράζοντα καὶ λέγοντα ὅτι σὺ εἶ ὁ [e] υἱὸς τοῦ
[e] θεοῦ. καὶ ἐπιτιμῶν οὐκ [f] εἴα αὐτὰ λαλεῖν, ὅτι ᾔδεισαν
τὸν χριστὸν αὐτὸν εἶναι. 42 [g] γενομένης δὲ ἡμέρας ἐξελθὼν
ἐπορεύθη εἰς ἔρημον τόπον, καὶ οἱ ὄχλοι [h] ἐπεζήτουν αὐτὸν
καὶ ἦλθον [i] ἕως αὐτοῦ, καὶ [k] κατεῖχον αὐτὸν [l] τοῦ μὴ
πορεύεσθαι ἀπ' αὐτῶν. 43 ὁ δὲ εἶπεν πρὸς αὐτοὺς ὅτι
καὶ ταῖς ἑτέραις πόλεσιν [m] εὐαγγελίσασθαί με δεῖ τὴν

u ch. ii. 9. Gen. xxiv. 43.
v Matt. ii. 9. Rev. vi. 8. xx. 3 al. 2 Kings i. 9.
w = Matt. viii. 26 ||. Ps. cv. 9.
x = Matt. iv. 11 reff.
y Matt. xxi. 19, 20 reff.
z || Mk. only. 3 Kings xxii. 6.
a Matt. iv. 23, 24 reff.
b = || Mk. Matt. iv. 24. 2 Tim. iii. 6. Tit. iii. 3 al.‡ (1 Chron. xxix. 2.)
c w. gen. part., ch. xvi. 5. Acts ii. 3. xvii. 27. xxi. 26. 1 Thess. ii. 11 al.
d Matt. viii. 29 al. fr. κραυγάζ., Matt. xii. 19 reff.
e see Matt. iv. 3 note.
f Matt. xxiv. 43 reff.
g ch. vi. 13 al.
h Matt. vi. 32 reff.
i = Acts ix. 38.
k = Philem. 13. Gen. xxiv. 56. xlii. 19.
l ch. xxiv. 16 reff.
m ch. xvi. 16. viii. 1.

39. επισταθεις D. aft αυτην ins ο πυρετος ℵ. for παρ. δε, και παρ. CL vulg lat-*b c* [*f ff*$_2$ *g*$_1$ *l q*] Syr.—παρ. ωστε αναστασαν αυτην διακονειν D.
40. δυσαντος D-gr : δυναντος UΛ Scr's d q r. απαντες BC 1. for οσοι, οι D¹-gr vulg lat-*b f ff*$_2$ *g*$_1$ [*l q*]. ειχαν D. ins και bef ηγ. A. for ηγαγον, εφερον D. om αυτων D vulg lat-*b c f ff*$_2$ *g*$_1$. επιθεις bef τ. χειρ. Cℵ coptt. rec επιθεις, with ACRℵ rel Orig$_1$: txt BDQΞ 69. rec εθεραπευσεν, with ACQRΞℵ rel Orig$_1$-mss : txt BD vulg lat-*a b c e f ff*$_2$ *g*$_1$ syrr.
41. εξηρχοντο CXℵ 1. 33 Orig$_1$. om απο ℵ. * κραυγάζοντα ADQ rel [Orig$_1$]: κραζοντα BCFKLMRSVXΛΞ[Π] ℵ(κραζοντων ℵ¹). rec ins ο χριστος bef ο υιος (*gloss*), with AQ rel lat-*f q* syrr goth : om BCDFLRXΞℵ 33 latt copt arm Orig Tert$_1$ Victorin. αυτον χρ. ειναι D vulg lat-*b f q* : αυτ. τον χρ. ειν. 69.
42. om τοπον ℵ¹(ins ℵ-corr¹). rec (for επεζ.) εζητουν, with EGHK[Π] : txt ABCDQRΞℵ rel Mcion Thl Euthym. επειχον D.
43. εις τας αλλας πολεις and pref δει με και (omg με δει below) D lat-*e*. δει bef με B(D) latt syrr æth. aft ευαγ. ins αυτ(αις ?) D(but erased). for την βασι-

count has only a slight additional detail, which is interesting however as giving another side of an eye-witness's evidence—it is **ἐπιστὰς ἐπάνω αὐτῆς.** Now this is implied in laying hold of her hand, as she was in bed; which particulars are both mentioned by Matt. and Mark:—this being one of those many cases where alteration (of κρατήσας τ. χειρ. . . . into ἐπιστ. ἐπ. αὐτ.) is utterly inconceivable. **38.] πενθερά,** anarthrous, being in fact predicative; as in all such cases of appellatives: see ch. x. 6. **πυρ. μεγάλῳ]** An epithet used by Luke, *as a physician*;—σύνηθες ἤδη τοῖς ἰατροῖς ὀνομάζειν . . . τὸν μέγαν τε καὶ μικρὸν πυρετόν. Galen de different. Febr. i. (Wetstein.) Bleek doubts this, and understands it only of the intensity of the fever. **40.] ἑνὶ ἑκάσ. αὐτ. τ. χ. ἐπ.** is a detail peculiar to Luke, and I believe indicating the same as above: as also the **κράζ. κ. λέγοντα** implied in the other Evangelists, but not expressed. **41.] λαλεῖν, ὅτι . . . to speak,** *because* **they knew,** &c.; not, 'to say that they knew:'—λαλεῖν is never '*to say*,' but '*to speak*,' '*to discourse*.'

42—44.] Jesus, being sought out in His retirement, preaches throughout Judæa. Mark i. 35—39. The dissimilitude in wording of these two accounts is one of the most striking instances in the Gospels, of variety found in the same narration. While the matter related (with one remarkable exception, see below) is nearly identical, the only words common to the two are εἰς ἔρημον τόπον. **42.] οἱ ὄχλοι** = Σίμων κ. οἱ μετ' αὐτοῦ, Mark. The great number of sick which were brought to the Lord on the evening before, and this morning, is accounted for by Schleierm. from His departure having been fixed on and known beforehand: but it is perhaps more simple to view it, with Mey., as the natural result of the effect of the healing of the dæmoniac in the syna-

n Matt. xix. 22 reff. o || Mk. reff. p Matt. xiii. 4 reff. q = here (John xi. 38 reff.) only. Job xix. 3. xxi. 27. r ver. 17 reff. 2 Kings i. 1. s here bis. ch. viii. 22, 23, 33. Rev. xix. 20. xx. 10, 14, 15. xxi. 8 only. Ps. cvi. 35. t John vi. 22, &c. reff.

[m] βασιλείαν τοῦ θεοῦ, ὅτι ἐπὶ τοῦτο ἀπεστάλην. 44 καὶ
[n] ἦν κηρύσσων [o] εἰς τὰς συναγωγὰς τῆς * Ἰουδαίας.
V. 1 Ἐγένετο δὲ [p] ἐν τῷ τὸν ὄχλον [q] ἐπικεῖσθαι αὐτῷ
καὶ ἀκούειν τὸν λόγον τοῦ θεοῦ, [r] καὶ αὐτὸς ἦν ἑστὼς
παρὰ τὴν [s] λίμνην Γεννησαρέτ, 2 καὶ εἶδεν δύο [t] πλοιάρια

...του θεου ℵ. ABCDE FGHKL MQRSU VXΓΔΛ Πℵ 1. 33. 69

λειαν, το ευαγγελιον ℵ[1](txt ℵ-corr[1]). for οτι ε. τ., ε. τ. γαρ D lat-*e*. rec (for επι) εις (|| *Mark*), with AC(D)QR rel: txt BLℵ. rec απεσταλμαι (*see* || *Mark*), with AQR rel: txt BCDLXℵ 1. 33. 69.

44. rec (for εις τας συναγωγας) εν ταις συναγωγαις (*more obvious*), with ACR rel: txt BDQℵ 69 ev-y. * rec γαλιλαίας, with AD rel latt Syr syr-mg goth æth arm; ιουδαιας BCLQRℵ 1 ev-y syr[-txt] copt.—(There is no reasonable doubt about the reading of B, but the editor regrets not having looked at it himself when at Rome.)

Chap. V. 1. for τον οχλ. επικεισθαι αυτω, συναχθηναι τον οχλον ℵ[1] [copt]. rec (for και) του, with CDQR rel vulg lat-*a b* &c syrr copt-wilk goth: txt ABLXℵ 1 lat-*c* copt-schw [æth] arm. for κ. αυτ. ην εστ., εστωτος αυτου D. om λιμνην ℵ[1].

2. πλ. bef δυο B lat-*a e* Syr copt: om δυο ℵ[1]. rec πλοια, with BC[3]Dℵ rel vulg

gogue, on the popular mind. **44.**] See Matt. iv. 23—25 and notes. **καὶ ἦν κηρ. . . .** is a formal close to this section of the narrative, and chronologically separates it from what follows. The reading **τῆς Ἰουδαίας** must, on any intelligible critical principles, be adopted; and Tregelles can hardly be acquitted of inconsistency with his own usual practice, in rejecting it. It is utterly inconceivable that it should have been a correction, seeing that Γαλιλαίας stands firm, with no various reading, in || Mark, from which the rec. reading here has come. (See however Mark i. 28, where ℵ[1] has Ἰουδαίας for Γαλιλαίας: and Isa. ix. 1, where *εἰς τὰ μέρη τῆς Ἰουδαίας* is added to the Hebrew, by Aℵ and one other uncial ms.) This view is confirmed by the fact that two evangelistaria here read *τοῖς Ἰουδαίοις*; one, *τῶν Ἰουδαίων*, both being attempts to escape from the difficulty of *τῆς Ἰουδαίας*; while one adopts *αὐτῶν*, part of the sentence in || Mark. So far, however, being plain, I confess that all attempts to explain the fact seem to me futile. The three Evangelists relate no ministry in Judæa, with this single exception. And our narrative is thus brought into the most startling discrepancy with that of St. Mark, in which unquestionably the same portion of the sacred history is related. Still, these are considerations which must not weigh in the least degree with the critic. It is his province simply to track out what *is* the sacred text, not what, in his own feeble and partial judgment, it *ought to have been*.

Chap. V. 1—11.] The miraculous draught of fishes. Call of Peter and the sons of Zebedee. The question at once meets us, whether this account, in its form here peculiar to Luke, is identical in its subject-matter with Matt. iv. 18—22, and Mark i. 16—20. With regard to this, we may notice the following particulars. (1) Contrary to Schleiermacher's inference (Trans. pp. 75, 76), it must be, I think, that of most readers, that a *previous and close relation had subsisted between our Lord and Peter*. The latter calls Him **ἐπιστάτα** (= ῥαββί), and **κύριε**: evidently (ver. 5, end) *expects a miracle*; and *follows Him, with his partners, without any present express command so to do*. Still all this might be, and yet the account might be identical with the others. For our Lord had known Peter before this, John i. 41 ff.; and, in all probability, as one of His disciples. And although there is here no express command to follow, yet the words in ver. 10 may be, and are probably intended to be, equivalent to one. (2) The Evangelist evidently intends this as the first *apostolic calling* of Peter and his companions. The expressions in ver. 11 could not otherwise have been used. (3) There is yet the supposition, that the accounts in Matthew and Mark may be a shorter way of recounting this by *persons who were not aware* of these circumstances. But then such a supposition will not consist with that high degree of authority in those accounts, which I believe them to have: see note on Mark. (4) It seems to me that the truth of the matter is nearly this:—that this event is *distinct from*, and *happened at a later period than*, the calling in Matt. and Mark; but

[u] ἑστῶτα παρὰ τὴν [s] λιμνην· οἱ δὲ [v] ἁλιεῖς ἀπ' αὐτῶν
[w] ἀποβάντες [x] ἔπλυνον τὰ [y] δίκτυα. 3 [z] ἐμβὰς δὲ εἰς ἓν τῶν
πλοίων ὃ ἦν Σίμωνος [a] ἠρώτησεν αὐτὸν ἀπὸ τῆς γῆς
[b] ἐπαναγαγεῖν ὀλίγον, [c] καθίσας δὲ ἐκ τοῦ πλοίου ἐδίδασκεν τοὺς ὄχλους. 4 ὡς δὲ [d] ἐπαύσατο λαλῶν, εἶπεν
πρὸς τὸν Σίμωνα [b] Ἐπανάγαγε εἰς τὸ [e] βάθος καὶ
[f] χαλάσατε τὰ [y] δίκτυα ὑμῶν [g] εἰς [h] ἄγραν. 5 καὶ ἀποκριθεὶς Σίμων εἶπεν αὐτῷ [i] Ἐπιστάτα, δι' ὅλης νυκτὸς
[j] κοπιάσαντες οὐδὲν ἐλάβομεν· [k] ἐπὶ δὲ τῷ ῥήματί σου
[f] χαλάσω τὸ [y] δίκτυον. 6 καὶ τοῦτο ποιήσαντες [l] συν-

...το βα. Q.
...βαθος G.
...σιμων ει[πεν] R.

u = here only. v Matt. iv. 18, 19 || Mk. only. Job xl. 26 (31). w = John xxi. 9 (ch. xxi. 13. Phil. i. 19) only ‡. x Rev. vii. 14. xxii. 14 only. Gen. xlix. 11. y Mark i. 18, 19 reff. z Matt. viii. 23 reff. a = ch. viii. 37 reff. b here bis & Matt. xxi. 18 (reff.) only. = 2 Macc. xii. 4. c intr., Matt. v. 1 reff. d L. P. H., exc. 1 Pet. iii. 10 (from Ps. xxxiii. 13). iv. 1. constr., Acts v. 42. Eph. i. 16. Heb. x. 2 al. Gen. xviii. 33. e = here only. (Matt. xiii 5 || Mk. al.) f Mark ii. 4 reff. g = ch. iii. 3. ver. 17. h ver. 9 only +. i ch. viii. 24, 45. ix. 33, 49. xvii. 13 only. L. 4 Kings xxv. 19. j Matt. xi. 28 al. Ps. cxxvi. 1. k = Acts iii. 16. Phil. iii. 9. Job xxix. 22. l Rom. xi. 32 Gal. iii. 22, 23 only. Exod. xiv. 3.

lat-*b c*: txt AC¹LQR 1¹. 33 lat-*a f*. (αλεεις ACLQℵ¹.) rec αποβαντες bef απ' αυτων (*απ' αυτων omd, then wrongly reinsd*), with AC³ rel lat-*c f* [syrr syr-jer] goth [æth arm]: om απ' αυτων R vulg lat-*b* ff_2 *l q*: om απ ℵ¹: txt BC¹DLℵ³ᵃ 33. rec απεπλυναν, with AC³R rel: επλυναν C¹LQXℵ: txt BD.

3. πλοιον (omg των) D latt. rec ins του bef σιμ. (*to suit* τον σ. *below*), with ACQR rel: om BDLℵ. επαναγαγειν bef απο της γης D lat-*a b c*.—επαναγειν A 1. for ολιγον, οσον οσον D. rec και καθισας (*to avoid repetn of* δε,—εμβ. δε, καθ. δε, ως δε), with ACDR rel: txt BLQℵ lat-*a* copt. rec εδιδασκεν bef εκ του πλοιου (*for perspicuity*), with ACQR rel latt: txt B(Dℵ).—for εκ του πλοιου, εν τω πλοιω (*for perspicuity*, aft καθισας) Dℵ.—for εκ, απο 1. 69.

4. for ως, οτε D lat-*a e*.

5. rec ins ο bef σιμων (*from* τον σιμ. *above*), with AC(D)R rel: om BLΔℵ.—ο πετρος X.—ο δε σιμ. αποκριθ.(αποκρεις, sic, D¹) ειπεν αυτω D.—ειπεν bef σιμων ℵ¹ om αυτω Bℵ lat-*e* copt. [for επιστ.] διδασκαλε *magister* D lat-*a* copt. rec aft ολης ins της, with CD rel: om ABLℵ 33. 131 Cyr_1. ελαβαμεν A. τα δικτυα (*from ver* 4) BLℵ 1 lat-*c* [*q* syr-jer] copt goth æth $Ambr_1$, and (but transpd to ver 6) D [lat-*e*]. for χαλ. τ. δικτ., ου μη παρακουσομαι(-σομεν D²) *non præteribo* D.

6. for τουτο ποιησαντες, ευθυς χαλασαντες τα δικτυα D [lat-*e*]. rec ιχθυων bef

that the four Apostles, when our Lord was at Capernaum, followed their occupation as fishermen. There is every thing to shew, in our account, that the calling had previously taken place; and the closing of it by the expression in ver. 11 merely indicates what there can be no difficulty in seeing even without it, that our present account is an imperfect one, written by one who found thus much recorded, and knowing it to be part of the history of the calling of the Apostles, appended to it the fact of their leaving all and following the Lord. As to the repetition of the assurance in ver. 10, I see no more in it than this, which appears also from other passages in the Gospels, that the Apostles, as such, were not called or ordained *at any special moment*, or by any *one word of power alone*; but that in their case as well as ours, there was line upon line, precept upon precept: and that what was said generally to all four on the former occasion, by words only, was repeated to Peter on this, not only in words, but by a miracle. Does his fear, as expressed in ver. 8, besides the reason assigned, indicate *some previous slowness*, or *relaxation of his usually earnest attachment*, of which he now becomes deeply ashamed? (5) It is also to be noticed that there is no chronological index to this narrative connecting it with what precedes or follows. It cannot well (see ver. 8) have taken place *after* the healing of Peter's wife's mother; and (ver. 1) must have been after the crowd had now become accustomed to hear the Lord teach. (6) Also, that there is no mention of *Andrew* here, as in ver. 10 there surely would have been, if he had been present. (7) It will be seen how wholly irreconcilable either of the suppositions is with the idea that Luke *used* the Gospel of Matt., or that of Mark, in compiling his own. **2.**] **ἔπλυνον**, 'ut peracto opere,' Bengel: see ver. 5.

4.] **ἐπανάγαγε**, to Peter alone, who was the steersman of his ship; **χαλάσατε**, to the fishermen in the ship collectively (Mey.). So below also, **χαλάσω**, of the

ἔκλεισαν πλῆθος ἰχθυων πολύ, [m] διερήσσετο δὲ τὰ [y] δίκ- ABCDE FHKL
τυα αὐτῶν. 7 καὶ [n] κατένευσαν τοῖς [o] μετόχοις ἐν τῷ MSUV
ἑτέρῳ πλοίῳ [p] τοῦ ἐλθόντας [q] συλλαβέσθαι αὐτοῖς· καὶ ΧΓΔΛΠ
ἦλθον καὶ ἔπλησαν ἀμφότερα τὰ πλοῖα ὥςτε [r] βυθίζεσθαι ℵ 1. 33. 69
αὐτά. 8 ἰδὼν δὲ Σίμων Πέτρος [st] προςέπεσεν τοῖς [t] γόνασιν
Ἰησοῦ λέγων [u] Ἔξελθε ἀπ' ἐμοῦ, ὅτι [v] ἀνὴρ [v] ἁμαρτωλός
εἰμι, κύριε. 9 [w] θάμβος γὰρ [x] περιέσχεν αὐτὸν καὶ πάντας
τοὺς σὺν αὐτῷ [y] ἐπὶ τῇ [z] ἄγρᾳ τῶν ἰχθύων * ᾗ [a] συνέλαβον·
10 [b] ὁμοίως [b] δὲ [b] καὶ Ἰάκωβον καὶ Ἰωάννην υἱοὺς Ζεβεδαίου, οἳ ἦσαν [c] κοινωνοὶ τῷ Σίμωνι. καὶ εἶπεν πρὸς τὸν
Σίμωνα Ἰησοῦς Μὴ φοβοῦ· [d] ἀπὸ τοῦ νῦν ἀνθρώπους

m ch. viii. 29 reff. n here only +. o Heb. i. 9 (from Ps. xliv. 7). iii. 1, 14. vi. 4. xii. 8 only. (-χή, 2 Cor. vi. 14.) p Matt. iii. 13 reff. q = Phil. iv. 3 only. Gen. xxx. 8 A. r 1 Tim. vi. 9 only +. 2 Macc. xii. 4 only +. (θός, 2 Cor. xi. 25.) s Mark iii. 11 reff. t here only. u = here only. v ch. xix. 7. Sir. x. 23. w ch. iv. 36 reff. x = here (Acts xxiii. 25. 1 Pet. ii. 6) only. Ps. xvii. 4. 2 Macc. iv. 16. y ch. ii. 47 al. z ver. 4 only +. a = here only. Ps. ix. 15, 16. (see Matt. xxvi. 55 reff.) b Matt. xxvii. 41 reff. c = 2 Cor. viii. 23. Philem. 17. (Matt. xxiii. 30 reff.) d ch. i. 48. xii. 52. xxii. [18] 69. 2 Cor. v. 16. Ps. cxii. 2.

πληθος, with D 69 latt: txt A[B]Cℵ rel copt goth arm [Eus_1]. (*The transposn, as Mey observes, has more prob been to bring* πληθος *and* πολυ *together, than to separate them.*) rec διερρηγνυτο, with X rel [Eus_1], διερηγνυτο A [Scr's g]: διερρητο C: txt B[1]L 33, διερρησ. B[2]ℵ.—ωστε τα δικτυα ρησσεσθαι D lat-*e f* [æth arm]. rec το δικτυον, with AC rel vulg lat-*b e* $g_{1.2}$ syrr [syr-jer]: txt B(D)Lℵ 1 lat-*a c f* ff_2 *l* [*q*] copt goth æth arm Eus_1.

7. κατενευον D E[1](perhaps) gat lat-*a e*: -σεν ℵ[1]. rec aft μετοχοις ins τοις, with AC rel: om BDLℵ lat-*a*. for του, τους ℵ[1](txt ℵ corr[1.3]). for συλλαβεσθαι, συνλαμβανεσθε ℵ[1](txt ℵ-corr[1.3]): βοηθειν D. ηλθαν Lℵ 435: for κ. ηλθ. κ., ελθοντες ουν D (lat-*e*). (B has επλησαν as in txt: see table at end of prolegomena.) αμφοτεροι ℵ[1](appy: but corrd by origl scribe) [M 33] 69 Scr's p. aft ωστε ins ηδη C[1]; παρα τι D Syr syr-mg [arm]. om αυτα D latt.

8. for ιδων δε, ο δε D: ιδων δε ο 69. om πετρος D 69 lat-*a b e*. rec ins του bef ιησου, with ACFLMXΛ 1. 33. 69: om Bℵ rel.—for τοις γονασιν ιησου, αυτου τοις ποσιν D lat-*e*: τοις ποσιν του ιησου 1 lat-*c* Syr copt. aft λεγων ins παρακαλω D lat-*c e f* Syr goth. om κυριε ℵ[1] [lat-*e*].

9. for αυτον, αυτους ℵ[1]. om και παντας τους συν αυτω D ev-47. * ὧν BDX goth: ᾗ ACℵ rel.

10. for ver, ησαν δε κοινωνοι αυτου ιακωβος και ιωαννης υιοι ζεβεδαιου ο δε ειπεν αυτοις δευτε και μη γεινεσθε αλιεις ιχθυων ποιησω γαρ υμας αλιεις ανθρωπων D lat-*e*.—om υιους ζεβεδαιου C[1]. ιακωβος και ιωαννης οι υιοι ℵ [lat-*a b c* ff_2 (*l*) *q*]. rec ins ο bef ιησ., with ACℵ rel: om BL.

director, **ποιήσαντες**, of the doers of the act. 5] **νυκτός**,—the ordinary time of fishing:—see John xxi. 3. 6.] **διερήσσ., was bursting—had begun to burst.** Similarly **βυθίζεσθαι**, ver. 7.

7.] They *beckoned*, on account of the distance; or perhaps for the reason given by Euthym.: μὴ δυνάμενοι λαλῆσαι ἀπὸ τῆς ἐκπλήξεως καὶ τοῦ φόβου. 8.] **ἔξελθε ἀπ' ἐμοῦ, depart from my ship.** The speech is in exact keeping with the quick discernment, and expression of feeling, of Peter's character. Similar sayings are found Exod. xx. 18, 19: Judg. xiii. 22: 1 Kings xvii. 18: Isa. vi. 5: Dan. x. 17. This sense of unworthiness and self-loathing is ever the effect, in the depths of a heart not utterly hardened, of the Divine Power and presence. "Below this, is the utterly profane state, in which there is no contrast, no contradiction felt, between the holy and the unholy, between God and man. Above it, is the state of grace, in which the contradiction is felt, the deep gulf perceived, which divides between sinful man and an holy God,—yet it is felt that this gulf is bridged over,—that it is possible for the two to meet,—that in One who is sharer with both, they have already been brought together." Trench on the Miracles, in loc. The same writer remarks of the miracle itself, "Christ here appears as the *ideal man*, the second Adam of the eighth Psalm; 'Thou madest him to have dominion over the works of Thy hands: Thou hast put all things under His feet .... the fowl of the air, and the fish of the sea, and what-

[e] ἔσῃ [f] ζωγρῶν. 11 καὶ [g] καταγαγόντες τὰ πλοῖα ἐπὶ
τὴν γῆν, [h] ἀφέντες ἅπαντα ἠκολούθησαν αὐτῷ.
12 [i] Καὶ ἐγένετο ἐν τῷ εἶναι αὐτὸν ἐν μιᾷ τῶν πόλεων,
[i] καὶ ἰδοὺ ἀνὴρ [j] πλήρης [k] λέπρας· καὶ ἰδὼν τὸν Ἰησοῦν,
[l] πεσὼν ἐπὶ [l] πρόσωπον ἐδεήθη αὐτοῦ λέγων Κύριε, ἐὰν
θέλῃς, δύνασαί με καθαρίσαι. 13 καὶ [m] ἐκτείνας τὴν [m] χεῖρα
ἥψατο αὐτοῦ εἰπὼν Θέλω, καθαρίσθητι. καὶ εὐθέως ἡ
[k] λέπρα ἀπῆλθεν ἀπ' αὐτοῦ. 14 καὶ αὐτὸς [n] παρήγγειλεν
αὐτῷ μηδενὶ εἰπεῖν, ἀλλὰ [o] ἀπελθὼν δεῖξον σεαυτὸν τῷ
ἱερεῖ, καὶ [p] προσένεγκε περὶ τοῦ [q] καθαρισμοῦ σου καθὼς
[r] προσέταξεν Μωυσῆς, [s] εἰς μαρτύριον αὐτοῖς. 15 [t] διήρχετο
δὲ μᾶλλον ὁ λόγος περὶ αὐτοῦ, καὶ συνήρχοντο ὄχλοι
πολλοὶ ἀκούειν, καὶ [u] θεραπεύεσθαι [u] ἀπὸ τῶν [v] ἀσθενειῶν
αὐτῶν· 16 αὐτὸς δὲ ἦν [w] ὑποχωρῶν ἐν ταῖς ἐρήμοις καὶ
προσευχόμενος.
17 [x] Καὶ ἐγένετο ἐν [y] μιᾷ τῶν [y] ἡμερῶν, [x] καὶ αὐτὸς ἦν

...πεσων F. ABCDE HKLM SUVXΓ ΔΛΠℵ 1. 33. 69

e constr., Matt. x. 22. xvi. 19. Mark xiii. 25. ch. i. 20. xvii. 35. 1 Cor. xiv. 9 al.
f 2 Tim. ii. 26 only. 2 Chron. xxv. 12.
g Luke only, exc. Rom. x. 6. = Acts xxi. 3. xxvii. 3 only ‡.
h Matt. iv. 11 al.
i ver. 17 reff.
j = ch. iv. 1 reff.
k here (bis) & || only. Lev. xiii. 2, 3.
l Matt. xvii. 6 reff. Gen. xvii. 3, 17.
m || Mt. reff.
n Mark viii. 6 reff.
o change of constr., Mark vi. 8, 9. Acts i. 4 al.
p Matt. ii. 11. Acts vii. 42 (from Amos v. 25) al. fr. principally in Heb. Paul, & other Epp., never.
q || Mk. reff.
r Matt. i. 24 reff. Levit. xiv. 2.
s || Mt. reff.
t Rom. v. 12. = 2 Chron. xxx. 5. Thuc. vi. 46.
u ch. viii. 2 reff.
v = Matt. viii. 17. ch. viii. 2. John xi. 4 al. 2 Macc. ix. 21, 22.
w ch. ix. 10 only. Judg. xx. 37 B. Sir. xiii. 9 only.
x vv. 1, 12. ch. [i. 15] viii. 1 al. Gen. xxiv. 30. Ruth i. 1. 1 Kings xvi. 23.
y ch. viii. 22. xvii. 22. xx. 1 only.

11. for ver, *οι δε ακουσαντες παντα κατελειψαν επι της γης και ηκολουθησαν αυτω* D lat-*e*. *παντα* B(D)Lℵ.

12. for *πληρης λεπρας*, *λεπρος* D. for *και ιδων*, *ιδων δε* Bℵ lat-*e* copt. for *πεσων*, *επεσεν*, and om *εδεηθη αυτου*, D lat-*e*.

13. for *και εκτ.*, *εκτ. δε* D. for *την χειρα*, *τας χειρας* ℵ[1](appy : txt ℵ-corr[1]). for *ειπων*, *λεγων* (*from* || *Matt*) BCDLX ℵ(λ is written above the line by ℵ[1] or corr[1]) 33. 69 arm Cyr_1 : txt A rel. for *η λεπ.* to *αυτου*, *εκαθαρισθη* D lat-*e*.

14. for *αλλα απελθων*, *απελθε δε και* D lat-*a e*. om *δειξον σεαυτον τω ιερει και* ℵ[1](ins ℵ-corr[1]). for *εις μαρτυριον αυτοις*, *ινα εις μαρτυριον η*(*ην* D[1]) *υμιν τουτο* D, simly lat-*a b c e ff*$_2$ *l q* $Tert_1$ $Ambr_1$. aft *αυτοις* ins *ο δε εξελθων ηρξατο κηρυσσειν και διαφημιζειν τον λογον ωστε μηκετι δυνασθαι αυτον φανερως εις πολιν εισελθειν αλλα εξω ην εν ερημοις τοποις και συνηρχοντο προς αυτον και ηλθεν παλιν εις καφαρναουμ* (*see* || *Mark*) D.

15. *ο λογος* bef *μαλλον* DMU Syr goth æth. om *περι* ℵ[1](ins ℵ-corr[1]). rec aft *θεραπευεσθαι* ins *υπ αυτου*, with C[2] rel syr goth; *απ' αυτου* A Scr's g: om BC[1]DLℵ 1. 69 latt Syr copt æth arm.

17. for *και αυτος ην διδασκων*, *αυτου διδασκοντος* D lat-*c* (*e*).

soever walketh through the paths of the seas' (vv. 6, 8)." **10. ἔσῃ ζωγρῶν]** Compare, and indeed throughout this miracle, the striking parallel, and yet contrast, in John xxi.—with its injunction, '*feed My lambs*,' '*shepherd My sheep*,' given to the same Peter; its net which *did not burst*: and the minute and beautiful appropriateness of each will be seen: this, at, or near, the commencement of the Apostolic course; that, at how different, and how fitting a time! It is perhaps too subtle, and hardly accordant with the rules of emphasis, to find (with Mey. and Stier) a fitness in **ζωγρῶν** as expressing the ethical catching of men. I prefer taking it as the word common to both acts—merely as **catch**.

12—16.] Healing of a leper. Matt. viii. 2—4. Mark i. 40—45. In Matt. placed immediately after the Sermon on the Mount; in Mark and here, without any note of time: see notes on Matt. **12.] πλήρης λ.** (a touch of medical accuracy from the beloved physician) implies the soreness of the disease. **14.]** A change of construction from the oblique to the direct: see reff. **15.]** The reason of this is stated in Mark, ver. 45, to be the disobedience of the leper to the Lord's command. **16.] καὶ προσευχ.** is peculiar to Luke, as often: see ch. iii. 21; vi.

z Acts v. 34. 1 Tim. i. 7 only †.
a constr., Rom. xiii. 4. 2 Cor. vii. 3.
b Mark vii. 4 reff.
c ver. 24. Acts viii. 7. ix. 33. Luke only, exc. Heb. xii. 12, from Isa. xxxv. 3. = 1 Macc. ix. 55.
d Matt. xii. 46 reff.
e Matt. vi. 13. ch. xi. 4. xii. 11. Acts xvii. 20. 1 Tim. vi. 7. Heb. xiii. 11 only. 4 Kings xxiii. 34.

διδάσκων, καὶ ἦσαν καθήμενοι Φαρισαῖοι καὶ [z] νομο- Ξ διδασκων...
διδάσκαλοι οἳ ἦσαν ἐληλυθότες ἐκ πάσης κώμης τῆς
Γαλιλαίας καὶ Ἰουδαίας καὶ Ἱερουσαλήμ, καὶ δύναμις
κυρίου [a] ἦν εἰς τὸ ἰᾶσθαι αὐτόν. 18 καὶ ἰδοὺ ἄνδρες ...αυτους H.
φέροντες ἐπὶ [b] κλίνης ἄνθρωπον ὃς ἦν [c] παραλελυμένος, ABCDE KLMS
καὶ [d] ἐζήτουν αὐτὸν [e] εἰσενεγκεῖν καὶ θεῖναι αὐτὸν [f] ἐνώπιον UVXΓΔ ΛΞΠℵ
αὐτοῦ. 19 καὶ μὴ [g] εὑρόντες [h] ποίας [e] εἰσενέγκωσιν αὐτον 1. 33. 69
διὰ τὸν ὄχλον, [i] ἀναβάντες [i] ἐπὶ τὸ [ik] δῶμα διὰ τῶν [l] κερά-
μων [m] καθῆκαν αὐτὸν σὺν τῷ [n] κλινιδίῳ εἰς τὸ μέσον ἔμπροσθεν τοῦ Ἰησοῦ. 20 καὶ ἰδὼν τὴν πίστιν αὐτῶν εἶπεν
Ἄνθρωπε, [o] ἀφέωνταί σοι αἱ ἁμαρτίαι σου. 21 καὶ ἤρξαντο

f ver. 25 al. Gen. xxiv. 51. g — ch. xix. 48. Acts iv. 21. h constr., see note. ch. xix. 4. i Acts x. 9. Josh. ii. 8. only. k as above (i). elsw. gen. aft. ἐπί, Matt. x. 27. xxiv. 17 ‖ Mk. ch. xii. 3. xvii. 31 l here only ‡. 2 Kings xvii. 28 only. m Acts ix. 25. x. 11. xi. 5 only. Exod. xvii. 11. n here bis only †. o = ‖. Matt. vi. 12. Lev. iv. 20.

ins *οι* bef *φαρισαιοι* BS copt-schw arm. for *κ. ησαν* to *νομοδ.*, *συνελθειν τους φ. κ. νομ.* D lat-*e*. ins *οι* bef *νομοδιδασκαλοι* B. for *οι ησαν*, *ησαν δε* D lat-*e*: om *οι* ℵ[1](ins ℵ-corr[1]) 33. **συνεληλυθοτες** (*συν perhaps error from -σαν preceding: so Mey*) A[1]D 1. 69 lat-*a* [arm]. aft *πασης* ins *της* B. om *και ιερ.* to *ην* D: om *και δυν. κυρ. ην* X. for *εις το*, *του* D. rec (for *αυτον*) *αυτους*, with ACD rel latt syrr [syr-jer] copt goth arm [Cyr_2]: *παντας* K Cyr_1: txt (*see note*) BLΞℵ.

18. *ανθρωπον* bef *επι κλινης*, and add *βεβληβλημενον*(sic) ℵ. *εισενεγκεν* bef *αυτον* D ev-47 lat-*a c e*. rec om 2nd *αυτον*, with ACDℵ rel [Cyr_1]: txt BLΞ syr-w-ob.

19. rec ins *δια* bef *ποιας*, with Scr's q r: om ABCDΞℵ rel Scr's-mss.—for *ποιας*, *ποθεν* 69: *πως* Scr's a l m n s. for *αναβαντες* to *κλινιδιω*, *ανεβησαν ε. τ. δ. και αποστεγασαντες τους κεραμους οπου ην καθηκαν τον κραβαττον συν τω παραλυτικω* D lat-*b*. for *του ιησ.*, *παντων* B.

20. aft *ιδων* ins *ο ιησους* CS 69 lat-ff_2 Syr arm-mss, *ιδων δε ιησους* D. for *ειπεν*, *λεγει* D. rec aft *ειπεν* ins *αυτω* (*gloss, as varr shew*), with A rel syr arm; *τω παραλυτικω* CD lat-*f* Syr copt goth Cyr_1; *τω ανθρωπω*, omg *ανθρωπε* below, 1 lat-*a b c g_1 l* [*q*]: om BLΞℵ 33 vulg lat-ff_2 g_2. *σου αι αμ.* (*from ‖ Matt Mark*) D-gr F(Wetst) ℵ.

12; ix. 18; xi. 1. This verse breaks off the sequence of the narrative.

17—26.] HEALING OF A PARALYTIC. Matt. ix. 2—8. Mark ii. 1—12. This miracle is introduced by the indefinite words, *καὶ ἐγ. ἐν μιᾷ τ. ἡμ.*: see reff. In Matt. viii. 5—ix. 1, a series of incidents are interposed. Our Lord there appears to have returned from the country of the Gadarenes and the miracle on the dæmoniac there, to '*His own city*,' i. e. Capernaum. The order in Mark is the same as here, and his narrative contains the only decisive note of sequence (ch. iv. 35), which determines his order and that in the text to have been the actual one, and the events in Matt. viii. to be related out of their order. **17.**] **ἐκ π. κώμ.** not to be pressed: as we say, **from all parts.** **δύν. κυρ.**] Does this mean *the power of God*—or *the power of the Lord*, i. e. Jesus? Mey. remarks that Luke uses *κύριος* frequently for Jesus, but always with the article: see ch. vii. 13; x. 1; xi. 39; xii. 42, al. fr.:—but the same word, without the article, for *the Most High*; see ch. i. 11, 38, 58, 66; ii. 9; iv. 19; whence we conclude that the meaning is, **the power of God** (working in the Lord Jesus) **was in the direction of His healing**: i. e. wrought so that He exercised the powers of healing: and then a case follows. For construction, see reff. **αὐτόν** has apparently been altered to *αὐτούς* from its difficulty. It might indeed be said that *-ους* may have been altered to *-ον* from the apparent difficulty of all these mentioned needing healing. So uncertain are merely subjective considerations either way: and so necessary is it to adhere in such cases, where any uncertainty exists, simply and faithfully to antiquity, as our best existing guide. **18.**] Borne of *four*, Mark. **19.**] This description is that of an eye-witness. For the genitive of place, which is mostly poetical, see Kühner, Gramm. § 523. **20.**] On **ἡ πίστις αὐτ.** see note on

[p]διαλογίζεσθαι οἱ γραμματεῖς καὶ οἱ Φαρισαῖοι λέγοντες
Τίς ἐστιν οὗτος ὃς [q]λαλεῖ [q]βλασφημίας; τίς δύναται
ἁμαρτίας [o]ἀφεῖναι εἰ μὴ μόνος ὁ θεός; 22 [r]ἐπιγνοὺς δὲ ὁ
Ἰησοῦς τοὺς [s]διαλογισμοὺς αὐτῶν, ἀποκριθεὶς εἶπεν πρὸς
αὐτοὺς Τί [p]διαλογίζεσθε ἐν ταῖς καρδίαις ὑμῶν; 23 τί
ἐστιν [t]εὐκοπώτερον, εἰπεῖν [o]Ἀφέωνταί σοι αἱ ἁμαρτίαι σου,
ἢ εἰπεῖν [u]Ἔγειρε καὶ περιπάτει; 24 ἵνα δὲ εἰδῆτε ὅτι ὁ
υἱὸς τοῦ ἀνθρώπου [v]ἐξουσίαν [v]ἔχει ἐπὶ τῆς γῆς [o]ἀφιέναι
ἁμαρτίας, εἶπεν τῷ [w]παραλελυμένῳ Σοὶ λέγω, [u]ἔγειρε, καὶ
R [κα]ι παραχρ. ... ἄρας τὸ [n]κλινίδιόν σου πορεύου εἰς τὸν οἶκόν σου. 25 καὶ
[x]παραχρῆμα ἀναστὰς ἐνώπιον αὐτῶν, ἄρας [y]ἐφ' [z]ὃ [a]κατ-
έκειτο ἀπῆλθεν εἰς τὸν οἶκον αὐτοῦ [b]δοξάζων τὸν θεόν.
26 καὶ [c]ἔκστασις [d]ἔλαβεν ἅπαντας, καὶ [b]ἐδόξαζον τὸν
θεόν, καὶ [e]ἐπλήσθησαν φόβου, λέγοντες ὅτι εἴδομεν [f]παρά-
δοξα σήμερον.
27 Καὶ μετὰ ταῦτα ἐξῆλθεν, καὶ ἐθεάσατο [g]τελώνην
ὀνόματι Λευεὶν καθήμενον ἐπὶ τὸ [h]τελώνιον, καὶ εἶπεν

p Matt. xvi. 7, 8 reff.
q here only, see Rev. xiii. 5.
r Matt. xiv. 25 reff.
s Matt. xv. 19 reff. Lam. iii. 60, 61.
t || Mt. reff.
u || Mt. Mk. John v. 8. Acts iii. 6.
v Matt. vii. 29 reff.
w ver. 18 reff.
x Luke only, exc. Matt. xxi. 19, 20 (reff.).
y acc., Matt. xiii. 2. Hom. Od. λ. 576. dat., Mark vi. 55.
z constr., Mark x. 40 reff.
a Mark i. 30 reff.
b ||. ch. ii. 20. vii. 16 al. Exod. xv. 2.
c Mark xvi. 8 reff. Zech. xiv. 13.
d = ch. vii. 16 reff.
e ch. iv. 28 reff.
f here only +. Sir. xliii. 25 al. (-ξάζειν, Exod. xi. 7.)
g Matt. v. 46 reff.
h || only +.

21. aft *φαρισαιοι* ins *εν ταις καρδιαις αυτων* D lat-*b* (*c*) *ff*$_2$ *g*$_{1.2}$ *l* [*q*]. for *τις εστιν ουτος ος*, *τι ουτος* D copt. rec *αφιεναι*, with ACℵ rel Cyr$_1$: txt BDΞ.—rec *αφ.* bef *αμαρτιας* (*from* || *Matt*), with ACℵ rel vulg lat-*a b f ff*$_2$ *g*$_1$ syrr [syr-jer] copt goth æth arm: txt BDLΞ 1 lat-*c e* Ambr$_1$. for *μονος*, *εἱς* C³ D-gr X lat-*a* syr-mg goth Cyr$_1$. om *ὁ* D¹(ins D-corr¹).
22. om *αποκριθεις* (*see* || *Matt Mark*) CD lat-*a b c ff*$_2$ *g*$_1$ *l* Syr-ed æth. for *ειπεν προς αυτους*, *λεγει αυτοις* D. aft *υμων* ins *πονηρα* D lat-*c e l* syr-jer æth.
23. *σου* bef *αι αμ.*, omg *σοι*, Dℵ ev-48: *σου αι αμ. σου* C F(Wetst) XΛ: *σοι αμ. σου*, omg *αι*, Ξ. rec **εγειραι**, with UXΔ: txt ABCDΞℵ rel.
24. rec *εξουσιαν εχει* bef *ο υιος του ανθρωπου* (|| *Matt Mark*), with ACDℵ rel lat-*a c e* syrr [syr-jer (copt)] goth æth arm [Mcion$_2$-e Cyr$_1$]: txt BKLΞ[Π] vulg lat-*b f ff*$_2$ *g*$_1$ *l q* [Cyr$_1$]. om *της* Λ Cyr$_1$: om *γης* D¹(ins D-corr¹). *αφιναι* (= *αφειναι*) D¹L¹. for *ειπεν*, *λεγει* D vulg lat-*a b e f g*$_1$. **παραλυτικω** CD F(Wetst) LMXΞℵ 33. 69 arm Cyr$_1$: txt AB rel. rec **εγειραι**, with LUΓ: txt ABCDΞℵ rel.
for *αρας*, *αρον*, and ins *και* bef *πορευου*, Dℵ 157 latt syrr [syr-jer] copt æth. for *κλινιδιον*, *κραβαττον* (|| *Mark*) D lat-*c* copt.
25. for *αυτων*, *αυτου* ℵ: *παντων* 69 [lat-*a* arm]. rec *εφ'* **ω** (*corrn to more obvious constr*, see reff), with RUΛ 69 (1, e sil): txt ABCΞℵ rel.—for *εφ ο κατεκ.*, *την κλεινην* D lat-*e* Syr, *lectum* [or *grabat.*] *in quo jacebat* vulg-clem lat-*a b c* syr [syr-jer].
26. om *και εκστασις* to *θεον* (*homœotel*) DMSX 69 lat-*e*. transp 2nd and 3rd clauses A. for *φοβου*, *θαμβου* D¹: *θαμβους* D². om *οτι* D. **ιδαμεν** C: *ιδωμεν* R. (*ιδ.* also AB²KLMVX[Π¹].)
27. for *και μετα* to *λευειν*, *και ελθων παλιν παρα την θαλασσαν τον ακολουθουντα αυτω οχλον εδιδασκεν και παραγων ειδεν λευει τον του αλφαιου* (*from* || *Mark*) D. for *εθεασατο*, *ειδεν* A(D)[Π²] 253 Scr's o; *ιδεν* K Scr's p w. aft *λευειν* (on the spelling, see prolegomena) ins *καλουμενον* C¹ 157. for *ειπεν*, *λεγει* (|| *Matt Mark*) Dℵ 69 vulg lat-*b f ff*$_2$ *g*$_1$ [*l q*].

Matt. ver. 2; also on **ἀφέωνται.** **24.**] **εἶπεν τῷ παρ.**, probably not parenthetic: see in Matt. **26.**] **παράδοξα** = *θαυμαστά, ἀπροσδόκητα*, Hesych. Compare the close of the accounts in Matt. and Mark.

27—39.] Calling of Levi. Question respecting fasting. Matt. ix. 9—17. Mark ii. 13—22. For all common matter,—the discussion of the identity of Matthew and Levi, &c.—see notes on Matt. and Mark. I here only notice what is peculiar to Luke. **27.**] **ἐθεάσ.**, not merely '*He saw*,' but **He looked on,**—He

i = Matt. xix. 5 reff. 3 Kings xix. 20.
k ||. Num. xxii. 20.
l ch. xiv. 13. Gen. xxvi. 30. Esth. i. 3.
m as above (l) only. Esth. v. 4 al.
n || Mk. Mark xiv. 3. 1 Cor. viii. 10.
o Matt. xx. 11 reff. Num. xvi. 41.
p Matt. vi. 8 reff.
q Gospp., Luke (vii. 10. xv. 27) only. Epp., Pastor. (1 Tim. i. 10. vi. 3. 2 Tim. i. 13. iv. 3. Tit. i. 9 al3.) only, exc. 3 John 2. Gen. xxix. 6.
r ch. iv. 23 reff.
s Matt. iv. 24.
t = ||. Num. xxiii. 11.
u ver. 8. Ps. iii. 7.
v Matt. iv. 2 reff.

αὐτῷ Ἀκολούθει μοι. 28 καὶ ⁱ καταλιπὼν πάντα ᵏ ἀναστὰς ᵏ ἠκολούθει αὐτῷ. 29 καὶ ˡ ἐποίησεν ˡᵐ δοχὴν μεγάλην Λευεὶς αὐτῷ ἐν τῇ οἰκίᾳ αὐτοῦ, καὶ ἦν ὄχλος πολὺς
ᵍ τελωνῶν καὶ ἄλλων οἳ ἦσαν μετ' αὐτῶν ⁿ κατακεί-
μενοι. 30 καὶ ᵒ ἐγόγγυζον οἱ Φαρισαῖοι καὶ οἱ γραμματεῖς αὐτῶν πρὸς τοὺς μαθητὰς αὐτοῦ λέγοντες Διὰ τί
μετὰ τῶν ᵍ τελωνῶν ἐσθίετε καὶ πίνετε; 31 καὶ ἀποκριθεὶς
ὁ Ἰησοῦς εἶπεν πρὸς αὐτοὺς Οὐ ᵖ χρείαν ᵖ ἔχουσιν οἱ
ᑫ ὑγιαίνοντες ʳ ἰατροῦ, ἀλλὰ οἱ ˢ κακῶς ˢ ἔχοντες. 32 οὐκ
ἐλήλυθα ᵗ καλέσαι δικαίους, ἀλλὰ ᵘ ἁμαρτωλοὺς εἰς μετάνοιαν. 33 οἱ δὲ εἶπαν πρὸς αὐτὸν Οἱ μαθηταὶ Ἰωάννου
ᵛ νηστεύουσιν ʷ πυκνὰ καὶ ˣʸ δεήσεις ʸ ποιοῦνται, ὁμοίως
καὶ οἱ τῶν Φαρισαίων, οἱ δὲ σοὶ ἐσθίουσιν καὶ πίνουσιν.
34 ὁ δὲ Ἰησοῦς εἶπεν πρὸς αὐτοὺς Μὴ δύνασθε τοὺς υἱοὺς
τοῦ ᶻ νυμφῶνος ᵃ ἐν ᾧ ὁ ᵇ νυμφίος μετ' αὐτῶν ἐστιν
ποιῆσαι ᵛ νηστεῦσαι; 35 ᶜ ἐλεύσονται δὲ ἡμέραι, ᵈ καὶ ὅταν

F εγογγυζον... ABCDE FKLM RSUVX ΓΔΛΞΠ ℵ1. 33. 69

H οι δε ειπον...

w Acts xxiv. 26. 1 Tim. v. 23 only. Ezek. xxxi. 3 A. 2 Macc. viii. 8 only. x ch. i. 13. ii. 37 al. 3 Kings viii 45. y Phil. i. 4. 1 Tim. ii. 1. z || only †. Tobit vi. 13, 16 only. a || Mk. John v. 7. Amos viii. 11. b || Mk. reff. c || Mt. reff. Jer. xxxi (xlviii.) 12. d a sim. use,

28. καταλειπων AELΓΔΛ[Π] 33. rec **απαντα**, with A rel: απαντα**ς**(but *s* erased) ℵ: απαν M: txt B C²(-τας¹) DLRΞ 33. rec ηκολουθ**ησεν** (|| *Matt Mark*), with ACRℵ rel syrr copt: txt BDLΞ 69 lat-*a*.

29. rec ins ο bef λευ.: om ABCDΞℵ rel Scr's-mss. λευει δοχ. αυτω μεγ. D: om αυτω [Δ]ℵ. rec τελωνων bef πολυς, with A rel: txt BCDLRΞℵ 1. 33. 69 latt syrr arm. om και αλλων ℵ¹. μετ αυτου B¹(Tischdf). for οι to κατακειμενοι, ανακειμενων D lat-*e*.

30. οι φαρ. κ. οι γραμματεις (αυτων) bef εγογγυζον D lat-*c e*.—εγογγυζ**αν** B¹(Tischdf) R.—rec transp οι φαρ. and οι γρ. αυτ. (|| *Mark*), with A rel (Syr) syr goth [(æth) Bas₁]: txt BCDLRΞℵ 1. 33 latt syr-jer (copt) arm.—om αυτων DFXℵ vulg-ms lat-*f* [*e l*] Syr copt æth. om αυτου C¹. rec om των (bef τελωνων), with V[Π] (S 33, e sil) [Bas₁-ed]: ins ABCDRΞℵ rel. rec aft τελωνων ins και αμαρτωλων (*from* ||), with ABC²Rℵ rel vss [Bas₁]: om C¹D Cyr₁.

31. for και αποκρ., αποκρ. δε D lat-*e*. om ὁ B. for προς αυτους, αυτοις LΞ 33. (αλλ**α**, so ABΞ.)

32. for εληλυθα, ηλθον (||) C³D 1. (Ξ has ηλ at end of a line, but ληλυθα in the next.) for αμαρτωλους, ασεβεις ℵ¹(txt ℵ-corr¹).

33. (ειπ**α**ν, so B¹CDLRΞ 33.) rec ins δια τι bef οι (*from* ||), with ACDR ℵ(erased but restored) rel latt goth [syrr æth arm]: om BLΞ 33 copt. aft ιωαννου ins και οι μαθ. των φαρισαιων (|| *Mark*), omg ομοιως και οι των φαρισαιων, D. for σοι, μαθηται σου (|| *Matt*) D lat-*b c e f ff₂* copt goth. for εσθιουσιν και πινουσιν, ουδεν τουτων ποιουσιν D lat-*e*.

34. rec om ιησους, with A rel: ins BCDLRXΞℵ 1. 33. 69 lat-*f* syr-mg copt æth. δυνανται οι υιοι, omg ποιησαι, (*from* ||) Dℵ¹ gat¹ lat-*a b c e ff₂ g₁* æth Tert₁ Ambr. εφ' οσον εχουσιν τον νυμφιον μεθ. εαυτων D lat-*e*. rec νηστευ**ειν** (*see* || *Mark*), with ACDRℵ¹ rel: txt BXΞℵ³ᵃ.

35. om και CFL M-txt ℵ 1. 69 vulg lat-*b c e f ff₂ g₁ l* [*q*] syrr copt arm: ins ABDRΞ

observed. **28.**] **κατ. πάντα**, not merely, '*having left his books and implements*,' but generally used, and importing not so much a present objective relinquishment, as the mind with which he rose to follow. **29.**] This fact is only expressly mentioned here—but may be directly inferred from Mark, and remotely from Matt. See on Matt. ver. 10. **33.**] On the difference in the persons who ask this question, see on Matt. and Mark. **καὶ δεήσεις ποι.**] See ch. xi. 1. These prayers must be understood in connexion with an ascetic form of life, not as only

[e] ἀπαρθῇ ἀπ' αὐτῶν ὁ νυμφίος, τότε [v] νηστεύσουσιν ἐν
ἐκείναις ταῖς ἡμέραις. 36 ἔλεγεν δὲ καὶ παραβολὴν πρὸς
αὐτοὺς ὅτι οὐδεὶς [f] ἐπίβλημα ἀπὸ ἱματίου καινοῦ [g] σχίσας
...παλαιον Ξ. ἐπιβάλλει ἐπὶ ἱμάτιον παλαιόν· [h] εἰ δὲ μήγε, καὶ τὸ καινὸν
[g] σχίσει, καὶ τῷ παλαιῷ οὐ [i] συμφωνήσει τὸ [f] ἐπίβλημα τὸ
ἀπὸ τοῦ καινοῦ. 37 καὶ οὐδεὶς [k] βάλλει οἶνον νέον εἰς
[l] ἀσκοὺς παλαιούς· [h] εἰ δὲ μήγε, [m] ῥήξει ὁ οἶνος ὁ νέος
τοὺς [l] ἀσκούς, καὶ αὐτὸς ἐκχυθήσεται καὶ οἱ [l] ἀσκοὶ ἀπο-
λοῦνται· 38 ἀλλὰ οἶνον νέον εἰς [l] ἀσκοὺς καινοὺς [n] βλη-
τέον. 39 καὶ οὐδεὶς πιὼν παλαιὸν [o] θέλει νέον· λέγει γὰρ
Ὁ παλαιὸς [p] χρηστός ἐστιν.

e || only ‡. Gen. xii. 9. Exod. xii. 37.
f here (bis) & || (Mt. w. ἐπιβάλλει) only. Isa. iii. 21 only.
g ch. xxiii. 45 || Mt. Mk. Mark i. 10 al. Zech. xiv. 4.
h || Mt. reff.
i = here (Matt. xviii. 19 reff.) only. (-νησις, 2 Cor. vi. 15.)
k Mark vii. 33. John xviii. 11. Ps. cxxv. 6 Ed-vat. ℵ[1]. (B def.)
l here (4 times) & | only. Josh. ix. 4, 13.
m || Mt. reff. Jer. xxiv. 2, 5.
n here (| Mk. v. r.) only †. o Matt. ix. 13 reff. p = here only. (Matt. xi. 30 reff.)

rel forj(with em ing) lat-*a* goth. ins και bef τοτε FMΔℵ 1. 69 lat-*b c e f ff*$_2$ *g*$_1$ *l* [*q*] goth arm-mss æth.

36. προς αυτους bef παραβολην [X]ℵ.—om δε και ℵ[1] : om και X lat-*c e* [copt]. rec om απο (*see* || *Matt Mark*), with ACR rel lat-*a f* goth [æth] Iren-int$_1$: ins BDLX [Ξ]ℵ 1. 33. 69 vulg lat-*b c e ff*$_2$ *g*$_1$ *l* [*q*] syrr copt [(arm) Cyr$_1$-p] Ambr$_1$. rec om σχισας (|| *Matt Mark*), with ACR rel latt syr goth æth arm Iren-int$_1$: ins BDLΞℵ 1. 33 Syr (copt) [Cyr$_1$-p]. om 2nd και ℵ[1] [copt-ms]. rec σχιζει (*see* ||), with A rel vulg lat-*b c f ff*$_2$ *g*$_1$ syrr copt goth æth arm : (. . .)ιζεται R : txt BCDLXℵ 33 ev-y lat-*a e*. rec συμφωνει (*see* ||), with R rel vulg lat-*b c f ff*$_2$ *g*$_1$ goth [&c] : txt ABC DLXℵ 33 lat-*a e* Mcion-e$_1$. rec (aft συμφων.) om το : om το επιβλημα AR rel goth æth : txt BCLXΛℵ 1. 33. 69 ev-y [latt syrr arm] copt.—ου συμφ. το απο τ. κ. επιβλ. D.

37. **επιβαλλει** C. ρησσει CΓΛ am lat-*b f* [*l*] *q* syrr goth. rec (for ο οιν. ο νε.) ο νεος οινος, with A rel : om ο νεος ℵ Scr's g : txt BCDLMRUXΛ 1. 33 latt. aft ασκους ins τους παλαιους D copt arm.

38. for βλητεον, βαλλουσιν (|| *Matt*) D ℵ[1](txt ℵ corr[1]) lat-*a b c e f ff*$_2$ *g*$_1$ [*l q*] syrr (copt) æth Dial$_1$. rec at end ins και αμφοτεροι συντηρουνται (*from* || *Matt : see digest on* || *Mark*), with AC(D)R rel latt syrr goth [æth arm Dial$_1$] (τηρουνται D lat-*a e*): om BLℵ 1. 33 copt.

39. om ver D lat-*a b c e ff*$_2$[1] *l* Eus-canon$_1$(perhaps). om και Bℵ[3a]. rec ins ευθεως bef θελει (*see note*), with AC[2]R vulg lat-*f* [*ff*$_2$] *g*$_{1.2}$ *q* syrr goth ; ευθυς X ev-y : om BC[1]Lℵ 1 copt æth arm. rec χρηστοτερος (*see note*), with ACR rel latt syr : txt BLℵ Syr copt.

the usual prayers of devout men.

34.] I have remarked on the striking contrast between **ποιῆσαι νηστεῦσαι** and **νηστεύσουσιν**, on Matt. ver. 15. **35. καὶ ὅταν . . .] yea, days when . . .**: so *τινας καὶ συχνούς*, Plato, Gorg. 455 C : *ὀλίγου τινὸς ἀξία καὶ οὐδενός*, ib. Apol. 23 A : see Hartung, Partikellehre, i. p. 145 f.

36.] The latter part of this verse is peculiar, and is to be thus understood : '*if he does, he both will rend the new garment*' (by taking out of it the *ἐπίβλημα*), '*and the piece from the new garment will not agree with the old.*' The common interpretation (which makes *τὸ καινόν* the nom. to *σχίσει*, and understands *τὸ παλαιόν* as its accus.) is inconsistent with the construction, in which *τὸ καινόν* is to be coupled with *ἱμάτιον*, not with *ἐπίβλημα*. In Matt. and Mark the mischief done is differently expressed. Our text is very significant, and represents to us the spoiling of both systems by an attempt to engraft the new upon the old :—the *new* loses its completeness; the *old*, its consistency. **39.**] This peculiar and important addition at once stamps our report with the very highest character for accuracy. Its apparent difficulty has perhaps caused its omission from Cod. D and mss. of the old Latin version. It contains the *conclusion of the discourse*, and the *final answer* to the question in ver. 33, which is not given in Matt. and Mark. The **πιόντες παλαιόν** are *the Jews*, who had long been habituated to the old system ;—the **νέος** is the new wine (see on Matt.) of the *grace and freedom of the Gospel :* and our Lord asserts that this new wine was *not palatable* to the Jews, who said **ὁ παλαιὸς χρηστός ἐστιν**. Observe (against De Wette, &c.) that even with the common reading *χρηστότερος* there is *no objective comparison whatever*

q constr., | Mk. vv. 6, 12 ch. iii. 21. r here only +.

VI. 1 q Ἐγένετο δὲ ἐν σαββάτῳ [r δευτεροπρώτῳ] ...εγενετο F. ABCDE HKLM RSUVX ΓΔΛΠℵ 1. 33. 69

CHAP. VI. 1. for εγ. δε, και εγ. D lat-*a e* (goth?) æth. αυτον bef εν σαβ. δευτ. διαπορ. D: om αυτον 33. om δευτεροπρωτω (*prob on acct of its difficulty, and as not being in* ||: *Tischdf omitted it in his* 1*st and* 2*nd edns, but restored it in the* 7*th* [*and* 8*th*]. *Mey holds it to be spurious*) BLℵ 1. 33. 69[1] (ev-y) lat-*b c e f*[2] *l q* Syr [syr-jer] copt æth: syr-marg notes that it is not in all the copies: ins ACDR rel vulg lat-*a f*[1] *ff*$_2$ *g*$_{1.2}$ syr-txt goth (arm) Cæs$_1$ Epiph$_2$ Chr$_1$ Isid$_1$ Thl$_1$ [Chron$_1$] Euthym$_1$ Ambr$_1$.—δευτερω πρωτω RΓ.

here between the old and new wine; the whole stress is on **θέλει** and **λέγει γάρ**, and the import of χρηστότερος is *subjective:—in the view of him who utters it.* And even if we were to assume such an objective comparison, it makes no difficulty. In time, the *new* wine will become *older:*—the man will become habituated to its taste, and the wine itself mellowed: and the comparison between the wines is not then which is the *older*, but which is intrinsically the *better*. Stier observes (i. 328), that the saying is a lesson for ardent and enthusiastic converts not to be disappointed, if they cannot at once instil their spirit into others about them.

As regards the *readings*,—the sentence seems to have been tampered with by some who wished to make it more obvious, and to bring out the *comparison* more strongly: εὐθέως being inserted, better to correspond with the fact, and the matter in question, and the comparative substituted for the positive: but the sentence loses much of its point and vigour by the change: the old wine is not *better than the new* (which has *not been tasted*), but merely **good**, i. e. *good enough:* therefore no new is desired.

CHAP. VI. 1—5.] THE DISCIPLES PLUCK EARS OF CORN ON THE SABBATH. Matt. xii. 1—8. Mark ii. 23—28. Between the discourse just related here and in Mark, and this incident, Matthew interposes *the raising of Jaeirus's daughter, the healing of the two blind and one dumb, the mission of the twelve, and the message of John.* I need not insist on these obvious proofs of independence in the construction of our Gospels. On the question of the arrangements, see on Matt. 1. **δευτεροπρώτῳ**] This word presents much difficulty. None of the interpretations have any certainty, as the word is found no where else, and can be only judged of by analogy. (1) It is not altogether clear that the word *ought to be here at all:*—see var. readd. Schulz supposes it to have arisen from putting together two separate glosses, in the margin of some MSS., one δευτέρῳ, the other πρώτῳ:—originally inserted,—the first, to distinguish this sabbath from that in ch. iv. 31,—the latter, from that in ver. 6. (2) Chrysostom, Hom. xxxix. on Matt., vol. vii. p. 431, says, ὁ δὲ Λουκᾶς φησιν Ἐν σαββάτῳ δευτεροπρώτῳ. τί δέ ἐστιν, ἐν **δευτεροπρώτῳ**; ὅταν διπλῆ ἡ ἀργία ᾖ, καὶ τοῦ σαββάτου τοῦ κυρίου, καὶ ἑτέρας ἑορτῆς διαδεχομένης. Paulus and Olsh. also take this interpretation. (3) Theophylact understands,—a sabbath, *the day before which* (παρασκευή) *had been a Feast-day.*

(4) Isidore of Pelusium, Euthym., and others, think that *the first day of unleavened bread* is meant, and is called δευτερόπ., because it is δευτέρα τοῦ πάσχα, which had been slain on the evening before. (5) Scaliger and Petavius interpret it to mean *the sabbath following the second day of the Passover*, from which the seven weeks to Pentecost were reckoned. This has been commonly followed; but is liable to the objection that the assumption, σάββ. δευτερόπρ. = σάββ. τῆς ἑβδομάδος δευτεροπρώτου = σάββ. τῆς ἑβδ. πρώτης μετὰ τὴν δευτέραν τῶν ἀζύμων, is an unjustifiable one. (6) To omit many other conjectures, I may mention that Wieseler (Chron. Synop. der 4 Evv., p. 231 ff.) suggests that it may mean the *first sabbath* in the *second* of the cycle of seven years, which completed the sabbatical period. He shews, by a passage from the κήρυγμα Πέτρου (Clem. Alex., Strom. vi. 5, p. 760 P.), that the Jews did call the first sabbath of the year πρῶτον—and that the years were reckoned as the first, second, &c., of the septennial cycle (see a decree of Jul. Cæsar in Jos. Antt. xiv. 10. 6). Thus the first sabbath of the first year would be πρωτόπρωτον or πρῶτον, that of the second δευτερόπρωτον, &c. And according to his chronology, which fixes this in A.U.C. 782, this year *was the second of the sabbatical cycle.* If we follow this conjecture, this day was the first sabbath in the month Nisan. The point so much insisted on, that this must have been *after the presentation of the first-fruits* which took place on the 16th of Nisan,—on account of the prohibition in Levit. xxiii. 14,—is of no weight, as it is very uncertain whether the action mentioned here is

[s] διαπορεύεσθαι αὐτὸν διὰ [t] σπορίμων, καὶ [u] ἔτιλλον οἱ
μαθηταὶ αὐτοῦ καὶ ἤσθιον τοὺς [v] στάχυας [w] ψώχοντες ταῖς
χερσίν. 2 τινὲς δὲ τῶν Φαρισαίων εἶπον Τί ποιεῖτε ὃ οὐκ
ἔξεστιν τοῖς [x] σάββασιν; 3 καὶ ἀποκριθεὶς πρὸς αὐτοὺς
εἶπεν ὁ Ἰησοῦς Οὐδὲ τοῦτο ἀνέγνωτε ὃ [y] ἐποίησεν Δαυεὶδ
[z] ὁπότε ἐπείνασεν αὐτὸς καὶ οἱ μετ᾽ αὐτοῦ ὄντες; 4 ὡς
εἰσῆλθεν εἰς τὸν οἶκον τοῦ θεοῦ καὶ τοὺς [a] ἄρτους τῆς
...εδωκεν C. [a] προθέσεως λαβὼν ἔφαγεν, καὶ ἔδωκεν τοῖς μετ᾽ αὐτοῦ,
οὓς οὐκ ἔξεστιν φαγεῖν εἰ μὴ μόνους τοὺς ἱερεῖς; 5 καὶ
ἔλεγεν αὐτοῖς ὅτι κύριός ἐστιν ὁ υἱὸς τοῦ ἀνθρώπου καὶ
τοῦ σαββάτου. 6 [b] Ἐγένετο δὲ [καὶ] ἐν ἑτέρῳ σαββάτῳ

s ch. xiii. 22. xviii. 36. Acts xvi. 4. Rom. xv. 24 only. Zeph. iii. 1 (ii. 15).
t ‖. Gen. i. 29 bis. Lev. xi. 37 only.
u ‖ only. Ezra ix. 3. Isa. xviii. 7 only.
v ‖. Mark iv. 28 bis only. Gen. xli. 5, 6. Deut. xxiv. 1 (xxiii. 25).
w here only †.
x Matt. xii. 1 reff.
y 1 Kings xxi. 6.
z here only †.
a ‖. Mk. reff.
b constr., ver. 1 reff.

for διαπ., πορευεσθαι C[1]X. rec ins των bef σποριμων (‖ *Matt Mark*), with CDRℵ[3a] rel copt arm [Chron$_1$]: om ABLΔΛ[1][Π]ℵ[1] 1. οι δε μαθηται αυτου ηρξαντο τιλλειν D lat-*b*. rec τους σταχυας bef και ησθιον, with AC[3] ℵ(but om τους) rel [latt syr syr-jer æth arm]: txt BC[1]LR.—τους σταχυας και ψωχοντες ταις χερσιν ησθιον D lat-(*a*) *e f* Syr copt æth arm. aft χερσ. ins αυτων CM[1] lat-*b c e* Syr copt-wilk[-dz] æth Ambr$_1$.

2. for ειπον, ελεγον D latt Syr. rec aft ειπ. ins αυτοις (*supplem, cf varr and* ‖), with AC[3]R rel; αυτω D: om BC[1]LXℵ 1 lat-*a c e* copt. for τι ποιειτε, ειδε τι ποιουσιν οι μαθηται σου (‖ *Matt Mark*) D. τοις σαββασιν bef ο ουκ εξεστιν D lat-*e*. rec aft εξεστιν ins ποιειν (*from* ‖ *Matt*), with ACℵ rel lat-*q* syr [syr-jer] copt goth [æth]; aft σαββ. L Syr: om BDR 69 latt arm. rec ins εν bef τοις σαββ. (‖ *Matt*), with AC rel vulg lat-$g_{1.2}$ [goth]: om BDLRUℵ 1. 69 [arm].

3. απ. δε ο ιησ. ελεγεν προς αυτους D. om ο (bef ιησ.) B. ο ιησ. ειπεν bef προς αυτους AC[3](D)KMRX[Π] 69 Syr, ο ιησ. ειπ. αυτοις 1 lat-*c f ff*$_2$: ο ιησ. πρ. α. ειπ. Lℵ vulg syr copt: πρ. α. ο ιησ. ειπ. 33 goth arm. for ουδε, ουδεποτε (‖ *Mark*) DHL. (om τουτο HL.) for οποτε, οτε (‖ *Matt Mark*) BCDLXΔℵ 1. 69: txt AR rel. (33 def.) for μετ᾽ αυτου, συν αυτω D. om οντες (‖) BDLXℵ 1. 33. 69 Syr [syr-jer] copt æth: ins ACR rel syr goth.

4. for ως, πως (*from* ‖ *Matt Mark*) L R(Treg, expr) Xℵ[3a] 1. 33. 69 copt arm: om BD Mcion-e$_1$: txt ACℵ[1] rel syr [syr-jer]. εισελθων D. προςθεσεως D-gr. rec (for λαβων) ελαβεν και, with AC[3]R rel latt syr goth: om (‖ *Matt Mark*) DK[Π]ℵ 1. 69 syr-jer æth arm Iren-int$_1$: txt BC[1]LX (33 Syr copt, appy). rec aft εδωκεν ins και (‖ *Mark*), with ADRℵ rel syr [syr-jer] æth Thl-ms: om BL 1 latt Syr copt goth arm Iren-int$_1$. for ους, οις D. for εξεστιν, εξον ην (‖ *Matt*) DM gat(with mm) lat-*b c e f* [*l q*] Syr Iren-int$_1$ Ambr$_1$. μονοις τοις ιερευσιν (‖ *Matt*) D 242-51 syr-mg goth.—μονον RΛ 237-48.

5. D reads this ver aft ver 10, and instead of it here, τη αυτη ημερα θεασαμενος τινα εργαζομενον τω σαββατω ειπεν αυτω ανθρωπε ει μεν οιδας τι ποιεις μακαριος ει ει δε μη οιδας επικαταρατος και παραβατης ει του νομου. om οτι Bℵ[1] 1 æth arm. του σαββατου bef ο υιος του ανθρωπου, omg και, (‖ *Matt*) Bℵ; simly Syr [syr-jer] copt æth.

6. for ver, και εισελθοντος αυτου παλιν εις την συναγωγην σαββατω εν η ην ανθρωπος ξηραν εχων την χειρα D. om 1st και BLXℵ 1. 33. 69 lat-*a b c e f ff*$_2$ g_1 *l* Syr copt

included in the prohibition. As regards the analogy of the word, δευτεροδεκάτη, sometimes cited from Jerome on Ezek. xlv., is not to the point: for that word represents the fact that "rursus ex ipsis decimis Levitæ, hoc est inferior ministrorum gradus, decimas dabant sacerdotibus:" so that it was not "the *second tenth*," as Wordsw., but a tenth of a tenth,—a second tithing of a tithe. **ψώχ. τ. χ.** is a detail peculiar to Luke: **rubbing them and blowing away the chaff.** **2.**] In Matt. and Mark, the Pharisees address our Lord, 'Why do Thy disciples,' &c. **3. οὐδὲ . . . .**] **Have ye not read so much as this?** E. V.: i. e. 'Are ye so utterly ignorant of the spirit of Scripture?' see Mark xii. 10, where the same expression occurs.

The remarkable substitution in D for ver. 5 seems to be an interpolation, but hardly an invention of a later time. Its

c constr., Esth. ii. 5. d = ‖. John v. 3 (reff.). e = ‖ Mk. ch. xiv. 1. xx. 20. Acts ix. 24 (Gal. iv. 10) only. Ps. xxxvi. 12. f see ch. v. 19 reff. g John v. 45 reff. h Matt. xv. 19 reff. i ch. v. 23 reff. j absol. = Matt. xiv. 6 reff. k Mark x. 2 reff. l ‖ Mk. (reff.) m = Matt. xxi. 41. xxii. 7 al.

εἰςελθεῖν αὐτὸν εἰς τὴν συναγωγὴν καὶ διδάσκειν, [c] καὶ ἦν
ἄνθρωπος ἐκεῖ [c] καὶ ἡ χεὶρ αὐτοῦ ἡ δεξιὰ ἦν [d] ξηρά.
7 [e] παρετηροῦντο δὲ οἱ γραμματεῖς καὶ οἱ Φαρισαῖοι εἰ ἐν
τῷ σαββάτῳ θεραπεύει, ἵνα [f] εὕρωσιν [g] κατηγορεῖν αὐτοῦ.
8 αὐτὸς δὲ ᾔδει τοὺς [h] διαλογισμοὺς αὐτῶν, εἶπεν δὲ τῷ ...αυτος R.
ἀνδρὶ τῷ [d] ξηρὰν ἔχοντι τὴν χεῖρα [i] Ἔγειρε καὶ στῆθι ..τω αν. H.
εἰς τὸ [j] μέσον. καὶ ἀναστὰς ἔστη. 9 εἶπεν οὖν ὁ Ἰησοῦς ABDE
πρὸς αὐτοὺς Ἐπερωτῶ ὑμᾶς [k] εἰ ἔξεστιν τῷ σαββάτῳ KLMS UVXΓΔ
[l] ἀγαθοποιῆσαι ἢ [l] κακοποιῆσαι, ψυχὴν σῶσαι ἢ [m] ἀπ- ΛΠℵ 1. 33. 69

æth arm Cyr$_1$: ins AR rel vulg lat-g_2 [q] syr goth. rec εκει bef ανθρωπος (‖ *Mark*), with A rel vulg lat-*a c* &c goth [syrr syr-jer arm]: txt BLRℵ 1. 33 copt Cyr$_1$.

7. rec παρετηρουν (‖ *Mark*), with ℵ rel: txt ABDLMRXΔ 1. 33. 69 Cyr$_1$. om δε D 69 copt. rec adds αυτον (*from* ‖ *Mark*), with BDLXℵ (33, e sil) 69(sic) syrr copt æth arm Cyr$_1$: om AR rel latt goth Tert$_1$. om εν (‖) DK[Π] am lat-*a b c* ff_2 *l*. rec θεραπευσει (*from* ‖ *Mark*), with B rel copt: txt ADL[Π]ℵ. (R def.) rec κατηγοριαν (*easier constr*), with Aℵ^{3a} rel [syr-mg] copt arm Cyr$_1$ κατηγορησαι D: txt BSXℵ^1 1 am(with fuld forj gat) lat-g_1 *q* syrr goth. (R def.) ins κατ' bef αυτου F(Wetst) KLRℵ^{3a} 33 syr-mg copt arm Cyr$_1$.

8. for ηδει, γεινωσκων *sciens* D lat-*b*. rec (for ειπ. δε) και ειπ. (‖ *Mark*), with A rel syr goth æth [Cyr$_1$]: λεγει D lat-*b f* copt: txt BLXℵ 1. 33. 69 lat-*a*. rec (for τω ανδρι) τω ανθρωπω (‖ *Mark*), with A rel: om D: txt BLℵ 1. 33 æth Cyr$_1$. ins την bef ξηραν Aℵ. τω τ. χ. εχ. ξ. D 33. rec εγειραι, with Γ: εγειρου D: txt AB [S(Tischdf)] ℵ rel. εν τω μεσω D lat-*a b c* [*f q*]. rec (for 2nd και) ο δε (*see below, ver* 10), with A rel syr [arm]: txt BDLXℵ 1. 33 latt (Syr) [syr-jer] copt goth æth Cyr$_1$. εσταθη D.

9. for ουν, δε (*see* ‖ *Matt, ver* 11) BDLℵ 33. 69 latt goth æth [Cyr$_1$]: om Syr copt arm: txt A rel syr. om ο (bef ιησ.) B [Cyr$_1$]. rec επερωτησω (*see ch* xx. 3: *Mark* xi. 29), with AD rel lat-*a b c* ff_2 g_1 *q* syrr æth arm: txt BLℵ 157 vulg lat-*e f l* [syr-jer] copt goth. rec (for ει) τι (*error*), with A rel lat-*q* syrr goth: txt BDLℵ 157 vulg lat-*a c e f* ff_2 g_1 *l* copt Cyr$_1$ Aug.—(rec υμας τι·, with Scr's v (o r evv-x-y, e sil) lat-*q* syr: υμας· τι AEKMSΓΛ[Π] Syr goth.) rec τοις σαββασι, with A rel vulg-ed lat-*a f* syr copt-wilk goth arm Mcion$_1$-t: txt BDLℵ am(with fuld em forj) lat-*c e* ff_2 (*l* ?) [Syr copt-schw æth Cyr$_1$]. (lat-*b* def.)

form and contents speak for its originality and, I am disposed to believe, its authenticity.

6—11.] Healing of the withered hand. Matt. xii. 9—14. Mark iii. 1—6. See on Matt. **6.**] The circumstances related in ch. xiv. 1—6 are very similar to these; and there Luke has inserted the question of Matt. vv. 11, 12. I should be disposed to think that Mark and Luke have preserved the exact narrative here. Matthew, as we see, describes the *watching* of the Pharisees (τοὺς διαλογισμοὺς αὐτῶν, Luke, ver. 8) as *words actually spoken,* and relates that *they* asked the question: which certainly arises from an imperfect report of what took place, the question itself being verbatim that which our Lord asked on that other occasion, Luke xiv. 3, and followed by a similar appeal about an animal. There can hardly be a doubt that in Matthew's narrative the two occurrences are blended: and this may have taken place from the very circumstance of the question about an animal having been asked on both occasions; Luke omitting it here, because he reports it there—Matthew joining to it the question asked there, because he was not aware of another similar incident. **ἡ δεξ.** is a mark of accuracy, and from an eye-witness. **9.**] The words in the rec. text, ἐπ. ὑμᾶς τί ἔξεστιν, admit of two constructions according as they are punctuated: 'I will ask you *what is allowable on the sabbath,—to do good, or to do evil?*' (ἐπ. ὑμ. τί ἔξ. κ.τ.λ.); or, 'I will ask you a certain thing: *Is it,*' &c. (ἐπ. ὑμ. τι· ἔξ. κ.τ.λ.) This latter is preferable, both on account of the future ἐπερ., and of its similarity to ἐρωτήσω ὑμᾶς κἀγὼ λόγον, ch. xx. 3. But the reading in the text is much preferable to either. After the question, Mark adds οἱ δὲ ἐσιώπων—as they did after the question just referred to in ch. xx., because they

ὀλέσαι ; 10 καὶ ⁿ περιβλεψάμενος πάντας αὐτοὺς εἶπεν n || Mk. reff.
αὐτῷ Ἔκτεινον τὴν χεῖρά σου. ὁ δὲ ἐποίησεν, καὶ ᵒ ἀπ- o || Mt. reff. p — ch. iv. 28 reff.
Q θη η χειρ... εκατεστάθη ἡ χεὶρ αὐτοῦ. 11 αὐτοὶ δὲ ᵖ ἐπλήσθησαν q 2 Tim. iii. 9 only. Prov. xxii. 15.
ᵠ ἀνοίας, καὶ ʳ διελάλουν πρὸς ἀλλήλους τί ἂν ποιήσαιεν r ch. i. 65 only +. Ps. lxxvi. 3 Symm.
τῷ Ἰησοῦ.
12 ˢ Ἐγένετο δὲ ἐν ταῖς ἡμέραις ταύταις ἐξελθεῖν αὐτὸν s constr., ver. 1 reff. t here only. Job ii. 9 only Jos. B. J. ii. 14. 7.
εἰς τὸ ὄρος προσεύξασθαι, καὶ ἦν ᵗ διανυκτερεύων ἐν τῇ

for απολεσαι, αποκτειναι (*from* || *Mark*) A F(Wetst) rel lat-*e* Syr-ms syr[-txt] æth : txt BDLXℵ 1. 69 vulg lat-*b c* &c Syr syr-mg [syr-jer] copt goth arm Mcion$_1$-t. (lat-*a* def.) add οι δε εσιωπων (*from* || *Mark*) DΛ(-πουν).

10. αυτους bef παντας DX lat-*b e f ff*$_2$ [*l*] *q* Syr. add εν οργη (|| *Mark*) DXΛ 1 lat-*a b c e ff*$_2$ *l* syr arm : μετ' οργης 69. for ειπεν, λεγει (*see* || *Mark*) D. rec (for αυτω) τω ανθρωπω (|| *Matt Mark*), with DLXℵ 1. 33. 69 latt syr-mg [syr-jer] copt æth arm-mss : txt AB rel syrr goth arm-ed. for ο δε, και (*see* || *Matt Mark*) D ev-48 latt Syr [syr-jer]. for εποιησεν, εξετεινεν (|| *Matt Mark*) DXℵ 1. 69 latt Syr syr-mg copt goth æth arm. rec adds ουτω, with K[Π] syr-w-ob [syr-jer] : om AB(Dℵ) rel (latt syrr copt goth æth arm). rec αποκατεσταθη, with BU : αποκατεστη 1 : απεκατεστη ℵ^1 243 : txt ADℵ^{3a} rel. rec adds υγιης (*from* || *Matt*), with E rel : om ABDKLQUXΔ[Π]ℵ 1. 33 latt syrr [syr-jer] copt goth arm. rec adds further ως η αλλη (*from* || *Matt*), with AQ rel lat-*b c f g*$_{1.2}$ [*q*] syrr [syr-jer] goth æth arm ; ως και η αλ. D 1 : om BLℵ 33 vulg lat-*a e ff*$_2$ *l* copt. D adds (*see ver* 5) και ελεγεν αυτοις οτι κυριος εστιν ο υιος του ανθρωπου και του σαββατου.

11. for διελαλουν, διελογιζοντο D. aft προς αλληλους ins λεγοντες AM syr-w-ob. rec ποιησειαν, with E rel, -σιαν QX : -σειεν A, -σιεν ℵ : txt BLΛ 1. 33(sic). 69.—for τι αν ποι. τω ιησ., πως απολεσωσιν αυτον (*see* || *Matt Mark*) D.

12. for ταυταις, εκειναις D copt. rec for εξελθειν αυτον, εξηλθεν (*because a lection begins with the word*), with Q rel Cypr [Ambr$_1$] : txt ABDLℵ 33 lat-*e*, εξελθειν but om αυτον X. (lat-*a* def.) for προσευξασθαι, και προσευχεσθαι D. for 2nd

were in a dilemma, and either answer would have convicted them.

10.] Mark adds μετ' ὀργῆς συλλυπούμενος ἐπὶ τῇ πωρώσει τῆς καρδίας αὐτῶν—one of the most striking and graphic descriptions in the Gospels. It was thus that He bare (see Matt. viii. 17), even while on earth, our sins and infirmities. *Their* hearts were hardened,—but *He* grieved for it. **11. ἀνοίας**] It does * not appear that this word can ever mean, as in some former editions, 'madness,' rage of a senseless kind: certainly it does not in reff., nor in Herod. vi. 69 or Thuc. iii. 48, there carelessly referred to. The proper meaning, 'senselessness,' 'wicked folly,' must be kept to. See Ellicott's note on 2 Tim. iii. 9, to which I owe this correction. **διελάλ.**, viz. the Pharisees and Herodians: Mark ver. 6, where see note.

12—19.] Calling and names of the twelve Apostles. *Peculiar* (in this form) *to Luke:* see Matt. xii. 15—21: Mark iii. 13—19. We may observe that Matt. does not relate the *choosing* of the Apostles, but only takes occasion to give a list of them on their being sent out, ch. x. 1 ff.; and that Mark and Luke agree in the time of their being chosen, placing it immediately after the healing on the sabbath,—but with no very definite note of time. **12.**] **ἐν τ. ἡμ. τ.** is vague in date, and may belong to any part of the period of our Lord's ministry now before us. I believe it to be a form of acknowledgment on the part of the Evangelist, that *he did not determine exactly into what part of this period to bring the incident so introduced.* Indeed the whole of this paragraph is of a supplementary and indefinite character, serving more as a preface to the discourse which follows, than as an integral part of the narration in its present sequence. This of course in no way affects the accuracy of the circumstances therein related, which nearly coincide in this and the cognate, though independent, account of Mark. **ἐξελθεῖν**—viz. from Capernaum. **τὸ ὄρος**] See on Matt. v. 1. **προσεύξ.**] See note on ch. v. 16. **κ. ἦν διαν. . . .**] and spent the night in prayer to God, see E. V. The whole context, and the frequency of the objective genitive (see Winer, § 30. 1, edn. 6), should have prevented the Commentators (Hammond, Olearius, &c.) from making the blunder of imagining **προσευχή** here to

u constr., see Mark xi. 22 reff. Num. xxvi. 9.
v = here only. (Matt. xi. 16 reff.) Jos. Antt. vii. 7. 4.
w John vi. 70. Acts i. 2 al. Gen. vi. 2.
x Acts i. 13. xxi. 20. xxii. 3. 1 Cor. xiv. 12. Gal. i. 14. Tit. ii. 14. 1 Pet. iii. 13 only. 2 Macc. iv. 2. LXX always w. θεός, Exod. xx. 5 al.
y here only of Judas. Acts vii. 52. 2 Tim. iii. 4 only †. 2 Macc. v. 15. x. 13, 22 only.
z here only. Deut. iv. 43. 2 Chron. i. 15.
a here only. Gen. xlix. 13. Deut. i. 7. vii. 35 reff.
b Heb. xii. 15 only. = Gen. xlviii. 1 al.
c = ch.

[u] προσευχῇ τοῦ θεοῦ. 13 καὶ ὅτε ἐγένετο ἡμέρα, [v] προσ- ABDE KLMQ
εφώνησεν τοὺς μαθητὰς αὐτοῦ, καὶ [w] ἐκλεξάμενος ἀπ' SUVXΓ ΔΠΙℵ
αὐτῶν δώδεκα, οὓς καὶ ἀποστόλους ὠνόμασεν, 14 Σίμωνα 1. 33. 69
ὃν καὶ ὠνόμασεν Πέτρον καὶ Ἀνδρέαν τὸν ἀδελφὸν
αὐτοῦ, καὶ Ἰάκωβον καὶ Ἰωάννην, καὶ Φίλιππον καὶ
Βαρθολομαῖον, 15 καὶ Μαθθαῖον καὶ Θωμᾶν, Ἰάκωβον
Ἀλφαίου καὶ Σίμωνα τὸν καλούμενον [x] ζηλωτήν, 16 καὶ
Ἰούδαν Ἰακώβου, καὶ Ἰούδαν Ἰσκαριὼθ ὃς ἐγένετο
[y] προδότης, 17 καὶ καταβὰς μετ' αὐτῶν ἔστη ἐπὶ τόπου
[z] πεδινοῦ, καὶ ὄχλος μαθητῶν αὐτοῦ, καὶ πλῆθος πολὺ
τοῦ λαοῦ ἀπὸ πάσης τῆς Ἰουδαίας καὶ Ἱερουσαλὴμ καὶ
τῆς [a] παραλίου Τύρου καὶ Σιδῶνος, οἳ ἦλθον ἀκοῦσαι
αὐτοῦ καὶ ἰαθῆναι ἀπὸ τῶν νόσων αὐτῶν, 18 καὶ οἱ [b] ἐν-
οχλούμενοι [c] ἀπὸ πνευμάτων ἀκαθάρτων ἐθεραπεύοντο. R [ε]θεραπευον[τ]ο...

εν, επι ℵ[1]. om του θεου D.

13. for προσεφ., εφωνησεν D 1 Eus_1. for ωνομασεν, εκαλεσεν D.

14. ins πρωτον bef σιμωνα D. for ωνομ. πετρ., πετρ. επωνομασεν D [arm]. rec om και (bef ιακ.), with AQ rel vulg lat-*e f ff₂* $g_{1.2}$ [syr] copt goth [æth Eus_1 Bas_1-2-mss]: ins BDKLΔ[Π]ℵ 33. 69 vulg-ms lat-*a b c* Syr arm. aft ιωαννην ins τον αδελφον αυτου ους επωνομασεν βοανηργες ο εστιν υιοι βροντης (*see Mark* iii. 17) D. rec om και (bef φιλιππον), with AQ rel vulg lat-*e f* ff_2 $g_{1.2}$ syr copt goth [Bas_1]: ins BDLℵ 33 lat-*a b c l* Syr æth arm Eus_1. om και βαρθολομαιον ℵ[1].

15. rec om 1st και, with AQ rel vulg [lat-*e* ff_2 $g_{1.2}$ syr] goth: ins BDLℵ lat-*a b c l q* Syr copt æth arm Eus_1. aft θωμαν ins τον επικαλουμενον διδυμον (*see John* xi. 16; xx. 24; xxi. 2) D. ins και bef ιακωβον D[1]Lℵ 33. 69 lat-*a b c l* Syr copt æth arm: om AB D-corr gr Q rel vulg lat-*e f* ff_2 g_1 [*q*] syr copt-ms goth [Bas_1]. rec ins τον του bef αλφαιου (*from Mark* iii. 18), with ADQ rel goth [Bas_1]: om BLℵ 1. 33. 69 arm.

16. rec om 1st και, with A rel am(with forj ing per tol) lat-*e f* g_1 *q* syr goth: ins BD F(Wetst) LQ 69 vulg-ed lat-*a b c* ff_2 *l* Syr copt æth arm [Bas_1.—om κ. ιου. ιακ. A em]. rec ισκαριωτην (‖ *Matt*), with AQℵ[3a] rel [vulg-clem syr copt goth arm-mss Bas_1] ($Mcion_1$-e): om lat-*a b*: txt BLℵ 33 $Mcion_1$-e, σκαριωθ D vulg[-mss] lat-*e f* g_1 *l* [*q*] Syr. rec aft ος ins και (*from* ‖ *Matt Mark*), with ADQ rel syr goth [Bas_1]: om BLℵ latt Syr copt æth arm $Mcion_2$-e.

17. aft οχλος ins πολυς (*usual addition*) BLℵ 1 Syr: om ADQ rel vss. om του λαου ℵ[1] 1. om της (aft πασης) D F(Wetst). for ιερουσ. κ. τ. π. τυρ. κ. σιδ. οι ηλθον, αλλων πολεων εληλυθοτων D. aft ιερουσ. ins και πιραιας ℵ[1] evv-H^1-z_1 [(lat-*a b c* ff_2 *l q* arm)].

18. rec (for ενοχλ.) οχλουμενοι, with DQ rel: txt ABLℵ 1. rec (for απο) υπο, with X[Π] 69 (KU 1. 33, e sil): txt ABDQℵ rel. rec ins και bef εθεραπευοντο, with X rel syrr goth: om ABDLQℵ 33 latt copt æth arm.

be a *proseucha* or *house of prayer*: see note on Acts xvi. 13. **13. προσεφ. τ. μ. αὐτ.**] Expressed in Mark, προσκαλεῖται οὓς ἤθελεν αὐτός—i. e. *He summoned to Him a certain larger number, out of whom He selected Twelve.* We are not to suppose that this selection was now first made out of a miscellaneous number—but now first formally announced; the Apostles, or most of them, had had each their special individual calling to be, in a peculiar manner, followers of the Lord, before this. **ὠνόμασεν**—not at a previous, or subsequent period, as Schleiermacher suggests (Trans. p. 89); but *at this time.* Mark (iii. 14) gives the substance, without the *form*, of the word **ἀπόστολος**—ἐποίησεν δώδεκα ἵνα . . . . . **ἀποστέλλῃ** αὐτοὺς κηρύσσειν . . . **14.**] On the catalogue, see notes on Matt. x. 1 ff.

16.] **Ἰούδαν Ἰακώβου**—usually, and I believe rightly, rendered Jude *the brother* of James: see Prolegg. to Jude. On the question *who this James was*, see on Matt. x. 3, and xiii. 55. **17.**] Having descended from the mountain, He stood on

19 καὶ πᾶς ὁ ὄχλος [d] ἐζήτουν ἅπτεσθαι αὐτοῦ, ὅτι [e] δύναμις παρ' αὐτοῦ ἐξήρχετο καὶ ἰᾶτο πάντας. 20 καὶ αὐτὸς
[f] ἐπάρας τοὺς ὀφθαλμοὺς αὐτοῦ εἰς τοὺς μαθητὰς αὐτοῦ
ἔλεγεν Μακάριοι οἱ [g] πτωχοί, ὅτι ὑμετέρα ἐστὶν ἡ βασιλεία
τοῦ θεοῦ. 21 μακάριοι οἱ [h] πεινῶντες νῦν, ὅτι [h] χορτασθή-
σεσθε. μακάριοι οἱ κλαίοντες νῦν, ὅτι [i] γελάσετε. 22 μακάριοί ἐστε ὅταν μισήσωσιν ὑμᾶς οἱ ἄνθρωποι, καὶ ὅταν
[k] ἀφορίσωσιν ὑμᾶς καὶ [l] ὀνειδίσωσιν καὶ [m] ἐκβάλωσιν τὸ

Ξ μακάριοι... P ὅτι χορτ....

d = Matt. xii. 46 reff.
e = Matt. xiv. 2 reff.
f Matt. xvii. 8 reff.
g Matt. v. 3 reff.
h Matt. v. 6 (reff.).
i ver. 25 only. Eccl. iii. 4. (-λως, James iv. 9.)
k = here only. (Matt. xiii. 49 reff.)
l Matt. v. 11 reff. 4 Kings xix. 16.
m = here only. Plato, Crito, § 6. see John ix. 34, 35. Hos. ix. 15.

19. rec εζητει, with ADQR rel vulg lat-*a c ff*$_2$ *g*$_1$ [*q*] syr [Mcion$_2$-e Cyr$_1$]: txt BLℵ am lat-*b e f* Syr goth. for απτεσθαι, αψασθε [= αψασθαι] D.

20. om αυτος D lat-*e* [Syr]. for επαρας, ετι αρας D. om 2nd αυτου D lat-*ff*$_2$ Orig$_1$. aft πτωχοι ins τω πνευματι (|| *Matt*) QX ℵ^{3a}(but erased) 1. 33. 69 gat lat-*a c f* syr-jer goth arm[(Griesb) Ambr-txt$_1$-com$_1$]: om ABDRℵ^1 rel vulg lat-*b e ff*$_2$ *g*$_{1.2}$ [*l q*] syrr copt [æth arm(Treg Tischdf)] Mcion$_1$-t Orig$_1$[int$_1$] Eus$_1$ Cyr$_{1expr}$ Ambr$_1$-comm.

21. χορτασθησονται ℵ$^{1 \cdot 3b}$[X 69 lat-*b e ff*$_2$ *l q* æth arm-ed Tert$_1$ Ambr$_2$]. om last clause D: transp 1st and 2nd clauses syr-jer.

22. μισησουσιν (*itacism?*) DPXΔ. om 2nd υμας D. transp ονειδισωσιν and εκβαλωσιν D lat-*a b c ff*$_2$ *g*$_1$ *l* [*q*] Cypr$_4$.

a level place—i.e. *possibly*, as has been suggested by some, *on a flat ledge or shelf on the side of the mountain;* but more naturally *below the mountain:* see on Matt. v. 1. Whether Luke could thus have written *with the Gospel of Matthew before him*, I leave the reader to judge: premising, that is, the identity of the two discourses. **19.**] Luke uses the same expression, of power going forth from our Lord, in ch. viii. 46.

20—49.] Sermon on the Mount (?). *Peculiar* (in this form) *to Luke*, answering to Matt. v.—vii. On the whole question of the identity or diversity of the two discourses, see on Matt. v. 1. In Matthew I cannot doubt that we have *the whole discourse much as it was spoken;* the connexion is intimate throughout; the arrangement wonderfully consistent and admirable. Here, on the other hand, the discourse is only reported in fragments—there is a wide gap between vv. 26 and 27, and many omissions in other parts; besides which, sayings of our Lord, belonging apparently to other occasions, are inserted: see vv. 39, 40, 45. At the same time we must remember, that such gnomic sayings would probably be frequently uttered by Him, and might very likely form part of this discourse originally. His teaching was not studious of novelty like that of men, but speaking with authority, as He did, He would doubtless utter again and again the same weighty sentences when occasion occurred. Hence may have arisen much of the difference of arrangement observable in the reports—because sayings known to have been uttered together at one time, might be thrown together with sayings spoken at another, with some one common link perhaps connecting the two groups. **20. εἰς τοὺς μ.**] The discourse was spoken to the disciples generally,—to the Twelve particularly,—to the people prospectively; and its subject, both here and in Matt., is, *the state and duties of a disciple of Christ.* **πτωχοί**] To suppose that Luke's report of this discourse refers *only to this world's* poverty, &c.—and the blessings to anticipated *outward* prosperity in the Messiah's Kingdom (De Wette, Meyer), is surely quite a misapprehension. Comparing these expressions with other passages in Luke himself, we must have concluded, *even without Matthew's report*, that they bore a *spiritual* sense: see ch. xvi. 11, where he speaks of '*the true* riches,' and ch. xii. 21, where we have **εἰς θεὸν πλουτῶν**. And who would apply such an interpretation to our ver. 21?

See on each of these beatitudes the corresponding notes in Matt. **ἡ βασ. τ. θ.** = ἡ βασ. τ. οὐρανῶν Matt., but it does not thence follow that οὐρανοί = θεός, but the two are different ways of designating the same kingdom—the one by its situation—*in heaven*, where its πολιτεία is (ἡ ἄνω Ἱερουσαλήμ, Gal. iv. 26), the other by *Him*, whose it is. **22.**] **ἀφορίσωσιν** and **ἐκβάλ.** must not be understood of Jewish excommunication only, but of all kinds of expulsion from society.

ὄνομα ὑμῶν ὡς πονηρὸν ἕνεκα τοῦ υἱοῦ τοῦ ἀνθρώπου.
23 χάρητε ἐν ἐκείνῃ τῇ ἡμέρᾳ καὶ [n] σκιρτήσατε· ἰδοὺ γὰρ
ὁ [o] μισθὸς ὑμῶν πολὺς ἐν τῷ οὐρανῷ· κατὰ τὰ αὐτὰ
γὰρ [p] ἐποίουν τοῖς προφήταις οἱ πατέρες αὐτῶν. 24 [q] πλὴν
οὐαὶ ὑμῖν τοῖς πλουσίοις, ὅτι [r] ἀπέχετε τὴν [s] παράκλησιν
ὑμῶν. 25 οὐαὶ ὑμῖν οἱ [t] ἐμπεπλησμένοι νῦν, ὅτι πεινάσετε.
οὐαὶ οἱ [u] γελῶντες νῦν, ὅτι [v] πενθήσετε καὶ [v] κλαύσετε.
26 οὐαὶ ὅταν [w] καλῶς ὑμᾶς [w] εἴπωσιν πάντες οἱ ἄνθρωποι·
κατὰ τὰ αὐτὰ γὰρ [p] ἐποίουν τοῖς [x] ψευδοπροφήταις οἱ
πατέρες αὐτῶν. 27 ἀλλὰ ὑμῖν λέγω τοῖς ἀκούουσιν,
ἀγαπᾶτε τοὺς ἐχθροὺς ὑμῶν, καλῶς ποιεῖτε τοῖς μισοῦσιν
ὑμᾶς, 28 [yz] εὐλογεῖτε τοὺς [za] καταρωμένους ὑμᾶς, προσευ-

H τε εν εκεινη... ...κατα Q. ABDE HKLM PRSUV XΓΔΛΞ Π ℵ 1. 33. 69

n ch. i. 42, 44 only. Mal. iv. 2. o = Matt. v. 12 reff. ver. 35. p ch. i. 49 reff. q = ver. 35. Matt. xi. 22, 24 al. Sir. xlv. 22. r Matt. vi. 2, 5. Phil. iv. 18. Gen. xliii. 23. s ch. ii. 25. 2 Thess. ii. 16. Isa. xxx. 7. t ch. i. 53 reff. u ver. 21 (reff.) only. v Mark xvi. 10 reff. w = here only. (ch. xx. 39.) see Acts xxiii. 5. x Matt. vii. 15 reff. y ch. ii. 34. Heb. vii. 1 al. Gen. xiv. 19. z Rom. xii. 14. Ps. cviii. 28. a Matt. xxv. 41 reff. dat. (see v. r.), 4 Kings ii. 24. Herod. iv. 184.

23. rec (for χαρητε) χαιρετε (*more usual*), with 218 Chr$_3$: txt ABD (PQ, Tischdf) RΞℵ rel Scr's-mss [Bas$_1$]. for ιδου γαρ, οτι (|| *Matt*) D 6-pe Syr [æth]. τοις ουρανοις (|| *Matt*) BR 69 lat-*e f* goth Cypr txt ADPQΞℵ rel [vss Bas$_1$-ms]. rec (for τα αυτα) ταῦτα, with EKLMUΓΛ[Π], ταυτα APRℵ rel vulg lat-*b* [*f ff*$_2$ *l q* syr] goth [æth Mcion$_1$-t] Orig$_1$: txt BDQXΞ 33 lat-*a c e* Syr copt(appy) arm Mcion$_2$-e. om 2nd γαρ D-gr 64 lat-*a* [*ff*$_2$ *l* Mcion-e$_2$-t$_1$] Ambr$_1$.

25. om υμιν [L]Ξ 1. 69 [Bas$_1$] Tert$_1$. rec om 1st νυν, with ADP rel latt Syr [Bas$_1$] Iren-int$_1$: ins BLQRXΔ^{1}ΛΞℵ 1. 33. 69 lat-*f* syr-w-ast copt goth æth arm [Ors$_1$]. rec aft 2nd ουαι ins υμιν (*as above*), with ADPQR rel latt [Bas$_1$ Chr$_1$] Orig-int$_1$ Hil$_1$: om BKL(S)Ξℵ 1. 69 Orig$_3$[int$_2$] Iren-int$_1$.—om οι γελ. νυν S.

26. rec aft ουαι ins υμιν, with DΔ 69 lat-*b* Syr copt æth arm [Mac$_1$] Chr$_6$ Iren-int$_1$: om ABPQRΞℵ rel vulg lat-*a c* syr goth Mcion$_1$-t Bas$_1$ Chr$_1$ Thl Orig-int$_1$ Ambr. υμας bef καλως B 33 lat-*e q*.—ειπωσιν bef υμας AHLℵ 33 vulg-ed(not am ing) [lat-*ff*$_2$ *g*$_1$ *l*] Syr [Mac$_1$ Bas$_1$ Chr$_2$] Iren-int$_1$.—for υμας, υμιν D Scr's d vulg lat-*a c*: om 69 ev-z$_1$. οι ανθρωποι bef παντες ℵ [copt Iren-int$_1$]: om παντες (*perhaps as seeming inconsistent with the other member of the comparison*, οι πατ. αυτ.) D F(Wetst) LSV ΓΔΛ vulg-ed Syr æth Mcion$_1$-t Mac$_1$ Thl Euthym: txt ABPQRΞ rel am(with fuld em forj ing mt per) lat-*a b c e f ff*$_2$ *g*$_1$ *l* [*q*] syr copt goth (arm ?) [Bas$_1$] Chr[$_{expr_1}$] Iren-int$_1$ Ambr Aug Bede. rec (for τα αυτα) ταυτα, with APℵ^1 rel vulg lat-*b f ff*$_2$ [*l q* æth] syr Iren-int$_1$ Tert$_1$: txt BDKRXΞ[Π] ℵ-corr^1 33 lat-*a c e* Syr copt goth [arm]. (Q def.) om γαρ D 29 am(with fuld em forj ing mt per tol) lat-*a b c e f ff*$_2$ *g*$_1$ *l* Mcion$_1$-t. om οι πατερες αυτων B.

27. (αλλα, so ABDPRΞℵ &c.)

28. rec (for 1st υμας) υμιν, with L rel vulg lat-*c f* Just$_1$ Orig$_1$: txt ABDKMPRXΓ Ξ[Π]ℵ 1. 33. 69 lat-*a b ff*$_2$ *g*$_1$ [*l q* Clem$_2$] Orig$_1$ Eus$_1$. rec ins και bef προσευχεσθε (*from* || *Matt*), with (Scr's b c i w, e sil) vulg lat-*ff*$_2$ Syr [Tert$_1$]: om ABDPRΞℵ rel

τὸ ὄν. ὑμ., literal: **your name**:—either your collective name as *Christians*,—to which Peter seems to refer, 1 Pet. iv. 14—16;—or, your individual name.

23.] **ἐν ἐκ. τ. ἡμ.**, not in the most solemn sense of the words (see Matt. vii. 22), but **in the day when men shall do thus to you.** **24.**] Of course (see Prolegg. ch. i.) I cannot assent to any such view as that taken by Meyer and others, that these 'woes' are inserted from later tradition (gehören zur Formation der spätern Ueberlieferung); in other words, *were never spoken by our Lord at all*:—either we must suppose that they ought to follow Matt. v. 12, which is from the context most improbable,—or that they, and perhaps the four preceding beatitudes with them, were on some occasion spoken by our Lord in this exact form, and so have been here placed in that form.

26.] Not said to the *rich*, but to the *disciples*. The very warning conveyed in **ψευδοπροφ.** shews this, and should have prevented Meyer from making the blunder. The mention of προφ. and ψευδοπροφ. has reference to the disciples' office as the salt of the earth. The address in ver. 27 is not (Meyer) a turning of the discourse to His own disciples, but **ὑμῖν λέγω τοῖς ἀκούουσιν** = ἐγὼ δὲ λέγω ὑμῖν, which introduces the same command Matt. v. 44,—

χεσθε περὶ τῶν [b] ἐπηρεαζόντων ὑμᾶς. 29 τῷ τύπτοντί σε
ἐπὶ τὴν [c] σιαγόνα [d] πάρεχε καὶ τὴν ἄλλην, καὶ ἀπὸ τοῦ
[e] αἴροντός σου τὸ ἱμάτιον καὶ τὸν χιτῶνα μὴ [f] κωλύσῃς.
30 παντὶ δὲ τῷ [g] αἰτοῦντί σε δίδου· καὶ ἀπὸ τοῦ [e] αἴροντος
τὰ σὰ μὴ [h] ἀπαίτει. 31 καὶ καθὼς θέλετε ἵνα [i] ποιῶσιν ὑμῖν
οἱ ἄνθρωποι, καὶ ὑμεῖς [i] ποιεῖτε αὐτοῖς ὁμοίως. 32 καὶ εἰ
ἀγαπᾶτε τοὺς ἀγαπῶντας ὑμᾶς, [k] ποία ὑμῖν [l] χάρις ἐστίν;
καὶ γὰρ οἱ ἁμαρτωλοὶ τοὺς ἀγαπῶντας αὐτοὺς ἀγαπῶσιν.
33 καὶ ἐὰν [m] ἀγαθοποιῆτε τοὺς [m] ἀγαθοποιοῦντας ὑμᾶς,
[k] ποία ὑμῖν [l] χάρις ἐστίν; καὶ γὰρ οἱ ἁμαρτωλοὶ τὸ αὐτὸ
ποιοῦσιν. 34 καὶ ἐὰν [n] δανείζετε παρ' ὧν ἐλπίζετε λαβεῖν,
ποία ὑμῖν χάρις ἐστίν; καὶ ἁμαρτωλοὶ ἁμαρτωλοῖς [n] δα-
νείζουσιν, ἵνα [o] ἀπολάβωσιν τὰ [p] ἴσα. 35 [q] πλὴν ἀγαπᾶτε
τοὺς ἐχθροὺς ὑμῶν, καὶ [m] ἀγαθοποιεῖτε, καὶ [n] δανείζετε
μηδὲν [r] ἀπελπίζοντες· καὶ ἔσται ὁ [s] μισθὸς ὑμῶν πολύς,

...καθως [θε] R.

b (Matt. v. 44 v. r.) 1 Pet. iii. 16 only †. (-ρεαστής, Ps. lvi. 2 Symm.)
c Matt. v. 39 only. Isa. l. 6. Hos. xi. 4.
d = here only. Aristoph. Ranæ 662.
e = Matt. xxi. 43. xxv. 28, 29. Isa. v. 23.
f constr., Acts x. 47. Gen. xxiii. 6.
g constr., Matt. v. 42 reff.
h here (ch. xii. 20 v. r.) only. Deut. xv. 2, 3.
i vv. 23, 26.
k = Matt. xxi. 23, &c. reff.
l = 1 Pet. ii. 19, 20. Sir. xx. 16. see ch. xvii. 9 reff.
m Mark iii. 4 reff.
n Matt. v. 42 reff.
o = ch. xviii. 13 reff.
p = Phil. ii. 6. Rev. xxi. 16. (Matt. xx. 12 reff.) Wisd. vii. 4. q = ver. 24. r here (Eph. iv. 19 v. r.) only. Isa. xxix. 19. 2 Macc. ix. 18. Sir. xxii. 21. = ? s = Matt. v. 12 reff. Gen. xv. 1.

am(with fuld em forj ing per) lat-*a b c* &c syr (copt ?) goth arm. rec (for περι) υπερ (*from* || *Matt*), with ADPR rel copt æth Just $Clem_1$ $Orig_1$ Eus_3: txt BLΞℵ.

29. [των B¹(Tischdf).] for επι, εις Dℵ¹ [$Clem_2$ $Orig_3$]. ins δεξιαν bef σιαγ. (|| *Matt*) E¹ℵ¹ 28 $Orig_1$ [Bas_1]: μιαν Scr's c. aft παρεχε ins αυτω (|| *Matt*) D vulg-sixt per lat-*a b c e f* ff_2 $g_{1.2}$ *l* Syr goth æth $Ambr_3$.—στρεψον αυτω 69. aft χιτωνα ins σου ΑΓ Syr copt.

30. om δε (|| *Matt*) BKLR[Π]ℵ 1 lat-*b* ff_2 *l* Syr æth arm $Barn_1$ $Clem_2$. om τω Bℵ $Barn_1$[-edd].

31. ποιουσιν υμας A. om και υμεις B lat-*a* ff_2 *l* Iren-int_1. om ομοιως D 248 lat-*e* $Clem_1$ Iren-int_1.

32. aft αμαρτωλοι ins τουτο ποιουσιν (*retaining follg clause*) D.

33. κ. **γαρ** εαν Bℵ¹, κ. ει D. αγαθοποιειτε (*itacism ?*) DHMP[S]ΓΔΛ 33. χαρις bef υμιν D; εστιν bef χαρις P. om γαρ (*see ver* 35) BΛℵ æth. om οι A[R ? (hom. και γαρ αμ. to αμ. next ver)]. for το αυτο, τουτο D vulg lat-*a* ff_2 [*l* Δ-lat].

34. καν D. rec δανειζητε, with [Π, and] (but each, according to Treg, e sil) MSUVΓ 1: δανει**σ**ητε B²Ξ: δανισητε B¹ℵ 157: txt ADP rel $Just_1$. for ων, ω ΓΞ. rec **απο**λαβειν (*from* απολαβωσιν *below*), with ADP rel: txt BLΞℵ $Just_1$. χαρις bef υμιν D. om εστιν B lat-*e*: ins ADPΞℵ rel. rec aft 2nd και ins γαρ, with ADP rel vulg lat-*a c*: om BLΞℵ copt. [R see above, ver 33.] rec ins οι bef αμαρτωλοι (*see ver* 32), with Ξ (HK 69, e sil) copt: om ABDPℵ rel goth. [R see above.] om τα ισα D lat-*a b c e* ff_2 *l q* $Ambr_1$.

35. μηδεν**α** Ξ[Π]ℵ [(syrr syr-jer)]. aft πολυς ins εν τοις ουρανοις A ℵ-corr¹ ev-y

and τοῖς ἀκούουσιν serves the purpose of the ἐγώ—**to you who now hear Me.** The discourse being mutilated, the strong antithesis could not be brought out. **29.**] See Matt. v. 39 ff. **31.**] Matt. vii. 12; but here it seems somewhat out of connexion, for the sense of vv. 29, 30, has been **resist not evil,** whereas this precept refers to the duty of man to man, injury being out of the question. **32.**] This verse again belongs to ver. 28, not to ver. 31: see Matt. v. 46 ff. **33 ff.**] **χάρις** corresponds to μισθός, Matt. (see note on Matt. v. 12). **35. ἀπελπίζοντες**] Three renderings have been given—(1) the ordinary one, μηδὲν ἀπ' αὐτῶν ἐλπίζοντες, Euthym.;—but this meaning of the word is unexampled, though agreeing with the context. (2) '*causing no one to despair,*' i. e. refusing no one (reading μηδέν': cf. Ξ[Π]ℵ in various readings);—so the Syr. renders it. (3) '*not despairing,*' i. e. '*without anxiety about the result.*' This last sense of the word is best supported by examples, both from Polybius (e. g. ἀπελπ. τὰ πράγματα, i. 19. 12,—τὴν σωτηρίαν, ii. 54. 7, al. freq., see Index), and the Apocrypha,—see reff. But as it is an ἅπαξ λεγόμενον in the N. T., perhaps the force of the context should

t Matt. v. 45. Sir. iv. 10. u Mark v. 7 reff. v = Rom. ii. 4. Eph. iv. 32. 1 Pet. ii. 3, from Ps. xxxiii. 8. w = Rom. xi. 22. Eph. ii. 7. Ps. cii. 17. x 2 Tim. iii. 2 only †. Wisd. xvi. 29. Sir. xxix. 17, 25 only. y here bis & James v. 11 only. Exod. xxxiv. 6. (-μός, Rom. xii. 1.)

καὶ ἔσεσθε [t] υἱοὶ [u] ὑψίστου, ὅτι αὐτὸς [v] χρηστός ἐστιν [w] ἐπὶ
τοὺς [x] ἀχαρίστους καὶ πονηρούς. 36 γίνεσθε [y] οἰκτίρμονες,
καθὼς καὶ ὁ πατὴρ ὑμῶν [y] οἰκτίρμων ἐστίν. 37 καὶ μὴ κρινετε, καὶ οὐ μὴ κριθῆτε· καὶ μὴ [z] καταδικάζετε, καὶ οὐ μὴ
[z] καταδικασθῆτε· [a] ἀπολύετε, καὶ [a] ἀπολυθήσεσθε· 38 δίδοτε,
καὶ δοθήσεται ὑμῖν· μέτρον καλὸν [b] πεπιεσμένον [c] σεσα-
λευμένον [d] ὑπερεκχυννόμενον δώσουσιν εἰς τὸν [e] κόλπον
ὑμῶν. τῷ γὰρ αὐτῷ μέτρῳ ᾧ [f] μετρεῖτε [g] ἀντιμετρηθήσεται ὑμῖν. 39 Εἶπεν δὲ καὶ παραβολὴν αὐτοῖς· [h] Μήτι

C και μη ...
ABCDE HKLM PSUVX ΓΔΛΞΠ ℵ 1. 33. 69

z Matt. xii. 7, 37. James v. 6 only. Ps. xxxvi. 33. a = (absol.) here only. 2 Macc. xii. 45. see ch. xxii. 68. b here only. Mic. vi. 15 only. c Matt. xi. 7. xxiv. 29. Ps. xvii. 7. d here only. Joel ii. 24 A only. (-χέειν, Prov. v 16.) e ch. xvi 22 reff. Ps. lxxviii. 12. f Matt. vii. 2 reff. w. dat. here only. Wisd iv. 8. g here only †. h Matt. vii. 16 reff.

lat-*c*, *in cœlo* lat-*a l* Ambr$_1$. rec ins του bef υψιστου, with (1, e sil) 69 [Bas$_1$]: om ABDPΞℵ rel.

36. rec aft γινεσθε ins ουν (*from Matt* v. 48), with AP rel vulg lat-*f g*$_{1.2}$ syrr [syr-jer] Orig-int$_1$ [Bas$_1$]: om BDLΞℵ 1. 33 lat-*a b c e ff*$_2$ *l q* copt goth æth arm Clem$_2$ Orig$_1$ [Ath Mac$_3$ Chr$_{sæpe}$ Cyr$_2$] Tert$_1$ Cypr$_1$. om και (*Matt* v. 48) BLΞℵ 1 lat-*c* D-lat copt æth Mcion$_1$-t Clem$_2$ [Ath$_2$] Chr$_7$: ins A D-gr P rel vulg lat-*a b* syrr [syr-jer] goth Just$_2$ Orig$_1$[int$_1$ Cyr$_2$ Bas$_1$] Cypr$_1$. ins ο ουρανιος bef οικτ. 69; aft εστιν ℵ-corr[1](om ℵ[3a]) [Just$_1$ Clem$_1$ Mac$_3$ Bas$_1$ Chr$_{alic}$ Cyr$_3$].

37. om 1st και (*see Matt* vii. 1) D 1 latt Syr copt arm Mcion-t. for 2nd και (omg ου), ινα (*from* ‖ *Matt*) AD Λ(Treg, expr) lat-*a c e f* goth æth (Polyc$_1$) Mcion$_1$-t Cypr$_1$ Ambr. rec om 3rd και, with ACDP rel [latt Syr copt Bas$_1$ Cyr$_1$] Tert$_1$: ins BLSXΞℵ syr [Bas$_1$]. [for καταδ. (twice)] δικαζ. and δικασθ. B. for 4th και (omg ου), ινα D lat-*a c e ff*$_2$ æth Bas$_1$ Tert$_1$ Cypr$_1$.

38. πεπιασμενον ℵ[1]. rec ins και bef σεσαλ., with ACP rel vulg lat-*f* syr goth Clem$_1$ Cyr$_2$[-ed]: om BDLℵ 1. 69 lat-*a b c e ff*$_2$ *g*$_1$ *l* [*q*] copt æth arm [Orig$_1$ Dial$_1$ Eus$_1$] Ambr$_2$.—om σεσαλευμενον Ξ [Tert$_1$]: σεσαλ. bef πεπιεσμενον D 1 [Orig$_1$ Eus$_1$] Dial. rec ins και bef υπερεκχ., with ACP rel vulg Syr goth æth [Cyr$_1$] Tert$_1$: om BDLΞℵ 1. 69 lat-*a b c e f ff*$_2$ *g*$_1$ *l* [*q*] copt arm Clem$_1$ Orig$_1$ [Dial] Eus [Cyr$_1$]. (33 def.) (υπερεκχυννομενον, so A B[1](Tischdf) CDPℵ &c.) for τω γαρ αυτω μετρω ω, ω γαρ μετρω (*from Matt* vii. 2) BDLΞℵ 1. 33 lat-*c e* (copt): om αυτω X 77. 259: om γαρ 69 lat-*a b l q* arm Mcion$_1$-t: txt ACP rel vulg lat-*f g*$_1$ syr goth. for αντιμετ., μετρηθησ. (‖ *Matt*) B[1](txt B-corr[1] appy, Tischdf) P lat-*b e q* æth(appy) arm. (33 def.)

39. ελεγεν D 69 latt. rec om και, with AP rel syr copt goth: ins BCD

prevail, and the ordinary interpretation be adopted, as there is nothing in analogy (ἀπαιτῶ, ἀπολαμβάνω, . . .) to forbid the meaning; and so Passow gives it in Lexic.

υἱοὶ ὑψίστου] Meyer maintains that this must mean 'sons of God' in the sense of partakers of the glory of the Messiah's Kingdom, but without reference to the state of believers in this life, which last he says is according to the usage of Paul, not of the three first Evangelists. But surely this is sufficiently answered by ὁ πατὴρ ὑμῶν in the next verse, where the actual present sonship to our heavenly Father is a reason why we should imitate Him.

36.] **οἰκτίρμ.** = τέλειοι Matt. v. 48, which last is the larger description, comprehending in it charity and mercy: see note there.

Vv. **37 f.** = Matt. vii. 1, 2. The saying is much enriched and expanded here; perhaps it was so uttered by our Lord on some other occasion; for the connexion is very strict in Matt., and would hardly bear this expansion of what is not in that place the leading idea. **38.**] The similitude is taken from a very full measure of some dry thing such as corn. That no *liquid* is intended by ὑπερεκχ., as Bengel supposes, is evident—for the three present participles all apply to the same **μέτ. καλ.** and form a climax. **δώσουσιν**] The subject of this verb answers to the unexpressed agents of ἀντιμετρηθήσεται; such agents being indefinite, and the meaning thereby rendered solemn and emphatic: see on ch. xii. 20. If we are to find a nom., it should be *the Angels*, who are in this matter the ministers of the divine purposes (so Meyer). This saying is found with a totally different import Mark iv. 24; one of the many instances how the Lord turned about, so to speak, the Light of Truth contained in His declarations, so as to shine upon different departments of life and thought. **39.**] From this verse to the end is in the closest

δύναται τυφλὸς τυφλὸν [i] ὁδηγεῖν; οὐχὶ ἀμφότεροι εἰς [k] βόθυνον [k] ἐμπεσοῦνται; 40 οὐκ ἔστιν μαθητὴς [l] ὑπὲρ τὸν διδά-
σκαλον· [m] κατηρτισμένος δὲ πᾶς ἔσται ὡς ὁ διδάσκαλος
αὐτοῦ. 41 τί δὲ βλέπεις τὸ [n] κάρφος τὸ ἐν τῷ ὀφθαλμῷ
τοῦ ἀδελφοῦ σου, τὴν δὲ [o] δοκὸν τὴν ἐν τῷ [p] ἰδίῳ ὀφθαλμῷ
οὐ [q] κατανοεῖς; 42 πῶς δύνασαι λέγειν τῷ ἀδελφῷ σου
Ἀδελφὲ [r] ἄφες ἐκβάλω τὸ [n] κάρφος τὸ ἐν τῷ ὀφθαλμῷ
σου, αὐτὸς τὴν ἐν τῷ ὀφθαλμῷ σου [o] δοκὸν οὐ βλέπων;
[s] ὑποκριτά, ἔκβαλε πρῶτον τὴν [o] δοκὸν ἐκ τοῦ ὀφθαλμοῦ
σου, καὶ τότε [t] διαβλέψεις τὸ [n] κάρφος τὸ ἐν τῷ ὀφθαλμῷ
τοῦ ἀδελφοῦ σου ἐκβαλεῖν. 43 οὐ γάρ ἐστιν δένδρον
καλὸν [u] ποιοῦν [u] καρπὸν [v] σαπρόν, οὐδὲ πάλιν δένδρον

...οφθαλμω σου P.

i Matt. xv. 14 reff. Exod. xiii. 17.
k Matt. xii. 11 (reff.).
l = Matt. x. 24. Phil. ii. 9. 1 Kings xv. 22.
m 1 Cor. i. 10. 2 Cor. xiii. 11. Heb. xiii. 21. 1 Pet. v. 10. Ezra iv. 13.
n here 3ce and Matt. vii. 3, 4, 5 only. Gen. viii. 11 only.
o N. T. as above (n) only. Gen. xix. 8 al.
p 2nd pers., 1 Thess. ii. 14. 1 Pet. iii. 1.
q Matt. vii. 3. ch. xii. 24, 27 al. Ps. xciii. 9.
r Matt. vii. 4 reff.
s Matt. vi. 2, 5 reff.
t Matt. vii. 5. Mark viii. 25 only +.
u Matt. iii. 8 reff.
v Matt. vii. 17, 18. xii. 33 bis. xiii. 48. Eph. 29 only +. σαπρία, Job vii. 5 al. fr.

F(Wetst) L[R]XΞℵ 33. 69 latt arm. ουκ ℵ. rec (for εμπεσ.) πεσουνται (*from Matt* xv. 14), with ACΞℵ rel vulg lat-*b c*: txt BDLP [R(appy)] 1 (69) ev-y lat-*a* copt(appy).

40. rec aft διδασκαλον ins αυτου, with ACP rel syrr copt goth [æth arm Cyr_1]: om BDLXΞℵ **1**. 33. 69 latt $Mcion_1$-t $Orig_1$ Iren-int_1. (*It is true, as Mey observes, that* αυτου *is wanting in Matt* x. 24: *but the probability of the mechanl addn of* αυτου (*esp with* ο διδασκαλος αυτου *in the same verse*) *is greater than any influence from* || *Matt; the balance of evidence is perhaps on the same side.*) om πας ℵ [lat-*b*]. for εσται, εστω F(Wetst) ℵ 239 [$Orig_1$ $Constt_1$].

41. om 2nd το D latt[not *e*] copt. την δε εν τ. σω οφθ. δοκ. (|| *Matt*) P 69: for ιδιω, σω D latt.

42. rec ins η bef πως (*from* || *Matt*), with ACDPΞ rel [vulg-ed(with fuld) lat-*a b c f* &c syrr copt goth]: ins και bef πως 251 am(with em forj ing per tol) lat-$g_{1.2}$: aft πως ins δε ℵ: om B lat-*e* ff_2. om αδελφε (|| *Matt*) D 157 lat-*a b c e* ff_2 *l q*. for το εν τω οφθαλμω (twice), εκ του οφθαλμου (|| *Matt*) D latt Syr [copt] æth arm. for αυτος to βλεπων, και ιδου η δοκος εν τω σω οφθαλμω υποκειται (|| *Matt*) D; simly lat-*a b c e* ff_2 *l* [*k*]. om 2nd την C. rec εκβαλειν bef το καρφος (|| *Matt*), with ACDΞℵ rel [vss]: aft το καρφος L **1**: txt B 69.

43. for ου γαρ, ουκ D lat-*a* Syr æth. καρπους σαπρους D latt Syr. rec om παλιν (*see Matt* vii. 18), with ACD rel lat-*a c* syrr goth æth: ins BLΞℵ **1**. 69 lat-*b* g_1

connexion, and it is impossible that it should consist of sayings thrown together and uttered at different times. The connexion with what went before is not so evident, indeed the εἶπεν δὲ π. αὐτ. seems to shew a break. The parabolic saying, implying the unfitness of an uncharitable and unjustly condemning leader (the Lord was speaking *primarily to His Apostles*) to perform his office, leads to the assertion (ver. 40) that no Christian ought to assume in this respect an office of judging which *his Master never assumed;* but rather will every well-instructed Christian strive to be humble as his Master was. Then follows the reproof of vv. 41—43; and vv. 44, 45 and 46—49 shew us, expanded in different images, what *the beam* in the eye is, to which our first efforts must be directed.

τυφλ. τ. ὁδ.] See this in quite another connexion, Matt. xv. 14, where Peter answers, φράσον ἡμῖν τὴν παραβολὴν [ταύτην]—meaning apparently *the last uttered words*, which the Lord however explains not specifically, but by entering into the whole matter. I believe this παραβολή to have been one of the usual and familiar sayings of our Lord.

40.] See above. **κατηρτισμένος** (see reff.)—fully instructed—perfect, in the sense of 'well-conditioned,' knowing what is his duty, and consistently endeavouring to do it. De Wette, Kuinoel, &c., have given a strange rendering of this clause, making **κατηρτ. ὡς ὁ δ. αὐτ.** the predicate—'every disciple will be instructed as his Master.' But if I mistake not, the position of κατηρτ. as first in the sentence forbids this rendering.

41.] De Wette imagines a break in the sense here, and a return to Matt. vii. 3 f.;—but the whole is in the strictest connexion: see above.

43.] The **καρπὸς**

v σαπρὸν u ποιοῦν u καρπὸν καλόν, 44 ἕκαστον γὰρ δένδρον ABCDE KLMSU
w ἐκ τοῦ ἰδίου καρποῦ w γινώσκεται. οὐ γὰρ ἐξ x ἀκανθῶν VXΓΔΛ ΞΠℵ
y συλλέγουσιν z σῦκα, οὐδὲ ἐκ a βάτου b σταφυλὴν c τρυγῶ- 1. 33. 69
σιν. 45 ὁ ἀγαθὸς ἄνθρωπος ἐκ τοῦ ἀγαθοῦ d θησαυροῦ
τῆς καρδίας αὐτοῦ e προφέρει τὸ ἀγαθόν, καὶ ὁ πονηρὸς
ἐκ τοῦ πονηροῦ e προφέρει τὸ πονηρόν· ἐκ γὰρ f περισ-
σεύματος καρδίας λαλεῖ τὸ στόμα αὐτοῦ. 46 τί δέ με
καλεῖτε Κύριε κύριε, καὶ οὐ ποιεῖτε ἃ λέγω; 47 πᾶς ὁ
ἐρχόμενος πρός με καὶ ἀκούων μου τῶν λόγων καὶ ποιῶν
αὐτούς, g ὑποδείξω ὑμῖν τίνι ἐστὶν ὅμοιος. 48 ὅμοιός
ἐστιν ἀνθρώπῳ οἰκοδομοῦντι οἰκίαν, ὃς h ἔσκαψεν καὶ
i ἐβάθυνεν καὶ k ἔθηκεν k θεμέλιον ἐπὶ τὴν πέτραν· l πλημμύρης δὲ γενομένης m προσέῤῥηξεν ὁ ποταμὸς τῇ οἰκίᾳ
ἐκείνῃ, καὶ οὐκ ἴσχυσεν n σαλεῦσαι αὐτήν, διὰ τὸ καλῶς
οἰκοδομεῖσθαι αὐτήν. 49 ὁ δὲ ἀκούσας καὶ μὴ ποιήσας
ὅμοιός ἐστιν ἀνθρώπῳ οἰκοδομήσαντι οἰκίαν ἐπὶ τὴν γῆν
χωρὶς θεμελίου· ᾗ m προσέῤῥηξεν ὁ ποταμός, καὶ εὐθὺς R [ευ] θεως...

w Matt. xiii. 33 reff. x Matt. vii. 16 reff. y Matt. vii. 16. xiii. 28 &c. only. Cant. vi. 1. z Matt. vii. 16. Mark xi. 13. James iii. 12 only. 4 Kings xx. 7. a ch. xx. 37 reff. b Matt. vii. 16. Rev. xiv. 18 only. Gen. xl. 10, 11. c Rev. xiv. 18, 19 only. Deut. xxiv. 23 (21). d Matt. ii. 11 reff. Isa. xxxiii. 6. e here (bis) only. Prov. x. 13. Tobit ix. 5 (not ℵ) only. f Matt. xii. 34. Mark viii. 8. 2 Cor. viii. 14 bis. Eccl. ii. 15 (only?). g ch. iii. 7 ‖ Mt. ch. xii. 5. Acts ix. 16. xx. 35 only. 2 Chron. xv. 3. h ch. xiii. 8. xvi. 3 only. Isa. v. 6 only. i here only. Ps. xci. 5. Jer. xxix. (xlix.) 8 only. k ch. xiv. 29. 1 Cor. iii. 10, 11. l here only. Job xl. 18 (23) only. m here bis only †. Ps. ii. 9 Aq. n Matt. xxiv. 19 reff.

q copt arm. καρπους καλους (*see Matt* vii. 18) D latt[not ff_2 g_2] Syr [Dial$_1$].

44. for 1st γαρ, δε Γ(Tischdf): om D Γ(Treg) 258 Scr's g tol lat-*a b c e* ff_2 *l q*. for ιδιου καρπου, καρπου αυτου D, *fructu suo* latt. εκλεγονται εξ ακανθων D[-gr] lat-*e*. for βατου, βλαστου ℵ^1(txt ℵ-corr^1). rec τρυγωσιν bef σταφυλην (*conformn to order of former clause*), with A rel latt Syr [copt] goth æth arm: txt BCDLXΞℵ 33. 69 ev-y syr.—σταφυλας (K)L 69 lat-*c e* syrr copt goth.

45. αυτου bef της καρδιας D[-gr]: om αυτου Bℵ. (*See digest on Matt* xii. 35.) om το (bef αγαθ.) D. rec aft πονηρος ins ανθρωπος (‖ *Matt*), with ACΞℵ^{3a} rel vulg lat-*c e f* ff_2 g_2 [*q*] syrr goth æth arm [Dial$_1$]: om BDLℵ^1 1 lat-*a b* g_1 *l* copt. rec aft πονηρου ins θησαυρου της καρδιας αυτου (*from* ‖ *Matt*), with AC rel [lat-*c e f* g_2 *q* syrr copt goth æth]; θησαυρου (alone) 69 vulg lat-*b* Dial: om BDLΞℵ 1 am(with forj tol) lat-*a* ff_2 g_1 arm. rec ins του bef περισσευματος, with CLMUΓ Dial: om AB D [S(Tischdf)] Ξℵ rel. rec ins της bef καρδιας (‖ *Matt*), with C rel Dial: om ABDΞℵ. το στομα (αυτου) bef λαλει (‖ *Matt*) Cℵ ev-y latt copt Dial.—om αυτου (‖ *Matt*) C F(Wetst) ev-y vulg lat-g_1 Syr copt æth Dial. for λαλει, καλει D-gr(txt D^4 and lat).

46. καλειτε bef με Ξ: με bef δε Δ. for καλειτε, λεγετε *dicitis* D 28 [Clem$_3$] Iren-int$_2$ [Orig-int$_1$] Gaud: λαλειτε K. for ἅ, ὅ B lat-*e* Syr goth.

47. τους λογους (*Matt* vii. 24) C F(Wetst) M, τ. λογους τουτους X lat-*b q* Syr-ms. aft λογων ins μου (retaing μου above) ℵ^1.

48. (πλημμυρης, so B^{1}LΞℵ 33. προσερηξεν (one ρ), so B^{1}DLℵ^1 [and B^1(D)L ver 49].) rec (for δια το καλως οικοδομεισθαι αυτην) τεθεμελιωτο γαρ επι την πετραν (*Matt* vii. 25), with ACD rel latt syrr goth [arm]: both are joined in æth: txt BLΞℵ 33 syr-mg copt [-μησθαι B^{1}LΞℵ].

49. οικοδομουντι (*from ver* 42) C 69. om ᾗ D lat-*a b c e* ff_2 g_1 *q*. συνερηξεν D. rec ευθεως, with AR rel: om (*Matt* vii. 27) D lat-*a c*: txt BCLΞℵ 33

σαπρός = the δοκὸς ἐν τῷ ὀφθ. If thy *life is evil*, it is in vain to pretend to *teach others*. **45.**] Again the closest connexion of sense and argument; nor is this verse (De Wette) put here because of the similarity of the preceding verses to Matt. xii. 33 reminding the compiler of ver. 35 there. Do these expositors suppose that our Lord *only once spoke* each of these *central* sayings, and with *only one reference*? **46—48.**] The connexion goes on here also—and our Lord descends into the closest personal searching of the life and heart, and gives His judicial declaration of the end of the hypocrite, whether teacher or private Christian: see notes on Matt. **48.**] **ἔσκαψεν κ. ἐβάθυνεν**—not a mere hendiadys for

[o] συνέπεσεν, καὶ ἐγένετο τὸ [p] ῥῆγμα τῆς οἰκίας ἐκείνης
μέγα.
VII. 1 Ἐπειδὴ [q] ἐπλήρωσεν πάντα τὰ ῥήματα αὐτοῦ
[r] εἰς τὰς [s] ἀκοὰς τοῦ λαοῦ, εἰσῆλθεν εἰς Καφαρναούμ.
2 ἑκατοντάρχου δέ τινος δοῦλος [t] κακῶς [t] ἔχων ἤμελλεν
τελευτᾶν, ὃς ἦν αὐτῷ [u] ἔντιμος. 3 ἀκούσας δὲ περὶ τοῦ
Ἰησοῦ ἀπέστειλεν πρὸς αὐτὸν [v] πρεσβυτέρους τῶν [v] Ἰουδαίων, [w] ἐρωτῶν αὐτὸν ὅπως ἐλθὼν [x] διασώσῃ τὸν δοῦλον
αὐτοῦ. 4 οἱ δὲ [y] παραγενόμενοι πρὸς τὸν Ἰησοῦν [z] παρεκάλουν αὐτὸν [a] σπουδαίως, λέγοντες ὅτι [b] ἄξιός ἐστιν
ᾧ [c] παρέξῃ τοῦτο· 5 ἀγαπᾷ γὰρ τὸ ἔθνος ἡμῶν, καὶ τὴν
συναγωγὴν αὐτὸς ᾠκοδόμησεν ἡμῖν. 6 ὁ δὲ Ἰησοῦς
ἐπορεύετο σὺν αὐτοῖς. ἤδη δὲ αὐτοῦ οὐ [d] μακρὰν [e] ἀπέχοντος ἀπὸ τῆς οἰκίας ἔπεμψεν πρὸς αὐτὸν φίλους
ὁ ἑκατόνταρχος λέγων αὐτῷ Κύριε μὴ [f] σκύλλου· οὐ

G των ιουδαιων ... ABCDE GHKL MRSU VXΓΔΛ ΞΠℵ 1. 33. 69

o here only. Ezek. xxx. 4 (see note).
p here only. Amos vi. 12.
q = Acts xix. 21. Rom. xv. 19. Col. i. 25.
r Gen. xx. 8.
s = Mark vii. 35 reff. 2 Tim. iv. 3, 4.
t Matt. iv. 24 reff.
u = Phil. ii. 29. 1 Pet. ii. 4, 6 (from Isa. xxviii. 16) only. (ch. xiv. 8.) 1 Kings xxvi. 21.
v E ra vi. 7, 8, 14. Esdr. vii. 2.
w w. ὅπως, ch. xi. 37. Acts xxiii. 20.
x = Matt. xiv. 36 only. (Luke [Acts xxiii. 24 al4.] only, exc. as above, and 1 Pet. iii. 20.) see Job xxi. 10.
y ver. 20. ch. viii. 19. Acts xx. 18 al. fr. chiefly Luke. Exod. ii. 18.
z Matt. viii. 5 al. 1 Kings xxii. 4.
a Phil. ii. 28. 2 Tim. i. 17. Tit. iii. 13 only †. Wisd. ii. 6 only. (-ος, 2 Cor. viii. 17, 22.)
b constr., here only.
c middle, Acts xix. 24. Col. iv. 1. Tit. ii. 7. Ps. xxxix. 7.
d Matt. viii. 30 reff.
e = Matt. xv. 8 reff. Ezek. xxii. 5.
f Matt. ix. 36. ch. viii. 49 ‖ Mk. only †.

ev-y. rec [for συνεπ.] επεσεν (*from Matt* vii. 27 ?), with AC rel vulg lat-*a c f ff*$_2$ *g*$_{1.2}$: txt BDLRΞℵ 1. 33. 69 ev-y tol lat-*b e l q*.

Chap. VII. 1. rec (for επειδη) επει δε, with C²RΞℵ rel vulg lat-*e f* [*g*$_2$] copt goth arm-zoh: επειδη δε K 239: και εγενετο οτε D lat-*b ff*$_2$ *g*$_1$ [*l*] *q*: txt A B(sic: see table) C¹X[Π]. for επληρωσεν, ετελεσεν D. for παντα, ταυτα D-gr: om παντα Xℵ¹ lat-*e* æth: for αυτου, ταυτα M 69. 243 Scr's d g [gat lat-*q*] Syr: om αυτου D lat-*a b c ff*$_2$ *g*$_1$ [*l*]. for εις τ. ακ. τ. λαου, λαλων D. om τας Ξ². ηλθεν D.

2. for δουλος, τις D¹-gr: παις *puer* D². om κακως εχων ℵ¹. for εντιμος, τιμειος D.

3. for ακουσ. δε, καὶ ακουσ. D 245 vulg lat-*b* [*e ff*$_2$ *q*] Syr. om προς αυτον D 69 lat-*a b c e f ff*$_2$ *g*$_{1.2}$ *l* [arm]. aft οπως ins αυτος ℵ.

4. for τον ιησ., αυτον C.—om προς τον ιησ. D lat-*a c e ff*$_2$ *l*. παρεκαλεσαν Λ copt-ms: ηρωτων DLΞℵ 1. 69: txt BCR rel. aft λεγοντες ins αυτω AC¹KΛ vulg lat-*f* æth: om BC²DRΞℵ rel [syrr syr-jer copt &c]. rec παρεξει, with GΓΛ(KMS UV ?): txt ABCDRΞℵ rel.

5. (οικοδομησεν C¹D: ωικ. Δ.)

6. επορευετο δε μετ' αυτων ο ιησ. D lat-*a* (*c e*) [*l*]. ου μακρ. απεχ. bef αυτου D. om απο Dℵ 1. 69 goth. om πρ. αυτον B ℵ¹(ins ℵ-corr¹).—for προς, επ' A. rec ὁ εκατοντ. bef φιλους, with ADR rel vulg lat-*a b* [*f l q* syrr arm] goth: om ὁ εκατοντ. Δ: txt BCLXΞℵ 33 lat-*c e* copt æth.—om ὁ L. [on εκατοντ. see proleg.] for αυτω, προς αυτον 69; om ℵ¹ [vulg lat-*b q*].

"dug deep," but, as Bengel observes, "crescit oratio:" he dug, and deepened as he dug: was not content with one digging, but kept going deeper.

49. συνέπεσεν] So we have συμπίπτει στέγη, Eur. Herc. Fur. 905: πόλιν . . . ὑπὸ σεισμοῦ . . . ξυμπεπτωκυῖαν, Thuc. viii. 41.

Chap. VII. 1—10.] Healing of the centurion's servant. Matt. viii. 5—13. In Matt. also placed after the Sermon on the Mount, but with the healing of the leper in our ch. v. 12 ff. interposed. Our narrative is fuller than that in Matt. in the beginning of the miracle, not so full at the end. See notes on Matt. **1.**] **τὰ ῥήματα . . . εἰς τ. ἀκ.** for τὰ ῥηθέντα εἰς . . . This, though there is no art. after αὐτοῦ, is better than to connect εἰς with ἐπλήρωσεν. **3.**] **πρεσβ.**, not elders of the *synagogue* (who in Luke are ἀρχισυναγωγοί, Acts xiii. 15), but of the *people*. **4.**] If the rec. reading παρέξει be retained, it must be remembered that it is *not the second person of* παρέξομαι (for which ὄψει, βούλει, οἴει are no precedents, being

g w. ἵνα, ‖ Mt. only. (Matt. iii. 4 reff.)
h ‖ Mt. reff.
i Matt. xxvii. 8. ch. i. 35.
k = here (Acts xv. 38. xxviii. 22. 2 Thess. i. 11. 1 Tim. v. 17. Heb. iii. 3. x. 29) only. L.P.H. Gen. xxxi. 28.
l ‖ Mt. only. (2 Macc. iii. 6.)
m = Rom. xiii. 1.
n constr., Acts vii. 31. Jude 16. Job xxxii. 22. see 2 Thess. i. 10.
o ch. ii. 20 reff.
p ch. v. 31 reff.
q ch. ix. 37. Acts xxi. 1. xxv. 17. xxvii. 18 only ‡. Deut. ii. 34. iii. 6.
r ch. xiv. 25 reff.

γὰρ [g] ἱκανός εἰμι ἵνα ὑπὸ τὴν [h] στέγην μου εἰσέλθῃς, ...εισελθης Ξ.
7 [i] διὸ οὐδὲ ἐμαυτὸν [k] ἠξίωσα πρός σε ἐλθεῖν· ἀλλὰ
εἰπὲ λόγῳ, καὶ ἰαθήτω ὁ παῖς μου. 8 καὶ γὰρ ἐγὼ
ἄνθρωπός εἰμι [l] ὑπὸ [l] ἐξουσίαν [m] τασσόμενος, ἔχων ὑπ' F ειμι...
ἐμαυτὸν στρατιώτας, καὶ λέγω τούτῳ Πορεύθητι, καὶ ABCDE FGHK
πορεύεται, καὶ ἄλλῳ Ἔρχου, καὶ ἔρχεται, καὶ τῷ δούλῳ LMRSU VXΓΔΛ
μου Ποίησον τοῦτο, καὶ ποιεῖ. 9 ἀκούσας δὲ ταῦτα ΠℵI. 33. 69
ὁ Ἰησοῦς [n] ἐθαύμασεν αὐτόν, καὶ στραφεὶς τῷ ἀκολου-
θοῦντι αὐτῷ ὄχλῳ εἶπεν Λέγω ὑμῖν, οὐδὲ ἐν τῷ Ἰσραὴλ
τοσαύτην πίστιν εὗρον. 10 καὶ [o] ὑποστρέψαντες οἱ πεμφ-
θέντες εἰς τὸν οἶκον εὗρον τὸν [ἀσθενοῦντα] δοῦλον
[p] ὑγιαίνοντα.

11 Καὶ ἐγένετο ἐν τῇ [q] ἑξῆς, ἐπορεύετο εἰς πόλιν καλουμένην Ναΐν, καὶ [r] συνεπορεύοντο αὐτῷ οἱ μαθηταὶ Ξ και συνεπορ. ...

rec ειμι bef ικανος (*see* ‖ *Matt*), with ACDRΞ rel [vulg lat-*a c* &c syr syr-jer copt goth æth arm]: txt Bℵ am(with ing forj) lat-*b l q*. μου bef υπο τ. στ. (‖ *Matt*) CDLMRXΓΞℵ 1. 33. 69 Chr Thl: txt AB rel vss.

7. om διο to ελθειν (*see* ‖ *Matt*) D 63. 240-4 lat-*a b c e* ff_2 *l*. ins μονον bef ειπε (‖ *Matt*) C 69 [lat-*l*] syr-w-ast. rec ιαθησεται (‖ *Matt*), with ACDℵ rel lat-*a b c*: txt BL.

8. for πορευθητι, πορευου DX.

9. ο ιησ. bef ταυτα C 157 am Syr. om αυτον (‖ *Matt*) DRX latt Syr-ms arm. ειπεν bef τω ακ. οχλω (omg αυτω) D lat-*e* syrr [syr-jer] copt æth. ins αμην bef λεγω (‖ *Matt*) DX 69 vulg lat-*a c e f* ff_2 $g_{1.2}$ *l* copt-dz-marg goth arm: om ABCRℵ rel lat-*b* [*q*] syrr copt æth. aft υμιν ins οτι AU syrr [syr-jer] arm. ουδεποτε D. τοσαυτην πιστιν ευρον bef εν τω ισραηλ D lat-*e*.

10. εις τον οικον bef οι πεμφθεντες BDFKLXℵ lat-*a b c e* [syr-jer æth] copt: txt AC rel vulg lat-*f* ff_2 [*l*] syrr goth arm.—om τον D^1(ins D^3).—D adds δουλοι. om ασθενουντα BLℵ 1 lat-*a b c e* ff_2 g_1 *l q* copt [syr-jer]. om δουλον D.

11. om εγενετο εν D lat-*e* [æth]. for τη, τω ABR$ℵ^{3a}$ rel vulg lat-*a b* $g_{1.2}$ *l* [*q*]: txt (*see note*) CDKM$ℵ^1$ (S, e sil) lat-*c e f* syrr copt goth æth arm. επορευθη BRℵ 69: txt ACD rel. om καλουμενην $ℵ^1$. om αυτω ARUXΛ 69: ins BCDΞ

peculiar conventional forms), but *third pers. fut. act.* The second person in -ει does not occur in later Greek, with the above exceptions. **5.] αὐτός, at his own expense. τὴν σ., our synagogue.** **7.] διό,** on account of his unworthiness; which unworthiness itself may be connected with the fact, that entering his house would entail ceremonial uncleanness till the evening. Matt. does not express this clause, having the narrative in a form which precludes it. See notes there. The **οὐδέ** brings into emphasis, not ἐμαυτόν, as distinguished from others, but the whole following clause; "neither did I adopt *that* course."

9.] After this there is an important addition in Matt. on the adoption of the Gentiles, and rejection of Israel who shewed no such faith. **10.]** Here Matt. simply states the fact of the healing, [apparently] not knowing of the οἱ πεμφθ.

11—16.] Raising of a dead man at Nain. *Peculiar to Luke.* **11. ἐν τῇ ἑξῆς]** With regard to the variety of reading here, Schulz remarks that St. Luke, when χρόνῳ is understood, uses **ἐν τῷ καθεξῆς**, see ch. viii. 1. On the other hand Meyer observes that when ἡμέρᾳ is understood, he never prefixes ἐν:—see reff.:—so that internal as well as external evidence is divided. Nain occurs no where else in the Bible. It was a town of Galilee not far from Capernaum, a few miles to the south of Mount Tabor, 'on the northern slope of the rugged and barren ridge of Little Hermon,' Stanley. A poor village has been found in this situation with ruins of old buildings. See Robinson, iii. 226. The κώμη καλουμένη Ναΐν (or Ναΐς) of Josephus, B. J. iv. 9. 4, on the borders of Idumea, is a different place. See Winer, Realw.; and Stanley's description, Sinai and Palestine, p. 357, edn. 3.

αὐτοῦ [ˢ ἱκανοὶ] καὶ ὄχλος πολύς. 12 ὡς δὲ ᵗ ἤγγισεν τῇ
πύλῃ τῆς πόλεως, ᵘ καὶ ἰδοὺ ᵛ ἐξεκομίζετο τεθνηκώς,
ʷ μονογενὴς υἱὸς τῇ μητρὶ αὐτοῦ, καὶ ˣ αὕτη ἦν χήρα·
καὶ ὄχλος τῆς πόλεως ˢ ἱκανὸς [ἦν] σὺν αὐτῇ. 13 καὶ
ἰδὼν αὐτὴν ὁ κύριος ʸ ἐσπλαγχνίσθη ἐπ' αὐτῇ, καὶ εἶπεν
αὐτῇ Μὴ κλαῖε. 14 καὶ προσελθὼν ἥψατο τῆς ᶻ σοροῦ·
οἱ δὲ ᵃ βαστάζοντες ᵇ ἔστησαν. καὶ εἶπεν ᶜ Νεανίσκε, ᵈ σοὶ
λέγω, ᵉ ἐγέρθητι. 15 καὶ ᶠ ἀνεκάθισεν ὁ νεκρὸς καὶ ἤρξατο
λαλεῖν. καὶ ἔδωκεν αὐτὸν τῇ μητρὶ αὐτοῦ. 16 ᵍ ἔλαβεν δὲ

s = Matt. xxviii. 12 reff. Acts v. 37. t ch. xv. 1 reff. Exod. xxxii. 19. u ch. ii. 21 reff. v here only +. = ἐκφέρω, Acts v. 6, 9, 10. w = ch. viii. 42. ix. 38. Heb. xi. 17 (John i. 14 reff.) only. (and constr.) Tobit iii. 15. x = ch. ii. 36. Acts ix. 36. y ch. x. 33. xv. 10. Matt. xiv. 14 al.+ z here only. Gen. l. 26. Job xxi. 32 A Ald. (σωρ. BℵF) only. a = Matt. iii. 11. Mark xiv. 13 al. b = Mark x. 49 reff. c Matt. xix. 20, 22 reff. d ch. v. 24 ‖ Mk. al. e = Matt. xxvii. 52 al. Isa. xxvi. 19. f Acts ix. 40 only +. g = ch. v. 26. 1 Cor. x. 13. Exod. xv. 15.

rel. om ικανοι (*as unusual with* οι μαθ. αυτου: *Mey suggests, because followed by* καιο) BDFLΞℵ vulg lat-*a e f ff*$_2$ *g*$_{1.2}$ *l* Syr syr-jer copt arm: ins ACR rel lat-*b c* [*q*] syr goth.

12. εγενετο δε ως D, simly lat-*b c ff*$_2$ [*e l*] *q*. ηγγιζεν D 69. om και ιδου D-gr (*et* D-lat) æth. om τεθνηκως A 54 lat-*c*: ins BCDRΞℵ rel. rec υιος bef μονογενης, with ACDR rel vulg lat-*a b* &c copt goth [syrr arm Bas-sel$_1$: om μον. æth]: txt BLXΞℵ lat-*c*. elz om 1st ην, with AC³R rel syr[-txt] goth: ins B(sic) C¹L V(S ?)Ξℵ 1. 33 latt Syr syr-mg [syr-jer] copt arm.—for και αυτη ην χηρα, χηρα ουση D. πολυς οχλ. τ. πολ. συνεληλυθι αυτη D, so (in part) lat-*c*. Steph om 2nd ην, with ACR rel latt syrr goth: ins BLΞℵ 33. 69 [syr-jer] copt æth arm.

13. for και ιδων, ιδων δε D lat-*e* Syr. om αυτην D [Syr]. for κυριος, ιησους D 1 forj(with gat) lat-*b f* Syr copt [(syr-jer goth] æth). επ' αυτην KRUX Γ[Π]ℵ 69 [Bas-sel$_1$].

14. νεανισκε is repeated in D lat-*a ff*$_2$.

15. for ανεκαθ., εκαθισεν B lat-*c e* Iren-int$_1$. απεδωκεν A 33 lat-*c f*.

This is one of the three greatest recorded miracles of our Lord: of which it has been observed, that He raised one (Jaeirus's daughter) when *just dead*,—one *on the way to burial*,—and one (Lazarus) *who had been buried four days*.

12. ἐξεκ.] The Jews ordinarily buried outside the gates of their cities. The kings however of the house of David were buried in the city of David; and it was a denunciation on Jehoiakim that he should be buried with the burial of an ass, drawn and cast forth *beyond the gates* of Jerusalem. Jer. xxii. 19. "One entrance alone Nain could have had; that which opens on the rough hill side in its downward slope to the plain. It must have been in this steep descent," &c. Stanley, ut supra. The usage of **μονογενής** with a dative is classical: cf. Herod. vii. 221, τὸν δὲ παῖδα . . . ἐόντα οἱ μαυνογενέα: Æsch. Agam. 872, μονογενὲς τέκνον πατρί.

αὔτ. χήρα] Some few cursive mss. read this in the dative (omg. ἦν), καὶ αὐτῇ χήρᾳ (see also the readg. of D): but even in this case it is more agreeable to Luke's usage to take it as a nominative. See ch. ii. 25, 36, and accentuate, as there, αὔτη.

14.] The **σορός** (= λάρναξ, Jos. Antt. xv. 3. 2) was an *open coffin*. There was something in the manner of our Lord which caused the bearers to stand still. We need not suppose any miraculous influence over them. All three raisings from the dead are wrought with words of power,—'Damsel, arise,'—'Young man, arise,'—'Lazarus, come forth.' Trench quotes an eloquent passage from Massillon's sermons (Miracles, p. 241),—'Elie ressuscite des morts, c'est vrai; mais il est obligé de se coucher plusieurs fois sur le corps de l'enfant qu'il ressuscite: il souffle, il se rétrécit, il s'agite: on voit bien qu'il invoque une puissance étrangère; qu'il rappelle de l'empire de la mort une âme qui n'est pas soumise à sa voix: et qu'il n'est pas lui-même le maître de la mort et de la vie. Jésus-Christ ressuscite les morts comme il fait les actions les plus communes: il parle en maître à ceux qui dorment d'un sommeil éternel: et l'on sent bien qu'il est le Dieu des morts comme des vivans,—jamais plus tranquille que lorsqu'il opère les plus grandes choses.'

15. ἔδ. αὐ. τῇ μ. αὐ.] Doubtless there was a deeper reason than the mere consoling of the widow (of whom there were many in Israel now as beforetime), that influenced our Lord to work this miracle: Olshausen (vol. i. p. 271) remarks, "A

φόβος πάντας, καὶ ἐδόξαζον τὸν θεὸν λέγοντες ὅτι προφήτης μέγας [h] ἠγέρθη ἐν ἡμῖν, καὶ ὅτι [i] ἐπεσκέψατο ὁ
θεὸς τὸν λαὸν αὐτοῦ. 17 καὶ [j] ἐξῆλθεν ὁ [k] λόγος οὗτος ἐν
ὅλῃ τῇ Ἰουδαίᾳ περὶ αὐτοῦ καὶ πάσῃ τῇ [l] περιχώρῳ.
18 Καὶ [m] ἀπήγγειλαν Ἰωάννῃ οἱ μαθηταὶ αὐτοῦ περὶ πάντων τούτων. 19 καὶ [n] προσκαλεσάμενος δύο [o] τινὰς τῶν
μαθητῶν αὐτοῦ ὁ Ἰωάννης ἔπεμψεν πρὸς τὸν κύριον
[p] λέγων Σὺ εἶ ὁ [q] ἐρχόμενος, ἢ ἄλλον [q] προσδοκῶμεν;
20 [r] παραγενόμενοι δὲ πρὸς αὐτὸν οἱ ἄνδρες εἶπαν Ἰωάννης ὁ βαπτιστὴς ἀπέσταλκεν ἡμᾶς πρός σε λέγων Σὺ
εἶ ὁ [q] ἐρχόμενος ἢ ἄλλον [q] προσδοκῶμεν; 21 ἐν ἐκείνῃ
τῇ [s] ὥρᾳ [t] ἐθεράπευσεν πολλοὺς [t] ἀπὸ νόσων καὶ [u] μασ-

…λαον αυτου C. ABDEF GHKL MRSUV ΧΓΔΛΞ Πℵ 1. 33. 69

h Matt. xxiv. 11, 24. Isa. xli. 25.
i = ch. i. 68, 78. Heb. ii. 6, from Ps. viii. 5. Gen. l. 24.
j 1 Cor. xiv. 36. Isa. ii. 3.
k = Matt. xxviii. 15. Mark i. 45. Acts xi. 22.
l Matt. xiv. 35 al. Gen. xix. 17.
m = Luke xiii. 1 reff.
n Matt. x. 1. Acts xxiii. 17, 18, 23 al. fr. Gen. xxviii. 1.
o = Acts xix. 14. xxiii. 23.
p = Mark xiv. 14.
q ‖ (reff.)
r ch. viii. 19. Acts xx. 18. Exod. ii. 17.
s ch. xii. 12. xx. 19 Dan. v. 5.
t ch. v. 15. viii. 2.
u = Mark iii. 10 reff.

16. rec απαντας, with ACFLRΓΞℵ (33, e sil): txt BD rel. rec εγηγερται (*apter sense*), with R rel: εξηγερθη D: txt ABCLΞℵ 1. 33.

17. ουτος bef ο λογος D vulg lat-*b e ff*$_2$ [*l q*]. και παση τη περιχωρω bef περι αυτου FLΞ 33 lat-*b c*: om περι αυτου ℵ[1](txt ℵ-corr[1]) [lat-*ff*$_2$ *l*]. rec ins εν bef παση, with ADR rel vulg lat-*a e f* [*q*]: om BFLΞℵ 1 [33, Tischdf] am(with fuld forj ing) lat-*b c* [*l*].

18, 19. D reads εν οις και μεχρι ιωανου του βαπτιστου ος και προσκαλεσαμενος δυο των μαθητων αυτου λεγει πορευθεντες ειπατε αυτω συ ει κ.τ.λ., simly lat-*e*.—τινας is also omd by vulg lat-*b c f ff*$_2$ *g*$_1$ *l* [*q*] Syr copt goth æth [Ambr$_1$].

18. (ιωαννει (*itacism?*) AB[1]ℵ, similarly elsewhere.)

19. om ὁ (bef ιωαννης) Ξ[1] 1. rec for (κυριον) ιησουν, with ADℵ rel vulg lat-*b c f* [*l q*] syrr copt goth [Cyr$_1$]: txt BLRΞ 33 am(with fuld tol) lat-*a ff*$_2$ *g*$_1$ æth arm, κυριον αυτου 69. for αλλον, ετερον (‖ *Matt*) BLRXΞℵ 33 Cyr$_3$: txt AD rel Orig$_2$.

20. om ver (*homœotel*) R 239 Scr's q[1] v[1] ev-x fuld lat-*g*$_1$ *l*. for παραγ. δε, και παραγ. D lat-*a* (*c*) *e* Syr. οι ανδρες bef προς αυτον D ℵ-corr[1] 33 lat-*a* syr: om οι ανδρες ℵ[1](ins ℵ-corr[1]). (ειπαν, so BDLΞℵ.) απεστειλεν Bℵ 258 Scr's p Cyr$_1$. for αλλον, ετερον (‖ *Matt, as in ver* 19) DLXΞℵ 1. 33 Cyr: txt AB rel.

21. rec (for εκεινη) αυτη, with ADRΞ rel 33(sic) vulg lat-*a b f ff*$_2$ *g*$_{1,2}$ [*l*] syrr [syr-jer] goth arm: txt BLℵ 1. 69 ev-y lat-*c e q* copt Cyr$_1$ Bas-sel$_1$. rec ins δε bef τη, with ADRΞ rel vulg lat-*e f g*$_{1.2}$ [*q*] syrr goth arm: om BLXℵ 1. 33. 69 ev-y lat-*a b c ff*$_2$ *l* copt Cyr$_1$. for ωρα, ημερα Lℵ[1] 69 Cyr$_1$. εθεραπευεν D-gr lat-*a b ff*$_2$ *q* [*l* Cyr$_1$].

reference in this miracle to the *raised man himself* is by no means excluded. Man, as a conscious being, can never be a *mere means* to an end, which would here be the case, if we suppose the consolation of the mother to have been the only object for which the young man was raised." He goes on to say that the hidden intent was probably the spiritual awakening of the youth; which would impart a deeper meaning to **ἔδωκεν αὐτ. τῇ μ. αὐ.** and make her joy to be a true and abiding one.

16.] **φόβος**, the natural result of witnessing a direct exhibition of divine power: compare ch. v. 8. **προφ. μέγ.**] For they had only been the *greatest of prophets* who had before raised the dead,—Elijah and Elisha; and *the* Prophet who was to come was doubtless in their minds. Bornemann supposes **ὅτι** in both cases to be not merely ὅτι loquentis, but 'for that,' and to be connected with ἐδόξαζον (but qu.?).

17.] Meyer refers **ὁ λόγος οὗτος** to the saying just cited: but it seems more natural to interpret it **this account**, viz. of the miracle. And so in reff. On the construction ἐξῆλθεν ἐν, Meyer cites Thuc. iv. 42, ἐν Λευκαδίᾳ ἀπήεσαν.

18—35.] Message of enquiry from the Baptist: our Lord's answer, and discourse to the multitudes thereon. Matt. xi. 2—19. The incident there holds a different place, coming after the sending out of the Twelve in ch. x.;—but neither there nor here is it marked by any definite note of time. πάντων τούτων here may extend very wide: so may τὰ ἔργα τοῦ χριστοῦ in Matt. On the common parts, see notes on Matt., where I have discussed at length the probable reason of the enquiry.

21.] This fact follows by inference from Matt. ver. 4: for they could not tell John ἃ ἔβλεπον, unless our

τίγων καὶ πνευμάτων [v] πονηρῶν, καὶ τυφλοῖς πολλοῖς
[w] ἐχαρίσατο βλέπειν. 22 καὶ ἀποκριθεὶς εἶπεν αὐτοῖς
Πορευθέντες ἀπαγγείλατε Ἰωάννῃ ἃ εἴδετε καὶ ἠκούσατε·
ὅτι τυφλοὶ ἀναβλέπουσιν, χωλοὶ περιπατοῦσιν, [x] λεπροὶ
[x] καθαρίζονται, κωφοὶ ἀκούουσιν, [y] νεκροὶ [y] ἐγείρονται, [z] πτωχοὶ [a] εὐαγγελίζονται, 23 καὶ μακάριός ἐστιν [b] ὃς ἐὰν μὴ
[c] σκανδαλισθῇ ἐν ἐμοί. 24 ἀπελθόντων δὲ τῶν ἀγγέλων
Ἰωάννου ἤρξατο λέγειν πρὸς τοὺς ὄχλους περὶ Ἰωάννου
Τί ἐξεληλύθατε εἰς τὴν ἔρημον [d] θεάσασθαι; [e] κάλαμον
ὑπὸ ἀνέμου [f] σαλευόμενον; 25 ἀλλὰ τί ἐξεληλύθατε ἰδεῖν;
ἄνθρωπον ἐν [g] μαλακοῖς ἱματίοις [h] ἠμφιεσμένον; ἰδοὺ οἱ ἐν
[i] ἱματισμῷ [k] ἐνδόξῳ καὶ [l] τρυφῇ [m] ὑπάρχοντες ἐν τοῖς [n] βα-
σιλείοις εἰσίν. 26 ἀλλὰ τί ἐξεληλύθατε ἰδεῖν; προφήτην;
ναί, λέγω ὑμῖν, καὶ [o] περισσότερον προφήτου. 27 οὗτός
ἐστιν περὶ οὗ γέγραπται [p] Ἰδοὺ ἀποστέλλω τὸν ἄγγελόν
μου πρὸ προσώπου σου, ὃς [q] κατασκευάσει τὴν ὁδόν σου
ἔμπροσθέν σου. 28 λέγω ὑμῖν, μείζων ἐν [r] γεννητοῖς
γυναικῶν [προφήτης] Ἰωάννου οὐδείς ἐστιν, ὁ δὲ [s] μικρότε-

...καθαρίζονται R.

...περισσότερον F.

v = (Luke) ch viii. 2 al. Acts xix. 12, &c.
w = Rom. viii. 32 al.† & constr., 2 Macc. iii. 31, 33.
x Matt. viii. 2 reff.
y Matt. x. 8 reff.
z ||. ch. iv. 8, from Isa. lxi. 1.
a constr., || reff.
b ||. ch. xviii. 17 || Mk. al.
c || reff.
d ch. xxiii. 55 reff.
e || reff.
f ||. ch. vi. 48. Ps. xvii. 7.
g || reff.
h Matt. vi. 30 reff.
i ch. ix. 29. John xix. 24, from Ps. xxi. 18. Acts xx. 33. 1 Tim. ii. 9 only.
k = here (ch. xiii. 17. 1 Cor. iv. 10. Eph. v. 27) only. see Isa. xxii. 17.
l 2 Pet. ii. 13 only. Gen. xlix. 20. Prov. xix. 10.
m = ch. xvi. 23. Phil. ii. 6.
n = here (1 Pet. ii. 9) only. Esth. ii. 13.
o || reff.
p Mal. iii. 1.
q Mark i. 2 reff. Num. xxi. 27.
r || only. Job xiv. 1.
s || reff.

πονηρων bef πνευματων D lat-*c e*: for πον., ακαθαρτων ℵ[1] : om και πν. πον. S Scr's g. rec ins το bef βλεπειν (*it appears from the weight of* MS *testimony, that* το *of* εχαρισατο *was mistaken for the article, and it thus became insd after the verb*), with (F, e sil) LUΛ ℵ-corr[1] 1. 33 [Cyr₁ Bas-sel₁]: om ABRΞℵ[1] rel.—και τυφλους εποιει βλεπειν D [lat-*e*].

22. rec aft αποκριθεις ins ο ιησους (|| *Matt*), with AR rel lat-*c f q* syrr [syr-jer] goth æth: om BDΞℵ vulg lat-*a b e ff₂ g₁.₂ l* copt arm Cyr₁. for απαγγειλατε, ειπατε D [tol Bas-sel]. for ειδετε και ηκουσατε, ειδον υμων οι οφθαλμοι(οφθι D[1]) και α ηκουσαν υμων τα ωτα D lat-*e*. om οτι (*see* || *Matt*) BLXΞℵ 1. 69 lat-*a b c ff₂ l q* (Orig₁) Did [Cyr₁ Bas-sel₁] Ambr₁. om χωλοι περιπατουσιν Ξ. ins και bef κωφοι (*from* || *Matt*) BDFΓΔ[1]Λℵ Syr æth arm-mss [Cyr₁ Bas-sel₁]: om AΞ rel latt syr [copt arm-ed Cyr₁]. ins και bef πτωχοι ℵ[FX 1. 33. 69 lat-*e* Syr syr-jer æth Cyr₁ Bas-sel₁].

23. for εαν, αν Dℵ [Cyr₁].

24. for προς τους οχλους, τοις οχλοις (|| *Matt*) DEFGHVΓΔΛℵ[1] copt: txt ABΞℵ[3a] rel [latt goth &c].—περι ιωαννου bef τοις οχλοις D am[with forj fuld ing] lat-*a f* [*ff₂ g₁.₂ l q*] copt. εξηλθατε (*from* || *Matt*) ABDLΞℵ 69: εξηλθετε K 1: txt E rel.

25. εξηλθατε (|| *Matt*) ABDLΞℵ 33. 69: εξηλθετε KM[Π] 1: txt E rel. for υπαρχοντες, διαγοντες D(*agent* D-lat) K[Π] Clem₁.

26. εξηλθατε (|| *Matt*) BDLΞℵ 69: εξηλθετε 1: txt A rel. at end ins οτι ουδεις μειζων εν γεννητοις γυναικων προφητης ιωανου του βαπτιστου D, omg the similar clause in ver 28; lat-*a* has them in both vv.

27. rec aft ιδου ins εγω (*from* || *Matt*), with A rel syrr goth æth Orig: om BDLΞℵ 1 latt copt arm Mcion[-e₂-t₁-ms] Orig₁-ms. om προ προσωπου σου Ξ.—om σου D-gr 57 Tert. for την, τον D. om εμπροσθεν σου (*Mark* i. 3) D 122[1] lat-*a l* Mcion-t.

28. rec aft λεγω ins γαρ, with A rel vulg lat-*f g₂ q* syr goth; δε D 69 lat-*a b c e ff₂ g₁ l*: pref αμην LXℵ syr-jer [æth] arm (*all corrns*): om BΞ 33 ev-y Syr copt. aft υμιν ins οτι D lat-*c e*. γεννηται (sic) ℵ[1](txt ℵ-corr[1](appy)[3a]): εκ γεννητης 69. om προφητης (*see* || *Matt*) BKLMXΞ[Π]ℵ 1. 33 lat-*a b c e ff₂ l* syr-mg syr-jer copt æth Orig₃: ins A (D ver 26) rel vulg lat-*f g₁.₂ q* syrr goth [arm] Clem₁ Mcion₁-t [Ambr₁].—om (but see ver 26) μειζων to ουδεις εστιν D. rec aft ιωαννου adds του βαπτιστου (*from* || *Matt*), with A (D ver 26) rel latt syrr goth æth Orig₂ Ambr₁ Quæst₁: om BLΞℵ 1 Syr-ms syr-jer copt arm Orig₁. om δε D(*see above*).

Lord were employed in works of healing at the time. Observe that Luke, himself a physician, distinguishes between the *diseased* and the *possessed*. **22 f.]**

ρὸς ἐν τῇ βασιλείᾳ τοῦ θεοῦ μείζων αὐτοῦ ἐστιν. 29 καὶ
πᾶς ὁ λαὸς ἀκούσας καὶ οἱ τελῶναι ᵗἐδικαίωσαν τὸν θεόν,
ᵘβαπτισθέντες τὸ ᵘβάπτισμα Ἰωάννου. 30 οἱ δὲ Φαρισαῖοι
καὶ οἱ ᵛνομικοὶ τὴν βουλὴν τοῦ θεοῦ ʷἠθέτησαν ˣεἰς
ἑαυτούς, μὴ βαπτισθέντες ὑπ' αὐτοῦ. 31 τίνι οὖν ʸὁμοι-
ώσω τοὺς ἀνθρώπους τῆς γενεᾶς ταύτης, καὶ τίνι εἰσὶν
ὅμοιοι; 32 ὅμοιοί εἰσιν παιδίοις τοῖς ἐν ᶻἀγορᾷ καθημέ- P παι-δίοις...
νοις, καὶ ᵃπροσφωνοῦσιν ἀλλήλοις λέγοντες ᵇΗὐλήσαμεν ABDE
ὑμῖν, καὶ οὐκ ᶜὠρχήσασθε· ᶜἐθρηνήσαμεν ὑμῖν, καὶ οὐκ GHKL MPSUV ΧΓΔΛΞ
ἐκλαύσατε. 33 ἐλήλυθεν γὰρ Ἰωάννης ὁ βαπτιστὴς μὴ Πℵ1. 33. 69
ᶜἔσθων ἄρτον μήτε ᶜπίνων οἶνον, καὶ λέγετε ᶜΔαιμόνιον
ᶜἔχει· 34 ἐλήλυθεν ὁ υἱὸς τοῦ ἀνθρώπου ᶜἐσθίων καὶ
πίνων, καὶ λέγετε Ἰδοὺ ἄνθρωπος ᵈφάγος καὶ ᵉοἰνοπότης,
φίλος τελωνῶν καὶ ἁμαρτωλῶν. 35 καὶ ᶠἐδικαιώθη ἡ
σοφία ᵍἀπὸ πάντων τῶν τέκνων αὐτῆς.
36 ʰἨρώτα δέ τις αὐτὸν τῶν Φαρισαίων ἵνα φάγῃ μετ

t = Matt. xi. 19. 1 Tim. iii. 16. Ps. l. 4.
u Acts xix. 4.
v = Luke (ch. x. 25 al.) only, exc. Matt. xxii. 35. Tit. iii. (9) 13 +.
w = ch. x. 16 reff.
x 2 Cor. xi. 10.
y Matt. vii. 24 reff.
z ‖. Matt. xx. 3. xxiii. 7 al. Cant. iii. 2.
a ‖ reff.
b ‖. 1 Cor. xiv. 7 only +. (-λητής, Matt. ix. 23.)
c ‖ (reff.)
d ‖ only +.
e ‖. Prov. xxiii. 20 only.
f ver. 29 reff.
g ‖. 1 Cor. i. 30. 2 Cor. vii. 13. James i. 13. Rev. xii. 6. Isa. xlv. 26.
h w. ἵνα, Mark vii. 26. ch. xvi. 27. John iv. 47. xvii. 15. 2 John 5.

aft μικροτερος ins αυτου D.

29. εδικαιωσαι D[1](txt D[2]).

30. om 2nd οι D. om εις εαυτους Dℵ 60. 243 æth.

31. rec at beg ins ειπε δε ο κυριος (*a lection beginning here*), with M-marg evv [vulg-cl] lat-*f* g_1; ουκετι εκεινοις ελεγετο αλλα τοις μαθηταις Ξ: om ABDℵ rel am(with fuld em forj gat harl ing jac mm mt per tol) syrr copt goth æth arm. for ουν, δε ℵ: om F(Wetst) ev-z [copt-schw-dz].

32. ins τοις bef παιδιοις D[1]. ins τη bef αγορα D. rec (for λεγοντες) και λεγουσιν (*see* ‖ *Matt*), with AP rel vulg lat-*f* g_1 [D-lat] syrr [goth]: α λεγει Bℵ[1] **1**: οι λεγουσιν Λ 262: λεγοντα Ξℵ[3a] 157: txt D-gr L 69 lat-*a b e* ff_2 *l q* copt. (*The varr have all been corrns of the harsh constr.*) om 2nd υμιν (*see* ‖ *Matt*) BDLΞℵ ev-y[1] vulg lat-*c e* $g_{1.2}$ *l* copt arm Ambr$_1$: ins AP rel lat-*a b f* ff_2 syrr goth æth [Bas$_1$].

33. (syr-cu contains Luke vii. 33—xv. 21.) rec (for μη) μητε, with AD rel [Orig$_1$ Oros$_1$]: txt BΞℵ. rec αρτον bef εσθιων and οινον bef πινων, with AP rel syr goth: om αρτον and οινον (‖ *Matt*) D **1**. 69 lat-*a b c e* ff_2 *l q* æth [arm] Orig$_1$ [Oros$_1$]: txt BLΞℵ vulg lat-*f* $g_{1.2}$ Syr copt. rec εσθιων, with APΞℵ rel: txt BD. μηδε ℵ.

34. [B[1] has εθιων; and δικαιωθη next ver.] rec τελωνων bef φιλος (‖ *Matt*), with HX (Clem$_1$): txt ABDPΞℵ rel vulg lat-*a c e f* ff_2 $g_{1.2}$ Thl Aug.

35. rec των τεκνων αυτης bef παντων, with APΞ rel syr copt goth: om παντων D F(Wetst) LMXℵ[3a] **1** syr-cu arm Iren-int$_1$ Ambr: txt B(ℵ[1]) 69 latt Syr. (*παντων being omd as in* ‖ *Matt, was restored in the wrong place.*)—for τεκνων, εργων (*see* ‖ *Matt, v. r.*) ℵ.

36. ηρωτησεν D lat-*a b c e f* ff_2 g_1 Amphil$_1$ [Ambr$_1$]. αυτον bef τις D **1** latt

Nearly verbatim as Matt. The expression **νεκροὶ ἐγ.** does not necessarily imply that more than one such miracle had taken place: the plural is generic.

24—28.] See Matt. **29, 30.**] It has been imagined that these words are a continuation of our Lord's discourse, (Grot., De Wette, Meyer, Bp. Wordsworth,) but surely they would thus be most unnatural. They are evidently a parenthetical insertion of the Evangelist, expressive not of what had taken place during John's baptism, but of the present effect of our Lord's discourse on the then assembled multitude. Their whole diction and form is *historical*, not belonging to discourse. Besides, if ἀκούσας were meant to signify '*when they heard him*' (John), then βαπτισθ. should be βαπτιζόμενοι.

31—35.] See on Matt. vv. 16—19.

36—50.] Anointing of Jesus' feet by a penitent woman. *Peculiar to Luke.* It is hardly possible to imagine that this history can relate to the same incident as that detailed Matt. xxvi. 6: Mark xiv. 3: John xii. 3: although such

...φαρισαιου Ξ. F αμαρτωλος...

αὐτοῦ· καὶ εἰςελθὼν εἰς τὸν οἶκον τοῦ Φαρισαίου
[i] κατεκλίθη. 37 καὶ ἰδοὺ γυνὴ ἥτις ἦν ἐν τῇ πόλει ἁμαρτωλὸς καὶ [k] ἐπιγνοῦσα ὅτι [l] κατάκειται ἐν τῇ οἰκίᾳ τοῦ
Φαρισαίου, [m] κομίσασα [n] ἀλάβαστρον [o] μύρου 38 καὶ στᾶσα
ὀπίσω [p] παρὰ τοὺς πόδας αὐτοῦ κλαίουσα, τοῖς δάκρυσιν

i ch. ix. 14. xiv. 8. xxiv. 30 only. 1 Kings xvi. 11. Judith xii. 15.
k = ch. xxiii. 7. Acts xxii. 29. xxviii. 1. Esth. iii. 5.
l = Mark ii. 15 reff.
m = here only. (Matt. xxv. 27 al.) Esdr. ix. 39, 40.
n Matt. xxvi. 7 ‖ Mk. only. 4 Kings xxi. 13 only.
o Matt. xxvi. 7 reff.
p ch. viii. 35. Acts xxii. 3.

[syrr goth] : *των φ.* bef *αυτ.* 33. rec **την οικιαν** (*more usual in the Gospels*), with AP rel: txt BDLΞℵ 1. 33. 69 Mcion$_2$-e Amphil$_1$. rec **ανεκλιθη**, with AP rel Amphil$_1$: *κατεκειτο* ℵ^1 : txt BDLXΞℵ^{3a} 1. 33 Mcion$_2$-e.

37. rec *εν τη πολει* bef *ητις ην*, with AP rel lat-*a b e q* syr goth Amphil$_1$: om *ητις ην* D æth : txt BLΞℵ vulg lat-*c f ff*$_2$ *l* (Syr syr-cu) [syr-jer] copt arm [Cyr$_1$-p] Ambr$_1$. rec om 2nd *και*, with DLΞ rel latt syr-cu [syr-jer] æth arm : ins ABFMPSVΔ [Π]ℵ 69 syrr copt goth. for *επιγν.*, *γνουσα* D. rec **ανακειται** (*cf ανεκλιθη ver* 36), with P rel : txt AB(D)LXΛΞℵ 33.—(aft *φαρισαιου* D lat-*c e* [syrr syr-cu].) *μυρου* bef *αλαβαστρον* D.

38. rec *παρα τους ποδας αυτου* bef *οπισω*, with AP rel syr goth : txt BDLXΔℵ 1. 33 latt Syr syr-cu [syr-jer] copt æth arm (Mcion$_1$-e) Orig-int$_1$ Ambr$_1$. for *αυτου*, *του*

an opinion has been entertained from the earliest times. Origen on Matt. xxvi. 6 ff., vol. iii. p. 892, mentions and controverts it. It has been held in modern times by Grotius, Schleiermacher, Ewald, and Hug: and recently by Bleek. But the *only particular common to the two* (unless indeed we account the *name of the host* to be such, which is hardly worth recounting), is *the anointing itself; and even that is not strictly the same.* The *character of the woman,*—the *description of the host,*—the *sayings uttered,*—the *time,*—all are different. And if the probability of this occurring twice is to be questioned, we may fairly say, that an action of this kind, which had been once commended by our Lord, was *very likely to have been repeated,* and especially at such a time as 'six days before the last Passover,' and by one anointing Him for His burial. I may add, that there is not the least reason for supposing the woman in this incident to have been Mary Magdalene. The introduction of her *as a new person* so soon after (ch. viii. 2), and what is there stated of her, make the notion exceedingly improbable. **36—38.**] The exact time and place are indeterminate—the occasion of Luke's inserting the history here may have been the φίλος τελωνῶν κ. ἁμαρτωλῶν in ver. 34. Wieseler places it *at Nain,* which certainly is the last πόλις that has been named: but it is more natural to suppose τῇ πόλει to refer only to τῇ οἰκίᾳ before—the city where the house was. Meyer thinks that the definite article points out Capernaum. The position of the words **ἐν τ. πόλει** in the amended text requires a different rendering from 'a woman in the city which was a sinner.' We must either render, 'which was a sinner in the city,' i. e. known as such in the place by public repute,—carrying on a sinful occupation in the place,—or (2) regard **ἥτ. ἦν ἐν τ. πόλ.** as parenthetic, 'a woman which was in the city, a sinner.' The latter seems preferable. **ἁμαρτωλός,** in the sense usually understood—*a prostitute:* but, by the context, *penitent.* **ἦν** is not however to be taken as a pluperfect. She *was,* even up to this time (see ver. 39), a prostitute (compare Augustine, Serm. xcix. (xxiii.) 2, vol. v. "Accessit ad Dominum immunda, ut rediret munda:" which cannot, as Wordsw., be explained away by what follows, "accessit confessa, ut rediret professa." The latter was a matter of course, otherwise she would not have come at all)—and this was the first manifestation of her penitence. "Quid mirum, tales ad Christum confugisse, cum et ad Johannis baptismum venerint?" Matt. xxi. 32 (Grotius). It is possible, that the woman may have just heard the closing words of the discourse concerning John, Matt. xi. 28—30; but I would not press this, on account of the obvious want of sequence in this part of our Gospel. The behaviour of the woman certainly implies that she had heard our Lord, and been awakened by His teaching. **ἀλάβ. μ.**] For the word, &c., see on Matt. xxvi. 7. Our Lord would, after the ordinary custom of persons at table, be reclining on a couch, on the left side, turned towards the table, and His feet would be behind Him. She seems to have embraced His feet (see Matt. xxviii. 9), as it was also the Jews' custom to do by way of honour and affection to their Rabbis (see Wetstein

ἤρξατο [q] βρέχειν τοὺς πόδας αὐτοῦ, καὶ ταῖς θριξὶν τῆς
κεφαλῆς αὐτῆς [r] ἐξέμασσεν, καὶ [s] κατεφίλει τοὺς πόδας
αὐτοῦ καὶ [t] ἤλειφεν τῷ [o] μύρῳ. 39 ἰδὼν δὲ ὁ Φαρισαῖος ὁ
[u] καλέσας αὐτὸν εἶπεν [v] ἐν ἑαυτῷ λέγων Οὗτος εἰ ἦν
προφήτης, ἐγίνωσκεν ἂν τίς καὶ [w] ποταπὴ ἡ γυνὴ ἥτις
ἅπτεται αὐτοῦ, ὅτι ἁμαρτωλός ἐστιν. 40 καὶ ἀποκριθεὶς
ὁ Ἰησοῦς εἶπεν πρὸς αὐτὸν Σίμων, [x] ἔχω σοί τι εἰπεῖν.
ὁ δὲ Διδάσκαλε, εἰπέ φησιν. 41 Δύο [y] χρεοφειλέται ἦσαν

q = ver. 44. Rev. xi. 6. (Matt. v. 45 reff.) Ps. vi. 6.
r ver. 44. John xi. 2. xii. 3. xiii. 5 only +. Sir. xii. 11. Ep. Jer. 13, 24 only.
s ver. 45. ch. xv. 20. Matt. xxvi. 49 || Mk. Acts xx. 37. Ruth i. 9, 14.
t Matt. vi. 17 reff.
u = Matt. xxii. 3, 9 reff. 18, 19. xxv. 26. xxviii. 19.
v Matt. iii. 9 reff.
w Matt. viii. 27 reff. +
x = Acts xxiii. 17,
y ch. xvi. 5 only. Job xxxi. 37. Prov. xxix. 13 only.

Ξ ουτος ... I_e εγινωσκεν...
ABDEF GHI_eK LMPSU VXΓΔΛ ΞΠℵ 1. 33. 69

ιησου AK[Π syr Amphil$_1$]. rec ηρξατο βρεχειν τους ποδας αυτου bef τοις δακρυσιν, with AP rel syr copt goth æth Amphil$_1$: txt B(D)Lℵ 33 latt syr-cu [syr-jer] arm Orig-int$_1$.—for ηρξατο βρεχειν, εβρεξε D. εξεμαξεν (*as in ver* 44 *and John* xii. 3) ADLXℵ^1 33 copt: txt BPℵ^{3a} rel latt syrr syr-cu [syr-jer] Orig-int$_1$ εξεμασεν E^{1}H^{1}Δ 69.

39. for ο καλεσας αυτον, παρ' ω κατεκειτο D lat-*e*. om λεγων DX 69 lat-*e* syr-txt arm Amphil$_1$ Orig-int$_1$ Aug$_2$. ins ο bef προφητης B^1(Tischdf) Ξ: om ADPℵ rel. ποδαπη D^1(txt D^8). for ητις απτεται, η απτομενη D Orig$_1$.

40. ειπεν bef ο ιησ. Ξ. rec φησι bef διδασκαλε ειπε, with P rel; so, but (for φησι) εφη, AD copt æth: txt BI_eLΞℵ 1.—ειπον D.

41. at beg ins ο δε ειπεν D syr-mg, simly X lat-*b c* syrr syr-cu copt[-schw æth arm].
(χρεοφειλεται, so A B(sic: see table) DI_e L(as corrd by origl scribe) Ξℵ &c.)

on this passage), and kissed them, and in doing so to have shed abundant tears, which, falling on them, she wiped off with her hair. It does not appear that this latter was an *intentional* part of her honouring our Lord: had it been, there would hardly have been an article before **δάκρυσιν.** As it stands, **τοῖς δάκρυσιν** is **the tears,** implied in κλαίουσα,—**the tears which she shed,**—not '*her tears*,' which would be δάκρυσιν only. The *ointment* here has a peculiar interest, as being the offering by a penitent of that which had been an accessory in her unhallowed work of sin. **39. εἶπ. ἐν ἑαυ. λέγων**] This phraseology is perhaps a mark of translation from the Hebrew. The Pharisee *assumes* that our Lord did not know who, or of what sort, this woman was, and thence doubts His being a prophet (see ver. 16);—the possibility of His *knowing this and permitting it*, never so much as occurs to him. It was the *touching* by an unclean person which constituted the defilement. This is all that the Pharisee fixes on: his *offence* is merely technical and ceremonial. **40.**] **ἀποκριθείς**—perhaps to the disgust manifested in the Pharisee's countenance; for that must have been the ground on which the narrative relates ver. 39. We must not however forget that in similar cases ἰδὼν ὁ Ἰησ. τὰς ἐνθυμήσεις αὐτῶν is inserted (Matt. ix. 4), and doubtless might also have been here. There is an *inner personal appeal* in the words addressing the Pharisee. The calling by name—the especial **ἔχω σοί τι εἰπεῖν,** refer to the *inner thoughts of the heart*, and at once bring the answer **διδάσ., εἰπέ,** so different from **οὗτος εἰ ἦν προφήτης.** **41.**] We must remember that our Lord is here setting forth the matter *primarily* with reference to Simon's subjective view of himself, and therefore not strictly as regards the actual comparative sinfulness of these two before God. Though however not to be pressed, *the case may have been so*: and, I am inclined to think, *was so*. The clear light of truth in which every word of His was spoken, will hardly allow us to suppose that such an admission would have been made to the Pharisee, if it had not really been so in fact. But see more below. **δύο χρ.**] The *debtors* are the prominent persons in the parable—the creditor is necessary indeed to it, but is *in the background*. And this remark is important—for on bearing it carefully in mind the right understanding of the parable depends. The Lord speaks *from the position of the debtors*, and applies to their case the considerations of ordinary gratitude and justice. And in doing so it is to be noticed, that he makes an assumption for the purpose of the parable:—*that sin = the sense of sin*, just as a debt is *felt* to the amount of the debt. The disorganization of our moral nature, the deadly sedative effect of sin in lulling the conscience, which renders the greatest sinner the least ready for penitence, *does not here come into consideration*; the examples being two persons, both *aware*

[z] δανειστῇ τινι· ὁ εἷς [a] ὤφειλεν δηνάρια πεντακόσια, ὁ δὲ
ἕτερος πεντήκοντα. 42 μὴ [b] ἐχόντων αὐτῶν [c] ἀποδοῦναι
ἀμφοτέροις [d] ἐχαρίσατο. [e] τίς οὖν αὐτῶν [, εἰπέ,] πλεῖον
ἀγαπήσει αὐτόν; 43 ἀποκριθεὶς ὁ Σίμων εἶπεν [f] Ὑπολαμβάνω ὅτι ᾧ [g] τὸ [g] πλεῖον [d] ἐχαρίσατο. ὁ δὲ εἶπεν αὐτῷ
[h] Ὀρθῶς ἔκρινας. 44 καὶ στραφεὶς πρὸς τὴν γυναῖκα
τῷ Σίμωνι ἔφη Βλέπεις ταύτην τὴν γυναῖκα; εἰσῆλθόν

z here only. 4 Kings iv. 1 al. (see ch. vi. 34, 35 reff.)
a = Matt. xviii. 28. Deut. xv. 2.
b = Matt. xviii. 25 reff.
c Matt. v. 26 reff.
d = 2 Cor. ii. 10. xii. 13. Col. ii. 13. L.P.+ (Sir. xii. 3 al.)
e = Matt. xxiii. 17, 19 reff.
f = Acts (i. 9) ii. 15 (ch. x. 30. 3 John 8) only. Job xxv. 3.
g sing., here only. Ps. lxxxix. 10. plur., Acts xix. 32. xxvii. 12. 1 Cor. ix. 19. x. 5 al. Exod. xxiii. 2 Ed-vat. (not B, Mai).
h Mark vii. 35 reff. Gen. xl. 16.

ins δηναρια bef πεντηκοντα D 69 lat-*a c* Syr syr-cu [aft, syr-jer].

42. rec aft εχοντων ins δε, with AI_eℵ rel lat-*b f* g_1 *q* syr copt goth æth arm [$Ambr_1$] (*et* insd in lat-*c e* Syr syr-cu [syr-jer]): om BDLPΞ vulg lat-*a* ff_2 g_2 *l* $Amphil_1$ $Orig_1$-int_1 Aug_1. om 2nd αυτων DI_e 69 latt æth arm $Ambr_1$: ins ABPΞℵ rel lat-*e f* Orig-int. om ειπε (*more likely to be dropped out than insd,* cf the mistake in A) BDLΞℵ 1 latt Syr syr-cu copt æth: ins I_eP rel syr goth, επι A. rec αυτον bef αγαπησει, with AI_eP rel tol lat-*f* goth: αυτον πλεον αγαπησει D (Scr's d) latt: om αυτον Δ (not Γ, Treg): txt BFLXΞℵ 33.

43. rec aft αποκριθεις ins δε, with AL[1]Pℵ rel lat-*a f q* syr [syr-jer] goth $Amphil_1$, and aft ο I_e 1 arm: txt BDL[2]Ξ vulg lat-*b c e* ff_2 $g_{1.2}$ *l* Syr copt.—om ο BLΓΞℵ. for πλειον, πλεον D.

44. for τω σιμωνι εφη, ειπεν τω σιμωνι D latt [syrr syr-cu syr-jer goth æth].

of their debt. This assumption itself is *absolutely necessary for the parable:* for if forgiveness is to awaken love in proportion to the magnitude of that which is forgiven, *sin* in such a connexion must be the *subjective debt* which is *felt* to exist, not the objective one, the magnitude of which *we* never can know, but God only: see on ver. 47 below. **πεντακόσια . . . πεντήκοντα**—a very different ratio from the ten thousand talents and the hundred pence in Matt. xviii. 21—35, because there it is intended to shew us how insignificant our sins towards one another are in comparison with the offence of us all before God. **42. μὴ ἐχόντων . . . . ἐχαρίσατο**] What depth of meaning there is in these words, if we reflect WHO said them, and by what means this forgiveness was to be wrought! Observe that the **μὴ ἐχ.** is pregnant with more than at first appears:—*how* is this incapacity discovered to the creditor in the parable? how, but *by themselves?* Here then is the *sense* and *confession* of sin; not a bare objective fact, followed by a decree of forgiveness: but the incapacity is an *avowed* one, the forgiveness is a *personal* one,—**ἀμφοτέροις.** **τίς οὖν . . ;**] The difficulty usually found in this question and its answer is not wholly removed by the subjective nature of the parable. For the sense of sin, if wholesome and rational, must bear a proportion, as indeed in this case it did, to the actual sins committed: and then we seem to come to the false conclusion, 'The more sin, the more love: let us then sin, that we may love the more.' And I believe this difficulty is to be removed by more accurately considering *what the love is,* which is here spoken of. It is an unquestionable fact, that the *deepest penitents* are, in *one kind* of love for Him who has forgiven them, the most devoted;—in that, namely, which consists in personal sacrifice, and proofs of earnest attachment to the blessed Saviour and His cause on earth. But it is no less an unquestionable fact, that *this love* is not the highest form of the spiritual life; that such persons are, by their very course of sin, incapacitated from entering into the length, breadth, and height, and being filled with all the fulness of Christ; that their views are generally narrow, their aims one-sided:—that though ἀγάπη be the greatest of the Christian graces, there are various kinds of it; and though the love of the reclaimed profligate may be and is intense of its kind, (and how touching and beautiful its manifestations are, as here!) yet *that kind* is not so high nor complete as the sacrifice of the *whole life,*—the bud, blossom, and fruit,—to His service to whom we were in baptism dedicated. For even on the ground of the parable itself, in that life there is a continually freshened sense of the need, and the assurance, of pardon, ever awaking devoted and earnest love. **43.**] In the **ὑπολαμβάνω** of Simon, we have, understood, "that is, if they feel as they ought."

44—46.] It would not appear

i see Mark xv. 24 ∥ J. Heb. xii. 10.
j ver. 38 (reff.).
k ch. xxii. 48. Rom. xvi. 16. 1 Cor. xvi. 20. 2 Cor. xiii. 12. 1 Thess. v. 26. 1 Pet. v. 14 only. Prov. xxvii. 6. Cant. i. 2 only.
l absol., = 2 Pet. iii. 4 only. 1 Macc. i. 11. see Acts xxiv. 11.

σου εἰς τὴν οἰκίαν, ὕδωρ μοι [i] ἐπὶ πόδας οὐκ ἔδωκας·
αὕτη δὲ τοῖς δάκρυσιν [j] ἔβρεξέν μου τοὺς πόδας καὶ ταῖς
θριξὶν αὐτῆς [j] ἐξέμαξεν. 45 [k] φίλημά μοι οὐκ ἔδωκας·
αὕτη δὲ [l] ἀφ' ἧς εἰσῆλθον οὐ [m] διέλιπεν [n] καταφιλοῦσά μου
τοὺς πόδας. 46 [o] ἐλαίῳ τὴν κεφαλήν μου οὐκ [op] ἤλειψας·
αὕτη δὲ [q] μύρῳ [p] ἤλειψεν τοὺς πόδας μου. 47 οὗ [r] χάριν,
λέγω σοι, [s] ἀφέωνται αἱ ἁμαρτίαι αὐτῆς αἱ πολλαί, ὅτι
ἠγάπησεν πολύ. ᾧ δὲ ὀλίγον [s] ἀφίεται, ὀλίγον ἀγαπᾷ.

ABDEF GHI$_e$K LMPSU VXΓΔΛ ΞΠℵ 1. 33. 69

...δε ολιγον α Ξ.

m here only. & constr., Jer. xvii. 8 al. n ver. 38 reff. o Mark vi. 13. James v. 14. 2 Kings xiv. 2. p Matt. vi. 17 reff. q vv. 37, 38. r Gal. iii. 19 al. 3 Kings xiv 16 A. [B def.] Sir. xxxvii. 5 al. s Matt. ix. 2 reff. Ps. xxiv. 18.

ins *και* bef *υδωρ* D 157. rec (for *μοι επι ποδας*) *επι τους ποδας μου*, with AI$_e^2$P rel vulg lat-*b c f g*$_2$ [æth] Amphil$_1$; *ποδας μου* I$_e^1$: *μου επι τους ποδας* LΞℵ copt : *μοι επι τους ποδας* X [33] : *επι ποδας μοι* D lat-*a ff*$_2$ *g*$_1$ *q* : *μοι επι ποδ. μου* goth [syr-jer] : txt B. (*The constr was perhaps gradually changed to suit the next clause.*) rec aft *θριξιν* ins *της κεφαλης* (*from ver* 38), with E rel syr-cu : om ABDI$_e$KLPXΞ[Π]ℵ 1 latt syrr [syr-jer] copt goth æth arm Ambr.

45. *εισηλθεν* L[1] 69 ev-y vulg lat-*a e ff*$_2$ *g*$_{1.2}$ [Syr syr-txt syr-jer] copt Amphil$_1$ Aug$_1$. *διελειπεν* AEGI$_e$KLM[S[2]]XΔΛΞ[Π]ℵ 33. 69 [Amphil$_1$]. *τους ποδας* bef *μου* P 259.

46. rec *μου* bef *τους ποδας* (*from last ver, as appears by the MS authority*), with KM S(e sil) XΔΛ[Π]ℵ : om *τους ποδας μου* DI$_e^1$ lat-*a b c e ff*$_2$ *l q* arm : om *μου* only I$_e^3$-marg(?) : txt ABPΞ rel vulg lat-*f*.—*τους ποδας μου* bef *ηλειψεν* LΞ Syr.

47. aft *οὑ χαριν* ins *δε* D-gr. for *λεγω*, *ειπον* ℵ[1]. for *αι αμαρτιαι αυτης αι πολλαι*, *αυτη πολλα* D lat-*ff*$_2$ *l* : *αυτη αι αμαρτιαι αυτης αι πολλαι* P [syrr syr-jer syr-cu arm], *ei peccata multa* vulg lat-*a c* [*f*$_1$ Orig-int$_1$ Ambr$_{alic}$] : *αυτης αι αμ. αι πολ.* AF (K)[Π]ℵ. om *οτι ηγ.* to *αγαπα* D lat-*e*. for *ω*, *ο* Ξ. aft *αφιεται* ins *και* B.

that Simon had been deficient in the ordinary courtesies paid by a host to his guests—for these, though marks of honour *sometimes* paid, were not (even the washing of the feet, except when coming from a journey) *invariably* paid to guests:—but that he had taken no *particular pains* to shew affection or reverence for his Guest. Respecting water for the feet, see Gen. xviii. 4: Judg. xix. 21. Observe the contrasts here:—**ὕδωρ**,—**δάκρυσιν** ('fudit lacrymas, sanguinem cordis,' Aug. Serm. xcix. (xxiii.) 1, vol. v.),—**φίλημα οὐκ ἔδωκ.** (on the *face*),—**καταφιλοῦσα τοὺς πόδας**:—**ἐλαίῳ τὴν κεφ.**,—**μύρῳ** (which was more precious) **τοὺς πόδας**. **ἀφ' ἧς εἰσῆλθ.**] These words will explain one difficulty in the circumstances of the anointing: how such a woman came into the guest-chamber of such a Pharisee. She appears by them to have entered *simultaneously with our Lord and His disciples.* Nor do vv. 36, 37 at all preclude this idea:—**ἐπιγνοῦσα ὅτι κατάκειται** may mean, 'having knowledge that He was going to dine,' &c. If she came in His train, the Pharisee would not exclude her, as He was accustomed to gather such to hear Him: it was the *touching* at which he wondered. **47.**] This verse has been found very difficult to fit into the lesson conveyed by the Parable. But I think there need be little difficulty, if we regard it thus. Simon had been offended at the uncleanness of the woman who touched our Lord. He, having given the Pharisee the instruction contained in the parable, and having drawn the contrast between the woman's conduct and his, now assures him, 'Wherefore, seeing this is so, I say unto thee, she is no longer unclean—her many sins are forgiven: *for* (thou seest that) *she loved much:* her conduct towards Me shews that love, which is a token that her sins are forgiven.' Thus the **ὅτι** is not the causative particle, '*because* she loved much;' but, as rightly rendered in E. V., **for she loved much**: '*for she has shewn that love, of which thou mayest conclude, from what thou hast heard, that it is the effect of a sense of forgiveness.*' Thus Bengel, 'Remissio peccatorum, Simoni non cogitata, probatur *a fructu*, ver. 42, qui est evidens et in oculos incurrit, quum illa sit occulta;'—and Calov., 'probabat Christus *a posteriori*.' But there is a deeper consideration in this solution, which the words of the Lord in ver. 48 bring before us. The *sense* of forgiveness of *sin* is not altogether correspondent to the sense of forgiveness of *a debt.* The latter must be altogether past, and a fact to be looked back on, to awaken gratitude: the former,

48 εἶπεν δὲ αὐτῇ [s] Ἀφέωνταί σου αἱ ἁμαρτίαι. 49 καὶ
...εαυτοις I_e. ἤρξαντο οἱ [t] συνανακείμενοι λέγειν [u] ἐν ἑαυτοῖς Τίς οὗτός
ἐστιν ὃς καὶ ἁμαρτίας [s] ἀφίησιν; 50 εἶπεν δὲ πρὸς
τὴν γυναῖκα Ἡ πίστις σου σέσωκέν σε, [v] πορεύου [v] εἰς
εἰρήνην.

VIII. 1 [w] Καὶ ἐγένετο [x] ἐν τῷ [xy] καθεξῆς, [w] καὶ αὐτὸς
[z] διώδευεν [a] κατὰ πόλιν καὶ κώμην κηρύσσων καὶ [b] εὐαγγελιζόμενος τὴν [b] βασιλείαν τοῦ θεοῦ, καὶ οἱ δώδεκα σὺν
αὐτῷ, 2 καὶ γυναῖκές τινες αἳ ἦσαν [c] τεθεραπευμέναι [c] ἀπὸ
πνευμάτων [d] πονηρῶν καὶ [e] ἀσθενειῶν, Μαρία ἡ καλου-
...επτα P. μένη Μαγδαληνή, ἀφ' ἧς δαιμόνια ἑπτὰ ἐξεληλύθει, 3 καὶ
Ἰωάννα γυνὴ Χουζᾶ [f] ἐπιτρόπου Ἡρώδου, καὶ Σουσάννα,
καὶ ἕτεραι πολλαί, [g] αἵτινες [h] διηκόνουν αὐτοῖς ἐκ τῶν
[i] ὑπαρχόντων αὐταῖς.

t Matt. xiv. 9 reff.
u ver. 39. Mark iii. 9 reff.
v ch. viii. 48 only. 1 Kings xx. 42. see Mark v. 34.
w ch. ii. 21 reff.
x here only. see ch. vii. 11 reff.
y ch. i. 3 reff.
z Acts xvii. 1 only. Gen. xiii. 17.
a Acts xiv. 23. xv. 21. xx. 23 al. fr.
b ch. iv. 43. xvi. 16. (Acts viii. 12.)
c ch. v. 15. vii. 21.
d = ch. vii. 21 reff.
e = ch. v. 15 reff.
f = Matt. xx. 8 (Gal. iv. 2) only †. 2 Macc. xi. 1. xiii. 2. xiv. 2 only.
g = Matt. vii. 15 reff. Deut. v. 26.
h = Matt. xx. 28 reff.
i w. dat., ch. xii. 15. Acts iv. 32 only. Gen. xxxi. 18 Ed-vat. [B def.] Job xx. 29 Bℵ. (gen., Matt. xix 21.)

48. *σοι* P 254 vulg lat-*b c* [*a e* g_1 *q*]. **49.** *εστιν* bef *ουτος* DP **1.** 69 latt copt.
50. aft *γυναικα* ins *γυναι* D. *εν ιρηνη in pace* D latt.

Chap. VIII. **1.** for *καθεξης*, *εξης* A. *διωδευσεν* ℵ 122(Sz) [Bas_1-ed]. for *συν αυτω*, *μετ' αυτου* D.

2. for *πονηρων*, *ακαθαρτων* ℵ. (*μαριαμ* ALP **1.** 33 Syr.) for *αφ*, *εξ* D. *επτα* bef *δαιμονια* D vulg(ed and some mss).—for *επτα*, *πολλα* H(sic): om F.

3. aft *αιτινες* ins *και* D lat-*a c* [*ff*$_2$ *l q*] $Mcion_1$-t. rec (for *αυτοις*) *αυτω* (*see Matt* xxvii. 55: *Mark* xv. 41), with ALMX[Π]ℵ **1.** 33 [vulg-clem](with fuld ing per) lat-*a b l* [*q*] syr-txt copt æth arm $Mcion_1$-t: txt BD rel am(with em forj gat jac san) lat-*c e f ff*$_2$ g_1 Syr syr-cu syr-mg goth Aug. rec (for *εκ*) *απο*, with X rel: txt A B(sic: see table) DKL[Π]ℵ **1.** 69 $Orig_1$. for *αυταις*, *αυτων* D ℵ[1](txt ℵ-corr[1](appy)·[3a]).

by no means so. The *expectation*, the *desire*, and *hope* of forgiveness, the *πίστις* of ver. 50, awoke this love; just as in our Christian life, the love daily awakened by a sense of forgiveness, yet is gathered under and summed up in a general faith and expectation, that 'in that day' all will be found to have been forgiven. The *ἄφεσις τῶν ἁμαρτιῶν*, into which we have been baptized, and in which we live, yet waits for that great *ἀφέωνταί σου αἱ ἁμαρτίαι*, which He will then pronounce.

The aorist **ἠγάπησεν** is in apposition with the aorists throughout vv. 44—46, as referring to the same facts.

Remark that the assertion regarding Simon is not *αἱ ὀλίγαι ἀφέωνται*, but *ὀλίγον ἀφίεται*; stamping the subjective character of the part relating to him:—he *felt*, or *cared about, but little forgiveness*, and his little love shewed this to be so: on the whole, see Bleek's note.

49.] This appears to have been said, not in an hostile, but a reverential spirit. Perhaps the **καί** alludes to the miracles wrought in the presence of John's messengers.

50.] See on ver. 47. The woman's faith embraced as her own, and awoke her deepest love on account of, that forgiveness, which the Lord now first formally pronounced. **εἰς εἰρήνην**, לְשָׁלוֹם 1 Sam. i. 17; not only 'in peace,' but implying the state of mind *to* which she might now look forward.

Chap. VIII. 1—3.] Jesus makes a circuit teaching and healing, with His twelve disciples, and ministering women. *Peculiar to Luke.* A general notice of our Lord's travelling and teaching in Galilee, and of the women, introduced again in ch. xxiii. 55; xxiv. 10, who ministered to Him. **2. δαιμόν. ἑπτά**] See ver. 30. **3.**] Prof. Blunt has observed in his Coincidences, that we find a reason here why Herod should say to his *servants* (Matt. xiv. 2), 'This is John the Baptist,' &c., viz.—because his *steward's wife* was a disciple of Jesus, and so there would be frequent mention of Him among the servants in Herod's court.

This is Herod Antipas. Johanna is mentioned again ch. xxiv. 10, and again

4 [j] Συνιόντος δὲ ὄχλου [k] πολλοῦ καὶ τῶν [l] κατὰ
πόλιν [m] ἐπιπορευομένων πρὸς αὐτὸν εἶπεν [n] διὰ παραβολῆς 5 Ἐξῆλθεν [o] ὁ σπείρων [p] τοῦ σπεῖραι τὸν [q] σπόρον
αὐτοῦ. καὶ ἐν τῷ σπείρειν αὐτόν, [r] ὃ μὲν ἔπεσεν παρὰ
τὴν ὁδόν, καὶ [s] κατεπατήθη, καὶ τὰ [t] πετεινὰ τοῦ οὐρανοῦ [u] κατέφαγεν αὐτό. 6 καὶ ἕτερον [v] κατέπεσεν ἐπὶ τὴν
πέτραν, καὶ [w] φυὲν [x] ἐξηράνθη διὰ τὸ μὴ ἔχειν [y] ἰκμάδα.
7 καὶ ἕτερον ἔπεσεν ἐν μέσῳ τῶν [z] ἀκανθῶν, καὶ [a] συμφυεῖσαι αἱ [z] ἄκανθαι [b] ἀπέπνιξαν αὐτό. 8 καὶ ἕτερον ἔπεσεν εἰς
τὴν γῆν τὴν ἀγαθήν, καὶ [w] φυὲν [c] ἐποίησεν [c] καρπὸν [d] ἑκατονταπλασίονα. ταῦτα λέγων [e] ἐφώνει Ὁ ἔχων ὦτα ἀκούειν
ἀκουέτω. 9 [f] ἐπηρώτων δὲ αὐτὸν οἱ μαθηταὶ αὐτοῦ [λέ-
γοντες] [g] Τίς [h] εἴη ἡ παραβολὴ αὕτη; 10 ὁ δὲ εἶπεν Ὑμῖν
[i] δέδοται [i] γνῶναι τὰ [i] μυστήρια τῆς βασιλείας τοῦ θεοῦ,
τοῖς δὲ λοιποῖς ἐν παραβολαῖς, ἵνα βλέποντες μὴ βλέπωσιν, καὶ ἀκούοντες μὴ συνιῶσιν. 11 [h] ἔστιν δὲ [k] αὕτη ἡ

Ξ ειπεν..
R [τον] σπορον..
...επι F.
ABDE GHKL MRSU VXΓΔΛ ΞΠℵ 1. 33. 69

j here only †. k Matt. xiv. 14. xx. 29 al. l ver. 1 reff. m here only. Lev. xxvi. 33. Ezek. xxxix. 14. 2 Macc. ii. 28 only. n = Acts xviii. 9. o || Mt. reff. p || Mt. al. Ps. cxlix. 7, 9. q ver. 11. Mark iv. 26, 27. 2 Cor. ix. 10 only. Lev. xxvi. 5. r see || Mt. reff. s Matt. v. 13 reff. t ||. Deut. xiv. 19, 20. u || Mt. reff. v Acts xxvi. 14. xxviii. 6 only. Neh. viii. 11. w here bis & Heb. xii. 15 (but intr.) only. Prov. xxvi. 9. x Matt. xxi. 19, 20. y here only. Job xxvi. 14. Jer. xvii. 8 only. z Matt. vii. 6 reff. Isa. v. 6. a here only †. Wisd. xiii. 13 only. (-φυτος, Rom. vi. 5) b || Mt. ver. 33 only †. Tobit iii. 8 (not ℵ) only. c Matt. iii. 8 reff. d Mark x. 30 (|| Mt. v. r.) only. 2 Kings xxiv. 3 only. e = ver. 54. ch. xvi. 24. xxi. 46. Dan. iv. 11 (14 Theod-F). f ch. ii. 46 reff. g = ch. xxiv. 17. John vii. 36. xvi. 17, 18. Ezek. xii. 22. h Matt. ix. 13 reff. i || Mt. (reff.) k = 1 John i. 5. 2 John 6 b.

4. *συνελθοντος* D 69 : *συνοντος* ℵ[1] 248-51 Scr's p. for *κατα*, *την* D-gr(*ad civitatem* D-lat). for *δια παραβολης*, *παραβολην τοιαυτην προς αυτους* D 39 lat-*b* [*l*] *q* æth.

5. om 1st *του* (*see* || *Mark*) DKΠ. *εαυτου* AMSVΓΔ. om *αυτον* D. for *ὅ*, *α* (|| *Matt*) B. for *παρα*, *επι* R. om *του ουρανου* (|| *Matt, cf* || *Mark*) D lat-*a b e ff*$_2$ *l q* Syr syr-cu. for *αυτο*, *αυτα* B, *αυτον* X.

6. for *ετερον*, *αλλο* (|| *Mark*) D. (So also in vv 7, 8.) rec (for *κατεπ.*) *επεσεν* (*from* || *Matt Mark*), with ADℵ rel : txt BLRΞ. for *επι*, *παρα* Ξ 248. om *την* B. aft *εξηρανθη* ins *και* ℵ[1](om ℵ-corr[1](appy)·[3a]).

7. for *εν μεσω*, *μεσον* D : *μεσω* 69 : *εμμεσω* ALPRΞ. for *συμφ.*, *φυεισαι* XΠ Scr's d ev-y. for *απεπν.*, *επνιξαν* ℵ[1].

8. for *επεσεν*, *εφυεν* (sic) ℵ[1]. rec (for *εις*) *επι* (*from* || *Matt, as the weight of MSS shews*), with D (Scr's g k q r ev-y, e sil) lat-*a c* Just$_1$: txt ABRΞℵ rel vulg lat-*b e f ff*$_2$ *g*$_{1.2}$ *l q* Hipp$_1$. aft *αγαθην* ins *και καλην* (*from* || *Matt Mark*) D lat-*a c e* Syr syr-cu arm. *εφυεν* L ℵ[1](txt ℵ-corr[1](appy)·[3a]). aft *φυεν* ins *και* D-gr ℵ[1](om ℵ-corr[1]) lat-*e f*.

9. om *αυτου* R lat-*a b c ff*$_2$ [arm]. om *λεγοντες* (*on acct of the indirect constr follg?*) BDLRΞℵ 1. 33 latt Syr syr-cu copt arm [Orig-int$_1$] : ins A rel lat-*f q* syr [syr-jer] goth æth. ins *το* bef *τις* D. om *ειη* LΓΞ. (*εἰ ἡ* (sic; Tischdf (N. T. Vat.) is in error) B[2].) *αυτη* bef *η παραβολη* LΞ 1 : bef *ειη* Bℵ.—for *τις* to *αυτη*, *περι της παραβολης* R. om *ἡ* B Scr's p.

10. *τα μυστ. τ. βασ. τ. θ.* bef *γνωναι* D. for *βλεπωσιν*, *ιδωσιν* DLΞ 1 : *βλεπωσιν και μη ιδωσιν* R. *ακουσαντες* A. aft *ακουοντες* ins *ακουσωσιν και* (|| *Mark*) R ℵ[1](om ℵ[3a], but restored) 69 copt.

in company with Mary Magdalene and others. Susanna is not again mentioned. **διηκ.**, providing food, and giving other necessary attentions.

4—15.] Parable of the Sower. Matt. xiii. 1—8, 18—23. Mark iv. 1—20. For the parable and its explanation, see notes on Matt., where I have also noticed the varieties of expression here and in Mark. On the relation of the three accounts to one another, see notes on Mark. Our Lord had retired to Capernaum,—and thither this multitude were flocking together to Him. **συνιόντος** is the present participle, which the E. V. overlooks. **τῶν κατὰ πόλιν**—'ex quavis urbe erat cohors aliqua,' Bengel. **ἐπιπορ.**, **coming up one after another.** It was

παραβολή. ὁ [l] σπόρος ἐστὶν ὁ λόγος τοῦ θεοῦ. 12 οἱ
δὲ παρὰ τὴν ὁδὸν εἰσὶν οἱ * ἀκούοντες, [m] εἶτα ἔρχεται ὁ
διάβολος καὶ αἴρει τὸν λόγον ἀπὸ τῆς καρδίας αὐτῶν,
ἵνα μὴ πιστεύσαντες σωθῶσιν. 13 οἱ δὲ ἐπὶ τῆς πέτρας, οἳ
ὅταν ἀκούσωσιν [n] μετὰ χαρᾶς [o] δέχονται τὸν λόγον, καὶ
οὗτοι ῥίζαν οὐκ ἔχουσιν, οἳ [p] πρὸς [p] καιρὸν πιστεύουσιν,
καὶ ἐν [q] καιρῷ [r] πειρασμοῦ [s] ἀφίστανται. 14 τὸ δὲ εἰς τὰς
[t] ἀκάνθας πεσόν, οὗτοί εἰσιν οἱ ἀκούσαντες, καὶ ὑπὸ
[u] μεριμνῶν καὶ πλούτου καὶ [v] ἡδονῶν τοῦ [w] βίου πορευόμενοι
[x] συνπνίγονται καὶ οὐ [y] τελεσφοροῦσιν. 15 τὸ δὲ ἐν τῇ
F αγαθη … καλῇ γῇ, οὗτοί εἰσιν [z] οἵτινες ἐν καρδίᾳ [a] καλῇ καὶ ἀγαθῇ
…εχουσ[ιν και] R. ἀκούσαντες τὸν λόγον [b] κατέχουσιν καὶ [c] καρποφοροῦσιν
ἐν [d] ὑπομονῇ. 16 Οὐδεὶς δὲ [e] λύχνον [e] ἅψας [f] καλύπτει
αὐτὸν [g] σκεύει ἢ [h] ὑποκάτω κλίνης τίθησιν, ἀλλ' ἐπὶ [i] λυχνίας τίθησιν, ἵνα οἱ [k] εἰςπορευόμενοι βλέπωσιν τὸ φῶς.

l ver. 5 reff. m = Mark iv. 17. James i. 15. n ||. ch. x. 17 al. 1 Chron. xxix. 22. o Acts viii. 14. xi. 1 al. p 1 Cor. vii. 5 only. Wisd. iv. 4. see 1 Thess. ii. 17. q = ch. i. 20. xix. 44. r ch. xxii. 28. James i. 2, 12. Deut. iv. 34. s = 1 Tim. iv. 1. t ver. 7. u || Mt. reff. v Tit. iii. 3. James iv. 1, 3. 2 Pet. ii. 13 only. Prov. xvii. 1. w = 2 Tim. ii. 4. 1 John ii. 16. x = || [Mk. bis] only †. (ver. 42.) y here only †. Ps. lxiv. 10 Symm. Jos. Antt. i. 6. 3.
z = Matt. vii. 15 reff. a see Heb. xiii. 18. b = 1 Cor. xi. 2. xv. 2. c ||. Mark iv. 28. Rom. vii. 4, 5. Col. i. 6, 10 only. Hab. iii. 17. Wisd. x. 7 only. d Gospp., here only. Rom. viii. 25. Heb. xii. 1. Rev. xiii. 10 al. e ch. xi. 33 (reff.). f Matt. viii. 24 reff. g Mark xi. 16. John xix. 29. Lev. vi. 28. h Matt. xxii. 44 reff. i ||. Heb. ix. 2. Rev. i. 12 al. Exod. xxv. 31. constr., see Matt. xxi. 7 reff. k = ch. xi. 33. xix. 30. Jer. xvii. 20.

11. aft λογος ins ο D.

12. * ἀκούσαντες B(sic) LUΞℵ: ακολουθουντες (*error*) D: ακουοντες A rel. for ειτα, ων *quorum* D. απο της καρδιας αυτων bef τον λογον D lat-*a b c f* [*l q*].

13. την πετραν D F(Wetst) Xℵ¹ Syr arm Orig₁. aft λογον ins του θεου ℵ¹. om 1st και ℵ¹. om ουτοι D lat-*e* syr-cu æth arm: **αυτοι** B¹.

14. om 2nd και D (not 69) lat-*c e f* æth. ins υπο bef ηδονων A 251 arm.

15. εις την καλην γην (|| *Matt*) D 157 Orig₁, *in bonam terram* latt (*in ter. bon.* D-lat). om καλη και D lat-*a b c e ff₂ l q* Ambr₁. aft τον λογον ins του θεου D. for καρποφορουσιν, τελεσφορουσιν (*from ver* 14) LΞ.

16. ins της bef κλινης D 346(Sz). for λυχνιας, την λυχνιαν (|| *Matt Mark*) DKM(U)XΠℵ. rec **επιτιθησιν** (*a similar corrn in* || *Mark*), with A rel: τιθι D: txt B(sic) FLΛΞℵ 1. 69 [Bas₁-ms]. om ινα to φως (|| *Mark*) B.

the desire of those who had been impressed by His discourses and miracles to be further taught, that brought them together to Him now. He spoke this parable sitting in a boat, and the multitude on the shore. **14.**] **ὑπό** must not be taken (Meyer) as belonging to **πορευόμενοι** (ὑπὸ μερ. ἀντὶ τοῦ μετὰ μερ., Euthym.), for no such usage of the preposition is found in the N. T., and the sense would be tame and frigid in the extreme; but ὑπό belongs to συνπνίγονται, and πορευόμενοι (which Meyer contends would have no meaning in this case) is in its ordinary sense of **going their way**, namely, *after having heard the word:* see for this usage of πορεύομαι Matt. ii. 8; ix. 13; xi. 4 al. (but not Mark, except xvi. 10 ff., where see note), and Luke vii. 22; ix. 13 al. freq. It is surprising that such a critic as Meyer should have upheld so absurd an interpretation as that impugned above. **τοῦ βίου** belongs to all three substantives. **15.**] It has been said, on Matt. ver. 23, that all *receptivity* of the seed is from God—and all men have receptivity enough to make it matter of condemnation to them that they receive it not in earnest, and bring not forth fruit:—but there is in this very receptivity a wide difference between men; some being false-hearted, hating the truth, deceiving themselves,—others being earnest and simple-minded, willing to be taught, and humble enough to receive with meekness the engrafted word. It is of these that our Lord here speaks; of this kind was Nathanael, the Israelite indeed in whom was no guile, John i. 48: see also John xviii. 37, "Every one that is of the truth, heareth My voice," and Trench on the Parables, in loc. **καλὸς καὶ ἀγαθός** has here nothing to do with its classical sense of εὐγενής, but is purely ethical,—and to be rendered as in E. V., **honest and good.** **ἐν ὑπομ.**]

17 οὐ γάρ ἐστιν κρυπτὸν ὃ οὐ φανερὸν γενήσεται, οὐδὲ ABDEF
[l] ἀπόκρυφον ὃ οὐ μὴ γνωσθῇ καὶ εἰς φανερὸν ἔλθῃ. GHKL MSUVX
18 [m] βλέπετε οὖν [m] πῶς ἀκούετε· ὃς ἂν γὰρ ἔχῃ, δοθήσε- ΓΔΛΞΠ ℵ 1.
ται αὐτῷ· καὶ ὃς ἂν μὴ ἔχῃ, καὶ ὃ δοκεῖ ἔχειν ἀρθή- 33. 69
σεται ἀπ' αὐτοῦ.
19 [n] Παρεγένοντο δὲ πρὸς αὐτὸν ἡ μήτηρ καὶ οἱ ἀδελφοὶ αὐτοῦ, καὶ οὐκ ἠδύναντο [o] συντυχεῖν αὐτῷ διὰ τὸν
ὄχλον. 20 [p] ἀπηγγέλη δὲ αὐτῷ [λεγόντων] Ἡ μήτηρ
σου καὶ οἱ ἀδελφοί σου ἑστήκασιν ἔξω ἰδεῖν σε θέλοντες.
21 ὁ δὲ ἀποκριθεὶς εἶπεν πρὸς αὐτοὺς Μήτηρ μου καὶ
ἀδελφοί μου οὗτοί [q] εἰσιν οἱ τὸν λόγον τοῦ θεοῦ [r] ἀκούοντες
καὶ [r] ποιοῦντες. ..ποιουντες Ξ.
22 Ἐγένετο δὲ ἐν [s] μιᾷ τῶν [s] ἡμερῶν, καὶ αὐτὸς [t] ἐνέβη

l ‖ Mk. reff.
m 1 Cor. iii. 10. Eph. v. 15.
n w. πρός, Matt. iii. 13. ch. vii. 4, 20. xi. 6. Acts xx. 18 only. Job ii. 11.
o here only†. 2 Macc. viii. 14 only.
p pass., here only. (ch. xiii. 1 al.) Josh. ii. 2.
q see Matt. xxvi. 26 reff.
r = ch. vi. 47, 49. Matt. vii. 24, 26.
s ch. v. 17 reff.
t Matt. viii. 23 reff.

17. for γενησεται, εσται D. rec ο ου γνωσθησεται (*from Matt* x. 26: *not as Mey, altered to txt, to corresp with* ελθη: *the rec reading was evidently originated by some scribe, who omitted to alter* ελθη *into accordance with it*), with A rel: ο ου μη γνωσθησεται F: αλλα ινα γνωσθη D: txt BLΞℵ 33 [Cyr$_2$]. (μη is over the line in L.)

18. rec γαρ bef αν, with DKUXΛ[Π] (S 1. 33, e sil); γαρ εαν A rel: txt BLΞℵ. αρθησεται απ' αυτων bef και ο δοκει εχειν D lat-*e*.

19. παρεγενετο BDX [copt]. aft η μητηρ ins αυτου Dℵ 69 ev-y lat-*c e* Syr syr-cu [syr-jer] copt Epiph$_2$.

20. rec (for απηγγ. δε) και απηγγ., with A rel vulg lat-*e f g$_2$* syrr syr-cu [syr-jer] goth æth arm Bas$_1$: txt BDLXΞℵ 33. 69 lat-*a b ff$_2$ g$_1$ l q* copt. om λεγοντων (*as unnecessary and harsh?*) BDLΔΞℵ 1. 33 latt Syr syr-cu [syr-jer] copt goth æth Bas$_1$. add οτι DLXℵ 1 ev-y lat-*a b c* [*e f ff$_2$ g$_1$ l q* syr syr-jer] goth Bas$_1$. om 1st σου ℵ. εξω bef εστηκασιν D lat-*c e* [æth] Bas$_1$ (Mcion$_1$-t). θελοντες bef σε BΞ: ζητουντες σε, omg ιδειν, (*see* ‖ *Matt*) D.

21. for πρ. αυτους, αυτοις D lat-*c e* [Bas$_1$]. ins η bef μητηρ and οι bef αδελφοι (‖ *Matt Mark*) DXΔ 69: om ABΞℵ rel. om του θεου ℵ. rec at end adds αυτον, with V(as corrd by origl scribe) X rel Syr syr-cu [syr-jer] copt Cyr$_1$ Mcion$_1$-t: om ABDH²LV¹ΞΠℵ 1. 33 latt syr goth æth arm Tit-bostr Thl Ambr.

22. rec (for εγεν. δε) και εγεν., with X rel syr-cu æth arm: txt ABDKLMUΠℵ 1. 33. 69 latt syrr copt goth. om εν ℵ¹(ins ℵ-corr¹). om και αυτος (D) ℵ¹(ins ℵ-corr¹).—αναβηναι αυτον D-gr. (ανεβη FLM 69.)

in patience—*consistently,* through the course of a life spent in duties, and amidst discouragements—ὁ ὑπομείνας εἰς τέλος, οὗτος σωθήσεται, Matt. xxiv. 13.

16—18.] Mark iv. 21—25, where see notes. The sayings occur in several parts of Matt. (v. 15; x. 26; xiii. 12), but in other connexions. Euthym. remarks well, εἰκὸς δὲ κατὰ διαφόρους καιροὺς τὰ τοιαῦτα τὸν χριστὸν εἰπεῖν. On the meaning of the separate sayings, see notes on the passages in Matt. Observe that ver. 18, **πῶς ἀκούετε** = τί ἀκούετε Mark, and **δοκεῖ ἔχειν** = ἔχει Mark.

19—21.] THE MOTHER AND BRETHREN OF JESUS SEEK TO SEE HIM. Matt. xii. 46-50. Mark iii. 31—35. The incident is introduced here without any precise note of sequence; not so in Matt., who says, after the discourse in ch. xii., ἔτι αὐτοῦ λαλοῦντος τοῖς ὄχλοις . . . . . and Mark καὶ ἔρχονται . . . . having before stated, ver. 21, that His relations went out to lay hold of Him,—for they said, "He is beside Himself." We must conclude therefore that *they* have it *in the exact place,* and that Luke only inserts it among the events of this series of discourses, as indeed it was, but *without fixing its place.* His account is abridged, and without marks of an eye-witness, which the others have.

20.] If we read λεγόντων, it may be observed that we have the same elliptic gen. absol. in Hom. Il. ε. 665 ff., οὔτις ἐπεφράσατ' οὐδ' ἐνόησε, μηροῦ ἐξερύσαι δόρυ μείλινον, ὄφρ' ἐπιβαίη, σπευδόντων:—Herod. i. 3, οὐδὲ ἐκδόντες ἀπαιτεόντων: see also οὐ προσδεχομένων, Thuc. iii. 34; ἐόντων,

εἰς πλοῖον καὶ οἱ μαθηταὶ αὐτοῦ, καὶ εἶπεν πρὸς αὐτοὺς
[u] Διέλθωμεν εἰς τὸ πέραν τῆς [v] λίμνης. καὶ [w] ἀνήχθησαν.
23 [x] πλεόντων δὲ αὐτῶν [y] ἀφύπνωσεν. καὶ [z] κατέβη [a] λαῖλαψ
ἀνέμου εἰς τὴν [v] λίμνην, καὶ [b] συνεπληροῦντο καὶ [c] ἐκινδύ-
νευον. 24 προσελθόντες δὲ [d] διήγειραν αὐτὸν λέγοντες
[e] Ἐπιστάτα ἐπιστάτα, ἀπολλύμεθα. ὁ δὲ ἐγερθεὶς [f] ἐπετίμησεν τῷ ἀνέμῳ καὶ τῷ [g] κλύδωνι τοῦ ὕδατος, καὶ
ἐπαύσαντο καὶ ἐγένετο [h] γαλήνη. 25 εἶπεν δὲ αὐτοῖς Ποῦ
ἡ πίστις ὑμῶν; φοβηθέντες δὲ ἐθαύμασαν, λέγοντες πρὸς
ἀλλήλους [i] Τίς ἄρα οὗτός ἐστιν, ὅτι καὶ τοῖς ἀνέμοις
[k] ἐπιτάσσει καὶ τῷ ὕδατι, καὶ ὑπακούουσιν αὐτῷ;
26 Καὶ [l] κατέπλευσαν εἰς τὴν χώραν τῶν Γερασηνῶν,
[m] ἥτις ἐστὶν [n] ἀντιπέρα τῆς Γαλιλαίας. 27 ἐξελθόντι δὲ
[o] αὐτῷ ἐπὶ τὴν γῆν [p] ὑπήντησεν [[o] αὐτῷ] ἀνήρ τις ἐκ τῆς

Ξ εθαυμασαν... R οτι και ...

u ‖ Mk. ch. ii. 15. Acts ix. 38. 3 Kings xviii. 5.
v ch. v. 1 reff.
w = here & Acts (xiii. 13 and passim) only.
x Gospp., here only. Acts xxi. 3. xxvii. 2, 6, 24. Rev. xviii. 17 only. Jon. i. 3.
y here only. Judg. v. 27 Ald. only.
z = Matt. vii. 25, 27 reff.
a ‖ Mk. 2 Pet. ii. 17 only. Jer. xxxii. (xxv.) 32.
b = here (ch. ix. 51. Acts ii. 1) only †.
c absol., 1 Cor. xv. 30 (Acts xix. 27, 40) only. Jon. i. 4.
d ‖ Mk. reff.
e ch. v. 5 reff. f ‖. Ps. cv. 9. g James i. 6 only. Jon. i. 4, 11, 12. h ‖ only †. Ps. cvi. 29 Symm.
i see ch. i. 66. Acts xii. 18. k = Mark i. 27 reff. l here only †. m = ch. ix. 30 reff.
n here only †. -ραν, Deut. xxx. 13 Aq. o constr., Matt. viii. 1 reff. p ‖ Mt. reff.

23. ειs την λιμνην bef ανεμου B lat-*a*. aft ανεμου ins πολλη D.
24. for επιστατα (twice), κυριε (‖ *Matt*) D: om 2nd επιστ. XΓ ℵ-corr(but reinsd) ev-y [latt syr-cu] copt goth arm-mss æth [Cyr_1]. **διεγερθειs** (*conformn to above and* ‖ *Mark*) BLℵ 33: txt AD rel. **του κλυδωνι** (sic) ℵ[1]. om του υδατοs D.
for επαυσαντο, επαυσατο EFGHℵ **1** vulg lat-*c f ff*$_2$ *g*$_{1.2}$ [*l*] syr-w-ob copt-ms [Cyr_1].
25. rec aft που ins εστιν, with D rel latt: om ABLXℵ **1** æth. for φοβηθ. δε, οι δε φοβηθεντεs Lℵ 33 syrr syr-cu. om προs αλληλουs ℵ ev-x: ins bef **λεγοντεs** LΞ 33 [vulg-cl] lat-*a b c* [*e ff*$_2$ *g*$_1$ *l q* syr]. om και υπακουουσιν αυτω B.
26. for και κατ., κατ. δε D am(with fuld em forj [tol]) lat-*a c* [*f ff*$_2$ *g*$_{1.2}$ *l q*]. κατεπλευσεν R Scr's (c) m. rec **γαδαρηνων**, with AR rel Syr syr-cu syr-txt goth: γεργεσηνων LXΞℵ (C[2]P in ver 37) **1**. 33 syr-jer copt æth arm [Cyr_1]: txt (*see prolegg*) BD (C[1] sah in ver 37) latt syr-mg. rec **αντιπεραν** (*cf* **περαν**, ‖ *Matt Mark*), with L: περαν MS: txt ABDRΞℵ rel.
27. κ. εξηλθον ε. τ. γ. και D. om 2nd αυτω BEΞℵ **1**. 33 arm [$Ps\text{-}Ath_1$]: ins ADR rel vss. τιs bef ανηρ B: om τιs D ev-y tol[1] lat-*a* (æth?).

Pind. Nem. i. 46, and other examples in Bernhardy, Syntax, p. 481. In ref. Josh. we have λέγοντες similarly placed.

22—25.] Jesus, crossing the lake, stills the storm. Matt. viii. 18, 23—27. Mark iv. 35—41. The chronology of this occurrence would be wholly uncertain, were it not for the precision of Mark, who has introduced it by ἐν ἐκείνῃ τῇ ἡμέρᾳ ὀψίας οὔσης,—i. e. *on the same day in which the preceding parables were delivered.* How it has come to be misplaced in Matthew, must ever be matter of obscurity. The fact *that it is so,* is no less unquestionable than the proof that it furnishes of the independence of the two other Evangelists. **22. ἐν μιᾷ τ. ἡμ.**] This serves to shew that Luke had no data by which he could fix the following events. If he had seen the Gospel of Mark, could this have been so?

23.] **ἀφύπ.** belongs to the later Greek, and even there more commonly signifies 'to awaken.' **κατέβη**—from the sky —or perhaps from the mountain valleys around: see Matt. vii. 27, and note on Acts xxvii. 14. **συνεπλ.**] **they** (= their ship) **were filling.** **24.**] See notes on Matt. **25.**] In Matt. this reproof comes *before* the stilling of the storm. But our account, and that in Mark, are here evidently exact.

26—39.] Healing of a dæmoniac in the land of the Gerasenes. Matt. viii. 28—34. Mark v. 1—20, in both of which places see notes. **26.**] **ἀντ. τ. Γ.**, a more precise description than τὸ πέραν Matt., or τὸ π. τῆς θαλ. Mark.

27.] **ἐκ τῆς πόλ.** belongs, not to ὑπήντ. (Meyer and E. V.), but to ἀνήρ τις—**a certain man of the city.** The man did not *come* from the city, but from the tombs. I put to any reader the question, whether it were possible for either

πόλεως, ὃς [q] εἶχεν δαιμόνια [r] ἐκ χρόνων [s] ἱκανῶν, καὶ ἱμάτιον οὐκ [t] ἐνεδιδύσκετο, καὶ ἐν οἰκίᾳ οὐκ [u] ἔμενεν, ἀλλ'
ἐν τοῖς [v] μνήμασιν. 28 ἰδὼν δὲ τὸν Ἰησοῦν [w] ἀνακράξας
[x] προσέπεσεν αὐτῷ καὶ φωνῇ μεγάλῃ εἶπεν [y] Τί ἐμοὶ καὶ
σοί, Ἰησοῦ υἱὲ τοῦ θεοῦ τοῦ [z] ὑψίστου; [a] δέομαί σου μή
με [b] βασανίσῃς. 29 [c] παρήγγελλεν γὰρ τῷ πνεύματι τῷ
ἀκαθάρτῳ ἐξελθεῖν ἀπὸ τοῦ ἀνθρώπου· [d] πολλοῖς γὰρ
[d] χρόνοις [e] συνηρπάκει αὐτόν, καὶ [f] ἐδεσμεῖτο [g] ἁλύσεσιν
καὶ [h] πέδαις φυλασσόμενος, καὶ [i] διαρήσσων τὰ [k] δεσμὰ
[l] ἠλαύνετο ὑπὸ τοῦ δαιμονίου εἰς τὰς ἐρήμους. 30 ἐπηρώτησεν δὲ αὐτὸν ὁ Ἰησοῦς λέγων Τί σοι ἐστὶν ὄνομα; ὁ
δὲ εἶπεν [m] Λεγεών, ὅτι δαιμόνια πολλὰ εἰσῆλθεν εἰς αὐτόν.

C -νη μεγαλη... ABCDE FGHKL MRSU VXΓΔΛ ΞΠℵ 1. 33. 69

q Matt. xi. 18 reff. (ch. iv. 33 reff.) r Acts ix. 33. John ix. 32. s of time, Luke only. ch. xx. 9. Acts viii. 11. ix. 23, 43 al. 2 Macc. i. 20. t (-διδύσκ.) ch. xvi. 19. Mark xv. 17 only. 2 Kings i. 24. u = John i. 39, 40 reff. v ‖ Mk. (bis) reff. w Mark vi. 49. ch. iv. 33 ‖ Mk. xxiii. 18. Judg. vii. 20. x = ‖ Mk. (reff.) y ‖. 2 Kings xvi. 10 al. z ‖ Mk. reff. a ch. v. 12. Gal. iv. 12 al. fr. L.P., exc. Matt. ix. 38. b ‖. 2 Pet. ii. 8. Rev. ix. 5 al. 1 Kings v. 3. c Mark viii. 6 reff. d dat., Acts viii. 11. Rom. xvi. 25. e Acts vi. 12. xix. 29. xxvii. 15 only. Prov. vi. 25. f here only †. Job xl. 20 Aq. g ‖ Mk. (3ce) reff. h ‖ Mk. bis only. Ps. civ. 18 al. i = Matt. xxvi. 65 ‖ Mk. ch. v. 6. Acts xiv. 14 only. Josh. vii. 6. k neut., Acts xvi. 26. xx. 23 only. (not LXX.) l = James iii. 4. 2 Pet. ii. 17 only. (Mark vi. 48 reff.) 2 Macc. ix. 4. m ‖ Mk. bis. Matt. xxvi. 53 only †.

for *ος ειχεν*, *εχων* Bℵ[1]. (not L, Treg.) for *εκ χρ.* to *ενεδ.*, *κ. χρονω ικανω ουκ ενεδυσατο ιματιον* BLΞ ℵ[1](txt (exc *ενεδ.*) ℵ[3a], but former reading restored) (1) 33 syr-mg syr-jer copt æth arm.—for *εκ*, *απο* D.—for *και*, *ος* D. *οικω* D. *εμεινεν* AL 1. *μνημειοις* D Scr's g.

28. rec ins *και* bef *ανακραξας*, with AR rel syr goth arm: om B(D)LXΞℵ 33 latt Syr syr-cu [syr-jer] copt æth.—*ανεκραξεν* and om *προσεπεσεν αυτω και* D(ins *και* D[2]-gr). om *ιησου* DR 1. 69 ev-y lat-*e* copt. om *του θεου* DΞ 1 lat-g_1 *l*.

29. rec *παρηγγειλε* (*corrn to aor, as so often*), with BFMSΛΞ 69: *ελεγεν* (‖ *Mark*) D lat-*e*: txt ACRℵ rel latt syrr syr-cu [syr-jer]. for *πνευματι*, *δαιμονιω* D lat-*e*. *εξελθε* [for *-θειν*] D lat-*e*. for *κ. εδεσμ.*, *εδεσμ. γαρ* D lat-*a b c*.—*εδεσμευετο* BLXΞℵ 33: txt ACDR rel. om 3rd *και* ℵ[1](ins ℵ-corr[1.3a]). (*διαρησσων*, so (with one *ρ*) AB[1]C(D)RUΔ 1.—*διερησσε* D lat-*c e* æth.) for *δεσμα*, *δεμονια* ℵ[1](txt ℵ-corr[1.3a]). aft *ηλαυνετο* ins *γαρ* D lat-*c e*. *απο* BΞ: txt ACDRℵ rel. rec *δαιμονος*, with AC[3]R rel lat-*a*: txt BC[1]DE[1]XΞℵ latt: *των δαιμονων* Λ Syr-ms syr-mg. *την ερημον* D [mm lat-*c f* ff_2] Syr syr-cu [syr-jer].

30. om *ο ιησους* ℵ[1]. om *λεγων* (*as* ‖ *Mark*) Bℵ 1 lat-*a b c e f* ff_2 *l q* Syr. ins *οτι* bef *σοι* Ξ[1](appy). *ονομα* bef *εστιν* BDLΞℵ 1. 33 latt Orig-int_1: *ον. σοι εστ.* C[2]: *ον. σοι*, omg *εστιν* (‖ *Mark*), C[1] [æth] (*hence the rearrangemts*): txt AC[3]R rel syr [arm] $Dial_1$. aft *λεγεων* ins *ονομα μοι* (‖ *Mark*) D lat-*c* syr-jer æth. for *οτι* to *εις αυτον*, *πολλα γαρ ησαν δαιμονια* D lat-(*a*) *c* (*f* ff_2).—*εισηλθεν* bef *δαιμονια πολλα* Bℵ vulg lat[-*q*] copt: txt ACRΞ rel lat-*a f* syrr [syr-jer] goth.

Mark or Luke to have drawn up their account from Matt., or with Matt. before them, seeing that he mentions *two possessed* throughout? Would no notice be taken of this? Then indeed would the Evangelists be but poor witnesses to the truth, if they could consciously allow such a discrepancy to go forth. Of the discrepancy itself, no solution has been proposed which can satisfy any really critical mind. That *one* should have been prominent, and the spokesman is of course *possible*, but such a hypothesis does not help us one whit. Where *two* healings take place, narrators do not commonly, being fully aware of this, relate in the singular: and this is the phænomenon to be accounted for. It is at least reasonable to assign accuracy in such a case to the more detailed and chronologically inserted accounts of Mark and Luke. **ἱμάτ. οὐκ ἐν.** is to be taken literally. The propensity to go entirely naked is a well-known symptom in certain kinds of raving madness: see Trench, Miracles, p. 167, note †. **29.**] **παρήγγελλεν, He was ordering,** imperf.: in the midst of this ordering, and as a consequence of it, the possessed man cried out, as in last verse. On **πολ. χρόνοις** see reff. Plutarch, Thes. 6, uses *χρόνοις πολλοῖς ὕστερον*:—not '*for many years*,' still less, '*oftentimes*,' E. V., Grot.;—but **during a long time. συνηρπ., it had seized him and carried him**: see reff. **ἐδεσμ.**] Notice the imperfect, giving the sense, **it was at-**

31 καὶ [n] παρεκάλουν αὐτὸν [n] ἵνα μὴ [o] ἐπιτάξῃ αὐτοῖς εἰς
τὴν [p] ἄβυσσον ἀπελθεῖν. 32 ἦν δὲ ἐκεῖ [q] ἀγέλη [q] χοίρων
[r] ἱκανῶν [s] βοσκομένων ἐν τῷ ὄρει· καὶ παρεκάλεσαν αὐτὸν
ἵνα [t] ἐπιτρέψῃ αὐτοῖς εἰς ἐκείνους εἰσελθεῖν. καὶ [t] ἐπέτρεψεν
αὐτοῖς. 33 ἐξελθόντα δὲ τὰ δαιμόνια ἀπὸ τοῦ ἀνθρώπου
εἰσῆλθον εἰς τοὺς [q] χοίρους, καὶ [u] ὥρμησεν ἡ [q] ἀγέλη κατὰ
τοῦ [v] κρημνοῦ εἰς τὴν [w] λίμνην καὶ [x] ἀπεπνίγη. 34 ἰδόντες
δὲ οἱ [s] βόσκοντες τὸ γεγονὸς ἔφυγον, καὶ ἀπήγγειλαν
εἰς τὴν πόλιν καὶ εἰς τοὺς ἀγρούς. 35 ἐξῆλθον δὲ
ἰδεῖν τὸ γεγονός, καὶ ἦλθον πρὸς τὸν Ἰησοῦν, καὶ εὗρον
καθήμενον τὸν ἄνθρωπον ἀφ' οὗ τὰ δαιμόνια ἐξεληλύθει
[y] ἱματισμένον καὶ [z] σωφρονοῦντα [a] παρὰ τοὺς πόδας
τοῦ Ἰησοῦ, καὶ ἐφοβήθησαν. 36 ἀπήγγειλαν δὲ αὐτοῖς

P και παρ... ...ορει F.

n Matt. xiv. 36 reff. o constr., Mark vi. 39 reff. p Rom. x. 7. Rev. ix. 1, 2, 11. xi. 7. xvii. 8. xx. 1, 3 only. Gen. i. 2. q || Mt. (reff.) r = Matt. xxviii. 12 reff. s || Mt. reff. t ||. Matt. viii. 21. Esth. ix. 14. u ||. Acts vii. 57. xix. 29 only. 1 Kings xv. 19. v || only. 2 Chron. xxv 12 bis only. w ch. v. 1, 2 reff. x ver. 7 || Mt. only †. Tobit iii. 8 (not ℵ) only. y || Mk. only †. z = || Mk. (reff.) 2 Cor. v. 13 only †. a ch. vii. 38. Acts xxii. 3.

31. for και παρ., παρ. δε D lat-*ff*$_2$. rec παρεκαλει (|| *Mark*), with APR U(Treg, expr) Ξ rel copt-ms goth: txt BCDFLSℵ 1. 33. 69 copt arm Cyr$_2$. om αυτον D.
32. om ικανων D 49 lat-*c*: for ικ., πολλων (|| *Matt*) X. βοσκομενη (*from* || *Matt Mark*) B D-gr KUΠℵ 69 lat-*a* Syr [syr-jer arm] æth: txt ACPRΞ rel vulg lat-*b c* [*f ff*$_2$ *g*$_{1.2}$ *l q*] D-lat syr-cu syr copt goth. for και παρ., παρ. δε D. rec παρεκαλουν (|| *Matt*), with AC[3]DPRℵ[1] rel vulg lat-*g*$_{1.2}$ [syrr syr-cu] copt: txt (|| *Mark, so that it is not easy to decide, except by txt being less usual*) BC[1]LΞℵ[3a] 1. 33 lat-*a b c f ff*$_2$ [*l*] *q* goth. aft ινα ins μη A. 1st αυτοις bef επιτρεψη LRΞ 33. for επιτρεψη to εισελθειν, εις τ. χοιρους εισελθωσιν D; simly lat-*a b ff*$_2$ *l q* [Syr syr-cu syr-jer]. for last και, ο δε D. om 2nd αυτοις ℵ[1] [Scr's f].
33. rec εισηλθεν, with U (S 1. 69, e sil): ωρμησαν *abierunt* D: txt ABCPRΞℵ rel. for και ωρμ., ωρμ. δε D. for λιμνην, θαλασσαν (||) ℵ 28. 435(Sz) [lat-*a c*]. απεπνιγοντο C lat-*b c ff*$_2$; απεπνιγησαν S Scr's g.
34. rec (for γεγονος) γεγενημενον, with X rel: txt ABCDKLPRUΞΠℵ 1. 33. 69. (εφυγαν DΛ.) rec ins απελθοντες (|| *Matt*) bef απηγγειλαν, with (Scr's c s, e sil) æth: om ABCDPRΞℵ rel latt syrr syr-cu [syr-jer] copt goth arm.
35. for ver, παραγενομενων δε εκ της πολεως και θεωρησαντων καθημενον τον δαιμονιζομενον σωφρονουντα και ιματισμενον καθημενον παρα τους ποδας του ιησου εφοβηθησαν D. for εξηλθ. δε, και εξηλθ. C[1](appy) 1 Syr syr-cu [syr-jer] æth. (ηλθαν and ευραν B[1].) τον ανθρωπον bef καθημενον P 1 vulg lat-*b c f ff*$_2$ *g*$_{1.2}$ [copt]. for εξεληλυθει, εξηλθεν B ℵ[1](-θον ℵ[3a]) lat-*f*. om του (bef ιησου) B.
36. for δε, γαρ D lat-*c*.—και απηγγ. C Syr syr-cu [syr-jer æth]. add λεγοντες ℵ.

tempted to bind him. **διαρ. τ. δ.**] The unnatural increase of muscular strength is also observed in cases of raving madness (as indeed also in those of any strong concentration of the will): see Trench as above. **30.**] Lightfoot (on Mark v. 9) quotes instances of the use of לגיון, for a great number, in the Rabbinical writings. The fact of *many dæmons* having entered into this wretched man, sets before us terribly the utter break-up of his personal and rational being. The words will not bear any figurative rendering, but must be taken literally (see ver. 2 of this chap., and ch. xi. 24 ff.); viz. that in the same sense in which other poor creatures were possessed by *one evil spirit* (see note on || Matt.), this man, and Mary Magdalene, were possessed by *many*. **31. τ. ἄβυσσον**] This word is sometimes used for Hades in general (Rom. x. 7), but more usually in Scripture for the abode of damned spirits: see reff. This last is certainly meant here—for the request is co-ordinate with the fear of torment expressed above (see Greswell on the Parables, v. (pt. 2) 365, and note on ch. xvi. 23). But, as Bp. Wordsw. remarks, we must distinguish between ἄβυσσος, the ad interim place of torment, and the lake of fire into which the devil will be cast by Christ at the end: see Rev. xx. 3, 10. **35.**] **ἐξῆλθ.**, viz. the people in the town and country = πᾶσα ἡ πόλις Matt.; here understood in ἀπήγ. εἰς τ. πόλ. κ. εἰς τ. ἀγ. **παρὰ τ. π. τ. Ἰη.**] This particularity denotes an eye-witness. The phrases common to Mark

[καὶ] οἱ ἰδόντες [b]πῶς [c]ἐσώθη ὁ [d]δαιμονισθείς. 37 καὶ ABCDE GHKL MPRSU VXΓΔΛ ΞΠℵ 1. 33. 69
[e]ἠρώτησεν αὐτὸν ἅπαν τὸ πλῆθος τῆς [f]περιχώρου τῶν
Γερασηνῶν ἀπελθεῖν ἀπʼ αὐτῶν, ὅτι φόβῳ μεγάλῳ
[g]συνείχοντο· αὐτὸς δὲ [h]ἐμβὰς εἰς πλοῖον [i]ὑπέστρεψεν.
38 [k]ἐδεῖτο δὲ αὐτοῦ ὁ ἀνὴρ ἀφʼ οὗ ἐξεληλύθει τὰ
δαιμόνια εἶναι σὺν αὐτῷ. [l]ἀπέλυσεν δὲ αὐτὸν λέγων
39 [i]Ὑπόστρεφε εἰς τὸν οἶκόν σου, καὶ [m]διηγοῦ ὅσα σοι
[n]ἐποίησεν ὁ θεός. καὶ ἀπῆλθεν [o]καθʼ [o]ὅλην τὴν [o]πόλιν
[p]κηρύσσων ὅσα [n]ἐποίησεν αὐτῷ ὁ Ἰησοῦς.
40 Ἐγένετο δὲ [q]ἐν τῷ [i]ὑποστρέψαι τὸν Ἰησοῦν, [r]ἀπ-
εδέξατο αὐτὸν ὁ ὄχλος· ἦσαν γὰρ πάντες [s]προςδοκῶντες
αὐτόν. 41 καὶ ἰδοὺ ἦλθεν ἀνὴρ ᾧ ὄνομα Ἰάειρος, καὶ
αὐτὸς ἄρχων τῆς συναγωγῆς ὑπῆρχεν· καὶ [t]πεσὼν παρὰ
τοὺς πόδας τοῦ Ἰησοῦ [u]παρεκάλει αὐτὸν εἰςελθεῖν εἰς

b 1 Mk. ch. xiv. 7 al. c = Matt. ix. 21 reff. d Matt. viii. 16 reff. e w. inf., ch. v. 3 John iv. 40. Acts iii. 3. x. 48. f Matt. xiv. 35 al. Deut. iii. 13, 14. g = Matt. iv. 24. ch. iv. 38. Job iii. 24. xxxi. 23. (Acts xviii. 5.) h Matt. viii. 23 reff. i ch. ii. 20 reff. k w. inf., Acts xxvi. 3. (2 Cor. x. 2.) l Matt. xiv. 15 reff. m Mark v. 16 reff. Ps. xlvii. 13. n ch. i. 49 al. o 2 Macc. v. 2. p = Mark i. 45. v. 20. vii. 36. q ch. iii. 21 reff. r = [ch. ix. 11.] Acts xviii 27 xxi. 17 xxviii. 30 2 Macc. iii. 9 al. s ch. i. 21 reff. t = Matt. iv. 9 reff. u Mark v. 17 reff.

om και BCDLPXℵ 33. 69 lat-*a b c f l* [*q*] Syr syr-cu [syr-jer] copt arm: ins AR rel vulg lat-ff_2 (g_1?) syr goth. for δαιμονισθεις, ο ληγαιων D^3, ο λιων D^1-gr, *a legione* vulg lat-*f* ff_2 $g_{1.2}$ *l q*.

37. for και ηρωτ., ηρωτ. δε D lat-*a* sah. rec ηρωτησαν, with DΞ rel vulg lat-*b c f* $g_{1.2}$ [*l q* Syr syr-cu syr-jer] coptt goth [æth Bas$_1$]: txt ABCKMPR S(Tischdf) Πℵ 33. 69 lat-*a* syr, επηρωτησεν X. for απαν, παν ℵ.—for αυ. απαν τ. πλ. τ. περ., τον ιησουν παντες και η χωρα D. rec γαδαρηνων, with AR ℵ^{3a}(but γεργεσ. restored) rel syrr syr-cu goth [Bas$_1$]: γεργεσηνων C^{2}LPXℵ^1 1. 33. 69 [syr-jer] copt æth arm: txt BC^{1}D latt sah. for οτι φοβω, φ. γαρ D lat-*c* goth. for αυτ. δε εμ., ενβας δε D: om δε A. rec ins το bef πλοιον, with AP rel [Bas$_1$]: om BCLRXℵ 1. 33 goth arm.—om εις πλ. D lat-*l* Ambr$_1$. επεστρεψαν V(Tischdf) ℵ^1: συνεστρεψεν ℵ-corr^1: txt ℵ^{3a}.

38. rec εδεετο, with C^{1}Rℵ^1 rel [Bas$_1$]: ηρωτα D: εδεειτο AP: txt BC^{2}LX ℵ-corr^1 (but -εε- restored) 33 Cyr$_1$. τα δαιμονια bef εξεληλυθει CRX 1. 69 vulg lat-*b c* sah goth. for ειναι, ινα η (*see* || *Mark*) P. rec aft αυτον ins ο ιησους, with ACPR rel vulg lat-(*a*) *f* ff_2 g_2 *q* syrr syr-cu goth: om BDLℵ 1 lat-*b c* g_1 *l* [syr-jer] coptt æth arm Cyr$_1$.

39. for υποστρεφε, πορευου D lat-*c*. for και διηγου, διηγουμενος D. rec εποιησε bef σοι, with AC^3 rel syrr copt goth: σοι ο θ. επ. D lat-*f*: σοι ο κυριος πεποιηκεν και ηλεησεν σε (|| *Mark*) C^1: txt BLP(R)Xℵ 1. 33 vulg lat-*a c l* Tit-bostr$_1$ Vict$_1$ (Cyr$_1$).—πεποιηκεν CR Cyr$_1$. απελθων κατα τ. πολιν εκηρυσσεν D.

40. εν bef δε, omg εγενετο, BLR ℵ^{3a}(but txt restored) 1. 33 Syr syr-cu coptt æth Mcion-e: txt ACDPℵ^1 rel latt syr goth [(arm)]. υποστρεφειν BRℵ. αποδεξασθαι and τον οχλον D. om ο C^1. for 2nd αυτον, τον θεον ℵ^1(txt ℵ-corr^1).

41. for ιδου ηλθεν, ελθων D lat-*c*. (ω to 1st και is omd by D^1-gr, the space having been occupied by της συναγ. πεσων (*from below*); supplied by D$^{8 \text{ or } 11}$.) ουτος (*from ignorance of reference of* αυτος) BDR 1. 69 lat-*a f* copt [goth æth]: txt APℵ vulg lat-*b* ff_2 $g_{1.2}$ [*l q*] syr [syr-jer] arm. (C uncert.) om υπηρχεν και D lat-*c* Syr. for παρα, υπο D. om του (bef ιησου) BP S(Tischdf) ℵ^1: ins ACDRℵ^{3a} rel [Damasc$_1$]. ινα εισελθη C^1(appy).

and Luke, e. g. ἱματ. καὶ σωφ., οἱ ἰδόντες, denote a common origin of the two narratives, which have however become considerably deflected, as comparison will shew. **38, 39.**] See notes on Mark.

40–56.] Raising of Jaeirus's daughter, and healing of a woman with an issue of blood. Matt. ix. 1, 18–26. Mark v. 21–43. Our account is that one of the three which brings out the most important points, and I have therefore selected it for full comment. **40.**] **ἐν τῷ ὑπ., when Jesus had returned. ἀπεδέξ., welcomed Him:** see reff. **ἦσαν γ.**] Here we have an eye-witness again. **41.**] **ἄρχων—a ruler,** = εἷς τῶν ἀρχισυναγώγων Mark;

τὸν οἶκον αὐτοῦ, 42 ὅτι θυγάτηρ [v] μονογενὴς ἦν αὐτῷ ὡς
[w] ἐτῶν δώδεκα, καὶ αὕτη [x] ἀπέθνησκεν. ἐν δὲ τῷ ὑπάγειν
αὐτόν, οἱ ὄχλοι [y] συνέπνιγον αὐτόν. 43 καὶ γυνὴ οὖσα
[z] ἐν [a] ῥύσει αἵματος [b] ἀπὸ ἐτῶν δώδεκα, ἥτις [c] ἰατροῖς
[d] προςαναλώσασα ὅλον τὸν [e] βίον οὐκ [f] ἴσχυσεν ἀπ'
οὐδενὸς θεραπευθῆναι, 44 προςελθοῦσα [g] ὄπισθεν ἥψατο
τοῦ [h] κρασπέδου τοῦ ἱματίου αὐτοῦ, καὶ [i] παραχρῆμα
[k] ἔστη ἡ [a] ῥύσις τοῦ αἵματος αὐτῆς. 45 καὶ εἶπεν ὁ Ἰησοῦς
Τίς ὁ ἁψάμενός μου; ἀρνουμένων δὲ πάντων εἶπεν ὁ

v ch. vii. 12 reff.
w ‖ Mk. reff.
x so -ων, Heb. xi. 21.
y = here (ver. 14 ‖ [Mk. bis]) only +.
z ‖ Mk. Mark i. 23. Rom. iv. 10.
a here (bis) & ‖ Mk. only. Lev. xv. 25.
b Rom. xv. 23.
c ch. iv. 23 reff.
d here only +.
e = Mark xii. 44 reff.
f = Matt. viii. 28 reff.
g Matt. xv. 23 reff.
h ‖ Mt. reff.
i Matt xxi. 19, 20 reff.
k = here only. Jon. i. 15.

την οικιαν D(appy).

42. for οτι to αυτω, ην γαρ θυγ. αυτω μονογ. D.—om ην ℵ[1]. om ως D 240 sah æth. for και αυτ. απεθ., αποθνησκουσα D(-σκον D[1] appy, but altered by origl scribe: Scriv) Syr syr-jer[2]. for εν δε τω υπαγειν, και εγενετο εν τω πορευεσθαι C[1]DP arm: txt ABC[3]Rℵ rel syrr syr-cu [syr-jer coptt] goth æth. συνεπνιγαν D: συνεθλιβον (‖ *Mark*) CL 33. 69, συνεθλιγον U.

43. for ητις to θεραπευθηναι, ην ουδε εις ισχυεν θεραπευσαι D sah.—ιατροις to βιον is also omd in B arm-zoh. rec (for ιατροις) εις ιατρους; εις τους ιατρους Orig: txt ACPRΞℵ rel Scr's-mss. aft βιον ins αυτης CX latt syrr [syr-cu syr-jer] copt goth æth arm-usc Ambr: εαυτης και ℵ[1]. rec (for απ') υπ', with PΞ[2]ℵ rel Orig$_1$, υπο C: παρ' 69: txt ABRΞ[1].

44. aft προςελθουσα ins δε C(appy) copt-dz. om οπισθεν D 258: ins aft ηψατο KΠ. om του κρασπεδου (‖ *Mark*) D lat-*a ff*$_2$ [*l*]. om αυτου A[1](perhaps).

45. for και to 1st μου, ο δε ιησους γνους την εξελθουσαν εξ αυτου δυναμιν επηρωτα

—in Matt. only ἄρχων. **42.**] **μονογ.**, peculiar to Luke, but perhaps implied in τὸ θυγάτριον of Mark. **ἀπέθν., was dying.** In Matt. she is represented as *already dead*. He is not aware of the subsequent message to Jaeirus, and narrates concisely and generally. The crowd seems to have followed to see what would happen at Jaeirus's house: see ver. 54.

43.] **προςαναλ.**, 'having, *besides all her suffering*, spent,' &c. But,—see notes on μὴ προςεῶντος τοῦ ἀνέμου, Acts xxvii. 7, and on συμμαρτυρεῖν, Rom. ii. 15; viii. 16; ix. 1,—**προς-** may denote the *direction* or tendency of her spending. Mark adds, that she grew nothing better, but rather worse. The omission of this clause, ἰατρ. προσαν. ὅλ. τ. β., in some of the best MSS., is curious. I have not ventured to exclude it, on account of the characteristic ἅπαξ λεγόμενον **προςαναλώσασα**, which seems to betray St. Luke's hand. The **ἀπ'** instead of ὑπ', which latter may have come from the ὑπὸ πολλῶν ἰατρῶν of St. Mark, conveys a slightly differing sense. ὑπό is more of direct agency, ἀπό of ultimate derivation. She could get no relief from any system of treatment adopted by any. **44.**] Her inner thoughts are given in Mark, ver. 28. There was doubtless a weakness and error in this woman's view;—she imagined that healing power flowed as it were magically out of the Lord's person; and she touched the fringe of his garment as the most *sacred*, as well as the most accessible part: see Matt. xxiii. 5: Num. xv. 37—40. But she *obtained what she desired*. She sought it, though in error, yet *in faith*. And she obtained it, because this faith was known and recognized by the Lord. It is most true objectively, that there did go forth healing virtue from Him, and from his Apostles (see Mark vi. 56: Luke vi. 19: Acts v. 15; xix. 12), but it is also true that, in ordinary cases, only those were receptive of this whose faith embraced the truth of its existence, and ability to heal them. The error of her view was overborne, and her weakness of apprehension of truth covered, by the strength of her faith. And this is a most encouraging miracle for us to recollect, when we are disposed to think despondingly of the ignorance or superstition of much of the Christian world: that He who accepted this woman for her faith even in error and weakness, may also accept them. **45.**] We are not to imagine that our Lord *was ignorant* of the woman, or any of the circumstances. The question is asked to draw out what followed. See, on the part of Jesus Himself, an undeniable instance of this, in ch. xxiv. 19—and note there. The healing took place *by His*

Πέτρος καὶ οἱ σὺν αὐτῷ [l] Ἐπιστάτα, οἱ ὄχλοι [m] συνέχουσίν
σε καὶ [n] ἀποθλίβουσιν [καὶ λέγεις Τίς ὁ ἁψάμενός μου;]
46 ὁ δὲ Ἰησοῦς εἶπεν Ἥψατό μού τις· ἐγὼ γὰρ ἔγνων
[op] δύναμιν [p] ἐξεληλυθυῖαν ἀπ᾽ ἐμοῦ. 47 ἰδοῦσα δὲ ἡ γυνὴ
ὅτι οὐκ [q] ἔλαθεν [r] τρέμουσα ἦλθεν, καὶ [s] προσπεσοῦσα αὐτῷ
δι᾽ ἣν αἰτίαν ἥψατο αὐτοῦ ἀπήγγειλεν [t] ἐνώπιον παντὸς
τοῦ λαοῦ, καὶ ὡς ἰάθη [i] παραχρῆμα. 48 ὁ δὲ εἶπεν αὐτῇ

...δυναμιν G. ABCDE HKLM PRSU VXΓΔΛ ΞΠℵ 1. 33. 69

l ch. v. 5 reff. m = here only. see ch. xix. 43. 1 Kings xxiii. 8. n here only. Num. xxii. 25 (only ?). o = Matt. xiv. 2 reff. p ‖ Mk. ch. vi. 19. q Mark vii. 24 reff. r ‖ Mk. 2 Pet. ii. 10 only. Isa. lxvi. 2 al. s Mark iii. 11 reff. t ch. xii. 9. 1 Kings xv. 30.

τις μου ηψατο (*see* ‖ *Mark*) D lat-*a*. om *και οι συν αυτω* BΠ 253 Scr's p w[1] syr-cu syr-jer sah.—rec (for *συν αυτω*) *μετ᾽ αυτου*, with X rel: txt ACDLPRUΞℵ 1. 33. 69. om *και λεγεις* to 2nd *μου* BLℵ 1 coptt arm: ins AC(D)PRΞ rel latt syrr syr-cu [syr-jer] goth æth.—for *ο αψ. μου*, *μου ηψατο* D vulg lat-*b c f*.

46. om *ιησους* DΞ lat-*a* Syr. (Tregelles expressly states that L 1 syr-cu syr do not omit *ιησους*.) rec (for *εξεληλυθυιαν*) *εξελθουσαν* (‖ *Mark*), with ACDPRΞ rel $Orig_1$ [Cyr_1]: txt BLℵ 33 $Orig_1$ [Cyr-jer_1].

47. om *ιδουσα* to *ηλθεν* ℵ[1](ins ℵ-corr[1]). for *τρεμουσα*, *εντρομος ουσα* D. om *δι ην αιτιαν ηψατο αυτου*, and for *απηγ.*, *διηγγειλεν* ℵ.—om *ηψατο αυτου* A[1]. rec aft *απηγγειλεν* ins *αυτω*, with C[1](appy) PR rel syr [sah] goth: om ABC[2]DLXΞ [Π]ℵ 1. 33. 69 latt Syr syr-cu copt æth arm. for *ως*, *οτι* D: *ευθεως* Ξ: *εως* 69 [omg *και*]: om Λ[1].

48. aft *ο δε* ins *ιησους* CMPRXΛ Syr goth. om *αυτη* ℵ fuld sah. rec aft *αυτη* ins *θαρσει* (*from* ‖ *Matt*), with ACPR rel lat-*q* syrr goth æth arm: om BDLΞℵ

will, and *owing to His recognition of her faith*: see similar questions, Gen. iii. 9, and 2 Kings v. 25. **ὁ Πέτ. κ. οἱ σ. αὐ.**] A detail contained only here. On the latter part of this verse many instructive remarks have been made in sermons—see Trench, Mir. p. 192, note (edn. 2)—to the effect that many press round Christ, but few touch Him, only the faithful. Thus Augustine, 'Sic etiam nunc est corpus ejus, id est, Ecclesia ejus. Tangit eam fides paucorum, premit turba multorum' (Serm. lxii. 3 (5), vol. v.). And Chrysostom, *ὁ πιστεύων εἰς τὸν σωτῆρα ἅπτεται αὐτοῦ· ὁ δὲ ἀπιστῶν θλίβει αὐτὸν καὶ λυπεῖ*. It is difficult to imagine how the miracle should be, as Bp. Wordsw., "a solemn warning to all who crowd on Christ:" or how such a forbidding to come to Him should be reconciled with *δεῦτε πρός με πάντες . . .* Rather should we say, seeing it was one of those that thus crowded on Him who obtained grace from Him, that it is a blessed encouragement to us not only to crowd on Him, but even to touch Him: so to crowd on Him as never to be content till we have grasped if it be but His garment for ourselves: not to despise or discourage any of the least of those who "make familiar addresses to Him in (so called) religious hymns," seeing that thus some of them may touch Him to the healing of their souls. I much fear that if my excellent friend had been keeping order among the multitude on the way to the house of Jaeirus, this poor woman would never have been allowed to get near to Jesus. But I hope and trust that he and I shall rejoice together one day in His presence amidst a greater crowd, whom no man can number, of all nations, and kindreds, and people, and tongues. **47.**] It is not necessary (though perhaps probable), from the **ἀρν. δὲ πάντων** ver. 45, that *the woman* should also have denied with them. She may have hidden herself among the crowd. Our Lord (Mark ver. 32) looked around to see *τὴν τοῦτο* **ποιήσασαν**—a wonderful precision of expression, by which His absolute knowledge of the whole matter is set before us. **τρέμ.** + *εἰδυῖα ὃ γέγονεν αὐτῇ* Mark; which is implied here. All this is omitted in Matt.; and if we had only his account, we should certainly *derive the wrong lesson* from the miracle; for there we miss altogether the reproof, and the shame to which the woman is put; and the words of our Lord look like an encomium on her *act itself*. Her confession **ἐνώπ. παν. τ. λ.**, is very striking here, as shewing us that Christ *will have Himself openly confessed, and not only secretly sought*: that our Christian life is not, as it is sometimes called, merely '*a thing between ourselves and God*;' but a *good confession*, to be witnessed *ἐνώπιον παν. τ. λ.* **48.**] How lovingly does our Lord re-assure the trembling woman; her faith saved her—not merely in the act of touching, but as now completed by

Θύγατερ, ἡ πίστις σου [u] σέσωκέν σε, [v] πορεύου εἰς εἰρήνην.
49 ἔτι αὐτοῦ λαλοῦντος ἔρχεταί τις παρὰ τοῦ [w] ἀρχισυναγώγου λέγων αὐτῷ ὅτι τέθνηκεν ἡ θυγάτηρ σου· μὴ
[x] σκύλλε τὸν διδάσκαλον. 50 ὁ δὲ Ἰησοῦς ἀκούσας ἀπεκρίθη αὐτῷ [λέγων] Μὴ φοβοῦ, [y] μόνον πίστευσον, καὶ
[u] σωθήσεται. 51 εἰσελθὼν δὲ εἰς τὴν οἰκίαν οὐκ [z] ἀφῆκεν
εἰσελθεῖν τινα σὺν αὐτῷ εἰ μὴ Πέτρον καὶ Ἰωάννην καὶ
Ἰάκωβον, καὶ τὸν πατέρα τῆς παιδὸς καὶ τὴν μητέρα.
52 ἔκλαιον δὲ πάντες καὶ [a] ἐκόπτοντο αὐτήν. ὁ δὲ εἶπεν
Μὴ κλαίετε· οὐ γὰρ ἀπέθανεν, ἀλλὰ [b] καθεύδει. 53 καὶ
[c] κατεγέλων αὐτοῦ, εἰδότες ὅτι ἀπέθανεν. 54 αὐτὸς δὲ

...μονον πι P. ...σωθησεται Ξ. F ιωαννην...

u = ver. 36.
v ch. vii. 50 reff.
w Mark v. 22 reff. see ver. 41.
x ‖ Mk. Matt. ix. 36. ch. vii. 6 only †.
y ‖ Mk. Matt. viii. 8.
z = ‖ Mk. reff.
a constr., ch. xxiii. 27. (Matt. xi. 17 reff.) Gen. xxiii. 2. Aristoph. Lysist. 397, κόπτεσθ' Ἄδωνιν.
b = ‖. see 1 Thess. v. 10. Dan. xii. 2.
c ‖ only. Gen. xxxviii. 23.

1 latt syr-cu syr-jer coptt. θυγατηρ BKL. εν ειρηνη D-gr latt coptt.

49. ερχονται and om τις (*both* ‖ *Mark*) DE[1] lat-*c* syr-cu. for παρα, απο (‖ *Mark*) AD 1 Damasc$_1$, *a* am lat-*a b* [*l q*]. λεγοντες D lat-*c* syr-cu. om αυτω (*see* ‖ *Mark*) BLXΞℵ 1. 33 lat-*e* [syr-jer] coptt: ins ACDPR rel latt syrr syr-cu goth [æth arm Damasc$_1$]. σου bef η θυγατηρ D-gr. μηκετι BDℵ syr-w-ast sah: txt ACPRΞ rel [vss Damasc$_1$]. (33 def.)

50. aft ακουσας ins τον λογον (‖ *Mark*) D vulg lat-*b c e f g*$_1$ [*l q*] syr-cu. for απεκριθη, ειπεν ℵ[1], *dixit* lat-*a c e* Syr [syr-cu] sah æth, *ait* lat-*b f g*$_1$. om λεγων BLXΛΞℵ 1. 33 vulg lat-*ff*$_2$ *l* syr-cu (Syr sah æth): ins ACDPR rel syr [syr-jer] copt goth arm. rec πιστευε (*from* ‖ *Mark*), with ACDRXℵ rel: txt BLΞ.

51. for εισελθων, ελθων (*to avoid repetn, from* ‖ *Matt and Mark*(*ver* 38)) ABCRℵ rel latt syrr syr-cu copt-schw sah goth Thl: txt DV copt-wilk æth arm. rec (for τινα) ουδενα (‖ *Mark*), with AC[3][L]R(ℵ) rel: txt B(sic: see table) C[1]DX 33. 69 latt coptt.—ουδενα αφηκεν συνεισελθειν αυτω ℵ. rec om συν αυτω, with AC[3]R rel syr-cu goth arm: ins bef τινα D latt: txt BC[1]LX 33. 69 (syrr) coptt æth. (ℵ see above.) rec transp ιωαννην and ιακωβον, with AL S(e sil) XΛℵ 33 vulg Syr syr-cu coptt goth æth arm: txt BCDR rel forj(with san tol) lat-*a b c e f* [*l q*] syr syr-jer Damasc Thl. for της παιδος, του κορασιου D.

52. rec (for ου γαρ) ουκ (*from* ‖ *Mark. This, in the very strong concurrence of* MSS, *is more prob, than that txt shd be from* ‖ *Matt*), with AR rel vulg lat-*b e* syr-mg Orig$_1$ Ambr$_1$: txt BCDFLXΔℵ 1. 33. 69 em(with per) lat-*a c* [*f ff*$_2$ *g*$_{1.2}$ *l q*] syrr syr-cu [syr-jer] coptt goth arm Cyr$_1$.

53. κατεγελουν (*itacism?*) D[1]KX.

54. rec aft αυτος δε ins εκβαλων εξω παντας και (*prob from* ‖ *Matt and Mark. Mey suggests that* εκβαλων εξω *may be a reminiscence from Acts* ix. 40), with C[3] rel; παντ. εκβ. εξω και AKRSUΠ 33 em lat-*f q* syrr [syr-jer] goth; εκβ. παντ. κ. (only) C[1]

the act of confession;—it saved her *mediately*, as the connecting link between herself and Christ: but the δύναμις ἐξεληλυθυῖα ἀπ' **αὐτοῦ**, working through that faith, saved her *energetically*, and as the working cause;—**τῇ χάριτι, διὰ** [**τῆς**] **πίστεως**, Eph. ii. 8. **εἰς εἰρ.**] See ch. vii. 50 and note. Mark's addition, ἴσθι ὑγ. ἀπὸ τ. μάστιγός σου, is important, as conveying to her an assurance that the effect which she felt in her body should be permanent; that the healing about which she might otherwise almost have doubted, as being surreptitiously obtained, was now openly ratified by the Lord's own word. **49.**] Little marks of accuracy come out in each of the two fuller accounts. Here we have **ἔρχεταί τις**, which was doubtless the *exact* fact:—in Mark ἔρχονται,—generally expressed. In Mark again we learn not only that Jesus heard,—but παρακούσας τὸν λόγον λαλούμενον, i. e. it was not *reported* to Him, but He *overheard it being said*, which is a minute detail not given here. Nothing could more satisfactorily mark the independent authority of the two narratives. **50.**] **καὶ σωθ.** is only here.

51.] Our Lord had entered the house, where He found θόρυβον, τοὺς αὐλητὰς καὶ τὸν ὄχλον (Matt., Mark), who were all following Him into the chamber of death. On this *He declared who were to follow Him* (οὐκ ἀφῆκεν, κ.τ.λ.), and uttered the words ἀναχωρεῖτε· οὐ γὰρ κ.τ.λ. Then He entered with His three Apostles and the parents. I say this, not for the sake of harmonizing,

d ||. Mark i. 31. Gen. xix. 16.
e = ver. 8 reff.
f voc., ch. xii. 32 reff.
g Judg. xv. 19. 3 Kings xvii. 21.
h vv. 44, 47.
i Matt. xi. 1 reff.
k Matt. xii. 23 reff.
l Mark viii. 6 reff.
m ch. xv. 6 reff.
n constr., ch. x. 19. Rev. vi. 8. xiii. 7. Sir. xxx. (xxxiii.) 19.
o = ch. xxii. 36. Acts xxi. 11. 2 Chron. xxxv. 3.
p ||. ch. x. 4. xxii. 35, 36 only. 4 Kings iv. 42 compl. Judith x. 5. xiii. 10, 15 only
q ch. x. 1 reff.

[d] κρατήσας τῆς χειρὸς αὐτῆς [e] ἐφώνησεν λέγων [f] Ἡ παῖς
ἔγειρε. 55 καὶ [g] ἐπέστρεψεν τὸ πνεῦμα αὐτῆς καὶ ἀνέστη
[h] παραχρῆμα, καὶ [i] διέταξεν αὐτῇ δοθῆναι φαγεῖν. 56 καὶ
[k] ἐξέστησαν οἱ γονεῖς αὐτῆς· ὁ δὲ [l] παρήγγειλεν αὐτοῖς
μηδενὶ εἰπεῖν τὸ γεγονός.

IX. 1 [m] Συγκαλεσάμενος δὲ τοὺς δώδεκα ἔδωκεν αὐτοῖς
δύναμιν καὶ [n] ἐξουσίαν ἐπὶ πάντα τὰ δαιμόνια καὶ νόσους
θεραπεύειν· 2 καὶ ἀπέστειλεν αὐτοὺς κηρύσσειν τὴν βασιλείαν τοῦ θεοῦ καὶ ἰᾶσθαι. 3 καὶ εἶπεν πρὸς αὐτοὺς
Μηδὲν [o] αἴρετε εἰς τὴν ὁδόν, μήτε ῥάβδον μήτε [p] πήραν
μήτε ἄρτον μήτε ἀργύριον, μήτε [[q] ἀνὰ] δύο χιτῶνας

Ξ συγκαλεσ.... ...επι R. ABCDE FHKL MSUV ΧΓΔΛΞ ΠℵΝ 1. 33. 69

coptt: txt BDLXℵ 1 latt syr-cu æth Ambr Bede. for αυτης, αυτη B[1]. rec εγειρου, with AR rel: txt BCDXℵ 1. 33, εγειραι (*itacism?*) L.

55. υπεστρεψεν D, *convertit* lat-*b*. om και ανεστη παραχρημα ℵ[1](ins ℵ-corr[1]). επεταξεν D. δοθηναι bef αυτη (|| *Mark*) DR 1. 33. 69 lat-*a* syrr syr-cu [syr-jer] æth arm.

56. οι δε γονεις αυτης θεωρουντες εξεστησαν D lat-*c*(omg θεωρ.). for ο δε παρηγγ., παρηγγ. δε D. for μηδενι, μηδε D[1]-gr(txt D[5]).

Chap. IX. 1. om δε C[3]H [S-marg] Ξ(once [it has the ver 3ce]). rec aft δωδεκα ins μαθητας αυτου (*from* || *Matt*), with C[3]EFHU lat-*b ff*$_2$ *g*$_1$ *l q*; αποστολους C[1]LXΛ Ξℵ 33. 69 vulg lat-*a c e f g*$_2$ syr [syr-jer] copt goth æth arm: om ABDR rel Syr syr-cu sah Dial$_1$ Thl Euthym. δεδωκεν ℵ. δυναμιν bef αυτοις B [copt]. πασαν(παντα D[10], *omne* D-lat) δαιμονιον D[1].

2. rec aft ιασθαι ins τους ασθενουντας, with C rel; τους ασθενεις ADLΞℵ 1. 33: om B syr-cu Dial$_1$.

3. om την (|| *Matt Mark*) CXΔ 69. rec ραβδους (*see note*, || *Matt*), with AC[3] Δ-gr rel goth: txt BC[1]DE[1]FKLM X(ραβδιον) Ξℵ 1. 33. 69 latt syrr syr-cu [syr-jer] sah æth arm [Eus$_1$] Cyr$_1$ [Tert$_1$ Aug$_1$]. for 4th μητε, μηδε ℵ. om ανα

but to bring out the sequence in our narrative here, which unless we get the right meaning for ἀφῆκεν, seems disturbed. **53.**] The maiden was *actually dead*, as plainly appears from the **εἰδότες ὅτι ἀπέθ.** The words οὐκ ἀπ. ἀλ. κ. are no ground for surmising the contrary: see note on Matt. ver. 24. **54.**] Mark gives the actual Aramaic words uttered by the Lord, ταλιθὰ κοῦμ. **55.**] **her spirit returned**: see reff., in the former of which death *had not* taken place, but in the latter it *had;* so that no inference adverse to her actual death can be derived from the use of the word. The command *to give her to eat*, shews that she was restored to actual life with its wants and weaknesses; and in that incipient state of convalescence, which would require nourishment. The testimony of Mark here precludes all idea of a recovery from a mere paroxysm—καὶ περιεπάτει. One who ἐσχάτως εἶχεν at the time of the father's coming, and then died, so that it could be said of the minstrels and others who had time to assemble, εἰδότες ὅτι ἀπέθανεν,—could not, supposing that they were mistaken and she was only in a trance, *have risen up and walked*, and been in a situation to take meat, in so short a time after. Every part of the narrative combines to declare that the death was *real*, and the miracle a *raising from the dead*, in the strictest sense. **56.**] The injunction, however, was not observed; for we read in Matt., ἐξῆλθεν ἡ φήμη αὔτη εἰς ὅλην τὴν γῆν ἐκείνην.

Chap. IX. 1—5.] Mission of the Twelve. Matt. x. 5—15. Mark vi. 7—13. Mark's account agrees nearly exactly with the text. The discourse is given at much greater length in Matt., where see notes. **1.**] **θεραπεύειν** belongs to **δύν. καὶ ἐξουσ.**, as in 1 Cor. ix. 5; some join it with **ἔδωκεν**, as in John v. 26: Matt. xiii. 11. **3.**] **μήτε [ἀνὰ] δύο χ. ἔχειν**—a mixed construction;—the former clause having been in the second person, this is added as if it had been in the infin., αἴρειν. The infinitive *for the imperative* would not be in place here,—see Winer, Gram. § 43, 5. d, edn. 6. It is remarkable that in

ἔχειν. 4 καὶ εἰς ἣν ἂν οἰκίαν εἰσέλθητε, ἐκεῖ μένετε καὶ ἐκεῖθεν ἐξέρχεσθε. 5 καὶ ὅσοι ἂν μὴ δέχωνται ὑμᾶς, ἐξερχόμενοι ἀπὸ τῆς πόλεως ἐκείνης τὸν r κονιορτὸν ἀπὸ τῶν
ποδῶν ὑμῶν s ἀποτινάσσετε εἰς t μαρτύριον t ἐπ' αὐτούς.
6 ἐξερχόμενοι δὲ u διήρχοντο κατὰ τὰς κώμας v εὐαγγελιζόμενοι καὶ θεραπεύοντες πανταχοῦ. 7 ἤκουσεν δὲ
Ἡρώδης ὁ w τετράρχης τὰ γινόμενα πάντα, καὶ x διηπόρει
διὰ τὸ λέγεσθαι ὑπό τινων ὅτι Ἰωάννης y ἐγήγερται
y ἐκ νεκρῶν, 8 ὑπό τινων δὲ ὅτι Ἡλίας ἐφάνη, ἄλλων
δὲ ὅτι προφήτης τις τῶν z ἀρχαίων a ἀνέστη. 9 εἶπεν δὲ
Ἡρώδης Ἰωάννην ἐγὼ b ἀπεκεφάλισα, τίς δέ ἐστιν οὗτος
περὶ οὗ ἐγὼ ἀκούω τοιαῦτα; καὶ c ἐζήτει ἰδεῖν αὐτόν.
10 Καὶ d ὑποστρέψαντες οἱ ἀπόστολοι e διηγήσαντο αὐτῷ

G της πολεως ... …ευαγγελιζομενοι και F.

r ‖ Mt. ch. x. 11. Acts xiii. 51. xxii. 23 only. Exod. ix. 9.
s Acts xxviii. 5 only. 1 Kings x. 2.
t 2 Thess. i. 10.
u = Acts viii. 4, 40 al. Ps. civ. 13.
v mid. absol., ch. xx. 1. Acts xiv. 7. Rom. xv. 20.
w ‖ Mt. ch. iii. 19. Acts xiii. 1 only †. (-χεῖν, ch. iii. 1.)
x (ch. xxiv. 4 v. r.) Acts ii. 12. v. 24. x. 17 only †. Dan. ii. 3 Symm.
y Matt. xvii. 9 reff.
z = ver. 19. Matt. v. 21, &c. 2 Pet. ii. 5. 3 Kings iv. 30.
a = Mark xvi. 9 al. fr.
b ‖ (Mk. bis) only. 1 Kings xxxi. 9 compl. Ps. cli. 7 only.
c ch. vi. 19. Exod. ii. 15.
d ch. ii. 20 reff. Josh. ii. 23.
e Mark v. 16 reff. Josh. ii. 23.

BC¹FL Δ-gr ΞΝ latt Syr syr-cu [syr-jer coptt] goth arm : ins AC³D rel syr. for εχειν, εχετε F(Wetst) L ℵ-corr¹ latt syrr syr-cu [syr-jer] (copt) arm : om (‖ *Matt*) ℵ¹ æth.

4. μινατε ℵ. κακειθεν D.

5. εαν CEFHM[S(Tischdf)]VXΓΔΞ 69. rec δεξωνται (*cf* ‖ *Matt Mark*), with C³D rel; δεξονται HΓΛ 69; *receperint* latt : txt ABC¹KLMUΞΠℵ 1. 33 goth. for 1st απο, εκ Dℵ, *de* latt. rec ins και bef τον κονιορτον, with AC³ rel vulg lat-*b e ff*$_2$ *g*$_1$ [*l q*] syrr syr-cu [syr-jer] goth [Ambr$_1$] : om BC¹DLXΞℵ 1. 33 lat-*a c f* coptt æth arm. om 2nd απο DU 248-54-9 Scr's a evv-47-P$^2_2$-y. rec αποτιναξατε, with A rel : εκτιναξατε (placed bef τ. κ. α. π. υμ.) D lat-*c* [*f*] : txt Bℵ 1. for επ αυτους, αυτοις ℵ¹(txt ℵ^{3a}, but ι replaced for υ; so X evv-47-49-P-z) 69 Scr's e lat-*a f* syr-cu arm.

6. for διηρχοντο κατα τας κωμας, κατα πολεις και ηρχοντο D, simly lat-*e*. om τας ℵ 237-45-54-9 Scr's a [Dial$_1$].

7. ακουσας D. om ο τετραρχης ℵ¹ : ins ℵ-corr¹(τετρααρχ. [so CΞ¹ copt]). γενομενα AX 1. 69. rec adds υπ' αυτου, with AC³ rel vulg lat-*c f g*$_{1.2}$ *q* goth [syrr æth] : om BC¹DLΞℵ 69 lat-*a b* [*e*] *ff*$_2$ *l* syr-cu coptt arm. om παντα DΓ tol. for κ. διηπ., ηπορειτο D. for εγηγερται, ηγερθη (*from* ‖ *Matt*) BCLΞℵ 1. 69. for εγη. εκ νεκρ., εκ νεκρ. ανεστη D.

8. for αλλων, αλλοι D 251 : υπο τινων LΞ. om 2nd δε Ξ. rec (for τις) εἷς (*see* ‖ *Mark*), with A rel vulg lat-*b c* [*f ff*$_2$ *g*$_1$ *l q* syr-cu æth (syr copt, appy)] : om D 69 lat-*a e* Syr : txt BCLXΔΞℵ 1. 33 ev-y syr goth [arm].

9. rec κ. ειπεν (*see* ‖ *Matt*), with A rel vulg syrr syr-cu [goth æth] : txt BCDLXΞℵ 1. 33. 69 latt coptt. rec ins ο bef ηρωδης, with BLXΞ (1. 33. 69, e sil) : om ACDℵ rel Thl. ins οτι bef ιωαν. CD coptt. om 2nd εγω BC¹LΞℵ lat-*e f ff*$_2$ coptt [æth]. for τοιαυτα, ταυτα D F(Wetst) LXΞ 69 lat-*e* Syr syr-cu sah.—τ. bef ακουω D. αυτον bef ιδειν D lat-*b l q* goth.

‖ Mark, there is also a mixed construction, ἵνα μηδὲν αἴρωσιν . . . . ἀλλ' ὑποδεδεμένους . . . . καὶ μὴ ἐνδύσησθε . . . . . (On **ἀνά**, see reff.) 5.] **ἐπ' αὐτούς, against them**;—more determinate than αὐτοῖς, Mark.

7—9.] Herod Antipas hears of the fame of Jesus through the doings of the Twelve. Matt. xiv. 1—12. Mark vi. 14—29. How inexplicable would be the *omission of the death of John the Baptist*, by the Evangelist who has given so particular an account of his ministry, (ch. iii. 1—20,) if Luke had had before him the narratives of Matt. and Mark. 7.] ὑπ' αὐτοῦ, of the rec., though a gloss, points to the right account of the matter. Herod (see Mark) heard the account of the miracles wrought by the Twelve; but even then it was τὸ ὄνομα **αὐτοῦ** which was spread abroad. These works were done in their Master's Name, and in popular rumour *passed for His*. 9.] The repetition of **ἐγώ** implies personal concern and alarm at the growing fame of Jesus: see notes on Matt.

10—17.] Return of the Apostles. Jesus retires to Bethsaida. Feed-

ὅσα ἐποίησαν. καὶ [f] παραλαβὼν αὐτοὺς [g] ὑπεχώρησεν
[h] κατ' [h] ἰδίαν εἰς πόλιν καλουμένην Βηθσαϊδά. 11 οἱ δὲ
ὄχλοι γνόντες ἠκολούθησαν αὐτῷ· καὶ [i] ἀποδεξάμενος αὐτοὺς ἐλάλει αὐτοῖς περὶ τῆς βασιλείας τοῦ θεοῦ, καὶ τοὺς
[j] χρείαν [j] ἔχοντας [k] θεραπείας ἰᾶτο. 12 ἡ δὲ ἡμέρα ἤρξατο
[l] κλίνειν· προςελθόντες δὲ οἱ δώδεκα εἶπον αὐτῷ [m] Ἀπόλυσον τὸν ὄχλον, ἵνα πορευθέντες εἰς τὰς [n] κύκλῳ κώμας R οχλον
καὶ ἀγροὺς [o] καταλύσωσιν καὶ [p] εὕρωσιν [q] ἐπισιτισμόν,
ὅτι ὧδε ἐν ἐρήμῳ τόπῳ ἐσμέν. 13 εἶπεν δὲ πρὸς αὐτοὺς
[r] Δότε αὐτοῖς [r] φαγεῖν ὑμεῖς. οἱ δὲ εἶπαν Οὐκ εἰσὶν ἡμῖν
πλεῖον ἢ πέντε ἄρτοι καὶ ἰχθύες δύο, [s] εἰ μή τι πορευθέντες

... ABCDE GHKL MRSU VXΓΔΛ ΞΠℵ 1. 33. 69

f Mark ix. 2 reff. g ch. v. 16 (reff.) only. h ‖ Mt. reff. i ch. viii. 40 reff. j Matt. vi. 8 reff. k = Rev. xxii. 2 (ch. xii. 42) only‡. Esth. ii. 12. l = ch. xxiv. 29 only. (Matt. viii. 20 reff.) Judg. xix. 11 A Ald. compl. Jer. vi. 4. m = ‖ Mt. reff. n Mark iii. 34 reff. Gen. xxxv. 5. o = ch. xix. 7 (xxi. 6 al.) only. Gen. xxiv. 23, 25. (-λυμα, ch. ii. 7.) only. Gen. xlii. 25. p = Acts vii. 11. [Rom. iv. 1.] 2 Tim. i. 18. Lam. i. 6. q here only. r ‖ Mt. reff. s 1 Cor. vii. 5. 2 Cor. xiii. 5 only.

10. for οσα, α ℵ coptt. εποιησεν ℵ[1](txt ℵ-corr[1](appy)). aft εποιησαν ins κ. οσα εδιδαξαν (*from* ‖ *Mark*) A. **ανεχωρησεν** D ev-y. (υπεχωρησεν as in txt is the reading of Cod B: see table.) rec (for πολιν καλουμενην) τοπον ερημον πολεως καλουμενης (*txt, not appearing to suit the requirements of the narrative follg, was amended from* ‖ *Matt and Mark: cf the varr*), with C rel: τοπον ερημον (omg βηθσ.) ℵ[1] [syr-cu]: ερημον τοπον 69: ερημ. τοπ. πολ. καλ. A 253-9 Scr's a c: τοπον πολ. καλ. 1: κωμην λεγομενην D: txt BLXΞ ℵ[3a](but former reading restored) 33 coptt.

11. rec (for αποδεξ.) δεξαμενος, with AC rel: txt BDLXΞℵ 1. 33. 69. ελαλησεν ℵ. aft θεραπειας ins αυτου παντας D. ιασατο CLΞ 1. 33. 69: txt ABDℵ rel latt syrr copt.

12. for η δε, ηδη B(sic: see table) lat-*e*[: και X] syr-cu. ηρξαντο ℵ[1]. **τους** οχλους ℵ[3a](but txt restored) 28 Scr's e k. rec (for πορευθεντες) απελθοντες (*from* ‖ *Matt Mark*), with X rel: txt ABCDLRΞℵ 33. 69. rec ins τους bef αγρους, with ACDRΞ rel coptt: om BEXℵ 1. 69 [goth]. om καταλ. και C[1](appy) lat-*f*. om και ευρ. επισιτ. D.

13. for πρ. αυτους, αυτοις LΞℵ. aft αυτους ins ο ῑς C lat-*f ff*$_2$ (g_1?) Syr syr-cu. αυτοιςυτοις(sic) D[1]. rec υμεις bef φαγειν (*from* ‖ *Matt Mark*), with ACDRΞℵ rel coptt: txt B lat-*b* [*l*[1]]. (ειπαν, so BCDLΞℵ 33.) for πλειον, πλεον DΓ[1]: **πλειονες** ℵ[1]: πλεους F(Wetst) M Scr's g. om η ℵ[1]. αρτοι bef πεντε Bℵ[1]. for πεντε, επτα (*mistake*) C, but πεντε below. rec δυο bef ιχθυες (‖ *Matt Mark*), with DLRΞ 33 vulg lat-*b c* [syrr syr-cu]: txt ABCℵ rel lat-*a* coptt

ING OF THE FIVE THOUSAND. Matt. xiv. 13—21. Mark vi. 30—44. John vi. 1—13. Compare the notes on each of these. **10.**] He went *in a ship* (Matt., Mark, John), of which our Evangelist seems not to have been aware; for we should gather from our text that it was *by land.* A great difficulty also attends the mention of Bethsaida here. At first sight, it would appear to be the well-known Bethsaida, on the western bank of the lake, not far from Capernaum. But (1) our Lord was *on this side before,*—see ch. viii. 37; and (2) Mark (vi. 45) relates that *after* the miracle of the loaves He caused His disciples to cross over to Bethsaida. But there were *two places* of this name:—another Bethsaida (Julias) lay at the top of the lake, on the Jordan: see Stanley, p. 381, edn. 3: Van de Velde, index, sub voce. Now it is very likely that our Lord may have crossed the lake to *this* Bethsaida, and St. Luke, finding that the miracle happened near Bethsaida, and *not being aware of the crossing of the lake,* may have left the name thus without explanation, as being that of the other Bethsaida. Mark gives us the exact account: that the Lord and the disciples, who went *by sea,* were perceived by the multitude who went *by land,* πεζῇ, and arrived before Him. How any of these accounts could have been compiled with a knowledge of the others, I cannot imagine.

11.] See note on Mark ver. 34. **ἀποδεξάμ.**] This word includes what Mark tells us of His going forth from His solitude, or perhaps landing from the ship, and seeing a great multitude, and having compassion on them; **having received them,** i. e. not sent them away.

12.] As the three agree in their account, and John differs from them, see the difference discussed in notes there. In

ἡμεῖς [t] ἀγοράσωμεν [u] εἰς πάντα τὸν λαὸν τοῦτον [t] βρώματα.
14 ἦσαν γὰρ [v] ὡσεὶ ἄνδρες πεντακισχίλιοι. εἶπεν δὲ πρὸς
τοὺς μαθητὰς αὐτοῦ [w] Κατακλίνατε αὐτοὺς [x] κλισίας [v] ὡσεὶ
[y] ἀνὰ πεντήκοντα. 15 καὶ ἐποίησαν οὕτως, καὶ [z] * ἀνέ-
κλιναν ἅπαντας. 16 λαβὼν δὲ τοὺς πέντε ἄρτους καὶ
τοὺς δύο ἰχθύας, [a] ἀναβλέψας εἰς τὸν οὐρανὸν [b] εὐλόγησεν
αὐτοὺς καὶ [c] κατέκλασεν, καὶ ἐδίδου τοῖς μαθηταῖς [d] παρα-
θεῖναι τῷ ὄχλῳ. 17 καὶ ἔφαγον καὶ [e] ἐχορτάσθησαν
πάντες, καὶ ἤρθη τὸ [f] περισσεῦσαν αὐτοῖς [g] κλασμάτων
[h] κόφινοι δώδεκα.
18 Καὶ ἐγένετο [i] ἐν τῷ εἶναι αὐτὸν προσευχόμενον
[k] καταμόνας, [l] συνῆσαν αὐτῷ οἱ μαθηταί. καὶ [m] ἐπηρώτη-

t || Mt. Gen. xlii. 7.
u ver. 3. Mark viii. 19, 20. John vi. 9.
v || (Mk. v. r.). ver. 28 al. Judg. iii. 29.
w ch. vii. 36 reff.
x here only. constr., Matt. xiii. 30.
y ch. x. 1 reff.
z act., ch. ii. 7 reff. (Matt. viii. 11 reff.)
a || Mt. reff.
b ||. Matt. xxvi. 26. 1 Cor. x. 16. Gen. i. 22, 28.
c || Mk. only. Ezek. xix. 12 only.
d || Mk. ch. x. 8. 1 Cor. x. 27 al. Gen. xliii. 31, 32.
e || Mt. Mk. Rev. xix. 21. Ps. xxxvi. 19.
f || Mt. reff.
g ||. Mark viii. 8 || Mt., 19, 20 only. Lev. ii. 6. Ezek. xiii. 19.
h || Mk. reff.
i ver. 51. Matt. xiii. 4 al. Ezek. ix. 8.
k Mark iv. 10 only. Ps. iv. 8.
l Acts xxii. 11 only. Jer. iii. 20. Esdr. vi. 2. 2 Macc. ix. 4 only.
m Matt. xii. 10 al.

goth æth. *ημεις* bef *πορευθεντες* D latt goth [Ambr$_1$].

14. for *γαρ*, *δε* L ℵ^1(txt ℵ^{3a}, but *δε* restored) vulg lat-*a e g*$_{1.2}$ copt. for *ωσει ανδρες*, *ανδρες ως* D; simly **1** Scr's i lat-*a e* [*f*]. rec om 2nd *ωσει*, with A rel [syrr syr-cu] copt [æth arm]: ins BCDLRΞℵ 33 lat-*e* sah Orig$_1$.

15. * *κατέκλιναν* BLΞℵ **1**. 33. 69: *ανεκλιναν* ACR rel.—om *και ανεκλιναν απαντας* DX. *παντας* LΞℵ 33.

16. ins *προσηυξατο και* bef *ευλογησεν* D. (*ηυλογησεν* A F(Wetst) Γ 33.) ins *επ'* bef *αυτους* D lat-*a b ff*$_2$ *g*$_{1.2}$ *l* [*q*] syr-cu Mcion$_3$-e. om *αυτους* Xℵ Syr æth arm. om *και κατεκλασεν* D. aft *τοις μαθηταις* ins *αυτου* LRΞ 33. 69 vulg lat-*c e* [*l*] Syr syr-cu syr-w-ast sah æth: om ABCDℵ rel lat-*a b f ff*$_2$ copt [arm]. rec (for *παραθειναι*) *παρατιθεναι*, with ADRΞ rel: *παρατεθηναι* 69: txt BCℵ **1**, *παραθηναι* X. *τοις οχλοις* D latt syrr syr-cu copt.

17. *περισσευμα* D-gr 69 lat-*e*. for *αυτοις*, *των* Dℵ[: om æth arm]. for *δωδεκα*, *δεκαδυο* D.

18. for *αυτον*, *αυτους* D sah-mnt: add *εν τοπω* (*see ch* xi. 1) ℵ-corr^1(but erased): *εκει και* Γ.—om *προσευχομενον* D lat-*a c e* syr-cu. *συνηντησαν* B^1(Tischdf, expr:

his account, the enquiry proceeds *from our Lord Himself*, and is addressed to Philip, and answered by Philip and Andrew.

13.] **εἰ μή τι—unless indeed we were to go and buy,** &c. On the construction see 1 Cor. ix. 11 (v. r.); xiv. 5: Rev. xi. 5 (rec.); and Winer, § 41. *b*. 2 prope fin., edn. 6. **14.**] **κλισίας—by companies**—the accusative of the *manner*, or *situation*, or *time, in which*: see Winer, § 32. 4, edn. 6. **ὡσεὶ ἀνὰ π.**] Mark gives *κατὰ ἑκατὸν καὶ κατὰ π.* with his usual precision. Besides these companies, there were the women and children *unarranged*: see on John vi. 10. **16.**] On the symbolic import of the miracle, see notes on John vi. **17.**] **κλασ.** in Matt. is joined with *τὸ περισσεῦον*,—in Mark with *κοφίνους πλήρεις*: here it may be taken with **τὸ περισ.** (ordinarily, and De Wette) or **κόφ.** (Meyer), but best, it appears to me, the *latter*,—because the article is not expressed as in Matt. Immediately after this miracle, Matt., Mark, and John relate the walking on the sea, which, and the whole series of events following as far as Matt. xvi. 12,—the healings in the land of Gennesaret, the discourse about unwashen hands, the Syrophœnician woman, the healing of multitudes by the sea of Galilee, the feeding of the 4000, the asking of a sign from Heaven, and the forgetting to take bread,—are *wholly omitted* by our Evangelist. Supposing him to have had Matt. before him, how is this to be explained? It is also an important observation, that the omission by Luke of the second miracle of feeding is not to be adduced against its historical reality, as has been done by Schleiermacher (transl. p. 144), since it is only omitted as *occurring in the midst of a large section, which the accounts gathered by Luke did not contain.* We see also, that the characteristic **κοφίνους** of the first feeding is preserved, without any confusion of terms: *σπυρίδας* being always used in relating and referring to the second,—Matt. xv. 37; xvi. 10: Mark viii. 8, 20.

18—26.] Confession of Peter.

σεν αὐτοὺς λέγων ⁿ Τίνα με οἱ ὄχλοι λέγουσιν εἶναι;
19 οἱ δὲ ἀποκριθέντες εἶπαν Ἰωάννην τὸν βαπτιστήν,
ἄλλοι δὲ Ἡλίαν, ἄλλοι δὲ ὅτι ° προφήτης τις τῶν ° ἀρχαίων ° ἀνέστη. 20 εἶπεν δὲ αὐτοῖς Ὑμεῖς δὲ τίνα με λέγετε
εἶναι; Πέτρος δὲ ἀποκριθεὶς εἶπεν Τὸν ᵖ χριστὸν τοῦ
ᵖ θεοῦ. 21 ὁ δὲ ᵍ ἐπιτιμήσας αὐτοῖς ʳ παρήγγειλεν μηδενὶ
λέγειν τοῦτο, 22 εἰπὼν ὅτι ˢ δεῖ τὸν ᵗ υἱὸν τοῦ ᵗ ἀνθρώπου
πολλὰ παθεῖν καὶ ᵘ ἀποδοκιμασθῆναι ᵛ ἀπὸ τῶν πρεσβυτέρων καὶ ἀρχιερέων καὶ γραμματέων, καὶ ἀποκτανθῆναι,
καὶ τῇ τρίτῃ ἡμέρᾳ ἀναστῆναι. 23 ἔλεγεν δὲ πρὸς πάντας
Εἴ τις θέλει ʷ ὀπίσω μου ἔρχεσθαι, ἀρνησάσθω ἑαυτὸν καὶ
ˣ ἀράτω τὸν ˣ σταυρὸν ˣ αὐτοῦ ʸ καθ' ἡμέραν, καὶ ἀκολουθείτω μοι. 24 ὃς γὰρ ἂν θέλῃ τὴν ᶻ ψυχὴν αὐτοῦ σῶσαι,
ἀπολέσει αὐτήν· ὃς δ' ἂν ἀπολέσῃ τὴν ψυχὴν αὐτοῦ
ἕνεκεν ἐμοῦ, οὗτος σώσει αὐτην. 25 τι γὰρ ᵃ ὠφελεῖται
ἄνθρωπος ᵇ κερδήσας τὸν κόσμον ὅλον, ἑαυτὸν δὲ ἀπο-

ABCDE GHKL MRSU VXΓΔΛ ΞΠℵ 1. 33. 69

n = ch. viii 25 al.
o ver. 8.
p see ch. ii. 26.
q ch. viii. 24 ||. Ps. cv. 9.
r Mark viii. 6 reff.
s = Matt. xxiv. 6 reff.
t Matt. viii. 20 reff.
u Matt. xxi 42 reff.
v = Matt xi. 19 reff.
w Matt. x. 38. 3 Kings xix. 20.
x ||. Mark x. 21.
y Matt. xxvi. 55 reff.
z = Prov. i. 19.
a Matt. xv. 5 reff. Prov. x. 2. xi. 4 A compl.
b || Mk. reff.

txt B-corr[1](appy)·[2]) 245 lat-*f*. ins *ο ῑς* bef *λεγων* Xℵ. rec *λεγουσιν* bef *οι οχλοι*, with CDℵ[3a] rel lat-*a c* syrr syr-cu : *λεγουσιν οι ανθρωποι* (|| *Matt Mark*) A 245-51 Scr's c lat-*e* g_1 : txt BLRΞℵ[1] 1.

19. (*ειπαν*, so BDℵ.) for *αλλοι* to *ανεστη*, *η ενα των πρ.* D lat-*e*.

20. rec *αποκρ. δε ο πετρ.* (*see* || *Matt Mark*), with ADR rel(several omit *ὁ*) vss : txt BCLΞℵ 1 syr-cu copt. aft *χριστον* ins *υιον* D lat-*e* (*f l* goth) $Orig_1$-ms. (*christus deus* copt.)

21. rec (for *λεγειν*) *ειπειν*, with R rel : txt ABCDKLMΞΠℵ 1. 33. 69 $Orig_1$.

22. *τον ῡν του ανθρωπου* bef *δει* ℵ[1]. **υπο** (|| *Mark*) D 1. for *τη τρ. ημ.*, *μεθ ημερας τρεις* D lat-*b* : simly Mcion[-e_2-t_1 $Dial_1$]. rec (for *αναστηναι*) *εγερθηναι* (*from* || *Matt, which also has τη τριτη ημ. It was thus more natural to subst the εγερ. of* || *Matt than the αναστ. of* || *Mark, which follows μετα τρ. ημ. This agst Mey*), with BRΞℵ rel : txt ACD F[1](Wetst) KΠ 1. 69[1] $Just_1$ $Orig_1$ [$Dial_1$] $Thaum_1$.

23. rec (for *ερχεσθαι*) *ελθειν* (|| *Matt*), with C[3]R ℵ-corr[1·3a] rel : txt ABC[1]DKLΞΠℵ[1] 1. 33. 69 $Orig_1$. rec **απαρνησασθω** (|| *Matt Mark*), with B[1]CR rel : txt A B[2](-corr[1] ?) DKLΞΠℵ 33 Orig. om *και αρατω τον σταυρον αυτου* D lat-*a l*. om *καθ ημεραν* (*see* || *Matt Mark*) CD rel vulg-ms lat-*a b c e* ff_2 *l q* syr-mg $Orig_1$ Jer : ins ABKLMRΞΠ ℵ[1](*marked for erasure, but marks removed*) 1. 33. 69 [vulg-ed](with am fuld em forj) lat-*f* $g_{1.2}$ Syr syr-cu syr-w-ast coptt goth æth[(aft *και*) arm] Chr Thl-ed mss-in-Jer.

24. for 1st *αν*, *εαν* CG H-corr[1] R S(Tischdf) UVXΓΔΛΞℵ 1 Thl.

25. for *ωφελειται*, *ωφελει* CDℵ. *ανθρωπον κερδησαι* and *απολεσαι η ζημιωθηναι* D[1] lat-*a c* $Cypr_1$: *ανθρωπος εαν κερδηση* and *απολεση η ζημιωθη* D-corr[1].

First announcement of the Passion and Resurrection. Matt. xvi. 13—28. Mark viii. 27—ix. 1. The Lord had gone into the neighbourhood of Cæsarea Philippi : see notes on Matthew. **19.** **ὅτι πρ. τις τ. ἀρχ. ἀν.**] See ver. 8. There is no improbability, nor contradiction to John's account that the multitudes sought to make Him a king, in our Lord's asking this question. We must remember that such enquiries were not made by Him *for information*, but as a means of drawing out the confession of others, as here. **20.**] See the important addition, the promise to Peter, in Matt. vv. 17—19. Ver. **22** as far as **ἀποκταν.** is nearly verbatim with Mark; the last clause nearly so with Matt. And yet, according to the Commentators, Mark has *compiled his account from Matt. and Luke*. The *almost* verbal agreement of the three in so solemn and sad an announcement, is what we might expect. Such words would not be easily forgotten. **23.**] **πρὸς πάντας**—'*having called the multitude with His disciples*,' Mark. There is no allusion to what He had said *to Peter* in this *πάντας*. **25.**] **ἑαυτόν**

λέσας ἢ [c] ζημιωθείς; 26 ὃς γὰρ ἂν [d] ἐπαισχυνθῇ με καὶ
P τουτον... τοὺς ἐμοὺς λόγους, τοῦτον ὁ υἱὸς τοῦ ἀνθρώπου [d] ἐπαισχυνθήσεται ὅταν ἔλθῃ [e] ἐν τῇ δόξῃ αὐτοῦ καὶ τοῦ πατρὸς
F αγγελων... καὶ τῶν [f] ἁγίων [f] ἀγγέλων. 27 λέγω δὲ ὑμῖν [g] ἀληθῶς,
εἰσίν τινες τῶν αὐτοῦ ἑστώτων οἳ οὐ μὴ [h] γεύσωνται θανάτου ἕως ἂν ἴδωσιν τὴν βασιλείαν τοῦ θεοῦ. 28 Ἐγένετο
δὲ μετὰ τοὺς λόγους τούτους [i] ὡσεὶ [k] ἡμέραι ὀκτὼ καὶ
[l] παραλαβὼν Πέτρον καὶ Ἰωάννην καὶ Ἰάκωβον ἀνέβη
...προσευξασθαι Ξ. εἰς τὸ ὄρος προσεύξασθαι. 29 καὶ ἐγένετο [m] ἐν τῷ προς-
εύχεσθαι αὐτὸν τὸ [n] εἶδος τοῦ προσώπου αὐτοῦ [o] ἕτερον
καὶ ὁ [p] ἱματισμὸς αὐτοῦ λευκὸς [q] ἐξαστράπτων. 30 καὶ
ἰδοὺ ἄνδρες δύο [r] συνελάλουν αὐτῷ, [s] οἵτινες ἦσαν Μωυσῆς καὶ Ἠλίας, 31 οἳ [t] ὀφθέντες [tu] ἐν δόξῃ [v] ἔλεγον τὴν
[w] ἔξοδον αὐτοῦ ἣν ἔμελλεν [x] πληροῦν ἐν Ἱερουσαλήμ. 32 ὁ

c ‖ Mt. reff. Prov. xxii. 3.
d (here bis) ‖ Mk. Rom. i. 16. 2 Tim. i. 8. Heb. ii. 11 al. Isa. i. 29 A$\aleph^{1\cdot 3b}$. Job xxxiv. 19 B$\aleph$ only.
e ‖. Matt. xxv. 31 al. Ps. ci. 6.
f ‖ Mk. reff.
g = ch. xii. 44. xxi. 3. John i. 48 al. Jer. xxxv. (xxviii.) 6.
h ‖. Heb. ii. 9 (there also w. θαν.). Ps. xxxiii. 8.
i ver. 14.
k constr., Matt. xv. 32 ‖ Mk. Acts v. 7.
l Matt. ii. 13. iv. 5, 8 al. Num. xxiii. 14.
m Matt. xiii. 4. Ezek. ix. 8.
n ch. iii. 22. John v. 37. 2 Cor. v. 7. 1 Thess. v. 22 only. Exod. xxiv. 17.
o = here only. see 1 Cor. xv. 40. Jude 7.
p ch. vii. 25 reff.
q here only. Ezek. i. 4, 7. Nah. iii. 3 only.
r ‖. ch. xxii. 4. iv. 36. Acts xxv. 12 only. Exod. xxxiv. 35.
s = ch. ii. 4. Acts xvi. 12. 1 Tim. iii. 15. Heb. ix. 2, 9 al.
t Ps. ci. 16.
u = Col. iii. 4.
v = Mark x. 32. Rom. iv. 6 al.
w = 2 Pet. i. 15 (Heb. xi. 22) only. Wisd. iii. 2.
x = Matt. i. 22 al. 3 Kings ii. 27.

26. εαν (*as* ‖ *Mark*) CLM 33. 69. εμε D Orig$_1$. om λογους D lat-*a e l* syr-cu Orig$_1$. aft πατρος ins αυτου D 65 coptt [Syr syr-cu æth].

27. ins οτι bef αληθως D: add οτι KMRΠ sah.—αληθως is joined to εισιν in ADHLSUΔΛ am lat-*f* Orig$_1$. rec (for αυτου) ωδε (*from* ‖ *Matt Mark*), with ACDPR rel Orig$_1$ Eus$_1$ Cæs$_1$ [Cyr$_1$]: txt BLΞ$\aleph$ 1 Cyr$_1$. rec εστηκοτων (‖ *Mark*), with BLRUXΓΞ$\aleph$ Cyr$_2$: txt ACDP rel Orig$_1$ Eus$_1$ [Cæs$_1$]. οιτινες AKΠ Orig Cæs. rec γευσονται, with HRΓΛ (G 69, e sil) Orig$_1$ Cæs: txt ABCDPΞ$\aleph$ rel Cyr$_1$. for τ. βασ. τ. θ., τον υιον του ανθρωπου ερχομενον εν τη δοξη αυτου (*see* ‖ *Matt*) D Orig$_{1certe}$.

28. εγενοντο P. om 1st και BH$\aleph^1$ forj lat-*a b* g_1 *l* syrr coptt goth æth arm: ins ACDPRΞ$\aleph^{3a}$ rel vulg lat-*c e f* ff_2 g_2 [*q*] syr-cu. (33 def.) rec ins τον bef πετρον (‖), with G-marg-eccles: om ABCDRΞ$\aleph$ rel. (F def.) transp ιωαν. and ιακ. (‖ *Matt Mark, and more usual order*) C^{3}DLMXΞ 33 [vulg] lat-ff_2 g_1 Syr syr-cu copt goth æth arm [Cyr$_1$-p]: txt ABC^{1}PR$\aleph$ rel [fuld(with forj tol)] lat-*a b c e f* g_2 syr sah. προσευχεσθαι $\aleph$: om L.

29. om εγενετο $\aleph^1$ [lat-*a*]. προσευξασθαι $\aleph^1$ 1[r]. for το ειδος, η ιδεα D Orig$_1$. ins εγενετο bef ετερον $\aleph$ lat-*a*. for ετερον και, ηλλοιωθη και D coptt: ετ. κ. ηλλ. syr-w-ast arm Orig.

30. οι ησαν C^1: ην δε D lat-*a* Arnob: ησαν δε latt: om syr-cu Mcion$_2$-e.

31. om οι D latt arm Orig$_2$. ins τη bef δοξη A. ins οι bef ελεγον P sah. aft ελεγον ins δε C^{1}D 69 lat-*c e* syrr: pref και C^{3}M vulg lat-*b f* ff_2 $g_{1.2}$ *l q* arm Arnob. ημελλεν AC$\aleph$, μελλει D. for ἐν, εἰς D.

= τὴν ψυχὴν αὐτοῦ Matt., Mark:—**his life**, in the highest sense. **26.**] After **λόγους**, Mark adds ἐν τῇ γεν. ταύτῃ τῇ μοιχαλίδι καὶ ἁμαρτωλῷ. Meyer remarks: 'the Glory is threefold: (1) *His own*, which He has to and for Himself as the exalted Messiah: (2) *the glory of God*, which accompanies Him as coming down from God's Throne: (3) *the glory of the angels*, who surround Him with their brightness.' **27.**] See note on Matt. ver. 28.

28–36.] The Transfiguration. Matt. xvii. 1—8. Mark ix. 2—8. I have commented on the relation of the three accounts in the notes on Mark, and on the Transfiguration itself in those on Matt., which treat also of the additional particulars found here. **28.**] **ἐγένετο—it was**, see reff. (k). **ὡσεὶ ἡμ. ὀκτώ** = μεθ' ἡμ. ἕξ Matt. and Mark, the one reckoning being *exclusive*, the other *inclusive*. **προσεύξ.**] See on ch. v. 16. This Gospel alone gives us the purpose of the Lord in going up, and His employment when the glorious change came over Him. **29.**] "St. Luke seems to have declined the use of μετεμορφώθη (employed

δὲ Πέτρος καὶ οἱ σὺν αὐτῷ ἦσαν [y] βεβαρημένοι ὕπνῳ,
[z] διαγρηγορήσαντες δὲ εἶδον τὴν δόξαν αὐτοῦ καὶ τοὺς
δύο ἄνδρας τοὺς [a] συνεστῶτας αὐτῷ. 33 καὶ ἐγένετο [b] ἐν
τῷ [c] διαχωρίζεσθαι αὐτοὺς ἀπ᾽ αὐτοῦ, εἶπεν ὁ Πέτρος
πρὸς τὸν Ἰησοῦν [d] Ἐπιστάτα, [e] καλόν ἐστιν ἡμᾶς ὧδε
εἶναι, καὶ ποιήσωμεν σκηνὰς τρεῖς, [f] μίαν σοὶ καὶ [f] μίαν
Μωυσεῖ καὶ [f] μίαν Ἠλίᾳ· μὴ εἰδὼς ὃ λέγει. 34 ταῦτα δὲ
αὐτοῦ λέγοντος [g] ἐγένετο [g] νεφέλη καὶ [h] ἐπεσκίαζεν αὐτούς,
ἐφοβήθησαν δὲ [b] ἐν τῷ εἰσελθεῖν αὐτοὺς εἰς τὴν νεφέλην.
35 καὶ φωνὴ [i] ἐγένετο ἐκ τῆς νεφέλης λέγουσα Οὗτός
ἐστιν ὁ υἱός μου ὁ [k] ἐκλελεγμένος, αὐτοῦ ἀκούετε. 36 καὶ
[b] ἐν τῷ [i] γενέσθαι τὴν φωνὴν [l] εὑρέθη Ἰησοῦς μόνος.
καὶ αὐτοὶ [m] ἐσίγησαν καὶ οὐδενὶ ἀπήγγειλαν ἐν ἐκείναις
ταῖς ἡμέραις οὐδὲν ὧν ἑώρακαν.
37 Ἐγένετο δὲ τῇ [no] ἑξῆς [o] ἡμέρᾳ, κατελθόντων αὐτῶν

y Matt. xxvi. 43 reff.
z here only †.
a = here only. 1 Kings xvii. 26 A [B def.]
b ver. 29.
c here only. Gen. xiii. 9, 11, 14.
d ch. v. 5 reff. L.
e Matt. xxvi. 24. 1 Cor. vii. 8. Job x. 3. Sir. xiv. 3.
f 1 Kings x. 3.
g ‖ Mk. Num. x. 34.
h ‖ Mk. ch. i. 35. Acts v. 15 only. Exod. xl. 29 (35).
i Acts ii. 6. xix. 34. Rev. xi. 15.
k Mark xiii. 20. ch. vi. 13. John vi. 70. Eph. i. 4 al. Num. xvii. 5.
l = Rev. xvi. 20. Gen. xviii. 26 A, 28, &c. [B def.]
m ch. xviii. 39 only.
n ch. vii. 11 reff.
o here only.

Ξ [διαγρη]γορησαντες ...
...τρεις Ξ.
...νεφελην F.
Frag.Par. ακουετε ...
...εν τω P
ABCDE GHKL MRSU VXΓΔΛ ΠΝ Frag.Par. 1. 33. 69

32. ειδαν LRℵ.
33. διαχωρισθηναι D. om ο (bef πετρος) AP rel: ins BCDKLMRXΔΞΠℵ. for προς τον ιησουν, τω ιησου D: om lat-*a b ff*$_2$. for 2nd και, θελεις (*see* ‖ *Matt*) D: om MU 69 lat-*l* sah. ποιησομεν ℵ Scr's p^2: ποιησω (‖ *Matt*) D^1(txt D^3). add ωδε (‖ *Matt*) D Tert. τρεις bef σκηνας D F(Wetst) KLΞ 33. 69 vulg lat-*c e f ff*$_2$ [*l*] Syr syr-cu coptt æth arm Tert$_1$. σοι bef 1st μιαν (‖) ℵ 1 Syr syr-cu. rec μω. bef 2nd μιαν (‖), with ℵ Syr syr-cu Tert$_1$: txt ABCDPR rel latt syr coptt goth æth arm. for ὅ, α D.
34. rec επεσκιασεν (‖ *Matt*), with ACDPR rel vulg lat-*b c*: txt BLℵ lat-*a*. rec εκεινους εισελθειν (*corrn to specify Moses and Elias, cf* Syr *below*), with ADPR rel syr(appy) sah goth: εκεινους ελθειν S: αυτους εισελθειν C: txt BLℵ copt æth (appy) arm.—*cum viderent Mosen et Eliam ascendentes* Syr.
35. for εγενετο, ηλθεν D. μου bef ο υιος P. rec (for εκλελεγμενος) αγαπητος (*from* ‖ *Matt Mark*), with ACDPR rel vulg lat-*b f* [*c e q* syrr syr-cu] goth [Mcion-e$_2$-t$_1$]: æth-rom has both: txt BLΞℵ gat lat-*a ff*$_2$ *l* syr-mg coptt æth-pl [arm]. add εν ω ευδοκησα C^{3}DM. ακουετε bef αυτου (‖ *Mark*) D lat-*c e*. (*so also* D *in* ‖ *Matt*(with Bℵ 1. 33) *and in* ‖ *Mark*(with BCLℵ 1. 33 Frag-cant vulg).)
36. rec ins ο bef ιησους, with C^{3}KLMXΔ (1. 33. 69, e sil): om ABC^{1}DRℵ rel. for και αυτοι, αυτοι δε D lat-*e* sah. om ουδεν D 239. rec εωρακασιν (*more usual form*), with AC^{1}Rℵ rel [Orig$_1$]: εθεασαν D^1, -αντο D-corr^1: εωρακεισαν G Scr's a: txt BC^{2}LX. (Π?)
37. rec ins εν bef τη εξης, with ACR rel vulg lat-*c* [*f*] copt: om B(sic: see table) LSℵ 1. 69 lat-*q*.—δια της ημερας D lat-*a b e ff*$_2$ *l* sah[*in eodem die*]. κατελθοντα αυτον D.

by the other two Evangelists here), that he might not awaken in his Greek readers any ideas or feelings connected with the fabulous *metamorphoses* of their heathen deities." Wordsw. **31.**] This **ἔξοδος** could be no other than His *death*—see reff. **πληροῦν—to fulfil** by divine appointment. **32.**] **διαγρ.**, not '*when they were awake*,' as E. V.—but **having kept awake** through the whole. The word occurs in this sense in Herodian iii. 4, πάσης τῆς νυκτὸς . . διαγρηγορήσαντες. It seems to be expressly used here to shew that it was *not merely a vision*, seen in sleep. **33.**] **while they were departing**—with a desire to hinder their departure. **μὴ εἰδ. ὃ λ.**, from fear and astonishment—ἔκφοβοι γὰρ ἐγένοντο, Mark. **34.**] There is no difference in the accounts, as Meyer thinks: the **ἐν τῷ διαχωρίζ. . .**, ver. 33, is only an additional particular, and the rest is exactly in accordance. Notice however the remarkable word **ἐκλελεγμένος** of the correct text: and compare the reff. **36.**] Luke gives the *result* of our Lord's command to them: the *command itself* is related in Matt. ver. 9, and Mark ver. 9.

37—42.] Healing of a possessed

ἀπὸ τοῦ ὄρους ᵖ συνήντησεν αὐτῷ ὄχλος πολύς. 38 καὶ
ἰδοὺ ἀνὴρ ἀπὸ τοῦ ὄχλου ᑫ ἐβόησεν λέγων Διδάσκαλε,
δέομαί σου ʳ ἐπιβλέψαι ἐπὶ τὸν υἱόν μου, ὅτι ˢ μονογενής μοί ἐστιν, 39 καὶ ἰδοὺ πνεῦμα ᵗ λαμβάνει αὐτὸν καὶ
ᵘ ἐξαίφνης κράζει καὶ ᵛ σπαράσσει αὐτὸν ʷ μετὰ ˣ ἀφροῦ,
καὶ ʸ μόγις ᶻ ἀποχωρεῖ ἀπ' αὐτοῦ ᵃ συντρίβον αὐτόν.
40 καὶ ἐδεήθην τῶν μαθητῶν σου ἵνα ἐκβάλωσιν αὐτό,
Ξ αποκριθεις ... καὶ οὐκ ἠδυνήθησαν. 41 ἀποκριθεὶς δὲ ὁ Ἰησοῦς εἶπεν
Ὦ ᵇ γενεὰ ᵇ ἄπιστος καὶ ᵇ διεστραμμένη, ᶜ ἕως πότε ἔσομαι
ABCDE GHKL MRSU VXΓΔΛ ΞΠℵ Frag.Par. 1. 33. 69
ᵈ πρὸς ὑμᾶς καὶ ᵉ ἀνέξομαι ὑμῶν; ᶠ προσάγαγε ὧδε τὸν
υἱόν σου. 42 ἔτι δὲ προσερχομένου αὐτοῦ ᵍ ἔρρηξεν αὐτὸν
τὸ δαιμόνιον καὶ ʰ συνεσπάραξεν· ⁱ ἐπετίμησεν δὲ ὁ Ἰησοῦς
τῷ πνεύματι τῷ ἀκαθάρτῳ, καὶ ἰάσατο τὸν παῖδα καὶ
ᵏ ἀπέδωκεν αὐτὸν τῷ πατρὶ αὐτοῦ. 43 ˡ ἐξεπλήσσοντο δὲ
...εξεπλησσοντο R. πάντες ᵐ ἐπὶ τῇ ⁿ μεγαλειότητι τοῦ θεοῦ. Πάντων δὲ
ᵒ θαυμαζόντων ᵐ ἐπὶ πᾶσιν οἷς ἐποίει εἶπεν πρὸς τοὺς
F υμων ... μαθητὰς αὐτοῦ 44 ᵖ Θέσθε ὑμεῖς εἰς τὰ ὦτα ὑμῶν τοὺς

p ch. xxii. 10 reff. Gen. xxxii. 1. q John i. 33 reff. r ch. i. 48. James ii. 3 only. Lev. xxvi. 9. 1 Kings i. 11. s ch. vii. 12 reff. t = ch. v. 26. vii. 16. Exod. xv. 15. u Mark xiii. 36 reff. v ‖ Mk. bis. Mark i. 26 only. 2 Kings xxii. 8. w see Matt. xxvii. 66. x here only †. (ἀφρίζειν, ‖ Mt. bis.) y here only †. Wisd. ix. 16 Aℵ (μόλις BC). z Matt. vii. 23. Acts xiii. 13 only. Jer. xxvi. (xlvi.) 5. 2 Macc. iv. 33 only. a Matt. xii. 20 reff. b ‖ Mt. reff. c ‖ bis. John x. 24. Rev. vi. 10 only. Ps. xciii. 3. d = Mark vi. 3 reff. e ‖. 2 Cor. xi. 1, 19. Eph. iv. 2. Isa. xlvi. 4. f Matt. xviii. 24. Acts xvi. 20. xxvii. 27. 1 Pet. iii. 18 only. Gen. xlviii. 9. g Matt. vii. 6 reff. h here only †. i ver. 55 reff. k ch. iv. 20. l Matt. vii. 28 reff. m = ch. i. 47 reff. n Acts xix. 27. 2 Pet. i. 16 only. Jer. xl. (xxxiii.) 9. Esdr. i. 5 only. o Mark xii. 17 reff. p = ch. xxi. 14. Acts v. 4. xix. 21. Hag. ii. 19

for συνηντησεν to πολυς, συνελθειν αυτω οχλον πολυν D.—συνηντησαν R.

38. rec ανεβοησεν, with AR rel: txt BCDLℵ 69. rec επιβλεψον (*corrn, -ψαι being mistaken for imperat-mid, whereas it is inf-aor-act*), with DXΛℵ Frag-par (E **1.** 33. 69, e sil): txt ABCR rel. rec εστι bef μοι, with R rel vulg lat-*b c f ff*$_2$ *g*$_1$ [*l q*] arm: txt ABCDLXℵ **1.** 33 lat-*a e* coptt goth.

39. for και ιδου to κραζει, λαμβανει γαρ αυτον εξαιφνης πνευμα D lat-*e*.—om ιδου ℵ [fuld Syr syr-cu]. add και ρησσει (*see* ‖ *Mark*) D(X) **1** vulg copt æth arm [syr-jer]; και ρασσει ℵ. om 2nd αυτον D [lat-*e*]. μολις BR. for συντριβον, και συντριβει D: συντριβουν ℵ¹(but corrd).

40. rec εκβαλλωσιν, with (**1**, e sil) 69: txt ABCRℵ rel.—απαλλαξωσιν D. αυτον D 3. 76. 247-marg evv-48-y.

41. om αποκ. δε C¹. απιστε D. for εσομαι προς υμας, μεθ υμων εσομαι (‖ *Matt*) ℵ. for προσαγαγε, προσενεγκε D. add μοι LXΞℵ³ᵃ Frag-par 33 syr-cu syr-w-ast æth. τον υιον σου bef ωδε (ωδε *omd and wrongly restored*) ACR rel syr-cu syr copt goth: om ωδε (‖) D am(with per): txt BLXΞℵ **1** [vulg] lat-(*a e*) *b c f* Syr [syr-jer] æth arm.

42. προσευχομενου ℵ¹. συνεταραξεν D ev-z. for τω πν. τω ακ., τω ακ. πν. D lat-*e*. for ιασατο to αυτον, αφηκεν αυτον και απεδωκεν τον παιδα D (lat-*e*).

43. παντ. δε εξ. D lat-*c e*. rec εποιησεν, with X rel: txt ABCDLΞℵ Frag-par **1.** 33. 69 latt syrr syr-cu [copt]. rec aft εποι. ins ο ιησους, with AC rel lat-*f q* syrr goth [æth]: om BDLΞℵ **1** latt syr-cu copt arm. om ειπεν ℵ¹(ins ℵ-corr¹). om αυτου Frag-par lat-*c*.

PERSON. Matt. xvii. 14—21. Mark ix. 14—29. The narrative in Mark is by far the most copious, and I have commented at length on it. **37. τ. ἑξ. ἡμ.**] The transfiguration probably took place *at night*,—see on Matt. xvii. 1,—and this was in the morning. Luke omits the whole discourse concerning Elias (Matt. and Mark, vv. 9—13). **38.] μον. μοί ἐστιν** is peculiar to Luke. **39.] κράζει**—i. e. the *child*—there is a rapid change of subject, see ch. xvii. 2; xix. 4 al. and Winer, § 67. 1. c, edn. 6. **συντρίβον** is perhaps literal—**bruising him.**

43—45.] OUR LORD'S SECOND ANNOUNCEMENT OF HIS DEATH. Matt. xvii. 22, 23. Mark ix. 30—32. **43, 44.**] **πάντες**—the multitude—in contrast with **ὑμεῖς** of ver. 44. **τοὺς λ. τ.**, not (Meyer), '*the foregoing discourses and*

λόγους τούτους· ὁ γὰρ υἱὸς τοῦ ἀνθρώπου μέλλει [q] παρα-
δίδοσθαι εἰς χεῖρας ἀνθρώπων. 45 οἱ δὲ [r] ἠγνόουν τὸ
ῥῆμα τοῦτο, καὶ ἦν [s] παρακεκαλυμμένον ἀπ' αὐτῶν [t] ἵνα
μὴ [u] αἴσθωνται αὐτό· καὶ ἐφοβοῦντο ἐρωτῆσαι αὐτὸν περὶ
τοῦ ῥήματος τούτου.
46 [a] Εἰσῆλθεν δὲ [b] διαλογισμὸς ἐν αὐτοῖς, [c] τὸ τίς ἂν
εἴη μείζων αὐτῶν. 47 ὁ δὲ Ἰησοῦς [d] ἰδὼν τὸν [b] διαλογισμὸν
τῆς καρδίας αὐτῶν, [e] ἐπιλαβόμενος παιδίον ἔστησεν αὐτὸ
[f] παρ' ἑαυτῷ 48 καὶ εἶπεν αὐτοῖς Ὃς ἐὰν δέξηται τοῦτο τὸ ...παρ εαυτω

q Matt. xxiv. 9 reff. Ezek. xxiii. 28. r = || Mk. reff. s here only. Isa. xliv. 8. Ezek. xxii. 26 only. t = John ix. 2. xii. 40. u here only. Isa. xxxiii. 11. a = here only. b = ch. xxiv. 38 reff. c ch. i. 62. xxii. 2, 4, 23, 24. Acts iv. 21. Rom. viii. 26. d = Matt. ix. 4. see Lam. iii. 60. e w. acc., ch. (xiv. 4) xxiii. 26. Acts ix. 27. xvi. 19. xviii. 17 only. (Prov. vii. 13.) w. gen., Matt. xiv. 31. Mark viii. 23 al. Joel ii. 9. f = John xix. 25. see ch. xix. 7.

Frag.Par. ABCDE FGHKL MSUV XΓΔΛΞ ΠΝ 1. 33 69

45. for παρακεκ., κεκαλυμμενον D. επερωτησαι (|| *Mark*) CDKMΠ: txt ABΞℵ rel. om αυτον D lat-*e* [*l q*].
46. om εισηλθεν to αυτοις D.
47. for ιδων, ειδως BFKΛΠℵ syrr syr-cu æth arm: txt ACDΞ [rel] latt copt goth Orig$_1$.—(γνους 1.) αυτων bef της καρδιας D. rec παιδιου, with AΞℵ rel: txt BCD Orig$_1$ [Cyr$_1$ (Frag-par ?)]. om αυτο D. παρ' εαυτον D.
48. om αυτοις D 157 lat-*a b c e ff*$_2$ *l* [*q*] syr-cu. for 1st εαν, αν DLΞ 33. 69

wonders:'—that would give no sense,—for the disciples were thinking exclusively of those already: nor strictly (Stier, but corrected in edn. 2) '*what I am about to tell you,*' so that τοὺς λ. τ. should be || with τὸ ῥῆμα below: but **these sayings**, of which this was now *the second;*—'these intimations which I make to you from time to time respecting My sufferings and death.' The *Resurrection*, expressly mentioned in the others, is omitted here.

45.] **ἵνα**—not to be evaded by forcing it to mean '*so that they did not . . . .,*' but to be rendered **that they might not**, as in Matt. i. 22 al. It was the *divine purpose*, that they should not at present be aware of the full significancy of these words.

46—50.] Jesus rebukes the disciples for their emulation and exclusiveness. Matt. xviii. 1—5. Mark ix. 33—40. The most detailed account is in Mark, where I have discussed the differences in the three narratives.

46.] There is not the least occasion to confine **διαλ.** to the sense of an inward doubt and questioning in the heart of each; indeed I will venture to say that no interpreter would have thought of doing so, had not the narratives of Matt. and Mark, by mentioning an outward expression of this thought, offered a temptation to *discover a discrepancy*,—of which Meyer, as usual, has not failed to avail himself. Had our narrative stood by itself, we should have understood it, as I do now, of a dispute which had taken place or was taking place, and which, though not actually spoken out before the Lord, was yet open to His discerning eye, so that not only the words, but the disputing of their thoughts, was known to Him. The idea of **τὸ τίς ἂν εἴη μ.** meaning that each one thought "Who is greater than I?" (Meyer, in loc.) is absurd enough. Still more absurd however is the harmonistic attempt of Greswell, to make two distinct events out of (1) the incident in Mark and Luke, and (2) that in Matthew; one, '*absente Petro,*' the other '*reverso Petro, discipuli sponte contentionem suam ad Jesum referunt; de qua Ille uti prius, sed uberius, disserit.*' (Harmony, p. 192, 3.) He has been led into this partly by the lower, literal-harmonistic spirit which pervades his school, and partly by the assumption which connects this strife and discourse immediately with the incident about the tribute-money,—for which there is *not the least ground* in the text of Matt.

48.] The discourse as here related has the closest connexion and harmony. The dispute had been, who (among the Twelve) should be greatest,—i. e. greatest *in the kingdom of heaven:* for other greatness is not to be thought of,—the minds of the disciples being always on this, as just about to appear (against De Wette and Meyer); and our Lord reminds them that no such precedence is to be thought of among those sent in His name; for that even a little child, if thus sent, is clothed with His dignity; and if there be any distinction among such, it is this, that he who is like that child, humblest and least, i. e. nearest to the spirit of his Lord, *he is the greatest.* "*The whole discourse in Luke is*

παιδιον [g] ἐπὶ τῷ ὀνόματί μου, ἐμὲ δέχεται· καὶ ὃς ἐὰν ἐμὲ
δέξηται, δέχεται τὸν ἀποστείλαντά με. ὁ γὰρ [h] μικρότερος ἐν πᾶσιν ὑμῖν ὑπάρχων, οὗτός ἐστιν μέγας. 49 ἀποκριθεὶς δὲ Ἰωάννης εἶπεν [i] Ἐπιστάτα, εἴδομέν τινα [j] ἐπὶ τῷ
ὀνόματί σου ἐκβάλλοντα δαιμόνια, καὶ [k] ἐκωλύσαμεν αὐτόν,
ὅτι οὐκ [l] ἀκολουθεῖ [l] μεθ' ἡμῶν. 50 εἶπεν δὲ πρὸς αὐτὸν
[ὁ] Ἰησοῦς Μὴ [k] κωλύετε· ὃς γὰρ οὐκ ἔστιν καθ' ὑμῶν
ὑπὲρ ὑμῶν ἐστιν.
51 Ἐγένετο δὲ [m] ἐν τῷ [n] συμπληροῦσθαι τὰς ἡμέρας τῆς

g = ‖. Matt. xix. 9. Acts iv. 21.
h Matt. xi. 11 reff.
i ch. v. 5 reff.
j ‖ Mk. Matt. xxiv. 5 ‖. Acts iv. 17, 18.
k ‖ Mk. ch. xi. 52. Acts xi. 17. Num. xi. 28.
l constr., Rev. vi. 8. xiv. 13.
m Matt. xiii. 4 al. Ezek. ix. 8.
n = Acts ii. 1 (ch. viii. 23) only †. (ρωσις, 2 Chron. xxxvi. 21.)

[Cyr_1]. το παιδιον bef τουτο D latt [syr-cu syr]. for 2nd εαν, αν BKLUΞ [33] 69: om ℵ 243: for 2nd δεξηται, δεχεται Xℵ: om ος to δεχεται D. om υπαρχων D [lat-*b* $Cypr_1$]. rec εσται, with AD rel lat-*e* syrr mss-in-Orig [Cyr_1] $Cypr_3$: txt BCLXΞℵ 1. 33 latt syr-cu copt [goth] $Orig_3$.

49. om δε C¹(perhaps). rec ins ο bef ιωαννης, with AC²Ξℵ rel: om B C¹(appy) D 69. for επιστατα, διδασκαλε (‖ *Mark*) C¹LΞ syr-mg copt. for επι, εν (‖ *Mark*) BLXΔΞℵ 1. 33. 69 copt: txt ACD rel. rec ins τα bef δαιμονια, with H(Treg, expr): om ABCDΞℵ rel goth arm. εκωλυομεν (‖ *Mark*) BLΞℵ lat-*a b e*.

50. rec (for ειπ. δε) και ειπ., with A rel vulg lat-*b f* [*l q*] syr[-txt] goth [æth] arm: txt BCDLXΞℵ 1. 33 lat-*a c e* copt syr-mg. om προς αυτον D tol¹ [lat-*e* copt-ms]. om ο Bℵ¹. (Ξ def.) aft κωλυετε ins αυτον (‖ *Mark*) CDFLMX em(with tol) copt [arm]: om ABΞℵ rel vulg lat-*b c e* [*l q*] syrr syr-cu copt-dz goth. ins ου γαρ εστιν καθ υμων bef ος γαρ LΞ 33 syr-w-ast copt. rec ημων υπερ ημων (‖ *Mark*), with Eℵ³ᵃ rel: υμων υπ. ημων AXΔℵ¹ (69): txt BCDKLMΞΠℵ³ᵇ 33 latt syrr syr-cu copt goth æth arm Tit-bostr Euthym Opt Aug Jer.

51. for συμπληρ., πληρουσθαι D.

without connexion." De Wette, strangely enough: who also says, κ. ὃς ἐὰν ἐμὲ δέξ. . . . . is borrowed from Matt. x. 40; and that ὁ γὰρ μικρ. . . . . οὗτος ἔσται . . . . ought to stand at the beginning of the discourse, as in Matt. I quote this as one among continually recurring specimens of the criticism which would cut our precious, and most truthful Gospels into fragments without meaning or connexion. We live in times when such criticisms are making way among shallow minds: let the student judge from the above sample, what they are generally worth. Schleiermacher has some excellent remarks on this discourse and the circumstances, Essay on Luke. translation, pp. 159—162.

49, 50.] On the connexion of this answer with the preceding, see on Mark. It is even more strikingly brought out here. Our Lord had declared the *absolute equality* of all sent in His name —and that if there were any difference, it was to be made by a *deeper self-renouncing.* Then arises the thought in the mind of the ardent son of Zebedee, of the *exclusive and peculiar dignity* of those who were thus sent, the ἀπόστολοι: and he relates what they had done, as a proof of his fully appreciating this exclusive dignity. The link to what has preceded, is in the words **ἐπὶ τῷ ὀν. σου** . . . see the rest in Mark.

51—Chap. XIX. 28.] Incidents during the Lord's last journey to Jerusalem. We now enter upon a long and most important portion of our Gospel, peculiar *in this form,* and most of it *entirely* peculiar, to Luke. At ch. xviii. 15 he again joins the narrative of Matt. and Mark within a few verses of where he parted from them. Respecting this portion, I will observe, without entangling myself in the harmonistic maze into which most of the interpreters have ventured, (1) that the whole of it is to be understood here as belonging to our Lord's *last journey from Galilee to Jerusalem:* see below on ver. 51. (2) that evidently that journey was *not a direct one* (see ch. x. 1; xiii. 22, 31; xvii. 11; xviii. 31, and notes), either in *time* or in the *road chosen.* (3) that in each of the two other Gospels there is a journey placed at this very time, described Matt. xix. 1, μετῆρεν ἀπὸ τῆς Γαλιλαίας καὶ ἦλθεν εἰς τὰ ὅρια τῆς Ἰουδαίας πέραν τοῦ Ἰορδάνου, and Mark x. 1, ἐκεῖθεν ἀναστὰς ἔρχεται εἰς τὰ ὅρια τῆς Ἰουδ. καὶ πέραν τοῦ Ἰορδάνου,—which, in their narrative also, is *the last*

o here only †. (-λαμβάνειν, Mark xvi. 19 reff.)
p = ch. ii. 21 reff.
q here only. Jer. xxi. 10. Ezek. vi. 2 al. see 4 Kings xii. 17.
r ch. xvi. 26. xxii. 32 al.
s Matt. xiii. 3 reff.
t constr., Matt. x. 1. xxvii. 1. ch. iv. 29. v. 7 al. Matth. G. G. § 532.

ᵒ ἀναλήμψεως αὐτοῦ, ᵖ καὶ αὐτὸς τὸ ᑫ πρόσωπον [αὐτοῦ]
ᑫʳ ἐστήρισεν ˢ τοῦ πορεύεσθαι εἰς Ἱερουσαλήμ. 52 καὶ ἀπέστειλεν ἀγγέλους πρὸ προσώπου αὐτοῦ, καὶ πορευθέντες
εἰσῆλθον εἰς κώμην Σαμαρειτῶν, ᵗ * ὥστε ἑτοιμάσαι αὐτῷ.

ABCDE FGHKL MSUVX ΓΔΛΞΠ ℵ 1. 33. 69

om 1st αυτου ℵ[1]. om 2nd αυτου BLΞ 1 lat-*c*: ins ACDℵ rel [vss]. rec εστηριξεν, with ADℵ rel: txt BCLVXΞ 33.—εστηρ. bef το πρ. LXΞ 33 lat-*a* copt. for εις, εν A Scr's c.

52. εαυτου AEGSVΛ 69[2]. for κωμην, πολιν ΓΛℵ[1] 69 latt(not *c*) [Tert₁ Op₁]. * ὡς Bℵ[1]: ωστε ACDΞℵ[3a] rel [Bas₁ Cyr₁].

journey from Galilee to Jerusalem. (4) that in John x. 22, we find our Lord at Jerusalem, at the feast of dedication, in the winter (about the end of December), without however any hint as to *how* or *whence* He came there. (5) that the whole time between that feast and His Passion is spent thus:—After the attempt to stone Him, John x. 31, He retired to Bethany *beyond Jordan;*—was summoned thence by the message from Martha and Mary to Bethany near Jerusalem, where He raised Lazarus;—again retired to Ephraim, somewhere beyond Jericho, on the borders of the desert;—six days before the passover came to Bethany, and the anointing took place, &c.; this whole time being *three months* and a few days. (6) I believe then that we have obtained a *fixed critical point* in all the four Gospels for the last journey from Galilee, after which He never returned (in the flesh) thither again. And this last journey was *to the feast of dedication,* or at all events brought Him in time for that feast (for it does not look like a journey specially *to a feast*) at Jerusalem. It was between the feast of tabernacles in John vii. 2, to which He went up privately (ib. ver. 10), and the occasion when we find Him in Solomon's porch, John x. 22. (7) The three first Evangelists relate nothing of the being in Jerusalem at the feast of dedication, *or indeed at all, except at the last passover.* We therefore find in them nothing of the retirements to Bethany (beyond Jordan) and Ephraim; but the removal of our Lord from Galilee to the confines of Judæa through the parts beyond Jordan is *described as uninterrupted.* (8) We are now I believe in a situation to appreciate the view with which our Evangelist inserts this portion. He takes this journey, beginning its narrative at the very same place where the others do, as comprehending—as indeed in strict historical fact it did—the last solemn farewell to Galilee (ch. x. 13—15), the final resolve of our Lord to go up to Jerusalem (ix. 51), and,—which in its wider sense it did,—all the records which he possessed of miracles and discourses between this time and the triumphal entry. (9) As to arranging or harmonizing the separate incidents contained in this portion, as the Evangelist himself has completely by his connecting words in many places *disclaimed* it (see ch. ix. 57; x. 1, 25, 38; xi. 1, 14; xii. 1; xiii. 1, 10, 22; xiv. 1, 25; xv. 1; xvii. 1, 5, 11, 20; xviii. 1, 9),—I do not suppose that we, at this distance of time, shall succeed in doing so. The separate difficulties will be treated of as they occur.

51.] **συμπλ.**, not *past*—not, **when the days** *were fulfilled;* but, **were being fulfilled**: i. e. approaching their fulfilment. '*When the time was come,*' E. V., is too strong: **when the days were come** would be better, for that would include the whole of the journey in those days. See reff. **ἀνάλημψις** can have but one meaning (which, as the word itself is not found elsewhere, must be determined by the sense of the cognate verb: see reff.), **His assumption**, i. e. ascension into heaven. *ἡμέρας τῆς ἀναλήψεως αὐτοῦ λέγει τὸν καιρὸν τὸν ἀφορισθέντα μέχρι τῆς ἀναλήψεως αὐτοῦ τῆς ἀπὸ γῆς εἰς οὐρανόν.* Euthym. **αὐτός** resumes the *subject,* not without some emphasis implying his own voluntary action. **τὸ πρός. [αὐ.] ἐστ.**, a Hebraism, see reff., implying determinate fixed purpose: cf. Isa. l. 7, the sense of which, as prophetic of the Messiah going to his sufferings, seems to be referred to in this expression. The LXX have there, *ἔθηκα τὸ πρόσωπόν μου ὡς στερεὰν πέτραν.* 52.] **ἀγγέλους**, who have been assumed without reason to have been James and John. **Σαμαρ.**] On the enmity of the Jews and Samaritans, see note, John iv. 9. The publicity now courted by our Lord is in remarkable contrast to His former avoidance of notice, and is a feature of the *close of His ministry,* giving rise to the accusation of ch. xxiii. 5. **ὥστε ἑτ. αὐτῷ** must

53 καὶ οὐκ [u] ἐδέξαντο αὐτόν, ὅτι τὸ [v] πρόσωπον αὐτοῦ ἦν
πορευόμενον εἰς Ἱερουσαλήμ. 54 ἰδόντες δὲ οἱ μαθηταὶ
[αὐτοῦ] Ἰάκωβος καὶ Ἰωάννης εἶπαν Κύριε, [w] θέλεις
[a] εἴπωμεν πῦρ [b] καταβῆναι ἀπὸ τοῦ οὐρανοῦ καὶ [c] ἀναλῶσαι
αὐτούς[, [d] ὡς καὶ Ἡλίας ἐποίησεν]; 55 [e] στραφεὶς δὲ
[f] ἐπετίμησεν αὐτοῖς*. 56 καὶ ἐπορεύθησαν εἰς ἑτέραν κώμην.

...Ιακωβος F.

u = Matt. x. 14 reff.
v see Jer. xlix. (xlii.) 15. 2 Kings xvii. 11.
w constr., Matt. xx. 32 reff. see Matt. vii. 4.
a = Mark v. 43 reff.
b Matt. vii. 25, 27 reff.
c Gal. v. 15 (2 Thess. ii. 8 v. r.) only. Joel ii. 3.
d 1 Kings i. 10, 12.
e Matt. vii. 6. xvi. 23 al.
f ver. 42. Matt. xvi. 22. Zech. iii. 3.

54. om *αυτου* Bℵ 1 lat-*e*. (*ειπαν*, so BCLΞℵ.) for *απο*, *εκ* CD 1 goth Bas$_1$ Chr$_2$: txt ABℵ rel, *απ'* LΞ. om *ως και ηλιας εποιησεν* (*see note*) BLΞℵ vulg lat-*e l* syr-cu copt-dz arm [Cyr$_1$] Jer$_1$: ins ACD rel lat-*a b c f* [*q*] syrr copt goth æth [Bas$_1$ Chr$_2$] (Tert ?).

55. * rec aft *αυτοις* adds καὶ εἶπεν Οὐκ οἴδατε οἵου πνεύματός ἐστε ὑμεῖς, with D F(Wetst) KMUΓΛΠ 1. 69 latt syrr syr-cu copt[-wilk æth arm] Clem$_1$(? see Tischdf) Did$_1$ Epiph$_1$(sic) Chr$_4$ Dion-areop$_1$ Antch$_2$ Thdor-stud$_1$[appy] Chrysoc$_1$ Cypr(appy) Op$_1$ Ambr$_1$ Aug (but of these DFUΓΛ 69 latt goth Chr$_2$ Antch$_2$ om *υμεις*) : om ABCΞℵ rel (*see note*) fuld(with gat) lat-*g*$_1$ *l* copt-schw æth Eus$_1$(appy) Bas$_1$ Cyr$_1$ Gaud [Jer$_1$].— for *οιου*, *ποιου* D 1 Scr's i q^1 w^2 ev-z$_1$ [Chr$_2$ Antch$_2$]. * rec adds further ὁ γὰρ υἱὸς τοῦ ἀνθρώπου οὐκ ἦλθεν ψυχὰς ἀνθρώπων ἀπολέσαι ἀλλὰ σῶσαι, with F(Wetst) KMUΓΛΠ 1. 69 latt syrr syr-cu [copt-wilk æth-ms] goth Antch$_1$ Cypr$_1$ Ambr$_1$ Quæst$_1$ (but of these UΓΛ 1. 69 vulg lat-*a e* Antch$_1$ Cypr$_1$ om *γαρ*, Γ has *ψυχην*, vulg lat-*c e* Syr syr-cu goth om *ανθρωπων*, and UΓ have *αποκτειναι* for *απολ.*) : om ABCDΞℵ rel [fuld(with gat)] lat-*g*$_{1.2}$ *l* copt-schw [æth-ed Chr$_1$].

mean something more, surely, than to provide board and lodging; there is a solemnity about the sentence which forbids that supposition. It must have been to announce the coming of Jesus as the Messiah, which He did not conceal in Samaria, as in Judæa and Galilee, see John iv. 26; and the refusal of the Samaritans must have been grounded on the jealousy excited by the preference shewn for the Jewish rites and metropolis. *They* expected that the Messiah would have confirmed their anti-Jewish rites and Gerizim temple, instead of going up solemnly to Jerusalem, and thereby condemning them. **54.**] The disciples whom He named 'sons of thunder,' Mark iii. 17. They *saw* some insult of manner, or actual refusal to allow the Lord to enter their village. That a collision of this kind did take place is plain from the last verse, and implied from the occasion alluded to by the two Apostles, where the fire was invoked in the presence of the offending persons. *It* happened also in Samaria. **πῦρ**, not *lightning*, but *fire*, as in the passage alluded to, and in 1 Kings xviii. 38. It is exceedingly difficult to determine the true reading in this passage, which seems to have been more than usually tampered with, or wrongly written. It is hardly conceivable that the shorter text, as edited by Tischdf., . . . ἀναλῶσαι αὐτούς; στραφεὶς δὲ ἐπετίμησεν αὐτοῖς. καὶ ἐπορεύθησαν . . . should have been the original, and all the rest, insertion. Homœoteleuton may have had some share in the omission of the latter debated portion, from ΚΑΙΕΙΠ to ΚΑΙΕΠ: but this does not touch ὡς καὶ Ἡλ. ἐπ. It has been suggested that those words may have been removed as involving indirect censure of Elias: but surely this lay too far off to create any offence. And their *insertion* into the text is quite inexplicable. In this great uncertainty, I have thought the candid way is to let my edited text reflect such uncertainty, and I have therefore printed these latter debatable words in the same type as the text, and have annotated on them. Let it be remembered that in both cases, versions far more ancient than our oldest MSS. contain these words. **55.**] [**οὐκ οἴδατε οἵου πνεύματός ἐστε.** Besides the *mistaken* ways of explaining these words of our Lord (e. g. '*Do you not see what a (bad) spirit you are shewing?*' Bornemann) there are two senses which they *may* bear. (1) Affirmative, as in E. V.,—'putatis vos agi Spiritu tali quali olim Elias . . . sed erratis. Habetis quidem ζῆλον sed οὐ κατ' ἐπίγνωσιν, et qui proinde humani est affectus, non divinæ motionis.' Grot.; or (2) interrogative—'*Know ye not what manner of spirit ye belong to (are of)?*' the spirit meant being the Holy Spirit. 'The Spirit in Elias was a fiery and

57 καὶ πορευομένων αὐτῶν ἐν τῇ ὁδῷ εἶπέν τις πρὸς αὐτὸν
Ἀκολουθήσω σοι ὅπου ἐὰν [g] ἀπέρχῃ [κύριε]. 58 καὶ
εἶπεν αὐτῷ ὁ Ἰησοῦς Αἱ [h] ἀλώπεκες [i] φωλεοὺς ἔχουσιν
καὶ τὰ [k] πετεινὰ τοῦ [k] οὐρανοῦ [l] κατασκηνώσεις, ὁ δὲ
[m] υἱὸς τοῦ [m] ἀνθρώπου οὐκ [m] ἔχει ποῦ τὴν κεφαλὴν [m] κλίνῃ.
59 εἶπεν δὲ πρὸς ἕτερον Ἀκολούθει μοι. ὁ δὲ εἶπεν Κύριε
[n] ἐπίτρεψόν μοι ἀπελθόντι πρῶτον θάψαι τὸν πατέρα
μου. 60 εἶπεν δὲ αὐτῷ [n] Ἄφες τοὺς νεκροὺς θάψαι τοὺς
ἑαυτῶν νεκρούς, σὺ δὲ ἀπελθὼν [o] διάγγελλε τὴν βασιλείαν
τοῦ θεοῦ. 61 εἶπεν δὲ καὶ ἕτερος Ἀκολουθήσω σοι κύριε·
πρῶτον δὲ ἐπίτρεψόν μοι [p] ἀποτάξασθαι τοῖς [q] εἰς τὸν

g = ‖ Mt. Matt. xiv. 25.
h ‖ Mt. ch. xii. 32 only. Judg. xv. 4.
i ‖ Mt. only +.
k Matt. vi. 26 reff.
l ‖ Mt. only. Ezek. xxxvi. 27. (-νοῦν, ch. xiii. 19.)
m = Mt. (reff.)
n = Mark v. 37 reff.
o Acts xxi. 26. Rom. ix. 17 (from Exod. ix. 16) only. 2 Macc. iii. 34.
p Mark vi. 46 reff.
q ch. xi. 7 reff

ABCDE GHKL MSUV XΓΔΛΞ ΠＡ 1. 33. 69

57. rec (for και) εγενετο δε (*beg of lection : cf* D *and* G *below*), with A rel vulg [lat-*b f l q*] syr goth [Ath_1] : και εγενετο D 346(Sz) lat-*a c e* [syr-jer] : txt BCLXΞא 33. 69 Syr syr-cu copt æth arm. rec (for εαν) αν, with Dא rel [Ath_1] : txt ABCKL S(Tischdf) UΞΠ 33. 69 Ath_2. for απερχῃ, υπαγεις D 157. om κυριε (*its unusual place at end of the clause and its non-occurrence in* ‖ *Matt account for the omission*) BDL Ξ(appy) א 1 vulg lat-*a c* copt arm $Mcion_1$-t Ath_2[-comm] : ins AC rel lat-*b f q* syrr [syr-jer] goth [Ath_1-txt, and aft σοι, syr-cu æth].
58. om 1st ο B.
59. om κυριε B¹(but corrd by origl scribe : see table : Tischdf says by B³) DV. πρωτον bef απελθοντι B D(-θοντα) א 33 : πρ. απελθειν και 1 latt Orig : απελθειν πρ. AKΠ : απελθειν, omg πρωτ., 69 [Thdrt] (*all more or less from* ‖ *Matt*) : txt CΞ rel syr æth. [Tischdf, ed 8, ascribes πρωτ. απελ. και to AKΠ latt Orig Bas_1, and απ. πρωτ. (without και) to 1 ev-y lat-*c* g_2 *l*.]
60. ο δε ειπ. D. rec aft αυτω ins ο ιησους (*cf* ‖ *Matt*), with AC rel [vss] : om B(D)LΞא 33 lat-*a* copt. for απελθων, πορευθεις D $Iren_1$.
61. επιτρ. δε μοι πρ. D Iren-gr. om τον (bef οικον) D.

judicial spirit, as befitted the times and the character of God's dealings then; but the Spirit in Me and mine is of a different kind —a spirit of love and forgiveness.' The latter of these is perhaps better suited to the context: but we seem to want an example in the Gospels of (οὐκ) οἴδατε used interrogatively: see Matt. vii. 11 ‖; xx. 22, 25 ‖; xxiv. 42 ‖; xxv. 13; xxvi. 2: Mark iv. 13 (doubtful, but the construction is direct): ch. xii. 56: John viii. 14; xiv. 4 al. I have therefore punctuated according to the former sense: which, indeed, seems more naturally followed by the γάρ of the clause following. It is very interesting to remember that this same John came down to Samaria (Acts viii. 14—17) with Peter, to confer the gift of the Holy Spirit on the Samaritan believers.]

57—62.] Matthew (viii. 19—22) relates the contents of vv. 57—60, but at a totally different period of our Lord's ministry, viz. His crossing the lake to go to Gadara. It is quite impossible to decide which Evangelist has placed the incidents in their proper chronological place. When we once begin to speculate on such things, it is easy to find a fitness, on whichever side of the argument we range ourselves. Only (see notes on Matt.) we must not adopt the wretched subterfuge of the harmonists, and maintain that the two events took place *twice, each time consecutively, and each time with the same reply from our Lord.* **57, 58.**] See notes on Matt.

59. ἀκολούθει μοι] This command is *implied* in Matthew, where the reply is, as here, κύριε, ἐπίτρεψόν μοι πρῶτον . . . which words could hardly be spoken without a reference in the πρῶτον to it.

60.] **διάγ.** κ.τ.λ., peculiar to Luke, and shews the independence of his source of information. Am I wrong in supposing also, that it connects this incident with the sending out of the Seventy, which follows immediately afterwards? **61, 62.**] Peculiar to Luke. **τοῖς εἰς . . .**, a mixture of two constructions—ἀπέρχεσθαι εἰς τ. οἰκ. μου καὶ ἀποτάξ. τοῖς ἐν τ. οἴκῳ μου. The meaning is, to *bid farewell to the persons,* not *to set in order the things,* as some have rendered it. The answer of our Lord again seems to refer to the sending out into the harvest (ch. x. 2), for which the present seventy were as it were the ploughmen, first breaking up the ground. The saying itself is to be ex-

οἶκόν μου. 62 εἶπεν δὲ ὁ Ἰησοῦς Οὐδεὶς [r] ἐπιβαλὼν τὴν χεῖρα αὐτοῦ ἐπ' [s] ἄροτρον καὶ βλέπων [t] εἰς τὰ ὀπίσω [u] εὔθετός ἐστιν τῇ βασιλείᾳ τοῦ θεοῦ.

X. 1 Μετὰ δὲ ταῦτα [v] ἀνέδειξεν ὁ κύριος [καὶ] ἑτέρους ἑβδομήκοντα, καὶ ἀπέστειλεν αὐτοὺς [w] ἀνὰ δύο πρὸ προς-

r = here only. Deut. xii. 7, 18 al. see Matt. xxvi. 50 reff.
s here only. Isa. ii. 4 al.
t Mark xiii. 16. ch. xvii. 31. John vi. 66. xviii. 6. xx. 14. Ps. ix. 3.
u ch. xiv. 35. Heb. vi. 7 only. Ps. xxxi. 6. Sus. 15 [Theod.] only.
v Acts i. 24 only. Hab. iii. 2. — 2 Macc. ix. 23. (-δειξις, ch. i. 80.)
w Matt. xx. 9, 10. ch. ix. [3,] 14 (| Mk. v. r.). John ii. 6. Rev. iv. 8. xxi. 21 only.

62. rec aft *ειπεν δε* ins *προς αυτον*, with LXΞℵ [latt] Syr copt goth æth arm: aft *ιησ.* AC rel [lat-*q* syr]: om B.—*ο δε ιησ. ειπ. αυτω* D lat-*e*. *ουδεις εις τα οπισω βλεπων και επιβαλλων την χειρα αυτου επ' αροτρον* D lat-*a b c e q* $Clem_1$ $Cypr_2$ Promiss Hil_1 Zeno.—om *αυτου* B 1 lat-*a b q* arm Iren-gr_1 $Orig_2$ Cyr_1 Bas_2 $Tert_1$.—*επιβαλλων* (*conformn to βλεπων*) ADL $Clem_1$. rec (for *τη βασιλεια*) *εις την βασιλειαν* (*prob as Mey, exegetical gloss on the dat, see ch* xiv. 35), with ACD rel Bas_3 Cyr_1 Chr_1[ed Savile $Antch_1$]: *εν τη β.* ℵ[3a] Iren-gr [Chr_1]: txt BLΞℵ[1] 1. 33 latt arm $Clem_1$ $Orig_2$[int_5] Iren-int [$Cypr_2$ Hil].

Chap. X. 1. for *μετα δε τ. ανεδ. ο κυρ., απεδειξεν δε* D lat-*a b c e*. om 1st *και* BLΞ Syr copt æth: ins ACDℵ rel latt syr-cu syr [syr-jer goth arm] Eus_1 [Bas_1] $Tert_1$. aft *εβδομηκοντα* ins *δυο* (*prob traditional corrn, to agree with the number of the members of the Sanhedrim*) BDM R(in index to chapters) vulg lat-*a c e l* syr-cu arm $Dial_2$ Clem $Epiph_1$ $Recog_1$ Aug_1 Prud Isid Bede: om ACΞℵ rel lat-*b f q* syrr [syr-jer] copt goth æth Eus_3 [Bas_1] Cyr_2 Thl Euthym Iren-int_2 $Tert_1$ $Ambr_1$ Jer. om *αυτους* B Eus_1. aft *ανα δυο* ins *δυο* BKΠ 69 syr-w-ob: om ACDΞℵ rel Eus_2 [Bas_1].

plained simply from agricultural operations—for he who has his hand on the plough, guiding it, must look on the furrow which his share is making—if he look behind, his work will be marred. Hesiod's precept is very similar, ἔργ. ii. 60, ἰθείην αὔλακ' ἐλαύνοι, **μηκέτι παπταίνων μεθ' ὁμήλικας** ἀλλ' ἐπὶ ἔργῳ θυμὸν ἔχων. **εὔθετος**, not '*fit*,' but **well adapted**, 'the right sort of workman.' The sense is more immediately applicable to the *ministry* of the gospel of Christ, which will least of all things bear a divided service and backward looks,—but of course affects also every private Christian, inasmuch as he too has a work to do,—ground to break, and a harvest to reap.

Chap. X. 1—16.] Mission of the Seventy. It is well that Luke has given us also the sending of *the Twelve;*—or we should have had some of the Commentators asserting that this was *the same* mission. The discourse addressed to the Seventy is in substance the same as that to the Twelve, as the similarity of their errand would lead us to suppose it would be. But there is, as Stier has well remarked (iii. 89, edn. 2), this weighty difference. The discourse in Matt. x. in its three great divisions (see notes there), speaks plainly of an office founded, and a ministry appointed, which was to involve a work, and embrace consequences, *co-extensive*, both in space and duration, *with the world*. Here, we have *no such prospective view* unfolded. The whole discourse is confined to the *first division* there (vv. 1—15), and relates entirely to *present duties*. Their sending out was not to prove and strengthen their own faith, as Hase supposes (Leben J. p. 194),—but to prepare the way for this solemn journey of the Lord, the object of which was the announcement of the near approach of the kingdom of God,—and the termination of it, the last events at Jerusalem. Their mission being thus temporary, and expiring with their return, it is not to be wondered at that we *hear nothing of them in the Acts*. This last is surely an absurd objection to bring against the historic truth of their mission, seeing that the Acts are written *by this same Evangelist*, and the omission is therefore an argument *for*, and not against, that truth. 1.] **μετὰ ταῦτα**—chronological—**after these things**, not '*besides these things*,' as Schleiermacher and Olsh. render it. **ἀνέδ.**, an official word: see reff. Bleek has observed, that ὁ κύριος, of our Lord, in narration, is peculiar to St. Luke, and to narrations which he alone gives. Cf. ch. vii. 13; xi. 39; xii. 42; xiii. 15; xvii. 5, 6; xviii. 6; xxii. 31, 61. But this is only true of the Synoptic Gospels. It occurs in the fragment at the end of St. Mark (xvi. 19), and in John (iv. 1 reff.). In the Acts, the usage is very general: see ii. 47; v. 9, 14; ix. 1, &c.;—and in St. Paul's Epistles: see 1 Cor. vi. 14, 17; vii. 10, &c. **[καὶ] ἑτ. ἑβδ.**, not '*other seventy also*,' but **others [also]**,

ώπου αὐτοῦ εἰς πᾶσαν πόλιν καὶ τόπον [x] οὗ ἤμελλεν
αὐτὸς ἔρχεσθαι. 2 ἔλεγεν δὲ πρὸς αὐτοὺς Ὁ μὲν
[a] θερισμὸς πολύς, οἱ δὲ [b] ἐργάται ὀλίγοι· δεήθητε οὖν τοῦ ...τςυ κυ H.
κυρίου τοῦ [a] θερισμοῦ, ὅπως [b] ἐργάτας [c] ἐκβάλῃ εἰς τὸν
[a] θερισμὸν αὐτοῦ. 3 ὑπάγετε· ἰδοὺ ἀποστέλλω ὑμᾶς
ὡς [d] ἄρνας ἐν μέσῳ [de] λύκων. 4 μὴ [f] βαστάζετε [g] βαλλάν- R [αρ]-νας...
τιον, μὴ [h] πήραν μὴ [i] ὑποδήματα· καὶ μηδένα κατὰ τὴν ABCDE GKLM
ὁδὸν ἀσπάσησθε. 5 εἰς ἣν δ' ἂν εἰςέλθητε οἰκίαν, πρῶτον RSUVX ΓΔΛΞΠ
λέγετε Εἰρήνη τῷ οἴκῳ τούτῳ. 6 καὶ ἐὰν ῇ ἐκεῖ [j] υἱὸς ℵ 1. 33. 69
εἰρήνης, [k] ἐπαναπαύσεται ἐπ' αὐτὸν ἡ εἰρήνη ὑμῶν· [l] εἰ
δὲ μήγε, ἐφ' ὑμᾶς [m] ἀνακάμψει. 7 ἐν αὐτῇ δὲ τῇ οἰκίᾳ

x = Matt. xxviii. 16. 1 Cor. xvi. 6. a John iv. 35 reff. b Matt. x. 10. xx. 1, al.+ Wisd. xvii. 17 al. c Mark i. 12. John x. 4. 1 Macc. xii. 27. d here only. Isa. lxv. 25. e Matt. vii. 15 reff. f = Matt. iii. 11. ch. xxii. 10. g ch. xii. 33. xxii. 35, 36 only. Job xiv. 17 only. h ch. ix. 3 al. xxii. 35, 36 only. 4 Kings iv. 42 compl. Judith x. 5. xvii. 10, 15 only. i Matt. iii. 11. ch. xxii. 35 al. Exod. xii. 11. j = ch. xvi. 8. John xii. 36. Eph. ii. 2. v. 6. k = here (Rom. ii. 17) only. Num. xi. 25, 26. l Matt. ix 17 reff. m Matt. ii. 12. Acts xviii. 21. Heb. xi. 15 only. Exod. xxxii. 27. Judg. xi. 39 A.

for *πασαν π. κ. τ.*, *παντα τοπον και πολιν* D lat-*a b c e l q* Syr syr-cu (Eus$_1$). (rec **εμελλεν**, with DKLΠ (S 1, e sil) Eus$_1$ [Bas$_1$] : txt ABCΞℵ rel. (33 def.)) om *αυτος* D latt Syr syr-cu [syr-jer copt-dz]. **εις**ερχεσθαι A 1 lat-*a e* syr-mg [syr-jer] Eus : *διερχ*. 69 Scr's g s.

2. rec (for 1st *δε*) *ουν*, with A rel syr-txt [Bas$_1$] : txt BCDLΞℵ 1. 33. 69 lat-*a c e q* syr-mg copt-schw goth arm. om *μεν* D lat-*a c* [*e*]. om *ουν* D-gr. rec *εκβ*. bef *εργατας* (*Matt* ix. 38), with ACΞℵ rel [vulg] lat-*a b c* : txt BD lat-*e*.—rec *εκβαλ***λ***η*, *εκβαλλει* Γ : txt A B(sic : see table) CDΞℵ rel Bas$_1$.

3. rec aft *ιδου* ins *εγω* (*from Matt* x. 16), with CDΞ rel [vulg] lat-*b c* [*f q* syrr syr-jer copt goth æth] : om ABℵ lat-*a e l* arm. for *αρνας*, *προβατα* (*Matt* x. 16) AM. for *εν μεσω*, *μεσον* D.

4. (*βαλ***λ***αντιον*, so ABCDΞℵ &c.) rec (for 3rd *μη*) *μηδε*, with ACR rel Clem$_1$: *μητε* M 69 vulg lat-*a b f* [*l q* Syr syr-cu syr-jer arm-ms] Ambr$_1$: txt BDLΞℵ 1 lat-*c e* syr [arm-ed]. om *και* Λ[1]ℵ[1] 33. 248.

5. *αν* bef *δε* D[1](txt D-corr[1]). rec *οικιαν* bef verb, with AC F(Wetst) LRXΞ rel vulg lat-*f* syrr [syr-jer] copt goth æth arm : txt B(D)ℵ 1 [Orig-int$_1$].—*πρωτον* between verb and *οικιαν* D[1]-gr, simly lat-*a b q* syr-cu, but om D-gr-corr(and lat) [lat-*e*].—*πολιν εισελθητε εις οικιαν* 69(sic).—rec (for *εισελθητε*) *εισερχεσθε*, with AR rel : txt BCD F(Wetst) LXΞℵ 1. 69.

6. *καν* D. rec aft *εαν* ins *μεν* (*Matt* x. 13), with (but e sil) Scr's d l m n s [Orig$_1$] : om ABCDRΞℵ rel Orig$_1$[int$_2$] Constt$_1$ Bas$_1$. *εκει* bef *η* B vulg lat-*a b f l* Orig$_1$. elz *ο* bef *υιος*, with ℵ[1](but erased) : om ABCDRΞ rel Scr's-mss goth arm Orig, Constt [Bas] Thl. *επαναπα***η***σεται* B[1](Tischdf) ℵ. ins *η ειρηνη υμων* bef *εφ' υμας* (|| *Matt*) R Syr-ed [syr-jer æth] copt Orig$_2$-int$_2$.—for *ανακαμψει*, *επιστρεψει η ειρ. υμ.* D.

seventy in number. The **ἑτέρους** may refer, either to the Twelve, ch. ix. 1, or perhaps, from the similarity of their mission, to the *ἄγγελοι* in ch. ix. 52. But perhaps the first is more probable, from the similarity of the discourses. The number of seventy might perhaps have reference to the *seventy elders* of Israel, Exod. xxiv. 1: Num. xi. 16:—all sorts of fanciful analogies have been found out and insisted on (and moreover forced into the text), which are not worth recounting. **οὗ** for *οἷ*,—see reff.

2.] See Matt. ix. 37 and notes. If **ἐκβάλλῃ** were read, the *pres.*, as usual, would have the force of the continually repeated act: as it is, the *aor.* (as in || Matt.) indicates the *whole mission*, considered as one great act. **3, 4.**] The time was now one of greater danger than at the mission of the Twelve; therefore ver. 3 is bound immediately up with their *present sending*, whereas in Matt. x. 16 it regards a time yet distant in the future; also one requiring greater haste,—which accounts for the addition, **μηδένα κ. τ. ὁδ. ἀσπ.** These reasons also account for *merely the healing the sick* being enjoined, ver. 9. **6.**] **υἱὸς εἰρ.**, **a** (or more probably, **the**,—as words like *πατήρ*, *μήτηρ*, *υἱός*, &c., are often definite though anarthrous) **son of peace**: i. e. persons receptive of your message of peace;—see reff. **7—12.**] See on Matt. x. 11—15. The particular directions here are different. **7.**] **ἐν αὐτῇ**

μένετε, ἔσθοντες καὶ πίνοντες ⁿ τὰ παρ' αὐτῶν· ᵒ ἄξιος γὰρ
ὁ ᵇ ἐργάτης τοῦ ᵖ μισθοῦ αὐτοῦ. μὴ ᑫ μεταβαίνετε ἐξ οἰκίας
εἰς οἰκίαν. 8 καὶ εἰς ἣν ἂν πόλιν εἰσέρχησθε καὶ δέχωνται
ὑμᾶς, ἐσθίετε τὰ ʳ παρατιθέμενα ὑμῖν, 9 καὶ θεραπεύετε
τοὺς ἐν αὐτῇ ἀσθενεῖς, καὶ λέγετε αὐτοῖς ˢ Ἤγγικεν ἐφ'
ὑμᾶς ἡ βασιλεία τοῦ θεοῦ. 10 εἰς ἣν δ' ἂν πόλιν εἰσέλθητε καὶ μὴ δέχωνται ὑμᾶς, ἐξελθόντες εἰς τὰς
ᵗ πλατείας αὐτῆς εἴπατε 11 Καὶ τὸν ᵘ κονιορτὸν τὸν
ᵛ κολληθέντα ἡμῖν ἐκ τῆς πόλεως ὑμῶν εἰς τοὺς πόδας
[ἡμῶν] ʷ ἀπομασσόμεθα ὑμῖν· ˣ πλὴν τοῦτο γινώσκετε, ὅτι
ˢ ἤγγικεν ἡ βασιλεία τοῦ θεοῦ. 12 λέγω ὑμῖν ὅτι
Frag.Par. μοις εν τη... Σοδόμοις ἐν τῇ ἡμέρᾳ ἐκείνῃ ʸ ἀνεκτότερον ἔσται ἢ τῇ
πόλει ἐκείνῃ. 13 οὐαί σοι Χοραζείν, οὐαί σοι Βηθσαϊδά,
ὅτι εἰ ἐν Τύρῳ καὶ Σιδῶνι ἐγενήθησαν ᶻ αἱ δυνάμεις αἱ
γενόμεναι ἐν ὑμῖν, ᵃ πάλαι ἂν ἐν ᵃ σάκκῳ καὶ ᵃ σποδῷ
καθήμενοι ᵇ μετενόησαν. 14 ˣ πλὴν Τύρῳ καὶ Σιδῶνι

n Mark v. 26. Phil. iv. 18.
o w. gen., Matt. x. 37, 38 reff.
p = Matt. xx. 8 reff.
q John vii. 3. xiii. 1 al.† Wisd. vii. 27 al.
r ch. ix. 16 reff. Gen. xviii. 8.
s Matt. iii. 2 reff. with ἐπί, here only. Ps. xxvi. 2.
t ch. xiv 21 reff. Prov. vii. 12.
u ch. ix. 5 reff.
v ch. xv. 15. Acts v. 13 al. = Ps. ci. 5.
w here only †. (ἐκμασσ., ch. vii. 38.)
x = Matt. xi. 22 reff.
y Matt. x. 15 (|| Mk. v. r.). xi. 22, 24 only †.
z = Matt. xi. 20, 21 reff.
a Matt. xi. 21 reff.
b Matt. iii. 2 reff.

7. rec εσθιοντες, with ACRΞℵ rel: txt BD. rec aft τ. μισθ. αυτ. ins εστι (*see Matt* x. 10), with ACR rel arm: om BDLXΞℵ. for εξ, απο D-gr.

8. rec aft ην ins δ' (*see ver* 10), with AKLXΛΠ (1, e sil): om BCDRΞℵ rel Orig$_2$ Constt Thl. δεχονται E¹KL¹MRUXΓΛ 69.

9. for τους, ους D¹(txt D³ ?). ασθενουντας D lat-*c e*. ηγγισεν Ξ.

10. rec (for εισελθητε) εισερχησθε (*from ver* 8: *see above, ver* 5), with AR rel [Eus$_1$ Bas$_1$]: txt BCDLΞℵ 1. 33. 69 latt. δεξωνται D ev-H [Bas$_1$].

11. for ημιν, υμιν D-gr² ℵ¹(txt ℵ-corr¹ ³ᵃ) Λ: om gat syr-cu arm. rec om εις τους ποδας ημων (*homœotel from* υμων *to* ημων), with ESVΓΔΛ vulg æth [Bas$_1$]: ins ABCDRΞℵ rel mm lat-*a b c e f i l* syrr syr-cu copt goth arm, but of these BDRℵ mm lat-*a b c e f i l* syr-cu(appy) om ημων. aft γινωσκ. ins υμεις ℵ¹(om ℵ-corr¹·³). rec aft ηγγικεν ins εφ' υμας (*from ver* 9), with ACR rel mm lat-*f l* syrr [syr-jer] copt-schw[-dz arm-mss Bas$_1$]: om BDLΞℵ 1. 33 ev-y latt syr-cu copt[-wilk] arm[-ed] Tert$_1$.—η (bef βασιλεια) is written twice in D.

12. rec aft λεγω ins δε, with DMVΞℵ (S, e sil) lat-*a f* [*q*] copt: om ABCR rel vulg lat-*b c e i* syrr syr-cu [syr-jer] goth æth arm. ανεκτοτερον εσται bef εν τη ημερα εκεινη A 69 Syr syr-cu arm; similar order in D lat-*e*.—for τη ημερα εκεινη, βασιλεια του θεου D lat-*e*, simly lat-*a b*.

13. (χοραζειν, so ABCGKLMSXΔΞℵ Frag-par: χοροζαιν D.) for 2nd ουαι σοι, και D. βηδσαιδα AB¹, βεδσ. D: βηθσαιδαν EUΓℵ 1. 69 [goth]. rec (for εγενηθησαν) εγενοντο (*from Matt* xi. 21), with ACR rel: txt BDLΞℵ 33. 69. rec καθημεναι (*amml corrn*), with D rel: txt ABCFLRXΓΞℵ Frag-par 33.

δὲ τῇ οἰκ., but in the (that) **house itself** (see ver. 5, where it was last spoken of, the *inhabitants* having been since mentioned) **remain.** Beware of rendering it *in the same house*, q. d. ἐν δὲ τῇ αὐτῇ οἰκ. **τὰ παρ' αὐτῶν**, the things which come from them; which are theirs, and by them set before you: cf. ver. 8.

9.] ἤγγικεν ἐφ' ὑμᾶς ἡ β. τ. θ. is a later announcement than generally ἤγγ. ἡ βασ. τ. οὐρ., Matt. x. 7. **11.] ἀπομασσόμεθα ὑμῖν** can hardly be with Wordsw., "*we wipe off from ourselves on you:*" the dat. pron. holds too slight and unemphatic a place for this, and is merely a dativus incommodi: '*against you,*' as E. V. Cf. Acts xiii. 51, where **ἐπ' αὐτούς** represents the same, and is similarly rendered in E. V. **13.]** In these words, which our Lord had uttered before (Matt. xi. 21 ff.), He takes His solemn farewell of the cities where the greatest number of His miracles had been done, and discourses uttered: they being awful examples of the **ἡ πόλις ἐκείνη** just described. It is wonderful how De Wette can write of these four verses falsche Reminiscenz, s. z. Matt. xi. 20—and this

c = ch. xi. 31, 32 || Mt. al. Ps. i. 5.
d Matt. xi. 23 reff.
e ch. i. 52. Acts xiii. 17. 2 Cor. xi. 7 al. 1 Chron. xvii. 17.
f Matt. xi. 23 reff.
g here (Matt. xi. 23 v. r.) only. Ezek. xxxi. 16 (w. εἰς ᾅδου).
h = ch. vii. 30. John xii. 48. Gal. ii. 21. 1 Thess. iv. 8. Isa. xxiv. 16.
i ch. ii. 20 reff.
k ch. viii. 13 reff.
l ch. ii. 51 reff.
m Mark xvi. 17 reff.
n ch. xxiv. 39. Mark iii. 11. John vi. 19. Acts vii. 56 al. Josh. viii. 20 (18) B. Ps. lxiii. 9.
o Matt. xxiv. 27 reff. Exod. xix. 16.
p Rev. viii. 10. ix. 1. (ἀπό, Matt. xxiv. 29.)

[y] ανεκτότερον ἔσται ἐν τῇ [c] κρίσει ἢ ὑμῖν.
15 καὶ σὺ Καφαρναοὺμ μὴ [d] ἕως τοῦ [d] οὐρανοῦ [e] ὑψωθήσῃ; [f] ἕως τοῦ [f] ᾅδου [g] καταβιβασθήσῃ.
16 ὁ ἀκούων ὑμῶν ἐμοῦ ἀκούει· καὶ ὁ [h] ἀθετῶν ὑμᾶς ἐμὲ [h] ἀθετεῖ· ὁ δὲ ἐμὲ [h] ἀθετῶν [h] ἀθετεῖ τὸν ἀποστείλαντά με.
17 [i] Ὑπέστρεψαν δὲ οἱ ἑβδομήκοντα [k] μετὰ χαρᾶς λέγοντες Κύριε, καὶ τὰ δαιμόνια [l] ὑποτάσσεται ἡμῖν [m] ἐν τῷ ὀνόματί σου.
18 εἶπεν δὲ αὐτοῖς [n] Ἐθεώρουν τὸν σατανᾶν ὡς [o] ἀστραπὴν [p] ἐκ τοῦ [p] οὐρανοῦ

...εμου ακο R.
ABCDE GKLM SUVX ΓΔΛΞ ΠΝ Frag.Par. 1. 33. 69

14. om εν τη κρισει D 253 Scr's c lat-*e* [*l*]: transpd in 1 lat-*a b q*. for η υμιν, υμιν CL: ημιν D[1](txt D[3]).

15. rec (for μη and υψωθηση) η and υψωθεισα (*see digest Matt* xi. 23), with ACR rel (69) vulg lat-*c f* g_1 *q* syrr goth [arm] Aug: η υψωθης (but txt restored) B[3](Tischdf = our B[2]): txt B[1]DLΞℵ lat-*a b e i l* [syr-cu] copt æth. om 1st του B[1]CDℵ: ins B(as corrd by origl scribe: Tischdf says by B[3]) RΞ rel. ins η bef 2nd εως C D[1] (and lat) 1 lat-*a b i l*. rec om 2nd του, with ACDRℵ rel Cæs: ins BL Frag-par. (*Prob the art is origl, cf ch* xvi. 23, *and was omd to suit* || *Matt.*) καταβηση (|| *Matt*) BD syr-cu [æth]: txt ACRΞℵ rel latt copt goth [syrr arm].

16. υμων bef ακουων A-corr(εμ. ακ. υμας A[1]) KΠ latt syrr [syr-cu] Ign_1 [$Constt_1$] $Iren\text{-}int_1$. aft ακουει add και ο εμου ακουων ακουει του πεμψαντος με Frag-par $Cypr_1$ [simly Ign_1]. for ο δε εμε to αποστειλαντα με, ο δε εμου ακουων ακουει του αποστειλαντος με D lat-[*a b*] *i l*.

17. μετα χαρας bef οι εβδομηκοντα AKΠ. aft εβδομηκοντα ins δυο (*see ver* 1) BD vulg lat-*a* [*c e l*] syr-mg arm.

18. εκ του ουρανου bef ως αστραπην B 254.

when he believes Luke to have had Matt. before him. **16.**] See Matt. x. 40 and notes.

17—24.] Return of the Seventy. As in ch. ix. 6—10, Luke attaches the return of the Seventy very closely to their mission. They probably were not many days absent. They say nothing of the reception of their message,—or it is not brought out in the Gospel, as not immediately belonging to the great central object of narration; they rejoice that more power seems to be granted to them than even His words promised, seeing that He commissioned them only to heal the sick, not to cast out devils, as He did the Apostles, ch. ix. 1. That this was a ground of joy not to be *prominently brought forward*, is the purport of our Lord's answer; the whole of which as far as ver. 24 incl. is in the strictest connexion, and full of most weighty and deep truth. **17.**] The **ἐν τῷ ὀν. σου** is perhaps too much lost sight of in the **ἡμῖν** here; though I would not lay so much stress on this as Stier has done.

18.] This verse has been generally misunderstood, and its force lost, by imagining it to refer to some triumph *just gained*, which our Lord announces as the reason for their newly manifested power. The truth is, that in this brief speech He sums up *proleptically*, as so often in the discourses in John, the whole great conflict with and defeat of the Power of evil, from the first even till accomplished by His own victory. The **ἐθεώρ. τ. σ.** refers to the original fall of Satan, when he lost his place as an angel of light, not keeping his first estate; which fall however had been proceeding ever since step by step, and shall do so, till all things be put under the feet of Jesus who was made lower than the angels. And this **ἐθεώρουν** belongs to the period before the foundation of the world when He abode in the bosom of the Father. He is to be (see ver. 22) the Great Victor over the Adversary, and this victory began when Satan fell from heaven. (I would not altogether erase the foregoing interpretation: but surely it is grammatically more correct, with Bleek, to refer the imperfect to the time just past,—to the Lord's prophetic sight at the time of the ministering of the Seventy. Cf. Acts xviii. 5 for a similar imperfect. If this view be correct, the words do not refer to any "*triumph just gained*," but to the Lord's glorious anticipations of final triumph, felt during the exercise of power by His servants.)

ὡς ἀστ.] Not the suddenness only

...πεσοντα Ξ. Η -τειν επανω...

[p] πεσόντα. 19 ἰδοὺ δέδωκα ὑμῖν τὴν [q] ἐξουσίαν τοῦ [r] πατεῖν
[s] ἐπάνω [t] ὄφεων καὶ [u] σκορπίων, καὶ ἐπὶ πᾶσαν τὴν δύναμιν
[v] τοῦ ἐχθροῦ, καὶ οὐδὲν ὑμᾶς οὐ μὴ [w] ἀδικήσει. 20 πλὴν
ἐν τούτῳ μὴ χαίρετε, ὅτι τὰ πνεύματα ὑμῖν [m] ὑποτάσσεται,
χαίρετε δὲ ὅτι τὰ ὀνόματα ὑμῶν [x] ἐγγέγραπται ἐν τοῖς
οὐρανοῖς. 21 ἐν αὐτῇ τῇ ὥρᾳ [y] ἠγαλλιάσατο τῷ πνεύματι τῷ ἁγίῳ καὶ εἶπεν [z] Ἐξομολογοῦμαί σοι, πάτερ

Ξ εν αυτη...

q constr., gen., Matt. x. 1 reff. ἐπί & acc., ch. ix. 1.
r ch. xxi. 24. Rev. xi. 2. xiv. 20. xix. 15 only. Isa. xlii. 5.
s Matt. v. 14. xxiii. 18, &c. Isa. xiv. 14.
t Mark xvi. 18.
u ch. xi. 12. Rev. ix. 3, 5, 10 only. Deut. viii. 15.
v = here only. see Matt. xiii. 28, 39.
w = here only, exc. Rev. vi. 6 al7. Isa. x. 20.
x 2 Cor. iii. 2, 3 only †. 1 Macc. xiii. 40 only.
y Matt. v. 12. Acts ii. 26 (from Ps. xv. 9). xvi. 34. Ps. ii. 11.
z = Matt. xi. 25. Rom. xiv. 11. xv. 9. 2 Kings xxii. 50.

19. rec διδωμι (*from misunderstanding, into which De W. also has fallen*: **δεδωκα** *does not apply merely to the* past, *but asserts an* abiding fact), with AC³D rel lat-*c* syrr syr-cu $Just_1$ Eus_1 $Iren\text{-}int_1$: txt BC¹LXℵ 1 vulg lat-*b e f* g_1 *i l q* syr-mg [syr-jer] goth æth [arm] $Orig_2$[int_5] Cyr_3 Chr [Bas_2] $Thdrt_1$ Mac $Epiph_1$ Hil_1 $Lucif_1$ Ambr $Cæs_4$. ins των bef οφεων and bef σκορπιων D. ins την bef του εχθρου B [$Orig_1$]. om ου μη D ℵ¹(ins ℵ-corr¹). Steph αδικηση (*ramml corrn or itacism?*), with BC rel : txt ADEHLMΓΛℵ 1. 33 $Orig_1$.

20. for πνευματα, δαιμονια (*gloss*) D 1 lat-*e f* syrr syr-cu copt-mss æth Eus_1 Bas_1 Cyr_1 $Thdrt_1$ $Orig\text{-}int_1$ $Ambr_{aliq}$ Ambrst Aug_1. rec aft δε ins μαλλον, with X Cyr_2: om ABCD [S(Tischdf)] ℵ rel latt [syrr syr-cu syr-jer copt goth æth arm] Eus_1 Bas_1 [$Orig\text{-}int_1$] Ambr. rec (for εγγεγραπται) εγραφη, with ACD rel Eus_1 : txt BLXℵ 1. 33 Eus_1 Constt Bas_1 Cyr_1 [$Thdrt_1$]. τω ουρανω D lat-*a b c* [*e f i l q*] $Constt_1$ Hil_1.

21. ταυτη ΑΔ copt [goth]. add δε DΛ lat-*f* [copt]. ins εν bef τω πνευματι D F(Wetst) LXΞℵ Frag-par 33 [vulg-sixt] lat-*a b c e* ff_2 *i l* [*q*] copt $Clem_1$. rec om τω αγιω, with A rel lat-*f* [*q*] goth ($Clem_1$) [Bas_1]: ins BCDKLXΞΠℵ 1. 33 latt syrr syr-cu syr-jer copt æth arm Aug Bede. rec adds ο ιησους, with AC rel [lat-*f q* syr goth Bas_1] : and bef τω πνευματι LX 33 lat-*c e* ff_2 Syr [syr-jer] æth arm : om

of the fall, but the brightness of the fallen Angel is thus set forth. The description is not figurative, but literal; i. e. as far as divine words can be said to be literal, being accommodated to our sensuous conceptions. See on this verse, Isa. xiv. 9—15, to which the words have a reference; and Rev. xii. 7—12.

19.] Our Lord here,—including all the evil and poison in nature in the **δύναμις τοῦ ἐχθ.**,—from the power given Him over that enemy, asserts the gift to them, extended afterwards to all believers (Mark xvi. 18), of authority to 'bruise the head of the serpent' (Gen. iii. 15). There is an evident allusion to Ps. xci. 13.

20.] The connexion is—'seeing that the power which I grant to you is so large, arising from my victory over the enemy,—make not one particular department of it your cause of joy, nor indeed the *mere subjection of evil to you at all*—but this,—the positive and infinite side of God's mercy and goodness to you, that He hath *placed you among His redeemed ones*.' **τὰ πνεύμ.** is something different from **τὰ δαιμόνια** in those words above, and denotes a wider range of influence—influence over *spirit* for good—whereby the πνευματικὰ τῆς πονηρίας are subjected to the believers in Christ. The **ἐγγέγραπται ἐν τοῖς οὐρανοῖς** is an expression in various forms frequent in Scripture, and is opposed to ἐπὶ τῆς γῆς γραφήτωσαν, Jer. xvii. 13, said of the rebellious. But no immutable predestination is asserted by it;—in the very first place where it occurs, Exod. xxxii. 32, 33, the contrary is implied, see Ps. lxix. 28: Isa. iv. 3: Dan. xii. 1: Phil. iv. 3: Heb. xii. 23: Rev. iii. 5; xiii. 8; xx. 12, 15. The **τὰ ὀνόμ. ὑμ.** seems to be a reference to **ἐν τῷ ὀν. σου** above, which perhaps was with them a *medium of self-praise*, as so often with Christians. Our Lord says, 'the true cause of joy for you is, not the power shewn forth by or in you *in My Name*, but that you, *your names*, are in the book of life'—as testified by the πνεῦμα which συμμαρτυρεῖ τῷ πν. ἡμῶν ὅτι ἐσμὲν τέκνα θεοῦ, Rom. viii. 16. And this brings us to ver. 21, where our Lord rejoices in the revelation of these things even to the babes of the earth by the will and pleasure of the Father:—*these things*—not, the power over the enemy—but all that is implied in **ἐγγέγραπται ἐν τ. οὐρ.** This, which is the true cause of joy to the believer, causes even the Saviour Himself to triumph, anticipating Isa. liii. 11.

21.] The words **τῷ ἁγίῳ** cannot well be excluded from the text; the expression as thus standing, forms an ἅπαξ λεγ., but is agreeable to the analogy of Scripture: cf.

a Matt. xi. 25. Acts xvii. 24. Gen. xxiv. 7.
b (Matt. xi. 25. xxv. 18 v. r.) 1 Cor. ii. 7. Eph. iii. 9. Col. i. 26 only. Ps. cxviii. 19.
c Matt. xi. 25 (reff.).
d Matt. xi. 26 reff.
e = Mark i. 24.
f absol., Matt. xi. 27 reff.
g Matt xiv. 23 reff.

[a] *κύριε τοῦ [a] οὐρανοῦ καὶ τῆς [a] γῆς, ὅτι [b] ἀπέκρυψας ταῦτα*
ἀπὸ [c] σοφῶν καὶ [c] συνετῶν, καὶ [c] ἀπεκάλυψας αὐτὰ [c] νηπίοις·
ναὶ ὁ πατήρ, ὅτι οὕτως [d] εὐδοκία ἐγένετο [d] ἔμπροσθέν σου.
22 [*καὶ στραφεὶς πρὸς τοὺς μαθητὰς εἶπεν*] *Πάντα μοι*
παρεδόθη ὑπὸ τοῦ πατρός μου, καὶ οὐδεὶς γινώσκει [e] τίς
ἐστιν [f] ὁ υἱὸς εἰ μὴ [f] ὁ πατήρ, καὶ τίς ἐστιν [f] ὁ πατὴρ εἰ
μὴ [f] ὁ υἱός, καὶ ᾧ ἂν βούληται [f] ὁ υἱὸς ἀποκαλύψαι. ...βουλ. ο υιος Frag.Par.
23 *καὶ στραφεὶς πρὸς τοὺς μαθητὰς [g] κατ' [g] ἰδίαν εἶπεν* ABCDE
Μακάριοι *οἱ ὀφθαλμοὶ οἱ βλέποντες ἃ βλέπετε.* 24 *λέγω* GHKL MSUV
γὰρ ὑμῖν ὅτι πολλοὶ προφῆται καὶ βασιλεῖς ἠθέλησαν ΧΓΔΛΞ Πℵ
ἰδεῖν ἃ ὑμεῖς βλέπετε καὶ οὐκ εἶδαν· καὶ ἀκοῦσαι ἃ 1. 33. 69
ἀκούετε καὶ οὐκ ἤκουσαν.

BDΞℵ vulg lat-*a b i l* syr-cu copt. transp σοφων and συνετων D. rec εγενετο bef ευδοκια (*from* ‖ *Matt*), with AC³Dℵ rel lat-*i* syrr syr-cu [syr-jer] copt goth æth arm: txt BC¹LXΞ 33 lat-*b c e ff*$_2$ *l q* [Clem$_1$ Iren-int$_1$] Eus$_1$ [Cyr$_1$-p].

22. elz om και to ειπεν, with BDLMΞΠℵ 1. 33. 69 vulg lat-*a b e f* syr-cu æth arm [Eus$_1$]: ins AC rel lat-*c ff*$_2$ *l q* syrr copt goth [æth-ms].—στραφεις δε Frag-par.—aft μαθ. ins αυτου C²(appy) Γ [lat-*c q* syrr goth]. rec παρεδοθη bef μοι, with vss [Eus$_1$]: txt ABCDΞℵ rel latt goth Orig$_1$ Eus$_1$. απο D. om μου D am(with forj per) lat-*a c l* arm (Just$_1$ [Eus$_1$] Iren-int$_1$). επιγινωσκει (‖ *Matt*) C F(Wetst) HΔ 33. rec εαν (‖ *Matt*), with ACΞℵ rel Eus$_1$: txt BD Frag-par 33. βουλεται AXΛ Frag-par 69.

23. for και στρ., στρ. δε D lat-*e*. om κατ' ιδιαν D latt(not *f*) [syr-cu]. aft ειπεν ins αυτοις D 1 [lat-*e*] copt. at end ins και ακουοντες α ακουετε D; simly tol lat-*c e f*.

24. om και βασιλεις D lat-*a e ff*$_2$ *i l* Meth$_1$ (Mcion$_1$-t): *et iusti* lat-*b q*. (ειδαν, so BCLΞℵ 33.) aft ακουσαι ins υου B. ins υμεις bef ακουετε D lat-*b c f* [*q* goth].

Rom. i. 4: Heb. ix. 14: 1 Pet. iii. 18: see also Rom. xiv. 17: 1 Thess. i. 6. The ascription of praise, and the verses following, are here *in the very closest connexion*, and it is perfectly unimaginable that they should have been inserted in this place arbitrarily. The same has been said of their occurrence in Matt. xi. 25; and, from no love of harmonizing or escaping difficulties, but from a deep feeling of the inner spirit of both discourses, I am convinced that our Lord did utter, *on the two separate occasions*, these weighty words; and I find in them a most instructive instance of the way in which such central sayings were repeated by Him. It was not a *rejoicing* before (in Matt.), but a *confession*: compare the whole discourse and notes. That the introductory words **ἐν αὐτῇ τ. ὥρᾳ**, = *ἐν ἐκ. τῷ καιρῷ*, may have been introduced from one passage into the other, and perhaps by some one who imagined them the same, I would willingly grant, if needful; not that, in the presence of such truths, such a trifle is worth mention, but that the shallow school of modern critics *do mention*, and *rest upon* such. On vv. 21, 22, see notes on Matt. xi. 25—27, observing here the gradual narrowing of the circle to which our Lord addresses himself, ver. 22, **στραφ. πρ. τ. μ.**,—then ver. 23 the same, with *κατ' ἰδίαν* added.

23.] This verse should not be marked off from ver. 22 by a new paragraph, as is done in the E. V.: much less, as in the Gospel for the 13th Sunday after Trinity, joined with what follows: except perhaps that the lesson taught us by its occurring there is an appropriate one, as shewing us how the *grace of Christian love*, which is the subject of the following parable, fulfils and abounds over, legal obedience. It is in connexion with the preceding, and comes as the conclusion after the thanksgiving in ver. 21. A similar saying of our Lord occurs Matt. xiii. 16, 17, but uttered altogether on a different occasion and in a different connexion.

24. προφ. κ. βασ.] David united both these, also Solomon. There may be an especial reference to the affecting last words of David, 2 Sam. xxiii. 1—5, which certainly are a prophecy of the Redeemer, and in which he says, ver. 5, "This is all my salvation, and all my desire, though he make it not to grow:"—see also Gen. xlix. 18.

25 Καὶ ἰδοὺ [h] νομικός τις [i] ἀνέστη [k] ἐκπειράζων αὐτὸν
λέγων Διδάσκαλε, τί ποιήσας [l] ζωὴν [l] αἰώνιον [lm] κληρονομήσω; 26 ὁ δὲ εἶπεν πρὸς αὐτὸν Ἐν τῷ νόμῳ τί γέγραπται; πῶς ἀναγινώσκεις; 27 ὁ δὲ ἀποκριθεὶς εἶπεν
Ἀγαπήσεις κύριον τὸν θεόν σου [n] ἐξ ὅλης τῆς καρδίας σου
καὶ ἐξ ὅλης τῆς ψυχῆς σου καὶ ἐξ ὅλης τῆς ἰσχύος σου
καὶ ἐξ ὅλης τῆς [o] διανοίας σου, καὶ τὸν [p] πλησίον σου
ὡς σεαυτόν. 28 εἶπεν δὲ αὐτῷ [q] Ὀρθῶς ἀπεκρίθης· τοῦτο
ποίει, καὶ ζήσῃ. 29 ὁ δὲ θέλων [r] δικαιῶσαι ἑαυτὸν εἶπεν

h ch. vii. 30 reff.
i = Mark xiv. 57, 60 reff.
k ch. iv. 12 reff.
l ch. xviii. 18 ‖ only.
m Matt. xxv. 34 reff.
n Mark xii. 30, 33. Eph. vi. 6. 1 Tim. i. 5. Deut. vi. 5. x. 12.
o Matt. xxii. 37 reff.
p Matt. v. 43. xix. 19 | Mk. Rom. xv. 2. Eph. iv. 25. Exod. xx. 17. Levit. xix. 18.
q ch. vii. 43 reff.
r Matt. xii. 37. 1 Cor. iv. 4. Gen. xliv. 16.

25. for *και ιδου νομ. τις ανεστη*, *ανεστη δε τις νομικος* D lat-(*c*) *e*. rec ins *και* bef *λεγων*, with ACD rel [vss]: om BLΞℵ lat-*e* [syr-cu] copt. om *διδασκαλε* D Mcion$_1$-t. aft *ποιησας* (sic) ins *ινα* ℵ[1](marked for erasure by origl scribe or ℵ-corr[1]).
26. om *τι* D[1]-gr(ins D-corr[1]) Scr's s.
27. (1st *σου* was at first omitted but afterwards supplied 1. m. in B: see table: Tischdf says by B[3].) *εν ολη τ. κ. σου* D 1 lat-*a b c ff*$_2$ *i* [*l q*] æth. om 1st *της* BΞ. *εν ολη τ. ψ. σ. κ. εν ολη τ. ισχ. σ. κ. εν ολη τ. δ. σ.* (*from Matt* xxii. 37) BLΞℵ 1 copt (æth?), and, omg *εν ολη τη διαν. σ.*, DΓ lat-*a b c ff*^{2} *i* [*l q*] Tert$_1$: txt AC rel vulg lat-*e f* syrr syr-cu [syr-jer] goth arm. for *σεαυτ.*, *εαυτον* AVX 69 Orig$_1$ [Bas$_2$].
28. *ζησεις* D.
29. rec *δικαιουν* (*more obvious tense*), with AC[3] rel: txt BC[1]DLXΞℵ Cyr$_1$ Isid$_2$.—*εαυτ.* bef *δικ.* D 243 lat-*c e* Cyr Isid. for *εαυτον*, *αυτον* L ℵ[1](txt ℵ-corr[1.3a]) Scr's c ev-47.

25—37.] Question of a lawyer: the parable of the good Samaritan. *Peculiar to Luke.* As Stier remarks (iii. 101, edn. 2), it is well that Luke has related the other incident respecting an enquiry of the same kind, for the critics would be sure to have maintained that this incident was another report of Matt. xix. 16. Such clear cases as this should certainly teach us caution, where *no such proof is given* of the independence of different narratives: and should shew us that both questions addressed to our Lord, and answers from Him, were, as matter of fact, repeated. See however a case to which this remark does not apply, ch. ix. 57 ff. **25.**] No immediate sequence from ver. 24 is implied. **νομικός**, a kind of scribe, = *νομοδιδάσκαλος*, ch. v. 17—whose especial office it was to teach the law, see Titus iii. 13; = *εἷς τῶν γραμματέων*, Mark xii. 28. There is no reason to suppose that the lawyer had any hostile intention towards Jesus,—rather perhaps a self-righteous spirit (see ver. 29), which wanted to see what this Teacher could inform *him, who knew so much already.* Thus it was a *tempting* or *trying* of Jesus, though not *to entangle* Him: for whatever had been the answer, this could hardly have followed. **τί ποιήσας**] He doubtless expects to hear of *some great deed;* but our Lord refers him back to the Law of which he was a teacher. **26. πῶς ἀν.;**] A common Rabbinical formula for eliciting a text of Scripture. **πῶς** is not merely = *τί*, but implies *how?* i. e. to what purport; so that the answer should contain a summary of his reading in the Law. **27.**] The first part of this, together with Deut. xi. 13 ff., the Jews had written on their phylacteries, and recited night and morning: but not the second; so that Kuinoel's idea that Jesus pointed to the phylactery of the lawyer, will not hold. Meyer thinks the man answered thus, because he had before heard our Lord cite these in connexion, and with an especial view to asking the question *τίς ἐστίν μου πλησίον;* It may have been so;—but I should rather believe the same spirit with which he began, to have carried him on to this second question. The words **θέλ. δικ. ἑαυτ.** seem to imply this, but see below. **29.**] Meyer explains this: The questioner, having been by our Lord's enquiry, *πῶς ἀναγ.*, himself thrown into the position of the answerer, yet, *θέλων δικ. ἑαυ.*, wishing to carry out the purpose with which he asked at first, and to cover what otherwise would be his shame at being answered by so simple a reply, and that his own,—asks **τίς ἐστίν μου πλησίον;**—I may observe that we need not take the

πρὸς τὸν Ἰησοῦν ˢ Καὶ τίς ἐστίν μου ᵗ πλησίον; 30 ᵘ ὑπολαβὼν δὲ ὁ Ἰησοῦς εἶπεν Ἄνθρωπός τις ᵛ κατέβαινεν ἀπὸ
Ἱερουσαλὴμ εἰς Ἱεριχώ, καὶ ʷ λῃσταῖς ˣ περιέπεσεν, οἳ καὶ
ʸ ἐκδύσαντες αὐτὸν καὶ ᶻᵃ πληγὰς ᶻ ἐπιθέντες ἀπῆλθον
ᵇ ἀφέντες ᶜ ἡμιθανῆ [ᵈ τυγχάνοντα]. 31 κατὰ ᵉ συγκυρίαν
δὲ ἱερεύς τις ᵛ κατέβαινεν ἐν τῇ ὁδῷ ἐκείνῃ, καὶ ἰδὼν
αὐτὸν ᶠ ἀντιπαρῆλθεν. 32 ᵍ ὁμοίως ᵍ δὲ ᵍ καὶ Λευείτης γενόμενος ʰ κατὰ τὸν τόπον, ἐλθὼν καὶ ἰδὼν ᶠ ἀντιπαρῆλθεν.
33 Σαμαρείτης δέ τις ⁱ ὁδεύων ἦλθεν ᵏ κατ' αὐτόν, καὶ ἰδὼν
ˡ ἐσπλαγχνίσθη· 34 καὶ προσελθὼν ᵐ κατέδησεν τὰ ⁿ τραύ-

ABCDE GHKL MSUV XΓΔΛΞ Πא 1. 33. 69

s interrog., ch. xviii. 26. 1 Cor. v. 2. 2 Cor. ii. 2. t without article, ver. 36 only. u = here only. (ch. vii. 43 reff.) Job ii. 4. iv. 1 al. v Mark iii. 22. ch. ii. 51 al. w Matt. xxi. 13 reff. x Acts xxvii. 41. James i. 2 only. 2 Kings i. 6. y Matt. xxvii. 28 reff. z Acts xvi. 23. Rev. xxii. 18. a ch. xii. 48. Acts xvi. 23, 33. 2 Cor. vi. 5. xi. 23. elsw., Rev. (ix. 18, 20 al.) only. b = Matt. iv. 11, &c. c here only. (= ἡμίθνητος, Wisd. xviii. 18.) d = here only. 2 Macc. iii. 9. e here only †. f here bis only †. Wisd. xvi. 10. g Matt. xxvii. 41 reff. h = Acts xv. 23. xxvii. 7. i here only. 3 Kings vi. 12 A (not in B). Tobit vi. 5 (not א) only. k constr., here only. l ch. vii. 13. Matt. xv. 32 al.† m here only. Ezek. xxxiv. 4, 16. n here only. Isa. i. 6. (-ματίζειν, ch. xx. 12.)

30. om δε B C¹(perhaps) א¹ copt-ms. aft ειπεν ins αυτω DΓ syrr syr-cu [syr-jer] copt[-wilk æth]. for κατεβαινεν, καταβανει C¹: καταβαινον Ξ. om 1st και C¹. om αυτον D lat-g_1. αφεικαν C¹ arm. om τυγχανοντα BDLΞא 1. 33 latt syrr syr-cu [syr-jer arm] æth Chr_1 $Vict_1$: ins AC rel copt.

31. for συγκυριαν, τυχα D: latt vary. om δε D-gr [lat-*a b e q*]. καταβαινων D [copt-dz]. om εν B(sic: see table) 1 vulg lat-*f* [*i*] *l q*.

32. om ver א¹. om γενομενος BLXΞא³ᵃ 1. 33 lat-*a c e f* copt æth(appy) arm. om ελθων D 243-53 Scr's p w vulg lat-*b e i* [ff_2 $g_{1.2}$ *l*] syr-cu Chr_1. aft ιδων ins αυτον (*see last ver*) ADΓΔ latt syrr syr-cu [syr-jer] copt: om BCΞא³ᵃ rel lat-*c* æth arm.

33. rec aft ιδων adds αυτον (*as above*), with ACD rel lat-*a* [*e f* vulg syrr syr-cu syr-jer] copt-wilk [æth Chr_1]: om BLΞא 1. 33 lat-*b c i l q* copt-schw.

whole of this explanation, but may well suppose that **δικαιῶσαι ἑαυτ.** may mean, 'to get himself out of the difficulty:' viz. by throwing on Jesus the definition of ὁ πλησίον, which was very narrowly and technically interpreted among the Jews, excluding Samaritans and Gentiles.

30] **ὑπολ., taking him up,** implies that the question was made an occasion of *saying more than the mere answer.* See Herod. vii. 101: Thucyd. v. 49. **κατέβ.,** both because Jerusalem was higher, and because 'to go up' is the usual phrase for journeying towards a metropolis. **ἀπὸ Ἱερ. εἰς Ἱεριχώ,** about 150 stadia distant. The road passed through a wilderness (Josh. xvi. 1) which was notorious for the robberies committed there. "Arabas . . . . quæ gens, latrociniis dedita, usque hodie incursat terminos Palestinæ, et descendentibus de Hierusalem in Hiericho obsidet vias, cujus rei et Dominus in Evangelio recordatur." Jerome, Comment. on Jer. iii. 2, vol. iv. p. 857. The same Father mentions that a part of the road was so infamous for murders, as to be called the red or bloody way, and that in his time there was a fort there garrisoned by Roman soldiers, to protect travellers (De locis Hebræis, under Adommim, vol. iii. p. 150). **περιέπ., exactly fell among.** They surrounded him. **ἐκδύσ.,** not merely of his clothing, but of all he had;—'despoliaverunt eum,' Vulg. **τυγχάνοντα** is not = ὄντα: ὄντα is understood with **ἡμιθ., in a state of (being) half-dead.**

31.] Many priests journeyed this way, for Jericho was a priestly city; this man is perhaps represented as having been up to Jerusalem in the order of his course, and returning (**κατέβαινεν**). The Law and Prophets enjoined the act of mercy which this priest refused (see Exod. xxiii. 4, 5: Deut. xxii. 1—4: Isa. lviii. 7); not, it is true, *literally,*—and therefore he neglected it. "The form συγκυρία is uncommon: Polybius has συγκύρημα and -ρησις." Bleek. **ἀντιπαρῆλθεν,** he did not even go up to him to examine him, but passed by on the opposite side of the road.

32.] The Levite, the inferior minister of the Law, did even worse; when he was at the place, he came and saw him;—came near, and then passed, as the other.

33—35.] The Samaritans were *entirely, not half,* Gentiles (= ἀλλογενής, ch. xvii. 18). Why our Lord mentions the name here, see below. **ἐσπλαγχν.**] This was *the*

F και οινον... ABCDE FGHKL MSUV ΧΓΔΛΞ Πℵ 1. 33. 69

μαта αὐτοῦ [o] ἐπιχέων ἔλαιον καὶ οἶνον· [p] ἐπιβιβάσας δὲ
αὐτὸν ἐπὶ τὸ ἴδιον [q] κτῆνος ἤγαγεν αὐτὸν εἰς [r] πανδοχεῖον καὶ [s] ἐπεμελήθη αὐτοῦ. 35 καὶ [t] ἐπὶ τὴν αὔριον
[ἐξελθὼν] [u] ἐκβαλὼν δύο [v] δηνάρια ἔδωκεν τῷ [w] πανδοχεῖ
καὶ εἶπεν [αὐτῷ] [s] Ἐπιμελήθητι αὐτοῦ, καὶ ὅ τι ἂν [x] προς-
δαπανήσῃς ἐγὼ [y] ἐν τῷ [z] ἐπανέρχεσθαί με [a] ἀποδώσω σοι.
36 τίς τούτων τῶν τριῶν [b] πλησίον δοκεῖ σοι γεγονέναι
τοῦ [c] ἐμπεσόντος εἰς τοὺς [d] λῃστάς; 37 ὁ δὲ εἶπεν Ὁ
[e] ποιήσας τὸ ἔλεος μετ' αὐτοῦ. εἶπεν δὲ αὐτῷ ὁ Ἰησοῦς
Πορεύου καὶ σὺ ποίει ὁμοίως.

P λῃσ-τας... ...ομοιως X.

o here only. Gen. xxviii. 18. p ch. xix. 35. Acts xxiii. 24 only. 2 Kings vi. 3. (see Matt. xxi. 5.) q Acts xxiii. 24. 1 Cor. xv. 39. Rev. xviii. 13 only. Num. xx. 4, 8, 11. r here only †. s 1 Tim. iii. 5 only. Gen. xliv. 21. (-λῶς, ch. xv. 8. -λεια, Acts xxvii. 3.) t constr., Mark xv. 1. Acts iii. 1. iv. 5. Esth. v. 8 F (not A[appy]). u = Matt. xii. 20, 35. xiii. 52. v Matt. xx. 2 reff. w here only †. x here only †. y Matt. xiii. 4 al. Ezek. ix. 8. z ch. xix. 15 only. Gen. l. 5. a ch. xix. 8. Matt. v. 26 al. Gen. xlii. 28. b vv. 27, 29 reff. c = 1 Tim. iii. 6, 7. vi. 9. Prov. xvii. 20. d ver. 30. e ch. i. 72 reff.

34. for επιβ. δε, και επιβ. D latt Syr syr-cu [syr-jer] æth. πανδοκιον Ξℵ[1].

35. for την, τη A. om εξελθων (*dropped out because of similar participle* εκβαλων?) BDLXΞℵ 1. 33 latt Syr syr-cu [syr-jer] copt æth $Vict_1$ Chr_1 Ambr: ins AC rel [lat-*q*] syr arm. aft εξ. ins και C[1]. δηναρια bef δυο D lat-*c e*. εδωκεν bef δυο δηναρια B. πανδοκει D[1](txt D-corr[1]) ℵ[1]. om αυτω BDLΞ 1. 33 vulg lat-*b c* [*e* ff_2 *i l*] syr-cu copt arm [Chr_1] $Ambr_1$: ins ACℵ rel lat-*a f* [*q*] syrr [syr-jer] æth. προσδαπανησεις (*itacism?*) DΛ. εν τω επανερχ. με bef εγω D, simly lat-*c e*: om εγω ℵ 1 arm Chr_1 $Ambr_1$ Aug. om σοι D.

36. for τις, τινα D. rec adds ουν, with ACD rel lat-*c e* syrr [syr-jer] copt æth arm: om BLΞℵ 1 vulg lat-*a b* syr-cu copt-ms [Bas_1 $Orig\text{-}int_1$]. om των ℵ[1](ins ℵ-corr[1.3a]) Γ (not B, see table): om τουτ. τ. τριων D. rec δοκει σοι bef πλησιον, with 1 latt syrr syr-cu arm $Orig\text{-}int_1$; δοκεις πλησιον D: txt A B(sic: see table) CΞℵ rel [Chr_1].—om π. δ. σοι 33.

37. rec (for 2nd δε) ουν, with AC[3]P rel lat-*q* syr-txt: om Scr's d lat-*c* Syr syr-cu arm: και ειπ. 77 vulg lat-*b f* [*i*] *l*: txt BC[1]DFLXΔΞℵ 1. 33. 69 lat-*a e* syr-mg copt. om αυτω DX copt-dz. om ο (bef ιησους) B[1].

great difference between the Samaritan and the others;—the actions which follow are but the expansion of this compassion. **ἔλαιον κ. οἶνον**] These were usual remedies for wounds in the East: Galen, cited by Wetstein in loc., prescribes thus for a wound in the head, ἐλαίας φύλλα τὰ ἁπαλώτατα τρίψας παράχει **ἐλαίου** καὶ **οἴνου** μέλανος καὶ κατάμασσε:—see also Isa. i. 6. **ἐπὶ τὸ ἴδ. κτ.**, thereby denying himself the use of it. **κτῆνος** is rarely found in the sing. in the classics: see an instance, Herod. ii. 132. **πανδοχεῖον**] The Attic form, as in the cognate words ἱεροδόκος, ξενοδοκεῖν, δωροδόκος, &c., is πανδοκεῖον. So Phryn.: οἱ διὰ τοῦ **χ** λέγοντες ἁμαρτάνουσιν· διὰ γὰρ τοῦ **κ** χρὴ λέγειν πανδοκεῖον κ. πανδοκεὺς κ. πανδοκευτρία:—p. 307, where see Lobeck's note. This is the only place where *an inn*, as we understand the word, *a house for reception of travellers kept by a host* as distinguished from an empty caravanserai, is mentioned. The Rabbinical writers frequently speak of such, but under a name adopted from this word, פונדק (Wetstein). Bleek remarks that this serves to shew, that there *were* such inns in that neighbourhood, though certainly they were not frequent. **ἐξελθ. . . . .**] **when he went on his journey.** **δύο δην.**] Some see in this, *two days' wages* (Matt. xx. 2).

36.] It will be observed that our Lord not only elicits the answer from the questioner himself, but that it comes *in an inverted form.* The lawyer had asked, *to whom* he was to understand himself obliged to fulfil the duties of neighbourship? but the answer has for its subject *one who fulfilled them to another.* The reason of this is to be found,—partly in the relation of neighbourship being *mutual*, so that if this man is my neighbour, I am his also;—but chiefly in the intention of our Lord to bring out a strong contrast by putting the hated and despised Samaritan in the *active* place, and thus to reflect back the **ὁμοίως** more pointedly. "Observe γεγονέναι, to have *become* neighbour. The neighbour Jews became strangers, the stranger Samaritan became neighbour, to the wounded traveller. It is not place, but love, which makes neighbourhood." Wordsworth.

37. πορεύου, κ.τ.λ.] The rendering is as

f constr., ch. ii. 21 reff.

38 f Ἐγένετο δὲ ἐν τῷ πορεύεσθαι αὐτοὺς f καὶ αὐτὸς ABCDE FGHKL MPSUV ΓΔΛΞΠ ℵ 1. 33. 69

38. for εγενετο δε εν τω, εν δε τω BLΞℵ 33 syr-cu copt: txt ACDP rel [latt] syrr [syr-jer æth(Tischdf) arm]. om αυτους D. om και BDLΞℵ 69 lat-*a* syr-cu

in E. V., **go and do thou likewise.** The καὶ σύ belongs, not to the πορεύου, but to the ποίει, which carries the main stress, the πορεύου being only secondary. The lawyer does not answer—'The Samaritan:' he avoids this; but he cannot avoid it in conviction and matter of fact. **ποίει ὁμ.**, i. e. 'count all men thy neighbours and love them as thyself.' The student accustomed to look at all below the surface of Scripture, will not miss the meaning which lies behind this parable, and which—while disclaiming all fanciful allegorizing of the text—I do not hesitate to say that our Lord Himself had in view when He uttered it. All acts of charity and mercy done here below, are but fragments and derivatives of *that one great act of mercy which* the Saviour came on earth to perform. And as He took on Him the nature of us all, being 'not ashamed to call us brethren,' counting us all His kindred,—so it is but natural that in holding up a mirror (for such is a parable) of the truth in this matter of duty, we should see in it not only the present and prominent group, but also Himself and His act of mercy behind. And thus we shall not (in spite of the scoffs which are sure to beset such an interpretation, from the superficial school of critics) give up the interpretation of the Fathers and other divines, who see in this poor traveller, going from the heavenly to the accursed city (Josh. vi. 26: 1 Kings xvi. 34),—*the race of man, the Adam who fell*;—in the robbers and murderers, *him who was a murderer from the beginning* (John viii. 44);—in the treatment of the traveller, the deep wounds and despoilment which we have inherited from the fall;—in the priest and the Levite passing by, the inefficacy of the law and sacrifice to heal and clothe us: Gal. iii. 21 (Trench remarks, Parables, p. 316, note, edn. 4, that the Church, by joining the passage Gal. iii. 16—23 as Epistle, with this Parable as Gospel for the 13th Sunday after Trinity, has stamped this interpretation with her approval):—in the good Samaritan, Him of whom it was lately said, "Say we not well that *thou art a Samaritan*, and hast a devil?" (John viii. 48)—who came to *bind up the broken-hearted*, to give them the *oil of joy for mourning* (Isa. lxi. 1 ff.);—who *for our sakes became poor, that we through His poverty might become rich*: who, though now gone from us, has left with us precious gifts, and charged His ministers to feed His lambs, promising them, when the chief Shepherd shall appear, a crown of glory that fadeth not away (1 Pet. v. 2, 4). Further perhaps it is well not to go;—or, if we do, only in our own private meditations, where, if we have the great clue to such interpretations,—*knowledge of Christ for ourselves*, and a *sound mind* under the guidance of His Spirit,—we shall not go far wrong. But minutely to allegorize, is to bring the sound spiritual interpretation into disrepute, and throw stumbling-blocks in the way of many, who might otherwise arrive at it.

38—42.] Entertainment of our Lord at the house of Martha and Mary. It surely never could be doubted who this Martha and Mary were, nor where this took place,—but that the harmonizing spirit has so beclouded the sight of our critics. Bengel believes them *not to be the sisters of Lazarus*, but another Martha and Mary somewhere else;—and this in spite of the deep psychological identity of characters which meets us in John xi. xii. Greswell, still more strangely, believes the *persons to be the same*, but that they had *another residence* in Galilee, and endeavours to establish this from John xi. 1 (where he says ἀπό only indicates residence, ἐκ origin; and the κώμη is not Bethany, but the village in Galilee: see notes there). I shall, as elsewhere, take the text in its most obvious and simple interpretation, and where nothing definite is inserted *in it*, throw light on it from what we know from other sources. And I believe most readers will agree with me in taking these for the sisters of Lazarus, and the village for Bethany. "As regards the name *Martha*, it is in Aramæan מרתא, from מר *dominus*, and answers to the Greek κυρία." Bleek. **38.**] **ἐν τῷ πορ.** need make no difficulty—the whole of the events related in this section of the Gospel are allotted, as in the widest sense they belonged, to *the last journey of our Lord from Galilee*, which ended in the triumphal entry into Jerusalem: see note on ch. ix. 51 ff. Jesus, as we know that He afterwards did, so now probably, when at Jerusalem (at the feast of Dedication), abode at Bethany. He 'loved'—(only used in this sense by John with regard to *this family*, and to *himself*)—Martha and Mary and Lazarus—and this

εἰσῆλθεν εἰς κώμην τινά· γυνὴ δέ τις ὀνόματι Μάρθα [g] ὑπεδέξατο αὐτὸν εἰς τὸν οἶκον αὐτῆς. 39 καὶ τῇδε ἦν ἀδελφὴ
καλουμένη Μαρία, ἣ καὶ [h] παρακαθεσθεῖσα [i] πρὸς τοὺς
πόδας τοῦ κυρίου ἤκουεν τὸν λόγον αὐτοῦ· 40 ἡ δὲ Μάρθα
[k] περιεσπᾶτο περὶ πολλὴν [l] διακονίαν. [m] ἐπιστᾶσα δὲ
εἶπεν Κύριε, οὐ μέλει σοι ὅτι ἡ ἀδελφή μου μόνην με κατέλειπεν διακονεῖν; [n] εἰπὲ οὖν αὐτῇ ἵνα μοι [o] συναντιλάβη-
ται. 41 ἀποκριθεὶς δὲ εἶπεν αὐτῇ ὁ Ἰησοῦς Μάρθα Μάρθα,
[p] μεριμνᾷς καὶ [q] θορυβάζῃ [r] περὶ πολλά· 42 ἑνὸς δέ ἐστιν

...συναντιλαβηται Ξ.

g ch. xix. 6. Acts xvii. 7. James ii. 25 only †. Tobit vii. 8. 1 Macc. xvi. 15 only.
h here only †.
i Mark v. 22. vii. 35. Rev. i. 17.
k here only. 2 Kings vi. 6. = Eccl. i. 13. cf. 1 Cor. vii. 35.
l = Heb. i. 14 ‡. (Esth. vi. 3 A. 1 Macc. xi. 58 only.)
m ch. ii. 38 al5. Acts xxii. 13 al10. 1 Thess. v. 3. 2 Tim. iv. 2, 6 only. L.P.
n w. ἵνα, Matt. iv. 3 reff.
o Rom. viii. 26 only. Ps. lxxxviii. 21 al.
p Matt. vi. 25 reff.
q here only †.
r = Acts xix. 25. Phil. ii. 23. 1 Tim. i. 19. vi. 4, 21. Tit. ii. 7.

copt: ins ACP rel. αυτον εισελθειν D. την οικιαν C^{1}LΞℵ 33: om εις τον οικον αυτης B. (αυτης (alone, appy) is supplied on the margin 2. m. [not noticed by Tischdf N.T. Vat.].)—om αυτης C^{1}LΞℵ^1 33: ins A[C^2]D ℵ-corr^1(but erased) rel [Bas$_1$], εαυτης P.

39. μαριαμ B^1(B^3 Tischdf) C^{1}LPΞℵ 1. 33 [copt-schw]. om η B^3(Tischdf) LΞ ℵ^1(insd by origl scribe or ℵ-corr^1). om 2nd και D lat-*a c* [*e*]. rec παρακαθισασα (*more usual form*), with C^{3}DP rel [Bas$_1$]: παρακαθησα K 69: txt ABC^{1}LΞℵ Mac$_1$. rec (for προς) παρα, with A B^2(qu? very uncertain) C^{3}DP rel [Bas$_1$]: txt B^{1}C^{1}LΞℵ 33 [Bas$_1$] Mac. rec (for κυριου) ιησου, with A B^1(perhaps: see table) C^{2}P rel lat-*b* syr-txt [Bas$_1$]: txt B^2 C^1(appy) DLΞℵ vulg lat-*a c* &c Syr syr-cu syr-mg copt æth arm. (Tischdf assigns παρα and ιησου to his B^3(= our B^2), but says that προς and κυριου were restored.) om αυτου D.

40. επισταθεις D. rec κατελιπε (*itacism?*), with B^{2}DΠ^{2}ℵ (FSUV, e sil): txt AB^{1}CPΞ rel. κατελειπεν bef με Ξ: κατ. με μονην D latt [Syr syr-cu syr-jer]. ειπον DLΞ 1. 33: ειπεν P: txt ABCℵ rel, εἶπε 69. for μοι συναντιλαβ., μου αντιλαβ. D.

41. ο ιησους bef ειπεν αυτη C^{3}DKUΠ 69 copt æth. for ιησους, κυριος B^1(Tischdf: ῑς B^3, but former reading restored) Lℵ vulg lat-*a i l* syr-mg [Bas$_1$(txt$_1$)] Ambr$_2$ Aug. om μεριμνας και D (Clem$_1$) Bas[-cat$_1$(txt$_1$)] Aug$_2$. rec (for θορυβαζη) τυρβαζη, with A B^3(Tischdf, but txt restored) P rel(-ζεις 69) Bas$_1$ Chr$_1$ [Antch$_1$] Damasc$_1$: txt B^{1}CDLℵ 1. 33 Bas[-cat$_1$] Evagr$_1$. om περι πολλα D.

42. for ενος δε εστιν χρεια, ολιγων δε εστιν χρεια η ενος B(χρεια εστιν) C^{2}L ℵ(om χρεια ℵ^1) 1. 33 syr-mg copt æth (arm) Orig$_1$ Bas$_2$ Jer$_1$: om D lat-*a b c e ff$_2$ i l* (Clem) Ambr$_3$(*the varr have arisen from understanding* ενος *to refer merely to the provisions then being prepared,—then softening it by* ολιγων, *and finally combining both*

word implies surely hospitality and intercourse. **γυνή τις**—it does not follow that Martha was a widow; the incident brings out the *two sisters*, and therefore no others are mentioned. She may have had a husband or a father living. At all events, it is a consistency belonging to real life, that we find the same person prominent in the family in John, as here.

39.] It does not appear that the meal *had begun*; far rather is it likely that Martha was busy about *preparing* it. Mary sat at Jesus' feet, as His disciple, while He was discoursing. **40.**] **περιεσπ.** (as also the form **παρακαθεσθεῖσα** above) is a word of later Greek. We have in Dion. Hal. ix. 43, περισπᾷ περὶ τὰς ἔξω στρατείας τὸν δῆμον: and in Jos. Antt. v. 1. 4, πρὸς τοσαύτας ὑπηρεσίας διασπώμενος. See also Diod. Sic. i. 74: Polyb. xv. 3. 4. It exactly answers to the Latin 'torqueor' used in the same connexion by Horace, Sat. ii. 8. 67, and to a midland provincial expression '*to be put about*,' meaning to be 'distracted with officious care.' See Phryn. ed. Lobeck, p. 415, who gives ἄσχολος εἶναι for the corresponding classical expression. **ἐπιστ.**, generally, but not always, used by Luke of a *sudden coming into presence*. It looks here as if our Lord were teaching in another apartment from that where the διακονία was going on:—this appears also in the **κατέλειπεν**. **41, 42.**] The repetition of her name indicates reproof. **μεριμνᾷς** expresses the inner anxiety (from μερίζω), **θορυβάζῃ** the outer bustle and confusion. The latter word is not elsewhere found in Greek. **πολλά, many things.** **ἑνός**, of one thing; perhaps we should not express the two words more definitely, for fear of narrowing the wide sense in which they are spoken. I can hardly doubt that our Lord, in the *first*

s = Heb. vii. 11. Sir. iii. 22.
t = here only. (Acts viii. 21. xvi. 12. 2 Cor. vi. 15. Col. i. 12 only. L.P.) Ps. lxxii. 26.
u ch. xiv. 7. Gen. xiii. 11.
v = Matt. ii. 6 al.
w ch. x. 35, 38 al.
x = Matt. vi. 10. 1 Pet. iii. 15. Isa. xxix. 23.

[s] χρεία. Μαρία [δὲ] τὴν ἀγαθὴν [t] μερίδα [u] ἐξελέξατο,
[v] ἥτις οὐκ ἀφαιρεθήσεται [ἀπ'] αὐτῆς.
XI. 1 Καὶ ἐγένετο [w] ἐν τῷ εἶναι αὐτὸν ἐν τόπῳ τινὶ
προσευχόμενον, ὡς ἐπαύσατο, εἶπέν τις τῶν μαθητῶν αὐτοῦ πρὸς αὐτὸν Κύριε δίδαξον ἡμᾶς προσεύχεσθαι, καθὼς
καὶ · Ἰωάννης ἐδίδαξεν τοὺς μαθητὰς αὐτοῦ.
2 εἶπεν δὲ
αὐτοῖς Ὅταν προσεύχησθε, λέγετε Πάτερ, [x] ἁγιασθήτω

XΞ και εγενετο.. ABCDE FGHKL MPSUV XΓΔΛΞ Πℵ 1. 33. 69

readings) : txt AC[1·3]P rel vulg lat-*f* *g*$_1$ *q* Syr syr-cu syr-txt Bas$_1$ Chr$_1$ [Mac$_1$ Antch$_1$] Damasc$_1$ Aug$_3$. μαριαμ B 1 [lat-*l*[1]]. om 2nd δε D latt syr-cu arm Orig-int$_1$ Jer$_1$ Ambr$_3$: ins ACP rel mm(with mt) lat-*f* *g*$_1$ *q* syrr [syr-jer] copt Clem$_1$ Bas$_1$ Chr$_1$ [Mac], γαρ BL X-comm Λℵ 1. 69 copt-ms Bas$_1$ Antch$_1$ Damasc$_1$. (33 def.) for ητις, η D. om απ' B D[-gr] Lℵ[1] lat-*a* *b* *c* *ff*$_2$ *i* *l* [*q*] : ins ACPℵ[3a] rel vulg lat-*c* *f* [D-lat] Clem$_1$ Bas$_2$ [Mac$_2$ Did$_1$].

CHAP. XI. 1. for και εγ., εγ. δε A 253 Scr's q r lat-*e*. προσευχομενον bef εν τοπω τινι P [Syr syr-cu] Orig$_1$[txt$_2$]. ins και bef ως επαυσατο DM lat-*a* *b* *c* [*e* *ff*$_2$ *i* *l* *q*]. om 2nd και Δℵ[1] 1. 69. 247-51 forj[with tol] lat-*a* *b* *c* *f* *l* [*i* *q*] syr-cu copt æth. om ιωαννης ℵ[1](insd by origl scribe or ℵ-corr[1]).

2. for ειπ. δε, ο δε ειπ. D lat-*e*. om αυτοις D. προσευχεσθε ACHMPΓΔΛΠ[1] 1. 33. 69. add μη βαττολογειτε ως οι λοιποι δοκουσιν γαρ τινες οτι εν τη πολυλογια αυτων εισακουσθησονται αλλα προσευχομενοι D (*see Matt* vi. 7 : D *throughout conforms many expressions to Matt*). rec aft πατερ ins ημων ο εν τοις ουρανοις (*from* ‖ *Matt*), with ACDP rel harl[1](with per) lat-*b* *e* syrr syr-cu copt [æth] : ins ημων (alone) L Scr's a [Cyr$_{sæpe}$-p] : ο εν τ. ουρ. (alone) 33(appy) lat-*a* *c* *ff*$_2$ *i* : om Bℵ 1 vulg Orig$_1$ Mcion$_1$(or

and *most obvious* meaning, indicated that simpler preparation would have been all that was needful, but the **πολλά** leads to the **ἕν**, and that to the **ἀγαθὴ μερίς**, the ἕν being the middle term of comparison between the *natural* πολλά and the *spiritual* ἀγαθὴ μερίς. So that the whole will imply—only *within* the circle of Christ's disciples, those who act from love (mistaken or otherwise) to Him—much as John vi. 27,—and will set before us the bread which perisheth on one hand, and that which endureth to everlasting life on the other. The **ἀγαθὴ μερίς, the good portion,** is the ἕν which is needful—see John vi. 53,—the *feeding on the bread of life by faith;* which faith cometh by hearing, and hearing by the ῥῆμα χριστοῦ, which Mary was now receiving into her soul, and which (John vi. 54) shall never be taken away, but result in everlasting life. The two types of character have ever been found in the Church; both, caring for Him, and for love to Him doing what they do: but the one busy and restless, anxious and stirring; the other quiet and humble, content to sit at His feet and learn. We see here which of the two He praises. But on the other hand we must not derive any argument hence against an active Christian life of doing good: *this is,* in fact, to sit at His feet and learn—to take His yoke on us, and learn of Him. It is the bustling about the πολλά of which there is no need, which is blamed: not the working out the fruits of the Spirit, which are needful, being parts themselves of the ἀγαθὴ μερίς.

CHAP. XI. 1—13.] JESUS TEACHES THE DISCIPLES TO PRAY. The locality and time of the following incident are alike indefinite. The only limits are those of the great journey which is the subject of this section. There is no reason for supposing this to be the *only occasion* on which the Lord delivered this prayer to His disciples. In the Sermon on the Mount, it stands in close connexion with what goes before;—and here also. In so weighty a summary of His teaching as that was, He was not likely, when speaking of prayer, to omit it;—when asked by His disciples to teach them to pray, He was not likely to depart from the form once given them. Such are ordinary probabilities, antecedent to every question affecting the two Gospels: and those critics who throw aside all such, are *far more prejudiced* in reality, than those who allow them full weight. "The peculiar and abridged form in Luke," says Meyer, "*is a proof that the apostolic Church did not use the Lord's prayer as a form.*" Rather, we may say, a proof of the fidelity with which our Evangelist reproduced his original reports, not correcting them as others after him did (see var. readd.) to suit the forms most probably in use. If

τὸ ὄνομά σου, ἐλθέτω ἡ βασιλεία σου· 3 τὸν ἄρτον ἡμῶν
τὸν [y] ἐπιούσιον δίδου ἡμῖν [z] τὸ [za] καθ' ἡμέραν· 4 καὶ [b] ἄφες
ἡμῖν τὰς ἁμαρτίας ἡμῶν, καὶ γὰρ αὐτοὶ ἀφίομεν παντὶ
ὀφείλοντι ἡμῖν· καὶ μὴ [c] εἰςενέγκῃς ἡμᾶς εἰς [d] πειρασμόν.
5 καὶ εἶπεν πρὸς αὐτοὺς Τίς ἐξ ὑμῶν ἕξει φίλον, καὶ
πορεύσεται πρὸς αὐτὸν [e] μεσονυκτίου καὶ εἴπῃ αὐτῷ Φίλε,
[f] χρῆσόν μοι τρεῖς [g] ἄρτους, 6 [h] ἐπειδὴ φίλος μου [i] παρ-

...ημιν Ξ. ...και μη P. R νηρου [και ε]ιπεν...

y Matt. vi. 11 only +. z ch. xix. 47. Acts xvii. 11 only. a Matt. xxvi. 55 reff. b = Matt. vi. 12. xii. 31, 32 al. Isa. xxii. 14. c = Matt. vi. 13 only. (ch. v. 18, 19 reff.) d ch. iv. 13. James i. 2, 12. Deut. iv. 34. e Mark xiii. 35. Acts xvi. 25. xx. 7 only. Ps. cxviii. 62. f here only. Exod. xii. 36. g = Matt. xiv. 17, 19 al. 1 Kings xxi. 3. h = Phil. ii. 26. Prov. i. 24. i ch. viii. 19 reff.

Tert). (Ξ def.) om το DKU. aft 1st σου ins εφ ημας D.—(Nyss and Max, simly Mcion(or Tert), say that St Luke for ελθετω η βασιλεια σου wrote ελθετω το αγιον πνευμα σου εφ' ημας και καθαρισατω ημας.) ελθατω CPΔℵ. 2nd σου bef η βασιλεια D. rec at end adds γενηθητω το θελημα σου ως εν ουρανω και επι της γης (*from* ‖ *Matt and liturgies*), with ACDPℵ rel harl(with tol per) lat-*a b c* syrr copt æth [Cyr-p] (but ουτω is insd bef και by ℵ[1], and της is omd in ACDMPΔ ℵ[1](insd by ℵ[3a], but erased) 69): om BL 1 vulg lat-ff_2 syr-cu arm $Orig_{expr}$ [$Tert_1$] Aug_{expr}. ℵ[3a] further adds και ρυσαι ημας απο του πονηρου.

3. for διδου, δος Dℵ 248 Scr's c g [$Orig_1$ Cyr_1]. for το καθ ημ., σημερον (‖ *Matt*) D Scr's g latt(but not am em gat mt per [tol] lat-g_2 *q*) syr-txt æth: om το ℵ[1] ev-P [$Orig_3$(ins_2)].

4. for τας αμαρτιας, τα οφειληματα *debita* D per tol lat-*b c* [ff_2]. for και γαρ αυτοι, ως και ημεις D mm lat-*b c* [*f* ff_2 *l* syr-cu]: ως και αυτοι ℵ[1] [lat-*i q*]. rec αφιεμεν, with FLMSUVXΞΠℵ $Clem_1$ $Orig_2$: txt ABCD ℵ[3a](Scr, Tischdf N. T., not Cod Sin) rel. for παντι οφειλοντι ημιν, τοις οφειλεταις ημων D mm lat-*b c* [ff_2 *l* copt] Ambr. rec at end adds αλλα ρυσαι ημας απο του πονηρου (*from* ‖ *Matt and liturgies*), with ACDR ℵ[3a](as far as απο τ, but erased: see ver 2) rel lat-*b c* syrr copt Thl: om BLℵ[1] 1 vulg arm $Orig_{expr2}$ [Cyr_{expr}-p $Tert_1$] Aug_{expr}.

5. om προς αυτους D lat-*c* $Mcion_2$-e. μεσονυκτιον X[1] Λ(Tischdf) ℵ-corr[1](but txt restored). for ειπη, ερει A D-gr KMPRΠ 69 latt Bas_1 $Damasc_1$: txt BCℵ rel lat-*f* ff_2 g_1 [D-lat] coptt $Orig_1$.

6. om μου (*on acct of repetns, μου, μοι, με*) CR rel lat-ff_2 Syr sah: ins ABLXℵ vulg lat-*a b* &c syr-cu syr copt æth arm $Orig_1$, μοι DM 69 lat-*c* Orig-int.

the apostolic Church did not use the Lord's Prayer as a form,—*when did its use begin*, which we find in every known Liturgy? (See Bingham, Antiqq. xiii. 7.) **1. καθ. κ. Ἰω. . . . .]** Of this fact we know nothing beyond the allusion here. **2.] ὅταν προς., λέγ. . . . .**, more definite than οὕτως προς. . . . . in Matt. On the prayer itself, see notes on Matt. vi. 9—13. The clauses not found in the text could hardly by any possibility have been *omitted* by any, had they ever formed a part of it. Stier's argument, that our text has not been conformed to Matt., because the doxology has never been inserted here, seems to me to tend in quite another direction: the doxology was inserted *there*, because *that was the form in general liturgical use*, and *not here*, because *this form was never used liturgically*. **3. τὸ καθ' ἡμ. . . . .]** for that day's need, or for that day, i. e. day by day. No substantive need be supplied after **τό**. **4.] καὶ γὰρ αὐτ. . . . .** expressed here more strongly than in Matt., as the plea for the exercise of the divine forgiveness to us,—'*for it is our own practice also to forgive*:' but notice, the difference—there is no **ἁμαρτία** here between man and man, only the ordinary business word of this world. **π. ὀφείλοντι ἡμ.]** This varied expression (see above) may serve to shew how far '*Luke's reporter*' (De Wette) was from misunderstanding the words of the Lord; that reporter, as Stier well observes, (Reden Jesu, iii. 126, edn. 2,) being no other than the *Holy Spirit Himself*, whose special guidance was promised in bringing to mind the things said by Jesus (John xiv. 26). **5.]** Now follows a parable on continuing instant in prayer, of the same nature as that in ch. xviii. 2 ff. In both parables, the argument is 'à fortiori:' "if *selfish man* can be won by prayer and importunity to give, and *unjust man* to do right, much more certainly shall the *bountiful* Lord bestow, and the *righteous* Lord do justice." Trench, Parables, in loc., who further remarks, that here *intercessory* prayer is the subject of the parable; there, *personal*. And, that we must remember that all reluctance on the part of God to answer our prayers is not

ἐγένετο [k]ἐξ ὁδοῦ πρός με, καὶ οὐκ [l]ἔχω ὃ [m]παραθήσω
αὐτῷ· 7 κἀκεῖνος ἔσωθεν ἀποκριθεὶς εἴπῃ Μή μοι [n]κό-
πους [n]πάρεχε· ἤδη ἡ [o]θύρα [o]κέκλεισται, καὶ τὰ παιδία
μου μετ' ἐμοῦ [p]εἰς τὴν [q]κοίτην εἰσίν· οὐ δύναμαι [r]ἀνα-
στὰς δοῦναί σοι. 8 λέγω ὑμῖν, εἰ καὶ οὐ δώσει αὐτῷ
[r]ἀναστὰς διὰ τὸ εἶναι φίλον αὐτοῦ, διά γε τὴν [s]ἀναίδειαν
αὐτοῦ [t]ἐγερθεὶς δώσει αὐτῷ ὅσων [u]χρῄζει. 9 κἀγὼ ὑμῖν
λέγω Αἰτεῖτε, καὶ δοθήσεται ὑμῖν· ζητεῖτε, καὶ εὑρήσετε·
[v]κρούετε, καὶ ἀνοιχθήσεται ὑμῖν. 10 πᾶς γὰρ ὁ αἰτῶν
λαμβάνει, καὶ ὁ ζητῶν εὑρίσκει, καὶ τῷ [v]κρούοντι ἀνοιχθήσεται. 11 τίνα δὲ ἐξ ὑμῶν τὸν πατέρα [w]αἰτήσει ὁ υἱὸς
ἄρτον, μὴ λίθον [x]ἐπιδώσει αὐτῷ; [y]ἢ καὶ ἰχθύν, μὴ [z]ἀντὶ

ABCDE FGHKL MRSUV ΧΓΔΛΠ ℵ 1. 33. 69

k = ch. xii. 36. John iv. 6 (?). l Matt. viii. 20 reff. m Mark vi. 41 reff. Gen. xviii. 8. n Matt. xxvi. 10 reff. o Matt. vi. 6. xxv. 10. John xx. 19, 26. 2 Chron. xxviii. 24. p = ch. iv. 23. vii. 1. ix. 61. xxi. 37. Mark i. 39. q = here (Rom. ix. 10. xiii. 13. Heb. xiii. 4) only. Exod. xxi. 18. r = Mark i. 35. ch. viii. 55 ‖ Mk. xxii. 46. s here only +. Sir. xxv. 22 only. t = Matt. ii. 13, &c. Gen. xli. 4, 7. u ch. xii. 30 reff. v Matt. vii. 7, 8 reff. w constr., Matt. vii. 9 reff. x Matt. vii. 9, 10 reff. y ch. xviii. 11. Rom. ii. 15. 1 Cor. ix. 8. xvi. 6 al. Job ix. 26. z = 1 Cor. xi. 15.

παρεστιν D[-gr]. for εξ οδου, απ αγρου D. om προς με D lat-*b* *i* [Bas_1] Orig-int.

7. και εκ. A : εκ. δε D sah. for ειπη, ερει D-gr lat-*b* [*l*] copt. om μου C[1]M 1 lat-*b* *c* ff_2 g_1 *i* [*l* *q*] syr-cu syr æth. εις την κοιτην bef μετ εμου ℵ [lat-*b* *l* *q* (sah)] : for εις την κοιτην, εν τη κοιτη D 57 latt sah $Clem_1$ Bas_1. for εισιν, εστιν D 254 Scr's c. add και ℵ.

8. om ει και D. rec αυτου bef φιλον, with E rel [$Damasc_1$] : αυτον φιλον AR : αυτον φιλον αυτου D : txt BCLXℵ 33 latt $Orig_2$ Bas_2 Chr_1 Mac_1. for γε, δε ℵ[1](txt ℵ-corr[1](?)[3a]) Scr's c [Chr_1]. om αυτω D-gr Syr-ed $Orig_1$. οσον DLℵ[3a] rel [sah] $Orig_1$ Bas_1-ms Mac [Damasc] : txt ABCKMRΠℵ[1] (33, e sil) [latt copt] $Orig_1$ Bas_2 [Chr].

9. [υμιν λε is written twice by B[1].] rec ανοιγησεται (*from* ‖ *Matt*), with ABCKLMRXΔΠℵ 1. 33. 69 $Clem_1$: txt D rel.

10. rec ανοιγησεται (*from* ‖ *Matt*), with CLMRXℵ 1. 33. 69 $Clem_1$: ανοιγεται (*corrn to* ευρισκει, *made by* B *in* ‖ *Matt also*) B D[-gr syrr syr-cu] : txt A rel.

11. for τινα, τις DLXℵ 33 vulg lat-*c* syr-mg $Orig_1$ Aug : txt ABCR rel lat-*f* [*b* ff_2 *i* *l* *q*] hom-Cl_1 [$Mcion_2$-e $Epiph_1$ $Dial_1$]. rec om εξ, with E rel : ins ABCDKLMRXΠℵ 33. 69 $Orig_1$ $Mcion_2$-e $Dial_1$. αιτησει bef τον πατερα B [syr-ms]. ο υιος bef αιτησει D 243 Scr's s [coptt $Orig_1$] : om ο υιος Lℵ vulg [not gat mm] lat-*c*. om αρτον to η και B lat-ff_2 *i* *l* sah [arm] $Orig_1$ $Mcion_2$-e. 1st αυτω bef επιδωσει D. rec (for ἤ) ει, with (but e sil) Scr's q r : txt ACDRℵ rel copt hom-Cl_1. om και [L]ℵ [33 vulg(with forj tol)] D-lat. ιχθην (sic) ℵ. aft ιχθυν ins αιτησει D lat-*b* *c* Syr syr-cu æth hom-Cl. for 2nd μη, και B 234(Sz) $Mcion_1$-e.

real, but *apparent* only, and arises from deeper reasons working for our good: whereas the reluctance in these two parables is *real*, arising from selfishness and contempt of justice. The interrogative form continues to **σοι**, ver. 7, 'Who of you shall be in these supposed circumstances?' **λέγω ὑμ.** . . . . . κ.τ.λ.

6. παρ. ἐξ ὁδ.] In the East it was and is the custom to travel late at night, for coolness' sake. Why **τρεῖς** ἄρτους, does not appear. I forbear to give the allegorical interpretations of the number, which abound: the significance of the *things asked for*, see below on ver. 13.

7.] We have an interesting fragment of domestic life here given us. The door is 'barred,' not only 'shut;' there is the trouble of unbarring it; the *father* and *children* are in bed (**εἰς τ. κ. εἰσ.** ellipt. for 'have gone εἰς τ. κ., and are ἐν τῇ κ.:' see reff.); (observe how in all the parables which place the Father, or the Husband, before us, the *Mother*, or the *Bride does not appear*;) and he cannot (i. e. will not, *cannot* from being overcome by reluctance) rise and give to him.

8.] **ἀναίδεια** is too mildly rendered by '*importunity*,' E. V. It should be **shamelessness**. It is presupposed here that the postulant goes on knocking and asking.

9.] What follows is in the closest connexion, and will not bear the idea that it is transferred here merely as being appropriate. The αἰτεῖν, ζητεῖν, κρούειν, all answer to the *features of the parable*. Ver. **10** declares to us not merely a result observable here among men, (in which sense it is *not universally true*,) but a *great law of our Father's spiritual Kingdom*: a clause out of the eternal covenant, which cannot be changed.

ἰχθύος ὄφιν αὐτῷ [x] ἐπιδώσει; 12 [y] ἢ καὶ [ἐὰν] αἰτήσει
[a] ᾠόν, μὴ [x] ἐπιδώσει αὐτῷ [b] σκορπίον; 13 εἰ οὖν ὑμεῖς
πονηροὶ [c] ὑπάρχοντες οἴδατε [d] δόματα ἀγαθὰ διδόναι τοῖς
τέκνοις ὑμῶν, πόσῳ μᾶλλον ὁ πατὴρ ὁ [e] ἐξ οὐρανοῦ δώσει
πνεῦμα ἅγιον τοῖς [f] αἰτοῦσιν αὐτόν;
14 Καὶ ἦν ἐκβάλλων δαιμόνιον[, καὶ αὐτὸ ἦν] [g] κωφόν.

a here only. Job xxxix. 14.
b ch. x. 19 reff.
c Acts xvi. 20 note.
d Matt. vii. 11. Eph. iv. 8 (from Ps. lxvii. 18). Phil. iv. 17 only.
2 Chron. xxi. 3.
e = here only. see Matt. xxiv. 17. 2 Cor. v. 2.
f constr., Matt. v. 42 reff.
g Mark vii. 32 reff.

rec 2nd επιδωσει bef αυτω (*corrn to precedg and* || *Matt*), with ACR$\aleph$ rel [vss Mcion$_1$-e Orig$_1$ Dial$_1$] : txt BDL lat-*c*.

12. C places this verse bef η και ιχθ. for η και [εαν], εαν δε και D : η ει R : om η C Syr syr-cu.—om εαν BL(R)$\aleph$ 1. 69 Dial$_1$: ins C rel, αν ΑΛ. Steph αιτηση (*gramml corrn* or *itacism?*), with E rel : txt ABCDHKL R(Treg, expr) ΓΔΛ$\aleph$ 1. 33 [Dial$_1$]. ωον bef αιτ. DRU fuld lat-*c*. om μη BL sah. transp επιδωσει and σκορπιον D.

13. for υπαρχοντες, οντες (|| *Matt*) DKMXΠ$\aleph$ Clem$_1$ Mcion$_2$-e Dial$_1$ Ath [Epiph$_1$] Cyr$_1$: txt ABCR rel [Antch$_1$]. rec αγαθα bef δοματα, with latt Clem$_1$ Orig-int$_1$ Hil$_1$: txt ABCDR$\aleph$ rel Scr's-mss Mcion-e [Dial$_1$ Epiph$_1$ Cyr$_1$ Antch$_1$]. aft ο πατηρ ins υμων (|| *Matt*) CU vulg [lat-*b e i l q*] Syr sah [æth arm Epiph$_1$ Cyr$_1$] Ambr Aug. om 2nd ὁ LX$\aleph$ 33 Syr syr-cu coptt. for πνευμα αγιον, αγαθον δομα D mss-in-Ambr lat-*b c ff$_2$ i l* [(arm)].

14. for ver, ταυτα δε ειποντος αυτου προσφερεται αυτω δαιμονιζομενος κωφος και εκβαλοντος αυτου παντες εθαυμαζον D lat-*c f*. om και αυτο ην A^1(appy) B(D)L$\aleph$

11—13.] Our Lord sets forth the certainty of our obtaining the Holy Spirit, (the *unspeakable gift*, in which all other δόματα ἀγαθά are included,) from our Father, by another 'à fortiori' argument, drawn from the love of earthly parents, so far less careful and tenderly wise than He is over His children. The construction, as before (ver. 5), is a mixed one: half interrogative, half hypothetical. For the rest, see notes on Matt. vii. 7 ff. The *egg* and *scorpion* are added here. The *serpent* and *scorpion* are the *positively mischievous:* the samples, ch. x. 19, of the δύναμις τοῦ ἐχθροῦ:—the *stone*, that which is simply *unfit for food*. So that God's answers to our prayers consist of neither useless nor mischievous things, but of His best gift—His Holy Spirit—in all the various and fitting manifestations of His guidance and consolation and teaching in our lives. This is (because this takes of and imparts to us by leading us continually to Him who is) the ἄρτος of the parable;—the 'paterfamilias' is our Father in Heaven, with whom however the night is as the day, who never slumbers nor sleeps. It has been noticed how by the hungry traveller coming to the man, may be imported, in the depth of the parable, the awakening in a man's own soul (which is so precious to him) of that hunger which he has nothing to satisfy, and which none but God can satisfy. The student may, as in the foregoing parable, follow out this clue for himself (provided it be done soberly) with much interest and profit. Notice that when *we address God* (Matt. vi. 9), He is ὁ πατὴρ ὁ ἐν τ. οὐρ.—when *He answers us*, He is ὁ πατὴρ ὁ ἐξ οὐρ. In the former case we go up into Him and His abode; in the latter He comes down to us. The construction is not (Meyer) ὁ ἐν οὐρανῷ ἐξ οὐρ. δώσει: but the one so common in good Greek, ὁ ἐκ Πελοποννήσου πόλεμος, denoting the quarter whence the influence implied in the *substantive* comes, which here is the result of that relation implied in πατήρ.

14—36.] Accusation of casting out devils by Beelzebub, and demand of a sign from heaven. Our Lord's discourse thereupon. Matt. xii. 22—45. Mark iii. 23—30. The reasonings of Greswell to shew that Luke relates an entirely different incident from Matt. and Mark, able and well conducted as they are, fail to carry conviction to my mind. The marks of identity are too many and striking to be mistaken; and on the plan of discrimination which he has adopted, I am persuaded that we might prove four distinct Crucifixions and Resurrections to have happened just as easily. Besides, it is quite impossible to carry the hypothesis throughout this section of Luke's Gospel: and when it has been once given up, a considerable difference is made in the way of regarding the various narrations. On the side of which Evangelist the strict accuracy lies, it is next to impossible for us now to decide. I am inclined to think with Schleiermacher (transl., p. 190), that the section from ch. xi. 14—xii. 53 (or rather perhaps 59) is a connected whole,

h = Acts xvii. 31. 1 Cor. vi. 2.
i Matt. xix. 3 al. 2 Chron. ix. 1.
k || Mt. reff.
l || Mk. ch. xii. 48.
m here only. Isa. lv. 9.
n pass., ch. xii. 52, 53. Acts ii. 3. act., ch. xxii. 17. Acts ii. 45. L. Isa. xxxiv. 17. mid., John xix. 24 (from Ps. xxi. 18) ||.
o || Mt. Rev. xvii. 16. xviii. 16, 19 only. Gen. xlvii. 19.
p ver. 15.

ABCDE FGHKL MRSUV XΓΔΛΠ ℵ 1. 33. 69

ἐγένετο δὲ τοῦ δαιμονίου ἐξελθόντος, ἐλάλησεν ὁ [g] κωφός.
καὶ ἐθαύμασαν οἱ ὄχλοι.
15 τινὲς δὲ ἐξ αὐτῶν εἶπαν [h] Ἐν Βεελζεβοὺλ τῷ ἄρχοντι τῶν δαιμονίων ἐκβάλλει τὰ δαιμόνια.
16 ἕτεροι δὲ [i] πειράζοντες [k] σημεῖον ἐξ οὐρανοῦ [l] ἐζήτουν [l] παρ' αὐτοῦ.
17 αὐτὸς δὲ εἰδὼς αὐτῶν τὰ [m] διανοήματα εἶπεν αὐτοῖς Πᾶσα βασιλεία ἐφ' ἑαυτὴν [n] διαμερισθεῖσα [o] ἐρημοῦται, καὶ οἶκος ἐπὶ οἶκον πίπτει.
18 εἰ δὲ καὶ ὁ σατανᾶς ἐφ' ἑαυτὸν [n] διεμερίσθη, πῶς σταθήσεται ἡ βασιλεία αὐτοῦ; ὅτι λέγετε ἐν Βεελζεβοὺλ ἐκβάλλειν με τὰ δαιμόνια.
19 εἰ δὲ ἐγὼ ἐν Βεελζεβοὺλ ἐκβάλλω τὰ δαιμόνια, οἱ υἱοὶ ὑμῶν [p] ἐν τίνι ἐκβάλλουσιν; διὰ τοῦτο

1. 33 copt æth arm. *εκβληθεντος* ACLX 33. 69 vulg lat-*b f i l* copt-ms: txt BRℵ rel. (for D's reading, see above.)

15. for *τινες δε, και τινες* D lat-*c* syr-cu. (*ειπαν*, so B(R ?).) rec om *τω* (*cf Matt* xii. 24), with DR rel: ins BCKLMΠℵ 33. 69 arm, *των* A. at end add (*from Mark* iii. 23) *ο δε αποκριθεις ειπεν πως δυναται σατανας σαταναν εκβαλλειν* A(D)KM(X)Π syr æth (*σαναν* D, *εκβαλειν* DX): om BCRℵ rel vss.

16. rec transp *εξ ουρανου* and *παρ' αυτου*, with R rel lat-*b q* syr: *εξ ουρ. εζητ.*, omg *παρ' αυτου*, X: txt ABCDLℵ 1. 33 (69) vulg lat-*c f ff₂ g₁ l* Syr syr-cu arm.

17. *τα διανοηματα* bef *αυτων* AKΠ vulg lat-*b c*. *διαμερισθεισα* bef *εφ' εαυτην* ADLℵ 33 Syr syr-cu copt: txt BR rel vss.—*μερισθεισα* (|| *Matt*) CFMXΓ. for *πιπτει*, *πεσιται* (sic, as often) D.

18. for *διεμερ.*, *εμερισθη* C(Γ)Λℵ. for *πως*, *ου* D. for *οτι*, *τι* ℵ[1](appy): txt ℵ-corr[1·3]).

19. om *οι* ADΓ: ins BCRℵ rel Orig$_1$. for *τινι*, *τι* D.

or, at all events, is intended to form such. But then the whole is introduced (ver. 14) without any mark of connexion with the preceding, and terminated as abruptly. On the other hand, the narrative in Matt. is introduced by his usual **τότε**, following upon a very general description of *a retirement* of our Lord, and His being pursued by multitudes, all of whom He healed; but whether the *οἱ ὄχλοι* are the same, and the *τότε* meant to specify that this incident occurred *then and there*, is by no means certain. Nor is the close of the section (xii. 50) bound very closely to xiii. 1, which commences *ἐν τῇ ἡμέρᾳ ἐκείνῃ*, and can hardly be said with certainty to define *the very same natural day*. We may observe that the attendant circumstances, as introduced and closed in Mark iii. 20; iv. 1, are equally indeterminate. I therefore leave the difficulty where I found it, and where I believe it will ever remain, during our present state of imperfection: only observing, that the important incident and discourse grounded on it is no way thereby invalidated in authority. It seems to have been a portion of the evangelic history, the position of which was not exactly and satisfactorily fixed; of which there have been already some instances (see ch. ix. 57—62), and there are, as will be seen, yet more as we proceed.

14.] **κωφόν**—*and blind*, Matt. ver. 22, where see notes on all the common matter. **15. τινὲς ἐξ αὐτ.**] No inference can here be drawn that these persons were not Pharisees (as Greswell has done), and consequently that the charge proceeded from a different quarter.

16.] This is not mentioned *here* by Matt., but further on in the discourse, ver. 38. No distinction (Gresw.) can be drawn between **σημ.** and **σημ. ἐξ οὐρ.**, for (1) our Lord answers the demand in both places *by the same reply*, the sign of Jonas,—see also Matt. xvi. 1—4; and (2) the ordinary Jewish idea attached to **σημ.** would imply **ἐξ οὐρ.**,—see notes on Matt. xvi. 1.

17. εἰδώς] So Matt. also, ver. 25. **οἰκ. ἐπὶ οἰκ.**] The ordinary rendering **and house** (divided) **against house, falleth**, is certainly right. Before Meyer charged this interpretation with having entirely arisen out of harmonistic considerations, he should have ascertained whether such an expression as a *kingdom* falling *οἶκος ἐπὶ οἶκον* is even tolerable. The ruling idea of the saying having been given by the **βασ. ἐφ' ἑαυτήν**, the emphatic pronoun need not be expressed again. Similarly we have, 1 Cor. ii. 11,

αὐτοὶ ὑμῶν κριταὶ ἔσονται. 20 εἰ δὲ ἐν [q] δακτύλῳ θεοῦ
ἐκβάλλω τὰ δαιμόνια, ἄρα [r] ἔφθασεν ἐφ' ὑμᾶς ἡ βασιλεία
τοῦ θεοῦ. 21 ὅταν [s] ὁ ἰσχυρὸς [t] καθωπλισμένος φυλάσσῃ
τὴν ἑαυτοῦ [u] αὐλήν, ἐν εἰρήνῃ ἐστὶν [v] τὰ ὑπάρχοντα αὐτοῦ·
22 [w] ἐπὰν δὲ [x] ἰσχυρότερος αὐτοῦ [y] ἐπελθὼν [z] νικήσῃ αὐτόν,
τὴν [a] πανοπλίαν αὐτοῦ αἴρει ἐφ' ᾗ [b] ἐπεποίθει, καὶ τὰ
[c] σκῦλα αὐτοῦ [d] διαδίδωσιν. 23 ὁ μὴ ὢν μετ' ἐμοῦ κατ'
ἐμοῦ ἐστιν, καὶ ὁ μὴ [e] συνάγων μετ' ἐμοῦ [f] σκορπίζει.
24 ὅταν τὸ ἀκάθαρτον πνεῦμα ἐξέλθῃ ἀπὸ τοῦ ἀνθρώπου,
διέρχεται δι' [g] ἀνύδρων τόπων ζητοῦν [h] ἀνάπαυσιν, καὶ μὴ

...διαδιδωσιν F.

Ξ και μη ...

q = here only. Exod. viii. 19. Ps. viii. 3.
r ‖ Mt. reff.
s art. = Matt. xxiv. 28. Rom. i. 17.
t here only. Jer. xxvi. (xlvi.) 9. 2 Macc. iv. 40. xv. 11 only.
u Matt. xxvi. 3 reff.
v = Matt. xix. 21 reff.
w ver. 34. Matt. ii. 8 only.
x ch. iii. 16 reff.
y = here only. 1 Kings xxx. 23.
z John xvi. 33 reff.
a Eph. vi. 11, 13 only. 2 Kings ii. 21.
b Mark x. 24 reff.
c here only. Zech. xiv. 1 al.
d ch. xviii. 22. John vi. 11. Acts iv. 35 (Rev. xvii. 13 v. r.) only. Josh. xiii. 6.
e = ch. xv. 13. John vi. 12. xv. 6. Exod. xxiii. 10.
f ‖ Mt. John x. 12. xvi. 32. 2 Cor. ix. 9 (from Ps. cxi. 9) only.
g ‖ Mt. 2 Pet. ii. 17. Jude 12 only. Ps. lxii. 1. Jer. ii. 6.
h Matt. xi. 29 reff.

rec transp *αυτοι* and *κριται*, with R rel: *κριται* bef *υμων* ACKLMUΠ 1. 33. 69 vulg lat-*ff*$_2$ *g*$_1$: *κριται εσονται* bef *υμων* א [lat-*b f i l q*]: txt BD [lat-*e*].

20. aft *ει δε* ins *εγω* (*from ver* 19) D 251 Scr's c ev-49 lat-*c* [copt æth Bas$_1$ Chr$_1$] Mcion$_1$-t; aft *θεου* (*from* ‖ *Matt*) BCLR א-corr$^{1.3}$ 33. 69 lat-*l* syr-w-ast [Bas$_1$]: om Aא^1 rel vulg lat-*b f ff*$_2$ [*i*] arm Eus$_1$ [Cyr$_1$].

21. om *ο* א^1(ins א-corr^1(?)^{3a}). *φυλασσει* (*itacism?*) DEMXΓΛ. for *εαυτ. αυλ.*, *αυλην αυτου* D. *εσται* Rא Scr's s.

22. for *επαν*, *εαν* D. rec ins *ο* bef *ισχυροτερος* (*from ο ισχυρος above: cf also ch* iii. 16 ‖ *Mark*), with ACR rel [Eus$_1$]: om BDLΓא copt arm. om 1st *αυτου* D. add *εστιν* א^1(marked for erasure by א-corr^1, and by origl scribe?) om *νικηση αυτον* D. for *επεποιθει*, *πεποιθεν* D. for last *αυτου*, *αυτο* D^1(txt D^2).

23. at end add *με* L א(marked for erasure by א^{3a}, but restored) 33 [gat] copt-wilk æth.

24. aft *οταν* ins *δε* DUX 1 lat-*b* syr copt[-wilk]. for *απο*, *εκ* R. for *δι ανυδρων*, *δια των υδρων* D-gr.

τίς οἶδεν ἀνθρώπων τὰ τοῦ ἀνθρώπου, εἰ μὴ τὸ πν. τοῦ ἀνθρώπου τὸ ἐν αὐτῷ; the ὁ ἄνθρ. being the same throughout.

20.] **ἐν δακτύλῳ θ.** = ἐν πνεύματι θ. Matt. No distinction can be established, as Gresw. attempts. The one expression explains the other. What was done (Hebraistically speaking) by the *finger* of God, was done by the Spirit of God. We have much greater variations than this in sayings demonstrably the same. And as to what the same author maintains about the relative magnitude of the works of the *finger, hand*, and *arm* of God, a reference to ref. Ps., where the *heavens* are 'the works of Thy *fingers*,' will sufficiently shew how little reliance is to be placed on such subtleties.

21.] This parabolic sentence is in close connexion with many prophetic sayings, Isa. xl. 10 marg.; liii. 12, and most pointedly Isa. xlix. 24, 25. It will be remembered that the Baptist called the Lord by this name, ὁ ἰσχυρότερος—placing after it, it is true, **μου**, but still using it as indicative of the Almightiness of the Son of God, rather than in comparison with himself. The **ἰσχυρός** is the adversary, Satan; his **αὐλή**, this present world,—John xii. 31; xiv. 30; xvi. 11. His goods, or tools, or spoils,—**τὰ ὑπάρχοντα** = τὰ σκεύη = τὰ σκῦλα,—are *the sons of men*,—2 Tim. ii. 26: 1 John v. 19 (Greek). With these is he clothed and armed, or rather with their *evil capacities*, which he furbishes and brightens for his use: with the πανοπλία τοῦ διαβόλου, compare by way of contrast, the πανοπλία τοῦ θεοῦ, Eph. vi. 11—20. Without these arms and tools he would be powerless: the evil one must have evil men—something receptive of evil—to work upon. But these the ἰσχυρότερος takes from him, and divides his spoils, Isa. liii. 12. He *divides his spoils*—turns to His own use and that of His followers all that good which the enemy had corrupted into evil. The Stronger had already come into the strong man's house—the *Saviour*, into the *world*—and was robbing him of his captives, and making them into His own disciples—e. g. Mary Magdalene and others: but the work was not fully completed yet, till the Lord, by and in His death, overcame him that had the power of death, i. e. the devil. And that His great victory is still proceeding;—He is still taking from him one and another,—rescuing the sons

i ‖ Mt. ch. xv. 8 only +.
j ‖ Mt. ch. xxi. 5. 1 Tim. ii. 9. Ezek. xxiii. 41.
k Matt. xvii. 1 reff.
l compar., ‖ Mt. only.
m ‖. 2 Pet. ii. 20. Rev. ii. 19. Ps. lxxii. 17.
n Matt. xiii. 4. Ezek. ix. 8.
o = Acts ii. 14. xiv. 11. xxii. 22. Judg. ix. 7.
p = ch. i. 15, &c. John iii. 4 al. Ps. xxi. 10.
q = here only.
r ch. xxiii. 29. Rev. i. 13 only.
s Job iii. 12. Joel ii. 16.
t = Matt. xxi. 16 (ch. xxi. 23 ‖ [xxiii. 29 v. r.]) only.
u = Phil. iii. 8. see Rom. ix. 20. x. 18.

εὑρίσκον λέγει Ὑποστρέψω εἰς τὸν οἶκόν μου ὅθεν
ἐξῆλθον. 25 καὶ ἐλθὸν εὑρίσκει [i] σεσαρωμένον καὶ [j] κεκοσμημένον. 26 τότε πορεύεται καὶ [k] παραλαμβάνει ἕτερα
πνεύματα [l] πονηρότερα ἑαυτοῦ ἑπτά, καὶ εἰςελθόντα κατοικεῖ ἐκεῖ, καὶ γίνεται [m] τὰ ἔσχατα τοῦ ἀνθρώπου ἐκείνου
χείρονα τῶν πρώτων.
27 Ἐγένετο δὲ [n] ἐν τῷ λέγειν αὐτὸν ταῦτα, [o] ἐπάρασά
τις [o] φωνὴν γυνὴ ἐκ τοῦ ὄχλου εἶπεν αὐτῷ Μακαρία ἡ
[p] κοιλία ἡ [q] βαστάσασά σε καὶ [rs] μαστοὶ οὓς [st] ἐθήλασας.
28 αὐτὸς δὲ εἶπεν [u] Μὲν οὖν μακάριοι οἱ ἀκούοντες τὸν

ABCDE GHKL MRSUV XΓΔΛΞ ΠΝ 1. 33. 69

...και μαστοι R.

ins τοτε bef λεγει (‖ *Matt*) BLXΞℵ[3a] 33 lat-*b l* syr copt Orig-int$_1$: om ACDRℵ[1] rel vulg lat-*c f i* Syr syr-cu æth arm.

25. ελθων CD(R) rel : txt A B(sic in cod : see table) ELMS[2]U V(e sil) ΔΞΠℵ.—εξελθων R. ins σχολαζοντα bef σεσαρωμενον (‖ *Matt*) BCLRΓΞℵ[3a] 1. 33. 69 lat-*f l* copt æth [Orig-int$_1$]. for και κεκοσμ., και κοσμ. L : om και DΓ copt. (*Both by homœotel from itacism.*)

26. om τοτε D (syr-cu) Orig-int$_1$. aft παραλαμβανει ins μεθ' εαυτου (*see* ‖ *Matt*) CX ℵ[1](or -corr[1]) 33. 69 [lat-g_1 *l* Orig-int$_1$].—rec επτα bef ετ. πν. πον. εαυτ. (‖ *Matt*), with ACR rel latt copt arm : αλλα επτα πν. πον. εαυ. D lat-*a* Vict-tun : ετ. επτ. πν. π. ε. G [Orig-int$_1$] : txt BLΞ(ℵ) 69. (ℵ had originally επτα before ετερα πν.: επτα having been erased μεθ εαυτου was written in the space.) for εισελθ., ελθοντα E rel : ελθων G : txt ABCDHKL[M]RXΞΠℵ [1. 33. 69] latt. om εκει C[1](appy) D 33 lat-*a b* [*e* ff_2 *i l q*].

27. rec γυνη bef φωνην, with ACRΞ rel copt arm : γ. τις επ. φω. D lat-*e* : εκ του οχλου bef φωνην γυνη KΠ 1 lat-*c* : txt BLℵ. om 1st ἡ ℵ. [σα of βαστασασα is omd in B(Tischdf).]

28. for αυτος δε, και αυτος C : ο δε D. rec μενουνγε, with B[2]CD rel : txt AB[1]LΔΞℵ.

of men by the power of His gospel, till the end, when He shall (Rev. xx. 1 ff.) bind him in the abyss; and though he be loosed for the final conflict by His sufferance, shall cast him overthrown into the lake of fire for ever. Rev. xx. 14.

23.] See on Matt. ver. 30. **24—26.**] See on Matt. xii. 43. **27, 28.**] This little but most instructive incident, here interposed, serves to shew the originality of Luke's account, and that, whatever its *position* may be, it is *itself* of the highest authority. The woman apparently was influenced by nothing but common-place and unintelligent wonder at the sayings and doings of Jesus:—and she broke out, with true womanly feeling, into a blessing of the mother who bare such a wonderful Teacher. Such seems to be the account of the incident itself. Our Lord's reply is indeed wonderful:—(1) In *reproof*. He corrects in her the unapprehensiveness of his word, which had caused her to go no further into the meaning of it than this ordinary eulogy imported,—and gives her an admonition how to profit better by it in future. (2) In *humility*. He disclaims all this kind of admiration for *his humanity*: and says not '*my word*,' but **the word of God**, which is in fact the same, but takes the view off from Him in his abasement, unto the Father who sent Him. (3) In *truth*. He does not deny the honour hereby pronounced upon his mother, but beautifully turns it to its true side—viz. that which was given her long since—μακαρία **ἡ πιστεύσασα**, ch. i. 45.

Her blessedness consisted not so much in being His mother, as in her lowly and faithful observance of the word of the Lord spoken to her: see ch. ii. 19, 51. Nor again does He deny that to have borne Him was an honour—**μὲν οὖν** is 'imo vero'—'yes, indeed, but.' (4) In *prophetic discernment*. It will be seen that this answer cuts at the root of all Mariolatry, and shews us in what the true honour of that holy woman consisted,—in *faith* and *obedience*. As the mother of the Lord, she represents our human race, unto whom a child is born, a son is given; no *individual* exclusive honour is due to her, any more than to Cornelius, who was singled out from the Gentile world, and honoured by an angelic message

λόγον τοῦ θεοῦ καὶ [v] φυλάσσοντες. 29 τῶν δὲ ὄχλων
[w] ἐπαθροιζομένων [x] ἤρξατο λέγειν Ἡ γενεὰ αὕτη γενεὰ
πονηρά ἐστιν· σημεῖον ζητεῖ, καὶ σημεῖον οὐ δοθήσεται
αὐτῇ εἰ μὴ τὸ σημεῖον Ἰωνᾶ. 30 καθὼς γὰρ ἐγένετο
...ση-μειον Ξ. Ἰωνᾶς τοῖς Νινευίταις σημεῖον, οὕτως ἔσται καὶ ὁ υἱὸς
τοῦ ἀνθρώπου τῇ γενεᾷ ταύτῃ. 31 [y] βασίλισσα [y] νότου
[z] ἐγερθήσεται ἐν τῇ [a] κρίσει μετὰ τῶν ἀνδρῶν τῆς γενεᾶς
ταύτης καὶ [b] κατακρινεῖ αὐτούς, ὅτι ἦλθεν ἐκ τῶν [c] περάτων
τῆς γῆς ἀκοῦσαι τὴν σοφίαν Σολομῶνος· καὶ ἰδοὺ [d] πλεῖον
Σολομῶνος ὧδε. 32 ἄνδρες Νινευὴ [e] ἀναστήσονται ἐν τῇ
[a] κρίσει μετὰ τῆς γενεᾶς ταύτης, καὶ [b] κατακρινοῦσιν αὐτήν,
ὅτι [f] μετενόησαν [g] εἰς τὸ [h] κήρυγμα Ἰωνᾶ· καὶ ἰδοὺ [d] πλεῖον
Ξ Ιωνα... Ἰωνᾶ ὧδε. 33 οὐδεὶς [ik] λύχνον [kl] ἅψας [m] εἰς [n] κρύπτην

v = Matt. xix. 20 reff.
w here only †.
x Matt. xi. 7 reff.
y || Mt. (reff.) 2 Chron. ix. 1.
z || Mt. 1 Cor. xv. 43. Isa. xxvi. 19.
a = ch. x. 14 reff.
b || Mt. Heb. xi. 7 al. Wisd. iv. 16.
c || Mt. Rom. x. 18 (Heb. vi. 16) only. Ps. xcvii. 3.
d = || Mt. Matt. vi. 25. Mark xii. 33. Heb. xi. 4.
e || Mt. Ps. i. 5.
f Matt. iii. 2 reff.
g = Matt. xviii. 20. 2 Tim. ii. 26.
h || Mt. reff.
i Matt. v. 15. ch. xv. 8 al. Exod. xxv. 31.
k ch. viii. 16. xv. 8. Exod. xxx. 8 A Ald. (ἐξάπτ., B F.)
l = as above [ch. xxii. 55 v. r.] & Acts xxviii. 2 only. Judith xiii. 13.
m = Acts xiii. 29. Rev. xi. 9.
n here only †. see note.

rec aft *φυλασσοντες* ins *αυτον*, with [B²(but erased, Tischdf)] X rel vulg-mss Lucif: *τον λογον του θεου* ℵ¹: om AB¹CDLΔΞ ℵ-corr¹·³ **1**. 33 am(with forj [per san tol]) lat-*a b c e f ff₂* syr æth arm Mcion₁-t.

29. rec om 2nd *γενεα*, with C rel Syr [æth]: ins A B(sic: see table) DLXΞℵ **1**. 33. 69 latt syr-w-ast [syr-cu syr-jer] copt arm. rec **επιζητει** (*from* || *Matt*), with CD rel: txt ABLΞℵ. rec aft *ιωνα* ins *του προφητου* (*from* || *Matt*), with AC rel [vulg-ed] lat-*e f q* syrr copt [æth]: om BDLΞℵ am(with em forj fuld jac mt per san [tol]) lat-*a b c ff₂ g₁·₂ i* syr-jer copt-ms arm.

30. om *γαρ* ℵ 239-45-58 ev-y [copt-wilk]. ins *ο* bef *ιωνας* BΛ. rec *σημειον* bef *τοις νινευιταις*, with AD rel latt [vss]: txt BCLXΞℵ 33. add *και καθως ιωνας εν τη κοιλια του κητους εγενετο τρεις ημερας και τρεις νυκτας ουτως και ο υιος του ανθρωπου εν τη γη* D, simly lat-*a* [*e*] *ff₂*.

31. om *εν τη κρισει* D lat-*ff₂*. for *ανδρων*, *ανθρωπων* ℵ¹: om *των ανδρων* (*see* || *Matt*) C 245 syr-cu æth. *πλεον* CD.

32. om ver D. rec *νινευι*, with K: *νινευιται* (*from* || *Matt, where there is no such var as here*) ABCℵ rel latt Syr syr-mg [syr-jer] arm: txt E¹HSVΔ.

33. rec aft *ουδεις* ins *δε*, with AΞ rel lat-*b f ff₂* syr æth: txt BCDUΓℵ 33 vulg lat-*a c* [*e i*] Syr syr-cu [syr-jer] copt-ms arm. Steph *κρυπτον*, with **1**: txt ABCD

relative to the divine purposes:—if she were, as there is every reason to conclude she was, a believer in her Son, *the Son of man*, she *bore Christ* in a far higher and more blessed sense than by being His mother in His humanity. And this honour may all believers in Him partake of with her; therefore the Lord says not *ἡ ἀκούουσα τ. λ. . . . . .* but *οἱ ἀκούοντες*. The last and boldest perversion of these words of our Lord by Father Newman, viz. that He thus does but still further exalt her honour, in that, besides being His mother, she heard His word, and kept it, need only be mentioned, to shew the follies to which able men are abandoned, who once desert truth and simplicity.

29.] This is now in answer to those who sought of Him a sign from Heaven. **τῶν ὄχλ. ἐπαθρ. . . . .** perhaps in expectation, as He paused in His discourse, that the sign was now about to be shewn:—see notes on Matt. for the main subject. Here we have one part of the sign of Jonas brought out, which is not touched on in Matt., viz. his *preaching after his resurrection* to the Ninevites, announcing—for that would necessarily be involved in that preaching—the wonderful judgment of God in bringing him there,—and thus *making his own deliverance*, that he might *preach to them, a sign* to that people; which sign (ver. 32) they received, and repented;—but a greater than Jonas, shewing and preaching a greater sign by far, this generation shall reject. **32. πλεῖον Ἰωνᾶ**] Not '*a greater than Jonas*,' or '*than Solomon*:' but Jonah = *the sign of* Jonah,—so that **πλεῖον** is *He who is the sign* to this generation:—a sign, *πλεῖον*, both in its *actuality*, its *significance*, and its *consequences*. The *order*, here, seems to be for the sake of climax;—

[m] τίθησιν οὐδὲ ὑπὸ [o] τὸν [o] μόδιον, ἀλλ᾽ ἐπὶ [o] τὴν [o] λυχνίαν, ...λυχνιαν Ξ.
ἵνα οἱ [p] εἰςπορευόμενοι τὸ φῶς βλέπωσιν. 34 ὁ [i] λύχνος ABCDE
τοῦ σώματός ἐστιν ὁ ὀφθαλμός σου· ὅταν ὁ ὀφθαλμός GHKL MSUVX
σου [q] ἁπλοῦς ᾖ, καὶ ὅλον τὸ σῶμά σου [r] φωτεινόν ἐστιν· ΓΔΛΠℵ 1. 33. 69
[s] ἐπὰν δὲ [t] πονηρὸς ᾖ, καὶ τὸ σῶμά σου [u] σκοτεινόν.
35 [v] σκόπει οὖν μὴ τὸ φῶς τὸ ἐν σοὶ σκότος [w] ἐστίν.
36 εἰ οὖν τὸ σῶμά σου ὅλον [r] φωτεινόν, μὴ ἔχον μέρος [τι]
[u] σκοτεινόν, ἔσται [r] φωτεινὸν ὅλον ὡς ὅταν ὁ [i] λύχνος τῇ
[x] ἀστραπῇ [y] φωτίζῃ σε. 37 [z] Ἐν δὲ τῷ λαλῆσαι [a] ἐρωτᾷ

o Matt. v. 15 (reff.). ver. 7. p ch. xix. 30. q Matt. vi. 22 (reff.) only. r here (3ce) & Matt. vi. 22. xvii. 5 only. Sir. xvii. 31. xxiii. 19 only. s ver. 22 reff. t = Matt. vi. 23. vii. 17, 18. Jer. xxiv. 2, 3, 8. u here (bis) & Matt. vi. 23 only. Prov. iv. 19. v = Gal. vi. 1. (Rom. xvi. 17. 2 Cor. iv. 18. Phil. ii. 4. iii. 17 only †. 2 Macc. iv. 5 only.) w indic., Gal. ii. 2. iv. 11. Col. ii. 8. Heb. iii. 12. Winer, § 56. 2. b. α. x = here only. (Matt. xxiv. 27 reff.) Hab. iii. 11. y trans., Rev. xviii. 1. xxi. 23. Ps. xvii. 28. z ch. iii. 21 (note). Ezek. ix. 8. a ch. vii. 3. Acts xxiii. 20.

S(Tischdf) Ξℵ rel. om ουδε υπο τον μοδιον LΓΞ 1. 69 arm[-zoh]. (αλλ᾽, so ABCΞℵ &c.) rec (for φως) φεγγος, with A rel: txt BCDXℵ 1. 33. 69. βλεπουσιν ℵ 33 Scr's i ev-z_1.

34. aft σωματος ins σου D latt(not *i q*) Syr copt æth. rec om 1st σου (‖ *Matt*), with Lℵ[3a] rel syr-cu arm: ins ABCDMℵ[1] latt syrr copt æth Jer. rec aft οταν ins ουν (*see Matt* vi. 22), with AC rel syrr syr-cu: om BDLΛℵ latt copt æth arm. η bef ο οφθαλμος D lat-*b e ff*$_2$ *q*. om 1st και (‖ *Matt*) CDΓ 69 latt[(exc *c*) copt-schw æth arm]. for ολον, παν D-gr. for επαν, οταν D 251. aft 2nd και ins ολον X ℵ[3a](but erased) 1. 253 lat-*f* (syr-cu copt) æth. aft σκοτ. ins εστιν D-corr lat-*e* copt æth. εσται KMUXΠ: εστιν both before and after D[1].

35. for ver, ει ουν το φως το εν σοι σκοτος το σκοτος ποσον (‖ *Matt*) D lat-*a b e ff*$_2$ *i* Aug. at end adds και ει το φως &c (as in D) syr-cu.

36. om ver (‖ *Matt*) D lat-*a b e ff*$_2$ *i* syr-cu. rec τι bef μερος, with ℵ rel vulg lat-*c*: om τι CLΓ: txt ABGKMXΠ 1. 33. 69 lat-*f*. om ο ℵ[1]. ins εν bef τη αστραπη B.

37. om εν δε τω λαλησαι D syr-cu. aft λαλησαι ins αυτον A; αυτον ταυτα 1. 69 lat-*c e f g*$_1$ *i*. for ερωτα(so ABMℵ 69) αυτον, εδεηθη δε αυτου D.

for the undervaluing and not appreciating His *wisdom*, will not lie so heavy on them in the judgment, as the *rejection* of His *preaching of repentance*.

33—36.] Our Lord goes on to speak of His teaching and miracles, which this generation despised, and demanded a sign from heaven in preference; He tells them that they will not see the significance of them, because they shut the eyes of their understanding, which should be the light of the soul;—this is set before them in a parable concerning the light of the body, which is the outward eye. The sentences are repeated from the Sermon on the Mount, see Matt. v. 15; vi. 22 f. (where see notes on all that is common), and ch. viii. 16; but, as has been shewn, the truth shines from a different side of them here. **33.**] **κρύπτην** (for so it should be accentuated), **a crypt**, or covered passage; τὴν ἀπόκρυφον οἰκίαν, Euthym. Athenæus, v. 205, describing a splendid ship built by Ptolemy Philopator, speaks of a κρύπτη φραγμοῖς καὶ θυρίσι περιεχομένη πάντοθεν.

35.] **σκόπει . . μὴ . .**, **take heed, lest . .**, and the **ἐστιν**, more forcible than ᾖ, implies the actual existence, in the hearers, of the state against which they are cautioned:—σκόπει μὴ ὁ νοῦς ὁ φωταγωγὸς τῆς ψυχῆς σου σκοτισθῇ ὑπὸ τῶν παθῶν, Euthym. **36.**] "*Tautological: the second member contains the same assertion as the first.*" (De Wette.)—Let us examine this. 'When thine eye is single (ver. 34),—i. e. *simple*,—straight and single-seeing,—thy whole body will be light.' Then (ver. 36),—'*if this be so*,—if thy whole body be light, having no part dark,—then it shall all be light as when a lamp with its brightness illuminates thee.' Of what is our Lord speaking? Of *His teaching*, as apprehended by the simple, single-seeing soul. If then the soul be so,—having no part darkened by prejudice or selfish lusts, and approach thus to His teaching, it shall be wholly illuminated by it, as by the candle of the Lord, searching its inward parts. So this saying, which, even as it stands, is not tautological,—for the second clause expresses the further result and waxing onward of the shining light, arising from the singleness of the eye,—becomes, in its spiritual significance, a weighty declaration of truth, answering to ch. viii. 15:—see also John viii. 12.

37—54.] DISCOURSE AGAINST THE

αὐτὸν Φαρισαῖος [a] ὅπως [b] ἀριστήσῃ [c] παρ᾽ αὐτῷ, εἰςελθὼν
δὲ [d] ἀνέπεσεν. 38 ὁ δὲ Φαρισαῖος ἰδὼν [e] ἐθαύμασεν ὅτι οὐ
πρῶτον [f] ἐβαπτίσθη πρὸ τοῦ [g] ἀρίστου. 39 εἶπεν δὲ ὁ
κύριος πρὸς αὐτὸν Νῦν ὑμεῖς οἱ Φαρισαῖοι [hi] τὸ ἔξωθεν τοῦ
[j] ποτηρίου καὶ τοῦ [k] πίνακος [l] καθαρίζετε, [im] τὸ δὲ ἔσωθεν
ὑμῶν [n] γέμει [o] ἁρπαγῆς καὶ [p] πονηρίας. 40 [q] ἄφρονες,

Θ_d xi. 40(appy) •••

b John xxi. 12, 15 only. Gen. xliii. 25. 1 Kings xiv. 24. 3 Kings xiii. 7 only.
c ch. xix. 17 reff.
d = ch. xiv. 10. xvii. 7. John xiii. 12 al. Judith xii. 16.
e John iii. 7 reff.
f = Mark vii. 4 only. 4 Kings v. 14.
g ch. xiv. 12 (15 v. r.). Matt. xxii. 4 only. 2 Kings xxiv. 15.
h here bis. Matt. xxiii. 25. 1 Tim. iii. 7. 1 Pet. iii. 3. Rev. xi. 2 only.
i Ezek. xli. 17.
j Matt. x. 42 al. Gen. xl. 11, &c.
k Matt. xiv. 8, 11 ‖ Mk. only +.
l Matt. viii. 2 al. Lev. xiv. 8.
m here [& 2 Cor. iv. 16] only.
n Matt. xxiii. 27 reff.
o Matt. xxiii. 25. Heb. x. 34 only. Isa. iii. 14.
p Matt. xxii. 18 reff. Isa. i. 16.
q ch. xii. 20. 1 Cor. xv. 36 al. L.P., exc. 1 Pet. ii. 15. Ps. xiii. 1.

rec aft *φαρισαιος* ins *τις*, with AC rel lat-*b e* [*q*] syrr syr-cu copt arm : pref DX vulg lat-*a c f ff*$_2$ [*i*] æth : om BLℵ 1. 69. for *οπως*, *ινα* D. for *παρ αυτω*, *μετ αυτου* D lat-*a ff*$_2$ [*b i*] *q*.

38. for *ιδων εθαυμασεν οτι*, *ηρξατο διακρεινομενος εν εαυτω λεγειν δια τι* D 251, simly latt syr-cu Tert$_1$.

39. aft *φαρισαιοι* ins *υποκριται* D lat-*b*.

Pharisees. There can be no antecedent improbability in the supposition that our Lord spoke on various occasions, and with various incidental references, the component parts of that great anti-pharisaic discourse contained in Matt. xxiii. *That was spoken* in the temple, during the last week of His ministry; it formed the *solemn close of His public teaching*,—and at the end of it He departed out of the temple to return no more. I do not think it possible to suppose any part of that discourse in Matthew to be related otherwise than in its true place; all probability is against such an idea,—and so is the character of the reports of discourses in that Gospel, in general so strictly coherent and exact. There is then but one supposition left, unless we suppose Luke to have put together at random a number of fragments, and to have inserted them here, *creating an occasion for them* (for it amounts to this), which is equally inconceivable. And that is, that our Lord *spoke at this meal*, the occasion being the wonder of the Pharisee at His not washing before sitting down to meat, *parts of that discourse*, with which He afterwards solemnly closed His public ministry. See throughout, notes on Matt. xxiii. **37.**] **ἀριστήσῃ**, the morning meal. **εἰςελθ. δὲ ἀνέπεσεν**, i. e. without any delay; as soon as He had entered, He sat down. **38.**] The *expression* of this wonder is not stated, but is probable. Our Lord would hardly have so suddenly begun, **ὑμεῖς οἱ Φ.**, unless something had been *said*, to which by assent they were parties. See His proceeding when *nothing was said*,—ch. vii. 39, 40. **ἐβαπτ. . . .**] This use of the word shews that it *did not imply necessarily immersion of the whole body*;—for it was only the hands which the Pharisees washed before meat. **39.**] There is not the least improbability or incongruity in our Lord's having thus spoken *as a guest at a meal* (as Strauss, Schleiermacher, De Wette, &c., maintain);—His solemn work of reproof and teaching was never suspended out of mere compliment,—nor were the intentions of the Pharisees towards Him so friendly as these invitations seem to imply. They were given mostly from deference to popular opinion, and from no love to Him;—sometimes even with a directly hostile object. See vv. 53, 54, and compare also ch. vii. 44—46. Observe also, that the *severest parts* of the discourse in Matt. (vv. 13—22, 33) were not uttered on this occasion. **νῦν**, i. e. as instanced by your present conduct—**Here is an instance of your, &c.** **τοῦ ποτ. κ. τ. πίν.**] Understand, 'in the proverb'—or perhaps the application is left to be enthymematically filled up, for the next clause presupposes it. **τὸ ἔξωθεν** and **τὸ ἔσωθεν** of a *man*, are not the outside and inside of the body—but the outside apparent *conduct*, and the inner unseen *motives*. Some difficulty has been found in the parallelism of *τὸ ἔξωθεν τοῦ ποτηρίου κ. πίνακος*, and *τὸ ἔσωθεν ὑμῶν*: and a proposal has been made (to which I am surprised to see Bleek giving his adhesion) to take *ὑμῶν* with what follows: "*the inside* (of the cup and platter) *is full of your plunder and wickedness.*" But surely all verisimilitude is against this, as well as the emphatic position thus given to *ὑμῶν*. The simple fact is, that the parable and its interpretation are intermixed throughout the whole, the mind of the hearer being left to find its own way in allotting each its part. Ver. **40** seems clearly to me to be a *ques-*

οὐχ ὁ ποιήσας [hi] τὸ ἔξωθεν καὶ [im] τὸ ἔσωθεν ἐποίησεν; ABCDE GHKL MSUVX ΓΔΘ$_d$ΛΠ ℵ 1. 33. 69
41 [r] πλὴν τὰ [s] ἐνόντα δότε [t] ἐλεημοσύνην, καὶ ἰδοὺ πάντα
καθαρὰ ὑμῖν ἐστιν. 42 ἀλλ' οὐαὶ ὑμῖν τοῖς Φαρισαίοις,
ὅτι [u] ἀποδεκατοῦτε τὸ [v] ἡδύοσμον καὶ τὸ [w] πήγανον καὶ
πᾶν [x] λάχανον, καὶ [y] παρέρχεσθε τὴν [z] κρίσιν καὶ τὴν
[a] ἀγάπην τοῦ [a] θεοῦ. ταῦτα ἔδει ποιῆσαι, κἀκεῖνα μὴ ...xi. 42 (appy) Θ$_d$.
[b] παρεῖναι. 43 οὐαὶ ὑμῖν τοῖς Φαρισαίοις, ὅτι ἀγαπᾶτε
τὴν [c] πρωτοκαθεδρίαν ἐν ταῖς συναγωγαῖς, καὶ τοὺς
[d] ἀσπασμοὺς ἐν ταῖς [e] ἀγοραῖς. 44 οὐαὶ ὑμῖν, ὅτι ἐστὲ ὡς

r = Matt. xi. 22 reff. Judg. iv. 9.
s here only. 1 Macc. v. 5.
t Matt. vi. 2, &c. reff.
u Matt. xxiii. 23. ch. xviii. 12. Heb. vii. 5 only. Gen. xxviii. 22.
v Matt. xxiii. 23 only +.
w here only +.
x Matt. xiii. 32 ∥ Mk. Rom. xiv. 2 only. Gen. ix. 3.
y = ch. xv. 29 only. (Matt. v. 18 reff.) Jer. xli. (xxxiv.) 18.
z = Matt. xxiii. 23 only. Deut. xxxii. 4.
a = John v. 42. 2 Thess. iii. 5. 1 John ii. 5, 15. iii. 17. iv. 12. v. 3.
b = here (Heb. xii. 12) only. Sir. xxiii. 2.
c ch. xx. 46 ∥ only +.
d ch. xx. 46 reff.
e ch. vii. 32 reff.

40. transp εξωθεν and εσωθεν CDΓ lat-*a c e* Petr$_1$ Cypr$_2$: txt ABΘ$_d$ℵ rel vulg lat-*b f ff*$_2$ *g*$_1$ *i* [*q*] syrr syr-cu copt æth arm [Archel$_1$] Cyr$_1$ Tert$_1$.

41. **εσται** DXΓ 1. 69 lat-*a* æth Bas-2-mss$_2$ Mcion$_1$-t.—**εστ.** bef υμιν D vulg lat-*b f* [*ff*$_2$ *i q*] syrr syr-cu æth.

42. **αλλα** B(Tischdf) DEGHLUΓΔΛℵ 69. (Θ$_d$?) ηδυσμον ℵ^1(txt ℵ^3). for παν, το V^2 ℵ^1(corrd by origl scribe or by corr^1): το παν Scr's e. παρερχετε Λ. (του θεου is written over the line in B by the origl scribe; see table: Tischdf says by B$^{2.3}$.) om ταυτα to παρειναι D lat-*b*. aft ταυτα ins δε (*from Matt* xxiii. 23) BCKLMXΘ$_d$Π ℵ-corr^1 33. 69 vulg lat-*c* Syr syr-w-ast syr-cu copt-wilk[-dz] æth: om ADℵ^1 rel lat-*a ff*$_2$ [*i*] copt-schw arm. for εδει, δει A [lat-*a*]. **ποιειν** Λ Scr's i: ποισαι (sic) ℵ. rec (for παρειναι) αφιεναι (*from Matt*), with B^2(but txt restored, Tischdf) C^1 rel: **αφειναι** ℵ^1 57 Scr's v^1 ev-y: παραφιεναι (*combn of readgs*) A: txt B^{1}Lℵ^{3a}.

43. for τοις φαρισαιοις, φαρισαιοι Dℵ lat-*a b c e ff*$_2$ *i* [*q* gat]. aft αγοραις ins και τας(om τας D) πρωτοκλισιας εν τοις δειπνοις (*from Matt* xxiii. 6) C(D) lat-*b q* [æth-ms]: aft συναγ. (but την -σιαν) 69.

44. rec aft υμιν ins γραμματεις και φαρισαιοι υποκριται (*from Matt* xxiii. 27), with A rel em lat-*b f q* syrr Cyr$_1$; γρ. κ. φαρ. (but not υποκρ.) D lat-*i* Lucif$_1$: om BCLℵ 1.

tion, and to mean, as E. V., **Did not He, who made the outside, make the inside also?**—i. e. if His works have become unclean and polluted through sin, what is the use of *only partially* purging them,—not *accomplishing* the purgation?—must not the cleansing, to be good for any thing, *extend to the whole?* The making **ὁ ποιήσας** to mean, '*he who has cleansed*,' and a negative, instead of an interrogative sentence—'ye fools, he who has cleansed the outside has not cleansed the inside also'—gives, especially as the same was more strongly implied in ver. 39, the most frigid sense imaginable; and I can only (still, after his second edition) wonder that Stier, after Kuinoel and others, should have adopted it. 41.] Here again I am compelled entirely to differ from Stier, who, with Erasmus, Lightfoot, Kuinoel, Schleiermacher, &c., understands this as *ironical—'but ye give alms of their contents, and behold, all things are clean* (in your estimation) *to you.*' But (1) this is inconsistent with the imperative **δότε**. (2) It would require ἐκ τῶν ἐνόντων, for the Pharisees did not give **τὰ ἐνόντα** in this sense. (3) It would be altogether irrelevant to the matter in hand, which was reproof to the Pharisees for their care *about outward cleanliness, when the inside was left unclean.* (4) It would be inconsistent with the emphatic position of **τὰ ἐνόντα**, which are thus pointed out as the *true material*, out of which to give alms. It would be altogether contrary to our Lord's usual habit of speaking about giving alms, to make Him cast a slur on it, as this would do: see Mark x. 21: ch. xii. 33, where the expression is very similar to this. The command is *a rebuke for their covetousness* (see ch. xvi. 14), which follows in close connexion with **ἁρπαγή** and **πονηρία**, ver. 39. The **τὰ ἐνόντα** are the *contents of the vessel*, which vessel (ver. 39: see note above) is **ὑμεῖς**: = therefore, in its meaning, the τὰ ὑπάρχοντα of ch. xii. 33,—and the **πάντα καθαρά ἐστιν** answers to the **θησαυρὸς** ἐν οὐρανῷ of that verse, the *result* of which is the **καρδία** ἐν οὐρανῷ: and such persons being **καθαροὶ** τῇ καρδίᾳ,—to them, as τοῖς καθαροῖς, **πάντα καθαρά** (Titus i. 15). **42.] But woe unto you, for ye do not this,—but make the most trifling payments, &c.** The con-

τὰ [f] μνημεῖα τὰ [g] ἄδηλα, καὶ οἱ ἄνθρωποι [οἱ] περιπατοῦντες [h] ἐπάνω οὐκ [i] οἴδασιν. 45 ἀποκριθεὶς δέ τις τῶν
[j] νομικῶν λέγει αὐτῷ Διδάσκαλε, ταῦτα λέγων καὶ ἡμᾶς
[k] ὑβρίζεις. 46 ὁ δὲ εἶπεν Καὶ ὑμῖν τοῖς [j] νομικοῖς οὐαί,
ὅτι [l] φορτίζετε τοὺς ἀνθρώπους [m] φορτία [n] δυςβάστακτα,
καὶ αὐτοὶ ἑνὶ τῶν δακτύλων ὑμῶν οὐ [o] προςψαύετε τοῖς
[m] φορτίοις. 47 οὐαὶ ὑμῖν, ὅτι οἰκοδομεῖτε τὰ [f] μνημεῖα
τῶν προφητῶν, οἱ δὲ πατέρες ὑμῶν ἀπέκτειναν αὐτούς.
48 ἄρα μάρτυρές ἐστε καὶ [p] συνευδοκεῖτε τοῖς ἔργοις τῶν
πατέρων ὑμῶν· ὅτι αὐτοὶ μὲν ἀπέκτειναν αὐτούς, ὑμεῖς δὲ
οἰκοδομεῖτε. 49 διὰ τοῦτο καὶ ἡ [q] σοφία τοῦ θεοῦ εἶπεν
Ἀποστελῶ εἰς αὐτοὺς προφήτας καὶ ἀποστόλους, καὶ

f Matt. viii. 28 al. fr. Gospp. only, exc. Acts xiii. 29. Gen. xxiii. 6, 9.
g 1 Cor. xiv. 8 only. Ps. l. 6 (8). (-λως, 1 Cor. ix. 26.)
h = ch. x. 19. Isa. iv. 14.
i = Mark iv. 27. John ii. 9 al.
j Matt. xxii. 35 reff.
k Matt. xxii. 6. ch. xviii. 32. Acts xiv. 5. 1 Thess. ii. 2 only. 2 Kings xix. 43.
l Matt. xi. 28 only. Ezek. xvi. 33 only.
m Matt. xi. 30. xxiii. 4. Acts xxvii. 10. Gal. vi. 5 only. 2 Kings xix. 35.
n here (Matt. xxiii. 4 v. r.) only. Prov. xxvii. 3 only.
o here only †.
p Acts viii. 1. xxii. 20. Rom. i. 32. 1 Cor. vii. 12, 13 only †. 1 Macc. i. 57. 2 Macc. xi. 24, 35 only.
q = here only. see Rom. xi. 33 al.

33 vulg lat-*a c e ff*$_2$ *g*$_{1.2}$ *l* syr-cu copt arm Mcion. om ως τα and 2nd τα D, simly lat-*a b c e ff*$_2$ *i* [*l q*] syr-cu [Lucif$_1$]. om 2nd οι AD rel: ins B(sic: see table) CLMℵ [syr]. επανω bef περιπατ. D æth.

46. ουαι bef τοις νομικοις D syr-cu. [τε of φορτιζετε is omd by B[1].] ins βαρεα και (*from Matt* xxiii. 4) bef δυςβαστακτα CX syr-mg [Bas$_1$-ms]. δυςβακτατα D[1] : δυσβακτα D-corr. aft. αυτοι ins υμεις B. for ενι, επι C 1. om τοις φορτιοις D lat-*b q*.

47. for οι δε, και οι Cℵ[1] [Mcion$_2$-e].

48. rec (for μαρτυρες εστε) μαρτυρειτε (*Matt* xxiii. 31), with ACD rel latt Chr$_1$ Lucif$_1$: txt BLℵ [æth(omg εστε)] Orig$_1$. for και συνευδοκειτε, μη συνευδοκειν D lat-*a b e q* Lucif$_1$. rec at end adds αυτων τα μνημεια, with AC rel; τους ταφους αυτων 1 Lucif$_1$; ins τ. ταφ. αυτ. bef οικ. 69: txt BDLℵ lat-*a b* (*e*) *i l*.

49. om και η σοφια του θεου ειπεν (*as Matt* xxiii. 34) D lat-*b* [Lucif$_1$]. αποστελλω (*Matt* xxiii. 34) D lat-*b* [*q*] Lucif. om 3rd και AKUΠ 1. 69 [D-lat] syrr syr-cu.

nexion, which is thus so close, is quite destroyed by the *ironical* interpretation of ver. 41. See note on Matt. xxiii. 23.

43.] Matt. xxiii. 6, 7. There doubtless was ample illustration of this at the time and place when it was spoken.

44.] See Matt. ver. 27;—but here the point of comparison is different. *There* (see note) *the sepulchres are whited, that men may not pass over them unawares:* and the comparison is to the outside fairness, and inside abomination. *Here,* the graves *are not seen,* and men thinking they are walking on clean ground *are defiled* by passing over them. Perhaps the difference of expression may have been occasioned by the greater wealth and splendour and display of the Pharisees *in the metropolis,* where Matt. xxiii. was spoken. **οἱ ἄνθρ. οἱ περ. ἐπ., the men who walk over them . . .; οἱ ἄνθρ. περ. ἐπ., men, when they walk over them.**

45.] This man appears to have been not a common Pharisee merely, but besides, a νομικός, whose duty it especially was to interpret the law. Perhaps he found himself involved in the censure of ver. 42; or generally among the other Pharisees.

46.] See on Matt. ver. 4.

47.] See on Matt. vv. 29—32.

48.] See on Matt. vv. 34—36. We have here a remarkable variation of expression in ver. 49, **ἡ σοφία τοῦ θεοῦ εἶπεν** here = ἐγώ Matt. Various explanations have been given of this. The difficulty is not the variation just noticed, so much as that *no such passage* exists in the O. T. But I have little doubt that the true explanation is this:—*the whole saying* is a reference to 2 Chron. xxiv. 18—22, and so marked a one, that I am surprised no Commentators but Olshausen and Stier should have observed it, and they not thoroughly. That passage opens with remarks of the sacred historian on the delinquency of Judah and Jerusalem after the death of Jehoiada the priest: then ver. 19, '*He sent prophets to them, to bring them again to the Lord; and they testified against them: but they would not give ear. And the Spirit of God came upon Zechariah the son of Jehoiada the priest, which stood above the people, and said unto them . . . . And they conspired against him, and stoned*

r Matt. xxiii. 34 reff.
s 1 Thess. ii. 15 only. Ps. cxviii. 157.
t = here bis (Acts xv. 17. Rom. iii. 11. Heb. xi. 6. xii. 17. 1 Pet. i. 10) only. 2 Kings iv. 11.
u Matt. xviii. 35 reff.
v Matt. xxv. 34 reff.
w Matt. xxiii. 18, &c. reff.
x abs., here only. 2 Chron. xxxv. 5.
y = Mark iv. 15. ver. 22.
z Matt. xvi. 19 reff.

ABCDE GHKL MSUVX ΓΔΛΠℵ 1. 33. 69

[r] ἐξ αὐτῶν ἀποκτενοῦσιν καὶ [[s] ἐκ]διώξουσιν, 50 ἵνα [t] ἐκ-
ζητηθῇ τὸ αἷμα πάντων τῶν προφητῶν τὸ [u] ἐκχυννόμενον
[v] ἀπὸ [v] καταβολῆς [v] κόσμου ἀπὸ τῆς γενεᾶς ταύτης, 51 ἀπὸ
αἵματος Ἄβελ ἕως αἵματος Ζαχαρίου τοῦ ἀπολομένου
μεταξὺ τοῦ [w] θυσιαστηρίου καὶ τοῦ [x] οἴκου. ναὶ λέγω
ὑμῖν, [t] ἐκζητηθήσεται ἀπὸ τῆς γενεᾶς ταύτης. 52 οὐαὶ
ὑμῖν τοῖς [j] νομικοῖς, ὅτι [y] ἤρατε τὴν [z] κλεῖδα τῆς [a] γνώσεως·
αὐτοὶ οὐκ εἰσήλθατε, καὶ τοὺς εἰσερχομένους [b] ἐκωλύσατε.
53 κἀκεῖθεν ἐξελθόντος αὐτοῦ ἤρξαντο οἱ γραμματεῖς καὶ
οἱ Φαρισαῖοι [c] δεινῶς [d] ἐνέχειν, καὶ [e] ἀποστοματίζειν αὐτὸν

a = ch. i. 77. Rom. ii. 20 al. 1 Kings ii. 3. b Matt. xix. 14 reff. c Matt. viii. 6 (reff.) only. d = Mark vi. 19 (Gal. v. 1) only. Gen. xlix. 23 (Ezek. xiv. 4) only. e here only +.

αποκτινουσιν ℵ[1]. διωξουσιν BCLXℵ : εκδ. AD rel.

50. for εκζητ., εκδικηθη L ℵ[3a](-δηκ.) ev-P [syr-ms]. (εκχυννομενον, so ACDE GLUΔΠℵ : εκκεχυμενον B 33. 69.) for 2nd απο, εως D lat-*a b c i l q* syr-cu Lucif.

51. rec aft απο ins του (*Matt* xxiii. 35), with A rel : om BCDLXℵ 1. 33. rec aft εως ins του (*see Matt*), with AC rel : om BDLXℵ 1. 33. aft ζαχαριου ins υιου βαραχιου (*from Matt*) D 251 syr-cu copt[-wilk]. for του απολομενου μεταξυ, ον εφονευσαν ανα μεσον (*from Matt*) D lat-*a* æth. for οικου, ναου *templi* D lat-*e* [arm].

52. for ηρατε, εκρυψατε D lat-*a* (*b*) *c e q* syr-cu arm : æth has both. κλειν D. ins και bef αυτοι D 69 lat-*a b c i l q* æth Orig-int$_2$ Ambr. rec εισηλθετε, with X rel Orig$_2$: txt ABC[2]DE[1]HLMΓΔℵ 33. 69. (C[1] uncert.) for εισερχ., εισπορευομενους D.

53. rec (for κακειθεν εξελθοντος αυτου) λεγοντος δε αυτου(om αυτου D) ταυτα προς αυτους, with A(D)X rel lat-(*a b*) *c e f i* Syr syr-cu [syr-txt] arm æth : om 69 : txt BCLℵ 33 copt.—add ενωπιον παντος του λαου D X(but οχλου for λαου) 254 Scr's i lat-*a b c e f* (*i*) *l* syr-mg syr-cu æth arm. (*The confusion has prob arisen from the seeming incongruity of the* αποστοματιζειν αυτον *&c after His departure.*) for οι γραμματεις και οι φαρισαιοι, οι φαρ. και οι νομικοι D vulg lat-*b c e f l* [*q*] : οι νομικοι κ. οι φαρ. 1 239 lat-*i*. επεχειν C : εχειν DS lat-*c e i* : συνεχ. H 241-6-52 Scr's d l m n u ev-y : txt ABℵ rel vulg copt æth arm. for αποστοματιζειν αυτον, συνβαλλειν αυτω D 69 lat-*b c e i l* [*q*].

him with stones at the commandment of the king in the court of the house of the Lord. . . . And when he died, he said, The Lord look upon it, **and require it.'** The words in our text are not indeed a *citation*, but an *amplification* of ver. 19 there—a paraphrase of them, giving the true sense of what the wisdom of God intended by them;—enlarging the mere historical notice which laid hold of God's purpose only by one thread let down to the earth, into the *divine revelation of the whole purpose* of God as the counsel of His will in heaven. In Matt. the *Lord Jesus Himself*, as became the solemnity of that final and awful close of His testimony to His own who received Him not, stands forth as the doer of this work, the sender of the Prophets and Apostles. (On *'son of Barachias'* see on Matt. ver. 35.) Perhaps the strangest solution of the difficulty above noticed is that of Meyer (second ed.), who supposes the words to have been inserted here from Matthew, and introduced as a quotation by ἡ σοφ. τ. θ. εἶπεν, which Luke *puts into the mouth of Jesus Himself*, läßt hier Jesum selbst reden. Bleek attributes the fact of our Lord having made this event the terminus historicus of their murders of the prophets to the position of the books of Chronicles at the end of the Hebrew Canon: and uses it as a proof that they *then* held the same place as now.

52.] **ἤρ. τὴν κλ. τῆς γν.** = κλείετε τὴν βασ. τ. οὐ. ἔμπροσθεν τ. ἀνθ. Matt. ver. 14, which words are the best explanation of our text:—**the key of knowledge** (i. e. not *of*, as *admitting to*, knowledge—but the key *is* the knowledge), being that right understanding of the Law and Prophets, which should shew Him to the people, of whom they testified; this the expounders of Scripture had taken away, neither themselves entering, nor permitting those to enter who were otherwise doing so,—and thus shutting the kingdom of heaven in men's faces.

53.] **ἐνέχ.** (αὐτῷ understood, see reff.) **to press vehemently upon Him** with a hostile view; a sense confined apparently to N. T. and LXX. **ἀποστ.]**

περὶ [f] πλειόνων, 54 [g] ἐνεδρεύοντες αὐτὸν [h] θηρεῦσαι τι ἐκ
τοῦ στόματος αὐτοῦ.
XII. 1 [i] Ἐν οἷς [j] ἐπισυναχθεισῶν τῶν [k] μυριάδων τοῦ
ὄχλου, ὥστε [l] καταπατεῖν ἀλλήλους, ἤρξατο λέγειν πρὸς
τοὺς μαθητὰς αὐτοῦ πρῶτον [m] Προσέχετε ἑαυτοῖς ἀπὸ τῆς
[n] ζύμης τῶν Φαρισαίων, [o] ἥτις ἐστὶν [p] ὑπόκρισις. 2 οὐδὲν
δὲ [q] συγκεκαλυμμένον ἐστὶν ὃ οὐκ [r] ἀποκαλυφθήσεται· καὶ
κρυπτὸν ὃ οὐ γνωσθήσεται. 3 [s] ἀνθ' ὧν ὅσα ἐν τῇ [t] σκοτίᾳ
εἴπατε, ἐν τῷ φωτὶ [u] ἀκουσθήσεται· καὶ ὃ πρὸς τὸ [v] οὖς
ἐλαλήσατε ἐν τοῖς [w] ταμείοις, κηρυχθήσεται ἐπὶ τῶν [x] δω-

...δωματων C.

f = Acts ii. 40. Heb. vii. 23 al. Num. ix. 19.
g Acts xxiii. 21 only. Deut. xix. 11. intrans., Judg. ix. 32.
h here only. Ps. lviii. 3.
i = here only.
j ch. xvii. 34 reff.
k Acts xix. 19. xxi. 20. Heb. xii. 22. Jude 14. Rev. v. 11 bis. ix. 16 only. Gen. xxiv. 60.
l Matt. v. 13 reff.
m Matt. vii. 15 reff. n Matt. xiii. 33 reff. o = ch. ii. 10 al. p Matt. xxiii. 28 reff.
q here only. 3 Kings xx. (xxi.) 4. r Matt. x. 26 reff. s = here only. (ch. i. 20 reff.) ἀντί = Eph. v. 31. t Matt. x. 27 reff. u Mark ii. 1 reff. v ch. ix. 44.
w Matt. vi. 6 reff. Deut. xxviii. 8. x Matt. x. 27 reff.

54. for ver, ζητουντες αφορμην τινα λαβειν αυτου ινα ευρωσιν κατηγορησαι αυτου D, simly lat-*a b c e f i l q*. om ενεδρευοντες αυτον D (258) lat-*a b c e i l q* syr-cu arm: om αυτον Xℵ 130 am copt. rec adds και, with (S, e sil) vulg syr æth arm: om ABCℵ rel latt Syr syr-cu copt. rec ins ζητουντες bef θηρευσαι, with AC rel vss [D, see above]: om BLℵ 1 copt æth. rec at end adds ινα κατηγορησωσιν αυτου (*expansive gloss, as is the readg of* D *above*), with AC rel latt syrr arm: om BLℵ copt æth.

Chap. XII. **1.** for εν οις to οχλου, πολλων δε οχλων συνπεριεχοντων κυκλω D, simly latt syr-mg. for καταπατειν αλληλους, αλληλους συνπνιγειν D. om αυτου D lat-*a i* [*l q*]. (πρωτον is joined to foregoing in ACDEHKΛΠℵ copt: to following in GLΔ 69 lat-[*b l*] *f i q* Syr syr-cu [æth] Lucif$_1$.) ητις εστιν υποκρισις bef των φαρισαιων BL lat-*e*.

2. for δε, γαρ D lat-*a* syr-cu syr-mg arm Iren-int: om ℵ 69. 239-45 [em]. for συγκεκ., κεκαλυμμενον C[1](aft εστιν) ℵ. for ουκ αποκαλυφθησεται, ου φανερωθησεται D.

3. ταμειεοις K 239-42-7-8 Scr's f w, ταμιοις AΓℵ 244-51-3 Scr's b.

ἀποστοματίζειν φασὶ τὸν διδάσκαλον, ὅταν κελεύει τὸν παῖδα λέγειν ἄττα ἀπὸ στόματος. Suidas. So it will mean, to *examine* Him,—to *question* Him,—especially, we may suppose, on such things as would require answers out of, or expository of, the Law, as they catechized in schools.

54. ἐνεδρ. αὐτόν] The accus. is Hellenistic, instead of the usual dative: so ἐνήδρευσαν τὰς παρθένους, Jos. Antt. v. 2. 12.

Chap. XII. 1—12.] Warning against hypocrisy. A discourse spoken immediately or very soon after the former, and in connexion with it;—consisting for the most part of sayings repeated from other occasions, and found nearly verbatim in Matt. It is impossible that there should be any reasonable doubt of this view, when we remember that some of them have appeared before, or appear again, in this very Gospel. While our Lord was in the house of the Pharisee, the multitudes appear to have assembled together again. If so, **ἐν οἷς** will mean, **during which things**, viz. those related above. He comes forth to them (ch. xi. 53) in the spirit of the discourse which He has just completed, and cautions his disciples against that part of the character of the Pharisees which was most dangerous *to them*. The connexion of these twelve verses may be thus enunciated:—*Beware of hypocrisy* (ver. 1), *for all shall be made evident in the end* (ver. 2), *and ye are witnesses and sharers in this unfolding of the truth* (ver. 3). *In this your work, ye need not fear men; for your Father has you in His keeping* (vv. 4—7)—*and the confession of my name is a glorious thing* (ver. 8), *but the rejection of it* (ver. 9), *and especially the ascription of my works to the evil one* (ver. 10), *a fearful one. And in this confession ye shall be helped by the Holy Spirit in the hour of need* (vv. 11, 12). **1. πρῶτον**] I am not convinced by Olsh., De Wette, and Meyer, that this belongs to **προσέχ.** . . . . Every instance which they quote of πρῶτον being thus used, is where *some definite matter is subsequent* to the thing said or done; e.g. Matt. vi. 33. But here is no *such matter*: πρ. would only mean, '*earnestly*,'—'*be sure that you*' . . . which meaning I do not think it bears. I have therefore coupled it with **τοὺς μ. αὐτ.**,

y Matt. x. 28 only. Lev. xxvi. 2. Jer. i. 17.
z (-νν-), Mt. x. 28 reff.
a ver. 48. ch. xx. 47 ‖ Mk. 1 Cor. xii. 23†. Dan. iv. 33 Theod.
b ch. iii. 7 ‖ Mt. vi. 47. Acts ix. 16. xx. 35 only. 2 Chron. xv. 3.
c Matt. vii. 29 reff.
d here only. Gen. xxxvii. 22.
e Matt. v. 22 reff.
f here bis & Matt. x. 29, 31 only. Eccl. xii. 4.
g Matt. x. 29 only†.
h pass., here only (Matt. xvi. 5 reff.). Isa. xxiii. 16.
i Matt. x. 30. Rev. vii. 9 only. Ps. cxlvi. 4.
k = Matt. vi. 26. x. 30. xii. 12. 2 Macc. xv. 13.
l constr., Matt. x. 32 bis only. = John xii. 42. Rom. x. 9, 10.

μάτων. 4 λέγω δὲ ὑμῖν τοῖς φίλοις μου, μὴ [y] φοβηθῆτε
[y] ἀπὸ τῶν [z] ἀποκτεννόντων τὸ σῶμα καὶ μετὰ ταῦτα μὴ R και μετα...
ἐχόντων [a] περισσότερόν τι ποιῆσαι. 5 [b] ὑποδείξω δὲ ABDEG
ὑμῖν τίνα φοβηθῆτε· φοβήθητε τὸν μετὰ τὸ ἀποκτεῖναι HKLM RSUVX
ἔχοντα [c] ἐξουσίαν [d] ἐμβαλεῖν εἰς τὴν [e] γέενναν, ναὶ λέγω ΓΔΛΠ ℵ 1. 33.
ὑμῖν τοῦτον φοβήθητε. 6 οὐχὶ πέντε [f] στρουθία πωλοῦνται 69
[g] ἀσσαρίων δύο; καὶ ἓν ἐξ αὐτῶν οὐκ ἔστιν [h] ἐπιλελησ- Q επιλελησμενον...
μένον ἐνώπιον τοῦ θεοῦ. 7 ἀλλὰ καὶ αἱ τρίχες τῆς κεφα-
λῆς ὑμῶν πᾶσαι [i] ἠρίθμηνται. μὴ φοβεῖσθε· πολλῶν F [ενω]πιων...
[f] στρουθίων [k] διαφέρετε. 8 λέγω δὲ ὑμῖν, πᾶς ὃς ἂν [l] ὁμολογήσῃ ἐν ἐμοὶ [m] ἔμπροσθεν τῶν ἀνθρώπων, καὶ ὁ υἱὸς
τοῦ ἀνθρώπου [l] ὁμολογήσει ἐν αὐτῷ [m] ἔμπροσθεν τῶν ἀγγέλων τοῦ θεοῦ. 9 ὁ δὲ [n] ἀρνησάμενός με [o] ἐνώπιον τῶν
ἀνθρώπων, [p] ἀπαρνηθήσεται ἐνώπιον τῶν ἀγγέλων τοῦ
θεοῦ. 10 καὶ πᾶς ὃς ἐρεῖ λόγον [q] εἰς τὸν υἱὸν τοῦ
ἀνθρώπου, [r] ἀφεθήσεται αὐτῷ· τῷ δὲ εἰς τὸ ἅγιον πνεῦμα
[s] βλασφημήσαντι οὐκ ἀφεθήσεται. 11 ὅταν δὲ [t] εἰςφέρωσιν
ὑμᾶς ἐπὶ τὰς συναγωγὰς καὶ τὰς [u] ἀρχὰς καὶ τὰς
[v] ἐξουσίας, μὴ [w] μεριμνᾶτε πῶς [ἢ τι] [x] ἀπολογήσησθε ἢ τί

m Matt. v. 16. vi. 1 al. n = Matt. x. 33 reff. o ch. viii. 47. xii. 9 al. p Mark xiv. 30, 31 reff. q = Matt. xviii. 15, 21. r Matt. vi. 12 reff. s w. εἰς, Mark iii. 29 reff. t ch. v. 18, 19 reff. u = Tit. iii. 1. v = Rom. xiii. 1. Tit. iii. 1 al. w = Matt. vi. 25 reff. x ch. xxi. 14. Acts xix. 33. xxiv. 10 al4. Rom. ii. 15. 2 Cor. xii. 19. L.P. Jer. xii. 1. xxxviii. (xxxi.) 6. 2 Macc. xiii. 26 only.

4. rec *αποκτεινοντων*, with B $Orig_1$ [Epiph] : *αποκτενοντων* DGHSXΛΠ 33. 69, *αποκταινοντων* M : txt Aℵ rel. for *και μετα τ. μη*, *την δε ψυχην μη δυναμενων αποκτειναι μηδε* D.—ℵ[1] omits *τα* of *μετα*. for *περισσοτερον*, *περισσον* ADKRΠ 33 : txt Bℵ rel $Orig_2$.

5. om *δε* ℵ Scr's b. om 2nd *φοβηθητε* Dℵ 69 lat-*a* Syr. rec *εξουσιαν* bef *εχοντα*, with E rel æth $Tert_1$: txt ABDKLRXΠℵ 1. 33. 69 latt syr arm $Orig_2$ $Mcion_2$-e. *εμβαλλειν* ℵ [Scr's w] : for *εμβαλειν εις την γεεν.*, *εις γεεν. βαλειν* D $Mcion_2$-e ($Thdot_1$). om *την* (D)R [Just ($Mcion_1$-e Thdot) $Orig_2$].

6. rec *πωλειται* (*gramml corrn*), with ADR rel $Orig_1$ [$Epiph_1$] Cyr_1 : txt Bℵ 69 $Epiph_1$.

7. *υμων πασαι* bef *της κεφαλης* D. for *ηριθμηνται*, *ηριθμημεναι εισιν* (*Matt* x. 30) D 259 ev-x $Clem_1$[txt_1]. rec aft *μη* ins *ουν* (‖ *Matt*), with ADQℵ rel vulg lat-*c e f* [*$g_{1.2}$ q*] syrr syr-cu [syr-jer] æth arm ($Orig_1$) : om BLR lat-*a b ff_2 i l* coptt $Ambr_1$. *φοβηθητε* D [$Orig_1$]. aft *πολλων* ins *γαρ* D (Syr ?) syr-cu arm. at end ins *υμεις* (‖ *Matt*) DFGKMΠ 33. 69 vulg[with tol (not am forj fuld em)] lat-*a e* æth.

8. aft *υμιν* ins *οτι* Dℵ. for *ομολογηση*, *ομολογησει* (*itacism* ?) AB[1]DR [S, Tischdf] ΓΔ. om *των αγγελων* ℵ[1](appy : ins ℵ-corr[1]) 259 [Mcion-e-t].

9. for 1st *ενωπιον*, *εμπροσθεν* (‖ *Matt*) ADKQΠ. for *απαρν.*, *αρνηθησεται* D Scr's h : *απαρνησεται* ℵ[1](txt ℵ-corr[1]). for 2nd *ενωπιον*, *ενπροσθεν* (‖ *Matt*) D 251 $Clem_1$.

10. aft *os* ins *αν* D 254. *εις δε το πν. τ. αγ.*, omg *τω* and, as 69 also does, *βλασφ.*, D. *βλασφημουντι* ℵ $Epiph_1$. aft *αφεθησεται* ins *αυτω ουτε εν τω αιωνι τουτω ουτε εν τω μελλοντι* (*see Matt* xii. 32) D lat-*c e* æth ($Lucif_1$).

11. rec **προσ***φερωσιν*, with AQR rel lat-*a* [D-lat Bas_1] : *φερωσιν* D[-gr] lat-*b q* $Clem_1$ $Orig_1$ Cyr-jer_1 : txt BLXℵ 1. 33 vulg lat-*e f i* [*l*] coptt. for *επι*, *εις* DRℵ 1. 69 $Clem_1$. *μεριμνησητε* (*gramml corrn, and* ‖ *Matt*) BLQRXℵ 1. 33. 69 $Orig_1$ Cyr-jer_1 : *προμεριμνατε* (*Mark* xiii. 11) D-gr $Clem_1$: txt A rel [Bas_1]. om 1st *η τι* D 157 lat-*a b c e ff_2 i l* [*q*] Syr syr-cu æth Clem $Orig_1$ Cyr-jer_1 : ins (*from* ‖ *Matt ?*) ABQRℵ rel vulg lat-*f* syr [syr-jer] copt [æth Bas_1].

as distinguishing this section from what follows spoken *to the crowd*, ver. 13 ff. On the rest, see on Matt. xvi. 6. **2—9.**] See on Matt. x. 26—33. **3. ἀνθ'**

εἴπητε· 12 τὸ γὰρ ἅγιον πνεῦμα διδάξει ὑμᾶς ἐν αὐτῇ τῇ
ὥρᾳ ἃ δεῖ εἰπεῖν. 13 Εἶπεν δέ τις αὐτῷ ἐκ τοῦ ὄχλου
[y] Διδάσκαλε, [z] εἰπὲ τῷ ἀδελφῷ μου [a] μερίσασθαι μετ᾽ ἐμοῦ
τὴν [b] κληρονομίαν. 14 ὁ δὲ εἶπεν αὐτῷ Ἄνθρωπε, τίς με
T ειπεν.. [c] κατέστησεν κριτὴν ἢ [d] μεριστὴν [e] ἐφ᾽ ὑμᾶς; 15 εἶπεν δὲ
πρὸς αὐτοὺς Ὁρᾶτε καὶ [f] φυλάσσεσθε [f] ἀπὸ πάσης
[g] πλεονεξίας· ὅτι οὐκ [h] ἐν τῷ [i] περισσεύειν τινὶ ἡ ζωὴ
...αυτω R. αὐτοῦ [k] ἐστιν ἐκ τῶν [l] ὑπαρχόντων αὐτῷ. 16 εἶπεν δὲ
παραβολὴν πρὸς αὐτοὺς λέγων Ἀνθρώπου τινὸς πλου-
σίου [m] εὐφόρησεν ἡ [n] χώρα. 17 καὶ [o] διελογίζετο ἐν ἑαυτῷ

ABDEF GHKL MQSTU VXΓΔΛ ΠΝ 1. 33. 69

y Matt. viii. 19 al.† 2 Macc. i. 10 only.
z constr., Mark v. 43. viii. 7 Exod. xxxv. 1.
a = Mark vi. 41. Rom. xii. 3. 1 Cor. vii. 17. Prov. xxix. 24.
b Matt. xxi. 38 ‖. Acts vii. 5 al. Josh. xvi. 8.
c = Acts vii. 10, 27, 35, from Exod. ii. 14. Heb. vii. 28.
d here only †.
e ch. i. 33. xix. 14.
f mid., 1 John v. 21 (2 Thess. iii. 2 act.) only. Deut. xxiii. 9.
g Mark vii. 22 al. Jer. xxii. 17. Ezek. xxi. 27.
h = 1 Cor. ii. 5.
i Mark xii. 44 reff.
k = John xviii. 36. Acts xix. 25.
l = ch. viii. 3 reff.
m here only †.
n = ch. xxi. 21. John iv. 35. James v. 4. Sir. xliii. 3.
o = Matt. xvi. 7, 8.

13. *εκ του οχλου* bef *αυτω* BFLQℵ 33: txt ADR rel am[with forj] syr coptt arm [Bas$_1$]. for *ειπε*, *ειπον* D.

14. aft *ο δε* ins *ῑς* R. rec (for *κριτην*) *δικαστην*, with AQR rel [Bas$_1$]: txt BDLℵ 1. 33 sah-gr.—om *η μεριστην* D lat-*a*(appy) *c* syr-cu Tert$_1$.—*κριτην η δικαστην* 69: *αρχοντα και δικαστην* 157. (*The element of confusion has been the αρχοντα κ. δικαστην of Acts* vii. 27, 35: *hence the varr.*) *υμων* ℵ^1.

15. rec (for *πασης*) *της*, with EGHVΓΔΛ (FS, e sil): txt ABDQRℵ rel latt syrr syr-cu coptt æth arm Clem$_1$ Bas$_1$ Antch$_1$ Tit-bostr Aug. *εστιν* bef *η ζωη* D lat-*c* [Clem$_1$]: bef *εν τω* K Π^1[at end of ver Π^2]: om *εστιν* RΠ^3.—om *αυτου* D Syr syr-cu. rec (for *αυτω*) *αυτου* (*repetn of foregoing*), with Aℵ^1 rel: txt BDFQRTℵ^{3a} 33 copt Bas$_1$ Cyr$_1$ [Antch$_1$].

16. *προς αυτους* bef *παραβολην* D sah. (*ηυφορησεν* ADGKLΓΛΠ 33.)

17. for *εαυτω*, *αυτω* BL^1.

ὧν] wherefore. **4. τοῖς φίλοις μου**] See John xv. 13—15. **10.**] See on Matt. xii. 31. **11, 12.**] See on Matt. x. 19, 20.

13—21.] ANSWER TO ONE WHO SOUGHT A DIVISION OF HIS INHERITANCE. *Peculiar to Luke.* **13.**] The man was evidently *not a disciple*, nor preparing to be one (as Schleierm. thinks), but *some hearer in the crowd*, whose mind had been working in him during our Lord's last sayings about the care of Providence for His friends, and he thought this was *just the care his circumstances wanted;* being, as appears, oppressed by his brother in the matter of his patrimony. Possibly too he had an idea that the Messias, or the great Rabbi to whom he was listening, was come to set all things right;—and with that feeling which we all have of the surpassing injustice of *our own* wrongs, broke out with this inopportune request. **14.**] **ἄνθρ.**, a word of solemn reproof: see Rom. ii. 1; ix. 20. The **ἄνθρ.** also forms a definite subject for **ὑμᾶς** to refer to, . . . '*men*,' i.e. mankind in general. This question is expressed in almost the very words of the Egyptian rejecting the arbitration of Moses, Exod. ii. 14;—and may shew us the essential difference of the two offices of Moses and Christ. **15.**] **αὐτούς**, i.e. *τὸν ὄχλον*. He saw into the covetousness of the man's disposition, and made it an instructive warning for his hearers. **πάσης πλ.**] There is a meaning in **πάσης**—**every kind of πλ.** *This kind*, of which they had an example before them, was by no means one of the worst; but *all* kinds must be avoided. **οὐκ ἐν τ. . . . .**] **not, because a man has abundance, does his life** (therefore) **consist in his goods.** That is, no man's life *ἐστιν ἐκ τῶν ὑπαρχ.* **consists in what he possesses** (*οὐκ ἐπ᾽ ἄρτῳ μόνῳ ζήσεται ἄνθρωπος*); . . . **nor** *ἐν τῷ περισσεύειν τινί*, **by his having abundance, can this be made to be the case.** Man's life is of *God*, not of *his goods, however abundant they may be.* And this is the lesson conveyed by the following parable, and lying at the foundation of the still higher lesson conveyed in ver. 21. **ζωή** is *life* in the pregnant sense, emphatically **his life**; including time and eternity. This is self-evident from the parable and its application.

16.] Our Lord in this parable sets before us one arrived at the very height of worldly prosperity, and that by no unfair means; 'non limite perturbato, non spoliato paupere, non circumvento simplice.' Aug. Serm. 178, c. 2, vol. v. It was *by*

λέγων Τί ποιήσω, ὅτι οὐκ [p] ἔχω ποῦ [q] συνάξω τοὺς καρπούς μου; 18 καὶ εἶπεν Τοῦτο ποιήσω· [r] καθελῶ μου τὰς
[s] ἀποθήκας καὶ μείζονας οἰκοδομήσω, καὶ [q] συνάξω ἐκεῖ
πάντα τὰ [t] γενήματά [μου] καὶ τὰ [u] ἀγαθά μου, 19 καὶ
ἐρῶ τῇ ψυχῇ μου Ψυχή, ἔχεις πολλὰ [u] ἀγαθὰ [v] κείμενα
[w] εἰς ἔτη πολλά· [x] ἀναπαύου, φάγε, πίε, [y] εὐφραίνου.
20 εἶπεν δὲ αὐτῷ ὁ θεὸς [z] Ἄφρων, ταύτῃ τῇ νυκτὶ τὴν
ψυχήν σου [a] αἰτοῦσιν [a] ἀπὸ σοῦ· ἃ δὲ ἡτοίμασας, τίνι
ἔσται; 21 οὕτως ὁ [b] θησαυρίζων ἑαυτῷ καὶ μὴ [c] εἰς θεὸν

...ερω F. ABDEG HKLM QSTUV XΓΔΛ Πℵ 1. 33. 69

p Matt. viii. 20 reff. q = Matt. iii. 12 reff. r = Judg. vi. 25. s Matt. iii. 12 reff. t = Matt. xxvi. 29 reff. u = ch. xvi. 25. Gen. xlv. 18, 20. v = here only. Ezra vi. 1. Xen. Œcon. vii. 36. w = Heb. vii. 3 al. fr. Exod. viii. 10. x Mark vi. 31 reff. y ch. xv. 23, 24, 29. xvi. 19. Rom. xv. 10 (from Deut. xxxii. 43) al. L.P., exc. Rev. xi. 10. xii. 12. xviii. 20. z ch. xi. 40 reff. a Matt. xx. 20 (reff.) only. b constr., Matt. v. 19, 20 (reff.). Rom. ii. 5. 2 Cor. xii. 14. Prov. i. 18. c = Eph. i. 5. ch. xvi. 8.

18. for *μειζονας οικοδομησω, ποιησω αυτας μειζονας* D lat-*e*. **ανοικοδομησω** ℵ[1] Orig-int$_1$. for *και σ. εκει, κακει συναξω* D latt. om *παντα* ℵ-corr[1](ins ℵ[3a]). for *γενηματα* (one *ν* ADQℵ[1] &c [Bas$_1$]) *τον σιτον* (*exegetl altern*) BLTX ℵ-corr[1·3a] 1. 69 coptt æth arm. om 2nd *μου* BLT 1 arm: ins ADQℵ rel latt syrr syr-cu [Bas$_1$]. om *και τα αγαθα μου* D ℵ[1](ins ℵ-corr[1·3a]) lat-*a b c e ff$_2$ i l q* syr-cu Euthym Ambr.

19. om from *κειμενα* to *πιε* D lat-*a b c e*.

20. om *ο* (bef *θεος*) T. for *θεος, κυριος* A Cypr$_1$(txt$_2$). elz-ed-1633 *αφρον* (*face gramml corrn*), with KM(S?)UVΓΠ 69 [Clem$_2$] Orig$_5$ [Ath$_1$ Bas$_1$]: txt A B(sic: see table) DLQℵ rel. rec **απαιτουσιν**, with ADℵ rel Clem$_2$ Orig$_4$ [Bas$_1$ Antch$_2$]: txt BLQT 33 sah(appy).—*απαιτ.* bef *τ. ψ. σου* D (69) lat-*c i* coptt æth Clem$_1$ Orig$_3$ Iren-int$_1$ Cypr$_3$. (F def.) for 2nd *δε, ουν* D lat-*c e* [*i l*] Cypr$_3$. **τινος** D lat-*a b c* Clem$_1$[txt$_1$] Antch$_1$ Iren-int$_1$ [Tert$_1$] Cypr.

21. om ver D lat-*a b*. for **εαυτω**, *αυτω* Bℵ[1] lat-*c e*. (*εν αυτω* L.)

God's blessing that he became thus rich, which might have been a *real* blessing, if he had known how to use it.

17.] 'Character animi sine requie quieti, egregie expressus.' Bengel. **οὐκ ἔχω ποῦ συν.**] '. . . Habes apothecas—inopum sinus, viduarum domus, ora infantum . . . Istæ sunt apothecæ quæ maneant in æternum.' Ambrose de Nabuthe, ch. vii. 37, vol. i. p. 575. **18, 19.**] "His folly is *fourfold*:—he forgets the Giver ('*my* fruits, *my* goods'),—he greedily reserves all for *himself* (**συνάξω ἐκεῖ πάντα**),—he imagines such things to be food for his *soul* (**ψυχή, . . . ἀναπ., φ., π., εὐφρ.**)—he forgets *death*, which is every day possible." (Stier, iii. 146, edn. 2.) A very striking similarity is found in Sir. xi. 18, 19, ἔστι πλουτῶν ἀπὸ προσοχῆς καὶ σφιγγίας αὐτοῦ, καὶ αὕτη ἡ μερὶς τοῦ μισθοῦ αὐτοῦ· ἐν τῷ εἰπεῖν αὐτὸν Εὗρον ἀνάπαυσιν, καὶ νῦν φάγωμαι ἐκ τῶν ἀγαθῶν μου, καὶ οὐκ οἶδε τίς καιρὸς παρελεύσεται, καὶ καταλείψει αὐτὰ ἑτέροις καὶ ἀποθανεῖται. Stier thinks this a convincing proof that our Lord did occasionally refer to the Apocrypha (?).

20.] **God said unto him,**—perhaps it is meant, by some unmistakable judgment; but more likely, as occurring in a parable, the words are to be literally taken. By supposing merely *a divine decree* to be meant, *without personal communication*, as Grotius, Kuinoel, and Trench do, we lose the impressive part of the parable, where the man's selfishness and folly is brought into immediate contact with the solemn truth of his approaching death, which certainly our Lord intends us to contemplate. **ἄφρων**, opposed to his *worldly prudence*;—**ταύτῃ τῇ ν.** to the **ἔτη πολλά**;—the **ψυχή** in the one case, at its ease, eating, drinking, and making merry, to the **ψυχή** in the other, demanded, rendered up, judged. **αἰτοῦσιν**, not strictly impersonal; there are those whose business it is, even *the angels*, the ministers of the divine purposes: see ch. vi. 38 and note. The merely impersonal sense may be defended: cf. ver. 48: but this saying seems so solemn, as to require something more. **ἃ ἡτοίμασας, which thou madest ready**; but *not for thyself*.

21.] **οὕτως, thus**: in utter confusion, and sudden destitution of all help and provision for eternity. There is no ἔσται: because the case, alas, is an every-day one in every place. **ἑαυτῷ . . . . εἰς θεὸν . . .**] The meaning of these expressions will be brought out thus: He who is rich *for himself*, laying up treasure *for himself*, is by so much robbing his real inward life, his life in and toward God, of its resources: he is laying up store

[d] πλουτῶν. 22 εἶπεν δὲ πρὸς τοὺς μαθητὰς αὐτοῦ Διὰ
τοῦτο λέγω ὑμῖν, μὴ [e] μεριμνᾶτε τῇ ψυχῇ τί φάγητε, μηδὲ
τῷ σώματι τί [e] ἐνδύσησθε. 23 ἡ [γὰρ] [e] ψυχὴ [e] πλεῖόν
ἐστιν τῆς τροφῆς, καὶ τὸ σῶμα τοῦ [f] ἐνδύματος. 24 [g] κατανοήσατε τοὺς [h] κόρακας, ὅτι οὔτε [i] σπείρουσιν οὔτε [i] θερί-
ζουσιν, οἷς οὐκ ἔστιν [k] ταμεῖον οὐδὲ [l] ἀποθήκη, καὶ ὁ θεὸς
τρέφει αὐτούς. πόσῳ [m] μᾶλλον ὑμεῖς [mn] διαφέρετε τῶν
[o] πετεινῶν; 25 τίς δὲ ἐξ ὑμῶν [[e] μεριμνῶν] δύναται [p] ἐπὶ
τὴν [q] ἡλικίαν αὐτοῦ [p] προσθεῖναι [r] πῆχυν; 26 εἰ οὖν οὐδὲ
ἐλάχιστον [s] δύνασθε, τί περὶ τῶν λοιπῶν μεριμνᾶτε;
27 [g] κατανοήσατε τὰ [t] κρίνα, [u] πῶς οὔτε [v] νήθει οὔτε
[w] ὑφαίνει· λέγω δὲ ὑμῖν, οὐδὲ Σολομῶν ἐν πάσῃ τῇ δόξῃ
αὐτοῦ [x] περιεβάλετο ὡς ἓν τούτων. 28 εἰ δὲ ἐν ἀγρῷ τὸν
[y] χόρτον ὄντα σήμερον καὶ [y] αὔριον εἰς [z] κλίβανον βαλ-
λόμενον ὁ θεὸς οὕτως [a] ἀμφιέζει, πόσῳ μᾶλλον ὑμᾶς,

...εν πασῃ τῃ G.

d 1 Tim. vi. 18. ch. i. 53.
e Matt. vi. 25 (reff.).
f Luke, here only. Matt. iii. 4 al6. only. Zeph. i. 8.
g Acts vii. 31, 32. Heb. iii. 1 al. Isa. v. 12.
h here only. Ps. cxlvi. 9.
i John iv. 36, 37 reff.
k = here only. (Matt. vi. 6 reff.) Deut. xxviii. 8.
l ver. 18.
m Matt. vi. 26 reff.
n ver. 7.
o Matt. vi. 26 reff.
p acc., Matt. vi. 27. Lev. xxvii. 15. dat., ch. iii. 20.
q Matt. vi. 27 reff.
r John xxi. 3 reff.
s constr., Mark ix. 22. 2 Cor. xiii. 8.
t Matt. vi. 28 only. Cant. ii. 16.
u = Matt. xii. 4. Mark v. 16.
v Matt. vi. 28 only. Exod. (only) xxxv. 25 al.
w here only. Judg. xvi. 13. (-αντός, John xix. 23.)
x Acts xii. 8. Rev. iii. 5, 18 al. Esth. v. 1.
y Matt. vi. 30 (reff.).
z Matt. vi. 30 || only. Gen. xv. 17.
a here only. see Matt. vi. 30 reff.

22. om *αυτου* B lat-*c e*. rec *υμιν* bef λεγω (|| *Matt*), with AQ rel lat-*a b c e* syrr arm: txt BDLXℵ 69 vulg lat-*f l q* syr-cu coptt æth. rec aft *τη ψυχη* ins *υμων* (|| *Matt*), with T rel lat-*a e* Syr syr-cu coptt $Clem_2$ [Ath_1]: om ABDLQℵ **1** am (with fuld em forj tol) lat-*b c f ff*$_2$ *g*$_1$ *i l* [*q*] syr arm $Ambr_1$. aft *σωματι* ins *υμων* (|| *Matt*) BT 33. 69 lat-*a* Syr coptt æth $Clem_1$.

23. rec om *γαρ*, with AQ rel vulg lat-*a f ff*$_2$ [*i q*]: ins BDLMSXℵ **1.** 69 lat-*b c e* Syr syr-cu syr-w-ast copt æth arm $Clem_2$.—*οτι η ψ.* T. for *πλειον*, *πλεον* D.

24. for *τους κορακας*, *τα πετεινα του ουρανου* D lat-*e l*. rec *ου σπ. ουδε* (*from || Matt, where there is no var*), with AB rel [$Clem_1$]: *ου σπ. ου* M: *ου σπ. ουγε* T: txt DLQℵ lat-*e*. **ουτε ταμ. ουτε** D. *ταμιον* ℵ: *ταμιειον* FMU **1.** 33. 69. **αυτα** D 69. for *ποσω μαλλον*, *ουχι* D mt lat-*c e ff*$_2$ *i* [*l*].

25. om *μεριμνων* D 225 ($Tert_1$): ins (*from || Matt?*) ABQℵ rel [vss] Eus_1. rec *προσθειναι* bef *επι την ηλικιαν αυτου* (*from || Matt*), with ADQTℵ rel Eus_1: txt B. rec aft *πηχυν* ins *ενα* (|| *Matt*), with AQT ℵ-corr¹ rel [vss Eus_1]: om B(sic: see table) Dℵ¹ lat-*i l* coptt.

26. for *ει* to *λοιπων*, *και περι των λοιπων τι* D lat-*a b c ff*$_2$ *i l*. rec *ουτε*, with A rel Eus_1: txt BLQTℵ **1.** 33 sah. aft *ελαχ.* ins *τι* ℵ¹.

27. rec (for *ουτε* to *υφαινει*) *αυξανει ου κοπια ουδε νηθει* (|| *Matt*), with ABQTℵ rel [vss]: txt D lat-*a* syr-cu $Clem_1$(quotes vv. 27-8 entire) $Mcion_1$-t(appy). aft *υμιν* ins *οτι* (|| *Matt*) ADLMXℵ **1.** 33. 69 lat-*b c e f ff*$_2$ *i* [*l q* syrr syr-cu] $Clem_1$: om BQT rel vulg lat-*a* æth arm.

28. rec ins *τω* bef *αγρω*, with E rel coptt arm: om ABLMQTUΛℵ [33 $Clem_1$].—rec *τον χορτον* bef *εν αγρω*, with E rel: *τον χορτον σημ.* bef *εν αγρω* AKMQTUΠ **1.** 33 vulg lat-*b c f g*$_1$ [*i l q*] syrr copt arm $Clem_1$: *τ. χορτ. του αγρου* (|| *Matt*) DG³HX vss Cyr-jer: txt BLℵ.—rec *σημερον* bef *οντα* (|| *Matt*), with ADQT rel vss $Clem_1$: txt BLΛℵ lat-*e* coptt. rec (for *αμφιεζει*) *αμφιεννυσι* (*from || Matt*), with AQℵ rel: txt DLT, *αμφιαζει* B.

for, providing for, the *flesh*; but the *spirit*, that which God looketh into and searcheth, is stripped of all its riches. These words may also, as remarked on ch. vi. 20, shew that Luke does not, as supposed by some recent critics, use '*riches*' as merely *this world's wealth*, but with a deeper spiritual meaning.

22—31.] Lessons of trust in God. In the closest connexion with the preceding;—**διὰ τοῦτο**, '*quæ cum ita sint*,' since worldly riches are of so little real use, &c.: see Matt. vi. 25—33, and notes. **24.**] **τοὺς κόρακας**, who are elsewhere spoken of in Scripture as the objects of the divine care: see Job xxxviii. 41: Ps. cxlvii. 9. **26. ἐλάχιστον**] This shews the truth of the interpretation of **ἡλικ.** given

b Matt. vi. 30. viii. 26. xiv. 31. xvi. 8 only †.
c here only ‡. Mic. iv. 1.
d Matt. vi. 32 reff.
e Matt. vi. 32. ch. xi. 8. Rom. xvi. 2. 2 Cor. iii. 1 only. Judg. xi. 7 B al. (only ?).
f = Matt. xi. 22 reff. Judg. iv. 9.
g Matt. vi. 33. ch. iii. 20. xii. 25. Tobit v. 15.
h voc., Matt. xxvii. 29 ||. Mark x. 47. ch. xviii. 11, 13 al.
i Acts xx. 28, 29. 1 Pet. v. 2, 3 only. Jer. xiii. 17.

ABDE HKLM QSTU VXΓΔΛ ΠΝ 1. 33. 69

[b] ὀλιγόπιστοι; 29 καὶ ὑμεῖς μὴ ζητεῖτε τί φάγητε ἢ τι
πίητε, καὶ μὴ [c] μετεωρίζεσθε. 30 ταῦτα γὰρ πάντα τὰ
ἔθνη τοῦ κόσμου [d] ἐπιζητοῦσιν, ὑμῶν δὲ ὁ πατὴρ οἶδεν
ὅτι [e] χρῄζετε τούτων. 31 [f] πλὴν [g] ζητεῖτε τὴν βασιλείαν
αὐτοῦ, καὶ ταῦτα [g] προστεθήσεται ὑμῖν. 32 μὴ φοβοῦ,
[h] τὸ μικρὸν [i] ποίμνιον, ὅτι [k] εὐδόκησεν ὁ πατὴρ ὑμῶν
δοῦναι ὑμῖν τὴν βασιλείαν. 33 πωλήσατε τὰ [l] ὑπάρχοντα
ὑμῶν, καὶ δότε [m] ἐλεημοσύνην. [n] ποιήσατε [n] ἑαυτοῖς [o] βαλλάντια μὴ [p] παλαιούμενα, [q] θησαυρὸν [r] ἀνέκλειπτον ἐν τοῖς
οὐρανοῖς, ὅπου κλέπτης οὐκ [s] ἐγγίζει οὐδὲ [t] σὴς [u] διαφθείρει.
34 ὅπου γάρ ἐστιν ὁ [q] θησαυρὸς ὑμῶν, ἐκεῖ καὶ ἡ καρδία P ἐκει και...
ὑμῶν ἔσται. 35 ἔστωσαν ὑμῶν αἱ [vw] ὀσφύες [wx] περιεζωσ-

k constr., Rom. xv. 26. 1 Cor. i. 21. Gal. i. 15, 16. Ps. lxvii. 16.
l = Matt. xix. 21 reff. Job xviii. 7. m Matt. vi. 2, &c. reff. n ch. xvi. 9. Exod. xx. 4, 23.
o ch. x. 4. xxii. 35, 36 only. Job xiv. 17 only. p Heb. i. 11 (from Ps. ci. 26). viii. 13 bis only. Josh. ix. 13.
q Matt. ii. 11 al. Neh. xiii. 12. r here only †. (-λιπής, Wisd. vii. 14. viii. 18.) s ch. xviii. 40. xix. 37, 41. xxiv. 15 al. Gen. xxvii. 26. t Matt. vi. 19, 20 only. Isa. li. 8. u 2 Cor. iv. 16. 1 Tim. vi. 5. Rev. viii. 9. xi. 18 bis only. 1 Kings xxiii. 10. v Matt. iii. 4 reff. w Exod. xii. 11. see Eph. vi. 14. 1 Pet. i. 13. x here bis. ch. xvii. 8. Eph. vi. 14. Rev. i. 13. xv. 6 only. Dan. x. 5.

29. om μη ℵ[1](ins ℵ-corr[1]) 237[1]. for η, και (*from Matt* vi. 25, *which our passage more resembles than ib. ver* 31) BLQTℵ 33 lat-*e* Syr syr-cu copt-schw Bas$_1$: txt AD rel latt syr copt-wilk sah [æth arm Clem$_1$ Ath$_1$. (Tischdf, ed 8, gives copt-schw-dz for txt, copt-wilk for και.)] aft πιητε ins μηδε τω σωματι (|| *Matt*) ℵ[1](but marked for erasure eadem manu).

30. rec επιζητει (*umml corrn, here and in* || *Matt*), with AQ rel [Bas$_1$ Ath$_1$]; ζητει D Clem$_1$: txt BLTXℵ 33. 69. for υμων to οιδεν, οιδεν γαρ ο πατηρ υμων (|| *Matt*) D lat-*a b c* [*e i l* æth Clem$_1$ (Tert$_1$)].

31. for πλην ζητ., ζητ. δε (|| *Matt*) D lat-*a* Mcion-e. rec (for αυτου) του θεου (*corrn here, and in* || *Matt*), with A D[1]-corr(and lat) QT rel vulg lat-*b e f ff$_2$ g$_{1.2}$ i* syrr syr-cu Clem$_1$ Mcion-e$_2$-t$_1$: txt B D[1](altered by origl scribe) Lℵ lat-*a c* coptt æth [Ath$_1$]. rec aft ταυτα ins παντα (*from* || *Matt*), with ADT ℵ-corr[1] rel vulg lat-*b c f ff$_2$ g$_{1.2}$ i* [*l q*] Syr syr-w-ast copt æth arm-mss Mcion$_2$-e [Ath$_1$] Ambr$_1$: om BEHL QSVΔΛℵ[1] lat-*a e* syr-cu sah arm Mcion$_1$-t.

32. aft οτι ins εν αυτω D lat-*e*. (ηυδοκησεν DΓ.) υμων bef ο πατηρ ℵ.

33. (βαλλαντια, so A B(sic: see table) DQTℵ &c.) διαφθερει D-gr Δ.

34. εσται bef και η καρδια υμων D(ημων D[1]) lat-*a b e f* [*l*]. om η TΔ.

35. for εστωσαν, εστω D. αι οσφυες bef υμων AKQTΠ latt Orig$_1$ Constt$_1$ Bas$_1$[(txt$_1$) Cyr$_1$(txt$_1$) Antch$_1$] Iren-int$_2$ Cypr.—υμων η οσφυς περιεζωσμενη D.

in the note on Matt. A *cubit* would not be ἐλάχιστον to add to the stature, but a very large increase: [whereas, as Trench observes, "a cubit would be infinitesimally small when compared to his length of life, that life being contemplated as a *course,* or *race,* which he may attempt, but ineffectually, to prolong."] **29.] μετεωρίζ.**, certainly not '*nolite in sublime tolli,*' Vulg.; which Meyer approves, and Luther has adopted. For what have *high thoughts* to do with the present subject,—which is, the duty of dismissing anxiety and over-carefulness, in confidence on God's paternal care? It is, **be not anxious**, 'at sea,' tossed about between hope and fear. So Thucyd. (ii. 8) describes Greece as being πᾶσα μετέωρος when the two first cities were at war. **32—34.**] Our Lord gives to his own disciples an assurance of the Father's favour as a ground for removing all fear from them, and shews them the true riches, and how to seek them. **32. τὸ μικ. π.**] Thus He sets himself forth as their Shepherd (John x. 1 ff.), and them (as in Isa. xli. 10—14) as a weak and despised people. **33.**] Meyer endeavours to evade the force of this, by supposing it addressed only to the Apostles and then existing disciples. But it is said to the μικρὸν ποίμνιον, who are *all the elect people of God.* **πωλ.**] This is the true way of investing worldly wealth:—'He that giveth to the poor, lendeth to the Lord.' See on Matt. vi. 19—21.

35—48.] Exhortations to watchfulness. The attitude and employment of the μικρὸν ποίμνιον is carried on, even to their duty of continual readiness for their Lord's coming. These verses are

μέναι καὶ οἱ [y] λύχνοι [y] καιόμενοι· 36 καὶ ὑμεῖς ὅμοιοι
ἀνθρώποις [z] προςδεχομένοις τὸν κύριον ἑαυτῶν πότε
[a] ἀναλύσῃ [b] ἐκ τῶν [c] γάμων, ἵνα ἐλθόντος καὶ [d] κρούσαντος
εὐθέως [e] ἀνοίξωσιν αὐτῷ. 37 μακάριοι οἱ δοῦλοι ἐκεῖνοι
οὓς ἐλθὼν ὁ κύριος εὑρήσει γρηγοροῦντας. ἀμὴν λέγω
ὑμῖν ὅτι [x] περιζώσεται καὶ [f] ἀνακλινεῖ αὐτοὺς καὶ [g] παρελθὼν [h] διακονήσει αὐτοῖς. 38 κἂν ἐν τῇ δευτέρᾳ κἂν ἐν
τῇ τρίτῃ [i] φυλακῇ ἔλθῃ, καὶ εὕρῃ [k] οὕτως, μακάριοί εἰσιν
[οἱ δοῦλοι] ἐκεῖνοι. 39 τοῦτο δὲ γινώσκετε, ὅτι εἰ ᾔδει
ὁ [l] οἰκοδεσπότης ποίᾳ ὥρᾳ ὁ κλέπτης ἔρχεται, [m] ἐγρη-

y = Matt. v. 15 reff.
z Matt. xv. 43 reff.
a here (Phil. i. 23) only †. Wisd. ii. 1.
b = ch. xi. 6. John iv. 6 (?).
c = Matt. xxii. 2, &c. reff.
d Matt. vii. 7, 8 reff.
e abs., Matt. xxv. 11. ch. xiii. 25
f act., ch. ii. 7 reff. (Matt. viii. 11 reff.) †
g = ch. xvii. 7. Acts xxiv. 7. Sir. xxix. 26.
h Mark x. 45 reff. ch. xvii. 8.
i Matt. xiv. 25 reff.
k see ch. xxii. 26. Ps. i. 4.
l Matt. x. 25 al. †
m Matt. xxiv. 42 reff.

36. αυτων D 1. 33. 69 $Clem_1$ $Orig_1$ $Meth_1$. rec αναλυσει (*somml corrn*), with GKXΓΛ Bas_1 [$Clem_1$ $Antch_1$ $Damasc_1$]: txt ABDPQTℵ rel $Meth_1$. aft κρουσαντος ins αυτου A 251. ανοιξουσιν D.

37. ο κυριος bef ελθων LQ 33. for ευρησει, ευρη D Clem. om και παρελθ. διακ. αυτοις ℵ¹(ins ℵ-corr¹) 251.

38. for 1st καν to ουτως, και εαν ελθη τη εσπερινη φυλακη και ευρησει ουτως ποιησει και εαν εν τη δευτερα και τη τριτη D, simly 1 lat-*c e* syr-cu $Iren\text{-}int_1$. rec (for κἂν twice) και εαν, insg ελθη bef εν τη δευτερα and adding φυλακη, with APQ rel vulg lat-*f* syr copt [Bas_1 $Damasc_1$]: txt BL(T)Xℵ (1) 33 [Cyr_1]. for ελθη και, και ελθων AKΠ. ευρησει (D)PΔ. om οι δουλοι BDLℵ gat(with mm) lat-*b e ff₂ i l* syr-cu copt-dz [Cyr_1] $Iren\text{-}int_1$: ins APQT rel vulg lat-*c f* [*q*] syrr copt æth arm. om εκεινοι ℵ¹(ins ℵ-corr¹·³) [gat(with mm) lat-*b ff₂ i l* $Iren\text{-}int_1$]. (lat-*a* is def vv. 38—59.)

39. om εγρηγορησεν αν και D ℵ¹(ins ℵ-corr¹(exc αν)·³) lat-*e i* syr-cu sah-woide

connected with ver. 32—'since your Father hath seen fit to give you the kingdom, be that kingdom, and preparation for it, your chief care.' There are continual *points* of similarity, in this part of the discourse, to Matt. xxiv. 42 ff., but *no more:* and the close connexion quite forbids us to imagine that the sayings have been collected merely by the Evangelist. **35.**] There is a slight reference to, or rather another presentation of the truth set forth in, the parable of the virgins, Matt. xxv. 1 ff. But the image here is of servants waiting for their Lord to *return from* the wedding;—left at home and bound to be in readiness to receive him. There is only a hint at the cause of his absence—he is gone to a wedding: **γάμοι** may mean almost any feast or entertainment—and the *main* thought here only is that he is away at a feast, and will return. But in the background lies the *wedding* in all its truth—not brought out here, but elsewhere, Matt. xxii. 1 ff.; xxv. 1 ff. **αἱ ὀσφ. περ.**] See reff., and John xiii. 4. **οἱ λύχνοι**] See note on Matt. xxv. 1. **36.**] **καὶ ὑμεῖς**—emphatic—distinguished from the **ὀσφ.** and **λύχ.** above:—**ye yourselves**, i.e. your whole conduct and demeanour. **κρούσαντος . . . αὐτῷ**—a very common construction of the gen. abs.: see ch. xvii. 12; xxii. 10 al.—and Winer, § 30. 11, rem., edn. 6, for classical examples. **37.**] See Rev. iii. 20, 21, where the same similitude is presented, and the promise carried on yet further,—to the *sharing of his Throne.* The Lord himself, in that great day of his glory,—the marriage-supper of the Lamb,—will invert the order of human requirements (see ch. xvii. 8), and in the fulness of his grace and love will serve his brethren:—the Redeemer, his redeemed,—the Shepherd, his flock. **παρελθ.**, coming in turn to each. Compare the washing of the disciples' feet in John xiii. 1 ff., which was a foreshewing of this last great act of self-abasing love. **38.**] Olsh. observes that the *first* watch is not named, because the marriage itself falls on it: but his view that because the *fourth* is not named, our Lord follows the ancient custom of the Jews and divides the night into three watches, is probably incorrect: it is more likely (Meyer) that the fourth is not named, because the return was not likely to be so long delayed;—for the *decorum* of the parable. **39.**] I am surprised that Schleiermacher can have imagined (transl. p. 198) that this verse has been inserted so as to break the connexion, and by a later hand. Nothing can be more exact and rigid than the connexion as it now stands. Our Lord transfers, to shew the unex-

n = Mark v. 37 reff. o Matt. vi. 19, 20 (reff.) only. p Matt. xxiv. 44 reff. q ch. xvi. 1, 3, 8 only in Gospp. 1 Cor. iv. 1, 2 al. L.P., exc. 1 Pet. iv. 10. Esth. i. 8. r Matt. vii. 24. xxv. 2, &c. Rom. xi. 25 al. Prov. xvii. 10. s Matt. xxiv. 45, 47 reff. t = here [and Matt. xxiv. 45 v. r.] only. (ch. ix. 11. Rev. xxii. 2 only.) Gen. xlv. 16. u Matt. xxiv. 45. ch. xx. 10. 1 Pet. v. 6. Ps. i. 3. v here only †. (-τρεῖν, Gen. xlvii. 12.)

γόρησεν ἂν καὶ οὐκ [n] ἀφῆκεν [o] διορυχθῆναι τὸν οἶκον
αὐτοῦ. 40 καὶ ὑμεῖς [p] γίνεσθε ἕτοιμοι, ὅτι ᾗ ὥρᾳ οὐ
δοκεῖτε ὁ υἱὸς τοῦ ἀνθρώπου ἔρχεται. 41 εἶπεν δὲ [αὐτῷ]
ὁ Πέτρος Κύριε, πρὸς ἡμᾶς τὴν παραβολὴν ταύτην
λέγεις, ἢ καὶ πρὸς πάντας; 42 καὶ εἶπεν ὁ κύριος Τίς
ἄρα ἐστὶν ὁ πιστὸς [q] οἰκονόμος ὁ [r] φρόνιμος ὃν [s] καταστήσει ὁ κύριος ἐπὶ τῆς [t] θεραπείας αὐτοῦ [τοῦ] διδόναι
[u] ἐν καιρῷ [v] σιτομέτριον; 43 μακάριος ὁ δοῦλος ἐκεῖνος
ὃν ἐλθὼν ὁ κύριος αὐτοῦ εὑρήσει ποιοῦντα οὕτως.
44 [w] ἀληθῶς λέγω ὑμῖν ὅτι [x] ἐπὶ πᾶσιν τοῖς [y] ὑπάρχουσιν
αὐτοῦ [s] καταστήσει αὐτόν. 45 ἐὰν δὲ εἴπῃ ὁ δοῦλος ἐκεῖνος
ἐν τῇ καρδίᾳ αὐτοῦ [z] Χρονίζει ὁ κύριος μου ἔρχεσθαι,
καὶ ἄρξηται τύπτειν τοὺς [a] παῖδας καὶ τὰς [b] παιδίσκας,
ἐσθίειν τε καὶ πίνειν καὶ [c] μεθύσκεσθαι, 46 ἥξει ὁ κύριος

R [οτ]ι η... ...ο δουλος Q. ...ερχεσθαι και P. ABDE HKLM RSTUV XΓΔΛ Πא 1. 33. 69

w ch. ix. 27 reff. x w. dat., = Matt. xxiv. 47 only. Gen. xli. 41 Ed-vat. (B def.) y Matt. xix. 21 reff. z Matt. xxiv. 48. xxv. 5. ch. i. 21. Heb. x. 37 (from Hab. ii. 3) only. Gen. xxxiv. 19. a = Matt. viii. 6 reff. b Matt. xxvi. 69. Acts xii. 13. Gal. iv. 22, &c. Gen. xx. 17. c Eph. v. 18. 1 Thess. v. 7 only. Prov. iv. 17. (-θύειν, Matt. xxiv. 49.)

arm[-zoh Tert$_1$]. rec aft ουκ ins αν (*Matt* xxiv. 43), with ADQTא rel Orig$_1$: om BKLPSΠ 1. 69. om αφηκεν διορυχθηναι τον οικον αυτου D. rec διορυγηναι (|| *Matt*), with APQT rel: txt BLא 33 [(Eus$_1$) Bas$_1$ Damasc$_1$].

40. rec aft υμεις ins ουν (*cf* || *Matt*, δια τουτο κ. υμ.), with AP rel D-lat syrr [Bas$_1$ Damasc$_1$]; δε D-gr: om BLQTא latt syr-cu coptt arm. aft η ωρα ins η D-gr L.

41. for ειπ. δε, και ειπ. D. om αυτω (*prob as superf: it seems impossible to give any account of its* insertion) BDLRX 33 lat-*b c e ff$_2$ g$_1$ i l* arm: ins APQTא rel vulg lat-*f* [*q*] syrr syr-cu coptt æth. λεγεις bef την παραβολην ταυτην D vulg lat-*c* [*b f ff$_2$ i* Syr syr-cu coptt]. om η και προς παντας D.

42. rec (for και ειπεν) ειπεν δε, with AQRT rel latt syr sah arm: txt BDLא 1. 33. 69 lat-*l* copt æth. εσται AKΠ. for οικονομος, δουλος א^1. rec (for ὁ bef φρονιμος) και (|| *Matt*), with ALMURXΓא [latt syrr syr-cu arm] Orig$_1$: txt BDPQT rel syr-mg sah [æth]. aft φρονιμος ins ο αγαθος D lat-*c e* syr-cu. κατεστησεν Tא^1 latt. την θεραπειαν D. om του DLQX Orig$_1$: ins (*from* || *Matt?*) ABPRTא rel Orig$_1$. for διδοναι, διαδουναι א^1: δουναι ev-y. add αυτοις R 69 vulg lat-*b c f i l* [*q*] syr-cu [copt] sah æth. rec ins το bef σιτομετριον, with APQRTא rel: om BD 69.

43. aft ευρησει ins αυτον D. ουτως bef ποιουντα LTXא 33. 69 ev-y vulg lat-*a b c e f i* æth Iren-int$_1$.

44. for αληθως, αμην (|| *Matt*) D 251 lat-*c*. for αυτου, αυτω MPTΓΛ lat-*c e*.

45. μου bef ο κυριος KΠ א^1(txt א^{3a}, but former order restored) [Orig$_1$]. for τυπτειν, τυπειν D. εσθιων τε και πεινων μεθυσκομενος, omg last και, D-gr.

pected nature of his coming, and the necessity of watchfulness, the relation between *Himself* and the *servants*, to that between the *thief* and the **οἰκοδεσπότης**. For the purposes of this verse, *they* represent the *οἰκοδεσπότης*—collectively, as put in charge with the Lord's house and household (thus the verse is intimately connected with ver. 42):—and in the further application, individually—each as the *οἰκοδεσπότης* of his own *σκεῦος*, to be kept with watchfulness against that day:—*He* is represented by the thief—*ἰδοὺ ἔρχομαι ὡς κλέπτης*, Rev. xvi. 15; iii. 3. Olshausen's view, that the *οἰκοδ.* is the *ἄρχων τοῦ κόσμ. τούτου*, is surely quite out of keeping with the main features of the parable. That *he* should be put in the place of the watching servants (**καὶ ὑμεῖς**) seems impossible: besides that the **πιστὸς οἰκονόμος** below is this very *οἰκοδ.*, being such in the absence of his Lord, but the **οἰκονόμος** when He appears. **41.**] **τὴν παρ. τ.**, not the two last verses (Stier), but *the whole*:—Who are they that are thus to wait and watch, and to be thus honoured at the Lord's coming? This question, coming in so suddenly and unconnectedly and remaining apparently unanswered, is among the many proofs of the originality and historic reality of this discourse (against De Wette, &c.).

τοῦ δούλου ἐκείνου ἐν [d] ἡμέρᾳ [e] ᾗ οὐ [d] προσδοκᾷ καὶ ἐν
ὥρᾳ [e] ᾗ οὐ γινώσκει, καὶ [f] διχοτομήσει αὐτόν, καὶ τὸ
[g] μέρος αὐτοῦ μετὰ τῶν ἀπίστων θήσει. 47 ἐκεῖνος δὲ ὁ
δοῦλος ὁ γνοὺς τὸ θέλημα τοῦ κυρίου αὐτοῦ καὶ μὴ
[h] ἑτοιμάσας μηδὲ ποιήσας πρὸς τὸ θέλημα αὐτοῦ [i] δαρήσεται [k] πολλάς· 48 ὁ δὲ μὴ γνοὺς ποιήσας δὲ [l] ἄξια
[lm] πληγῶν [i] δαρήσεται [k] ὀλίγας. [n] παντὶ δὲ ᾧ ἐδόθη πολύ,
πολὺ [o] ζητηθήσεται παρ' αὐτοῦ· καὶ ᾧ [p] παρέθεντο πολύ,
[q] περισσότερον [r] αἰτήσουσιν [r] αὐτόν. 49 πῦρ ἦλθον [s] βαλεῖν

d Matt. xxiv. 50 al. Lam. ii. 16.
e attr., Mark vii. 13 reff.
f Matt. xxiv. 51 only. Exod. xxix. 17 only.
g Matt. xxiv. 51 reff.
h = (absolute) here only.
i Matt. xxi. 35 reff.
k constr. acc., 2 Thess. ii. 15. Mark x. 38. Rev. xvi. 9. Winer, edn. 6, § 32. 5. ellips., 2 Cor. xi. 24.
l (but of the person) Deut. xxv. 2.
m ch. x. 30 reff.
n constr., Mark vi. 16 reff.
o ch. xi. 16 || Mk.
p = ch. xxiii. 46. Acts xx. 32. 1 Tim. i 18. 2 Tim. ii. 2. 1 Pet. iv. 19. Tobit iv. 20.
q ver. 4 reff.
r constr., Matt. vii. 9, 10 reff.
s = ch. xiii. 19 reff.

46. for *του δουλου εκεινου*, *αυτου* D lat-*e* Iren-int$_1$. *θησει* bef *μετα των απιστων* D [Syr syr-cu coptt Dial (Cæs)].

47. rec (for 1st *αυτου*) *εαυτου*, with AR rel [Bas$_2$]: txt BDE[1]KLTXΠℵ 1. 33. 69 [Bas$_1$-mss Cyr$_2$ Antch$_1$]. om *ετοιμασας μηδε* D 69 [Bas$_1$ Chr$_1$ Cyr$_1$ Antch$_2$] (Orig$_1$ Dial$_1$ Iren-int$_1$): om *μηδε ποιησας* L lat-*b f ff*$_2$ *i* Syr syr-cu Jer: for *μηδε*, *η* BTℵ 33 sah.

48. om 3rd *δε* ℵ[1](ins ℵ-corr[1.3]) copt-wilk. for *εδοθη*, *εδωκαν* D. om 2nd *πολυ* ℵ[1](ins ℵ-corr[1.3]).—for *πολυ* to *αυτου*, *ζητησουσιν απ αυτου περισσοτερον* D lat-*ff*$_2$ æth.—for *παρ'*, *απ'* R 1. for *περισσοτερον*, *πλεον* D. **απαιτησουσιν** DU Just$_1$ (Clem$_1$) Constt$_1$ Epiph$_1$ Bas$_5$ Mac$_1$ [Antch$_1$].

42 ff.] Our Lord does not answer the question directly, but proceeds with His discourse, so as to furnish it with an answer;—viz. that in its highest sense it applies to his Apostles and ministers, inasmuch as to them most has been given as the *οἰκονόμοι*—but that its application is gradationally downwards through all those who know their Master's will, even to the lowest, whose measure both of responsibility and of reward is more limited. For the comment on vv. 42—46 see on Matt. xxiv. 45—51. Notice that **ἀπίστων** here = *ὑποκριτῶν* in Matt.

47, 48.] *Primarily*, in reference to the question in ver. 41, **οἱ γνόντες** = **ἡμεῖς**, the disciples. **οἱ μὴ γνόντες** = **πάντες**, the multitude:—but the application is not limited to this: the truth is one of universal extent. The 47th verse needs little explanation:—after both *πολλάς* and *ὀλίγας*, **πληγάς** is to be supplied, see reff.: and cf. Aristoph. Nub. 959, *ἐπετρίβετο τυπτόμενος πολλάς*.

ἑτοιμ., not *ἑαυτόν*, but, **matters**, *πρὸς τ. θ. αὐ.*: almost in the absolute sense of 'making ready:'—it refers back to the *γίνεσθε ἕτοιμοι* of ver. 40; this readiness being not only preparing *himself*, but the matters over which he has charge, ver. 35. There is reference to Deut. xxv. 2.

ὁ δὲ μὴ γν.] The case is of one (a disciple in the first reference, but then generally of all men) who bona fide is ignorant of his Lord's will. That such persons *shall be punished*, is both the sentence of the law, see Levit. v. 17—19, and an inference from the truth set forth ver. 57, and Rom. i. 19, 20, 32; ii. 14, 15,—that the *natural conscience* would have prevented the *μὴ ποιῆσαι*. (Observe that the two classes, *not included here*, are *ὁ γνοὺς καὶ ποιήσας*, and *ὁ μὴ γνοὺς καὶ ποιήσας*, as far as that can be said (see Rom. ii. 14);—the reference *here* being only to the *μὴ ποιήσας* in both cases, or rather to the *μὴ π.* in the first case and its equivalent *π. ἄξια πληγῶν* in the second.) But the difficulty seems to be to assign *a spiritual meaning* to the **δαρήσεται ὀλίγας**. *That such will be the case*, would *à priori* be consonant to the justice of the Judge of all the earth: and we have it here declared, that *it shall be so*: but *how*, is not revealed to us. It is in vain for the sinner to encourage himself in sin from such a declaration as this: for the very knowledge of the declaration excludes him from the exemption. "Our ears have heard the voice divine; We cannot be as they." (Christian Year.)

παντὶ ᾧ, attr. for *παρὰ παντός*, *ᾧ*.

πολὺ . . πολύ] The second *πολύ* is not the *πολύ* that has been given, but a proportionable amount of result of diligence, a *πολύ* which he is to render.

περισσ.] Perhaps, *more than from others*: but more likely *more than had been deposited with him*, viz. that, and the interest of it: see Matt. xxv. 15 ff.

49—53.] The connexion appears to be this:—the immense and awful difference between the faithful and unfaithful servants brings our Lord to the *ground* of

* ἐπὶ τὴν γῆν, καὶ τί θέλω; [t] εἰ ἤδη [u] ἀνήφθη. 50 [v] βάπτισμα δὲ [w] ἔχω βαπτισθῆναι, καὶ [x] πῶς [y] συνέχομαι ἕως
ὅτου [z] τελεσθῇ. 51 δοκεῖτε ὅτι εἰρήνην [a] παρεγενόμην
[b] δοῦναι ἐν τῇ γῇ; οὐχὶ λέγω ὑμῖν, [c] ἀλλ' ἢ [d] διαμερισμόν.

ABDE HKLM RSTUV XΓΔΛ Πא 1. 33. 69

t see ch. xiii. 9 reff. Winer, edn. 6, § 53. 8. e.
u James iii. 5 (Acts xxviii. 2 v. r.) only. 2 Chron. xiii. 11.
v = Mark x. 38, 39 (‖ Mt. v. r.).
w = 2 Cor. iv. 1. Phil. i. 30. Acts xviii. 18.
x = John xi. 36.
y = Acts xviii. 5. 2 Cor. v. 14. Phil. i. 23. see Matt. iv. 24 reff.
z John xix. 30.
a ch. xix. 16. John iii. 23. Acts v. 21 al. fr. Josh. xviii. 8.
b = ch. i. 77. Lev. xxvi. 6.
c 2 Cor. i. 13. Num. xiii. 29.
d here only. Ezek. xlviii. 29. Mic. vii. 12 bis only.

49. * rec εἰς, with D R(Tischdf) rel $Meth_1$ [Bas_1 Chr_1]: επι (*from Matt* x. 34 ?) ABKLM R^1(Treg) TUXΠא 1. 33. 69 syr-mg $Clem_1$ $Orig_6$[int_2] $Eus_{sæpe}$ Tit-bostr Chr_5 [Ath_2 Bas_1 Cyr_3-p $Antch_1$] Hil_1 Jer Aug_1.
50. rec (for οτου) ου, with X rel [$Orig_1$-ed]: txt ABDKLMRTUΠא 33. 69 $Orig_2$[ms_1 $Dion_1$]. συντελεσθη $א^{3a}$(but συν erased) 195(Sz).
51. for δουναι, ποιησαι D lat-*e* syr-cu. for αλλ η, αλλα D 69 coptt.

that difference, and its necessary development in the progress of His kingdom on earth. **49. πῦρ**] It is extraordinary that the official announcement of the Baptist (ch. iii. 16)—αὐτὸς ὑμᾶς βαπτίσει ἐν πν. ἁγ. **καὶ πυρί**—connected with the mention of a baptism here,—with the promise Acts i. 5, and the appearance Acts ii. 3, so strikingly expressed as **διαμεριζόμεναι** γλῶσσαι ὡσεὶ **πυρός**,—have not kept the Commentators in general (Bleek is an exception) from falling into the blunder of imagining here that the *fire* is synonymous with, and means no more than, the *discord* and *division* which follow. The fire is, *the gift of the Holy Spirit,*—the great crowning result of the sufferings and triumph of the Lord Jesus. To follow this out in all its references belongs to another place: see notes on Mark ix. 49, and Acts ii. 3. This fire, in its purifying and separating effects on the mass of mankind, causes the **διαμερισμός** afterwards spoken of.

The *construction* of **τί θέλ. εἰ ἤδ. ἀν.** has been ever a matter of dispute, while the *meaning* is on all hands nearly agreed. The three prevalent explanations of it are: (1) which is Origen's (appy), and is adopted by Grot., and defended by Meyer [formerly] and Stier,—making εἰ = εἴθε, and rendering, **and what will I? would that it were already kindled!** Certainly thus there is nothing forced in the *construction;* we have εἰ for '*utinam*' joined with aorist in Josh. vii. 7;—but the abrupt short ejaculation seems unlike the usual character of our Lord's discourses. It is true the structure of John xii. 27 affords an instance of a similar question, καὶ τί εἴπω; . . . and under similar circumstances, of *His soul being troubled.* (2) which Theophyl., Kuinoel, Olsh., De Wette, Bleek, &c. [so Meyer, edn. 5, see Moulton's Winer, p. 562, note 3] adopt, taking τί = ὡς, as some do, adopting that reading, in Matt. vii. 14 (but see note there), and εἰ = ὅτι, and rendering, How I wish that it were already kindled! But here we have serious difficulties of an *idiomatic* kind:—τί is apparently never thus used—and εἰ only after words of wondering, being grieved, &c.: see Mark xv. 44. (3) That of Euthym., Beza, &c., and the E. V., 'What will I, if it be already kindled?' i. e. τί πλεῖον θέλω ἐὰν ἀνήφθῃ; τί πλεῖον ἀναμένω ἐν τῷ κόσμῳ; Euth. This also presents no constructional, but a very great contextual difficulty; for by ver. 50 it evidently *was not yet kindled;* and even if this were overcome, the expression, evidently a *deep one of personal anxiety* (and be it remembered Who said it), would be vapid and unmeaning in the extreme. All things then being considered, I prefer the first explanation. **50.**] The symbolic nature of Baptism is here to be borne in mind. *Baptism = Death.* The figure in the Sacrament is the *drowning,*—the *burial,* in the water, of the *old man* and the *resurrection* of the *new man:* see 1 Pet. iii. 20—22, and notes. *The Lord's Baptism* was *His Death,* in which the Body inherited from the first Adam (ἐν ὁμοιώματι σαρκὸς ἁμαρτίας) was buried, and the new Body (τὸ σῶμα τῆς δόξης αὐτοῦ) raised again: see Rom. vi. 1—11, but especially ver. 10. And He was **straitened** (the best possible rendering) till this was accomplished:—i. e. in anxiety and trouble of spirit. The δέ here implies, **but first,** i. e. before that *fire* can be shed abroad. Here we have then, as Stier expresses it, a 'passio inchoata' of our Lord; the first utterance of that deep anguish, which afterwards broke forth so plentifully,—but coupled at the same time with holy zeal for the great work to be accomplished.

51—53.] The work of *this fire,* as it burns onward in the world, will not be peace, but division: see Mal. iii. 2, 3, 18; iv. 1, where we have the separating effect

...νυν πεν R. G [πεν]-τε...

52 ἔσονται γὰρ [e] ἀπὸ τοῦ [e] νῦν πέντε ἐν ἑνὶ οἴκῳ [f] διαμεμε-
ρισμένοι, τρεῖς [g] ἐπὶ δυσὶν καὶ δύο [g] ἐπὶ τρισὶν 53 [f] διαμε-
ρισθήσονται, πατὴρ [g] ἐπὶ υἱῷ καὶ υἱὸς [g] ἐπὶ πατρί, μήτηρ
[h] ἐπὶ θυγατέρα καὶ θυγάτηρ [h] ἐπὶ τὴν μητέρα, [i] πενθερὰ
[h] ἐπὶ τὴν νύμφην αὐτῆς καὶ νύμφη [h] ἐπὶ τὴν [i] πενθεράν.
54 Ἔλεγεν δὲ καὶ τοῖς ὄχλοις Ὅταν ἴδητε [[k] τὴν] νεφέλην
[l] ἀνατέλλουσαν ἀπὸ [m] δυσμῶν, εὐθέως λέγετε ὅτι [n] ὄμβρος
ἔρχεται, καὶ γίνεται οὕτως. 55 καὶ ὅταν [op] νότον [pq] πνέοντα,
λέγετε ὅτι [r] καύσων ἔσται, καὶ γίνεται. 56 ὑποκριταί, τὸ
[s] πρόσωπον τῆς γῆς καὶ τοῦ οὐρανοῦ [t] οἴδατε [u] δοκιμάζειν,
τὸν δὲ καιρὸν τοῦτον [v] πῶς * οὐ [u] δοκιμάζετε; 57 τί δὲ καὶ

e ch. v. 10 reff. f ch. xi. 17, 18 reff. g = Rom. x. 19 (from Deut. xxxii. 21). h = ch. xi. 17 ‖. Matt. xxiv. 7 al. i ch. iv. 38 reff. k = Rev. xi. 12. l = Matt. iv. 16 reff. m Matt. viii. 11 reff. Isa. xlv. 6. n here only. Deut. xxxii. 2. o = Acts xxvii. 13. xxviii. 13 only. (Matt. xii. 42 reff.) p Sir. xliii. 16. q John iii. 8 reff.

r Matt. xx. 12. James i. 11 only. Jon. iv. 8. s = [Matt. xvi. 3.] James i. 11. Ps. ciii. 30. see ch. xxi. 35. t Matt. vii. 11. Phil. iv. 12 al. 3 Kings v. 6. u Rom. ii. 18. Phil. i. 10. Job xxxiv. 3. v Matt. xvi. 11. Mark iv. 40.

52. om 1st clause, except final νοι, ℵ[1](ins ℵ-corr[1]). εν ενι οικω bef πεντε D. rec οικω bef ενι, with AT rel vulg lat-*b f* [*l q*] D-lat syrr arm Eus$_1$: txt B D-gr L ℵ-corr[1] lat-*c e ff*$_2$ syr-cu Hil$_1$. τρεις bef διαμεμερισμενοι D. for επι, εν (twice) D lat-*c e*.

53. rec διαμερισθησεται, with A rel syrr syr-cu sah-mnt æth arm Mcion$_1$-t : txt BDLTUℵ vulg lat-*b c e f ff*$_2$ copt Eus$_1$ Hil$_1$. rec (for 1st επι) εφ', with ADKLΠ 1. 69 : txt BTℵ rel Eus$_1$. aft πατρι ins αυτου D lat-[*b l*] *c e i q* : και ℵ. ins διαμερισθησονται *dividetur* bef μητηρ D lat-*b c e i* [*l*] *q* Ambr$_1$. rec (for θυγατερα) θυγατρι (*conformn to foregoing*), with A rel : txt BDℵ, την θυγατερα LT 1 Eus$_1$. rec (for την μητερα) μητρι, with A rel : txt BDL 1 Eus$_1$, μητερα (omg την) Tℵ. for 1st αυτης, εαυτης T : om Δℵ[1] copt-wilk Eus$_1$ Tert$_1$. rec aft πενθεραν ins αυτης, with ATℵ[3a] rel latt syrr syr-cu : om BDLℵ[1] copt-ms Eus$_1$ Mcion$_1$-t.

54. om την ABLXΔℵ 1. 33. 69 arm : ins DT rel [Bas$_1$]. for απο, επι BLℵ : txt ADT rel. rec om οτι (*see Matt* xvi. 3), with D rel vulg lat-*b f g*$_2$: ins ABKL UXΠℵ 33. 69 lat-*c e ff*$_2$ syrr syr-cu coptt arm Bas$_1$.

55. πλεοντα D-gr. om οτι DLℵ[1] æth. for εσται, ερχεται ℵ[1](txt ℵ-corr[1.3]) [lat-*l*].

56. aft το ins μεν D ev-y lat-*b q* copt-wilk. transp της γης and του ουρανου (*more usual order*) DKLTXΠℵ[3a] 33 vulg-ed lat-*b c* Syr syr-cu coptt [æth arm Tert$_1$]: txt ABℵ[1] rel am(with harl) Syr-mss syr [Bas$_1$]. for τον δε καιρον, πλην τον καιρον D 157; τον κ. L : τ. κ. δε B. om πως D lat-*c e i* syr-cu. * οὐκ οἴδατε δοκιμάζειν BLTℵ 33 lat-*ff*$_2$ [*l*] syr-mg coptt æth : ου δοκιμαζετε AD rel latt Syr syr-cu [syr-txt] arm.—om last clause (*homœotel?*) X.

57. om τι δε D lat-*b*(appy) syr-cu.

of this fire in its completion at the great day: see also Matt. iii. 12. On the passage itself, see notes on Matt. x. 35, 36.

54—59.] Reproaches for blindness to the signs of the times. The connexion of this with the foregoing is natural and close. ἀπὸ τοῦ νῦν (ver. 52), the distinction shall begin to be made;—the discord and division between those who discern τὸν καιρὸν τοῦτον (ver. 56) and those who do not. Our Lord then turns to the crowd (**καί.** He not only said to the disciples the foregoing, but also to the crowd the following) and reproaches them (1) for their *blindness*, in not being able to discern it, as they did the signs in the natural heavens; and (2) for their *want of prudence* (vv. 57—59), in not repenting and becoming reconciled to the law of God while yet there was time. Schleiermacher and De Wette can discover no connexion, and yet the latter thinks Luke inserted the sayings of vv. 54—56 out of Matt. xvi., because of vv. 49 ff.

54.] There is a somewhat similar saying of our Lord at Matt. xvi. 2 ff., but differing both in its occasion and its substance. **τὴν νεφ.**, just as τὰς νεφέλας, —**the cloud,**—that usually rises there: see 1 Kings xviii. 44. The west, in Judæa, would be the direction of the sea.

55.] **ὅταν**, sc. ἴδητε. 56.] **τὸ πρ. τῆς γῆς**—perhaps referring to other signs of rain or heat from the appearance of the hills, &c. **τὸν δὲ κ. τ. . . . . .**] The signs of this time were very plain;—the

w ἀφ' ἑαυτῶν οὐ x κρίνετε τὸ δίκαιον ; 58 y ὡς γὰρ z ὑπάγεις
μετὰ τοῦ a ἀντιδίκου σου b ἐπ' ἄρχοντα, ἐν τῇ ὁδῷ c δὸς
d ἐργασίαν e ἀπηλλάχθαι ἀπ' αὐτοῦ, μήποτε f κατασύρῃ
σε πρὸς τὸν κριτήν, καὶ ὁ κριτής σε g παραδώσει τῷ
h πράκτορι, καὶ ὁ h πράκτωρ σε i βαλεῖ εἰς i φυλακήν. ...βαλη E.
59 λέγω σοι, οὐ μὴ ἐξέλθῃς ἐκεῖθεν ἕως οὗ καὶ τὸ ἔσχατον
k λεπτὸν ἀποδῷς.
XIII. 1 Παρῆσαν δέ τινες ἐν αὐτῷ τῷ καιρῷ l ἀπαγγέλλοντες αὐτῷ περὶ τῶν Γαλιλαίων ὧν τὸ αἷμα Πιλάτος

ABDG HKLM STUVX ΓΔΛΠℵ 1. 33. 69

w John v. 19 reff. x = 1 Cor. x. 15. y = John xii. 35, 36. z = ch. xix. 20. John vi. 21 ‡. a Matt. v. 25 bis. ch. xviii. 3. 1 Pet. v. 8 only. 1 Kings ii. 10. b = Matt. x. 18. ch. xxi. 12. xxiii. 1 al. c = here only. d = here only. (Acts xvi. 16, 19. xix. 24, 25. Eph. iv. 19 only. Ps. cvi. 23 al.) e = Heb. ii. 15 (Acts xix. 12) only. Job ix. 34. f here only. Jer. xxix. (xlix.) 10. g Matt. v. 25. xxvii. 26 ‖. Ezek. xxiii. 28. h here bis only. Isa. iii. 12 only. i John iii. 24 reff. k ch. xxi. 2 ‖ Mk. only +. (-πτός, Gen. xli. 4.) l Matt. viii. 33. ch. vii. 18, 22. viii. 20 al. Gen. xiv. 13.

58. for τη, τω D. απαλλαχθαι ΑΔ, απαλαχθαι X ; απαλλαγηναι D. om απ' B Bas_1. for κατασυρη, κατακρινη D lat-*b* ff_2 *i l q* syr-cu $Ambr_1$. rec (for παραδωσει) παραδω (*see Matt* v. 25), with L rel : txt ABDTℵ 69 $Mcion_2$-c.—π. bef σε D 157 latt. rec βαλλη, with T Scr's q^2 : βαλη A rel Bas_1 : βαλλει 69 lat-*e* : txt BDXΓℵ 33 ev-y.—βαλ. bef σε D [1] 241-5-52 Scr's q^2 latt.

59. for οὗ, του A : αν (‖ *Matt*) T : om BLℵ 1 $Orig_1$: txt D rel. for και to end, αποδοις τον εσχατον κοδραντην (*see* ‖ *Matt*) D lat-*b c* [*e*] Syr $Mcion_1$-t.—for το, τον (*influence of Matt* v. 26 : *cf Luke* xxi. 2) Aℵ[3a] rel Orig : txt BMTΓℵ[1].

CHAP. XIII. 1. om εν D 69 lat-*a e* g_2.

sceptre had departed from Judah;—the general expectation of the coming of the Messiah is testified even by profane authors;—the prophets had all spoken of Him, and the greatest of them, the Baptist, had announced His arrival.

57.] In what follows, our Lord takes occasion from the *request about the inheritance*, which had begun this discourse, to pass to infinitely more solemn matters. There is, I think, no denying that the **κρίνειν τὸ δίκ.** and the **ὁ ἀντίδικός σ.** have *a* reference to that request, in the ability and duty of every man to 'judge what is right:'—but the sense of the words far outruns that reference, and treats of loftier things. '*Why do ye not discern of yourselves your true state—that which is just—the justice of your case as before God? You are going* (the course of your life is the journey) *with your adversary* (the just and holy law of God) *before the magistrate* (God Himself); *therefore by the way take pains* (δὸς ἐργ., *da operam*—a Latinism: there is no reference to interest of money, as Thl.,—who also has the other interpretation,—supposes) *to be delivered from him* (by repentance, and faith in the Son of God, see Ps. ii. 12), *lest he drag thee to the judge* (κριτής—who adjudges the case and inflicts the fine; that is, the Son, to whom all judgment is committed), *and the judge deliver thee to the* ***exactor*** (see Matt. xiii. 41), *and the exactor* ***cast thee into prison***' (ditto, ver. 42).

59.] See on Matt. v. 25, and, on λεπτόν, Mark xii. 42.

CHAP. XIII. **1—9.**] ANSWER TO INTELLIGENCE OF THE MURDERED GALILÆANS, AND PARABLE THEREUPON. *Peculiar to Luke.* **1.**] **ἐν αὐτ. τ. καιρ.** *may mean* **at that very time**—viz. as He finished the foregoing discourse: but it is not *necessary* to interpret thus;—for, Matt. xii. 1; xiv. 1, the similar expression, ἐν ἐκείνῳ τ. κ. is certainly *indefinite*. **παρ. . . . . ἀπαγγ., came with the news,**—not, as Stier supposes, '*were in the crowd, and remarked to the Lord concerning these Galilæans*,' in consequence of what He had said ch. xii. 57:—such a finding of connexion is too fine-drawn, and is a fault which we may *excuse* in Stier, for his many services in interpreting our Lord's discourses, but must not *imitate*. It is obvious that no connexion is intended between this incident and the foregoing discourse. **περὶ τ. Γ.**] The historical fact is otherwise unknown. The way of speaking here shews that it was well known to the writer. It must have occurred at some feast in Jerusalem, on which occasions riots often took place (see Jos. Antt. xvii. 9. 3; 10. 2), and in the outer court of the temple. Such slaughters were frequent, and would not be particularly recorded by the historians. This mingling of their blood with their sacrifices seems to have been thought by the narrators evidence that they were very depraved sinners: for this

[m] ἔμιξεν μετὰ τῶν θυσιῶν αὐτῶν. 2 καὶ ἀποκριθεὶς εἶπεν
αὐτοῖς Δοκεῖτε ὅτι οἱ Γαλιλαῖοι οὗτοι ἁμαρτωλοὶ [n] παρὰ
πάντας τοὺς Γαλιλαίους ἐγένοντο, [o] ὅτι * τοιαῦτα πε-
πόνθασιν; 3 οὐχὶ λέγω ὑμῖν, ἀλλ' ἐὰν μὴ [p] μετανοῆτε,
πάντες ὁμοίως ἀπολεῖσθε. 4 ἢ ἐκεῖνοι οἱ δέκα [καὶ]
ὀκτὼ ἐφ' οὓς ἔπεσεν ὁ [q] πύργος ἐν τῷ Σιλωὰμ καὶ ἀπέκτεινεν αὐτούς, δοκεῖτε ὅτι αὐτοὶ [r] ὀφειλέται ἐγένοντο
[n] παρὰ πάντας τοὺς ἀνθρώπους τοὺς [s] κατοικοῦντας Ἱερουσαλήμ; 5 οὐχὶ λέγω ὑμῖν, ἀλλ' ἐὰν μὴ [p] μετανοήσητε,
πάντες [t] ὡσαύτως ἀπολεῖσθε. 6 ἔλεγεν δὲ ταύτην τὴν παρα-

m Matt. xxvii. 34. Rev. viii. 7. xv. 2 only. 4 Kings xviii. 23.
n = Rom. i. 25. xiv. 5. Ps. cxxxiv. 5.
o = Matt. ii. 18. v. 3 al. fr.
p Matt. iii. 2 reff.
q Matt. xxi. 33 reff.
r = Matt. vi. 12 (reff.).
s constr., Matt. xxiii. 21 reff.
t Matt. xx. 5. xxi. 30, 36 al. Judg. viii. 8 B.

2. rec aft *αποκριθεις* ins *ο ιησους*, with AD rel lat-*c* [*f*] *ff*$_2$ *q* syrr syr-cu copt æth: om BLTℵ vulg lat-*a b e i l* copt-dz sah arm. *ουτοι* bef *οι γαλιλαιοι* D 69 latt Syr syr-cu. *παρα π. τ. γαλ. εγενοντο* bef *αμαρτωλοι* D (latt). om 2nd *οτι* T.
* ταῦτα BDLℵ [lat-*e*]: *τοιαυτα* AT rel [latt Chr$_1$].

3. *αλλα* D, *αλλ η* L. *μετανοησητε* ADMXΓ 1. 69 vulg lat-*a c e f ff*$_2$ Bas$_1$ Chr$_2$ Antch Vict-tun: txt BLTℵ rel lat-*b q* [Bas$_1$-ms]; *μετανοειτε* HV. rec (for *ομοιως*) *ωσαυτως*, with A rel arm [Bas$_1$]: txt BDLTℵ 1. 33. 69 syr-mg [Chr$_1$].

4. om 1st *και* B D-gr Lℵ^1 sah [Epiph$_1$] Cyr$_1$: ins ATℵ^{3a} rel vulg lat-*a c f ff*$_2$ [Bas$_1$ Epiph$_1$ Chr$_1$]. *επεπεσεν* ℵ. for *εν τω*, *του* D-gr. rec *ουτοι* (*conformn to ver* 2), with E rel copt [Bas$_1$]: om D 240-1 lat-*e* Syr syr-cu: txt ABKLTXΠℵ (33) 69 latt syr sah Chr$_1$. rec om *τους*, with X rel: ins ABDLMTΛℵ 69 sah Bas$_1$. *ενοικουντας* D lat-*a*. rec ins *εν* bef *ιερουσαλημ*, with ATℵ rel latt syrr syr-cu coptt arm [Bas$_1$]: om BDLX 1 lat-*e* [æth] Chr$_1$. (33 def.)

5. aft *λεγω* ins *δε* D. *αλλα* KTΠ, *αλλ η* L: *οτι* D: om lat-*c e f i l* [*q*]. rec *μετανοητε* (*see ver* 3), with B ℵ^{3a}(but txt restored) rel [Bas$_1$]: txt ADLMTUXℵ^1 1. 69 vulg lat-*a c* sah Epiph$_2$ Chr$_1$ Euthym. rec (for *ωσαυτως*) *ομοιως*, with ADT rel: txt BLMℵ 1. 33 syr-mg Bas$_1$ Chr$_1$.

was their argument, and is unconsciously that of many at this day,—'the worse the affliction, the more deserved:' see Gen. xlii. 21: Acts xxviii. 4. **2, 3.**] Our Lord perceives this to be their reasoning —they did not *express* it, as is plain by the **δοκεῖτε ὅτι . . .** He does not deny that all the Galilæans were sinners, and deserved God's judgments, but *that these were pre-eminently so.* The **ὁμοίως** (the force of which is lost in the E. V., '*likewise*') should be rendered **in like manner,** as indeed the Jewish people did perish by the sword of the Romans. **4, 5.**] Our Lord introduces this incident as shewing that whether the hand of man or (so called) accidents, lead to inflictions of this kind, it is in fact but one Hand which doeth it all—Amos iii. 6. There is also a transference from the Galilæans—a despised people—to the *inhabitants of Jerusalem,* on whom the fulness of God's wrath was to be poured out in case of impenitence. Of the incident itself, or of the *tower in Siloam* (probably the district in which the fountain, John ix. 7, was situated,—though on the whole matter, and the situation of the fountain itself, there is considerable uncertainty), we know nothing. Josephus says of the wall of the ancient city, *πρὸς νότον ὑπὲρ τὴν Σιλωὰμ ἐπιστρέφον πηγήν,* B. J. v. 4. 2: see also Neh. iii. 15. In B. J. vi. 7. 2, he uses *μέχρι τοῦ Σιλωάμ,* as here, meaning apparently a district of the city: see on John l. c. **ὀφειλέται, sinners,**—see Matt. vi. 12;—perhaps the same thought may be traced as pervading the saying, as in vv. 58, 59, of the last chapter. (No such idea as that the tower was a *prison for debtors* is for a moment to be thought of.) **ὡσαύτως**] See on *ὁμοίως* above,—**similarly**—in the ruin of your whole city. This does not render it necessary that these words should have been spoken to actual dwellers in Jerusalem: for nearly the whole nation was assembled there at the time of the siege. **6—9.**] This Parable has perhaps been interpreted with hardly enough reference to its own peculiar context, or to the symbolic language of Scripture in other places. Ordinarily (also in Trench, Par. in loc.) the owner of the vineyard is explained to be the *Eternal Father:* the dresser and intercessor, the *Son of God:* the fig-tree, the *whole Jewish people:* the vineyard, the *world.* But it may be objected to this, that the owner *comes* to seek the fruit, which can be properly said

u Matt. xxiv. 32 reff. v Matt. xv. 13 reff. w Matt. xx. 1, &c. reff. x here only. 2 Chron. xxvi. 10. y ver. 16 reff. z = ver. 25. ch. xxiv. 21. Rev. xvi. 18. Hos. x. 9. see ch. vii. 45.

βολήν. [u] Συκῆν εἶχέν τις [v] πεφυτευμένην ἐν τῷ [w] ἀμπελῶνι αὐτοῦ, καὶ ἦλθεν ζητῶν καρπὸν ἐν αὐτῇ καὶ οὐχ
εὗρεν. 7 εἶπεν δὲ πρὸς τὸν [x] ἀμπελουργὸν [y] Ἰδοὺ τρία
ἔτη ἀφ᾽ οὗ [z] ἔρχομαι ζητῶν καρπὸν ἐν τῇ [a] συκῇ ταύτῃ
καὶ οὐχ εὑρίσκω· [b] ἔκκοψον αὐτήν· [c] ἵνα τί καὶ τὴν γῆν
[d] καταργεῖ; 8 ὁ δὲ ἀποκριθεὶς λέγει αὐτῷ Κύριε, [e] ἄφες

ABDG HKLM STUVX ΓΔΛΠℵ 1. 33. 69

a pres., John xv. 27. 2 Pet. iii. 4. 1 John iii. 8. Jer. i. 5. b Matt. iii. 10. vii. 19 al. Dan. iv. 11 (14 Theod.-F). c Matt. ix. 4 reff. d elsw. P. only (Rom. iii. 3. 1 Cor. xiii. 8 al.), exc. Heb. ii. 14. Ezra iv. 21, 23. v. 5. vi. 8 only. e = Matt. xxiv. 2. 4 Kings xxiii. 18.

6. *τις* bef *ειχεν* DKΠ lat-*e* [æth] $Ambr_1$. rec *εν τω αμπελωνι αυτου* bef *πεφυτευμενην* (*more usual order*), with A rel: txt BDLXℵ 1. 33 latt syrr coptt arm $Petr_1$ [Bas_1 Cyr_2].—om *τω* ℵ[1]. rec *καρπον* bef *ζητων*, with Scr's g(e sil) lat-*c ff*$_2$ *i l* [arm]: txt ABDTℵ rel vulg lat-*a b e f g*$_1$ [*q* syrr syr-cu] coptt æth Petr Bas_1 &c. for *εν αυτη*, *απ αυτης* D-gr. for *ουχ ευρεν*, *μη ευρων* D 157 lat-*e l*.

7. om *δε* D lat-*e l*. *ετη* bef *τρια* D vulg lat-*b c f* [*i l q*]. om *αφ ου* A rel syrr sah $Orig_1$ [Bas_2] $Iren\text{-}int_1$: ins BDLTℵ 69 latt syr-cu copt [æth] arm $Petr_1$ Ambr. ins *φερε την αξεινην* bef *εκκοψον* D. aft *εκκοψον* ins *ουν* ALTX 33. 69 latt syr coptt æth arm: om BDℵ rel lat-*e* Syr syr-cu Orig $Petr_1$ [Bas_2 Cyr_2-p]. for *την γην*, *τον τοπον* B[1](txt B[2.3], Tischdf).

only of Him who εἰς τὰ ἴδια ἦλθεν—who is even in Matt. ὁ κληρονόμος—and by implication there, the *possessor of the vineyard* ὅταν ἔλθῃ (for that destruction He universally represents as *His* coming). The other objections will come out in the direct exposition of the Parable, which I take to be this:—The link which binds it to the foregoing is ἐὰν μὴ μετανοῆτε . . .; and it is addressed rather to individuals than to the whole nation—though of course to the whole nation as made up of individuals. The vineyard is not *the world*, which would be wholly inconsistent with Scripture symbolism (for Matt. xiii. 24 the comparison is to ἡ βασ. τ. οὐρ.—*the gospel dispensation*, in which the field—*not the vineyard*—is the whole world); but, as in Isa. v. 7, *the house of Israel and the men of Judah* (see notes on Matt. xxi. 33 ff.). The fig-tree planted in the vineyard—among the vines—(a usual thing) denotes an individual application, fixing each man's thought upon one tree—and that one, *himself*; just as the guest without the wedding-garment in Matt. xxii. He who had the tree planted in His vineyard (—'All things that the Father hath, are Mine'—John xvi. 15), came seeking fruit, and found it not: see Matt. xxi. 19 and note. (The vinedresser, see below.) He commands it to be cut down, as encumbering the soil (exhausting it, rendering it inactive: see reff.); three years has He been coming and seeking fruit in this tree, and he findeth none. Then, at the intercession of the vinedresser, He consents (for this is implied) to spare it this year also, until it has been manured; if that fail, the Intercessor himself has no more plea to urge—it is to be cut down. Now *who is this Intercessor?* First look at the matter of fact. *Who were the vinedressers* of God's vineyard? They were many. Moses, the Prophets, the Baptist, the Lord Himself, the Apostles and Teachers after Him. But what *one Personality* might be set forth as pervading all these, 'striving with man' in them all—as being **ὁ ἀμπελουργός**? Clearly, it seems to me, *the Holy Spirit of God*. In the passage just alluded to, Gen. vi. 3, we can hardly but recognize the main features of our present parable; especially when the Days of Noah are compared by the Lord Himself to His own coming to vengeance. The intercessory office of the Spirit (ὁ παράκλητος, see on John xiv. 16), pleading with man and for man, and resigning that blessed conflict when met with inveterate obduracy, is often set before us in Scripture. (See the whole history of Saul; Zech. vii. 12—14: Prov. i. 23—32: Isa. lxiii. 10: Neh. ix. 20: Rom. viii. 26, 27.)

7. τρία ἔτη] I have little doubt (against Bleek, al.) that an *allusion* is intended to the *three years of our Lord's ministry*. The objection to this, that the cutting down ought then to have taken place *at the end of* τοῦτο τὸ ἔτος, does not apply; for all is left indefinite in the request and the implied answer. In the individual application, *many thousands did bear fruit this very year;* and of those who did not, who shall say *when* the Spirit ceased pleading with them, and the final sentence went forth? **καὶ τ. γ. κατ.**] **Why, besides bearing no fruit, is it impoverishing the soil** [rendering the

αὐτὴν καὶ τοῦτο τὸ ἔτος [f] ἕως [f] ὅτου [g] σκάψω περὶ αὐτήν,
καὶ [h] βάλω [i] κόπρια. 9 [k] κἂν μὲν [l] ποιήσῃ [l] καρπὸν [m] εἰς
τὸ μέλλον· [n] εἰ δὲ μήγε, ἐκκόψεις αὐτήν.
10 [o] Ἦν δὲ διδάσκων ἐν [p] μιᾷ τῶν συναγωγῶν ἐν τοῖς
[q] σάββασιν. 11 καὶ ἰδοὺ γυνὴ [r] πνεῦμα ἔχουσα [r] ἀσθενείας ἔτη δέκα [καὶ] ὀκτώ, καὶ ἦν [s] συγκύπτουσα καὶ μὴ
δυναμένη [t] ἀνακύψαι εἰς τὸ [u] παντελές. 12 ἰδὼν δὲ αὐτὴν
ὁ Ἰησοῦς [v] προσεφώνησεν καὶ εἶπεν αὐτῇ Γύναι, [w] ἀπο-
λέλυσαι τῆς ἀσθενείας σου. 13 καὶ ἐπέθηκεν αὐτῇ τὰς
χεῖρας, καὶ [x] παραχρῆμα [y] ἀνορθώθη καὶ ἐδόξαζεν τὸν

E νησεν ...

f ch. xv. 8 reff.
g ch. vi. 48. xvi. 3 only. Isa. v. 6 only.
h ver. 19 reff.
i here only †. Jer. xxxii. (xxv.) 33. 1 Macc. ii. 62 A only. (-ρία, ch. xiv. 35.)
k aposiop., ch. xix. 42. xxii. 42. Acts xxiii. 9. 1 Kings xii. 14.
l Matt. iii. 8 reff.
m 1 Tim. vi. 19 only.
n Matt. ix. 17 reff.
o constr., Matt. xix. 22 reff.
p = ch. v. 17 al. Deut. xix. 5.
q Matt. xii. 1 reff.
r see (Acts xvi. 16 v. r.) 2 Tim. i. 7.
s here only. Job ix. 27. Sir. xii. 11. xix. 26 only.
t ch. xxi. 28 [John viii. 7, 10 rec.] only. Job x. 15 only.
u Heb. vii. 25 only (there also w. εἰς) †. Jos. Antt. vi. 2. 3. (-λῶς, 2 Macc. iii. 12.)
v Matt. xi. 16 reff.
w = here only. Tobit iii. 6 (w. ἀπό, ℵ). 2 Macc. vi. 22.
x Matt. xxi. 19, 20 reff.
y Acts xv. 16. Heb. xii. 12 only. Ps. xvii. 35.

8. for και to ετος, ετι τουτον τον ενιαυτον D arm. aft σκαψω ins τα T $Petr_1$. Steph κοπριαν, with GHKΠ: κοπρον 1. 69: κοφινον κοπριων D lat-*a b c f* ff_2 *i l* [*q*]: txt ABTℵ rel vulg lat-*e* $Orig_1$ $Petr_1$ [$Epiph_2$] Cyr_1.
9. και εαν D Scr's c: και T. rec ει δε μηγε bef εις το μελλον, with AD rel latt syrr syr-cu arm $Petr_1$: εις το μελλον αφησεις ει δε μη γε T sah: εις το μελλον δε ει μη ποιηση 69: txt BLℵ 33 coptt æth [Cyr_1].
10. om 2nd εν DT 1. 69 latt. for τοις σαββασιν, σαββατω D [lat-*i*] coptt.
11. rec aft γυνη ins ην, with A rel lat-*e* [Syr syr-cu æth]: transpd in D: om BLTXℵ 33 latt syr [syr-jer] coptt arm.—for πνευμα εχουσα ασθενειας, εν ασθενεια ην πνευματος D. om ετη B^1(ins $B^{2\cdot3}$, Tischdf). om και (bef οκτω) B(but ins in ver 16) Tℵ 1 sah.—ιη′ D [copt]. συνκαπτουσα D^1: -καμπτ. D^4: -κυμπτ. X.
12. om προσεφωνησεν και D lat-*e*. aft απολελυσαι ins απο ADXℵ 33 syrr syr-cu [syr-jer]: om BLT rel $Orig_1$ [Cyr_1].
13. τας χειρας bef αυτη D Syr syr-cu coptt. rec ανωρθωθη, with EG^1KTUΠℵ (SV 1, e sil): txt A B(Tischdf) D rel. εδοξασεν D lat-*c* Syr copt-wilk: -ζον (appy) $ℵ^1$(but altered to txt by origl scribe).

neighbouring ground useless]? **8.] σκ. καὶ βάλ. κ., dig holes about the root, and cast in manure,** as is done (Trench in loc.) to orange-trees in the south of Italy: and to hops in England. **9.]** After **καρπόν,** λείπει, τὸ εὖ ἔχει, Euthym.; but not without reason: to fill up the aposiopesis *did not belong to the purpose of this parable.* **εἰς τὸ μέλλον,** not ἔτος (Meyer), but indefinite (see reff.), **hereafter**:—and purposely so;—because, *in the collective sense,* the sentence lingered. **ἐκκόψεις, Thou shalt cut it down**—not ἐκκόψω; and I find in this an additional proof of the correctness of the foregoing interpretation. It is the κύριος τ. ἀμπελῶνος who ὅταν ἔλθῃ, κακοὺς κακῶς ἀπολέσει αὐτούς. *All judgment is committed to* THE SON:—it is not the work of the Holy Spirit to cut down and destroy, for He is the Giver of *life.* The above interpretation is partially given by Stier, who has however in my view (in his 2nd edn. also) quite missed the ἀμπελουργός, understanding by him *the husbandmen in Matt.* xxi., forgetting that they are *destroyed* in the sequel of that parable, and that their position, that of the *tenants* of the vineyard, does not appear at all in this, any more than does the ἀμπελουργός in that.

10—21.] HEALING OF A WOMAN ON THE SABBATH: DISCOURSE THEREUPON. *Peculiar to Luke,* except the parables, which are in Matt. xiii. 31—33: Mark iv. 31—34. **10.]** Time and place alike indefinite. **11. πν. ἀσθ.]** Her weakness was the effect of permitted power of the evil one (ver. 16); but whether we are to find here a direct instance of *possession,* seems very doubtful. There is nothing in our Lord's words addressed to her, to imply it: and in such cases He did not *lay on His hands, or touch,*—but only in cases of sickness or bodily infirmity. **εἰς τὸ παντελές** belongs to ἀνακύψαι, not to δυναμ.: see note on ref. Heb. **12.]** There is no reason to suppose any eminence of faith in her—though we may fairly conclude that she was there with *some expectation* of a cure: see ver. 14. **ἀπολέλ.** expresses the setting

θεόν. 14 [z] ἀποκριθεὶς δὲ ὁ [a] ἀρχισυνάγωγος, [b] ἀγανακτῶν
ὅτι τῷ σαββάτῳ ἐθεράπευσεν ὁ Ἰησοῦς, ἔλεγεν τῷ ὄχλῳ
ὅτι ἓξ ἡμέραι εἰσὶν ἐν αἷς δεῖ [c] ἐργάζεσθαι· ἐν αὐταῖς οὖν
ἐρχόμενοι θεραπεύεσθε, καὶ μὴ τῇ [d] ἡμέρᾳ τοῦ [d] σαββάτου.
15 ἀπεκρίθη δὲ αὐτῷ ὁ κύριος καὶ εἶπεν Ὑποκριταί,
ἕκαστος ὑμῶν τῷ σαββάτῳ οὐ [e] λύει τὸν βοῦν αὐτοῦ ἢ
τὸν [f] ὄνον ἀπὸ τῆς [g] φάτνης καὶ ἀπαγαγὼν [h] ποτίζει;
16 ταύτην δὲ θυγατέρα Ἀβραὰμ οὖσαν, ἣν ἔδησεν ὁ σατανᾶς [i] ἰδοὺ δέκα καὶ ὀκτὼ ἔτη, οὐκ ἔδει λυθῆναι ἀπὸ τοῦ
[k] δεσμοῦ τούτου τῇ [d] ἡμέρᾳ τοῦ [d] σαββάτου; 17 καὶ ταῦτα
λέγοντος αὐτοῦ [l] κατῃσχύνοντο πάντες οἱ [m] ἀντικείμενοι
αὐτῷ, καὶ πᾶς ὁ ὄχλος [n] ἔχαιρεν [n] ἐπὶ πᾶσιν τοῖς [o] ἐνδόξοις
τοῖς γινομένοις ὑπ᾽ αὐτοῦ. 18 ἔλεγεν οὖν Τίνι ὁμοία ἐστὶν

F σαββατω... ABDEF GHKL MSTUV ΧΓΔΛ Πℵ 1. 33. 69

z = Matt. xi. 25 reff. a Mark v. 22 reff. b Matt. xx. 24 reff. c = Acts xviii. 3. 1 Cor. iv. 12. 2 Thess. iii. 8, &c. Exod. xx. 9. d see ch. iv. 16 reff. e = Matt. xxi. 2 ‖ Mk. f Matt. xxi. 2, 5 ‖ J., 7 (ch. xiv. 5 v. r., w. βοῦς) only. Isa. i. 3. g ch. ii. 7, 12, 16 only. Job xxxix. 9. h Matt. xxv. 35, &c. xxvii. 48 ‖ Mk. Gen. xxi. 19. i = ver. 7. ch. xv. 29. Acts ii. 7 al. Judg. iv. 14 A. k Mark vii. 35. Phil. i. 13 al. Ps. cvi. 14. l Gospp., here only. Rom. v. 5. ix. 33 (& 1 Pet. ii. 6, from Isa. xxviii. 16). x. 11. 1 Cor. i. 27 bis. xi. 4, 5, 22. 2 Cor. vii. 14. ix. 4. 1 Pet. iii. 16 only. m ch. xxi. 15. 1 Cor. xvi. 9. Gal. v. 17. Phil. i. 28. 2 Thess. ii. 4. 1 Tim. i. 10. v. 14 only. L.P. Zech. iii. 1. n Matt. xviii. 13 reff. o = here only. (ch. vii. 25 reff.) Exod. xxxiv. 10.

14. om *ο* (bef *ιησ.*) D. *ελεγεν τω οχλω* bef *οτι τω σαββατω* D lat-*a e*. rec om 2nd *οτι*, with ADT rel: ins BLℵ gat. (33 def.) (*εν αις* is written over the line in B *a prima manu*.) om *εν αις δει εργαζεσθαι* ℵ[1](ins ℵ-corr[1]). rec *ταυταις*, with D rel latt syrr syr-cu: txt ABLTXΠℵ 1. 69. for *ουν ερχομ.*, *συνερχομ.* A: om *ουν* U 241 Scr's p Syr syr-cu æth arm.
15. rec (for *δε*) *ουν*, with AT rel lat-*q* syr coptt: txt BDLℵ 1. 69 latt Syr [syr-jer]. for *κυριος*, *ιησους* D-gr FUΓ 1. 69 forj Syr syr-cu: txt ABTℵ rel syr [arm-ms]. rec (for *υποκριται*) *υποκριτα* (*corrn to αυτω*), with DVX lat-*f* Syr syr-cu [syr-jer] sah-mnt arm: txt ABTℵ rel latt syr coptt [æth] $Hipp_1$ $Iren\text{-}int_1$. *ημων* T. ins *εν* bef *τω σαββατω* AT coptt: om *τω σαβ.* ℵ[1]. for *ἤ*, *και* D. for *τον* (bef *ονον*), *την* AV. *απαγων* B[1](sic, see table: txt B[2](appy), Tischdf) ℵ[1] 1.
16. ins *του* bef *αβρααμ* D. *ετη ιη'* D.
17. om *ταυτα λεγοντος αυτου* D lat-*e*. *κατησχυνθησαν* D-gr lat-*e* sah. *εν πασιν οις εθεωρουν ενδοξοις υπ αυτου γεινομενοις* D lat-*e f l*. *γενομενοις* B: *γιγν.* T: *λεγομενοις* ℵ[1].
18. rec (for *ουν*) *δε*, with ADT rel lat-*c q* Syr arm: txt BLℵ 69 vulg lat-*a b* &c syr-mg coptt.

free of her muscles from the power which bound them down,—and then, ver. 13, the laying on of the divine hands confers upon her strength to rise and stand upright. It would be, in such a case, one thing to be loosed from the stiffening of years,—and another to have strength at once conferred to stand upright. **14.**] The ruler speaks not either to Jesus or to the woman; but covertly and cowardly, to the *multitude*. Stier notices the self-stultification of this speech, in making *θεραπεύεσθαι*, a reception of divine grace and help, a species of *ἐργάζεσθαι*.
15. ὑποκριταί] The Lord saw the real thoughts of his heart, that they were false, and inconsistent with his pretended zeal, and addressed the multitude as represented by him, their leader. A man hardly could give forth a doctrine so at variance with common sense and common practice, without some by-end, with which he covered his violation of truth. That by-end *here* was enmity to and jealousy of Jesus. The instance chosen *exactly fits* the circumstances. A beast tied to the manger is confined down as this poor woman was. **16.**] The contrast is strongly drawn—between a *dumb animal*, and (not merely a human creature, but) a *daughter of Abraham*—one of the chosen people (I cannot see any necessity for a *spiritual daughtership* (Gal. iii. 7) being here implied),—between a *few hours*, since the last watering, and 'lo these *eighteen years*' (compare ver. 7, *ἰδοὺ τρ. ἔτ.*).
17.] So far am I from thinking a description of this kind to be a mere general close, put in by the Evangelist, that I would take it as an accurate and graphic account of the immediate effect of our Lord's power and irresistible words, and the following parables as spoken *immediately thereupon*, shewing the people the ultimate conquest which the Kingdom of God should obtain over all opposition,

ἡ βασιλεία τοῦ θεοῦ, καὶ τίνι [p] ὁμοιώσω αὐτήν; 19 ὁμοία
ἐστὶν [q] κόκκῳ [q] σινάπεως, ὃν λαβὼν ἄνθρωπος [r] ἔβαλεν εἰς
[s] κῆπον ἑαυτοῦ· καὶ [t] ηὔξησεν καὶ [u] ἐγένετο εἰς δένδρον
[μέγα] καὶ τὰ [v] πετεινὰ τοῦ [v] οὐρανοῦ [w] κατεσκήνωσεν ἐν
τοῖς [x] κλάδοις αὐτοῦ. 20 καὶ πάλιν εἶπεν Τίνι [p] ὁμοιώσω
τὴν βασιλείαν τοῦ θεοῦ; 21 ὁμοία ἐστὶν [x] ζύμῃ, ἣν [x] λαβοῦσα γυνὴ ἔκρυψεν εἰς [y] ἀλεύρου [z] σάτα τρία, ἕως οὗ
[a] ἐζυμώθη ὅλον.

22 Καὶ [b] διεπορεύετο κατὰ πόλεις καὶ κώμας διδάσκων
καὶ [cd] πορείαν [d] ποιούμενος εἰς Ἱερουσαλήμ. 23 εἶπεν δέ
τις αὐτῷ Κύριε, [e] εἰ ὀλίγοι οἱ [f] σωζόμενοι; ὁ δὲ εἶπεν
πρὸς αὐτοὺς 24 [g] Ἀγωνίζεσθε [h] εἰςελθεῖν διὰ τῆς [i] στενῆς
θύρας· ὅτι πολλοί, λέγω ὑμῖν, ζητήσουσιν εἰςελθεῖν
καὶ οὐκ [k] ἰσχύσουσιν. 25 [l] ἀφ᾽ οὗ ἂν [m] ἐγερθῇ ὁ [n] οἰκο-

...θυρας F.

p Mark iv. 30 reff.
q || Mt. reff.
r = ver. 8. ch. xii. 49. Matt. x. 34. Mark iv. 26. Ps. cxxv. 6.
s John xviii. 1 reff. Deut. xi. 10.
t see || Mt. reff.
u ch. xx. 17 reff.
v Matt. vi. 26 reff.
w ||. Acts ii. 26 only. Ps. ciii. 12.
x || Mt. (reff.)
y || only. Num. v. 15.
z || only ‡. Gen. xviii. 6 Aq. Symm.
a ||. 1 Cor. v. 6. Gal. v. 9 only. Hos. vii. 4.
b ch. vi. 1 reff. Gen. xxiv. 62 Ed-vat. (B def.).
c James i. 11 only. Jon. iii. 3, 4.
d 2 Macc. xii. 10. see Mark ii. 23.
e = Matt. xii. 10. xix. 3. 2 Kings xii. 19.
f = Matt. x. 22 al.
g John xviii. 36 reff.
h John x. 2, 9. Matt. xix. 24. vii. 13.
i Matt. vii. 13, 14 only. Isa. xlix. 30.
k = Mark ix. 18.
l ver. 7 reff.
m = Mark iii. 3. x. 49 al.
n Matt. x. 25 al.†.

19. elz (for *ον*) *ο*, with 243: txt ABDTא rel Scr's-mss. *εισβαλεν* (sic, but corrd) א[1]. ins *τον* bef *κηπον* D א-corr[1] Scr's q r. for *εαυτου*, *αυτου* DFKL XΠא. om *εις* D 1 lat-*a b e ff*$_2$ *i l* [Syr] syr-cu copt-ms sah arm. om *μεγα* (|| *Matt*) BDLTא lat-*a b e ff*$_2$ *i l* syr-cu syr-jer copt-dz-txt sah arm Ambr$_1$: ins A rel vulg lat-*c f* [*q*] syrr copt æth. *κατεσκηνωσαν* D(Γ): *κατεσκηνουν* A 69. for *εν τ. κλ.*, *υπο τους κλαδους* D sah.

20. for ver, *η τινι ομοια εστιν η βασιλεια του θεου και τινι ομοιωσω αυτην* D. om *και* (*see Matt* xiii. 33) A rel Syr syr-cu sah: ins BGLTא 1. 69 latt copt æth arm.

21. rec *ενεκρυψεν* (|| *Matt*), with ADTא rel Eus$_1$: txt BKLUΠ. *ζυμωθη* D-gr.

22. ins *τας* bef *πολεις* LTX 1 sah. [*πορειαν* is repeated by B[1].] *ιεροσολυμα* B(*ερυσ.* B[1], Tischdf) Lא.

23. aft *ολιγοι* ins *εισιν* D 300(Sz) latt[not *q*] copt arm [Orig-int$_1$(om$_1$)]. ins *αποκριθεις* bef 2nd *ειπεν* D. om *προς αυτους* D 69.

24. rec (for *θυρας*) *πυλης* (*Matt* vii. 13), with A rel Orig$_2$ [Bas$_1$ Mac$_1$]: txt BDLא 1 arm Orig$_1$.—*δια τ. θυρας στηνης πυλης* T. for *ουκ ισχυσουσιν*, *ουχ ευρησουσιν* D syr(appy).

25. for *οὗ*, *οτου* D. *εαν* T 69 [Bas$_1$]. for *εγερθη ο οικ.*, *ο οικ. εισελθη* D.

however strong. On the parables themselves, see on Matt. xiii. 31—33.

[18—21.] These two parables, found in Matthew as above, and the former of them in Mark iv. 30—32, seem to have been again spoken by our Lord at this time, in reference to the progress of His Gospel indicated in ver. 17. **οὖν**, ver. 18, is important, as pointing out the connexion.]

22—30.] Answer to the question as to the number who shall be saved. Our Lord repeats, occasion being given by a question peculiar to Luke, parts of His discourses spoken elsewhere, as referred to below. **22.**] This notice includes what follows in the cycle of this last journey, but disclaims any definiteness of place or time for it. But certainly it seems to follow in natural order after our Lord's solemn warnings to repentance at the beginning of this chapter. The enquirer can hardly have been a disciple of Jesus (see ver. 28), but most likely a *Jew from the multitude*, who had heard his discourses, and either from Jewish pride, or perhaps from real desire to learn from Him, put this question. **23.**] On **οἱ σωζόμενοι**, see note, Acts ii. 47. Here, the implication of final salvation is obvious. **αὐτούς**, the multitude. Similar sayings have occurred in the Sermon on the Mount, but the connexion here is intimate and strict. **24.**] See on Matt. vii. 13. The description of *the broad and narrow ways* is not here inserted, as probably by this time, *ἡ στενὴ θύρα* (or *πύλη*) was a familiar image. **ζητ. εἰς. κ. οὐκ ἰσχ.**, not, 'shall seek to enter *by it*, and shall not be able:'—the emphasis of the command is, **seek to enter** *at the strait door*: **for many shall seek to** *enter* (elsewhere), **and shall not be able.**

δεσπότης καὶ ᵒ ἀποκλείσῃ τὴν θύραν, καὶ ᵖ ἄρξησθε ἔξω
ἑστάναι καὶ ᑫ κρούειν τὴν θύραν λέγοντες Κύριε ἄνοιξον
ἡμῖν, καὶ ἀποκριθεὶς ἐρεῖ ὑμῖν Οὐκ οἶδα ὑμᾶς πόθεν ἐστέ,
26 τότε ᵖ ἄρξεσθε λέγειν Ἐφάγομεν ἐνώπιόν σου καὶ
ἐπίομεν, καὶ ἐν ταῖς ʳ πλατείαις ἡμῶν ἐδίδαξας. 27 καὶ
ἐρεῖ Λέγω ὑμῖν, οὐκ οἶδα πόθεν ἐστέ. ˢ ἀπόστητε ἀπ' ἐμοῦ
πάντες ᵗ ἐργάται ᵘ ἀδικίας. 28 ἐκεῖ ἔσται ὁ ᵛ κλαυθμὸς καὶ
ὁ ᵛ βρυγμὸς τῶν ὀδόντων, ὅταν ὄψησθε Ἀβραὰμ καὶ
Ἰσαὰκ καὶ Ἰακὼβ καὶ πάντας τοὺς προφήτας ἐν τῇ
βασιλείᾳ τοῦ θεοῦ, ὑμᾶς δὲ ʷ ἐκβαλλομένους ʷ ἔξω.
29 καὶ ἥξουσιν ἀπὸ ˣ ἀνατολῶν καὶ ˣ δυσμῶν καὶ [ἀπὸ]
ʸ βοῤῥᾶ καὶ ᶻ νότου, καὶ ᵃ ἀνακλιθήσονται ἐν τῇ βασιλείᾳ

R σθε λεγειν... ABDE GHKL MRST UVXΓΔ ΛΠℵ 1. 33. 69

o here only. Gen. xix. 10.
p Matt. iv. 17 al. Gen. xi. 6.
q Matt. vii. 7, 8 reff. constr., Acts xii. 13. Judith xiv. 14.
r ch. xiv. 21 reff. Prov. vii. 6.
s = ch. ii. 37. iv. 13 al. Ps. vi. 8.
t = here only. (2 Cor. xi. 13. Phil. iii. 1.) 1 Macc. iii. 6. τῶν καλῶν καὶ σεμνῶν ἐργάτην, Xen. Mem. ii. 1. 27.
u = Acts i. 18. 1 Kings iii. 13, 14.
v Matt. viii. 12 reff.
w John vi. 37 reff.
x Matt. viii. 11 reff. Isa. xlv. 6.
y Rev. xxi. 13 only. Gen. xiii. 14.
z Matt. xii. 42 reff. Eccl. i. 6.
a Matt. viii. 11 reff.

om εξω εσταναι και ℵ^1(ins ℵ-corr$^{1\cdot3}$). om 2nd την θυραν D lat-*b q* sah-mnt. rec ins a 2nd κυριε (*from Matt* xxv. 11), with ADT rel [lat-*b f i q*] syrr syr-cu [syr-jer copt-dz æth arm] Bas$_1$ Lucif$_1$: om BLℵ vulg lat-*a c e* [*ff*$_2$ *g*$_{1.2}$] *l* coptt.

26. αρξησθε (*from ver* 25) ADKLM S(Tischdf) TXΓΔΠℵ 69: txt B rel. aft λεγειν ins κυριε D.

27. λεγων B(sic: see table) T: om ℵ latt Syr coptt arm-usc [Lucif$_1$]. rec aft οιδα ins υμας (*so Matt* vii. 23; xxv. 12), with Aℵ rel vulg lat-*a c f ff*$_2$ [*q*] Orig$_2$: om BLRT tol lat-*b i l*.—ουδεποτε ειδον υμας D. om ποθεν εστε D 56-8 sah-mnt Orig$_1$ (appy). rec ins οι bef εργαται (*Matt* vii. 23), with AKMTUΓΠ 1. 33. 69 [coptt arm]: om BDRℵ rel Cyr$_1$ (Clem-rom$_1$ Just$_2$ Orig Epiph$_1$). rec ins της bef αδικιας, with AT rel coptt (Epiph$_2$) Cyr$_1$: om B(D)LRℵ arm Orig.—for αδικιας, ανομιας D ev-x [Just$_2$] Orig$_1$ Epiph$_2$.

28. οψεσθε B^1 D-gr X 69: ιδητε ℵ [Mcion$_2$-e]: txt A B^2[B^2(appy)$^{\cdot3}$, Tischdf] RT rel. ισακ DLℵ^1 [lat-*a b e i*]. for του θεου, αυτου A.

29. om 2nd απο A D-gr ℵ rel vulg lat-*b c e ff*$_2$ *i l* syr coptt: ins BLR(T) lat-*a f q* D-lat (Syr syr-cu) [syr-jer].—om 3rd και T.

After **εἰςελθ.**, is to be supplied in both places, *εἰς σωτηρίαν*, or *εἰς τ. βασ. τ. θεοῦ*. This remark will dispose of the punctuation of Lachmann and Tischendorf in his earlier editions, who place only a comma at *ἰσχύσουσιν*, and connect it with *ἀφ' οὗ*. **25.**] A reason why this *ἀγωνίζεσθαι* is so important:—because there will be a day when the gate will be *shut*. The figure is the usual one,—of a *feast*, at which the householder entertains (in this case) the members of his family. These being assembled, he rises and shuts the door, and none are afterwards admitted. The **ἀφ' οὗ** extends to **ἐστέ**, end of ver. 25—and the second member of the sentence begins with **τότε**. **ἔξω ἑστάναι** and **κρούειν** both depend on **ἄρξησθε**:—*Hearing that the door is shut,* **ye begin to stand without and knock.** On the spiritual import, see note on Matt. xxv. 11. **οὐκ οἶδ. π. ἐστέ**, *'ye are none of my family—have no relationship with me.'*

26. ἐφάγ. ἐνώπ. σου κ. ἐπ.] As applied to the *then assembled crowd,* these words refer to the miracles of feeding,—perhaps also to His having so often sat at meat in the houses of various persons (the **κ. ἐπίομεν** must not be pressed as meaning any thing different from **ἐφάγ.**:—the expression is a general one for taking a meal);—as applied to *Christians,* to *the eating and drinking* whereof those miracles were anticipatory. Both these are **ἐνώπιόν σου** merely,—*in His presence*;—very different from the drinking **μεθ' ὑμῶν** of which He speaks Matt. xxvi. 29, and from the *δειπνήσω μετ' αὐτοῦ καὶ αὐτὸς μετ' ἐμοῦ*, Rev. iii. 20. **ἐν τ. πλ. ἡμ. ἐδ.**, applicable directly to those to whom the words were spoken; and further, in its fuller sense, to all among whom the gospel is preached, even till the end.

27. ἐργάται ἀδικ.] This unusual expression seems to mean, *persons engaged in the hire and receiving the wages* of unrighteousness: see Matt. vii. 23, where *οἱ ἐργαζόμενοι τ. ἀνομίαν* answers to it. This meaning of *ἐργάτης* is peculiar: see reff. **28, 29.**] See Matt. viii. 11, 12, and notes. The verses occur here in

τοῦ θεοῦ. 30 καὶ ἰδοὺ εἰσὶν ἔσχατοι οἳ ἔσονται πρῶτοι,
καί εἰσιν πρῶτοι οἳ ἔσονται ἔσχατοι.
31 Ἐν αὐτῇ τῇ ὥρᾳ προςῆλθάν τινες Φαρισαῖοι λέγοντες
αὐτῷ Ἔξελθε καὶ πορεύου ἐντεῦθεν, ὅτι Ἡρώδης θέλει σε
...αυτοις T. ἀποκτεῖναι. 32 καὶ εἶπεν αὐτοῖς [b] Πορευθέντες εἴπατε τῇ
[c] ἀλώπεκι ταύτῃ Ἰδοὺ ἐκβάλλω δαιμόνια καὶ [d] ἰάσεις
[e] ἀποτελῶ [f] σήμερον καὶ [f] αὔριον, καὶ [g] τῇ τρίτῃ [h] τελειοῦμαι.

b = Matt. ii. 8. ix. 13 al.
c = here only (ch. ix. 58 || Mt. only. Judg. xv. 4.)
d Acts iv. 22, 30 only. Prov. iii. 8.
e James i. 15 only †. 2 Macc. xv. 39 only.
f James iv. 13. Exod. xix. 10.
g elliptic fem., Acts xxvii. 19. ch. x. 35. John i. 29. Exod. xxi. 29.
h = Heb. ii. 10. Phil. iii. 12. Wisd. iv. 13.

31. ταυτη DKMTΠ coptt. rec (for ωρα) ημερα, with B²T rel latt syrr coptt æth arm: txt AB¹DL R(appy) Xℵ syr-mg. (*Cf ch* ii. 38; vii. 21; x. 21; xii. 12; xx. 19; xxiv. 33: *this may have been conformed to those places, but the evidence is very strong, and* ημερα *is read in* vii. 21 *by* Lℵ¹ 69. *Notwithstanding the evidence of the ancient versions, Tregelles seems hardly consistent with his principles here in editing* ημερα.) (προςηλθαν, so B¹DL.) αυτω τινες των φαρισαιων λεγοντες D (latt Syr syr-cu). for θελει, ζητει D 253-9 [syr-cu] sah.

32. rec (for αποτ.) επιτελω (*commoner word*), with AR rel: αποτελουμαι D: txt BLℵ 33 $Clem_1$. aft τριτη ins ημερα B 56 latt [Syr syr-cu] copt æth arm.

a different connexion: '*Ye Jews, who neglect the earnest endeavour to enter* now, *shall weep and gnash your teeth when ye see all the saints, Jews and Gentiles, in the Kingdom of God, and yourselves excluded*' (see ch. xvi. 23). In these two verses is the real answer to the question of ver. 23 given :—'*they shall be* MANY—*but what is that to* you, *if you be not among them?*' **30.**] As the words here stand—somewhat different from those in Matt. xx. 16—they seem to be a prophetic declaration of what shall be in the course of the ingathering of these guests; —viz. that some who were the first, or among the first to believe, shall fall from their high place, and vice versa. This former has, as Stier notices (iii. 200), been remarkably the case with the Oriental Churches, which were the first founded and flourishing :—and, we may add, with the mother Church of Jerusalem, which has declined, while her Gentile offsets have flourished.

31—35.] WARNING OF HEROD'S ENMITY; OUR LORD'S REPLY. *Peculiar to Luke*:—the apostrophe in vv. 34, 35 was spoken by our Lord also on another occasion, Matt. xxiii. 37—39. **31.**] **ἐν αὐτῇ τῇ ὥρᾳ** is not necessarily *definite*. These Pharisees appear to have been sent by Herod for the purpose of getting rid of Jesus out of his jurisdiction. Considering his character, it is hardly possible that he should really have wished to kill *one who was so popular*;—he refused to do so when Jesus was in his power afterwards in Jerusalem;—but, as great multitudes were now following Him about, and superstitious fears, as we know, agitated Herod, he wished to be quit of Him, and took this means of doing so. I think this view is necessary to justify the epithet applied to Herod, which certainly implies *cunning on his part.* Stier thinks the Pharisees *invented* the tale about Herod: but then how can the *epithet applied to him* be explained? I cannot for a moment believe, as he does, that our Lord saw through the lie of the Pharisees, and yet *adopted* it, meaning the ἀλώπηξ to signify themselves. "That Jesus in a public discourse uses such an expression of the ruler of his country, is not to be judged of by the manners, and ways of speech, of our times. The free-spokenness of the ancient world, which we meet with especially in the Hebrew prophets, allowed such strong expressions, without any thing peculiarly offensive being found in them." Bleek.

32, 33.] The interpretation of this answer is difficult, for two reasons—(1) that the signification of the **σήμ.**, **αὔρ.**, and **ἡ τρίτη** is doubtful—(2) that the meaning of **τελειοῦμαι** is also doubtful. The days mentioned are ordinarily supposed to be proverbially used; **σήμ.** for His present working—**αὔριον**, for that between the present time and his arrival at Jerusalem—**ἡ τρ.**, for that arrival, and the end of his work and course by his Death. Against this, is (1) the positive use of the *three days*, in an affirmative sentence,—of which no instance can be brought where the proverbial meaning is implied :—(2) the πορεύεσθαι belonging to *all three* in ver. 33, whereas thus it only belongs to the two first. The interpretation adopted by Meyer (and Bleek) is this :—In three days (literal days) the Lord's working of miracles in Galilee would be ended, which had excited the apprehension of Herod: and then He would leave the

i = Matt. xi. 22, 24 reff. Judg. iv. 9. k = Mark i. 38 reff. l = ch. i. 6 reff. m here only +. 2 Macc. xi. 18 only. (ἐχομένως, 2 Macc. xiii. 26.) n Acts xiv. 19. xxi. 5, 30. Neh. xiii. 20. o Matt. xxi. 35 reff. p = Matt. xxiii. 37. Rev. xviii. 24. Isa. xxii. 16 Heb. see ch. i. 45. q ch. xvii. 34 reff. r Matt. xxiii. 37 only. 3 Kings iv. 23 A B (not Ed vat.) only. s here only. (= νόσσια, Matt. xxiii. 37.) Gen. vi. 14. t Matt. xxiii. 37 reff. u = Matt. iv. 11, &c.

ABDE GHKL MRSUV XΓΔΛΠ ℵ 1. 33. 69

33 [i] πλὴν δεῖ με [f] σήμερον καὶ [f] αὔριον καὶ τῇ [k] ἐχομένῃ
[l] πορεύεσθαι, ὅτι οὐκ [m] ἐνδέχεται προφήτην ἀπολέσθαι
[n] ἔξω Ἱερουσαλήμ. 34 Ἱερουσαλὴμ Ἱερουσαλήμ, ἡ ἀποκτείνουσα τοὺς προφήτας καὶ [o] λιθοβολοῦσα τοὺς ἀπεσταλμένους πρὸς [p] αὐτήν, [q] ποσάκις ἠθέλησα [q] ἐπισυνάξαι τὰ
τέκνα σου [q] ὃν τρόπον [r] ὄρνις τὴν ἑαυτῆς [s] νοσσιὰν ὑπὸ
τὰς [t] πτέρυγας, καὶ οὐκ ἠθελήσατε; 35 ἰδοὺ [u] ἀφίεται
ὑμῖν ὁ οἶκος ὑμῶν. λέγω δὲ ὑμῖν [ὅτι] οὐ μὴ ἴδητέ με

33. ins *τη* bef *αυριον* D: om *αυριον και* ℵ[1]. *ερχομενη* DΛℵ 69. *απολεσθαι* bef *προτην* (sic, with *σ* written above the line) D.

34. (*αποκτεννουσα* AKU[1]: *-κτενουσα* XΔ 1.) for *αυτην*, *αυτον* ℵ[1]. *ορνιξ* Dℵ: *ορης* L. *τα εαυτης νοσσια* (|| *Matt*) AKMΠ 1 sah arm: *τα νοσσια αυτης* D lat-*c* Iren-int: *την εαυτου νοσσιαν* ℵ[1].

35. rec aft *υμων* ins *ερημος* (*Matt* xxiii. 38), with D rel vulg-ed lat-*a b c f* (g_1 *l*?) [*q*] syrr syr-cu copt-wilk æth [$\text{Chr}_{\text{ubique}}$] Iren-int_2: om ABKLRSVΓΛΠℵ 69 am(with fuld bodl em forj jac san tol trev) lat-*e* ff_2 g_2 *i* copt-schw[-dz] sah arm Orig_2 Epiph_1. rec (for *λεγω δε*) *αμην δε λεγω*, with Scr's o(e sil): *λεγω* alone Lℵ[1] lat-*b c* ff_2 [*i*] *l* syr-cu sah æth: txt ABDRℵ[3a] rel Scr's-mss vulg lat-*f q* syr copt arm. om *οτι* (|| *Matt*) BDHLRℵ 1 gat(with mm) lat-*b c e i l q*: ins A rel vulg lat-*a f* ff_2. rec *με* bef *ιδητε* (|| *Matt*), with DL rel lat-*b c e q*: txt ABKMRΠℵ 69 vulg lat-*a f i l*

territory, not for fear of Herod, but because He was going to Jerusalem to die. The objection to this is, that the sense—of *ending these present works of healing*, &c. does not seem a sufficient one for τελειοῦμαι. Meyer takes it as *middle*—but qu., is a *middle present* ever thus placed alone? Is not such a form, when standing thus, necessarily passive? And though the word τελειοῦμαι is not found earlier than the writings of the Fathers in the sense of '*suffering martyrdom*,' it is found in that of '*being perfected*'—which, as applied to the Lord, *included his Death*:—see reff. I own that neither of the above interpretations satisfies me,—and still less the various modifications of them which have been proposed (e. g. by Stier and Wieseler; De Wette adopts none). Nor can I suggest any less open to objection:—but merely state my conviction, (1) that the days mentioned must have some *definite fixed reference to three actual days*: (2) that τελειοῦμαι is the *pres. pass.*, and is used in the solemn sense elsewhere (reff.) attached to the word. If this Gospel had been a chronological calendar of our Lord's journey, the meaning would probably have been clear: but as we have none such, it is, and I believe must remain, obscure. Bp. Wordsworth's note is much to the point: "It must be remembered that Herod was ruler of Peræa as well as of Galilee: and that John the Baptist had been put to death at Machærus, where Herod had a palace, about ten miles E. of Jericho, and thirty E. of Jerusalem. St. Matt., xix. 1, and St. Mark, x. 1, 46, speak of our Lord being in Peræa, whence He passed over the river Jordan, and so came to Jericho, and thence to Bethany and Jerusalem for His Passion. Herod had put John to death not in Galilee but in Peræa: and if our Lord was now, as seems probable, in Peræa or near it, it was very likely that the Pharisees should endeavour to intimidate Him with a threat of Herod's anger." **τῇ ἐχ.** = τῇ τρίτῃ above, and is not *less precise* (Stier). **πορεύεσθαι, to journey**—the very word in which they had addressed Him, **πορ.** ἐντεῦθεν. **οὐκ ἐνδ.**, a monopoly not without exceptions, for John had been put to death by Herod out of Jerusalem. But our Lord's saying is not to be so literally pressed;—He states the general rule, which in His own case was to be fulfilled. There is no reference to the power of the Sanhedrim to judge and condemn false prophets (as Grot., Lightf., &c. think), for the fact of **ἀπολέσθαι** only is here in question;—and our Lord never would place himself in such a category (Meyer). **34, 35.**] These verses are in too close connexion with the preceding to allow of the supposition that they are inserted unchronologically, as Grot., Mey., De W., Neander, and even Schleierm. suppose: and their variations from those in Matthew (xxiii. 37—39) are striking and

ἕως [v ἥξει ὅτε] εἴπητε w Εὐλογημένος ὁ ἐρχόμενος ἐν
ὀνόματι κυρίου.

...τω ελθειν R. XIV. 1 Καὶ ἐγένετο ἐν τῷ ἐλθεῖν αὐτὸν εἰς οἶκόν
τινος τῶν ἀρχόντων [τῶν] Φαρισαίων σαββάτῳ φαγεῖν
ἄρτον, x καὶ αὐτοὶ y ἦσαν z παρατηρούμενοι αὐτόν. 2 καὶ
ἰδοὺ ἄνθρωπός τις ἦν a ὑδρωπικὸς b ἔμπροσθεν αὐτοῦ.
3 καὶ ἀποκριθεὶς ὁ Ἰησοῦς εἶπεν πρὸς τοὺς c νομικοὺς καὶ
Φαρισαίους λέγων Ἔξεστιν τῷ σαββάτῳ d θεραπεῦσαι ἢ
οὔ; 4 οἱ δὲ e ἡσύχασαν, καὶ f ἐπιλαβόμενος ἰάσατο αὐτὸν
καὶ g ἀπέλυσεν, 5 καὶ [ἀποκριθεὶς] πρὸς αὐτοὺς εἶπεν Τίνος

v = John ii. 4. 2 Pet. iii. 10. Ps. xxxvi. 13. [constr. see Rev. xiii. 17, Moulton's Winer, p. 370, note 3.]
w Matt. xxi. 9 reff. Psa. cxvii. 26.
x ch. ii. 21 reff. passim in Luke.
y Matt. xix. 22 reff.
z ch. vi. 7 reff.
a here only +.
b Matt. v. 16 al. 2 Kings iii. 31 A.
c = Matt. xxii. 35 reff.
d = ch. vi. 7. ix. 6 al.
e = Acts xi. 18. xxi. 14 (ch. xxiii. 56. 1 Thess. iv. 11) only. Neh. v. 8.
f = Matt. xiv. 31. Acts ix. 27. Judg. xix. 25.
g = Matt. xiv. 15 reff.

coptt Epiph$_2$. rec aft *εως* ins *αν*, with Aℵ rel: om BDKLRΠ. om *ηξει οτε* (‖ *Matt*) BLMRXℵ 1. 69 gat(with mm) lat-*e i* Syr coptt arm: om *ηξει* KΠ: ins AD rel. (*ηξει*, so ADVΔΛ ev-y.)

Chap. XIV. 1. *εισελθειν* DM 69 latt coptt arm (Syr æth ?). ins *τον* bef *οικον* A. om 2nd *των* BK¹ℵ.

2. om *τις* D 1 mt lat-*b c ff_2 i* [*l q*].

3. om *λεγων* D am lat-*a b e q* Syr syr-cu. rec ins *ει* bef *εξεστιν* (*from Matt* xii. 10), with A rel [vulg-clem](with fuld forj san) lat-*a b c e ff_2* syrr syr-cu arm: om BDLℵ am lat-*f* syr-jer [copt-wilk æth]. rec *θεραπευειν* (*from Matt* xii. 10), with A rel: txt BDLℵ 1. rec om *η ου* (*Matt ib*), with A rel vulg lat-*a c ff_2* [*i l*] Syr sah-woide arm: ins BDLℵ 1. 69 mm lat-*b e f q* syr-cu syr-w-ast syr-jer coptt æth Cyr$_1$.

4. aft *επιλαβομενος* ins *αυτον και* D lat-*e* Syr syr-cu; *αυτου* 1. 69 lat-*b c ff_2 l* coptt æth arm. *ιασαμενος* D. om *αυτον* D 69 am lat-*e*. om last *και* D.

5. om *αποκριθεις* (*not in Matt* xii. 11) BDKLΠ 1. 69 lat-*a b c e ff_2 i l* Syr syr-cu coptt æth arm: ins A ℵ(marked for erasure, but marks removed) rel vulg lat-*f* syr [syr-jer]. (33 def.) *ειπεν* bef *προς αυτ.* (*Matt*) ADKΠ lat-*a b c e f ff_2 i l* [*q* syrr] coptt æth arm: txt Bℵ rel vulg. for *αυτους*, *αυτον* ℵ¹. aft *τινος* ins *εξ* D

characteristic. For *γάρ*, which *there* accounts for the *ἐρημία* of the temple, then for the last time left by our Lord, *does not appear here*, but *δέ*, introducing a fresh saying, *having* I believe *another meaning*: and the words *ἀπ' ἄρτι*, which follow *ἴδητε there*, marking *that moment* as the *commencement* of the dereliction, are here omitted. Surely these differences indicate an uttering of the words *prophetically*, previous to their utterance in the act of departure. Our Lord overleaps in prophetic foresight the death just set forth as certain, and speaks of the ages to come, during which the holy city should be desolate and trodden down of the Gentiles. That the very words **εὐλ. ὁ ἐρχ.** *κ.τ.λ. were used by the multitude* at the Lord's entry into Jerusalem, I should much rather ascribe to a misunderstanding by them and the disciples of this very declaration, than for a moment suppose that these words found any sufficient *fulfilment* in that entry (Erasmus, Paulus, Wieseler).

Chap. XIV. 1—6.] Healing of a dropsical man on the Sabbath. *Peculiar to Luke.* 1.] **ἐν τῷ ἐλθ. αὐτ.**, viz. during the *πορεύεσθαι*, ch. xiii. 33. **τ. ἀρχ. [τ.] Φ.**, of the **chief men of the Pharisees**; or, if the **τῶν** be omitted, of the **Pharisees who were rulers.** Though the Pharisees had no official rulers as such, they had men to whom they looked up, as Hillel, Schammai, Gamaliel, &c. (Meyer.) **φ. ἄρτ.**] The Jews used to give entertainments on the Sabbath, see Neh. viii. 9—12: Tobit ii. 1. The practice latterly became an abuse,—'Hodiernus dies sabbati est: hunc in præsenti tempore otio quodam corporaliter languido et fluxo et luxurioso celebrant Judæi.' Aug. in Ps. xci. 1, Enarr. § 2, vol. iv. Again, 'observa diem Sabbati, non Judaicis deliciis . . . .' in Ps. xxxii. 2, Enarr. ii. § 6. **καί**, usual after *ἐγένετο*: not '*also*,' or '*even*.' 2.] **ἔμπρ. αὐτ.**, not *as a guest*: see ver. 4, and compare ch. vii. 37, and note on ib. ver. 45. *ἦν ἱστάμενος καὶ μὴ τολμῶν μὲν ζητῆσαι θεραπείαν διὰ τὸ σάββ. καὶ τοὺς Φαρ. φαινόμενος δὲ μόνον, ἵνα ἰδὼν οἰκτειρήσῃ τοῦτον ἀφ' ἑαυτοῦ καὶ ἀπαλλάξῃ τοῦ ὕδρωπος.* Euthym. It does not appear, though it is certainly possible, that

h John iv. 11, 12. Rev. ix. 1, 2 (3ce) only. Gen. xvi. 14 al.
i Acts xi. 10 only. Hab. i. 15.
k see ch. iv. 16 reff.
l = Matt. viii. 28 reff.
m Rom. ix. 20 only. Judg. v. 29 A. Job xvi. 8. xxxii. 12 only.
n = Matt. xxii. 3, &c. reff.
o = Acts iii. 5. (ix. 22. Phil. ii. 16.) 1 Tim. iv. 16 only. Sir. xxxi. (xxxiv.) 2. constr., here only.

ABDE GHKL MSUV XΓΔΛΠ ℵ 1. 33. 69

ὑμῶν υἱὸς ἢ βοῦς εἰς [h] φρέαρ πεσεῖται, καὶ οὐκ εὐθέως
[i] ἀνασπάσει αὐτὸν ἐν τῇ [k] ἡμέρᾳ τοῦ [k] σαββάτου; 6 καὶ
οὐκ [l] ἴσχυσαν [m] ἀνταποκριθῆναι πρὸς ταῦτα. 7 ἔλεγεν
δὲ πρὸς τοὺς [n] κεκλημένους παραβολήν, [o] ἐπέχων πῶς τὰς
[p] πρωτοκλισίας [q] ἐξελέγοντο, λέγων πρὸς αὐτούς 8 Ὅταν
[n] κληθῇς ὑπό τινος εἰς [r] γάμους, μὴ [s] κατακλιθῇς εἰς τὴν
[p] πρωτοκλισίαν, μήποτε [t] ἐντιμότερός σου ᾖ [n] κεκλημένος
ὑπ' αὐτοῦ, 9 καὶ ἐλθὼν ὁ σὲ καὶ αὐτὸν [n] καλέσας ἐρεῖ σοι
[u] Δὸς τούτῳ [u] τόπον, καὶ τότε ἄρξῃ μετὰ [v] αἰσχύνης τὸν
ἔσχατον τόπον [w] κατέχειν. 10 ἀλλ' ὅταν [n] κληθῇς, πορευ-

p = here bis. ch. (xi. 43 v. r.) xxi. 6 | only +. q ch. x. 42. Gen. xiii. 11. r Matt. xxii. 2 reff. s ch. vii. 36 reff. t ch. vii. 2 reff. u Rom. xii. 19. Eph. iv. 27 only. Sir. iv. 5. xxxviii. 12. v 2 Cor. iv. 2. Phil. iii. 19. Heb. xii. 2. Jude 13. Rev. iii. 18 only. 2 Chron. xxxii. 21. w = here [Matt. xxi. 38 v. r.] only. (ch. iv. 42. viii. 15 al.) Ezek. xxxiii. 24.

copt-ms. rec (for *υιος*) *ονος* (*see note*), with KLXΠℵ 1. 33. 69(*ορος*) latt copt [syr-jer æth] arm: *προβατον* D: txt AB rel lat-*e f q* syrr (syr-cu) sah Thl Euthym.—pref *ὁ* A S(Tischdf) U.—aft *βους* add *η ονος* syr-cu. rec **εμπεσειται** (*Matt*), with D rel: txt ABLΠℵ 1. 69. for *αυτον*, *αυτο* A. om *εν* ADKLXΔΠ 69 vulg lat-*b c l*: ins Bℵ rel lat-*a e f* [*q*]. *τη ημ. τ. σαβ.* bef *και ουκ ευθ. αν. αυ.* D Syr syr-cu. om *τη* (bef *ημερα*) Bℵ[1].

6. for *και* to *ανταπ.*, *οι δε ουκ απεκριθησαν* D 47 lat-*e*. for *ανταπ.*, *αποκριθηναι* Λℵ 1. 243-51 Scr's i. rec adds *αυτω*, with A rel (latt): om BDLℵ 1 lat-*e l*.

7. aft *ελεγεν δε* ins *και* D vulg lat-*a* arm.

8. om *υπο τινος* D vulg lat-*e i* syr-cu $Clem_1$. *γαμον* D. for *ῇ κεκλημενος*, *ηξει* D. om *υπ' αυτου* D lat-*a b c* ff_2 *i l* Syr syr-cu copt æth: om *υπ'* L ℵ[1](ins ℵ-corr[1 or ?a]).

9. for *αρξη*, *εση* D-gr lat-*e*. (**μετα**, so ABDℵ &c.) om *τον* D[1](ins D[4]).

10. *κληθεις* B[1](sic: see table). om *πορευθεις* D 251 lat-*e* [$Clem_1$].

he was set there by the Pharisees *on purpose.* This was *before* the meal (ver. 7). **5.**] There is a strict propriety in the comparison: the accident and disease are *analogous.* **υἱὸς ἢ βοῦς**] This reading, which evidently was the original, seemed incompatible with the supposed argument *à minori ad majus*: *υἱός* was therefore altered to *ὄνος* (as in ch. xiii. 15) or *πρόβατον* (Mill and Bornemann conjectured *ὄϊς*). But our Lord's argument is of another and a far deeper kind. The stress is on *ὑμῶν*: and the point of comparison is the ownership, and consequent tender care, of the object in question. '*Those who are in* your *possession and care, whether belonging to your* families, *or your* herds, *are cared for, and rescued from perishing: am I* (*the possessor of heaven and earth,*—this lies in the background) *to let mine perish without care or rescue?*' There may be in the words the meaning '*son, or* even *ox;*' but I prefer rendering them simply.

7—24.] Sayings of our Lord at this Sabbath feast. **7—11.**] It does not appear that the foregoing miracle gave occasion to this saying; so that it is no objection to it, that it has no connexion with it. Our Lord, as was His practice, founds His instructions on what He saw happening before Him. As Trench remarks (Par. in loc.), it is probable this was a splendid entertainment, and the guests distinguished persons (ver. 12).

7.] **πρωτοκλ.**, see Matt. xxiii. 6, the middle place in the triclinium, which was the most honourable. At a large feast there would be many of these. **8.**] The whole of this has, besides its plain reference, a *deeper one,* linked into it by the pregnant word **γάμους**, *relating to the Kingdom of God.* Both meanings are obvious, and only one remark needed;—that all that *false* humility, by which men put themselves lowest and dispraise themselves *of set purpose to be placed higher,* is, by the very nature of our Lord's parable, *excluded*: for that is not *bona fide ταπεινοῦν ἑαυτόν.* The exaltation at the hands of the Host is not to be a *subjective end* to the guests, but will follow true humility.

9.] **σὲ καὶ αὐτόν**, not, '*thyself also,*' (see ch. ii. 35,) **but thee and him,** as E. V. **ἐρεῖ**, not dependent on **μή**, but future. **ἄρξῃ . . . κατ.**] The form of expression sets forth the reluctance and

θεὶς [x] ἀνάπεσε εἰς τὸν ἔσχατον τόπον, ἵνα ὅταν ἔλθῃ ὁ
[n] κεκληκώς σε εἴπῃ σοι Φίλε, [y] προσανάβηθι ἀνώτερον·
τότε ἔσται σοι δόξα [z] ἐνώπιον πάντων τῶν [a] συνανακειμένων
σοι. 11 ὅτι πᾶς ὁ [b] ὑψῶν ἑαυτὸν [b] ταπεινωθήσεται, καὶ
ὁ [b] ταπεινῶν ἑαυτὸν [b] ὑψωθήσεται. 12 ἔλεγεν δὲ καὶ τῷ
[n] κεκληκότι αὐτὸν Ὅταν [c] ποιῇς [d] ἄριστον ἢ δεῖπνον, μὴ
[e] φώνει τοὺς φίλους σου μηδὲ τοὺς ἀδελφούς σου μηδὲ
τοὺς [f] συγγενεῖς σου μηδὲ [g] γείτονας πλουσίους· μήποτε
R αυτοι ... καὶ αὐτοὶ [h] ἀντικαλέσωσίν σε, καὶ γένηται [i] ἀνταπόδομά
σοι. 13 ἀλλ᾽ ὅταν [c] ποιῇς [k] δοχήν, [l] κάλει πτωχούς,
[m] ἀναπείρους, χωλούς, τυφλούς· 14 καὶ μακάριος ἔσῃ, ὅτι
P ανταποδοθησεται... οὐκ ἔχουσιν [n] ἀνταποδοῦναί σοι· [n] ἀνταποδοθήσεται γάρ
σοι ἐν τῇ [o] ἀναστάσει τῶν δικαίων.

x ch. xi. 37 reff.
y here only. Exod. xix. 23.
z = Acts vi. 5 al. Num. xiii. 34.
a Matt. ix. 10 reff.
b Matt. xxiii. 12 reff.
c = Matt. xxii. 2 reff. Gen. xxi. 8.
d ch. xi. 38. Matt. xxii. 4 only. 2 Kings xxiv. 15.
e = here only. see ch. xvi. 2 al. fr.
f Mark vi. 4 reff.
g ch. xv. 6, 9. John ix. 8 only. Exod. xii. 4 al.
h here only +.
i Rom. xi. 9 only. Ps. xxvii. 4. (-δοσις, Col. iii. 24.)
k ch. v. 29 (reff.) only.
l vv. 7, &c.
m ver. 21 only +. 2 Macc. viii. 24 only.
n here bis. Rom. xi. 35. xii. 19 (& Heb. x. 30, from Deut. xxxii. 35). 1 Thess. iii. 9. 2 Thess. i. 6 only. Isa. lxiii. 7.
o see John v. 29. Rev. xx. 5, 6.

rec αναπεσον, with 236: αναπεσαι (*see ch* xvii. 7) B²(sic) GLMXΔΛ Scr's q r s: αναπειπτε D [Clem₁]: txt A B¹(sic: see table) ℵ rel. ε. τ. εσχ. τοπ. bef αναπ. D lat-*e* [Clem₁]. for ειπη, ερει (*mechanl repetn*) BLXℵ: txt AD rel [Antch₁]. [α only of ανωτερον is written by B¹.] ins και bef τοτε D. om 2nd σοι ℵ¹(ins bef εσται ℵ-corr¹·³ (so appy, but Tischdf's account is not clear) 248) 234 Scr's f. rec om παντων, with D rel latt goth arm: ins ABLXℵ 1. 33. 69 syrr syr-cu [syr-jer] coptt æth [Antch₁]. om 3rd σοι D 258 latt syr-cu.

11. ταπεινουται and υψουται D-gr.

12. κεκληκυντι A. om 1st σου D lat-*a* Iren-int₁. om μηδε τ. αδ. σ. L [1] 69 Iren-int₁. om μηδε τους συγγενεις σου D ev-48 lat-*a e* Cypr₁: om σου ℵ 254 vulg lat-*b c ff₂* Iren-int₁. for 3rd μηδε, μη B. ins τους bef γειτονας D (69). ins μηδε τους bef πλουσιους D lat-*a b c* [*ff₂ i l*] arm Cypr₁. rec σε bef αντικαλεσωσιν, with A rel latt arm [Bas₁]: txt BDLRXℵ 1. 69 mt lat-*e f* syrr copt goth Iren-int₁ Cypr₁ [Damasc₁]. rec σοι bef ανταποδομα, with A rel vulg lat-*b c* syrr syr-cu goth [Bas₁ Damasc₁] Cypr₁: txt B(sic: see table) DLRℵ lat-*a e* copt.

13. δοχην bef ποι. Bℵ. ποιησης Mℵ 258. (αναπειρους (*η and ει are very commonly confounded in MSS*), so AB¹DE¹LRℵ ev-y.)

14. for γαρ, δε ℵ¹ 1. 69 lat-*c e f ff₂ i l* [*q*] æth arm Cypr₁: om 253.

lingering with which it is done. **10.**] **ἵνα**, not expressing the view with which *thou* art to do it (Meyer, bezeichnet die Absicht des ἀνάπεσε), but a consequence which may follow: the view with which the act, as an objective fact, happens: the effect, of which it is (however the actor may be unaware of this) the cause; as the μήποτε in ver. 8. **11.**] As an example of the first clause, see Isa. xiv. 13—15; of the second, Phil. ii. 5—11.

12—14.] The *composition of the company before Him* seems to have given occasion for this saying of our Lord. The Pharisee his host had doubtless, with the view (of watching Him) mentioned in ver. 1, invited the principal persons of the place, and with the intention of *courting their favour*, and *getting a return*. The Lord rebukes in him this spirit:—and it has been well remarked, that the intercourse and civilities of social life among *friends* and *neighbours* are here *pre-supposed*, (inasmuch as for them there takes place an ἀνταπόδομα, and they are struck off the list by this means,) with this caution,—that our means are not to be *sumptuously laid out upon them*, but upon *something far better*,—the providing for the poor and maimed and lame and blind. When we will make a sacrifice, and provide at some cost, let us not throw our money away, as we should if an ἀνταπόδομα is made to us in this world: but give it to the poor, i. e. lend it to the Lord; and then, as in ver. 14, there will be an ἀνταπόδ. ἐν τ. ἀναστ. τ. δικ.,—which shall not be a mere equivalent, but a rich reward. See an excellent note in Bleek. **14.**] **ἀναστ. τ. δικ.**, the *first* resurrection, here distinctly asserted by our Lord; otherwise τ. δικ. would be vapid and unmeaning. See 1 Cor. xv. 22 f.: 1 Thess. iv. 16: Rev. xx. 4, 5.

15 Ἀκούσας δέ τις τῶν [p] συνανακειμένων ταῦτα εἶπεν
αὐτῷ Μακάριος ὅστις [q] φάγεται ἄρτον ἐν τῇ βασιλείᾳ τοῦ
θεοῦ. 16 ὁ δὲ εἶπεν αὐτῷ Ἄνθρωπός τις [c] ἐποίει δεῖπνον
μέγα καὶ ἐκάλεσεν πολλούς, 17 καὶ ἀπέστειλεν τὸν δοῦλον
αὐτοῦ τῇ ὥρᾳ τοῦ δείπνου εἰπεῖν τοῖς [l] κεκλημένοις Ἔρχεσθε, ὅτι ἤδη ἕτοιμά ἐστιν [πάντα]. 18 καὶ ἤρξαντο [r] ἀπὸ
[r] μιᾶς πάντες [s] παραιτεῖσθαι. ὁ πρῶτος εἶπεν αὐτῷ Ἀγρὸν
[t] ἠγόρασα, καὶ [u] ἔχω [u] ἀνάγκην [v] ἐξελθὼν [w] ἰδεῖν αὐτόν·
ἐρωτῶ σε [x] ἔχε με [s] παρῃτημένον. 19 καὶ ἕτερος εἶπεν
[y] Ζεύγη βοῶν ἠγόρασα πέντε, καὶ πορεύομαι [z] δοκιμάσαι
αὐτά· ἐρωτῶ σε [x] ἔχε με [s] παρῃτημένον. 20 καὶ ἕτερος

p ver. 10. Matt. ix. 10 reff. q = ver. 1 al. Exod. ii. 20. fut., ch. xvii. 8. John ii. 17. James v. 3. r here only. see Matt. xviii. 35. Rom. xi. 25 al. s here 3ce. Acts xxv. 11. 1 Tim. iv. 7. v. 11. 2 Tim. ii. 23. Tit. iii. 10. Heb. xii. 19, 25 bis only. L.P.H. see 1 Kings xx. 6, 28. Esth. iv. 8. t Matt. xiii. 44. 2 Chron. xxxiv. 11. u [ch. xxiii. 17.] 1 Cor. vii. 37. Heb. vii. 27. Jude 3 only. v = Matt. xviii. 28. xx. 1, &c. w = John xii. 21. Josh. ii. 1. x constr., here bis. ch. xix. 20. Mark iii. 1. viii. 17. y ch. ii. 24 only. Lev. v. 11. z = 1 Cor. iii. 13. 2 Cor. viii. 8. 1 Thess. v. 21. 1 Pet. i. 7 al. Ps. xxv. 2. Prov. xvii. 3.

F [πα]-ρητη-μενον... ABDEF GHKL MPRSU VXΓΔΛ Πℵ 1. 33. 69

15. *ταυτα* bef *των συναν.* D ℵ-corr¹ [copt]: om *ταυτα* ℵ¹ Scr's g [lat-*e f*]. om *ειπεν* to *ειπεν* next ver ℵ¹(ins ℵ-corr¹, except *αυτω*, which is added by ℵ³ᵃ). rec (for *οστις*) *ος*, with AD rel $Clem_1$ [Eus_2 Bas_1] $Epiph_1$: txt BLPRX ℵ-corr 1. 69 syr-mg copt [Eus_5].

16. for *ο δε*, *ουδε* D-gr. om *αυτω* D 253 lat-*a b e* [arm-ed]. om *τις* P $Orig_1$. rec *εποιησεν* (*commoner tense in narration*), with ADP rel [syrr $Clem_1$] $Orig_1$ Bas_1 [Eus_1 $Tert_1$]: txt BRℵ 1 syr-cu $Orig_1$. *μεγαν* B²(but corrd, Tischdf) DΛΠ² 69 $Clem_1$: txt AB¹PRℵ rel $Orig_2$ Eus_2 [Bas_1]. (om X lat-*e* arm Tert.)

17. *τους δουλους* P 259 Scr's c. om *τη ωρα του δειπνου* P 259. *ερχεσθαι* (*itacism?*) ADKLPR Δ(Treg) Γ ℵ. for *εστιν*, *εισιν* LRℵ. om *παντα* BLRℵ¹ lat-*b c ff₂ i l q*: ins AP ℵ-corr¹(appy, but erased) rel vulg lat-*f*, and (but bef *ετοιμα* (*as in Matt* xxii. 4) D lat-*a e* Syr syr-cu [syr-jer] copt.

18. rec *παραιτεισθαι* bef *παντες*, with AP rel syr copt goth æth Bas_1: om *παντες* syr-cu: txt BDLRXℵ 1 latt Syr arm. ins *και* bef *ο πρωτος* P lat-*c e*. om *αυτω* D 1 lat-*a b c e* ff_2 *i l* [*q*] copt[-dz] goth arm. *αναγκην* bef *εχω* DP latt: txt A B(-*κη* B¹) Rℵ rel. rec *εξελθειν*, with APR rel: txt BDLℵ. rec aft *εξελθ.* ins *και*, with AP rel: om BDGLRℵ Syr syr-cu copt [æth] arm. om *σε* ℵ¹(ins ℵ-corr¹).

19. for *ερωτω κ.τ.λ.*, *διο ου δυναμαι ελθειν* D lat-*a c* ff_2 *i q* (*b l*) mss-in-Orig(*κ. δια τουτο . . .*).

20. for *ετερος*, *αλλος* D latt.

15—24.] *Parable of the Great Supper.* One of the guests takes this literally, and imagines *the great feast to which the Jews looked forward* to be meant. He spoke *as a Jew*, and probably with an idea that, as such, his admission to this feast was *sure and certain.* Our Lord answers him by the parable following, which shewed him that true as his assertion was, (and He does not deny it,) the blessedness would not be *practically* so generally acknowledged nor entered into. The Parable, whatever analogy it may bear with that in Matt. xxii. 1 ff., is *wholly different from that in many essential points.*

15.] **φάγεται** is a well-known future, contracted from *φαγήσεται*: see reff.

16.] The **δεῖπ. μέγα** is the *βασιλεία τ. θεοῦ*, the feast of fat things in Isa. xxv. 6; completed in the marriage-supper of the Lamb; but fully prepared when the glad tidings of the gospel were proclaimed. **ἐκάλ. πολ.**] These first *κεκλημένοι* are the Pharisees and Scribes and learned among the Jews.

17.] The **δοῦλος** is one *spirit*, one *message*; but not necessarily, in the three cases, one and the same *person*. The three messages were delivered (1) by John the Baptist and our Lord; (2) by our Lord and the Apostles; (3) by the Apostles and those who came after. The elder prophets cannot be meant, for **ἕτοιμά ἐστιν πάντα** was the message, = *ἤγγικεν ἡ βασ. τ. οὐρ.*

18—20.] **ἀπὸ μιᾶς**, supply *γνώμης*: so *ἀπὸ τῆς ἴσης*, Thucyd. i. 15; so (ch. vii. 30) they had rejected John's baptism, and (John vii. 48) the Lord himself. The saying is not to be taken strictly without exception, e. g. Nicodemus: but generically. So also ver. 24. The *temper* of these self-excusers is threefold; the

εἶπεν Γυναῖκα ἔγημα, καὶ διὰ τοῦτο οὐ δύναμαι ἐλθεῖν.
21 καὶ [a] παραγενόμενος ὁ δοῦλος [b] ἀπήγγειλεν τῷ κυρίῳ
αὐτοῦ ταῦτα. τότε [c] ὀργισθεὶς ὁ [d] οἰκοδεσπότης εἶπεν τῷ
δούλῳ αὐτοῦ Ἔξελθε [e] ταχέως εἰς τὰς [f] πλατείας καὶ
[g] ῥύμας τῆς πόλεως, καὶ τοὺς πτωχοὺς καὶ [h] ἀναπείρους
καὶ τυφλοὺς καὶ χωλοὺς εἰςάγαγε ὧδε. 22 καὶ εἶπεν ὁ
δοῦλος Κύριε, [i] γέγονεν ὃ [j] ἐπέταξας, καὶ ἔτι [k] τόπος
ἐστίν. 23 καὶ εἶπεν ὁ κύριος πρὸς τὸν δοῦλον Ἔξελθε εἰς
τὰς ὁδοὺς καὶ [l] φραγμούς, καὶ [m] ἀνάγκασον εἰςελθεῖν, ἵνα
[n] γεμισθῇ μου ὁ οἶκος. 24 λέγω γὰρ ὑμῖν ὅτι οὐδεὶς
τῶν ἀνδρῶν ἐκείνων τῶν κεκλημένων [o] γεύσεταί μου τοῦ
δείπνου.

25 [p] Συνεπορεύοντο δὲ αὐτῷ ὄχλοι πολλοί. καὶ [q] στρα-

a see ch. xi. 6 reff.
b Matt. ii. 8 al. Gen. xiv. 13.
c Matt. v. 22 reff.
d ch. xii. 39 al.†
e ch. xvi. 6. John xi. 31 only in Gospp. 1 Cor. iv. 19 al. 4 Kings i. 11.
f Matt. vi. 5. xii. 19. ch. x. 10. xiii. 26. Acts v. 15. Rev. xi. 8. xxi. 21. xxii. 2 only. Isa. xv. 3. Tobit xiii. 17.
g Matt. vi. 2. Acts ix. 11. xii. 10 only. Prov. xxxi. 23 ℵ. Isa. xv. 3. Tobit xiii. 18 (not ℵ). Sir. ix. 7 only.
h ver. 13.
i = Matt. vi. 10. ch. xxiii. 24. Rev. xvi. 17. Gen. i. 3, &c.
j Mark vi. 27, 39 al. Gen. xlix. 33.
k = ver. 9. ch. ii. 7. Gen. xxiv. 23, 25.
l Matt. xxi. 33 reff.
m Matt. xiv. 22 reff.
n Mark iv. 37 reff.
o Matt. xxvii. 34. John ii. 9. Acts xxiii. 14 al. Job xii. 11.
p Mark x. 1. ch. vii. 11. xxiv. 15 only. Exod. xxxiii. 15, 16. Judg. xi. 8 A.
q ch. vii. 9 al.

for εγημα, ελαβον D. for και δια τουτο, διο D.

21. rec aft ο δουλος ins εκεινος (*see Matt* xxii. 10), with X rel syrr syr-cu [syr-jer]: om ABDKLPRΠℵ 1. 69 latt copt goth æth arm Bas_1. (33 def.) aft αυτου ins παντα D (arm-usc). for τοτε, και D lat-*e*. τω δουλω αυτου bef ειπεν D 131(Sz). om τους (bef πτωχους) D: for τους, οσους εαν ευρητε ℵ-corr[1](txt ℵ[1·3a]). (αναπειρους, so AB[1]DL ev-y: αναπιρους PRℵ.) rec transp τυφλους and χωλους, with R rel Syr syr-cu [arm]: om και χωλους A 69 syr-jer: txt BDFKLMPUΠℵ 33 latt syr copt goth æth Eus_1 Bas_1. for εισαγαγε, ενεγκε D.

22. ο δουλος bef ειπεν D lat-*e*. aft ειπεν ins αυτω A. om κυριε D lat-*c e*. rec (for ὃ) ὡς, with AP rel latt syrr [syr-jer] goth æth: txt BDLRℵ 1 lat-*e* syr-cu syr-mg copt arm.

23. aft δουλον add αυτου D lat-*a b* Syr syr-cu æth Bas_1. rec ο οικος bef μου, with P rel latt: txt ABDKLRXΠℵ lat-*e* syr-cu syr-mg copt arm Aug_1.

24. for ανδρων, ανθρωπων Dℵ spec. om εκεινων D-gr spec.

25. om πολλοι D lat-*a b c e ff*$_2$ *l* syr-cu.

excuses themselves are threefold; their *spirit is one.* The first alleges an ἀνάγκη,—he *must* go and see his land: the second not so much as this, only his own plan and purpose—πορεύομαι: the third not so much as either of these, but rudely asserts οὐ δύναμαι (i. e. οὐ βούλομαι) ἐλθεῖν. Also the *excuses themselves* are threefold. The first has his *worldly possession* ('one to his farm,' Matt. xxii. 5) to go and see: the second his purchase ('another to his merchandise,' ibid.) of stock to prove: the third his home engagements and his lust to satisfy. *All* are detained by *worldliness,* in however varied forms. **21.**] **τῆς πόλεως**, still, *in the city* (Matt. xxii. 7); still, *among the Jews.* **πλατ. κ. ῥύμ.**, the broad and narrow streets: perhaps the πόλεις κ. κῶμαι through which the Lord and his Apostles journeyed preaching. Here appear again the very persons of ver. 13; the representatives of the wretched and despised; = ὁ πολὺς ὄχλος, Mark xii. 37: not perhaps without a hint, that only those who knew themselves to be spiritually poor and maimed and halt and blind would come to the gospel feast. **22.**] The palace is large, and the guest-room: 'nec natura nec gratia patitur vacuum,' Bengel. **23.**] The calling of the Gentiles, *outside the city; in the country* (Matt. xxii. 9, 10). **ἀνάγκ. εἰςελθ.**] Is there not here *an allusion to Infant Baptism?* for remember, the εἰςελθόντες are *good and bad.* (Matt. l. c.) **24.**] I think with Stier (iii. 202, edn. 2), that our Lord here speaks *in his own Person:* **ὑμῖν** will fit no circumstance in the parable; for the householder and his servant are alone: the guests are not present. Our Lord speaks, with His usual λέγω γὰρ ὑμῖν, *to the company present:* and half continuing the parable, half expounding it, substitutes *Himself* for the master of the feast, leaving it hardly doubtful who **ἄνδρες ἐκεῖνοι οἱ κεκλημένοι** are.

25—35.] DISCOURSE TO THE MULTITUDES. Our Lord is, at some time further

φεὶς εἶπεν πρὸς αὐτοὺς 26 Εἴ τις ἔρχεται πρός με, καὶ
οὐ [r] μισεῖ τὸν πατέρα αὐτοῦ καὶ τὴν μητέρα καὶ τὴν
γυναῖκα καὶ τὰ τέκνα καὶ τοὺς ἀδελφοὺς καὶ τὰς ἀδελ-
φάς, [s] ἔτι τε καὶ τὴν ἑαυτοῦ [t] ψυχήν, οὐ δύναται εἶναί μου
μαθητής. 27 [καὶ] ὅςτις οὐ [u] βαστάζει τὸν σταυρὸν ἑαυτοῦ
καὶ ἔρχεται ὀπίσω μου, οὐ δύναται εἶναί μου μαθητής.
28 τίς γὰρ ἐξ ὑμῶν θέλων [v] πύργον οἰκοδομῆσαι οὐχὶ πρῶτον [w] καθίσας [x] ψηφίζει τὴν [y] δαπάνην, εἰ ἔχει [z] εἰς [a] ἀπ-
αρτισμόν; 29 [b] ἵνα [b] μήποτε [c] θέντος αὐτοῦ [c] θεμέλιον καὶ μὴ
[d] ἰσχύοντος [e] ἐκτελέσαι, πάντες οἱ [f] θεωροῦντες ἄρξωνται

...προς αυτους P.

...εχει τα προς (?) F.

ABDE GHKL MRSU VXΓΔΛ Πℵ 1. 33. 69

r = Matt. vi. 24. ch. xvi. 13. John xii. 25. Gen. xxix. 31.
s Acts xxi. 28.
t = Matt. vi. 25. xvi. 25. ch. xvii. 33. John xii. 25 al. Exod. xxi. 23.
u = John xix. 17. Acts xv. 10. Gal. vi. 2, 5.
v Matt. xxi. 33 reff.
w = ver. 31. ch. xvi. 6. Matt. xiii. 48. Isa. xxx. 8.
x Rev. xiii. 18 only †.
y here only. Ezra vi. 4, 8. (-νᾶν, ch. xv. 14.)
z = 2 Cor. x. 5. 2 Tim. ii. 20, 21.
a here only †. Dion. Hal. de comp. verb. 24 only. (τίζειν, Ps. vii. 10 Symm.)
b here only.
c ch. vi. 48. 1 Cor. iii. 10, 11.
d Matt. viii. 28 reff.
e here bis only. Deut. xxxii. 45 B. 2 Chron. iv. 5. 2 Macc. xv. 9 only.
f = Matt. xxvii. 55. Acts xix. 26. Ps. xxi. 7.

for *προς αυτους*, *αυτοις* D.

26. for *με*, *εμε* ℵ. for *μισει*, *πεισει* D[1](txt D-corr[1·2]). rec (for *αυτου*) *εαυτου*, with BLRΓ: txt ADℵ rel [Bas_4]. aft *μητερα* ins *αυτου* D [Bas_1]. rec (for *τε*) *δε*, with A D-gr ℵ rel vulg lat-*c f* (*ff_2*?): txt BLRΔ. *ψυχην* bef *εαυτου* Bℵ (69) latt Hil. rec *μου μαθητης* bef *ειναι*, with AD rel lat-*a b c e f ff_2* Syr syr-cu goth $Orig_1$ Hil_1: *μου ειν. μαθ.* KΠ 69 vulg Eus_1 Bas_3 Orig-int_1 Hil_1: txt BLMR S(Treg) Xℵ fuld syr copt æth.

27. om ver (*homœotel*) M[1]RΓ 69. om *και* BLℵ[1] copt (æth). for *οστις*, *ος* D Iren-gr. aft *οστις* ins *ουν* B. (*ου* is written over the line in B by the origl scribe; see table: by B[3](= our B[2]) appy, Tischdf.) rec (for *εαυτ.*) *αυτου*, with DL[1]ℵ rel Iren-gr_1 [Bas_1]: txt ABL[2]M[2]Δ. for *ερχεται*, *ακολουθει* KΠ 243-53-9 Scr's d w copt Iren-gr_1 Bas_1. rec *μου* bef *ειναι*, with AKM[2]UΠ vulg am[1] lat-*c ff_2*: *μου μαθ.* bef *ειν.* D: txt BLℵ rel am[2](with fuld forj) lat-*b e f q* goth Bas_1.

28. for *γαρ*, *δε* D [lat-*e*]. rec aft *εχει* ins *τα*, with Aℵ rel lat-*a f* goth (arm): om BDLR vulg lat-*b c e ff_2* [*l q*] syrr syr-cu copt æth(appy) [$Ephr_1$] Orig-int_1. rec (for *εις*) *προς* (*see ver* 32), with VXΠ (F 1, e sil) Bas_2 [$Ephr_1$]: txt ABDRℵ rel.

29. for *και μη ισχυοντος εκτελεσαι*, *μη ισχυση οικοδομησαι και* D lat-*e*.

on in the journey, going forward, and speaking to the multitude on counting the cost before any man becomes his disciple.

26, 27.] See Matt. x. 37, 38, and note. The remark there made of the *strangeness* of this sound of *the Cross*, still applies: our Lord had not yet announced his death *by crucifixion*. **μισεῖ**] It is well to enquire what sense this word here bears. That no such thing as *active hatred* can be meant, is plain: our Lord himself is an example to the contrary, John xix. 25—27: the *hate* is the *general*, not *personal*, feeling of alienation in the inmost heart,—so that this world's relationships, as belonging to *the state of things in this world*, are not the *home* and *rest* of the heart. This is evident from the **ἔτι τε κ. τ. ἑαυ. ψυχήν** which follows. Let the *hate begin here*, and little explanation will be further wanted. This addition also shews that the saying was not meant only for those times, in which more perhaps of the disruption of earthly ties was required, but *for all time:* for ἡ ἑαυτοῦ ψυχή is equally dear to every man in every age. It hardly need be observed that *this hate* is not only consistent with, but *absolutely necessary to* the very highest kind of love. It is that element in love which makes a man *a wise and Christian friend*,—not for time only, but for eternity. Beware of thinking, with Wordsw., that in εἶναί μου μαθητής, there is any emphasis on μου. Rather is it in the *least* emphatic place in the sentence, in order to throw all the stress on the verb εἶναι: cf. ἵνα γεμισθῇ μου ὁ οἶκος, ver. 23; καταφαγών σου τὸν βίον, ch. xv. 30. In ver. 33, the collocation is different, and μου has a secondary emphasis. See remarks on this idea of Wordsworth's, in note on Matt. xvi. 18.

28—30.] Peculiar to Luke. *The same caution* is followed out in this parable. This is to be borne in mind, or it will be misinterpreted. The ground of the parable is, that *entire self-renunciation* is requisite, to become a disciple of Christ. This man wishes to build a tower: to raise that building (see 1 Cor. iii. 11—15), which we must rear on the one Foundation, and which shall be tried in the day of the Lord. He is advised to count the cost, to see whether he have enough

αὐτῷ [g] ἐμπαίζειν 30 λέγοντες ὅτι οὗτος ὁ ἄνθρωπος ἤρξατο
οἰκοδομεῖν καὶ οὐκ [d] ἴσχυσεν [e] ἐκτελέσαι. 31 ἢ τίς βασιλεὺς
πορευόμενος ἑτέρῳ βασιλεῖ [h] συμβαλεῖν εἰς πόλεμον οὐχὶ
[i] καθίσας πρῶτον [k] βουλεύεται εἰ δυνατός ἐστιν [l] ἐν δέκα
[m] χιλιάσιν [n] ὑπαντῆσαι τῷ μετὰ εἴκοσι [m] χιλιάδων ἐρχομένῳ ἐπ' αὐτόν; 32 [o] εἰ δὲ μήγε, ἔτι αὐτοῦ [p] πόῤῥω ὄντος
[q] πρεσβείαν ἀποστείλας [r] ἐρωτᾷ τὰ [s] πρὸς εἰρήνην. 33 οὕτως οὖν πᾶς ἐξ ὑμῶν ὃς οὐκ [t] ἀποτάσσεται πᾶσιν τοῖς
ἑαυτοῦ [u] ὑπάρχουσιν, οὐ δύναταί μου εἶναι μαθητής.
34 καλὸν οὖν τὸ [v] ἅλας· ἐὰν δὲ καὶ τὸ [v] ἅλας [w] μωρανθῇ,

g Matt. xxvii. 29, 31, 41. Judg. xvi. 25.
h = here only. (ch. ii. 19 reff.) 2 Macc. viii. 23. Jos. Antt. vi. 5. 3, σ. εἰς μάχην.
i = ver. 28 reff.
k John xii. 10 reff.
l = Acts vii. 14. Jude 14. 1 Macc. xi. 15. see 1 Cor. iv. 21 al. fr.
m here bis. Acts iv. 4. 1 Cor. x. 8, from Num. xxv. 9. Rev. v. 11. vii. 4, &c. al4.
n ch. viii. 27 al. Gospp. only, exc. Acts xvi. 16†. Toibt vii. 1 (not ℵ) al.
o Matt. ix. 17 reff.
p Matt. xv. 8 reff.
q ch. xix. 14 only. 2 Macc. iv. 11 only. (-εύειν, 2 Cor. v. 24.)
r = ver. 18.
s (ver. 28 v. r.) Acts xxviii. 10. 2 Pet. i. 3.
t Mark vi. 46. ch. ix. 61. Acts xviii. 18, 20. 2 Cor. ii. 13 only ‡. Jos. Antt. viii. 13. 7.
u Matt. xix. 21 reff.
v Matt. v. 13 reff.
w = Matt. v. 13 only. (Rom. i. 22. 1 Cor. i. 20 only. 2 Kings xxiv. 10.)

for αρξ. αυτ. εμ. λεγ., μελλουσιν λεγειν D lat-*e* Aug$_1$. rec εμπαιζειν bef αυτω, with Δ rel vulg lat-*f* syrr syr-cu goth Petr Bas$_1$: txt A(sic) BKLRUXΠℵ 1 Bas$_1$ [Ephr$_1$].

30. om οτι D 253-9 Scr's a syr-cu [Petr$_1$ Ephr$_1$] Ambr.

31. rec συμβ. bef ετερω βασιλει, with E rel latt syr copt goth æth arm Bas$_1$: txt ABDLRXℵ 33. συμβαλλειν ℵ. for ουχι, ουκ ευθεως D. βουλευσεται Bℵ lat-(*a* [*ff*$_2$ *i l*]) *b q*. rec απαντησαι, with L rel Bas$_1$: txt ABDRXΔℵ 1. 33. 69². τω μ. ε. χιλ. ερχ. επ' αυτον bef υπαντησαι D.

32. πορρω bef αυτου AR rel goth Bas$_1$ Damasc$_1$: txt BDLXℵ 1. 69 latt. αποστ. bef πρεσβ. D lat-*e* copt goth. om τα BΓℵ¹. for προς, εις BKΠ.

33. aft ουν ins και D. εξ υμων bef πας D. om πασιν DR: ins ABℵ rel vss. for εαυ. υπαρχ., υπαρχ. αυ. DKMΠ. ειναι bef μου (*see ver* 27) BLRℵ 33 lat-*a* [syrr copt] goth [Orig-int$_1$]: μαθητης bef ειναι DU¹ lat-*b c e ff*$_2$ *i q*: txt A rel vulg lat-*f* arm [Ath$_1$] Bas$_2$ Orig-int$_3$.

34. rec om ουν (*see Mark* ix. 50), with ADR(Γ) rel latt copt-[schw-]dz: ins BLXℵ 69 copt[-wilk]. for 1st αλας, αλα Dℵ¹. rec om και (*cf Matt* v. 10: *Mark* ix. 50), with AR rel vulg-ed lat-*e f ff*$_2$ *i* [syrr coptt æth arm]: ins BDLXℵ am(with most other mss of vulg) Syr syr-cu Bede. for 2nd αλας, αλα Dℵ.

thoroughly to finish it. If he begin, lay the foundation,—however seemingly well it may be done, it is *not well done*, because he has not enough to complete it: and the attempt can only lead to shame. So it is with one who would be Christ's disciple: but with this weighty difference, lying in the background of the parable—that in his case the counting the cost must *always* issue in a discovery of the utter inadequacy of his own resources, and the going *out of himself* for strength and means to build. **31—33.**] This same lesson is even more pointedly set before us in the following parable, which, as well as the other, is frequently misunderstood. The *two kings* here are,—the *man desirous to become a disciple*, to work out his salvation,—and God, with whose just and holy law he is *naturally at variance*;—it is his ἀντίδικος, see ch. xii. 58, and note:—these two are going to engage in war: and the question for each man to sit down and ask himself is, 'Can I, with (**ἐν**,—*clad in,—surrounded by, all that I have,* all my instrument of war) my ten thousand, stand the charge of Him who cometh against me with (**μετά**, being *only as many as He pleases to bring with Him* for the purpose, see Ps. lxviii. 17, E. V.) twenty thousand?'—see Job xv. 24—26. Here the inadequacy of man's resources is *plainly set forth*, not left, as in the former parable, to be inferred. Then, finding that he has no hope of prevailing,—**ἔτι αὐτοῦ πόῤῥω ὄντος**, while there is yet time,—he sends an embassy, and sues for peace, abandoning the conflict: throwing himself upon the mere mercy and grace of God;—**ἀποτασσόμενος πᾶσιν τοῖς ἑαυτοῦ ὑπάρχουσιν**, in both cases. The ordinary misinterpretation of this parable is in taking the king with twenty thousand to be the ἄρχων τοῦ κόσμου τούτου—which *destroys all the sense*:—for with him the *natural man is at peace*, but the *disciple of Christ at war*. **31.**] **εἰς πόλ.** belongs to **συμβ.**, not to **πορευόμ.** συμβαλεῖν πρὸς μάχην occurs Polyb. x. 37. 4 (the instance from Xen. Cyrop. vii. 1. 20, cited by Meyer,

x Matt. v. 13. Mark ix. 50. Heb. x. 29.
y Mark ix. 50. Col. iv. 6 only +. Cant. viii. 2 Symm.
z here only. 1 Kings ii. 8. (-ριος, ch. xiii. 8.)
a ch. ix. 62. Heb. vi. 7 only. Ps. xxxi. 6. Sus. 15 [Theod.] only.
b Matt. v. 13 reff. xxvii. 26.

x ἐν τίνι y ἀρτυθήσεται ; 35 οὔτε εἰς γῆν οὔτε εἰς z κοπρίαν
a εὔθετόν ἐστιν· b ἔξω b βάλλουσιν αὐτό. ὁ ἔχων ὦτα
ἀκούειν ἀκουέτω. XV. 1 c Ἦσαν δὲ αὐτῷ d ἐγγίζοντες
πάντες οἱ τελῶναι καὶ οἱ ἁμαρτωλοὶ ἀκούειν αὐτοῦ. 2 καὶ ...και οι R.
e διεγόγγυζον οἵ τε Φαρισαῖοι καὶ οἱ γραμματεῖς λέγοντες ABDE
ὅτι οὗτος ἁμαρτωλοὺς f προσδέχεται καὶ g συνεσθίει αὐτοῖς. GHKL MSUVX
3 εἶπεν δὲ πρὸς αὐτοὺς τὴν παραβολὴν ταύτην, λέγων ΓΔΛΠℵ 1. 33. 69
4 Τίς ἄνθρωπος ἐξ ὑμῶν ἔχων ἑκατὸν πρόβατα καὶ

c Matt. xix. 22 reff. d constr., ver. 25. ch. vii. 12. xxii. 47. Acts ix. 3 al. Gen. e ch. xix. 7 only. Exod. xv. 24. f = Rom. xvi. 2. Phil. ii. 29. Isa. xlii. 1. g Acts x. 41. xi. 2. 1 Cor. v. 11. Gal. ii. 12 only. Gen. xliii. 32. Ps. c. 5 only.

35. aft 1st *εις* ins *την* D 69.

Chap. XV. **1.** rec *εγγιζ.* bef *αυτω*, with D rel vss(of which vulg lat-*b c l* [*q*] Syr syr-cu om *παντες*) : *παντ.* bef *εγγιζ.* LR : txt ABKMUΠℵ 1. 69 goth Bas$_1$. om 2nd *οι* DU [arm].

2. rec om *τε*, with A rel copt [Bas$_1$] : ins BDLℵ. transp *φαρισ.* and *γραμμ.* A 69 Scr's i Syr syr-cu [æth]. om *ουτος* ℵ.

3. om *λεγων* D 69 lat-*b e* Syr syr-cu arm.

4. for *εχων*, *ος εξει* D.

does not apply, being *συμβ. πρὸς τὸ μαχόμενον*). **32. τὰ πρὸς εἰρ.**] So *τὰ πρὸς πόλεμον*, Xen. Anab. iv. 3. 10, but there, 'the *resources* of war ;'—here, **conditions, preliminaries, of peace.**

34, 35.] For the third time, our Lord repeats the saying concerning salt: see Matt. v. 13: Mark ix. 50, and notes. The **οὖν** and **καί**, here restored to the text, are both valuable; the former as importing the recurrence of a saying known before, the latter as giving force to the supposition. The *salt*, in Scripture symbolism, is the whole life-retaining antiseptic influence of the Spirit of God:—this, working in the *εἶναί μου μαθητής*, is good: but if even this be corrupted—if the mere appearance of this, and not the veritable salt (which is the *savour*), be in you—wherewith, &c.? Such a disciple is **ἔξω βλητέος.** Salt was not used for *land*, Ps. cvii. 34, nor for *mingling with manure;* it is of no use for either of those purposes, but must be utterly cast out.

Chap. XV. Parables, setting forth God's mercy to sinners. **1—7.**] The lost sheep. It does not appear where or when this [gathering of publicans and sinners to hear him] happened,—but certainly in the progress of this same journey, and, we may well believe, consecutively on the discourses in the last chapter. This first parable had been spoken by our Lord before, Matt. xviii. 12—14: but, as Trench has remarked, (Par. in loc.,) with a different view: there, to bring out *the preciousness of each individual little one in the eyes of the good Shepherd;* here, to shew *that no sheep can have strayed so widely, but He will seek it and rejoice over it when found.* The second is peculiar to Luke. **1.**] **ἦσαν ἐγγ., were busied in drawing near—were continually about Him,** struck perhaps with penitence,—found, by His seeking them:—having come from the husks of a life of sin, to the bread of life;—so the three parables seem to imply. **πάντες,** a general term, admitting of course of exceptions, see ch. xiii. 33 and note. **2.**] **προσδέχ.,** into His circle of adherents—**συνεσθ.,** allows them to sit at meat with Him;—on the journey, or at entertainments, as in Matt. ix. 10. Stier remarks (iii. 214, edn. 2) that this **ἁμαρτ. προσδέχ.** is an important and affecting testimony, from the mouth of the enemies of our Lord, to His willingness to receive sinners.

The **διεγόγγ.** implies either **throughout the journey;**—or rather, **one to another,**—**responsively.** **3—7.**] The man having the hundred sheep, is plainly *the Son of God, the Good Shepherd.* This had been his prophetic description, and that *in this very connexion,*—of *seeking the lost,* Ezek. xxxiv. 6, 11 ff. This it is which gives so peculiar an interest to David as a type of Christ—that he was *a shepherd:* ibid. ver. 23. Our Lord plainly declares then by this parable—and that I take to be the reason why it is placed *first* (see below)—that the matter in which they had found fault with Him was the *very pursuit most in accordance with his divine Office of Shepherd.*

4.] It is the *Owner Himself* who goes to seek, see Ezek., ver. 11—*God in Christ.*

The **ἑκατὸν πρόβ.** are the house of

ἀπολέσας ἐξ αὐτῶν [h] ἕν, οὐ [i] καταλείπει τὰ [j] ἐννενηκονταεννέα ἐν τῇ ἐρήμῳ καὶ πορεύεται [k] ἐπὶ τὸ ἀπολωλός, ἕως
εὕρῃ αὐτό; 5 καὶ εὑρὼν ἐπιτίθησιν ἐπὶ τοὺς [l] ὤμους αὐτοῦ
χαίρων, 6 καὶ ἐλθὼν εἰς τὸν οἶκον [m] συγκαλεῖ τοὺς φίλους
καὶ τοὺς [n] γείτονας, λέγων αὐτοῖς [o] Συγχάρητέ μοι, ὅτι
εὗρον τὸ πρόβατόν μου τὸ ἀπολωλός. 7 λέγω ὑμῖν ὅτι
οὕτως χαρὰ ἐν τῷ οὐρανῷ ἔσται [p] ἐπὶ ἑνὶ [q] ἁμαρτωλῷ
[r] μετανοοῦντι [s] ἢ ἐπὶ [t] ἐννενηκονταεννέα δικαίοις [u] οἵτινες
οὐ [v] χρείαν [v] ἔχουσιν [w] μετανοίας. 8 ἢ τίς γυνὴ [x] δραχμὰς

h Matt. xviii. 12. xxii. 35 reff. i = Acts xviii. 19. 1 Thess. iii. 1. Zech. xi. 17. j ver. 7. Matt. xviii. 12, 13 only. Gen. xvii. 1 only. k = Matt. xxvi. 55 ‖. l Matt. xxiii. 4 only. Judg. xvi. 3. m ver. 9. ch. ix. 1. xxiii. 13. Acts v. 21. x. 24. xviii. 17. Luke only, exc. Mark xv. 16. Exod. vii. 11. n ch. xiv. 12 reff. o ch. i. 58 reff. p ch. i. 47 reff. q 1 Pet. iv. 18, from Prov. xi. 31. r Matt. iii. 2 reff. 1 Kings xv. 29. s constr., Matt. xviii. 8, 9 reff. t ver. 4. u Matt. vii. 15 reff. v Matt. vi. 8 reff. Prov. xviii. 2. w Mark i. 4 reff. x here (3ce) only. Gen. xxiv. 22.

απολεση B[2·3](Tischdf in N. T. Vat.: the reverse is stated, with 'sic' in his N. T. ed 8 since published) D Meth: txt AB[1]ℵ rel. rec ἑν bef εξ αυτων, with A rel [vulg] lat-*a b c* syrr syr-cu [Meth$_1$ Bas$_1$ Bas-sel$_1$]: txt B D-gr ℵ 1. 69 lat-*e*. for ου καταλειπει, ουκ αφιησι D sah Meth$_1$. for πορευεται επι το απολωλος, απελθων το απολωλος ζητει D, simly lat-*a e f* syr-cu coptt. aft εως ins ου AMUΔΛℵ 1. 69 arm Bas$_1$. (Some fragments of F remain in vv. 4—12.)

5. rec εαυτου, with A rel: txt BDFKLXΓΛΠℵ 1. 69 Meth$_1$ [Bas-sel$_1$].

6. ελθω(-θων D[2]) δε D (sah). om τον D[1](ins D[2]). συγκαλειται (*see ver* 9) DFΛ 1. 69 Meth$_1$ Bas$_1$ Bas-sel$_1$.

7. aft λεγω ins δε D syr-cu. rec εσται bef εν τω ουρανω, with AD rel latt syrr syr-cu coptt goth æth (arm) Cypr$_1$: txt BLℵ 33(appy). εχουσιν bef χρειαν D.

Israel, see Matt. x. 6; but in the *present* application, mankind (not, '*believers in Christ*:' see on ver. 7). The argument is to *their self-interest*: but the act on the part of the good Shepherd is, from the nature of the case, one of *love*: or, as Stier remarks, also human love for *his own*; for in Him, Love, and His glory, are one and the same thing.

καταλ. τὰ ἐνν.] These pass altogether into the background, and are lost sight of. The character of the good Shepherd is a sufficient warrant for their being well cared for. The **ἔρημος** is not a barren place, but one abounding in pastures (John vi. 10, compared with Matt. xiv. 15). **5.**] Not mere self-interest, but *love* comes forward here: see Isa. xl. 11. No blows are given for the straying—no hard words; mercy to the lost one,—and joy, within himself,—are the Shepherd's feeling; the sheep is weary with long wanderings,—He gives it rest. Matt. ix. 36; xi. 28. **6.**] In this return to His house, must be understood the whole course of seeking and finding which the good Shepherd, either by Himself or His agents, now pursues in each individual case, even until He brings the lost sheep home into heaven to himself—not in *reality*, so that it should not take place till the *death* of the penitent—but *proleptically*,—till the *name is written in heaven*;—till the sinner is penitent. This is clear from the interpretation in ver. 7. The **φίλοι καὶ γείτονες** = the angels (and spirits of just men made perfect?).

τὸ πρόβ. τὸ ἀπολωλός breathes a totally different thought from *τ. δραχμὴν ἣν ἀπώλεσα*. There is pity and love in it, which, from the nature of the case, the other does not admit of. **7. λέγω ὑμῖν**] In these words the Lord often introduces His revelations of the unseen world of glory: see Matt. xviii. 10.

On these **δίκαιοι**, see note at Matt. ix. 12, 13. They are the *subjectively* righteous, and this saying respects their own view of themselves. (Or if it be required that the words should be literally explained, seeing that these ninety-nine *did not err*,—then I see no other way but to suppose them, in the deeper meaning of the parable, to be the *worlds that have not fallen*;—and the one that has strayed, our human nature, in this our world.) But we have yet to enquire, *what sort of sinner* this parable represents: for each of the three sets before us a *different type* of the sinner sunk in his sin. Bengel, in distinguishing the three, says, 'Ovis, drachma, filius perditus—peccator (1) stupidus,—(2) sui plane nescius,—(3) sciens et voluntarius.' This one is the *stupid* and *bewildered* sinner, erring and straying away in ignorance and self-will from his Shepherd, but sought by the Shepherd, and fetched back with joy.

y = ch. xi. 33 reff.
z ch. xi. 25 ‖ Mt. only +.
a here only. Gen. vi. 5. (λεῖσθαι, ch. x. 34, 35. -λεια, Acts xxvii. 3.)
b ch. xiii. 8. xxii. 16. John ix. 18. 1 Kings xxx. 4.
c = mid., here only.
d so Rev. iii. 5. xiv. 10. see Isa. lii. 10.

ἔχουσα δέκα, ἐὰν ἀπολέσῃ [x] δραχμὴν μίαν, οὐχὶ [y] ἅπτει
[y] λύχνον, καὶ [z] σαροῖ τὴν οἰκίαν καὶ ζητεῖ [a] ἐπιμελῶς [b] ἕως ...επιμελως E.
[b] ὅτου εὕρῃ; 9 καὶ εὑροῦσα [c] συγκαλεῖται τὰς φίλας καὶ
[n] γείτονας, λέγουσα [o] Συγχάρητέ μοι, ὅτι εὗρον τὴν
[x] δραχμὴν ἣν ἀπώλεσα. 10 οὕτως, λέγω ὑμῖν, γίνεται
χαρὰ [d] ἐνώπιον τῶν [d] ἀγγέλων τοῦ θεοῦ [p] ἐπὶ ἑνὶ ἁμαρτωλῷ [r] μετανοοῦντι. 11 εἶπεν δὲ Ἄνθρωπός τις εἶχεν
δύο υἱούς. 12 καὶ εἶπεν ὁ νεώτερος αὐτῶν τῷ πατρὶ

ABDG HKLM SUVX ΓΔΛΠℵ 1. 33. 69

8. εχουσα bef δραχμας D latt syrr syr-cu æth. for εαν απολεση, και απολεσασα D. om δραχμην D lat-*a b c e ff$_2$ i l* [*q*] Syr syr-cu coptt. for οτου, ου Bℵ 1. 33, σου LX: om D 69: txt A rel.

9. συγκαλει (*see ver* 6) BKLUXΔΠℵ: txt AD rel. rec ins τας bef γειτονας, with A rel; τους M Scr's g s: om BLℵ.—τας γειτ. κ. φιλ. D. ην απωλεσα bef δραχμην, omg την, D lat-*e*.

10. rec χαρα bef γινεται, with A rel [syr sah goth]: χαρα εσται (*ver* 7) D 69 latt arm: txt BLXℵ 33(appy) Syr [(syr-cu æth)] copt Vict-tun$_2$. om των B.

8—10.] The lost piece of money. In the following wonderful parable, we have the next class of sinners set before us, sought for and found by the power and work of the Spirit in the Church of Christ. It will be seen, as we proceed, how perfectly this interpretation comes out, not as a fancy, but as the *very kernel and sense* of the parable. The **γυνή** cannot be *the Church absolutely,* for the Church herself is a lost sheep at first, sought and found by the Shepherd. Rather is the **οἰκία** here the Church—as will come out by-and-by,—and the **γυνή** the *indwelling Spirit,* working in it. All men belong to this Creator-Spirit; all have been *stamped with the image of God.* But the sinner lies in the dust of sin and death and corruption—'sui plane nescius.' Then the Spirit, lighting the candle of the Lord (Prov. xx. 27: Zeph. i. 12), searching every corner and sweeping every unseen place, *finds out* the sinner; restores him to his true value as made for God's glory. This lighting and sweeping are to be understood of the office of the Spirit in the Church, in its various ways of seeking the sinner—by the preaching of repentance, by the Word of God read, &c. Then comes the joy again. **9.**] **αἱ φίλαι κ. γείτονες** are invited—but there is *no return home* now—nor in the explanation, ver. 10, is there any *ἐν οὐρανῷ,* because the Spirit *abides in the Church*—because the *angels are present in the Church,* see 1 Cor. xi. 10:—nor is it *ἔσται* (as in ver. 7 at the return of the Redeemer then future), but **γίνεται**—the ministering spirits rejoice over every soul that is brought out of the dust of death into God's treasure-house by the searching of the blessed Spirit. In this parable then we have set before us the sinner who is unconscious of *himself* and *his own real worth;* who is lying, though in reality a precious coin, in the mire of this world, lost and valueless, till he is searched out by the blessed and gracious Spirit. And that such a search will be made, we are here assured. **11—32.**] The Prodigal Son. *Peculiar to Luke.* 'If we might venture here to make comparisons, as we do among the sayings of *men,* this parable of the Lord would rightly be called, *the crown and pearl of all His parables.*' Stier, iii. 227, edn. 2. We have here the glad and welcome reception of the returning sinner (sinner under the most aggravating circumstances) in the bosom of his heavenly Father: and agreeably to the circumstances under which the discourse was spoken, the *δίκαιοι* who murmured at the publicans and sinners are represented under the figure of the elder son: see below. The parable certainly was spoken on the same occasion as the preceding, and relates to the same subject. Bp. Wordsworth, who for the sake of upholding the patristic interpretation denies this, seems to me to have entirely missed the scope of the parable: see below. **11.**] **ἄνθ. τις**—*our heavenly Father,* the Creator and Possessor of all: *not Christ,* who ever represents Himself *as a Son,* although frequently as a possessor or lord. **δύο υἱούς,** *not,* in any *direct* or primary sense of the Parable, *the Jews and the Gentiles:* that there may be an ulterior application to this effect, is only owing to the parable grasping the *great central truths,* of which the Jew and Gentile were, in their relation,

Πάτερ, δός μοι τὸ [e] ἐπιβάλλον μέρος τῆς [f] οὐσίας. ὁ δὲ
[g] διεῖλεν αὐτοῖς τὸν [h] βίον. 13 καὶ μετ' οὐ πολλὰς ἡμέρας
P παντα ... [i] συναγαγὼν πάντα ὁ νεώτερος υἱὸς [k] ἀπεδήμησεν εἰς
R ος υιος ... χώραν [l] μακράν, καὶ ἐκεῖ [m] διεσκόρπισεν τὴν [f] οὐσίαν αὐτοῦ
Q εγενετο ... ζῶν [n] ἀσώτως. 14 [o] δαπανήσαντος δὲ αὐτοῦ πάντα ἐγένετο
[p] λιμὸς [q] ἰσχυρὰ κατὰ τὴν χώραν ἐκείνην, καὶ αὐτὸς
ἤρξατο [r] ὑστερεῖσθαι, 15 καὶ πορευθεὶς [s] ἐκολλήθη ἑνὶ τῶν

e = here only ‡. 1 Macc. x. 30. see note. f here bis only †. Tobit xiv. 13' (not ℵ) only. g 1 Cor. xii. 11 only. Josh. xviii. 5. (διαίρεσις, 1 Cor. xii. 4, 5, 6.) h = Mark xii. 44 reff. i ch. xi. 23. John vi. 12. xv. 6. Exod. xxiii. 10. k Matt. xxi. 33 reff. l = ch. xix. 12. (xx. 47 ‖ [Mt v. r.]) only. Prov. vii. 19. m = ch. xvi. 1 (Matt. xxv. 24, 26 reff.) only. see Ps. cxi. 9. n here only †. (-τος, Prov. vii. 11. -τία, Eph. v. 18. Prov. xxviii. 7.) o James iv. 3. Mark v. 26. Acts xxi. 24. 2 Cor. xii. 15 only †. Judith xii. 4. (-νη, ch. xiv. 28.) p fem., Acts xi. 28. 1 Macc. ix. 24 A. q = Gen. xli. 31. see Matt. xiv. 30. r = 2 Cor. xi. 8. Phil. iv. 12. Deut. xv. 8 A. Cant. vii. 3. s Acts v. 13. viii. 29 al. 2 Kings xx. 2.

12. om πατερ ℵ[1](ins ℵ[3b]). aft επιβαλλον ins μοι D (13. 64. 124. 346, Sz) latt syrr syr-cu (coptt) goth æth. rec (for ο δε) και, with Dℵ[1] rel latt syrr syr-cu [syr-jer] goth æth arm [Ps-Chr$_1$]: txt ABLℵ[3a] copt.

13. for μετ' ου, ου μετα D 157(Sz) [Ps-Chr$_1$]. rec **απαντα**, with Aℵ rel [Ps-Chr$_1$]: txt BDP. for και εκει, κακει DG 69 [Ps-Chr$_1$]. **εαυτου** ℵ: for την ουσιαν αυτου, εαυτου τον βιον D-gr. for ζων ασωτως, εις χωραν μακραν ℵ[1](txt ℵ-corr[1]).

14. rec ισχυρ**ος**, with PQ R(Tischdf, expr) rel [Ps-Chr$_1$]: txt ABDLℵ **1**. 33. ins του bef υστερεισθαι AGMSΓΛ.

illustrations,—and of which such illustrations are furnished wherever such differences occur. The two parties standing in the *foreground* of the parabolic mirror are, *the Scribes and Pharisees* as the elder son, the *publicans and sinners* as the younger;—all, *Jews:* all belonging to God's family. The mystery of the admission of the Gentiles into God's Church was not yet made known in any such manner as that they should be represented as of one family with the Jews;—not to mention that this interpretation fails in the very root of the Parable; for in strictness the Gentile should be the *elder,* the Jew not being constituted in his superiority till 2000 years after the Creation. The upholders of this interpretation forget that when we speak of the Jew as elder, and the Gentile as younger, it is in respect not of birth, but of *this very* return to and reception into the Father's house, which is *not to be considered yet.* Bp. Wordsworth's objections (in loc.) do not touch the reasons here given. The relations of elder and younger have a peculiar fitness for the characters to be filled by them, and are I believe chosen on that account; νεώτερον δὲ ὀνομάζει τὸν ἁμαρτωλὸν ὡς νηπιόφρονα καὶ εὐεξαπάτητον. Euthym. **12—20.**] The part of the parable relating to the prodigal himself divides itself into three parts—1. *his sin:* 2. *his misery:* 3. *his penitence.* In vv. 12, 13 his *sin* is described. It consists in a desire to depart from his Father's house and control, and to set up for himself,—to live a life of what the carnal man calls *liberty.*

12.] **τὸ ἐπιβάλλον μέρος** is classical Greek —ἀπολαχόντες τῶν κτημάτων τὸ ἐπιβάλλον, Herod. iv. 115. Such a request as this is shewn by Orientalists to have been known in the East, though not among the Jews. **βίος = οὐσία**:—no distinction is implied, as some (Paulus, Stier) have thought. The first-born had *two-thirds* of the property, see Deut. xxi. 17. The father, as implied in the parable, reserves to himself the power during his life over the portion of the first-born, see ver. 31. The parable sets before us very strikingly the *permission of free will* to man. **13.**] **μακράν**—probably not adverbial (Stier), but agreeing with **χώραν**, see reff., and Æsch. Prom. 814: Xen. Cyr. v. 4. 47: compare however ἔθνη μακράν, Acts xxii. 21. The images of both the preceding parables are united here:—in **ἀπεδήμησεν** we have the straying sheep; in *his state when he got into the far country,* the lost piece of money. But in this case the search is to be carried on *within him*—we are now on *higher ground* than in those two parables. 'Regio longinqua est oblivio Dei,' Augustine. (Trench, in loc.) **ἀσώτως**] The old English word **retchlessly** expresses perhaps best the meaning, which is not '*unsparingly*' (in which sense of '*saving money*' I doubt σώζω ever being used), but **incorrigibly**, past hope of reclaim: —ἄσωτος, ὁ δι' αὑτὸν ἀπολλύμενος, Aristot. Eth. iv. 1. **14—16.**] *His misery* is set forth in these verses. He soon spends all:—there is a fine irony, as Stier remarks, in **δαπανήσαντος**, as compared with **διεσκόρπισεν** before—he *spent*

t ch. xix. 14 Acts xxi. 39. Heb. viii. 11 (from Jer. xxxviii. 34 Bℵ) only.
u Matt. viii. 30, &c. reff.
v Mark iv. 37 reff.
w see Prov. xviii. 20. xxiv. 15. Jer. xxviii. (li.) 34.
x here only †.
y abs., Matt. v. 42. x. 8 al.
z = here only. see Acts xii. 11.

ABDGH KLMPQ RSUVX ΓΔΛΠℵ 1. 33. 69

[t] πολιτῶν τῆς χώρας ἐκείνης, καὶ ἔπεμψεν αὐτὸν εἰς
τοὺς ἀγροὺς αὐτοῦ [u] βόσκειν [u] χοίρους. 16 καὶ ἐπεθύμει
[vw] γεμίσαι τὴν [w] κοιλίαν αὐτοῦ ἀπὸ τῶν [x] κερατίων ὧν
ἤσθιον οἱ [u] χοῖροι, καὶ οὐδεὶς [y] ἐδίδου αὐτῷ. 17 [z] εἰς ἑαυτὸν
δὲ ἐλθὼν εἶπεν Πόσοι [a] μίσθιοι τοῦ πατρός μου [b] περισ-
σεύονται ἄρτων· ἐγὼ δὲ ὧδε λιμῷ ἀπόλλυμαι. 18 [c] ἀναστὰς πορεύσομαι πρὸς τὸν πατέρα μου καὶ ἐρῶ αὐτῷ
Πάτερ, [de] ἥμαρτον [d] εἰς τὸν οὐρανὸν καὶ [e] ἐνώπιόν σου·

here only. a ver. 19 only. Lev. xxv. 50. b subjective, Phil. iv. 12, 18. 2 Cor. ix. 8. constr., here only. c Mark vii. 24 reff. Gen. xxii. 19. d Matt. xviii. 15 reff. see 2 Kings xii. 13. e = here only. 1 Kings xx. 1.

15. om *αυτου* D 34 Syr syr-cu æth.

16. for *γεμισαι την κοιλιαν αυτου, χορτασθηναι* (*euphemism*) BDLRℵ 1. 69 lat-*e f* [syr-jer] sah goth(appy) æth; *manducare* syr-cu: txt APQ rel latt syrr copt arm [Ps-Chr$_2$].—for *απο*, *εκ* BDLRℵ: txt APQ rel. for *αυτω*, *τω* D[1](txt D-corr[1]).

17. for *ειπεν*, *εφη* BLℵ 69 [Ps-Chr$_1$]. rec *περισσευουσιν* (*more usual*), with DQRℵ rel [Ps-Chr$_1$]: txt ABP 1. rec om *ωδε* (*homœotel*, *εγωδεωδε*), with APQ rel sah goth: ins DRU 1 latt Syr [syr-cu syr-jer] copt æth arm [Ps-]Chr$_2$ Ambr$_1$ Jer Aug; aft *λιμω* (*i. e. restored in wrong place*) BLℵ lat-*e* syr.

18. aft *αναστας* ins *δε* ℵ[1] [syr-cu].

his money for that which was no bread. **14. λιμὸς ἰσχ.**] On *λιμός* fem., see note on ref. Acts. This famine is the shepherd seeking his stray sheep—the woman sweeping to find the lost. The famine, in the interpretation, is to be *subjectively* taken; he begins to *be in want* (no stress on *αὐτός*, which is inserted on account of the change of subject from the last clause),—to *feel* the emptiness of soul which precedes either utter abandonment or true penitence. **15.**] He sinks lower and lower—becomes the despised servant of an alien (is there here any hint at the situation of the *publicans?*) who employs him in an office most vile and odious to the mind of a Jew. **ἐκολλήθη**—no emphasis, see reff., **he attached himself.** Notice the abrupt change of subject, *ἐκολλήθη . . . ἔπεμψεν.* See ch. xix. 4. **16.**] **ἐπεθύμει**—not *merely* **he desired,** see ch. xvi. 21, where the fact is surely implied that Lazarus *did eat* of the crumbs. The mistake has arisen from supplying a wrong object to **ἐδίδου,** and that from misunderstanding **κεράτια.** 'These are not the husks or pods of some other fruit, as of peas or beans, but *themselves a fruit*, that of the *carob* (or *caruba*, found not only in the East, but in South Europe, e. g. in abundance on the Riviera between Nice and Genoa. H. A.) tree (*κερατωνία*) . . . . They are in shape something like a bean-pod, though larger and more curved, thence called *κεράτιον* or little horn, ... they have a hard dark outside and a dull sweet taste . . . . the shell or pod alone is eaten.' Trench, Par. in loc. His appetite even drove him to these for food;—**for**-**καί** (implying his state of destitution)—**no man gave** (aught) **to him.** Meyer, De Wette, Greswell, and others supply *κεράτια* after *ἐδίδου*, but wrongly, I think; the *absolute* use of *δίδωμι* being very frequent, and the other construction harsh and unusual. We see him now in the depth of his misery,—the sinner reaping the consequences of his sin in utter shame and extremity of need. **17—20.**] *His penitence.* And here we have a weighty difference between the permitted rational free will of man, and the stupid wandering on of the sheep, or the inanimate coin lying till it is picked up,—both these being however true, *did not God seek and save the sinner:* 'the grace of God by Christ preventing us that we may have a good will, and working with us when we have that good will.' Article X. of the Church of England. **17. εἰς ἑαυτὸν ἐλθών**] Similar expressions seem to occur in the Heb. Deut. xxx. 1 (where Syr. renders "Redi in temetipsum;" but Gesen. understands an accus. "si revocabis ea"); 1 Kings viii. 47: Isa. xlvi. 8. Before this, he was *beside himself*. The most dreadful torment of the lost, in fact that which constitutes their state of torment, will be this *εἰς ἑαυτὸν ἐλθεῖν*, when too late for repentance. He now recalls the peace and plenty of *his Father's house.* **μίσθιοι,** for he now was a *μίσθιος*, but in how different a case! **18. ἀναστάς**] See ver. 24, *νεκρὸς ἦν καὶ ἀνέζησεν* [it was truly a resurrection from the dead]. This reso-

19 οὐκέτι εἰμὶ [f] ἄξιος κληθῆναι υἱός σου, [g] ποίησόν με ὡς
ἕνα τῶν [h] μισθίων σου. 20 καὶ [c] ἀναστὰς ἦλθεν πρὸς τὸν
πατέρα ἑαυτοῦ. ἔτι δὲ αὐτοῦ [i] μακρὰν [k] ἀπέχοντος εἶδεν
αὐτὸν ὁ πατὴρ αὐτοῦ καὶ [l] ἐσπλαγχνίσθη, καὶ δραμὼν
[mn] ἐπέπεσεν ἐπὶ τὸν [no] τράχηλον αὐτοῦ καὶ [p] κατεφίλησεν
αὐτόν. 21 εἶπεν δὲ ὁ υἱὸς αὐτῷ Πάτερ, [de] ἥμαρτον [d] εἰς τὸν
οὐρανὸν καὶ [e] ἐνώπιόν σου· οὐκέτι εἰμὶ [f] ἄξιος κληθῆναι
υἱός σου. 22 εἶπεν δὲ ὁ πατὴρ πρὸς τοὺς δούλους αὐτοῦ
Ταχὺ [q] ἐξενέγκατε [r] στολὴν τὴν [s] πρώτην καὶ [t] ἐνδύσατε
αὐτόν, καὶ [uv] δότε [vw] δακτύλιον εἰς τὴν χεῖρα αὐτοῦ
καὶ [x] ὑποδήματα εἰς τοὺς πόδας, 23 καὶ [y] φέρετε τὸν

E ειπεν δε... ABDE GHKL MPQRS UVXΓ ΔΛΠℵ 1. 33. 69

f constr., Acts xiii. 25. Rev. iv. 11. v. 2, &c. Wisd. xviii. 4.
g = Matt. iv. 19 al. Gen. xlv. 8.
h ver. 17 only.
i Mark xii. 34. Acts xxii. 21 al. Zech. x. 9.
k = Matt. xv. 8 reff. Isa. lv. 9.
l Matt. ix. 36 reff.
m Mark iii. 10 reff.
n Acts xx. 37 only. Gen. xlv. 14. xlvi. 29.
o Mark ix. 32 reff.
p ch. vii. 38 reff. Gen. xlv. 15.
q Mark viii. 23. Acts v. 6, &c. 1 Tim. vi. 7. Heb. vi. 8 only. 4 Kings x. 22.
r Mark xii. 38 reff.
s = Matt. xxii. 38. Acts xvii. 4. Dan. x. 13.
t act., Matt. xxvii. 28, 31 ‖ Mk. Ezek. xvi. 10.
u = ch. xix. 23. Lev. xxv. 37. 1 Kings xx. 40.
v Esth. iii. 10.
w here only. (see James ii. 2.) Gen. xli. 42.
x Matt. iii. 11 ‖. x. 10 al. Gen. xiv. 23.
y = Mark xi. 2, 7. Gen. xlvii. 16.

19. rec ins *και* bef *ουκετι*, with GMPX (69, e sil) am(with forj fuld mt [ing tol]) syrr syr-cu arm [Ps-Chr$_1$]: om ABDQRℵ rel vulg-ed(with em gat) lat-*a b c e f ff$_2$ g$_2$* [syr-jer] coptt goth æth [Ps-Chr-comm$_1$]. *σου* bef *υιος* D-gr. om from *υιος σου* to *υιος σου* in ver 21 (*homœotel*) R^1.

20. for *εαυτ.*, *αυτου* DHKLMPQR^{r}XΛΠℵ 69. ins *ου* bef *μακραν* PX 33. *ενεπεσεν* D: *επεσεν* 1. 69 arm [Ps-Chr$_1$]. om last *και* D^1-gr(ins D^2) ev-y.

21. rec *αυτω* bef *ο υιος*, with APQR^{r}ℵ rel latt: txt B(D)L 1 (syr-cu) copt.—*ο δε υιος ειπεν αυτω* D syr-cu. om *και* P. rec ins *και* bef *ουκετι*, with PQR^r rel syrr syr-cu [goth arm-ed] Constt$_1$: om ABDKLΠℵ 1 latt [syr-jer] coptt æth arm-mss. *σου* bef *υιος* D-gr. add *ποιησον με ως ενα των μισθιων σου* (*from ver* 19) BDUXℵ 33 bodl(with gat mm tol) syr æth. (*Contra*, Aug, who says, *Non addit quod in illa meditatione dixerat "Fac me sicut unum de mercenariis tuis."*)

22. for 1st *αυτου*, *εαυτου* ℵ. rec om *ταχυ*, with APQ rel syrr sah [Damasc$_1$]: ins BLXℵ latt syr-jer copt goth æth arm, *ταχεως* D (13. 157. 346, Sz). *εξενεγκαντες*, and om *και*, A. rec ins *την* bef *στολην*, with D^{2}R rel arm [Ps-Chr$_1$ Damasc$_1$]: om ABD^{1}K^{1}LPQΠℵ. aft *ποδας* ins *αυτου* DGPX 69 vulg lat-*a b f* [*i*] *l* syr [syr-jer] coptt goth æth arm [Ps-Chr$_1$].

23. rec (for *φερετε*) *ενεγκαντες* (*emendn of constr*), with AP rel [goth Ps-Chr$_1$]:

lution is a further step than his last reflection. In it he *no where gives up his sonship: this*, and the **πάτερ**, lie at the root of his penitence:—it is the thought of having sinned against (in the parable *itself*, Heaven and) Thee, which works now in him. And accordingly he does not resolve to ask to be made ἕνα τῶν μισθ. but **ὡς** ἕνα τ. μ.:—still a *son*, but *as* an hireling. "And what is it that gives the sinner now a sure ground of confidence, that returning to God he shall not be repelled, nor cast out? The adoption of sonship which he received in Christ Jesus at his baptism, and his faith that the gifts and calling of God are *without repentance* or recall." Trench, Par. in loc. **20—24.**] *His restoration.* **20.**] What he has resolved, he does: a figure not of the *usual*, but of the *proper* course of such a state of mind. **μακρ. ἀπέχ.**] Who can say whether *this itself was not a seeking?* whether his courage would have held out to the meeting? On what follows, see especially Jer. iii. 12: James iv. 8: Gen. xlvi. 29: 2 Sam. xiv. 33. **21.**] The intended close of his confession is not uttered;—there is no abatement of his penitence, for all his Father's touching and reassuring kindness,—but his filial confidence is sufficiently awakened to prevent the request, *that he might be as an hired servant.* **22.**] All these gifts belong to his reception, not as a servant, but as a son: the *first* (best) *robe*, for him who came in rags,—Isa. lxi. 10: Rev. iii. 18:—not—*the robe which he used to wear—his former robe*—this would not be consistent with the former part of the parable, in which he was not turned out with any disgrace, but left *as a son* and *of his own accord*: but **a robe**, (yea) **the first and goodliest.** The **ring**,—a token of a distinguished and free person, see James ii. 2: Gen. xli. 42. The **shoes**, also the mark

z here, &c. (3ce.) Heb. ix. 12, 19. Rev. iv. 7 only. Gen. xx. 14.
a (N.T. & LXX alw. w. μόσχ.) vv. 27, 30 only. Judg. vi. 25 & 28 A. Jer. xxvi. (xlvi.) 21 only.
b = Matt. xxii. 4 reff.
c ch. xii. 19 reff. Deut. xiv. 26.
d Rom. vii. 9 (ver. 32. Rom. xiv. 9. Rev. xx. 5 v. r.) only †.

[z] μόσχον τὸν [a] σιτευτόν· [b] θύσατε, καὶ φαγόντες [c] εὐφραν-
θῶμεν· 24 ὅτι οὗτος ὁ υἱός μου νεκρὸς ἦν καὶ [d] ἀνέζησεν,
ἦν [e] ἀπολωλὼς καὶ εὑρέθη. καὶ ἤρξαντο [c] εὐφραίνεσθαι.
25 ἦν δὲ ὁ υἱὸς αὐτοῦ ὁ πρεσβύτερος ἐν ἀγρῷ· καὶ ὡς
ἐρχόμενος [f] ἤγγισεν τῇ οἰκίᾳ, ἤκουσεν [g] συμφωνίας καὶ
[h] χορῶν. 26 καὶ προσκαλεσάμενος ἕνα τῶν [i] παίδων
[k] ἐπυνθάνετο [k] τί [ἂν] εἴη ταῦτα. 27 ὁ δὲ εἶπεν αὐτῷ
ὅτι ὁ ἀδελφός σου ἥκει· καὶ [l] ἔθυσεν ὁ πατήρ σου τὸν
[l] μόσχον τὸν [l] σιτευτόν, ὅτι [m] ὑγιαίνοντα αὐτὸν [n] ἀπέλα-
βεν. 28 [o] ὠργίσθη δὲ καὶ οὐκ ἤθελεν εἰςελθεῖν. ὁ δὲ

ABDE GHKL MPQRS UVXΓΔ ΛΠℵ 1. 33. 69

e = Matt. xv. 24. xviii. 11. Ezek. xxxiv. 4, 6. f constr., ver. 1 reff. g here only. Dan. iii. 15 (5, 7 LXX, Theod.-A, 10 Theod.-A) only. h here only. Exod. xv. 20. i = Matt. viii. 6, 8 reff. k = ch. xviii. 36. l ver. 23. m ch. v. 31 reff. n = ch. xviii. 30 reff. o abs., ch. xiv. 21. Matt. (v. 22) xviii. 34. xxii. 7. Eph. iv. 6. Rev. xi. 18 (xii. 17) only. Esth. i. 12.

ενεγκοντες GQVΔ : ενεγκατε D [Damasc_1] : txt BLRXℵ latt syrr [syr-jer] coptt æth arm. τ. σιτ. μ. D lat-*e*. ins και bef θυσατε DX latt syr [syr-jer] æth arm. for φαγοντες, φαγωμεν και D latt syrr [syr-jer] copt æth arm.

24. μου bef ο υιος ΑΠ Scr's w : ο υιος μου bef ουτος Kℵ 69. 243 Scr's p. for ανεζ., εζησεν (*see ver* 32) B Syr copt arm. rec aft ανεζησεν ins και (*see ver* 32), with E rel syrr [syr-jer] goth æth : om ABDLPQRXℵ 1. 69 latt copt arm [Ephr_1 Ps-Chr_1 (Bas_1)] Damasc_1. rec απολωλ. bef ην, with Pℵ[3a] rel [Ps-Chr_1 Damasc_1] : om ην DQR 69 [Ephr_1 Bas_1] : txt ABLℵ[1] copt.—απολωλος MRXΓ [G(KSΠ[1], Tischdf)] ℵ 69. ins αρτι bef ευρεθη D. om last και ℵ.

25. for κ. ως ερχ. ηγγ., ελθων δε κ. εγγισας D.—ηγγιζεν AM 69.

26. Steph aft παιδων ins αυτου, with sah : om ABDPQRℵ rel. rec om αν, with ADℵ rel vulg-ed : ins BPQRX 1. 69 lat-*a b e f*.—for τι αν, τινα LΛ lat-*c* ff_2 g_1 *i* [*l q*] am[with forj fuld em ing mt tol]. for ειη ταυτα, θελει τουτο ειναι D 42, ειη τουτο ΚΜΠ.

27. om αυτω D. τον σειτευτον μ. and adds αυτω D.

28. ηθελησεν ALPQRX lat-*a c* ff_2 *i* [*l q* gat] : txt BDℵ rel vulg lat-*b e f* syrr [syr-jer]. rec (for 2nd δε) ουν, with PQ rel vulg syr : txt ABDLRXℵ 1. 33 lat-*a b c e*

of a free man (for slaves went barefoot), see Zech. x. 12: Eph. vi. 15. These are the gifts of grace and holiness with which the returned penitent is clothed by his gracious Father, see Zech. iii. 4, 5.

23. τ. μόσχ. τ. σιτ.] So, Judg. vi. 25, Gideon is commanded to kill τὸν μόσχον τὸν ταῦρον ὅς ἐστιν τῷ πατρί σου (τ. μ. τ. σιτευτὸν τοῦ πατρός σου A):—some calf fatted for a particular feast or anniversary, and standing in the stall. No allusion must be thought of to the *sacrificing of Christ*:—which would be *wholly out of place* here,—and is *pre-supposed* in the whole parable. **εὐφρανθ.**] So ver. 6, 'joy in heaven;'—*all rejoice.* Some of these are δοῦλοι who have entered into the *joy of their Lord*: Matt. xxv. 21, 23. **24.**] **νεκ. κ. ἀνέζ.**,—*the lost money*: **ἀπολωλ. καὶ εὑρέθη**,—*the lost sheep*: see 1 John iii. 14: Eph. ii. 5: 1 Pet. ii. 25. **ἤρξαντο**, a contrast to the ἤρξατο in ver. 14. **25—28.**] As far as regards *the penitent*, the parable is finished:—but those who murmured at his reception, who were the proud and fault-less elder son,—always in the house and serving, but not, as will appear, either over-affectionate or over-respectful,—they too must act their part, in order to complete the instruction. As regards the penitent, this part of the parable sets forth the reception he meets with from his *fellow-men*, in contrast to that from his *father*: see Matt. xviii. 27, 30.

25.] **ἐν ἀγρῷ**—probably *working*, in the course of his δουλεύειν, as he expresses it, ver. 29. **ἐρχόμ.**, at meal-time. **συμφ. κ. χορ.**] This is one of those by-glances into the lesser occupations and recreations of human life, by which the Lord so often stamps his tacit approval on the joys and unbendings of men. Would these festal employments have been here mentioned by Him on so solemn and blessed an occasion, if they really were among those works of the devil which He came into the world to destroy?

28—32.] Stier well remarks (iii. 255, edn. 2) that this elder is now the *lost son*: he has lost all childlike filial feeling; he betrays the hypocrite within. The love

πατὴρ αὐτοῦ ἐξελθὼν [p] παρεκάλει αὐτόν. 29 ὁ δὲ ἀποκριθεὶς εἶπεν τῷ πατρὶ αὐτοῦ Ἰδοὺ [q] τοσαῦτα ἔτη [r] δουλεύω
σοι καὶ οὐδέποτε ἐντολήν σου [s] παρῆλθον, καὶ ἐμοὶ οὐδέποτε ἔδωκας [t] ἔριφον, ἵνα μετὰ τῶν φίλων μου [u] εὐφρανθῶ·
30 ὅτε δὲ ὁ υἱός σου οὗτος ὁ [v] καταφαγών σου τὸν [w] βίον
μετὰ τῶν πορνῶν ἦλθεν, [x] ἔθυσας αὐτῷ τὸν [x] σιτευτὸν
[x] μόσχον. 31 ὁ δὲ εἶπεν αὐτῷ Τέκνον, σὺ πάντοτε μετ'
ἐμοῦ εἶ, καὶ πάντα τὰ ἐμὰ σά ἐστιν· 32 [u] εὐφρανθῆναι δὲ
καὶ χαρῆναι [y] ἔδει, ὅτι ὁ ἀδελφός σου οὗτος νεκρὸς ἦν καὶ
ἔζησεν, καὶ [z] ἀπολωλὼς καὶ εὑρέθη.

...αυτω Q.

p = Matt. xviii. 32 reff. see Gen. xxxvii. 35.
q = Matt. xv. 33. John xii. 37. (xiv. 9. Heb. iv. 7.)
r = Phil. ii. 22.
s = ch. xi. 42. Jer. xli. (xxxiv.) 18.
t [illegible] (-φιον, ib. ver. 33) only. Gen. xxvii. 9.
u ch. xii. 19 reff.
v Matt. xiii. 4. — (-εσθίειν) ch. xx. 47 (|| Mk. v. r.). 3 Kings xviii. 38.
w Mark xii. 44 reff.
x ver. 23.
y = Matt. xviii. 33. xxiii. 33. xxv. 27 al.
z ver. 24 reff.

f ff$_2$ *l* [*i q*] copt goth arm. for παρεκαλει, ηρξατο (sic) D-gr, *cœpit rogare* lat-*a b c*: *rogabat* D-lat.

29. rec om αυτου, with Qℵ rel syr goth arm [Ps-Chr$_1$]: ins A B(sic: see table) DG PR(Δ)Λ 69 latt Syr coptt. for εντ. σου παρηλθον, παρεβην σου εντολην D. for εμοι ουδ. εδωκας, ουδ. εδωκας μοι D [simly latt Syr sah]. εριφιον B. aft εριφ. ins εξ αιγων D coptt. for ευφρανθω, αριστησω D goth, *æpularer* vulg lat-*a b c*.

30. for ver, τω δε υιω σου τω καταφαγοντι παντα μετα των πορνων και ελθοντι εθυσας τον σιτευτον μοσχον D lat-*e*. om τον (bef βιον) P. rec om των, with BPXℵ rel: ins ADLQR coptt. om αυτω D lat-*a e*. rec (for τον σιτ. μ.) τον μοσχον τον σιτευτον (*from ver* 23), with AP rel latt: txt B(sic) DLQRℵ lat-*e*.

31. om τεκνον D lat-*a*.

32. εδει bef και χαρηναι D(KΠ) lat-*a c f* Syr Constt$_1$.—for χαρ., αγαλλιαθηναι KΠ. rec ανεζησεν (*from ver* 24), with ADPℵ^{3a} rel latt syr [syr-jer] goth æth [Constt$_1$ Ps-Chr$_1$ Antch$_1$]: txt BLRΔℵ^1 Syr coptt arm. om 3rd και DXℵ 1. 69 latt coptt arm Antch$_1$. απολωλος (*see digest ver* 24) KMR S(Tischdf) XΓΠ^{1}ℵ^{3a} 69. rec aft απολωλως ins ην, with Pℵ rel Syr (coptt?) [arm-ms Ps-Chr$_1$ Antch$_1$]: om AB DLRX 1. 33(appy) 69 goth [arm-ed] Constt$_1$.

and forbearance of the father are eminently shewn—the utter want of love and humility in the son strongly contrasted with them. **29.**] **ἰδ. τοσ. ἔτη δουλ. σοι**, the very manner of speech of a Pharisee: as is the continuation—**οὐδέπ. ἐντ. σου παρ.** Could the *Jewish nation* be introduced saying this, even in the falsest hypocrisy? **ἐμοὶ οὐδέποτε ἔδωκας** answers to the younger son's *δός μοι* in ver. 12;—it is a separation of the individual son from his father, and, as there pointed out, the very root and ground of sin. **ἔριφον**, of less value than a calf. **τ. φίλ. μου**—who are these? this elder son also then has *friends, who are not his father's friends*: see Matt. xxii. 16, τ. *μαθητὰς αὐτῶν* **μετὰ** τῶν **Ἡρωδιανῶν.** **30.**] **ὁ υἱ. σου οὗτος**, the last degree of scorn and contempt,—just such as was shewn by the Pharisees towards the publicans and sinners (see ch. xviii. 11). 'I will not count such an impure person *my brother.*' **σου τ. βίον**, a covert reproach of his father for having given it to him. **μετὰ τῶν πορνῶν**, a charitable addition on the part of the elder brother, such as those represented by him always take care to make under similar circumstances. Even supposing it a necessary inference from the kind of life which he had been leading, it was one which nothing but the bitterest jealousy would have uttered at such a time. **ἔθυ. αὐ. τ. σ. μ.** parallel with *ἁμαρτωλοὺς προσδέχεται, καὶ συνεσθίει αὐτοῖς*, ver. 2. 'Thou hast not only made him equal to me, but hast received him into superior favour.' **31.**] **πάντοτε μ. ἐμ. εἶ**, as a reason why no *extraordinary* joy should be shewn over *him;* other reasons might be assigned, and lie indeed in the background, suggested by his tone and words: but this is the soft answer to turn away wrath. **πάντα τὰ ἐμὰ σά ἐσ.**, because the portion of goods which remained was *his.* **32.**] **ἔδει**—not **σε**, but generally —**it was right.** The Father still asserts the restored sonship of his returned prodigal—**ὁ ἀδελ. σου οὗτος.** We may remark that the difficulties which have been found in the latter part of the parable, from the *uncontradicted* assertion in ver. 29, if the *Pharisees* are meant,—and the great pride and uncharitableness shewn, if *really righteous persons* are

a ch. xii. 42 reff. b here only. Dan. iii. 8 (vi. 24 Theod.). 2 Macc. iii. 11 only. c = ch. xv. 13 (Matt. xxv. 24, 26 reff.) only. see Ps. cxi. 9. d Matt. xix. 21 reff.

XVI. 1 Ἔλεγεν δὲ καὶ πρὸς τοὺς μαθητὰς Ἄνθρωπός τις ἦν πλούσιος ὃς εἶχεν [a] οἰκονόμον, καὶ οὗτος
[b] διεβλήθη αὐτῷ ὡς [c] διασκορπίζων τὰ [d] ὑπάρχοντα αὐτοῦ.

ABDE GHKL MPRSU VXΓΔΛ ΠΝ 1. 33. 69

CHAP. XVI. 1. rec aft μαθητας ins αυτου, with AP rel [latt] syrr copt goth æth: om BDLRℵ 69 lat-*e* arm. om ος ℵ[1]. οικονομους B[1].

meant,—are considerably lightened by the consideration, that the contradiction of that assertion would have been *beside the purpose of the parable;* that it was the very thing on which the Pharisees prided themselves; that, besides, it *is* sufficiently contradicted *in fact,* by the spirit and words of the elder son. He was breaking his Father's commandment even when he made the assertion,—and the making it is part of his hypocrisy. The result of the Father's entreaty is left purposely uncertain (see Trench, Par. in loc.):—is it possible that this should have been the case, had the *Jewish nation* been meant by the elder brother? But now, as he typifies a set of individuals who might themselves be (and many of them were) won by repentance,—it is thus broken off, to be closed by each individual for himself. For we are all in turn examples of the cases of both these brothers, containing the seeds of both evil courses, in our hearts: but, thanks be to God, under that grace, which is sufficient and willing to seek and save us from both.

CHAP. XVI. 1—8.] PARABLE OF THE UNJUST STEWARD. *Peculiar to Luke.* No parable in the Gospels has been the subject of so much controversy as this: while, at the same time, the general stream of interpretation is well defined, and, in the main, satisfactory. It would be quite beyond the limits of a note to give any thing like a recension of the views respecting it: the principal ones which differ from that which I have adopted, will appear in the course of my remarks. 1.] **ἔλεγεν δὲ καί**—a continuation, I believe, of the foregoing:—certainly closely connected in subject with it, as is the second parable in this chapter also: see below. **πρὸς τ. μαθ.**, not to the *Twelve only,* but to the *multitude of the disciples;* and more immediately perhaps to the *Publicans,* whose reception by Him had been the occasion of this discourse. I say this because I believe them to hold *a* place, though not a principal or an exclusive one, in the application of the parable which follows. **ἄνθρ. τ. ἦν πλούσ. . . . .**] The history in this parable is, in itself, purely *worldly.* The *master* is a *υἱὸς τοῦ αἰῶνος τούτου,* as well as his steward: *bear this in mind:*—the whole parabolic machinery is *from the standing-point of the children of this world.* In the interpretation, this rich man is *the Almighty Possessor of all things.* This is the *only tenable view.* Meyer, who supposes him to be *Mammon* (defending it by the consideration that *dismissal from his service = being received into everlasting habitations,* which it *does not,*—see below), is involved in inextricable difficulties further on. Olshausen's view, that he = the *Devil,* the *ἄρχων τοῦ κόσμου τούτου,* will be found equally untenable. Schleiermacher's, that the *Romans* are intended, whose stewards the Publicans were, and that the debtors = the Jews, hardly needs refuting;—certainly not *more* refuting, than any consistent exposition will of itself furnish. **οἰκονόμον**, a general overlooker—very much what we understand by *an agent,* or 'a man of business,' or, in the larger sense, **a steward.** They were generally of old, *slaves:* but this man is a *freeman,* from vv. 3, 4. This steward = especially the *Publicans,* but also *all the disciples,* i. e. *every man in Christ's Church.* We are all God's stewards, who commits to our trust His property:—each one's office is of larger or smaller trust and responsibility, according to the measure entrusted to him. I say, *especially the Publicans,* because the Twelve, and probably others, had *relinquished all and followed Christ,* and therefore the application of the parable to them would not be *so direct:* and also because I cannot but put together with this parable, and consider as perhaps prompted by it or the report of it, the profession of Zacchæus, ch. xix. 8. Other interpretations have been—*the Pharisees* (Vitringa, and more recently Zyro, Theol. Stud. und Krit. for 1831)—but then the parable should have been *addressed to them,* which it was not,—and this view entirely fails in the application:—*Judas Iscariot* (Bertholdt), of the vindication of which view I am not in possession, and therefore can only generally say, that it is perfectly preposterous:—*Pontius Pilate* &c. &c. **διεβλήθη**—not *wrongfully,* which the word does not imply necessarily—but *maliciously,* which it does imply:

2 καὶ [e] φωνήσας αὐτὸν εἶπεν αὐτῷ Τί τοῦτο ἀκούω περὶ
σοῦ; [f] ἀπόδος τὸν [f] λόγον τῆς [g] οἰκονομίας σου, οὐ
γὰρ [h] δύνῃ ἔτι [i] οἰκονομεῖν. 3 [k] εἶπεν δὲ ἐν ἑαυτῷ ὁ
F αφαιρειται... [a] οἰκονόμος Τί ποιήσω, ὅτι ὁ κύριός μου [l] ἀφαιρεῖται τὴν
[g] οἰκονομίαν ἀπ' ἐμοῦ; [m] σκάπτειν οὐκ [n] ἰσχύω· [o] ἐπαιτεῖν
[p] αἰσχύνομαι. 4 [q] ἔγνων τί ποιήσω, ἵνα ὅταν [r] μετασταθῶ ἐκ

e = Matt. xx. 32 reff. f Matt. xii. 36. Acts xix. 40 [Rom. xiv. 12] al. Dan. vi. 2 Theod. g here, &c. 3ce. 1 Cor. ix. 17. Eph. i. 10. iii. 2, 9. Col. i. 25. 1 Tim. i. 4 only. Isa. xxii. 19, 21 only. h = Mark i. 45. Gen. xix. 22. i here only. Ps. cxi. 5. 2 Macc. iii. 14 only. k Matt. ix. 3 reff. Esth. vi. 6. l mid., Rom. xi. 27 (from Isa. xxvii. 9) only. m ch. vi. 48. xiii. 8 only. Isa. v. 6 only. n = Matt. viii. 28 reff. o ch. xviii. 35 only. Ps. cviii. 10 only. p Gospp., here only. 2 Cor. x. 8. Phil. i. 20. 1 Pet. iv. 16. 1 John ii. 28 only. Ezra viii. 22. q constr., ch. x. 22. xix. 15. r Acts xiii. 22. xix. 26. 1 Cor. xiii. 2. Col. i. 13 only. L.P. 3 Kings xv. 13.

2. om αυτον D-gr 69 Scr's f arm. om αυτω ℵ. om 2nd σου (*σου ου has confused the transcribers*) ADKLPRΠ copt-wilk[-dz] : ins Bℵ rel latt syrr copt-schw goth. ετι bef δυνη ℵ. rec δυνησῃ, with AR rel : txt BDPℵ 1 (69) lat-*e ff*$_2$ syrr goth(Treg).

3. απ' εμου bef την οικονομιαν LR vulg lat-*b c f ff*$_2$ *g*$_1$ [*i l q*] Syr : με της οικονομιας KΠ Scr's p w.—for απ' εμου, μου D. ins και bef επαιτειν B copt [Syr æth].

4. for οταν, αν ℵ. rec om εκ, with APR rel [arm] : ins B(sic : see table) Dℵ 1. 69 syrr copt æth.—for εκ, απο LX 33(appy) vulg lat-*b c e f ff*$_2$ *i l* [*q*] : *de* lat-*a*.

see Dan. vi. 24. The reason why it has come so generally to signify '*wrongful* accusation,' is, that malicious charges are so frequently slanderous. The steward himself does not deny it. Meyer (see above) in carrying out his view, would interpret this charge as an accusation by the Pharisees against the disciples that they *wasted the goods of Mammon by entering the service of Christ*:—but then (1) *this other service* never once appears on the face of the parable; and (2) surely it would hardly be within the bounds of decorum that this διασκορπίζειν should = the entering Christ's service;—this would bring a train of false interpretations with it, and even hold up the ἀδικία of the steward, *as such*, for imitation. **διασκορπίζων**—not that he *had wasted* (E. V.), but **was wasting**, his goods, ὡς διασκορπίζων = ὅτι διεσκόρπιζεν. So διέβαλλον ὡς λυμαινόμενον τὴν πολιτείαν, Xen. Hell. ii. 3. 23. In this charge (spiritually) we may see the real guilt of every man who is entrusted with the goods of our heavenly Father. We are all 'scattering His goods.' If some one is to be found to answer to οἱ διαβάλλοντες, the analogy of **ὁ διάβολος**, 'the accuser of the brethren,' is too striking to escape us.

2. τί τοῦτο . . . .] It makes very little difference either in admissibility of construction or of sense, whether we render, '*why* do I hear this of thee?' i. e. 'what is the ground of this report?—what occasion hast thou given for this being brought to me?' or, '*What is this that* I hear of thee?' i. e. 'give some account of it.' There is the same ambiguity in Mark xi. 3, τί ποιεῖτε τοῦτο; I prefer rather the former, because no opportunity of explanation *what* it is, is given him, but he is commanded to produce his books, to shew *how* it has arisen. **ἀπόδος . . . .**] **give up the account of thy stewardship; for** (taking for granted the correctness of the report, the steward not denying it) **thou wilt not be able to retain thy stewardship any longer,**—in ordinary English, **thou** *canst* not, &c. **οὐ δύνῃ**—in the *nature of things*—**thou art precluded from.** The interpretation of this announcement to the steward, is *the certainty*, spoken by God in every one of our consciences, *that we must give up and give an account of our stewardship at death.* The great truth lies in the background, that that dismissal, death itself, is the consequence of the διασκορπίζειν τὰ ὑπάρχοντα αὐτοῦ,—the *wages of sin.* **3.**] The steward sets before himself the certainty of poverty and misery. He has not by his waste of his lord's property been laying up any store *for himself*;—that is not the point of the parable;—he has lived softly and effeminately, and cannot do an honest day's work:—**σκάπτειν**, for *all manual labours*; so Aristoph. Av. 1432, σκάπτειν γὰρ οὐκ ἐπίσταμαι. This speech, of digging and begging, must not be sought for in the interpretation; it belongs to the truth of the parable itself as introducing the scheme which follows, but has no ulterior meaning. **4.**] **ἔγνων**—not = ἔγνωκα, which would be, '*I know*, as part of my stock of knowledge, I am well aware,'—but implying, **I have just arrived at the knowledge,—an idea has just struck me—I have a plan.**

s = ver. 9. ch. ix. 53. Acts iii. 21. see Eur. Med. 505.
t w. gen. part., ch. iv. 40 reff.
u ch. vii. 41 only. Job xxxi. 37. Prov. xxix. 13 only.
v = here only ‡. (3 Kings v. 11.) Isa. v. 10 Aq. Symm. &c. (see ch. xx. 37.)
w = ch. ii. 28. xxii. 17. Eph. vi. 17.
x = here bis only. Jos. Antt. xviii. 6. 3, ἐπὶ γράμματι καὶ πίστει τῇ αὐτοῦ.

τῆς [g] οἰκονομίας, [s] δέξωνταί με εἰς τοὺς οἴκους ἑαυτῶν.
5 καὶ προσκαλεσάμενος [t] ἕνα [t] ἕκαστον τῶν [u] χρεοφειλετῶν
τοῦ κυρίου ἑαυτοῦ, ἔλεγεν τῷ πρώτῳ Πόσον ὀφείλεις τῷ
κυρίῳ μου; 6 ὁ δὲ εἶπεν Ἑκατὸν [v] βάτους ἐλαίου. ὁ δὲ
εἶπεν αὐτῷ [w] Δέξαι σου τὰ [x] γράμματα καὶ [y] καθίσας
[z] ταχέως γράψον πεντήκοντα. 7 ἔπειτα ἑτέρῳ εἶπεν Σὺ
δὲ πόσον ὀφείλεις; ὁ δὲ εἶπεν Ἑκατὸν [a] κόρους σίτου.
λέγει αὐτῷ Δέξαι σου τὰ [x] γράμματα καὶ γράψον ὀγδο-
ήκοντα. 8 καὶ [b] ἐπῄνεσεν ὁ κύριος τὸν [c] οἰκονόμον τῆς
[d] ἀδικίας, ὅτι [e] φρονίμως ἐποίησεν· ὅτι οἱ [f] υἱοὶ τοῦ

ABDE FGHK LMPRS UVXΓΔ ΛΠℵ 1. 33. 69

y = ch. xiv. 28 reff. z ch. xiv. 21 reff. a here only. 3 Kings iv. 22. b Rom. xv. 11 (from Ps. cxvi. 1). 1 Cor. xi. 2, 17, 22 only. Gen. xii. 15. c ver. 1. d constr., here bis. ch. xviii. 6. Rom. vi. 6. vii. 24. Col. ii. 11. Isa. xxxiii. 6. e here only †. f ch. xx. 34, 36 (reff.).

rec (for ἑαυτ.) *αυτων*, with AD rel: txt BPRXℵ.

5. (*χρεοφειλετων*, so ABDPRℵ &c.) for *εαυτ.*, *αυτου* DFGMXΛ ℵ^1(txt$^{3a\cdot b}$) 1. 69.

6. aft 1st *ειπεν* ins *αυτω* ℵ 254. for *βατους*, *καδους* D^1 Scr's b ev-z vulg lat-*e f l* Chr$_1$-mss; *καβους* D^2 ev-48; *βαδους* LXℵ Orig$_1$. rec (for 2nd *ὁ δε*) *και*, with P rel [vulg lat-*c ff$_2$ l* syr] goth æth: txt ABLRℵ 69 copt.—for *ο δε ειπ.*, *ειπ. δε* D lat-*a b e f* [*q*]. rec *το γραμμα* (*because but one sum is mentnd*), with APR rel: *το γραμματειον* X Chr$_1$: *cautionem* vulg lat-*a f* Jer: *chirografum* lat-*e* [*l*]: txt BDLℵ lat-*b c ff$_2$ q* copt goth Gaud. (So again in ver 7, but there R vulg also have txt.) om *καθισας ταχεως* D. *γραψον* bef *ταχεως* B lat-*e* syr-w-ast æth arm.

7. ins *τω* bef *ετερω* D. om *συ* to 2nd *ειπεν* D-gr. rec ins *και* bef *λεγει*, with AP rel syr goth æth arm; *ο δε* D: om BLR 69 vulg lat-*b c e ff$_2$ q* Syr copt, *λεγει δε* ℵ [lat-*a*].

8. for 2nd *οτι*, *διο λεγω υμιν* D; *dixit autem ad discipulos suos* gat(with mm mt)

δέξωνται—viz. those who are about to be spoken of, the χρεοφειλέται. He has them in his mind. Observe, the aim of his scheme is that they may receive him into their houses,—*give him shelter*. This is made use of afterwards in the interpretation, for which see on ver. 9. **5.**] It is more natural to suppose that these χρεοφειλέται *had borrowed*, i. e. not yet paid for these articles of food out of the stores of the rich man, than that they were *contractors* to the amounts specified. **τοῦ κ. ἑαυτοῦ, of his own lord,**—shewing the unprincipled boldness of his plan for saving himself; as we express the same when we say, 'he robbed his own father.' **6. βάτους**] ὁ δὲ βάτος δύναται χωρῆσαι ξέστας ἑβδομήκοντα δύο, Jos. Antt. viii. 2. 9;—the same for liquids as the ephah for solids. See Ezek. xlv. 10, 11, 14, where the LXX represent the Heb. בַּת by χοῖνιξ and κοτύλη. **δέξαι σ. τ. γρ.**] The steward, not yet out of office, has all the vouchers by him, and returns each debtor his own bond, for him to alter the figure (not, to *make another*, which would imply the *destruction* of the old bond, not its *return*). **σου** is not emphatic, as Wordsworth, who has several times fallen into this mistake: see note, ch. xiv. 26, 27: but entirely unemphatic; almost expletive. **καθ. ταχ.**] καθίσας is graphic. ταχέως implies the hurry with which the furtive business is transacted. The debtors seem to be all together, that all may be implicated and none may tell of the other.

7. κόρους] ὁ δὲ κόρος δύναται μεδίμνους ἀττικοὺς δέκα, Jos. Antt. xv. 9. 2. There does not appear to be any designed meaning in the variation of the amount deducted. We may easily conceive a reason, if we will, in the different circumstances of the debtors. **8.**] **ὁ κύριος**—of course, *the lord of the steward*. The E. V. ought to have been expressed **his lord**, and there would have been no ambiguity. **τ. ο κ. τῆς ἀδ.**, not '*the steward for his injustice*,' but (see reff.) **the unjust steward.** He is not praised 'for his *injustice*:' see below.

ὅτι φρονίμως ἐπ., *because he had acted shrewdly, cleverly for his own interest.* The point brought out is not merely the shrewdness of the steward, but *his lord*, whose injury was wrought by this very shrewdness, *praising it*: for, our Saviour adds, **the sons of this world,** — to which category *both* belonged—*he who conceived* and *he who praised* the shrewd-

[f] αἰῶνος τούτου [g] φρονιμώτεροι [h] ὑπὲρ τοὺς [fi] υἱοὺς τοῦ [i] φωτὸς [k] εἰς τὴν γενεὰν τὴν ἑαυτῶν εἰσιν.
9 καὶ ἐγὼ ὑμῖν
λέγω, [l] ἑαυτοῖς [l] ποιήσατε φίλους ἐκ τοῦ [m] μαμωνᾶ τῆς
[d] ἀδικίας, ἵνα ὅταν [n] ἐκλίπῃ, [o] δέξωνται ὑμᾶς εἰς τὰς
αἰωνίους [p] σκηνάς.
10 ὁ πιστὸς ἐν ἐλαχίστῳ καὶ ἐν πολλῷ

g ch. xii. 42 reff. compar., here only. Gen. xli. 39 only.
h = Heb. iv. 12. 2 Cor. xii. 13. 3 Kings xix. 4.
i John xii. 36. 1 Thess. v. 5. see Eph. v. 8.
k = ch. xii. 21. Eph. i. 5.
l = ch. xii. 33. Exod. xx. 4, 23.
m Matt. vi. 24. vv. 11, 13 only †.
n ch. xxii. 32. Heb. i. 12 (from Ps. ci. 27) only. Gen. xxv. 8. xlix. 33. Tobit xiv. 11.
o ver. 4.
p = here only. (-νος, 2 Cor. v. 1, 4.)

lat-*a b c* (*e*) *l*. φρονιμωτεροι bef οι υιοι τ. αι. τουτου ℵ. for 2nd την, ταυτην ℵ[1](but corrd eadem manu): ταυτην την Scr's c.

9. rec (for και εγω) καγω, with ADP rel: txt BLRℵ **1**. λεγω bef υμιν DM lat-*a c ff*$_2$ *g*$_{1.2}$ Syr æth. rec ποιησατε bef εαυτοις, with ADP ℵ-corr[1·3] rel latt syrr copt goth æth arm [Clem$_1$ Bas$_1$ Thdrt$_1$] Iren-int [Orig-int$_2$ Tert$_1$]: txt BLRℵ[1]. for μαμ. της αδικιας, αδικου μαμωνα D lat-*a* [Chr$_1$(txt$_5$)] Orig-int$_2$[txt$_1$] Ambr$_1$. rec εκλιπητε, with P (FU, e sil) ℵ[3a](but txt restored) vulg lat-*b c f ff*$_2$ *g*$_{1.2}$ [*l*^{2} *q*] syr goth æth-ms Clem$_2$ Meth$_1$ Bas$_1$ Chr$_2$ Iren-int$_1$ Orig-int$_2$; εκλειπητε E rel Chr$_2$: εκλειπη AB[2]X 69 lat-*a* Syr syr-mg copt æth arm [Cyr$_1$]: txt B[1]DLRΠℵ[1] **1**. aft σκηνας ins αυτων P lat-*b* Syr æth Chr$_3$ Cyr$_1$ [Thdrt$_1$] Ambr$_2$.

ness—**are more shrewd, εἰς τ. γ. τ. ἑαυ.**, **for the purposes of** *their* **self-interest, —than the sons of light.** But this very **τὴν ἑαυ.** indicates that there *is a better and a higher* **γενεά**, *the family of light* (John xii. 36: Rom. xiii. 12: Eph. v. 8: 1 Thess. v. 5), whose interests require a higher and better wisdom and foresight. It is hardly necessary to add that the *discovery* of the steward's trick by the master is essential to the parable, as exemplifying the φρονίμως and φρονιμώτεροι. Had the master (as Wordsw.) merely seen the *result*, that the debtors received him into their houses, the praise could hardly have been put in this form. The aor. ἐποίησεν too seems to point at the past device, rather than the permanent result. **9.**] We now pass to the application at once—from the mouth of our Lord Himself. All that is dishonest and furtive in the character of the steward belonged entirely to him as a υἱὸς τοῦ αἰῶνος τούτου: but even in this character there was a point to praise and imitate. And the dishonesty itself is not inserted without purpose—viz. to shew us *how little the* υἱοὶ τ. αἰ. τ. *scruple to use it, and how natural it is to them. Now*, however, we stand on higher ground: καθαροῖς πάντα καθαρά:—in bringing up the example into the purer air which the sons of light breathe, its grosser parts drop off, and the finer only remain.
καὶ ἐγὼ ὑμῖν λ. seems to recognize a necessary difference in the two situations: —'although *you* are sons of the light and the day, and *can do no such furtive acts, yet* I *say to* YOU' . . . . . This view will explain how we may make **φίλους ἐκ τοῦ μαμ. τῆς ἀδ.** just as we can make an example for ourselves out of the **οἰκονόμος τῆς ἀδικ.**—that which is of itself **τῆς ἀδικίας**—which belongs to, is part of a system of, ἀδικία,—which is the very ῥίζα πάντων τῶν κακῶν, the result, and the aptest concretion, of that system of meum and tuum (see ch. xv. 12) which is itself the result of sin having entered into the world. And we are to use this Mammon of unrighteousness to make ourselves, —not palaces, nor barns, nor estates, nor treasures,—but *friends*; i. e. to bestow it on the poor and needy—(see ch. xii. 33, which is the most striking parallel to our text—compare **ὅταν ἐκλίπῃ**, with θησαυρὸν ἀνέκλειπτον there) **that when it shall fail,—they**, i. e. the φίλοι—(compare the joy in heaven ch. xv. 7, 10, and Baxter's remark cited there by Stier—'Is there joy in heaven at thy conversion, and will there be none at thy glorification?') **may receive you into the** (or their) **everlasting tabernacles.** See also ch. xiv. 13, 14. God repays in their name. They receive us there with joy, if they are gone before us: they receive us there by making us partakers of their prayers, which 'move the Hand that moves the world,' even during this life. Deeds then of charity and mercy are to be our spiritual shrewdness, by which we may turn to our account the ἄδικον μαμωνᾶ,—providing ourselves with friends out of it;—and the debtors are here perhaps to be taken in their literal, not parabolic sense—we are to lighten their burdens by timely relief —the only way in which a son of light can change the hundred into fifty, or fourscore: see Isa. lviii. 6—8.
10—12.] Closely connected with the foregoing (against De Wette and Strauss):

q ver. 9. r = John i. 9 reff. s = Rom. iii. 2. 1 Cor. ix. 17. (John ii. 24.) Wisd. xiv. 5. t Matt. xvii. 25. John x. 5 al. Prov. xxvii. 10. u Acts x. 7. Rom. xiv. 4. 1 Pet. ii. 18 only. Gen. ix. 25, 26. v Matt. vi. 24 reff. w 2 Tim. iii. 2 only +. (-ρία, 1 Tim. vi. 10. -ρεῖν, 2 Macc. x. 20.) x Gospp., Luke only. = ch. xxiii. 50, Acts ii. 30. iii. 2. Phil. ii. 6 al. y ch. xxiii. 35 only. Ps. ii. 4. xxi. 7 al. z = ch. x. 29. see ch. xviii. 14. a = Acts iv. 19. 1 Tim. iii. 2. v. 4. 1 John iii. 10. 3 Kings iii. 10. b Ps. cxxxviii. 23. see Acts i. 24. xv. 8. c = Rom. xii. 16. 1 Kings ii. 3. d Matt. xxiv. 15 || Mk. Rev. xvii. 4, 5. xxi. 27 only. Prov. xi. 1.

ABDE FGHK LMPRS UVXΓΔ ΛΠℵ 1. 33. 69

πιστός ἐστιν, καὶ ὁ ἐν ἐλαχίστῳ ἄδικος καὶ ἐν πολλῷ ἄδι-
κός ἐστιν. 11 εἰ οὖν ἐν τῷ ἀδίκῳ q μαμωνᾷ πιστοὶ οὐκ
ἐγένεσθε, τὸ r ἀληθινὸν τίς ὑμῖν s πιστεύσει; 12 καὶ εἰ ἐν
τῷ t ἀλλοτρίῳ πιστοὶ οὐκ ἐγένεσθε, τὸ ὑμέτερον τίς ὑμῖν
δώσει; 13 οὐδεὶς u οἰκέτης δύναται δυσὶ κυρίοις v δουλεύειν·
ἢ γὰρ τὸν v ἕνα v μισήσει καὶ τὸν v ἕτερον v ἀγαπήσει, ἢ v ἑνὸς
v ἀνθέξεται καὶ τοῦ v ἑτέρου v καταφρονήσει. οὐ δύνασθε
θεῷ δουλεύειν καὶ q μαμωνᾷ. 14 Ἤκουον δὲ ταῦτα πάντα
[καὶ] οἱ Φαρισαῖοι, w φιλάργυροι x ὑπάρχοντες, καὶ y ἐξ-
εμυκτήριζον αὐτόν. 15 καὶ εἶπεν αὐτοῖς Ὑμεῖς ἐστε οἱ z δικαιοῦντες ἑαυτοὺς a ἐνώπιον τῶν ἀνθρώπων, ὁ δὲ θεὸς
b γινώσκει τὰς b καρδίας ὑμῶν, ὅτι τὸ ἐν ἀνθρώποις c ὑψηλὸν d βδέλυγμα ἐνώπιον τοῦ θεοῦ. 16 ὁ νόμος καὶ οἱ προ-

10. for 2nd ελαχιστω, ολιγω D 1 vulg lat-*b c e f* [*i*] *q*. for 2nd εστιν, γινεται D.
12. ημετερον BL lat-*e i l* $Orig_1$ $Tert_2$: txt ADPRℵ rel vulg lat-*a c f* ff_2 $g_{1.2}$ [*q*] syrr [syr-jer copt] goth [Bas_1] Orig-int_2 $Cypr_1$. δωσει bef υμιν DLRℵ 33 latt Syr [syr-jer] æth (Iren ?) $Orig_1$[int_2] $Mcion_1$-t $Cypr_1$: txt ABP rel syr goth arm [Bas_1].
13. for 1st η, ει (*itacism ?*) ℵ Scr's f.
14. παντα bef ταυτα KΠ vulg [lat-*q*] syr: om παντα D 60. 245 Scr's b ev-H lat-*i* æth $Orig_1$. om 1st και BDLR(ℵ) latt Syr [syr-jer] copt æth arm $Orig_2$: ins APX rel syr goth.—om οι φαρισαιοι also ℵ[1](ins ℵ-corr[1]).
15. for ανθρωποις, ανθρωπω B[1]. for του θεου, κυριου B. rec adds εστιν, with X rel vss: om ABDKLPRSV[2]ΔΠℵ goth æth Ign Constt Thl.

—the 'faithfulness in the least' is the same as the prudence and shrewdness just spoken of;—in the case of the children of light they run up into one—τίς ἐστιν ὁ **πιστὸς** οἰκονόμος **καὶ φρόνιμος**, ch. xii. 42;—the **ἐλάχιστον** = ὁ ἄδικος (see above: not "*fallacious*," as Wordsw.) μαμωνᾶς = **τὸ ἀλλότριον**—*the wealth of this present world*, which is not the Christian's own, nor his proper inheritance. The **πολύ** = **τὸ ἀληθινόν** = **το ὑμέτερον** = *the true riches of God's inheritance*: of which the earth (see Matt. v. 5) forms a part, which ὁ θεός (implied in the τίς—for there will be none to give it you if you be untrue during this state of probation;—He will not be your God) shall give to you. The wealth of this world is ἀλλότριον—forfeited by sin—only put into our hands to try us, and to be rendered an account of. **13.**] See note on Matt. vi. 24. The connexion here is,—that we must, while put in trust with the ἄδικος μαμωνᾶς, be serving *not it, but God*. The saying here applies (as Olshausen remarks) admirably to the Pharisees and Publicans: the former were, to outward appearance, the servants of God, but inwardly served Mammon;—the latter, *by profession* in the service of Mammon, were, by coming to Jesus, shewing that they inwardly served God.

14—31.] By occasion of the covetous Pharisees deriding Him, our Lord speaks the parable of the rich man and Lazarus. The Pharisees were not slow in perceiving that the scope of **ταῦτα πάντα** was to place this world's goods, and all that the covetous seek after, at a very low price. It will be observed that the sayings which follow, are in reference to matters mentioned during the discourses, or arising out of the character of the Pharisees as commented on in them. **15.**] See last note, end. **δικαιοῦντες .... ἐνώπ. τ. ἀνθρ.**, a contrast to ἥμαρτον ἐνώπιόν σου, ch. xv. 18: and **βδέλυγ. ἐνώπιον τ. θεοῦ** to χαρὰ ἐνώπιον τ. ἀγγ. τοῦ θεοῦ, ch. xv. 10.. **16.**] See Matt. xi. 12 and note. After **προφ.** supply προεφήτευσαν, not (Meyer) ἐκηρύσσοντο, which would be inapplicable to the law and the prophets. The connexion is,—'*Ye are they that justify yourselves before men; ye are no publicans and sinners,—no poor and needy,—but righteous, and increased with this world's*

φῆται μέχρι Ἰωάννου· [e]ἀπὸ τότε ἡ βασιλεία τοῦ θεοῦ
[f]εὐαγγελίζεται καὶ πᾶς εἰς αὐτὴν [g]βιάζεται. 17 [h]εὐκο-
πώτερον δέ ἐστιν τὸν οὐρανὸν καὶ τὴν γῆν [i]παρελθεῖν ἢ
τοῦ νόμου μίαν [k]κεραίαν [l]πεσεῖν. 18 πᾶς ὁ [m]ἀπολύων
τὴν γυναῖκα αὐτοῦ καὶ γαμῶν ἑτέραν [n]μοιχεύει· καὶ
ὁ [m]ἀπολελυμένην ἀπὸ ἀνδρὸς γαμῶν [n]μοιχεύει. 19 Ἄνθρωπος δέ τις ἦν πλούσιος, καὶ [o]ἐνεδιδύσκετο [o]πορφύραν

...πας εις R.

e Matt. v. 17 reff.
f constr. pass., Gal. i. 11. 1 Pet. i. 25. iv. 6 (Matt. xi. 5 reff.). act., Rev. xiv. 6.
g = here (Matt. xi. 12) only. Exod. xix. 24.
h ch. v. 23 reff.
i = Matt. v. 18 reff.
k Matt. v. 18 only +.
l = 1 Cor. xiii. 8. Josh. xxiii. 14.
m Matt. v. 32 reff.
n Matt. v. 27 (from Deut. v. 18) al.
o Mark xv. 17 (reff.).

16. rec (for μεχρι) εως (|| *Matt*), with ADP rel Mcion$_2$-e Orig$_1$: txt BLRXℵ 1. 69 Clem$_1$ Orig$_1$. aft ιωαννου ins επροφητευσαν (|| *Matt*) D mm. om το(of τοτε) D[1](ins D[2]). om και πας to βιαζεται (*homœotel*) G ℵ[1](ins ℵ[3a], adding και βιασται αρπαζουσιν αυτην).

17. κεραιαν bef μιαν B [syrr] sah.

18. 1st και is repeated by D[2]. rec aft 2nd και ins πας (*mechanl repetn*), with APℵ rel syrr goth: om BDL 69 latt coptt (æth) arm Tert$_1$. om απο ανδρος D 28 Syr copt goth arm.

19. at beg ins ειπεν δε και ετεραν παραβολην D bodl. om δε DXΔ vulg lat-*a*

goods. But, since John, a kingdom has been preached, into which every one, publicans and sinners too (πᾶς || πάντες, ch. xv. 1) *are pressing in. The true relation however of that kingdom to the law is not as ye suppose, to destroy the law* (Matt. v. 17), *but to fulfil.*' Then, as an example, our Lord reiterates the decision which He had before given on a point much controverted among the Jews—the law of adultery. But this He does, not *without occasion given*, and close connexion with the circumstances, and with what had before been said. As early as Tertullian, cont. Marc. iv. 34, vol. ii. p. 443, it was remarked, that an allusion was meant here to the adultery of Herod Antipas with his brother Philip's wife, which the Pharisees had tacitly sanctioned, thus allowing an open breach of that law which Christ came to fulfil. To this mention of Herod's crime the μέχρι Ἰωάννου gave relevance. Still the idea must not be too lightly assumed. Bleek's remark is worth notice, that, had such an allusion been intended, the last words of the verse would have been otherwise expressed. Antipas had not *married a divorced woman*, but abduced a married woman from her husband. See on Matt. v. 32. **19–31.**] Our Lord, in this closing parable, grasps the whole covetous and self-seeking character of the Pharisees, shews them a case in which it is carried to the utmost, by one who '*made no friends*' with the unrighteous Mammon;—places in contrast with it a case of extreme destitution and poverty,—the very thing which the φιλάργυρος most abhorred;—and then passes over into the region beyond the grave, shewing them the contrast there also—and ending with a mysterious prophetic hint at the final rejection of the Kingdom of God and Himself by those for whom the law and prophets were insufficient to bring them to repentance. And while it does not appear that the φιλαργυρία of the Pharisees shewed itself in this particular way, our Lord here grasps the depravity by its root, which is, *a godless and loveless self-seeking*—saying in the heart, 'There is no God'—and acting accordingly.

The explanation of particular points see below. **19.**] **δέ** connects this directly with what goes before; being an answer, not immediately to *any thing said* by the Pharisees, but to their *scoffs* at Him;—q. d. '*hear now a parable.*' **ἄνθρ. πλ.**] Tertullian thought (l. c.) that *Herod* was meant, and by Lazarus *John;* and this view has been taken by Paulus and Schleiermacher also: but surely with no probability. Our Lord might hint with stern rebuke at the present notorious crime of Herod, but can hardly be thought to have spoken thus of him. That the circumstances *will in some measure apply to these two*, is owing, as above in ch. xv., to the parable taking the *general case*, of which theirs was a particular instance. Zeller (refuted by Bleek in loc.) thinks that the rich man sets forth the Jews and the poor man the Gentiles. In my view, the very name of the poor man (see below) is a sufficient answer to this.

Observe, that this rich man is *not accused of any flagrant crimes:*—he lives, as the world would say, *as became his means and station;* he does not oppress

καὶ [p] βύσσον, [q] εὐφραινόμενος [r] καθ' ἡμέραν [s] λαμπρῶς.
20 πτωχὸς δέ τις ὀνόματι Λάζαρος [t] ἐβέβλητο πρὸς
τὸν [u] πυλῶνα αὐτοῦ [v] εἱλκωμένος 21 καὶ [w] ἐπιθυμῶν
[xy] χορτασθῆναι [y] ἀπὸ τῶν [z] πιπτόντων ἀπὸ τῆς [z] τραπέζης
τοῦ πλουσίου· ἀλλὰ καὶ οἱ κύνες ἐρχόμενοι [a] ἐπέλειχον
τὰ [b] ἕλκη αὐτοῦ. 22 [c] ἐγένετο δὲ ἀποθανεῖν τὸν πτωχὸν καὶ [d] ἀπενεχθῆναι αὐτὸν ὑπὸ τῶν ἀγγέλων εἰς τὸν

ABDEF GHKL MPSUV XΓΔΛ ΠΝ 1. 33. 69

p here (Rev. xviii. 12 v. r.) only. 2 Chron. ii. 14.
q ch. xii. 19 reff. Deut. xiv. 26.
r Matt. xxvi. 55 reff.
s here only †. (-ρός, Rev. xviii. 14. Sir. xxix. 22.)
t see Matt. viii. 6, 14. ix. 2. Mark vii. 30.
u Matt. xxvi. 71. Acts x. 17 al. Gen. xliii. 19.
v here only †.
w ch. xv. 16. Isa. lviii. 2.
x ch. ix. 17 || Mt. Mk. Ps. xvi. 15.
y here (ch. xv. 16 v. r.) only. Ps. ciii. 13.
z Matt. xv. 27.
a here only †.
b Rev. xvi. 2, 11 only. Job ii. 7.
c constr., Matt. xviii. 13. Mark ii. 23. ch. iii. 21. vi. 1, 6. Acts iv. 5 al. fr.
d Mark xv. 1 reff. Hos. x. 6.

b e f [*q*] æth arm. ins και bef ευφραινομενος D-gr [Syr] goth.

20. rec aft τις ins ην, with AP² rel vulg lat-(*b c* [*ff*$_2$ *g*$_{1.2}$]) *i* syrr sah[Treg] goth: om BDLP¹Xℵ 33(appy) lat-*a e f* coptt æth arm Clem$_1$ Dial$_1$. rec aft λαζαρος ins ος, with AP rel vulg lat-*b c f* [*ff*$_2$ *g*$_{1.2}$ *l q*] syr goth: om BDLXℵ 33 lat-*a e f i* coptt [æth arm] Clem$_1$ Dial$_1$. for προς, εις PΓ. rec ηλκωμενος, with KMSUVΓΠ 1: txt ABDPℵ rel.

21. rec ins των ψιχιων bef των πιπτοντων (*from Matt* xv. 27 || *Mark*), with A(D) Pℵ^3a rel vulg lat-*a f g*$_1$ syrr copt-wilk Ephr$_1$ Chr$_1$: om BLℵ¹ lat-*b c e ff*$_2$ *i l q* syr-jer copt-schw[-dz] sah Clem Dial Ambr Gaud.—τ. ψιχων D. rec απελειχον, with P rel: ελειχον D 1 Dial$_1$ (Ephr$_1$): txt ABLXℵ 33.

nor spoil other men: he is simply a *υἱὸς τοῦ αἰῶνος τούτου*, in the highest form. **πορφ. κ. βύσ.**, the Tyrian costly purple—and the fine linen (for under clothing) from Egypt. **εὐφρ. λαμπ.**] Probably the E. V. is right—**fared sumptuously**: '*epulabatur splendide*,' Vulg. Others render it '*enjoyed himself sumptuously*.' **20.**] The significant name Lazarus (= Eleazarus = אֶלְעָזָר, *Deus auxilium*) should have prevented the expositors from imagining this to be *a true history*. Perhaps by this name our Lord may have intended *to fill in the character of the poor man*, which indeed must otherwise be understood to be that of one who feared God. **ἐβέβ., was, or had been, cast down,** i. e. was placed there on purpose to get what he could of alms. **πυλῶνα**, see on ref. Matt.: it was the portal, which led out of the *προαύλιον* into the *αὐλή*. **21.**] It would seem that he *did* obtain this wish, and that, as in ch. xv. 16, the **ἐπιθ.** must mean, he **looked for it, willingly took** it. The **ἀλλὰ καί** seems also to imply, that he *got the crumbs*: this verse, relating the two points of contrast to the rich man: his only food, the crumbs, with which he longed to fill his belly, but could not:—his only clothing, nakedness and sores, and instead of the boon companions of the rich man, none to pity him but the dogs, who **ἐπέλειχον**—certainly in pity, not '*dolorem exasperantes*' (Bengel)—his sores, as they do their own. Such was the state of the two in this world. **22.**] The *burial* of Lazarus is not mentioned, *διὰ τὸ ἀτημέλητον τῆς τῶν πτωχῶν ταφῆς*, Euthym. This is the only admissible reason. Meyer rejects it as arbitrary, and not consistent with the received notions about Hades, in which not the soul only, but the whole man was after death—believing it to be meant that the angels carried Lazarus *bodily* into Paradise. But then his interpretation halts, when he comes to the burial of the rich man, whom he makes go down out of his grave into hell. The fact is, that in both cases the material corpse remains on this earth, buried or unburied; while that personality, to which universal consent rightly attributes sensibility to bliss and woe, and the feelings and parts of the body, the man's real *self*, is translated into the other world. (If, when parts of the body are removed, we still believe that we possess those limbs, and feel pain in them, why may not the disembodied spirit still subjectively exist in, and feel the sensations of, that corporeal system from which it is temporarily separated?) **ἀπενεχθ. αὐτ. . . . .**] In the whole of this description, the following canon of interpretation may be safely laid down:—Though it is unnatural to suppose that our Lord would in such a parable formally *reveal* any *new truth* respecting the state of the dead,—yet, in conforming himself to the ordinary language current on these subjects, it is impossible to suppose that He, whose essence is Truth, could have assumed as existing any thing which does not exist. It would destroy the truth of our Lord's

... αβρααμ P.

[e] κόλπον Ἀβραάμ. ἀπέθανεν δὲ καὶ ὁ πλούσιος καὶ ἐτάφη,
23 καὶ ἐν τῷ [f] ᾅδῃ [g] ἐπάρας τοὺς [g] ὀφθαλμοὺς αὐτοῦ,
[h] ὑπάρχων ἐν [i] βασάνοις, ὁρᾷ Ἀβραὰμ [k] ἀπὸ [k] μακρόθεν,
καὶ Λάζαρον ἐν τοῖς [l] κόλποις αὐτοῦ. 24 καὶ αὐτὸς
[m] φωνήσας εἶπεν Πάτερ Ἀβραάμ, ἐλέησόν με καὶ πέμψον
Λάζαρον, ἵνα [n] βάψῃ τὸ [o] ἄκρον τοῦ δακτύλου αὐτοῦ
[p] ὕδατος καὶ [q] καταψύξῃ τὴν γλῶσσάν μου, ὅτι [r] ὀδυνῶμαι
ἐν τῇ [s] φλογὶ ταύτῃ. 25 εἶπεν δὲ Ἀβραὰμ Τέκνον, μνήσ-

e = ver. 23. ch. vi. 38. John i. 18. xiii. 23 (Acts xxvii. 39) only. Deut. xiii. 6.
f Matt. xi. 23 reff. Ps. xv. 10.
g = Matt. xvii. 8 reff.
h ver. 16 reff.
i Matt. iv. 24. ver. 28 only. Wisd. iii. 1. xix. 4.
k Matt. xxvi. 58 reff.
l ver. 22. plur., here only. Prov. xvi. 33. m = ch. viii. 8 reff. n John xiii. 26 bis. Rev. xix. 13 only. Num. xix. 18. o Matt. xxiv. 31 || Mk. Heb. xi. 21 (from Gen. xlvii. 31) only. Deut. iv. 32. p constr., Matt. xvi. 28. Mark v. 30 al. see Winer, edn. 6, § 30. 8. c. and Exod. xii. 22. q here only. Gen. xviii. 4. Ezek. xxvi. 19 Ald. only. r here bis. ch. ii. 48. Acts xx. 38 only. Isa. xl. 29. s Gospp., here only. (elsw. in N. T. always w. πῦρ, Acts vii. 30. 2 Thess. i. 8. Heb. i. 7. Rev. i. 14 al2.) Isa. v. 24.

22. *εις τον κολπον αβρααμ* bef *υπο των αγγελων* D 142(Sz). rec ins *του* bef *αβρααμ*, with 69 : om ABDPℵ rel Mcion$_1$-e Orig Dial Ephr$_1$ [Chr$_1$].
23. om 1st *και* ℵ[1] lat-*q*. rec ins *τον* bef *αβρααμ*, with A rel Orig$_1$ Ephr$_1$ [Chr$_1$] : om BDLXℵ Orig$_1$ Dial$_1$. *τω κολπω* D-gr latt [Syr syr-jer] coptt. aft 2nd *αυτου* ins *αναπαυομενον* D lat-*b c e q* arm.
24. *ενφωνησας exclamans* D lat-*a b* (*e*) *f*. *υδατι* ℵ : *υδατον* D[1].
25. *μνησθητι* bef *τεκνον* ℵ.

sayings, if we could conceive Him to have used popular language which *did not point at truth*. And accordingly, where *such* language was current, we find Him not adopting, but protesting against it: see Matt. xv. 5. The bearing of the spirits of the just into bliss by the holy angels is only analogous to their other employments: see Matt. xiii. 41: Heb. i. 14. **τ. κόλπ. Ἀβραάμ**] The above remark does not apply here—for this, as a form of speech among the Jews, was not even by themselves understood in its strict literal sense; and though the *purposes of the parable* require this, ver. 23, no one would think of pressing it into a truth, but all would see in it the graphic filling up of a state which in itself is strictly actual. The expression בחיקו של אברהם signified the *happy side of Hades*, where all the Fathers were conceived as resting in bliss. In Joseph. de Macc. § 13 we have *οὕτω γὰρ θανόντας ἡμᾶς Ἀβραὰμ κ. Ἰσ. κ. Ἰακ. ὑποδέξονται εἰς τοὺς κόλπους αὐτῶν.* No pre-eminence is signified, as in John xiii. 23;—*all the blessed* are spoken of as in Abraham's bosom. See also John i. 18.

The death of the rich man *last* should be remarked; Lazarus was taken soon from his sufferings; Dives was left longer, that he might have space to repent. **κ. ἐτάφη**] There can be no doubt that the *funeral* is mentioned as being congruous to his station in life,—and, as Trench observes, 'in a sublime irony,'—implying that he had all things *properly cared* for; the purple and fine linen which he wore in life, not spared at his obsequies. See Meyer's interpretation above. **23. ἐν τ. ᾅδῃ**] Hades, שְׁאוֹל, is the abode of *all disembodied spirits* till the resurrection; not, the place of torment,—much less *hell*, as understood commonly, in the E. V. Lazarus was *also in Hades*, but separate from Dives; one on the blissful, the other on the baleful side. It is the *gates of Hades, the imprisonment of death*, which shall not prevail against the Church (Matt. xvi. 18);—the Lord holds the *key of Hades*, (Rev. i. 18);—Himself went into the same Hades, of which Paradise is a part. **ἐν βασάνοις**—not *eternal condemnation*;—for the judgment has not yet taken place; men can only be judged *in the body*, for the deeds *done in the body*:—but, *the certainty and anticipation of it*. **ἐπάρας**, not necessarily *to a higher place*, though that *may* be meant:—see reff. **24.**] '*Superbus temporis, mendicus inferni.*' Aug. (Trench, Par. in loc.) On **πάτερ Ἀβρ.** see Matt. iii. 9. **φλογί**, not subjective *only*, though perhaps mainly. The omission of the article before *βασάνοις* points no doubt to *subjective* torments;—but where lies the limit between inner and outer to the disembodied? Hardened sinners have died crying 'Fire!'—Did the fire leave them, when they left their bodies? **25.**] The answer is solemn, calm, and fatherly;—there is no mocking, as is found in the Koran under the same circumstances; no grief, as is sometimes represented affecting the blessed spirits for the lot of the lost. (Klopstock, cited by Stier, iii. 319, edn. 2: Wehmuth der Himmlischen die verlorenen Seelen be=

θητι ὅτι [t] ἀπέλαβες τὰ [u] ἀγαθά σου ἐν τῇ ζωῇ σου, καὶ
Λάζαρος ὁμοίως τὰ κακά· νῦν δὲ ὧδε [v] παρακαλεῖται, σὺ
δὲ [r] ὀδυνᾶσαι. 26 καὶ [w] * ἐπὶ πᾶσιν τούτοις [x] μεταξὺ ἡμῶν
καὶ ὑμῶν [y] χάσμα μέγα [z] ἐστήρικται, ὅπως οἱ θέλοντες
[a] διαβῆναι [b] ἔνθεν πρὸς ὑμᾶς μὴ δύνωνται, μηδὲ [οἱ]
ἐκεῖθεν πρὸς ἡμᾶς [c] διαπερῶσιν. 27 εἶπεν δὲ [d] Ἐρωτῶ σε
οὖν, πάτερ, ἵνα πέμψῃς αὐτὸν εἰς τὸν οἶκον τοῦ πατρός
μου· 28 ἔχω γὰρ πέντε ἀδελφούς· ὅπως [e] διαμαρτύρηται
αὐτοῖς, ἵνα μὴ καὶ αὐτοὶ ἔλθωσιν εἰς τὸν τόπον τοῦτον
τῆς [f] βασάνου. 29 λέγει δὲ [αὐτῷ] Ἀβραὰμ Ἔχουσιν
[g] Μωυσέα καὶ τοὺς [g] προφήτας· [h] ἀκουσάτωσαν αὐτῶν.

ABDEF GHKL MSUVX ΓΔΛΠℵ 1. 33. 69

t ch. xv. 27. xxiii. 41. Gal. iv. 5 al. Num. xxxiv. 14.
u = ch. xii. 18, 19. Gen. xlv. 18, 20.
v = Acts xx. 12 al. Gen. xxiv. 67.
w = ch. iii. 20. Col. iii. 14. 2 Chron. xxix. 10.
x = Matt. xxiii. 35. ch. xi. 51. Acts xii. 6.
y here only. 2 Kings xviii. 17 (Num. xvi. 30 Ald.) only (?).
z = here only. Gen. xxxviii. 12. see ch. ix. 51.
a Acts xvi. 9. Heb. xi. 29 only. 1 Kings xiii. 7.
b Matt. xvii. 20 only.
c Matt. ix. 1 reff.
d = ch. vii. 36 reff.
e Gospp., here only. Acts ii. 40 al8. 1 Thess. iv. 6. 1 Tim. v. 21. 2 Tim. ii. 14. iv. 1. Heb. ii. 6 only. L.P.H. Gen. xliii. 2(3) A. (B def.) Exod. xix. 21.
f ver. 23 reff.
g ch. xxiv. 27, 44. John i. 46. see ver. 16.
h = Matt. xvii. 5. Isa. xlviii. 18.

rec aft απελαβες ins συ, with X rel lat-*b* syr Dial$_1$ Chr$_2$ Orig-int$_3$; aft τα αγαθα σου A: om BDGHLΠ[1]ℵ 69 vulg lat-*a c* &c Syr [syr-jer] coptt æth arm Ps-Ath$_1$ Ephr$_1$ Chr$_{sæpe}$ [Bas$_3$ Orig-int$_1$] Thl Cypr$_1$ Hil Ambr Aug Fulg Paulin. rec (for ωδε) οδε, with **1**: txt ABDℵ rel syrr coptt æth arm. (*hic* latt [Orig-int$_1$] Cypr Hil.)

26. * ἐν πᾶσι BLℵ, *in his omnibus* vulg lat-*b c* [*e f ff$_2$ g$_{1.2}$ i l* (*q*) D-lat] copt: επι πασιν AEXΓΔΛ, επι πασι D[-gr] KMU[Π Dial$_1$ Chr$_1$ Ephr$_1$]. rec (for ενθεν) εντευθεν (*more usual*), with KΠ 1: om D lat-*c e* Dial spec: txt ABℵ rel [Chr$_1$ Ephr$_1$]. om οι B(D)ℵ[1]: ins Aℵ[3a] rel copt arm [Dial Chr Ephr].—for last clause, μητε εκειθεν ωδε διαπερασαι D latt Ambr.

27. rec ουν bef σε, with LXℵ rel [arm] Dial$_1$ Ephr$_1$ spec: txt ABD 69 syr. aft πατερ ins αβρααμ DX mt Aug$_2$.

28. om ινα D Dial$_1$. τουτον bef τον τοπ. D vulg-clem lat-*a c* [*e ff$_2$ g$_1$ l*] Dial$_1$: om τουτ. Λ.

29. for λεγει, ειπεν D lat-*a* spec. rec om δε, with EGHMSΓΛ lat-*e* Syr Dial$_1$: *et ait* vulg lat-*b c*: txt ABDℵ rel lat-*a* syr copt Ephr. om αυτω BLℵ D-lat [arm] Ephr: ins A D-gr rel latt syrr [syr-jer æth] copt Dial$_1$.

gleitet.) **μνήσθητι . . .**] Analogy gives us every reason to suppose, that in the disembodied state the whole life on earth will lie before the soul in all its thoughts, words, and deeds, like a map of the past journey before a traveller. **ἀπέλαβες**—not sufficiently expressed by '*receivedst*,' E. V.:—it is analogous to **ἀπέχουσιν**, Matt. vi. 2, 5, 16,—and expresses the receipt *in full*, the exhaustion of all claim on. Those that were good things *to thee*, **τὰ ἀγ. σου**, *came to an end* in thy lifetime: there are no more of them. What a weighty, precious word is this **σου**: were it not for it, De Wette and the like, who maintain that the only meaning of the parable is, '*Woe to the rich, but blessed are the poor*'—would have found in this verse at least a specious defence for their view:—though even then **τὰ ἀγ.** would have implied the same, in fair interpretation. **τὰ κακά**—not αὐτοῦ—for to him *they were not so*. **παρακαλ.**] See ch. vi. 24. **26.**] *Even if it were not so,*—however, and for whatsoever reason, God's decree hath placed thee there—thy wish is *impossible*. **χάσμα μέγα**] In the interpretation,—the irresistible decree—*then* truly so, but *no such on earth*—by which the Almighty Hand hath separated us and you, **in order that**, not merely *so that*, none may pass it. In the graphic description, a yawning chasm impassable. **ἐστήρικται**, is *fixed* for ever. This expression precludes all idea that the following verse indicates the beginning of a better mind in the rich man. **27.**] This is the *believing and trembling* of James ii. 19. His eyes are now opened to the truth; and no wonder that his natural sympathies are awakened for his brethren. That a *lost spirit* should feel and express such sympathy, is not to be wondered at; the misery of such will be very much heightened by the awakened and active state of those higher faculties and feelings which selfishness and the body kept down here. **29.**] ἡ πίστις ἐξ ἀκοῆς, ἡ δὲ ἀκοὴ διὰ ῥήματος χριστοῦ. Rom. x. 17. 'Auditu fideli salvamur, non apparitionibus.' Bengel. This verse furnishes a weighty tes-

30 ὁ δὲ εἶπεν Οὐχὶ πάτερ Ἀβραάμ, ἀλλ᾽ ἐάν τις ἀπὸ
νεκρῶν πορευθῇ πρὸς αὐτούς, [i] μετανοήσουσιν. 31 εἶπεν
δὲ αὐτῷ Εἰ [g] Μωυσέως καὶ τῶν [g] προφητῶν οὐκ ἀκούουσιν,
οὐδ᾽ ἐάν τις [k] ἐκ νεκρῶν [k] ἀναστῇ [l] πεισθήσονται.
XVII. 1 Εἶπεν δὲ πρὸς τοὺς μαθητὰς αὐτοῦ [m] Ἀνένδεκτόν ἐστιν [n] τοῦ τὰ [o] σκάνδαλα μὴ [p] ἐλθεῖν, οὐαὶ δὲ [q] δι᾽
οὗ [p] ἔρχεται. 2 [r] λυσιτελεῖ αὐτῷ εἰ λίθος [s] μυλικὸς [t] περίκειται περὶ τὸν [u] τράχηλον αὐτοῦ καὶ [v] ἔῤῥιπται εἰς τὴν
θάλασσαν, [w] ἢ ἵνα [x] σκανδαλίσῃ τῶν [y] μικρῶν τούτων

i. Matt. iii. 2 reff.
k Mark vi. 14 reff.
l absol., Acts xvii. 4. xxi. 14. Esth. iv. 4 B (not Aℵ).
m here only †.
n constr., Acts x. 25. [Rev. xii. 7.]
o Matt. xiii. 41 reff. Hos. iv. 17.
p = Matt. xviii. 7 bis only.
q ellips., Mark x. 40. ch. v. 25. Rom. vi. 21.
r here only †. Tobit iii. 6 al.
s here only †. (-ινός, Rev. xviii. 21.)
t Mark ix. 42. Acts xxviii. 20. Heb. v. 2. xii. 1. †
u Mark ix. 42 reff.
v = ch. iv. 35. (Matt. xv. 30 reff.) Gen. xxi. 15.
w constr., Matt. xviii. 8, 9 reff.
x Matt. v. 29, 30 reff.
y = Matt. x. 42. Acts viii. 10 al.

30. πατηρ D. for απο, εκ DF 1 latt Dial [Ephr] Thl Iren-int$_1$. for πορευθη, αναστη ℵ: αναστη και πορ. 69: *surrexerit*, or *resurrexerit* (omg πρ. αυτ.) lat-*a b c ff$_2$ i* [*l q*].

31. (ουδ᾽, so ABD.) aft αναστη ins και απελθη προς αυτους D Iren-int. for πεισθησονται, πιστευουσιν D Ephr$_1$.

Chap. XVII. **1.** rec om αυτου, with E rel lat-*e* [Damasc$_1$] Tert: ins ABDFLMUXℵ 69 latt Syr syr-w-ast [æth arm]. elz om του: ins ABDℵ rel Scr's-mss Orig$_1$ Chr$_1$ Damasc$_1$. rec μη ελθειν bef τα σκανδαλα (*to connect* αν. εστιν *or* του *with the inf, or to avoid* του τα), with AD rel latt Orig$_1$ [Chr$_1$ (Damasc$_1$)]: txt BLXℵ lat-*e*. for ουαι δε, πλην ουαι (*from Matt* xviii. 7) BDLℵ 1. 33. 69 lat-*a b c e ff$_2$ i* [*q*] syr-mg copt: txt A rel vulg lat-*f* [*l*] syrr arm [Damasc].

2. for λυσιτελει, συνφερει δε, D[-gr]. rec (for λιθος μυλικος) μυλος ονικος (*from Matt* xviii. 6), with A rel syrr [æth Damasc$_1$] Dial: txt BDLℵ 1. 69 latt syr-mg copt arm Mcion$_1$-t. περιεκειτο and εριπτο D (εριπτετο D^5). rec ενα bef των μικρων τουτων (*from Matt* xviii. 6), with ADℵ^{3a} rel vss: txt BLℵ^1.

timony from our Lord Himself of the sufficiency *then* of the O. T. Scriptures for the salvation of the Jews. It is *not so now.*

30, 31.] **οὐχί**—not, '*they will not hear them:*' he could not tell that, and besides, it would have taken away much of the ground of the answer of Abraham:—the word deprecates leaving their salvation in *such uncertainty*, as the chance of their hearing Moses and the Prophets seems to him to imply.—'*Leave it not so, when it might be at once and for ever done by sending them one from the dead.*' Abraham's answer, besides opening to us a depth in the human heart, has a plain application to the Pharisees, to whom the parable was spoken. They would not hear Moses and the Prophets:—Christ rose from the dead, but He did not go to *them;*—this verse is not *so* worded, 'they would have rejected Him, had He done so:'—the *fact* merely is here supposed, and that in the very phrase which so often belongs to His own resurrection. They were not persuaded—did not believe, though One rose from the dead. To deny altogether this allusion, is to rest contented with merely the surface of the parable.
Observe, Abraham does not say, 'they will not *repent*' but, 'they will not *believe, be persuaded:*' which is another and a deeper thing. Luther does not seem to conclude rightly, that this *disproves* the possibility of appearances of the dead. It only says, that such appearances will not bring about *faith* in the human soul: but that they may not serve other ends in God's dealings with men, it does not assert. There is no gulf between the *earth* and Hades: and the very form of Abraham's answer, setting forth no impossibility in this second case, as in the former, would seem to imply its *possibility*, if requisite. We can hardly pass over the identity of the *name* Lazarus with that of him who *actually was recalled from the dead*, but whose return, far from persuading the Pharisees, was the immediate exciting cause of their crowning act of unbelief.

Chap. XVII. **1—10.**] Further discourses. The discourse appears to proceed onward from the foregoing.
1.] **τὰ σκ.** is perhaps owing to some *offence* which had happened;—the departure of the Pharisees in disgust, or some point in their conduct; such as the previous chapter alluded to. **ἀνένδεκτόν ἐστιν** = οὐκ ἐνδέχεται, ch. xiii. 33. **2.**] See Matt. xviii. 6, 7, and notes. **τῶν μικ. τ.**, perhaps the publicans and sinners of ch. xv. 1;—perhaps also, repeated with

ἕνα. 3 ᶻ προσέχετε ᵃ ἑαυτοῖς. ἐὰν ἁμάρτῃ ὁ ἀδελφός σου
ᵇ ἐπιτίμησον αὐτῷ, καὶ ἐὰν ᶜ μετανοήσῃ, ᵈ ἄφες αὐτῷ.
4 καὶ ἐὰν ᵉ ἑπτάκις τῆς ἡμέρας ᶠ ἁμαρτήσῃ ᶠ εἰς σὲ καὶ
ᵉ ἑπτάκις ᵍ ἐπιστρέψῃ πρός σε λέγων ᶜ Μετανοῶ, ᵈ ἀφήσεις
αὐτῷ. 5 καὶ εἶπαν οἱ ἀπόστολοι τῷ κυρίῳ ʰ Πρόσθες ἡμῖν
πίστιν. 6 εἶπεν δὲ ὁ κύριος Εἰ ἔχετε πίστιν ὡς ⁱ κόκκον
ⁱ σινάπεως, ἐλέγετε ἂν τῇ ᵏ συκαμίνῳ ταύτῃ ˡ Ἐκριζώθητι
καὶ ᵐ φυτεύθητι ἐν τῇ θαλάσσῃ, καὶ ὑπήκουσεν ἂν ὑμῖν.
7 τίς δὲ ἐξ ὑμῶν δοῦλον ἔχων ⁿ ἀροτριῶντα ἢ ᵒ ποιμαί-

ABDEF GHKL MSUV XΓΔΛ Πℵ 1. 33. 69

z ch. xii. 1. xxi. 34. Acts v. 35. xx. 28. Gen. xxiv. 6.
a Matt. iii. 9 reff.
b Mark viii. 32, 33 reff.
c Matt. iii. 2 reff.
d Matt. vi. 12 reff.
e Matt. xviii. 21, 22 only. Ps. cxviii. 164 al.
f Matt. xviii. 15 reff.
g ch. xxii. 32. Acts xiv. 15. Deut. xxx. 2.
h = ch. xii. 31 reff.
i Matt. xiii. 31 reff.
k here only. 1 Chron. xxvii. 28 al. see ch. xix. 4.
l Matt. xiii. 29. xv. 13. Jude 12 only. Jer. i. 10.
m Matt. xv. 13 reff.
n 1 Cor. ix. 10 bis only. Deut. xxii. 10.
o lit., 1 Cor. ix. 7 only. (Matt. ii. 6 al.) 1 Kings xxv. 16.

3. rec aft 1st εαν ins δε (*from Matt* xviii. 15), with A rel syr: om BDLXℵ 33 latt Syr [syr-jer] copt goth æth arm Clem₁ spec. αμαρτησῃ (|| *Matt*) DXΔΠ 69. rec adds εις σε (|| *Matt*), with D rel vulg-ed lat-*c e q* syr-ms arm-usc [Antch₁]: om ABLℵ 1 am(with fuld em forj gat jac mt tol) lat-*a b f ff*₂ *g*₁.₂ *i l* syrr [syr-jer] copt goth arm-zoh Clem₁ Damasc₁ spec. aft και εαν ins μεν A 67 evv-49-H.

4. rec αμαρτη (*repetn from ver* 3), with Fℵ rel Clem₁ Orig₁: txt ABDLXΔ vulg [Antch₁ Damasc₁] spec. (αναστησῃ 69.) ins εαν bef 2nd επτακις (*from above*) AKΠ lat-*b*; το D Clem₁. rec adds της ημερας (*from above*), with A rel vulg lat-*f g*₁.₂ syrr goth æth [Antch₁] spec: om BDLXℵ mt lat-*a b c i l q* syr-jer copt arm Clem₁ Orig₁ Vict-tun. rec (for προς) επι, with 1(e sil): txt ABDLXΛℵ latt syrr copt arm Clem [Antch].—om προς σε (*omd as unnecessary, cf Matt* xiii. 15: *Luke* xxii. 32: *Acts* iii. 19, *al: and then variously reinsd*) E rel mt lat-*f i* goth æth Orig₁ Damasc₁ spec. (Π? 33 def.) μετανοησω D¹. for αφησεις, αφες DHΛ latt Syr [syr-jer] copt-dz Clem.

5. (ειπαν, so BDLXℵ.)

6. ο δε ειπεν αυτοις, omg κυριος, D, simly lat-*a b c e ff*₂ *i* [*q*]. rec ειχετε, with DEGH latt: txt ABℵ rel. (εχητε M 248 Scr's g.) aft ελεγετε αν ins τω ορει τουτω μεταβα εντευθεν εκει και μετεβαινεν και (*Matt* xvii. 20) continuing τῃ συκαμινω μεταφυτευθητι εις την θαλασσαν D. om ταυτῃ (D)LXℵ copt. om 2nd αν A.

7. om εξ D-gr L latt. εχων bef υμων δουλον D.

reference to what took place, Matt. l. c. **3, 4.**] See on Matt. xviii. 15, 21, 22. The **προσέχετε ἑαυτ.** here is to warn them not to be too readily dismayed at σκάνδαλα, nor to meet them in a brother with an unforgiving spirit. **ἐπιτίμ.**] 'ἀγάπη begins with ἀληθεύειν,' Stier:—who remarks, that in the Church, as in the world, the love of many waxing cold,—not being strong or warm enough for this ἐπιτίμησον,—is the cause why offences abound. **5.**] **πρόσθ. ἡμ. πίστ.**, '*increase our faith*,' of the E. V., is not exact: **give us more faith**, is more literal and simpler. Wordsw.'s rendering, "Give faith in addition to our other privileges, powers, and virtues," is not so probable, seeing 1) that faith is not the crowning item in such a list, but the first and most elementary: and 2) that, had this been intended, it would most probably have been expressed πρόσθ. ἡμῖν καὶ πίστιν. This is the only example in the Gospels in which *the Apostles* are marked out as requesting or saying any thing to the Lord. They are amazed at the greatness of the faith which is to overcome σκάνδαλα and forgive ἁμαρτήματα as in vv. 3, 4:—and pray that *more faith* may be added to them. **6.**] See on Matt. (xvii. 20) xxi. 21. On this occasion some particular tree of the sort was close at hand, and furnished the instance, just as the Mount of Transfiguration in the former of those passages, and the Mount of Olives in the latter. **συκάμινος** is *the mulberry-tree;* not very common in Palestine, but still found there. It must not be confounded with συκομορέα, ch. xix. 4, which is the Egyptian fig. See note there. Notice the different tenses with **ἄν**: ἐλέγετε ἄν, *ye would say:* ὑπήκουσεν ἄν, *it would* (even while you were speaking) *have obeyed.* **ἐκριζώθ.**] 'Cum ipsis radicibus, in mari mansura. Tale quiddam fit ipsis fidelibus.' Bengel. **7—10.**] The connexion is,—'Ye are *servants* of your Master; and therefore endurance is required of you,—faith and trust to endure out your day's work before you enter into your rest. Your Master will enter into His, but

νοντα, ὃς εἰςελθόντι ἐκ τοῦ ἀγροῦ ἐρεῖ αὐτῷ Εὐθέως
p παρελθὼν q ἀνάπεσε, 8 ἀλλ' οὐχὶ ἐρεῖ αὐτῷ Ἑτοίμασον
r τί s δειπνήσω, καὶ t περιζωσάμενος u διακόνει μοι ἕως
φάγω καὶ πίω, καὶ μετὰ ταῦτα φάγεσαι καὶ πίεσαι σύ;
9 μὴ ἔχει v χάριν τῷ δούλῳ ὅτι ἐποίησεν τὰ w διαταχθέντα;
10 οὕτως καὶ ὑμεῖς, ὅταν ποιήσητε πάντα τὰ w διαταχθέντα
ὑμῖν, λέγετε ὅτι. δοῦλοι x ἀχρεῖοί ἐσμεν, ὃ y ὠφείλομεν
ποιῆσαι πεποιήκαμεν.
11 Καὶ ἐγένετο z ἐν τῷ πορεύεσθαι [αὐτὸν] εἰς Ἱερου-

p ch. xii. 37 reff.
q ch. xi. 37 reff.
r = Matt. xv. 32 ||. 1 Pet. v. 8.
s ch. xxii. 20. 1 Cor. xi. 25. Rev. iii. 20 only. Prov. xxiii. 1. Tobit viii. 1 (not ℵ) only.
t ch. xii. 35, 37 reff.
u = Mark x. 45 reff.
v 1 Tim. i. 12. 2 Tim. i. 3. Heb. xii. 28 only. 2 Macc. iii. 33.
w ch. iii. 13. Acts xxiii. 31. Judg. v. 9.
x Matt. xxv. 30 only. 2 Kings vi. 22. Ep. Jer. 17 (15) B only.
y = John xiii. 14. xix. 7 al.
z Matt. xiii. 4 reff.

ins *μη* bef *ερει* D lat-*e l* copt. rec om *αυτω*, with A rel goth Cypr$_1$: ins BDLXℵ **1**. 69 latt Syr syr-w-ast [syr-jer] copt æth arm. (DKMUΔΠ join *ευθ.* with *ερει* : ELΛ with *παρελθ.*) rec *αναπεσαι*, with AMΔ (1, e sil) 33. 69[1] [Antch$_1$], *αντπεσαι* L, *αναπαυσαι* X : *αναπεσον* Γ [(Chr$_1$)] : txt BDℵ rel.

8. om *ουχι* D lat-*a b c* (*e* ?) *f ff$_2$ i l q* Syr Cypr$_1$ Ambr. aft *ετοιμ.* ins *μοι* ℵ lat-*a b f q* [copt-ms]. aft *εως* ins *αν* AKLMXΠ 33 [Antch$_1$]. *συ* bef *και πιεσαι* D [Antch$_1$].

9. rec *χαριν* bef *εχει*, with A rel vulg lat-*b c f ff$_2$* syrr (goth) arm [Antch$_1$] : txt BDLℵ lat-*a e* copt æth Cypr$_1$. rec aft *τω δουλω* ins *εκεινω* (*cf ch* xii. 37, *and see ch* xiv. 31 *al*), with E rel vulg lat-*e f i* syr goth (æth) arm [Antch$_1$] Cypr Aug : pref KΠ : om ABDLX(ℵ) lat-*a b c ff$_2$ l q* copt Ambr.—om *τω δουλω* also ℵ[1](ins ℵ-corr[1]). rec aft *τα διαταχθεντα* ins *αυτω*, with DX 69 latt Syr copt æth Cypr$_1$: om AB ℵ-corr[1] rel lat-*e* syr [syr-jer arm] goth Antch$_1$. (ℵ[1] see below.) rec at end adds *ου δοκω*, with AD rel vulg lat-*b c* syrr goth [Antch$_1$] : om BLX ℵ-corr[1] **1** lat-*a e* [syr-jer] copt æth arm Cypr. (ℵ[1] see below.)

10. om *ουτως* to *διαταχθεντα* (*homœotel ?*) ℵ[1](ins ℵ-corr[1]). for *παντα* to *υμιν*, *οσα λεγω* D. om *παντα* ℵ-corr[1](ins ℵ[3a]) [lat-*a b e ff$_2$ i l* Cypr$_1$]. aft *παντα* ins *ταυτα* A 28. om *οτι* AX **1** latt (Syr æth ?) Bas$_1$(ins$_1$) Cypr$_2$. *αχρειοι* bef *δουλοι* U 69 Scr's a o [Bas$_1$(txt$_1$) Chr$_{sæpe}$ Antch] : *εσμεν* bef *αχρ.* D-gr 220(Sz) Syr Ign Philast. rec ins *οτι* bef *ο ωφειλομεν*, with X rel syrr : om ABDLℵ **1** latt [syr-jer] copt æth arm Orig$_1$[int$_1$] Epiph$_1$ Bas$_1$ Antch Cypr$_1$. *ωφειλαμεν* ℵ[1](txt ℵ-corr[1.3]).

11. om *αυτον* BLℵ.

your time will not yet come; and all the service which you can meanwhile do Him, is but that which is your bounden duty to do,—seeing that your body, soul, and spirit are His.' **7.**] **εὐθέως** in the E. V. is wrongly joined with **ἐρεῖ**: it corresponds to **μετὰ ταῦτα** in ver. 8. 'Construendum; *cito accumbe: cito* cupiunt *accumbere* qui missis cæteris officiis fidem sibi summam conferri oportere putant.' Bengel. **8.**] **ἕως φ. κ. π.**, **till I shall have eaten and drunken**: see ch. xii. 37, where a different assurance seems to be given. But our Lord is here speaking of what we in our state of *service* are to *expect;* there, of what in our state of *manumission* ('mensæ servos adhibere manumissionis erat species.' Grotius, citing from Ulpian) and *adoption*, the *wonders of His grace will confer on us.* Here the question is of *right;* there, of *favour.* **9.**] Our Lord is not laying down rules for the behaviour of an earthly master to his servants,—but (see above) is speaking of the rightful state of relation *between us, and Him whose we are, and whom we serve.* **10.**] This shews the sense of the parable, as applying to our own thoughts of ourselves, and the impossibility of any *claim* for our services to God. In Rom. vi. 23 (see also the foregoing verses) we have the true ground on which we look for eternal life set before us;—viz. as the *gift* of God *whose servants we are,*—not the *wages*, as in the case of sin, *whose we are not.* In the case of *men* this is different; a good servant is *εὔχρηστος* (Philem. 11), not *ἀχρεῖος*, i. e. *οὗ μὴ ἔχει τις χρείαν*,—Etym. Mag. See Acts xvii. 25. The case supposed introduces an argument à fortiori: '*how much more, when ye have failed in so many respects.*' 'Miser est quem Dominus *servum inutilem* appellat, Matt. xxv. 30; beatus qui se ipse.' Bengel. Thus closes the series of discourses which began with ch. xv. 1.

11—19.] Healing of ten lepers. It does not appear to what part of the last journey this is to be referred. There is no

σαλήμ, [a] καὶ αὐτὸς διήρχετο διὰ μέσον Σαμαρείας καὶ
Γαλιλαίας. 12 καὶ εἰςερχομένου αὐτοῦ εἴς τινα κώμην
[b] ἀπήντησαν [αὐτῷ] δέκα [c] λεπροὶ ἄνδρες, οἳ ἔστησαν
[d] πόῤῥωθεν· 13 καὶ αὐτοὶ [e] ἦραν [e] φωνὴν λέγοντες Ἰησοῦ
[f] ἐπιστάτα, ἐλέησον ἡμᾶς. 14 καὶ ἰδὼν εἶπεν αὐτοῖς
Πορευθέντες [g] ἐπιδείξατε ἑαυτοὺς τοῖς ἱερεῦσιν. καὶ
ἐγένετο [z] ἐν τῷ ὑπάγειν αὐτούς, ἐκαθαρίσθησαν. 15 εἷς ...αυτους F.
δὲ ἐξ αὐτῶν ἰδὼν ὅτι ἰάθη, [h] ὑπέστρεψεν [i] μετὰ φωνῆς ABDEG
μεγάλης [k] δοξάζων τὸν θεόν, 16 καὶ [l] ἔπεσεν ἐπὶ πρόσωπον HKLM SUVXΓ
παρὰ τοὺς πόδας αὐτοῦ [m] εὐχαριστῶν αὐτῷ· καὶ αὐτὸς ἦν ΔΛΠℵ 1. 33. 69
Σαμαρείτης. 17 [n] ἀποκριθεὶς δὲ ὁ Ἰησοῦς εἶπεν Οὐχὶ οἱ

a red., ch. v. 17 reff.
b Matt. xxviii. 9 reff.
c Matt. viii. 2 reff.
d Heb. xi. 13 only. Isa. xxxiii. 13.
e Acts iv. 24 only. Judg. xxi. 2 B. 1 Kings xxx. 4.
f ch. v. 5 reff.
g Matt. xvi. 1 reff. Isa. xxxvii. 26, but not =.
h ch. ii. 20 reff.
i Matt. xxiv. 31. Heb. v. 7.
k = Matt. v. 16 al. fr. Isa. xliii. 23.
l Matt. xvii. 6 reff. 2 Chron. vii. 3.
m ch. xviii. 11. John xi. 41. Acts xxvii. 35. Rom. xvi. 4 al.† Judith viii. 25.
n red., Matt. xi. 25 reff.

for *δια*, *ανα* **1.** 69 : om D. rec *μεσου*, with A rel : txt B(D)Lℵ (1. 69).

12. *υπηντησαν* Lℵ 1. 69. 239 Scr's g [Bas_1 $Damasc_1$] : *οπου ησαν* (*error*) D lat-*e*; *et ecce* lat-*a b c ff₂ i l q*. om *αυτω* B(D)L : ins Aℵ rel. *ανδρες* bef *λεπροι* D 157(Sz) latt syrr. om *οι εστησαν πορρωθεν* ℵ[1] [$Damasc_1$]. for *οι*, *και* D Syr copt[-schw-dz]. *ανεστησαν* BF.

13. for *αυτοι ηραν φωνην λεγοντες*, *εκραξαν φωνη μεγαλη* D (lat-*e*). ins *την* bef *φωνην* ℵ.

14. aft *ιδων* ins *αυτους* D 69 (latt) Syr æth arm. aft *αυτοις* ins *τεθεραπευεσθε* (but 4th *ε* marked for erasure) D. for *και εγ.*, *εγ. δε* D.

15. for *ιαθη*, *εκαθαρισθη* D 254 vulg lat-*b f l* Syr [syr-jer] goth(appy) æth. *μεγαλης* bef *φωνης* D vulg lat-*b c* [*ff₂ i l q*] copt.

16. ver is written twice by ℵ[1], but the 2nd copy marked for erasure. for *παρα*, *προς* D. om *ευχαριστων αυτω* D, om *αυτω* Λ latt(not *b q*). for *και αυτος ην*, *ην δε* D.

17. om 1st *δε* A. aft *ειπεν* ins *αυτοις* D. for *ουχι οι*, *ουτοι* D lat-*a b c e ff₂*

reason for supposing it to have been subsequent to what has just been related:—this is not implied. It may have been at the very beginning of the journey. From the circumstance that these lepers were a mixed company of Jews and Samaritans, **διὰ μέσον Σ. κ. Γ.** probably means '*between* Samaria and Galilee,' on the frontiers of both. Meyer supposes **αὐτός** to mean 'He for his part'—separate from the others going up to the feast, who would go direct through Samaria. Xen. has *διὰ μέσου δὲ ῥεῖ τούτων ποταμός*, i. e. '*between* these walls.' Anab. i. 4. 4. This seems to be ‖ with Matt. xix. 1. The journey mentioned there would lead Him *διὰ μέσ.* **Σ. κ. Γ.** **12. πόῤῥωθεν**] See Levit. xiii. 46: Num. v. 2. The Rabbinical prescriptions as to *the distance* are given in Wetstein. Their misery had broken down the national distinction, and united them in one company.

On the nature of leprosy and its significance, see on Matt. viii. 2. **14.**] One of our Lord's first miracles had been the healing of a leper; then He touched him and said, 'Be thou clean:' now He *sinks* as it were *the healing*, and keeps it in the background;—and why so? There may have been reasons unknown to us; but one we can plainly see, and that is, to bring out for the Church the lesson which the history yields. In their going away, in the absence of Jesus they are healed: what need to go back and give Him thanks? Here was a trial of their *love: faith* they had, enough to go, and enough to be cleansed: but *love* (with the one exception)—gratitude, they had not.

ἐπιδείξ.] See note on Matt. viii. 4.

ἐν τῷ ὑπ. αὐτ.] i. e. **while on their way**;—the meaning evidently being that they had not gone far, and that the whole took place within a short time. They had not been to the priests, as some suppose. **15.**] The **ἰδὼν ὅτι ἰάθη**, and **ὑπέστ. μ. φ. μεγ. δ. τ. θεόν**, set before us something immediate, and, I should be inclined to think, witnessed by the narrator. **16. αὐτ. ἦν Σαμ.**] Strauss supposes (and Hase, but doubtfully) from this, that the whole narrative arose out of a parable about Jews and Samaritans. Such an absurd notion is however not without its use for believers. Every miracle *is a parable:* our Lord did not

δέκα ἐκαθαρίσθησαν; οἱ δὲ ἐννέα ποῦ; 18 οὐχ [o] εὑρέθησαν
[h] ὑποστρέψαντες [p] δοῦναι [p] δόξαν τῷ θεῷ, εἰ μὴ ὁ [q] ἀλλο-
γενὴς οὗτος; 19 καὶ εἶπεν αὐτῷ [r] Ἀναστὰς πορεύου·
ἡ πίστις σου σέσωκέν σε.
20 [s] Ἐπερωτηθεὶς δὲ ὑπὸ τῶν Φαρισαίων πότε [t] ἔρχεται ἡ βασιλεία τοῦ θεοῦ, ἀπεκρίθη αὐτοῖς καὶ εἶπεν
Οὐκ ἔρχεται ἡ βασιλεία τοῦ θεοῦ [u] μετὰ [v] παρατηρήσεως,
R η βασ. ... 21 οὐδὲ ἐροῦσιν Ἰδοὺ ὧδε ἢ ἐκεῖ· ἰδοὺ γὰρ ἡ βασιλεία τοῦ
θεοῦ [w] ἐντὸς ὑμῶν ἐστίν. 22 εἶπεν δὲ πρὸς τοὺς μαθητὰς

o = Matt. i. 18. 2 Cor. v. 3. 1 Kings xiii. 15.
p John ix. 24 reff. Ps. lxv. 2.
q here only. Job xv. 19.
r Acts ix. 6. Gen. xxii. 3, 19.
s Matt. xii. 10. ch. ii. 46 al. Judg. i. 1.
t constr. pres., ver. 30. Matt. xi. 3. xvii. 11. John iv. 25. vi. 14.
u 2 Cor. viii. 4 al.
v here only +. Exod. xii. 42 Aq. (-ρεῖν, ch. vi. 7.)
w = here (Matt. xxiii. 26) only. Ps. cviii. 22.

i q [ουχ οι B(Tischdf N. T. Vat.) ev-y].—aft δεκα ins ουτοι AΠ 254 Scr's d p w. om 2nd δε AD lat-*a b c i l* [*q*] Syr copt Orig-int$_1$.

18. for ουχ to δουναι, εξ αυτων ουδεις ευρεθη υποστρεφων ος δωσει D, simly latt Ambr$_1$.

19. ins οτι bef η πιστις D latt[not *i*]. om last clause B.

21. rec ins ιδου bef εκει (*see ver* 23), with AD rel latt [syr] goth Orig$_1$: om BLℵ lat-*e ff$_2$ g$_{1,2}$ i l* arm. D adds μη πιστευσητε (|| *Matt Mark*). εστιν bef εντος υμων R[1] Petr.

22. for δε, ουν D 157. aft μαθητας ins αυτου AX vulg-ed(not am forj) lat-*a b c*

work mere feats of supernatural power, but *preached by His miracles* as well as by His discourses. **17.**] **Were not the ten cleansed? but** (of those ten) **the nine, where** (are they)? **18. ὁ ἀλλογ. οὗτ.**] The Samaritans were *Gentiles*;—not a *mixed race*, as is sometimes erroneously supposed. They had a *mixed religion*, but were themselves originally from other countries: see 2 Kings xvii. 24–41. There may have been a reason for the nine Jews not returning,—that they held the ceremonial duty imposed on them to be paramount, which the Samaritan might not rate so highly. That he was going to Mount Gerizim does not appear: from his being found with Jews, he probably would act as a Jew. **19.**] **σέσωκέν σε**—in a higher sense than the mere cleansing of his leprosy—*theirs* was merely the beholding of the brazen serpent with the outward eyes,—but his, with the eye of inward faith; and this faith saved him;—not only healed his body, but his soul.

20–37.] Prophetic answer to the Pharisees. In this discourse we have several sayings which our Lord afterwards repeated in His last prophetic discourse to the four apostles on Mount Olivet; but much also which is peculiar to Luke, and most precious (eine köstliche Perle, De Wette). **20.**] The question certainly is asked by the Pharisees, as all their questions were asked, with no good end in view: to entangle our Lord, or draw from Him some direct announcement which might be matter of accusation. **μετὰ παρατηρ.**] **with** (accompanied with) **anticipation,** or **observation.** The cognate verb is used ch. xiv. 1 of the Pharisees 'watching' Jesus. **21. οὐδὲ ἐρ. . . . .**] Its coming shall be so gradual and unobserved, that none during its waxing onward shall be able to point here or there for a proof of its coming. **ἰδοὺ γάρ**] **for behold the kingdom of God is (already) among you.** The misunderstanding which rendered these words '*within you,*' meaning this in a spiritual sense, '*in your hearts,*' should have been prevented by reflecting that they are addressed to the *Pharisees,* in whose hearts it certainly *was* not. Nor could the expression in this connexion well bear this spiritual meaning *potentially*—i. e. is in its nature, within your hearts. The words are too express and emphatic for this. We have the very expression, Xen. Anab. i. 10. 3,—ἀλλὰ καὶ ταύτην ἔσωσαν (οἱ Ἕλληνες) καὶ ἄλλα ὁπόσα **ἐντὸς αὐτῶν** καὶ χρήματα καὶ ἄνθρωποι ἐγένοντο πάντα ἔσωσαν:—see also John i. 26; xii. 35, both of which are analogous expressions. See the two renderings compared in Bleek's note. The kingdom of God was *begun among them,* and continues thus making its way in the world, without observation of men; so that whenever men can say 'lo here or lo there,'—whenever great '*revivals*' or 'triumphs of the faith' can be pointed to, they stand self-condemned as *not belonging to that kingdom.* Thus we see that every such marked event in the history of the Church is by God's own hand as it were *blotted* and *marred,* so as

x Matt. ix. 15 reff. y ch. v. 17 reff. z John viii. 56. 1 Pet. iii. 10, from Ps. xxxiii. 12. see Amos v. 18. a = Matt. viii. 19 reff. John xii. 19. b absol., Phil. iii. 12. Hag. i. 9. c Matt. xxiv. 27 reff. d ch. xxiv. 4 only. 2 Kings xxii. 15 Ed-vat. (not AB). Ps. cxliii. 6. Wisd. xi. 18 only. e ellips., Deut. xxv. 19. Job ii. 2 al. see ch. vii. 11 al.

ABDE GHKL MRSU VXΓΔΛ Πℵ 1. 33. 69

[x] Ἐλεύσονται [x] ἡμέραι ὅτε ἐπιθυμήσετε [y] μίαν τῶν [yz] ἡμερῶν
τοῦ υἱοῦ τοῦ ἀνθρώπου [z] ἰδεῖν, καὶ οὐκ ὄψεσθε. 23 καὶ
ἐροῦσιν ὑμῖν Ἰδοὺ ἐκεῖ ἢ ἰδοὺ ὧδε· μὴ [a] ἀπέλθητε μηδὲ
[b] διώξητε. 24 ὥσπερ γὰρ ἡ [c] ἀστραπὴ [ἡ] [d] ἀστράπτουσα
ἐκ [e] τῆς ὑπὸ τὸν οὐρανὸν εἰς [e] τὴν ὑπ' οὐρανὸν [f] λάμπει,
οὕτως ἔσται ὁ υἱὸς τοῦ ἀνθρώπου ἐν τῇ ἡμέρᾳ αὐτοῦ.
25 πρῶτον δὲ δεῖ αὐτὸν πολλὰ παθεῖν καὶ [g] ἀποδοκιμασθῆναι ἀπὸ τῆς γενεᾶς ταύτης. 26 καὶ [h] καθὼς ἐγένετο
ἐν ταῖς ἡμέραις Νῶε, οὕτως ἔσται καὶ ἐν ταῖς ἡμέραις τοῦ
υἱοῦ τοῦ ἀνθρώπου. 27 ἤσθιον, ἔπινον, ἐγάμουν, [i] ἐγα-
μίζοντο, [k] ἄχρι [k] ἧς [k] ἡμέρας εἰςῆλθεν Νῶε εἰς τὴν [l] κιβωτόν, καὶ ἦλθεν ὁ [m] κατακλυσμὸς καὶ [n] ἀπώλεσεν πάντας.

f Matt. v. 15, 16. xvii. 2. Acts xii. 7. 2 Cor. iv. 6 (bis) only. Prov. iv. 18. g Matt. xxi. 42 reff. h ch. vi. 31 al. fr. Eccl. v. 14. i Matt. xxii. 30 reff. k Matt. xxiv. 38 reff. l Matt. xxiv. 38. Heb. ix. 4. xi. 7. 1 Pet. iii. 20. Rev. xi. 19 only. Gen. vi. 14, &c. m Matt. as above, & 2 Pet. ii. 5 only. Gen. vi. 7, &c. n = Matt. xxi. 41.

(not *e f*) [syrr] copt æth. επιθυμησητε B¹MΛ 1 : for οτε επιθ., του επιθυμησαι υμας D 69 arm. aft ημερων ins τουτων D goth. om ιδειν D mt.

23. rec transp εκει and ωδε (*see ver* 21), with A(D)R rel : txt B²Lℵ copt.—for εκει, ωδε B¹(Tischdf). om η D[-gr] KLXΠ¹ 33. 69 : for η, και Mℵ Syr æth. for μηδε, μητε ℵ : om απελθητε μηδε B 69. (syr-cu contains Luke xvii. 23 to xxiv. 44.)

24. om 2nd η B(see table) LXΓℵ 1. 69 [arm] : ins ADR rel. rec (for υπο τον) υπ', with L rel : txt ABDKRΠℵ 33. om εις την υπ' ουρανον D Scr's e g ev-y. for λαμπει, αστραπτει D. rec aft εσται ins και (*to suit ver* 26 : *so also rec in Matt* xxiv. 27), with D lat-*b c e* [*i*] æth arm : om ABRℵ rel vulg lat-*a f ff*₂ [*l*] *q* syrr syr-cu copt goth. om εν τη ημερα αυτου (*homœotel,* πoυ *and* του : *had the clause been added, it wd have been* εν τη παρουσια αυτου, *cf Matt, and below : so also Mey*) BD lat-*a b c e i* æth : ins ARℵ rel vulg lat-*f* [*q*] syrr copt goth arm.

25. πολλα παθειν bef αυτον AKΠ lat-*e*.

26. rec ins του bef νωε, with 1(e sil) Scr's g : om ABDRℵ rel (Clem₁) Damasc Thl.

27. rec εξεγαμιζοντο (*Matt* xxiv. 38), with AR rel : txt BDLVXℵ 69¹. for ηλθεν ο, εγενετο D lat-*e*. for απωλεσεν, ηρεν (*Matt*) ℵ 248 Scr's g i. rec απαντας (*Matt*), with ARℵ rel : txt BDLX.

not to deceive us into thinking that the kingdom has come. So it was at the Pentecostal era:—so at that of Constantine;—so at the Reformation. The meaning 'among you,' includes of course the deeper and personal one 'within each of you,' but the two are not convertible.

22.] This saying is *taken up from* ἐντὸς ὑμῶν ἐστίν. '*He is among you, who is the Bridegroom,—the Son of Man;*' —during whose presence ye cannot mourn, but when He shall be taken from you, you shall wish in vain for one of these days of His presence. Stier (iii. 362) thinks this addressed to the Pharisees also, and to apply to their recognizing too late in their future misery the Messiahship of Jesus:—but this does not appear from the text. Meyer tries to prove this interpretation altogether wrong, from the ἐν τ. ἡμέραις τ. υἱ. τ. ἀνθ., ver. 26. But the words have the general meaning of *the days of the Son of Man's presence,* and this extends on to His *future* presence, or παρουσία, as well. Of course, if they *hereafter* desired to see one of the days of His presence, it would be a second or future presence.

23. καὶ ἐρ. ὑμ.] 'Ye shall not see one;—therefore do not run after false reports of my coming.' A warning to all so-called expositors, and followers of expositors, of prophecy, who cry ἰδοὺ ἐκεῖ and ἰδοὺ ὧδε, every time that war breaks out, or revolutions occur. See on these verses, 23, 24, Matt. xxiv. 23—27 and notes. **24. ἐκ τῆς . . . εἰς τὴν . . .**] Supply χώρας . . . χώραν. **25—30.**] The events which must precede the coming: and (1) ver. 25, as regards *the Lord Himself,*—His sufferings and rejection, primarily by this generation,—but in implication, by the world;—and (2) vv. 26—30, which unfold this implication as regards the whole world, which shall be in its state of carelessness and sensuality at that time: see notes on Matt. xxiv. 37—39. The example of *the days of Lot*

28 ὁμοίως [h] καθὼς ἐγένετο ἐν ταῖς ἡμέραις Λώτ· ἤσθιον,
ἔπινον, [o] ἠγόραζον, [o] ἐπώλουν, [p] ἐφύτευον, ᾠκοδόμουν· 29 ᾗ
δὲ ἡμέρᾳ ἐξῆλθεν Λὼτ ἀπὸ Σοδόμων, [q] ἔβρεξεν πῦρ καὶ
[r] θεῖον ἀπ' οὐρανοῦ καὶ ἀπώλεσεν πάντας· 30 κατὰ
τὰ αὐτὰ ἔσται ᾗ ἡμέρᾳ ὁ υἱὸς τοῦ ἀνθρώπου [s] ἀποκαλύπτεται. 31 ἐν ἐκείνῃ τῇ ἡμέρᾳ ὃς ἔσται [t] ἐπὶ τοῦ
[u] δώματος καὶ τὰ [v] σκεύη αὐτοῦ ἐν τῇ οἰκίᾳ, μὴ καταβάτω
ἆραι αὐτά, καὶ ὁ ἐν ἀγρῷ ὁμοίως μὴ [w] ἐπιστρεψάτω [x] εἰς
τὰ ὀπίσω. 32 [y] μνημονεύετε τῆς γυναικὸς Λώτ. 33 ὃς
ἐὰν [z] ζητήσῃ τὴν [a] ψυχὴν αὐτοῦ [b] περιποιήσασθαι, ἀπολέσει αὐτήν, καὶ ὃς ἂν ἀπολέσῃ, [c] ζωογονήσει αὐτήν.
34 λέγω ὑμῖν, ταύτῃ τῇ νυκτὶ ἔσονται δύο ἐπὶ κλίνης

o abs., Matt. xxi. 12. Rev. xiii. 17. Isa. xxiv. 2.
p Matt. xv. 13 reff.
q Matt. v. 45. ch. vii. 38, 44. James v. 17 bis. Rev. xi. 6 only. Gen. xix. 24. Ps. lxxvii. 27.
r Rev. ix. 17, 18 al4. Gen. l. c. Ezek. xxxviii. 22.
s = Rom. viii. 18. pres., ver. 20 reff.
t = Matt. xxiv. 17. Eph. i. 10 al.
u Matt. x. 27 reff.
v = Matt. xii. 29 ‖. Gen. xxxi. 37.
w = Matt. xii. 44. xxiv. 17 ‖ Mk. 2 Pet. ii. 22. Ezek. vii. 13.
x ch. iv. 62 reff.
y gen., John xv. 20 al. 1 Chron. xvi. 15. acc., Matt. xvi. 9. Isa. xliii. 18.
z = Matt. xii. 46, 47 reff.
a = Matt. xiv. 26 reff.
b Acts xx. 28. 1 Tim. iii. 13 only. Gen. xxxi. 18. Isa. xxxi. 5.
c Acts vii. 19. 1 Tim. vi. 13 only. Exod. i. 17, 18, 22. 4 Kings vii. 4 al.

28. rec (for *καθως*) *και ως*, with AD rel Clem$_1$ Iren-int$_1$: txt BLRXℵ 69 vulg lat-*f i* syr-cu.

29. om *δε* D lat-*a e* copt-wilk. transp *πυρ* and *θειον* ADKMΠ 69: om *και θειον* lat-*a b e ff*$_2$ [*i l q*] syr-cu [Eus$_1$] Iren-int$_1$. rec **απαντας**, with ARℵ rel: txt BDLΔΛ [Eus$_1$].

30. rec (for *τα αυτα*) *ταυτα*, with Aℵ[1] rel vulg lat-*b c e f* [*ff*$_2$ *i l q*]: *αυτα* R: txt (*cf ch* vi. 23) BDKXΠℵ[3a] lat-*a* syrr syr-cu copt æth Eus$_1$. for *η ημ. ο υι. τ. ανθρ.*, *εν τη ημερα του υιου του ανθρωπου η* D lat-*c ff*$_2$ *i l*, simly lat-*b q* Aug. *αποκαλυπτηται* B: *-λυπται* L: *αποκαλυφθη* D.

31. om *εν* D gr lat-*e*. aft *οικ.* ins *αυτου* ℵ. rec ins *τω* bef *αγρω*, with ADR rel: om BLℵ 69 goth. *επιστραφητω* D. om *εις τα* R[1](appy).

33. ins *δ αν* bef *εαν* ℵ[1](marked for erasure by ℵ-corr[1](appy)[3a]). for 1st clause, *os αν θεληση ζωογονησαι την ψυχην αυτου* D. rec (for *περιποιησασθαι*) *σωσαι* (*from ch* ix. 24 *al*), with ARℵ rel: txt BL lat-*b c i q*. for *και os*, *os δ'* (*see ch* ix. 24 *al*) BLℵ 69: txt ADR rel vss.—om *και* to *αυτην* X. rec (for *αν*) *εαν*, with AR rel: txt BDLℵ 69. for *απολεση*, *απολεσει* (*itacism?*) ALR S(Tischdf) ΓΔΛΠ[1]ℵ. rec adds *αυτην* (*ch* ix. 24 *al*), with A rel [latt syrr copt æth]: om BDRℵ **1. 33** lat-*a* arm.

34. *δυο* bef *εσονται* (*Matt* xxiv. 40) AKMRUΠ 69 lat-*q* syrr syr-cu goth æth [Bas$_1$]

is added here,—and thereby the sanction of the Lord of Truth given to another part of the sacred record, on which modern scepticism has laid its unhallowed hands. **28.**] Bornemann joins *ὁμοίως* with the former verse—but thus the parallelism (see ver. 29, end) is broken.

29.] **ἔβρεξεν**, impersonal, not *ὁ θεὸς ἔβρ.* That such an expression as *ὁ θεὸς βρέχει* is used Matt. v. 45, is no proof that when *βρέχει* is used impersonally the sacred name is to be supplied. Ver. **31** refers immediately to the example of Sodom just related. In Matt. xxiv. 16—18 it finds its place by a reference to the destruction of Jerusalem, see there.

32.] A solemn caution is here added, binding the warning to the example before,—**μὴ ἐπιστρεψάτω**—*remember her who did.* **33.**] See on Matt. x. 39, and ch. ix. 24. In connexion here, it leads the way to vv. 34, 35. **ζητήσῃ** should be rendered as a *futurus exactus*, as an aorist conjoined with a future always must be:—**shall have sought,** i. e. 'during his preceding life,'—**shall lose it** *then.* "**ζωογονήσει**, *vivipariet* (Acts vii. 19): an expressive word, derived from animal parturition, bringing forth to air and life what was before concealed in the womb. That day shall come as the pains of labour (*ὠδῖνες*) on a woman in travail (Matt. xxiv. 8): but to the saints of God it shall be the birth of the soul and body to life and glory everlasting. See St. Ignatius ad Rom. c. 6." Wordsw. **34—36.**] See on Matt. xxiv. 40, 41. Here, there are two references: (1) to the servants of the Lord in the midst of the world out of which they shall be separated: (2) to the separation of the faithful and unfaithful among *themselves.* Ver. **34** indicates a closer relationship than that of mere fellow-workmen, and

d Matt. vi. 24 reff. e Matt. xxiv. 40, 41 reff. f = Matt. iv. 11, 20. Judg. ii. 23. g Matt. xxiv. 41 only. Num. xi. 8. Judg. xvi. 21. Eccl. xii. 3, 4 only. h Matt. xxii. 34 reff. i = Matt. xiv. 12. Heb. xiii. 11. 1 Kings xxxi. 10, 12. k Matt. xxiv. 28. Rev. iv. 7. viii. 13. xii. 14 only. Job ix. 26. Prov. xxx. 17. l ch. xii. 1. xiii. 34. Matt. xxiii. 37. xxiv. 31 ‖ Mk. Mark i. 33 only. 2 Chron. xx. 26. m constr., here only. Jer. xxxiv. (xxvii.) 10. πρός, see ch. xii. 41. n 2 Cor. iv. 1, 16. Gal. vi. 9. Eph iii. 13. 2 Thess. iii. 13 only. L.P.† Prov. xiii. 11 Theod.

μιᾶς, [d] εἷς [e] παραλημφθήσεται καὶ ὁ [d] ἕτερος [f] ἀφεθήσεται. Q ται και ...
35 ἔσονται δύο [g] ἀλήθουσαι [h] ἐπὶ τὸ [h] αὐτό, ἡ [d] μία [e] παρα- ABDE
λημφθήσεται, ἡ δὲ [d] ἑτέρα [f] ἀφεθήσεται. 37 καὶ ἀπο- GHKL MQRSU
κριθέντες λέγουσιν αὐτῷ Ποῦ, κύριε; ὁ δὲ εἶπεν αὐτοῖς VXΓΔ ΛΠℵ
Ὅπου τὸ [i] σῶμα, ἐκεῖ καὶ οἱ [k] ἀετοὶ [l] ἐπισυναχθήσονται. 1. 33. 69
XVIII. 1 Ἔλεγεν δὲ [καὶ] παραβολὴν αὐτοῖς [m] πρὸς
τὸ δεῖν πάντοτε προσεύχεσθαι αὐτοὺς καὶ μὴ [n] ἐγκακεῖν,

Ambr: εσ. επ. κλ. μ. δυο D Scr's d. om μιας B lat-*c*. rec ins ο bef εις (*Matt*), with Bℵ (1. 69, e sil) [Eus_1]: om ADR rel Bas_1 [Cyr_1]. παραλαμβανεται D-gr GKΠ. for αφεθησεται, αφιεται DK goth.

35. om ver (*homœotel*) ℵ[1](ins ℵ-corr[1]) [lat-*l*]. rec δυο bef εσονται, with AQR rel vulg lat-*f i* [syrr]: txt BDL ℵ-corr[1] [syr-cu]. Steph om η (bef μια) (*so Matt* xxiv. 41), with AQ rel copt-wilk arm [Bas_1] Thl: ins BDR ℵ-corr[1] 1. 69 lat-*a* copt-schw. rec (for η δε) και η (*from foregoing and Matt*), with ADQ rel latt: txt BLR ℵ-corr[1] 69 [Eus_1].

[**36.** elz δυο εσονται εν τω αγρω ο εις παραληφθησεται και ο ετερος αφεθησεται (*from Matt* xxiv. 40; *the futures adapted to the context here. The* MS *authority against it is too weighty to suppose an omission through homœotel*), with (DU) 33. 69 latt syrr syr-cu arm Victorin $Ambr_1$ Aug_1 Bede: om ABQRℵ rel lat-g_1 copt goth æth Bas_1 Thl Euthym Op_1 Max_1.—om εσονται D Scr's h i evv-H-z vss; for εν τω αγρω, εγρω (sic) D[1], εν αγρω D-corr[1 or 2]; om ο (bef εις) DU.]

37. om αυτω D. rec (aft εκει) om και, with A D-gr QR rel am(with other mss) lat-*a c e f i* Syr syr-cu goth [æth Cyr_1]: ins BLUΛℵ 69 vulg-ed lat-*b* D-lat syr copt arm Eus_1 Bas_1 Thl $Ambr_1$. rec (for επισυναχθ.) συναχθησονται, with ADR rel latt syrr syr-cu copt Eus [Cyr_1]: txt BLQℵ arm.—placed in rec aft εκει (*as Matt* xxiv. 28), with ADQR rel [latt syrr syr-cu æth Cyr_1]: txt BLℵ 69 ev-y arm.

Chap. XVIII. 1. om και BLMℵ 69 lat-*a b c* (copt æth, appy) $Orig_2$ [Bas_1]: ins ADQ rel vulg lat-*e f* ff_2 $g_{1.2}$ *i* syrr syr-cu goth arm [Chr_1 $Antch_1$]. rec om αυτους (*prob from the* generality *of the parable that follows*), with DEGHΛ ℵ[3a](but restored) (1, e sil) $Orig_1$ [Eus_1 $Antch_1$: Tischdf gives also Bas_1 Chr_1 $Damasc_1$ for the omn, not for the insn]: ins ABQR S(Tischdf) ℵ[1] rel copt arm $Orig_1$ Bas Chr Damasc. rec εκκακειν, with R rel $Orig_2$ Eus_1 [Bas_1 $Damasc_1$]: ενκ. AB[1]DHKQℵ 69: txt B[2]LUΔΠ.

sets forth the division of even families in that day. **37.**] **ποῦ**, not '*how?*' (Kuinoel) but literal—**where shall this happen?** The disciples know not the univercality of this which our Lord is announcing to them, and which His dark and awful saying proclaims, see note on it, Matt. xxiv. 28. Observe, there is *not a word*, except so far as the greater coming includes the lesser, in all this, of the destruction of Jerusalem. The future παρουσία of the Lord is the *only subject*: and thus it is an entirely distinct discourse from that in Matt. xxiv., or our ch. xxi.

Chap. XVIII. 1—8.] The unjust judge. This parable, though not perhaps spoken in immediate unbroken sequence after the last discourse, evidently arose out of it:—perhaps was the fruit of a conversation with the disciples about the day of His coming and the mind with which they must expect it. For observe that in its *direct* application it is ecclesiastical; and not individual, but by a legitimate accommodation. The widow is the Church; the judge, her God and Father in heaven. The argument, as in the parable of the steward τῆς ἀδικίας, so in this of the κριτὴς τῆς ἀδικίας, is *à fortiori*: 'If such be the power of earnest entreaty, that it can win right even from a man sunk in selfishness and fearing neither God nor men, how much more will the right be done by the just and holy God in answer to the continued prayers of his elect:' even though, when this very right is asserted in the world by the coming of the Son of Man, He may hardly find among his people the power to believe it – though few of them will have shewn this unweariedness of entreaty which the poor widow shewed?

1.] **πρός, with reference to.** **πάντοτε**] See 1 Thess. v. 17. The *mind* of prayer, rather than, though of

2 λέγων Κριτής τις ἦν ἔν τινι πόλει τὸν θεὸν μὴ φοβούμενος καὶ ἄνθρωπον μὴ [o] ἐντρεπόμενος. 3 χήρα δὲ ἦν ἐν τῇ
πόλει ἐκείνῃ, καὶ ἤρχετο πρὸς αὐτὸν λέγουσα [p] Ἐκδίκησόν
με ἀπὸ τοῦ [q] ἀντιδίκου μου. 4 καὶ οὐκ ἤθελεν [r] ἐπὶ χρόνον,
μετὰ ταῦτα δὲ εἶπεν ἐν ἑαυτῷ Εἰ καὶ τὸν θεὸν οὐ φοβοῦμαι
καὶ ἄνθρωπον οὐκ [o] ἐντρέπομαι, 5 διά γε τὸ [s] παρέχειν
μοι [s] κόπον τὴν χήραν ταύτην, [p] ἐκδικήσω αὐτήν, ἵνα μὴ
[t] εἰς τέλος ἐρχομένη [u] ὑπωπιάζῃ με. 6 εἶπεν δὲ ὁ κύριος
Ἀκούσατε τί ὁ κριτὴς [v] τῆς ἀδικίας λέγει· 7 ὁ δὲ θεὸς οὐ
μὴ [wx] ποιήσῃ τὴν [xy] ἐκδίκησιν τῶν [z] ἐκλεκτῶν αὐτοῦ τῶν
[a] βοώντων αὐτῷ [b] ἡμέρας καὶ [b] νυκτός, καὶ [c] μακροθυμεῖ

o = Matt. xxi. 37 reff.
p here bis. Rom. xii. 19. 2 Cor. x. 6. Rev. vi. 10. xix. 2 only. Ps. xxxvi. 28.
q ch. xii. 58. Matt. v. 25 bis. 1 Pet. v. 8 only. 1 Kings ii. 10.
r Acts xviii. 20. Rom. vii. 1 al.
s Matt. xxvi. 10 ‖ Mk. Gal. vi. 17. Sir. xxix. 4 Aℵ.
t Matt. x. 22 reff. Ps. cii. 9.
u = here (1 Cor. ix. 27) only +. Aristoph. Pax 533, πόλεις . . . δαιμονίως ὑπωπιασμέναι. (-πιον, Prov. xx. 30.)
v constr., ch. xvi. 8 reff.
w = John v. 27. Jude 15.
x here bis. Acts vii. 24. Judg. xi. 36. Mic. v. 15.
y as above (x). ch. xxi. 22. Rom. xii. 19 al.
z Matt. xxiv. 31. Col. iii. 12. Tit. i. 1. Ps. cv. 23.
a w. dat., here only. (John i. 23 reff.)
b Mark v. 5 reff.
c and constr., Matt. xviii. 26, 29. James v. 7. Sir. xviii. 11. xxxii. (xxxv.) 18. (-μός, Acts xxvi. 3.)

2. om λεγων D 1 Syr syr-cu $Orig_1$ Bas_1. for τινι, τη DLX 33[τινι τη].

3. elz aft χηρα δε ins τις, with Λ 1 latt copt [Syr syr-cu syr-jer æth arm $Hipp_1$] : om ABDQRℵ rel lat-*e* syr goth Bas_1 Chr_1 $Damasc_1$.

4. rec ηθελησεν, with E rel: txt ABDLQRXΛℵ 1. 33. 69 $Hipp_1$ [Bas_1] Chr_1 $Damasc_1$. aft χρονον ins τινα D. rec δε bef ταυτα, with ADRℵ rel syr: txt BLQ. for ειπεν εν εαυτω, ηλθεν εις εαυτον και λεγει D (æth Vig). om 2nd και D lat-*a b c ff*$_2$ *i* [*l q*] Syr syr-cu [syr-jer]. for και ανθρωπον ουκ, ουδε ανθρωπον BLXℵ latt $Hipp_1$: txt ADQR rel [lat-*q* goth Bas_1 Chr_1 $Damasc_1$].

5. παρενοχλειν ℵ[1] [($Hipp_1$)]. κοπους E[1]GRℵ[1] 1. 69 Scr's c f i s[1]. ins απελθων bef εκδικησω D.

6. om ακουσατε Λ[1] ℵ[1](ins ℵ-corr[1]).

7. rec ποιησει, with AEHKLRSΛ [Mac_1] $Antch_1$: txt BDQℵ rel [Bas_1 Chr_1 $Damasc_1$]. rec (for αυτω) προς αυτον, with AR rel [Mac_1 Bas_1 Chr_1 Antch $Damasc_1$]: txt BLQℵ lat-*e*.—βοωντων αυτων, omg των, D-gr. transp ημερας and νυκτος D Scr's c [Mac_1 $Antch_1$]. rec μακροθυμων, with R(Tischdf, expr) rel lat-*a b c ff*$_2$ *i* [*l q*] syrr [$Damasc_1$]: txt ABDLQXΠℵ 1 lat-*e* syr-cu goth(appy) arm Chr_1 $Antch_2$.

course including, the outward act, is here intended. The earnest desire of the heart is prayer. **ἐγκακεῖν** (= ἐκκακεῖν, rec.: see note 2 Cor. iv. 1)—**to languish,**—to give up through the weight of overpowering evil. **2.**] See Deut. xvi. 18 and Matt. v. 21, 22. **τὸν θ. μὴ φ. κ. ἄνθ. μὴ ἐντ.**] A common form of expression for an unprincipled and reckless person, see instances in Wetstein. **3. ἐκδίκ.**] **deliver me from**—the justice of her cause being presupposed—this adversary being her oppressor on account of her defenceless situation, and she wanting a sentence from the judge to stop his practices. **4.**] **ἐπὶ χρ. . . . . for some time,** not, '*for a long time.*' τλῆτε, φίλοι, καὶ μείνατ' ἐπὶ χρόνον, Il. β. 299:—**for a while,** E. V. The point of this part of the parable is, the extortion of *right* from *such a man* by importunity. *His act* was not an act of justice, but of injustice; his very ἐκδίκησις was ἀδικία, because he did it from *self-regard,* and *not from a sense of duty.* He, like the steward above, was τῆς ἀδικίας,—*belonging to, being of,* the iniquity which prevails in the world. **5.**] **εἰς τέλος** belongs to **ἐρχομένη,** as in E. V., but has a stronger force than there—**lest coming for ever, she . . . ὑπωπιάζῃ,** from ὑπώπιον, the part of the cheek immediately beneath the eyes, signifies literally **to smite in the face;**—and proverbially (see reff.), **to mortify** or **incessantly annoy.** It answers exactly to the Latin *obtundo,* which Terence has in this sense, '*Ne me obtundas hac de re sæpius,*' Adelph. i. 2. 33; and al. fr.—Livy, '*Neque ego obtundam, sæpius eadem nequicquam agendo,*' ii. 15. The Greek word does not appear to be any where used in this sense;—so that the use of it here may be a Latinism, as Grotius thought. Meyer interprets it literally—'*lest at last she should become desperate and come and strike me in the face.*' It has been observed that the Apostles acted from this very motive when they besought the Lord to send away the Syrophœnician woman,—'for she *cried after them.*' Matt. xv. 23. **6.**] On **ὁ κρ. τ. ἀδ.** see above, and on ch. xvi. 9. **7.**] The poor

ἐπ' αὐτοῖς; 8 λέγω ὑμῖν ὅτι [wx] ποιήσει τὴν [xy] ἐκδίκησιν αὐτῶν ἐν [d] τάχει. [e] πλὴν ὁ υἱὸς τοῦ ἀνθρώπου ἐλθὼν [f] ἆρα
εὑρήσει [g] τὴν πίστιν ἐπὶ τῆς γῆς; 9 Εἶπεν δὲ καὶ [h] πρός
τινας τοὺς [i] πεποιθότας ἐφ' ἑαυτοῖς ὅτι εἰσὶν δίκαιοι καὶ
[k] ἐξουθενοῦντας τοὺς λοιπούς, τὴν παραβολὴν ταύτην·
10 Ἄνθρωποι δύο [l] ἀνέβησαν εἰς τὸ ἱερὸν προσεύξασθαι, εἷς
Φαρισαῖος καὶ ὁ ἕτερος τελώνης. 11 ὁ Φαρισαῖος σταθεὶς ...ο ετερος R.
πρὸς ἑαυτὸν ταῦτα προσηύχετο· [m] Ὁ θεός, [n] εὐχαριστῶ

ABDE GHKL MQSUV ΧΓΔΛ Πℵ 1. 33. 69

d N. T. always w. ἐν, Acts xii. 7. Rom. xvi. 20. Rev. i. 1 al. Deut. xxviii. 20.
e = Matt. xi. 22. Judg. iv. 9.
f Gal. ii. 7 (ἆρά γε, Acts viii. 30. Gen. xxvi. 9 Ed-vat. [B def. ἆρα γε F]) only.
g Acts vi. 7. 2 Tim. v. 8.
h = ch. xii. 41. xix. 9 al.
i Mark x. 24 reff.
k ch. xxiii. 11. Rom. xiv. 3, 10 al. L.P. Prov. i. 7.
l = John vii. 14. Acts iii. 1. Isa. ii. 3.
m voc., Matt. xi. 26 reff.
n ch. xvii. 16 reff.

εν αυτοις D-gr latt.

8. ins ναι bef λεγω GMR 69 copt arm Mac_1 $Antch_1$ $Iren\text{-}int_1$. om οτι DG 69 tol[1] lat-*b c ff₂ i l* Mac_1 $Iren\text{-}int_1$. αρα bef ο υι. τ. ανθ. ελθων D: om αρα 243. om την (bef πιστιν) D 240-4 arm.

9. om 1st και A rel fuld[2] lat-*b c e l q* syr syr-cu coptt goth Bas_1: ins BDLMQRXΔℵ 1. 33 vulg [lat-*a f*]. εξουθενουντες B 259 Scr's d g: εξουδ. ℵ. aft λοιπους ins ανθρωπους and om την παραβολην ταυτην D.

10. δυο bef ανθρωποι D latt Syr syr-cu [æth]. rec ins ο bef εἷς, with AQℵ rel [coptt arm $Orig_1$ Bas_1]: om BDRX. for ο ετερος, εἷς D lat-*c* [*e ff₂ q*] $Cypr_1$ [Opt].

11. aft 1st ο ins δε QX copt. ταυτα bef προς εαυτον BLℵ[3a] 1 vulg lat-*e* [syr-jer] arm $Orig_1$ $Cypr_1$: om πρ. εαυτ. ℵ[1] [lat-*b c f ff₂ i l q* sah æth.—for προς, καθ D.] προσηυξατο A[Π] 1.

widow in this case (the forsaken Church, contending with her adversary the devil, 1 Pet. v. 8) has this additional claim, in which the right of her cause consists,—that she is the Elect of God,—His Beloved. **ἡμέρας κ. νυκτός**] This answers to the πάντοτε in ver. 1, but is an amplification of it. **κ. μακροθυμεῖ . . . . . . and He delays his vengeance in their case:—and He, in their case, is long-suffering.** '*Est in hac voce dilationis significatio, quæ ut debitori prodest, ita gravis est ei qui vim patitur.*' Grotius. The rec. reading, **μακροθυμῶν**, conveys the same meaning, **καί** being understood as καίπερ. This is perhaps what the E. V. means by '*though He bear long with them,*' which is ambiguous as it stands. The μακροθ. has no doubt a *general reference* also to God's dealing with man: see 2 Pet. iii. 9, 15.

8.] **ἐν τάχει** will not bear the meaning '*swiftly,*' i. e. '*suddenly, when it comes,*' but (see reff.) is **shortly—soon, speedily,** as E. V. And this is no inconsistency with μακροθυμεῖ: see 2 Pet. iii. 8, 9. **πλὴν . . . .**] See the beginning of this note. This can hardly be, as Meyer interprets it, that the painful thought suddenly occurs to the Lord, how many there will be even at His coming who will not have received Him as the Messiah: for **ἡ πίστις**, though 'faith' generally, is yet here faith *in reference to the object of the parable*—faith which has endured in prayer without fainting. Or the meaning may be general and objective; as in reff.

9—14.] The Pharisee and the Publican. This parable is spoken not *to* the Pharisees, for our Lord would not in their presence have chosen a Pharisee as an example: nor *concerning* the Pharisees, for then it would have been *no parable*—but to the people, and with reference to some among them (then and always) **τοὺς πεπ. ὅτι εἰσὶν δίκ.**, who trusted in themselves that they were righteous, and despised other men. The parable describes an every day occurrence: the parabolic character is given by the concurrence and grouping of the two, and by the fact that each of these represents psychologically a class of persons.

9.] **πρός**, to, not *concerning*: it was concerning them, it is true:—but this word expresses that it was spoken *to* them. The usage of πρός in ver. 1 is no example for the sense *concerning*, for it is not there so used of *persons*, but *with a neuter article and infinitive*: εἶπεν πρὸς αὐτοὺς παρ. is too general a phrase, to allow of any other interpretation than the ordinary one, where the context will bear it. **πεποιθ. ἐφ' ἑαυτ.**, not, '*were persuaded of themselves,*' as Greswell renders; but as E. V., **trusted in themselves**: see reff. **10, 11.**] **πρὸς ἑαυτόν** belongs to **προσηύχ.** (cf. Mark xiv. 4), not to **σταθείς**: that would be καθ' ἑαυτόν, see James ii. 17. **He stood** (in the ordinary place), **and prayed thus with himself,** as E. V.,—'*apud animum suum:*'—such a prayer he would not dare to put up aloud (Meyer). The Church has ad-

σοι ὅτι οὐκ εἰμὶ ὥσπερ οἱ [o] λοιποὶ τῶν ἀνθρώπων, [p] ἅρπαγες, ἄδικοι, [q] μοιχοί, ἢ καὶ ὡς οὗτος ὁ τελώνης·
12 [r] νηστεύω [s] δὶς τοῦ [t] σαββάτου, [u] ἀποδεκατῶ πάντα ὅσα [v] κτῶμαι.
13 καὶ ὁ τελώνης μακρόθεν ἑστὼς οὐκ ἤθελεν οὐδὲ τοὺς ὀφθαλμοὺς [w] ἐπᾶραι εἰς τὸν οὐρανόν, ἀλλ' ἔτυπτεν [[x] εἰς] τὸ [y] στῆθος ἑαυτοῦ λέγων [m] Ὁ θεός, [z] ἱλάσθητί μοι [a] τῷ [b] ἁμαρτωλῷ.
14 λέγω ὑμῖν, [c] κατέβη οὗτος [d] δεδικαιωμένος εἰς τὸν οἶκον αὐτοῦ [e] παρ' ἐκεῖνον.

P μοι τω ...

o constr., Rev. ix. 20. xii. 17. xx. 5. p Matt. vii. 15. 1 Cor. v. 10, 11. vi. 10 only. Gen. xlix. 27 only. q 1 Cor. vi. 9. Heb. xiii. 4 (James iv. 4 v. r.) only. Job xxiv. 15. r Matt. iv. ? reff. s Mark xiv. 30 reff. t = Mark xvi. 9. 1 Cor. xvi. 2.

u Matt. xxiii. 23. ch. xi. 42. Heb. vii. 5 only. Gen. xxviii. 22. v Matt. x. 9 reff. w ch. vi. 20. John vi. 5. xvii. 1. Ezek. xviii. 6. see Isa. li. 6. x Matt. xxvii. 30. Prov. xxvi. 22. y ch. xxiii. 48. John xiii. 25. xxi. 20. Rev. xv. 6 only. Exod. xxviii. 23 (29). z constr., here (Heb. ii. 17) only. Ps. xxiv. 11. a ch. vi. 24. xi. 46. Rev. iii. 17. b Matt. ix. 13. Prov. xi. 31. c Mark xiii. 15. Acts viii. 38 al. 3 Kings xx. (xxi.) 16. d = here only in Gospp. Acts xiii. 39 (Paul). Rom. ii. 13 and (Paul) passim. James ii. 21, 24, 25. Gen. xxxviii. 26. e = ch. xiii. 2, 4. Rom. xiv. 5 al.

for ωσπερ, ως DLQ Orig$_3$ [Cyr$_1$ Antch$_1$]. ο τελωνης bef ουτος AK[Π] lat-*e* Cypr$_1$ Aug$_3$ Vict-tun.

12. αποδεκατευω Bℵ[1].

13. for και ο, ο δε BGLℵ 69 lat-*e* Syr syr-cu coptt [æth Antch$_1$] Cypr$_1$ Aug$_2$ [Vict-tun]. rec εις τον ουρανον bef επαραι, with AD rel vulg lat-*a* syrr [syr-cu arm Bas$_1$ Ambr$_1$] Cypr$_1$: txt BLQXℵ 33 lat-*b c* [*ff*$_2$] *q* [syr-jer æth] coptt goth. om 2nd εις (*as unnecessary; see also ch* xxiii. 48, *where no* εις *is insd : it hardly can have been insd to suit Matt* xxvii. 30) BDKLQX[Π]ℵ 1. 33 latt arm Orig$_1$ Cyr$_2$ Antch$_1$ Cypr$_1$: ins A rel syrr syr-cu coptt goth [Bas$_1$]. rec (for εαυτου) αυτου, with ADℵ rel [Bas$_1$ Antch$_1$]: om 1 : txt B(sic : see table) Q Orig$_1$. om ο θεος ℵ[1].

14. aft υμιν ins οτι KQU[Π] lat-*a b c f ff*$_2$ *i l* [*q*] syrr syr-cu [syr-jer] coptt Antch$_1$ Hil$_1$. om εις τον οικον αυτου D sah.—εαυτου BL[2]. rec (for παρ εκεινον) η εκεινος (*gloss : παρ' εκ. being misunderstood, as e.g. by* vulg, *which renders it* 'ab illo'), with 69 arm [Antch$_1$]; η γαρ εκεινος (*combination of the two,* ΓΑΡ *being a mistake for* ΠΑΡ) APQ rel syr goth Bas$_1$-ms : μαλλον παρ' εκεινον τον φαρισαιον (*gloss*)

mirably fitted to this parable the declaration of thankfulness in 1 Cor. xv. 9, 10 (the two being the Epistle and Gospel for the Eleventh Sunday after Trinity), also made *by a Pharisee,* and also on the ground '*that he was not as other men :*'—but how different in its whole spirit and effect! There, in the deepest humility, he ascribes it to the *grace of God* that he laboured more abundantly than they all;—**yet,** *not I,* **but the grace of God that was with me.** **12. νηστ. δὶς τ. σ.**] This was a *voluntary* fast, on the Mondays and Thursdays; the only prescribed fast in the year being the great day of atonement, see Levit. xvi. 29: Num. xxix. 7. So that he is boasting of his *works of supererogation.* **ἀποδ. πάντα**] Here again, the law perhaps (but cf. Abraham's practice, Gen. xiv. 20; and Jacob's, Gen. xxviii. 22) only required tithe of the fruit of the field, and the produce of the cattle: see on Matt. xxiii. 23. **κτῶμαι**] Not *I possess,* which would be κέκτημαι—but **I acquire;—of all my increase**: see Deut. xiv. 22. His speech shews admirably what his πεποίθησις ἐφ' ἑαυτῷ was. **13.**] **μακρόθεν**—far from the Pharisee;—a contrast in spirit to the other's *thanks* that he was not as other men, is furnished by the poor Publican in his humility acknowledging this by an *act.* **οὐδὲ τ. ὀφθ.**] Another contrast,—for we must here suppose that the Pharisee prayed with all significance of gesture, with eyes and hands uplifted (see Matt. vi. 5). There is a slight but true difference also in **σταθείς** of the Pharisee—'being put in position' (answering to 'being seated' of the other usual posture), and **ἑστώς** of the publican, —'standing;'—coming in merely and remaining, in no studied place or posture. So Tacitus, Hist. iv. 72, '*stabant conscientia flagitii mœstæ fixis in terram oculis :*'—see also Ezra ix. 6. **ἔτυπ. [εἰς] τ. στ.**] See ch. xxiii. 48, '*præ dolore animi : ubi dolor, ibi manus.*' Bengel. There may be a stress on **τῷ** bef. **ἁμαρτ.**, '*me the sinner.*' Gresw. But see reff., where, as probably here, the art. is generic. It seems to me that any emphatic comparison here would somewhat detract from the solemnity and simplicity of the prayer (agst. Stier, iii. 384, edn. 2). The **τῷ** rather implies, not comparison with others, but intense self-abasement: "sinner that I am." Nor are we to find any doctrinal meanings in **ἱλάσθ.**: WE *know* of *one only way,* in which the prayer could be accomplished: but the words here *have no reference to that, nor could they have.* **14.**] The sense is,

f Matt. xxiii. 12 reff. g Matt. vii. 6 al. h ch. i. 41, 44 reff. 1 Macc. i. 64. i ‖ Mk. Mark viii. 22 al. k Matt. xii. 16 reff. l = Mark v. 37 reff. m ‖ Mt. reff. n Matt. v. 18 reff. o ch. viii. 13. 2 Cor. vi. 1.

ὅτι πᾶς ὁ [f] ὑψῶν ἑαυτὸν [f] ταπεινωθήσεται, ὁ δὲ [f] ταπεινῶν I_d νωθησεται ο δε... F εαυτον υψ....
ἑαυτὸν [f] ὑψωθήσεται.
15 Προσέφερον δὲ αὐτῷ καὶ [g] τὰ [h] βρέφη, ἵνα αὐτῶν
[i] ἅπτηται· ἰδόντες δὲ οἱ μαθηταὶ [k] ἐπετίμων αὐτοῖς. ...ιδοντες Q.
16 ὁ δὲ Ἰησοῦς προσεκαλέσατο αὐτὰ λέγων [l] Ἄφετε τὰ ABDEF
παιδία ἔρχεσθαι πρός με, καὶ μὴ [m] κωλύετε αὐτά· τῶν GHI_dK LMPS
γὰρ τοιούτων ἐστὶν ἡ βασιλεία τοῦ θεοῦ. 17 [n] ἀμὴν λέγω UVXΓΔ ΛΠℵ
ὑμῖν, ὃς ἂν μὴ [o] δέξηται τὴν βασιλείαν τοῦ θεοῦ ὡς 1. 33. 69
παιδίον, οὐ μὴ εἰσέλθῃ εἰς αὐτήν.

p = Matt. xii. 10 al. q ‖ Mt. reff. r Matt. xxv. 34 reff. Num. xxvi. 55. s = ‖ Mk. reff. t Exod. xx. 12—16. Deut. vi. 16—20. u ‖ Mt. reff.

18 Καὶ [p] ἐπηρώτησέν τις αὐτὸν ἄρχων λέγων Διδάσκαλε
ἀγαθέ, τί ποιήσας [q] ζωὴν [q] αἰώνιον [r] κληρονομήσω; 19 εἶπεν
δὲ αὐτῷ ὁ Ἰησοῦς Τί με [s] λέγεις ἀγαθόν; οὐδεὶς ἀγαθός,
εἰ μὴ εἷς θεός. 20 τὰς ἐντολὰς οἶδας, [t] Μὴ μοιχεύσῃς,
μὴ φονεύσῃς, μὴ κλέψῃς, μὴ [u] ψευδομαρτυρήσῃς, τίμα τὸν
πατέρα σου καὶ τὴν μητέρα. 21 ὁ δὲ εἶπεν Ταῦτα πάντα

D Syr: txt BLℵ 1 coptt $Orig_1$. for 1st εαυτ., αυτον D[1](txt D[2]). for ο δε, και ο (*see ch* xiv. 11: *Matt* xxiii. 12) A 1 latt Syr syr-cu [syr-jer] æth $Cypr_2$.

15. om και D 25(Sz) lat-*a b* [*l*] Syr-ed copt goth. om τα D 1. 69. 247 arm $Orig_1$. for βρεφη, παιδια D. απτηται bef αυτων I_d(X).—αψηται P[X].—(αυτων is written over the line by the origl scribe in B: see table.) rec επετιμησαν (‖ *Matt prob: cf digest* ‖ *Mark*), with AI_dP rel [lat-*e* Syr]: επετιμουν 69: txt BDGLℵ 1 [(latt) syr syr-cu copt].

16. rec προσκαλεσαμενος αυτα ειπεν, with A rel: προσεκαλειτο αυτα λεγων D[G], txt Lℵ lat-*a* copt, and, but omg αυτα, B. (ειπεν *from* ‖ *and* προσεκ. *altered to suit the constr.*) κωλυσηται D.

17. aft αμην ins γαρ D 248-52[1]. rec εαν (‖ *Mark*), with AI_dP rel [$Orig_1$]: txt BDLXℵ 69.

18. om λεγων (‖ *Mark*) D am.

19. for ειπ. δε αυ. ο ιησ., ο δε ειπεν αυτω DG. rec ins ο bef θεος (‖ *Mark*), with A B[2](but marked for erasure, so Tischdf) Dℵ[3a] rel [$Orig_{1expr}$]: om B[1]ℵ[1].

20. aft οιδας ins ο δε ειπεν ποιας ειπεν δε ο ιησους το D [lat-*e*]. for μη (four times) ου (with futures) D latt. ψευδομαρτυρης B. rec aft μητερα ins σου, with ℵ rel lat-*a b c* Syr syr-cu [syr-jer] copt æth [$Orig_1$ $Dial_1$]: om $ABDI_dKLMPX$[Π] 1. 33 vulg [lat-*e f ff*$_2$ *i l q* syr] goth arm.

21. παντα bef ταυτα AI_dK[Π] lat-*e* [syr].

One returned home in the sight of God with his prayer answered, and that prayer had grasped the true object of prayer,—the forgiveness of sins (so that **δεδ.** is in the usual sense of the Epistles of Paul, **justified before God**—see reff.), the other prayed not for it, and obtained it not. Therefore he who would seek justification before God must seek it by humility and not by self-righteousness. **ὅτι πᾶς ὁ ὑψῶν ἑαυτ.** has been illustrated in the demeanour of the Pharisee;—**ταπεινωθ.** in his failure to obtain justification from God:—**ταπεινῶν ἑαυτόν** in that of the Publican;—**ὑψωθήσ.** in his obtaining the answer to his prayer, which was *this justification*. Thus the particular instance is bound up with the general truth.

15—17.] Little children brought to Christ. Here the narrative of Luke again falls in with those of Matthew and Mark, after a divergence of nearly nine chapters: see note on ch. ix. 51. Matt. xix. 13—15. Mark x. 13—16. The *narrative* part of our text is distinct from the two; the words of our Lord are verbatim as Mark: see notes on Matt. The place and time indicated here are the same as before, from ch. xvii. 11.

15.] **καὶ τὰ βρέφη**—**their infants also**; not the people came only, but also brought their children. Or, the art. may be merely generic, as in E. V. **βρ.** points out more distinctly the tender age of the children than παιδία.

18—30.] Question of a rich ruler: our Lord's answer, and discourse thereupon. Matt. xix. 16—30. Mark x.

[v] ἐφύλαξα [w] ἐκ [w] νεότητος. 22 ἀκούσας δὲ ὁ Ἰησοῦς εἶπεν
R ετι... αὐτῷ Ἔτι ἕν σοι [x] λείπει· πάντα ὅσα ἔχεις πώλησον καὶ
[y] διάδος πτωχοῖς, καὶ ἕξεις [z] θησαυρὸν ἐν τοῖς οὐρανοῖς καὶ
[a] δεῦρο ἀκολούθει μοι. 23 ὁ δὲ ἀκούσας ταῦτα [b] περίλυπος
ἐγενήθη, ἦν γὰρ πλούσιος [c] σφόδρα. 24 ἰδὼν δὲ αὐτὸν ὁ
Ἰησοῦς εἶπεν [d] Πῶς [e] δυςκόλως οἱ τὰ χρήματα ἔχοντες
..ευκοπω I_d. εἰς τὴν βασιλείαν τοῦ θεοῦ εἰςπορεύονται· 25 [f] εὐκοπώτερον
γάρ ἐστιν [g] κάμηλον διὰ [h] τρήματος [i] βελόνης [j] εἰςελθεῖν
ἢ πλούσιον εἰς τὴν βασιλείαν τοῦ θεοῦ εἰςελθεῖν. 26 εἶπον
δὲ οἱ ἀκούσαντες [k] Καὶ τίς δύναται σωθῆναι; 27 ὁ δὲ εἶπεν
Τὰ ἀδύνατα [l] παρὰ ἀνθρώποις δυνατὰ παρὰ τῷ θεῷ ἐστιν.
...πετρος ι F. 28 εἶπεν δὲ [ὁ] Πέτρος Ἰδοὺ ἡμεῖς [m] ἀφέντες [n] τὰ [n] ἴδια
ἠκολουθήσαμέν σοι. 29 ὁ δὲ εἶπεν αὐτοῖς Ἀμὴν λέγω ὑμῖν
ὅτι οὐδείς ἐστιν ὃς [m] ἀφῆκεν οἰκίαν ἢ γυναῖκα ἢ ἀδελφοὺς ἢ γονεῖς ἢ τέκνα ἕνεκεν τῆς βασιλείας τοῦ θεοῦ, 30 ὃς
οὐχὶ μὴ [o] ἀπολάβῃ [p] πολλαπλασίονα ἐν τῷ [q] καιρῷ τούτῳ,
καὶ ἐν τῷ [r] αἰῶνι τῷ [r] ἐρχομένῳ [s] ζωὴν [s] αἰώνιον.

v act. = ‖ Mt. ch. xi. 28. John xii. 47. Acts vii. 53 al. Eccl. xii. 13.
w ‖ Mk. reff.
x act., Tit. i. 5. iii. 13 (pass., James i. 4, 5. ii. 15) only. = Wisd. xix. 4 only.
y ch. xi. 22 reff.
z Matt. ii. 11 reff. Josh. vi. 19.
a = ‖ Mt. reff.
b Matt. xxvi. 38 reff.
c Matt. ii. 10 reff.
d = Matt. xxi. 20 reff.
e ‖ only †. (-λος, Mark x. 24.)
f ‖. ch. v. 23 ‖. xvi. 27 only †. Sir. xxii. 25. 1 Macc. iii. 18 only.
g ‖ Mt. reff.
h here only †. (-ητός, Sir. xxviii. 14, 15 v. r.)
i here only †.
j w διά, Matt. vii. 13 reff.
k = ch. x. 29 reff.
l ‖. (ch. i. 37.) Gen. xviii. 14.
m = Matt. iv. 20, 22. Exod. ix. 21.
n John i. 11 reff.
o = ch. vi. 34. xv. 27. Rom. i. 27 al. Num. xxxiv. 14. 2 Macc. (iv. 46. vi. 21) viii. 6 only.
p ‖ Matt. only †.
q ‖ Mk. Rom. iii. 26. viii. 18. Eph. ii. 12.
r ‖ Mk. only. see ch. xx. 35. Heb. vi. 5.
s ver. 18.

rec εφυλαξαμην (‖ *Mark, which our txt more nearly approaches than* ‖ *Matt*), with DI_dP rel: txt ABLℵ 1 $Dial_1$. rec aft νεοτητος ins μου (‖ *Mark*), with AI_dPℵ rel latt [syrr syr-jer æth]: om BD lat-*l* syr-cu $Mcion_1$-t $Dial_1$.

22. rec aft ακουσας δε ins ταυτα, with AI_dP rel syr [goth æth arm]: om BDLℵ 1. 33. 69 lat-*e* Syr syr-cu [syr-jer] copt. for ετι, οτι FHVℵ¹. for διαδος, δος (‖ *Matt Mark*) $ADI_dLMR\Delta$ℵ 1. 33 $Dial_1$. ins τοις bef πτωχοις D Scr's f. rec εν ουρανω (‖ *Mark*), with I_dP rel vulg lat-*b c* goth [arm Bas_1] $Dial_1$: εν ουρανοις (‖ *Matt*) ALRℵ: txt BD lat-*a e* copt.

23. aft ταυτα ins παντα Γℵ. rec εγενετο (*more usual form*), with ADI_dPR rel [Cyr_1]: txt BLℵ.

24. om ὁ B. rec ins περιλυπον γενομενον bef ειπεν, with ADI_dPR rel [vulg syrr syr-cu &c]: om BLℵ 1 copt.—ειπεν bef ο ιησους D. rec εισελευσονται (‖ *Matt Mark*) ε. τ. β. τ. θ., with AI_dP rel: ε. τ. β. τ. θ. εισελευσονται DRℵ 33 lat-*a b c*: txt BL.

25. rec (for τρηματος) τρυμαλιας (‖ *Mark*), with AP rel: τρυπηματος LR: txt BDℵ. rec (for βελονης) ραφιδος (‖ *Matt Mark*), with APR rel: txt BDLℵ 1 (69) $Clem_1$. for 1st εισελθειν, διελθειν (‖ *Mark*) ADMP 1 latt syr-cu syr(εισελθ. in marg) goth [æth arm] Thl. 2nd εισελθ. bef εις τ. β. τ. θ. (‖ *Matt*) D vulg lat-*b c f* $g_{1.2}$ syr-cu [syr jer] copt æth.

26. ειπαν Rℵ. ακουοντες D-gr L latt.

27. rec εστι bef παρα τω θεω (‖ *Mark*), with A(P)R rel vulg lat-*b c f* [ff_2 *i l q*] syr copt goth Iren-int_2: txt B(D)Lℵ 1 lat-*a e* Jer_1.—om τω D[P].

28. om ὁ AP rel: ins (‖ *Matt Mark*) BDLRUXℵ (1. 69, e sil). rec (for αφ. τα ιδ.) αφηκαμεν παντα και (‖ *Matt Mark*), with APRℵ¹ rel [syrr syr-cu goth æth]: txt B(D)Lℵ^3a syr-mg copt [arm].—τα ιδ. bef αφ. D. at end add τι αρα εσται ημιν (‖ *Matt*) Xℵ^3a lat-*l*.

29. om οτι DΔℵ¹ latt [$Cypr_1$]. οικιας (‖ *Matt*) DH 69 Syr arm-ed. rec η γον. η αδ. η γυν., with AP rel [vss]; so, but insg η αδελφας aft αδελφους, DXΔ $Cypr_1$: txt BLℵ copt. [aft τεκνα ins εν τω καιρω τουτω D.] εινεκεν Bℵ.

30. rec (for ος ουχι) ος ου, with APR rel: εαν D [arm]: txt B(sic: see table) Lℵ 1. for απολαβη, λαβη (‖ *Matt Mark*) BDM arm: txt APRℵ rel. επταπλασιονα D lat-*a b c e* ff_2 *i* [*l q*] syr-ms-mg Iren-int $Cypr_4$ Ambr Aug Bede.

17—31. The only addition in our narrative is that the young man was *a ruler,*—perhaps of the synagogue: see notes on Matt. and Mark.

31 [t] Παραλαβὼν δὲ τοὺς δώδεκα εἶπεν πρὸς αὐτοὺς
[u] Ἰδοὺ ἀναβαίνομεν εἰς Ἱερουσαλήμ, καὶ [v] τελεσθήσεται
πάντα τὰ [w] γεγραμμένα [w] διὰ τῶν προφητῶν [x] τῷ υἱῷ τοῦ
ἀνθρώπου· 32 [y] παραδοθήσεται γὰρ τοῖς ἔθνεσιν, καὶ [z] ἐμ-
παιχθήσεται καὶ [a] ὑβρισθήσεται καὶ [b] ἐμπτυσθήσεται, 33 καὶ
[c] μαστιγώσαντες ἀποκτενοῦσιν αὐτόν, καὶ τῇ ἡμέρᾳ τῇ
τρίτῃ ἀναστήσεται. 34 καὶ αὐτοὶ οὐδὲν τούτων συνῆκαν, Q και αυτοι...
καὶ ἦν τὸ ῥῆμα τοῦτο κεκρυμμένον ἀπ' αὐτῶν, καὶ οὐκ ABDEF GHKL
[d] ἐγίνωσκον τὰ λεγόμενα. MQRSU VXΓΔ ΛΠℵ 1. 33. 69
35 Ἐγένετο δὲ [e] ἐν τῷ [f] ἐγγίζειν αὐτὸν εἰς Ἱεριχώ,
τυφλός τις ἐκάθητο παρὰ τὴν ὁδὸν [g] ἐπαιτῶν· 36 ἀκούσας δὲ ὄχλου [h] διαπορευομένου, [i] ἐπυνθάνετο [i] τί εἴη τοῦτο.
37 [k] ἀπήγγειλαν δὲ αὐτῷ ὅτι Ἰησοῦς ὁ Ναζωραῖος [l] παρ-

t Mark ix. 2 reff.
u ch. xxiv. 49 al. Mal. iii. 1.
v ch. xxii. 37. Rev. x. 7. Ezra i. 1.
w = Matt. ii. 5 only. see Acts xv. 23. 2 Cor. ii. 4.
x constr., Jude 14. 3 Kings xxii. 18. see Matt. xiii. 14. Winer, § 31. 4, edn. 6 [and Moulton's note p. 265, 3].
y = ‖ al. Ezek. xxiii. 28.
z ‖. Matt. xxvii. 29 ‖. Gen. xxxix. 17.
a ch. xi. 45 reff.
b Matt. xxvi. 67 reff.
c Matt. x. 17 reff.
d = Mark iv. 13. John iii. 10 al. Job ix. 11.
e Matt. xiii. 4 al. Ezek. ix. 8.
f ch. xix. 29 ‖ Mt. Mk. xxiv. 28. Ps. xxvi. 2.
g ch. xvi. 3 only. Ps. cviii. 10 only.
h ch. vi. 1 reff. Gen. xxiv. 62.
i ch. xv. 26.
k ch. xiii. 1 al.
l = Mark vi. 48. Judg. xi. 17.

31. for *προς αυτους, αυτοις* D vulg lat-*c* [*f ff*$_2$ *i l*]. (*ιερουσαλημ*, so BDLRℵ Orig$_1$.) for *τω υιω, περι του υιου* D 69 latt syrr syr-cu copt arm Epiph$_2$: *του υιου* (*itacism?*) Δ.
32. for *παραδ. γαρ, οτι παραδ.* D lat-*e*. om *και υβρισθησεται* DL lat-*a b c ff*$_2$ *i* [*q*] syr[-txt: has it w-ast] arm-zoh. om *και εμπτυσθησεται* (‖ *Matt*) PR arm-zoh.
33. *αποκτεινουσιν* D-gr.
34. for *και αυτοι, αυτοι δε* DU lat-*e* Syr æth. *τουτων* bef *ουδεν* D. for 2nd *και, αλλ'* D 1 lat-*a b c e f i* [*q* syr-mg-ms] Syr syr-cu. om *τουτο* D 1 lat-*a b c* [*ff*$_2$ *l q*] syr-cu copt-dz arm.
35. rec **προσ***αιτων* (*cf* ‖ *Mark*), with APQR rel: txt BDLℵ[1] Orig$_1$. *επαιτων* bef *εκαθητο π. τ. οδ.* (‖ *Mark*) D lat-*e* Dial$_1$.
36. **παρα***πορευομενου* DX latt. ins *αν* bef *ειη* DKLMQRX[Π] 1. 69 Orig$_2$ Dial$_1$: om ABPℵ rel.
37. for *απ. δε αυτω, οι δε απηγγειλαν* ℵ[1]. *ναζαρηνος* D-gr 1 vulg lat-*a* (*e i l*) Orig$_1$.

31—34.] Fuller declaration of his sufferings and death. Matt. xx. 17—19. Mark x. 32—34. The narrative of the journey now passes to *the last section of it*,—the going up to Jerusalem, properly so called; that which in Matt. and Mark forms *the whole journey*. We know from John xi. 54 that this journey took place from Ephraim, a city near the desert. **31.**] The dative (commodi) **τῷ υἱῷ** belongs to **γεγραμμένα**—as in E. V.: see Winer in reff. **32.**] The *betrayal* is omitted here, which is unaccountable if Luke saw Matthew's account, as also the omission of the *crucifying*, this being the *first* announcement of it: see a similar omission in ch. ix. 45. **34.**] Peculiar to Luke. **οὐδὲν τούτων**—i. e. neither the sufferings nor the resurrection. All was as yet hidden from them, and it seems not to have been till very shortly before the event itself that they had any real expectation of its happening.

35—43.] Healing of a blind man at the entrance into Jericho. Matt. xx. 29—34. Mark x. 46—52, where see notes. I have on Matt. spoken of the discrepancy of his narrative from the two others. The supposition that they were two miracles is perfectly monstrous; and would at once destroy the credit of Matthew as a truthful narrator. If further proof of their identity were wanting to any one, we might find it in the fact that the following expressions are common to Mark and Luke. In Matt. of course they are in the plural, as he has *two* blind men.—*ἐκάθητο παρὰ τ. ὁδὸν ἐπαιτῶν* (*προσαίτης ἐκαθ. π. τ. ὁδ.*)—*Ιησοῦς ὁ Ναζωραῖος* (*-αρηνός*)—*ἐπετίμων αὐτῷ ἵνα σιγήσῃ* (*σιωπ.*)—*αὐτὸς* (*ὁ*) *δὲ πολλῷ μᾶλλον ἔκραζεν υἱὲ Δ. ἐλέησόν με—τί σοι θέλεις ποιήσω* (*θ. π. σ.*)—*κύριε* (*ῥαββουνί* Mark as usual) *ἵνα ἀναβλέψω—ἡ πίστις σου σέσωκέν σε.* **36. τί εἴη**] Luke generally inserts **ἄν**—see ch. ix. 46: Acts v. 24; x. 17 al. and var. readings.

ἔρχεται. 38 καὶ [m] ἐβόησεν λέγων Ἰησοῦ [n] υἱὲ [n] Δαυείδ,
ἐλέησόν με. 39 καὶ οἱ [o] προάγοντες [p] ἐπετίμων αὐτῷ ἵνα
...υιε δαδ P. [q] σιγήσῃ· αὐτὸς δὲ πολλῷ μᾶλλον ἔκραζεν [n] Υἱὲ [n] Δαυείδ,
ἐλέησόν με. 40 σταθεὶς δὲ ὁ Ἰησοῦς ἐκέλευσεν αὐτὸν
ἀχθῆναι πρὸς αὐτόν. [r] ἐγγίσαντος δὲ αὐτοῦ [s] ἐπηρώ-
Fποιησω ... τησεν αὐτὸν 41 Τί σοι [t] θέλεις [tu] ποιήσω; ὁ δὲ εἶπεν
Κύριε, [v] ἵνα [w] ἀναβλέψω. 42 καὶ ὁ Ἰησοῦς εἶπεν αὐτῷ
[w] Ἀνάβλεψον· ἡ πίστις σου σέσωκέν σε. 43 καὶ [x] παραχρῆμα [w] ἀνέβλεψεν, καὶ ἠκολούθει αὐτῷ δοξάζων τὸν
...θεω X. θεόν. καὶ πᾶς ὁ λαὸς ἰδὼν [y] ἔδωκεν [z] αἶνον τῷ θεῷ.
XIX. 1 Καὶ εἰσελθὼν διήρχετο τὴν Ἱεριχώ. 2 καὶ ἰδοὺ
ἀνὴρ [a] ὀνόματι [a] καλούμενος Ζακχαῖος, καὶ αὐτὸς ἦν
[b] ἀρχιτελώνης, [c] καὶ [c] αὐτὸς πλούσιος· 3 καὶ [d] ἐζήτει ἰδεῖν
τὸν Ἰησοῦν [e] τίς ἐστιν, καὶ οὐκ ἠδύνατο [f] ἀπὸ τοῦ ὄχλου,
ὅτι τῇ [g] ἡλικίᾳ μικρὸς ἦν. 4 καὶ [h] προδραμὼν [[i] εἰς τὸ]
ἔμπροσθεν [k] ἀνέβη ἐπὶ [l] συκομορέαν, ἵνα ἴδῃ αὐτόν, ὅτι

m John i. 23 reff. n ch. xx. 41 reff. o = Matt. xxi. 9 al.† Wisd. xix. 11. p Matt. xvi. 22. Zech. iii. 2. w. ἵνα, Matt. xii. 16 reff. q ch. ix. 36. xx. 26 only in Gospp. Acts xii. 17. xv. 12, 13. Rom. xvi. 25. 1 Cor. xiv. 28, 30, 34 only. L.P. Exod. xiv. 14. r ch. xii. 33 reff. s Matt. xii. 10 al. t see ‖ Mt. reff. u dat., ch. i. 49 al. v ‖. John vi. 7. xvii. 24. w Matt. xi. 5 reff. x ch. i. 64 reff. y John ix. 24 reff. Ps. lxv. 2. z Matt. xxi. 16 (from Ps. viii. 2) only. Ezra iii. 11. a ch. i. 61.

b here only †. c ch. xx. 28. d = Matt. xii. 46, 47 reff. e Mark i. 24. John viii. 53. f = Matt. xviii. 7 al. 2 Chron. v. 6. g = ch. ii. 52 (?). Eph. iv. 13 only. (Matt. vi. 27 reff.) E ek. xiii. 18. h John xx. 4 only. 1 Kings viii. 11. Tobit xi. 3 only. i = ver. 28. Phil. iii. 13 only. Gen. xxxii. 16. [εἰς τὸ ἔμπ., here only.] k = ch. v. 19. l here only †. (-ρος, Amos vii. 14 Aq. Symm.]

38. for και, ο δε D lat-*e* [*f*] goth. for εβοησεν, εκραξεν P. om ιησου AEK[Π] Orig$_1$.

39. οι δε D lat-*e* Mcion$_1$-t. for προαγ., παραγοντες AK[Π lat-*a*]. επετιμουν AΓ 69. rec σιωπηση (‖ *Mark Matt*), with AQRℵ rel Orig$_1$: txt BDLPX Orig$_1$. for αυτος, ο (‖ *Mark*) ℵ [lat-*a d e*]. om πολλω D lat-*c* [Syr syr-cu]. aft εκραζεν ins ιησου Uℵ 1. 69. υιος D : υυ̅ (sic) ℵ[1].

40. om ο ιησους A Dial$_1$.—om ο BD. om προς αυτον D 1 lat-*a e ff*$_2$ *i l* syr-cu Dial$_1$. aft 2nd αυτον ins ο ιησους QX 69.

41. rec ins λεγων bef τι, with AQR X(Treg, expr) rel : om BDLℵ lat-*e* copt Dial$_1$.

42. for ιησ., αποκριθεις D (Orig$_1$).

43. αυτον ℵ[1]. for λαος, οχλος Q[Λ] 69 Orig$_1$. for αινον, δοξαν D.

Chap. XIX. **2.** om καλουμενος DG (latt) Syr syr-cu æth. for 1st και αυτος, ουτος D lat-*e* [*f*] *i* goth[appy] : και ουτος 69. rec (for 2nd αυτος) ουτος, with AQR rel : om Lℵ syr-cu [syr-jer] copt goth : txt BKU[Π] 1. 69.—rec adds ην, with AQRℵ rel syr-cu syr-mg [syr-jer] copt goth : om BK[Π] 1. 69 latt arm.—om και αυτος D lat-*e*.

3. εδυνατο B[1]K[Π].

4. προςδραμων (*see digest on Matt* xxvi. 39) (E ?)FGHLRVΓ [Π(not R, Tischdf)] Naz-ms : προλαβων D. rec om εις το, with AD rel : ins BLℵ lat-*e*. Steph and elz-1633 συκομωραιαν (*by itacism ?*), with E[1]GKU[Π Cyr$_1$] : -ωμοραιαν A Naz-ms : -ομοραιαν E[2]FHMSVΓΛ : -ομωρεαν DQ : txt BLΔℵ [copt. -κομορ- only remains in R]. for ινα ιδη, του ιδειν ℵ[1].

39.] **οἱ προάγ.** = ὁ ὄχλος Matt. = πολλοί Mark. **43.**] Peculiar (except **ἠκολούθει αὐτῷ**, which all three relate) to Luke;—his usual way of terminating such narrations, as it certainly was the result of such a miracle: see ch. xiii. 17; ix. 43; v. 26. He, of the three Evangelists, takes most notice of the glory given to God on account of the miraculous acts of the Lord Jesus.

Chap. XIX. 1—10.] Zacchæus the publican. *Peculiar to Luke*, and indicating that though in the main his narrative is coincident with, yet it is wholly independent of those of Matt. and Mark.

2.] **Ζακχαῖος** = זַכַּי, 'pure,' Ezra ii. 9: Neh. vii. 14; also found in the Rabbinical writings, see Lightfoot. He was not a Gentile, as Tertullian supposed, (contr. Marc. iv. 37, vol. ii. p. 451,) but a Jew, see ver. 9. **ἀρχιτ.**] Probably an administrator of the revenue derived from *balsam*, which was produced in abundance in the neighbourhood.

[m] ἐκείνης ἤμελλεν διέρχεσθαι. 5 καὶ ὡς ἦλθεν ἐπὶ τὸν
τόπον, [n] ἀναβλέψας ὁ Ἰησοῦς [εἶδεν αὐτόν, καὶ] εἶπεν
πρὸς αὐτὸν Ζακχαῖε, [o] σπεύσας [p] κατάβηθι· [q] σήμερον γὰρ
ἐν τῷ οἴκῳ σου [r] δεῖ με μεῖναι. 6 καὶ [o] σπεύσας [p] κατέβη,
καὶ [s] ὑπεδέξατο αὐτὸν χαίρων. 7 καὶ ἰδόντες πάντες [t] διεγόγγυζον λέγοντες ὅτι [u] παρὰ [v] ἁμαρτωλῷ [v] ἀνδρὶ εἰσῆλθεν
[w] καταλῦσαι. 8 [x] σταθεὶς δὲ Ζακχαῖος εἶπεν πρὸς τὸν
κύριον Ἰδοὺ τὰ [y] ἡμίσειά μου τῶν [z] ὑπαρχόντων, κύριε, τοῖς
πτωχοῖς δίδωμι· καὶ εἴ τινός τι [a] ἐσυκοφάντησα, [b] ἀποδίδωμι
[c] τετραπλοῦν. 9 εἶπεν δὲ πρὸς αὐτὸν ὁ Ἰησοῦς ὅτι σήμερον

ABDEF GHKL MQRS UΓΔ ΛΠℵ 1. 33. 69

m constr., see ch. v. 19.
n = Matt. xiv. 19 reff.
o ch. ii. 16 reff. Acts xxii. 18. Gen. xviii. 6.
p = Matt. xxiv. 17 al.
q Matt. vi. 11 al. Gen. iv. 14.
r ch. xiii. 33.
s ch. x. 38. Acts xvii. 7. James ii. 25 only +. Tobit vii. 8. 1 Macc. xii. 15 only.
t ch. xv. 2 only. Exod. xv. 24.
u = ch. xi. 37. John i. 40. Acts x. 6.
v ch. v. 8. Sir. x. 23.
w = ch. ix. 12 (reff.) only.
x = ch. xviii. 11. Acts ii. 14. v. 20 al.
y here only. (-συ, Mark vi. 23.)
z = Matt. xix. 21 reff.
a ch. iii. 14 only. Eccl. iv. 1 al.
b = ch. x. 35. Matt. v. 26 al. Gen. xlii. 28.
c here only +. (-πλῶς, 3 Kings vi. 31 [33].)

rec ins δι bef εκεινης, with Λ 1. 69: om AB(D)Qℵ rel.—εκεινη D.

5. for ως ηλθεν to ιησ., εγενετο εν τω διερχεσθαι αυτον D, simly lat-*a b c e ff$_2$ i l q*. om ὁ B. om ειδεν αυτον και (*passing from* ει- *to* ει-?) BLℵ 1 copt æth(appy) arm: ins AQR rel vulg lat-*f* syrr (syr-cu) goth, ειδον και (omg αυτον) D. for προς αυτον, αυτω D lat-*a e*. σπευσον D-gr Λ lat-*e q* copt. for σημ. γαρ, οτι σημ. D latt æth Iren-gr$_1$.

7. rec απαντες, with (KM[Π], e sil) 1: txt ABDQR [S(Tischdf)] ℵ rel Thl. (οι φαρισαιοι 69.) om λεγοντες D lat-*a e ff$_2$ i l* syr-cu. ανδρι bef αμαρτ. ℵ [latt].

8. ins ο bef ζακχαιος Dℵ 1. rec ημιση, with E rel Clem$_1$ Bas$_1$, ημυση D^8: ημισυ (retaining τα) ARΔ 69, ημυσοι (-οι *itacism for* υ) D^1: txt BLQℵ.—(ημισια B^1[Q]ℵ.) rec των υπαρχοντων bef μου, with A(D)R rel latt Clem$_1$ [Bas$_1$] Iren-int$_1$ Cypr$_1$: txt BLQℵ 1 copt.—for μου, μοι D^1(txt D^8) 242-5 Scr's h q r s evv-H-x-y-z. rec διδωμι bef τοις πτωχοις, with AR rel latt syrr syr-cu goth [copt æth arm] Bas$_1$ Iren-int$_1$ Cypr: txt (B)DLQℵ 1. 33 [Antch$_1$].—om τοις B 248 Scr's g.

9. ο ιησ. bef προς αυτον D latt.—om ο (bef ιησ.) B. προς αυτους R lat-*a b c ff$_2$*

4. **προδρ. ἔμπρ.**] So Jos. Antt. vii. 8. 5, προέπεμψεν ἔμπροσθεν. **συκομορ.**] The Egyptian fig, a tree (Pliny xiii. 14: Dioscor. i. 182, cited by Winer) like the mulberry in appearance, size, and foliage, but belonging generically to the fig-trees. It grows to a great size and height: see Winer, Realwörterbuch, under Maulbeer-feigenbaum. See also on ch. xvii. 6. Notice the changes of subject here,—ἀνέβη (Ζακχ.) . . . . ἵνα ἴδῃ αὐτόν, ὅτι ἐκείνης ἤμελλεν (ὁ Ἰησ.) διέρ. . . . . κ. σπεύσας (Ζακχ.). See ch. xv. 15:—and a curious and characteristic note in Wordsw. here. 5.] The *probability* is, that our Lord's supernatural knowledge of man (see John i. 48—50) is intended to be understood as the means of his knowing Zacchæus: but the narrative does not absolutely exclude the supposition of a personal knowledge of Zacchæus on the part of some around Him. But of what possible import can such a question be, when the narrative plainly shews us that Jesus saw into his *heart?* Cannot He who knows the thoughts, call by the name also? **μεῖναι,** probably over the night. See John i. 40. **δεῖ, it is my purpose,** or even more, **I must;** for especially in these last days of our Lord's ministry, every event is fixed and determined by a divine plan. 7.] The murmurers are Jews who were accompanying Him to Jerusalem, on the road to which Zacchæus's house lay (see ver. 1). **παρὰ ἁμ. ἀνδρί** belongs to **καταλῦσαι.** His profession in life, and perhaps an unprincipled exercise of his power in it, had earned him this name with his fellow-countrymen. Cf. his confession in the next verse. 8.] This need not have taken place *in the morning;* much more probably it was immediately on our Lord's entrance into the house, while the multitude were yet murmuring in the court, and in their presence. Our Lord's answer, **σήμερον . . . . τῷ οἴκῳ τούτῳ,** looks as if He were just entering the house, not just leaving it; and the **σήμ.** must be the same with that in ver. 5. **σταθείς** has something formal and predetermined about it: he stood forward, with some effort and resolve: see on ch. xviii. 11 ff. **τὰ ἡμ. . . . πτωχ. δίδ.**] See note on ch. xvi. 9. Zacchæus may well have heard of that parable from one of his publican acquaintances, or perhaps repentance may have led him at once to

σωτηρία τῷ οἴκῳ τούτῳ [d] ἐγένετο, [e] καθότι καὶ αὐτὸς [f] υἱὸς
[f] Ἀβραάμ ἐστιν. 10 ἦλθεν γὰρ ὁ υἱὸς τοῦ ἀνθρώπου
[g] ζητῆσαι καὶ σῶσαι τὸ [h] ἀπολωλός. 11 Ἀκουόντων δὲ
αὐτῶν ταῦτα [i] προςθεὶς εἶπεν παραβολήν, διὰ τὸ ἐγγὺς
εἶναι Ἱερουσαλὴμ αὐτὸν καὶ δοκεῖν αὐτοὺς ὅτι [k] παραχρῆμα
…μελλει η βα Q. μέλλει ἡ βασιλεία τοῦ θεοῦ [l] ἀναφαίνεσθαι. 12 εἶπεν οὖν
Ἄνθρωπός τις [m] εὐγενὴς ἐπορεύθη εἰς χώραν [n] μακρὰν
λαβεῖν ἑαυτῷ βασιλείαν καὶ [o] ὑποστρέψαι. 13 καλέσας δὲ
δέκα δούλους ἑαυτοῦ, ἔδωκεν αὐτοῖς δέκα [p] μνᾶς καὶ εἶπεν

d = dat., Mark ix. 21. w. ἐπί, ch. iii. 2. κατά, ch. x. 32. πρός, John x. 35.
e ch. i. 7 reff.
f Gal. iii. 7. see Matt. iii. 9.
g = Matt. xviii. 12. ch. xv. 8.
h Matt. xviii. 11 reff.
i = ch. xx. 11, 12 reff.
k ch. i. 64 reff.
l Acts xxi. 3 only. Cant. vi. 4.
m Acts xvii. 11. 1 Cor. i. 26 only. Job i. 3. 2 Macc. x. 13 only. (-νῶς, 2 Macc. xiv. 42. -νεια, Wisd. viii. 3.)
n = ch. xv. 13 (reff.).
o = ch. ii. 20 reff.
p here, &c. (7 times) only. 3 Kings x. 17.

i l [*q*] syr-mg. ins εν bef τω οικω AD copt-dz. om εστιν LR$\aleph^1$.
10. απο of απολωλος is repeated in ℵ.
11. rec αυτον bef ειναι ιερουσαλημ, with AR rel : ειν. αυτ. ιερ. Q : ειν. αυτ. εγ. ιερ. D (*attempts to escape the harshness of txt*) : txt BLℵ. δοκει (sic) $\aleph^1$. om αυτους D : αυτοις $\aleph^1$ Scr's d p. μελλει bef παραχρημα D : aft η βασ. τ. θ. ℵ.
12. for ουν, δε DL goth. επορευετο DH (copt ?). om εαυτω D lat-*a b e* g_1 *i l* [*q*] syr-cu copt Lucif$_1$.
13. for εαυτου, αυτου DΓ.

this act of self-denial. **ἐσυκοφ.**] There is no *uncertainty* in εἴ τι : it = ὅ τι : **whatever I have unfairly exacted from any man.** See note on ch. iii. 14.
9.] **πρός, to him,** not *'concerning him.'* The announcement is made *to him,* though not in the second person. **σωτηρία,** in the stronger sense, **salvation.**
υἱὸς Ἀβ. ἐστιν] Not, *has become* (γέγονεν) *a son of Abraham by his repentance* (Kuinoel, &c.), but **is a son of Abraham** : though despised by the multitude, has his rights as a Jew, and has availed himself of them by receiving his Lord in faith and humility. 10.] For, the greater sinner he may have been, the more does he come under the description of those (sheep) whom the good Shepherd came to seek and save (Matt. xv. 24).
11—27.] Parable of the minæ. *Peculiar to Luke.* By the introductory words, the parable must have been spoken *in the house of Zacchæus,* i. e. perhaps in the open room looking into the court, where probably many of the multitude were assembled. A parable very similar in some points to this was spoken by our Lord in His last great prophetic discourse, Matt. xxv. 14—30. Many modern Commentators (Calv., Olsh., Meyer (on Matt.), but not Schleierm. or De Wette) maintain that the two parables represent one and the same : if so, we must at once give up, not only the pretensions to *historical* accuracy on the part of our Gospels, (see ver. 11,) but all idea that they furnish us with the words of our Lord any where : for *the whole structure and incidents of the two are essentially different.* If oral tradition thus varied before the Gospels were written, *in the report of our Lord's spoken words,* how can we know that He spoke *any thing which they relate?* If the Evangelists themselves *altered, arranged,* and *accommodated* those discourses, not only is the above the case, but their honesty is likewise impugned (see Prolegomena to Gospels). Besides, we shall here find the parable, in its very root and point of comparison, *individual and distinct.* Compare throughout the notes on Matt.
11.] The distance of Jericho from Jerusalem was 150 stadia = 18 English miles and 6 furlongs. **ὅτι παραχρ.**] They imagined that the present journey to Jerusalem, undertaken as it had been with such publicity and accompanied with such wonderful miracles, was for the purpose of revealing and establishing the Messianic kingdom. **12.**] The groundwork of this part of the parable seems to have been derived from the history of Archelaus, son of Herod the Great. The kings of the Herodian family made journeys to Rome, to receive their βασιλείαν. On Archelaus's doing so, the Jews sent after him a protest, which however was not listened to by Augustus. Jos. Antt. xvii. 11. 1 ff. The situation was appropriate; for at Jericho was the royal palace which Archelaus had built with great magnificence. Jos. Antt. xvii. 13. 1. **13. δέκα**] See on Matt. xxv. 1. The giving the μνᾶ *to each,* is a

πρὸς αὐτοὺς [q] Πραγματεύσασθε, [r] ἐν ᾧ ἔρχομαι. 14 οἱ δὲ ABDEF GHKL
[s] πολῖται αὐτοῦ ἐμίσουν αὐτόν, καὶ ἀπέστειλαν [t] πρεσβείαν MRSUV ΓΔΛΠℵ
ὀπίσω αὐτοῦ λέγοντες Οὐ θέλομεν τοῦτον [u] βασιλεῦσαι 1. 33. 69
[uv] ἐφ' ἡμᾶς. 15 καὶ ἐγένετο [w] ἐν τῷ [x] ἐπανελθεῖν αὐτὸν
λαβόντα τὴν βασιλείαν, [y] καὶ [z] εἶπεν [a] φωνηθῆναι αὐτῷ
τοὺς δούλους τούτους οἷς δεδώκει τὸ ἀργύριον, ἵνα
γνοῖ τί [b] διεπραγματεύσαντο. 16 [c] παρεγένετο δὲ ὁ πρῶτος
λέγων Κύριε, ἡ [d] μνᾶ σου δέκα [e] προσηργάσατο [d] μνᾶς.
17 καὶ εἶπεν αὐτῷ [f] Εὖγε ἀγαθὲ δοῦλε, ὅτι [g] ἐν ἐλαχίστῳ
πιστὸς ἐγένου, [h] ἴσθι ἐξουσίαν [i] ἔχων [k] ἐπάνω δέκα πόλεων.
18 καὶ ἦλθεν ὁ δεύτερος λέγων Ἡ [d] μνᾶ σου, κύριε, [l] ἐποίησεν
πέντε [d] μνᾶς. 19 εἶπεν δὲ καὶ τούτῳ Καὶ σὺ [k] ἐπάνω γίνου

q here only. 1 Kings x. 22 (ix. 19) only. (-τεία, 2 Tim. ii. 4.)
r = John v. 7 reff. see ver. 15.
s ch. xv. 15. Acts xxi. 39. Heb. viii. 11 only. Prov. xi. 9.
t ch. xiv. 32 only. 2 Macc. iv. 11 only. (-εύειν, Eph. vi. 20.)
u ver. 27. ch. i. 13. Gen. xxxvii. 8.
v ch. xii. 14.
w ch. iii. 21 reff. and note.
x ch. x. 35 only. Gen. l. 5.
y ch. ii. 21 reff. Gen. xxiv. 30.
z = Mark v. 43 reff. a w. dat., = here only. b here only †. c ch. xii. 51 reff. d ver. 13. e here only †. f here only. Ezek. xxxvi. 2. see Matt. xxv. 21, 23 reff. g see Matt. xvii. 12 reff. h constr., Matt. v. 25. Sir. v. 10. i Matt. vii. 29 reff. k = here bis. John iii. 31 bis only. Job xxxiii. 12. l = Matt. xxv. 16. Deut. viii. 18.

πραγματευεσθε DΛ 1 : -τευσθε U. rec (for εν ω) εως, with E rel : ως 69 : txt ABDKLR[Π]ℵ 1 Orig$_1$.

14. om 1st αυτου D 254 lat-*b* *ff*$_2$ *l* Lucif. for απεστειλαν, ενεπεμψαν D^1 : επεμψ. D-corr.

15. om εν τω DΔ. for αυτω, αυτου (*itacism ?*) DΓ lat-*a* : om Δ vulg lat-*b* *c* æth arm Lucif$_1$. om τουτους D 1 latt(not *f*) æth arm Orig Lucif. rec (for δεδωκει) εδωκε, with AR rel vulg lat-*b* *c* *f* Lucif$_1$: txt BDLℵ 1 lat-*a* *e* arm. rec γνω, with A rel Orig : txt BDLℵ 33. (R def.) rec ins τις bef τι, with AR rel syrr goth arm Lucif$_1$: om BDLℵ lat-*e* syr-cu copt æth.—rec διεπραγματευσατο (for -σαντο), with A rel syrr goth arm : txt BDLRℵ lat-*e* syr-cu copt (æth) [Orig$_1$].

16. μνας B^{2}EFHKMR^{2}Λ 1. 33. rec προς. bef δεκα, with AR rel syr copt goth : μνας bef πρ. D latt Syr [syr-cu arm] Lucif$_1$: txt BLℵ 1 lat-*a* *e*. rec προσειργασατο, with B^{2}ℵ^{3a} rel : προσηργασα ℵ^1 : txt AB^{1}DE^{1}LR.

17. for και, ο δε D lat-*e*. rec (for ευγε) ευ (*from Matt* xxv. 21), with ARℵ rel Syr syr-cu syr-mg-gr [Eus$_1$] : txt BD latt Orig$_1$ Lucif$_1$. δουλε bef αγαθε Mℵ 1. 69 lat-*c* *f* *i* *l* (arm) Eus$_1$ Orig-int$_1$.

18. for ηλθεν ο δευτ. λεγων, ο ετερος ελθων ειπεν D. rec κυριε bef η μνα σου, with AD rel latt syrr syr-cu copt goth æth Lucif$_1$: txt BL R(appy) ℵ.—μνας (so ver 20) EFHMRΛℵ^{3a} 1. 33. πεντε bef εποιησεν D Syr syr-cu.

19. rec γινου bef επανω, with AR rel Orig$_1$ [Eus$_1$] Lucif$_1$: bef και συ D (copt) : txt BLℵ 1.

totally different thing from giving to one *five*, to another *two*, and to a third *one* talent. The sums given are here all the *same*, and all *very small*. The (Attic) mina is $\frac{1}{60}$ of a talent, and equal to about £3 of our money. In Matt. the man gives his *whole property* to his servants: here he makes trial of them with these small sums (ἐλάχιστον, see ver. 17). **πραγμ.** = ἐργάζεσθαι Matt. **ἐν ᾧ ἔρχ.**] **while I go and return**;—till I come. **14.**] The nobleman, son of a king, **εὐγενής**, is the Lord Jesus; the kingdom is that over his own citizens, the Jews. They sent a message after Him; their cry went up to Heaven, in the persecutions of his servants, &c.; **we will not have this man to reign over us.** The parable has a double import: suited both to the disciples (οἱ δοῦλοι ἑαυτοῦ), and the multitude (οἱ πολῖται αὐτοῦ). **15. διεπρ.**] **what business they had carried on**: not, '*what they had gained*.' Dion. Hal., iii. 72, has the word signifying '*to arrange a matter*,' which however was not then executed. 'The sons of Ancus having often arranged (διαπραγματευσαμένων) a plot to kill Tarquinius' . . . . **16—23.**] See on Matt. It is observable here, however, how exactly and minutely in keeping is every circumstance. *Thy pound* **hath gained ten pounds**; the humility with which this is stated, where no account of ἡ ἰδία δύναμις is taken as in Matt., and then the proportion of the reward,—**δέκα πόλεις**—so according with the nature of what the Prince went to receive, and the

πέντε πόλεων. 20 καὶ ὁ ἕτερος ἦλθεν λέγων Κύριε, ἰδοὺ
ἡ [d] μνᾶ σου ἣν εἶχον [m] ἀποκειμένην ἐν [n] σουδαρίῳ. 21 ἐφο-
βούμην γάρ σε, ὅτι ἄνθρωπος [o] αὐστηρὸς εἶ, [p] αἴρεις ὃ
οὐκ [q] ἔθηκας καὶ [r] θερίζεις ὃ οὐκ ἔσπειρας. 22 λέγει
αὐτῷ Ἐκ τοῦ στόματός σου κρινῶ σε, πονηρὲ δοῦλε.
ᾔδεις ὅτι ἐγὼ ἄνθρωπος [o] αὐστηρός εἰμι, [p] αἴρων ὃ οὐκ
[q] ἔθηκα καὶ [r] θερίζων ὃ οὐκ ἔσπειρα· 23 καὶ διὰ τί οὐκ
[s] ἔδωκάς μου τὸ ἀργύριον ἐπὶ [t] τράπεζαν, κἀγὼ ἐλθὼν
σὺν [u] τόκῳ ἂν αὐτὸ [v] ἔπραξα; 24 καὶ τοῖς παρεστῶσιν
εἶπεν Ἄρατε ἀπ' αὐτοῦ τὴν [w] μνᾶν, καὶ δότε τῷ τὰς δέκα
[w] μνᾶς ἔχοντι. 25 καὶ εἶπαν αὐτῷ Κύριε, ἔχει δέκα [w] μνᾶς.
26 λέγω ὑμῖν, ὅτι παντὶ τῷ ἔχοντι δοθήσεται, ἀπὸ δὲ
τοῦ μὴ ἔχοντος καὶ ὃ ἔχει ἀρθήσεται. 27 [x] πλὴν τοὺς
ἐχθρούς μου τούτους τοὺς μὴ θελήσαντάς με [y] βασιλεῦσαι
[y] ἐπ' αὐτοὺς ἀγάγετε ὧδε καὶ [z] κατασφάξατε αὐτοὺς [a] ἔμ-

m Col. i. 5. 2 Tim. iv. 8. Heb. ix. 27 only. Gen. xlix. 10. Job xxxviii. 23. 2 Macc. xii. 45 only.
n John xi. 44. xx. 7. Acts xix. 12 only †.
o here bis only †. 2 Macc. xiv. 30 only.
p = Mark xv. 24.
q ch. xiv. 19. see John x. 18.
r Matt. vi. 26. James v. 4 al. Ruth ii. 4.
s ch. xv. 22. Lev. xxv. 37.
t = Matt. xxi. 12 ‖ Mk. John ii. 15.
u Matt. xxv. 27 only. Exod. xxii. 25.
v = ch. iii. 13. Dan. xi. 20 Theod. (?). 1 Macc. x. 35 (?).
w ver. 13. x = Matt. xi. 22 reff. Judg. iv. 9. y ver. 14. z here only. Zech. xi. 5.
a = Matt. v. 16. ch. xiv. 2 al.

20. rec om ὁ (*the word not here implying 'the second'*), with A rel: *οτερος* (sic) א^1: txt BDLRא^{3a} 69 ev-y syr-w-ast arm.

21. for *εφοβουμην γαρ, οτι εφοβηθην* D gat(with mm) lat-*a b c e ff$_2$ i* Lucif$_1$. for *οτι ανθρ., ανθρ. γαρ* D lat-*e*. *ει* bef *αυστηρος* D lat-*e*.

22. rec aft *λεγει* ins *δε* (*Matt* xxv. 26), with A rel lat-*q* [arm]: om BE^{1}GLMRS^1 UΛא 1. 69 vulg lat-*a* syrr syr-cu copt.—for *λεγει, ο δε ειπεν* D. for *αιρων, αιρω* DF lat-*a b c e ff$_2$ i* syrr syr-cu Lucif. for *θεριζων, θεριζω* D lat-*a b c e ff$_2$ i* syrr syr-cu Lucif.

23. for *και δια τι, δια τι ουν* D lat-*e*. rec *το αργυριον* bef *μου*, with DR rel latt Lucif$_1$: txt ABLא 33. rec ins *την* bef *τραπεζαν* (*cf τοις τραπεζιταις Matt*), with K Scr's i ev-z: om ABDRא rel. (rec *και εγω*, with AR rel: txt BDא.) aft *ελθων* ins *ουν* א^1. rec *επραξα* bef *αυτο*, with DR rel latt syr goth Lucif$_1$: *αυτο ανεπραξα* A: txt BLא lat-*f*.

24. for *και τ. παρ. ειπεν, ειπεν δε τ. παρ.* D. for *αρατε, αρε* א^1. om *την μναν* D lat-*a e*. for *δοτε, απενενκατε* D.

25. om ver D 69 lat-*b e g$_2$* syr-cu Lucif$_1$. (*ειπαν*, so BL[א].) (In B *κε̄* is written over the line by the origl scribe: see table.)

26. rec aft *λεγω* ins *γαρ* (*from Matt* xxv. 29), with ADR rel syr-cu syr goth: om BLא lat-*a* Syr copt æth. om *υμιν* א^1(ins א-corr^1). for *δοθησεται, προστιθεται* D. rec aft *αρθησεται* ins *απ' αυτου* (*from Matt* xxv. 29), with ADRא^{3a} rel latt syrr syr-cu goth Ephr$_1$ [Cyr$_1$]: om BLא^1 Lucif$_1$. (*N.B.* lat-*b* is def from xix. 26 to xxi. 29.)

27. rec (for *τουτους*) *εκεινους*, with A(D)R rel latt Syr syr-cu goth [æth] Orig$_1$ [Eus$_1$] Lucif$_1$: txt BKLM[Π]א copt Did$_1$.—*εκειν.* bef *τ. εχ.* D lat-*e*. *θελοντας* D[-gr] R 1. 69 [lat-*e* Chr$_1$]. *βασιλευειν* D. *αγαγατε* D. *κατασφαξετε* MSא 69. rec om *αυτους*, with AD rel latt goth [Eus$_1$]: ins BFLRא 33 ev-y Syr syr-cu syr-w-ast copt æth Chr$_3$.

occasion of his return. **20.**] **σουδάριον** is *sudarium*, from 'sudor,' one of those Latin words which entered, with Roman habits, into the language of the East. Buxtorf, Lex. Talm. p. 1442, gives an account of various usages of the word in the Targums. Schöttg., in loc., shews by Rabbinical citations that the Jews used the *σουδάριον* for wrapping and keeping their money in. Ver. **25** is parenthetical, spoken by *the standers-by in the parable*, in surprise at such a decision: then in ver. **26**, the King answers them.

27.] This command brings out both comings of the Lord,—at the destruction of Jerusalem, and at the end of the world; for we must not forget that even now *'He is gone to receive a Kingdom and return:'* 'we see not yet all things put under His feet.'

b = ver. 4.
c = Matt. xx. 17, 18 reff.
d || Mt. Mk. ch. xviii. 35. Ps. xxvi. 2.
e ch. xxi. 37. Acts i. 12 only. see || Mt. reff.
f || Mk. reff.
g intr., Matt. xxiii. 2 reff. 2 Kings vii. 1.
h = || Mt. Mk. ch. xiii. 15.
i Matt. vi. 8 reff. Prov. xviii. 2.
k = Matt. ix. 37 reff. Exod. xxi. 28.
l = here (met., 1 Pet. v. 7, from Ps. liv. 22) only. Num. xxxv. 20, 22.
m (see || Mt.) ch. x. 34. Acts xxiii. 24. 2 Kings vi. 3.
n here only. Isa. lviii. 5. Sir. iv. 27 only.
o Mark v. 11 reff.
p here only. Josh. viii. 24.
q see ver. 29.

ABDEF GHKL MRSUV ΓΔΛΠℵ 1. 33. 69

προσθέν μου. 28 καὶ εἰπὼν ταῦτα ἐπορεύετο ᵇ ἔμπροσθεν,
ᶜ ἀναβαίνων εἰς Ἱεροσόλυμα. 29 Καὶ ἐγένετο ὡς ᵈ ἤγγισεν
εἰς Βηθφαγὴ καὶ Βηθανιὰ πρὸς τὸ ὄρος τὸ καλούμενον
ᵉ Ἐλαιών, ἀπέστειλεν δύο τῶν μαθητῶν 30 * εἰπὼν Ὑπάγετε εἰς τὴν ᶠ κατέναντι κώμην· ἐν ᾗ εἰσπορευόμενοι εὑρήσετε πῶλον δεδεμένον, ἐφ᾽ ὃν οὐδεὶς πώποτε ἀνθρώπων
ᵍ ἐκάθισεν, καὶ ʰ λύσαντες αὐτὸν ἀγάγετε. 31 καὶ ἐάν τις
ὑμᾶς ἐρωτᾷ Διὰ τί ʰ λύετε; οὕτως ἐρεῖτε [αὐτῷ], ὅτι ὁ
κύριος αὐτοῦ ⁱ χρείαν ⁱ ἔχει. 32 ἀπελθόντες δὲ οἱ ἀπεσταλμένοι εὗρον καθὼς εἶπεν αὐτοῖς· 33 ʰ λυόντων δὲ
αὐτῶν τὸν πῶλον εἶπαν οἱ ᵏ κύριοι αὐτοῦ πρὸς αὐτοὺς Τί
ʰ λύετε τὸν πῶλον; 34 οἱ δὲ εἶπαν ὅτι ὁ κύριος αὐτοῦ
ⁱ χρείαν ⁱ ἔχει. 35 καὶ ἤγαγον αὐτὸν πρὸς τὸν Ἰησοῦν,
καὶ ˡ ἐπιρίψαντες αὐτῶν τὰ ἱμάτια ἐπὶ τὸν πῶλον ᵐ ἐπεβί-
βασαν τὸν Ἰησοῦν. 36 πορευομένου δὲ αὐτοῦ ⁿ ὑποστρών-
νυον τὰ ἱμάτια αὐτῶν ἐν τῇ ὁδῷ. 37 ἐγγίζοντος δὲ αὐτοῦ ...εγγιζοντος F.
ἤδη ᵒ πρὸς τῇ ᵖ καταβάσει τοῦ ὄρους τῶν ᵠ ἐλαιῶν ἤρξαντο

at end ins *και τον αχρειον δουλον εκβαλετε εις το σκοτος το εξωτερον εκει εσται ο κλαυθμος και ο βρυγμος των οδοντων* (*see Matt* xxv. 30) D.

28. om *εμπροσθεν* D 40(Sz) lat-*a c e ff*$_2$ *i l q*. *αναβ. δε εις ιερουσαλημ* D lat-*e*.

29. [*νε* of *εγενετο* is omd by B¹.] *βηθσφαγη* B[³(Tischdf)] U(Γ 69) goth. rec *βηθανιαν*, with A D²-gr ℵ³ᵃ rel vulg: txt B D¹(and lat) ℵ¹ am lat-*e*. for *το καλ. ελ.*, *των ελαιων καλουμενον* D [om *ελαιων* B¹: ins B²(Tischdf)]. rec aft *μαθητων* ins *αυτου* (|| *Mark*), with ADR rel vss [Orig-int$_1$]: om BLℵ lat-*e l* Orig$_1$ Ambr$_1$.

30. * λέγων (*from* || *Matt*) BDLℵ 69 Orig$_1$ [Syr syr-cu]: *ειπων* AR rel. for *εν η*, *και* D. om *δεδεμενον* D. om *πωποτε* DH lat-*a c e f ff*$_2$ *i l q* [syr-cu æth] Ambr$_1$. rec om *και* (|| *Matt Mark*), with ARℵ rel latt syrr syr-cu [goth]: ins BDL copt-ms. om *αυτον* DL: ins aft *αγαγετε* AK[Π] lat-*e* syrr syr-cu: txt BRℵ rel. *αγαγατε* D.

31. for *εαν*, *αν* D. om *δια τι λυετε* D lat-*c e ff*$_2$ *l*. add *αυτον* ℵ³ᵃ(but erased). om *αυτω* (*cf* || *Matt Mark*) BDFLRℵ lat-*c e ff*$_2$ *i l* [*q*] copt æth Orig$_3$: ins A rel vulg lat-*a f* Syr syr-cu syr(Treg, expr) goth arm Orig-int$_1$.

32. for *απελθ. δε*, *και απελθ.*, omg the rest of ver, D.

33. om ver D. (*ειπαν*, so BLℵ 33 Orig$_2$, and in ver 34 BLℵ Orig$_1$.)

34. for *οι δε ειπαν*, *απεκριθησαν* D syr-cu. rec om *οτι*, with R rel lat-*c e i* goth æth arm: ins ABDKLM[Π]ℵ 69 vulg lat-*a f ff*$_2$ [*l q*] syrr syr-cu copt Orig$_2$.

35. for *ηγαγον* to *και*, *αγαγοντες τον πωλον* D (lat-*e*): om FV. *επεριψαν* D 1 lat-*c e f ff*$_2$ *i* æth. (*επιριψ.* (one *ρ*), so AB¹DEGLRΔℵ.) rec *εαυτων*, with AR rel: txt BDL [Δ]ℵ.—*τα ιματια* bef *αυτων* D. for *επι τον πωλ.*, *επ᾽ αυτον* D lat-*c e ff*$_2$ syr-cu (arm). ins *και* bef *επεβιβασαν* D 1 lat-*c e f ff*$_2$ *i* Syr syr-cu æth. [*επεβισαν* B¹(Tischdf).]

36. *εαυτων* ABK[RUΠ] 1. om *εν τη οδω* D 229(Sz).

37. *εγγιζοντων δε αυτων* D syr-cu æth. om *ηδη* DMΓ lat-*a e* Syr syr-cu æth. *την καταβασιν* D 115(Sz). for *ηρξαντο*, *ηρξατο* DLR [S-corr¹(Tischdf)]

28.] Not *immediately* after saying these things—see on ver. 5: unless they were said in the morning on his departure.

29—38.] Triumphal entry into Jerusalem. Matt. xxi. 1–9. Mark xi. 1–10. John xii. 12—19, where see notes. **29.**] The name, when thus put, must be accentuated **ἐλαιών**, for when it is the genitive of ἐλαία the article is prefixed (ver. 37). Luke uses this same expression elsewhere, see reff. Josephus has διὰ τοῦ ἐλαιῶνος ὄρους, Antt. vii. 9. 2. **33.**] τινὲς τῶν ἐκεῖ ἑστηκότων said this, as in the probably more concise account of Mark;—**οἱ κύριοι αὐτ.** is the *natural inference* as to who they were.

37.] **πρὸς τ. κ.**, not merely local, '*at the declivity of*,' but expressing the result of ἐγγίζοντες—**just about to descend the Mount of Olives.**

ἅπαν τὸ πλῆθος τῶν μαθητῶν χαίροντες [r] αἰνεῖν τὸν θεὸν
φωνῇ μεγάλῃ περὶ πασῶν ὧν εἶδον [s] δυνάμεων, 38 λέγοντες [tu] Εὐλογημένος ὁ [u] ἐρχόμενος βασιλεὺς [u] ἐν ὀνόματι
κυρίου· ἐν οὐρανῷ εἰρήνη καὶ [v] δόξα ἐν [vw] ὑψίστοις. 39 καί
τινες τῶν Φαρισαίων ἀπὸ τοῦ ὄχλου εἶπαν πρὸς αὐτὸν
Διδάσκαλε, [x] ἐπιτίμησον τοῖς μαθηταῖς σου. 40 καὶ ἀποκριθεὶς εἶπεν Λέγω ὑμῖν ὅτι ἐὰν οὗτοι [y] σιωπήσουσιν, οἱ
λίθοι κράξουσιν. 41 καὶ ὡς [z] ἤγγισεν, ἰδὼν τὴν πόλιν
[a] ἔκλαυσεν [a] ἐπ' αὐτήν, 42 λέγων ὅτι [b] εἰ ἔγνως [c] καὶ σὺ
[[d] καί [d] γε] ἐν τῇ [e] ἡμέρᾳ [σου] ταύτῃ [f] τὰ πρὸς εἰρήνην
C σου ὅτι... [σου]· νῦν δὲ [g] ἐκρύβη ἀπὸ ὀφθαλμῶν σου. 43 ὅτι

r ch. ii. 13 reff. s = Matt. vii. 22 reff. t ‖ Mt. reff. u ch. xiii. 35 al. v ch. ii. 14. w ‖ Mt. reff. (see Ps. xcii. 4.) x Matt. xvi. 22. Zech. iii. 3. y Matt. xx. 31 reff. z abs., ch. xii. 33 al. a ch. xxiii. 28 reff. b = ch. xii. 49. Josh. vii. 7. c = Matt. x. 30. Mark i. 27. d Acts ii. 18 (from Joel ii. 29 Aℵ[3a]). xvii. 27 (1 Cor. iv. 8) only. Josh. ix. 4. 10. 2 Pet. i. 3. e ch. i. 80. 2 Cor. vi. 2, from Isa. xlix. 8. f ch. xiv. 32. Acts xxviii. g Matt. xi. 25. John xii. 36. Deut. vii. 20.

UVΛ 69 Orig$_1$. παν [for απαν] D 57. 254. om φωνη μεγαλη D lat-*l*. for πασων, παντων BD [Meth$_1$] : txt ARℵ rel Orig. for δυναμεων, γεινομενων D : om syr-cu.

38. om ερχομ. ℵ[1][H lat-*e l* Orig$_1$]. ins ο bef βασιλευς B. aft κυριου ins ευλογημενος ο βασιλευς, omg βασ. above, D lat-*a c ff$_2$ i* æth. rec ειρηνη bef εν ουρανω, with ADR rel vss [Tit$_1$] : txt BLℵ Orig$_1$.—ουρανοις A.—ins εν bef ειρηνη ℵ[1].

39. for και τ., τ. δε D lat-*e*. (**ειπαν**, so ABDLℵ Orig$_1$.)

40. for και αποκ., αποκ. δε D. for ειπεν, λεγει D. rec adds αυτοις, with ADR rel latt [syrr goth æth] : om BLℵ copt arm Orig$_1$. om οτι B[1] 69 lat-*a c* [*e ff$_2$ i l*] Orig$_1$. rec σιωπησωσιν (*gramml emendn*), with E rel latt : σειγησουσιν D : txt A B(sic : see table) LRΔℵ [Orig$_3$-ed Cyr$_1$], *tacebunt* fuld lat-*e i*. rec κεκραξονται (*common with* LXX : *cf Ps* xxvii. 1), with AR rel Orig-ms$_1$[ed$_2$] : κραξονται D Scr's b : txt BLℵ Orig-ed$_2$.

41. rec (for αυτην) αυτη, with E rel Orig$_{1 \text{ or } 2}$ Eus : txt ABDHLRΓΔ[Π]ℵ 1. 69 Iren-gr$_1$ Orig$_{2 \text{ or } 3}$ Bas$_1$.

42. [και γε] εν τη ημερα [σου] ταυτη bef και συ BLℵ (æth) Orig$_1$: [om και συ Syr syr-cu :] txt ADR rel latt syr copt goth Iren-gr$_1$ Eus$_1$ Orig-int$_2$. om και γε BDLℵ lat-*e f* [*q*] copt goth æth Orig[-int$_2$] Iren-int : ins AR rel vulg lat-*a* (*c*) *i* syrr syr-cu arm Eus$_1$. om 1st σου ABDLℵ 1 lat-*e f i q* syr-cu copt æth arm Orig[-int$_2$] Eus$_2$ Bas$_1$ Iren-int$_1$: ins R rel vulg lat-*a c* syrr goth. om 2nd σου (*influence of ch* xiv. 32 ?) BLℵ Orig$_1$ Iren-int : ins AR rel lat-*a* syrr syr-cu copt goth æth arm Orig$_1$ Eus$_2$ [Bas$_1$ Cyr$_1$], σοι D 69 vulg lat-*c e f i* [*l q*] Eus$_1$ Orig-int$_2$.

τὸ πλῆθ. τ. μ., in the widest sense; = *οἱ ὄχλοι* Matt. The *δύναμις*, which dwelt mostly on their minds, was *the raising of Lazarus*, John xii. 17, 18:—but as this perhaps was not known to Luke, we must understand him to mean, *all that they had seen during their journey with Him.* **38.**] **ἐν οὐρανῷ = ἐν ὑψίστοις**, and was probably added by them to fill out the parallelism.

39, 40.] The Pharisees murmur: our Lord's reply. *Peculiar to Luke.* **39.**] These Pharisees could hardly in any sense be *μαθηταί* of Jesus. Their spirit was just that of modern Socinianism: the prophetic expressions used, and the lofty epithets applied to Him, who was merely in their view a *διδάσκαλος*, offended them. **40.**] A proverbial expression —but probably not without reference to Hab. ii. 11.

41—44.] Our Lord weeps over Jerusalem. *Peculiar* (in this form) *to Luke.* **41.**] Our Lord stood on the lower part of the Mount of Olives, whence the view of the city even now is very striking. What a history of divine Love and human ingratitude lay before him!

When He grieved, it was for the *hardness of men's hearts:* when He wept, in Bethany and here, it was over the *fruits of sin.* **42.**] **εἰ ἔγνως**—*εἰώθασιν οἱ κλαίοντες ἐπικόπτεσθαι τοὺς λόγους ὑπὸ τῆς τοῦ πάθους σφοδρότητος*, Euthym. Perhaps in the *actual words* spoken by the Lord there may have been an allusion to the *name Jerusalem:*—'Utinam quæ diceris Jerusalem re ipsa esses Jerusalem, ac videres ea, quæ pacem tibi præstare possent.' Wetstein. **καὶ σύ, thou also**, as well as these My disciples. [**καί γε**, *et quidem*—**even**: Hartung remarks, Partikellehre i. 397, that this expression is confined to the Attic dialect.

[h] ἥξουσιν ἡμέραι [h] ἐπὶ σὲ [i] καὶ [k] * περιβαλοῦσιν οἱ ἐχθροί ABCDE GHKL MRSUV ΓΔΛΠℵ 1. 33. 69
σου [l] χάρακά σοι καὶ [m] περικυκλώσουσίν σε καὶ [n] συνέξου-
σίν σε [o] πάντοθεν, 44 καὶ [p] ἐδαφιοῦσίν σε καὶ τὰ τέκνα σου
ἐν σοί, καὶ οὐκ [q] ἀφήσουσιν λίθον ἐπὶ λίθον ἐν σοί, [r] ἀνθ'
ὧν οὐκ [s] ἔγνως τὸν καιρὸν τῆς [t] ἐπισκοπῆς σου.
45 Καὶ εἰςελθὼν εἰς τὸ ἱερὸν ἤρξατο ἐκβάλλειν τοὺς
πωλοῦντας, 46 λέγων αὐτοῖς Γέγραπται [u] Καὶ ἔσται ὁ
οἶκός μου [v] οἶκος [v] προσευχῆς· ὑμεῖς δὲ αὐτὸν ἐποιήσατε
[w] σπήλαιον [x] ληστῶν.
47 Καὶ [y] ἦν διδάσκων [z] τὸ καθ' ἡμέραν ἐν τῷ ἱερῷ·
οἱ δὲ ἀρχιερεῖς καὶ οἱ γραμματεῖς [a] ἐζήτουν αὐτὸν ἀπολέσαι, καὶ οἱ [b] πρῶτοι τοῦ λαοῦ, 48 καὶ οὐχ [c] εὕρισκον Q λαου ...

h Matt. xxiii. 36 reff. i = Matt. xxvi. 45. Mark xv. 25 al. k — here only. (Matt. vi. 29 reff.) Ezek. iv. 2. παρεμβάλλειν, here v. r. only. l here only. Ezek. iv. 2 al. m here only. 4 Kings vi. 14. n — here only. (ch. viii. 45.) 1 Kings xxiii. 8. o Mark i. 45 reff. p here only. Isa. iii. 26. Hos. x. 14 al. (-φος, Acts xxii. 7.) q = Matt. xxiv. 2 reff. r ch. i. 20 reff. s = John i. 10. Rom. vii. 7. t = 1 Pet. ii. 12 [v. 6 v. r.] (Acts i. 20. 1 Tim. iii. 1) only. Job x. 12. Jer. vi. 15. see ch. i. 68. u Isa. lvi. 7. Jer. vii. 11. v ||. Isa. lx. 7. w ||. John xi. 38. Heb. xi. 38. Rev. vi. 5 only. Gen. xix. 30 al. x || Mt. reff. y Matt. xix. 22 reff. z ch. xi. 3. Acts xvii. 11. a = ch. v. 18. vi. 19. Exod. ii. 15. b = Mark vi. 21 reff. c = ch. v. 19 reff.

43. * παρεμβαλοῦσιν C^1Lℵ 33 [$Eus_{1 \text{ or } 2}$]: βαλουσιν D: περιβαλουσιν ABR rel. —και βαλουσιν bef επι σε D. [om σοι D lat-*a e ff*$_2$ Eus_1.] om 2nd σε Lℵ[1] [$Orig_1$]. om 3rd σε ℵ[1] Scr's e [D-lat].

44. om 1st εν σοι D 1 $Orig_1$ Eus_1. rec 2nd εν σοι bef λιθον επι λ., with ACR rel vulg lat-*f* syrr syr-cu goth: txt B(sic: see table) DLℵ 1 ev-y lat-*a c* [*e ff*$_2$ *i l q*] copt æth [arm $Orig_1$].—ins ολη bef σοι D lat-*c* (*e*) *ff*$_2$ *i* arm. rec (for 2nd λιθον) λιθω, with AC rel: txt BDLRΛ[1][Π]ℵ 1. 33 ev-y $Orig_1$. om τον CD.—εις καιρον επισκ. σου D.

45. for κ. εισελθ., ελθων δε D lat-*e*. rec aft πωλουντας ins εν αυτω (|| *Matt Mark*), with ADR rel latt syrr syr-cu goth: om BCLℵ 1. 69 lat-*e l* copt arm $Orig_2$.—rec adds further και αγοραζοντας (|| *Matt Mark*), with A C(κ. τους α.) DR rel: om BLℵ 1 copt $Orig_3$(ἐν οἷς ἤρξατο ἐκβάλλειν μόνους τοὺς πωλοῦντας, οὐχὶ δὲ καὶ τοὺς ἀγοράζοντας). add και τας τραπεζας των κολλυβιστων εξεχεεν και τας καθεδρας των πωλουντων τας περιστερας DΛ lat-*a c e ff*$_2$ *g*$_2$ *i* [*l q* æth] syr-w-ast.

46. rec om και, with ℵ[1] rel lat-*a e ff*$_2$ *i*: for και, οτι (|| *Mark*) ACDKM[Π] 33 vulg lat-*f g*$_{1.2}$ syrr syr-cu copt goth (æth): txt BLRℵ[3a] 1. 69 lat-*c* $Orig_1$. rec om εσται, with AC^1Dℵ[1] rel vulg lat-*a* (*e*) *f ff*$_2$ *g*$_{1.2}$ syrr syr-cu goth: ins BLRℵ[3a] 1. 69 lat-*c* arm $Orig_1$.—rec aft προσευχης ins εστιν, with AC^1D rel vulg lat-*a f ff*$_2$ *g*$_{1.2}$ syrr syr-cu goth: κληθησεται C^2 lat-*e* æth [$Epiph_2$]: om BLRℵ 1. 69 lat-*c* arm $Orig_1$. εποιησατε bef αυτον D 237 Scr's a f ev-y vulg lat-*c e f ff*$_2$ *g*$_{1.2}$ [*i l q*] $Orig_1$ $Epiph_2$.

47. om ιερω οι δε ℵ[1](ins ℵ-corr[1.3]). om 2nd οι $AK^1Λ$. κ. οι πρωτ. τ. λ. bef εζητ. αυτ. απολ. D latt syrr syr-cu copt æth arm $Orig_1$.

But in classic Greek the emphatic word always intervenes between καί and γε,—so καί σέ γε ἐν τούτοις λέγω, Æsch. Prom. 1009: whereas in Latin *et quidem* is usually found undivided.] **43.**] ὅτι declares, not '*the things hidden from thine eyes,*' so that it should be rendered, '*namely, that the days shall come,*' &c.: but the awful reason which there was for the fervent wish just expressed—**for,** or **because.** **χάρακα,** a mound with palisades. The account of its being built is in Jos. B. J. v. 6. 2. When the Jews destroyed this, Titus built a wall round them (ib. 12. 2),—see Isa. xxix. 2, 3, 4,—to which our Lord here tacitly refers. **44.**] **ἐδαφ.** is used in *two meanings*:—**shall level thy buildings to the foundation, and dash thy children against the ground:** see reff. **τὰ τέκνα** is not '*infants,*' but **thy children,** in general. **οὐκ ἀφήσ.**] See ref. Matt. and note there. **ἀνθ' ὧν . . . .**] Not, '*because of thy sins and rebellions;*'—those might be all blotted out, hadst thou known, recognized, the time of thy visiting by Me. **ἐπισκ.** is a word of ambiguous meaning—**visitation,** either for good or for evil: see reff. It brings at once here before us the *coming seeking fruit,* ch. xiii. 7—and the *returning of the Lord of the vineyard,* ch. xx. 16. It is however the first or favourable meaning of ἐπισκοπή that is here prominent.

45, 46.] Cleansing of the temple. See on Matt. xxi. 12, 13: Mark xi. 15—17.

47, 48.] A general description of His

[d]τὸ τί ποιήσωσιν· ὁ λαὸς γὰρ ἅπας [e]ἐξεκρέματο αὐτοῦ
ἀκούων.
XX. 1 Καὶ ἐγένετο ἐν [f]μιᾷ τῶν ἡμερῶν, διδάσκοντος
αὐτοῦ τὸν λαὸν ἐν τῷ ἱερῷ και [g]εὐαγγελιζομένου, [h]ἐπ-
έστησαν οἱ ἱερεῖς καὶ οἱ γραμματεῖς σὺν τοῖς πρεσβυτέροις, 2 καὶ εἶπαν πρὸς αὐτὸν Εἰπὸν ἡμῖν, [i]ἐν [k]ποίᾳ
ἐξουσίᾳ ταῦτα ποιεῖς, ἢ τίς ἐστιν ὁ δούς σοι τὴν ἐξουσίαν
ταύτην; 3 ἀποκριθεὶς δὲ εἶπεν πρὸς αὐτοὺς Ἐρωτήσω
ὑμᾶς κἀγὼ [l]λόγον, καὶ εἴπατέ μοι. 4 τὸ βάπτισμα
Ἰωάννου ἐξ οὐρανοῦ ἦν ἢ ἐξ ἀνθρώπων; 5 οἱ δὲ [m]συνελο-
γίσαντο πρὸς ἑαυτοὺς λέγοντες ὅτι ἐὰν εἴπωμεν Ἐξ οὐρανοῦ, ἐρεῖ Διὰ τί οὐκ ἐπιστεύσατε αὐτῷ; 6 ἐὰν δὲ εἴπωμεν
Ἐξ ἀνθρώπων, ὁ λαὸς ἅπας [n]καταλιθάσει ἡμᾶς· [o]πε-
πεισμένος γάρ [o]ἐστιν Ἰωάννην προφήτην εἶναι. 7 καὶ

d see Mark ix. 23 reff.
e here only. Gen. xliv. 30 (Judith viii. 24 [21] Ald. compl.) only.
f ch. v. 17 reff.
g = ch. ix. 6 reff.
h ch. ii. 9, 38. xxiv. 4. Acts iv. 1. xii. 7. Luke only, exc. 1 Thess. v. 3. 2 Tim. iv. 2, 6.
i ||. Acts iv. 7. ch. i. 17. iv. 14 al.
k ||. Matt. xix. 18. xxii. 36 al. 2 Kings xv. 2.
l ||. 2 Kings iii. 13. see ch. xxiii. 9. Acts xxviii. 25. Jer. xlv. (xxxviii.) 14.
m here only. Isa. xliii. 18.
n here only †.
o constr., Acts xxvi. 26.

48. om το DUΓ¹Δ **1.** 69 arm Orig$_1$. aft ποιησωσιν ins αυτω D vulg lat-*c f* &c(not *a e*) Syr syr-cu syr-w-ast. γαρ bef λαος D 69 Orig$_1$. εξεκρεμετο (*itacism?*) Bℵ Orig: εκρεματο D. ακουειν DM 69 copt-ms.—ακ. bef αυτου D 248 ιv-y latt [copt].

Chap. XX. **1.** for και εγ., εγ. δε D lat-*e*. rec aft των ημερων ins εκεινων, with ACR rel syr goth arm: om BDLQℵ **1** latt Syr syr-cu [syr-jer] copt æth Mcion$_1$-e. εν τω ιερω bef τον λαον D lat-*e* Syr syr-cu. ευαγγελιζομενοι (sic) ℵ¹. rec αρχιερεις (*so* || *and ch* xix. 47), with BCDLMQRℵ **1.** 33. 69 vss: txt A [S(Tischdf)] rel lat-*a e* goth Thl. om 2nd οι AGVΓΔ arm.
2. (ειπαν, so BLRℵ 69.) rec aft προς αυτον ins λεγοντες (|| *Matt*), with AQR rel lat-*a* syr goth: pref BLℵ **1** vulg lat-*c ff$_2$ i l* Syr syr-cu: om CD lat-*e f q* [syr-jer] copt æth arm. rec (for ειπον) ειπε, with ADQ rel: txt BLR ℵ-corr¹·³ **1.** 33.—om ειπ. ημ. (|| *Matt Mark*) C ℵ¹(ins ℵ-corr¹·³). for ἤ, και D lat-*a e* Syr. ταυτην bef την εξουσιαν D latt Hil$_1$.
3. aft αποκριθεις δε ins ο ιησους C 130(Sz) vulg-clem [lat-*i l q*] Syr. αυτον ℵ¹: om πρ. αυ. 69. επερωτησω D Scr's v. rec ins ενα bef λογον (|| *Mark*), with CDQ rel [syr-jer] goth (æth); aft λογον (|| *Matt*) AKMU¹[SΠ] vulg lat-*f g$_1$* syr-w-ast arm: om BLRℵ **1.** 33. 69 forj(with tol) lat-*a c e ff$_2$ i q* Syr copt. for και, ον D.
4. ins το bef ιωαννου (|| *Mark*) DLRℵ: om ABCQ rel.
5. συνελογιζοντο (*imperf as in* ||) CDℵ latt syrr syr-cu [syr-jer]: txt ABQR rel lat-*e* copt goth. for εαυτ., αυτους ℵ¹ Scr's e. om οτι C Scr's h i lat-*e ff$_2$ i q* syr-cu. rec aft δια τι ins ουν (*from* || *Matt*), with ACDKMQ[Π] **1.** 33 vulg lat-*a e f g$_{1.2}$ q* syr arm: om BR [S(Tischdf)] ℵ rel harl¹(with mm) lat-*c ff$_2$ i l* Syr syr-cu [syr-jer] copt æth.
6. for εαν δε, και εαν D lat-*a c* [*i l q* syr-jer] syr-cu. ins οτι bef εξ C¹ syr-cu. for εξ, απο των *ab* D lat-*a c* [*e ff$_2$*]. rec (for ο λαος απας) πας ο λαος, with ACQ rel lat-*a f ff$_2$* syr-cu syr [goth] arm, απας ο λαος R: txt BDLℵ **1.** 33 vulg lat-*c* [*i l q* syr-jer] Syr copt.—λιθασει(for καταλ.) ημας bef ο λαος απας D. πεπεισμενοι γαρ εισιν D-gr Scr's c latt. for ειναι, γεγονεναι D 69 lat-*a c e f ff$_2$ i l q*

employment during these last days, the particulars of which follow. It is rightly however placed at the *end* of a chapter, for it forms a close to the long section wherein the last journey to Jerusalem has been described.

Chap. XX. 1—8.] His authority questioned. His reply. Matt. xxi. 23—27. Mark xi. 27—33, where see notes. (The *history of the fig-tree* is not in our text.) **1. τῶν ἡμ.]** of the days, viz. of this His being in Jerusalem. **ἐπέστ.** without a dative (see ch. ii. 38) does not signify any *suddenness* of approach. **2.] ἤ—or (to speak more definitely).**

ἀπεκρίθησαν μὴ εἰδέναι πόθεν. 8 καὶ ὁ Ἰησοῦς εἶπεν
αὐτοῖς Οὐδὲ ἐγὼ λέγω ὑμῖν [i] ἐν [k] ποίᾳ ἐξουσίᾳ ταῦτα ποιῶ.
9 [p] ἤρξατο δὲ πρὸς τὸν λαὸν λέγειν τὴν παραβολὴν ταύτην. Ἄνθρωπος [q] ἐφύτευσεν [r] ἀμπελῶνα καὶ [s] ἐξέδετο
αὐτὸν [t] γεωργοῖς, καὶ [u] ἀπεδήμησεν χρόνους [v] ἱκανούς.
10 καὶ [w] καιρῷ ἀπέστειλεν πρὸς τοὺς [t] γεωργοὺς δοῦλον,
ἵνα [x] ἀπὸ τοῦ καρποῦ τοῦ [r] ἀμπελῶνος δώσουσιν αὐτῷ. οἱ
δὲ [t] γεωργοὶ [y] ἐξαπέστειλαν αὐτὸν [z] δείραντες κενόν. 11 καὶ
[a] προσέθετο ἕτερον πέμψαι δοῦλον· οἱ δὲ κἀκεῖνον [z] δείραντες καὶ [b] ἀτιμάσαντες [y] ἐξαπέστειλαν κενόν. 12 καὶ
[a] προσέθετο τρίτον πέμψαι· οἱ δὲ καὶ τοῦτον [c] τραυμα-
τίσαντες [d] ἐξέβαλον. 13 εἶπεν δὲ ὁ κύριος τοῦ [r] ἀμπελῶνος Τί ποιήσω; πέμψω τὸν υἱόν μου τὸν [e] ἀγαπητόν·
[f] ἴσως τοῦτον [ἰδόντες] [g] ἐντραπήσονται. 14 ἰδόντες δὲ
αὐτὸν οἱ [h] γεωργοὶ [i] διελογίζοντο πρὸς ἀλλήλους λέ-

ABCDE GHLK MQRSU VΓΔΛ Πא 1. 33. 69

F τριτον ...

p = Matt. iv. 17. Gen. xviii. 27.
q Matt. xv. 13 reff. Deut. xx. 6.
r Matt. xx. 1 reff.
s | (Mt. bis) only. Exod. ii. 21. Sir. vii. 25.
t || Mt reff.
u ||. ch. xv. 13. Matt. xxv. 14 only +.
v ch. viii. 27 reff.
w without ἐν (absol., here only), 2 Cor. vi. 2 (from Isa. xlix. 8). Gal. vi. 9. 1 Tim. ii. 6. vi. 15. Tit. i. 3 only. with ἐν, Matt. xxiv. 45. 1 Pet. v. 6. Ps. i. 3.
x || Mk. [ch. xxiv. 42.] John xxi. 10. cf. Matt. xxv. 8.
y ch. i. 53 reff.
z || Mt. reff.
a = ch. xix. 11. Acts xii. 3 only. Gen. iv. 2. viii. 12. xviii. 29.
b || Mk. reff.
c Acts xix. 16 only. Ezek. xxviii. 16.
d ||. John ix. 34, 35. xii. 31. Gen. iii. 24.
e || Mk. Matt. iii. 17 reff.
f here only. Gen. xxxii. 20. 1 Kings xxv. 21 (only ?).
g || Mt. reff.
h ver. 9.
i Matt. xvi. 7, 8 reff.

7. om *μη* א[1](ins א-corr[1·3]). aft *ειδεναι* ins *αυτους* CD. ins *το* bef *ποθεν* D 69.

8. for *ο ιησους*, *αποκριθεις* א[1].

9. for *ηρξατο*, *ελεγεν*, and om *προς τον λαον λεγειν* D lat-*e*. *λεγειν* bef *πρ. τ. λαον* Q vulg lat-*c* ff_2 *i l* [*q*] syr copt: om *λεγειν* א[1](txt א-corr[1]) lat-*a*. rec aft *ανθρωπος* ins *τις*, with A 69 lat-g_1 Syr syr-cu syr-w-ast [arm]: om BCDQRא rel latt copt goth æth Orig_1. *αμπελωνα* bef *ανθρωπος εφυτευσεν* C: *αμπ. εφ. ανθ.* (|| *Mark*) D lat-*a c f* [*i l q*]: txt ABQא rel (Orig). (*εξεδετο*, so AB[1]CLא[1].) for last *και*, *αυτος δε* D lat-*e*. (*ικανους* only on margin in B.)

10. rec ins *εν* bef *καιρω*, with AR rel; *εν τω* CQ copt: om BDLא [33].—for *και καιρω*, *καιρω δε* D. *τους καρπους* (retaining *απο*) Λ ev-y: om א. rec (for *δωσουσιν*) *δωσιν*, with CDR rel: *δωσει* 69: txt ABLMQא. om *οι δε γεωργοι* and aft *δειραντες* ins *δε* D (syr-cu). rec transp *εξαπεστειλαν* and *δειραντες*, with AC (D)QR rel: txt BLא.

11. for *προσεθετο*, *εθετο* א[1](txt א-corr[1]): *επεμψεν* (omg *πεμψαι*) D lat-*e*. aft *προσεθετο* ins *αυτοις* Q copt: aft *πεμψαι* C[1](perhaps) syr. rec *πεμψαι* bef *ετερον*, with CQR rel syrr syr-cu (copt) goth æth arm: txt ABL[U]א lat-*a c* ff_2 *i* [*l q*], but for *ετερον*, *υστερον* (*by itacism οιστερον*) L. (D see above.)

12. rec *πεμψαι* bef *τριτον*, with ACQR rel syrr copt goth: txt BLא latt arm.—*τριτον επεμψεν*, omg [*και*] *προσεθετο*, D lat-*e* (æth). om *οι δε* D lat-*a c e* ff_2 *i* [*l*]. for *και τουτον*, *κακεινον* (|| *Mark*) AK[Π] latt (syr-mg): txt BCDQRא rel. for *εξεβαλον*, *εξαπεστειλαν κενον* (*from ver* 10) D lat-*f i q*.

13. *ο δε κ. τ. αμπ. ειπεν* D lat-*e*. [om *τι ποιησω* B[1]: ins B[2·3](Tischdf).] for *ισως*, *τυχον* D. om *ιδοντες* (|| *Matt Mark*) BCDLQא 1. 33 lat-*a c* ff_2 *i l* [*q*] syr-cu syr-mg copt arm Ambr_2: ins AR rel vulg lat-*e f* syrr goth (æth).

14. om 1st *αυτον* Mא[1]. om *οι γεωργοι* D lat-*e*. *διελογισαντο* (*more usual historical tense*) AK[Π] latt: txt BCDQRא rel lat-*e* syrr syr-cu copt. rec (for *αλληλους*) *εαυτους* (|| *Mark Matt*), with ACQ rel syrr arm-ms: txt BDLRא 1. 33

9—19.] Parable of the vineyard let out to husbandmen. Matt. xxi. 33—46. Mark xii. 1—12. See notes on Matt. for the sense; and for comparison of the reports, on Mark. **9.**] The parable was spoken **πρός**, **to**, the *people*—but (ver. 19), *πρός*, at, with reference to, *the chief priests and scribes.* Bengel suggests that He addressed it to the people, to guard against interruption on the part of the chief priests.

11.] **προσέθ. π.**, a Hebraism: see reff. Gen., Hebrew and LXX. **14. ἰδόντ. δέ**] This is taken up from the **τοῦτον ἰδόντες** of the verse before, and is emphatic—**On the contrary, when they saw**

γοντες Οὗτός ἐστιν ὁ [k] κληρονόμος· ἀποκτείνωμεν αὐτόν,
ἵνα ἡμῶν γένηται ἡ [l] κληρονομία. 15 καὶ [d] ἐκβαλόντες
αὐτὸν ἔξω τοῦ [h] ἀμπελῶνος ἀπέκτειναν. τί οὖν ποιήσει
αὐτοῖς ὁ κύριος τοῦ [h] ἀμπελῶνος; 16 ἐλεύσεται καὶ [m] ἀπολέσει τοὺς [h] γεωργοὺς τούτους, καὶ δώσει τὸν [h] ἀμπελῶνα
ἄλλοις. ἀκούσαντες δὲ εἶπαν [n] Μὴ γένοιτο. 17 ὁ δὲ
[o] ἐμβλέψας αὐτοῖς εἶπεν [p] Τί οὖν ἐστιν τὸ γεγραμμένον
τοῦτο, Λίθον ὃν [q] ἀπεδοκίμασαν οἱ οἰκοδομοῦντες, οὗτος
[rs] ἐγενήθη [s] εἰς [r] κεφαλὴν [rt] γωνίας; 18 πᾶς ὁ πεσὼν ἐπ'
ἐκεῖνον τὸν λίθον [u] συνθλασθήσεται, ἐφ' ὃν δ' ἂν πέσῃ,
[v] λικμήσει αὐτόν. 19 καὶ [w] ἐζήτησαν οἱ γραμματεῖς καὶ οἱ
ἀρχιερεῖς [x] ἐπιβαλεῖν ἐπ' αὐτὸν τὰς χεῖρας ἐν [y] αὐτῇ τῇ
[y] ὥρᾳ, καὶ ἐφοβήθησαν τὸν λαόν· ἔγνωσαν γὰρ ὅτι [z] πρὸς
αὐτοὺς εἶπεν τὴν παραβολὴν ταύτην.

20 Καὶ [a] παρατηρήσαντες ἀπέστειλαν [b] ἐγκαθέτους [c] ὑπο-
κρινομένους ἑαυτοὺς δικαίους εἶναι, ἵνα [d] ἐπιλάβωνται
αὐτοῦ [e] λόγου, [f] ὥςτε [g] παραδοῦναι αὐτὸν τῇ [h] ἀρχῇ καὶ

...τι ουν Q.

...δικαιους R.

k || Mk. reff. l || Mt. reff. m = Matt. x. 28. xxii. 7 al. n here only in Gospp. Rom. iii. 4, &c. L.P. Gen. xliv. 7. Josh. xxii. 29. o Mark x. 21 reff. p = ch. viii. 9. xviii. 36. q || Mt. reff. Psa. cxvii. 22. r ||. Acts iv. 11, & 1 Pet. ii. 7, from l. c. s as above (r). ch. xiii. 19. Rom. xi. 9, from Ps. lxviii. 22. Rev. viii. 11. t as above (r). Matt. vi. 5. Acts xxvi. 26. Rev. vii. 1. xx. 8 only. u || Mt. only. Ps. lvii. 6. Mic. iii. 3. v || Mt. only. Job xxvii. 21. Dan. ii. 44 Theod. w = Matt. xii. 46, 47 reff. x Matt. xxvi. 50 reff.

y ch. xii. 12. z = Rom. x. 21. Heb. i. 7, 8. a ch. vi. 7 reff. b here only. = Job xix. 12 (xxxi. 9) only. Jos. B. J. vi. 5. 2. c here only ‡. 2 Macc. v. 25. d = ver. 26 only. (ch. xxiii. 26 reff.) e = Matt. v. 37. xxii. 15. f = ch. ix. 5 reff. g Matt. xvii. 22 reff. h = ch. xii. 11. Tit. iii. 1.

syr-mg copt arm. rec ins δευτε bef αποκτεινωμεν (*from* ||), with CDRℵ rel tol lat-*e* Syr syr-cu syr-w-ast copt æth(appy) Orig$_1$: om ABKMQ[Π] 1 latt goth arm. for ινα ημων γενηται, και ημων εσται (|| *Mark*) C 1 forj lat-*c e i* [*l*] *q* Syr syr-cu. η κληρ. bef γεν. L.

15. for εκβαλοντες, λαβοντες (|| *Matt Mark*) CL. aft αυτον ins εξεβαλον, and aft αμπελωνος ins και (|| *Matt*) C. om 1st του αμπελωνος Q. om αυτοις (|| *Mark*) D 29 forj lat-*a c e q*.

16. om τους γεωργους ℵ^1 Scr's g. for τουτους, εκεινους 1. 69 lat-*f* æth : om (|| *Mark*) D 76. 247 lat-*e* copt. for ακ. δε, οι δε ακ. AD lat-*e* : txt BCQRℵ rel. (ειπαν, so BDGLQRℵ 33.)

19. εζητουν (|| *Mark*) CD vulg lat-*c f ff$_2$ i* Syr syr-cu copt arm : txt ABRℵ rel lat-*a e* syr goth. rec transp γραμματεις and αρχιερεις (|| *Matt*), with DRℵ rel latt Syr syr-cu : txt ABC K(Treg, expr) LMU[Π] 1. 33 lat-*e* syr copt goth æth arm. om εν D latt. for και εφοβ., εφοβ. δε D lat-*e*. om εγνωσαν γαρ ℵ^1(ins ℵ-corr^1). rec την παραβ. ταυτ. bef ειπεν (|| *Mark*), with ACR rel syr goth arm : txt B(D)GLℵ 69 latt Syr copt.—ειρηκεν D.

20. for παρατηρησαντες, αποχωρησαντες D lat-*a c e f ff$_2$ g$_1$ i l* goth æth. αποκρινομενους ℵ^1(txt ℵ^{3b}). om ειναι D[-gr]. for αυτου λογου, αυτον λογον C : αυτους λογους L : αυτου λογον KΓ : αυτου των λογων D lat-*a c e ff$_2$ i l* (arm) : txt A B(sic : see table) ℵ rel. (R def.) rec (for ωστε) εις το (*never used by Luke*), with A rel : txt BCDLℵ ev-y. for 1st τη to ηγεμονος, τω ηγεμονι D lat-*e* syr-cu : om lat-*i*.—om 2nd τη ℵ evv-H-z.

him . . . . 17.] The **οὖν** infers the negation of **μὴ γένοιτο**—'*How then, supposing your wish to be fulfilled, could this which is written come to pass?*' 19.] **καί** before ἐφοβήθ. is not *but:* the clause signifies the state of mind in which this their attempt was made: **and they did so in fear of the people.**

20—26.] Reply concerning the lawfulness of tribute to Cæsar. Matt. xxii. 15—22. Mark xii. 13—17, where see notes as before. 20.] **παρατηρ., having watched an opportunity. ἐγκαθ.,** see reff., **men suborned,** *instructed and arranged for that purpose.* **ἐπιλάβ.,** not the spies, but the chief priests. **αὐτοῦ** is not the genitive after **λόγου,** as in E. V., but after **ἐπιλ.,** as in ἐπιλαμβάνεται αὐτοῦ τῆς ἴτυος, Xen. Anab. iv. 7. 12:—**that they might lay hold of him by some saying;** = αὐτὸν ἀγρεύσωσιν λόγῳ, Mark.

i = ch. xxii. 53. Rev. xii. 10.
k Matt. xii. 10 al. fr.
l ch. vii. 43 reff.
m Gal. ii. 6 only. Ps. lxxxi. 2 (see Acts x. 34. James ii. 1, 9).
n ‖ Mk. ch. iv. 25. Acts iv. 17. x. 34 al. Deut. xxii. 30. (ἐν ἀλ., ‖ Mt. reff.)
o ‖. (Acts xviii. 26 v. r.) see Ps. cxviii. 15 al.
p ch. xxiii. 2. Rom. xiii. 6, 7 only. Judg. i. 28.
q = ‖. ch. xxiii. 2. Heb. vii. 4.
r = Matt. vii. 3. Isa. v. 12.
s 1 Cor. iii. 19. 2 Cor. iv. 2. xi. 3. Eph. iv. 14 only. Josh. ix. 4. (-γος, 2 Cor. xii. 16.)

τῇ [i] ἐξουσίᾳ τοῦ ἡγεμόνος. 21 καὶ [k] ἐπηρώτησαν αὐτὸν ... καὶ ε F.
λέγοντες Διδάσκαλε, οἴδαμεν ὅτι [l] ὀρθῶς λέγεις καὶ διδάσκεις, καὶ οὐ [m] λαμβάνεις [m] πρόσωπον, ἀλλ' [n] ἐπ' [n] ἀληθείας P και ου
τὴν [o] ὁδὸν τοῦ [o] θεοῦ διδάσκεις. 22 ἔξεστιν ἡμᾶς Καίσαρι ABCDE GHKL
[p] φόρον [q] δοῦναι, ἢ οὔ; 23 [r] κατανοήσας δὲ αὐτῶν τὴν MPSUV ΓΔΛΠ
[s] πανουργίαν εἶπεν πρὸς αὐτούς 24 Δείξατέ μοι [t] δη- ℵ 1. 33. 69
νάριον. τίνος ἔχει [u] εἰκόνα καὶ [v] ἐπιγραφήν; ἀποκριθέντες δὲ εἶπαν Καίσαρος. 25 ὁ δὲ εἶπεν πρὸς αὐτούς
[w] Τοίνυν [x] ἀπόδοτε τὰ Καίσαρος Καίσαρι, καὶ τὰ τοῦ θεοῦ
τῷ θεῷ. 26 καὶ οὐκ [y] ἴσχυσαν [z] ἐπιλαβέσθαι τοῦ ῥήματος
[a] ἐναντίον τοῦ λαοῦ, καὶ θαυμάσαντες [b] ἐπὶ τῇ [c] ἀποκρίσει
αὐτοῦ [d] ἐσίγησαν. 27 Προσελθόντες δέ τινες τῶν Σαδδουκαίων, οἱ [ef] ἀντιλέγοντες [g] ἀνάστασιν [f] μὴ εἶναι, ἐπηρώτησαν αὐτὸν 28 λέγοντες Διδάσκαλε, Μωυσῆς ἔγρα- ...αυτον C.
ψεν ἡμῖν, [h] ἐάν τινος ἀδελφὸς ἀποθάνῃ ἔχων γυναῖκα,

t Matt. xx. 2 reff. u ‖ only in Gospp. Rom. i. 23. Heb. x. 1. Gen. i. 26 al. v ‖. ch. xxiii. 38 ‖ Mk. only †. w 1 Cor. ix. 26. Heb. xiii. 13 (James ii. 24 v. r.) only. Isa. iii. 10. v. 13. x ‖ Rom. xiii. 7. Deut. xxiii. 21. y = Matt. viii. 28 reff. z = ver. 20 only. a = Mark ii. 12 reff. b ‖ Mk. reff. Isa. lii. 15. c ch. ii. 47. John i. 22. xix. 9 only. Job xxxv. 3. d ch. xviii. 39 reff. e ch. ii. 34 reff. f here only. see 1 John ii. 22. g ‖ Mt. reff. h Deut. xxv. 5.

21. λεγεις bef *ορθως* D lat-*a e*. for *ου*, *ουδενος* (‖ *Matt Mark*) D Aug Promiss.
22. rec **ημιν** (*more usual*), with CDP rel vss [Bas_1]: txt ABLℵ 33. 69. for *δουναι*, *διδοναι* DM.—*φορ. δ.* bef *καισαρι* D vulg[-clem] lat-*a q*.
23. for *κατανοησας*, *επιγνους* D lat-*e*. for *πανουργιαν*, *πονηριαν* (‖ *Matt*) C^1D [lat-*a e l*]: txt ABC^3Pℵ rel Syr. rec at end ins *τι με πειραζετε* (‖ *Matt Mark*), with ACDP rel [vss Bas_1]: om BLℵ 1 lat-*e* copt arm.—C adds further *υποκριται* (*from* ‖ *Matt*).
24. rec **επιδειξατε** (‖ *Matt*), with C rel: txt ABDLMPℵ 33. 69 [Bas_2]. for *δηναριον*, *το νομισμα* D Orig-int_1. add *οι δε εδειξαν και ειπεν* (*gloss founded on* ‖) CL 1. 33. 69 (lat-*c*) syr copt arm: *οι δε εδειξ. αυτω κ. ειπ.*(*ειπαν* $ℵ^1$) ℵ: om ABDP rel vulg lat-*a* Syr syr-cu goth æth(Treg) [Bas_2]. om *και επιγραφην* P: ins *την* bef *επιγρ.* D. for *αποκριθεντες δε*, *οι δε* (‖ *Mark*) BLℵ 33 Syr syr-mg copt [Bas_1]: *αποκριθεντες*, omg *δε* (‖ *Matt*), DΓ 1 latt: *και απ.* G Scr's f: txt ACP rel lat-*f* syr[-txt] goth [Bas_1]. (*ειπαν*, so BCLℵ 33.)
25. for *ο δε ειπεν*, *ειπεν δε* D. rec (for *προς αυτους*) *αυτοις* (‖ *Matt Mark*), with ACDP rel: txt BLℵ 1. 69 lat-*e*. rec *αποδοτε* bef *τοινυν*, with ACP rel vulg lat-*c f* ff_2 syrr: om *τοινυν* D lat-*a e i l q* syr-cu [æth]: txt BLℵ 69 copt goth arm. ins *τω* bef *καισαρι* C^1DL: om ABC^3Pℵ rel [Bas_1]. (*Cf digest on* ‖ *Matt Mark.*)
26. for *και ουκ ισχυσαν*, *ουκ εισχυσαν δε* D. rec for 1st *του*, *αυτου* (*see ver* 20), with AC(D) rel: txt BLℵ.—for *ρηματος*, *ρημα*, and *αυτου ρ.* bef *επιλαβεσθαι*, D latt(not *e*).
27. for *αντιλεγοντες*, *λεγοντες* (*from* ‖ *Matt Mark*) BCDLℵ 1. 33 lat-*e* Syr syr-cu copt goth æth: txt AP rel syr (arm). *επηρωτων* (‖ *Mark*) B lat-*a* syr, *επηρωτουν* 69.

τῇ ἀρχῇ, to the Roman power (genus)—**τῇ ἐξ. τ. ἡ.**, to the authority of the governor (species). The *second article* renders the separation of the two necessary. **22.**] **φόρον** = κῆνσον, see on Matt.:—differs from τέλος, '*vectigal*,' customs duties.

27—40.] Reply to the Sadducees respecting the resurrection. Matt. xxii. 23—33: Mark xii. 18—27, and notes.

27.] **οἱ ἀντιλέγοντες** refers to τῶν Σαδ., not to τινες. The main subject of the sentence is sometimes put in the nom., even when the construction requires another case: so Ἀνδρομάχη, θυγάτηρ μεγαλήτορος Ἠετίωνος, Ἠετίων, ὃς ἔναιεν . . . . Hom. Il. ζ. 395. See also κ. 437, and more examples in Bernhardy, Syntax, p. 68. The use of ἀντιλέγ. μή (or τὸ μή) is frequent in Xenophon, see Wetstein: and cf. Thucyd. i. 95, ἀπολύεται τοῦ μὴ ἀδικεῖν,—ii. 49, ἀπορίᾳ τοῦ μὴ

καὶ οὗτος [i] ἄτεκνος ᾖ, ἵνα [k] λάβῃ ὁ ἀδελφὸς αὐτοῦ
τὴν γυναῖκα καὶ [l] ἐξαναστήσῃ σπέρμα τῷ ἀδελφῷ αὐτοῦ.
29 ἑπτὰ [m] οὖν ἀδελφοὶ ἦσαν. καὶ ὁ πρῶτος [k] λαβὼν
γυναῖκα [n] ἀπέθανεν [in] ἄτεκνος, 30 καὶ ὁ δεύτερος 31 καὶ ὁ
τρίτος [k] ἔλαβεν αὐτήν· [o] ὡσαύτως δὲ καὶ οἱ ἑπτὰ οὐ [p] κατέλιπον τέκνα, καὶ ἀπέθανον. 32 [q] ὕστερον καὶ ἡ γυνὴ
R αυτων ἀπέθανεν. 33 ἡ γυνὴ οὖν ἐν τῇ ἀναστάσει τίνος αὐτῶν
... γίνεται γυνή; οἱ γὰρ ἑπτὰ [r] ἔσχον αὐτὴν γυναῖκα.
Q οι υιοι 34 καὶ εἶπεν αὐτοῖς ὁ Ἰησοῦς Οἱ [st] υἱοὶ τοῦ [t] αἰῶνος τούτου
... γαμοῦσιν καὶ [u] γαμίσκονται, 35 οἱ δὲ [v] καταξιωθέντες τοῦ
[wx] αἰῶνος [x] ἐκείνου [y] τυχεῖν καὶ τῆς [z] ἀναστάσεως τῆς [z] ἐκ
[z] νεκρῶν οὔτε γαμοῦσιν οὔτε [u] γαμίσκονται. 36 οὐδὲ γὰρ

i here 3ce only. Isa. xlix. 21.
k ‖ Mk. Gen. iv. 19. Hos. i. 2, 3.
l = ‖ Mk. (aor. intr., Acts xv. 5) only. Gen. xix. 32, 34.
m = John iv. 5. 1 Cor. vii. 26.
n Lev. xx. 20, 21. Sir. xvi. 3.
o Matt. xx. 5. ch. xxii. 20. Judg. viii. 8 B.
p Mark xii. 19. Deut. xxviii. 54.
q Matt. iv. 2 reff. Jer. xxxvi. (xxix.) 2.
r = Matt. xiv. 4 reff.
s = ch. x. 6. John xii. 36. Eph. ii. 2. Ezra ii. 2.
t ch. xvi. 8.
u here bis (‖ Mk. v. r.) only +.
v and constr., (ch. xxi. 36 v. r.) Acts v. 41. 2 Thess. i. 5 only +. (Gen. xxx. 28 compl.? 2 Macc. xiii. 12 only, but not =.)
w = Mark x. 30 reff.
x here only.
y = Acts xxiv. 3. xxvi. 22. xxvii. 3. 2 Tim. ii. 10. Heb. viii. 6. xi. 35 only. 2 Macc. iv. 6.
z Acts iv. 2. 1 Pet. i. 3. see Matt. xxii. 31 reff. Phil. iii. 11.

28. homœotel in א[1] *και* to *και* (ins א-corr[1]). *ατεκνος* bef *εχων γυναικα*, omg *και ουτος*, D. rec (for *ῇ*) *αποθανη*, with A rel lat-*e f i* syr goth: om D: txt BLPא[3a] **1.** 33 vulg lat-*a ff*$_2$ *g*$_1$ *l* [*q*] (Syr syr-cu) copt (æth) arm, *ην* א-corr[1]. *εξαναστησει* (*itacism*) AEHΡΓΛ 69.

29. transp *ησαν* to beg, addg *παρ ημειν* and omg *ουν*, (‖ *Matt*) D. aft *ησαν* ins *παρ ημιν* (D) א-corr[1] 245-9 lat-*c ff*$_2$ *l* [*q*] æth.

30. rec aft *και* ins *ελαβεν*, and aft *ο δευτερος* ins *την γυναικα και ουτος απεθανεν ατεκνος*, with AP rel syrr syr-cu: om BDLא lat-*e*.

31. om *ελαβεν αυτην* (‖ *Matt*) D lat-*a e* copt æth [arm]: *ελαβον* א[3a]. *ωσαυτως* is written twice in AE[H]VΓΛ goth. om *δε και* D. elz ins *και* bef *ου κατελιπον*, with GHKMP[2]Γ[Π] **1.** 69: om ABDא rel lat-*e ff*$_2$ *i q* copt æth. for *ου κατελιπον*, *ουκ αφηκαν* D. **τεκνον** D-gr Γ lat-*a e* copt: *σπερμα* P[1].

32. rec aft *υστερον* ins *δε παντων* (‖ *Matt*), with AP rel lat-*f q* syr-w-ast: ins *παντων* (only) EHSΔΛ 69 vulg lat-*g*$_1$ goth arm-usc: ins *δε* (only) Lא[3a] **1** (syr-cu) copt: txt BDא[1] lat-*c ff*$_2$ *i* Syr. (om ver lat-*a e*.) rec *απεθανεν* bef *και η γυνη* (‖ *Matt: so also rec in* ‖ *Mark*), with AP rel latt syrr syr-cu copt goth æth arm: txt (‖ *Mark*) BDLא **1.** 33.

33. rec om *η γυνη*, and places *εν τη* bef *ουν* (*see* ‖ *Matt*), with ADPא[3a] rel [vulg lat-*f q* syrr copt]: om *η γυνη ουν* א[1] [lat-*a e ff*$_2$ *i l* syr-cu]: txt BL (lat-*a*) syr-mg. om *αυτων* א[1] [lat-*a e ff*$_2$]. for *γινεται*, *εσται* (‖ *Matt Mark*) DGLא **1.** 33 latt Syr syr-cu copt æth arm: txt ABP rel syr goth.

34. rec aft *και* ins *αποκριθεις* (*from* ‖ *Matt: see also in* ‖ *Mark*), with APR rel syr goth æth arm: om BDLא latt Syr syr-cu copt. for *αυτοις*, *προς αυτους* D lat-*e*. om *ο ιησ.* D lat-*e i*. aft *τουτου* ins *γεννωνται και γεννωσιν* D mm lat-*a* syr-cu syr-mg(stating "not in greek"). rec **εκγαμισκονται**, with QR rel: *εκγαμιζονται* AKMPUΓΔ[Π] 69 [Bas$_1$]: *γαμουνται* D: txt BLא 33 Clem$_1$ Orig$_1$ Eus$_1$.

35. rec **εκγαμισκονται**: *εκγαμιζονται* AP rel [Bas$_1$]: *γαμιζονται* DLQRΔא **1.** 33 Clem$_1$: txt B 240-4.

36. rec *ουτε*, with QRא rel [Bas$_1$]: txt ABDLP.

ἡσυχάζειν. See also Herod. i. 68: Soph. Œd. Tyr. 57. **28. καὶ οὗτος**] See ch. xix. 2. **29.**] **οὖν, well then**— i. e. '*as an example of this law, . . .*'

31.] The **οὐ κατ. τέκ.** coming before **καὶ ἀπέθ.** is by a mixture of constructions—**and they had no children by her, and died, leaving none**:—not merely from the emphasis being on the leaving no children (as in Meyer). It is meant to express the absence of offspring *before* their death, *and after*. **34, 35. οἱ υἱοὶ . . . .**] Peculiar to Luke, and important. For this present state of men, marriage is an ordained and natural thing; but in *τῷ αἰῶνι ἐκείνῳ*, which is by the context the state of the *first resurrection* (nothing being said of the rest of the dead, though the *bare fact* might be predicated of them also), they who are

a here only +. b Matt. v. 9 reff. c Matt. x. 8 reff. d Exod. iii. 6. e John xi. 57. Acts xxiii. 30. 1 Cor. x. 28 only +. 2 Macc. iii. 7. vi. 11. xiv. 37 only. f = ‖ Mk. only. see Acts xxiv. 20. compare ἐν, Rom. xi. 2. g ‖ Mk. ch. vi. 44. Acts vii. 33, 35 only. Exod. iii. 2 (3ce), 3, 4. Deut. xxxiii. 16. Job xxxi. 40 only.

ἀποθανεῖν ἔτι δύνανται, [a] ἰσάγγελοι γάρ εἰσιν καὶ [b] υἱοί
εἰσιν [b] θεοῦ, τῆς ἀναστάσεως [s] υἱοὶ ὄντες. 37 ὅτι δὲ [c] ἐγείρονται οἱ [c] νεκροὶ καὶ [d] Μωυσῆς [e] ἐμήνυσεν [f] ἐπὶ τῆς [g] βάτου, ὡς [h] λέγει κύριον τὸν θεὸν Ἀβραὰμ καὶ θεὸν Ἰσαὰκ
καὶ θεὸν Ἰακώβ· 38 θεὸς δὲ οὐκ ἔστιν νεκρῶν, ἀλλὰ ζών-
των· πάντες γὰρ αὐτῷ [i] ζῶσιν. 39 ἀποκριθέντες δέ τινες
τῶν γραμματέων εἶπαν Διδάσκαλε, καλῶς εἶπας. 40 οὐκέτι γὰρ ἐτόλμων [k] ἐπερωτᾶν αὐτὸν οὐδέν. 41 Εἶπεν δὲ
πρὸς αὐτοὺς [l] Πῶς λέγουσιν τὸν χριστὸν εἶναι [m] Δαυεὶδ
[m] υἱόν, 42 καὶ αὐτὸς Δαυεὶδ λέγει ἐν [n] βίβλῳ [n] ψαλμῶν

ABDE GHKL MPQRS UVΓΔ ΛΠℵ 1. 33. 69

h Mark x. 18 reff. Rom. vi. 10. Ps. xxi. 29. k ver. 21. l = John iv. 9. vii. 15. 1 Cor. xv. 12. m Matt. i. 1. xx. 30, 31 al. n Acts i. 20. see ch. xxiv. 44.

for δυνανται, μελλουσιν D-gr lat-*a e* syr-mg Tert$_1$. om και υιοι εισιν (*homœotel*) D lat-*a c e ff$_2$ i l* (Tert) Cypr$_1$. ins οι bef υιοι A ev-y. rec ins του bef θεου, with (D)PQR rel [Bas$_1$]: om ABL(ℵ).—τω θεω (*itacism?*) D.—θεου bef 2nd εισιν ℵ.

37. om 1st και D lat-*a c e ff$_2$ i* [*l q*] (Cypr$_1$). for εμηνυσεν, εδηλωσεν D. rec ins τον bef 2nd and 3rd θεον, with APQ rel [syr-mg-gr]: om BDLRℵ Orig$_1$.

38. νεκρων bef ουκ εστιν, omg δε, D.

39. for γραμματεων, σαδδουκαιων Q. (ειπαν, so BDLQℵ.) add αυτω ℵ.

40. rec (for γαρ) δε, with ADPQR rel syr goth [arm]: txt BLℵ 33 copt.

41. aft λεγουσιν ins τινες AKM[Π] syr-w-ast. rec transp ειναι and υιον, with APQR rel am lat-*a c ff$_2$ i* syr copt goth arm Tert$_1$: om ειναι D: υιον bef δαυειδ G: txt BLℵ.

42. for και αυτος, αυτος γαρ (*see digest* ‖ *Mark*) BL R(Treg, expr) ℵ 1. 33 lat-*l* copt [Cyr$_1$]: και αυτος γαρ Q: txt ADP rel latt syrr syr-cu goth. for βιβλω, τη βυβλω D. ins των bef ψαλμων DP 69.

found worthy to obtain that state of life and the resurrection from the dead, are no longer under the ordinance of marriage: for neither can they any more die; i. e. they will have no need of a succession and renewal, which is the main purpose of marriage. **36.**] The **ἰσάγγ. γάρ εἰσιν** is alleged, not as shewing them to be ἀπαθεῖς κ. ἀφιλήδονοι (Euthym.), but as setting forth their *immortality*. **υἱοὶ θ.** is here used, not in its *ethical sense*, as applied to believers in this world,—but its *metaphysical sense*, as denoting the *essential state* of the blessed after the resurrection:—'they are, by their resurrection, *essentially* partakers of the divine nature, and so cannot die.' When Meyer says that the Lord *only* speaks of the *risen*, and has not here in His view the 'quick' at the time of His coming, it must be remembered that the 'change' which shall pass on them (1 Cor. xv. 51—54) shall put them into precisely the same ἀφθαρσία as the risen (compare ibid. ver. 42). **37.**] **καὶ M.**, *that very* Moses, whom you allege as shewing by inference the contrary. **38.**] On **πάντ. γ. αὐτ. ζ.** see on Matt. vv. 31—33: but we have in this argument even a further generalization than in Matt. and Mark. There, it is a *covenant relation* on which the matter rests: here, a life of *all*, living and dead, *in the sight of God*,—so that none are annihilated,—but in the regard of Him who inhabiteth Eternity, the being of *all* is a *living one*, in all its changes. **39, 40.**] Peculiar to Luke;—implied however in Matt. ver. 34, and Mark ver. 28.

41—44.] Question respecting Christ and David. Matt. xxii. 41—46: Mark xii. 35—37, where see notes. Luke omits the question of the lawyer, which occurred *immediately* on the gathering together of the Pharisees after the last incident. This question of our Lord seems to have followed close on that, which (and not that in vv. 27 ff. here) was their *last to Him*, Mark xii. 34. **41.**] **πρὸς αὐτούς**, i. e. the Scribes. The same thing is signified by πῶς λέγουσιν οἱ γρ. in Mark. In Matt. the question is addressed to the Pharisees. I mention these things as marks of the independence of the accounts. The underlying *fact* is, the Lord addressed the Pharisees and Scribes on a view which they (the Scribes, the Pharisees agreeing) entertained about the Messiah. Hence the three accounts diverge.

42.] On **ἐν βίβλῳ ψαλμ.**, Wordsw. says,

[o] Εἶπεν Κύριος τῷ κυρίῳ μου Κάθου [p] ἐκ δεξιῶν μου 43 ἕως
ἂν [q] θῶ τοὺς ἐχθρούς σου [r] ὑποπόδιον τῶν ποδῶν σου;
44 Δαυεὶδ οὖν αὐτὸν κύριον καλεῖ, καὶ πῶς αὐτοῦ υἱός
ἐστιν; 45 ἀκούοντος δὲ παντὸς τοῦ λαοῦ εἶπεν πρὸς
αὐτοὺς 46 [s] Προσέχετε ἀπὸ τῶν γραμματέων τῶν θελόντων περιπατεῖν ἐν [t] στολαῖς, καὶ [u] φιλούντων [v] ἀσπασμοὺς ἐν ταῖς [w] ἀγοραῖς καὶ [x] πρωτοκαθεδρίας ἐν ταῖς
συναγωγαῖς καὶ [y] πρωτοκλισίας ἐν τοῖς δείπνοις· 47 οἳ
[z] κατεσθίουσιν τὰς οἰκίας τῶν χηρῶν, καὶ [a] προφάσει
[b] μακρὰ προσεύχονται. οὗτοι λήμψονται [c] περισσότερον
[d] κρίμα. XXI. 1 [e] Ἀναβλέψας δὲ εἶδεν τοὺς [f] βάλλοντας εἰς τὸ [g] γαζοφυλάκιον τὰ δῶρα αὐτῶν πλουσίους,
2 εἶδεν δέ τινα [καὶ] χήραν [h] πενιχρὰν [f] βάλλουσαν [i] ἐκεῖ

X πρωτοκλισιας... ...λημψ R.

o Psa. cix. 1. p Matt. xx. 21, 23 reff. q - [‖ v. r.] Acts ii. 35, & Heb. i. 13. x. 13, from l. c. Rom. iv. 17, from Gen. xvii. 5. Heb. i. 2. r Matt. v. 35 reff. s Matt. vii. 15 reff. t ‖ Mk. reff. u = Matt. v. 5. xxiii. 6. Rev. xxii. 15. Prov. xxix. 3. v ‖. elsw. L.P. only. ch. i. 29, 41, 44. xi. 43. 1 Cor. xvi. 21. Col. iv. 18. 2 Thess. iii. 17 †. w ch. vii. 32 reff. x ‖. ch. xi. 43 only †. y ‖. ch. (xi. 43 v. r.) xiv. 7, 8 only †. z ‖ Mk. (Mt. v. r.) 2 Cor. xi. 20. Gal. v. 15. Rev. xi. 5 only. Isa. ix. 12. (-φαγεῖν, Matt. xiii. 4 reff.) a ‖ Mk. reff. b = ‖ Mk. [Mt. v. r.] only. (see ch. xv. 13. xix. 12.) c ‖ Mk. reff. d ‖ Mk. ch. xxiii. 40. xxiv. 20. Deut. xxi. 22. e = Matt. xiv. 19 reff. f = ‖. Matt. xxvii. 6. John xii. 6. g ‖ Mk. (3ce.) John viii. 20 only. Neh. x. 37. 2 Macc. v. 18 al. h here only. Exod. xxii. 25 al. i = Matt. ii. 22 reff.

for ειπεν, λεγει (‖ *Mark*) D lat-*a c ff*$_2$. rec ins ο bef κυριος (*corrn to* LXX: *so also in* ‖ *Matt Mark, which cf*), with APQRℵ rel [Cyr$_1$]: om BD.

43. for αν θω, τιθω D. for υποποδιον, υποκατω (‖ *Matt Mark*) D lat-*a c e ff*$_2$ *i l* [*q*] Syr syr-cu copt.

44. om ουν (‖ *Mark*) D Scr's b[1] lat-*a i* goth [Cyr$_1$]. rec κυριον bef αυτον (‖ *Matt*), with DPℵ rel latt (syr) [(Tert$_1$)]: txt ABKLMQRU[Π] 33 lat-*f* copt goth arm Cyr$_1$. καλει bef αυτον κυριον R Syr copt. for καλει, λεγει D-gr. om και D lat-*c e ff*$_2$ *i l* Syr syr-cu arm. rec υιος bef αυτου (*so also in* ‖ *Mark: from* ‖ *Matt*), with DPQRℵ rel latt [Cyr$_1$]: txt ABKM[Π] 1 copt.

45. rec (for προς αυτους) τοις μαθηταις αυτου, with APRℵ rel [latt &c]: τοις μαθηταις BD arm: txt Q. (*An eccl lection begins at* ειπεν: προς αυτους *was therefore variously specified,* τοις μαθηταις αυτου *being borrowed from Matt* xxiii. 1.)

46. εν στολαις bef περιπατειν (‖ *Mark*) AGLRℵ 1. 33. 69 arm.

47. κατεσθιοντες PX, κατεσθοντες (‖ *Mark*) D: txt ABQRℵ rel syrr [Bas$_1$]. om και D latt. μακραν A[1](appy) LX. προσευχομενοι (‖ *Mark*) DPR 69 lat-*e*: txt ABQℵ rel copt.

Chap. XXI. 1. rec τα δωρα αυτων bef εις το γαζοφυλακιον (*after* ‖ *Mark*), with APQ rel latt syr-cu syr copt æth arm [Bas$_1$]: txt BDLXℵ 1. 33. 69 lat-*e* Syr [syr-jer] Orig$_3$. ins τους bef πλουσιους D.

2. rec και bef τινα, with DP vulg lat-*a e f* Syr syr-cu syr-w-ast copt arm: aft A rel: om και BKLMQX Γ(Treg) ℵ 33 lat-*c ff*$_2$ *i* [*l q* syr-jer] æth Orig$_2$ Bas$_1$. (*The unusual position of* και *may have occasioned its transposn and omn.*) om εκει D 44(Sz) latt Syr syr-cu æth Orig$_3$.

"added here as conveying information necessary to Gentile readers." This might be well, did the words occur in the Evangelist's narrative: but surely not, when they are in a discourse of our Lord. If His words were so loosely reported as this, where is any dependence on the accuracy of the Evangelists?

45—47.] Denunciation of the Scribes. Matt. xxiii. 6, 7. Mark xii. 38—40, with which latter our text almost verbally agrees: see notes there.

45.] This particular, **ἀκούοντ. δὲ π. τ. λ.,** is only in Luke.

Chap. XXI. 1—4.] The widow's mites. Mark xii. 41—44, where see notes.

1. **ἀναβλέψας**] Our Lord as yet has been surrounded with His disciples (see ch. xx. 45), and speaking to them and the multitude. He now lifts up His eyes, and sees at a distance, &c. **πλουσ.** belongs to **τοὺς βάλ.**, and ὄντας is not to be supplied, nor a comma put after **γαζ.** It was not the *rich only*, which that would imply—but ὁ ὄχλος (Mark), who were casting gifts in.

δύο [k] λεπτά, 3 καὶ εἶπεν [l] Ἀληθῶς λέγω ὑμῖν ὅτι ἡ χήρα
ἡ πτωχὴ αὕτη πλείω πάντων [f] ἔβαλεν· 4 ἅπαντες γὰρ
οὗτοι ἐκ τοῦ [m] περισσεύοντος αὐτοῖς [f] ἔβαλον εἰς τὰ
δῶρα, αὕτη δὲ ἐκ τοῦ [n] ὑστερήματος αὐτῆς ἅπαντα τὸν
[o] βίον ὃν εἶχεν [f] ἔβαλεν. 5 Καί τινων λεγόντων περὶ
τοῦ ἱεροῦ, ὅτι λίθοις καλοῖς καὶ [p] ἀναθήμασιν [q] κεκόσμηται,
εἶπεν 6 [r] Ταῦτα ἃ [s] θεωρεῖτε, [t] ἐλεύσονται ἡμέραι ἐν αἷς
οὐκ [u] ἀφεθήσεται λίθος ἐπὶ λίθῳ ὃς οὐ [v] καταλυθήσεται.
7 ἐπηρώτησαν δὲ αὐτὸν λέγοντες Διδάσκαλε, πότε οὖν
ταῦτα ἔσται; καὶ τί τὸ [w] σημεῖον ὅταν μέλλῃ ταῦτα
γίνεσθαι; 8 ὁ δὲ εἶπεν [x] Βλέπετε μὴ [y] πλανηθῆτε· πολλοὶ
γὰρ ἐλεύσονται [z] ἐπὶ τῷ ὀνόματί μου λέγοντες [ὅτι]
[a] ἐγώ εἰμι· καὶ Ὁ καιρὸς [b] ἤγγικεν. μὴ πορευθῆτε

..αληθως P.
ABDE GHKL MQSUV XΓΔΛ Πℵ 1. 33. 69

..πολλοι γαρ Q.

k ||. ch. xii. 59 only †. (-πτός, Gen. xli. 3, &c.)
l — ch. ix. 27 reff.
m || Mk. reff.
n (-ησις, || Mk.) here only in Gospp. 2 Cor. viii. 13, 14 al. L.P. Judg. xvii. 10.
o || Mk. reff. Cant. viii. 7.
p here only. (Lev. xxvii. 28, 29 v. r.) = (& with κοσμεῖν) 2 Macc. ix. 16 only.
q ch. xi. 25 || Mt. 1 Tim. ii. 9. Ezek. xxiii. 41.
r constr., see Rom. viii. 3. 2 Cor. xii. 17. Gal. i. 20. Heb. viii. 1.
s ch. x. 18 reff.
t Matt. ix. 15 reff. Jer. xvi. 14.
u ||. Judg. ii. 23.
v || Mt. reff.
w ||. Matt. xii. 38. Exod. iii. 12.
x || Mt. reff.
y ||. Matt. xxii. 29. John vii. 47. Isa. xli. 10.
z ||. ch. ix. 49. Acts iv. 17, 18.
a ellips., || Mk. John viii. 58. xviii. 5, 6, 8. Deut. xxxii. 39.
b = Matt. xxi. 34. ver. 20. ch. xxii. 1.

λεπτα bef δυο (|| *Mark*) BLQXℵ 33 vulg lat-*c f* Syr syr-cu [syr-jer] copt Orig$_2$: txt ADP rel lat-*a e* syr-mg-gr [æth arm Bas$_1$]. at end ins ο εστιν κοδραντης (|| *Mark*) D.

3. αυτη bef η πτωχη (|| *Mark*) BDLQℵ 33. 69 vulg lat-*c f ff*$_2$ *l* arm [Bas$_1$]: txt A rel lat-*a* syr Orig$_2$. rec πλειον (|| *Mark*), with AB rel Orig$_2$ [Bas$_1$]: πλεον ℵ: πλειονα L: txt DQX.

4. for απαντες, παντες (|| *Mark*) BDΔℵ Orig$_1$: txt AQ rel [Bas$_1$]. rec aft τα δωρα ins του θεου, with ADQ rel latt syrr [arm Bas$_1$]: om BLXℵ 1 syr-cu syr-jer copt. for απαντα, παντα (|| *Mark*) BDLQXℵ 33. 69 Orig$_1$: txt A rel [Bas$_1$].

5. for καλοις, μεγαλοις (but txt restored) ℵ-corr^1. κεκοσμηται bef και αναθ. D. αναθεμασιν ADXℵ 1: txt BQ rel syr-mg-gr.

6. om ἃ DL lat-*a c ff*$_2$ *i* [*l*] *q* syr-cu æth arm. ins ωδε (|| *Matt*) bef λιθος X 1. 33 lat-*e* syr-cu æth arm: aft λιθω BLℵ 69 copt: aft λιθω ins εν τοιχω ωδε D lat-*a c ff*$_2$ *i l q*: om AQ rel vulg lat-*f* [$g_{1.2}$] syrr. for λιθω, λιθον LXℵ^{3a} 1. 33. 69.

7. aft αυτον ins οι μαθηται (|| *Matt*) D 252-marg. om ουν D 1 latt Syr syr-cu copt æth arm. for οταν to γινεσθαι, της σης ελευσεως D.

8. om οτι (*so* || *Matt*: *cf* D *in* || *Mark*) BLXℵ lat-*c* æth (Mcion$_1$-t): txt AD rel [latt] copt. om ο καιρος ηγγικεν μη ℵ^1. rec aft μη ins ουν, with A rel vulg lat-*f* ($g_{1.2}$ *l*?) syr: om BDLXℵ lat-*a c e ff*$_2$ *i* [*l* syr-jer] syr-cu copt [æth] arm.

4.] **εἰς τὰ δῶρ., among (into) the gifts**; not *quæ donarent* (Beza), '*as*,' or, '*for, gifts*,' which would require the omission of the article:—nor so that τὰ δῶρ. = τὸ γαζ.

5—36.] PROPHECY OF HIS COMING, AND OF THE TIMES OF THE END. Matt. xxiv. 1—51 (xxv. 1—46). Mark xiii. 1—37. See notes on both, but especially on Matt. Meyer says truly in loc. that there is no trace in Luke of the discourse being delivered on *the Mount of Olives*—but he adds, that it belongs to the discourses *in the temple*, which begin ch. xx. 1, and that therefore Luke alone mentions ἀναθήματα. He seems to have overlooked the *break* at ver. 7, corresponding to the change of scene. All three speak of the *opening incident* as happening while He was departing from the temple; and Matt. and Mark, of the enquiry being made *afterwards*, on the Mount of Olives,—i. e. in the evening, when He had retired thither (ver. 37).

5.] Meyer has made the same mistake here, and spoken of the τινές as those to whom the *discourse* was delivered. The **ἀναθήματα** were many and precious. Tacitus, Hist. v. 8, calls it *immensæ opulentiæ templum*: and Jos., B. J. v. 5. 4, gives an account of the gilding, and golden vines (presented by Herod the Great) with bunches of grapes as large as a man, &c. in the temple: see also Antt. xv. 11. 3.

6.] **ταῦτα ἃ θ.**,—absolute: see reff.

7.] That Luke's account *alone* gives us no trace of a different scene or a different auditory, is a proof of its independence of the others; for how could any rational writer have omitted

[c] ὀπίσω αὐτῶν. 9 ὅταν δὲ [d] ἀκούσητε πολέμους καὶ
[e] ἀκαταστασίας, μὴ [f] πτοηθῆτε· [g] δεῖ γὰρ [g] γενέσθαι ταῦτα
πρῶτον, ἀλλ' οὐκ εὐθέως τὸ [h] τέλος. 10 τότε ἔλεγεν
αὐτοῖς [i] Ἐγερθήσεται ἔθνος ἐπ' ἔθνος καὶ βασιλεία ἐπὶ
βασιλείαν, 11 σεισμοί τε μεγάλοι καὶ [k] κατὰ τόπους
[l] λοιμοὶ καὶ λιμοὶ ἔσονται, [m] φόβηθρά τε καὶ σημεῖα ἀπ'
οὐρανοῦ μεγάλα ἔσται. 12 πρὸ δὲ τούτων πάντων [n] ἐπι-
βαλοῦσιν ἐφ' ὑμᾶς τὰς χεῖρας αὐτῶν καὶ [o] διώξουσιν, [p] παραδιδόντες εἰς [τὰς] συναγωγὰς καὶ [q] φυλακάς, [r] ἀπαγομέ-
R και ηγ... νους [s] ἐπὶ βασιλεῖς καὶ ἡγεμόνας, [t] ἕνεκεν τοῦ [t] ὀνόματός
μου. 13 [u] ἀποβήσεται [δὲ] ὑμῖν [v] εἰς μαρτύριον. 14 [w] θέτε
οὖν ἐν ταῖς καρδίαις ὑμῶν μὴ [x] προμελετᾶν [y] ἀπολογη-
θῆναι· 15 ἐγὼ γὰρ δώσω ὑμῖν στόμα καὶ σοφίαν, ᾗ οὐ

c = Matt. iv. 19 reff. 3 Kings xix. 20.
d = ||. Matt. xi. 2. Acts xxiii. 16 al.
e here only in Gospp. 1 Cor. xiv. 33. 2 Cor. vi. 5. xii. 20. James iii. 16 only. Prov. xxvi. 28. Tobit iv. 13 (not in א) only.
f ch. xxiv. 37 only. Deut. xxxi. 6.
g = || Mt. reff.
h Matt. xxiv. 14 reff.
i ||. Isa. xix. 2.
k || Mt. reff.
l [|| Mt. v. r.] = here (Acts xxiv. 5) only. Jer. xxxiv. [xxvii.] 8 & xxxv. [xxviii.] 8 compl. xxxix. [xxxii.] 24 Ald. compl. only. (Ps. i. 1 al.)
m here only. Isa. xix. 17 only.
n = Matt. xxvi. 50 reff.
o = Matt. v. 10, 11 reff.
p Matt. xvii. 22 reff.
q = Matt. xxv. 36 reff.
r Matt. xxvi. 57. Acts xii. 19 al.
s ||. Acts ix. 21 al.
t Matt. xix. 29 only. see ver. 17.
u = Phil. i. 19 (ch. v. 2. John xxi. 9) only. Job xiii. 16.
v Matt. viii. 4 reff. Zeph. iii. 8.
w ch. i. 16 reff.
x here only †.
y = ch. xii. 11 reff.

9. for πτοηθητε, φοβηθητε D lat-*q*. rec ταυτα bef γενεσθαι (|| *Matt*), with BLא rel lat-*a e* [*l* (*c f i q*)] : txt ADX.

10. om τοτε ελεγεν αυτοις D lat-*a e ff*$_2$ *i l* Syr syr-cu. aft εγερθησεται ins γαρ D evv-H-y$_1$-z lat-*a c e ff*$_2$ *i l* Syr syr-cu. (επ', so ADLXא 1. 33.)

11. om τε AL am[with forj] D-lat. rec κατα τοπους bef και (*cf* ||), with AD rel latt [syrr syr-cu] : txt BLא 33 copt æth arm. rec transp λοιμοι and λιμοι (λιμοι *coming aft the verb in* ||), with ADLא rel lat-*e* syrr [syr-jer arm] copt : om λοιμοι και X ev-y [æth] : om και λιμοι 69 : txt B (130-57, Sz) latt syr-cu Mcion$_1$-t. rec φοβητρα, with ALא rel : txt BD. απ' ουρ. bef σημεια B : απ' ουρανου bef και σημεια D latt [syr-cu] : μεγαλα bef απ' ουρανου Lא 33. 69 arm (*all corrns : txt is characteristic*) : txt A rel Tert$_1$.

12. rec **απαντων** (with Scr's l m n s, e sil) : txt ABDא rel Scr's-mss. for εφ υμας, επ αυτους א[1](txt א corr[1]). rec om τας (*see* || *Mark*), with A rel : ins BDא. rec (for απαγ.) αγομενους, with A rel : txt BDLא 1 lat-*e*. **ενεκα** D Scr's g.

13. om δε BDא[1].

14. rec (for θετε) θεσθε (*gramml corrn*), with B[2] rel Orig$_1$: txt AB[1]DLMRX[Π]א 33. om ουν א[1] [Cypr$_2$]. rec (for εν τ. κ.) εις τας καρδιας, with R rel Orig$_1$: txt ABDLXא 1. 33 latt Cyr$_1$ Did$_2$ Cypr. **προμελετωντες** D.

15. υμιν bef δωσω D.

so interesting a matter of accurate detail, if he had been aware of it? **οὖν**, on account of what our Lord had said, ver. 6.

8.] **ὁ κ. ἤγγ.**, i. e. the *time of the Kingdom*. They are the words, not of our Lord, but of the **πολλοί**: see on Matt. vv. 4, 5. **10.**] **τότε ἔλ. αὐτ.** perhaps implies a break in the discourse which the other reports do not notice.

11.] **ἀπ' οὐρ.** belongs to both **φόβηθ.** and **σημ.**: so does **μεγάλα**. **φόβηθρα** cannot stand alone, especially with **τε καί**.

12.] Why the words **πρὸ δὲ τ. π.** should have made any difficulty, I am at a loss to imagine. The prophecies of vv. 7, 8 in Matt.,—ver. 8 in Mark,—and vv. 10, 11 here,—are a parenthetical warning of what shall happen *before the* **τέλος**. And then having stated, ἀρχὴ ὠδίνων ταῦτα,—these things shall be the *very beginning of the actual pangs themselves* (see note on Matt.), the prophetic chronology is resumed from οὔπω τὸ τέλος in all three accounts; here, by distinct statement, πρὸ δὲ τούτων πάντων: in Mark by implication, βλέπετε δὲ ὑμ. ἑαυ. παρ. ὑμ., by which δέ, the following words are thrown back to the βλέπετε before:—in Matthew by the gathering up of the parenthetical announcements as πάντα ταῦτα, and thus casting them off, as the ἀρχὴ ὠδίνων belonging to the τέλος, before the discourse proceeds with the **τότε** taken up from ver. 6. The whole difficulty has arisen from not rightly apprehending the force of **ὠδίνων**, *as the death-throes of the end*. **13.**] **εἰς μαρτ.**, viz. of *your* faithfulness, and (Mark) *αὐτοῖς*, 'against

δυνήσονται [z] ἀντιστῆναι ἢ [a] ἀντειπεῖν ἅπαντες οἱ [b] ἀντικείμενοι ὑμῖν. 16 παραδοθήσεσθε δὲ καὶ ὑπὸ γονέων καὶ
ἀδελφῶν καὶ συγγενῶν καὶ φίλων, καὶ [c] θανατώσουσιν
[d] ἐξ ὑμῶν, 17 καὶ ἔσεσθε μισούμενοι ὑπὸ πάντων [e] διὰ τὸ
[e] ὄνομά μου. 18 καὶ [f] θρὶξ ἐκ τῆς κεφαλῆς ὑμῶν οὐ μὴ
ἀπόληται. 19 ἐν τῇ [g] ὑπομονῇ ὑμῶν [h] κτήσεσθε τὰς [i] ψυχὰς
ὑμῶν. 20 ὅταν δὲ ἴδητε [k] κυκλουμένην ὑπὸ [l] στρατοπέδων
Ἱερουσαλήμ, τότε γνῶτε ὅτι [m] ἤγγικεν ἡ [n] ἐρήμωσις αὐτῆς.
21 τότε οἱ ἐν τῇ Ἰουδαίᾳ φευγέτωσαν εἰς τὰ ὄρη, καὶ οἱ ἐν C τοτε οι...
μέσῳ αὐτῆς [o] ἐκχωρείτωσαν, καὶ οἱ ἐν ταῖς [p] χώραις μὴ ABCDE GHKL
εἰσερχέσθωσαν εἰς αὐτήν. 22 ὅτι [q] ἡμέραι [r] ἐκδικήσεως MRSUV ΧΓΔΛ
αὗταί εἰσιν, [s] τοῦ [t] πλησθῆναι πάντα τὰ γεγραμμένα. ΠΝ 1. 33. 69
23 οὐαὶ ταῖς [u] ἐν [u] γαστρὶ [u] ἐχούσαις καὶ ταῖς [v] θηλαζούσαις
ἐν ἐκείναις ταῖς ἡμέραις· ἔσται γὰρ [w] ἀνάγκη μεγάλη ἐπὶ
τῆς γῆς καὶ ὀργὴ τῷ λαῷ τούτῳ, 24 καὶ [x] πεσοῦνται

z Matt. v. 39. Acts vi. 10 al. Jer. xxvii. (l.) 24.
a Acts iv. 14 only. Esth. viii. 8.
b ch. xiii. 17 reff.
c || Mk. 2 Cor. vi. 9. Exod. ix. 15 B. 2 Kings viii. 2.
d = Matt. xxiii. 34. ch. xi. 49. 3 Kings x. (ix.) 22.
e John xv. 21 reff.
f Acts xxvii. 34. 1 Kings xiv. 45. Dan. iii. 27.
g Rom. ii. 7. v. 3, 4. Jer. xvii. 13.
h Matt. x. 9 reff.
i = Heb. x. 39. James i. 21 al.
k John x. 24. Acts xiv. 20. Heb. xi. 30 (Rev. xx. 9 v. r.) only. Isa. xxxvii. 33.
l here only. Jer. xlviii. (xli.) 12.
m ver. 8 reff.
n Matt. xxiv. 15 || Mk. only. Jer. vii. 34.
o here only. Num. xvi. 45.
p = ch. xii. 16. plur., John iv. 35. James v. 4 only.
q = Rom. ii. 5. Eph. iv. 30 al.
r ch. xviii. 7, 8 reff.
s = ch. xxii. 31.
t = here only. see ch. i. 23, 57. ii. 6.
u Matt. i. 18 reff.
v = || Mk. (reff.)
w = 1 Cor. vii. 26. 2 Cor. vi. 4 al. Ps. xxiv. 17.
x = Heb. iii. 17. Num. xiv. 32. Jer. xx. 4.

rec *αντειπειν ουδε αντιστηναι*, with X rel lat-*f* Syr æth; *αντειπειν η αντιστηναι* AKM R[Π] 1: txt BLℵ 69 lat-*e f* arm $Orig_1$.—om *η αντειπειν* D lat-*a c ff$_2$ i* syr-cu copt-dz $Cypr_2$. rec (for *απαντες*) *παντες*, with ADRℵ rel $Orig_1$ [Cyr_1]: txt BL.

16. *συγγενεων* A 1.

19. rec *κτησασθε*, with DRℵ rel [Cyr_1]: txt AB 33 latt syrr syr-cu copt[-schw-dz æth] arm $Orig_1$ Mac_1 $Tert_1$.

20. rec ins *την* bef *ιερουσαλημ* (*to shew that ιερ. is the accusative*), with AL rel $Orig_1$ Eus_3: om BDRℵ $Orig_2$ Eus_1-ms. *ιερουσαλημ* bef *υπο στρατοπεδων* D [Eus_1-mss]. for *γνωτε*, *γνωσεσθε* DX lat-*e* $Orig_1$ Eus_1: *γινωσκεται* R Eus_2-ms(txt_1 in ed), *γινωσκετε* 1 Eus_1. *ηγγισεν* A 1 $Orig_3$.

21. ins *μη* bef *εκχωρ.* D tol.

22. om *εισιν* ℵ. rec *πληρωθηναι*, with CX: txt ABDRℵ rel.

23. rec aft *ουαι* ins *δε* (|| *Matt Mark*), with ACRℵ rel vulg lat-*f* syrr syr-cu copt [æth arm] Eus_1: om BDL lat-*a c e ff$_2$ i* [*l q*]. *θηλαζομεναις* D-gr [*ενθηλαζουσαις* L]. aft *γαρ* ins *εν εκειναις ταις ημεραις* ℵ[1]. rec ins *εν* bef *τω λαω*, with E rel syr æth Eus_1: om ABCDKLMRX[Π]ℵ 1. 33. 69 latt copt arm Eus_1.

them:' the dativus incommodi.

15.] Luke only. **ἀντειπ.** corresponds to **στόμα, ἀντιστ.** to **σοφία.** **16.**] **καί**—'non modo ab alienis,' Bengel. **θαν. ἐξ ὑμ.**, of the Apostles. One of the four who heard this discourse was put to death, Acts xii. 2. **18.**] Not *literally*, but *really* true; not corporeally, but in that real and only *life* which the disciple of Christ possesses. **19.**] **By your endurance** (of all these things), **ye shall acquire** (not, *possess*, which is only the sense of the perf. *κέκτημαι*) **your souls**: this endurance being God's appointed way, **ἐν** (in and by) which your salvation is to be put in your possession. **κτήσ.** as **εὑρήσει**, Matt. xvi. 25—*σῶσαι*, ch. ix. 24.

20.] **κυκλ.**, not *circumdari*, but participial, graphically setting forth the scene now before them, as it should then appear. On the variation of expression from Matt. and Mark, see note on Matt. ver. 15. **21.**] **αὐτῆς** belongs to the *αὐτῆς* of ver. 20, and signifies not Judæa, but *Jerusalem*. **ταῖς χώρ.**, **the fields**—not '*the provinces*:' see reff. **22.**] **ἐκδικ.**, a hint perhaps at ch. xviii. 8. The latter part of the verse alludes probably to the prophecy of Daniel, which Luke has omitted, but referred to in *ἡ ἐρήμωσις αὐτῆς*, ver. 20. **23.**] **ἐπὶ τ. γ.**, general; **τῷ λ. τούτῳ**, particular. The distress on all the earth is not so distinctly the result of the divine anger, as that which shall befall this nation. **24.**] A most important addition, serving to fix the meaning of the other two Evangelists,—see notes there,—and carrying

[y] στόματι [y] μαχαιρας καὶ [z] αἰχμαλωτισθήσονται εἰς τὰ ἔθνη
πάντα, καὶ Ἱερουσαλὴμ [a] ἔσται [b] πατουμένη ὑπὸ ἐθνῶν,
ἄχρι οὗ [c] πληρωθῶσιν [d] καιροὶ ἐθνῶν. 25 καὶ ἔσονται
[e] σημεῖα ἐν ἡλίῳ καὶ σελήνῃ καὶ [f] ἄστροις, καὶ ἐπὶ τῆς
γῆς [g] συνοχὴ ἐθνῶν [h] ἐν [i] ἀπορίᾳ [k] ἤχους θαλάσσης καὶ
[l] σάλου, 26 [m] ἀποψυχόντων ἀνθρώπων [n] ἀπὸ φόβου καὶ
[o] προσδοκίας τῶν [p] ἐπερχομένων τῇ [q] οἰκουμένῃ· αἱ γὰρ
[r] δυνάμεις τῶν οὐρανῶν [s] σαλευθήσονται. 27 καὶ τότε
ὄψονται τὸν [t] υἱὸν τοῦ [t] ἀνθρώπου [u] ἐρχόμενον ἐν [u] νεφέλῃ
F αρχομενων... [v] μετὰ δυνάμεως καὶ δόξης πολλῆς. 28 ἀρχομένων δὲ
τούτων γίνεσθαι [w] ἀνακύψατε καὶ [x] ἐπάρατε τὰς κεφαλὰς
ὑμῶν, [y] διότι [z] ἐγγίζει ἡ [a] ἀπολύτρωσις ὑμῶν. 29 καὶ
εἶπεν παραβολὴν αὐτοῖς· Ἴδετε τὴν [b] συκῆν καὶ πάντα

y Heb. xi. 34 only. Josh. xix. 48 al. z Rom. vii. 23. 2 Cor. x. 5. 2 Tim. iii. 6 only. L.P. 3 Kings viii. 46. a ch. v. 10 reff. b ch. x. 19. Rev. xi. 2. xiv. 20. xix. 15 only. Isa. xlii. 5. Zech. xii. 3. Dan. viii. 13. c = Mark i. 15. Acts vii. 23, 30 al. Gen. xxv. 24. d = 2 Thess. ii. 6. Rev. xi. 18. e ver. 7. Exod. iii. 12. f Acts vii. 43 (from Amos v. 26). xxvii. 20 Heb. xi. 12 only. L.H. Deut. i. 10. g 2 Cor. ii. 4 only. L.P. Job xxx. 3. (see ch. xii. 50 reff.) h = ch. xiv. 31. Matt. xxii. 37. Rom. v. 17, 21. Jude 14 al. 1 Macc. xi. 15. i here only. Lev. xxvi. 16. (-ρεῖν, ch. xxiv. 4.) k here only. Ps. lxxvi. 17. see ch. iv. 37. Acts ii. 2. Heb. xii. 19. l here only. Jon. i. 15. m here only †. n = Matt. xiv. 26. ch. xxii. 45. Heb. v. 7. Ps. cxviii. 28. o Acts xii. 11 only. L. Gen. xlix. 10. (-κᾶν, ch. i. 21.) p = [ver. 35 v. r.] James v. 1. Judg. ix. 57. q Matt. xxiv. 14 reff. r ‖ Mt. reff. s ‖. Matt. xi. 7 al. Ps. xvii. 7. t Matt. viii. 20 reff. u ‖ Mt. reff. v ‖. Acts xxvi. 12. Isa. xxxiii. 17. Dan. vii. 13. w ch. xiii. 11 [John viii. 7, 10 rec.] only. Job x. 15 only. x Matt. xvii. 8 reff. y ch. i. 13 reff. z ver. 8 reff. a Gospp. here only. Rom. viii. 23. Heb. xi. 35. L.P.H. Dan. iv. 32 (LXX) only. (-τροῦν, Exod. xxi. 8. Zeph. iii. 1. see also Ps. lxviii. 18. Isa. lxiii. 4.) b ‖ Mt. reff.

24. ins εν bef στοματι DR latt syrr syr-cu Eus_2: om ABCℵ rel. μαχαιρης $B^1Δ$: ρομφαιας D. rec παντα bef τα εθνη, with ACD rel vulg lat-*c e f ff₂ i* syr-cu syr [æth] arm Eus_2 : txt BLRℵ lat-*a* copt. (αχρις CDR 69 [Eus].) rec om ου, with A rel Eus_1 : ins BCDLRℵ 33. 69 Eus_1. ins και εσονται bef καιροι εθνων B : aft καιροι L syr-mg copt-ms : om ACRℵ rel vss Eus_2.—om καιροι εθνων D.

25. rec (for εσονται) εσται (*gramml corrn*), with ACR rel Eus_1 : txt BDℵ. σεληνης R. for 2nd εν, και D harl Syr, και εν ℵ. rec (for ηχους) ηχουσης, with D rel (æth) Eus_1 : txt ABCLMRXℵ 1. 33. 69 latt syrr copt arm $Tert_1$.

26. ins των bef ανθρωπων R. επαρχομ. $ℵ^1$. for των ουρανων, αι(η D^1) εν τω ουρανω D lat-*a c ff₂ l* $Ambr_1$.

27. νεφελαις C 239-43-7-54 Scr's c k lat-*c e f i l* Syr syr-cu syr-mg $Tert_1$ $Ambr_1$. for μετα δυναμ. κ. δοξης πολλης, και δυναμει πολλη κ. δοξη D æth.

28. ερχομενων D-gr 13(Sz). om 1st υμων D lat-*i* $Tert_1$.

on the prophetic announcements, past our own times, even close to the days of the end. **πεσοῦνται . . . αἰχμ.**, viz. *this people.* **ἔσται πατ.**] See Rev. xi. 2. The *present* state of Jerusalem. Meyer maintains that the whole of this was to be consummated *in the lifetime of the hearers,* on account of the ἀνακύψατε, &c. ver. 28. What views of the discourses of our Lord must such an expositor have!

πληρ. καιροὶ ἐθν.] Who could suppose that καιροὶ ἐθνῶν should have been interpreted (by Meyer) the appointed time *until the Gentiles shall have finished this judgment* of wrath—to be ended by the παρουσία, within the lifetime of the hearers? The **καιρ. ἐθν.** (see reff.) are the *end of the Gentile dispensation,*—just as the καιρός of Jerusalem was the *end,* fulfilment, *of the Jewish dispensation:*—the *great rejection of the Lord by the Gentile world,—answering to its type, His rejection by the Jews,—being finished, the* **καιρός** *shall come, of which the destruction of Jerusalem was a type.* καιροί = καιρός : no essential difference is to be insisted on. It is plural, because the ἔθνη are plural : each Gentile people having in turn its καιρός. **25, 26.**] The greater part of these signs are peculiar to Luke. **ἀπορίᾳ ἤχους, despair on account of the noise**—so Herodian (see Mey.) iv. 14. 1, ἐν ἀπορίᾳ . . . . τοῦ πρακτέου. By no possibility can ἤχους be gen. after σημεῖα, as Wordsw.: the καί after ἄστροις having since its occurrence taken up a new subject in apposition. **καί bef. σάλου**—'vocem angustiorem annectit latiori.' Kypke, Observv. in loc. The same may be said of the **καί** bef. **προσδοκ.** in ver. 26.

28.] **ἀπολ.**, i. e. **the completion of it**

c = here (Acts xix. 33) only. (Prov. xxvi. 18 al.) Jos. Antt. iv. 8. 19.
d John v. 19 reff.
e ‖ only. Gen. viii. 22.
f = Matt. v. 18 reff. Ps. lxxxix. 5. Jer. viii. 20.
g ch. xvii. 3 reff.
h Matt. xxvi. 43 reff.
i = 2 Pet. ii. 18.
k here only †. (-λᾶν, Isa. xxix. 9.)
l Gospp., here only. Rom. xiii. 13. Gal. v. 21 only. L.P. Hag. i. 6.
m Matt. xiii. 22 reff.
n 1 Cor. vi. 3, 4 only †.
o = 1 Thess. v. 3. 2 Tim. iv. 6 only. see ch. xx. 1 reff.
p 1 Thess. v. 3 only †. Wisd. xvii. 15. 2 Macc. xiv. 1. (-ως, 2 Macc. v. 5.)
q Matt. vii. 22 reff.
r Rom. xi. 9 (from Ps. lxviii. 22). 1 Tim. iii. 7. vi. 9. 2 Tim. ii. 26 only.
s here only †. 1 Macc. xvi. 16 only.
t Matt. iv. 16. ch. i. 79. Jer. xxxii. (xxv.) 29, 30.
u Mark xiii. 33. Eph. vi. 18. Heb. xiii. 17 only. Job xxi. 32. (-πνία, 2 Cor. vi. 5.)
v Eph. vi. 18 only. Ps. cv. 3.
w Matt. xvi. 18. ch. xxiii. 23 only. Isa. xxii 4. Wisd. xvii. 5.
x Acts xvi. 27. xix. 16. Rom. ii. 3. 2 Cor. xi. 33. 1 Thess. v. 3. Heb. ii. 3. xii. 25 only. Judg. vi. 11.
y see Rev. vi. 17. Wisd. v. 1.
z = Matt. v. 16 al.
a ver. 27.
b constr., Matt. xix. 22 reff.
c constr., ch. ii. 37. Matt. xii. 40.

ABCDE FGHKL MRSUV ΧΓΔΛ ΠΝ 1. 33. 69

τὰ δένδρα. 30 ὅταν ^{c}προβάλωσιν ἤδη, βλέποντες ^{d}ἀφ᾽
ἑαυτῶν γινώσκετε ὅτι ἤδη ἐγγὺς τὸ ^{e}θέρος ἐστίν.
31 οὕτως καὶ ὑμεῖς ὅταν ἴδητε ταῦτα γινόμενα, γινώσκετε
ὅτι ἐγγύς ἐστιν ἡ βασιλεία τοῦ θεοῦ. 32 ἀμὴν λέγω
ὑμῖν ὅτι οὐ μὴ ^{f}παρέλθῃ ἡ γενεὰ αὕτη ἕως ἂν πάντα
γένηται. 33 ὁ οὐρανὸς καὶ ἡ γῆ ^{f}παρελεύσονται, οἱ δὲ
λόγοι μου οὐ μὴ ^{f}παρελεύσονται. 34 ^{g}προσέχετε δὲ
ἑαυτοῖς, μήποτε ^{h}βαρηθῶσιν ὑμῶν αἱ καρδίαι ^{i}ἐν ^{k}κραι-
πάλῃ καὶ ^{l}μέθῃ καὶ ^{m}μερίμναις ^{n}βιωτικαῖς, καὶ ^{o}ἐπιστῇ
ἐφ᾽ ὑμᾶς ^{p}αἰφνίδιος ἡ ^{q}ἡμέρα ἐκείνη 35 ὡς ^{r}παγίς·
^{s}ἐπεισελεύσεται γὰρ ἐπὶ πάντας τοὺς ^{t}καθημένους ἐπὶ
πρόσωπον πάσης τῆς γῆς. 36 ^{u}ἀγρυπνεῖτε δὲ ^{v}ἐν παντὶ
^{v}καιρῷ δεόμενοι ἵνα ^{w}κατισχύσητε ^{x}ἐκφυγεῖν ταῦτα πάντα
τὰ μέλλοντα γίνεσθαι, καὶ ^{y}σταθῆναι ^{z}ἔμπροσθεν τοῦ
^{a}υἱοῦ τοῦ ^{a}ἀνθρώπου.
37 ^{b}Ἦν δὲ τὰς ^{c}ἡμέρας ἐν τῷ ἱερῷ ^{b}διδάσκων, τὰς δὲ

30. aft προβαλωσιν ins τον καρπον αυτων D lat-*e* syr-cu. om ηδη βλεποντες αφ᾽ εαυτων D(but aft γινωσκ. ins ηδη D^1) syr-cu: om βλεποντες latt Syr: aft βλεπ. ins αυτων ℵ^1(om ℵ-corr^1).—for αφ εαυτ., απ αυτων [L] ℵ^{3a}(but txt restored) [Syr (syr) syr-jer copt arm: εφ εαυ. F]. γινωσκετε is repeated by ℵ^1. [add ηδη D^1(and lat).] for οτι, διοτι A. εγγυς bef 2nd ηδη DLR 33: aft το θερος M 69 lat-*e*: om ηδη KX[Π] vulg lat-*a c* Syr syr-cu [æth arm]: εγγυς εστιν ηδη το θερος ℵ [syr-jer].
31. aft ουτως ins ουν R. om γινομενα D (‖ *Matt*) lat-*a*.
32. om αν Dℵ 33. ins ταυτα bef παντα (‖ *Matt Mark*) D 69 lat-*l* (Syr) syr-cu copt (æth arm).
33. for 1st παρελευσονται, παρελευσεται (‖ *Matt*) CK[Π] 1 lat-*a e q*. rec (for 2nd παρελευσονται) παρελθωσι (‖ *Matt*), with ACR rel: txt BDLℵ 33 copt.
34. om δε Dℵ 1. 69 lat-*l* æth Iren-int$_2$. rec βαρυνθωσιν, with D H(Treg, expr) 69 [Meth$_1$ Bas$_1$ Cyr$_1$]: txt ABCRℵ rel Bas$_1$ Cyr$_1$. αι καρδιαι bef υμων ABX 69 latt Iren-int: txt CDRℵ rel copt Meth$_1$ Epiph$_1$ [Bas$_2$ Cyr$_1$]. rec transp επιστη and αιφνιδιος, with C rel syr arm [Bas$_1$]; αιφ. επ. εφ υμ. A Syr copt [Bas$_1$] Iren-int$_1$ (*both appy to put αιφν. in emphatic place*): om εφ υμας X: txt BDLRℵ latt syr-cu æth (Meth$_1$) Mcion$_1$-t.—εφνιδιος (*itacism*) A D(ενιφνιος D^1, εφνιος D-corr) FKLMXΔ [Cℵ], εφνιδιως RΓ[Π] 1. 33. 69 æth Bas$_{1 \text{ or } 2}$. om η DV.
35. rec γαρ bef επεισελευσεται, putting a colon at end of ver 34, with ACR rel vulg lat-*f* syrr syr-cu [syr-jer] arm Eus$_1$ [Bas$_1$] Iren-int$_1$: txt BDLℵ lat-*a b c e ff$_2$ i* copt Meth$_1$ (Cyr$_1$) Mcion$_1$-t.—rec επελευσεται, with ACR ℵ-corr rel Eus$_1$ [Bas$_1$]: ελευσ. 67-9 Scr's p ev-H^1: txt BDℵ^1 lat-*a e*. (*The double compound is characteristic of Luke.*) om παντας D. της γης bef πασης AKU^2[Π].
36. rec (for δε) ουν (*so* ‖ *Mark*), with ACR rel vulg lat-*b c f ff$_2$* [*i l q* syr-jer-ms] syrr syr-cu copt æth arm: txt BDℵ lat-*a e* copt-ms. rec (for κατισχυσητε) καταξιωθητε, with ACDR rel latt syrr syr-cu arm Tert$_1$: txt BLXℵ 1. 33 [syr-jer] copt æth. παντα bef ταυτα AC^{1}M lat-*a e i* syr [syr-jer] Tert$_1$: om ταυτα C^{3}Rℵ^1 rel am: txt BDLX Δℵ^{3a} 1. 33. 69 vulg lat-*b c f* [*ff$_2$ l q*]. for σταθηναι, στησεσθε D lat-*a b c e ff$_2$ i l* [*q*].
37. διδασκων bef εν τω ιερω BK vulg lat-*b c e f g$_{1,2}$ i l* [*q*] Syr syr-cu [æth]: om διδασκων G: txt ACDRℵ rel lat-*a* syr copt. om τας δε νυκτας εξερχομενος D.

by My appearing. **34—36.**] Peculiar to Luke. **34.**] **ἑαυτοῖς** and **ὑμῶν** are emphatic, recalling the thoughts to *themselves*, after the recounting of these outward signs. **35.**] There is meaning in **καθημ.**,—**sitting securely.**

[c] νύκτας ἐξερχόμενος [d] ηὐλίζετο [e] εἰς τὸ ὄρος τὸ καλούμενον [f] Ἐλαιών. 38 καὶ πᾶς ὁ λαὸς [g] ὤρθριζεν πρὸς
αὐτὸν ἐν τῷ ἱερῷ ἀκούειν αὐτοῦ.
XXII. 1 [h] Ἤγγιζεν δὲ ἡ ἑορτὴ τῶν [i] ἀζύμων ἡ λεγομένη [k] πάσχα· 2 καὶ ἐζήτουν οἱ ἀρχιερεῖς καὶ οἱ γραμματεῖς [l] τὸ πῶς [m] ἀνέλωσιν αὐτόν, ἐφοβοῦντο γὰρ τὸν
λαόν. 3 εἰςῆλθεν δὲ σατανᾶς εἰς Ἰούδαν τὸν καλούμενον Ἰσκαριώτην, ὄντα ἐκ τοῦ ἀριθμοῦ τῶν δώδεκα·
4 καὶ ἀπελθὼν [n] συνελάλησεν τοῖς ἀρχιερεῦσιν καὶ [o] στρατηγοῖς [l] τὸ πῶς αὐτοῖς [p] παραδῷ αὐτόν. 5 καὶ ἐχάρησαν,
καὶ [q] συνέθεντο αὐτῷ ἀργύριον δοῦναι· 6 καὶ [r] ἐξωμο-

...αυτον 33. ABCDE FGHKL MRSUV ΧΓΔΛΠ ℵ 1. 69

P εις-ηλθεν... ..δωδεκα F.

d Matt. xxi. 17 only. Judg. xix. 6, &c.
e = ch. xi. 7 reff.
f ch. xix. 29 reff. and note.
g here only. Gen. xix. 27 al.
h = ch. xxi. 8 reff.
i ‖ Mk. reff.
k ‖ Mt. reff.
l ch. ix. 46 reff.
m Matt. ii. 16. ch. xxiii. 32 al. Exod. xxi. 29.
n ch. iv. 36. ix. 30 ‖. Acts xxv. 12 only. Exod. xxxiv. 35.
o ver. 52. Acts iv. 1. v. 24, 26. xvi. 20, &c. only. L. Neh. ii. 16.
p Matt. xvii. 22 reff.
q John ix. 22. Acts xxiii. 20 (xxiv. 9 v. r.) only. 1 Kings xxii. 13.
r = here only. (Matt. xi. 25 al. 1 Chron. xvi. 4.)

εις το ορος bef *ηυλ.* D. *ηυλησετο* D[1] : *ηυληζετο* D-corr[1] : *διηλιζετο* A.
38. for *ιερω*, *ορει* C[1](perhaps) U. *ακουειν αυτου* bef *εν τω ιερω* D. (at end 13. 69. 124. 346 ins John vii. 53—viii. 11.)

Chap. XXII. **1.** *ηγγισεν* DL lat-*b e* g_1 *i* [*l*] *q*.
2. *οι δε αρχιερεις και γραμματεις* bef *εζητουν* (omg 1st *και* and 2nd *οι* and insg *δε*) D lat-*e*. om *το* D 254. for *ανελωσιν*, *απολεσωσιν* D. *εφοβουντο* D[1](txt D-corr[1 or 2]). for *γαρ*, *δε* D 254 vulg lat-*b c* ff_2 g_1 *i* [*q*] æth arm.
3. rec ins *ο* bef *σατανας*, with U copt Eus_1 : om ABCDP R[appy] ℵ rel $Orig_1$. ins *τον* bef *ιουδαν* D. rec *επικαλουμενον* (*more usual*), with ACPR rel $Orig_1$ Eus_1 : txt BDLXℵ 69 syr-ms copt arm. (om *τον καλουμενον* G.) *ισκαριωδ* D-gr, *-ριωθ* lat-*a* D-lat syr-cu Orig. aft *αριθμου* ins *εκ* D[1][-gr].
4. aft *αρχιερευσιν* ins *και τοις γραμματευσιν* (*prob a mere mechanl addn; as Mey*) C P(omg *τοις*) lat-*a b c e* ff_2 *i l* [*q*] syrr syr-cu æth arm Eus_2: om ABDRℵ rel vulg lat-*f* [syr-jer] copt. rec ins *τοις* bef *στρατηγοις*, with C (S, e sil) UΛ Eus_1 : om ABPRℵ rel $Orig_1$ Eus_1.—om *και στρατηγοις* D lat-*a b c e* ff_2 *i l q* syr-cu æth. add *του ιερου* (*see ver* 52: *Acts* iv. 1; v. 24) CP syrr Eus_2. om *το* D arm. rec transp *αυτοις* and *αυτον* (*cf* ‖ *Matt Mark*), with AP rel vulg lat-*b c f* [*q*] arm Orig Eus_2 $Mcion_2$-e : txt BCGKL[Π]ℵ, *παραδοι αυτον* (omg *αυτοις*) D lat-*a*.
5. *αργυρια* (‖ *Matt*) ACKUX[Π] 69 syr Eus_1 : txt BDPRℵ rel Eus_1.
6. om *και εξωμολογησεν* C ℵ[1](ins ℵ[3b]) evv-H_1[1]-48 lat-*a b c* ff_2 *i l q* Eus_2.—*ωμολ.* D;

36.] **σταθ.**, **to be set**, i. e. *by the angels*—see Matt. ver. 31—before the glorified Son of Man.

37, 38.] *Peculiar to Luke.* These verses close the scene of our Lord's discourses in Jerusalem which began ch. xx. 1. It does not appear, as Meyer will have it, that Luke believed our Lord to have taught *after this* in the temple. Nothing is said to imply it—a general closing formula like this applies to what *has been* related. **38.**] **ὤρθρ.** is literal,—not figurative, '*came eagerly*,' as De Wette, &c. think, from several places in the LXX. There is no occasion for a figure here. Luke relates nothing of any visits to *Bethany*. He has the name, incidentally only, in ch. xix. 29 and ch. xxiv. 50, where see note. On the whole question regarding the history of the woman taken in adultery (see digest), compare notes, John viii. 1 ff.

Chap. XXII. **1, 2.**] Conspiracy of the Jewish authorities to kill Jesus. Matt. xxvi. 1—5. Mark xiv. 1, 2. The account of Matt. is the fullest: see notes there. The words here give us a mere compendium of what took place.

3—6.] Compact of Judas with them to betray Him. Matt. xxvi. 14—16. Mark xiv. 10, 11. Our account is strikingly peculiar and independent of the others. The expression **εἰςῆλθ. δὲ σατ.** is found in John xiii. 27,—and certainly *in its proper place*. Satan had not yet *entered into* Judas,—only (John xiii. 2) put it into his heart to betray our Lord. **4.**] **καὶ στρατηγοῖς** is peculiar to Luke: the others have merely *the chief priests*. On **στρατ.**, see Acts iv. 1. The Levitical guard of the temple would be consulted, because it had been of late especially *in the temple* that our Lord

λόγησεν, καὶ ἐζήτει [s] εὐκαιρίαν [t] τοῦ παραδοῦναι αὐτὸν
[u] ἄτερ [v] ὄχλου αὐτοῖς. 7 Ἦλθεν δὲ ἡ ἡμέρα τῶν [w] ἀζύμων,
ᾗ ἔδει [x] θύεσθαι τὸ [x] πάσχα· 8 καὶ ἀπέστειλεν Πέτρον καὶ
Ἰωάννην εἰπὼν [y] Πορευθέντες ἑτοιμάσατε ἡμῖν τὸ πάσχα,
ἵνα φάγωμεν. 9 οἱ δὲ εἶπαν αὐτῷ Ποῦ θέλεις ἑτοιμάσωμεν; 10 ὁ δὲ εἶπεν αὐτοῖς Ἰδοὺ εἰσελθόντων ὑμῶν εἰς
τὴν πόλιν [z] συναντήσει ὑμῖν ἄνθρωπος [a] κεράμιον ὕδατος
[b] βαστάζων· ἀκολουθήσατε αὐτῷ εἰς τὴν οἰκίαν εἰς ἣν
εἰσπορεύεται. 11 καὶ ἐρεῖτε τῷ [c] οἰκοδεσπότῃ τῆς οἰκίας
Λέγει σοι ὁ [d] διδάσκαλος Ποῦ ἐστιν τὸ [e] κατάλυμα, ὅπου
τὸ [f] πάσχα μετὰ τῶν μαθητῶν μου [f] φάγω; 12 κἀκεῖνος
ὑμῖν δείξει [g] ἀνάγαιον μέγα [h] ἐστρωμένον· ἐκεῖ [i] ἑτοιμάσατε. 13 ἀπελθόντες δὲ εὗρον καθὼς εἰρήκει αὐτοῖς,

...δουναι R. F [αυ]τοις... ...ιωαν F. R πορευθεντες... F[κερα]μιον... ...της F. ABCDE GHKL MPRSU VXΓΔΛ ΠΝ 1. 69 F [αυ]τοις...

s ‖ Mt. (reff.) only. t ch. x. 19. Acts xxvii. 20. Rom. xv. 23. 1 Cor. ix. 10 al. u ver. 35 only†. 2 Macc. xii. 15 only. v = Acts xxiv. 18. w ver. 1. x ‖ Mk. reff. y Matt. ii. 8 al. Josh. xxiii. 16. z ch. ix. 37. Acts x. 25. xx. 22. Heb. vii. 1, 10 only. Num. xxiii. 16. a ‖ Mk. only. Isa. v. 10. Jer. xlii. (xxxv.) 5 only. b = ‖ Mk. Matt. iii. 11. John xix. 17 al.
c Matt. x. 25 al.† d = ‖. John xi. 28. e ‖ Mk. ch. ii. 7 only. 1 Kings ix. 22.
f ‖ Mk. reff. g ‖ Mk. only †. h = ‖ Mk. Acts ix. 34 only. (Matt. xxi. 8 reff.) Ezek. xxiii. 41.
i abs., ‖ Mk. ch. ix. 52. Gen. xliii. 16.

ομ. P. for *του παραδουναι, ινα παραδω* (‖ *Matt*) P. rec *αυτοις* bef *ατερ οχλου*, with P rel lat-*c f ff*$_2$ [*q*] syrr syr-cu copt æth arm Eus$_2$: om *αυτοις* D vulg lat-*a e l*: txt ABCLℵ lat-*b i* [*l*].

7. om ἡ ACΔ. for *των αζυμων, του πασχα* D lat-*a b e ff*$_2$ *i l* Syr syr-cu. rec ins *εν* bef ἡ, with APℵ rel latt Eus$_1$: om BCDL.

8. ins *τον* bef *πετρον* D.

9. (*ειπαν*, so BCDLℵ.) aft *ετοιμασωμεν* ins *σοι* DP gat lat-*c e ff*$_2$ sah æth; *σοι φαγειν το πασχα* (‖ *Matt*) B syr-mg-ms.

10. om *αυτοις* D lat-*e*. for *εισελθοντων, εισερχομενων* D. **υπαντησει** CLX; **απαντησει** D 29. 248 Scr's g [Orig$_1$]: txt ABPRℵ rel. *βασταζων* bef *κεραμιον υδατος* D: om *υδατος* ℵ[1](ins ℵ[3b]). rec (for *εις ην*) *οὗ*, with D rel Syr syr-cu(appy): *ου εαν* (*cf* ‖ *Mark, οπου αν*) AKMPR[Π]: txt BCLℵ latt syr [syr-jer coptt] arm, *εν η* X.

11. aft *οικιας* ins *λεγοντες* ℵ. om *σοι* (‖ *Matt Mark*) DUX lat-*q* Syr syr-cu. aft *καταλυμα* ins *μου* Cℵ sah arm.

12. for *κακεινος, εκεινος* D Orig$_1$. (**αναγαιον**, so ABDEGHKLMPR S-marg V[ΔΠ[1]]ℵ: *αναγεον* C 1.) for *μεγα, οικον* D sah. **κακει** LXℵ vulg lat-*f i* æth arm-ed.

13. rec *ειρηκεν*, with APR rel: txt BCDLℵ 69 lat-*a*. (*ειπεν* X 240-4-8 Scr's g evv-x-z$_1$.) for *αυτοις, αυτος* D[1][-gr](txt D-corr[1]).

had become obnoxious to them (see ver. 53 and ch. xxi. 37, 38). **5, 6.**] The words **συνεθ.** and **ἐξωμολ.** here seem clearly to imply that the money was *not now paid, but afterwards*, when the treachery was accomplished;—see note on Matt. xxvi. 15. **ἄτερ ὄχλ.** = *καταμόνας* Theophyl., or perhaps *χωρὶς θορύβου*, Euthym.

7—14.] Preparation for celebrating the Passover. Matt. xxvi. 17—19. Mark xiv. 12—16. Our account is the fullest of the three, related however nearly to Mark's. **7.**] **ἦλθεν** is not '*appropinquabat*,' but '*venit*.' On this whole subject see notes on Matt. xxvi. 17, and John xviii. 28. **ᾗ ἔδει**, the *legal time* of the Passover being sacrificed. So the narrators in the three Gospels evidently intend. **8, 9.**] It was a solemn message, and for it were chosen the two chief Apostles. In the report of Matthew, the suggestion is represented as coming from the disciples themselves. The question, **ποῦ θέλ.** *was* asked, but only in reply to the command of our Lord. **10.**] There can, I think, be no question that this direction was given in superhuman foresight, just as that in ch. xix. 30: see also 1 Sam. x. 2—8, and Matt. xvii. 27. This person carrying water would probably be a *slave*, and the time, towards evening, the usual hour of fetching in water. **11, 12.**] The **οἰκοδεσπ.** was a man of some wealth, and could not be *identical with* the water-carrier (see notes on Matt.). **κατάλ.** is not here, as in ch. ii. 7, an *inn*, but a room set apart at this season of the feast, by residents in Jerusalem, in which parties

καὶ ἡτοίμασαν τὸ πάσχα. 14 Καὶ ὅτε ἐγένετο ἡ [k] ὥρα,
[l] ἀνέπεσεν, καὶ οἱ ἀπόστολοι σὺν αὐτῷ. 15 καὶ εἶπεν πρὸς
αὐτοὺς [m] Ἐπιθυμίᾳ ἐπεθύμησα τοῦτο τὸ [f] πάσχα [f] φαγεῖν
μεθ᾽ ὑμῶν [n] πρὸ τοῦ με [o] παθεῖν· 16 λέγω γὰρ ὑμῖν ὅτι οὐ
μὴ φάγω αὐτὸ ἕως [p] ὅτου [q] πληρωθῇ ἐν τῇ βασιλείᾳ τοῦ
θεοῦ. 17 καὶ [r] δεξάμενος ποτήριον [s] εὐχαριστήσας εἶπεν
Λάβετε τοῦτο καὶ [t] διαμερίσατε εἰς ἑαυτούς· 18 λέγω γὰρ
ὑμῖν, οὐ μὴ [u] πίω [[v] ἀπὸ τοῦ νῦν] ἀπὸ τοῦ [w] γενήματος
τῆς [x] ἀμπέλου ἕως οὗ ἡ βασιλεία τοῦ θεοῦ ἔλθῃ. 19 Καὶ

...ειπεν F. ...επιθυμια R. ...βασιλεια P. F τηριον ...

k = Matt. xxvi. 45. John xvi. 4. l = ch. xi. 37 reff. m constr., John iii. 29. Acts iv. 17. v. 28. xxiii. 14. Gen. xxxi. 30. n constr., Matt. vi. 8 reff. Acts xxiii. 15 al. o = (see note) Acts i. 3. iii. 18. Heb. xiii. 12. p ch. xv. 8 reff. q = John iii. 29. 2 Cor. x. 6 al. r = ch. ii. 28. xvi. 6. Eph. vi. 17. Jer. xxxii. (xxv.) 28. s absol., here (bis) & ||. Matt. xv. 36 || Mk. al. Wisd. xviii. 2. t ch. xi. 17, 18 reff. Judg. v. 30. u w. ἀπό here only. ἐκ, || Mt. reff. v ch. v. 10 reff. w || Mt. reff. x John xv. 1 reff.

14. rec ins δωδεκα bef αποστολοι (*see* ||), with ACPRℵ[3b] rel vulg lat-*f q* syrr [syr-jer] copt æth arm $Epiph_2$: om BDℵ[1] lat-*a b c e ff*$_2$ *i l* syr-cu sah.—οι δωδεκα, omg αποστολοι, LXℵ[3a].

16. om οτι C[1](perhaps) DX. rec ins ουκετι bef ου μη (*from Mark* xiv. 25), with C[2]P rel vulg lat-*c e* syrr syr-cu [syr-jer] æth arm [$Orig_1$] : for ου, ουκετι D : txt ABC[1]HLℵ 1 lat-*a* coptt. **φαγομαι** D. rec (for αυτο) εξ αυτου (*from* ||), with AC[2]P rel lat-*f* syr-txt [syr-jer] æth arm : απ᾽ αυτου (*from below*) D 69 : txt B C[1](appy) Lℵ 1 latt syr-mg coptt $Epiph_1$ [$Orig\text{-}int_1$]. for πληρωθη, καινον βρωθη D.

17. ins το bef ποτηριον (*see ver* 20) ADKMU[Π] : om BCLℵ rel coptt. om τουτο ℵ[1] [vulg lat-*e*]. om και D[-gr lat-*e*] syr-cu syr-jer coptt. rec (for εις εαυτους) εαυτοις (*from John* xix. 24 : *Ps* xxi. 18), with AD rel syr : αλληλοις ℵ[1] : txt BC(L)Mℵ[3a] 1. 69 latt arm.—αυτοις L.

18. rec aft υμιν ins οτι (*Matt* xxvi. 29 || *Mark*), with Aℵ rel latt syrr syr-cu syr-jer [coptt arm] : om BCDGL 1 mt lat-*e* æth. rec om απο του νυν, with AC rel Syr Iren-int : ins bef ου μη πιω DG 1 lat-e_1 syr-cu arm : txt BKLM[Π]ℵ lat-e_1 syr syr-jer coptt æth. (rec γενν., with K (S, e sil) : txt ABCDℵ rel.) rec (for ου) οτου, with AD rel : om C[1](appy) : txt BC[1]FLℵ 1. ελθη bef η β. τ. θ. D [Syr syr-cu syr-jer].

coming from the country might eat the Passover. The question therefore would be well understood;—and the room being **ἐστρωμένον**, and as Mark adds, ἕτοιμον, would be no matter of surprise.

14.] The **ὥρα** was *evening*, see above on ver. 10, and Matt. xxvi. 20.

15—18.] *Peculiar to Luke.* The desire of our Lord to eat this His last Passover may be explained from ch. xii. 50: not *merely* from his depth of love for His disciples, though this formed an element in it,—see John xiii. 1 sq. The **γάρ** in ver. 16 gives us the leading reason. **15. παθεῖν**] This is *the only instance in the Gospels, of the absolute use of* **πάσχω**, as in the Creed, '*He suffered.*' We have several times πολλὰ παθεῖν, ch. ix. 22; xvii. 25: Matt. xvi. 21 al. ταῦτα παθεῖν, ch. xxiv. 26, and οὕτως παθεῖν, ditto ver. 46.

16.] The full meaning of this declaration is to be sought in the words **τοῦτο** τὸ πάσχα. It was *that particular* Passover, not *merely* the Passover generally—though of course that also,—that was to receive its fulfilment in the kingdom of God. And to this fulfilment our Lord alludes again in ver. 30, ἵνα ἔσθητε καὶ πίνητε ἐπὶ τῆς τραπέζης μου ἐν τῇ βασιλείᾳ μου. It is to this marriage supper of the Lamb, that the parable Matt. xxii. 1—14 in its ultimate application refers: nor can we help thinking on the faithless Apostle at this very supper, in ib. vv. 11—13: see notes there.

17.] Some (e. g. De Wette) suppose that it is here implied that our Lord *did not drink of the cup Himself.* But surely this cannot be so. The two members of the speech are strictly parallel: and if He desired to *eat* the Passover with them, He would also *drink of the cup*, which formed a usual part of the ceremonial. This seems to me to be implied in **δεξάμενος**: λαβών is the word used by all *afterwards*, when He did *not* partake of the bread and wine. This most important addition in our narrative, amounts I believe to a solemn declaration of the *fulfilment of the Passover rite*, in both its usual divisions,—the eating the flesh of the lamb, and drinking the cup of thanksgiving. Henceforward, He who fulfilled the Law for man will no more eat and drink of it. I remark this, in order further to observe that *this division of the cup* is not only not *identical with*, but has *no reference to*, the subsequent one in ver. 20. That was the *institution of a new rite*;—this the *abro-*

λαβὼν ἄρτον [s] εὐχαριστήσας [y] ἔκλασεν καὶ ἔδωκεν αὐτοῖς
λέγων Τοῦτό [z] ἐστιν τὸ σῶμά μου τὸ ὑπὲρ ὑμῶν διδόμενον·
τοῦτο ποιεῖτε [[a] εἰς] τὴν [b] ἐμὴν [c] ἀνάμνησιν. 20 καὶ τὸ ...εις την C.
ποτήριον [d] ὡςαύτως [e] μετὰ τὸ [f] δειπνῆσαι, λέγων Τοῦτο
τὸ ποτήριον ἡ [g] καινὴ [g] διαθήκη [h] ἐν τῷ αἵματί μου τὸ
ὑπὲρ ὑμῶν [i] ἐκχυννόμενον. 21 [k] πλὴν ἰδοὺ ἡ χεὶρ τοῦ T εκχυν ...
παραδιδόντος με μετ᾽ ἐμοῦ ἐπὶ τῆς τραπέζης. 22 ὅτι ὁ ABDEF
[l] υἱὸς μὲν τοῦ [l] ἀνθρώπου κατὰ τὸ [m] ὡρισμένον [n] πορεύεται, GHKL MSTUV
[k] πλὴν οὐαὶ τῷ ἀνθρώπῳ ἐκείνῳ δι᾽ οὗ παραδίδοται. ΧΓΔΛΠ ℵ 1. 69
23 καὶ αὐτοὶ ἤρξαντο [o] συνζητεῖν πρὸς ἑαυτοὺς [p] τὸ τίς
ἄρα [q] εἴη ἐξ αὐτῶν ὁ τοῦτο μέλλων πράσσειν. 24 ἐγένετο

y || Matt. xiv. 19. xv. 36 al. Jer. xvi. 7.
z = Matt. xiii. 37. John xv. 1. 1 Cor. x. 4. Gen. xli. 26, 27. Exod. xii. 11. Ezek. xxxvii. 11.
a = Matt. viii. 34. Mark i. 4. xiv. 9.
b (= ἐμοῦ) || 1 Cor. bis. John xv. 9.
c || 1 Cor. bis. Heb. x. 3 only. L.P.H. Num. x. 10.
d ch. xx. 31 reff.
e Matt. xxvi. 32 reff. Gen. v. 4, &c.
f ch. xvii. 8 reff.
g || [Mt.]. 2 Cor. iii. 6. Heb. viii. 8, from Jer. xxxviii. (xxxi.) 31.
h Heb. ix. 22, 25. 1 John v. 6. Zech. ix. 11.
i Matt. xxiii. 35 reff.
k = Matt. xi. 22 al. Judg. iv. 9.
l Matt. viii. 20 reff.
m Acts ii. 23. x. 42. xi. 29. xvii. 26, 31. Rom. i. 4. Heb. iv. 7 only. L.P.H. Num. xxxiv. 6.
n = Gen. xv. 2 Symm. (see John xiv. 2, 28.)
o Mark i. 27 reff.
p vv. 2, 4.
q opt., ch. ix. 46. xv. 26. see Acts xvii. 27. xxiv. 19. Winer, edn. 6, § 41. 4. c.

19. aft λεγων ins λαβετε A. om εις B[1](sic: see table): ins AB[2]CDℵ rel.
19, 20. om το υπερ ver 19 to end of ver 20 D lat-*a b e ff*$_2$ *i l*: lat-*b e* read instead vv. 17, 18, omg them above: similarly syr-cu substitutes vv. 17, 18 for ver 20.
20. rec ωσαυτως bef και το ποτηριον (*aft* || 1 *Cor*), with A rel [vulg lat-*c f g*$_{1.2}$ *q* syrr &c Bas$_1$]: txt BLℵ copt [syr-jer]. (εκχυννομενον, so AB[1]ELUΔ[ΤΠ]ℵ.)
21. om μετ᾽ εμου D 57 Syr.
22. rec (for οτι) και, with A rel vulg lat-*c* [*b e f ff*$_2$ *i l q*] syrr syr-cu [syr-jer æth arm]: om lat-*a i* D-lat Orig$_1$: txt B D-gr LTℵ coptt. rec μεν bef υιος (|| *Matt Mark*), with A rel: μεν bef ο υιος D: om μεν ℵ[1]: txt BLTℵ[3a] D-lat coptt. rec πορευεται bef κατα το ωρισμενον (||), with A rel lat-*f* syrr syr-cu coptt æth: txt BDGLTℵ 69 latt [syr-jer] arm Orig. om τω ανθρωπω D lat-*e* syr-cu Tert$_1$.
23. for και αυτοι, αυτοι δε D lat-*e f* sah. om το DL sah(appy) Orig$_1$. om εξ αυτων D 142[1](Sz) lat-*a b e ff*$_2$ *i* [*l q*] syr-cu. aft αυτων ℵ[1] repeats ειη. μελλων bef τουτο DL 241-5.

gation of an old one, now fulfilled, or about to be so, in the person of the true Lamb of God. This is generally supposed to have been the *first* cup in the Passover-meal, with which the whole was introduced. On the possible connexion of this speech of our Lord with the celebration of the Passover at this particular time, see note on Matt. xxvi. 17.

After these verses, in order of time, follows *the washing of the disciples' feet* in John xiii. 1—20, referred to in our ver. 27.

19, 20.] Institution of the Lord's Supper. Matt. xxvi. 26—29. Mark xiv. 22—24. 1 Cor. xi. 23—25. See notes on Matthew. **20. τὸ ὑπὲρ ὑμῶν ἐκχυννόμενον**] These words cannot be said of ποτήριον, '*nam poculum plenum non effunditur, sed bibitur*' (Bengel), but are said πρὸς τὸ σημαινόμενον, which is the wine poured out from the grapes (τὸ γέννημα τῆς ἀμπέλου) and represents the Blood poured out from the Lord's Body. Here follows, in Matt. ver. 29, Mark ver. 25, a second declaration, respecting *not drinking any more of this fruit of the vine.*

21—23.] Announcement of a betrayer. See notes on Matt. xxvi. 20—25. I would not venture absolutely to maintain that this announcement is *identical* with that one; but I own the arguments of Stier and others to prove them distinct, fail to convince me. The expression **πλὴν ἰδού** bears marks of verbal accuracy, and inclines us to believe that this announcement was made *after the institution of the cup*, as here related. 'Notwithstanding this My declaration of love, in giving My Body and Blood for you, there is one here present who shall betray Me.' **ἐπὶ τ. τρ.**, viz. in dipping into the dish with the Lord. **πορεύεται**] A somewhat similar πορεύεσθαι to this occurs ch. xiii. 33; but that is used of our Lord's ministerial progress; this of His progress through suffering to glory.

24—30.] Dispute for pre-eminence. Our Lord's reply. Without attempting to decide the question whether this incident is strictly narrated in order of time, or identical with one of those strifes on this point related Matt. xviii. 1; xx. 20, I will offer one or two remarks on it as it here stands. (1) Its having happened at this time is not altogether unaccountable.

δὲ καὶ [r] φιλονεικία ἐν αὐτοῖς [p] τὸ τίς αὐτῶν [s] δοκεῖ εἶναι
μείζων. 25 ὁ δὲ εἶπεν αὐτοῖς Οἱ βασιλεῖς τῶν ἐθνῶν
[t] κυριεύουσιν αὐτῶν, καὶ οἱ [u] ἐξουσιάζοντες αὐτῶν [v] εὐεργέται καλοῦνται. 26 ὑμεῖς δὲ οὐχ [w] οὕτως, ἀλλ' ὁ [x] μείζων
ἐν ὑμῖν γινέσθω ὡς ὁ νεώτερος, καὶ ὁ [y] ἡγούμενος ὡς
ὁ [z] διακονῶν. 27 τίς γὰρ μείζων, ὁ [a] ἀνακείμενος ἢ ὁ
Q -σω υμων... [z] διακονῶν; οὐχὶ ὁ [a] ἀνακείμενος; ἐγὼ δὲ [b] ἐν μέσῳ ὑμῶν
εἰμι ὡς ὁ [z] διακονῶν. 28 ὑμεῖς δέ ἐστε οἱ [c] διαμεμενηκότες
μετ' ἐμοῦ ἐν τοῖς [d] πειρασμοῖς μου. 29 κἀγὼ [e] διατίθεμαι
ὑμῖν καθὼς [e] διέθετό μοι ὁ πατήρ μου βασιλείαν, 30 ἵνα
[f] ἔσθητε καὶ πίνητε [f] ἐπὶ τῆς τραπέζης μου ἐν τῇ βασιλείᾳ

r here only †. 2 Macc. iv. 4 only (-κος, 1 Cor. xi. 16. -κεῖν, Prov. x. 12.)
s = 1 Cor. xi. 16. Gal. ii. 6.
t Gospp., here only. elsw. Paul (Rom. vi. 9, 14. vii. 1. xiv. 9. 2 Cor. i. 24. 1 Tim. vi. 15) only. Gen. iii. 16.
u 1 Cor. vi. 12. vii. 4 bis only. Eccl. ix. 17.
v here only †. Wisd. xix. 4. 2 Macc. iv. 2 only. (-τεῖν, Acts x. 38.)
w see ch. xii. 21, 38. x comp., Sir. i. 4. y = Acts xv. 22 al. 1 Chron. xvi. 5. z Mark x. 45 reff. a Matt. xxii. 10, 11 reff. b ch. ii. 46. Matt. xviii. 20. c ch. i. 22 reff. d ch. iv. 13. viii. 13. James i. 2. Deut. iv. 34. e Gospp., here bis only. Acts iii. 35. Heb. viii. 10 & x. 16 (from Jer. xxxviii. [xxxi.] 33). ix. 16, 17 only. Gen. xv. 18. f 2 Kings ix. 11, 13.

24. om *και* ℵ 127(Sz) [gat(with mm tol) lat-*a b c e ff₂ i l q*] $Orig_1$. εις εαυτους ℵ[1] [*εν εαυτοις* A[1] T(Tischdf) 69]. om *αυτων*, and for *δοκει ειναι*, *αν ειη* D lat-*a f* Syr syr-cu (coptt).
25. for *εξουσιαζοντες αυτων*, *αρχοντες των εξουσιαζουσιν αυτων και* (sic) ℵ[1].
26. rec *γενεσθω*, with A rel [Bas_1] : txt BDLTℵ 1 [Damasc-ms_1]. om 2nd *ο* D 69. for *νεωτερος*, *μικροτερος* D vulg lat-*a c ff₂ i l*. διακονος D.
27. for ver, *μαλλον η ο ανακειμενος εγω γαρ εν μεσω υμων ηλθον ουχ ως ο ανακειμενος αλλ' ως ο διακονων και υμεις ηυξηθητε εν τη διακονια μου ως ο διακονων* D. ins *ο* bef *μειζων* ℵ[1]. rec *ειμι* bef *εν μεσω υμων*, with A rel [lat-*a b e q* Bas_1 Chr_1 Orig-int_2] : om *ειμι* D(as above) : txt BLTℵ vulg lat-*c f ff₂* [*i l*] Eus_1.
28. om *υμεις δε εστε* D.
29. *διατιθημι* A 1. aft *υμ.* ins *διαθηκην* A. om *μου* DΓ 248 lat-*e*.
30. rec *εσθιητε*, with A D-corr[1] Qℵ rel Eus_1 : txt BD[1]T.

They had been just enquiring *among themselves* (ver. 23), *who among them should do this thing*. May it not reasonably be supposed, that some of them (Judas *at least*) would be anxiously employed in *self-justification*, and that this would lead, in some part of the table, to a dispute of the kind here introduced? The natural effect of the Lord's rebuke would be to give rise to a different spirit among them, and the question "*Lord, is it I?*" may have been the offspring of this better mind;—but see note on Matt. vv. 20—25. (2) It is surprising to find the very declaration of our Lord on the former strife related in this Gospel (ch. ix. 46—48), repeated as having been made *at this Paschal meal*,—by John (xiii. 20). May not this lead us to suppose that there has been a transposition of some of the circumstances regarding these various contentions among the Apostles, and that these words occurring in John may possibly *point to a strife of this kind?* (3) The *ἐγώ εἰμι ἐν μέσῳ ὑμῶν ὡς ὁ διακονῶν* is too clear an allusion to the *washing of their feet by the Lord*, to have escaped even those Commentators who are slow to discern such hints (e. g. De Wette). The appeal, if *it had taken place*, is natural and intelligible; but not otherwise. (4) The diction is repeatedly allusive to their *then* employment: *ἀνακείμενος — διατίθεμαι — ἔσθειν καὶ πίνειν—ἐν τῇ βασιλείᾳ μου*—all these have reference to things present, or words spoken, during that meal.

I therefore infer that the strife *did happen at this time, in the order related here.*

25.] See on Matt. xx. 25. The expression here **οἱ ἐξουσ. αὐτ. εὐεργ. καλ.** also seems to be connected with what had just taken place. 'Among *them*, the *εὐεργέται* are those who *ἐξουσιάζουσιν αὐτῶν*—but among *you*, I, your *εὐεργέτης* (see vv. 19, 20, *ὑπὲρ ὑμῶν*, bis), *do not so*, but am in the midst of you as your servant.' Ptolemy *εὐεργέτης* at once occurs to us;—numerous other examples are given by Wetstein. **26.**] **οὕτως**, i. e. *ἔσεσθε*.

27.] Compare John xiii. 13—17.

28.] These words could hardly have been spoken except on this occasion, when *τὸ περὶ ἐμοῦ τέλος ἔχει*, ver. **37.**

29, 30.] See above, and note on Matt. xix. 28, see also Rev. ii. 27. The word *βασιλείαν* belongs to both verbs—not, '*I appoint to you* (as my Father hath appointed to me a kingdom) *that ye*

μου, καὶ κάθησθε ἐπὶ θρόνων [g] κρίνοντες τὰς δώδεκα
φυλὰς τοῦ Ἰσραήλ· 31 Σίμων Σίμων, ἰδοὺ ὁ σατανᾶς
[h] ἐξῃτήσατο ὑμᾶς, τοῦ [i] σινιάσαι ὡς τὸν σῖτον· 32 ἐγὼ δὲ
[k] ἐδεήθην [l] περὶ σοῦ, ἵνα μὴ [m] ἐκλίπῃ ἡ πίστις σου· καὶ σὺ
[n] ποτὲ [o] ἐπιστρέψας [p] στήρισον τοὺς ἀδελφούς σου. 33 ὁ δὲ
εἶπεν αὐτῷ Κύριε, μετὰ σοῦ ἕτοιμός εἰμι καὶ εἰς φυλακὴν
καὶ εἰς θάνατον πορεύεσθαι. 34 ὁ δὲ εἶπεν Λέγω σοι,

ABDEF GHKL MQSTU VXΓΔΛ Πא 1. 69

g = Matt. xix. 28. 1 Cor. vi. 2, 3. Gen. xlix. 16 al. see Dan. vii. 22. h here only +. Jos. Antt. v. 2. 9. i here only +. k with περί, here only. Gen. xxv. 21. with ὑπέρ, Acts viii. 24. l = ch. iv. 38. John xvi. 26. xvii. 9, 20. Isa. xlv. 11. m ch. xvi. 9. Heb. i. 12 (from Ps. ci. 27) only. n Rom. i. 10. Phil. iv. 10 al. o = Matt. xiii. 15 reff. (?) p = Acts xviii. 23. Rom. i. 11. xvi. 25. 1 Pet. v. 10. 2 Pet. i. 12. Ps. l. 12. (-ιγμός, 2 Pet. iii. 17.)

om 2nd μου D am(with forj [ing] tol) lat-*e l* syr-cu. rec **καθισησθε**, with H: **καθεζησθε** D-gr: **καθησεσθε** AB²GLQ[Π¹]א 1. 69 (-σθαι AL): καθισεσθε (*see Matt* xix. 28) X rel: txt B¹T, **καθησθαι** B(as corrected by origl scribe, see table) Δ. (*The* -σθαι *is too obvious an itacism to bring the infin seriously into question, as in Mey.*) ins δωδεκα bef θρον. (|| *Matt*) X (Dא³ᵃ ιβ) lat-*a b f* [*l q* syr-jer] syr-cu syr-w-ast sah arm Orig$_1$; aft θρον. 69 lat-*c* [*ff*$_2$ mm]. θρον**ους** (|| *Matt*) D 69. om τας D¹(ins D-corr¹ ?). τας δωδεκα φυλας bef κρινοντες BT lat-*i*.

31. rec at beg ins ειπε δε ο κυριος (*to mark the supposed beginning of a new subject*), with ADQא rel [Bas$_2$]: om BLT coptt. om 2nd σιμων א.

32. rec εκλ**ει**πη, with AQ rel: txt BDKLMTUX[Π]א 1 [Bas$_2$ Chr$_{sæpe}$ Cyr$_1$]. for και συ ποτε επιστρεψας, συ δε επιστρεψον και D lat-*e* Gelas. rec στηρι**ξ**ον, with D rel [Bas$_1$]: txt ABKLMQT[Π]א 1. (X doubtful, see Treg.)

33. for ο δε ειπεν, ειπεν δε A lat-*a b f ff*$_2$ *i* [*l*] *q*.

&c.,' but, **I appoint to you, as my Father hath appointed to me, a kingdom, that ye** &c. **ἐπὶ τῆς τρ.**] See above, ver. 21, and note on ver. 16.

31—34.] Appeal to Peter: his confidence, and our Lord's reply. (See Matt. xxvi. 30—35: Mark xiv. 26—31: John xiii. 36—38.) The speech appears to *proceed continuously*. There are marks in these words of our Lord, of close connexion with what has gone before. *His* way which the Father διέθετο to Him, is *to His kingdom*—but it is *through* πειρασμοί. To *these*, who have been with Him in these trials, He διατίθεται βασιλείαν,—but *His* way to it must be *their* way, and here is the πειρασμός,—the sifting as wheat. The sudden address to Simon may perhaps have been occasioned by some remark of his,—or, which I think more probable, may have been made in consequence of some part taken by him in the preceding strife for precedence. Such sudden and earnest addresses spring forth from deep love and concern awakened for another. **31. ἐξῃτήσ.**] Not only '*hath desired to have you,*' E. V., but **hath obtained you**;—'his desire is granted.' **ὑμᾶς**—*all*. This must include Judas, though it does not follow that he was present—the sifting separated the chaff from the wheat, which chaff he was, see Amos ix. 9. **32.**] **ἐγὼ δὲ ἐδ. π. σοῦ**] As Peter was the *foremost* (the rest are here addressed through him), so he was in the greatest danger. It must not be supposed that our Lord's prayer was not heard, because Peter's faith *did fail*, in his denial; **ἐκλίπῃ** implies a *total extinction* which Peter's faith *did not suffer*. Though the **ὑμᾶς** included Judas, he is not included in the *prayer*: see John xvii. 6—12. We may notice here, that our Lord speaks of the total failure of *even an Apostle's faith*, as *possible*. **ἐπιστρέψας**] There can, I think, be little doubt that this word is here used in the general N. T. sense, of *returning as a penitent* after sin, turning to God; and not in the almost expletive meaning which it has in such passages as Ps. lxxxiv. 6, ὁ θεός, σὺ ἐπιστρέψας ζωώσεις ἡμᾶς (although even here it may have a somewhat similar sense to the above—see Joel ii. 14: Acts vii. 42). **στήρισον**] The use of this word and the cognate substantive *thrice by Peter in his two epistles* (see reff.), and in the first passage in a connexion with the mention of *Satan's temptations*, is remarkable. **33, 34.**] Whether these words are in close connexion with the preceding, may I think be doubted. They may represent the same reply of our Lord as we have recorded in John xiii. 38. One thing seems clear, without any attempt at minutely harmonizing: that *two announcements were made* by our Lord to Peter of his future denial, occasioned by *two very different professions of his*. One,—*during the last meal*, i. e. before going out, and occasioned by Peter's professed

Πέτρε, οὐ [q] φωνήσει σήμερον [r] ἀλέκτωρ ἕως τρὶς [s] ἀπαρνήσῃ
[μὴ] εἰδέναι με. 35 καὶ εἶπεν αὐτοῖς Ὅτε ἀπέστειλα ὑμᾶς
[t] ἄτερ [u] βαλλαντίου καὶ [v] πήρας καὶ [w] ὑποδημάτων, μή
τινὸς [x] ὑστερήσατε; οἱ δὲ εἶπαν Οὐθενός. 36 εἶπεν οὖν
αὐτοῖς Ἀλλὰ νῦν ὁ ἔχων [u] βαλλάντιον [y] ἀράτω, ὁμοίως
καὶ [v] πήραν· καὶ ὁ μὴ [z] ἔχων πωλησάτω τὸ ἱμάτιον αὐτοῦ
καὶ [a] ἀγορασάτω μάχαιραν. 37 λέγω γὰρ ὑμῖν ὅτι τοῦτο

q = ‖ & vv. 60, 61 ‖ only. Jer. xvii. 11.
r here, &c. ‖ only. Prov. xxx. 31 only.
s ‖. ch. xii. 9. Isa. xxxi. 7 only. see Gal. v. 7. 1 John ii. 22. [with μή, here only.]
t ver. 6 only †. 2 Macc. xii. 15 only.
u here bis. ch. x. 4. xii. 33 only. Job xiv. 17 only.
v ch. ix. 3 reff.
w Matt. x. 10. ch. x. 4. Exod. xii. 11.
x = Rom. iii. 23. Eccl. vi. 2.
y = ch. x. 3. xix. 21. Mark xv. 24.
z ellips., ch. iii. 11. 1 Cor. xi. 22.
a Matt. xiii. 44. 2 Chron. xxxiv. 11.

34. rec aft *ου* ins *μη* (*see John* xiii. 38), with AD rel: om BLQTXℵ. rec (for *εως*) *πριν η* (*from* ‖ *Mark*), with A rel syr-txt æth [arm]: *πριν* (‖ *Matt*) Q 251: *εως ου* (‖ *John*) KMX[Π]; *εως οτου* D: txt BLTℵ 69 latt Syr syr-mg [syr-jer] coptt. *με* bef *απαρνηση* BLTℵ 69: *με* bef *ειδεναι* Q 1 lat-*f*; *με απαρνηση μη ειδεναι με* D syr-cu: txt A rel vulg syrr sah. om *μη* BLMQTX[Π¹]ℵ 1 copt: ins AD rel Syr syr-cu [syr-jer æth] sah arm.
35. (*βαλλαντιου*, so ABDQ [T(Tischdf)] ℵ &c.) *μηρας* ℵ¹(txt ℵ³ᵃ or earlier). for *τινος*, *τι* ℵ¹. (*ειπαν*, so BDL [T(Tischdf)].) (rec *ουδενος*, with DL T[Alf]UΛℵ 1(e sil) Orig [Chr]: txt ABQ [T(Tischdf)] rel.)
36. for *ουν*, *δε* BL [T(Tischdf)] ℵ³ᵃ 69 coptt: txt AQ T[Alf] rel [syrr arm].—*ο δε ειπεν* Dℵ¹ lat-*e* [syr-jer Chr_1]. om *αυτοις* D 1 lat-*a b e ff₂ i* [arm]. *αρει* D. *πωλησαι* D: *πωλησει* EGHSVΔΛ 69 arm [Chr_1(txt_1)]. *αγορασει* DEFHSUVΓΛ 69 Chr_2 Thl.
37. om *υμιν* D lat-*b*. rec ins *ετι* bef *τουτο*, with T[Alf] rel vulg lat-*a c e i* syrr

readiness to go to prison and to death (= to lay down his life) for and with the Lord:—the other,—*on the way to the Mount of Olives*, after the declaration that all should be offended, and occasioned by Peter's profession that though all should be offended, yet would not he. Nothing is more natural or common than the repetition, by the warm-hearted and ardent, of professions like these, in spite of warning:—and when De Wette calls such an interpretation eine Nothhülfe, all that we can say is to disclaim any wish to clear up difficulties, except by going into their depths and examining them honestly and diligently. If the above view be correct, I conceive that the account in John of this profession and our Lord's answer, being in strict coherence, and arising out of the subject of conversation, must be taken as the *exact* one: and Luke must be supposed to have inserted them here *without being aware of the intermediate remarks* which led to them. This is the only place in the Gospels where our Lord addresses Peter by the name Πέτρε. And it is remarkable as occurring in the very place where He forewarns him of his approaching denial of Himself.

35—38.] Forewarning of perils at hand. *Peculiar to Luke.* The meaning of our Lord in this much controverted passage appears to be, *to forewarn the Apostles of the outward dangers which will await them henceforward in their mission*:—unlike the time when He sent them forth without earthly appliances, upheld by His special Providence, they must now make use of common resources for sustenance, yea and even of the sword itself for defence. This they misunderstand, and point to the two swords which they have,—for which they are rebuked (see below). **35.**] See ch. ix. 3; x. 4; also Matt. x. 9. **36.**] **αἴρειν** was the very word used in the prohibition before. There is a question what should be supplied after **μὴ ἔχων.** Very many authorities make *μάχαιραν* understood (as in E. V.);—but the simpler construction and better sense is to place *μὴ ἔχων* in contrast with *ἔχων*, **he who has a purse,** &c., **and he who has none, let him** &c., see reff. Thus the sense will be complete—for he who *has a purse*, can buy a sword, *without selling his garment.* **μάχαιρα** must be here used in the sense of **a sword,**—compare ver. 49:—and not a *knife to eat with*, which some have understood. The 'sword of the Spirit' (Olshausen and others) is *wholly out of the question.* The saying is both a description to them of their altered situation with reference to the world without, and a declaration that self-defence and self-provision would henceforward be necessary. It forms a *decisive testimony, from the mouth of the Lord Himself, against the views of the Quakers and some other sects on these points.* But it does not warrant *aggression* by Christians, nor, as some R. Catholics (see the bull "Unam sanctam" of

τὸ γεγραμμένον [b] δεῖ [c] τελεσθῆναι [d] ἐν ἐμοί, [e] τὸ Καὶ μετὰ
[f] ἀνόμων [g] ἐλογίσθη· [h] καὶ γὰρ [i] τὸ περὶ ἐμοῦ [k] τέλος [k] ἔχει.
38 οἱ δὲ εἶπαν Κύριε, ἰδοὺ μάχαιραι ὧδε δύο. ὁ δὲ εἶπεν
αὐτοῖς [l] Ἱκανόν ἐστιν. 39 Καὶ ἐξελθὼν ἐπορεύθη [m] κατὰ
τὸ [m] ἔθος εἰς τὸ [n] ὄρος [n] τῶν [n] ἐλαιῶν, ἠκολούθησαν δὲ
αὐτῷ καὶ οἱ μαθηταί. 40 γενόμενος δὲ [o] ἐπὶ τοῦ τόπου
εἶπεν αὐτοῖς [p] Προςεύχεσθε μὴ εἰςελθεῖν εἰς πειρασμόν.
41 καὶ αὐτὸς [q] ἀπεσπάσθη ἀπ' αὐτῶν [r] ὡςεὶ λίθου [s] βολήν,

ABDEF GHKL MQSTU VXΓΔΛ Πℵ 1. 69

b = Matt. xxiv. 6 reff. c = ch. xviii. 31. Rev. x. 7. Ezra i. 1 d = ch. xxiii. 31. Matt. xvii. 12. John xiv. 30. 1 Cor. ix. 15. e Matt. xix. 18. Gal. v. 14. f = (Acts ii. 23. 1 Cor. ix. 21 3ce.) 2 Thess. ii. 8. 1 Tim. i. 9. 2 Pet. ii. 8 only. Isa. liii. 12. g Rom. viii. 36 (from Ps. xliv. 22). ix. 9. h Matt. xxvi. 73. Mark x. 45 al. i ch. xxiv. 27. Acts xxiv. 10. xxviii. 23, 31. Phil. ii. 19, 20. k Mark iii. 26 (Heb. vii. 3) only. Jos. Antt. ii. 5. 3, ταῦτα . . . τέλος ἔλαβε. l = 2 Cor. ii. 6. Gen. xxx. 15. m ch. i. 9 reff. n Matt. xxi. 1 reff. o Mark ix. 3 al. p constr., here only. see James v. 17. q = Acts xxi. 1 (Matt. xxvi. 51. Acts xx. 30) only. 2 Macc. xii. 10, 17. r = ch. i. 56. Judg. iii. 29. s here only. Gen. xxi. 16.

syr-cu arm: om ABDHLQ [T(Tischdf)] Xℵ 1 lat-*b f* coptt [syr-jer] æth. for 2nd το, οτι A lat-*a c e ff₂ i* [*l* D-lat] Ambr₁. ins των bef ανομων D. om 2nd γαρ D lat-*a e ff₂ i* [*l*] syr-cu: ins A B(sic: see table) ℵ rel syr coptt. rec (for το bef περι) τα, with A rel Syr syr-mg [æth arm]: txt BDLQ(T)ℵ 1 lat-*b* syr-cu syr [syr-jer] coptt.—το bef γαρ T.

38. (ειπαν, so BDLQ [T(Tischdf) ℵ.) ιδου bef κυριε D: om κυριε ℵ[1]. δυο bef μαχαιραι ωδε D em. for ικανον εστιν, αρκει D.

39. επορευετο D evv-H₂-z₂-48₂. (και (bef οι μαθηται) is written over the line by the origl scribe in B: see table [om και V 69 æth].) rec aft οι μαθηται ins αυτου (‖ *Matt*), with Q rel lat-*a b c* Syr syr-cu [syr-jer] sah æth: om ABDLM²T[Δ²]ℵ 1 vulg lat-*q* syr copt arm.

40. γενομενοις T. om δε T. om του D. εισελθητε D ev-y latt: εμπεσειν 69: ελθειν Δ-gr. (εισελθειν is written over the line by the origl scribe in B: see table: Tischdf says by B²(appy)³.)

41. for και αυτος, αυτος δε D sah. for απεσπασθη, απέσπαθη ℵ¹(txt ℵ-corr¹·³) Scr's n: απεσταθη D: απεστη G 157(Sz) lat-*c f l*.

Boniface VIII., cited in Wordsw. ad loc.), *spreading the gospel by the sword.*

37.] The connexion is this: 'Your situation among men will be one of neglect and even of danger;—for I myself (see Matt. x. 24, 25) am about to be reckoned among transgressors.' By the very form of the expression it is evident, that the sword alluded to could have no reference to *that night's danger,* or the *defending Him from it.* **τὸ περὶ ἐμ. τέλος ἔχει**] The prophecy cited closes the section of Isaiah, which eminently predicts the Lord's sufferings (ch. lii. 13—liii. 12). **τὸ περὶ ἐμοῦ**—supply γεγραμμένον, or perhaps more generally, 'determined in the counsel of God.' **τέλος ἔχει** does not merely mean '*must be fulfilled,*' which would be an assertion without any special reference here—but (as E. V.) **have an end**;—are coming to the *completion* of their accomplishment. So **τετέλεσται,** John xix. 30. **38.**] Two of them were armed,—either from excess of zeal to defend Him, excited by His announcement of His sufferings during this feast,—or perhaps because they had brought their weapons from Galilee as protection by the way. The road from Jericho to Jerusalem (see ch. x. 30) was much infested with robbers;—and it was the custom for the priests, and even the quiet and ascetic Essenes, to *carry weapons* when travelling. Chrysostom (Hom. in Matt. lxxxiv. vol. vii. p. 797) gives a curious explanation of the two swords: εἰκὸς οὖν καὶ μαχαίρας εἶναι ἐκεῖ διὰ τὸ ἀρνίον. This certainly agrees with the number of the disciples sent to get ready the Passover: but it has nothing else to recommend it. They exhibit their swords, misunderstanding His words and supposing them to apply to that night. Our Lord breaks off the matter with **ἱκανόν ἐστιν,**—'*It is enough*;' not '*they are sufficient*;'—but, **It is well,**—**we are sufficiently provided**—'it was not to this that My words referred.' The rebuke is parallel with, though milder than, the one in Mark viii. 17,—as the misunderstanding was somewhat similar.

39—46.] Christ's Agony at the Mount of Olives. Matt. xxvi. 36—46. Mark xiv. 32—42. John xviii. 1. For all comment on the general narrative, see notes on Matthew. Our account is compendious, combines the three prayers of our Lord into one, and makes no mention of the Three Apostles being taken apart from the rest. On the other hand it in-

R -ερ ει βουλει... καὶ [t] θεὶς τὰ [t] γόνατα προςηύχετο 42 λέγων Πάτερ, [u] εἰ
βούλει [v] παρενεγκεῖν τοῦτο τὸ ποτήριον ἀπ᾽ ἐμοῦ· [w] πλὴν
μὴ τὸ [x] θέλημά μου ἀλλὰ τὸ σὸν [x] γινέσθω. 43 [y] ὤφθη
...αυτον F. δὲ αὐτῷ ἄγγελος ἀπ᾽ οὐρανοῦ [z] ἐνισχύων αὐτόν. 44 καὶ

t Mark xv. 19 reff. u aposiop., ch. xiii. 9 reff. v = ‖ Mk. (reff.) only. w = ver. 21. x ‖ Mt. Matt. vi. 10. Acts xxi. 4. y Matt. xvii. 3 al. Exod. iii. 2. z = here only. 2 Kings xxii. 40 al. intr., Acts ix. 19 only. Gen. xlviii. 2.

προςευχετο D: προςευξατο T: προςηυξατο ΓΝ [Damasc$_1$].

42. *μη* to *γενεσθω* bef *ει βουλει* to *απ᾽ εμου*, omg *πλην*, D lat-*a c e ff*$_2$. for *παρενεγκειν*, *παρενεγκε* (‖ *Mark*) B D-gr T 1 latt syr [arm Dion$_1$] Orig$_1$ Damasc$_1$ Ambr, *παρενεγκαι* KLMR[Π]ℵ 69: txt AQ rel Dion[-comm$_1$] Bas$_1$. (*παρενεγκαι may be a substantive reading, but -αι is probably an itacism for -ε, see ‖ Mark, where it* must *be so.*) rec *το ποτηριον* bef *τουτο* (‖ *Matt Mark*), with AR rel latt [syrr syr-cu Dion Damasc] Orig Bas$_1$: txt BDLQT ℵ-corr[1] lat-*f ff*$_2$ coptt.—*τουτο τ. π. τουτο* ℵ[1].
rec *γενεσθω*, with B^2(sic: see table, not as Tischdf) DEXΛ 69 [Constt$_1$]: txt QR [S(Tischdf)] T rel [Bas-2-mss$_1$ Damasc-ms$_1$], *γειν.* AB^{1}Δℵ.

Vv. 43, 44 om BRT ℵ-corr[1] 124 lat-*f* copt-wilk sah-woide arm-mss, and A(which has nevertheless the Ammonian section marked) 69(but ins "with all known evangelistaria" (Scriv) aft Matt xxvi. 39) Hil$_1$ Jer$_1$: ins DQℵ$^{1\cdot 3}$ rel(and the mass of cursives) latt syrr syr-cu syr-jer copt-schw[-dz] sah-ms(Zoega) æth arm Just$_1$ Iren$_1$-gr Hipp$_1$ Dion$_1$ Eus-canon Cæs$_1$ Arius-in-Epiph$_2$ Tit-bostr Chr$_1$ &c, but in L the Ammonian section and Eusebian canon are wanting, and in ESVΔ[Π] 24. 36. 161-6. 274 they are marked with asterisks, and in Γ 123. 344 Scr's d o with obeli. (The chief details of the patristic evidence are as follows:—

I. On the side of the omission. Hilary, after saying that Luke subjoins the two facts as above, adds *Nec sane ignorandum a nobis est et in græcis et in latinis codicibus complurimis, vel de adveniente angelo vel de sudore sanguinis nil scriptum reperiri* (de Trinitate, lib x. 41, vol ii. p. 349). The verses are not commented upon in Cyril's homilies on this Gospel, edited in the Syriac by Rev. R. Payne Smith [now Dean of Canterbury]. Jerome says *In quibusdam exemplaribus tam græcis quam latinis invenitur scribente Luca "Apparuit illi angelus"* &c. (cont. Pelag. lib ii. 16, vol ii. p. 760).

II. In support of the passage. Justin Martyr (cont. Tryph. 103, p. 199) ἐν γὰρ τοῖς ἀπομνημονεύμασι ἅ φημι ὑπὸ τῶν ἀποστόλων αὐτοῦ καὶ τῶν ἐκείνοις παρακολουθησάντων συντετάχθαι, ὅτι "ἱδρὼς ὡσεὶ θρόμβοι" κατεχεῖτο αὐτοῦ εὐχομένου καὶ λέγοντος κ.τ.λ. Irenæus (lib iii. cap 22, p. 219) οὐδ᾽ ἂν ἵδρωσε θρόμβους αἵματος. Hippolytus (cont. Noet. cap 18, p. 828) ἀγωνιῶν ἱδροῖ, καὶ ὑπ᾽ ἀγγέλου ἐνδυναμοῦται ὁ ἐνδυναμῶν τοὺς εἰς αὐτὸν πιστεύοντας; and again (quoted in Theod as given by Tregelles) ὅτε "ὡσεὶ θρόμβοι αἵματος" εἰπών, οὐ θρόμβους ἱδρῶτος ἀπεφήνατο αἵματος, and lower down, τοιοῦτόν ἐστι κἀκεῖνο τὸ εἰρημένον, ὡς ἄγγελος ἦν παρεστηκὼς τῷ σωτῆρι καὶ ἐνισχύων αὐτόν. Epiphanius (Ancoratus 31, vol ii. (iii., Migne) p. 36) ἀλλὰ καὶ "ἔκλαυσε" κεῖται ἐν τῷ κατὰ Λουκᾶν εὐαγγελίῳ (usually but erroneously referred to ch xix. 41) ἐν τοῖς ἀδιορθώτοις ἀντιγράφοις καὶ κέχρηται τῇ μαρτυρίᾳ ὁ ἅγιος Εἰρηναῖος ἐν τῷ κατὰ αἱρέσεων πρὸς τοὺς δοκήσει τὸν χριστὸν πεφηνέναι λέγοντας. ὀρθόδοξοι δὲ ἀφείλοντο τὸ ῥητὸν φοβηθέντες καὶ μὴ νοήσαντες αὐτοῦ τὸ τέλος καὶ τὸ ἰσχυρότατον· καὶ γενόμενος ἐν ἀγωνίᾳ ἵδρωσε, καὶ ἐγένετο ὁ ἱδρὼς αὐτοῦ ὡς θρόμβοι αἵματος, καὶ ὤφθη ἄγγελος ἐνισχύων αὐτόν.)

43. for *απ᾽*, *απο του* DQU 69 copt-dz. *επησχυων* L.

serts the very important additional details of vv. 44, 45, besides the particularity of ὡσεὶ λίθου βολήν, ver. 41. **42.**] **εἰ** is not to be *rendered* 'utinam,' but '**si**,' and the sentence is broken off at **ἐμοῦ**: thus rendering the meaning equivalent to a wish. Some suppose **παρενεγκεῖν** to be an inf. *for an imperative*, but incorrectly. **43.**] The principal testimonies of the Fathers, &c. against and for vv. 43, 44, are collected in the digest. With the early and weighty evidence there cited in favour of the passage, it is impossible that it should have been an apocryphal insertion. It was perhaps, as Epiph. states of ἔκλαυσε, expunged by the orthodox, who imagined they found in it an inconsistency with the divine nature of our Lord. We have reason to be thankful, that orthodoxy has been better understood since. The strengthening by means of the angel is *physical*—and the appearance likewise. See an interesting reply to the scoffs of Julian on this point, in Theodore of Mopsuestia, in loc. ed. Migne, p. 723. It is strange how Olshausen can

a here only †. 2 Macc. iii. 14, 16. xv. 19 only. b Acts xii. 5. 1 Pet. i. 22 only. Jon. iii. 8. (-νής, 1 Pet. iv. 8. -νία or -νεία, Judith iv. 9.) c here only. Gen. iii. 19. 2 Macc. ii. 27 only. d = Matt. iii. 16. Acts ii. 3. e here only †. f = Matt. vii. 25, 27. ch. ix. 54. Job xxxviii. 30. g = Matt. xxviii. 13 reff. 4 Kings iv. 20 al. fr. h = Matt. xiii. 44 reff. i Mark x. 1. Gen. xxii. 3, 19. k ||. = Heb. iii. 11. l ver. 28. m constr., Mark vi. 33 only ‡. see ch. i. 17. n constr., ch. xv. 1 reff. o = ||. Gen. xxvii. 26, 27.

γενόμενος ἐν [a] ἀγωνίᾳ [b] ἐκτενέστερον προσηύχετο. καὶ ἐγένετο
[ὁ] [c] ἱδρὼς αὐτοῦ [d] ὡσεὶ [e] θρόμβοι αἵματος [f] καταβαίνοντος
ἐπὶ τὴν γῆν. 45 καὶ ἀναστὰς ἀπὸ τῆς προσευχῆς, ἐλθὼν
πρὸς τοὺς μαθητὰς εὗρεν [g] κοιμωμένους αὐτοὺς [h] ἀπὸ τῆς
λύπης, 46 καὶ εἶπεν αὐτοῖς Τί καθεύδετε; [i] ἀναστάντες ...και ειπεν Q.
προσεύχεσθε ἵνα μὴ [k] εἰσέλθητε εἰς [l] πειρασμόν. ABDE GHKL
47 Ἔτι αὐτοῦ λαλοῦντος ἰδοὺ ὄχλος, καὶ ὁ λεγόμενος MRSTU
Ἰούδας, εἷς τῶν δώδεκα, [m] προήρχετο αὐτούς, καὶ [n] ἤγγισεν VXΓΔΛ Πℵ
τῷ Ἰησοῦ [o] φιλῆσαι αὐτόν. 48 Ἰησοῦς δὲ εἶπεν αὐτῷ 1. 69

44. γεναμενος ℵ. rec (for και εγεν.) εγενετο δε, with DQ rel: txt VXℵ 1 Scr's c latt Syr syr-cu [syr-jer] copt-dz[-schw æth (arm)] Epiph$_1$. om ο ℵ. for ωσει, ως D [Epiph$_1$]: ως αι Λ. rec καταβαινοντες, with DQ rel [forj mm lat-*b e i* syr æth]: txt Xℵ vulg lat-*a c ff$_2$ g$_{1.2}$* copt-dz[-schw syr-jer arm]. της γης QU.
45. for προς, επι D. elz aft μαθητας ins αυτου, with 1 latt Syr syr-cu syr-w-ast coptt æth: om ABDQRTℵ rel lat-*f* [syr-jer] arm. rec αυτους bef κοιμωμενους (|| *Matt Mark*), with AQR rel latt syrr syr-cu: txt BDLTℵ 69.
46. om τι D. εις πειρασμον bef εισελθητε D.
47. rec aft ετι ins δε, with DEHSVΓΔ lat-*b c e* [*ff$_2$ i*] arm: om AB R(appy) Tℵ rel vulg lat-*l q* syr copt. aft οχλος ins πολυς D syr-cu. for λεγομενος, καλουμενος D 1. aft ιουδας ins ισκαριωθ D [(lat-*l*)]. for προηρχετο, προηγεν D 1. 69 Syr. rec (for αυτους) αυτων: αυτοις ΓΛ Scr's c f ev-y: txt ABD[T]ℵ rel. for last clause, και εγγισας εφιλησεν τον ιησουν D lat-*a b c e ff$_2$ i* syr-cu copt-mss [(æth arm)]. add τουτο γαρ σημειον δεδωκει αυτοις ον αν φιλησω αυτος εστιν (|| *Matt Mark*) DEHX 69 lat-*b c* syrr æth arm.
48. rec (for ιησ. δε) ο δε ιησους (|| *Matt*), with ADR rel: txt BLTXℵ. for

have so far deceived himself as to imagine that **ὤφθη αὐτῷ** can imply a merely inward and spiritual accession of strength from above. It is strange likewise that the analogy of the ministration of angels in the Lord's former temptation should not have occurred to those modern Commentators who have objected to this circumstance as improbable. This strengthening probably took place *between the first and the second prayer*;—and the effect of it is the **ἐκτενέστερον προσηύχετο** of ver. 44, and the entire resignation expressed in the second and third prayer of Matthew's narrative.

44.] The intention of the Evangelist seems clearly to be, to convey the idea that the sweat was (not *fell* like, but *was*) *like drops of blood*;—i. e. *coloured with blood*,—for so I understand the ὡσεί, as just distinguishing the drops *highly coloured with blood*, from *pure blood*. Aristotle, speaking of certain morbid states of the blood, says, ἐξυγραινομένου δὲ λίαν νοσοῦσιν· γίνεται γὰρ ἰχωροειδές, καὶ διοῤῥοῦται, οὕτως ὥστε ἤδη τινὲς ἴδισαν **αἱματώδη ἱδρῶτα**, Hist. Anim. iii. 19. To suppose that it only *fell like drops of blood* (why not drops of any thing else? and drops of blood *from what*, and *where?*) is to nullify the force of the sentence, and make the insertion of αἵματος not only superfluous but absurd. We must not forget, in asking on what testimony this rests, that the marks of such drops would be visible after the termination of the agony. An interesting example of a sweat of blood under circumstances of strong terror, accompanied by loss of speech, is given in an article by Dr. Schneider in Casper's Wochenschrift for 1848: and cited in the Medical Gazette for December of that year. **45.**] **ἀπὸ τῆς λύπης**—the effect of anxiety and watching. The words *may possibly* express an inference of the Evangelist (Meyer): but I would rather understand them as exactly describing the cause of their sleeping.

47—53.] Betrayal and apprehension of Jesus. Matt. xxvi. 47—56. Mark xiv. 43—52. John xviii. 2—11. Our narrative is here distinguished even more than before by minute and striking details (see on the whole the notes to Matt.). The first of these is the address to Judas ver. 48, calling the traitor by name, and setting before him the whole magnitude of his crime in the very words in which the treason had

Ἰούδα, [p] φιλήματι τὸν [q] υἱὸν τοῦ [q] ἀνθρώπου παραδίδως;
49 ἰδόντες δὲ [r] οἱ περὶ αὐτὸν τὸ [s] ἐσόμενον, εἶπαν Κύριε,
[t] εἰ [uv] πατάξομεν [vw] ἐν [v] μαχαίρῃ; 50 καὶ [u] ἐπάταξεν [x] εἷς
[x] τις ἐξ αὐτῶν τοῦ ἀρχιερέως τὸν δοῦλον, καὶ [y] ἀφεῖλεν τὸ
οὖς αὐτοῦ τὸ δεξιόν. 51 ἀποκριθεὶς δὲ ὁ Ἰησοῦς εἶπεν
[z] Ἐᾶτε [a] ἕως τούτου. καὶ ἀψάμενος τοῦ [b] ὠτίου ἰάσατο
αὐτόν. 52 εἶπεν δὲ Ἰησοῦς πρὸς τοὺς [c] παραγενομένους
ἐπ' αὐτὸν ἀρχιερεῖς καὶ [d] στρατηγοὺς τοῦ ἱεροῦ καὶ πρεσβυτέρους Ὡς ἐπὶ [e] λῃστὴν ἐξεληλύθατε [f] μετὰ μαχαιρῶν
καὶ [g] ξύλων. 53 [h] καθ' ἡμέραν ὄντος μου μεθ' ὑμῶν ἐν τῷ
ἱερῷ οὐκ [i] ἐξετείνατε τὰς χεῖρας ἐπ' ἐμέ. ἀλλὰ αὕτη ἐστὶν
ὑμῶν ἡ [k] ὥρα καὶ ἡ [lm] ἐξουσία τοῦ [mn] σκότους.
54 [o] Συλλαβόντες δὲ αὐτὸν ἤγαγον καὶ εἰςήγαγον εἰς

p ‖. ch. vii. 45 reff. Cant. i. 2. q Matt. viii. 20 reff. r Mark iv. 10 reff. s = ch. xii. 55. Matt. xxiv. 3 al. t = Matt. xii. 10 reff. ch. xiv. 3. Acts xix. 2. 3 Kings i. 27. u Matt. xxvi. 31 reff. v Jer. xxxiii. (xxvi.) 23. w = Matt. xii. 24, 27, 28 al. x Matt. xiv. 51. John xi. 49. y ‖ Mt. Mk. 1 Kings v. 4. z Matt. xxiv. 43 reff. absol., here only. a = Mark vi. 23. xiv. 34 al. 2 Kings vii. 18. b ‖ Mt. (Mk. v. r.) John xviii. 26 only. Deut. xv. 17. c w. ἐπί, here only. 2 Macc. iv. 34. (see ch. viii. 9 reff. John viii. 2 al.) d ver. 4 reff. e ‖. Matt. xxi. 13 ‖. John x. 1, 8. Ezek. xxii. 9. f ‖. Acts xxiv. 18. g = ‖. (Mt. bis) only. h ‖ Mt. reff. i = here only. (Matt. viii. 3 reff.) Jer. xxviii. (li.) 25. k see John ii. 4 reff. l = ch. xx. 20. Rev. xii. 10. m Col. i. 13. n = Eph. v. 8, 11. vi. 12. o Matt. xxvi. 48 reff.

αυτω, τω D. om ιουδα ℵ[1].

49. for *εσομενον, γενομενον* D 106(Sz) lat-*ff*$_2$ Syr syr-mg copt arm. (*ειπαν*, so BDLTXℵ.) rec ins *αυτω* bef *κυριε*, with AR rel latt syrr syr-cu: om BLTXℵ lat-*ff*$_2$ *i l q* coptt.—for *κυριε, τω κυριω* D. (*μαχαιρη*, so B[1]DLTℵ.)

50. rec *τον δουλον* bef *του αρχιερεως* (*from* ‖), with ADR T[Alf] rel latt: txt BL [T(Tischdf)] ℵ 69. *αφειλατο* D. rec *αυτου* bef *το ους* (*from* ‖), with AR rel; *αυτου το ωτιον* DK: txt BLTℵ 69.

51. om *δε* A sah[-ms]. om *ὁ* B. for *αψαμενος* to *αυτον, εκτεινας την χειρα ηψατο αυτου και απεκατεσταθη το ους αυτου* D lat-*a e ff*$_2$ (*i l*). rec aft *ωτιου* ins *αυτου*, with A rel: om BLRTℵ [1 arm].

52. rec ins *ο* bef *ιησους*, with R T[Alf] rel: om AB [T(Tischdf)] ℵ.—om *ο ιησ.* D 1 lat-*e* syr-cu arm. for *επ, προς* GHRΔℵ[1]. for *ιερου, λαου* D. for *εξεληλυθατε, εξηλθατε* (*from* ‖) BDLRTℵ 69: *-θετε* KMX[Π] 1 Orig$_1$ Eus Bas-sel: txt A rel.

53. ins *το* bef *καθ ημεραν* D. *εν τω ιερω* bef *μεθ' υμων* D 248 Scr's h ev-H [copt]. *εξεστινατε* D[1]. (*αλλα*, so DEGL T[Alf] UΔΛ.) rec *υμων* bef *εστιν*, with A rel: om *υμων* ℵ[1] ev-48: om *εστιν* H: txt BDGKLMRTX[Π]ℵ[3a]. om 2nd *ἡ* D Scr's g. for *του σκοτους, το σκοτος* D-gr.

54. om *και εισηγαγον* DΓ 1 vulg lat-*a b e f ff*$_2$ *i l* Syr syr-cu æth (Eus). rec aft *εισηγαγον* ins *αυτον*, with X rel syr-w-ob coptt æth: om AB(D)KLMRT[Π]ℵ 1 latt Syr [arm] Orig$_1$ Eus$_1$.

lately (Matt. ver. 45: Mark ver. 41) and so often (Matt. xxvi. 2; xx. 18; xvii. 22) been announced. Another is in ver. 49, where the disciples seeing **τὸ ἐσόμενον**, ask **Κύριε, εἰ πατάξ. ἐν μαχαίρῃ**; which question refers to, and is the filling up of their misunderstanding of our Lord in ver. 38. Again ver. 51 is peculiar to Luke. **51.**] **ἐᾶτε ἕως τούτου** I understand as addressed, not to the disciples, but to the multitude, or rather *to those who were holding Him*;—His hands were held,—and He says, **Suffer, permit me, thus far**: i. e. to touch the ear of the wounded person. If this interpretation be correct, it furnishes an additional token of the truthfulness of our narrative—for the previous laying hold of Jesus has not been mentioned here, but in Matthew (ver. 50) and Mark (ver. 46). **53.**] There is an important addition here to the other reports of our Lord's speech;—**ἀλλὰ . . . . σκότους.** It stands here instead of the declaration that *this was done that the Scriptures might be fulfilled* (Matt. ver. 56: Mark ver. 49). The inner sense of those words is indeed implied here—but we cannot venture to say that our report is of the same saying. Our Lord here distinguishes between the power exercised over Him by *men*, and that by *the Evil One*:—but so as to make the *ἐξουσία* which rules over *them* to be that of darkness—while His own assertion of this shews that all was by the determinate counsel and foreknowledge of God. In the word **σκότος** there is also an allusion

τὴν οἰκίαν τοῦ ἀρχιερέως. ὁ δὲ Πέτρος ἠκολούθει [p] μα-
κρόθεν· 55 [q] περιαψάντων δὲ πῦρ ἐν μέσῳ τῆς [r] αὐλῆς
καὶ [s] συγκαθισάντων ἐκάθητο ὁ Πέτρος [t] μέσος αὐτῶν.
56 ἰδοῦσα δὲ αὐτὸν [u] παιδίσκη τις καθήμενον [v] πρὸς τὸ ...καθημενον R.
[v] φῶς καὶ [w] ἀτενίσασα αὐτῷ εἶπεν Καὶ οὗτος σὺν αὐτῷ ἦν. ABDE
57 ὁ δὲ [x] ἠρνήσατο [αὐτὸν] λέγων Οὐκ οἶδα αὐτόν, γύναι. GHKL MSTUV
58 καὶ [y] μετὰ [yz] βραχὺ ἕτερος ἰδὼν αὐτὸν ἔφη Καὶ σὺ [a] ἐξ ΧΓΔΛΠ א 1. 69
αὐτῶν εἶ. ὁ δὲ Πέτρος ἔφη Ἄνθρωπε, οὐκ εἰμί. 59 καὶ
[b] διαστάσης [c] ὡσεὶ ὥρας μιᾶς ἄλλος τις [d] διϊσχυρίζετο
λέγων [e] Ἐπ' ἀληθείας καὶ οὗτος μετ' αὐτοῦ ἦν, καὶ γὰρ
Γαλιλαῖός ἐστιν. 60 εἶπεν δὲ ὁ Πέτρος, Ἄνθρωπε, οὐκ
οἶδα ὃ λέγεις. καὶ [f] παραχρῆμα ἔτι λαλοῦντος αὐτοῦ
[g] ἐφώνησεν [g] ἀλέκτωρ· 61 καὶ [h] στραφεὶς ὁ κύριος [i] ἐν-
έβλεψεν τῷ Πέτρῳ· καὶ [k] ὑπεμνήσθη ὁ Πέτρος τοῦ λόγου

p ch. xviii. 13. xxiii. 49 only. (elsw. ἀπὸ μ., || Mt. reff.) Gen. xxi. 16.
q here only †. (3 Macc. iii. 7.) = Phalar. Ep. v. p. 28 (said of the *bull*), περιήψαμεν, ὡς αὐτὸς ὑπεξέθετο πίμπρασθαι.
r Matt. xxvi. 3 reff.
s intr., here (tr., Eph. ii. 6) only. Exod. xviii. 13.
t = John i. 26 reff.
u ch. xii. 45 reff.
v = Mark xiv. 54 (reff.).
w ch. iv. 20 reff.
x Matt. x. 33 reff.
y here only.
z of time, Acts v. 34. xxvii. 28 (Heb. ii. 7, 9, from Ps. viii. 5?) only. (John vi. 7. Heb. xiii. 22 only.) Isa. lvii. 17.
a ||. John i. 24. Acts xxi. 8 and freq.
b ch. xxiv. 51. Acts xxvii. 28 only ‡. Isa. lix. 2. (-στημα, Acts v. 7.)
c ver. 41.
d Acts xii. 15 only †.
e = ch. iv. 25. (Mark xii. 14 reff.)
f ch. i. 64 reff.
g ver. 34 (reff.).
h Matt. vii. 6 al.
i Mark x. 21 reff.
k pass., here only. John xiv. 26. 2 Tim. ii. 4. Tit. iii. 1. 2 Pet. i. 12. 3 John 10. Jude 5 only. Wisd. xviii. 22 (only?). (-μνησις, 2 Tim. i. 5.)

rec τον οικον, with ADR rel: txt BKLMT[Π]א 1 $Orig_1$ Eus_1. aft ηκολ. ins αυτω D 69 em lat-*b* [*e f ff*$_2$ *i l q* Syr syr-cu syr-w-ast æth arm] copt (sah). ins απο bef μακροθεν DΛ.

55. rec (for περιαψ.) αψαντων, with ADR rel: txt BLTא Eus_1. περικαθισαντων DG 1 vulg lat-*b f ff*$_2$ [*c e i l q*] arm: txt ABRTא rel lat-*a*. rec adds αυτων, with A rel vulg lat-*f*; aft δε R: om BDKLTΛא lat-*a b e ff*$_2$ *l* [*c q*] arm. ins και bef ο πετρος D lat-*b c f i* [*l q*] copt arm. rec (for μεσος) εν μεσω, with (AR, εμμεσω) Xא rel: μετ' D: txt BLT 1. aft αυτων ins θερμαινομενος (|| *Mark*) D.

57. om 1st αυτον (|| *Matt Mark*) B D-corr-gr KLMSTX[Π]א 1 lat-*a b c f ff*$_2$ *l* Syr syr-cu coptt æth arm: ins A D[1](and lat) rel vulg syr. rec γυναι bef ουκ οιδα αυτον, with A rel latt syrr syr-cu; om γυναι D: txt BLTXא coptt (æth) arm.

58. aft βραχυ ins παλιν א-corr[1] (om א[3a]). for εφη και συ εξ αυτων ει, ειπεν το αυτο D syr-cu. om πετρος D (lat-*a b ff*$_2$ *i* [*l q*]). rec (for 2nd εφη) ειπεν, with A(D) rel: txt BKLMT[Π]א 69.

59. [διαστησας D.] for λεγων επ' αληθειας, επ' αληθειας λεγω D. om ην א[1](ins א-corr[1]).

60. for ὅ, τι Dא, *quid* latt. aft ετι ins αυτου (but erased) א-corr[1]. rec ins ο bef αλεκτωρ, with sah: om ABDTא rel Scr's-mss copt arm.

61. for και στρ., στρ. δε D sah. ins πετρος bef κυρ. (but marked as if thought to be an interpolation) T. for κυριος, ιησους D Scr's c h ev-z Syr syr-txt copt[-wilk: κυριε T(Tischdf)]. om ο πετρος D 157(Sz) gat. for λογου, ρηματος (|| *Matt Mark*) BLTXא: txt AD rel.

to the time—midnight. Compare with this declaration of the power of darkness over Him, the declaration, in ch. iv. 13, that the devil left Him ἄχρι καιροῦ.

54.] Matt. xxvi. 57. Mark xiv. 53. John xviii. 13. Our narrative leaves it undecided *who this high-priest was,*—inasmuch as, ch. iii. 2, *Annas and Caiaphas* are mentioned as high-priests. From John we find that it was *Annas;* who having questioned Jesus, sent Him bound to Caiaphas, before whom His trial took place. Luke omits this trial altogether—or perhaps gives the substance of it in the account (vv. 66—71) of the morning assembly of the Sanhedrim. See notes on Matt.

55—62.] Peter's three denials of Jesus. Matt. xxvi. 69—75. Mark xiv. 66—72. John xviii. 17, 18, 25—27. See throughout, table and notes in Matthew.

58. ἕτερος] In Matt. it is ἄλλη,—in Mark ἡ παιδίσκη. **61.**] See extract from Robinson's notes on Matt. ver. 69. If, as there supposed, the trial was going on *in an open chamber looking on the court* (αὐλή), the look might well have been given from a considerable distance. *We* need not enquire, *how* our Lord could hear what was going on round the fire in

τοῦ κυρίου ὡς εἶπεν αὐτῷ ὅτι πρὶν [g] ἀλέκτορα [g] φωνῆσαι
σήμερον, [g] ἀπαρνήσῃ με τρίς. 62 καὶ ἐξελθὼν ἔξω [ὁ
Πέτρος] ἔκλαυσεν [l] πικρῶς.
63 Καὶ οἱ ἄνδρες οἱ [m] συνέχοντες αὐτὸν [n] ἐνέπαιζον
αὐτῷ [o] δέροντες· 64 καὶ [p] περικαλύψαντες αὐτὸν [q] ἐπηρώτων λέγοντες [r] Προφήτευσον, τίς ἐστιν ὁ [s] παίσας σε;
65 καὶ ἕτερα πολλὰ [t] βλασφημοῦντες ἔλεγον [u] εἰς αὐτόν.
66 Καὶ ὡς ἐγένετο ἡμέρα, [v] συνήχθη τὸ [w] πρεσβυτέριον τοῦ
λαοῦ, ἀρχιερεῖς τε καὶ γραμματεῖς, καὶ [x] ἀπήγαγον αὐτὸν
εἰς τὸ [y] συνέδριον αὐτῶν λέγοντες Εἰ σὺ εἶ ὁ χριστός,

l || Mt. (reff.) only.
m = here only. (Matt. iv. 24 al.) 2 Kings xx. 3.
n Matt. ii. 16. xxvii. 29 al. Gen. xxxix. 17.
o Matt. xxi. 35 reff.
p || Mk. Heb. ix. 4 only. Exod. xxviii. 30. 3 Kings vii. 42. viii. 7 only.
q ch. xxiii. 6 reff.
r = || only.
s || Mt. reff.
t Mark xv. 29. Acts xxvi. 11. 4 Kings xix. 4, 6, 22.
u Mark iii. 29. 2 Macc. vii. 31.
v Matt. xiii. 2 reff. Ps. ii. 2.
w Acts xxii. 5. 1 Tim. iv. 13 only +. Sus. 50 Theod.-A only.
x ch. xxiii. 26 reff.
y Luke, here only. Matt. xxvi. 3, 59 al. Prov. xxii. 10.

om οτι D lat-*a b c e ff*$_2$ *i* arm. aft πριν ins η B. rec om σημερον (|| *Matt Mark*), with AD rel latt Syr syr-cu [arm] : ins BKLMTX[Π]ℵ (69 fuld lat-*b f l*) syr-w-ast copt sah-woide-txt (æth). τρις bef απαρνηση με D [syr-cu]. at end ins μη ειδεναι με D.

62. om ο πετρος (*see* || *Matt Mark*) BDKLMTX[Π]ℵ 1 syr-cu coptt arm : ins A rel vulg lat-*c f g*$_{1.2}$ *q* syrr æth.

63. for και οι, οι δε D lat-*c* sah [om οι T(Alf : om 2nd οι, Tischdf)]. rec (for αυτον) τον ιησουν, with A rel Syr syr-cu syr-txt æth : txt BDLMT[Π]ℵ latt Syr-ms syr-mg coptt arm. ενεπεζαν ℵ[1]. om δεροντες D 69 lat-*a b e* [*i q*] Syr.

64. om αυτον (but see below) ℵ. rec aft αυτον ins ετυπτον αυτου το προσωπον και (*for* αυτον, αυτου το πρ. *from* || *Mark, then united with txt,* ετυπτον *being insd to account for* παισας *below*), with A rel vulg lat-*f* syrr ; αυτου το προσωπον 1 ; αυτου το προσωπον ετυπτον αυτον και D 131(Sz) lat-*a q* arm [æth] : txt BKLMT[Π]ℵ lat-*b c e ff*$_2$ *i l* copt. rec aft επηρωτων ins αυτον, with Aℵ rel : om B(D)KLMTX[Π] lat-*b*. for επηρωτων λεγοντες, ελεγον D (lat-*b ff*$_2$ *q*) Syr syr-cu.

65. for ετερα, αλλα D. for αυτον, εαυτους D-gr.

66. ημερα bef εγεν. ℵ 1 lat-(*a*) *c* [(coptt) Orig$_1$]. for αρχ. τε, και αρχ. D 116(Sz) lat-*a b c* : om τε EGHSUΓΔΛ [arm : om αρχ. τε V]. rec ανηγαγον, with A rel : txt BDKTℵ 69 syr-mg Orig$_1$. rec εαυτων, with AΔ : txt BDTℵ rel sah Orig$_1$. om ει DL.

the court, as some Commentators have done. But even were such an enquiry necessary, I see no difficulty in answering it. The anathemas of Peter, spoken to οἱ παρεστῶτες with vehemence, and the crowing of the cock,—were not these audible? But our Lord needed not these to attract His attention.

63—65.] He is mocked. Luke does not, as some Commentators say, place this mocking *before the trial* in Caiaphas's house, but in the same place as Matt. vv. 67, 68, and Mark ver. 65, viz. *after* what happened there. The trial he *omits altogether,* having found no report of it. How those who take this view of Luke's arrangement can yet suppose him to have had Matt. and Mark before him while writing, I am wholly at a loss to conceive.

66—71.] Hearing before the council. (Probably) Matt. xxvii. 1. Mark xiv. 1. It seems probable that Luke here gives us an account of a *second and formal judgment held in the morning.* The similarity of the things said at the two hearings may be accounted for by remembering that they were both more or less formal processes in legal courts, one the precognition, the other, the decision, at which the things said before would be likely to be nearly repeated. **66. ὡς ἐγ. ἡμ.**] Some trace of a meeting of the Sanhedrim after daylight I believe our Evangelist to have found, see Matt. xxvii. 1—and to have therefore related as then happening, the following account of what really took place at the former meeting.

λέγοντες—but first took place the μαρτυρία referred to in ver. 71; and the person who said this was the high-priest, and with an adjuration, Matt. ver. 63. The ordinary rendering is the most natural and correct: **If thou art** (not if thou *be*) **the Christ, tell us.** The others, '*Tell us whether thou be the Christ;*' and, '*Art thou the Christ? tell us*' (see the question in ver. 49), are forced

z Matt. xviii. 27 reff. a ch. v. 10 reff. b constr., Matt. xvi. 19 bis. xviii. 18 bis. ch. vi. 40. xii. 52. Heb. ii. 13, from Isa. viii. 17. c Matt. viii. 20 reff. d = Matt. xx. 21, 23 reff. Psa. cix. 1. e = ∥ only. f Matt. iv. 3 note. g see ch. xxiii. 3 reff. h ch. xxi. 8 reff. i Matt. vi. 8 reff. k Mark xiv. 55, 56, 59. Acts xxii. 18. 1 Tim. iii. 7.

εἰπὸν ἡμῖν. 67 εἶπεν δὲ αὐτοῖς Ἐὰν ὑμῖν εἴπω, οὐ μὴ
πιστεύσητε· 68 ἐὰν δὲ ἐρωτήσω, οὐ μὴ ἀποκριθῆτέ [μοι
ἢ [z] ἀπολύσητε]. 69 [a] ἀπὸ τοῦ νῦν δὲ [b] ἔσται ὁ [c] υἱὸς τοῦ
[c] ἀνθρώπου καθήμενος [d] ἐκ δεξιῶν τῆς [e] δυνάμεως τοῦ θεοῦ.
70 εἶπαν δὲ πάντες Σὺ οὖν εἶ ὁ [f] υἱὸς τοῦ [f] θεοῦ; ὁ δὲ πρὸς R ειπαν
αὐτοὺς ἔφη Ὑμεῖς [g] λέγετε ὅτι [h] ἐγώ εἰμι. 71 οἱ δὲ εἶπαν ÄBDEG
Τί ἔτι [i] ἔχομεν [k] μαρτυρίας [i] χρείαν; αὐτοὶ γὰρ ἠκούσα- HKLM RSTUV
μεν ἀπὸ τοῦ στόματος αὐτοῦ. XXIII. 1 Καὶ [l] ἀναστὰν ΧΓΔΛΠ ℵ 1. 69
ἅπαν τὸ [m] πλῆθος αὐτῶν ἤγαγον αὐτὸν ἐπὶ τὸν Πιλάτον.
2 ἤρξαντο δὲ κατηγορεῖν αὐτοῦ λέγοντες Τοῦτον εὕραμεν
[n] διαστρέφοντα τὸ ἔθνος [ἡμῶν] καὶ [o] κωλύοντα [p] φόρους

Tit. i. 13 only, exc. John passim. Prov. xxv. 18. l Mark vii. 24 reff. m John xviii. 35 reff. n ch. ix. 41 ∥ Mt. Acts xiii. 8, 10. xx. 20. Phil. ii. 15 only. 3 Kings xviii. 17. o = Matt. xix. 14 reff. 1 Tim. iv. 3. p ch. xx. 22. Rom. xiii. 6, 7 only. Judg. i. 28.

rec ειπε, with A rel: txt BLTℵ.—om ειπον ημιν D.

67. for ειπεν δε, ο δε ειπεν D. om υμιν ℵ[1] ev-z sah.

68. rec aft εαν δε ins και, with A T[Alf] rel vulg lat-*f* syr copt: om BL [T(Tischdf)] ℵ Syr æth arm Cyr_1, om δε also D lat-*a b ff₂ i q*. om μοι η απολυσητε (*homœotel?*) BLTℵ copt: om η απολυσητε 1 forj sah: ins AD rel vss.

69. rec om δε, with E rel Syr copt-dz sah: ins ABDLTXℵ vulg lat-*a b e f i l* [*q*] syr-w-ast copt æth arm Cyr_1.

70. (ειπαν, so BLTℵ.) for δε, ουν AKM[Π] 1. 69. om ουν DKΛ 69 lat-*a* syr-cu sah-ms. for προς αυτους εφη, ειπεν αυτοις D.

71. (ειπαν, so BDLRTXℵ.) rec χρειαν bef εχομεν μαρτυριας (∥ *Matt Mark*), with ADℵ rel: txt BLT.—μαρτυρων (∥ *Matt Mark*) D 69 sah. ηκουσαμεν γαρ, omg αυτοι, D lat-*a b c e* [*i l*].

Chap. XXIII. **1.** αναστάντες D 239-47 Syr syr-cu sah. for απαν, παν R: ολον L.—om απαν το πληθος αυτων D. rec ηγαγεν (*gramml corrn*), with (but e sil) 1 Scr's c d g o q r s: txt ABDRTℵ rel syrr syr-cu coptt arm. om τον D (157, Sz).

2. rec ευρομεν, with AB[2] D[5](and lat) R T[Alf] ℵ rel: ευρον D[1]-gr: txt B[1]L [T(Tischdf)] X 1. rec om ημων, with A rel $Mcion_2$-e Eus_1 Cyr_1 $Thdrt_1$: ins (*perhaps a reminiscence of ch* vii. 5) BDHKLMRT[Π]ℵ 69 latt syrr syr-cu coptt

and unusual. **68.**] I believe these words to have been said as a formal protest on the part of our Lord against the spirit and tendency of the question asked Him, before He gives an answer to it: and as such, I regard them as an original and most valuable report.—'*It is with no view to examine and believe, that you ask this question: nor, were I to attempt to educe from your own mouths my innocence, would you answer Me* [*or release Me*]. *I am well aware of the intention of this question:* BUT (πλήν, Matt. ver. 64) *the time is come for the confession to be made:*—**ἀπὸ τοῦ νῦν κ.τ.λ.**' **69.**] On **ἀπὸ τ. ν.** = ἀπ' ἄρτι, see notes on Matt. **καθ. ἐκ δ. τ. δυν.** is common to all Three: only Luke adds **τοῦ θεοῦ**.

70.] We find **ὁ υἱὸς τ. θ.** used as synonymous with **ὁ υἱ. τ. ἀνθ. καθ. ἐκ δεξ. τῆς δυν. τοῦ θ.**, i.e. with the glorified Messiah. On **ὑμ. λέγ. . . . .** see note on Matt., ver. 64. **71.**] How would it have been possible that these words should have been said, if no μαρτυρία had been brought forward at this examination, and if the *very same question* had been asked at the termination of the former one?

Chap. XXIII. 1—5.] He is accused before Pilate. Matt. xxvii. 2, 11—14. Mark xv. 1—5. John xviii. 28—38. Our account, not entering at length into the words said, gives a particular and original narrative of the things transacted at this interview. **2.**] This charge was intended to represent the result of their previous judgment, **εὕραμεν**;—whereas, in fact, *no such matter had been before them*: but they falsely allege it before Pilate, knowing that it was the point on which his judgment was likely to be most severe. The words themselves which they use are not so false, as the spirit, and impression which they convey. The **κωλύοντα φ. Κ. διδ.** was, however, *false entirely* (see ch. xx. 22 ff.); and is just one of those instances where those who are determined

Καίσαρι [q] διδόναι, [καὶ] λέγοντα ἑαυτὸν χριστὸν βασιλέα
εἶναι. 3 ὁ δὲ Πιλάτος ἠρώτησεν αὐτὸν λέγων Σὺ εἶ
ὁ βασιλεὺς τῶν Ἰουδαίων; ὁ δὲ ἀποκριθεὶς αὐτῷ ἔφη
[r] Σὺ [r] λέγεις. 4 ὁ δὲ Πιλάτος εἶπεν πρὸς τοὺς ἀρχιερεῖς
καὶ τοὺς ὄχλους Οὐδὲν εὑρίσκω [s] αἴτιον ἐν τῷ ἀνθρώπῳ
τούτῳ. 5 οἱ δὲ [t] ἐπίσχυον λέγοντες ὅτι [u] ἀνασείει τὸν
λαόν, διδάσκων [v] καθ᾽ ὅλης τῆς Ἰουδαίας, [καὶ] [w] ἀρξάμενος [w] ἀπὸ τῆς Γαλιλαίας [x] ἕως ὧδε. 6 Πιλάτος δὲ
ἀκούσας [Γαλιλαίαν] [y] ἐπηρώτησεν εἰ ὁ ἄνθρωπος Γαλιλαῖός [z] ἐστιν, 7 καὶ [a] ἐπιγνοὺς ὅτι ἐκ τῆς [b] ἐξουσίας
Ἡρώδου [z] ἐστίν, [c] ἀνέπεμψεν αὐτὸν πρὸς Ἡρώδην, ὄντα

q = ch. xx. 22 reff.
r = ‖ (and plur., ch. xxii. 70) only.
s vv. 14, 22. Acts xix. 40 only +.
t here only +. Sir. xxix. 1. 1 Macc. vi. 6 only.
u Mark xv. 11 only +. Job ii. 3 Aq.
v ch. iv. 14. Acts ix. 31, 42. x. 37.
w Matt. xx. 8 reff.
x Mark xiv. 54. xv. 38 ‖ Mt. John ii. 7. 2 Chron. xxvi. 8.
y Matt. xii. 10 al. fr. in Gospp. elsw. Acts (i. 6 v. r.) v. 27. xxiii. 34. Rom. x. 20, from Isa. lxv. 1. 1 Cor. xiv. 35 only.
z constr., John i. 40 reff.
a = ch. vii. 37 reff.
b = Eph. ii. 2. 4 Kings xx. 13.
c vv. 11, 15. Acts xxv. 21. Philem. 11 only +.

æth arm Aug. rec *καισαρι* bef *φορ.*, with AR T[Alf] rel syr Eus_1 Thdrt: *διδοναι* bef *καισαρι* D: txt BL [T(Tischdf)] ℵ latt Syr syr-cu $Constt_1$.—*φορον* AKMR[Π] syr coptt Eus_1 $Thdrt_2$. om 2nd *και* A R(appy) rel lat-*a c* coptt [$Thdrt_1$]: ins BLTℵ vulg lat-*b e f* [*ff_2 i l q*] syrr syr-cu [arm].—for [*και*] *λεγ.*, *λεγ. δε* D. for *εαυτον*, *αυτον* BGT.

3. rec *επηρωτησεν* (‖ *Matt Mark*), with AD rel: txt BRTℵ. om *ο* (bef *βασιλευς*) T[Alf]. for *αποκριθεις αυτω εφη*, *απεκριθη αυτω λεγων* D (1 lat-*a*), for *εφη*, *λεγει* ℵ.

5. *ενισχυον* DH 69. om *οτι* D T^1(appy [not so Tischdf]) vulg lat-*a b e f ff_2* [*i l q*] syr-cu æth. *αναςι* (sic) $ℵ^1$. for *λαον*, *οχλον* Lℵ Scr's v. om *διδασκων* $ℵ^1$ lat-*b c e i l* [*q*]. for *ιουδαιας*, *γης* D. om *και* ADR rel [latt copt-schw-dz sah]: ins BLTℵ am(with em [forj] fuld ing) syrr syr-cu copt[-wilk and ms].

6. for *πιλ. δε ακ.*, *ακουσας δε ο πιλατος* D lat-*c*. om *γαλιλαιαν* BLTℵ copt: ins ADR rel vss.—pref *την* D. for *ο ανθρωπος γαλιλαιος*, *απο της γαλιλαιας ο ανθρωπος* D lat-*a b e ff_2 i* [*q*].—(ὁ is written over by the origl scribe in B: see table.)

7. for *και επιγν.*, *επιγν. δε* D. ins *τον* bef *ηρωδην* B [T(Tischdf)].—for *προς* to 2nd *αυτον*, *τω ηρωδι οντι αυτω* D: for *και*, *κατ* $ℵ^1$(but corrd).

to effect their purpose by falsehood, do so, in spite of the fact having been precisely the contrary to that which they assert. 3.] This question is related in all four Gospels. But in John the answer is widely different from the distinct affirmation in the other three, amounting perhaps to it in substance—at all events affirming that He was 'a King'—which was the form of their charge. I believe therefore that the Three give merely the general import of the Lord's answer, which John relates in full. It is hardly possible, if Jesus had affirmed the fact so strongly and barely as the Three relate it, that Pilate should have made the avowal in ver. 4—which John completely explains. 4.] The preceding question had been asked *within* the prætorium—a fact which our narrator does not adduce,—representing the whole as a continuous conversation in presence of the Jews: see John, ver. 38. We may remark (and on this see Matt., ver. 18: Mark, ver. 10) that Pilate must have known well that a man who had really done that, whereof Jesus was accused, would be *no such object of hatred to the Sanhedrim.* This knowledge was doubtless accompanied (as the above-cited verses imply) with a previous acquaintance with some of the sayings and doings of Jesus, from which Pilate had probably formed his own opinion that He was *no such King* as His foes would represent Him. This is now confirmed by His own words (as related by John); and Pilate wishes to dismiss Him, finding no fault in Him. 5.] Possibly they thought of the matter mentioned ch. xiii. 1, in introducing Galilee into their charge. ἐπίσχ.] **they strengthened, redoubled, the charge**—or perhaps intransitive, **they became urgent.**

6—12.] He is sent to Herod, and by him returned to Pilate. *Peculiar to Luke:* see remarks on ver. 12. Pilate, conscious that he must either do the duty of an upright judge and offend the Jews, or sacrifice his duty to his popu-

καὶ αὐτὸν ἐν Ἱεροσολύμοις ἐν ταύταις ταῖς ἡμέραις.
8 ὁ δὲ Ἡρώδης ἰδὼν τὸν Ἰησοῦν [d] ἐχάρη [de] λίαν· [f] ἦν
γὰρ ἐξ [g] ἱκανῶν χρόνων θέλων ἰδεῖν αὐτὸν [h] διὰ τὸ
ἀκούειν περὶ αὐτοῦ, καὶ ἤλπιζέν τι [i] σημεῖον ἰδεῖν ὑπ'
αὐτοῦ [k] γινόμενον. 9 ἐπηρώτα δὲ αὐτὸν ἐν [l] λόγοις
[m] ἱκανοῖς, αὐτὸς δὲ οὐδὲν ἀπεκρίνατο αὐτῷ. 10 εἱστήκεισαν
δὲ οἱ ἀρχιερεῖς καὶ οἱ γραμματεῖς [n] εὐτόνως [o] κατηγο-
ροῦντες αὐτοῦ. 11 [p] ἐξουθενήσας δὲ αὐτὸν ὁ Ἡρώδης
σὺν τοῖς [q] στρατεύμασιν αὐτοῦ καὶ [r] ἐμπαίξας, [s] περι-
βαλὼν [tu] ἐσθῆτα [uv] λαμπρὰν [w] ἀνέπεμψεν αὐτὸν τῷ Πιλάτῳ.
12 ἐγένοντο δὲ φίλοι ὅ τε Ἡρώδης καὶ ὁ Πιλάτος ἐν αὐτῇ

ABDEG HKLM RSTUV XΓΔΛΠ ℵ 1. 69

...επεμψεν R. F ηρωδης ...

d 2 John 4. 3 John 3 only. e Matt. ii. 16. Mark i. 35. ix. 3. Gen. i. 31. f Matt. xix. 22 reff. g ch. viii. 27 reff. h Matt. xiii. 5 reff. i ch. xxi. 7, 25 al. Exod. iii. 12. k ch. x. 13. Acts viii. 13. Gen. ii. 4. l ch. xx. 3 ||. Acts ii. 40. xxviii. 25. m = Matt. xxviii. 12 reff. n Acts xviii. 28 only. Josh. vi. 7. (-νος, 2 Macc. xii. 25. -νία, Eccl. vii. 8 Aℵ.) o John v. 45 reff. p ch. xviii. 9 reff. q Matt. xxii. 7 reff. r Matt. ii. 16. xx. 19 al. Exod. x. 2. Ps. ciii. 26. s Matt. vi. 29, 31 reff. t ch. xxiv. 4 only in Gospp. Acts (i. 10 v. r.) x. 30. xii. 21. James ii. 2 bis, 3 only +. 2 Macc. viii. 35 al. u Acts x. 30. James ii. 2, 3. v as above (u). Rev. xv. 6. xix. 8 al.3 only +. Sir. xxix. 22 al. Cant. v. 10 Symm. w = Philem. 11 only. (ver. 7 reff.)

for ταυταις, εκειναις D latt [syr-cu copt-wilk-schw] : αυταις ℵ[1].

8. om δε ℵ[1] [sah-woide-txt]. rec (for εξ ικανων χρονων θελων) θελων εξ ικανου, with AR rel; θελων εκ ικανου χρονου HM[Π] 1 : εξ ικανου χρονου θελων X 69 : txt B(DL)Tℵ lat-*c*.—om θελων L.—θελων ιδειν αυτον bef εξ ικανων χρονων D lat-*b e f i* Syr syr-cu. rec aft ακουειν ins πολλα, with AR T[Alf] rel latt syrr [arm] : om BDKLM [T(Tischdf) Π]ℵ 1 syr-cu coptt æth. ελπιζειν T.

9. om 1st δε Gℵ[1]. om αυτον T. for ουδεν, ουκ ℵ Scr's p. for ουδεν απεκρινατο αυτω, ουκ απεκριθη αυτον ουδεν D lat-*e*.—απεκριναντο (sic) ℵ[1].

11. for δε, τε ℵ. om αυτον ℵ[1]. ins και bef ο ηρωδης L [T(Tischdf)] Xℵ 69 lat-*a* copt-[wilk and] ms. rec aft περιβαλων ins αυτον, with AD rel lat-*b c e f* ff_2 [*l q*] coptt; αυτω RSUΓ 69 : om BLTℵ vulg lat-*a*. for ανεπεμψεν, επεμψεν LRℵ[1] lat-*c*. om τω AM[Π].

12. for ver, οντες δε εν αηδια ο πιλατος και ο ηρωδης εγενοντο φιλοι εν αυτη τη ημερα D lat-*c*. rec transp ηρωδης and πιλατος, with A(D) rel syrr copt arm : txt BLTℵ

larity, first attempts to get rid of the matter altogether by sending his prisoner to Herod, on occasion of this word *Galilee.* This was Herod Antipas, tetrarch of Galilee and Peræa (see ch. iii. 1 and note on Matt. xiv. 1), who had come up to keep the feast. **7. ἀνέπεμψεν**] "Propriam Romani juris vocem usurpavit. Nam *remittitur* reus qui alicubi comprehensus mittitur ad judicem aut originis aut habitationis. Itaque Pilatus Herodi, ut Tetrarchæ ejus loci unde esse Jesus dicebatur, potestatem permisit Jesum abducendi in Galilæam, ibique, si vellet, cognoscendi de ejus causa: ut fieri inter Romanos provinciarum rectores solebat." Grotius. So Vespasian, in judging the inhabitants of Tarichææ (Jos. B. J. iii. 10. 10), allowed Agrippa to dispose of those ἐκ τῆς ἑαυτοῦ βασιλείας. **8, 9.**] The reason of our Lord's silence is sufficiently shewn, in the account of Herod's feelings at seeing Him. "Noluit Christus miraculis et sermonibus, ut non ad auditorum curiositatem aut propriam jactantiam, ita nec ad suam ipsius a morte liberationem uti." Drusius. **10.**] The accusations, of *worldly kingship* and of *blasphemy,* would probably be here *united,* as Herod was a Jew, and able to appreciate the latter. **11.**] **στρατ.** are the *body-guard in attendance upon Herod.*

ἐσθῆτα λαμπρ.] Variously interpreted :—either *purple,* as befitting a king,—and why should this not be the very χλαμὺς κοκκίνη afterwards used by Pilate's soldiers (Matt. xxvii. 28; ἱμάτιον πορφυροῦν, John xix. 2)?—or *white,* as λαμπρ. is rendered by some (but see note), Acts x. 30. **12.**] The cause of the quarrel is uncertain: apparently something concerning Herod's power of jurisdiction, which was conceded by Pilate in this sending Jesus to him, and again waived by Herod in sending Him back again. From chap. xiii. 1, Pilate appears to have encroached on that jurisdiction. The remarks of some Commentators about their *uniting in enmity against Christ* (so even, recently, Wordsworth), are quite beside the purpose. The present feeling of Pilate was any thing but hostile to the person of Christ; and Herod, by his treatment of Him, shews that he thought Him beneath

τῇ ἡμέρᾳ [x] μετ' ἀλλήλων· [y] προϋπῆρχον γὰρ ἐν ἔχθρᾳ
ὄντες πρὸς αὐτούς. 13 Πιλάτος δὲ [z] συγκαλεσάμενος
τοὺς ἀρχιερεῖς καὶ τοὺς ἄρχοντας καὶ τὸν λαὸν 14 εἶπεν
πρὸς αὐτοὺς [a] Προσηνέγκατέ μοι τὸν ἄνθρωπον τοῦτον
ὡς [b] ἀποστρέφοντα τὸν λαόν, καὶ ἰδοὺ ἐγὼ [c] ἐνώπιον
ὑμῶν [d] ἀνακρίνας οὐδὲν εὗρον [e] ἐν τῷ ἀνθρώπῳ τούτῳ
[f] αἴτιον ὧν [g] κατηγορεῖτε κατ' αὐτοῦ. 15 ἀλλ' οὐδὲ
Ἡρώδης· [h] * ἀνέπεμψα γὰρ ὑμᾶς πρὸς αὐτόν, καὶ ἰδοὺ
οὐδὲν [i] ἄξιον θανάτου ἐστὶν πεπραγμένον αὐτῷ. 16 [k] παιδεύσας οὖν αὐτὸν [l] ἀπολύσω. [17 [m] ἀνάγκην δὲ [m] εἶχεν
[l] ἀπολύειν αὐτοῖς [n] κατὰ ἑορτὴν ἕνα.] 18 [o] ἀνέκραγον δὲ

x = Matt. xx. 2. 1 Cor. vi. 6.
y Acts viii. 9 only. Job xlii. 17 only (?).
z ch. xv. 6 reff.
a = here [ch. xii. 11 v. r.] only.
b = here only. Josh. xxii. 16 al.
c = ch. v. 25.
d Gospp., here only. = Acts iv. 9. xii. 19. xxiv. 8. xxviii. 18. (1 Cor. ii. 14 al. L.P. 1 Kings xx. 12.) Sus. 48, 51 only.
e vv. 4, 22. Acts xxiii. 9. xxiv. 20 al.
f ver. 4 reff.
g constr., here only. (Matt. xxvii. 12 reff.)
h ver. 7 reff.
i = ch. xii. 48. Acts xxiii. 29. xxv. 25. xxvi. 31.
k = ver. 22. 2 Cor. vi. 9. Heb. xii. 6, 7, 10. 2 Chron. x. 11. Prov. xix. 18.
l Matt. xviii. 27 reff.
m ch. xiv. 18. 1 Cor. vii. 37. Heb. vii. 27. Jude 3 only.
n ||. ch. ii. 41.
o Mark i. 23. vi. 49. ch. iv. 33. viii. 28 only. Judg. vii. 20.

vulg lat-*a b e f ff*$_2$ syr-cu sah æth. προυπηρχοντο ℵ[1]. rec εαυτους, with A rel: txt BLTℵ.

13. for πιλ. δε συγκαλεσαμενος, ο δε πιλατος συνκαλεσας D. ins παντα bef τον λαον D lat-*c* syr-cu.

14. προσηνεγκα (sic) T[Alf].—κατηνεγκατε D. for και ιδου εγω, καγω δε D. ανακρινας bef ενωπιον υμων D Syr syr-cu copt. ουθεν B [T(Tischdf)] ℵ 1. for εν τω ανθρωπω τουτω αιτιον, αιτιον εν αυτω D [sah]. om ων to αυτου D.—om κατ' ALΛℵ 1 latt.

15. * ἀνέπεμψεν γὰρ αὐτὸν πρὸς ἡμᾶς (*to suit ver* 11?) BKLMT[Π]ℵ 69 lat-*f* coptt: ανεπεμψα γαρ υμας προς αυτον AD rel latt (syrr syr-cu).—υμας 69 gat(with mm) syr-mg. om ιδου D Scr's e syr-cu. πεπραγμενον bef εστιν D latt. ins εν bef αυτω DXΓ 69 lat-*c*.

17. om ver ABKLT[Π] fuld lat-*a* copt-dz sah: ins Xℵ rel vulg lat-*b c e f* [*g*$_{1.2}$ *l q*] syrr copt-wilk æth-ms, and (aft ver 19) D syr-cu æth-ed. (*The evidence of the best Greek mss* (ℵ excepted), *if taken alone, would lead to the erasure of the verse as an interpolation founded on the other Gospels. But* 1, *the words are very different from those in* ||: 2, *they contain an idiom in Luke's manner*, αναγκην ειχεν, *which an interpolator would hardly have substituted for the* ||: 3, *they might have been erased here as occurring too soon, and insd aft ver* 19 *as in* D, *and thus have dropped out*: 4, *the words* ΑΝΑΓΚΗΝΔΕ *and* ΑΝΕΚΡΑΓΟΝΔΕ *may have occasioned omn by homœotel.*) κατα εορτην bef απολυειν αυτοις D. for ενα, ινα ℵ[1](corrd eadem manu).

18. rec ανεκραξαν, with AD rel: txt BLTℵ lat-*a* Cyr$_1$. om δε T[1] 69 [sah].

his judicial notice. This remission of Jesus to Herod seems not to have been known to either of the other three Evangelists. It is worthy of notice that they all relate the mocking by the soldiers of Pilate, which Luke omits,—whereas he gives it as taking place before Herod. This is one of the very few cases where the nature of the history shews that *both* happened. Let the student ask himself, How could John, if he composed his Gospel with that of Luke before him, have here given us a narrative in which so important a fact as this is not only not related, but absolutely *cannot find any place of insertion?* Its *real place* is after John ver. 38;—but obviously nothing was further from the mind of that Evangelist, for he represents Pilate as speaking continuously.

13—25.] Further hearing before Pilate, who strives to release Him, but ultimately yields to the Jews. Matt. xxvii. 15—26. Mark xv. 6—15. John xviii. 39, 40. Our account, while entirely distinct in *form* from the others, is in *substance* nearly allied to them. In a few points it approaches John very nearly, compare ver. 18 with John ver. 40, also ἕνα ver. 17, with John ver. 39. The second declaration of our Lord's innocence by Pilate is in John's account united with the first, ver. 38. In the three first Gospels, as asserted in our ver. 14, the questioning takes place in the presence of the Jews: not so, however, in John (see xviii. 28).

15.] ἐστὶν πεπ. αὐτῷ—is done by him— not '*to* him,' see ch. xxiv. 35, ἐγνώσθη

[p] παμπληθεὶ λέγοντες [q] Αἶρε τοῦτον, [1] ἀπόλυσον δὲ ἡμῖν
τὸν Βαραββᾶν,
19 ὅςτις [r] ἦν διὰ [s] στάσιν τινὰ γενομένην
ἐν τῇ πόλει καὶ φόνον [[t] βληθεὶς] [tu] ἐν τῇ φυλακῇ.
20 πάλιν
δὲ ὁ Πιλάτος [v] προςεφώνησεν θέλων ἀπολῦσαι τὸν P λατος
Ἰησοῦν.
21 οἱ δὲ [w] ἐπεφώνουν λέγοντες Σταύρου σταύ- ...τον T.
ρου αὐτόν.
22 ὁ δὲ [x] τρίτον εἶπεν πρὸς αὐτούς Τί γὰρ ABDEF GHKL
κακὸν ἐποίησεν οὗτος; οὐδὲν [y] αἴτιον θανάτου εὗρον MPSUV XΓΔΛΠ
ἐν αὐτῷ· [z] παιδεύσας οὖν αὐτὸν ἀπολύσω.
23 οἱ δὲ ℵ 1. 69
[a] ἐπέκειντο φωναῖς [b] μεγάλαις [c] αἰτούμενοι αὐτὸν σταυρωθῆναι, καὶ [d] κατίσχυον αἱ φωναὶ αὐτῶν [καὶ τῶν ἀρχ-
ιερέων]·
24 καὶ Πιλάτος [e] ἐπέκρινεν γενέσθαι τὸ [f] αἴτημα
αὐτῶν,
25 ἀπέλυσεν δὲ τὸν διὰ [g] στάσιν καὶ φόνον [h] βεβλημένον [h] εἰς φυλακήν, ὃν ᾐτοῦντο, τὸν δὲ Ἰησοῦν [i] παρ- C εις την ...
έδωκεν τῷ [k] θελήματι αὐτῶν.
26 Καὶ ὡς [l] ἀπήγαγον
αὐτόν, [m] ἐπιλαβόμενοι Σίμωνά τινα Κυρηναῖον ἐρχό- 33 επιλαβομενοι...

p here only †. (-θής, 2 Macc. x. 24.)
q = Matt. xxiv. 39. Acts xxi. 36. Isa. lvii. 1.
r constr. w. aor. part., here only.
s = ‖ Mk. ver. 25. Acts xxiv. 5. Prov. xvii. 14.
t here only. see ver. 25.
u = John iii. 35 reff.
v Matt. xi. 16 reff.
w Acts xii. 22. xxi. 34. xxii. 24 only †. Esdr. ix. 47. 2 Macc. i. 23 only.
x Mark xiv. 41 reff.
y ver. 4 reff.
z ver. 16 reff.
a = here only. (John xi. 38 reff.)
b Matt. xxiv. 31 al.
c constr., Acts iii. 14 (vii. 46). 3 Kings xix. 4.
d Matt. xvi. 18. ch. xxi. 36 only. Exod. xvii. 11.
e here only †. 2 Macc. iv. 47 only.
f Phil. iv. 6. 1 John v. 15 only. 1 Kings i. 17.
g = ver. 19.
h Matt. v. 25 al.
i Matt. xvii. 22. Ezek. xxiii. 28.
k = John i. 13. 2 Pet. i. 21. Sir. viii. 15.
l = Matt. xxvi. 57. ch. xxi. 12. xxii. 26. Ep. Jer. 18. abs., Acts xii. 19.
m constr., ch. ix. 47 reff.

απανπληθει T : πανπλ. [ADEHMΔ]ℵ. αιρε τουτον twice in D. om τον A rel Thl : ins BDLTXℵ 1. 69 $Orig_1$ Cyr_1.

19. rec βεβλημενος εις φυλακην, with AD(1) rel: βεβλημενος εν τη φυλακη X ℵ-corr[1·3]: εν τη φυλ. (only) ℵ[1] : βληθεις εν τη φυλακη BL(T).—(ins την 1 : om τη T[Alf].)

20. rec (for δε) ουν, with X rel syr : txt ABDLTℵ latt Syr coptt. aft προσεφωνησεν ins αυτοις BL [T(Tischdf)] ℵ Aug ; αυτους D ; προς αυτους 69 vulg lat-*b c e f* ff_2 g_1 *l* : om AP T[Alf] rel syrr arm.

21. for επεφωνουν, εκραξαν D lat-*c*. [om λεγοντες D.] rec (for σταυρου σταυρου) σταυρωσον σταυρωσον (*from* ‖ *Mark*), with AP rel : txt BDℵ Coisl-oct-marg $Orig_6$ Eus_2 Cyr_1. for αυτον, τον D[1](txt D[5]).

22. for ουδεν αιτιον, ουδεμιαν αιτιαν D vss, ουδεν αξιον L evv-48_2-49-z_1 lat-*a c* syr-cu syr-mg. for ευρον, ευρισκω D 243 vulg lat-*b c e f* ff_2 *l* syr-cu. απολυσω bef αυτον D.

23. for επεκ., εκειντο ℵ. for σταυρωθηναι, σταυρωσαι B.—σταυρωθηναι bef αυτον D. om και των αρχιερεων (*homœotel ?*) BLℵ vulg lat-*a b e* ff_2 $g_{1.2}$ *l* coptt : ins ADP rel lat-*c f* syrr syr-cu arm.—των is written twice by D[1].

24. rec (for και) ο δε, with AP rel lat-*f* syrr sah arm : txt BLℵ vulg lat-*a b e* ff_2 syr-cu copt æth.—for κ. π. επεκρ., επεκρεινεν δε ο πειλατος D.

25. rec aft απελυσεν ins αυτοις (‖ *Matt Mark*), with KM[Π] 1. 69 vulg lat-*b c* &c Syr syr-cu syr-w-ob æth arm : om ABDPℵ rel lat-*a* coptt. for δια to φονον, ενεκα φονου D. rec ins την bef φυλακην, with ACP rel coptt : om BDFKℵ 69 arm $Orig_1$.

26. for και ως, ως δε D. for απηγαγον, απηγον B Scr's c f. rec σιμωνος τινος κυρηναιου του ερχομενου (*prob gramml corrn, and* του *mistake from the precedg* -ου), with Scr's g(e sil), and (omg του) AP rel Scr's-mss : 69 combines both (-να τινα -αιον, -ενου) : txt B(CDL)Xℵ 33 (om τινα L, τινα bef σιμωνα (‖ *Mark*) CD).

αὐτοῖς. **16.**] ‘*Hic cœpit nimium concedere Pilatus,*’ Bengel. If there be no fault in Him, why should He be *corrected at all ?*—the Jews perceive their advantage, and *from this moment follow it up.* **23.**] **κατίσχυον**—got the upper hand, prevailed : see reff.

25. τὸν δ. σ. κ.τ.λ.] The description is inserted for the sake of contrast ;—see Acts iii. 14. Luke omits the scourging and mocking of Jesus. It is *just possible* that he might have omitted the mocking, because he had related a similar incident before Herod ; but how shall we say this of the scourging, if he had seen any narratives which contained it ? The break between vv. 25 and 26 is harsh in the extreme, and if Luke had any materials wherewith to fill it up, I have no doubt he would have done so.

26—33.] He is led forth to Crucifixion. Matt. xxvii. 31—34. Mark

μενον ἀπ' ἀγροῦ, [n] ἐπέθηκαν αὐτῷ τὸν σταυρὸν φέρειν
[o] ὄπισθεν τοῦ Ἰησοῦ. 27 ἠκολούθει δὲ αὐτῷ πολὺ πλῆθος
τοῦ λαοῦ, καὶ γυναικῶν, αἳ [p] ἐκόπτοντο καὶ [q] ἐθρήνουν
αὐτόν. 28 στραφεὶς δὲ πρὸς αὐτὰς Ἰησοῦς εἶπεν [r] Θυγατέρες Ἱερουσαλήμ, μὴ [s] κλαίετε [t] ἐπ' ἐμέ, [u] πλὴν [t] ἐφ'
ἑαυτὰς [s] κλαίετε καὶ [t] ἐπὶ τὰ τέκνα ὑμῶν, 29 ὅτι ἰδοὺ
[v] ἔρχονται [v] ἡμέραι ἐν αἷς ἐροῦσιν Μακάριαι αἱ [w] στεῖραι,
καὶ αἱ [x] κοιλίαι αἳ οὐκ [y] ἐγέννησαν, καὶ [z] μαστοὶ οἳ οὐκ
Q -ειν τοις... [a] ἔθρεψαν. 30 τότε [b] ἄρξονται λέγειν τοῖς ὄρεσιν Πέσατε

n John xix. 2. Acts xv. 28. Exod. xxii. 25.
o = Matt. xv. 23 (reff.) only. Gen. xviii. 10.
p Matt. xi. 17 reff. Gen. xxiii. 2.
q constr., here only. (Matt. xi. 17 reff.) Jer. xxii. 10.
r = Matt. xxi. 5, from Zech. ix. 9. Ps. cxxxvi. 8. Isa. x. 2.
s w. ἐπί, here bis. ch. xix. 41 only.
t = Rev. i. 7. Matt. xv. 32. Acts vii. 54.
u Matt. xi. 22. Judg. iv. 9.
v Matt. ix. 15 reff.
w ch. i. 7. Gal. iv. 27 (from Isa. liv. 1) only. Gen. xi. 30.
x = ch. i. 41, 42, 44. John iii. 4. Ps. xxi. 10.
y = ch. i. 13, 57. John xvi. 21. Gal. iv. 24.
z ch. xi. 27. Rev. i. 13 only. Job iii. 12.
a = here only (Matt. vi. 26 reff.) ‡.
b Matt. xxvi. 22. ch. xiii. 26 al. Gen. xviii. 27.

απο D. επεθηκεν א[1]. for φερειν, αιρειν (*see* ||) א-corr[1] : om א[1] : txt א[3a].
27. for αυτω πολυ πληθ., το πληθος αυτω D. γυναικες D 243 lat-*c f* Syr syr-cu. om αι א [L(αι κοπτ. for αι εκοπτ.)] 69. rec aft αι ins και, with C[3]P rel syr : om ABC[1]DLXא 33 latt Syr syr-cu coptt æth arm. αυτον bef και εθρηνουν D [syr-cu].
28. rec ins ο bef ιησ., with ACDP א[3a](but erased) rel : om BLא[1].—om ιησ. also Γ.—ο ιησ. bef προς αυτας C ev-y [Syr-ms syr-cu] ; ο ιησ. ειπεν bef προς αυτας D Scr's c [arm]. om επ, εφ, and επι D lat-*b* [*a e ff*$_2$ *l*] Ambr. aft εμε ins μηδε πενθειτε D. for πλην, αλλ' D latt Ambr Jer Leo.
29. om ιδου D 69 lat-*a b e ff*$_2$ [*l*] syr-cu æth arm Leo. ημεραι bef ερχονται CXא sah : ελευσονται ημεραι D 69 latt. om 1st αι (*homœotel*) א. rec om 2nd αι (*homœotel*), with ADP rel arm : ins BCXא 1. 69 coptt. μαζοι C, μασθοι D[1]FGΓ. rec (for εθρεψαν) εθηλασαν, with AP rel vulg lat-*f* syrr syr-cu æth : εξεθρεψαν C[2]D 1 : txt BC[1]Lא syr-mg.
30. αρξωνται APΔ 33. rec πεσετε, with ABC[2]DPא[1] rel : txt C[1]LQXΔא[3a] [Cyr$_3$-p].

xv. 20—23. John xix. 16, 17. Our account is original—containing the affecting narrative vv. 27—32, peculiar to itself. **26. ἐρχόμενον ἀπ' ἀγρ.**] See on Mark. **ὄπισθεν τ. Ἰη.** is peculiar to Luke, and a note of accuracy.

27.] These were not the women who had followed Him from Galilee, but the ordinary crowd collected in the streets on such occasions, and consisting, as is usually the case (and especially at an execution), *principally of women.* Their weeping appears to have been of that kind of well-meant sympathy which is excited by any affecting sight, such as that of an innocent person delivered to so cruel a death. This description need not of course exclude many who may have wept from deeper and more personal motives, as having heard Him teach, or received some benefit of healing from Him, or the like.

28.] **στραφείς**—after He was relieved from the burden of the cross. This word comes from an eye-witness. **ἐπ' ἐμέ**—*His* future course was not one to be bewailed—see especially on this saying, Heb. xii. 2,—ὃς ἀντὶ τῆς προκειμένης αὐτῷ χαρᾶς ὑπέμεινεν σταυρόν, αἰσχύνης καταφρονήσας. Nor again were His sacred sufferings a mere popular tragedy for street-bewailing; the sinners should weep for *themselves*, not for *Him.* **ἐφ' ἑαυτὰς . . . καὶ ἐπὶ τὰ τέκνα ὑμῶν**] See Matt. ver. 25, where the people called down the vengeance of His blood on themselves καὶ ἐπὶ τὰ τέκνα ἡμῶν. *Many of those who now bewailed Him perished in the siege of Jerusalem.* Those who now were young wives, would not be more than *sixty* when (A.D. 70) the city was taken. But to *their children* more especially belonged the miseries of which the Lord here speaks. **29. ἔρχονται ἡμ.**] Between this and then would be time for *that effectual weeping*, which might save both themselves and their children: see Acts ii. 37, 38,—but of which few availed themselves. These few are remarkably hinted at in the change to the third person, which excludes them—**ἐροῦσιν,** i.e. not *'men in general,'* nor *'My enemies,'*—but 'the impenitent among you,—those who weep merely tears of idle sympathy for Me, and none of repentance for themselves;—those who are *in Jerusalem* and its misery, which My disciples *will not be.*' On the saying itself, compare the whole of Hosea ix., especially vv. 12—16. **30.**] This is cited from the next chapter of Hosea (ref.). It was partially and primarily accomplished, when multitudes of the

c ch. iii. 5 (from Isa. xl. 4) only. 1 Kings x. 13. Hosea x. 8 al.
d Matt. viii. 24 reff.
e Matt. xvii. 12. ch. xxii. 37. John xiv. 30. 1 Cor. ix. 15.
f here only. Judg. xvi. 7, 8. Job viii. 16 only. = χλωρ., Ezek. xx. 47.
g = Rev. ii. 7. xxii. 2, 14, 19 only. (ch. xxii. 52 ‖ al.) Exod. ix. 25. Xen. Anab. vi. 4. 4, 5.
h = here only. (John v. 3 reff.) Ezek. xvii. 24.
i ver. 39. 2 Tim. ii. 9 only. Prov. xxi. 15. Sir. xi. 33. xxx. (xxxiii.) 26 only.
k = Matt. ii. 16. Exod. xxi. 29.
l ‖ (Mt. reff.) only.
m Matt. xiii. 8 reff.
n Matt. xx. 21, 23 reff.
o Matt. vi. 3. Mark x. 37. 2 Cor. vi. 7 only. 1 Chron. xii. 2.
p = Matt. vi. 12 reff.

ἐφ᾽ ἡμᾶς, καὶ τοῖς [c] βουνοῖς [d] Καλύψατε ἡμᾶς. 31 ὅτι εἰ
[e] ἐν τῷ [f] ὑγρῷ [g] ξύλῳ ταῦτα ποιοῦσιν, [e] ἐν τῷ [h] ξηρῷ τί
γένηται; 32 ἤγοντο δὲ καὶ ἕτεροι * δύο [i] * κακοῦργοι σὺν
αὐτῷ [k] ἀναιρεθῆναι. 33 Καὶ ὅτε ἦλθον ἐπὶ τὸν τόπον τὸν
καλούμενον [l] Κρανίον, ἐκεῖ ἐσταύρωσαν αὐτὸν καὶ τοὺς
[i] κακούργους, [m] ὃν μὲν [n] ἐκ [n] δεξιῶν [m] ὃν δὲ ἐξ [o] ἀριστερῶν.
34 ὁ δὲ Ἰησοῦς ἔλεγεν Πάτερ, [p] ἄφες αὐτοῖς· οὐ γὰρ

...οτε P. ABCDE FGHKL MQSUV XΓΔΛ Πℵ 1. 33. 69

31. om 1st τω BC: ins ADPQℵ rel. ξυλαω (but corrd) ℵ[1]. for ταυτα, τουτο C Ambr$_2$. for γενηται, γενησεται DK[2]Λ: γινεται EFS ev-y.
32. * κακοῦργοι δύο Bℵ coptt: δυο κακ. ACDPQ rel [latt &c].
33. rec απηλθον, with A rel [Damasc$_1$]: txt BCDLQℵ 33. 69 latt Syr syr-cu syr-mg. —ηλθαν D. for καλουμενον, λεγομενον (‖ *Matt*) CGXΛ Mcion$_e$-e. aft κακουργους ins ομου D. for αριστερων, ευωνυμων (‖ *Matt Mark*) C[1]LQ 33. 69.
34. om ο δε to ποιουσιν B D[1](and lat) ℵ-corr[1](but restored) lat-*a b* copt-dz sah: ins

Jews towards the end of the siege sought to escape death by hiding themselves in the subterranean passages and sewers under the city . . . . οὓς δ᾽ ἐν τοῖς ὑπονόμοις ἀνηρεύνων, καὶ τὸ ἔδαφος ἀναῤῥηγνύντες ὅσοις μὲν ἐνετύγχανον ἀνεῖλον. εὑρέθησαν δὲ καὶ ἐκεῖ νεκροὶ πλείους δισχιλίων, Jos. B. J. vi. 9. 4. But the words are too solemn, and too often used in a more awful connexion, for a further meaning to escape our notice: see Isa. ii. 10, 19, 21, and Rev. vi. 16, where is the striking expression ἀπὸ τῆς ὀργῆς **τοῦ ἀρνίου**—of Him who now was the victim about to be offered. And the whole warning—as every other respecting the destruction of Jerusalem—looks through the type to the antitype, the great day of His wrath. *Now,* **ἔρχονται ἡμέραι**—then **ἦλθεν ἡ ἡμέρα** ἡ μεγάλη τῆς ὀργῆς αὐτοῦ, Rev. vi. 17. It is interesting to see how often David, who had passed so long in hiding among the rocks of the wilderness from Saul, calls the Lord *his Rock* (see Ps. xviii. 2, 46; xlii. 9, &c.). They who have this defence, will not need to call on the rocks to hide them.

31.] This verse—*the solemn close of our Lord's teaching on earth*—compares His own sufferings with that awful judgment which shall in the end overtake sinners, the unrepentant human kind—the *dry tree.* These things—**ταῦτα**—were *a* judgment on sin;—He *bore our sins;*—He,—the vine, the *green tree,* the fruit-bearing tree,—of Whom His people are the branches,—if He, if they in Him and *in* themselves, are so treated, so tried with sufferings,—*what shall become of them who are cast forth as a branch and are withered?* Read 1 Pet. iv. 12—18;—ver. 18 is a paraphrase of our text. Theophylact's comment is excellent: εἰ ταῦτα ποιοῦσιν ἐν ἐμοὶ ἐγκάρπῳ καὶ ἀειθαλεῖ καὶ ἀειζώῳ διὰ τὴν θεότητα, τί γένηται ἐν ὑμῖν ἀκάρποις καὶ πάσης δικαιοσύνης ζωοποιοῦ ἐστερημένοις; The explanations which make the green-tree = the young, and the dry = the old (Bengel),—or the green-tree = the women, comparatively innocent, the dry = the guilty (Baumgarten-Crusius), at the destruction of Jerusalem—seem to me unworthy of the place which the words hold, though the latter agrees with the symbolism of Ezek. xx. 47, compared with xxi. 4.

32.] The digest shews that the reading **ἕτεροι κακοῦργοι δύο** has diplomatically almost as great claims to be the true one as that in the text: and if we take the probabilities of alteration into account, it has even stronger claims. Of course it can bear but one meaning—**two other malefactors.** That this should have been substituted for **ἕτεροι δύο κακοῦργοι,** which may mean **two other, malefactors** (as rendered in E. V.), is simply inconceivable; that the transposition took place vice versa, is highly probable. This having now appeared by the additional evidence of the Codex Sinaiticus, it is impossible to annotate as was done in my earlier Editions.

33—49.] The Crucifixion, mocking, last words, and death of Jesus. Matt. xxvii. 35—50. Mark xv. 24—37. John xix. 18—30; with however some particulars inserted which appear later in the other Gospels.

34.] Spoken apparently *during the act of the crucifixion,* or

οἴδασιν τί ποιοῦσιν. [q] διαμεριζόμενοι δὲ τὰ ἱμάτια αὐτοῦ
[r] ἔβαλον [r] κλήρους. 35 καὶ εἱστήκει ὁ λαὸς θεωρῶν. [s] ἐξ-
εμυκτήριζον δὲ καὶ οἱ ἄρχοντες λέγοντες Ἄλλους ἔσωσεν,

q || Mt. reff.
r || only. Joel iii. 3. Obad. 11. Jon. i. 7. see Acts i. 26.
s ch. xvi. 14 only. Ps. ii. 4 al.

[AC] D[10]-marg Q$\aleph^1$ rel vulg lat-*c e f ff*$_2$ syrr syr-cu [syr-jer æth arm] copt Eus Eus-canon hom-Clem$_1$ Constt$_1$ Chr$_{sæpe}$ [Thdrt$_2$ Damasc$_1$] Iren-int$_1$ Orig-int$_1$ Hil$_1$ Ambr Jer. (*The non-occurrence of the words in the other Gospels had probably something to do with the omission: the citation of them by Irenæus and their occurrence in the ancient versions seems to prove that we have here a grave error in Cod. Vat. or in the* MS *from which it was derived.*) for ιησ., κυριος Q syr-mg. for ελεγεν, ειπεν AKM[Π syr-cu]. om πατερ A. διεμεριζοντο D sah. for εβαλον, βαλοντες (|| *Matt Mark*) D lat-*c*. rec κληρον (*from Matt Mark John*), with BCDQℵ rel lat-*b c* [Syr syr-mg æth]: txt AX 1. 33 vulg lat-*a e f ff*$_2$ syr[-txt syr-jer] arm Aug$_{expr}$ (*Lucas dicendo sortes . . . . quamvis nonnulli codices sortem reperiantur habere*).

35. for θεωρων εξεμυκτ., ορων εμυκτηριζον D. aft δε ins αυτον D 1. 69 latt syrr syr-cu arm Eus$_1$.—om 2nd και Dℵ 1 lat-*a c*. om οι αρχοντες D. rec aft αρχοντες ins συν αυτοις (*to shew, aft* ||, *that* the people also *derided Him*), with A rel vulg lat-*f* syr-cu syr Eus$_1$: om BCDLQXℵ 33. 69 lat-*b c e ff*$_2$ *l* Syr [syr-jer] copt æth. for λεγοντες, και ελεγαν αυτω D æth. εσωσας and σεαυτον σωσον D lat-*c*.

immediately that the crosses were set up. Now first, in the fullest sense, from the wounds in His Hands and Feet, is His Blood shed, εἰς ἄφεσιν ἁμαρτιῶν (Matt. xxvi. 28), and He inaugurates His intercessional office by a prayer for His murderers, —**ἄφες** αὐτοῖς. This also is a fulfilment of Scripture, Isa. liii. 12;—where the contents of our verses 33, 34 are remarkably pointed out. His *teaching* ended at ver. 31. His *High-Priesthood* is now begun. His first three sayings on the Cross are *for others*: see ver. 43: John xix. 26, 27. **πάτερ**] He is the *Son of God*, and He speaks in the fulness of this covenant relation. ἐγὼ ᾔδειν ὅτι πάντοτέ μου ἀκούεις:—it is not merely *a prayer*—but *the* prayer of the Great Intercessor, which is always heard. Notice that though on the Cross, there is no alienation, no wrath of condemnation, between the Father and the Son. **ἄφες αὐτοῖς**—*who are here intended?* Doubtless, first and directly, *the four soldiers,* whose work it had been to crucify Him. The **ποιοῦσιν** points directly at this: and it is surely a mistake to suppose that they *wanted no forgiveness,* because they were merely *doing their duty*. Stier remarks, "This is only a misleading fallacy, for they were sinners even as others, and their obedient and unsuspecting performance of their duty was not without a sinful pleasure in doing it, or at all events formed part of their entire standing as sinners, included in that *sin of the world,* to which the Lord here ascribes His Crucifixion" (vi. 403, edn. 2). But not only to *them,* but to them as the representatives of that sin of the world, does this prayer apply. The nominative to **ποιοῦσιν** is οἱ ἄνθρωποι—*mankind,*—the Jewish nation, as the next moving agent in His death,—but all of us, inasmuch as for our sins He was bruised. **οὐ γὰρ οἴδασιν τί ποιοῦσιν,** primarily, as before, spoken of the *soldiers,*—then of the *council,* who delivered Him up, see John xi. 49, ὑμεῖς **οὐκ οἴδατε** οὐδέν,—then of *all,* whose sin is from lack of knowledge of the truth, of *what sin is,* and what it *has done*—even the crucifixion of the Lord. But certainly from this intercession is excluded *that one sin*—strikingly brought out by the passage thus cited as committed by him who said it, viz. Caiaphas, and hinted at again by our Lord, John xix. 11—and perhaps also by the awful answer Matt. xxvi. 64, σὺ **εἶπας**—'thou *saidst* it'—viz. in prophecy, John xi. 49: see also Matt. xxvi. 25,—and on the sin alluded to, Matt. xii. 31: 1 John v. 16. Observe that between the two members of this prayer lies the work of the Spirit leading to repentance—the prayer that they may have their eyes opened, and *know* what they have done: which is the necessary subjective condition of forgiveness of sins, see 2 Tim. ii. 25, 26. **35.**] The insults of *the people* are by no means excluded, even with σὺν αὐτοῖς omitted: nay they are implied, by the δὲ καί which follows. To find a discrepancy with Matt. and Mark here, is surely unfair (Meyer, De Wette):—the people's *standing looking on,* does not describe their mind towards Jesus: Luke reports no more than he had before him: and the inference may be drawn that those whom he has related to have cried out an hour ago, 'Crucify him,'—would not have stood by in silence. On ver. 48, see note there. **οἱ ἄρχοντες** are the chief priests and members of the Sanhedrim: Matt.

σωσάτω ἑαυτόν, εἰ οὗτός ἐστιν ὁ χριστὸς τοῦ θεοῦ ὁ
[t] ἐκλεκτός. 36 [u] ἐνέπαιξαν δὲ αὐτῷ καὶ οἱ στρατιῶται
προσερχόμενοι, [v] ὄξος προσφέροντες αὐτῷ 37 καὶ λέγοντες
Εἰ σὺ εἶ ὁ [w] βασιλεὺς τῶν [w] Ἰουδαίων, σῶσον σεαυτόν.
38 ἦν δὲ καὶ [x] ἐπιγραφὴ ἐπ' αὐτῷ [[y] γράμμασιν Ἑλληνικοῖς
καὶ Ῥωμαϊκοῖς καὶ Ἑβραϊκοῖς], Ὁ [w] βασιλεὺς τῶν [w] Ἰουδαίων οὗτος. 39 εἷς δὲ τῶν [z] κρεμασθέντων [a] κακούργων
[b] ἐβλασφήμει αὐτὸν Οὐχὶ σὺ εἶ ὁ χριστός; σῶσον σεαυτὸν
καὶ ἡμᾶς. 40 ἀποκριθεὶς δὲ ὁ ἕτερος [c] ἐπιτιμῶν αὐτῷ ἔφη
Οὐδὲ φοβῇ σὺ τὸν θεόν, ὅτι ἐν τῷ αὐτῷ [d] κρίματι εἶ;
41 καὶ ἡμεῖς μὲν [e] δικαίως· [f] ἄξια γὰρ ὧν ἐπράξαμεν

t = 1 Pet. ii. 4, 6, from Isa. xxviii. 16. see Matt. xxiv. 22 reff.
u ver. 11.
v Matt. xxvii. 34 reff.
w Matt. xxvii. 11 reff.
x ‖ Mk. ch. xx. 24 ‖ only †.
y = Gal. vi. 11 only. (ch. xvi. 6 al.)
z ch. xviii. 6 reff.
a vv. 32, 33 reff.
b ‖ Mt. reff.
c Mark viii. 32, 33 reff.
d ch. xx. 47 ‖ Mk. xxiv. 20. Deut. xxi. 22.
e 1 Cor. xv. 34. 1 Thess. ii. 10. Tit. ii. 12 1 Pet. ii. 23 only. Deut. i. 16. f = Matt. iii. 8. Acts xxvi. 20. Job xxxiii. 27.

...ενεπαιξ. δε F.

R γραμμασιν...

ABCDE GHKL MQRSU VXΓΔΛ Πא 1. 33. 69

for ουτος, υιος BD: for χριστος, υιος 69. for εστιν, εἶ D lat-*c*. rec ο bef του θεου, with AC^3Q rel; both bef and aft $א^1$: ο εκλεκτος bef του θεου C^1 lat-*c* ff_2: του θεου ει χριστος εἶ ο εκλεκτος D: txt BL א-$corr^{1.3}$ 1 (69) [syr syr-jer coptt arm] Eus_1.—(B does not om ὁ as Mai ed 1: see table.)

36. rec ενεπαιζον (*conforming to* εξεμυκτηριζον *above*), with ACDQ rel vss: txt BLא sah. om και א. rec ins και bef οξος, with C^3Q rel vulg lat-*b c e f* syrr æth arm: om $ABC^1Lא$ lat-*a* coptt.—aft οξος ins τε D. προσεφερον and om αυτω D[-gr] (lat-*b e* ff_2 [*l q* syr-jer sah(appy)]).

37. om και D am[with fuld ing forj em] lat-*b* [*e* ff_2 *l q*] copt-dz sah. aft λεγοντες ins χαιρε D lat-*c* syr-cu. om 1st ει (*error, supposing it repeated?* ει συ ει) A 1 lat-*a e* ff_2.—om ει συ ει D lat-*c*. om σωσον σεαυτον and ins περιθεντες αυτω και ακανθινον στεφανον D (lat-*c* syr-cu).

38. ins η bef επιγραφη (‖ *Mark*) CDGSU. rec ins γεγραμμενη bef επ' αυτω (‖ *Matt*), with C^3 rel syrr syr-cu æth arm; aft επ' αυτω C^1X 33. 69: ins επιγεγραμμενη bef επ' αυτω (‖ *Mark*) ADQ lat-*b*: om BLא coptt. om γραμμασιν ελληνικοις και ρωμαικοις και εβραικοις (*gloss founded on* ‖ *John?*) BC^1L $א^{3a}$(but restored) lat-*a* syr-cu coptt: ins A(D)QR($א^1$) rel latt syrr æth arm.—om και (twice: *as* ‖ *John*) $Dא^1$. rec ουτος, subjoining εστιν, bef ο βασιλευς των ιουδαιων (‖ *Matt*), with AQR rel vulg lat-*b* [*f q*] syrr syr-cu copt æth arm $Orig_1$: om ουτος C lat-*c*: txt BDLא lat-*a e* ff_2.—add εστιν D lat-*e* ff_2.—(B does not om ὁ as Mai ed 1: see table.)

39. om κρεμασθεντων D ev-z_1. rec aft αυτον ins λεγων, with ACQRא rel [vss] Orig-int_1: om B(D)L lat-*l*.—om further ουχι to end of ver D. rec (for ουχι) ει (*see ch* iv. 3 *and* ‖ *Matt*), with AC^3QR rel [vulg lat-*c f q* syrr Orig-int_1]: txt $BC^1Lא$ lat-*a b* ff_2 syr-cu [syr-jer] coptt æth arm.

40. rec επετιμα and (for εφη) λεγων (*to avoid the two participles* αποκριθεις *and* επιτιμων), with AC^3DQR rel latt syr (æth) arm: (επετιμησεν E^1 syr-cu:) txt $BC^1LXא$ copt. for ουδε, οτι ου D: ου $Gא^1$ ev-47 [lat-*c f* Orig-int_1 Aug_1 Vict-tun_1]. for ει, εσμεν C^1 syr-cu syr-jer coptt æth Chr_5. at end ins και ημεις εσμεν D.

41. om και C^1 coptt.

ver. 41. **τ. θ. ὁ ἐκλ.**, either **the Christ of God, His elect one,—or, the elect Christ of God**; I prefer the former: but either way, χρ. τ. θεοῦ must be taken together, not as in rec. **36.**] A different incident from that related Matt. ver. 48: Mark ver. 36: John vv. 28, 29. It was about the time of the mid-day meal of the soldiers,—and they in mockery offered Him their posca or sour wine, to drink with them. **38.**] See on Matt. ver. 37. **ἐπ' αὐτῷ, over Him**, on the projecting upright beam of the cross.

39—43.] Peculiar to Luke. Matthew and Mark have merely a general and less precise report of the same incident. All were now mocking; the soldiers, the rulers, the mob:—and the evil-minded thief, perhaps out of bravado before the crowd, puts in his scoff also.

40.] Bengel supports the notion that this penitent thief was a *Gentile*. But surely this is an unwarranted assumption. What should a Gentile know of Paradise, or of the kingdom of the Messiah as about to come? The silence of the penitent is broken by the **ἡμᾶς** of the other compromising him in the scoff. **οὐδέ** alludes to the multitude—**Dost** *thou too* **not fear God? ὅτι**—(as thou oughtest to

[g] ἀπολαμβάνομεν· οὗτος δὲ οὐδὲν [hi] ἄτοπον [i] ἔπραξεν. 42 καὶ
ἔλεγεν Ἰησοῦ μνήσθητί μου, ὅταν [j] ἔλθῃς ἐν τῇ βασιλείᾳ
σου. 43 καὶ εἶπεν αὐτῷ [k] Ἀμήν σοι λέγω, σήμερον μετ'
ἐμοῦ ἔσῃ ἐν τῷ [l] παραδείσῳ. 44 Καὶ ἦν [ἤδη] [m] ὡσεὶ

g ch. xvi. 25 reff. h Acts xxv. 5. xxviii. 6. 2 Thess. iii. 2 only. Job iv. 8. i Job xxvii. 6. j Matt. xvi. 28. k Matt. v. 18 reff. l 2 Cor. xii. 4. Rev. ii. 7 only. Gen. ii. 8 and fr. m = ch. i. 56. xxii. 41, 59. Judg. iii. 29.

for *απολαμβανομεν*, *απελαβαμεν* C. for *ατοπον*, *πονηρον* D.

42. rec ins *τω* bef *ιησου*, with $AC^3QR\aleph^{3a}$ rel: om $BC^1L\aleph^1$ coptt.—for *ελεγεν ιησου*, *στραφεις προς τον κυριον ειπεν αυτω* D. rec aft *μου* ins *κυριε* (*addn, from ιησου being mistaken for dative*), with AC^2R rel lat-*b* [*q*] syrr æth arm Eus_1 Orig-int_1 Hil_2: bef *μνησθητι* Q [vulg] lat-*c e f ff₂ l* syr-cu Hil_1: om $BC^1DLM^1\aleph$ lat-*a* syr-jer coptt $Orig_1$ [int_1]. om *οταν ελθης* (D, see below) Q [Chr_2 Bas-sel_1]. for *εν τη βασιλεια*, *εις την βασιλειαν* (*see note*) BL vulg [lat-*c e f* ff_2 *l* Orig-int_4] Hil Ambr: txt $ACQR\aleph$ rel [lat-*a b q*] $Orig_2$ Eus_1 [Chr_1].—*εν τη ημερα της ελευσεως σου*, omg *οταν ελθης*, D.

43. rec aft *αυτω* ins *ο ιησους*, with AC(D)QR rel [latt syrr syr-cu &c]: om $BL\aleph$ lat-e^1 coptt.—for *και* to *λεγω*, *αποκριθεις δε ο ιησους ειπεν αυτω τω επλησοντι*(*επιπλ.* D^4) *θαρσει* D. rec *λεγω* bef *σοι*, with $AC^3QR\aleph$ rel latt syrr syr-cu coptt æth: txt BC^1L arm.

44. rec (for *και ην*) *ην δε*, with AC^3QR rel vulg lat-*f* syrr arm: txt $BC^1DL\aleph$ lat-*a b e* ff_2 [*l*] *q* copt Orig-int_1. rec om *ηδη*, with $AC^3DQR\aleph$ rel latt Syr syr-cu [syr-jer] sah arm Orig-int_1: ins BC^1L syr (copt) Orig-int_1.

do), **seeing that . . . .** **41. ἡμεῖς**] He classes himself with the other in condemnation, but not in his prayer afterwards. **ἄτοπον, unseemly.** This is a remarkable testimony to the innocence of Jesus from one who was probably executed for his share in those very tumults which He was accused of having excited. **42.**] The thief had heard of the announcements which Jesus had made,—or at all events of the popular rumour concerning his Kingdom. His faith lays hold on the truth that this *is* the King of the Jews in a higher and immortal sense. There is nothing so astounding in this man's faith *dogmatically* considered, as De Wette thinks; he merely *joins* the common belief of the Jews of a Messianic Kingdom, in which the ancient Fathers were to rise, &c.,—with the conviction, that *Jesus is the Messiah.* What is *really* astounding, is the *power* and *strength* of that faith, which, amidst shame and pain and mockery, could thus lift itself to the apprehension of *the Crucified* as this King. This thief would fill a conspicuous place in a list of the triumphs of faith supplementary to Heb. xi. **ἐν τῇ βασ.**] The Vulgate, which is followed by Luther,—and the E. V.,—renders this as if it were *εἰς τὴν βασ.* (see var. readd.), which is a sad mistake, as it destroys the force of the expression. It is *in* **thy Kingdom—with thy Kingdom,** so *ἔλθῃ ἐν τῇ δόξῃ αὐτοῦ*, Matt. xxv. 31, which we (E.V.) have translated rightly. The above mistake entirely loses **ἔλθῃς**—making it merely '*comest into*,' just as we say to '*come into*' an estate: whereas it is the chief word in the clause, and *ἐν τῇ β. σου* its qualification, **at Thy coming in Thy Kingdom.** It will be seen that there is no necessity for supposing the man to have been *a disciple*, as some have done.

It is remarkable how, in three following sayings, the Lord appears as Prophet, Priest, and King: as *Prophet*, to the *daughters of Jerusalem*;—as *Priest*, interceding for forgiveness;—as *King*, acknowledged by the penitent thief, and answering his prayer. **43. ἀμήν σοι λέγω . . . .**] The Lord surpasses his prayer in the answer; the *ἀμήν σοι λέγω*, **σήμερον**, is the reply to the uncertain **ὅταν** of the thief. **σήμερον**] **this day**: *before the close of this natural day.* The attempt to join it with *σοὶ λέγω*, considering that it not only violates common sense, but destroys the force of our Lord's promise, is surely something worse than silly: see below. **μετ' ἐμοῦ ἔσῃ** can bear no other meaning than **thou shalt be with Me**, in the ordinary sense of the words, 'I shall be in Paradise, and thou with Me.' **ἐν τῷ παρ.**] On these words rests the whole exegesis of the saying. *What is this* PARADISE? The *word* is used of the *garden of Eden* by the LXX, Gen. ii. 8, &c., and subsequently became, in the Jewish theology, the name for that part of Hades, the abode of the dead, where the souls of the righteous await the resurrection. It was also the name for a supernal or heavenly abode, see reff. N. T. The *former of these* is, I believe, here primarily to be understood;—but only as *introductory, and that immediately, to the latter.* By the death of Christ only was *Paradise* first opened, in the *true sense of the word.* He Himself, when speaking of Lazarus (ch. xvi. 22), does not place him in Para-

n Matt. xxiv. 29 reff. o = ‖ Mt. Mk. ch. v. 36. Isa. xlviii. 21. p ‖ Mt. Mk. Heb. vi. 19. ix. 3. x. 20 only. Exod. xxvi. 35 al. xiv. 18.

ὥρα ἕκτη, καὶ σκότος ἐγένετο ἐφ' ὅλην τὴν γῆν ἕως ὥρας
ἐνάτης. 45 καὶ [n] ἐσκοτίσθη ὁ ἥλιος, καὶ [o] ἐσχίσθη τὸ
[p] καταπέτασμα τοῦ ναοῦ [q] μέσον. 46 καὶ [rs] φωνήσας [s] φωνῇ
[s] μεγάλῃ ὁ Ἰησοῦς εἶπεν Πάτερ, εἰς χεῖράς σου [t] παρα-

q = Acts i. 18. Gen. xv. 10. r = ch. viii. 8 reff. s Acts xvi. 28. Rev. t ch. xii. 48 reff. Psa. xxx. 5.

P -ταπετασμα... ABCDE GHKL MPQRS UVXΓΔ ΛΠℵ 1. 33. 69

ωρα bef ωσει ℵ 253. om 2nd και ℵ[1].

45. for και εσκοτισθη ο ηλιος, του ηλιου εκλειποντος B C[1](appy) syr-mg coptt(appy) Orig("*in quibusdam exemplaribus*"), so, but -λιπ-, Lℵ [Orig$_2$] : om C[2](appy) 33 : txt AC[3](D)QR rel latt syrr syr-cu [syr-jer] æth (arm) Orig-int$_1$("*secundum pleraque exemplaria*") Mcion$_1$-e.—for και εσκ., εσκ. δε D.—(Origen (iii. 923) says *Et forsitan ausus est aliquis quasi manifestius aliquid dicere volens pro "Et obscuratus est sol" ponere "Deficiente sole:" existimans quod non aliter potuissent fieri tenebræ nisi sole deficiente.* This is confirmed by the "Acta Pilati" (ed Tischdf A. xi. 2) ἔκλειψις ἡλίου γέγονεν κατὰ τὸ εἰωθός.) for και εσχισθη, εσχισθη δε (*in pursuance of former alteration*) BC[1]Lℵ 1. 33 : txt AC[3]QR rel latt syrr syr-cu arm.—om last clause (but see next ver) D.

46. ο ιησ. bef φωνη μεγαλη C(D) Syr syr-cu [syr-jer æth] coptt.—μεγαλη bef φωνη D-gr. rec (for παρατιθεμαι) παραθησομαι (*from* LXX), with L rel [Dial$_1$] : παρατιθημι D[1](παρατιθειμι D[4]) R 1 Constt$_2$ Ath$_1$ Bas$_1$ Epiph$_1$ Thdrt$_4$ Thl : txt ABCKMPQ

dise, but in Abraham's bosom—in that place which the Jews *called* Paradise, but by an anticipation which our Lord did not sanction. I believe the matter to have been thus. Our Lord spoke (as Grotius has remarked) to the thief so as He knew the thief would understand Him; but He spoke with a fuller and more blessed meaning than he could understand then. For *that day, on that very evening,* was 'Paradise' truly 'regained'—opened by the death of Christ. We know (1 Pet. iii. 18, 19, where see note; iv. 6) that our Lord went down into the depths of death,—announced His triumph (for His death was His triumph) to the imprisoned spirits,—and in that moment—for change of *state,* to the *disembodied,* is all that *change of place* implies—they perhaps were in the Paradise of God,—in the blessed heavenly place, implied by the word, 2 Cor. xii. That this is not *fulness* of glory as yet, is evident;—for the glorified *body* is not yet joined to their spirits,—they are not yet perfect (Heb. xi. 40); but it is a degree of bliss compared to which their former degree was but as imprisonment.

This work of the Lord I believe to have been accomplished *on the instant of His death,* and the penitent to have followed Him at *his death*—some little time after—into the Paradise of God. That our Lord *returned* to take his glorified Body, was in accordance with His design, and He became thereby the *first-fruits of the holy dead,* who shall like Him put on the body of the resurrection, and be translated from disembodied and imperfect bliss in the Paradise of God, to the perfection of glorified humanity in His glory, and with Him, *not in Paradise,* but *at God's right hand.*

44—46.] Our account is very short and epitomizing—containing however, peculiar to itself, the *last word of our Lord on the cross.* The impression conveyed by this account, if we had no other, would be that the veil was rent *before* the death of Jesus;—but the more detailed account of Matthew corrects this.

45.] The words **ἐσκοτ. ὁ ἥλ.** are probably added to give solemnity to the preceding, assigning its reason; so that the gloss τοῦ ἡλ. ἐκλείποντος shews a right apprehension of the words. It can hardly be, as Mey., that the *earth* was darkened till the ninth hour, and *then* the *sun* became dark also.

46.] The use of **φωνῇ μεγάλῃ** shews that *this was the cry* to which Matt. and Mark allude. The words are from the LXX, varying however from the common reading παραθήσομαι, and giving the verb in the present, which is also the rendering of the Hebrew (אַפְקִיד).

These words have in them an important and deep meaning. They accompany that, which in our Lord's case was strictly speaking the *act* of death. It was *His own act*—not 'feeling the approach of death,' as some, not apprehending the matter, have commented; but a *determinate delivering up of His spirit to the Father.*—παρέδωκεν τὸ πνεῦμα, John: see John x. 18—οὐδεὶς αἴρει αὐτὴν ἀπ' ἐμοῦ, ἀλλ' ἐγὼ **τίθημι αὐτὴν ἀπ' ἐμαυτοῦ.** None of the Evangelists say 'He *died:*' although that expression is ever after used of His death stated as one great fact:—but it is, ἀφῆκεν τὸ πν., Matt.; ἐξέπνευσεν, Mark, Luke; παρέδωκεν τὸ πνεῦμα, John.

τίθεμαι τὸ [u] πνεῦμά μου. τοῦτο δὲ εἰπὼν [v] ἐξέπνευσεν.
47 ἰδὼν δὲ ὁ ἑκατόνταρχος τὸ γενόμενον [w] ἐδόξαζεν τὸν
θεὸν λέγων [x] Ὄντως ὁ ἄνθρωπος οὗτος δίκαιος ἦν. 48 καὶ
πάντες οἱ [y] συνπαραγενόμενοι ὄχλοι [z] ἐπὶ τὴν [a] θεωρίαν
ταύτην, [b] θεωρήσαντες τὰ γενόμενα, τύπτοντες τὰ [c] στήθη
[d] ὑπέστρεφον. 49 εἱστήκεισαν δὲ πάντες οἱ [e] γνωστοὶ αὐτῷ
[f] μακρόθεν, καὶ γυναῖκες αἱ [g] συνακολουθοῦσαι αὐτῷ ἀπὸ
τῆς Γαλιλαίας, ὁρῶσαι ταῦτα.
50 Καὶ ἰδοὺ ἀνὴρ [h] ὀνόματι Ἰωσήφ, [i] βουλευτὴς [k] ὑπ-

...γνωστοι Q

u = || Mt. J. Acts vii. 59. Eccl. xii. 7.
v || Mk. bis only †.
w ch. v. 25, 26 reff.
x Mark xi. 32. 1 Tim. v. 3 al. Num. xxii. 37 only.
y 2 Tim. iv. 16 only. Ps. lxxxii. 8 only.
z = Matt. iii. 7 (note).
a here only †. 2 Macc. v. 26. xv. 12 only.
b Matt. xxvii. 55. xxviii. 1. Mark iii. 11 al6. ch. x. 18 al5. John ii. 23 al22. Acts iii. 16 al13. Rev. xi. 11, 12. Epp., Heb. vii. 4. 1 John iii. 17 only. Josh. viii. 20 (18) B. Ps. lxiii. 9.
c John xiii. 25 reff.
d ch. ii. 20 reff.
e = ch. ii. 44 (reff.).
f ch. xxii. 54 reff.
g Mark v. 37. xiv. 51 only. Num. xxxii. 11 Ald. (συνεπακ. AB.) 2 Macc. ii. 4 only. pres. part., Mark i. 4. vi. 14.
h ch. i. 5 al. fr.
i || Mk. only. Job iii. 14. xii. 17 only.
k ch. xvi. 14 reff.

U[XΠ]ℵ 33 Just$_1$ Orig$_1$ Thdot Eus$_2$ Cyr-jer$_1$. rec (for τουτο δε) και ταυτα, with AC^{3}QR rel vulg lat-*f ff*$_2$ syr arm : και τουτο KMP[Π] 69 lat-*b e l q* [D-lat] copt-[wilk-dz æth Bas$_1$] Ambr$_1$: om δε L Syr sah : txt BC^1 D[-gr] ℵ lat-*c* copt-schw. (om clause X.) εξεπν(. .)σεσθαι Q. at end ins (omg last clause of ver 45) και το καταπετασμα του ναου εσχισθη D.

47. for ιδων δε, και D. τα γενομενα R ev-48 Orig-int$_2$; το γεγονος C^1: φωνησας D. rec εδοξασε, with ACPQ rel vulg lat-*a f* Syr syr-cu [syr-jer] copt-dz sah Orig-int$_2$: txt BDLRℵ lat-*c e ff*$_2$ *q* copt Cyr. aft λεγων ins οτι ℵ. δικαιος ην bef ο ανθρωπος ουτος D [sah æth Orig-int$_1$].

48. (συνπαραγενομενοι, so AB^{1}CDELPQRΔℵ.) for οχλοι to ταυτην, επι θεωρεια οχλοι D lat-*c*. for επι, εις ℵ : om 69. rec θεωρουντες (*joining it to foregoing*), with PQ rel vulg lat-*a b* D-lat : txt BC D-gr LRXℵ 33 lat-*c* syrr syr-cu.—om θεωρ. τα γενομενα A. rec ins εαυτων bef τα στηθη (*reminiscence of ch* xviii. 13, *where see digest*), with C^{2}QR rel ; αυτων UXΓ 69 ; ins εαυτων bef στηθη P : om ABC^{1}DLℵ 1 forj arm. aft στηθη ins και τα μετωπα D. υπεστρεφαν D.

49. rec (for 1st αυτω) αυτου, with CDRℵ rel latt syr copt : txt ABLP 33. ins απο bef μακροθεν (*from* || *Matt Mark*) BDLℵ 1. 33 latt coptt : om ACPR rel. aft και ins αι B sah. rec συνακολουθησασαι, with ADP rel : συνακολουθησαι Δ : txt BCLRXℵ 33.

The **πνεῦμα** here is the *Personality* —the human soul informed by the Spirit, *in union :* not separated, so that His soul went to Hades, and His spirit to the Father (Olshausen). Both are delivered into the hand of the Father—by Whom quickened (but ζωοποιηθεὶς πνεύματι of 1 Pet. iii. 18 is to be rendered 'quickened *in* the spirit'—*by the Father* is understood in ζωοποιηθείς) He worked His great victory over death and Hell. See again 1 Pet. iii. 18, 19, and notes, and Rom. viii. 10, 11. The latter part of the verse in Ps. xxxi., '*for Thou hast redeemed me, O Lord, thou God of truth,*' is not applicable here. The whole Psalm is not strictly prophetic, but is applied by the Lord to Himself. **47—49.**] Our account, as well as that of Mark, ascribes the impression made on the centurion to that which took place at the death of Jesus, —i. e. ὅτι οὕτως ἐξέπνευσεν. Something in the manner and words convinced him that this man was the Son of God ; which expression he uses doubtless with reference to what he had before heard, but especially to the words just uttered— "*Father,* into Thy hands I commend my spirit." Luke has not expressed the words exactly the same,—but the E. V. has wrongly and ungrammatically rendered what he relates the centurion to have said, and made 'a righteous man' (Luke) stand in the place of 'the Son of God' (Mark) ; —whereas they only give the *general sense* of the persuasion of the centurion. **Truly, this man was innocent** :—and if innocent (nay, more, δίκαιος, **just, truthful**), *He was the Son of God, for He had asserted it.* **48.**] Peculiar to Luke. **τὰ γενόμενα** are the darkness and other prodigies, after which we have no more *raillery* :—men's tempers are changed, and we here see the result. **τύπτοντες** . . . . a sign of self-accusation, at least for the time,—which is renewed on the preaching of Peter, Acts ii. 37. **49.**] See on Matt. and Mark.

50—56.] Burial of the body of Jesus by Joseph of Arimathæa. Matt. xxvii. 57—61. Mark xv. 42—47. John xix. 38—42. See notes on Matt.

ἄρχων, ἀνὴρ ἀγαθὸς καὶ δίκαιος, 51 οὗτος οὐκ ἦν
[l] συγκατατεθειμένος τῇ [m] βουλῇ καὶ τῇ [n] πράξει [o] αὐτῶν,
ἀπὸ Ἀριμαθαίας πόλεως τῶν Ἰουδαίων, ὃς [p] προςεδέχετο
τὴν βασιλείαν τοῦ θεοῦ, 52 οὗτος προςελθὼν τῷ Πιλάτῳ
[q] ᾐτήσατο τὸ σῶμα τοῦ Ἰησοῦ· 53 καὶ [r] καθελὼν [s] ἐνετύλιξεν αὐτὸ [t] σινδόνι, καὶ ἔθηκεν αὐτὸν ἐν [u] μνήματι
[v] λαξευτῷ, οὗ [w] οὐκ [x] ἦν οὐδεὶς οὔπω κείμενος. 54 καὶ
ἡμέρα ἦν [y] παρασκευῆς, καὶ [z] σάββατον [a] ἐπέφωσκεν.
55 [b] κατακολουθήσασαι δὲ γυναῖκες, αἵτινες [c] ἦσαν [c] συν-
εληλυθυῖαι ἐκ τῆς Γαλιλαίας αὐτῷ, [d] ἐθεάσαντο τὸ μνημεῖον
καὶ ὡς ἐτέθη τὸ σῶμα αὐτοῦ, 56 [e] ὑποστρέψασαι δὲ ἡτοίμασαν [f] ἀρώματα καὶ [g] μύρα. καὶ τὸ μὲν σάββατον [h] ἡσύχα-

...ουκ ην R.
F -ριμαθαιας...
...και καθ F.
F σαββατον...
ABCDE FGHKL MPSUV ΧΓΔΛ Πא 1. 33. 69

l here only. = Exod. xxiii. 1. (-θεσις, 2 Cor. vi. 16.)
m = Acts xxvii. 12, 42. Gen. xlix. 6.
n Matt. xvi. 27 reff.
o indef. pron., John viii. 44 reff.
p = || Mk. ch. ii. 25, 38. Tit. ii. 13. Jude 21. Ps. liv. 8.
q = Matt. xxvii. 20 reff.
r || Mk. Acts xiii. 29. Josh. viii. 29.
s || Mt. John xx. 7 only +.
t Mark xiv. 51, 52 reff.
u Mark v. 3, 5 reff.
v here only. Deut. iv. 49 only. (-εύειν, Exod. xxxiv. 1, 4. -ευτήριον. Ps. lxxiii. 6.)
w Acts viii. 39 al.
x constr., Matt. xix. 22 reff.
y || Mt. reff.
z no art., John v. 9.
a Matt. xxviii. 1 only. Job xli. 9 (10) A (ἐπιφαυσκ. Bא) only.
b Acts xvi. 17 only. Jer. xvii. 16. 1 Macc. vi. 23 only.
c = Acts i. 21. ix. 39. x. 23. xxi. 16.
d Matt. vi. 1 al3. (Mark xvi. 11, 14 only.) ch. v. 27. vii. 24. John i. 14 al6. Acts i. 11 al2. Paul, Rom. xv. 24 only. 1 John i. 1 al2. 2 Chron. xxii. 6. 2 Macc. ii. 4. iii. 36 only.
e ver. 48.
f here (bis) & || Mk. John xix. 40 only. 4 Kings xx. 13.
g Matt. xxvi. 7 reff. Exod. xxx. 25.
h = here only. (ch. xiv. 4 reff.)

50. ins *και ο* bef 2nd *ανηρ* C; *και* LXא 33. om 2nd *ανηρ* DΓ lat-*a b e ff*$_2$ [*l*] *q*. om *και* (bef *δικαιος*) B sah.

51. *συνκατατιθεμενος* (for *-τεθειμενος*) CDLXΔא 1. 69: txt ABP rel.—(*συνκ.*, so AB[1]CDHLPΔא 33.) rec ins *και* bef *προσεδεχετο*, with A rel syr; *και αυτος* (|| *Matt Mark*) KMPUX[Π] arm: om BCDLא 1. 33. 69 vulg lat-*a b e f ff*$_2$ *l* coptt.—rec aft *προσεδεχετο* further ins *και αυτος*, with A rel vulg lat-*f ff*$_2$ syr æth: om BCDL Γא[KMPUXΠ] 69 lat-*a b e l* Syr syr-cu copt.

52. for *ουτος*, *και* D(above the line) æth.

53. rec aft *καθελων* ins *αυτο*, with AP rel lat-*o* syrr syr-cu [coptt arm]; *αυτον* U Scr's e lat-*q*: om BCDLא 33. 69 latt. for *αυτο*, *το σωμα του ιησου εν* D. rec (for *αυτον*) *αυτο* (*repetn of precedg*), with AP rel lat-*c*: om 1. 69 lat-*e* arm: txt B(sic: see table) CDא vulg lat-*a b f ff*$_2$ [*l q*]. for *μνηματι λαξευτω*, *μνημειω λελατομημενω* (|| *Mark*) D. rec (for *ουδεις ουπω*) *ουδεπω ουδεις* (|| *John*), with X rel syr-cu arm Orig-int$_1$: *ουδεποτε ουδεις* Λ: *ουδεις ουδεπω* CKMPU[Π]א 33. 69: *ουπω ουδεις* D Orig$_1$: txt ABL 1 syrr. add *και θεντος αυτου επεθηκεν τω μνημειω λιθον ον μογις εικοσι εκυλιον* D lat-*c* sah: *και προσεκυλισε λιθον μεγαν επι την θυραν του μνημειου* (|| *Matt Mark*) U copt æth-mss.

54. for ver, *ην δε η ημερα προσαββατου* D: so lat-*c*, adding *cenæ puræ*. rec (for *παρασκευης*) *παρασκευη*, with AC[2]P rel lat-*f ff*$_2$ Eus$_1$: txt BC[1]Lא vulg [lat-*a b e l q*]. om *και* (bef *σαββατον*) AC[2]P rel lat-*c* sah: ins BC[1]LΛא 1. 33. 69 latt Syr syr-cu syr-w-ob copt arm Eus$_1$.

55. *κατηκολουθησαν* D lat-*c ff*$_2$ syrr. rec ins *και* bef *γυναικες*; *αι* BLPX 1. 33. 69 [syrr] syr-cu coptt; *δυο* D lat-*a b e ff*$_2$ *q*: om ACא rel Eus$_2$. rec *αυτω* bef *εκ της γαλιλαιας*, with AC[2]P rel vss Eus$_3$: om *αυτω* C[1](appy) D lat-*c* æth: txt BLא Eus$_1$.—for *εκ*, *απο* D lat-*c f* Eus$_3$. ins *και* bef *εθεασαντο* D lat-*c* [Syr]. *το μνημα αυτου*, omg *και ως ετεθη το σωμα*, D.

56. om *δε* C[1] æth: *και υποστρ.* C[2] vulg lat-*b c e f ff*$_2$ Syr syr-cu Mcion$_2$-e.

51. οὗτος . . . .] Peculiar to Luke. The meaning is, he had absented himself, and taken no part in their (the council's) determination against Jesus.

53.] Notice the similarity of our *οὐκ ἦν οὐδεὶς οὔπω κείμενος* to St. John's *οὐδέπω οὐδεὶς ἐτέθη*. **54.**] **παρασκευή**—'the day before the sabbath,'—which now **ἐπέφωσκεν, drew on**;—a *natural* word, used of the *conventional* (Jewish) day beginning at sunset. There is no reference to the lighting of candles in the evening or on the sabbath. Lightfoot (in loc.) has shewn that such use of the word was common among the Jews, who called the evening (the beginning) of a day אוֹר, 'light.' **55.**] Only Mary Magdalene and Mary, the mother of Joses ('the other Mary,' Matt.),—Mark. **56.**] They bought their spices, &c. *in the short time before sunset*. The **μέν** before σάβ. answers to **δέ**, ch. xxiv. 1, which ought therefore to continue the sense, as I have punctuated it in the text.

σαν κατὰ τὴν [i] ἐντολήν, [XXIV.] 1 τῇ δὲ [k] μιᾷ τῶν
...βαθεος P. σαββάτων [l] ὄρθρου [m] βαθέως ἦλθον ἐπὶ τὸ [n] μνῆμα φέρου-
σαι ἃ ἡτοίμασαν [f] ἀρώματα. 2 εὗρον δὲ τὸν λίθον [o] ἀπο-
κεκυλισμένον ἀπὸ τοῦ [p] μνημείου. 3 εἰςελθοῦσαι δὲ οὐχ
...εγενετο F. εὗρον τὸ σῶμα τοῦ κυρίου Ἰησοῦ. 4 καὶ ἐγένετο [q] ἐν τῷ
[r] ἀπορεῖσθαι αὐτὰς περὶ τούτου, [s] καὶ ἰδοὺ ἄνδρες δύο
[t] ἐπέστησαν αὐταῖς ἐν [u] ἐσθῆτι [v] ἀστραπτούσῃ. 5 [w] ἐμφόβων
Fκλινουσων... δὲ γενομένων αὐτῶν καὶ [x] κλινουσῶν τὸ πρόσωπον εἰς τὴν

i Matt. xix. 17. 1 Tim. vi. 14. k = Acts xx. 7. 1 Cor. xvi. 2. Gen. i. 5. Ezra iii. 6. l [John viii. 2.] Acts v. 21 only. Esth. v. 14. (-ρινός, ver. 22.) m = here only. see note. n Mark v. 3, 5 reff. o || Mt. Mk. (bis v. r.) only. Gen. xxix. 3, 8, 10. Judith xiii. 9 only. p ch. xi. 44 reff. Isa. xxvi. 19. q Matt. xiii. 4. Ezek. ix. 8. r John xiii. 22 reff. s ch. viii. 1 al. Gen. xxiv. 30. t ch. ii. 9 reff. xx. 1. u ch. xxiii. 11 reff. (-ησις, Acts i. 10.) v ch. xvii. 24 (reff.) only. w ver. 37. Acts x. 4. xxii. 9. xxiv. 23. Rev. xi. 13 only †. Sir. xix. 24. 1 Macc. xiii. 2 B [εκφ. Aℵ] only. x John xix. 30. (Matt. viii 20 reff.)

om κατα την εντολην D.

CHAP. XXIV. 1. for τη δε μια, μια δε D. ορθου (sic) ACℵ. (rec βαθεος, with EKP (S, e sil) UV[Π² Dion₁ Eus$_{\rm alic}$]: txt ABCDℵ rel Eus₁.) επι το μνημα bef ηλθον B[-θαν B¹] L(ℵ) Dion₁ [Eus₂]: txt A(CD) rel vulg lat-*f* [*ff*₂] syrr syr-cu coptt [Eus₁] Tert₁.—for ηλθον, ηρχοντο D.—for μνημα, μνημειον (|| *Mark John*) C¹FX Δℵ Eus₂. om αρωματα D lat-*a b c e ff*₂ *l* syr-cu sah. rec at end adds και τινες συν αυταις (*harmonistic insn, cf Mark* xvi. 1, *and our ver* 10), with AC³D [rel] lat-*f q* (syrr syr-cu) æth-pl arm Eus₁: om BC¹Lℵ 33 latt copt æth-rom Dion₁ Eus₁ Aug.

2. for ευρ. δε, ελογιζοντο δε εν εαυταις τις αρα αποκυλισει τον λιθον ελθουσαι δε ευρον (*see* || *Mark*) D lat-*c* sah. for απο, εκ C¹H Eus₁.

3. rec (for εισελθ. δε) και εισελθ. (|| *Mark*), with AC³ rel vulg lat-*f q* syrr syr-cu æth arm: txt BC¹DLℵ 1. 33 lat-*a b c e ff*₂ *l* coptt Eus₂. om του κυριου ιησου D lat-*a b e ff*₂ *l* Eus₁: om του κυριου 42 lat-*f* Syr syr-cu. (*Tischdf* (ed 7) *followed* D &c, *but they do not carry weight enough alone to decide: besides* (1), το σωμα *is not used absolutely in Luke's narrative; and* (2), ο κυριος ιησους *is a very common expression with our Evangelist—see Acts* i. 21; iv. 33; vii. 59; viii. 16; xi. 20 *&c* [in ed 8 he reads as in txt].)

4. for και εγ., εγ. δε C copt-dz sah. rec διαπορεισθαι, with A rel [Eus₁], διαπορειν 1: txt BCDLℵ. for τουτου, αυτου D Eus₁. om και D vulg lat-*a c f ff*₂ syr-cu coptt. rec δυο bef ανδρες, with D lat-*b c e ff*₂ [*l q* vulg syr-jer] Syr syr-cu Eus₆: txt ABCℵ rel lat-*a f* syr coptt arm Eus₁. for επεστησαν, παρειστηκεισαν C¹. rec (for εσθητι αστραπτουση) εσθησεσιν αστραπτουσαις, with AC rel syr [syr-jer arm] coptt; εσθησεσιν λευκαις L: txt BDℵ latt Orig Eus₆.

5. for εμφοβων to κλινουσων, ενφοβοι δε γενομεναι εκλειναν D lat-*c*. for το προσωπον, τα προσωπα (*altern to suit the other plurals: cf* αυτων *of* C¹ &c) BC¹DGL X[Π]ℵ 1. 33 syrr syr-cu [syr-jer arm]: txt AC³ rel latt copt. (om το Δ.)—add αυτων C¹ D-lat coptt [arm].

CHAP. XXIV. 1—12.] THE WOMEN COMING TO THE SEPULCHRE LEARN THAT HE IS RISEN, AND ANNOUNCE IT TO THE APOSTLES, BUT ARE NOT BELIEVED. Matt. xxviii. 1—10. Mark xvi. 1—8. John xx. 1—10. See notes on Matt. 1.] **ὄρθρ. βαθ.**, **deep dawn**, i. e. just beginning to dawn (in Plato, Crito, § 1, we have *οὐ πρῲ ἔτι ἐστίν; πάνυ μὲν οὖν. πηνίκα μάλιστα; ὄρθρος βαθύς*) = *σκοτίας ἔτι οὔσης*, John, and *τῇ ἐπιφωσκ. εἰς μίαν σαβ.*, Matt., and *λίαν πρωΐ*, Mark; but not *ἀνατείλαντος τοῦ ἡλ.*, Mark also: see notes there. **βαθέως** may be an old form of the gen. as rendered above, or the adv. **ἦλθον**—the same women as those afterwards mentioned (ver. 10) who told the Apostles the intelligence. The reference is to *γυναῖκες αἵτινες*, &c. ch. xxiii. 55. **ἀρώματα**, which (ch. xxiii. 56) they had made ready before the sabbath; in Mark xvi. 1, had bought the evening before, *διαγεν. τοῦ σαβ.* 2.] This agrees with the more detailed account in Mark;—and, as regards the majority of the women, may also with that in Matt.:—but not as regards the two Maries.

4.] **ἐπέστ.** does not determine the *position* of the angels. It is merely **came upon them** under ordinary circumstances;—**appeared to them**, in a supernatural connexion: see reff. On the *two* angels here, see note on Mark ver. 5; to which I will just add, that the Harmonistic view, as represented by Greswell [Diss. vi., vol. 3], strangely enough puts together the angel in Matthew,

y = ch. xi. 7. xv. 29, 30. xxii. 37.
z constr., John viii. 54 reff.
a ch. ii. 20 reff. xxiii. 56.
b | Mt. (J. v. r.) Matt. viii. 33. Mark xvi. 10.
c see note.
d plur., Matt. vi. 28. John xix. 31. 1 Cor. x. 11. Rev. i. 19. iii. 2. Ps. cxliv. 10. Winer, edn. 6, § 58. 3. *a.*
e ch. i. 15 reff.
f = Matt. iii. 16. Acts ii. 3.
g here only †. (-ρώδης, 2 Macc. xii. 44,)
h ver. 41 reff.
i Mark vii. 24 reff.
k = Matt. xxi. 19. ch. xii. 5.

γῆν, εἶπαν πρὸς αὐτάς Τί ζητεῖτε τὸν ζῶντα [y] μετὰ τῶν
νεκρῶν; 6 οὐκ ἔστιν ὧδε, ἀλλὰ ἠγέρθη. μνήσθητε ὡς
ἐλάλησεν ὑμῖν ἔτι ὢν ἐν τῇ Γαλιλαίᾳ, 7 [z] λέγων τὸν [z] υἱὸν
τοῦ ἀνθρώπου [z] ὅτι δεῖ παραδοθῆναι εἰς χεῖρας ἀνθρώπων ...ανθρωπου C.
ἁμαρτωλῶν, καὶ σταυρωθῆναι, καὶ τῇ τρίτῃ ἡμέρᾳ ἀνα- ABDEF
στῆναι. 8 καὶ ἐμνήσθησαν τῶν ῥημάτων αὐτοῦ, 9 καὶ GHKL MSUVX
[a] ὑποστρέψασαι ἀπὸ τοῦ μνημείου [b] ἀπήγγειλαν ταῦτα ΓΔΛΠ ℵ
πάντα τοῖς ἕνδεκα καὶ πᾶσιν τοῖς λοιποῖς. 10 [ἦσαν δὲ] 1. 33. 69
ἡ Μαγδαληνὴ Μαρία καὶ Ἰωάννα καὶ Μαρία [ἡ] [c] Ἰακώβου καὶ αἱ λοιπαὶ σὺν αὐταῖς [αἳ] ἔλεγον πρὸς τοὺς
ἀποστόλους ταῦτα. 11 καὶ [d] ἐφάνησαν [e] ἐνώπιον αὐτῶν I_e -λους
[f] ὡσεὶ [g] λῆρος τὰ ῥήματα ταῦτα, καὶ [h] ἠπίστουν αὐταῖς. ταυτα...
12 ὁ δὲ Πέτρος [i] ἀναστὰς ἔδραμεν [k] ἐπὶ τὸ μνημεῖον, καὶ

ins οι δε bef ειπ. D lat-*c*. (ειπαν, so BCDLℵ $Mcion_2$-e.)

6. om ουκ to ηγερθη D lat-*a b e ff₂ l*. (αλλα, so BLXℵ 33 : om (|| *Matt*) C¹ lat-g_2 Syr.) aft μνησθητε ins δε D. for ως, οσα D lat-*c* ff_2 Syr syr-cu Mcion-e_2-t_1.

7. om λεγων D lat-*c* ff_2 æth. rec οτι δει bef τον υιον του ανθρωπου, with AC³Dℵ³ᵃ rel vss [$Mcion_2$-e] $Tert_1$: txt B C¹(appy) Lℵ¹ lat-*a* syr-cu. om αμαρτωλων D lat-*b e* ff_2 *l*.

9. om απο του μνημειου D lat-*a b c e* ff_2 *l* arm. παντα bef ταυτα Dℵ rel lat-*c* : om παντα syr-cu sah æth : txt ABGLM (S, e sil) **1. 33** [latt Cyr_1] Eus_1.

10. om ησαν δε AD [Γ(sic, Tischdf)] syr-cu copt[-wilk] æth : for ησαν, ην KU[Π] **1.** 69 vulg lat-*a b f* ff_2 *q* copt-[schw-]dz sah : txt Bℵ rel lat-*c* Syr syr-w-ast arm Eus_2. (μαριαμ (1st) ℵ **1.**) μαρια bef η μαγδαληνη D latt coptt. rec om 2nd η, with EFGH²LΛ copt : ins ABDℵ rel syr sah Eus. (*The insn may be from Matt* xxvii. 56 : *Mark* xvi. 1 : *without the art, it is more in Luke's manner, see ch* vi. 16 : *Acts* i. 13.) om 2nd αι ABDEFGHL[M]ΓΔℵ¹ lat-*b e* ff_2 *q* syr-cu [æth] : ins Xℵ³ᵃ rel vulg lat-*a c f* Syr syr-w-ast copt arm. for τους, αυτους D¹-gr.

11. rec (for ταυτα) αυτων, with AI_e rel lat-*f* syr arm : txt BDLℵ latt Syr syr-cu syr-mg [syr-jer] coptt (æth) Eus_1.

12. om ver D [fuld] lat-*a b e l* syr-jer(ins in marg) Eus-canon (*see note*).

and the angel in Mark, and makes the *two* angels in Luke : see Acts i. 10. **ἄνδρες**—to all appearance; the Evangelist does not mean that they *were* such, as clearly appears from what follows.

5.] τὸν ζῶντα, simply **the living,—Him who liveth**, as addressed to the women ; but Olshausen's view of a deeper meaning in the words (Bibl. Com. ii. 47) should be borne in mind ;—τὸ κυρίως ζῆν παρὰ μόνῳ κυρίῳ τυγχάνει, Orig. in Joan. tom. ii. 11, vol. iv. p. 71. **6, 7.]** See ch. ix. 22; xviii. 32. The mention of *Galilee* is remarkable, as occurring in the angelic speeches in Matt. and Mark in quite another connexion. Here it is said to the women, as *being from Galilee*, see ch. xxiii. 55—and meaning, 'when He was yet with you.' **9.]** See note on Mark ver. 8. **10.]** It seems as if the testimony of one of the disciples who went to Emmaus had been the ground of the whole former part—perhaps of the whole—of this chapter. We find consequently this account exactly agreeing with his report afterwards, ver. 23, 24. Joanna was the wife of Chuza, Herod's steward, ch. viii. 2. On Μαρία [ἡ] Ἰακώβου, and the questions connected with it, see Prolegg. to Vol. IV. ch. ii. § i. 4. It will be observed (see var. readd.) that the omission of the second αἵ (as in Lachm.), will make this verse mean : 'It was Mary, &c. ; also the rest with them told the Apostles these things.' **11.] ἐφάνησαν**, a plural, with **τὰ ῥήμ.**, is not without meaning. The ῥήματα were the (perhaps slightly differing) accounts of many persons. **12.]** This verse cannot well be interpolated from John xx., for the only reason for the insertion would be, to tally with ver. 24, and in that case it certainly *would not mention Peter alone*. That Cleopas says, ver. 24, **some of [them that were with] us went**, &c. must not be pressed too much, although it does

[l]παρακύψας βλέπει τὰ [m]ὀθόνια [κείμενα [n]μόνα], καὶ ἀπῆλθεν [o]πρὸς ἑαυτὸν θαυμάζων τὸ [p]γεγονός. 13 Καὶ ἰδοὺ
δύο ἐξ αὐτῶν [q]ἦσαν πορευόμενοι ἐν αὐτῇ τῇ ἡμέρᾳ εἰς
κώμην [r]ἀπέχουσαν [s]σταδίους ἑξήκοντα ἀπὸ Ἱερουσαλήμ,
ᾗ ὄνομα Ἐμμαούς, 14 καὶ αὐτοὶ [t]ὡμίλουν πρὸς ἀλλήλους
περὶ πάντων τῶν [u]συμβεβηκότων τούτων. 15 καὶ ἐγένετο [v]ἐν τῷ [t]ὁμιλεῖν αὐτοὺς καὶ [w]συνζητεῖν, [x]καὶ αὐτὸς

ℵ -χουσαν... P και αυτοι...

l John xx. 5, 11. James i. 25. 1 Pet. i. 12 only. Gen. xxvi. 8.
m John xix. 40. xx. 5, 6, 7 only. Judg. xiv. 13 B. Hos. ii. 5, 9 only.
n John xvi. 32. 2 Kings xviii. 24.
o = ‖ J. only. Num. xxiv. 25.
p Mark v. 14. ch. viii. 35, 56. Esth. iv. 4.
q Matt. xix. 22 reff.
r = Matt. xv. 8 reff. Ezek. xxii. 5.
s John vi. 19 reff.
t here bis. Acts xx. 11. xxiv. 26 only. Prov. xxiii. 30.
u Mark x. 32 reff.
v ver. 4.
w Mark ix. 10 reff.
x red., ch. viii. 1 al. Gen. xxiv. 30.

om κειμενα μονα $\aleph^1$: ins I_e rel : om κειμενα (*homœotel?*) $B\aleph^{3b}$ 243 syr-cu coptt Eus_1 : μονα bef κειμενα L vulg lat-*c* [ff_2 æth] arm : om μονα (*homœotel?*) AK[Π] 69 am(with harl mt). απηλθον (*John* xx. 10) A. for εαυτον, αυτον (*see* BL *in John*) BL : txt Aℵ rel Eus_1. (I_e def.)

13. for και to πορευομενοι, ησαν δε δυο πορευομενοι εξ αυτων D lat-*e*. aft ησαν ins δε (D) $\aleph^1$(om ℵ-$corr^1$(?)$^{\cdot 3}$). εν αυτη τη ημερα bef ησαν B(ℵ).—τη αυτη ημ. ℵ.—for ημερα, ωρα AG. ins εκατον bef εξηκοντα $I_eK^1N^1$[Π]ℵ fuld lat-g_1 syr-mg-ms syr-jer. for η ονομα εμμαους, ονοματι ουλαμμαους D.

14. for και αυτοι ωμ., ωμ. δε D lat-*c e* (sah). for αλληλους, εαυτους D : om Λ lat-*a b* ff_2 [*l*]. om των D^1(ins D^4).

15. (συνζητειν, so AB^1DGLNPΔℵ.) om 3rd και B^1 lat-*c e* syr-cu sah. (και is written over in B, possibly only *secunda manu:* see table.) for αυτος, αυτους B^1 [Tischdf ascribes και αυτος to his B^2] : om D lat-*a c e* syr-cu sah æth.

certainly look as if he knew of more than one (see note there). The similarity in diction to John xx. 5, 10 (παρακύψας βλέπει τὰ ὀθόνια κείμενα, and ἀπῆλθ. πρὸς ἑαυτ., being common to the two passages) indicates a common origin, and, if I mistake not, one distinct from the rest of the narrative in this chapter. The meaning of **πρὸς ἑαυτόν**, as belonging to ἀπῆλθεν and not to θαυμάζων, is fixed by the expression in John, l. c.

13—35.] Jesus appears to two of the disciples at Emmaus. *Peculiar to Luke:*—the incident (but from another source) is alluded to in the fragmentary addition to Mark xvi. (ver. 12). **13.] ἐξ αὐτῶν**, not of the *Apostles*—the last-mentioned were οἱ ἕνδεκα καὶ πάντες οἱ λοιποί, ver. 9: see also ver. 22, ἐξ ἡμῶν. One of them, ver. 18, was called Kleopas (= Κλεόπατρος, probably a different name from Κλωπᾶς, John xix. 25 (חלפי): see note on Matt. x. 3). Who the other was, is idle to conjecture. Origen, in several places, calls him Simon; apparently from having read λέγοντες in ver. 34, and referring ὤφθη τ. Σ. to the present appearance. Epiphanius says it was Nathanael; Theophylact, Luke himself. This may shew what such reports are worth. Wieseler (Chron. vol. i. p. 431) believes the two to have been, James the son of Alphæus or Clopas or Cleopas (but see above) journeying *with his father*, and the appearance on the road to Emmaus to be the same as ὤφθη Ἰακώβῳ, 1 Cor. xv. 7. Our narrative seems to have been from the report of Cleopas. **Ἐμμαούς]** Joseph., B. J. vii. 6. 6, mentions this Emmaus as sixty stades from Jerusalem. There were two other places of the same name: (1) a town afterwards called Nicopolis, twenty-two Roman miles from Jerusalem, where Judas Maccabæus defeated the Syrian general Gorgias: see 1 Macc. iii. 40—57. (2) Another Emmaus is mentioned Jos. B. J. iv. 1. 3, πρὸ τῆς Τιβεριάδος—where he adds, μεθερμηνευομένη δὲ Ἀμμαοῦς θερμὰ λέγοιτ' ἄν, ἔστι γὰρ ἐν αὐτῇ πηγὴ θερμῶν ὑδάτων πρὸς ἄκεσιν ἐπιτήδειος. This was the case also with the other places of the name. Our Emmaus is now called Cubeibi (?).

15.] καὶ ἐγέν. . . . . καὶ . . ., the ordinary construction. The last καί does not mean '*also*.' **αὐτὸς Ἰη.] Jesus Himself**, of whom they had been speaking. But this expression forbids the supposition that He was here, *strictly speaking*, ἐν ἑτέρᾳ μορφῇ, as we find it less precisely expressed in Mark xvi. 12. The reason why they did not know Him was (ver. 16), that *their eyes were supernaturally influenced, so that they could not:*—see also ver. 31. No change took place in *Him*—nor apparently in *them*, beyond a power upon them, which prevented the recognition just so much as to delay it till aroused by the well-known action and manner of His breaking the bread. The *cause* of this was the will of the Lord himself, who would not be seen by them till the time

Ἰησοῦς [y] ἐγγίσας [z] συνεπορεύετο αὐτοῖς· 16 οἱ δὲ ὀφθαλμοὶ αὐτῶν [a] ἐκρατοῦντο [b] τοῦ μὴ [c] ἐπιγνῶναι αὐτόν.
17 εἶπεν δὲ πρὸς αὐτοὺς [d] Τίνες οἱ λόγοι οὗτοι, οὓς [e] ἀντι-
βάλλετε πρὸς ἀλλήλους περιπατοῦντες[; καὶ ἐστάθησαν]
[f] σκυθρωποί[.]; 18 ἀποκριθεὶς δὲ εἷς ὀνόματι Κλεόπας,
εἶπεν πρὸς αὐτὸν Σὺ [g] μόνος [h] παροικεῖς Ἱερουσαλὴμ καὶ
οὐκ ἔγνως τὰ γενόμενα ἐν αὐτῇ ἐν ταῖς ἡμέραις ταύταις;
19 καὶ εἶπεν αὐτοῖς Ποῖα; οἱ δὲ εἶπον αὐτῷ [i] Τὰ περὶ
Ἰησοῦ τοῦ Ναζαρηνοῦ, ὃς ἐγένετο [k] ἀνὴρ προφήτης [l] δυνατὸς ἐν [l] ἔργῳ καὶ [l] λόγῳ [m] ἐναντίον τοῦ θεοῦ καὶ παντὸς
τοῦ λαοῦ, 20 ὅπως τε [n] παρέδωκαν αὐτὸν οἱ ἀρχιερεῖς καὶ

ABDEF GHI$_e$K LMNPS UVXΓΔ ΛΠℵ 1. 33. 69

...οι F. ...θεου I$_e$

y ch. xii. 33 reff. z ch. vii. 11. xiv. 25. Mark x. 1 only. Exod. xxiii. 15. Judg. xi. 8 A. a = here only. b ch. iv. 42. Acts x. 47. xiv. 18. Rom. vi. 6 al. Gen. xx. 6. c = Matt. xiv. 35 reff. d = Mark vi. 2. ch. viii. 9 reff. e here only †. 2 Macc. xi. 13 only. f Matt. vi. 16 only. Gen. xl. 7. Sir. xxv. 23 only. Dan. i. 10 Theod. g = 1 Cor. xiv. 36. Col. iv. 11. 2 Tim. iv. 11. h Heb. xi. 9 only. Gen. xii. 10. xvii. 8. Exod. vi. 4. i ch. xxii. 37. Acts xxiv. 10. Phil. i. 27. ii. 19, 20 al. k Acts iii. 14. Judg. vi. 8. l Acts vii. 22. m Mark ii. 12 reff. n ch. xii. 58 reff.

rec ins *ο* bef *ιησ.*, with DNP rel: om ABLℵ. (I$_e$ def.) at end ℵ[1] adds *ιν* (sic, but marked for erasure).

17. for *ειπεν δε*, *ο δε ειπεν* D lat-*c e* Orig$_1$. om *προς αυτους* D. for *αλληλους*, *εαυτους vos* D. rec (aft *περιπ.*) *και εστε*, with A I$_e$[appy] NP rel; *κ. εστησαν* L; *και εσταθησαν* Bℵ: om D Cyr$_1$.—(*και εσται* (= *και εστε*), followed by an erasure of five letters, A[1].)

18. rec ins *ὁ* bef *εις*, with A rel: om BDE[1]LNPΛℵ 1. 69 [arm]. (I$_e$ def.)—*τις* X. add *εξ αυτων* I$_e$P 33. 69 gat lat-*a b f ff$_2$ l* [D-lat] syrr syr-cu syr-jer copt-wilk sah æth arm Cyr$_1$. rec (for *ονοματι*) *ω ονομα*, with ADP rel [latt]: txt BLNXℵ lat-*b*. (I$_e$ def.) *μονοις* (*ι* over the line) D-gr. rec ins *εν* bef *ιερουσαλημ*, with Λ 69 latt Orig$_1$ Sevrn$_1$ Hil$_1$: om AB D-gr I$_e$NPℵ rel Cyr$_1$ Thl. om *και* D lat-*a b c e ff$_2$* [*l*] Syr syr-cu. ins *ταυτα* bef *ουκ* ℵ.

19. for *και ειπεν αυτοις*, *ο δε ειπεν αυτω* D. om *οι δε ειπον αυτω* D.—*ειπαν* BI$_e$ℵ 33. rec *ναζωραιου*, with ADNP rel Orig$_1$[-ed Huet]: txt BI$_e$Lℵ Orig$_1$[ed Delarue]. transp *εργω* and *λογω* Dℵ Syr æth. ins *εν* bef *λογω* A lat-*c*. for *εναντιον*, *ενωπιον* D lat-*c e l* Aug$_1$.

20. for *οπως τε*, *ως* D lat-*a b c e f* [*l*] copt [Aug$_1$(txt$_1$)]. *αυτον* bef *παρεδωκαν* AKP[Π] 1. 69 latt; *τουτον παρ.* D.

when He saw fit. **ἐγγίσας**—from *behind:* see ver. 18, where they take Him for an inhabitant of Jerusalem. **17.**] He had apparently been walking with them some little time before this was said. **ἀντιβάλλειν λόγους** implies to dispute with some earnestness: but there is no *blame* implied in the words. Possibly, though both were sad, they may have taken *different views:*—and in the answer of Cleopas we have that of the one who was most disposed to abandon all hope.

18. μόνος παρ.] They took Him (but we must not think of a *peculiar dialect* as giving that impression) for one who had been at Jerusalem at the feast:—and asked, **Dost thou lodge alone at Jerusalem?** **παροικ.** (with or without *ἐν*, see reff.) in the LXX is **to sojourn in**—not to *dwell in.* **19–24.**] Stier well remarks, that the Lord here gives us an instructive example how far, in the wisdom of love, we may carry *dissimulation, without speaking untruth.* (See the citation from Jer. Taylor below, on ver. 29.) He does not assert, that he was one of the strangers at this feast at Jerusalem, nor does He deny that he knew what had been done there in those days, but He puts the question by, with **What things?** **οἱ δὲ εἶπ.**] Either, one spoke and the other assented; or perhaps each spoke, sometimes one and sometimes the other;—only we must not break up these verses and allot an imagined portion to each. They contain the substance of what was said, as the reporter of the incident afterwards put it together. **ὃς ἐγ. ἀν. πρ. κ.τ.λ.**] See a similar general description of Him to the Jewish people, Acts ii. 22. They had repeatedly acknowledged Him as a Prophet: see especially Matt. xxi. 11, 46. The phrase **δυν. ἐν λόγοις κ. ἔργοις** occurs of Moses, ref. Acts. **ἐγένετο, was,** not *became* (or *was becoming*), as Meyer renders it. They speak of the whole life of Jesus as a thing past. **20.**] **ὅπως** depends on **οὐκ ἔγνως,**

οἱ ἄρχοντες ἡμῶν εἰς [o] κρῖμα θανάτου καὶ ἐσταύρωσαν
αὐτόν. 21 ἡμεῖς δὲ ἠλπίζομεν ὅτι αὐτός ἐστιν ὁ μέλλων
[p] λυτροῦσθαι τὸν Ἰσραήλ. ἀλλά γε καὶ [q] σὺν πᾶσιν τούτοις τρίτην ταύτην ἡμέραν [r] ἄγει [σήμερον] [s] ἀφ' οὗ
ταῦτα ἐγένετο. 22 [t] ἀλλὰ καὶ γυναῖκές τινες ἐξ ἡμῶν
[v] ἐξέστησαν ἡμᾶς, [w] γενόμεναι [x] ὀρθριναὶ [y] ἐπὶ τὸ μνημεῖον,
23 καὶ μὴ εὑροῦσαι τὸ σῶμα αὐτοῦ ἦλθον λέγουσαι καὶ
[z] ὀπτασίαν ἀγγέλων ἑωρακέναι, οἳ λέγουσιν αὐτὸν ζῆν.
24 καὶ [a] ἀπῆλθόν τινες τῶν σὺν ἡμῖν ἐπὶ τὸ μνημεῖον, καὶ
εὗρον οὕτως [b] καθὼς αἱ γυναῖκες εἶπον, αὐτὸν δὲ οὐκ
εἶδον. 25 καὶ αὐτὸς εἶπεν πρὸς αὐτοὺς Ὦ [c] ἀνόητοι καὶ
[d] βραδεῖς τῇ καρδίᾳ [e] τοῦ πιστεύειν [f] ἐπὶ πᾶσιν οἷς ἐλάλησαν οἱ προφῆται. 26 οὐχὶ ταῦτα [g] ἔδει παθεῖν τὸν χρι-

...τριτην ταυτην Ν.

o ch. xx. 47 ‖ Mk. xxiii. 10. Deut. xxi. 22.
p Tit. ii. 14. 1 Pet. i. 18 only. Exod. vi. 6. Ps. cvi. 2. cxxix. 8. Isa. xli. 4. Jer. xxxviii. (xxxi.) 11. (-τρωσις, ch. i. 68.)
q = here only. Neh. v. 18. 3 Macc. i. 22.
r = [Matt. xiv. 6 v. r.] Acts xix. 38 only. 2 Macc. ii. 16.
s ch. xiii. 7 reff.
t Matt. xxi. 21. John v. 18.
v tr., Acts viii. 9 only. (Matt. xii. 23 reff.) Job xii. 17.
w = Matt. xxvi. 6. ch. xxii. 40.
x here only. (-ρος, ver. 1. -ριος, Job xxix. 7. -ρίζειν, ch. xxi. 38.)
y ch. xxiii. 48.
z ch. i. 22 reff.
a = Matt. xiv. 25 reff.
b ch. vi. 31 al. fr. Eccl. v. 14.
c here only in Gospp. elsw. Paul (Rom. i. 14. Gal. iii. 1, 3. 1 Tim. vi. 9. Tit. iii. 3) only. Prov. xvii. 28.
d James i. 19 bis only †. see Exod. iv. 10.
e constr., Acts xxiii. 15. 1 Cor. xvi. 4.
f constr., Rom. iv. 18. Num. xiv. 11. w. pers., Rom. ix. 33 (from Isa. xxviii. 16 Aℵ) al.
g = Matt. xxiv. 6 reff.

21. *ελπιζομεν* ΡΔΛ[Π]ℵ 69: *ηλπιζωμεν* X: *ηλπιζαμεν* B[1] (sic: see table). for *εστιν*, *ην* D lat-*c e* Aug Ambrst. rec om *και*, with ANP rel vss: ins BDLΔℵ 1. 33 syr-mg arm. om *ταυτην* D 42 Scr's g latt syr [Aug_2]. om *αγει* ℵ[1]. om *σημερον* BD[11][L]ℵ 1 Syr syr-cu copt arm: *σημεραν* (sic) bef *αγει* D[1]. for *εγενετο*, *γεγονεν* D.

22. om *εξ ημων* D æth. *γεναμεναι* B Scr's f. rec for (*ορθριναι*) *ορθριαι*, with P rel: txt ABDK[1]LΔ[Π]ℵ 1.

23. *ηλθαν* B. om 2nd *και* D lat-*c e* Syr syr-cu coptt æth.

24. ins *εκ* bef *των* D latt syrr syr-cu [arm Aug_1]. for *καθως*, *ως* D. rec ins *και* bef *αἱ*, with APℵ rel syr copt: om BD latt Syr syr-cu [syr-jer] sah æth arm. *ειπον* bef *αι γυναικες* D lat-*c e* Syr syr-cu [syr-jer]. *ειδομεν* D lat-*e*.

25. for *και αυτος*, *ο δε* D lat-*c e*. for *αυτους*, *εαυτους* A. om *του πιστευειν* D.

26. for *ουχι*, *οτι* D $Dial_1$.

ver. 18. **ἡμῶν**] Therefore the two disciples were *Jews*, not Hellenists, as some have supposed. That "they say **our**, not as excluding, but as including the stranger," as alleged in some former Editions, is not a safe view from the evidently exclusive use of *ἡμεῖς* in the next verse. **παρέδωκαν**, to Pilate. **21.**] **ἠλπ.** is a word of weakened trust, and shrinking from the avowal that they 'believed' this. **λυτροῦσθαι**—in the theocratic sense—including both the spiritual and political kingdom: see ch. i. 68, 69, 74, 75, and compare Acts i. 6. **σὺν π. τ.**, rightly rendered in E. V. **beside all this**: see reff. **ἄγει**, not *impersonal* (as al. and recently Wordsw.), nor to be supplied with a nom. case *θεός* or *ὁ ἥλιος*, &c., but spoken of *Jesus*. **He is now in the third day, since** &c. This is the usage of later Greek:—and the words are spoken not without a reference, in the mind of the speaker, to His promise of rising on the third day. **22.**] **ἀλλὰ καί**, **but, moreover**—equivalent to 'certainly, thus much has happened, that' . . . . **ὀρθριναί** is the later form, for which the Attic *ὄρθριαι* has been substituted: see var. readd. **ἐξ ἡμῶν**—'disciples, as we are.' The *Apostles* are distinguished presently as *οἱ σὺν ἡμῖν*, ver. 24. **23.**] This agrees exactly with Luke's own narrative, but not with Matthew's, in which they had seen *the Lord Himself*. There seems however to be some hint that the *women* had made some such report in the *αὐτὸν δὲ οὐκ εἶδον* said below of the *τινὲς τῶν σὺν ἡμῖν*. **24. ἀπῆλθόν τινες**] See ver. 12 and note. It is natural, even in accordance with ver. 12, that the antithesis to *τινές* before, and the loose way of speaking to a stranger, who (they believed) was not acquainted with any among them, might cause them here to use *τινές*, without any reference to Peter being *accompanied*. But what wonder, if the reports of such a day of anxiety and confusion were themselves disjointed and confused? **25.**] **ἀνόητοι**, **without under-**

h Matt. xx. 8 reff. i ch. xvi. 29, 31. k Acts ix. 36. 1 Cor. xii. 30. xiv. 5, 13, 27 only L.P.† 2 Macc. i. 36 only. (-νευτής, 1 Cor. xiv. 28.) l = John v. 39 reff. m ch. xxii. 37 reff. n = ch. xix. 29 || Mt. Mk. Ps. xxvi. 2. o ch. x. 1 reff.

ABDEG HKLM PSUVX ΓΔΛΠℵ 1. 33. 69

στὸν καὶ εἰςελθεῖν εἰς τὴν δόξαν αὐτοῦ; 27 καὶ [h] ἀρξάμενος
ἀπὸ [i] Μωυσέως καὶ ἀπὸ πάντων τῶν [i] προφητῶν [k] διερμή-
νευσεν αὐτοῖς ἐν πάσαις ταῖς [l] γραφαῖς [m] τὰ περὶ ἑαυτοῦ.
28 καὶ [n] ἤγγισαν εἰς τὴν κώμην [o] οὗ ἐπορεύοντο, καὶ αὐτὸς
[p] προσεποιήσατο [q] πορρώτερον πορεύεσθαι, 29 καὶ [r] παρ-
εβιάσαντο αὐτὸν λέγοντες Μεῖνον μεθ' ἡμῶν, ὅτι [s] πρὸς
[t] ἑσπέραν ἐστὶν καὶ [u] κέκλικεν ἤδη ἡ ἡμέρα. καὶ εἰςῆλθεν
[v] τοῦ μεῖναι σὺν αὐτοῖς. 30 καὶ ἐγένετο [w] ἐν τῷ [x] κατα-

so ἐκεῖ, Matt. ii. 22 al. Gen. xx. 13. p here [John viii. 6 v. r.] only. = 1 Kings xxi. 13 (Job xix. 14. Sir. xxxiv. [xxxi.] 30) only. q Matt. xv. 8 reff. compar., here only †. r Acts xvi. 15 only. Gen. xix. 9. s = here only. Num. ix. 3. t Acts iv. 3. xxviii. 23 only. Gen. i. 5, &c. u = ch. ix. 12 only. Judg. xix. 11 A Ald. compl. Jer. vi. 4. (Matt. viii. 20 reff.) v Matt. iii. 13 reff. w Matt. xiii. 4 al. Ezek. ix. 8. x ch. vii. 36. ix. 14. xiv. 8 only 1 Kings xvi. 11. Judith xii. 15.

27. ins *ην* bef *αρξαμενος* D gat(with mm) lat-*a b c e* ff_2 g_2 Aug_1. om 2nd *απο* D latt. rec (for *διερμηνευσεν*) *διηρμηνευεν*, with EHK (SV, e sil) [Π]: *διερμηνευεν* A rel: txt BLUℵ[3a].—*ερμηνευειν* D: *και διερμηνευειν* ℵ[1]. aft *αυτοις* ins *τι ην* Lℵ 1. 33. om *πασαις* Dℵ lat-g_1 copt-ms. elz (for *εαυτ.*) *αυτου*, with DELMVX 1. 33. 69: txt A B(sic: see table) ℵ rel.

28. *ηγγικαν* B. rec *προσεποιειτο*, with P rel lat-*a* syrr: txt ABDLℵ 1 vulg lat-*b c e f* ff_2 g_1 [syr-cu syr-jer]. rec *πορρωτερω*, with DLP ℵ(-*τερωτερω* ℵ[1]) rel: txt AB.

29. *παρεβιαζοντο* MP. om *εστιν* D forj(with mm tol) lat-*a b c e* ff_2 *l* Syr. rec om *ηδη*, with ADP rel gat[1] lat-*c* [*l*] syr-cu sah æth arm: ins BLℵ 1. 33 latt Syr syr-w-ob copt. om *του* (bef *μειναι*), and for *συν αυτοις*, *μετ αυτων* D.

standing;—βρ. τ. κ. sluggish—in disposition—**to believe**: these were both shewn in their not having apprehended, from the fulfilment of the sufferings and death of Christ, the sequel of that death, the resurrection. **26. παθεῖν καὶ εἰςελθ.**] The sufferings were the appointed way by which Christ should enter into His glory. *παθεῖν καὶ εἰςελθ.* = *παθόντα εἰςελθ.* It was not the *entering into His glory*, but the *suffering*, about which they wanted persuading. **27.**] **ἀρξάμ.** belongs to *both* the following clauses, and cannot, as Stier would take it, stand by itself, leaving **ἀπό** in both clauses to be construed with **διερμ.** A similar expression is found Acts iii. 24. He began with Moses first;—He began with each as He came to them. **τὰ π. ἑαυτοῦ**] De Wette remarks, "It were much to be wished that we knew what prophecies of the death and triumph of Jesus are here meant. There are but few that point to the subject." But I take the **τὰ περὶ ἑαυτοῦ** to mean something very different from mere *prophetical passages.* The *whole Scriptures* are a *testimony to Him*: the whole history of the chosen people, with its types, and its law, and its prophecies, is a *shewing forth of Him*: and it was here the *whole,*—**πᾶσαι αἱ γρ.**,—that He laid out before them. This general leading into the meaning of the whole, *as a whole*, fulfilled in Him, would be much more opportune to the place, and the time occupied, than a direct exposition of selected passages. **The** *things* **concerning Himself** (E. V.) is right: not, 'the *parts* concerning Himself.' Observe the testimony which this verse gives to the divine authority, and the Christian interpretation, of the O. T. Scriptures: so that the denial of the references to Christ's death and glory in the O. T. is henceforth *nothing less than a denial of His own teaching.* **29.**] **παρεβ., they constrained Him.** It is not implied that He *said* any thing to indicate that He would go further—but simply, that He was passing on. "Our blessed Saviour pretended that He would pass forth beyond Emmaus: but if he intended not to do it, yet He did no injury to the two disciples, for whose good it was that He intended to make this offer: and neither did He prevaricate the strictness of simplicity and sincerity, because they were persons with whom He had made no contracts; to whom He had passed no obligation; and in the nature of the thing, it is proper and natural, by an offer, to give an occasion to another to do a good action: and in case it succeeds not, then to do what we intended not; and so the offer was conditional." Jer. Taylor, Sermon on Christian Simplicity. Works (Heber), vi. 156. **μεθ' ἡμῶν** does not imply that they lived at Emmaus; merely **in the same quarters with us.** **30.**] I believe that there was something in the manner of His breaking the bread, and helping and

κλιθῆναι αὐτὸν μετ᾽ αὐτῶν, λαβὼν τὸν ἄρτον [y] εὐλόγησεν
καὶ [z] κλάσας [a] ἐπεδίδου αὐτοῖς· 31 αὐτῶν δὲ [b] διηνοίχθησαν
οἱ ὀφθαλμοί, καὶ [c] ἐπέγνωσαν αὐτόν· καὶ αὐτὸς [d] ἄφαντος
ἐγένετο ἀπ᾽ αὐτῶν. 32 καὶ εἶπαν πρὸς ἀλλήλους Οὐχὶ
ἡ καρδία ἡμῶν [e] καιομένη ἦν [ἐν ἡμῖν] ὡς ἐλάλει ἡμῖν
ἐν τῇ ὁδῷ, ὡς [f] διήνοιγεν ἡμῖν τὰς [g] γραφάς; 33 καὶ
[h] ἀναστάντες αὐτῇ τῇ ὥρᾳ [i] ὑπέστρεψαν εἰς Ἱερουσαλήμ,
καὶ εὗρον [k] ἠθροισμένους τοὺς ἕνδεκα καὶ τοὺς σὺν αὐτοῖς,
34 λέγοντας ὅτι [l] ὄντως ἠγέρθη ὁ κύριος καὶ [m] ὤφθη Σίμωνι.

y Matt. xiv. 19. 1 Cor. xiv. 16. 1 Kings ix. 13.
z Matt. xiv. 19 al. Jer. xvi. 7.
a Matt. vii. 9, 10 reff.
b ch. i. 23, from Exod. xiii. 2. vv. 32, 45. Acts vii. 56. xvi. 14. xvii. 3. Luke only, exc. Mark vii. 34, 35. 4 Kings vi. 17.
c ver. 16.
d here only +.
e = here only. see Ps. xxxviii. 3.
f vv. 31, 45.
g ver. 27.
h Mark vii. 24 reff.
i ch. ii. 20 reff.
k here only. 1 Kings vii. 5. Num. xx. 2 B. (συνηθρ. A. συν., Acts xii. 12. xix. 25 only. Deut. i. 41.)
l ch. xxiii. 47 reff.
m ch. xxii. 43. Matt. xvii. 3 al. Exod. iii. 2.

30. om *μετ αυτων* D lat-*e* syr-cu. ins *και* bef *λαβων* ℵ. om *τον* D 131(Sz) Eus$_1$. om *κλασας* D. **προσ**εδιδου D : εδιδου ℵ.

31. for 1st clause, *λαβοντων δε αυτων τον αρτον απ᾽ αυτου ηνυγησαν οι οφθ. αυτ.* D lat-*c e* (Orig$_1$). *διηνυγησαν* (= -*νοιγ*-) ℵ[1]. om *και επεγνωσαν αυτον* (*passing from* και *to* και) ℵ[1] (ins ℵ-corr[1.3]).

32. for *και*, *οι δε* D lat-*c e*. (*ειπαν*, so BLℵ 33.) for *αλληλους*, *εαυτους* D. for *ημων καιομενη ην*, *ην ημων κεκαλυμμενη* D lat-*c l*. om *εν ημιν* BD tol[1] lat-*c e* syr-cu Orig$_3$: ins APℵ rel vss Orig$_{sæpe}$. for *ελαλει*, *ελαλησεν* A. rec ins *και* bef 2nd *ως*, with AP rel vulg lat-*f ff*$_2$ syrr [Orig$_3$] : om BDLℵ 33 lat-*a b c e* syr-cu coptt. for *διηνοιγεν*, *ηνυγεν* D.

33. aft *αναστ.* ins *λυπουμενοι* D lat-*c e* sah. rec **συνηθροισμενους**, with AP rel Cyr$_1$: txt BDℵ 33 Eus$_1$.

34. *λεγοντες* D. rec *ηγερθη ο κυριος* bef *οντως*, with A rel vulg syr : txt BDLPℵ 1 lat-*a c f* Syr syr-cu [syr-jer copt] æth arm [Eus$_1$ Chr$_1$]. ins *τω* bef *σιμωνι* ℵ.

giving it to them, which was his own appointed means of opening their eyes to the recognition of Him. But we must not suppose any reference to, much less any celebration of, the Sacrament of the Lord's Supper. *Neither of these disciples was present at its institution* (but see Wieseler's conjecture, which is at all events worth consideration, in note on ver. 13); and certainly it had never been celebrated since. With this simple consideration will fall to the ground all that Romanists have built on this incident, even to making it a defence of administration in one kind only. See Wordsw., who gives, in reply, a solution as artificial and unwarranted as the argument of the R. Catholics: shewing the danger of departing from the plain sense of Holy Scripture in search of fanciful allusions. The analogy of such a breaking and giving with His institution of that holy ordinance becomes lost, when we force the incident into an example of the ordinance itself. The Lord at their meal takes on Him the office of the *master of the house* (which alone would shew that it was not *their house*, but an inn), perhaps on account of the superior place which His discourse had won for Him in their estimation:—and as the Jewish rule was, that "three eating together were bound to give thanks" (Berac. 45. 1, cited by Meyer), He fulfils this duty. In doing so, perhaps the well-known manner of His taking bread, &c., perhaps the marks of the nails in His hands, then first noticed, or these together, as *secondary* means,—but certainly *His own will and permission to be seen by them*, opened their eyes to know Him.

31.] **ἄφαντος**, not *αὐτοῖς*, which would imply His Body to have remained, but *invisible to them*: but *ἀπ᾽ αὐτῶν*, implying, besides the supernatural disappearance, a real objective *removal from them*.

32.] 'Was there not something heart-kindling in His discourse by the way, which would have led us to suppose that it was none but the Lord Himself?' not that they *did* suppose it,—but the words are a sort of self-reproach for not having done so. Compare Matt. vii. 29. **ἐλάλει ἡμῖν**, as Bengel remarks, is more than *συνελάλει ἡμ.*:—**He spoke to us**, not merely, '*with us*,' as E. V.

33.] 'Jam non timent iter nocturnum, quod antea dissuaserant ignoto comiti.' Bengel. The *whole eleven* were not there—Thomas was not present, if at least the appearance which follows be the same as that in John xx. 19, which there seems no reason to doubt. Some have derived an argument from this incompleteness in their number, for the

35 καὶ αὐτοὶ [n] ἐξηγοῦντο τὰ ἐν τῇ ὁδῷ, καὶ ὡς ἐγνώσθη
[o] αὐτοῖς ἐν τῇ [p] κλάσει τοῦ ἄρτου.
36 Ταῦτα δὲ αὐτῶν λαλούντων αὐτὸς ἔστη ἐν μέσῳ
αὐτῶν, καὶ λέγει αὐτοῖς [q] Εἰρήνη ὑμῖν. 37 [r] πτοηθέντες
δὲ καὶ [s] ἔμφοβοι γενόμενοι ἐδόκουν [t] πνεῦμα [u] θεωρεῖν.
38 καὶ εἶπεν αὐτοῖς Τί [v] τεταραγμένοι ἐστέ, καὶ διὰ τί
[w] διαλογισμοὶ [x] ἀναβαινουσιν ἐν τῇ καρδίᾳ ὑμῶν; 39 ἴδετε
τὰς χεῖράς μου καὶ τοὺς πόδας μου, ὅτι ἐγώ εἰμι αὐτός.

...θεωρειν P. ABDE GHKL MSUVX ΓΔΛΠ ℵ 1. 33. 69

n John i. 18 reff. Judg. vii. 13. o dat., 2 Cor. xii. 20. p Acts ii. 42 only +. q ch. x. 5. John xx. 19, 21, 26. r ch. xxi. 9 only. Deut. xxxi. 6. (-ησις, 1 Pet. iii. 6.) s ver. 5 reff. t = John iv. 24 reff. u ch. xxiii. 48 reff. v Matt. ii. 3. Mark vi. 50. John xii. 27. xiii. 21 al. Esth. vii. 6. w Matt. xv. 19 al. = ch. ix. 46. Phil. ii. 14. 1 Tim. ii. 8. Sir. ix. 15. x = Acts vii. 23. Isa. lxv. 16.

35. for ωs, οτι D lat-*c e*.

36. rec aft αυτος ins ο ιησους (*beg of eccl lection*), with A rel am syrr copt arm; aft εστη P vulg-ed lat-*ff*$_2$; ο κυριος H lat-*c*: om BDLℵ lat-*a b e* syr-cu sah Ambr. for εστη, εσταθη D. om και to υμιν D lat-*a b e ff*$_2$ *l*. (Possibly *from* || *John: but as the whole is nearly related to that narrative, and the authority for the omn weak, Tischdf* (ed 7 [and 8]) *is certainly not justified in expunging it.*) at end add (*from* || *John*) εγω ειμι μη φοβεισθε GP vulg lat-*c f g*$_{1.2}$ syrr [syr-jer] copt[-wilk] æth arm Ambr Aug.

37. for πτοηθ. δε, αυτοι δε πτοηθεντες D.—for πτοηθεντες, θροηθεντες B: φοβηθεντες ℵ. for πνευμα, φαντασμα D Mcion$_1$-t.

38. for 1st και, ο δε D lat-*c e*. for δια τι, τι (*mechanl repetn*) BΛ² Mcion$_1$-t: ινατι DL Dial$_1$. rec (for τη καρδια) ταις καρδιαις, with Aℵ rel vulg lat-*f* syrr syr-cu [syr-jer] copt [Cyr$_1$] Tert$_1$ Hil [Aug$_1$]: txt BD gat(with mm) lat-*a b c e ff*$_2$ *l* sah æth.

39. transp τας χ. and τους π. ℵ. rec αυτος bef εγω ειμι, with A rel am[with fuld ing tol] syr Eus$_1$ Thdrt$_2$ Hil: αυτος bef ειμι D vulg lat-*c e ff*$_2$ [arm Tert$_1$]: txt BLℵ 33 lat-*a b f i* Dial$_1$ [Ath$_1$ Cyr$_1$] Ambr$_1$.

second of the travellers being also an Apostle: see above on ver. 13. Who these οἱ σὺν αὐτοῖς are, we learn from Acts i. 14. **34.**] This *appearance to Simon* (i. e. Peter—the other Simon would not be thus named without explanation: see ch. v. 3 ff.) is only hinted at here,—but is asserted again, 1 Cor. xv. 5, in immediate connexion with that which here follows. It is not clear whether it took place before or after that on the way to Emmaus. **35.**] **And they**—the travellers, distinguished from the others—not '*they also*,' for thus we should leave the clause without a copula. **ἐν τῇ κλ.**] We can hardly after **ἐγνώσθη** exclude that sense of **in**, which gives that which follows a share in the instrumentality: being the element, in and by means of which. The example cited by De Wette, ἐν τῇ ἀναστάσει, Matt. xxii. 28, for the sense, '*during* the breaking,' &c. does not apply, inasmuch as in that case there is no verb: John xiii. 35 is far more to the point, and almost decides for the other sense. That this should have been so, does not exclude the supernatural opening of their eyes: see above, on ver. 31.

36—49.] Appearance of Jesus to the disciples. Mark xvi. 14. John xx. 19—23. The identity of these appearances need hardly be insisted on. On Mark's narrative, see notes there. That of John presents no difficulties, on one supposition,—*that he had not seen* this of Luke. The particulars related by him are mostly additional, but not altogether so. **36.**] **ἔστη ἐν μέσῳ**—while they were speaking of these things,—possibly not entirely crediting the account, as seems hinted at in Mark xvi. 13,—the Lord appeared, the doors being shut, in the midst (John xx. 19 and notes). **εἰρ. ὑμ.**, the ordinary Jewish salutation, שָׁלוֹם לָכֶם, see ch. x. 5, but of more than ordinary meaning in the mouth of the Lord: see John xiv. 27. **37.**] On account of His sudden appearance, and the likeness to one whom they knew to have been dead. **πνεῦμα** is a *ghost* or *spectre*—an appearance of the dead to the living; not exactly as φάντασμα, Matt. xiv. 26, which might have been *any* appearance of a supernatural kind. **38.**] **διαλογ.**, not merely '*thoughts*,' as E. V., but **questionings**. **39.**] There seems to be some doubt whether the reference to His hands and feet was on account of the *marks of the nails*, to prove His *identity*,—or as being the *uncovered parts* of His body, and to prove His *corporeity*. Both views seem supported by the text, and I think both were united. The sight of the Hands and Feet, which they recognized as His, might at once con-

N πνευ-μα... [y] ψηλαφήσατέ με καὶ ἴδετε, ὅτι [t] πνεῦμα σάρκα καὶ [z] ὀστέα
οὐκ ἔχει [a] καθὼς ἐμὲ [b] θεωρεῖτε ἔχοντα. 40 καὶ τοῦτο
εἰπὼν [[c] ἐπ]έδειξεν αὐτοῖς τὰς χεῖρας καὶ τοὺς πόδας.
41 ἔτι δὲ [d] ἀπιστούντων αὐτῶν [e] ἀπὸ τῆς χαρᾶς καὶ
...θαυ-μαζον-των G. θαυμαζόντων εἶπεν αὐτοῖς Ἔχετέ τι [f] βρώσιμον [g] ἐνθάδε;
42 οἱ δὲ [h] ἐπέδωκαν αὐτῷ ἰχθύος [i] ὀπτοῦ μέρος [καὶ [k] ἀπὸ
[l] μελισσίου [m] κηρίου]. 43 καὶ λαβὼν [n] ἐνώπιον αὐτῶν
ἔφαγεν. 44 εἶπεν δὲ πρὸς αὐτοὺς Οὗτοι οἱ λόγοι μου

y Acts xvii. 27. Heb. xii. 18. 1 John i. 1 only. Gen. xxvii. 12.
z Matt. xxiii. 27. John xix. 36, from Num. ix. 12. [Eph. v. 30.] Heb. xi. 22 only. Gen. ii. 23.
a ch. vi. 31 al. fr. Eccl. vi. 4.
b ver. 37.
c Matt. xvi. 1. xxii. 19. ch. xvii. 14. Isa. xxxvii. 26, but not =.
d ver. 11. Matt. xvi. 11, 16. Acts xxviii. 24. Rom. iii. 3. 2 Tim. ii. 13 only +. Wisd. x. 7 al.
e = Matt. xiii. 44 reff.
f here only. Lev. xix. 23. Neh. ix. 25. Ezek. xlvii. 12 only. Æsch. Prom. 479.
g John iv. 15, 16 reff. +
h ver. 30.
i here only. Exod. xii. 8, 9. Isa. xliv. 16 F(not A) Ald. only.
k = ch. xx. 10.
l here only +. (-σσα, Deut. i. 44. -σσών, 1 Kings xiv. 27.)
m here only. 1 Kings xiv. 27. Prov. xvi. 24.
n = ch. i. 19. Gen. xxiv. 51.

om *με* D vulg lat-*a b* syr-cu syr[has it]-w-ob syr-jer Hil. for *οτι*, *το* D-gr. *οστα ουκ εχει και σαρκας* D. ins *και* bef *σαρκα* B[1] Iren-int. *σαρκας* D ℵ[1](but corrd) [Dial, Iren-int$_1$]. for *θεωρ.*, *βλεπετε* D.

40. om ver D lat-*a b e ff$_2$ l* (see above on ver 36. *Had this been interpolated from* || *John, we certainly should have found* *ποδας* *by some altered to* *πλευραν*, *either here only, or in ver* 39 *also*). for *επεδειξεν*, *εδειξεν* (*from* || *John, where there is no var*) BGHLNXℵ 1. 33 Cyr Damasc Thl: txt A rel [Chr$_1$].

41. for *αυτων*, *αυτω* A. *και θαυμαζοντων* bef *απο της χαρας* A latt(not gat lat-*f*) Cyr$_2$. om *αυτοις* D vulg lat-*a b l.* for *ενθαδε*, *ωδε* ℵ[1].

42. for *οι δε*, *και* D lat-*e* syr-cu. om *και απο μελισσιου κηριου* (*homœotel:* ΚΑΙΑ *to* ΚΑΙΛ) ABDL[Π]ℵ lat-*e* copt-dz Clem$_1$ Orig$_2$ Eus$_2$ Epiph$_1$ Ath$_1$ Cyr$_7$: ins N rel [latt] Syr syr-cu syr-w-ast [syr-jer] copt æth arm Ps-Just$_1$ [Cyr$_1$].

43. for *αυτων*, *παντων* A. aft *εφαγεν* ins *και τα επιλοιπα εδωκεν αυτοις* K[Π[1]] vulg lat-*c l* syr-cu syr-w-ob syr-jer copt[-wilk] æth arm Aug$_1$.

44. for *ειπεν δε*, *και ειπεν* D vulg lat-*a c f ff$_2$* [*e l q* syr-jer] Syr æth. rec (for *προς αυτους*) *αυτοις*, with ADN rel lat-*a e*: txt BLXℵ 33 vulg lat-*b c* [*f ff$_2$ l q*]. rec om *μου*, with ℵ rel latt syrr [syr-jer] copt-schw[-dz arm] Iren-int$_1$ [Cypr$_1$] Aug$_1$: ins ABDKLNX[Π] 33 copt[-wilk] æth Hil.

vince them of the *reality* of the appearance, and the identity of the Person. The account of John confirms the idea that He shewed them the marks of the nails, both by *His side* being added, and by the expressions of Thomas which followed. The same seems also implied in our ver. 40.

The assertion of the Lord must not be taken as representing merely 'the popular notion concerning spirits' (Dr. Burton); *He who is the Truth, does not speak thus of that which He knows, and has created.* He declares to us the truth, that those appearances to which He was now likened by the disciples, and spirits in general, have not flesh and bones. Observe *σάρκα κ. ὀστέα* —but not *αἷμα*. This the resurrection Body probably *had not,*—as being the *animal life:* see notes on John vi. 51, and John xx. 27. **41.**] **ἀπὸ τῆς χ.**, **from their joy**: the joy which they felt. Wetstein quotes Livy, xxxix. 49, *vix sibimet ipsi præ necopinato gaudio credentes.* **42.**] This was done to convince them further of his real corporeity. The omission of the words **καὶ . . . . κηρίου** in the best MSS. is remarkable: see var. readd. It may possibly have arisen from an idea in some transcriber that this meal is the same as that in John xxi. 9. The words could hardly have been an interpolation. **44.**] Certainly, from the recurrence of **δέ**, which implies immediate sequence, Luke, at the time of writing his Gospel, was not in possession of records of any Galilæan appearances of the Lord, nor indeed of any later than this one. That he corrects this in Acts i., shews him meantime to have become acquainted with some other sources of information, not however perhaps including the Galilæan appearances (see Prolegg. to Luke, § iv. 2).

The following discourse apparently contains a summary of many things said during the last forty days before the ascension;—they cannot have been said *on this evening;* for after the command in ver. 49, the disciples would not have gone away into Galilee. Whether *the Evangelist regarded* it as a summary, is to me extremely doubtful. Knowing apparently of no Galilæan appearances, he seems to relate the command of ver. 49, both here and in the Acts, as intended to apply to the

οὓς ἐλάλησα πρὸς ὑμᾶς ἔτι ὢν σὺν ὑμῖν, ὅτι δεῖ πληρω- F υμας...
θῆναι πάντα τὰ γεγραμμένα ἐν τῷ νόμῳ [o] Μωυσέως καὶ
[o] προφήταις καὶ [p] ψαλμοῖς περὶ ἐμοῦ. 45 τότε [q] διήνοιξεν
αὐτῶν τὸν [r] νοῦν [s] τοῦ [t] συνιέναι τὰς [u] γραφάς, 46 καὶ C και
εἶπεν αὐτοῖς ὅτι οὕτως γέγραπται παθεῖν τὸν χριστὸν ειπεν... ABCDE
καὶ [v] ἀναστῆναι ἐκ νεκρῶν τῇ τρίτῃ ἡμέρᾳ, 47 καὶ [w] κηρυχ- FHKL MNSUV
θῆναι [x] ἐπὶ τῷ ὀνόματι αὐτοῦ [y] μετάνοιαν καὶ [z] ἄφεσιν XΓΔΛ ΠΝ
ἁμαρτιῶν εἰς πάντα τὰ ἔθνη, [a] ἀρξάμενοι [a] ἀπὸ Ἱερουσαλήμ. 1. 33. 69
48 ὑμεῖς [b] μάρτυρες τούτων. 49 καὶ ἰδοὺ ἐγὼ [c] ἐξαποστέλλω
τὴν [d] ἐπαγγελίαν τοῦ πατρός μου ἐφ᾽ ὑμᾶς· ὑμεῖς δὲ ...δε N.

o see ver. 27. p = ch. xx. 42. q vv. 31, 32. r = Phil. iv. 7. Rev. xiii. 8. s Matt. iii. 13 reff. ver. 16. t Matt. xiii. 14, 15 (from Isa. ix. 9, 10), 51. ch. ii. 50. Hos. xiv. 10. u vv. 27, 32. v = Mark vi. 14. ch. xvi. 13 al. fr. Isa. xxvi. 19. w ch. iii. 3 al. Exod. xxxii. 5. x = Matt. xxiv. 5 ||. Acts iv. 17, 18 al. y Mark i. 4 reff. z ch. i. 77. iii. 3. Matt. xxvi. 28. Deut. xv. 2, 3. a Matt. xx. 8 reff. b Gospp., Matt. xviii. 16. xxvi. 65 || Mk. only. constr., Acts i. 8, 22. ii. 32 al. fr. c ch. i. 53 reff. d here only in Gospp. Amos ix. 6. = Acts i. 4. ii. 33. Gal. iii. 14.

for ετι ων, εν ω ημην D Iren-int. πλησθηναι D[1](txt D[2]). απαντα B. for 1st και, εν τοις ℵ [και τοις B copt : και εν τοις L]. ψαλμοι ℵ[1](corrd ℵ-corr[1][?]·[3a]).

45. συνειναι B[1].

46. rec aft γεγραπται ins και ουτως εδει (εδει *was substd for* γεγραπται, *from ver* 26, *then both readings were adopted and united by* και), with AC[2]N rel vulg lat-*f q* [syrr] $Cypr_1$ Aug_1 : om BC[1]DLℵ gat(with mm) lat-*a b c e* ff_2 *l* copt æth [syr-jer] Hil_1. τον χριστον bef παθειν D latt copt Iren-int Cypr Hil. om εκ νεκρων D.

47. for 2nd και, εις Bℵ [Syr] copt. for εις, ως επι D lat-*c e*. rec αρξαμενον, with AC[3] rel syrr, -νων DΔ[2] syr-mg-ms ("*from* one *greek ms*"): -νος S ev-47 lat-*a c l* Aug_1 : -νην 1: txt BC[1]LNXℵ 33 copt æth.

48. at beg ins και D. rec aft υμεις ins δε, with AC[2]DN rel latt syr Aug: om BC[1]Lℵ mt [syr-jer] copt. rec ins εστε bef μαρτυρες, with AC[3]ℵ rel am[with fuld forj ing mt tol] lat-*a b c e f* syrr copt arm : aft μαρτυρες C[1] vulg-ed lat-ff_2 : om BD æth Aug_1.

49. om ιδου D latt Syr copt, for και ιδου εγω, καγω Lℵ 33 : εγω bef ιδου 1. rec (for εξαποστ.) αποστελλω, with ACDNℵ[1] rel : txt B (L[-ελω]) XΔℵ[3a] 33. om του πατρος D.

whole time between the Resurrection and the descent of the Holy Ghost. **οὗτοι οἱ λ.**, 'behold the realization of the words,' &c. **οὓς ἐλ.**] See ch. xviii. 31—33; xxii. 37 : Matt. xxvi. 56 al.; but doubtless He had often said things to them on these matters, which have not been recorded for us. So in John x. 25, we have perhaps a reference to a saying not recorded. This threefold division of the O. T. is the ordinary Jewish one, into the Law (תּוֹרָה), Prophets (נְבִיאִים), and Hagiographa (כְּתוּבִים)—the first containing the Pentateuch; the second Joshua, Judges, the four books of Kings, and the Prophets, except Daniel; the third the Psalms, and all the rest of the canonical books,—Daniel, Esther, Ezra, and Nehemiah being reckoned as one book, and the Chronicles closing the canon.

47. **ἀρξάμενοι**] See reff. The substance of the preaching of the Gospel literally corresponded to this description—see Acts ii. 38 : *μετανοήσατε, καὶ βαπτισθήτω ἕκαστος ὑμῶν ἐπὶ τῷ ὀν. Ἰησοῦ χρ. εἰς ἄφεσιν ἁμαρτιῶν*,—were the words of the first sermon preached at Jerusalem.

48. **ὑμεῖς**] From what follows, Acts i. 22, if these words are to be taken in their strict sense, they must have been spoken *only to the Apostles;*—they may however have been more general, and said to all present. 49.] This promise is explained (Acts i. 5) to be the *baptism with the Holy Ghost,*—and the time is limited to 'not many days hence.'

ἐγὼ ἐξαποστ.] The procession of the Holy Spirit from the Son is clearly here declared, as well as that from the Father. And consequently we find Peter, in Acts ii. 33, referring back to *these very words*, in ascribing the outpouring of the Spirit to the now exalted Saviour. In that verse, the *ἐγώ* of this is filled up by *τῇ δεξιᾷ τοῦ θεοῦ ὑψωθείς*—the proper supplement of it here also. The promise itself is not found in the three Gospels, but expressly and frequently in John xiv.—xvi. : see xiv. 16—26; xv. 26; xvi. 7—11, 13, 14. The present, **ἐξαποστέλλω**, is not = a future, but implies that the actual work is done, and the state brought in, by which that sending is accomplished;—viz. the giving of the

[e] καθίσατε ἐν τῇ πόλει [f] ἕως οὗ [g] ἐνδύσησθε ἐξ [h] ὕψους
[i] δύναμιν. 50 [kl] ἐξήγαγεν δὲ αὐτοὺς [[l] ἔξω] ἕως πρὸς Βηθανίαν, καὶ [m] ἐπάρας τὰς [m] χεῖρας αὐτοῦ [n] εὐλόγησεν
αὐτούς. 51 καὶ ἐγένετο [o] ἐν τῷ εὐλογεῖν αὐτὸν αὐτούς,
[p] διέστη ἀπ' αὐτῶν καὶ [q] ἀνεφέρετο εἰς τὸν οὐρανόν.
52 καὶ αὐτοὶ [r] προςκυνήσαντες αὐτὸν [s] ὑπέστρεψαν εἰς
Ἱερουσαλὴμ [t] μετὰ χαρᾶς μεγάλης, 53 καὶ ἦσαν [u] διὰ

e = Acts xviii. 11. Exod. xvi. 29 Ed-vat. (not B). Judg. xi. 17.
f Matt. i. 25. ch. xii. 50 al. Gen. viii. 7.
g = 1 Cor. xv. 53, 54. Col. iii. 10, 12. Ps. xcii. 1. cxxxi. 9, 16. Isa. li. 9.
h = ch. i. 79 (reff.).
i = ch. x. 19. Rom. xv. 19. 1 Cor. ii. 4.
k Mark xv. 20. John x. 3. Acts v. 19. vii. 36, 40 (from Exod. xxxii. 1) al.
l here (Mark viii. 23 v. r.) only. Gen. xv. 5. xix. 17.
m = 1 Tim. ii. 8. Ps. lxii. 4 (6).
n ver. 30.
o Matt. xiii. 4 al. Ezek. ix. 8.
p ch. xxii. 59. Acts xxvii. 28 only. Exod. xv. 8.
q pass., here only. (Matt. xvii. 1 reff.)
r w. acc., Matt. iv. 10 ||. John iv. (22,) 23, 24. Rev. ix. 20. xiii. 8, 12, 15. xiv. 9, 11. xx. 4 bis only. Judg. vii. 15 A.
s ch. ii. 20 reff. xxiii. 48.
t ch. viii. 12 reff.
u Matt. xviii. 10 reff. Prov. xiii. 9.

rec aft *πολει* ins *ιερουσαλημ* (*gloss*), with AC^2 rel lat-*f q* syrr [syr-jer] æth arm Chr$_1$: om BC^{1}DLא latt copt Gaud Vig Promiss Fulg. for *ου*, *οτου* D **1**. rec *δυναμιν* bef *εξ υψους*, with AC^{2}D rel latt syrr [syr-jer] æth Chr$_1$ [Cyr-jer$_1$ Thdrt$_1$]: txt BC^{1}Lא **1**. 33 Eus$_2$ [Cyr-jer$_1$] Aug.

50. om *εξω* BC^{1}Lא **1**. 33 lat-*a e* Syr [syr-jer] copt arm [Cosm$_1$] Aug$_1$: ins AC^{3}D rel vulg lat-*b c* [*f ff$_2$ l q*] syr æth [Aug$_1$]. om *εως* D vulg lat-*b c e ff$_2$ l*. rec (for *προς*) *εις*, with AC^3 rel vulg lat-*b c f ff$_2$ l* [*q* Aug$_1$]: txt BC^{1}DLא **1** lat-*a* [Cosm$_1$]. for *και επ.*, *επ. δε* D. om *αυτου* D lat-*ff$_2$*.

51. **απεστη** D. om *και ανεφερετο εις τον ουρανον* (*homœotel: -νκαι to -νκαι. To exclude the words, as Griesb, Tischdf, is rash in the extreme, in the known inaccuracy, in this matter, of* Dא) Dא^1 lat-*a b e ff$_2$ l* Aug$_1$.

52. om *προσκυνησαντες αυτον* (*homœotel: αυτοι to αυτον*) D lat-*a b e ff$_2$ l* Aug$_1$. (*μεγαλης* is written on margin in B by the origl scribe.)

πᾶσα ἐξουσία ἐν οὐρανῷ κ. ἐπὶ γῆς, Matt. xxviii. 18. No stress need be laid on **καθίσατε**: see reff. The word Ἱερουσ. is probably interpolated by some who, believing these words to represent the Galilæan discourse, placed it here for an explanation: or perhaps Acts i. 4 gave occasion to it. This command must have been (historically) uttered *after the return from Galilee*: see above. **ἐνδύσ.**] Though the verb is used in the O. T. (see Judg. vi. 34: 2 Chron. xxiv. 20: 1 Chron. xii. 18) of *inspiration by the Spirit*, it here has its full meaning, of *abiding upon and characterizing*, as a garment does the person: this, as Stier remarks, was the true and complete clothing of the nakedness of the Fall. **50.**] The Ascension appears to be related as taking place *after the above words were spoken*—but there is an uncertainty and want of specification about the narrative, which forbids us to conclude that it is intended as following immediately upon them. This however can only be said as taking the other Gospels and Acts i. into account:—if we had *none but the Gospel of Luke* we should certainly say that the Lord ascended *after the appearance to the Apostles and others on the evening of the day of His resurrection.* **ἐξήγ.** [**ἔξω**], i. e. probably, after the words *ἐν τῇ πόλει* just occurring, outside *Jerusalem*, as in ref. Mark: but the *ἔξω* might only apply to the house in which they were, see the other reff., and Matt. xxvi. 75. **ἕως πρὸς Β.**] Not quite to the village itself, but over the brow of the Mount of Olives where it descends on Bethany: see Acts i. 12. (The synonymousness of these two expressions may shew that the same is meant, when, Mark xi. 11, our Lord is said to have gone out at night *to Bethany*, and, Luke xxi. 37, *to the Mount of Olives.*) **51.**] **διέστη**—not, '*He went a little distance from them previous to His ascension,*'—as Meyer would interpret it; but the two verbs belong to one and the same incident,—**He was parted from them and borne up into heaven.** We need not understand, '*by an angel,*' or '*by a cloud,*' nor need **ἀνεφ.** be middle; the *absolute passive* is best. The tense is *imperfect*, signifying the *continuance of the going up* during the **προσκυν.** of the next verse. The more particular account of the Ascension is given Acts i. 9—12, where see notes. That account is in perfect accordance with this, but supplementary to it. *
52. προσκ.] This had been done before by the women, Matt. xxviii. 9, and by the disciples on the mountain in Galilee. This however was a more solemn act of worship, now paid to Him as exalted to God's right hand. **53.**] **διὰ παντός, continually,**—not '*all* their time;'—daily, at the hours of prayer: see Acts i. 13, 14; iii. 1.

v ch. ii. 13 al. Luke only, exc. Rom. xv. 11 (from Ps. cxvi. 1.) Rev. xix. 5.
w ch. i. 64 reff.

παντὸς ἐν τῷ ἱερῷ [v αἰνοῦντες καὶ] w εὐλογοῦντες τὸν θεόν. ABCDE FHKL MSUVX ΓΔΛΠℵ 1. 33. 69

ΚΑΤΑ ΛΟΥΚΑΝ.

53. om εν τω ιερω A[1]. om αινουντες και (*homœotel: the eye passing, before copying, from -ουντες to -ουντες*) BC[1]Lℵ: ins AC[2](D) rel vss. om και ευλογουντες (*homœotel*) D bodl(with gat) lat-*a b e ff*$_2$ *l* copt Aug$_1$. rec at end adds αμην, with ABC[2] rel vulg(with am ing tol) lat-*c f* syrr æth: om C[1](appy) DL[Π[1]]ℵ 1. 33 fuld(with forj) lat-*a b e ff*$_2$ *l* syr-jer copt arm.

Subscription: ευαγγελιον κατα λουκαν A[2]CKLSUΔΛ[Π]ℵ 33: ευαγγ. κ. λ. επληρωθη αρχεται κατα μαρκον D: om A[1]FMXΓ 69: ευαγγ. κ. λ. εξεδοθη μετα χρονους ιε της του χ̄υ αναληψεως KS: txt B.

A few words must be appended here on a point which has been much stirred in Germany, even among the more orthodox Commentators; THE HISTORIC REALITY OF THE CIRCUMSTANCES OF THE ASCENSION. On those among them who doubt *the fact of an Ascension at all,* I have nothing to say, standing as I do altogether on different ground from them. *The Lord Himself foretold* His Ascension, John vi. 62; xx. 17:—it was immediately after His disappearance from the earth *expressly announced by the Apostles,* Acts ii. 33, 34; v. 31:—*and it continued to be an article of their preaching and teaching,* 1 Pet. iii. 22: Eph. ii. 6; iv. 10: 1 Tim. iii. 16. *So far* should we have been assured of it, had we *not possessed* the testimonies of Luke, here and in the Acts:—for the fragment superadded to the Gospel of Mark merely *states the fact,* not the *manner of it.* But, to take first the *a priori* view,—*is it probable that our Lord would have left so weighty a fact in His history on earth, without witnesses?* And might we not have concluded from the wording of John vi. 62, that our Lord must have intended an ascension *in the sight of some of those to whom He spoke,* and that the Evangelist himself *gives that hint, by recording those words without comment, that he had seen it?* Then again, is there any thing in the bodily state of our Lord after His resurrection which raises any even the least difficulty here? He appeared suddenly, and vanished suddenly, when He pleased; when it pleased Him, He ate, He spoke, He walked, but His Body was the Body of the Resurrection; only not yet his σῶμα τῆς δόξης (Phil. iii. 21), because He had *not yet assumed* that glory: but that He *could* assume it, and did assume it at His Ascension, will be granted by all who believe in Him as the Son of God. So that it seems, *on à priori grounds,* probable that, *granted the fact of the Ascension,* it did take place in some such manner as our accounts relate:—*in the sight of the disciples,* and *by the uplifting of the risen Body of the Lord towards that which is to those on this earth the visible heaven.* This being so, let us now, secondly, regard the matter *à posteriori.* We possess two accounts of the circumstances of this ascension, written by the same person, and that person a contemporary of the Apostles themselves. Of the *genuineness* of these accounts there never was a doubt. How improbable that Luke should have related *what any Apostles or apostolic persons might have contradicted?* How improbable that the universal Church, founded by those who are said to have been eyewitnesses of this event, should have *received these two accounts as authentic, if they were not so?* That *these accounts themselves* are never referred to in the Epistles, is surely no argument against them. If an occasion had arisen, such as necessitated the writing of 1 Cor. xv., there can be little doubt that St. Paul would have been as particular in the circumstances of the Ascension, as he has been in those of the Resurrection. The fact is, that by far the greatest difficulty remains to be solved by those who can imagine a myth or fiction on this subject to have arisen in the first age of the Church. Such a supposition is not more repugnant to our Christian faith and reverence, than it is to common sense and historical consistency.

G ευαγγ.
...

ΕΥΑΓΓΕΛΙΟΝ

ΚΑΤΑ ΙΩΑΝΝΗΝ.

Frag. Mosq. εν αρχη ... ...και ο λογος F. ABDEGHKLMSUVXΓΔΛΠא Frag. Mosq. 1. 33. 69

I. 1 [a]Ἐν ἀρχῇ ἦν ὁ [b]λόγος, καὶ ὁ [b]λόγος [c]ἦν [c]πρὸς

a = Gen. i. 1. (Acts xi. 15.) see 1 John i. 1. b = besides here, Rev. xix. 13. 1 John i. 1 (see note there). John only. c = Mark vi. 3 || Mt. ix. 19 || L. 2 Thess. ii. 5. 1 John i. 2. (see 1 Cor. xvi. 6, 7. Gal. i. 18. iv. 18.)

TITLE: Steph το κατα ιωαννην ευαγγελιον: elz το κ. ιω. αγιον ευαγ.: κατα ιωαννην B(one ν) Dא: ευαγ. εκ του κ. ι. 69: [ευαγ. του κ. ι. αγιου ευαγγελιου Γ:] txt A C(top of pages) rel. [Π ?]

CHAP. I. **1—18.**] Prologue: in which is contained the substance and subject of the whole Gospel. THE ETERNAL WORD OF GOD, THE SOURCE OF ALL EXISTENCE, LIFE, AND LIGHT, BECAME FLESH, DWELT AMONG US, WAS WITNESSED TO BY JOHN, REJECTED BY HIS OWN PEOPLE, BUT RECEIVED BY SOME, WHO HAD POWER GIVEN THEM TO BECOME THE SONS OF GOD. HE WAS THE PERFECTION AND END OF GOD'S REVELATION OF HIMSELF; WHICH WAS PARTIALLY MADE IN THE LAW, BUT FULLY DECLARED IN JESUS CHRIST.

1—5.] THE ETERNAL PRÆ-EXISTENCE OF THE **λόγος**: HIS PERSONAL DISTINCTNESS; BUT ESSENTIAL UNITY WITH GOD. HIS WORKING IN CREATION, AND IN THE ENLIGHTENING OF MEN BEFORE HIS MANIFESTATION IN THE FLESH; HIS NON-APPREHENSION BY THEM.

Before commenting on the truths here declared, it is absolutely necessary to discuss the one word on which the whole turns: viz. **ὁ λόγος**. This term is used by John *without explanation*, as bearing a meaning well known to his readers. The enquiry concerning that meaning must therefore be conducted on *historical*, not on mere *grammatical* grounds. And the most important elements of the enquiry are, (I.) *the usage of speech as regards the word*, by John himself and other biblical writers: and (II.) *the purely historical information* which we possess on the *ideas attached to the word.*

I. (α) From the first consideration we find, that in other biblical authors, as well as in John, the word is never used to signify the divine *Reason* or *Mind;* nor indeed those of any human creature. These ideas are expressed by πνεῦμα or καρδία, or νοῦς, or ἡ σοφία τοῦ θεοῦ. In the classics the word λόγος never signifies the *subjective faculty* of reason, but the *reason to be given, objectively*, of any thing or things. The usual Scripture meaning of λόγος is *speech* or *word.* **ὁ λόγος τοῦ θ.** is *the creative, declarative, injunctive Word of God.* (β) That this is also the import in our prologue, is manifest, from the evident relation which it bears to the opening of the history of creation in Genesis. **ὁ λόγος** is not an *attribute* of God, but an *acting reality*, by which the Eternal and Infinite is the great first cause of the created and finite.

(γ) Again this **λόγος** is undoubtedly in our prologue, *personal:*—not an abstraction merely, nor a personification,—not the speaking word of God, once manifested in the Prophets but afterwards fully declared in Christ, as Luthardt (i. 280 ff.), comparing our prologue with Heb. i. 1,—but a PERSON: for ὁ λόγος **ἦν πρὸς τὸν θεόν**, and ὁ λόγος **σὰρξ ἐγένετο**: also **θεὸς ἦν** ὁ λόγος, not θεοῦ

τὸν θεόν, καὶ θεὸς ἦν ὁ [b] λόγος. 2 οὗτος [c] ἦν ἐν ἀρχῇ

ABDE GHKL MSUVX ΓΔΛΠℵ Frag. Mosq. 1. 33. 69

CHAP. I. 1. ins ο bef θεος L Nyss$_1$(om$_2$).

ἦν,—which certainly would be said of none but a PERSON. (δ) Moreover, the λόγος is *identical with* JESUS CHRIST, as the præ-existing Son of God. A comparison of vv. 14 and 15 will place this beyond doubt. (ε) And Jesus Christ is the Word of God, not because He *speaks the word* (as if ὁ λόγος = ὁ λέγων, which is contrary to all usage, in which it = not ὁ λέγων, but τὸ λεγόμενον);—nor because He is the One promised or spoken of, = ὁ λεγόμενος,—which is even less according to analogy;—nor because He is the Author and source of the λόγος as spoken in the Scriptures, &c.,—any more than his being called ζωή and φῶς implies only that He is the *Giver* of life and light: but because *the Word dwells in and speaks from him*, just as the Light dwells in and shines from, and the Life lives in and works from, Him. (ζ) This **λόγος** which became flesh, *is not from, nor of, Time or Space* (ch. iii. 31; viii. 58); but *eternally præ-existent*,— and *manifested in Time and Space*, for the gracious ends of divine Love in Redemption (ch. iii. 16, 17). (η) This **λόγος** spoke in the Law and Prophets, yet partially and imperfectly (ver. 17; ch. v. 39, 46); but in the personal λόγος, spoke forth in fulness of grace and truth. It was He who made the worlds (ver. 3); He, who appeared to Isaiah (Isa. vi., compare ch. xii. 41); He, whose glory is manifested in His power over nature (ch. ii. 11); He, by reception of whom the new birth is wrought (ch. i. 12, 13); who has power over all flesh (ch. xvii. 2),—and can bestow eternal life (ibid.); whose very sufferings were His glory, and the glorifying of God (ch. xvii. 1 al.); and who, after those sufferings, resumed, and now has, the glory which He had with the Father before the world began (ch. xviii. 5, 24).

(θ) Luthardt, in his Commentary on this Gospel, has propounded (vol. i. p. 280 ff.) the following view of the word λόγος and its usage: Jesus Christ is the fulness of that word of God which was fragmentarily manifested in the Prophets (Heb. i. 1). But in this prologue, ὁ λόγος is not to be taken as *identical with* Jesus not yet incarnate, nor is He the subject of vv. 1 ff. And he urges ch. x. 35, 36 (see note there, where I have discussed this) as a key text to the meaning of λόγος. It seems to me, that while much of his view is true and sound, that part of it will not hold which denies the identity of the præ-existent λόγος with Jesus, in the Apostle's mind. Had he intended by the λόγος of vv. 1—4 any other than the personal Son of God who in ver. 14 became flesh, I do not see how ἦν πρὸς τὸν θεόν, and θεὸς ἦν, could be used of ὁ λόγος. Nor again can I consent with him to disconnect the use of λόγος by St. John from its previous history. The reasons given in this note for believing such use, as matter of fact, to have been prepared by the Alexandrine philosophy, are no way affected by the objections which he alleges, the difference between the λόγος of St. John and that of Philo, and the corrupt character of the philosophy itself. II. (α) We are now secondly to enquire, how it came that St. John found this *word* **λόγος** *so ready made to his hands, as to require no explanation*. The answer to this will be found by tracing the *gradual personification* of the *Word*, or *Wisdom of God*, in the O. T. and Jewish writings.

(β) We find faint traces of this personification in the *book of Psalms:* see Ps. xxxiii. 4, 6; cxix. 89, 105; cvii. 20; cxlvii. 15, 18. But it was not the mere offspring of poetic diction. For the whole form and expression of the O. T. revelation was that of the *Word of God*. The Mosaic history opens with '*God said*, Let there be light.' *Spoken* commands, either openly, or in visions, were the communications from God to man. It is the Word, in all the Prophets; the Word, in the Law; in short, the Word, in all God's dealings with his people: see further, Isa. xl. 8; lv. 10, 11: Jer. xxiii. 29 al.

(γ) And as the *Word* of God was the constant idea for his revelations *relatively to man*, so was the *Wisdom* of God, for those which related to *His own essence and attributes*. That this was a later form of expression than the simple recognition of the divine Word in the Mosaic and early historical books, would naturally be the case, in the unfolding of spiritual knowledge and divine contemplation. His Almightiness was first felt, before His Wisdom and moral Purity were appreciated. In the books of Job (ch. xxviii. 12 ff.) and the Proverbs (ch. viii., ix.) we find this *Wisdom of God* personified; in the latter in very plain and striking terms; and this not poetically only, but practically; ascribing to the

F αυτου εγ... [c] πρὸς τὸν θεόν· 3 πάντα [d] δι᾽ αὐτοῦ [e] ἐγένετο, καὶ [f] χωρὶς

d Col. i. 16. + Heb. i. 2. e = Heb. iv. 3. xi. 3. Gen. ii. 4. Ps. cxlviii. 5. f = ch. xv. 5. Eph. ii. 12.

Wisdom of God all his revelation of Himself in His works of Creation and Providence. So that this *Wisdom* embraced in fact in itself the *Power* of God; and there wanted but the highest divine attribute, *Love*, to complete the idea. But this was reserved for the N. T. manifestation. (δ) The next evidences of the gradual personification of the *Wisdom of God* are found in the two Apocryphal Books, the Wisdom of Jesus the Son of Sirach, and the Wisdom of Solomon. The first of these, *originally written in Hebrew* (see Winer, Realwörterbuch, s. v.), belongs probably to the latter half of the second century before Christ. In ch. i. 1, Wisdom is said to be παρὰ κυρίου, καὶ μετ᾽ αὐτοῦ εἰς τὸν αἰῶνα: and in ver. 4, προτέρα πάντων ἔκτισται σοφία. Then in ch. xxiv. 9—21, the same strain is continued: πρὸ τοῦ αἰῶνος ἀπ᾽ ἀρχῆς ἔκτισέν με κ.τ.λ., and the passage concludes with these remarkable words, οἱ ἐσθίοντές με ἔτι πεινάσουσιν, καὶ οἱ πίνοντές με ἔτι διψήσουσιν. In the book of the Wisdom of Solomon, dating probably about 100 A.C., we find (in ch. vi. 22—ch. ix.) a similar personification and eulogy of Wisdom. In this remarkable passage we have Wisdom called πάρεδρος τῶν σῶν θρόνων (ch. ix. 4)—said to have been παροῦσα ὅτε ἐποίεις τὸν κόσμον (ch. ix. 9)—parallelized with ὁ λόγος σου (ch. ix. 1, 2: see also ch. xvi. 12). In ch. xviii. 15, 16, the παντοδύναμος λόγος is set forth as an Angel coming down from heaven, and destroying the Egyptians.

It seems highly probable that the author's monotheistic views were confused by the admixture of Platonism, and that he regarded Wisdom as a kind of soul of the world. He occasionally puts her for God, occasionally for an attribute of God. But he had not attained that near approach to a *personal* view which we shall find in the next step of our enquiry. (ε) The large body of Jews resident in Alexandria were celebrated for their *gnosis*, or religious philosophy. The origin of this philosophy must be referred to the mixture of the Jewish religious element with the speculative philosophies of the Greeks, more especially with that of Plato, and with ideas acquired during the captivity from Oriental sources. One of these Alexandrine writers in the second century A.C. was Aristobulus, some fragments of whose works have been preserved to us. He tells us that by the θεία φωνή we are not to understand a ῥητὸν λόγον, but ἔργων κατασκευάς—the whole working of God in the creation of the world. But the most complete representation of the Judæo-alexandrine gnosis has come down to us in the works of Philo, who flourished cir. A.D. 40—50. It would be out of the province of a note to give a review of the system of Philo: the result only of such review (see Lücke, vol. i. 272—283) will be enough. He identifies the λόγος with the σοφία of God; it is the εἰκὼν θεοῦ (Mangey, vol. i. p. 6 al. fr.); the ἀρχέτυπος κ. παράδειγμα φωτός, αὐτὸς δὲ οὐδενὶ τῶν γεγονότων ὅμοιος (i. 632): ὁ πρεσβύτερος τῶν γένεσιν εἰληφότων (i. 437): πρεσβύτερος υἱὸς τοῦ τῶν ὄντων πατρός (i. 414): ὁ πρωτόγονος αὐτοῦ, ὁ ἄγγελος πρεσβύτατος, ὡς ἀρχάγγελος πολυώνυμος ὑπάρχων (i. 427): σκιὰ θεοῦ, ᾧ καθάπερ ὀργάνῳ χρησάμενος ἐκοσμοποίει (i. 106): δι᾽ οὗ ὁ κόσμος κατεσκευάσθη (i. 162): τῷ δὲ ἀρχαγγέλῳ κ. πρεσβυτάτῳ λόγῳ δωρεὰν ἐξαίρετον ἔδωκεν ὁ τὰ ὅλα γεννήσας πατήρ, ἵνα μεθόριος στὰς τὸ γενόμενον διακρίνῃ τοῦ πεποιηκότος.—ἀγάλλεται δὲ ἐπὶ τῇ δωρεᾷ, ... οὔτε ἀγέννητος ὡς ὁ θεὸς ὤν, οὐδὲ γεννητὸς ὡς ὑμεῖς, ἀλλὰ μέσος τῶν ἄκρων, ἀμφοτέροις ὁμηρεύων (i. 501 f.): δύο γάρ, ὡς ἔοικεν, ἱερὰ θεοῦ, ἓν μὲν ὅδε ὁ κόσμος, ἐν ᾧ καὶ ἀρχιερεὺς ὁ πρωτόγονος αὐτοῦ θεῖος λόγος (i. 653): ὁ τοῦ θεοῦ ὕπαρχος (i. 308): περιέχει πάντα καὶ πεπλήρωκεν (ii. 655): δεύτερος θεός, ὅς ἐστιν ἐκείνου λόγος (ii. 625, fragment, from Eusebius, Præp. Evang. vii. 13, vol. iii. p. 545). These instances, the number of which might be much enlarged, will serve to shew how remarkably near to the diction and import of some passages in our Gospel Philo approached in speaking of the λόγος.

At the same time there is a *wide and unmistakeable difference* between his λόγος and that of the Apostle. He does not distinguish it from the *Spirit of God* (Lücke, i. p. 278), nor does he connect it with any Messianic ideas, though these latter were familiar to him. Besides, his views are strangely compounded of Platonism and Judaism. The λόγος seems to be one comprehending, or ruling, the δυνάμεις or ἰδέαι of God, which, although borrowed from Plato, he judaically calls ἄγγελοι, and the λόγος their ἀρχάγγελος. We see by this however how fixed and prepared *the term*, and many of its attributes, were in the religious philosophy of the Alexandrine Jews. (On the question

g Matt. xxvii. 14 reff.
h ch. v. 26. 1 John i. 2. v. 11.

αὐτοῦ [e] ἐγένετο [g] οὐδὲ [g] ἓν ὃ [e] γέγονεν. 4 ἐν αὐτῷ [h] ζωὴ

C.-δε εν. ABCDE FGHKL MSUVX ΓΔΛΠℵ Frag. Mosq. 1. 33. 69

3. for ουδε εν, ουδεν Dℵ[1] 1. (Clem Orig Eus have both.) ο γεγονεν is joined *to follg* in A[appy] C^1 G^1(appy) L Frag-mosq[1][appy] em[with jac] lat-*a b e f ff*$_2$ syr-cu syr-jer sah Ptol Val_1 $Heracl_2$ $Thdot_2$ Iren-gr $Clem_2$ $Orig_{sæpe}$ Eus_{alic} Ath_2 Cyr-jer_3 Cyr_1 Hil_2 Ambr(discusses the two ways) [Aug_1] : *to foregoing* in C^3 &c vulg lat-*c* syrr[-edd] copt Ign_1 $Epiph_3$ Chr_1 Thl_1 Cypr Arnob Jer_1 : D(Scr) has a point both before and after. (*See note.*)

whether the λόγος of Philo is to be taken as strictly *personal*, see Dorner's remarks on Lücke, in his Lehre von der Person Christi, i. p. 22 note.) (ζ) Meanwhile the Chaldee paraphrasts of the O. T. had habitually used such expressions as יְקָרָא, or שְׁכִינָה, or מֵימְרָא, 'the glory,' or 'the presence,' or 'the word,' of God,—in places where nothing but His own agency could be understood. The last of these—the Memra, or word of God,—is used in so strictly personal a sense, that there can be little doubt that the Paraphrasts understood by it a divine Person or Emanation. (η) From these elements, the Alexandrine and Jewish views of the λόγος or σοφία of God, there appear to have arisen very early among Christians, both orthodox and heretic, formal expressions, in which these or equivalent terms were used. Of this the Apostle Paul furnishes the most eminent example. His teacher Gamaliel united in his instruction both these elements, and they are very perceptible in the writings of his pupil. But *we do not find in them any direct use of the term* **λόγος**, *as personally applied to the Son of God*. This shews him to have spoken mainly according to the Jewish school,—among whom, as Origen states, he could find none who held τὸ τὸν λόγον εἶναι τὸν υἱὸν τοῦ θεοῦ (Cont. Cels. ii. 31, vol. i. p. 413). (θ) We find a much nearer approximation to the Alexandrine method of speech in the Epistle to the Hebrews, written evidently by some disciple intimately acquainted with the Alexandrine gnosis (see the opening verses, and especially φέρων τὰ πάντα τῷ ῥήματι τῆς δυνάμεως αὐτοῦ). But even there *we have not the* **λόγος** *identified personally with the Lord Jesus Christ,* nor indeed *personally spoken of at all,*—however near some passages may seem to approach to this usage (ch. iv. 12, 13; xi. 3). (ι) The Alexandrine gnosis was immediately connected with Ephesus, where the Gospel of John was probably written. Apollos (Acts xviii. 24) came thither *from Alexandria;* and Cerinthus is related by Theodoret (Fab. Hær. ii. 3, vol. iv. p. 389) to have studied and formed his philosophic system in Egypt, before coming to Ephesus. (κ) These notices will serve to account for the term **λόγος** being already found by St. John framed to his use; and the anti-Gnostic tendency of his writings will furnish an additional reason why he should rescue such important truths as the præ-existence and attributes of the divine λόγος from the perversions which false philosophy had begun to make of them. (λ) In all that has been said in this note, no insinuation has been conveyed that either the Apostle Paul, or the writer to the Hebrews, or John, *adopted in any degree their* TEACHING *from the existing philosophies.* Their teaching (which is totally distinct from any of those philosophies, as will be shewn in this commentary) is that of the Holy Spirit;—and the existing philosophies, with all their follies and inadequacies, must be regarded, *in so far as they* by their terms or ideas subserved the work which the Spirit had to do by the Apostles and teachers of Christianity, as so many providential preparations of the minds of men to receive the fuller effulgence of the Truth as it is in Jesus, which shines forth in these Scriptures.

The substance of this note has been derived from Dr. Lücke's Commentary, vol. i. p. 249—294: De Wette's Handbuch, on John i. 1: Dorner, Lehre von der Person Christi, i. p. 15 ff.: Olshausen, Comm. ii. p. 30 ff.

1.] **ἐν ἀρχῇ** = πρὸ τοῦ τὸν κόσμον εἶναι, ch. xvii. 5. The expression is indefinite, and must be interpreted relatively to the matter spoken of. Thus in Acts xi. 15, it is 'the beginning of the Gospel:' and by the same principle of interpretation, *here* it is **the beginning of all things,** on account of the πάντα δι' αὐτ. ἐγ. ver. 3.

These words, if they do not *assert,* at least *imply,* the *eternal præ-existence* of the Divine Word. For ἐν ἀρχῇ **ἦν** is not said of an *act done* ἐν ἀρχῇ (as in Gen. i. 1), but of a *state existing* ἐν ἀρχῇ, and therefore without beginning itself.

ἦν, not equivalent to ἔστιν (see ἐγώ εἰμι, ch. viii. 58 al.), as Euthymius and others have supposed; but Origen has given the true reason for the indefinite past being used,—ἦν μὲν κυριώτερον ἐπὶ

...ζωη ην Frag. Mosq. ἦν, καὶ ἡ [h] ζωὴ ἦν τὸ φῶς τῶν ἀνθρώπων· 5 καὶ τὸ

4. for 1st ην, εστιν Dℵ mss-in-Orig-Aug gat(with mm) lat-*a b c* &c(not *g*) syr-cu sah [$Thdot_1$] $Clem_1$ Val-in-$Iren_1$ Hil_2 [$Cypr_1$-mss Aug_1]. (των ανθρωπων is omd in the text of B, but is added on the marg by the origl scribe.)

τοῦ θεοῦ λόγου τὸ **ἔστιν** *εἰπεῖν· ἀλλ' ἐπεὶ πρὸς διαφορὰν τῆς ἐνανθρωπήσεως γενομένης ἔν τινι καιρῷ, ἀντὶ τοῦ* **ἔστιν** *τῷ* **ἦν** *ὁ εὐαγγελιστὴς κέχρηται* (in Catena, Lücke, p. 296). The existence of an enduring and unlimited state of being, implied in ἦν, is contrasted with ἐγένετο in ver. 3, and especially in ver. 14. **καὶ ὁ λ. ἦν πρὸς τ. θ.**] The usage of πρός here, as **with** (i.e. 'chez'), is sufficiently borne out by the reff. Basil remarks (Lücke, i. 297) that John says πρὸς τὸν θ., not ἐν τῷ θ., ἵνα τὸ **ἰδιάζον** τῆς ὑποστάσεως παραστήσῃ, ... ἵνα μὴ πρόφασιν δῷ τῇ συγχύσει τῆς ὑποστάσεως. Both the inner substantial union, and the distinct personality of the λόγος are here asserted. The former is distinctly repeated in the next words. **κ. θ. ἦν ὁ λ.**] **and the Word was God.** As regards the *form* of the sentence, it is strictly parallel with πνεῦμα ὁ θεός, ch. iv. 24. But the *sense* to be conveyed here is as weighty a consideration as the form of the sentence. Had John intended to say, '*God was the Word*,'—what meaning could his assertion possibly have conveyed? None other than a contradiction to his last assertion, by which he had distinguished God from the Word. And not only would this be the case, but the assertion would be inconsistent with the whole historical idea of the λόγος, making this term to signify merely an attribute of God, just as when it is said ὁ θεὸς ἀγάπη ἐστίν. Not to mention the unprecedented inversion of subject and predicate which this would occasion; ὁ λόγος *having been the subject before*, and again *resumed as the subject afterwards*.

The *rendering* of the words being then as above, their *meaning* is the next question. The omission of the article before θεός is not *mere usage*; it could not have been here expressed, whatever place the words might hold in the sentence. ὁ λόγος ἦν ὁ θεός would give a sense liable to the objections first stated, and destroy the idea of the λόγος altogether. θεός must then be taken as implying **God**, *in substance and essence*,—not ὁ θεός, 'the Father,' *in Person*. It does not = θεῖος, nor is it to be rendered *a God*—but, as in **σὰρξ ἐγένετο**, σάρξ expresses that *state* into which the Divine Word entered by a definite act, so in **θεὸς ἦν**, θεός expresses that *essence* which was His ἐν ἀρχῇ:—that He was *very God*. So that this first verse might be connected thus: the Logos was from eternity,—was with God (the Father),—and was Himself God.

2.] In order to direct the mind to the difference (in unity) between this λόγος and ὁ θεός, John recalls the reader's attention to the two first clauses of ver. 1, which he now combines, in order to pass on to the *creative work*, which distinctly belongs to the λόγος. Thus also this verse fixes the reference of αὐτοῦ in ver. 3, which might otherwise, after the mention of θεός, have seemed ambiguous.

3.] **πάντα** = τὰ Πάντα (1 Cor. viii. 6: Col. i. 16), = ὁ κόσμος, ver. 10. This parallelism of itself refutes the Socinian interpretation of πάντα, 'all Christian graces and virtues,' 'the whole moral world.' But the history of the term λόγος forbids such an explanation entirely. For Philo (i. 162) says εὑρήσεις αἴτιον μὲν αὐτοῦ (τοῦ κόσμου) τὸν θεόν, ὑφ' οὗ γέγονεν· ὕλην δέ, τὰ τέσσαρα στοιχεῖα, ἐξ ὧν συνεκράθη· **ὄργανον δέ, λόγον θεοῦ, δι' οὗ κατεσκευάσθη**: see also Col. i. 16, and Heb. i. 2. Olshausen observes, that we never read in Scripture that 'Christ made the world;' but 'the Father made the world διά the Son,' or 'the world was made ὑπό the Father, and διά the Son:' because the Son *never works of Himself*, but always *as the revelation of the Father*; His work is the Father's *will*, and the Father has no Will, except the Son, who is *all His will* (ἐν ᾧ εὐδόκησεν). The Christian Fathers rightly therefore rejected the semi-Arian formula, 'The Son was begotten by an act of the Father's will;' for He is *that Will Himself*. **καὶ χωρ. αὐτ.**] This addition is not merely a Hebraistic parallelism, but a distinct denial of the eternity and uncreatedness of matter as held by the Gnostics. They set *matter*, as a separate existence, over against God, and made it the origin of evil:—but John excludes any such notion. Nothing was made without Him (the λόγος); all matter, and *implicitly* evil itself, in the deep and inscrutable purposes of creation (for it οὐκ ἦν ἐν τῇ ἀρχῇ **ἀλλὰ γέγονεν**), **δι' αὐτοῦ ἐγένετο**. The punctuation at the end of the verse is uncertain, if we regard solely manuscript authority, but rests on the sense of the passage, which is rendered weak, and inconsistent with analogy,

φῶς ἐν τῇ ⁱσκοτίᾳ ᵏφαίνει, καὶ ἡ ⁱσκοτία αὐτὸ οὐ ˡκατέλαβεν.

ABCDE FGHK LMSUV ΧΓΔΛ ΠＮ 1. 33. 69

i = 1 John ii. 8. John only, exc. Matt. iv. 16. x. 27. Luke xii. 3. Job xxviii. 3 only. k = ch. v. 35. 1 John ii. 8. Rev. i. 16. l = Phil. iii. 12, 13. see Acts iv. 13. x. 34.

5. (B does not read αυτō as Bch, on the authority of Blanchini: so Tischdf, expr.)

by placing the period after οὐδὲ ἕν:—*weak*, because in that case we must render 'That which was made by Him was life (i.e. having life), and that life was the light of men;' but *how* was that life, i.e. that living creation which was made by Him, the light of men?—*inconsistent with grammatical analogy*, for John never uses γενέσθαι ἐν for 'to be made by.' [But Cyr-Alex., who adopts this punctuation, renders the passage thus: 'that which was made, therein was life.'] Besides which, John's usage of beginning a sentence with ἐν and a demonstrative pron. should have its weight: cf. ch. xiii. 35; xv. 8; xvi. 26: 1 John ii. 3, 4, 5; iii. (8,) 10, 16, 19, 24; iv. 2 al. fr. Compare also ἐν τούτῳ ἡ ἀλήθεια οὐκ ἔστιν, 1 John ii. 4,—ἁμαρτία ἐν αὐτῷ οὐκ ἔστιν, ib. iii. 5. I have determined therefore for the ordinary punctuation. It is said to have been first adopted owing to an abuse of the passage by the Macedonian heretics, who maintained that if the exclusion was *complete*, the Holy Spirit can also not have been without His creating power, i.e. was created by Him. But this would be refuted without including ὃ γέγονεν, for the Holy Spirit **ἦν**, not **ἐγένετο**.

4. **ἐν αὐτῷ ζωὴ ἦν**] Compare 1 John v. 11; i. 1, 2, and ch. vi. 33. **ζωή** is not merely '*spiritual life*,' nor '*the recovery of blessedness*,'—as Tholuck, Kuinoel, &c. explain it:—the λόγος is the source of *all life* to the creature, not indeed ultimately, but mediately (see ch. v. 26: 1 John v. 11). **κ. ἡ ζωὴ ἦν τ. φῶς τ. ἀνθ**] This is not to be understood of the *teaching of the Incarnate Logos*, but of the *enlightening and life-sustaining influence of the eternal Son of God*, in Whom was life. In the material world, light, the offspring of the Word of God, is the condition of life, and without it life degenerates and expires:—so also in the spiritual world that *life* which is in Him, is to the creature the very condition of all development and furtherance of the life of the spirit. All knowledge, all purity, all love, all happiness, spring up and grow from this life, which is the light to them all. It is not φῶς, but **τὸ** φῶς:—because this is *the only* true light: see ver. 9, also 1 John i. 5. 5.] As *light* * and *life* are closely connected ideas, so are *death* and *darkness*. The whole world, lying in death and in darkness, is the **σκοτία** here spoken of:—not merely the ἐσκοτωμένοι (Eph. iv. 18; see ib. v. 7, 8), but the *whole mass*, with the sole exception (see below, ver. 12) of ὅσοι ἔλαβον αὐτόν (compare ch. iii. 19: 1 John v. 19). This **φαίνει** is not merely the historical present, but describes the whole process of the light of life in the Eternal Word shining in this evil and dark world; both by the O. T. revelations, and (see ch. x. 16; xi. 52) by all the scattered fragments of light glittering among the thick darkness of heathendom. **καὶ . . . κατέλ.**] **and the darkness comprehended** (understood, apprehended) **it not.** That this is the meaning, will be clear from the context. John states here as a *general* fact, what he afterwards states of the appearance of the Incarnate Word to the chosen people, ver. 11. The sentences are strictly parallel. τὸ φ. ἐν τῇ σκ. φαίνει || εἰς τὰ ἴδια ἦλθεν, and κ. ἡ σκ. αὐτὸ οὐ κατέλ. || καὶ οἱ ἴδιοι αὐτὸν οὐ παρέλαβον. In the first, he is speaking of the *whole shining of this light over the world;* in the second, of its *historical manifestation to the Jews.* In both cases, *the Divine Word was rejected.* παρέλαβον is used in the second case as expressing the personal assumption to oneself as a friend or companion: see reff. Lücke observes (i. 313), that the almost tragic tone of this verse is prevalent through the Gospel of John and his First Epistle, see ch. iii. 19; xii. 37 ff. al.: and is occasionally found in Paul also, see Rom. i. 18 ff. The other interpretation of κατέλαβεν, '*overtook*,' '*came upon*' (for that of '*overcame*' (Orig., Theophyl., Euthym.) is not admissible, the word never importing this), is unobjectionable as far as the *usage* of the word is concerned (see ch. xii. 35: Mark ix. 18); but yields no sense in the context.

The connexion of the two members of our verse by **καί** is not, 'The Light shineth in the darkness, *and therefore* (i.e. because darkness is the opposition to light, and they exclude one another) the darkness comprehended it not;' but, 'The Light shineth in the darkness, *and yet* (notwithstanding that the effect of light in darkness is so great and immediate in the physical world) the darkness comprehended it not:' see *καί* below, ver. 11.

6 [m] Ἐγένετο ἄνθρωπος ἀπεσταλμένος [n] παρὰ θεοῦ,
[o] ὄνομα αὐτῷ Ἰωάννης· 7 οὗτος ἦλθεν [p] εἰς [q] μαρτυρίαν,
ἵνα [r] μαρτυρήσῃ περὶ τοῦ [s] φωτός, ἵνα πάντες πιστεύσωσιν
δι' αὐτοῦ. 8 οὐκ ἦν ἐκεῖνος τὸ [s] φῶς, ἀλλ' [t] ἵνα [r] μαρτυρήσῃ περὶ τοῦ [s] φωτός. 9 [u] ἦν τὸ φῶς τὸ [v] ἀληθινόν, ὃ
[w] φωτίζει πάντα ἄνθρωπον, [ux] ἐρχόμενον εἰς τὸν [x] κόσμον.

m Judg. xix. 1. see ch. iii. 1. n = Matt. xxi. 42, from Ps. cxvii. 23. Luke ii. 1. 2 Tim. i. 18. o ch. iii. 1. (xviii. 10.) Rev. vi. 8. ix. 11. 1 Kings i. 1. Jos. Antt. xx. 9. 1. see Matt. xxvii. 32. Luke i. 27. ii. 25. p = Matt. iii. 11. xxvi. 13, 28. 1 Kings ix. 14. q = ver. 19. ch. iii. 11, &c. Acts xxii. 18. 1 John v. 9. Rev. i. 2, 9. xii. 11, 17 al. r w. περι, John only, ver. 15. ch. ii. 25 and passim. see Acts xxiii. 11. s = John only. ch. iii. 19, &c. 1 John ii. 8, 9, 10. t constr., ch. ix. 3. xiii. 18. Mark xiv. 49. u constr., Mark i. 6, 22. xv. 43. ver. 28. Acts viii. 28. xxi. 3 al. fr. v ch. iv. 23. vi. 32. 1 John ii. 8. Heb. viii. 2. ix. 24. Jer. ii. 21. w = Eph. i. 18. iii. 9. Ps. cxviii. 130. x ch. xii. 46. xvi. 28. 1 Tim. i. 15.

6. for *θεου, κυριου* D[1](txt D-corr[1]). (*N.B.* D lat def as far as ch. iii. 16.) ins *ην* bef *ονομα* D[1]ℵ[1](om D-corr[1] ℵ-corr[1](?)·[3a]), simly latt Iren-int &c. *ιωαννην* D[1](txt D-corr[1]).

7. *πιστευσουσιν* D ev-H.

6—18.] The manifestation and working of the Divine Word, Jesus Christ, the Son of God, incarnate in our flesh. **6.**] The Evangelist now passes to the *historic manifestation* of the Word. *μετεληλυθὼς ἐπὶ τὴν ἐπιφάνειαν τοῦ υἱοῦ, τίνα ἂν εὗρεν ἀρχὴν ἑτέραν, ἢ τὰ κατὰ τὸν Ἰωάννην;* (Theodor. Mopsuest. in loc. p. 729, ed. Migne.) He *enunciates* briefly in these verses 6, 7, what he afterwards, vv. 19—36, narrates with historical detail. **ἐγένετο**—not belonging to **ἀπεσταλμένος**, but to **ἄνθρ.**: the ordinary opening of an historical period, see Luke i. 5. No stress on *ἐγένετο*, as distinguished from *ἦν*, ver. 1 (Olshausen), see ch. iii. 1. **There was—a man sent,** &c. In **ἀπεστ. παρὰ θεοῦ** we have possibly a reference to Mal. iii. 1.
7.] The purpose of John's coming was to *bear witness to a fact,* which fact (ver. 33) was made known to him by divine revelation. **εἰς μαρτυρίαν**, not as E. V., '*for a witness,*' but **for witness**, for the purpose of bearing witness: so A. V. R. **ἵνα μαρτ.** *κ.τ.λ.* is an expansion of **εἰς μαρτ.**:—the subject of his testimony was to be **the Light,**—and the aim of it, **that all might believe** (*εἰς τὸ φῶς*, see ch. xii. 36) **through** *him* (i. e. John: not *τοῦ φωτός* (Grot.), which confuses the whole, for then we must understand *εἰς* **θεόν** after **πιστ.** which is here out of place).

8.] John was himself **ὁ λύχνος** *ὁ καιόμενος καὶ φαίνων* (ch. v. 35), see note on Matt. v. 14, but not **τὸ φῶς.** On **ἵνα**, see reff.: it belongs to **ἦν**, not to *ἦλθεν* above. And thus there is no ellipsis of '*came*' or 'was sent:' John simply *was,* in order to &c. **9.**] The word **ἀληθινόν** (see reff.) in this connexion imports **original**, 'archetypal,' and is used of the true genuine sources and patterns of those things which we find here below only in fragmentary imitations and derivations. Such an *original* was the Light here spoken of;—but John was only a derived light,—not lumen *illuminans,* but lumen *illuminatum.* The construction of this verse has been much disputed. Is **ἐρχόμενον εἰς τ. κ.** to be taken with **ἄνθρωπον** (as latt syrr copt Orig Eus$_2$ Epiph Chr Cyr Thl Euthym and most of the ancient Commentators and E. V.), or does it belong to **τὸ φῶς τὸ ἀλ.**? The former construction can only be defended by a Rabbinical usage, by which כָּל בָּאֵי עוֹלָם means 'all men' (Schöttgen, i. 223). But it is very questionable whether John ever speaks thus. Certainly he does not, in any of the passages commonly cited to defend this rendering, ch. xviii. 37 (which is spoken by Christ of Himself and His Mission); xvi. 21, 28; xii. 46. And even if he had thus spoken, how harsh and how unmeaning is the sentence; whether with Euthym. we lay an emphasis on *ἦν*, or with E. V. &c. supply *τοῦτο* before it. If this latter had been intended, surely it would have been more distinctly expressed; and even when it is supplied, we have in this verse only a less forcible repetition of ver. 4. It seems then that we must join **ἐρχ. εἰς τ. κ.** with **τ. φῶς τ. ἀληθ.** But even then, three ways of rendering are apparently open to us. The first of these, which is that of Socinus, takes **ἐρχόμ.** *κ.τ.λ.* as meaning, '*at its coming into the world.*' This however—besides the sense being inconsistent with ver. 4—leaves the opening clause without a demonstrative pronoun, as before. Then, secondly, **ἐρχόμενον** might seem to be used in the sense in which we frequently have *ἐρχόμενος*, as a quasi-future, 'who was, or is, to come:' see Matt. xi. 3: Mark x. 30 al. fr.: ch. vi. 14; xi. 27, in which last two places it is joined, as

10 ἐν τῷ κόσμῳ ἦν, καὶ ὁ κόσμος δι' αὐτοῦ [y] ἐγένετο, καὶ ...και H.
ὁ κόσμος αὐτὸν οὐκ ἔγνω. 11 εἰς [z] τὰ [z] ἴδια ἦλθεν, καὶ
[a] οἱ [a] ἴδιοι αὐτὸν οὐ [b] παρέλαβον. 12 ὅσοι δὲ [c] ἔλαβον
αὐτόν, [d] ἔδωκεν αὐτοῖς [de] ἐξουσίαν [f] τέκνα [f] θεοῦ γενέσθαι,
τοῖς [gh] πιστεύουσιν [gh] εἰς τὸ [h] ὄνομα αὐτοῦ, 13 οἳ οὐκ [i] ἐξ H -του οι ουκ...

ABCDE FGHK LMSUV ΧΓΔΛ ΠΝ 1. 33. 69

y ver. 3. z ch. viii. 44. (xv. 9.) xvi. 32. xix. 27. Luke xviii. 28. Acts xxi. 6. 1 Thess. iv. 11 only. Esth. v. 10. a ch. xiii. 1. Acts iv. 23. xxiv. 23. 1 Tim. v. 8 only. 2 Macc. xii. 22. b Matt. i. 20, 24. Cant. viii. 2. c = ch. v. 43. xiii. 20 (3ce). Matt. xiii. 20 ‖ Mk. d Matt. xxviii. 18 reff. ch. v. 27. xvii. 2. Rev. ii. 26. vi. 8. ix. 8 al. 1 Macc. i. 13. e ch. x. 18. xix. 10 bis, 11. f ch. xi. 52. Rom. viii. 16, (17,) 21. ix. 8. Phil. ii. 15. 1 John iii. 1, 2, 10. v. 2 only. g ch. ii. 11 reff. h ch. ii. 23. iii. 18. 1 John v. 13 only. i = Matt. i. 18, 20. 1 Cor. viii. 6. xi. 8.

10. for αυτου, αυτον ℵ[1].
12. om δε D lat-*e* Tert$_1$ Cypr$_1$. ελαβαν B[1]. for εδωκεν, εδων D[1](txt D[2]).
13. om οι D[1](txt D[2]) lat-*a*.

here, with εἰς τὸν κόσμον. But if this be adopted (which even constructionally is very doubtful), the only sense will be that the true light, &c. *was to come;* i. e. *had not yet come;* which manifestly is not correct;—for it *had come,* when John gave his witness; and the whole of these verses 6—13 relate to the time when He *had appeared,* and *come* to His own. We are driven then to the only legitimate rendering, which is to take ἦν ἐρχόμενον as equivalent to an imperfect came:—this usage being frequent in the N. T., see reff.:—i. e. at the time when John bore this witness, the true light which lighteth every man, came—was in process of manifesting Himself,—into the world. Tholuck objects to this construction that ἦν is too far from ἐρχόμενον:—but Lücke answers, that ἦσαν and νηστεύοντες are nearly as far separated in Mark ii. 18. **ὃ φωτ. πάντα ἄνθ.** is a further expansion of **τὸ ἀληθινόν.** 10.] The **κόσμος** is the created **world,** into which He came (ver. 9), which was made by Him (ver. 3), which nevertheless (i. e. as here represented by *man,* the only creature who γινώσκει) knew, recognized Him not. **καί** is as in ver. 5. **αὐτόν,** not αὐτό, because though τὸ φῶς has been the subject, yet the **δι' αὐτοῦ ἐγένετο** brings in again the creative λόγος, Who *is* the Light. The three members of the sentence form a climax;—**He was in the world** (and therefore the world should have known Him), **and the world was made by Him** (much more then should it have known Him), **and the world knew Him not.** 11.] **τὰ ἴδια** here cannot well mean *the world,* or **οἱ ἴδιοι** *mankind in general:* it would be difficult to point out any Scripture usage to justify such a meaning. But abundance of passages bear out the meaning which makes **τὰ ἴδια** His own inheritance or possession, i. e. Judæa; and **οἱ ἴδιοι,** the Jews: compare especially the parable Matt. xxi. 33 ff., and Sir. xxiv. 7 ff. And thus **ἦλθεν** forms a nearer step in the approach to the declaration in ver. 14. He *came to* His own. On **παρέλ.** see reff.,—and above on ver. 5. 12.] The **ὅσοι** . . . . primarily refers to the ἐκλογή *among the Jews* who have just been spoken of: but also, by implication, being opposed to both **ὁ κόσμος** and **οἱ ἴδιοι,** the ἐκλογή in all the world. **ἔλαβον** = **παρέλαβον** above—as many as recognized Him as that which He was—the Word of God and Light of men. **ἔδωκεν αὐτ. ἐξουσ.**] ἐξουσ. is not merely *capability* = δύναμιν (Lücke),—still less *privilege* or *prerogative* (Chrysost. and others),—but **power** (De Wette); involving all the actions and states needful to their so becoming, and removing all the obstacles in their way (e. g. the wrath of God, and the guilt of sin). **τέκνα θ. γενέσθαι**] The spiritual life owes its beginning to a *birth from above,* ch. iii. 3—7. And this birth is owing to the Holy Spirit of God; so that this is equivalent to saying, 'As many as received Him, to them gave He His Holy Spirit.' And we find that it was so: see Acts x. 44. **τέκνα θ.** is a more comprehensive expression than υἱοὶ τ. θ., which brings out rather our *adoption,* and hope of inheritance (Rom. viii. 14 ff.), whereas the other involves the *whole generation and process* of our life in the Spirit, as being from and of God, and consequently our *likeness* to God, walking in light as He is in light (1 John i. 5—7)—free from sin (ib. iii. 9; v. 18) and death (ch. viii. 51). **τοῖς πιστ. εἰς τ. ὄν. αὐτ.**] τὸ ὄνομα αὐτ. is *His manifestation as that which He has given Himself out to be,* i. e. *as a Saviour from sin:* see Matt. i. 21, καλέσεις **τὸ ὄνομα αὐτοῦ** Ἰησοῦν· αὐτὸς γὰρ σώσει τὸν λαὸν αὐτοῦ ἀπὸ τῶν ἁμαρτιῶν αὐτῶν. 13.] The Jews grounded their claim to be children of God on their descent from Abraham. John here negatives any such claim, and asserts the exclusive divine birth of all who become

[k] αἱμάτων, οὐδὲ [i] ἐκ [l] θελήματος [l] σαρκός, οὐδὲ ἐκ θελήματος ἀνδρός, ἀλλ' ἐκ θεοῦ [m] ἐγεννήθησαν. 14 καὶ
ὁ [n] λόγος [o] σὰρξ ἐγένετο, καὶ [p] ἐσκήνωσεν ἐν ἡμῖν,
καὶ [q] ἐθεασάμεθα τὴν [r] δόξαν αὐτοῦ, δόξαν [s] ὡς [t] μονο-

k [Acts xvii. 26.] pl. = here only. l Eph. ii. 3 only. m w. ἐκ, Matt. i. 3, 5, 6, 16 (xix. 12). ch. iii. 5, 6 bis, 8. viii. 41. 1 John ii. 29. iii. 9 bis. iv. 7. v. 1 bis, 4, 18 bis only. Ezra x. 44. n ver. 1 reff. o = 1 Tim. iii. 16. Heb. ii. 14. 1 John iv. 2. 2 John 7. p Rev. vii. 15. xxi. 3. xii. 12. xiii. 6 only. J. Gen. xiii. 12. Judg. viii. 11 B only. q Luke xxiii. 55 reff. r = Luke ix. 32. 2 Pet. i. 17. s = Matt. vii. 29. 2 Cor. ii. 17. t = ver. 18. ch. iii. 16, 18. 1 John iv. 9 only. (Luke vii. 12 al[2]. Heb. xi. 17 only. Ps. xxi. 20.)

om ουδε εκ θελ. ανδρ. (*homœotel*) B[1]-txt 17[1] Eus_1 Chr_2 $Cypr_1$: ins B[1]-marg rel [$Cyr\text{-}p_2$]. om 2nd εκ D[1](ins D[2]) ℵ[1]. εγενηθησαν AB[1]Δ 69[1]. (The 2nd ν is B[2], not B[1] : see table.)

children of God by faith. It is to be noticed that the conjunctions here are not the merely disjunctive ones οὔτε . . . . οὔτε, which would necessitate the ranging the clauses as co-ordinate and parallel, but **οὐδὲ . . . . οὐδέ**, which rise in climax from one clause to another,—'*not* ἐξ αἱμάτων, *nor yet* ἐκ θελ. σαρκ. *nor yet* ἐκ θελ. ἀνδ., *but* ἐκ θεοῦ' (see examples of οὔτε, Matt. xii. 32: of οὐδέ, Matt. vi. 26). Many interpreters have seen in θέλημα ἀνδρός the male, and in θέλημα σαρκός the female side of human concupiscence (so Augustine, Theophylact, &c.); or in the former the higher and more conscious, in the latter the lower and animal side (Bleek, Luthardt). Besides the above, other objections lie against both these interpretations,—(1) that σάρξ is never so used (Eph. v. 29 is no instance in point); (2) that θέλημα is ascribed to *both*. Euthymius seems to give the right interpretation: εἰπὼν δὲ ὅτι οὐκ ἐξ αἱμάτων, ἐπήγαγε φανερώτερον ὅτι οὐδὲ ἐκ θελήματος σαρκός· εἶτα καὶ τοῦτο τελεώτερον ἑφηρμήνευσε, προσθεὶς ὅτι οὐκ ἐκ θελήματος ἀνδρός· αἷμα γὰρ καὶ σάρξ, ὁ ἀνήρ· θέλημα δὲ νῦν νοεῖ τὴν ἐπιθυμίαν, τὴν συνουσίαν: in loc. ii. 421. Or perhaps this may be carried somewhat further, and we may better satisfy the climax by regarding the ἐξ αἱμάτων as indicating the mere phenomena of physical generation wherever found: then rising to ἐκ θελήματος σαρκός, the instigation of that capacity by sexual desire: then rising still higher to the most exalted instance of that desire, ἐκ θελήματος ἀνδρός. The plural usage of **αἱμάτων** is only found in one other place in this signification,—Eurip. Ion 693 Dind., 705 Herm., ἔχει δόλον τύχαν θ' ὁ παῖς | ἄλλων τραφεὶς ἀφ' αἱμάτων. The other usage of the plural, for *murder*, is frequent in the LXX and the classics. **ἀνήρ**, in the sense of *man* generally, is not uncommon; we have in plur. πατὴρ ἀνδρῶν τε θεῶν τε, in Hom. passim; and in sing. Il. ν. 321; σ. 432, 433. **ἐκ**, remarks De Wette, denotes, the first time, the *material*—the second and third time, the *mediate* cause,—the fourth time, the *immediate* cause, of the generation. **14.**] **καί** must not be understood (Chrysost., Grot., Lampe, Theophylact, al.) as giving a reason for the verse before; it is only the same copula as in vv. 1, 3, 4, 5; passing on to a further assertion regarding the Word. **σὰρξ ἐγ.**, became *flesh*: the most general expression of the great truth that He became *man*. He became that, of which man is in the body compounded. There is no *reference* here to the doctrine of the Lord Jesus being the second Adam, as Olshausen thinks; but although there may be no *reference* to it, it *lies at the ground* of this wideness of expression. The doctrine *in this form* may have been, as Lücke observes, alien to John's habits of thought, but not *that which is implied in the doctrine*, the taking of the *nature of man* by the Eternal Word. The simplicity of this expression is no doubt directed against the Docetæ of the Apostle's time, who maintained that the Word *only apparently* took human nature. Therefore he says σὰρξ **ἐγένετο**, absolutely and literally *became* flesh: see ref. 1 John. The expression is not guarded against the interpretation of the Apollinarian heretics, who held that the Lord had not a human *soul* (ψυχή); but this error was not in the Apostle's view, and is abundantly refuted elsewhere (see Matt. xxvi. 38 and note on 36—46, and the references there made to John's Gospel). **ἐσκήνωσεν**, '*sojourned*,' or '*tabernacled*,' in us. There is no reference to the flesh being the *tabernacle* of the Spirit;—but the word is one technically used in Scripture to import the *dwelling of God among men.* See besides reff., Levit. xxvi. 11, 12: Ezek. xliii. 7; xxxvii. 27: Sir. xxiv. 8, 10.

ἡμῖν—" hominibus, qui caro sumus," Bengel. **καὶ ἐθ. τ. δόξ. αὐτ.**] **we saw**—see 1 John i. 1: 2 Pet. i. 16.

u ch. vii. 29. see Mark iii. 21.
v John vv. 16, 17. 2 John 3. Rev. i. 4. xxii. 21 only. elsw., princ. L.P., passim.
w ch. iv. 24. xvii. 17. 1 John i. 6 al.
x ver. 7 reff.
y perf., here only. Isa. xv. 4.

γενοῦς [u] παρὰ πατρός, πλήρης [v] χάριτος καὶ [w] ἀληθείας.
15 Ἰωάννης [x] μαρτυρεῖ [x] περὶ αὐτοῦ, καὶ [y] κέκραγεν λέ-

ABCDE FGHK LMSUV ΧΓΔΛ ΠℵN 1. 33. 69

14. πληρη D 5 Thl. (*pleni* (viz *unigeniti*) Aug_1; *plenum* (viz *verbum*) vulg lat-*b c* $Iren\text{-}int_2$ Hil : *plenus* lat-*a e* $Novat_1$.) om last και B^1. (ins B^2, not B^1-corr : see **table.**)

This is the Apostle's testimony *as such*, see Acts i. 21. The mention of **δόξα** seems to be suggested by the word **ἐσκήνωσεν**, so frequently used of the divine Presence or *Shechinah*, and cognate in its very form with it: "eædem litteræ in שכינה et σκηνή." Bengel. This glory was seen by the disciples, ch. ii. 11; xi. 4: also by Peter, James, and John, specially, on the mount of transfiguration: to which occasion the words ὡς μονογενοῦς παρὰ πατρός seem to refer: but mainly, in the whole converse and teaching and suffering of the Lord, who was full of grace and truth: see below. On **ὡς** Chrysostom remarks (Hom. xii. in Joan., vol. viii. p. 66), οὐχ ὁμοιώσεως, οὐδὲ παραβολῆς, ἀλλὰ βεβαιώσεως καὶ ἀναμφισβητήτου δωρισμοῦ· ὡσανεὶ ἔλεγεν Ἐθ. δόξαν **οἵαν ἔπρεπε καὶ εἰκὸς ἔχειν** μονογενῆ καὶ γνήσιον υἱὸν ὄντα τοῦ πάντων βασιλέως θεοῦ (see reff.). **μονογ.**] This word applied to Christ is peculiar to John: see reff. In the N. T. usage it signifies the *only* son;—in the LXX, Ps. xxi. 20, the *beloved*, and Ps. xxiv. 16, one *deserted, left alone*. It has been attempted to render the word in John, according to the usage in Ps. xxi. 20. But obviously in the midst of ideas reaching so far deeper than that of regard, or love, of the Father for the Son, the word cannot be interpreted except in accordance with them. It refers to, and contrasts with, the τέκνα τοῦ θεοῦ in vv. 12, 13. *They* receive their divine birth by faith in Him and through Him; but He is the μονογενής of the Father in the higher sense, in which He is γεννηθείς the Son of God. **παρὰ πατρός** belongs to μονογενοῦς; not to **δόξαν**, as Theophyl., Erasm., Grot. suppose. The ellipse is to be supplied by considering the state in which the λόγος here appears,—that of having become σάρξ and dwelling among us. **πλήρ. χάρ. κ. ἀλ.**] These words have been variously connected. The view of Erasmus, who places the period at πατρός, and connects these words with Ἰωάννης, scarcely needs refutation, whether we regard the construction, or the meaning of the sentence. The reading πλήρη has probably arisen from a correction, to connect the adj. with δόξαν. Some do this even with πλήρης, but both the construction and the sense are against it. It was not the δόξα, but He Himself, that was πλήρης χ. κ. ἀλ.: see below, ver. 17. Others suppose πλήρης to refer directly to μονογενοῦς, and justify this by Eph. iii. 17, 18. But besides the unnecessary harshness of this, the sense is against it also; for it cannot be said, 'we saw His glory, the glory as of one who was full of grace and truth;' we must have the ὡς referring, in the sense of οἵαν ἔπρεπε (see above), to some mysterious hidden character which the glory testified, whereas the πλήρης χ. κ. ἀλ. is itself a *mere matter of fact*, to which the Apostles themselves could (ver. 17) bear witness. Another construction is (as usually done and in E. V.) to take καὶ . . . . πατρός as parenthetical, and connect πλήρης immediately with ἐσκήνωσεν. Such parentheses are common in the style of this Gospel: see ch. vi. 22—24; xi. 2; xix. 23, 24; ib. ver. 31. But by far the best is, to regard πλήρης as referring to αὐτοῦ, by an anomaly in concord often found in the N. T. (see Luke xx. 27 note; xxiv. 47), and especially in the Apocalypse,—cf. Rev. i. 4 al. fr. **χάρ. κ. ἀλ.**] Not = χάριτος ἀληθινῆς, which destroys the precision of the expression, and itself conveys no sense whatever; but *setting out the two sides* of the divine manifestation in Christ,—**χάρις**, as the result of Love to mankind,—**ἀλήθεια** (see reff. and ch. xiv. 6), as the unity, purity, and light of His own Character. **15.**] The testimony of John, so important as being the fulfilment of the very object for which he was ἀπεσταλμένος παρὰ θεοῦ, is in this prologue ranged, so to speak, parallel with the assertions and testimony of the Evangelist himself. So that this verse does not interrupt the train of thought, but confirms by this important testimony the assertion ὁ λόγος σὰρξ ἐγ., shewing that John *bore witness to His præ-existence*. Then (ver. 16) the πλήρ. χ. κ. ἀλ. is again taken up. Euthymius paraphrases: εἰ καὶ μὴ ἐγώ, φησί, δοκῶ τισιν ἴσως ἀξιόπιστος, ἀλλὰ πρὸ ἐμοῦ ὁ Ἰωάννης μαρτυρεῖ περὶ τῆς θεότητος αὐτοῦ, Ἰωάννης ἐκεῖνος, οὗ τὸ ὄνομα μέγα καὶ περιβόητον παρὰ πᾶσι τοῖς Ἰουδαίοις. **μαρτυρεῖ**, present, for solemnity—as part of the testimony to

γων Οὗτος ἦν ὃν [z] εἶπον Ὁ [a] ὀπίσω μου ἐρχόμενος, [b] ἔμπροσθέν μου γέγονεν, ὅτι [c] πρῶτός μου ἦν.
16 ὅτι
...παντες D. ἐκ τοῦ [d] πληρώματος αὐτοῦ ἡμεῖς πάντες [e] ἐλάβομεν,

z constr., ch. viii. 54. x. 36. Matt. iii. 3. xxiv. 15.
a = Matt. iii. 11 ∥ Mk. only. Neh. xiii. 19.
vv. 27, 30
b = ver. 30 only. Gen. xlviii. 20.
c = ver. 30. ch. xv. 18.
d John, here only. — Eph. iii. 19. Rom. xv. 29. see Ps. xxiii. 1.
e Matt. x. 8. Rom. i. 5.

15. om *λεγων* D ℵ[1](ins ℵ-corr[1]) lat-*b*. *ο ειπων* B[1]C[1] ℵ-corr[1] Orig[-Huet] : *ον ειπων* ℵ[2](?) : *ον ελεγον* C[3] : om ℵ[1] : txt B[2](sic) ℵ[3b] &c [$Orig_1$]. aft *ειπον* ins *υμιν* D[2]X am(with fuld) lat-*f* æth $Epiph_2$. aft *ερχομενος* ins *ος* ℵ[1] [lat-*c*].

16. rec (for *οτι*) *και* (*possibly the occurrence of οτι thrice following gave offence*), with AC[3] rel vulg lat-*c f* syrr syr-cu $Orig_2$ Chr_1 [Aug_1] : txt BC[1]DLXℵ 33 lat-*a b e ff*$_2$ *ç* syr-jer copt æth arm $Hipp_1$ $Orig_3$[int_1] Eus_1 Cyr_{alic} Hil_1.

Him, not only once given, but still subsisting. **κέκραγεν**] **crieth** (the *perfect* being, in sense, *present; 'hath cried,'* so that the voice is still sounding), see ch. vii. 37: "clamat Johannes cum fiducia et gaudio, uti magnum præconem decet." Bengel. **οὗτος ἦν ὃν εἶπον . . . .**] This form of the words seems to shew, as indeed would appear from the announcement of his own office by the Baptist, that he had uttered these words in the power of the Spirit concerning Him whose forerunner he was *before he saw and recognized Him in the flesh.* Then, *on doing so,* he exclaimed, **This was He of whom I said,** &c. This view seems to be borne out by his own statement, ver. 33, and by the order of the narrative in Matt. iii. 11, 12, 13. **ὀπίσω μ. ἐρχ.**] In point of *time;* **not** of *birth* merely or principally, nor of *commencement of official life:* but, inasmuch as John was His *Forerunner,* on account of official *position.* **ἔμπροσθέν μ. γέγονεν**] The E. V. is here very accurate,—**is preferred before me;** the **γέγονεν** setting forth the advancement to official dignity before which John's office waned and decreased (ch. iii. 30), which took place even while John's course was being fulfilled. The only objection to *'preferred'* is, its possible ambiguity. Even Dr. Johnson has fallen into the mistake, in his Dictionary, of quoting this passage as an instance of the sense "to love more than another." [*'Taketh place,'*] *' is advanced,'* 'hath come to be' (which however again is ambiguous), are other possible renderings. This sense of **ἔμπροσθεν** (besides reff.) is justified by classical usage in Plato, who uses *ἔμπροσθεν τιθέναι* for *præponere,* Legg. vii. 805. See also i. 631; v. 743. Also Demosthenes, *κατὰ Διονυσοδώρου,* p. 1296. 26, ... *τὰς αἰτίας τῶν ἠδικηκότων ἔμπροσθεν οὔσας τοῦ δικαίου.* **ὅτι πρῶτός μου ἦν**] The only sense which these words will bear, is, **because** (or, **for,** but better *because*) **He** *was* (not *ἐγένετο,* but **ἦν** as in ver. 1) **before Me;** i. e. 'He *existed,* was in being, before me.' The question raised by Lücke and De Wette, whether it is probable that the Baptist had, or expressed such views of the præ-existence of Christ, is not one for us to deal with, in the face of so direct a testimony as is given to the *fact,* here and in ch. iii. 27 ff. In all probability, the Evangelist was himself a disciple of the Baptist: and if he has given us a fuller and somewhat differing account of his testimony to Christ, it is because his means of information were ampler than those of the other Evangelists. The questioners seem to forget that the Baptist was divinely raised up and commissioned, *and full of the Holy Ghost,* and *spoke in that power;* his declarations were not therefore merely conclusions which he had arrived at by natural means,—the study of the prophecies, &c. (Lücke, p. 353): but *inspirations and revelations of the Spirit.* This last is fully recognized by Olshausen (ii. 61). **16.**] Origen (in Evang. Johan. tom. vi. 2, vol. iv. p. 102) blames Heracleon for terminating the testimony of John at the end of ver. 17, and makes it continue to the end of ver. 18. But it can hardly be that his testimony extends beyond ver. 15, for *ἡμεῖς πάντες* would bear no very definite meaning, and the assertions in ver. 17 would be alien from the character of the Baptist, belonging as they do to the more mature development of Christian doctrines. I cannot doubt that this and the following verses *belong to the Evangelist,* and are a carrying onwards of his declarations concerning the divine Word. Ver. 15 is not parenthetical, but confirmatory of ver. 14, and this verse *grounds itself on the fact* of ver. 14, *corroborated by the testimony* of ver. 15,—*that He dwelt among us, and that we saw His glory, full of grace and truth.* **τὸ πλήρωμα** is *that of which He was* **πλήρης,** ver. 14, and is not connected with the Gnostic *pleroma* at all. See reff. **ἡμεῖς πάντες**] All who believe on Him: see ver. 12. **ἐλάβομεν, καί**] **received,**

καὶ χάριν [f] ἀντὶ χάριτος· 17 ὅτι ὁ νόμος [g] διὰ Μωυσέως [h] ἐδόθη, ἡ [i] χάρις καὶ ἡ [i] ἀλήθεια διὰ Ἰησοῦ
χριστοῦ [k] ἐγένετο. 18 [l] θεὸν οὐδεὶς [l] ἑώρακεν [l] πώποτε·

ABCEF GHKL MSUVX ΓΔΛΠℵ 1. 33. 69

f = here only. see Isa. lvii. 19.
g Matt. i. 22. Gal. iii. 19 al.
h ch. vii. 19, 22. Acts vii. 8. Gal. iii. 21. Ezek xx. 11 al.
i ver. 14.
k = Luke iii. 2. ch. x. 35. Acts x. 37.
l see 1 John iv. 12, 20

17. om χριστου ℵ[1]. [**18.** εορακεν B[1](Tischdf, expr) EFGHKX.]

and that . . . . 'our relation to Him has been that of recipients out of His fulness, and the thing received has been' . . . . So Herod. i. 102, ἔχων δύο ταῦτα ἔθνεα, καὶ ἀμφότερα ἰσχυρά. **χάριν ἀντὶ χάριτος**] The ancient interpretation, τὴν καινὴν διαθήκην ἀντὶ τῆς παλαιᾶς (Euthym.), is certainly wrong, for the ἐλάβομεν is spoken entirely of *the times of the Incarnate Word:* and besides, ὁ νόμος and χάρις are distinctly *opposed* to one another in the next verse. The prep. **ἀντί** is properly used of any thing which *supersedes* another, or occupies its place. This is in fact its ordinary usage when *exchange* is spoken of: the possession of the thing gotten succeeds to, supersedes, the possession of the thing given in exchange, and I possess τοῦτο ἀντὶ ἐκείνου. Thus also we have received χάριν ἀντὶ χάριτος, *continual accessions of grace;* new grace coming upon and superseding the former. Thus in Theognis, Sentt. 343 ff. (Lücke), τεθναίην δ' εἰ μή τι κακῶν ἄμπαυμα μεριμνέων | εὑροίμην, δοίης δ' **ἀντ' ἀνιῶν ἀνίας**. And Chrysostom, de Sacerdotio, 6. 13, vol. i. p. 435, σὺ δέ με ἐκπέμπεις, **ἑτέραν ἀνθ' ἑτέρας** φροντίδα ἐνθείς. Also Philo, i. 254, speaking of this very word χάρις:—τὰς πρώτας ἀεὶ χάριτας . . . . ἐπισχὼν καὶ ταμιευσάμενος εἰσαῦθις **ἑτέρας ἀντὶ ἐκείνων** καὶ **τρίτας ἀντὶ δευτέρων**, καὶ ἀεὶ **νέας ἀντὶ παλαιοτέρων**, τότε μὲν διαφορούσας, τότε δ' αὖ καὶ τὰς αὐτὰς ἐπιδίδωσι. **17.**] The connexion of this verse with the foregoing lies in the words τοῦ πληρώμ. αὐτοῦ (ver. 16), and in χάρις κ. ἀλ. (ver. 14). 'We received from His fulness continual additions of grace, *because that fulness is not, like the law, a positive enactment, finite and circumscribed,* of which it could be said that it **ἐδόθη**, but the *bringing in of grace and truth,* which **ἐγένετο** by Jesus Christ.' **ἐδόθη** and **ἐγένετο** have been variously distinguished,—αὐθεντικὸν μὲν **τὸ ἐγένετο**, δουλικὸν δὲ **τὸ ἐδόθη**, Theophyl. Similarly Bengel, "Mosis non sua est lex; Christi sua est gratia et veritas." Clem. Alex. Pæd. i. 7, p. 134 P, says: διὸ καί φησιν ἡ γραφὴ "ὁ νόμος **διὰ** Μωυσέως ἐδόθη," οὐχὶ **ὑπὸ** Μωυσέως, ἀλλὰ ὑπὸ μὲν τοῦ λόγου, διὰ Μωυσέως δὲ τοῦ θεράποντος αὐτοῦ· διὸ καὶ πρόσκαιρος ἐγίνετο, ἡ δὲ ἀΐδιος χάρις καὶ ἡ ἀλήθεια διὰ Ἰησοῦ χριστοῦ ἐγένετο, κ.τ.λ. Origen (in Joan. tom. vi. c. 3, vol. iv .p. 107) speaks very similarly. But the distinction laid down above, which is hinted at by De Wette, seems to me to be the most obvious, and best suited to the context, where the **πλήρωμα** of Christ is set against the *narrowness of positive enactment* in the law. Certainly, the distinction must not be lost sight of, nor denied, as Lücke attempts to do: for Bengel truly observes: "Nullus philosophus tam accurate verba ponit, differentiamque eorum observat, quam Johannes, in hoc præsertim capite." **χάρις κ. ἀλ.**] I must again caution the student against any such wholly inadequate explanations as that these words are put 'per hendiadyn' for χάρις ἀληθινή. It is in this way that the depths of Scripture have been covered over by the rubbish of expositors. Such was not the method of investigation pursued by the great men of former centuries: witness Origen in loc.: εἰ γὰρ Ἰησοῦς ἐστιν ὁ φάσκων "ἐγώ εἰμι ἡ ἀλήθεια," πῶς ἡ ἀλήθεια διὰ Ἰησοῦ χριστοῦ γίνεται; αὐτὸς γάρ τις δι' ἑαυτοῦ οὐ γίνεται. ἀλλὰ νοητέον ὅτι ἡ αὐτοαλήθεια ἡ οὐσιώδης καὶ ἵν' οὕτως εἴπω πρωτότυπος τῆς ἐν ταῖς λογικαῖς ψυχαῖς ἀληθείας . . . . οὐχὶ διὰ Ἰησοῦ χριστοῦ ἐγένετο, οὐδ' ὅλως διά τινος, ἀλλ' ὑπὸ θεοῦ ἐγένετο· ὡς καὶ ὁ λόγος οὐ διά τινος, ὁ ἐν ἀρχῇ πρὸς τὸν θεόν, καὶ ἡ σοφία, ἣν ἔκτισεν ἀρχὴν ὁδῶν αὐτοῦ ὁ θεός, οὐ διά τινος, οὕτως οὐδὲ ἡ ἀλήθεια διά τινος. ἡ δὲ παρ' ἀνθρώποις ἀλήθεια διὰ Ἰησοῦ χριστοῦ ἐγένετο· οἷον ἡ ἐν Παύλῳ ἀλ. καὶ τοῖς ἀποστόλοις διὰ Ἰησοῦ χριστοῦ ἐγένετο (vol. iv. p. 107). **18.**] The connexion is: 'Moses could not give out of the πλήρωμα of grace and truth, for he had no *immediate* sight of God, and no man can have: there is but One who can ἐξηγεῖσθαι θεόν, the μονογενὴς υἱός, who is no mere *man*, but abides in the bosom of the Father.' **θεὸν οὐδ. ἑώρ. π.**] The *sight of God* here meant, is not only bodily sight (though of that it is true, see Exod. xxxiii. 20: 1 Tim. vi. 16), but *intuitive* and *infallible knowledge,* which enables Him who has it to declare the nature and will of God: see ch. iii. 11; vi. 46; xiv. 7. The Evangelist speaks in this verse in accord-

* ὁ [m] μονογενὴς * υἱός, ὁ ὢν [n] εἰς τὸν [o] κόλπον τοῦ πατρός, [p] ἐκεῖνος [q] ἐξηγήσατο.

m ver. 14. n constr., Matt. ii. 23. Mark i. 21, 39. xiii. 16. o Luke xvi. 22 reff. p = ver. 33. ch. v. 11. ix. 37. x. 1 al. q John, here only. Luke xxiv. 35. Acts x. 8. xv. 12, 14. xxi. 19 only. Lev. xiv. 57. 1 Chron. xvi. 24.

* μονογενὴς θεός BC¹Lℵ 33 Syr syr-mg copt æth-rom Thdot Clem Ep-syn-Ancyr $Epiph_3$ Did_2 (pref ὁ ℵ[3a] $Clem_1$) : ο μονογενης υιος A rel (and apparently all other mss) latt syr-cu syr-txt syr-jer æth-pl arm $Hipp_1$ Ps-Ign Ep-syn-Ant $Eus_{5\ or\ 6}$ Eustath Ath_7 $emp\text{-}Julian_2$(apud Cyr) Naz_1 Chr_3 Thdor-mops $Thdrt_4$ $Damasc_3$ $Thdor\text{-}stud_2$ Thl $Euthym_3$ Ps-Archel-int $Tert_2$ Hil_7 Phœb $Ambr_7$ Jer Aug_3 Maximin-arian Vig-taps. [A detailed account of the most important parts of the patristic testimony is in this case very necessary.

Tertullian wrote against Praxeas (cap xv. vol ii. pp. 172 ff. ed Migne) as follows: *Ecce enim et in Evangeliis et in Apostolis visibilem et invisibilem deum deprehendo; sub manifesta et personali distinctione conditionis utriusque. Exclamat quodammodo Johannes: "Deum nemo vidit unquam," utique nec retro. Ademit enim temporis quæstionem, dicendo deum nunquam visum. Confirmat et Apostolus de deo: "Quem nemo vidit hominum sed nec videre potest," scilicet quia morietur, qui videbit. . . . . . Et ideo quoniam sermonem dei deum dixerat* (John i. 1) *ne* (al *ut*) *adjuvaret adversariorum præsumptionem quasi patrem ipsum vidisset, ad distinguendum inter invisibilem patrem et filium visibilem, superdicit ex abundanti: "Deum nemo vidit unquam." Quem deum: sermonem? Atquin "vidimus et audivimus et contrectavimus de sermone vitæ" prædictum est. Sed quem deum? scilicet patrem apud quem deum erat sermo, "unigenitus (scilicet) filius qui in sinum* (al *est in sinu*) *patris ipse disseruit." . . . . . Filius ergo visus est semper, et filius conversatus est semper, et filius operatus est semper, ex auctoritate patris et voluntate: quia "filius nihil a semetipso potest facere, nisi viderit patrem facientem;" in sensu scilicet facientem. Pater enim (in) sensu agit. Filius vero, quod in patris sinu est videns perficit. Sic "omnia per filium facta sunt et sine illo factum est nihil."* There cannot therefore be the smallest doubt that Tertullian really read *filius*. Equally clear is the evidence of Hippolytus: ὁρῶν δὲ τὸν θεὸν οὐδ' εἷς εἰ μὴ μόνος ὁ παῖς, καὶ τέλειος ἄνθρωπος, καὶ μόνος διηγησάμενος τὴν βουλὴν τοῦ πατρός. λέγει γὰρ καὶ Ἰωάννης "Θεὸν οὐδεὶς ἑώρακεν πώποτε· μονογενὴς υἱός, ὁ ὢν εἰς τὸν κόλπον τοῦ πατρός, αὐτὸς διηγήσατο." (Cont. Hær. Noeti, c. v. p. 812, Migne, Patrol. vol x.) On the same side is the Synodical Epistle of the Antiochene Council which condemned Paul of Samosata: ἀλλὰ μὴν καὶ τὸν νόμον ὁμοίως Μωυσῇ φαμὲν δεδόσθαι διακονοῦντος τοῦ υἱοῦ τοῦ θεοῦ (Gal iii. 19: Exod iii. 2, 4, 16; iv. 1) . . . . (Exod xxxiii. 17--19) ὅπερ τελειοῦται οὕτως . . . (xxxiv. 5, 6) ὁ γὰρ ἄνω παρελεύσεσθαι ἐπαγγειλάμενος, ὁ υἱὸς τοῦ θεοῦ κύριος· καὶ ἐκάλεσεν ἐν ὀνόματι κυρίου τοῦ πατρός. οὗτός ἐστιν ὃς καὶ ἀληθεύει λέγων . . . (John vi. 46 and 37). καὶ "Θεὸν οὐδεὶς ἑώρακε πώποτε· ὁ μονογενὴς υἱὸς ὁ ὢν εἰς τὸν κόλπον τοῦ πατρός, ἐκεῖνος ἐξηγήσατο." καὶ ὁ ἀπόστολος ἐν ἄλλῳ. . . . (1 Tim i. 17). τὸν δὲ υἱόν, παρὰ τῷ πατρὶ ὄντα θεὸν μὲν καὶ κύριον τῶν γενητῶν ἁπάντων κ.τ.λ. (was sent from heaven and became incarnate). Routh, Rel. Sacr. iii. pp. 295—297, ed 1846. With regard to Eusebius, the facts seem to be as follows:—that he distinctly "quotes the passage with the "reading υἱός not less than six times. In one case indeed (De Eccles. Theol. lib i. c. "9, vol vi. p. 840) the words ἡ μονογενὴς θεός are added after ὁ μονογενὴς υἱός. This "passage *alone*, however, when carefully examined with the *context*, seems enough "to disprove this claim; and when it is taken in connexion with at least *five* other "unequivocal quotations in which Eusebius reads υἱός, there really appears to be no "room for doubt." (Mr. E. Abbot in the Andover "Bibliotheca Sacra," Oct. 1861.) The summary of the chapter in which the passage above referred to occurs is "that the Son does not subsist in the same way as τὰ πολλὰ κτίσματα." After quoting "This is my beloved Son," Eusebius goes on: αὐτοῦ τοιγαροῦν τοῦ τῶν ὅλων θεοῦ ταύτην αὐτῷ τὴν μαρτυρίαν παρασχομένου τοῦ τε εὐαγγελιστοῦ διαῤῥήδην αὐτὸν υἱὸν μονογενῆ εἶναι διδάσκοντος δι' ὧν ἔφη "Θεὸν οὐδεὶς ἑώρακε πώποτε· ὁ μονογενὴς υἱός, ἡ μονογενὴς θεός, ὁ ὢν εἰς τὸν κόλπον τοῦ πατρός, ἐκεῖνος ἐξηγήσατο." "Athanasius "apparently knew of no other reading but υἱός: he distinctly quotes the text 4 times, "and refers to it thrice in addition. Hilary has *commented* on his quotation

ance with the sayings of the gnosis whose phraseology he has adopted: τίς ἑώρακεν αὐτὸν καὶ ἐκδιηγήσεται; Sir. xliii. 31.

ὁ μον. υἱός] As regards the reading μονογενὴς **θεός**, the authorities for and against it will be found in the digest. It

r constr., Rom. xi. 27, from Isa. xxvii. 9. s ver. 7.

19 Καὶ ʳ αὕτη ἐστὶν ἡ ˢ μαρτυρία τοῦ Ἰωάννου, ʳ ὅτε ABCEF GHKL MSUVX ΓΔΛΠℵ 1. 33. 69

"of John i. 18 (De Trin. lib vi. cap 39, vol ii. p. 163) in such a way as to demon-"strate that he read *Filius*. He remarks: *Naturæ fides non satis explicata vide-"batur ex nomine 'Filii,' nisi proprietatis extrinsecus virtus per exceptionis signifi-"cantiam adderetur. Præter 'Filium' enim, et 'unigenitum' cognominans, suspi-"cionem adoptionis penitus exsecuit.* The only passage, so far as I know, in all "Hilary's writings, which has even the appearance of supporting the reading *uni-"genitus Deus* is in his work De Trin. lib xii. cap 24, vol ii. p. 422. Having quoted "Exod iii. 14, '*Misit me ad vos is qui est*' (ὁ ὤν, LXX), and remarking *Deo proprium "esse* id quod est *non ambigens sensus est*, he goes on to argue that this expression "implies eternity, and then says: *Quod igitur et per Moysen de Deo significatum "....id ipsum unigenito Deo esse proprium Evangelia testantur: cum in principio* "erat *verbum* (John i. 1), *et cum hoc apud Deum* erat, *et cum* erat *lumen verum* (ver "9), *et cum unigenitus Deus in sinu Patris* est (ver 18), *et cum Jesus Christus super "omnia Deus* est (Rom ix. 5). 'Erat' *igitur atque* 'est;' *quia ab eo est, qui quod "est semper est.* From this it will be perceived that Hilary's argument rests wholly "on the word '*est.*'" (Notwithstanding this, however, the impression naturally derived from the passage is that Hilary is here just as distinctly quoting John i. 18 (with the reading θεός) as Rom ix. 5 immediately below. H. A.) "The *expression "'unigenitus Deus'* is a favourite one with Hilary. It occurs in his treatise De "Trinitate about one hundred and four times." (Abbot, *ut supra.*) The following is Abbot's list of the seven places in which Hilary quotes the passage with the reading *Filius*: Tract. in Psalmum cxxxviii. cap 35, vol i. p. 578, Migne: De Trin. lib ii. cap 23, vol ii. p. 40; lib iv. capp 8, p. 76; 42, p. 101; lib v. capp 33, 34, pp. 125, 126; and lib vi. cap 39, p. 163.

The concurrent testimony of Hippolytus, the Synodical Epistle from Antioch, Eusebius, Athanasius, and apparently the whole of the Latin Fathers, is very strong. On the other side we have the Excerpta Theodoti, Epiphanius, Didymus, and perhaps Clement of Alexandria and the Synod of Ancyra A.D. 358.

THEODOTUS says, John i. 1 is interpreted by the Valentinians thus: ἀρχὴν μὲν γὰρ τὸν μονογενῆ λέγουσιν, ὃν καὶ θεὸν προσαγορεύεσθαι, ὡς καὶ ἐν τοῖς ἑξῆς ἄντικρυς θεὸν αὐτὸν δηλοῖ λέγων "Ὁ μονογενὴς θεός, ὁ ὢν εἰς τὸν κόλπον τοῦ πατρός, ἐκεῖνος ἐξηγήσατο." (Excerpta Theod. inter Opp. Clem. Alex. § 6, p. 958 P: but see Theod. § 9, p. 959.) CLEMENT OF ALEXANDRIA, speaking of the difficulty of knowing God and of the impossibility of declaring God in words, brings forward Rom xi. 33: 1 Cor ii. 6, 7: Col ii. 2, 3: Ps lxxvii.: and Matt xiii. 11, 33: having added quotations from Solon and Empedocles, he goes on: καὶ Ἰωάννης ὁ ἀπόστολος "Θεὸν οὐδεὶς ἑώρακεν πώποτε· ὁ μονογενὴς θεός, ὁ ὢν εἰς τὸν κόλπον τοῦ πατρός, ἐκεῖνος ἐξηγήσατο." τὸ δ' ἀόρατον καὶ ἄῤῥητον, κόλπον ὀνομάσας θεοῦ. . . . . . τοῦ δὲ ἀγεννήτου οὐδὲν προϋπάρχει. λείπεται δὴ θείᾳ χάριτι καὶ μόνῳ τῷ παρ' αὐτὸν λόγῳ τὸ ἄγνωστον νοεῖν· καθὸ καὶ ὁ Λουκᾶς . . . . (Acts xvii. 22, 23). (Strom. v. 12, pp. 695, 696 P.) The only other passage in which Clement quotes John i. 18 is in "Quis dives salvetur," the opening words of ch xxxvii., p. 946 P: τί γὰρ ἔτι δεῖ θεῷ τὰ τῆς ἀγάπης μυστήρια; καὶ τότε ἐποπτεύσεις τὸν κόλπον τοῦ πατρός, ὃν ὁ μονογενὴς υἱὸς θεὸς μόνος ἐξηγήσατο. It appears then that Clement knew of and used a reading or interpretation (it may be only the latter) of John i. 18 which sanctioned the use of the term μονογενὴς θεός.

"EPIPHANIUS has quoted the passage three times with the reading θεός (Hær. "lxv. cap 5 (*bis?*), vol i. (ii. Migne) p. 612, and lxx. cap 7, p. 817). In the remark, "however, which follows the quotation in the first passage, θεός and υἱός are inter-"changed:—καί φησι, 'Ὁ μονογενὴς θεός·' ὁ μὲν γὰρ λόγος ἐστὶν ἐκ πατρὸς γεννηθείς, "ὁ πατὴρ δὲ οὐκ ἐγεννήθη· διὰ τοῦτο μονογενὴς υἱός. DIDYMUS has quoted the "passage twice with the reading θεός (De Trinit. lib i. cap 26, p. 393, and lib ii. cap "5, p. 495). He also says ὁ υἱὸς κέκληται μονογενὴς θεὸς λόγος, καὶ εἷς κύριος Ἰησοῦς "χριστός (lib i. c. 15, p. 313). But here it may be doubted whether a comma should "be placed after μονογενής, or after θεός, or after neither. The SECOND (semi-"arian) SYNOD OF ANCYRA *may* have read θεός in John i. 18, but the evidence is not "decisive. After quoting Prov viii. 22 &c., Col i. 15 &c., and the first verses of the

seems to have arisen from a confusion of the contracted forms of writing, ΥC and ΘC. The question, which reading to adopt, is one which, in the balance of authorities, must be provisionally decided by the consideration that as far as we can see, we

ἀπέστειλαν πρὸς αὐτὸν οἱ ᵗ Ἰουδαῖοι ἐξ Ἱεροσολύμων ᵗ – (see note) ch. ii. 18, 20. v. 10 al. fr.

"Proem to the Gospel of John, without any allusion, however, to John i. 18 . . . . "ὡς ἔχειν τὴν ἐπὶ στόματος δύο καὶ τριῶν μαρτύρων εἰς ἀπόδειξιν τῆς κατ' οὐσίαν πρὸς "πατέρα τοῦ υἱοῦ ὁμοιότητος. ὁ μὲν γὰρ (Solomon) τοῦ σοφοῦ τὴν σοφίαν υἱόν· ὁ δὲ "(John) τοῦ θεοῦ τὸν λόγον μονογενῆ θεόν· ὁ δὲ (Paul) τοῦ θεοῦ τὸν υἱὸν εἰκόνα φησί "(Apud Epiph. Hær. lxxiii. cap 8, vol i. (ii. Migne) p. 854). We have no reason to "suppose, *à priori*, that the reference to John is verbally accurate any more than "that to Proverbs, where we find neither the word υἱός, nor the expression ἡ "σοφία τοῦ σοφοῦ. It is not uncommon with the Fathers to give as the language "of Scripture, expressions formed from several passages combined, or which they "regard as fully authorized by Scripture though not occurring there in so many "words." (Abbot, *ut supra.*)

The evidence from Irenæus, Origen, Basil, and Cyril of Alexandria, is contradictory and uncertain. It is hardly possible to decide what was the reading of the copies known to IRENÆUS: he quotes the passage three times; *unigenitus Filius Dei* in Hær. iii. 11. 6, p. 189, *unigenitus Filius* ib iv. 20. 6, p. 255, *unigenitus Deus* ib iv. 20. 11, p. 256. In no case is either word absolutely inconsistent with his context; as far as Irenæus' argument is concerned we might read 'He who is in the bosom of the Father hath declared Him.' In the two first cases we have *Filius* in the immediate context; in the third, *Verbum*, though *Filius Dei* is not far off. On the one hand, the translator *may* have conformed two of the quotations to the received Latin version. On the other hand, had Irenæus read θεός, his subject ("seeing God") must almost have compelled him to give some distinct exposition of its bearing.

"ORIGEN has θεός, In Joan. tom ii. c. 29, vol iv. p. 89, and xxxii. c. 13, "p. 438. In both (only the former in Migne) these passages, however, the very literal "version of Ferrari, made from a ms now lost, reads *unigenitus* alone, without either "*Deus* or *Filius*. On the other hand we have υἱός, Cont. Cels. lib ii. c. 71, vol i. "p. 440 . . . . So De la Rue and Lommatsch from two mss; the earlier edn of "Hœschel founded on a single ms, instead of ὁ μονογενὴς υἱός reads καὶ μονογενής "γε ὢν θεός. . . . υἱὸς τοῦ θεοῦ occurs In Joan. tom vi. cap 2, p. 102, as edited "by De la Rue and Lommatsch from the Bodleian ms; the earlier edn of Huet, which "was founded on a single ms, reads υἱὸς θεός. A little after, in two allusions to the "passage, ὁ μονογενής is used alone. BASIL . . . has θεός once, and in another "passage mentions υἱὸς ἀληθινός, μονογενὴς θεός, δύναμις θεοῦ, σοφία, and λόγος as "names given to Christ in Scripture; but he twice quotes the text in question with "the reading υἱός. CYRIL OF ALEXANDRIA, as edited by Aubert, has θεός four "times, and υἱός three times. His commentary on the passage, as printed, favours "θεός, but its evidence is somewhat weakened by various readings." (Abbot, *ut supra.*)]

om ο ων ℵ[1](ins ℵ[2] ?) [lat-*a*].

19. rec om προς αυτον, with C[3]ℵ rel Orig$_2$ [Cyr$_1$-txt]: ins BC[1] 33 lat-*a b c* Syr syr-cu

should be introducing great harshness into the sentence, and a new and strange term into Scripture, by adopting θεός: a consequence which ought to have no weight whatever where authority is overpowering, but may fairly be weighed where this is not so. The "præstat procliviori ardua" finds in this case a legitimate limit.

ὁ ὢν εἰς τ. κόλπον] The expression must not be understood as referring to the custom of reclining ἐν τῷ κόλπῳ, as in ch. xiii. 23: for by this explanation confusion is introduced into the imagery, and the real depth of the truth hidden. The expression signifies, as Chrysostom observes, συγγένεια καὶ ἑνότης τῆς οὐσίας:—and is derived from the fond and intimate union of children and parents. The *present* participle, as in ch. iii. 13, is used to signify *essential truth*, without any particular regard to time. On the use of εἰς, see reff. It is not 'put for' ἐν: indeed it would be well for the student to bear in mind as a general rule, that *no word or expression is ever 'put for' another:* words are the index of thoughts, —and where an unusual construction is found, it points to some reason in the mind of the writer for using it, which reason is lost in the ordinary shallow method of accounting for it by saying that it is 'put for' some other word. So here, εἰς τὸν κόλπον is not = ἐν τῷ κόλπῳ, but is a carrying on of the thought expressed in ver. 1, by πρὸς τὸν θεόν: it is a pregnant construction, involving in it the begetting of the Son and His being the λόγος of the Father,—His

u = Matt. vii. 23. Tit. i. 16. 2 Macc. vi. 6.
v Matt. xxvi. 70, 72 reff.
w Matt. vii. 23. Heb. xi. 13. 1 John iv. 15 only. see 2 Macc. vii. 37.

ἱερεῖς καὶ Λευείτας ἵνα ἐρωτήσωσιν αὐτὸν Σὺ τίς εἶ;
20 καὶ [u] ὡμολόγησεν καὶ οὐκ [v] ἠρνήσατο· καὶ [uw] ὡμολόγησεν
[w] ὅτι ἐγὼ οὐκ εἰμὶ ὁ χριστός. 21 καὶ ἠρώτησαν αὐτὸν Σὺ

ABCEF GHKL MSUVX ΓΔΛΠℵ 1. 33. 69

copt (æth) arm Chr$_1$, and (aft λευειτας) AX 69 vulg lat-*e f ff$_2$ l q* syr [Aug$_1$]. επερωτησωσιν ℵ.

20. om 3rd και C^{2}L 1. 33 lat-*b f* æth: om και ωμολογησεν ℵ [lat-*e l* syr-cu]. rec ουκ ειμι bef εγω, with C^3 rel vulg lat-*c f* [*ff$_2$ l*] syrr Hipp$_1$ [Epiph$_1$] Aug$_1$: [om εγω Π:] txt ABC^{1}LXΔℵ 33 forj lat-*a b e q* syr-cu syr-jer arm Orig$_3$ Chr$_1$-δ-ε-ζ-λ-π Cyr$_2$-comm.

21. επηρωτησαν ℵ^1(txt ℵ-corr$^{1 \cdot 3}$). for αυτον, παλιν ℵ^1: αυτον παλιν ℵ^{3a} [lat-*a*

proceeding forth from God. It is a similar expression, on the side of His Unity with the Father, to εἰμὶ παρὰ τοῦ θεοῦ, on the side of His manifestation to men. We have similar expressions, uniting the verb of rest with the preposition of motion, in ἐς θρόνους ἕζοντο, Od. δ. 51; εἰς ἀνάγκην κείμεθ', Eur. Iph. T. 624: see Kühner, Gr. Gr. § 622. **ἐκεῖνος**] '**He**, and none else:' an emphatic exclusive expression. **ἐξηγήσατο**] **declared**, better than '*hath declared*,' as E. V. ἐξηγέομαι, ἐξήγησις, and ἐξηγητής (Gen. xli. 8, 24), are technical terms used of the declaration of divine matters. Wetstein has collected abundance of passages in illustration of this usage. See also Müller's Eumenides, Excursus D, on the ἐξηγηταί. But Lücke (and I think rightly) believes it more in accordance with the simple style of John to take the word here in its ordinary, not its technical meaning. The object to be supplied after the verb is most likely αὐτόν, i. e. τὸν θεόν. De Wette thinks this too definite, and supplies 'that which He has seen,' as in ch. iii. 11. Lücke supplies τὴν χάριτα κ. ἀλ., as *being* 'that which He has seen;' but De Wette well observes that χάρις is more matter of revelation *by act*, than of ἐξήγησις. Euthymius's explanation, ἐδίδαξεν ὅτι θεὸν οὐδεὶς ἑώρακε πώποτε, is certainly wrong. See Matt. xi. 27.

19—II. 11.] Introduction of Christ to the world: by the witness of John (vv. 19—40): by Himself (ver. 41—ii. 11).

19—28.] *The first witness borne by John to Jesus: before the deputation from the Sanhedrim.*

19.] **αὕτη** is the predicate, **ἡ μαρτυρία** the subject, in the present form of the sentence. So very frequently in St. John, where commonly the mistake is made of supposing the demonstrative pronoun to be the subject, whereas it is ever the predicate of identification. Euthym., αὕτη . . . περὶ ἧς εἰπεῖν μέλλει προϊών, ... ἡ γενομένη δηλονότι ὅτε ἀπεστ. κ.τ.λ.

οἱ Ἰουδαῖοι] John alone of the Evangelists uses this expression;—principally as designating *the chiefs of the Jewish people*, the members of the Sanhedrim. It is an interesting enquiry, what this usage denotes as to the author or date of our Gospel. Prof. Bleek, Beiträge, pp. 245—249, has satisfactorily shewn that no inference can be deduced from it *against the Jewish origin* of the author, as Bretschneider and Fischer endeavoured to do: but it is rather confirmatory of the belief that the Gospel was written after the Jews had ceased to be politically a nation,—and among Gentiles;—the author himself contemplating these last as his readers. **ἐξ Ἱερ.** does not belong to οἱ Ἰουδ.,—nor to ἱερ. κ. Λευ.,—but to ἀπέστειλαν:—**sent from Jerusalem priests**, &c.: so ἐξαποστέλλω, Acts vii. 12; xi. 22 al. **ἱερ. κ. Λ.**] This was a *formal deputation*;—priests and Levites, constituting the two classes of persons employed about the service of the temple (see Josh. iii. 3), are sent (Matt. xxi. 23) officially to enquire into the pretensions of the new Teacher (ver. 25), who had collected about him such multitudes (Matt. iii. 5), and had awakened popular expectation that he was the Messiah (Luke iii. 15). **σὺ τίς εἶ**;—with reference to the popular doubts respecting him; asked in an unbelieving and inquisitorial spirit,—compare Matt. iii. 7 ff., which had already taken place. Even among the learned, as well as among the people, there were considerable differences as to the prophecies respecting the Messiah: see ch. vii. 40—52. **20.**] **ὡμολόγησεν**, he openly and formally confessed. This emphatic notice of his declaration seems to be introduced *not with any view of removing too high an estimate of John's work and office*, as sometimes supposed, but rather *to shew the importance of his testimony*, which was so publicly and officially delivered,—that the Messiah was come (see ch. v. 33—35); and the way in which he depreciated *him-*

οὖν τί; Ἡλίας εἶ; καὶ λέγει Οὐκ εἰμί. [x] Ὁ προφήτης
εἶ σύ; καὶ ἀπεκρίθη [y] Οὔ. 22 εἶπαν οὖν αὐτῷ Τίς εἶ;
ἵνα [za] ἀπόκρισιν [a] δῶμεν τοῖς πέμψασιν ἡμᾶς. τί λέγεις
περὶ σεαυτοῦ; 23 ἔφη Ἐγὼ [b] φωνὴ [c] βοῶντος ἐν τῇ
ἐρήμῳ [d] Εὐθύνατε τὴν ὁδὸν κυρίου, καθὼς εἶπεν Ἠσαΐας
ὁ προφήτης. 24 καὶ ἀπεσταλμένοι ἦσαν ἐκ τῶν Φαρι-

x ver. 25. ch. vi. 14. vii. 40. Deut. xviii. 15.
y = ch. xxi. 5. Matt. xiii. 29 only. see Acts xvi. 37. Rom. iii. 9.
z ch. xix. 9. Luke ii. 47. xx. 26 only. Prov. xv. 1.
a = ch. xix. 9. Job xxxv. 3.
b Isa. xl. 3.
c Mark i. 3 ||. xv. 34. Luke ix. 38. xviii. 7, 38. Acts viii. 7. xvii. 6. xxv. 24. Gal. iv. 27 (from Isa. liv. 1) only.
d = here only. (James iii. 4 only. Num. xxii. 23.) Sir. ii. 6.

b e ff$_2$ *l* Syr]. rec τι ουν ηλιας ει συ, with AC^3 rel vulg lat-(*b c*) *f* [*q*] syr [Chr$_1$]: τι ουν συ ηλ. ει C^1 33 forj lat-(*e*) *ff*$_2$ *l* Orig$_5$: τι ουν ηλ. ει Lא lat-*a* Syr [Cyr$_1$]: txt B. om 2nd και א [lat-*a b* copt]. om ο (bef προφητης) א^1 69.

22. (ειπαν, so BC^{1}Δ.)

24. rec ins οι bef απεσταλμενοι, with (A)C^3 א^{3b}(appy) rel latt syrr syr-jer [æth arm] (Orig$_1$) Chr$_1$: om BC^{1}Lא^1 copt (Orig$_1$).—οι απε re-written *prima manu* in A.

self in comparison with Him who came after him. **21.**] **σὺ οὖν τί**; equivalent to τί λέγεις περὶ σεαυτοῦ; ver. 22. **Ἡλίας εἶ;**] The whole appearance of John reminded them of Elias:—see Matt. iii. 4, and compare 2 Kings i. 8. Besides, his announcement that *the Kingdom of God was at hand*, naturally led them to the prophecy Mal. iv. 5. Lightfoot cites from the Rabbinical books testimonies that the Jews expected a general purification or baptism before the coming of the Messiah (from Ezek. xxxvi. 25, 26, and Zech. xiii. 1), and that it would be administered by Elias. **κ. λ. Οὐκ εἰμί**] The right explanation of this answer seems to be the usual one,—that the deputation asked the question in a mistaken and superstitious sense, meaning Elias bodily come down from heaven, who was expected to forerun and anoint the Messias. (Our Lord seems to refer to the same extravagant notion in Matt. xi. 14, **εἰ θέλετε δέξασθαι,** αὐτός ἐστιν Ἡλ. ὁ μέλλων ἔρχεσθαι.) *In this sense*, John was not Elias; nor indeed in any other sense, *was* he Elias:—but only (Luke i. 17) ἐν πνεύματι καὶ δυνάμει Ἡλίου. **ὁ προφ. εἶ σύ;**] From the prophecy of Moses, Deut. xviii. 15, 18, the Jews expected some particular prophet to arise,—distinct from the Messiah (this distinction however was not held by all, see ch. vi. 14),—whose coming was, like that of Elias, intimately connected with that of the Messiah Himself: see ch. vii. 40, 41. In Matt. xvi. 14 we have 'Jeremiah, or one of the prophets' apparently = this expected prophet. There seem to have been various opinions about him;—all however agreeing in this, that he was to be *one of the old prophets raised from the dead* (see also 2 Macc. ii. 1—8). This John *was not*: and he therefore answers this also in the negative. **22.**] Notice—they ever ask about his *person*: he ever refers them to his *office*. He is no one—a *voice* merely: it is the work of God, the testimony to Christ which is every thing. So the formalist ever in the church asks *Who* is he? while the witness for Christ only exalts, only cares for Christ's work. **23.**] These words, which by the other Evangelists are spoken *of* John as the fulfilment of the prophecy, appear from this place to have been first so used *by himself*. They introduce the great closing section of the prophecy of Isaiah (ch. xl.—lxvi.) so full of the rich promises and revelations of the Messiah and His kingdom. **εὐθύνατε** is used as compendiously expressing ἑτοιμάσατε . . . . εὐθείας ποιεῖτε. By implication, the Baptist, quoting this opening prophecy of himself, announces the approaching fulfilment of the whole section. **24.**] The reason of this explanation being added is not very clear. Lücke, with whom De Wette agrees, refers it to the apparent hostility of the next enquiry: but I confess I cannot see that it is more hostile than the preceding. Luthardt thinks that it imports, there were some ἀπεσταλμένοι present, who belonged to the sect of the Pharisees (ἦσαν δὲ καὶ ἐκ τῶν Φαρ. ἀπεσταλμένοι), which the words will hardly bear: see below. Might it not be to throw light on their question about *baptizing*, as the Pharisees were the most precise about all ceremonies, lustrations, &c.? Origen makes this *a new deputation*: but he is plainly wrong: see the **οὖν** below. Euthymius gives another reason yet: ἐπεσημήνατο καὶ τὴν αἵρεσιν αὐτῶν, ἐμφαίνων τὸ περίεργον τούτων καὶ σκολιόν. Abandoning the *οἱ* (see var. readd.), we must render, **And they** (i. e. the whole deputation) **were** (or **had been**) **sent by the Pharisees**; which will make it more

e vv. 20, 21. f see Matt. vi. 7. Mark v. 2. Eph. vi. 2. Isa. iv. 4. g = Matt. xiv. 24. Luke xxii. 55. Num. xxxv. 5. h ver. 15 reff. i Matt. iii. 12 reff. j constr., here only. k Mark i. 7 || L. Acts xxii. 25 only. Job xxxix. 10. Isa. v. 18, 27. Sir. xxx. (xxxiii.) 26 only. l Matt. x. 10 al8. Exod. iii. 5. m Matt. xix. 22 reff. ch. x. 41.

T_b i. 25 (appy)... ABCEF GHKL MST_bU VXΓΔΛ ΠΝ 1. 33. 69

σαίων· 25 καὶ ἠρώτησαν αὐτὸν καὶ εἶπαν αὐτῷ Τί οὖν βαπτίζεις, εἰ σὺ οὐκ εἶ ὁ ᵉχριστὸς οὐδὲ ᵈἩλίας οὐδὲ ὁ ᵉπροφήτης; 26 ἀπεκρίθη αὐτοῖς ὁ Ἰωάννης λέγων Ἐγὼ βαπτίζω ᶠἐν ὕδατι· ᵍμέσος ὑμῶν στήκει ὃν ὑμεῖς οὐκ οἴδατε, 27 [ὁ] ʰὀπίσω μου ἐρχόμενος, ⁱοὗ οὐκ εἰμὶ ἐγὼ ʲἄξιος ἵνα λύσω ⁱαὐτοῦ τὸν ᵏἱμάντα τοῦ ˡὑποδήματος. 28 ταῦτα ἐν Βηθανίᾳ ἐγένετο πέραν τοῦ Ἰορδάνου, ὅπου ᵐἦν [ὁ] Ἰωάννης βαπτίζων.

25. om ηρωτησαν αυτον και (*homœotel*) ℵ [lat-*a e*] syr-cu. (ειπαν, so BC¹LX 33 Orig₁.) rec ουτε (twice), with E rel [Chr Cyr]: txt ABCL[T_b] X(Treg, expr) ℵ 1. 33 $Orig_5$ [$Cyr\text{-}p_1$]. om ο (bef προφητης) CΔ.

26. [απεκρινατο LT_bU 33 $Orig_1$.] om ο A Scr's c ev-z_1. ins τω bef υδατι ℵ¹(om ℵ³). rec aft μεσος ins δε, with AC³ rel [vss] $Orig_2$ Chr_1 [Eus_1]: om BC¹L[T_b]ℵ lat-*ff₂* arm $Heracl_1$ $Orig_{sæpe}$. rec εστηκεν, with AC rel $Orig_{sæpe}$: εστηκει Gℵ $Orig_2$: txt BL[T_b] 1 lat-*a b e f ff₂* [*l q*] syrr syr-cu syr-jer copt [$Cyr\text{-}p_1$] $Orig_2$-int_4 $Cypr_1$.

27. rec at beg ins αυτος εστιν (*to fill out the constr, and refer to vv.* 15, 30), with AC³ rel vulg lat-*b c f q* syrr [syr-jer] $Orig_2$[int_1]; ουτος εστιν G 244-9 Chr_1: αυτος εστιν ον ειπον (*ver* 30) S lat-*e ff₂ l* $Cypr_1$: om BC¹L[T_b]ℵ 1. 33 lat-*a* syr-cu copt æth [arm] $Orig_5$[int_2] Cyr_1. om ο (bef οπισω) Bℵ¹ $Orig_2$: ins AC[T_b]ℵ³ᵃ rel $Orig_4$. rec aft ερχομενος ins ος εμπροσθεν μου γεγονεν (*from vv* 15, 30), with AC³ rel lat-*a c* [*e f ff₂ q* vulg] syrr syr-jer arm-usc æth-pl [Chr_1] $Cypr_1$: om BC¹ L[T_b]ℵ 1. 33 lat-*b l* syr-cu copt æth[-rom] arm-zoh $Orig_4$[int_1] Chr-μ Cyr_1 Non_1 [Aug_1]. rec εγω bef ουκ ειμι (εγω *omd, see below, and reinsd*), with A rel latt: om εγω CLℵ 33 lat-*q* copt æth-rom arm $Heracl_1$ $Clem_1$ $Orig_2$ Chr_2 $Cypr_1$ Ambr: txt B[T_b]X 69 syr-jer $Orig_4$ Aug_1.

28. εγενετο bef εν βηθ. ℵ. rec (for βηθανια) βηθαβαρα, with C²KUΛ[T_b Π-corr¹] 1. 33. 69 syr-cu mss-in-Chr-Euthym arm and the approval of Orig Eus Suid Jer &c, in many of whom the variation is noticed: 237-46-52 æth Epiph have both, βηθαραβα ℵ³ᵇ syr-mg [(βηανια and βηαραβα: syr-ms-mg βιθαρα) $Orig_1$]: txt ABC¹ℵ¹ rel latt syrr syr-jer copt arm Heracl Chr_2 Cyr_1. εγενοντο A 262. aft ιορδανου ins ποταμου ℵ [syr-cu]. rec om ὁ, with A rel $Orig_1$ [Chr_1 Cyr_1]: ins BCℵ. aft βαπτιζων ins το πρωτον C.

probable that the explanation refers to the *nature* of the following question. ἀποστέλλομαι . . . . ἐκ has occurred above, ver. 19, which gives additional probability to the reading of the text. **25.**] On **οὐδὲ . . . . οὐδέ**, see note on ver. 13. This question shews probably that they did not interpret Isa. xl. 3 of any herald of the Messiah. They regarded baptism as a significant token of the approach of the Messianic Kingdom, and they asked, 'Why baptizest thou, if thou art no forerunner of the Messiah?' **26, 27.**] **[ὁ] ὀπίσω μου ἐρχ.** is the *subject* of the sentence; **He that cometh after me,** &c., **stands among you.** The insertions (see var. readd.) have been made by some one not aware of this, and wishing to square the verse with vv. 15, 30.

The answer of the Baptist seems not to correspond to the question in ver. 25. This was noticed as early as Heracleon (Origen in Joan. tom. vi. 15, vol. iv. p. 131), who said, ἀποκρίνεται ὁ Ἰωάννης τοῖς ἐκ τῶν Φαρισαίων πεμφθεῖσιν, οὐ πρὸς ὃ ἐκεῖνοι ἐπηρώτων, ἀλλ' ὃ αὐτὸς ἐβούλετο. This however is impugned at some length by Origen, but not on very convincing grounds. The truth seems to have been apprehended by Olshausen,—that the declaration of John that the Messiah was standing among them at that moment unknown to them, *was an answer to their question demanding a legitimation of his prophetic claims;*—a σημεῖον that he was sent from God:—see ch. ii. 18. Olsh. also suggests that this may clear up the saying of the Jews in ch. x. 41 (see note there). In repeating this saying at other times (see Matt. iii. 11 and ||), the Baptist plainly states of the Messiah, that he should baptize them with the Holy Ghost (and fire), as here in ver. 33. Here, in speaking to those learned in the offices of the Messiah, he leaves that to be supplied.

λύσω αὐτοῦ τ. ἱμ. . . .] See note on Matt. iii. 11. **28.**] The common reading, **Βηθαβαρᾷ**, is owing to a conjecture of Origen, the grounds of which he thus

P ερχο-μενον...

29 Τῇ [n] ἐπαύριον βλέπει τὸν Ἰησοῦν ἐρχόμενον πρὸς

n Matt. xxvii. 62. Mark xi. 12. vv. 35, 44. ch. vi. 22. xii. 12. Acts x. 9 al. Num. xi. 32.

29. rec aft βλεπει ins ο ιωαννης (*a lection beginning at* βλεπει), with C³EFGH[ΓΛ] vulg lat-*b c* [*e ff*$_2$] Syr Orig$_1$ [Cypr$_1$]: om ABC¹א rel mt lat-*a q* syr-cu syr copt æth arm Orig$_1$ Chr$_1$ [Cyr$_2$] Thl. [T$_b$?]

states:—ὅτι μὲν **σχεδὸν ἐν πᾶσι τοῖς ἀντιγράφοις** κεῖται "ταῦτα ἐν Βηθανίᾳ ἐγένετο" οὐκ ἀγνοοῦμεν, καὶ ἔοικε τοῦτο καὶ ἔτι πρότερον γεγονέναι· καὶ παρὰ Ἡρακλέωνι γοῦν Βηθανίαν ἀνέγνωμεν. ἐπείσθημεν δὲ μὴ δεῖν **Βηθανίᾳ** ἀναγινώσκειν, ἀλλὰ **Βηθαβαρᾷ**, γενόμενοι ἐν τοῖς τόποις ἐπὶ ἱστορίαν τῶν ἰχνῶν Ἰησοῦ καὶ τῶν μαθητῶν αὐτοῦ καὶ τῶν προφητῶν. Βηθανία γάρ, ὡς ὁ αὐτὸς εὐαγγελιστής φησι, ἡ πατρὶς Λαζάρου καὶ Μάρθας καὶ Μαρίας, ἀπέχει τῶν Ἱεροσολύμων σταδίους δέκα πέντε· ἧς πόῤῥω ἐστὶν ὁ Ἰορδάνης ποταμός, ὡς ἀπὸ σταδίων πλατεῖ λόγῳ ρπ΄ (180). ἀλλ᾽ οὐδὲ ὁμώνυμος τῇ Βηθανίᾳ τόπος ἐστὶν περὶ τὸν Ἰορδάνην· **δείκνυσθαι δὲ λέγουσι** παρὰ τῇ ὄχθῃ τοῦ Ἰορδάνου τὰ Βηθαβαρᾶ, ἔνθα ἱστοροῦσι τὸν Ἰωάννην βεβαπτικέναι (In Joan. vi. 24, p. 140). He goes on to shew from the *etymology of the names* that it must have been Bethabara; an argument which modern criticism will not much esteem. It will be seen that his testimony is decisive for the universality and authority of Βηθανίᾳ, while for the other he only produces a tradition, and that only at second-hand; "*they say* that such a place is shewn." That no Bethany beyond Jordan was known in his time proves but little;—for 300 eventful years had changed the face of Palestine since these events, and the names and sites of many obscure places may have been forgotten. I abstain from enumerating modern conjectures on the identity of the two, or the etymology of the names, as being indecisive and unprofitable. The objection of Paulus, that πέραν τοῦ Ἰορδάνου the Sanhedrim had no authority, appears not to be founded in fact: see Lücke's Comm. i. 394 ff. The question whether this testimony of the Baptist is identical with that given by the three other Evangelists, especially by Luke (iii. 16), is, after all that has been said on it (Lücke, De Wette, Olshausen, &c.), not of great importance. The whole series of transactions here recorded, from ver. 15 onwards, certainly happened *after* the baptism of our Lord;—for before that event John *did not know Him* as ὁ ἐρχόμενος: and μέσος ὑμῶν στήκει ver. 26 shews that *he had so recognized Him* (see below on τῇ ἐπαύρ.): whereas the testimony in Luke iii. 16 and ||, is as certainly given *before* the baptism. But since the great end of John's mission was to proclaim Him who was coming after him, it is not only probable, but absolutely necessary to suppose, that he should have delivered this testimony *often*, and under varying circumstances: *before* the baptism, in the form given by Luke, **ἔρχεται** ὁ ἰσχυρ. μου κ.τ.λ., and *after* it in this form, οὗτος ἦν ὃν εἶπον (ver. 15), where his former testimony is distinctly referred to. And among John's disciples and the multitudes who frequented his baptism, many reports of such his sayings would naturally be current. So that there is neither a real nor even an apparent contradiction between John and the other Evangelists. It is a far more important question, *in what part of this narration the forty days' Temptation is to be inserted.* From ver. 19 to ch. ii. 1 there is an unbroken sequence of days distinctly marked. Since then ver. 19 must be understood as happening after the baptism, it must have happened *after the Temptation* also. And in this supposition there is not the slightest difficulty. But when we have made it, it still remains to say whether at that time our Lord had returned from the Temptation or not. The general opinion of Harmonists has been, that the approach of Jesus to John in ver. 29 *was His return after the Temptation.* But this I think questionable, on account of the μέσος ὑμῶν στήκει, ver. 26; which I can only understand literally. I therefore believe that the return from the Temptation to Bethany beyond Jordan had taken place before the deputation arrived.

29—34.] *Second witness borne by John to Jesus:* apparently before his disciples. **29.] τῇ ἐπαύριον, the day after.** Those who wish to introduce the Temptation between vv. 28 and 29, interpret it, '*on some day after.*' Thus Euthym. **τῇ ἐπ.**, μετὰ τὴν ἀπὸ ἐρήμου κάθοδον αὐτοῦ δηλονότι. But this sense of τῇ ἐπ., although certainly found in the LXX,—see Gen. xxx. 33,—is not according to the usage of John (see reff.), and would be quite alien from the precision of this whole portion of the narrative, which, ver. 40, specifies even the hours of the day. I understand it therefore literally, both here and in vv. 35 and 44. **ἐρχ. π. αὐτ.]** It is not said *whence*, or *why*, or whether

αὐτὸν καὶ λέγει Ἴδε ὁ [o] ἀμνὸς τοῦ θεοῦ ὁ [p] αἴρων τὴν

ABCEF GHKL MPST$_b$ UVXΓΔ ΛΠא 1. 33. 69

o ver. 36. Acts viii. 32. 1 Pet. i. 19 only. Isa. liii. 7.
p = 1 John iii. 5. Col. ii. 14. 1 Kings xv. 25. xxv. 28. see Exod. xxviii. 34 (38). Lev. x. 17.

for the purpose of an interview, or not; *the fact* merely is related, for the sake of the testimony which follows. I mention this, because on these points difficulties have been raised. **ἴδε ὁ ἀμν. τ. θ.**] This is one of the most important and difficult sayings in the N. T. *The question to be answered* is, in calling Jesus by so definite a name as **ὁ ἀμνὸς τοῦ θεοῦ**, *to what* did John refer? And this question is intimately connected with that of the meaning of the following words, **ὁ αἴρων τὴν ἁμαρτίαν τοῦ κόσμου.** (*α*) The title must refer to *some known and particular lamb*, and cannot be a mere figure for a just and holy man, as Kuinoel and Gabler suppose. It is inconceivable, that *ὁ ἀμνὸς τοῦ θεοῦ* should in a testimony so precise and formal as this of the Baptist, be *nothing but an hyperbole*, and that one *wholly unprecedented*, and to his hearers *unintelligible*. Had no doctrinal considerations been at stake, we may safely say that this interpretation would never have been proposed. In its bearing on the latter clause of the verse, it is equally untenable. These interpreters make *ὁ αἴρων τ. ἁμ. τ. κόσ.* to mean, "qui pravitatem hominum per vitam suam graviter quidem etsi innocens experietur, sed agni instar mala sibi inflicta patiente et mansueto animo sustinebit" (Gabler); or, "Hic removebit peccata hominum, i. e. pravitatem e terra." The first of these meanings of *αἴρειν* is *altogether without example*:—that cited from 1 Macc. xiii. 17, not being applicable. The second, though common enough in other connexions, is never found with *ἁμαρτίαν*: see reff. The commonsense account of this part of the matter is:—John wished to point out Jesus as *the Messiah*: he designates Him as *the Lamb of God*; he therefore referred to some definite lamb,—revealed by God, sent by God, pleasing to God, or in some meaning especially, **τοῦ θεοῦ.** *Whence did this idea come?* (*β*) Can John have referred to the *paschal lamb*? Further than that the very use of the name brings in with it the general typical use of the animal, and that thus this particular use may lie in the background, *I think not*,—and for this reason:—The *dominant idea* in the paschal sacrifice has no connexion, in any sense of the words, with *αἴρειν τὴν ἁμαρτίαν*. However by the light *now* thrown back on it since the Spirit has opened the things of Christ, *we* discern this typical meaning in the sprinkling of the blood (see 1 Cor. v. 7),—in the *Jewish mind*, no mention being made of sin or the removing of sin in any connexion with the paschal lamb, the two could not be brought forward, in such an announcement as this, in close connexion with one another.

(*γ*) Can the reference be to the *lamb of the daily morning and evening sacrifice?* or to the *sacrificial lamb* generally? With the same reservation as above, *I think not*: for (1) this expression is too definite to have so general and miscellaneous a reference; (2) of many animals which were used for sacrifice, the lamb was *only one*, and that one *not by any means so prominent as to serve as a type for the whole*: and (3) the lamb (with only two exceptions, Levit. iv. 32: Num. vi. 14, in both which cases it was to be a *female*, as if for express distinction from the ordinary use of the lamb) was *never used for a sin-offering*, properly so called and known. The *question is not*, whether Christ be not typified by all these offerings, which we *now know* to be the case (1 Pet. i. 19 al.), but whether *the Baptist is likely to have referred to them in such words as these*.

(*δ*) There remains but one reference, and that is, to the *prophetic announcement in Isa.* liii. 7. The whole of that latter section of Isaiah, as before remarked on ver. 23, is Messianic, and was so understood by the Jews (see my Hulsean Lectures for 1841, pp. 62—66). We have there the servant of God (= the Messiah) compared to *a lamb brought to the slaughter* (liii. 7), and it is said of Him (ib. ver. 4), *οὗτος* **τὰς ἁμαρτίας** *ἡμῶν* **φέρει** *καὶ περὶ ἡμῶν ὀδυνᾶται*—ver. 5, *αὐτὸς δὲ ἐτραυματίσθη* **διὰ τὰς ἁμαρτίας ἡμῶν**—ver. 6, *καὶ κύριος παρέδωκεν αὐτὸν* **ταῖς ἁμαρτίαις ἡμῶν**—ver. 8, *αἴρεται ἀπὸ τῆς γῆς ἡ ζωὴ αὐτοῦ, ἀπὸ τῶν ἀνομιῶν τοῦ λαοῦ μου ἤχθη εἰς θάνατον*—ver. 12, *καὶ αὐτὸς* **ἁμαρτίας πολλῶν ἀνήνεγκε** *καὶ διὰ τὰς ἀνομίας αὐτῶν παρεδόθη*. So that here, and here only, we have the connexion of which we are in search,—between *the lamb*, and the *bearing or taking away of sin*,—expressly stated, so that it could be formally referred to in a testimony like the present. And I have therefore no doubt that *this was the reference*. (*ε*) We have now to enquire into the specific meaning of **ὁ αἴρων τὴν ἁμαρτίαν τοῦ κόσμου** (see above under (*α*)). **αἴρειν** answers to the Heb. נָשָׂא, which is used frequently in the O. T. in connexion with חֵטְא or עָוֹן, in the sense of *peccati pœnas luere*:—see Levit. xxiv. 15:

ἁμαρτίαν τοῦ κόσμου. 30 οὗτός ἐστιν [q] ὑπὲρ οὗ ἐγὼ εἶπον q — 2 Cor. i. 8. viii. 23.
Ὀπίσω μου ἔρχεται ἀνὴρ ὃς [r] ἔμπροσθέν μου γέγονεν, ὅτι 2 Thess. ii. 1. r ver. 15 (reff.).
[r] πρῶτός μου ἦν. 31 κἀγὼ οὐκ [s] ᾔδειν αὐτόν, ἀλλ' ἵνα s Isa. xlv. 5.

30. rec (for *υπερ*) *περι* (*corrn to more obvious*), with AC³P[T_b]ℵ²⁽?⁾·³ᵃ rel $Orig_1$ Eus_1 Chr_1 [Cyr_2] : txt BC¹ℵ¹ $Orig_2$.

Num. v. 31; xiv. 34: Ezek. iv. 5; xxiii. 35 al.:—and variously rendered in the LXX by ἀναφέρειν, as above, Isa. liii. 11, 12, or φέρειν, ib. ver. 4,—or λαμβάνειν, Ezek. iv. 5; xviii. 19: Num. v. 31; xiv. 34: Levit. xxiv. 15. ἀφαιρεῖν (which though not a compound of αἴρειν, seems to have almost been adopted as such, the actual compound ἀπαίρειν being intransitive) is used in the sense of '*taking away of sin and its guilt*,' but taking it away *by expiation*: see Exod. xxxiv. 7: Levit. x. 17: Num. xiv. 18. The word in our verse will bear either of these meanings, or both conjoined; for if the Lamb is to suffer the burden of the sins of the world, and to take away sin and its guilt by expiation, this result must be accomplished by the *offering of Himself*. But (ζ) it is objected, that this view of a suffering Messiah and of expiation by the sufferings of *one*, was *alien from the Jewish expectations*;—and that the Baptist (see Matt. xi. 2 ff. and note) cannot himself have had any such view. But the answer to this may be found in the fact that the view, though not generally prevalent among the Jews, was by no means unknown to many. The application by the early Jewish expositors of Isa. liii. to the Messiah, could hardly have been made, without the idea of the suffering and death of their Messiah being presented to their minds. The same would be the case in the whole sacrificial œconomy:—the removal of guilt (which was universally ascribed to the Messiah) by suffering and death would be familiarized to their minds. Traces of this are found in their own writings. In 2 Macc. vii. 37, 38, the last of the seven brethren thus speaks before his martyrdom: ἐγὼ δὲ καθάπερ οἱ ἀδελφοί μου καὶ σῶμα καὶ ψυχὴν προδίδωμι περὶ τῶν πατρίων νόμων, ἐπικαλούμενος τὸν θεὸν ἵλεων ταχὺ τῷ ἔθνει γενέσθαι, καὶ σὲ μετὰ ἐτασμῶν καὶ μαστίγων ἐξομολογήσασθαι, διότι μόνος αὐτὸς θεός ἐστιν. ἐν ἐμοὶ δὲ καὶ τοῖς ἀδελφοῖς μου στῆναι τὴν τοῦ παντοκράτορος ὀργὴν τὴν ἐπὶ τὸ σύμπαν ἡμῶν γένος δικαίως ἐπηγμένην. And Josephus, de Maccab. § 17 (4 Macc. xvii. 22), says of these same martyrs, that they were ὥσπερ ἀντίψυχον τῆς τοῦ ἔθνους ἁμαρτίας. καὶ διὰ τοῦ αἵματος τῶν εὐσεβῶν ἐκείνων καὶ (τοῦ) ἱλαστηρίου τοῦ θανάτου αὐτῶν ἡ θεία πρόνοια τὸν Ἰσραὴλ προκακωθέντα διέσωσε. The whole history of the sacrifices and devotions of the heathen world abounds with examples of the same idea variously brought forward; and to these the better-informed among the Jews could be no strangers. And as to the Baptist himself, we must not forget that the power of the Holy Spirit which enabled him to recognize by a special sign the Redeemer, also *spoke in him*, and therefore his words would not be the result of education merely, or his own reasoning, but of that kind of intuitive perception of divine truth, which those have had who have been for any special purpose the organs of the Holy Ghost. And as regards Matt. xi. 3, the doubt on the mind of John there expressed does not appear to have touched at all on the matter now in question,—but to have rather been a form of expressing his impatience at the slow and quiet progress of Him of whom he expected greater things and a more rapid public manifestation. See this whole enquiry pursued at greater length in Lücke's Commentary, vol. i. pp. 401—416, from whence the substance of this note is taken. **30.**] See on ver. 15.

31.] On the apparent discrepancy between this statement, **οὐκ ηδειν αὐτόν**, and St. Matthew's narrative, I have stated my view on Matt. iii. 14. Both accounts are entirely consistent with the supposition that John had been from youth upwards acquainted with our Lord, and indeed may have in his own mind believed Him to be the Christ:—but having (ver. 33) *a special sign appointed him*, by which to recognize Him as such,—until that sign was given, he, like the rest of the people (κἀγώ, **I also**, see ver. 26), had no certain knowledge of Him. Lücke's whole note proceeds upon the unworthy view of the historical character of the Gospels which his school has adopted. The same may be said of Neander, Leben Jesu, pp. 86 ff. De Wette gives the sense well: "This testimony (ver. 30) does not rest upon my long personal acquaintance with Him, but on that which happened during my work of baptizing." **ἀλλ' ἵνα φαν.**] Justin Martyr represents Trypho the Jew saying, χριστὸς δὲ εἰ καὶ γεγέννηται, καὶ

t = ch. vii. 4. 2 Cor. iii. 3. 1 John ii. 19.
u ver. 26.
v Luke xxiii. 55 reff.
w Matt. iii. 16 ||. Isa. lxiii. 14.
x Matt. iii. 16 reff.
y constr., Matt. xiii. 2. Luke ii. 25, 40. Rev. vii. 15
z ver. 18 reff.
a ch. xix. 35.
b ch. iii. 28. iv. 39, 44. v. 36. vii. 7 al. fr.
c see Matt. iv. 3 and note.

ABCEF GHKL MPST$_b$ UVXΓΔ ΛΠℵ 1. 33. 69

[t] φανερωθῇ τῷ Ἰσραήλ, διὰ τοῦτο ἦλθον ἐγὼ [u] ἐν [τῷ]
ὕδατι βαπτίζων. 32 καὶ ἐμαρτύρησεν Ἰωάννης λέγων
ὅτι [v] τεθέαμαι τὸ πνεῦμα [w] καταβαῖνον ὡς [x] περιστερὰν ἐξ
οὐρανοῦ, καὶ ἔμεινεν [y] ἐπ' αὐτόν. 33 κἀγὼ οὐκ [s] ᾔδειν
αὐτόν, ἀλλ' ὁ πέμψας με βαπτίζειν [u] ἐν ὕδατι, [z] ἐκεῖνός
μοι εἶπεν Ἐφ' ὃν ἂν ἴδῃς τὸ πνεῦμα [w] καταβαῖνον καὶ
μένον [y] ἐπ' αὐτόν, οὗτός ἐστιν ὁ βαπτίζων [u] ἐν πνεύματι
ἁγίῳ. 34 κἀγὼ [a] ἑώρακα, καὶ [ab] μεμαρτύρηκα ὅτι οὗτός
ἐστιν ὁ [c] υἱὸς τοῦ [c] θεοῦ.

31. εγω bef ηλθον C[1] 157(Sz) lat-*b* [copt]. om 2nd τω (*perhaps conformn to vv.* 26, 33) BCGLP[T$_b$]Λℵ **1.** 33. 69 Orig$_3$ Chr Cyr$_1$: ins A rel.
32. om λεγων ℵ[1](ins ℵ[2], appy) [lat-*e*]. rec ωσει, with KMPUXΔΛ[Π] **1** : txt ABCℵ rel Orig$_2$. ως περιστεραν bef καταβαινον ℵ [lat-*a b e g*]. for εξ, εκ του ℵ [1]. for εμεινεν, μενον ℵ [lat-*b e q* Chr$_1$ Ambr$_1$ Jer$_1$].
33. και εγω ℵ. ins τω bef υδατι ℵ 1 Orig$_2$. αυτος A lat-*b e q*. at end ins και πυρι (*Matt* iii. 11) C[1] Orig$_3$ Non$_1$.
34. for υιος, εκλεκτος ℵ[1] 77(e sil) 218 lat-*e* syr-cu [Ambr$_1$].

ἔστι που, ἄγνωστός ἐστι, καὶ οὐδὲ αὐτός πω ἑαυτὸν ἐπίσταται, οὐδὲ ἔχει δύναμίν τινα, μέχρις ἂν ἐλθὼν Ἠλίας χρίσῃ αὐτὸν καὶ **φανερὸν πᾶσι ποιήσῃ**, § 8, p. 110. But our narrative is not built upon any such Jewish belief, for it is evidently only as a *spiritual preparation*, through repentance, for the knowledge of Him, that John regarded his baptism, not as any thing ἐκεῖνον φανερὸν πᾶσι ποιοῦν. **ἐν [τῷ] ὕδ.**, hardly distinguishable in English from ἐν ὕδ., but importing, 'in the water which it is my custom to use,'—'in the water in which you see I do baptize.' **32, 33.**] "Quæ sequuntur, erant *testimonii*: quæ ex ver. 29 sq. dicuntur, erant *demonstrationis ex testimonio*. Cohærentibus Baptistæ verbis Evangelista quasi parenthesin interponit: καὶ ἐμαρτύρησεν Ἰωάννης λέγων." Bengel. The occurrence related by John happened *at the baptism* of Jesus, which is therefore here *pre-supposed as known*. Although this has been questioned (Usteri, Nachrichten über den Täufer J. u.s.w., cited by Lücke, i. 423), I cannot see how it can be reasonably doubted. We cannot surely suppose that such a sign was *twice* shewn. On the appearance itself, see note Matt. iii. 16. The account here given confirms the view which I have there maintained, that the appearance was confined to our Lord and the Baptist: *he* was to receive the sign, and then to testify to the others, who were not themselves yet the bearers, but the recipients of testimony:—κατά τινα πνευματικὴν θεωρίαν ὤφθη μόνῳ τῷ Ἰωάννῃ. Theod. Mops. p. 736. **τεθέαμαι**, perf. **I have seen**, in reference to the sign divinely intimated to him, in the abiding fulfilment of which he now stood. So again below, ver. 34. **ἔμεινεν ἐπ' αὐτ.**] By some appearance which is not described, the Holy Spirit was manifested to John as *not removing from Jesus again, but abiding on Him*. But we are not to understand that he had seen the Spirit descending on *others*, and *not abiding*; for (see ch. vii. 39: Acts i. 5; xix. 2 ff.) the gift of the Holy Spirit did not ordinarily accompany John's baptism, but only in this one case; and its occurrence was to point out to him the Messiah. **οὗτ. ἐστ. ὁ βαπτ. ἐν πν. ἁγ.**] Here again we seem to have a reference to the synoptic cycle of narratives, for our Evangelist has not before mentioned this office of the Messiah. **34.**] A solemn reiteration of his testimony, after the mention of the giving of this token by Him who sent him;—**And I have seen (accordingly)** &c. The token must have been given to the Baptist *by a special revelation*, which also revealed to him his own errand and office; so Luke iii. 2, ἐγένετο ῥῆμα θεοῦ ἐπὶ Ἰωάννην τὸν Ζαχ. υἱὸν ἐν τῇ ἐρήμῳ. **μεμαρτύρηκα** is stronger than μαρτυρῶ—**I have seen** (on the perf. see above, ver. 32) **and have borne testimony**—it is a reference to his testimony at the time, as a thing on record in their memories, and as still continuing. **ὁ υἱ. τ. θεοῦ** (see ver. 18) = the **λόγος** made flesh, the Messiah. On the import of the descent of the Spirit on Jesus at His baptism, those who can do so should consult Lücke's very able Excursus, i. 433—443. In this commentary, see notes on Luke ii. 41—52. I may just remark, that the Personal Logos, Who σὰρξ ἐγένετο in

35 Τῇ [d] ἐπαύριον πάλιν εἱστήκει Ἰωάννης καὶ ἐκ τῶν
μαθητῶν αὐτοῦ δύο, 36 καὶ [e] ἐμβλέψας τῷ Ἰησοῦ περι-
πατοῦντι λέγει Ἴδε ὁ [f] ἀμνὸς τοῦ θεοῦ. 37 καὶ ἤκουσαν
αὐτοῦ οἱ δύο μαθηταὶ λαλοῦντος, καὶ ἠκολούθησαν τῷ
Ἰησοῦ. 38 στραφεὶς δὲ ὁ Ἰησοῦς καὶ [v] θεασάμενος αὐτοὺς
ἀκολουθοῦντας λέγει αὐτοῖς 39 Τί ζητεῖτε; οἱ δὲ εἶπαν
αὐτῷ [g] Ῥαββί (ὃ λέγεται [h] μεθερμηνευόμενον διδάσκαλε)
ποῦ [i] μένεις; 40 λέγει αὐτοῖς Ἔρχεσθε καὶ ὄψεσθε. ἦλθαν
οὖν καὶ εἶδαν ποῦ [j] μένει καὶ [k] παρ' αὐτῷ ἔμειναν τὴν
ἡμέραν ἐκείνην· ὥρα ἦν ὡς δεκάτη. 41 ἦν Ἀνδρέας ὁ

d ver. 29 reff.
e Mark x. 21 reff. Luke xxii. 61 al. Isa. li. 1, 2.
f ver. 29 reff.
g ver. 50. ch. iii. 2, 26. iv. 31. vi. 25. ix. 2. xi. 8. Matt. xxiii. 8 reff. (-βουνί, ch. xx. 16.)
h Mark v. 41 reff.
i = ch. iv. 40. Acts xvi. 15. xxviii. 16, 30 al. 1 Macc. xi. 40.
j constr., ch. ii. 9. iv. 1. Matt. xx. 30. Mark v. 14 al. fr. Judg. xiii. 6. Winer, § 40. 2. c.
k = Acts ix. 43 al.

35. rec ins *ο* bef *ιωαννης*, with ACP[T_b]ℵ rel $Orig_3$: om BL.
36. aft *θεου* ins *ο αιρων τ. αμαρτιαν τ. κοσμου* C[1] 235(Sz) forj(with [fuld] mt) lat-*a ff*$_2$ æth Cyr_1 Ammon.
37. om 1st *και* ℵ[1] 1. *οι δυο* bef *αυτου* C[1]L[T_b]X 33 Syr copt, *οι δ. μ. αυ.* Bℵ lat-*b* Syr: txt AC[3]P rel vulg lat-*c f* [*l*] syr [Chr_1-txt Cyr_1].
38. om *δε* ℵ[1](ins ℵ-corr[1 or 2]) [EFHMVΓΛ arm $Orig_1$]. om *αυτοις* ℵ[1].
39. (*ειπαν*, so BC[1].) rec (for *μεθερμ.*) *ερμηνευομενον*, with Pℵ[1] rel: txt ABCLXℵ[3a] 33 $Orig_1$. (*ερμηνευεται* 1 copt [lat-*b c e q*].) [T_b?]
40. rec (for *οψεσθε*) *ιδετε* (*from ver 47, where there is no var: txt is certainly not a gloss, as Mey*), with AC[3]Pℵ rel latt copt [arm] $Epiph_1$ Chr_1: txt BC[1]L[T_b] 1. 33 syrr syr-cu [syr-jer] $Orig_1$ [$Cyr\text{-}p_1$]. (*ηλθαν* and *ειδαν*, so B[1]C.) rec om *ουν*, with P rel vulg lat-*c f* [*q*] arm: ins ABCLX Λ(Treg, expr) ℵ 33 lat-*a e* copt syr-mg [syr-jer] Cyr_1 [*και ηλθ. ουν* T_b]. rec aft *ωρα* ins *δε*, with 218 vulg lat-*a c* [*l*] syr copt: om ABCP[T_b]ℵ rel Scr's-mss fos lat-*q* æth $Epiph_1$ Cyr_1. for *δεκατη*, *εκτη* A.
41. aft *ην* ins *δε* AΛ vulg lat-*a c* [*e ff*$_2$ *l*] Syr syr-w-ast copt.

our Lord, and was subjected to all the laws of human development in infancy, childhood, youth,—evermore in an especial degree under the leading of the Holy Spirit, by whose agency the Incarnation had taken place,—was the Recipient (*τὸ δεχόμενον*) of this fulness of the indwelling of the Holy Ghost: and that herein consisted the real depth and propriety of this sign;—the abiding of the Spirit *without measure* (ch. iii. 34) on Him indicated beyond doubt that He was the *λόγος σὰρξ γεγονώς*,—for no mere human intelligence could be thus receptive of the Holy Spirit of God;—*we* receive Him only *as we can*, only as far as our receptivity extends,—*by measure*; but HE, into the very fulness and infinite capacities of His Divine Being.

35—43.] *On account of the testimony of John, first Andrew, and another of his disciples, and through Andrew, Simon Peter, become acquainted with Jesus.*

35. τῇ ἐπ.] See on ver. 29. I can hardly suppose with De Wette, that these two had been absent on the preceding day. Rather, what they then heard seems to have made a powerful impression on their minds, so that the repetition of the notice is now the signal for them to follow Jesus. (On the second disciple, see below on ver. 41.)

37.] We must not understand **ἠκολ.** in the narrower sense which it bears when they *left all and followed* Him; but here only of *mechanical going after* Him, *βουλόμενοι πεῖραν λαβεῖν αὐτοῦ*, Euthym.

39.] On **τί ζητ.** Euthym. remarks, *οὐκ ἀγνοῶν, ὁ τοῖς λογισμοῖς τῶν ἀνθρώπων ἐμβατεύων, ἀλλ' ἵνα διὰ τῆς ἐρωτήσεως οἰκειώσηται τούτους, καὶ παράσχῃ θαῤῥεῖν. εἰκὸς γὰρ αὐτοὺς ἐρυθριᾶν ἔτι καὶ ἀγωνιᾶν, ὡς ἀγνῶτας.*

40.] They ask **ποῦ μ.**, *βουλόμενοι καταμόνας ἐντυχεῖν αὐτῷ καὶ μεθ' ἡσυχίας.* Euthym. They enquire after *His place of lodging for the night*, intending to visit Him there; or perhaps He was then apparently going thither, as it was late in the day. But He furthers their wish by inviting them to follow, and they will see. **ὡς δεκάτη**] i. e. 4 P.M., according to the Jewish reckoning; not, as some have thought, 10 A.M., according to that of the Romans. Our Evangelist appears always to reckon according to the Jewish method, see ch. iv. 6, 52; xix. 14, and notes, but especially ch. xi. 9. And as Lücke remarks (i. 446), even among the Romans, the division of the day into twelve equal hours was, though not the *civil*, the popular way of

l ch. vi. 45 al5. Acts x. 22. 2 Tim. i. 13. ii. 2 only. Xen. Anab. i. 2. 5.
m pres., ver. 29, and John passim. see Rev. xii. 2, 4 al. fr.
n ch. iv. 25 only.
o see Dan. ix. 25 Theod.
p Mark x. 21 reff.
q elsw. Paul (1 Cor. i. 12. iii. 22. ix. 5. xv. 5. Gal. i. 18. ii. 9, 11, 14) only.
r (ver. 39 v. r.) ch. ix. 7. Heb. vii. 2 only. Ezra iv. 7 only.
s ver. 29 reff.
t = ch. v. 40 al. fr. in John.
u Matt. xi. 7. xxii. 10 al.

ἀδελφὸς Σίμωνος Πέτρου εἷς ἐκ τῶν δύο τῶν [l] ἀκουσάντων
[l] παρὰ Ἰωάννου καὶ ἀκολουθησάντων αὐτῷ. 42 [m] εὑρίσκει
οὗτος πρῶτον τὸν ἀδελφὸν τὸν ἴδιον Σίμωνα, καὶ [m] λέγει
αὐτῷ Εὑρήκαμεν τὸν [n] μεσσίαν (ὅ ἐστι [g] μεθερμηνευόμενον
[o] χριστός). 43 ἤγαγεν αὐτὸν πρὸς τὸν Ἰησοῦν. [p] ἐμβλέψας αὐτῷ ὁ Ἰησοῦς εἶπεν Σὺ εἶ Σίμων ὁ υἱὸς Ἰωάννου·
σὺ κληθήσῃ [q] Κηφᾶς (ὃ [r] ἑρμηνεύεται Πέτρος).
44 [s] Τῇ ἐπαύριον [t] ἠθέλησεν [u] ἐξελθεῖν [u] εἰς τὴν Γαλιλαίαν, καὶ [m] εὑρίσκει Φίλιππον καὶ λέγει αὐτῷ ὁ Ἰησοῦς

...ιωαννου C. ...αυτω P. .. i. 42 (app) T_b. ABEFG HKLM SUVXΓ ΔΛΠℵ 1. 33. 69

om 2nd *των* Cℵ[1][: om *των δυω* T_b].

42. rec *πρωτος*, with Lℵ[1] rel: txt ABM[T_b]Xℵ[3a] 1. 69 latt syrr [syr-jer copt arm] æth $Orig_{appy}$ Gaud. (33 def.) rec ins *ο* bef *χριστος*, with Scr's g copt arm: om ABℵ rel Scr's-mss $Orig_2$ Epiph Chr.

43. rec ins *και* bef *ηγαγεν*, with A rel vulg lat-*a c* syrr syr-cu [syr-jer] æth; *ουτος* G 1 arm $Epiph_1$: om BLℵ copt. rec aft *εμβλεψας* ins *δε*, with XΔΛ (S 33, e sil) [Π[2](but erased)] vulg lat-*b c* [*f l*] syr-w-ast copt: pref *και* 46 lat-*a e* Syr Chr: om ABℵ rel arm [$Epiph_1$-ms]. rec *ιωνα* (*corrn from Matt* xvi. 17: *cf ch* xxi. 15 *var readd*), with AB[2] rel vulg-ed lat-*c q* syrr [syr-jer arm] æth-pl $Epiph_1$ Chr Cyr_1: *iohanna* am: txt B[1](*-ανου*) Lℵ 33 lat-*a b f* ff_2 *l* copt æth-rom [Non_1] Jer Aug. for *ὅ*, *os* A.

44. rec aft *ηθελησεν* ins *ο ιησους*, with FGH U(Treg, expr) [Γ] Syr: om ABℵ rel latt syr copt æth arm $Orig_1$ $Epiph_3$ Chr_1[-txt] Cyr_1 Thl. rec (aft *αὐτῷ*) om *ο ιησ.*, with FHM[Γ] am(with fuld) lat-*e* Syr syr-jer copt-dz $Orig_1$ Chr_1[-txt]: ins AB(ℵ) rel vulg-ed(with forj san [em ing]) lat-*a b c f* ff_2 *l* [*q*] syr copt (æth) arm $Epiph_2$ [Cyr_1].—om *ὁ* ℵ[1].

computing time. So Persius, Sat. iii. 3: "Stertimus . . . quinta dum linea tangitur umbra." They remained with Him *the rest of that day*, which would be four or five hours, and need not strictly be limited by sunset. **41.**] Who the other disciple was, is not certain: but considering (1) that the Evangelist *never names himself* in his Gospel, and (2) that this account is so minutely accurate as to specify even the hours of the day, and in all respects *bears marks of an eye-witness*, and again (3) that this other disciple, from this last circumstance, certainly *would have been named*, had not the name been suppressed *for some especial reason*, we are justified in inferring that it was *the Evangelist himself*. And such has been the general opinion. Euthymius gives an alternative which is hardly probable: ἢ διότι οὐκ ἦν τῶν ἐπισήμων καὶ γνωρίμων ἐκεῖνος, ἢ ὅτι αὐτὸς ἦν ὁ ταῦτα γράφων. **42.**] **ἴδιον**, not merely "*for the possessive pronoun*" (according to Winer, § 22. 7), but referring to **πρῶτον**, and furnishing a reason for it.

μεσσίαν = מָשִׁיחַ = not **ὁ** χριστός, but *χριστός*: being the identification simply of the two *words*, not here of the two *titles*. **43.**] This is evidently the *first bestowal of the new name* on Simon: and it is done from our Lord's prophetic knowledge of his future character: see note on Matt. xvi. 18. **Κηφᾶς** = כֵּיפָא Aramaic, כֵּף Hebrew, **a stone**. The Greek name *Peter* became the prevalent one in the apostolic Church very soon: Paul uses both names indiscriminately. I own I cannot but think with Bengel, Paulus, and Strauss, that the knowledge of Simon shewn by the Lord is *intended to be miraculous*. So also Stier, i. 31 f. edn. 2, "I know who and what thou art from thy birth till thy present coming to me. . . . . I name thee, I give thee a new name, I know what I will make of thee in thy following of Me and for my Kingdom." The emphatic use of ἐμβλέψας here (it is not so emphatic in ver. 36, but still even there may imply fixed contemplation, in the power of the Spirit, who suggested the testimony) is hardly accountable except on this explanation of supernatural knowledge. Similarly Abram, Sara, Jacob, received new names in reference to the covenant and promises of God to them.

44—52.] *The calling of Philip and Nathanael.* **44. τῇ ἐπαύρ**] Apparently, the day after the naming of Peter; and if so, the next but one after the visit of Andrew and the other disciple, and the

Ἀκολούθει μοι. 45 ἦν δὲ ὁ Φίλιππος [vw] ἀπὸ Βηθσαϊδά,
[wx] ἐκ τῆς πόλεως Ἀνδρέου καὶ Πέτρου. 46 [m] εὑρίσκει
Φίλιππος τὸν Ναθαναήλ, καὶ λέγει αὐτῷ Ὃν [y] ἔγραψεν
Μωυσῆς ἐν τῷ νόμῳ καὶ οἱ προφῆται εὑρήκαμεν, Ἰησοῦν
τὸν υἱὸν τοῦ Ἰωσὴφ τὸν [v] ἀπὸ Ναζαρέτ. 47 καὶ εἶπεν
αὐτῷ Ναθαναὴλ Ἐκ Ναζαρὲτ δύναταί τι ἀγαθὸν εἶναι;
λέγει αὐτῷ ὁ Φίλιππος Ἔρχου καὶ ἴδε. 48 εἶδεν Ἰησοῦς
τὸν Ναθαναὴλ ἐρχόμενον πρὸς αὐτόν, καὶ λέγει περὶ
αὐτοῦ Ἴδε [z] ἀληθῶς [a] Ἰσραηλίτης, ἐν ᾧ δόλος οὐκ ἔστιν.

v Matt. xv. 1. xxi. 11. xxvii. 57 ||. ch. xii. 21. xxi. 22.
w ch. xi. 1. see vv. 46, 47. ch. vii. 42.
x Luke xxiii. 7. ch. iv. 7 al.
y constr., Rom. x. 5. see Luke xviii. 31.
z Luke ix. 27. xii. 44. ch. iv. 42 al. Gospp. only exc. Acts xii. 11. 1 Thess. ii. 13. 1 John ii. 5. Jer. xxxv. (xxviii.) 6.
a Gospp., here only. Acts ii. 22 al4. Rom. ix. 4. xi. 1. 2 Cor. xi. 22.

45. om δε ο ℵ[1] : om ο F[1] 69 Scr's b c. βηθσαιδαν ℵ[1] (8. 127, Sz). om εκ ℵ[1] (ins ℵ[3a], but erased) [vulg].
46. om τον (bef υιον) Bℵ 33 $Orig_1$ $Epiph_1$ Cyr_{aliq}. om του ΑΚΜΔ[Π[1]] 33 Chr Cyr.
47. om 1st και ℵ Scr's g lat-*a b e* Syr [arm Chr_1-6-mss]. αγαθον bef τι ℵ[1]. rec om ο (*see ver* 46, *where none ins* ο), with Aℵ rel [$Epiph_1$-ms] Chr Cyr_1 : ins BL 33 $Epiph_1$[-ed].
48. for ειδεν, ιδων ℵ[1] (124, Sz) [foss lat-*a b e* ff_2 *l* $Epiph_1$]. rec ins ο bef ιησ., with Aℵ rel : om BH[SΓ]. (33 def.) om και ℵ[1]. for αυτου, του ναθαναηλ ℵ[1].

fourth day *after* ver. 19. Our Lord is on the point of setting out from the valley of the Jordan to Galilee, and finds Philip, with whom there is every reason to believe He was previously acquainted (see ver. 45). Here we find Jesus himself *calling* a disciple, for the first time. But **ἀκολούθει** does not here bear its strict apostolic sense; the εὑρήκαμεν afterwards, and the going to search for others to be disciples, unites Philip to the company of those who have been before mentioned, who we know were not immediately or inseparably attached as followers to Jesus.

45.] On the futility of Mr. Greswell's distinction between **ἀπό** as signifying *mere habitation*, and **ἐκ**, *nativity*, see reff. and note on ch. xi. 1. This is Bethsaida on the *Western* bank of the lake of Gennesareth; another Bethsaida (Julias) lay at the top of the lake, on the Jordan. See note on Luke ix. 10.

46.] It does not appear where Nathanael was found: but he is described, ch. xxi. 2, as ὁ ἀπὸ Κανὰ τῆς Γαλιλαίας: and as we find Jesus there, ch. ii. 1, it is probable the call may have taken place in its neighbourhood. Nathanael ("נְתַנְאֵל, i. q. Θεόδωρος, gift of God." Wordsw.) is mentioned *only in these two places*. From them we should gather that *he was an Apostle*; and as his name is no where found in the catalogues of the Twelve, but Philip is associated in three of them (Matt. x. 3 : Mark iii. 18 : Luke vi. 14) with *Bartholomew*, it has been supposed that Nathanael and Bartholomew *were the same person* (see note on Matt. x. 3). This is however mere conjecture.

Μωυσῆς ἐν τ. ν., probably in Deut. xviii. 15; but also in the promises to Abraham, Gen. xvii. 7 al.: and in the prophecy of Jacob, Gen. xlix. 10, and the Prophets, passim : see the reff. in E. V. **τὸν υἱὸν τοῦ Ἰωσ. τ. ἀπὸ** N.] This expression seems to shew previous acquaintance on the part of Philip with Jesus. No stress can be laid, as has been most unfairly done by Lücke, De Wette, and others, on Jesus being called by Philip, **the son of Joseph**, as indicating that the history of His birth and childhood, as related by Matt. and Luke, was *unknown to John*. Philip *expresses what was the prevailing belief, in the ordinary words*, as Olshausen remarks. In an admirable note, Leben Jesu, p. 23 ff., Neander remarks, that by combining the two declarations of John, that *in Jesus the Eternal Word of God became flesh* (ver. 14), and that '*that which is born of the flesh is flesh*' (ch. iii. 6), we cannot escape the inference, that a *supernatural working of God in the conception of the Man Christ Jesus is implied.*

47.] As Lücke observes, the meaning of this question is simpler than at first sight appears. It is impossible that Nathanael, himself a Galilæan, could speak from any feeling of contempt for Galilee generally: and we have no evidence that Nazareth was held in contempt *among the Galilæans.* He alluded therefore to the smallness and insignificance of the town in proportion to the great things which were now predicated of it. Nazareth is never named in the O. T. nor in Josephus.

48.] The Evangelist certainly intends a supernatural

49 λέγει αὐτῷ Ναθαναὴλ [b] Πόθεν με γινώσκεις; ἀπεκρίθη ABEFG
Ἰησοῦς καὶ εἶπεν αὐτῷ [c] Πρὸ τοῦ σε Φίλιππον [d] φωνῆσαι HKLM SUVXΓ
ὄντα [e] ὑπὸ τὴν [f] συκῆν εἶδόν σε. 50 ἀπεκρίθη αὐτῷ Ναθα- ΔΛΠℵ 1. 33. 69
ναὴλ Ῥαββί, σὺ εἶ ὁ [g] υἱὸς τοῦ [g] θεοῦ, σὺ [h] βασιλεὺς εἶ
τοῦ [h] Ἰσραήλ. 51 ἀπεκρίθη Ἰησοῦς καὶ εἶπεν αὐτῷ Ὅτι
εἶπόν σοι ὅτι Εἶδόν σε [i] ὑποκάτω τῆς [f] συκῆς, πιστεύεις;

b = Matt. xiii. 27, 54, 56. Mark xii. 37. Luke i. 43.
c constr., Matt. vi. 8 reff. Gen. xxvii. 7.
d = Matt. xx. 32. Luke xvi. 2. ch. iv. 16. Acts ix. 41. x. 7. Tobit v. 8 (not ℵ).
e 3 Kings xiii. 14. f Matt. xxiv. 32 reff. g ver. 3. h ch. xii 13. Matt. xxvii. 42 || Mk. only.
i Mark vi. 11. Luke viii. 16. Rev. v. 3, 13. Ezek. xxiv. 5. Mic. iv. 4.

49. rec ins *ο* bef *ιησ.*, with E[1] [Π[2](but erased)] ℵ (**1**. 69, e sil). om AB rel Cyr.
50. rec (for *αυτω ναθ.*) *ναθ. και λεγει αυτω*, with A rel syrr [syr-jer copt] Chr_1 Cyr_1; *ναθ. και ειπεν αυτω* [Γ]Δ 28. 254 ev-z lat-ff_2 *q*; *ναθ. και ειπεν*, omg *αυτω*, ℵ: txt B(sic in cod: see table) L(X) 33.—add *κ. ειπεν* X ev-49 vulg lat-*a f l* $Epiph_1$. rec ins *ο* bef *βασιλευς*, with Xℵ rel: om ABL **1**. 33. rec *ει* bef (*ὁ*) *βασιλευς*, with Xℵ rel latt copt Chr_1 Cyr_1 Thdor-$mops_1$ Iren-int_1 Hil_1: txt ABL **1**. 33 [Cyr-p_{alic}].
51. rec om 2nd *οτι*, with X rel vulg lat-*c e f* ff_2 [*l q*] æth: ins ABGLℵ lat-*a* [*b*]

insight by the Lord into Nathanael's character to be here understood; and there is probably no reference at all to the question which Nathanael had just asked. To suppose that Jesus *overheard that question*, is just one of those perfectly gratuitous assumptions which the very Commentators who here make this supposition are usually the first to blame. Compare ch. ii. 25. **ἀληθ. Ἰσρ.**] 'An Israelite who truly answers to the inner and honourable meaning of the name.' When we reflect what was contained in that name, and Who it is that speaks, we can hardly agree with De Wette that the words are spoken merely in the spirit in which every nation attaches some peculiar virtue, and especially those of openness and straightforwardness, to itself, as deutsch herausſagen, deutsche Treue, or Cicero's "Romano more loqui." Our Lord probably referred to Ps. xv. **49.**] The remark was overheard by Nathanael, and recognized as indicating perfect knowledge of his character. The question **πόθ. με γιν.** is one of astonishment, but not perhaps yet of suspicion of any thing supernatural. Our Lord's answer first opens this to him. **πρὸ τοῦ** *κ.τ.λ.*] It would be doubtful whether **ὄντα ὑπὸ τ. συκ.** belong to **φωνῆσαι** or to **εἶδόν σε**, did not ver. 51 decide for the latter construction. The whole form of our Lord's answer seems to indicate that the place where Philip called Nathanael was not *now* in sight, nor had been. The declaration that Jesus had seen him there, at once brings the conviction which he expresses in the next verse. This would not have been the case, unless the sight had been evidently and unquestionably supernatural: and unless the words ὄντα ὑπὸ τὴν συκῆν involved this. Had Jesus merely seen Nathanael without being seen by him, (De Wette,) or had εἶδόν σε only expressed '*I knew thy character*,' at first sight, '*although at a distance*' (Lücke), *no such immediate conviction would have followed.* **ὄντα ὑπὸ τὴν συκῆν**, says Wordsw., "is something more than ὑπὸ τῇ συκῇ—the accusative indicates retirement thither as well as concealment there,—perhaps for purposes of prayer and meditation." In fact it contains in it, 'when thou wentest under the fig-tree, and while thou wert there.'
Ver. **50** = 'Thou art the Messiah:' see Ps. ii. 7. ch. xi. 27: Matt. xvi. 16: Luke xxii. 70. Olshausen (ii. 77 ff.) maintains that **ὁ υἱ. τ. θ.** was not a Jewish appellation for the Messiah,—on account of the Jews taking up stones to cast at Jesus when He so called Himself, ch. x. 33. But as Lücke observes (i. 456, note), it was not for the *mere use* of this Name,—but for using it in a *close and literal sense* which was unintelligible and appeared blasphemous to them, ἐγὼ κ. ὁ πατὴρ ἕν ἐσμεν,—that they wished to stone Him: see note on ch. x. 36. It was certainly not so common a name as 'the Son of David,' for the Messiah. Nathanael can hardly have meant the name in other than its popular meaning; and the synonymous and better known appellation which he adds, confirms this. **51.**] Our Lord says this not in blame, rather in praise of the simple and honest expression of Nathanael's conviction; but principally to shew him, that if he believed by reason of this comparatively small proof of His divine power, his faith would increase from strength to strength at the greater proofs which should from that time forward be given. It is perhaps best to set a question at πιστεύεις; but see notes

μείζω τούτων ὄψῃ. 52 καὶ λέγει αὐτῷ [k]Ἀμὴν ἀμὴν λέγω
ὑμῖν, ὄψεσθε τὸν [l]οὐρανὸν [lm]ἀνεῳγότα, καὶ τοὺς [n]ἀγγέ-
λους τοῦ θεοῦ [n]ἀναβαίνοντας καὶ [n]καταβαίνοντας ἐπὶ
τὸν [o]υἱὸν τοῦ [o]ἀνθρώπου.

II. 1 Καὶ τῇ τρίτῃ ἡμέρᾳ [p]γάμος ἐγένετο ἐν Κανᾷ

k see Matt. v. 18 reff.
l = Matt. iii. 16 ||. Acts vii. 56. x. 11. Rev. xix. 11.
m perf. midd., 1 Cor. xvi. 9. 2 Cor. vi. 11 only.
n Gen. xxviii. 12.
o Matt. viii. 20 reff.
p Matt. xxii. 2, &c. xxv. 10. Luke xii. 36. xiv. 8. Heb. xiii. 4. Rev. xix. 7, 9 only. Gen. xxix. 22.

syrr copt [arm] Cyr_1. μειζονα ℵ [$Epiph_1$-ms]. rec οψει, with U[ΓΠ[1]] 1.69: txt ABℵ rel.

52. rec ins απ' αρτι bef οψεσθε, with A rel lat-*e q* syrr Chr_1 Cyr_1 [Aug_1] (*prob from Matt* xxvi. 64. *The referring what follows to the angelic appearances at the passion and resurrection would not occasion its omn, for, as Lücke has observed, the most ancient interpretation of the saying was the* spiritual one, *e. g. in Orig, who omits it*): om BLℵ latt copt æth arm $Orig_1$[int_2] $Epiph_1$ Cyr[$_2$-ms_1-p] Promiss Zeno. ηνεωγοτα ℵ[1].

Chap. II. 1. rec τη ημερα τη τριτη, with Aℵ rel (vulg lat-*a c* [$Epiph_1$ Chr_1 Cyr_1]): τη τριτη (alone) M: txt BU 69 lat-*b e q* $Epiph_3$.

on the similar sentences, ch. xvi. 31, and xx. 29. **52.**] **ἀμὴν ἀμήν** is peculiar to John. The other Evangelists use ἀμήν *once* only in such asseverations. The LXX do not use it in this sense. Stier remarks (i. 36, edn. 2), that the **Verily, verily, I say unto you** of the Lord, is spoken in His coequality with the Father: not as the 'Thus saith the Lord' of the Prophets. **ὑμῖν**] The words following are then spoken to all the disciples present, not only to Nathanael. With or without ἀπ' ἄρτι, the meaning will be much the same. The glories of a period beginning from the opening of the Lord's public ministry, and *at this day not yet completed*, are described. For it is not the outward visible opening of the material heavens, nor ascent and descent of angels in the sight of men, which our Lord here announces; but the series of glories which was about to be unfolded in His Person and Work from that time forward. Lüther, cited by Lücke, i. 458, beautifully says: "When Christ became man and had entered on His ministerial office and begun to preach, then was the heaven opened, and remains open; and has from that time, since the baptism of Christ in the Jordan, never been shut, and never will be shut, although we do not see it with our bodily eyes . . . Christ says this: 'Ye are now heavenly citizens, and have your citizenship above in the heavenly Jerusalem, and are in communion with the holy angels, who shall without intermission ascend and descend about you.'" The **opening of heaven** is a symbolical expression, signifying the imparting of divine grace, help, and revelation. See Gen. xxviii. 10–17: Ezek. i. 1. Isa. vi. 1: Mal. iii. 10: Isa. lxiv. 1: also Deut. xi. 17: 1 Kings viii. 35. The words have a plain reference to the *ladder of Jacob*, and imply that what he then saw was now to receive its fulfilment: that He, the Son of Man, was the dwelling of God and the gate of Heaven, and that *through* Him, and *on* Him in the first place, was to descend all communication of help and grace from above. That no allusion is meant to the Transfiguration, or the Agony, is plain; for *all* those here addressed did not witness these appearances, but Peter and John only; nor to the Ascension, for they did not see heaven opened, nor did angels ascend nor descend. The above has (remarks Olsh. ii. 79) been the interpretation of all Commentators of any depth in all times: Origen as well as Augustine, Luther as well as Calvin, Lücke as well as Tholuck: and I may add, De Wette as well as Stier. **τὸν υἱ. τ. ἀνθ.**] An expression originally (as appears) derived, in its Messianic sense, from Dan. vii. 13, 14, and thenceforward used as one of the titles of the Messiah (see ch. xii. 34). It is never predicated of our Lord by any but Himself, except in Acts vii. 56 by Stephen, in allusion apparently to Matt. xxvi. 64, and—which is hardly an exception—in the passages of the Revelation (ch. i. 13; xiv. 14) which are almost citations from Daniel.

Chap. II. **1—11.**] *The miracle of turning water into wine: the first fulfilment of the announcement in* ch. i. 51: see ver. 11. **1.**] **τῇ τρίτῃ**—reckoned from the day of Nathanael's calling. There would thus be but one day between that event and the marriage.

Κανᾷ τ. Γ.] See ch. iv. 46;—not far from Capernaum. Josephus (Life, § 16) calls it κώμη τῆς Γαλιλαίας. There is a Kanah in Josh. xix. 28, in the tribe of

q = Matt. xxii. 3, &c. Luke xiv. 7, &c. Esth. v. 12.
r = Mark x. 21. Isa. li. 14 F (not A). Ald. compl. (from Theod.)
s Mark v. 7 ‖. 2 Kings xvi. 10 al.

ABEFG HKLM SUVXΓ ΔΛΠℵ 1. 33. 69

τῆς Γαλιλαίας, καὶ ἦν ἡ μήτηρ τοῦ Ἰησοῦ ἐκεῖ. 2 q ἐκλήθη
δὲ καὶ ὁ Ἰησοῦς καὶ οἱ μαθηταὶ αὐτοῦ εἰς τὸν p γάμον.
3 καὶ r ὑστερήσαντος οἴνου λέγει ἡ μήτηρ τοῦ Ἰησοῦ πρὸς
αὐτὸν Οἶνον οὐκ ἔχουσιν. 4 καὶ λέγει αὐτῇ ὁ Ἰησοῦς s Τί

3. for *υστερησαντος οινου*, *οινον ουχ ειχον οτι συνετελεσθη ο οινος του γαμου ειτα* ℵ[1](txt ℵ-corr[1]) lat-*a b* ff_2 (syr-mg æth). for *οινον ουκ εχουσιν*, *οινος ουκ εστιν* ℵ[1] [(Syr syr-jer æth)].

4. rec om 1st *και*, with EFHMSV[Γ]Λℵ[1] forj lat-*a* Syr : ins AB ℵ[3a](but erased) rel vulg lat-*b c* syr [syr-jer] copt æth arm Cyr_1 Non_1.

Asher, which must be distinct from this. Jerome however in his Onomasticon believes it to have been the same. It was the residence, and probably birth-place, of Nathanael. If his calling took place in its neighbourhood, our Lord may have gone on and spent the intervening day at Nazareth. Dr. Robinson, Bib. Res. iii. 204 ff., satisfactorily establishes that Kâna-el-Jelîl, about 3 hours N. ½ E. from Nazareth, is the site of this miracle. The name is identical, and so stands in the Arabic version of the N. T. He shews this to have been recognized in early tradition, and its honour to have been only recently usurped by Kefr Kenna, a village 1½ hour N.E. from Nazareth, on one of the roads to Tiberias. [See a very interesting description of Kâna-el-Jelîl in "The Land and the Book," pp. 426, 427.]

ἡ μήτηρ τ. Ἰ.] John *never names* her, as being already well known (Lücke): or perhaps more probably from his own intimate connexion with her, in pursuance of the injunction ch. xix. 26, 27. He never names either himself, or his own brother, James. **2.**] **ἐκλήθη**, not for a pluperfect:—**was invited**: the historical past. **κ. οἱ μαθ. αὐτ.**] It does not appear *who these were*, unless we assume that they were those called in ch. i., which seems most probable. John himself was most likely present. He does not relate so circumstantially any thing which he had not witnessed. In this case, there must have been some other reason for the invitation, besides mere previous acquaintance. This would be the probable reason for *Jesus Himself* being invited; but the *disciples*, being from various places in the district, can hardly *all have been* (De Wette) *friends of the family*. The fact of Jesus having attached disciples to Himself must have been known, and they were doubtless invited *from consideration to Him*. Our Lord at once opens His ministry with the character which He gives of himself Matt. xi. 18, 19, as distinguished from the asceticism of John. He also, as Trench admirably remarks (Miracles, edn. 2, p. 98, note), gives us his own testimony against the tendency which our indolence ever favours, of giving up those things and occasions to the world and the devil, which we have not Christian boldness to mingle in and purify. Even Cyprian, for instance, proscribes such festivals,—"nuptiarum festa improba et convivia lasciva vitentur, quorum periculosa contagio est." De Habitu Virginum, ch. xxi. p. 460. And such is the general verdict of modern religionism, which would keep the leaven distinct from the lump, for fear *it* should become *unleavened*. The especial honour conferred upon *marriage* by the Lord should also be noticed. "He here adorned and beautified it with his presence, and first miracle that He wrought." **3.**] There is no necessity to suppose that the feast had lasted several days, as De Wette and Lücke do. It has been suggested that the unexpected presence of the disciples may have occasioned a failure in the previously sufficient supply: a gloss in the old latin cod. Rhedigerianus has, "*et factum est per multam turbam vocatorum vinum consummari.*" The mother of Jesus evidently is *in a position of authority* (see ver. 5) in the house, which was probably that of a near relative. The conjectures and traditions on the subject are many, but wholly unsatisfactory. A graver question arises as to the intent with which this **οἶνον οὐκ ἔχ.** was said. She cannot have had *from experience* any reason to suppose that her Son would work a miracle, for this (ver. 11) *was His first.* Chrysostom suggests (so also Theophyl., Euthym., and Neander, L. J. p. 271) that, knowing Him to be Who He was, she had been by the recent divine acknowledgment of Him and His calling disciples to Himself, led to expect the manifestation of his Messianic power about this time; and here seemed an occasion for it. Some of the other explanations are: "that she had always found Him a wise counsellor, and mentioned the want to Him merely that He might suggest some way of remedying it." Cocceius, cited by Trench. "Velim discedas, ut ceteri item discedant,

ἐμοὶ καὶ σοί, γύναι; οὔπω [t] ἥκει ἡ [u] ὥρα μου. 5 λέγει ἡ
μήτηρ αὐτοῦ τοῖς [v] διακόνοις Ὅ τι ἂν λέγῃ ὑμῖν, ποιήσατε.
6 ἦσαν δὲ ἐκεῖ [w] λίθιναι [x] ὑδρίαι ἓξ κατὰ τὸν [y] καθαρισ-

t [Luke xiii. 35.] 2 Pet. iii. 10. Gen. vi. 13.
u = ch. vii. 30. viii. 20. xiii. 1. (xvi. 21.)
v Matt. xxiii. 11 reff.
w 2 Cor. iii. 3. Rev. ix. 20 only. Gen. xxxv. 14.
x here bis & ch. iv. 28 only. Eccl. xii. 6.
y ch. iii. 25. Luke ii. 22. v. 14 || Mk. Heb. i. 3. 2 Pet. i. 9 only. 1 Chron. xxiii. 28.

5. for ο τι, οτι ο ℵ [Chr-3-mss].
6. rec υδριαι bef λιθιναι (*more usual order*), with A rel lat-*a b e f* [*l q*] Chr_1 Cyr_1:

antequam penuria patefiat." Bengel. "Ut pia aliqua exhortatione convivis tædium eximeret, ac simul levaret pudorem sponsi." Calvin, cited by Lücke. "Jesus had wrought miracles, but in secret, before this." Tholuck. On the whole, the most probable explanation is that of Lücke, which somewhat modifies the first here mentioned,—that our Lord Himself had recently given some reason to expect that He would shew forth His glory by wonderful works. So, very nearly, Stier, R. J. i. 38, edn. 2. 4.] The answer of our Lord is beyond question *one of reproof,* and *disclaimer of participation in the grounds on which the request was made.* See instances, besides reff., in Josh. xxii. 24: Mark i. 24. And so all the early expositors understood it. Irenæus (iii. 16. 6, p. 206) says, "Dominus repellens ejus intempestivam festinationem, dixit," &c.;—and Chrysostom, ἐβούλετο . . . . ἑαυτὴν λαμπροτέραν ποιῆσαι διὰ τοῦ παιδός, and therefore He σφοδρότερον ἀπεκρίνατο. Hom. xxi. in Joh., vol. viii. p. 122. The Romanist expositors mostly endeavour to divest the answer of any aspect of rebuke, and maintain that it was so uttered for *our sakes* alone, to teach us that He did not perform His miracles from regard to human affinity, but solely from love and His object of manifesting His glory. So Maldonatus. And this is true:—but first among those to be taught this, was *she herself, who had tempted Him to work a miracle from that regard.*

It has perhaps not been enough noticed, that in this answer the Lord declares His period of subjection to her as His earthly parent to be at an end. Henceforth His thoughts are not her thoughts. At twelve years of age, see Luke ii. 49, He answers 'thy father and I,' by 'My Father:'—now, He is to be no longer before the world *as Mary's son,* but as sanctified by the Father and sent into the world:—compare Matt. xii. 48—50, and Luke xi. 27, 28, and see Stier's admirable remarks, R. J. i. 39, edn. 2, also Olshausen's, ii. 81. **γύναι**] There is no reproach in this term: but rather respect. The Lord henceforth uses it towards her, not calling her 'mother,' even on the Cross (see ch. xix. 26), doubtless for the reason alleged above. **οὔπω ἥκ. ἡ ὥρα μου**] * This expression is generally used in John of the time of the *Death* of Christ: see reff. But it is only so used because His death is in those passages the subject naturally underlying the narrative. It is, *any fixed or appointed time;*—and therefore here, the appointed time of His self-manifestation by miracles. This time was not yet come, but was close at hand. Some have supposed that the wine was not yet wholly exhausted, and that our Lord would wait till the miracle should be undoubted (so Trench, p. 192): but Stier well remarks that the known *depth* of all His early sayings forbids us from attaching only this meaning to it;—and he sees in it a reference to the great marriage-feast and the new fruit of the vine in the Kingdom of God (i. 41, edn. 2). If this be so, it can be only in the background; the words must have had a present meaning, and I believe it to be, '*My time, the time at which, from the Father's appointment and my own concurring will, I am to begin miraculous working, is not yet arrived: forestall it not.*' Very similarly He speaks, ch. vii. 6, to His brethren, and yet afterwards goes up to the feast. The notion that ἡ ὥρα μου refers to the hour of our Lord's human infirmity on the Cross when (ch. xix. 27) He "acknowledged her as His mother," Wordsw., seems wholly unfounded. Where do we find any such special acknowledgment there? And why should we go out of our way for a fanciful sense of words which bear an excellent meaning as referring to circumstances then present?

5.] There certainly seems beneath this narrative to lie *some incident which is not told us.* For not only is Mary *not repelled* by the answer just given, but she is *convinced that the miracle will be wrought,* and she is not without an anticipation of the *method of working it:* for how should He require the aid of the servants, except the miracle were to take place according to the form here related? I believe we shall find, when all things are opened to us, that there had been

μὸν τῶν Ἰουδαίων [z] κείμεναι, [a] χωροῦσαι [b] ἀνὰ [c] μετρητὰς
δύο ἢ τρεῖς. 7 λέγει αὐτοῖς ὁ Ἰησοῦς [d] Γεμίσατε τὰς
[x] ὑδρίας ὕδατος. καὶ [d] ἐγέμισαν αὐτὰς [e] ἕως ἄνω. 8 καὶ
λέγει αὐτοῖς [f] Ἀντλήσατε νῦν καὶ φέρετε τῷ [g] ἀρχιτρι-
κλίνῳ. οἱ δὲ ἤνεγκαν. 9 ὡς δὲ [h] ἐγεύσατο ὁ [g] ἀρχιτρίκλινος τὸ ὕδωρ οἶνον [i] γεγενημένον, καὶ οὐκ ᾔδει πόθεν
[k] ἐστίν· οἱ δὲ [l] διάκονοι ᾔδεισαν οἱ [f] ἠντληκότες τὸ ὕδωρ·

T_b ii. 9 (appy)... ABEFG HKLM ST_bUV ΧΓΔΛ Πℵ 1. 33. 69

z = ch. xix. 29. xxi. 9. Rev. iv. 2. Jer. xxiv. 1.
a = ch. xxi. 25. Mark ii. 2. 3 Kings vii. 38.
b Matt xx. 9, 10 reff.
c here only. 2 Chron. iv. 5.
d here bis. Mark iv. 37. xv. 36. Luke xiv. 23. xv. 16. ch. vi. 13. Rev. viii. 5. xv. 8 only. Gen. xlv. 17.
e w. adv., Mark xiv. 54. xv. 38 ‖ Mt. Luke xxiii. 5. 2 Chron. xxvi. 8.
f here bis and ch. iv. 7, 15 only. Gen. xxiv. 13, 20. (-τλημα, ch. iv. 11.)
g here 3ce only +.
h w. acc., Heb. vi. 5. 1 Kings xiv. 29. Job xii. 11.
i = Matt. iv. 3 ‖ L. Rev. viii. 8. Exod. iv. 3.
k pres., ch. i. 40 reff.
l ver. 5.

txt BLXℵ 33 vulg lat-*c*. rec κειμεναι bef κατα τ. καθ. τ. ιουδ., with A rel vulg lat-*c* syrr [syr-jer Cyr_1]; bef υδρ. lat-*b f*; bef εξ 69 lat-*l* Chr_1: om κειμ. ℵ[1] ev-47 lat-*a e* arm: txt BLXℵ[3a] 33 æth.

7. at beg ins και Xℵ (lat-*a e* ff_2 *l*) [æth].

8. rec (for οι δε) και, with A rel vulg lat-*b c f* syrr sah-mnt æth [Chr_1]: om clause X: txt BKL[Π]ℵ 1. 33 lat-*a* syr-mg [syr-jer] copt arm.

[9. for ποθεν, που T_b.]

a previous hint given her,—where or how I would not presume to say,—by our Lord, of His intention and the manner of performing it, and that her fault was, *the too rash hastening on of what had been His fixed purpose.* 6.] These vessels were for the washings usual at feasts: see Mark vii. 4. There could be no collusion or imposture here, as they were *water-vessels,* and could have no remnants of wine in them (see also ver. 10). And the large quantity which they held could not have been brought in unobserved. The **μετρητής** is probably = the Jewish בַּת (which, Jos. Antt. viii. 2. 9, held 72 ξέσται = the Attic μετρητής = 8 gallons 7·4 pints), and stands for it in the LXX, ref. 2 Chron. According to this, the quantity of wine thus created would = 6 × (2 or 3) × (8 gallons 7·4 pints) = 6 × (between 17 and 25 gallons) = say, 6 × 21 gallons = 126 gallons. The large quantity thus created has been cavilled at by unbelievers. We may leave them to their cavils with just one remark,—that He who creates abundance enough in this earth to "put temptation in men's way," acted on this occasion *analogously with His known method of dealing.* We may answer an error on the other side (*if it be on the other side*), by saying, that the Lord here most effectually and once for all stamps with His condemnation that false system of moral reformation, which would commence by *pledges to abstain from intoxicating liquors.* He pours out His bounty *for all,* and He vouchsafes His grace to *each* for guidance; and to endeavour to evade the work which He has appointed for each man,—by *refusing the bounty, to save the trouble of seeking the grace,* is an attempt which must ever end in degradation of the individual motives, and in social demoralization,—whatever present apparent effects may follow its first promulgation. One visible sign of this degradation, in its intellectual form, is the miserable attempt made by some of the advocates of this movement, to shew that the wine here and in other places of Scripture is unfermented wine, not possessing the power of intoxication.

The filling with water, and drawing out wine, is all that is related. "The *moment* of the miracle," says Lücke, "is rather understood than expressed. It seems to lie between vv. 7 and 8" (i. 471). The *process* of it is wholly out of the region of our imagination. In order for wine to be produced, we have the growth and ripening of the grape; the crushing of it in proper vessels; the fermentation;—but here all these are in a moment brought about in their *results,* by the same Power which made the laws of nature, and created and unfolded the capacities of man. See below on ver. 11.

8.] The **ἀρχιτρίκλινος** (συμποσίαρχος, ἐπιμελητὴς τοῦ συμποσίου, Euthym.) seems to be the same with the ἡγούμενος spoken of, Sir. xxxv. (xxxii.) 1, and with the Latin *rex,* or *magister, convivii.* It would seem (from Sir. l. c.) that he was *one of the guests* raised to the post of presiding over the arrangements of the feast. This is however doubted by the older Commentators (Severus in the Catena, Lücke, i. 472), who make him not one of the guests, but a person *holding this especial office, and attending on feasts.* Here, he *tastes the wine;* and therefore probably was a guest himself. Lücke quotes from

[m] φωνεῖ τὸν [n] νυμφίον ὁ [g] ἀρχιτρίκλινος 10 καὶ λέγει αὐτῷ
Πᾶς ἄνθρωπος πρῶτον τὸν καλὸν οἶνον [o] τίθησιν, καὶ
ὅταν [p] μεθυσθῶσιν, [τότε] τὸν [q] ἐλάσσω· σὺ [r] τετήρηκας
τὸν καλὸν οἶνον [s] ἕως ἄρτι. 11 ταύτην ἐποίησεν [t] ἀρχὴν
τῶν [u] σημείων ὁ Ἰησοῦς ἐν Κανᾷ τῆς Γαλιλαίας, καὶ
[v] ἐφανέρωσεν τὴν [w] δόξαν αὐτοῦ· καὶ [x] ἐπίστευσαν [x] εἰς
αὐτὸν οἱ μαθηταὶ αὐτοῦ.

m ch. i. 49 reff.
n Matt. ix. 15 ‖. xxv. 1, 5, 6, 10. ch. iii. 29 (3ce). Rev. xviii. 23 only. Ps. xviii. 5.
o = here only. Bel & Dr. 11 Theod.
p pass., Rev. xvii. 2 only. 1 Kings i. 14 al. elsw. neut., Matt. xxiv. 49. Acts ii. 15. 1 Cor. xi. 21. 1 Thess. v. 7. Rev. xvii. 2, 6 only.
q = here (Rom. ix. 12, from Gen. xxv. 23. Heb. vii. 7) only. (= -ττον, adv., 1 Tim. v. 9.)
r = ch. xii. 7. 2 Pet. ii. 17. Jude 6.
s Matt. xi. 12. ch. v. 17.
t = Matt. xxiv. 8. Mark i. 1. Ruth i. 22.
u = Mark xvi. 17, 20. Luke xxiii. 8. Acts iv. 16, 22. viii. 6. John, ch. xii. 37. xx. 30 al. fr.
v ch. i. 31 reff.
w ch. i. 14 al. fr.
x ch. i. 12 al. fr. in John. elsw., Matt. xviii. 6 (‖ Mk. v. r.). Acts x. 43. xiv. 23. xix. 4. Rom. x. 14. Gal. ii. 16. Phil. i. 29. 1 Pet. i. 8, 21 only †.

10. om *αυτω* ℵ. om *τοτε* BL[T_b]ℵ[1] lat-*a e ff*$_2$ *l* copt æth Orig-int$_1$ Gaud$_1$: ins Aℵ[3a] rel lat-*b c f* [vulg syr-jer] syrr arm [Chr$_1$ Cyr$_1$]. aft *σν* ins *δε* GΛℵ 69 vulg-ed lat-*a b e f ff*$_2$ [*l q* syr-jer] Syr syr-w-ast copt æth Orig-int$_1$.
11. rec ins *την* bef *αρχην*, with ℵ rel Eus$_1$[-mss]: om ABL[T_b]Λ 1. 33 [arm] Orig$_1$ Eus$_2$ [Cyr-p$_1$] Chron$_1$. aft *γαλιλαιας* ins *πρωτην* ℵ[1](om ℵ-corr[1 or 2·3]). om 1st *αυτου* ℵ[1]. *οι μαθ. αυ.* bef *εις αυτον* ℵ[1].

Petronius "triclinarches." **9. οἱ ἠντληκότες**] This is the participle of the pluperf. (as well as of the perf.), and is here to be so rendered—**who had drawn the water.** **10.**] The saying of the ἀρχ. is a general one, not applicable to the company then present. We may be sure that the Lord would not have sanctioned, nor ministered to, *actual drunkenness*. Only those who can conceive *this*, will find any difficulty here; and they will find difficulties every where. The account of the practice referred to is, that the palates of men become after a while dull, and cannot distinguish between good wine and bad. Pliny (Nat. Hist. xiv. 13) speaks of persons "qui etiam convivis (vina) alia quam sibimetipsis ministrant, *aut procedente mensa subjiciunt*." But the practice *here* described is not precisely that of which Pliny speaks, nor is there any meanness to be charged on it: it is only that, when a man has some kinds of wine choicer than others, he naturally produces the choicest, to suit the most discriminating taste. With regard to the word **μεθυσθῶσιν**, while there is no reason here to *press* its ordinary meaning, so neither is there any to shrink from it, as uttered by the ἀρχιτρίκλινος. The safest rendering is that of Tyndall and Cranmer, "*when men be dronke;*" "*cum inebriati fuerint*," Vulg. **11.**] Without the article before ἀρχήν (see rec. in digest) it is **This wrought Jesus as the beginning of his miracles**:—ἀρχή being the predicate. This assertion of John excludes all the apocryphal miracles of the Gospel of the Infancy, and such like works, from credit. **σημεῖον**, which occasionally occurs in the other Gospels and the Acts in this absolute sense of *a miracle* (see reff.), is St. John's ordinary word for it. Cf. Luthardt, p. 62. **τὴν δόξαν αὐτ.**] The glory, namely, which is referred to in ch. i. 14, where see note. It was a miracle eminently shewing forth the glory of the λόγος, δι' οὗ πάντα ἐγένετο, in His state of having become flesh. And this '*believing on Him*,' here predicated of the disciples, was certainly a higher faith than that which first led them to Him. They obtained new insight into His power;—not yet reflectively, so as to infer what all this implied, but so as to increase their faith and trust in Him. Again and again '*they believed*:' new degrees of faith being attained; just as this has since been the case, and will continue to be, in the Church, in the continual providential development of the Christian spirit,—the leavening of the whole lump by degrees. This important miracle, standing as it does *at the very entrance of the official life of Christ*, has been the subject of many doubts, and attempts to get rid of, or explain away, the power which was here manifested. But never did a narrative present a more stubborn inflexibility to the wresters of Scripture:—never was simple historical veracity more strikingly stamped on any miracle than on this. And doubtless this is providentially so arranged: see the objections to it treated, and some admirable concluding remarks, in Lücke, i. 478. To those who yet seek some sufficient *cause* for the miracle being wrought, we may—besides the conclusive answer that we are not in a position to treat this question satisfactorily,—assign the unmistakeable spiritual import of the change here made, as indicating the general nature of

y = Mark iii. 22. Luke x. 30. Gen. xii. 10. z = ch. vi. 4. vii. 2. Matt. xxiv. 32. Rev. i. 3. xxii. 10. Isa. xiii. 6. a ch. (vi. 4) xi. 55 only. see Matt. xxvi. 2 reff. b = Matt. xx. 18 reff. c Matt. iii. 16 reff. d here only †. e here only †. (-λλοῦν, Matt. xxvii. 26.) f Acts xxvii. 32 only. 2 Kings viii. 2. g = Matt. xxi. 12. ix. 25 ‖ Mk. Acts ix. 40 al. Gen. iii. 24. h Matt. xxi. 12 ‖ only †. i Matt. ix. 17 (‖ Mk. v. r.). Acts i. 18. Judg. vi. 20. j here only †.

12 Μετὰ τοῦτο [y] κατέβη εἰς Καφαρναοὺμ αὐτὸς καὶ ἡ
μήτηρ αὐτοῦ καὶ οἱ ἀδελφοὶ [αὐτοῦ] καὶ οἱ μαθηταὶ αὐτοῦ,
καὶ ἐκεῖ ἔμειναν οὐ πολλὰς ἡμέρας. 13 καὶ [z] ἐγγὺς ἦν τὸ
[a] πάσχα τῶν [a] Ἰουδαίων, καὶ [b] ἀνέβη εἰς Ἱεροσόλυμα ὁ
Ἰησοῦς. 14 καὶ εὗρεν ἐν τῷ ἱερῷ τοὺς πωλοῦντας βόας
καὶ πρόβατα καὶ [c] περιστερὰς καὶ τοὺς [d] κερματιστὰς καθημένους. 15 καὶ ποιήσας [e] φραγέλλιον ἐκ [f] σχοινίων πάντας [g] ἐξέβαλεν ἐκ τοῦ ἱεροῦ, τά τε πρόβατα καὶ τοὺς βόας,
καὶ τῶν [h] κολλυβιστῶν [i] ἐξέχεεν τὰ [j] κέρματα καὶ τὰς

P και εγγυς... ABEF GHKL MPST$_b$ UVXΓΔ ΛΠℵ 1. 33. 69

12. om 2nd αυτου BL[T$_b$] lat-*a c e* Orig$_4$: ins Aℵ rel vulg lat-*b f* [*l* syr-jer] syrr copt æth arm. [om 3rd αυτου L T$_b$(appy) Orig$_4$:] om και οι μαθηται αυτου ℵ 245-9 Scr's e q[1] r v lat-*a b e ff$_2$ l* [*q* arm]: ins bef κ. οι αδ. αυ. K[Π[1]] 258 Scr's p w. εμεινεν AFGH[2]Λ 1 lat-*b* [syr-jer] copt arm Orig$_1$ Non$_1$.
13. for και εγγυς, εγγυς δε ℵ.
14. for βοας και προβ., και τα προβ. και βοας ℵ[1].
15. for και ποιησας, εποιησεν ℵ[1]. aft σχοινιων ins και ℵ[1]. om τε ℵ[1] [lat-*a e l q*]: for τε, και ℵ[3a](but erased). rec (for τα κερματα) το κερμα, with APℵ rel:

the beneficent work which the Lord came on earth to do. So Cornelius a Lapide (Trench, p. 113, edn. 2, note): "Christus initio suæ prædicationis mutans aquam in vinum significabat se legem Mosaicam, instar aquæ insipidam et frigidam, conversurum in Evangelium gratiæ quæ instar vini est, generosa, sapida, ardens, et efficax." Similarly Eusebius, Augustine, Bernard, and Gregory the Great. Trench, ibid.

12—IV. 54.] First manifestation of Himself as the Son of God:—and herein, ii. 13—iii. 36, in Jerusalem and Judæa. 12.] **κατέβη**, because Capernaum lay on the lake,—Cana higher up the country. There is no certainty as to this visit, whether or not it is the same with that hinted at in Luke iv. 23: so that no chronological inferences can be built on the hypothesis with any security. On **οἱ ἀδελφοὶ** [**αὐτοῦ**] see Matt. xiii. 55 and note. Notice the transition from His private to His public life. His mother and brethren are still with Him, attached merely by nature: His disciples, newly attached by faith. In the next verse He has cast off His mere earthly ties for His work. Also in the **οὐ πολλὰς ἡμ.**, notice less a mere chronological design, than one to shew that He lost no time after His first miracle, in publicly manifesting Himself as the Son of God.

13—22.] *The first official visit to Jerusalem, at a Passover: and cleansing of the Temple.* 13.] No data are given to determine whether the reason of the short stay at Capernaum was the near approach of the Passover. Nothing is said of those who accompanied Jesus: but at all events, *His already called disciples* would be with Him (see ver. 22, and ch. iii. 22), and among them in all probability the Evangelist himself:—but *not the rest of the Twelve*, who were not yet called. Of this visit, the synoptic narrative records nothing. 14.] On the distinctness of this cleansing from that related in Matt. xxi. 12 ff., see note there.

ἐν τῷ ἱερῷ] In the court of the Gentiles, the *ἔξωθεν ἱερόν*, as distinguished from the *ναός*, the inner temple. This market appears to have sprung up since the captivity, with a view to the convenience of those Jews who came from a distance, to provide them with the beasts for offering, and to change their foreign money into the sacred shekel, which alone was allowed to be paid in for the temple capitation-tax (Matt. xvii. 24 ff.). This tax was sometimes, as in Matt. l. c., paid elsewhere than in Jerusalem; but generally there, and in the temple. The very fact of the market being held there would produce an unseemly mixture of sacred and profane transactions, even setting aside the abuses which would be certain to be mingled with the traffic. It is to the *former* of these evils that our Lord makes reference in this *first* cleansing; in the *second*, to the *latter*.

15.] The **σχοινία** were probably *the rushes* which were littered down for the cattle to lie on. That our Lord used the scourge on the beasts only, not on the sellers of them, is almost necessarily contained in the form of the sentence here: the *τά τε πρόβατα κ. τ. βόας* being as it stands with *τε* and *καί*, merely epexegetical

[k] τραπέζας [l] ἀνέστρεψεν, 16 καὶ τοῖς τὰς [c] περιστερὰς πω-
λοῦσιν εἶπεν Ἄρατε ταῦτα [m] ἐντεῦθεν· μὴ ποιεῖτε τὸν οἶκον
τοῦ πατρός μου οἶκον [n] ἐμπορίου. 17 [o] ἐμνήσθησαν οἱ
μαθηταὶ αὐτοῦ ὅτι γεγραμμένον ἐστὶν Ὁ [p] ζῆλος τοῦ οἴκου
σου [q] καταφάγεταί με. 18 [r] ἀπεκρίθησαν οὖν οἱ Ἰουδαῖοι καὶ
εἶπαν αὐτῷ Τί [s] σημεῖον δεικνύεις ἡμῖν [t] ὅτι ταῦτα ποιεῖς;
19 ἀπεκρίθη Ἰησοῦς καὶ εἶπεν αὐτοῖς [u] Λύσατε τὸν ναὸν

Frag. Ath_a. ii. 17...

k = Matt. xxi. 12 ||. Luke xix. 23 only.
l trans., = here only. intrans., Acts v. 23 (Matt. xvii. 22 reff.).
m Luke xiii. 31. ch. vii. 3. xiv. 31.
n here only. Deut. xxxiii. 19. Isa. xxiii. 17. Ezek. xxvii. 3 only. (-ρία, Matt. xxii. 5.)
o w. ὅτι, Matt. v. 23. xxvii. 63. Luke xvi. 25. ver. 22. ch. xii. 16 only.
p Psa. lxviii. 9. constr., Rom. x. 2. see Acts xxii. 3.
q Luke viii. 5 ||. xv. 30. Rev. x. 9, 10. xii. 4. xx. 9 only. = Aristoph. Vesp. 287, μηδ' οὕτως σεαυτὸν ἔσθιε. (κατεσθ., Luke xx. 47 reff.) fut., Luke xiv. 15. xvii. 8. James v. 3.
r = Matt. xi. 25 reff. ch. v. 17.
s = Matt. xii. 38, 39. 1 Cor. i. 22. Exod. iv. 8.
t Matt. xvi. 8.
u = Eph. ii. 14. 2 Pet. iii. 10, 11, 12. Esdr. i. 55 (52).

txt BL[Γ_b]X 33 lat-*b q* copt arm $Orig_8$ Eus_1. for ανεστρ., ανετρεψεν BX[Π^2 Cyr_1] $Orig_1$: κατεστρεψεν ℵ 69¹-marg: κατορθωσε 69-txt [$Epiph_1$].

16. ins και bef μη ποιειτε AUX 1. 69 vulg lat-*a b e q* [*l* syr-jer] syrr æth arm Cyr-jer_1 [Eus_2].

17. rec aft εμνησθησαν ins δε, with AP rel vulg lat-*b c* syr; δε και M: om BL[Γ_b]Xℵ copt Eus_2 [Cyr_1]. εστιν bef γεγραμμενον B Chr_1. add οτι X Frag-ath_a Scr's t $Orig_1$(om_1) [$Epiph_1$]. rec κατεφαγε (*conformn to* LXX), with 69 latt syrr [Eus_2] $Epiph_2$ Hil: txt ABP[Γ_b]ℵ rel copt Cyr_3.

18. (ειπαν, so BL 33 $Orig_2$.)

19. rec ins ο bef ιησους, with Kℵ 69 (1. 33, e sil): om ABP rel $Orig_2$ Cyr. [Γ_b?]

of πάντας, not conveying new particulars. So that it should be rendered as in A. V. R., "He drove all out of the temple, both the sheep and the oxen." (ἐξέχεεν is the aor., not the resolved form of the imperfect: cf. Aristoph. Nub. 75, and see Lobeck's note on Phryn. p. 222.) It has been imagined, that He dealt more mildly with those who sold the doves, which were for the offerings *of the poor*. But this was not so: He dealt alike with all. No other way was open with regard to them, than to order them to take their birds away. This cleansing of the temple was in the direct course of His manifestation as the Messiah. Immediately after the prophetic announcement of the Forerunner, Mal. iii. 1, is that of the Lord's *coming suddenly to His temple, and purifying it*. This act also answers (but like the fulfilment last mentioned, only in an *imperfect* and *still prophetic* sense) to the declaration of the Baptist "Whose fan is in His hand," &c., Matt. iii. 12. His proceeding was not altogether unexampled nor unauthorized, even in an uncommissioned person: for all had the right to reform an abuse of this sort, and the zealots put this right in practice. The disciples by their allusion in ver. 17 seem to refer the action to this latter class.

16. τοῦ πατρός μου] The coincidence with Luke ii. 49 is remarkable. By this expression thus publicly used, our Lord openly announces His Messiahship. Nathanael had named Him 'the Son of God' with this meaning—see on ch. i. 50,—and these words, coupled with the expectation which the confession of John the Baptist would arouse, could leave no doubt on the minds of the Jews as to their import: see on ch. iii. 2. **οἶκ. ἐμπ.**] Not yet σπήλαιον λῃστῶν, as at the end of His ministry: see above on ver. 14.

17.] **ἐμνήσθησαν**, *at the time*, not afterwards, which would have been expressed, as in ver. 22. But the very remembrance itself was prophetic. The καταφαγεῖν spoken of in that passion-Psalm, was the marring and wasting of the Saviour's frame by His zeal for God and God's Church, which resulted in the buffeting, the scourging, the Cross. **καταφάγεται** is a well-known future, contracted from καταφαγήσεται: see reff. and cf. the prophecy, 4 Kings ix. 36, καταφάγονται οἱ κύνες τὰς σάρκας Ἰεζάβελ.

18.] On the demand of the Jews, see Deut. xiii. 1—3. It was not only to justify His having driven out the abomination; this any one might have done;—but to justify the mission and the whole course of action which the words τοῦ πατρός μου implied. They used the same expression at the end of His ministry, Matt. xxi. 23.

19.] This answer of our Lord has been involved in needless difficulty. That [in uttering the words τὸν ναὸν τοῦτον] He *pointed to* His own Body, is inconceivable;—for thus both the Jews and His own disciples must have understood Him, which (see vv. 20, 22) neither of them did. That He implied [in saying Λύσατε τ. ν. τ.] *that their lawless proceedings in the temple would at last bring it to an end*, is equally inconceivable;

v Eph. v. 14. James iv. 7, 8. Rev. ii. 10. w = here (bis) only, but see ver. 22. (-σις, Esdr. v. 62 [59].) x John here only. elsw. passim. tense, see note.

τοῦτον, [v] καὶ ἐν τρισὶν ἡμέραις [w] ἐγερῶ αὐτόν. 20 εἶπαν
οὖν οἱ Ἰουδαῖοι Τεσσεράκοντα καὶ ἓξ ἔτεσιν [x] ᾠκοδομήθη

ABEF GHKL MPST$_b$ UVXΓΔ ΛΠא Frag. Ath$_a$. 1. 33. 69

om εν B Orig.

20. (ειπαν, so B Orig$_1$. [T$_b$?]) οικοδομηθη B[1][T$_b$]א Frag-ath$_a$ [33].

both on account of the latter part of His declaration, which would thus have no meaning,—and because of the use of the word **ναός**,—which was *the holy and the holiest place*, the *temple itself*,—as distinguished from **τὸ ἱερόν**, the whole enceinte of the sacred buildings. Stier has well remarked (i. 48, 49, edn. 2) that our Lord in this saying *comprehended in the reality*,—His own Body, *its type and symbol*,—the temple then before them. That temple, with all its ordinances and holy places, was but the shadow of the Christian Church;—that, the type of the Body of the Lord, represented the Church, which is *veritably His Body*. And so the saying was fulfilled by the slaying of His actual Body, in which rejection of Him the destruction of the Jewish temple and city was involved,—and the raising of that Body after three days, in which resurrection we, all the members of His new glorified Body, are risen again. It is for want of keeping in mind this width and depth of the Lord's sayings, that so many Commentators have fallen into error here and elsewhere in interpreting them. Most of the best German expositors, e. g. Lücke, Neander (L. J. 283), and even Olshausen, find insuperable difficulty in the *exposition given by the Evangelist of these words*, and even contend that it *could not have been the right one*. But surely those who believe the Apostles to have been under the special influence of the Holy Spirit in their work of witnessing to and bringing out the truth of the sayings and doings of the Lord, cannot take this ground. It is a wholly distinct matter from a chronological inaccuracy, or a report of the same occurrence varying in minor details; such things the Spirit may have, and has as matter of fact, for special reasons permitted in the Evangelists; but we have here,—assumed the genuineness of our Gospel, on which none of these writers have a doubt,—*the positive declaration of an Apostle* (and what an Apostle) *of the meaning of the Lord's saying*;—which I do not think we are at liberty to question, on any, even the most moderate view, of the inspiration of the Scriptures. The difficulties attending the interpretation are,—besides the double meaning which I have treated above,—(1) *the use of the imperative, as applied to the death of Christ*. Olshausen contends that it must be mandatory, and cannot be hypothetical. But surely Matt. xii. 33 is an instance in point, as adduced by De Wette, for the hypothetical meaning: and usages exactly like that in our text are found in the reff. (v): see Winer, Gram. edn. 6, § 43. 2. (2) *The words* **ἐγερῶ αὐτόν**,—seeing that the resurrection of the Lord is ever spoken of as *the work of the Father*. Yes,—but by power committed to Christ Himself: see ch. x. 18, where this is distinctly asserted; and ch. vi. 39, 40, 44, where it is implied, for He is the first fruits of them that sleep,—and (though the whole course of His working was after the will of the Father,—and in the Spirit, which wrought in Him) strictly and truly *raised Himself* from the dead in the sense here intended. (3) *The utterance of such a prophecy at so early a period of His official life*. But it was not a prophecy known and understood,—but a *dark saying*, from which no one could then draw an inference as to His death or resurrection. The disciples did not understand it; and I cannot agree with Stier that the Jews could have had any idea of such being His meaning. Chrys. (Hom. xxiii. in Joan. p. 134) says, *πολλὰ τοιαῦτα φθέγγεται τοῖς μὲν τότε οὐκ ὄντα δῆλα, τοῖς δὲ μετὰ ταῦτα ἐσόμενα. τίνος δὲ εἵνεκεν τοῦτο ποιεῖ; ἵνα δειχθῇ προειδὼς ἄνωθεν τὰ μετὰ ταῦτα, ὅταν ἐξέλθῃ καὶ τῆς προῤῥήσεως τὸ τέλος, ὃ δὴ καὶ ἐπὶ τῆς προφητείας ταύτης γέγονεν.* Lücke remarks, that the circumstance of the words being spoken so long before his trial by the Sanhedrim, would make it more easy for the false witnesses to distort them. This they did, but not so as to agree with one another. They reported it, 'I can destroy,' &c., which makes a wide difference, and represents our Lord as an enemy of the temple (Matt. xxvi. 61), and some added to **τὸν ν. τ.**,—*τ. χειροποίητον*, and that He would raise another **ἀχειροποίητον** (Mark xiv. 58). **20.**] The building of the temple by Herod the Great is stated by Josephus, in Antt. xv. 11. 1, to have been begun in the *eighteenth* year of his reign; in B. J. i. 21. 1, in the *fifteenth*: the difference being made by counting his reign from the death of Antigonus, or from his appointment by the Romans, see

ὁ ναὸς οὗτος, καὶ σὺ ἐν τρισὶν ἡμέραις [w] ἐγερεῖς αὐτόν; [y] Matt. xvii. 9 reff.
21 ἐκεῖνος δὲ ἔλεγεν περὶ τοῦ ναοῦ τοῦ σώματος αὐτοῦ. [z] ver. 17. [a] constr., Luke i. 20. ch. iv. 50 al. 2 Chron. ix. 6.
22 ὅτε οὖν [y] ἠγέρθη ἐκ [y] νεκρῶν, [z] ἐμνήσθησαν οἱ μαθηταὶ
αὐτοῦ ὅτι τοῦτο ἔλεγεν, καὶ [a] ἐπίστευσαν τῇ γραφῇ, καὶ [b] constr., ch. iv. 5, 50. Tit. iii. 5. Rev. i. 20.
...ο ιησους X. τῷ λόγῳ [b] ὃν εἶπεν ὁ Ἰησοῦς.
23 Ὡς δὲ ἦν ἐν [c] τοῖς [c] Ἱεροσολύμοις ἐν τῷ [d] πάσχα ἐν [c] ch. v. 2 reff. [d] ch. vi. 4. (xiii. 1.)
τῇ [d] ἑορτῇ, πολλοὶ [e] ἐπίστευσαν [e] εἰς τὸ [e] ὄνομα αὐτοῦ [f] θεω- [e] ch. i. 12 reff. [f] Luke xxiii. 48 reff.
ροῦντες αὐτοῦ τὰ σημεῖα ἃ ἐποίει. 24 αὐτὸς δὲ Ἰησοῦς οὐκ [g] see Luke xvi. 11. Rom. iii. 2. 1 Cor. ix. 17.
...παντας και P. [g] ἐπίστευεν αὐτὸν αὐτοῖς, διὰ τὸ αὐτὸν γινώσκειν πάντας,
25 καὶ ὅτι οὐ [h] χρείαν εἶχεν [h] ἵνα τὶς μαρτυρήσῃ περὶ τοῦ [h] ch. xvi. 30. 1 John ii. 27 only. see Matt. iii. 14 reff.
ἀνθρώπου· αὐτὸς γὰρ ἐγίνωσκεν τί ἦν ἐν τῷ ἀνθρώπῳ.

om εν ℵ [lat-*a c*. εγειρεις T_b^1 ev-47 lat-*b* (*e*).]
21. om αυτου ℵ¹ 47. 63. 253.
22. rec aft ελεγεν ins αυτοις, with K[Π]: om ABP[T_b]ℵ rel latt syrr [syr-jer] copt æth arm $Orig_3$ Chr Cyr Thdrt Thl. rec (for ον) ᾧ, with A rel: txt BL[T_b]ℵ $Frag\text{-}ath_a$ $Orig_5$.
23. rec om τοις (with 33 evv-H-P-X-Y-Z, e sil): ins AB[T_b]ℵ rel $Orig_3$ Chr Cyr. (Treg queries M and P.) om 3rd εν B.
24. rec ins ο bef ιησ., with APℵ rel $Orig_3$ [Did_1 Chr_1 $Cyr\text{-}p_2$(not ad loc)]: om BL $Frag\text{-}ath_a$ [om ιησ. also T_b Scr's i¹ lat-*e*]. επιστευσεν A $Frag\text{-}ath_a$ Scr's f¹ p (w¹ ?) $Orig_3$. rec (for 1st αυτον) εαυτον, with A²ℵ³ᵃ rel $Orig_2$ [Chr_1 Cyr_1]: txt A¹BLℵ¹ $Orig_1$ [Cyr_1]. (P def. [T_b?]) om 2nd αυτον ℵ [lat-*a b q*].
25. om οτι A[T_b] Syr copt (æth?) Did. for ου χρ., χρ. ουκ ℵ. τι ην εν is repeated by ℵ¹.

Antt. xvii. 8. 1. Reckoning from this latter, we shall have twenty years till the birth of Christ, and thirty years since that event, from which fifty, however, four must be taken, since our era is four years too late. This gives forty-six. The temple was not completed till A.D. 64, under Herod Agrippa II., and the procurator Albinus; so that **ᾠκοδομήθη, was in building**, must refer to the greater part of the work now completed. The sense of this aor. is curiously illustrated by a passage in Ezra v. 16, τότε Σαβανασὰρ ἐκεῖνος ἦλθε καὶ ἔδωκε θεμελίους τοῦ οἴκου τοῦ θεοῦ ἐν Ἱερουσαλήμ, καὶ ἀπὸ τότε ἕως τοῦ νῦν ᾠκοδομήθη καὶ οὐκ ἐτελέσθη.

22.] **τῇ γραφῇ**, by all analogy, must mean *the O. T. scriptures*. That the resurrection of the Lord is the subject of O. T. prophecy, we find in several passages of the N. T., see ch. xx. 9: Luke xxiv. 26, 27: 1 Cor. xv. 4. At first sight it appears difficult to fix on any passage in which it is directly announced: but with the deeper understanding of the Scriptures which the Holy Spirit gave the Apostles and still gives the Christian Church, such prophecies as that in Ps. xvi. are recognized as belonging to Him in Whom alone they are properly fulfilled: see also Hosea vi. 2.

23—25.] Many believe on Jesus at the Passover: His knowledge of their character, and withholding of Himself from them. **23.**] As analogous with **ἐν τῷ πάσχα ἐν τῇ ἑορτῇ**, see ch. vi. 4. **θεωρ. αὐτ. τὰ σημ. ἃ ἐπ.**] ἐπίστευον εἰς αὐτόν, ἀλλ' οὐ βεβαίως. ἐκεῖνοι γὰρ ἀκριβέστερον ἐπίστευον, ὅσοι μὴ διὰ τὰ σημεῖα μόνον, ἀλλὰ καὶ διὰ τὴν διδασκαλίαν αὐτοῦ ἐπίστευον. Euthym. *What miracles* these were, is not related:—certainly some notable ones, see ch. iii. 2. The mention of them precludes us from understanding ch. iv. 54, as indicating that the healing of the ruler's son was *absolutely His second* miracle.

24, 25.] The repetition of **ἐπίστ.** has been regarded (Lücke, De Wette) as a sort of play on the word. But I should rather set it down to the simplicity of John's style. The meaning is, **He did not trust himself to them,**—i. e. treat them as true and earnest disciples: they entered into no spiritual relation with Him, and He in consequence into none with them. The fact of this being narrated shews that it made an impression on the Evangelist, and led him perhaps first to the conclusion which he here expresses, and which higher knowledge enabled him afterwards to place, as he here does, on its right ground:—His *knowing what was in man*. Nothing less than *divine knowledge* is here set forth; the words are even

i ch. i. 6 reff. j = Luke xviii. 18. ch. vii. 26, 48. xii. 42. Acts iii. 17 al. k Matt. ii. 14. xxviii. 13. ch. xix. 31. l ch. i. 39 reff. m Luke i. 66. Acts vii. 9. x. 38. Judg. vi. 12.

ABEFG HKLM ST_bUV ΓΔΛΠℵ Frag. Ath_a. 1. 33. 69

III. 1 Ἦν δὲ ἄνθρωπος ἐκ τῶν Φαρισαίων, Νικόδημος [i] ὄνομα αὐτῷ, [j] ἄρχων τῶν Ἰουδαίων. 2 οὗτος ἦλθεν πρὸς αὐτὸν [k] νυκτὸς καὶ εἶπεν αὐτῷ [l] Ῥαββί, οἴδαμεν ὅτι ἀπὸ θεοῦ ἐλήλυθας διδάσκαλος· οὐδεὶς γὰρ δύναται ταῦτα τὰ σημεῖα ποιεῖν ἃ σὺ ποιεῖς, ἐὰν μὴ ᾖ ὁ θεὸς [m] μετ᾽ αὐτοῦ.

Chap. III. 1. for *ονομα αυτω, ονοματι* ℵ[1](txt ℵ[2]) [lat-*b c f l*].

2. *νυκτος* bef *προς αυτον* ℵ (ev-z) [lat-*l*]. rec (for *αυτον*) *τον ιησουν*, with EFG HM[Γ] vulg-ed lat-*a e f* Syr [syr-jer] copt: txt AB[T_b]ℵ rel am[with fuld forj ing em tol] lat-*b c l* [*q*] syr æth arm Chr_1 Cyr_1 Thl Aug. for *ουδεις γαρ, και ουδεις* ℵ [lat-*e*]. rec *ταυτα τα σημεια* bef *δυναται*, with E rel syr Chr_1: txt ABL[T_b]ℵ Frag-ath_a 33 latt Syr [syr-jer] copt arm $Orig_1$ [Chr_1].

stronger than if *τῶν ἀνθ.* and *ἐν τοῖς ἀνθ.* had been used. Then some reference might have been imagined to the persons here mentioned; but now, the singular is, and must be on all hands, *purely generic*,—as in E. V.

Chap. III. 1—21.] *The Lord's discourse with Nicodemus,—one of these believers on account of His Miracles—on the spiritual nature of the kingdom of God and the necessity of the new birth.* 1.] We have in the Talmud (see Lightfoot, Hor. Heb. in loc.) a Nicodemus ben Gorion, who was properly called Bonai, and said to have been a disciple of Jesus: but he is found living at the destruction of Jerusalem. This might certainly have been; still it must be quite uncertain whether he be the same with this Nicodemus. He is mentioned again ch. vii. 50; xix. 39. He was a member of the Sanhedrim (**ἄρχων**, see reff.), and, besides, a *νομοδιδάσκαλος* (ver. 10). 2.] **νυκτός**—*for fear of the Jews:* see ch. xii. 42. The discourse seems to have taken place between Jesus and Nicodemus *alone*,—and may have been related by our Lord to the Evangelist afterwards. If this be deemed improbable (though I do not see why it should),—of the two other alternatives I would rather believe that John was present, than that Nicodemus should have so minutely related a conversation which in his then position he could not understand. **οἴδαμεν**] This plural may be merely an allusion to others who had come to the same conclusion, e. g. Joseph of Arimathea; or it may express that Nicodemus was sent in the name of several who wished to know the real character of this Person who wrought such miracles. It is harsh, in this private conversation, to take the plural as merely of singular import, as Lightfoot seems to do. His other rendering, "*vulgo agnoscitur*," is better,—but not satisfactory; for the common people did not generally confess it, and Nicodemus, as an *ἄρχων*, would not be likely to speak in their name (see ch. vii. 49). I would rather take it to express *the true conviction respecting Jesus, of that class to which Nicodemus belonged*—the *ἄρχοντες*: and see in it an important fact, that their persecutions and murder of the Prince of Life hence found their greatest aggravation, that they were carried on *against the conclusions of their own minds*, out of bitter malice, and worldly disappointment at His humble and unobtrusive character, and the spiritual purity and self-sacrifice which He inculcated. Still this must not, though undoubtedly it has truth in it, be carried too far: cf. Acts iii. 17 note, and Acts xiii. 27: 1 Cor. ii. 8. *Some degree of ignorance* there must necessarily have been in all of them, even Caiaphas included, of our Lord's Office and Person. Stier (iv. 11 ff., edn. 2) seems to think that Nicodemus, by using the plural, is sheltering himself from expressing *his own* conviction, so as to be able to draw back again if necessary. **ἐλήλυθας**] Stier (and Schleiermacher, cited by Stier, iv. 12, edn. 2, note) thinks that there is involved in this word a *recognition* by Nicodemus *of the Messianic mission of Jesus:* —that it expresses His being *ὁ ἐρχόμενος* (Matt. xi. 3 al.). It is never used of any but the Messiah, except by the Lord Himself, when speaking of John the Baptist as the subject of prophecy (see Matt. xi. 14 al.). **διδάσκαλος**] In this and the following words, Nicodemus seems to be cautiously withdrawing from his admission being taken as expressing too much. For who of the Jews ever expected a *teacher* to come from God? They looked for a *King*, to sit on David's throne,—a *Prophet*, to declare the divine will;—but the Messiah was never designated as a *mere teacher*, till the days of modern Socinianism. So that he seems trying to qualify or recall his *ἐλήλυθας* by this addition. The following words exhibit the same cautious inconsistency. **No one**

...ειπεν F. ...iii. 4 (appy) T_b.

3 ἀπεκρίθη Ἰησοῦς καὶ εἶπεν αὐτῷ [n] Ἀμὴν [n] ἀμὴν [n] λέγω
σοι, ἐὰν μή τις [o] γεννηθῇ [p] ἄνωθεν, οὐ δύναται [q] ἰδεῖν τὴν
[r] βασιλείαν τοῦ [r] θεοῦ. 4 λέγει πρὸς αὐτὸν ὁ Νικόδημος
Πῶς δύναται ἄνθρωπος γεννηθῆναι [s] γέρων ὤν; μὴ δύναται εἰς τὴν [t] κοιλίαν τῆς μητρὸς αὐτοῦ δεύτερον εἰσελθεῖν
καὶ γεννηθῆναι; 5 ἀπεκρίθη [ὁ] Ἰησοῦς [n] Ἀμὴν [n] ἀμὴν

n ch. i. 52 al. fr. J. see Matt. v. 18 reff.
o = here, &c. 5 times. ch. i. 13. 1 John ii. 29. iii. 9. iv. 7. v. 1, 4, 18 only. see 1 Pet. i. 3, 23.
p ver. 31. ch. xix. 11, 23. James i. 17. iii. 15, 17. Job iii. 4. see also Gal. iv. 9. Wisd. xix. 6.
q = Luke ii. 26. 1 Pet. iii. 10, from Ps. xxxiii. 12 al.
r John, ver. 5 (Rev. xii. 10) only. Gospp. & Paul, passim.
s here only. Job xxxii. 9. Prov. xvii. 6. xxxi. 23 B-txt ℵ[1]. Sir. viii. 9 al[3], only.
t = Luke i. 41. xi. 27. Ps. xxi. 10.

3. rec ins *ο* bef *ιησ.*, with AHℵ rel: om BEFGKLM[T_bΓΠ] Frag-ath_a 1 Cyr_1. (E and H as Treg, expr.) om *και ειπεν αυτω* ℵ[1]. [for *ιδειν*, *εισελθειν εις* T_b.]
4. om *ὁ* BE[1]GL Frag-ath_a. (33 def.) *γερων ων* bef 1st *γεννηθηναι* ℵ.
5. om *ὁ* A[S(Tischdf)]ℵ rel Cyr_1: ins BLU 33. 69 [Chr_1]. aft *ιησ.* ins *και ειπεν αυτω* KM[Π] 258 Scr's o p v w Syr syr-mg [syr-jer] copt-ms æth arm, *και ειπεν* L ℵ[3a] (but erased) Frag-ath_a lat-*f* syr-jer copt-ed. om 2nd *αμην* A ev-z.

can do, &c. unless—we expect some strong expression of the truth, such as we had from Nathanael in ch. i. 50, but the sentence drops to merely—'*God be with him*,' which is a very poor and insufficient exponent of ἀπὸ θ. **ἐλήλυθας**. Against this inconsistency,—the inner knowledge that the Kingdom of God was come, and He who was to found it, on the one hand,—and the rationalizing endeavour to reduce this heavenly kingdom to *mere learning*, and its Founder to a *mere teacher*, on the other,—is the following discourse directed.

3.] We are not to imagine that any thing is wanting to complete the sense or connexion. Our Lord replies, It is not *learning*, but *life*, that is wanted for the Messiah's Kingdom; and *life* must begin by *birth*. Luther (Stier, iv. 17, edn. 2) says: "My teaching is not of *doing* and *leaving undone*, but of a *change in the man* (nicht von Thun und Lassen, sondern von Werden);—so that it is, not *new works* done, but a *new man* to do them; not another *life* only, but another *birth*." And *only by this means* can Nicodemus gain the teaching for which he is come,—**ἰδεῖν** τ. β. τ. θ.,—'become a disciple of Christ:' —**ἴδοι**, τουτέστι νοήσοι, Thl.,—'*understand, by sharing*'—'have any conception of.' **ἄνωθεν**—οἱ μὲν "ἐκ τοῦ οὐρανοῦ" φασιν, οἱ δὲ "ἐξ ἀρχῆς." Chr.,—who, as also Euthym., explains **γεν. ἄνωθ.** by παλιγγενεσία:—Orig., Cyr., and Thl. taking the other meaning. The true meaning is to be found by taking into account the answer of Nicodemus, who obviously understood it of a *new birth in mature life*. **Born afresh** would be a better rendering than 'born *again*,' being closer to the meaning of ἄνωθεν, 'from the very beginning;'—'unless a man begin his life anew altogether (πάλιν ἄνωθεν, Gal. iv. 9), he cannot' &c. It is not possible that the other meaning may *lie beneath this*,—as the βασιλεία is **τοῦ θεοῦ**, and so must the birth be;—but Grotius has remarked that in Hebrew and Aramaic (in one of which languages our Lord, discoursing with a Rabbinical Jew, probably spoke) there is no word of double meaning corresponding to ἄνωθεν:—so that He must have expressed it, as Nicodemus understood it, of an *entirely new* birth. That John never uses the word elsewhere in this sense (Lücke) is here of little weight, for he uses it only three times more, and never with a verb cognate to γεννάομαι. The Evangelist most likely chose the Greek expression **γεν. ἄνωθ.** as strictly corresponding to the term ἀναγεννᾶσθαι, which, when he wrote, was in common use in the Church: see 1 Pet. i. 3, 23. Justin Martyr, as Bp. Wordsworth reminds us, quotes as our Lord's saying, Apol. i. 61, p. 79, ἂν μὴ ἀναγεννηθῆτε, οὐ μὴ εἰσέλθητε εἰς τ. βασιλείαν τῶν οὐρανῶν: probably mixing this with Matt. xviii. 3. On the birth itself, see below, ver. 5.

4.] It is impossible that Nicodemus can have so entirely and stupidly *misunderstood* our Lord's words, as his question here would seem to imply. The idea of new birth was by no means alien from the Rabbinical views. They described a proselyte when baptized as "sicut parvulus jam natus." Lightfoot in loc. I agree with Stier in thinking that there was something of the spirit that *would not* understand, and the disposition to turn to ridicule what he heard. But together with this there was also considerable *real ignorance*. The proselyte might be regarded as born again, when he became one of the seed of Abraham: this figure would be easily explained on the Judaical view: but that *every* man should need this, was beyond Nicodemus's comprehension. He

u w. ἐκ, ch. i. 13 reff.
v Rom. i. 4. Heb. xi. 35.
w ver. 3.

[n] λέγω σοι, ἐὰν μή τις [ou] γεννηθῇ [v] ἐξ ὕδατος καὶ πνεύματος,
οὐ δύναται εἰςελθεῖν εἰς τὴν [w] βασιλείαν τοῦ [w] θεοῦ. 6 τὸ
[ou] γεγεννημένον ἐκ τῆς σαρκὸς σάρξ ἐστιν, καὶ τὸ [ou] γεγεν-

ABEG HKLM SUVΓΔ ΛΠℵ Frag. Ath$_a$. 1. 33. 69

for γενν., γενηθη A. εξ υδατος και πνευματος bef γεννηθη ℵ. for εισελθειν, ιδειν Mℵ[1]. om εις ℵ. for του θεου, των ουρανων ℵ[1] Scr's c lat-*e* Hipp$_1$ Eus$_1$ [Constt$_1$ hom-Clem$_1$ Chr$_3$] Orig-int$_2$ Tert$_1$.

6. elz (for γεγεννημ.) γεγενημ. (twice), with A(2nd doubtful) H 258 Scr's q.

therefore rebuts the assertion with a reductio ad absurdum, which in spirit expresses, as in ch. vi. 60,—'This is an hard saying; who can hear it?' **γέρων ὤν**] Probably he himself was old, and he instances his own case. 5.] Our Lord passes by the question of Nicodemus without notice, further than that this His second assertion takes as it were the ground from under it, by explaining the token and means of the new birth.

There can be no doubt, on any honest interpretation of the words, that **γεννηθῆναι ἐξ ὕδατος** refers to the token or outward sign of baptism,—**γ. ἐκ πνεύματος** to the thing signified, or inward grace of the Holy Spirit. All attempts to get rid of *these two plain facts* have sprung from doctrinal prejudices, by which the views of expositors have been warped. Such we have in Calvin: "spiritum, qui nos repurgat, et qui virtute sua in nos diffusa vigorem inspirat cœlestis vitæ;"—Grotius: "spiritum aquæ instar emundantem;"—Cocceius: "gratiam Dei, sordes et vitia abluentem;"—Lampe: "obedientiam Christi;"—Tholuck, who holds that not Baptism itself, but only its *idea*, that of *cleansing*, is referred to;—and others, who endeavour to resolve ὕδατος καὶ πνεύματος into a figure of ἓν διὰ δυοῖν, so as to make it mean '*the cleansing or purifying Spirit.*' All the better and deeper expositors have recognized the coexistence of the two, *water* and the *Spirit*. So for the most part the ancients: so Lücke (in his last edition), De Wette, Neander, Stier, Olshausen, &c. This being then recognized, *to what does ὕδωρ refer?* At that time, two kinds of baptism were known: that of the *proselytes*, by which they were received into Judaism,—and that of *John*, by which, as a preparatory rite, symbolizing repentance, the people were made ready for Him who was to baptize them with the Holy Ghost. But both these were significant of *one and the same truth;* that namely of the *entire cleansing of the man* for the new and spiritual life on which he was to enter, symbolized by water cleansing the outward person. Both were appointed means,—the one by the Jewish Church,—the other, stamping that first with approval, by God Himself,—towards their respective ends. John himself declared his baptism to be *incomplete*,—it was *only with water;* One was coming, who should baptize *with the Holy Ghost. That declaration of his is the key to the understanding of this verse.* Baptism, *complete*, with *water* and the *Spirit*, is the admission into the kingdom of God. Those who have received *the outward sign and the spiritual grace*, have entered into that Kingdom. And this entrance was fully ministered to the disciples when the Spirit descended on them on the day of Pentecost. So that, as spoken to Nicodemus, these words referred him to the baptism of John, which probably (see Luke vii. 30) he had slighted. But they were *not only* spoken to him. The words of our Lord have in them life and meaning for all ages of His Church: and more especially these opening declarations of His ministry. He here unites together the two elements of a complete Baptism which were sundered in the words of the Baptist, ch. i. 33—in which united form He afterwards (Matt. xxviii. 19, 20: Mark xvi. 16) ordained it as a Sacrament of His Church. Here He speaks of spiritual Baptism, as in ch. vi. of spiritual Communion, and in both places in connexion with the outward conditions and media of these sacraments. It is observable that here, as ordinarily (with a special exception, Acts x. 44 ff.), the outward sign comes first, and then the spiritual grace, vouchsafed in and by means of it where duly received. **εἰςελθεῖν εἰς** is more than ἰδεῖν above, though no stress is to be laid on the difference. The former word was perhaps used because of Nicodemus's expectation of *teaching* being all that was required: but now, the necessity of a real vital change having been set forth, the expression is changed to a practical one—the *entering into* the Kingdom of God.

6.] The neuter denotes not only the universal application of this truth, but (see Luke i. 35) the very first beginnings of life in the embryo, before sex can be predicated. So Bengel: "notat ipsa prima stamina vitæ." The Lord here answers Nicodemus's hypothetical question

νημένον ἐκ τοῦ πνεύματος πνεῦμά ἐστιν. 7 μὴ [x] θαυμάσῃς
ὅτι εἶπόν σοι [y] Δεῖ ὑμᾶς [o] γεννηθῆναι [z] ἄνωθεν. 8 τὸ
[ab] πνεῦμα ὅπου θέλει [bc] πνεῖ, καὶ τὴν [d] φωνὴν αὐτοῦ ἀκούεις,
ἀλλ' οὐκ οἶδας πόθεν ἔρχεται καὶ [e] ποῦ ὑπάγει· οὕτως
ἐστὶν πᾶς ὁ [ou] γεγεννημένος ἐκ τοῦ πνεύματος. 9 ἀπεκρίθη
Νικόδημος καὶ εἶπεν αὐτῷ Πῶς δύναται ταῦτα γενέσθαι;

. ανωθεν Frag. Ath$_a$. T$_b$ iii. 8 (appy)...

x w. ὅτι, ch. iv. 27. Luke xi. 38. Gal. i. 6 only. y = ch. iv. 20, 24. ix. 4. Acts v. 29 al. z ver. 3. a = here only. Gen. viii. 1. Eccl. xi. 5. b here only. Isa. xl. 7 only. c Matt. vii. 25, 27. Luke xii. 55. ch. vi. 18. Acts xxvii. 40. Rev. vii. 1 only. Ps. cxlvii. 18 (7). d = Matt. xxiv. 31. Rev. xiv. 2. xviii. 22 al. Joel ii. 5. e = ch. vii. 35. viii. 14. xii. 35. Heb. xi. 8. Gen. xvi. 8.

8. αλλα B. for 2nd και, η A Scr's c latt syr-mg [syr-jer] arm Ambr$_1$ Aug. ins του υδατος και bef του πνευματος ℵ lat-*a b e ff*$_2$ syr-cu Hil.

of ver. 4, by telling him that *even could it be so*, it would not accomplish the birth of which He speaks. In this **σάρξ** is included *every part* of that which is born after the ordinary method of generation: even the spirit of man, which, receptive as it is of the Spirit of God, is yet in the natural birth *dead*, sunk in trespasses and sins, and in a state of wrath. Such 'flesh and blood' cannot inherit the Kingdom of God, 1 Cor. xv. 50. But when the man is born again of the Spirit (the water does not appear any more, being merely the outward form of reception,—the less included in the greater), then just as flesh generates flesh, so spirit generates spirit, after its own image, see 2 Cor. iii. 18 fin.; and since the Kingdom of God is a spiritual kingdom, such only who are so born can enter into it. **7.**] The weightiest word here is **ὑμᾶς**. The Lord did not, could not, say this of *Himself*. Why?—Because in the full sense in which the flesh is incapacitated from entering the kingdom of God, He was *not born of the flesh*. He inherited the weakness of the flesh, but His spirit was not, like that of sinful man, alien from holiness and God; and therefore on Him no second birth passed; when the Holy Spirit descended on Him at His baptism, the words spoken by the Father were indicative of *past approval*, not of *renewal*. His obedience was accepted as perfect, and the good pleasure of the Father rested on Him. Therefore He includes not Himself in this necessity for the new birth. The **μὴ θαυμάσῃς** applies to the next verse, in which Nicodemus is told that he has things as wonderful around him every day in the natural world. **8.**] Our Lord might have chosen any of the mysteries of nature to illustrate the point:—He takes *that one*, which is above others symbolic of the action of the *Spirit*, and (which in both languages, that in which He spoke, as well as that in which His speech is reported) is expressed by *the same word* as it. So that the words as they stand apply themselves at once to the Spirit and His working, without any figure;—*spiritus ubi vult spirat.* Bengel, after Origen and Augustine, takes **τὸ πν.** of the *Holy Spirit* exclusively: but this can hardly be. The *form* of the sentence, as well as its import, is against it. The **πνεῖ, ἀκούεις, οἶδας**, are all said of well-known facts. And the comparison would not hold on that supposition—'As *the Spirit* is in His working on those born of Him, so is *every one that is born of the Spirit*.' But on the other interpretation, we have **The wind breatheth**, &c.:—**so is**, i. e. '*so it is with*' (see a similar construction Matt. xiii. 45) **every one born of the Spirit.** Notice it is not ὁ ἄνεμος here, but **τὸ πνεῦμα**, the gentle breath of the wind;—and it is heard, not felt;—a case in which the **οὐκ οἶδας** κ.τ.λ. is more applicable than in that of a violent wind steadily blowing. It is one of those sudden breezes springing up on a calm day, which has no apparent direction, but we hear it rustling in the leaves around. The **ὅπου θέλει**, *in the application*, implies the *freedom* (2 Cor. iii. 17) and *unrestrained working of the Spirit* (1 Cor. xii. 11). **πᾶς ὁ γεγ.**] Our Lord can hardly, as Stier explains (iv. 48, edn. 2), mean *Himself* by these words; or, if He does, only *inclusively*, as being **γεγ. ἐκ τ. πν.**,—not principally. He describes *the mystery of the spiritual life:* we see its *effects*, in ourselves, and others who have it; but we cannot trace its beginnings, nor can we prescribe to the Holy Spirit His course: He works in us and leads us on, accompanying us with His witness,—*His voice*, spiritually discerned. "*Homo in quo spiritus spirat, e spiritu respirat.*" Bengel. This saying of the Lord—in contradiction to all so called Methodism, which prescribes the time and manner of the working of the Spirit—assures us of the manifold and undefinable variety of both these. "The physiognomies of those who are born again, are as various as those of natural men" (Dräseke, cited by Stier, iv. 50, edn. 2). **9.**] The question of Nicodemus is evidently still one of un-

f = here only. see James v. 6.
g vv. 32, 33. 1 John v. 9.
h = ch. i. 12. v. 43. Matt. xiii. 20.
i 1 Cor. xv. 40 bis. 2 Cor. v. 1. Phil. ii. 10. iii. 19. James iii. 15 only +.
j in Gospp., Matt. xviii. 35 (reff.) only. Eph. i. 3. Phil. ii. 10 al.

10 ἀπεκρίθη Ἰησοῦς καὶ εἶπεν αὐτῷ Σὺ εἶ [f] ὁ διδάσκαλος ABEG
τοῦ Ἰσραήλ, καὶ ταῦτα οὐ γινώσκεις; 11 ἀμὴν ἀμὴν λέγω HKLM ST_bUVΓ
σοι ὅτι ὃ οἴδαμεν λαλοῦμεν καὶ ὃ ἑωράκαμεν μαρτυροῦμεν, ΔΛΠℵ 1. 33. 69
καὶ τὴν [g] μαρτυρίαν ἡμῶν οὐ [gh] λαμβάνετε. 12 εἰ τὰ [i] ἐπίγεια
εἶπον ὑμῖν καὶ οὐ πιστεύετε, πῶς ἐὰν εἴπω ὑμῖν τὰ
[j] ἐπουράνια πιστεύσετε; 13 καὶ οὐδεὶς [k] ἀναβέβηκεν εἰς
τὸν οὐρανόν, εἰ μὴ ὁ ἐκ τοῦ οὐρανοῦ [k] καταβάς, ὁ [l] υἱὸς

k Eph. iv. 9. Prov. xxx. 4. l Matt. viii. 20 reff.

10. rec ins ο bef ιησ., with ℵ 69: om AB rel Cyr Thl [om απεκρ. ιησ. T_b].
[**11.** πιστευετε (for -σετε) T_bΛ lat-*b* *ff*$_2$ *l* copt-dz.]

belief, though no longer of frivolity: see ver. 12. **10.**] I believe the E. V. is right in rendering **ὁ διδ. a master**; the article is inserted as required by τοῦ before Ἰσραήλ, which is expressed as giving a solemnity to Ἰσρ. as the people of God. Or is it possible that ὁ διδάσκαλος may merely be meant as *one of οἱ διδάσκαλοι*? I prefer either of these reasons for the presence of the article, to supposing it to have any emphatic meaning. Nicodemus was manifestly in no supereminent place among the ἄρχοντες: see ch. vii. 50—52. Still less can I with Bp. Middleton, Gr. Art. pp. 242-3, believe any *blame conveyed in the title*. [Dean Alford afterwards preferred rendering ὁ διδάσκαλος **the teacher**; see N. T. for English Readers, and N. T. Authorized Version Revised.]

11.] Henceforward the discourse is an answer to the *unbelief*, and in answering that, to the *question* (**πῶς δύν. τ. γεν.**) of Nicodemus: by shewing him the appointed means of this new birth, and of being upheld in the life to which it is the entrance, viz. *faith in the Son of God*. **ὃ οἴδαμεν λ. . . .**] *Why these plurals?* Various interpretations have been given: ἢ περὶ ἑαυτοῦ **καὶ τοῦ πατρὸς** τοῦτό φησιν, ἢ περὶ ἑαυτοῦ μόνου (Euthym.);—"Loquitur de se et *de Spiritu*" (Bengel);—of Himself and *the Prophets* (Beza, Tholuck);—of Himself and *John the Baptist* (Knapp);—of *Teachers like Himself* (Meyer);—of *all the born of the Spirit* (Lange, Wesley);—of the *three Persons in the Holy Trinity* (Stier);—or, the plural is *only rhetorical* (Lücke, De Wette). I had rather take it as a *proverbial* saying; q. d. 'I am one of those who,' &c. Our Lord thereby brings out the unreasonableness of that unbelief which would not receive *His witness*, but made *it* an exception to the general proverbial rule. **οὐ λαμβάνετε**, addressed still to Nicodemus, and through him to the Jews: not to certain others who were present, as Olsh. supposes. **12.**] The words **μαρτυρίαν λαμβάνειν** prepared the way for the new idea which is brought forward in this verse—**πιστεύειν**. Faith is, in the most pregnant sense, 'the receiving of testimony;' because it is the making *subjectively real* the contents of that testimony. So the πιστεύειν **εἰς αὐτόν** [see ver. 15] is, *the full reception of the Lord's testimony*; because the burden of that testimony is, *grace and truth and salvation by Himself*. This faith is neither reasoning, nor knowledge, but a *reception* of divine Truth declared by One who came from God; and so it is *far above* reasoning and knowledge:—**πιστεύομεν** above **οἴδαμεν**. But what are the **ἐπίγεια**? The matters relating to the new birth which have hitherto been spoken of;—called so because *that side of them* has been exhibited which is *upon earth*, and happens among men;—**ἃ** τοῖς ἐπὶ γῆς ἔτι διατρίβουσιν ἀνθρώποις δυνατὰ ὑπάρξαι τε καὶ νοηθῆναι, Origen. That the *parable about the wind* is not intended, is evident from **κ.** οὐ **πιστεύετε**, which in that case would be 'do not *understand*.' And the **ἐπουράνια** are the things of which the discourse goes on to treat *from this point*: viz. the *heavenly side* of the new birth and salvation of man, in the eternal counsels of God regarding His only-begotten Son. Stier supposes a reference in this verse to Wisd. ix. 16, καὶ μόλις εἰκάζομεν τὰ ἐπὶ τῆς γῆς, καὶ τὰ ἐν χερσὶν εὑρίσκομεν μετὰ πόνου, τὰ δὲ ἐν οὐρανοῖς τίς ἐξιχνίασεν;

13.] The whole verse seems to have * intimate connexion with and reference to Prov. xxx. 4; and as spoken to a learned doctor of the law, would recall that verse,—especially as the further question is there asked, 'Who hath gathered *the wind* in His fists?' (מִי אָסַף־רוּחַ בְּחָפְנָיו), and 'What is His name, and what His Son's name?' See also Deut. xxx. 12, and the citation, Rom. x. 6—8. All attempts to explain away the plain sense of this verse are futile and ridiculous. The Son of Man, the Lord Jesus, the Word made Flesh, *was*

τοῦ [l] ἀνθρώπου ὁ [m] ὢν ἐν τῷ οὐρανῷ. 14 καὶ καθὼς
F εν τη ... Μωυσῆς [n] ὕψωσεν τὸν [o] ὄφιν ἐν τῇ ἐρήμῳ, οὕτως [n] ὑψωθῆναι

m Exod. iii. 14. Rev. i. 4.
n = ch. viii. 28. xii. 32, 34 only. met., Matt. xi. 23 al.
o Matt. vii. 10. 1 Cor. x. 9 al. Num. xxi. 9.

13. om *ο ων εν τω ουρανω* (*carelessness or misunderstanding?*) BL[T_b]ℵ 33 copt-dz æth Eus_2 [*Cyr*-p] Orig-int_1: ins (A: "*ων* prius omissum. Erasit manus antiqua et rescripsit addito *ων*." Cowper) rel latt syrr syr-cu [syr-jer] copt arm $Hipp_1$ [Did_1 Chr_2] Orig-int_2 $Novat_1$ Hil_3(certissime$_2$) $Lucif_1$ [Jac-$nisib_1$].—om *ων* A^1(appy) ev-44: *qui erat* lat-*e*: contra, Orig on Rom x. 6 (*non dixit "qui fuit" sed "qui est" in cælo*).

14. ins *ο* bef *υψωθ.* $ℵ^1$(marked for erasure *eadem manu*).

in, came down from, heaven,—and was *in heaven* (heaven about Him, heaven dwelling on earth, ch. i. 52), *while here,* and ascended up into heaven when He left this earth;—and by all these proofs, speaking in the prophetic language of accomplished Redemption, does the Lord establish, that *He alone* can speak of τὰ ἐπουράνια to men, or convey the blessing of the new birth to them. Be it remembered, that He is here speaking *proleptically*, of *results* of His course and sufferings on earth,—of the way of regeneration and salvation which God has appointed by Him. He regards therefore throughout the passage, the great facts of redemption *as accomplished,* and makes announcements which could not be literally acted upon till they had been so accomplished. See vv. 14 ff., whose sense will be altogether lost, unless this **ἀναβέβηκεν** be understood of His exaltation to be a Prince and a Saviour. **ὁ ὢν ἐν τῷ οὐρ.**] See ch. i. 18 and note. Doubtless the meaning involves '*whose place is in heaven;*' but it also asserts the **being in heaven** of the *time then present:* see ch. i. 52. Stier (iv. 68, edn. 2) speaks well of the majestic ὁ ὢν ἐν τῷ οὐρανῷ, by which the Lord characterizes His whole life in the flesh between the καταβαίνειν and the ἀναβαίνειν. As uniting in Himself God, whose dwelling is heaven, with man whose dwelling is on earth, He ever was in heaven. And nearly connected with this fact is the transition to His being the fountain of eternal life, in vv. 14 ff.: cf. 1 Cor. xv. 47—50, where the same connexion is strikingly set forth. To explain such expressions as ἀναβαίνειν εἰς τ. οὐρ., &c., as mere *Hebrew metaphors* (Lücke, De Wette, &c.) is no more than saying that Hebrew metaphors were founded on deep insight into divine truth:—these words in fact express *the truths on which Hebrew metaphors were constructed.* Socinus is quite right, when he says that *those who take* ἀναβ. εἰς τ. οὐ. *metaphorically, must in all consistency take* ὁ καταβὰς ἐκ τ. οὐρ. *metaphorically also;* "qualis descensus, talis etiam ascensus." **14.**] From this point the discourse passes to the *Person* of Christ, and Redemption by His Death. The Lord brings before this doctor of the Law the mention of Moses, who in his day by divine command lifted up a symbol of forgiveness and redemption to Israel. **καθώς**] We must avoid all such ideas as that our Lord *merely compares* His death to the elevation of the brazen serpent, as if only a *fortuitous likeness* were laid hold of by Him. This would leave the *brazen serpent itself meaningless,* and is an explanation which can only satisfy those who do not discern the typical reference of all the ceremonial dispensation to the Redeemer. It is an important duty of an expositor here, to defend the obvious and only honest explanation of this comparison against the tortuous and inadequate interpretations of modern critics. The comparison lies between the *exalted serpent of brass,* and the *exalted Son of Man. The brazen serpent* sets forth *the Redeemer.* This by recent Commentators (Lücke, De Wette, and others) is considered impossible: and the tertium comparationis is held to be only 'the lifting up.' But this does not satisfy the construction of the comparison. 'The brazen serpent was lifted up: every one who looked on it, lived,' = 'The Son of Man must be lifted up: every one who believes on Him, shall live.' The *same thing* is predicated of the two;—both are lifted up; cognate consequences follow,—*body-healing* and *soul-healing* (as Erskine, On the Brazen Serpent). There must then be *some reason* why the *only two members of the comparison yet unaccounted for* stand where they do,—considering that the brazen serpent was lifted up not for any physical efficacy, but by command of God alone. *Now on examination we find this correspondence fully established.* The 'serpent' is in Scripture symbolism, *the devil,*—from the historical temptation in Gen. iii. downwards. But *why* is the devil set forth by the *serpent?* How does the bite of the serpent operate? It *pervades with its poison the frame of its victim:* that frame *becomes poisoned:*—and *death ensues.* So sin, *the poison of the devil,* being instilled into our nature,

δεῖ τὸν [l] υἱὸν τοῦ [l] ἀνθρώπου, 15 ἵνα πᾶς ὁ [p] πιστεύων ἐν
αὐτῷ ἔχῃ [q] ζωὴν [q] αἰώνιον. 16 [r] οὕτως γὰρ ἠγάπησεν ὁ θεὸς

ABEF GHKL MST_bU VΓΔΛ Πא 1. 33. 69

p w. ἐν, Mark i. 15 only. Ps. lxxvii. 22. Jer. xii. 6.
q Matt. xix. 16 ||, 29 ||. xxv. 46. Luke x. 25. John, passim. Acts xiii. 48. Paul, Rom. ii. 7 al7. Jude 21. Dan. xii. 2. ἡ ἀ. ζ., ch. xvii. 3. Acts xiii. 46. 1 Tim. vi. 12 only.
r Acts xiv. 1 only.

δει bef υψωθηναι A ev-26 lat-*a* $Lucif_1$.

15. rec (for εν αυτω) εις αυτον (*from ver* 16, *and John's usage elsw*), with א rel vulg lat-*a b e f* [*q*] Chr_1 Cyr_1 [$Thdrt_3$] $Lucif_1$: επ' αυτον A : επ' αυτω L $Thdrt_1$: txt B[T_b] am(with em [fuld] harl ing mt) lat-*c g* [*l*] $Fulg_1$. rec ins μη αποληται αλλ' bef εχη (*from ver* 16), with A rel [latt syrr æth-pl arm-usc] Chr_1 $Thdrt_{sæpe}$: om BL[T_b]א 1. 33 lat-*a f* syr-cu syr-jer copt æth[-rom] arm[-zoh] Cyr_1 Non_1 $Cypr_1$ $Lucif_1$.

that nature has become σὰρξ ἁμαρτίας, a *poisoned nature*,—a *flesh of sin*. Now the brazen serpent was made *in the likeness of the serpents* which had bitten them. It *represented to the children of Israel the poison* which had gone through their frames, and it was hung up there on the banner-staff, as a trophy, to shew them that *for the poison, there was healing*;—that the plague had been overcome. In *it*, there was *no poison*; only the *likeness* of it. Now was not the Lord Jesus made ἐν ὁμοιώματι σαρκὸς ἁμαρτίας, Rom. viii. 3? Was not He made 'Sin for us, who knew no sin' (2 Cor. v. 21)? Did not He, on His Cross, make an open shew of, and triumph over, the Enemy, so that it was *as if the Enemy himself had been nailed to that Cross* (Col. ii. 15)? Were not Sin and Death and Satan crucified, when *He was crucified*? ἐκεῖ μέν, ἐπεὶ δι' ὄφεως ἡ βλάβη, δι' ὄφεως καὶ ἡ θεραπεία· ἐνταῦθα δέ, ἐπεὶ δι' ἀνθρώπου ὁ θάνατος εἰσῆλθεν εἰς τὸν κόσμον, δι' ἀνθρώπου καὶ ἡ ζωὴ παρεγένετο, Euthym. **δεῖ, it is necessary,** in the Father's counsel—it is decreed, but not arbitrarily;—the very necessity of things, which is in fact but the evolution of the divine Will, made it requisite that the pure and sinless Son of Man should thus be uplifted and suffer: see Luke xxiv. 26. **ὑψωθῆναι**] In this word there is more than the mere crucifixion. It has respect in its double meaning (of which see a remarkable instance in Gen. xl. 13, 19, E. V.) to the exaltation of the Lord on the Cross, and through the Cross to His Kingdom; and refers back to ἀναβέβηκεν εἰς τ. οὐρ. before. Stier quotes the Christian proverb, '*Crux scala cœli*.'

* **15.**] The corresponding clause applying to the type is left to be supplied—'And as every one who looked on it was healed, so . . . .' **πιστ. ἐν αὐτῷ**] This expression, here only used by John, *implies His exaltation*,—see ch. xii. 32. It is *a belief in* (*abiding in*, see note on ver. 18) *His Person being what God by His sufferings and exaltation hath made Him to be, and being that* TO ME. This involves, on the part of the believer, the anguish of the bite of the fiery serpent,—and the earnest looking on Him in Whom sin is crucified, with the inner eye of faith. **ἔχῃ ζ. αἰ.**] Just as in the type, God did not remove the fiery serpents,—or not all at once,—but healing was to be found in the midst of them by looking to the brazen serpent (πᾶς ὁ δεδηγμένος ἰδὼν αὐτὸν ζήσεται, LXX),—so the temptations and conflicts of sin shall *not leave* the believer,—but *in the midst of these*, with the Eye of Faith fixed on the uplifted Son of Man, he *has eternal life*; perishes not of the bite, but ζήσεται. See on this verse the remarkable passage, Wisd. xvi. 5—13, where as much of the healing sign is opened as could be expected before the great Antitype Himself appeared. **16.**] Many Commentators—since the time of Erasmus, who first suggested the notion—have maintained *that the discourse of our Lord breaks off here*, and the rest, to ver. 21, consists of the remarks of the Evangelist. (So Tholuck, Olshausen, Lücke, De Wette; which last attributes vv. 13, 14 also to John.) But to those who view these discourses of our Lord as intimately connected *wholes*, this will be as inconceivable, as the idea of St. Matthew having combined into one the insulated sayings of his Master. This discourse would be altogether fragmentary, and would have left Nicodemus *almost where he was before*, had not this most weighty concluding part been also spoken to him. This it is, which expands and explains the assertions of vv. 14, 15, and applies them to the present life and conduct of mankind. The principal grounds alleged for supposing the discourse to break off here seem to be (α) *that all allusion to Nicodemus is henceforth dropped*. But this is not conclusive, for it is obvious that the natural progress of such an interview on his part would be *from questioning to listening*: and that even had he joined in the dialogue, the Evangelist would not have been bound to relate all his remarks, but only those which, as vv. 2, 4 and 9, were important to bring out his mind and standing-point. (β) *That*

τὸν κόσμον, [rs] ὥςτε τὸν υἱὸν αὐτοῦ τὸν [t] μονογενῆ ἔδωκεν,
ἵνα πᾶς ὁ πιστεύων εἰς αὐτὸν μὴ [u] ἀπόληται ἀλλ' ἔχῃ
[q] ζωὴν [q] αἰώνιον. 17 οὐ γὰρ [v] ἀπέστειλεν ὁ θεὸς τὸν [v] υἱὸν
[αὐτοῦ] [v] εἰς τὸν κόσμον ἵνα [w] κρίνῃ τὸν κόσμον, ἀλλ' ἵνα
σωθῇ ὁ κόσμος δι' αὐτοῦ. 18 ὁ πιστεύων εἰς αὐτὸν οὐ

s John, here only. constr. Gal. ii. 13 only. Winer, § 41. 5, rem. 1.
t ch. i. 14 reff.
u = ch. x. 28. 1 Cor. i. 18. 2 Thess. ii. 10.
v 1 John iv. 8. see ch. x. 36.
w = ch. xii. 47, 48. James v. 9.

16. om *αυτου* B$\aleph^1$. om *εδωκεν* $\aleph^1$(ins $\aleph$-corr[1]). [*επ αυτον* T_b: *επ αυτω* L.] *απολλυηται* A. **αλλα** B.

17. om 1st *αυτου* (*see above, ver* 16) BL[T_b]$\aleph$ **1** *Cyr*[-p] : ins A rel D-lat vss $Tert_1$ Hil_2 $Lucif_1$.

henceforth past tenses are used ; making it more probable that the passage was added after the great events alluded to had taken place. But does not our Lord speak here, as in so many other cases, *proleptically,* of the fulness of the accomplishment of those designs, which *in the divine counsels were* accomplished? Is not this way of speaking natural to a discourse which is treating of the *development* of the new birth, itself not yet brought in till the Spirit was given? See a parallel instance, with the Evangelist's explanation, ch. vii. 37—39. (γ) *On account of this use of* **μονογενής**, vv. 16, 18, which is peculiar to John. But, as Stier well enquires (iv. 84, edn. 2), *whence did John get this word,* but from the lips of his Divine Master? Would he have ventured on such an expression, except by an authorization from Him? (δ) *It is asserted that John often continues our Lord's discourses with additions of his own ;*—and ver. 31, and ch. i. 16, are alleged as instances. Of these, ch. i. 16 is *beside the question ;*—for the whole prologue is spoken in the person of the Evangelist, and the Baptist's testimony in ver. 15 is merely confirmatory of ver. 14, and then the connexion goes on with ver. 16. On the untenableness of the view with regard to vv. 31 ff., see notes there.
It would besides give us a very mean idea of the honesty or reverence of one who sets forth so sublime a view of the Divinity and Authority of our Lord, to suppose him capable, *in any place,* of attributing to his Master words and sentiments of his own invention. And that the charge amounts to this, every simple reader can bear testimony. The obvious *intention* of the Evangelist here is, *that the Lord shall have said these words.* If our Lord did not say them, but the Evangelist, we cannot stop with the view that he has *added his own remarks* to our Lord's discourse, but must at once pronounce him *guilty of an imposture and a forgery.* (See Stier, iv. 81 ff., edn. 2.) I conclude therefore on all these grounds that the words following, to ver. 21, cannot be otherwise regarded than as *uttered by our Lord in continuation of His discourse.* **ἠγάπησεν**] The indefinite signifying the universal and eternal existence of that love which God Himself *is* (1 John iv. 8). **τὸν κόσμον, the world,** in the most general sense, as represented by, and included in, man,—Gen. iii. 17, 18, and i. 28 ;—not, *the elect,* which would utterly destroy the force of the passage: see on ver. 18. The Lord here reveals *Love* as the *one ground of the divine counsel* in redemption,—*salvation* of men, as its *one purpose with regard to them.* **τὸν υἱὸν . . . ἔδωκεν**] These words, whether spoken in Hebrew or in Greek, seem to carry a reference to the offering of Isaac; and Nicodemus in that case would at once be reminded by them of the love *there required,* the *substitution there made,* and the *prophecy there uttered* to Abraham, to which **ἵνα πᾶς ὁ πιστ.** so nearly corresponds. **ἔδωκεν** – absolute, not merely *τῷ κόσμῳ*—gave up,—*παρέδωκεν,*—Rom. viii. 32; where as Stier remarks, we have again, in the *οὐκ ἐφείσατο,* an unmistakeable allusion to the *οὐκ ἐφείσω,* said to Abraham, Gen. xxii. 16. **ἵνα . . .**] By the repetition of this final clause verbatim from ver. 15, we have the identity of the former clauses established: i. e. the uplifting of the Son of Man like the serpent in the wilderness *is* the manifestation of the Divine Love in the gift of the Son of God:—*ὁ υἱὸς τοῦ ἀνθρώπου* of ver. 14, = in the strictest sense, *ὁ υἱὸς αὐτ. ὁ μονογ.* of ver. 16.

17.] The **κόσμος,**—the Gentile world,—was according to Jewish ideas to be judged and condemned by the Messiah. This error our Lord here removes. The assertion ch. ix. 39, **εἰς κρίμα** *ἐγὼ εἰς τ. κόσ. τοῦτ. ἦλθον,* is no contradiction to this. The *κρῖμα* there, as here, results from the separation of mankind into two classes,—those who will and those who will not come to the light; and that result itself is not the *purpose why* the Son of God came into the world, but is evolved in the ac-

x ch. i. 12 reff. y constr., 1 John v. 9, 11. z = ch. v. 29. Matt. xxiii. 33. a see ch. i. 9. b John, here and 1 John i. 6 only. Matt. vi. 23 al. fr. Gen. i. 4. c ch. vii. 7. Col. i. 21. 2 John 11. (2 Tim. iv. 18.) d ch. v. 29. Rom. ix. 11. Tit. ii. 8. James iii. 16 only. Prov. xxii. 8. e Eph. v. 11, 13. Jude 15. Jer. ii. 19.

[w] κρίνεται· ὁ μὴ πιστεύων ἤδη [w] κέκριται, ὅτι μὴ [x] πε- ABEF
πίστευκεν [x] εἰς [x] τὸ ὄνομα τοῦ [t] μονογενοῦς υἱοῦ τοῦ θεοῦ. GHKL MST$_b$U
19 [y] αὕτη δέ ἐστιν ἡ [z] κρίσις, [y] ὅτι τὸ [a] φῶς ἐλήλυθεν ΥΓΔΛ Πℵ
εἰς τὸν κόσμον, καὶ ἠγάπησαν οἱ ἄνθρωποι μᾶλλον τὸ 1. 33. 69
[b] σκότος ἢ τὸ φῶς· ἦν γὰρ αὐτῶν [c] πονηρὰ τὰ [c] ἔργα.
20 πᾶς γὰρ ὁ [d] φαῦλα πράσσων μισεῖ τὸ φῶς καὶ οὐκ
ἔρχεται πρὸς τὸ φῶς, ἵνα μὴ [e] ἐλεγχθῇ τὰ ἔργα αὐτοῦ·

18. rec aft 2nd ὁ ins δε, with A[T$_b$] rel D-lat vss [Cyr$_2$] Iren-int$_1$ Orig-int$_1$ Hil$_2$ Lucif$_1$: om Bℵ lat-*ff*$_2$ *l* Orig$_1$ Tert$_1$ Cypr$_2$.
19. *οι ανθρωποι* bef *ηγαπησαν* ℵ. *μαλλον* bef *οι ανθρ.* 1. 258 (lat-*e*). *το σκοτος* bef *μαλλον* ℵ 245 ev-H. rec *πονηρα* bef *αυτων*, with E rel Ambr$_1$: txt AB GKLUΛℵ[T$_b$Π) 1. 33. 69 vulg lat-*c e f ff*$_2$ D-lat Ath$_1$ Chr$_1$ Cyr$_1$[-p].
20. om *και ουκ ερχεται προς το φως* (*homœotel*) ℵ[1]. *αυτου* bef *τα εργα* (*see next ver*) AK[Π] 1 Chr$_1$: txt B[T$_b$]ℵ rel Iren-int [Orig-int] Lucif.

complishment of the higher purpose, viz. Love, and the salvation of men. Observe, the latter clause does not correspond to the former—it is not ἵνα **σώζῃ τὸν κόσμον,**—but **ἵνα σωθῇ ὁ κόσμος δι' αὐτοῦ**:—the *free will* of the *κόσμος* is by this strikingly set forth, in connexion with vv. 19, 20. Not that the Lord is not the *σωτὴρ τοῦ κόσμου* (ch. iv. 42), but that the peculiar cast of this passage required the other side of the truth to be brought out. **18.**] On **πιστ. εἰς αὐτ.** (which is John's usual phrase) the remarks above on ver. 15 apply with little distinction; *εἰς* giving more the *direction* of the belief *towards*, and its *resting upon*, *ἐν* its *abiding in*, Jesus as the Saviour. **οὐ κρίνεται**] See ch. v. 24, where the same assertion is made more fully; and note there. **ἤδη κέκριται,** implying,—*by no positive act of judgment of mine*,—but by the very nature of things themselves. God has provided a remedy for the deadly bite of sin; this remedy the man has not accepted, not *taken*: he must then perish in his sins: he is *already judged and sentenced*. **μὴ πεπίστευκεν**] The perfect implies more than 'that faith is a definite act in time' (Lücke, De Wette); it sets before us the deliberate choice of the man, q. d. 'he hath not chosen to believe' (Lange, in Stier, iv. 93, edn. 2): see 2 Thess. ii. 11, 12. **εἰς τὸ ὄν.**, not without meaning: that name was Ἰησοῦς, *αὐτὸς γὰρ σώσει τὸν λαὸν αὐτοῦ ἀπὸ τῶν ἁμαρτιῶν αὐτῶν*, Matt. i. 21. The **μονογενοῦς** also here sets before us the *hopelessness of such a man's state*: he has no *other* Saviour. **19.**] The particular *nature* of this decided judgment is now set forth,—**that the Light** (see ch. i. 4, 5, 7, and notes) **is come into the world** (*ἐλήλυθεν*, in reference perhaps to *ἐλήλυθας*, ver. 2), **and men** (= *ὁ κόσμος*, men in general; an awful revelation of the future reception of the Gospel) **loved** (the perversion of the affections and will is the deepest ruin of mankind) **the darkness** (see note on ch. i. 5; = the state of sin and unbelief) **rather than** (not = '*and not*,' but as Bengel says, "Amabilitas lucis eos perculit, sed obhæserunt in amore tenebrarum," see ch. v. 35; xii. 43: 2 Tim. iii. 4) **the light, because their deeds were evil** (their habits, thoughts, practices,—all these are included,—were perverted). **ἠγάπησαν** and **ἦν** are the *indefinite aorists*, implying the general usage and state of men, when and after the *φῶς ἐλήλυθεν εἰς τ. κόσ.* **20.**] This verse analyses the psychological grounds of the preceding. The *φῶς* is not here 'the common light of day,' nor light in general: but as before, **the Light**; i. e. *the Lord Jesus*, and His salvation: see ver. 21 fin. There is here a difference between *φαῦλα* **πράσσειν,** and **ποιεῖν** *τὴν ἀλήθειαν*, which is too remarkable to be passed over,—especially as the same distinction is observed in ch. v. 29,—*οἱ τὰ* **ἀγαθὰ ποιήσαντες** *εἰς ἀνάστασιν ζωῆς, οἱ δὲ τὰ* **φαῦλα πράξαντες** *εἰς ἀν. κρίσεως.* Bengel, who noticed this, hardly I think gives the right reason for it: "malitia est *irrequieta*, est quiddam operosius quam veritas;" nor does Stier fully reach it, "that *πράσ.* signifies more a subordination, a being the *servants* of sin, *ἐργάται ἀδικίας*, Luke xiii. 27." I think the distinction is rather perhaps this,—that *πράσσειν* is more the *habit of action*; so that we might say '*he that practises evil*;' but *ποιεῖν* the true *doing* of good, *good fruit*, good that *remains*. He who **πράσσει,** has nothing but his *πρᾶγμα*, which is an event, a thing of the past, a source to him only of condemnation, for he

21 ὁ δὲ ποιῶν τὴν [f] ἀλήθειαν ἔρχεται πρὸς τὸ φῶς, ἵνα
[g] φανερωθῇ αὐτοῦ τὰ ἔργα ὅτι [h] ἐν θεῷ ἐστιν εἰργασμένα.
22 Μετὰ ταῦτα ἦλθεν ὁ Ἰησοῦς καὶ οἱ μαθηταὶ αὐτοῦ
εἰς τὴν [i] Ἰουδαίαν γῆν, καὶ ἐκεῖ [j] διέτριβεν μετ᾽ αὐτῶν καὶ
ἐβάπτιζεν. 23 [k] ἦν δὲ καὶ Ἰωάννης [k] βαπτίζων ἐν Αἰνὼν
[l] ἐγγὺς τοῦ Σαλείμ, ὅτι [m] ὕδατα πολλὰ ἦν ἐκεῖ, καὶ

f = 1 Cor. v. 8. xiii. 6. Eph. iv. 21. vi. 14.
g ch. ii. 11. w. ὅτι, 2 Cor. iii. 3. 1 John ii. 19.
h 1 Cor. vii. 39. xi. 11. 1 John iv. 16.
i adj., Mark i. 5. Acts xvi. 1. xxiv. 24 only.
j John, here (ch. xi. 54 v. r.) only. elsw., Acts (only) xii. 19 al7. Lev. xiv. 8.
k constr., Matt. xix. 22 reff.
l w. gen., ch. xi. 18, 54. xix. 20. Rom. x. 8 (from Deut. xxx. 14). xiii. 11? Heb. vi. 8. viii. 13 only. w. dat., Acts ix. 38. xxvii. 8. (Luke xix. 11. Acts i. 12.)
m plur., Matt. viii. 32. Mark ix. 22. Rev. viii. 10. xiv. 7. xvi. 4. xvii. 1. Exod. xv. 27.

21. om ο δε ποιων την αληθειαν ερχεται προς το φως ινα φανερωθη αυτου τα εργα (*homœotel: see next var*) א[1]. τα εργα bef αυτου LUא[3a] 33. 69 vulg-clem lat-(*a*) *b e f l* [*q*] D-lat Iren$_1$ Cyr[-p$_1$] Lucif$_1$. ειργασμενον א[1](txt א-corr[1·3a]).
22. om ο A[Π] 3 Scr's h k p. εις την ιουδαιαν γην bef και οι μαθηται αυτου א (Chr-6-mss). κακει א.
23. ins ο bef ιωαννης B : om Aא 1(Treg, expr) rel [Orig$_1$].

has nothing to shew for it, for it is also φαῦλον, worthless; whereas he that **ποιεῖ**, has his ποίημα,—he has abiding fruit; *his works do follow him.* So that the expressions will not perhaps here admit of being interchanged. (See however Rom. vii. 15—20, where the two verbs are certainly interchanged more than once.) There may possibly be a hint [in the mention of σκότος ver. 19] at the *coming by night* of Nicodemus, but surely only by a distant implication. He might gather this from what was said, that it would have been better for him to make open confession of Jesus; but we can hardly say that our Lord reproves him for coming even as he did. **21.**] Who is this **ποιῶν τ. ἀλήθ.**? the end of ch. i. will best explain to us,—ἐν ᾧ δόλος οὐκ ἔστιν, see also Luke viii. 15, and Ps. xv. The πράσσων πονηρά is crooked and perverse; he has a light, which he does not follow; he knows the light, and avoids it; and so there is no truth, singleness, in him; he is a man at variance with himself. But the simple and single-minded is he who knowing and approving the light, comes to it; and comes that he may be carried onward in this spirit of truth and single-mindedness to higher degrees of communion with and likeness to God. "The good man seeks the light, and to place his works in the light, not from a vain love of praise, but from a desire for communion wherein he finds strength and security," De Wette. But this is not all: the *manifesting his works, that they are wrought in God,* is and can be only by the candle of the Lord being kindled within him, and he himself born again in the Kingdom of God: see Ps. cxxxix. 23, 24.

We hear nothing of the effect produced on Nicodemus by this interview. It certainly did not alienate him from Jesus, see ch. vii. 50; xix. 39, also ch. xii. 42. "It speaks for the simplicity and historic truthfulness of our Evangelist, that he adds nothing more, and even leaves untold the immediate result which the discourse had." (Baumgarten-Crusius, in Stier, iv. 102, edn. 2.)

22—36.] *Removal of Jesus and His disciples into the neighbourhood of the Baptist, who, upon occasion given, bears another notable testimony to Him.*

22. μετὰ ταῦτα] The sequence is not *immediate;* for this, John uses μετὰ τοῦτο, see ch. xi. 7, 11; xix. 28.

τὴν Ἰουδαίαν γῆν, the rural districts of Judæa, in distinction from the metropolis. **ἐβάπτ.**, viz. by means of His disciples: see ch. iv. 2, and note. The place is not named: perhaps He did not remain in one fixed spot.

23.] The situation of these places is uncertain. Eusebius and Jerome place Salim eight Roman miles south of Scythopolis, and Ænon at the same distance, on the Jordan. If Scythopolis was the ancient Bethshan, both places were in *Samaria:* and to this agree Epiphanius and the Samaritan chronicle called Abul Phatach. In Judith iv. 4, we find mention of ὁ αὐλὼν Σαλήμ in Samaria (see note on Heb. vii. 1). An Ænon in the wilderness of Judah is mentioned Josh. xv. 61 [(56) B], and ib. ver. 32, שִׁלְחִים and עַיִן, Σελεεὶμ κ. Ἀίν (F., om κ. Ἀίν AB), both in Judah, where it is certainly more probable, both from the text here and from *à priori* considerations, that John would have been baptizing, than in Samaria. The name עֵינָן, is an intensitive form of עַיִן, a fountain, which answers to the description here given. Both places

[n] παρεγίνοντο καὶ ἐβαπτίζοντο. 24 οὔπω γὰρ ἦν [o] βε-
βλημένος εἰς τὴν [o] φυλακὴν [ὁ] Ἰωάννης. 25 ἐγένετο
οὖν [p] ζήτησις [q] ἐκ τῶν μαθητῶν Ἰωάννου μετὰ Ἰουδαίου
περὶ [r] καθαρισμοῦ. 26 καὶ ἦλθαν πρὸς τὸν Ἰωάννην καὶ
εἶπαν αὐτῷ Ῥαββί, ὃς ἦν μετὰ σοῦ πέραν τοῦ Ἰορδάνου, ᾧ σὺ [s] μεμαρτύρηκας, ἴδε οὗτος βαπτίζει, καὶ πάντες
ἔρχονται πρὸς αὐτόν. 27 ἀπεκρίθη Ἰωάννης καὶ εἶπεν
Οὐ δύναται ἄνθρωπος λαμβάνειν οὐδέν, ἐὰν μὴ ᾖ δεδομένον αὐτῷ ἐκ τοῦ οὐρανοῦ. 28 αὐτοὶ ὑμεῖς μοι [st] μαρτυρεῖτε

n John, here [ch. viii. 2 rec.] only. Luke xii. 51 al7. Acts v. 21 and freq. Job ii. 11.
o Matt. v. 25. xviii. 30. Luke xii. 58. xxiii. 19, 25. Acts xvi. 37.
p Acts xv. 2. xxv. 20. 1 Tim. i. 4. vi. 4. 2 Tim. ii. 23. Tit. iii. 9 only +.
q = Acts v. 38, 39. Rom. ii. 29. xii. 18. Rev. ii. 9.
r ch. ii. 6 reff.
s w. dat., Matt. xxiii. 31 reff.
t w. ὅτι, ch. i. 34 reff.

D ραβ-βει... ABDEF GHKL MST_bU VΓΔΛΠ ℵ 1. 33. 69

24. om ὁ Bℵ Eus_1 : ins A [T_b(e sil)] rel $Orig_2$ [Cyr_1].
25. for ουν, δε ℵ[1] 47 vulg-ed Syr [syr-cu syr-jer] copt[-wilk]. for ζητ., συνζητησις ℵ[1]. aft μαθητων ins των B. rec ιουδαιων, with GΛ[2] [Π[2](but txt restored)] ℵ[1](sic) 1. 69 latt syr-cu copt goth æth arm[-usc] $Orig_1$: txt ABℵ[3a] rel syrr arm-zoh Chr_1 Cyr_1 Thl Euthym. [T_b ?]
26. (ηλθαν and ειπαν, so B[1].) for ᾧ, ως ℵ[1](but corrd) ev-P : ον ev-y. ιδου D 1.
27. for λαμβ., λαβιν ℵ. ουδε εν αν B syr-cu.
28. om μοι EFHM[VΓ]ℵ harl.

were West of the Jordan: see ver. 26, and compare ch. i. 28. **παρεγ. κ. ἐβ.**, i. e. the multitudes. **24.**] There is much difficulty, which probably never will be cleared up, about the *date of the imprisonment* of John, and its reference to the course of our Lord's ministry. Between Matt. iv. 11 and 12, there seems to be a wide hiatus, in which (see note there) the first chapters of this Gospel should be inserted. But the records from which the three synoptic Gospels have arisen were apparently unconscious of any such interval. Our Evangelist seems here to refer to such records, and to insert this remark, that it might not be imagined, as it would be from them, that our Lord's public ministry (in the wider sense, see below on ver. 26) began with the imprisonment of the Baptist. **25.**] The circumstances under which this dispute arose seem to have been these:—John and our Lord were baptizing near to one another. (On the relation of their baptisms, see below on ver. 26.) They were both watched jealously (see ch. iv. 1) by the Pharisees. One of these (**Ἰουδαῖος**, i. e. Ἰουδ. τις) appears to have entered into dispute with the disciples of John about the relative importance of the two baptisms; *they* perhaps maintaining that their master's καθαρισμός preparatory to the Messiah was absolutely necessary for all, and *he* (the Ἰουδαῖος) pointing out to them the apparent inconsistency of this Messiah himself authorizing a baptism in his name, and alleging that if so, their master's baptism was rendered superfluous. We are driven to these conjectures, because the text gives us no further insight into the fact than what the circumstances and the answer of John render probable. **26.**] Compare ch. i. 28. **πάντες ἔρχ.**] Not, probably, any who had been baptized already by John; but multitudes of persons. The baptism now carried on by the disciples appears to have stood very much in the same position as that of John. It was preparatory to the *public ministry* of our Lord *properly so called*, which began in Galilee after the imprisonment of John. It was *not accompanied with the gift of the Spirit*, see ch. vii. 39. As John's commission was now on the wane, so our Lord's was expanding. The solemn cleansing of the temple was its opening; and now it is proceeding onwards, gathering multitudes around it (see ch. iv. 1). **27.**] The subject of this answer is,—*the divinely appointed humiliation and eclipsing of the Baptist himself before the greater majesty of Him who was come after him.* Accordingly he begins in this verse by answering to the zeal of his disciples, 'that he cannot go beyond the bounds of his heaven-appointed mission.' "Non possum mihi arrogare et capere quæ deus non dedit." (Wetstein.) Some apply the words to Jesus:—εἰ δὲ λαμπρότερα τὰ ἐκείνου, καὶ πάντες πρὸς αὐτὸν ἔρχονται, θαυμάζειν οὐ χρή. τοιαῦτα γὰρ τὰ θεῖα. Chrys. But the whole tone of the answer makes the other view more likely. Of course the remark, being general, may in the background have reference to the greater mission of Jesus; but not primarily. The parallelism of ἄνθρωπος here and himself as the subject of εἶπον in the next verse, also supports this view: see Heb. v. 4. **28.**] 'Not only so, but I have always given the same consistent

ὅτι εἶπον Οὐκ εἰμὶ ἐγὼ ὁ χριστός, ἀλλ' ὅτι ἀπεσταλμένος
εἰμὶ [u] ἔμπροσθεν ἐκείνου. 29 ὁ ἔχων τὴν [v] νύμφην [w] νυμφίος
ἐστίν· ὁ δὲ φίλος τοῦ [w] νυμφίου, ὁ ἑστηκὼς καὶ ἀκούων
αὐτοῦ, [x] χαρᾷ [x] χαίρει [y] διὰ τὴν φωνὴν τοῦ [w] νυμφίου.
αὕτη οὖν ἡ [z] χαρὰ ἡ ἐμὴ [z] πεπλήρωται. 30 ἐκεῖνον δεῖ
[a] αὐξάνειν, ἐμὲ δὲ [b] ἐλαττοῦσθαι. 31 ὁ [c] ἄνωθεν ἐρχόμενος

u = Luke xix. 4, 28. ch. x. 4. Gen. xxiv. 7.
v = Rev. xviii. 23. xxi. 2, 9. xxii. 17 only. Jer. ii. 32. (Matt. x. 35. Luke xii. 53 bis only.)
w ch. ii. 9 reff. [and constr.]
x Isa. lxvi. 10 Bℵ. (Matt. ii. 10. 1 Thess. iii. 9. Jon. iv. 6.) constr., Luke xxii. 15. Ps. cxxxi. 16.
y 1 Thess. iii. 9.
z = ch. xvi. 24. xvii. 13. Phil. ii. 2. 1 John i. 4. 2 John 12.
a intr., see Mark iv. 8 reff.
b Heb. ii. 7 (from Ps. viii. 5), 9 only. Jer. xxxvii. (xxx.) 19.
c ver. 3 reff.

aft ειπον ins εγω B am lat-*c* [syr-jer : pref T_b(appy)] syr-cu. om εγω (bef ο χς) D lat-*a*(appy) *l* syr-cu Cypr [Firm].

29. for εστηκως, εστως D $Thdot_1$ [$Orig_1$]. αυτου bef και ακουων ℵ.

testimony; that I was only the forerunner of One greater than myself.' **ἐκείνου** does not refer to *ὁ χριστός*, in which case it would have been *αὐτοῦ* (see, however, apparent exceptions to this, ch. vii. 45: Acts iii. 13; see also Winer, Gr., edn. 6, § 23. 1): but *to Jesus*, as the subject of ver. 26; and thus is not merely a *general* testimony with regard to the Messiah, but a *personal* one to Jesus.

29.] Here first, (and here only in our Gospel,) comes from the mouth of the Forerunner, this great symbolical reference which is so common in the other Gospels and in the Epistles. It is remarkable that our Lord brings it forward in His answer *to the disciples of John* respecting fasting, Matt. ix. 15: where see note on the further import of the terms used. The **φίλος τοῦ νυμφίου** (Heb. שׁוֹשְׁבִּן) was the regular organ of communication in the preliminaries of marriage, and had the ordering of the marriage feast. It is to this last time, and not to any ceremonial custom connected with the marriage rites, that this verse refers. The friend rejoices at hearing the **φωνὴ τοῦ νυμφίου**, (see Jer. vii. 34; xvi. 9; xxv. 10: Rev. xviii. 23,) in his triumph and joy, *at the marriage*. He **χαρᾷ χαίρει** (see reff.: 1 Thess. iii. 9 is not a parallel case as to *construction*, for ᾗ there is only by attraction) because he hears in the voice of the Bridegroom an assurance of the happy completion of his mission, and on account of the voice itself,—*τὴν οὕτω γλυκεῖαν, τὴν οὕτως ἐπέραστον, τὴν οὕτω σωτήριον*. **ἑστηκὼς καί** belongs merely to the graphic setting forth of the similitude. **αὕτη . . . πεπλήρ.**] *παραδόντος ἐκείνῳ τὴν νύμφην, καὶ πεπληρωκότος, ὡς εἴρηται, τὴν ἐγχειρισθεῖσάν μοι διακονίαν*. Euthym. **30.**] **ἐλαττοῦσθαι**,—*ὡς ἡλίου ἀνατείλαντος ἑωσφόρον*. Euthym. See note on Matt. xi. 2 ff.

31.] Many modern critics, beginning with Bengel and Wetstein, and including Lücke, Kuinoel, Olshausen, Tholuck, De Wette, and others, maintain that after ver. 30 we have the words, *not of the Baptist, but of the Evangelist*. Lücke and De Wette assume that the Evangelist has put his own thoughts into the Baptist's mouth, or at least mixed them with his words. The reason of this arbitrary proceeding is, (α) *that the sentiments of the following verses seem to them not to be congruous with the time and position of the Baptist*. But some of them confess (e. g. Lücke, De Wette) that this very position of the Baptist is to them yet unexplained, and are disposed to question the applicability to their idea of it of very much which is undoubtedly recorded to have been said by him. So that we cannot allow such a view much critical weight, unless it can be first clearly shewn, *what were* the Baptist's convictions concerning the Person and Office of our Lord. (β) *That the diction and sentiments of the following verses are so entirely in the style of our Evangelist*. But first, I by no means grant this, in the sense which is here meant. It will be seen by the reff. that the Evangelist does not so frequently repeat himself as in most other passages of equal length. And even were this so, the remark made above on vv. 16—21, would apply here also; that the Evangelist's peculiar style of theological expression was formed on some model; and on what more likely than in the first place the discourses of his Divine Master, and then such sententious and striking testimonies as the present? But there is a weightier reason than these for opposing the above view, and that arises from what modern criticism has been so much given to overlook,—the *inner coherence of the discourse itself*; in which John explains to his disciples the *reason why* HE must increase; whereas his own dignity was to be eclipsed before Him. This will be seen below as we proceed. And there is nothing inconsistent with what the Lord himself says of the Baptist in these verses. He (the Baptist) ever speaks not *as a disciple* of Jesus, not as *within* the Kingdom,

[d] ἐπάνω πάντων ἐστίν. ὁ ὢν [e] ἐκ τῆς γῆς ἐκ τῆς γῆς ἐστιν
καὶ [f] ἐκ τῆς γῆς [f] λαλεῖ· ὁ ἐκ τοῦ οὐρανοῦ ἐρχόμενος [d] ἐπάνω
πάντων ἐστίν. 32 ὃ ἑώρακεν καὶ ἤκουσεν, τοῦτο [g] μαρτυρεῖ·
καὶ τὴν [g] μαρτυρίαν αὐτοῦ οὐδεὶς [gh] λαμβάνει· 33 ὁ [gh] λαβὼν
αὐτοῦ τὴν [g] μαρτυρίαν [i] ἐσφράγισεν ὅτι ὁ θεὸς [j] ἀληθής ἐστιν. c την μαρτυριαν...
34 ὃν γὰρ ἀπέστειλεν ὁ θεὸς τὰ ῥήματα τοῦ θεοῦ λαλεῖ· οὐ
γὰρ [k] ἐκ [kl] μέτρου δίδωσιν τὸ πνεῦμα. 35 ὁ πατὴρ ἀγαπᾷ τὸν
υἱὸν καὶ πάντα [m] δέδωκεν [mn] ἐν τῇ [o] χειρὶ αὐτοῦ. 36 ὁ [p] πιστεύων εἰς τὸν υἱὸν ἔχει [q] ζωὴν αἰώνιον· ὁ δὲ [r] ἀπειθῶν τῷ

ABCDE FGHKL MST$_b$U VΓΔΛΠ ℵ 1. 33. 69

d = Luke xix. 17, 19 only. Job xxxiii. 12. see Matt. ii. 9. Mark xiv. 5. e ch. viii. 23, 44. 1 John ii. 16. iv. 1, &c. f Matt. xii. 34. ch. viii. 44. xii. 49. 1 John iv. 5. g ver. 11. h = ch. i. 12 reff. i = and constr., here only. (ch. vi. 27 reff.) j subj., ch. vii. 18. viii. 26. Matt. xxii. 16 al. k here only. l = 1 Cor. vii. 5. xii. 27. m = 2 Cor. i. 22. viii. 16. Judg. viii. 7. Ezek. xxxvi. 26, 27. see Judg. iii. 28. n = Luke xxiii. 19. o Matt. xvii. 22. Luke xxiii. 46 al. see Gen. xxxix. 4. p ch. ii. 11 reff. q ver. 15. r here only in Gospp. Acts xiv. 2. 1 Pet. ii. 7, 8. Exod. xxiii. 21. (-θής, Luke i. 17.)

31. aft 2nd *ο* ins *δε* Dℵ[1] mt lat-*a b l q* [syr-jer] Quæst$_1$: *και ο* Syr syr-cu. for 1st *εκ*, *απο* D 69: *επι* ℵ[1] [lat-*a e*]. om 2nd *επανω παντων εστιν* Dℵ[1] 1 lat-*a b e ff$_2$ l* syr-cu arm Eus$_1$ Non$_1$ Tert$_1$ Hil$_1$ Quæst$_1$.
32. rec at beg ins *και*, with A rel vulg lat-*c f* (*ff$_2$*?) *g$_2$* [*q* syrr goth æth Orig$_1$(ed Delarue)-int$_1$ Chr$_1$ Aug$_2$]: om BDL[T$_b$]ℵ 33 lat-*a b e l* syr-cu [syr-jer] copt arm Eus$_1$ Non$_1$ Tert$_1$ Hil$_1$ Quæst$_1$. for ὅ, *ον* ℵ[1](txt ℵ[2]). om *τουτο* Dℵ 1 lat-*a b e ff$_2$ l* Syr (copt?) æth arm Eus$_1$ [Orig-int$_1$] Hil$_1$ Quæst$_1$.
34. rec aft *διδωσιν* ins *ο θεος*, with AC[2]D rel vulg lat-*a* (*c*) [*ff$_2$ g$_2$ q*] syrr (copt) æth arm Orig$_1$(int$_2$) Cyr-jer$_1$ [Did$_1$] Chr$_1$ Aug$_1$: om BC[1]L[T$_b$]ℵ 1. 33 lat-*b e f* [*l*] *Cyr*[-p]. (*το πνευμα* is written on marg in B *a prima manu*.)
35. for *δεδ.*, *εδωκεν* DK.
36. at beg ins *ινα* and (for *εχει*) *εχη* D. om *δε* ℵ[1] [lat-*a e ff$_2$ l* Tert$_1$ Cypr$_1$].

—but as knowing the blessedness of those who should be within it; as *standing by*, and hearing the Bridegroom's voice. Nor again is there any thing inconsistent with the frame of mind which prompted the question sent by John to our Lord afterwards in the onward waning of his days in prison: see note on Matt. xi. 2. **ὁ ἄνωθ. ἐρχ.**] This gives us *the reason why* He must increase: His power and His words are not from below, temporary, limited; but are divine and inexhaustible; and, ver. **32**, His witness is not, like John's, only of what he has been forewarned to expect, but of that which he has seen and heard. But **οὐδείς**,—i. e. in reference to the *κόσμος* into which He is come, the *σκοτία* in which His light shines,—*no one comparatively*,—receives His testimony. The state of men's minds at Jerusalem with regard to Jesus must ere this have been well known to the Baptist. Notice in ver. 31 the collocation of the words as regards emphasis: *ὁ* **ὢν** *ἐκ τῆς γῆς* **ἐκ τῆς γῆς** *ἐστιν*, **κ. ἐκ τῆς γῆς** *λαλεῖ*. **33, 34.**] This exception shews the correctness of the sense just assigned to *οὐδείς*. *ὁ λαβὼν αὐτοῦ τὴν μαρτυρίαν καὶ πιστεύων αὐτῷ, ἐβεβαίωσεν, ἔδειξεν, ὅτι ὁ θεὸς ἀληθής ἐστιν ὁ ἀποστείλας αὐτόν, οὗτινός ἐστι τὰ ῥήματα ἃ λαλεῖ· ὁ δὲ μὴ λαβὼν αὐτὴν καὶ ἀπιστῶν αὐτῷ, τοὐναντίον ποιεῖ, καὶ οὐδὲν ἕτερον ἢ προδήλως θεομαχεῖ.* Euthym.

The middle *σφραγίζομαι* is more usual in this signification. See instances in Wetstein. **ἀληθής**, not as Wetstein, "Deum veracem esse, et quæ per Prophetas promiserat, præstitisse;" this does not suit the context, and besides would require *πιστός*, not *ἀληθής* (see 1 John i. 9): but, as above from Euthym., **true**. **οὐ γὰρ ἐκ μ. . . .**] Seeing that the contrast is between the *unlimited* gift of the Spirit to Him that comes from above, and the *limited* participation of Him by those who are of the earth; we must not understand the assertion generally, but supply *αὐτῷ*, as has usually been done, after **δίδωσιν**. "Spiritus sanctus non habitavit super Prophetas, nisi mensura quadam; quidam enim librum unum, quidam duos vaticiniorum ediderunt." (Vajikra Rabba, in Wetstein.) This unmeasured pouring of the Spirit on Him accounts for his speaking the words of God. **35.**] This, again, is the *ground why* the Father **gives not the Spirit by measure (to Him)**: see Matt. xi. 27—29, with which this verse forms a remarkable point of connexion, shewing that what is commonly known as John's form of expression was not confined to him, but originated higher, having its traces in the synoptic narrative, which is confessedly, in its main features, independent of him. **36.**] Compare ch. i. 12, 13; ver. 15. **ἀπειθῶν** may mean **disbelieving**, see reff. Unbelief implies

υἱῷ οὐκ [s]ὄψεται ζωήν, ἀλλ' ἡ [t]ὀργὴ τοῦ θεοῦ [u]μένει ἐπ' αὐτόν.

IV. [1] Ὡς οὖν ἔγνω [v]ὁ *κύριος ὅτι ἤκουσαν οἱ Φαρισαῖοι ὅτι Ἰησοῦς πλείονας [w]μαθητὰς [wx]ποιεῖ καὶ βαπτίζει ἢ Ἰωάννης· [2] [y]καίτοιγε Ἰησοῦς αὐτὸς οὐκ ἐβάπτιζεν, ἀλλ' οἱ μαθηταὶ αὐτοῦ· [3] [z]ἀφῆκεν τὴν Ἰουδαίαν καὶ ἀπῆλθεν πάλιν εἰς τὴν Γαλιλαίαν. [4] [a]ἔδει δὲ αὐτὸν [b]διέρχεσθαι [b]διὰ τῆς Σαμαρείας. [5] ἔρχεται [c]οὖν εἰς πόλιν τῆς Σαμαρείας λεγομένην Συχάρ, [d]πλησίον τοῦ [e]χωρίου [f]ὃ

s = here only. (see ἰδεῖν, ver. 3 reff.) Ps. lxxxviii. 48.
t Gospp., Luke iii. 7 ‖. xxi. 23 only. Rom. i. 18. Rev. vi. 16, 17 al.
u ch. i. 32.
v in John, = ch. vi. 23. xi. 2. xx. 2, 18, 20, 25. xxi. 7 bis, 12 only. in Luke passim.
w here only. see Matt. xxviii. 19.
x pres., ch. i. 40 reff.
y Acts xiv. 17 (xvii. 27 v. r.) only +. Xen. Mem. i. 2. 3.
z = Matt. iv. 11 al.
a = Luke xx. 29. 1 Cor. xi. 19.
b Luke xvii. 11.
c — Luke xx. 29. 1 Cor. vii. 26.
d w. gen., = here only. Num. xxxiii. 37. Deut. xi. 30.
e Matt. xxvi. 36 reff.
f constr., ch. ii. 22. ver. 50. Tit. iii. 5. Rev. i. 20.

for οψεται, εχει ℵ-corr[1a] [Iren-int$_1$ Cypr$_1$]. (μενεῖ M[ΓΠ] lat-*b e g* Syr copt æth Iren-int$_1$ Tert$_1$ Cypr$_1$: μένει EHK[S]V 69 vulg lat-*a c f ff$_2$* [*l q*] D-lat (syr-cu syr ?) arm.) επ' αυτον bef μενει ℵ [lat-*b*].

Chap. IV. 1. * Ἰησοῦς DΛℵ 1 latt syrr syr-cu copt arm Chr$_1$: κυριος ABC[T$_b$] rel lat-*f q* syr-mg æth [Cyr$_1$ Non$_1$]. om η AB[1]L[ΓΓ] : ins B(as corrd by origl scribe) CDℵ rel.

2. καιτοι, omg γε, C. αυτος bef ιησ. ADK[Π] 33 gat(with mm) lat-*ff$_2$* Chr$_1$ Cyr$_1$. —ins ο bef ιησ. K 69.

3. aft την ιουδαιαν ins γην D 1. 69 Scr's d e k q[1] r s foss(with gat mm) lat-*a b e ff$_2$ l* æth arm Chr. om παλιν A B[1]-txt rel lat-*q* syr (Orig$_1$) Chr$_1$: ins B[1]-marg CDLM [T$_b$]ℵ 1. 33. 69 latt Syr syr-cu copt [æth arm].

5. om ερχεται to σαμαριας (*homœotel*) ℵ[1](ins in marg ℵ-corr[1]). elz σιχαρ, with 69 vulg lat-*c* Non$_1$: txt A B(sic) ℵ rel am(with forj fuld harl) lat-*a* (*b e*) *f l q* coptt Chr$_1$ Cyr$_1$. for ὅ, ου C[1]DLMS 1. 33 Chr$_1$: ὧ [Γ] 69(sic) : txt ABC[2][T$_b$]ℵ rel Cyr$_1$.

disobedience. **μένει**] It was on him, see ver. 18, in his state of darkness and nature,—and can only be removed by faith in the Son of God, which he *has not*.

Chap. IV. 1—54.] Manifestation of Himself as the Son of God in Samaria and Galilee. 1—42.] *On his way back to Galilee through Samaria, he discourses with a Samaritan woman. Confession of his Messiahship by the Samaritans.* 1.] An inference may be drawn from this, that our Lord knew the anger of the Pharisees to be more directed against Him than against the Baptist,—probably on account of what had passed in Jerusalem. **ὅτι Ἰησοῦς**, not ὅτι αὐτὸς . . . . because the report which the Pharisees had heard is given verbatim: the **ὅτι** is 'recitantis' merely. 2.] Probably for the same reason that Paul did not baptize usually (1 Cor. i. 14—16); viz. because His office was to preach and teach;—and the disciples as yet had no office of this kind. To assume a further reason, e.g. that there might not be ground for those whom the Lord himself had baptized to boast of it, is arbitrary and unnecessary. "Johannes, minister, sua manu baptizavit; discipuli ejus, ut videtur, neminem. At Christus baptizat Spiritu Sancto." Bengel. 4.] If He was already on the borders of Samaria, not far from Ænon (see note on ch. iii. 23), the direct way was through Samaria. Indeed without this assumption, we know that the Galilæans ordinarily took this way (Jos. Antt. xx. 6. 1, beginning). But there was probably design also in the journey. It could not have been mere speed (πάντως ἔδει τοὺς ταχὺ βουλομένους ἀπελθεῖν δι' ἐκείνης πορεύεσθαι, Jos. Vit. 52),—since He made two days' stay on the way. 5.] Sychar is better known by the O. T. name of Sychem (**Συχέμ**), or τὰ Σίκιμα (Josephus, Euseb., &c.), or ἡ Σικίμα (LXX, 3 Kings xii. 25). It was a very old town on the range of Mt. Ephraim, in a narrow valley between Mt. Ebal and Mt. Gerizim, Judg. ix. 7. The name Sychar has been variously derived: from שֶׁקֶר, a lie, or שִׁכֹּר, *drunken* (Isa. xxviii. 1), by some (Reland, Lightfoot), who believe it to have originally been an opprobrious name given by the Jews, but by this time to have lost its signification, and become the usual appellation: by others from **Συχέμ**, by mere corruption of the terminating liquid μ into ρ, Olsh. Very near it was afterwards built Flavia Neapolis (**Συχέμ, νῦν ἔρημος, δείκνυται δὲ ὁ τόπος ἐν προαστείοις νέας**

g Gen. xlviii. 22. Josh. xxiv. 32.
h here bis. ver. 14. Mark v. 29. James iii. 11 (12 v. r.). 2 Pet. ii. 7. Rev. vii. 17 al4. only. Exod. xv. 27.
i = Matt. xi. 28. Rev. ii. 3 only. (ver. 38 reff.) Isa. xl. 31.
k = Luke xi. 6. xii. 36. ch. xiii. 4, or Matt. xv. 5. 2 Cor. vii. 9.
l 2 Cor. xi. 26 only †. 1 Macc. vi. 41. (-ρεῖν, Acts x. 8.)
m Matt. xxvi. 55 reff.
n = Acts xx. 11. xxvii. 17. see Heb. vi. 15.
o ver. 15. ch. ii. 8, 9 only. Gen. xxiv. 13, 20.
p Matt. xxvii. 34. Rev. xvi. 6. Prov. xxxi. 6.
q plur., here only. 2 Chron. xi. 23.
r = Luke xx. 41. ch. vii. 15. 1 Cor. xv. 12.

g ἔδωκεν Ἰακὼβ Ἰωσὴφ τῷ υἱῷ αὐτοῦ. 6 ἦν δὲ ἐκεῖ h πηγὴ ABCDE
τοῦ Ἰακώβ. ὁ οὖν Ἰησοῦς i κεκοπιακὼς k ἐκ τῆς l ὁδοι- FGHKL
πορίας m ἐκαθέζετο n οὕτως ἐπὶ τῇ h πηγῇ. ὥρα ἦν ὡς ἕκτη. MST$_b$U
7 ἔρχεται γυνὴ ἐκ τῆς Σαμαρείας o ἀντλῆσαι ὕδωρ. λέγει VΓΔΛΠ
αὐτῇ ὁ Ἰησοῦς p Δός μοι p πεῖν. 8 οἱ γὰρ μαθηταὶ αὐτοῦ ℵ 1. 33. 69
ἀπεληλύθεισαν εἰς τὴν πόλιν ἵνα q τροφὰς ἀγοράσωσιν. Frag. Ath$_b$. ερχεται ...
9 λέγει οὖν αὐτῷ ἡ γυνὴ ἡ Σαμαρεῖτις r Πῶς σὺ Ἰουδαῖος

ins τω bef ιωσηφ Bℵ.

6. rec ωσει, with E ℵ^{3a}(but txt restored) rel Chr Cyr: ως η H^1 69: txt ABCD L[Π^2]ℵ^1 33. [T$_b$?]

7. aft ερχεται ins τις ℵ [lat-*b* coptt]. rec πιειν, with AB$^?$C^{3}ℵ^{3a} rel: txt B^{1}C^1 D[L] ℵ^1(πιν). (So vv. 9, 10, exc that in ver 9 A also has πιν. [T$_b$ def., but has πειν vv. 9, 10. Frag-ath$_b$ also def., but has πιειν there.])

9. om ουν V^{1}ℵ^1 1 [not Frag-ath$_b$, as Tischdf] Syr syr-cu copt [æth arm] Cyr$_1$. συ ιουδ

πόλεως, Euseb. Onomasticon, in Winer, sub voce). There is a long and interesting history of Sychem and the Samaritan worship on Gerizim, and the Christian church in the neighbourhood, in Robinson's Palestine, iii. 113—136. [See also Dr. Thomson, The Land and the Book, p. 472 ff. He thinks that Sychar and Shechem are not the same, because at Shechem (Nablus) there are delicious fountains of water, which the woman would hardly have left to draw from a deep well two miles off.] **τοῦ χωρ. ὃ ἔδωκ. . . . .**] This is traditional: it finds however support from Gen. xxxiii. 19, where we find Jacob buying a field near Shechem, and Josh. xxiv. 32, where, on the mention of Joseph's bones being laid there, it is said that it became the inheritance of the children of Joseph. *This form* of the tradition is supposed to have arisen from the translation by the LXX of Gen. xlviii. 22, ἐγὼ δὲ δίδωμί σοι Σίκιμα ἐξαίρετον (שְׁכֶם אַחַד, 'one share') ὑπὲρ τοὺς ἀδελφούς σου: and of Josh. xxiv. 32, ἐν τῇ μερίδι τοῦ ἀγροῦ οὗ ἐκτήσατο Ἰακὼβ παρὰ τῶν Ἀμοῤῥαίων τῶν κατοικούντων ἐν Σικίμοις . . . καὶ ἔδωκεν αὐτὴν Ἰωσὴφ ἐν μερίδι, where they apparently read or mistook וַיְהִיוּ for וַיְּהָבֵהוּ (3 sing. fut. Kal. w. suffix of יָהַב, a verb which only occurs in the imperative mood, unless it be in the very doubtful place of Hosea iv. 18). Our Lord does not allude to it in the conversation, though the woman does. **6.**] Robinson (iii. 112) can only solve the difficulty of the present well standing in a spot watered by so many natural fountains, by supposing that it may have been dug, according to the practice of the patriarchs, by Jacob, in connexion with the plot of ground which he bought, to have an independent supply of water.

οὕτως—see reff.—refers to **κεκοπιακὼς ἐκ τ. ὁδ.**, and may be rendered **accordingly.** There is no authority for the meaning ἁπλῶς ὡς ἔτυχε, 'just as he was,' or 'just as it happened,' i. e. on the bare stone. **ὥρα . . . ἕκτη, mid-day.** Townson supposed the sixth hour, according to John, to mean *six in the evening,* "after the way of reckoning in Asia Minor;"—but, as Lücke observes (i. 580), this way of reckoning in Asia Minor is a pure invention of Townson's. A decisive answer however to such a supposition here, or any where else in our Evangelist, is, that he would naturally have specified whether it was 6 A.M. or P.M. The *unusualness* of a woman coming to draw water at midday is no argument against its *possibility;* indeed the very fact of her being *alone* seems to shew that it was not the common time. This purely arbitrary hypothesis of St. John's way of reckoning the hours has been recently again upheld by Bp. Wordsworth: but it has only harmonistic grounds to rest on. The passage which he urges as supporting it, Martyr. Polycarp, c. 21, p. 1044, ed. Migne, does not in reality give it the least countenance. The ὥρα ὀγδόη there mentioned is much more probably according to the usual Roman computation. **7.**] **ἐκ τ. Σ.**, i. e. a Samaritan—so γυνὴ Χαναν. ἀπὸ τῶν ὁρίων ἐκείνων, Matt. xv. 22. **8.**] The disciples had probably taken with them the baggage, among which would be the ἄντλημα,—see ver. 11. The Rabbis say that a Jew might not eat the bread or drink the wine of a Samaritan: but that appears from this verse to be exaggerated. **9. Ἰουδαῖος ὤν**] She knew this

ὢν [s] παρ' ἐμοῦ πεῖν [s] αἰτεῖς γυναικὸς Σαμαρείτιδος οὔσης;
οὐ γὰρ [t] συγχρῶνται Ἰουδαῖοι Σαμαρείταις. 10 ἀπεκρίθη
Ἰησοῦς καὶ εἶπεν αὐτῇ Εἰ ᾔδεις τὴν [u] δωρεὰν τοῦ θεοῦ,
καὶ τίς ἐστιν ὁ λέγων σοι [p] Δός μοι [p] πεῖν, σὺ ἂν [v] ᾔτησας
αὐτόν, καὶ ἔδωκεν ἄν σοι [w] ὕδωρ [wx] ζῶν. 11 λέγει αὐτῷ
[ἡ γυνὴ] Κύριε, [y] οὔτε [z] ἄντλημα ἔχεις [y] καὶ τὸ [a] φρέαρ
ἐστὶν βαθύ· πόθεν οὖν ἔχεις τὸ ὕδωρ τὸ ζῶν; 12 μὴ σὺ

s Acts iii. 2. ix. 2. James i. 5. 1 John v. 15 only. Judg. i. 14 al. (ἀπό, Matt. xx. 20. Luke xii. 20.)
t here only †.
u Gospp., here only. Acts viii. 20. xi. 17. Rom. v. 15, 17 al. Wisd. xiii. 25.
v w. acc., Matt. v. 42 reff.
w ch. vii. 38. Rev. vii. 17. Zech. xiv. 8. see Rev. xxi. 6. xxii. 1, 17.
x = ch. vi. 51. Acts vii. 38. 1 Pet. i. 3.
y ch. v. 37, 38. 3 John 10.
z here only †.
a here bis. Luke xiv. 5. Rev. ix. 1, 2 (3ce) only. Gen. xvi. 14 al.

ων bef *πως* D lat-*a b e ff*$_2$ [*l*] syr-cu arm. rec *ουσης* bef *γυν. σαμ.*, with C³ rel latt: om *ουσης* D [arm]: txt A B(sic in cod: see table) C¹L[T$_b$]ℵ Frag-ath$_b$[sic] 33. om last clause Dℵ¹(ins ℵ-corr¹) lat-*a b e*.

10. ins *ο* bef *ιησ.* D [Π²(but erased)] 69. for *συ αν ητησας*, *συνητησας* D¹(txt D-corr¹). om *αυτον* Frag-ath$_b$[sic].

11. for *η γυνη*, *εκεινη* ℵ¹: om B. *ουδε* D. om *ουν* Dℵ Scr's c foss lat-*a b* [*e ff*$_2$ *l*] Syr syr-cu [syr-jer]. om *το* (twice, bef *υδωρ* and bef *ζων*) D 49. 91 Syr.

perhaps by his dress, more probably by his dialect. There seems to be a sort of playful triumph in the woman's question, q. d. 'even a Jew, when weary and athirst, can humble himself to ask drink of a Samaritan woman.' **οὐ γὰρ συγχρ.** . . . . are the words of the Evangelist to explain her question. *συγχράομαι* is properly spoken of *trade*,—but here is in a wider signification. Wetstein quotes from Polybius, *παρὰ Ταραντίνων καὶ Λοκρῶν συγχρησάμενοι πεντηκοντόρους καὶ τριήρεις.* Notice, 1) that this explanatory clause is omitted by Dℵ¹, and certainly *may* have been a gloss originally: but the authority is not enough to justify us in bracketing it: 2) that **Ἰουδ.** and **Σαμ.** are both anarthrous—'Jews have no dealings with Samaritans.' The fact is abundantly illustrated in the Rabbinical writings: see Schöttg. h. l. The question of the woman shews a lively naïve disposition, which is further drawn out and exemplified by Him who knew what is in man, in the following dialogue. **10.**] The important words **the gift of God** have been misunderstood by many Commentators. Some suppose them to mean '*our Lord himself*,' and to be in apposition with the next clause, *καὶ τίς ἐστιν κ.τ.λ.* Others, '*this opportunity of speaking with me.*' Doubtless both these meanings *are involved*,—especially the former: but *neither of them is the primary one*, as addressed to the woman. The WATER *is, in this first part of the discourse, the subject*, and serves as a point of connexion, whereby the woman's thoughts may be elevated, and her desire aroused. The process of the discourse in this particular is similar to that in Acts xiv. 17. From recognizing *this water* as the gift of God, in its *limitation*, ver. 13, and its *parabolic import*, ver. 14, her view is directed to Him who was speaking with her, and the Gift which He should bestow,—THE GIFT OF THE HOLY SPIRIT: see ch. vii. 37—39. **τίς ἐστιν**] These pregnant words form the *second step* in our Lord's declaration. He who speaks with thee is no ordinary Ἰουδαῖος, nor any ordinary man, but One who can give thee the gift of God; One sent from God, and God Himself. All this lies in the words, which however only serve to arouse in the woman's mind the question of ver. 12 (see below). **ὕδωρ ζῶν**] Designedly used in a double sense by our Lord, that the woman may lay hold of the *material* meaning, and by it be awakened to the *higher one* (see reff.). The words bring with them, and in our Lord's inner meaning involved, the performance of all such prophetic promises as Ezek. xxxvi. 25: Zech. xiii. 1 (see also Jer. ii. 13); but, as regarded the woman, the *ordinary sense* was that intended for her to fasten on, which she does accordingly. On the question, how this living water could be *now* given, before Jesus was glorified, see on ch. vii. 38, 39. **11, 12.**] Though **κύριε** is not to be pressed as emphatic, it is not without import; it surely betokens a different regard of the stranger than **σὺ Ἰουδαῖος ὢν** did;—*κύριον αὐτὸν προσηγόρευσε, νομίσασα μέγαν εἶναί τινα.* Euthym. The course of her thoughts appears to be:—'*Thou canst not mean living water* (*ἀναβλύζον καὶ ἁλλόμενον*, Euthym.), *from* this *well, because thou hast no vessel to draw with, and it is deep; whence then hast thou* (knowest thou of, drawest thou) *the living water of which thou speakest? Our father Jacob was contented with*

μείζων εἶ τοῦ πατρὸς ἡμῶν Ἰακώβ, ὃς ἔδωκεν ἡμῖν τὸ
[a] φρέαρ καὶ αὐτὸς [b] ἐξ αὐτοῦ [b] ἔπιεν καὶ οἱ υἱοὶ αὐτοῦ καὶ
τὰ [c] θρέμματα αὐτοῦ; 13 ἀπεκρίθη Ἰησοῦς καὶ εἶπεν αὐτῇ
Πᾶς ὁ [b] πίνων [b] ἐκ τοῦ ὕδατος τούτου [d] διψήσει πάλιν·
14 ὃς δ' ἂν [b] πίῃ [b] ἐκ τοῦ ὕδατος οὗ ἐγὼ δώσω αὐτῷ οὐ μὴ
[d] διψήσει [e] εἰς τὸν αἰῶνα, ἀλλὰ τὸ ὕδωρ ὃ δώσω αὐτῷ
γενήσεται ἐν αὐτῷ [f] πηγὴ ὕδατος [g] ἁλλομένου εἰς [h] ζωὴν
[h] αἰώνιον. 15 λέγει πρὸς αὐτὸν ἡ γυνή Κύριε, δός μοι

b Matt. xxvi. 27, 29 reff.
c here only†. Jos. Antt. vii. 7. 3.
d ch. vi. 35. vii. 37. Matt. v. 6. xxv. 35, &c. Isa. xlix. 10. Sir. xxiv. 21.
e = ch. viii. 51, 53. xiii. 8. 1 Cor. viii. 13. Gen. vi. 3.
f ver. 6 reff.
g Acts iii. 8. xiv. 10 only. Isa. xxxv. 6.
h ch. iii. 15 reff.

ABCDE FGHKL MST$_b$U VΓΔΛ ΠℵFrag. Ath$_b$. 1. 33. 69

...iv. 14 (appy) T$_b$.
..αιωνιον Frag. Ath$_b$.

12. μειζον ℵ¹. for ος, οστις ℵ. **δεδωκεν** C 69 Orig$_1$. αυτος bef και ℵ¹. om last αυτου D.

13. rec ins ο bef ιησ., with Λ [Π²(but erased)] 69 Orig$_1$: om ABCD[T$_b$]ℵ rel Chr$_1$ Cyr$_1$. (33 def.)

14. for ος δ' αν πιη, ο δε πινων Dℵ¹ [Orig$_1$(txt$_5$)] Eus$_1$[txt$_3$] : ος δ' αν πινη ℵ^{3a}. om ου μη διψ. ε. τ. αι. αλ. τ. υδ. ο δ. αυτ. (i.e. αυτω to αυτω, *homœotel*) C¹ lat-*l* sah Orig$_2$ Eus$_3$ Ambr$_1$. om μη D. rec διψηση (*gramml corrn*), with C³ rel [Orig$_1$ Eus$_1$] Thdrt$_1$: διψει Δ : txt ABDLM[T$_b$Γ]ℵ 1. 33. 69 Orig$_2$ Heracl$_1$ Chr$_1$ Cyr$_1$ Thdrt$_3$. (Frag-ath$_b$ def.) ins εγω bef 2nd δωσω DM[T$_b$]ℵ 33. 69 vulg(so am &c ; not em ing tol &c) lat-*a b* &c(not *c q*) arm [syr syr-jer Thdrt$_2$ Orig-int$_1$]. (Frag-ath$_b$ def.) om 2nd αυτω ℵ [Quæst$_1$].

this, *used it, and bequeathed it to us: if thou hast better water, and canst give it* (notice the ἔδωκεν in both verses), *thou must be greater than Jacob.*' There is something also of Samaritan nationality speaking here. Claiming Jacob as her father (ὅταν μὲν εὖ πράττοντας βλέπωσι τοὺς Ἰουδαίους, συγγενεῖς ἀποκαλοῦσιν, ὡς ἐξ Ἰωσήπου φύντες, ὅταν δὲ πταίσαντας ἴδωσιν, οὐδαμόθεν αὐτοῖς προσήκειν λέγουσιν, Jos. Antt. ix. 14. 3), she expresses by this question an appropriation of descent from him, such as almost to exclude, or at all events set at a greater distance, the Jews, to one of whom she believed herself to be speaking.

13, 14.] Our Lord, without noticing this, by His answer leaves it to be implied, that, *assuming what she has stated,* He *is greater* than Jacob: for his (Jacob's) gift was of water which cannot satisfy: but the water which He should give has *living power,* and becomes an eternal fountain within. This however, 'that *He was greater than Jacob,*' lies only in the background: *the water* is the subject, as before. The words apply to every similar quenching of desire by earthly means: the desire springs up again;—is not *satisfied,* but only *postponed.* The manna was as insufficient to satisfy hunger,—as this water, thirst, see ch. vi. 49, 58: it is only the ὕδωρ **ζῶν**, and the ἄρτος **τῆς ζωῆς**, which can *satisfy.* The **ὁ πίνων** sets forth the recurrence, the interrupted seasons, of the drinking of earthly water;—the **ὃς δ' ἂν πίῃ**—the *once having tasted,* and ever continuing in the increasing power, and living forth-flowing, of that life-long draught. **οὐ μὴ διψήσει**, shall never have to go away and be exhausted, and come again to be filled;—but shall have the spring at home, in his own breast,—so that he can "*draw water with joy out of the wells of salvation*" (Isa. xii. 3) at his pleasure. "Ubi sitis recurrit, hominis, non aquæ, defectus est." Bengel. **γενήσεται πηγή**] All earthly supplies have access only into those lower parts of our being where the desires *work themselves out*—are but *local applications;* but the heavenly gift of spiritual life which Jesus gives to those who believe on Him, enters into the *very secret* and *highest place of their personal life,* the *source whence the desires spring out;*—and, its nature being living and spiritual, it does not merely *supply,* but it *lives* and waxes onward, unto everlasting life, *in duration,* and also *as producing and sustaining it.* It should not be overlooked, that this discourse had, besides its manifold and wonderful meaning for us all, an especial moral one as applied to the woman,—who, by successive draughts at the 'broken cistern' of carnal lust, had been vainly seeking solace:—and this consideration serves to bind on the following verses (ver. 16 ff.) to the preceding, by another link besides those noticed below.

15.] This request seems to be made still under a misunderstanding, but not so great an one as at first sight appears. She apprehends this water as something not requiring an ἄντλημα to draw it;—as something whose

τοῦτο τὸ ὕδωρ, ἵνα μὴ [d] διψῶ μηδὲ [i] διέρχωμαι [k] ἐνθάδε
[l] ἀντλεῖν. 16 λέγει αὐτῇ [m] Ὕπαγε [n] φώνησόν σου τὸν
ἄνδρα καὶ ἐλθὲ [k] ἐνθάδε. 17 ἀπεκρίθη ἡ γυνὴ καὶ εἶπεν
[αὐτῷ] Οὐκ [o] ἔχω [o] ἄνδρα. λέγει αὐτῇ ὁ Ἰησοῦς [pq] Καλῶς
[q] εἶπας ὅτι [o] ἄνδρα οὐκ [o] ἔχω. 18 πέντε γὰρ [o] ἄνδρας [o] ἔσχες,
καὶ νῦν ὃν ἔχεις οὐκ ἔστιν σου ἀνήρ· τοῦτο ἀληθὲς εἴρηκας.

i = here only. (ver. 4 al.) 4 Kings iv. 42.
k = here bis. Acts xxv. 17 only. (Luke xxiv. 41. Acts x. 18 al3. only. 2 Macc. xii. 27 Ed-vat. [not AB] only.)
l ver. 7.
m Matt. iv. 10 reff.
n ch. i. 49 reff.
o = Gal. iv. 27, from Isa. liv. 1. see Matt. xxii. 28 al.
p ch. xiii. 13 reff.
q Luke xx. 39.

15. for διψω, δειψησω D^1. rec (for διερχ.) ερχωμαι, with ACDSUVΔ[ΓΠ] (1, e sil) [Chr_1 $Cyr\text{-}p_1$], ερχομαι $L\aleph^{3a}$ rel: txt $\aleph^1$ $Orig_4$, διερχομαι B(sic: see table) $Orig_1$. for ενθαδε, ωδε $\aleph^1$.

16. rec aft αυτη ins ο ιησους, with $C^2D[\Pi^2]\aleph^{3a}$ rel, ιησ. $A[\Pi^{1\cdot3}]\aleph^1$ 1: om BC^1 33 lat-*a* $Heracl_1$ $Orig_1$. ins καλ (sic) bef υπαγε $\aleph^1$(corrd $\aleph^{1\cdot3}$). rec τον ανδρα bef σου, with ACDℵ rel: txt B 69 $Orig_3$.

17. om και ειπεν $\aleph^1$. rec om αυτω, with ADℵ rel vulg lat-*c e f* [*q*] syr copt $Orig_2$: ins BCEFGH 33 lat-*a b l* Syr syr-cu sah æth (arm). ανδρα bef ουκ εχω $C^1DL\aleph$ Cyr_1: txt ABC^3 rel [latt Chr_1] $Orig_2$. ειπες $B^1\aleph$ [Chr_1(and 4-mss) Cyr_1]. for 2nd εχω, εχεις Dℵ lat-*b c e l* $Heracl_1$.

18. αληθως E(Tischdf) ℵ Scr's t.

power shall never fail;—which shall quench thirst for ever;—and half in banter, half in earnest, wishing perhaps besides to see whether the gift would after all be conferred, and how,—she mingles in with the τοῦτο τὸ ὕδωρ,—implying some view of its distinct nature,—her 'not coming hither to draw,'—her willing avoidance of the toil of her noonday journey to the well. We must be able to enter into the complication of her character, and the impressions made on her by the strange things which she has heard, fully to appreciate the spirit of this answer. **16.**] The connexion of this verse with the foregoing has been much disputed; and the strangest and most unworthy views have been taken of it. Some (e. g. Grotius) have strangely referred it to the supposed indecorum of the longer continuance of the colloquy with the woman alone; some more strangely still (Cyril Alex. in Catena, Lücke, p. 588) to the incapacity of the female mind to apprehend the matters of which He was to speak. Both these need surely no refutation. The band of women from Galilee, "last at the cross, and earliest at the tomb," are a sufficient answer to them. Those approach nearer the truth, who believe the command to have been given *to awaken her conscience* (Maldonatus and al.); or to shew her the divine knowledge which the Lord had of her heart (Meyer). But I am persuaded that the right account is found, in viewing this command, as the *first step of granting her request*, δός μοι τοῦτο τὸ ὕδωρ. The first work of the Spirit of God, and of Him who here spoke in the fulness of that Spirit, is, to *convince of sin*. The 'give me this water' was not so simple a matter as she supposed. The heart must first be laid bare before the Wisdom of God: the secret sins set in the light of His countenance; and this our Lord here does. The command itself is of course given in the fulness of knowledge of her sinful condition of life. In every conversation which our Lord held with men, while He connects usually one remark with another by the common links which bind human thought, we perceive that He knows, and sees through, those with whom He speaks. Euthymius, though not seeing the whole bearing of the command, expresses well this last remark:—ἐγκειμένης καὶ ζητούσης λαβεῖν, λέγει Ὕπαγε κ.τ.λ. προσποιούμενος ὅτι χρὴ κἀκεῖνον κοινωνῆσαι ταύτῃ τοῦ δώρου. καὶ ὅτι μὲν οὐκ ἔχει ἄνδρα νόμιμον ἐγίνωσκεν, ὡς πάντα εἰδώς· ἐβούλετο δὲ ταύτην εἰπεῖν ὅτι οὐκ ἔχω ἄνδρα, ἵνα λοιπόν, προφάσεως δραξάμενος, προφητεύσῃ τὰ κατ' αὐτὴν καὶ διορθώσηται ταύτην. θέλει γὰρ τῶν προῤῥήσεων καὶ τῶν θαυμάτων τὰς ἀφορμὰς παρ' αὐτῶν λαμβάνειν τῶν προσιόντων, ὥστε καὶ τὴν τοῦ κενοδοξεῖν ὑπόνοιαν διαφεύγειν, καὶ οἰκειοῦσθαι μᾶλλον αὐτούς. **17.**] This answer is not for a moment to be treated as something unexpected by Him who commanded her (Lücke). He *has before Him her whole life of sin*, which she in vain endeavours to cover by the doubtful words of this verse. **18.**] There was *literal* truth, but no more, in the woman's answer: and the Lord, by His divine knowledge, detects the hidden falsehood of it. Notice it is ἀληθές, not ἀληθῶς: this *one word* was *true*: further shewn by the emphatic position of ἄνδρα in our Lord's answer. **πέντε γὰρ ἄνδ. ἔσχες**] These five *were certainly lawful*

r = and constr., ch. xii. 19. Acts xxvii. 10. 2 Macc. ix. 23. see ch. vi. 40. ix. 8. xiv. 17.
s = ch. xii. 20. Acts viii. 27. xxiv. 11.
t constr., ch. v. 24 reff.
u ch. v. 25, 28. xvi. 2, 25, 32.
v w. dat., Matt. ii. 2 reff. w. acc., Luke xxiv. 52 reff.

19 λέγει αὐτῷ ἡ γυνὴ Κύριε, [r] θεωρῶ ὅτι προφήτης εἶ σύ.
20 οἱ πατέρες ἡμῶν ἐν τῷ ὄρει τούτῳ [s] προςεκύνησαν, καὶ
ὑμεῖς λέγετε ὅτι ἐν Ἱεροσολύμοις ἐστὶν ὁ τόπος ὅπου
[s] προςκυνεῖν δεῖ. 21 λέγει αὐτῇ ὁ Ἰησοῦς [t] Πίστευέ μοι,
γύναι, ὅτι [u] ἔρχεται ὥρα ὅτε οὔτε ἐν τῷ ὄρει τούτῳ οὔτε ἐν
Ἱεροσολύμοις [v] προςκυνήσετε τῷ πατρί. 22 ὑμεῖς [v] προς-

ABCDE FGHKL MSUV ΓΔΛΠℵ 1. 33. 69

19. om *κυριε* ℵ[1] 245. om *συ* D lat-*a b e l* Hil$_1$.

20. rec *τουτω* bef *τω ορει*, with (244 Scr's g, e sil) lat-*a b e* [D-lat syr-jer] Syr syr-cu Orig-int$_1$ Tert$_1$: txt ABC D[-gr] ℵ rel Scr's-mss vulg lat-*c f ff*$_2$ *l* [*q*] syr Orig$_4$ Chr$_1$ Cyr[-p] Thdrt$_1$ Thl Hil$_1$. om *ο τοπος* ℵ [(Tert$_1$)]. rec *δει* bef *προσκυνειν*, with C[3] rel lat-*e* syrr coptt arm Epiph$_1$ Chr$_1$ Thdrt$_1$ Tert$_1$: txt ABC[1]DLℵ 33 latt Orig$_2$[int$_1$] Cyr[-p] Hil$_1$.

21. rec *γυναι* bef *πιστ. μοι*, with AC[3]D rel vulg lat-*a*(appy) *c e f* syrr syr-cu copt arm Thdrt$_1$: txt BC[1]Lℵ lat-*b q* sah [syr-jer æth] Heracl$_1$ Orig$_1$ Ath$_1$ Cyr[-p] Hil$_1$.—om *γυν.* F.—om *μοι* Δ.—rec *πιστευσον*, with AC[3] rel: txt BC[1]DLℵ 1. 69 sah-gr Orig$_1$ [Heracl$_1$ Ath$_1$ *Cyr*-p]. (33 def.) for *οτε*, *οτι* AV[Γ]Λ 69. *τουτω* bef *τω ορει* D lat-*a b e* Syr syr-cu Hil$_1$.

husbands; they are distinguished from the sixth, who *was not;*—probably the woman had been separated from some by divorce (the law of which was but loose among the Samaritans),—from some by death,—or perhaps by other reasons more or less discreditable to her character, which had now become degraded into that of an openly licentious woman. The conviction of sin here lies beneath the surface: it is not pressed, nor at the moment does it seem to have worked deeply, for she goes on with the conversation with apparent indifference to it; but our Lord's words in vv. 25, 26 would tend to infix it more deeply, and we find at ver. 29, that it had been working during her journey back to the city. **19.**] In speaking this her conviction, she virtually confesses all the truth. That she should pass to another subject immediately, seems, as Stier remarks (iv. 125, edn. 2), to arise, not from a wish to turn the conversation from a matter so unpleasing to her, but from a real desire to obtain from this Prophet the teaching requisite that she may pray to God acceptably. The idea of her endeavouring to *escape from the Lord's rebuke*, is quite inconsistent with her recognition of Him as a prophet. Rather we may suppose a pause, which makes it evident that He does not mean to proceed further with His laying open of her character. Obs., not *σύ* (Wordsw.), but *προφήτης*, is the word of primary emphasis. *σύ* has the secondary emphasis, by its very *expression.* **20.**] **ἐν τῷ ὄρει τούτῳ**—Mount Gerizim, on which once stood the national temple of the Samaritan race. In Neh. xiii. 28 we read that the grandson of the high-priest Eliashib was banished by Nehemiah because he was son-in-law to Sanballat, the Persian satrap of Samaria. Him Sanballat not only received, but (Jos. Antt. xi. 8. 2—4) made him high-priest of a temple which he built on Mount Gerizim. Josephus makes this appointment sanctioned by Alexander, when at Tyre;—but the chronology is certainly not accurate, for between Sanballat and Alexander is a difference of nearly a century. This temple was destroyed 200 years after by John Hyrcanus (B.C. 129), see Jos. Antt. xiii. 9. 1; but the Samaritans still used it as a place of prayer and sacrifice, and to this day the few Samaritans resident in Nablus (Sychem) call it the holy mountain, and turn their faces to it in prayer.

They defended their practice by Deut. xxvii. 4, where our reading and the Hebr. and LXX is Ebal, but that of the Samaritan Pentateuch, Gerizim (probably an alteration): also by Gen. xii. 6, 7; xiii. 4; xxxiii. 18, 20: Deut. xi. 26 ff. **Our fathers** most likely mean *not the patriarchs*, but the ancestors of the then Samaritans. **ὁ τόπος**] The definite place spoken of Deut. xii. 5. She pauses, having suggested, rather than asked, a question,—seeming to imply, 'Before I can receive this gift of God, it must be decided, *where* I can acceptably pray for it;' and she leaves it for Him whom she now recognizes as a prophet, to resolve this doubt. **21.**] Our Lord first raises her view to a higher point than her question implied, or than indeed she, or any one, without His prophetic announcement, could then have attained. **οὔτε .... οὔτε** are *exclusive:* **Ye shall worship the Father, but not (only) in this mountain,**

κυνεῖτε ὃ οὐκ οἴδατε· ἡμεῖς [v] προςκυνοῦμεν ὃ οἴδαμεν, ὅτι
ἡ [w] σωτηρία ἐκ τῶν Ἰουδαίων ἐστίν. 23 ἀλλὰ [ux] ἔρχεται
ὥρα [x] καὶ νῦν ἐστίν, ὅτε οἱ [y] ἀληθινοὶ [z] προςκυνηταὶ προς-
κυνήσουσιν τῷ πατρὶ ἐν [a] πνεύματι καὶ [b] ἀληθείᾳ. καὶ
γὰρ ὁ πατὴρ τοιούτους [c] ζητεῖ τοὺς [v] προςκυνοῦντας αὐτόν.
24 [d] πνεῦμα ὁ θεός, καὶ τοὺς [v] προςκυνοῦντας αὐτὸν ἐν

...πνευματι και F.

w John, here only. Luke i. 69, 71, 77. xix. 9 only in Gospp. Acts xiii. 47 (from Isa. xlix. 6) al.
x ch. v. 25 only.
y ch. i. 9 reff.
z here only †.
a = 1 Cor. xiv. 15, 16. Eph. vi. 18.
b 2 Cor. vii. 14. 1 Tim. ii. 7. 1 John iii. 18.
c — ch. i. 38. ver. 27. 2 Cor. xii. 14.
d = Luke xxiv. 38, 39. Heb. xii. 23. 1 Pet. iii. 19.

23. (αλλα, so ABDℵ.) αυτω ℵ[1] [αυτων Γ].
24. om αυτον D[1](ins D[3]) ℵ[1] $Heracl_1$ $Novat_1$.

nor in Jerusalem:—had it been οὐδὲ .... οὐδέ, it would have meant, '*Ye shall not worship the Father, either in this mountain, or even in Jerusalem.*' The **προςκυνήσετε**, though embracing in its wider sense *all mankind*, may be taken primarily as foretelling the success of the gospel in Samaria, Acts viii. 1—25.
τῷ πατρί, as implying the One God and Father of all. There is also, as Calvin remarks (Stier, iv. 129, edn. 2), a "tacita oppositio" between **ὁ πατήρ**,—and ὁ π. ἡμ. **Ἰακώβ**, ver. 12, οἱ πατέρες ἡμῶν, ver. 20.

22.] But he will not leave the temple of Zion and the worship appointed by God without His testimony. He decides her question not merely by affirming, but by *proving* the Jewish worship to be the right one. In the Samaritan worship there was no leading of God to guide them, there were no prophetic voices revealing more and more of His purposes. The neuter **ὃ** is used to shew the want of personality and distinctness in their idea of God:—the second **ὃ**, merely as corresponding to it in the other member of the sentence. Or perhaps better, *both*, as designating merely the abstract *object of worship*, not the personal God. The **ἡμεῖς** is remarkable, as being the *only instance* of our Lord thus speaking. But the nature of the case accounts for it. He never elsewhere is speaking to one so set in opposition to the Jews on a point where Himself and the Jews stood together for God's truth. He now speaks *as a Jew*. The nearest approach to it is in His answer to the Canaanitish woman, Matt. xv. 24, 26. **ὅτι, because**: this is *the reason* why we know what we worship, because the promises of God are made to us, and we possess them and believe them: see Rom. iii. 1, 2.
ἡ σωτ. ἐκ τ. Ἰ. ἐστ.] It was in this point especially, expectation of the promised salvation by the great Deliverer (see Gen. xlix. 18), that the Samaritan rejection of the prophetic word had made them so deficient in comparison of the Jews. But not only this;—the Messiah Himself was to spring from among the Jews, and *had sprung* from among them;—not **ἔσται**, but **ἐστίν**, the abstract present, but perhaps with a reference to what was then happening. See Isa. ii. 1—3. **23.**] The discourse returns to the ground taken in ver. 21, but not so as to make ver. 22 parenthetical only: the spiritual worship now to be spoken of is the carrying out and consequence of the σωτηρία just mentioned, and could not have been brought in without it. **καὶ νῦν ἐστίν**] "Hoc (versu 21 non additum) nunc additur, ne mulier putet, sibi tantisper sedem in Judæa quærendam esse." Bengel. **οἱ ἀληθ. προςκ.**, as distinguished (1) from *hypocrites*, who have pretended to worship Him: (2) from *all* who went before, whose worship was necessarily imperfect.
The **ἐν πνεύματι καὶ ἀληθείᾳ** (not without an allusion to **ἐν τούτῳ τῷ ὄρει**) is, in its first meaning, opposed to ἐν ἔθει καὶ ψεύδει,—and denotes the *earnestness of spirit* with which the true worshippers shall worship: so Ps. cxliv. 18, ἐγγὺς κύριος πᾶσιν τοῖς ἐπικαλουμένοις αὐτὸν **ἐν ἀληθείᾳ**. A deeper meaning is brought out where the ground of this kind of worship is stated, in the next verse. **ζητεῖ**—not only 'requires,' from His very nature, **but seeks,—is seeking**. This seeking on the part of the Father naturally brings in the idea, in the woman's answer, of the Messiah, *by Whom* He seeks (Luke xix. 10) His true worshippers to gather them out of the world. **τοὺς προσκ.**] The construction is, the Father is seeking for such to be οἱ προσκυνοῦντες αὐτόν,—'*for* οἱ προσκ. αὐτ. *of this kind*.' **τοιούτους** *may be* the predicate—'*such the Father seeketh his worshippers to be*:' or it may be the object—'*such the Father seeketh as* (or *to be*) *his worshippers*.'

24.] **πνεῦμα ὁ θεός** was the great Truth of Judaism, whereby the Jews were distinguished from the idolatrous people around them. And the Samaritans held even more strongly than the Jews the pure monotheistic view. Traces of this, remarks

e ch. i. 42 only. f pres., Luke xvii. 20 reff. g = ch. xvi. 13, 14, 15. Acts xx. 20, 27. 1 Pet. i. 12. Josh. iv. 10. h ch. viii. 24, 58. xviii. 5, 6, 8. Deut. xxxii. 39. i = 2 Cor. vii. 4. Eph. iv. 26. 1 Thess. iii. 7. Deut. xxiv. 17 (15).

[a] πνεύματι καὶ [b] ἀληθείᾳ δεῖ προσκυνεῖν. 25 λέγει αὐτῷ ἡ
γυνὴ Οἶδα ὅτι [e] μεσσίας [f] ἔρχεται, ὁ λεγόμενος χριστός·
ὅταν ἔλθῃ ἐκεῖνος, [g] ἀναγγελεῖ ἡμῖν ἅπαντα. 26 λέγει αὐτῇ
ὁ Ἰησοῦς [h] Ἐγώ εἰμι, ὁ λαλῶν σοι. 27 Καὶ [i] ἐπὶ τούτῳ

ABCDE GHKL MSUV ΓΔΛΠא 1. 33. 69

for και αληθεια, αληθειας א[1]. προσκυνειν bef δει Dא[1] lat-*a* Novat$_1$ Hil$_1$ [Victorin$_1$].

25. οιδαμεν GLΛא[3a] 33. 69 syr-mg coptt Orig$_1$ [*Cyr*-p]. αναγγελλει D-gr א[1]. rec (for απαντα) παντα, with AC[2]D rel [Chr$_1$ Cyr-p$_2$]: txt BC[1]א 1 Orig$_3$.

26. om 1st ο A.

27. for επι, εν Dא[1] [copt].

Lücke (from Gesenius), i. 599 note, are found in the alterations made by them in their Pentateuch, long before the time of this history. This may perhaps be partly the reason why our Lord, as Bengel remarks, "Discipulis non tradidit sublimiora," than to this Samaritan woman. God being pure **spirit** (perhaps better not '*a* Spirit,' since it is His *Essence*, not His Personality, which is here spoken of), cannot dwell in particular spots or temples (see Acts vii. 48; xvii. 24, 25); cannot require, nor be pleased with, earthly material offerings nor ceremonies, as such: on the other hand, is only to be approached in *that part of our being, which is spirit*,—and even there, inasmuch as He is pure and holy, with no by-ends nor hypocritical regards, but in truth and earnestness. But here comes in the deeper sense alluded to above. How is the spirit of man to be brought into communion with God? "In *templo* vis orare; in *te ora*. Sed prius *esto* templum Dei." Aug. (Stier, iv. 137, edn. 2.) And how is this to be? *Man cannot make himself the temple of God.* So that here comes in the *gift of God*, with which the discourse began,—*the gift of the Holy Spirit*, which Christ should give to them that believe on Him: thus we have '*praying* ἐν πνεύματι ἁγίῳ,' Jude 20. So beautifully does the expression **ὁ πατήρ** here bring with it the new birth by the Spirit,—and for us, the readers of the Gospel, does the discourse of ch. iii. reflect light on this. And so wonderfully do these words form the conclusion to the great subject of these first chapters: 'GOD IS BECOME ONE FLESH WITH US, THAT WE MIGHT BECOME ONE SPIRIT WITH HIM.' **25.**] These words again seem uttered under a complicated feeling. From her λαλιά, ver. 29, she certainly had some suspicion (in her own mind, perhaps over and beyond His own assertion of the fact: but see note there) that He who had told her all things, &c., *was the Christ*; and from her breaking in with this remark after the weighty truth which had been just spoken, it seems as if she thought thus, '*How these matters may be, I cannot understand;—they will be all made clear when the Christ shall come.*' The question of ver. 20 had not been answered to her liking or expectation: she therefore puts aside, as it were, what has been said, by a remark on that suspicion which was arising in her mind. It is not certain what expectations the Samaritans had regarding the Messiah. The view here advanced might be well derived from Deut. xviii. 15;—and the name, and much that belonged to it, might have been borrowed from the Jews originally. **ὁ λεγόμ. χριστός** appear to me to be the words of the woman, *not of the Evangelist*; for in this latter case he would certainly have used ὁ μεσσίας again in ver. 29. See also the difference of expression where he inserts an interpretation, ch. i. 42; xix. 13, 17. It is possible that the name ὁ χριστός had become common in popular parlance, like many other Greek words and names. **ἀναγγέλλω** is used especially of *enouncing* or *propounding* by *divine or superior authority*,—see reff. **26.**] * Of the *reasons* which our Lord had, thus to declare Himself to this Samaritan woman and through her to the inhabitants of Sychem (ver. 42), as the Christ, thus early in his ministry, we surely are not qualified to judge. There is nothing so opposed to true Scripture criticism, as to form a preconceived plan and rationale of the course of our Lord in the flesh, and then to force recorded events into agreement with it. Such a plan *will be formed* in our own minds from continued study of the Scripture narrative:—but by the arbitrary and procrustean system which I am here condemning, the very facts which are the chief data of such a scheme, are themselves set aside. When De Wette says, "This early and decided declaration of Jesus is in contradiction with Matt. viii. 4, and xvi. 20,"—he forgets the very different circumstances under which both those injunctions were spoken:—while he

ἦλθον οἱ μαθηταὶ αὐτοῦ, καὶ [k] ἐθαύμαζον ὅτι μετὰ γυναικὸς
ἐλάλει· οὐδεὶς μέντοι εἶπεν Τί ζητεῖς; ἢ Τί λαλεῖς μετ'
αὐτῆς; 28 [l] ἀφῆκεν οὖν τὴν [m] ὑδρίαν αὐτῆς ἡ γυνὴ καὶ
ἀπῆλθεν εἰς τὴν πόλιν, καὶ λέγει τοῖς ἀνθρώποις 29 Δεῦτε
ἴδετε ἄνθρωπον ὃς εἶπέν μοι πάντα ὅσα ἐποίησα· [n] μήτι
οὗτός ἐστιν ὁ χριστός; 30 ἐξῆλθον ἐκ τῆς πόλεως, καὶ
ἤρχοντο πρὸς αὐτόν. 31 [o] Ἐν τῷ [o] μεταξὺ [p] ἠρώτων
αὐτὸν οἱ μαθηταὶ λέγοντες Ῥαββί, φάγε. 32 ὁ δὲ εἶπεν
αὐτοῖς Ἐγὼ [q] βρῶσιν ἔχω φαγεῖν ἣν ὑμεῖς οὐκ οἴδατε.
33 ἔλεγον οὖν οἱ μαθηταὶ πρὸς ἀλλήλους [r] Μή τις ἤνεγκεν
T_b iv. 34 (appy)... αὐτῷ [s] φαγεῖν; 34 λέγει αὐτοῖς ὁ Ἰησοῦς Ἐμὸν [t] βρῶμά

k ch. iii. 7 reff.
l = Matt. iv. 11 al.
m ch. ii. 6, 7 only. Gen. xxiv. 14, &c.
n Matt. vii. 16 reff.
o here only. see Acts xiii. 42.
p = Matt. xv. 23 reff.
q = ch. vi. 27 bis, 55. Rom. xiv. 17. 1 Cor. viii. 4. 2 Cor. ix. 10. Col. ii. 16. Heb. xii. 16 (Matt. vi. 19, 20) only. Gen. xlvii. 24.
r ch. vii. 48 only.
s see Matt. xiv. 16 reff. ver. 7.
t Matt. xiv. 15. Luke iii. 11. 1 Cor. x. 3 al. Ps. lxviii. 21.

επηλθαν ℵ[1] [lat-*e q*]: ηλθαν B[1]. rec εθαυμα**σαν** (*conformn to foregoing aor*), with E rel [syr] sah: txt ABCDGKLM[Π]ℵ 1. 33 latt Syr [syr-cu syr-jer arm] copt $Orig_2$ Chr_1 Cyr_1 Thl. aft ειπεν ins αυτω Dℵ lat-*a* (*b*) [ff_2 foss syr-cu copt æth].

28. η γυνη bef την υδριαν αυτης D lat-*b l* [*e q* syr] syr-cu sah arm.—**ε**αυτης D.

29. for οσα, **α** BC[1]ℵ lat-*a e q* [D-lat] coptt $Orig_1$-mss [Cyr-p_1]. for **ουτος**, **εκεινος** D [lat-*q*].

30. rec aft εξηλθον ins **ουν**, with Λℵ (1. 69, e sil) vulg-ed lat-*e f* [*l q*] coptt: [δε $Π^2$ $Orig_1$:] pref **και** CD lat-*b* syrr syr-cu æth: om AB rel am(with em forj. fuld [ing] tol) [lat-*c g*] arm $Orig_2$ [Cyr-p_1].

31. rec aft εν ins δε, with AC[3] rel lat-*b f q* syr [syr-cu] copt [$Orig_1$] Chr_1: om BC[1]DLℵ vulg lat-*a*(appy) *c e g* [*l* syr-jer] $Orig_2$ [Cyr-p_1]. ηρωτου**ν** C 69.

33. for ελεγον, λεγουσιν ℵ[1] [lat-*b* $Quæst_1$].—for ουν, δε D-gr lat-*a b q* [syr-jer]: om ℵ[1] lat-*e* D-lat Syr syr-cu. for οι μαθ. **προς** αλλ., εν εαυτοις οι μαθ. D-gr lat-ff_2.

is forced to confess that it is in agreement with the whole spirit of the Sermon on the Mount. He who knew what was in man, varied His revelations and injunctions, as the time and place, and individual dispositions required. **ἐγώ εἰμι**] The verb involves in it the predicate. **ὁ λαλῶν σοι** has a reference to her words, ἀναγγελεῖ ἡμ. πάντα—**I am He, who am now speaking to thee**—fulfilling part of this *telling all things*: see also her confession ver. 29.

27.] **μετὰ γυν., with a woman.** No inference, it is true, can be drawn as to the indefiniteness of the noun, from the omission of the article *after a preposition*, see Bp. Middleton, ch. vi. § 1: but the position of μετὰ γυναικός before the verb throws an emphasis on the words, and makes it probable that the meaning is as above. **τί ζητεῖς; κ.τ.λ.**] Either—*to the woman*—**What seekest thou?** and to the Lord, **Why talkest thou with her?**—or perhaps both questions *to Him*: and then we must suppose a mixture of two constructions, of τί ζ. παρ' αὐτῆς;—and τί λαλεῖς μετ' αὐτῆς;—I rather prefer the former interpretation. **28—30.**] She does not mention to the men *His own* announcement of Himself,—but as is most natural under such circumstances, rests the matter on the testimony likely to weigh most with them,—*her own*. We often, and that unconsciously, put before another not *our* strongest, but what is likely to be *his* strongest reason. At the same time she shews how the suspicion expressed in ver. 25 arose in her own mind. **30.**] * **ἤρχοντο—were coming,**—had not arrived, when what follows happened.

31, 32.] The bodily thirst (and hunger probably, from the time of day) which our Lord had felt before, had been and was forgotten in the carrying on of His divine work in the soul of this Samaritan woman. Although **ἐγώ** and **ὑμεῖς** are emphatic, the words are not spoken in *blame*, for none was deserved: but in fulness and earnestness of spirit;—in a feeling analogous to that which comes upon us when called from high and holy employment to the supply of the body or business of this world. **βρῶσις**, generally distinguished, as 'eating,' from βρῶμα, 'food' (see ref. 1 Cor.),—is here equivalent to it.

33.] It is very characteristic of the first part of this Gospel to bring forward instances of unreceptivity of spiritual meaning: compare ver. 11; ch. ii. 20; iii. 4; vi. 42, 52. The disciples probably have the woman in their thoughts.

34.] Christ alone could properly

u Matt. vii. 21 reff.
v = ch. v. 36. xvii. 4. Acts xx. 24. 2 Chron. viii. 16.

ἐστιν ἵνα [u] ποιήσω τὸ [u] θέλημα τοῦ πέμψαντός με καὶ
[v] τελειώσω αὐτοῦ τὸ ἔργον. 35 οὐχ ὑμεῖς λέγετε ὅτι ἔτι
[w] τετράμηνός ἐστιν καὶ ὁ [x] θερισμὸς ἔρχεται; ἰδοὺ λέγω

ABCDE GHKL MST_bU ΥΓΔΛΠ ℵ 1. 33. 69

w here only. Judg. xix. 2 & xx. 47 A. see Heb. xi. 23. x Matt. ix. 37, 38 bis. xiii. 30 bis, 39. Mark iv. 29. Luke x. 2 (3ce). 1 Cor. ix. 11. Rev. xiv. 15 only. Gen. viii. 22.

34. rec (for ποιησω) ποιω, with Aℵ rel $Hipp_1$ $Orig_1$ [Bas_2 $Antch_1$]: txt BCDKL [T_bΠ] 1. 33 arm(appy) Clem $Orig_6$ [*Cyr*-p].

35. om ετι (*homœotel*) DL[Π[1]] 1. 69 syr-cu $Orig_5$ Chr_1 Cyr[-p_1]. rec τετραμηνον (*cf Heb* xi. 23), with H Scr's p: txt ABC[2]D[T_b]ℵ rel $Orig_8$ Chr[-4-mss_1] Cyr_1 Thl.—(In C[1] it appears to have been written τραμηνος by mistake, or perhaps τριμηνος as in 14.)

say these words. In the believer on Him, they are partially true,—true as far as he has received the Spirit, and entered into the spiritual life;—but in Him they were absolutely and fully true. His whole life was the doing of the Father's will. We can 'eat and drink, &c. to the glory of God,'—but in Him the hallowing of the Father's name, doing His will, bringing about His Kingdom, was His *daily bread*, and superseded the thoughts and desires for the other, needful as *it* was for His humanity. ἵνα is not = ὅτι. The latter would imply what was true (but not here expressed), that *the absolute doing*, &c. was His food;—as it now stands, it implies that it was His food to *carry onward* to completion that work: to be ever, step after step, having regard to its being completed. **My meat is** (not *to do*, as E. V., but) **that I may do**, &c. In the **τελειώσω αὐτοῦ τὸ ἔργον**, the way is prepared for the idea introduced in the next verse. These words give an answer to the questioning in the minds of the disciples, and shew *that He had been employed in the Father's work during their absence*. **35.**] The sense of these much-controverted words will be best ascertained by narrowly observing the form of the sentence. **οὐχ ὑμεῖς λέγετε ὅτι . . . .** surely *cannot be the introduction to an observation of what was matter of fact at the time*. Had the words been spoken *at a time when it wanted four months to the harvest*, and had our Lord *intended to express this*,—is it conceivable that He should have thus introduced the remark? Would not, *must* not, the question have been a *direct* one in that case—'*are there not four months?*' &c. I know not how to account for this οὐχ ὑμεῖς λέγετε ὅτι . . . . except that it introduces *some common saying* which the Jews, or perhaps the people of Galilee only, were in the habit of using. **Are not ye accustomed to say, that . . . . ?** That we hear of no such proverb elsewhere, is not to the point;—for such unrecorded sayings are among every people. That we do not know whence to date the four months, is again no objection:—there may have been, in the part where the saying was usual (possibly in the land west of the lake of Tiberias, for those addressed were from thence, and the emphatic ὑμεῖς seems to point to some particular locality), *some fixed period* in the year,—the end of the sowing, or some religious anniversary,—when it was *a common saying, that it wanted four months to harvest*. And this might have been the first date in the year which had regard to the harvest, and so the best known in connexion with it.

If this be so, all that has been built on *this* saying, as giving a chronological date, must fall to the ground. (Lightfoot, Meyer (1), Wieseler, i. p. 215 ff., and others, maintain, that since the harvest began on the 16th of Nisan, we must reckon four months back from that time for this journey through Samaria, which would bring it to the middle of Chisleu, i. e. the beginning of December.)

To get the meaning of the latter part of the verse, we must endeavour to follow, as far as may be, the train of thought which pervades the discourse. He that soweth the good seed is the Son of Man: our Lord had now been employed in this His work. But not as in the natural year, so was it to be in the world's lifetime. One-third of the year may elapse, or more, before the sown seed springs up; but the *sowing by the Son of Man* comes late in time, and the harvest should immediately follow. The fields were whitening for it; these Samaritans (not that I believe He *pointed to them approaching*, as Chrys. and most expositors, but had them in his view in what he said), and the multitudes in Galilee, were all nearly ready. In the discourse as far as ver. 38, He is ὁ σπείρων, the disciples (see Acts viii.) were οἱ θερίζοντες:—He was the κεκοπιακώς, they were the εἰς τὸν κόπον αὐτοῦ εἰσεληλυθότες. The *past* is used, as descriptive of the office which each held, not of the actual thing done. I cannot also but see an allusion to the words spoken by Joshua (xxiv.

ὑμῖν [y] ἐπάρατε τοὺς [y] ὀφθαλμοὺς ὑμῶν καὶ [z] θεάσασθε τὰς
[a] χώρας, ὅτι λευκαί εἰσιν [b] πρὸς [x] θερισμὸν ἤδη. 36 ὁ
[c] θερίζων [d] μισθὸν λαμβάνει, καὶ [e] συνάγει καρπὸν εἰς
[f] ζωὴν [f] αἰώνιον· ἵνα [καὶ] ὁ [g] σπείρων [h] ὁμοῦ χαίρῃ καὶ ὁ
[cg] θερίζων. 37 [i] ἐν γὰρ τούτῳ ὁ λόγος [l] ἐστὶν [ὁ] [k] ἀληθινός,
ὅτι ἄλλος ἐστὶν ὁ [g] σπείρων καὶ ἄλλος ὁ [cg] θερίζων. 38 ἐγὼ
F υμας... ἀπέστειλα ὑμᾶς [c] θερίζειν ὃ οὐχ ὑμεῖς [l] κεκοπιάκατε· ἄλλοι
...iv. 38 (appy) T_b. [l] κεκοπιάκασιν, καὶ ὑμεῖς εἰς τὸν [m] κόπον αὐτῶν [n] εἰσεληλύ-

y Matt. xvii. 8 reff. z Luke xxiii. 55 reff. a = Luke xii. 16. xxi. 21. James v. 4. Sir. xliii. 3. b = 2 Cor. x. 4. Tit. iii. 1 al. c w. σπείρ., as below (g). otherwise, here bis. Gal. vi. 9. James v. 4. Rev. xiv. 15 bis, 16. Ruth ii. 4. partic., as Matt. iv. 3. d = Matt. xx. 8. Prov. xi. 12. e = Matt. iii. 12 || L. xiii. 30. Ps. xxxviii. 6. f ch. iii. 15 reff. g here bis. Matt. vi. 26. xxv. 24, 26 || L. Luke xii. 24. 1 Cor. ix. 11. 2 Cor. ix. 6 bis. Gal. vi. 7, 8 bis. Jer. xii. 13. h ch. xx. 4 reff. i see ch. i. 4. 1 John v. 11. k = ch. xix. 35. Rev. xv. 3. xvi. 7 al. 2 Chron. ix. 5. l = Matt. vi. 28. Luke v. 5 al. (ver. 6 reff.) Josh. xxiv. 13. m = 1 Cor. iii. 8. xv. 58. 2 Cor. vi. 5 al. (Matt. xxvi. 10 reff.) Wisd. x. 17. n = here only. see Heb. iii. 11, &c.

AC¹DEL [ℵ³(Tischdf)] lat-*b l q* syr-cu Eus_1 $Thdrt_2$ [(Iren-int_1)] join ηδη with what follows: txt (*see note*) C²GHKUΔΛ[ΣΓΠ²] syr copt-wilk Orig Eus: om ηδη lat-*a* syr-jer copt-dz æth [arm] Chr_1 Hil_2.

36. rec at beg ins και, with AC² rel vulg lat-*c f ff*₂ Syr syr-cu copt-ed æth arm $Cyr\text{-}jer_1$ Chr_1 [Cyr-p_1]: om BC¹DL[T_b]ℵ 33 lat-*a b e l q* copt-dz $Orig_5$ Cyr_1 Iren-int_1. om και (bef ο σπ.) BCL[T_b]U 1. 33 lat-*e g* syr [syr-jer] copt arm $Orig_4$ $Heracl_1$ [Cyr_1]: ins ADℵ rel. και ο θερ. bef ομου χ. D Syr syr-cu [syr-jer] æth Iren-int_1. χαρη D.

37. εστιν bef ο λογος D 301 Scr's p latt copt arm $Heracl_1$ Iren-int_1. om ο (bef αληθινος) BC¹KLΔ[T_bΠ¹] 1. 33 arm $Orig_3$ $Heracl_1$ Chr[-6-mss_1] Cyr_1 Thl: ins AC³Dℵ rel.

38. απεσταλκα Dℵ. om ο D¹(ins D³) L lat-*e*. εκοπιασατε and εκοπιασαν D.

13), *on this very spot;*—'I have given you a land for which ye did not labour'—ἐφ' ἣν οὐκ **ἐκοπιάσατε** ἐπ' αὐτῆς (αὐτήν A). Taking this view, *I do not believe there was any allusion to the actual state of the fields at that time.* The words **ἐπάρατε** κ.τ.λ. are of course to be understood *literally;*—they were to lift up their eyes and look on the lands around them;—and then came the assurance; 'they are whitening already towards the harvest.' And it seems to me that on *this view*—of the Lord speaking of spiritual things to them, and announcing to them the approach of the spiritual harvest, *and none else,—the right understanding of the following verses depends.* It is of course *possible* that it *may have been seed-time;*—possible also, that the fields may have been *actually whitening for the harvest;*—but to lay down either of these as certain, and build chronological inferences on it, is quite unwarranted. **ἤδη** belongs certainly to ver. 35, and refers back to **ἔτι.** Taken with ver. 36, it would not agree with the *truth* of the comparison. The harvest was *not yet come.* The ancient MSS. are not trustworthy guides in division and punctuation, which rather form matter of criticism, in which we stand on the same ground as they. **36.**] The **μισθός** of the **θερίζων** is in the χαρά here implied, in having gathered many into eternal life, just as the βρῶσις of the σπείρων was His joy already begun in His heavenly work. See Matt. xx. 1—16 and notes. **37.**] ὁ λόγ. **ἐστιν** [ὁ] ἀλ., i. e. **has place,—applies** = συμβέβηκεν in 2 Pet. ii. 22. So Winer, Meyer (1), Stier, but contr. Lücke, De Wette, who question the propriety of the art. and take [ὁ] ἀληθινός for the predicate, and as = ἀληθής. John's usage however is to join ὁ λόγ. ὁ ἀληθινός: see ch. xv. 1. We may also take the words, without doing any violence to the art. before ἀληθινός, 'Herein is that saying the true one.' But I still prefer the other way. If we regard the bracketed article as omitted, the sense will of course be, 'Herein is that saying true.' Such however is not St. John's usage: see above. **38.**] Here, as often, our Lord speaks of the office and its work as *accomplished,* which is but beginning (see Isa. xlvi. 10). By **ἄλλοι** here He cannot mean the O. T. Prophets (Grotius, Bengel, Lange), for then His own place would be altogether left out;—and besides, all Scripture analogy is against the idea of the O. T. being the *seed* of which the N. T. is the *fruit:*—nor can it be *right,* as Olshausen maintains, to leave Him out, as being the *Lord of the Harvest:*—for He is certainly *elsewhere,* and was by the very nature of the case *here, the Sower.* The plural is I believe merely inserted as the correspondent word to ὑμεῖς in the explanation, as it was ἄλλος—ἄλλος, in the proverb. (So Lücke, Tholuck, Stier. De

θατε. 39 Ἐκ δὲ τῆς πόλεως ἐκείνης πολλοὶ ἐπίστευσαν
εἰς αὐτὸν τῶν Σαμαρειτῶν, διὰ τὸν λόγον τῆς γυναικὸς
ᵒ μαρτυρούσης ὅτι εἶπέν μοι πάντα ἃ ἐποίησα. 40 ὡς οὖν
ἦλθον πρὸς αὐτὸν οἱ Σαμαρεῖται, ᵖ ἠρώτων αὐτὸν ᑫ μεῖναι
παρ' αὐτοῖς. καὶ ᑫ ἔμεινεν ἐκεῖ δύο ἡμέρας. 41 καὶ πολλῷ
πλείους ἐπίστευσαν διὰ τὸν λόγον αὐτοῦ, 42 τῇ τε γυναικὶ
ἔλεγον ὅτι οὐκέτι διὰ τὴν σὴν ʳ λαλιὰν πιστεύομεν· αὐτοὶ
γὰρ ˢ ἀκηκόαμεν, καὶ οἴδαμεν ὅτι οὗτός ἐστιν ᵗ ἀληθῶς ὁ
ᵘᵛ σωτὴρ τοῦ ᵛ κόσμου.
43 Μετὰ δὲ τὰς δύο ἡμέρας ἐξῆλθεν ἐκεῖθεν εἰς τὴν
Γαλιλαίαν. 44 αὐτὸς γὰρ Ἰησοῦς ᵒ ἐμαρτύρησεν ὅτι

o ch. i. 34 reff.
p = and constr., Luke viii. 37 reff.
q ch. i. 39, 40 reff.
r ch. viii. 43. Matt. xxvi. 73 only. Ps. xviii. 3.
s perf., ch. v. 37. xviii. 21. Acts vi. 11, 14. Rom. xv. 21 (from Isa. lii. 15.) 1 John i. 3, 5. iv. 3 only. Job v. 27.
t ch. i. 48 reff.
u Luke ii. 11. Acts xiii. 23 al. fr.
v 1 John iv. 14.

T_b iv. 42 (appy)... ABCDE FGHKL MST_bU VΓΔΛΠ ℵ 1. 33. 69

39. των σαμαρ. bef εις αυτ. 1 : om εις αυτον ℵ¹ Scr's p [lat-*a e* $Orig_1(ins_1)$]. rec (for ἅ) οσα, with AC³D rel vulg lat-*c f ff₂* [*g*] syr arm [$Orig_2$ Chr_1 Cyr_1] : txt BC¹ Lℵ lat-*b e l q* Syr syr-cu copt æth $Orig_2$.

40. (ως is written over the line and also συν above ουν ηλθον *a prima manu* in B : ηλθον ουν B².) for παρ αυτοις, προς αυτους C. for εκει, παρ' αυτοις ℵ Scr's g [Syr syr-cu syr-jer]. ημερας bef δυο ℵ.

42. for τε, δε DE Λ(Treg, expr) foss lat-*a e ff₂ l q* syr $Orig_1$.—και ελεγον τη γυναικι ℵ¹. om οτι B(sic) lat-*b f* Syr æth $Orig_1$ Iren-int_1. for σην λαλ., λαλ. σου B $Orig_2$: σην μαρτυριαν Dℵ¹ lat-*b l*. for αυτοι, αυτου D lat-*a*. aft ακηκ. ins παρ' αυτου ℵ [Π²(but erased) 1. 69 syr-cu [syr-jer] arm. αληθως bef ουτος εστιν ℵ [am fuld syr-cu $Orig_1$ Aug_1] : om αληθως K¹[Π] Scr's g lat-*ff₂* $Heracl_1$ $Victorin_1$. rec at end ins ο χριστος, with AC³D 69(sic) rel lat-*e f q* syrr [syr-jer²] : om B(sic in cod : see table) C¹[T_b]ℵ latt syr-cu syr-jer¹ copt æth arm $Orig_4$ $Heracl_1$ [Eus_1 Cyr-p_1] Iren-int_1 $Victorin_1$ Aug_1.

43. rec aft εκειθεν ins και απηλθεν, with A rel vulg Syr syr-mg æth arm [Chr_2] ; και ηλθεν L 106 gat(with mm) [lat-*g*] syr[-txt] : om BCD[T_b]ℵ 69 lat-*a b e f ff₂ l q* syr-cu copt $Orig_3$ Cyr_1.

44. rec ins ο bef ιησ., with LMΛ[Π²] 69 : om ABCDℵ rel $Orig_5$ Thl. [T_b ?]

Wette denies their interpretation, but gives none of his own.) **39—42.**] The truth of the saying of ver. 35 begins to be manifested. These Samaritans were the foundation of the church afterwards built up there. It does not seem that any miracle was wrought there : αὐτοὶ ἀκηκόαμεν was enough to raise their faith to a point never attained by the Jews, and hardly as yet by the disciples,—that He was the Saviour of *the world*. Their view seems to have been less clouded by prejudice and narrow-mindedness than that of the Jews; and though the conversion of this people lay not in the plan of the official life of our Lord, or working of His Apostles during it (see Matt. x. 5),—yet we have abundant proof from this history, of His gracious purposes towards them. A trace of this occurrence may be found ch. viii. 48, where see note. Compare throughout Acts viii. 1—25. (In ver. 42 λαλιά is perhaps not to be distinguished from λόγος before : see ch. viii. 43. But it is hardly possible not to see in the word something of allusion to the woman's eager and diffuse report to them.)

43—54.] *The second miracle of Jesus in Galilee. The healing of the Ruler's son.* **43.**] **τάς** should have been expressed in E. V.,—**after the two days.** We find no mention of the *disciples* again till ch. vi. 3. **44.**] Much difficulty has been found in the connexion of this verse, but unnecessarily. Some have supposed that the Evangelist means *Judæa* by ἡ ἰδία πατρίς (Orig., Lücke (second edn., but see below), Ebrard, &c.),—which cannot be, for there is no allusion to Judæa at all here, as He came *from Samaria*, and the verse manifestly alludes to His journey *into* Galilee :—some, that Capernaum is meant, or Nazareth, and 'He went into Galilee,' as distinguished from one or other of these places (Chrys., Euthym., Cyril, Olsh.) ;—but neither can this be, for our Evangelist does not so lightly pass over the reasons of the remarks he makes, and there is no allusion to any city *in Galilee*, but to His going into Galilee in general. Some again suppose it to be a reason why He did not go into Galilee before, but remained in Judæa and Sa-

προφήτης ἐν τῇ ἰδίᾳ [w] πατρίδι τιμὴν οὐκ ἔχει. 45 ὅτε w Matt. xiii. 54, 57 reff.
οὖν ἦλθεν εἰς τὴν Γαλιλαίαν, [x] ἐδέξαντο αὐτὸν οἱ Γαλι- x = Matt. x. 14 reff.
λαῖοι, πάντα ἑωρακότες ὅσα ἐποίησεν ἐν Ἱεροσολύμοις
ἐν τῇ ἑορτῇ· καὶ αὐτοὶ γὰρ ἦλθον εἰς τὴν ἑορτήν. y = ch. v. 11 reff.
46 Ἦλθεν οὖν πάλιν εἰς τὴν Κανᾶ τῆς Γαλιλαίας, z = here bis only ‡. (Acts xii. 20, 21. James ii. 8 only. Num. xx. 17 al.)
ὅπου [y] ἐποίησεν τὸ ὕδωρ οἶνον. καὶ ἦν τις [z] βασιλικός,
οὗ ὁ υἱὸς [a] ἠσθένει ἐν Καφαρναούμ. 47 οὗτος ἀκούσας a = Matt. x. 8 al.

45. for οτε, ως Dℵ[1] [Chr$_1$]. εξεδεξαντο D. om εδεξαντο αυτον and γαλιλαιοι ℵ[1]. εωρακοτες bef παντα ℵ[1] [lat-*a b f* syr-mg Orig$_1$(txt$_2$)]. rec (for οσα) α (*see ver* 29), with D[T$_b$]ℵ[1] rel [latt syrr syr-cu æth] Orig$_2$: txt ABCL [Π[2](but α restored)] ℵ[3a] 1. 33. 69 syr Orig$_4$ Chr$_1$ Cyr$_1$. ιερουσαλημ and om εν (bef τη εορ.) D. for ηλθον, εληλυθισαν ℵ [latt].

46. ηλθαν ℵ. rec ins ο ιησ. bef παλιν, with Chr$_1$: aft A rel lat-*f q* syrr : om BCDLℵ 33 latt syr-cu copt æth arm Orig$_1$ Cyr$_1$. [T$_b$?] for εις την, εν B. (καναν ℵ[1].) εποιησαν (sic) ℵ[1]. for και ην, ην δε DL[T$_b$]ℵ 33 lat-*b e f ff*$_2$ [*l*] *q* copt-ms [Chr$_1$ Cyr$_1$] Gaud. βασιλισκος D ev-31[2] Chron$_1$ Synop$_1$, *basiliscus* lat-*a*. (so also in ver 49 D ev-y.)

47. om ουτος ℵ[1].

maria (Theophyl., Meyer (1), and somewhat similarly Neander, L. J. 385, and Jacobi); this however would be equally alien from the simplicity of John's style, and not in accordance with the fact of almost all His teaching and working being in Galilee. Nor is **γάρ** to be rendered '*although*' (Kuinoel)—a sense (Lücke, i. 613) which it never has. One admissible view is (Tholuck, Lücke (third edn.), De Wette), that this verse refers to the next following, and indeed to the whole narrative which it introduces. It stands as a preliminary explanation of the 'Except ye see signs and wonders, ye will not believe;' and as indicating the contrast between the Samaritans, who believed on Him for His *word*,—and His own countrymen, who only received Him because they *had seen the miracles* which He did at Jerusalem. Such use of **γάρ** is not unexampled (see Hartung, Partikellehre, i. p. 467; Lücke, 467; Thol.; De Wette; and Matthiæ, Gr. Gr. § 615). In Herod. i. 124 we have ὦ παῖ Καμβύσεω, σὲ γὰρ θεοὶ ἐπορέωσι· οὐ γὰρ ἄν κοτε ἐς τοσοῦτον τύχης ἀπίκευ· σὺ νῦν Ἀστυάγεα τὸν σεωυτοῦ φονέα τίσαι. Soph. Antig. 393: ἀλλ', ἡ γὰρ ἐκτὸς καὶ παρ' ἐλπίδας χαρὰ | ἔοικεν ἄλλῃ μῆκος οὐδὲν ἡδονῇ, | ἥκω κ.τ.λ. And thus the *οὖν* in the next verse will be a particle connecting it with this preliminary reason given. But **ἐμαρτύρησεν** is not to be taken as a pluperfect. A simpler view still is this: the reason (ver. 1) why He left Judæa for Galilee was, because of the publicity which was gathering round Himself and his ministry. He betakes Himself to Galilee therefore, to avoid fame, testifying that His own country (Galilee) was that where, as a prophet, He was least likely to be honoured. **45.**] They received Him, but in accordance with the proverbial saying just recorded;—not for any honour in which they themselves held Him, or value which they had for His teaching; but *on account of His fame in Jerusalem*, the metropolis,—which set them the fashion in their estimate of men and things. **καὶ αὐτοὶ γάρ**, inserted for those readers who might not be aware of the practice of the Galilæans to frequent the feasts at Jerusalem. **46.**] **οὖν**, perhaps (see above) because of the receptivity of Him from signs and wonders merely,—not as a Prophet from His teaching. But it is hardly safe in this Gospel to mark the inference in *οὖν* so strongly: it is St. John's habitual particle of sequence, even where that sequence is not strictly logical, only temporal, and thus in God's purposes, no doubt, consequential.

βασιλικός] ἢ ἐκ γένους βασιλικοῦ, ἢ ὡς ἀξίωμά τι κεκτημένος ἀφ' οὗπερ ἐκαλεῖτο βασιλικός (Euthym., Chrys.), ἢ ὡς ὑπηρέτης βασιλικός (Euthym.). Origen thinks he may have been one of the household of Cæsar, having some business in Judæa at that time. But the usage of Josephus is perhaps our surest guide. He uses **βασ.** to distinguish the soldiers, or courtiers, or officers of the *kings* (Herods or others), from those of *Rome*,—but never to designate the royal family: see B. J. vii. 5. 2: Antt. xv. 8. 4. So that this man was probably an officer of Herod Antipas. He *may* have been Chuza, Herod's steward, Luke viii. 3: but this is pure conjecture. The man seems to have been a Jew: see below. **47, 48.**] This miracle is a notable instance of our

ὅτι Ἰησοῦς ἥκει ἐκ τῆς Ἰουδαίας εἰς τὴν Γαλιλαίαν,
[b] ἀπῆλθεν πρὸς αὐτὸν καὶ [c] ἠρώτα ἵνα [d] καταβῇ καὶ ἰάση-
ται αὐτοῦ τὸν υἱόν· ἤμελλεν γὰρ ἀποθνήσκειν. 48 εἶπεν
οὖν ὁ Ἰησοῦς πρὸς αὐτὸν Ἐὰν μὴ [e] σημεῖα καὶ [f] τέρατα
ἴδητε, οὐ μὴ πιστεύσητε. 49 λέγει πρὸς αὐτὸν ὁ [z] βασι-
λικὸς Κύριε, [d] κατάβηθι πρὶν ἀποθανεῖν τὸ παιδίον μου.
50 λέγει αὐτῷ ὁ Ἰησοῦς Πορεύου· ὁ υἱός σου [g] ζῇ. [h] ἐπίστευσεν ὁ ἄνθρωπος τῷ [h] λόγῳ [i] ὃν [h] εἶπεν αὐτῷ ὁ Ἰησοῦς,
καὶ ἐπορεύετο. 51 ἤδη δὲ αὐτοῦ [d] καταβαίνοντος, οἱ δοῦλοι
αὐτοῦ [k] ὑπήντησαν αὐτῷ [καὶ [l] ἀπήγγειλαν] λέγοντες ὅτι

ABCDE FGHKL MST$_b$U VΓΔΛΠ ℵ 1. 33. 69

...iv. 50 (appy) T$_b$.

b = Matt. xiv. 25 reff. c Luke vii. 36 reff. d see Luke iv. 31. e ch. ii. 11 reff. f in N. T. alw. w. σημ., Matt. xxiv. 24 ‖ Mk. Acts ii. 19, 22, 43 al6. Rom. xv. 19. 2 Cor. xii. 12. 2 Thess. ii. 9. Heb. ii. 4 only. Deut. xiii. 12. g = vv. 51, 53. Mark v. 23 (‖ Mt.?) only. 4 Kings i. 2. h ch. ii. 22 (reff.). i constr., ver. 5 reff. k ch. xi. 20, 30. xii. 18. Matt. viii. 28 al.+ Tobit vii. 1 (not ℵ) al. l John here only, exc. 1 John i. 2, 3. Luke (Gosp. and Acts) passim. Paul, 1 Cor. xiv. 25. 1 Thess. i. 9 only. Heb. ii. 12.

ins *ο* bef *ιησ.* ℵ Scr's c evv-P-y. for *απηλθ.*, *ηλθεν* Cℵ[1] 1. 33. 69 lat-*a b e ff*$_2$ [*l*] syr-cu copt-ms æth arm Chr$_1$. add *ουν* ℵ[1]. rec aft *ηρωτα* ins *αυτον*, with A rel: om BCDL[T$_b$]ℵ 33. 69 fos lat-*a e l q* arm Orig$_1$ Chr$_2$ [Cyr$_1$].—(om *κ. ηρωτα* G.)

49. for *το παιδιον*, *τον υιον* A 69 Chr-mss$_1$: *τον παιδα* ℵ. om *μου* D 1 lat-*b e ff*$_2$ *l* Syr syr-cu.

50. om *ο ιησ.* E 157 Scr's c. rec ins *και* bef *επιστευσεν*, with AC rel lat-*a b e f ff*$_2$ [*q* syr-jer] syrr syr-cu copt æth arm (L[T$_b$] add *δε*): om BDℵ vulg lat-*c l* Cyr$_1$. rec (for ὅν) ᾧ, with D rel: *ων* F: txt ABCL[T$_b$](ℵ[3a]).—for *ον ειπ. αυτω ο ιησ.*, *του ιῡ* ℵ[1] syr-cu, *του ιῡ ον ειπ. αυτω* ℵ[3a]. rec om *ο* (bef *ιησ.*), with S(e sil): ins ABCD rel Cyr$_1$. [T$_b$?]

51. om 2nd *αυτου* D-gr Lℵ 1 latt. rec **απηντησαν**, with A rel Orig$_1$ Chr$_1$ Cyr$_1$: txt (*always used by John, see reff*) BCDKLℵ 1. *υπηντ.* bef *οι δουλοι* D (arm). for *αυτω*, *αυτον* A. om *κ. απηγγ.* BL (syr-jer) copt æth-rom [Orig$_1$(appy)

Lord 'not quenching the smoking flax:' just as His reproof of the Samaritan woman was of His 'not breaking the bruised reed.' The little spark of faith in the breast of this nobleman is by Him lit up into a clear and enduring flame for the light and comfort of himself and his house. **καταβῇ**] See on ch. ii. 12. The charge brought against them, **ἐὰν μὴ** κ.τ.λ., does not imply, as some (Raphel and Storr) think, that they would not believe signs and wonders *heard of*, but required to *see* them (thus laying the stress on **ἴδητε**)—for in this case the expression would certainly have been fuller, ἴδητε τοῖς ὀφθαλμοῖς, or something similar;—and it would not accord with our Lord's known low estimate of all *mere miracle-faith*, to find Him making so weighty a difference between faith from miracles *seen* and faith from miracles *heard*. The words imply the contrast between the Samaritans, who believed *because of His word*, and the Jews (the plural reckoning the βασιλικός among them), who would not believe but *through signs and prodigies*: see 1 Cor. i. 22. And observe also that it is not implied that even when they had seen signs and wonders, they would believe:—they required these as a condition of their faith, but even these were rejected by them: see ch. xii. 37. But even with such inadequate conceptions and conditions of faith, our Lord receives the nobleman, and works the sign rather than dismiss him. It was otherwise in Matt. xvi. 1 ff. **49.**] Here is the same weakness of faith,—but our Lord's last words have made visible impression. It is like the Syrophœnician woman's rejoinder,—'Yea, Lord; but . . . ,' only the faith is of a far less noble kind than hers. He seems to believe it necessary that Jesus should be on the spot;—not that there was any thing strange or blameable in this, for Martha and Mary did the same, ch. xi. 21, 32:—and to think that it would be too late when his child *had expired*;—not imagining that He to whom he spoke could *raise the dead*. **50.**] The bringing out and strengthening of the man's faith by these words was almost as great a spiritual miracle, as the material one which they indicated. We may observe the difference between our Lord's dealing here and in the case of the centurion (Matt. viii. 6 ff. and ‖). There, when from humility the man requests Him to speak the word only, He offers to go to his house: here, when pressed to go down, He speaks the word only. Thus (as Trench observes, after Chrysostom) the weak faith

ὁ παῖς αὐτοῦ [m] ζῇ. 52 [n] ἐπύθετο οὖν τὴν ὥραν παρ' αὐτῶν
ἐν ᾗ [o] κομψότερον [p] ἔσχεν. εἶπον οὖν αὐτῷ ὅτι [q] ἐχθὲς
I_d [εβδο]μην... [r] ὥραν ἑβδόμην [s] ἀφῆκεν αὐτὸν ὁ [st] πυρετός. 53 ἔγνω
οὖν ὁ πατὴρ ὅτι [u] ἐν ἐκείνῃ τῇ ὥρᾳ ἐν ᾗ εἶπεν αὐτῷ ὁ
Ἰησοῦς Ὁ υἱός σου [m] ζῇ, καὶ ἐπίστευσεν αὐτὸς καὶ ἡ
[v] οἰκία αὐτοῦ ὅλη. 54 τοῦτο [δὲ] [w] πάλιν δεύτερον

m ver. 50.
n with acc., Acts xxiii. 20 only. w. παρά, Matt. ii. 4 only. otherwise, Luke xv. 26. xviii. 36. Acts iv. 7 al5. only.
o here only +.
p = Mark xvi. 18.
q Acts vii. 28. Heb. xiii. 8 only. Exod. v. 14 A B1(Mai, not Ed-vat). Josh. iii. 4.
r acc., Acts x. (3 v. r.) 30. Rev. iii. 3.
s Matt. viii. 15 |.
t as above (s). Acts xxviii. 8 only. Deut. xxviii. 22 only.
u ellips. (?, see Winer, p. 513, edn. 2.), 2 Cor. i. 6.
v = Matt. x. 13. xii. 25. 1 Cor. xvi. 15. Gen. l. 8. Josh. xxiv. 15.
w ch. xxi. 16. Matt. xxvi. 42. Acts x. 15.

Chr_1]: *κ. ανηγγ.* K[Π] 1. 33: *κ. ηγγειλαν αυτω* (omg *λεγοντες*) D ℵ[omg *αυτω*] lat-*b*. om *ο* (bef *παις*) C¹. for *παις, υιος* DKLU[Π] 33. 69 latt Syr syr-cu syr-mg [syr-jer] copt æth Cyr_1. rec (for 3rd *αυτου*) *σου*, with D-gr rel lat-*a b e* [*q*] syrr syr-cu syr-jer copt æth $Orig_2$: txt ABCℵ 1 vulg lat-*c f* ff_2 *g l* [D-lat] arm.

52. rec *παρ' αυτων* bef *την ωραν* (*to bring the governed case close to the verb*), with L rel Chr_1 Cyr_1: txt ACDKU[Π]ℵ 1. 33. 69 latt: for *παρ αυτ.*, *εκεινην* B. rec (for *ειπ. ουν*) *και ειπ.*, with ADℵ rel latt syr [syr-jer] æth Chr_1 Cyr_1: txt BCL 1. 33 arm. rec *χθες*, with B² rel [Chr_1 Cyr_1]: om 69: txt AB¹CDKL[Π]ℵ. *αυτην* B(sic in cod: see table) [Λ].

53. aft *ο πατηρ* ins *αυτου* C 69 lat-*e f* syrr syr-cu copt [æth arm]. om 1st *εν* BCℵ¹ 1. om *ο ιησ.* ℵ¹ [foss]. rec ins *οτι* bef *ο υιος*, with DI_d rel lat-*e f* [*l q*] syrr syr-cu arm [Cyr_1]: om ABCLℵ 1. 33 latt [syr-jer] copt æth Cyr[-p_1].

54. for *τουτο*, *του* D¹(txt D³). rec om *δε*, with AC²DI_dℵ rel latt syrr [syr-cu syr-jer] copt-dz arm: ins BC¹G 69 copt $Orig_3$.

of the nobleman is strengthened, while the humility of the centurion is honoured. **51.**] He appears [see below] to have gone leisurely away,—for the hour (1 P.M.) was early enough to reach Capernaum the same evening (twenty-five miles): in confidence that an amendment was taking place, which he at present understood to be only a gradual one. **52, 53.**] **κομψῶς ἔχειν** in this sense is found in Arrian. Dissert. Epictet. iii. 10, cited by most of the Commentators. ὅταν ὁ ἰατρὸς εἰσέρχηται, μὴ φοβεῖσθαι τί εἴπῃ· μηδ' ἂν εἴπῃ, **κομψῶς ἔχεις**, ὑπερχαίρειν . . . . . . μηδ' ἂν εἴπῃ, **κακῶς ἔχεις**, ἀθυμεῖν . . . . **ἀφῆκεν αὐτ. ὁ πυρ.**] This was probably more than he expected to hear; and the coincidence of so sudden a recovery with the time at which Jesus had spoken the words to him (after ἐκείνῃ τῇ ὥρᾳ understand ἀφῆκεν αὐτὸν ὁ πυρετός), raises his faith at length into a full belief of the Power and Goodness and the Messiahship of Him, who had by a word commanded the disease, and it had obeyed. The **ἐπίστευσεν**, *absolutely*, implies that in the fullest sense he and all his *became disciples of Jesus.* It is very different from ἐπίστευσεν τῷ λόγῳ ὃν εἶπ. Ἰησ. in ver. 50—as believing on HIM must be always different from believing on *any thing else in the world*, be it *even His own word or His own ordinances.* Here the advocates of the (imaginary—see above on ver. 6) Asiatic division of the hours by St. John, suppose him to have put that division into the mouth of Jews in Galilee. But that division would in reality not help the narrative here at all, as they maintain. The βασιλικός probably set out, as indeed the narrative implies, immediately on hearing our Lord's assurance, and *spent the night on the way.* Indeed, curiously enough, Bp. Wordsw. makes him do this, and yet maintains the seventh hour to have been 7 P.M. **54.**] The *meaning* of the Evangelist clearly is, that this was the second *Galilæan* miracle (see ch. iii. 2, and ver. 45). But (1) how is that expressed in the words? The σημεῖα which He did at Jerusalem in the feast being omitted, the πάλιν δεύτερον σ. naturally carries the thoughts back to a former one related; and the clause added (ἐλθὼν κ.τ.λ.) shews, not that a miracle prior to this, during this return visit, has been passed over,—but that as the scene of this second was in Galilee, so that former one, to which δεύτ. refers, must be sought in Galilee also. And then (2) *why* should this so particularly be stated? Certainly, it seems to me, on account of the part which this miracle bore in the calling out and assuring of faith by the manifestation of His glory, as that first one had done before. By that (ch. ii. 11), His disciples had been convinced: by this, one (himself a type of the weak and unworthy in faith) outside the circle of His own. By both, half-belief was strengthened into faith in Him: but in each case it is of a different kind. It is an interesting

x = ch. ii. 11 reff. Exod. iv. 30.

y = Matt. xx. 17, 18 reff.

ABCDE FGHI$_d$ KLMSU VΓΔΛΠ ℵ 1. 33. 69

[x] σημεῖον ἐποίησεν ὁ Ἰησοῦς ἐλθὼν ἐκ τῆς Ἰουδαίας εἰς τὴν Γαλιλαίαν.

V. 1 Μετὰ ταῦτα ἦν ἑορτὴ τῶν Ἰουδαίων, καὶ [y] ἀνέβη

εποιησεν bef σημειον ℵ [Chr$_1$].

Chap. V. 1. ins η bef εορτη (*prob to specify the feast*) CEFH I$_d$(appy) LMΔ[Π]ℵ

question, whether or not this miracle be the same as the healing of the centurion's servant (or *son*, Matt. ?) in Matt. viii. 5: Luke vii. 1. Irenæus *appears* to hold the two narratives to be the same history (*appears* only; for his words are, "Filium centurionis absens verbo curavit dicens Vade, filius tuus vivit," Hær. ii. 22. 3, p. 147: which remark may be simply explained by his having cited from memory, and thus either made this βασιλικός a centurion,—or, which is more probable, having understood the παῖς in Matt. viii. as a *son*, and made our Lord there speak very similar words to those really uttered by Him, but which are in reality found here): so Eusebius also in his canons. Chrysostom notices, but opposes the view:—and it has never in modern times gained many advocates, being only held by Semler, Seiffarth, and the interpreters of the Straussian school. Indeed, the internal evidence is all against it: not only (Chrys.) ἀπὸ τοῦ ἀξιώματος, ἀλλὰ καὶ ἀπὸ τῆς πίστεως, does the man in one case differ from the man in the other. The inner kernel of the history is, in our case here,—*the elevation of a weak and mere wonder-seeking faith into a deep conviction of the personal power and love of our Lord;* in the other, the commendation of a noble confession of our Lord's divine power, indicating great strength and grasp of faith, and inducing the greatest personal humility. And the external point brought out in the commendation, οὐδὲ ἐν τῷ Ἰσραήλ, is not only different from, but stands in absolute contrast with, the depreciating charge here, ἐὰν μὴ σημεῖα καὶ τέρατα ἴδητε, οὐ μὴ πιστεύσητε. Olshausen (whose commentary on John is far less elaborate than on the other Gospels, which may account for my referring less often to it) well remarks, that this narrative may be regarded as a sequel to the foregoing one.

Chap. V.—XII. *Second great division of the Gospel.* Jesus in conflict with the Jews. V., VI. Jesus the life. *Beginning of the conflict.*

Chap. V. 1—47.] *Healing of a cripple at the pool of Bethesda, during a feast; and the discourse of Jesus occasioned by the persecution of the Jews arising thereupon.* **1. μετὰ ταῦτα**] Lücke remarks that when John wishes to indicate immediate succession, he uses μετὰ τοῦτο, ch. ii. 12; xi. 7, 11; xix. 28: when mediate, after an interval, μετὰ ταῦτα, ch. iii. 22; v. 14; vi. 1; vii. 1; xix. 38. So that apart from other considerations which would lead us to the same conclusion, we may infer that some interval has elapsed since the last verse of ch. iv. **ἑορτὴ τ. Ἰουδ.**] Few points have been more controverted, than the question, *what this feast was.* I will give the principal views, and then state my own conclusion. (I have abridged the following statement principally from Lücke's note, ii. 1—15.) (1) Irenæus understands it (Hær. ii. 22. 3, p. 147) to be the *second Passover of our Lord's ministry.* Origen (whose commentary on this chapter is lost) mentions this view (tom. xiii. 39, vol. iv. p. 250), but apparently does not approve it. (ms. Λ reads ην εορτη των αζυμων κ.τ.λ.) This is the view of Luther, Calovius, Scaliger, Grotius, Lightfoot, Lampe, Kuinoel. (2) Cyril Alex. and Chrysostom think it to be *the Pentecost;* similarly Euthym. and Theophyl. This opinion prevailed in the Greek Church; and has been defended by Erasmus, Calvin, Beza, &c., and more recently by Bengel in his Harmony. (3) Kepler first suggested the idea that it might be *the feast of Purim,* (Esth. ix. 21, 26,) almost immediately preceding the Passover (the 14th and 15th of Adar). This was adopted by Petavius, and has been the general view of the modern chronologists. So Lamy (Apparat. Chronol.), Hug, Lücke (1st edn.), Olshausen, Meyer, Wieseler, Stier, Neander, Winer. (4) The *feast of Tabernacles* has been suggested by Cocceius, and is supported by one ms. (131, which adds ἡ σκηνοπηγία.) (5) Kepler and Petavius thought it also possible that the *feast of Dedication* (see ch. x. 22) might be meant. So that *almost every Jewish feast* finds some supporters. I believe with Lücke (3rd edn.), De Wette, and Tholuck, *that we cannot with any probability gather what feast it was.* Seeing as I do no distinct datum given in ch. iv. 35, nor again in ch. vi. 1, and finding nothing in this chapter to determine the nature of this feast, I cannot attach any weight to most of the elaborate

Ἰησοῦς εἰς Ἱεροσόλυμα. 2 ἔστιν δὲ ἐν [z] τοῖς [z] Ἱεροσολύμοις [a] ἐπὶ τῇ [b] προβατικῇ [c] κολυμβήθρα ἡ [d] ἐπιλεγομένη
[e] Ἑβραϊστὶ Βηθεσδά, πέντε [f] στοὰς ἔχουσα. 3 ἐν ταύταις

z ch. ii. 23. x. 22. xi. 18 only. a = Matt. xxiv. 33 ‖. Acts iii. 11. v. 9. b here only. Neh. iii. 1, 32. xii. 39 only. c ver. (4 v. r.) 7. ch. ix. 7 (11 v. r.) only. Isa. vii. 3. d = here only ‡. (Acts xv. 40 only. Exod. xvii. 9 al.) e ch. xix. 13 reff. f ch. x. 23. Acts iii. 11. v. 12 only. Ezek. xlii. 3.

1. 33 coptt Cyr_1 : om ABD rel $Orig_1$ Chr_1. rec ins ο bef ιησ., with Cא rel $Orig_1$ Chr_1 Cyr_1 : om $ABDHI_dKL$[TΠ[1]] $Chron_2$.

2. for επι, εν ADGLא[3a] lat-*q* Non_1 : om επι τη א[1] [vulg(with forj tol) æth Chr_1]. for η επιλεγ., το λεγομενον א[1].—for επιλεγ., λεγ. DV **1.** 33 lat-*a b* [*e* ff_2 *l q* foss]. βηθσαιδα B vulg lat-*c* syr-txt [and mg-gr] coptt æth $Tert_1$: βελζεθα D, *belzatha* lat-*a*: βηθζ. א 33 : βηζαθα L lat-*e l* Eus_1 [Cyr-p_1].

3. aft ταυταις ins ουν D [Chr_1].

chronological arguments which have been raised on the subject. It can hardly have been a Passover, both on account of the omission of the article before ἑορτή (see ch. vi. 4), and because if so, we should have an interval of a whole year between this chapter and the next, which is not probable. Nor can it have been the Dedication, in the winter; for then the multitude of sick would have hardly been waiting in the porches of Bethesda. The feast of Purim would nearest agree with the subsequent events; and it seems as if our Lord did not go up to Jerusalem at the Passover next following (ch. vi. 4; vii. 1), so that no difficulty would be created by the proximity of the two feasts, unless, with De Wette, we believe that the interval was too little for what is related ch. vi. 1—3 to have happened. But it may be doubted, (1) whether it was a general practice to go up to Jerusalem at the Purim: (2) whether our Lord would be likely to observe it, even if it was.

No reason need be given why John does not name the feast; it is quite in accordance with his practice of mentioning nothing that does not concern his subject-matter. Thus the Passover is mentioned ch. ii. 13, because of the *buying and selling in the temple;* again, ch. vi. 4, to account for the *great multitude,* and as eminently suiting (see notes) the subject of His discourse there; the feast of Tabernacles, ch. vii. 2, because of the practice alluded to by our Lord in ver. 37; that of the Dedication, ch. x. 22, to account for His being in Solomon's porch because it was winter; but in this chapter, where there is nothing alluding to the time or nature of the feast, it is not specified.

Ἰησοῦς—and probably His disciples: for the same expression is used ch. ii. 13, whereas we find, ch. iii. 22, that His disciples were with Him: compare also ch. vii. 10 and ch. ix. 2. **2.**] **ἔστιν** has been thought by Bengel and others to import that John wrote his Gospel *before the destruction of Jerusalem.* But this must not be pressed. He might have spoken in the present without meaning to be literally accurate at the moment when he was writing (see Prolegg. to John, § iv. 6). **ἐπὶ τῇ προβ.**, probably **near the sheep-gate,**—mentioned by Nehemiah, see reff. The situation of this gate is unknown;—it is traditionally supposed to be the same with that now called St. Stephen's gate; but inaccurately, for no wall existed in that quarter till the time of Agrippa (Robinson, i. 472). Eusebius, Jerome, and the Itinerarium Hieros. speak of a προβατικὴ κολυμβήθρα, so also *probatica piscina,* Vulg. The reading λεγομένη would be more usual; perhaps **ἐπιλ.** implies that it had another name. **Βηθεσδά** = Syr. בֵּית חֶסְדָּא, **the house** (place) **of mercy, or of grace.** Its present situation is very uncertain. Robinson established by personal inspection the fact of the subterranean connexion of the pool of Siloam (see ch. ix. 7, note; and the supplementary note at the end of this volume) and that called the Fountain of the Virgin (i. 501 ff.); and has made it probable that the Fountain under the grand Mosk is also connected with them (i. 509 ff.); in fact that all these are but one and the same spring. (See also some interesting particulars respecting an attempt made subsequently to prove this connexion, and mention of a fourth fountain with the same peculiar taste as the water of Siloam, in Williams's Holy City, pp. 381 ff.) Now this spring, as he himself witnessed, (i. 506,) is an *intermittent* one, as indeed had been reported before by Jerome (on Isa. viii. 6), Prudentius (in Trench, Mir. p. 247, edn. 2), William of Tyre, and others. There might have been then, it is obvious, some artificially constructed basin in connexion with this spring, the site and memory of which have perished, which would present the phænomenon here described: see below. The spot now traditionally

g = ver. 6. Mark i. 30. ii. 4. Luke v. 25 (29 reff.). Acts ix. 33. xxviii. 8 only. Prov. v. 9 only. Judith xiii. 15. Wisd. xvii. 7.
h John, here only. Matt. xv. 30, 31 al.
i = Matt. xii. 10. Mark iii. 3. Luke vi. 6, 8 only. (Matt. xxiii. 15. Luke xxiii. 31. Heb. xi. 29 only. Isa. lvi. 3.)

[g] κατέκειτο πλῆθος τῶν ἀσθενούντων, τυφλῶν, [h] χωλῶν,
[i] ξηρῶν. 5 ἦν δέ τις ἄνθρωπος ἐκεῖ τριάκοντα καὶ ὀκτὼ

ABCDE FGHI$_d$ KLMSU VΓΔΛΠ ℵ 1. 33. 69

κατεκειντο DΛ² lat-[l^1] q^2 sah. rec aft πληθος ins πολυ, with AI$_d$ rel vulg lat-*c f* [*ff*$_2$] syrr arm [Chr$_1$] Cyr$_1$: om BCDLℵ 33 lat-*a b e l q* syr-cu [syr-jer] coptt Chr$_2$-mss. aft ξηρων ins παραλυτικων (*addn because this man was paralytic*) D lat-*a b l*. rec at end ins [k] εκδεχομενων την του υδατος [l] κινησιν (*see note*), with A²C³DI$_d$ [Π(but marked with asterisks)] rel [latt syrr syr-jer copt-wilk æth arm] Chr$_2$ Cyr$_1$ Euthym Thl Tert Ambr : om A¹BC¹Lℵ lat-*q* syr-cu copt-dz sah.

[4. rec ins ἄγγελος γὰρ [m] κατὰ [m] καιρὸν κατέβαινεν [n] ἐν τῇ [o] κολυμβήθρᾳ καὶ [p] ἐτάρασσε τὸ ὕδωρ· ὁ οὖν πρῶτος [q] ἐμβὰς μετὰ τὴν [r] ταραχὴν τοῦ ὕδατος [s] ὑγιὴς [s] ἐγίνετο [t] ᾧ δήποτε [u] κατείχετο [v] νοσήματι (*insn to complete that implied in the narrative with reference to the popular belief : see notes*), with AC³I$_d$L [SΠ with ast: Λ with ob] rel latt Syr syr-w-[ast to υδωρ, the rest w-]ob [syr-jer arm-ed] copt-wilk ; κατὰ τὴν ἡμέραν τῆς ἁγίας πεντηκοστῆς ἄγγελοι καταφοιτῶντες ἐξ οὐρανοῦ τὸ τῆς κολυμβήθρας ἐξετάραττον ὕδωρ Cyr$_1$:—aft αγγελος ins κυριου AKL[ΔΠ] vulg lat-*a c* [*g* æth] arm ; aft γαρ 69 : for γαρ, δε L latt [arm] : καιρω L : for κατεβ., ελουετο A[Π] 42 forj(with foss) syr æth, ἐλουετον K : εταρασσετο C¹GHI$_d$MUVΛ¹[Π] : εγενετο FL 69 : for ω δηπ., οιωδηποτουν A, ουδηποτε L, ω δ' αν K(= 42 ?)[Π] : κατηχετο L Scr's b f i ev-y, κατηχετω C³ :—om BC¹Dℵ 33 harl¹(with san) lat-*f l q* syr-cu copt-dz sah arm-mss.]

5. om τις D 11 lat-*a b* [*l q*] arm. om εκει ℵ : εκει bef ανθρ. F lat-*a b* [*q*]. rec om και, with BKΛ[ΓΠ] (SV, e sil) am lat-*a* [*l* coptt Orig$_1$] Chr$_2$: ins ACDI$_d$ℵ rel

k Acts xvii. 16. 1 Cor. xi. 33. xvi. 11. Heb. x. 13. xi. 10. James v. 7 only ‡. Gen. xliii. 9 al.
l here only. Job xvi. 6.
m = here only. (Rom. v. 6.) see Num. ix. 13.
n ch. iii. 35 reff.
o ver. 2 reff.
p ver. 7.
q = here only. Nah. iii. 14. of embarking, Matt. viii. 23 reff. ch. vi. 17 al.
r = here only. (Mark xiii. 8 only.) Isa. xxiv. 19.
s ver. 6 reff.
t here only.
u = here only. see Rom. vii. 6. Jer. xiii. 21.
v here only †.

known as Bethesda is a part of the fosse round the fort or tower Antonia, an immense reservoir or trench, seventy-five feet deep. But, as Robinson observes (i. 489), there is not the slightest evidence that can identify it with the Bethesda of the N. T. This pool is not mentioned by Josephus. **πέντε στοὰς ἔχ.**] Probably these were for the shelter of the sick persons, and were arches or porticos, opening upon and surrounding the reservoir. *στοά ἐστιν ἡ παρ' ἡμῖν λεγομένη καμάρα, ἢ καὶ ὁ θόλος.* Euthym. 3.] **ξηρῶν**, those who were afflicted with the loss of vital power in any of their limbs by stiffness or paralysis. Of this kind was the man on whom the miracle was wrought.

[**ἐκδεχ. . . . κίνησιν**, and ver. 4. The spuriousness of this controverted passage seems to me more clear than when I prepared my Second Edition. The very reasons which Stier and De Wette allege in its favour, and which then weighed with me, will on more consideration be found to range themselves on the other side. Let us conceive of the matter thus. The facts, of the assemblage of sick persons round the pool, and of the answer of the sick man in ver. 7, were recorded in the sacred text as we now find them, and nothing else. In the background, and explanatory of both, was the popular belief of the Jews, not alleged by the Evangelist. In very early times, this deficiency was supplied by the insertion of the spurious passage. I say, in very early times: for Tertullian refers to it in a way which leaves no doubt that he read it entire. "Piscinam Bethsaidam (cf. digest on ver. 2) angelus interveniens commovebat: observabant qui valetudinem querebantur. Nam si quis prævenerat descendere illuc, queri post lavacrum desinebat." De Bapt. c. 5, vol. i. p. 1205. So that the fact of so many different kinds of sick persons being mentioned here (Stier), and that of the connexion of the account almost requiring this passage as its explanation (De Wette), points to the reason why it was put in, to clear up a narrative otherwise obscure. I would not lay much stress on the variations in the passage, which are only such as are perpetually meeting us in the undoubted text: but the fact that there are no less than seven words used either here only, or here only in this sense, is strong against its genuineness: as is the concurrence of B, C, D, and ℵ in omitting it. Of N. T. critics, Griesb. brackets it, Tischdf., Meyer, and Treg. omit it,—while Lachm. retains it in his text. De Wette, Lücke, and Luthardt, are undecided, but inclined more or less strongly against it. As a marginal gloss, it certainly does good

ἔτη [w] ἔχων ἐν τῇ [x] ἀσθενείᾳ αὐτοῦ. 6 τοῦτον ἰδὼν ὁ Ἰησοῦς
[y] κατακείμενον, καὶ γνοὺς ὅτι πολὺν ἤδη χρόνον [w] ἔχει,
λέγει αὐτῷ Θέλεις [za] ὑγιὴς [a] γενέσθαι; 7 ἀπεκρίθη αὐτῷ ὁ
ἀσθενῶν Κύριε, ἄνθρωπον οὐκ ἔχω, [b] ἵνα ὅταν [c] ταραχθῇ
τὸ ὕδωρ, [d] βάλῃ με εἰς τὴν [e] κολυμβήθραν· [f] ἐν ᾧ δὲ
ἔρχομαι ἐγώ, ἄλλος πρὸ ἐμοῦ καταβαίνει. 8 λέγει αὐτῷ
ὁ Ἰησοῦς [g] Ἔγειρε ἆρον τὸν [h] κράβαττόν σου καὶ περι-

w = ch. viii. 57 reff. x = Luke v. 15 reff. y ver. 3 reff. z Matt. xii. 13 reff. a vv. (4 v. r.) 9, 14 only. b = ver. 36 al. c lit., here (ver. 4 v. r.) only. Ezek. xxxii. 2. d = Mark vii. 33. James iii. 3 al. e ver. 2 reff. f = Luke v. 34 ‖ Mk. xix. 13. g Matt. ix. 5. Mark ii. 11. iii. 3. Eph. v. 14 al. h here, &c. 5 times (& ver. 12 v. r.). Mark ii. 4, 9, 11, 12. vi. 55. Acts v. 15. ix. 33 only†.

vulg lat-*b c* [*e f q* syr-jer] syr-cu syrr æth arm [Chr$_2$] Cyr$_1$ Iren-int$_1$-mss. rec om αυτου (*overlooked between* -α *and* του- : *so Mey*), with AC^{3}I$_d$ rel lat-*b f q* [syrr] Orig$_1$ Aug$_1$: ins BC^{1}DL[Π^2]ℵ 1. 33 vulg lat-*a c e l* [syr-jer] coptt arm Chr$_1$ Cyr$_1$.

6. ιδως A. ανακειμενον ℵ^1. om ηδη ℵ 253 [lat-*e* syr-jer] Syr syr-cu æth : ins aft χρονον 1 Scr's p.

7. for απεκριθη, λεγει A^{2}D. ins ναι bef κυριε C^{2}EFGH 33 syrr syr-jer [Cyr-jer$_1$] Chr$_2$. rec βαλλη (with Scr's c i q, e sil) ; βαλει G 69 Scr's e : εμβαλη C^1 : txt ABC^{2}Dℵ rel Cyr-jer$_1$ Chr$_2$. (I$_d$ 33 def.) προς B^{1}L : txt A B^2[Tischdf ascribes the correction to his B$^{2\cdot3}$] CDI$_d$ℵ rel.

8. rec εγειραι, with UV[Γ]Δ : txt ABCDℵ rel. (I$_d$ 33 def.) ins και bef αρον ADK[Π] lat-*a b e ff$_2$* æth. (κραβαττον, so AB^{1}CD ℵ(-κτον sic : in vv. 9—11 corrd to -ττον by ℵ^{3a}) &c.)

service, as explaining both the obscure points—the assemblage of sick, and the answer in ver. 7. **κατὰ καιρόν,** here, apparently, **at intervals**: and those irregular ones, or the sick need not have *waited* there for them. **κατέβαινεν, was in the habit of descending**: the imperfects continue throughout.] **5.**] There are two ways of taking the construction of **ἔχων**: (1) to regard ἔχων ἐν τῇ ἀσθ. as = ἀσθενῶς ἔχων, and τριάκοντα ὀκτὼ ἔτη as the *accus. of duration;* which is objectionable on account of the article τῇ, (not on account of the present participle, as De Wette, for it is often found with duration of time,) and as being alien from John's usage, which is (2) to place ἔχω in this sense with *an accusative of the time:* see reff., and ver. 6. So that the construction is ἔχων τριάκ. ὀκτὼ ἔτη ἐν τῇ ἀσθ. Observe, he had *been lame* thirty-eight years, not *at Bethesda* all that time. **6.**] **γνούς,** i. e. ἐν ἑαυτῷ, as on other similar occasions. Our Lord singled him out, being conscious of the circumstances under which he lay there, by that superhuman knowledge of which we had so striking an example in the case of the woman of Samaria. **θέλεις ὑγ. γεν.**] Lightfoot and Semler would supply, "licet sit sabbatum." But this is very improbable, see ver. 17. Our Lord did not thus appeal to his hearers' prejudices, and make His grace dependent on them. Besides, the ὑγιὴς γενέσθαι had in the mind of the man no reference to a healing such as there would be any objection to on the Sabbath; but to the cure *by means of the water,* which he was there to seek.

The question is one of those by which He so frequently testified his compassion, and established (so to speak) a point of connexion between the spirit of the person addressed, and his own gracious purposes. Possibly it may have conveyed to the mind of the poor cripple the idea that at length a compassionate person had come, who might put him in at the next troubling of the water. It certainly is possible that the man's long and apparently hopeless infirmity may have given him a look of lethargy and despondency, and the question may have arisen from this: but there is no ground for supposing (Schleiermacher) *blame* conveyed by it, still less that he was an impostor labouring under some trifling complaint (Paulus and others), and wishing to represent it more important than it was. **7.**] The man's answer implies the popular belief which the spurious but useful insertion in vv. 3, 4 expresses. Bauer asks why the person who *brought him there every day,* could not have put him in? But no such person is implied. The same slow motion which he describes here, would suffice for his daily coming and going. **8.**] The **ἆρον τ. κρ. σου** has been treated (Stier, iv. 168, edn. 2: Trench, Mir. 251, edn. 2) as making a difference between the man lame from his birth in Acts iii. 8, who *walked* and *leaped* and *praised God;* and this man, who, since sin had been the cause of his disease (ver. 14), is ordered to carry his bed, "a present memento of his past sin." Possibly; but our Lord must have had in

i ver. 6.
k Matt. xxii. 23. Josh. vi. 26.
l John, ch. xviii. 31 only. = Matt. xii. 2 al. fr.
m = ch. iv. 46. vi. 15. Matt. iv. 19. v. 36. Acts ii. 36. Gen. xlv. 9.
n ver. 15. ch. vii. 23 only.
o pres., ch. i. 40 reff.
p here only. Judg. iv. 18 (3ce) & xviii. 26 A. 2 Kings ii. 24. xxiii. 16 only.

πάτει. 9 καὶ εὐθέως [i] ἐγένετο [i] ὑγιὴς ὁ ἄνθρωπος, καὶ
ἦρεν τὸν [h] κράβαττον αὐτοῦ καὶ περιεπάτει. ἦν δὲ σάββατον [k] ἐν ἐκείνῃ τῇ ἡμέρᾳ. 10 ἔλεγον οὖν οἱ Ἰουδαῖοι τῷ
τεθεραπευμένῳ Σάββατόν ἐστιν· καὶ οὐκ [l] ἔξεστίν σοι ἆραι
τὸν [h] κράβαττον. 11 ἀπεκρίθη αὐτοῖς Ὁ [mn] ποιήσας με
[n] ὑγιῆ, ἐκεῖνός μοι εἶπεν Ἆρον τὸν [h] κράβαττόν σου καὶ
περιπάτει. 12 ἠρώτησαν αὐτὸν Τίς ἐστιν ὁ ἄνθρωπος
ὁ εἰπών σοι Ἆρον καὶ περιπάτει; 13 ὁ δὲ ἰαθεὶς οὐκ
ᾔδει τίς [o] ἐστιν· ὁ γὰρ Ἰησοῦς [p] ἐξένευσεν ὄχλου ὄντος

...[περι]πατει I_d. ABCDE FGHKL MSUV ΓΔΛΠℵ 1. 33. 69

9. om *και ευθεως* ℵ (ins ℵ[3a·b]) : om *ευθεως* D lat-*l* arm. *υγιης* bef *εγενετο* D **1** latt(not *q*). ins *εγερθεις* bef *ηρεν* (*cf Matt* ix. 7) D **1**. 69 lat-*ff*$_2$ Syr arm : *ηγερθη και* ℵ [lat-*a b e* syr-w-ast]. *εαυτου* C[1]. *περιπατει* (for *περιεπ.*) AL. om *εν εκ. τ. ημ.* D lat-*e*.

10. rec om *και*, with C[3] rel vulg lat-*c f* [*q* syr-cu] syrr Chr$_1$ Hil$_1$: ins A B(see table) C[1]DGLV[Γ]ℵ **1**. 33. 69 lat-*a b e l* [syr-jer] coptt æth arm Chr$_1$ Cyr$_1$. aft *τ. κρ.* ins *σου* C[1]DLΛ[Π]ℵ 69 latt(exc *e*) Syr syr-cu syr-w-ast [syr-jer coptt æth arm] Chr$_1$ Cyr$_1$.

11. ins *ος δε* bef *απεκ.* AB ; *ο δε* C[1]GKLΔΛ[Π]ℵ foss lat-*f* syrr [syr-jer] copt [Cyr-p$_1$]: om C[3]D rel latt syr-cu (æth) arm. (33 def.) *απεκρινατο* ℵ[1]. (*υγιην* ℵ[1].) *αραι* ℵ[1]. om *σου* ℵ[1]. *περιπατειν* ℵ[1].

12. rec aft *ηρωτησαν* ins *ουν*, with AC rel vulg lat-*c* syr : om BDℵ foss lat-*a e ff*$_2$ syr-cu sah arm. *αραι* ℵ[1]. rec aft *αρον* ins *τον κραββατον σου* (*from above*), with AC[3]D rel latt syrr syr-cu copt æth arm Chr : om BC[1]Lℵ sah. *περιπατειν* ℵ[1].

13. om *δε* D[1][and lat](ins D-corr[1]). for *ιαθεις*, *ασθενων* (*from ver* 7) D foss lat-*b l*. for *εστιν*, *ην* D latt. *ενευσεν* D[1](txt D-corr[1]) ℵ[1].

his view what was to follow, and have ordered it also to bring about this his first open controversy with the Jews.

10.] **οἱ Ἰουδαῖοι**, never the *multitude*, but always those in authority of some kind, whom John ever puts forward as the representatives of the whole people in their rejection of the Lord. **οὐκ ἔξεστιν]** The bearing of burdens on the Sabbath was forbidden not only by the glosses of the Pharisees, but *by the law itself*. See Neh. xiii. 15—19: Exod. xxxi. 13—17: Jer. xvii. 21, 22. And our Lord does not, as in another case (Luke xiii. 15, 16), appeal here to the reasonableness of the deed being done on the Sabbath, *salvo sabbato*, but takes altogether loftier ground, as being One greater than the Sabbath. The whole kernel of this incident and discourse is *not, that it is lawful to do works of mercy on the Sabbath :* but *that the Son of God* (here) *is Lord of the Sabbath.*

11.] The man's excuse is simple and sufficient; and for us, important, inasmuch as it goes into the depth of the matter, and is by the Jews themselves accepted. He who had power to make him whole, had power to suspend that law which was, like the healing, God's work. The authority which had overruled one appointment of Providence, could overrule another. I do not mean that this reasoning was *present to the man's mind ;*—he very likely spoke only from intense feeling of obligation to One who had done so much for him ;—but it lay *beneath the words*, and the Jews recognized it, by transferring their blame, *from the man, to Him who healed him.*

12.] Not, 'who is he that *healed thee?*' but they carefully bring out the unfavourable side of what had taken place, as malicious persons always do.

13.] Difficulty has been found here from the supposed improbability that some should not have told him, seeing that Jesus was by this time well known in Jerusalem. But this is wholly unnecessary. His fame had not been so spread yet, but that He might during the crowd of strangers at the feast pass unnoticed. **ἐξένευσεν, passed on unobserved :** just spoke the healing words, and then went on among the crowd; so that no particular attention was attracted to Himself, either by the sick man or others. *The context requires this interpretation :* being violated by the ordinary one, that Jesus '*conveyed himself away*, because a multitude was in the place :' for that would imply that attention had been attracted towards him which He wished to avoid; and in that case he could hardly fail to have been known to the man and to others. Observe, ἐξένευσεν has for its understood *object, the man* subjectively *:—escaped his notice, a crowd*

ἐν τῷ τόπῳ. 14 μετὰ ταῦτα εὑρίσκει αὐτὸν ὁ Ἰησοῦς
ἐν τῷ ἱερῷ, καὶ εἶπεν αὐτῷ Ἴδε [i] ὑγιὴς [i] γέγονας· μηκέτι
ἁμάρτανε, ἵνα μὴ [q] χεῖρόν σοί τι γένηται. 15 ἀπῆλθεν ὁ
ἄνθρωπος, καὶ [r] ἀνήγγειλεν τοῖς Ἰουδαίοις ὅτι Ἰησοῦς
[o] ἐστὶν ὁ [s] ποιήσας αὐτὸν [s] ὑγιῆ. 16 καὶ διὰ τοῦτο [t] ἐδίωκον
...σαβ-βατω C. οἱ Ἰουδαῖοι τὸν Ἰησοῦν, ὅτι ταῦτα ἐποίει ἐν σαββάτῳ.
17 ὁ δὲ Ἰησοῦς [u] ἀπεκρίνατο αὐτοῖς Ὁ πατήρ μου [v] ἕως
ἄρτι [w] ἐργάζεται, κἀγὼ ἐργάζομαι. 18 διὰ τοῦτο οὖν
...εζη F. μᾶλλον [x] ἐζήτουν αὐτὸν οἱ Ἰουδαῖοι ἀποκτεῖναι, ὅτι

q Matt. ix. 16 reff.
r ch. iv. 25 reff.
s ver. 11.
t = Matt. v. 10, &c. reff.
u = Matt. xi. 25 reff.
v Matt. xi. 12. ch. ii. 10. xvi. 24. 1 Cor. iv. 13. viii. 7. xv. 6. 1 John ii. 9 only.
w = Rom. iv. 4, 5. 1 Cor. ix. 6.
x = Matt. xii. 46, 47 reff.

for τοπω, μεσω ℵ[1].

14. for αυτον ο ιησ., ο ῑς τον τεθεραπευμενον ℵ[1], simly syr-cu [syr-jer] æth. om ὁ B. for ειπεν, λεγει ℵ. rec τι bef σοι, with DEK[Π]ℵ 1. 33. 69 lat-*a b e f* [*l q*] arm Orig$_1$[int$_3$ Bas$_1$] Chr$_2$ Iren-int$_2$ Cypr$_4$: txt ABC rel vulg lat-*c* Syr Cyr-jer$_2$ Cyr$_1$.

15. ins και bef απηλθεν A foss lat-*b f* [*q*] syrr syr-cu [syr-jer] æth: add ουν DΛℵ[3a] copt Chr$_1$ Cyr$_1$: om BCℵ[1] rel. for ανηγγειλεν, ειπεν CLℵ lat-*a e q* Syr syr-cu [syr-jer] copt Cyr$_1$: txt AB rel vulg lat-*b c f ff$_2$* syr æth arm, απηγγειλεν DKUΔ 33. 69 Chr$_1$. for αυτον, με DΛ[2] 1 lat-*a e ff$_2$ l q* syr-cu copt-dz arm.

16. rec τον ιησουν bef οι ιουδαιοι, with A rel lat-*a e q* syr copt-wilk arm: txt BCD LUℵ 33. 69 vulg lat-*b c f g* [*l*] Syr syr-cu [syr-jer] copt-schw æth Hil$_1$. rec adds και εζητουν αυτον αποκτειναι (*to justify ver* 18), with A rel lat-*e f q* syrr copt-wilk æth: om BCDLℵ 1. 33. 69 latt syr-cu copt-schw arm Chr$_1$ Non$_1$. om εν D lat-*a b e q* Tert Hil$_1$.

17. om ιησ. Bℵ. απεκρινετο ℵ: απεκριθη D ev-47.

18. om ουν Dℵ forj lat-*a b* [*c e f l* syr-jer] arm Hil$_1$. οι ιουδαιοι bef εζητουν αυτον D [syr-cu Tert$_1$] Hil$_1$.

being in the place: not referring to any thing which Jesus had *done* himself.

14.] The knowledge of our Lord extended even to the sin committed thirty-eight years ago, from which this long sickness had resulted, for so it is implied here. The **χεῖρόν τι**, as Trench observes (Mir. 254, edn. 2), "gives us an awful glimpse of the severity of God's judgments:"—see Matt. xii. 45.

15.] The man appears to have done this partly in obedience to the authorities; partly perhaps to complete his apology for himself (Bengel). We can hardly imagine ingratitude in him to have been the cause; especially as ὁ ποιήσας αὐτὸν ὑγιῆ speaks so plainly of the benefit received: compare ver. 11 and note.

16.] **ἐδίωκον** is not used in the sense of *legal prosecution* in the N. T.:—**persecuted** is the best word for it.

17.] The *true keeping* of the rest of the Sabbath was not that otiose and unprofitable cessation from even good deeds, which they would enforce: the Sabbath was *made for man*;—and, in its Jewish form, for man in a mere state of legal discipline (which truth could not yet be brought out to them, but is implied in this verse, because His people are even as He is—in the liberty wherewith He hath made them free); whereas He, the only-begotten of the Father, doing the works of God in the world, *stands on higher ground*, and hallows, instead of breaking the Sabbath, by thus working on it. "He is no more a breaker of the Sabbath than God is, when He upholds with an energy that knows no pause the work of His creation from hour to hour, and from moment to moment; 'My Father worketh hitherto, and I work;' My work is but the reflex of His work. Abstinence from outward work belongs not to the idea of a Sabbath, it is only more or less the necessary condition of it for beings so framed as ever to be in danger of losing the true collection and rest of the spirit in the multiplicity of earthly toil and business. Man indeed must cease from *his* work if a higher work is to find place in him. He scatters himself in his work, and therefore he must collect himself anew, and have seasons for so doing. But with Him who is one with the Father, it is otherwise. In Him the deepest rest is not excluded by the highest activity." (Trench, Mir. p. 257, edn. 2.)

18.] The ground of the charge is now shifted; and by these last words (ver. 17), occasion is given for one of our Lord's most weighty discourses.

The Jews understood His words to mean nothing short of *peculiar personal*

y = Matt. v. 19. ch. vii. 23. x. 35 only.	οὐ μόνον [y]ἔλυεν τὸ σάββατον, ἀλλὰ καὶ πατέρα [z]ἴδιον	ABDEG
	[a]ἔλεγεν τὸν θεόν, [bc]ἴσον ἑαυτὸν [b]ποιῶν τῷ [c]θεῷ. 19 ἀπ-	HKLMS UVΓΛΔ
z ch. i. 42. Rom. viii. 32. 1 Cor. vii. 2.	εκρίνατο οὖν ὁ Ἰησοῦς καὶ εἶπεν αὐτοῖς Ἀμὴν ἀμὴν	Πℵ 1. 33. 69
a = Mark x. 18 reff.	λέγω ὑμῖν, οὐ δύναται ὁ υἱὸς ποιεῖν [d]ἀφ' ἑαυτοῦ οὐδέν,	
b Matt. xx. 12 only. 2 Macc. ix. 15.	ἐὰν μή τι βλέπῃ τὸν πατέρα ποιοῦντα· ἃ γὰρ ἂν ἐκεῖνος	
c Phil. ii. 6. ἴσ., Matt.	ποιῇ, ταῦτα καὶ ὁ υἱὸς ὁμοίως ποιεῖ. 20 ὁ γὰρ πατὴρ	
Phil. as above. Mark xiv. 56, 59.	φιλεῖ τὸν υἱόν, καὶ πάντα δείκνυσιν αὐτῷ ἃ αὐτὸς ποιεῖ·	
Luke vi. 34. Acts xi. 17.	καὶ μείζονα τούτων δείξει αὐτῷ ἔργα, ἵνα ὑμεῖς θαυμά-	
Rev. xxi. 16 only. Ezek. xl. 5.	ζητε· 21 ὥςπερ γὰρ ὁ πατὴρ [e]ἐγείρει τοὺς νεκροὺς καὶ	

d ver. 30. ch. x. 18. xvi. 13. Luke xii. 57. xxi. 30. 2 Cor. iii. 5. x. 7 al. e Matt. x. 8 reff.

19. απεκριθη D 33: ελεγεν ℵ[1]. for ο ιησ. και ειπ. αυτ., αυτοις ο ῑς ℵ[1].—om ο ιησ. B Scr's c.—for ειπεν, ελεγεν BLℵ[3a] [Tert$_1$]. om 2nd αμην ℵ[1] 237. aft ο υιος ins του ανθρωπου D 69 arm. aft ποιειν ins τι, omg ουδεν below, D. for εαν, αν Bℵ. ποιουντα bef τον πατερα D[-gr]. om αν A D-gr L[Π] lat-*e* [*q* Tert$_1$]. for ποιη, ποιει AE[1]Λ[ΓΠ] lat-*b e* Orig$_1$ Chr: ποιησῃ (but ποιει at first) D. ποιει bef ομοιως Dℵ lat-*a b l* Orig-int$_2$ Hil$_8$ [Novat$_1$ Ambr$_1$].

20. for φιλει, αγαπα D Orig$_1$ Chr$_1$. for δεικνυσιν, δεικνυει D: διγνυσιν A. c. αν αυτος ποιη D 16. εργα bef δειξει αυτω ℵ [lat-*b* Cyr$_1$ Tert$_1$ Hil$_2$]. for δειξει, δεικνυσιν D 28 lat-*e* [syr-cu arm]. θαυμαζετε Lℵ 69 ev-y.

21. for ωσπερ, ως ℵ.

Sonship, and thus equality of nature with God. And that this their understanding *was the right one*, the discourse testifies. *All might in one sense*, and *the Jews did in a closer sense*, call God *their*, or *our*, *Father;* but they at once said that the individual use of 'MY FATHER' by Jesus had a totally distinct, and in their view a blasphemous, meaning: this latter especially, because He thus made God a participator in his crime of breaking the sabbath. Thus we obtain from the adversaries of the faith a most important statement of one of its highest and holiest doctrines. **19.**] The discourse is a wonderful setting forth of the Person and Office of the Son of God in His Ministrations as the Word of the Father. It still has reference to the charge of working on the Sabbath, and the context takes in our Lord's answer both to this, ver. 17, and to the Jews' accusation, ver. 18. In this verse, He states that He cannot work any but the works of God: *cannot*, by his very relationship to the Father, by the very nature and necessity of the case;—the **ἀφ' ἑαυτοῦ** being an impossible supposition, and purposely set here to express one:—the Son *cannot* work of Himself, because *He is* the Son: His very Person presupposes the Father's will and counsel as *His* will and counsel,—and His perfect *knowledge* of that will and counsel. And this, because every *creature* may abuse its freedom, and *will contrary to God:* but THE SON, standing in essential unity with God, cannot, even when become Man, commit sin,—break the Sabbath; for His whole Being and Working is in and of God. **ἃ γὰρ ἂν . . .**] This clause *converts* the former proposition, and asserts its truth when thus converted. '*For* it is the very nature of the Son to do whatever the Father doeth.' Also, to do these works **ὁμοίως**—after the same plan and proceeding, so that there can be no discord, but unity. **20.**] **For** (this last is ensured by the fact, that) **the Father loves the Son, and shews to Him** (in this the Lord sets forth to us the unfolding of the will and purposes of the Father to (Mark xiii. 32: Acts i. 7) and by Him, in His Mediatorial office) **all things which He Himself does** (all the purposes of His secret counsel;—for with the Father, *doing* is *willing;* it is *only the Son who acts in time*); and this manifestation will go on increasing in majesty, that the wonder which now is excited in you by these works may be brought out to its full measure (in the acceptation or rejection of the Son of God—wonder leading naturally to the *τιμή* of ver. 23). **21.**] It is very important to observe the distinction here between the working of the Eternal Son (in creation, e. g.) as He is *ἐν οὐρανῷ*, with God, and His working in the state of His humiliation in which the Father should by degrees advance Him to exaltation and put His enemies under His feet. Of the *latter of these* mention is made (ver. 20) in the *future*, of the *former* in the *present*. The former belong to the Son as His proper and essential work: the latter are

[f] ζωοποιεῖ, οὕτως καὶ ὁ υἱὸς οὓς θέλει [f] ζωοποιεῖ.
22 οὐδὲ γὰρ ὁ πατὴρ [g] κρίνει οὐδένα, ἀλλὰ τὴν [hi] κρίσιν
πᾶσαν [i] δέδωκεν τῷ υἱῷ, 23 ἵνα πάντες τιμῶσιν τὸν υἱὸν
καθὼς τιμῶσιν τὸν πατέρα. ὁ μὴ τιμῶν τὸν υἱὸν οὐ
τιμᾷ τὸν πατέρα τὸν πέμψαντα αὐτόν. 24 [j] ἀμὴν ἀμὴν
λέγω ὑμῖν ὅτι ὁ τὸν λόγον μου ἀκούων καὶ [k] πιστεύων
τῷ πέμψαντί με ἔχει [l] ζωὴν [l] αἰώνιον· καὶ εἰς κρίσιν οὐκ
[m] ἔρχεται, ἀλλὰ [n] μεταβέβηκεν ἐκ τοῦ [n] θανάτου εἰς τὴν

f here bis. ch. vi. 63. Rom. iv. 17. viii. 11. 1 Cor. xv. 22, 36, 45. 2 Cor. iii. 6. Gal. iii. 21. 1 Pet. iii. 18 only. 4 Kings v. 7.
g 1 Cor. v. 12, 13. 1 Pet. iv. 5. Gen. xviii. 25.
h ver. 27. 2 Thess. i. 5. Jude 15.
i Dan. vii. 22 LXX. see Rev. xx. 4.
j ch. iii. 3, 5, 11. vi. 26, &c. see Matt. v. 18 reff.
k constr., Matt. xxi. 25 ‖, &c. Mark xvi. 13, 14. vv. 38, 46 ch. iv. 21. x. 37. Acts viii. 12. xvi. 34. Tit. iii. 8. 1 John v. 10.
l ch. iii. 15 reff.
m = Acts xix. 27. Job xxxiii. 28 BCℵ F(not A).
n 1 John iii. 14.

24. om *οτι* D 240-4 Clem$_1$. om *την* D^1(ins D^2).

opened out before Him in the process of His passing onward in the humanity which He has taken. And the unfolding of these latter shall all be in the direction of, and in accordance with, the eternal attributes of the Son: see ch. xvii. 5: resulting in His being exalted to the right hand of the Father. So here,—as it is the Father's essential work to vivify the dead (see Rom. viii. 11: 1 Sam. ii. 6 al.), so the Son vivifies whom He will: this last **οὓς θέλει** not implying any selection out of mankind, nor said merely to remove the Jewish prejudice that their own nation alone should rise from the dead,—but meaning, that in every instance where *His will is to vivify*, the result invariably follows. Observe, this **ζωοποιεῖ** lays hold of life in its innermost and deepest sense, and thus finds its illustration in the waking both of the *outwardly* and the *spiritually* dead.

22.] In the **οὐδὲ γάρ** is implied that as the Father does not Himself, by His own proper act, *vivify* any, but commits all quickening power to the Son:—so is it with judgment also. And *judgment* contains eminently in itself the *οὓς θέλει*,—when *ζωοπ.* is understood—as it must be *now*—of *bestowing everlasting life.* Again, the raising of the *outwardly dead* is to be understood as a sign that He who works it is appointed Judge of quick and dead, for it is a part of the office of that Judge;—*in the vivifying, the judgment is made:* see below, ver. 29, and Ps. lxxii. 1—4.

23.] This being so, the end of all is, *the honour of the Father in and by the Son.* He (the Son) is the Lord of life, and the Judge of the world;—all must honour Him with equal honour to that which they pay to the Father:—and whosoever does not, however he may imagine that he honours or approaches God, does not honour him at all;—because *He can only be known or honoured by us as* 'THE FATHER WHO SENT HIS SON.'

24.] What follows, to ver. 30 incl., is an expansion of the two assertions in vv. 21, 22,—the **ζωοποιεῖν** and the **κρίνειν**,—intimately bound up as they are together. There is a parallelism in vv. 24 and 25 which should be noticed for the right understanding of the words. *ὁ τὸν λόγον μου* **ἀκούων** in one, answers to *οἱ νεκροὶ* **ἀκούσονται** *τῆς φωνῆς τοῦ υἱοῦ τοῦ θεοῦ* in the other. It is a kind of *hearing* which awakens to life,—one accompanied by *πιστεύειν τῷ πέμψαντί με*. And this last is not barely 'Him who sent Me,' but Him, *the very essence of belief in Whom is in this,* THAT HE SENT ME (see ch. xii. 44). And the *dative* here after *πιστεύω* expresses that belief in the *testimony* of God that He hath sent His Son, which is dwelt on so much 1 John v. 9—12, where, ver. 10, we have the same *ὁ μὴ πιστεύων τῷ θεῷ.*

ἔχει ζ. αἰ.] So 1 John v. 12, 13. The **πιστεύων** and the **ἔχει ζ. αἰ.** are *commensurate*:—where the faith is, the possession of eternal life is:—and when the one remits, the other is forfeited. But here the faith is set before us as an *enduring* faith, and its effects described *in their completion* (see Eph. i. 19, 20). **εἰς κρίσιν οὐκ ἔρχεται,**—*κρίσις* being the *separation*,—the effect of which is to gather out of the Kingdom *all that offendeth;*—and thus regarding especially the *damnatory* part of judgment,—he who believes *comes not into*, has no concern with, *κρίσις*. Compare Ps. cxlii. 2 LXX. The reckoning which ends with *εὖ ἀγαθὲ δοῦλε*, is not *κρίσις*: *the reward is of free grace.* In this sense, the believers in Christ will not be judged according to their works: they are justified before God by faith, and *by God*—*θεὸς ὁ δικαιῶν, τίς ὁ κατακρίνων;* Their 'passage over' from death into life *has already taken place,*—from the state of spiritual death into that *ζωὴ αἰώνιος*, which in their believing state they *ἔχουσι*

o ch. iv. 23. p see Matt. iv. 3 note. q = Matt. ix. 18 reff. r ch. vi. 53 reff. s Matt. xiii. 11 reff. t ch. i. 12 reff. u Jude 15 only. Gen. xviii. 25. v = Luke xviii. 7, 8 reff. w with obj. acc., Luke vii. 9. xxiv. 12. Acts vii. 31. Jude 16 only. Lev. xix. 15. Dan. viii. 27 Theod. x ch. iv. 21 reff. y Matt. viii. 28 al. Gen. xxiii. 6, 9.

ABDEG HKLMS UVΓΔΛ Πℵ 1. 33. 69

n ζωήν. 25 k ἀμὴν ἀμὴν λέγω ὑμῖν ὅτι o ἔρχεται ὥρα καὶ
νῦν ἐστιν ὅτε οἱ νεκροὶ ἀκούσονται τῆς φωνῆς τοῦ p υἱοῦ
τοῦ p θεοῦ, καὶ οἱ ἀκούσαντες q ζήσουσιν. 26 ὥσπερ γὰρ ὁ
πατὴρ r ἔχει r ζωὴν ἐν ἑαυτῷ, οὕτως καὶ τῷ υἱῷ s ἔδωκεν
r ζωὴν r ἔχειν ἐν ἑαυτῷ· 27 καὶ t ἐξουσίαν t ἔδωκεν αὐτῷ
u κρίσιν uv ποιεῖν, ὅτι υἱὸς ἀνθρώπου ἐστίν. 28 μὴ w θαυμάζετε
τοῦτο· ὅτι x ἔρχεται ὥρα, ἐν ᾗ πάντες οἱ ἐν τοῖς y μνη-

25. om *και νυν εστιν* ℵ[1] lat-*a b* [Tert$_2$ Ambr$_1$]. ακουσουσιν (for -σονται) B 22. 357 Chr$_2$ [Cyr-p$_1$] : -σωσιν Lℵ 1. 33. 69 Chr-mss [Cyr-p$_1$]: txt AD rel [Hipp$_2$]. om 2nd *οἱ* ℵ[1] [(lat-*l* Tert$_1$)]. rec ζησονται (*more usual*), with A rel Hipp$_2$: txt BDLℵ 1. 33 Chr-5-mss$_2$.

26. *ως* Dℵ[1] [Eus$_1$]. aft *πατηρ* ins *ο ζων* D. *ζωην* bef *εχει* ℵ 254 [Eus$_3$ Did$_1$ Epiph$_1$(txt$_1$) Novat$_1$]. rec *εδωκεν* bef *και τω υιω*, with AD rel vulg lat-*a*(appy) *c e* [*f q* syr-jer] syrr syr-cu copt arm [Did$_1$ Chr$_1$] : txt BLℵ[3a] lat-*b l* æth Eus$_2$ [Cyr-jer] Epiph$_2$ Cyr[-p(but *εδωκε*)] Orig-int$_1$ Tert$_1$ Hil$_{sæpe}$.—om last clause (*homœotel*) ℵ[1].

27. transp *εξουσιαν* and *κρισιν* ℵ[1]. rec ins *και* bef *κρισιν*, with D-gr rel am(with fuld em forj ing mt &c) lat-*f g q* syrr [Chr$_1$ Cyr$_1$] : om ABLℵ 33 vulg lat-*b c e l* D-lat syr-cu syr-jer copt æth arm Orig$_5$ Did$_1$ [Thdrt$_1$] Leo Vig.

already. It is to be observed that our Lord speaks in very similar terms of the unbelieving being *condemned already*, in ch. iii. 18. The *perfect* sense of **μεταβέβηκεν** must not be weakened nor explained away,—see ref. **25.**] This verse continues to refer to *spiritual* awakening from the dead. The **ἔρχεται ὥρα κ. νῦν ἐστιν** is an expression (see ref.) used of those things which are to characterize the spiritual Kingdom of Christ, which was even now begun among men, but not yet brought (until the day of Pentecost, Acts ii.) to its completion. Thus it **cometh**, in its fulness,—and **even now is begun.** **οἱ νεκροί,**—in reference to *ἐκ θανάτου* of the preceding verse —**the** *spiritually* **dead**:—see below on ver. 28. **τῆς φωνῆς,** His *call to awake*, in its widest and deepest sense;—by His own preaching, by His Apostles, His ministers, &c. &c. In all these He speaks to the spiritually dead. **οἱ ἀκούσ.**] Not *ἀκούσαντες merely*, which would be 'and having heard it, shall live:' but **οἱ** *ἀκούσ.*, **and** THEY WHO **have heard it** (or, **who hear it**) **shall live.** *This determines the verse to be spoken of spiritual, not bodily* awakening. **οἱ ἀκούσαντες** are the persons to whom the Lord cried so often *ὁ ἔχων ὦτα ἀκούειν, ἀκουέτω*:—the persons who stand opposed to those addressed in ver. 40, *οὐ θέλετε ἐλθεῖν πρός με, ἵνα ζωὴν ἔχητε.* **ζήσουσιν** is explained in the next verse. **26, 27.**] We have here again *ζωοποιεῖν* and *κρίνειν* bound together as the two great departments of the Son's working;—the former, as substantiating the *ζήσουσιν* just uttered; the latter, as leading on to the great announcement of the next verse. But the two departments spring from *two distinct sources*, united in the Person of the Incarnate Son of God. The Father hath given Him to have life in Himself, *as He is* THE SON OF GOD. *We* have none of us *life in ourselves: in Him* we live and move and have our being. But He, as the Father is, is the *source* of Life. Then again the Father hath given Him power to pass judgment, *because He is* THE SON OF MAN; man is to be judged by Man,—by that Man whom God hath appointed, who is the inclusive Head of humanity, and to whom mankind, and man's *world*, pertain by right of covenant-purchase. This *κρίσιν* **ποιεῖν** leads the thought to the *great occasion* when judgment shall be executed; which accordingly is treated of in the next verse. **28, 29.**] **μὴ θαυμ.**, as ch. iii. 7, introduces a matter of even *greater* wonder to them;—the astounding proof which shall be given in the face of the universe that this is so. **ἔρχεται ὥρα,** but not *καὶ νῦν ἐστιν* this time,—because He is *now speaking* of the great day of the resurrection: when not merely *οἱ νεκροί*, but **πάντες οἱ ἐν τοῖς μνημείοις,** shall hear His voice, and **οἱ** *ἀκούσαντες* are not specified, because *all* shall *hear* in the fullest sense. Observe that here, as elsewhere, when the judgment according to *works* is spoken of, it is the great *general* resurrection of Matt. xxv. 31—46, which (and the notes) compare. So here we have not *οἱ πιστεύσαντες* and *οἱ*

μείοις ἀκούσονται τῆς φωνῆς αὐτοῦ
29 καὶ [z] ἐκπορεύσονται,
οἱ τὰ ἀγαθὰ ποιήσαντες εἰς [a] ἀνάστασιν [b] ζωῆς, οἱ τὰ
[c] φαῦλα πράξαντες εἰς [a] ἀνάστασιν [bd] κρίσεως.
30 οὐ δύνα-
μαι ἐγὼ ποιεῖν [e] ἀπ' ἐμαυτοῦ οὐδέν. καθὼς ἀκούω κρίνω,
καὶ ἡ κρίσις ἡ ἐμὴ δικαία ἐστίν, ὅτι οὐ [f] ζητῶ τὸ θέλημα
τὸ ἐμὸν ἀλλὰ τὸ θέλημα τοῦ πέμψαντός με.
31 ἐὰν ἐγὼ
[g] μαρτυρῶ [g] περὶ ἐμαυτοῦ, ἡ μαρτυρία μου οὐκ ἔστιν
ἀληθής.
32 ἄλλος ἐστὶν ὁ [g] μαρτυρῶν [g] περὶ ἐμοῦ, καὶ

z Luke iii. 7. Rev. xvi. 14 al.
a Luke xiv. 14. Rev. xx. 5, 6.
b gen., Mark i. 4 ‖ L.
c ch. iii. 20 reff.
d = Matt. xxiii. 33. Heb. x. 27. 2 Pet. ii. 4. Rev. xviii. 10.
e ver. 19.
f ch. vii. 18. viii. 50. 1 Cor. x. 24, 33 al. Neh. ii. 10.
g ch. i. 7, 8 reff.

28. ακουσουσιν B 157 [Chr$_1$]: -σωσιν LΔℵ 33 [Cyr-p$_3$]: txt AD rel [Bas$_1$ Chr$_1$ [Cyr-p$_1$]].

29. for εκπορ., εξελευσονται D [Cyr-p$_2$]. rec aft 2nd οι ins δε, with ADℵ rel vulg lat-*b c f* [*l q* syr-jer] syr [Cyr-p$_2$]: *et qui* Syr syr-cu copt Iren-int$_1$: txt B lat-*a e ff*$_2$ Tert$_1$ Aug$_3$. om 2nd τα D. πρασσοντες D.

30. απ' εμαυτου bef ποιειν D 13. 249 vulg lat-*b c f* [*ff*$_2$ *l q*] Syr (syr-cu) Eus$_1$: ποιειν bef εγω ℵ 33 Scr's t. om και ℵ[1](appy: ins ℵ-corr[1.3]). (με is not omd in B as Btly: see table.) rec at end ins πατρος, with E rel em(with tol) lat-*b c* [Bas$_1$ Cyr$_1$]: om ABDKLΔΛℵ 1. 33 vulg lat-*a e f* copt æth arm Orig$_3$ Eus$_2$ Chr$_2$ Ambr$_1$ Aug$_1$.

μὴ πιστεύσαντες, but the categories reach far wider, including indeed in this most general form the first resurrection unto life also—and the two great classes are described as **οἱ τὰ ἀγ. ποιήσαντες** and **οἱ τὰ φαῦλα πράξαντες.** On the difference between ποιέω and πράσσω, see note on ch. iii. 20, 21. Observe, that **ζωή** and **κρίσις** stand opposed here, as in ver. 24:—not that there is *no such thing* as an ἀνάστασις θανάτου (Schleiermacher, in Stier, iv. 194, edn. 2), but that *it is involved* in this κρίσις. Olshausen observes (ii. 153) that this, and Acts xxiv. 15, are the only *direct* declarations in the N. T. of a *bodily resurrection of the unjust* as well as of the just. It is implied in some places, e. g. Matt. x. 28, and less plainly in Matt. xxv. 34 ff.: Rev. xx. 5, 12, and directly asserted in the O. T., Dan. xii. 2. In 1 Cor. xv.,—as the object was to convince *believers in Christ* of the truth of the resurrection of *their* bodies,—no allusion is made to those who are not believers. **30.**] Here begins (see Stier, iv. 195, edn. 2) *the second part of the discourse*,—but bound on most closely to the first (ver. 23),—treating of the *testimony by which these things were substantiated, and which they ought to have received.* This verse is, however, perhaps rather a point of transition to the next, at which the testimony is first introduced. As the Son does nothing of Himself,—but His working and His judgment all spring from His deep unity of will and being with the Father,—this His great and last judgment, and all His other ones, will be just and holy (He being not separate from God, but one with Him); and therefore His witness given of Himself ver. 17, and called by them blasphemy, is true and holy also.

Observe, the discourse here passes into the *first person*, which was *understood* before, because he had called himself the Son of God,—but is henceforth used *expressly.* **31.**] This assertion is not to be trifled away by an accommodation, or supposed to be introduced by '*Ye will say to Me:*'—see by all means ch. viii. 12—14 and notes. The words are said in all earnestness, and are *strictly true.* If such a separation, and independent testimony, as is here supposed, *could take place*, it would be a falsification of the very conditions of the Truth of God as manifested by the Son, Who being the **λόγος**, speaks, not of himself, but of the Father. And in this sense ch. viii. 14 is eminently true also, the φῶς being the ἀπαύγασμα τῆς δόξης τοῦ πατρός. **32.**] **ἄλλος** can, by the inner coherence of the discourse, be no other than THE FATHER, of Whom so much has been said in the former part, but Who is hinted at rather than mentioned in *this* (πατρός in ver. 30 is spurious). *It cannot be John*,—from whom (ver. 34) our Lord *took not his testimony.* Similar modes of alluding to the Father occur ch. viii. 50: see also ch. viii. 18, and Matt. x. 28 and ‖. Many interpreters however understand it of *John*,—Chrysostom, Nonnus, Theophylact, Euthym.:—and lately De Wette has defended the view with some acuteness. But he has certainly missed the inner coherence of the passage. The reason why our Lord mentions John is not 'as ascending from the lesser witness to the greater,' but *purposely to remove the idea that He meant*

οἶδα ὅτι ἀληθής ἐστιν ἡ μαρτυρία ἣν [g] μαρτυρεῖ [g] περὶ
ἐμοῦ. 33 ὑμεῖς ἀπεστάλκατε πρὸς Ἰωάννην, καὶ [hi] μεμαρτύρηκεν τῇ [i] ἀληθείᾳ. 34 ἐγὼ δὲ οὐ [j] παρὰ ἀνθρώπου τὴν
μαρτυρίαν [j] λαμβάνω, ἀλλὰ ταῦτα λέγω ἵνα ὑμεῖς σωθῆτε.
35 ἐκεῖνος ἦν ὁ [k] λύχνος ὁ [k] καιόμενος καὶ [l] φαίνων, ὑμεῖς
δὲ [m] ἠθελήσατε [n] ἀγαλλιαθῆναι [o] πρὸς [o] ὥραν ἐν τῷ φωτὶ
αὐτοῦ. 36 ἐγὼ δὲ ἔχω τὴν μαρτυρίαν [p] μείζων [q] τοῦ

ABDEG HKLMS UVΓΔΛ ΠℵI. 33. 69

g dat., Matt. xxiii. 31 reff. h = ch. xviii. 37. (3 John 3.) i see note. j = vv. 41, 44. see Acts ii. 33. Rev. ii. 27. k Matt. v. 15 reff. Sir. xlviii. 1. l intr., John only (ch. i. 5. 1 John ii. 8. Rev. i. 16. viii. 12. xxi. 23), exc. 2 Pet. i. 19. Gen. i. 17. m ver. 40. 2 Tim. iii. 12. Heb. xiii. 18. n w. ἐν, 1 Pet. i. 6. Ps. ii. 11. Hab. iii. 18. o 2 Cor. vii. 8. Gal. ii. 5. Philem. 15 only. see 1 Thess. ii. 17. q constr., 1 Cor. i. 25. see Matt. v. 20. 1 John ii. 2, and Winer, § 66. 2.

32. οιδατε Dℵ[1] lat-*a e q* syr-cu arm. aft η μαρτυρια ins μου D[1]-gr lat-*e*; αυτου D-corr[1] 254 tol lat-*b g* Syr syr-cu copt [æth] (Chr$_2$).
34. ανθρωπων DΛ[2] mn copt-wilk arm [Cyr-p$_1$].
35. λυχλον D[1](-λος D[2]). om δε ℵ[1] 253. rec αγαλλιασθηναι, with BL 1. 69 Chr$_2$: txt ADℵ rel Chr-mss [*Cyr*-p]. προς ωραν bef αγαλ. A Scr's c h s vulg (not am forj fuld &c) lat-*a ff*$_2$ Chr$_1$ Hil$_1$ Aug.
36. om την ℵ Chr-3-mss. rec (for μειζων) μειζω, with ℵ rel [Cyr$_1$]: μειζονα D

him only or principally by these words, and to set his testimony in its right place: then at ver. 36 He returns again to the ἄλλος μαρ. περὶ ἐμοῦ. **καὶ οἶδα . . . .**] This is the Son's testimony to the Father's truth: see ch. (iii. 33) vii. 28; viii. 26, 55. It testifies to the full consciousness on the part of the Son, even in the days of his humiliation, of the righteousness of the Father: and (for the testimony of the Father to the Son is contained in the Scriptures) also to His distinct recognition and approval (Ps. xl. 6—8) of psalm and type and prophecy, as applied to Himself and His work. **33.**] See ch. i. 19. The connexion is,—**another testifies of Me** (ver. 32)—'not John only, although he, when sent to, did certainly testify to the truth; for' &c. **τῇ ἀληθείᾳ,** not merely (Grot.) "*modeste* dictum;"—but *necessarily.* ἐμοί would have been asserting what the next verse denies. **34.**] '**I take not my testimony** (the testimony to Me of which I have spoken) **from man,** but I mention John's testimony that you may make the intended use of it, to be led to Me for salvation.' **35.**] This **ἦν** shews, as Stier rightly observes, that John *was now cast into prison,* if not executed.
ὁ λύχνος] The article has been taken by some (e. g. Bengel, Lücke, Stier) to point to the prophecies concerning John. But we have no passage in the O. T. which designates Elias in such terms. In ref. Sirach we read of him, ἀνέστη προφήτης ὡς πῦρ, καὶ ὁ λόγος αὐτοῦ ὡς λαμπὰς ἐκαίετο, which Stier thinks may be referred to here. We may, as indeed he also suggests, believe that those words represent or gave rise to a common way of speaking of Elias, as certain Rabbis were called 'The candle of the Law,' &c. (Lightf.) De Wette takes the article as meaning, '*the lamp which was to lead you,*' &c.
καιόμενος, not καίων, as it is ὁ λύχνος, not τὸ φῶς: *lumen illuminatum,* not *lumen illuminans:* see note on Matt. v. 14.
καὶ φαίνων (lit up), **and shining.** The description sets forth the *derived,* and *transitory* nature of John's light.
ὑμεῖς δὲ . . . .] See Ezek. xxxiii. 30, 32. 'But you wished only to disport yourselves in his light for a time—came out to him in crowds at first,—and—like silly children who play with the fire till it burns and hurts them, and then shrink from and loathe it,—when he began to speak of deep repentance as the preparation for God's Kingdom, and laid the axe to the root of the trees, you left him.' No one cared, when he was imprisoned and put to death. And even those few who remained true to him, did not follow his direction to Christ. For the mass of the people, and their leaders, his mission was in vain (Lücke, ii. 75). **36. ἔχω τὴν μ. μείζων**] Literally, **I have my witness greater** (μείζων being probably a solœcism like πλήρης in ch. i. 14, a nominative in concord with an accusative) . . . . **τοῦ Ἰωάννου,** not [perhaps], 'than *that of* John;'—but, **than John** *himself.* John *was* a testimony. **τὰ γὰρ ἔργα,** not *His miracles* alone, although those principally; but *the whole of His life and course of action,* full as it was of holiness, in which, and as forming harmonious parts of which, His miracles were testimonies of His divine mission. His *greatest work* (ch. vi. 29) was the awakening of faith, the ζωοποιεῖν of which we have heard before, to which the miracles were but as means to an end.

Ἰωάννου· τὰ γὰρ [r] ἔργα ἃ [r] δέδωκέν μοι ὁ πατὴρ [r] ἵνα
[s] τελειώσω αὐτά, αὐτὰ τὰ ἔργα ἃ ποιῶ, [g] μαρτυρεῖ [g] περὶ
ἐμοῦ ὅτι ὁ πατήρ με ἀπέσταλκεν. 37 καὶ ὁ πέμψας με
πατήρ, ἐκεῖνος [g] μεμαρτύρηκεν [g] περὶ ἐμοῦ· [t] οὔτε φωνὴν
αὐτοῦ πώποτε [u] ἀκηκόατε, οὔτε [v] εἶδος αὐτοῦ ἑωράκατε,
F [αυ]-του ουκ.. 38 [t] καὶ τὸν λόγον αὐτοῦ ουκ ἔχετε ἐν ὑμῖν [w] μένοντα, ὅτι ὃν
ἀπέστειλεν ἐκεῖνος, τούτῳ ὑμεῖς οὐ πιστεύετε. 39 [x] ἐραυνᾶτε

r ch. xvii. 4. s = ch. iv. 34 reff. t see ch. iv. 11. 3 John 10. u w. acc., Matt. vii. 24, 26 reff. perf., ch. iv. 42 reff. v Luke iii. 22. ix. 29. 2 Cor. v. 7. 1 Thess. v. 22 only. Exod. xxiv. 17. w = John only. ch. xv. 7. 1 John ii. 14, 24. iii. 9, 17 al. x ch. vii. 52. Rom. viii. 27. 1 Cor. ii. 10. 1 Pet. i. 11. Rev. ii. 23 only. Gen. xxxi. 35. see Ps. cxviii. 2.

Chr$_1$: *μειζον* 69 : txt ABEGMΛ 33. rec εδωκε (*mechanl repetn from vv.* 26, 27), with AD rel Chr$_1$: txt BL[Γ]ℵ 1. 33. 69 Ath$_1$ [Cyr-p$_1$]. rec ins εγω bef ποιω, with Δ-gr rel vulg lat-*c e f* [*q* syr-jer] syr goth [Bas$_1$] : om ABDLℵ 1. 33 lat-*b* Δ-lat copt æth arm Cyr$_1$ Hil$_1$. εμε ℵ. απεστειλεν D 241-5-8-53-8 Scr's c g ev-x [Bas$_1$] Chr$_2$.

37. rec (for εκεινος) αυτος, with A rel vulg lat-*b c e f ff*$_2$ [*l q* syrr syr-jer copt &c] Chr$_1$ Cyr$_1$ Tert$_1$ Hil$_2$; εκεινος αυτος D (αυτος, *insd to give the sense of 'Himself,' afterwards absorbed the origl* εκεινος) : txt BLℵ lat-*a* Ath$_1$. for μεμαρτυρηκεν, μαρτυρει D lat-*b c* [*a f l q* syr-jer] syrr syr-cu (æth) Orig$_1$ [Did$_1$] Aug. rec ακηκοατε bef πωποτε, with E rel copt Chr$_1$ Cyr[-p$_1$] Tert$_1$ Quæst : txt ABDKL[Π]ℵ 33. 69 latt syrr syr-cu [syr-jer] goth arm [Syn-ep-Ant] Ath$_1$ Cyr[-p$_3$].

38. rec μενοντα bef εν υμιν, with AD rel lat-*a e q* syrr syr-cu goth arm Chr$_1$: txt BLℵ 1. 33 ev-y vulg lat-*b c f ff*$_2$ *g l* æth [syr-jer Ath$_1$] Cyr Hil. απεσταλκεν D ev-H.

39. (εραυνατε, so B[1]ℵ.)

ἃ δέδωκεν . . . . ἵνα τελ.] See ch. xvii. 4 and note. **αὐτὰ τὰ ἔργα ἃ ποιῶ**] The repetition is to shew that His life and working was an exact fulfilment of the Father's will. **The works which the Father hath given Me to do, those very works which I am doing, ...**

37—39.] The connexion of these verses has been much disputed. I believe it will be found to be this: 'The works of which I have spoken, are only *indirect* testimonies; the Father Himself, who sent Me, has given *direct* testimony concerning Me. Now that testimony cannot be derived by you, nor any man, by direct *communication* with Him; for ye have never heard His voice nor seen His shape. (Or perhaps have not heard His voice, as your fathers did from Sinai,—nor seen His visional appearance, as the Prophets did.) Nor (ver. 38), *in your case,* has it been given by that *inward witness* (ch. iii. 33: 1 John iv. 13, 14) which those have (and had in a measure, even before the gift of the Spirit—see inter al., Ps. li. 11) in whom His word abides; for ye have not His word abiding in you, not believing on Him whom He hath sent. Yet (ver. 39) there is *a form* of this direct testimony of the Father, accessible even to you;—'*search the Scriptures,*' &c. Chrysostom, Euthymius, Lampe, Bengel, &c., understand **φωνή** to refer to *the voice at our Lord's baptism:* but, as Lücke observes, **πώποτε** forbids this. I may also add that the perfect, **ἀκηκόατε,** excludes it. Had reference been to a *distinct event,* it must have been ἠκούσατε,—and (Lücke) τὴν φωνήν. Observe that the testimony in the Scriptures is not the only, nor the chief one, *intended* in ver. 37, but (as De Wette well maintains) the direct testimony *in the heart of the believer;*—which, as the Jews *have not,* they are directed to *another form* of the Father's testimony, *that in the Scriptures.*

ἐραυνᾶτε, either *indicative* (Cyril, Erasm.,* Beza, Lampe, Bengel, Kuinoel, Lücke, Tholuck, Olshausen, De Wette), '*Ye search the Scriptures, for ye believe ye have &c., and they are they that testify of Me, and* (*yet,* ver. 40) *ye will not come to Me that ye may have life:*' or *imperative* (Chrys., Theophyl., Euthym., August., Luther, Calvin, Wetst., Paulus, Stier), in which case generally a period has been placed after **ἐμοῦ,** and a fresh sentence begins at **καὶ οὐ θέλ.** I believe the *imperative sense only* will be found to cohere with the previous verses:—see above, where I have given the context. And no other sense will suit the word ἐραυνᾶτε, which cannot be used, as in the indicative it would be, with blame attached to it,—'*ye make nice and frivolous search into the letter of Scripture;*' but, as ἐξερευν. in ref. Ps., implies *a thorough search* (see also 1 Pet. i. 11) *into the contents and spirit* of Scripture. Besides, the emphatic position of ἐραυνᾶτε before τὰς γραφάς, while it does not absolutely necessitate the imper. sense, makes it much

τὰς [y] γραφάς, ὅτι ὑμεῖς [z] δοκεῖτε ἐν αὐταῖς [a] ζωὴν [a] αἰώνιον
ἔχειν· καὶ ἐκεῖναί εἰσιν αἱ [b] μαρτυροῦσαι [b] περὶ ἐμοῦ.
40 καὶ οὐ [c] θέλετε ἐλθεῖν πρός με, ἵνα [d] ζωὴν [d] ἔχητε.
41 [e] δόξαν [f] παρὰ ἀνθρώπων οὐ [f] λαμβάνω. 42 ἀλλὰ
[g] ἔγνωκα ὑμᾶς ὅτι τὴν [h] ἀγάπην τοῦ [h] θεοῦ οὐκ [i] ἔχετε
ἐν [j] ἑαυτοῖς. 43 ἐγὼ [k] ἐλήλυθα ἐν τῷ ὀνόματι τοῦ πατρός
μου, καὶ οὐ [l] λαμβάνετέ με· ἐὰν ἄλλος ἔλθῃ ἐν τῷ ὀνό-

ABDEF GHKL MSUV ΓΔΛΠℵ 1. 33. 69

y Matt. xxi. 42. xxii. 29 ∥ Mk. xxvi. 54, 56. Luke xxiv. 27, &c. Acts xvii. 2, 11 al.
z Matt. iii. 9.
a ch. iii. 15 reff.
b ch. i. 7, 8 reff.
c ver. 35. James ii. 20.
d ch. vi. 53 reff.
e = 1 Thess. ii. 6.
f ver. 34.
g constr., Matt. xxv. 24.
h Luke xi. 12 reff.
i Mark iv. 17.
j 2nd pers., Matt. iii. 9 reff.
k Matt. xxi. 9 al.
l ch. 1. 12 reff.

εχειν bef εν αυτ. ζ. αι. D. for αι μαρτυρουσαι, αμαρτανουσαι D[1]-gr(corrd *eadem manu*).

40. aft ζωην ins αιωνιον D 69. 244 lat-*e g* Syr Chr_2.

41. ανθρω**που** AK[Π] copt Chr_1 Cyr_1.

42. (αλλ**α**, so BDL 33.) ουκ εχετε bef την αγαπην τ. θ. D lat-*b e q* [$Cyr\text{-}p_1$]: in both places ℵ[1].

43. om 2nd εν ℵ.

more probable than the indic., which would be conveyed by τὰς γρ. ἐραυνᾶτε. Luthardt (ii. 21) remarks, that the almost unanimous verdict of the *Greek* Fathers (Cyril however is a remarkable exception) for the imper. decides him in its favour. **ὅτι ὑμ. δοκ.**] *Ye* (emphatic) **imagine that** *in them* (emphatic) **ye have eternal life** (Schöttgen quotes testimonies from the Rabbis: "*Qui acquirit sibi verba legis, is acquirit sibi vitam æternam, &c.*");—but they, like all other secondary ordinances, have a spiritual end in view, and that end is to testify, from first to last (it is *their office, ἐκεῖναί εἰσιν* **αἱ μαρτυροῦσαι**) of Me. **40.**] I would connect these words with the former, and regard them as describing the inconsistency of those who think that they ζωὴν ἔχειν in the Scriptures, and yet will not come to Him of whom they testify, ἵνα ζωὴν ἔχωσιν. So that **καί** will be spoken in a fine irony, **And ye will not come to Me!** Observe, this command to the Jews to *search* their Scriptures, applies *à fortiori* to Christians; who are yet, like them, in danger of idolizing a mere written book, believing that *in the Bible* they have eternal life, and missing the personal knowledge of Him of whom the Scriptures testify. The **οὐ θέλετε** here sets forth strikingly *the freedom of the will,* on which the unbeliever's condemnation rests: see ch. iii. 19.

41—44.] The connexion seems to be;—the standing-points of our Lord and of the Jews were not only *different,* but were *inconsistent with* and *exclusive of* one another. He sought not glory from below, from man's praise or report: *the Father testified to Him,* in all the ways which have been specified; but this testimony they could not receive, nor discover Him in their Scriptures, because human regards and ambition and intrigue had blinded their eyes, and they had not the love of God (the very first command in their law, Deut. vi. 4, 5) in their hearts.

41.] **οὐ λαμβ.**, not merely, '*I do not desire,*' '*non capto;*'—but, '**I do not** *receive;*'—'no such praise nor testimony accrues to Me, nor has in Me that on which it can lay hold.' 'My glory is altogether from another source.'

42.] **ἀλλά** draws forcibly the distinction, setting Himself and them in strong contrast. **ἔγνωκα ὑμ.**] By long trial and bearing with your manners these many generations; and personally also:—"*Hoc radio penetrat corda auditorum.*" Bengel. **ἀγάπην**] Luthardt remarks, perhaps refining somewhat too much,—**τὴν ἀγάπην**, because "*the love which ye ought to have*" is imported: **τοῦ θεοῦ**—"*of* (for) *your God the God of Israel.*" So that the words are spoken, not of an ungodly mind in general, but of an absence of that love which God's covenant people should have for Him. "They would none of Jesus: for they were not true Israelites." This love, if they had it, would teach them,—the whole heart, and soul, and mind, and strength being given to God,—to seek honour *only from Him,*—and thus to appreciate the glory which He hath given to His Son, and His testimony concerning Him.

43.] The first clause is clear. In the latter we have a prophetic declaration regarding the Jews in the latter days. This **ἄλλος** is in strong contrast with the ἄλλος of ver. 32. 'The testimony of that Other, who is greater than I, ye will not receive; but if another come in his own name, him ye will receive.' The words are perhaps spoken primarily of the false

ματι τῷ ἰδίῳ, ἐκεῖνον [l]λήμψεσθε. 44 πῶς δύνασθε ὑμεῖς
πιστεῦσαι, δόξαν [f]παρ' ἀλλήλων [f]λαμβάνοντες, καὶ τὴν
[m]δόξαν τὴν παρὰ τοῦ [n]μόνου [n]θεοῦ οὐ [m]ζητεῖτε; 45 μὴ
δοκεῖτε ὅτι ἐγὼ [o]κατηγορήσω ὑμῶν [p]πρὸς τὸν πατέρα·
ἔστιν ὁ [o]κατηγορῶν ὑμῶν Μωυσῆς, εἰς ὃν ὑμεῖς [q]ἠλπίκατε.
46 εἰ γὰρ [r]ἐπιστεύετε Μωυσεῖ, [r]ἐπιστεύετε ἂν ἐμοί· περὶ
γὰρ ἐμοῦ ἐκεῖνος ἔγραψεν. 47 εἰ δὲ τοῖς ἐκείνου [s]γράμμα-
σιν οὐ πιστεύετε, πῶς τοῖς ἐμοῖς ῥήμασιν πιστεύσετε;

m 1 Thess. ii. 6. (ch. vii. 18 bis.)
n 1 Tim. i. 17. Jude 25 (ch. xvii. 3. Rom. xvi. 27) only.
o Matt. xii. 10 ⁝. Luke xxiii. 2, 10, 14. Rom. ii. 15 +. 1 Macc. vii. 6, 25.
p = 1 John ii. 1.
q constr., 2 Cor. i. 10. 1 Pet. iii. 5 only. Ps. cxliv. 15. Isa. li. 5 bis. see Acts xxiv. 15. Rom. xv. 12 al. perf., 1 Cor. xv. 19. 2 Cor. i. 10. 1 Tim. iv. 10. v. 5. vi. 17 only.
r w. dat., ver. 24 reff.
s = 2 Tim. iii. 15. Esth. vi. 1.

44. πιστευειν AL 1. 33 Chr_1 Cyr[-p_2]. (παρ', so BDK[Γ 1.] 69 $Orig_1$.) om θεου (*homœotel*) B lat-*a b* copt-dz arm-mss $Orig_1$ Eus. **ζητουντες** $ℵ^1$ 47. 248-9 [lat-*e l* $Ephr_1$ Bas_2 Chr_1 Aug_1].

45. for 1st υμων, υμας D^1(txt D^2) Scr's c: υμιν L Scr's s ev-y. ins προς τον πατερα bef μωυσης B.

46. (μωυσει, so ABD(ℵ) &c.) εμου bef γαρ D Scr's l m n t. **γεγραφεν** $ℵ^1$.

47. πιστευετε (for -σετε) BV ℵ("sic" Tischdf's notes, but txt in facsimile and both edns [also in N. T. edn 8]) fos lat-ff_2 *l* [*f* syr-cu] Orig-ms Chr-$montf_1$ [Cyr-p_1] Iren-int-mss_1: -σητε DGSΔ 1. 69 Orig-ms_1 Chr-mss_1.

or Idol-Messiah, the Antichrist, who shall appear in the latter days (2 Thess. ii. 8—12); whose appearance shall be κατ' ἐνέργειαν τοῦ σατανᾶ (their *father*, ch. viii. 44), **ἀποδεικνὺς ἑαυτὸν ὅτι ἐστὶν θεός**, 2 Thess. ii. 4;—and doubtless, *in* that their final reference, embrace also all the cases in which the Jews *have* more or less *received* those false Messiahs who have been foreshadowers of the great Antichrist, and indeed all the cases in which *such a spirit* has been shewn by them, even in the absence of false Messiahs. **44.**] **πῶς δύνασθε** (emphatic) is grounded on οὐ θέλετε—is the consequence of the carnal regards in which they lived. **λαμβάνοντες** *here* implies '*captantes*' also. **παρὰ τοῦ μόνου θεοῦ**, not '*from God only*' (E. V. and De Wette), which is ungrammatical (requiring μόνου to be either *after* θεοῦ, see Matt. iv. 4; xii. 4; xvii. 8, or *before* τοῦ θεοῦ, Luke v. 21; vi. 4: Heb. ix. 7. Lücke); but **from the only God**: in contradistinction to the *idolatry of the natural heart*, which is ever setting up for itself other sources of honour, worshipping *man*, or *self*,—or even, as in the case alluded to in the last verse, *Satan*,—instead of God. The words τοῦ μόνου θεοῦ are very important, because they form the point of passage to the next verses; in which the Jews are accused of not believing the *writings of Moses*, the very pith and kernel of which was *the unity of God*, and *the having no other gods but Him*. **45.**] The work of Christ is not **κατηγορεῖν**, even as He is Judge;—but **κρίνειν**, by the appointment of the Father. And therefore—though He has said so much of the unbelief of the Jews, and charged them in the last verse with breach of the central law of God—*He will not accuse* them; nay, it is not needful;—for Moses, whom they disbelieved, while vainly hoping in him (see above on ver. 39),—ἐπαναπαυόμενοι νόμῳ, Rom. ii. 17,—*already accused them*: see Deut. xxxi. 21, 26, and ch. vii. 19. **46.**] The former part of this verse should not be rendered as in E. V. '*had ye believed Moses, ye would have believed me*;' but **if ye believed Moses, ye would believe me.** The imperfects render this necessary: the other rendering would require aorists. **περὶ ἐμοῦ ἔγραψεν**—"*nusquam non.*" Bengel. This is an important testimony by the Lord to the *subject* of the whole Pentateuch;—it is **περὶ ἐμοῦ.** It is also a testimony to *the fact*, of Moses *having written those books*, which were then, and are still, known by his name. **47.**] **γράμμασιν** here does not, *in the sense*, = γραφαῖς: for ταῖς ἐκείνου γραφαῖς could not be used;—the **γραφή** being ἡ θεία γραφή, not (ἡ τοῦ) Μωυσέως γραφή,—but the **γράμματα** were those of Moses; the outward expression of the γραφή,—the letters, and words, as found on paper:—just as the ῥήματα in the other case are the outward expression of the λόγος. The meaning is: 'men give greater weight to what is written and published, the letter of a book, than to mere word of mouth;—and ye in particular give greater honour to Moses, than to Me: if then ye believe not what *he* has written, which comes down to

t John (ver. 23. ch. xxi. 1) only. Jos. Antt. xviii. 2. 3.
u Luke x. 18 reff.
v ch. ii. 11 reff.
w constr., here only.
x Gal. i. 18 only. 3 Kings xiii. 12. Judg. xxi. 8 Ald. only.
y = ch. ii. 13 reff.

ABDEF GHKL MSUV ΓΔΛΠℵ 1. 33. 69

VI. 1 Μετὰ ταῦτα ἀπῆλθεν ὁ Ἰησοῦς πέραν τῆς
θαλάσσης τῆς Γαλιλαίας τῆς [t] Τιβεριάδος· 2 ἠκολούθει δὲ
αὐτῷ ὄχλος πολύς, ὅτι [u] ἐθεώρουν τὰ [v] σημεῖα ἃ ἐποίει
[w] ἐπὶ τῶν ἀσθενούντων· 3 [x] ἀνῆλθεν δὲ εἰς τὸ ὄρος Ἰησοῦς,
καὶ ἐκεῖ ἐκάθητο μετὰ τῶν μαθητῶν αὐτοῦ· 4 ἦν δὲ [y] ἐγγὺς

Chap. VI. 1. ins εις τα μερη bef της τιβεριαδος D 77²(Treschow) 249 lat-*b e* syr-mss Chr_1.

2. rec (for ηκολ. δε) και ηκολ., with A rel vulg lat-*f* [*g q* syr-jer] syrr syr-cu æth arm Chr_1 $Chron_1$: txt BDLℵ 1. 33. 69 lat-*a b c e* ff_2 *l* copt Cyr_1. πολυς bef οχλος ℵ [Iren-int_1]. rec (for εθεωρουν) εωρων, with Δℵ rel: txt BDL 33. 69 Cyr_1, εθεωρων A 13. rec ins αυτου bef τα σημεια (*from ch* ii. 23), with E[F] rel Chr_1: om ABDKLSΛ[Π]ℵ 69 latt syrr syr-cu [syr-jer] copt goth æth arm Chr_2 Cyr Chron. for επι, περι ℵ.

3. απηλθεν Dℵ¹ lat-*a* ff_2 [*l*] copt Chr_1. for δε, ουν D 1. 69 latt goth: om δε, insg και at beg, ℵ¹ Syr syr-cu [syr-jer æth]. rec ins ο bef ιησ., with Aℵ³ᵃ rel [Chr Cyr Chron]: om BDℵ¹.—om ιησ. also Δ. εκαθ. bef εκει DU 1 Scr's q¹ r æth: om εκει ℵ¹ 248-9-51-3-9 Scr's g.—εκαθηζετο D: εκαθεζετο ℵ¹ 69.

4. εγγ. δε ην D.

you hallowed by the reverence of ages,—how can you believe the words which are uttered by Me, to whom you are hostile?' This however is not all:—*Moses leads to Christ*:—is one of the witnesses by which the Father hath testified of Him: 'if then ye have rejected the *means*, how shall ye reach the *end*?' 'If your unbelief has stopped the path, how shall ye arrive at Him to whom it leads?' Meyer is quite right in maintaining that the opposition does not lie between *γράμμασιν* and *ῥήμασιν*, but between *ἐκείνου* and *τοῖς ἐμοῖς*. Those who can, should by all means consult Stier, whose exposition of the above important discourse is very elaborate and valuable:—Reden Jesu, vol. iv. pp. 170—233, 2nd edn.

Chap. VI. Jesus the life in the flesh. 1—15.] *Miraculous feeding of five thousand men.* Matt. xiv. 13—21. Mark vi. 30—44. Luke ix. 10—17,—in each of which compare the notes throughout. Here we have another example of John relating a miracle with the view of introducing a discourse, and that discourse carries on the testimony of Jesus to Himself. In the last, He was the Son of God, testified to by the Father, received by faith, rejected by unbelief: here He is son of man, the incarnate Life of the world, and we have the unbelief of the Jews and His own disciples set in strong contrast with the feeding on and participating in Him as the Bread of Life. 1.] **μετὰ ταῦτα** gives us no fixed date: see on ch. v. 1. As Lücke remarks, the **ἀπῆλθ. πέραν τῆς θαλ. . . .**, if connected with the preceding discourse, would be unintelligible,—and can only be understood by the fragmentary character of this Gospel as relates to mere narration, and the well-known fact being presupposed, that His Ministry principally took place in Galilee.

Matt. gives this passage over the lake *in connexion with the execution of John the Baptist*: Mark and Luke, *with the return of the Twelve from their mission.* (The Twelve were probably gathered, or their gathering finished, in the interval since ch. v. 47, during which time their *mission* also had taken place.)

τῆς Γ. τῆς Τιβ.] The last appellation is probably inserted for the sake of Gentile readers, to whom it was best known by that name: thus Pausan. v. 7. 3, *αὐτὸς οἶδα Ἰόρδανον λίμνην Τιβερίδα ὀνομαζομένην διοδεύοντα*: but it was more usually called, as by Josephus, *Γεννησάρ* or *Γεννησαρῖτις*, 1 Macc. xi. 67: Strabo xvi. 2 (Ptolem. v. 15, Lücke). **τῆς Τιβ.** cannot mean that He *came from Tiberias*, however true that may have been. That would have been *ἀπὸ* or *ἐκ Τιβεριάδος*. It is possible, though not likely, that **τῆς Τιβ.** may have been a gloss, and have found its way into the text very early. But at all events we must not adopt the reading of D &c., *εἰς τὰ μέρη τ. Τιβ.*,—for the fact was just otherwise: compare vv. 2 and 23. 2.] It is evident from this that a circuit in Galilee and works of healing are presupposed (see Matt. ver. 13: Mark, ver. 33: Luke, ver. 11).

3.] **τὸ ὄρος**, perhaps 'the hill country' on the shore of the lake = *ἔρημον τόπον κατ' ἰδίαν*, Matt. The expression is used by John only here and in ver. 15, but no inference can be drawn from that, for this is the only portion of the Galilæan Ministry related by him. 4.] This will

τὸ [z] πασχα η [z] ἑορτὴ τῶν Ἰουδαίων. 5 [a] ἐπάρας οὖν τοὺς
[a] ὀφθαλμοὺς ὁ Ἰησοῦς καὶ [b] θεασάμενος ὅτι πολὺς ὄχλος
[c] ἔρχεται πρὸς αὐτόν, λέγει πρὸς Φίλιππον Πόθεν ἀγοράσωμεν [d] ἄρτους ἵνα φάγωσιν οὗτοι; 6 τοῦτο δὲ ἔλεγεν
[e] πειράζων αὐτόν· αὐτὸς γὰρ ᾔδει τί ἔμελλεν ποιεῖν.

z ch. ii. 23.
a Matt. xvii. 8 reff.
b Luke xxiii 55 reff. w. ὅτι, 1 John iv. 14 (Acts viii. 18 v. r.) only.
c pres., ch. i. 40 reff.
d plur., Matt. iv. 3 reff.
e = Acts v. 9. 2 Cor. xiii. 5. Deut. xiii. 3.

5. rec ο ιησ. bef τους οφθαλμους, with E rel Syr [syr-jer]: txt ABDKLM[Π](א) 1. 33. 69 latt syr-cu syr copt goth æth arm Cyr_1.—om ο $א^1$. οχλος bef πολυς Dא vulg lat-*a b c f* ff_2 [*l*]. ins και bef λεγει D-gr Syr syr-cu [syr-jer] æth. rec ins τον bef φιλιππον, with A rel [Bas_1]: om BDLΔא 33 Cyr_1. rec αγορασομεν, with KU (V, e sil) [Bas_1] Cyr[-p]: txt ABDא rel. ουτοι bef φαγωσιν Gא lat-*a*.
6. transp δε and γαρ $א^1$. ημελλεν DEFGMUV[Γ]Λ 1.

account, not for so great a multitude *coming to Him*, but perhaps (?) for the circumstance that the people at that time were gathered in multitudes, ready to set out on their journey to Jerusalem. We must remember also that the reference of the following discourse to the Passover being so pointed, the remark would naturally be here inserted by the Evangelist: but I would not, with Luthardt (i. 80; ii. 41) insist on this as the *only* reason for his making it. **5.**] Here there is considerable difficulty, on account of the variation from Matt., Mark, and Luke, who relate that the disciples came to the Lord after He had been teaching and healing the multitudes, and when it was now evening,—and asked him to dismiss the multitudes, that they might buy food; —whereupon He commanded, 'Give ye them to eat;'—whereas here apparently, on their first coming, the Lord Himself suggests the question, how they were to be fed, to Philip. This difference is not to be passed over, as it has usually been by English Commentators, without notice. Still less are we to invent improbable and hardly honest harmonistic shifts to piece the two narratives together. There can be no doubt, fairly and honestly speaking, that the narratives, *in their mere letter*, disagree. But those who are not slaves to the mere letter will see here that inner and deeper accordance of which Augustine (De Consensu Evang. ii. 46, vol. iii. pt. i.) speaks in commenting on this passage: "Ex qua universa varietate verborum, rerum autem sententiarumque concordia, satis apparet salubriter nos doceri, nihil quærendum in verbis nisi loquentium voluntatem; cui demonstrandæ invigilare debent omnes veridici narratores, cum de homine vel de angelo vel de Deo aliquid narrant." I repeat the remark so often made in this Commentary,—that if we were in possession of the facts as they happened, there is no doubt that the various forms of the literal narrations would fall into their places, and the truthfulness of each historian would be apparent:—but as we cannot at present reconcile them in this way, the humble and believing Christian will not be tempted to handle the word of God deceitfully, but to admire the gracious condescension which has given us the evidence of so many independent witnesses, whose very difference in detail makes their accordance in the great central truths so much the more weighty. *On every point of importance here, the four sacred historians are entirely and absolutely agreed.* That every minor detail related by them had its ground in historical fact, we fully believe; it is the *tracking it to* this ground in each case, which is now *beyond our power;* and here comes in the simplicity and reliance of faith: and the justification of those who believe and receive each Gospel as they find it written. **πρὸς Φ.**] Why to *Philip*, does not appear; perhaps some reason lay in the **πειράζων αὐτόν**, which is now lost to us. From his words in ch. xiv. 8, we cannot infer, as has been done by Chrys. (Hom. xlii. 1, in Joann. vol. viii. p. 249) and others, that he was weaker in faith, or tardier in spiritual apprehension, than the rest. Of all the Apostles who appear in the sacred narrative, something might be quoted shewing equal unreadiness to believe and understand. I would take the circumstance as simple matter of fact, implying perhaps that Philip was nearest to our Lord at the moment. We must not fall into the mistake of supposing that Philip being *of Bethsaida the city of Andrew and Peter* (ch. i. 45) throws any light on the question: for the Bethsaida near which our Lord now was, Luke ix. 10, was *another place*, see notes there. **πόθεν**—**whence**—'from what store.' Hence Philip's answer. **6.**] **He knew:** —by this St. John must be understood not only to rescue our Lord from the imputation of asking counsel of Philip, but

7 ἀπεκρίθη αὐτῷ Φίλιππος Διακοσίων [f] δηναρίων ἄρτοι
οὐκ [g] ἀρκοῦσιν αὐτοῖς ἵνα ἕκαστος [h] βραχύ [τι] λάβῃ.
8 λέγει αὐτῷ εἷς ἐκ τῶν μαθητῶν αὐτοῦ Ἀνδρέας ὁ ἀδελφὸς Σίμωνος Πέτρου 9 Ἔστιν [i] παιδάριον [[j] ἓν] ὧδε,
[k] ὃς ἔχει πέντε ἄρτους [l] κριθίνους καὶ δύο [m] ὀψάρια·
ἀλλὰ ταῦτα τί ἐστιν [n] εἰς τοσούτους; 10 εἶπεν ὁ Ἰησοῦς
[o] Ποιήσατε τοὺς ἀνθρώπους [p] ἀναπεσεῖν. ἦν δὲ χόρτος
πολὺς ἐν τῷ τόπῳ. [p] ἀνέπεσαν οὖν οἱ ἄνδρες τὸν ἀριθμὸν
[q] ὡς πεντακισχίλιοι. 11 ἔλαβεν οὖν τοὺς ἄρτους ὁ

ABDEF GHKL MSUV ΓΔΛΠℵ 1. 33. 69

f constr., here only. see Mark vi. 37. g = ch. xiv. 8. Matt. xxv. 9. 2 Cor. xii. 9 (Luke iii. 14. 1 Tim. vi. 8. Heb. xiii. 5. 3 John 10) only. Exod. xii. 4. Num. xi. 22. h = Heb. ii. 7 (from Ps. viii. 5), 9. xiii. 22. 1 Kings xiv. 29. i here (Matt. xi. 16 v. r.) only. Gen. xxxiii. 14. j = John, here only. Matt. viii. 19 al. Gen. xxii. 13. k constr., Gal. iv. 19. Philem. 10. 2 John 1. l ver. 13 only. Num. v. 15. Judg. vii. 13. 4 Kings iv. 42. Ezek. iv. 12 only. (-θή, Rev. vi. 6.) m ver. 11. ch. xxi. 9, 10, 13 only+. (ὄψος, Num. xi. 22.) n = Mark viii. 19, 20. xiv. 8. ch. xiii. 29. o = Mark i. 17. vii. 37. Acts iii. 12 al. p Matt. xv. 35 reff. q = Mark v. 13. Luke viii. 42. ch. i. 40. iv. 6. Acts i. 15 al.

7. αποκρινεται D-gr ℵ[1]. for αυτω, ουν ℵ[1](txt ℵ[3a]: ουν αυτω ℵ[3b]?). ins ο bef φιλιππος Lℵ 239-58 Scr's v[2]. ουκ αρκουσιν αυτοις bef αρτοι D: om αυτοις ℵ Chr-7-mss$_1$. rec aft εκαστος ins αυτων, with D rel Syr [syr-jer]: om ABL[Π]ℵ 33. 69 latt syr copt goth æth arm Chr$_1$ Cyr$_1$. om τι (*as superfl*) BD lat-*b e ff$_2$ l q* copt goth: ins Aℵ rel [vulg lat-*c f g* syr arm Chr$_1$ Cyr$_1$].

9. om ἓν (*easily overlooked aft ον*) BDL[Π[1]]ℵ 1. 69 lat-*a b e l* syr-cu æth Orig$_1$ Chr$_1$ Cyr$_1$: ins A rel vulg lat-*c f* [*ff$_2$ g* syr-jer] syrr goth arm. (33 def.) rec (for ὅς) ὅ (*gramml emendn*), with D[10]ℵ rel Orig$_1$ [Cyr$_1$]: txt ABD[1]GUΛ. (33 def.) om τι D[1](ins D[8]).

10. rec aft ειπεν ins δε, with A rel lat-*b* [*q*] syr goth; ουν DG vulg lat-*c e f g* [*ff$_2$ l*]: om BLℵ foss lat-*a* Syr syr-cu arm Orig$_1$. for χορτος, τοπος ℵ[1]. (ανεπεσαν, so ABDℵ &c.) om οι DL 1. 33 Cyr$_1$. ins ανθρωποι bef ανδρες AK[Π[1]]. (rec ωσει, with A rel: om Syr syr-cu copt: txt BDLℵ.) τρισχιλιοι ℵ[1].

11. rec (for ουν) δε, with ℵ[1] rel lat-*b* syr-txt goth [arm Bas$_1$]: txt ABDLℵ[3a] vulg lat-*c e f ff$_2$ g* [*l*] *q* syr-ms-mg copt Cyr$_1$.—και λαβων G 1. 69 (Syr syr-cu [syr-jer] æth). ins πεντε bef αρτους D.

to refer the miraculous act, on His part, to His purpose of exhibiting Himself as the Son of Man the Life of the World in the flesh. **7.**] See notes on Mark.

8.] Meyer remarks, that *εἷς ἐκ τῶν μαθητῶν αὐτοῦ* may seem strange, seeing that Philip also was this: but that it has its pragmatic value, seeing that, Philip having been asked in vain, one from among the circle of the disciples answers, and is afterwards specified as having been Andrew. In the three other Gospels, the loaves and fishes appear as the disciples' own;—and we have thus a very simple but very instructive instance of the way in which differences in detail arose. They were their own,—but not till they had bought them. **9.**] **κριθίνους**, the usual barley bread of the lower orders. **ὀψάρια** = *ἰχθύδια*, Suidas, but of later Greek usage:—at first used to signify any thing subsidiary to bread as a relish, such as meat of all kinds, and condiments. Later however, from fish being, in the deeply coast-indented country of Greece, the most common animal food, it came to be applied to that alone or principally—(see art. Opsonium in the Dictionary of Gr. and Rom. Antiquities).

10.] **χόρτος πολύς**, in accordance with the time of year, the latter end of spring, after the rainy season. On **ἀναπεσεῖν** see Mark and Luke, who describe the manner. **οἱ ἄνδρες**] This is a particular touch of accuracy in the account of an eye-witness which has not I think been noticed. Why in the other accounts should mention be made only of the *men* in numbering them? Matt. has, it is true, *χωρὶς γυν. κ. παιδ.*, leaving it to be inferred that there was some means of distinguishing;—the others merely give [ὡσεὶ] *ἄνδρες πεντακισχ.* without any explanation. But here we see how it came to be so—the *men alone* were arranged in companies, or alone arranged so that *any account* was taken of them: the women and children being served promiscuously; who indeed, if the multitude were a paschal caravan (?), or parts of many such, would not be likely to be very numerous;—and here again we have a point of minute truthfulness brought out.

11.] On the process of the miracle, see notes on Matt. John describes the *διάδοσις* as being the act of the Lord Himself, and leaves the intervention of the disciples to be understood.

Ἰησοῦς καὶ [r] εὐχαριστήσας [s] διέδωκεν τοῖς [t] ἀνακειμένοις,
ὁμοίως καὶ ἐκ τῶν [u] ὀψαρίων ὅσον ἤθελον. 12 ὡς δὲ [v] ἐνε-
πλήσθησαν, λέγει τοῖς μαθηταῖς αὐτοῦ [w] Συναγάγετε τὰ
Θg vi. 13 (appy)... [x] περισσεύσαντα [y] κλάσματα, ἵνα μή τι [z] ἀπόληται. 13 [w] συνήγαγον οὖν, καὶ [a] ἐγέμισαν δώδεκα [b] κοφίνους [y] κλασμάτων
ἐκ τῶν πέντε ἄρτων τῶν [c] κριθίνων, ἃ [d] ἐπερίσσευσαν τοῖς
[e] βεβρωκόσιν. 14 οἱ οὖν ἄνθρωποι ἰδόντες ὃ ἐποίησεν [f] σημεῖον, ἔλεγον ὅτι οὗτός ἐστιν [g] ἀληθῶς ὁ [h] προφήτης ὁ
...vi. 14 (appy) ΘgII. [i] ἐρχόμενος εἰς τὸν κόσμον. 15 Ἰησοῦς οὖν γνοὺς ὅτι
[k] μέλλουσιν ἔρχεσθαι καὶ [l] ἁρπάζειν αὐτὸν ἵνα [m] ποιήσωσιν
βασιλέα, [n] ἀνεχώρησεν πάλιν εἰς [o] τὸ [o] ὄρος αὐτὸς μόνος.
16 Ὡς δὲ [p] ὀψία ἐγένετο, [q] κατέβησαν οἱ μαθηταὶ αὐτοῦ

r Luke xxii. 19 reff.
s Luke xi. 22. xviii. 22. Acts iv. 35 (Rev. xvii. 13 v. r.) only. Josh. xiii. 6.
t = Matt. ix. 10 reff.
u ver. 9 reff.
v Luke i. 53. vi. 25. Acts xiv. 17. Rom. xv. 24 only. Ps. lxxvii. 29.
w — Luke xv. 13 reff.
x = Matt. xiv. 20 reff.
y here (bis) & ‖. Mark viii. 8 ‖, 19, 20 only. Lev. ii. 6. Judg. ix. 53 al.
z Luke xxi. 18
a Mark iv. 37 reff.

b ‖. Matt. xvi. 9 ‖ only. Judg. vi. 19 B. Ps. lxxx. 6 only. c ver. 9 (reff.) only. d w. dat., ‖ L. Luke xii. 15. xxi. 4. Tobit iv. 16. [א def.] e here only. Josh. v. 12 al. f ch. ii. 11 reff. g ch. i. 48 reff. h ch. i. 21 reff. i Matt. xi. 3 reff. ch. i. 9. k pres., ch. i. 40 reff. l = Acts viii. 39. 2 Cor. xii. 2, 4. 1 Thess. iv. 17. Rev. xii. 5. Judg. xxi. 21. m = ch. v. 11 reff. n Matt. ii. 12, &c. reff. o John, ver. 3 only. p John, ch. xx. 19 only. elsw., Matt. (viii. 16 al.) & Mark (i. 3 al.) only +. Judith xiii. 1 only. q = ch. ii. 12.

ευχαριστησεν και D(ηυχ.) א [lat-*a b e q* Syr syr-cu syr-jer]. for διεδ., εδωκεν D[Γ]א 69 lat-*b e q* syr Orig$_1$ [Chr$_1$]. rec ins τοις μαθηταις οι δε μαθηται bef τοις ανακειμενοις (*to correspond with* ‖), with Dא^{3b} rel lat-*b e* [æth-pl]: om ABL[Π]א^1 1. 33 vulg lat-*a c f ff$_2$ l* [*q*] syrr syr-cu syr-jer copt goth æth-rom arm Orig$_1$ Bas$_1$ [Chr$_1$ *Cyr*-p] Non$_1$ Aug$_1$. aft ομοιως ins δε DM.

12. περισσευοντα B 63. 248-53 Scr's g. at end add εξ αυτων D lat-(*b* [*l*]) *f* copt (æth).

13. for ουν, δε DΛ lat-*b*. rec επερισσευσεν (*gramml corrn*), with Aא rel: txt BD[Θg].

14. α επ. σημεια B[Θg] lat-*a* copt arm. rec aft σημ. ins ο ιησους (*beg of a lection*), with A rel lat-*f* [*q* syr-jer] syrr copt goth æth: om BDא am(with em forj foss fuld ing jac mt) lat-*a b c g* [*l*] syr-cu arm. om οτι א Scr's h [lat-*a b q* arm]. om αληθως D. εις τον κοσμον bef ερχομενος DMא lat-*a b ff$_2$* [*l* foss].

15. for ινα ποιησ., και αναδικνυναι א^1. rec aft ποιησ. ins αυτον, with D rel latt syrr syr-cu [syr-jer] coptt goth æth arm [Chr$_1$]: om ABLא 1. 33 lat-*q* Orig$_1$ Cyr$_1$. for ανεχωρησεν, φευγει א^1 [vulg lat-*a c ff$_2$ g l q* syr-cu]. (ανεχωρησεν, so B, not as Btly: see table.) om παλιν E rel Syr coptt æth Orig$_1$ Chr$_1$ Non$_1$: ins ABDKLΛא 1. 33 latt syr-cu syr [syr-jer] goth arm. μονος bef αυτος א. aft μονος ins κακει προσηυχετο D.

εὐχαριστήσας here answers to εὐλόγησεν in the other Gospels. It was the '*grace*' of the father of the family; perhaps the ordinary one in use among the Jews. John seems to connect with it the idea brought out by Luke, εὐλ. **αὐτούς**, i. e. τοὺς ἄρτους: see ver. 23. **12.**] Peculiar to John. The command, one end of which was certainly to convince the disciples of the power which had wrought the miracle, is given by our Lord a moral bearing also. They collected the fragments *for their own use*, each in his κόφινος, the ordinary furniture of the travelling Jew ("*quorum cophinus fœnumque supellex*," Juv. Sat. iii. 14), to carry his food, lest he should be polluted by that of the people through whose territory he passed: see note on Matt. xv. 32. Observe, that here the 12 baskets are filled with the fragments of the *bread alone:* but in Mark, with those of the fishes also. We must not altogether miss the reference to the twelve tribes of Israel, typifying the Church which was to be fed with the bread of life to the end of time. **14.**] On **ὁ προφ.** see note on ch. i. 21,—ὁ προφ. εἶ σύ; **15.**] After such a recognition, nothing was wanting but that the multitudes who were journeying to the Passover should take Jesus with them and proclaim Him king of the Jews in the holy City itself. The other three Evangelists, while they do not give any intimation of this reason of our Lord's withdrawal, relate the *fact*, and Luke preserves in the very next verse *a trace of its motive*, by the question '*Whom do the people say that I am?*' and the answer, expressing the very confession of the people here.

16—21.] *Jesus walks on the sea.*

ἐπὶ τὴν θάλασσαν, 17 καὶ [r] ἐμβάντες εἰς πλοῖον ἤρχοντο ABDEF
πέραν τῆς θαλάσσης εἰς Καφαρναούμ. καὶ [s] σκοτία ἤδη GHKL MSUV
ἐγεγόνει, καὶ οὔπω ἐληλύθει πρὸς αὐτοὺς ὁ Ἰησοῦς, 18 ἥ ΓΔΛℵ 1. 33. 69
τε θάλασσα [t] ἀνέμου μεγάλου [t] πνέοντος [u] διεγείρετο.
19 [v] ἐληλακότες οὖν [w] ὡς [x] σταδίους εἰκοσιπέντε ἢ τριάκοντα,
[y] θεωροῦσιν τὸν Ἰησοῦν [z] περιπατοῦντα [z] ἐπὶ τῆς θαλάσσης
καὶ [a] ἐγγὺς τοῦ πλοίου γινόμενον· καὶ ἐφοβήθησαν. 20 ὁ
δὲ λέγει αὐτοῖς [b] Ἐγώ εἰμι, μὴ φοβεῖσθε. 21 [c] ἤθελον οὖν
[d] λαβεῖν αὐτὸν εἰς τὸ πλοῖον, καὶ εὐθέως ἐγένετο τὸ
πλοῖον ἐπὶ τῆς γῆς εἰς ἣν ὑπῆγον.

r Matt. viii. 23 reff.
s = ch. xx. 1 (i. 5 reff.).
t Matt. vii. 25, 27 reff.
u = here (Mark iv. 39 reff.) only. (ἐξεγ., Jon. i. 13.)
v = Mark vi. 48 (reff.) only.
w ver. 10 reff.
x Luke xxiv. 13. ch. xi. 18. 1 Cor. ix. 24. Rev. xiv. 20. xxi. 16 only +. 2 Macc. xi. 5 B. xii. 9, 10, 16, 29 only.
y Luke xxiii. 48 reff.
z ||. Job ix. 8.
a gen., ch. iii. 23 reff.
b ||. ch. xviii. 5, 8.
c = ch. i. 44. v. 35. viii. 44.
d = ch. xix. 27. 2 John 10.

17. **αναβαντες** AK Chr$_1$. rec ins το bef πλοιον, with AD rel [Chr$_1$]: om BLΔℵ 33 goth [Cyr$_1$]. **ερχονται** ℵ. ins εις το bef περαν D 69 ev-y Chr$_1$. for και σκ. ηδ. εγ., κατελαβεν δε αυτους η σκοτια Dℵ. rec (for ουπω) ουκ, with A rel vulg lat-*c* *ff*$_2$ syrr syr-cu: txt BDLℵ 33. 69 lat-*a* *b* *e* *f* [*l* *q*] syr-jer copt goth æth arm Cyr$_1$ Non$_1$. προς αυτους bef εληλυθει B. (B has not εληλυθεν as Btly.) ὁ ιησ. bef προς αυτους D ℵ(omg ὁ [as does L]) 80 lat-*a* [syr-jer] æth.

18. for τε, δε D-gr vulg lat-*b* *c* *f* [*l* *q*] syrr copt goth æth. rec διηγειρετο, with ADℵ rel [Chr$_1$ Cyr$_1$]: txt B(sic: see table) GLUVΛ 69.

19. ωσει A D(but aft σταδ.) 1. **σταδια** *stadia* D ℵ^1(txt ℵ-corr$^{1 \text{ or } 2 \cdot 3}$) 106.

20. for ο δε, και ℵ.

21. for ηθελον, ηλθον ℵ. αυτον bef λαβειν D 69 lat-*e* goth Aug$_1$. rec το πλοιον bef εγενετο, with (D)ℵ rel [vulg-clem lat-*a* *b* *f* *ff*$_2$ syrr syr-cu goth]: txt ABGL 1. 33. 69 am(with forj foss fuld ing mt) lat-*c* *e* *g* *l* *q* coptt æth arm Orig$_1$ Cyr$_1$ Aug$_1$. **εγενηθη** D. την γην ℵ^1 28. 69. 251 Orig$_1$. for υπηγον, υπηντησεν ℵ^1.

Matt. xiv. 22—33. Mark vi. 45—52. Omitted by Luke. An important and interesting question arises, WHY is this miracle here inserted by St. John? That he ever inserts for the mere purpose of narration, I cannot believe. The reason seems to me to be this: to give to the Twelve, in the prospect of so apparently strange a discourse respecting His Body, a view of the truth respecting that Body, that it and the things said of it were not to be understood in a gross corporeal, but in a supernatural and spiritual sense. And their very terror, and reassurance, tended to impress that confidence in Him which kept them firm, when many left Him, ver. 66. **16.**] **ὀψία**, here, will be during the time between the ὀψία of Matt. xiv. 15, and that of ib. ver. 23. [The Jews commonly reckoned two evenings: see the introductory note on Matt. xxvi. 17—19.] **κατέβησαν**—by the command of Jesus (Matt., Mark). **17.**] **ἤρχοντο**—denoting the unfinished action—**they were making for the other side of the sea, in the direction of Capernaum**; πρὸς Βηθσαϊδάν, Mark, which would be the same thing. It would appear as if the disciples were lingering along shore with the expectation of taking in Jesus: but night had fallen, and He had not come to them, and the sea began to be stormy (ver. 18). Having therefore (**οὖν**) set out (ver. 19), and rowed, &c. The **οὖν** seems to me to render this supposition necessary,—to bind their having rowed twenty-five or thirty stadia, with the fact that the Lord had not come, and it was dark, and the sea swelling into a storm. The lake is (Jos. B. J. iii. 10. 7) forty stadia wide: so that, as we can hardly assume the passage to have been to a point *directly opposite*, they were somewhere about μέσον τῆς θαλάσσης, Matt. ver. 24. **18.**] **διεγείρετο**, was becoming thoroughly agitated: **was rising.** **19—21. περ. ἐπὶ τῆς θαλ.**] There surely can be no question in the mind of an unprejudiced reader, that it is John's intention to relate a *miracle*;—nor again,—that there could be in the minds of the disciples *no doubt about* that miracle,—*no chance of a mistake* as to what they saw. I have treated of **ἐπὶ τῆς θαλ.** on Matthew, ver. 25. They were afraid:—but upon being reassured by His voice, they were willing to take Him into the ship; and upon their doing so, the ship in a comparatively short time (or perhaps *immediately, by miracle*, but I prefer the other) was at the land to which they had been going, viz. by the storm ceasing, and the ship making smooth way (ἐκόπασεν ὁ ἄνεμος, Matt., Mark). It seems to me that the above interpretation

22 Τῇ [e] ἐπαύριον ὁ ὄχλος ὁ ἑστηκὼς πέραν τῆς θαλάσσης εἶδον ὅτι [f] πλοιάριον ἄλλο οὐκ ἦν ἐκεῖ εἰ μὴ ἕν, καὶ
ὅτι οὐ [g] συνειςῆλθεν τοῖς μαθηταῖς αὐτοῦ ὁ Ἰησοῦς εἰς τὸ
Θ_g vi. 22 (appy)... πλοῖον, ἀλλὰ μόνοι οἱ μαθηταὶ αὐτοῦ ἀπῆλθον· 23 ἄλλα
[δὲ] ἦλθεν [f] πλοιάρια ἐκ [h] Τιβεριάδος [a] ἐγγὺς τοῦ τόπου
ὅπου ἔφαγον τὸν ἄρτον [i] εὐχαριστήσαντος τοῦ [k] κυρίου·
...vi. 24 (appy) Θ_g. 24 ὅτε οὖν εἶδεν ὁ ὄχλος ὅτι Ἰησοῦς οὐκ [l] ἔστιν ἐκεῖ οὐδὲ οἱ
μαθηταὶ αὐτοῦ, [m] ἐνέβησαν αὐτοὶ εἰς τὰ [f] πλοιάρια καὶ ἦλθον
εἰς Καφαρναοὺμ ζητοῦντες τὸν Ἰησοῦν. 25 καὶ εὑρόντες
αὐτὸν πέραν τῆς θαλάσσης εἶπον αὐτῷ Ῥαββί, πότε ὧδε

e ch. i. 29 reff.
f here 3ce. Mark iii. 9. (iv. 36 v. r.) Luke v. 2. ch. xxi. 8 only †.
g ch. xviii. 15 only. Exod. xxi. 3. Esth. ii. 13. Sir. xxxix. 2 only.
h ver. 1.
i ver. 11.
k = ch. iv. 1 reff.
l pres., ch. i. 40 reff.
m ver. 17.

22. for εστηκως, εστως ℵ ev-z. rec (for ειδον) ιδων, with E rel: ειδων Δ[-gr]: ιδον L: ειδεν D[-gr] ℵ (ev-y?) vulg lat-*b c* [ff_2 *g* Δ-lat] arm Chr-comm [Aug_1]: txt AB lat-*a f* [*l q* D-lat syr-jer] syrr copt goth æth. rec aft εν ins εκεινο εις ο ενεβησαν οι μαθηται αυτου (*explanation*), with ($D\aleph^1$) E rel lat-(*a*) *e* syrr (syr-cu [syr-jer] sah arm Chr) Cyr_1 (om εν $\aleph^1$: om εκεινο D 33 ev-y lat-*a* syr-cu arm Chr_3:—ον ανεβ. Δ[-gr Cyr]:—for αυτου, του ιησου D-corr $\aleph^1$ 69 lat-*a* syr-cu sah arm, αυτου ιησ. D^1): om $ABL\aleph^{3a.b}$ 1 vulg lat-*c f* ff_2 *g l* [*q* Δ-lat] copt goth æth Non_1. for συνεισηλθεν τοις μαθ. αυτου, συνεληλυθι αυτοις $\aleph^1$. ο ιησους bef τοις μαθ. αυτου A. rec (for πλοιον) πλοιαριον (*as above*), with E rel lat-*a f q*: πλοιαν $\aleph^1$ (ο added above α): txt ABDKL[Θ_g] 1. 33. 69 vulg lat-*b c e* ff_2 [*l*] goth Chr Cyr. μονον D 248 lat-*a* [*q*]. om απηλθον $\aleph^1$(ins $\aleph^2$) 56-8 [lat-ff_2 *l*].

23. for αλ. δ. ηλθ. πλ., αλλων πλοιαριων ελθοντων D lat-*b* syr-cu arm: επελθοντων ουν των πλοιων $\aleph^1$.—om δε BL[Θ_g] 33 lat-*e* [syr-jer] copt: ins A rel vulg lat-*a c f* ff_2 syrr goth æth [Cyr.—ηλθον $KLM\Gamma\Theta_g$ 1. 33 ev-y].—for πλοιαρια, πλοια B 157 ev-32 vulg lat-*c* [*b f* ff_2 *g l*. ℵ see above]. ins της bef τιβεριαδος B 245-8-53 Scr's g i ev-P^2. for του τοπου, ουσης $\aleph^1$. ins και bef εφαγον $\aleph^1$. om τον ℵ. om ευχ. τ. κυρ. D 69^1 lat-*a e* syr-cu arm.

24. for οτε to εκει, και ιδοντες οτι ουκ ην εκει ο ῑς $\aleph^1$ [syr-cu]. om αυτου $\aleph^1$. rec ins και bef αυτοι, with UΓ (1. 33, e sil): om AB(Dℵ) rel lat-*q* syrr syr-cu copt æth Cyr_1.—om αυτοι $S\aleph^1$ goth arm.—for ενεβ. αυτ. εις τα, ελαβον εαυτοις D lat-*b* ff_2 *l*.—ανεβησαν [L]$\aleph^1$ 1. 245-9-54 Scr's s t evv-47-8-53-z. rec (for τα πλοιαρια) τα πλοια, with A rel: το πλοιον $\aleph^1$ [simly lat-ff_2 syr-cu]: txt $BDL\aleph^{3a}$ 33. 69 latt syr-mg Cyr_1.

of **ἤθελον οὖν λαβεῖν** is absolutely necessary to account for the **οὖν**, and quite in accordance with John's usage of θέλω (see reff.). Some of the German Commentators (even De Wette among them) have created a difficulty, by strangely rendering ἤθελον, '*they wished*' (implying, '*but did not*'), *but* (καί) *the ship was immediately*, &c.—i. e. they were already close to the land, and so there was no occasion. Prof. Bleek (Beiträge, pp. 103-4) half adopts this view:—adding to it, I am sorry to see, that perhaps Jesus was on the land, and the disciples in the storm and darkness thought Him to be on the sea.

22—59.] *The multitudes follow Jesus to Capernaum, where, in the synagogue, He discourses to them on Himself as the Bread of Life.* 22—24.] These verses are involved and parenthetical in construction, but very characteristic of the minute care with which the Evangelist will account for every circumstance which is essential to his purpose in the narrative. **ὁ ὄχλος**] We are not to understand *the whole multitude who were fed*,—but that portion of them which had remained on the coast over the night. Many had probably dispersed to the villages about, or perhaps taken up their night quarters more inland. **πέραν τ. θαλ.**, i. e. on the east coast. We are supposed to be at Capernaum. **ἦν** is not pluperfect in sense—the meaning is regulated by εἶδον—**they were aware that there was no other ship there but one, and that Jesus did not,** &c. Then the **ἦλθεν** afterwards, belonging to the same set of facts, is in the same tense, but not pluperfect: **came**, not '*had come*.' The **πλοιάρια** had perhaps brought some of them thither; or the spot **ἐγγὺς τ. τόπου,** &c. might have been some landing-place of merchandise. 25.] **πέραν τ. θαλ.** is *now* the *west* bank;—we have been crossing the sea with the multitude. **πότε**, as Stier remarks, includes πῶς in its meaning. Our Lord leaves the question unanswered,

n = Luke x. 32.
o ch. v. 24, 25 reff.
p = ch. ii. 11 reff.
q = vv. 50, 51 [Luke xxii. 16 v. r.] only. (Mark xi. 14. Heb. xiii. 10. Rev. ii. 7.) Deut. xxviii. 31. see 1 Cor. ix. 7.
r Matt. xiv. 20 ‖ Mk. L. James ii. 16. Ps. xvi. 15.
s = 2 John 8 only ‡.

[n] γέγονας; 26 ἀπεκρίθη αὐτοῖς ὁ Ἰησοῦς καὶ εἶπεν [o] Ἀμὴν
[o] ἀμὴν [o] λέγω ὑμῖν, ζητεῖτέ με οὐχ ὅτι εἴδετε [p] σημεῖα, ἀλλ'
ὅτι [q] ἐφάγετε [q] ἐκ τῶν ἄρτων καὶ [r] ἐχορτάσθητε. 27 [s] ἐργάζεσθε μὴ τὴν [t] βρῶσιν τὴν [u] ἀπολλυμένην, ἀλλὰ τὴν
[t] βρῶσιν τὴν μένουσαν εἰς ζωὴν αἰώνιον, ἣν ὁ [v] υἱὸς τοῦ
[v] ἀνθρώπου ὑμῖν δώσει· τοῦτον γὰρ ὁ πατὴρ [w] ἐσφράγισεν
ὁ θεός. 28 εἶπον οὖν πρὸς αὐτὸν Τί ποιῶμεν, ἵνα [x] ἐργα- T ειπον
ζώμεθα τὰ ἔργα τοῦ θεοῦ; 29 ἀπεκρίθη ὁ Ἰησοῦς καὶ εἶπεν ... ABDEF GHKL
αὐτοῖς [y] Τοῦτό ἐστιν τὸ ἔργον τοῦ θεοῦ, [y] ἵνα [z] πιστεύητε MSTUV ΓΔΛℵ 1. 33. 69

t ch. iv. 32 reff. u = Heb. i. 11, from Ps. ci. 26. James i. 11. 1 Pet. i. 7. v Matt. viii. 20 reff. w ch. iii. 33. Matt. xxvii. 66. Rom. xv. 28. 2 Cor. i. 22. Eph. i. 13. iv. 30. Rev. vii. 3 al7. (17 v. r.) 3 Kings xx. (xxi.) 8. x ch. iii. 21. Matt. xxvi. 10 reff. y John (vv. 39, 40. ch. xv. 12. xvii. 3. 1 John iii. 11, 23. iv. 21. v. 3, 2 John 6) only. see ch. xv. 8. 1 John iv. 17. z ch. ii. 11 reff.

25. for *γεγονας*, *εληλυθας* D; *ηλθες* ℵ; simly latt Syr syr-cu [syr-jer] sah-mnt goth arm: æth has both.

26. om *ὁ* ℵ. om *ζητειτε με* ℵ[1]. *ειδατε* D. aft *σημεια* ins *και τερατα* D foss(with gat) lat-*a b f* goth.

27. 1st *βρωσιν* bef *μη*, omg *την*, ℵ [lat-*b* Hil_1]. om 2nd *την βρωσιν* EFGHℵ 69 vulg lat-*c* [*l*] $Clem_2$ $Constt_1$ $Epiph_1$ Aug_1. for *υμιν δωσει*, *διδωσιν υμιν* Dℵ foss lat-*e* ff_2 syr-cu goth Chr_1: *δωσει υμ.* 69 Chr_1 Hil_1. *εσφραγ.* bef *ο πατηρ* L: om *εσφραγισεν* ℵ[1](txt ℵ-corr[1]).

28. om *ουν* A Syr syr-cu syr-jer arm. Steph *ποιουμεν*, with (ESΓ 1. 33, e sil [so Treg: Tischdf cites ESΓ for txt]) [*Cyr*-p]: *-ησομεν* 69 latt sah Chr_1: *-ησωμεν* DG: txt ABLTℵ rel $Orig_1$ Chr_1 Cyr_1.—transp *ποι.* and *εργ.* D.

29. om *ὁ* ℵ rel: ins ABDKLTΛ. *τα εργα* T. rec *πιστευσητε*, with D

because it was not for *a sign to these people* that He had miraculously crossed the lake.

26.] The seeking Him, on the part of these people,—to Him, who saw the hearts,—was merely a low desire to profit by His wonderful works,—not a reasonable consequence of deduction from His miracles that He was the Saviour of the world. And from this low desire of mere satisfaction of their carnal appetite, He takes occasion in the following discourse to raise them to spiritual desire after HIMSELF, THE BREAD OF LIFE. The discourse forms a parallel with that in ch. iv.

27.] **ἐργάζ.**, imperative: another instance of the construction which I have advocated in ch. v. 39. The E. V., '*Labour not for*,' does not give the sense of *ἐργάζ.* They had not *laboured* in this case for the *βρῶσις ἀπολλυμένη*, but it had been furnished miraculously. A better rendering would be, **Busy not yourselves about,—Do not weary yourselves for,**—which they were doing, by thus coming after our Lord: [but best of all **Work not for**: so as to preserve the connexion between verses 27, 29, 30.] **τὴν ἀπολλ.** "*whose nourishing power passes away*," De Wette. Rather perhaps more literally, **which perisheth,** E. V.:—the *useless* part of it, in being cast out;—the *useful*, in becoming part of the body which perishes (see 1 Cor. vi. 13). **ἀλλὰ τ. βρ.**] It is important to bear in mind that the *ἐργάζεσθαι* spoken of above, which also applies to this, was not a '*working for*,' or '*bringing about of*,' but a following Christ in order to obtain. So the meaning will be, **but seek to obtain,** by following after Me . . . . And thus *μὴ* . . . . *ἀλλά* keeps its true literal force, **Do not . . . . but.** **τὴν μένουσαν εἰς ζ. αἰ.**] See ch. iv. 14. If this *βρῶσις remains to eternal life*, it must be *spiritual food*. **ἣν . . . . δώσει**] See ch. iv. ib. **ἥν** agrees with **βρῶσιν**, not with **ζωήν**. **δώσει**, future, because the great Sacrifice was not yet offered: so in ch. iv. **ὁ υἱὸς τ. ἀνθρ.**, emphatic here and belonging to this discourse, since it is of His *Flesh* that He is about to speak. **τοῦτον γὰρ . . . .**] **for Him the Father sealed, even God.** **ἐσφράγ.**, by *undoubted testimony*, as at His baptism; and since, *by His miracles*, see ch. x. 36: not, 'stamped with the image of His Person,' which is altogether beside the present subject, and inconsistent with the meaning of *σφραγίζω*.

28.] The people understand His *ἐργάζεσθε literally*, and dwell upon it. They quite seem to think that the food which is to endure for ever is to be spiritually interpreted; and they therefore ask this question,—referring the *ἐργάζ.* to the works of the law. **τὰ ἔργα τοῦ θεοῦ** must not be taken to mean '*the works which God works*,' but, as in Jer. xlviii. 10 (xxxi. 10 LXX): 1 Cor. xv. 58, **the**

[z] εἰς ὃν ἀπέστειλεν ἐκεῖνος. 30 εἶπον οὖν αὐτῷ Τί οὖν
ποιεῖς σὺ [a] σημεῖον, ἵνα ἴδωμεν καὶ [b] πιστεύσωμέν σοι; τί a ch. ii. 11 reff. b constr., ch. v. 24 reff.
ἐργάζῃ; 31 οἱ πατέρες ἡμῶν τὸ [c] μάννα ἔφαγον ἐν τῇ ἐρήμῳ, c ver. 49. Heb. ix. 4. Rev. ii. 17 only.
καθώς ἐστιν γεγραμμένον [d] Ἄρτον ἐκ τοῦ οὐρανοῦ [e] ἔδωκεν Num. xi. 6, 7, 9.
αὐτοῖς [e] φαγεῖν. 32 εἶπεν οὖν αὐτοῖς ὁ Ἰησοῦς Ἀμὴν ἀμὴν d Psa. lxxvii. 24.
λέγω ὑμῖν, οὐ Μωυσῆς ἔδωκεν ὑμῖν τὸν ἄρτον ἐκ τοῦ e Matt. xiv. 16 reff.
οὐρανοῦ· ἀλλ' ὁ πατήρ μου δίδωσιν ὑμῖν τὸν ἄρτον ἐκ τοῦ
οὐρανοῦ τὸν [f] ἀληθινόν. 33 ὁ γὰρ ἄρτος τοῦ θεοῦ ἐστὶν f = ch. i. 9 reff. g = Acts x. 11. Rev. xvi. 21
ὁ [g] καταβαίνων ἐκ τοῦ οὐρανοῦ καὶ ζωὴν διδοὺς τῷ al. Isa. lv. 10.

rel: txt ABTℵ 1. 33 Orig Bas$_1$ Cyr[-p], πιστευειτε L. απεσταλκεν ΤΓ.

30. ειπεν D[1](txt D[2]). om 2nd ουν Lℵ 33 foss lat-*l* Syr [syr-jer] copt arm [æth Cyr$_1$]. συ bef ποιεις D vulg lat-*c e* [*b q*]: om συ 69. 245-54 Scr's e g i m q[1] r ev-z arm [foss lat-*l* Chr$_1$ Cyr$_1$]: σημειον bef συ ℵ.

31. εστ. γεγρ. εστ. (but 1st εστ. erased) D. om αρτον ℵ[1].

32. (rec δεδωκεν, with AT ℵ(so also in ver 31) rel Orig$_1$ Eus$_1$ [Chr$_1$ Cyr$_1$]: txt BDL Clem$_1$ Eus$_1$ [Chr$_1$].)

33. ins ο bef του θεου Dℵ: om ABT rel Clem$_1$ Orig$_1$ Eus$_1$ [Chr Cyr]. διδους bef ζωην AK 33 vulg lat-*c f ff*$_2$ syrr [syr-jer] coptt goth æth Eus$_1$: txt BDTℵ rel lat-*a b e* [*q*] syr-cu arm Clem$_1$ Orig$_3$ Eus$_3$ [Chr$_1$ *Cyr*-p].

works well pleasing to God. **29.**] The meaning is not,—that faith is *wrought in us by* God, is *the work of God;* but that the truest way of working the work of God is to believe on Him whom He hath sent. **ἔργον**, not ἔργα, because there is but this one, properly speaking, and all the rest are wrapt up in it (see James i. 25). This is a most important saying of our Lord, as containing the germ of that teaching afterwards so fully expanded in the writings of Paul. "I know not," says Schleiermacher (cited by Stier, iv. 231, edn. 2), "where we can find any passage, even in the writings of the Apostles, which says so clearly and significantly, that all eternal life in men proceeds from nothing else than faith in Christ." **30, 31.**] This answers to ch. iv. 12, '*Art thou greater than our father Jacob,*' &c. It is spoken in unbelief and opposition; not, as many have supposed, as a request for the Bread of Life, meaning *it* by the sign, but in the ordinary sign seeking spirit of the Jews. Stier says well, "They have been hesitating between better and worse thoughts, till at last unbelief prevails." The **σημεῖον** here demanded is the *sign from heaven,* the proof of the sealing by God; such a proof would be, in their estimation, compared with His present miracles, as the manna (bread *from heaven*) was, compared to the multiplied loaves and fishes. The manna was extolled by the Jews as the greatest miracle of Moses. Josephus calls it θεῖον καὶ παράδοξον βρῶμα: see also Wisd. xvi. 20, 21. "They forgot that their fathers disbelieved Moses almost from the time when they began to eat the manna; and that the Psalm from which they quote most strongly sets forth this;—that they despised the manna, and preferred ordinary meat to it." Stier. Observe our Lord's πιστ. **εἰς** and their πιστ. **σοι.** The former, the casting their whole hopes and faith on Him, is what He requires: but they will not even give the latter, common credence, to Him. Their **τί ἐργάζῃ;** Meyer remarks, is a retort of our Lord's command, ver. 27. There is no σύ expressed, but the stress is on the **τί.**

32.] Our Lord lays open the course of their argument. They have not *mentioned* Moses,—nor was the giving of the manna a miracle performed by Moses;—but He knew that the comparison between Moses and Himself was in their minds, and answers by exposing the error which represented Moses as the giver of the manna. Neither again was that the true bread from heaven. It was, in one sense, bread from heaven;—but not in *this* sense. It was a type and shadow of the true bread from heaven, **which My Father is giving** (δίδωσιν,—or perhaps the abstract present,—**giveth**) **to you.** Our Lord does not here *deny*, but *asserts* the miraculous character of the manna. **33.**] **ὁ ἄρτος τοῦ θεοῦ** = ὁ ἄρτος ὃν δίδωσιν ὁ πατήρ μου. The words **ὁ καταβ. . . .** are the predicate of ὁ ἄρτος, and do *not apply, in the construction of this verse, to Christ personally,* however truly they apply to Him in fact. The E. V. is here wrong: it should be, **The bread of God is** *that* (not *He*) **which cometh,** &c. *Not*

κόσμῳ. 34 εἶπον οὖν πρὸς αὐτὸν Κύριε, πάντοτε δὸς ἡμῖν
τὸν ἄρτον τοῦτον. 35 εἶπεν αὐτοῖς ὁ Ἰησοῦς Ἐγώ εἰμι
ὁ ἄρτος τῆς ζωῆς· ὁ ἐρχόμενος πρὸς ἐμὲ οὐ μὴ πεινάσῃ,
καὶ ὁ [h] πιστεύων [h] εἰς ἐμὲ οὐ μὴ [i] διψήσει πώποτε. 36 ἀλλ'
εἶπον ὑμῖν ὅτι καὶ ἑωράκατέ με καὶ οὐ πιστεύετε. 37 πᾶν
ὃ δίδωσίν μοι ὁ πατὴρ πρὸς ἐμὲ ἥξει, καὶ τὸν ἐρχόμενον
πρός με οὐ μὴ [k] ἐκβάλω [k] ἔξω, 38 ὅτι καταβέβηκα ἀπὸ
τοῦ οὐρανοῦ οὐχ ἵνα [l] ποιῶ τὸ [l] θέλημα τὸ ἐμὸν ἀλλὰ τὸ

h ver. 29.
i ch. iv. 13, &c. reff.
k Matt. xxi. 39 ||. Luke iv. 29. xiii. 28. ch. ix. 34, 35. xii. 31. Acts vii. 58. ix. 40. Rev. xi. 2 only.
l Matt. vii. 21 reff.

ABDEF GHKL MSTUV ΓΔΛℵ 1. 33. 69
Π vi. 36 (appy)...
C ω το θελημα ...

34. παντοτε bef κυριε ℵ.
35. rec aft ειπεν ins δε, with A rel vulg lat-*c* syr-mg Cyr_1; ουν DΓℵ 33. 69 syr-txt sah : om BLT foss lat-*a b e* Syr syr-cu copt arm. (rec (for εμε) με, with AD rel $Orig_1$ Eus_1 [Chr_1 Cyr_1] : txt BTℵ.) πεινασει DHT 1 Eus_1 Chr. add πωποτε D(Scr). rec διψηση, with B² rel Orig : διψασει D : txt AB¹HLTΔℵ 1. 33 Eus Chr.
36. om με Aℵ gat lat-*a b e q* [syr-cu] : ins BD T[μη] rel. aft κ. ου ins μη T. [at end ins μοι AΠ² Chr_1(om_1).]
37. for με, εμε EKTΔℵ. om εξω Dℵ¹ lat-*a b e* syr-cu Hil_1 : ins BT rel [vulg lat-*e f* ff_2 *q* syrr syr-jer &c].
38. ins ου bef καταβεβηκα, omg ουχ, ℵ¹ [lat-*b e* $Cypr_3$ $Novat_2$ $Quæst_1$ (Aug_1)]. rec (for απο) εκ (*from vv.* 33, 41, 51, *where there is no var : see on ver* 42), with Dℵ rel Ign_1 Eus_1 Bas_1 Ath_3 [Did_1 *Cyr*-p $Antch_1$] : txt ABLT 33. 69 (sah ?). ποιησω D L¹(appy) ℵ Ath_3 Euthym.

till ver. 35 does Jesus first say, 'I AM the bread of life.' The *manna* is still kept in view—ὅταν κατέβη ἡ δρόσος . . . . . **κατέβαινεν** τὸ μάννα ἐπ' αὐτῆς, Num. xi. 9. And the present participle, here used in reference to the manna, is dropped when the Lord Himself is spoken of : see vv. 38, 41, 58, and especially the distinction between ver. 50 and ver. 51 (so Lücke, De Wette, Stier, Bengel). **34.**] Ch. iv. 15 is exactly parallel. The Jews understand this bread, as the Samaritan woman understood the water, to be some miraculous kind of sustenance which would bestow life everlasting :—perhaps they thought of the heavenly manna, which the Rabbis speak of as prepared for the just in the future world : see quotations in Lücke, ii. 132, also Rev. ii. 17. **πάντοτε,** emphatic :—not now only, but always. **35.**] As in ch. v. 30, so here, our Lord passes from the indirect to the direct form of speech. Henceforward it is 'I,' 'Me,' throughout the discourse.
In the genitive **τῆς ζωῆς** is implied ὁ καταβὰς ἐκ τοῦ οὐρ. καὶ ζωὴν διδοὺς τῷ κόσμῳ. So ὕδωρ ζῶν in ch. iv.
On the assurance of *never hungering or thirsting,* see note at ch. iv. 14. It is possible that our Lord placed the all-satisfying bread of life in contrast to the manna, which was *no sooner given,* Exod. xvi., *than* the people *began to thirst,* Exod. xvii. ;—but I would not lay any stress on this. **ὁ ἐρχόμ. πρ. ἐμέ** is in the same sense as in ch. v. 40—that of acceptance of and faith in Him. **36.**] **εἶπον ὑμῖν**—πότε δὲ τοῦτο εἶπεν αὐτοῖς; εἰκὸς τοῦτο ῥηθῆναι μὲν μὴ γραφῆναι δέ. Euthym. But perhaps, as Euthym. himself seems to suggest, and as Lücke and De Wette are inclined to think, the reference may be to ch. v. 37—44, and the **ὑμῖν** may be said generally. Stier and others think that ver. 26 is referred to : but this is far-fetched. We have instances of reference to sayings not recorded, in ch. x. 26 ; xii. 34. **ἑωράκατέ με**] 'Ye have seen the true Bread from heaven, the σημεῖον greater than the manna, *even Me Myself :* and yet have not believed.' **37.**] The whole body of believers on Christ are spoken of by Him, here and in ch. xvii., *as given to Him by the Father.* But Bengel's observation is very important : "**πᾶν**—vocula momentosissima, et, collatis iis quæ sequuntur, consideratu dignissima. Nam in sermonibus Jesu Christi, quod Pater ipsi dedit, id, et singulari numero et neutro genere, appellatur *omne ;* qui ad ipsum, *Filium,* veniunt, ii masculino genere vel etiam plurali numero describuntur,— *omnis,* vel *illi.* Pater Filio totam quasi massam dedit, ut omnes quos dedit unum sint ; id universum Filius singulatim evolvit, in exsecutione. Hinc illud in xvii. 2, ut *omne quod dedisti* ei, *det eis* vitam æternam." See also 1 John v. 4. See further on πᾶν ὃ δίδωσίν μοι ὁ πατήρ, ver. 44. **οὐ μὴ ἐκβ. ἔξω** does not refer here to the office of the Son of God *as Judge ;* but is another way of expressing the grace and readiness with which He will receive all who come to Him.
38—40.] His reception of men is not

...εστιν το θε F.

θέλημα τοῦ πέμψαντός με. 39 [m] τοῦτο δέ ἐστιν τὸ θέλημα
τοῦ πέμψαντός με, [m] ἵνα [n] πᾶν ὃ δέδωκέν μοι, μὴ [o] ἀπολέσω
[p] ἐξ αὐτοῦ, ἀλλὰ [q] ἀναστήσω αὐτὸ τῇ [r] ἐσχάτῃ [r] ἡμέρᾳ.
40 [ms] τοῦτο γάρ ἐστιν τὸ [s] θέλημα τοῦ πατρός μου, [m] ἵνα
πᾶς ὁ [t] θεωρῶν τὸν υἱὸν καὶ [u] πιστεύων [u] εἰς αὐτὸν ἔχῃ
ζωὴν αἰώνιον, καὶ [q] ἀναστήσω αὐτὸν ἐγὼ τῇ [r] ἐσχάτῃ
[r] ἡμέρᾳ. 41 [v] ἐγόγγυζον οὖν οἱ Ἰουδαῖοι περὶ αὐτοῦ, ὅτι
εἶπεν Ἐγώ εἰμι ὁ ἄρτος ὁ [w] καταβὰς [w] ἐκ τοῦ οὐρανοῦ,
42 καὶ ἔλεγον Οὐχ οὗτός ἐστιν Ἰησοῦς ὁ υἱὸς Ἰωσήφ, οὗ

m ver. 29 reff.
n constr., ch. xvii. 2. Rev. ii. 26. Ps. x. 5.
o = ch. xviii. 9.
p = 2 John 4. Rev. v. 9. xi. 9.
q act., = here, &c. (4 times) & Acts (ii. 24 al.) only. pass., ch. xi. 23, 24 al.
r — here, &c. 4 times. ch. (vii. 37.) xi. 24. xii. 48 only. J.
s 1 Thess. iv. 3.
t = ch. xii. 45 bis. xiv. 17.
u ch. ii. 11 reff.
v here bis & ver. 61. ch. vii. 32. Matt. xx. 11. Luke v. 30. 1 Cor. x. 10 bis, only. Num. xiv. 27.
w see ver. 33.

at end add *πατρος* D 33 [lat-*a e* (*b ff*$_2$)] syr-cu syr-jer Did$_1$ [Bas$_1$ (Tert$_1$)].

39. om 1st clause (*homœotel*) C ℵ(ins ℵ^{3a}, but erased) Scr's g.—rec aft *πεμψαντος με* ins *πατρος*, with E rel vulg lat-*a c* syr syr-jer [æth arm Cyr$_1$ Aug$_1$]: om ABDL T(ℵ^{3a}) 1 lat-*b e f q* Syr syr-cu coptt goth Ath$_1$ Chr$_1$ Cyr$_3$ Ambr$_1$ Aug. for *εξ αυτου*, *μηδεν* D. for *αλλα*, *αλλ' ινα* D [foss lat-*f*]. rec ins *εν* bef *τη εσχατη*, with ADK[Π]ℵ 69 (S 33, e sil) latt coptt Ath [in Cyr mss vary]: om BCLT rel am [with fuld forj ing] lat-*e* Ath-ms.

40. rec (for *γαρ*) *δε* (*from ver* 39), with E rel syr(Tischdf) Chr$_1$ Chrom$_1$: [om T arm:] txt ABCDKLU[Π]ℵ 1. 33. 69 am(with em foss fuld ing jac [mm] mt tol) lat-*a b c* [*e f ff*$_2$ *g q*] syrr syr-cu coptt. rec (for *πατ. μου*) *πεμψαντος με* (*from ver* 39), with A rel Did$_1$ Chr$_1$: *πεμψ. με πατρος* Δ 69 ev-y vulg lat-*c f ff*$_2$ *g* syr-jer Aug$_1$ Chrom$_1$: txt BCDLTUℵ 1. 33 lat-*a b e q* syrr syr-cu coptt æth arm Clem$_1$ Ath-ms$_1$ Chr$_1$ Non$_1$ Tert$_2$ Hil$_2$ Victorin$_1$. om *εγω* AD 1 foss(with tol) lat-*b f* copt Clem$_1$ Chr$_1$ Tert$_1$ Hil$_1$: ins BCTℵ rel vulg lat-*a c e ff*$_2$ *g* [*q* syr-jer] syrr syr-cu sah goth æth arm. ins *εν* bef *τη εσχατη* ADKLSU[Π]ℵ latt coptt goth Clem [Aug$_1$]: om BCT rel lat-*e* Tert.

41. for *ουν*, *δε* D-gr Syr syr-cu goth.

42. *ουχι* BT. ins *του* bef *ιωσηφ* D.

capricious, nor even of His own arbitrary choice; but as He came into the world to do the Father's will, and that will is that all who come to Him by faith shall have life, so He receives *all such*;—loses none of them;—and will raise them all up (here, *in the fullest* and *blessed sense*) at the last day. (**ἀπολέσω** again is not '*destroy*,' '*condemn*,' but lose: see ch. xii. 25; xvii. 12. ἵνα μὴ ἐξ ἐμῆς αἰτίας ἀπόληταί τις, Euthym.) Olshausen remarks, that "in ch. iv. we had only the inexhaustible refreshing of the *soul* by the water of life; but this discourse goes further;—that not even death itself shall destroy the *body* of him who has been nourished by this bread of life" (ii. 167). **ἀναστήσω** refers to the only resurrection which is the completion of the man in his glorified state;—it does not set aside the ἀνάστασις κρίσεως, but that very term is a debasement of ἀνάστασις: its true sense is only ἀνάστασις ζωῆς. Bengel has beautifully given the connexion of this last promise with what went before: "hic finis est, ultra quem periculum nullum." But there is much more than this in it. In this declaration (vv. 39, 40) is contained the key of the following discourse, vv. 44—59. The *end* of the work of God, as regards man, is the glorification of his restored and sanctified nature,—*body, soul, and spirit*,—in eternity. Without this,—salvation, restitution, would be incomplete. The adoption cannot be consummated without the redemption of the body. Rom. viii. 18—23. And the glorification of the body, soul, and spirit,—of the whole man,—cannot take place but by means of *the glorified Body of the second Adam*. "He who does not see this, will never understand either the Holy Communion, or this testimony of the Lord in its inner meaning." Stier, iv. 243, edn. 2. The **θεωρῶν** here is a different thing from the mere ὁρᾶν of ver. 36. It is the awakening of the attention preparatory to faith, answering to the looking on the serpent of brass: τοῖς ὀφθαλμοῖς τῆς ψυχῆς, Euthym.; but afterwards he makes the θεωρεῖν = πιστεύειν, to which it is only preparatory.

41.] Not different hearers, nor does the scene of the discourse here change: they were the same,—perhaps the principal among them, the official superintendents of the synagogue:—for John generally uses οἱ Ἰουδαῖοι in this official sense. **42.**] They rightly supposed

ἡμεῖς οἴδαμεν τὸν πατέρα καὶ τὴν μητέρα; πῶς νῦν
λέγει ὅτι [w] ἐκ τοῦ οὐρανοῦ [w] καταβέβηκα; 43 ἀπεκρίθη ὁ
Ἰησοῦς καὶ εἶπεν αὐτοῖς Μὴ [v] γογγύζετε [x] μετ᾽ ἀλλήλων.
44 οὐδεὶς δύναται ἐλθεῖν πρὸς ἐμέ, ἐὰν μὴ ὁ πατὴρ
ὁ πέμψας με [y] ἑλκύσῃ αὐτόν, κἀγὼ [z] ἀναστήσω αὐτὸν
ἐν τῇ ἐσχάτῃ ἡμέρᾳ. 45 ἔστιν γεγραμμένον [a] ἐν τοῖς
προφήταις Καὶ ἔσονται πάντες [b] διδακτοὶ [c] θεοῦ. πᾶς ὁ

ABCDE GHKL MSTUV ΓΔΛΠℵ 1. 33. 69

x Matt. xviii. 23. xxv. 19. Mark vi. 50. y = ch. xii. 32 only. (John [xviii. 10. xxi. 6, 11] only, exc. Acts xvi. 19.) Jer. xxxviii. (xxxi.) 3. z vv. 39, 40 reff. a Mark i. 2 reff. b 1 Cor. ii. 13 only. Isa. liv. 13. 1 Macc. iv. 7 only. see 1 Thess. iv. 9. c gen., Matt. xxv. 34. Philem. 1. Winer, edn. 6, § 30. 2.

aft *οιδαμεν* ins *και* ℵ[1]. om *και την μητερα* (*homœotel*) ℵ[1] lat-*b* syr-cu arm-ed. rec (for *νυν*) *ουν*, with ADℵ rel vulg lat-*b c f ff*$_2$ *g* syr Ath[-ed$_1$ (Cyr varies)]: om lat-*a e*: txt BCT [syr-jer] copt goth arm Ath-2-mss$_1$. rec aft *λεγει* ins *ουτος*, with A rel vulg lat-*c f* syrr goth: pref ℵ [lat-*b e f* syr-jer]: om BCLT 1. 33. 69 lat-*a ff*$_2$ [*q*] syr-cu coptt æth arm Chr Cyr.—*λεγει εαυτον απο τ. ȣ. καταβεβηκεναι* D Chr$_1$.—for *οτι, εγω* ℵ: om 69 Chr-6-mss.

43. rec aft *απεκριθη* ins *ουν*, with ADℵ rel vulg lat-*b c* syr [syr-jer]: om BCKLT[Π] 33. 69 lat-*a e* Syr coptt arm Cyr$_1$. om *ο* BLTℵ 1. 33 [Cyr$_1$]: ins ACD rel. *αυτοις* bef *και ειπεν* ℵ. *μετα* B.

44. rec (for *εμε*) *με*, with ACDTℵ rel Hipp$_1$ Orig$_1$ Did$_1$ Chr$_1$ Cyr[-p]: txt BEMU VΔ. om *ὁ πατηρ* A Scr's q r. rec *και εγω*, with A rel Chr: *εγω* T: txt BCDLℵ 1. 33 [Did$_1$] Cyr. rec om *εν*, with Δℵ am(with [forj fuld] ing[2]) lat-*e*: ins ABCDT rel (latt) coptt goth [Did$_1$] Cyr.

45. rec ins *του* bef *θεου*, with Scr's t[1]: om ABCDTℵ rel Scr's-mss Chr$_1$ Cyr$_1$ Thl. rec aft *πας* ins *ουν*, with A rel lat-*q* (syrr syr-cu): om BCDLSTℵ 69 latt coptt

that this **καταβῆναι ἐκ τοῦ οὐρανοῦ** must imply some method of coming into the world diverse from ordinary generation. Meyer gathers from the *οἴδαμεν*, that our Lord's reputed father was then still alive. But surely the verb will bear the sense of knowing as matter of fact who they were, and need not be confined to personal knowledge. **43.**] Our Lord does not answer their objection, because it lay far from His present purpose to disclose aught of those mysteries which the answer must have indicated. It was not till the faith of the apostolic Christians was fully fixed on Him as the Son of God, and the outline of the doctrine of His Person was firmly sketched out, that the Spirit brought out those historical records which assure us of His supernatural conception (see Nitzsch, cited by Stier, iv. 244, edn. 2). **44.**] The connexion seems to be this: They were not to murmur among themselves because He had said this; for the right understanding of what He had said is only to be gained by being taught of God, by being drawn by the Father, who alone can give the desire to come to Christ, and bring a man to Him. That this 'drawing is not *irresistible grace*, is confessed even by Augustine himself, in his Tractatus on this passage. "Si trahitur, ait aliquis, invitus venit. Si invitus venit, nec credit: si non credit, nec venit. Non enim ad Christum ambulando currimus, sed credendo; nec motu corporis sed voluntate cordis accedimus, ... Noli te cogitare invitum trahi; trahitur animus et amore." And just before; "Intrare quisquam ecclesiam potest nolens, accedere ad altare potest nolens, accipere sacramentum potest nolens:—*credere non potest, nisi volens.*" He quotes, "trahit sua quemque voluptas" (Virg. Ecl. ii. 65), to shew that the drawing is that of delight and choice, not of obligation and necessity. Calvin (?), Beza, and Lampe understand *irresistible grace* to be here meant: "Falsum est et profanum, non nisi volentes trahi" (Calv., Lücke, ii. 144 note). The Greek expositors, Cyril, Chrysostom, Euthymius, Theophylact, take the view which I have adopted above. Chrysostom says, *ὃ καὶ αὐτὸ οὐ τὸ ἐφ᾽ ἡμῖν ἀναίρει, ἀλλὰ μᾶλλον ἐμφαίνει ἡμᾶς βοηθείας δεομένους.* See Article X. of the Church of England, *in fine.* This *drawing towards Christ* may be exemplified in the legal dispensation, which was to the Jews a *παιδαγωγία εἰς χριστόν.* It now is being exerted on all the world,—in accordance with the Lord's prophecy ch. xii. 32 (see note there), and His command Matt. xxviii. 19, 20,—by Christian preaching and missions; but, after all, the *individual will* must be turned to Christ by the Father, Whose covenanted promise is, that He will so turn it in answer to prayer. "Nondum traheris? ora ut traharis" (Augustine, ut supra). The same solemn and joyous *refrain*, as Meyer well calls it, follows, as in vv. 39, 40. **45.**] **ἐν τοῖς προφ.** may be a general form of citation

[d]ἀκούσας [d]παρὰ τοῦ πατρὸς καὶ μαθὼν ἔρχεται πρός
με. 46 [e]οὐχ [e]ὅτι τὸν πατέρα ἑώρακέν τις, εἰ μὴ ὁ [f]ὢν
παρὰ τοῦ θεοῦ· οὗτος ἑώρακεν τὸν πατέρα. 47 ἀμὴν
ἀμὴν λέγω ὑμῖν, ὁ [g]πιστεύων [εἰς ἐμὲ] ἔχει ζωὴν αἰώνιον.
48 ἐγώ εἰμι ὁ ἄρτος τῆς [h]ζωῆς. 49 οἱ πατέρες ὑμῶν ἔφαγον ἐν τῇ ἐρήμῳ τὸ [i]μάννα καὶ ἀπέθανον· 50 οὗτός ἐστιν
ὁ ἄρτος ὁ [k]ἐκ τοῦ οὐρανοῦ [k]καταβαίνων, ἵνα τὶς [l]ἐξ
αὐτοῦ [l]φάγῃ καὶ μὴ ἀποθάνῃ. 51 ἐγώ εἰμι ὁ ἄρτος ὁ
[m]ζῶν ὁ [k]ἐκ τοῦ οὐρανοῦ [k]καταβάς· ἐάν τις [l]φάγῃ [l]ἐκ τούτου τοῦ ἄρτου, [n]ζήσεται [n]εἰς τὸν [n]αἰῶνα. [o]καὶ ὁ ἄρτος

...καταβαινω A.

d ch. i. 41. vii. 51. viii. 26, 40. xv. 15. Acts x. 22. xxviii. 22. 2 Tim. i. 13. ii. 2.
e = 2 Cor. i. 24. iii. 5. Phil. iii. 12. iv. 11, 17. 2 Thess. iii. 9 only.
f ch. vii. 29 reff.
g absol., John, ch. i. 7. iii. 18. iv. 41, 42, 53 al. w. εἰς, ch. ii. 11 reff.
h = ch. viii. 12. Rev. ii. 7. vii. 17 al.
i ver. 31.
k ver. 33.
l ver. 26 reff.
m = ch. iv. 10, 11. Acts vii. 38.
n = ver. 58. see Rev. i. 18. iv. 9, 10. xv. 7. Dan. vi.
o Matt. x. 18. ch. viii. 16, 17. xv. 27. Acts iii. 24. 1 John i. 3. 2 Macc. v. 15 Ed-vat. [not B].

æth arm $Orig_2$. *ακουων* (*cf ch* v. 24) D rel foss(with gat mm) lat-*a b e g q* syr-mg goth Cyr Hil_1: txt ABCKLT[Π]ℵ 1. 33. 69 vulg lat-*c f* ff_2 $Orig_2$ [Cyr_2]. aft *μαθων* ins *την αληθειαν* A. *εμε* BTℵ $Orig_1$: txt ACD rel $Orig_1$. (33 def.)

46. rec *τις* bef *εωρακεν*, with A rel syr coptt [Syn-ep-Ant_1] Did_2 $Thdrt_2$ Chr_1: txt BCDLTℵ 33 latt Syr syr-cu goth $Orig_1$ [Cyr-jer_1] *Cyr*[-p]. *εορακε* (twice) B^1(Tischdf [N. T. Vat., not N. T. ed 8]). om *του* B. for *θεου*, *πατρος* ℵ Syn-ep-Ant Chr-5-mss. for *πατερα*, *θεον* D$ℵ^1$ lat-*a b e* [Cyr-jer_1(txt_1)] $Novat_1$ $Quæst_1$.

47. ins *οτι* bef *ο πιστευων* ℵ 124(Sz). om *εις εμε* BLTℵ arm-zoh: ins (*cf ver* 35 *&c*) ACD rel latt syrr coptt goth æth arm-usc [Cyr-p_1] Hil_1.

49. aft *εφαγον* ins *τον αρτον* D lat-*a b e.* rec *το μαννα* bef *εν τη ερημω*, with Aℵ rel vulg lat-*a* syrr coptt goth æth arm Thdrt Cyr[-p] Ambr: txt BCDT am(with [fuld] ing san tol) lat-*b c e* ($Orig_1$) Eus_1 Chr_1 Aug_1.

50. ins *και* bef *καταβαινων* D^1-gr. ins *εαν* bef *τις* D^3(and lat) vulg lat-*a b c f* [ff_2] *g*. *αποθνησκη* B Eus_1.

51. aft *εαν* ins *ουν* D-gr. *του αρτου* bef *τουτου* D-gr arm [Chr_2 *Cyr*-p]: *του εμου αρτου* (omg *τουτου*) ℵ lat-*a e* Eus_2 $Cypr_1$ Hil_1. *ζησει* DLℵ 33 $Orig_3$: txt BCT rel $Orig_3$ [Eus_2]. om *και* $ℵ^1$ [lat-*a b e q* sah $Orig_1$ Ath_1].

(Mark i. 2: Acts vii. 42; xiii. 40), or may mean that the sense is found in several places of the prophets: see besides reff., Jer. xxxi. 33, 34. This clearly intimates the *kind of drawing* meant in the last verse;—the opening the eyes of the mind by divine teaching. **ἀκούσας κ. μαθών** is an expansion of *διδακτός*. **ἔρχ. πρός με**] This is the final decision of the human will, acted on by the divine attraction to Christ. *The beginning* is, the Father draws him: *the progress*, he hears and learns—here is the consenting will—'Speak, Lord, for thy servant heareth:'—*the end*, he cometh to Christ—here is the will acting on the whole man.

46.] The connexion is: the mention of *ἀκούσας παρὰ τοῦ πατρός* might lead them to think of a personal communication from the Father to each man, and thus the necessity of the mission of the Son might be invalidated. This was the only way in which a Jew could misunderstand ver. 45; he could not dream of a seeing of the Father with bodily eyes. **ὁ ὢν παρὰ τ. θεοῦ** is Jesus Himself: see ch. vii. 29. His knowledge of the Father is *complete* and immediate; ours, *partial*, and derived through Him only.

47.] Our Lord now recurs to the subject of their murmurs, and gives the answer for which He has been preparing the way, repeating nearly ver. 40, and adding,

48.] If *so*, (see ver. 47,) there is full reason for my naming Myself the Bread of Life.

49.] *That* bread from heaven had no power to keep off death, and that, *death owing to unbelief:*—our Lord by thus mentioning *οἱ πατέρες* **ὑμῶν** and their death, certainly hints at the *similar unbelief* of these Jews. And the same dubious sense of *ἀποθάνῃ* prevails in ver. 50. Death is regarded as being swallowed up in the glory of the resurrection, and the second death—which was hidden in the former *ἀπέθανον*—has over him who eats this Bread of Life, *no power:* nay, he is brought, even *here*, into a resurrection state from sin and death: see Rom. vi. init. and Col. iii. init.

51.] **ὁ ζῶν**, 'containing life in itself,' not merely supplying the waste of life with lifeless matter: see on ch. iv. 13, 14. **καὶ ὁ ἄρτος . . . .**] From this time we hear no more of *ἄρτος*: this figure is dropped, and the reality takes its place. Some

° δὲ ὃν ἐγὼ δώσω ἡ σάρξ μου ἐστὶν ὑπὲρ τῆς τοῦ κόσμου BCDE GHKL MSTUV ΓΔΛΠℵ 1. 33. 69

om δε DΓℵ lat-*a b c* [*ff*$_2$ vulg copt Syr syr-cu syr-jer æth arm Ammon$_1$] Clem$_1$ Aug. rec aft εστιν ins ην εγω δωσω, with E rel lat-*f q* syrr [syr-jer] copt goth arm Clem$_1$ Orig$_2$ [Cyr-p$_2$] : om BCDLTℵ 33 latt syr-cu sah æth Orig$_2$ Ath$_1$ *Cyr*[-p] Tert$_1$ Cypr$_1$.—υπερ της του κοσμου ζωης bef η σαρξ μου εστιν ℵ [Tert$_1$].

difficult questions arise regarding the sense and reference of this saying of our Lord. (1) Does it refer to His Death? and, (2) is there any reference to the Ordinance of the Lord's Supper?

(1) In treating this question I must at once reject all metaphorical and side-interpretations, as, that the *teaching* of Christ is the Bread, and to be *taught by Him* is feeding upon it (so Grotius, and the modern rationalists): that the *divine Nature of Christ*, or His *sending of the Holy Spirit*, or His *whole life of doing good on earth*, can be meant: all such have against them the plain sense of the words, which, as Stier observes, are *very simple ordinary words;* the only difficulty arising, when we come to enquire into their application to His own Person. The Bread of Life is *Himself:* and, strictly treated, when we come to enquire *what*, of that body, soul, and spirit, which constituted Himself, this Bread specifically is, we have His answer that it is *His Flesh* which He will give (for this will be the meaning, whether the words ἣν ἐγὼ δώσω are to be regarded as part of the text or not) on behalf of the life of the world. We are then specifically directed to *His Flesh* as the answer. Then, *what does that Flesh import?* The flesh of animals is the ordinary food of men; but *not the blood.* The blood, which is the life, is spilt at death, and is not in the flesh when eaten by us. Now this distinction must be carefully borne in mind. The *flesh* here, (see ver. 53,) and the *eating of the flesh, are distinct from the blood,* and *the drinking of the blood.* We have no generalities merely, to interpret as we please: but the terms used are *precise and technical.* It is then *only through or after the Death of the Lord,* that by any propriety of language, His Flesh could be said to be eaten. Then another distinction must be remembered: The flesh of animals which we eat is *dead* flesh. It is already the prey of corruption; we eat it, and die (ver. 49). But *this* Bread is *living Bread;* not dead flesh, but living Flesh. And therefore *manducation by the teeth materially is not to be thought of* here; but some kind of eating by which the *living Flesh of the Son of God* is made the *living sustenance* of those who partake of it. Now His Flesh and Blood were *sundered* by Death. Death was the shedding of His precious Blood, which *He did not afterwards resume:* see ch. xx. 27, and Luke xxiv. 39. His Flesh is the glorified substance of His Resurrection-Body, now at the right hand of God. It is then in His *Resurrection form only* that His Flesh can be eaten, and be living food for the living man. I cannot therefore see how *any thing short of His Death* can be here meant. By that Death, He has given His Flesh for the *life of the world:* not merely that *they who believe on Him* may, in the highest sense, have life; but that **ὁ κόσμος** may have life. *The very existence of all the created world* is owing to, and held together by, that Resurrection-Body of the Lord. In Him *all things* are gathered together and reconciled to God: τὰ πάντα ἐν αὐτῷ **συνέστηκεν**, Col. i. 17. (2) The question *whether there is here any reference to the* Ordinance of the Lord's Supper, has been *inaccurately put.* When cleared of inaccuracy in terms, it will mean, *Is the subject here dwelt upon, the same as that which is set forth in the ordinance of the Lord's Supper?* And of this there can surely be no doubt. To the *ordinance itself*, there is here *no reference;* nor *could* there well have been any. But the spiritual verity which underlies the ordinance is one and the same with that here insisted on; and so considered, the discourse is, as generally treated, most important towards a right understanding of the ordinance. On the *history* of the exegesis of this passage, see Lücke ii. pp. 149—159 (3rd edn.), and Excursus ii., in his 2nd edn. (omitted in his 3rd);—also Tholuck and Olshausen, in loc. To attempt to recount the various opinions, would exceed the limits of a note in an edition of the whole Testament: for the present subject is one in which the manifold dogmatical variations of individual belief have influenced Commentators to such an extent as to render accurate classification impossible. I may roughly state, that three leading opinions may be traced: that of those who hold (*a*) that *no reference* to the Holy Communion is intended,—among whom are Origen and Basil, of the ancients; and of the moderns, the Swiss Reformers, Zwingle and Calvin (the former however not very

ζωῆς. 52 [p] ἐμάχοντο οὖν πρὸς ἀλλήλους οἱ Ἰουδαῖοι
λέγοντες Πῶς δύναται οὗτος ἡμῖν [q] δοῦναι τὴν σάρκα
φαγεῖν; 53 εἶπεν οὖν αὐτοῖς ὁ Ἰησοῦς Ἀμὴν ἀμὴν λέγω
ὑμῖν, ἐὰν μὴ φάγητε τὴν σάρκα τοῦ [r] υἱοῦ τοῦ [r] ἀνθρώπου
καὶ πίητε αὐτοῦ τὸ αἷμα, οὐκ [st] ἔχετε [s] ζωὴν ἐν [tu] ἑαυτοῖς.

p = Acts iii. 26. 2 Tim. ii. 24. James iv. 2 only. Neh. xiii. 11.
q Matt. xiv. 16 reff.
r Matt. viii. 20 reff.
s ch. v. 26 bis, 40. x. 10. xx. 31. 1 John v. 12 bis, 13.
t ch. v. 42. Mark iv. 7 bis.
u = Matt. iii. 9 reff.

52. *οι ιουδαιοι* bef *προς αλληλους* CD **1**. 33. 69 vulg lat-*a c e* [*q* syr-jer] syrr syr-cu æth: txt BTℵ rel lat-*b f* coptt goth arm $Orig_1$. aft *πως* ins *ουν* ℵ. *ημιν* bef *ουτος* Cℵ 1 $Orig_1$ [$Cyr\text{-}p_1$]: aft *δουναι* U: *τ. σ. δου. ημ.* 69. *την σαρκα* bef *δουναι* DK[Π] lat-*a c e* [ff_2 *q* vulg]. aft *σαρκα* ins *αυτου* BT latt syrr syr-cu [syr-jer] coptt æth arm Chr_1 [$Cyr\text{-}p_2$] $Orig\text{-}int_1$: om CDℵ rel lat-ff_2 goth $Orig_1$ [$Cyr\text{-}p_1$].
53. om *ὁ* B. [om 2nd *αμην* CΔ.] for *εαν*, *αν* ℵ. for *φαγητε*, *λαβητε* D lat-*a* $Victorin_1$. *το αιμα* bef *αυτου* ℵ: transp *πιητε* and *το αιμα* D lat-*a* Hil. *εν εαυ. την ζωην* D. aft *ζωην* ins *αιωνιον* ℵ [Chr_1].

decidedly, see Olsh. ii. 173 note), Luther, Melanchthon. (β) That the whole passage regards *exclusively* the Holy Communion,—among whom are Chrysostom, Cyril, Theophylact, Euthymius, the Schoolmen, and the Roman Catholic expositors, with a few exceptions. (γ) That the *subject* and *idea* of the Holy Communion, not the ordinance is referred to: to which class belong the best modern Commentators in Germany, e. g. Lücke, Tholuck, Olshausen, Stier. Bengel's note to the same effect is important: "Jesus verba sua scienter ita formavit, ut statim et semper illa quidem de spirituali fruitione sui agerent proprie; sed posthac eadem consequenter etiam in augustissimum S. Cœnæ mysterium, quum id institutum foret, convenirent. Etenim ipsam rem hoc sermone propositam in S. Cœnam contulit; tantique hoc sacramentum est momenti, ut facile existimari possit, Jesum, ut proditionem Judæ ver. 71, et mortem suam hoc versu, ita etiam S. Cœnam, de qua inter hæc verba certissime secum cogitavit, uno ante anno prædixisse, ut discipuli possent prædictionis postea recordari. Tota hæc de carne et sanguine J. C. oratio Passionem spectat, et cum ea S. Cœnam. Hinc separata carnis et sanguinis mentio constanter. Nam in passione sanguis ex corpore eductus est, Agnusque mactatus." **52.**] The inference conveyed in **φαγεῖν**, which *first comes from the Jews themselves*, is yet a right one. If He is the Bread, and that Bread is His Flesh, we must *eat His Flesh*, though not in the sense here meant by them. They contended against one another, probably some having more insight into the possibility of a spiritual meaning than others. **53.**] Our Lord not only ratifies their *φαγεῖν*, but adds to it a more wonderful thing; that they must also do that against which a prohibition might seem to have existed from Noah downwards,—*drink His Blood*. But observe, this Blood is not to be *eaten* in the Flesh, *which was the forbidden thing* (Gen. ix. 4: Levit. xvii. 10—16), in its strict literal form: but to be *drunk*, separate from the flesh: again *presupposing death*. Now as the Flesh of Christ (see above) is the Resurrection-Body which He now has, and in which all things consist: so is His Blood ("the blood is the *life*." Levit. xvii. 11, 14) the Life which He gave up, paid down, as the penalty for the sin of the world. By the shedding, pouring forth, of that Blood, is remission of sin. It is quite impossible that these words should, as De Wette maintains, be merely an expansion of *τὴν σάρκα φαγεῖν*. Even had the idea of *τὸ αἷμα πίνειν* been one familiar to the Jews, the construction would not have allowed such an interpretation;—but *new as it was*, and *abhorrent from their habits and law*, we must regard it as specially and purposely added. But *what* is this eating and drinking? Clearly, not *merely faith*: for faith answers to the *hand reached forth for the food*,—but is *not the act of eating*. Faith is a *necessary condition* of the act: so that we can hardly say with Augustine, "crede, et manducasti;" but 'crede et manducabis.' Inasmuch as Faith will necessarily in its energizing lead to this partaking, we sometimes incorrectly say that it *is* Faith:—but for strict accuracy this is not enough. To eat the flesh of Christ, is *to realize, in our inward life, the mystery of His Body now in heaven,—to digest and assimilate our own portion in that Body*. To drink His Blood, is *to realize, in our inward life, the mystery of His satisfaction for sin,—to digest and assimilate our own portion in that satisfaction, the outpouring of that Blood*. And both these definitions may be gathered into one, which is: The eating of His

v vv. 56. 57, 58. Matt. xxiv. 38. ch. xiii. 18 only †. w ch. iii. 15, 16, 36. v. 24. 1 John iii. 15 al. x vv. 39, 40 reff. y ch. iv. 32 reff. z Rom. xiv. 17. Col. ii. 16 only. Dan. i. 10 only. a ver. 54 reff. b = ch. v. 38 reff. c Rom. ix. 26, from Hos. i. 10. 2 Cor. iii. 3 al. d see 1 John iv. 9. e ver. 51 (reff.).

BCDE GHKL MSTUV ΓΔΛΠℵ 1. 33. 69

54 ὁ v τρώγων μου τὴν σάρκα καὶ πίνων μου τὸ αἷμα w ἔχει
w ζωὴν w αἰώνιον, κἀγὼ x ἀναστήσω αὐτὸν τῇ x ἐσχάτῃ
ἡμέρᾳ. 55 ἡ γὰρ σάρξ μου ἀληθής ἐστιν y βρῶσις, καὶ
τὸ αἷμά μου ἀληθής ἐστιν z πόσις. 56 ὁ a τρώγων μου
τὴν σάρκα καὶ πίνων μου τὸ αἷμα b ἐν ἐμοὶ b μένει, κἀγὼ
ἐν αὐτῷ. 57 καθὼς ἀπέστειλέν με ὁ c ζῶν πατήρ, κἀγὼ
ζῶ διὰ τὸν πατέρα· καὶ ὁ a τρώγων με, κἀκεῖνος d ζήσει
d δι' ἐμέ. 58 οὗτός ἐστιν ὁ e ἄρτος ὁ e ἐξ οὐρανοῦ καταβάς,

54. for *μου, αυτου* (twice) D lat-*e* Victorin$_1$. *σαρκαν* D. (rec *και εγω*, with T rel Orig$_1$ Eus$_1$: txt BCDGKLU[Π]ℵ 1 Orig$_2$ Chr$_1$ Cyr$_2$ Bas$_2$.) ins *εν* bef *τη εσχατη* CKMTVΔΛ [S(Tischdf) Π] 69 vulg lat-*b c f* [*q*] arm Orig$_2$ Eus$_1$ Chr Cyr[-p$_2$] spec: om BDℵ rel lat-*a e* [*ff*$_2$ Orig$_1$(Tischdf)].

55. rec (twice) *αληθως* (*-θης seemed inappropriate: so Orig has αληθινη*), with (Dℵ[1], once) rel latt syrr syr-cu [syr-jer] goth Orig$_1$-int$_4$ Hil$_1$ Ambr Aug: txt BCKLT ℵ[3a](but 2nd *-θως* restored) **1.** 69 [Π Coisl-oct-marg] tol(with mm) lat-*q* coptt æth Clem$_1$ Orig$_4$ Eus$_1$ Bas$_3$ Chr$_1$ *Cyr*[-p].—om latter clause D.—om from 1st *αληθ.* to 2nd (*homœotel*) ℵ[1]. for *ποσις, ποτον* ℵ[1].

56. aft *αυτω* ins *καθως εν εμοι ο πατηρ καγω εν τω πατρι αμην αμην λεγω υμειν εαν μη λαβητε το σωμα του υιου του ανθρωπου ως τον αρτον της ζωης ουκ εχετε ζωην εν αυτω* D, simly lat-*a ff*$_2$.

57. *απεσταλκεν* D 69. om *ζω* T. for *τρωγων, λαμβανων* D Victorin$_1$. rec *ζησεται*, with E rel [Cyr-p$_1$]: *ζη* C[1](appy) D-gr, *vivit* lat-*b q* Ambr$_2$: txt BC[2]K LT[Π]ℵ 33. 69 Orig$_1$ Eus$_2$ Chr$_1$ *Cyr*[-p], *vivet* latt.

58. om *ουτος* ℵ[1]. rec (for *εξ*) *εκ του*, with Dℵ rel Orig$_1$ [Eus$_1$] Chr$_1$ Cyr$_1$: txt BCT. for *καταβας, καταβαινων* ℵ[1].

Flesh and drinking of His Blood import the making to ourselves and using as *objectively real*, those two great Truths of our Redemption in Him, of which our Faith *subjectively* convinces us.
And of this realizing of Faith He has been pleased to appoint certain symbols in the Holy Communion, which He has commanded to be received; to signify to us the spiritual process, and to assist us towards it. **οὐκ ἔχ. ζωὴν ἐν ἑαυτ.**] 'Ye have not in you that spring of life, which shall overcome death, and lead (ver. **54**) to the resurrection in the true sense:' see above, ver. 44, and notice again the solemn *refrain*. **τρώγων**] It is not necessary to see any more literal 'eating' in the word than in *φαγών*:—it expresses the *present* of *φαγών*, which must be either *τρώγων* or *ἐσθίων*,—and the real sense conveyed is, that by the very act of inward realization, which is the 'manducatio,' the possession of eternal life is certified.
55.] **ἀληθής** is here not = *ἡ ἀληθινή*, nor is the sense, '*My Flesh is the true meat* &c.,' but **My flesh is true meat**, i. e. *really* TO BE EATEN, which they doubted. Thus *ἀληθῶς* is a gloss, which falls short of the depth of the adjective. This verse is decisive against all explaining away or metaphorizing the passage. Food and drink are not here mere metaphors;—rather are our common material food and drink mere shadows and imperfect types of this only real reception of refreshment and nourishment into the being. **56.**] **He who thus lives upon Me, abides in Me** (see ch. xv. 5 and note);—**and I** (that living power and nourishment conveyed by the *ἄρτος τῆς ζωῆς* which = *ἐγώ*) **abide in him.** Beware of imagining, as Bp. Wordsw. again (see note on Matt. xvi. 18), that there is any especial emphasis on **μου** *because of its position*. **57.**] The same expanded further—see ch. v. 26. The two branches of the feeding on Christ are now united under the general expression, **τρώγων με.**
διά expresses the *efficient cause*. The Father is the Fountain of all Life: the Son lives in and by the Father: and all created being generally, lives (*in the lower sense*) in and by Him; but he that eateth Him shall (*eternally and in the highest sense*) live by Him. Ver. **58** forms the solemn conclusion of the discourse, referring back to the Bread with which it began and to its difference from the perishable food which they had extolled:—and setting forth the infinite superiority of its effects over those of that sustenance.
οὗτός ἐστιν, such is. **καταβάς,—**

οὐ καθὼς ἔφαγον οἱ [f] πατέρες καὶ ἀπέθανον· ὁ [a] τρώγων
τοῦτον τὸν ἄρτον [e] ζήσει [e] εἰς τὸν αἰῶνα. 59 Ταῦτα εἶπεν
ἐν συναγωγῇ διδάσκων ἐν Καφαρναούμ.
60 Πολλοὶ οὖν ἀκούσαντες ἐκ τῶν μαθητῶν αὐτοῦ εἶπον
[g] Σκληρός ἐστιν ὁ λόγος οὗτος· τίς δύναται αὐτοῦ
[h] ἀκούειν; 61 [i] εἰδὼς δὲ ὁ Ἰησοῦς [i] ἐν ἑαυτῷ ὅτι [k] γογγύ-
ζουσιν περὶ τούτου οἱ μαθηταὶ αὐτοῦ, εἶπεν αὐτοῖς Τοῦτο
ὑμᾶς [l] σκανδαλίζει; 62 ἐὰν οὖν [m] θεωρῆτε τὸν [n] υἱὸν τοῦ
[n] ἀνθρώπου [o] ἀναβαίνοντα ὅπου ἦν [p] τὸ [p] πρότερον; 63 τὸ
F το πνευμα.. πνεῦμά ἐστιν τὸ [q] ζωοποιοῦν, ἡ σὰρξ οὐκ [r] ὠφελεῖ οὐδέν·

f ch. vii. 22 reff.
g = Jude 15 (Matt. xxv. 24. Acts [ix. 5 v. r.] xxvi. 14. James iii. 4) only. Gen. xxi. 11. xlii. 7, 30 al.
h see ch. x. 20.
i here only. see Mark v. 30.
k vv. 41, 43 reff.
l Matt. v. 29, 30 reff.
m Luke xxiii. 48. xxiv. 39.
n Matt. viii. 20 reff.
o ch. iii. 13. xx. 17. Eph. iv. 8 (from Ps. cxvii. 18), 9, 10. Rev. xi. 12.
p ch. ix. 8. Gal. iv. 13. 1 Tim. i. 13 only. Jer. xxxvii. (xxx.) 20. see Heb. x. 32. 1 Pet. i. 14.
q ch. v. 21 reff.
r ch. xii. 19. Matt. xxvii. 24. Sir. xxxi. (xxxiv.) 23.

οι πατερες bef εφαγον ℵ. rec aft οι πατερες ins υμων, with D 69-corr[1] rel [latt syrr syr-cu syr-jer sah goth æth arm Cyr Non$_1$] Chr; ημων Γ 69[1] Scr's e ev-P: om BCLTℵ copt Orig$_1$. rec adds further το μαννα, with E rel latt syrr syr-jer goth arm [Cyr Non$_1$]: om BCDLTℵ 33 lat-*e* syr-cu coptt æth. rec ζησεται, with DHK MUΓ[Π] 69 Thdrt$_1$[freely]: txt BCTℵ rel Orig Chr Cyr.

59. ins τη bef συναγωγη D arm [Cyr$_1$]. at end ins σαββατω D lat-*a ff*$_2$ Aug.

60. εκ τ. μαθ. αυτ. bef ακουσαντες D lat-*q* syr-cu. ειπαν D. rec ουτος bef ο λογος, with E rel latt syr [syr-jer]: txt BCDKLT[Π]ℵ 1. 33 lat-*e q* Syr syr-cu Chr$_1$ Cyr$_2$[-p].

61. for ειδως δε, ως ουν εγνω D Chr$_1$: εγνω ουν ℵ[1] 69 (lat-*b e*): ιδων δε C[1] copt. om ὁ ℵ[1]. for εν εαυτω οτι, οτι εν εαυτοις D Chr$_1$. ins και bef ειπεν ℵ[1] 69 Syr.

62. om ουν ℵ[1] ev-P[1]. for οπου, ου D. αναβ. bef τ. υι. τ. ανθ. ℵ.

63. om 1st το ℵ[1].

past, *now:* because He has clearly identified it with *Himself.* **καθώς** must = τοιοῦτος, ὅν: if ὑμῶν τὸ μάννα (see digest) is to stand, the construction must be filled up οὐ καθὼς τὸ μ. ὃ ἔφ. κ.τ.λ.

60-65.] *Murmuring of some of the disciples at the foregoing discourse, and the answer of Jesus to them.*

60.] Lampe shews by reff. and other citations that σκληρός "non tam *absurditatem* quam *impietatem* designat." It seems clear that it was not the *difficulty,* so much as the *strangeness* of the saying, which scandalized them. It is the whole discourse,—the turn given to it,—the doctrine of the Bread of Life,—the giving His Flesh and Blood to eat,—at which they take offence. **ἀκούειν, to listen to it**—'Who can stay and hear such sayings as this?' not, '*to understand it.*' 61.] **ἐν ἑαυτῷ**, by His divine knowledge. 62.] **ἐὰν οὖν θεωρ., what then, if ye see . . .** not meaning '*will ye not then be much more scandalized?*' or, '*what will ye say* (or *do*), *then?*'—but appealing to an event which they should witness, as a *certain proof of one part* of the σκληρὸς λόγος, with which indeed *the rest of it was bound up,*—His having *descended from heaven.* All attempts (as those of Lücke, De Wette, and others) to explain this otherwise than of His ascent into heaven, are simply *dishonest,*—and spring from laxity of belief in the historical reality of that event. That it is not recorded by John, is of no moment here: see Prolegomena. And that none but the Twelve saw it, is unimportant; for how do we know that our Lord was not here speaking to some among the Twelve? To explain it of His *death,* as part of His going up where He was before, is hardly less disingenuous. Lücke maintains that θεωρεῖν need not mean bodily sight: which is true enough in some constructions in John (ch. viii. 51 al.); but surely, as joined with ἀναβαίνοντα, it must. The whole exegesis of the passage in the above-named Commentators is a remarkable instance of the warping of the judgment by unsoundness of belief in the historical truth of the evangelistic testimony. 63.] **πνεῦμα, σάρξ**, do not mean the *spiritual* and *carnal sense of the foregoing discourse,* as many Commentators explain them: for our Lord is speaking, not of *teaching* merely, but of *vivifying:* He is explaining the *life-giving principle* of which He had been before speaking. 'Such eating of My flesh as you imagine and find hard to listen to, could profit you nothing,—for *it* will have ascended up, &c.; and besides, generally, it is only the *Spirit* that can vivify the spirit of man: the *flesh* (in whatever way

s = here only. t ch. viii. 12. x. 10. xx. 31. Deut. xxxii. 47. u ch. xvi. 4 only. see Acts xxvi. 24. 1 John i. 1 al. v pres., ch. i. 40 reff. w = ch. xix. 11. Matt. xiii. 11 reff. x = ch. iii. 27. y = ch. xix. 12 only. see 1 John iv. 6. z Luke ix. 62. xvii. 31 ‖ Mk. ch. xviii. 6 xx. 14 only. Isa. i. 4 Ald. compl. F(not A). a Rev. iii. 4 only. b ch. vii. 47 reff. c = ch. xii. 11. xviii. 8 al.

τὰ ῥήματα ἃ ἐγὼ λελάληκα ὑμῖν, [s] πνεῦμά ἐστιν καὶ
[t] ζωή ἐστιν. 64 ἀλλ' εἰσὶν ἐξ ὑμῶν τινὲς οἳ οὐ πιστεύουσιν. ᾔδει γὰρ [u] ἐξ ἀρχῆς ὁ Ἰησοῦς, τίνες [v] εἰσὶν οἱ μὴ
πιστεύοντες καὶ τίς [v] ἐστιν ὁ παραδώσων αὐτόν. 65 καὶ
ἔλεγεν Διὰ τοῦτο εἴρηκα ὑμῖν ὅτι οὐδεὶς δύναται ἐλθεῖν
πρός με, ἐὰν μὴ ᾖ [w] δεδομένον αὐτῷ [x] ἐκ τοῦ πατρός.
66 [y] Ἐκ [y] τούτου πολλοὶ [ἐκ] τῶν μαθητῶν αὐτοῦ ἀπῆλθον
[z] εἰς τὰ ὀπίσω, καὶ οὐκέτι [a] μετ' αὐτοῦ [a] περιεπάτουν.
67 εἶπεν οὖν ὁ Ἰησοῦς τοῖς δώδεκα [b] Μὴ καὶ ὑμεῖς θέλετε
[c] ὑπάγειν; 68 ἀπεκρίθη αὐτῷ Σίμων Πέτρος Κύριε, πρὸς

BCDEF GHKL MSTUV ΓΔΛΠℵ 1. 33. 69

...υπαγειν T.

rec λαλω (*force of the perfect not perceived: cf ch* xiv. 10), with E rel: txt BCDKLTU[Π]ℵ 1. 33. 69 latt syrr syr-cu [syr-jer] copt goth æth arm Orig$_1$-int$_2$ Eus$_2$ Ath$_1$ Cyr-jer$_1$ Bas Did$_1$ Chr$_1$ Cyr$_1$ Tert$_1$ Ambr Gaud Aug Vig-taps. om και D[1](ins D[2]) Tert$_1$. om 3rd εστιν ℵ ev-47 [lat-*b f* arm Ath$_1$ Chr$_1$].

64. αλλα DL. τινες bef εξ υμων ST vulg lat-*f ff*$_2$ Chr$_1$: εξ υμων bef εισιν Dℵ lat-*a b e* [*q*]. for 2nd εξ, απ' ℵ. for ιησ., σωτηρ ℵ. om μη Gℵ 240-4-59 am(with forj tol). for last clause, και (add τις ℵ[3a]) ην ο μελλων αυτον παραδιδοναι ℵ. for παραδωσων, παραδιδους D 47. 56 ev-47.

65. εμε Cℵ. om αυτω ℵ[1]. rec aft πατρος ins μου, with C[3] rel vulg lat-*c e f* [*q*] syrr goth arm Bas$_2$ Chr$_2$ Cyr$_1$: om BC[1]DLTℵ lat-*a b ff*$_2$ *l* syr-cu syr-jer copt æth Cypr$_1$.

66. aft εκ τουτου ins ουν Dℵ 69 foss lat-*b c f l*. rec om 2nd εκ, with CDℵ rel vulg lat-*c* [*ff*$_2$ *g l* Bas$_2$ Chr$_1$ Cyr$_1$]: ins BGT 1. 33 lat-*a b e f q* Bas$_1$. rec απηλθον bef [εκ] των μαθητων αυτου, with E rel syr copt goth [Bas$_2$ Chr Cyr Cosm$_1$]: txt BCDKLT[Π](ℵ) 1. 33. 69 latt Syr syr-cu [syr-jer] æth arm.—om αυτου ℵ Scr's f[1].

67. for ουν, δε D lat-*b*.

68. for απεκριθη, ειπεν D. rec adds ουν, with E rel vulg lat-[*g l*] *q* syr Bas$_1$: δε D: om BCKLΛℵ 1. 33. 69 (GU, Treg [and Tischdf, ed 8]) lat-*a c e f* [*ff*$_2$ syr-jer] Syr syr-cu coptt arm Bas$_1$ Cyr$_1$ Cypr$_1$.

used) can profit nothing towards this.' He does not say '*My* Flesh profiteth nothing,' but '*the* flesh.' To make Him say this, as the Swiss anti-sacramentalists do, is to make Him contradict His own words in ver. 51. **τὰ ῥήμ. ἃ ἐγὼ λελάληκα**—*viz. the words* **μου τὴν σάρκα** *and* **μου τὸ αἷμα**, *above.* They are πνεῦμα and ζωή:—spirit, not flesh only:—*living food,* not *carnal* and *perishable.* This meaning has been missed by almost all Commentators: Stier upholds it, iv. 281 (2nd edn.): and it seems to me *beyond question the right one.* The common interpretation is, '*the words which I have spoken,*' i. e. '*My discourses,*' are πνεῦμα, '*to be taken in a spiritual sense,*' (? this sense of πνεῦμα,) '*and are life.*' But this is any thing but precise, even after the forcing of πνεῦμα.

64. ἀλλ' εἰσὶν . . . .] 'This accounts for your murmuring at what I said, that *ye do not believe.*' **ᾔδει γὰρ . . .**] De Wette remarks, that the *foreknowledge* of our Lord with regard to Judas renders it impossible to apply the ordinary rules of moral treatment,—as 'Why did He then continue him as an Apostle? Why did He give him the charge of the purse, knowing him to be a thief? &c.,'—to the case: and it is therefore better not to judge at all on the matter. The fact is, we come here to a form of the problem of *divine foreknowledge* and *human free-will,* which, in any of its endless combinations of expression, it is equally impossible for us to solve. **ἐξ ἀρχῆς**, from their first coming to Him;—the first beginning of their connexion with Him. **65.**] These unbelievers had not that *drawing to Christ,* which leads (ver. 44) to true coming to Him. Observe the parallelism between ᾖ δεδομένον αὐτῷ here, and ὃ δίδωσίν μοι, ver. 37. Both these gifts are in the Father's power.

66—71.] *Many of the disciples leave Him. The confession of the Twelve through Peter: and the Lord's warning to them.* **66. ἐκ τούτου**] upon this. The *temporal* meaning prevails, but does not exclude the *causal.* **πολλοί**, viz. of the μὴ πιστεύοντες: but not all. **67.**] The first mention of *the Twelve* by John. The question is asked in order to extract from them

τίνα ἀπελευσόμεθα; [d] ῥήματα [d] ζωῆς αἰωνίου ἔχεις· 69 καὶ
ἡμεῖς [e] πεπιστεύκαμεν, καὶ [e] ἐγνώκαμεν ὅτι σὺ εἶ ὁ [f] ἅγιος
τοῦ [f] θεοῦ. 70 ἀπεκρίθη αὐτοῖς ὁ Ἰησοῦς Οὐκ ἐγὼ ὑμᾶς
τοὺς δώδεκα [g] ἐξελεξάμην, καὶ ἐξ ὑμῶν εἷς [h] διάβολός ἐστιν;
71 [i] ἔλεγεν δὲ τὸν Ἰούδαν Σίμωνος Ἰσκαριώτου· οὗτος γὰρ
[k] ἔμελλεν παραδιδόναι αὐτόν, εἷς ἐκ τῶν δώδεκα.

d Acts v. 20. see Phil. ii. 16. 1 John i. 1.
e 1 John iv. 16.
f Mark i. 24 || only. see Acts iii. 14. 1 John ii. 20.
g Luke x. 42. xiv. 7. ch. xiii. 18. xv. 16. Num. xvi. 7.
h see note. Esth. vii. 4. Ps. cviii. 6.
i = Mark xiv. 71.
k = Matt. ii. 13. Luke x. 1 al. fr.

69. aft *εγνωκαμεν* ins *σε* D. rec (for *ο αγιος*) *ο χριστος ο υιος* (*from Matt* xvi. 16), with C³(see Tischdf N. T.) rel [latt] syrr goth arm [Cyr-p] Tert: *ο υιος* 17 lat-*b* syr-cu [$Cypr_1$]: txt BC¹DLℵ Non_1 $Cosm_1$. rec aft *του θεου* ins *του ζωντος* (*from Matt* xvi. 16), with E rel lat-ff_2 syrr [syr-jer] goth Bas_2 Chr [Cyr-p_2] $Cypr_2$: om BC DLℵ 1¹. 33 latt syr-cu coptt æth arm Non_1 $Cosm_1$.

70. om *αυτοις* Dℵ lat-*a b c e* copt arm: *αυτω* 69 forj(with foss) lat-*g q*. om *ὁ* ℵ. aft *ιησ.* ins *και ειπεν αυτοις* ℵ [lat-*a* ff_2 æth: *λεγων* D (coptt)]. for *ουκ*, *ουχι* ℵ [$Epiph_1$] Chr-5-mss. *εξελεξαμην* bef *υμ. τ. δωδ.* G: bef (*τους*) *δωδεκα* ℵ. (om *τους* ℵ¹.) *εἷς* bef *εξ υμων* Dℵ³ᵃ 248 lat-*b c e f* [*q*] Chr_1: om *εἷς* ℵ¹.

71. om *τον* DKℵ¹ 1. rec *ισκαριωτην* (*more usual*), with E rel vulg-ed goth Cyr_1: *σκαριωθ* D san lat-*a b* ff_2: *απο καριωτου* 69. 124 syr-mg[and -gr], *απο καρυωτου* ℵ¹ (*attempts at explanation*): txt BCGL [Π²(but *την* restored)] ℵ³ᵃ 33 am(with forj gat harl) lat-*f g* coptt. aft *γαρ* ins *και* ℵ. rec *ημελλεν*, with D rel: *εμελλον* ℵ¹: txt BCKLU[SΠ]ℵ³ᵃ 1. 69 Cyr_1. rec *αυτον* bef *παραδιδοναι*, with ℵ rel lat-*a* [*l*] Cyr_1: txt BCDL 69 vulg lat-*b c e f g* arm. rec ins *ων* bef *εκ* (*from Mark* xiv. 43: *had ων been omd to suit Matt* xxvi. 47, *εκ would also have been omd*), with C²ℵ rel latt syr coptt goth arm Cyr: om BC¹DL Syr syr-cu æth.

the confession which follows, and thus to bind them closer to Himself. We must not forget likewise, in the mystery of our Lord's human nature, that at such a moment of desertion, He would seek comfort in the faith and attachment of His chosen ones. **68.**] Peter answers quickly and earnestly for the rest, as in Matt. xvi. 16. **πρὸς τίνα**] What they had heard and seen had awakened in them the desire of being led on by some teacher towards eternal life; and to whom else should they go from Him who *had*, and brought out of His stores for their instruction, *the words* (see ver. 63) of eternal life? **69.**] **πεπιστεύκαμεν** seems to be used absolutely, as in ver. 64: **we believe, and have long done so.** In the following words the readings vary; the common text having been to all appearance introduced from Matt. xvi. 16. The circumstance of the Lord not being elsewhere called *ὁ ἅγιος τ. θεοῦ* by John, is of course *in favour* of the reading. The idea however is found (ch. x. 36). I regard the coincidence with the testimony of the dæmoniacs, reff. Mark ||, as a remarkable one. *Their* words appear to have been the first plain declaration of the fact, and so to have laid hold on the attention of the Apostles. **70.**] The selection of the Twelve by Jesus is the consequence of the giving of them to Him by the Father, ch. xvii. 6,—in which there also Judas is included. So that *His selecting, and the Father's giving and drawing, do not exclude final falling away.* Meyer observes, that the solemn addition, **τοὺς δώδεκα** after *ὑμᾶς*, heightens the contrast to the opposite result which follows. **διάβολος**] It is doubtful in what sense this word should be taken. Whether we render it *διαβολικός* (= *τοῦ διαβόλου ὑπουργός*), or *ἐπίβουλος*, (both given by Euthym.,) it will be an *ἅπαξ λεγόμενον* in the N. T. Of the two however the latter is the harsher, and less analogous to N. T. diction. Certainly, in the dark act here prophesied, Judas was under the immediate instigation of and yielded himself up to Satan (cf. our Lord's reply to Peter, Matt. xvi. 23); and I would understand this expression as having reference to that league with and entertainment of the Evil One in his thoughts and purposes, which his ultimate possession by Satan implies. This meaning can perhaps hardly be rendered by any single word in another language. The E. V. '*a devil*' is certainly too strong; **devilish** would be better, but not unobjectionable. Compare *ὁ υἱὸς τῆς ἀπωλείας* ch. xvii. 12.

71.] On the name *Ἰσκαριώτης* (here applied to Simon, Judas's father), see on Matt. x. 4. **ἔμελλεν**, not, '*intended*,' see ch. xiii. 2: but simply *future*, = *ἦν ὁ παραδώσων αὐτόν*, see ver. 64; ch. vii. 39; xi. 51 al.

l Mark xi. 27. ch. x. 23. Rev. ii. 1. Esth. ii. 11.
m = vv. 19, &c. Mark xiv. 1. Luke vi. 19. Exod. ii. 15.
n ch. ii. 13 reff.
o ch. v. 1. vi. 4 only.
p here only. Deut. xvi. 16. xxxi. 10. Zech. xiv. 16, 18, 19.
q Luke x. 7. ch. xiii. 1 al.+ Wisd. vii. 27 al.
r constr., Eph. vi. 3. Rev. xxii. 14 al.

VII. 1 Καὶ μετὰ ταῦτα [l] περιεπάτει ὁ Ἰησοῦς ἐν τῇ
Γαλιλαίᾳ· οὐ γὰρ ἤθελεν ἐν τῇ Ἰουδαίᾳ [l] περιπατεῖν, ὅτι
[m] ἐζήτουν αὐτὸν οἱ Ἰουδαῖοι ἀποκτεῖναι. 2 Ἦν δὲ [n] ἐγγὺς
ἡ [o] ἑορτὴ τῶν [o] Ἰουδαίων ἡ [p] σκηνοπηγία. 3 εἶπον οὖν πρὸς
αὐτὸν οἱ ἀδελφοὶ αὐτοῦ [q] Μετάβηθι ἐντεῦθεν καὶ ὕπαγε
εἰς τὴν Ἰουδαίαν, [r] ἵνα καὶ οἱ μαθηταί σου [r] θεωρήσουσιν
τὰ ἔργα σου ἃ ποιεῖς· 4 οὐδεὶς γάρ τι [s] ἐν κρυπτῷ ποιεῖ
καὶ ζητεῖ αὐτὸς [t] ἐν [tu] παῤῥησίᾳ εἶναι. εἰ ταῦτα ποιεῖς,
[v] φανέρωσον σεαυτὸν τῷ κόσμῳ. 5 οὐδὲ γὰρ οἱ ἀδελφοὶ

X και μετα... ...ινα και C. BDEF GHKL MSUV ΧΓΔΛ Πℵ 1. 33. 69

s Matt. vi. 4 bis, 6 bis (18 bis v. r.). ver. 10. ch. xviii. 20. Rom. ii. 29 only. Ps. cxxxviii. 15 Symm.
t Eph. vi. 19. Phil. i. 20. Col. ii. 15. Wisd. v. 1. u = ch. xi. 54. v ch. i. 31 reff.

CHAP. VII. 1. om *και* C^{2}Dℵ^1 latt Syr syr-cu sah : ins BC^1 ℵ^{3a}(but erased) rel lat-*q* syr [syr-jer] copt [æth arm Bas$_1$ Cyr-p$_1$]. rec *περιεπ. ο ιησ.* bef *μετα ταυτα*, with E rel [lat-*q*] syr goth [Bas$_1$] : om *μετα ταυτα* Γ ev-y : txt BCDGKLX[Π]ℵ 1. 33. 69 latt Syr syr-cu [syr-jer] coptt æth arm [Cyr$_1$]. om *ὁ* B.

3. *οι αδ. αυ.* bef *προς αυτον* ℵ [Syr syr-cu]. for *ιουδαιαν*, *γαλιλαιαν* D-gr. rec *θεωρησωσιν* (*gramml corrn*), with B^{2}X rel [Bas$_1$ Chr$_1$ Cyr$_1$] : *θεωρουσιν* ℵ^1 : txt B^{1}DLMΔℵ^{3a}. *σου* bef *τα εργα* B : om *σου* DG[U]ℵ^1 1 lat-*a b c e ff$_2$ l^1* [*q*] Syr syr-cu sah [arm] Bas$_1$ Chr$_1$ Cyr$_1$: txt Lℵ^{3a} rel vulg lat-*f* [*l^2* syr-jer] syr copt goth.—aft *ἅ* ins *συ* G 1.

4. rec *εν κρυπτω* bef *τι*, with D rel vulg lat-*a c f ff$_2$ g* [*l^2 q*] syr goth arm : om *τι* æth : txt BKLX[Π]ℵ (lat-*b ff$_2$*) Syr syr-cu ([syr-jer] coptt). *ποιων*, omg *και*, ℵ. for *αυτος*, *αυτο* BD^1 copt : *αυτον* E^1 : txt D^{s}Lℵ rel vulg lat-*a c f ff$_2$ g* [*l*] syr goth arm.—*εν παρρησια* bef *αυτ.* D 69.

5. for *ουδε*, *οιδε* D : *ου* 69.

CHAP. VII.—X.] JESUS THE LIGHT OF THE WORLD. *The conflict at its height.*

VII. 1—52.] JESUS MEETS THE UNBELIEF OF THE JEWS AT JERUSALEM. *The circumstances* (vv. 1—13). 1.] The chronology of this period is very doubtful. I have remarked on it in my note on Luke ix. 51. Thus much we may observe here, that **μετὰ ταῦτα** cannot apply emphatically to ch. vi., but must be referred back to ch. v., as indeed must the Jews seeking to kill Him, and the miracle alluded to in ver. 23. But it will not follow from this, that ch. vi. is not in its right place : it contains an independent memoir of a miracle and discourse of our Lord in Galilee which actually happened in the interval, and only serves to shew us the character of this Gospel as made up of such memoirs, more or less connected with one another, and selected by the Evangelist for their higher spiritual import, and the discourses arising from them. I would understand this verse as merely carrying on the time from ch. v. and ch. vi.,—and its contents as introductory to the account of Jesus not going up at first to the feast. Ch. vi. is in some measure presupposed in our ver. 3, as indicating that He had not constantly observed the festal journeys of late.

2.] See Deut. xvi. 13—17. Josephus, Antt. viii. 4. 1, calls this ἑορτὴ ἁγιωτάτη καὶ μεγίστη. It began on the 15th (evening of 14th) of Tisri [Sept. 28], and lasted till the evening of the 22nd [Oct. 6]. 3—5.] Respecting the BRETHREN OF THE LORD, see note on Matt. xiii. 55. They seem to have had at this time *a kind of belief* in the Messianic character of Jesus, but of the very lowest sort, not excluding the harsh and scoffing spirit visible in these words. They recognized his miracles, but despised his apparent want of prudence and consistency of purpose, in not shewing himself to the world. In the **ἵνα καὶ οἱ μαθ. σου** *κ.τ.λ.* there is perhaps a reference to the desertion of many of his disciples just before. Nay, more than this : the indication furnished by this verse of the practice of our Lord with regard to His miracles up to this point is very curious. He appears as yet to have made His circuits in Galilee, and to have wrought miracles there, in the presence of but a small circle of disciples properly so called : and there would seem to have been a larger number of disciples, in the wider sense, in Judæa, or to be gathered in Judæa by the feast, who yet wanted assuring, by open display, of the reality of His wonderful works. In ver. **5** (as well as by *οἱ μαθηταί σου*, ver. 3), we have these brethren *absolutely excluded from the number of the Twelve* (see ch. vi. 69); and it is impossible to modify the meaning

αὐτοῦ [w] ἐπίστευον εἰς αὐτόν. 6 λέγει οὖν αὐτοῖς ὁ Ἰησοῦς w ch. ii. 11 reff.
T ουπω ... Ὁ [x] καιρὸς ὁ ἐμὸς οὔπω πάρεστιν· ὁ δὲ [x] καιρὸς ὁ ὑμέτερος x = Matt. xxvi. 18.
πάντοτέ ἐστιν [y] ἕτοιμος. 7 οὐ δύναται ὁ κόσμος μισεῖν Luke xxi. 24. 2 Thess.
ὑμᾶς, ἐμὲ δὲ μισεῖ, ὅτι ἐγὼ [z] μαρτυρῶ [z] περὶ αὐτοῦ ὅτι τὰ ii. 6. Jer. xxvii. (l.) 31. y = 1 Pet. i. 5.
[a] ἔργα αὐτοῦ [a] πονηρά ἐστιν. 8 ὑμεῖς [b] ἀνάβητε εἰς τὴν ἑορ- z ch. l. 7, 8 reff.
τήν· ἐγὼ οὐκ [b] ἀναβαίνω εἰς τὴν ἑορτὴν ταύτην, ὅτι ὁ ἐμὸς a ch. iii. 19 reff. b see Matt. xx. 17, 18 reff.
[x] καιρὸς οὔπω [c] πεπλήρωται. 9 ταῦτα δὲ εἰπὼν αὐτοῖς c = Mark i. 15.
ἔμεινεν ἐν τῇ Γαλιλαίᾳ. 10 ὡς δὲ [b] ἀνέβησαν οἱ ἀδελφοὶ d Mark i. 45.
αὐτοῦ εἰς τὴν ἑορτήν, τότε καὶ αὐτὸς [b] ἀνέβη, οὐ [d] φανε- Acts x. 3 only †.

[*επιστευσαν* DL lat-*q*.] aft *αυτον* add *τοτε* D-gr foss lat-*a c* ff_2 *q* syr-cu Jer.
6. om *ουν* D-gr ℵ[1] lat-*e* foss Syr syr-cu arm. om *ὁ* (bef *ιησ.*) ℵ[1] for *ουπω*, *ου* ℵ[1]. for *εστιν*, *παρεστιν* B.
7. *ο κοσμος* bef *ου δυναται* ℵ[1]. om *εγω* ℵ. *μαρτυρον* T. *περι αυτ.* bef *μαρτ.* 33 : om *περι αυτου* ℵ.
8. rec aft 1st *εορτην* ins *ταυτην* (*conformn to follg : if omd from homœotel, as Mey, why is the omn so general and not found in any* MS *in the follg* *εορτ. ταυ.*?), with ℵ[1](marked for erasure, but marks removed) rel vulg lat-*f g* [*l*[2]] *q* syrr syr-cu goth Ammon : om BDKLTX[Π] 1 lat-*a b c e* ff_2 coptt [Bas$_1$] Chr$_1$ Cyr[-p$_1$]. rec (for *ουκ*) *ουπω* (*to avoid offence : Porphyry, e.g., charged our Lord with fickleness on account of* *ουκ*), with BLT rel some-mss-of-vulg lat-*f g q* syrr [syr-jer] sah goth [Bas$_1$] : txt DKM[Π]ℵ 33 latt syr-cu copt æth [arm] Porph-in-Jer$_1$ Epiph$_1$ Chr$_1$ Cyr[-p$_1$] Jer$_1$. rec *ο καιρ. ο εμ.* (*corrn to ver* 6), with E rel [Bas$_1$] Chr$_1$: txt BDLTUX(ℵ) 1. 33. 69 Cyr[-p$_1$].—om *ὁ* ℵ[1].
9. om *δε* DK[Π]ℵ 1. 33 latt Syr syr-cu arm Chr$_1$ Cyr$_1$: ins BT rel lat-*f* syr [syr-jer goth] coptt. for *αυτοις*, *αυτος* (*corrn from next ver*) D[1]KL T(Bch) X[Π]ℵ 1 vulg lat-*b l* coptt arm Cyr$_1$: om 248-53-9 lat-*e* Syr syr-cu : txt B D-corr[1](Scr) T(Georgi [and Tischdf]) 33(sic) rel lat-*f q* syr [syr-jer] goth æth [Bas$_1$]. *εις την γαλιλαιαν* D ev-2 lat-*b c* [*f* ff_2] : *in judæa* lat-*a*.
10. rec *τοτε και αυτος ανεβη* bef *εις την εορτην*, with D rel latt syr-cu syr goth arm [Bas$_1$] : txt BKLTX[Π]ℵ 33 Syr syr-jer coptt æth Cyr$_1$. (*τοτε* not omd in B : see table.)

of *ἐπίστευον* so as to suppose that they may have been of the Twelve, but not believers in the highest sense. This verse also excludes *all* of His brethren : it is inconceivable that John should have so written, if *any among them* believed at that time. The attempt to make the words mean, that *some of his brethren did not believe on him*, is in my view quite futile. In that case we should certainly have had some such expression as *ἦσαν γὰρ καὶ ἐκ τῶν ἀδελφῶν αὐτοῦ, οἳ οὐκ ἐπίστευον εἰς αὐτόν*. No such attempt would ever have been made by a Greek scholar,—except for the fiction which has been so long, and, strange to say, is still upheld with regard to our Lord's brethren.

The emphatic expression, **οὐδὲ γὰρ οἱ ἀδ.**, is a strong corroboration of the view that they were really and literally *brethren* : see also Ps. lxix. 8.

6—9.] **ὁ καιρ. ὁ ἐμ.** can hardly be taken as directly meaning '*the time of my sufferings* and death,'—but as *ἡ ὥρα μου* in ch. ii. 4 : 'My time for the matter of which you speak, viz. manifestation to the world.' That (ch. xii. 32) was to take place in a very different manner. But *they*, having no definite end before them, no glory of God to shew forth, but being of the world, always had their opportunity ready of mingling with and standing well with the world. Then (ver. 7), '*you* have no hatred of the world in *your* way : but its hatred to Me on account of my testimony against it, causes me to exercise this caution which you so blame.' In ver. 8, it is of little import (see var. readd.) whether we read **οὐκ** or **οὔπω** : the sense will be the same, both on account of the present, *ἀναβαίνω* (not *ἀναβήσομαι*, which would express the disavowal of *an intention* to go up), and of *οὔπω* afterwards. **οὐκ** *ἀναβ.* would mean, **I am not** (at present) **going up.** Meyer attributes to our Lord change of purpose, and justifies his view by the example of His treatment of the Syrophœnician woman, whom He at first repulsed, but afterwards had compassion on. Matt. xv. 26 ff. The same Commentator directs attention to the emphatic *ταύτην*, as implying that our Lord had it

ρῶς, ἀλλὰ ὡς [e] ἐν κρυπτῷ. 11 οἱ οὖν Ἰουδαῖοι ἐζήτουν BDEF
αὐτὸν ἐν τῇ ἑορτῇ καὶ ἔλεγον Ποῦ ἐστιν ἐκεῖνος; 12 καὶ GHKL MSTUV
[f] γογγυσμὸς περὶ αὐτοῦ ἦν πολὺς ἐν τοῖς ὄχλοις. οἱ XΓΔΛ Πℵ
μὲν ἔλεγον ὅτι ἀγαθός ἐστιν· ἄλλοι δὲ ἔλεγον Οὔ, ἀλλὰ 1. 33. 69
[g] πλανᾷ τὸν ὄχλον. 13 οὐδεὶς μέντοι [h] παῤῥησίᾳ ἐλάλει
περὶ αὐτοῦ διὰ τὸν φόβον τῶν Ἰουδαίων.
14 Ἤδη δὲ τῆς ἑορτῆς [i] μεσούσης [k] ἀνέβη Ἰησοῦς εἰς
τὸ ἱερόν, καὶ ἐδίδασκεν. 15 ἐθαύμαζον οὖν οἱ Ἰουδαῖοι
λέγοντες [l] Πῶς οὗτος [m] γράμματα οἶδεν μὴ μεμαθηκώς;
16 ἀπεκρίθη οὖν αὐτοῖς ὁ Ἰησοῦς καὶ εἶπεν Ἡ ἐμὴ [n] διδαχὴ
οὐκ ἔστιν ἐμή, ἀλλὰ τοῦ πέμψαντός με· 17 ἐάν τις [o] θέλῃ

e ver. 4 reff. f Acts vi. 1. Phil. ii. 14. 1 Pet. iv. 9 only. Exod. xvi. 7, 8, 9. (-σις, Num. xiv. 27.) g Matt. xxiv. 4, &c. 1 Cor. vi. 9. 1 John i. 8. Isa. xlvi. 8. h ver. 26. ch. xviii. 20. Mark viii. 32. 2 Cor. iii. 12. Prov. i. 20. i here only. Exod. xii. 29. k Luke xviii. 10. Acts iii. 1. 4 Kings xx. 8. l = Luke xx. 41. ch. iv. 9. 1 Cor. xv. 12. m 2 Tim. iii. 15. ch. v. 47. Acts xxvi. 24. Isa. xxix. 11, 12. Dan. i. 4. n Matt. vii. 28. xxii. 33. Mark i. 22 || L. al. Ps. lix. tit. only. o ch. viii. 44.

(αλλα, so BT.) om ως Dℵ lat-*a b e* [syr-cu sah].

12. ην bef περι αυτου D[ℵ] 33 [syr-cu syr syr-jer arm (Chr_1)]. rec transp περι αυτου and πολυς, with E[ℵ] rel vulg lat-*f g* [syrr syr-cu syr-jer coptt]: om πολυς D lat-*a c e* ff_2 [arm]: txt BLTX lat-*b q* [Chr_1] Cyr_1. τω οχλω Dℵ 33 latt Syr syr-cu [syr-jer] copt goth. om δε Dℵ rel lat-*b e q* goth arm: ins BTX 1. 33. 69 vulg lat-*c f* ff_2 [*q*].—pref *et* lat-*a* Syr syr-cu. ουχι KT.

13. (παρησια B[1](as elsewhere) [so Tischdf N. T. edd 7, 8; παρρ. N. T. Vat., but παρησ. ver 4] DL[1].) περι αυτου bef ελαλει ℵ [lat-*q*]: om π. αυ. L.

14. μεσαζουσης D 1. 69 [Epiph-ms]. rec ins ο bef ιησ., with D rel [Chr_1 Cyr_1]: om BLTUXℵ.

15. rec (for εθαυμ. ουν) και εθαυμ., with E rel vulg lat-*f* syrr syr-cu [syr-jer æth arm]: txt BDLTXℵ 1. 33 lat-*a c e* ff_2 *l* syr-mg coptt Cyr_1.

16. rec om ουν, with DLX vulg lat-*a* [*e* ff_2 *l*] Syr syr-cu copt [arm] Cyr_1: ins BTℵ rel syr sah goth. om ὁ Bℵ 33 [Cyr].

in His mind to go up to some future feasts, but not to *this one*. **οὔπω πεπλήρ., is not yet fully come**: see Luke ix. 51 and note. **10.**] **οὐ φαν.**, i. e. not in the usual caravan-company, nor probably by the usual way. Whether the Twelve were with Him, we have no means of judging: probably so, for they appear ch. ix. 2; and after their becoming once attached to the Person of our Lord as Apostles, we find no trace of his having been for any long time separated from them, except during their mission Matt. x., which was long ago accomplished.

11.] These **Ἰουδ.** are, as usual, the ἄρχοντες, as distinguished from the multitudes. Their question itself (**ἐκεῖνος**) shews a hostile spirit. **12.**] **οἱ ὄχλ.** (the different groups of which ὁ ὄχλος was composed) would include the Galilæan disciples, and those who had been baptized by the disciples in Judæa,—whose view **ἀγαθός ἐστιν** would represent,—as expressed mildly in protest against His enemies. **πλανᾷ τὸν ὄχλον**, possibly in reference to the feeding of and then the discourse to the multitude, which had given so much offence. **13. παῤῥ.**] This was true only of the side who said **ἀγαθός ἐστιν**: *they* dared not speak their mind: the others spoke plainly enough. Here again *οἱ* Ἰουδ. are distinguished from the ὄχλοι. **14—39.**] *Jesus testifies to Himself in the Temple.* **15—24.**] *His teaching is from the Father.*

14, 15.] **τ. ἑορ. μεσ., about the middle of the feast.** Probably *on a sabbath* (see Wieseler, Chron. i. 309). It appears to have been the first time that He ἐδίδασκεν publicly at Jerusalem;—whence (**οὖν**) the wonder of the Jews, i. e. the rulers of the hierarchy. **γράμματα**—generally **letters**; but also particularly, **scripture-learning**—perhaps because this was *all the literature* of the Jews: see reff. Probably His teaching consisted in *exposition of the Scripture*. **μὴ μεμ.**, never having been the scholar of any Rabbi. He was θεοδίδακτος. These words are spoken in the true bigotry and prejudice of so-called 'learning.' These words of His enemies, testifying to matter of fact well known to them, are, as Meyer observes, decisive against all attempts of unbelievers to attribute our Lord's knowledge to education in any human school of learning. Such indications are not without their value in these times. **16.**] Here only does our Lord call His teaching διδαχή, as being now among the διδάσ-

τὸ [p] θέλημα αὐτοῦ [op] ποιεῖν, γνώσεται περὶ τῆς [n] διδαχῆς, p Matt. vii. 21 reff.
[q] πότερον [r] ἐκ τοῦ θεοῦ ἐστιν, ἢ ἐγὼ [s] ἀπ' ἐμαυτοῦ λαλῶ. q here only. Job vii. 12. xiii. 7, 11.
18 ὁ [s] ἀφ' ἑαυτοῦ λαλῶν τὴν δόξαν τὴν ἰδίαν ζητεῖ· ὁ δὲ r Matt. xxi. 25. ch. i. 13.
ζητῶν τὴν δόξαν τοῦ πέμψαντος αὐτόν, οὗτος ἀληθής s ch. v. 19 reff.
ἐστιν, καὶ ἀδικία ἐν αὐτῷ οὐκ ἔστιν. 19 οὐ Μωυσῆς
[t] ἔδωκεν ὑμῖν τὸν νόμον; καὶ οὐδεὶς ἐξ ὑμῶν [u] ποιεῖ τὸν t ch. i. 17 reff. u = Rom. ii. 14. Gal. v. 3.
νόμον· τί με [v] ζητεῖτε ἀποκτεῖναι; 20 ἀπεκρίθη ὁ ὄχλος v ver. 1 reff.
[w] Δαιμόνιον [w] ἔχεις· τίς σε [v] ζητεῖ ἀποκτεῖναι; 21 ἀπεκρίθη w Matt. xi. 18 ‖. Luke viii. 27. ch. viii. 48, 49, 52. x. 20 only.
Ἰησοῦς καὶ εἶπεν αὐτοῖς Ἓν ἔργον ἐποίησα, καὶ πάντες

17. om του (bef θεου) Dℵ. **18.** for ο δε, και ο ℵ [syr-cu].
19. rec δεδωκεν, with Tℵ rel : txt BDH[Π²].
20. rec aft οχλος ins και ειπεν (*see ver* 21, *where there is no var*), with D rel latt syrr [syr-jer] Cyr₁ : om BLTXℵ 33 coptt Aug₁.—απεκριθησαν οι ιουδ. κ. ειπον αυτω K[Π] Scr's p t (w) syr-mg.
21. rec ins ο bef ιησ., with DKLTUΛ[Π] Cyr₁ : om Bℵ rel. om αυτοις D lat-*a e* [*l* arm]. for παντες, υμεις D.

καλοι, the Rabbis, in the temple. It is often so called by the Evangelists, see reff. The words may bear two meanings: —either, '*the sense of Scripture which I teach is not my own, but that in which it was originally penned as a revelation from God*;' or, **My teaching** (generally) **is not mine, but that of Him who sent me.** The latter is preferable, as agreeing better with what follows, and because the former assumes that He was expounding Scripture, which, though probable, is not asserted. **17.**] **θέλειν τὸ θέλ. αὐτ. ποιεῖν** is equivalent to τὴν ἀγάπην τοῦ θεοῦ ἔχειν ἐν ἑαυτοῖς, ch. v. 42. The **θέλειν** should not have been slurred over in the E. V., for it is important. **If any man's will be, to do His will,** &c. As it now stands in the E. V., *a wrong idea is conveyed:* that the *bare performance of God's outward commands* will give a man sufficient acquaintance with Christian doctrine:—whereas what our Lord asserts to the Jews is, that if the *will* be set in His ways, if a man be really anxious to do the will of God, and thus to fulfil this first great commandment of the law,—be, as Meyer expresses it, in ethical harmony with God,—the singleness of purpose, and subjection to the will of God, will lead him on to faith in the promised and then apparent Messiah, and to a just discrimination of the divine character of his teaching. **18.**] This gives us the reason why he, who wishes to do God's will, will know of the teaching of Christ: viz. because both are seeking one aim—the glory of God:—and the humility of him, whose will it is to do God's will, can best appreciate that more perfect humility of the divine Son, who speaks not of himself, but of Him that sent him,—see ch. v. 41—44, of which this verse is a repetition with a somewhat different bearing. In its *general* sense, it asserts that self exaltation and self-seeking necessarily accompany the unaided teaching of man, but that all true teaching is from God. But then we must remember that, simply taken, the latter part of the sentence is only true of the Holy One Himself; that owing to human infirmity, purity of motive is no sure guarantee for correctness of doctrine;—and therefore in this second part it is not τοῦ θεοῦ, which would generalize it to all men, but **τοῦ πέμψ. αὐτόν**, which confines it to Himself. **19.**] There is a close connexion with the foregoing. Our Lord now takes the *offensive* against them. The θέλειν τὸ θέλημα αὐτοῦ ποιεῖν was to be the great key to a true appreciation of His teaching: but of this there was no example among *them:* and therefore it was that they were no fair judges of the teaching, but bitter opponents and persecutors of Jesus, of whom, had they been anxious to fulfil the law, they would have been earnest and humble disciples (ch. v. 46). The law was to be read before all Israel every seventh year in the feast of tabernacles (Deut. xxxi. 10—13):—whether this was such a year is uncertain: but this verse may allude to the practice, even if it was not. **ζητεῖτε ἀποκτ.**] In their killing the Lord of Life was summed up all their transgression of God's law. It was the greatest proof of their total ignorance of and disobedience to it. **20.**] The multitude, not the rulers, replied this. Indeed their question, τίς σε ζητεῖ ἀποκτεῖναι; shews their ignorance of the purpose of their rulers,

θαυμάζετε. 22 διὰ τοῦτο Μωυσῆς [t] δέδωκεν ὑμῖν τὴν
[x] περιτομήν, οὐχ ὅτι ἐκ τοῦ Μωυσέως ἐστίν, ἀλλ' ἐκ τῶν
[y] πατέρων, καὶ ἐν σαββάτῳ [z] περιτέμνετε ἄνθρωπον. 23 εἰ
[x] περιτομὴν [a] λαμβάνει ἄνθρωπος ἐν σαββάτῳ ἵνα μὴ
[b] λυθῇ ὁ νόμος Μωυσέως, ἐμοὶ [c] χολᾶτε ὅτι [d] ὅλον ἄνθρωπον [e] ὑγιῆ [e] ἐποίησα ἐν σαββάτῳ; 24 μὴ [fg] κρίνετε [g] κατ'

BDEF GHKL MSTUV ΧΓΔΛ ΠN 1. 33. 69

x here only in Gospp. Acts vii. 8 al2. Epp., Paul passim.
y absol., = ch. vi. 58. Acts vii. 19. xiii. 32. xxvi. 6. Rom. ix. 5. xi. 28. xv. 8. Heb. i. 1. 2 Pet. iii. 4 only.
z Luke i. 59. ii. 21. Acts vii. 8 (from Gen. xxi. 4). xv. 1, 5, 24 al2. 1 Cor. vii. 18 bis. Gal. ii. 3 al5. Col. ii. 11 only.
a = Rom. iv. 11. b = Matt. v. 19. ch. v. 18. x. 35. c here only +. 3 Macc. iii. 1 B. d = ch. xiii. 10. Zech. iv. 2. see ch. ix. 34. e ch. v. 11, 15 only. f = Matt. vii. 1 reff. g ch. viii. 15. xviii. 31, 1 Pet. i. 17 al.

22. om δια τουτο א[1]. ins ο bef μωυσης א [Cyr-p_1]. εδωκεν(so also L) υμιν bef μωυσης D. om του D. aft αλλ' ins οτι א [syr-cu Cyr-p_1]. om εν B lat-*b* *e* [*ff*$_2$].

23. aft ει ins ουν D 29 lat-*a f* arm. ins ο bef ανθρωπος B 33. ins ο bef μωυσεως(sic) א[Π[2]]. ins πως bef εμαι D [simly lat-*f*] coptt æth.

which our Lord had just exposed and charged them with. It would not now be *their* policy to represent Him as possessed.

21.] The **one work** was the sabbath-healing in ch. v. **22.**] **διὰ τοῦτο** is variously placed; either at the end of ver. 21, so as to come after θαυμάζετε, (Cod. X, lat.-*q*, Theophyl., Beza, and many of the moderns, Lücke, De Wette, Stier, Lachmann, &c.,)—or at the beginning of this verse (Codd. D, E, G, K, L, T, U, Δ, Λ, [H, S, Γ, Π,] vulg., the syriac versions, coptt., goth., Euthym., Chrys., Cyril, Grotius, &c.). I prefer the latter arrangement: because (1) I believe τοῦτο would not be used in the sense required by the other, but αὐτό (nor can I see that the ἓν ἔργον makes the τοῦτο any more applicable (see Stier, edn. 2, iv. 315); nay, it seems to me to take the attention off from the particular work done, and fix it on the mere ἓν ἔργ. ποιῆσαι, abstractedly—'Ye wonder that I have acted at all'): and (2) because I find διὰ τοῦτο joined with ὅτι to be a usual mode of speaking with our Evangelist, see ch. v. 16, 18; viii. 47 (θαυμάζειν διά τι is used Mark vi. 6; Rev. xvii. 7; see also John iii. 29). (3) I see an appropriateness of meaning in ver. 22 with the διὰ τοῦτο, which it has not without it. **Moses** *on this account* **gave you circumcision, not because it is of Moses, but of the fathers**; (the repetition of ἐκ τ. Μωυ. ἐστ. does not necessarily imply a parenthesis: John constantly uses these formal repetitions: this in answer to Stier, iv. 315, edn. 2)—i. e. it is no part of the law *of Moses*, properly so called,—but was adopted by Moses, and thereby becomes part of his law. The meaning of οὐχ ὅτι, '*not that*,' implying 'I mean not, that,' does not seem to suit the context so well, because it would leave the preceding διὰ τοῦτο without any thing to refer to. **Now you circumcise on the Sabbath, to avoid breaking the law of Moses, &c.** If our Lord had said these last words (in ver. 23) *merely*, the argument would not have been strict: they might have answered, that circumcision was not only a command of the law, but anterior to it: whereas ver. 22 takes this answer from them; reminding them that though they regarded its sanction as derived from Moses, it was in fact older,—and tacitly approving their doing it on the Sabbath. Then the argument is, *If this may be done on the Sabbath*:—if an ordinance *strictly Mosaic* (which *the Sabbath* in its Jewish mode of observance was) may be set aside by another, Mosaic also, but more ancient, and borrowed from a more general and direct command of God ("circumcisio est antiquior rigido otio sabbati per Mosen imperato"—Grotius), *how much more may it* by *a deed of mercy*, a benevolent exercise of divine power, the approval of which is anterior to and deeper than all ceremonial enactment?

23.] **ἵνα μὴ λυθῇ**—not,—"*ita ut non solvatur*"—"*salva lege*;" which is ungrammatical;—but **in order that the Law of Moses may not be broken**, viz. that which (after the fathers) ordains circumcision on the eighth day. **ὅλον ἄνθρ.**] The distinction is between circumcision, which purified only part of a man, by which he received (ἔλαβεν) ceremonial cleanness,—and that perfect and entire healing which the Lord bestowed on the cripple. Stier (after Bengel) thinks the ὅλον refers to *body and soul*,—see ch. v. 14,—whose healing is a much greater benefit than circumcision, even viewed as a sacrament; "nam circumcisio est *medium*, sanatio animæ *finis*." But this is perhaps too subtle. The Jews could not have appreciated this meaning, and the argument is especially addressed *to them*. Besides, it is by no means certain from that passage that such was the case.

h ὄψιν, ἀλλὰ τὴν δικαίαν i κρίσιν i κρίνετε. 25 ἔλεγον οὖν
τινὲς ἐκ τῶν k Ἱεροσολυμιτῶν Οὐχ οὗτός ἐστιν ὃν l ζητοῦσιν l ἀποκτεῖναι; 26 καὶ ἴδε m παῤῥησίᾳ λαλεῖ, καὶ οὐδὲν
αὐτῷ λέγουσιν. n μήποτε o ἀληθῶς ἔγνωσαν οἱ ἄρχοντες
ὅτι οὗτός ἐστιν ὁ χριστός; 27 ἀλλὰ τοῦτον οἴδαμεν p πόθεν
ἐστίν· ὁ δὲ χριστὸς ὅταν ἔρχηται, οὐδεὶς γινώσκει p πόθεν
ἐστίν. 28 q ἔκραξεν οὖν ἐν τῷ ἱερῷ διδάσκων ὁ Ἰησοῦς
...οιδατε και F. καὶ λέγων Κἀμὲ οἴδατε, καὶ οἴδατε p πόθεν εἰμί· καὶ r ἀπ'
ἐμαυτοῦ οὐκ ἐλήλυθα· ἀλλ' ἔστιν s ἀληθινὸς ὁ πέμψας
μέ, ὃν ὑμεῖς οὐκ οἴδατε· 29 ἐγὼ οἶδα αὐτόν, ὅτι t παρ'

h ch. xi. 44. Rev. i. 16 only. = Gen. xxiv. 16. Thucyd. vi. 46.
i here only. Deut. xvi. 18. constr., as Col. ii. 19.
k Mark i. 5 only.
l ver. 1.
m ver. 13 reff.
n = here only.
o = ch. xvii. 8. Acts xii. 11 only. Exod. xxiii. 16.
p = Matt. xxi. 25. ch. ix. 29, 30. xix. 9. 2 Kings i. 13.
q ver. 37. ch. xii. 44.
r ch. v. 19 reff.
s = Heb. x. 22. Rev. iii. 14. xix. 11.
t ch. vi. 46. ix. 16, 33. Luke x. 7. Phil iv. 18

24. rec (for 2nd *κρινετε*) *κρινατε*, with ℵ rel: txt BDLT Constt$_1$ Cyr[-p$_1$]. (33 def.)
25. om *εκ* Γℵ.
26. for *μηποτε*, *μητι numquid* Dℵ 49. 108 vulg lat-*a b* Chr$_1$. *οι αρχοντες* bef *εγνωσαν* D arm.—for *αρχοντες*, *αρχιερεις* ℵ Scr's g [lat-*a*]. rec aft *εστιν* ins *αληθως*, with E rel lat-*f q* syrr [syr-jer] goth æth Chr-txt [Cyr-p$_1$]: om BDKLTX[Π]ℵ 1. 69 latt syr-cu coptt arm Orig$_2$ Epiph$_1$ Chr$_1$-comm *Cyr*[-p]. (33 def.)
27. om *δε* ℵ[1](ins ℵ[3a], but erased) [lat-*e* Orig$_1$(ins$_2$)]. aft *χριστος* ins *οταν ελθη μη πλιονα σημια ποιησει η* ℵ[1]. elz *ερχεται*, with HXΔ[1]ℵ 69 (F, e sil): *ελθη* G Scr's g [Cyr$_1$]: txt BDT rel latt Orig$_3$ [Chr$_1$]. aft *γινωσκει* ins *αυτον* ℵ.
28. *εκραζεν* D latt. *ο ιησ.* bef *εν τ. ιερ. διδ.* ℵ 1. 69 vulg lat-*b e l* æth arm: *εν τ. ι. ιησ. δ.* T 251 lat-*q*: *ο ιησ. δ. εν τ. ι.* D Scr's i [Syr syr-jer Cyr$_1$]: om *ο ιησ.* Δ.—om *ο* (bef *ιησ.*) B[2][Tischdf ascribes the erasure to his B[2.3]] T. *και εμε* ℵ [Orig$_1$ Chr$_1$]. *αλλα* ℵ. *αληθης* ℵ 435(Sz) Chr-5-mss.
29. rec aft *εγω* ins *δε*, with DXℵ [1. 33] lat-*b c f ff$_2$* Syr syr-cu syr-w-ast [syr-jer]

24.] No stress must be laid on the article (**τήν**) with *κρίνετε*: it is merely expressive of habit,—Let your judgment (**ἡ** *κρ. ὑμῶν*) be a just one. **κρίνετε** implies *habit*—in all your judgments: whereas the *aorist* (see var. readd.) would enjoin right judgment on the present occasion, directing the attention on what had just happened.

25—31.] He Himself is from the Father. **25, 26.**] The inhabitants of Jerusalem know better than the *ὄχλος* the mind of their rulers towards Jesus; and suspect some change in their purpose, on account of His being thus permitted to teach freely. **27.**] Perhaps they refer to the idea (see Justin Mart., Dial. c. Tryph. 8, 110, pp. 110, 203) that the Messiah would not be known (*ἄγνωστός ἐστι καὶ οὐδὲ αὐτός πω ἑαυτὸν ἐπίσταται*) until anointed by Elias, when He would suddenly come forth from obscurity.
They may allude to Isa. liii. 8. The *place* of the Messiah's *birth* was known, ver. 42. At all events we see here, that the Jews regarded their Messiah not as a mere man, but one to be supernaturally sent into the world. **28, 29.**] **ἔκραξεν**,—in the same open undisguised manner referred to in *παῤῥησίᾳ λαλεῖ* above; but *διδάσκων*, in the course of His teaching. **κἀμὲ οἴδατε . . . .**] It has been questioned whether these words are to be taken ironically, interrogatively, or affirmatively. I incline to the last view, for this reason:—obviously no very high degree of knowledge **whence He was** is implied, for they knew not Him that sent Him (see also ch. viii. 14, 19), and therefore could not know **whence He was**, in this sense. The answer is made *in their own sense*:—they knew that He was from Nazareth in Galilee, see ver. 41,—and probably that He was called the son of Joseph. In this sense they knew **whence He was**; but further than this they knew not.
καὶ ἀπ' ἐμ. . . . . **and moreover—and besides this**—not = *but*. The sense of **ἀληθινός** must be gathered from the context. **I have not come of Myself, but He who sent Me is** *ἀληθινός*—**ye know Him not; I know Him,—for I came from Him, and He sent Me.** The matter here impressed on them is the *genuineness*, the *reality* of the fact:—that Jesus *was sent*, and *there was one who sent Him*, though they knew Him not, and consequently knew not *πόθεν ἐστίν*. The nearest English word would be **real**: but this would not convey the meaning perspicuously to the ordinary mind;—perhaps the E. V. **true** is better, provided it be explained to mean *objectively*, not *subjectively*, true;

αὐτοῦ εἰμί, κἀκεῖνός με ἀπέστειλεν. 30 ἐζήτουν οὖν αὐτὸν
[u] πιάσαι· καὶ οὐδεὶς [v] ἐπέβαλεν ἐπ' αὐτὸν τὴν [v] χεῖρα, ὅτι
οὔπω ἐληλύθει ἡ [w] ὥρα αὐτοῦ. 31 ἐκ τοῦ ὄχλου δὲ πολλοὶ
[x] ἐπίστευσαν [x] εἰς αὐτόν, καὶ ἔλεγον Ὁ χριστὸς ὅταν
ἔλθῃ μὴ πλείονα [y] σημεῖα ποιήσει [z] ὧν οὗτος ἐποίησεν;
32 ἤκουσαν οἱ Φαρισαῖοι τοῦ ὄχλου [a] γογγύζοντος περὶ
αὐτοῦ ταῦτα, καὶ ἀπέστειλαν οἱ ἀρχιερεῖς καὶ οἱ Φαρισαῖοι
[b] ὑπηρέτας ἵνα [c] πιάσωσιν αὐτόν. 33 εἶπεν οὖν ὁ Ἰησοῦς
Ἔτι [d] χρόνον [d] μικρὸν μεθ' ὑμῶν εἰμι, καὶ ὑπάγω πρὸς

BDEG HKLM STUV ΧΓΔΛ ΠΝ 1. 33. 69

u vv. 32, 44. ch. viii. 20 al4. Rev. xix. 20. John only, exc. Acts iii. 7. xii. 4. 2 Cor. xi. 32. Cant. ii. 15. Sir. xxiii. 21 BN F(not A) only.
v Matt. xxvi. 50 reff.
w ch. ii. 4 reff.
x ch. ii. 11 reff.
y Matt. xvi. 1. ch. ii. 11, 18, 23 al.
z attr., Mark vii. 13 reff.
a ch. vi. 41, 43 reff. b = Matt. xxvi. 58 || Mk. vv. 45, 46. ch. xviii. 3, &c. Acts v. 22, 26. c ver. 30.
d ch. xii. 35. Rev. [vi. 11] xx. 3. Isa. liv. 7.

copt goth æth Cyr_1 Hil: om BT rel vulg lat-*a e g* [*l*] *q* sah arm $Orig_1$ $Tert_1$. for αυτου, αυτω ℵ[1] [lat-*e* $Tert_1$ $Phœb_1$]. απεσταλκεν Dℵ 131.

30. for εζητ. ουν, οι δε εζητ. ℵ. for επεβ., εβαλεν T, *misit* vulg lat-*a c* [*e f* ff_2 *g l q*]. (εληλυθει, so B: see table.)

31. rec transp εκ του οχλου and πολλοι, with E rel lat-*q* syrr [syr-cu] goth arm; πολλοι δε επιστ. εκ τ. οχλ. Dℵ [coptt]: txt BKLTX[Π] 1 (33) 69 latt æth Cyr_1. ελεγαν D. rec aft ελεγον ins οτι, with E rel syr: om BDLTUX[Δ]ℵ 1. 33. 69 latt Syr syr-cu coptt goth arm [Chr_1] Cyr_1. rec (for μη) μητι, with Δ rel [$Cyr\text{-}p_1$]: txt BDEKLTXℵ 1. 33 Chr. πλεονα DΔ. rec ins τουτων bef ποιησει (*to fill out the constr*), with E rel syrr syr-cu coptt [goth]: bef σημ., M Scr's d s: om BDKLTX[Π]ℵ 1. 33. 69 latt sah-georgi æth arm Chr Cyr. for εποιησεν, ποιει Dℵ[1] 69 vulg lat-*a c e* [ff_2 *g* l^2 q^1 arm-ed] Syr syr-cu.

32. aft ηκουσαν ins ουν KMU[Π] 1 lat-*a f* ff_2 sah; δε Dℵ lat-*c e* goth arm. ταυτα bef περι αυτου ℵ: om ταυτα DL[1] 1 lat-*a b c e l* syr-cu arm Chr_1. υπηρ. bef οι αρχ. D ℵ(prefg τους) rel lat-*a q* syr goth: om υπηρ. syr-cu: txt BGKLTUX[Π] 1. 33. 69 vulg lat-*c f* ff_2 [*g l* coptt æth arm] Syr $Cyr[\text{-}p_1]$.—rec transp αρχ. and φαρ., with E rel lat-*a q* syr goth: txt BDGKLTUX[Π]ℵ 1. 33. 69 vulg lat-*c f* ff_2 [*g*] *l* syr-cu coptt æth arm $Cyr[\text{-}p_2]$.

33. rec aft ουν ins αυτοις, with T (1, e sil) vulg-ed lat-(*c*) *g* æth [sah]: om BDℵ rel am[with forj fuld foss ing mt tol] lat-*a b c f* ff_2 *l* [*q* syr-jer] syrr syr-cu copt goth arm. rec μικρον bef χρονον, with D rel vss Chr_1 $Cyr[\text{-}p_2]$: txt BLTXℵ 69 lat-*e q*.

really existent, not '*truthful*,' which it may be questioned whether the word ἀληθινός will bear, although it is so maintained by Euthym., Cyril, Chrys., Theophylact, Lampe, Baumgarten-Crusius, Tholuck, and many others. See on this, ch. viii. 16 and note. With the **δέ** of the rec. omitted the sense becomes more emphatic. It was probably inserted on account of the apparent want of connexion, as has been the case very frequently throughout the Gospel. We have here an instance of a usage of ἐκεῖνος which is very common in St. John, as emphasizing the main subject, not (as more commonly) diverting the attention to one more removed. In ignorance of this usage, Hilgenfeld, "Die Evangelia nach ihrer Entstehung, u. s. w.," has argued from ch. xix. 35, that the writer of this Gospel cannot himself have been an eye-witness of the crucifixion, because he there distinguishes that witness by ἐκεῖνος from himself. In consequence of this assertion, an article appeared in the Stud. u. Kritik. for 1859, pt. 3, by G. E. Steiss, in which the use of ἐκεῖνος by St. John is gone into, and Hilgenfeld's mistake (which Köstlin had committed before him) was exposed. Referring to that article for the full treatment of the subject, I merely cite from among many other instances of the usage, ch. i. 18, 33; v. 11; vi. 57; x. 1; xii. 48; xiv. 12, 21, 26; xvii. 24.

30.] Namely, *the rulers*,—instigated by what had been above remarked by the people, vv. 25, 26. There was some secondary hindrance to their laying hands on Him,—possibly the fear of the people: but the Evangelist passes at once to the real cause;—that God's appointed time was not yet come. **31.**] The **δέ** here contrasts with what went before—**nay, many** &c. The indefiniteness of **ὅταν ἔλθῃ** implies their belief that the Christ had come.

32—36.] HE WILL RETURN TO THE FATHER. **32.**] The wavering of the multitude appears to the Pharisees a dangerous sign: and the Sanhedrim (οἱ ἀρχ. κ. οἱ Φ.) send officers specially to lay hold on Him. **33, 34.**] The omission or insertion of αὐτοῖς makes very little difference.

τὸν πέμψαντά με. 34 [e] ζητήσετέ με, [e] καὶ [e] οὐχ εὑρήσετε
με· καὶ ὅπου εἰμὶ ἐγὼ ὑμεῖς οὐ δύνασθε ἐλθεῖν. 35 εἶπον
οὖν οἱ Ἰουδαῖοι [f] πρὸς ἑαυτοὺς [g] Ποῦ οὗτος μέλλει
πορεύεσθαι, ὅτι ἡμεῖς οὐχ εὑρήσομεν αὐτόν; μὴ εἰς
τὴν [h] διασπορὰν τῶν [i] Ἑλλήνων μέλλει πορεύεσθαι καὶ
διδάσκειν τοὺς [i] Ἕλληνας; 36 [k] τίς ἐστιν ὁ λόγος οὗτος
ὃν εἶπεν [e] Ζητήσετέ με, [e] καὶ [e] οὐχ εὑρήσετέ με, καὶ ὅπου
εἰμὶ ἐγὼ ὑμεῖς οὐ δύνασθε ἐλθεῖν;
37 Ἐν δὲ τῇ ἐσχάτῃ ἡμέρᾳ τῇ [l] μεγάλῃ τῆς ἑορτῆς

e = Ps. ix. 15 (36). xxxvi. 10. Isa. xli. 12.
f = Mark x. 26. ch. xii. 19 al.
g = ch. iii. 8 reff.
h James i. 1. 1 Pet. i. 1 only. Ps. cxlvi. 2.
i here bis & ch. xii. 20 only in Gospp. Acts xiv. 1. xviii. 4. Rom. i. 16 al.
k = Luke viii. 9 reff.
l = ch. xix. 31. Acts ii. 20, from Joel ii. 31. Jude 6. Rev. vi. 17. Mal. iv. 5.

34. rec om 2nd *με*, with Dℵ rel latt goth arm [Chr_1 Cyr-p]: ins BTX **1** syrr syr-cu coptt æth. at end ins *εκει* B(sic in cod: see table).
35. om *προς εαυτους* ℵ[1] [lat-*e*]. *μελλει* bef *ουτος* DLX Syr (syr-cu). om *ημεις* Dℵ 249 latt(not *f q*). for *μη*, *μητι* D 124, *numquid* latt.
36. for *τις*, *τι* ℵ. rec *ουτος* bef *ο λογος*, with E-corr[1] ℵ rel latt syrr: om T 57. 91 harl: txt B D-gr E[1][appy] KLX[Π] **1**. 33. 69 syr-cu arm. for *ον*, *οτι* T. rec om 2nd *με*, with Dℵ rel latt goth arm: ins BGT X(Treg, expr) Syr syr-cu syr-w-ob coptt æth.
37. *τη ημ. τη μεγ.* **τη** *εσχ.* D.

The words were spoken, not to the officers only, but to all the people. **ἔτι χρ. μικ. . . . .**] This appears to be said in reference to ver. 30, to shew them the uselessness of their attempting to lay hands on Him till His hour was come, which it soon would be. **πρὸς τ. πέμψ. με**] It has been asked, 'If Jesus thus specified where He was going, how could the Jews ask the question in ver. 35?' but De Wette answers well, that the Jews knew not *τὸν πέμψαντα αὐτόν*, and therefore the saying was a dark one to them. **ζητ. με, κ. οὐχ εὑρ.**] These words must not be pressed too much, as has been done by many interpreters (Chrysost., Theophyl., Euthym., Meyer, Tholuck, but not in his 6th edn.), who would make them mean, '*Ye shall seek My help and not find it*' (viz. in your need, at the destruction of Jerusalem); for this would not be true even of the Jews, any one of whom might have at any time turned and looked on Him whom he had pierced, by faith,—and have been saved;—nor again must it be taken as meaning, '*Ye shall seek to lay hands on Me, and shall not be able*' (Orig., Grot.), —which is vapid and unmeaning. Neither of these interpretations, nor their cognates, will agree with the parallel place, ch. xiii. 33, where the same words are used to the *disciples*. The meaning is simply (as in reff.), 'My bodily presence will be withdrawn from you; I shall be personally in a place inaccessible to you:' see ch. xiii. 36. **εἰμί, am**; not *εἶμι*, '*go*,' which is never used in the N. T. Nor need we supply *τότε*; the present tense is used in the solemn sense of ch. i. 18, and ch. iii. 13, to signify *essential truth*. Compare *οὐ δύνασθε* addressed to the Jews, with *οὐ δύνασαί μοι νῦν ἀκολ.*, *ἀκολουθήσεις δὲ ὕστερον* to Peter, ch. xiii. 36, and it will be evident that the Lord had their *spiritual state* in view: 'Ye cannot, as ye are now, enter there.' On the whole, see Luke xvii. 22. **35, 36.**] The Jews understood not *his death* to be meant, but some journey which he would take in the event of their rejecting him.

The **διασπ. τ. Ἑλλ.** must not be interpreted 'the Hellenistic Jews,' for the *Ἕλληνες* are always distinguished from the Jews; and this would convey hardly any meaning. The sense of *διασπορά* is,—see reff. James, 1 Pet.,—'the country where Jews lay scattered,' as qualified by the succeeding genitive, where one occurs, as here. So here **ἡ δ. τ. Ἑλ.** means '*the dispersed in the Gentile world*;'—and their intent is, to convey contempt and mockery. They do not however *believe* the hypothesis; but ask again, **τίς ἐστιν ὁ λόγος οὗτος**;

37—52.] Jesus the Giver of the Spirit (37—39). Consequences of the discourse (40—52). **37, 38.**] It is not certain what is meant by this **ἡ ἐσχ. ἡμ. ἡ μεγ.** The command, Levit. xxiii. 34, 35, was to keep the feast seven days; the *first* to be a solemn assembly and a feast-sabbath,—then on the *eighth* day another solemn assembly and a feast-sabbath:—so also ib. ver. 39. (But in Deut. xvi. 13 nothing is said of the *eighth* day.) In Neh. viii. 18 the feast is

m ver. 28.
n ch. iv. 13, &c. reff.
o ch. ii. 11 reff.
p = sing., ver. 42. ch. x. 35. xx. 9 al. pl., ch. v. 39 reff.

εἱστήκει ὁ Ἰησοῦς, καὶ [m] ἔκραξεν λέγων Ἐάν τις [n] διψᾷ,
ἐρχέσθω πρός με καὶ πινέτω· 38 ὁ [o] πιστεύων [o] εἰς ἐμέ,
καθὼς εἶπεν ἡ [p] γραφή, ποταμοὶ ἐκ τῆς κοιλίας αὐτοῦ

BDEG HKLM STUV ΧΓΔΛ Πℵ 1. 33. 69

εκραζεν Dℵ 1. 69 Chr_1, *clamabat* latt coptt. $Victorin_1$ Aug_1. εμε B : om προς με $Dℵ^1$ lat-*b e* $Cypr_2$

kept seven days, and on the eighth is a solemn assembly, "*according unto the manner*." In Num. xxix. 12—38, where minute directions are given for every day of the feast, the eighth day is reckoned in, as usual. Josephus, Antt. iii. 10. 4, gives a similar account. In 2 Macc. x. 6, we read ἡμέρας ὀκτώ, σκηνωμάτων τρόπον. But the eighth day was not properly one of the *feast days;* the people ceased to dwell in the tabernacles on the seventh day. Philo says of it, ἑπτὰ δὲ ἡμέραις ὀγδόην ἐπισφραγίζεται, καλέσας ἐξόδιον αὐτήν, οὐκ ἐκείνης ὡς ἔοικε μόνον τῆς ἑορτῆς, ἀλλὰ πασῶν τῶν ἐτησίων ὅσας καθηριθμήσαμεν· τελευταία γὰρ ἐστι τοῦ ἐνιαυτοῦ. De Septenario, § 24. And though this, as Lücke observes (ii. 224), may be pure conjecture, it is valuable, as shewing *the fact* the reason of which is conjectured; viz. that the *eighth day was held in more than ordinary estimation.* The *eighth* day then seems here to be meant, and **the last of the feast** to be popularly used, as in some of the citations above. But a difficulty attends this view. Our Lord certainly seems to allude here to the custom which prevailed during the seven days of the feast, of a priest bringing water in a golden vessel from the pool of Siloam with a jubilant procession to the temple, standing on the altar and pouring it out there, together with wine, while meantime the Hallel (Ps. cxiii.—cxviii.) was sung. This practice was by some supposed—as the dwelling in tabernacles represented their life in the desert of old—to refer to the striking of the rock by Moses;—by others, to the rain, for which they then prayed, for the seed of the ensuing year:—by the elder Rabbis (Maimonides, cited by Stier, iv. 331, edn. 2), to Isa. xii. 3, and the effusion of the Holy Spirit in the days of the Messiah. But it was universally agreed (with the single exception of the testimony of R. Juda Hakkadosh, quoted in the tract Succa, which itself distinctly asserts the contrary), that on the eighth day this ceremony *did not* take place. Now, out of this difficulty I would extract what I believe to be the right interpretation. It *was* the eighth day, and the pouring of water *did not* take place. But is therefore (as Lücke will have it) all allusion to the ceremony excluded? I think not: nay, I believe it is the more natural. For seven days the ceremony had been performed, and the Hallel sung. On the eighth day the Hallel was sung, but the outpouring of the water did not take place: "desideraverunt aliquid." '*Then Jesus stood and cried,* &c.' Was not this the most natural time? Was it not probable that He would have said it at such a time, rather even than while the ceremony itself was going on? An attempt has been made to alter the punctuation thus: ἐάν τις διψᾷ, ἐρχέσθω πρός με, καὶ πινέτω ὁ πιστεύων εἰς ἐμέ· καθὼς εἶπεν ἡ γρ., ποταμοὶ κ.τ.λ. Of this I can only say, that it is surprising to me how any one accustomed to the style of our Evangelist can for a moment suppose it possible. The harshness of καὶ πινέτω ὁ π. εἰς ἐμέ is beyond all example. The ordinary punctuation, making ὁ πισ. εἰς ἐμέ a nom. abs., see ch. vi. 39, is the *only admissible one,*—even were it beset with far greater difficulties than it is. (The punctuation above mentioned is strongly upheld against this note in Stier, edn. 2. In spite of what he there says, I cannot think it can ever make way among Biblical scholars. It introduces *two subjects* into the first part of the sentence, viz. ὁ διψῶν and ὁ πιστεύων εἰς ἐμέ, to the utter confusion of both sense and metaphor. The distinction, insisted on by Stier, between the believer on Christ, who was not only to *come,* but to *drink,*—and the people at the feast, who only witnessed the outpouring of the water,—and which he gives as a reason why πινέτω must stand emphatically *before* ὁ πιστ. its qualifying subject, will be quite as marked with the usual punctuation: nay even more so.) On the first clauses, see notes on ch. iv. 13, 14. **καθὼς εἶπ. ἡ γρ.**] These words must apply to ποταμοὶ ἐκ τ. κ. . . . , since ὁ πιστ. εἰς ἐμέ could not form part of the citation. But we look in vain for such a text in the O. T., and an apocryphal or lost canonical book is out of the question.

I believe the citation to be intimately connected with the ceremony referred to, and that we must look for its place by consulting the passages where the *flowing out of water from the temple* (see above) is spoken of. The most remarkable of these is found in Ezek. xlvii. 1—12.

q ῥεύσουσιν ὕδατος r ζῶντος. 39 τοῦτο δὲ εἶπεν περὶ τοῦ q here only. Job xxxviii. 30.
πνεύματος * οὗ ἔμελλον λαμβάνειν οἱ o πιστεύσαντες o εἰς r ch. iv. 10, 11 reff.
...ουπω γαρ ην V. αὐτόν· οὔπω γὰρ ἦν πνεῦμα [ἅγιον], ὅτι Ἰησοῦς οὔπω s = ch. xii. 16, 23. xiii. 31. xvii. 1.
s ἐδοξάσθη. 40 t ἐκ τοῦ ὄχλου οὖν ἀκούσαντες τῶν λόγων t = ch. vi. 39. 2 John 4. Rev. v. 9. ix. 10.
τούτων ἔλεγον [ὅτι] οὗτός ἐστιν u ἀληθῶς v ὁ προφήτης.
41 ἄλλοι ἔλεγον Οὗτός ἐστιν ὁ χριστός. οἱ δὲ ἔλεγον u ch. i. 48 reff. v ch. i. 21 reff.

39. for ειπεν, ελεγεν א 249 [lat-*c ff*$_2$ *l q* Did$_1$ Chr$_1$ Cyr$_1$ Thdrt$_1$ Hil$_1$]. * ὅ BEKM[S]UVΛ : οὗ Dא rel. rec πιστευοντες, with Dא rel [Did$_1$ Chr Cyr] Hil : txt BLT. ins το bef πνευμα D : aft also D[2]. om αγιον KT[Π]א latt Syr coptt arm Orig$_4$[int$_1$] Eus$_1$ [Cyr-p$_2$] Cypr : ins BD rel lat-*e f q* syr [syr-jer] goth æth Chr [Cyr-p$_1$] Or g-int$_1$. add further δεδομενον B latt Syr syr-w-ast syr-jer sah Eus$_1$; επ αυτοις D[1] lat-*f* goth; επ αυτους D[2]: om KT[Π]א rel fuld(with harl[1] san) copt arm Orig$_4$[int$_1$] Ath$_1$ Cyr$_4$ Hesych$_1$. rec ins ο bef ιησ. (with S Scr's g, e sil): om BDTא rel vulg Orig$_3$ Chr Cyr Did$_1$ [Ath Hesych]. rec ουδεπω, with T rel Orig$_1$ [Ath$_1$ Chr Cyr Hesych Thdrt]; ουδεπωτε L: txt BDא Orig$_1$. δεδοξαστο א[1].

40. rec (for εκ τ. οχλ. ουν) πολλοι ουν εκ του οχλου, with E rel lat-*f q* syrr [syr-jer (goth æth)]: txt BDLTXא 1 vulg [lat-*a b*] coptt arm. aft ακουσ. ins αυτου Dא[1] syr-txt. rec τον λογον, with [S]XΔ[2]Λ 69 sah-mnt æth [Cyr$_1$]: txt BDTא rel latt syrr [syr-jer] coptt goth arm Orig$_1$. rec om τουτων, with E rel Syr: ins BDLTUא 1. 33 latt syr-mg [syr-jer] coptt goth arm, and (bef τ. λογ.) G; τουτον X æth [Cyr$_1$], αυτου K[Π]. om οτι Tא rel vss Orig$_1$: ins BD. αληθως bef ουτος εστιν א.

41. aft 1st αλλοι ins δε T 1. 69 lat-*b c f* coptt Orig$_1$. ins οτι bef ουτος DLX 69 lat-*g* syr-w-ast [Cyr$_1$]: om BTא rel Orig. rec (for οι) αλλοι, with Dא rel syrr coptt goth: txt BLTX 1. 33 vulg lat-*a c f ff*$_2$ (æth) arm Orig$_1$. om δε Dא rel syrr goth: ins BLTX 1. 33 vulg lat-*a c e f ff*$_2$ coptt (æth) arm Orig$_1$ Cyr$_1$. ελεγαν D[1](txt D[2]).

There a ποταμός of water of life (see ver. 9 especially) *flows from under the threshold of the temple.* Again in Zech. xiv. 8, ἐξελεύσεται ὕδωρ ζῶν ἐξ Ἱερουσαλήμ. I believe these expressions to be all to which the citation applies, and the ἐκ τῆς κοιλίας αὐτοῦ to be the interpretation of the corresponding words in the prophecies. For the temple was symbolic (see ch. ii. 21) of the Body of the Lord; and the Spirit which dwells in and flows forth from His glorified Body, dwells in and flows forth from His people also, who are made like unto Him, Gal. iv. 6: Rom. viii. 9—11: 1 Cor. iii. 16. **39.**] The difficulties raised concerning this interpretation of the saying of our Lord have arisen from a misapprehension. John does not say that the words were a prophecy of *what happened* on the day of Pentecost; but of *the Spirit,* which the believers were about to receive. Their *first reception* of Him must not be illogically put in the place of *all His indwelling and working,* which are here intended. And the symbolism of the N. T. is fully satisfied by the interpretation. Granted that the water is the *water of life*—what is that life but the life of the Spirit? τὸ φρόνημα τοῦ πνεύμ., ζωή, Rom. viii. 6; and again, **τὸ πνεῦμα, ζωή**, ib. ver. 10. It is lamentable to see such able and generally right-minded Commentators as Lücke carping at the interpretation of an Apostle, and the one Apostle who perhaps of all men living had the deepest insight into the wonderful analogies of spiritual things. **οὔπω ἦν**] The additions δεδομένον, δοθέν, ἐπ' αὐτοῖς, are all *glosses*, to avoid a misunderstanding which no intelligent reader could fall into. Chr. in loc. quotes the verse thus: ὁ εὐαγγελιστὴς ἔλεγεν, Οὔπω γὰρ ἦν πνεῦμα ἅγιον, τουτέστι δοθέν, ἐπεὶ Ἰησοῦς οὔπω ἐδοξάσθη· δόξαν καλῶν τὸν σταυρόν. It is obvious that ἦν cannot refer to the *essential existence* of the Holy Spirit, as this would be not only in flat contradiction to ch. i. 32, 33; iii. 5, 8, 34, but to the whole O. T., in which the agency of the Spirit in the *outward world* is recognized even more vividly than in the N. T. The ἦν implies not exactly δεδομένον, but rather ἐνεργοῦν, or some similar word: **was not,—had not come in**; *'the dispensation of the Spirit was not yet.'* **ἐδοξάσθη**, *through death.* The glorified Body of the Lord is the temple from under whose threshold the Holy Spirit flows forth to us: see ch. i. 16: Rom. viii. 11: Col. ii. 9. **40.**] **ὁ προφήτης** is here clearly distinguished from **ὁ χριστός**: see note on ch. i. 21, and Deut. xviii. 15. **41—43.**] The mention of the question about Bethlehem seems to me rather to corroborate our belief that the Evangelist was well aware how the fact stood, than (De Wette) to imply that he was ignorant of it. That no more re-

w = ch. ix. 30. Matt. xxvii. 23.
x = here bis only.
y pres., Matt ii. 4. xi. 3 reff.
z ver. 38.
a = Matt. xxii. 24 al. Psa. cxxxi. 11.
b ch. xi. 1 reff.
c ch. xi. 1, 30. Matt. ix. 35. Luke x. 38 al. fr.
d = Mark ix. 19 ||.
e Mark ii. 21 reff.
f ver. 30.
g = here only. (ch. xx. 25, 27.)
h ver. 32.
i ver. 52. ch. vi. 67. xviii. 17, 25.
k ver. 12 reff.
l ch. iv. 33 only.
m ch. ii. 11 reff.
n here only †.

BDEG HKLM STUX ΓΔΛΠℵ 1. 33 69

Μὴ [w] γὰρ [x] ἐκ τῆς Γαλιλαίας ὁ χριστὸς [xy] ἔρχεται;
42 οὐχ ἡ [z] γραφὴ εἶπεν ὅτι [x] ἐκ τοῦ [a] σπέρματος Δαυεὶδ
καὶ [b] ἀπὸ Βηθλεέμ, τῆς [c] κώμης ὅπου [d] ἦν Δαυείδ,
[xy] ἔρχεται ὁ χριστός; 43 [e] σχίσμα οὖν ἐγένετο ἐν τῷ ὄχλῳ
δι᾽ αὐτόν. 44 τινὲς δὲ ἤθελον ἐξ αὐτῶν [f] πιάσαι αὐτόν,
ἀλλ᾽ οὐδεὶς [g] ἔβαλεν ἐπ᾽ αὐτὸν τὰς [g] χεῖρας.
45 Ἦλθον οὖν οἱ [h] ὑπηρέται πρὸς τοὺς ἀρχιερεῖς καὶ
Φαρισαίους· καὶ εἶπον αὐτοῖς ἐκεῖνοι Διὰ τί οὐκ ἠγάγετε
αὐτόν; 46 ἀπεκρίθησαν οἱ [h] ὑπηρέται Οὐδέποτε ἐλάλησεν
οὕτως ἄνθρωπος [ὡς οὗτος ὁ ἄνθρωπος]. 47 ἀπεκρίθησαν
αὐτοῖς οἱ Φαρισαῖοι [i] Μὴ καὶ ὑμεῖς [k] πεπλάνησθε; 48 [l] μή
[l] τις ἐκ τῶν ἀρχόντων [m] ἐπίστευσεν [m] εἰς αὐτὸν ἢ ἐκ τῶν
Φαρισαίων; 49 ἀλλὰ ὁ ὄχλος οὗτος ὁ μὴ γινώσκων τὸν
νόμον [n] ἐπάρατοί εἰσιν. 50 λέγει Νικόδημος πρὸς αὐτούς,

42. rec *ουχι*, with Dℵ rel [Cyr-p$_2$]: txt B^{2}TL Orig$_1$; *ουκ* B^1. for *ειπεν*, *λεγει* D 235(Sz). om *του* DU 1. 69 Orig. ins *ο* bef 2nd *δᾱδ* ℵ. rec *ο χριστος* bef *ερχεται* (*repetn from above*), with (D)ℵ rel [lat-*a b f l q* syr goth Cyr-p$_2$]: txt BLT 33 vulg lat-*c ff$_2$ g* Syr [syr-jer] æth arm Chr$_1$.—*ερχ. ο χρ.* bef *οπου ην δ.* D.

43. rec *εν τω οχλω* bef *εγενετο*, with E rel lat-*q* goth: txt B(D)LTXℵ 33 latt syrr [syr-jer] coptt [(arm)].—*εις τον οχλον* D-gr.

44. for *ηθελον*, *ελεγον* ℵ^1. rec *επεβαλεν* (*from ver* 30), with Dℵ rel lat-*e f* Chr$_1$ Cyr$_1$: txt BLT vulg lat-*a c*. for *επ᾽ αυτον*, *αυτω* ℵ^1: *επ᾽ αυτω* U.

45. for *ειπον*, *λεγουσιν* ℵ [lat-*e* (Chr$_1$)].

46. aft *απεκρ.* ins *δε* D.—*οι δε υπηρ. απεκρ.* ℵ. rec *ουτως* bef *ελαλησεν*, with E rel vulg lat-*c* [*f ff$_2$ l q* syrr goth æth Chr-txt$_1$ Thdrt$_1$]: *ουτως ανθρωπος* bef *ελαλησεν* Dℵ^1: txt BLTXℵ^{3a} 33 Orig$_1$ Chr$_2$ Cyr[-p]. om *ως ουτος ο ανθρωπος* (*homœotel?*) BLTℵ^{3a} forj copt Orig$_1$ Chr-comm$_2$ Cyr[-p]: ins X rel vulg lat-*e f* [*l q*] syr sah goth æth arm [Chr-txt$_1$ Thdrt$_1$], *ως ουτος λαλει* D lat-*c ff$_2$*: *ως ουτος λαλει ο ανθρωπος* ℵ^1 [Syr syr-jer].

47. rec aft *απεκρ.* ins *ουν*, with BT rel vulg lat-*f g* [*l q*] syr [Cyr$_1$]: om Dℵ 1. 33 lat-*a c e ff$_2$* Syr sah goth arm. om *αυτοις* BK 69 foss lat-*l* arm: ins DTℵ rel vss.

48. for *επιστευσεν*, *πιστευει* Dℵ^1.

49. (**αλλα**, so BDLT 33.) rec **επικαταρατοι** (*more common, cf Gal* iii. 10, 13), with D rel: txt BTℵ 1. 33 Orig$_1$ Chr-comm$_1$ Cyr[-p$_1$].

50. for *λεγει*, *ειπεν δε* ℵ [lat-*f* (syr-jer æth)].

marks are appended, is natural. John had one great design in writing his Gospel, and does not allow it to be interfered with by explanations of matters otherwise known. Besides, we may note that De Wette's "*probability, that John knew nothing of the birth at Bethlehem,*" reaches much further than may appear at first. If John knew nothing of it, and yet the mother of the Lord lived with him, the inference must be that *she* knew nothing of it,—in other words, that it never happened.

σχίσμα implies a *violent dissension,*—some taking up His cause, some wishing to lay hands on Him. **44.**] These were from among the multitude. Those who wished to lay hands on Him were, as Euthymius remarks, *invisibly restrained*.

45—52.] *Return of the officers to the Sanhedrim; consultation on their report.* Either these officers had been watching Jesus for some days, or the present section goes back a little from what has preceded. The latter is more probable.

49.] There is no intention to pronounce a formal ban upon the followers of Jesus;—the words are merely a passionate expression of contempt. The putting a stop at **νόμον**, and supplying *ἐπίστευσεν εἰς αὐτόν*, and then making **ἐπάρ. εἰσιν!** an *exclamation* (Paulus, Kuinoel), is not to be thought of. **50.**] The Jews had, since the sabbath-healing, condemned Jesus, and were seeking to kill him. But in Exod. xxiii. 1, 2: Deut. i. 16, 17, justice is commanded to be done in the way here insisted on by Nicodemus. On the consistency, and development, of the character of Nicodemus, Luthardt has some valuable remarks, pp. 125 ff. [see on ch. xix. 39].

ὁ ἐλθὼν πρὸς αὐτὸν πρότερον, εἷς ὢν ἐξ αὐτῶν, 51 Μὴ ὁ
νόμος ἡμῶν κρίνει [o] τὸν ἄνθρωπον, ἐὰν μὴ [p] ἀκούσῃ πρῶτον
παρ' αὐτοῦ καὶ γνῷ τι ποιεῖ; 52 ἀπεκρίθησαν καὶ εἶπαν
αὐτῷ Μὴ καὶ σὺ ἐκ τῆς Γαλιλαίας εἶ; [qr] ἐραύνησον καὶ
[r] ἴδε· ὅτι ἐκ τῆς Γαλιλαίας προφήτης οὐκ [s] ἐγείρεται.

o gen. art., Matt. xv. 11. Mark iv. 21 reff.
p ch. vi. 45 reff.
q ch. v. 39 reff. Gen. xliv. 12.
r 4 Kings x. 23.
s = Matt. xi. 11. xxiv. 11, 24 al.

om ο ελθ. προς αυτ. προτ. א^1: εις ων εξ αυτ. bef ο ελθ. D [(syr)].—rec ins νυκτος bef προς αυτ., with E rel: aft DKUXΔ[Π] 33 vulg lat-*c f l q* syrr goth æth arm [Bas$_1$]: om BLTא^{3a} lat-*a* syr-jer sah [Cyr$_1$].—rec om προτερον, with E rel vulg lat-*f* Syr goth [Bas$_1$]: ins BTא^{3a}, το προτερον LX **1**. 33(sic Treg) 69 lat-(*a*) *c e l* syr-w-ast syr-jer sah-mnt arm æth, το πρωτον D.

51. rec παρ' αυτου προτερον, with E rel vulg lat-*q* [syr-jer Bas$_1$] Chr$_1$: παρ. αυτ. πρωτον K **1**. 69: πρωτον, omg παρ' αυ., X(bef ακ.) א^1: txt BDLTא^{3a} 33 [lat-*a c ff$_2$ q* syrr coptt arm] Orig$_1$ Bas$_1$ Cyr$_1$. **επιγνωσθη** D. **εποιησεν** D lat-*c* Lucif.

52. (ειπαν, so BDKT 33.) (εραυνησον, so B^{1}Tא.) aft ιδε ins τας γραφας D 229; *scrutare scripturas* vulg-ed(not am em forj gat ing^2 mm san) lat-*a c e ff$_2$ l* (not *f g q*) sah. rec προφητης bef εκ τ. γ., with Dא rel am(with forj fuld ing san &c) lat-*a c* [*e f l q* syrr coptt arm] goth: txt BLTX vulg-ed [æth] Orig$_1$ Chr$_4$ Cyr$_1$. rec εγηγερται (*cf Luke* vii. 16: *to say, as Mey, that the pres was substd* to remove the historical difficulty, *is absurd, for it* does not *remove it*), with L rel: **εγειγερται** EG[H]M: txt BDK S-marg ΓΓΔ[Π]א **1**. 33 vulg lat-*a c* [*f ff$_2$ g q* syr-jer] syrr goth æth Orig$_1$ [Non$_1$, ερχεται U].

Ver 53 to ch. viii. 11 is omitted in ABCLTXΔא 33 ev-y 2-pe Scr's a^1 b 3. 9^1. 12-5. 21-2. 36. 44-9. 72. 87. 95-6-7. 106-8-23-31-4-9-43-9-57-68-9-79^1-81-6-94-5. 210-3-28-32^1-49-50-3-5-61-2^2-9-84^1. 314-31-53^1-88-92. 401[-16] (and about 90 evangelisteria: but see Scriv. Introd. to Crit. p. 441) lat-*a b^2 f l* [*q*] syrr coptt goth arm-6-mss Orig Apollin Thdor-mops Chr Bas Cyr Cosm Non Thl Tert(see Treg on the Printed Text p. 239 note) Cypr Juv. A and C are defective, but from the quantity of space it is *certain* that they could not have contained the passage. LΔ leave a space, but not sufficient for the whole. viii. 3—11 is omitted in 77. 242. 324.

It is marked as doubtful in EMSΛ [Π(to viii. 5)] Scr's k l m n 4. 8. 14-8. 24. 34-5. [83.] 109-25-41-5-8^2-56-61-4-6-7-78-89-96-8. 202-12-5-26-30-1^2-41-6-71-4-7-85. 338-55-60-1-3-76-91^2-4. 40[7-]8[-15]-36, and viii. 3—11 in 128-37-47. It is placed at the end of the Gospel in 237, which however has vii. 53 to viii. 2 here as well; 37 (102 ?) 105 retain vii. 53 to viii. 2 here, but place viii. 3—11 at the end of the Gospel; 259 (and 102?) omits vii. 53 to viii. 2 altogether and inserts the rest at the end of the Gospel. The whole passage is inserted at the end of this Gospel in **1**. 19. 20. 129-35. 207 [-15]. 30[0-]1-47 ev-86 leips-tisch-iv arm-mss; at the end of Luke xxi. in 13. 69. 124. 346; aft John vii. 36 in 225.

It is contained in D (F, partly) GHKUΓ and about 290 cursive mss vulg lat-*b^1 c e ff$_2$ g* [*h*] *l*-marg [syr-2-mss] syr-jer [copt-wilk] æth 5-later-mss-of-arm. (Scholz numbers 469 cursive mss of the Gospels: of these all but those named above and the following contain the disputed passage. The following either do not contain St. John's Gospel or are mere fragments, 41. 92-4-9. 136-46-97. 222-3-4-38-43-56-7-88. 302-3-4-5-10-1-2-3-20-3-34-6-7-54-6-62-6-9-78-81.400-17-8-23-4-6-7-32-4. The following are also defective at this point, 67. 176. 221. 317-72 evv-37-42-3-4. The following numbers ought for various reasons (see in Prolegg) to be considered as in abeyance, 42. 81-2. 93. 110. 203. 321-6-7-8-98-9. 440-1-2. It is hardly safe to reckon 64. 90. 101-21 as distinct witnesses. We have no information concerning the reading of 104-14-32. 216-33. 318-48-50-64-73. 437-8-9. In ms 115 the pericope is found, but with ver 12 written both before and after it. The remaining 270 (about) certainly contain the passage without any mark of doubt: to these we must add Scr's-15-mss and evv-18-19-20-37-41-67.)

In evangelio secundum Johannem in multis et Græcis et Latinis codicibus invenitur de adultera muliere quæ accusata est apud dominum, Jer. adv. Pelag. ii. 17,

51.] There is no need of supplying κριτής before ἀκούσῃ and γνῷ—the judge is implied in ὁ νόμος. He is only its representative and mouthpiece. **ἐὰν μὴ ἀκ.**] See Deut. i. 16. **52.**] They taunt him with being disposed to join those (mostly Galilæans) who had attached themselves to Jesus. Whether we read ἐγείρεται or ἐγήγερται, the assertion is much the same: for προφ. cannot mean *the* Prophet, or the Messiah. It was *not historically true*;—for two Prophets at least had arisen from Galilee: Jonah of Gathhepher, and the greatest of the Prophets, Elijah of Thisbe;

VIII. 12 Πάλιν οὖν αὐτοῖς ἐλάλησεν ὁ Ἰησοῦς λεγων BDEFG HKLM STUX ΓΔΛΠℵ 1. 33. 69

vol ii. p. 762. *Sed hoc videlicet infidelium sensus exhorret ita ut nonnulli modicæ fidei vel potius inimici veræ fidei credo metuentes peccandi impunitatem dari mulieribus suis illud quod de adulteræ indulgentia Dominus fecit, auferrent de codicibus suis, quasi permissionem peccandi tribuerit qui dixit jam deinceps noli peccare,* Aug. de Conj. Adult. ii. 7, vol vi. Euseb. H. E. iii. 39 says: ἐκτέθειται δὲ καὶ ἄλλην ἱστορίαν περὶ γυναικὸς ἐπὶ πολλαῖς ἁμαρτίαις διαβληθείσης ἐπὶ τοῦ κυρίου, ἣν τὸ καθ' ἑβραίους εὐαγγέλιον περιέχει, which history can hardly be other than this. Nicon (cent x.) says that the Armenians expunged it, thinking βλαβερὰν εἶναι τοῖς πολλοῖς τὴν τοιαύτην ἀκρόασιν.

Chap. VIII. 12. rec ο ιησ. bef αυτ. ελαλ.: αυτοις ο ῑς ελ. E rel Scr's-mss: ελ. αυτοις ο ῑς D [1] 33 lat-*a f ff$_2$ g l* Syr copt æth arm: txt (B)LSTUXℵ [69] Scr's k lat-*b* [*c q*], and (omg αυτοις) Scr's s.—om ο B. (om ο ιησ. Scr's c q r.)

and perhaps also Nahum and Hosea. Their contempt for Galilee made them lose sight of historical accuracy. (Bretschneider absurdly lays the inaccuracy to the charge of the Evangelist.)

12—59.] The conflict between

HISTORY OF THE WOMAN TAKEN IN ADULTERY. [VII. 53.

[53 καὶ ἐπορεύθησαν ἕκαστος εἰς τὸν οἶκον αὐτοῦ. 1 Ἰησοῦς δὲ DGHK UΓ (EMΛΠ 1.69 with ast, S with ob.)

53. rec επορευθη, with E rel [syr-uss-bars æth]: απηλθεν U 69; -θον Λ: txt DMSΓ 1 [vulg lat-*c e g l*^{2} copt-wilk] syr-jer arm[-usc]. for τ. οικ., τον τοπον 1 copt-wilk arm[-usc]: τα ιδια 69.

1. for ιησ. δε, και ο ιησ. UΓ [Λ(omg ο)] 69.

[53—Chap. VIII. 11.] The history of the woman taken in adultery.—See var. readd.; and a very complete discussion of the authorities for and against the passage in Lücke (edn. 3), ii. 243—256. The critical examination of the genuineness of this passage is attended with many and complicated difficulties. Setting aside here purely diplomatic evidence (for which see var. readd.), we may observe (1) that *at first sight*, the reasons given by Aug. and Nicon seem enough to warrant the inference that it was expunged on account of the supposed licence given by it to sin. And this has been the hypothesis generally adopted by those who would override critical difficulties by strong autocratic assertion. Even Stier and Ebrard decide thus, without pausing to examine the real complications of the question. But (2) granting that such an hypothesis might be admissible as regards ch. viii. 3—11, I do not see how the whole passage can be involved in it, especially the opening verse 53, which would naturally appear to form a sequel to what has preceded, and would surely never have been expunged with the offensive paragraph. (3) No such hypothesis as this will account for the coexistence of so many distinct and independent texts, apparently none of which owes its origin to any attempt to remove matter of offence. This phænomenon (not that of the *abundance of various readings,* from which it is totally distinct) points undoubtedly to some inherent defect in the text of the passage itself, irrespective of all treatment subsequent to its establishment as a part of the sacred narrative. (4) At the same time it is an embarrassing circumstance, that the contents of the passage are of such a kind, as to give every countenance to the supposition above dealt with. Had they been otherwise, we should have been much more free in pronouncing a critical decision for or against it. (5) Another difficulty is presented by the very general concurrence of the mss. containing the passage, in placing it *here.* If it was not originally found in the text, why should this place, of all others, have been selected for its insertion? It has no connexion with the context: belongs, apparently, to another portion of our Lord's ministry: what could induce the interpolators to place it here? (6) Nor are we helped much by its variations of position in some mss. The end of Luke xxi. seems most to approve itself as the fitting place. but if it was the original one, it is totally inexplicable that we should find no trace of the fact *there,* except in four of the (best) cursive mss. Its occurrence *here* then, seems to me much *in its favour.* (7) After all, the most weighty argument *against* the passage is found in its *entire*

Ἐγώ εἰμι τὸ [a] φῶς τοῦ [a] κόσμου· ὁ ἀκολουθῶν ἐμοὶ

a = ch. ix. 5. see Matt. v. 14.

φως bef ειμι, omg το, $\aleph^1$. for εμοι, μοι BT $Orig_1$: txt DLℵ rel [Chr_1 Cyr_1].

JESUS AND THE JEWS, AT ITS HEIGHT. 12—20.] *Testimony to Himself as the Light.* 12.] The attempts of Bengel, Schulthess, and Stier, to establish a connexion with the passage concerning the woman taken in adultery

---

VIII. 1, 2.] HISTORY OF THE WOMAN TAKEN IN ADULTERY.

ἐπορεύθη εἰς τὸ [a] ὄρος [a] τῶν ἐλαιῶν. 2 [b] ὄρθρου δὲ πάλιν [c] παρα-

a Matt. xxi. 1 reff. John, here only.
b Luke xxiv. 1. Acts v. 21 only. Prov. vii. 18 al. [w. βαθ., see digest, there only.]
c w. εἰς, Matt. ii. 1. Acts ix. 26. xiii. 14. xv. 4 only. 1 Kings x. 16, 17. see ch. iii. 23.

επορευετο S Scr's e k s. at end add μονος Γ 272 Scr's f.
2. for ορθρου δε, και οτε Γ 272. aft παλιν ins βαθεως U Scr's e f w^2.

diversity from the style of narrative of our Evangelist. It is not merely that many words and idioms occur which John never uses, but that the whole cast and character of the passage is alien from his manner, in whichever of the existing texts we read it. (It would be hardly worth while to cite an opinion which affirms that "such a course of argument is very fallacious, leads to nothing but endless *logomachies,* and can never settle a question of this kind" (Bloomf. edn. 9),—were it not earnestly to remind my readers, that the more the sacred text is *really studied,* the more such considerations, duly and cautiously weighed, will be urged and appreciated.) (8) Balancing all these difficulties, I am almost disposed, as a desperate resource, to adopt the following hypothesis; not as by any means satisfying or even recommending itself to me, but as really the only one which seems at all to shew us a way out of the ænigma: That the Evangelist may have, in this solitary case, incorporated a *portion of the current oral tradition* into his narrative: that this portion may have been afterwards variously corrected, from the Gospel of the Hebrews, or other traditional sources: that being seen in early times to be alien from John's diction, it may have been by some replaced in the synoptic narrative, in its apparent chronological place, at Luke xxi. fin.: or inserted variously in this Gospel from the mere fact of having dropped out here. Then again the contents of the passage would operate with the above causes to its exclusion altogether from many MSS.: and the fact of some excluding only ch. viii. 3—11, seems certainly to shew that the *moral* element *did operate* in the matter. (9) Dropping all idea of the hypothesis just suggested, our conclusion on the data must I think be, *to retain the passage,* as we retain Mark xvi. 9 ff., with a distinction from the rest of the text. With regard to the question, *what text of the passage itself to adopt,* it would seem idle to attempt to unite into one by critical processes texts which seem to be due to different sources. Our solution of the question must be merely formal and diplomatic. And, thus solving it, it has been thought best in this Edition to give the text as it is found in the only one of our most ancient MSS. which contains it: the amount and nature of the variations being fully seen in the accompanying Digest. In adopting this plan, it will be observed that no judgment whatever is given on the purity of the text thus adopted,—no approval whatever of the Codex Bezæ as a *fons lectionum:* our proceeding is simply a formal and objective one, adopted as a necessity where no other seemed even moderately satisfactory. 53.] The circumstance that this verse is included in the dubious passage is remarkable, and seems to shew, as remarked above, that the doubt *has not arisen from the ethical difficulty,* as Aug. hints (var. readd.),—for then the passage would have begun with ch. viii. 1. Nor can this verse have been expunged to keep up the connexion with ch. viii. 12—for that is just as good *with it,*—if understood, as usually, of the members of the Sanhedrim. We must now regard it as fragmentary, forming the beginning of the account of the woman taken in adultery. It is therefore not clear to what the words apply. Taken in conjunction with what follows (see on ch. viii. 5), I should say that they indicate some time during the last days of the Lord's ministry, when He spent the nights on the Mount of Olives, as the date of the occurrence. Certainly the end of Luke xxi. seems to be its fitter place. CHAP. VIII. 1.] John *never elsewhere mentions the Mount of Olives* (not even in ch. xviii. 1): and when he

b ch. xii. 35. see Isa. ix. 2.
c ch. i. 5 reff.

οὐ μὴ [b] περιπατήσῃ ἐν τῇ [bc] σκοτίᾳ, ἀλλ' ἕξει τὸ φῶς

BDEFG HKLM STUX ΓΔΛℵ 1. 33. 69

rec περιπατησει, with DEHMΔ (S 1, e sil) Cyr[-p_2]: txt BTℵ rel $Orig_1$ Cyr[-p_2]. αλλα D. εχει ℵ[1].

are forced and harsh. It was, say they, the early morning (ver. 2) and the sun was just rising, to which these words τὸ φῶς τοῦ κόσ. allude,—and the walking in darkness is an allusion to the woman, whose deed of darkness had been detected in the night. But not to dwell on other objections to this view,—e. g. that such an allusion to the woman would be wholly out of character after our Lord's previous treatment of her,—how come these Pharisees, who on the hypothesis of the above Commentators are *the same as those who accused the woman,* to be *again so soon present?* Was this at all likely? We cannot escape from this difficulty with Stier, iv. 363, edn. 2, by supposing a multitude of the people to have been witnesses on both occasions: the οἱ Φαρισαῖοι of the one must surely extend through the other, if *this connexion* is to be maintained. On the other hand, this discourse comes in very well after ch. vii. 52. The last saying of Jesus (ch. vii. 37, 38) had referred to a festal usage then just over: He now adds another of the same kind. It was the custom during the first night, if not during every night, of the feast of tabernacles (see authorities in Wetstein), to light up two large golden chandeliers in the court of the women, the light of which illuminated all Jerusalem. All that night they held a festal dance by the light. Now granted that this was on the first night only,—what is there improbable in the supposition that our Lord—standing in the very place where the candlesticks had been or perhaps actually were—should have alluded to that practice, as He did to the outpouring of water in ch. vii. 37, 38? Surely to say in both cases, as Lücke and De Wette do, that the allusion could not have been made unless the usage *took place on that day,* is mere trifling. *While the feast lasted,* and the remembrance of the ceremonies was fresh, the allusion would be perfectly natural.

τὸ φῶς τ. κόσ.] See on ch. i. 9, and xi. 9, 10. See also Isa. xlii. 6: Mal. iv. 2;

HISTORY OF THE WOMAN TAKEN IN ADULTERY. [VIII.

f w. ἐπί, = here only.

γίνεται εἰς τὸ ἱερόν, καὶ πᾶς ὁ λαὸς ἤρχετο πρὸς αὐτόν. 3 ἄγουσιν
δὲ οἱ γραμματεῖς καὶ οἱ Φαρισαῖοι ἐπὶ ἁμαρτίᾳ γυναῖκα [f] εἰλημ-

DGHK UΓ (EM ΛΠ 1. 69 with ast, S with ob.)

d part., princ. Luke, v. 2. xiv. 28, 31. xvi. 6. Acts xii. 21. xvi. 13. xxv. 6, 17. Matt. v. 1. xiii. 48. Mark ix. 35. xii. 41 only. [John, here only.] Num. xi. 4 al.
e Matt. xv. 19 (reff.). Mark vii. 21 only.

rec παρεγενετο, with E rel: ηλθεν UΛ 69 syr-uss[-bars, *venit* latt arm]: txt D. add ο ιησους U Scr's d e f s. om last clause 69. for ο λαος, ο οχλος GSU: om Γ 272. om προς αυτον EGHK[Π]: ins D U(Treg, expr) rel. rec at end adds και [d] καθισας εδιδασκεν αυτους, with E rel syr-jer: om D.

3. for αγουσιν δε, προσηνεγκαν αυτω Λ^2 69. om δε UΓ arm. for γραμματεις, αρχιερεις **1** copt-wilk arm. rec aft φαρισαιοι ins προς αυτον, with E rel lat-*c* (*ff*$_2$) copt-wilk (æth arm): om DM[S]UΓΛ 1. 69 vulg lat-*e* [*g*] l^2 syr-uss[-bars] arm. rec (for επι αμαρτια γυν.) γυν. εν [e] μοιχεια, with EGHK[Π]: γυν. επι μοιχεια M rel: txt D. rec

introduces a new place, it is his habit to give explanations (see ch. i. 45; v. 2, and λεγομένην ch. iv. 5; xix. 13, 17). (Stier, who says (iv. 348, edn. 2), "The simple answer to Alford's remark is, *that John here, and here only, mentions the Mt. of Olives,*" omits all allusion to this habit of the Evangelist, which *alone gives weight* to my remark.) πορεύομαι with εἰς is not found elsewhere in John; but (in the Gospels) only in Matt. and Luke, and the frag. Mark xvi. fin. Nor is ὄρθρον, nor παραγίνομαι εἰς nor ὁ λαός *in this sense,* but always ὁ ὄχλος (see ὁ λαός ch. xi. 50; xviii. 14): nor such an expression as καθίσας ἐδίδασκεν αὐτούς (v. r.):—but all these are found in Luke. It is not in John's manner to relate that *Jesus taught them,* without relating *what* He taught.

3.] John does not usually connect with δέ, more commonly with οὖν: but δέ is found thus used *here,* vv. 1, 2, 3, (5, where the conjunction of δὲ . . . δέ is not in St. John's manner, see Gal. ii. 20,) 6 (twice v. r.), 7, 9, 10, 11 (twice v. r.). Thence, there is not one δέ of *mere connexion* (ver. 35 is no exception) through the remaining forty-eight verses of the

[d] τῆς ζωῆς. 13 εἶπον οὖν αὐτῷ οἱ Φαρισαῖοι Σὺ [e] περὶ

d ch. i. 4. vi. 48.
e ch. i. 7, 8 reff.

and on τὸ φῶς τῆς ζωῆς, ch. i. 4, and vi. 48. 13.] See ch. v. 31. The assertion there was, that His own *unsupported* witness (*supposing that possible*) would not

3—5.] HISTORY OF THE WOMAN TAKEN IN ADULTERY.

μένην· καὶ [g] στήσαντες αὐτὴν [gh] ἐν μέσῳ 4 λέγουσιν αὐτῷ [i] ἐκπειράζοντες αὐτὸν οἱ ἱερεῖς ἵνα ἔχωσιν [k] κατηγορίαν αὐτοῦ
Διδάσκαλε, αὕτη ἡ γυνὴ [l] κατείληπται [m] ἐπ' αὐτοφώρῳ [n] μοιχευο-
...viii. 5 (appy) Π. μένη, 5 Μωϋσῆς δὲ ἐν τῷ νόμῳ ἐκέλευσεν τὰς τοιαύτας [p] λιθάζειν.

g Matt. xviii. 2 ‖ Mk. Acts iv. 7 only.
h absol., ver. 9. Matt. xiv. 6. = εἰς τὸ μέσον, Ps. lxxvii. 18. Exod. xxii. 4. Lev. xx. 10. trans., Matt. v. 28. ch. xx. 19, 26.
i Luke iv. 12 ‖ Mt. (from Deut. vi. 16). x. 25. 1 Cor. x. 9 only.
k [Luke vi. 7 v. r.] ch. xviii. 29. 1 Tim. v. 19. Tit. i. 6 only +.
l = here [bis v. r.] only.
m here only +. Thucyd. vi. 38.
n pass., here and Matt. v. 32 v. r. only.
p ch. x. 31 reff., &c. [λιθοβολ., see digest, Matt. xxi. 35 reff.]

[l] κατειλημμενην, with M rel: καταληφθεισαν EGHK[Π]: txt D. aft εν ins τω Λ 69.

4. for λεγουσιν, ειπον UΛ 69 latt. rec om εκπειρ. αυτ. οι ιερ. ινα εχ. κατ. αυτ. (*but see ver* 6), with U rel [latt syr-uss-bars copt-wilk æth arm-usc]: ins D: πειραζοντες (alone) EGHK[Π] arm[-mss]. for αυτη to μοιχευομενη, ταυτην ευρομεν επ αυτοφωρω μοιχευομενην U.—η γυνη bef αυτη M. rec [l] κατειληφθη; κατεληφθη EGHK[ΓΠ]: ειληπται MΛ[S] 69: txt D 1. [επ αυτω τω φωρω 346 (Burgon).]

5. rec εν bef δε and εν δε τω νομω bef μω., with E rel [for εν δε, και εν Γ]: txt D.—rec aft μω. ins ημιν, with E rel: [bef, Λ 1. 69 lat-*e*:] bef τας U: ins ημων bef μω. S[Γ æth]: om DH syr-uss syr-jer copt. rec (for εκελευσεν) [o] ενετειλατο, with E rel: txt D. rec (for λιθαζειν) [p] λιθοβολεισθαι, with E rel: txt DMSUΛ 1. 69.

o constr. w. inf. pass., here only. inf. act., Matt. xix. 7. Gen. xlii. 25.

chapter. Nor does he ever mention οἱ γραμματεῖς elsewhere, but usually calls the opponents of Jesus οἱ Ἰουδαῖοι, or οἱ ἄρχοντες. οἱ γρ. κ. οἱ Φ. is a very common expression in the synoptic narrative.

The account gives no light as to the *capacity in which* these Scribes and Pharisees acted when they brought the woman. Probably, *only* as tempting Jesus, and not in the course of any legal proceedings against her. Such would have required (Levit. xx. 10: Deut. xxii. 22) that the *man also* should have been put to death.

4.] The λέγουσιν αὐτῷ ἐκπειράζοντες αὐτόν savours much more of the synoptic Gospels than of John: see Matt. xvi. 1; xix. 3; xxii. 18, 35: Mark viii. 11; x. 2; xii. 15, &c. Obviously our ch. vi. 6 is no example to the contrary. (So Luthardt.) The difficulty is even greater than the last, to say, *in what sense this was a temptation, to lead to His accusation.* The principal solutions of it have been, (1) that the command of the law had fallen into disuse from the frequency of the crime, and to re-assert it would be contrary to the known mildness of Jesus (Michaelis (first part), Aug., Euthym.). But what reason had any of His sayings,—who came to fulfil the Law, not to destroy it,—given them to expect such mildness in this case? And suppose He had re-asserted the law,—how could they have *accused Him?* (2) That some political snare was hereby laid for Him, whereby the Roman power might have been brought to bear against Him (Grotius and others). But this does not in any way appear; for (α) the Romans certainly allowed to the Jews (by connivance) the power of putting to death according to their law,—as they did in the case of Stephen: (β) our Lord's answer need not have been so worded as to trench upon this matter: and (γ) the accusers would have been more deeply involved than Himself, if such had been the case, being by the law the prominent persons in the execution. So that I leave the difficulty unsolved. Lücke (whose discussion on it see, ii. 261 ff.) observes: "Since Jesus seems to avoid every kind of decision on the question put to Him, it follows that He found in it no reference to the great subjects of His teaching, but treated it as a purely civil or political matter, with which in His ministry He had no concern. *Some kind of civil or political collision* the question certainly was calculated to provoke: but from the brevity of the narration, and our want of more accurate knowledge of criminal proceedings at the time, it is impossible to lay down definitely, wherein the collision would have consisted." p. 267. 5.] I

σεαυτοῦ [e] μαρτυρεῖς· ἡ μαρτυρία σου οὐκ ἔστιν ἀληθής. BDEFG HKLM STUX ΓΔΛℵ 1. 33. 69

be trustworthy, but that His testimony *was* supported by, and in fact coincident with, that of the Father. The very same argument is here used, but *the other side of it*

HISTORY OF THE WOMAN TAKEN IN ADULTERY. [VIII.

σὺ δὲ νῦν τί λέγεις; 6 ὁ δὲ Ἰησοῦς κάτω [r] κύψας τῷ [s] δακτύλῳ
[t] κατέγραφεν εἰς τὴν γῆν. 7 ὡς δὲ [v] ἐπέμενον ἐρωτῶντες, [w] ἀν-
έκυψεν καὶ εἶπεν αὐτοῖς Ὁ [x] ἀναμάρτητος ὑμῶν πρῶτος ἐπ' αὐτὴν

DGHK UΓ(EM Λ 1. 69 with ast, S with ob.)

r [here bis, v. r.] Mark i. 7 only. Exod. vi. 31.
s Matt. xxiii. 4 reff.
t here bis only. Exod. xvii. 14.
v [John, here only.] elsw., Luke (Acts x. 48 al.) & Paul (Rom. vi. 1 al.) only. Exod. xii. 39 B. (only?). constr., Acts xii. 16 only.
w here bis. Luke xiii. 11. xxi. 28 only. Job x. 15 only. [ἀναβλέπ., see digest. = John, here bis (ch. ix. 11, &c.) only. Matt. xiv. 19 reff.]
x here only. Deut. xxix. 19. 2 Macc. viii. 4. xii. 42 only.

q John, ch. vi. 6. Rev. ii. 2, 10. iii. 10 only. = Matt. xvi. 1 ‖ al.
u Luke xxiv. 28 only. = 1 Kings xxi. 13. (Job xix. 14. Sir. xxxiv. [xxxi.] 30) only.

rec om 2nd δε, with E rel: ins D lat-*c ff*$_2$. [rec ουν, with E rel: txt D.] aft λεγεις ins περι αυτης MSUΛ 69 lat-*c ff*$_2$ æth arm.
6. rec at beg ins τουτο δε ελεγον [q] πειραζοντες αυτον ινα εχωσι κατηγορειν αυτου, with E rel: om D(*but see ver* 4) M(here: but ins aft ver 11).—(for ελεγον, ειπον S[Γ] syr-uss[-bars], ειπαν M.—for εχωσιν, ευρωσι 1 [σχωσιν SΓ].—for κατηγορειν, κατηγοριαν κατ' MSUΛ 69 arm [κατηγορησαι Γ].) om τω δακτυλω Λ syr-uss[-bars]. rec (for κατεγρ.) εγραφεν, with K rel (-ψεν 69): txt DEGHM[S]. at end ins μη [u] προσποιουμενος EGHK.
7. επερωτωντες M[S] 1. rec adds αυτον, with E rel: om D. rec (for ανεκυψεν και) ανακυψας, with E rel: [w] αναβλεψας UΛ 69 arm: txt DMS 1 [latt]. rec (for αυτοις) προς αυτους, with E rel: om M: txt DSU[Γ]Λ 1. 69 latt. πρωτον EGH. rec επ' αυτη: txt D[S] rel.

will just remark that the very fact of their questioning thus, 'Moses commanded, . . . but what sayest *Thou?*' belongs to the *last days* of the Lord's ministry, and cannot well be introduced chronologically where it here stands: nor does John any where introduce these questions between the law of Moses and Jesus; but the synoptic Gospels often do. The command here mentioned is not to be found, unless 'putting to death' generally, is to be interpreted as = *stoning:* compare Exod. xxxi. 14 and xxxv. 2, with Num. xv. 35, 36, in which the special order given by God would sanction such a view. But the Rabbis taught "omne mortis supplicium in scriptura absolute positum esse *strangulationem.*" Tract. Sanhedr. ch. x. (Lücke, De Wette.) The passage Ezek. xvi. 38, 40 proves nothing, or proves too much; for it is added, "and thrust thee through with their swords." I would rather suppose that from Deut. xxii. 21, 23, 24, an inference was drawn *what kind of a death* was intended in ver. 22, the crime being regarded as the same; "*he hath humbled his neighbour's wife.*" We have similar indefiniteness in ib. ver. 25, where evidently the same punishment is meant: see the whole matter discussed in Lücke, ii. 257 ff. **6. κατέγ. εἰς τ. γῆν**] ὅπερ εἰώθασι πολλάκις ποιεῖν οἱ μὴ θέλοντες ἀνακρίνεσθαι πρὸς τοὺς ἐρωτῶντας ἄκαιρα καὶ ἀνάξια. γνοὺς γὰρ αὐτῶν τὴν μηχανὴν **προσεποιεῖτο** γράφειν εἰς τὴν γῆν, καὶ μὴ προσέχειν οἷς ἔλεγον. Euthym. The habit was a usual one to signify pre-occupation of mind, or intentional inattention: see instances in Wetstein and Lücke. The one ordinarily cited from Ælian is irrelevant: see Lücke, ii. 269 note. The additions προσποιούμενος or μὴ προσπ. are glosses. It does not follow that any thing was actually written. Stier refers to Jer. xvii. 13, but perhaps without reason. This minute circumstance speaks strongly for the *authenticity* of the narration. **7.**] **ἀναμάρτ.** is common in the classics: see instances in Lücke. It is not here used in the general sense, '*without sin*' (E. V.), nor in the strictest, '*free from the crime of adultery*' (it can hardly be that any of the Pharisees should have held themselves *sinless,*—or that all should have been *implicated in adultery*):—but—as ἁμαρτωλός, Luke vii. 37,—of the *sin of uncleanness* generally. Stier, who contends strongly for the *genuineness* of this narrative *in this place,* finds in ver. 46 an allusion to this saying. I cannot say that his attempts to establish a connexion with the subsequent discourse are to me at all satisfactory: I am much more inclined to think with Luthardt (i. 16), that the whole arrangement and plan of our Gospel is broken by

14 ἀπεκρίθη Ἰησοῦς καὶ εἶπεν αὐτοῖς Κἂν ἐγὼ [e] μαρτυρῶ

14. ins ο bef ιησ. Dℵ 69 Orig$_1$.—ειπεν αυτοις ο ις, omg απεκ. and και, ℵ.

presented to us. He *does* witness of Himself, *because* His testimony is the testimony of the Father;—He being the λόγος τοῦ θεοῦ, and the Father *witnessing in Him.*

6—11.] HISTORY OF THE WOMAN TAKEN IN ADULTERY.

βαλέτω λίθον. 8 καὶ πάλιν [y] κατακύψας τῷ δακτύλῳ [t] κατέγραφεν
εἰς τὴν γῆν. 9 ἕκαστος δὲ τῶν Ἰουδαίων ἐξήρχετο, [c] ἀρξάμενοι
[c] ἀπὸ τῶν πρεσβυτέρων, ὥστε πάντας ἐξελθεῖν· καὶ [d] κατελείφθη
μόνος καὶ ἡ γυνὴ ἐν μέσῳ οὖσα. 10 [w] ἀνακύψας δὲ ὁ Ἰησοῦς
εἶπεν τῇ γυναικὶ Ποῦ εἰσιν; οὐδείς σε [i] κατέκρινεν; 11 κἀκείνη

F (θεασαμενος ...) ειπεν ...

y here only. 4 Kings ix. 32 only.
c Matt. xx. 8 reff. [John, here only.]
d = Luke xv. 4. Acts xvii. 19. 1 Thess. iii. 1.
i Matt. xx. 18 reff. [John, here bis only.]

rec ins τον bef λιθον, with E rel: om DU[Γ]Λ 1. 69.—rec (τον) λιθον bef επ' αυτ. βαλετω (with Scr's r s, e sil): (τ.) λιθ. bef βαλ. E rel latt [Aug$_1$]: transp επ' αυτ. and (τ.) λιθ. UΛ 69 æth arm: βαλ. bef επ' αυτ. [M] syr-uss[-bars] syr-jer: txt D 1.—βαλλετω EGHK 1.

8. rec κατω [r] κυψας, with E rel: κυψας H[1][Γ]: txt D 1. rec om τω δακτυλω, with E rel: ins D lat-*ff*$_2$. rec (for κατεγρ.) εγραφεν, with E rel; εγραψεν M: txt D. for εις, επι M. at end ins ενος εκαστου αυτων τας αμαρτιας U.

9. rec (for εκαστος δε των ιουδ.) οι δε ακουσαντες, with E rel: ακουσαντες δε 1 [vulg lat-*l*] arm: om Λ 69 syr-jer: txt D. rec adds και υπο της [z] συνειδησεως [a] ελεγχομενοι, with E rel copt-wilk: om DMU[Γ]Λ 1. 69 vulg lat-*c e ff*$_2$ *l* syr-uss[-bars] syr-jer æth arm. rec εξηρχοντο, with E rel: ανεχωρησαν [M:] και εξηλθον 69: και[om Tischdf] εξηλθεν Λ: txt D. rec adds [b] εις καθ' εις, with E rel: pref M vulg lat-*e* [*c ff*$_2$ *g l*]: εις εκαστος αυτων 1: om D. αρξαμενος E[1]. rec (for ωστε παντ. εξελθ.) εως των εσχατων, with S rel: om EGHKM[Γ] vulg lat-*e* [*g*] *l* syr-uss[-bars]: txt D (lat-*c ff*$_2$). om μονος 69. aft μονος ins ο ιησους, with E rel: pref ιησους U lat-*e*: [ο ιησ. Γ:] om D 1 am[with forj fuld ing em harl] lat-*c* syr-uss syr-jer. rec (for ουσα) εστωσα, with 1 (F, e sil) vulg lat-*c* [*l* æth] syr-jer: txt D rel lat-*ff*$_2$ syr-uss[-bars copt-wilk].

10. [w] αναβλεψας Λ 69. rec ins και μηδενα [e] θεασαμενος [f] πλην της γυναικος bef ειπεν, with E (F, appy) rel; ειδεν αυτην και UΛ 69 æth: om DMS[Γ] 1 vulg lat-*c e* [*ff*$_2$ *g l*] syr-uss[-bars] syr-jer copt-wilk arm. rec (for τη γυναικι) αυτη, with E rel vulg lat-*e ff*$_2$ [*g l* æth arm] syr-jer: om UΛ 69: txt D (lat-*c*) syr-uss[-bars]. rec ins [g] η γυνη bef που: γυναι MSU[Γ]Λ 1. 69: om D rel syr-uss[-bars]. rec aft εισιν ins εκεινοι οι [h] κατηγοροι σου, with E rel copt-wilk æth; οι κατ. σοι, omg εκεινοι, H[S]U 69 [vulg-ed]: om DMΛ 1 am[with san] lat-*c e* syr-uss syr-jer arm.

z Gospp., here only. Rom. ii. 15. ix. 1 al.‡ Eccl. x. 20. Wisd. xvii. 10 only.
a = ver. 46. ch. xvi. 8. 2 Tim. iv. 2. Job xv. 6.
b Mark xiv. 19. Rev. iv. 8 only. (Rom. xii. 5. 3 Macc. v. 34.)
e Luke xxiii. 55 reff.
f = Mark xii. 32 al. (John, Rev. ii. 25 only.)
g voc., Luke xii. 32 reff.
h Acts xxiii. 30, 35. [xxiv. 8.] xxv. 16, 18 only. Prov. xviii. 17. 2 Macc. iv. 5 only. (-γωρ, Rev. xii. 10.)

the insertion of this passage. The Lord Jesus was not sent to be a ruler and a judge in this or that particular case of crime, see Luke xii. 14; but the Ruler and Judge of *all:* and His answer expresses this, by convicting them *all* of sin before Him. τόν (see digest), if genuine, refers to the *first* stone, which by Deut. xvii. 7 the *witnesses* were to cast.

8.] ἵνα μή, βλέποντος εἰς αὐτούς, αἰσχύνωνται, ῥᾷον οὕτως ἐλεγχθέντες, καὶ ἵνα, ὡς αὐτοῦ δῆθεν ἀσχολουμένου εἰς τὸ γράφειν, ἐξῇ αὐτοῖς ὑπαναχωρῆσαι πρὸ φανερωτέρας καταγνώσεως· καὶ αὐτῶν γὰρ ἐφείδετο δι' ὑπερβολὴν χρηστότητος. Euthym. The gloss in U (see var. readd.) is curious.

9.] They had said, **τὰς τοιαύτας**—they now perceive that they themselves were τοιοῦτοι. There is no historical difficulty in this conduct of the Pharisees, as Olshausen finds;—they were struck by the power of the word of Christ. It was a case somewhat analogous to that in which His ἐγώ εἰμι struck His foes to the ground, ch. xviii. 6.

The variations of reading are very wide (see digest) in the latter part of the verse. We can hardly (with some) lay any stress on **πρεσβυτέρων**, as indicating the *natural order* of conviction of sin. If the consciences of older sinners have heavier loads on them, those of younger

f ch. iii. 8 reff. g 2 Cor. xi. 18 only. κ. σάρκα, Rom. i. 3. v. 1. ix. 3, 5 al. h ch. vii. 24. i ch. vi. 51 reff. j Rev. xv. 3. xvi. 7 al. Isa. lix. 4.

[e] περὶ εμαυτοῦ, ἀληθής ἐστιν ἡ μαρτυρία μου, ὅτι οἶδα BDEF
πόθεν ἦλθον καὶ [f] ποῦ ὑπάγω· ὑμεῖς δὲ οὐκ οἴδατε πόθει GHKL MSTU
ἔρχομαι ἢ ποῦ ὑπάγω. 15 ὑμεῖς [gh] κατὰ [g] τὴν [g] σάρκα ΧΓΔΛℵ 1. 33. 69
[h] κρίνετε, ἐγὼ οὐ κρίνω οὐδένα. 16 [i] καὶ ἐὰν κρίνω [i] δὲ
ἐγώ, ἡ κρίσις ἡ ἐμὴ [j] ἀληθινή ἐστιν, ὅτι μόνος οὐκ εἰμί,

η μαρτ. μου bef *αληθ. εστιν* B lat-*b* sah arm Orig$_1$ Chr$_1$ Did$_2$ Faust-in-Aug: *αληθινη μου εστ. η μαρτ.* D. om last clause (*homœotel*) M[SΓ]Δ 33. 69 syr-jer Orig$_2$ Cyr$_1$ Aug. om *δε* FHKℵ lat-*a* [Novat$_1$]. rec (for *η*) *και* (*from above*), with ℵ rel lat-*a b c e* [D-lat] Syr æth arm-mss [Cyr-p$_1$]: txt B D[-gr] KTUXΛ 1. 33 vulg lat-*f ff$_2$ l q* syr coptt goth arm-ed.
16. for *και εαν*, *καν* ℵ. rec **αληθης** (*from vv.* 13, 14), with ℵ rel Orig$_1$: txt BDLTX 33 Orig$_1$. aft *μονος* ins *εγω* D ev-40 (sah).

14. ὅτι οἶδα *κ.τ.λ.*] See on ch. vii. 29. This reason binds His testimony to that of the Father; for He came forth from the Father, ch. xvi. 28, and was returning to Him. "*Lumen*," says Augustine (Tract. in Joan. xxxv. 4) "*et alia demonstrat et seipsum . . . . Testimonium sibi perhibet lux: aperit sanos oculos et sibi ipsa testis est, ut cognoscatur lux.*" Then again, he only who *knows* can witness: and Jesus only *knew* this. Notice **ἦλθον** and **ἔρχομαι**,—**I know whence I** *came*:—this goes back to the *ἐν ἀρχῇ ἦν* of ch. i. 1; **but ye know not whence I** *come*,—'do not recognize even My present mission.' We must not for a moment understand **κἂν ἐγὼ μαρτ.** with Grotius, "*even though I should witness*," &c.: "*etiamsi nulla essent de me prægressa prophetarum, nulla Joannis Baptistæ testimonia.*" It does not *suppose a case*, but *allows the fact*.
15, 16.] There is no allusion to the foregoing history; the train of thought is *altogether another*. 'The end of all *testimony*, is the forming, or pronouncing, of *judgment*. Ye do this by fleshly rules, concerning me and my mission: I judge no man, i. e. it is not the object nor habit of this My mission on earth; but even if I be called on to exercise judgment, my judgment is decisive:' not exactly *ἀληθής*, but

HISTORY OF THE WOMAN TAKEN IN ADULTERY.

k Luke v. 10 reff. [John, here only.]

εἶπεν αὐτῷ Οὐδεὶς κύριε. ὁ δὲ εἶπεν Οὐδὲ ἐγώ σε [i] κατακρίνω. DFGH
ὕπαγε, [k] ἀπὸ τοῦ νῦν μηκέτι ἁμάρτανε.] KUΓ (EMΛ 1. 69 with ast, S with ob.)

11. rec (for *κακ. ειπ. αυτω*) *η δε ειπεν*, with E rel: txt D. rec (for *ο δε ειπεν*) *ειπεν δε ο ιησους*, with E rel vulg (syr-uss[-bars]): *ο δε ιησ. ειπεν* Λ: *και ο ιησ. ειπεν* 69: *ειπεν αυτη ο ιησ.* U: txt D. rec adds *αυτη*, with Λ[(U)] lat-*c* (*e*) *ff$_2$ g* syr-jer æth: om D rel vulg lat-*l* syr-uss [-bars] syr-jer arm. for *κατακ.*, *κρινῶ* EFGK. rec (for *υπαγε*) *πορευου*, with E rel: txt D. rec (for *απο του νυν*) *και*, with E rel: om 69: txt DM 1 (am) lat-*c* [*l* vulg] (syr-uss[-bars]) syr-jer copt-wilk æth, and (prefg *και*) lat-*ff$_2$* arm. [Tischdf (ed 8) gives *και* as omd only by D-gr lat-*ff$_2$* copt-wilk arm.]

ones are more tender. **μόνος**, i. e. with the multitude and the disciples; the woman standing between Him and the disciples on one hand,—and the multitude on the other. **10, 11.**] **πλήν** (v. r.) is only found here in John, Gosp. and Epp. **κατακρίνω** also is not found elsewhere in John, who uses *κρίνω* in its strict sense for it. The question is evidently so worded for the sake of *οὐδὲ ἐγώ σε κατακρίνω*: but it expresses the truth in the depth of their hearts. The Lord's challenge to them would lead to a condemnation *by comparison* with themselves, if they condemned at all: which they had not done. The words of Jesus were in fact a far deeper and more solemn testimony against the sin than could be any mere penal sentence. And in judging of them we must never forget that He who thus spoke knew the hearts,—and what was the peculiar state of this woman as to penitence. We must not apply in all cases a sentence, which requires *His divine knowledge* to make it a just one.]

ἀλλ' ἐγὼ καὶ ὁ πέμψας με πατήρ. 17 [i] καὶ ἐν τῷ νόμῳ
[i] δὲ τῷ ὑμετέρῳ γέγραπται ὅτι δύο ἀνθρώπων ἡ μαρτυρία
ἀληθής ἐστιν. 18 ἐγώ εἰμι ὁ [e] μαρτυρῶν [e] περὶ ἐμαυτοῦ,
καὶ [e] μαρτυρεῖ [e] περὶ ἐμοῦ ὁ πέμψας με πατήρ. 19 ἔλεγον
οὖν αὐτῷ Ποῦ ἐστιν ὁ πατήρ σου; ἀπεκρίθη Ἰησοῦς
Οὔτε ἐμὲ οἴδατε οὔτε τὸν πατέρα μου· εἰ ἐμὲ ᾔδειτε, καὶ
τὸν πατέρα μου ἂν ᾔδειτε. 20 ταῦτα τὰ ῥήματα ἐλάλη- k Luke xxi. 1 || Mk. (3ce)
σεν ἐν τῷ [k] γαζοφυλακίῳ διδάσκων ἐν τῷ ἱερῷ, καὶ only. Neh. xiii. 4, 5.
οὐδεὶς [l] ἐπίασεν αὐτόν, ὅτι οὔπω ἐληλύθει ἡ [m] ὥρα αὐτοῦ. l ch. vii. 30 reff. m ch. ii. 4 reff.
21 Εἶπεν οὖν πάλιν αὐτοῖς Ἐγὼ ὑπάγω, καὶ ζητήσετέ n here bis. ch. xiii. 33, 36.
με, καὶ ἐν τῇ ἁμαρτίᾳ ὑμῶν ἀποθανεῖσθε· [n] ὅπου ἐγὼ xiv. 4. Rev. xiv. 4 only.

om πατηρ Dℵ[1].

[17. γεγραμμενον εστιν ℵ.]

19. rec ins ο bef ιησ., with ℵ 69 (S 33, e sil) $Orig_1$: om BDT rel.—και ειπεν added in ℵ [foss]: και ειπεν αυτοις D lat-*b* (*e*). for 2nd ουτε, ουδε T $Orig_1$. om 2nd μου ℵ. rec ηδειτε bef αν, with ℵ rel lat-*q*: om αν D lat-*b e* ff_2 Victorin: txt BLTX 1. 33 (vulg) lat-*c* æth arm $Orig_5$ *Cyr*[-p] Ambr.

20. rec aft ελαλησεν ins ο ιησους, with E rel vulg-ed lat-ff_2 *q* [arm-ed]: om BDKL Tℵ am[with forj ing san] lat-*a b c e f l* syrr [syr-jer] coptt goth æth arm-mss $Orig_2$ Chr-comm Cyr_1. om διδασκων εν τω ιερω ℵ.

21. for ειπεν, ελεγεν ℵ. om παλιν ℵ. rec aft αυτοις ins ο ῑς, with E rel vulg lat-*a* (*c*) *f* (copt) sah Chr_1: om BDLTXℵ lat-*b e* $Orig_1$ [Cyr_1]. ζησετε D[1](txt D[5]). αποθανησεσθε T.

ἀληθινή, which rather means, **genuine**; which a judgment can only be by being *true* and final: see ch. v. 30 and note.

17.] The **ὑμετέρῳ** seems to give this sense to the clause:—'So that if you will have the mere letter of the law, and judge my testimony by it, I will even thus satisfy you:' **ὑμετ.** thus implying, 'The law which you have made so completely *your own* by your kind of adherence to it.'

19.] Augustine (in Joan. Tract. xxxvii. 2, vol. iii. pt. ii.) and others imagine that the Jews thought of a *human father*, in thus speaking. But surely before this, as Stier remarks (iv. 370, edn. 2), the Jews must have become accustomed to ὁ πατήρ μου too well to mistake its meaning. It is rather a question asked in mere scorn, by persons who know, but will not recognize, the meaning of a word uttered by another. **εἰ ἐμὲ ᾔδειτε**] See ch. xiv. 9 ff. and note.

20. τῷ γαζοφυλακίῳ] See Luke xxi. 1, and note on Mark xii. 41. It was in the court of the women. **οὔπω ἐληλύθει ἡ ὥρα αὐτοῦ**] See ch. vii. 8, 30.

21—59.] *Further discourses of Jesus. The Jews attempt to stone Him.* This forms the great conclusion of the series of discourses to the Jews. In it our Lord testifies more plainly still to His divine origin and sinlessness, and to the cause of their unbelief; until at last their enmity is worked up to the highest pitch, and they take up stones to cast at Him. It may be divided into four parts: (1) vv. 21—24,—*announcing to them the inevitable consequence of persistence in their unbelief on His withdrawal from them:* (2) vv. 25—29,—*the things which He has to say and judge of them, and the certainty of their own future recognition of Him and His truthfulness:* (3) vv. 30—47,—*the first springing up of faith in many of them is by Him corrected and purified from Jewish pride, and the source of such pride and unbelief detected:* (4) vv. 48—58,—*the accusation of the Jews in ver.* 48, *gives occasion to Him to set forth very plainly His own divine dignity and præexistence.*

21.] The time and place of this discourse are not definitely marked; but in all probability they were the same as before. Only no stress must be laid on the **οὖν** as connected with ver. 20, for it is only the accustomed carrying forward by the Evangelist of the great self-manifestation of Jesus. **ζητ. με** includes the idea 'and shall not find me,' which is expressed in ch. vii. 34, 36:—**ye shall continue seeking Me. καὶ ἐν τ. ἁμ. . . . . and shall die** (perish) **in** (not *because of* (Lampe, Kuinoel)) **your sin.** This sin is not *unbelief*, for, ver. 24, it is clearly *distinguished from that:* but, 'your *state of sin, unremoved,* and therefore *abiding and*

o Matt. vii. 16. ch. iv. 29 al. Mal. iii. 8 Bℵ1.
p ch. iii. 31 reff.
q here only.
r Gal. iv. 26. Phil. iii. 14. Col. iii. 1, 2 only.
s 1 Cor. xv. 17. ch. ix. 34.
t ch. iv. 26 reff.
u ch. i. 19.
v = (see note) here only ‡. (Gen. xliii. 20. Dan. viii. 1 Theod.)

BDEF GHKL MSTU XΓΔΛℵ 1. 33. 69

n ὑπαγω ὑμεῖς οὐ δύνασθε ἐλθεῖν. 22 ἔλεγον οὖν οἱ
Ἰουδαῖοι o Μήτι ἀποκτενεῖ ἑαυτόν, ὅτι λέγει n Ὅπου ἐγὼ
n ὑπάγω, ὑμεῖς οὐ δύνασθε ἐλθεῖν; 23 καὶ ἔλεγεν αὐτοῖς
Ὑμεῖς p ἐκ q τῶν q κάτω ἐστέ, ἐγὼ p ἐκ r τῶν r ἄνω εἰμί·
ὑμεῖς ἐκ τούτου τοῦ κόσμου ἐστέ, ἐγὼ οὐκ εἰμὶ ἐκ τοῦ
κόσμου τούτου. 24 εἶπον οὖν ὑμῖν ὅτι ἀποθανεῖσθε s ἐν
ταῖς s ἁμαρτίαις ὑμῶν· ἐὰν γὰρ μὴ πιστεύσητε ὅτι t ἐγώ
εἰμι, ἀποθανεῖσθε s ἐν ταῖς s ἁμαρτίαις ὑμῶν. 25 ἔλεγον
οὖν αὐτῷ u Σὺ τίς εἶ; εἶπεν αὐτοῖς ὁ Ἰησοῦς v Τὴν

22. ελεγαν D[1]. αυτον D[1](txt D-corr[1]) [Γ]Λ 69 Orig$_1$. aft οπου ins αν ℵ[1].
23. rec (for ελεγεν) ειπεν, with E rel lat-*f q* syrr: txt BDLTXℵ 69 latt syr-mg [syr-jer] Orig$_1$ Cyr$_1$.—for και ελ., ελ. ουν ℵ[1](txt ℵ[3a], but former readg restored). aft εγω ins δε D-gr lat-*f q* copt goth [æth]. rec 1st του κοσμου bef τουτου (*conformed to follg*), with Dℵ rel vulg [lat-*l*] syr Orig$_2$ Chr$_2$ [Cyr-p$_1$]: txt BT 69 lat-*a b c* [*e f q*] Syr coptt goth Orig$_1$.
24. om ουν ℵ 240-4 [lat-*a e*]. aft πιστευσητε ins μοι Dℵ 69 lat-*e* æth.
25. om ουν [Γ ℵ 249 Scr's t[1]. rec ins και bef ειπεν, with E rel lat-*f* [*l*] *q* syr goth æth: om BL [T(sic, Tischdf)] X(Dℵ) 1. 33. 69 latt Syr coptt Cyr.—add ουν D-gr ℵ 249. om ο B Scr's h[1].

proving your ruin' (see on ver. 24). The words do not refer to the destruction of Jerusalem, but to *individual perdition.* In these discourses in John, the *public* judgment of the Jews is not prominently brought forward, as in the other Evangelists. **ὅπου ἐγὼ ὑπ. . . . . .** is the *consequence*, not the *cause* (by any absolute decree) of their dying in their sins (see ch. vii. 34; xiii. 33). This latter sense would have required ὅπου **γάρ**. **22.**] It is at least probable that they allude to the idea mentioned by Josephus, himself a Pharisee, in his speech at Jotapata, B. J. iii. 8. 5:—ὅσοις δὲ καθ' ἑαυτῶν ἐμάνησαν αἱ χεῖρες, τούτων μὲν **ᾅδης** δέχεται τὰς ψυχὰς **σκοτιώτερος**:—and with the bitterest malice taunt Him with thus being about to go where they, the children of Abraham, could never come. ὁ Ἡρακλέων . . . . . φησὶν ὅτι πονηρῶς διαλογιζόμενοι οἱ Ἰουδαῖοι ταῦτα ἔλεγον, καὶ μείζονας ἑαυτοὺς ἀποφαινόμενοι τοῦ Σωτῆρος καὶ ὑπολαμβάνοντες ὅτι αὐτοὶ μὲν ἀπελεύσονται πρὸς τὸν θεὸν εἰς ἀνάπαυσιν αἰώνιον, ὁ δὲ Σωτὴρ εἰς φθορὰν καὶ εἰς θάνατον ἑαυτὸν διαχειρισάμενος ὅπου ἑαυτοὺς οὐκ ἐλογίζοντο ἀπελθεῖν. Orig. tom. xix. c. 4, vol. iv. p. 302. De Wette thinks this too refined, and that such a meaning would, if intended, have been marked in our Lord's answer. **23.**] 'Ye cannot come where I am going, because we both shall return thither whence we came: I to the Father from Whom (**ἐκ τῶν ἄνω**) I came: ye to the earth and under the earth (for that more awful meaning surely is not excluded) whence ye came' (**ἐκ τῶν κάτω**). Then **ὁ κόσμος οὗτος** of course does not *only* imply '*this present state of things*,' but involves the deeper meaning, of the *origin* of that state of things (see ver. 44) and its *end*, ver. 24.

24.] Since this (ver. 23) is the case, —**if ye do not believe that I am He**, the Deliverer,—and be renewed by Faith, **ye shall die in your sins** (plural here, as struck nearer home to their consciences, and implying individual acts of sin, the results of the carnal state). On **ἐγώ εἰμι** see note, ver. 58. **25.**] Their question follows on **ἐγὼ ἐκ τῶν ἄνω εἰμί**, ver. 23, and the dubious elliptical expression **ἐγώ εἰμι** of the last verse. It is intended to bring out a plain answer on which their enmity might fasten. Our Lord's reply has been found difficult, principally from the ambiguity of ὅτι and ὅ τι. No sense can however be given by ὅτι which will at all harmonize with the context, notwithstanding Luthardt's defence of it. Lücke's interpretation (edn. 3) after Euthym., "*Why do I speak with you at all?*" is not only ungrammatical, but most alien from the whole character of our Lord's discourses. I assume then that ὅ τι is to be read. Then comes another question: what does **λαλῶ** mean? It has been usually rendered '*say*,' or '*tell*:' '*even the same that I said unto you from the beginning*,' E. V. But as De Wette has observed, λαλῶ will not bear this. It is never '*to say*' simply, but '*to discourse*,' or '*to hold converse*,' '*to speak*.' Again, what is **τὴν ἀρχήν**? not to be taken substantively (as Aug., Ambr., Vulg. *princi-*

ἀρχὴν ὅ τι καὶ λαλῶ ὑμῖν. 26 πολλὰ ἔχω περὶ ὑμῶν
λαλεῖν καὶ κρίνειν· ἀλλ' ὁ πέμψας με ἀληθής ἐστιν, κἀγὼ
ἃ [w] ἤκουσα [w] παρ' αὐτοῦ, ταῦτα λαλῶ [x] εἰς τὸν κόσμον. w ch. vi. 45 reff. x constr., Mark i. 21, 39 al.
27 οὐκ ἔγνωσαν ὅτι τὸν [y] πατέρα αὐτοῖς [y] ἔλεγεν. 28 εἶπεν y constr., Phil. iii. 18.
οὖν ὁ Ἰησοῦς Ὅταν [z] ὑψώσητε τὸν υἱὸν τοῦ ἀνθρώπου, z ch. iii. 14. xii. 32, 34.
τότε γνώσεσθε ὅτι [a] ἐγώ εἰμι, καὶ [b] ἀπ' ἐμαυτοῦ ποιῶ a vv. 24, 58. b ch. v. 19 reff.

26. att *με* ins *πατηρ* ℵ. ins *και* bef *καγω*(sic) T [copt]. *αυτω* $ℵ^1$. rec (for *λαλω*) *λεγω*, with E rel: txt BDKLTUXΔℵ 33. 69 latt syrr [syr-jer] goth Cyr[-p_2].

27. for *αυτοις*, *αυτου* D Scr's g h k r vulg(not am san) lat-*l*. *λεγει* DF Chr_1. add *τον θεον* $Dℵ^1$ vulg(not am forj harl san) lat-(*b*) *c e ff*$_2$ *g* [*l*].

28. rec aft *ουν* ins *αυτοις*, with (D)Eℵ rel vulg lat-*b c e f ff*$_2$ [*g l*] *q*: om BLT 1 lat-*a*.—aft *αυτ.* ins *παλιν* D syrr [syr-jer] sah-woide: aft *ο ι̅ς* ℵ. ins *οτι* bef *οταν* B.

pium), so as to mean '*The beginning*, as I, &c,' (so recently, Bp. Wordsw.): but adverbially, with *all Greek interpreters* (see reff.). And adverbially it may mean (1) '*in the beginning*,' '*from the beginning*,' but not '*firstly*:' (2) '*generally*,' '*at all*,' '*omnino*,' usually with a negative clause, but sometimes with an affirmative. Thus Soph. Antig. 92, ἀρχὴν δὲ θηρᾶν οὐ πρέπει τἀμήχανα: Herod. i. 9, ἀρχὴν γὰρ ἐγὼ μηχανήσομαι οὕτω: iv. 25, τοῦτο οὐκ ἐνδέκομαι τὴν ἀρχήν: Plato, Lysis, p. 265, πῶς οὖν οἱ ἀγαθοὶ τοῖς ἀγαθοῖς ἡμῖν φίλοι ἔσονται τὴν ἀρχήν; See many more examples in Hermann on Viger, p. 722. The common rendering takes the first of these meanings;—but the above remarks on λαλῶ will set that rendering aside;—and together with the assumption of λαλῶ = ἔλεξα, the meaning, '*in the beginning*,' or '*at first*,' or '*from the beginning*,' falls to the ground. We have then the second meaning of τὴν ἀρχήν, **generally**, or 'traced up to its principle,'—for such is the account to be given of this meaning of the word. The rendering of καί, '*even*,' and placing it before τὴν ἀρχ., as done in E. V., is ungrammatical. It must be taken with λαλῶ, being inseparable from it by its position between the relative ὅ τι and the verb: as in the clause, ὃς καὶ παρέδωκεν αὐτόν.
This being premised, the sentence must be rendered (literally) thus: **Essentially, that which I also discourse unto you:** or **In very deed, that same which I speak unto you.** He is the **λόγος**—His *discourses* are the *revelation of Himself*. And there is especial propriety in this:—When Moses asked the name of God, "*I am that which* I AM," was the mysterious answer; the hidden essence of the yet unrevealed One could only be expressed by self-comprehension; but when God manifest in the flesh is asked the same question, it is 'I am that which I SPEAK:' what He *reveals* Himself to be, that He *is* (see on next verse). The above sense is maintained by De Wette, and strikingly expanded and illustrated by Stier, iv. 378 ff., edn. 2. The meaning maintained by Meyer, "*Do ye ask, what I have been long telling you?*" is ingenious, but seems to be by implication refuted by what has been said above. He gives a good *résume* of the interpretations. **26.**] He is, that which He speaks; and that, He has received from the Father;—He has His definite testimony to give, and His work to do: and therefore, though He has much that He could speak and judge about the Jews, He does it not, but overlooks their malice,—not answering it,—that He may go forward with the **λαλεῖν εἰς τὸν κόσμον**, the revelation of Himself: the ἀλήθεια of which is all-important, and excludes less weighty things. **εἰς τ. κόσ., out into the world**, as εἰς τὸν ἀέρα λαλοῦντες, 1 Cor. xiv. 9: see Mark xiii. 10: Luke xxiv. 47. This verse is in the closest connexion with the foregoing.
27.] They did not identify ὁ πέμψας με with ὁ πατήρ μου. However improbable this may be after ὁ πέμψας με πατήρ, ver. 18 (De Wette), it is *stated as a fact*; and the Evangelist certainly would not have done so without some sure ground:—εἰκὸς αὐτοὺς διαπορεῖν πρὸς ἀλλήλους λέγοντας Τίς ἐστιν ὁ πέμψας αὐτόν; Euthym. There is no accounting for the *ignorance of unbelief*, as any minister of Christ knows by painful experience. **28.**] This connects (**οὖν** being the continuation of the foregoing, see above on ver. 21) with ver. 26, and also with ver. 27, as the **τότε γνώσεσθε** shews, referring to the **οὐκ ἔγνωσαν.** On ὑψ. see ch. iii. 14. 'When ye shall have been the instruments of accomplishing that death by which He shall enter into His glory:' for

c = ch. xiv. 18. xvi. 32.
d Acts vi. 2. xii. 3. 1 John iii. 22 only. Gen. xvi. 6.
e ch. ii. 11 reff.
f constr., ch. v. 24 reff.
g ch. xv. 9, 10. 1 Tim. ii. 15. 1 John ii. 10. 2 Macc. viii. 1.
h ch. i. 48 reff.
i 2 John 1.
k ch. xvii. 19. Rom. i. 18 al.
l John, ver. 36 only. Rom. vi. 18, 22. viii. 2, 21. Gal. v. 1 only +. (Sir. l. 23 [25] Tromm. [but ? δευτεροῦν ABℵ &c.]) 2 Macc. i. 27. ii. 22 only.
m = Rom. ix. 7. Gal. iii. 29. Isa. xli. 8.
n John, here only. = Acts vii. 7, from Gen. xv. 14.

BDEF GHKL MSTU XΓΔΛℵ 1. 33. 69

οὐδέν, ἀλλὰ καθὼς ἐδίδαξέν με ὁ πατήρ, ταῦτα λαλῶ.
29 καὶ ὁ πέμψας με μετ' ἐμοῦ ἐστιν· οὐκ [c] ἀφῆκέν με
μόνον, ὅτι ἐγὼ τὰ [d] ἀρεστὰ αὐτῷ ποιῶ πάντοτε.
30 ταῦτα αὐτοῦ λαλοῦντος πολλοὶ [e] ἐπίστευσαν [e] εἰς αὐτόν.
31 Ἔλεγεν οὖν ὁ Ἰησοῦς πρὸς τοὺς [f] πεπιστευκότας αὐτῷ
Ἰουδαίους Ἐὰν ὑμεῖς [g] μείνητε ἐν τῷ λόγῳ τῷ ἐμῷ, [h] ἀληθῶς μαθηταί μου ἐστέ, 32 καὶ [i] γνώσεσθε [k] τὴν [ik] ἀλήθειαν,
καὶ ἡ ἀλήθεια [l] ἐλευθερώσει ὑμᾶς. 33 ἀπεκρίθησαν πρὸς
αὐτὸν [m] Σπέρμα Ἀβραάμ ἐσμεν, καὶ οὐδενὶ [n] δεδουλεύκαμεν

rec aft *πατηρ* ins *μου*, with B rel lat-*f q* syrr coptt goth arm: om DLTXℵ 69 latt [syr-jer] æth Eus$_1$ Cyr$_1$ Thdrt$_1$ Hil$_1$. for *ταυτα*, *ουτως* ℵ ev-H [lat-*a e*].

29. *ουκ αφ. με μονον* bef *μετ' εμου εστιν* ℵ^1. rec aft *μονον* ins *ο πατηρ*, with E rel lat-*f q* syrr [goth]: om BDLTXℵ 1. 69 latt syr-jer coptt æth arm Eus$_1$ Chr$_1$ Cyr$_1$ Hil$_1$. (33 def.)

31. om *ὁ* (bef *ιησ.*) ℵ^1. for *μεινητε*, *μενητε* TΔ. *εμω* bef *λογω*, omg 2nd *τω*, D Eus$_1$. om *μου* ℵ^1.

33. rec (for *προς αυτον*) *αυτω*, with E rel vulg lat-*a b f*: txt BDLTXℵ 33 lat-*e ff$_2$ l q*. add *και ειπαν* D 1 lat-*e* (*b c ff$_2$* coptt æth) [syr-jer] arm. *δεδουλευκαμεν* bef *ουδενι*, prefg *ου*, D.

the latter idea is clearly implied here. **τότε γνώσ.**] Perhaps, in different ways:—some, by the power of the Holy Spirit poured out after the exaltation of Christ, and to their own salvation; others by the judgments which were to follow ere long, and to their own dismay and ruin. The construction and connexion of the following appears to be this: **καὶ ἀπ' ἐμαυτοῦ . . . .** depends on **ὅτι**, and is an expansion of **ἐγώ εἰμι**: whereas ver. 29 is an independent assertion. The interchange of **ποιῶ** and **λαλῶ** is remarkable. The construction is not elliptical, so that **ποιῶ κ. λαλῶ** should be understood in both cases; but the declaration of ver. 25 is still in the Lord's mind, His **ποιεῖν** being all *a declaration of the Father*,—a **λαλεῖν** in the widest sense. Cf. Bengel: "cognoscetis ex *re*, quod nunc ex verbo non creditis." **29.**] **ἀφῆκεν**, aor. referring to the *appointment* of the Father by which His work was begun, and which the **μετ' ἐμοῦ ἐστιν** carries on through that work: see ch. xvi. 32. **ὅτι, because**;—not 'for,' as if what follows were merely a *token* that it is so (Olsh.). The **τὰ ἀρεστὰ αὐτ. ποιῶ πάντ.** is the very essential being of the Son, and is the *cause why* the Father is ever with Him. **30.**] They believed on Him with a higher degree of faith than those in ch. ii. 23, inasmuch as faith wrought by hearing is higher than that by miracles; but still wanted confirming. **31.**] **ἐν τῷ λ. τῷ ἐμῷ** = *ἐν ἐμοί*, ch. xv. 7, though that perhaps is spoken of a deeper entrance into the state of union with Christ. *Remaining in His word* is not merely *obeying His teaching*, but is the inner conviction of the truth of that revelation of Himself, which is his *λαλιά* or *λόγος*. **ἐστέ**, for probably they had given some outward token of believing on Him, e. g. that of ranging themselves among His disciples. **32.**] In opposition to the mere *holding* of the truth. The *knowing* of the truth answers to the *feeding* on Christ;—is the inner realization of it in the man. And in the continuing increase of this comes true freedom from all fear and error and bondage. **33.**] The answerers are the *πεπιστευκότες*, not some others among the hearers, as many Commentators (Lampe, Kuinoel, De Wette, Lücke, edn. 3) have maintained;—see, as a proof of this, ver. 36, addressed to these same persons. They had not yet become *ἀληθῶς μαθηταί*, were not yet distinct from the mass of the unbelieving; and therefore, in speaking to them, He ascribes to them the sins of their race, and addresses them as part of that race. **σπέρμα Ἀβ. ἐσμ.**] See Matt. iii. 9. The assertion **οὐδενὶ δεδ. πώπ.** was so contrary to historical truth, that we must suppose some technical meaning to have been attached to **δεδουλεύκαμεν**, in which it may have been correct. The words cannot be meant of *that generation only*, for *πώποτε* connects with *σπέρμα Ἀβ. ἐσ.*, and generalizes the assertion. As usual (see ch. iii. 4; iv.

πώποτε· πῶς σὺ λέγεις ὅτι ἐλεύθεροι γενήσεσθε; 34 ἀπ-
C πας ο ... εκρίθη αὐτοῖς ὁ Ἰησοῦς Ἀμὴν ἀμὴν λέγω ὑμῖν ὅτι πᾶς ὁ
[o] ποιῶν τὴν [o] ἁμαρτίαν δοῦλός ἐστιν τῆς ἁμαρτίας. 35 ὁ
δὲ δοῦλος οὐ [p] μένει ἐν τῇ οἰκίᾳ [p] εἰς τὸν αἰῶνα· ὁ υἱὸς
[p] μένει [p] εἰς τὸν αἰῶνα. 36 ἐὰν οὖν ὁ υἱὸς ὑμᾶς [q] ἐλευθερώσῃ,
[r] ὄντως ἐλεύθεροι ἔσεσθε. 37 οἶδα ὅτι [m] σπέρμα Ἀβραάμ
ἐστε· ἀλλὰ [s] ζητεῖτέ με ἀποκτεῖναι, ὅτι ὁ λόγος ὁ ἐμὸς οὐ
[t] χωρεῖ ἐν ὑμῖν. 38 ἐγὼ ἃ ἑώρακα [u] παρὰ τῷ πατρὶ
λαλῶ· καὶ ὑμεῖς οὖν ἃ [v] ἠκούσατε [v] παρὰ τοῦ πατρὸς

o 2 Cor. xi. 7. James v. 15 1 Pet. ii. 22. 1 John iii. 4, 8, 9 only. 3 Kings xvi. 19.
p here bis. ch. xii. 34. 2 Cor. ix. 9, from Ps. cxi. 9. Heb. vii. 24. 1 Pet. i. 25, from Isa. xl. 8. 1 John ii. 17 only.
q ver. 32 reff.
r Mark xi. 32 al. Num. xxii. 37 only.
s Matt. xii. 46, 47 reff.
t = here only. Wisd. vii. 23. 2 Macc. iii. 40. xv. 37.
u Matt. vi. 1. Acts ix. 43 al.
v ch. vi. 45 reff.

34. om *ο* (bet *ιησ.*) B. om *της αμαρτιας* D lat-*b* Clem$_1$ Orig$_1$ Faustin$_1$.
35. *εις την οικιαν* D. aft 2nd *ὁ* ins *δε* DT vulg[not am fuld forj ing tol] lat-*a* [*ff*$_2$ *g* syr-jer] Syr syr-w-ob (æth) arm Cyr Cypr$_1$. om last clause (*homœotel*) X[Γ]ℵ 33 Clem$_1$.
36. *ελευθερωσει* (*itacism*) DHMΔ. [**37.** *αποκτ.* bef *με* B-corr (Tischdf N. T. Vat.).]
38. rec (for *ἅ*) *ὅ* (twice), with T rel lat-*a c ff*$_2$ *q* syrr [syr-jer] goth æth: 1st K [**1.** 33 vulg] lat-*b e* [*f g l*]: 2nd Lℵ^{3a}: txt BCDXℵ^1 69 lat-*f* copt Orig$_3$ Chr$_1$ Cyr$_1$ Tert. —1st *ἅ* bef *εγω* (*more usual order*) BCℵ copt Orig$_3$ Chr, *ὅ* bef *εγω* **1**: *εγω δε ἅ* 69.
rec aft *πατρι* ins *μου*, with Dℵ rel vulg-ed(with forj san) lat-*a b c e f ff*$_2$ [*q* copt] syrr goth æth-pl Tert$_1$ spec: om BCLTX am(with em foss [fuld] harl^1 ing jac) lat-*g*$_1$ *l* [syr-jer] æth-rom Orig$_{3(1\ expr)}$ Cyr$_1$. ins *ταυτα* bef *λαλω* D 33 [Cyr-jer] Chr. rec (for *ηκουσατε παρα του πατρος*) *εωρακατε παρα τω πατρι* (*both for uniformity with preceding*), with D rel latt syrr æth-pl Tert$_1$: *ηκουσατε παρα τω πατρι* 69: *εωρακατε παρα του πατρος* Tℵ^1: txt BCKLXℵ^{3a} **1.** 33 lat-*f* syr-mg [syr-jer] coptt goth æth-rom Orig$_{sæpe(1\ expr)}$ Chr$_1$ Cyr$_1$. rec adds *υμων*, with CDℵ rel vss Chr Tert$_1$: om BLT sah æth-rom Orig$_{sæpe(1\ expr)}$ Cyr$_1$.

11; vi. 52), they take the words of our Lord in their outward literal sense. Perhaps this was not always an *unintentional* misunderstanding. **34.**] **ποιῶν τὴν ἁμαρτ.**, not = *ἁμαρτάνων*, for that *all do*; but = *ἐργαζόμενος τὴν ἀνομίαν*, Matt. vii. 23. It implies **living in the practice of sin,—doing sin**, as a habit: see reff. The mere moral sentiment of which this is the spiritual expression, was common among the Greek and Roman philosophers. See Wetstein: also Rom. vi. 12: 2 Pet. ii. 19. **35.**] I believe, with Stier and Bengel, the reference to be to Hagar and Ishmael, and Isaac: the *bond* and the *free*. They had spoken of themselves as the *seed of Abraham*. The Lord shews them that there may be, of that seed, *two kinds*; the *son*, properly so called, and the *slave*. The latter does not abide in the house for ever: it is not his right nor his position—'Cast out the bondwoman and her son.' 'But the *son* abideth ever.' For the application, see on following verses. **ὁ** *δοῦλος* and **ὁ** *υἱός* are in this verse generic merely.

36.] Ye then, being in sin, are carnal: the sons of the bondwoman, and therefore need liberation. Now comes in the *spiritual reality*, into which the discourse passes from the figure. This liberation can only take place by means of Him of whom Isaac was the type—the Seed according to promise; those only who of His Spirit are born again, and after His image, are **ὄντως ἐλεύθεροι**—truly sons of God, and no longer children of the bondwoman, but of the free. See by all means Gal. iv. 19 (where the subject really begins, not at ver. 21) to end, which is the best commentary on this verse. There neither is, nor can be here, any allusion either to the liberation of the sabbatical year (Œcolampadius); or to the subject of Heb. iii. 5, 6 (Euthym., after Chrys.). **37.**] 'Ye are Abraham's seed, according to the flesh and the covenant: but'—and here the distinction appears—'ye *ποιεῖτε τὴν ἁμαρτίαν* by seeking to kill Me, because My **λόγος** (see above on ver. 31) **οὐ χωρεῖ**—does not work (spread, go forward,—'ne marche pas') *in* you' (not, *among* you). Herodian, v. 3. 31, says of a report, *ὥστε εἰς πᾶν* **χωρῆσαι** *τὸ στρατιωτικόν*, 'it *spread through* the whole army.' Such expressions as *τὰ πράγματα χωρεῖ κατὰ λόγον*, Polyb. xxiii. 15. 12,—*ταῦτα καλῶς κατὰ νοῦν ἐχώρει αὐτῷ*, ib. x. 15. 4,—*πῶς οὖν οὐ χωρεῖ τοὔργον;* Aristoph. Pax 464,

ποιεῖτε. 39 ἀπεκρίθησαν καὶ εἶπαν αὐτῷ Ὁ πατὴρ ἡμῶν
Ἀβραάμ ἐστιν. λέγει αὐτοῖς ὁ Ἰησοῦς Εἰ τέκνα τοῦ
Ἀβραὰμ ἔστε, τὰ ἔργα τοῦ Ἀβραὰμ ἐποιεῖτε. 40 νῦν
δὲ [s] ζητεῖτέ με ἀποκτεῖναι, ἄνθρωπον ὃς τὴν ἀλήθειαν ὑμῖν
λελάληκα, ἣν [v] ἤκουσα [v] παρὰ τοῦ θεοῦ· τοῦτο Ἀβραὰμ
οὐκ ἐποίησεν. 41 ὑμεῖς ποιεῖτε τὰ ἔργα τοῦ πατρὸς ὑμῶν.
εἶπον αὐτῷ Ἡμεῖς ἐκ [w] πορνείας οὐκ [x] ἐγεννήθημεν· ἕνα

w Matt. xv. 19 al. Hos. ii. 4.
x w. ἐκ, ch. i. 13 reff.

Π viii. 39(appy) ... BCDEF GHKL MSTUX ΓΔΛΠℵ 1. 33. 69

ins ταυτα bef ποιειτε D.

39. (ειπαν, so BCDℵ 33 $Orig_1$.) for λεγει αυτοις, ειπεν ουν D lat-*e*: απεκριθη αυτοις ℵ. om 2nd ὁ B. rec (for εστε) ητε, with C rel vss(" ut vid." Treg) $Orig_3$ Eus_3 $Cyr\text{-}jer_1$ Bas_1 Did_1 Cyr[-p]: txt BDLTℵ vulg lat-ff_2 $Orig_{10}$ Aug_1. rec aft εποιειτε ins αν, with CKLMXΔ[Π]ℵ[3a] 1. 33 lat-*b* æth $Orig_1$-int_2 [Did_1 $Cyr\text{-}p_1$]: om B D-gr Tℵ[1] rel $Orig_{12}$ Eus_2 $Cyr\text{-}jer_1$ $Epiph_1$ Bas_1 Chr_1. [Tischdf ed 8 gives ποιειτε B[1] lat-ff_2 $Orig_{7\text{ or }8}$ Chr_1.]

40. λελαληκα bef υμιν D 69 lat-*a b c e l* [*q*] copt æth Orig-int_2 $Tert_2$. ηκουσεν D[1.8](and lat: txt D-corr[1]) lat-*e* ff_2 $Tert_1$.

41. aft υμεις ins δε D [Π[2](but erased) ℵ[3](Tischdf ed 8)] 1 lat-[*b e*] *l* Syr (æth). (ειπαν Dℵ.) rec aft ειπον ins ουν, with CD rel vulg lat-*f* syr-w-ast sah goth $Orig_1$ Cyr_1: om BLTℵ foss lat-*a b e* (ff_2?) *l q* Syr [syr-jer] copt æth arm. rec (for ουκ εγεννηθημεν) ου γεγεννημεθα, with CD[2]ℵ[3a] rel $Orig_4$: ουκ εγεννημεθα LTℵ[1]: txt BD[1.8].

seem also to illustrate this meaning. **38.**] We have the same remarkable relation between λαλεῖν and ποιεῖν, as in ver. 28: except that here the ποιεῖν is applied to the Jews only; λαλεῖν being used in the same comprehensive sense as there.

But notice the distinction in the restored text between ἑώρακα παρὰ τῷ πατρί and ἠκούσατε παρὰ τοῦ πατρός, ὁ πατήρ being a common term, and the articles possessive. [The speaking and doing were in each case from the father of each. But] Jesus was πρὸς τὸν θεόν, in a relation of abiding unity with His Father: they were ἐκ τοῦ πατρὸς τοῦ διαβ.,—he was the suggester of their course, the originator of their acts. Jesus was the υἱός, who remains in the house and sees the father's acts: they the δοῦλοι, merely prescribed to and under bondage. The **οὖν** implies **accordingly,—by the same rule.** **39, 40.**] There is a distinction between **σπέρμα** and **τέκνα.** The former our Lord grants that they were (ver. 37), but the latter (by implication—see below on the construction) He denies them. See Rom. ix. 7, οὐ γὰρ πάντες οἱ ἐξ Ἰσραήλ, οὗτοι Ἰσραήλ· οὐδ' ὅτι εἰσὶν **σπέρμα** Ἀβραάμ, πάντες **τέκνα.** The latter betokens *likeness*, true genuine descent in character and habits.

The reading in the text is remarkable as connecting together the present ἔστε and the imperfect ἐποιεῖτε. In such a case there must be a suppressed change of meaning between the protasis and the apodosis. The εἰ ἔστε concedes, in a certain sense: the ἐποιεῖτε denies, by making an assumption at variance with present fact. The sentence is in fact a combination of a protasis of one form with an apodosis of another. It might have been, (a) εἰ ἔστε . . . ., ποιεῖτε; or, (b) εἰ ἦτε . . . ., ἐποιεῖτε. But as it stands, protasis (a) is joined with apodosis (b): and thereby the τέκνα τοῦ Ἀβραὰμ εἶναι in any worthy sense is denied, while in the mere formal sense it is conceded. **τοῦτο, this**; not, 'tale quid:' and **ἐποίησεν**, fecit, not 'fecisset:' for the statement is one of a *fact*:—**this did not Abraham,** as E. V.: see Gen. xviii. **41.**] **ποιεῖτε**—not imperative, which destroys the sense. **ἐκ πορν.**] Stier remarks, that they now let fall Abraham as their father, being convicted of unlikeness to him. They see that a *spiritual* paternity must be meant, and accordingly refer to God as their Father. This consideration will rule the sense of **ἐκ πορν.**, which must therefore be spiritual also. And spiritually the **τέκνα πορνείας**, ref. Hosea, are idolaters. πολύθεος ὁ ἐκ πόρνης, τυφλώττων περὶ τὸν ἀληθῆ πατέρα, καὶ διὰ τοῦτο πολλοὺς ἀνθ' ἑνὸς γονεῖς αἰνιττόμενος. Philo de Migr. Abr. 13, vol. i. p. 447. Ishmael cannot well be alluded to; for they would not call the relation between Abraham and Hagar one of πορνεία. Still less can Origen's interpretation be adopted, ἔλεγον Ἡμεῖς μᾶλλον ἕνα πατέρα ἔχομεν τὸν θεόν, ἤπερ σύ, ὁ φάσκων μὲν ἐκ παρθένου γεγεννῆσθαι, ἐκ πορνείας δὲ γεγεννημένος, καὶ διὰ τὸ αὐχεῖν τὸ ἐκ παρθένου γεγεννῆσθαι λέγων ἕνα πατέρα ἔχειν μόνον, τὸν θεόν (tom. xx. 14, p.

πατέρα ἔχομεν τὸν θεόν. 42 εἶπεν αὐτοῖς ὁ Ἰησοῦς Εἰ
ὁ θεὸς πατὴρ ὑμῶν ἦν, ἠγαπᾶτε ἂν ἐμέ· ἐγὼ γὰρ ἐκ
τοῦ θεοῦ [y] ἐξῆλθον καὶ ἥκω· οὐδὲ γὰρ [z] ἀπ' ἐμαυτοῦ
ἐλήλυθα, ἀλλ' ἐκεῖνός με ἀπέστειλεν. 43 διὰ τί τὴν
[a] λαλιὰν τὴν ἐμὴν οὐ [b] γινώσκετε; ὅτι οὐ δύνασθε
[c] ἀκούειν τὸν λόγον τὸν ἐμόν. 44 ὑμεῖς [d] ἐκ τοῦ πατρὸς
τοῦ [e] διαβόλου [d] ἐστέ, καὶ τὰς [f] ἐπιθυμίας τοῦ πατρὸς
ὑμῶν [g] θέλετε ποιεῖν. ἐκεῖνος [h] ἀνθρωποκτόνος ἦν [i] ἀπ'
ἀρχῆς, καὶ ἐν τῇ ἀληθείᾳ οὐχ [k] ἕστηκεν, ὅτι οὐκ ἔστιν

...εκ του T.

y = Mark i. 38. z ch. v. 19 reff. a ch. iv. 42 reff. b = ch. iii. 10. Mark iv. 13. c = ch. ix. 27. Matt. xiii. 13, &c. Rev. ii. 7, 11 al. d ch. iii. 31 reff. e = Matt. iv. 1 reff. see ch. vi. 70. f Mark iv. 19. Rom. vii. 7, 8 al. g ch. v. 35, 40. vii. 17. h 1 John iii. 15 (bis) only †. i Matt. xix. 4, 8 al. fr. Eccl. iii. 11. k = Rom. v. 2. 1 Cor. xv. 1.

42. rec aft ειπεν ins ουν, with DMUXΔℵ 69 (S, e sil) vulg lat-*f* sah: om BCT rel lat-*a b c e ff*$_2$ [*l q* syr-jer] syrr copt goth arm Orig$_1$. om ο (bef ιησ.) B. ins ο bef πατηρ B. ημων (*carelessly*) Gℵ ev-y. for ουδε, ου D-gr G 69 lat-*c e f ff*$_2$ [*l*] *q* syr. εληλυθον D$^{1\cdot 8}$(txt D^2). (αλλα D.)
43. for λαλιαν, αληθειαν D^1-gr(txt D^2).
44. rec om του (bef 1st πατρος), with (33, e sil) goth arm: ins BCDℵ rel Clem$_1$ Heracl Orig$_{sæpe}$ Dion Nyss Epiph Bas Chr Cyr Thl. (om του πατρος K 44(Sz) em Orig$_1$.) αληθεια bef ουκ εστιν D[Γ] lat-*q* Syr Orig$_1$ Cypr$_1$.

327),—for our Lord never proclaimed this of Himself. There may possibly be a reference to the *Samaritans* (ver. 48), who completely answered in the spiritual sense to the children of fornication: see Deut. xxxi. 16: Isa. i. 21: Ezek. xvi. 15 ff.; xx. 30 al. **42.**] 'If you were the children of God, the *ethical proof* (as Luthardt well calls it) of such descent would be, that you would love Me, who am κατ' ἐξοχήν the Son of God, and who am come by the mission, and bearing the character, of God.' **ἥκω** conveys the result of **ἐξῆλθον**, as Meyer; who also remarks that mere *sending* will not exhaust ἐξῆλθον, which must be taken metaphysically, of the proceeding forth of the Eternal Son from the essence of the Father. **43.**] **λαλιὰν γινώσκειν** is to *understand the idiom or dialect* in which a man speaks, **λαλ.** being his **manner of speech**: see Matt. xxvi. 73, and Cant. iv. 3, LXX. **Why do ye not understand my speech?** as E. V. But this of course does not here refer to the mere outward expression of the Lord's discourses, but to the *spiritual idiom* in which He spoke, and which can only be spiritually understood. Then **ὁ λόγος ὁ ἐμός** is the *matter* of those discourses, the Word itself. The connexion of the two clauses is, **Why,** &c.? **Because ye** *cannot* **receive**, hear with the inner ear (see reff., and ch. vi. 60), **that which I say.** And the verification and ground of this 'cannot' is in the next verse. Meyer remarks, that in questions and answers, the emphatic words come *last*—being here **γινώσκετε** and **τὸν λόγον τ. ἐμόν.** **44.**] The first article τοῦ is important, and to be rendered (against Meyer) as in E. V., **your father the devil.** This verse is one of the most decisive testimonies for the *objective personality* of the devil. It is quite impossible to suppose an accommodation to Jewish views, or a metaphorical form of speech, in so solemn and direct an assertion as this. **θέλετε ποιεῖν** is important, and should have been in E. V. more marked: **Your will is to do**: or, as A. V. R. "**ye love to do**" [**or, are inclined to do**]. It indicates, as in ch. v. 40, the *freedom of the human will*, as the *foundation of the condemnation of the sinner*.
ἀνθρωποκτόνος] The most obvious reference seems to be, to the murder of Abel by Cain: see the Apostle's own comment on these words, 1 John iii. 12, 15. But this itself was only a result of the introduction of death by sin, which was the work of the devil: Adam and Eve were the *first* whom he murdered. But then again both these were only *manifestations* of the fact here stated by divine omniscience respecting him: that he was ἀνθρωποκτόνος. **ἀπ' ἀρχῆς**, the author and bringer in of that hate which is ἀνθρωποκτονία, 1 John iii. 15. The mention of **murder** is introduced because the Jews went about to kill Jesus; and the *typical* parallel of Cain and Abel is certainly hinted at in the words: see Lücke's note, ii. 338 ff., and Stier, iv. 414 (edn. 2) ff. **οὐχ ἕστηκεν**, not '*abode* not,' E. V.; a sense which ἕστηκα will not bear, being always *present* in meaning, and = 'I have placed myself,' i. e. I *stand*: see Matt. xii. 47; xx. 6:

ἀλήθεια ἐν αὐτῷ. ὅταν λαλῇ τὸ [l] ψεῦδος, [m] ἐκ [n] τῶν
[n] ἰδίων [m] λαλεῖ· ὅτι [o] ψεύστης ἐστὶν καὶ ὁ πατὴρ [p] αὐτοῦ.
45 ἐγὼ δὲ ὅτι τὴν ἀλήθειαν λέγω, οὐ [q] πιστεύετέ μοι. 46 τίς
ἐξ ὑμῶν [r] ἐλέγχει με περὶ ἁμαρτίας; εἰ ἀλήθειαν λέγω,

BCDEF GHKL MSUX ΓΔΛΠℵ 1. 33. 69

l Eph. iv. 25. Rev. xxi. 27 al. Ps. v. 6. m ch. iii. 31 reff. n ch. i. 11 reff. o ver. 55. 1 John i. 10 al. John only, exc. Rom. iii. 4. 1 Tim. i. 10. Tit. i. 12. Ps. cxv. 11. p indef. pron., Rom. ii. 26. Luke xxiii. 51. 1 Pet. iii. 14. Jude 24 al. q ch. v. 24 reff. r (ver. 9.) w. περί, ch. xvi. 8—11. Luke iii. 19. Jude 15 only.

45. om δε D lat-*a b c e ff*$_2$ [*l q*] (not B: see table). for λεγω, λαλω D. aft λεγω ins υμιν C[1](appy) 253 lat-*b f* copt [æth] Cyr$_1$. at end ins υμεις D.
46. om ver (*homœotel*) D Scr's v. rec aft ει ins δε, with E rel copt-ms æth: om BCLX[Π]ℵ 1. 33. 69 latt syr syr-jer coptt goth arm Orig$_1$ Cyr[-p].

Mark ix. 1; xi. 5: John iii. 29: Acts i. 11; vii. 33: Rom. v. 2; xi. 20 al. fr.: whereas the pluperfect, εἱστήκειν, 'I had placed myself,' i. e. I *stood*, is *imperfect* in sense: see Matt. xii. 46. And that this place forms no exception, is shewn by ὅτι οὐκ ἔστιν (not ἦν) immediately following. But as the account of this *present* sense shews, it is not a *mere* present, but a present dependent on and commencing with an implied past fact. And that fact here is, the *fall* of the devil, which was not an insulated act, but in which state of apostasy from the truth he **ἕστηκεν**,—it is his *status*. So Euthym.: ἐμμένει, ἀναπαύεται. **ἡ ἀλήθεια**, as De Wette remarks, is *objective: the* **truth** of God:—in this **he standeth not,** *because* **there is no truth** ('*truthfulness,*' *subjective*) **in him.** His *lie* has become his very nature, and therefore he is thoroughly alien from the truth of God. To take **ὅτι** as 'not the cause, but the proof' (*for,* i. e. 'for we see it by this, that' . . . . .) is not only to do violence to construction, but to overthrow the whole sense of the passage. **τὸ ψεῦδος, a lie**; generic: we in English have retained the article in the expression 'to speak the truth,' but not in the corresponding one. He ἐλάλει τὸ ψεῦδος to Eve. **ἐκ τ. ἰδ., of his own,** as E. V., not, '*according to his character*' (De Wette),—but 'out of his own resources,' 'treasures:' see Matt. xii. 35. **ὁ πατ. αὐτοῦ**] i. e. either τοῦ ψεύδους—(absolutely, or as understood in ψεύστης,—Orig., Euthym., Theophyl., &c. Nitzsch (Theol. Zeitschrift, 1822), De Wette, Lücke, Wordsw., and Winer, § 22. 3. b),—or τοῦ ψεύστου (= τῶν ψευστῶν), *of the liar generally*. The former is *not the fact*,—for the devil is not the father **τοῦ ψεύδους**, but **τῶν ψευστῶν**, by being himself one whose very nature has become τὸ ψεῦδος. Certainly by this he has become the author, promoter, of falsehood among men; but this kind of paternity is not here in question: the object being to shew that he was the father of these lying Jews. I therefore hold the latter interpretation, with Bengel, Meyer, and Stier. The construction of this passage with the art. before πατήρ has presented insuperable difficulty to Bp. Middleton and others: see Midd. in loc. The rendering which he proposes is this: "When (any of you) speaks that which is false, he speaks after the manner of his kindred (ἐκ τῶν ἰδίων!), for he is a liar, and so also is his father," i. e. the devil. To which the late Prof. Scholefield proposes an emendation, to take away the comma after ἐστίν, and translate, "For his father also is a liar," not knowing, apparently, that this was the ancient heretical interpretation according to which the πατὴρ αὐτοῦ was the Demiurge: see Meyer, edn. 3, and Hilgenfeld, referred to by him as supporting this rendering. It is really almost incredible that learned men, students of our Lord's discourses, should seriously uphold an interpretation so utterly absurd and preposterous. It is only an instance how the judgment may be warped by the adoption of canons respecting the article grounded on insufficient observation. The instances which Middleton adduces to prove that according to the ordinary rendering, the article must be omitted before πατήρ, none of them touch the question. The article here is *emphatic*, and could not be omitted, any more than in the sentence ἐγώ εἰμι ὁ ἄρτος τῆς ζωῆς. The simple account to be given of this construction, is that it = ὅτι ψεύστης ἐστίν, καὶ ὁ πατὴρ αὐτῶν: but by ψεύστης being singular, the pronoun is attracted into the singular also. **45.**] 'And the very reason why ye do not believe *Me* (as contrasted with *him*) is, *because I speak the truth*;—you *not being of the truth*, but of him who is falsehood itself.' This implies a charge of wilful striving against known and recognized truth. Euthymius fills up the context—εἰ μὲν ἔλεγον ψεῦδος, ἐπιστεύσατέ μοι ἄν, ὡς τὸ ἴδιον τοῦ πατρὸς ὑμῶν λέγοντι: see ch. v. 43. **46.**] **ἁμαρτία** here is strictly **sin**: not '*error in argument,*' or '*falsehood.*' These two latter meanings are found in classical Greek, but

διὰ τί ὑμεῖς οὐ [q] πιστεύετέ μοι; 47 ὁ [s] ὢν [s] ἐκ τοῦ θεοῦ τὰ s vv. 23, 44.
ῥήματα τοῦ θεοῦ ἀκούει· διὰ τοῦτο ὑμεῖς οὐκ ἀκούετε,
ὅτι [s] ἐκ τοῦ θεοῦ οὐκ [s] ἐστέ. 48 ἀπεκρίθησαν οἱ Ἰουδαῖοι
καὶ εἶπαν αὐτῷ Οὐ [t] καλῶς λέγομεν ἡμεῖς ὅτι Σαμαρείτης t = ch. xiii. 13 reff.
εἶ σὺ καὶ [u] δαιμόνιον [u] ἔχεις; 49 ἀπεκρίθη Ἰησοῦς Ἐγὼ u ch. vii. 20 reff.
[u] δαιμόνιον οὐκ [u] ἔχω, ἀλλὰ τιμῶ τὸν πατέρα μου, καὶ
ὑμεῖς [v] ἀτιμάζετέ με. 50 ἐγὼ δὲ οὐ ζητῶ τὴν δόξαν μου· v Mark xii. 4 reff.
ἔστιν ὁ ζητῶν καὶ κρίνων. 51 [w] ἀμὴν ἀμὴν λέγω ὑμῖν, ἐάν w ch. v. 24, 25 reff.

47. om last clause (*passing from* -ετε *to* εστε) DG.
48. rec aft απεκρ. ins ουν, with E rel vulg lat-*f g q* syr [Chr_1]: om BCDLXℵ **1**. 33. 69 foss lat-*a b c e ff*$_2$ *l* Syr coptt arm $Orig_1$ Cyr_1. (ειπαν, so BCDℵ 33 $Orig_1$.) ημεις bef λεγ. DL [lat-*c* Eus_1]. om συ ℵ[1] **1** syr-txt $Orig_1$(ins_4).
49. ins ο bef ιησ. D[Π^2] 69 Chr. aft ιησ. ins και ειπεν Gℵ **1**. 69 [syr-jer] copt æth (arm). μου bef τον πατερα D.

never in the N. T. or LXX. And besides, they would introduce in this most solemn part of our Lord's discourse, a vapid tautology. The question is an appeal to His *sinlessness of life*, as evident to them all,—as a pledge for His truthfulness of word: which word asserted, be it remembered, that *He was sent from God.* And when we recollect that He who here challenges men to convict him of sin, never could have upheld *outward* spotlessness merely (see Matt. xxiii. 26–28), the words amount to a declaration of His absolute sinlessness, in thought, word, and deed. Or, the connexion may be as stated by Euthym.: εἰ μὴ διότι τὴν ἀλήθειαν λέγω ἀπιστεῖτέ μοι, εἴπατε, τίς ἐξ ὑμῶν ἐλέγχει με περὶ ἁμαρτίας ὑπ' ἐμοῦ γενομένης, ἵνα δόξητε δι' ἐκείνην ἀπιστεῖν;

εἰ ἀλ. λέγω] And **if** it be thence (from the impossibility of convicting me of sin) evident, that **I speak the truth,** *why* **do ye not believe Me?** (not πιστ. **εἰς ἐμέ**, but simply **μοι, give credence to Me.**)

Ver. **47** gives the answer to the **διὰ τί,** and concludes the discourse with the final disproof of their assertion, ver. 41,—with, as it were, a 'quod erat demonstrandum.' This verse is cited 1 John iv. 6.

48.] The Jews attempt no answer, but commence reviling Him. These are now properly **οἱ Ἰουδ.**,—the principal among the Jews. **Σαμ.**] So they called 'outcasts from the commonwealth of Israel:' and so afterwards they called the Christians כותיים, from כּוּתָה (2 Kings xvii. 24). They imply, that He differed from their interpretation of the law,—or perhaps, as He had convicted them of not being the genuine children of Abraham, they cast back the charge with a senseless 'Tu quoque.' There may perhaps be a reference to the occurrence related in ch. iv. 5 ff.; but Schöttgen (p. 371) has shewn that "*Samaritanus es*" is found in the Rabbis as addressed to one whose word is not to be believed. **κ. δαιμ. ἔχ.**] "As in the first clause they sundered Him from the communion of Israel, so now from that of Israel's God." Stier. Or perhaps they mean the reproach more as expressing aggravated madness owing to dæmoniacal possession. The **καλῶς λέγομεν** connects with the charge twice brought against Him by the Pharisees, 'of casting out devils by the prince of the devils.'

49.] The former term of reproach Jesus passes over ("cum jam inter Samaritanos haberet, qui in eum credebant." Lampe; but qu.?), and mildly answers (1 Pet. ii. 23) the malicious charge of having a devil, by an appeal to his whole life and teaching (see ch. iv. 34), which was not the work of one having a devil. There is no *retort of the charge* in the emphatic **ἐγώ**, as Cyr. and Lücke; this, as Meyer observes, would have required *οὐκ ἐγώ*. At present the **ἐγώ** followed by **ὑμεῖς** only brings out the two parties into stronger contrast.

κ. ὑμ. ἀτιμ. με] The **ἐγώ** and **ὑμεῖς** correspond strictly to the *ἡμεῖς* and *σύ* of the preceding verse. 'Our mutual relation is not that, but this: that I honour Him that sent me, and ye, in dishonouring me, dishonour Him.' It is the same contrast, the *ἐκ τοῦ θεοῦ* and *οὐκ ἐκ τοῦ θεοῦ*, as before, ver. 47, which lies at the root.

50.] 'Ye dishonour me;—not that I seek my own honour, but His who sent me. There is One who seeketh my honour (ch. v. 23), and will have me honoured; and who judgeth between me and you, between truth and falsehood.' Supply *τ. δόξαν μου* after *ζητῶν*, but not after *κρίνων*. **51.**] There is no pause (De Wette) between ver. 50 and this. This is the direct carrying on of the discourse, arising out of **κρίνων** in the last

x here 3ce. ch. xiv. 23, 24. xv. 20. xvii. 6. 1 John ii. 4. Rev. iii. 8, 10. xxii. 7, 9. J. 1 Kings xv. 11 B.
y = Matt. xix. 17. xxiii. 3. xxviii. 20 al.
z = here only. see Luke ii. 26. Ps. lxxxviii. 48.
a (ver. 35 reff.) ch. iv. 14. vi. 51, 58. x. 28. xi. 26. xiii. 8. xiv. 16. Matt. xxi. 19 || Mk. Mark iii. 29. 1 Cor. viii. 13. Heb. (i. 8) v. 6. vi. 20. vii. 17, 21, 28. 2 John 2. Jude 13 only. Ps. xxx. 1.

τις τὸν ἐμὸν [x] λόγον [xy] τηρήσῃ, θάνατον οὐ μὴ [z] θεωρήσῃ
[a] εἰς τὸν αἰῶνα. 52 εἶπον αὐτῷ οἱ Ἰουδαῖοι Νῦν ἐγνώκαμεν ὅτι [u] δαιμόνιον [u] ἔχεις. Ἀβραὰμ ἀπέθανεν καὶ
οἱ προφῆται, καὶ σὺ λέγεις Ἐάν τις τὸν [x] λόγον μου A λεγεις
[xy] τηρήσῃ, οὐ μὴ [b] γεύσηται [b] θανάτου [a] εἰς τὸν αἰῶνα. 53 μὴ ABCDE
σὺ [c] μείζων εἶ τοῦ πατρὸς ἡμῶν Ἀβραάμ, [d] ὅστις ἀπέθα- FGHK LMSUX
νεν; καὶ οἱ προφῆται ἀπέθανον· τίνα σεαυτὸν [e] ποιεῖς; ΓΔΛΠℵ 1. 33. 69
54 ἀπεκρίθη Ἰησοῦς Ἐὰν ἐγὼ [f] δοξάσω ἐμαυτόν, ἡ δόξα
μου [g] οὐδέν ἐστιν· ἔστιν ὁ πατήρ μου ὁ [f] δοξάζων με, [h] ὃν
ὑμεῖς λέγετε ὅτι θεὸς ἡμῶν ἐστιν, 55 καὶ οὐκ ἐγνώκατε
αὐτόν, ἐγὼ δὲ οἶδα αὐτόν· καὶ ἐὰν εἴπω ὅτι οὐκ οἶδα
αὐτόν, ἔσομαι [i] ὅμοιος * ὑμῶν [j] ψεύστης· ἀλλὰ οἶδα αὐτὸν

b Matt. xvi. 28 ||. Heb. ii. 9 only. c ch. iv. 12. Gen. xlviii. 19. d Matt. ii. 6. xxii. 2 al. Deut. v. 26. e = ch. x. 33. xix. 7, 12. 1 John i. 10. v. 10. f = Matt. vi. 2. Luke iv. 15. Rev. xviii. 7. Lam. i. 8. g = Matt. xxiii. 16, 18 reff. h constr., Luke xxiv. 7. ch. ix. 19. x. 36. i w. gen., here only. Sir. xiii. 16. ὅμοια τοῦ Ἡφαίστου, Herod. iii. 37 j ver. 44 reff.

51. for *εαν τις, ος αν* D Syr sah (æth?). rec (for *τον εμον λογ.*) *τον λογ. τον εμον*, with E rel: txt BCDLXℵ 33 Orig$_1$ Cyr[-comm$_1$]. *τηρησει* M[Γ]ℵ. *θεωρησει* M[Γ]ℵ 1 Orig$_2$ [Chr$_1$].

52. (*ειπαν* Dℵ.) rec aft *ειπ.* ins *ουν*, with DL rel vulg lat-*c f* [*ff*$_2$ *l q*] syr sah goth: om BCℵ lat-*a b e* Syr [syr-jer] copt arm Orig$_1$. *μου* bef *τις τον λογον* D [bef *τ. λογ.* L]. *τηρησει* (*itacism*) DM[Γ]. rec *γευσεται*, with EFH: txt ACDℵ rel Orig$_2$ Cyr$_1$.—for *ου μη γευ. θαν.*, *θανατον ου μη θεωρηση* (*from ver* 51) B [lat-*e*].—om *θανατου* ℵ[1]. om *εις τον αιωνα* D 249 lat-*b c ff*$_2$[1] [*l*] Non$_1$.

53. om *πατρος ημων* D lat-*a b c e ff*$_2$ *l.* for *οστις*, *οτι* D lat-*a*. rec aft *σεαυτον* ins *συ*, with X(Treg, expr) rel goth (arm): om ABCDGKLΔ[ΓΠ]ℵ 1. 33 latt (syrr?) coptt Orig$_2$ Chr$_2$ Cyr[-p].

54. ins *ο* bef *ιησ.* DΔ[1] [Π[2](but erased)] ℵ 69 Orig$_1$. rec *δοξαζω* (*more obvious: cf δοξαζων below*), with AC[2]L ℵ[3a](but txt restored) rel vulg lat-*b f* Chr-montf$_1$ Cyr$_1$: txt BC[1]Dℵ[1] 1. 69 lat-*a c e ff*$_2$ *l q* Orig$_2$ Chr-mss$_1$ Ambr$_1$. rec *υμων*, with B DFXℵ 69(as corrd 1. m.) [vulg-ed] lat-*a b c e ff*$_2$ *l q* Chr$_1$ Tert$_1$: txt A B[2.3](Tischdf) C rel am(with fuld em forj gat ing jac mm mt san tol) lat-*f g* syrr coptt goth æth arm.

55. (for *και εαν*, *καν* BDℵ.) *ομοιος* bef *εσομαι* D. * *ὑμῖν* (*more usual*) ABD 1: *υμων* Cℵ rel. (*αλλα*, so BDX.)

verse, and forming a "novum tentamen gratiæ" (Lampe). 'Ye are *now* children of the devil, but if ye keep My word ye shall be rescued from that *ἀνθρωποκτόνος*.' **τὸν ἐμ. λόγ. τηρ.**, as *ἐν τῷ λόγῳ τῷ ἐμῷ μένειν*, ver. 31, is not only outward obedience, but the endurance in, and obedience of faith. **θεωρεῖν θάν.**, as *γεύεσθαι θαν.*, is a Hebraism for *to die*,—see reff.,—and must not be pressed to mean, 'shall not *feel* (the bitterness of) death,' in a temporal sense, as has been done by Stier (iv. 433, edn. 2). The *death of the body* is not reckoned as *death*, any more than the *life of the body* is *life*, in our Lord's discourses: see ch. xi. 25, 26, and notes. Both words have a deeper meaning. **52, 53.**] The Jews, not knowing what death really imports, regard the saying as a decisive proof of their surmise ver. 48. "Their misunderstanding (says De Wette) keeps to the well-known type (ch. iii. 4; iv. 11 ff.), but this time theocratic pride is added to carnal sensuousness:—'the O. T. Saints died!'"

54, 55.] The argument in these verses is: 'The same God who is the God of Abraham, is my Father;—He it is who honours (glorifies) me, and it is His word that I keep. I was promised by Him to Abraham.' **δοξάσω**, 'glorify myself to this high designation, of being able to deliver from death.' **ὃν λέγ.**] Whom you are in the habit of calling *your* God (for so of course the *θεὸς ἡμῶν* imports)—i. e. the God of Israel. A most important identification, from the mouth of our Lord Himself, of *the Father*, with the *God of Israel* in the O. T. The **καί** here is not '*but*,' nor '*although*;' the sense is, **of Whom ye say 'He is our God,' and know Him not.** Then what follows sets forth

καὶ τὸν [x] λόγον αὐτοῦ [xy] τηρῶ. 56 Ἀβραὰμ ὁ πατὴρ ὑμῶν
[k] ἠγαλλιάσατο [l] ἵνα [m] ἴδῃ τὴν [n] ἡμέραν τὴν ἐμήν, καὶ
εἶδεν καὶ ἐχάρη. 57 εἶπον οὖν οἱ Ἰουδαῖοι πρὸς αὐτὸν
Πεντήκοντα ἔτη οὔπω [o] ἔχεις, καὶ Ἀβραὰμ ἑώρακας;
58 εἶπεν αὐτοῖς ὁ Ἰησοῦς Ἀμὴν ἀμὴν λέγω ὑμῖν, πρὶν

k Matt. v. 12. Luke x. 21. Rev. xix. 7 al. Ps. lii. 6.
l = ch. xi. 15. xii. 23. 1 John i. 9.
m Luke xvii. 22. 1 Pet. iii. 10, from Ps. xxxiii. 12.
n Luke xvii. 24. Acts ii. 20, from Joel ii. 31.
o = ch. v. 5, 6. ix. 21, 23. xi. 17.

56. for ιδη, ειδη (*itacism*) A B[1][Tischdf ascribes ιδη to his B[2·3]] D-corr[1] Xℵ 69 Orig$_1$ [ηδη Γ]. (for ειδεν, ιδεν ACKLMX[ΓΠ[1]].)
57. (ειπαν Dℵ.) ουδεπω D. for εωρακας, εωρακεν σε ℵ[1] [sah]: εορακες B[1](Tischdf).
58. aft ειπεν ins ουν DGKX 1. 69 sah: pref και L Scr's d syr [æth]. om ὁ BC.

the contrast between them, the pretended children of Abraham, who know not Abraham's God (the *liars*), and Him who knows Him, and keeps His word, so that His word works in and by Him; yea, He *is* ὁ λόγος τοῦ θεοῦ. His *allowing their denial* of this state of knowledge and union would be *as great a lie in Him*, as their *assumption* of it was *in them*. ὅμοιος **ὑμῶν** (instead of the more usual ὑμῖν) signifies the being 'one of them;' as we say, 'the like of them.' **56.**] The Lord does not deny them their *outward* title of children of Abraham:—it is of spiritual things that He has been speaking, in refusing them the *reality* of it. **ἠγαλλ. ἵνα ἴδῃ, rejoiced, that He should see**; not (Grotius, Calov., Kuin., &c.) "wished that he might see." The object of his joy is treated as its purpose. The intent is to shew that Abraham did in his time keep Christ's word, viz. by a *prospective realizing faith;* and *therefore* that he, in the sense of ver. 51, *had not seen death.* This is expressed by **κ. εἶδεν κ. ἐχάρη**: see below. But what is **τ. ἡμ. τ. ἐμήν**? Certainly, the day of Christ's appearance in the flesh (ὁ τῆς ἐπιδημίας αὐτοῦ καιρός, Cyril Alex.). *When that was over,* and the attention was directed to another and future appearance, the word came to be used of His *second coming,* 1 Cor. i. 8, &c. &c. But this, as well as *the day of His Cross* (Euthym., al.), is out of the question *here;*—and the word Rabbinically was used for the time of the Messiah's appearance. So we have it, Luke xvii. 22, 26: but here as there, the expression must not be limited *exclusively* to the former appearance. From the sense it is evident that Abraham saw by faith and will see in fact, not the first coming only, but that which it introduces and implies, the second also. Technically however, in the form of the sentence here, the First is mainly in view. And to *see* that day, is to be present at, witness, it;—to have experience of it. **κ. εἶδεν κ. ἐχάρη**, viz. in his Paradisiacal state of bliss. Maldonatus has a striking note here (ii. 710): "Cum dicit, *vidit,* haud dubium quin eo modo vidisse dicat, quo videre dixerat tantopere concupivisse. Non autem concupiverat sola videre fide . . . . quia fide *jam* Christi diem *videbat.* . . . . Vidit ergo diem Christi *re ipsa,* quemadmodum et ille et patres omnes videre concupiverant. Non quod vivus viderit, sed quod mortuus Christum venisse noverit, tempusque illud exactum esse quod usque ad ejus adventum a Deo constitutum fuisse sciebat. Quod enim dicit, Exsultavit ut videret diem meum, perinde valet ac si diceret, Cupivit ut veniret dies meus: venit, et gavisus est. Quis enim dubitet Abraham et cæteros patres qui cum eo erant (sive ex revelatione, quam in hac vita habuissent, sive ex revelatione, quam tunc, quum Christus venit, habuerint de ejus adventu) *non ignorasse Christum venisse,* etiam antequam ad eos post mortem veniret?" Only that I would rather believe, as Stier does (iv. 444 f. edn. 2), that the 'seeing of Christ's day' was not *by revelation,* but *actual*—the seeing of a witness. 'Abraham then has not seen death, but lives through my word;—having believed and rejoiced in the promise of Me, whom he has now seen manifest in the flesh.' Meyer quotes the Socinian interpretation as a specimen of "monstrous perversion:" "*exultaturus fuisset . . . . et si vidisset, omnino fuisset gavisurus.*" **57.**] No inference can be drawn from this verse as to the age of our Lord at the time, according to the flesh. Fifty years was with the Jews the completion of manhood. The reading **τεσσαράκοντα**—found in Cod. Λ, and read by Chrys., of which Euthym. says, ὅπερ δοκεῖ ἀκριβέστερον,—has probably been introduced for that very reason. **58.**] As Lücke remarks, all unbiassed exegesis of these words must recognize in them a declaration of the essential præ-existence of Christ. All such interpretations of **πρὶν Ἀβραὰμ γενέσθαι,** as

p pres., ch i. 18. xiv. 9. xv. 27. Col. i. 17. Ps. lxxxix. 2. Jer. i. 5.
q Rev. xviii. 21.
r [ver. 7.] see Rev. xviii. 19.
s ch. xii. 36. Deut. vii. 20.
t Matt. ix. 9 reff.
u here only. Lev. xxv. 47 only.

ABCDE FGHK LMSU ΧΓΔΛ Πא 1. 33. 69

Ἀβραὰμ γενέσθαι [p] ἐγὼ εἰμί. 59 [q] ἦραν οὖν [q] λίθους ἵνα
[r] βάλωσιν ἐπ᾽ αὐτόν· Ἰησοῦς δὲ [s] ἐκρύβη καὶ ἐξῆλθεν ἐκ
τοῦ ἱεροῦ.
IX. 1 Καὶ [t] παράγων εἶδεν ἄνθρωπον τυφλὸν ἐκ [u] γενετῆς. 2 καὶ ἠρώτησαν αὐτὸν οἱ μαθηταὶ αὐτοῦ λέγοντες
Ῥαββί, τίς ἥμαρτεν, οὗτος ἢ οἱ γονεῖς αὐτοῦ, [v] ἵνα

v = Mark iv. 12. Luke ix. 45. ch. xii. 40.

om *γενεσθαι* D lat-*a b c e ff*$_2$ *l q* Ign(ad Magn 9) Epiph$_{sæpe}$ Ps-Ath [Cyr-p$_{expr}$] Orig-int Victorin Novat: ins ABCא rel vulg lat-*f* Orig$_3$ Eus$_2$ Iren-int.

59. for *ηραν ουν*, *τοτε ηραν* D. om *δε* B. rec aft *ιερου* ins *διελθων δια μεσου αυτων και παρηγεν ουτως* (*from Luke* iv. 30: *the last words to introduce ch* ix.), with A rel lat-*f q* syr [goth æth] Thdor-heracl; so, but ins *και* bef *διελθ.* and aft *αυτων* ins *επορευετο*, CLX א^{3a}(*επορ. κ. παρ. αυ.* erased but 1st *και* retained א^{3b}) [Syr (syr has *επορ.* with ast) copt] Ath Cyr[-p$_1$]: aft *εξηλθ.* ins *απ᾽ αυτων δια μεσου* 69: om BDא^1 latt sah arm Orig$_1$ Chr$_{appy}$ Cyr[-p$_1$].

Chap. IX. **1.** at end ins *καθημενον* D Ps-Ath$_1$.
2. om *αυτου λεγοντες* D lat-*e* [*l*].

"*before Abraham became Abraham,*" i. e. father of many nations (Socinus and others), and of **ἐγὼ εἰμί**, as "*I was predetermined, promised by God*" (Grotius and the Socinian interpreters), are little better than *dishonest quibbles.* The distinction between *γενέσθαι* and *εἰμί* is important. "Antequam *nasceretur* Abraham, ego *sum*" (Erasmus). The present **εἰμί** expresses *essential existence,* as in reff., especially Col. i. 17, and was often used by our Lord to assert His Divine Being. In this verse *the Godhead of Christ is involved;* and this the Jews *clearly understood, by their conduct to Him.* **59.**] Probably there were stones (for building) lying about in the outer court of the temple, where these words seem to have been spoken. The reason of the Jews' doing this is given by them on a similar occasion, ch. x. 33, *ὅτι σὺ ἄνθρωπος ὢν* **ποιεῖς σεαυτὸν θεόν.**

There does not appear to be any *miraculous* escape intended here, although certainly the assumption of one is natural under the circumstances. Jesus was probably surrounded by His disciples, and might thus hide himself (see ch. xii. 36), and go out of the temple.

Chap. IX. X.] Jesus the light, for the healing of the world and the judgment of the Jews. IX. 1—41.] *Manifestation of Jesus as the Light by a miracle. Judgment of the Jews by the healed man, and by Jesus.* **1.**] This, if the concluding words of ch. viii. in the rec. are genuine, would appear to have happened on the same day [as the incidents there related], which is hardly likely, for we should thus have the whole incidents from ch. vii. 37 (omitting ch. vii. 53—viii. 12), belonging to one day, and that day a sabbath (ver. 14). And besides, the circumstances under which Jesus here appears are too usual and tranquil to have succeeded immediately to His escape in ch. viii. 59. I would rather therefore suppose that there is a break before this verse: how long, we cannot of course say. Thus we have the commencement of a new narrative here, as in ch. vi. 1, and vii. 1. This is the view of Lücke, Tholuck, and De Wette; Olshausen, Meyer, and Stier believe it to have been the same day; and the former refers the *ἦν σάβ.* (ver. 14) to its being the last day of the feast (ch. vii. 37, where see note). The blind man was sitting begging (ver. 8), possibly proclaiming the fact of his having been so born; for otherwise the disciples could hardly have asked the following question. The incident may have been in the neighbourhood of the temple (Acts iii. 2): but doubtless there were other places where beggars sat, besides the temple entrances.

2.] According to Jewish ideas, every infirmity was the punishment of sin (see ver. 34). From Exod. xx. 5, and the prevailing views on the subject, the disciples may have believed that the man was visited for the sins of his parents: but how could *he himself have sinned* before his birth? Beza and Grotius refer the question to the doctrine of metempsychosis; that he may have sinned in a former state of existence; this however is disproved by Lightfoot and Lampe. The Pharisees believed that the *good souls only* passed into other bodies, which would exclude this case (see Jos. Antt. xviii.

τυφλὸς γεννηθῇ; 3 ἀπεκρίθη Ἰησοῦς Οὔτε οὗτος ἥμαρτεν οὔτε οἱ γονεῖς αὐτοῦ, ἀλλ' [w] ἵνα [x] φανερωθῇ τὰ ἔργα
τοῦ θεοῦ [x] ἐν αὐτῷ. 4 * ἐμὲ δεῖ [y] ἐργάζεσθαι τὰ ἔργα
τοῦ πέμψαντός με, [z] ἕως ἡμέρα ἐστίν· ἔρχεται νύξ, ὅτε
οὐδεὶς δύναται ἐργάζεσθαι. 5 [a] ὅταν ἐν τῷ κόσμῳ ὦ, [b] φῶς
εἰμι τοῦ κόσμου. 6 ταῦτα εἰπὼν [c] ἔπτυσεν [d] χαμαί, καὶ
ἐποίησεν [e] πηλὸν ἐκ τοῦ [f] πτύσματος, καὶ [g] ἐπέχρισεν

w = ch. xi. 4. Matt. i. 22 al
x so 1 John iv. 9.
y ch. iii. 21. Matt. xxvi. 10 reff. Num. viii. 19.
z ch. xxi. 22, 23. 1 Tim. iv. 13. see ch. xii. 35, 36. Xen. Anab. ii. 6. 2.
a = here only.
b Matt. v. 14. ch. i. 4. viii. 12.
c Mark vii. 33. viii. 23 only. Num. xii. 14. Sir. xxviii. 12 only.
d ch. xviii. 6 only. Job i. 20. Dan. viii. 12. Judith xii. 15. xiv. 18 only. see Esdr. viii. 91 (88).
e here bis. vv. 11, 14, 15. Rom. ix. 21 only. Job iv. 19.
f here only †.
g ver. 11 only †.

3. rec ins ο bef ιησ., with D [Π²(but erased)] Scr's i Cyr_1: om ABCℵ rel.

4. * ἡμᾶς B(D)Lℵ¹ [syr-jer] coptt æth-rom Cyr[-p_{expr}] Non_1: εμε AC ℵ-corr¹ or ² rel latt æth-pl Hil.—δει bef ημ. D. for με, ημας L ℵ¹(txt ℵ-corr¹ or ²) copt æth-rom Cyr[-p].

5. ω bef εν τω κοσμω DLX 1. 33 vulg lat-*a b g* [*e l*] Chr_1 Cyr_1.

6. for επεχρ., επεθηκεν B C¹(appy).

1. 3, and B. J. ii. 8. 14). Lightfoot, Lücke, and Meyer refer it to the possibility of sin *in the womb;* Tholuck to *predestinated sin,* punished by anticipation: De Wette to the general doctrine of the præ-existence of souls, which prevailed both among the Rabbis and Alexandrians: see Wisd. viii. 19, 20 (the applicability of which passage is doubted by Stier, iv. 455 note, edn. 2). So Isidore of Pelusium in the Catena (Lücke, ii. 372), οὗτος, **ὥς φασιν** Ἕλληνες,—ἢ οἱ γονεῖς αὐτοῦ, **ὥς φασιν Ἰουδαῖοι.** The question may have been asked vaguely without any strict application of it to the circumstances, merely taking for granted that *some sin* must have led to the blindness, and hardly thinking of the non-applicability of one of the suppositions to this case. Or perhaps, as Stier inclines to suppose, the **οὗτος, ἤ** may mean, 'this man, or, *for that is out of the question* (dieser selbst, oder, da uns dies doch nicht denkbar ist, ...), his parents?'
ἵνα as a *cause* why he should be . . . . ,—used τελικῶς:—not ἐκβατικῶς (Olsh.), expressing the mere consecution of events. **3.**] After **αὐτοῦ** supply **ἵνα τυφ. γεν.**: 'neither of these was the cause; but τυφ. ἐγεννήθη, in order that . . . .' But how so? οὐ κολαστικῶς, ἀλλ' οἰκονομικῶς. Euthym. In the economy of God's Providence, his suffering had its place and aim, and this was to bring out the **ἔργα τ. θεοῦ** in his being healed by the Redeemer (see Rom. xi. 11 and note). So Lücke:—De Wette denies the interpretation, and refers the saying merely to the view of our Lord to bring out his own practical design, to make use of this man to prove His divine power. But see ch. xi. 4, which is strictly parallel. **4.**] Connected by **ἐργάζ. τὰ ἔργα** to the former verse. There certainly seems to be some reference to its being the sabbath; see the similar expressions in ch. v. 17. From **ὅταν . . . .**, in ver. 5, it seems evident that **ἡμέρα** is the appointed course of the working of Jesus on earth, and **νύξ** the close of it (see the parallel, ch. xi. 9, 10). It is true, that, according to John's universal diction, the death of Jesus is ***His*** glorification; but the similitude *here* regards the *effect on the world,* see ver. 5; and the language of Rom. xiii. 12 is in accordance with it, as also Luke xxii. 53: John xiv. 30. **5.**] This partly explains the ἡμ. and νύξ of the former verse, partly alludes to the nature of the healing about to take place. As before the raising of Lazarus (ch. xi. 25), He states that He is *the Resurrection and the Life;* so now, He sets forth Himself as the source of the archetypal spiritual light, of which the natural, now about to be conferred, is only a derivation and symbol.
6.] See reff. Mark. The virtue especially of the saliva *jejuna,* in cases of disorders of the eyes, was well known to antiquity. Pliny, H. N. xxviii. 7, says, "Lippitudines matutina quotidie velut inunctione arceri." In both accounts (Suet. Vesp. 7: Tacitus, Hist. iv. 8) of the restoring of a blind man to sight attributed to Vespasian, the use of this remedy occurs. See also Wetstein in loc. (Trench, Miracles, 293 note, edn. 2). The use of clay also for healing the eyes was not unknown. Serenus Samonicus (in the time of Caracalla) says: "Si tumor insolitus typho se tollat inani, Turgentes oculos vili circumline cœno."

No rule can be laid down which our Lord may seem to have observed, as to using, or dispensing with, the ordinary human means of healing. He Himself determined by considerations which are

αὐτοῦ τὸν [e] πηλὸν ἐπὶ τοὺς ὀφθαλμούς, 7 καὶ εἶπεν αὐτῷ
Ὕπαγε [h] νίψαι [i] εἰς τὴν [k] κολυμβήθραν τοῦ Σιλωάμ, ὃ
[l] ἑρμηνεύεται ἀπεσταλμένος. ἀπῆλθεν οὖν καὶ [h] ἐνίψατο,
καὶ ἦλθεν βλέπων. 8 Οἱ οὖν [m] γείτονες καὶ οἱ θεωροῦντες
αὐτὸν [n] τὸ [n] πρότερον ὅτι [o] προςαίτης ἦν, ἔλεγον Οὐχ
οὗτός ἐστιν ὁ καθημενος καὶ [p] προςαιτῶν; 9 ἄλλοι ἔλεγον
ὅτι οὗτός ἐστιν· ἄλλοι ἔλεγον Οὐχί, ἀλλ᾽ ὅμοιος αὐτῷ

ABCDE FGHK LMSU ΧΓΔΛ ΠΝ 1. 33. 69

h vv. 11 bis, 15. ch. xiii. 5, &c. John, Gosp. only, exc. Matt. vi. 17. xv. 2 ‖ Mk. 1 Tim. v. 10. 2 Chron. iv. 6.
i Mark i. 9, 39. ch. i. 18 al.
k ch. v. 2, &c. only. Isa. vii. 3.
l ch. i. (39 v. r.) 43. Heb. vii. 2 only. Ezra iv. 7 only.
m Luke xiv. 12. xv. 6, 9 only. Ps. xxx. 11.
n ch. vi. 62 reff.
o Mark x. 46 only †.
p here (Mark x. 46 ‖ L. v. r.) only. Job xxvii. 14 only.

rec om *αυτου*, with C¹ rel latt Syr Ps-Ath: ins ABC²Lℵ 1. 33 copt (goth æth), *αυτω* D. rec aft *οφθαλμους* ins *του τυφλου*, with AC rel lat-*b e f* syrr: *αυτου* D lat-*a c* ff_2: om BLℵ 1. 33.

7. om *αυτω* D forj lat-*a e l*. om *νιψαι* A¹(ins aft *σιλωαμ* A²) lat-*a b*. **μεθερμηνευεται** D. om *ουν κ. ενιψ. κ. ηλθεν* (*homœotel*) B.

8. rec (for *προsαιτης*) *τυφλος*, with C³ rel: [*τυφλ. προsαιτης* Π¹:] *τυφλος ην και προsαιτης* 69 (lat-*a b c e l* syr-jer): txt ABC¹DKLX[Π²]ℵ 1. 33 vulg lat-*f* ff_2 *g* [*q*] syrr coptt goth æth arm Ps-Ath$_1$ Chr-comm$_1$ Cyr[-p$_1$].

9. om 1st *οτι* ℵ¹ 237 Scr's a [lat-*a b c e* ff_2 *l* Cyr$_1$ Ps-Ath$_1$]. for 2nd *αλλοι*, *ετεροι* D. rec (for *ελεγον ουχι αλλ᾽*) *δε οτι*, with AD rel lat-(*a c e* [ff_2 *q*]) *f* [*l*] syr

hidden from us. Whatever the means used, the healing was not in *them*, but in Him alone. The 'conductor' of the miraculous power was generally the *faith* of the recipient: and if such means served to awaken that faith, their use would be accounted for. 7.] The *reason* of his being sent to Siloam is uncertain. It may have been as *part of the cure*,—or merely to wash off the clay. The former is most probable, especially as the **εἰς** must be taken with *νίψαι*, not with *ὕπαγε*, and thus would imply immersion in the pool. So Athen. x. p. 438 F (in Meyer), *λούεσθαι εἰς λουτρῶνας*. A beggar blind from his birth would know the localities sufficiently to be able to find his way; so that there is no necessity to suppose a partial restoration of sight before his going. The situation of the fountain and pool of Siloam is very doubtful. Robinson makes both at the mouth of the ancient Tyropœon, S.E. of the city. He himself explored a subterranean passage from this spot to the Fountain of the Virgin higher up on the banks of the Kedron. Josephus, B. J. v. 4. 1, says, *ἡ δὲ τῶν τυροποιῶν προςαγορευομένη φάραγξ . . . καθήκει μέχρι Σιλωάμ· οὕτω γὰρ τὴν πηγήν, γλυκεῖάν τε καὶ πολλὴν οὖσαν, ἐκαλοῦμεν.* Jerome sets it "ad radices montis Zion" (on Isa. viii. 6), and mentions its intermittent character: but he also says (on Matt. x. 28), "ad radices montis Moria, *in quibus* Siloa fluit:" so that his testimony exactly agrees with Josephus and Robinson (see Robins. i. 493 ff., and The Land and the Book, pp. 659 ff.). It is mentioned Neh. iii. 15: Isa. viii. 6. On the subject of a recent suggestion respecting the identity of Siloam and Bethesda, see supplementary note at the end of this volume. **ὃ ἑρμ. ἀπεστ.**] The reason of this derivation (Σιλωάμ = שִׁלֹחַ) being stated has been much doubted. Some (e. g. Lücke) consider the words to have been inserted as an early gloss of some allegorical interpreter. But there is no external authority for this; every MS. and version containing them, except the Syr. and Pers. Euthym. says, *οἶμαι διὰ τὸν ἀπεσταλμένον ἐκεῖ τότε τυφλόν.* So also Nonnus: *ὕδωρ στελλομένοιο προώνυμον ἐκ σέο πομπῆς*: and Meyer takes this view. But it would be a violent transfer,—of the name of the fountain, to the man who was sent thither. I should rather regard the healing virtue imparted to the water to be denoted, as symbolical of *Him who was sent*, and whose mission it was to give the healing water of life. Aug., Chrys., Thl., Erasm., Beza, Calvin, &c., and Ebrard and Luthardt, similarly refer *ἀπεσταλ.* to the Lord Jesus: Stier, to the Holy Spirit,—but as one with, and proceeding from Christ. **ἦλθεν, came back**;—apparently to his own house, by the next verse. 8.] **θεωροῦντες** belongs to **τὸ πρότερον**, and thus expresses the present relatively to that time,—*οἳ ἦσαν τὸ πρότ. θεωροῦντες.* The choice of the word *θεωροῦντες* implies attention and habit. The reading *τυφλός* was most likely a correction of some one who thought *προsαίτης* did not express plainly enough the change in him. The question of identity would be much more likely to turn on whether

ἐστιν. ἐκεῖνος ἔλεγεν ὅτι q ἐγώ εἰμι. 10 ἔλεγον οὖν
αὐτῷ Πῶς [οὖν] r ἠνεῴχθησάν σου οἱ r ὀφθαλμοί; 11 ἀπεκρίθη ἐκεῖνος [Ὁ] ἄνθρωπος [ὁ] λεγόμενος Ἰησοῦς
s πηλὸν ἐποίησεν καὶ t ἐπέχρισέν μου τοὺς ὀφθαλμοὺς καὶ
...ειπε C. εἶπέν μοι Ὕπαγε εἰς τὸν Σιλωὰμ καὶ u νίψαι. ἀπελθὼν
οὖν καὶ u νιψάμενος v ἀνέβλεψα. 12 εἶπαν αὐτῷ Ποῦ ἐστιν
ἐκεῖνος; λέγει Οὐκ οἶδα. 13 Ἄγουσιν αὐτὸν πρὸς τοὺς
Φαρισαίους τὸν w ποτὲ τυφλόν. 14 ἦν δὲ σάββατον ἐν
ᾗ ἡμέρᾳ τὸν s πηλὸν ἐποίησεν ὁ Ἰησοῦς καὶ r ἀνέῳξεν
αὐτοῦ τοὺς r ὀφθαλμούς. 15 πάλιν οὖν ἠρώτων αὐτὸν

q constr., ch. xviii. 6.
r Matt. ix. 30. xx. 33. ch. x. 21. xi. 37. Isa. xxxv. 5.
s ver. 6 reff.
t ver. 6 only.
u ver. 7 reff.
v = Matt. xi. 5 al.‡ but see 1 Kings xiv. 27. Isa. xlii. 18. (-ψις, Luke iv. 18.)
w = Rom. vii. 9. xi. 30. Gal. i. 13, 23 al.

goth: txt BCLXℵ 1. 33 vulg lat-*b g* Syr syr-mg [syr-jer] coptt æth arm Cyr_1. [Of these ℵ syr-mg syr-jer copt arm retain δε.]—(αλλα C.) aft εκεινος ins δε AC^2KUX[ΓΠ] $ℵ^1$ (marked for erasure, but marks removed) 33. 69 latt Syr syr-w-ast [syr-jer] coptt æth arm: om BC^1D rel am(with forj san) syr goth Cyr. om last οτι $Lℵ^{corr}$ lat-*a b c e* ff_2.

10. for ελεγον, ειπον D lat-*b*: ελεγαν $ℵ^1$. aft 1st ουν ins οι ιουδαιοι $ℵ^1$(marked for erasure *eadem manu*). rec om 2nd ουν, with AB rel vulg lat-*b c e f* ff_2 *g* [*q* Syr] coptt goth: ins CDLXℵ lat-*a l* syr-w-ast [syr-jer] arm. rec ανεωχθησαν, with AKU[Π] Chr Cyr: txt B(sic: see table) CDℵ rel. [S ?] elz σοι, with (Scr's a o, e sil) vulg lat-*a c e f* ff_2 *g* [*l q*] D-lat: txt ABC D-gr ℵ rel foss(with tol) lat-*b* syrr syr-jer [goth æth] arm Chr Cyr Thl Aug_1.

11. rec aft εκεινος ins και ειπεν, with A rel lat-*a b f* [*q*] syrr syr-jer copt goth æth: om BCDLℵ 1. 33 vulg lat-*c e* ff_2 *l* sah arm Cyr_1 Aug_1. rec om ὁ (twice), with AD rel goth arm: om 1st ὁ C: ins BLℵ 1. 33 vulg lat-*c e* [*l*] syr-w-ast. aft μοι ins οτι BLℵ syr-jer coptt: om AD rel latt. rec (for τον) την κολυμβηθραν του, with A rel vulg lat-*e f g* [*q*] syr goth æth Chr_1 [$Ps\text{-}Ath_1$]: txt BDLXℵ 1 lat-*a b c* ff_2 [*l*] syr-jer coptt arm Cyr_1 $Iren\text{-}int_1$. rec (for ουν) δε, with A rel syr[-txt] goth: txt BDLXℵ 1. 33 syr-mg coptt Cyr_1. (B does not omit και bef νιψαμενος: see table.) for last clause, απηλθον ουν και ενιψαμην και ηλθον βλεπων D.

12. (ειπαν, so BDℵ.) rec aft ειπ. ins ουν, with D rel foss lat-*a c* [ff_2 *q* goth] syr: pref και BLXℵ 1. 33 vulg-ed lat-*l* [syr-jer] æth Cyr_1: om A am(with forj ing) lat-*e* Syr coptt arm Aug. aft λεγει ins αυτοις D 69 foss lat-*b* Syr [syr-jer] æth arm.

13. ins και bef αγουσιν D [lat-*c* syr-jer] Syr æth.

14. rec (for εν η ημερα) οτε, with AD rel vulg lat-*e f* [*l q*] syrr coptt goth: txt BLXℵ 33 mm lat-*a b c* ff_2^* *g* syr-mg [syr-jer] Cyr_1. for ανεωξεν, ηνυξεν (i. e. ηνοιξεν) D 249.

15. επηρωτων D.

he was really *the person who had sat and begged* (the blindness being involved in it), than on the fact of his having been blind.

11.] ἀνέβλ., strictly speaking, is inappropriate in the case of one *born* blind. Lücke refers to Aristotle as using the word thus, and cites Pausanias, who speaks of Ὀφιονέα . . . . τὸν ἐκ γενετῆς τυφλόν, whom ἐπέλαβε τῆς κεφαλῆς ἄλγημα ἰσχυρόν, καὶ **ἀνέβλεψεν** ἀπ' αὐτοῦ. Sight being natural to men, the deprivation of it is regarded as a *loss*, and the reception of it, though never enjoyed before, as a *recovery*. So Grotius: "nec male *recipere* quis dicitur, quod communiter tributum humanæ naturæ ipsi abfuit." There is no emphasis on μου here (as Bp. Wordsw.) nor in vv. 15, 30: nor on σου in vv. 10, 17, 26. See on Matt. xvi. 18, and compare Luke xii. 18. 13.] The neighbours appear to have brought him to the *Pharisees*, out of hostility to Jesus (see ver. 12): and ver. 14 alleges the reason of this:—or perhaps from fear of the sentence alluded to in ver. 22. The '*Pharisees*' here may have been the court presiding over the synagogue, or one of the lesser local courts of Sanhedrim. Lücke inclines to think they were an assembly of the great Sanhedrim, whom John sometimes names οἱ Φαρ.: see ch. vii. 47; xi. 46: Meyer regards them as some formal section of the *Pharisees, as a body*: but were there such? 14.] Lightf. cites from a Rabbinical treatise on the Sabbath, "sputum etiam super palpebras poni prohibitum." But the *making the clay*, as a servile work, seems to be here prominently mentioned. Meyer notices,—and it is interesting, as a minute mark of accuracy,—that the man only relates what he himself, as being blind, had felt: he says nothing of the spittle. 15.] **πάλιν** refers to ver. 10. The enquiry was official,

καὶ οἱ Φαρισαῖοι πῶς [v] ἀνέβλεψεν. ὁ δὲ εἶπεν αὐτοῖς ABDEF GHKL MSUX ΓΔΛΠℵ
[s] Πηλὸν ἐπέθηκέν μου ἐπὶ τοὺς ὀφθαλμούς, καὶ [u] ἐνιψάμην,
καὶ βλέπω. 16 ἔλεγον οὖν ἐκ τῶν Φαρισαίων τινὲς Οὐκ 1. 33. 69
[x] ἔστιν οὗτος παρὰ θεοῦ ὁ ἄνθρωπος, ὅτι τὸ σάββατον
οὐ [y] τηρεῖ. ἄλλοι ἔλεγον Πῶς δύναται [z] ἄνθρωπος ἁμαρτωλὸς τοιαῦτα [a] σημεῖα ποιεῖν; καὶ [b] σχίσμα ἦν ἐν αὐτοῖς.
17 λέγουσιν οὖν τῷ τυφλῷ πάλιν Τί σὺ λέγεις περὶ
αὐτοῦ [c] ὅτι ἠνέῳξέν σου τοὺς [d] ὀφθαλμούς; ὁ δὲ εἶπεν
ὅτι προφήτης ἐστίν. 18 οὐκ [e] ἐπίστευσαν οὖν οἱ Ἰουδαῖοι
περὶ αὐτοῦ, ὅτι ἦν τυφλὸς καὶ [f] ἀνέβλεψεν, [g] ἕως ὅτου
[h] ἐφώνησαν τοὺς γονεῖς αὐτοῦ τοῦ [f] ἀναβλέψαντος 19 καὶ
ἠρώτησαν αὐτοὺς λέγοντες Οὗτός ἐστιν ὁ υἱὸς ὑμῶν, [i] ὃν
ὑμεῖς λέγετε ὅτι τυφλὸς ἐγεννήθη; πῶς οὖν βλέπει
[k] ἄρτι; 20 ἀπεκρίθησαν οἱ γονεῖς αὐτοῦ καὶ εἶπαν Οἴδαμεν
ὅτι οὗτός ἐστιν ὁ υἱὸς ἡμῶν καὶ ὅτι τυφλὸς ἐγεννήθη·
21 πῶς δὲ νῦν βλέπει οὐκ οἴδαμεν, ἢ τίς [d] ἤνοιξεν αὐτοῦ
τοὺς [d] ὀφθαλμοὺς ἡμεῖς οὐκ οἴδαμεν· αὐτὸν ἐρωτήσατε,

x ch. vii. 29 reff.
y = ch. viii. 51 al.
z = Matt. xiii. 45, 52. xviii. 23 al.
= ch. ii. 11 reff.
b Mark ii. 21 reff.
c = ch. ii. 18.
d vv. 10, 14 reff.
e constr., here only. see ch. xiv. 10. Acts ix. 26.
f vv. 11, 15.
g Luke xv. 8 reff.
h = Matt. xx 32 reff.
i constr., ch. viii. 54. x. 36. Gal. v. 21.
k Matt. iii. 15 al.

rec *επι τους οφθ.* bef *μου*, with D (33, e sil) lat-*a b* [Syr syr-jer arm]: *μου επεθηκεν επι τους οφθαλμους* A vulg: txt BLℵ rel. (Δ doubtful: *μοι* H.)

16. [*ελεγαν* ℵ[1].] rec (for *ουκ* to *ο ανθρωπος*) *ουτος ο ανθρωπος ουκ εστι παρα του θεου*, with A rel [lat-*a b f q* syrr coptt goth æth], but of these AGK[Π] 69 om *του*: *ο ανθρ.* bef *ουτ. π. θεου* 33 vulg lat-*c e* [*ff*$_2$ *g*] arm [Orig-int$_1$]: txt BDLXℵ lat-*l* [syr-jer Cyr$_1$]. aft *αλλοι* ins *δε* BDℵ 1. 69 vulg-ed(not am) lat-*c* [*ff*$_2$ syr-jer] Syr coptt.

17. for *λεγουσιν*, *ελεγον* D lat-*a b c e*. rec om *ουν*, with E rel lat-*q* Syr copt goth [æth arm]: ins ABDLXℵ 1. 69 latt syr-w-ast Cyr$_1$. ins *ποτε* bef *τυφλω* ℵ. om *παλιν* D lat-*a b c ff*$_2$. aft *παλιν* ins *ουν* ℵ[1]. rec *συ* bef *τι*, with AD rel vss: txt BLXℵ copt Cyr$_1$. for *αυτου*, *σεαυτου* ℵ: *εαυτου* D-gr. rec *ηνοιξεν*, with ADℵ rel: *ανεωξεν* KL[Π] 1: txt BXΔ. (33 def.)

18. om *ουν* D 69 ev-y lat-*a b f ff*$_2$ *l* copt (æth arm). rec *τυφλος* bef *ην* (*more usual order*), with A rel vulg lat-*a c e f ff*$_2$: txt BLℵ lat-*b* copt Chr$_1$. (33 def.)—om *οτι* to *ανεβλ.* D [lat-*l*]. for *οτου*, *ου* DX Chr$_1$. om 2nd *αυτου* D ev-54 sah-mnt arm.

19. *επηρωτησαν* D. for *λεγοντες*, *ει* ℵ[1](lat-*a b c ff*$_2$ *l*) Syr. for *ουτος εστιν*, *ει εστιν ουτος* D. rec *αρτι* bef *βλεπει*, with A rel vulg lat-*a e f g* [*q*]: txt BDL U(Treg, expr) ℵ 33 lat-*b c ff*$_2$ *l* Cyr$_1$.

20. aft *απεκρ.* ins *ουν* Bℵ; *δε* A rel lat-*f q* syrr goth: om DGLUX[Π 1. 33] 69 latt coptt [arm]. rec ins *αυτοις* bef *οι γονεις*, with AD rel vulg lat-*b c* [*l q*] syr (sah) goth: om BLXℵ 33. 69 lat-*a e f ff*$_2$ Syr copt æth arm Cyr. (*ειπαν*, so BLℵ 33.)

21. *ηνεωξεν* A 1. 33: txt BDLℵ rel. *αυτου* bef *ηνοιξεν* D [vulg] lat-*b* (*f*). rec aft 2nd *οιδαμεν* ins *αυτος*, with Aℵ[1] rel lat-*q* Syr goth: om B(sic: see table) DLXℵ[3a] 1. 33 latt [syr syr-jer] æth Ps-Ath Cyr.—rec *ηλικιαν εχει* bef *αυτον ερωτησατε*

as addressed to the chief witness in the matter. We cannot hence infer with Lücke that no one else was present at the healing but Jesus and His disciples.

16. τινὲς . . ἄλλοι] Among the latter party would be such as Nicodemus, Joseph, (Gamaliel?); who probably (Joseph certainly, Luke xxiii. 51) at last withdrew, and left the majority to carry out their hate against Jesus. **17.]** The question is but *one*, as in E. V., **What sayest thou of him, that he hath opened** (i. e. for having opened) **thine eyes?** The stress is on **σύ**—'What hast *thou* to say to it, seeing we are divided on the matter?' Both parties are anxious to have the man's own view to corroborate theirs. **προφ.**, and therefore παρὰ τοῦ θεοῦ. **18.]** The hostile party (**οἱ Ἰουδαῖοι**,—those in authority among these variously-minded Pharisees), disappointed at his direct testimony against them, betake themselves to sifting more closely *the evidence of the fact*. The parents are summoned as wit-

[l] ἡλικίαν [m] ἔχει· αὐτὸς περὶ αὐτοῦ λαλήσει. 22 ταῦτα
εἶπον οἱ γονεῖς αὐτοῦ, ὅτι ἐφοβοῦντο τοὺς Ἰουδαίους·
ἤδη γὰρ [n] συνετέθειντο οἱ Ἰουδαῖοι ἵνα ἐάν τις αὐτὸν
[o] ὁμολογήσῃ χριστὸν [p] ἀποσυνάγωγος γένηται. 23 διὰ
τοῦτο οἱ γονεῖς αὐτοῦ εἶπαν ὅτι [l] ἡλικίαν [m] ἔχει, αὐτὸν
ἐρωτήσατε. 24 [q] ἐφώνησαν οὖν τὸν ἄνθρωπον [r] ἐκ δευτέρου ὃς ἦν τυφλός, καὶ εἶπαν αὐτῷ [s] Δὸς δόξαν τῷ θεῷ·
ἡμεῖς οἴδαμεν ὅτι ὁ ἄνθρωπος οὗτος ἁμαρτωλός ἐστιν.
25 ἀπεκρίθη οὖν ἐκεῖνος [t] Εἰ ἁμαρτωλός ἐστιν οὐκ οἶδα·
ἓν οἶδα, ὅτι τυφλὸς ὢν [u] ἄρτι βλέπω. 26 εἶπον οὖν
αὐτῷ Τί ἐποίησέν σοι; πῶς [v] ἤνοιξέν σου τοὺς [v] ὀφθαλμούς;

l = Matt. vi. 27 reff.
m = ch. viii. 57 reff.
n Luke xxii. 5. Acts xxiii. 20 (xxiv. 9 v. r.) only. 1 Kings xxii. 13.
o = and constr., Wisd. xviii. 13. see Rom. x. 9. 1 John iv. 2, 3. 2 John 7.
p ch. xii. 42. xvi. 2 only †.
q ver. 18.
r Matt. xxvi. 42 reff.
s Luke xvii. 18. Acts xii. 23. Rom. iv. 20. Rev. xi. 13 al. Josh. vii. 19.
t = Acts xix. 2. 1 Cor. i. 16. vii. 16. Joel ii. 14. Jonah iii. 9.
u ver. 19.
v vv. 10, &c.

(*as in ver* 23), with A rel syrr goth: om αυτ. ερωτησ. $\aleph^1$ lat-*b* sah [Chr$_1$]: txt BDL X$\aleph^{3a}$ **1.** 33 vulg lat-*a c e f g* [syr-jer] copt æth arm.—επερωτησατε D. om αυτος $\aleph^1$. for αὑτου, εαυτου ABEKMX[Γ]Λℵ **1.** 33: txt D rel.

22. (ειπαν ℵ.) for συνετεθειντο, συνετεθεντο AM syr-mg-gr: συνετιθεντο G[Γ] 247-51 Scr's k ev-y [Cyr$_1$]: συνετιθοντο 69. ομολ. bef αυτον DK 69. aft χριστον ins ειναι D lat-*e* [Cyr-p$_2$].

23. (ειπαν, so BDℵ.) om οτι DL fuld lat-*a c e l* æth. om εχει $\aleph^1$. ins και bef αυτον A. επερωτησατε Bℵ: ερωτατε D.

24. rec εκ δευτ. bef τον ανθρ., with A rel vulg lat-*a f* syr [syr-jer æth] goth: txt B(D)Lℵ 33 lat-*b c e ff$_2$ l q* Syr coptt.—for ανθρωπον, αυτον D. (ειπαν, so BDℵ.) ουτος bef ο ανθρ. BL(ℵ) latt Syr [syr-jer] goth Chr$_1$ [Cyr-p$_2$]: txt AD rel lat-*e* Syr. ο [is insd bef αμαρτ. but] marked for erasure by $\aleph^1$(or -corr^1)$^{\cdot 3}$.

25. rec aft εκεινος ins και ειπεν, with E rel Syr [syr-jer] copt æth Chr: om ABDLℵ **1.** 33 latt syr sah goth arm Cyr$_1$. aft εν ins δε $\aleph^1$ [copt Ps-Ath$_1$]. for ων, ημην και DL **1.** 33 lat-*a e f ff$_2$* [*l q* syr-jer] Syr *Cyr*[-p].

26. (ειπαν ℵ.) rec (for ουν) δε, with A rel syr æth: om $\aleph^1$ lat-*a e* Syr copt arm: txt BDKLX$\aleph^{3a}$ **1.** 33. 69 vulg lat-*b c* [*f ff$_2$ g q* sah] goth Cyr$_1$. rec aft αυτω ins παλιν, with A$\aleph^{3a}$ rel lat-*f q* syrr goth arm [æth Cyr$_1$]: om BD$\aleph^1$ latt coptt [syr-jer] Non$_1$. εποιησαν $\aleph^1$(txt ℵ-corr^1, see Tischdf's Cod. Sin., large edn). ins και bef πως D lat-*c* æth.

nesses. **19.**] The question is threefold, and in strict legal formality: 'Is this your son? Was he born blind? How is it that he now sees?' **21.**] Notice the emphatic **αὐτοῦ—ἡμεῖς—αὐτόν—αὐτός.** **22.**] It is not said when this resolution was come to; and this also speaks for an interval between ch. vii. viii., and this incident. It could hardly have been before the council at the conclusion of ch. vii. **ἀποσυν.**] Probably the first of the three stages of Jewish excommunication,—the being shut out from the synagogue and household for thirty days, but without any anathema. The other two,—the repetition of the above, accompanied by a curse,—and final exclusion,—would be too harsh, and perhaps were not in use so early. Trench (Mirr. 299, edn. 2) regards the resolution not as a token that the Sanhedrim had pronounced Him a false Christ, but as shewing that they forbade a private man to anticipate their decision on this point by confessing Him (?). **24. δὸς δ. τ. θεῷ**] Not, 'Give God the praise' (E. V.), i. e. 'the glory of thy healing:' for the Pharisees want to overawe the man by their authority, and make him deny the miracle altogether. The words are a form of *adjuration* (see ref. Josh.), *to tell the truth,* q. d. 'Remember that you are in God's presence, and speak as unto Him.'

25. ὤν] See on ver. 8. The man shrewdly evades the inference and states again the simple fact. Bear in mind, that **ὤν** must here be strictly kept to its *present sense,* as being joined with a *present verb* βλέπω: the rule for the construction of a pres. part. being, that it is contemporaneous with the verb which rules the time of the sentence. So that we must render, not '*whereas I* WAS *blind, now I see,*' as E. V.: but as A. V. R., **being a blind man** [or, **though a blind man**], **now I see.** The shrewd and naïve disposition of the man furnishes the key to the ænigmatical expression. He puts it to them as the problem, the fact of which he knows for certain but the reason of which it was for them to solve, that he, whom they all

27 ἀπεκρίθη αὐτοῖς Εἶπον ὑμῖν ἤδη, καὶ οὐκ [w] ἠκούσατε·
τί πάλιν θέλετε ἀκούειν; [x] μὴ καὶ ὑμεῖς θέλετε αὐτοῦ
μαθηταὶ γενέσθαι; 28 [y] ἐλοιδόρησαν αὐτὸν καὶ εἶπον Σὺ
μαθητὴς εἶ ἐκείνου, ἡμεῖς δὲ τοῦ Μωυσέως ἐσμὲν μαθηταί.
29 ἡμεῖς οἴδαμεν ὅτι Μωυσεῖ [z] λελάληκεν ὁ θεός, τοῦτον
δὲ οὐκ οἴδαμεν [a] πόθεν ἐστίν. 30 ἀπεκρίθη ὁ ἄνθρωπος
καὶ εἶπεν αὐτοῖς Ἐν τούτῳ [b] γὰρ [c] θαυμαστόν ἐστιν, ὅτι
ὑμεῖς οὐκ οἴδατε [a] πόθεν ἐστίν, καὶ [v] ἀνέῳξέν μου τοὺς
[v] ὀφθαλμούς. 31 οἴδαμεν ὅτι ὁ θεὸς ἁμαρτωλῶν οὐκ ἀκούει,
ἀλλ' ἐάν τις [d] θεοσεβὴς ᾖ καὶ τὸ [e] θέλημα αὐτοῦ [e] ποιῇ,
τούτου ἀκούει. 32 [f] ἐκ τοῦ [f] αἰῶνος οὐκ [g] ἠκούσθη ὅτι
[v] ἤνοιξέν τις [v] ὀφθαλμοὺς τυφλοῦ γεγεννημένου. 33 εἰ μὴ
ἦν οὗτος [h] παρὰ θεοῦ, οὐκ ἠδύνατο ποιεῖν οὐδέν. 34 ἀπεκρίθησαν καὶ εἶπαν αὐτῷ [i] Ἐν [i] ἁμαρτίαις σὺ ἐγεννήθης
[k] ὅλος, καὶ σὺ διδάσκεις ἡμᾶς; καὶ [l] ἐξέβαλον αὐτὸν [l] ἔξω.

...γαρ H.
ABDE FGKL MSUX ΓΔΛΠℵ 1. 33. 69

w = ch. viii. 43 reff.
x ch. vii. 47, 52.
y Acts xxiii. 4. 1 Cor. iv. 12. 1 Pet. ii. 23 only. Deut. xxxiii. 8. (-ρος, 1 Cor. v. 11. -ρία, 1 Tim. v. 14.)
z Exod. iv. 30 al. fr.
a ch. vii. 27 bis, 28 reff.
b = ch. vii. 41. Matt. xxvii. 23.
c Matt. xxi. 42 || Mk., from Ps. cxvii. 23. (2 Cor. xi. 14 v. r.) 1 Pet. ii. 9. Rev. xv. 1, 3 only. Exod. xxxiv. 10.
d here only. Exod. xviii. 21. (-βεια, 1 Tim. ii. 10.)
e Matt. vii. 21 reff. Ps. xxxix. 8.
f here only. ἀπ' αἰ., Luke i. 70. Acts iii. 21. xv. 18. Isa. lxiv. 4.
g = Mark ii. 1 reff.
h ch. vii. 29 reff.
i ch. viii. 24 bis. 1 Cor. xv. 17.
k ch. vii. 23.
l ch. vi. 37 reff. 2 Chron. xxix. 16.

27. for απεκρ. αυτ., ο δε ειπεν D. aft τι ins ουν B æth. θελετε bef παλιν D lat-*a e* syr. ακουσαι D. μαθηται bef αυτου DLX[Γ]Δℵ 33 latt Chr_1 *Cyr*[-p]: txt AB rel.

28. rec aft ελοιδ. ins ουν, with 69 vulg-ed lat-*c* goth: pref και Bℵ[1] [syr-jer] sah æth Cyr_1 $Ambr_1$: pref οι δε DLℵ[3a] 1. 33 (lat-*a f*) Syr syr-w-ast copt: om A rel am(with fuld em forj foss ing jac tol) [arm] Aug_1. (ειπαν Dℵ.) rec ει bef μαθητης, with E rel lat-*e f g* [*l*] *q* goth æth arm Chr_1 $Ps\text{-}Ath_1$: εκεινου bef ει D 157(Sz) latt: om ει L copt: txt ABℵ 1 (33) Chr-mss [$Cyr\text{-}p_3$]. om δε D lat-*b c e* ff_2 *l* [goth] arm.

29. for λελ., ελαλησεν A. aft ο θεος ins και οτι θεος(ο θεος D-corr[1]) αμαρτωλων ουκ ακουει D.

30. om αυτοις D 59 lat-*b c* [*e l* æth]. rec γαρ bef τουτω, with A rel: txt BLℵ vulg lat-*f g* syr Chr_1 Cyr_1.—for γαρ, ουν D [Syr]. ins το bef θαυμαστον BLℵ 1. 33 Chr_1 Cyr_1: om AD rel arm. ηνοιξεν BDLℵ Cyr[-p_2]: ηνεωξεν X: txt A rel.

31. rec aft οιδαμεν ins δε, with A rel vulg lat-*f* syrr [syr-jer æth] goth; γαρ 69 Hil_1: om BDGLℵ 1. 33 foss lat-*a b c e* ff_2 *l* coptt arm Cyr_1. rec αμαρτωλων bef ο θεος, with Aℵ rel vulg lat-*b c f* [ff_2 *g l q* syr-jer] syr æth arm $Orig\text{-}int_1$ Hil_1: txt BDΛ lat-*a e* Syr coptt goth arm Chr_1 $Cypr_1$. [αλλα B.]

32. ηνεωξεν BXΔ Ath_1. οφθαλμου A. γεγενημ. AX[Γ].

33. ουτος παρα θεου bef ην D sah.

34. (ειπαν, so BDℵ.) αυτω bef κ. ειπ. D lat-*a*.

knew as a blind man, now saw. So that the ὢν carries not so much present matter of fact, as common designation and title.

26.] They perhaps are trying to shake his evidence,—or to make him state something which should bring out some stronger violation of the sabbath.

27.] **οὐκ ἠκούσατε** must be in its special meaning of 'did not heed it.' The latter clause is of course ironical: 'you seem so anxious to hear particulars about Him, that you must surely be intending to become His disciples.' **29.**] **λελάληκεν**, not ἐλάλησεν, is important: it betokens the abiding finality of God's revelation to Moses, in their estimation: q. d. '*We stand by* God's revelation to Moses.' **πόθεν**—'whether from God or not.' But see ch. vii. 27, 28, where a very different reason is given for disbelieving Him to be the Christ.

30.] **ἐν τ. γάρ** is well expressed in E. V., **Why herein is** &c. Cf. Klotz, p. 242: "γάρ respicit ad ea quæ alter antea dixerat, et continet cum affirmatione conclusionem, quæ ex rebus ita comparatis facienda sit." **ὑμεῖς**, you, whose business it is to know such things. **31.**] He expresses a general popular conviction, that one who could do these things, must be a *pious man:* and (ver. 32) *very eminently so*, since this miracle was unprecedented. Ver. 32, says Meyer, is the minor proposition: ver. 33, the conclusion;

35 Ἤκουσεν ὁ Ἰησοῦς ὅτι [l] ἐξέβαλον αὐτὸν [l] ἔξω· καὶ εὑρὼν
αὐτὸν εἶπεν [αὐτῷ] Σὺ [m] πιστεύεις [m] εἰς τὸν υἱὸν τοῦ * θεοῦ;
36 ἀπεκρίθη ἐκεῖνος [καὶ εἶπεν] [n] Καὶ τίς ἐστιν, κύριε, ἵνα
[m] πιστεύσω εἰς αὐτόν; 37 εἶπεν αὐτῷ ὁ Ἰησοῦς Καὶ ἑώρακας
αὐτόν, καὶ ὁ [o] λαλῶν μετὰ σοῦ ἐκεῖνός ἐστιν. 38 ὁ δὲ ἔφη
[p] Πιστεύω, κύριε. καὶ [q] προσεκύνησεν αὐτῷ. 39 καὶ εἶπεν
ὁ Ἰησοῦς Εἰς [r] κρῖμα ἐγὼ εἰς τὸν κόσμον τοῦτον ἦλθον,
ἵνα οἱ μὴ [s] βλέποντες βλέπωσιν καὶ οἱ βλέποντες [t] τυφλοὶ
γένωνται. 40 ἤκουσαν ἐκ τῶν Φαρισαίων ταῦτα οἱ μετ'

m ch. ii. 11 reff.
n interrog., Luke x. 29. xviii. 26. 1 Cor. v. 2. 2 Cor. ii. 2.
o ch. iv. 27. Mark vi. 50.
p Mark ix. 24.
q Matt. viii. 2 al. fr.
r Matt. vii. 2. 1 Tim. iii. 6 al. Job xiii. 18.
s Matt. xiii. 13, 14, from Isa. vi. 9.
t = Matt. xv. 14 al.

35. ins *και* bef *ηκουσεν* Dℵ[1] Syr æth. om *ὁ* Bℵ[1]. om *εξω* D. *ευρεν* and aft *αυτον* ins *και* D lat-*a b q* Syr. om *αυτω* BDℵ[1] lat-*e* copt-ms : ins A rel [vss].
* ἀνθρώπου BDℵ sah æth-rom Chr-2-mss$_1$: *θεου* A rel latt syrr [syr-jer] copt goth æth-pl arm Tert$_1$ Hil$_2$.
36. om *απεκρ.* to *ειπεν*, and aft *εστιν* ins *εφη*, B : *και ειπεν* is also omd in A 68 lat-*a* copt-wilk : ins Dℵ rel vss. rec om *και* (bef *τις*), with AL latt [Syr coptt sah Chr$_1$] : ins BD [ℵ(above the line 1. m.)] rel syr goth arm Chr$_2$ Cyr$_1$.—*κε̄* bef *και τις εστιν* ℵ. (*κυριε and και were easily confounded by the scribes, each being frequently written κε.*)
37. for *ειπεν*, *απεκριθη* D syr-mg : *εφη* ℵ. rec aft *ειπ.* ins *δε*, with A rel lat-*q* goth : om BDXℵ 33 lat-*a b e* syrr [syr-jer] coptt arm. om 1st *ὁ* A. *μετα σου* bef *λαλων* D [lat-*l*] Hil$_2$.
38. om ver ℵ[1]. *αυτον* D Scr's e.
39. om *και ειπ. ο ιησ.* ℵ[1](om *ο* ℵ[3a]). *εγω* bef *εις κριμα* D. *ηλθον* bef *εις τ. κοσμ. τουτ.* D lat-*a b c f* [*q*] æth (arm) Orig-int$_{aliq}$.
40. rec ins *και* bef *ηκουσαν*, with A rel latt syrr [syr-jer] goth æth : add *δε* D lat-*ff*$_2$ *g*$_1$: om BLXℵ 33 coptt arm Cyr$_1$. om *ταυτα* D ℵ[1](ins ℵ[3a], but erased) 253 lat-*ff*$_2$

both in a popular form. **33.**] **οὐδέν,** nothing of this kind, much less such a thing as this. **34.**] See on ver. 2. **ὅλος, altogether,**—deeply and entirely, as thy infirmity proved. "They forget that the two charges,—one that he had never been born blind, and so was an impostor,—the other, that he bore the mark of God's anger in a blindness that reached back to his birth,—will not agree together." (Trench, Mirr. 305, edn. 2, note.) **ἐξέβ.**] They excommunicated him : see on ver. 22. It cannot merely mean, '*they cast him out of the court*' (Chrys., Mald., Grot., Fritzsche, Tholuck, Meyer); see next verse, where it would hardly be stated that Jesus heard of it, unless it had been some public formal act. **35.**] "Tune ille es, qui propter fidem in Jesum quem dicunt Christum, acerbitatem nostrorum magistrorum expertus est? An tu post has molestias etiamnum in filium Dei credis?" Lampe in loc. **36.**] This **υἱὸς τ. θεοῦ** surpasses his present comprehension : and therefore, true to his simple and guileless character, he asks for further information about Him. **καὶ τίς**] See reff. and Mark x. 26. **37.**] These words **καὶ ἑώρακας αὐτ.** serve to remind the man of the benefit he has received, and to awaken in him the liveliest gratitude : compare Luke ii. 30. They do not refer to a *former seeing*, when he was healed : this was the first time that he had *seen* his Benefactor. **39.**] There seems to be an interval between the last verse and this, and the narrative appears to be taken up again at some subsequent time when this miracle became again the subject of discourse. The blind man had recovered sight in two senses,—bodily and spiritual. And as our Lord always treats of the spiritual as paramount, *including* the bodily, so here He proceeds to speak of spiritual sight. **κρῖμα,** the effect of *κρίσις*, not merely *distinction*, but **judgment**; the following out of the divine *εὐδοκία*, Matt. xi. 25, 26. "We are all, according to the spirit of nature, no better than persons born blind; and to know and confess this our blindness, is our first and only true *sight*, out of which the grace of the Lord can afterwards bring about a complete *receiving of sight*. The '*becoming blind*,' on the other hand, is partly an ironical expression for remaining blind, but partly also has a real meaning in the increasing darkening and hardening which takes place through unbelief." (Stier, iv. 568; 475, edn. 2.) The **βλέ-**

αὐτοῦ ὄντες, καὶ εἶπον αὐτῷ [u] Μὴ καὶ ἡμεῖς τυφλοί ἐσμεν; ABDE
41 εἶπεν αὐτοῖς ὁ Ἰησοῦς Εἰ τυφλοὶ ἦτε, οὐκ ἂν [v] εἴχετε FGKL
ἁμαρτίαν· νῦν δὲ λέγετε ὅτι βλέπομεν· ἡ ἁμαρτία ὑμῶν MSUX
μένει. X. 1 ἀμὴν ἀμὴν λέγω ὑμῖν, ὁ μὴ [w] εἰςερχόμενος ΓΔΛΠℵ 1. 33. 69
διὰ τῆς θύρας εἰς τὴν [x] αὐλὴν τῶν προβάτων, ἀλλὰ
[y] ἀναβαίνων [z] ἀλλαχόθεν, ἐκεῖνος [ab] κλέπτης ἐστὶν καὶ
[bc] λῃστής. 2 ὁ δὲ [w] εἰςερχόμενος διὰ τῆς θύρας ποιμήν

u ver. 27.
v ch. xv. 22, 24. xix. 11. (Acts xxiii. 29.) 1 Tim. v. 12. 1 John i. 8.
w Matt. vii. 13 reff.
x = ver. 16 only ‡. (Matt. xxvi. 3 reff.)
y = Acts viii. 31. Rev. xx. 9. Ruth iii. 3. iv. 1.
z here only. Esth. iv. 14 Ald. compl. only. (-χοῦ, Mark i. 38.)
a Matt. vi. 19, 20 al.
b ver. 8. Obad. 5.
c Matt. xxi. 13 reff.

[*b c e f* $g_{1.2}$ *l* copt] sah-mnt arm. rec οντες bef μετ' αυτου, with A rel goth æth arm: txt BDLXℵ 1. 33 latt Cyr. (ειπαν Dℵ.)

41. aft ειπεν ins ουν D 237-49 ev-y: δε S[Γ] Scr's f g k: pref και Δ 69. 245-58 Scr's q[1] r lat-*g l* æth. om ὁ B. [ο ιησ. bef αυτοις D coptt.] om αν DK 69. rec ins ουν bef αμαρτ., with A rel [lat-*a l*] syrr goth æth: om BDKLXℵ 1. 33. 69 vulg lat-*b c e f* ff_2 *g q* coptt Cyr [Orig-int]. αι αμαρτιαι and μενουσιν DLX ℵ[3a] (but txt restored) 33 syr-mg [syr-jer arm] Cyr_1.

Chap. X. 1. υμιν bef λεγω B. αλλαχοθεν bef αναβαινων D arm.

2. for ποιμην εστιν, αυτος εστιν ο ποιμην D (lat-*b c f* ff_2 *q* [*l* foss] copt) sah Chr_1.

ποντες here answer to the *ἰσχύοντες* and *δίκαιοι* of Matt. ix. 12, 13: see note there.

40.] They ask the question, not understanding the words of Jesus in a bodily sense, but well aware of their meaning, and scornfully rejoining, 'Are then *we* meant by these blind, *we*, the leaders of the people?' **41.**] The distinction in expression between the two clauses must be carefully borne in mind. Our Lord is referring primarily to the unbelief of the Pharisees and their rejection of Him. And He says, 'If ye were really blind (not, '*confessed yourselves* blind:' Kuinoel, Stier, De Wette), ye would not have incurred guilt; but now ye say, "We see;" ye believe ye have the light, and boast that ye know and use the light; and *therefore* your guilt abideth, remaineth on you.' Observe there is a middle clause understood, between 'ye would never have incurred guilt,' and 'your guilt remaineth;' and that is, '*ye have incurred guilt;*' which makes it necessary to take the **λέγετε ὅτι βλέπομεν** as in a certain sense implying *βλέπετε*: viz. 'by the Scriptures being committed to you, by God's grace, which ought to have led you to faith in me.' Chap. X. 1—21.] *Of true and false shepherds. Jesus the good Shepherd.* This discourse is connected with the preceding miracle; and the conduct of the Pharisees towards the man who had been blind, seems to have given occasion to this description of false shepherds, which again introduces the testimony of Jesus to Himself as the true Shepherd. So that, as Meyer remarks, the paragraph should begin at ch. ix. 35 properly. The more we study carefully this wonderful Gospel, the more we shall see that the idea of this close connexion is never to be summarily dismissed as imaginary, and that our Evangelist never "passes without notice to an entirely different and disjointed occurrence or discourse," as I stated in some of my earlier editions. See on the whole subject of the parable, Jer. xxiii. 1—4: Ezek. xxxiv.: Zech. xi. 4—17. These opening verses (to ver. 5) set forth the distinction between *false and true shepherds.* Then (vv. 7, 8, 9) He brings in *Himself*, as *the door*, by which both shepherds and sheep enter the fold. Then (ver. 10) He returns to the imagery of the first verses, and sets forth Himself as The Good Shepherd; and the rest (to ver. 18) is occupied with the results and distinctions dependent on that fact.

1. τὴν αὐλ.] *ὁ περιτετειχισμένος κ. ὕπαιθρος τόπος* (Phavorinus, Lücke ii. 403); just answering, except in this being a *permanent* enclosure, to our **fold.** This fold is *the visible Church of God*, primarily, as His people Israel were His peculiar fold; the possibility of there being *other folds* has been supposed to be alluded to in ver. 16: but see note there.

The terms in this first part are *general,* and apply to *all leaders* of God's people; in ver. 1, to those who enter that office without having come in by the door (i. e. Christ, in the large sense, in which the O. T. faithful looked to and trusted in Him, as the covenant promise of Israel's God); and in ver. 2 to those who do enter this way; and whosoever does is the shepherd of the sheep (not emphatic,—not, '*the Good Shepherd,*' as below, ver. 11, but here it is merely predicated of one

ἐστιν τῶν προβάτων. 3 τούτῳ ὁ [d] θυρωρὸς ἀνοίγει, καὶ
τὰ πρόβατα τῆς φωνῆς αὐτοῦ ἀκούει, καὶ τὰ [e] ἴδια πρόβατα [f] φωνεῖ [g] κατ' ὄνομα καὶ [h] ἐξάγει αὐτά. 4 ὅταν τὰ
ἴδια πάντα [i] ἐκβάλῃ, [k] ἔμπροσθεν αὐτῶν πορεύεται, καὶ
τὰ πρόβατα αὐτῷ ἀκολουθεῖ, ὅτι [l] οἴδασιν τὴν φωνὴν
αὐτοῦ. 5 [m] ἀλλοτρίῳ δὲ οὐ μὴ ἀκολουθήσουσιν, ἀλλὰ
φεύξονται ἀπ' αὐτοῦ, ὅτι οὐκ [l] οἴδασιν τῶν [m] ἀλλοτρίων
τὴν φωνήν. 6 ταύτην τὴν [n] παροιμίαν εἶπεν αὐτοῖς ὁ
Ἰησοῦς· ἐκεῖνοι δὲ οὐκ ἔγνωσαν [o] τίνα ἦν ἃ ἐλάλει αὐτοῖς.
7 εἶπεν οὖν πάλιν ὁ Ἰησοῦς Ἀμὴν ἀμὴν λέγω ὑμῖν [ὅτι]

d Mark xiii. 34. ch. xviii. 16, 17 only. 4 Kings vii. 11.
e Matt. xxv. 14. ch. i. 42 al.
f ch. i. 49 reff.
g 3 John 15 only.
h Mark xv. 20. Acts v. 19 al.
i Mark i. 12. Luke x. 2. 1 Macc. xii. 27.
k = ch. iii. 28 reff.
l = Matt. xxv. 12 al.
m = here bis only. Job xix. 13. Prov. xxvii. 12. (Luke xvi. 12. Acts vii. 6. Rom. xiv. 4. Heb. xi. 34 al.)
n = here only. (ch. xvi. 25 bis, 29. 2 Pet. ii. 22 only. Prov. i. 1 al2. Sir. vi. 35 al4. only.)
o = Luke viii. 9 reff. Acts xvii. 19.

3. for τα ιδ. προβ., τα προβ. τα ιδ. D. rec (for φωνει) καλει, with E rel: txt ABDLXℵ 1. 33 Cyr_1.

4. rec ins και bef οταν, with AD rel vulg lat-*a e* [*f*] $Lucif_1$: add δε K[Π1·3] lat-*b c* ff_2 *l* [*q*] copt Cyr_1: om BL[Π2]ℵ 1. 33 sah. rec (for παντα) προβατα, with A rel vulg lat-*f* [*q*] syrr: om ℵ1: txt BDLX [ℵ3a(but erased)] 1. 33 lat-*a e* coptt (æth) arm Cyr Lucif. αυτου bef την φωνην D lat-*b c* ff_2 [*l*] *q*.

5. rec ακολουθησωσιν, with ℵ rel [Bas_1]: txt ABDEFGΔ Chr_1 Cyr_1.

6. for εκεινοι δε, και ℵ1. for ην, η B(Tischdf: but see table) EFG 69.

7. rec aft παλιν ins αυτοις, with D rel lat-*a* sah goth; pref AKΛ[Π] ℵ-corr1(appy) vulg lat-*b c* syrr [syr-jer æth arm]; aft ο ῑς X 33: om B ℵ1(appy).—om παλιν ℵ1(appy)·3a(but reinsd by ℵ3b) 1. 69 lat-*e* [Cyr_1] $Lucif_1$. om ὁ B. υμιν bef λεγω B. om οτι BGKLUX[Π1] 33 mm lat-*a* æth arm Cyr_1 $Lucif_1$.

who thus enters, that he is the shepherd of that particular fold: it is the attribute of a shepherd thus to enter). The sheep throughout this parable are not the mingled multitude of good and bad; but the *real* sheep, the faithful, who *are*, what all in the fold *should be*. The false sheep (*goats*, Matt. xxv. 32) do not appear; for it is not the character of the *flock*, but that of the *shepherd*, and the relation between him and his sheep, which is here prominent. **3.**] Perhaps the **θυρωρός** should not be too much pressed as significant; but certainly *the Holy Spirit* is especially He who opens the door to the shepherds: see frequent uses of this symbolism by the Apostles, Acts xiv. 27: 1 Cor. xvi. 9: 2 Cor. ii. 12: Col. iv. 3;—and instances of the θυρωρός shutting the door, Acts xvi. 6, 7. (So Theodorus Heracleota, and Stier, iv. 482, edn. 2.) **τὰ πρόβ. τ. φων. αὐτ. ἀκ.**] The voice of *every such true shepherd* is heard (heeded, understood) by *the sheep* (generally): and he calls by name *his own* sheep, that portion of the great flock entrusted to him, and leads them out to pasture, as his office is. This distinction between τὰ πρόβ. and **τὰ ἴδια** πρόβ. has given rise to exegetical and doctrinal mistakes, from not observing ποιμήν above. It has been imagined that Christ is here spoken of, and that therefore these two descriptions of sheep must be different, and so the whole exposition has been confused. Even Stier has fallen into this mistake. **4.**] When he has led forth (**ἐκβάλλειν** = ἐξάγειν) to pasture *all* his sheep (there shall not an hoof be left behind), he goes before them (see The Land and the Book, p. 202); in his teaching pointing out the way to them; they follow him, because they know his voice; his words and teaching are familiar to them. But observe that the expression here becomes again more general; not τὰ ἴδ. πρ., but τὰ πρ. as in ver. 3. *The sheep* know the voice of every true shepherd. **5.**] So that the **ἀλλότριος** is not *the shepherd of another section* of the flock, but an *alien*: the λῃστής of ver. 1;—and **τῶν** ἀλλ. is *generic*, as in E. V. Meyer takes it as merely meaning a *stranger*, one who is *not their Shepherd*: but this hardly seems strong enough for the context. **6.**] **παροιμία** is not = παραβολή, as so generally set down. This is not properly a parable: but rather a parabolic allegory. The *parable* requires *narrative* to set it forth; and John relates *no such*. The right word for παροιμία would be *allegory*: etymologically it is, any saying diverging from the common way of speech (παρ' οἶμον): cf. Meyer. We have other examples in ch. xv. 1 ff. and in Matt. ix. 37, 38. **7.**] What follows is not so much an exposition, as an

ἐγώ εἰμι ἡ θύρα τῶν προβάτων. 8 πάντες ὅσοι ἦλθον
πρὸ ἐμοῦ p κλέπται εἰσὶν καὶ p λῃσταί· ἀλλ' οὐκ q ἤκουσαν
αὐτῶν τὰ πρόβατα. 9 ἐγώ εἰμι ἡ θύρα· δι' ἐμοῦ ἐάν τις
r εἰςέλθῃ, σωθήσεται, καὶ r εἰςελεύσεται καὶ ἐξελεύσεται,
καὶ s νομὴν t εὑρήσει. 10 ὁ κλέπτης οὐκ ἔρχεται εἰ μὴ
ἵνα κλέψῃ καὶ u θύσῃ καὶ v ἀπολέσῃ· ἐγὼ ἦλθον ἵνα w ζωὴν
w ἔχωσιν, καὶ x περισσὸν ἔχωσιν. 11 ἐγώ εἰμι ὁ ποιμὴν ὁ

ABDE FGKL MSUX ΓΔΛΠℵ 1. 33. 69

p ver. 1. q = Matt. xvii. 5 al. Deut. xviii. 15. r vv. 1, 2. s = here (2 Tim. ii. 17) only. Gen. xlvii. 4. t = Luke ix. 12. Rev. ix. 6. Exod. xv. 22. u = Matt. xxii. 4. Luke xv. 23, 27, 30. Acts x. 13. xi. 7 only. (Mark xiv. 12 reff.) 1 Kings xxviii. 24. v = Matt. ii. 13 al. w ch. vi. 53 reff. x = here only. see Mark vi. 51.

8. om παντες D foss lat-*b* Did$_1$ Quæst$_1$. rec προ εμου bef ηλθον, with **1** (Treg, expr) foss arm Orig$_1$ Non Quæst: om προ εμου (*possibly on account of the misuse of the expression by the Gnostics and Manichees as applying to the O. T.*) ℵ[1] rel latt Syr-ed syr-jer sah goth Bas$_1$ Chr$_1$ *Cyr*[-p Thdor-heracl Manichæans-in-Thl] Thl Euthym Aug$_{expr}$: txt ABDKLXΛ[Π]ℵ[3a] 33. 69 gat Syr-ms syr-w-ast copt æth arm Orig$_3$ Clem$_2$ Did$_1$ Isid-pel$_1$ Hesych$_1$ Lucif$_1$ Faust$_1$ Jer$_3$ Quæst. αλλα DX.

10. aft εγω ins δε D lat-*a* copt(not [schw] dz) goth æth Chr. aft ζωην ins αιωνιον ℵ. om και περισσον εχωσιν (*homœotel*) D.

expansion of the allegory. The key to this verse is the right understanding of what went before. Bear in mind, that vv. 1—5 were of *shepherds in general.* But these shepherds themselves go into and out of the fold *by the same door as the sheep:* and Christ *is that door;* THE DOOR OF THE SHEEP: the *one* door both for sheep and shepherds, into the fold (see **ἡ θύρα,** absol. ver. 9), into God's Church, to the Father. **8.**] I believe that the right sense of these words, **ὅσοι ἦλθον πρὸ ἐμοῦ,** has not been apprehended by any of the Commentators. First, they can only be honestly understood of *time:* all **who came** *before* **me** (not, "*without regard to me,*" Olsh. &c., nor "*passing by me as the door,*" Camer., nor "*instead of me,*" Lampe, &c.: nor "*pressing before me,*" ch. v. 7, which would have been ἔρχονται, not ἦλθ.: nor "before taking the trouble to find me, the door," Stier, iv. 492, edn. 2: nor any other of the numerous shifts which have been adopted). *What pretended teachers then came before* Christ? Remember the connexion of these discourses. He has taught the Jews that Abraham and the Prophets *entered by Him* (ch. viii. 56): but He has set in strong opposition to Himself and His, them (these Jews) and their father, *the Devil* (ib. ver. 44). *He* was "the first thief who clomb into God's fold;" and all his followers are here spoken of inclusively in the language of the allegory, as coming in by and with *him.* His was the first attempt to lead human nature, *before* Christ came; before the series of dispensations of grace began, in which pasture and life is offered to man by Him. Meyer understands the Pharisees, &c. who taught the people before Christ *appeared* as the Door of the sheep: but this does not seem to reach the depth of the requirements of the saying. **εἰσίν,** not ἦσαν, because their essential nature as belonging to and being of the evil one is set forth, and the inclusion of these present Pharisees in their ranks. **ἀλλ' οὐκ . . .**] This of course cannot be understood absolutely,—'*the sheep never for one moment listened to them;*' but, did not listen to them in the sense of becoming their disciples eventually. So that the fall of our first Parents would be no exception to this; whom of all men we must conclude, by the continuing grace and mercy of God to them after that fall, to have been of His real sheep. And since then, the same is true; however the sheep may for a while listen to these false shepherds, they do not *hear them,* so as to follow them. Those who do, belong not to the true flock.

Ver. **9** expands and fixes ver. **7.** "Non est salutaris aditus in ecclesiam, nisi per me, sive pastor esse velis, sive ovis." Erasmus, Paraphr. See Num. xxvii. 16, 17. The sequel of the verse shews that this combined meaning is the true one. Meyer, who understands it all of *shepherds alone,* finds great difficulty in the interpretation of the latter words: "shall go in and out *before the sheep,* and find pasture *for them.*" Ver. **10** shews the gracious intent of the Saviour in this;—to *give life,* and in *abundance.* This verse forms the transition from Him as ἡ θύρα, to Him as ὁ ποιμήν. He is here set in opposition to ὁ κλέπτης (see on ver. 8), and thus insensibly passes into the place of a ποιμήν, who has been hitherto thus opposed. Then the **ζωὴν ἔχωσιν** binds on to νομὴν εὑρήσει—

[y] καλός. ὁ ποιμὴν ὁ καλὸς τὴν [z] ψυχὴν αὐτοῦ [z] τίθησιν
[a] ὑπὲρ τῶν προβάτων· 12 ὁ [b] μισθωτὸς δὲ καὶ οὐκ ὢν
ποιμήν, [c] οὗ οὐκ ἔστιν τὰ πρόβατα [c] ἴδια, θεωρεῖ τὸν
[d] λύκον ἐρχόμενον καὶ [e] ἀφίησιν τὰ πρόβατα καὶ φεύγει·
καὶ ὁ [d] λύκος [f] ἁρπάζει αὐτὰ καὶ [g] σκορπίζει [τὰ πρό-
βατα]· 13 ὅτι [b] μισθωτός ἐστιν καὶ οὐ [h] μέλει αὐτῷ
[h] περὶ τῶν προβάτων. 14 ἐγώ εἰμι ὁ ποιμὴν ὁ [y] καλός·
καὶ γινώσκω τὰ ἐμὰ καὶ γινώσκουσίν με τὰ ἐμά. 15 καθὼς
γινώσκει με ὁ πατὴρ κἀγὼ γινώσκω τὸν πατέρα· καὶ τὴν
[i] ψυχήν μου [i] τίθημι ὑπὲρ τῶν προβάτων. 16 καὶ ἄλλα

y = 1 Tim. iv. 6. 2 Tim. ii. 3. 1 Pet. iv. 10.
z = vv. 15, 17, 18. ch. xiii. 37, 38. xv. 13. 1 John iii. 16 bis only. J.
a = 2 Cor. v. 15. 1 Tim. ii. 6. Heb. ii. 9 al.
b here bis and Mark i. 20 only. Exod. xii. 45. (-θιος, Luke xv. 17, 19.)
c constr., Acts i. 19. 2 Pet. iii. 16.
d here bis. Matt. vii. 15. x. 16. Luke x. 16. Acts xx. 29 only. Jer. v. 6. Ezek. xxii. 27.
e = Matt. iv. 11 al.
f = here only. Ps. vii. 2.
g Luke xi. 23 ‖. ch. xvi. 32. 2 Cor. ix. 9 only. 2 Kings xxii. 15. (-διασκορπ., Matt. xxvi. 31.)
h Matt. xxii. 16 reff.
i ver. 11 reff.

11. for τιθησιν, διδωσιν Dℵ[1] vulg lat-*c* [syr-jer] Aug$_1$.

12. δε bef μισθωτος DXΔℵ 33. 69 Constt$_1$ *Cyr*[-p]: om δε BGL **1** am(with fuld forj ing mt) lat-*a* copt-dz (Lucif$_1$). rec (for εστιν) εισι (*cf* ηκουσαν *above: but there the sheep are the* agents), with D rel [Chr-montf]: txt ABLXℵ **1**. 33. 69 Eus$_1$ Constt Chr Cyr. om ερχομ. A[1]. om αυτα D vulg lat-*b ff$_2$ g l* syrr sah-mnt Aug$_1$. om last τα προβ. BDL[Π]ℵ **1**. 33 syr-jer (coptt æth) arm Lucif$_1$ [*Cyr*-p]: ins A rel latt syrr sah-mnt goth.

13. rec at beg ins ο δε μισθωτος φευγει, with A[corr] rel latt syrr goth: om BDLℵ **1**. 33 syr-jer coptt æth arm [*Cyr*-p] Lucif$_1$.—A has ο δε μισθωτος φευγει οτι μισθος(sic) εστιν και ου μελει, the words from φευγει to ου με being written on an erasure.

14. for ο π. ο καλ., ο καλ. π. D [Eus$_1$]. rec (for γινωσκ. με τα εμα) γινωσκομαι υπο των εμων, with A rel syrr arm: txt BLℵ latt [syr-jer] coptt goth æth Eus$_1$ Epiph$_1$ Cyr$_1$ Non$_1$, γεινωσιν(txt D[5]) εμε τα εμα D.

15. om μου D. for τιθημι, διδωμι Dℵ[1].

16. aft και αλλα ins δε D 346(Sz) syrr.

and **καὶ περισ. ἔχ.**: q. d. not merely as a door to pass through, but actively, abundantly, to *bestow* abundance of life. We are thus prepared for (ver. **11**) the announcement of Himself as **ὁ ποιμὴν ὁ καλός**—the great antagonist of ὁ κλέπτης—the pattern and Head of all good shepherds, as *he* of all thieves and robbers: the Messiah, in His best known and most loving office: cf. Ezek. xxxiv. 11—16, 23; xxxvii. 24, and Isa. xl. 11. But He is **ὁ π. ὁ κ.** in this verse, as having most eminently *the qualities* of a good shepherd, one of which is to *lay down His life* for the sheep. These words here are not so much a prophecy, as a declaration, implying however that which ver. 15 asserts explicitly. **12.**] The imagery is here again somewhat changed. The false shepherds are here compared to hirelings, i. e. those who serve *merely* for gain; the μισθωτός who fulfils the character implied by the word. The idea is brought in by τὴν ψυχ. αὐτ. τίθ. ὑπὲρ τ. πρ., which introduces a time of danger, when the true and false shepherds are distinguished. **τ. λύκον**] The purposes of this **wolf** are the same as those of the thief in ver. 10, and in the allegory he is the same;—*the great Foe of the sheep of Christ.* Lücke and De Wette deny this, and hold 'any enemies of the theocracy' to be meant;—but no deep view of the parable will be content with this,—see Matt. vii. 15, where the λύκοι ἅρπαγες are ψευδοπροφῆται, the κλέπται κ. λῃσταί of ver. 8;—and their chief and father would therefore be **ὁ λύκος**, just as **ὁ ποιμήν** is *the* Shepherd. **14, 15.**] The knowledge of His sheep here spoken of is more than the mere *knowing by name:* it is a knowledge corresponding to the Father's knowledge of Him;—i. e. entire, perfect, all-comprehensive: and *their* knowledge of *Him* corresponds to His of the Father,—i. e. is intimate, direct, and personal: both being bound together by holy and inseparable Love. Beware of rendering [the former clause of] ver. 15 as in E. V. as an independent sentence, '*As my Father knoweth me, even so know I the Father:*' it is merely the sequel to ver. 14, and should stand, **as the Father knoweth me and I know the Father.** **ὑπὲρ τ. προβ.**] for those **my sheep**—not, for *all;* that, *however true*, is not *the point* brought out *here:* the Lord lays down His life strictly and properly, and in the depths of the Divine counsel, *for those who are His sheep.* **16.**] The **ἄλλα πρόβ.** are the *Gentiles;*—not the dispersion of the Jews,

πρόβατα ἔχω, ἃ οὐκ ἔστιν ἐκ τῆς [k] αὐλῆς ταύτης· κἀκεῖνα δεῖ με [l] ἀγαγεῖν, καὶ τῆς φωνῆς μου ἀκούσουσιν,
καὶ γενήσονται μία [m] ποίμνη, εἷς ποιμήν.
17 διὰ τοῦτό με ὁ πατὴρ ἀγαπᾷ, ὅτι ἐγὼ [i] τίθημι τὴν [i] ψυχήν μου
ἵνα πάλιν [n] λάβω αὐτήν.
18 οὐδεὶς αἴρει αὐτὴν ἀπ' ἐμοῦ,
ἀλλ' ἐγὼ τίθημι αὐτὴν [o] ἀπ' ἐμαυτοῦ. [p] ἐξουσίαν ἔχω
θεῖναι αὐτήν, καὶ [p] ἐξουσίαν ἔχω πάλιν [n] λαβεῖν αὐτήν·
ταύτην τὴν [q] ἐντολὴν [q] ἔλαβον παρὰ τοῦ πατρός μου.
19 [r] Σχίσμα πάλιν ἐγένετο ἐν τοῖς Ἰουδαίοις διὰ τοὺς
λόγους τούτους.
20 ἔλεγον δὲ πολλοὶ ἐξ αὐτῶν [s] Δαιμόνιον [s] ἔχει καὶ [t] μαίνεται· τί αὐτοῦ ἀκούετε;
21 ἄλλοι
ἔλεγον Ταῦτα τὰ ῥήματα οὐκ ἔστιν [u] δαιμονιζομένου·
μὴ δαιμόνιον δύναται τυφλῶν [v] ὀφθαλμοὺς [v] ἀνοῖξαι;
22 Ἐγένετο δὲ τὰ [w] ἐγκαίνια ἐν [x] τοῖς Ἱεροσολύμοις.

ABDE FGKL MSUX ΓΔΛΠℵ 1. 33. 69

k ver. 1. l = Matt. xxi. 7. ch. vii. 45. m Matt. xxvi. 31, from Zech. xiii. 7. Luke ii. 8. 1 Cor. ix. 7 bis only. Gen. xxxii. 16 bis only. n = Heb. v. 4. Rev. xi. 17. o ch. v. 19 reff. p ch. i. 12. xix. 10. Rev. ix. 10. xi. 6. 1 Macc. x. 35. q Acts xvii. 15. Col. iv. 10. 2 John 4 only. r Mark ii. 21 reff. s ch. vii. 20 reff. t Acts xii. 15. xxvi. 24, 25. 1 Cor. xiv. 23 only. Jer. xxxvi. (xxix.) 26. Wisd. xiv. 28 only. u John, here only. Matt. iv. 24 al6. Mark i. 32 al3. Luke viii. 36 only +. Ps. xc. 6 Aq. v ch. ix. 10, &c. reff. w here only. Ezra vi. 16, 17 al. (-νίζειν, Heb. ix. 18. x. 20. -νισμός, Num. vii. 84. -νισις, ib. 88 A [-νωσις Bl.]) x ch. v. 2 reff.

rec με bef δει, with A rel Eus$_1$ [Bas$_1$ Chr$_1$] Thdrt$_{sæpe}$ Cyr[-p$_1$] : txt BDLΔ[Π]ℵ 1. 33. 69 latt syrr [syr-jer Cyr-p$_2$] Orig-int$_2$. ακουσωσιν AGXΔΛℵ 33. 69 Eus$_1$. rec γενησεται, with Aℵ[1] rel [latt syrr] Eus$_1$ [Bas$_1$] Cypr : txt BDLXℵ[3a] 1. 33 forj lat-*f* syr-mg [syr-jer] coptt goth arm Clem$_1$ Chr-2-mss$_1$ [Cyr-p$_3$].

17. rec ο πατηρ bef με, with A rel goth Thdrt$_1$: txt BDLXℵ 33 latt.

18. for αιρει, ηρεν Bℵ[1] : txt ADℵ[3a] rel vss Orig$_{sæpe}$ Eus$_5$ [Did$_1$] Cypr$_1$ Hil$_1$. om from εμου to εμαυτου D 251 lat-*l* goth [Eus$_4$]. for λαβειν, αραι D lat-*c*. om την B. om μου D lat-*a b* Chr$_2$ Tert$_1$ Hil$_2$ Novat$_1$.

19. rec aft σχισμα ins ουν, with AD rel tol syr copt Chr : om BLXℵ latt sah arm. om παλιν D 225(Sz) tol copt Chr$_1$.

20. [ελεγαν ℵ[1].] for δε, ουν D ℵ[1](txt ℵ[3a], but ουν restored) 1. ins οτι bef δαιμονιον D [Chr].

21. aft αλλοι ins δε ℵ 69. transp ταυτα and ουκ εστ. D. οφθ. bef τυφλων D 245 lat-*ef*. rec ανοιγειν, with AD rel : txt BLXℵ 1. 33. 69 Orig Chr$_2$.

22. εγενοντο D. for δε, τοτε (*error from* -το δε) BL 33 (gat) coptt arm. om τοις Dℵ rel Chr$_1$: ins ABL 33.

who were already in God's αὐλή. By these wonderful words, as by those in Acts xviii. 10, and by the conclusion of Matt. xxv. (see notes there), our Lord shews that, dark and miserable as the Gentile world was, *He had sheep even there.* Observe they are not *in other folds,* but scattered : see ch. xi. 52. Cf. also Eph. ii. 14 ff.

δεῖ με ἀγ. . . . . .] i. e. in the purpose and covenant of the Father. The Lord speaks of *His* bringing them, and their hearing *His* voice : meaning that His servants in His name and by His power would accomplish this work. Admirably illustrative of the converse method of speaking which He employs Matt. xxv. 40, 45. The **μία ποίμνη** is remarkable—*not* **μία αὐλή**, *as characteristically, but erroneously rendered in E. V. :*—not ONE FOLD, but ONE FLOCK; no one exclusive enclosure of an outward church,—but one flock, all knowing the one Shepherd and known of Him. On **εἷς ποιμήν** compare Heb. xiii. 20.

17.] The λαλεῖν ἐν παροιμίαις is now over, and He speaks *plainly*,—**My Father.** In this wonderful verse lies the mystery of the love of the Father for the Son;—*because* the Son has condescended to the work of humiliation, and to earn the crown through the cross (see Phil. ii. 8, 9, **διό**). The **ἵνα** here is strictly τελικόν,—**in order that.** "Without this purpose in view," says Stier (iv. 504, edn. 2), "the Death of Christ would neither be lawful nor possible."

18.] The truth of this voluntary rendering up was shewn by His whole sufferings, from the falling of His enemies to the ground in the garden (ch. xviii. 6) to His last words, **παρατίθεμαι τὸ πν. μου**, Luke xxiii. 46 (see note there). His resurrection also was eminently His own work, by virtue of the Spirit of the Father dwelling in and filling Him : the ἐξουσία in both these cases being the ἐντολή, appointment, ordinance of the Father, from the counsel of whose will the whole media-

[y] χειμὼν ἦν, 23 καὶ περιεπάτει ὁ Ἰησοῦς ἐν τῷ ἱερῷ ἐν τῇ
[z] στοᾷ Σολομῶνος. 24 [a] ἐκύκλωσαν οὖν αὐτὸν οἱ Ἰουδαῖοι, καὶ ἔλεγον αὐτῷ [b] Ἕως πότε τὴν ψυχὴν ἡμῶν
[c] αἴρεις ; εἰ σὺ εἶ ὁ χριστός, εἰπὲ ἡμῖν [d] παῤῥησίᾳ. 25 ἀπεκρίθη αὐτοῖς ὁ Ἰησοῦς Εἶπον ὑμῖν, καὶ οὐ πιστεύετε.
Η τα εργα... τὰ ἔργα ἃ ἐγὼ ποιῶ ἐν τῷ ὀνόματι τοῦ πατρός μου, ταῦτα
[e] μαρτυρεῖ [e] περὶ ἐμοῦ· 26 ἀλλὰ ὑμεῖς οὐ πιστεύετε· οὐ
γάρ [f] ἐστε [f] ἐκ τῶν προβάτων τῶν ἐμῶν[, καθὼς εἶπον

y Matt. xxiv. 20 reff.
z ch. v. 2 reff.
a Luke xxi. 20. Acts xiv. 20. Heb. xi. 30. (Rev. xx. 9 v. r.) only. Ps. cxvii. 10.
b Matt. xvii. 17 (bis) ||. Rev. vi. 10 only. Ps. xii. 1.
c = here only ‡. see Ezek. xxiv. 25.
d = ch. xi. 14. xvi. 25, 29. Mark viii. 32.
e ch. i. 7, 8 reff.
f = Matt. xxvi. 73 ||. ch. vi. 64 al.

rec ins *και* bef *χειμων*, with A [Π²(but erased)] rel: om BDGLX[Π¹]א 1. 33 coptt æth Chr-ms.

23. *περιπατει* (for *περιεπ.*) AL. om *ὁ* B. rec ins *του* bef *σολ.*, with BLX (33, e sil): om ADא rel Chr_1.

24. *εκυκλευσαν* B. om *αυτον* א¹ 249. *ειπον* א¹(txt א^{3a} but *-ον* restored).

25. om *αυτοις* Dא¹ goth. (*ο* is insd in B, possibly *prima manu*, Tischdf [N. T. Vat.].) for *ειπον*, *λαλω* D vulg lat-*b c e ff₂ g l* $Tert_1$. *ουκ επιστευσατε* B 248-59 Scr's g Chr-2-mss_1. add *μοι* D 69 sah arm Chr_1. om *τω* א. for *ταυτα*, *αυτα* D lat-*a e* [*l*] $Tert_1$.

26. (*αλλα*, so A B(sic) LΔא.) for *ου γαρ*, *οτι ουκ* BDLXא 1. 33. 69 vulg lat-*b f ff₂ g l* Syr syr-mg [syr-jer] goth æth $Orig_1$ Chr_1 Cyr_1. om *καθως ειπον υμιν* BKLM¹[Π¹·³]א 33 vulg lat-*c g* coptt arm. [lat-*ff₂ l* ins, but join with follg.]

torial office of Christ sprung: see ch. xii. 49. **19—21.**] The concluding words bind this discourse to the miracle of ch. ix., though not necessarily in *immediate* connexion.

22—39.] *Discourse at the Feast of Dedication.* It may be, that Jesus remained at, or in the neighbourhood of, Jerusalem during the interval (two months) between the Feast of Tabernacles and that of the Dedication. Had He *returned to Galilee*, we should have expected some mention of it. Still, by the words ἐν τοῖς Ἱεροσολύμοις, it would seem as if a fresh period and a new visit began; for why should such a specification be made, if the narrative proceeded continuously? See on Luke ix. 51 ff. **22.**] This feast had become usual since the time when Judas Maccabæus purified the temple from the profanations of Antiochus. It was held on Chisleu (December) 25, and seven following days: see 1 Macc. iv. 41—59: 2 Macc. x. 1—8: Jos. Antt. xii. 7. 7. **χειμ. ἦν**] **it was winter** (not *'stormy weather,'* as Lampe, al.: Matt. xvi. 3): see above. The notice is inserted to explain to Gentile readers the reason of our Lord's walking in Solomon's portico. This latter was on the east side of the temple, called also by Jos. στοὰ ἀνατολική. He says, Antt. xx. 9. 7, that it was an original work of Solomon, which had remained from the former temple. **24.**] **ψυχὴν αἴρεις** is generally explained, *'keep us in doubt,'* αἰωρεῖς, ἀναρτᾷς μεταξὺ πίστεως κ. ἀπιστίας, Euthym. But there is some question whether ψ. αἴρ. is ever so used. In Josephus, it signifies *'to uplift the soul,' 'raise the courage;'* ἐπὶ τὸν κίνδ. τὰς ψ. ἠρμένοι, Antt. iii. 2. 3; 5. 1. So also Aquila, Prov. xix. 18, πρὸς τὸ θανατῶσαι αὐτὸν μὴ ἄρῃς ψ. σου. See also Ps. lxxxv. 4; cxlii. 8 (LXX). These usages, however, as all the examples adduced in the comm., are confined to the act of a man on *his own* soul: when the term applies to effects produced on *another*, it seems to imply any strong excitement of mind, whether for hope or fear. **How long dost thou excite our minds?**

25.] He had often told them, in unmistakable descriptions of Himself; see ch. v. 19; viii. 36, 56, 58, &c. &c. But the great reference here is to His *works*, as in ver. 37. Observe the sharp contrast of **ἐγώ** and **ὑμεῖς**. **26.**] The difficulty of καθὼς εἶπον ὑμῖν is considerable warrant for its genuineness: and it comes much more naturally with this than with the following verse. I believe it to refer more to the *whole allegory*, than to any explicit saying of this kind; and this is shewn to my mind by the following words in ver. 27:—the minor proposition, *'but ye hear not my voice,'* being understood. This was a corollary from the allegory, and thus it might be said **καθὼς εἶπον ὑμῖν**. This reference to the allegory some two months after it was spoken, has been used by the rationalists as an argument against the authenticity of the narrative. But, as Meyer observes, it in reality implies that

g plur., Matt. vi. 28 reff. h ch. viii. 51 reff. i = Matt. xiii. 19. Jude 23. 2 Kings xxiii. 21. k comp., Matt. xiii. 32. 1 Cor. xv. 19. Judg. vi. 15. l ch. xvii 11, 21, 22. 1 Cor. iii. 8. see Eph ii. 14. (1 John v. 8.) m = here only. n here 3ce. ch. [viii. 5] xi. 8. Acts v. 26. xiv. 19. 2 Cor. xi. 25. Heb. xi. 37 only. 2 Kings xvi. 6, 13 only. o Matt. v. 16 reff.

ὑμῖν]. 27 τὰ πρόβατα τὰ ἐμὰ τῆς φωνῆς μου [g] ἀκουου-
σιν, κἀγὼ γινώσκω αὐτά, καὶ ἀκολουθοῦσίν μοι, 28 κἀγὼ
δίδωμι αὐτοῖς ζωὴν αἰώνιον, καὶ οὐ μὴ ἀπόλωνται [h] εἰς
τὸν [h] αἰῶνα, καὶ οὐχ [i] ἁρπάσει τις αὐτὰ ἐκ τῆς χειρός μου.
29 ὁ πατήρ μου ὃ δέδωκέν μοι πάντων [k] μεῖζον ἐστίν,
καὶ οὐδεὶς δύναται [i] ἁρπάζειν ἐκ τῆς χειρὸς τοῦ πατρός.
30 ἐγὼ καὶ ὁ πατὴρ [l] ἕν ἐσμεν. 31 [m] ἐβάστασαν οὖν πάλιν
λίθους οἱ Ἰουδαῖοι, ἵνα [n] λιθάσωσιν αὐτόν. 32 ἀπεκρίθη
αὐτοῖς ὁ Ἰησοῦς Πολλὰ [o] καλὰ [o] ἔργα ἔδειξα ὑμῖν ἐκ τοῦ
πατρός· [p] διὰ [q] ποῖον αὐτῶν ἔργον ἐμὲ [n] λιθάζετε; 33 ἀπ- ...δια F.
εκρίθησαν αὐτῷ οἱ Ἰουδαῖοι [r] Περὶ [o] καλοῦ [o] ἔργου οὐ ABDE GHKL MSUX
[n] λιθάζομέν σε, ἀλλὰ [r] περὶ [s] βλασφημίας, καὶ ὅτι σὺ ΓΔΛΠℵ 1. 33. 69

p = ch. xi. 15, 42. xvi. 21 al. fr. q = Acts iv. 7. xxiii. 34 al. 2 Kings xv. 2. r = Acts xix. 23 al. s Matt. xii. 31. Luke v. 21. Rev. ii. 9 al. Ezek. xxxv. 12.

27. rec (for *ακουουσιν*) *ακουει*, with AD rel Clem$_1$ Orig$_2$ hom-Cl-ed$_1$ Eus$_2$: txt BLXℵ 33. 69 Orig$_4$ hom-Cl-ms$_1$ [Cyr-p$_4$]. for *καγω*, *και* ℵ.

28. rec *ζωην αιων.* bef *διδ. αυτοις*, with AD rel latt syr goth arm[Treg] Orig$_1$ Eus$_1$ [Bas$_2$] : txt BLM[1]Xℵ 33 Syr [syr-jer] coptt æth [arm(Tischdf) Cyr-p$_4$]. *απολητai* ℵ[1]. for *ουχ*, *ου μη* DLXℵ 69 Bas$_1$. *αρπαση* (*itacism?*) DELMXℵ.

29. om *μου* ℵ[1] 13(Sz) [lat-*a b c e ff$_2$ l* syr-jer Bas$_1$ Dial$_1$] Chr-3-mss$_1$ [Tert$_1$ Hil$_2$]. rec (for *ὅ*) *ὅς*, with AB[2] rel sah æth [Bas$_1$ Dial$_1$ Chr$_3$ Cyr$_2$] Tert-ms; *ους* Λ: txt B[1](D)Lℵ latt copt goth Tert-ms Hil$_2$.—*δεδωκως* D. rec *μειζων*, with Dℵ rel [Bas Dial Chr Cyr$_2$] Tert-ms : txt ABX latt [syr-jer] copt goth Tert-ms$_1$ Hil$_2$ Ambr Jer Aug Fulg. rec *μειζ.* bef *παντ.*, with A rel vulg lat-*b c* [&c syr syr-jer copt goth]: *εστιν* bef *μειζ.* X : txt BDLℵ Syr Cyr[-p$_3$]. rec aft *του πατρος* ins *μου*, with AD rel vss [Cyr-p$_1$] Hil : om BLℵ [syr-jer] Orig$_1$ [Cyr-p$_1$].

31. om *ουν* BLℵ 33 am(with fuld em forj ing jac mt) lat-*ff$_2$ g* sah[-woide] goth arm [Ath$_1$] Aug$_4$. om *παλιν* D 69 latt[not *f*] copt.

32. *εργα* bef *καλα* AKΛ[Π]ℵ 1. 33 am(with fuld forj foss ing) lat-*a c e f* [*l*] syrr [syr-jer æth] coptt arm Ath$_1$ [Quæst$_1$] : *εργα εδ. υμιν* bef *καλα* B. rec aft *πατρος* ins *μου*, with Aℵ[3a] rel : om BDℵ[1] lat-*e* [syr-jer] Ath$_1$. rec (for *εμε λιθ.*) *λιθαζετε με*, with AD rel lat-*c f* syrr [syr-jer] goth Epiph$_1$ Thdrt$_1$ Hil$_1$: txt BLℵ 33 vulg lat-*a b e*.

33. rec aft *ιουδαιοι* ins *λεγοντες*, with D rel lat-*e* [syr-jer æth arm-mss]: om ABKL M[1]X[Π]ℵ 1. 33. 69 latt [coptt goth] Hil$_1$. om *και* ℵ [lat-*c* coptt Cyr-p$_4$ Thdrt$_3$]. om *συ* DK[Π] vulg-ms lat-*e* Syr [syr-jer] Chr$_1$ Quæst$_1$.

the conflict with the Jewish authorities is here again taken up after that interval, during which it had not broken out. **27—29.**] This leads to a further description of these sheep. The form of the sentence is a climax; rising through the **ἐγὼ** *δίδωμι* and *ἐκ τ. χ.* **μου**, to **ὁ πατήρ μου** *ὃ δέδωκέν μοι* and *ἐκ τ. χ.* **τοῦ πατρός.** Then the apparent diversity of the two expressions, *ἐκ τ. χ.* **μου** and *ἐκ τ. χ.* **τοῦ πατ. μου**, gives occasion to the assertion in ver. **30**, that Christ and the Father are ONE; one in *essence* primarily, but therefore also one in *working*, and POWER, and in *will*. *ἓν κατὰ δύναμιν, ἤγουν ταυτοδύναμοι*, Euthym.; who adds, *εἰ δὲ ἓν κατὰ δύναμιν, ἓν ἄρα καὶ κατὰ τὴν θεότητα καὶ οὐσίαν καὶ φύσιν*. This certainly is *implied* in the words, and so the Jews understood them, ver. 33. Bengel remarks after Augustine, "per *sumus* refutatur Sabellius, per *unum*, Arius." It is perhaps more than is actually contained in the words: but, as Meyer says, they are *founded on* the unity of essence of the Son and the Father, and so *presuppose* the homousian doctrine. **ἕν**, not *εἷς*: not *personally* one, but *essentially*. **31.**] i. e. as having spoken blasphemy, Levit. xxiv. 10 ff. "**ἐβάστασαν**, *sustulerunt* (Vulg.)—*they lifted up in the air*, in act to throw at him. It is more than *αἴρειν*, ch. viii. 59. Cf. Hom. Od. λ. 594 (*λᾶαν βαστάζοντα πελώριον ἀμφοτέρῃσιν*), Polyb. xv. 26. 3 (*βαστάσας τὸ παιδίον*)." Meyer. **32.**] See Mark vii. 37. **ἐκ τοῦ πατρός μου**, because (cf. vv. 37, 38) He Himself proceeded forth from the Father, and the Father wrought in Him. **ἔδειξα**, because they were part of the manifestation of Himself as the Son of God. **λιθάζετε,**

ἄνθρωπος ὢν [t] ποιεῖς σεαυτὸν θεόν. 34 ἀπεκρίθη αὐτοῖς ὁ
Ἰησοῦς Οὐκ ἔστιν γεγραμμένον ἐν τῷ νόμῳ ὑμῶν ὅτι ἐγὼ
εἶπα [u] θεοί ἐστε; 35 εἰ ἐκείνους εἶπεν θεοὺς πρὸς οὓς ὁ
λόγος τοῦ θεοῦ [v] ἐγένετο, καὶ οὐ δύναται [w] λυθῆναι ἡ
[x] γραφή· 36 ὃν ὁ πατὴρ [y] ἡγίασεν καὶ [z] ἀπέστειλεν [z] εἰς τὸν
κόσμον ὑμεῖς [a] λέγετε ὅτι βλασφημεῖς, ὅτι εἶπον [b] Υἱὸς
τοῦ θεοῦ εἰμι; 37 εἰ οὐ ποιῶ τὰ ἔργα τοῦ πατρός μου, μὴ
πιστεύετέ μοι· 38 εἰ δὲ ποιῶ, κἂν ἐμοὶ μὴ πιστεύητε, τοῖς
ἔργοις πιστεύσατε, ἵνα γνῶτε καὶ γινώσκητε ὅτι ἐν ἐμοὶ ὁ
πατὴρ κἀγὼ ἐν τῷ πατρί. 39 ἐζήτουν [οὖν] πάλιν αὐτὸν

t ch. viii. 53 reff.
u Psa. lxxxi. 6.
v = Luke iii. 2. xix. 9. Isa. ii. 1.
w = ch. vii. 23. v. 18. Matt. v. 19.
x ch. vii. 38 reff.
y ch. xvii. 17, 19 al. fr. = Jer. i. 5. Sir. xlix. 7.
z ch. iii. 17. 1 John iv. 8.
a constr., ch. i. 15. viii. 54, 55. ix. 19. Gal. v. 21.
b Matt. iv. 3 and note.

34. om ὁ B. aft *ο ιησ.* ins *και ειπεν* D copt [æth]. om *υμων* D ℵ[1](ins ℵ-corr[1]) lat-*b c e ff*$_2$ *l* Eus$_1$ Tert$_1$ Cypr$_1$ Hil$_1$ &c. rec om *οτι*, with A rel lat-*f* goth æth arm Ath Thdrt$_1$ Tert$_1$: ins BDLXℵ 33 latt [syrr syr-jer] sah Eus$_2$ Ath-ms Cypr Hil. om *εγω* ℵ[1](ins ℵ[3b], appy) [lat-*l*[1]]. *ειπον* ADMSUΔ 33. 69: txt Bℵ rel.

35. *εγεν.* bef *του θεου* D lat-*a b e ff*$_2$ *l* Eus$_2$ [Damasc$_1$] Hil$_1$.

36. om *του* DEGℵ 69 (goth?) Eus$_1$ Did$_1$ Chr$_1$ Cyr[-p$_2$(ins$_1$)] Damasc$_1$.

38. for *πιστευητε*, *πιστευετε* AEGH [S(Tischdf)] UXΔΛℵ 1[1]. 33. 69 [Bas$_1$]: *θελετε πιστευειν* D latt Tert$_1$ Cypr$_1$ Hil Zeno. for *πιστευσατε*, *πιστευετε* BDKLU[Π]ℵ 1. 33 [Cyr-p$_4$]. rec (for *γινωσκητε*) *πιστευσητε* (*see note*), with A rel vulg lat-*f g* syrr goth [Bas$_1$], *πιστευητε* ℵ: txt BLX 1. 33 coptt arm Ath$_2$ [Ps-Ath$_1$] Hil$_3$.—om *και γινωσκητε* D lat-*a b c e ff*$_2$ *l* Tert$_1$ Cypr$_1$ Zeno. rec (for *τω πατρι*) *αυτω* (*not noticing the emphasis*), with A rel lat-*b f ff*$_2$ [*l*] syr-txt goth [Bas$_1$] Cypr$_1$ Hil$_2$ Zeno: txt BDLXℵ 33 vulg lat-*a c e g* Syr syr-mg [syr-jer] coptt æth arm Eus$_2$ Ath$_1$ Damasc$_1$ Orig-int$_1$ Hil$_6$.

39. om *ουν* BEGHMUΛ [S(appy, Tischdf) Γ] copt goth arm: ins Aℵ rel syr sah.—for *εζητουν* [*ουν*], *και εζητουν* D Syr [syr-jer] æth. *αυτον* bef *παλιν* AKLXΔ[Π]ℵ[3a] 1. 33 lat-*f* goth: om *παλιν* Dℵ[1] 69 latt [syr-jer] Chr: txt B rel [syrr]. (*πιασαι* bef *αυτον* U [sah] æth.)

are ye stoning (preparing to stone) **Me?**

33.] **θεόν** = *ἴσον τῷ θ.*, ch. v. 18.

34.] **νόμος** here is in its widest acceptation,—the whole O. T.,—as ch. xii. 34; xv. 25. The Psalm (lxxxii.) is directed against the injustice and tyranny of judges (not, the *Gentile rulers* of the world (De Wette), nor, the *angels* (Bleek)) in Israel. And in the Psalm reference is made by **εἶπα** to previous places of Scripture where judges are so called, viz. Exod. xxi. 6; xxii. 9, 28. 35.] **πρὸς οὓς ὁ λόγ. τ. θεοῦ ἐγ., to whom God** (in those passages) **spoke.** We can hardly build on this passage, as Luthardt has done, a theory as to the distinction between those to whom *ὁ λόγος τοῦ θεοῦ* came merely *in utterance*, and those to whom He came *in Person*. See below on ver. 36. The expression, **καὶ οὐ δύν. λυθ. ἡ γρ.** (which is not a parenthesis, but constructionally part of the sentence, depending on **εἰ**), implies, 'and if you cannot *explain this expression away*,—if it cannot mean nothing,—for it rests on the testimony of God's word,' . . .

36.] The argument is *à minori ad majus*. If in any sense they could be called **gods**,—how much more properly He, whom &c. They were only officially so *called*, only **λεγόμενοι** *θεοί*—but He, the only One, sealed and hallowed by the Father, and sent into the world (the aorists refer to the time of the Incarnation), is essentially **θεός**, inasmuch as He is **υἱὸς τοῦ θεοῦ**. The deeper aim of this argument is, to shew them that the idea of *man and God being one*, was not alien from their O. T. spirit, but set forth there in types and shadows of Him, the real God-Man. Observe **ὑμεῖς**, set in emphatic contrast to the authority of Scripture,—as **ὃν ὁ πατὴρ ἡγίασεν . . .** is to **ἐκείνους** above. 37, 38.] Having put the charge of *blasphemy* aside, our Lord again has recourse to the testimony of *His works*, at which He hinted ver. 32; and here, to their *character*, as admitted by them in ver. 33. 'If they bear not the character of the Father, believe Me not: but if they do (which even yourselves admit), though ye may hate and disbelieve Me, recognize the unquestionable testimony of the works:—that ye may be led on to the higher faith of the unity of Myself and the Father.' **γνῶτε κ. γινώσκητε**] The distinction lies in the force of the present as denoting the continuance of a state, whereas the aorist

c ch. vii. 30 reff.
d = here only. see 2 Cor. vi. 17.
e Acts xii. 11. 2 Chron. xxxii. 13, 14.
f Matt. xix. 22 reff. ch. i. 28.
g ch. xii. 16. xix. 39 only.
h = ch. ii. 11 al.
i ch. ii. 11 reff.
k = ch. vii. 42. xii. 21. xix. 38. xxi. 2. Matt. xxi. 11 al.
l = ch. i. 45. vii. 42. Luke ii. 4 (b). viii. 27. xxiii. 7. ἐκ = ἀπό, Acts xxiii. 34.
m ch. vii. 42 reff.
n Matt. vi. 17. Mark vi. 13. xvi. 1. Luke vii. 38, 46 bis. ch. xii. 3. James v. 14 only. Gen. xxxi. 13.
o Matt. xxvi. 2 reff.
p Luke vii. 38 reff.

[c] πιάσαι· καὶ [d] ἐξῆλθεν [e] ἐκ τῆς χειρὸς αὐτῶν, 40 καὶ
ἀπῆλθεν πάλιν πέραν τοῦ Ἰορδάνου εἰς τὸν τόπον ὅπου [f] ἦν
Ἰωάννης [g] τὸ πρῶτον βαπτίζων, καὶ ἔμεινεν ἐκεῖ. 41 καὶ
πολλοὶ ἦλθον πρὸς αὐτόν, καὶ ἔλεγον ὅτι Ἰωάννης μὲν
[h] σημεῖον ἐποίησεν οὐδέν· πάντα δὲ ὅσα εἶπεν Ἰωάννης περὶ
τούτου ἀληθῆ ἦν. 42 καὶ πολλοὶ [i] ἐπίστευσαν [i] εἰς αὐτὸν ἐκεῖ.
XI. 1 Ἦν δέ τις ἀσθενῶν Λάζαρος [k] ἀπὸ Βηθανίας,
[l] ἐκ τῆς [m] κώμης Μαρίας καὶ Μάρθας τῆς ἀδελφῆς αὐτῆς·
2 ἦν δὲ Μαρία ἡ [n] ἀλείψασα τὸν κύριον [o] μύρῳ καὶ [p] ἐκ-
μάξασα τοὺς πόδας αὐτοῦ ταῖς θριξὶν αὐτῆς, ἧς ὁ ἀδελφὸς
Λάζαρος ἠσθένει. 3 ἀπέστειλαν οὖν αἱ ἀδελφαὶ πρὸς αὐτὸν

F προς... ABDEF GHKL MSUX ΓΔΛΠℵ 1. 33. 69

40. for και απηλθεν, απηλθεν ουν A. om εις τον τοπον ℵ[1] 245 [Chr_1]. for πρωτον, προτερον Δℵ 69 lat-*a e f ff*$_2$ [Chr]. for εμεινεν, εμενεν B lat-*a b c e ff*$_2$.
41. om οτι Dℵ 245 [lat-*c e*]. ιωαννης bef ειπεν D [lat-*b f l*].
42. rec επιστ. bef πολλοι, with A rel syr goth: txt BDLM X(Treg, expr) ℵ 1. 33 latt Syr [syr-jer] coptt æth arm Chr_1. rec εκει bef εις αυτον, with E rel: om 16 latt Syr Chr: txt ABDKLMUX[Π]ℵ 1. 33. 69 syr [syr-jer] coptt goth æth arm.

Chap. XI. **1.** ins της bef μαριας Dℵ. ins της bef μαρθας D[1]. αυτου A ev-32.
2. μαριαμ B 33. om αυτου D. aft ης ins και D.
3. προς αυτον bef αι αδελφαι ℵ 249 [Scr's c coptt arm]: om αι αδ. lat-*b l*. aft αδελφαι ins αυτου DS 1 [$Andr_1$]. for αυτον, τον ιησουν D lat-*b c e l* Syr [syr-jer æth $Andr_1$].

implies an act of a moment. The nearest approach to it in English would perhaps be, **that ye may perceive** (the introductory act) **and know** (the abiding state). This distinction between the tenses not being appreciated, γινώσκητε has been awkwardly changed to πιστεύσητε. Cf. Plato, Legg. viii. p. 849 A, τῶν δὲ ἐν ἄστει κατὰ τὰ αὐτὰ ἐπιμεληθῆναι καὶ ἐπιμελεῖσθαι τὴν τῶν ἀστυνόμων ἀρχήν.

39.] The attempt to stone Him seems to have been abandoned, but (see ch. vii. 30) they tried again to take Him into custody: and, as before, He (miraculously?) withdrew Himself from them.

40—42.] *Jesus departs to Bethany beyond Jordan, and is there believed on by many.* **40.**] See ch. i. 28 and note.

41.] The locality reminds them of John and his testimony. The remark seems to have a double tendency;—to relate their now confirmed persuasion, that though John did not fulfil their expectations by shewing a sign or working miracles, yet he was a *true* prophet, and really, as he professed, the forerunner of this Person, who in consequence must be, what John had declared Him to be, the Messiah. And (ver. 42) the result followed:—*many believed on Him.* "The **Ἰωάννης** repeated, ver. 42, belongs to the simplicity of the speech, which is reproduced *literatim*, and expresses the honour paid by the people to the holy man whose memory still lived among them." Meyer.

Chap. XI., XII.] Jesus, delivered to death, the Resurrection, and the Life, and the Judgment. XI. 1—44.] *The raising of Lazarus.* On the omission of this, the chief of our Lord's miracles, by the three other Evangelists, see Prolegg. ch. i. § v. 1. **1.**] **δέ**, not transitional,—but expressing a contrast to the sojourn in Peræa, and thus conveying the reason why our Lord's retirement (see ch. x. 40) was broken in upon. Meyer (but not in edns. 2, 3), and Greswell, maintain that **ἀπό** means *present residence,*—**ἐκ**, *nativity.* But this distinction is *wholly untenable:* and all the inferences drawn from it in Mr. G.'s dissertation (vol. ii. p. 481 ff.) fall to the ground (see reff., especially last). Bethany is designated as 'the village of Martha and Mary,' to distinguish it from that Bethany beyond Jordan, which has just been alluded to (not named, perhaps to avoid the confusion), ch. x. 40. Mary and Martha are mentioned as already well known from the current apostolic teaching (see Prolegg. to John, § ii. 11). **2.**] Another reference to a fact which, as our Lord prophesied,

λέγουσαι Κύριε, [q] ἴδε ὃν φιλεῖς ἀσθενεῖ. 4 ἀκούσας δὲ ὁ
Ἰησοῦς εἶπεν Αὕτη ἡ ἀσθένεια οὐκ ἔστιν [r] πρὸς θάνατον,
ἀλλ' [s] ὑπὲρ τῆς δόξης τοῦ θεοῦ, [t] ἵνα [u] δοξασθῇ ὁ υἱὸς τοῦ
θεοῦ δι' αὐτῆς. 5 ἠγάπα δὲ ὁ Ἰησοῦς τὴν Μάρθαν καὶ
τὴν ἀδελφὴν αὐτῆς καὶ τὸν Λάζαρον. 6 ὡς οὖν ἤκουσεν
ὅτι [v] ἀσθενεῖ, τότε μὲν ἔμεινεν ἐν ᾧ ἦν τόπῳ δύο ἡμέρας.
7 ἔπειτα μετὰ τοῦτο λέγει τοῖς μαθηταῖς [w] Ἄγωμεν εἰς
C γουσιν αυτω... τὴν Ἰουδαίαν πάλιν. 8 λέγουσιν αὐτῷ οἱ μαθηταὶ Ῥαββί,
[x] νῦν [y] ἐζήτουν σε [z] λιθάσαι οἱ Ἰουδαῖοι, καὶ πάλιν ὑπάγεις
[a] ἐκεῖ; 9 ἀπεκρίθη Ἰησοῦς Οὐχὶ δώδεκα ὧραί εἰσιν τῆς

q = ch. iii. 26 al. r = ch. iv. 35. 2 Cor. i. 20. Col. ii. 23. Rev. xiii. 3. see 4 Kings xx. 1. s = Acts v. 41. ix. 16. Rom. xv. 8, 9 al. t = ch. ix. 3. u ch. viii. 54 al. v pres., ch. i. 40 reff. w = Matt. xxvi. 46. Mark i. 38. vv. 15, 16. ch. xiv. 31. x w. imperf., here only. Xen. Cyr. iv. 5. 48. y Matt. xii. 46, 47 reff. z ch. x. 31, &c. reff. a = Matt. ii. 22. xvii. 20. Luke xxi. 2. ch. xviii. 3. Rom. xv. 24 only. Deut. i. 37.

4. om 1st ὁ D. aft *ασθενεια* ins *αυτου* D 69 æth. ins *αλλ'* bef *ινα* ℵ.
5. for *ηγαπα*, *εφιλει* *amabat* D lat-*a e*.
6. aft *εμεινεν* ins *ο ιησους* D lat-*b* (*c*) *l*. for *εν ω ην*, *επι τω* D (sah).
7. for *επειτα*, *ειτα* D 435(Sz) Chr_1. aft *μαθ.* ins *αυτου* ADKΔΛ[ΓΠ] 69 lat-*b c f* [*ff*$_2$ *g l*^{2} syr-jer] syrr coptt æth : om Bℵ rel lat-*a* goth Chr_1 $Andr_1$. **πολιν** A ev-y : om ℵ[1] [sah-ming Chr_1 : ins bef *εις τ. ιου.* 1. 69 foss lat-*a c e ff*$_2$ Syr copt sah-woide æth arm Thdor-mops].
8. aft *μαθηται* ins *αυτου* D[Γ] Scr's e lat-*a c e* syrr [syr-jer] coptt æth.
9. rec ins ὁ bef *ιησ.*, with U (1, e sil) [$Andr_1$] : om ABCDℵ rel. rec *εισιν* bef *ωραι*, with E rel vulg-ed [lat-*ff*$_2$ *g*] syr goth : txt ABCKLMX[ΓΠ]ℵ 1. 33. 69 latt Syr

was known wherever the gospel was preached. This reference containing, as it does, the expression *τὸν κύριον* (= **our Lord**), q. d. 'as we all well know,'—is a striking illustration of that prophecy. John himself relates the occurrence, ch. xii. 3, being necessary for the course of his narrative. **3.**] The message (see vv. 21, 32) evidently was *to request the Lord to come and heal him:* and implies that the sickness was of a dangerous kind. **4.**] The only right understanding of this answer, and our Lord's whole proceeding here is,—that *He knew and foresaw all from the first,*—as well the termination of Lazarus's sickness and his being raised again, as the part which this miracle would bear in bringing about the close of His own ministry. **αὕτη ἡ ἀσθ.**] "Ostendit Christus, notum sibi, quod tanquam nescienti indicabatur." Grot. **οὐκ ἔστ. πρὸς θάν.**] Its *result* as regards Lazarus will not be *death* (see Matt. ix. 24 ||, and notes):—but (see ch. ii. 11; ix. 3) it has a higher purpose,—the glory of God;—the glorification, by its means, of the Son of God. And this **δοξασθῇ**—how was it accomplished? By *this miracle leading to his death,*—which in John's diction is so frequently implied in that word. (It need hardly be remarked, with Olsh. and Trench, that the glorifying of the Son of God in Lazarus *himself* is subordinately implied. Men are not mere tools, but temples, of God.) It is doubtful whether these words were the answer sent back to the sisters, or were said to the disciples. In either case, they evidently carried a double meaning, as again those in ver. 11. Ver. **5** explains **ὃν φιλεῖς**. Observe **ἠγάπα** here; while we have **ὃν φιλεῖς** in ver. 3, where there was no possibility of misunderstanding the import: cf. note on Matt. v. 46, and Trench, New Test. Synonyms, p. 45. **6.**] **οὖν** connects with ver. 4, 'Having then said this,—although He loved, &c., He abode,' &c.: *μέν* pointing on to *ἔπειτα μ. τ.* in next verse. In all probability Lazarus *was dead*, when He spoke the words ver. 4;—or at all events before the messenger returned. **7.**] If the **οὖν** in ver. 6 referred to this verse, the connexion must have been made by *καὶ μετὰ τ.*: the **ἔπειτα** cuts off all connexion (Gal. i. 18), and throws back the **οὖν** as explained above. The question, why our Lord did not go at once on receiving the message, is not to be answered by any secondary reasons, such as the trial of the faith of those concerned, or the pressing nature of His own ministry in Peræa,—but by referring back to ver. 4,—because, for the glory of God, He would have the miracle happen as it did and no otherwise. Compare Meyer. **8.**] **νῦν** = *ἀρτίως*—**but now. ἐζήτουν, were seeking: ὑπάγεις, art thou going?** **9, 10.**] Our Lord's answer is first general, vv. 9, 10,—then particular,

b = but trans., Matt. iv. 6 || L. from Ps. xc. 12. (Matt. vii. 27.) Jer. xiii. 16. met., Rom. ix. 32. xiv. 21. 1 Pet. i. 8 only.
c = 1 John i. 8, 10. ii. 10.
d = Matt. xxviii. 13. Luke xxii. 45. Acts xii. 6 only, or Matt. xxvii. 52. 1 Cor. xv. 6 al. 3 Kings xiv. 31.
e here only. 3 Kings iii. 15. Job xiv. 12 only. (-πνός, Acts xvi. 27.)

ἡμέρας; ἐάν τις περιπατῇ ἐν τῇ ἡμέρᾳ, οὐ [b] προσκόπτει, ABCDE
ὅτι τὸ φῶς τοῦ κόσμου τούτου βλέπει· 10 ἐὰν δέ τις FGHK LMSUX
περιπατῇ ἐν τῇ νυκτί, [b] προσκόπτει, ὅτι τὸ φῶς οὐκ [c] ἔστιν ΓΔΛΠℵ 1. 33. 69
ἐν αὐτῷ. 11 ταῦτα εἶπεν, καὶ μετὰ τοῦτο λέγει αὐτοῖς
Λάζαρος ὁ φίλος ἡμῶν [d] κεκοίμηται· ἀλλὰ πορεύομαι ἵνα
[e] ἐξυπνίσω αὐτόν. 12 εἶπον οὖν [οἱ μαθηταὶ] αὐτῷ Κύριε,
εἰ [d] κεκοίμηται, [f] σωθήσεται. 13 εἰρήκει δὲ ὁ Ἰησοῦς περὶ
τοῦ θανάτου αὐτοῦ· ἐκεῖνοι δὲ ἔδοξαν ὅτι περὶ τῆς [g] κοι-
μήσεως τοῦ ὕπνου [h] λέγει. 14 τότε οὖν εἶπεν αὐτοῖς ὁ
Ἰησοῦς [i] παῤῥησίᾳ Λάζαρος ἀπέθανεν, 15 καὶ χαίρω [k] δι'
ὑμᾶς, [l] ἵνα πιστεύσητε, ὅτι οὐκ ἤμην ἐκεῖ. ἀλλὰ [m] ἄγωμεν

ch. i. 40 reff. f as Matt. ix. 21 al. g here only †. Sir. xlvi. 19. xlviii. 13 only. h pres., i = ch. x. 24 reff. k = ch. x. 32 al. l = 1 Cor. v. 2. m ver. 7.

[syr-jer] Chr_1 Cyr_1.—ωρας εχει η ημερα D. for τουτου, του ℵ[1].

10. for αυτω, αυτη D[1](and lat : txt D-corr[1]) sah[-woide].

11. κοιμαται D[-gr]. for ινα εξυπ., του εξυπνισαι D [εξυπνησαι(omg του) Γ].

12. (ειπαν ℵ.) om οι μαθηται A [lat-ff_2 *l* $Andr_1$] : ins BC rel vulg lat-*e f* syr copt goth, and (but aft αυτω) DK[Π]ℵ lat-*b* Syr syr-mg [syr-jer æth] sah arm. rec αυτου, with C[2] rel vulg lat-*e f* syr-txt goth : txt ABC[1]DKXℵ 33 lat-*b* coptt arm. for κεκοιμηται, κοιμαται *dormit* D latt.

13. om αυτου (*homœotel?*) ℵ[1] Scr's c.

14. om ουν A 249 lat-*a* Syr [syr-jer (not sah, Tischdf expr)] copt æth arm. (ο insd above the line ℵ[1], appy.) aft λαζαρος ins ο φιλος ημων D.

15. (αλλα, so ACDEFGHLMUΛ[Π]ℵ 33.)

ver. 11. **οὐχὶ δώδ.**] See on ch. ix. 4, where the same thought is expressed. But here it is carried further,—'I have a fixed time during which to work, appointed me by my Father; during that time I fear no danger, I walk in His light, even as the traveller in the light of this world by day: and (by inference) ye too are safe, walking in this light, which light to you is Myself,—walking with Me:—whosoever walks without this light,—without Me,—without the light of the divine purpose illumining the path of duty, stumbles,—because he has no light in him.' **In him,** for 'the light of the body is the eye,' and the light must be *in us* in order to guide us. Shut it out by blinding the eyes, and we are in darkness. So too of spiritual light.

The twelve-hour division of the day was common among the Jews by this time, being probably borrowed from Babylon (*οἱ Ἕλληνες τὰ δυώδεκα μέρεα τῆς ἡμέρας παρὰ Βαβυλωνίων ἔμαθον*, Herod. ii. 109). As the day in Palestine varied in length from 14h. 12m. in summer to 9h. 48m. in winter, these hours must also have varied considerably in length at the different seasons (see Winer, Realwört. art. 'Tag'). I may remark that this verse refutes the fancy of Townson and others, also upheld by Bp. Wordsworth (who passes this verse without remark), that St. John adopts the so-called Asiatic method of reckoning time: see on ch. i. 40; iv. 6 al.

Notice **δώδεκα** emphatically prefixed, implying (as Bengel,—"jam multa erat hora, sed tamen adhuc erat dies") that though the conflict was far spent, there were yet more hours of daylight, and it could not yet be said *ἐλήλυθεν ἡ ὥρα*, ch. xvii. 1. Cf. ch. vii. 30; viii. 20; xii. 27: and consult Meyer's able and exhaustive note.

11.] The *special reason* for going, which the disciples appear not to have borne in mind, having probably supposed from ver. 4 that Lazarus would recover.

ὁ φίλ. ἡμ.] "Quanta humanitate Jesus amicitiam suam cum discipulis communicat!" Bengel. And the **ἡμῶν** gives a reason why *they* should go too. This **κεκοίμ.** might have recalled to *three at least* of the disciples that other saying, Matt. ix. 24. But the former *οὐ πρὸς θάν.* had not been understood,—and that error ruled in their minds. **ἐξυπνισθῆναι** *οὐ χρὴ λέγειν, ἀλλ'* **ἀφυπνισθῆναι.** Phryn. ed. Lobeck, p. 224.

12.] They evidently understand the sleep announced to them by Jesus as a physical fact,—**if he has fallen asleep,**—and a token of a favourable crisis, and **σωθήσεται** (as in E. V. **he shall do well**), = his recovery,—will probably be the result.

15.] "Notice that Jesus rejoices not over the

πρὸς αὐτόν. 16 εἶπεν οὖν Θωμᾶς ὁ [n] λεγόμενος [o] δίδυμος
τοῖς [p] συμμαθηταῖς [m] Ἄγωμεν καὶ ἡμεῖς, ἵνα ἀποθάνωμεν
μετ' αὐτοῦ. 17 ἐλθὼν οὖν ὁ Ἰησοῦς εὗρεν αὐτὸν τέσσαρας
ἤδη ἡμέρας [q] ἔχοντα ἐν τῷ [r] μνημείῳ. 18 ἦν δὲ ἡ Βηθανία
[s] ἐγγὺς [t] τῶν Ἱεροσολύμων, ὡς [u] ἀπὸ [v] σταδίων [w] δεκα-
πέντε· 19 πολλοὶ δὲ ἐκ τῶν Ἰουδαίων ἐληλύθεισαν πρὸς
* τὴν Μάρθαν καὶ Μαριάμ, ἵνα [x] παραμυθήσωνται αὐτὰς
περὶ τοῦ ἀδελφοῦ. 20 ἡ οὖν Μάρθα ὡς ἤκουσεν ὅτι
Ἰησοῦς [h] ἔρχεται, [y] ὑπήντησεν αὐτῷ· Μαρία δὲ ἐν τῷ

n = Matt. xxvii. 33. ch. i. 39. iv. 25. xx. 16, 24. xxi. 2. Acts ix. 36.
o ch. xx. 24. xxi. 2 only. LXX, plur. only, Gen. xxv. 24 al.
p here only +. Plato, Euthyd. p. 272 c.
q = ch. viii. 57 reff.
r Matt. viii. 28 al. Gen. xxiii. 6, 9.
s ch. iii. 23 reff.
t ch. v. 2 reff.
u = ch. xxi. 8. Rev. xiv. 20 only. J. Jos. Antt. xviii. 3. 2.
v ch. vi. 19 reff.
w Acts xxvii. 28. Gal. i. 18. Gen. vii. 20 A. [B def.]
x ver. 31. 1 Thess. ii. 11. v. 14 only +. 2 Macc. xv. 9 only. (-θία, 1 Cor. xiv. 3. -θιον, Phil. ii. 1.)
y Luke viii. 27 || Mt. (Mk. v. r.) xiv. 31. ver. 30. ch. iv. 51. xii. 18. Acts xvi. 16 only +. Tobit vii. 1 (not ℵ) al.

16. aft *συμμαθηταις* ins *αυτου* D tol lat-*f ff*$_2$ coptt goth.

17. *ηλθεν* and *και ευρεν* C[1](appy) D latt(not *f*). aft *ο ιησ.* ins *εις βηθανιαν* A[1]-corr DXΛℵ[3b] 33 Syr [syr-jer] æth: om [A[1]]BCℵ[1] rel vss. [*τεσσαρες* Δℵ.] rec *ημερας* bef *ηδη*, with A[2]C[3]ℵ rel vulg lat-*b c f* syr Andr$_1$: om *ηδη* A[1]D foss lat-*e* Syr coptt æth arm: txt BC[1] 69 (lat-*a g l*) goth. (*ηδηημ seems to have produced the confusion, and ηδη being omd was variously reinsd: so Mey.*) *εν τω μνημ.* bef *εχοντα* DL vulg lat-*b c ff*$_2$ *l*.

18. om ἡ Bℵ[1]. om *ως* D.

19. rec (for *πολλ. δε*) *και πολλοι*, with A rel lat-*f* syrr goth æth: txt BCDLXℵ 33 latt [syr-jer] coptt. for *ιουδ.*, *ιεροσολυμων* D. *rec τὰς περί, with AC[3] rel: om D: *τας*, omg *περι*, M: *την* BC[1]LXℵ 33 latt Syr coptt goth æth arm. (*μαριαμ*, so BCDLΔ.) rec aft *αδελφου* ins *αυτων*, with AC rel: om BDLℵ lat-*l* arm.

20. rec ins *ὁ* bef *ιησ.*, with M ev-z: om ABCD[ℵ] rel [Andr$_1$] Thl.

sad event itself, but that *He was not there*, which might prove salutary to the disciples' faith." Meyer. The **ἵνα πιστ.** is not to be taken as the *great end* of the miracle (expressed in ver. 4), but the end as regarded *them*. Beware of the imaginary *ecbatic ἵνα*, which does not exist. **ἀλλά** breaks off: "indicat, satis argumentorum allatum esse." Herm. ad Viger. p. 811. **16.**] **Θωμᾶς**, in Aramaic תְּאֹמָא = *δίδυμος*. The remark means, **Let us also go** (with our Master, implied in the **καί**), **that we may die with Him** (not, with Lazarus, as Grot.). This is in exact accord with the character of Thomas, as shewn in ch. xiv. 5; xx. 25;—ever ready to take the dark view, but deeply attached to his Lord. **17.**] Jesus remained two days after the receipt of the message: one day the journey would occupy: so that Lazarus must have died on the day of the messenger's being sent, and have been buried that evening, according to Jewish custom: see ver. 39, and Acts v. 6—10. **18.**] The geographical notice is given, to account for the occurrence detailed in the next verse. A stadium = $\frac{1}{8}$ of a Roman mile. Meyer remarks, that **ἦν** does not *necessarily* imply that the places no longer existed when the Apostle wrote, but may arise from the word occurring in context with a history which is past. So Xen. Anab. i. 4. 9, *αἱ δὲ κῶμαι ἐν αἷς ἐσκήνουν Παρυσάτιδος ἦσαν.* But seeing that *John alone* uses this form of designation (cf. ch. xviii. 1; xix. 41), and that he probably wrote after the destruction of Jerusalem, it is more natural (as Meyer himself confesses) to explain the past tense by his regarding Jerusalem and its neighbourhood as laid waste at the time when he published his Gospel. **19.**] Lightfoot (Hor. Hebr. in loc.) gives an account of the ceremonies practised during the thirty days of mourning. The rec. reading, **τὰς περὶ Μ. κ. Μ.**, would mean Martha and Mary and their friends—the women mourning with them. The expression is foreign to N. T. diction elsewhere, and might be used here for decorum, seeing that they were *men* who came: or as indicating that the house was one of large hospitality and acquaintance.

20.] The behaviour of the two sisters is quite in accordance with their character, Luke x. 38—42: and thus we have a most interesting point of connexion between two Gospels so widely various in their contents and character. Stier thinks (v. 19, edn. 2), as also Trench (Mirr. 398, edn. 2), that Mary *did not hear* of the

οἴκῳ [z] ἐκαθέζετο. 21 εἶπεν οὖν ἡ Μάρθα πρὸς τὸν Ἰησοῦν
Κύριε, [a] εἰ ἦς ὧδε, οὐκ ἂν ἐτεθνήκει ὁ ἀδελφός μου·
22 καὶ νῦν οἶδα ὅτι ὅσα ἂν [b] αἰτήσῃ τὸν θεὸν δώσει
σοι ὁ θεός. 23 λέγει αὐτῇ ὁ Ἰησοῦς [c] Ἀναστήσεται ὁ
ἀδελφός σου. 24 λέγει αὐτῷ ἡ Μάρθα Οἶδα ὅτι [c] ἀναστήσεται ἐν τῇ [d] ἀναστάσει ἐν τῇ [e] ἐσχάτῃ [e] ἡμέρᾳ. 25 εἶπεν
αὐτῇ ὁ Ἰησοῦς Ἐγώ εἰμι ἡ [d] ἀνάστασις καὶ ἡ ζωή. ὁ
[f] πιστεύων [f] εἰς ἐμὲ κἂν ἀποθάνῃ ζήσεται, 26 καὶ πᾶς ὁ
ζῶν καὶ [f] πιστεύων [f] εἰς ἐμὲ οὐ μὴ ἀποθάνῃ [g] εἰς τὸν αἰῶνα.

ABCDE FGHK LMSUX ΓΔΛΠℵ 1. 33. 69

z Matt. xxvi. 55 reff.
a constr. chiefly John, ch. xv. 19 al. Luke vii. 39. Acts xviii. 14. 1 Cor. xii. 19.
b Matt. xxi. 22. ch. xv. 7. 1 John iii. 22. v. 14, 15. Josh. xv. 18. of our Lord, here only.
c Matt. xx. 19. 1 Thess. iv. 16 al. Isa. xxvi. 19.
d Matt. xxii. 23, &c. reff.
e ch. vi. 39, 40 reff.
f ch. ii. 11 reff.
g ch. viii. 51 reff.

21. om ἡ A rel: ins BCDKLX[Π]ℵ 1. 33. om τον Bℵ. om κυριε (*see ver* 32) B C^1(appy): ins AC^2Dℵ rel. rec ο αδελφ. μου bef ουκ αν (*from ver* 32), with C^2 rel vulg lat-*b c e f* [ff_2] syr coptt arm [Chr_1]; bef the verb AD: order of txt BC^1LXℵ 1. 33 lat-*a g* [*l*] Syr goth æth Chr_2.—for ετεθνηκει, απεθανεν (*from ver* 32, *where none vary*) BC^1DKLX[Π]ℵ 1. 33 Chr_2 [$Andr_1$]: txt AC^3 rel.
22. rec at beg ins αλλα, with AC^3Dℵ^{3a} rel vulg lat-*b c e f* ff_2 [syrr coptt &c]: om BC^1Xℵ^1 1. 33 lat-*a* Chr_1 [$Andr_1$]. (εαν CMℵ. αιτησει M[Γ]ℵ.)
23. om 1st ὁ A. σου bef ὁ αδελφος D.
24. rec om η, with AC^3ℵ rel: ins BC^1DKLX[Π] 33 Chr.
25. aft ειπεν ins δε ℵ^1 1 lat-*b* Scr's c ev-y goth; ουν X 247-8-53-9 Scr's q ev-z.

approach of Jesus, and that we must not bring the characters to bear on this case (?). **21.**] This saying has evidently been the leading thought of the four days since their brother's death. Mary repeats it, ver. 32. **22.**] She seems to express some expectation of the raising of her brother; but it is too great a thing for her to venture to mention:—possibly she had not dared to form the thought fully, but had some vague feeling after help, such as she knew He would give. I can hardly see, as some have done, a "verbum minus dignum" (Bengel) in the form of her expression, ὅσα ἂν αἰτήσῃ τὸν θ. κ.τ.λ. It was said in the simplicity of her faith, which, it is true, was not yet a fully ripened faith: but it differs little from our Lord's own words, ver. 41.
The repetition of **ὁ θεός** after **τὸν θεόν** is to be noticed, as expressive of her faith in the unity of purpose and action between Jesus and God. **23.**] I believe these words of our Lord to contain no allusion to the *immediate* restoration of Lazarus; but to be pædagogically used, to lead on to the requisite faith in her mind. I have to learn whether ἀναστήσεται in this direct absolute sense could be used of his *recall into human life.*
24.] She understands the words rightly, but gently repels the insufficient comfort of his ultimate resurrection.
25, 26.] These words, as Stier observes, are the *central point* of the history; the *great testimony to Himself,* of which the subsequent miracle is *the proof.* The *intention* of the saying seems to have been, to awaken in Martha the faith that He could raise her brother from the dead, in its highest and proper form. This He does by announcing *Himself* (**ἐγώ, I, and no other . . .**) as 'THE RESURRECTION' (q. d.—that resurrection in the last day shall be only *by my Power,* and therefore I can raise now as well), and more than that, THE LIFE ITSELF: so that **he that believeth in me** (= Lazarus, *in her mind*), **even though he have died** (ἀποθάνῃ, past) **shall live; and he that liveth** (physically, 'is not yet dead') **and believeth in me, shall never die:** i. e. 'faith in Me is the source of *life,* both here and hereafter; *and those who have it, have Life, so that they shall* NEVER DIE;' *physical death* being overlooked and disregarded, in comparison with that which is really and only *death.* Compare 4 Macc. vii. 19. The **ζῶν** *must* be (against Lampe, Olshausen, and Stier) taken of *physical life,* for it stands opposed to **κἂν ἀποθάνῃ**. **ὁ πιστ. εἰς ἐμέ** is the subject of both clauses; in the former it is said that he κἂν ἀποθ., ζήσεται: in the second, that he ζῶν, οὐ μὴ ἀποθάνῃ. Olshausen's remark, that ζῶν and ἀποθ. in the second clause must *both* be physical, *if one is,* is wrong; the antithesis consisting, in both clauses, in the reciprocation of the two senses, physical and spiritual; and serving in the latter clause, as a key hereafter to the condition of Lazarus, *when raised* from the dead.
There can hardly be any reference

[h] πιστεύεις τοῦτο; 27 λέγει αὐτῷ Ναὶ κύριε· ἐγὼ πεπίστευκα ὅτι σὺ εἶ ὁ χριστὸς ὁ υἱὸς τοῦ θεοῦ ὁ εἰς τὸν
κόσμον [i] ἐρχόμενος. 28 καὶ τοῦτο εἰποῦσα ἀπῆλθεν καὶ
[k] ἐφώνησεν Μαριὰμ τὴν ἀδελφὴν αὐτῆς [l] λάθρα εἰποῦσα
Ὁ [m] διδάσκαλος [n] πάρεστιν καὶ [k] φωνεῖ σε. 29 ἐκείνη
[δὲ] ὡς ἤκουσεν, ἠγέρθη ταχὺ καὶ ἤρχετο πρὸς αὐτόν.
30 οὔπω δὲ ἐληλύθει ὁ Ἰησοῦς εἰς τὴν [o] κώμην, ἀλλ' ἦν
[ἔτι] ἐν τῷ τόπῳ ὅπου [p] ὑπήντησεν αὐτῷ ἡ Μάρθα. 31 οἱ
οὖν Ἰουδαῖοι οἱ ὄντες μετ' αὐτῆς ἐν τῇ οἰκίᾳ καὶ [q] παρα-
μυθούμενοι αὐτήν, ἰδόντες τὴν Μαριὰμ [r] ὅτι [s] ταχέως
ἀνέστη καὶ ἐξῆλθεν, ἠκολούθησαν αὐτῇ [t] δόξαντες ὅτι
[u] ὑπάγει εἰς τὸ μνημεῖον ἵνα κλαύσῃ ἐκεῖ. 32 ἡ οὖν

h acc., Acts xiii. 41, from Hab. i. 5. 1 Cor. xiii. 7. 1 John iv. 16.
i Matt. xi. 3 reff.
k = Matt. xx. 32 reff.
l Matt. i. 19. ii. 7. Acts xvi. 37 only. Deut. xiii. 6.
m Matt. viii. 19. xii. 38. xxvi. 18 ||, al.+ 2 Macc. i. 10 only.
n Matt. xxvi. 50 reff.
o ver. 1.
p ver. 20 reff.
q ver. 19.
r constr., Mar xii. 34.
s Luke xiv. reff.
t Matt. vi. 7 reff.
u pres., ch. i. 40 reff.

27. om *αυτω* D-gr 57 copt. for *ναι κυριε, ο ιησους* A. for *πεπιστευκα, πιστευω* B¹(corrd *eadem manu,* Tischdf) Scr's c t: *επιστευσα* E¹. *κοσμος* D¹(txt D⁴).

28. rec (for *τουτο*) *ταυτα,* with AD rel latt syrr [syr-jer] sah arm: txt BCLXℵ copt goth æth. (33 def.) (*μαριαμ,* so ABCDKLΔ[Π] 33.) *την αδελφ. αυτ.* bef *μα.* D. for *λαθρα, σιωπη* D latt. for 2nd *ειπουσα, ειπασα* BC¹: txt AC²Dℵ rel [Andr$_1$]. (33 def.) add *οτι* D.

29. rec om *δε,* with AC²D rel vulg lat-*a c e* [*g*] arm: ins BC¹LXℵ 33. 69 lat-*f* syr-w-ast [syr-jer] coptt goth. rec (for *ηγερθη*) *εγειρεται,* with AC³ rel vulg [lat-*l*] syrr: txt BC¹DL X(Treg, expr) ℵ 33 [foss mt] lat-*a b c e f ff$_2$ l* syr-mg goth æth arm Andr. rec *ερχεται,* with AC³D rel vulg lat-*c e f* [*g*] syr copt: txt BC¹L X(Treg, expr) ℵ 33 lat-*a b ff$_2$ l* Syr goth æth (arm).

30. for *ουπω, ου* D-gr. for *δε, γαρ* D latt (copt?) goth. *ιησ.* bef *εληλυθει,* omg *ὁ,* D [Andr$_1$]. (*αλλα* D.) rec om *ετι,* with AD rel syrr æth: *ετι* bef *ην* F lat-*a e* sah Andr: txt BCXℵ 1. 33 latt copt goth arm Aug. om *ἡ* D Scr's c.

31. om *και* (bef *παραμυθ.*) D foss lat-*f l* [*b e ff$_2$* Syr syr-jer arm]. (*μαριαμ,* so BC¹DKLΔ[Π] 33.) rec (for *δοξαντες*) *λεγοντες,* with AC² rel latt syr[-txt syr-jer] sah goth: txt B C¹(appy) DLXℵ 1. 33 Syr syr-mg copt æth arm Andr Non$_1$. ins *ῑς* bef *υπαγει* ℵ¹(marked for erasure *eadem manu*).

in ver. 26 to the *state of the living faithful at the Lord's coming* (*πάντες οὐ κοιμηθησόμεθα, πάντες δὲ ἀλλαγησόμεθα,* 1 Cor. xv. 51),—for although the Apostle there, speaking of believers primarily and especially, uses the first person,—the saying would be equally true of unbelievers, on whose bodies the change from *τὸ φθαρτόν* to *ἀφθαρσία* will equally pass, and of whom the *οὐ μὴ ἀποθάνῃ* here would be equally true,—whereas the saying is one setting forth an exclusive privilege of *ὁ ζῶν κ. πιστεύων εἰς ἐμέ.* Besides, such an interpretation would set aside all reference to Lazarus, or to present circumstances.

27.] Her confession, though embracing the great central point of the truth in the last verse, does not enter fully into it. Nor does she (ver. 40) seem to have adequately apprehended its meaning. *ὅτι μὲν μεγάλα περὶ ἑαυτοῦ εἶπεν, ἔγνω·* **πῶς δὲ ταῦτα εἶπεν,** *ἠγνόησε· διὰ τοῦτο ἕτερον ἐρωτηθεῖσα, ἕτερον ἀποκρίνεται,* Euthym. **ἐγώ,** I, for my part: **πεπίστευκα,** 'have convinced myself, and firmly believe.' **ὁ ἐρχ.**] Who should come: see reff. **28.**] Her calling her sister is characteristic of one who (as in Luke x. 40) had not been much habituated herself to listen to His instructions, but knew this to be the delight of Mary. Besides this, she evidently has hopes raised, though of a very faint and indefinite kind. *προσδοκήσασά τι ἀγαθὸν ἀπὸ τῶν λόγων αὐτοῦ.* Euthym. **λάθρα**] *ἵνα μὴ οἱ παρόντες Ἰουδαῖοι τοῦτο γνῶσι, καὶ ἴσως καταμηνύσωσιν αὐτὸν τοῖς ἐπιβουλεύουσιν.* Euthym. This fear was realized (ver. 46). **φωνεῖ σε**] This is not recorded. Stier thinks that the Lord had not actually asked for her, but that Martha sees such an especial fitness for her hearing in the words of vv. 25, 26, that she uses this expression. But is it not somewhat too plainly asserted, to mean only *calling by inference?* Meyer regards the **φωνεῖ σε** as proving it to have been a fact.

31.] **ἵνα κλ. ἐκεῖ**—as is the custom

v see Mark v. 40. ch. vi. 62. xxi. 18 bis. w Mark v. 22. Acts v. 10. Rev. i. 17 only. see Mark vii. 25. x constr., Mark xiv. 53, or Luke xxiii. 55. Acts ix. 39 al. y ver. 38. Matt. ix. 30. Mark i. 43. xiv. 5 only+. Isa. xvii. 13 Symm. (-μημα, Lam. ii. 6.) z = Mark ii. 8 reff. a = ch. xii. 27. xiii. 21. xiv. 1, 27. Matt. ii. 3 al. Gen. xliii. 30. b = Mark xv. 47. xvi. 6. ch. xix. 42 ‖ Mt. L. xx. 2, 13, 15. Acts ix. 37.

Μαριὰμ ὡς v ἦλθεν v ὅπου v ἦν Ἰησοῦς, ἰδοῦσα αὐτὸν w ἔπε- ABCDE
σεν αὐτοῦ w πρὸς τοὺς w πόδας λέγουσα αὐτῷ Κύριε, εἰ ἦς FGHK
ὧδε, οὐκ ἄν μου ἀπέθανεν ὁ ἀδελφός. LMSUX ΓΔΛΠℵ 1. 33. 69
33 Ἰησοῦς οὖν
ὡς εἶδεν αὐτὴν κλαίουσαν καὶ τοὺς x συνελθόντας αὐτῇ
Ἰουδαίους κλαίοντας, y ἐνεβριμήσατο τῷ z πνεύματι καὶ
a ἐτάραξεν ἑαυτὸν
34 καὶ εἶπεν Ποῦ b τεθείκατε αὐτόν;

32. (*μαριαμ*, so BC¹E¹L [33].) rec ins *ο* bef *ιησ.*, with C³Lℵ^3a rel [Andr]: om ABC^1.2DKX[Π^1.3]ℵ¹ 33.—*ιησ.* bef *ην* C¹(appy). om *αυτον* D. rec *εις τους ποδας* bef *αυτου*, with D latt arm Chr₁: txt ABCℵ rel [lat-*f*] goth Andr.—rec (for *προς*) *εις*, with AC³ rel: txt BC¹DLXℵ Andr. om *αυτω* DX lat-*a* copt arm. *ωδε* bef *ης* D [lat-*a b c e*]. rec *απεθανεν* bef *μου*, with AC³ rel: *ο αδελφ.* bef *απεθ.* D: *απ. ο αδελφ.* bef *μου* 69 latt [arm]: txt BC¹LΔℵ 33.

33. om *ως* ℵ¹. for *τους* to *κλαιοντας*, *τους ιδοιους*(sic D¹-gr, *ιουδαιους* D³) *κλαιοντας τους συνεληλυθοτας μετ' αυτης* D lat-*a b c e ff₂* [*g*] *l*. for *ενεβριμ.* to *εαυτ.*, *εταραχθη τω πν. ως ενβρειμουμενος* D 1 sah-mnt arm. *εβριμησατο* A ℵ¹(txt ℵ-corr^1 or 2.3).

even now in the East [see an affecting account in Lamartine's Pilgrimage to the Holy Land. English Translation, vol. ii. pp. 76—78]. **32.**] The words of Mary are fewer, and her action more impassioned, than those of her sister: she was perhaps interrupted by the arrival of the Jews: cf. ver. 33. Kühner, Gram. § 627, Anm. 4, remarks that when the genitive of the enclitic personal pronoun is prefixed to its substantive, a slight sense of the *dativus commodi* is given: "non mihi frater mortuus esset." **33.**] In explaining this difficult verse, two things must be borne in mind: (1) that **ἐμβριμάομαι** can bear but one meaning, that of *indignor* ("infremuit," Vulg.),—the expression of *indignation* and *rebuke, not of sorrow.* This has been here acknowledged by all the expositors who have paid any attention to the usage of the word. (2) That both from **ὡς εἶδεν**, &c.,—from **καὶ ἐτάραξ. ἑαυτ.**, and ver. 35,—the feeling in the Lord was clearly one of *rising sympathy*, which vented itself at last in tears.

These two things being premised, I think the meaning to be, that Jesus, with the tears of sympathy already rising and overcoming His speech, *checked them, so as to be able to speak the words following.* I would read *ἐνεβρ. τ. πν., καὶ ἐτ. ἑαυ., καὶ εἶπεν* in immediate connexion, as expressing the temporary check given to the flow of His tears,—*the effort used to utter the following question.* And I would thus divest the self-restraint of all stoical and unworthy character, and consider it as *merely physical*, requiring indeed an act of the will, and a self-troubling,—a complication of feeling,—but implying no deliberate disapproval of the rising emotion, which indeed immediately after is suffered to prevail. What minister has not, when burying the dead in the midst of a weeping family, felt the emotion and made the effort here described? And surely this was one of the things in which He was made like unto His brethren. Thus Bengel: "Ita Jesus austeriore affectu lacrymas hic cohibuit, et mox ver. 38 abrupit. Eoque major earum fuit auctoritas." Meyer's explanation deserves mention: that our Lord was indignant at seeing the Jews, His bitter enemies, mingling their hypocritical tears (Crocodilsthränen) with the true ones of the bereaved sister. But, not to say how unworthy this seems of the Person and occasion, the explanation will find no place in ver. 38: for surely the question of the Jews in ver. 37 is not enough to justify it. Still perhaps any contribution to the solution of this difficult word is not to be summarily rejected. **τῷ πν.** is not the dat. after **ἐνεβρ.**, '*rebuked His spirit,*'—but **in Spirit**: see *ἐν ἑαυτῷ* ver. 38. Indignation over unbelief and sin, and death the fruit of sin, doubtless lay in the background; but to see it *in the words* (with Olsh., Stier, and Trench), seems unnatural. **ἐτάραξεν ἑαυτόν** is understood by Meyer, and perhaps rightly, as describing an outward motion of the body,—**He shuddered**: and so Euthym.: *διέσεισε* (not, as Bloomf. somewhat confidently asserts, a blunder of the scribes for *διεσείσθη*, but the (so-called) intrans. sense of *σείω*, in which it was used of this very act of 'shaking' bodily: cf. Xen. Cyneg. iii. 4, *αἱ δὲ τὰ ὦτα μὲν ἀκίνητα ἔχουσιν, ἄκρᾳ δὲ τῇ οὐρᾷ σείουσιν*: ib. vi. 15, *ταχὺ ταῖς οὐραῖς διασείουσαι*: cf. also the impersonal usage, Thuc. iv. 52, *τοῦ αὐτοῦ*

λέγουσιν αὐτῷ Κύριε, ἔρχου καὶ ἴδε. 35 c ἐδάκρυσεν ὁ
Ἰησοῦς. 36 ἔλεγον οὖν οἱ Ἰουδαῖοι Ἴδε πῶς ἐφίλει αὐτόν.
37 τινὲς δὲ ἐξ αὐτῶν εἶπον Οὐκ ἐδύνατο οὗτος ὁ d ἀνοίξας
τοὺς d ὀφθαλμοὺς τοῦ τυφλοῦ ³ ποιῆσαι e ἵνα καὶ οὗτος
μὴ ἀποθάνῃ; 38 Ἰησοῦς οὖν πάλιν f ἐμβριμώμενος ἐν
ἑαυτῷ ἔρχεται εἰς τὸ μνημεῖον· ἦν δὲ g σπήλαιον, καὶ
λίθος h ἐπέκειτο ἐπ' αὐτῷ. 39 λέγει ὁ Ἰησοῦς Ἄρατε τὸν
λίθον. λέγει αὐτῷ ἡ ἀδελφὴ τοῦ τετελευτηκότος Μάρθα
Κύριε, ἤδη i ὄζει· k τεταρταῖος γάρ ἐστιν. 40 λέγει αὐτῇ

c here only. Job iii. 24. d ch. ix. 10, &c. reff. e = Col. iv. 10. Rev. iii. 9. xiii. 12, [15,] 16. Eccl. iii. 14. f ver. 33 reff. g Matt. xxi. 13 ||. Heb. xi. 38. Rev. vi. 15 only. Gen. xix. 30. h = ch. xxi. 9 only. 2 Macc. i. 21. (Luke v. 1. xxiii. 23. Acts xxvii. 20. 1 Cor. ix. 16. Heb. ix. 10 only. Job xix. 3.) i here only. Exod. viii. 14 (ἐπόζ., Ald., &c.) only(?). k here only. Herod. ii. 89. (Xen. Anab. vi. 4. 9, πεμπταῖοι, of the dead.)

35. ins και bef εδακρυσεν Dℵ 69 latt Syr [syr-jer] copt goth æth arm. om ὁ ℵ¹.
[36. ελεγαν ℵ¹.]
37. for ειπον, [ειπαν ℵ¹:] ελεγον AK[Π] Chr-mss₁: ειπ. bef εξ ων(sic D¹, αυτων D²) D [am(with fuld forj ing) lat-*a b c e ff₂*]. (εδυνατο, so B¹CDK[Π].)
38. εμβριμουμενος (*itacism?*) AUℵ 69: εμβριμησαμενος C¹X Andr₁. for εις, επι D. om επ' Lℵ¹ Scr's f v (latt).
39. om ὁ AD[Π¹]: ins BCℵ rel. μαρθα bef η αδελφη D(prefg ἡ) vulg lat-*a f g* syrr coptt æth arm. rec (for τετελευτ.) τεθνηκοτος, with C² rel: txt ABC¹DKL[Π]ℵ 33 syr-mg Andr. om γαρ D [Epiph₁].

μηνὸς ἱσταμένου, ἔσεισε)· συμβαίνει γὰρ τινάσσεσθαι τὰ ἀνώτερα μέρη τῶν οὕτως ἐμβριμωμένων. Cyril's comment is, ἐπειδὴ οὐ μόνον θεὸς κατὰ φύσιν ἀλλὰ καὶ ἄνθρωπος ἦν ὁ χριστός, πάσχει καὶ νῦν τὸ ἀνθρώπινον· ἀρχομένης δέ πως ἐν αὐτῷ κινεῖσθαι τῆς λύπης, καὶ νευούσης ἤδη πρὸς τὸ δάκρυον τῆς ἁγίας σαρκός, οὐκ ἐφίησιν αὐτὴν τοῦτο παθεῖν ἐκλύτως, καθάπερ ἔθος ἡμῖν, ἐμβριμᾶται δὲ τῷ πνεύματι, τουτέστι τῇ δυνάμει τοῦ ἁγίου πνεύματος ἐπιπλήττει τρόπον τινὰ τῇ ἰδίᾳ σαρκί· ἡ δέ, τὸ τῆς ἑνωθείσης αὐτῇ θεότητος οὐκ ἐνεγκοῦσα κίνημα, τρέμει τε καὶ θορύβου πλάττεται σχῆμα καὶ συγχέεται. πένθος γὰρ οἶδεν ἀναῤῥιπίζειν. τοῦτο γὰρ οἶμαι σημαίνειν τὸ **ἐτάραξεν ἑαυτόν.**

35—38.] It is probable that the second set of Jews (ver. 37) spoke with a scoffing and hostile purport: for John seldom uses δέ as a mere copula, but generally as **but**: see vv. 46, 49, 51. It is (Trench, p. 407, edn. 2) a mark of accuracy in the narrative, that these dwellers in Jerusalem should refer to a miracle so well known among themselves, rather than to the former raisings of the dead in Galilee (Strauss has made this very point an objection), of which they probably may have heard, but naturally would not thoroughly believe on rumour only. Again, of *raising* Lazarus none of them seem to have thought, only of preventing his death. This second ἐμβριμᾶσθαι of our Lord I would refer to the same reason as the first. ἐδάκρυσε μέν, **ἀφεὶς** τὴν φύσιν ἐνδείξασθαι τὰ ἑαυτῆς· . . . . εἶτα πάλιν ἐμβριμᾶται τῷ πάθει. Euthym. Only he assigns a didactic purpose, to teach us moderation in our tears; I should rather believe the self-restraint to have been exercised as a preparation for what followed. The caves were generally horizontal, natural or artificial, —with recesses in the sides, where the bodies were laid. There is no necessity here for supposing the entrance to have been otherwise than horizontal, as the word σπήλαιον would lead us to believe. Graves were of both kinds: we have the vertically sunk mentioned Luke xi. 44. See on the whole subject, Winer, Realw. art. 'Gräber:' and cf. Isa. xxii. 16: 2 Chron. xvi. 14: 2 Kings xxiii. 16. Probably, from this circumstance, as from 'the Jews' coming to condole,—and the costly ointment (ch. xii. 3),—the family was wealthy.

39.] The corpse had not been embalmed, but merely 'wrapped in linen clothes with spices, as the manner of the Jews is to bury,'—see ch. xix. 40, and ver. 44 below. ἡ ἀδελφὴ τοῦ τετελευτηκότος, as Meyer remarks, notes the natural horror of the *sister's heart* at what was about to be done. There is no reason to avoid the assumption of the plain fact (see below) stated in **ἤδη ὄζει.** I cannot see that any monstrous character (Olsh., Trench) is given to the miracle by it; any more than such a character can be predicated of *restoring the withered hand*. In fact, the very *act* of death is the beginning of decomposition. I have no hesitation, with almost all the ancient,

ὁ Ἰησοῦς Οὐκ εἶπόν σοι ὅτι ἐὰν πιστεύσῃς ὄψῃ τὴν
[l] δόξαν τοῦ θεοῦ; 41 ἦραν οὖν τὸν λίθον. ὁ δὲ Ἰησοῦς ...θεου F.
[m] ἦρεν τοὺς [m] ὀφθαλμοὺς ἄνω καὶ εἶπεν Πάτερ, [n] εὐχα- ABCDE GHKL
ριστῶ σοι ὅτι ἤκουσάς μου. 42 ἐγὼ δὲ ᾔδειν ὅτι πάντοτέ MSUX ΓΔΛΠℵ
μου ἀκούεις· ἀλλὰ [o] διὰ τὸν ὄχλον τὸν [p] περιεστῶτα 1. 33. 69
εἶπον, ἵνα πιστεύσωσιν ὅτι σύ με ἀπέστειλας. 43 καὶ ταῦτα
εἰπὼν φωνῇ μεγάλῃ [q] ἐκραύγασεν Λάζαρε, [r] δεῦρο ἔξω.
44 ἐξῆλθεν ὁ τεθνηκὼς [s] δεδεμένος τοὺς [s] πόδας καὶ τὰς
[s] χεῖρας [t] κειρίαις, καὶ ἡ [u] ὄψις αὐτοῦ [v] σουδαρίῳ [w] περιεδέ-

l see Rom. vi. 4. m here only. Zech. i. 18 al. see ch. iv. 35. Luke xvii. 13. Acts iv. 24. Judg. xxi. 2. Ps. cxxii. 1. n w. ὅτι, 1 Cor. i. 14. 2 Thess. ii. 13. Rev. xi. 17 al. Wisd. xviii. 2. o ch. x. 32 reff. p = Acts xxv. 7 (2 Tim. ii. 16. Tit. iii. 9) only. 2 Kings xiii. 31. q ch. xviii. 40 reff. r Acts vii. 34, from Exod. iii. 10. Rev. xvii. 1. xxi. 9. s Matt. xxii. 13. t here only. Prov. vii. 16 only. u = Rev. i. 16 (ch. vii. 24) only. Cant. ii. 14. v Luke xix. 20. ch. xx. 7. Acts xix. 12 only †. w here only. Job xii. 18 Bℵ only.

40. om ὁ A 1. rec οψει (*itacism?*), with KU[ΓΠ¹]: txt ABCDℵ rel $Orig_3$.
41. for ηραν ουν, οτε ουν ηραν D lat-*e* arm. rec aft λιθον ins ου ην ο τεθνηκως κειμενος, with C³ rel $Chr\text{-}montf_1$; ου ην AK[Π] 1 lat-*f* syr goth: om BC¹DLXℵ 33 latt Syr syr-jer æth arm $Orig_4$ $Chr\text{-}mss_1$. for ο δε, και D. aft οφθαλμους ins αυτου D 33. 69 $Orig_1$ Eus_2 Chr_1.
42. om δε D (69) lat-*c*.
43. εκραξεν C¹ Chr_1: εκραυγαζεν ℵ¹. for λαζαρε, λαζαρ ℵ¹.
44. rec ins και bef εξηλθεν, with AC³ℵ rel lat-*a b c* [syrr &c] $Iren\text{-}int_1$; και ευθυς D vulg lat-*f* $Andr_2$: om BC¹L sah $Orig_1$ transp τ. ποδας and τ. χειρας AΛ 69 foss(with gat) lat-*a b c* syrr æth $Andr_2$. κηριαις (*itacism*) AXΔΛ 33. περιδεδετο

and many of the best modern Commentators, in assuming ἤδη ὄζει as *a fact*, and indeed with Stier, believing it to be spoken *not as a supposition*, but *as a* (sensible) *fact*. The entrances to these vaults were not *built up*,—merely defended, by a stone being rolled to them, from the jackals and beasts of prey. **40.**] I can hardly think she supposed merely that Jesus desired to *look on the face of the dead*;—she expected *something* was about to be done, but in her anxiety for decorum (Luke x. 40) she was willing to avoid the consequence of opening the cave. This feeling Jesus here rebukes, by referring her to the plain duty of simple faith, insisted on by Him before (vv. 25, 26? or in some other teaching?) as the condition of beholding the glory of God (not merely in the event about to follow,—for that was seen by many who did not believe,—but in a deeper sense,—that of the unfolding of the ἀνάστασις κ. ζωή in the personal being). **41, 42.**] In the filial relation of the Lord Jesus to the Father, all power is *given* to Him: the Son can do nothing of Himself:—and during His humiliation on earth, these acts of power were done by Him, not by that glory of His own which He had laid aside, but by the mighty working of the Father *in Him*, and in answer to His prayer: the difference between Him and us in this respect being, that His prayer *was always heard*, —even (Heb. v. 7) that in Gethsemane. And this **ἤκουσάς μου** He states here for the benefit of the standers-by, that they might know the truth of His repeated assertions of His mission from the Father. At the same time He guards this, ver. 42, from future misconstruction, as though He had no more power than *men* who pray, by ἐγὼ δὲ ᾔδειν ὅτι πάντοτέ μου ἀκούεις, 'because Thou and I are One.'

When He prayed, does not appear. Probably in Peræa, before the declaration in ver. 4. **43.**] Some (Chrys., Lampe) suppose that the revivification had taken place before εὐχαριστῶ σοι,—and these words were *merely a summoning forth*. But this is highly improbable. The comparison of ch. v. 25, 28, which are analogically applicable, makes it clear that **ἀκούσαντες** ζήσονται is the physical as well as the spiritual order of things. **κραυγάζειν** was not His wont: see Matt. xii. 19. This cry signified *that greater one*, which all shall hear, ch. v. 28.

44.] **κειρία**, εἶδος ζώνης ἐκ σχοινίων, παρεοικὸς ἱμάντι, ᾗ δεσμοῦσι τὰς κλίνας (see ref.), Suidas. κειρία ὁ τῶν νηπίων δεσμός, ἤγουν ἡ κοίνως φασκία (fascia), καὶ ᾗ δεσμοῦσι τοὺς νεκρούς, Moschopulus (in Kuinoel). It does not appear whether the bands were wound about each limb, as in the Egyptian mummies, so as merely to *impede* motion,—or were loosely wrapped round both feet and both hands, so as to hinder any free movement altogether. The latter seems most probable, and has been supposed by many, e.g. Basil, Homil. de gratiar. actione, c. 5, vol. iii. p. 29, ὁ νεκρὸς

δετο. λέγει αὐτοῖς ὁ Ἰησοῦς [x] Λύσατε αὐτὸν καὶ [y] ἄφετε
αὐτὸν ὑπάγειν.
45 Πολλοὶ οὖν ἐκ τῶν Ἰουδαίων οἱ ἐλθόντες πρὸς τὴν
Μαριὰμ καὶ [z] θεασάμενοι ὃ ἐποίησεν, [a] ἐπίστευσαν [a] εἰς αὐτόν.
46 τινὲς δὲ ἐξ αὐτῶν ἀπῆλθον πρὸς τοὺς Φαρισαίους καὶ
...εποιησεν ις C. εἶπον αὐτοῖς ἃ ἐποίησεν Ἰησοῦς. 47 [b] συνήγαγον οὖν οἱ
ἀρχιερεῖς καὶ οἱ Φαρισαῖοι [c] συνέδριον, καὶ ἔλεγον [d] Τί
[d] ποιοῦμεν; ὅτι οὗτος ὁ ἄνθρωπος πολλὰ ποιεῖ [e] σημεῖα.
48 ἐὰν [f] ἀφῶμεν αὐτὸν οὕτως, πάντες [a] πιστεύσουσιν [a] εἰς
αὐτόν· καὶ ἐλεύσονται οἱ Ῥωμαῖοι καὶ [g] ἀροῦσιν ἡμῶν

x = Acts xxii. 30. Rev. ix. 14, 15. Jer. xlvii. (xl.) 4.
y = Mark v. 37 reff.
z Luke xxiii. 55 reff.
a ch. ii. 11 reff.
b = Matt. ii. 4. xxii. 10. Rev. xiii. 10 al. 2 Chron. xxiv. 5.
c John, here only. Matt. xxvi. 59. Acts v. 41 al. Prov. xxii. 10.
d Mark xi. 5 reff.
e = ch. ii. 11 reff.
f = Matt. xv. 14. Mark xiv. 6. 4 Kings iv. 27.
g Matt. xxi. 21. ch. ii. 16. xx. 1. 1 Macc. v. 2.

D¹(txt D²). ὁ ιησ. bef αυτοις (B)L am[with forj fuld ing²] coptt $Orig_2$: txt A C(appy) Dℵ rel vulg-ed lat-*c ff*$_2$ syrr æth.—om ὁ B $Orig_1$. rec om 2nd αυτον, with AC²Dℵ rel latt syrr sah goth arm $Andr_3$ Iren-int_1: ins BC¹L 33 copt æth $Orig_4$ Chr_1.

45. for ουν, δε L[Sz] ℵ sah. om εκ D **1** (copt?) $Orig_1$. for οι ελθ., των ελθοντων D. for και θεασ., εωρακοτες D. (μαριαμ, so BCDL 33.) rec (for ὅ) ἅ, with A¹ℵ rel latt [copt arm] $Orig_6$: txt A²BCD **1** lat-*e* sah goth æth. rec aft εποιησ. add ο ιησ., with C²·³D rel vulg-ed lat-*a f ff*$_2$ *g* Syr [syr-jer] æth $Orig_3$ [$Andr_1$]: ιησους ℵ: om AB C¹(appy) LX **1** am(with fuld em forj foss gat ing jac mm tol) lat-*b c* (*e*) [*l*] coptt goth arm $Orig_3$.

46. (απηλθαν D.) (ειπαν Dℵ.) for ἅ, ὅ CDM 69 lat-*b e* copt goth æth: οσα A[Π] Syr: txt Bℵ rel vulg lat-*a c f* [*ff*$_2$ *g*] syr sah arm $Orig_3$. (S omits ver.) rec ins ο bef ιησ., with Aℵ rel $Orig_3$: om BCDL.

47. om οτι D. for πολλα, τοιαυτα D lat-*b c e ff*$_2$. rec σημεια bef ποιει, with D rel vss [Chr]: txt ABLMXℵ 33 sah Orig Ath.

48. ins και bef εαν D 245 Syr [syr-jer] copt-wilk æth. πιστευουσιν ℵ¹ 258 [-σωσιν GHLXΓΔ 1. 33. 69].

ἐζωοποιεῖτο καὶ ὁ δεδεμένος περιεπάτει· θαῦμα ἐν θαύματι, κειρίαις δεδέσθαι τοὺς πόδας, καὶ μὴ κωλύεσθαι πρὸς κίνησιν. Ancient pictures represent Lazarus gliding forth from the tomb, not stepping: and that apparently is right. The **σουδάριον** appears to have tied up his chin. **ὑπάγειν**, probably, to his home.

45—57.] The death of Jesus the life of the world. *Consequences of the miracle. Meeting of the Sanhedrim and final determination, on the prophetic intimation of the High Priest, to put Jesus to death. He retires to Ephraim.*

46.] Meyer, with his usual philological acumen, takes pains to set right the understanding of this. In the last verse, it is not πολλοὶ . . . . τῶν ἐλθόντων, but πολλοὶ . . . **οἱ ἐλθόντες**: thus identifying the πολλοί with those that came: 'many . . to wit, *those that came*.' All these ἐπίστευσαν εἰς αὐτόν (see a similar case in ch. viii. 30 ff.). Then, τινὲς ἐξ αὐτῶν, viz. the ἐλθόντων, and πιστευόντων, went, &c. The **δέ** (see on ver. 37) certainly shews that this was done with a hostile intent: not in *doubt* as to the miracle, any more than in the case of the blind man, ch. ix., but with a view to stir up the rulers yet more against Him. This Evangelist is very simple, and at the same time very consistent, in his use of *particles:* almost throughout his Gospel the great subject, the manifestation of the Glory of Christ, is carried onward by **οὖν**, whereas **δέ** as generally prefaces the development of the antagonist manifestation of hatred and rejection of Him. If it seem strange that this hostile step should be taken by πιστεύοντες εἰς αὐτόν, we at least find a parallel in the passage above cited, ch. viii. 30 ff. 47.] Their words may be read two ways; with, or without, a question after **ποιοῦμεν**. (1) is the ordinary way. (2) as in A. V. R., 'What do we, seeing that,—because,—this man doeth many miracles?' 48.] They evidently regarded the result of 'all believing on Him,' as likely to be, that He would be *set up as king:* which would soon bring about the ruin here mentioned. Augustine (in Joan. Tract. xlix. 26) understands it differently: that, all men being persuaded by Him to peaceful lives, they would have no one to join them in revolt against the Romans; but this seems forced: for no ἐλεύσονται would in that

καὶ τὸν [h] τόπον καὶ τὸ ἔθνος. 49 [i] εἷς δέ [i] τις ἐξ αὐτῶν
Καϊάφας, ἀρχιερεὺς ὢν τοῦ ἐνιαυτοῦ ἐκείνου, εἶπεν αὐτοῖς
Ὑμεῖς οὐκ οἴδατε οὐδέν, 50 οὐδὲ [k] λογίζεσθε ὅτι [l] συμφέρει ὑμῖν ἵνα εἷς ἄνθρωπος [m] ἀποθάνῃ [m] ὑπὲρ τοῦ [n] λαοῦ
[o] καὶ μὴ ὅλον τὸ [p] ἔθνος ἀπόληται. 51 τοῦτο δὲ [q] ἀφ' ἑαυτοῦ
οὐκ εἶπεν, ἀλλὰ ἀρχιερεὺς ὢν τοῦ ἐνιαυτοῦ ἐκείνου [r] ἐπροφήτευσεν ὅτι ἤμελλεν Ἰησοῦς [m] ἀποθνήσκειν [m] ὑπὲρ τοῦ
ἔθνους, 52 καὶ οὐχ ὑπὲρ τοῦ ἔθνους μόνον, ἀλλ' ἵνα καὶ
τὰ [s] τέκνα τοῦ θεοῦ τὰ [t] διεσκορπισμένα [u] συναγάγῃ [v] εἰς

I_a συμφερει... ABDE GHI$_a$K LMSU XΓΔΛ Πℵ 1. 33. 69

h Rev. ii. 5. vi. 14. xii. 14. Ps. cii. 16.
i Mark xiv. 51. Luke xxii. 50.
k Gospp., Luke xxii. 37 (from Isa. liii. 12) only. (Mark xi. 31 & xv. 28 v. r.) = Rom. ii. 3. viii. 18 al.
l constr., ch. xvi. 7. Matt. v. 29, 30. xviii. 6 only. (w. inf., Matt. xix. 10 reff.) see ch. xviii. 14.
m Rom. v. 6, &c. xiv. 15. 2 Cor. v. 14, 15 bis.
n 1 Thess. v. 10. = ch. xviii. 14. Matt. ii 4. xxvii. 25. Acts xxi. 28. xxvi. 17, 23. xxviii. 17.
o Matt. v. 29, 30 reff.
p see ch. xviii. 35 reff. 1 Pet. ii. 9.
q ch. v. 19 reff.
r Matt. xv. 7 al. fr.
s ch. i. 12 reff.
t Matt. xxvi. 31 || Mk. from Zech. xiii. 7 A[ℵ$^{3a.b}$]. Luke i. 51. Acts v. 37.
u = Matt. iii. 12. xiii. 30. ch. iv. 36. Isa. xxvii. 12.
v ch. xvii. 23 only. (1 John v. 8.)

om *και* (bef *τον τοπον*) DK[Π] vulg-ed(not am) lat-*a b c e f l* [*ff*$_2$ syr-jer] Syr.—*τον τοπον* bef *ημων* D lat-*a e f*.

50. rec **δια**λογιζεσθε, with X rel: txt ABDLℵ 1. 69 Orig$_2$ Chr$_1$-2-mss Cyr$_1$ Thdrt$_1$. rec **η**μιν, with AI$_a$ rel am lat-*c f g* syrr [syr-jer] sah æth arm Orig$_7$ [Cyr$_1$]: om ℵ 252 [Chr Thdrt$_2$]: txt BDLMX[Γ] vulg-ed lat-*a b e ff*$_2$ *l* [Orig-int$_3$].

51. om *εκεινου* D-gr. (rec *εμελλεν*, with [B[1](Tischdf N. T. Vat.)] ℵ rel Orig: txt A B[[2.3](Tischdf)] DI$_a$LUΔ 1. 33. 69.) rec ins *ο* bef *ιησ.*, with [Π[2]] 69 (33, e sil): om ABDI$_a$ℵ rel Orig$_6$. *ιησ.* bef *ημελλ.* D.

52. aft *εθνους* ins *δε* ℵ[3a](but erased) [X 33]. *του θεου* bef *τεκνα* A. for *διεσκ.*, *εσκορπισμενα* D. *εις εν* bef *συναγαγη* D lat-*a e*.

case be provoked. **τὸν τόπον**, not, *the temple* (sc. ἅγιον, Acts vi. 13. 2 Macc. v. 19 hardly applies, being *the place* which the Lord chose to put His Name there, not ὁ τόπος **ἡμῶν**) but **our place**, as in reff.: i. e. our *local habitation*, and our *national existence*. Both these literally came to pass. Whether this fear was earnestly expressed, or only as a covert for their enmity, does not appear. The **ἡμῶν** is emphatic, detecting the real cause of their anxiety. Respecting this man's pretensions, they do not pretend to decide: all they know is that if he is to go on thus, THEIR status is gone. **49—52.**] The counsel is given in subtilty, and was intended by Caiaphas in the sense of political expediency only. But it pleased God to make him, as High Priest, the special though involuntary organ of the Holy Spirit, and thus to utter by him a prophecy of the death of Christ and its effects. That this is the only sense to be given, appears from the consideration that the *whole* of vv. 51, 52 cannot for a moment be supposed to have been in the mind of Caiaphas; and to divide it and suppose the latter part to be the addition of the Evangelist, is quite unjustifiable. **ἀρχ. τ. ἐνιαυτοῦ ἐκείνου**—repeated again, ch. xviii. 13. He was High Priest during the whole Procuratorship of Pontius Pilate, eleven years: Jos. Antt. xviii. 2. 2, and 4. 3. In **τοῦ ἐν. ἐκ.** there is no intimation conveyed that the High Priesthood was changed every year, which it *was not*: but we must understand the words as directing attention to '*that* (*remarkable*) *year*,' without any reference to time past or to come. THAT YEAR *of great events* had Caiaphas as its High Priest. See on ver. 57. **οὐκ οἶδ. οὐδ.**] Probably various methods of action had been suggested. Observe **λαός** here, the usual term for the chosen people (reff.), and then ἔθνος, when it is regarded as a nation among the nations: cf. also ver. 52. Meyer otherwise: but Scripture usage is as above. **ἀφ' ἑαυτ. οὐκ εἶπ.**] **not** *merely* **of himself**, but under the influence of the Spirit, who caused him to utter words, of the full meaning of which he had no conception. **ἀρχ. ὢν ἐπροφ.**] There certainly was a belief, arising probably originally from the use of the Urim and Thummim, that the High Priest, and indeed every priest, had some knowledge of dreams and utterance of prophecy. We find it in Jos. B. J. iii. 8. 3, and Philo de Creat. Principum, 8, vol. ii. p. 367. The latter says ὁ πρὸς ἀλήθειαν ἱερεὺς εὐθύς ἐστι προφήτης. That this belief existed, may account for the expression here; which however does not confirm it in all cases, but asserts the fact that the Spirit *in this case* made use of him, as High Priest, for this purpose. This confirms the above view of **τοῦ ἐνιαυτοῦ ἐκείνου**, here again

[v] ἔν. 53 ἀπ' ἐκείνης οὖν τῆς ἡμέρας [w] συνεβουλεύσαντο ἵνα
ἀποκτείνωσιν αὐτόν. 54 ὁ οὖν Ἰησοῦς οὐκ ἔτι [x] παῤῥησίᾳ
[y] περιεπάτει ἐν τοῖς Ἰουδαίοις, ἀλλὰ ἀπῆλθεν ἐκεῖθεν εἰς
τὴν χώραν [z] ἐγγὺς τῆς ἐρήμου, εἰς Ἐφραῒμ λεγομένην
πόλιν, κἀκεῖ ἔμεινεν μετὰ τῶν μαθητῶν. 55 ἦν δὲ [a] ἐγγὺς
τὸ [a] πάσχα τῶν [a] Ἰουδαίων· καὶ ἀνέβησαν πολλοὶ εἰς
Ἱεροσόλυμα ἐκ τῆς χώρας πρὸ τοῦ πάσχα, ἵνα [b] ἁγνί-
σωσιν ἑαυτούς. 56 ἐζήτουν οὖν τὸν Ἰησοῦν, καὶ ἔλεγον
μετ' ἀλλήλων ἐν τῷ ἱερῷ ἑστηκότες Τί δοκεῖ ὑμῖν; ὅτι οὐ
μὴ ἔλθῃ εἰς τὴν ἑορτήν; 57 [cd] Δεδώκεισαν δὲ οἱ ἀρχιερεῖς
καὶ οἱ Φαρισαῖοι [d] ἐντολὰς ἵνα ἐάν τις γνῷ ποῦ ἐστιν,
[e] μηνύσῃ, ὅπως [f] πιάσωσιν αὐτόν.

w (and constr.) Matt. xxvi. 4 (ch. xviii. 14. Acts ix. 23. Rev. iii. 18) only. (3 Kings xii. 8.)
x = ch. vii. 4.
y = ch. vii. 1 reff.
z ch. iii. 23 reff.
a ch. ii. 13 (reff).
b Acts xxi. 24, 26. xxiv. 18 (met., James iv. 8. 1 Pet. i. 22. 1 John iii. 3) only. 2 Chron. xxx. 17.
c ch. i. 17 reff.
d ch. xii. 49. xiii. 34. xiv. 31. 1 John iii. 23 only.
e Luke xx. 37 (reff.) Acts xxiii. 30. 1 Cor. x. 28 only †.
f ch. vii. 30 reff.

53. for συνεβ., εβουλευσαντο BDא 69 $Orig_1$ Chr Ath: txt AI_a rel $Orig_2$ Cyr[$_{expr}$(but?)] Chron.

54. rec (for ο ουν ιησ.) ιησ. ουν, with ADI_a rel: txt BLMXא 1 $Orig_2$ Ath_1. om εκειθεν (*homœotel*) D 250 Scr's e f k latt[not *f*] æth $Orig_1$ Non. aft χωραν ins σαμφουρειν *sapfurim* D; *longinquum* lat-*b*; *proximam* lat-*f*. rec (for εμεινεν) διετριβε (*see ch* iii. 22), with ADI_a rel latt Syr [syr-jer Chron]: txt BLא syr-mg $Orig_3$. rec aft μαθητων ins αυτου, with A rel vss Chr Chron: om BDI_aL[Γ]Δא 1 am(with fuld) arm $Orig_3$.

55. transp ην and εγγυς D vulg lat-*b c* [ff_2 *l*]. for και ανεβ., ανεβ. ουν D foss lat-*b c* ff_2. εις ιεροσολυμα bef πολλοι D. for προ του, πριν το D.

56. ins και bef τον ιησ. D. (ελεγαν Dא.) εστωτες D. for δοκει υμιν, δοκειτε D.

57. rec aft δεδ. δε ins και (*see note*), with DI_a rel sah[?]: om ABKLMUXΔ[ΛΠ]א 1. 69 latt syrr copt (æth?) arm $Orig_1$ $Chron_1$. rec εντολην (*because* but one *is mentioned*), with AD rel latt syr[-txt] coptt Chron: txt BI_aMא 1 syr-mg $Orig_2$. for εαν, αν D. γνοι D^1(txt D^5).

repeated. See on ver. 49. **ὅτι ἤμελ. . . .**, the purport (unknown to himself) of his prophecy. And τοῦ ἔθν. is guarded from misunderstanding by what follows. **τὰ τέκ. τ. θεοῦ . . .** are the τασσόμενοι εἰς ζωὴν αἰώνιον, the τέκνα θ. of ch. i. 12, among all nations: see ch. x. 16.

53.] The *decision*, to put Him to death, is *understood:* and from that day they plotted **that they might slay Him** (not, *how* they might slay Him).

54.] Observe the Ἰουδαῖοι here as the official body. He was still among *Jews* at Ephraim. This city is mentioned 2 Chron. xiii. 19 in connexion with Bethel, as also by Jos. B. J. iv. 9. 9. **ἐγγ. τ. ἐρ.**, near the desert of Judah. Its situation is at present unknown (see Winer, Realw. edn. 3, sub voce). Robinson (Harmony, p. 204) supposes it to be the same with Ophrah (Josh. xviii. 23: 1 Sam. xiii. 17: not Judg. vi. 11, 24; viii. 27) and Ephron of the O. T. (2 Chron. xiii. 19, עֶפְרַיִן, Keri; עֶפְרוֹן, Cetibh), and the modern et-Taiyibeh, twenty R. miles from Jerusalem. See also Van de Velde, Memoir to accompany the Map of the Holy Land, under Ophrah, p. 338: and Stanley's Sinai and Palestine, p. 214.

55.] **ἐκ τ. χώρ.**, not '*from that country*,'—the connexion with εἰς τὴν χώραν above having been severed by the note of time, ἦν δὲ ἐγγὺς κ.τ.λ.:—but, **from the country** generally. **ἵνα ἁγν. ἑαυτ.**] To purify themselves from any Levitical uncleanness, that they might be able to keep the Passover: see Num. ix. 10; and reff. 2 Chron. and Acts.

56.] **τί δοκ. ὑμ.**, and **ὅτι οὐ μὴ ἔλθῃ . . . .**; are *two separate questions*, as in E. V. The making them *one*, is hardly grammatical, seeing that **οὐ μὴ ἔλθῃ** must have a *future* sense, whereas in that case it would be *past:* 'What think ye, that He is not (i. e. of His not having) come to the feast?'

57.] The import of this verse depends on the insertion or omission of the **καί** before οἱ ἀρχιερεῖς. *Without* it, it is merely an explanation of the people's question: **For the chief priests** &c.: *with* it, it would mean, 'And besides, the chief priests' &c.; i. e. 'not only did the people question, but' &c.

XII. 1 Ὁ οὖν Ἰησοῦς [g] πρὸ ἓξ ἡμερῶν τοῦ πάσχα
ἦλθεν εἰς Βηθανίαν, ὅπου ἦν Λάζαρος [ὁ τεθνηκὼς] ὃν
[h] ἤγειρεν [h] ἐκ νεκρῶν ὁ Ἰησοῦς. 2 [i] ἐποίησαν οὖν αὐτῷ
δεῖπνον ἐκεῖ, καὶ ἡ Μάρθα [k] διηκόνει· ὁ δὲ Λάζαρος εἷς
ἦν ἐκ τῶν [l] ἀνακειμένων σὺν αὐτῷ. 3 ἡ οὖν Μαρία
λαβοῦσα [m] λίτραν [n] μύρου [o] νάρδου [p] πιστικῆς [q] πολυτίμου Q πολυτιμου...
[r] ἤλειψεν τοὺς πόδας τοῦ Ἰησοῦ καὶ [s] ἐξέμαξεν ταῖς θριξὶν
αὐτῆς• τοὺς πόδας αὐτοῦ· ἡ δὲ οἰκία [t] ἐπληρώθη ἐκ τῆς F αυτης ...
[u] ὀσμῆς τοῦ [n] μύρου. 4 λέγει οὖν Ἰούδας ὁ Ἰσκαριώτης

ÄBDEF GHI_aK LMQSÜ XΓΔΛ Πא 1. 33. 69

g constr., here only. (2 Cor. xii. 2. 2 Tim. i. 9. Tit. i. 2.) Amos i. 1. iv. 7. 2 Macc. xv. 36.
h Matt. xvii. 9 reff.
i = Matt. xxii. 2. Mark vi. 21. Gen. xxi. 8.
k abs., Matt. xx. 28. Luke x. 40 †.
l ch. vi. 11. Matt. ix. 10. xxvi. 7 al.† Esdr. iv. 10 only.
m ch. xix. 39 only †. n ‖ Mt. reff. o ‖ Mk. only. Cant. i. 12. iv. 13, 14 only. p ‖ Mk. only †. q (‖ v. r.) Matt. xiii. 46. 1 Pet. i. 7 only †. r ch. xi. 2 reff. s ch. vii. 38 reff. t = Acts ii. 2. v. 28. w. ἐκ, here only. πλέα ἀπ' αὐτῶν, Xen. Cyr. i. 3. 5. u 2 Cor. ii. 14, 16. Eph. v. 2. Phil. iv. 18 only. 2 Macc. ix. 10, 12.

CHAP. XII 1. om ο τεθνηκως (*as superfluous, the fact being sufficiently indicated without it*) BLXא lat-*a c e* Syr syr-jer sah æth Chr-2-mss$_1$ Ps-Chr$_1$: ins ADI_a rel vulg lat-*b f ff*$_2$ *g* syr copt goth arm. rec om ο ιησ., with H rel lat-*a b c e* Chron: ins A(B)DEGI_aLΔΛ²[Π] vulg lat-*ff*$_2$ *g* syrr [syr-jer] coptt[bef ηγειρ.] goth, and bef εκ א [lat-*f* æth].—om ο Bא¹.

2. for εποι. ουν, και εποι. D lat-*c e* Syr æth. διηκονει bef μαρθα, omg ἡ, D arm. rec om εκ, with ADI_a rel: ins BL[א] latt syrr [syr-jer] Orig$_1$. rec (for ανακειμ. συν) συνανακειμενων, with Scr's g: συνακ. συν 33: txt ABDI_aא rel Orig$_1$.

3. for λαβουσα, λαυβανει and ins και bef ηλειψεν D vulg-ed(not am) lat-*a b c e f*. πιστικης bef μυρου, omg ναρδου, D lat-*e*. om [1st] του B. ins της κεφαλης bef αυτης I_aX coptt [Orig-int$_1$]. for η δε, και η D latt[not *f*]. επλησθη B.

4. for ουν, δε (*from* ‖, *Matt* xx. 8: *Mark* xiv. 4) Bא copt goth: om L 33 lat-*a e* [foss sah arm]. rec aft ιουδ. ins σιμωνος (*see ch* vi. 71; xiii. 2, 26), with AI_aQ rel foss lat-*f ff*$_2$[Blanch] syr goth æth-ms: σιμων E¹(appy) FGHU lat-*b c ff*$_2$[Sabat] copt-wilk: om BDLא 1. 33 vulg lat-*g* Syr syr-jer copt-dz sah æth arm Aug$_1$. rec om 1st ὁ, with AI_aQ rel: ins ABEFGHLUא [1] 33.—for ο ισκ., απο καρυωτου D. rec εἱς εκ των μαθ. αυτ. bef ιουδ. ο ισκ., with ADI_aQ rel [latt] syr copt goth arm: txt

The former is in my view most probable; for the command, having been given, would satisfactorily account for the questioning, and not be stated merely as coordinate with it.

CHAP. XII. 1—36.] PROPHETIC ANTICIPATIONS OF THE LORD'S GLORIFICATION BY DEATH. 1—11.] *The anointing at Bethany.* Matt. xxvi. 6—13. Mark xiv. 3—9, where see notes. 1.] On **πρὸ ἓξ ἡμ.**, see reff. It is an expression frequent in later Greek; so μετὰ τριάκοντα ἡμ. τῶν γάμων, Dio lix. 20; μετὰ δέκα ἔτη τοῦ οἰκῆσαι Ἀβραὰμ ἐν γῇ Χαναάν, Philo de Congressu, 14, vol. i. p. 529. See numerous instances in Greswell, vol. iii. Diss. 1, where he defines the expression to be *exclusive* of the period named as the limit *ad quem* or *a quo* (according as πρό or μετά is used), but *inclusive* of the day or month or year of the occurrence specified. Thus the arrival, and anointing, at Bethany, will be on the eighth of Nisan, if the passover was on the fourteenth. That day was a Sabbath; but this makes no difficulty, as we know not from what point our Lord came, or whether He arrived at the commencement of the Sabbath, i. e. sunset,—or a little after, on Friday evening, from Jericho. 2. **ἐποίησαν**] It is not said *who*. It was (Matt., Mark) in the house of *Simon the leper*. From Lazarus being there, and Martha serving, he may have been a near relative of theirs. See notes on Matt. Lazarus is mentioned throughout the incident, as forming an element in the unfolding of the hatred of the Jews which issued in the Lord's death: notice the climax, from mere connecting mention in ver. 1, then nearer connexion in ver. 2,—to his being the cause of the Jews flocking to Bethany in ver. 9,—and the joint object with Jesus of the enmity of the chief priests, in ver. 10. 3. **λίτραν**] What weight is imported, is uncertain: hardly (see ch. xix. 39) so much as a Roman pound. The word, originally Greek, was adopted into the Aramaic, and is found in the Rabbinical writings as equivalent to a mina; see Friedlieb, Archäologie der Leidensgeschichte, p. 33. On **νάρδ. πιστ.**, see note on Mark. **ἤλ. τ. πόδ.**] His *head*, according to Matt. and Mark. See note on Luke vii. 38. 4.] For *Judas*, we have οἱ μαθ. αὐτοῦ, Matt.,—τινές, merely, Mark. See note on Matt. ver. 8.

εἷς ἐκ τῶν μαθητῶν αὐτοῦ, ὁ μέλλων αὐτὸν παραδιδόναι
5 Διὰ τί τοῦτο τὸ [n] μύρον οὐκ [v] ἐπραθη [w] τριακοσίων
δηναρίων καὶ ἐδόθη πτωχοῖς; 6 εἶπεν δὲ τοῦτο οὐχ ὅτι
[x] περὶ τῶν πτωχῶν [x] ἔμελεν αὐτῷ, ἀλλ' ὅτι [y] κλέπτης ἦν
καὶ τὸ [z] γλωσσόκομον ἔχων τὰ [a] βαλλόμενα [b] ἐβάσταζεν.
7 εἶπεν οὖν ὁ Ἰησοῦς [cd] Ἄφες αὐτὴν [d] ἵνα εἰς τὴν ἡμέραν
τοῦ [e] ἐνταφιασμοῦ μου [f] τηρήσῃ αὐτό. 8 τοὺς πτωχοὺς
γὰρ πάντοτε ἔχετε μεθ' [g] ἑαυτῶν, ἐμὲ δὲ οὐ πάντοτε
ἔχετε. 9 Ἔγνω οὖν ὄχλος πολὺς ἐκ τῶν Ἰουδαίων ὅτι

v ||. Mt. xiii. 46 reff. w and constr., || Mk. constr., || Mt. x Matt. xxii. 16 reff. y ch. x. 1 reff. z ch. xiii. 29 only. 2 Chron. xxiv. 8, 10, 11 bis only. Jos. Antt. vi. 1. 2. a = Matt. xxvii. 6. Mark xii. 41, 43, 44 ||. b = ch. xx. 15. see Mark xiv. 13. Acts xxi. 35. c = Matt. xv. 14. ch. xi. 48. 4 Kings iv. 27. d Mark xi. 16 only. e || Mk. only †. (-άζειν, || Mt.) f and constr., Acts xxv. 21. g = Matt. iii. 9 reff. Acts xiii. 46.

BLℵ 33 Syr [syr-jer] sah æth. om εκ BLQ 33 : ins ADI$_a$ℵ rel latt Syr. *os ημελλεν παραδουναι αυτον* D lat-*b c ff*$_2$.

5. ins τοις bef πτωχοις D 33.

6. transp ειπεν and τουτο D lat-*a c e f* Syr [syr-jer] copt goth. (B has not εμελλεν as Mai, Verc.) rec (for εχων) ειχεν και, with AI$_a$ rel mm lat-*a b c* [*e f* arm] goth : txt BDLQℵ **1**. 33 vulg [lat-*g*] (coptt) [Orig$_1$]. (*το γλωσσοκ. εχων was supposed to be a joint predicate with κλεπτης, and thus και was insd after it, and it afterwards became corrd to ειχεν : this agst Mey, Lücke, and De W., who hold εχων to be a gramml corrn.*)

7. rec om ινα, and (for τηρηση) τετηρηκεν (*see note*), with AI$_a$ rel lat-*f* Syr syr-txt goth : txt BDKLQX[Π]ℵ 33 latt syr-mg [syr-jer] coptt æth arm Non$_1$. om μου (*homœotel*) D, erased in 33.

8. om ver D (*prob from the influence of* ||).

9. for εγνω to ιουδ., οχλ. δε πολ. εκ τ. ιουδ. ηκουσαν D lat-*a*. ins ο bef οχλος B^{1}Lℵ.

ὁ μέλλων αὐτὸν παραδιδόναι is not inserted, nor are any such notices in St. John without significance. It has a pragmatic connexion with the narrative in hand. Only one with thoughts alien from Jesus could have originated such a murmur. And on the other hand, it may well be, as some have supposed, that by the rebuke of the Lord on this occasion, the traitorous scheme of Judas, long hidden in his inmost soul, may have been stimulated to immediate action. **5. τριακοσ. δην.**] Common (with the slight difference of the insertion of ἐπάνω) to our narrative and Mark. The sum is about 9*l*. 16*s*. of our money (Friedlieb, p. 31). **6.**] **γλωσσόκομον,** ἀγγεῖον τῶν αὐλητικῶν γλωττῶν, Phryn. (De Wette), to keep the reeds, or *tongues,* of wind instruments:—thus, generally, any kind of pouch, or money-chest. See LXX, and Josephus, in reff. **ἐβάσταζεν**] It seems hardly possible, with St. John's use of **βαστάζειν** in ch. xx. 15 before us, altogether to deny that the sense of *carrying off*, i. e. *purloining,* may be here intended. And we have examples in Josephus somewhat analogous: e. g. Antt. vii. 15. 3, where Hyrcanus the High Priest, wishing to give Antiochus Eusebes money to raise the siege, καὶ ἀλλαχόθεν οὐκ εὐπορῶν, ἀνοίξας ἕνα οἶκον τῶν ἐν τῷ Δαυίδου μνήματι, καὶ **βαστάσας** τρισχίλια τάλαντα, μέρος ἔδωκεν Ἀντιόχῳ . . . . See also ib. ix. 4. 5; xii. 5. 4: and Polyb. i. 48. 2. And so Origen, Theophyl., al.; contra Lücke, De Wette, Tholuck, al. **7.**] See note on Matt. ver. 12. To suppose that it was a remnant from that used at the burial of Lazarus, is not only fanciful, but at variance with the character of the deed as apparent in the narrative. The rec. reading, *εἰς τ. ἡμ. τ. ἐντ. μου τετήρηκεν αὐτό,* seems to be an adaptation to Mark xiv. 8, in order to escape from the difficulty of understanding how she could *keep for His burial,* what she *poured out now.* Meyer understands the text of the *remnant:* but Luthardt rightly observes that the history clearly excludes the idea of a remnant: cf. ἐπράθη and ἐδόθη. He himself, with Baumg.-Crusius, takes τηρήσῃ as past, "*Let her have kept it,*" i. e. blame her not for having kept it: but this is vapid in sense, and ungrammatical. I understand the words, which, like all our Lord's proleptical expressions, have something enigmatical in them, of her whole act, not regarded as a thing past, but spoken of in the abstract as to be allowed or disallowed: **Let her keep it for the day of my burial:** not

ἐκεῖ [h] ἐστιν, καὶ ἦλθον οὐ [i] διὰ τὸν Ἰησοῦν μόνον, ἀλλ'
ἵνα καὶ τὸν Λάζαρον ἴδωσιν ὃν [k] ἤγειρεν [k] ἐκ νεκρῶν. ...λαζαρον I.
10 [l] ἐβουλεύσαντο δὲ οἱ ἀρχιερεῖς ἵνα καὶ τὸν Λάζαρον ABDEF
ἀποκτείνωσιν, 11 ὅτι πολλοὶ δι' αὐτὸν [m] ὑπῆγον τῶν GHKL MQSUX
Ἰουδαίων καὶ [n] ἐπίστευον [n] εἰς τὸν Ἰησοῦν. ΓΔΛΠℵ 1. 33. 69
12 [o] Τῇ ἐπαύριον ὄχλος πολὺς ὁ ἐλθὼν εἰς τὴν ἑορτήν,
ἀκούσαντες ὅτι [h] ἔρχεται Ἰησοῦς εἰς Ἱεροσόλυμα, 13 ἔλαβον τὰ [p] βαΐα τῶν [q] φοινίκων καὶ [r] ἐξῆλθον [r] εἰς [s] ὑπάντησιν αὐτῷ, καὶ [t] ἐκραύγαζον [u] Ὡσαννά, [u] εὐλογημένος ὁ
ἐρχόμενος ἐν ὀνόματι κυρίου, καὶ ὁ [v] βασιλεὺς τοῦ [v] Ἰσραήλ.
14 [w] εὑρὼν δὲ ὁ Ἰησοῦς [x] ὀνάριον [y] ἐκάθισεν ἐπ' αὐτό,
καθώς ἐστιν γεγραμμένον 15 [z] Μὴ φοβοῦ θυγάτηρ Σιών· ...εστι F.
ἰδοὺ ὁ βασιλεύς σου ἔρχεται καθήμενος ἐπὶ [a] πῶλον [b] ὄνου.

h pres., ch. i. 40 reff.
i ch. x. 32 reff.
k ver. 1.
l Luke xiv. 31. (ch. xi. 53 v. r.) Acts v. 33. xxvii. 39. 2 Cor. i. 17 bis, only. Esth. iii. 6.
m ch. vi. 67.
n ch. ii. 11 reff.
o ch. i. 29 reff. here only +.
p 1 Macc. xiii. 51 only.
q Rev. vii. 9 only. Ps. xci. 12.
r Matt. viii. 34. xxv. 6.
s Matt. xxv. 1 only. Judg. xi. 34 B.
t ch. xi. 43 reff.
u || Mt. (reff.)
v ch. i. 50 (reff.).
w = Acts xxi. 2. xxvii. 6.
x here only +.
y intr., Matt. v. 1 reff. xiii. 15 (xiv. 5 v. r.) only. Gen. xxxii. 15.
z Zech. ix. 9.
a || (Mt. 3ce, Mk., L., 4 times) only.
b || Mt. 3ce. Luke

(ηλθαν D., om μονον D 245 lat-*b e*. om 2nd και D latt(not tol *f*) Vig. aft ηγειρεν ins ιησους D; aft νεκρων ins ο ιησ. A 33: om BQℵ rel. ins των bef νεκρων D.

10. aft δε ins και B.

11. των ιουδ. bef δι' αυτ. υπηγ. D lat-*a c e ff*$_2$ Syr [syr-jer arm].

12. ins ο bef οχλος BL. om ὁ (bef ελθων) Δℵ[1]. rec ins ο bef ιησ., with B[Γ] (69, e sil) Orig$_1$ [Cyr$_1$]: om ADLQℵ rel.—ιησ. bef ερχεται ALX 33 lat-*a c e* syrr [syr-jer] coptt.

13. συναντησιν DGLX 69: απαντησιν AKU[Π] Orig$_2$: txt BQℵ rel. αυτου D. rec (for εκραυγαζον) εκραζον (*from || Matt Mark*), with A rel Orig$_1$: txt B[3(Tischdf)] DLQℵ[, εκραυγασαν B[1](Tischdf, expr)]. add λεγοντες ADKQX[Π]ℵ 1: om B rel vulg lat-*b c* [*e f g* syr-txt] sah goth Orig$_1$. ευλογητος D. rec om 3rd και, with AD rel latt sah: ins BLQℵ(marked for erasure, but marks removed) copt æth Orig$_1$. om ο (bef βασιλευς) A rel Thl: ins BDKLQX[Π]ℵ (1, e sil). (33 def.)

15. rec θυγατερ, with ℵ rel Orig$_2$: η θυγατηρ B[2.3](Tischdf): txt AB[1]DKLQXΔΛ[Π]. om σου A [sah-mnt].

meaning a *future* day or act, but the present one, as one to be allowed. **8.**] See note on Mark, vv. 7, 8. **γάρ** implies the ἔργον καλὸν εἰργάσατο εἰς ἐμέ of Matt. ver. 10. **9 ff.**] Remember, here as elsewhere in John, the Ἰουδαῖοι are not *the people*, but the rulers, and persons of repute: the representatives of the Jewish *opposition* to Jesus. **10.**] **ἐβουλ.**, not, '*came to a* (formal) *resolution*,' but **were in the mind,—had an intention:** see Acts v. 33; xv. 37. The chief priests, named here and in ch. xi. 57, were of the sect of the Sadducees; and therefore disbelieved the *fact* of the raising of Lazarus; only viewing him as one whom it would be desirable to put out of the way, as an object of popular attention in connexion with Jesus. **11.**] **ὑπῆγον, went away** (to Bethany); there is something in the **ὑπ-** which almost always implies *away, out from under*, the persons or the place in the narrative. And so here, the ἀρχιερεῖς being the main subject of the sentence, the word gets the sense of '*fell away:*' scil. from under their hand or power.

12—19.] *The triumphal entry into Jerusalem.* Matt. xxi. 1—17. Mark xi. 1—11. Luke xix. 29—44. On the chronology, see note on Matt. xxi. 1. **12.**] **τῇ ἐπ.**, i. e. on the *Sunday:* see on ver. 1. **ἀκούσ.**, from the multitude who had returned from Bethany, ver. 9. The order of the narrative seems to require that these people should have visited Bethany late on the Sabbath, after sunset, and the anointing. **13. τὰ β. τ. φοιν.**] The articles shew that the palm-trees were on the spot: **the branches of the palm-trees:** or perhaps (Lücke) that the custom was usual at such festivities. **βαΐα**] The classical word is βάϊς, from the Coptic *bai*. **14—16.**] The Evangelist seems to suppose his readers already acquainted with the circumstances of the triumphal entry, and therefore relates it thus compendiously. **εὑρών** does not involve any discrepancy with the three Evangelists, but is a compendious term implying

16 ταῦτα οὐκ ἔγνωσαν οἱ μαθηταὶ αὐτοῦ [c] τὸ πρῶτον,
ἀλλ' ὅτε [d] ἐδοξάσθη Ἰησοῦς, τότε ἐμνήσθησαν ὅτι ταῦτα
ἦν [e] ἐπ' αὐτῷ [e] γεγραμμένα καὶ ταῦτα ἐποίησαν αὐτῷ.
17 [f] ἐμαρτύρει οὖν ὁ ὄχλος ὁ ὢν μετ' αὐτοῦ, ὅτε τὸν Λάζαρον [g] ἐφώνησεν ἐκ τοῦ μνημείου καὶ [h] ἤγειρεν αὐτὸν
[h] ἐκ νεκρῶν· 18 διὰ τοῦτο καὶ [i] ὑπήντησεν αὐτῷ ὁ ὄχλος,
ὅτι [j] ἤκουσαν τοῦτο αὐτὸν πεποιηκέναι τὸ [k] σημεῖον. 19 οἱ
οὖν Φαρισαῖοι εἶπον [l] πρὸς ἑαυτούς [m] Θεωρεῖτε [m] ὅτι οὐκ
[n] ὠφελεῖτε οὐδέν; ἴδε, ὁ κόσμος [o] ὀπίσω αὐτοῦ [o] ἀπῆλθεν.
20 Ἦσαν δὲ Ἕλληνές τινες ἐκ τῶν [p] ἀναβαινόντων

c ch. x. 40. xix. 39 only.
d ch. vii. 39 reff.
e w. dat., here only. acc., Mark ix. 12, 13. see Rev. x. 11.
f ch. i. 32. xiii. 21. xv. 27. xix. 35. 1 John v. 6 al.
g = Matt. xx. 32 reff. constr., here only.
h ver. 1. Matt. xvii. 9 reff.
i ch. xi. 20 reff.
j w. acc. and inf., 1 Cor. xi. 18 only.
k ch. ii. 11 reff.
l Mark x. 26 reff.
m constr., Mark xvi. 4. ch. iv. 19. (ix. 8.) Acts xxvii. 10 only. 2 Macc. ix. 23. see Acts xxi. 20. Heb. vii. 4.
n Matt. xxvii. 24. ch. vi. 63. Heb. xiii. 9. Sir. xxxi. (xxxiv.) 23.
o Mark i. 20.
p = ch. vii. 8, 10. Acts xviii. 22 al. Neh. vii. 6.

16. rec aft ταυτα ins δε, with AD rel lat-*a c f* copt [syrr goth Cyr_1] $Orig_{11}$: om BL Qℵ vulg lat-*b e* [ff_2 *g l* syr-jer] sah. for εγνωσαν, ενοησαν D. αυτου bef οι μαθ. Bℵ : om K[Π]. rec ins ο be. ιησ., with DHΛ : om ABQℵ rel. for επ' αυτω, περι αυτου D latt : επ αυτ. bef ην ℵ.

17. elz οτι, with DE^1KL[Π] lat-*a b c e* ff_2 Syr coptt arm : txt ABQℵ rel vulg lat-*f* [*g* syr-jer] syr goth æth. (33 def.)

18. om και B^1EHΔΛ tol lat-*a b c e* ff_2 *l* Syr coptt goth : ins A $B^{2\cdot 3}$(Tischdf) D Q(appy) ℵ rel vulg lat-*f* syr æth. υπηντησαν αυτω οχλοι D lat-*c* Syr. ins και bef ο οχλος B. for ο οχλος, οχλος πολυς ℵ. rec ηκουσε, with EGHU[Γ]Δ syr : txt ABDQℵ rel latt Syr [syr-jer] coptt. αυτον bef τουτο ℵ ev-y.

19. (ειπαν Bℵ.) for εαυτους, αυτους D Scr's g ev-H_1 lat-*a c e* Chr. aft ο κοσμος ins ολος DLQX 33 latt Syr syr-w-ast syr-jer copt æth arm Cyr[-p_1(appy)] Non_1 $Andr_1$.

20. aft ησαν δε ins και D Syr æth. rec τινες bef ελληνες, with A rel vulg lat-*a g* syr arm goth Chr_1 : txt BDLMQXℵ 1. 33 am[with fuld forj ing] lat-*b c e f* ff_2 [Syr].

their details. **15.**] The prophecy is more fully cited by Matt. **16.**] Important, as shewing that this, and probably other prophetic citations under similar circumstances, were the effect of the light poured into the minds of the Apostles by the Holy Spirit after the Ascension. **ἐπ' αὐτῷ**] So Æsch. Eum. 343, γιγνομέναισι λάχη τάδ' ἐφ' ἁμῖν ἐκράνθη: Soph. Trach. 997, οἵαν ἐπί μοι χάριν ἠνύσω; Plato, Euthyd. 278 A, ὄνομα ἐπ' ἀνθρώποις ἐναντίως ἔχουσι κείμενον. **ταῦτα ἐποίησαν αὐτῷ**—viz. the going out to meet Him, strewing clothes and branches in the way, and shouting 'Hosanna' before Him: also perhaps, the setting Him on the ass, implied in the concise narrative. Notice the thrice-repeated **ταῦτα**, each time signifying *'this which was written by the Prophet,' 'the above citation.'* **17.**] The testimony which they bore is given in Luke xix. 37, 38. Meyer regards the ἐφώνησεν ἐκ τοῦ μνημείου κ. ἤγειρεν ἐκ νεκρῶν as *an echo of their song of triumph.* **18.**] I see no necessity for supposing this multitude distinct from that in the last verse. We have had no account of any multitude *coming from Bethany with Him,* nor does this narrative imply it: and surely **ὁ ὄχλος** in the two verses must mean the same persons. The **καί** here does not imply another ὄχλος, but **And on this account the multitude also went out to meet Him**: i. e. their coming out to meet Him and their μαρτυρία on the Mount of Olives, had one and the same cause,—the raising of Lazarus. **19. κόσμος**] κόσμον τὰ πλήθη λέγουσιν. Euthym. **ἀπῆλθεν** can hardly be altogether without allusion to the fact, or likelihood, of *apostasy from Judaism.* It is used to signify entire devotion to Him whithersoever He might lead them, as in ref.: and thus implies *escape* and alienation from themselves.

20—36.] Future spread of the kingdom of God among Gentiles from the death of Jesus. *Some Greeks desire to see Jesus. His discourse thereupon.* **20.**] These **Ἕλληνες** were not *Grecian Jews,*—who would not have been so called: but *Gentiles,* 'proselytes of the gate,' who were in the habit (implied by the pres. part. **ἀναβαινόντων**) of coming up to the feast: see ch. vii. 35 reff. and

ἵνα [q] προσκυνήσουσιν ἐν τῇ ἑορτῇ· 21 οὗτοι οὖν προσῆλθον Φιλίππῳ τῷ [r] ἀπὸ Βηθσαϊδὰ τῆς Γαλιλαίας καὶ
ἠρώτων αὐτὸν λέγοντες Κύριε, θέλομεν τὸν Ἰησοῦν ἰδεῖν.
22 ἔρχεται ὁ Φίλιππος καὶ λέγει τῷ Ἀνδρέᾳ· ἔρχεται
Ἀνδρέας καὶ Φίλιππος, καὶ λέγουσιν τῷ Ἰησοῦ. 23 ὁ δὲ
Ἰησοῦς ἀπεκρίνατο αὐτοῖς λέγων Ἐλήλυθεν ἡ [s] ὥρα [t] ἵνα
[u] δοξασθῇ ὁ [v] υἱὸς τοῦ [v] ἀνθρώπου. 24 [w] ἀμὴν ἀμὴν λέγω
ὑμῖν, ἐὰν μὴ ὁ [x] κόκκος τοῦ σίτου [y] πεσὼν [y] εἰς τὴν γῆν
ἀποθάνῃ, αὐτὸς μόνος μένει· ἐὰν δὲ ἀποθάνῃ, πολὺν
[z] καρπὸν [za] φέρει. 25 ὁ φιλῶν τὴν [b] ψυχὴν αὐτοῦ ἀπολέσει αὐτήν, καὶ ὁ [b] μισῶν τὴν [b] ψυχὴν αὐτοῦ ἐν τῷ

...εν τη εορτη Q. — F μισων ...

q = ch. iv. 20. Acts viii. 27.
r ch. xi. 1 reff.
s = Mark xiv. 41.
t ch. xiii. 1. xvi. 2, 32.
u ver. 16.
v Matt. viii. 20 reff.
w ch. v. 24, 25 reff.
x (=) Matt. xiii. 31 ||. xvii. 20 ||. 1 Cor. xv. 37 only. (Lam. iv. 5 only.)
y = Mark iv. 8 || L. only.
z ch. xv. 2, &c. (7 times) only. J. Ezek. xvii. 8 only. (ποιεῖν κ., Matt. iii. 8. διδόναι κ., Matt. xiii. 8. ἀποδιδ. κ., Rev. xxii. 2. καρποφορεῖν, Matt. xiii. 23.)
a — Mark iv. 8.
b Luke xiv. 26 reff.

ABDFF GHKL MSUX ΓΔΛΠℵ 1. 33 69

rec προσκυνησωσιν, with ABQℵ rel: txt DLΔ.
21. (προσηλθαν D.) ins τω bef φιλιππω D.
22. rec om ὁ, with ADℵ rel: ins BLX[Π[2]] 33. rec (for 2nd ερχεται) και παλιν, omg και bef λεγουσιν, with X rel; παλιν ο, omg και, D; κ. παλ. κ. H: και παλιν ερχεται, retaining και bef λεγ., ℵ: txt ABL 33 lat-*a e* syr-jer æth.
23. αποκρινεται BLXℵ 33: txt AD rel latt syrr [syr-jer &c].
25. for απολεσει, απολλυει BLℵ 33: txt AD rel vss $Clem_1$ $Cypr_1$ $Lucif_1$.

note; also Acts viii. 27. **21.**] For what reason *Philip* was selected, it is impossible to say. The Greek form of his name may imply some connexion with Hellenistic Jews, who may have been friends or relatives of these Greeks. If they were *from the neighbourhood of Bethsaida*, they would indeed have been familiar with the person of Jesus:—but what they here requested was evidently a private interview. **22.**] Andrew (ch. i. 45) was of the same city as Philip: and this reason of Philip conferring with him is perhaps implied in the **τῷ ἀπὸ Β. τ. Γ.** Bengel remarks on this touch of nature: "*cum sodali, audet.*" **ἔρχεται**—so ἔπεμψέ με Ἀριαῖος κ. Ἀρτάοζος, Xen. Anab. ii. 4. 16. **23.**] *Did the Greeks see* (i. e. speak with) *Jesus, or not?* Certainly *not*, if I understand His discourse rightly. But they may have been present at, and have understood it. The substance of His answer (**αὐτοῖς**, to Philip and Andrew, not to the Greeks) is, that the time was now come for His glorification, which should draw all nations to Him:—but that glorification must be accomplished by His Death. The very appearance of these Greeks is to Him a token that His glorification is at hand. Stier strikingly says, "These men from the West at the end of the Life of Jesus, set forth the same as the Magi from the East at its beginning;—but they come to the *Cross* of the King, as those to His *cradle*." (R. J. v. 69, edn. 2.) The rejection of the Jews for their unbelief is the secondary subject, and is commented on by the Evangelist, vv. 37—43. **ἵνα**, not 'eventual,' nor 'for' any thing, but *most strictly* of the *purpose*—**the hour has come, that** (whose object of preparation, and aim, in the eternal counsels, it has been, that) **the Son of Man should be glorified.** **24.**] Meyer thinks, that our Lord begins His declaration with the double asseveration **ἀμὴν ἀμήν**, on account of the unreceptivity of the mind of the disciples for the announcements of His Death. But St. John *always* uses ἀμὴν ἀμήν. The *grain of wheat* perishes, and is *not apparent* (as the seeds of dicotyledonous plants *are*) *in the new plant*: see 1 Cor. xv. 36. The saying is more than a mere parabolic similitude: the divine Will, which has fixed the law of the springing up of the wheat-corn, has also determined the law of the glorification of the Son of Man, and the one in analogy with the other: i. e. both *through Death*. The symbolism here lies at the root of that in ch. vi., where Christ is **ὁ ἄρτος** τῆς ζωῆς. **αὐτὸς μόνος, by itself alone**, with its life uncommunicated, lived only within its own limits, and not passing on. **25.**] And this same divine Law prevails for *the disciples*, as well as for their Master: see Matt. x. 39 and note. But the saying here proclaims more plainly its true extent,—by its immediate connexion with ver. 24, and by **εἰς ζ. αἰών.** **ψυχή** is not *really* in a double sense: as the wheat-corn retains its identity, though it die, so the ψυχή: so that the two senses are, in their depth, but

κόσμῳ τούτῳ εἰς ζωὴν αἰώνιον [c] φυλάξει αὐτήν. 26 ἐὰν
ἐμοί τις [d] διακονῇ, ἐμοὶ ἀκολουθείτω· καὶ ὅπου εἰμὶ ἐγώ,
ἐκεῖ καὶ ὁ [e] διάκονος ὁ ἐμὸς ἔσται· ἐάν τις ἐμοὶ [d] διακονῇ,
τιμήσει αὐτὸν ὁ πατήρ. 27 Νῦν ἡ ψυχή μου [f] τετάρακται,
καὶ τί εἴπω; πάτερ, [g] σῶσόν με ἐκ τῆς [h] ὥρας ταύτης·
ἀλλὰ διὰ τοῦτο ἦλθον εἰς τὴν [h] ὥραν ταύτην. 28 πάτερ,
[ik] δόξασόν σου τὸ [k] ὄνομα. ἦλθεν οὖν [l] φωνὴ [l] ἐκ τοῦ
[l] οὐρανοῦ Καὶ [i] ἐδόξασα καὶ πάλιν δοξάσω. 29 ὁ οὖν

c = and constr., 2 Tim. i. 12.
d Matt. xxv. 44. Acts xix. 22 al.†
e Matt. xxiii. 11 reff.
f = ch. xi. 33 reff. Psa. xli. 6.
g constr., Heb. v. 7. James v. 20. Jude 5 only. Ps. xxx. 7. 2 Macc. i. 11.
h = Mark xiv. 35.
i = ch. xvii. 5.
k Rev. xv. 4. Mal. i. 11.
l Matt. iii. 17 ||. Rev. x. 4, 8. xiv. 2, 13. Dan. iv. 28 LXX.

om *φυλαξει αυτην* ℵ[1](ins ℵ-corr[1]).

26. rec 1st *διακονη* bef *τις*, with E rel: for *εμοι τις*, *τις μοι* D **1**. 33 latt arm; *τις* bef *εμοι* 69: txt ABK L(*μοι*) MUX[Π]ℵ syrr [syr-jer] copt goth Chr_1. aft *οπου* ins *αν* D. *εγω* bef *ειμι* D lat-*a b c* Syr. om *εκει* D. rec ins *και* bef 2nd *εαν*, with A rel lat-*f* syr copt goth æth: om BDLXℵ **1**. 33. 69 latt Syr [syr-jer arm] sah.

28. for *σου*, *μου* B 5(Sz). add *εν τη δοξη η ειχον παρα σοι προ του τον κοσμον γενεσθαι* (*see ch* xvii. 5) D Aug_1 Jer_1. for *ηλθεν ουν*, *και εγενετο* D. aft *ουρανου* ins *λεγουσα* D[$Π^2$] lat-*a c e* syr [syr-jer] copt æth.

29. om *ουν* B lat-*a*.

one. ψυχή is *the life* in both cases;—not the *soul*, in the present acceptation of that term. **26.**] Connexion:—The ministering to, or intimate union with, Christ (the position of Philip and Andrew and the rest, and that into which these Greeks seemed desirous to enter) implies *following* Him,—and that, through tribulation to glory. **εἰμί**, the *essential* present—in My true place, i. e. (ch. xvii. 24) in the glory of the Father. **τιμήσει**—by glorifying him in My glorification, ch. xvii. 24. **27.**] "Concurrebat horror mortis et ardor obedientiæ" (Bengel). And to express both these *together* in human speech was impossible: therefore **τί εἴπω;** The following words must not be taken interrogatively (as by Theophyl., Grot., Tholuck, al.) [as if our Lord were doubting whether to say them or not]: for thus the whole sense is destroyed, besides the sentiment being most unworthy of Him who uttered it. The prayer is a *veritable prayer;* and answers to the prophetic Messianic prayers in the Psalms, which thus run—"My soul is troubled; Lord, help me" (Ps. lxix. 1; xl. 12, 13; xxv. 17; vi. 3, 4 al.); and to that prayer afterwards in Gethsemane, Matt. xxvi. 39. **διὰ τοῦτο**] The misunderstanding of these words has principally led to the erroneous punctuation just noticed. διὰ τοῦτο = **ἵνα σωθῶ** ἐκ τῆς ὥρας ταύτης. 'I came to this hour for this very purpose,—*that I might be saved from* this hour:' i. e. '*the going into, and exhausting this hour, this cup, is the very appointed way of my glorification.*' Das Hineinkommen ist selbst das Hindurchkommen, das Leiden selbst die Erlösung! Stier, v. 77, edn. 2: so also Lampe. This interpretation does not, as Luthardt says, *fall* with the interrogative punctuation of the previous clause, but holds equally good when that is relinquished. The other interpretation, that of Meyer, al., is, *that Thy Name may be glorified.* But surely this is to do violence to the order of thought. This particular does not come in till the next clause, and cannot without an improbable trajection be drawn into this. **28.**] The glorifying *the Name* of the *Father* can only take place by the glorification of *the Son;* and this latter only by *His death:* so that this is the "ardor obedientiæ" triumphant. **φωνή**] This 'voice' can no otherwise be understood, than as a plain articulate sound, miraculously spoken, heard by all, and variously interpreted. So all the ancients, and the best of the modern expositors, Meyer, Stier, Luthardt, &c. On the saying of the crowd (ver. 29) has been built the erroneous and unworthy notion, that it *was* only thunder, but understood by the Lord and the disciples to mean as here stated. The Jewish Bath Kol has no applicability here. **ἐδόξασα**] In the manifestation hitherto made of the Son of God, imperfect as it was (see Matt. xvi. 16, 17); in all O. T. type and prophecy; in creation; and indeed (Aug. in Joan. Tract. lii. 4) "antequam facerem mundum." **πάλιν** is here no mere repetition, but an intensification of the δοξάζειν, a **yet once more** [: and this time fully and finally]. **29.**] Some *heard words*, but did not apprehend their meaning; others *a sound*, but no words. I should rather believe this difference to

m Mark iii. 17. Rev. xi. 19 al9. only. Job xxvi. 14.
n ch. x. 32 reff.
o ch. xvi. 8, 11. Matt. x. 15 al. Isa. xxxiv. 8.
p ch. xiv. 30. xvi. 11 J. see 2 Cor. iv. 4. Eph. ii. 2. vi. 12.
q ch. vi. 37 reff.
r = ch. iii. 14. viii. 28 only.
s Ps. ix. 13.
t = ch. vi. 44 (xviii. 10. xxi. 6, 11. Acts xvi. 19) only. Jer. xxxviii. (xxxi.) 3.

ὄχλος ὁ ἑστὼς καὶ ἀκούσας ἔλεγεν ^m βροντὴν γεγονέναι. ABDEF
ἄλλοι ἔλεγον Ἄγγελος αὐτῷ λελάληκεν. GHKL
30 ἀπεκρίθη MSUX
Ἰησοῦς καὶ εἶπεν Οὐ ^n δι' ἐμὲ ἡ φωνὴ αὕτη γέγονεν, ἀλλὰ ΓΔΛΠℵ 1. 33. 69
δι' ὑμᾶς.
31 νῦν ^o κρίσις ἐστὶν τοῦ κόσμου τούτου· νῦν ὁ ^p ἄρχων τοῦ ^p κόσμου τούτου ^q ἐκβληθήσεται ^q ἔξω.
32 κἀγὼ ἐὰν ^{rs} ὑψωθῶ ^s ἐκ τῆς γῆς, πάντας ^t ἑλκύσω πρὸς

εστηκως ADGKMX[Π] 33. 69: txt Bℵ rel. om και Dℵ 1. 69 lat-*l* coptt goth. for βροντ. γεγ., οτι βροντη γεγονεν D. ins οτι bef αγγελος D 69 coptt.

30. rec ins ο bef ιησ., with A U(Treg, expr) rel: om BDGKXℵ[SΓΠ] 33. 69. και ειπ. bef ιησ. BL: om και ειπ. ℵ: txt AD rel vss. rec αυτη bef η φωνη, with E rel vulg-ed lat-*g* syrr (goth ?) Tert$_1$: txt ABDLMU²Xℵ 1. 33 am(with fuld forj [ing]) [lat-*a b c e f* syr-jer] Chr$_1$ Cyr[-p$_2$] Hil$_2$. for γεγονεν, ηλθεν D.

31. om 1st τουτου D 248 vulg lat-*b g l* syr-jer sah[-mnt]. om νυν ο αρχ. τ. κ. τουτου (*homœotel*) ℵ¹(ins ℵ-corr^{1.3a}) 69. ins και bef εκβληθησ. ℵ.

32. και εγω D 69. for εαν, αν B. for εκ, απο DL vulg lat-*b c e f ff$_2$ g* [*l* Cæs$_1$] Chr$_1$. for παντας, παντα Dℵ¹ 56 latt [syr-jer æth] goth Iren-int$_1$ Aug$_{expr}$. ελκ. bef παντ. D [coptt æth].

have been proportioned to each man's inner relation to Christ, than fortuitous. **30.**] The voice had been heard by those, who did not apprehend its meaning, *as thunder.* But αὕτη ἡ **φωνή** could not by any possibility have been said to them, *if it had only thundered.* Our Lord does not say that the assurance was *not made* for *His* sake;—He had prayed, and His prayer had been answered:—but that it had not been thus *outwardly expressed* for *His*, but for *their* sake. This is likewise true in the case of all testimonies to Him; and especially those two other voices from heaven,—at His Baptism and His Transfiguration. **ὑμᾶς** is the whole multitude, not merely the disciples. All heard, and all *might have* understood the voice: see ch. xi. 42. **31.**] All this is a comment on ἐλήλυθεν ἡ ὥρα, ver. 23: and now a different side of the subject is taken up, and one having immediate reference to the occasion: viz. the drawing of the Gentile world to Him. **νῦν**] He speaks of Himself as having actually entered the hour of His passion, and views the result as already come. **κρίσις**, not (Chrys., Cyril, Aug., Grot.) "the *deliverance* of this world from the devil;"—nor, "decision concerning this world," *who* is to possess it (Bengel):—but (see ch. xvi. 11) **judgment**, properly so called, the work of the Spirit who was to come, on the world, which ὅλος ἐν τῷ πονηρῷ κεῖται, 1 John v. 19. **ὁ ἄρχ. τ. κόσ. τ.**] The שַׂר הָעוֹלָם of the Jews, Satan, the ὁ θεὸς τοῦ αἰῶνος τούτου of 2 Cor. iv. 4: see also Eph. ii. 2; vi. 12. Observe it is **ἐκβληθήσεται**, not ἐκβάλλεται, because the casting out (ἔξω, ἐκ τῆς ἀρχῆς, Euthym., Grot., or better perhaps, out of ὁ κόσμος οὗτος, his former place) shall be gradual, as the *drawing* in the next verse. But after the death of Christ the casting out *began*, and its first-fruits were, the coming in of the Gentiles into the Church. **32.**] See reff. Here there is more perhaps implied in **ὑψ.** than in either of those places: viz. *the Death, with all its consequences.* The Saviour crucified, is in fact the Saviour glorified; so that the exalting to God's right hand is set forth by that uplifting on the Cross. There is a fine touch of pathos, corresponding to the feeling of ver. 27, in **ἐὰν ὑψωθῶ.** Hermann's description of the meaning of ἐὰν τοῦτο γένηται exactly gives it: "sumo hoc fieri, et potest omnino fieri, sed utrum vere futurum sit necne, experientia cognoscam." Viger, p. 832. The Lord Jesus, though *knowing all this*, yet in the weakness of his humanity, puts himself into this seeming doubt, 'if it is so to be:' cf. Matt. xxvi. 42. All this is missed by the shallow and unscholarlike rendering '*when*,' which I need hardly remind my readers ἐάν can never bear. See on ch. xiv. 3: 1 John iii. 2. **ἑλκύσω**—by the diffusion of the Spirit in the Church: manifested in the preaching of the Word mediately, and the pleading of the Spirit immediately. Before the glorification of Christ, the Father drew men to the Son (see ch. vi. 44 and note), but now the Son Himself to Himself. Then it was, 'no man can come except the Father draw Him:' now the Son draws *all.* And, *to Himself*, as thus uplifted, thus exalted;—the great object of

ἐμαυτόν. 33 τοῦτο δὲ ἔλεγεν [u] σημαίνων ποίῳ [v] θανάτῳ
ἤμελλεν [v] ἀποθνήσκειν. 34 ἀπεκρίθη οὖν αὐτῷ ὁ ὄχλος
Ἡμεῖς [w] ἠκούσαμεν [w] ἐκ τοῦ νόμου ὅτι ὁ χριστὸς [x] μένει
[x] εἰς τὸν αἰῶνα· καὶ πῶς λέγεις σὺ ὅτι δεῖ [r] ὑψωθῆναι τὸν
υἱὸν τοῦ ἀνθρώπου; τίς ἐστιν οὗτος ὁ υἱὸς τοῦ ἀνθρώπου; 35 εἶπεν οὖν αὐτοῖς ὁ Ἰησοῦς Ἔτι [y] μικρὸν [y] χρόνον
τὸ [z] φῶς [a] ἐν ὑμῖν ἐστιν. περιπατεῖτε [b] ὡς τὸ [z] φῶς ἔχετε,
ἵνα μὴ [c] σκοτία ὑμᾶς [d] καταλάβῃ· καὶ ὁ [e] περιπατῶν ἐν
τῇ [ce] σκοτίᾳ οὐκ οἶδεν [f] ποῦ ὑπάγει. 36 [b] ὡς τὸ [z] φῶς
ἔχετε, [g] πιστεύετε [g] εἰς τὸ φῶς, ἵνα [h] υἱοὶ φωτὸς γένησθε.
ταῦτα ἐλάλησεν Ἰησοῦς, καὶ ἀπελθὼν [i] ἐκρύβη ἀπ' αὐτῶν.
37 Τοσαῦτα δὲ αὐτοῦ [k] σημεῖα πεποιηκότος [l] ἔμπροσθεν

u ch. xviii. 32. xxi. 19. Acts xi. 28. xxv. 27. Rev. i. 1 only. 2 Macc. xi. 17.
v ch. xviii. 32 only. see Jer. xvi. 4.
w constr., 2 Cor. xii. 6.
x ch. viii. 35 (bis) reff.
y ch. vii. 33 reff.
z ch. i. 7 reff.
a = Acts iv. 43 al. fr.
b = Luke xii. 58.
c ch. i. 5 reff.
d = 1 Thess. v. 4. Num. xxxii. 23.
e ch. viii. 12.
f ch. iii. 8 reff.
g ch. ii. 11 reff.
h 1 Thess. v. 5. Luke x. 6. Eph. ii. 2. v. 6. (8.)
i ch. viii. 59. Deut. vii. 20.
k ch. ii. 11 reff.
l = Matt. v. 16 al. 2 Kings iii. 31 A.

33. τουτον ℵ[1](corrd *eadem manu*). (εμελλεν HK [S(Tischdf)]UX[ΓΠ]ℵ 1.)

34. rec om *ουν*, with AD rel latt syrr [syr-jer arm] copt Chr_1 : ins BLXℵ syr-mg sah. rec *συ* bef λεγεις, with ADℵ rel latt sah arm Ath_1 Cypr : txt BLX syrr copt Chr_1 [$Victorin_1$]. aft *εστιν* ins *ουν* D.

35. rec (for *εν υμιν*) *μεθ' υμων*, with A rel Syr [syr-jer æth arm] sah(appy) Chr_1 : txt BDKLMX[Π]ℵ 1. 33. 69 latt syr copt goth Cyr[-p_1] Non_1. aft *περιπατειτε* ins *ουν* D lat-*e* copt Aug_1. rec (for *ως*) *εως* (*from ε preceding*), with ℵ rel latt syrr [syr-jer] goth arm Cypr : txt ABDKLX[Π] 1. 33 syr-mg coptt[appy] Did. *υμας* bef *σκοτια* D vulg-ed(not am [fuld forj ing]) lat-*a* Cypr spec.—ins *η* bef *σκοτια* [KLUXΠ]ℵ[3a].

36. rec (for *ως*) *εως*, with E rel [(vss as ver 35) Cyr_1] : txt ABDL[Π]ℵ [æth] Did_1 Ath-mss_1. rec ins *ο* bef *ιησ.*, with Aℵ[3a] rel : om BDL ℵ[1](perhaps). for *απελθων*, *απηλθεν και* D latt.

Faith : see ch. xi. 52. **33.**] **ποίῳ θαν.** can hardly mean more than **by what manner of death.** Lampe ("non nude significat *quo genere mortis*, sed in sensu latiori *qualitatem mortis*, etiam *internam* involvit, adeoque ad fructus etiam hujus mortis respicit") and Stier find in the word the whole consequences and character of His Death : but see ch. xviii. 32. John does not say that this was *all* that ὑψωθῶ meant, but that it was its first and obvious reference. **34.**] In such passages as Ps. lxxxix. 36, and perhaps cx. 4 : Dan. vii. 13, 14. **τοῦ νόμου**] The O. T. : see ch. x. 34. The actual words **ὅτι δεῖ ὑψ. τ. υἱ. τ. ἀνθ.** had not been on this occasion used by Jesus; but in His discourse with Nicodemus, ch. iii. 14, and perhaps in other parts of His teaching which have not been recorded. **τίς ἐστιν . . . .**] They thought some other Son of Man, not the Messiah, was meant; because this lifting up (which they saw implied *taking away*) was inapplicable to their idea of the Messiah, usually known as the Son of Man.

35.] He does not answer them, but enjoins them to make use of the time of His presence yet left them. **ὡς, as,** not exactly '*while*:' walk, according to your present state of privilege in possessing the Light : which indeed can only be done *while it is with you.* **τὸ φῶς,** 'Myself' —see ch. vii. 33; viii. 12; ix. 4, 5. **ἐν ὑμ., among you** : see ref., and ch. xv. 24 (or in the deeper meaning of ch. xi. 10, which see, and note). The *light* is an easy transition from their question, if, as above supposed, Ps. lxxxix. 36 was alluded to : "His (David's) seed shall endure for ever, and his throne *as the sun* before Me." **περιπατ.,** i. e. '*make use of* the Light, do your work in it, and by it.' **οὐκ οἶδ. ὑπ. π.,** 'has no guide nor security, no principle to lead him.' **36.**] It is by believing on the Light, that men become sons of Light : see ch. i. 12.

Our Lord probably went to Bethany, Luke xxi. 37.

37—50.] Final judgment on the unbelief of the Jews. **37—43.**] *The Evangelist's judgment on their unbelief* (37—41), *and their half-belief* (42, 43). I do not regard these verses as forming the conclusion to the narrative of the public ministry of the Lord, on account of vv. 44—50 (where see note) : but doubtless the *approaching close* of that ministry *gives occasion* to them, and is the time to which they refer. **37.**] **τοσαῦτα, so many** : not, *so great* : see ch. vi. 9 :

αὐτῶν οὐκ [g]ἐπίστευον [g] εἰς αὐτόν· 38 [m] ἵνα ὁ λόγος Ἡσαΐου ABDEF
τοῦ προφήτου [m] πληρωθῇ ὃν εἶπεν, Κύριε, τίς [n] ἐπίστευσεν GHKL MSUX
τῇ [o] ἀκοῇ ἡμῶν; καὶ ὁ [p] βραχίων κυρίου τίνι [q] ἀπεκα- ΓΔΛΠℵ 1. 33. 69
λύφθη; 39 διὰ τοῦτο οὐκ ἠδύναντο πιστεύειν· ὅτι πάλιν
εἶπεν Ἡσαΐας 40 [r] Τετύφλωκεν αὐτῶν τοὺς ὀφθαλμούς,
καὶ [s] ἐπώρωσεν αὐτῶν τὴν καρδίαν, [t] ἵνα μὴ ἴδωσιν τοῖς
ὀφθαλμοῖς καὶ [u] νοήσωσιν τῇ καρδίᾳ καὶ [v] στραφῶσιν
καὶ ἰάσομαι αὐτούς. 41 ταῦτα εἶπεν Ἡσαΐας ὅτι εἶδεν
τὴν [w] δόξαν αὐτοῦ· καὶ ἐλάλησεν περὶ αὐτοῦ. 42 [xy] ὅμως
[y] μέντοι καὶ ἐκ τῶν [z] ἀρχόντων πολλοὶ [a] ἐπίστευσαν [a] εἰς
αὐτόν, ἀλλὰ διὰ τοὺς Φαρισαίους οὐχ [b] ὡμολόγουν, ἵνα μὴ
[c] ἀποσυνάγωγοι γένωνται. 43 [d] ἠγάπησαν γὰρ τὴν [e] δόξαν
[f] τῶν ἀνθρώπων μᾶλλον [g] ἤπερ τὴν δόξαν [f] τοῦ θεοῦ.

m Matt. i. 22 al.
n dat., Luke i. 20. ch. ii. 22 al. Isa. liii. 1.
o = Rom. x. 16, from l. c. 1 Thess. ii. 13. Heb. iv. 2. 2 Kings xiii. 30.
p Luke i. 51. Acts xiii. 17 only. Deut. v. 15.
q Matt. x. 26. Rom. i. 17, 18 al. 1 Kings iii. 7.
r 1 John ii. 11. 2 Cor. iv. 4 only. Isa. xlii. 19 only. (Isa. vi. 10.)
s Mark vi. 52. viii. 17. Rom. xi. 7. 2 Cor. iii. 14 only. Job xvii. 7 B only.
t = Mark iv. 12. ch. ix. 2. u Matt. xv. 17. 1 Tim. i. 7 al. Prov. i. 2, 6. v = Matt. xviii. 3 reff.
w Isa. vi. 1. x 1 Cor. xiv. 7. Gal. iii. 15 only. 2 Macc. xv. 5. y here only. Herod. i. 189 end.
z = ch. iii. 1 reff. a ch. ii. 11 reff. b ch. ix. 22. Rom. x. 10. c ch. ix. 22. xvi. 2 only.
d = 2 Tim. iv. 10. 1 Pet. iii. 10, from Ps. xxxiii. 12. Rev. xii. 11. e = ch. v. 41, 44. 1 Thess. ii. 6.
f gen., 1 Pet. iii. 14. g here only †. 2 Macc. xiv. 42.

39. for *οτι παλιν, και γαρ* D copt-ms.

40. om *τους οφθαλμους* to *αυτων* (*homœotel*) D. rec πεπαρωκεν (*conformn to preceding*), with B?(sic: see table) rel Eus$_1$ Chr$_1$ Thdrt$_1$: txt AB[1]KLX 33. 69 Eus$_1$, επηρωσεν [Π[2](επηρωτησεν Π[1])] ℵ Scr's p[2] w. ins *μη* bef *νοησ.* D vulg-ed lat-*a* [*e f l*]. (-σουσιν D 69.) for *νοησ. τη καρδια, τη καρδια συνωσιν* K[Π]ℵ Scr's p w. rec επιστραφωσι, with AD[4] rel; επιστρεψωσι (*so* LXX) KLMX[Π] Eus$_2$ Did, -ψουσι [*so* LXX-ℵ] 69: txt BD[1]ℵ 33. rec *ιασωμαι* (*conformn to foregoing: the authority is too strong, to suppose the fut to be from* LXX), with LU[2][Γ] (1, e sil) Eus$_2$: txt ABDℵ rel lat-*b* Eus-ms$_2$ Did$_1$.

41. aft *ταυτα* ins *δε* D Did$_1$ Chr$_1$ Hil$_1$. rec *οτε*, with D rel latt syrr [syr-jer] goth æth Eus$_3$ Chr$_1$ Hil$_1$: txt ABLMXℵ 1. 33 lat-*e* coptt arm Epiph$_1$ [Cyr-p$_2$]. for 1st *αυτ.*, *του θεου* 69 [gat syr-txt syr-jer coptt æth-mss]: *του θεου αυτου* D.

43. υπερ LXℵ 1. 33. 69 Chr-ms$_1$.

xxi. 11. **οὐκ ἐπίστ.**, i. e. the *generality* did not;—they did not, *as a people*: see ver. 42. **38.**] On **ἵνα πλ.** see note, Matt. i. 22: beware of the '*ecbatic*' or 'eventual' sense, which has no existence.

39.] **διὰ τοῦτο** refers to the last verse, and **ὅτι** sets forth the reason more in detail: see ch. v. 16: 1 John iii. 1: Matt. xxiv. 44. The common interpretation (Theophyl., Vulg., Lampe, Tholuck, Olsh., al.), by which *διὰ τοῦτο* is referred forward to *ὅτι*, would require some particle, *καί*, or *δέ*, to denote a transition to the fresh subject. De Wette, Meyer, Lücke, edn. 3, Grot. al. **οὐκ ἠδύν.**] **could not**—i. e. it was otherwise ordained in the divine counsels. No attempt to escape this meaning (as "*nolebant*," Chr., Thl. &c.) will agree with the prophecy cited ver. 40. But the *inability*, as thus stated, is coincident with the fullest freedom of the human will: compare *οὐ θέλετε*, ch. v. 40. **ὅτι**, not '*for*,' but **because.** A more special ground is alleged why they could not believe: see above.

40.] The prophecy is freely cited, after neither the Heb. nor the LXX, which is followed in Matt. xiii. 14 f. What God *bids* the Prophet *do*, is here described as *done*, and by Himself: which is obviously *implied* in the Heb. text. The reading *αὐτῶν* (Morus) supplying *ὁ λαὸς οὗτος* as the subject of *τετύφ.* and *πεπώρ.*, is out of the question,—as ungrammatical, and inconsistent with the context, which will only allow of *ὁ κύριος* (i. e. Jehovah) as the *subject*. **41.**] **ὅτι εἶδ.**, **because he saw.** "This apocalyptic vision was the occasion of that prophecy." Meyer. **αὐτοῦ**, *of Christ.* The Evangelist is giving his judgment,—having (Luke xxiv. 45) had his understanding opened to understand the Scriptures,—*that the passage in Isaiah is spoken of Christ.* And indeed, strictly considered, the glory which Isaiah saw *could only* be that of the Son, Who is the *ἀπαύγασμα τῆς δόξης* of the Father, Whom no eye hath seen. **κ. ἐλάλ. π. αὐτ.** does not depend on *ὅτι*: **and he spake concerning Him.** **42.**] e. g. Nicodemus, Joseph, and others like them. On *ἀποσυν.* see note, ch. ix. 22. Ver. **43** is a reference

44 Ἰησοῦς δὲ [h] ἔκραξεν καὶ εἶπεν Ὁ [a] πιστεύων [a] εἰς ἐμὲ
οὐ [a] πιστεύει [a] εἰς ἐμέ, ἀλλὰ εἰς τὸν πέμψαντά με· 45 καὶ ὁ
[i] θεωρῶν ἐμὲ [i] θεωρεῖ τὸν πέμψαντά με. 46 ἐγὼ [j] φῶς [k] εἰς
τὸν κόσμον [k] ἐλήλυθα, ἵνα πᾶς ὁ [a] πιστεύων [a] εἰς ἐμὲ ἐν τῇ
[l] σκοτίᾳ μὴ [m] μείνῃ. 47 καὶ ἐάν τις [n] μου [n] ἀκούσῃ τῶν [n] ῥημάτων καὶ μὴ [o] φυλάξῃ, ἐγὼ οὐ [p] κρίνω αὐτόν· οὐ γὰρ
ἦλθον ἵνα κρίνω τὸν κόσμον, ἀλλ᾽ ἵνα σώσω τὸν κόσμον.
48 ὁ [q] ἀθετῶν ἐμὲ καὶ μὴ [r] λαμβάνων τὰ ῥήματά μου ἔχει
τὸν κρίνοντα αὐτόν· ὁ λόγος ὃν ἐλάλησα, ἐκεῖνος κρινεῖ
αὐτὸν ἐν [s] τῇ ἐσχάτῃ ἡμέρᾳ. 49 ὅτι ἐγὼ [t] ἐξ ἐμαυτοῦ οὐκ
[t] ἐλάλησα, ἀλλ᾽ ὁ πέμψας με πατὴρ αὐτός μοι [u] ἐντολὴν
[u] δέδωκεν τί εἴπω καὶ τί λαλήσω· 50 καὶ οἶδα ὅτι ἡ ἐντολὴ
αὐτοῦ ζωὴ αἰώνιός [v] ἐστιν. ἃ οὖν ἐγὼ λαλῶ, καθὼς
εἴρηκέν μοι ὁ πατήρ, οὕτως λαλῶ.

h ch. i. 15. vii. 28, 37.
i = ch. vi. 40. xiv. 17.
j ch. i. 7 reff.
k ch. i. 9 reff.
l ch. i. 5 reff.
m 1 John iii. 14. 1 Cor. vii. 20, 24.
n constr., Acts xxii. 1.
o = Luke xi. 28. Ps. cxviii. 9. see ch. viii. 51.
p = ch. iii. 18 bis. James v. 9.
q John, here only. = Luke vii. 30. x. 16. Gal. ii. 21. 1 Thess. iv. 8. Isa. xxiv. 16.
r = Matt. xiii. 20. ch. iii. 11, 32, 33. xvii. 8.
s ch. vi. 39, 40 reff.
t ch. viii. 44 end. iii. 31. Matt. xii. 34.
u = ch. xi. 57 reff.
v = ch. xvii. 3. vi. 63. 1 John ii. 20.

44. for δε, *ουν* D 240-4. for εκραξεν κ. ειπεν, εκραζεν[so A[1] but corrd appy eadem manu] κ. ελεγεν D 69 lat-*b c ff*$_2$ [*l*] *q* Eus$_1$. (αλλα, so BDLΔℵ.)
45. om *και* D. **46.** om *πας* B.
47. for *εαν*, *αν* D. om *μη* D foss lat-*a b c ff*$_2$ *l*[1] Ambr$_1$. rec (for φυλαξη) *πιστευση*, with E rel lat-*f q* syr-mg goth: txt ABDKLX[Π]ℵ 1. 33. 69 latt syrr [syr-jer] coptt æth arm Ath$_1$ Non$_1$. for αλλ ινα, αλλα D[1]-gr(txt D[2]).
49. εξ εμαυτου bef εγω D: om εγω G. rec (for δεδωκεν) εδωκεν, with D rel Chr$_1$: txt ABMXℵ 1. 33. 69 Did$_2$ [Cyr[-p].
50. αιων. εστ. bef ζωη D: εστ. bef αι. 69. rec λαλω bef εγω, with Δ rel sah: om εγω D[Γ] em lat-*a*: txt ABLMXℵ 1. 33. 69 vulg lat-*b c f ff*$_2$ *g* [*q*] copt arm Bas$_1$ Tert$_1$.

to ch. v. 44. περ (in ἤπερ), in this case, augments the disjunctive force of ἤ. See Kühner, ii. § 747, Anm. 4, where many examples are given. **44—50.**] *Proof of the guilt of their unbelief, from the words of Jesus Himself.* It was by the older Commentators generally thought that these verses formed part of some other discourse delivered at this period. But this is improbable, from no occasion being specified,—from ver. 36,—and from the form and contents of the passage, and its reference to the foregoing remarks of the Evangelist. I take it—with almost all modern Commentators—to be a *continuation of those remarks, substantiating them by the testimony of the Lord Himself.* The words are taken mostly, but not altogether, from discourses *already given* in this Gospel. **44, 45.**] **ἔκρ. κ. εἶπ.** not pluperf. (nor ever), but indefinite, as ἐπίστευσαν, ὡμολ., and ἠγάπ. above. **ἔκρ.** is used of open public teaching, see reff. On the close connexion with the Father, see ch. v. 24, 38; viii. 19, 42; xiv. 10. The words are in logical sequence to ver. 41, in which the Evangelist has said that *the glory of Jehovah* and His *glory* were *the same.* **46.**] See ver. 35; ch. viii. 12; ix. 5. The **μείνῃ** here expresses that all are *originally in darkness,*—as μένει, ch. iii. 36. **47.**] See ch. iii. 17; v. 45; viii. 15. The omission of μή (see var. readd.) appears to have been occasioned by a mistaken idea that vv. 48 and 47 were in contrast to one another. **48.**] See ch. iii. 18, also v. 45 ff., and Heb. iv. 12. On **ἀθετῶν** and **μὴ λαμβ.** see reff.: and on the emphatic **ἐκεῖνος**, referring to the primary subject, cf. note on ch. vii. 29, also on ch. iii. 28. **49.**] See ch. v. 30; vii. 16, 17, 28, 29; viii. 26, 28, 38. On **ἐντολή**, ch. x. 18. There does not appear to be any real difference here, though many have been suggested, between **εἴπω** and **λαλήσω**: both are summed up in λαλῶ in the next verse: compare Matt. x. 19. **50.**] See ch. vi. 63 (and note), 68. On **οἶδα**, ch. iii. 11; v. 32; viii. 55.

The **ἐντολὴ αὐτοῦ** *is*, results in, not as a means merely, but in its accomplishment and expansion, *eternal life*: see ch. iii. 15; v. 24; vi. 40. Thus all who do not believe are without excuse;—because Jesus is not come, and speaks not, of Himself, but of the Father, Whose will and commandment respecting Him is, that He should be, and give, Life to all. They

w Matt. xxvi. 2 reff. x ch. ii. 4 reff. y ch. xii. 23 reff. z Luke x. 7. ch. vii. 3 al.† Wisd. vii. 27 al. a ch. i. 11 reff. b Matt. x. 22. xxiv. 13 || Mk. Luke xviii. 5. 1 Thess. ii. 16 only. Ps. ix. 18. ἕως, 1 Cor. i. 8. 2 Cor. i. 13. ἄχρι, Heb. iii. 6, 14. μέχρι, Heb. vi. 11. Rev. ii. 26. c Matt. iv. 1 reff. d = here only. Hom. Od. α. 201. see ch. xii. 6 reff. e ch. vi. 71. xii. 4 al. form, see Mark v. 43 reff. f Luke xv. 22. Ezek. x. 7.

ABDEF GHKL MSUX ΓΔΛΠℵ 1. 33. 69

XIII. 1 Πρὸ δὲ τῆς ἑορτῆς τοῦ [w] πάσχα, εἰδὼς ὁ
Ἰησοῦς ὅτι ἦλθεν αὐτοῦ ἡ [x] ὥρα [y] ἵνα [z] μεταβῇ ἐκ τοῦ
κόσμου τούτου πρὸς τὸν πατέρα, ἀγαπήσας [a] τοὺς [a] ἰδίους
τοὺς ἐν τῷ κόσμῳ, [b] εἰς τέλος ἠγάπησεν αὐτούς. 2 καὶ
δείπνου γενομένου, τοῦ [c] διαβόλου ἤδη [d] βεβληκότος εἰς
τὴν καρδίαν ἵνα [e] παραδοῖ αὐτὸν Ἰούδας Σίμωνος Ἰσκαριώτης, 3 εἰδὼς ὅτι πάντα [f] δέδωκεν αὐτῷ ὁ πατὴρ [f] εἰς

Chap. XIII. 1. rec (for ηλθ.) εληλυθεν (*from ch* xii. 23), with E rel: παρην D: txt ABKLMX[Π]ℵ 1. 33. 69 $Orig_1$ Chr_1 Cyr[-p_1]. for ιδιους, ιουδαιους ℵ[1].

2. γινομενου (*because supper was not ended: but see note*) BLX æth $Orig_4$ [Non_1]; γεινομενου ℵ[1]: txt A D-gr ℵ[3a] rel latt $Orig_1$ Chr_1 Cyr_1. ins τε bef διαβ. A. rec καρδ. ιουδα σιμ. ισκαριωτου ινα αυτ. παρ. (*rearrangement to escape difficulty of constr, see note*), with A (D[παρ. bef αυτ.]) rel lat-*a c e f q* syrr [syr-jer] æth $Orig_2$ [int_4]: txt B(LM)Xℵ vulg lat-*b g* [*ff_2 l*] (copt) arm $Orig_7$.—σιμων M.—ισκαριωτου LM vulg lat-*g* arm: απο καριωτου D.—rec παραδω, with A D-corr[1] rel: txt BD[1]ℵ.

3. rec aft ειδως ins ο ιησ., with A rel lat-*b f q* syrr [syr-jer sah-mnt] copt $Orig_2$ [Chr_1]: om BDLXℵ vulg lat-*a c e ff_2* æth $Orig_2$ [Cyr-p_1]. for δεδωκεν, εδωκεν

who reject Him, reject Life, and (ch. iii. 19) prefer darkness to Light.

Chap. XIII.—XX.] *Third division of the Gospel.* Jesus and His own.

XIII.—XVII.] His Love and the faith of His own. XIII. 1—30.] His Love in Humiliation. 1—11.] *His condescension in washing their feet.* On the chronological difficulties, see notes on Matt. xxvi. 17, and ch. xviii. 28. There can be no reasonable doubt that this meal was the same as that at which the Lord's Supper was instituted, as related in the three Evangelists. The narrative proceeds without any break until ch. xvii. 26, after which our Lord and the disciples go to Gethsemane. **1. πρὸ τ. ἑορ. τ. π.**] *How long,* is not said: but probably, a very short time;—not more than one day at the most: see ch. xviii. 28 and note. The words belong to the whole narrative following, not to εἰδώς or ἀγαπήσας. **εἰδώς**] The view with which our Lord washed His disciples' feet, is shewn by the repeated εἰδώς and by ἀγαπήσας . . . . αὐτούς. The connexion is:—"Jesus loved His own even to the end (of His life in the flesh), and gave them in the washing of their feet a proof of His love; and to this act He was induced by the knowledge that He must soon leave this world; and although this knowledge was united (ver. 3) with the highest consciousness of His divine mission and speedy glorification, yet this latter did not prevent Him from giving this proof of His self-humiliating love" (De Wette). **τοὺς ἰδ. τ. ἐν τ. κ.**] See ch. xvii. 11.

2. δείπ. γεν.] Not as E. V. '*supper being ended,*' for (ver. 12) He *reclined again,* and in ver. 26, the supper is *still going on*:—but, **supper having begun,** or **having been served**—see Ἰησ. γενομένου ἐν Βηθ. Matt. xxvi. 6, 'When Jesus had arrived at B.;'—and πρωΐας **γενομένης,** 'when it had become morning,' ch. xxi. 4. Cf. also γενομένου σαββάτου, Mark vi. 2. **τοῦ δ. ἤδη βεβ.**] The construction of the text, according to the true reading, is involved and difficult. But its *meaning* will be immediately perceived, if we render βεβληκότος εἰς τὴν καρδίαν, **suggested,—proposed,** viz. to the mind of Judas. **The devil having by this time suggested** (to Judas) **that Judas Iscariot the son of Simon** (i. e. that he) **should betray Him.** The interpretation of βεβλ. εἰς τ. κ., "*having conceived in his* (the devil's) *mind*" (Meyer), is wholly unworthy of a scholar, and simply absurd. Judas had before this covenanted with the Sanhedrim to betray Him, Matt. xxvi. 14 and ||, which must here be meant by *the devil having put it into his heart*:—the thorough self-abandonment to Satan which led to the actual deed, being designated ver. 27. Luke (xxii. 3) expresses the steps of his treasonable purpose otherwise,—meaning the same. The fact is here stated, to enhance the love which Jesus shewed in the following action. **3.**] See above. He did what follows with a full sense of the glory and dignity of His own Person. "Præfatio gloriæ est instar protestationis, ne quid indignum fecisse existimetur Dominus pedes suorum lavans." Bengel.

τὰς χεῖρας, καὶ ὅτι ἀπὸ θεοῦ ἐξῆλθεν καὶ πρὸς τὸν θεὸν
[g] ὑπάγει, 4 [h] ἐγείρεται ἐκ τοῦ δείπνου καὶ [i] τίθησιν τὰ
ἱμάτια, καὶ λαβὼν [k] λέντιον [l] διέζωσεν ἑαυτόν· 5 εἶτα
βάλλει ὕδωρ εἰς τὸν [m] νιπτῆρα, καὶ ἤρξατο [no] νίπτειν τοὺς
[o] πόδας τῶν μαθητῶν καὶ [p] ἐκμάσσειν τῷ [k] λεντίῳ ᾧ ἦν
...διεζωσμενος X. [l] διεζωσμένος. 6 ἔρχεται οὖν πρὸς Σίμωνα Πέτρον·
λέγει αὐτῷ Κύριε, σύ μου [no] νίπτεις τοὺς [o] πόδας; 7 ἀπεκρίθη Ἰησοῦς καὶ εἶπεν αὐτῷ Ὃ ἐγὼ ποιῶ σὺ οὐκ
C λεγει ... [q] οἶδας ἄρτι, γνώσῃ δὲ μετὰ ταῦτα. 8 λέγει αὐτῷ Πέτρος
Οὐ μὴ [no] νίψῃς μου τοὺς [o] πόδας [r] εἰς τὸν αἰῶνα. ἀπ-

g ch. vii. 33 xvi. 5, 10 al.
h = ch. xi. 29. Matt. ix. 19 al.
i = here only. see ch. x. 11, &c.
k here bis only†.
l here bis & ch. xxi. 7 only. Ezek. xxiii. 15 A only.
m here only†.
n ch. ix. 7 reff.
o here, &c. (7 times) & 1 Tim. v. 10 only. Gen. xliii. 24.
p Luke vii. 38 reff.
q = Matt. xx. 22.
r ch. viii. 51 reff. esp., 1 Cor. viii. 13.

BKLℵ 1 Orig$_{sæpe}$ [Bas$_2$ Cyr$_1$]: txt AD rel Orig$_1$. ins οτι bef προς D.
4. aft τα ιματια ins αυτου D 124(Sz) vulg lat-*a c f g* syrr [syr-jer] æth Bas$_1$ Hil$_1$.
5. aft ειτα ins λαβων, also υδωρ bef βαλλει D 69 arm. aft μαθ. ins αυτου D foss lat-*c f q* Syr [syr-jer] copt æth.
6. for σιμ. πετρ., τον πετρ σιμ. D lat-*a* [*l*]. rec ins και bef λεγει, with Aℵ rel latt syr æth arm: om BDL lat-*e l* Syr [syr-jer] copt Orig$_1$ spec. rec aft αυτω ins εκεινος, with ADℵ^{3a} rel lat-*ff*$_2$ [*l*] syr Chr$_1$ spec: om Bℵ^1 lat-*b* [syr-jer] æth Orig$_1$ Cyr$_1$. om κυριε ℵ^1.
7. for ὃ, α ℵ^1. [for μετα ταυτα, μετ αυτα B^1(Tischdf).]
8. aft πετρ. ins κυριε D[Π^2]. νιψεις (*itacism?*) D 1 Orig$_1$. rec τους ποδας bef μου, with Aℵ rel lat-*a* [*l*] Orig$_1$ Chr$_1$: μου bef νιψ. D 1. 69: txt BCL vulg lat-*b c*

The perfect, **δέδωκεν**, and present, **ὑπάγει**, are used indefinitely: *of things fixed in the counsel of God:* or perhaps, rather, as consistent with the historical *presents*, ἐγείρεται, τίθησιν, to give life and presence to the whole scene. **4.] τὰ ἱμ.**, "eas, quæ lotionem impedirent." Bengel. He put Himself into the ordinary dress of a servant. Or, which is far more probable, on the deepest grounds, did He not humble Himself so far as *literally* to divest Himself, and gird Himself merely, as the basest of slaves? **5.] τὸν νιπ.**, the vessel usually at hand for such purposes. The context seems to shew that He had washed the feet of one or more before the incident of the next verse: were it not so, **ἤρξατο** might merely express his doing something unusual and unlooked for. **ᾧ** is perhaps by attraction for ὅ, which would be the ordinary case after διεζωσμένος, cf. Rev. i. 13; xv. 6: or it may be dative by construction, as in Hom. Il. κ. 77, πὰρ δὲ ζωστὴρ κεῖτο παναίολος, ᾧ ῥ' ὁ γεραιὸς Ζώννυθ', and other examples in Meyer. **6.]** And (the οὖν taking up the narrative again at the ἤρξατο, q. d., 'in pursuance of this intention') He comes to Simon Peter; not *first*, as some have maintained, both with and without reference to the primacy of Peter:—for that would be hardly consistent (see on the preceding verse) with the context, which seems to require that the washing should have begun and been going on, before He came to Peter. **νίπτεις] art** *Thou* **washing** (intending to wash) **my feet?** He thinks the act unworthy of the Lord; even as many think that great act of Love to have been, which was typified by it. Notice that **μου** is enclitic, *not emphatic*, in which case it would be **ἐμοῦ**. The having his feet washed is a matter of course: it is the Person who is about to do it that offends him. **7.]** Hitherto our Lord had been silent. He emphasizes the **ἐγώ** and **σύ**, but so as to set forth Himself as the Master, Peter as the disciple, not wholly cognizant of His will and purpose, and therefore more properly found in subjection to it. **ὃ ἐγὼ ποιῶ**, i. e. (1) *this washing itself*, as a lesson of humility and love, ver. 14. (2) Its *symbolical meaning*, vv. 9, 10. (3) The *great Act of Love*, the laying aside my glory, and becoming in the form of a servant, that the washing of the Holy Spirit may cleanse men. **μετὰ ταῦτα]** (1) was known very soon, but (2) and (3) not till after the Spirit was given. **8.]** The rash and self-opinionated Apostle opposes to μετὰ ταῦτα his **οὐ μὴ . . . εἰς τ. αἰῶνα.** In interpreting our Lord's answer, we must remember, that He replies more to the *spirit* of Peter's objection, than to his words. The same well-meaning but false humility would prevent him (and does prevent many) from stooping to receive at the hands of the Lord that spiritual washing which is ab-

εκρίθη Ἰησοῦς αὐτῷ Ἐὰν μὴ νίψω σε, οὐκ [s] ἔχεις [s] μέρος ABCDE
μετ' ἐμοῦ. 9 λέγει αὐτῷ Σίμων Πέτρος Κύριε, μὴ τοὺς FGHK
πόδας μου μόνον, ἀλλὰ καὶ τὰς χεῖρας καὶ τὴν κεφαλήν. LMSU
10 λέγει αὐτῷ ὁ Ἰησοῦς Ὁ [t] λελουμένος οὐκ [u] ἔχει [u] χρείαν ΓΔΛΠℵ
εἰ μὴ τοὺς [v] πόδας [v] νίψασθαι, ἀλλ' ἔστιν καθαρὸς [w] ὅλος· 1. 33. 69
καὶ ὑμεῖς καθαροί ἐστε, ἀλλ' [x] οὐχὶ πάντες. 11 ᾔδει γὰρ
τὸν παραδιδόντα αὐτόν· διὰ τοῦτο εἶπεν ὅτι οὐχὶ πάντες
καθαροί ἐστε. 12 Ὅτε οὖν [v] ἔνιψεν τοὺς [v] πόδας αὐτῶν
καὶ [y] ἔλαβεν τὰ ἱμάτια αὐτοῦ καὶ [z] ἀνέπεσεν πάλιν, εἶπεν
αὐτοῖς Γινώσκετε τί πεποίηκα ὑμῖν; 13 ὑμεῖς [a] φωνεῖτέ με
[b] Ὁ διδάσκαλος καὶ ὁ κύριος, καὶ [c] καλῶς λέγετε, εἰμὶ

s Rev. xx. 6 only. (see Luke xi. 36. xii. 46. Acts viii. 21.)
t Acts ix. 37. xvi. 33. Heb. x. 22. 2 Pet. ii. 22. Rev. i. 5 only. Exod. ii. 5.
u Matt. iii. 14 reff.
v vv. 5, &c. reff.
w = ch. vii. 23. Zech. iv. 2. see ch. ix. 34.
x ch. xiv. 22. 1 Cor. v. 2 al. Num. xxiv. 17.
y ch. x. 17, 18 reff.
z Luke xi. 37 reff.
a = here only.
b nom., Luke xix. 20. 1 Kings ix. 9. Ps. lxxxvi. 5 A(not F)Bℵ &c.
c = ch. iv. 17. viii. 48. Matt. xv. 7 al. Jer. i. 12.

e f ff$_2$ [*g*] *q* Orig$_7$ [Cyr-p$_1$]. rec (for *ιησ. αυτω*) *αυτω ο ιησ.*, with ℵ rel; *αυτω ιησ.* GK[EΠ$^{1\cdot3}$]: om *αυτω* C^{3}D lat-*b e* [*l*] copt arm spec: txt A B(sic: see table) C^{1}L am (with [fuld] forj) Orig$_1$.

9. *πετρος* bef *σιμων* B: om *σιμων* D: txt ACℵ rel vss Orig$_1$. om *κυριε* ℵ^1 253. *μονον* bef *τους ποδας* D latt[not *e*] copt. om *μου* DEGH 69 lat-*a b c e ff*$_2$ *l* Ambr spec.

10. om *ο* (bef *ιησ.*) B Orig$_1$. rec *ου χρειαν εχει*, with C^{3}D rel Chr$_1$ Cyr$_1$ Ambr$_2$: txt ABC^{1}ℵ lat-*a e q* Orig$_6$ Tert$_1$ [Aug$_1$]. add *την κεφαλην νιψασθαι* D. rec (for *ει μη*) *ἤ*, with AC^3 rel: om E^{2}FHℵ: txt BC^{1}DL [K(*η μη*) Π] 13. 33. 69 Orig$_1$ Chr$_1$.—om *τους ποδας* also ℵ lat-*c*. for *νιψασθαι*, *μονον* D. for *αλλ' εστιν*, *εστιν γαρ* D Syr [syr-jer] arm.—*αλλα* ℵ.

11. aft *γαρ* ins *ιησ.* D Syr [arm]. om 2nd clause D [syr-jer]. rec om *οτι*, with Aℵ rel vulg lat-*e g* Orig$_1$ spec: ins BCL 33 lat-*a b c f ff*$_2$ *l* [*q*] syrr Cyr$_1$.

12. om *και* (bef *ελαβεν*) A C^2(appy) Lℵ 33 ev-y foss lat-*a b c* [*f ff*$_2$ *g l* spec] Syr copt æth arm: ins BC$^{1\cdot3}$D [rel vulg lat-*e q* syr syr-jer goth Orig$_1$ Bas$_1$ Chr$_1$ Cyr$_1$]. for *αυτου*, *αυτων* ℵ^1: om D lat-*b e* spec. rec om 2nd *και*, with D rel mm: ins ABC^{1}Lℵ 33 Syr copt æth Orig$_1$. rec *αναπεσων* (*it was not perceived that the apodosis began at ειπεν: hence the omn of και bef ελαβ., and the other changes*), with ADℵ^{3a} rel vulg lat-*b c* [*f ff*$_2$ *g l q*] syr goth arm Chr$_1$ spec: txt BC^{1}ℵ^1 lat-*a e* Syr [syr-jer] copt æth Orig$_1$. (*και αναπεσων παλιν ειπεν αυτοις* written on the margin of A, possibly by the origl scribe.)

solutely necessary in order to have any part in Him, Rom. viii. 9, '*If I wash thee not, thou hast no part in Me;*' but the affirmative proposition is not equally true; witness the example of Judas, who *was washed, but yet had no part* in Jesus. In the *spiritual sense* of washing, this is not so. Whoever is washed by Jesus, has part in Him. We are here in the realm of another and deeper logic: the act being no longer symbolic, but veritable.

9.] The warm-hearted Peter, on learning that *exclusion* would be the consequence of not being washed, can hardly have enough of a cleansing so precious. There surely is implied in this answer an incipient apprehension of the meaning of our Lord's words. The **ἐὰν μὴ νίψω σε** has awakened in him, as the Lord's presence did, Luke v. 8, a feeling of his own want of cleansing, his entire pollution. This sense (Stier, Bengel, Baumgarten-Crusius) is denied by Lücke and Olsh.

10.] Reference appears to be made to the fact that one who *has bathed*, after he has reached his home, needs not entire washing, but only to have his feet washed from the dust of the way. This bathing, the bath of the new birth, but only yet in its foreshadowing, in the purifying effect of faith working by love, the Apostles, with one exception, *had;* and this *foot-washing* represented to them, besides its lesson of humility and brotherly love, their *daily need of cleansing from daily pollution, even after spiritual regeneration*, at the hands of their Divine Master. See 2 Cor. vii. 1: James i. 21: Acts xv. 8, 9: 2 Pet. ii. 22. On **καθ. ἐστε**, see note, ch. xv. 3.

11.] **τὸν παραδιδόντα**, as *ὁ ἐρχόμενος*, **him that should betray Him**, the indefinite characteristic present.

12—20.] *This act, a pattern of self-denying love for His servants.*

12. **γινώσκ. τί π. ὑ.**] These words are uttered, not so much in expectation of an answer, as to direct their attention to the following.

13.] **ὁ διδάσκ.** and **ὁ κ.** are titular

γάρ. 14 εἰ οὖν ἐγὼ [v] ἔνιψα ὑμῶν τοὺς [v] πόδας ὁ κύριος
καὶ ὁ διδάσκαλος, καὶ ὑμεῖς [d] ὀφείλετε ἀλλήλων [v] νίπτειν
τοὺς [v] πόδας. 15 [e] ὑπόδειγμα γὰρ ἔδωκα ὑμῖν [f] ἵνα
Frag.-nitr. καθὼς ἐγὼ ἐποίησα ὑμῖν καὶ ὑμεῖς ποιῆτε. 16 ἀμὴν ἀμὴν
δουλος .. λέγω ὑμῖν, οὐκ ἔστιν δοῦλος [g] μείζων τοῦ κυρίου αὐτοῦ,
οὐδὲ [h] ἀπόστολος [g] μείζων τοῦ πέμψαντος αὐτόν. 17 εἰ
...αυτα ταῦτα οἴδατε, μακάριοί ἐστε ἐὰν ποιῆτε αὐτά. 18 οὐ περὶ
Frag.-nitr. πάντων ὑμῶν λέγω· ἐγὼ οἶδα τίνας [i] ἐξελεξάμην· ἀλλ'
[k] ἵνα ἡ γραφὴ πληρωθῇ Ὁ [l] τρώγων μου τὸν ἄρτον
[m] ἐπῆρεν [n] ἐπ' ἐμὲ τὴν [o] πτέρναν αὐτοῦ. 19 [p] ἀπ' ἄρτι

d Luke xvii. 10 ch. xix. 7 al.
e Heb. iv. 11. viii. 5. ix. 23. James v. 10. 2 Pet. ii. 6 only +. Sir. xliv. 16. 2 Macc. vi. 28, 31 only.
f ver. 34.
g = Matt. xi. 11. ch. xiv. 28. xv. 20 al. Gen. xlviii. 19.
h = 2 Cor. viii. 23. Phil. ii. 25. 3 Kings xiv. 6 A, &c. only. see Herod. i. 21. v. 38.
i ch. vi. 70 reff.
k constr., ch. i. 8. ix. 3. Mark xiv. 49.
l Matt. xxiv. 38. ch. vi. 54—58 only +.
m (Psa. xl. 9) = here only. (Luke xxi. 28. xxiv. 50 al.) 1 Kings xx. 33.
n = 2 Thess. ii. 4. Ps. cv. 26.
o here only. Gen. iii. 15. (-νισμός, Ps. l. c.)
p Matt. xxiii. 39. xxvi. 29, 64. ch. (i. 52 v. r.) xiv. 7. Rev. xiv. 13 only.

14. [*ει ουν* to *διδασκαλος* is written twice by B[1](Tischdf).] *τους ποδας* bef *υμων* DK[Π] vulg lat-*a c e ff*$_2$ [*l q* spec] syr. ins *ποσω μαλλον* bef *και υμεις* D lat-*a ff*$_2$ *g* [*l* spec] (Syr). *νιπτ.* bef *αλληλ.* ℵ.
15. δεδωκα AKM[Π]ℵ 33. 69 [Bas$_2$] Cyr$_1$. ποιειτε (*itacism?*) DEFGHMΛ 1.
18. aft *εγω* ins *γαρ* AK[Π]ℵ 69 lat-*c l q* Syr copt arm Cyr[-p$_1$]. rec (for *τινας*) *ους*, with AD rel Eus$_2$: txt BCLMℵ 33 Orig$_4$ Cyr[-p$_1$]. *πληρ.* bef *η γραφη* D vulg lat-*b c* goth [arm]. rec (for *μου*) *μετ' εμου*, with ADℵ rel vulg lat-*a b* [*c e f ff*$_2$ *g l*] syrr copt goth arm Orig$_1$ Eus$_1$: txt BCL tol æth Orig$_3$ Eus$_1$ Cyr-comm[-p]. επηρκεν AU[Π]ℵ 1. om *επ'* B.

nominatives, as in reff. (Winer, § 29. 1, edn. 6.) **14.**] [The command here given must be understood in the full light of intelligent appreciation of the circumstances and the meaning of the act.] "Pedilavium, quod Dominus discipulis adhibuit, pertinebat et ad beneficium conferendæ puritatis totalis, et ad *παιδείαν* docendæ dilectionis humilis, ver. 34, coll. ver. 1. Inde pedilavium discipulorum inter se eo pertinet, ut alter alterum quoquo modo adjuvet ad consequendam puritatem animæ; et ut alter alteri pedes lavet,—*vel* proprie, 1 Tim. v. 10, idque serio, si scil. accidat, ut opus sit: est enim præceptum affirmativum, obligans semper, sed non ad semper: quale etiam illud, 1 Joh. iii. 16—*vel* synecdochice, per omne genus officiorum, quæ alter alteri etiam servilia et sordida, modo opportuna, præstare potest. Dominus igitur per ipsum pedilavium purificavit discipulos: quare etiam Petrum amanter coëgit: sed discipulis pedilavium mutuum non hoc nomine præcepit; neque adeo tanta est pedilavii literatenus imitandi necessitas, quantam nonnulli statuerunt: quum Johannes v. gr. Thomæ pedes nusquam laverit; et tamen major pedilavii Dominici et fraterni similitudo, quam plerique agnoscunt. Hodie pontifices et principes pedilavium ad literam imitantur; magis autem admirandus foret, v. gr. pontifex, unius regis, quam duodecim pauperum pedes, seria humilitate lavans." Bengel. The custom of literally and ceremonially washing the feet in obedience to this command, is not found before the fourth century. **15.**] **καθώς**, not *ὅ*, *ἐγὼ ἐπ.* Our Lord's action was symbolical, and is best imitated in His followers by endeavouring, "if a man be overtaken in a fault, to restore (*καταρτίζειν*) such an one in the spirit of meekness:" Gal. vi. 1. **16, 17.**] The proverbial expression **οὐκ ἔστιν δ. . . .** is used here in a different sense from ch. xv. 20. Here it is, 'if the Master thus humble Himself, much more should His servants and messengers:' see Matt. x. 24: Luke vi. 40; and on ver. 17, Luke xii. 47, 48. The *mere recognition* of such a duty of humility, is a very much more easy matter than the *putting it in practice.* **18.**] **I say it not** (viz. the *ἐὰν ποιῆτε αὐτά*) **of you** *all*: for there is one who can never be *μακάριος*. Our Lord repeats His *ἀλλ' οὐχὶ πάντες* of ver. 10, and the sad recollection leads to His trouble in spirit, ver. 21. **ἐγὼ οἶδα**] The **ἐγώ** is emphatic; and the reason of its emphasis is given in ver. 19. Connexion: 'It might be supposed that this treachery has come upon Me unawares; but it is not so: I (for my part) know whom I have selected (viz. *the whole twelve,* see ch. vi. 70; not only the true ones (Stier), as in ch xv. 16, said when Judas was not present): but this has been done by the determinate counsel and foreknowledge of God, declared in the Scriptures.' On the citation, see

q ch. iv. 26 reff.
r ch. i. 12 reff.
s ch. xvi. 23. xx. 23 bis only.
t ch. xi. 33 reff.
u Mark ii. 8 reff.
v = ch. xii. 17 reff.
w Mark vi. 20 v. r. Luke xxiv. 4. Acts xxv. 20. 2 Cor. iv. 8. Gal. iv. 20 only. Gen. xxxii. 7.
x Matt. xx. 10, 11 reff.
y Luke xvi. 22 reff. 2 Kings xii. 3.
z = ch. xi. 5. Gen. xliv. 20.

λέγω ὑμῖν πρὸ τοῦ γενέσθαι, ἵνα πιστεύσητε ὅταν γένηται Frag.-nitr.
ὅτι [q] ἐγώ εἰμι. 20 ἀμὴν ἀμὴν λέγω ὑμῖν, ὁ [r] λαμβάνων οταν...
[s] ἄν [s] τινα πέμψω, ἐμὲ [r] λαμβάνει· ὁ δὲ ἐμὲ [r] λαμβάνων Χ αμην αμην...
[r] λαμβάνει τὸν πέμψαντά με. ...τον
21 Ταῦτα εἰπὼν Ἰησοῦς [t] ἐταράχθη τῷ [u] πνεύματι, Frag.-nitr.
καὶ [v] ἐμαρτύρησεν καὶ εἶπεν Ἀμὴν ἀμὴν λέγω ὑμῖν ὅτι εἷς
ἐξ ὑμῶν παραδώσει με. 22 ἔβλεπον εἰς ἀλλήλους οἱ
μαθηταὶ [w] ἀπορούμενοι περὶ τίνος λέγει. 23 ἦν [x] ἀνακείμενος εἷς ἐκ τῶν μαθητῶν αὐτοῦ ἐν τῷ [y] κόλπῳ τοῦ Frag.-nitr.
Ἰησοῦ, ὃν [z] ἠγάπα ὁ Ἰησοῦς· 24 [a] νεύει οὖν τούτῳ Σίμων εις...

a Acts xxiv. 10 only. Prov. iv. 25 only. (ἐννεύειν, Luke i. 62.)

ABCDE FGHK LMSUX ΓΔΛΠℵ Frag.-nitr. 1. 33. 69

19. rec *οταν γεν.* bef *πιστ.*, with ACD rel vulg-ed lat-*c f ff*$_2$ *q* [syrr arm] goth Orig$_2$ Thdrt$_1$: txt BLℵ Frag-nitr am(with fuld forj ing mt) lat-*a b e g* [*l*] copt Orig$_3$ Cyr$_1$. —*πιστευητε* BC Orig$_3$: txt ADℵ rel [Orig$_2$]. (Frag-nitr def.)

20. (rec *εαν*, with D rel Orig$_2$ [Chr$_1$] : txt ABCKLMX[Π]ℵ Frag-nitr 33 Cyr$_1$.) *και ο λαμ. εμε* D Syr Chr$_1$ (not 33 as Tischdf [ed 7]).

21. rec ins *ὁ* bef *ιησ.*, with ACD rel : om BLℵ. *υμιν* bef *λεγω* B.

22. rec aft *εβλεπον* ins *ουν*, with ADL ℵ(*ουν ουν* ℵ[1] : om 2nd *ουν* ℵ[3a.b]) rel [latt syr copt goth] Cyr$_1$; *δε* Scr's m n t lat-*a* Syr æth Orig$_1$: om BC lat-*e* arm Orig$_1$. ins *οι ιουδαιοι* bef *εις αλληλ.* ℵ[1](marked for omission by ℵ-corr[1]). *απορουντες* D 69.

23. rec aft *ην* ins *δε*, with AC[2]Dℵ rel lat-*a c f ff*$_2$ [*q*] Syr syr-w-ast copt goth [arm] : om BC[1]L Orig$_2$. rec om *εκ*, with EFGHU[Γ]Λ (S 1, e sil) goth Orig$_1$: ins ABCDℵ Frag-nitr rel latt Syr coptt æth Orig$_2$ Cyr. aft *ον* ins *και* D. om *ὁ* B.

24. om *ουν* C[1] Λ(Treg, expr) 69 lat-*c ff*$_2$[Sabat] Syr arm.

LXX. The words here are given freely, the LXX having ἐμεγάλυνεν ἐπ' ἐμὲ πτερνισμόν. This is another instance of the direct and unhesitating application of the words of the Psalms by our Lord to Himself. **τὴν πτ.**] "Congruit hic sermo imprimis ad lotionem *pedum*, et ad morem veterum discumbentium ad *panem* edendum." Bengel. **19.**] '*Now, from this time*, I announce it to you, that when it shall have happened, you may believe that I am (the Christ).' See ch. xvi. 1, and above on ἐγὼ οἶδα, ver. 18. **20.**] See Matt. x. 40. The connexion is very difficult, and variously set down. It has been generally supposed (Euthym., &c.) that the words were to comfort the Apostles for the disgrace of their order by Judas, or in prospect of their future labours. But then would not ἄν τινα π. have been expressed by ὑμᾶς? Another view is to refer back to vv. 16, 17, and suppose the connexion to have been broken by the allusion to Judas. But is this likely, in a discourse of our Lord? I rather believe that the saying sets forth the dignity of that office from which Judas was about to fall: q. d. 'not only was he in close intercourse with Me (ver. 18), but invested with an ambassadorship for Me, and in Me, for the Father; and yet *he* will lift up his heel against Me.' And the consideration of this dignity in all its privileges, as contrasted with the sad announcement just to be made, leads on to the ἐταράχθη τῷ πν. of the next verse.

21—30.] *Contrast of the manifestations of love and hate.* See notes on Matt. xxvi. 21—25. Mark xiv. 18—21. Luke xxii. 21—23. **21.**] See above. One of those mysterious troublings of spirit, which passed over our Lord,—ch. xi. 33 and xii. 27. **ἐμαρτ.** implies the delivery of some solemn and important announcement. This was the first time He had ever spoken so plainly. All four Evangelists agree in the substance of the announcement.

22.] In Matt. and Mark they express their questioning in *words*. St. Luke's συνζητεῖν πρὸς ἑαυτούς would appear to imply the same. We seem called on here to decide a much-controverted question,—*where in John's narrative the institution of the Lord's supper is to be inserted?* I believe certainly *before* this announcement, as in Luke: and if before it, *perhaps before the washing of the disciples' feet:* for I see no break which would admit it between our ver. 1 and ver. 21. **23.**] Since the captivity, the Jews lay at table in the Persian manner, on divans or couches, each on his left side, with his

Πὲτρος καὶ λέγει αὐτῷ Εἰπὲ τίς ἐστιν περὶ οὗ λέγει.
25 [b] ἀναπεσὼν ἐκεῖνος [c] οὕτως ἐπὶ τὸ [d] στῆθος τοῦ Ἰησοῦ
λέγει αὐτῷ Κύριε, τίς ἐστιν; 26 ἀποκρίνεται οὖν ὁ Ἰησοῦς
Ἐκεῖνός ἐστιν ᾧ ἐγὼ [ef] βάψω τὸ [fg] ψωμίον καὶ δώσω
αὐτῷ. [ef] βάψας οὖν τὸ [fg] ψωμίον λαμβάνει καὶ δίδωσιν
Ἰούδᾳ Σίμωνος Ἰσκαριώτου. 27 καὶ μετὰ τὸ [g] ψωμίον,
τότε [h] εἰςῆλθεν εἰς ἐκεῖνον ὁ [h] σατανᾶς. λέγει οὖν αὐτῷ
Ἰησοῦς Ὃ ποιεῖς ποίησον [i] τάχιον. 28 τοῦτο δὲ οὐδεὶς

...ου λεγει Frag.-nitr. Frag.-nitr. ιουδα... ...ποιεις Frag.-nitr.

b Luke xi. 37 reff.
c = ch. iv. 6.
d Luke xviii. 13. xxiii. 48. ch. xxi. 20. Rev. xv. 6 only. Dan. ii. 32.
e here bis. Luke xvi. 24. Rev. xix. 13 only. Num. xix. 18 al.
f see Ruth ii. 14.
g here, &c. (4 times) only †. (μίζειν, Rom. xii. 20, from Prov. xxv. 21.)
h Luke xxii. 3.
i ch. xx. 4. 1 Tim. iii. 14. Heb. xiii. 23 only †. Wisd. xiii. 9. 1 Macc. ii. 40 only.

πετρους D^{1}-gr. rec (for *κ. λεγ. αυτω ειπε τις εστ.*) *πυθεσθαι τις αν ειη* (*see note*), with A D(adding *ουτος*) rel syrr copt[om *τις αν ειη*] goth [arm] Cyr$_1$: *πυθ. τις αν ειη περι ου ελεγεν και λεγει αυτω ειπε τις εστιν* ℵ(retaining *περι ου λεγει* afterwards): txt BCLX Frag-nitr 33 [latt(exc *e*)] æth Orig$_{alic}$.

25. rec *επιπεσων* (*from Luke* xv. 20, *αναπ. not seeming appropriate*), with AC^{3}Dℵ^{1} rel: txt BC^{1}KLX[Π^{1}]ℵ^{3a} 33 Orig$_2$. rec adds *δε*, with A rel lat-*ff$_2$ q* syr[-txt] copt-dz goth [æth arm] Cyr$_1$; *ουν* DLMXΔℵ 1. 33. 69 vulg [lat-*a b c f g l*] syr-mg copt-wilk [sah-mnt]: om BC lat-*e* Orig$_1$. rec om *ουτως*, with AD[Π]ℵ 1. 69 vss Orig$_1$: ins BC rel goth Euthym. (*ουτος* [*itacism ?*] KSU[Γ]Λ.)

26. rec om *ουν*, with AC^{3}Dℵ^{1} rel vulg lat-*b c*: for *ουν*, *αυτω* D 69 lat-*e*: txt BC^{1} LXℵ^{3a} lat-*a* syr-mg Orig$_1$ [Cyr$_1$]. om *ὁ* B(sic: see table) M. aft *ιησ.* ins *και λεγει* Dℵ 69 Syr copt æth [arm]. ins *αν* bef *εγω* D 1. rec *βαψας το ψωμιον επιδωσω*, omg *και* (*corrn for elegance; επιδ., which Mey thinks genuine, from its not being elsw used by John, might well be a copier's reminiscence of such passages as Matt* vii. 9, 10 ‖, *or even Luke* xxiv. 30, 42), with ℵ rel; so, but *εμβαψας* (*from* ‖ *Matt Mark*) ADK[Π] 1. 69: *βαψ. το ψ. δωσω αυτω* MX: txt BCL copt æth arm Orig$_3$(*οὐ γέγραπται Ἐκεῖνός ἐστιν ᾧ ἐγὼ δώσω τὸ ψ., ἀλλὰ μετὰ προsθήκης τοῦ Βάψω· Βάψω γάρ, φησί, τὸ ψ. κ. δώσω*). rec (for *βαψας ουν*) *και εμβαψας*, with A rel: *και βαψ.* D 69 Orig$_2$: txt BC^{1}LXℵ (lat-*a*) Orig$_2$ Cyr$_1$ [*εμβ. ουν* Π^{2}]. om 2nd *το* B. rec om *λαμβ. και*, with ADℵ^{1} rel latt syrr [copt]: ins BCLMX ℵ^{3a}(but erased) 33 syr-mg æth Orig$_4$. rec *ισκαριωτη* (*as ch* vi. 70), with A rel copt [goth arm]: *απο καρυωτου* D: txt BCLMX[Π^{2}]ℵ Frag-nitr 33 lat-*g* Orig$_3$-mss.

27. om *μετα το ψωμιον* D lat-*e*. om *τοτε* DLℵ vulg-ed(not am forj foss [fuld ing]) lat-*a b c* [*ff$_2$ l*] copt Orig$_4$(ins$_3$) Cyr$_1$. om *ὁ* D^{1}(ins D^{4}) Δ. for *λεγει ουν*, *και λεγει* D [lat-*e* æth] Syr arm. rec ins *ο* bef *ιησ.*, with ACDℵ Frag-nitr rel: om BL. for *ποιησον*, *ποιης* D^{1}(txt D^{4}).

28. om *δε* B 248

face towards the table, his left elbow resting on a pillow and supporting his head. Thus the second guest to the right hand lay with his head near the breast of the first, and so on (Lücke ii. 565). **ὃν ἠγάπα ὁ Ἰησ.**] The disciple meant is John himself, see ch. xxi. 20; also designated thus, ch. xix. 26; xxi. 7 (see Prolegomena to John, § i. 6). **24—26.**] See note on Matt. ver. 23. Peter characteristically imagines that John, as the beloved disciple, would know: but he, not knowing, asks of the Lord. It is an argument for the reading in the text, that (Schulz) John never uses the *optative*.

25.] **ἀναπεσών, leaning back on the bosom of Jesus. οὕτως,** as in ref. I understand it, that John, who was before lying *close to* the bosom (*ἐν τῷ κόλπῳ*) of Jesus, now leaned his head absolutely *upon* His breast, to ask the question. This escaped the notice of the rest at the table: see on Matt. as above.

26.] This = Matt. ver. 23, Mark, ver. 20. Meyer remarks, that the *ἐγώ* is *expressed* as a contrast to the *ἐκεῖνος*. **τὸ ψωμ.,** probably a piece of the unleavened bread, dipped in the broth made of bitter herbs. **27.**] "*Post* offulam, non *cum* offula." Bengel. Observe the **ψωμίον** stands for the act in which it played a principal part. This giving the sop was one of the closest testimonies of friendly affection. **τότε** carries a graphic power and pathos with it: **at that moment. εἰςῆλθ. εἰς ἐκ. ὁ σ.**] See ver. 2 and note. Satan *entered fully* into him, took full possession of him, —so that his will was not only bent upon doing the deed of treachery, but fixed and determined to do it *then and there*. The words must be understood literally, not as

ἔγνω τῶν [k] ἀνακειμένων [l] πρὸς τί εἶπεν αὐτῷ· 29 τινὲς
γὰρ ἐδόκουν, ἐπεὶ τὸ [m] γλωσσόκομον εἶχεν Ἰούδας, ὅτι
λέγει αὐτῷ Ἰησοῦς Ἀγόρασον ὧν [n] χρείαν [n] ἔχομεν [o] εἰς
τὴν ἑορτήν· ἢ τοῖς πτωχοῖς [p] ἵνα τὶ δῷ. 30 λαβὼν οὖν
τὸ ψωμίον ἐκεῖνος ἐξῆλθεν εὐθύς. ἦν δὲ νύξ. 31 ὅτε
οὖν ἐξῆλθεν, λέγει Ἰησοῦς Νῦν [q] ἐδοξάσθη ὁ υἱὸς τοῦ

ABCDE FGHK LMSUX ΓΔΛΠא 1. 33. 69

k ver. 23. l here only. cf. εἰς τί, Matt. xiv. 31. xxvi. 8 al. m ch. xii. 6 (reff.) only. n constr., Matt. vi. 8 reff. o = Matt. xxvi. 28. xxvii. 7 al. p arrangement of words, Acts xix. 4. Rom. xi. 31. 1 Cor. ix. 15. xiv. 9. 2 Cor. ii. 4. Gal. ii. 10. q ch. vii. 39 reff.

29. for επει, οτι D, *quia* latt. rec ins ὁ bef ιουδ., with CD rel Cyr: om ABF LMUXא 1. 33. 69 $Orig_1$. rec ins ὁ bef ιησ., with ACD rel [Cyr_1]: om Bא $Orig_1$. (δοι D.)

30. rec ευθ. bef εξηλθεν, with A rel lat-*a f q* syrr goth: txt BCDLMXא 33. 69 vulg lat-*b c* [ff_2 *g l* æth] copt arm $Orig_2$.—rec ευθεως, with A rel: txt BCDLXא $Orig_3$ [Cyr_1].

31. om ουν (*joining for the most part* οτε εξ. *to ver* 30) A rel foss syrr goth Chr_1 [Cyr_1]: ins BCDLXא 1. 33. 69 copt arm $Orig_1$ Cyr_1. rec ins ὁ bef ιησ., with AD rel [Cyr_1]: om BLΔא.

Theod. Mops., as merely betokening *τὴν κύρωσιν τῶν καταθυμίων τῷ διαβόλῳ λογισμῶν.* **ὃ ποιεῖς . . . . .**] These words are not to be evaded, as being *permissive* (Grot.) or *dismissive* (*οὐδὲ προστάττοντος οὐδὲ συμβουλεύοντος, ἀλλ' ὀνειδίζοντος καὶ δεικνύοντος ὅτι αὐτὸς μὲν ἐβούλετο διορθώσασθαι, ἐπειδὴ δὲ ἀδιορθώτως εἶχεν,* **ἀφίησιν** *αὐτόν.* Chrys. Hom. in Joan. lxx. 1. 2). They are like the saying of God to Balaam, Num. xxii. 20,—and of our Lord to the Pharisees, Matt. xxiii. 32. The *course of sinful action is presupposed*, and the command to go on is but the echo of that mysterious appointment by which the sinner in the exercise of his own corrupted will becomes the instrument of the purposes of God. Thus it is not ὅ, or εἴ τι, **ποιήσεις**, but **ὃ ποιεῖς**:—**that which thou art doing**, hast just now fully determined to put in present action, **do more quickly**—'than thou seemest willing:'—or perhaps better 'than thou wouldst otherwise have done,' which seems the account to be ordinarily given of this use of the comparative:—reproving his lingering, and his pretending (Matt. ver. 25) to share in the general doubt. **28.**] Not even John: who knew he was the traitor, but had no idea the deed was so soon to be done (Lücke, De Wette). Stier supposes John to exclude himself in saying *οὐδεὶς τ. ἀνακ.*, and that *he* knew. **29.**] The *first* supposition agrees with ver. 1,—that it was *πρὸ τῆς ἑορτῆς τοῦ πάσχα.* Had it been the night of the passover, the next day being hallowed as a sabbath, nothing *could have been bought.* On the whole question see notes on Matt. xxvi. 17, and ch. xviii. 28. On the *second* supposition, see ch. xii. 5. The gift to the poor might be, to *help them to procure their paschal lamb.* **30.**] The remark **ἦν δὲ νύξ** (which certainly concludes this period, see *ὅτε οὖν*, ver. 12) seems to be added to bring the whole narrative from ch. xiii. 1 to ch. xviii. 3 into precision, as happening on one and the same night. It is perhaps fanciful to see, as Orig., Olsh., Stier, &c. have done, an allusion to the *σκοτία* in Judas's soul, or to *ὑμῶν . . ἡ ὥρα καὶ ἡ ἐξουσία τοῦ σκότου*, Luke xxii. 53; though doubtless *there* the Lord alludes to its being *also night*: but I quite feel, with Meyer, that there is something awful in this termination—**it was night.**

31—XVI. 33.] HIS LOVE IN KEEPING AND COMPLETING HIS OWN. And herein, **31—XIV. 31.**] *He comforts them with the assurance that He is going to the Father.*

31—38.] *Announcement of the fact—its effect on Peter.* Here commences that solemn and weighty portion of the Gospel (ch. xiii. 31—xvii. 26) which Olshausen not without reason calls Allerheiligstes—'the most holy place.' He beautifully remarks, "These were the last moments which the Lord spent in the midst of His own before His passion, and words full of heavenly meaning flowed during them from His holy lips:—all that His heart, glowing with love, had yet to say to His own, was compressed into this short space of time. At first the conversation with the disciples takes more the form of usual dialogue: reclining at the table, they mournfully reply to and question Him. But when (ch. xiv. 31) they had risen from the supper, the discourse of Christ took a higher form: surrounding their Master, the disciples listened to the Words of Life, and seldom spoke (only ch. xvi. 17, 29). Finally, in the sublime prayer of the great High Priest, the whole Soul of Christ flowed forth in earnest intercession for His own to His

ἀνθρώπου, καὶ ὁ θεὸς [q] ἐδοξάσθη ἐν αὐτῷ. 32 [εἰ ὁ θεὸς
ἐδοξάσθη ἐν αὐτῷ,] καὶ ὁ θεὸς δοξάσει αὐτὸν ἐν ἑαυτῷ,
καὶ εὐθὺς δοξάσει αὐτόν. 33 [r] τεκνία, [s] ἔτι [st] μικρὸν μεθ'
ὑμῶν εἰμι. ζητήσετέ με, καὶ καθὼς εἶπον τοῖς Ἰουδαίοις,
ὅτι [uv] ὅπου ἐγὼ [v] ὑπάγω, ὑμεῖς οὐ δύνασθε ἐλθεῖν, καὶ ὑμῖν
λέγω ἄρτι. 34 [w] ἐντολὴν καινὴν [w] δίδωμι ὑμῖν, [x] ἵνα ἀγαπᾶτε ἀλλήλους· καθὼς ἠγάπησα ὑμᾶς, ἵνα καὶ ὑμεῖς ἀγα-

...καθως F.

r John (1 John ii. 1, 12, 28. iii. 7, 18. iv. 4. v. 21) only, exc. Gal. iv. 19 +.
s ch. xiv. 19. Heb. x. 37 only. Jer. xviii. 33. see ch. vii. 33.
t as above (s). ch. xvi. 16, &c. (7 times). Matt. xxvi. 39, 73 || Mk. 2 Cor. xi. 1, 16 only.
u = Matt. viii. 19. Mark vi. 10.
v here bis. ch. viii. 21, 22. xiv. 4. Rev. xiv. 4 only.
w ch. xi. 57 reff.
x ver. 15. ch. xv. 12. Matt. xii. 16 al.

32. om ει to αυτω (*homœotel ?*) BC¹DLX[Π]א¹ 1 fuld(with harl) lat-*a b c ff₂ g* [*l*¹] syr æth-mss Tert₁ Ambr₂: ins AC²א³ᵃ rel vulg-ed lat-*e f* [*l*² *q* syr-jer] Syr coptt goth æth-rom [arm] Orig₂ Hil₄. for εαυτω, αυτω BHΛ א¹(txt א³ᵃ, but ε erased) Orig₂. aft ευθυς ins και ευς (but erased) D¹.

33. aft μικρον ins χρονον LX[Γ]א ev-y lat-*c f l* Eus₁. om οτι Dא 249 vulg lat-*b c e ff₂* [*l*] æth Cyr. rec υπαγω bef εγω, with EFGHS[Γ]ΔΛ lat-*a b q* syrr Chr₁: txt ABCDא rel vulg lat-*c f ff₂* [*g*] *l* goth arm Orig₄.

34. aft καθως ins καγω D. om 2nd ινα א Scr's p.

Heavenly Father." Olsh. ii. 329. **31. νῦν ἐδοξ.**] It was not that the *presence of* Judas, as some have thought, hindered the great consummation imported by **ἐδοξ.**, but that the work on which he was gone out, was the ACTUAL COMMENCEMENT *of that consummation:* "ab hinc enim passiones Christi initium capiebant." Lampe. It is true that his presence hindered the *expression* of these gracious words: "jam quasi obice rupto torrentes gratiæ a labiis Jesu effunduntur." Id. **ἐδοξάσθη**—spoken proleptically as if accomplished, because the deed was actually in doing, which was to accomplish it. The glorifying spoken of here, and in δοξάσει, ver. 32, is not the same. *This* is the glorifying of God by Christ on earth, in His course of obedience as the Son of Man, which was completed by His death (ὑπήκοος μέχρι θανάτου, Phil. ii. 8). And His death was the transition-point between God being glorified in Him, and He being glorified in God—manifested to be the Son of God with power by His resurrection, and received up to the Father, to sit at the right hand of God. This latter (ver. 32) is spoken of by Him here as future, but immediate (εὐθύς) on His death, and leads on to the address in ver. 33. **ἐν ἑαυτῷ** is in *God* (the Father), not in Christ. ἑαυτ. reflects back on the *subject* of the sentence: and ἐν is not '*by means of*,' but in, by the resurrection of Him into that glory, which He had indeed before, but now has *as the Son of Man*, with the risen Manhood; so **παρὰ σεαυτῷ**, ch. xvii. 5. Grotius compares 1 Sam. ii. 30 (τοὺς δοξάζοντάς με δοξάσω LXX). ἀντιδωρεῖται αὐτῷ ὁ πατὴρ τὸ μεῖζον οὗ ὁ υἱὸς τοῦ ἀνθρώπου πεποίηκεν. Origen. in Joan. tom. xxxii. 18, vol. iv. p. 451.

33.] **τεκνία**—*here only* used by Christ—affectingly expresses His not only brotherly, but fatherly love (Isa. ix. 6) for His own, and at the same time their immature and weak state, now about to be left without Him. **καθὼς εἶπ.**] "Noluit discipulis citius hoc dicere: infidelibus dixit citius." Bengel. But naturally the two clauses, 'Ye shall seek Me and not find Me, and shall die in your sins,' also spoken to the Jews (ch. vii. 33; viii. 21), are here omitted: and by this omission the connexion with ver. 34 is supplied;—'Ye shall be left here: but, unlike the Jews, ye shall seek Me and shall find Me, and the way is that of Love,—to Me, and to one another (so Stier, v. 140 ff. edn. 2)—forming (ver. 35) an united Body, the Church, in which all shall recognize My presence among you as My disciples.'

34.] The καινότης of this commandment consists in its *simplicity* and (so to speak) *unicity*. The same *kind* of love was prescribed in the O. T. (see Rom. xiii. 8):—'as thyself' is the *highest* measure of love, and it is therefore not in *degree* that the new commandment differs (Cyr., Euthym., Theod. Mops.) from the old, nor in *extent*, but in being *the* commandment of the new covenant,—the first-fruit of the Spirit in the new dispensation (Gal. v. 22): see 1 John ii. 7, 8 (and note), where καινή is commented on by the Apostle himself. I cannot agree with Stier (v. 148, edn. 2), that **ἵνα** in the second sentence is not || with **ἵνα** in the first, but signifies ('I have loved you') "in order that &c." The sentence is analogous to ver. 14, and the *new* point in it is the καθὼς ἠγ. ὑμ., which is therefore

y 1 John ii. 3 & passim. = 1 Cor. iv. 6. Gen. xlii. 33.
z Mark ix. 50. Rom. i. 12. xv. 5 only.
a = ch. iii. 8 reff.
b Matt. ix. 11, 14 al.
c ch. x. 11 reff.
d Matt. xxvi. 34 (reff.).
e constr., Luke xii. 59.
f Matt. x. 33 reff.
g ch. xi. 33 reff.
h ch. ii. 11 reff.

πᾶτε ἀλλήλους. 35 ʸ ἐν τούτῳ γνώσονται πάντες ὅτι ἐμοὶ ABCDE
μαθηταί ἐστε, ἐὰν ἀγάπην ἔχητε ᶻ ἐν ᶻ ἀλλήλοις. 36 λέγει GHKL MSUX
αὐτῷ Σίμων Πέτρος Κύριε, ᵃ ποῦ ὑπάγεις; ἀπεκρίθη ΓΔΛΠℵ 1. 33. 69
Ἰησοῦς ᵘᵛ Ὅπου ᵛ ὑπάγω οὐ δύνασαί μοι νῦν ἀκολουθῆσαι,
ἀκολουθήσεις δὲ ὕστερον. 37 λέγει αὐτῷ Πέτρος Κύριε,
ᵇ διὰ τί οὐ δύναμαί σοι ἀκολουθῆσαι ἄρτι; τὴν ᶜ ψυχήν
μου ὑπὲρ σοῦ ᶜ θήσω. 38 ἀποκρίνεται Ἰησοῦς Τὴν ᶜ ψυχήν
σου ὑπὲρ ἐμοῦ ᶜ θήσεις; ἀμὴν ἀμὴν λέγω σοι, οὐ μὴ
ᵈ ἀλέκτωρ ᵈ φωνήσῃ, ᵉ ἕως οὗ ᶠ ἀρνήσῃ με τρίς.
XIV. 1 Μὴ ᵍ ταρασσέσθω ὑμῶν ἡ καρδία· ʰ πιστεύετε

35. aft *εν τουτω* ins *γαρ* D lat-*c*. *μετ' αλληλων* ℵ.
36. for *απεκριθη*, *λεγει* D latt. rec aft *απεκρ.* ins *αυτω*, with AC^{3}Dℵ rel fuld (with foss) lat-*q* syrr æth: om BC^{1}L [latt syr-jer] copt goth arm. rec ins *ὁ* bef *ιησ.*, with C^{3}Dℵ rel Chr Cyr: om ABC^{1}L. aft *οπου* ins *εγω* D S-marg UXℵ 33. 69 latt [syr-jer copt sah-mnt arm] goth Orig$_2$ Chr Cyr Thl. for *νυν ακολ.*, *συνακολ.* D^1(Scr): *συ νυν ακολ.* D^4(?): *συ ακολ.* D^r lat-*e c*: *ακολ.* (only) ΔU^1. aft *ακολουθησαι* add *αρτι* (*see ver* 37) D lat-*e*. rec transp *ακολουθησεις* and *υστερον*, with AC^{3}D rel vss: txt BC^{1}LXℵ 1. 33 latt Orig$_4$ Chr$_1$ Cyr$_1$.—rec aft *ακολ.* ins *μοι*, with C^3 rel: pref D: om ABC^{1}LXℵ 1. 33.
37. rec ins *ὁ* bef *πετρος*, with BL^{1}M 69 (1. 33, e sil) Cyr$_1$: om ACℵ rel.—om *πετρος* D 22(Sz). om *κυριε* ℵ^1 33. 249 vulg[(not tol) copt]. *δυνασαι μοι* A. add *νυν* (*see ver* 36) C^{1}DLX: om ABC^{3}ℵ rel. *ακολουθειν* BC^1: txt AC^{3}Dℵ rel. om *αρτι* C^{1}LX. *υπερ σου* bef *την ψυχ. μου* Xℵ.
38. rec *απεκριθη*, with C^{3}D rel: txt ABC^{1}LXℵ 1. 33. 69 syr. rec adds *αυτω*, with C^{3}EGHSU[Γ]ΔΛ^2 vulg-ed lat-*b f q* Syr copt æth: om ABC^{1}ℵ rel am[with em fuld forj ing] lat-*a e ff*$_2$ syr goth arm. rec ins *ὁ* bef *ιησ.*, with C^3 rel [Cyr$_1$]: om ABC^{1}DKLX[Π]ℵ 33. 69. add *και ειπεν αυτω* D lat-*c* (*ff*$_2$) [syr-jer]. ins *οτι* bef *ου μη* D lat-*c* syrr goth. rec *φωνησει*, with CD rel Orig$_1$ Cyr: txt ABGK UXΔ[ΓΠ]ℵ 33. rec **απαρνηση** (*from* ||), with ACℵ rel: txt BDLX 1 Orig$_1$ [Cyr$_1$].

CHAP. XIV. **1.** pref *και ειπεν τοις μαθ. αυτου* D lat-*a c*.

set first, and should be (as in E. V.) retained so. **35.**] **πάντες,—all the world,**—and the object is to be, not mere vain praise or display before the world, but that men may be attracted by the exhibition of the Spirit of Christ, and won over to Him. The world, notwithstanding this proof of His presence among them, shall hate them: see 1 John iii. 10—15. But among *πάντες* they themselves are also included—brotherly love is the true sign to them of being children of God, 1 John ii. 3—5.
36.] This announcement of Peter's denial is probably the same with that in Luke xxii. 33 ff., where see notes: but distinct from that on the way to Gethsemane, Matt. xxvi. 34: Mark xiv. 30. **ἀκ. δὲ ὕστ.**, alluding probably both to the future reception of His Apostle into His glory, and to the particular path by which he should come to that glory;—as in ch. xxi. 18, 19. **37.**] Peter understands our Lord's *death* to be meant [as the time of his following]: see Luke, ver. 33.
38.] The **διὰ τί** is not answered—but Peter's boast solemnly questioned. See a somewhat similar question, ch. i. 51. There was at the same time a startling *inversion* of the subsequent facts, in this boast; to which our Lord, I think, alludes in His question,—*τ. ψ.* **σου** *ὑπὲρ* **ἐμοῦ** *θήσεις;* The **οὐ μὴ ἀλέκ. φων.** necessarily implies, as it *was night*, *ἐν τῇ νυκτὶ ταύτῃ* [Matt., Mark],—and binds the whole events of this chapter to ch. xviii. CHAP. XIV. 1–31.] This first division of the great discourse (see above on ch. xiii. 31) is spent in more directly comforting the disciples for their Lord's departure, by the assurance of His going to the Father, and its consequences.
1—10.] HE, *in his union with the Father, will take His own to Him.*
1.] A pause has intervened; "Peter is humbled and silent" (Lücke); the rest are *ταρασσόμενοι τῇ καρδίᾳ* on account of the sad things of which they had been hearing;—Judas's treachery,—Peter's denial,—the Lord's departure from them.

εἰς τὸν θεόν, καὶ [h] εἰς ἐμὲ [h] πιστεύετε. 2 ἐν τῇ οἰκίᾳ τοῦ
N μοναι … πατρός μου [i] μοναὶ πολλαί εἰσιν· εἰ δὲ μή, εἶπον ἂν
ὑμῖν· ὅτι πορεύομαι [jk] ἑτοιμάσαι [k] τόπον ὑμῖν. 3 καὶ ἐὰν
πορευθῶ καὶ [jk] ἑτοιμάσω [k] τ όπον ὑμῖν, πάλιν [l] ἔρχομαι καὶ
Q -μας προς… [m] παραλήμψομαι ὑμᾶς πρὸς ἐμαυτόν, ἵνα ὅπου εἰμὶ ἐγὼ

i ver. 23 only †. 1 Macc. vii. 38 only.
j = Heb. xi. 16. 2 Kings vii. 12.
k here bis & Rev. xii. 6 only. 1 Chron. xv. 3.
l pres., Matt. xxvii. 63 reff.
m Mark ix. 2 reff. Cant. viii. 2.

2. om αν א. rec om οτι (*mistaken for the mere* οτι recitantis, *and so, as often, overlooked*), with C^2N rel lat-*a e f q* goth æth Chr_1 [$Orig\text{-}int_1$] : ins ABC^1DKLX[Π]א 33. 69 vulg lat-*b c* ff_2 *g* syrr [syr-jer] copt arm Cyr_1.
3. for και εαν, καν D. om και (bef ετοιμ.) ADEGHKM[Γ]Δ lat-*f* Syr (copt) goth $Phot_1$: ins B(sic : see table) CNא rel latt syr [syr-jer] æth arm. ετοιμασαι DM lat-*f q* Syr copt [Cyr_1]. rec υμιν bef τοπον, with AC rel vulg lat-*b c f* ff_2 *g* : txt BDKLNX[ΓΠ]א 1. 33 copt Cyr_2 Thdrt ερχ. bef παλιν D.

πιστεύετε *both times* is *imperative.* So Cyr., Nonn., Thl., Euth., Aug., Hil.,—Lampe, Lücke, De Wette, Stier, Tholuck (edn. 6), and A. V. R. Many (Erasmus, Beza, Grot., Olsh., also E. V.) take the first as indic., the second as imper., '*Ye believe in God : believe also in me.*' But this is inconsistent with the whole tenour of the discourse, which presupposes a want of belief in God in its full and true sense, as begetting *trust* in Him. Luther takes *both* as indicative. The command is intimately connected with ch. xiii. 31, 32—*faith in the glorification of Christ in the Father,* and *of the Father in Him.*

2.] This comfort—of being reunited to their Lord—is administered to them as τεκνία, in forms of speech simple, and adapted to their powers of apprehension of spiritual things. The **οἰκία** is Heaven : Ps. xxxiii. 13, 14 : Isa. lxiii. 15. In it are many (in number—not in degree of dignity, as Clem. Alex., Basil., Theod., Chrys., Theophylact, Tert., Hil., Aug., &c., at least no such meaning is *here* conveyed) abiding-places; *room enough for them all ;*—ἱκαναὶ δέξασθαι καὶ ὑμᾶς συνεσομένους ἡμῖν ἀεί. Euthym. If not,—if they could not follow Him thither, He would not have concealed this from them. This latter assurance is one calculated to beget entire trust and confidence ; He would not in any matter hold out vain hopes to them ;—His word to them would plainly state all difficulties and discouragements,—as indeed He does, ch. xv. 18 ; xvi. 1, 4 ; which last verse ἵνα μνημ. . . . . ὅτι **ἐγὼ εἶπον ὑμῖν**, is decisive for the above interpretation here, against those who would join ὅτι πορεύομαι . . . . . with εἶπον ἂν ὑμῖν (Euthym., Aug., Erasm., Luther, Bengel) :—which besides does violence to the next verse, where the 'going to prepare a place' is stated as a *fact.* The **ὅτι** may, it is true, have been inserted as a ὅτι *recitantis,* to favour the view just controverted : but it is much more probably genuine, signifying **because**, and belongs to the whole sense of vv. 1, 2, as a reason why their heart should not be troubled.

The sense confidently proposed for the **many mansions** by a correspondent,—that He was going to *one part* of His Father's house, while they would remain in *another,* that house being not Heaven, but the Universe,—is entirely put out of the question, as being frigid in the extreme under the solemn circumstances,—as being contrary to all Scripture analogy of expression,—and as inconsistent with the **πορεύομαι ἑτοιμάσαι τόπον ὑμῖν**, where the τόπος is of necessity correlative with the μοναί, which are in that οἰκία whither He is going. Besides, their earthly μικρὸς χρόνος could in no sense be called a **μονή**. The **ἑτοιμάσαι τόπον** is that of which we sing,—" When Thou hadst overcome the sharpness of death, Thou didst open the Kingdom of Heaven to all believers :" see note on Luke xxiii. 43. And thus it is **τόπον**, not τὰς μονάς :—*the place* as a whole, not *each man's place* in it.

3.] On **ἐάν** (not '*when,*' here or any where), see note, ch. xii. 32. Here there is no translation of feeling : only in the extract from Hermann there, we may read 'experientiâ (vestrâ) cognos*cetur.*'

In order to understand this, we must bear in mind what Stier well calls the 'perspective' of prophecy. The *coming again of the Lord* is not one single act,—as His resurrection, or the descent of the Spirit, or His second personal advent, or the final coming to judgment ; but the *great complex* of all these, the result of which shall be, His taking His people to Himself to be where He is. This **ἔρχομαι** is *begun* (ver. 18) in His Resurrection—*carried on* (ver. 23) in the *spiritual life* (see also ch. xvi. 22 ff.), the making *them* ready for the place prepared ;—*further advanced* when each by death is fetched

n ch. xiii. 33, 36 reff.
o see ch. i. 14 reff.
p = ch. xi. 25. Col. iii. 4. 1 John i. 2. v. 20.
q ch. (i. 52 v. r.) xiii. 19. Matt. xxiii. 39. xxvi. 29, 64. Rev. xiv. 13 only +.
r — Matt. xxv. 9 reff. impers., here only. Prov. xxx. 16.
s Heb. iv. 7 only. see Luke xv. 29.
t pres., ch. vi. 58 reff.

καὶ ὑμεῖς ἦτε. 4 καὶ [n] ὅπου ἐγὼ [n] ὑπάγω οἴδατε τὴν ὁδόν.
5 λέγει αὐτῷ Θωμᾶς Κύριε, οὐκ οἴδαμεν ποῦ ὑπάγεις,
καὶ πῶς οἴδαμεν τὴν ὁδόν; 6 λέγει αὐτῷ ὁ Ἰησοῦς Ἐγώ
εἰμι ἡ ὁδὸς καὶ ἡ [o] ἀλήθεια καὶ ἡ [p] ζωή· οὐδεὶς ἔρχεται
πρὸς τὸν πατέρα, εἰ μὴ δι' ἐμοῦ. 7 εἰ ἐγνώκειτέ με, καὶ
τὸν πατέρα μου ἂν ᾔδειτε· [q] ἀπ' ἄρτι γινώσκετε αὐτὸν
καὶ ἑωράκατε [αὐτόν]. 8 λέγει αὐτῷ Φίλιππος Κύριε,
δεῖξον ἡμῖν τὸν πατέρα, καὶ [r] ἀρκεῖ ἡμῖν. 9 λέγει αὐτῷ
ὁ Ἰησοῦς [s] Τοσοῦτον [s] χρόνον μεθ' ὑμῶν [t] εἰμι, καὶ οὐκ

...εωρακατε C. ABDE GHKL MNQSU XΓΔΛ Πא 1. 33. 69

for ητε, εσθαι *eritis* D.

4. om εγω DLX 1. 69 lat-*a b e ff*$_2$ *q* [æth] arm Chr$_1$. rec ins και bef την οδον and aft it ins (a 2nd) οιδατε (*mistaken filling up of sense*), with AC^{3}DN rel [latt(exc *a*)] syrr goth Chr$_1$ Cyr$_1$: txt BC^{1}LQXא 33 copt (æth) [Non$_1$].

5. aft θωμας ins ὁ λεγομενος διδυμος D 76 Non$_1$. om και BC^{1}L lat-*a b* [æth]. rec (for οιδ. τ. οδον) δυναμεθα την οδον ειδεναι, with AC^{2}NQ(א) rel [vulg lat-*c* &c syrr syr-jer (arm)] : txt BC^1(D) lat-*a b e* [æth] Cyr Tert$_1$.—(δυνομεθα N.—τ. οδ. ειδ. δυν. א : τ. οδ. δυν. ειδ. K arm.—τ. οδ. bef οιδ. D lat-*b e* Tert.)

6. om ὁ C^{1}Lא : ins ABC^{3}DNQ rel.

7. εγνωκατε D^1(txt D^2) א [copt Cyr-p$_2$]. εμε Dא Chr$_1$: om A. rec (for αν ηδειτε) εγνωκειτε αν, with AC^{3}D^{2}N rel : γνωσεσθαι D^{1}א : txt BC^{1}LQ[X] 1. 33 Cyr$_1$ [Bas$_1$ Ps-]Ath$_1$. rec ins και bef απ' αρτι, with AC^{3}DNא rel vulg lat-*b c e f ff*$_2$ Iren-int$_2$ Tert Novat Hil spec : om BC^{1}LQX 1 lat-*a*. for γινωσκετε, γνωσεσθαι (sic) א [*cognoscetis* vulg lat-*f q*]. om last αυτον BC^1 Iren-int$_1$: ins AC^{3}DNQא rel latt Iren-int-mss$_1$ Tert$_1$.

8. ins ο bef φιλιππος א.

9. om 1st ὁ AL[Π$^{1\cdot3}$]. τοσουτω χρονω DLQא^1 Cyr[-p varies] Marcell$_1$ Iren-int$_1$ Orig-int$_1$, but L^1(appy) had τοσουτον : txt ABN א^{3a}(but former reading restored) rel Hipp$_1$ Orig$_1$.

away to be with Him (Phil. i. 23); *fully completed* at His coming in glory, when they shall for ever be with Him (1 Thess. iv. 17) in the perfected resurrection state.

4.] **And where** (whither) **I go ye know the way.** They might have known, and doubtless did know in some sense; but, as Lampe remarks, "interdum quis laudatur ut officii sui moneatur." We use thus '*you know*,'—leaving to be supplied, '*if you would give the matter thought*.' ὅπου, *to the Father*; **τὴν ὁδόν** (in our Lord's own case, of which *this* verse treats), *His death*. 5.] Thomas is slow of belief and apprehension. The answer to ποῦ ὑπάγεις; ch. xiii. 37, which Peter seems to have apprehended, was not sufficient for him: see ch. xx. 25: ᾤετο γάρ, says Euthym., αἰσθητὸν εἶναί τινα τόπον ὅπου ὑπάγει, καὶ ὁδὸν ὁμοίως τοιαύτην. 6.] Our Lord, as Lücke (after Bengel) remarks (ii. 596), inverts the order of Thomas's question, and in answering it practically, *for them*, speaks of 'the Way' first. *He* is THE WAY; not merely the Forerunner; which would imply on our part only an outward connexion with Him as His *followers*:—but *the way*, in and on which we must go, having an inner union with and in Him (De Wette): see Heb. x. 20. **ἡ ἀλήθεια**—more than ὅτι ἀληθεύω κ. πάντως ἔσται ταῦτα, Euth. It is another side of the same idea of *the Way*;—God being true, and only approached by and in truth. Christ IS THE TRUTH, in Whom only (Col. ii. 3) that Knowledge of Him is gained, which (ch. xvii. 3) is eternal life. **ἡ ζωή**—not merely because οὐδὲ ὁ θάνατος διαστήσει ὑμᾶς ἐμοῦ, Euthym.,—but as being THE LIFE (see ver. 19: Gal. ii. 20) of all His, in Whom only they who live can come to the living Father (ch. vi. 57). **οὐδεὶς ἔρχ. . . .**] This plainly states the ποῦ ὑπάγω, and the way also. **δι' ἐμοῦ**—as τῆς ὁδοῦ. 7.] See ch. viii. 19. **ἀπ' ἄρτι**] There is no difficulty, if we bear in mind the **νῦν** of ch. xiii. 31. The **henceforth** is the future time, beginning with our Lord's glorification, which was now at hand. Lücke remarks: "ἀπ' ἄρτι is not entirely future nor entirely present, but the moment of transition, the identification of the present and future. Christ speaks here proleptically, in reference to the hour of His glorification being come" (ii. 598). 8.] Philip misunderstands **ἑωρ.** to mean '*seeing in a vision*,'—and intimates that

ἔγνωκάς με, Φίλιππε; ὁ ἑωρακὼς ἐμὲ ἑώρακεν τὸν πατέρα·
καὶ πῶς σὺ λέγεις Δεῖξον ἡμῖν τὸν πατέρα; 10 οὐ
πιστεύεις ὅτι ἐγὼ ἐν τῷ πατρὶ καὶ ὁ πατὴρ ἐν ἐμοί ἐστιν;
τὰ ῥήματα ἃ ἐγὼ λέγω ὑμῖν [u] ἀπ' ἐμαυτοῦ οὐ λαλῶ, ὁ δὲ u ch. v. 19 reff.
...μενων αυτος N. πατὴρ [ὁ] ἐν ἐμοὶ [v] μένων ποιεῖ τὰ ἔργα αὐτοῦ. 11 πι- v = John only. ch. vi. 56. xv. 5 al.
στεύετέ μοι ὅτι ἐγὼ ἐν τῷ πατρὶ καὶ ὁ πατὴρ ἐν ἐμοί·
εἰ δὲ μή, [w] διὰ τὰ ἔργα αὐτὰ πιστεύετέ μοι. 12 ἀμὴν w constr., ch. iv. 39, 40, 41 al.
ἀμὴν λέγω ὑμῖν, ὁ [x] πιστεύων [x] εἰς ἐμέ, τὰ ἔργα ἃ ἐγὼ x ch. ii. 11 reff.
ποιῶ κἀκεῖνος ποιήσει, καὶ μείζονα τούτων ποιήσει, ὅτι

om και (bef πως) BQℵ latt Iren-int$_1$ Hil$_2$ Ambr$_1$ Aug: ins ADN rel lat-*f* [*q* syr-jer] syrr goth arm. aft λεγεις ins οτι ℵ[1].

10. πιστευσεις B[1](sic). rec (for λεγω) λαλω, with AQℵ rel [Cyr-p$_3$]: λελαληκα D 3. 218 æth (*to conform to follg: or perhaps from ch* vi. 63, *where rec has* λαλω, *and txt* λελαλ.): txt BLNX lat-*e* syr-mg copt [Cyr-p$_1$]. (λεγω over the line 1. m. in B: see table: Tischdf [N. T. Vat.] says by B[3] appy.) om ὁ (bef εν) BL vulg lat-*b e ff*$_2$ *g* Orig$_1$ Did$_1$ [Ath$_1$ Cyr$_1$] Aug$_1$: ins ADQℵ rel lat-*a c f* syrr syr-cu [syr-jer]. rec ins αυτος bef ποιει, omg αυτου, with ANQ rel vulg syrr syr-cu goth arm Orig$_1$ Ath$_1$ Chr$_1$: for αυτου, αυτος LX 33 *Cyr*[-p]: txt BDℵ [Cyr-p$_1$].

11. transp εγω εν τω πατρι and ο πατηρ εν εμοι (and for και εγω, καγω) D: om και ο πατηρ εν εμοι A [Ath-2-mss$_1$]. elz aft εν εμοι ins εστιν, with 1. 69[1] vulg lat-*c e* [*g* syr-cu goth arm-usc Ath$_1$] Iren-int Hil$_1$: om (A)BDNQℵ rel(H—Treg, expr) 33. 69[1] Chr Cyr$_1$ Tert$_1$ Hil$_{sæpe}$. μηγε D. om δια ℵ[1]. for αυτα, αυτου B æth. om μοι (*as not logically corresponding to the* μοι *before*) DLℵ 33 vulg lat-*c e f g* Syr syr-cu syr-jer Tert$_1$ Hil$_5$ Ambr$_1$.

one such sight of God would set at rest all their fears, and give them perfect confidence. **9.**] The Son is the only Exponent of the Father to men: see ch. xii. 44, 45: Col. i. 15: Heb. i. 3: 1 Tim. vi. 16. This seeing of the Father in Him, is not only seeing His bodily presence, but *knowing* Him (οὐκ **ἔγνωκάς** με). **10.**] See ch. x. 30, 38, and for the latter clause ch. viii. 28, where the contrast is, as here, purposely inexact in *diction,—words* being placed in one member and *works* in the other: and, as there, **ἔργα** and **ῥήματα** are taken as correlative and co-extensive; —all the working of the Lord Jesus being a λαλιά, a *revelation of the Father.* De Wette supposes both ἔργα and ῥήμ. to be understood in *both places.* Without the [ὁ], the sense will be, of course, the Father, abiding in Me . . . . **ποιεῖ τὰ ἔργα αὐτοῦ**] **doeth His works**: they are not Mine, but His, done in and by Me: but ἐν ἐμοί, present and abiding, so that ὁ ἑωρακὼς ἐμὲ ἑώρακεν τὸν πατέρα.

11—24.] *Jesus will make proof of His abiding union with the Father, in His union with His own:* and this, vv. 12—14, *in answering prayer:* vv. 15—17, *in the sending of the Spirit:* vv. 18 ff., *as a pledge of the completion of this union in His personal return.* The Lord now unfolds out of this **ποιεῖ τὰ ἔργα αὐτοῦ**, the great promise of the Paraclete. **διὰ τὰ ἔργα αὐτά**] See ch. x. 38. The object here seems to be, to fix their attention on the *works* as a plain testimony even to such as could not simply believe so deep a thing on His assertion (**πιστ. μοι**), and one which (ver. **12**) should become subjective in themselves hereafter,—by virtue of their living union with Him who is gone to the Father, and become the dispenser and channel of the Spirit. "Qui Christo de se loquenti credit, in Christum credit." Bengel. **μείζ. τούτων**] This word **μείζ.** is not to be evaded (so as to = πλείονα, Lampe), but taken in its full strict sense. And the keys to its meaning will be found ch. i. 51; v. 20. *The* works which Jesus did, His Apostles also did,— scil., raising the dead, &c.;—*greater works than those,* they did,—not in *degree,* but *in kind: spiritual* works, under the dispensation of the Spirit, which *had not yet come in.* But they did them, *not as separate from* Him: but *in* Him, and *by* Him; and so (ch. v. 21) *He* is said to do them. The work which He did by Peter's sermon, Acts ii., was one of these μείζονα τούτων,—the first-fruits of the unspeakable gift. This union of them with and in Him is expressed here by τὰ ἔρ. **ἃ ἐγὼ** ποιῶ, **κἀκεῖνος** ποιήσει. "He has sown, we reap; and the harvest is greater than the seed-time," Stier. v. 189, edn. 2.

13.] I have retained the period after

y Mark xvi. 17 reff. ch. xv. 16. xvi. 23, 24, 26 al.
z constr., ch. xiii. 31, 32.
a Matt. xix. 17 (reff.).
b ver. 26. ch. xv. 26. xvi. 7. 1 John ii. 1 only †. Job xvi. 2 Aq.

ἐγὼ πρὸς τὸν πατέρα πορεύομαι. 13 καὶ ὅ τι ἂν αἰτήσητε ABDE GHKL MQSUX ΓΔΛΠℵ 1. 33. 69
y ἐν τῷ ὀνόματί μου, τοῦτο ποιήσω, ἵνα z δοξασθῇ ὁ
πατὴρ ἐν τῷ υἱῷ. 14 ἐάν τι αἰτήσητε y ἐν τῷ ὀνόματι
μου, ἐγὼ ποιήσω. 15 ἐὰν ἀγαπᾶτέ με, τὰς a ἐντολὰς τὰς
ἐμὰς a τηρήσατε. 16 κἀγὼ ἐρωτήσω τὸν πατέρα, καὶ
ἄλλον b παράκλητον δώσει ὑμῖν, ἵνα ᾖ μεθ' ὑμῶν εἰς τὸν

12. rec aft πατερα ins μου, with E rel lat-*e* syrr: om ABDLQX[Π]ℵ 1. 33. 69 latt [syr-jer] copt goth æth arm Chr$_2$ Non$_1$ [Novat$_1$] Aug. πορευσομαι H^1Q copt.
13. for αιτησητε, αιτηται B, αιτητε Q.
14. for εαν, αν D. aft αιτησητε ins με BEH U(Treg, expr) [Γ]Δℵ 33 vulg lat-*c f* Syr-ed syr goth arm-usc: om ADQ rel lat-*a e g* [*q*] Syr-ms copt [æth]. for εγω, τουτο (*from last ver*) A B(sic: see table) L[$Λ^2$] 33 vulg lat-*c g q* copt arm[-usc æth] Cyr$_1$ Aug$_1$: εγω τουτο M: txt DQℵ rel [lat-*a e f ff$_2$* syrr goth].
15. om με ℵ^1(ins ℵ^{3b}). τηρησετε BL Eus$_1$ [Melet$_1$]: τηρησητε ℵ 33. 69[1] ev-y [Cyr-p$_1$].
16. (καγω, so BDQℵ 1 [*Cyr*-p].) for ερωτησω, τηρησω ℵ^1(sic). rec (for ᾖ) μενη (*from ver* 17), with AD rel Eus Cyr-jer: txt (B)LQX(ℵ) 33 lat-*a b c e f ff$_2$ q* Syr syr-cu syr-mg copt goth [Eus$_3$] Cyr-jer$_1$ Did$_1$ Ambr Hil$_1$ Lucif.—μεθ' υμ. εις τ. αι. bef ᾖ B [lat-*b*]: μεθ' υμων bef η ℵ [lat-*a c f ff$_2$ q* Eus$_1$ Cyr-jer$_1$]. εις τ. αιωνα bef μεθ υμων D [Eus$_1$].

πορεύομαι (Grot., Griesb., Lachm., Knapp, Lücke, Meyer, Stier place a comma only and connect this verse with the **ὅτι**), because the sense remains much the same, and the style is better preserved.

αἰτήσητε, scil. τὸν πατέρα: so ch. xv. 16; xvi. 23. But this does not exclude, but *distinctly includes*, prayer to Christ; so blended are these two (as the ὁρᾷν, ver. 9), that we have not ποιήσει, but **ποιήσω**, and, ver. 14, emphatically **ἐγὼ** ποιήσω. He who prays to the Father, prays to the Son. This ποιήσω answers to the ποιήσει in ver. 12; *the reason why you shall do these greater works, is, on account of the all-powerful Spirit of grace and supplication which My going to the Father shall bring down upon the Church; in answer to which Spirit, I will do by you whatever in My Name* (i. e. in union with Me, as being Mine, manifesting forth Jesus *as the Son of God*) *ye shall ask. And the end of this is, that by these* **μείζονα τούτων**, *the wonders of grace and triumphs of the Spirit, the Father may be glorified* (His glory shewn forth) *in and by the Son.* Ver. **14** solemnly repeats *as a promise*, what was incidentally asserted before: 'For this is a truth, that whatever' &c. And besides, adds the **ἐγώ**: **it is I that will do it**: shewing that the use of the first person before was emphatic. "ἐγώ hoc jam indicat gloriam."—Bengel.

Ver. **15** is a following out of the ἐν τῷ ὀνόματί μου: 'That *way of prayer* is the way of *loving obedience*, in which the Spirit is ever found, and which is only trodden by His help:'—and also of ἵνα δοξ. ὁ π. ἐν τῷ υἱ., 'As the Father is honoured in the Son, so must the Son be honoured in you:' see ch. xv. 10.

16.] And *then* the Spirit shall proceed forth upon you. Not αἰτήσω, but **ἐρωτήσω**—"familiaris petendi modus," Bengel:—rather perhaps, a manner of asking implying *actual presence and nearness*,—and here used of the mediatorial office in Christ's *ascended state*. **παράκλητον**] Olshausen remarks that the interpretations of this word range themselves in *two classes*, which again by no means exclude one another:—those of 'COMFORTER,' and those of 'ADVOCATE.' * ("*Teacher*" (Theodore of Mopsuest. and Ernesti) is out of the question.) The etymology of the word requires the latter as its strict meaning, and in this strict meaning it satisfies 1 John ii. 1, **παράκλητον** ἔχομεν πρὸς τὸν πατέρα Ἰησοῦν χριστόν: but not so all the places where it is used *of the Holy Spirit*,—nor this verse, where of the Son and Spirit both. And therefore the other meaning,—**Comforter**, including as it does in its fulness (see Rom. viii. 26, where both, the συναντιλαμβάνεσθαι and the ὑπερεντυγχάνειν, are united) the *Advocate* also, has been both here and in Germany (Tröster, Luther) sanctioned by Christian usage as the most adequate rendering. See Archdeacon Hare's Mission of the Comforter, vol. ii. note J a. He shews that Wicliff, from whom we have our **Comforter**, often used "comfort" for the Latin *comfortari*, as e. g. Luke xxii. 43: Acts ix. 19 al. Thus the idea of *help and strength* is conveyed by it, as well as of consolation. It was this office (comfortari) which Jesus

αἰῶνα, 17 τὸ [c] πνεῦμα τῆς [c] ἀληθείας, ὃ ὁ κόσμος οὐ
δύναται [d] λαβεῖν, ὅτι οὐ [e] θεωρεῖ αὐτὸ οὐδὲ γινώσκει
αὐτό· ὑμεῖς γινώσκετε αὐτό, ὅτι [f] παρ' ὑμῖν [f] μένει καὶ
ἐν ὑμῖν ἐστίν. 18 οὐκ [g] ἀφήσω ὑμᾶς [h] ὀρφανούς, [i] ἔρχομαι πρὸς ὑμᾶς. 19 [k] ἔτι [k] μικρὸν καὶ ὁ κόσμος με οὐκ
ἔτι [e] θεωρεῖ, ὑμεῖς δὲ [e] θεωρεῖτέ με. ὅτι ἐγὼ ζῶ, καὶ ὑμεῖς
ζήσετε. 20 ἐν ἐκείνῃ τῇ ἡμέρᾳ ὑμεῖς γνώσεσθε ὅτι ἐγὼ ἐν

c = ch. xv. 26. xvi. 13. see 1 John iv. 6.
d = ch. i. 12 reff.
e = ch. vi. 40. xii. 45.
f ch. i. 40. Acts ix. 43 al.
g = ver. 27. ch. viii. 29. xvi. 32. Matt. v. 24 al.
h James i. 27 only. Ps. ix. 14, 18 (35, 38).
i pres., ver. 3.
k ch. xiii. 33 reff.

17. for ὅ, ον ℵ[3a](but ν erased). αυτον (3 times) D[1]L, and (1st) M ℵ[3a](but txt restored) 69, (2nd) 69, (3rd) G[2]MU :—om 2nd αυτο Bℵ lat-*a* Lucif$_1$. rec aft υμεις ins δε, with AD rel vulg lat-*c e f ff*$_2$ *g* [*q* syr-cu syrr syr-jer copt &c] Cyr-jer$_1$ Did$_1$: om BQℵ lat-*a b* Lucif$_1$ Quæst$_1$. rec εσται, with AD[2]Qℵ rel vulg syr syr-jer copt æth arm: txt BD[1] 1. 69 tol lat-*a b c e f ff*$_2$ Syr syr-cu goth Lucif Ambr Quæst.
19. om 2nd με LQ. rec ζησεσθε (*more usual*), with ADQℵ rel Chr$_1$ *Cyr*[-p] Hil: txt BLX.
20. rec γνωσ. bef υμεις, with Dℵ rel lat-*a c e* [*ff*$_2$ *g q*] syr copt goth arm: om υμεις

had filled to His disciples while with them:—and which the Holy Spirit was to fill even more abundantly (and in a higher sense, because their state would be higher) on the removal of Jesus from them.

17.] τὸ πν. τ. ἀλ., not 'the true Spirit,'—but 'THE SPIRIT OF TRUTH;'—the Spirit *Who is truth*, 1 John v. 6,—of Whom all truth comes, and who alone leads into *the whole truth*, the truth of God, ch. xvi. 13. **ὁ κόσμος** = οἱ ψυχικοί, 1 Cor. ii. 14, those who live according to the desires of the flesh and the mind, and have no receptivity of the things of God.

θεωρεῖ sometimes = γινώσκει, but not here, as being separated from it by οὐδέ: '*recognizes not* in His operations (obj.) *nor knows* (subj.);'—**has neither sight nor knowledge of. γινώσκετε**—present, but spoken of their state as disciples opposed to the world,—and proleptically, as before. They were even now not of the world (ch. xv. 19), and are therefore viewed in the completion of their state as opposed to it. **μένει** (not μενεῖ as Vulg. and some other vss.) is rightly explained by De Wette to be future in *signification*, as any present predication of permanence must necessarily be; **abideth**, as μένει, ch. viii. 35. Euthym. understands παρ' ὑμ. μένει of the Spirit abiding *in Jesus*, Who was among them: but wrongly.

ἐστίν] This was perhaps corrected to the future, because, though their knowledge of the Spirit proper to their complete state, and His dwelling, remaining, among them, had in some inferior sense begun,—His dwelling *in* them had not. See Hare, Mission of the Comforter, ii. note I. With the reading **ἐστίν**, the prolepsis is still stronger. **18.] ὀρφ. should be orphans,** as in the E. V. marg. The office of the παράκλ. is to connect the disciples with the Father: if therefore they had Him not, they would be *fatherless*. The expression connects with τεκνία ch. xiii. 33, and as Euthym., springs from πατρικὴ εὐσπλαγχνία. This makes ἔρχομαι, **I am coming**, plain, as applying to the coming by the Spirit, who is one with Christ;—not only the ultimate personal coming, which is but the last step of the ἔρχομαι, nor only the bodily coming again to them and not to the world at the Resurrection, which was but a pledge of His lasting presence in the Spirit: see on ver. 3. ἔρχομαι is (as there) the complex of these —the *great Revisitation*, in all its blessed progress. The absence of any connecting particle as γάρ, with ἔρχομαι, arises (Meyer) from the depth of affection in the Lord's heart. **19—21.]** This ἔρχομαι is explained to consist in His presence among them by the life of His Resurrection, which is theirs; by (ver. 20) the witness of the Spirit in their hearts; and (ver. 21) their sanctification by the Spirit in love, and the consequent manifestation of Jesus to them.

Luthardt (ii. p. 309 f.) attempts to confine ἔρχομαι (and this whole passage) to the παρουσία, in spite of the plain sense of vv. 19, 20, relying on the analogy of Rev. xxii. 17, and saying that on the common interpretation, the Church would have no cause to long for her Lord: and so Aug., Maldon., Hofm., al. But manifestly the context is against him: and he must thus explain away many other passages (e. g. Matt. xviii. 20). The presence of Christ by the Spirit is none the less *real*, for being *incomplete*. **19.]** The *immediate reference* of this θεωρεῖτε is to the forty days (see Acts x. 41)—but only as leading on to its wider and deeper

l = ch. v. 38.
m ver. 15.
n ch. i. 18 reff.
o act., here bis. Acts xxiii. 15, 22. xxiv. 1. xxv. 2, 15. Heb. xi. 14 only. Exod. xxxiii. 13. pass., Matt. xxvii. 53. Heb. ix. 24. Wisd. i. 2.
p Acts vii. 40, from Exod. xxxii. 1.
q ch. viii. 51, 52, 55 reff.
r ver. 2 only †. 1 Macc. vii. 38 only. *μονὴν ποιεῖσθαι*, Thuc. i. 131. Jos. Antt. viii. 13. 7.

τῷ πατρί μου καὶ ὑμεῖς ἐν ἐμοὶ κἀγὼ ἐν ὑμῖν. 21 ὁ [l] ἔχων
τὰς ἐντολάς μου καὶ [m] τηρῶν αὐτάς, [n] ἐκεῖνός ἐστιν ὁ
ἀγαπῶν με· ὁ δὲ ἀγαπῶν με ἀγαπηθήσεται ὑπὸ τοῦ
πατρός μου, κἀγὼ ἀγαπήσω αὐτὸν καὶ [o] ἐμφανίσω αὐτῷ
ἐμαυτόν. 22 Λέγει αὐτῷ Ἰούδας, οὐχ ὁ Ἰσκαριώτης,
Κύριε, [καὶ] [p] τί γέγονεν ὅτι ἡμῖν μέλλεις [o] ἐμφανίζειν ...εμφανιζειν σε Q.
σεαυτὸν καὶ οὐχὶ τῷ κόσμῳ; 23 ἀπεκρίθη Ἰησοῦς καὶ
εἶπεν αὐτῷ Ἐάν τις ἀγαπᾷ με, τὸν [q] λόγον μου [q] τηρήσει,
καὶ ὁ πατήρ μου ἀγαπήσει αὐτόν, καὶ πρὸς αὐτὸν ἐλευ-
σόμεθα καὶ [r] μονὴν παρ' αὐτῷ ποιησόμεθα. 24 ὁ μὴ ἀγαπῶν με τοὺς [q] λόγους μου οὐ [q] τηρεῖ· καὶ ὁ λόγος ὃν

ABDE GHKL MSUX ΓΔΛΠℵ 1. 33. 69

A lat-*b* Syr æth Chr_1 Cyr[-p_4] Victorin: txt BLM^1QX 33 vulg lat-*f*. και εγω $E^2GMU\Delta$[S(Tischdf)Π^2] Chr.

21. (καγω, so BDGLQX[Γ]Λℵ 1.) ενφωνησω D^1(txt D-$corr^1$(?)).

22. for ισκαριωτης, απο καρυωτου D. rec om 1st και (*as unnecessary and misunderstood: or perhaps from κε̄ preceding*), with ABDELX 33 latt Syr syr-cu [syr-jer] coptt goth æth arm Cyr_1 Orig-int_1: ins Qℵ rel lat-*q* syr Chr_1. for γεγονεν, εστιν D Chr_1. μελλεις bef ημιν D. εμφανιζεις A lat-*a* Lucif.

23. rec ins ο bef ιησ., with MXΛ 69 $Orig_1$: om ABDℵ rel Cyr_1. for 1st αυτω, αυτοις $ℵ^{3a}$(but txt restored). ελευσομαι D lat-*e* syr-cu. for μονην παρ' αυτω, προς αυτον μονην D Syr. rec ποιησομεν (*more usual*), with A rel $Orig_1$ Ath_3 $Epiph_3$; ποιησωμεν M[Γ]ΔΛ: ποιησομαι D lat-*e* syr-cu: txt BLX[Π^2]ℵ 1. 33. 69 $Orig_5$ Eus_3 Ath-ms_1 Did_2 $Epiph_1$ Chr-ms_1 Cyr[-p_4] $Thdrt_1$.

24. τηρησει D copt. aft ο λογος ins ο εμος D lat-*a e* syr [syr-jer] arm $Gaud_1$.

reference to the spiritual life. **ζῶ**, not *ζήσω*—the principle of Life being immanent in Him. **ζήσετε**, in all its fulness, including the most blessed sense of **ζωή**,—the Life of the Spirit,—here and hereafter. See Meyer's note. **20.**] **ἐκ. τῇ ἡμ.**, *no particular day*: but 'each of these periods, as its continually increasing light breaks upon you, shall bring increased knowledge of your unity in Me with the Father, and my dwelling in you by the Spirit.' If any particular day is to be thought of, it would naturally be the Pentecost. **21.**] **ἔχων κ. τηρῶν**, "qui habet in memoria et servat in vita." Aug. in loc. Or perhaps more accurately (with Stier), "He who *has* my commandments, as being my disciple by outward profession (not thus only: but *holds* them, by the inner possession of a living faith. So Meyer), and *keeps* them:" see Luke xi. 28. And **τηρ.** is more of the inner *will* to keep them, than the absolute observance, which can only follow on high degrees of spiritual advancement.

ἐμφ. αὐτ. ἐμ., by the Holy Spirit: see ch. xvi. 14. This (as Stier observes) is *the highest promise which can be made to man* (see ver. 23), and yet it is made to *every man* who *ἔχει κ. τηρεῖ* the commandments of the Lord Jesus. Cf. Exod. in reff.

22.] **Ἰούδας, οὐχ ὁ Ἰσκ.** = *Ἰούδας Ἰακώβου* of Luke vi. 16: see note on Matt. x. 2 ff. Meyer remarks that the **οὐχ ὁ Ἰσκαριώτης** is *pragmatically* superfluous, after ch. xiii. 30, but is added by St. John from his deep horror of the Traitor who bore the same name. The question seems to be put with the Jewish idea, that the Messiah, the King and Judge of the nations, must necessarily *manifest himself to the world*. [**καί** preceding an interrogation, expresses astonishment at what has just been said, and, assuming it, connects to it a conclusion which appears to refute or cast doubt on it. So Eur. Med. 1388, —*ὦ τέκνα φίλτατα! "μητρί γε, σοὶ δ' οὔ." κἄπειτ' ἔκτας;* See more examples in Hartung, i. p. 146, and cf. Kühner on Xen. Mem. p. 117.] **τί γέγ. ὅτι**] **What has happened, that . . . ?** i. e. **how is it, that . . . ?** **23, 24.**] These verses contain the answer to the question in both its parts:—**ἡμῖν**, because love to Christ, leading to the keeping of His word, is the necessary condition of the indwelling and manifestation in man of the Father and the Son;—**οὐχὶ τῷ κόσμῳ**, because want of love to Christ, leading to neglect of His words, necessarily excludes from communion with the Father and the Son, and the Spirit, who reveals the Son in man. "The

ἀκούετε οὐκ ἔστιν ἐμός, ἀλλὰ τοῦ πέμψαντός με πατρός.
25 Ταῦτα λελάληκα ὑμῖν [s] παρ' ὑμῖν [s] μένων· 26 ὁ δὲ
[t] παράκλητος, τὸ πνεῦμα τὸ ἅγιον, ὃ πέμψει ὁ πατὴρ ἐν
τῷ ὀνόματί μου, [u] ἐκεῖνος ὑμᾶς διδάξει πάντα, καὶ [uv] ὑπομνήσει [u] ὑμᾶς [u] πάντα ἃ εἶπον ὑμῖν. 27 εἰρήνην [w] ἀφίημι
ὑμῖν, εἰρήνην τὴν ἐμὴν [x] δίδωμι ὑμῖν· οὐ καθὼς ὁ κόσμος
δίδωσιν, ἐγὼ δίδωμι ὑμῖν. μὴ [y] ταρασσέσθω ὑμῶν ἡ
καρδία μηδὲ [z] δειλιάτω. 28 ἠκούσατε ὅτι ἐγὼ εἶπον ὑμῖν
Ὑπάγω καὶ [a] ἔρχομαι πρὸς ὑμᾶς. εἰ ἠγαπᾶτέ με, ἐχάρητε
ἂν ὅτι πορεύομαι πρὸς τὸν πατέρα, ὅτι ὁ πατὴρ [b] μείζων

s ver. 17 reff.
t ver. 16 reff.
u constr., 2 Tim. ii. 14. Wisd. xviii. 22.
v as above (u). Luke xxii. 61. Tit. iii. 1. 2 Pet. i. 12. 3 John 10. Jude 5 only†.
w ver. 18.
x ch. x. 28 al.
y ver. 1. ch. xi. 33 reff.
z here only. Deut. i. 21 al. fr. (-λός, Matt. viii. 26. -λία, 2 Tim. i. 7.)
a pres., vv. 3, 18. Matt. xvii. 11. xxvi. 2.
b = ch. iv. 12. viii. 53. Gen. xlviii. 19.

26. πεμψει bef το πν. το αγ. ℵ[1].—for ὅ, ον LXℵ[3a] Chr-mss$_1$: om ℵ[1]. aft ο πατηρ ins μου D [Π[2](but erased)] lat-*g* Syr syr-cu copt-wilk Eus$_3$ Gaud$_1$. for ειπον, αν ειπω D[Π] 254 latt. aft υμιν ins εγω BL : om ADℵ rel vss Orig.
27. aft διδωσιν ins υμιν ℵ.
28. αγαπατε D[1](txt D[2]) HL 69. rec aft 2nd οτι ins ειπον (*cf preceding clause*), with E rel Ath$_1$ Ambr$_1$: om ABDK[1]LX[Π]ℵ 1. 33. 69 latt syrr syr-cu syr-jer copt goth [æth arm] Orig [Eus$_1$] Chr Cyr[-p$_1$]. rec aft πατηρ ins μου, with D[5] ℵ[1](marked for erasure, but marks removed) rel lat-*a f* syrr Eus$_1$: om ABD[1]LX 1. 33 vulg lat-*b c e ff*$_2$ *g l* æth Chr$_2$ Cyr[-p$_2$] Iren-int$_1$ Orig-int$_1$ Tert$_1$ Cypr$_1$ Hil$_5$.

addition **πρὸς αὐτὸν ἐλευσ. κ. μονὴν παρ' αὐτῷ ποιησ.** makes this incapacity still plainer and more deeply felt." Meyer. For (**καί**, and hence you may infer what I am setting forth) **the word which ye hear** (and which the world *οὐ τηρεῖ = ἀθετεῖ*), **—is not Mine, but the Father's** (*not, 'non tam . . . quam'*). On the gracious and wonderful promise of ver. 23, see Rom. viii. 15. **25—31.**] *His farewell, and the parting bequest of His Love.* **25.**] **λελάληκα** is proleptic, referring, as εἶπον (ver. 26), to the futures, διδάξει and ὑπομνήσει. Meyer supposes that a *pause* took place here, and the Lord looks back on what He had said to them. But this does not seem so natural. **26.**] q. d. 'I know that ye do not understand them yet: but' &c. **τὸ πν. τὸ ἅγ.**] The Paraclete is now more closely defined by this well-known Name, —and, by ὃ πέμψει ὁ πατήρ, and ἐκεῖνος . . . , designated *personally*, as One sent, and One acting on them. **ἐν τῷ ὀν. μου**, not, 'in My stead,' but **in regard of Me**—'in answer to My prayer, and prayers in My name,—to those who bear My name,—and as a means of manifesting Me.' **διδάξ. πάντα** stands by itself, not with ἃ εἶπον:—**shall teach you all things**;—'all that can and may be learnt by you, all that belongs to your work and life in Me.' **ὑπομνήσει**] What is *not understood* is liable to be *forgotten*;—and therefore in this word is implied the giving them a right understanding of, as well as recalling, what Jesus had said to them: see ch. ii. 22; xii. 16. *It is on the fulfilment of this promise to the Apostles, that their sufficiency as Witnesses of all that the Lord did and taught, and consequently* THE AUTHENTICITY OF THE GOSPEL NARRATIVE, *is grounded.* **27.**] This is introduced by ver. 25, which suggests the speedy close of the discourse. It was customary to take leave with wishes of peace:—so 1 Sam. i. 17: Luke vii. 50: Acts xvi. 36: 1 Pet. v. 14: 3 John 15. Also, to reassure by such words, see Gen. xliii. 23: Judg. vi. 23. But our Lord distinguishes *His* peace, *true* peace, '*the peace which I have and give*' (see ch. xv. 11), from the mere empty word used in the world's form of greeting. Peace (in general) He *leaves* with them;—*His* peace He *gives* to them, over and above that other. The καθὼς ὁ κ. δίδ. must refer, I think (with Lampe, Lücke, and Stier), to the world's *manner of giving*,—not to the unreality of the world's peace, of which, however true, there is no direct mention here. The world can only give peace in empty formulæ, saying 'Peace, peace,' when there is no peace: Jer. vi. 14. al.

Ver. **28** as far as ὑμᾶς is a reason why their heart should not be troubled;—then the rest of the verse removes all ground of δειλία, since it is an *exaltation* of Him whom they loved, which is about to happen; and therefore a ground of joy, and not of fear. **μείζων**] And therefore the *going* of Jesus *to the Father* is an

μοι ἐστίν. 29 καὶ νῦν εἴρηκα ὑμῖν [c] πρὶν γενέσθαι, ἵνα ABDE
ὅταν γένηται, πιστεύσητε. 30 οὐκ ἔτι πολλὰ λαλήσω GHKL MSUX
μεθ' ὑμῶν· ἔρχεται γὰρ [d] ὁ τοῦ [d] κόσμου [d] ἄρχων, καὶ [e] ἐν ΓΔΛΠℵ 1. 33. 69
ἐμοὶ οὐκ ἔχει οὐδέν· 31 ἀλλ' [f] ἵνα γνῷ ὁ κόσμος ὅτι ἀγαπῶ
τὸν πατέρα, καὶ καθὼς [g] ἐνετείλατό μοι ὁ πατήρ, οὕτως
ποιῶ. [h] ἐγείρεσθε, [i] ἄγωμεν ἐντεῦθεν.

c constr., Matt. xxvi. 34 al. Isa. xlvi. 10. d ch. xii. 31. xvi. 11 only. see Eph. ii. 2. vi. 12. e Luke xxii. 37. xxiii. 31. 1 Cor. ix. 15. f ellips., ch. ix. 3. xv. 25. g w. dat., ch. xv. 14, 17. Acts i. 2. xiii. 47 al. Exod. xii. 28. (w. πρός, Heb. ix. 20.) h = Matt. ix. 19. ch. xi. 29. = ch. xi. 7 reff.

29. aft *πιστευσητε* ins *μοι* D.

30. rec aft *του κοσμου* ins *τουτου*, with 1 latt copt Orig$_{sæpe}$ Ath$_3$ [Chr$_1$ (Hipp$_1$ Bas$_1$ Mac$_1$ Cyr-p$_4$)] Thdrt$_1$ Hil$_3$: om AB D-gr ℵ rel syrr Cyr[-comm-p] Thdrt Thl-comm Non Hil$_2$ Aug$_1$. aft *ουδεν* ins *ευρειν* D lat-*a*.

31. om *και* A¹E lat-*b* *ff*$_2$. for *ενετειλατο*, *εντολην εδωκεν* (*cf ch* xii. 49) BLX (1. 33) latt æth-pl Cyr$_1$: txt ADℵ rel syrr [syr-jer] goth(appy) arm. om *ο πατηρ* D lat-*e* *l*¹ æth[-rom].

advancement. This word **greater**, as Luther well remarks (Stier, v. 228, edn. 2), is not here used as referring to the *Nature or Essence of the Son as related to the Father,*—but as indicating that particular subordination to the Father in which the Lord Jesus then was,—and the cessation of the state of humiliation, and entering into His glory, which would take place on His being received up to the Father. So also Calvin: "Non confert hic Christus Patris Divinitatem cum sua, nec humanam suam naturam divinæ Patris essentiæ comparat, sed potius statum præsentem cœlesti gloriæ ad quam mox recipiendus erat." And Cocceius: "Non intelligitur hic minoritas secundum naturam humanam, — quia intelligitur minoritas quæ per profectionem ad Patrem *deponitur*" (Stier, ibid. Similarly, De Wette, Tholuck). And this removes all reason for fear, as *they* will be exalted in *Him*.

The whole doctrinal controversy which has been raised on these words (especially by the Fathers against the Arians, see Suicer, Thes. ii. pp. 1368-9), seems not to belong to the sense of the passage. That *there is a sense* in which the Father is greater than even the *glorified* Son, is beyond doubt (see especially 1 Cor. xv. 27 f.); but as on the one hand that concession is no concession to Arianism, because it is not in the essential being of the Son, but in His Mediatorial office that this *minoritas* consists, —so on the other hand this verse implies in itself *no such* minoritas, the discourse being of *another kind*. **29.] εἴρηκα**— viz. 'the prophecies of My Resurrection and Ascension,' &c. **πιστεύσητε]** See ch. xiii. 19, where *ὅτι ἐγώ εἰμι* is supplied. **That ye may believe**, in the fullest sense of the word. "Neque enim Eum Dei Filium non et ante credebant: sed cum in Illo factum esset quod ante prædixit, fides illa quæ tunc quando illis loquebatur fuit parva, et cum moreretur pæne jam nulla, et revixit et crevit." Aug. in Joann. Tract. lxxix. 1. **30.] οὐκ ἔτι πολλὰ λαλ.**:— then, as Stier remarks, He had *some* words more to say, and was not about to break off at ver. 31, as some have supposed: cf. Grotius: "q. d., temporis angustiæ abripiunt verba." **ὁ τ. κόσ. ἄρχων]** i. e. Satan:—not, Satan in Judas, but *Satan himself*, with whom the Lord was in conflict during His passion: see Luke iv. 13 (and note), and xxii. 53. **ἐν ἐμοὶ οὐκ ἔχ. οὐδ.]** "Nullum scilicet omnino peccatum." Aug. ibid. 2. This is the only true interpretation: **has nothing in Me**—no point of appliance whereon to fasten his attack. But Meyer well observes, that this is rather *the fact to be assumed* as the *ground* of what is here said, than the *thing itself* which is said. De Wette, Lücke, Tholuck, and many others render it, "*has no power over me,*"—*οὐδὲν αἴτιον θανάτου*, Euthym. **31.]** 'But my Death is an act of voluntary obedience, that it may be known that I love and obey the Father—that the glory of the Father in and by Me may be manifested.'

The construction is elliptic: supply, 'But (his power over Me for death will be permitted by Me) that,' &c. And set a period at *ποιῶ*, as usually done. Meyer, al., and Luthardt, would carry on the sense from *ποιῶ*, "*But that the world may know that I love the Father, and as the Father commanded me, thus I do, arise, let us go hence.*" I need only put it to the inner feeling of any who have learned to appreciate the majesty and calmness of our Lord's discourses, whether a sentence so savouring of theatrical effect is likely to have been spoken by Him. We may notwithstanding safely believe that the *ἐγ.*

XV. 1 Ἐγώ εἰμι ἡ [k] ἄμπελος ἡ [l] ἀληθινή, καὶ ὁ πατήρ
μου ὁ [m] γεωργός ἐστιν. 2 πᾶν [n] κλῆμα ἐν ἐμοὶ μὴ [o] φέρον
[o] καρπόν, [p] αἴρει αὐτό· καὶ πᾶν τὸ [o] καρπὸν [o] φέρον, [q] καθαίρει

k Matt. xxvi. 29 ||. vv. 4, 5. James iii. 12. Rev. xiv. 18, 19 only. Isa. v. 2.
l = ch. i. 9. iv. 23. Heb. viii. 2 al. Jer. ii. 21.
m = Matt. xxi. 33, &c. ||. (2 Tim. ii. 6. James v. 7) only.
n vv. 4, 5, 6 only. Ezek. xv. 2.
o ch. xii. 24 reff.
p ch. xi. 48 reff.
q = here only. Heb. x. 2 only. see Lev. xix. 23.

Chap. XV. 1. om 2nd ὁ DΔ.
2. φερων (twice) A 33, 1st H[Γ²]. for καρπ. φερ., καρποφορον D (Clem). καθαριει D vulg lat-*b c e ff₂ g l* [*q*] copt Orig-int₁ Hil₁.

ἄγ. ἐντ., *without this connexion*, does undoubtedly express the holy boldness of the Lord in going to meet that which was to come upon Him, and is for that reason inserted by St. John. **ἐγείρ., ἄγ. ἐντ.**] These words imply a movement from the table to depart. Probably the rest of the discourse, and the prayer, ch. xvii., were delivered when now all were standing ready to depart. There would be some little pause, in which the preparations for departure would be made. But the *place* is clearly the same, see ch. xviii. 1, ταῦτα εἰπὼν ὁ Ἰησοῦς ἐξῆλθεν:—besides which, we can hardly suppose (Grot., &c.) discourses of a character like those in ch. xv. xvi. to have been delivered to as many as eleven persons, while *walking by the way*, and in a time of such publicity as that of the Paschal Feast. Still less is the supposition of Bengel and Beausobre probable,—that ch. xiii. xiv. happened outside the city, and that between ch. xiv. and xv. the paschal meal takes place. Compare also ch. xiii. 30, which is decisive against this idea.

Chap. XV. 1—27.] *Injunction to vital union in love with Jesus and one another.*

1—11.] *Their relation to Him.* Various suggestive circumstances have been imagined, but none of them are satisfactory. The vineyards on the way to Gethsemane (Lampe),—the carved vine on the great doors of the temple (Rosenmüller, Bibl. Exeget. Repert. i. 166 (Lücke),—see Jos. B. J. v. 5. 4: Antt. xv. 11. 3); a vine trained about the window of the guest-chamber (Knapp, Lücke conj., Tholuck, 6), are all fanciful, and the two first (see on ch. xiv. 31) inapplicable. The *cup*, so lately partaken (Meyer, Stier), is certainly nearer,—see below. But I believe with Lücke that most probably the Lord did not take the similitude from any outward suggesting occasion, but as a means of illustrating the great subject, *the inner unity of Himself and His.* Occasion enough was furnished, by the O. T. symbolism of the vineyard and the vine,—Isa. v. 1 ff.: Jer. ii. 21: Ezek. xix. 10 ff., and especially Ps. lxxx. 8—19: by the intimate analogy of vegetable life (of which the tree bearing fruit is the highest kind, and of such trees the vine the noblest) with spiritual, and perhaps also by the γέννημα τῆς ἀμπ. having been so recently the subject of their attention and the Lord's prophecy, Luke xxii. 18||.

1.] The Vine and branches stand in a much nearer connexion than the Shepherd and the sheep, or the lord of the vineyard and the vines; and answer to the Head and members in Eph. v. 23, 30: Col. ii. 19, linked together by a common organization, and informed by one and the same life. **ἡ ἀληθινή**, not only, 'by which prophecy is fulfilled:' not only, "in which the organism and qualities of the vine are most nobly realized" (Tholuck), but as in ch. i. 9, **true**, i. e. **original**, *archetypal.* The material creations of God are only inferior examples of that finer spiritual life and organism in which the creature is raised up to partake of the divine nature; only **ἀντίτυπα τῶν ἀληθινῶν**, Heb. ix. 24; ὑποδείγματα τῶν ἐν τοῖς οὐρ., ib. 23: see ch. vi. 32. **ὁ γεωργός**, not only the tiller of the land, but the vine-planter and dresser; He who has originated the relation between the vine and branches by planting the Vine in this earth (the nature of man), and who looks for and ensures the bringing forth of fruit. **2.**] The Vine contains *fruitful*, and *unfruitful* branches. Who are these unfruitful branches? *Who are the branches?* Clearly, all those who, adopting the parallel image, are made *members* of Christ by baptism, Rom. vi. 3, 4: compare **σύμφυτοι**, ib. ver. 5, also Rom. xi. 17 ff. The Vine is *the visible Church here*, of which Christ is the *inclusive* Head: the Vine *contains* the branches; hence the unfruitful, as well as the fruitful, are **ἐν ἐμοί.** Every such unfruitful branch (notice the **μή** in an hypothesis, not οὐ) the Father **αἴρει**,—pulls off and casts away: and every one that beareth fruit He **καθαίρει** (an allusion to αἴρει, but only in the Greek (?): "suavis rhythmus," Bengel), prunes, by cleansing it of its worthless parts, and shortening its rank growth, that it may ripen and enlarge its fruit better. Cf. Æsch. in Ctes. (ill. 166, quoting Demos-

ABDE GHKL MSUX ΓΔΛΠℵ 1. 33. 69

r = Rom. xiv. 15. xv. 15. 1 Cor. vii. 5. s ver. 2 reff. t ch. v. 19 reff. u ver. 1 reff. v ch. i. 3. Eph. ii. 12. w Matt. v. 13 reff. x gen., Matt. x. 16 al. fr. y Matt. xxi. 19, 20 reff. z = Luke xv. 13 reff. a = Matt. xiii. 40. Rev. xix. 20. xxi. 8. Deut. iv. 11.

αὐτὸ ἵνα ° καρπὸν πλείονα ° φέρῃ. 3 ἤδη ὑμεῖς καθαροί
ἐστε r διὰ τὸν λόγον ὃν λελάληκα ὑμῖν. 4 μείνατε ἐν ἐμοί,
κἀγὼ ἐν ὑμῖν. καθὼς τὸ s κλῆμα οὐ δύναται ° καρπὸν
° φέρειν t ἀφ' ἑαυτοῦ, ἐὰν μὴ μείνῃ ἐν τῇ u ἀμπέλῳ, οὕτως
οὐδὲ ὑμεῖς, ἐὰν μὴ ἐν ἐμοὶ μένητε. 5 ἐγώ εἰμι ἡ u ἄμπελος, ὑμεῖς τὰ s κλήματα. ὁ μένων ἐν ἐμοὶ κἀγὼ ἐν
αὐτῷ, οὗτος ° φέρει ° καρπὸν πολύν· ὅτι v χωρὶς ἐμοῦ οὐ
δύνασθε ποιεῖν οὐδέν. 6 ἐὰν μή τις μένῃ ἐν ἐμοί, w ἐβλήθη
w ἔξω ὡς x τὸ s κλῆμα καὶ y ἐξηράνθη, καὶ z συνάγουσιν
αὐτὰ καὶ εἰς τὸ πῦρ βάλλουσιν, καὶ a καίεται. 7 ἐὰν

for 2nd αυτο, αυτον [G]ℵ. rec πλειονα bef καρπον, with AD rel $Orig_1$ [Bas_1] $Thdrt_1$: txt BLM¹X(ℵ) 33 latt [Eus_1 Cyr_1 Orig-int_2] Hil Novat.—πλειω ℵ Clem.

3, 4. om ηδη to φερειν (*passing by mistake from* φερη *ver* 2 *to* φερειν *ver* 4) D¹[and lat].

4. for μεινη, μενη BLℵ lat-*a*. rec (for μενητε) μεινητε, with D rel Eus_1: txt ABLℵ.

5. aft εγω ins γαρ D¹(and lat) lat-*a*. om εν (bef εμοι) D¹-gr(ins D²). om ουδεν D¹(and lat: ins D³): ουδε εν B.

6. rec μεινη, with ℵ³ᵃ rel Cyr_1: txt ABDℵ¹. επληθη D¹. αυτο DLXΔ[Π]ℵ 1. 33. 69 vulg lat-*e g q* Syr [syr-jer] æth arm Cyr: txt AB rel am[with forj ing] lat-*a b c f* ff_2 syr copt. rec om το (bef πυρ) (*less usual, cf Matt* iii. 10; vii. 19: *Luke* iii. 9), with DHX $Orig_1$ Cyr_1 $Thdrt_2$: ins ABℵ rel Chr_1.

thenes), ἀμπελουργοῦσί τινες τὴν πόλιν, ἀνατετμήκασί τινες τὰ κλήματα τοῦ δήμου. The two, **πᾶν κλ., καὶ πᾶν . . . .**, are pendent nominatives, a construction usual with John in connexion with πᾶν, see ch. vi. 39; xvii. 2. **3. καθαροί**] See ch. xiii. 10. In Eph. v. 26, we have both the washing διὰ τὸν λόγον, and the word (ἐν ῥήματι), united. The *word* of Christ dwelling in them by Faith (see ver. 7) is the purifying principle (ch. xvii. 17). But the καθαροί here is not = κεκαθαρμένοι, *pruned*, in the sense of ver. 2. The ἤδη limits it to their present capacities and standing. There was more pruning at hand, when the sap should begin to flow,—when the Spirit should be shed abroad; and this future handling of the γεωργός is indicated by μείνατε ἐν ἐμοί . . . . **4.**] **κἀγὼ** ἐν ὑμ. must not (with Euthym., Meyer, and Lücke) be taken as a *promise*, which (see on ἐν ἐμοί above) would be contrary to the sense: but (with Aug., Tholuck, Bengel, Stier, who however modifies it by rendering "*so* abide in Me that I may abide in you") as a clause dependent on μείνατε ἐν ἐμοί, 'Take care that ye abide in Me and I in you:' *both these* being necessary to the bringing forth fruit: see ver. 5, where the two are similarly bound together.

Here the natural strictness of the similitude is departed from. The branch cannot sever itself from the vine: but, *such a case supposed*, every one will see the inevitable consequence. Bengel says well, "Hic locus egregie declarat discrimen naturæ et gratiæ." It is *the permitted free-will of the creature* which makes the difference between the branches in the two cases. **5.**] The interpretation of the allegory which each mind was forming for itself, the Lord solemnly asserts for them. Notice **οὗτος**—he and no other: 'it is he, that . . . .' **χωρὶς ἐμ.** is more than '*without Me*,' it = χωρισθέντες ἀπ' ἐμοῦ (Mey.), **separate from Me**, from being in Me and I in you. The **ὅτι** regards what is *implied* in χωρὶς ἐμ. οὐ δ. π. **οὐδ.** rather than the word themselves: *because* union with Me (μένειν ἐν ἐμοί) is the sole efficient cause of fruit being produced, you having no power to do any thing (not, ποιεῖν καρπόν: for φέρειν is here used throughout), to bring any thing to perfection, to do any of the ἀρεταί of that which ye are, separate from Me. **6.**] This verse is a most important testimony against supra-lapsarian error, shewing us that *falling from grace is possible*, and pointing out the steps of the fall. Observe this is *not said of the unfruitful branch*, which the Father *takes away* (in judgment): but of one who *will not abide* in Christ, becomes separate from Him: (1) is *cast out* (of the vineyard, or of the Vine) like a (**τὸ κλῆμα**, scil. τὸ ἄχρηστον, Euth.) branch in such a case: (2) becomes *dried up*, having lost the supply of life-giving sap ("quenched the Spirit," 1 Thess.

[b] μείνητε ἐν ἐμοὶ καὶ τὰ ῥήματά μου ἐν ὑμῖν [c] μείνῃ, ὃ ἐὰν
θέλητε αἰτήσασθε, καὶ γενήσεται ὑμῖν. 8 ἐν [d] τούτῳ
[e] ἐδοξάσθη ὁ πατήρ μου, [d] ἵνα [o] καρπὸν πολὺν [o] φέρητε,
καὶ γένησθε ἐμοὶ μαθηταί. 9 καθὼς ἠγάπησέν με ὁ πατήρ,
κἀγὼ ὑμᾶς ἠγάπησα· [f] μείνατε ἐν τῇ ἀγάπῃ τῇ [g] ἐμῇ.
10 ἐὰν τὰς [h] ἐντολάς μου [h] τηρήσητε, μενεῖτε ἐν τῇ ἀγάπῃ
μου· καθὼς ἐγὼ τοῦ πατρὸς τὰς [h] ἐντολὰς [h] τετήρηκα, καὶ
μένω αὐτοῦ ἐν τῇ ἀγάπῃ. 11 ταῦτα λελάληκα ὑμῖν ἵνα ἡ

b ch. xiv. 10 reff.
c ch. v. 38 reff.
d 1 John iv. 17. see ver. 12. ch. vi. 39 reff.
e ch. xiv. 13.
f ch. viii. 31.
g = ch. iii. 29. v. 30. see ver. 11.
h Matt. xix. 17 reff.

7. aft εαν ins δε D foss lat-*f* [Syr syr-jer] copt goth [μη B¹(Tischdf: om B²·³)]. for μεινη, η ℵ¹. for ο, οσα ℵ. θελετε A 248 Scr's i Cyr-comm₁. rec αιτησεσθε, with ℵ rel [Chr-montf]: txt ABDLMX[Γ] 1 lat-*b e ff*₂ [*q* syr-jer] goth æth arm Chr. (-σθαι AD[Γ] lat-*a c f* Syr.) om υμιν D¹(ins D³) [lat-*e*].
8. πολυν bef καρπον D. rec γενησεσθε, with Aℵ rel [Chr₁]: txt BDLMX[Λ] 1 latt æth Chr₁ Amphil₁ [Cyr-p₁]. for εμοι, μου D¹(txt D²) 254: μοι Lℵ 33 evv-P₁-x₁.
9. rec ηγαπησα bef υμας, with AD⁶ℵ rel vulg lat-*c f* [*ff*₂ *g*] goth Novat₁: txt BD¹L 1. 33 lat-*a b e q*.
10. om εαν to αγαπη μου (*possibly homœotel*) ℵ¹. for 1st μου, τας εμας A. [τηρησετε Lℵ³ᵃ ev-P₁¹.] for 2nd μου, τη εμη Xℵ³ᵃ. καγω D[-gr] ℵ [latt syr-jer copt arm Cyr₁]. rec τας εντ. bef του πατρος (*conformn to foregoing*), and adds μου, with AD rel lat-*c e f q* goth Cyr[-p₁]: txt B(ℵ) lat-*a b ff*₂ [*g*] Chr-mss Novat₁.—ins μου ℵ¹(om ℵ-corr¹(appy)³). for τετ., ετηρησα ℵ.
11. aft ταυτα ins δε D syr.

v. 19): (3) is gathered up with other such (Matt. xiii. 40) by the angels at the great day: (4) is cast into the fire, as the result of that judgment; and finally (5) '*burneth*;' not 'is burned,' in any sense of being *consumed; und muß brennen*, Luther. The aorists I take with Meyer as a consequence of the whole being spoken by our Lord as if the great day were come: hence also the presents, βάλλουσιν and καίεται. **7.**] All bringing forth fruit is the result of answered prayer for the assisting grace of God: and therefore the answer of all prayer is here promised to those who abide in Christ and have His word (Heb. vi. 5) abiding in them. **αἰτήσασθε** is the imperative used proleptically of the future time. This not having been seen, it has probably been altered to αἰτήσεσθε: see ch. xiv. 13. **ὃ ἐὰν θέλητε**, in the supposed case, is necessarily *in the way of God's will*, and as tending to πολὺν καρπὸν φέρειν.
8.] **ἐν τούτῳ** belongs to the following, not the preceding: ἐν τούτῳ, ἵνα .... as in E. V., see reff. **ἐδοξάσθη** again is proleptic, representing that in the spiritual dispensation the fact is habitually so. See on this sense of the aorist, Winer, edn. 6, § 40. 5. b. 2. The **πολὺς καρπός** is not merely 'large success in the apostolic mission,' but 'individual advance in bringing forth the fruits of the Spirit.' **καὶ γένησθε**] **and that ye may become My** (true) **disciples**, ἀπαρτισθήσεσθε, Euthym. (reading the *future*, see below.) "Fundamentum Christianismi, fieri discipulum Christi: fastigium, esse discipulum Christi." Bengel. According to the reading γενήσεσθε, the actual result of what precedes is stated: *and so ye shall become* . . . **9.**] The Love between the Father and Christ is compared with that between Christ and His disciples. The sense is best served by placing a colon (as in E. V.) after ὑμᾶς ἠγάπησα, making μείνατε κ.τ.λ. a separate injunction, and κἀγώ = οὕτως. With only a comma at ἠγάπησα, that which is the great assertion of the sentence, is suffered to slip by unnoticed; viz. that 'as the Father hath loved the Son, so the Son His disciples.' **τῇ ἀγ. τῇ ἐμῇ** may be rendered *the love of Me*, as in Luke xxii. 19 || 1 Cor.,—but the sense is not good, and the expression is not parallel with τῇ ἀγ. μου in ver. 10; so that I prefer **my love**, the love which I have towards you; remain in it: do not cast yourselves out of it. The other sense is *implied* in this, but not expressed.
10.] The way thus to remain is prescribed; even that way of simple obedience to *His* Will, which He followed to the Will of the Father. On **τῇ ἀγάπῃ μου**, see above: in the *last* clause, αὐτοῦ is *prefixed*, as Meyer well says, to denote the high consciousness of bliss and dignity in abiding in the Father's love.
11.] **λελάλ.** again proleptic, hastening to

i constr., ch. xiv. 27, or Matt. xxv. 21.
k = ch. iii. 29 reff. see Luke xxii. 16.
l vv. 8, 17. ch. xiii. 15, 34. Matt. xiii. 34 al.
m ch. x. 11 reff.
n Luke xii. 4.
o ch. xiv. 31 reff.
p Mark x. 18 reff.
q ch. vi. 45 reff.
r ch. xvii. 26. Luke ii. 15. Acts ii. 28, from Ps. xv. 11. Rom. ix. 22 al. Ezek. xliv. 23.
s ch. vi. 70 reff.

[i] χαρὰ ἡ ἐμὴ ἐν ὑμῖν ᾖ, καὶ ἡ χαρὰ ὑμῶν [k] πληρωθῇ.
12 αὕτη ἐστὶν ἡ ἐντολὴ ἡ ἐμή, [l] ἵνα ἀγαπᾶτε ἀλλήλους
καθὼς ἠγάπησα ὑμᾶς. 13 μείζονα ταύτης ἀγάπην οὐδεὶς I_a καθως ...
ἔχει, ἵνα τὶς τὴν [m] ψυχὴν αὐτοῦ [m] θῇ ὑπὲρ τῶν φίλων
αὐτοῦ. 14 ὑμεῖς [n] φίλοι μου ἐστέ, ἐὰν ποιῆτε ἃ ἐγὼ [o] ἐντέλ-
λομαι ὑμῖν. 15 οὐκέτι [p] λέγω ὑμᾶς δούλους, ὅτι ὁ δοῦλος N δουλος...
οὐκ οἶδεν τί ποιεῖ αὐτοῦ ὁ κύριος· ὑμᾶς δὲ εἴρηκα φίλους, ABDE
ὅτι πάντα ἃ [q] ἤκουσα [q] παρὰ τοῦ πατρός μου [r] ἐγνώρισα GHI$_a$K LMNSU
ὑμῖν. 16 οὐχ ὑμεῖς με [s] ἐξελέξασθε, ἀλλ' ἐγὼ [s] ἐξελεξάμην XΓΔΛ ΠΝ 1. 33. 69

rec (for ᾖ) μεινη, with ℵ rel lat-*f* [Chr$_1$ Cyr-p$_1$]: txt ABD 1 (33 latt) syrr [syr-jer] goth æth arm [Cyr-p$_2$].

13. ουδε εις B. om τις D[1](ins D[4]) ℵ[1] lat-*a b c e ff*$_2$ arm Cypr$_1$ Lucif$_1$.

14. aft υμεις ins γαρ D[1][and lat] ℵ[1]. ποιησητε D[1] latt. rec (for ἃ) οσα, with AI$_a$ rel syrr: ὃ B lat-*a e q* goth æth Cypr$_1$ Lucif$_2$: txt DLXℵ 1. 69 vulg lat-*b c f ff*$_2$ *g* [*q*] syr-mg [syr-jer] copt.

15. rec υμας bef λεγω, with D-gr I$_a$ rel lat-*q* goth [æth Chr$_1$] Orig$_1$: txt ABLXℵ 33 latt syrr [syr-jer arm] Constt$_1$ Orig$_1$-int$_4$ Chr-mss Cyr$_1$ Iren-int$_1$ Cypr$_2$ Hil$_1$ Lucif$_3$. for ἃ, οσα D[1]S 33 vulg lat-*b c f* [*ff*$_2$ *g* Cyr-p$_1$(txt$_{3 \text{ or } 4}$)] Chr$_1$.

16. (αλλα D.)

the end of the discourse, and treating it as ended. **ἡ χαρὰ ἡ ἐμή**, not "*joy concerning Me*" (Euthym.), nor "*joy derived from Me*" (De Wette), nor "*My joy over you*" (Aug., Lampe, Lücke, former edd.), but **My joy**, properly speaking (see 2 Cor. ii. 3, ὅτι ἡ ἐμὴ χαρὰ πάντων ὑμῶν ἐστιν): "His own holy exultation, the joy of the Son in the consciousness of the love of God, of His Unity with the Father: see ver. 10." (Lücke, 3rd edn.) **κ. ἡ χ. ὑμ. πλ.**] That their joy might, by the indwelling of that *His Joy*, be uplifted and ennobled (πληρωθῇ) even to fulness,—to the extreme of their capability and satisfaction,—and might remain so.

12—17.] *Union in love with one another enjoined on them.* **12.**] That He may shew them that it is no rigid code of keeping commandments in the legal sense, ver. 11 is inserted, and now *the* commandment (as including all others) is again explained (see ch. xiii. 34) to be, *mutual love,*—and that, after His example of Love to them. **13.**] A difficulty has been unnecessarily found in this verse, because St. Paul, Rom. v. 6 ff., cites it as a nobler instance of love, that Christ died for us *when we were enemies.* But manifestly *here* the example is from common life, in which if a man did lay down his life it would naturally be for his friends; and would be, and is cited as, the greatest example of love. Nor again is there any doctrinal difficulty: our Lord does not assert of himself, that He laid down his life *only* for his friends (as defined in the next verse), but puts forward *this side* of his Love as a great and a practical example for his followers. His own great Sacrifice of Himself lies in the background of this verse; but only in the background, and with but one side of it seen, viz. his Love to *them.* See 1 Tim. iv. 10, and compare 1 John iii. 16. **ἵνα,** as in ver. 8, depends on αὕτη, not on any *will* implied in ἀγάπη (De Wette), nor used ἐκβατικῶς (Olsh.),—and answers to 'scilicet, ut:' see on this use of ἵνα, note on 1 Cor. xiv. 13. Ver. **14** parallel to ver. 10,—and, like it, guarded, in vv. 15, 16, 17, from legal misinterpretation.

Ver. **15** *proleptically* spoken, of the state in which He would place them under the Spirit. Nor is there any discrepancy with ch. xiii. 13, 16, and ver. 20 here, which are also spoken of their future condition: for in that sense both relations subsist together. It is the *lower sense* of δοῦλος which is brought out in this verse. The proleptical character of the saying is clearly shewn in the οὐκ οἶδεν τί ποιεῖ ὁ κ., for this was precisely their *present* condition, but was after His Ascension changed into light and knowledge. **ἐγνώρισα ὑμ.**] Here again the allusion must be (see ch. xvi. 12) to their future state under the dispensation of the Spirit: nay, even to the fulness and completion of *it,* as Aug. remarks, Tract. lxxxvi. 1, vol. iii. pt. ii.: compare the confession of one of the greatest Apostles, 1 Cor. xiii. 10. "Sicut immortalitatem carnis et salutem animarum futuram exspectamus, quamvis

ὑμᾶς, καὶ [t] ἔθηκα ὑμᾶς ἵνα ὑμεῖς [u] ὑπάγητε καὶ [v] καρπὸν
[v] φέρητε καὶ ὁ καρπὸς ὑμῶν [w] μένῃ· ἵνα ὅ τι ἂν αἰτήσητε
τὸν πατέρα [x] ἐν τῷ ὀνόματί μου δῷ ὑμῖν. 17 ταῦτα ἐντέλ-
λομαι ὑμῖν, [y] ἵνα ἀγαπᾶτε ἀλλήλους.
18 Εἰ ὁ κόσμος ὑμᾶς μισεῖ, γινώσκετε ὅτι ἐμὲ [z] πρῶτον
ὑμῶν μεμίσηκεν. 19 εἰ [a] ἐκ τοῦ κόσμου ἦτε, ὁ κόσμος ἂν
[b] τὸ ἴδιον ἐφίλει· ὅτι δὲ [a] ἐκ τοῦ κόσμου οὐκ ἐστέ, ἀλλ'
ἐγὼ [s] ἐξελεξάμην ὑμᾶς ἐκ τοῦ κόσμου, διὰ τοῦτο μισεῖ ὑμᾶς

t = Acts xx. 28. 1 Cor. xii. 28. 1 Tim. i. 12. 2 Tim. i. 11. Heb. i. 2. Ps. xc. 9.
u Matt. xiii. 44.
v ch. xii. 24 reff.
w = 2 Cor. iii. 11. Heb. xii. 27. 1 Pet. i. 23.
x ch. xiv. 14 reff.
y ver. 12.
z = ch. i. 15, 30.
a ch. iii. 31 reff.
b neut. sing. = here only. see ch. i. 11 reff.

ins πολυ (sic) bef καρπον A (Ambr$_2$). for 2nd ινα, και 69 arm : om א^1. (εαν Λא.) for αιτησητε, αιτητε BL [Cyr-p$_1$]. for δω, δωσει א 247 Scr's d^2 w^2 ev-y [Cyr$_1$] : δωη EGHNXΛ 33, δωει M : txt ABDI$_a$ rel.

17. om ινα D lat-*e*.

18. μισει bef υμας N Orig-int$_1$. om υμων Dא^1 lat-*a b c e ff$_2$* copt æth arm Cypr$_2$. for μεμισηκεν, εμισησεν N Scr's j : εμισηκεν א^1.

19. om δε D lat-*e*. for ουκ εστε, ητε D^1[and lat](txt D^4) (Orig$_1$). ο κοσμος bef μισει υμας א [copt syr-jer].

jam pignore accepto salvi facti esse dicamur: ita omnium notitiam quæcumque Unigenitus audivit a Patre, futuram sperare debemus, quamvis hoc jam se fecisse dixerit Christus." Aug. ut supra.

16.] See 1 John iv. 10, 19. Further proof of His love, in his choosing His, when they had not chosen Him. **ἔθηκα**] **appointed**: see Acts xiii. 47: 1 Thess. v. 9, and reff. Euth., Chrys., Thl. explain it ἐφύτευσα, in the parabolic sense. But the parable seems to be no further returned to than in the allusion implied in καρπός. '*Ordained*,' in E. V., is objectionable, as conveying a wrong idea. **ὑπάγ. κ. καρ. φέρ.**] ὑπ. probably merely expresses (see ref. and Matt. xviii. 15; xix. 21, and πορευόμενοι, Luke viii. 14) the activity of living and developing principle; not the missionary journeys of the Apostles (Grot., Lampe, Meyer). The καρπός is not the Church, to be founded by the Apostles, and endure;—this is evident, for *here* the fruit is spoken of with reference to *themselves*, and their ripening into the full stature of Christ. Much of their fruit will be necessarily the winning of others to Christ: but that is not *the prominent* idea here. **μένῃ**] See 2 John 8: Rev. xiv. 13. **ἵνα ὅ τι ἂν . . .**] This ἵνα is parallel with the former one, not the result of it; the two, the bringing forth of fruit and the obtaining answer to prayer, being co-ordinate with each other; but (vv. 7, 8) the bearing fruit to God's glory is of these the greater, being the result and aim of the other. **17.**] **ταῦτα** refers (as almost always in John, see vv. 11, 21; xvi. 1, 25, 33; xvii. 1; xviii. 1 al.) back to what has gone before. 'The object of my enjoining these things on you is (for all since ver. 12 has been an expansion of **καθὼς ἠγ. ὑμ.**) that ye love one another' (see 1 John iv. 11). Then from the indefiniteness of this word ἀλλήλους our Lord takes occasion to forewarn them that however wide their love to one another, they cannot bring all within this category; there will be ὁ κόσμος, which will hate them.

18—27.] *Their relation to the world*: and, vv. 18—21, *ground of the world's hatred*. On the connexion, see above. **18.**] See ch. vii. 7. **γινώσκετε**, most probably *imperative*, **know ye . . . .** The *assertion* of their knowledge of the fact would in all likelihood be conveyed in the past tense, οἴδατε, or ἔγνωτε, or ἐγνώκατε: cf. for the imperative, ch. xxiv. 43: Luke x. 11; xii. 39: Gal. iii. 7: Heb. xiii. 23; for the indicative, ch. xiv. 17: Acts xx. 34: 2 Cor. viii. 9: Phil. ii. 22: 1 John ii. 29 (see note there); iv. 2; for both combined, Matt. xxiv. 32, 33 ||; for the past tense in assertion, Luke xvi. 4: ch. v. 42; vi. 69; viii. 52, 55 al. The great proof of this hatred to Him was yet to come, but is viewed as past. This knowledge brings comfort, 1 Pet. iv. 12, 13. Ver. **19** not only explains this hatred, but derives additional comfort from it, as a sign that they were not (any longer) *of the world*; but chosen out of it by Him, and endued with a new life from above. In **τὸ ἴδιον** ἐφίλει, not ὑμᾶς ἐφ., we have the true practice of the world hinted at, and the false character of the world's love, as a mere φιλαυτία, set forth. "*Suum* dicitur pro *vos*, atque sic notatur *Interesse* mundi," Bengel. In this 'loving their own,' the children of this world fall into hating one another.

ὁ κόσμος. 20 [c] μνημονεύετε τοῦ λόγου [d] οὗ ἐγὼ εἶπον
ὑμῖν, Οὐκ ἔστιν δοῦλος μείζων τοῦ κυρίου αὐτοῦ. εἰ ἐμὲ
[e] ἐδίωξαν, καὶ ὑμᾶς [e] διώξουσιν· εἰ τὸν [f] λόγον μου [f] ἐτήρησαν, καὶ τὸν ὑμέτερον [f] τηρήσουσιν. 21 ἀλλὰ ταῦτα
πάντα ποιήσουσιν εἰς ὑμᾶς [g] διὰ τὸ [g] ὄνομά μου, ὅτι οὐκ
[h] οἴδασιν τὸν πέμψαντά με. 22 εἰ μὴ ἦλθον καὶ ἐλάλησα
αὐτοῖς, ἁμαρτίαν οὐκ εἴχοσαν· νῦν δὲ [ij] πρόφασιν οὐκ
[j] ἔχουσιν [k] περὶ τῆς ἁμαρτίας αὐτῶν. 23 ὁ ἐμὲ μισῶν καὶ
τὸν πατέρα μου μισεῖ. 24 εἰ τὰ ἔργα μὴ ἐποίησα ἐν

...δε N. ABDE GHI_aK LMSUX ΓΔΛΠℵ 1. 33. 69

c gen., ch. xvi. 4, 21. Luke xvii. 32 al. 1 Chron. xvi. 15.—acc., Matt. xvi. 9. 1 Thess. ii. 9. (1 Tim. ii. 8.) Rev. xviii. 5 only. 1 Chron. xvi. 12, and usually in LXX.
d attr., Mark vii. 13 reff.
e = Matt. v. 10, 11. Acts vii. 52 al. Ps. vii. 1.
f ch. viii. 51, 52, 55 reff.
g Matt. x. 22. xxiv. 9 ||. 1 John ii. 12. Rev. ii. 3 only. διὰ τοῦ ὀν., Acts iv. 30. 1 Cor. i. 10. ὑπὲρ τοῦ ὀν., Acts v. 41. ix. 16. xv. 26. xxi. 13. Rom. i. 5. 3 John 7. ἕνεκεν, Matt. xix. 29. Luke xxi. 12.
h = ch. i. 26 al.
i = here only. ἀγὼν προφάσεις οὐκ εἰςδέχεται, Plato, Crat. 421 D. (Mark xii. 40 ||. L. Acts xxvii. 30. Phil. i. 18. 1 Thess. ii. 5 only. Ps. cxl. 4.)
j here only. Dem. p. 526. 15. Plato, Rep. 5, p. 469 C. Xen. Cyr. iii. 1. 27.
k = Heb. x. 6, &c. 1 Pet. iii. 18. 1 John ii. 2. iv. 10. Lev. xiv. 19.

20. τους λογους ους D: τον λογον ον ℵ. aft λογου ins μου EGI_a[Γ]ΔΛ vulg lat-[ff_2] *g q* syr æth. for εγω ειπον, ελαλησα ℵ. (for υμιν, υμας ιν ℵ[1], but *as* dotted 1. m. and erased.) ins μου bef δουλος D[1]-gr. τηρησωσιν ℵ Scr's c evv-P-z_1.
21. om παντα DX arm Chr-ms. rec (for εις υμας) υμιν, with AD^2I_aN rel vulg lat-*a e f* [*g q*] syr[-txt syr-jer] copt goth $Novat_1$: υμας X ev-y_1 : om ℵ[1] : txt BD[1]L ℵ-corr[1] 1. 33 (lat-*b c* ff_2 [*l*]) Syr syr-mg [Petr] Chr.
22. rec (for ειχοσαν) ειχον, with $AD^2I_aN^2$[$Π^{1.3}$] rel $Orig_5$ [Chr_{alic} Cyr-p_1] : ειχαν D[1] : txt BLN^1[$Π^2$]ℵ 1. 33 $Orig_2$-mss Cyr[-$p_{2 \text{ or } 3}$]. om δε ℵ[1] [lat-*e*].

Meyer remarks the solemnity of *κόσμος* thus repeated five times.
20.] Ch. xiii. 16, but with a different reference: the sense here being, 'Remember the saying, for it is true in this matter also:' see Matt. x. 24, where it is used in the same sense. The subject of *ἐδίωξαν* is *ὁ κόσμος* as a noun of number. A difficulty has been raised on *ἐτήρησαν . . . τηρήσουσιν*, and some have wanted to give this word a hostile sense, (as *παρατηρεῖν*,) quoting Matt. xxvii. 36, and Gen. iii. 15 (which is altogether an exceptional use, the reading being undoubtedly genuine): see also Jer. xx. 13. But in John this cannot be. Nor is *irony* (Lampe, Stier) in this latter clause at all in keeping with the solemnity of the discourse. The words simply mean (as Thl.), 'the keeping My word and the keeping yours are intimately joined, and when you find the world or any part of the world do the first, you may infer the other.' The issue of *εἰ τ. λ. μ. ἐτήρ.* was to be proved by their rejection and killing of the Lord Jesus. Beware of rendering as Kuinoel, "*If they had kept my word, they would keep yours,*" which is ungrammatical. The only idiomatic rendering in English is that of the E. V., **If they have kept** [or rather, **If they kept**] **my word they will keep yours.** **21.**] **ἀλλά**—nay, so far is this from being so, that it is on this very account, *because* ye belong to Me, that they will thus treat you. **ταῦτα πάντα**—all that is implied in *μισεῖν* and *διώκειν*. **τ. π.**, 'these things, all of them:' not *π. τ.*, 'all, every one of, these things:' the former order gives the *ταῦτα* in the gross,—'all this treatment,'—the latter in the particular, so that not one is excepted from the category. It was on account of bearing the Name of Christ that the Christians were subjected to persecution in the early ages, and that they are even now hated by those who know Him not: but this is to them comfort and joy, see Acts v. 41: 2 Cor. xii. 10: Gal. vi. 17: 1 Pet. iv. 14. **οὐκ οἴδασιν**, not, '*They know Him not as having sent Me*'—but **they know not** (absolutely) **Him who has sent Me.** Ignorance of God (not desiring the knowledge of His ways) is the great cause of hostility to Christ and His servants. **22.**] *The sinfulness of this hate.* See ch. ix. 41 and note. **ἐλάλησα, discoursed**, generally: not, acquainted them with their sin. The *sin* spoken of is, not the generally sinful state of the world,—nor the sin of unbelief in Christ, which they of course could not have committed, had He never come: but *the sin of hatred to Him and His*, which might have been excused otherwise, but now that He had come and discoursed with them, had no excuse, since He had plainly shewn them the proofs of his mission from the Father. Euthym. says well, *ἀποστερεῖ τοὺς Ἰουδαίους πάσης συγγνώμης ἐθελοκακοῦντας.* **23.**] See ch. xiv. 9. Human regards, whether of

αὐτοῖς ἃ οὐδεὶς ἄλλος ἐποίησεν, ἁμαρτίαν οὐκ εἴχοσαν·
νῦν δὲ καὶ ἑωράκασιν καὶ μεμισήκασιν καὶ ἐμὲ καὶ τὸν
πατέρα μου· 25 ἀλλ' [l] ἵνα πληρωθῇ ὁ λόγος ὁ ἐν τῷ
..δωρεαν ℵ. νόμῳ αὐτῶν γεγραμμένος, ὅτι ἐμίσησάν με [m] δωρεάν.
26 ὅταν [δὲ] ἔλθῃ ὁ [n] παράκλητος ὃν ἐγὼ πέμψω ὑμῖν παρὰ
τοῦ πατρός, τὸ [o] πνεῦμα τῆς [o] ἀληθείας ὃ παρὰ τοῦ πατρὸς
[p] ἐκπορεύεται, ἐκεῖνος μαρτυρήσει περὶ ἐμοῦ. 27 [q] καὶ

l ellips., ch. ix. 3. xiv. 31.
m = Psa. xxxiv. 19. lxviii. 4. Gal. ii. 21. see Matt. x. 8 reff.
n ch. xiv. 16 reff.
o ch. xiv. 17 reff.
p w. παρά, here only. ἐκ, Mark vii. 15, &c. ||. xiii. 1 al. ἀπό, Matt. xx. 29 || Mk.
q ch. vi. 51 reff.

24. rec (for εποιησεν) πεποιηκεν, with E rel: txt ABDI$_a$KLX[Π]ℵ 1. 33. 69 Chr$_1$. rec (for ειχοσαν) ειχον, with AD[2]I$_a$[Π[1.3]] rel [Chr]: ειχαν D[1]: txt BL[1][Π[2]]ℵ(1) 33. for και εμε, με D lat-*a c e ff*$_2$ [*l q*] copt arm-mss.

25. rec γεγραμμενος bef εν τω νομω αυτων, with AI$_a$ rel syrr [syr-jer] goth arm: txt BDGLXℵ 1. 33 latt (æth) Orig$_1$ Cyr$_1$.—(for νομω, κοσμω ℵ!)

26. om δε BΔℵ lat-*e* [*l* syr-jer] copt[-dz] Novat$_1$ Hil$_1$ spec: ins AD rel vulg lat-*f* [*g q*], *ergo* lat-*a b c ff*$_2$. πεμπτω D lat-*ff*$_2$ goth. [ον εγω πεμ. υμ. παρα is written by B[1] over an erasure.] aft 1st πατρος ins μου D [A[1](appy) Π[1]] 33 lat-*a c* Syr copt [Did$_1$] Novat spec. aft 2nd πατρος ins μου D 33 lat-*a b c* Syr Novat$_1$ Hil$_1$.

love or of hatred, towards Him who is the only manifestation of the Father to His creatures, are in fact directed towards the Father Himself: see Ps. lxix. 9, cited in Rom. xv. 3. **24.**] He refers to the testimony of His *works* among them also, as leaving them again without excuse;—they had had ocular witness of His mission. **ἐν αὐτοῖς**—not *to* them (as Aug.), but as Acts ii. 22, *ἐν μέσῳ ὑμῶν*. **ἐποίησεν** is, not only by external evidence, but also by internal, the right reading. πεποίηκεν (as Lücke remarks, ii. 643) would imply that the **ἄλλοι** referred to were contemporaries of our Lord,—or, at all events, that their works still lasted. **ἑωράκασιν** does not refer to *the works* (as Lücke), but to *καὶ ἐμὲ καὶ τὸν πατέρα μου*, see ch. xiv. 9. **25.**] **ἀλλ'**,—but all this not as an *accidental* thwarting of My word and work among them, but as a matter predicted in Scripture. **ἵνα**, with the fullest sense of *purpose*, as always, and most especially in this formula. Beware of the evasive ecbatic sense. **ἐν τῷ νόμῳ αὐτῶν**] See ch. x. 34 and note. To suppose any irony in these words, as De W. does ("they are *true followers-out of their law*"), is manifestly against the whole spirit of our Lord's reference to the law. It is '*their* law,'—"quem assidue terunt et jactant," Bengel,—as condemning them, though their boast and pride. **δωρεάν**, not, "*to no purpose*," as Bengel (vergeblich), but as E. V., **without a cause**, answering to *πρόφασιν οὐκ ἔχουσιν*, ver. 22. The citation is probably from the Messianic Psalm lxix. **26.**] This assurance carries on the testimony concerning Christ,—which the world should see and hear, and yet reject and hate Him,—even to the end of time, by means of the Spirit of Truth: so that on the one hand this **seeing and hating** must not be expected to cease as long as the Spirit bears this witness,—and on the other, He, the Spirit of Truth, will never cease to overcome the hating world by this His testimony. **ὁ παράκλ.**] See ch. xiv. 16 and note. **ὃν ἐγὼ πέμψω**] Stier (whose comment on this verse should be consulted) dwells on the accurate division of the clauses here, *ὁ παράκλ.* **ὃν** *ἐγὼ πέμψω*,—but *τὸ πνεῦμα τ. ἀληθ.* **ὃ** *παρὰ τ. πατρὸς ἐκπορεύεται*. The first clause he regards as spoken œconomically, of the Spirit in His office as Paraclete, sent from the Father by the glorified Son (or, by the Father in the Son's name, ch. xiv. 26), and bringing in the dispensation of the Spirit;—the second ontologically, of the essential nature of the Spirit Himself, that He *proceeded forth from the Father*. (And if from the Father, from the Son also,—see ch. xvi. 15, and those passages where the Spirit is said to be *His* Spirit, Rom. viii. 9: Gal. iv. 6: Phil. i. 19: 1 Pet. i. 11: also Rev. xxii. 1.) Perhaps however it is better to take *the whole* œconomically, as Luthardt has done. Then *ὃν ἐγὼ πέμψω παρὰ τ. π.* is *parallel with ὃ παρὰ τοῦ π. ἐκπορεύεται*, and the procession from the Father *is* the sending by the Son. At all events, *this passage*, as Beza remarks, cannot be alleged either one way or the other in the controversy with the Greek Church on the procession of the Holy Spirit. See this done in the interest of the Greek view, by Theodor. Mops. in loc. **ἐκεῖνος**, as opposed to the world which hates Christ. On the

ὑμεῖς [q] δὲ μαρτυρεῖτε, ὅτι [r] ἀπ' [r] ἀρχῆς μετ' ἐμοῦ [s] ἐστε.
XVI. 1 Ταῦτα λελάληκα ὑμῖν, ἵνα μὴ [t] σκανδαλισθῆτε.
2 [u] ἀποσυναγώγους [v] ποιήσουσιν ὑμᾶς· [w] ἀλλ' [x] ἔρχεται
ὥρα [y] ἵνα πᾶς ὁ ἀποκτείνας ὑμᾶς δόξῃ [z] λατρείαν [a] προς-
φέρειν τῷ θεῷ. 3 καὶ ταῦτα ποιήσουσιν, ὅτι οὐκ ἔγνωσαν
τὸν πατέρα οὐδὲ ἐμέ. 4 ἀλλὰ ταῦτα λελάληκα ὑμῖν, ἵνα
ὅταν ἔλθῃ ἡ ὥρα αὐτῶν, [b] μνημονεύητε αὐτῶν, ὅτι ἐγὼ

r = Luke i. 2. 1 John ii. 7, 24. iii. 11. 2 John 5, 6.
s pres., ch. viii. 58 reff.
t Matt. xi. 6. xiii. 21. xxiv. 10 al.†. Sir. ix. 5. xxiii. 8. xxxv. (xxxii.) 15 only.
u ch. ix. 22. xii. 42 only†.
v = ch. v. 11 reff.
w = 2 Cor. i. 9. vii. 11 (often). Phil. iii. 8. x ch. iv. 21, 23 reff. y constr., ver. 32. ch. xii. 23. xiii. 1.
z Rom. ix. 4. xii. 1. Heb. ix. 1, 6 only. Exod. xii. 25, 26. a = Acts vii. 42, from Amos v. 25. Heb. xi. 4 al. Num. xxxi. 50. b ch. xv. 20 reff.

...αποσυναγωγους Γ_a.
Y -γνωσαν τον ...
ABDE GHKL MSUY ΓΔΛΠℵ 1. 33. 69

27. om δε D 254 ev-y_1 latt syrr(exc 3 mss of syr).

CHAP. XVI. 1. om μη ℵ[1].
2. aft αποσυναγωγους ins γαρ ℵ. ποιησωσιν ℵ Scr's c evv-P_1-x_1-y_1-z_1. (αλλα ℵ.) om 2nd υμας B. for θεω, κυριω A.
3. ποιησωσιν ℵ 33 evv-y_1-z_1. rec aft ποιησ. ins υμιν, with DLℵ 1. 69 lat-*a c f* ff_2 *g* syr-w-ast [syr-jer æth arm] copt; εις υμας 33. 63: om AB rel am(with em forj foss [fuld] gat mm mt tol) lat-*b e l q* syrr goth Chr_1 Cyr_1 $Cypr_3$ Lucif.
4. om αλλα D[1][and lat](ins D[6]) lat-*a e l* Syr Chr_1. for οταν, αν ℵ[1]; εαν Lℵ[3a]. rec om 1st αυτων, with Dℵ rel [lat-*a* syr-jer arm] copt: ins ABL[Π] 33. 69 vulg lat-*b c e f* ff_2 *g l* [*q*] syrr goth $Cypr_2$. for μνημονευητε, μνημονευτε D[1]; μνημονευσητε D-corr[1] [Π[1]] 69. om 2nd αυτων DL[Π[2]] (ℵ-corr, marked for erasure, but marks removed) 69 vulg lat-*b c e* ff_2 *g l* [*q*].

emphatic use of this pronoun as identifying the chief subject of the sentence, see note, ch. vii. 29. **27.**] The disciples are not, as some have supposed, here mentioned as witnesses *separate from* and *working with* the Holy Spirit. The witness is *one and the same*—the Spirit will witness in and by them; the ὅταν ἔλθῃ ὁ παρ. belongs to the whole: see Luke xxiv. 48, 49, where this is strongly expressed. This verse alludes to the historical witness which the Holy Ghost in the ministers and eye-witnesses of the word, Luke i. 2, should enable them to give,—which forms the *human side* (**καὶ ὑμ. δέ**, "quin et vos," Erasm.) of this great testimony of the Spirit of truth, and OF WHICH OUR INSPIRED GOSPELS ARE THE SUMMARY: the *divine side* being, His own indwelling testimony in the life and heart of every believer in all time. But both the one and the other are given *by the self-same* SPIRIT;—neither of them inconsistent with, or superseding the other. Beware of taking μαρτυρεῖτε imperative as Hofmann, Schriftb. ii. 2, p. 15. It would thus be very abrupt and unnatural. The καὶ . . . δέ, and the reason, ὅτι κ.τ.λ., seem decisive against it. **ἀπ' ἀρχῆς**, as in reff., and in the sense of Acts i. 21:—'from the beginning of the Lord's ministry.' The present tenses set forth the connexion between the being (continuing to be) witnesses, and the being (having been throughout) companions of the Lord in His ministry. Cf. ἀπ' ἀρχῆς ὁ διάβολος ἁμαρτάνει, 1 John iii. 8.

CHAP. XVI. 1—33.] *The promise of the Comforter expanded in its fulness.* And herein, vv. 1—15, *the conditions of His coming and His office.* **1.**] **ταῦτα**, scil. ch. xv. 18—27,—not only the warning of the hatred of the world, but the promise of the testifying Spirit (Stier). **2.**] On **ἀποσυν.** see reff. **ἀλλ'**, **yea, and**,—see reff. It introduces a yet more grievous and decisive proof of their nature. **ἵνα**] "That which shall happen in the ὥρα, is regarded as the *object of its coming.*" Meyer. **προσφέρειν**, the technical word for offering a sacrifice—see reff. **λατρείαν**] "Quisquis effundit sanguinem impii, idem facit ac si sacrificium offerat." Jalkut Schimeoni, cited by De Wette, &c., see 1 Cor. iv. 13. But the sense of 'sacrificium' must not be too much pressed, as Stier remarks, to mean in every case an expiatory offering: see reff. **3.**] See Luke xxiii. 34: ch. xv. 21: Acts iii. 17: and 1 Tim. i. 13. **4.**] **ἀλλά** here indicates no contrast, but only breaking off the mournful details, and passing back to the subject of ver. 1. Cf. Æsch. Agam. 507—9. Hartung, Partikellehre, ii. p. 35. If we are to seek any contrast, it will be between the οὐκ ἔγνωσαν of the world, and the μνημονεύητε of the Church. The one know not what they are doing: the other know well what they are suffering. **ἡ ὥρα αὐτῶν**, the time of their happening **ἐγώ** before εἶπον is emphatic, 'I

εἶπον ὑμῖν. ταῦτα δὲ ὑμῖν [c] ἐξ [c] ἀρχῆς οὐκ εἶπον, ὅτι μεθ' c ch. vi. 64 only.
ὑμῶν ἤμην. 5 νῦν δὲ [d] ὑπάγω πρὸς τὸν πέμψαντά με, d ch. xiii. 1. see ch. xiv. 12.
καὶ οὐδεὶς ἐξ ὑμῶν ἐρωτᾷ με [e] Ποῦ ὑπάγεις; 6 ἀλλ' ὅτι e ch. iii. 8. viii. 14. xii. 35. Heb. xi. 8. Gen. xvi. 8.
ταῦτα λελάληκα ὑμῖν, ἡ λύπη [f] πεπλήρωκεν ὑμῶν τὴν
[f] καρδίαν. 7 ἀλλ' ἐγὼ τὴν ἀλήθειαν λέγω ὑμῖν, [g] συμφέρει f = Acts v. 3. Eccl. ix. 3.
ὑμῖν ἵνα ἐγὼ ἀπέλθω· ἐὰν γὰρ [ἐγὼ] μὴ ἀπέλθω, ὁ g constr., Matt. v. 29, 30. ch. xi. 50.
[h] παράκλητος οὐκ ἐλεύσεται πρὸς ὑμᾶς· ἐὰν δὲ [i] πορευθῶ, h ch. xiv. 16 reff.
i Acts i. 10, 11. 1 Pet. iii. 22.

$Cypr_2$. om 2nd υμιν א[1]. εξ αρχης bef 3rd υμιν D [33] 254 Chr[-ms_1].
5. ins εγω bef υπαγω א. for υπαγεις, υπαγει א[1]
6. om αλλ' A.
7. rec om 3rd εγω (*as not in the opposed clause below: this is more prob than that it should have been insd from the clause preceding, which is not so nearly connected*), with BDLYא 1 (S, e sil) vulg lat-ff_2 *g* [*l*] syr copt Cyr[-p_7] spec: ins A rel lat-(*a b c*) *e f* [*q* syr-jer] Syr goth æth arm Cyr-jer_1 Bas_1 Chr_1 Did_1 [Cyr-p_1] Phot Thl $Novat_1$ Ambr. for ουκ, ου μη BL 33 Chr [Cyr-p_6(txt_1)]. for 1st υμας, א[1] Scr's t.

MYSELF:'—**that it was I** MYSELF **who told you.** A difficulty has been found in the latter part of the verse, because our Lord had repeatedly announced to them future persecutions, and that at least as plainly as here, Matt. v. 10; x. 16, 21—28 al. freq. And hence, De Wette, Meyer, and Lücke, and even Olsh., find ground for supposing that the chronological order of the discourses has not been followed in the Synoptic Gospels. But there is in reality no inconsistency, and therefore no need for such a supposition. This declaration, *as here meant*, was *not made before*, because He was with them. Then clearly it *is now made*, in reference to His immediate departure. And if so, to what will **ταῦτα** most naturally refer? To *that full and complete account* of the world's motives, and their own office, and their comfort under it, which He has been giving them. This He had *never before done* so plainly, though occasional mention has been made even of the help of the Spirit under such trials, see Matt. x. 19, 20. **μεθ' ὑμ. ἤμ.**] While the Lord was *with them* (cf. Matt. ix. 15), the malice of the world was mainly directed against *Him*,—and they were overlooked: see ch. xviii. 8. In **ἤμην** we have the proleptical character of the discourse again manifest. **5.**] This is occasioned by the foregoing, but in fact begins the new subject, *the condition of the Comforter's coming*. **καὶ οὐδ.**] They had (see ch. xiii. 36; xiv. 5) asked this *verbally* before: our Lord therefore cites the question here in some other and deeper sense than they had used it there. I believe the meaning to be: 'None of you enquires into the NATURE (ποῦ being emphatic) *of My departure*, so as to appear anxious to know what advantages are to be derived from it; but (ver. 6) you are all given up to grief on account of what I have said, "expavescitis, neque reputatis quo discedam aut in quem finem." Calvin. **6. ἡ λύπη πεπλ. ὑμ. τ. κ.**] 'Your grief (or abstract, 'grief') has filled, entirely occupied, your heart (not τὰς κ., but singular, as common to all, see Rom. i. 21), to the exclusion of any regard of my object in leaving you.' "These are the same disciples who afterwards when their risen Lord had ascended to heaven,—without any pang at parting with Him, returned with great joy to Jerusalem, Luke xxiv. 52" (Stier). "Subest huic blandæ increpationi tacita consolatio. Dum enim improbat, quod quæstionem, quo vaderet, negligant, sibi id optime perspectum esse docet. Dum negligentiæ incusat, ad excusationem tamen affert, quod ea ex tam vehementi affectu tristitiæ oriunda sit." Lampe. **7.**] **ἀλλά** refers to the last clause (**notwithstanding, or nevertheless**, as E. V.): **ἐγώ**, to οὐδεὶς ἐξ ὑμ. κ.τ.λ. I *Myself* tell you the real state of the case. **συμφέρει ὑμ.** implies that the dispensation of the Spirit is a more blessed manifestation of God than was even the bodily presence of the risen Saviour.
Every rendering of this verse ought to keep the distinction between ἀπέλθω and πορευθῶ, which is not sufficiently done in E. V. by '*go away*' and '*depart*.' **Depart** and **go** would be better: the first expressing merely the *leaving them*, the second, the *going up* to the Father. The **ἐγώ** before ἀπέλθω is again emphatic: 'that I, for my part, should leave you.' This οὐκ ἐλεύσεται ... is a convincing proof, if one more were needed, that *the gift of the Spirit at and since the day of Pentecost, was and is something* TOTALLY DISTINCT

j constr., ch. viii. 46. Luke iii. 19. Jude 15 only. k = John chiefly (ch. vii. 4, 7. xiv. 17, &c. xv. 18, 19. 1 John ii. 15 al.). Heb. xi. 7, 38. James i. 27. 1 Pet. ii. 5. l ch. ii. 11 reff.

πέμψω αὐτὸν πρὸς ὑμᾶς. 8 καὶ ἐλθὼν ἐκεῖνος [j] ἐλέγξει
τὸν [k] κόσμον περὶ ἁμαρτίας καὶ περὶ δικαιοσύνης καὶ περὶ
κρίσεως. 9 περὶ ἁμαρτίας μέν, ὅτι οὐ [l] πιστεύουσιν [l] εἰς

ABDE GHKL MSUY ΓΔΛΠℵ 1. 33 69

9. om *ου* ℵ[1].

from any thing before that time: a new and loftier dispensation. **8—11.**] We have here, in a few deep and wonderful words, *the work of the Spirit on the world* set forth. This work He shall begin **ἐλθών**, scil. πρὸς ὑμᾶς: not, however, merely *'by your means,'* but personally: so that it is *not the work and witness of the Apostles* which is spoken of, except in so far as they are servants of the Holy Spirit, but (ἐκεῖνος) *His own immediate* personal working. **ἐλέγξει**] It is difficult to give in one word the deep meaning: *'convince'* approaches perhaps the nearest to it, but does not express the double sense of ἐλέγχειν, which is manifestly here intended—of a *convincing* unto salvation, and a *convicting* unto condemnation:—*'reprove'* is far too weak, conveying merely the idea of an objective rebuke, whereas ἐλέγξει reaches into the heart, and works subjectively in both the abovementioned ways. See the whole question amply discussed in Archdeacon Hare's Mission of the Comforter, vol. ii. note K.

Lücke's comment is valuable: "The testimony of the Holy Ghost in behalf of Christ as opposed to the unbelieving world (ch. xv. 26) is essentially a *refutation*, ἔλεγχος, a demonstration of its wrong and error. All the apostolic preaching, as addressed to the world, takes necessarily this polemical form (1 Tim. v. 20: 2 Tim. iv. 2; iii. 16: Titus i. 9, 13; ii. 15). And the more difficult was the disciples' conflict against the power of this world with only the Word for their weapon, the more comfort was it for them, that the power of God the Spirit working by this ἔλεγχος was their help. In Matt. x. 19, 20: Luke xii. 11, 12, the apologetic side of their conflict, which was in close connexion with the polemical, is brought into view. In ἐλέγχειν is always implied the refutation, the overcoming of an error, a wrong,—by the truth and the right. And when, by means of the ἔλεγχος, the truth detects the error, and the right the wrong, so that a man becomes conscious of them,—then arises the feeling of *guilt*, which is ever painful. Thus every ἔλεγχος is a chastening, a punishment. And hence this office has been called the Strafamt (punitive office) of the Spirit. The *effect* of the ἔλεγχος of the Divine Spirit in the world may be *to harden:* but its *aim* is the *deliverance* of the world. ὁ κόσμος, in John, includes those who are not yet delivered (from the power of Satan to God), who *may be yet delivered,*—not the condemned. If the ἔλεγχος of the world is a moral process, its result may just as well be conversion, as non-conversion. *Only thus* did the ἔλεγχος of the Spirit answer the end of Christ's coming;—only thus could it be a cheering support to the Apostles. Certainly, the κρίσις with which the ἔλεγχος closes is *condemnation*, not however of the *world*, but of the *Prince of the world*" (ii. 649 f.). De Wette denies the *salutary* side of this ἐλέγχειν—but he is certainly wrong: see below.

These three words, **ἁμαρτία, δικαιοσύνη, κρίσις**, comprehend the three great steps of advance in spiritual truth among men. Of itself the world does not know what *Sin* is, what *Righteousness* is, what *Judgment* is. Nor can either of these be revealed to any man except by the Spirit of God working within him. Each man's conscience has some glimmering of light on each of these; *some* consciousness of guilt, *some* sense of right, *some* power of judgment of what is transitory and worthless: but all these are unreal and unpractical, till the ἔλεγχος of the Spirit has wrought in him (see Stier, v. 306, edn. 2).

9.] And the great opening of *Sin* to the world is to shew them that its root and essence is, *unbelief in Christ as the Son of God.* UNBELIEF:—for, mankind being alien from God by nature, the first step towards their recovery must be to lay hold on that only safety which He has provided for them; and that laying hold is *faith*, and the not doing it, when revealed and placed before them, is *sin*. Beforetime, it was also *unbelief;*—"The fool hath said in his heart, There is *no God:*"—but now,—for we can only believe as God has revealed Himself,—it is unbelief in *Christ the Son of God,*—the οὐ **θέλετε** ἔρχεσθαι πρός με: see this pointedly asserted 1 John v. 10—12. Remember, this unbelief is not a mere want of historical faith,—but unbelief *in its very root,*—the want of a personal and living recognition of Jesus as the Lord (1 Cor. xii. 3), which, wherever the Spirit has "opened His commission" by the planting of the visible

ἐμέ· 10 περὶ δικαιοσυνης δέ, ὅτι πρὸς τὸν πατέρα [μου]
m ὑπάγω καὶ οὐκ ἔτι θεωρεῖτέ με· 11 περὶ δὲ κρίσεως, ὅτι m ver. 5.
ὁ n ἄρχων τοῦ n κόσμου τούτου κέκριται. 12 ἔτι πολλὰ n ch. xii. 31 reff.

10. om μου BDLℵ 1. 33 vulg lat-*a b e ff₂ g l* [syr-jer] coptt æth Chr₁ Cyr₁ Victorin₁: ins A rel lat-*c f q* syrr goth [arm].

Church, is *the condemning sin* of the world. Of this He shall *convince* those who are brought out of the world, and ultimately *convict* those who remain in it and die in their sins (see Hare, Mission of the Comforter, vol. ii. note Q).

10.] **δικαιοσ.** cannot be *only* the righteousness *of Christ*, the mere conviction of which would only bring condemnation to that world which rejected and crucified Him: but, as Stier remarks rightly (v. 312, edn. 2), τοῦ κόσμου must be supplied after each of the three ἁμαρτία, δικαιοσύνη, κρίσις:—the conviction being of a sin that is *theirs*, a righteousness that is (or, in the case of condemnation, might have been) *theirs*, a judgment which is *theirs* (see below). Then, *what is the world's righteousness?* Not their own, but that of the accepted Man Christ Jesus standing at the right hand of God (seen by us no more, but by that very withdrawal testified to be the Son of God, THE RIGHTEOUS ONE), manifested in the hearts of men by the Spirit to be *their only* righteousness;—and thereby that righteousness, which they had of their own before, is demonstrated to be worthless and as filthy rags. It is the ὑπάγειν πρὸς τὸν πατέρα by which this righteousness is assured to us, and by the effect of which, the Spirit, the conviction respecting it is wrought in our hearts (see Hare, as above, note T). The *condemnatory* side of this part of the ἔλεγχος is,—that *remorse*, wherewith they whose day of grace is past shall look on the perfect righteousness which might have been theirs, and on the miserable substitute with which they contented themselves.

11.] As δικαιοσύνη was *the world's righteousness*, and the ἔλεγχος of it was the manifesting to them how worthless it (their δικαιοσύνη after its old conception) was of their own by nature, but how perfect and complete it (the same as now newly and more worthily apprehended) is in and by Christ,—so now κρίσις is *the world's judgment:—on the one side, their judgment* or estimate, or discrimination of things,—on the other side, *God's judgment*, to which it is opposed. This their judgment by nature they form in subjection to the prince of this world, the Devil, of whose power they are not conscious, and whose existence they even deny: but the Spirit of God ἐλέγξει, shall convict this judgment of wrong;—shall shew them how erroneous and destructive it is, and what a bondage they have been under;—shall detect to them the Prince of this world reigning in the children of disobedience, and give them *a better judgment*, by which they shall "not be ignorant of his devices" (2 Cor. ii. 11). But this better judgment itself is that very truth of God manifested in the Lord Jesus, by which (ch. xii. 31) *the Prince of this world is cast out;*—by which the follower of Christ is enabled to say, "Get thee behind me, Satan;" by which the unbelieving world, and its Prince, are finally condemned in *the judgment* hereafter (see Hare, as above, note V). I have preferred giving pointedly what I believe to be the sense of this most important passage, to stringing together a multitude of opinions on it: seeing that of even the best Commentators no two bring out exactly the same shade of meaning, and thus classification is next to impossible. I sincerely recommend the student to read the notes in Archdeacon Hare's work, where he will find the whole literature of the subject, with the exception of Stier's second edition, and Luthardt's commentary, which have been published since. It will be seen that in my view the subjective and objective bearing of the three words are *both* to be kept in sight, and that the great convictive work of the Spirit is to bring man OUT OF HIMSELF INTO CHRIST, Who (in His objective manifestation) must be *made unto him* (subjectively), (1) **ἀπολύτρωσις**, (2) **δικαιοσύνη**, (3) **σοφία** (the fourth, ἁγιασμός, not being here treated of, as being another part of the Spirit's work, and on those who are no longer the κόσμος, see ch. xvii. 16, 17); and to condemn those who remain in the world finally, in all these points, as having rejected Christ. And this convictive work of the Spirit is a *complex* and *progressive* work; including the ministry of the Apostles, and every step taken towards divine truth in the history of the Church, as well as the conversion of individuals, and condemnation of the unbelieving.

12.] The **πολλά** are the things belonging to πᾶσα ἡ ἀλήθεια in the next verse, which were gradually

o = Matt. viii. 17. xx. 12. 4 Kings xviii. 14.
p ch. xiv. 17 reff.
q Matt. xv. 14. Luke vi. 39. Acts viii. 31. Rev. vii. 17 only. Ps. xxiv. 5. lxxxv. 11. cxviii. 35.
r Mark v. 33.
u ch. xii. 28.

ἔχω ὑμῖν λέγειν, ἀλλ᾽ οὐ δύνασθε ° βαστάζειν ἄρτι· 13 ὅταν
δὲ ἔλθῃ ἐκεῖνος, τὸ p πνεῦμα τῆς p ἀληθείας, q ὁδηγήσει
ὑμᾶς εἰς τὴν ἀλήθειαν r πᾶσαν· οὐ γὰρ λαλήσει s ἀφ᾽
ἑαυτοῦ, ἀλλ᾽ ὅσα ἀκούσει λαλήσει, καὶ τὰ ἐρχόμενα t ἀναγγελεῖ ὑμῖν. 14 ἐκεῖνος ἐμὲ u δοξάσει, ὅτι v ἐκ τοῦ ἐμοῦ
λήμψεται, καὶ t ἀναγγελεῖ ὑμῖν. 15 πάντα ὅσα ἔχει ὁ

ABDE GHKL MSUY ΓΔΛΠא 1. 33. 69. Frag. Nitr. vv. 12, 13.

s ch. v. 19 reff. t ch. iv. 25. Acts xx. 20, 27. 1 Pet. i. 12. Isa. xliv. 7. v constr., ch. i. 16.

12. rec *λεγειν* bef *υμιν*, with AD Frag-nitr rel lat-*a* syrr [syr-jer arm] copt goth $Orig_1[int_1]$ Eus_2 Did_1 Chr_1 $Thdrt_1$ $Tert_3$ Hil_1: txt BLYא 33 vulg lat-*b c e f* [*ff_2 g l*] $Orig_1[int_2]$ $Tert_2$ Hil_1 spec. ins *αυτα* bef *βασταζειν* D lat-*a b c e ff_2* copt [$Orig\text{-}int_3$] $Tert_{alic}$ Hil_2. om *αρτι* $א^1$.

13. om *δε* D Scr's d ev-y_1 lat-*e* arm $Orig_1$ $Tert_3$ Hil_1. aft *αληθ.* ins *εκεινος* D (lat-*a*) Syr [syr-jer] ($Orig\text{-}int_2$ $Tert_1$ $Novat_1$). *υμας* bef *οδηγ.* D lat-*a* $Tert_{alic}$ $Novat_1$ Vig. rec *πασαν* bef *την αληθ.*, with Frag-nitr rel vulg lat-*a f* Bas_1 $Epiph_1$ Chr_1 $Thdrt_1$ $Tert_{alic}$ Novat Hil_2: *εν τη αληθεια παση* (*εν is more common aft οδηγεω, see reff to Psalms: and thus the copyist substd it*) DL א(but om *παση* $א^1$) 1. 33 mss-in-Aug lat-*b c e ff_2*[Sabat] *l* [arm] Cyr[-p_1 $Victorin_1$]: txt ABY Petr $Orig_2$ Eus Cyr[-p_2]. [*αλλα* D.] rec aft *οσα* ins *αν*, with D^2 rel, *εαν* AK[Π]: om BD^1Lא 1 $Orig_1$ $Marcell_1$ Ath_2 $Cyr\text{-}jer_1$ $Epiph_1$ [$Cyr\text{-}p_1$]. rec *ακουση*, with A rel Eus: txt BDE^1HY 1 $Orig_1$ [$Marcell_1$] Eus_1 Ath_1 $Cyr\text{-}jer_1$ $Epiph_1$, *ακουει* Lא 33 [$Cyr\text{-}p_1$] $Ambr_1$. (for *υμιν*, *ημιν* א-corr, appy.)

15. om ver (*homœotel*) $א^1$.

unfolded after the Ascension, by the Spirit. **13.**] **ἐκεῖνος**, emphatical, as in ver. 8: see note, ch. vii. 29. **τὴν ἀλήθ. πᾶσαν**] **all the truth**, viz. on those points alluded to in ver. 12. Lücke observes that the rec. reading connects πᾶσαν more with ὁδηγήσει, the other with ἀλήθ. The Lord had ever told them *the truth*, and *nothing but the truth*, in spiritual things,—but not yet *the whole truth*, because they could not bear it. This the Spirit should lead them into, open the way to it, and unfold it by degrees. No promise of universal knowledge, nor of infallibility, is hereby conveyed; but a promise to them and us, that the Holy Spirit shall teach and lead us, not as children, under the tutors and governors of legal and imperfect knowledge, but as sons (Gal. iv. 6), making known to us the whole truth of God. This was in an especial manner fulfilled to *them*, as set to be the founders and teachers of the Churches. **οὐ γὰρ λαλ. ἀφ᾽ ἑαυτ.**] The Spirit does not, any more than the Son, work or speak *of Himself:* both are sent, the one from the Father, the other from the Father and Son: the one to testify ὅσα ἀκούσει of the Father, the other of the Father and the Son. **ὅσα ἀκ.**, from God, the Father and the Son. **τὰ ἐρχ. ἀναγ. ὑμ.**] As the *direct* fulfilment *to the Apostles* of the leading into the whole truth was the unfolding before them those truths which they have delivered down to us in their Epistles,—so, though scattered traces of the fulfilment of *this part* of the promise are found in the Acts and those Epistles, its complete fulfilment was the giving of the Apocalypse, in which τὰ ἐρχόμενα are distinctly the subject of the Spirit's revelation, and with which His *direct* testimony closes: see Rev. i. 1; xxii. 6, 20. On the whole of this verse, see Eph. iv. 7—16. **14.**] Notice the emphatic **ἐμέ**, prefixed to the verb. This is in connexion with ver. 12—and sets forth that the *Spirit guiding into* truth is in fact *the Son declaring* the truth, for He shall shew forth the glory of Christ, by revealing the matters of Christ,—the riches of the Father's love in Him (ver. 15). "Œconomia trium testium: patrem glorificat filius, filium Spiritus sanctus." Bengel. This verse is decisive against all additions and pretended revelations subsequent to and besides Christ; it being the work of the Spirit to testify to and declare THE THINGS OF CHRIST; not any thing new and beyond Him. And this declaration is coincident with inward advance in the likeness and image of Christ (2 Cor. iii. 17, 18), not with a mere external development. **15.**] Here we have given us a glimpse into the essential relations of the Blessed Trinity. The Father hath given the Son to have life and all things in Himself (Col. i. 19; ii. 2, 3), the relation being, that the Son glorifies not Himself but the Father, by revealing the Father, whom He alone knows (Matt. xi.

Frag. Nitr. contains vv. 15, 16.

πατὴρ ἐμά ἐστιν· διὰ τοῦτο εἶπον ὅτι [v] ἐκ τοῦ ἐμοῦ λαμβάνει καὶ [t] ἀναγγελεῖ ὑμῖν.
16 [w] Μικρὸν καὶ [x] οὐκέτι θεωρεῖτέ με, καὶ πάλιν [w] μικρὸν
καὶ [y] ὄψεσθέ με. 17 Εἶπον οὖν [z] ἐκ τῶν μαθητῶν αὐτοῦ
πρὸς ἀλλήλους [a] Τί ἐστιν τοῦτο ὃ λέγει ἡμῖν, [w] μικρὸν
καὶ οὐ θεωρεῖτέ με, καὶ πάλιν [w] μικρὸν καὶ [y] ὄψεσθέ με; καὶ
ὅτι [b] ὑπάγω πρὸς τὸν πατέρα; 18 ἔλεγον οὖν Τοῦτο τί
ἐστιν ὃ λέγει [w] μικρόν; οὐκ [c] οἴδαμεν τί λαλεῖ. 19 ἔγνω
Ἰησοῦς ὅτι ἤθελον αὐτὸν ἐρωτᾶν, καὶ εἶπεν αὐτοῖς Περὶ
τούτου [d] ζητεῖτε μετ᾽ ἀλλήλων, ὅτι εἶπον [w] Μικρὸν καὶ οὐ
θεωρεῖτέ με, καὶ πάλιν [w] μικρὸν καὶ [y] ὄψεσθέ με; 20 ἀμὴν
ἀμὴν λέγω ὑμῖν ὅτι κλαύσετε καὶ [e] θρηνήσετε ὑμεῖς, ὁ δὲ

Frag. Nitr. contains vv. 18, 19.

w ch. xiii. 33 reff.
x ver. 10.
y Matt. v. 8. Luke iii. 6, from Isa. xl. 5. ch. iii. 36. Rom. xv. 21. Heb. xii. 14. 1 John iii. 2.
z ch. ix. 40. 2 John 4. Rev. ii. 10 al.
a = Luke viii. 9 reff.
b vv. 5, 10.
c = Mark iv. 13 al.
d = here only. (-τησις, ch. iii. 25 reff.) see 1 Pet. i. 10.
e Matt. xi. 17 ‖ L. Luke xxiii. 27 only. Jer. ix. 17.

aft *ειπον* ins *υμιν* Lℵ^{3a} 249 lat-*a e f* [*q* syr-jer] syrr copt-dz æth arm [Cyr-jer$_1$ Cyr$_1$ Non$_1$. *αναγγελλει* ℵ^{3a} goth].

16. rec (for *ουκετι*) *ου*, with A rel lat-*a e f q* [D-lat] Syr copt goth(Treg) æth Chr-montf[-txt] Cyr[-com-p$_2$]: txt B D-gr LΛℵ Frag-nitr **1.** 33 vulg lat-*b c ff*$_2$ *g* syr arm Orig$_1$ Chr[-com$_1$] Cyr[-p$_3$] Non$_1$. rec adds at end *οτι εγω υπαγω προς τον πατερα* (*to suit ver* 17: *see on εγω there*), with A Frag-nitr rel vulg lat-*c f q* [*ff*$_2$(Blanch) *g* syr-jer] syrr copt goth æth-pl Cyr[-p$_{expr}$], but of these all but Y [lat-*f*] copt arm om *εγω*: om BDLℵ lat-*a b e ff*$_2$[Sabat] sah æth-mss Orig$_1$.

17. om 1st *μικρον* to *παλιν* (*homœotel*) ℵ^1. for *ου*, *ουκετι* D-gr 33. for *θεωρειτε*, *οψεσθε* D. for *οτι*, *ω* ℵ^1. rec ins *εγω* bef *υπαγω* (*from ch* xiv. 12), with D rel lat-*f* syr: om ABLMΛ[Π]ℵ 33 vulg lat-*b* &c æth.

18. om *ελεγον ουν* D^1[and lat](ins D^6-gr) Scr's g lat-*a b e*. *τι εστιν* bef *τουτο* (*more usual arrangement*) BD^{1}LY[Π^2]ℵ **1.** 33. 69 latt [Syr syr-jer copt æth arm] Orig$_1$: txt A D^6-gr Frag-nitr rel syr goth. om *ο λεγει* D^1(ins D^6-gr) ℵ^1. rec ins *το* bef *μικρον*, with AD[ℵ] rel arm: om BLY Orig. (Frag-nitr def.) for *τι λαλει*, *ο λεγει* D^1(txt D^6) lat-*c*: om B æth.

19. rec aft *εγνω* ins *ουν*, with A Frag-nitr rel; *δε* U[Π] Scr's p w vulg lat-*f g q* syrr goth: om BDLℵ **1.** 33 lat-*a b* copt arm. rec ins *ο* bef *ιησ.*, with ADℵ Frag-nitr rel: om BL. for *ηθελον*, *ημελλον* ℵ 69 lat-*c ff*$_2$. for *ερωταν*, *επερωτησαι περι τουτου* D. om *αυτοις* A 96 gat.

20. *θρηνησητε* ℵ^1(but corrd *eadem manu*).

27). And this Revelation, the Revelation of the Father by Christ—is carried on by the blessed Spirit in the hearts of the disciples of Christ; Who takes (**λαμβάνει**, indefinite, of the *office* of the Spirit) of the things of Christ, and declares, proclaims, to them. **διὰ τοῦτο**] **For this cause I** (rightly) **said . . . .** i. e. 'this was the ground of My asserting:'—not the reason *why it was said*, but the justification of it when said. This verse contains the plainest proof by inference of the orthodox doctrine of the Holy Trinity.

16—24.] *The Lord speaks of His withdrawal, and its immediate mournful, but ultimate* (and those soon to begin) *joyful consequences for His disciples.* The connexion is: "Very soon will the Spirit, the Comforter, come to you: for I go to the Father, without any real cessation of the communion between you and Me." Lücke. **16.**] The mode of expression is (purposely) enigmatical;—the **θεωρεῖτε** and **ὄψεσθε** not being co-ordinate;—the first referring merely to physical, the second also to spiritual sight. So before, ch. xiv. 19, where see note. The *ὄψεσθε began to be fulfilled* at the Resurrection;—then received its *main fulfilment* at the day of Pentecost;—and shall have its *final completion* at the great return of the Lord hereafter. Remember again, that in all these prophecies we have a perspective of continually unfolding fulfilments presented to us: see note on ch. xiv. 3. **17, 18.**] The disciples are perplexed by this *μικρόν*, as connected with what our Lord had before asserted ver. 10, *ὑπάγω πρὸς τ. πατέρα*. *That* seemed to them a long and hopeless withdrawal: how was it then to be reconciled with what he now said of a short absence? What was this **μικρόν**? This connexion not being observed has led to the insertion of *ὅτι ἐγὼ ὑπάγω πρ. τ. πατ.* in ver. 16.

19.] The real difficulty being in

κόσμος χαρήσεται· ὑμεῖς λυπηθήσεσθε, ἀλλὰ ἡ λύπη ὑμῶν εἰς χαρὰν [f] γενήσεται. 21 ἡ γυνὴ ὅταν [g] τίκτῃ, [h] λύπην [h] ἔχει, ὅτι [i] ἦλθεν ἡ [i] ὥρα αὐτῆς· ὅταν δὲ γεννήσῃ τὸ παιδίον, οὐκ ἔτι [k] μνημονεύει τῆς [l] θλίψεως, διὰ τὴν χαρὰν ὅτι ἐγεννήθη ἄνθρωπος εἰς τὸν κόσμον. 22 καὶ ὑμεῖς οὖν νῦν μὲν [h] λύπην [h] ἔχετε· πάλιν δὲ [m] ὄψομαι ὑμᾶς, καὶ [n] χαρήσεται ὑμῶν ἡ [n] καρδία, καὶ τὴν χαρὰν ὑμῶν οὐδεὶς

ABDE GHKL MSUY ΓΔΛΠℵ 1. 33. 69

C οτι εγενηθη ...

f Matt. xxi. 42 ||, from Ps. cxvii. 22. Acts v. 36. Rev. viii. 11. xvi. 19.
g Matt. i. 21 reff.
h here bis. 2 Cor. ii. 3. Phil. ii. 27 only.
i see ch. vii. 30 al.
k ch. xv. 20 reff.
l = here only. see Jer. vi. 24.
m of a divine person, here only. (see Heb. xiii. 23.)
n Isa. lxvi. 14. Zech. x. 7 bis.

rec ins δε bef λυπηθ. (*to contrast with ο κοσμ. χαρ.*), with Aℵ[3a] rel vulg lat-*g* syr Orig$_1$[int$_1$] Cyr$_1$: om BDΛℵ[1] 1 lat-*a b c* [*e ff$_2$ q*] syr-jer copt goth arm [Tert$_1$] Cypr$_2$. (αλλα, so DLUYΓΛ.)

21. for ωρα, ημερα D 248 lat-*a b c e ff$_2$* Syr. for γενν., γενηση A. for θλιψεως, λυπης D foss lat-*c* Ambr$_1$. for εγενν., εγενηθη C: txt A[B]Dℵ rel. ins ο bef ανθρωπος ℵ[1](corrd ℵ[(1 ?)]-corr[1·3]).

22. rec transp νυν and λυπην, with AC[3] rel: νυν μεν ουν λυπην ℵ[1]: txt BC[1]DL MYℵ[3a] 1. 33 vulg lat-*b c e f ff$_2$* [*q*] syrr (copt goth arm) Chr-ms$_1$ Hil$_1$. εξετε (*conformn to fut above, ver* 20) ADLℵ[3a] 33 am(with fuld mt) lat-*a b e* Antch$_1$ Chr-

μικρόν, our Lord applies himself only to this, not noticing the other part of the question: which confirms the view of the connexion taken above. **20.**] **κλαύσ. κ. θρην.** are to be literally taken: see Luke xxiii. 27. They would mourn for Him as dead: see also ch. xx. 11. **ὑμεῖς**, emphatic, as opposed to **ὁ κόσμος**. And the joy of the world found its first exponent in the scoffs of the passers-by at the crucifixion. **λυπηθ.**] This goes deeper than the weeping and wailing before: and plainly shews that the whole does not *only* refer to the grief while the Lord was in the tomb, but to the grief continually manifesting itself in the course and conflict of the Christian, which is turned into joy by the advancing work of the Spirit of Christ:—and, in the completion of the sense, to the grief and widowhood of the Church during her present state, which will be turned into joy at the coming of her Lord. **εἰς χαρ. γεν.**, not merely *changed for* joy, but **changed into** so as *itself to become*,—so that the very matter of grief shall become matter of joy; as Christ's Cross of shame has become the glory of the Christian, Gal. vi. 14.

21.] The 'tertium comparationis' is ἡ λύπη εἰς χαρὰν γενήσεται: but the comparison itself goes far beyond this mere similitude. **ἡ γυνή** is not merely generic, but allusive to the frequent use and notoriety of the comparison. We often have it in the O. T.,—see Isa. xxi. 3; xxvi. 17, 18; xxxvii. 3; lxvi. 7, 8: Hosea xiii. 13, 14: Micah iv. 9, 10.

τίκτῃ] **is bringing forth**, viz. παιδίον, expressed in **τὸ π.** below. **ἡ ὥρα αὐτ.**] **her** (appointed) **time.** **τὸ παιδ.** not necessarily masculine ("non puella sed puer," Aug.), but indefinite. The deeper reference of the comparison has been well described by Olshausen: "Here arises the question, how are we to understand this similitude? We might perhaps think that the suffering Manhood of Christ was *the woman in her pangs*, and the same Christ glorified in the Resurrection, *the Man born;* but the Redeemer (ver. 22) applies the pangs to the *disciples:* how then will the ἄνθρωπος who is born apply to them?" Then, after condemning the shallow and unsatisfactory method of avoiding deep research by asserting that the details of parables are not to be interpreted, he proceeds: "Hence the proper import of the figure seems to be, that the Death of Jesus Christ was as it were an anguish of birth belonging to all Humanity (ein schmerzvoller Geburtsact der ganzen Menschheit) in which the perfect Man was born into the world; and in this very birth of the new man lies the spring of eternal joy, never to be lost, for all, inasmuch as through Him and His power the renovation of the whole is rendered possible" (ii. 379). And indeed the same is true of every Christian who is planted in the likeness of Christ. His passing from sorrow to joy—till "Christ be formed in him," is this birth of pain. And the whole Church, the Spouse of Christ,—nay, even the whole Creation, συνωδίνει, till the number of the elect be accomplished, and the eternal joy brought in. And thus the meaning which Luthardt insists on as against the above remarks of Olshausen, viz. *the new birth of the Church*, is in inner truth the same as his.

22.] **ὄψομαι**—in the same manifold

X εν εκεινη... ἀρεῖ ἀφ' ὑμῶν, 23 καὶ ἐν ἐκείνῃ τῇ ἡμέρᾳ ἐμὲ οὐκ ἐρωτή-
σετε οὐδέν. ἀμὴν ἀμὴν λέγω ὑμῖν, [o] ἄν τι αἰτήσητε τὸν
πατέρα, δώσει ὑμῖν [p] ἐν τῷ ὀνόματί μου· 24 [q] ἕως ἄρτι οὐκ
ᾐτήσατε οὐδὲν [p] ἐν τῷ ὀνόματί μου· αἰτεῖτε, καὶ λήμψεσθε,
ἵνα ἡ [r] χαρὰ ὑμῶν ᾖ [r] πεπληρωμένη. 25 Ταῦτα ἐν [s] παροιμίαις λελάληκα ὑμῖν· [t] ἔρχεται ὥρα ὅτε οὐκ ἔτι ἐν
[s] παοοιμίαις λαλήσω ὑμῖν, ἀλλὰ [u] παῤῥησίᾳ περὶ τοῦ

o ch. xiii. 20. xx. 23 (bis) only.
p ch. xiv. 13, 14 reff.
q Matt. xi. 12. ch. ii. 10 al.
r ch. iii. 29 reff.
s = here bis. ver. 29. (ch. x. 6.) 2 Pet. ii. 22 only. Prov. i. 1.
t ch. iv. 21, 23 reff.
u = ch. x. 24 reff.

mss$_1$, εξητε L. rec αιρει, with AC D^1-corr ℵ rel am[fuld] lat-*b e f* [*q*] syrr(Treg) goth [Antch$_1$]: txt BD^{1}Γ vulg lat-*a c ff$_2$* copt æth [Cyr-p$_1$] Orig-int$_1$ Cypr$_1$ Hil$_1$.

23. (ερωτησηται (*itacism*) ℵ [Λ(-τε)].) rec aft υμιν ins οτι, with AD^{4}ℵ rel lat-*a c* syrr(Treg) goth Chr$_1$: om BCD^{1}LY vulg lat-*b* [*e ff$_2$ g q*] Orig$_1$ Cyr$_2$[Quæst$_1$]. rec (for αν τι) οσα αν, with E rel Syr, οσα εαν KM Chr$_1$: αν (alone) A: ο εαν X[Π] 33 syr [syr-jer] goth æth: ο αν ℵ Scr's d p: txt BCLY^1 copt latt Orig$_1$ [Cyr-p$_1$] Ambr, εαν τι DY^2 Orig$_1$ Ath$_1$. rec εν τω ον. μου bef δωσει υμιν (*see ch* xiv. 13), with AC^{3}D rel vss Chr$_1$: txt BC^{1}LXYΔℵ sah[-mnt] Orig$_2$ Cyr[-p$_2$].

24. for ητησατε, ητησασθε A ev-z Cyr$_1$. for αιτειτε, αιτησασθαι ℵ^1.

25. rec ins αλλ' bef ερχεται, with AC^{3}D^6[Π$^{1.3}$] rel lat-*c f ff$_2$ q* syr goth æth Orig$_1$ Ath$_1$: om BC^{1}D^{1}LXY[Π^2]ℵ 1. 33. 69 vulg lat-*a b e g* [syr-jer] coptt arm [Cyr-p$_1$] Orig[-int$_1$] Aug$_1$ [ερχ. δε Syr]. for οτε, οπου ℵ^1: [οτι Γ:] om 1. ins εν bef

meaning as before noticed—**will see you**—at My Resurrection—by My Spirit—at My second Advent. **23.**] **ἐν ἐκείνῃ τῇ ἡμ.**, in its full meaning, cannot import *the forty days*: for, Acts i. 6, they did then *ask* the Lord *questions* (the sense of ἐρωτᾶν, see vv. 19, 30, not ver. 26, where the construction is different);—nor this present dispensation of the Spirit, during which we have only the first-fruits, but not the full understanding so as not to need to ask any thing: (for is not *prayer itself* an *asking?*)—but that great completion of the Christian's hope, when he shall be with his Lord, when all doubt shall be resolved, and prayer shall be turned into praise. The Resurrection-visiting and the Pentecost-visiting of them, were but foretastes of this. Stier well remarks, "The connexion of the latter part of this verse is,—The way to οὐδὲν ἐρωτᾶν any more, is to ask and to pray the more diligently, till that day comes." It has been supposed wrongly that ἐμέ and τὸν πατέρα are in opposition in this verse, and thence gathered (Origen de Orat. § 15, vol. i. p. 222, λέγεται (al. λείπεται) τοίνυν προσεύχεσθαι μόνῳ τῷ θεῷ τῷ τῶν ὅλων πατρί· ἀλλὰ μὴ χωρὶς τοῦ ἀρχιερέως, κ.τ.λ.) that it is not lawful to address prayer to Christ. But such an opposition is contrary to the whole spirit of these discourses,—and *asking the Father in Christ's name*, is in fact *asking* HIM.

In the latter clause, notice the right reading: **He shall give it you in my name**, He being, as Luthardt expresses it, the *element*, the *region*, of all communication between God and the Church. Cf. Rom. i. 8, where *thanks* are offered διὰ Ἰησοῦ χριστοῦ. **24.**] It was impossible, up to the time of the glorification of Jesus (ἕως ἄρτι, proleptical, as before), to pray to the Father in His Name. It is a fulness of joy peculiar to the dispensation of the Spirit, to be able so to do, Eph. ii. 18. **αἰτεῖτε**] See Matt. vii. 7, and mark the difference between the command then and now,—that ἐν τῷ ὀν. μου is added.

25—33.] *Their present real weakness and imperfection, though fancied strength: their future high blessedness and share in His triumph, though in tribulation in the world.* **25.**] **παροιμία**, properly, a *proverb*:—but implying generally in Scriptural and oriental usage something dark and enigmatical: see especially Sir. vi. 35; viii. 8; xxxix. 3; xlvii. 17: "in dictis tectioribus," Bengel. This is true of the whole discourse—and of the discourses of the Lord in general, as they must then have seemed to them, before the Holy Spirit furnished the key to their meaning. **ἔρχεται ὥρα**, viz. the same as that indicated in vv. 16 and 23;—but here again, not one ὥρα only exclusive of all others, but to be understood of the several steps of spiritual knowledge. Olshausen finely remarks, that all human language is a παροιμία, only able to hint at, not to express fully, the things of God; and that the Lord contrasts the use of this weak and insufficient medium, with the inward teaching of the Holy Spirit. This inward teaching, because it is a real imparting of the divine Nature and Life, brings with it not only *prayer in the name of Jesus*, but a *free access to the Father*

πατρὸς [v] ἀπαγγελῶ ὑμῖν. 26 ἐν ἐκείνῃ τῇ ἡμέρᾳ [p] ἐν τῷ ABCDE GHKL
ὀνόματί μου αἰτήσεσθε, καὶ οὐ λέγω ὑμῖν ὅτι ἐγὼ [w] ἐρωτήσω MSUX
τὸν πατέρα περὶ ὑμῶν· 27 αὐτὸς γὰρ ὁ πατὴρ φιλεῖ ὑμᾶς, ΥΓΔΛ Πא
ὅτι ὑμεῖς ἐμὲ πεφιλήκατε, καὶ πεπιστεύκατε ὅτι ἐγὼ παρὰ 1. 33. 69
τοῦ πατρὸς [x] ἐξῆλθον. 28 [x] ἐξῆλθον ἐκ τοῦ πατρὸς καὶ
[y] ἐλήλυθα [y] εἰς τὸν κόσμον· πάλιν [z] ἀφίημι τὸν κόσμον καὶ
[a] πορεύομαι [a] πρὸς τὸν [a] πατέρα. 29 Λέγουσιν οἱ μαθηταὶ
αὐτοῦ Ἴδε νῦν ἐν [b] παῤῥησίᾳ λαλεῖς, καὶ [c] παροιμίαν

v John, ch. iv. 51. 1 John i. 2, 3 only. Mt. Mk. L. (Gosp. & Acts), passim. 1 Cor. xiv. 25. 1 Thess. i. 9. Heb. ii. 12.
w constr., Luke iv. 38. ch. xvii. 9, 20. Isa. xlv. 11.
x w. παρά, ch. xvii. 8. Num. xvi. 35. ἐκ, ch. viii. 42.
y ch. i. 9 reff.
z = Matt. iv. 11 al. a ch. xiv. 12, 28. b ver. 25. ch. vii. 4. Eph. vi. 19. Phil. i. 20. Col. ii. 15 only. Wisd. v. 1. c ver. 25.

παρησια(sic) D. rec αναγγελω (*from vv.* 13, 14, 15), with C² rel Chr_1 Cyr_1 : txt ABC¹DKLMUXY[Π] א(-λλω) 33 [Cyr-p_1].

26. αιτησασθαι(sic, א) bef εν τω ον. μου א 1 copt. aft πατερα ins μου D.

27. for εμε, με Lא. om του Aא 33 Chr-montf-mss_1[txt_1]. rec (for πατρος) θεου (*from ch* xiii. 3), with AC³א¹ rel latt [syr-jer] goth æth arm [Chr] Hil_3: txt BC¹DLX א³ᵃ(but former reading restored) Syr syr-ms coptt Cyr[-p_1] Did_2.

28. rec (for εκ) παρα (*repetn of preceding*), with AC²א rel: txt BC¹LX 33 copt $Hipp_1$ $Epiph_1$.—om εξηλθ. εκ τ. πατ. D lat-*b* *ff*₂ Orig-int_2(appy). for εληλυθα, ηλθον D.

29. rec aft λεγουσιν ins αυτω, with AC³ D(Scr: D³ Kipling) rel Syr syr-mg [syr-jer æth arm] Cyr_1 Hil[-ed_1] : om BC¹ D¹(Kipl) Λ[Π]א 1 lat-*e* *q* syr[-txt] goth Hil-ms_1.—for αυτου, αυτω (*itacism?*) א¹ [add αυτω copt]. rec om εν (*overlooked after* νυν, *or conformn to ver* 25), with A rel Chr_1 Cyr_1 : ins BCDא.

Himself. This παῤῥησίᾳ λαλεῖν however, he continues, is spoken of here by the Lord in its ideal perfection (as it will hereafter be): and is only approximated to on earth; for, as long as the *old man* yet lives in us, we require still the Lord's intercessory prayer (ch. xvii. 15), daily washing from the pollution of the world; by which Intercession alone the faithful man notwithstanding his imperfection can enjoy in peace the grace of God vouchsafed to him. **26.**] "The more knowledge, the more prayer in the name of Jesus," Lücke. "Cognitio parit orationem," Bengel. The approaching the Father through Him shall be a characteristic of their higher state under the dispensation of the Spirit.

οὐ λέγω ὑμ.] This has been variously understood. Grotius's rendering, "prætereo hoc quasi minus eo quod jam inferam," comes I believe the nearest to the truth, though it does not express the whole meaning. The Lord is now describing the fulness of their state of communion with Himself and the Father by the Spirit. He is setting in the strongest light their reconciliation and access to the Father. He therefore says, **Ye shall ask the Father in My name: and I do not now say to you,**—I do not now state it in this form,—**that I will ask the Father for you**—as if there were no relation of love and mercy *between the Father and yourselves:*—(27) **for the Father** *Himself* (αὐτός, i. e. αὐτοκέλευτος (Nonnus)—'proprio motu') **loveth you;**—why? **Because ye love and believe on Me.** The whole mind of the Father towards mankind is *Love:* both in Redemption itself (ch. iii. 16),—and then in an especial manner by drawing those who come to Christ (vi. 44),—and again by this fuller manifestation of His love to those who believe on and love Christ. The aim of this saying is to shew them that His intercession (which is still going on under the dispensation of the Spirit, 1 John ii. 1) does not imply their *exclusion from access* to the Father, but rather *ensures that access,* by the especial love which the Father bears to them who believe in and love His Son: CHRIST being still the efficient cause of the Father's love to them, and the channel of that Love. No stress must be laid (Lücke) on πεφιλήκατε here coming before πεπιστεύκατε, as to Faith coming after Love: probably πεφιλ. is placed first as corresponding to φιλεῖ just before:—and it might be said with just as much reason that καὶ πεπιστεύκατε . . . contains the ground of the πεφιλ., as the converse. **28.**] "Recapitulationem maximam habet hic versus," Bengel. 'And your belief is sound: for I did indeed come forth' . . . . see ch. xiii. 3. "Exiit a Patre, quia de Patre est; in mundum venit, quia mundo suum corpus ostendit quod de virgine assumpsit; reliquit mundum corporali discessione, perrexit ad Patrem hominis adscensione, nec mundum deseruit præsentiæ gubernatione." Aug. Tract.

οὐδεμίαν λέγεις. 30 νῦν οἴδαμεν ὅτι οἶδας πάντα καὶ οὐ
[d] χρείαν [d] ἔχεις [d] ἵνα τίς σε ἐρωτᾷ· [e] ἐν τούτῳ πιστεύομεν
ὅτι [f] ἀπὸ θεοῦ [f] ἐξῆλθες. 31 ἀπεκρίθη αὐτοῖς Ἰησοῦς,
Ἄρτι πιστεύετε· 32 ἰδοὺ [g] ἔρχεται ὥρα καὶ ἐλήλυθεν, [h] ἵνα
[i] σκορπισθῆτε ἕκαστος εἰς [j] τὰ [j] ἴδια κἀμὲ μόνον [k] ἀφῆτε·
[l] καὶ οὐκ εἰμὶ μόνος, ὅτι ὁ πατὴρ μετ' ἐμοῦ ἐστιν. 33 ταῦτα
λελάληκα ὑμῖν, ἵνα ἐν ἐμοὶ εἰρήνην ἔχητε. ἐν τῷ κόσμῳ
[mn] θλῖψιν [n] ἔχετε· ἀλλὰ [o] θαρσεῖτε, ἐγὼ [pq] νενίκηκα τὸν
[q] κόσμον.

d constr., ch. ii. 25. 1 John ii. 27 only.
e = Matt. vi. 7. 2 Cor. viii. 20.
f ch. xiii. 3. see ref. (x) above.
g ver. 25.
h = ver. 2 (see note there).
i Luke xi. 23 ||. ch. x. 12. 2 Cor. ix. 9 (from Ps. cxi. 9) only. 2 Kings xxii. 15.
j ch. i. 11 reff.
k = ch. xiv. 18 reff.
l = ch. vii. 28.
m John (Gosp)., ver. 21 only.
n 1 Cor. vii. 28. Rev. ii. 10. Sir. li. 3.
o Matt. ix. 2, 22. xiv. 27 || Mk. Mark x. 49. Acts xxiii. 11 only. Gen. xxxv. 17.
p Gospp., Luke xi. 22 only. Rom. iii. 4 (from Ps. l. 4 [6]). xii. 21 bis. 1 John ii. 13, 14 al[4]. Rev. ii. 7 al[15].
q 1 John v. 4 bis, 5.

30. for *απο*, *παρα* D.
31. rec ins *ο* bef *ιησ*., with ADℵ rel [Bas$_1$]: om BC.—(om *ιησ*. S 47. 56-8.)
32. rec ins *νυν* bef *εληλ*. (*cf ch* v. 25), with C^{2}D^4 rel latt syrr goth (æth) [Bas$_1$] Hil$_1$: om ABC^{1}D^{1}LXℵ 33 [syr-jer arm] coptt Constt$_1$. aft *εληλ*. ins *η ωρα* ℵ^1. (*καμε*, so BC^{1}Lℵ 1.)
33. rec (for *εχετε*) *εξετε*, with D 69 latt goth(Treg) æth arm Orig$_3$ Eus$_1$ Chr$_1$ [Cyr-p$_3$] Cypr$_1$ Hil$_1$: txt ABCℵ rel forj(with foss mm san) (lat-*e*) syrr copt Orig-mss$_2$ Constt$_1$ Eus$_2$ Bas$_1$ [Cyr-p$_1$] Thdrt$_1$.

cii. 6. **29, 30.**] The stress is on **νῦν**: q. d. why announce that as *future*, which Thou art doing *now?* The hour was not yet come for the *ἐν παῤῥησίᾳ λαλεῖν*: so that we must understand the disciples' remark to be made in weakness, however true their persuasion, and heartfelt their confession. "Usque adeo non intelligunt, ut nec saltem se non intelligere intelligant. Parvuli enim erant." Aug. Tract. ciii. 1. "Dolent, se a Magistro pro imperitis haberi, qui conciones ejus non intelligant, alioque doctore, promisso Spiritu, indigeant. Quare eo usque progrediuntur, ut Christo contradicant, et clarissima ejus verba invertant, eumque parœmiastice locutum esse negent." Lampe, vol. iii. 350. But by *νῦν* they probably only mean, in ver. 26—28. **30.**] 'Thou hast spoken so clearly of our feeling towards Thee, and of Thyself, that we have no occasion to ask Thee any thing;—and this was what Thou didst announce would be;—we know therefore, by its being so, that Thou knowest the secrets of our hearts (*πάντα* by inference),—and hence believe that Thou camest forth from God:' the whole being a misunderstanding of what had gone before, vv. 23, 25. **31.**] Our Lord does not clear up their misunderstanding, but leaves that for the coming day of the Spirit. He only assures them that their belief, though sincere and loving, was not so deeply grounded in knowledge of Him and His appointed course as they imagined.

ἄρτι πιστ. is *not a question:* this very belief was by our Lord recognized and commended, see ch. xvii. 8, also Matt. xvi. 17, 18. And as Stier remarks (v. 369, edn. 2), "it was the aim and purpose of the whole prophetic office of Jesus, to prepare some first disciples (not the Apostles alone) for the reception of the Spirit of Truth and the fruits of His Death, by grounding in them firm belief in His Person." He therefore recognizes their faith; but shews them how weak it as yet was.

32.] See Matt. xxvi. 31, to which same prophecy the reference here is.

εἰς τὰ ἴδ., "quæ antea propter Me reliquistis." Bengel: see Luke xviii. 28.

καὶ οὐκ εἰμὶ μ.] **and** (not *but:* it is a pathetic use of the copulative, and a favourite one with St. John: cf., besides ref., ch. iii. 11, 32; vi. 70; vii. 19; viii. 38, 49; x. 25; xiii. 33; xiv. 30; xvii. 11, 14, 25) **I am not alone**: the Father can never leave the Son, even in the darkest hour of His human suffering:—the apparent desertion implied in the cry "Why hast Thou forsaken me?" being perfectly consistent with this, see note, Matt. xxvii. 46.

33.] On the first clause, especially **ἐν ἐμοί,** see ch. xv. 7. This presupposes the return from the scattering in ver. 32,—the branches again gathered in the vine.

ἔχετε, of their normal state in the world. This **θλῖψις** is not only persecution *from the world*, but trouble, inward distress, *while we are in the world*,—ch. xvii. 11;—a comforting sign that we are not *of* the world (see Stier, v. 373, edn. 2). And this latter idea is implied *between* the two clauses: 'Be of good cheer; for ye belong not to the world, but to Me, who have (proleptically again, by that which is

r Matt. xvii. 8 reff. see Isa. li. 6. s ch. xvi. 21. t = ch. vii. 39 reff. u = Matt. v. 16. ix. 8, &c.

XVII. 1 Ταῦτα ἐλάλησεν ὁ Ἰησοῦς, καὶ r ἐπάρας τοὺς
ὀφθαλμοὺς αὐτοῦ εἰς τὸν οὐρανὸν εἶπεν Πάτερ, s ἐλήλυθεν
ἡ ὥρα· t δόξασόν σου τὸν υἱόν, ἵνα ὁ υἱός [σου] u δοξάσῃ

ABCDE GHKL MSUX ΥΓΔΛ Πℵ 1. 33. 69

Chap. XVII. 1. λελαληκεν ℵ ev-y_1. om ο [bef ιησ.] Bℵ. rec (for επαρας) επηρεν and ins και bef ειπεν, with AC³ rel lat-*c e f ff*$_2$ *q* syrr [syr-jer] goth æth arm Chr_1 [Non_1]: txt BC¹DL M-marg-eccles Xℵ 1. 33. 69 [vulg] lat-*a b g* copt $Orig_1$ Cyr_1. rec aft ινα ins και, with C³ rel lat-*q* sah æth arm $Orig_1$ Chr_2 Cyr[-p]: om ABC¹Dℵ 1 latt syrr copt goth $Orig_1$ Non_1[?] Hil_2 [$Victorin_1$]. (B does not omit ὁ bef υιος as the Btly collation states.) om σου (*to avoid repetn, but the repetn belongs to the solemnity of the style*) BC¹ℵ lat-*e ff*$_2$ [D-lat] $Orig_1$ [Cyr-p_1 Hil_2] $Victorin_1$: ins AC³ D-gr rel latt $Orig_1$[int_2 Cyr-p_3] Hil_3.

now at hand) overcome the world, so that it shall have no power over you, externally by persecution, or internally by temptations or discouragements.' See 1 John v. 4, 5.

Chap. XVII. 1—26.] His love in the glorification of the Son of God. *The parting prayer of the Lord Jesus:* and herein, *for Himself* (1—5): *for His disciples* (6—19): *for all believers, that they may be one* (20, 21),—*that they may be glorified in the completion of that unity* (22—24),—*for their abiding in the union of love, the perfection of divine knowledge* (25, 26). "Hoc caput in tota scriptura est verbis facillimum, sensibus profundissimum." Bengel. "Poterat Dominus noster unigenitus et coæternus Patri in forma servi et ex forma servi, si hoc opus esset, orare silentio; sed ita se Patri exhibere voluit precatorem, ut meminisset, nostrum se esse doctorem. Proinde eam, quam fecit, orationem pro nobis, notam fecit et nobis: quoniam tanti Magistri non solum apud ipsos sermocinatio, sed etiam ipsius pro ipsis ad Patrem oratio discipulorum est edificatio. Et si illorum qui hæc dicta erant audituri, profecto et nostra, qui fueramus conscripta lecturi." Aug. Tr. civ. 2. 1.] **ταῦτα,** the foregoing discourse. St. John very seldom depicts the gestures or looks of our Lord, as here. But this was an occasion of which the impression was indelible, and the upward look could not be passed over. **εἰς τὸν οὐρ.**] Nothing hereby is determined as to the locality. The guest-chamber no doubt was the place of this prayer. The eyes may be lifted to heaven in as well as out of doors; *heaven* is not the sky, but that upper region, above our own being and thoughts, where we all agree in believing God to be especially present; and which we indicate when we direct our eyes or our hands upward. The Lord, being in all such things like as we are, lifted up His eyes to heaven when addressing the Father (not His *hands,* for He prays not here as a suppliant—but as an intercessor and a High Priest, standing between earth and heaven, see ver. 24, **θέλω ἵνα . . . . .**). **καὶ εἶπεν**] It is impossible to regard the following prayer otherwise than as the *very words of our Lord Himself,*—*faithfully rendered by the beloved Apostle in the power of the Holy Spirit.* The view which has led so many of the best German Commentators (even Olshausen) to see in parts of it the words of the Evangelist, and not of our Lord, is, it seems to me, inconsistent with any earnest reception of the Gospels as truthful. If such a promise as ch. xiv. 26 was made, *and fulfilled,* then these must be the words of the Lord Himself;—and the *Greek form* of them only (and query whether even that? see Prolegg. ch. ii. § ii. (π)) can be regarded as bearing evidence of the style and manner of John. **πάτερ,** not, *Our* Father,—which He never could say,—nor, *My* Father,—which would be too great a separation between Himself and His for such a prayer (see Matt. xxvi. (39,) 42, where He prays for Himself only)—but simply Father; that Great Name in which all the mystery of Redemption is summed up. "Sic patrem absolute appellat in hac oratione dulci et prolixa quater, et cum epitheto bis, in universum nonnisi sexies, idque fere ineunte nova sermonis parte, vv. 1, 5, 11, 21, 24, 25. Talis simplicitas appellationis ante omnes decuit filium Dei." Bengel. **ἐλήλ. ἡ ὥρα**] See ch. xii. 23, 28; xiii. 31, 32. The Glorification is—the exaltation by Death and Resurrection: He prays in the Manhood and for the exaltation of the Manhood, but in virtue of His Godhead, ver. 5. **τὸν υἱόν**] He prays first objectively, to set the great matter forth in all its majesty; then subjectively, δόξασόν με σύ, ver. 5, putting *Himself* into the place of τὸν υἱόν here. **ἵνα . . .**] "These words are a proof that the Son is equal to the Father as touching His Godhead. What

σέ· 2 καθὼς ἔδωκας αὐτῷ v ἐξουσίαν πάσης σαρκός, ἵνα
w πᾶν ὃ δέδωκας αὐτῷ, x δώσει αὐτοῖς ζωὴν αἰώνιον.
3 y αὕτη δέ z ἐστιν ἡ αἰώνιος ζωή, y ἵνα a γινώσκωσίν σε
τὸν b μόνον c ἀληθινὸν b θεόν, καὶ ὃν ἀπέστειλας d Ἰησοῦν

v w. gen. obj., Matt. x. 1 reff. 1 Cor. ix. 12. Sir. x. 4. w constr., ch. vi. 39. xv. 2. Rev. ii. 26. x fut. ind. w. ἵνα, Gal. ii. 4. Rev. iii. 9. xxii. 14. 1 Pet. iii. 1 al. Exod. i. 11 A (not F). Winer, § 41. b. 1. b. y = ch. vi. 29 reff. z ch. xii. 50. 1 John v. 20. a = ch. xiv. 7. xvi. 3 al. b see ch. v. 44 reff. c 1 Thess. i. 9. 1 John v. 20. d Matt. i. 1, 18. Mark i. 1. ch. i. 17. Acts & Epp. passim. Rev. i. 1, 2, 5.

2. rec δωσῃ, with ACℵ3a rel: δωσω ℵ1: txt BEHUYΓΔΛ 1. 69.—δως L: for δωσει αυτοις, εχῃ D. for αυτοις, αυτω ℵ1 1[1] lat-*e f* Syr Hil4 [Victorin1].
3. γινωσκουσιν ADGLYΔΛ 33: txt BCℵ rel.

creature could stand before his Creator and say, 'Glorify Thou me, that I may glorify Thee?'" (Stier.) This glorifying of the Father by the Son is, the whole great result of the glorification of the Son by the Father,—the manifestation of God to and in men by the Son through the Spirit.

2.] "The causal connexion expressed by **καθώς** is this, that the glorification, the *end*, must correspond to the *beginning*, to the sending, the preparation, and office of the Son." (Lücke.) We must also bear in mind that the 'giving of power' in this verse is the *ground*, as well as the *type*, of the glorification, see Rom. i. 28: 1 Cor. i. 6: so Stier (v. 383, edn. 2). **πᾶσα σάρξ** is not only 'all mankind,' but (see Gen. vii. 15, 16, 21) *all that has life*, all that is subject to death, all that is cursed on account of sin. But of this all, *mankind* is the head and crown, and in the *full* blessings of the Lordship of Christ mankind only can participate. πᾶσα σάρξ is given by the Father from before the foundation of the world to Christ; the *whole creation* is His to rule, His to judge, by virtue of His being, in the root of that human nature, to which sovereignty over the world was given, THE SECOND AND RIGHTEOUS ADAM. But in this wide gift, there is a *more special gift*,—ὃ δέδωκας αὐτῷ in the stricter sense,—*the chosen*, they who believe on Him. And to them, and them only, He imparts the further and ineffable gift consequent on union with Him their God in the Spirit,—viz. ETERNAL LIFE (compare ch. v. 26, 27; also vi. 37).

3.] See a similar definition of a term just used, in ch. iii. 19. **δέ**, as there, is transitional; bringing out, in fact, the contrast between the incidental mention of the word, and its more solemn definition. **ἐστιν—is**; not *is the way to*. The knowledge spoken of is no mere head or heart knowledge,—the mere information of the mind, or excitation of the feelings,—but that living reality of knowledge and personal realization,—that oneness in will with God, and partaking of His nature, which IS itself life eternal:—the knowledge, love, enjoyment, of Him who is infinite, being themselves infinite. ἡ ὕπαρξις τῆς ζωῆς ἐκ τῆς τοῦ θεοῦ περιγίνεται μετοχῆς· μετοχὴ δὲ θεοῦ ἐστι τὸ γινώσκειν θεὸν καὶ ἀπολαύειν τῆς χρηστότητος αὐτοῦ. Iren. adv. Hær. iv. 20. 5, p. 254. The accusatives after γινώσκ. are purely accusatives of the person, and the emphasis is on γινώσκ. From not seeing this, various mistakes have arisen—e.g. the making τὸν μόν. ἀλ. θεόν the predicate, '*Thee to be the only true God*,' and similarly with χριστόν (which would require **τὸν χρ.**) or with ὃν ἀπέστειλας,—'*Jesus, whom Thou hast sent, to be* (*the*) *Christ*,'—or '*Jesus Christ to be Him whom Thou hast sent*.' It is rightly rendered in E. V.

The Latin Fathers (Aug., Amb., Hil.), anxious to avoid the inference unwarrantably drawn by some from this verse against the Godhead of Christ, construed: ἵνα γιν. σε κ. Ἰ. χ. ὃν ἀπ., τὸν μόνον ἀλ. θεόν,—which is of course inadmissible. Others (Chrys., Euth.), construing rightly, yet regarded Jesus Christ as included in the words μόν. ἀληθ. θεόν. But all such violences to the text are unnecessary. For, first, the very juxtaposition of Jesus Christ here with the Father, and the knowledge of *both* being defined to be eternal life, is a proof by implication of the Godhead of the former. The knowledge of *God and a creature* could not be eternal life, and the juxtaposition of the two would be inconceivable. Secondly, the **ὃν ἀπέστειλας** most distinctly expresses the ἐξελθεῖν from God, ver. 8—implies the ἡμεῖς ἕν of ver. 22, and cannot, in connexion with what follows, possibly be understood in a Socinian, or an Arian sense. I do not scruple to use and preach on the verse as a plain proof of the co-equality of the Lord Jesus in the Godhead. A difficulty has been found in the use of the name JESUS CHRIST *by the Lord Himself*:—and inferences have been hence made that we have

e ch. iv. 34. v. 36. Acts xx. 24. Neh. vi. 16.
f constr., ch. v. 36.
g = Rev. ii. 13. Matt. vi. 1. Prov. ii. 1.
h attr., ver. 11. Mark vii. 13 reff.
i Matt. vi. 8 reff. Prov. viii. 24.
k ch. i. 31 reff.

[d] χριστόν. 4 ἐγώ σε [u] ἐδόξασα ἐπὶ τῆς γῆς τὸ ἔργον
[e] τελειώσας ὃ [f] δέδωκάς μοι [f] ἵνα ποιήσω· 5 καὶ νῦν
δόξασόν με σὺ πάτερ [g] παρὰ σεαυτῷ τῇ δόξῃ [h] ᾗ εἶχον
[i] πρὸ τοῦ τὸν κόσμον εἶναι [g] παρὰ σοί. 6 [k] ἐφανέρωσά
σου τὸ ὄνομα τοῖς ἀνθρώποις οὓς δέδωκάς μοι ἐκ τοῦ

ABCDE GHKL MSUX ΥΓΔΛ Πא 1. 33. 69

at end ins εις τουτον τον κοσμον D.

4. ins και bef το εργον D. rec (for τελειωσας) ετελειωσα, with D rel vulg lat-*c e g l q* [*a f*] Syr goth arm $Hipp_1$ [$Marcell_1$] Did_1 Ath_1 Bas_1 Chr_1 [$Cyr\text{-}p_1$] $Cypr_1$ Hil_3 : txt ABCL[Π]א 1. 33 (lat-*b* ff_2) syr-w-ast [syr-jer] copt æth [$Hipp\text{-}ms_1$] Hil_2. for δεδ., εδωκας CDK[Π] Hipp Bas. for μοι, με א[1].

5. πατηρ D[1](txt D[2]). for ᾗ, ην א[1] $Orig_1$(txt_2) Eus_1 : om 69[1]. παρα σοι προ του γενεσθαι τον κοσμον D.

6. το ονομα bef σου D latt Hil_3. for 1st δεδωκας, εδωκας A B(sic : see table) DK[Π]א Eus_1 : txt C rel $Orig_1$.

John's own language here:—but surely without any ground. He who said σου τὸν υἱόν, ver. 1, might well here, before the ἐγώ of ver. 4, use that prophetic Name [**Ἰησοῦς**] which had been divinely given Him as the Saviour of men, and its weighty adjunct **χριστός** (= υἱὸς τοῦ θεοῦ, 1 John v. 1, 5), in which Names are all the hidden treasures of that knowledge of which He here speaks.
And as to the later use of the two names together having led to their insertion here by the Apostle (gegen das geschichtliche Decorum, De Wette; similarly Lücke, and even Olshausen),—what if *the converse were the case*, and this solemn use of them by our Lord had given occasion to their subsequent use by the Church? This is to me much more probable than the other. **4.**] The past tenses are proleptical. In the rendering of this whole chapter they should be kept indefinite, not made into *perfects* as in E. V., which destroys this proleptical character. **I glorified Thee . . . I finished . . .** What view of the aorist has led to Bp. Wordsworth's explanation here,—"the aorist is used, not the perfect, inasmuch as the work of glorification was still going on, and not to be completed before His Passion, when He would say τετέλεσται,"—I am quite unable to imagine. That the aorist implies *present continuance*, is at least a startling doctrine. The force of it here surely is, that our Lord stands by anticipation at the end of His accomplished course, and looks back on it all as past, as historically gathered up in one act: which is the very sense and propriety of the aorist. **τὸ ἔργον** is not only the ministerial life of our Lord, but the *whole* Life, with all its appointed manifestations of humility and purity,—the perfect righteousness which by that life He has planted in our nature,—and His prophetic and declarative office, terminated by His Passion and Death. **5. δόξασόν με**] Notice the correlation, which Meyer has pointed out, between **ἐγώ σε** before and **με σύ** now. The same Person (ἐγώ) who had with the Father glory before the world, also glorified the Father in the world, and prays to be again received into that glory. *A decisive proof of the unity of the Person of Christ*, in His three estates of eternal præ-existence in glory, humiliation in the flesh, and glorification in the Resurrection Body. This direct testimony to the eternal præexistence of the Son of God has been evaded by the Socinian and also the Arminian interpreters, by rendering **εἶχον**,—"habebam *destinatione tua*," Grot., Wetst. On the identity of the δόξα in ver. 22 with this δόξα, see note there. **εἶχον**] "*Hic* non dicit *accepi*. Semper habebat: nunquam cœpit habere." Bengel. **πρὸ τοῦ τ. κ. εἶν.**, before the καταβολὴ κόσμου, ver. 24;—'before all creation.' "Antequam fieret mundus, gloriam illam habebat Filius; sed cum fieret mundus, gloria illa se cœpit (?) exserere." Bengel. **παρὰ σοί** = πρὸς τὸν θεόν, ch. i. 1; εἰς τὸν κόλπον τοῦ πατρός, ch. i. 18. **6—19.**] *He prays for His disciples.* **6.**] This verse particularizes ver. 4, and forms the transition to the intercessory prayer.
σου τὸ ὄνομα] Thy Name of FATHER, which was so constantly on the lips of our Lord;—and which derived its living meaning and power from His teaching: see Exod. xxiii. 21. No especial emphasis on σου: it carries on the strain of address, and points to the emphatic **σοί** which follows, and the equally emphatic **παρὰ σοῦ** in ver.

κόσμου· [l] σοὶ ἦσαν, καὶ ἐμοὶ αὐτοὺς δέδωκας, καὶ τὸν
λόγον σου [m] τετήρηκαν· 7 νῦν ἔγνωκαν ὅτι πάντα ὅσα
δέδωκάς μοι [n] παρὰ σοῦ [o] εἰσίν, 8 ὅτι τὰ ῥήματα ἃ [p] ἔδωκάς
μοι δέδωκα αὐτοῖς, καὶ αὐτοὶ [q] ἔλαβον, καὶ ἔγνωσαν [r] ἀληθῶς ὅτι [s] παρὰ σοῦ [s] ἐξῆλθον, καὶ ἐπίστευσαν ὅτι σύ με
ἀπέστειλας. 9 ἐγὼ [t] περὶ αὐτῶν [t] ἐρωτῶ· οὐ [t] περὶ τοῦ
κόσμου [t] ἐρωτῶ, ἀλλὰ περὶ ὧν δέδωκάς μοι, ὅτι [u] σοί εἰσιν.

l Matt. vii. 3, 22. Mark ii. 18. ch. iv. 42 al.
m ch. viii. 51, 52, 55 reff.
n ch. vii. 29 reff.
o plur., Matt. vi. 28 reff.
p = ver. 14. Acts vii. 38.
q = ch. i. 12 reff.
r = ch. vii. 26. Acts xii. 11 only. Exod. xxxiii. 16.
s ch. xvi. 27 reff.
t ch. xvi. 26 reff.
u ver. 6.

καμοι BY 1. 33 (*but* και εμοι *here perhaps belongs to the solemnity of the style*) : txt ACDℵ rel. for 2nd δεδωκας, εδωκας ABDKL[Π]ℵ 1 : txt C rel $Orig_1$ Eus_1. rec τετηρηκασι, with AC rel : ετηρησαν ℵ 33 : txt BDL.

7. εγνωσαν UX 33. 69 [Chr_1] : εγνωκασιν S 122(Sz) : εγνων ℵ. for δεδωκας, εδωκας A 1, εδωκες B. rec (for εισιν) εστιν, with AD rel : txt BCLXYℵ 1. 33.

8. aft τα ρημ. ins σου D. rec δεδωκας, with Lℵ rel Cyr_1 : txt A B(-κες) CD[Π¹]. om και εγνωσαν ADℵ¹ lat-*a e q* goth Hil_1 (*it is not a gloss, as Mey : Luthardt rightly observes that such* circumstantiality of expression *belongs to this prayer*) : ins BCℵ^{3a} rel. επιστευσας ℵ¹.

9. εδωκας D.

7. **οὓς δέδ.**] The Father gave them to Christ, by *leading* them to Christ, see ch. vi. 37, 44, 45. **σοὶ ἦσαν**] **Thine** (**σοί**, from *σός*) **they were**—*Israelites—Thy people, before*:—not only outwardly, but Israelites indeed, see ch. i. 48, and thus prepared to receive Christ (so Stier, v. 411 ff., edn. 2). And thus the **ἐκ τοῦ κόσμου** answers to λαβεῖν ἑαυτῷ ἔθνος ἐκ μέσου ἔθνους, Deut. iv. 34. But see the fuller sense below, on ver. 9. **τὸν λ. σου τετήρηκαν**] **They have observed Thy word**—walked in the path of Thy commandments;—for so λόγον τηρεῖν means: see ch. xiv. 23—and reff. Stier understands their walking in the O. T. ordinances blameless, as Luke i. 6,—and thus (compare ch. i. 42, 46) recognizing Christ as the Messiah when He came. But this is perhaps hardly likely to have been set at the *end* of the sentence, *after* ἐμοὶ αὐτοὺς δέδωκας. It is more likely that τὸν λόγον σου = τὰ ῥήματα ἃ δέδωκάς μοι, ver. 8, and is proleptically spoken. **7.**] **πάντα ὅσα δέδ. μοι**, 'My whole words and works:' **εἰσίν**, as contemplated in their separate meanings and testimonies: q. d. 'are *all* from Thee:'—the *collective* assertion see at ver. 10. On this their conviction, which however had not reached its ripeness yet, see ch. xvi. 30. **8.**] Notice particularly here, as indeed throughout, the marked difference between the aorists and the perfects. **τὰ ῥ. . . δέδ. αὐτοῖς**, and the similar sayings ch. xv. 15 al., seem to be a reference to Deut. xviii. 18, 19, where it is said that the Prophet "shall speak unto them all that I shall command Him." The imparting to them of these *ῥήματα* was the efficient cause of their faith:—see their confession ch. vi. 68, 69, where πεπιστεύκαμεν and ἐγνώκαμεν are connected as here. On the two last clauses we may notice that **παρὰ σοῦ ἐξῆλθον** is more a matter of *conviction from inference* (see ch. iii. 2),—**ἔγνωσαν**:—whereas the other side of the same truth, **σύ με ἀπέστειλας**, the act of the Father unseen by us, is more a matter of *pure faith*,—**ἐπίστευσαν**. In the first, the ἔγνωσαν **ἀληθῶς** stamps our Lord's approval on *their* knowledge, and distinguishes it from such knowledge as the bare οἴδαμεν [ch. iii. 2] of Nicodemus and his colleagues. **9.**] Stier remarks, that the Lord *here begins to fulfil His promise* Matt. x. 32. **οὐ περὶ τ. κόσμου ἐρ.**] The misconceptions which have been made of this verse (Calvin, Lampe, and even Luther, who elsewhere corrects himself, see Tholuck on John, edn. 6, p. 352) as implying a decree of exclusion for the vessels of wrath, may be at once removed by considering the usage of **ὁ κόσμος** in this Prayer. The Lord *does pray* distinctly for ὁ κόσμος, vv. 21, 23, that they may believe and know that the Father hath sent Him. He cannot therefore mean here that He does not pray (absolutely) for the world, but that He is not *now* asking for the world, does not pray *this thing* for the world. *These* (οὓς δέδωκάς μοι) *have already* believed and known; the prayer for them is therefore a different one, viz. that in vv. 11, 15. The mistake would be at once precluded for English readers by the paraphrase, **I am praying for them; I am not praying for the world.** **ὅτι σοί εἰσιν**—

v ch. xiii. 31, 32. xiv. 13 reff.
w = 1 Thess. v. 23 al. Prov. iv. 6. constr., Jude 21.
x attr., ver. 5. Mark vii. 13 reff.
y ch. x. 30 reff.

10 καὶ τὰ ἐμὰ πάντα [u] σά ἐστιν, καὶ τὰ [u] σὰ ἐμά, καὶ [v] δε-
δόξασμαι ἐν αὐτοῖς. 11 καὶ οὐκ ἔτι εἰμὶ ἐν τῷ κόσμῳ,
καὶ οὗτοι ἐν τῷ κόσμῳ εἰσίν, κἀγὼ πρός σε ἔρχομαι.
πάτερ ἅγιε, [w] τήρησον αὐτοὺς ἐν τῷ ὀνόματί σου [x] ᾧ
δέδωκάς μοι, ἵνα ὦσιν [y] ἓν καθὼς ἡμεῖς. 12 ὅτε ἤμην μετ'

ABCDI GHKL MSUX ΥΓΔΛ Πℵ 1. 33. 69

10. for τα εμα to σα εμα, εμοι αυτους εδωκας ℵ. aft σα εμα ins εστιν D vulg lat-*a c* Syr coptt æth. for δεδοξασμαι, εδοξασας με D.

11. εν τω κοσμω bef ειμι A: ins εν τουτω bef τω κοσμω D. for ουτοι, αυτοι Bℵ. (rec και εγω (*prob in this case corrn to corresp to* και ουτοι), with AC³ rel: txt BC¹DLXℵ 1. 33 Orig₂ Cyr.) aft ερχομαι ins ουκετι ειμι εν τω κοσμω και εν τω κοσμω ειμι D; and, except last clause, lat-*c*. πατηρ B. aft ονοματι σου ins και οτε ημην μετ' αυτων (add εν τω κοσμω D³-gr) εγω ετηρουν αυτους εν τω ονοματι σου (and repeat again in ver 12) D. rec (for ᾧ) οὓς, with D³ vulg lat-*f g q* goth æth Ath₁: ὃ D¹UX fuld: txt ABCℵ rel syrr syr-jer copt æth-ms arm Ath[-mss₁] Cyr[-p] Thl Euthym. εδωκας LMℵ. ins και bef ημεις B¹MSUY[Π²] 69 vulg lat-*f g* syr [syr-jer₁] arm Ath₂: om A B²[²·³(Tischdf)] CD[Π¹·³]ℵ rel [lat-*q* syr-jer₁] Syr coptt goth æth [Cyr-p₂].

in a fuller sense than σοὶ ἦσαν, ver. 6. That was their *preparation for* Christ; this is their *abiding in* Him, which is abiding in the Father, see next verse.

10.] Compare ch. xvi. 15 and note. "It were not so much if He had only said, 'All Mine is Thine;' for that we may all say, that all we have is God's. But this is a far greater thing, that He inverts this and says, 'All Thine is Mine.' This can no *creature* say before God." Luther, Stier, v. 418, edn. 2. The E. V.,—'All Mine *are* Thine,' &c.,—gives the erroneous impression that *persons* only are meant, whereas it is *all things*, in the widest meaning,—*the Godhead itself included*,—of which this is asserted. **ἐν αὐτοῖς**, not '*by their means*,' **but in them**; by that ἐγὼ ἐν αὐτοῖς of ver. 23, the life of the vine in the branches; so that the fruit of the branches is the glory of the vine, by the sap of the vine living in the branches. All this again is proleptic.

11.] The *occasion*, and *substance* of His prayer for them. **οὐκ ἔτι εἰμὶ ἐν τῷ κ.**] This shews us that ὁ κόσμ. is not said of *place* alone, for the Lord Jesus is still *here*; but of *state*, the *state of men in the flesh*; sometimes viewed on its darker side, as overcoming men and bringing in spiritual death,—sometimes, as here, used in the most general sense. **καί**, not *but*; it expresses the simultaneous state of the Lord and His, see ch. xvi. 32, and note. **ἅγιε**] *Holy*, as applied to God, peculiarly expresses that *penetration of all His attributes by* LOVE, which He only who here uttered it sees through in its length, breadth, and height:—which angels (Isa. vi. 3: Rev. iv. 8) feel and express:—which men are privileged to utter, but can never worthily feel:—but which devils can neither feel nor worthily utter (see Mark i. 24). They know His Power and His Justice only. But His Holiness is especially employed in this work of **τηρεῖν** now spoken of. **ἐν τῷ ὀν. σου**, not '*through* Thine own Name,' as E. V. which yet renders '*in* Thy Name' ver. 12 (so Chrys., Theophyl., Euthym.),—but in the ὄνομα of vv. 6 and 12: see below. **ᾧ**] Not only the best supported, but the *best* reading, though Stier maintains that it can bear no meaning χριστοπρεπῶς.

The *Name* of God is that which was to be *in the Angel of the Covenant*, Exod. xxiii. 21, see also Isa. ix. 6: Jer. xxiii. 6.

This Name,—not the essential Godhead, but the covenant name, JEHOVAH OUR RIGHTEOUSNESS,—the Father hath *given to Christ*, see Phil. ii. 9; and it is the being kept in this, the truth and confession of this, for which He here prays. "That which the Son has given to His disciples is no other than that which He himself has received from the Father, viz. the essential revelation of the Father." Luthardt. Cf. Matt. x. 27. **ἵνα ὦσιν ἓν καθ. ἡμεῖς**] The oneness here is not merely harmony of will or of love,—as some have interpreted it, and then tried to weaken the Oneness of the Godhead by the καθώς,—but oneness by the indwelling of the Spirit of Christ, the gift of the covenant (1 Cor. vi. 17), and ultimately [as the close union implied by καθώς requires] oneness of nature, 2 Pet. i. 4, where the ἐπαγγέλματα δεδώρηται answers to the ὄνομα ὃ δέδωκάς μοι here. "Non ait, ut *nobiscum* sint *unum*,—aut *simus unum* ipsi et nos, sicut unum sumus nos,—sed ait, ut sint unum sicut et nos." Aug. Tract. cvii. 5. **12. ἐφύλαξα**] See ch. x. 28—30. The aor. should be adhered to again: I

αὐτῶν, ἐγὼ [w] ἐτήρουν αὐτοὺς ἐν τῷ ὀνόματί σου [x] ᾧ δέδωκάς μοι, καὶ [z] ἐφύλαξα, καὶ οὐδεὶς ἐξ αὐτῶν [a] ἀπώλετο,
εἰ μὴ ὁ [b] υἱὸς τῆς [bc] ἀπωλείας, ἵνα ἡ γραφὴ πληρωθῇ.
13 νῦν δὲ πρός σε ἔρχομαι, καὶ ταῦτα λαλῶ ἐν τῷ κόσμῳ,
ἵνα ἔχωσιν τὴν [d] χαρὰν τὴν ἐμὴν [d] πεπληρωμένην ἐν ἑαυτοῖς. 14 ἐγὼ [e] δέδωκα αὐτοῖς τὸν λόγον σου, καὶ ὁ κόσμος
ἐμίσησεν αὐτούς, ὅτι οὐκ [f] εἰσὶν ἐκ τοῦ κόσμου καθὼς ἐγὼ
οὐκ [f] εἰμὶ ἐκ τοῦ κόσμου. 15 οὐκ [g] ἐρωτῶ ἵνα [h] ἄρῃς
αὐτοὺς ἐκ τοῦ κόσμου, ἀλλ᾽ ἵνα [i] τηρήσῃς αὐτοὺς ἐκ τοῦ
[k] πονηροῦ. 16 ἐκ τοῦ κόσμου οὐκ [f] εἰσίν, καθὼς ἐγὼ οὐκ

z 2 Pet. ii. 5. Jude 24.
a ch. x. 29.
b 2 Thess. ii. 3. see Eph. v. 6.
c = Matt. vii. 13 al. Isa. lvii. 4.
d ch. iii. 29 reff.
e ver. 8.
f ch. iii. 31 reff.
g w. ἵνα, Luke vii. 36 reff.
h constr., Mark xiii. 15. 1 Cor. v. 2. see Acts viii. 33. xxii. 22.
i w. ἐκ, Rev. iii. 10 only. w. ἀπό, Prov. vii. 5.
k see note. Matt. xiii. 19, 28. Eph. vi. 16.

12. rec aft *μετ᾽ αυτων* ins *εν τω κοσμω* (*from ver* 11), with AC³ rel lat-*f q* syrr goth [syr-jer æth] (arm Chr_1): om BC¹DLא 1 latt coptt Cyr[-p_2] Hil_2 Aug_1. rec *οὕς* (*see above, ver* 11), with AC³D rel latt syrr goth æth $Orig\text{-}int_1$ Hil_1: txt BC¹L 33 syr-jer coptt arm Cyr[-p], *ο* א³ᵃ.—om *ω δεδωκας μοι* א¹. *εδωκας* C. rec om *και* (bef *εφυλαξα*) (*to suit arrangement*), with AC³ D-gr E rel latt syrr copt goth: ins BC¹Lא 33 D-lat syr-jer sah arm Cyr_2 Hil_1. *εφυλασσον* א¹.
13. ins *τουτω* bef *τω κοσμω* D. *πεπληρωκενην* (sic) א¹. rec (for *εαυτοις*) *αυτοις*, with C³D rel syrr: txt ABX[Π] א(*ε* above the line 1. m.).—*τ. καρδιαις εαυτων* C¹ [sah-mnt].
14. for 1st clause, *εγω δε εδωκα τ. λογ. σ. εν αυτοις* D. for *εμισησεν*, *μισει* D 63. 77. 253-9 lat-*a e q*. ins *τουτου* bef 1st *του κοσμου* D lat-*a c f* [*q*]. om *καθως* to *κοσμου* (*homœotel*) D[Π¹] 69 lat-*b c e*. om 2nd *εγω* א¹.
15. for *πονηρου*, *κοσμου* B¹. (There are other mistakes in B at this point: see table.)
16. aft 1st *εκ* ins *τουτου* D. for *εγω*, *καγω* D 69 vulg lat-*c f* coptt [syr-jer] Orig-int.

kept them. The Lord here, as Cyril remarks, compares *His* keeping of His own, to that by *the Father*,—in a way only accountable by both Persons being of equal Power and Dignity. **οὐδεὶς . . εἰ μὴ . . .**] So that Judas was of the number *οὓς δέδωκάς μοι* of ver. 9,—shewing us (1) the sense in which those words must be understood (see above); and (2) that of such persons it is true that there is for them no 'gratia irresistibilis,' no 'keeping in God's Name' independently of their 'keeping God's word,' ver. 6, which Judas did not do. **ὁ υἱ. τ. ἀπ.**] See ref. 2 Thess. As the other disciples by true *τήρησις* of the divine *ῥήματα* given to them, rose from being natural men to be the children of God, so Judas, through want of the same, sunk from the state of the natural man to that of the lost—the children of the devil (Olsh. nearly). Remark, it is not *οὐδένα* . . . . . **ἀπώλεσα**, *εἰ μὴ τὸν υἱὸν τῆς ἀπ.*: Christ did not lose him (compare ch. xviii. 9, where there is no exception), but *he lost himself*.

ἡ γραφή—in which this was indicated, viz. the passages alleged by Peter, Acts i. 20: see ch. xiii. 18. Beware again of any evasion of the full telic sense of *ἵνα*. **13.**] **νῦν δέ**, opposed to *ὅτε ἤμην* ver. 12, implying, 'But I shall be here to keep them no more. And therefore I pray this prayer in their hearing, that' &c.

On **ἡ χ. ἡ ἐμή** see ch. xv. 11; xvi. 24; also the reference to these words in 1 John i. 4. **14—16.**] See ver. 8.

Ver. **14** contains the manner in which He *ἐφύλαξεν αὐτούς*, *by giving them the Divine Word*;—and the reason of the *τήρησις* prayed for, viz., because they would be objects of hatred to the world: *ἐγώ* and *ὁ κόσμος* being opposed. **καθὼς ἐγώ**] See ch. xv. 18. **15. οὐκ ἐρωτῶ**] Said mostly for their sakes, for whom it was necessary that they should abide yet in the flesh, to do God's work, and (ver. 17) to be sanctified by God's truth. **τοῦ πον.**] Not '*from the evil*,' as E. V.; but **from the evil One**, see the usage of our Apostle in 1 John ii. 13, 14, *ὅτι νενικήκατε τὸν πονηρόν*,—ib. v. 18, and compare ib. iii. 12. **16.**] Repeated, as the ground both of the *οὐκ ἐρωτῶ*,—for they are already not of the world, above the world, so that they need not be *removed from it* in order to distinction from it;—and of the *ἀλλ᾽ ἵνα*,—for they are clean (ch. xiii. 10); 'Keep them from the polluter.' This leads on to (vv. 17—19) *the process of sanctification*

[f] εἰμὶ ἐκ τοῦ κόσμου. 17 [l] ἁγίασον αὐτοὺς ἐν τῇ ἀληθείᾳ·
ὁ λόγος ὁ σὸς [m] ἀλήθειά ἐστιν. 18 καθὼς ἐμὲ ἀπέστειλας
εἰς τὸν κόσμον, κἀγὼ ἀπέστειλα αὐτοὺς εἰς τὸν κόσμον·
19 καὶ [n] ὑπὲρ αὐτῶν ἐγὼ [o] ἁγιάζω ἐμαυτόν, ἵνα ὦσιν καὶ
αὐτοὶ [l] ἡγιασμένοι ἐν ἀληθείᾳ. 20 Οὐ [p] περὶ τούτων δὲ
[p] ἐρωτῶ μόνον, ἀλλὰ καὶ περὶ τῶν [qr] πιστευόντων [q] διὰ
τοῦ λόγου αὐτῶν [r] εἰς ἐμέ, 21 ἵνα πάντες [s] ἓν ὦσιν, καθὼς

ABCDE GHKL MSUX ΥΓΔΛ Πℵ 1. 33. 69

l ch. x. 36 al. Lev. xi. 44. w. ἐν, Rom. xv. 16. 1 Cor. i. 2. vii. 14. Heb. x. 29.
m = 2 Cor. vii. 14. Ps. cxviii. 142.
n = Heb. xiii. 17. Col. iv. 12. Eph. vi. 20.
o = Rom. xv. 16. Lev. xxii. 2. Deut. xv. 19.
p ver. 9.
q ch. i. 7. 1 Cor. iii. 5. see 1 Pet. i. 21.
r ch. ii. 11 reff.
s ch. x. 30 reff.

rec εκ του κοσμου bef ουκ ειμι (*conformn to former clause*), with E rel syr goth: txt ABCDLXΔℵ 33 latt Syr [syr-jer] coptt arm Chr_1 Cyr_1.

17. om τη B. rec aft τη αληθεια ins σου (*conformn to ονοματι σου, ver* 11), with $C^3ℵ^{3a}$ rel lat-*q* syrr copt æth arm: om $ABC^1DL[Π^2]ℵ^1$ 1 latt [syr-jer] sah goth Did_1. om ο λογος ο σος αληθεια $ℵ^1$. ins η bef αληθεια B.

18. ins τουτον bef τον κοσμον (twice) D lat-*a b c* [*f q*] Ambrst. [The 2nd clause is repeated by B^1.]

19. om εγω Aℵ 248 Scr's g foss lat-*b c e q* [sah Chr_1] Ath_1 Did_1. rec και αυτοι bef ωσιν, with C^3 rel syr sah: txt $ABC^1DKLXY[Π]ℵ$ 1. 33. 69 latt [Syr syr-jer æth] copt goth arm Ath_3 Did_2 Cyr_1.

20. rec πιστευσοντων, with D^{10}(and lat) vulg lat-*a c* [*e f g q* æth] sah [Orig-int_1] $Cypr_1$ Hil_1: txt $ABCD^1ℵ$ rel lat-*b* syrr copt goth arm Ath_1 Bas_3 Chr_1 Cyr[-p_2] Non Thl.

21. om ἓν C^1.

through the knowledge of the truth imparted to them by Christ, and expanded in them by the Spirit. **17.**] **ἁγιάζειν** here and in ver. 19 carries the meaning, which unites the two uses, of *consecration to God.* (1) In *them,* this setting apart for Him was a long and gradual process, to be accomplished by conflicts, and the deeper sinking in of the Truth by the blows of affliction, and the purifying fire of the Spirit: in *them* it was strictly *sanctification,* the *making holy:* but (2) in HIM it was that pure and entire self-consecration by His submission to the Father's holy will, the entire possession of His sinless humanity with the living and speaking Truth of God, which should be at the same time the efficient cause of their sanctification and their Pattern. Such an High Priest *became us* (see Heb. vii. 26), who are to be ourselves priests unto God. Rev. xx. 6. **ἐν**, not 'by,' but **in**: see on ver. 11. The truth is the *element in which* the ἁγ. takes place. **ὁ λόγ. ὁ σός**] Compare Acts xx. 32. Thy word, in its inner subjective power. Ver. **18** is proleptic,—and received its fulfilment ch. xx. 21. He does not merely *leave* them in the world, but *sends* them into it, to witness to this same truth of God: see ch. xv. 16. **19.**] See above on ver. 17. Notice, says Meyer, the emphatic correlation of **αὐτῶν—ἐγὼ ἐμαυτόν—καὶ αὐτοί.** It is clear against all Socinian inferences from this verse, that all that part of ἁγιάζειν implied in ch. x. 36 is here excluded: and only that intended which is expressed Heb. ii. 10 by διὰ παθημάτων τελειῶσαι. Of this, His death was the crowning act, and was also the one to which the ὑπὲρ αὐτῶν most directly applies; but the whole is included. The confining the meaning to *His sacrifice* (Chrys., Euthym.), and the ἵνα καὶ αὐτοὶ . . . . to *their martyrdom,* or their spiritual *self-offering,* Rom. xii. 1 (Euthym.), is insufficient for the depth of the words. **ἐν ἀληθ.**] **in truth:** *what* truth, is evident from ver. 17, where, in the repetition, ὁ λόγ. ὁ σὸς ἀλήθειά ἐστιν, the article is also wanting: see also ch. i. 14; iv. 24: 3 John 3,—for ἀλήθ. without the article. But the distinction is perhaps somewhat obscured after a preposition. **20.**] The connexion is the ἀπέστειλα αὐτοὺς εἰς τ. κόσμον, ver. 18. The present part. expresses the *state* of faith in which all believers are found: the future (of the rec.) would refer more to the act of belief by which that state is begun. But perhaps it is best to take the pres. as proleptic. It is strikingly set forth here that *all* subsequent belief on Christ would take place through the apostolic word: see Rom. x. 16, 17. **21.**] The **ἵνα** here hardly can regard the subject-matter of the **ἐρωτῶ**, ver. 20, but rather we should supply after that word ταῦτα, and understand this ἵνα as expressing the *object of the prayer* respecting both. The subject-matter of the prayer is, that they may be kept in God's name and sanctified in God's truth; and if this be so, their unity with the Son and the

σὺ πατὴρ ἐν ἐμοὶ κἀγὼ ἐν σοί, ἵνα καὶ αὐτοὶ ἐν ἡμῖν ὦσιν,
ἵνα ὁ κόσμος πιστεύσῃ ὅτι σύ με ἀπέστειλας. 22 κἀγὼ
τὴν δόξαν ἣν δέδωκάς μοι δέδωκα αὐτοῖς, ἵνα ὦσιν [s] ἓν
καθὼς ἡμεῖς ἕν, 23 ἐγὼ ἐν αὐτοῖς καὶ σὺ ἐν ἐμοί, ἵνα ὦσιν
[t] τετελειωμένοι [u] εἰς [u] ἕν, ἵνα γινώσκῃ ὁ κόσμος ὅτι σύ με
ἀπέστειλας καὶ ἠγάπησας αὐτοὺς καθὼς ἐμὲ ἠγάπησας.
24 Πατήρ, ὃ δέδωκάς μοι, θέλω ἵνα ὅπου εἰμὶ ἐγὼ κἀκεῖνοι

t 1 John ii. 5. iv. 12, 17, 18. Heb. x. 14.
u ch. xi. 52 only. (1 John v. 8.)

(rec πατερ, with ACℵ rel Clem$_1$ Orig$_1$ [Eus$_2$ Bas$_1$] : txt BD Eus$_1$.) rec aft εν ημιν ins ἕν, with AC^{2}ℵ rel vulg lat-*f* [*g q* syr-jer] syrr copt goth (æth) Clem Orig$_3$[int$_{sæpe}$ Bas$_1$ *Cyr*-p] Eus$_1$ Thdrt$_1$ Cypr$_1$ Hil$_1$ Jer Ambr Aug Leo : txt BC^{1}D lat-*a b c e g* sah arm Eus$_2$ Ath-mss$_1$ Hil$_3$. for πιστευσῃ, πιστευῃ BC^{1}ℵ^1 Clem$_1$ Eus$_1$: txt AC^{3}Dℵ^{3a} rel Orig$_1$ [Cyr$_1$].

22. (καγω, so BC^{1}DLX[U]ℵ 1. 33.) εδωκας AD[UΠ] Clem Hipp$_1$ Eus$_2$ Chr. εδωκα AKM[Π]ℵ Hipp$_1$ Chr$_1$. aft ωσιν ins το D. om 2nd ἕν ℵ^1. rec at end ins εσμεν, with AC^{2}ℵ^{3a} rel latt syrr [coptt goth arm] Eus$_2$ Orig-int$_3$ Hil$_1$: om BC^{1}DLℵ^1 1. 33 lat-*e* [syr-jer] æth Clem Hipp$_1$ Eus$_2$ *Cyr*[-p].

23. for 1st clause, συ εν εμοι καγω εν αυτοις D 59. ins το bef ἕν D Eus$_2$ Chr$_1$. rec ins και bef 2nd ινα (*not seeing the dependence of 2nd* ινα *on 1st*), with Aℵ rel vulg lat-*b c f* syrr sah goth : om BCDLX 33. 69 lat-*a e g* copt Hipp$_1$ Chr Cyr. om 2nd ινα ℵ 1 lat-*b c* [vulg syr-jer] æth arm. for 1st ηγαπησας, ηγαπησα D 42. 237-51 gat lat-*a b* Syr-mss syr-txt [syr-jer arm] copt æth Chr$_1$. for εμε, συ με D [lat-*a b*].

24. rec πατερ, with CDℵ rel : txt AB. rec (for ὁ) οὓς, with AC rel vss : txt BDℵ copt goth. for 1st δεδ., εδωκας A[Π^2] Scr's w [Clem] Chr Thdrt. (και

Father follows, 1 John i. 3. But here it is not merely 'with,' but in, the Son and the Father;—because the Spirit proceeds from *the Father and the Son*, and 'He that is joined to the Lord, is one Spirit:' see ver. 11. This unity has its true and only *ground* in faith in Christ through the Word of God as delivered by the Apostles; and is therefore not mere outward uniformity, nor can such uniformity produce it. At the same time its effects are to be real and visible, such that the world may see them. **ἵνα πιστ.**] Not parallel with the former ἵνα, as if πιστ. ὁ κόσμος meant the same as πάντες ἓν ὦσι, that all may be brought to believe. Nor again can the words mean that the *unbelieving and condemned world, at the end*, may be persuaded 'that Thou hast sent Me.' Such a rendering would surely be repugnant to the spirit of the prayer, and the use of the word πιστεύω in our Gospel. Rather is it,—'that this their testimony, being borne by them all, and in all ages, may continue to convince the world, so that many in the world may believe,' &c. The **ὅτι σύ με ἀπέστειλας** implies belief in the whole Work and Office of Christ. Here our Lord certainly *prays for the world*,—see above on ver. 9. See a remarkable parallel, Rev. iii. 9, where, as Stier truly remarks, the persons spoken of are *penitents*.

22, 23.] Grotius and others interpret this **δόξα**, "potestas faciendi miracula," and refer to ch. ii. 11 and ch. xi. 40; but wrongly:—for if so, the αὐτοῖς must mean the Apostles only, whereas it is distinctly referred to the believers *of all time*. The δόξα is (Lücke, De Wette, Stier:—Meyer understands it of the heavenly glory, Rom. viii. 17) *the glory of Christ as the only-begotten Son* (ch. i. 14), full of grace and truth (see ver. 5 and note), which by virtue of His exaltation and the unity of all believers in Him through the Spirit, has become (not, *shall be*) theirs, Eph. i. 18; ii. 6: Rom. viii. 30: not yet fully, nor *as it is His*, but as each can receive and shew it forth. The perfection of it is spoken of, ver. 24. We have the same recurrences of ἵνα as in ver. 21, and the same dependence (see var. readd.). The second of them here expresses not merely the similarity of their unity to that of the Son and Father,—but the *actuality of its subsistence*, in Christ abiding in them and the Father in Christ. On **τετελ. εἰς ἕν**, see reff. **γινώσκῃ** here, parallel as it is to **πιστεύσῃ** above, cannot be interpreted of a bare recognition, or of a recognition at the final judgment,—but must be taken to mean that salutary knowledge by which from time to time the children of the world are by God called to become the children of light. See the same words, and note, ch. xiv. 31, also ch. xiii. 35, and observe that in all three places the recognition is that of *love*;—in ch. xiii. 35, of the

v πρό, Eph. i. 4. 1 Pet. i. 20 only. ἀπό, Matt. xxv. 34 reff. w = here only in Gospp. Rom. iii. 26. 2 Tim. iv. 8. 1 John ii. 29. Rev. xvi. 5. x ch. xv. 15 reff. y Eph. ii. 4. 2 Kings xiii 15.

ABCDE GHKL MSUX ΥΓΔΛ ΠΝ 1. 33. 69

ὦσιν μετ' ἐμοῦ· ἵνα θεωρῶσιν τὴν δόξαν τὴν ἐμήν, ἣν
δέδωκάς μοι, ὅτι ἠγάπησάς με πρὸ v καταβολῆς v κόσμου.
25 πατὴρ w δίκαιε, καὶ ὁ κόσμος σε οὐκ ἔγνω, ἐγὼ δέ σε
ἔγνων, καὶ οὗτοι ἔγνωσαν ὅτι σύ με ἀπέστειλας, 26 καὶ
x ἐγνώρισα αὐτοῖς τὸ ὄνομά σου καὶ x γνωρίσω· ἵνα ἡ
y ἀγάπη y ἣν y ἠγάπησάς με ἐν αὐτοῖς ᾖ, κἀγὼ ἐν αὐτοῖς.

XVIII. 1 Ταῦτα εἰπὼν Ἰησοῦς ἐξῆλθεν σὺν τοῖς μα-

εκεινοι AKU[Π¹] Thdrt₁.) om την εμην D [Eus-ms₁] Cypr₁. rec (for 2nd δεδ.) εδωκας, with B rel Clem Thdrt₁ : txt ACDHLMXΔℵ[UΠ²] 1. 33. 69 Hipp Eus₁ Cyr.

25. rec πατερ, with CDℵ rel Clem₁ Hipp₁ : txt AB. om 1st και D vulg(not am fuld forj ing) lat-*b* [*c f q* syr-jer] coptt(not copt-dz). [Tischdf ed 8 states that copt-wilk and sah ins και, and that it is omd by copt-schw-dz.] aft ο κοσμος ins τουτος (sic) D (lat-*a f*). om 2nd σε A. for εγνων, εγνωκα D.

26. for ἥν, ᾗ D-gr, *qua* latt(*quam* D-lat). for με, αυτους ℵ.

Chap. XVIII. 1. rec ins ο bef ιησ., with ACD rel : om BL¹ℵ. (τοις written

disciples one to another; in ch. xiv. 31, of Jesus to the Father; here, of the Father to believers, as perfected into unity in the Son of His love. "Observe," says Meyer, "how the glance of the Intercessor reaches in these verses even to the highest aim of His work on earth, when the *world* shall be believing, and Christ Himself actually the Saviour *of the world*, ch. iv. 42, cf. ch. x. 16." **24. ὃ δέδωκάς μοι**] The neuter has a peculiar solemnity, uniting the whole Church together as *one gift* of the Father to the Son: see ch. vi. 39, note. Then the κἀκεῖνοι resolves it into the great multitude whom no man can number, and comes home to the heart of every individual believer with inexpressibly sweet assurance of an eternity with Christ. **θέλω** is not the θέλω of ch. xii. 21: 1 Cor. vii. 7, but more like that of Mark vi. 25,—an expression of will founded on acknowledged right: compare διατίθεμαι, Luke xxii. 29. Compare also the θέλω and ὃ δέδωκ. μοι, with ch. v. 21; vi. 44. **ὅπου εἰμὶ ἐγώ**] i. e. in the glorified state: see ch. xii. 26 and note: also ch. xiv. 3. **ἵνα θεωρ.**] This is the completion of ver. 22,—the open beholding of His glory, spoken of 1 John iii. 2, which shall be coincident with our being changed into His perfect image. **θεωρ.** is to *behold* and *partake*—the very case supposes it. No *mere spectator could behold* this glory. See Rom. viii. 17 end, and 2 Cor. iii. 18. **ὅτι ἠγ. με . . . .**] The most glorious part of this sight of glory will be to behold the whole mystery of redemption unfolded in the glory of Christ's Person,—and to see how, before the being of the creature, that eternal Love was, which gave the glory to Christ of which all creation is but the exponent. On **κατ. κόσ.** see reff. **25, 26.**] **δίκαιε** is connected with the final clause of ver. 24. The Righteousness of the Father is witnessed by the beginning (πρὸ κατ. κόσ.) of Redemption, and (κἀκεῖνοι ὦσιν) by the glorification of the elect from Christ; but also by ὁ κόσμος σε οὐκ ἔγνω,—the final distinction made by His justice between the world and His. The first **καί** is in the quasi-disjunctive usage so common with our Evangelist, see ch. xvi. 32, note, —and contrasts with the **δέ** immediately following: the more classical construction would be τε—δέ (Lücke). The second **καί** merely couples the preceding to the following, as depending upon it: see Matt. xi. 27. This **ἔγνω, ἔγνωσαν, ἐγνώρισα, γνωρίσω**, shew that our Lord spoke here of the then present time and disciples again, at the close of His prayer. The **γνωρίσω** is by the whole work and testimony of the Spirit completed in the Kingdom of God. This promise has been in fulfilment through all the history of the Church. And the great result of this manifestation of the Father's name is, that the wonderful Love wherewith He loved Christ, may dwell in (not the Apostles merely — the future γνωρίσω has again thrown the meaning onward to the great body of believers) them,—i. e. the perfect, living knowledge of God in Christ, which reveals, and in fact is, this love. And this can only be by κἀγὼ ἐν αὐτοῖς—Christ dwelling in their hearts by faith, and renewing and enlightening them by His Spirit. He does not say, '*Thou* in them'—but **I in them and Thou in Me**; see ver. 23.

Chap. XVIII.—XX.] Final manifestation of Jesus as the Lord, in reference to the now accomplished rejection of Him by the unbelief of Israel, and the sorely tried but eventually confirmed faith of His

θηταῖς αὐτοῦ πέραν τοῦ [z] χειμάῤῥου τῶν [a] κέδρων, ὅπου ἦν [b] κῆπος, εἰς ὃν εἰςῆλθεν αὐτὸς καὶ οἱ μαθηταὶ αὐτοῦ.
2 ᾔδει δὲ καὶ Ἰούδας ὁ [c] παραδιδοὺς αὐτὸν τὸν τόπον· ὅτι πολλάκις [d] συνήχθη Ἰησοῦς ἐκεῖ μετὰ τῶν μαθητῶν αὐτοῦ.
3 Ὁ οὖν Ἰούδας λαβὼν τὴν [e] σπεῖραν καὶ ἐκ τῶν ἀρχιερέων καὶ [τῶν] Φαρισαίων [f] ὑπηρέτας ἔρχεται [g] ἐκεῖ μετὰ [h] φανῶν καὶ [i] λαμπάδων καὶ [k] ὅπλων.
4 Ἰησοῦς οὖν

...συνήχθη Η. (between this and ver. 18, some fragments remain.)

z here only. 4 Kings x. 33 al.
a here only. 2 Kings xv. 23.
b ver. 26. ch. xix. 41 bis. Luke xiii. 19 only. Cant. v. 1.
c pres., Matt. xxvi. 25. Luke xxii. 21. ch. xiii. 11.
d constr., Matt. xxviii. 12.
e ver. 12. Matt. xxvii. 27 || Mk. Acts x. 1. xxi. 31. xxvii. 1 only +. Judith xiv. 11. 2 Macc. viii. 23. xii. 20, 22 only.
f = Matt. xxvi. 58. ch. vii. 32 al.
g = ch. xi. 8 reff.
h here only +.
i Matt. xxv. 1, &c. reff.
k Gospp., here only. Rom. vi. 13 bis. xiii. 12. 2 Cor. vi. 7. x. 4 only. 2 Chron. xxiii. 10.

αυτοις but corrd ℵ¹.) for των κεδρων, του κεδρων ASΔ vulg-ed(with forj foss gat mm) lat-*c f ff*$_2$ *g* [*q* goth arm(appy)] Ambr$_1$ [Aug$_1$]: του κεδρου Dℵ¹ lat-*a b* sah: txt BCℵ^{3a} rel Orig$_1$ Chr$_1$ Cyr$_1$.

2. παραδιδων D. rec ins ο bef ιησ., with ACD rel: om BLXΛℵ. εκει bef (ο) ιησ. D lat-*a* [*b c f g* vulg syr æth arm]: μετα των μαθ. αυ. bef εκει B.

3. aft 2nd και ins εκ DL ℵ(marked for erasure, but marks removed) forj(with foss) Cyr[-p$_1$]. om 2nd των, with AC rel Orig$_2$ [Chr$_1$]: ins BDL ℵ(marked for erasure, but marks removed) copt [Cyr-p$_1$]. om εκει ℵ¹.

4. for ουν, δε DLXℵ 1. 33 (69) foss(with mt) lat-*a b c f* [*q* syr-jer] Syr copt goth (æth) [Chr$_1$] Cyr$_1$.

own. And herein XVIII. 1—XIX. 16.] *His voluntary submission of Himself to His enemies and to the unbelief of Israel.* 1—11.] *His betrayal and apprehension.* 1—3.] Matt. xxvi. 30—47. Mark xiv. 26—43. Luke xxii. 39—53. On the omission by John of the conflict of the Redeemer's soul in Gethsemane, I would remind the reader of what has been said in the Prolegomena on the character of this Gospel. The attempt to find in this omission a discrepancy between the setting forth of the Redeemer by John and the synoptic Gospels, is, as usual, unsuccessful. John presents us with most striking instances of the troubling of the human soul of Christ by the suffering which was before Him: see ch. xii. 23—27; xiii. 21. Compare notes on Matt. ver. 36, and throughout the section. **1. τῶν κέδρων**] This is evidently a Greek corruption of the Hebrew (קִדְרוֹן); and coincides with the LXX in ref. and 3 Kings xv. 13, where however F (not A) has τοῦ κέδρων. If there were cedars in the ravine, the corruption would be easily accounted for. Suidas, under Ἰαβίν, quotes Ps. lxxxii. 9 thus, Ἰαβὶν ἐν τῷ χειμάῤῥῳ τῶν κισσῶν. Instances of the practice of changing foreign names into other words bearing sense in the new language are common in all countries. This being so, it is perhaps safer to follow the best mss., even against our own conviction, that St. John can hardly have written τῶν κέδρων. Josephus calls it χειμ. κεδρῶνος, or φάραγξ κεδρῶνος. Antt. viii. 1. 5; ix. 7. 3: see 2 Kings xxiii. 6, 12. The ravine in the bottom of which flows the Kidron, is to the East of Jerusalem, between the city and the Mount of Olives. **κῆπος**] Lücke suggests that the owner of this garden may have been friendly to (or a disciple of?) Jesus. It was called Gethsemane,—Matt., Mark. Traditions as to its site are, as usual, various. A square plot of ground in the depth of the ravine is now usually pointed out, and seems to have been fixed on at the time when the empress Helena visited Jerusalem, A.D. 326. Euseb. says Gethsemane was *at* the Mount of Olives: Jerome, *at the foot of* the mount. The language of Luke xxi. 37 leads to a belief that it may have been higher up the mount. Robinson, i. 346.

2.] **often,**—see Luke xxi. 37 [ch. viii. 1]. These accurate notices of our Evangelist are especially found in this last portion of his Gospel: cf. vv. 13, 24, 28; ch. xix. 14, 20, 41, &c. **3.**] See, on this band of men, note on Matt. ver. 47. Lücke refers to Dion. Hal. ix. (ἐξέτρεχον ἅπαντες ἐκ τῶν σκηνῶν ἀθρόοι, φανοὺς ἔχοντες κ. λαμπάδας) to shew that lanterns and torches were part of the utensils of military on a night march. **φανοί** appear to be strictly **torches,**—any blazing substance held in the hand;—and **λαμπάδες, lights,** fed with oil. The weapons were swords and staves,—Matt., Mark. The fact of its being full moon did not make the lights unnecessary, as, in searching for a prisoner, they might have to enter dark places. **4—11.**] Matt. xxvi.

l – Matt. xxiii. 35. Rev. iii. 10. Ps. liv. 5.
m ch. iv. 26 reff.
n Mark xiii. 16. Luke ix. 62. xvii. 31. ch. vi. 66. xx. 14 only.
4 Kings xx. 10, 11.
o ch. ix 6 (reff.) only.

εἰδὼς πάντα τὰ [l] ἐρχόμενα ἐπ᾽ αὐτόν, ἐξῆλθεν καὶ λέγει
αὐτοῖς Τίνα ζητεῖτε; 5 ἀπεκρίθησαν αὐτῷ Ἰησοῦν τὸν
Ναζωραῖον. λέγει αὐτοῖς [m] Ἐγώ εἰμι. εἱστήκει δὲ καὶ
Ἰούδας ὁ [e] παραδιδοὺς αὐτὸν μετ᾽ αὐτῶν. 6 ὡς οὖν εἶπεν
αὐτοῖς ὅτι [m] ἐγώ εἰμι, ἀπῆλθαν [n] εἰς τὰ ὀπίσω καὶ ἔπεσαν
[o] χαμαί. 7 πάλιν οὖν ἐπηρώτησεν αὐτοὺς Τίνα ζητεῖτε;
οἱ δὲ εἶπον Ἰησοῦν τὸν Ναζωραῖον. 8 ἀπεκρίθη Ἰησοῦς

...αυτον G. ABCDE KLM SUXY ΓΔΛΠℵ 1. 33. 69

for ειδως, ιδων D(ειδων) 69 syr-jer æth-rom [arm Non_1]. rec (for εξηλθ. κ. λεγει) εξελθων ειπεν, with AC[3]ℵ rel lat-*f* copt goth: txt BC[1]D 1 vulg lat-*a c* [*e g q* syrr] sah[-mnt æth arm] $Orig_2$.

5. ναζαρηνον D vulg lat-*a e* [*c* Orig-int_1]. rec aft *αυτοις* ins *ο ῑς*, with AC rel [lat-*c f q* syrr syr-jer copt &c]: *ῑς* ℵ: aft *ειμι* ins *ῑς* B lat-*a*: om D ev-H[1] lat-*b e* $Orig_1$.

6. om *ουν* A 13(Sz) æth arm. om *αυτοις* ℵ[1]. om *οτι* (*as ver* 5) ABDLX[Π]ℵ 1. 33 latt copt æth $Orig_1$: ins C rel syrr goth arm $Orig_1$ [Cyr-p_1]. (απηλθαν, so BDℵ.) [επεσαν, so BCDE[1]LXℵ 1. 33.]

7. rec *αυτους* bef *επηρωτ.*, with Dℵ rel am(with fuld forj ing) lat-*a b c* goth $Orig_1$: txt ABCLUXY (33) 69 lat-*e f q* [vulg-ed syr-jer] syrr coptt æth arm $Orig_1$ Cyr_1. ins *λεγων* bef *τινα* D sah [(syr-jer æth)]. *ειπαν* D[X]. add *παλιν* D [$Orig_1$].

8. aft *απεκριθη* ins *αυτοις* DX 1. 69 foss lat-*f q* [Syr (syr-jer æth)] sah arm $Orig_1$. rec ins *ο* bef *ιησ.*, with DX[Π[2]] 1. 69 $Orig_1$: om ABCℵ rel.

48—56. Mark xiv. 44—52. Luke xxii. 48—53. 4.] On **εἰδὼς πάντα τὰ ἐρχ.** see Matt. xxvi. 45. **ἐξῆλθεν**—probably, from the shade of the trees into the moonlight;—hardly, as De Wette and Lücke suggest, from some building in the garden. **τίνα ζητ.**, spoken,—as was the saying *ἐφ᾽ ὃ πάρει*, Matt. xxvi. 50,—to carry reproof to the conscience of those addressed: and also to obtain for so solemn an act as the delivering Himself up to them, the formal declaration of their intention to take Him. "When men sought Him to make Him a king, He fled: now that they seek Him to put Him to death, He goes forth to meet them." Stier, vi. 252, edn. 2. 5.] Some among them knew Him (Matt. xxvi. 55), others probably not. This answer may have been given by some one in authority among the Roman soldiers, who had it in command 'to apprehend Jesus of Nazareth.' **εἱστήκει . . . . μετ᾽ αὐτῶν**] I believe these words to be the description of an eye-witness;—John detected Judas standing among them, and notices the detail, as is his constant habit, by way of enhancing the tragic character of the history. The synoptic narrative related the kiss which presently took place: but this self-tradition of our Lord was not related in it. John therefore adds this touch of exactness, to shew that the answer Ἰησοῦν τ. N. was not given because they were ignorant of His Person, so as *not to be able* to say 'Thee;'—but because they *feared* to say it. 6.] The question on the miraculous nature of this incident is not whether it were a miracle *at all* (for it is evident that it must be regarded as one), but whether it were an act *specially intended* by our Lord, or a result of the superhuman dignity of His person and the majestic calmness of His reply. I believe the latter alternative to be the right one. Commentators cite various instances of the confusion of the enemies of *innocent men* before the calmness and dignity of their victims. how much more was this likely to be the case when He in whom was no sin, and who spake as never man spake, came forth to meet His implacable foes as the self-sacrificing Lamb of God. So that I regard it rather as a miracle *consequent upon* that which Christ said and did, and the state of mind in which His enemies were,—than as one, in the strict sense, *wrought by* Him: bearing however always in mind, that to Him nothing was *unexpected*, or a *mere result*, but every thing foreknown. With this view what follows is also consistent, rather than with the other. The distinction is an important one, as the view which we take of our Lord's mind towards His captors must enter, as an element, into our understanding of the whole of this scene, and indeed of the solemn occurrences which follow. Such incidents as this are not related by the Evangelists, and least of all by St. John, as mere astounding facts, but as grounds on which we are to enquire, and determine for ourselves, as to the "glory, full of grace and truth," which was in Him, whom, not having seen, we love. 8.] Bengel strikingly says of this *ἐγώ εἰμι* "*Tertio*

Εἶπον ὑμῖν ὅτι [p] ἐγώ εἰμι· εἰ οὖν ἐμὲ ζητεῖτε, [q] ἄφετε τούτους [r] ὑπάγειν. 9 ἵνα πληρωθῇ ὁ λόγος ὃν εἶπεν, ὅτι
[s] οὓς δέδωκάς μοι, οὐκ [s] ἀπώλεσα [s] ἐξ αὐτῶν οὐδένα.
10 Σίμων οὖν Πέτρος ἔχων [t] μάχαιραν [u] εἵλκυσεν αὐτὴν
καὶ [v] ἔπαισεν τὸν τοῦ ἀρχιερέως δοῦλον καὶ [w] ἀπέκοψεν
αὐτοῦ τὸ [x] ὠτάριον τὸ δεξιόν· ἦν δὲ ὄνομα τῷ δούλῳ
Μάλχος. 11 εἶπεν οὖν ὁ Ἰησοῦς τῷ Πέτρῳ [y] Βάλε τὴν
[t] μάχαιραν εἰς τὴν [z] θήκην. τὸ [a] ποτήριον ὃ [b] δέδωκέν μοι
ὁ πατήρ, οὐ μὴ πίω αὐτό;
12 Ἡ οὖν [c] σπεῖρα καὶ ὁ [d] χιλίαρχος καὶ οἱ [e] ὑπηρέται
τῶν Ἰουδαίων [f] συνέλαβον τὸν Ἰησοῦν καὶ ἔδησαν αὐτόν,

p vv. 5, 6.
q = Matt. xxiii. 14 al. 2 Kings xvi. 11.
r = Matt. viii. 13 al. fr.
s ch. vi. 39.
t ‖ al. Gen. xxvii. 40.
u = here only ‡. (ch. vi. 44 reff.)
v = ‖ Mk. (Matt. xxvi. 68 ‖ L. Rev. ix. 5) only. 2 Kings xx. 10. Xen. Cyrop. viii. 5. 12.
w ver. 26. Mark ix. 43, 45. Acts xxvii. 32. Gal. v. 12 only. Deut. xxiii. 1.
x ‖ Mk. only †.
y = Mark vii. 33. ch. xx. 25 bis, 27 al.
z here only. Exod. xxv. 27 (xxxvi. 34 & xxxvii. 14 F [not AB]). Isa. vi. 13 only.
a = Matt. xx. 22, 23 reff.
b = 2 Cor. xii. 7.
c ver. 3 reff.
d Mark vi. 21. Acts xxi. 31—xxv. 23 (18 times). Rev. vi. 15. xix. 18 only. Zech. ix. 7.
e ver. 3.
f = ‖. Acts i. 16. xii. 3. Josh. viii. 23.

9. εδωκας D 42 Scr's w. εξ αυτ. ουδενα bef απωλεσα D. αυτου A.
10. for σιμ. ουν, τοτε σιμ. D. δουλον bef του αρχ. Dℵ 242 lat-*a b c* [*e f*]. rec (for ωταριον) ωτιον (*prob from ‖ Matt, here and in ‖ Mark*), with AC³D rel: txt BC¹LXℵ syr-mg [e contra syr-bars], *auriculam* latt. ins το bef ονομα DX. for τω δουλω, του δουλου εκεινου (*reminiscence of Matt* xviii. 27) D 29 lat-*a*.
11. rec aft μαχαιραν ins σου (*from ‖ Matt*), with 69 (1, e sil) vulg-ed(with foss gat mm [mt] tol) lat-*e* sah[-mnt æth] Cyr[-p_1] Orig-int_1 Hil_2: om ABCDℵ rel am(with fuld em forj [ing]) lat-*a b c f g* [*ff*$_2$ *q* syr-jer] syrr copt goth arm Non_1. εδωκεν DΔ Chr_1.

dicet *olim*." And Augustine, "Quid judicaturus faciet, qui judicandus hoc fecit? Quid regnaturus poterit, qui moriturus hoc potuit?" Tract. cxii. 3. **ἄφετε τούτους**, "quos illi cæci adoriebantur." Bengel. This saying was sufficient to shew Peter and the rest what was the appointed course for them;—the ἄφ. τούτ. ὑπάγειν to the band, is ὑπάγετε ὑμεῖς to the Apostles. **9.**] See ch. xvii. 12. An unquestionable proof, if any were wanted, that the words of ch. xvii. are no mere description of the mind of our Lord at the time, nor free arrangement of His words, but his very words themselves. This is recognized even by De Wette. On the *application* of the saying, we may remark that the words unquestionably had a much deeper meaning than any belonging to this occasion; but that the remarks so often made in this commentary on the fulfilment of prophecies must be borne in mind;—that to '*fulfil*' a prophecy is not to *exhaust* its capability of being again and again fulfilled:—that the words of the Lord have many stages of unfolding;—and that the temporal deliverance of the Apostles now, doubtless was but a part in the great spiritual safe-keeping which the Lord asserted by anticipation in these words. **10.**] At this time took place the kiss of Judas, in accordance with the agreement entered into, and to assure the captors that the person thus offering Himself was indeed Jesus of Nazareth, and no substitute for him: see note on Matt. ver. 49. The other view, that the kiss took place first, before the incidents of our vv. 4—9 (Friedlieb, Archäologie der Leidensgeschichte, p. 68), is to me quite inconceivable. On Peter's act, see Matt. ver. 51. The *names* of Peter and Malchus are only found *here*:—τὸ **δεξιόν** only here and in Luke. The (external) ear, though severed, was apparently still hanging on the cheek;—for our Lord is said in Luke xxii. 51, to have touched τοῦ ὠτίου αὐτοῦ in performing the healing. **11.**] **τὴν θήκ.** = τὸν τόπ. αὐτῆς, Matt., where see notes. **τὸ ποτ.**] A striking allusion to the prayer in Gethsemane; for the image does not elsewhere occur in our Evangelist. See Matt. xx. 22 and ‖. **οὐ μὴ πίω**] **am I not to drink it?** "*non vis ut bibam?*" Vulg. Sixt. "Huc enim tendebat pugna Petri." Bengel.

12—24.] *Jesus before the Jewish High Priests.—Peculiar to John.* See below. **12.**] See Acts xxi. 31 al. The **ὑπηρ. τ. Ἰ.** were the officers sent by the Sanhedrim. Luthardt remarks: "He before whose aspect, and ἐγώ εἰμι, the whole band had been terrified and cast to the ground, now suffers himself to be taken, bound, and led away. This contrast the Evangelist has in mind here. To appre-

13 καὶ [[g] ἀπ]ήγαγον αὐτὸν πρὸς Ἄνναν πρῶτον· ἦν γὰρ
[h] πενθερὸς τοῦ Καϊάφα, ὃς ἦν [i] ἀρχιερεὺς τοῦ [i] ἐνιαυτοῦ
ἐκείνου. 14 ἦν δὲ Καϊάφας ὁ [k] συμβουλεύσας τοῖς Ἰουδαίοις
ὅτι [l] συμφέρει ἕνα ἄνθρωπον ἀποθανεῖν ὑπὲρ τοῦ [m] λαοῦ.
15 ἠκολούθει δὲ τῷ Ἰησοῦ Σίμων Πέτρος καὶ [ὁ] [n] ἄλλος
[n] μαθητής. ὁ δὲ μαθητὴς ἐκεῖνος ἦν [o] γνωστὸς τῷ ἀρχιερεῖ,
καὶ [p] συνεισῆλθεν τῷ Ἰησοῦ εἰς τὴν [q] αὐλὴν τοῦ ἀρχιερέως,
16 ὁ δὲ Πέτρος εἱστήκει [r] πρὸς τῇ θύρᾳ ἔξω. ἐξῆλθεν οὖν
ὁ [n] μαθητὴς ὁ [n] ἄλλος ὁ [o] γνωστὸς τοῦ ἀρχιερέως, καὶ εἶπεν
τῇ [s] θυρωρῷ καὶ [t] εἰσήγαγεν τὸν Πέτρον. 17 λέγει οὖν

..εκεινου D. ABCE KLM SUXY ΓΔΛΠℵ 1. 33. 69

g = Matt. xxvi. 57 || Mk. xxvii. 2 al. 4 Kings xi. 4. see Acts xii. 19.
h here only. Gen. xxxviii. 13. (-ρά, Matt. x. 35 reff.)
i ch. xi. 49, 51.
k act., Rev. iii. 18 only. Exod. xviii. 19. mid., Matt. xxvi. 4. ch. xi. 53. Acts ix. 23 only.
l Matt. xix. 10. pres., ch. i. 40 reff.
m = ch. xi. 50 reff.
n here bis. ch. xx. 2, 3, 4, 8.
o Luke ii. 44 reff.
p ch. vi. 22 (reff.) only.
q Matt. xxvi. 2 reff. 1 Chron. ix. 22, 25.
r Mark v. 11 reff.
s fem., here bis only. 2 Kings iv. 6. Jos. Antt. vii. 2. 1. see Acts xii. 13. masc., ch. x. 3. Mark xiii. 34 only.
t Luke ii. 27. xiv. 21. Gospp. & Acts only, exc. Heb. i. 6. Gen. xlvii. 7.

13. ηγαγον BDℵ[1] 69 lat-*a* Syr(appy) copt goth(appy): απηγαγον ACℵ[3a] rel vulg lat-*b c f g* syr(appy) æth. om αυτον (|| *Matt*) BC[1]DXΔℵ 33 lat-*a c ff*$_2$ Chr$_1$ Cyr$_1$: ins AC[3] rel vulg lat-*b f g* [*q* syr-jer] syrr copt sah-mnt. καιφα D latt(not am fuld[varies]).

14. [aft δε ins και C.] rec (for αποθανειν) απολεσθαι, with AC[3] rel syr[-txt] goth: txt BC[1]D[r]LXℵ [1] 33. 69 [vss] Chr$_1$ Cyr[-p$_1$] Non$_1$ Chron$_1$.

15. for τω ιησου, αυτοις C[1]. om ο (bef αλλος) ABD[r]ℵ[1] coptt arm-mss Non$_1$: ins Cℵ[3b] rel [Chr$_1$ Cyr$_1$]. γνωστος bef ην B lat-*a c f* [*q* syr-jer] Syr.

16. εξω bef προς τη θυρα ℵ [lat-*a* Syr coptt]. rec (for ο γνωστ. τ. αρχ.) ος ην γνωστος τω αρχιερει (*from ver* 15), with AC[2]ℵ rel: txt BC[1]L. for εισηγαγεν, εισηνεγκε ℵ.

hend and bind ONE, all gave their help: the cohort, the chiliarch, and the Jewish officers. This the Evangelist brings prominently forward, to shew how deep the impression of that previous incident still was: only *by the help of all* did they feel themselves secure. And thus it was ordered, that the disciples might escape with the more safety." **13.**] On Annas, see note Luke iii. 2. The influence of Annas appears to have been very great, and Acts iv. 6, he is called *the High Priest,* in the year following this. The whole matter is discussed in Friedlieb, Arch. der Leid. § 22. He ends by saying that the narrative evidently rests upon some arrangement with regard to the High Priesthood now unknown to us, but accountable enough by foreign influence and the deterioration of the priestly class through bribes and intrigues, to which Josephus and the Talmud sufficiently testify. This *hearing* is entirely distinct from that in the other Gospels. *There,* no questions are asked of Jesus about His disciples or doctrine (ver. 19): *there* witnesses are produced, and the whole proceedings are after a legal form. That hearing was in a public court of justice, before the assembled Sanhedrim; this was a private and informal questioning. That Annas should be so often called 'the High Priest,' is no objection to this view: see on Luke as above: see also note on ver. 24. The *two* hearings are maintained to be *one and the same* by Luther, Grot., Bengel, Lampe, Tholuck, Lücke, De Wette, Friedlieb, Wordsworth, &c.; —the view here taken is maintained by Chrys., Aug., Euthym., Olsh., Neander, Baumgarten-Crusius, Meyer, Ebrard, Wieseler, Hase, Lange, Hess, von Meyer, von Gerlach, Luthardt, and Stier (vi. 284, edn. 2). **14.**] See ch. xi. 49—52 and notes; also on τοῦ ἐνιαυτοῦ ἐκείνου, ver. 13. **15.**] [ὁ] **ἄλλος μαθ.** is here mentioned for the first time. There is no reason to doubt the universal persuasion that by this name John intends *himself,* and refers to the mention in ch. xiii. 23 of a disciple whom Jesus loved. The idea that it was *Judas Iscariot* (Heumann), is surely too absurd to need confutation. The [ὁ] ἄλλος, συνεισ. τῷ Ἰησ., ἦν γνωστὸς τῷ ἀρχ. (as a matter of individual notice), and the whole character of the incident, will prevent any real student of St. John's style and manner from entertaining such a supposition for a moment. How John was *known to the High Priest* we have no means of forming a conjecture. The palace of the High Priest was probably the dwelling of both Annas and Caiaphas.

16. τῇ θυρ.] It was not unexampled to have female porters among the Jews: see reff. **17.**] See the whole subject

τῷ Πέτρῳ ἡ [u] παιδίσκη ἡ [s] θυρωρὸς [v] Μὴ καὶ σὺ ἐκ τῶν
μαθητῶν εἶ τοῦ ἀνθρώπου τούτου; λέγει ἐκεῖνος Οὐκ
εἰμί. 18 εἱστήκεισαν δὲ οἱ δοῦλοι καὶ οἱ ὑπηρέται [w] ἀν-
H -τι ψυχος... θρακιὰν πεποιηκότες, ὅτι [x] ψῦχος ἦν, καὶ [y] ἐθερμαίνοντο·
ἦν δὲ καὶ ὁ Πέτρος μετ' αὐτῶν ἑστὼς καὶ [y] θερμαινό-
G τον ιησ... μενος. 19 Ὁ οὖν ἀρχιερεὺς ἠρώτησεν τὸν Ἰησοῦν περὶ
τῶν μαθητῶν αὐτοῦ καὶ περὶ τῆς [z] διδαχῆς αὐτοῦ. 20 ἀπεκρίθη αὐτῷ ὁ Ἰησοῦς Ἐγὼ [a] παῤῥησίᾳ λελάληκα τῷ
κόσμῳ· ἐγὼ πάντοτε ἐδίδαξα ἐν συναγωγῇ καὶ ἐν τῷ
ἱερῷ, ὅπου πάντες οἱ Ἰουδαῖοι [b] συνέρχονται, καὶ [c] ἐν
[c] κρυπτῷ ἐλάλησα οὐδέν· 21 τί με ἐρωτᾷς; ἐρώτησον
τοὺς ἀκηκοότας, τί ἐλάλησα αὐτοῖς· ἴδε οὗτοι οἴδασιν ἃ
εἶπον ἐγώ. 22 ταῦτα δὲ αὐτοῦ εἰπόντος εἷς [d] παρεστηκὼς
τῶν ὑπηρετῶν [e] ἔδωκεν [f] ῥάπισμα τῷ Ἰησοῦ, εἰπὼν Οὕτως

u ‖. Luke xii. 45. Gal. iv. 22, &c. Gen. xx. 17.
v ch. vii. 47 reff.
w ch. xxi. 9 only †. Sir. xi. 32 only. (-θραξ, Rom. xii. 20.)
x Acts xxviii. 2. 2 Cor. xi. 27 only. Gen. viii. 22.
y here bis. ver. 25. Mark xiv. 54, 67. James ii. 16 only. Hag. i. 6.
z ch. vii. 16 reff.
a = ch. x. 24 reff.
b w. ἐνθάδε, Acts xxv. 17.
c ch. vii. 4 reff.
d Mark xiv. 47, 69. Acts i. 10 al. Num. xi. 28.
e = ch. xix. 3. Luke vii. 45. Rev. xiii. 16.
f Mark xiv. 65. ch. xix. 3 only. Isa. l. 6 only. (-ίζειν, Matt. v. 39.)

17. rec η παιδ. η θυρ. bef τω πετρω, with AC³ℵ rel [lat-*a* syrr syr-jer coptt goth æth arm]: txt BC¹LX 33 vulg lat-*b c* [*f*] *ff*₂ *g* Cyr₁.

18. om 1st δε L [lat-*ff*₂ copt-dz] arm. aft 1st δε ins και ℵ. rec μετ' αυτων bef ο πετρος and om preceding και, with A rel [lat-*f g* syr-txt goth]: txt BCLXℵ 1. 33 lat-*a* Syr [syr-jer sah] arm Cyr.

20. at beg ins και ℵ. om αυτω C foss[addg *et dixit ei*] lat-*a b*: ῑς bef αυτω ℵ¹. om ο (bef ιησ.) BDʳLℵ: ins AC rel [Bas₁ Cyr₁]. rec (for λελαληκα) ελαλησα, with C³ rel Chr₁ [Bas₁]: txt ABC¹LXYΔ[Π²]ℵ 1. 33 Cyr. rec ins τη bef συναγωγη, with Λ 69-marg (1, e sil) [Bas₁]: om ABCℵ rel. Steph (for παντες) παντοτε, with C³Dʳ rel lat-*q* syr goth: elz παντοθεν: txt ABC¹LX[Π]ℵ 1. 33. 69 latt Syr [syr-jer] coptt æth arm Bas₁ Cyr₁ Orig-int₁.

21. rec επερωτας (*see ver* 7), with C³Dʳ rel Chr-montf: txt ABC¹LXY[Π²]ℵ 33 Chr-mss₁ Cyr₁. rec επερωτησον (*ver* 7), with AC³Dʳ rel: txt BC¹LX[Π²]ℵ 1. 69 Chr Cyr[-p₁].

22. rec των υπηρ. bef παρεστ., with AC³ rel syr sah goth arm: εις τ. παρεστωτων υπ. C¹LX(Yℵ³ᵃ) lat-*b c f* copt: txt Bℵ¹ vulg lat-*a ff*₂ *g* Cyr.—παρεστηκοτων Yℵ³ᵃ.

of Peter's denials discussed in notes on Matt. vv. 69—75. This first denial was to all appearance rashly and almost inadvertently made, from a mere feeling of shame. Lücke suggests that Peter may have set himself among the servants of the High Priest *to bear out his denial*. The μὴ **καὶ σύ** (ver. 25), as Luthardt remarks, implies that the other disciple had already been recognized as a follower of Jesus, and had escaped annoyance. **19.**] This preliminary enquiry seems to have had for its object to induce the prisoner to criminate himself, and furnish matter of accusation before the Sanhedrim. **τῶν μαθ.**, His party, or adherents, as the High Priest would understand His disciples to be; how many, and who they were, and with what object gathered together;—and what His customary teaching of them had been. Of *these*, Jesus says nothing: compare vv. 8, 9. But He substitutes for them ὁ κόσμος, to which He had spoken plainly. **20.**] **ἐγώ**, emphatic: q. d. **I am one, who . . . . παῤῥησίᾳ, plainly** (subjective): not *openly*, in an objective sense, which the word will not bear (Mey.). **ὁ κόσμος** here = πάντες οἱ Ἰουδ., or perhaps rather, all who were there to hear. By the omission of the art. before **συναγ.**, the distinction is made between synagogues, of which there were many, and **τὸ ἱερόν**, which was but one. **ἐν κρ. ἐλ. οὐδ.**] Stier thinks there was an allusion in these words to Isa. xlv. 19; xlviii. 16,—in the last of which places the Messiah is speaking. **21.**] See ch. v. 31, which appears to have been a legal maxim. **οὗτοι**, demonstrative: "videtur innuere quod digito extenso ad circumstantes provocaverit." Bengel. The ὑπηρέται of ch. vii. 46 may have been present: see next verse. **22.**] See Acts xxiii. 2. **εἷς παρεστ. τ. ὑπ.** was probably one of the band who took Jesus (cf. ὑπηρέται, ver. 12), and had brought Him hither. **ῥάπισμα**—uncertain whether with the hand or a staff. ῥαπίσαι, ῥαβδῷ

ἀποκρίνῃ τῷ ἀρχιερεῖ; 23 ἀπεκρίθη αὐτῷ Ἰησοῦς Εἰ
[g] κακῶς ἐλάλησα, [h] μαρτύρησον [h] περὶ τοῦ κακοῦ· εἰ δὲ
[i] καλῶς, τί με [j] δέρεις; 24 Ἀπέστειλεν οὖν αὐτὸν ὁ
Ἄννας δεδεμένον πρὸς Καϊάφαν τὸν ἀρχιερέα.
25 Ἦν δὲ Σίμων Πέτρος ἑστὼς καὶ [k] θερμαινόμενος·
εἶπον οὖν αὐτῷ [l] Μὴ καὶ σὺ ἐκ τῶν μαθητῶν αὐτοῦ εἶ;
ἠρνήσατο ἐκεῖνος, καὶ εἶπεν Οὐκ εἰμί. 26 λέγει εἷς ἐκ τῶν
δούλων τοῦ ἀρχιερέως, [m] συγγενὴς ὢν οὗ [n] ἀπέκοψεν Πέτρος τὸ [o] ὠτίον, Οὐκ ἐγώ σε εἶδον ἐν τῷ [p] κήπῳ μετ'
αὐτοῦ; 27 πάλιν οὖν ἠρνήσατο Πέτρος, καὶ εὐθέως
[q] ἀλέκτωρ [q] ἐφώνησεν.
28 Ἄγουσιν οὖν τὸν Ἰησοῦν ἀπὸ τοῦ Καϊάφα εἰς τὸ
[r] πραιτώριον. ἦν δὲ [s] πρωΐ· καὶ αὐτοὶ οὐκ εἰσῆλθον εἰς

ABCE GHKL MSUX ΥΓΔΛ ΠN 1. 33. 69

g = Acts xxiii. 5 (from Exod. xxii. 28). James iv. 3 only. 1 Macc. vii. 42.
h ch. i. 7, 8 reff. v. 36. x. 25.
i Heb. xiii. 18.
j = Matt. xxi. 35. Luke xii. 47 al.‡ 2 Chron. xxix. 34 A only.
k ver. 18 reff.
l ch. vii. 47 reff.
m Mark vi. 4 reff.
n ver. 10 reff.
o Matt. xxvi. 51 ‖ L. (Mk. & ver. 10 v. r.) only. Deut. xv. 17.
p ver. 1 reff.
q Matt. xxvi. 34 (reff.).
r here bis. ver. 33. ch. xix. 9. Matt. xxvii. 27 ‖ Mk. Acts xxiii. 35. Phil. i. 13 only †.
s Matt. xvi. 3. Mark i. 35 al. Gen. xxxii 24.

23. for *απεκρ. αυτω ιησ.*, *ο δε ιησ. ειπεν αυτω* ℵ 69 (arm). rec ins *ὁ* bef *ιησ.*, with AC³Dr(ℵ) rel: om BC¹L. for *ελαλησα*, *ειπον* ℵ¹.
24. [Steph] om *ουν* [with] AC³ rel lat-*q*: ins BC¹LXΔ[Π²] 1. 33 lat-*a b f ff₂* syr arm Cyr; *δε* ℵ 69. 247-51 Syr sah. om *ὁ* DrΓ.
25. for *αυτου ει*, *ει εκεινου* C¹; *ει του ανθρ. εκεινου* C². for *ειπεν*, *λεγει* A 33.
27. rec ins *ὁ* bef *πετρος*, with C²HMSUX[Π²]ℵ 69: om ABC¹ rel Cyr₁.
28. rec (for *πρωι*) *προια*, with EGHKYΓ[Π¹] (S, e sil) Chr₁: txt ABCℵ rel Cyr.

πλῆξαι ἢ ἀλοῆσαι, Hesych.;—*πατάξαι τὴν γνάθον ἁπλῇ τῇ χειρί*, Suidas: see Matt. v. 39. *ῥάπισμα* is not good Greek: see Phryn. p. 175, and Lobeck's note. They had staves, and perhaps thus used them: see note on Matt. xxvi. 67. This blow was a signal for the indignities which followed. **23.] μαρτύρ.** in a legal way. **εἰ δέ** "vim habet affirmandi," Bengel. It has been often and well observed, that our Lord here gives us the best interpretation of Matt. v. 39—that it does not exclude the remonstrating against unjust oppression, provided it be done calmly and patiently. **24.]** From what has been above said, it will be seen that I cannot acquiesce in the *pluperfect* rendering of *ἀπέστειλεν*, to bring about which the **οὖν** has apparently been omitted. I believe the verse simply to describe what followed on the preceding: **—Annas therefore sent Him bound to Caiaphas the High Priest.** *εἶτα, μηδὲ οὕτως εὑρίσκοντές τι πλέον, πέμπουσιν αὐτὸν δεδεμένον πρὸς Καϊάφαν*, Chrys. There is no real difficulty in this rendering, if Annas and Caiaphas lived in one palace, or at all events transacted public affairs in one and the same. They would naturally have different apartments, and thus the sending from one to the other would be very possible; as also would the incident related by Luke xxii. 61: see the extract from Robinson, Matt. xxvi. 69, note. "The Evangelist had no need to relate the hearing before Caiaphas, for he has related ch. xi. 47 ff.: and we have ere this been familiarized with the habit of our Evangelist not to narrate any further the outward process, where he has already by anticipation substantially given us its result." Luthardt. **25—27.]** Matt. xxvi. 71—74. Mark xiv. 69—72. Luke xxii. 58—61:—see note on Matt. xxvi. 69. Peter was in the court-yard of the house—the *αὐλή*. **26.]** This was about an hour after the former,—Luke, ver. 59. Notice the emphatic **ἐγώ**: as we say, *with my own eyes*.

28—XIX. 16.] *Jesus before the Gentile governor.* Matt. xxvii. 2, 11—30. Mark xv. 1—19. Luke xxiii. 1—25. Before this comes in the section of Luke, ch. xxii. 66—71, containing the close of the examination before the Sanhedrim, which did not happen till the morning. This undesigned agreement between Luke and John further confirms the justice of the view respecting the *two hearings* maintained above: see note on Luke, as above. **28—40.]** *Pilate's first attempt to deliver Him.* **28. κ. αὐτοὶ οὐκ εἰσῆλθ.]** I have already discussed the difficulties attending the subject of our Lord's last Passover, in the note on Matt. xxvi. 17—19. I will add here some remarks of Friedlieb's, Arch. der Leid. § 30. "The Jews would not enter the Præ-

τὸ [r] πραιτώριον, ἵνα μὴ [t] μιανθῶσιν, ἀλλὰ [u] φάγωσιν
τὸ [v] πάσχα. 29 ἐξῆλθεν οὖν ὁ Πιλάτος ἔξω πρὸς αὐτοὺς

t Tit. i. 15 bis. Heb. xii. 15. Jude 8 only. = Lev. v. 3.
u Matt. xxvi. 17 ||.
v Matt. xxvi. 2 reff.

rec (for αλλα) αλλ' ινα, with C^2 rel vulg[-ed] lat-*a e f ff*$_2$ [*q*] syr: txt $ABC^1D^r\Delta$ℵ 1 [am fuld forj ing] lat-*b* (*c*) *g* (Syr) sah goth.

29. rec om εξω, with AC^3 rel [lat-*q*] coptt: ins BC^1LX[Π]ℵ 1 [33] forj Syr syr-w-ast (goth) æth, and (but aft αυτους) 69. 254 latt [syr-jer arm] Aug.—προς αυτους bef ο πιλατος εξω ℵ.

torium that they might not be defiled, but that they might eat the Passover. For the entrance of a Jew into the house of a Gentile made him unclean till the evening. It is surprising, that according to this declaration of the Holy Evangelist, the Jews *had yet to eat the Passover*, whereas Jesus and His disciples had already eaten it in the previous night. And it is no less surprising, that the Jews in the early morning should have been afraid of rendering themselves unclean for the Passover,—since the Passover could not be kept till *evening*, i. e. *on the next day*, and the uncleanness which they dreaded did not, by the law, last till the next day. For this reason, the passage in John labours under no small exegetic difficulties, which we cannot altogether solve, from want of accurate knowledge of the customs of the time. Possibly the law concerning Levitical defilements and purifications had in that age been made more stringent or otherwise modified; possibly, they called some other meal, besides the actual Passover, by its name. This last we certainly, with our present knowledge of Hebrew antiquities, must assume; for the law respecting uncleanness will not allow us to interpret this passage of the *proper* Passover on the evening of the 14th of Nisan, nor indeed of any *evening meal* at all." The whole depends on this: can **φαγεῖν τὸ πάσχα** *mean any thing else besides eating the paschal lamb in the strict sense?* This is a question which in our day we have no power of answering; and, as De Wette has shewn (in loc.), none of the instances cited on the affirmative side are applicable. See note on ch. xix. 14.

Mr. Wratislaw, in his little volume of Sermons and Dissertations (Lond. J. W. Parker, 1859), has proposed a solution of the difficulties which is at least very ingenious. Its chief point is, that the Jews, reckoning their days from evening to evening, and also holding *two* evenings, the former beginning at 3 P.M., the other at sunset, the space between the evenings, during which the passover was to be sacrificed (Exod. xii. 6), might be reckoned indifferently, sometimes as part of the preceding, sometimes as part of the following day. Then he thinks that in order to avoid any mistake, they considered the 14th Nisan to begin at 3 P.M. on Thursday, and to end at sunset on Good Friday, thus extending the day to its utmost possible limit. He instances similar confusion between the 14th and 15th Nisan, or rather Abib, in Exod. xii. 18 and Levit. xxiii. 6, arising from the space between the evenings being reckoned in the one case as belonging to the former, and in the other as belonging to the latter day; and suggests that the same ambiguity will account for Josephus's statement that the Jews kept the feast of unleavened bread for *eight* days. Thus, he says, any time after 3 P.M. on Thursday might be called by St. Mark "the first day of unleavened bread, when they sacrificed the passover," and by St. Luke, "the day of unleavened bread, when the Passover must be killed," it being killed after the first and before the second evening on Friday, and thus, loosely speaking, within the day, which commenced at 3 o'clock, and, strictly speaking, within that which commenced at sunset on Thursday. Similarly any time after 3 or sunset on the Thursday might be called the παρασκευή or preparation of the passover, which was to be eaten at some time after sunset on the Friday. Then he understands, that the disciples made all preparations on Thursday afternoon for the passover, which was to be killed the next afternoon, and eaten the following night: and that the passover of which our Lord so earnestly desired to partake, was that which was thus prepared, but of which He knew He was not Himself destined to partake. This he supports by the true reading (omitting the οὐκέτι) in Luke xxii. 16. "If this view," he adds, "be accepted, there is no longer any question, *as far as the passover is concerned*, about reconciling St. John with the synoptical Gospels. The eucharist will thus have been instituted at an ordinary meal, eaten the evening before the paschal feast in the same room in which it was intended afterwards to celebrate the passover." See this more fully illustrated in the vol. above alluded to, pp.

w w. κατά, 1 Tim. v. 19. Gen. xliii. 18 schol. [gen. pers., (Luke vi. 7 v. r.) ch. viii. 4.] gen. thing, Tit. i. 6 only.
x = Acts xxv. 18. 2 Pet. ii. 11. 2 John 10. Jer. xlvi. (xxxix.) 16.

καί φησιν Τίνα [w] κατηγορίαν [x] φέρετε κατὰ τοῦ ἀνθρώπου
τούτου ; 30 ἀπεκρίθησαν καὶ εἶπαν αὐτῷ Εἰ μὴ ἦν οὗτος
[y] κακὸν [y] ποιῶν, οὐκ ἄν σοι παρεδώκαμεν αὐτόν. 31 εἶπεν
οὖν αὐτοῖς Πιλάτος Λάβετε αὐτὸν ὑμεῖς, καὶ [z] κατὰ τὸν
νόμον ὑμῶν [z] κρίνατε αὐτόν. εἶπον αὐτῷ οἱ Ἰουδαῖοι
Ἡμῖν οὐκ [a] ἔξεστιν ἀποκτεῖναι οὐδένα· 32 ἵνα ὁ λόγος τοῦ

Θ_c xviii. 29... ABCE GHKL MSUX ΥΓΔΘ_c ΛΠℵ 1. 33. 69

y particip., 1 Pet. iii. 12, from Ps. xxxiii. 16. z ch. vii. 24. a ch. v. 10 reff.

rec (for φησιν) ειπεν (*corrn of tense to* εξηλθεν), with AC³ rel latt : txt BC¹LXℵ 1. 33 Cyr₁. om κατα B ℵ¹(ins ℵ-corr¹) [lat-*e* (*q*). (Θ_c def, but hardly has space enough.)]

30. (ειπαν, so BCℵ.) rec (for κακον ποιων) κακοποιος (*corrn of constr ; the word from* 1 *Pet* ii. 12, 14 ; iii. 16 ; iv. 15), with AC³[Θ_c] rel vulg lat-*b c f* [*ff*₂ *g q* Chr₁] Eus₁ : κακον ποιησας ℵ¹ : κακοποιων C¹ 33 lat-*a* [Cyr-p₁] : txt BLℵ³ᵃ lat-*e*. παρεδωκειμεν (sic) ℵ [*tradidissemus* latt(not *b e q*)].

31. rec ins ὁ bef πιλατος, with AC³[Θ_c]ℵ rel : om BC¹. om 2nd αυτον [Θ_c]ℵ¹ 1 lat-*c* arm [Cyr-comm₁]. rec aft ειπον ins ουν, with ℵ rel vulg [lat-*a b c f ff*₂ *g* syr-jer] Chr Cyr ; δε ADʳKU[Θ_cΠ] 1 syr goth [æth] : om BC lat-*e* [*q*] Syr coptt arm. (aft ουδενα ins ιουδενα (sic) ℵ : corrd ℵ¹(appy)·³ᵇ.)

168—175. The main objections to it seem to me to be, 1) the total absence of any trace of such an usage, of eating a preliminary solemn meal in the passover-chamber ; 2) the plain and undeniable impression on the mind of every unbiassed reader of the synoptic Gospels, that the meal of our Lord and the Twelve *was* a passover, and that His ἐπιθυμίᾳ ἐπεθύμησα describes, not that which He desired to do, owing however to His predetermined course would not do,—but that which He was then doing in the fulfilment of that His earnest desire. So that I am afraid Mr. Wratislaw's ingenious solution leaves us, for all essentials of the question, where we were before : merely, by suggesting the introduction of possible new elements of confusion, giving us an additional warning not to be rash in assuming a discrepancy between the Evangelists, where computations of time may have been so vague and various.

29.] Though Pilate, having granted the service of the σπεῖρα to the Sanhedrim, must have been aware of the circumstances under which Jesus was brought before him, he demanded a formal accusation on which legally to proceed : "se scire dissimulabat," Rupert. in Meyer. **30.**] They do not mention the charge of blasphemy brought against Him by the Sanhedrim, for fear of the entire rejection of their cause, as by Gallio, Acts xviii. 16. The Procurators in such cases had a discretionary power. On what they did say, Grot. observes, "Quod probationibus deerat, id supplere volunt sua auctoritate."

31.] This answer is best regarded as an ironical reproach founded on their apparently proud assertion in ver. 30—and amounting to this :—'If you suppose I am to have such implicit confidence in your judgment concerning this prisoner as to take his guilt on your word, take him and put him to death (for κρίνατε must be thus understood,—see below) according to your law ;' reminding them that the same Roman power which had reserved capital cases for his jurisdiction, also expected proper cognizance to be taken of them, and not that he should be the mere executioner of the Sanhedrim. **ἡμ. οὐκ ἔξ.**] From the time when Archelaus was deposed (A.D. 6 or 7), and Judæa became a Roman province, it would follow by the Roman law that the Jews lost the power of life and death. Josephus tells us, Antt. xx. 9. 1, that οὐκ ἐξὸν ἦν χωρὶς τῆς ἐκείνου (the Procurator's) γνώμης καθίσαι συνέδριον,—i. e. to hold a court of judgment in capital cases. Some have thought that this power was reserved to them in religious matters, as of blasphemy and sacrilege ; but no proof has been adduced of this ; the passages commonly alleged—Jos. Antt. xiv. 10. 2 : B. J. vi. 2. 4, and Acts vii. 58, not applying (see note on Acts ut supra). The Talmud relates that this had taken place forty years (or more, see Lücke, ii. 737 note) before the destruction of Jerusalem. Biscoe, on the Acts, pp. 134—167, argues at great length that the Jews had this power ; and that the words here merely mean that they could not put to death *on the Sabbath*, which, according to the usual custom of executing the next day after judgment, would now have been the case. But this treatment of the word is unjustifiable. Can we suppose for a moment that this can have been meant, when there is not a word in the text to imply it ? We may hope that the day for such forced interpretations

Ἰησοῦ πληρωθῇ, ὃν εἶπεν ^b σημαίνων ^b ποίῳ ^b θανάτῳ
ἤμελλεν ^b ἀποθνήσκειν. 33 εἰςῆλθεν οὖν πάλιν εἰς τὸ
^c πραιτώριον ὁ Πιλάτος καὶ ^d ἐφώνησεν τὸν Ἰησοῦν καὶ
εἶπεν αὐτῷ Σὺ εἶ ὁ ^e βασιλεὺς τῶν ^e Ἰουδαίων; 34 ἀπεκρίθη Ἰησοῦς ^f Ἀπὸ σεαυτοῦ σὺ τοῦτο λέγεις, ἢ ἄλλοι
...xviii. 35 Θc. εἶπόν σοι περὶ ἐμοῦ; 35 ἀπεκρίθη ὁ Πιλάτος ^g Μήτι ἐγὼ
Ἰουδαῖός εἰμι; ^h τὸ ἔθνος τὸ σὸν καὶ οἱ ἀρχιερεῖς παρ-
έδωκάν σε ἐμοί· τί ἐποίησας; 36 ἀπεκρίθη Ἰησοῦς Ἡ

b ch. xii. 33 (reff.).
c ver. 28.
d ch. i. 49 reff.
e ‖ Mt. reff.
f ch. v. 19 reff.
g Matt. vii. 16 reff.
h of Jews, John always, ch. xi. 48, 50, 51, 52 only. Luke vii. 5. xxiii. 2. Acts x. 22. xxiv. 3, 10, 17. xxvi. 4. xxviii. 19 only.

32. om ον ειπεν ℵ¹.

33. rec εις το πραιτ. bef παλιν, with Aℵ rel syr: om παλιν C³ 33 Syr sah: txt BC¹DʳLXYΔ latt [syr-jer] copt arm Cyr₁. [Θc ?] for αυτω, αυτοις A.

34. απεκρινατο ADʳU[ΘcΠ] 1. 33. rec aft απεκ. ins αυτω, with C³ℵ rel lat-c Syr [syr-jer æth]: om ABC¹DʳLMUXY 1. 33 [latt goth arm] syr coptt Cyr₁. [Θc ?] rec ins ὁ bef ιησ., with A[Θc]ℵ rel: om BLX 1 Cyr₁. rec αφ' εαυτου, with AC²[Θc] rel: txt BC¹Lℵ Chr₁ Cyr₁. om συ Dʳℵ¹ [latt (not *b e q*) æth] sah arm Chr. for λεγεις, ειπας ℵ¹. rec σοι bef ειπον, with AC³[Θc]ℵ rel am(with fuld forj ing) lat-*a b c e f* goth arm [(Chr)]: txt BC¹DʳL vulg-ed syrr [syr-jer] coptt Cyr.

35. for μητι, μη ℵ¹ [1]. for οι αρχ., ο αρχιερευς ℵ¹ [lat-*b e*]. for εμοι, μοι A.

36. rec ins ὁ bef ιησ., with Δ[Π²(but erased)] 69: om ABC¹ℵ rel Cyr₁.

is fast passing away. Friedlieb (§ 31) gives the most consistent account of the matter. In the Roman provinces generally the Proprætor or Proconsul conducted judicial proceedings. But Judæa, which belonged to the province of Syria, was an exception. There was a Procurator cum potestate, who exercised the right of judicial cognizance. Jerusalem however possessed the privilege of judging all lighter causes before the *three-and-twenty*, and heavier causes, with the sole exception of judicia de capite, before the great Sanhedrim: so that none but these reserved cases remained for the Procurator. Pilate seems to have judged these cases at his visits during the festivals; which would fall conveniently for the purpose, it being the custom in Jerusalem, to execute great criminals at the Feasts. In other provinces the governors made circuits and held assizes throughout their jurisdictions. See on this subject Lücke's note, ii. 736.

32.] See Matt. xx. 19 al.: ch. xii. 32, 33. Had the Jews taken Him and judged Him, He would have been *stoned*, not crucified. And this whole section, vv. 28—32, serves to shew how the divine purpose was accomplished. **33.**] This question probably arose out of what Pilate had previously heard, not from any charge to this effect being made between our vv. 31 and 34. Had such a charge been made, our Lord's question ver. 34 would be unnatural. Pilate summoned Jesus in, who had been as yet outside with the Jews. This was the formal *reception* of the case before him;—as the Roman soldiers must now have formally taken charge of Jesus, as servants of the Roman authorities: having previously, when granted by Pilate to the Chief Priests, acted as *their* police. The judgments of the Romans were always public and sub dio, see ch. xix. 13;—but the enquiries and examinations might be private. In this case Pilate appears to have wished to obtain an account from Jesus apart from the clamours of the chief priests and the mob. **34.**] On this whole interview, see note on Luke vv. 3, 4. I regard this question **ἀπὸ σεαυτ. κ.τ.λ.** as intended to distinguish the senses of the word *King* as applied to Jesus: and of course not (De Wette, Lücke) for the information of Him who asked it, but to bring out this distinction in Pilate's mind. If he asked *of himself*, the word could certainly have but one meaning, and that one would be wrongly applied;—if from information derived from the Jews, this very fact would open the way to the true meaning in which He was King of the Jews. Stier and Ebrard think there may be some reference in ἀπὸ σεαυτοῦ to a momentary earnestness in Pilate's own mind,—a suspicion that his prisoner *was* what he was charged with being (see ch. xix. 8, 12), from the mention of which he immediately (ver. 35) recoils, and implies the other side of the dilemma. **35.**] Pilate at once repudiates the idea of *his* having any share in Jewish expectations, or taking any personal interest in Jewish matters: all his information he has derived from the public accusation of the people and chief

βασιλεια ἡ ἐμὴ οὐκ ἔστιν [i] ἐκ τοῦ κόσμου τούτου. εἰ [i] ἐκ
τοῦ κόσμου τούτου ἦν ἡ βασιλεία ἡ ἐμή, οἱ ὑπηρέται ἂν
οἱ ἐμοὶ [k] ἠγωνίζοντο ἵνα μὴ παραδοθῶ τοῖς Ἰουδαίοις· νῦν
δὲ ἡ βασιλεία ἡ ἐμὴ οὐκ ἔστιν [l] ἐντεῦθεν. 37 εἶπεν οὖν
αὐτῷ ὁ Πιλάτος [m] Οὐκοῦν βασιλεὺς εἶ σύ; ἀπεκρίθη [ὁ]
Ἰησοῦς [n] Σὺ λέγεις, ὅτι βασιλεύς εἰμι [ἐγώ]. ἐγὼ [o] εἰς
τοῦτο γεγέννημαι καὶ [o] εἰς τοῦτο ἐλήλυθα εἰς τὸν κόσμον,
ἵνα [p] μαρτυρήσω τῇ [p] ἀληθείᾳ. πᾶς ὁ [q] ὢν [qr] ἐκ τῆς

..κοσμου του C. ABEG HKLM SUXY ΓΔΛΠℵ 1. 33. 69

i ch. iii. 31 reff. k Luke xiii. 24. Col. i. 29. iv. 12. 1 Tim. vi. 12. 2 Tim. iv. 7. 1 Cor. ix. 25 only +. Sir. iv. 28 al. Dan. vi. 14 Theod. l Luke iv. 9. James iv. 1 al. m here only +. n :: only. o Mark i. 38. Acts ix. 21. 1 John iii. 8. p = ch. v. 33 (3 John 3). constr., 3 John 6 al. q 1 John iii. 19. r = Rom. ii. 8. iii. 26. iv. 12, 14. Gal. iii. 7.

for η βασ. η εμη, η εμη βασ. (3 times) ℵ, and (2nd time) Dr Chr-ms. ins και bef οι υπηρ. ℵ. οι εμοι ηγωνιζ. bef αν B[[2](om αν B[1])] LXℵ 1. 33. 69 arm $Orig_3$ Chr_1 Cyr[-p_1]: txt A rel æth $Orig_1$.

37. om ὁ (bef ιησ.) LXΓΔ 33: ins AB[Λ(sic)]ℵ rel Cyr_1. om 1st εγω (*easily passed over*) BD[r]LYℵ 1. 33. 69 foss lat-*a c* arm Chr_1 Cyr[?] $Cypr_1$ $Ambr_1$: ins A rel vulg lat-*b f* ff_2 *g* [*q* syr-jer] syrr coptt goth. μαρτυρηση ℵ[1](txt ℵ[1] or -corr[1]). for τη αληθεια, περι της αληθιας ℵ[1]. om εκ ℵ[1].

priests. Then in **τί ἐπ.** is implied, 'There is no definiteness in their charge: let me have thine own account, thy ex-parte statement, that I may at least know *something* definite of the case.'

36.] This answer goes to explain the injustice of the charge of διαστρέψαι τὸ ἔθνος (Luke xxiii. 2), and to shew Pilate something of the nature of the kingdom which Jesus really came to establish. **οὐκ .... ἐκ τοῦ κόσ. τούτου**] **not belonging to** (ch. viii. 23; x. 16) **this world**; not springing from, arising out of this world;—and therefore not to be supported by this world's weapons. There is no denial that His Kingdom is *over* this world—but that it is to be established by this world's power. The words not only deny, they affirm: if not of this world, then *of another world.* They assert this other world before the representative of those who boasted of their 'orbis terrarum.' Notice the solemn repetition of **ἐκ τοῦ κόσμου τούτου.**

οἱ ὑπηρ., certainly not *angels* (as Stier) nor *angels and disciples* (as Lampe). This sentence is elliptical, and οἱ ὑπηρ. is included under the supposition introduced by εἰ. 'If &c.,—I should have had servants, and those servants would have fought.' **παραδοθῶ**] This delivering up is referred to ch. xix. 16—*παρέδωκεν αὐτὸν αὐτοῖς.* The **νῦν** has been absurdly pressed by the Romanist interpreters to mean that at some time His Kingdom would be ἐντεῦθεν—i. e. ἐκ τοῦ κόσμου τούτου—as if its essential character could ever be changed. **νῦν** implies, 'as the case now stands;'—a demonstratio ad oculos from the fact that no servants of His had contended or were contending in his behalf: see similar usages of νῦν, ch. viii. 40; ix. 41; xv. 22, 24: Rom. vii. 16, 17 al.

37.] It is best to take **οὐκοῦν β. εἶ σύ** as interrogative, **Art Thou then a King?** on account of what follows. **σύ**, emphatic and sarcastic. **σὺ λέγεις**] A formula neither classical nor found in the LXX, but frequent in the Rabbinical writings: see Schöttgen, Hor. Hebr. on Matt. xxvi. 25. It seems best to punctuate at λέγεις, and regard **ὅτι** as the reason for the affirmation conveyed in σὺ λέγεις. This agrees best with the order of the words, β. εἰμ. [ἐγώ], and with the continued affirmation which follows. The first ἐγώ, if genuine, refers to Pilate's σύ. **ἐγὼ .... τῇ ἀληθείᾳ**] Our Lord here preached the Truth of his mission, upholding that side of it best calculated for the doubting philosophic mind of the day, of which Pilate was a partaker. He declares the unity and objectivity of Truth;—and that Truth must come from above, and must come through a Person sent by God, and that that Person was Himself. **ἐγώ**, both times emphatic, and majestically set (see above) against the preceding scornful **σύ.** **εἰς τοῦτο γεγέννημαι** implies that He was *born* a King, and that He was born with a definite purpose. The words are a pregnant proof of an Incarnation of the Son of God. This great truth is further expressed by **ἐλήλυθα εἰς τ. κ.**: 'I have been born, but not therein commencing my being—I *have come into* the world.' Thus certainly are the words to be understood, and not of his public appearance, his ἀνάδειξις (as Lücke, De Wette), nor as synonymous with γεγέννημαι. It is this saying which began the *fear* in Pilate,

[q] ἀληθείας [s] ἀκούει μου τῆς [s] φωνῆς. 38 λέγει αὐτῷ ὁ
Πιλάτος Τί ἐστιν ἀλήθεια ; καὶ τοῦτο εἰπὼν πάλιν ἐξῆλθεν πρὸς τοὺς Ἰουδαίους, καὶ λέγει αὐτοῖς Ἐγὼ οὐδεμίαν
εὑρίσκω ἐν αὐτῷ [t] αἰτίαν. 39 ἔστιν δὲ [u] συνήθεια ὑμῖν
[v] ἵνα ἕνα ὑμῖν [w] ἀπολύσω ἐν τῷ πάσχα· [x] βούλεσθε οὖν
ὑμῖν [wx] ἀπολύσω τὸν βασιλέα τῶν Ἰουδαίων ; 40 [y] ἐκραύγασαν οὖν πάλιν πάντες λέγοντες Μὴ τοῦτον, ἀλλὰ τὸν
Βαραββᾶν. ἦν δὲ ὁ Βαραββᾶς [z] λῃστής. XIX. 1 Τότε

s = ch. x. 3, 16, 27. t = ch. xix. 4, 6. Acts xiii. 28. xxviii. 18. Prov. xxviii. 17. u 1 Cor. (viii. 7 v. r.) xi. 16 only †. Prov. xvii. 9 Symm. (-θης, 2 Macc. iii. 31.) v = Matt. x. 25. ch. ii. 25 al. w = ||. ch. xix. 10, 12 bis. Matt. xviii. 27. Acts iii. 13 al. Sus. 53. x constr. w. βούλεσθαι, here only. see Isa. xlii. 21. w. θέλειν, Matt. xiii. 28. see Mark xiv. 12. y ch. xix. 6 al. John only, exc. Matt. xii. 19. xv. 22. (Luke iv. 41 v. r.) Acts xxii. 23. Ezra iii. 13. z Matt. xxi. 13 ||, from Jer. vii. 11. Luke x. 30 al.

38. τις ℵ[1]. rec αιτιαν bef ευρ. εν αυτω, with Aℵ rel lat-*q* syrr [syr-jer goth arm] Chr_1 : txt BLX vulg lat-*b c e ff*$_2$ *g* [Cyr-p_1].

39. απολυσω bef 2nd υμιν (*conformn to order in subseq clause in* || *Matt Mark*) BD[r]KLUXΔ[Π]ℵ 1. 33 latt syrr [syr-jer] copt arm Cyr[-p_1] : txt A rel goth æth. om εν B. aft ουν ins ινα KUY[Π]ℵ. απολυσω bef 3rd υμιν (*order in* || *Matt Mark*) ABD[r]KLUXY[Π]ℵ 1. 33. 69 latt syrr [syr-jer] coptt goth arm Cyr[-p_1] : txt E rel.

40. om παντες (*confusion seems to have arisen from the similar* beginnings *of* παλιν *and* παντες, *and the same* endings *of* παντες *and* λεγοντες) BLXℵ : ins A rel vss. (λεγοντες bef παντες D[r].)

which the charge of the Jews, ch. xix. 7, increased. **τῇ ἀληθείᾳ**, not τὴν ἀλήθειαν: not 'the truth,' so that what He said should be *true*,—but **to the Truth**, in its objective reality: see ch. xvii. 17, 19, of which deep saying this is the popular exposition for his present hearer. The Lord, besides, sets forth here in the depth of these words, the very idea of all kinghood. The *King* is the representative of the truth: the truth of dealing between man and man;—the truth of that power, which in its inmost truth belongs to the great and only Potentate, the King of Kings. Again, the Lord, the King of manhood and the world, the second Adam, came to testify to the *truth* of manhood and the world, which sin and Satan had concealed. This testimony to the Truth is to be the weapon whereby His Kingdom will be spread;—'every one who is of the truth,' i. e. here in the most general sense, every one who is a true dealer with his own heart, who has *an ear to hear*,—'of such are my subjects composed:—they hear my voice.' But for the putting this true dealing on its *proper and only ground*, see ch. viii. 47; vi. 44.

38.] To this number Pilate did not belong. He had no ear for Truth. His celebrated question is perhaps more the result of indifferentism than of scepticism; it expresses, not without scoff and irony, a conviction *that truth can never be found:* and is an apt representative of the state of the polite Gentile mind at the time of the Lord's coming. It was rather an inability than an unwillingness to find the truth. He waits for no answer, nor did the question require any. Nay, it was no real question, any more than τί ἐμοὶ κ. σοί, or any other, behind which a negation lies hid. **ἐγὼ οὐδεμ. αἰτ. . . . .**] ἐγώ, opposed to ὑμεῖς, who had found fault in Him. Pilate mocks both—the Witness to the Truth, and the haters of the Truth. His conduct presents a pitiable specimen of the moral weakness of that spirit of worldly power, which reached its culminating point in the Roman empire.

39.] At this place comes in Matt. xxvi. 12—14;—the repeated accusation of Jesus by the chief priests and elders, to which He answered nothing;—and Luke xxiii. 5—16, the sending to Herod, and second proclamation of His innocence by Pilate,—after which he adopts this method of procuring His release (Luke, ver. 17). **ἔστιν συνήθ.**] See note Matt. xxvii. 15, and compare, for an instructive specimen of the variations in the Gospel narratives, the four accounts of this incident.

40.] They have not before cried out in this narrative: so that some circumstances must be pre-supposed which are not here related: unless vv. 30 and 31 be referred to. **ἦν δὲ ὁ Β. λ.**,—in Mark xv. 7 and Luke xxiii. 19, a rioter;—but doubtless also a robber, as such men are frequently found foremost in civil uproar. There is a solemn irony in these words of the Apostle—a *Robber!* See the contrast strongly brought out, Acts iii. 14.

οὖν [a] ἔλαβεν ὁ Πιλάτος τὸν Ἰησοῦν καὶ [b] ἐμαστίγωσεν.
2 καὶ οἱ στρατιῶται [c] πλέξαντες [d] στέφανον ἐξ [e] ἀκανθῶν
[f] ἐπέθηκαν αὐτοῦ τῇ κεφαλῇ, καὶ ἱμάτιον [g] πορφυροῦν
[h] περιέβαλον αὐτόν, 3 καὶ ἤρχοντο πρὸς αὐτὸν καὶ ἔλεγον
Χαῖρε [i] ὁ [k] βασιλεὺς τῶν [k] Ἰουδαίων· καὶ [l] ἐδίδοσαν αὐτῷ
[l] ῥαπίσματα. 4 καὶ ἐξῆλθεν πάλιν ἔξω ὁ Πιλάτος, καὶ
λέγει αὐτοῖς Ἴδε ἄγω ὑμῖν αὐτὸν ἔξω, ἵνα γνῶτε ὅτι
[m] αἰτίαν ἐν αὐτῷ οὐδεμίαν εὑρίσκω. 5 ἐξῆλθεν οὖν ὁ ...εν αυτω G.
Ἰησοῦς ἔξω, [n] φορῶν τὸν [o] ἀκάνθινον [p] στέφανον καὶ τὸ
[p] πορφυροῦν ἱμάτιον. καὶ λέγει αὐτοῖς Ἰδοὺ ὁ ἄνθρωπος.
6 ὅτε οὖν εἶδον αὐτὸν οἱ ἀρχιερεῖς καὶ οἱ ὑπηρέται, [q] ἐκραύ-

ABEH KLMS UXY ΓΔΛΠℵ 1. 33. 69

a = Matt. xiii. 31. Luke xxiv. 43 al.
b Matt. x. 17. xx. 19 ||. xxiii. 34. Heb. xii. 6 (from Prov. iii. 19) only. Jer. v. 3.
c || only. Exod. xxviii. 14. Isa. xxviii. 5 only.
d ||, & ver. 5 only in Gospp. 1 Cor. ix. 25. Rev. ii. 10 al.
e Matt. vii. 16 reff. Ps. cxvii. 12.
f constr., Luke xxiii. 26 al. see || Mt.
g here & ver. 5. (-ρα, || Mk. reff.) Rev. xvii. 4. xviii. 16 only. Esth. i. 6. see Num. iv. 13.
h Matt. vi. 29, 31 reff. constr., Luke xxiii. 11.
i ||. Mark x. 47. Luke xii. 32. xviii. 11, 13 al.
k || Mt. reff.
l ch. xviii. 22 (reff.).
m ch. xviii. 38 reff.
n Matt. xi. 8. Rom. xiii. 4. 1 Cor. xv. 49 bis. James ii. 3 only. Prov. xvi. 23, 27. Sir. xi. 5. xl. 4 only.
o Mark xv. 17 only. Isa. xxxiv. 13 Bℵ only.
p ver. 3 (reff.).
q ch. xviii. 40 reff.

CHAP. XIX. 1. λαβων and om και LXℵ 33 lat-*a* coptt.

2. επεθηκεν ℵ[1]. for τη κεφαλη, επι την κεφαλην A(G)U[Π].

3. rec om και ηρχ. προς αυτον (*i. e. from* αυτον *to* αυτον; *but see note*), with A rel lat-*f q* Syr goth: ins BLUXΛ[Π]ℵ 33. 69 latt syr syr-jer coptt æth arm Cyr_1 Non_1[appy]. for ο βασ., βασιλευ ℵ. rec εδιδουν, with A rel: txt BLXℵ 1 Cyr_1.

4. rec (for και εξηλθ.) εξηλθεν ουν, with Δ rel vulg-ed lat-*b* ff_2 Chr: εξηλθεν (only) D^rΓℵ 1 ev-y am(with fuld em forj foss gat ing mt) lat-*a c e f g q* syr coptt goth arm: txt ABKLX[Π] 33 Syr æth Cyr_1. ο πιλατος bef εξω LXℵ 69 vulg [lat-*a b c f* ff_2 *g q* syr-jer æth arm]: εξω bef παλιν Y. rec εν αυτω ουδεμ. bef αιτιαν, with D^r rel am(with fuld foss mt tol) syr goth: ουδεμ. εν αυτω αιτ. ευρ. A 122(Sz): ουδ. αιτ. ευρ. εν αυτω B 33 [1 coptt æth]: αιτιαν ουδεμ. ευρισκω εν αυτω ℵ-corr[1a](the origl scribe of parts of the Codex, Tischdf: see ch. xxi. 25 digest): αιτιαν ουχ ευρισκω (omg εν αυτω) ℵ[1](appy, Tischdf): εν αυτω ουχ ευρ. αιτ. 69: txt LXY. (*I adopt txt, with Tischdf* (edn 7), *as more probably having originated the other transposns, than a transposn itself.*)

5. om ὁ (bef ιησ.) B. om το ℵ. rec ιδε, with A rel: txt BLXY[$Π^2$]ℵ 1. 33 Cyr_1 $Hesych_1$. om ὁ (bef ανθρωπος) B.

Luthardt (after Krafft) remarks on the parallelism with Levit. xvi. 5—10. Thus was Jesus "the goat upon which the Lord's lot fell, to be offered for a sin-offering." See the same idea expanded by Mr. Wratislaw, in the first of the sermons in his volume. CHAP. XIX. 1.] The reason or purpose of this scourging does not here appear; but in Luke xxiii. 21—23 we read that after the choice of Barabbas, Pilate asked them what should be done with Jesus? And when they demanded that He should be crucified, Pilate, after another assertion of his innocence, said παιδεύσας αὐτὸν ἀπολύσω. Thus it is accounted for. **2, 3. κ. ἤρχοντο πρ. αὐτ.**] This has been perhaps erased as not being understood. It was their mock-reverential approach, as to a crowned king: coming probably with obeisances and pretended homage. In the χαῖρε ὁ β. τ. Ἰουδαίων, "non tam Christum derident, quam Judæis insultant:" Lampe. See notes on Matt. vv. 27—30;—and on πορφύραν, Mark ver. 17. **4.**] The unjust and cruel conduct of Pilate appears to have had for its object to satisfy the multitude by the mockery and degradation of the so-called King of the Jews: and with that view he now brings forth Jesus. His speech is equivalent to—'See what I have done purely to please *you*—for *I* believe Him innocent.' Ver. **5** is the accurate and graphic delineation of an eye-witness, and intimately connected with the speech of Pilate which follows. For the **ἰδοὺ ὁ ἄνθ.** is to move their contempt and pity;—'See this man who submits to and has suffered these indignities—how can He ever stir up the people, or set Himself up for King? Now cease to persecute Him; your malice surely ought to be satisfied.' **6.**] This had been cried before, see Matt. ver. 22 and parallels. Possibly St. John had not heard the cry. According as men have been in different parts of a mob, they will naturally report differently, according as those nearest to

γασαν λέγοντες Σταύρωσον σταύρωσον. λέγει αὐτοῖς ὁ
Πιλάτος Λάβετε αὐτὸν ὑμεῖς καὶ σταυρώσατε· ἐγὼ γὰρ
...ουχ Γ. οὐχ εὑρίσκω ἐν αὐτῷ [m] αἰτίαν. 7 ἀπεκρίθησαν αὐτῷ οἱ
Ἰουδαῖοι Ἡμεῖς νόμον ἔχομεν, καὶ κατὰ τὸν νόμον [r] ὀφείλει
ἀποθανεῖν, ὅτι υἱὸν θεοῦ ἑαυτὸν [s] ἐποίησεν. 8 ὅτε οὖν
ἤκουσεν ὁ Πιλάτος τοῦτον τὸν λόγον, μᾶλλον ἐφοβήθη,
9 καὶ εἰσῆλθεν εἰς τὸ [t] πραιτώριον πάλιν, καὶ λέγει τῷ
Ἰησοῦ [u] Πόθεν εἶ σύ; ὁ δὲ Ἰησοῦς [v] ἀπόκρισιν οὐκ ἔδωκεν
αὐτῷ. 10 λέγει [οὖν] αὐτῷ ὁ Πιλάτος Ἐμοὶ οὐ λαλεῖς;
οὐκ οἶδας ὅτι [w] ἐξουσίαν ἔχω [x] ἀπολῦσαί σε, καὶ [w] ἐξουσίαν

r = Luke xvii. 10. ch. xiii. 14 al.
s = Matt. xx. 12. ch. v. 18 al.
t ch. xviii. 28 reff.
u Luke xx. 7. ch. vii. 27 bis. ix. 29, 30. 2 Kings i. 13.
v Luke ii. 47. xx. 26. ch. i. 22 only. Job xxxiii. 5.
w Matt. ix. 6 ||. Mark iii. 15. ch. v. 27. 1 Macc. x. 35.
x ch. xviii. 39 reff.

6. εκραξαν ℵ[1]. om λεγοντες Yℵ [lat-*a b e ff*$_2$]. aft 2nd σταυρωσον ins αυτον (*from* || *Mark Luke and ver* 15) Aℵ rel [vss] Chr$_1$: om BL **1** am(with em forj [fuld] ing mt tol) lat-*e* Cyr[-p$_2$ Aug$_1$] Hil$_1$. ins και bef λεγει ℵ.
7. om αυτω ℵ **1** lat-*b c e f ff*$_2$ æth Orig$_1$. rec aft νομον ins ημων, with A rel vss [Chr$_1$] : om BD[r]LΔℵ latt Orig$_1$[int$_2$] Hil$_1$ Aug$_1$. elz ins του bef θεου : om ABℵ rel Orig Chr Cyr. rec εαυτον bef υιον θεου, with A rel vss : txt BLMXYℵ **1**. 33. 69 vulg lat-*c e f ff*$_2$ *g* (æth) Orig Cyr[-p$_1$].
8. τον λογον bef τουτον ℵ Scr's b p t[1] ev-P.
9. om παλιν ℵ[1](ins ℵ-corr[1]) evv-47-49 sah-ms æth.
10. om ουν Aℵ[1] 69 ev-y lat-*q* Syr copt arm : ins Bℵ[3a] rel vulg syr sah. rec transp απολυσαι and σταυρωσαι, with L rel : txt AB E-corr[1] ℵ lat-*e* Syr.

them cried out. **λάβ. αὐτ. ὑμ.**] The words of Pilate shew vacillation between his own sense of the innocence of Jesus and his fear of displeasing the Jews and their rulers. He now, but in ironical mockery, as before, ch. xviii. 31, delivers the matter entirely into their hands: perhaps after having received the message from his wife, Matt. ver. 19.

7.] In consequence of this taunt, they now declare the cause of their condemnation of Him—see Levit. xxiv. 16—and their demand that, though found innocent by the governor, He should die. **8.**] This charge served to increase the fear which Pilate had before: see note on ch. xviii. 37. The name **υἱὸς θεοῦ** served also to confirm the omen already furnished by the dream of his wife. That this fear was not a fear *of the Jews*, nor *of acting unjustly*, but of the Person of Jesus, is evident from what follows. **9.**] He entered, taking Jesus with him.

πόθεν—i. e. not 'from what province?'—for he knew this, Luke xxiii. 6, 7: nor, 'of what parents?'—but **whence?** in reference to υἱὸς θεοῦ: cf. πόθεν γένος εὔχεται εἶναι, Hom. Od. ρ. 373. Observe that the fear of Pilate is not mere superstition, nor does it enter into the Jewish meaning of υἱὸς θ.: but arises from an indefinite impression made on him by the Person and bearing of our Lord. We must not therefore imagine any fear of Him as being a 'son of the gods,' in Pilate's mind (so even Luthardt): this gives a wrong direction to his conduct, and misses the fine psychological truth of the narrative. Our Lord, in His silence, was acting according to His own precept, Matt. vii. 6. Notwithstanding Pilate's fear of Him, he was not in earnest;—not determined to be led by his conscience, but had already given way to the unjust demands of the people; and He who saw his heart, knew how unworthy he was of an answer to so momentous a question. Besides, this silence was the most emphatic answer to all who had ears to hear it;—was a reference to what He had said before, ch. xviii. 37, and so a witness to His divine origin. Would any *mere man*, of true and upright character, have refused an answer to such a question, so put? Let the modern rationalist consider this. **10.**] As in ch. xviii. 35, Pilate at once recoils from his better conscience into the state-pride of office. "Objurgans increpatio timori præcedenti plane contraria." Lampe. This very boast was a self-conviction of injustice. No just judge has any such power as this, to punish or to loose (see 2 Cor. xiii. 8); but only patiently to enquire and give sentence according to the truth.

ἐμοί, emphatic: it perhaps being implied, 'Thou hast, I know, refused to reply to others before.' **ἀπολῦσαι** *first* seems most natural, as appealing most to the prisoner: **σταυρῶσαι** follows, as the alter-

ἔχω σταυρῶσαί σε ; 11 ἀπεκρίθη [αὐτῷ] Ἰησοῦς Οὐκ εἶχες
[y] ἐξουσίαν κατ᾽ ἐμοῦ οὐδεμίαν, εἰ μὴ ἦν [z] δεδομένον σοι I_a ην σοι
[a] ἄνωθεν. διὰ τοῦτο ὁ παραδιδούς μέ σοι μείζονα ἁμαρ- ABEH
τίαν [b] ἔχει. 12 [c] ἐκ τούτου ὁ Πιλάτος [d] ἐζήτει [x] ἀπολῦσαι I_aKLM SUXY
αὐτόν. οἱ δὲ Ἰουδαῖοι ἔκραζον λέγοντες Ἐὰν τοῦτον ΔΛΠℵ 1. 33. 69

y w. κατά, = here only. ἐπί, w. acc., Luke ix. 1. Rev. xvi. 9. xxii. 14. ἐπί, w. gen., Rev. vi. 6. ἐπάνω, Luke xix. 17. gen. only, ch. xvii. 2. z ch. i. 12. v. 27. Rev. ii. 26 al. a ch. iii. 3 reff. b ch. ix. 41 reff. c = ch. vi. 66 only. see 1 John iv. 6. d = ch. v. 18. Matt. xii. 46, 47 reff.

11. om *αυτω* A rel vulg lat-*b e f ff*$_2$ [*q*] syr copt goth arm: ins BD^{r}Lℵ **1.** 33 lat-*a c* Syr sah Cyr$_1$. rec ins *ὁ* bef *ιησ.*, with ALMY^{2}ΔΛℵ 69 Cyr: om B [S(Tischdf)] rel. for *ειχες*, *εχεις* AD^{r}LYΛℵ[XΠ] copt: txt B rel sah æth [Chr$_1$(not ms) Thdrt$_1$ Cyr$_1$] Iren-int$_1$ Orig-int$_1$ Cypr Hil. rec *ουδεμ.* bef *κατ' εμου*, with A rel syrr goth: *κατ εμ. εξ. ουδ.* Y[Π] Scr's w lat-*q* [Orig-int$_2$: om *ουδεμ.* Λ^1 Scr's p Hil$_1$]: txt BD^r [K]LXℵ **1.** 33 vulg [lat-*a b c ff*$_2$ *g* syr-jer æth] arm. rec *σοι* bef *δεδομ.*, with AI$_a$ rel vulg lat-*b f* [*g*] goth arm [Cyr-p$_2$] Orig-int$_1$: om *σοι* X: txt BD^{r}LYℵ lat-*a c e q* [*ff*$_2$ Cyr-p$_2$] Iren-int$_1$ Orig-int$_1$ Cypr$_2$ Hil. for *παραδιδ.*, *παραδους* BEΔℵ [-*δος* Λ].

12. rec *εζητει* bef *ο πιλατος*, with AI$_a$ rel vulg lat-*f* [*q* syrr æth arm]: *εζ. απ. αυ. ο πι.* K[Π]: txt BLMXℵ 33 lat-*a c e ff*$_2$ *g* coptt [syr-jer(p 372, Tischdf) Cyr$_1$]. *εκραυγαζον* (*from ver* 6 *and ch* xviii. 40, *whence also εκραυγασαν literatim*) I$_a$Y[Π] **1.** 69 [Orig$_1$], *εκρυγαζον* A, *εκραυαζον* LM, *εκραυγασαν* BD^r 33 [lat-*a* syr-jer]: om ℵ^1: txt ℵ^{3a} rel [Chr$_1$]. for *λεγοντες*, *ελεγον* ℵ^1. [for *εαν*, *αν* B.]

native in case the other is rejected.

11.] This last testimony of our Lord before Pilate is a *witness to the truth:* opening in a wonderful manner the secret of Pilate's vaunted power, of His own humble submission, and the sinfulness of His enemies. This saying, observes Meyer, breathes truth and grace. The great stress is on the word **ἄνωθεν**, on which Grotius strikingly says (ungewöhnlich treffend, Stier), "inde scilicet, unde ortus sum!" so that it answers remarkably to the *πόθεν* above. We must not dream of any allusion to *Rome*, or the *Sanhedrim*, in this ἄνωθεν, as the sources of Pilate's power;—the word was not so meant, nor so understood: see ver. 12. **δεδομένον**, not δεδομένη:—the neuter is more general, requiring the supply, as Meyer, of τὸ ἐξουσιάζειν κατ' ἐμοῦ,—and embraces in itself the whole delegation from above, power included—q. d. *except by appointment from above.* Lampe (in loc.) remarks: "Concedit Pilato (1) *potestatem.* Agnoscebat fori humani authoritatem, quia regnum ejus non erat terrenum, humanos magistratus destruens. Neque Pilato et Romanis jus in Judæos disputabat. . . . . (2) Exaggerat illam potestatem, *ut superne datam.* Hæc est doctrina Christiana, omnem potestatem esse a Deo (Rom. xiii. 1, 2). . . . . (3) Agnoscit potestatem illam se *in Seipsum* extendere, cum omnia secum ex decreto divino agerentur (Acts iv. 28)."

διὰ τοῦτο] **on this account**, viz. because of what has just been asserted, **οὐκ εἶχες** κ.τ.λ. The connexion is somewhat difficult. I take it to be this: 'God has given to thee *power over* me;—not insight into the character which I claim, that of being the son of God—but simply *power:* that insight belonged to others, viz. the Sanhedrim, and their president, whose office it was to judge that claim; *they* have judged against the clearest evidence and rejected me, the Son of God; thy sin, that of blindly exercising thy *power*, sin though it be, is therefore *less than theirs*, who being God's own people, and with God's word of prophecy before them (and the High Priest, with his own prophetic word before him,—see ch. xviii. 14), deliberately gave me over into thy hand.' It is important to this, which I believe to be the only right understanding of the words, to remember that Pilate, from ver. 6, was making himself simply their tool;—He was the sinful, but at the same time the blind instrument of their deliberate malice. Nearly so Lücke and De Wette. Bengel and Stier understand "quia Me non nosti" as the subject of **διὰ τοῦτο**, but Lücke rightly says that **δεδομ.** ἄνωθεν, and nothing else must be that subject. So Meyer also. **ὁ παραδιδ.**, beyond question, *Caiaphas*,—to whom the initiative on the Jewish side belonged; "cujus authoritate omnia agebantur," Lampe. At the same time the whole Sanhedrim are probably included under the guilt of their chief. In this ἁμαρτίαν is an implied reference to a higher Judge—nay, that Judge Himself speaks. **12.**] **ἐκ τ.**, **from this time;** so De W., Lücke, &c.: Meyer, Stier, and Luthardt render it "*on this account;*" arguing that Pilate had before been endeavouring to deliver Him: but the words imply that from this time, he *entirely set*

[x] ἀπολύσῃς, οὐκ εἶ φίλος τοῦ Καίσαρος. πᾶς ὁ βασιλέα
ἑαυτὸν [e] ποιῶν [f] ἀντιλέγει τῷ Καίσαρι. 13 Ὁ οὖν Πιλάτος ἀκούσας τῶν λόγων τούτων ἤγαγεν ἔξω τὸν Ἰησοῦν,
καὶ [g] ἐκάθισεν ἐπὶ [h] βήματος [i] εἰς τόπον λεγόμενον [k] Λιθό-
στρωτον, [l] Ἑβραϊστὶ δὲ Γαββαθά· 14 ἦν δὲ [m] παρασκευὴ
τοῦ πάσχα. ὥρα ἦν ὡς ἕκτη, καὶ λέγει τοῖς Ἰουδαίοις

e = ch. v. 18. viii. 53. x. 33.
f Luke ii. 34 reff. Isa. l. 5.
g intr., Matt. v. 1 al.
h = Matt. xxvii. 19. Acts xii. 21. xviii. 12, 16, 17. xxv. 6, 10, 17. Rom. xiii. 10. 2 Cor. v. 10 (Acts vii. 5) only ‡. 2 Macc. xiii. 26. see Neh. viii. 4.
i Matt. ii. 23. ch. ix. 7 al. fr.
k here only. 2 Chron. vii. 3. Esth. i. 6. Cant. iii. 10 only.
l vv. 17, 20. ch. v. 2. xx. 16. Rev. ix. 11. xvi. 16 only †. see Acts xxi. 40. 4 Kings xviii. 26.
m (=) Matt. xxvii. 62. Mark xv. 42. Luke xxiii. 54. vv. 31, 42 only ‡. (Exod. xxxv 24 Ed-vat. [κατασκ. AB]. xxxix. 42 A [ἀποσκ. B]. 2 Macc. xv. 21 only.) Jos. Antt. xvi. 6. 2.

rec (for εαυτον) αυτον : txt ABI$_a$ℵ rel syrr goth æth arm Orig Constt Chr Cyr.

13. rec τουτον τον λογον (*from ver* 8), with KU Syr æth Chron$_1$, τον λογον τουτον Λ[Π] Scr's w Cyr$_1$: txt ABℵ, τον λογων τουτων L, των λογον τουτων M 33, τουτων των λογων D^{r}EHI$_a$YΔ [S(Tischdf) Γ] Aug. rec ins του bef βηματος, with E rel : om ABD^{r}I$_a$LUX[Π]ℵ 1. 33 Cyr$_1$ [Chron$_1$]. om δε D^{r}ℵ^1. for γαββαθα, γολγοθα ℵ^1 !

14. rec (for 2nd ην) δε, with EHI$_a$SYΛ[Γ lat-*ff*$_2$] syr arm : δε ην K 127(Sz) : txt ABℵ rel lat-*a c* copt. rec ωσει, with D^{r}HMUΔ 1. 69 : txt AB [S(Tischdf)] ℵ rel. for εκτη, τριτη D^r-gr L X(txt but not comm) Δℵ^{3a} Chron$_2$(καθὼς τὰ ἀκριβῆ ἀντίγραφα περιέχει, αὐτό τε τὸ ἰδιόχειρον τοῦ εὐαγγελιστοῦ) Non$_1$ Sev$_1$(in a schol often found, appealing to Eus-ad-Marin, vol iv. p. 1009) Ammon$_1$ Thl$_1$ (*see note*).

himself to deliver Him. Pilate himself was deeply struck by these words of majesty and mildness, and almost sympathy for his [own] weakness, and made a last, and, as **ἐκ τ.** seems to imply, a somewhat longer attempt than before, to deliver Him. **φίλος τ. Κ.**] There does not seem to be any allusion to a title of honour, *amicus Cæsaris;* indeed, to judge from the citations in Wetstein, a good deal of fancy has been employed in making out the fact of such a title having been in use, any further than that the appellation would naturally arise and be accounted honourable. **φίλ. τ. Κ.** here is 'well affected to Cæsar.' This was a terrible saying, especially under Tiberius, with whom (Tacit. Ann. iii. 38) "majestatis crimen omnium accusationum complementum erat." **πᾶς ὁ β. . . . .**] This was true: their application of it to Christ a lie. But *words,* not *facts,* are taken into account by tyrants, and this Pilate knew. **13.**] **τ. λόγων τούτων** —viz. these two last remarks. "In such a perplexity, a man like Pilate could not long hesitate. As Caiaphas had before said, it were better that one even innocent man should die, than that all should perish: so now in like case Pilate decided rather to sacrifice Jesus though innocent, than to expose himself to so great danger." Friedlieb, Arch. der Leid. § 34. **ἔξω**] See on ch. xviii. 33. The **βῆμα** was in front of the prætorium, on an elevated platform; —Gabbatha, probably from גָּבַהּ, *altus fuit,* —which was paved with a tessellated pavement. Such a pavement Julius Cæsar carried about on his expeditions, Suet. Cæs. c. 46. **14. παρασκευὴ τοῦ π.**] The signification, 'Friday in the Passover week' (using παρασκευή for 'day before the sabbath,' as reff. Matt., Luke, and τοῦ π. as in σάββατον τοῦ π. Ps.-Ign. ad Philip. c. 13, p. 937, ed. Migne), has found many and some recent defenders: see especially Wieseler, Chron. Synops. i. 335 ff. But this is not its natural meaning, nor would it ever have been thought of in this place, but for the difficulty arising from the whole Passover question, which I have discussed on Matt. xxvi. 17—19, and on ch. xviii. 28. **παρ. τοῦ π.** answers to עֶרֶב הַפֶּסַח, and is '*the vigil of the Passover,*' i.e. the day preceding the evening when the passover was killed. And so it must be understood here, especially when connected with ch. xviii. 28. See on the whole matter the notes above referred to. **ὥρα ὡς ἕκτη**] There is an insuperable difficulty as the text now stands. For Mark relates, ch. xv. 25, that the *crucifixion* took place at the *third hour:* and that it certainly was so, the whole arrangement of the day testifies. For on the one hand, the judgment could hardly have taken the whole day till noon: and on the other, there will not thus be time left for the rest of the events of the day, before the sabbath began. We must certainly suppose, as did Eusebius, Theophylact, and Severus (in the Catena, Lücke, ii. 750), that there has been some very early erratum in our copies; whether the interchange

n Mark iii. 34. ch. i. 29 al. o ch. xviii. 40 reff. p Luke xxiii. 18 reff. see ch. xvii. 15 reff. q = ch. x. 10. 2 Cor. xii. 13. Eph. iv. 9. r = Acts xvi. 33. xxi. 24 al. s = Luke xiv. 27. Acts xv. 10. Gal. vi. 2, 5. constr. w. dat., here only. t || only. Judg. ix. 53. 4 Kings ix. 35 only. u ver. 13 reff. v here (Rev. xxii. 2 v. r.) only. Dan. xii. 5 Theod. see Ezek. xl. 34, 37. w = Luke xxii. 55. ch. i. 26. 2 Macc. x. 30.

[n] Ἴδε ὁ βασιλεὺς ὑμῶν. 15 [o] ἐκραύγασαν οὖν ἐκεῖνοι
[p] Ἆρον ἆρον, σταύρωσον αὐτόν. λέγει αὐτοῖς ὁ Πιλάτος
Τὸν βασιλέα ὑμῶν σταυρώσω; ἀπεκρίθησαν οἱ ἀρχιερεῖς
Οὐκ ἔχομεν βασιλέα [q] εἰ μὴ Καίσαρα. 16 τότε οὖν παρέδωκεν αὐτὸν αὐτοῖς ἵνα σταυρωθῇ.

[r] Παρέλαβον οὖν τὸν Ἰησοῦν· 17 καὶ [s] βαστάζων
αὐτῷ τὸν σταυρὸν ἐξῆλθεν εἰς τὸν λεγόμενον [t] κρανίου
τόπον, ὃ λέγεται [u] Ἑβραϊστὶ Γολγοθᾶ· 18 ὅπου αὐτὸν
ἐσταύρωσαν, καὶ μετ᾽ αὐτοῦ ἄλλους δύο [v] ἐντεῦθεν καὶ
ἐντεῦθεν, [w] μέσον δὲ τὸν Ἰησοῦν. 19 Ἔγραψεν δὲ καὶ

...βασταζων τον Δ. ABEH I$_a$KLM SUXY ΓΛΠℵ 1. 33. 69

15. rec (for εκρ. ουν εκεινοι) οι δε εκρ., with AI$_a$ rel vulg lat-*a* (*c f ff*$_2$) [copt æth arm]: οι δε ελεγον ℵ^1: εκρ. ουν, omg εκεινοι, 33: txt BLXℵ^{3a} lat-*b e q* Cyr$_1$.—εκραυγασον A: εκραυγαζον D^{r}KY[Π]: εκραυασαν L. [om 1st αρον ℵ^{3a}(but marks of erasure removed) lat-*c*.]

16. αυτοις bef αυτον ℵ [latt(not *a e*) Cyr$_1$]. rec (for 2nd ουν) δε, with AI$_a$ rel vulg lat-*g* syr [Chr$_1$ Cyr-ms]: txt BD^{r}LX 33 foss lat-*a b c e ff*$_2$ *q* copt [Cyr].—οι δε λαβοντες ℵ^1 [sah], so (but παραλ.) M 1: παραλαβοντες ουν ℵ^{3a} evv-H$_1$-P$_1$-Z$_1$ Orig$_1$. rec aft ιησ. ins και απηγαγον, with A vulg-ed [lat-*g q*] syr sah æth; απηγαγον MU[Π^2]ℵ 1 arm: και ηγαγον D^{r}EHI$_a$KSYΔΛ[ΓΠ$^{1.3}$] am(with foss mt) lat-*f* Chr Cyr-ms: om BLX 33. 69 lat-*a b c e ff*$_2$ syr-jer copt Orig Cyr. ins further αυτον ℵ.

17. rec (for αυτω τ. στ.) τον σταυρον αυτου, with E rel; τον στ. εαυτου AI$_a$UY Chr [Cyr-ms]: εαυτου τ. στ. D^r 239: txt BX(L[Π]ℵ 1) 33 latt [syr-jer] Orig(κατὰ τ. Ἰωαν. Ἰησοῦς ἑαυτῷ βαστάζει τ. στ.) Cyr$_1$, but of these L[Π]ℵ 1 Cyr$_1$ have εαυτω. rec (for ὃ) ὅς, with I$_a$ rel lat-*e* syr: txt A[B]Kℵ ev-y lat-*a c f q* [syr-jer] Cyr.—om ο λεγεται LX 33 vulg lat-*b ff*$_2$ *g* Syr coptt Chr.

of Γ′ (3) and ς′ (6), or some other, cannot now be determined. Lücke and Friedlieb defend the *sixth* hour: but the above difficulties seem to me decisive against it. We certainly may approximate the two accounts by recollecting that as the crucifixion itself certainly did not (as in Mark) take place *exactly* at the third hour, and as here it is ὥρα ὡς ἕκτη, some intermediate time may be described by both Evangelists. But this is not satisfactory: see note on Mark xv. 25. The solution given by Bp. Wordsworth after Townson and others, that St. John's reckoning of the hours is different, and like our own, so that the sixth hour = 6 A.M., besides being unsupported by any authority (see ch. i. 39; iv. 6, 52; xi. 9, and notes), would leave here the difficulty that there must thus elapse three hours between the hearing before Pilate and the Crucifixion. Besides which, we may ask, is it possible to imagine St. John, with the other Gospels before him as these expositors believe him to have had, adopting without notice an independent reckoning of his own which would introduce utter confusion into that history which (again on their hypothesis) he wrote his Gospel to complete and clear up? The words **ἴδε ὁ βασ. ὑμ.** seem to have been spoken in irony to the Jews—in the same spirit in which afterwards the title was written over the cross:—partly perhaps also, as in that case, in consequence of the saying in ver. 12,—to sever himself altogether from the suspicion there cast on him. **15.] οὐκ ἔχ. βασ. εἰ μὴ Κ.**,—a degrading confession from the *chief priests* of that people of whom it was said, "The Lord your God is your King." 1 Sam. xii. 12. "Jesum negant usque eo, ut omnino Christum negent," Bengel. However, it furthered the present purpose, and to this all was sacrificed, including truth itself; for the confession was not only degrading, but false in their mouths. Some of those who now cried this, died miserably in rebellion against Cæsar forty years afterwards. **16.]** Here the scourging seems (Matt., Mark) to have taken place, or perhaps to have been renewed, since the former one was not that customary before execution, but conceded by Pilate to the mob in hope of satisfying them.

16 b—42.] *Jesus surrenders himself to death.* Matt. xxvii. 31—61. Mark xv. 20—47. Luke xxiii. 26—56. Compare the notes on the four throughout. **16.] παρέλ.**, viz. the chief priests. **17—22.]**

ˣ τίτλον ὁ Πιλάτος καὶ ἔθηκεν ἐπὶ τοῦ σταυροῦ. ἦν δὲ
γεγραμμένον, Ἰησοῦς ὁ ʸ Ναζωραῖος ὁ βασιλεὺς τῶν
Ἰουδαίων. 20 τοῦτον οὖν τὸν ˣ τίτλον πολλοὶ ᶻ ἀνέγνωσαν
τῶν Ἰουδαίων, ὅτι ᵃ ἐγγὺς ἦν ὁ τόπος τῆς πόλεως ὅπου
ἐσταυρώθη ὁ Ἰησοῦς· καὶ ἦν γεγραμμένον ᵇ Ἑβραϊστὶ
ᶜ Ῥωμαϊστὶ ᵈ Ἑλληνιστί. 21 ἔλεγον οὖν τῷ Πιλάτῳ οἱ
ἀρχιερεῖς τῶν Ἰουδαίων Μὴ γράφε, Ὁ βασιλεὺς τῶν
Ἰουδαίων· ἀλλ' ὅτι ἐκεῖνος εἶπεν Βασιλεύς τῶν Ἰουδαίων
εἰμί. 22 ἀπεκρίθη ὁ Πιλάτος Ὃ γέγραφα γέγραφα. 23 Οἱ
οὖν στρατιῶται, ὅτε ἐσταύρωσαν τὸν Ἰησοῦν, ἔλαβον
τὰ ἱμάτια αὐτοῦ, καὶ ἐποίησαν τέσσερα μέρη, ἑκάστῳ
Td xix. 23(appy) στρατιώτῃ μέρος, καὶ τὸν ᵉ χιτῶνα. ἦν δὲ ὁ ᵉ χιτὼν
ᶠ ἄραφος, ᵍ ἐκ τῶν ᵍ ἄνωθεν ʰ ὑφαντὸς ⁱ δι' ὅλου. 24 εἶπον
οὖν πρὸς ἀλλήλους Μὴ ᵏ σχίσωμεν αὐτόν, ἀλλὰ ˡ λάχω-
μεν περὶ αὐτοῦ, τίνος ἔσται. ἵνα ἡ γραφὴ πληρωθῇ
...διεμερισαν-[το] Ia. ἡ λέγουσα ᵐ Διεμερίσαντο τὰ ἱμάτιά μου ⁿ ἑαυτοῖς, καὶ
ἐπὶ τὸν ᵒ ἱματισμόν μου ᵖ ἔβαλον ᵖ κλῆρον. Οἱ μὲν οὖν
στρατιῶται ταῦτα ἐποίησαν· 25 ᑫ εἱστήκεισαν δὲ ʳ παρὰ

x here bis only †. y so Matt., Luke (Gosp. xviii. 37 [but not iv. 34. xxiv. 19], and Acts), John. Ναζαρηνός, Mark i. 24. x. 47. xiv. 67. xvi. 6. z = Matt. xxiv. 15. Acts viii. 28, 30 al. Deut. xvii. 19 al. a ch. iii. 23 reff. b ver. 13 reff. c here only. d Acts xxi. 37 only. e here bis. Matt. v. 40. x. 10 ||. Mark xiv. 63. Luke iii. 11. ix. 3. Acts ix. 39. Jude 23 only. Gen. xxxvii. 3. f here only †. g here only. ἀπό, Matt. xxvii. 51 || Mk. h here only. Exod. xxviii. 6. (-αίνειν, Luke xii. 27.) i similarly, but of time, Luke v. 5. k ch. xxi. 11. Matt. xxvii. 51 (bis) ||. Isa. xxxvii. 1. l here only. Diod. Sic. iv. 63. (Luke i. 9 reff.) m Psa. xxi. 18. = ||. Luke xxii. 17. Acts ii. 45. n refl. pron. aft. mid. voice, Tit. ii. 7. Isa. vii. 11. Xen. Cyr. viii. 1. 2, 9. Winer, edn. 6, § 38. 6. o Luke vii. 25. ix. 29. Acts xx. 33. 1 Tim. ii. 9 only. Ps. xliv. 9. p || only. Joel iii. 3 al. see Acts i. 26. q Matt. xii. 46. ch. i. 35. vii. 37 al. Josh. iv. 10. Dan. xii. 5. r Luke ix. 47.

19. επεθηκεν (|| *Matt*) AK[Π] coptt.
20. om ver and ver **21** to 2nd ιουδαιων (*homœotel*) ℵ¹(ins ℵ-corr¹).—om 1st clause (*homœotel*) 69. rec της πολεως bef ο τοπος, with 1. 69 latt Syr [syr-jer] coptt arm : txt ABIa ℵ-corr¹ rel lat-*q* syr æth Cyr₁. rec ελληνιστι bef ρωμαιστι, with AIa rel latt syrr : txt BLX ℵ-corr¹ 33 lat-*e* [syr-jer arm] coptt æth Cyr[-p₁].
21. rec ειμι bef 3rd των ιουδ., with AIaℵ rel latt [sah] : txt BLX 33 æth.
23. for οτε εσταυρ., οι σταυρωσαντες ℵ. (rec τεσσαρα, with BIa rel : txt AL Mℵ.) om και τον χιτωνα ℵ¹ lat-*a b c ff*₂ Syr. (αραφος, so all MSS but B(sic : see table).)
24. (ειπαν LXℵ [Eus₁ Ps-Ath-ms₁].) for αλληλους, αυτους ℵ¹, εαυτους ℵ³ᵃ. om η λεγουσα Bℵ lat-*a b c e ff*₂ sah Eus₁ [Ps-Ath₁] (*aft ch* xiii. 18, *and ver* 36). μου bef τα ιματια ℵ.

His Crucifixion. **17.**] See on Matt. ver. 33. **αὐτῷ** is dat. commodi: 'carrying the cross for himself.' **19.**] Matt., ver. 37. **20—22.**] The same spirit of mockery of the Jews shewed itself in the title, as before, ver. 14. They had prevailed on Pilate by urging this point, that Jesus had set Himself up for a king; and Pilate is willing to remind them of it by these taunts. Hence their complaint and his answer. The Latin was the official language, the Greek that usually spoken,—the Hebrew (i. e. Aramaic) that of the common people. **ὃ γέγ. γέγ.**] The first perfect denotes the past action; the second that it was complete and unalterable. **23—30.**] *His death.* **23, 24.**] **οὖν** goes back to ver. 18. There were four soldiers, a τετράδιον, Acts xii. 4, *and* a centurion?—"centurio supplicio præpositus," Seneca de Ira, 16 (Friedlieb). The garments of the executed were by law the perquisite of the soldiers on duty. Dig. xlviii. 20. 6 (Friedlieb). The tunic was the so-called 'toga ocellata,' or 'byssina.' It reached from the neck to the feet, and was fastened round the throat with a clasp. It was properly a priest's garment (see Jos. Antt. iii. 7. 4), and was woven of linen, or perhaps of wool (Friedlieb). The citation is verbatim from the LXX. In it, ἱμάτια = the upper garments, ἱματισμός the tunic. Again, beware of any evasion of ἵνα. **25.**] In Matt. xxvii. 55, 56 ||, we learn that two of these were looking on afar off, after Jesus had expired, with Salome. Considering then that John's

τῷ σταυρῷ τοῦ Ἰησοῦ ἡ μήτηρ αὐτοῦ, καὶ ἡ ἀδελφη
τῆς μητρὸς αὐτοῦ, Μαρία ἡ τοῦ Κλωπᾶ, καὶ Μαρία ἡ
Μαγδαληνή. 26 Ἰησοῦς οὖν ἰδὼν τὴν μητέρα καὶ τὸν
μαθητὴν [s] παρεστῶτα ὃν [t] ἠγάπα, λέγει τῇ μητρὶ [αὐτοῦ]
Γύναι, ἰδὲ ὁ υἱός σου. 27 εἶτα λέγει τῷ μαθητῇ Ἰδὲ
ἡ μήτηρ σου. καὶ [u] ἀπ' ἐκείνης τῆς ὥρας ἔλαβεν ὁ
μαθητὴς αὐτὴν εἰς [v] τὰ [v] ἴδια. 28 Μετὰ τοῦτο εἰδὼς ὁ
Ἰησοῦς ὅτι ἤδη πάντα τετέλεσται, ἵνα [w] τελειωθῇ ἡ

s ch. xviii. 22 reff. t ch. xiii. 23. u Matt. xxii. 46. ch. xi. 53. Acts xx. 18 al. v = ch. xvi. 32. Acts xxi. 6. Esth. vi. 12. (ch. i. 11 reff.) w = here only. see Luke xviii. 31. xxii. 37. Rev. xvii. 17.

G μαθη-τη... ...xix. 27(appy) T_d. ABEG HKLM SUXY ΓΛΠℵ 1. 33. 69

26. om *ιησ. ουν ιδων την μητερα* ℵ[1](ins ℵ-corr[1], reading *δε* for *ουν* [as do foss lat-*a b c e f ff*$_2$ Syr coptt]). [ins *και* bef *λεγει* ℵ[1] : om ℵ-corr[1·3].] om *αυτου* (*as not expressed before*) BLXℵ 1 lat-*b e* arm [Cyr_1] : ins A rel vulg lat-*a c f* syrr $Orig_1$. [T_d ?] rec (for *ιδε*) *ιδου* (*not so common in John, only ver* 5; *ch* iv. 35; xvi. 32; *and* xii. 15, *from* LXX), with Aℵ rel : txt BD[r]M[T_d]XΛ 33(appy) $Orig_1$ Chr_1 Cyr_1.

27. rec **ιδου**, with A rel : txt BL[T_d]ℵ 33 Chr_1 Cyr_1. [om *και* T_d lat-*a e* sah.] for *ωρας*, *ημερας* A E[1](appy) 33. 69 sah. rec *αυτην* bef *ο μαθητης*, with D[r]U[T_dΓ]ℵ 1. 69 latt copt : txt AB rel lat-*e* sah arm Cyr.

28. *ιησ.* bef *ειδως*, omg *ὁ*, B. rec *παντα* bef *ηδη*, with ℵ rel lat-*f* [*q* arm] syr : om *ηδη* 1 Scr's d g t evv-H_1-P_2-y_1-z_2 vulg[-ed(with forj) syr-jer] Syr sah æth Chr_1 Hil_1 : txt ABD[r]LUXY[Π] 33 am(with em [fuld] ing mm) [copt] Did. for *τελ.*, *πληρωθη* D[r]ℵ 1. 69 [Eus_2].

habit of not naming himself might extend to his mother (he names his father, ch. xxi. 2), we may well believe that ἡ ἀδελφὴ τ. μητρὸς αὐτοῦ here represents *Salome*, and that *four* women are designated by this description. So Wieseler and Meyer, Luthardt opposing them. So also Ewald: and, which is no mean evidence, the Peschito, inserting a καί between αὐτοῦ and Μαρία. **ἡ τοῦ Κλωπᾶ**, wife of Klopas (Alphæus, see Matt. x. 3, and Prolegg. to Ep. of James, § i. 4), the mother of James the Less and Joses: Matt., Mark. **26. ἰδὲ ὁ υἱός σου**] The relationship in the flesh between the Lord and His mother was about to close; hence He commends her to another son who should care for and protect her. Thus,—as at the marriage in Cana, when His official independence of her was to be testified, so now,—He addresses her as γύναι. **27.**] The solemn and affecting commendation of her to John is doubly made,—and thus bound by the strongest injunctions on both. The Romanist idea, that the Lord *commended all His disciples, as represented by the beloved one, to the patronage of His mother*, is simply absurd. The converse is true: He did solemnly commend the care of her, especially indeed to the beloved disciple, but in him to the whole cycle of disciples, among whom we find her, Acts i. 14. No certain conclusion can be drawn from this commendation, as to the 'brethren of the Lord' believing on Him or not at this time. The reasons which influenced Him in his selection must ever be far beyond our penetration:—and *whatever relations to Him we suppose those brethren to have been*, it will remain equally mysterious why He passed them over, who were so closely connected with His mother. Still the presumption, that they did not then believe on Him, is one of which it is not easy to divest one's self; and at least may enter as an element into the consideration of the whole subject, beset as it is with uncertainty. **ἀπ' ἐκ. τ. ὥρας** is probably to be taken literally,—**from that time**;—so that she was spared the pangs of witnessing what was to follow. If so, John returned again to the Cross, ver. 35.

εἰς τὰ ἴδια need not imply that John had a house *in Jerusalem*. It would equally apply to his lodging during the feast; only meaning, that henceforth, wherever he was, she was an inmate with him; and certainly that his usual habitation was fixed, and was his own.

Ewald remarks (see Meyer in loc.), "It was for the Apostle in his later years a sweet reward to recall vividly every such minute detail,—and for his readers a sign that he alone could have written all this."

28.] **μετὰ τοῦτο** is generally, but not necessarily, immediate. Here we must suppose the ἐλωΐ ἐλωΐ to have been said meantime, and the three hours' darkness to have taken place. Perhaps during some of this time John was absent: see above. **ἵνα τελ. ἡ γρ.**] Various needless objections have been raised to the

ˣ γραφή, λέγει ʸ Διψῶ. 29 ᶻ σκεῦος ᵃ ἔκειτο ᵇ ὄξους ᶜ μεστόν·
ᵈ σπόγγον οὖν ᶜ μεστὸν τοῦ ᵇ ὄξους ᵉ ὑσσώπῳ ᶠ περιθέντες
ᵍ προσήνεγκαν αὐτοῦ τῷ στόματι. 30 ὅτε οὖν ʰ ἔλαβεν τὸ
ᵇ ὄξος ὁ Ἰησοῦς, εἶπεν ⁱ Τετέλεσται, καὶ ʲ κλίνας τὴν κεφαλὴν ᵏ παρέδωκεν τὸ ˡ πνεῦμα. 31 Οἱ οὖν Ἰουδαῖοι, ἐπεὶ
ᵐ παρασκευὴ ἦν, ἵνα μὴ μείνῃ ἐπὶ τοῦ σταυροῦ τὰ σώματα
ⁿ ἐν τῷ σαββάτῳ (ἦν γὰρ ᵒ μεγάλη ἡ ᵖ ἡμέρα ἐκείνου

x sing., ch. vii. 38 reff. Psa. lxviii. 21.
y ch. iv. 13, &c. reff.
z Mark xi. 16. Luke viii. 16 al. Lev. vi. 28.
a = ch. ii. 6. xx. 5, 6. xxi. 9. Rev. iv. 2. Jer. xxiv. 1.
b Matt. xxvii. 34 reff.
c here bis. ch. xxi. 11. Matt. xxiii. 28. Rom. i. 29. xv. 14. James iii. 8, 17. 2 Pet. ii. 14 only. Ezek. xxxvii. 1.
d ‖ Mt. Mk. only †.
e Heb. ix. 19 only. Exod. xii. 22 al.
f Matt. xxvii. 28 reff. Gen. xxvii. 16.
g = here only.
h = Mark xv. 23. Acts ix. 19. 1 Tim. iv. 4.
i = Luke xii. 50. Rev. x. 7. Ezra vii. 12.
j = Luke xxiv. 5. (Matt. viii. 20 reff.)
k = Acts xv. 40.
l = ‖ Mt. L. Eccl. xii. 7.
m ver. 14 reff.
n = Matt. xii. 2 al. fr.
o = ch. vii. 37 reff
p here only. Neh. x. 31. see Luke iv. 16 reff

29. rec aft *σκευος* ins *ουν*, with Dʳ rel vulg lat-*c f g q* syr; *δε* ℵ [syr-jer coptt arm]: om ABLX foss lat-*a b e*. rec (for *σπογγον ουν μεστον του οξους*) *οι δε πλησαντες σπογγον οξους και* (*the ver has been corrd aft Matt* xxvii. 48 *and Mark* xv. 36, *and the ουν transposed to suit*), with A rel vulg lat-*f g* syrr (copt æth) arm: txt BL(Xℵ) 1. 33 lat-*b e ff*$_2$ (sah [Eus$_2$]) Cyr Hil$_1$. (om *του* Xℵ[1] Eus$_2$.)

30. om *ὁ* (bef *ιησ.*) B. om *ιησ.* also ℵ[1] [em] lat-*a*: *ο ιησ.* bef *το οξ.* E 69 vulg lat-*b c* [*e f ff*$_2$ *g q* æth] arm Eus$_2$ Hil.

31. rec *ινα* to *σαββατω* bef *επει παρασκευη ην*, with A(Dʳ) rel syr: txt BLXYℵ 33. 69 latt Syr [syr-jer arm] coptt æth Chr$_1$ Cyr$_1$ Non$_1$ [Hesych$_1$], *επι παρασκευι*, omg *ην*, Dʳ. om *ἡ* AE[Γ]ℵ. elz *εκεινη*, with [B[1](Tischdf (N. T. Vat.), expr] H 33 (69) vulg lat-*c f g* syr: txt A B[[3](Tischdf)] ℵ rel lat-*a b e ff*$_2$ *q* Syr coptt æth arm

application of these words to the saying of the Lord which follows, and attempts have been made (by Luthardt and Meyer among others: see on the other hand Ewald) to connect them with *τετέλεσται* (*τετέλεσται, ἵνα τελειωθῇ*). That St. John does use *ἵνα* . . . . as applying to what *follows*, ch. xiv. 31 shews. And so here,—'that the Scripture might be *accomplished*' (not *πληρωθῇ*),—having it in view to leave no pre-appointed particular of the circumstances of his suffering unfulfilled, Jesus, speaking doubtless also in intense present agony of thirst, but only speaking because He so willed it, and because it was an ordained part of the course which He had taken upon Him, said this word. "Nec hoc levamentum petiisset, nisi scivisset id quoque ad *κριτήρια* Messiæ secundum Prophetas spectare. Unde hæc altera motiva additur: *ut consummaretur Scriptura*." Lampe in loc. **29.**] The **ὄξος** was the posca, the sour wine, or vinegar and water, the common drink of the Roman soldiers. **ὑσσώπῳ**—an aromatic plant growing on walls, common in the south of England and on the Continent, with blue or white flowers, and having stalks about 1½ foot long, which would in this case be long enough, the feet of the crucified person not being ordinarily raised above that distance from the ground. It was much used for sprinkling, Exod. xii. 22: Levit. xiv. 4 &c.: Ps. li. 7. **30.**] **τετέλεσται** expresses the fulfilling of that appointed course of humiliation, obedience, and suffering, which the Lord Jesus had undertaken. ("Verbum *τελέω* convenit rebus, *τελειόω* scripturæ sacræ," Bengel.) That was now over,—the redemption of man accomplished,—and from this time "the joy that was set before Him" begins. It is beyond the purpose of a note to bring out the many meanings of this most important and glorious word. There is an admirable sermon on it by Schleiermacher (vol. ii. serm. 10); and Stier's Comment, vi. 473 ff., should be read. **κλίνας τ. κεφαλήν**] We have the minuteness of an eye-witness, on whom every particular of this solemn moment made an indelible impression. **παρέδωκεν τὸ πνεῦμα**—viz. in the words given by Luke, *πάτερ, εἰς χεῖράς σου παρατίθεμαι τὸ πνεῦμα*,—which was also the *φωνὴ μεγάλη* of Matt. and Mark. This *παραδιδόναι* was strictly a voluntary and determinate act—no *coming on* of death, which had no power over Him,—see ch. x. 18, and note on Luke xxiii. 46. **31—42.**] *Jesus in Death*: and herein, **31—37.**] *Proof of His Death.* **31.**] On the Jewish custom, see note, Matt. xxvii. 57. **ἦν γὰρ μεγ. . . . . .**, being as it was (see note on ch. xviii. 28, and Matt. xxvi. 17) *a double sabbath*: the coincidence of the first day of unleavened bread (Exod. xii. 16) with an ordinary sab-

q Luke vii. 36 reff.
r here 3ce and Matt. xii. 20 only. Deut. xxxiii. 11. 2 Kings xxii. 35. Jer. xxxi. (xlviii.) 25. Hab. iii. 12 only. plur., Luke xxiv. 11 reff.
s here 3ce only. Amos iii. 12 al.
t ch. xi. 48 reff.
u Matt. xxvii. 44 ‖ Mk. Rom. vi. 6. Gal. ii. 20 only †.

τοῦ [p] σαββάτου), [q] ἠρώτησαν τὸν Πιλάτον ἵνα [r] κατ-
εαγῶσιν αὐτῶν τὰ [s] σκέλη καὶ [t] ἀρθῶσιν. 32 ἦλθον οὖν οἱ
στρατιῶται, καὶ τοῦ μὲν πρώτου [r] κατέαξαν τὰ [s] σκέλη
καὶ τοῦ ἄλλου τοῦ [u] συνσταυρωθέντος αὐτῷ, 33 ἐπὶ δὲ τὸν
Ἰησοῦν ἐλθόντες ὡς εἶδον ἤδη αὐτὸν τεθνηκότα, οὐ [r] κατέαξαν αὐτοῦ τὰ [s] σκέλη, 34 ἀλλ' εἷς τῶν στρατιωτῶν
[v] λόγχῃ αὐτοῦ τὴν [w] πλευρὰν [x] ἔνυξεν, καὶ [y] ἐξῆλθεν εὐθὺς
αἷμα καὶ [z] ὕδωρ. 35 καὶ ὁ [a] ἑωρακὼς [ab] μεμαρτύρηκεν, καὶ
[c] ἀληθινὴ αὐτοῦ ἐστὶν ἡ [d] μαρτυρία, κἀκεῖνος οἶδεν ὅτι

Δ οτι αληθη... ABEG HKLM SUXY ΓΔΛΠℵ 1. 33. 69

v here only. 1 Kings xvii. 7 al. w ch. xx. 20, 25, 27. Acts xii. 7 only. Gen. ii. 21, 22. x here only †. Sir. xxii. 19 bis only. y = Rev. xiv. 20. Exod. xvii. 6. z = here only. see 1 John v. 6. a ch. i. 34. b = Acts xxiii. 11. Heb. x. 15. c = ch. iv. 37 reff. d ch. i. 7 reff.

[Cyr-p$_1$] Hesych$_1$. aft *ηρωτ.* ins *ουν* Lℵ[1].

33. for *ως ειδον*, *ευρον* [insg *και* bef *ου*] ℵ[1] [lat-*f*]. rec *αυτον* bef *ηδη*, with Aℵ rel latt Syr coptt [Cyr$_1$]: txt BL Orig$_1$.

34. rec *ευθυς* bef *εξηλθεν*, with A rel vulg lat-*c f* [*ff*$_2$ *g* syrr coptt &c] Chron: txt BLXYℵ 33 lat-*a b* [syr-jer] Orig$_1$ Eus$_1$.—(*ευθεως* D[r]GMUY[Γ] 69 Chron.)

35. for *αληθινη*, *αληθης* ℵ [Chr$_1$]. (*και εκεινος* BY 1 Orig$_1$ Cyr$_1$: txt Aℵ rel Orig$_1$.)

bath. **ἵνα κατεαγ.**] The *crurifragium* was sometimes appended to the punishment of crucifixion, see Friedlieb, p. 164,—but does not appear to have been inflicted for the purpose of causing death, which indeed it would not do. Friedlieb supposes that the term involved in it the '*coup de grâce*,' which was given to all executed criminals, and that the piercing with the spear was this death-blow, and was also inflicted on the thieves.

34.] The lance must have penetrated deep, for the object was to *ensure* death,—and, see ch. xx. 27, probably into the *left* side, on account of the position of the soldier, and of what followed.

αἷμα κ. ὕδωρ] The spear perhaps pierced the pericardium or envelope of the heart, in which case a liquid answering the description of *ὕδωρ* may have flowed with the blood. But the quantity would be so small as scarcely to have been observed. It is hardly possible that the separation of the blood into placenta and serum should so soon have taken place, or that, if it had, it should have been by an observer described as *αἷμα καὶ ὕδωρ*. It is more probable that the fact, which is here so strongly testified, was a consequence of the extreme exhaustion of the Body of the Redeemer. The medical opinions on the point are very various, and by no means satisfactory. Meyer's note is well worth consulting. His view after all seems to be the safe and true one—that the circumstance is related as a miraculous sign, having deep significance as to the work of the Redeemer, and shewing Him to be more than mortal. It can be no reason against this, that, as Ewald urges, St. John does not *here* dwell on any such typical significance, nor can I see how, as he maintains, 1 John v. 6 ff. can be understood without reference to this fact: see note there.

35.] This emphatic affirmation of the fact seems to regard rather the whole incident than the mere outflowing of the blood and water. It was the object of John to shew that the Lord's Body was a *real body*, and *underwent real death*. And both these were shewn by what took place: not so much by the phænomenon of the water and blood, as by the infliction of such a wound,—after which, even had not death taken place before, there could not by any possibility be life remaining. So Lücke: except that he seems to refer *ἑωρακώς* more to the whole circumstances of the death of Jesus.

The third person gives solemnity. [It is, besides, in accordance with St. John's way of speaking of himself throughout the Gospel.] Meyer is for keeping **ἀληθινή** here to its strict sense, not *true*, but *genuine, real*. Perhaps the best account to be given of the word is to be found in the use of **ἀληθῆ** immediately afterwards of the matter of the testimony. The things related are *ἀληθῆ*: the narrative of them is *ἀληθινή*, a narrative of truth.

Some have fancied that by the use of **ἐκεῖνος** here, the narrator necessarily signifies not himself, but some third person. But it has been shewn above (see note on ch. vii. 29) that St.

ἀληθῆ λέγει, [e] ἵνα καὶ ὑμεῖς πιστεύσητε. 36 ἐγένετο γὰρ
ταῦτα, ἵνα ἡ [f] γραφὴ πληρωθῇ [g] Ὀστοῦν οὐ [h] συντριβή-
σεται αὐτοῦ. 37 καὶ πάλιν ἑτέρα [f] γραφὴ λέγει [i] Ὄψονται εἰς ὃν [j] ἐξεκέντησαν. 38 Μετὰ δὲ ταῦτα [k] ἠρώτησεν
τὸν Πιλάτον Ἰωσὴφ [l] ἀπὸ Ἀριμαθαίας, ὢν μαθητὴς τοῦ
Ἰησοῦ, [m] κεκρυμμένος δὲ διὰ τὸν [n] φόβον τῶν Ἰουδαίων,
ἵνα [o] ἄρῃ τὸ σῶμα τοῦ Ἰησοῦ· καὶ [p] ἐπέτρεψεν ὁ Πιλάτος.
ἦλθεν οὖν καὶ [o] ἦρεν τὸ σῶμα αὐτοῦ. 39 ἦλθεν δὲ καὶ
Νικόδημος, ὁ ἐλθὼν πρὸς αὐτὸν [q] νυκτὸς [r] τὸ πρῶτον,
φέρων [s] μίγμα [t] σμύρνης καὶ [u] ἀλόης, ὡς [v] λίτρας ἑκατόν.

e ch. xx. 31.
f sing., ch. vii. 38 reff.
g Matt. xxiii. 27. Luke xxiv. 39. [Eph. v. 30.] Heb. xi. 22 only. Exod. xii. 46. Num. ix. 12.
h Matt. xii. 20 reff.
i constr., here only. 1 Kings xvi. 7. (Zech. xii 10.)
j Rev. i. 7 only. Judg. ix 54.
k constr., Luke vii. 36 reff.
l ch. xi. 1 reff.
m = here only Ezek. xii. 6, 7, 12
n constr., ch. vii. 13. xx. 19. Heb. ii. 15. Rev. xviii. 10, 15. Esth. viii. 17.
o ver. 31. 3 Kings xiii. 29.
p Mark v. 13 ‖ L. 1 Cor. xvi. 7. Heb. vi. 3.
q ch. iii. 2 reff.
r ch. x. 40. xii. 16 only.
s here only +. Sir. xxxviii. 8 only.
t Matt. ii. 11 only. Ps. xliv. 8. Cant. v. 5. (-νίζειν, Mark xv. 23. -νινος, Esth. ii. 12.)
u here only. Cant. iv. 14 ℵ Ald. only. there also w. σμύρν. so Aq.
v ch. xii. 3 only +.

rec om και (bef υμεις), with EGMSY[Γ]Δ copt : ins A B(Tischdf) ℵ rel latt syrr [syr-jer] sah arm $Orig_1$ Cyr. for πιστευσητε, πιστευητε B ℵ[1](txt ℵ-corr[1]) $Orig_1$.

36. ins απ' bef αυτου [Γ]ℵ 33. 69 (latt) syr sah æth [Non_1].

38. rec ins ο bef ιωσηφ, with AHSYΔΛ : om Bℵ rel. rec ins ο bef απο, with ℵ rel [syrr syr-jer] Chr Cyr Thdrt : om ABD[r]L. (*The art would be more usual in indicating a well-known person : but cf* λαζ. απο βηθ., *ch* xi. 1.) om του (bef 1st ιησ.) B. om κ. επετρ. to end of ver (*i. e., prob, from* ιησ. *to* ιησ.) A. ηλθον and ηραν ℵ[1], simly lat-*a b c e* ff_2 [foss sah] syr-jer arm[-zoh]. rec (for αυτου) του ιησου (*specification : cf next ver*), with D[r] rel vulg lat-*f g q* syrr copt æth-pl $Thdrt_1$ (A see above) : txt BLXΛℵ[3a] 33 sah æth-rom Cyr.—for το σωμα αυτου, αυτον ℵ[1] [foss lat-*a b c e* ff_2 syr-jer arm].

39. rec (for αυτον) τον ιησουν, with D[r] U(Treg, expr) ℵ rel [vss] : txt ABLXY sah-mnt Cyr_1. for φερων, εχων ℵ. for μιγμα, ελιγμα Bℵ[1]. σζμυρνης ℵ. rec ωσει, with AUXY 69 (1. 33, e sil) : txt Bℵ rel.

John constantly uses ἐκεῖνος merely as emphatically taking up again the main subject of the sentence. The use of **πιστεύειν** in John makes it probable that he lays the weight on the proof of the *reality* of the death, as above. The **ἵνα** depends on the three preceding clauses, without any parenthesis, as the final aim of what has gone before: **in order that**; not, '*so that.*'

36.] 'For'—i. e. as connected with the true Messiahship of Christ, 'these things were a fulfilment of Scripture.' It is possible that Ps. xxxiii. 20 (LXX) may be also referred to;—but no doubt the primary reference is to the Paschal Lamb of Exod., as in reff. : see 1 Cor. v. 7.

37.] LXX, ἐπιβλέψονται πρός με, ἀνθ' ὧν κατωρχήσαντο—but the Evangelist has given the literal and, as now acknowledged (Lücke), true sense of the word דָּקַר. The **ὄψονται** does not refer to the Roman soldiers,—but to the repentant in the world, who, at the time the Gospel was written, had begun to fulfil the prophecy : and is not without a prophetic reference to the future conversion of Israel, who were here the real *piercers*, though the act was done διὰ χειρὸς ἀνόμων.

38—42.] *His Burial.*

38.] **μετὰ ταῦτα**—not, 'immediately after this'—but 'soon after.' The narrative implies, though it does not mention (as Mark and Luke do), that Joseph himself took down the Body from the cross. Lücke thinks the soldiers would have done this : but their duty seems only to have extended to the ascertaining of the fact of death. The **ἀρθῶσιν** of ver. 31 need not imply, 'by their hands.'

It was customary to grant the bodies of executed persons to their friends. "Percussos sepeliri carnifex non vetat," Quintil. Declam. vi. On Joseph, and the other particulars, see notes on Matt. **ἦλθεν**—to Golgotha.

39.] John alone mentions Nicodemus. The Galilæan narrative had no previous trace of him, and does not recognize him here. Joseph bore too prominent a part not to be mentioned by all. Luthardt beautifully remarks on the contrast between these men's secret and timid discipleship before, and their courage now, "Their love to Jesus was called out by the might of His love. His Death is the

40 ἔλαβον οὖν τὸ σῶμα τοῦ Ἰησοῦ καὶ [w] ἔδησαν αὐτὸ
[x] ὀθονίοις [y] μετὰ τῶν [z] ἀρωμάτων, καθὼς [a] ἔθος ἐστὶν τοῖς
Ἰουδαίοις [b] ἐνταφιάζειν. 41 ἦν δὲ ἐν τῷ τόπῳ ὅπου
ἐσταυρώθη [c] κῆπος, καὶ ἐν τῷ [c] κήπῳ [d] μνημεῖον καινὸν ἐν ...τω κηπω Y.
ᾧ οὐδέπω οὐδεὶς ἐτέθη. 42 ἐκεῖ οὖν διὰ τὴν [e] παρασκευὴν ABEG
τῶν Ἰουδαίων, ὅτι [f] ἐγγὺς ἦν τὸ [d] μνημεῖον, ἔθηκαν τὸν HKLM SUX
Ἰησοῦν. ΓΔΛΠℵ 1. 33. 69

XX. 1 Τῇ δὲ [g] μιᾷ τῶν σαββάτων Μαρία ἡ Μαγ-

w = ch. xi. 44. x Luke xxiv. 12. ch. xx. 5, 6, 7 only. Judg. xiv. 13 B. Hos. ii. 5, 9 only. y Matt. xxvii. 66. Luke ix. 39. z Mark xvi. 1. Luke xxiii. 56. xxiv. 1 only. 4 Kings xx. 13. a Luke i. 9 reff. constr., Acts xxv. 16. Heb. x. 25.
b Matt. xxvi. 12 only. Gen. l. 2 bis only. (-ασμός, ch. xii. 7.) c ch. xviii. 1 reff. d Luke xi. 44 reff. e ver. 14 reff. f absol., = Eph. ii. 13, 17. Matt. xxiv. 33. Exod. xiii. 17.
g ‖. = Acts xx. 7. 1 Cor. xvi. 2. Gen. i. 5. Ezra iii. 6.

40. for *ιῡ*, *θῡ* A. ins *εν* bef *οθονιοις* A rel foss lat-*q* sah $Nyss_1$: om BKLXY [$Π^{1.3}$]ℵ 69. for *εστιν*, *ην* ℵ[1] [$Nyss_1$].
41. *ουδεις* bef *ουδεπω* ℵ [syr-jer]. for *ετεθη*, *ην τεθειμενος* (‖ *Luke*) Bℵ Cyr_1.
42. ins *οπου* bef *εθηκαν* ℵ[1] ev-y.

Power which constrains men. And thus this act of love on the part of both these men is a testimony for Jesus, and for the future effect of His death. Hence also it appears why the Evangelist mentions the weight of the spices, as a proof of the greatness of their love, as Lampe observes." **σμύρνης**, myrrh,—the gum of an aromatic plant, not indigenous in Palestine, but in Arabia Felix, see reff. and Exod. xxx. 23 : Prov. vii. 17 (Hebr. and E. V.): Cant. iii. 6, and Winer, Realwörterbuch, ii. 126 (edn. 3). **ἀλόης**, the name of various sorts of aromatic wood in the East,—see Winer, Realw. i. 54. Both materials appear to have been pulverized (the wood by scraping or burning?) and strewed in the folds of the linen in which the body was wrapped (De Wette). The quantity is large; but perhaps the whole Body was encased, after the wrapping, in the mixture, and an outer wrapper fastened over all. The proceeding was hurried, on account of the approaching Sabbath: and apparently an understanding entered into with the women, that it should be more completely done after the Sabbath was over. This plentiful application of the aromatic substances may therefore have been made with an intention to prevent the Body, in its lacerated state, from incipient decomposition during the interval.

40.] See ch. xi. 44. Little is known with any certainty, except from these passages, of the Jews' ordinary manner of burying. Winer, Friedlieb. **41.**] See note on Matt. ver. 60. The words *ἐν τῷ τόπῳ ὅπου ἐσταυρώθη* are *so far* in favour of the traditional site of the Holy Sepulchre, that Calvary and the Sepulchre are close together, under the roof of the same church. And those who have found an objection in that circumstance have forgotten this testimony of John. **καινὸν . . . .**, and therefore *given for the purpose*—so that the additional particular not here mentioned, that it *belonged to Joseph*, is almost implied. The *newness* of the tomb was important, that it should be seen "neminem præter Jesum, neque Jesum alterius virtute, ut olim circa sepulchrum Elisæi acciderat, resurrexisse" (Lampe): so that (Luthardt) no room might be left for the evasions of unbelief. **42.**] **τὴν παρασκ. τ. Ἰουδ.** seems to indicate clearly the *παρασκ.* *of the Passover*, as I have before maintained that the words mean; not the mere day of the week so called, which, as it was by the Christians also in the Apostles' time named *παρασκευή*, *would not be qualified* by *τῶν Ἰουδ.* The words **ὅτι ἐγγ. ἦν τὸ μν.** certainly at first sight appear as if John were not aware that the tomb belonged to Joseph; but it is more likely that the thought of asking for the body may have been originally suggested to Joseph by his possessing a tomb close to the place of crucifixion, and so *ὅτι ἐγγ. ἦν τὸ μν.* may have been the real original reason of the whole proceeding: and John, not anxious to record every particular, may have given it as such.

CHAP. XX. **1—29.**] JESUS ALIVE FROM THE DEAD. COMPLETION OF THE DISCIPLES' FAITH WROUGHT THEREBY. And herein, **1—18**] *Contrast between His former life, within the conditions of the flesh, and His present, in which His communion with His own partakes of His new relation to the Father.* Compare Matt. xxviii. 1 : Mark xvi. 1 : Luke xxiv. 1. On the chronology of the events of the Resurrection, see note on Matt. xxviii. 1. *I attempt no harmony of the ac-*

δαληνὴ ἔρχεται [h] πρωῒ [i] σκοτίας ἔτι οὔσης εἰς τὸ μνημεῖον,
καὶ βλέπει τὸν λίθον ἠρμένον ἐκ τοῦ μνημείου. 2 τρέχει
οὖν καὶ ἔρχεται πρὸς Σίμωνα Πέτρον καὶ πρὸς τὸν [k] ἄλλον
[kl] μαθητὴν [l] ὃν [l] ἐφίλει ὁ Ἰησοῦς, καὶ λέγει αὐτοῖς Ἦραν
τὸν κύριον ἐκ τοῦ μνημείου, καὶ οὐκ οἴδαμεν ποῦ ἔθηκαν
αὐτόν. 3 ἐξῆλθεν οὖν ὁ Πέτρος καὶ ὁ [k] ἄλλος [k] μαθητής,
καὶ ἤρχοντο εἰς τὸ μνημεῖον. 4 ἔτρεχον δὲ οἱ δύο [m] ὁμοῦ·
καὶ ὁ [k] ἄλλος [k] μαθητὴς [n] προέδραμεν [o] τάχιον τοῦ Πέτρου
καὶ ἦλθεν πρῶτος εἰς τὸ μνημεῖον, 5 καὶ [p] παρακύψας
βλέπει [q] κείμενα τὰ [r] ὀθόνια, οὐ μέντοι εἰσῆλθεν. 6 ἔρχε-

h ch. xviii. 28 reff.
i = ch. vi. 17 (ch. i. 5 reff.).
k here 3ce. ver. 8. ch. xviii. 15, 16.
l here only. elsw. ἀγαπᾷ, ch. xiii. 23 al.
m ch. iv. 36. xxi. 2. Acts ii. 1 (xx. 18 v. r.) only. Ezra ii. 64.
n Luke xix. 4 only. 1 Kings viii. 11. Tobit xi. 3 only. Xen. Anab. iv. 7. 10.
o ch. xiii. 27 reff.
p ‖ L. ver. 11. James i. 25. 1 Pet. i. 12 only. Gen. xxvi. 8.
q = ch. xix. 29 reff.
r ch. xix. 40 reff.

Chap. XX. 1. ins *απο της θυρας* bef *εκ* ℵ (1 lat-*f* D-lat coptt æth arm).

2. ins *τον* bef *σιμωνα* ℵ. aft *κυριον* ins *μου* X[Δ] fuld mt [$Eus_2(om_1)$] Chr_1 Aug_1(*nonnulli codices etiam græci habent "tulerunt dominum* meum," *quod videri dictum potest propensiore caritatis vel famulatus affectu: sed hoc in pluribus codicibus quos in promtu habuimus non invenimus.* In Joan. Tract. cxx. 6).

3. om *ηρχοντο εις το μνημειον* ℵ[1].

4. for *ετρ. δε*, *και ετρ.* ℵ[1]. for *και ο*, *ο δε* (*for contrast*) AU 33 lat-*a f ff*$_2$ Syr sah.—om *και ο αλλος μαθητης* and aft *προεδ.* ins *δε* ℵ[1](om *ο* ℵ[3a] also). *εις το μνημειον* bef *πρωτος* ℵ [om *πρωτ.* lat-*e*].

5, 6. ℵ[1] has only the first clause of ver 5, i. e. the scribe passed from *τα οθονια κειμενα* ver 5 to *τα οθ. κειμ.* ver 6.

5. *τα οθονια* bef *κειμενα* (*see ver* 6) AXℵ mt lat-*c* [*ff*$_2$ syrr] coptt æth arm: om *κειμενα* Λ: txt B rel [Cyr_1].

counts:—I believe all such attempts to be fruitless;—and *I see in their failure strong corroboration of the truth of the evangelic narratives.* It is quite impossible that so astounding an event, coming upon various portions of the body of disciples from various quarters and in various forms, should not have been related, by four independent witnesses, in the scattered and fragmentary way in which we now find it. In the depth beneath this varied surface of narration rests the great central fact of the Resurrection itself, unmoved and immoveable. As it was THIS above all other things to which the Apostles bore their testimony, so, in their testimony to this, we have the most remarkable proof of each having faithfully elaborated into narrative those particular facts which came under his own eye or were reported to himself by those concerned. Hence the great diversity in this portion of the narrative:—and hence I believe much that is now dark might be explained, were the facts themselves, in their order of occurrence, before us. Till that is the case, (and I am willing to believe that it will be one of our delightful employments hereafter, to trace the *true* harmony of the Holy Gospels, under His teaching of whom they are the record,) we must be content to walk by faith, and not by sight. We must also remember in this case, that our Evangelist is selecting his points of narration with a special purpose,—to shew us how the belief of the disciples was brought out and completed, after the unbelief of Israel: cf. vv. 30, 31.

1, 2. Μαρ. ἡ Μαγδ.] She was not alone (Matt., Mark, Luke). Does this appear in the **οἴδαμεν** below? This is not, as Meyer says, precluded by the *οἶδα* in ver. 13. Mary there speaks in her own person, which she might do however accompanied. Still, probably not. She uses the plural as involving all the disciples in her own feeling of ignorance and of consequent sorrow. So Meyer: and it is more natural to take it thus. One thing we may conclude for certain, that *she*, for some reason, *did not see* the vision related in Matt., Mark, and Luke.

3.] Luke, ver. 12, speaks only of *Peter's* going. Meyer directs attention to the interchange of aorists and graphic imperfects in this and the following verse.

4—8.] Full of most interesting and characteristic detail. John, probably the younger, outruns Peter;—but when there, reverently (not "*ne pollueretur*," as Wetst.) abstains from entering the sepulchre. The ardent and impetuous Peter goes directly in—John follows—and *believes.* What can exceed the inner truth of this description? And what is *not* re-

ται οὖν καὶ Σίμων Πέτρος ἀκολουθῶν αὐτῷ, καὶ εἰςῆλθεν
εἰς τὸ μνημεῖον, καὶ θεωρεῖ τὰ [r] ὀθόνια [q] κείμενα, 7 καὶ τὸ
[s] σουδάριον ὃ ἦν ἐπὶ τῆς κεφαλῆς αὐτοῦ οὐ μετὰ τῶν
[r] ὀθονίων [q] κείμενον, ἀλλὰ [t] χωρὶς [u] ἐντετυλιγμένον εἰς ἕνα
τόπον. 8 τότε οὖν εἰςῆλθεν καὶ ὁ [v] ἄλλος [v] μαθητὴς ὁ
ἐλθὼν πρῶτος εἰς τὸ μνημεῖον, καὶ εἶδεν καὶ ἐπίστευσεν·
9 οὐδέπω γὰρ ᾔδεισαν τὴν [w] γραφήν, ὅτι [x] δεῖ αὐτὸν ἐκ
νεκρῶν [y] ἀναστῆναι. 10 ἀπῆλθον οὖν πάλιν [z] πρὸς ἑαυτοὺς οἱ μαθηταί. 11 Μαρία δὲ [a] εἱστήκει [b] πρὸς τῷ μνημείῳ
ἔξω κλαίουσα. ὡς οὖν ἔκλαιεν, [c] παρέκυψεν εἰς τὸ
μνημεῖον, 12 καὶ θεωρεῖ δύο ἀγγέλους [d] ἐν λευκοῖς [e] καθεζο-

Frag. Mosq. απηλθον ...

...καθεζομενους H. ABEG KLMSU ΧΓΔΛ Πℵ Frag. Mosq. 1. 33. 69

s Luke xix. 20. ch. xi. 44. Acts xix. 12 only †.
t adv., here only ‡. Xen. Cyr. iv. 1. 18.
u Matt. xxvii. 59 || L. only †.
v vv. 2, &c.
w sing., ch. vii. 38 reff.
x = Matt. xxiv. 6 reff. pres., ch. i. 40 reff.
y = Mark vi. 14 al. Isa. xxvi. 19.
z — || L. only. Num. xxiv. 25.
a ch. xix. 25 reff.
b Mark v. 11 reff.
c ver. 5.
d see Exod. xxxiii. 4.
e Matt. xxvi. 55 reff.

6. rec om 1st *και*, with A D^r(sic) rel latt syrr [syr-jer Cyr$_1$]: ins BLXℵ^{3a} 33 (lat-*a* coptt). (The reading of the xith century supplement of the Codex Bezæ was ascertained by personal inspection of the ms itself.)
9. for *ηδεισαν*, *ηδει* ℵ^1 [gat mm lat-*b c e q*].
10. for *εαυτους*, *αυτους* BLℵ^1: txt Aℵ^{3a} rel [Chr$_1$].
11. for *προς*, *εν* ℵ. rec **το μνημειον**, with KUX Frag-mosq 69 (S 33, e sil) Cyr: txt AB(ℵ) rel Nyss Chr-mss Sev. (for *τω*, *το* (*itacism*) D^{r}HL.) rec *κλαιουσα* bef *εξω*, with D^r rel lat-*q* syr Sev: om *εξω* Aℵ^1 lat-*a b c e ff$_2$* Syr sah: txt BLXΔℵ^{3a} Frag-mosq 1. 33 vulg lat-*f g* D-lat Nyss Cyr Ambr.
12. om *δυο* ℵ^1. *καθεζομενους* bef *εν λευκοις* ℵ.

lated, is as full of truth as that which is. For, vv. 6, 7, we seem to hear the very voice of Peter describing to his companion the inner state of the tomb. On **σουδ.** see reff. Notice **βλέπει**, of the cursory glance of John, who did not go in,—**θεωρεῖ**, of the exhaustive gaze of Peter who did. Notice also that John when he stooped and looked in saw only the *ὀθόνια*, which seem to have been lying where the Feet were, nearer the entrance, whereas Peter, on going in, saw the *σουδάριον* which was perhaps deposited further in, near the place of the Head. Nor should, as Meyer observes, the minute distinction of *κείμενα τὰ ὀθόνια* in ver. 5 and *τὰ ὀθόνια κείμενα* in ver. 6, be altogether overlooked. **8. ἐπίστευσεν**] Nothing is said of Peter—did he *believe* too? I think *not*;—and that John modestly suppresses it. But *what* did John believe? Was it merely, "corpus fuisse translatum, ut dixerat Maria?" (Bengel, so August., Erasm., Grot., Stier, Ebrard.) Surely not; the facts which he saw would prevent this conclusion: nor does John so use the word *πιστεύειν*. He believed *that Jesus was risen from the dead*. He received into his mind, embraced with his assent, THE FACT OF THE RESURRECTION, for the first time. He did this, on the *ocular testimony before him*; for as yet neither of them *knew the Scripture*, so as to be *à priori* convinced of the certainty that it would be so. But (see above) Peter does not seem to have as yet received this fact;—accounting probably for what he saw as Mary had done. Lampe beautifully says "Concludimus, ab hoc momento in ipsis monumenti tenebris animum Joannis fide salvifica resurrectionis Jesu, tanquam novo quodam orti solis justitiæ radio, collustratum fuisse." **10.**] Luke has the very same expression, *ἀπῆλθεν πρὸς ἑαυτόν*. This is remarkable, as he evidently has a fragment of the same incident. **πρὸς ἑαυτ.**, to their lodging. **11.**] She had come with them, but more slowly. **εἱστήκει, was standing,** strictly imperfect: not '*had been standing*.' **12.**] From what has been said above, my readers will not expect me to compare the angelic appearances in the four Gospels. What wonder, if the heavenly hosts were variously and often visible on this great day, when "the morning stars sang together, and all the sons of God shouted for joy?" What can be more accurate in detail than this description of the vision of Mary? Every word was no doubt carefully related to the Apostle, and as carefully recorded. And all is significant: they are in *white*, because from the world of light: they *sit*, as not defending, but peacefully watching the Body: at the *Head* and the *Feet*, for

μενους, ἕνα [g] πρὸς τῇ κεφαλῇ καὶ ἕνα [g] πρὸς τοῖς ποσίν,
ὅπου ἔκειτο τὸ σῶμα τοῦ Ἰησοῦ. 13 καὶ λέγουσιν αὐτῇ
. κλαιεις Frag. Mosq. D τινα ζητεις... ἐκεῖνοι Γύναι, τί κλαίεις; λέγει αὐτοῖς Ὅτι [f] ἦραν τὸν [f] ch. xix. 31, 38.
κύριόν μου, καὶ οὐκ οἶδα ποῦ ἔθηκαν αὐτόν. 14 ταῦτα
εἰποῦσα [g] ἐστράφη [h] εἰς τὰ ὀπίσω, καὶ θεωρεῖ τὸν Ἰησοῦν [g] Matt. vii. 6. Luke vii. 9 al.
ἑστῶτα, καὶ οὐκ ᾔδει ὅτι Ἰησοῦς [i] ἐστιν. 15 λέγει αὐτῇ [h] ch. xviii. 6 reff.
Ἰησοῦς Γύναι, τί κλαίεις; τίνα ζητεῖς; ἐκείνη δοκοῦσα [i] pres., ch. i. 40 reff.
Frag. Mosq. λεγει... ὅτι ὁ [j] κηπουρός ἐστιν, λέγει αὐτῷ Κύριε, εἰ σὺ [k] ἐβάστασας [j] here only †. (-πος, ch. xix. 41.)
αὐτόν, εἰπέ μοι ποῦ ἔθηκας αὐτόν, κἀγὼ αὐτὸν [l] ἀρῶ. [k] = here only. [l] ch. xix. 38 reff.
16 λέγει αὐτῇ Ἰησοῦς Μαριάμ. [m] στραφεῖσα ἐκείνη λέγει [m] ver. 14.

13. om 1st και א [vulg(not foss) lat-*a b f g* D-lat sah]. ins και bef λεγει B æth: τινα ζητεις (*ver* 15) D 69 æth. **τεθεικαν** D(X) Cyr-jer$_1$.

14. rec ins και bef ταυτα, with E rel ⌊syr-jer] æth Chr$_1$ Sev$_1$: om ABDSX[Π]א **1.** 33 latt syrr coptt arm Cyr$_1$.—ταυτα δε L. rec ins ὁ bef ιησ., with Λ: om ABDא rel Eus$_1$ Cyr Sev.

15. rec ins ὁ bef ιησ., with AD rel: om BLא. aft εκεινη ins δε א[1] [foss lat-*c f* syrr syr-jer] coptt [Sev$_1$]. for εβαστασας, ηρες *sustulisti* D vulg lat-*b c* [*f ff*$_2$ *g*]: ει ο βαστασας א[1]. rec αυτον bef εθηκας, with EΔ[Π] lat-*q*: txt ABDא rel latt Cyr Sev Thl. [S, usually cited e sil for rec, is omitted altogether by Tischdf ed 8.]—**τεθεικας** D[Π[2]].

16. rec ins ὁ bef ιησ., with Aא rel Cyr: om BDL M[1](appy) Frag-mosq. (μαριαμ, so BL[Π]א Frag-mosq **1.** 33 coptt.) aft στραφεισα ins δε D[Π[2] lat-*e* copt arm] א sah.

the Body of the Lord was from head to foot in the charge of His Father and of His servants. (Luthardt.) **13.**] Here again the finest psychological truth underlies the narrative. The other women (Mark, ver. 5: Luke, ver. 5) *were afraid* at the vision; but now Mary, having but one thought or desire, to recover the lost Body of her Lord (τὸν κύριόν **μου**), *feels no fear*. The angels doubtless are proceeding further to assure her as they did the women before:—but this is broken off by the appearance of the Lord Himself, or perhaps by Mary's turning away.

14.] **ἐστράφη**—having her attention attracted by the consciousness of some one [being] present near her—not perhaps by the *approach* of Jesus. Or it might be (Stier, Ebrard) with intent to go forth and weep again, or further to seek her Lord. Chrysostom's reason is very beautiful, but perhaps hardly probable: καὶ ποία αὕτη ἀκολουθία, πρὸς ἐκείνους διαλεγομένην, καὶ μηδέπω μηδὲν ἀκούσασαν παρ' αὐτῶν, στραφῆναι πρὸς τὰ ὀπίσω; ἐμοὶ δοκεῖ ταῦτα λεγούσης αὐτῆς, ἄφνω φανεὶς ὁ χριστὸς ὄπισθεν αὐτῆς ἐκπλῆξαι τοὺς ἀγγέλους, κἀκείνους θεασαμένους τὸν δεσπότην, καὶ τῷ σχήματι, καὶ τῷ βλέμματι, καὶ τῷ κινήματι εὐθέως ἐμφῆναι, ὅτι τὸν κύριον εἶδον· καὶ τοῦτο τὴν γυναῖκα ἐπέστρεψε, καὶ εἰς τὰ ὀπίσω στραφῆναι ἐποίησεν. Homil. in Joann. lxxxvi. 1. We need not surely enquire too minutely, *why* she did not know Him. The fact may be psychologically accounted for—she did not *expect Him to be there*, and was wholly preoccupied with other thoughts: or, as Dräseke (cited by Stier, vii. 12, edn. 2) says, "Her tears wove a veil, which concealed Him who stood before her. The seeking after the Dead prevents us from seeing the Living."

15.] The same kind of repetition by the Lord of what the angel had before said is found in Matt. xxviii. 7—10.

It is idle to enquire *why* she thought Him to be the gardener (see specimens of such speculations in Lücke and Stier in loc.): but I may once for all observe that we must believe the clothing of His risen Body to have been *that which He pleased to assume*; not earthly clothing, but perhaps some semblance of it. Certainly, in this case, He *was clothed*;—or she must at once have recognized Him. But see on στραφεῖσα below.

κύριε, the appellation of courtesy to an unknown person. **σύ**, emphatic.

κἀγὼ αὐτ. ἀρῶ] She forgets her lack of strength for this, in the overbearing force of her love. (Meyer.)

16.] With one word, and that one word *her name*, the Lord awakens all the consciousness of His presence: calling her in that tone doubtless in which her soul had been so often summoned to receive divine knowledge and precious comfort.

n ch. xix. 13 reff. o Mark x. 51 only †. p = ch. i. 39. iv. 25. xi. 16. Acts ix. 36. q = ch. vi. 62. Eph. iv. 8 (from Ps. lxvii. 18), 9, 10. Rev. xi. 12. Tobit xii. 20. r = Matt. xxv. 40. xxviii. 10 al. s = Matt. vii. 21. x. 32, 33. xi. 27. xii. 50. ch. ii. 16. xiv. 2, 20 al. fr. t = Matt. v. 16, &c. x. 20, 29 al. fr. John, here only. u = Rev. [ii. 7] iii. 2, 12 (4 times) only. v here only. see Ezra vii. 17, 18.

αὐτῷ [n] Ἑβραϊστὶ [o] Ῥαββουνί, ὃ [p] λέγεται διδάσκαλε.
17 λέγει αὐτῇ Ἰησοῦς Μή μου ἅπτου· οὔπω γὰρ [q] ἀνα-
βέβηκα πρὸς τὸν πατέρα· πορεύου δὲ πρὸς τοὺς [r] ἀδελφούς μου, καὶ εἰπὲ αὐτοῖς [q] Ἀναβαίνω πρὸς τὸν [s] πατέρα
[s] μου καὶ [t] πατέρα [t] ὑμῶν καὶ [u] θεόν [u] μου καὶ [v] θεὸν

I_d προς τους ... ...θεον υμων Frag. Mosq.

ABDE GI_dKL MSUX ΓΔΛΠℵ 1. 33. 69

rec om εβραιστι, with A rel vulg lat-*a f g* [*q*] : ins BDLXΔ[Π¹]ℵ Frag-mosq 33 lat-*b c e ff*$_2$ syrr syr-jer coptt æth arm. ins κυριε bef διδασκαλε D, simly lat-*e ff*$_2$. at end ins και προσεδραμεν αψασθαι αυτου ℵ^{3a}(ℵ^{3b} disapproving [gat mm lat-*g* syr syr-jer Cyr$_1$].

17. rec ins ὁ bef ιησ., with Aℵ rel Cyr : txt BDL. (M¹ uncertain : see Treg. [Frag-mosq ?]) απτου bef μου B arm Tert$_1$. (txt Orig$_7$ Eus$_6$ [Cyr-p$_1$ Sevrn$_1$] Iren-int$_1$.) rec aft 1st πατερα ins μου, with A rel vulg lat-*a* [*c f ff*$_2$ *g q*] Orig$_3$ Eus$_3$ Cyr$_1$ [Sevrn$_1$ Non$_1$] Thdrt$_1$ Tert$_1$: om B(sic : see table) Dℵ lat-*b e* [syr-jer] Orig$_2$ Iren-int$_1$. for δε, ουν DL ℵ^{3a}(but txt restored) Frag-mosq lat-*q* : om A Orig$_1$ Did$_1$: txt Bℵ¹ rel vss Orig$_2$ Eus$_1$ Hil$_1$. om 2nd μου Dℵ¹ lat-*e* Orig-ms$_1$ Iren-int$_1$. aft αυτοις ins ιδου ℵ.

στραφεῖσα seems to imply that she had not been looking full at Him before. **ῥαββουνί**] See ref.: רַבּוֹנִי, either **my Master**,—or only **Master**, the ׳ being merely paragogic; which last appears (from διδάσκαλε) to be the case here. That she gives way to no impassioned exclamations, but pours out her satisfaction and joy in this one word, is also according to the deepest psychological truth. The addition of και προσέδραμεν ἅψασθαι αὐτοῦ (see digest: so also, but with προέδραμεν, the cursives 13, 346) is an explanatory gloss to μή μου ἅπτου —but doubtless a correct one. "It was the former name with which He called her: His former appellation in which she replied; and now she seeks to renew the former intercourse." (Luthardt.)

* **17.**] The connexion between the prohibition and its reason is difficult, and has been very variously given. See a complete discussion of the exegetical literature of the passage in Stier, vi. 640—667. The sense seems to me to be connected with some gesture of the nature alluded to in the gloss above quoted, but indicating that she believed she had now gotten him again, never to be parted from Him. This gesture He reproves as unsuited to the time, and the nature of His present appearance. 'Do not thus—for I am not yet restored finally to you in the body—I have yet to ascend to the Father.' This implies in the background *another and truer touching*, when He should have ascended to the Father. "Vis me tangere, Maria; vis omnino frui amicitia mea : id nunc non licet, quum tantum οἰκονομικῶς, ad fidem vestram roborandam me do conspiciendum. At ubi ad Patrem ascendero, veniet tempus quum frui mea amicitia perfectissime poteris, non terrestri contactu, sed tali qui loco illi, i. e. cœlo conveniat, *spirituali*." Grotius. With this my view nearly agrees, not confining (as indeed neither does he) the latter enjoyment to *in cœlo*, but understanding it to have begun here below. So Leo the Great, Serm. lxxiv. (al. lxxii.) 4, p. 295: "Hinc illud est quod post resurrectionem suam Dominus Mariæ Magdalenæ personam Ecclesiæ gerenti cum ad contactum ipsius properaret accedere dicit; *Noli me tangere, nondum enim ascendi ad Patrem meum:* hoc est, nolo ut ad me corporaliter venias, nec ut me sensu carnis agnoscas : ad sublimiora te differo, majora tibi præparo: cum ad Patrem ascendero, tunc me perfectius veriusque palpabis, apprehensura quod non tangis, et creditura quod non cernis." The two renderings of ἅπτου to be guarded against are, (1) a laying hold of to *retain* (= μή με κράτει), (2) a laying hold of to *worship* (ἐκράτησαν αὐτοῦ τοὺς πόδας Matt. xxviii. 9). Neither of these senses can be extracted from the word without forcing.

πορεύου δέ] Stier remarks that this was a far greater honour than that which had been forbidden her;—just as the handling of the Lord allowed to Thomas was a far less thing than the not seeing and yet believing. **τοὺς ἀδελφ. μου**] By this term He testifies that He has not put off his humanity, nor his love for his own, in his resurrection state : see Heb. ii. 11.

πατ. μου κ. πατ. ὑμῶν] This distinction, **μου κ. ὑμῶν**, when ἡμῶν *seems* so likely to have been said, has been observed by all Commentators of any depth, as indicating an *essential difference in the relations*. Cyr.-jer. (Stier),—ἄλλως ἐμοῦ,

[v] ὑμῶν. 18 ἔρχεται Μαριὰμ ἡ Μαγδαληνὴ [w] ἀγγέλλουσα
τοῖς μαθηταῖς ὅτι ἑώρακα τὸν κύριον καὶ ταῦτα εἶπεν
αὐτῇ.
19 Οὔσης οὖν [x] ὀψίας τῇ ἡμέρᾳ ἐκείνῃ τῇ [y] μιᾷ σαββάτων, καὶ τῶν θυρῶν κεκλεισμένων ὅπου ἦσαν οἱ
μαθηταὶ διὰ τὸν [z] φόβον τῶν Ἰουδαίων, ἦλθεν ὁ Ἰησοῦς
καὶ ἔστη [a] εἰς τὸ μέσον καὶ λέγει αὐτοῖς [b] Εἰρήνη ὑμῖν.
Frag. Mosq. 20 καὶ τοῦτο εἰπὼν ἔδειξεν καὶ τὰς χεῖρας καὶ τὴν
[c] πλευρὰν αὐτοῖς. ἐχάρησαν οὖν οἱ μαθηταὶ ἰδόντες
εχαρησαν... τὸν κύριον. 21 εἶπεν οὖν αὐτοῖς [ὁ Ἰησοῦς] πάλιν

w here only †. (-λία, 1 John i. 5. iii. 11 only.)
x ch. vi. 16 reff. w. οὔσης, here only.
y ver. 1 reff.
z constr., ch. xix. 38 reff.
a constr., ver. 26. Mark iii. 3 ‖ L. xiv. 60.
b here (bis) & ‖ L. ver. 26. Luke x. 5.
c ch. xix. 34 reff.

18. (μαριαμ, so BLא 1. 33 sah.) rec απαγγελλουσα, with Dא[3a] rel vulg lat-*b c f ff*$_2$: αναγγ. EG [S(Tischdf)] Δ 33 : txt ABI$_d$Xא[1]. aft τ. μαθ. ins αυτου D æth. rec εωρακεν, with ADI$_d$ rel lat-*b c e f* [*q*] syrr [syr-jer arm], εωρακαμεν S 33 : txt BXא [vulg] lat-*a ff*$_2$ *g* coptt æth. for ταυτα ειπ. αυτη, α ειπεν αυτη εμηνυσεν αυτοις D lat-*c e* æth.

19. om 2nd τη א[1]. rec ins των bef σαββατων (*see ver* 1), with D rel *Cyr*[-p] : om ABI$_d$Lא 33. rec ins συνηγμενοι bef δια, with L א-corr[1] rel vulg lat-*b c e f ff*$_2$ [(syr-w-ast) syr-jer] coptt æth arm Cyr : om ABDI$_d$Λ[1]א[1] am(with fuld gat harl[1]) lat-*a q* Syr. om ὁ DI$_d$. om αυτοις א[1] 245 [syr-jer].

20. rec aft εδειξεν ins αυτοις, reading αυτου aft πλευραν, with L rel [vss Eus$_1$] Cyr$_1$: txt ABDI$_d$א lat-*q*. rec om και (bef τας χειρας), with Dא rel latt Syr [syr-jer coptt æth arm Cyr] Eus$_1$: ins AB syr. aft οι μαθηται ins αυτου D 127(Sz) æth.

21. for ειπ. ουν, και ειπ. LX א[3a](but txt restored) Frag-mosq copt æth. om ο ιησους DLXא Frag-mosq 69 vulg lat-*a c e g q* coptt arm Eus$_1$ Cyr : ins ABI$_d$ rel lat-*b*

κατὰ φύσιν· ἄλλως ὑμῶν, κατὰ θέσιν. Aug. :—"Non ait, Patrem *nostrum ;* aliter ergo meum, aliter vestrum ; natura meum, gratia vestrum. Et, Deum meum et Deum vestrum. Neque hic dixit Deum *nostrum ;* ergo et hic aliter meum, aliter vestrum. Deum meum, sub quo et Ego sum homo ; Deum vestrum, inter quos et Ipsum Mediator sum." Tract. cxxi. 3. The **μου** is the ground and source of the **ὑμῶν**,—therefore the Lord so speaks. Stier, vii. 32, edn. 2. "Nos, per Illum : Ille, singularissime et primo." Bengel. But the θεόν **μου** indicates that He is still man : cf. Eph. i. 3 and passim : 1 Cor. iii. 23 : and especially Heb. ii. 11. In the ἀναβαίνω is included His temporary stay which He was now making with them—**I am ascending**—q. d. 'I am on my way.'

19—23.] *In the freedom of His spiritual and triumphant life, He appears to and commissions His own.* Compare Luke xxiv. 36—49 : Mark xvi. 14—18.

19.] The circumstance of the doors being shut is mentioned here and in ver. 26, to indicate *what sort of appearances* these were. Suddenly, unaccounted for by any approach,—the Lord rendered Himself visible to His disciples. Nor did this affect the truth of that resurrection Body, any more than his withdrawing himself from mortal sight occasionally affected the truth of His fleshly Body. Both were done by that supernatural power dwelling in Him, by which His other miracles were wrought. It seems to have been the normal condition of His fleshly Body, to be visible to mortal eyes :—of His risen Body, not to be. But both these He could suspend when He pleased, without affecting the substance or truth of either. **διὰ τ. φόβ. τ. Ἰουδ.**] This was natural enough ;—the bitter hatred of the Jews (both people and rulers) to their Master,—and his own prophetic announcements,—would raise in them a dread of incipient persecution, now that He was removed. **ἦλθεν**—not, by ordinary approach ; nor, *through* the closed doors ;—nor in any visible manner ;—but (*subjectively*, of *Himself*) the word describes that *unseen arrival among them* which preceded His becoming visible to them. **ἔστη εἰς τ. μ.**] Compare Luke, ver. 36, ἔστη ἐν μέσῳ. The **εἰς**, as in ch. xxi. 4, denotes the *coming*, and *standing*, *in one*—the standing *without motion thither*, which in ordinary cases would be standing as the *result of motion thither ;*—so that in this case **ἔστη** itself is the verb of motion. **εἰρ. ὑμ.**] See on Luke ver. 36, and ch. xiv. 27. Ver. **20** answers to Luke, ver. 39. **ἐχάρησαν**] The first and partial fulfilment of ch. xvi. 20—22 ; see notes there. The dis-

[b] Εἰρήνη ὑμῖν· καθὼς ἀπέσταλκέν με ὁ πατὴρ κἀγὼ
πέμπω ὑμᾶς. 22 καὶ τοῦτο εἰπὼν [d] ἐνεφύσησεν καὶ λέγει
αὐτοῖς [e] Λάβετε [e] πνεῦμα [e] ἅγιον. 23 [f] ἄν τινων [g] ἀφῆτε

d here only. Gen. ii. 7. Wisd. xv. 11 al.
e ch. vii. 39. xiv. 17. Acts viii. 15, 17, 19. xix. 2.
f here bis. ch. xiii. 20. xvi. 23 only.
g = Matt. vi. 12. ix. 2 al. Isa. xxii. 14.

ABDE GI_dKL MSUX ΓΔΛΠℵ Frag. Mosq. 1. 33. 69

f ff$_2$ syrr æth. for πεμπω, αποστελλω D[1]Lℵ[3a] Frag-mosq 33 Cyr: txt ABD[3] I_d(appy) ℵ[3b] rel Eus_1 [Chr], πεμψω ℵ[1] [lat-*c*].
22. om και D-gr latt. aft ενεφυσησεν ins αυτοις D Syr [syr-jer] (coptt) æth arm.
23. (εαν (twice) AD, 2nd ℵ[1].) **τινος** (twice) B vulg lat-*a e f* Syr Eus_1 $Orig\text{-}int_1$

ciples seem to have *handled* Him: see Luke, ver. 39: 1 John i. 1, and below, ver. 25. **21.**] 'Peace be unto you' is solemnly repeated, as the introduction of the sending which follows. The ministers and disciples of the Lord are messengers of *peace*. This view is more natural than that of Euthym.: ὑπὸ πολλῆς χαρᾶς ὡς εἰκὸς θορυβοῦντας καταστέλλει, ἵνα προσέχωσιν οἷς μέλλει ἐρεῖν.
καθώς] He confirms and grounds their Apostleship on the present glorification of Himself, whose Apostleship (Heb. iii. 1) on earth was now ended, but was to be continued by this sending forth of them. This commission was not now first given them, but now first fully assured to them: and their sending forth by Him their glorified Head, was to be, in character and process, like that of Himself by the Father. **22.**] To understand this verse as the outpouring of the Spirit, the fulfilment of the promise of the Comforter, is against all consistency, and most against John himself: see ch. xvi. 7, and ch. vii. 39. To understand it rightly, we have merely to recur to that great key to the meaning of so many dark passages of Scripture, the manifold and gradual unfolding of promise and prophecy in their fulfilment. The presence of the Lord among them *now* was a slight and temporary fulfilment of His promise of returning to them; and so the imparting of the Spirit *now*, was a symbol and foretaste of that which they should receive at Pentecost:—just as, to mount a step higher, *that itself*, in its present abiding with us, is but the first-fruits and pledge (Rom. viii. 23: 2 Cor. i. 22) of the fulness which we shall hereafter inherit. "The relation of this saying to the effusion of the Spirit is the same which chap. iii. bears to Baptism, chap. vi. to the Lord's Supper, chap. xvii. 1 to the Ascension, &c." (Luthardt.) Further: this giving of the Spirit was not the Spirit's personal imparting of Himself to them, but only a partial instilling of His influence. He proceeds forth in His work (as in His essence) from the Father and the Son: this breathing of His influence was an imparting of Him from the Son in His risen Body, but that Body had not yet been received up, without which union of the God-manhood of the Son to the glory of the Father the Holy Spirit would not come. *What* was now conferred is plain from our ver. 23—by which authority to discern spirits and pronounce on them is re-assured (see Matt. xviii. 18)—and from Luke, ver. 45, by which a discerning of the mind of the Spirit is given to them. We find instances of both these gifts being exercised by Peter in Acts i., in his assertion of the sense of Scripture, and his judgment of Judas. Both these however were only temporary and imperfect. That *no formal gifts of Apostleship were now formally conferred, is plain by the absence of Thomas,* who in that case would be no apostle in the same sense in which the rest were.
ἐνεφύσησεν (see reff.) was the word expressing the act of God in the original infusion of the spirit of life into man. This act is now by God incarnate repeated, sacramentally (see λάβετε, Matt. xxvi. 26 ||), representing the infusion of the new life, of which He is become by His glorified Humanity the source to his members: see Job xxxiii. 4: Ps. xxxiii. 6: 1 Cor. xv. 45. **23.**] The *present* meaning of these words has been spoken of above. They reach forward however beyond that, and extend the grant which they re-assure to all ages of the Church. The words, closely considered, amount to this: that with the gift and real participation of the Holy Spirit, comes the conviction, and therefore the *knowledge*, of *sin*, of *righteousness*, and *judgment*;—and this knowledge becomes more perfect, the more men are filled with the Holy Ghost. Since this is so, they who are pre-eminently filled with His presence are pre-eminently gifted with the discernment of sin and repentance in others, and hence by the Lord's appointment authorized to pronounce pardon of sin and the contrary. The Apostles had this in an especial manner, and by the full indwelling of the Spirit were enabled

τὰς ἁμαρτίας, [g] ἀφίενται αὐτοῖς· [f] ἄν τινων [h] κρατῆτε,
[h] κεκράτηνται. 24 Θωμᾶς δὲ εἷς ἐκ τῶν δώδεκα, ὁ [i] λεγόμενος [i] δίδυμος, οὐκ ἦν μετ' αὐτῶν ὅτε ἦλθεν Ἰησοῦς.
25 ἔλεγον οὖν αὐτῷ οἱ ἄλλοι μαθηταὶ Ἑωράκαμεν τὸν
κύριον. ὁ δὲ εἶπεν αὐτοῖς Ἐὰν μὴ ἴδω ἐν ταῖς χερσὶν
αὐτοῦ τὸν [k] τύπον τῶν [l] ἥλων καὶ [m] βάλω τὸν δάκτυλόν
μου εἰς τὸν [k] τύπον τῶν [l] ἥλων καὶ [m] βάλω μου τὴν
χεῖρα εἰς τὴν [n] πλευρὰν αὐτοῦ, οὐ μὴ πιστεύσω. 26 Καὶ
μεθ' ἡμέρας ὀκτὼ πάλιν ἦσαν [o] ἔσω οἱ μαθηταὶ αὐτοῦ,
καὶ Θωμᾶς μετ' αὐτῶν. ἔρχεται ὁ Ἰησοῦς τῶν [p] θυρῶν
[p] κεκλεισμένων, καὶ [p] ἔστη [p] εἰς τὸ μέσον καὶ εἶπεν [p] Εἰρήνη

...ο ιη-σους Frag. Mosq.
Η των ηλων...
C και μεθ...
...και θω I_d.

h = here bis only. see Rev. vii. 1.
i ch. xi. 16 (reff.).
k = (and Gospp.) here bis only ‡. (Acts vii. 43 al.)
l here bis only. Josh. xxiii. 13.
m = ch. xviii. 11. Mark vii. 33. James iii. 3.
n ch. xix. 34 reff.
o = Acts v. 23. Gen. xxxix. 11.
p ver. 19.

$Cypr_4$: txt ADℵ rel vulg lat-*b c g* [*q* syr-jer] syr coptt æth arm $Orig_2$ [Cyr-jer Bas_1] $Novat_1$. αφεωνται ADXℵ[3a] Frag-mosq **1** [Chr_3 $Cyr\text{-}p_2$]; αφεονται L: αφειονται B[1]: αφεθησεται ℵ[1]: txt B[2]I_d rel $Orig_2$-int_1 Cyr-jer_1 Bas_1 Ath_1. for αν, εαν δε ℵ[1] [(syr-jer)]. for κρατητε, κρατησητε D: κρατηνται ℵ[1].

24. om ὁ D [Chr_1]. aft οτε ins ουν ℵ[1]. rec ins ὁ bef ιησ., with AI_d rel: om BDℵ.

25. om ουν ℵ[1] 433(Sz) [arm]. om αλλοι ℵ[1] 122(Sz) [Syr copt]. aft μαθηται ins οτι D arm. [εορακεν B[1](Tischdf) EGI_dKLMXΓΔΠ[1].] for εν ταις χερσιν, εις τας χειρας D lat-*c*. om 1st αυτου ℵ[1]. μου bef τον δακτυλον D[-gr(om μου D-lat) L] ℵ 33. for 2nd τυπον, τοπον AI_d latt syrr [syr-jer arm] $Orig_1$ Hil_1 $Ambr_1$.—κ. βαλω . . πλευρ. αυτ. bef κ. βαλω . . ηλων D.—for 2nd τον τυπον των ηλων, την χειραν αυτου ℵ[1]. rec την χειρα bef μου, with AI_d rel [Cyr]: txt BDLℵ 33.—τας χειρας D æth.

26. om αυτου ℵ **1**. 69 Scr's c lat-*a b c e* Syr [syr-jer] sah. ins ὁ bef θωμας D 69. aft ερχεται ins ουν D **1** copt.

to discern the hearts of men, and to give sentence on that discernment: see Acts v. 1—11; viii. 21; xiii. 9. And this gift belongs to the Church in all ages, and especially to those who by legitimate appointment are set to minister in the Churches of Christ: not *by successive delegation* from the Apostles,—*of which fiction I find in the N. T. no trace*,—but by their mission from Christ, the Bestower of the Spirit for their office, when *orderly and legitimately conferred upon them by the various Churches*. Not however to them exclusively,—though for decency and order it is expedient that the outward and formal declaration should be so:—but in proportion as *any disciple* shall have been filled with the Holy Spirit of wisdom, is the inner discernment, the κρίσις, his.

κρατεῖν here (see ref.) corresponds to **δέειν** in Matt. xvi. 19 (see the distinction there); xviii. 18, **ἀφιέναι** to **λύειν**.

24—29.] *He proves Himself to His own to be Lord and God, to be believed on by them, though not seen. Thomas's doubt, and its removal.—Peculiar to John.*

24.] **οὐκ ἦν**—for what reason does not appear. Euthym. says, εἰκὸς γὰρ αὐτὸν μετὰ τὸ διασκορπισθῆναι τοὺς μαθητάς, ... μήπω συνελθεῖν αὐτοῖς. I incline, with Stier (vii. 117, edn. 2), to think that it could not have been accidentally (Lücke), nor "negotio aliquo occupatus" (Grot.). On such a day, and in such a man, such an absence must have been *designed*. Perhaps he had abandoned hope;—the strong evidence of his senses having finally convinced him that the pierced side and wounded hands betokened such a death that revivification was impossible. **25.**] He probably does not name the Feet, merely because the Hands and Side would more naturally offer themselves to his examination than the Feet, to which he must stoop. He requires no more than had been granted to the rest: but he had *their testimony in addition*, and therefore ample ground for faith to rest on. Olshausen calls him the "Rationalist among the Apostles." Meyer lays some stress on τόπον being used (see var. readd.) instead of τύπον in the second place: "τύπος *videtur*, τόπος *impletur*," Grot.;—he would *see* the τύπος, but place his finger in the τόπος. *Valeat quantum:* but meantime the authority is but weak, and the mistake so obvious, that we can hardly with any safety adopt τόπον. **26.**] There is not the least reason for supposing, with

ὑμῖν. 27 εἶτα λέγει τῷ Θωμᾷ [q] Φέρε τὸν δάκτυλόν σου ABCDE
ὧδε καὶ ἴδε τὰς χεῖράς μου, καὶ [q] φέρε τὴν χεῖρά σου καὶ GHKL MSUX
[m] βάλε εἰς τὴν [n] πλευράν μου, καὶ μὴ γίνου [r] ἄπιστος ΓΔΛΠℵ 1. 33. 69
ἀλλὰ [s] πιστός. 28 ἀπεκρίθη Θωμᾶς καὶ εἶπεν αὐτῷ
[t] Ὁ κύριός μου καὶ [t] ὁ θεός μου. 29 λέγει αὐτῷ ὁ Ἰησοῦς
Ὅτι ἑώρακάς με, πεπίστευκας· μακάριοι οἱ μὴ ἰδόντες [u] καὶ
πιστεύσαντες.

q = here bi only.
r Matt. xvii. 17 ||. Luke xii. 46 al. Isa. xvii. 10.
s = 2 Cor. vi. 15 (there also w. ἄπιστ.). Gal. iii. 9.
t constr., Matt. xi. 26 reff.
u ch. xxi. 23 reff.

27. for *γινου*, *ισθι* D.

28. rec ins *και* bef *απεκρ.*, with AC³ rel lat-*q* syrr [syr-jer] æth: om BC¹DGLXℵ 1. 33(appy) 69 latt copt-[schw-dz-]ms sah arm Cypr₁. rec ins *ὁ* bef *θωμας*, with Lℵ 33: om ABCD rel Cyr. om *ὁ* (bef *θεος*) D.

29. for *λεγει*, *ειπεν* ℵ¹ 69 [*dixit* vulg(not am fuld ing &c) lat-*g*]. add *δε* ℵ 69 (lat-*e*). om *ὁ* B. rec aft *με* ins *θωμα*, with vulg-ed(with foss mm mt); *και* ℵ¹ [gat lat-*g q* copt-ms arm]: om ABCDℵ³ᵃ rel am(with fuld em ing jac) lat-*a b c e f* syrr syr-jer coptt æth Chr₁ Cyr₁ Cypr₁ Hil spec. aft *ιδοντες* ins *με* ℵ¹ [foss gat syr-jer] syrr.

Olshausen, that this appearance was in Galilee. The whole narrative points out the same place as before. The eight days' interval is the first testimony of the recurring day of the Resurrection being commemorated by the disciples:—but, it must be owned, a weak one;—for in all probability they had been thus assembled every day during the interval. It forms however an interesting opening of the history of THE LORD'S DAY, that the Lord Himself should have thus selected and honoured it. **27.**] Our Lord says nothing of the *τύπος τῶν ἥλων*—He does not recall the malice of his enemies. The words imply that the marks were no *scars*, but *the veritable wounds themselves*;—that in His side being large enough for a hand to be thrust into it. This of itself would shew that the resurrection Body was *bloodless*. It is *φέρε κ. ἴδε* in the case of the *hands*, which were exposed—but merely *φέρε κ. βάλε* in the case of the *side*, which was clothed. So Meyer: but query? **μὴ γ. ἄπιστ.**, not merely, 'Do not any longer disbelieve in my Resurrection;'—but **Be not** (do not become)—as applied generally to the spiritual life, and the reception of God's truth—**faithless, but believing.** The E. V. is excellent. That Thomas *did not* apply his finger or his hand, is evident from *ὅτι ἑώρακάς με* below.

28.] The Socinian view, that these words, *ὁ κύρ. μου κ. ὁ θεός μου*, are *merely an exclamation*, is refuted—(1) By the fact that no such exclamations were in use among the Jews. (2) By the *εἶπεν* **αὐτῷ**. (3) By the impossibility of referring *ὁ κυριός μου* to another than Jesus: see ver. 13. (4) By the N. T. usage of expressing the vocative by the nom. with an article. (5) By the utter psychological absurdity of such a supposition: that one just convinced of the presence of Him whom he deeply loved, should, instead of addressing Him, break out into an irrelevant cry. (6) By the further absurdity of supposing that *if such were* the case, the Apostle John, who of all the sacred writers most constantly keeps in mind the object for which he is writing, should have recorded any thing so *beside that object*. (7) By the intimate conjunction of *πεπίστευκας*—see below. Dismissing it therefore, we observe that this is *the highest confession of faith which has yet been made*;—and that it shews that (though not yet *fully*) the meaning of the previous confessions of His being '*the Son of God*' was understood. Thus John, in the very close of his Gospel (see on vv. 30, 31) iterates the testimony with which he began it—to the Godhead of the Word who became flesh: and by this closing confession, shews how the testimony of Jesus to Himself had gradually deepened and exalted the Apostles' conviction, from the time when they knew Him only as *ὁ υἱὸς τοῦ Ἰωσήφ* (ch. i. 46), till now when He is acknowledged as their LORD and their GOD. **29.**] The **ὅτι ἑώρ.** blames the slowness and required ground of the faith: the **πεπίστευκας** recognizes and commends the soundness of that faith just confessed.

Meyer remarks on the perf. *πεπίστευκας*, "*thou hast become believing and now believest*," and the aorr. *ἰδόντες* and *πιστεύσαντες*, which are not usitative (an usage never occurring in the N. T.), but indicate the state of those described from the time of the *μακαριότης* predicated of them, "*who never saw, and yet became believers.*" The aorists, as often in such

T_d xx.30 (appy)... 30 Πολλὰ μὲν οὖν καὶ ἄλλα [v] σημεῖα ἐποίησεν ὁ
Ἰησοῦς [w] ἐνώπιον τῶν μαθητῶν, ἃ οὐκ ἔστιν γεγραμμένα
ἐν τῷ [x] βιβλίῳ τούτῳ. 31 ταῦτα δὲ γέγραπται [y] ἵνα
[z] πιστεύσητε ὅτι [z] Ἰησοῦς ἐστιν ὁ χριστὸς ὁ [z] υἱὸς τοῦ
θεοῦ, καὶ ἵνα πιστεύοντες [a] ζωὴν [a] ἔχητε [b] ἐν τῷ ὀνόματι
...xx.31 (appy) αὐτοῦ.

T_d. P ἐφανερωσεν ... XXI. 1 Μετὰ ταῦτα [c] ἐφανέρωσεν ἑαυτὸν πάλιν τοῖς
μαθηταῖς [d] ἐπὶ τῆς θαλάσσης τῆς [e] Τιβεριάδος, [c] ἐφανέρωσεν
δὲ [f] οὕτως. 2 ἦσαν [g] ὁμοῦ Σίμων Πέτρος καὶ Θωμᾶς

v = ch. ii. 11 reff.
w = Luke i. 19. Gen. xxiv. 51.
x Luke iv. 17, 20. ch. xxi. 25 al. 2 Chron. xxxvi. 8.
y ch. xix. 35.
z 1 John (iv. 15) v. 5.
a ch. vi. 53 reff.
b = Mark xvi. 17 reff. Acts iv. 10. 1 Cor. vi. 11.
c = (see note) ver. 14. pass., ch. i. 31 al.
d = Matt. xxi. 19. Luke xxii. 30. (dat., ch. iv. 6. v. 2.)
e ch. vi. 1.
f = Acts vii. 6. xiii. 47 al.
g ch. xx. 4 reff.

30. (ἅ is not added aft σημεια in B: see table.) om ὁ D. rec aft μαθητων ins αυτου, with CDℵ rel latt Syr syr-w-ast [syr-jer] copt æth arm Chr_1 Cyr_2: om AB EKSΔ Λ[(Treg) Π] lat-*f* [sah-mnt]. βιβλω D.

31. for πιστευσ., πιστευητε Bℵ[1]. rec ins ὁ bef ιησ. (with 33, e sil): om ABCDℵ rel Cyr_2. for εστιν to υιος, χρ. υιος εστιν, omg ὁ twice, D. om και ℵ[1]. aft ζωην ins αιωνιον C[1]DL[T_d]ℵ 33. 69 gat lat-*b e f g* [*q*] Syr syr-w-ast [copt] æth arm Chr_1 Non_1 Iren-int_1.

Chap. XXI. 1. παλιν bef εφαν. εαυτ. D 235(Sz) copt [æth] arm; bef εαυτον ℵ [Syr]. rec ins ο ιησ. bef τοις μαθ., with Aℵ rel(bef παλιν 69) [Cyr]; ιησους BC (*an eccl lection beginning at* εφανερωσεν): om DM lat-*e* Chr. aft μαθ. ins αυτου C[3]DGH MUX[Γ] 69 lat-*a b c f g q* Syr [syr-jer] coptt æth arm.

sentences (see a remarkable coincidence Luke i. 45), indicate the present state of those spoken of, grounded in the past. Wonderful indeed, and rich in blessing for us who have not seen Him, is this, the closing word of the Gospel. For these words cannot apply to the *remaining Ten:* they, like *Thomas, had seen and believed.* "All the appearances of the forty days," says Stier (vii. 139, edn. 2), "were mere preparations for the believing without seeing." *On the record of them,* we now believe: see 1 Pet. i. 8.

30, 31.] Formal close of the Gospel (see notes on ch. xxi.). 30.] **μὲν οὖν—yea, and,**—or, **moreover:** meaning, 'This book must not be supposed to be a complete account.' **καί, and indeed: —many and other signs.** **σημεῖα,** not, as Theophyl., Euthym., Lücke, Olsh., "proofs of His resurrection,"—but, as ch. xii. 37 and elsewhere in this Gospel, **miracles** in the most general sense—these after the Resurrection included:—for John is here reviewing his whole narrative, **τὸ βιβλίον τοῦτο.** 31.] The mere *miracle-faith,* so often reproved by our Lord, is not that intended here. This is faith in *Himself,* as the Christ the Son of God: and the Evangelist means, that enough is related in this book to be a ground for such a faith, by shewing us His glory manifested forth (see ch. ii. 11). **πιστ. ζωὴν ἔχ.**] Thus he closes almost in the words of his prologue, ch. i. 4, 12. **ἐν τῷ ὀν. αὐτ.** (see reff. Acts, 1 Cor.) is the whole standing of the faithful man in Christ,—by which and in which he has life eternal.

Chap. XXI. 1—23.] The Appendix. The glimpse into the future. And herein, **1—8**] *The significant draught of fishes.* I reserve the remarks on this chapter to the end, thereby better to put the reader in possession of the evidence which I shall there gather up into one, but which will present itself as we go on. I will only state here, that whether written by John himself or not, *it is evidently an appendix to the Gospel, which latter has already concluded by a formal review of its contents and object at* ch. xx. 30, 31.

1. **μετὰ ταῦτα**] Compare ch. v. 1; vi. 1: **at a subsequent time.** **ἐφαν. ἑαυτ.**] This expression is no where else used by John of the Lord's appearances, but only in Mark xvi. 12, 14. We have however φανέρωσον σεαυτόν, ch. vii. 4; and ἐφ. τὴν δόξαν αὐτοῦ, ch. ii. 11; and the passive of φανερόω is very usual with him. The use of the verb here indicates that the usual state of the Lord at this time was not manifestation, but invisibility to them. **ἐπὶ τῆς θ.,** elsewhere, see reff., used by John with a *dative* in this sense. The expression indicates the *locality,* not the *manner,* of the appear-

h ch. xi. 16 reff.
i constr., here only.
j here only. Jer. xvi. 16 only. (-εύς, Luke v. 2.)
k = Matt. viii. 23 reff.
l = ver. 10. Rev. xix. 20 only. (ch. vii. 30 reff.) Cant. ii. 15.
m Matt. xxi. 18. xxvii. 1. (ch. xviii. 28 v. r.) only. Lam. iii. 23.
n ch. xx. 19, 26.
o Matt. xiii. 2 reff.
p pres., ch. i. 40 reff.

ABCDE GHKL MPSUX ΓΔΛΠℵ 1. 33. 69

ὁ [h] λεγόμενος [h] δίδυμος καὶ Ναθαναὴλ ὁ ἀπὸ Κανᾶ τῆς
Γαλιλαίας καὶ οἱ τοῦ Ζεβεδαίου καὶ ἄλλοι ἐκ τῶν μαθητῶν αὐτοῦ δύο. 3 λέγει αὐτοῖς Σίμων Πέτρος [i] Ὑπάγω
[j] ἁλιεύειν. λέγουσιν αὐτῷ Ἐρχόμεθα καὶ ἡμεῖς σὺν σοί.
ἐξῆλθον καὶ [k] ἐνέβησαν εἰς τὸ πλοῖον, καὶ ἐν ἐκείνῃ τῇ
νυκτὶ [l] ἐπίασαν οὐδέν. 4 [m] πρωΐας δὲ ἤδη γενομένης ἔστη
Ἰησοῦς [n] εἰς τὸν [o] αἰγιαλόν· οὐ μέντοι ᾔδεισαν οἱ μαθηταὶ
ὅτι Ἰησοῦς [p] ἐστιν. 5 λέγει οὖν αὐτοῖς Ἰησοῦς [q] Παιδία,
μή τι [r] προσφάγιον ἔχετε; ἀπεκρίθησαν αὐτῷ Οὔ. 6 ὁ
δὲ εἶπεν αὐτοῖς Βάλετε εἰς τὰ δεξιὰ μέρη τοῦ πλοίου τὸ

q 1 John ii. 13, 18. (iii. 7 v. r.) r here only †.

2. for 2nd ὁ, *ος ην* D. aft *οι* ins *υιοι* D(E)ℵ latt Syr [syr-jer] copt æth : aft *ζεβ.* C : om ABP rel syr arm [Cyr_1]. om *του* Dℵ. aft *αυτου* ins *του* D[1].
3. for *αυτοις*, *τουτοις* D. ins *και* bef *εξηλθ.* AP vulg lat-*b c f g* Syr syr-w-ast [syr-jer] copt æth : aft *εξηλθ.* ins *ουν* GLX[Π[2]]ℵ : om BCD[Π[1·3]] rel lat-*a e* [*q*] arm [Cyr_1]. (*εξηλθαν* D.) rec *ανεβησαν*, with ΔΛ Cyr : txt ABCDℵ rel. rec aft *πλοιον* ins *ευθυς*, with AC[3]P rel syr Cyr : om BC[1]DLXΔℵ 1. 33. 69 latt Syr [syr-jer] coptt æth arm. *εκοπιασαν* ℵ[1](txt ℵ-corr[1·3]). *ουδε εν* C[1].
4. om *ηδη* ℵ[1] 69 ev-H vulg-cl lat-*a c e* Syr copt æth arm. *γινομ.* C[1]EL, *γειν.* AB. rec ins ὁ bef *ιησ.*, with L rel : om ABCDEPℵ[Π[1].—om ῑς also S(Tischdf)]. for *εις*, *επι* ADLMUXℵ 33 latt $Clem_1$ Orig : txt BC rel. for *ηδεισαν*, *εγνωσαν* LXℵ 33 vulg lat-*b c* [*f g*] Cyr : txt ABCDP rel.
5. rec ins ὁ bef *ιησ.*, with [A[2](from here to *τι προς* is written over an erasure)] CDP rel : om Bℵ.—om *ιησ.* also A[1](appy) lat-*a*. om *τι* ℵ[1].
6. for *ο δε ειπεν*, *λεγει* ℵ[1](txt ℵ[3a], but former readg restored) [simly vulg lat-*b c g* Syr syr-jer copt arm].

ance; *on*, i. e. on the shore of the sea of Galilee: see note on Matt. xiv. 25. **ἐφαν. δὲ οὕτως** must not be too rashly cited as unlike John's style. We must remember that, in adding an appendix, expressions of this kind would occur, which the narrative itself would not contain.

2.] Nathanael is named *by John only*, see ch. i. 46 ff.: Thomas also *by John only*, except in the catalogues of the Apostles. The junction of ἀπό with a proper name is in John's style: see ch. i. 45; xi. 1; xix. 38. **οἱ τοῦ Ζεβ.** are *no where else named by John*;—they may however be here mentioned as in reminiscence of the *draught of fishes which occurred before*: see Luke v. 1 ff. **ἐκ τ. μαθ. αὐτοῦ δύο**] The same words occur ch. i. 35, with reference to John the Baptist. Who these were does not appear. Probably (as Luthardt) some two not named in the Gospel, and therefore not specified in its appendix.

3.] The disciples returned to their occupation of fishing, probably as a means of livelihood, during the time which the Lord had appointed them in Galilee between the feasts of the Passover and Pentecost. This seems to be the first proposal of so employing themselves. **καὶ ἡμεῖς**] See ch. xi. 16. **ἐξῆλθον**—from the house where they were together. **ἐπίασαν οὐδέν**—as before, Luke v. 5. The correspondence of this account with that is very remarkable—as is also their entire distinctness in the midst of that correspondence. The disciples must have been powerfully reminded of that their former and probably last fishing together. And after the "*fishers of men*" of that other occasion, the whole could not but bear to them a spiritual meaning in reference to their apostolic commission:—their powerlessness without Christ,—their success when they let down the net at His word. Their present part was not to go fishing of themselves, but *περιμένειν τ. ἐπαγγελίαν τοῦ πατρός*, Acts i. 4 (Luthardt).

4. ἔστη εἰς] See reff. A sudden appearance is indicated by the words. The **ἐστιν** after **ᾔδεισαν** is quite in John's manner: see reff.

5.] λέγ. **οὖν** is in John's manner. **παιδία**] See reff. In ch. xiii. 33 we have *τεκνία*. **προσφάγιον** is said by the grammarians to be the Hellenic form equivalent to the Attic *ὄψον*, signifying any thing eaten as an additament to bread, but especially *fish*. So that here the best rendering would be as in A.V.R.,

[s] δίκτυον, καὶ [t] εὑρήσετε. ἔβαλον οὖν, καὶ οὐκ ἔτι αὐτὸ
[u] ἑλκύσαι [v] ἴσχυον [w] ἀπὸ τοῦ πλήθους τῶν [x] ἰχθύων.
7 λέγει οὖν ὁ [y] μαθητὴς ἐκεῖνος [y] ὃν [y] ἠγάπα ὁ Ἰησοῦς τῷ
Πέτρῳ Ὁ κύριός ἐστιν. Σίμων οὖν Πέτρος, ἀκούσας
ὅτι ὁ κύριός ἐστιν, τὸν [z] ἐπενδύτην [a] διεζώσατο, ἦν γὰρ
γυμνός, καὶ ἔβαλεν ἑαυτὸν εἰς τὴν θάλασσαν· 8 οἱ δὲ
ἄλλοι μαθηταὶ τῷ [b] πλοιαρίῳ ἦλθον, οὐ γὰρ ἦσαν [c] μακρὰν
ἀπὸ τῆς γῆς, ἀλλὰ ὡς [d] ἀπὸ [e] πηχῶν διακοσίων, [f] σύροντες
τὸ [g] δίκτυον τῶν [x] ἰχθύων. 9 ὡς οὖν [h] ἀπέβησαν εἰς τὴν
γῆν, βλέπουσιν [i] ἀνθρακιὰν [j] κειμένην καὶ [k] ὀψάριον [l] ἐπι-
κείμενον καὶ ἄρτον. 10 λέγει αὐτοῖς ὁ Ἰησοῦς Ἐνέγκατε
ἀπὸ τῶν [k] ὀψαρίων ὧν [m] ἐπιάσατε νῦν. 11 [n] ἀνέβη οὖν
Σίμων Πέτρος καὶ [o] εἵλκυσεν τὸ δίκτυον εἰς τὴν γῆν
..μεστον P. [p] μεστὸν [q] ἰχθύων μεγάλων ἑκατὸν πεντηκοντατριῶν· καὶ

s Mark i. 18, 19 reff. t absol., Matt. vii. 7.=Luke ix. 12 al. u = ver. 11 only. (ch. vi. 44 reff.) v Matt. viii. 28 al. 1 Chron. xxix. 14. w = Matt. xiii. 44 reff. x John, here bis & ver. 11 only. y ch. xiii. 23. z here only. 1 Kings xviii. 4 A (B def.). 2 Kings xiii. 18 only. (-δύεσθαι, 2 Cor. v. 2, 4.) a ch. xiii. 4, 5 only. Ezek. xxiii. 15 A Ald. only. b ch. vi. 22, &c. reff. dat., 1 Cor. ix. 7. xi. 5. 2 Cor. i. 15. c Matt. viii. 30. Acts xvii. 27. Judg. xviii. 7. d = ch. xi. 18. Rev. xiv. 20 only. e Matt. vi. 27. Luke xii. 25. Rev. xxi. 17 only. Gen. vi. 15, 16. f Acts viii. 3. xiv. 19. xvii. 6. Rev. xii. 4 only. 2 Kings xvii. 13. g ellips., Mark xiv. 13. h = Luke v. 2 (xxi. 13. Phil. i. 19) only. i ch. xviii. 18 only†. Sir. xi. 32 only. j = ch. xix. 29 reff. k here bis. ver. 13. ch. vi. 9, 11 only†. (ὄψος, Num. xi. 22.) l = ch. xi. 38 (reff.). m ver. 3. n = Matt. xiv. 32 reff. o ver. 6. p ch. xix. 29 (bis) reff. q vv. 7, 8.

aft ευρησετε ins οι δε ειπον δι ολης της νυκτος εκοπιασαμεν και ουδεν ελαβομεν επι δε τω σω ρηματι βαλουμεν (*Luke* v.5) ℵ3a(ℵ3b disapproving) [em mm] lat-*g* æth [Cyr_1]. for εβαλον ουν, οι δε εβαλον Dℵ copt. (ειλκυσαι D(Δ), ιλκ. ℵ.) rec ισχυσαν (*to suit* εβαλον), with AP rel lat-*e q* Syr copt: txt BCDLΛ[Π]ℵ 1. 33 latt [syr syr-jer] Cyr.

7. om ὁ (bef ιησ.) D. aft ο κυρ. εστ. ins ημων D. for εβαλ. εαυτ., ηλατο D¹, ηλλατο D².

8. ins αλλω bef πλοιαριω ℵ. πλοιω P. (ηλθαν D.) (αλλα, so ABCℵ.) πηχεων A Cyr_1.

9. ανεβησαν Hℵ¹ [Syr]. for εις, επι LX ℵ3a(but txt restored). for βλεπουσιν, ειδαν P vulg lat-*b c* [*f g*].

10. om ὁ B. for απο, εκ DL.

11. ενεβη Lℵ 1 arm Cyr_1. rec om ουν, with ADP rel vulg lat-*a b* [*e ff₂ g* arm]: ins BCLX[Π²]ℵ 1. 33 syr [syr-jer] copt Cyr. rec (for εις την γην) επι της γης, with E rel: επι την γην D 1. 69: txt ABCLPXΔℵ[Π 33].—μεστον bef ε. τ. γ. D lat-*b*. μεγαλων bef ιχθυων A D(μεγων D¹) GLXΔ 1. 33 vulg lat-*a b* [*f ff₂ g*]: txt BCℵ rel lat-*c* Cyr.

Have ye any fish? 6.] See Luke v. 6. 7.] The **οὖν** here seems distinctly to allude to the former occasion—the similarity of the incident having led the beloved Apostle to scrutinize more closely the person of Him who spoke to them. διορατικώτερος μὲν ὁ Ἰωάννης . . . . θερμότερος δὲ ὁ Πέτρος. διὸ γνωρίζει μὲν αὐτὸν ὁ Ἰωάννης πρὸ τοῦ Πέτρου· ἔξεισι δὲ πρὸς αὐτὸν ὁ Πέτρος πρὸ τοῦ Ἰωάννου. Euthym. **τὸν ἐπενδ. διεζ.**] He bound round him his fisher's coat or shirt, to facilitate his swimming. **ἦν γὰρ γυμ.**, i. e. as above, he was stripped for his fisher's work;—[some say] without his upper garment. Some [more probably] take it literally, and understand that he girt round him his ἐπενδύτης as a subligaculum. Theophyl.,—ἐπενδ. λινοῦν τι ὀθόνιον, ὃν οἱ Φοίνικες κ. οἱ Σύροι ἁλιεῖς περιελίττουσιν ἑαυτοῖς. 8.] 200 cubits = 100 yards. The lake was about five miles broad—Jos. B. J. iii. 10. 7: according to Stanley (Sinai and Palestine, p. 369), six in the widest part: according to Dr. Thomson (The Land and the Book, p. 400) nine. **ὡς ἀπό**] See reff.: a mode of speech peculiar to John.

9—14.] *The significant meal*: see below on ver. 14. 9.] The rationalist and semi-rationalist interpreters have taken great offence at the idea of a miracle being here intended. But is it possible to understand the incident otherwise? As Stier says, let any child reading the chapter be the judge. And what difficulty is there in such a fire and fish being provided either by the Lord Himself, or by the ministry of angels at His bidding? **ὀψάριον**] See reff.: a word peculiar

r ch. xix. 24 reff. s ver. 15. Luke xi. 37 (reff.) only. t John, here only. Luke xx. 40 || al. u Matt. ii. 8. x. 11 only. Deut. xix. 18. v pres., ch. i. 40 reff. w vv. 9, 10 reff. x 2 Cor. [xii. 14.] xiii. 1 only. Judg. xvi. 15. y as above (x). ver. 17 (bis). Matt. xiv. 41. Luke xxiii. 22. 1 Cor. xii. 28 only. z see ver. 1 reff. & note. a Matt. xvii. 9 reff. see Sir. xlviii. 5. b ver. 12.

ABCDE GHKL MSUX ΓΔΛΠℵ 1. 33. 69

τοσούτων ὄντων οὐκ [r] ἐσχίσθη τὸ δίκτυον.
12 λέγει αὐτοῖς ὁ Ἰησοῦς Δεῦτε [s] ἀριστήσατε. οὐδεὶς [t] ἐτόλμα τῶν
μαθητῶν [u] ἐξετάσαι αὐτὸν Σὺ τίς εἶ; εἰδότες ὅτι ὁ κύριος
[v] ἐστίν. 13 ἔρχεται Ἰησοῦς καὶ λαμβάνει τὸν ἄρτον καὶ
δίδωσιν αὐτοῖς, καὶ τὸ [w] ὀψάριον ὁμοίως. 14 [x] τοῦτο ἤδη
[xy] τρίτον [z] ἐφανερώθη Ἰησοῦς τοῖς μαθηταῖς [a] ἐγερθεὶς [a] ἐκ
νεκρῶν.
15 Ὅτε οὖν [b] ἠρίστησαν, λέγει τῷ Σίμωνι Πέτρῳ ὁ

12. om 1st ὁ B. rec aft *ουδεις* ins *δε*, with ADℵ rel [syrr syr-jer copt arm Cyr_1]: om BC.

13. rec aft *ερχεται* ins *ουν*, with A rel lat-*f ff*$_2$ syr copt: om BCDLXℵ 1. 33 foss (with gat) lat-*a b e* sah[-mnt] arm Cyr_1. rec ins ὁ bef *ιησ.*, with Aℵ rel [Cyr]: om B C(appy) D. om 2nd *και* D-gr. for *διδωσιν*, *ευχαριστησας εδωκεν* D [mm lat-*f g*] syr-jer.

14. aft *τουτο* ins *δε* GLXℵ 33 [syr-jer] copt. rec ins ὁ bef *ιησ.*, with Aℵ rel [Cyr_1]: om BCD. rec aft *μαθ.* ins *αυτου*, with D rel vulg [lat-*b c f*] syrr [syr-jer æth] copt Cyr: om ABCLℵ 1. 33 am(with fuld mt) lat-*a e ff*$_2$ arm.

15. *ο ιησ.* bef *τω σιμωνι πετρω* D tol lat-*a c* syrr [syr-jer] copt [æth Chr_1].

to John, and = ἰχθύδια, Matt. xv. 34: Mark viii. 7. It is probably here not '*a fish*,' but **fish**. **11.**] **ἀνέβη**, into the boat, which apparently was now on the beach, in the shallow water. **ἑκατὸν πεντ.**] This enumeration is singular, and not to be accounted for by any mystical significance of the number, but as betokening the careful counting which took place after the event, and in which the narrator took a part. **οὐκ ἐσχίσθη τὸ δίκτ.**, herein differing from what happened Luke v. 6, when it *was broken*.

12. ἀριστ.] Hereby is implied the *morning meal:* see vv. 3, 4. **οὐδεὶς ἐτ.**] I take these words to imply that they sat down to the meal in silence,—wondering at, while at the same time they well knew, Him who was thus their Host. Chrys. says, *οὐκέτι γὰρ τὴν αὐτὴν παῤῥησίαν εἶχον . . . . ἀλλὰ μετὰ σιγῆς καὶ δεοῦς πολλοῦ καὶ αἰδοῦς ἐκαθέζοντο προσέχοντες πρὸς αὐτόν, ... τὴν δὲ μορφὴν ἀλλοιοτέραν ὁρῶντες καὶ πολλῆς ἐκπλήξεως γέμουσαν, σφόδρα ἦσαν καταπεπληγμένοι, καὶ ἐβούλοντό τι περὶ αὐτῆς ἐρωτᾶν· ἀλλὰ τὸ δέος καὶ τὸ εἰδέναι αὐτοὺς ὅτι οὐχ ἕτερός τις ἦν ἀλλ' αὐτός, ἐπεῖχον τὴν ἐρώτησιν.* Hom. in Joann. lxxxvii. 2. **τολμᾶν** and **ἐξετάζειν** are *not elsewhere in John*. **ἐξετάσαι**, more than '*ask:*' to question or prove Him. **ἐστίν** again, after *ἐτόλμα*, in John's manner. **13.**] **ἔρχεται**,—from the spot where they had seen Him standing, to the fire of coals. **λαμβ. κ. δίδωσιν** bears evident trace of the *λαβὼν ἐδίδου* of another occasion, and reminds us of the similar occurrence at Emmaus, Luke xxiv. 30. **14. τοῦτο ἤδη τρίτον**] Compare *τοῦτο [δὲ] πάλιν δεύτερον*, ch. iv. 54: and 2 Cor. xiii. 1. The number here is clearly not that of *all* appearances of Jesus up to this time, for that to Mary Magdalen is not reckoned; but only those *to the disciples*,—i. e. any considerable number of them together. This one internal trait of consistency speaks much for the authenticity and genuineness of the addition. **ἐγερθεὶς**] The participle is not found elsewhere in John, but the participial construction is found in ch. iv. 54. Without agreeing with all the allegorical interpretations of the Fathers, I cannot but see much depth and richness of meaning in this whole narrative. The Lord appears to His disciples, busied about their occupation for their daily bread; speaks and acts in a manner wonderfully similar to His words and actions on a former memorable occasion, when we know that by their toiling long and taking nothing, but at his word enclosing a multitude of fishes, was set forth what should befall them as fishers of men. Can we miss that application at this far more important epoch of their apostolic mission? Besides, He graciously provides for their present wants, and invites them to be His guests: why, but to shew them that in their work hereafter they should never want but He would provide? And as connected with the parable, Matt. xiii. 47 ff., has the net *enclosing a great multitude and yet not broken*, no meaning? Has the 'taking the bread and giving to

Ἰησοῦς Σίμων Ἰωάννου, ἀγαπᾷς με [c] πλέον τούτων; c = (πλεῖον) Matt. v. 20. Luke vii. 42 only.
...κυριε L. λέγει αὐτῷ Ναὶ κύριε, σὺ οἶδας ὅτι φιλῶ σε. λέγει d ver. 17. Matt. viii. 30, 33 ||. Luke
αὐτῷ [d] Βόσκε τὰ [e] ἀρνία μου. 16 λέγει αὐτῷ πάλιν xv. 15 only. 3 Kings xii. 16. Ezek. xxxiv. 3, 14.
e here only, exc. Rev. v. 6 al. fr. Ps. cxiii. 4, 6. Jer. xi. 19. xxvii. (l.) 45 only.

rec (for ιωαννου, here and vv. 16, 17) ιωνα (*from Matt* xvi. 17), with AC[2·3] rel syrr [syr-jer] æth arm [Bas$_1$] Chr Cyr$_1$ Thdrt$_1$: txt BC[1]DL(א) vulg lat-*a b* [*e ff*$_2$ *g*] coptt Non$_1$ Jer (*cf ch* i. 43). (om ιωνα here א[1] : ins א-corr[1·3].) rec πλειον, with A rel [Bas$_1$] : txt BCDLSXΛא 33 lat-*a b c e* Chr. ins ο ιησ. bef βοσκε DU gat(with mm) Syr. for αρνια, προβατα C[1]D Chr$_1$.

16. παλιν bef 1st λεγει αυτω Cא lat-*b f* [syr-jer] copt arm : om παλιν D lat-*c e*.

them, and the fish likewise' no meaning, which so closely binds together the miraculous feeding, and the institution of the Lord's Supper, with their future meetings in His Name and round His Table? Any one who recognizes the *teaching* character of the acts of the Lord, can hardly cast all such applications from him;—and those who do not, have yet the first rudiments of the Gospels to learn. **15—23.**] *The calling, and its prospect.* **15. ὅτε οὖν ἠρ.**] There appears to have been nothing said during the meal. Surely every word would have been recorded. One great object of this appearance, observes Stier, certainly was the confirmation, and encouragement of the "*fisher of men*," in his apostolic office. **Σίμων Ἰωάννου**] A reminiscence probably of his own name and parentage, as distinguished from his apostolic name of honour, Cephas, or Peter, see ch. i. 43. Thus we have **Σ.** *βαριωνᾶ*, Matt. xvi. 17, connected with the mention of his natural state of flesh and blood, which had not revealed to him the great truth just confessed—and Luke xxii. 31, "Simon, Simon," when he is reminded of his natural weakness. See also Mark xiv. 37, and Matt. xvii. 25, where the significance is not so plain. **πλέον τούτων**] **more than these thy fellow-disciples**: compare Matt. xxvi. 33: Mark xiv. 29, "Though *all* should be offended, yet not I." That John does not record this saying, makes no difficulty here; nor does it tell against the genuineness of this appendix to the Gospel. The narrator tells that which he heard the Lord say, and tells it faithfully and literally. That it coincides with what Peter is related to have said elsewhere, is a proof of the *authenticity*, not of the *connexion*, of the two accounts. **τούτων** has been strangely enough understood (Whitby, Bolten) of the *fish*, or the "employment and furniture of a fisherman:"—Olshausen sees a reference to the pre-eminence given to Peter, Matt. xvi. 19,—and regards the words as implying that on that account he really did love Jesus more than the rest;—but surely this is most improbable, and the other explanation the only likely or true one. Perhaps there is also a slight reference to his present just-shewn zeal, in leaping from the ship first to meet the Lord. 'Has thy past conduct to Me truly borne out thy former and present warmth of love to Me above these thy fellows?' "Mira Christi sapientia, qui tam paucis vocibus efficit, ut Petrus et sibi satisfaceret, quem ter negaverat, et collegis quibus se prætulerat;—exemplum dans disciplinæ ecclesiasticæ." Grot. Peter's answer shews that he understood the question as above. He says nothing of the πλέον τούτων—but dropping all comparison of himself with others, humbly refers to the Searcher of hearts the genuineness of his love, however the past may seem to have called it in question.

The distinction between **ἀγαπᾶν** and **φιλεῖν** must not here be lost sight of, nor must we superficially say with Grotius, "Promiscue hic usurpavit Johannes ἀγαπᾶν et φιλεῖν ut mox βόσκειν et ποιμαίνειν (see below). Neque hic quærendæ sunt subtilitates." If so, why do the Lord's two first questions contain ἀγαπᾷς while Peter's answers have φιλῶ—whereas the third time the question and answer both have φιλεῖν? This does not look like accident. The distinction seems to be that ἀγαπᾶν is more used of that reverential love, grounded on high graces of character, which is borne towards God and man by the child of God;—whereas φιλεῖν expresses more the personal love of human affection. Peter therefore uses a less exalted word, and one implying a consciousness of his own weakness, but a persuasion and deep feeling of personal love. (Hence it will be seen that in the sublimest relations, where, all perfections existing, love can *only be personal*, φιλεῖν only can be used, see ch. v. 20.) Then in the third question, the Lord adopts the word of Peter's answer, the closer to press the meaning of it home to him. The **σὺ οἶδας**, the *two first* times, seems to

Matt. ii. 6. Acts xx. 28. 1 Pet. v. 2. 2 Kings vii 7.
g = ch. x. 1, &c. Matt. x. 6 al. fr. Ezek. xxxiv. passim.
h see ver. 14 reff.
i ch. xvi. 20. Matt. xvii. 23 reff.
j ver. 15.
k here only +.
l Acts v. 6. 1 Pet v. 5 al. Judg. viii. 20.

δεύτερον Σίμων Ἰωάννου, ἀγαπᾷς με; λέγει αὐτῷ Ναὶ
κύριε, σὺ οἶδας ὅτι φιλῶ σε. λέγει αὐτῷ [f] Ποίμαινε τὰ
[g] πρόβατά μου. 17 λέγει αὐτῷ τὸ [h] τρίτον Σίμων Ἰωάννου,
φιλεῖς με; [i] ἐλυπήθη ὁ Πέτρος ὅτι εἶπεν αὐτῷ τὸ [h] τρίτον
Φιλεῖς με; καὶ εἶπεν αὐτῷ Κύριε, πάντα σὺ οἶδας· σὺ
γινώσκεις ὅτι φιλῶ σε. λέγει αὐτῷ Ἰησοῦς [j] Βόσκε τὰ
[k] προβάτιά μου. 18 ἀμὴν ἀμὴν λέγω σοι, ὅτε ἦς [l] νεώτερος,

ABCDE GHKM SUX ΓΔΛΠℵ 1. 33. 69

om δευτερον ℵ[1](ins, prefixing το, ℵ-corr[1.3]) [latt(not *c e*) arm]. aft δευτ. ins ο κυριος D. om ναι ℵ[1]. μου bef τα προβατα D. προβατια BC, *oviculas* lat-*b*.
17. om το (bef 1st τριτον) C. aft ελυπηθη ins δε ℵ[1]. ins και bef φιλεις ℵ[1](marked for erasure by ℵ-corr[1.3]). om και A am lat-*a b*. for 2nd ειπεν, λεγει ADXℵ 1. 33 am lat-*a b c e f g*. om αυτω (bef κυριε) B 249. rec συ bef παντα, with AC[3] rel vulg lat-*f* æth [syr-jer Bas_1] : txt BC[1]Dℵ 33 tol lat-*a e* ff_2 syrr $Ambr_1$ spec. ins και bef λεγει ℵ. rec ins ὁ bef ιησ., with A rel [Bas_1 Cyr_1]: om BC ev-y.—om ιησ. also Dℵ 1. 33 latt copt. rec (for προβατια) προβατα (*repetition from ver* 16 ?), with Dℵ rel [latt Cyr] : αρνια Λ em(with gat mm) : txt ABC syrr.
18. οτι C[1] ev-y.

refer to the Lord's *personal* knowledge of Peter's heart—in His having given him that name, ch. i. 43, in Matt. xvi. 17: Luke xxii. 31, and the announcement of his denial of Him. The *last* time, he widens this assertion 'Thou knowest *me*,' into 'Thou knowest *all things*,' being grieved at the repetition of a question which brought this Omniscience so painfully to his mind. **βόσκε τὰ ἀρν. μου**] This and the following answers of the Lord can hardly be regarded as the *reinstating* of Peter in his apostolic office, for there is no record of his ever having lost it: but as a further and higher setting forth of it than that first one Matt. iv. 18 ff., both as belonging to all of them on the present occasion, and as tending to comfort Peter's own mind after his fall, and reassure him of his holding the same place among the Apostles as before, owing to the gracious forgiveness of his Lord.

We can hardly with any deep insight into the text hold *βόσκειν* and *ποιμ.* to be synonymous (Grot. above, Lücke, De Wette, Trench), or *ἀρνία, πρόβατα,* and *προβάτια.* The sayings of the Lord have not surely been so carelessly reported as this would assume. Every thing here speaks for a *gradation* of meaning. The variety of reading certainly makes it difficult to point out exactly the steps of that gradation, and unnecessary to follow the various interpreters in their assignment of them: but that there *is such*, may be seen from Isa. xl. 11: 1 John ii. 12, 13. Perhaps the *feeding of the lambs* was the furnishing the apostolic testimony of the Resurrection and facts of the Lord's life on earth to the first converts; the *shepherding* or ruling *the sheep*, the subsequent government of the Church as shewn forth in the early part of the Acts; the *feeding of the προβάτια*, the choicest, the loved of the flock, the furnishing the now maturer Church of Christ with the wholesome food of the doctrine contained in his Epistles. But those must strangely miss the whole sense, who dream of an exclusive primatial power here granted or confirmed to him. A sufficient refutation of this silly idea, if it needed any other than the **ἐλυπήθη** of this passage, is found in the *συμπρεσβύτερος* of 1 Pet. v. 1, where he refers apparently to this very charge: see note on Matt. xvi. 17 ff. "Illud, *'plus his'* (*πλέον τούτων*), indicio est, Petrum hic restitui in locum suum, quem amiserat per abnegationem (but see above) simulque *quiddam ei præ condiscipulis* tribui, sed nihil a quo cæteri excludantur. Nam sane etiam hi amabant Jesum. Desinat tandem hoc ad se, et ad se unum rapere, qui nec amat nec pascit, sed depascit, per successionis Petrinæ simulationem. Non magis Roma, quam Hierosolyma aut Antiochia aut quivis alius locus ubi apostolum Petrus egit, Petrum sibi vindicare potest: imo Roma minime, caput *gentium:* nam Petrus erat in apostolis *circumcisionis.* Unum Romæ proprium est, quod apostolorum, etiam Petri sanguis in ea reperietur." Bengel. **16. πάλιν δεύτερον**] The words are found together in John iv. 54. **17. φιλεῖς**] See above on ver. 15. **ἐλυπήθη**—not merely on account of the repetition of the question, but because of **τὸ τρίτον**, the number of his own denials of Christ. **πάντα**

m ἐζώννυες σεαυτὸν καὶ περιεπάτεις ὅπου ἤθελες· ὅταν δὲ
n γηράσῃς, o ἐκτενεῖς τὰς χεῖράς σου, καὶ ἄλλος m ζώσει σε
καὶ οἴσει ὅπου οὐ θέλεις. 19 τοῦτο δὲ εἶπεν p σημαίνων
ποίῳ θανάτῳ q δοξάσει τὸν θεόν. καὶ τοῦτο εἰπὼν λέγει
αὐτῷ Ἀκολούθει μοι. 20 r ἐπιστραφεὶς ὁ Πέτρος βλέπει
τὸν s μαθητὴν s ὃν s ἠγάπα ὁ Ἰησοῦς ἀκολουθοῦντα, ὃς καὶ
t ἀνέπεσεν u ἐν τῷ δείπνῳ ἐπὶ τὸ v στῆθος αὐτοῦ καὶ εἶπεν

m here bis and Acts xii. 8 only. Neh. iv. 18.
n Heb. viii. 13 only. Ps xxxvi. 25.
o John, here only. Matt. viii. 3 reff. Sir. xv. 16.
p ch. xii. 33 reff.
q = here only. see Luke xxiii. 47.
r Mark v. 30. viii. 33. 1 Kings x. 9.
s ver. 7. ch. xiii. 23.
t = Luke xi. 37. ch. xiii. 12 al. Tobit ii. 1.
u = Matt. xxvi. 5 al.
v ch. xiii. 25 reff.

την χειραν א^1 [syr-jer]. αλλοι C^{2}D[Π]א 1. 33 syr-mg [syr-jer] arm Chr$_1$ Cyr[-p$_1$ Non$_1$]. rec σε bef ζωσ., with AD rel: txt BC^{2}א. [C^1?] ζωσουσιν [Π]א 1. 33 syr-mg [syr-jer] arm [Chr Cyr-p$_1$], ζωσωσιν C^2, ζωσουσει D: txt ABC^1 rel [latt syrr æth]. οισουσιν C^2 33; αποισουσιν σε [Π]א^{3a} 1 syr-mg Cyr[-p$_1$]: απαγουσιν σε D: οισει σε A em lat-*a c ff*$_2$ syrr copt æth: for οισει οπου, ποιησουσιν σοι οσα א^1. for ου, συ D^1[-gr], συ ου D^3 [latt(exc foss mt)].

19. for 1st τουτο, ταυτα D Orig$_1$.

20. rec aft επιστραφεις ins δε, with Dא rel [lat-*f* syr copt Cæs$_1$ Cyr$_1$]: om ABC[Π^1] 33 vulg lat-*b c e g* arm. om ὁ (bef ιησ.) D. om ακολουθουντα א^1(ins א-corr$^{1 \cdot 3}$). om ος א^1. for αυτου, του ιησου C(appy) lat-*a f*. for ειπεν, λεγει א^1

οἶδας] See above. **18.**] The end of his pastoral office is announced to him:—a proof of the *πάντα οἶδας* which he had just confessed;—a contrast to the denial of which he had just been reminded;—a proof to be hereafter given of the here recognized genuineness of that love which he had been professing. There is no implied *question*, as Lücke thinks:—the futures are prophetic. **ἀμὴν ἀμήν**] John's manner again. **ὅτε ἦς νεώτερος**—[may be merely] in contrast to **ὅταν δὲ γηρ.** [Or] it perhaps includes his life up to the time prophesied of. **ἐζώνν. σ.**,—as in ver. 7, he had girt his fisher's coat to him: but not confined in its reference to that girding alone—'thou girdedst thyself up for My work, and wentest hither and thither—but hereafter there shall be a service for thee "paullo constrictior"—**ἐκτενεῖς τὰς χ. σου**, but not as just now, in swimming; in a more painful manner, on the transverse beam of the cross; and another—the executioner—shall gird thee, —with the cords binding to the cross'—("tunc Petrus ab altero vincitur, cum cruci adstringitur," Tertull. Scorp. 15, vol. ii. p. 151). Such is the traditionary account of the death of Peter, Euseb. ii. 25; iii. 1, where see notes in Heinichen's edn. Cf. also Prolegg. to 1 Pet. § ii. 9 ff. **οἴσει**, viz. in the lifting up after the fastening to the cross—or perhaps, by a *ὕστερον πρότερον*, in making thee go the way to death, bearing thy cross. **ὅπου οὐ θέλ.**] "Quis enim vult mori? Prorsus nemo: et ita nemo ut B. Petro diceretur, Alter te cinget, et feret quo tu non vis." Aug. Serm. clxxiii. 2. Prof. Bleek (Beiträge zur Evangelien-kritik, p. 235, note) suggests an interpretation of this prophecy which is surely contrary to ver. 19:—that the former part, *ὅτε ἦς ν. . . .* applies to the life of Peter before his calling,—the latter *ἐκτενεῖς . . .* to his life in the service of the Lord, who is the *ἄλλος*—who was to strengthen him for his work (*ζώσει*),—that he was to stretch out his hands in the sense of his own weakness, not merely in the feebleness of old age (in prayer?), and finally this *ἄλλος*, the Lord whom he served, would carry him whither he would not, i. e. to a death of martyrdom. But this says nothing of **ποίῳ** *θανάτῳ*, on which the stress evidently is, and which Bleek, while he recognizes, endeavours to get rid of by strangely supposing the idea to have arisen after the death of Peter.

19.] This remark is entirely in John's manner, see ch. ii. 21; vi. 6; vii. 39; xii. 33; as may be also the *δοξάζειν τ. θ.* used of such a death, see ch. xiii. 31 f.; xvii. 1. **ἀκολούθει μοι**] Not to be understood I think of any present gesture of the Lord calling Peter aside;—but, from the next verse, followed perhaps by a motion of Peter towards Him, in which John joined. The words seem to be a plain reference to ch. xiii. 36;—and the *following*,—a following through the Cross to glory: see Matt. xvi. 24: Mark x. 21. Now, however, *ἄρας τὸν σταυρόν* is omitted. He had made this so plain, that it needed not expressing. There was also a forcible reminding Peter of the first time when he had heard this command on the same shore, Matt. iv. 19.

20.] The details necessary to complete the narrative are obscure, and only hinted

w ellips., Matt. xxvi. 8. Mark xiv. 36 end. x = 1 Cor. xv. 6. Phil. i. 25. y ch. ix. 4. 1 Tim. iv. 13. see Luke xix. 13. z Matt. xxvii. 4. a = Matt. ix. 26. Mark i. 28. Rom. x. 18, from Ps. xviii. 4.

Κύριε, τίς ἐστιν ὁ παραδιδούς σε; 21 τοῦτον οὖν ἰδὼν ὁ
Πέτρος λέγει τῷ Ἰησοῦ Κύριε, οὗτος δὲ w τί; 22 λέγει
αὐτῷ ὁ Ἰησοῦς Ἐὰν αὐτὸν θέλω x μένειν y ἕως ἔρχομαι,
z τί z πρὸς σέ; σύ μοι ἀκολούθει. 23 a ἐξῆλθεν οὖν οὗτος

...xxi. 22 (appy, but continued by a later hand?) Π. ABCDE GHKM SUX ΓΔΛℵ 1. 33. 69

[Chr]. add αυτω CDℵ 33 foss lat-ff_2 [syr-jer] copt æth Cyr: om AB rel Orig. om κυριε C[1] 435(Sz); και (κε̄ *itacised?*) G. παραδιδων D.

21. rec om ουν, with A rel Syr æth arm: ins BCDℵ 33 latt syr-w-ast copt $Orig_1$ Cyr_1. for λεγει, ειπεν ℵ [vulg(not am fuld em) lat-*f g*] Chr-4-mss. for τω, αυτω D[1][-gr]. om κυριε ℵ.

22. aft μενειν ins ουτως D lat-ff_2. aft συ ins δε C[1 or 2] [copt]. rec ακολουθει bef μοι, with C[3] rel lat-*f* copt: txt ABC[1]Dℵ 1. 33 latt Orig Cyr_1.

at in the background. It seems that Peter either was at the time of the foregoing conversation walking with Jesus, and turned round and saw John following,—or that he moved towards Him on the termination of it (but certainly not from a misunderstanding of the words ἀκολ. μοι, see ver. 21). I can hardly conceive Him *moving away* on uttering these words, and summoning Peter away in private. It seems in the highest degree unnatural. The description of the disciple whom Jesus loved is evidently inserted to justify his following, and is a strong token of John's hand having written this chapter: see ch. xiii. 23. **21.**] Peter's question shews that he had rightly understood the Lord's prophecy respecting him. He now wishes to know what should befall his friend and colleague,—*ἀποδιδοὺς αὐτῷ τὴν ἀμοιβὴν* (for *his* similar service in ch. xiii. 23 just referred to) *καὶ νομίσας αὐτὸν βούλεσθαι ἐρωτᾶν τὰ καθ' αὐτόν, εἶτα μὴ θαῤῥεῖν, αὐτὸς ἀνεδέξατο τὴν ἐρώτησιν.* Chrysost. (Stier vii. 198, edn. 2.) This was not mere *idle* curiosity, but that longing which we all feel for our friends; of which Bengel says,—"Facilius nos ipsos voluntati divinæ impendimus, quam curiositatem circa alios, æquales præsertim aut suppares, deponimus." *οὐκ ἀκολουθήσει σοι; οὐ τὴν αὐτὴν ἡμῖν ὁδὸν τοῦ θανάτου βαδιεῖται;* Euthym. **22.**] The words **τί πρὸς σέ;** imply a rebuke;—not perhaps however so sharp a one as has been sometimes seen in them. They remind Peter of the distinctness of each man's position and duty before the Lord; and the **σύ μοι ἀκ.**, which follows, directs his view along that course of duty and suffering, which was appointed for him by his Divine Master. Notice the emphatic expression of *σύ*, and the emphatic position of *μοι*: q. d. '*His* appointed lot is no element in *thy* onward course: it is ME that *thou* must follow.'

On the **ἐὰν θέλω . . . .**, three opinions have been held (for that which refers the words to John's remaining where he then was, on the shore, till the Lord returned from His colloquy with Peter, is not worth more than cursory mention): (1) that of Aug., Maldon., Grot., Lampe, Olsh., &c. (it being allowed on all hands, that *μένειν* means **to remain in this life**: see reff. and ch. xii. 34), "If I will that he remain till I fetch him," i. e. by a *natural death.* But this is frigid, and besides inapplicable here. Peter's death, although by the hands of an *ἄλλος*, was just as much the Lord's '*coming for him,*' as John's, and there would thus be no contrast. (2) That that 'coming of the Lord' is meant which is so often in the three Gospels alluded to (see especially notes on Matt. xxiv.), viz. the establishment in full of the dispensation of the Kingdom by the destruction of the nation and temple of the Jews. This is the view of some mentioned by Theophyl., of Bengel (see below), Stier, Dräseke, Jacobi, &c.—and is upheld by the similar place, Matt. xvi. 28. (3) That the Lord here only puts a case,—"Even should I will that he remain upon earth till My last coming—what would that be to thee?" This view is upheld by Trench, Miracles, p. 466, edn. 2; but I think must be rejected on maturer consideration of the character of the words of our Lord, in whose mouth such a mere hypothetical saying would be strangely incongruous, especially in these last solemn days of his presence on earth. The second view seems then to remain, and I adopt it with some qualification. At the destruction of Jerusalem began that mighty series of events of which the Apocalypse is the prophetic record, and which is in the complex known as the 'COMING OF THE LORD,' ending, as it shall, with His glorious and personal Advent. This the beloved Apostle alone lived to see, according to ancient and undoubted tradition (Euseb. H. E. iii. 23). When De Wette (whom Lücke in the main follows: see also Mr. Elliott, Apocal. Alf. p. 160)

ὁ λόγος εἰς τοὺς [b] ἀδελφοὺς ὅτι ὁ μαθητὴς ἐκεῖνος οὐκ
[c] ἀποθνήσκει· [d] καὶ οὐκ εἶπεν αὐτῷ ὁ Ἰησοῦς ὅτι οὐκ
ἀποθνήσκει, ἀλλ' Ἐὰν αὐτὸν θέλω [x] μένειν [y] ἕως ἔρχομαι,
[z] τί [z] πρὸς σέ;
24 Οὗτός ἐστιν ὁ μαθητὴς ὁ [e] μαρτυρῶν [e] περὶ τούτων
καὶ [ὁ] γράψας ταῦτα, καὶ [f] οἴδαμεν ὅτι ἀληθὴς αὐτοῦ ἡ
μαρτυρία ἐστίν. 25 ἔστιν δὲ καὶ ἄλλα πολλὰ ἃ ἐποί-

b = in Gospp., here only. Acts ix. 30. xi. 1, 12 al. fr. see Matt. xxiii. 8.
c pres., Matt. xxvii. 63 reff.
d = Matt. xi. 17 bis. xii. 43. ch. i. 5. xx. 29 al.
e ch. i. 7 reff.
f 1 John v. 18, 19, 20.

23. rec ο λογος bef ουτος, with A rel vulg syr arm: txt BCDℵ 1. 33 gat lat-*a b c e f ff*₂ [*q* syr-jer] Syr. aft αδελφους ins και εδοξαν D arm. for και ουκ ειπ., ουκ ειπ. δε BCℵ 33 (lat-*c* Syr) [syr-jer Chr] Orig: txt AD rel [latt] syr æth arm. for αυτω, αυτο *illud* D. om 2nd οτι D[Λ] vulg lat-*a b e*. αποθνησκεις D lat-*e*. (αλλα D.) om τι D-gr.—om τι προς σε ℵ[1](ins ℵ-corr[1]) 1 lat-*a e* arm [Chr-5-mss$_1$].

24. ins και bef μαρτυρων B [Cyr$_1$]. om 3rd ὁ ACℵ[1] rel [Syr syr-jer Chr$_1$] Orig: ins BD lat-(*a*) *b* (*ff*₂) copt æth, and (but bef και) ℵ-corr[1.3b](appy) 33. 69 lat-*c* syr-w-ast arm [Cyr]. rec transp αυτου and 2nd εστιν, with AC[3]ℵ rel latt Chr [Cyr-p$_1$]: εστιν bef αυτου η μαρτ. D: αυτ. εστ. η μ. 33: txt BC[1].

25. Tischdf states that ver 25 and the subscription in ℵ are written not by the same hand as that which precedes, but by ℵ-corr[1a]. rec (for ἅ) οσα, with AC[2]D

calls this interpretation ganz nichtig, and would interpret this answer by the current idea in apostolic times, that His coming was very near, he is assuming (1) that this *was* the idea of the Apostles themselves (see 2 Thess. ii. 2, 3: 2 Pet. iii. 3, 4, 8, 9); (2) that this answer is not that of our Lord, but apocryphal. If all that he says about the early expectations of the Church were granted, it would not follow that the view above taken is erroneous. And as to the chapter having been written after the death of John and the destruction of Jerusalem, see below. **23.**] **τοὺς ἀδελφούς** is an expression of later date than any usually occurring in the Gospels. It is however frequent in the Acts: see reff. **ἐξῆλθ. εἰς** (see reff.) is more in the manner of the other Gospels. **καὶ οὐκ εἶπ. . . . .**] This *καί* is much in John's manner, see ch. xvi. 32; not meaning *but*,—rather, **and yet.** The following words are to me a proof that this chapter was written during John's lifetime. If written by another person after John's death, we should certainly, in the refutation of this error, have read, *ἀπέθανεν γάρ, καὶ ἐτάφη*, as in Acts ii. 29. This notion of John's not having died, was prevalent in the early Church,—so that Augustine himself seems almost to credit the story of the earth of John's tomb heaving with his breath. Tract. cxxiv. 2. "The English sect of the 'seekers' under Cromwell expected the reappearance of the Apostle as the forerunner of the coming of Christ," Tholuck. See Trench on the Miracles, edn. 2, p. 467 note. The simple recapitulation of the words of the Lord shews that their sense remained dark to the writer, who ventured on no explanation of them; merely setting his own side of the apostolic duty over against that of Peter, who probably had already by following his Master through the Cross, glorified God, whereas the beloved disciple was, whatever that meant, to tarry till He came.

24, 25.] Identification of the Author, and conclusion. See remarks below. **24.**] **περὶ τούτων** and **ταῦτα** certainly refer to the whole Gospel, not merely to the Appendix—and are quite in John's style: see ch. xii. 41; xx. 31. **οἴδαμεν** is in John's style—see reff.: also 1 John iv. 14, 16 al. fr. On **ὅτι ἀλ. ἐστ. . . . .** see 3 John 12, and ch. v. 32. **25.**] The purpose of this verse seems to be to assert and vindicate the fragmentary character of the Gospel, considered merely as a historical narrative:—for that the doings of the Lord were so many,—His life so rich in matter of record,—that, in a popular hyperbole, we can hardly imagine the world containing them all, if singly written down; thus setting forth the superfluity and cumbrousness of any thing like a perfect detail, in the strongest terms,—and in terms which certainly looked as if fault had been found with this Gospel for want of completeness, by some objectors.

The reader will have perceived in the foregoing comment on the chapter a manifest leaning to the belief that it was written by John himself. *Of this I am fully convinced.* In every part of it, his hand is

ησεν ὁ Ἰησοῦς, [g] ἅτινα ἐὰν γράφηται [h] καθ᾿ [h] ἕν, οὐδ᾿ αὐτὸν
[i] οἶμαι τὸν κόσμον [k] χωρῆσαι τὰ [l] γραφόμενα βιβλία.

ABCDE GHKM SUX ΓΔΛℵ 1. 33 69

ΚΑΤΑ ΙΩΑΝΝΗΝ.

g = Acts x. 41 al. fr. h 1 Cor. xiv. 31. Eph. v. 33 only. Xen. Anab. iv. 7. 8. i Phil. i. 17. James i. 7 only. Job xi. 2. 1 Macc. v. 61. 2 Macc. v. 21. vii. 24 only. k = ch. ii. 6. Mark ii. 2 only. 2 Chron. iv. 5. l pres., ver. 23. Matt. xxvii. 63 reff.

rel syr-mg-gr: txt BC¹Xℵ 33 vulg lat-*c f* [*q*] $Orig_1$ Chr Cyr. ins *χριστος* bef *ιησ.* D. (*ουδ᾿*, so BDΔℵ 1 [69 $Orig_1$].) *χωρησειν* BC¹ℵ: txt AC²D rel syr[-mg-gr $Orig_2$ Chr Cyr]. rec at end adds *αμην*, with E rel am lat-*c f* syr[and -mg-gr]: om AB C(appy) Dℵ 1. 33 [vulg-ed] fuld(with ing &c) lat-*a b* [*e ff₂ g q*] Syr syr-mss syr-jer [coptt] æth arm $Orig_1$ Chr_2.

Subscription. *κατα ιωαννην* B: *ευαγγελιον κατα ι.* ACEΔΛ ℵ[-corr¹] 33: *εναγγ. κ. ι. ετελεσθη αρχεται ευαγγ. κ. λουκαν* D, simly lat-*a b e f* ff_2 [*q*]: om KMUX[Γℵ¹] 69: *ευ. κ. ι. εξεδοθη μετα χρονους λβ της του χυ αναληψεως* S Scr's k l m n p [so G, but with *κ* for *λβ* and *αναλυσεως*]: *τελος του κ. ιω. ευαγγελιου* H [Π-suppl(insg *αγιου* bef *ευαγ.*) Scr's d].

plain and unmistakeable: in every part of it, his character and spirit is manifested in a way which none but the most biassed can fail to recognize. I believe it to have been added some years probably after the completion of the Gospel; partly perhaps to record the important miracle of the second draught of fishes, so full of spiritual instruction, and the interesting account of the sayings of the Lord to Peter;—but principally to meet the error which was becoming prevalent concerning himself. In order to do this, he gives a complete account, with all minute details,—even to the number of the fish caught,—of the circumstances preceding the conversation,—and the very words of the Lord Himself; not pretending to put a meaning on those words, but merely asserting that they announced no such thing as that he should not die. Surely nothing can be more natural than this. External evidence completely tallies with this view. The chapter is contained in *all the principal* MSS.: and there is no greater variety of reading than usual. In these respects it differs remarkably from John vii. 53—viii. 11, and indeed from even Mark xvi. 9—20. Internal evidence of style and diction is nearly balanced. It certainly contains several words and constructions not met with elsewhere in John; but, on the other hand, the whole cast of it is his;—the copulæ are his;—the train of thought, and manner of narration. And all allowance should be made for the double alteration of style of writing which would be likely to be brought about, by lapse of time, and by the very nature of an appendix,—a fragment,—not forming part of a whole written continuously, but standing by itself. The last two verses, from their contents, we might expect to have more of the epistolary form; and accordingly we find them singularly in style resembling the Epistles of John.

On the whole, I am persuaded that in this chapter we have a fragment, both *authentic* and *genuine*, added, for reasons apparent on the face of it, *by the Apostle himself*, bearing evidence of his hand, but in a 'second manner,'—a later style;—probably (as I think is shewn, inter alia, in the simplicity of the *οἶμαι* in ver. 25) in the decline of life. I cannot, with Luthardt, regard the last two verses as an addition by the Ephesian Church. If, as he thinks, the *οἴδαμεν* favours this view, does not the *οἶμαι* as much disfavour it? Nor does the ingenious reasoning of Bp. Wordsworth at all convince me that this chapter originally formed a part of the Gospel, or that the view here advocated arises from a "non-apprehension of the connexion between the 20th and 21st chapters." His *à priori* reason, that had it been an appendix afterwards added, we should have had two distinct editions of the Gospel, whereas now all the MSS. contain it, is not reliable, in the uncertainty which rests on the origin of our present MSS., and also on the length or shortness of the interval during which it may have been wanting to the Gospel.

NOTE ON CH. V. 2.

An interesting notice has been forwarded me respecting the probable locality of the pool of Bethesda. My correspondent believes that it must have been identical with Siloam, and thinks he has obtained evidence on the spot which renders this exceedingly probable. I subjoin an extract from his letter:—

"The excavation, near the Mosque of Omar, which from a comparatively recent date has been designated 'Bethesda,' lays claim to that title only from its proximity to the modern 'St. Stephen's Gate,' which is *supposed* to be near the site of the 'Sheep Gate' mentioned in Nehemiah, which again is only *presumed* to be the locality referred to in St. John as τῇ προβατικῇ.

"The greater number of eye-witnesses reject this 'ditch of Antonia' on the evidence of a first impression, which being so general, is not to be despised. Dr. Robinson, the first to upset many similar legends, came at once to the conclusion, that wherever Bethesda had been, it was never in *that ditch*, and setting himself to discover a more probable substitute, unluckily pitched upon an even more unlikely spot, to wit, the 'Fountain of the Virgin,' which could never have been within Jerusalem or near to the 'Sheep Gate,' and, being a cave, into which you descend by a flight of steps, can by no stretch of imagination answer the requirements of a 'pool having five porches.' But he was directed to this spot from the singular coincidence presented by the phænomenon for which that fountain is celebrated. It seems curious that, having himself explored the narrow tunnel, which connects this cave with the well-established pool of Siloam; and having remarked that the pool, being supplied with water from the cave, necessarily shares the phænomenon, he should not have erected his porches upon the more eligible spot. For the Pool of Siloam, for any thing to the contrary in Nehemiah or Josephus, might have been within the city wall; nay there is a strong probability that it *was* so, founded on the only intelligible use of the connecting conduit, namely, to supply the city with water in times of siege, and (as appears from its formation) without the knowledge of the besiegers. The solution seems to be that, as there was no necessity to upset the Pool of Siloam for the *substitution* of Bethesda or any thing else, its *identity* with any other spot never occurred to him.

"Dr. Kitto, who I believe never visited the places about which he so ably wrote, refused Robinson's theory, 1st, on the proper grounds of distance, and impossibility of porching the Virgin's cave; 2ndly, on the less reasonable objection, of an inconsistency between a *regular* descent of the angel, and an *irregular* action of the syphon. But upon a reference to the original this second objection falls through, for the expression there used, κατὰ καιρόν, simply conveys an impression of *recurrence*, and indeed our translation 'at a certain season' does not seem to imply *regularity*.

"Armed therefore with Robinson's (in this respect) unimpeached hypothesis, and conceiving that a pool may have both a topographical and an eleemosynary designation—nay, *concluding*, that it had more names than one, from the expression ἐπιλεγομένη, we proceed to erect our στοάς over this pool of Siloam, to see how better *it* will steer clear of Kitto's *first*, and more reasonable, objection. And lo! we find the requisites for such a structure appear (I would rather say have never *dis*appeared),—the remains of four columns built into the (north) *east wall* of the pool, and the remains of four corresponding columns, yet visible down the *centre* of the pool, as in the subjoined sketch,—

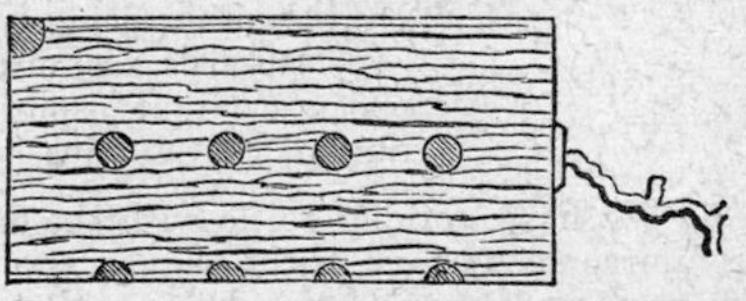

clearly shewing that at a former period Siloam was *half covered over*. And it is something more than a coincidence, when we perceive that by such an arrangement the colonnade would be divided into exactly *five equal portions*, the whole being neither more nor less than a κολυμβήθρα πέντε στοὰς ἔχουσα. I need not say that this fact alone at sight, produced in my mind the strongest conviction.

"The taste of the water of Siloam resembles flat Seltzer, and from Wilde's narrative we find its analysis is as near as possible the same as Harrogate, which you are aware is famed as a specific in cutaneous disorders. Dr. Wilde mentions that the people about believe in the efficacy of this water in similar diseases, particularly *eye* disorders; and of this I satisfied myself on the spot, though I was not fortunate enough to *see* it so used or to witness the bubbling.

"To this day such springs are as common in the East as with us. Invalids in great numbers resort to the hot springs at Tiberyeh (Tiberias), and there is something of the kind at Panias (Cæsarea Philippi). That the water should have been considered more efficacious immediately after the bubbling, seems not unnatural, and that such bubbling should have been ascribed to supernatural agency is much less so, when we remember, that the phænomenon defied explanation, until a quite late date,—at that date it could be scarcely supposed otherwise."

On this I may make one or two remarks, both by way of illustration, and as referring to objections which may be made to the supposition.

1. No meaning has ever been assigned to ἐπὶ τῇ προβατικῇ which should affect this or any other view of the site of Bethesda.

2. It is perhaps hardly fair to lay stress on ἐν τοῖς Ἱεροσολύμοις as implying that Bethesda was within the walls. The expression may be a wide one, as in ch. x. 22: Luke xiii. 4: Acts ii. 5, &c.

3. On the other hand the long and crooked tunnel connecting the two fountains, which Robinson explored, would seem as if it could have served no other purpose than that of a secret means of water-supply unknown to besiegers; and if so, then perhaps it may be allowable to claim for the words ἐν τοῖς Ἱεροσολύμοις, as my correspondent does, the above meaning.

4. The fact of the two pools, the Fountain of the Virgin and Siloam, being simultaneously intermittent, was established by Robinson.

5. I am informed, that the "troubling of the pool" is exactly similar to what might be expected from a rush of water up through a narrow tunnel: and occurs at irregular intervals of from two or three days to a fortnight: depending on the quantity of rain that has recently fallen.

6. Robinson observed the drums of pillars under the water, but makes no comment on them, nor does he mention their number.

7. Irenæus, Hær. iv. 8. 2, p. 236, says of our Lord, "Et Siloâ etiam sæpe Sabbatis curavit: et propter hoc assidebant ei multi die Sabbatorum." And Prudentius (*Contra Homuncionitas*, 129 ff.) says:—

"Variis Siloa refundit
Momentis latices, nec fluctum semper anhelat,
Sed vice distincta largos lacus accipit haustus.
Agmina languentum sitiunt spem fontis avari,
Membrorum maculas puro ablutura natatu:
Certatim interea roranti pumice raucas
Expectant scatebras, et sicco margine pendent."

And again, Enchiridion Vet. et Nov. Test. xxxiii.,—

"Morborum medicina latex, quem spiritus horis
Eructat variis, fusum ratione latenti,
Siloam vocitant: sputis ubi conlita cæci
Lumina Salvator jussit de fonte lavari."

8. We have nothing to do with the descent of the angel, nor with the existence of any miraculous power in the water: the former existing only in the spurious part of the passage, and the latter being merely implied as matter of popular belief in the speech of the paralytic, ver. 7: see note there.

9. One objection will suggest itself: if the pools of Bethesda and Siloam were but one, why should St. John call it in ch. v. 2 by one name, and in ch. ix. 7 by another? An answer may perhaps be suggested: that the latter appellation is chosen by the Evangelist in ch. ix. 7, because of the mystical meaning there predicated of the word, ὃ ἑρμηνεύεται ἀπεσταλμένος.

THE

GREEK TESTAMENT.

VOL. II.

THE ACTS OF THE APOSTLES,
THE EPISTLES TO THE ROMANS AND CORINTHIANS.

CONTENTS OF THE PROLEGOMENA.

CHAPTER I.

OF THE ACTS OF THE APOSTLES.

CHAPTER II.

OF THE EPISTLE TO THE ROMANS.

CHAPTER III.

OF THE FIRST EPISTLE TO THE CORINTHIANS.

CHAPTER IV.

OF THE SECOND EPISTLE TO THE CORINTHIANS.

CHAPTER V.

APPARATUS CRITICUS.

PROLEGOMENA.

CHAPTER I.

THE ACTS OF THE APOSTLES.

SECTION I.

ITS AUTHORSHIP.

1. The Author of this book is identical with that of the third Gospel, as plainly appears from the circumstance that in its address, to a certain Theophilus, reference is made to a former work, on the acts and words of Jesus, similarly addressed. Compare Acts i. 1, Luke i. 3. That Author is traditionally known as Lucas or Luke, spoken of Col. iv. 14, and again Philem. 24, and 2 Tim. iv. 11. For notices respecting him, see Prolegg. to Vol. I. ch. iv. § i.

2. Nor is there any reason to reject the testimony of tradition in this matter. In chapters xxvii. and xxviii. we find our Author (see below, par. 4) accompanying Paul to Rome. In the passages above cited, all written from Rome, we find that Luke was there, in the company of that Apostle. So far at least there is nothing inconsistent with Luke having written this book ; and if this book, the Gospel.

3. That *no other writer has here assumed the person of the Author of the Gospel*, may be gathered from the diction of this book strongly resembling that of the other. Supposing the student to consult the references in this Edition, he will be continually met by words and phrases either peculiar to the two books and not met with elsewhere (about fifty of these occur),—or mostly found in the two.

4. That *no writer other than the Author of the rest of the book* has furnished the parts in which the narrative proceeds in the *first person*, will be plain, if the matter be thus considered. (*a*) We have evidence, both by his own assertion (Luke i. 3), and from the contents of the Gospel and this book, that Luke was a careful and painstaking writer. Now it would bespeak a degree of carelessness wholly unexampled,—for one who compiled a continuous memoir, to leave its component parts, derived from various sources, in their original fragmentary state,

some in the third, others in the first person. Unquestionably such a writer would in such a case have translated the whole into the third person. (β) Seeing that Luke *does* use the first person in Acts i. 1, and that the first person is resumed ch. (xiv. 22) xvi. 10—17 ; xx. 5—15 ; xxi. 1—18 ; xxvii. 1—xxviii. 16, it is but a fair inference that in one and the same book, and that book betokening considerable care of writing and arrangement, the speaker implied by the use of the first person is one and the same throughout.

5. That the author never names himself, either *as* the author, or otherwise, can of itself not be urged as an objection to any hypothesis of authorship, unless by the occurrence of some mention, from which the authorship by *another* may be fairly inferred. But, if we have in this book no mention of Luke, we have as certainly no hint of any other person having furnished the narrative. On the other hand we have a hint by which it appears that some one other than all the specified companions of Paul on a certain occasion (Acts xx. 4, 5) was with him, and was the author of the narrative. After the mention by name of Sopater, Aristarchus, Secundus, Gaius, Timotheus, Tychicus, and Trophimus, we read, 'These having gone forward waited for *us* at Troas :' this pronoun including Paul and the writer, at least (see note there).

6. That Paul himself, in Epistles written during the journeys here described, does not name Luke, cannot be alleged as any argument why Luke should not have been the author of our narrative. For (a), we have undoubted examples of Paul sometimes merely alluding generally to those who were with him, as Phil. iv. 21, 22 ;—sometimes sedulously suppressing their names while speaking of services performed by them, as 2 Cor. viii. 18 : sometimes not mentioning or alluding to them at all, as in the Epistles to the Galatians and to the Ephesians :—and (β) strictly speaking, no Epistles appear to have been written by Paul while our writer was in his company, before his Roman imprisonment. For he does not seem to have joined him at Corinth, ch. xviii., whence the two Epistles to the Thessalonians were written :—or to have been with him at Ephesus, ch. xix.,—whence (probably) the Epistle to the Galatians was written ;—nor again to have wintered with him at Corinth, ch. xx. 3, at the time of his writing the Epistle to the Romans, and (possibly) that to the Galatians.

7. But independently of the above arguments to establish the identity of the author throughout, we may infer the same from the similarity of diction and style, which do not vary through the book. Here again we have, as will be seen abundantly in the references, terms *peculiar to the writer* occurring in various parts of the book ;—favourite terms and phrases occurring in all parts of the book ; which could not well have been the case, had he merely incorporated the memoirs of others. For

compendious statements of these, the whole of which have been inserted in my references, I refer the reader to Dr. Davidson's Introd. to the N. T. vol. ii. pp. 4, 5.

8. And again, the notes will be found repeatedly to point out cases where the narrator takes up again (with his characteristic μὲν οὖν or otherwise) the thread of history previously dropped (see e. g., and compare, ch. xi. 16, i. 5 : xi. 19, viii. 1—4 : xxi. 8, vi. 5, viii. 5 ff. : xxii. 20, vii. 58, viii. 1, &c.).

9. Another interesting source of evidence on this head is pointed out by Mr. Smith, in his valuable work on the Voyage and Shipwreck of St. Paul. He has shewn that in the various narratives of sea voyages in this book, and in that of the stilling of the storm in the Gospel, Luke has, with remarkable consistency, shewn himself to be just so much acquainted with the phrases and habits of seamen, as a landsman well habituated to the sea, but himself no seaman, might be expected to be. To specify instances would be beyond my limits, besides that Mr. Smith's very interesting and ingenious argument and illustrations would be spoiled by abridgment. I can only refer my reader to his work[1].

10. To the same class belong the intimations, slight indeed but interesting, discoverable here and in the Gospel in the descriptions of diseases, that the author was one well acquainted with them and with the technical language of the medical profession. Of this kind are συνεχομένη πυρετῷ μεγάλῳ, Luke iv. 38 ; πυρετοῖς κ. δυσεντερίῳ συνεχόμενον, Acts xxviii. 8 : see also Luke viii. 43, 44,—Acts iii. 7, xii. 23, xiii. 11, and compare Col. iv. 14.

11. It will be necessary to mention the various hypotheses which have substituted some other narrator for Luke in the parts of the Acts where the first person is used, or have merged his personality in that of some other companion of Paul : and, irrespective of the above arguments, to deal with them on their own merits. (*a*) Bleek and De Wette hold TIMOTHEUS, *and not Luke, to have been the companion of Paul and the narrator in the first person,—and Luke to have inserted those portions from a journal kept by Timotheus, and without alteration.* But this is not consistent with ch. xx. 4, 5 : where, when the companions of Paul have been named, and Timotheus among them, it is said οὗτοι προελθόντες ἔμενον ἡμᾶς ἐν Τρωάδι : the escape from this objection attempted by making οὗτοι refer to Tychicus and Trophimus only, being on all ordinary rules of construction, inadmissible. This reason is, to my mind, sufficient : those who wish to see others brought out, and the supports of the hypothesis (which are entirely negative and inferential)

[1] A second edition of Mr. Smith's book appeared in 1856, enlarged with much interesting detail. See the excursus below "On the city of Lasæa."

invalidated, may consult Dr. Davidson's Introduction to the N. T., vol. ii. pp. 9 ff.

(β) SILAS *was the narrator in the first person, and indeed the author of the latter part of the book, beginning with ch.* xv. 13 (30 ?), *in the form of personal memoirs, which then were worked up.* This hypothesis, which has not any thing resembling evidence to support it, is sufficiently refuted by the way in which the mention of Silas is introduced ch. xv. 22 (included by the hypothesis in *his own work*) as being a 'chief man among the brethren.' If it be answered that this notice of him was inserted by Luke,—Is it, I would ask, likely, that an author who was at no more pains in his work than to leave the *first person* standing in the narrative of another which he used, would have added to the mention of new individuals notices of this kind ?

(γ) More ingenious, and admitting of more plausible defence, is the hypothesis, which *identifies Luke himself with Silas.* The latest and ablest vindication of this view is contained in an article by the Author of the literary history of the N. T. in Kitto's Journal of Sacred Lit. for Oct. 1850. The chief arguments by which he supports it are these :—

(1) "The author of the Acts appears, in the early part of his history, to have been well acquainted with the acts and sayings of Peter, as he was afterwards with those of Paul. Now the only persons whom this description would fit, are *Silvanus* (or Silas), and *Mark* (see 1 Pet. v. 12, 13). That Mark did not after Acts xv. travel with Paul, we know : but Silas did, and from that time we find greater precision in the narrative as regards the history of that Apostle."

But to this it may be answered,—that the difference between the kind of acquaintance which the historian possesses with Peter and his sayings and doings, and that with Paul and his history, is very observable even to a cursory reader. No where in the first part of the book does he use the first person : and no where, although the testimony has plainly come in many parts from autoptic authority, does the narrator himself appear as the eye-witness. In fact, all that the above argument insists on, is easily and naturally satisfied, by the long and intimate companionship of Luke and Silvanus as fellow-travellers with Paul, during which time Luke may have gathered, if Silvanus must be considered as his authority, all that we now find in the former parts of our history [2].

[2] I do not notice in the text the untenableness of the author's hypothesis that Silvanus accompanied Peter from Jerusalem into the East, and became the bearer of his first Epistle to the Christians of Asia Minor, *before* the commencement of his own connexion with Paul : i. e. before the gospel had ever been preached to many of those addressed by Peter, which it *had already been*,—see 1 Pet. i. 12, 25, and remark the aorists in both places. This extraordinary hypothesis is not necessary to his theory of the identity of Luke and Silas : indeed that theory is better without it, as then the

(2) "Luke and Silvanus (Silas) are no where mentioned *together*. Luke is never mentioned in the Acts: Silas is never coupled with Luke in the addresses or salutations of the Epistles. And the two names, Silvanus from *silva*, and Lucanus from *lucus*, are so cognate that they might well be the appellations of one and the same person."

This ingenious argument, if well weighed, will be found to have but little force. As to Luke not being named in the Acts, the fact itself goes for nothing. If it have any prima facie weight, it would be against the hypothesis. That one who was careful to insert an explanatory notice respecting one so well known as Σαῦλος ὁ καὶ Παῦλος, should take no notice at all of the fact hereafter likely to occasion so much confusion,—that he who was named Silas in the history, was known by Paul, and mentioned in his Epistles, as Lucas,—is hardly probable. But let us observe the occasions on which Silvanus and Lucas have been mentioned by Paul. In 1 Thess. i. 1, and 2 Thess. i. 1, we have Silvanus joined with Paul and Timotheus. In 2 Cor. i. 19, we have an allusion to the preaching of Christ at Corinth by Paul, Silvanus, and Timotheus. Accordingly in Acts xviii. 5, we find that Silas and Timotheus came from Macedonia and joined Paul at Corinth: this occurring in a part of the history when (I am speaking according to the ordinary and prima facie inference, from the disuse of the first person since xvi. 17) the author was *absent* from Paul. Now let us turn to Col. iv. 14, Philem. 24[3]. These Epistles belong to a time when we know by the latter chapters of the Acts, that the writer of the history *was with Paul*. Accordingly I find *Lucas* mentioned in both places. So far at least is in remarkable accordance with the common view that Silas and Lucas were not one, but two persons, and that the latter was the author of the Acts, and not the former. It may be said that Paul called the same person Lucas whom he had previously called Silvanus: and this may be supported by his variations between Peter and Cephas. But (1) I conceive that the case of Peter was too exceptional an one (both names having apparently been given him and used by our Lord Himself) to found an analogy upon: and (2) Peter's names are forms of the same meaning in two different languages, not words of similar meaning in the same language.

But the principal argument in my mind against this hypothesis (over and above that from ch. xv. 22) is, that it would introduce unaccountable confusion into the form and expression of a history, which on the common view is lucid and accountable enough. Imagine Silas to be the speaker in ch. xvi., and Luke to be merged in Silas. Then '*we*,' from ver. 10 to ver. 18, = Silas and Timotheus. In ver. 19, it would be

silence of the Acts on Peter's proceedings after Acts xii. is accountable, which on that hypothesis it would not be.

[3] I omit at present 2 Tim. iv. 11.

natural to desert the first person, in order to express what happened to Paul and Silas, and not to Timotheus. The same specification of Paul and Silas might, for the same reason, be continued during the stay at Philippi, i. e. to the end of that chapter. But is it conceivable, that the '*we*' should not be resumed when the journey begins again ch. xvii. 1, —that it should not be used ch. xviii. 11, seeing that from 2 Cor. i. 19 it was Paul, Silvanus, and Timotheus, who were preaching during that time at Corinth—in fact, that it should never be resumed till ch. xx. 5, at the very place (Philippi) where it was dropped before ?

The argument from the similarity of *silva* and *lucus* is too unsubstantial to deserve serious attention. And that built on the assumption that the author of the third Gospel and the Acts must have held a place of greater honour than we find assigned to Lucas, is purely arbitrary, and sufficiently answered by observing that he is ranked with Marcus, apparently his fellow-Evangelist, in Philem. 24. Rather would it seem probable, that the men of *word* and *action*, in those times of the living energy of the Spirit, would take the highest place ; and that the work of securing to future generations the word of God would not be fully honoured, till from necessity, it became duly valued.

12. I shall now endeavour to sketch out the personal history of the author of the Acts, as for as it can be gathered, during the events which he relates.

The first direct intimation of his being in the company of Paul, occurs ch. xvi. 10, at Troas, when Paul was endeavouring (looking for a ship) to sail into Macedonia. Now at this time, Paul had been apparently detained in Galatia by sickness, and had just passed through (preaching as he went, see ch. xviii. 23) that country and Phrygia. It is hardly probable that he had visited Colossæ, as it lay far out of his route, but he *may*, in the then uncertainty of his destination, have done so. (See Col. ii. 1 and note.) I say this, because it is remarkable that in sending Luke's salutation to the Colossians (Col. iv. 14), he calls him ὁ ἰατρὸς ὁ ἀγαπητός. This designation might recall to their minds the relation in which Luke had stood to Paul when in their country ; or more probably may have been an effusion of the warm heart of Paul, on recollection of the services rendered to him on that journey by his loving care. At all events such a designation, occurring in such a place, is not inconsistent with the idea that Luke about that time became Paul's companion on account of the weak state of his health. Further to establish this is impossible : but what follows is not inconsistent with it. We find him in the Apostle's company no further than to Philippi, the object perhaps of his attendance on him having been then fulfilled [4].

[4] He may have been put in charge with the church at Philippi, but the conjecture is not very probable.

13. If we seek for any trace of *previous* connexion between Luke and Paul, we find nothing but the very slightest hint, and that perhaps hardly to be taken as such. In ch. xiv. 21, 22 we read, that Paul, after the stoning at Lystra, departed with Barnabas to Derbe, and returned through Lystra and Iconium and Antioch (in Pisidia) confirming the souls of the disciples, exhorting them to remain in the faith, καὶ ὅτι διὰ πολλῶν θλίψεων δεῖ ἡμᾶς εἰςελθεῖν εἰς τ. βασιλεῖαν τοῦ θεοῦ. This ἡμᾶς may be, as commonly understood, spoken by the writer as a Christian, and *of all* Christians: but it *may also be indicative of the writer's presence*[5]: and I cannot help connecting it with the tradition that Luke was a native of *Antioch*[6]: though Antioch in Syria is there meant. Certainly, in the account (ch. xiii.) of the events at Antioch in Pisidia, there is remarkable particularity. Paul's speech is fully reported: the account of its effect vv. 44—49 given with much earnestness of feeling:—and one little notice is added after the departure of Paul and Barnabas, ver. 52, which looks very like the testimony of one who was left behind at Antioch. Whether this may have been the place of Luke's own conversion, we know not; but a peculiar interest evidently hangs about this preaching at Antioch in the mind of the narrator, be he who he may: and Mark had departed, who might have supplied the *Cyprian* events (see ver. 13).

14. After the second junction with Paul and his company, ch. xx. 5, we find him remaining with the Apostle to the end of our history. It would not be necessary to suppose this second attachment to him to have had the same occasion as the first. That which weakness of body at first made advisable, affection may subsequently have renewed. And we have reason to believe that this was really the case. Not only the epithet ἀγαπητός, Col. iv. 14, but the fact, that very late in the life of the Apostle (see Prolegg. to the Pastoral Epistles, § ii.) when "all in Asia were turned away from him" (2 Tim. i. 15), and Demas, Crescens, and Titus had for various reasons left him, the faithful Luke still remained (2 Tim. iv. 11), bespeaks an ardent and steady attachment to the person of him who in all probability was his father in the faith.

15. Of the subsequent history and death of Luke nothing is known.

[5] The idea that ἡμᾶς can by any possibility be applied to the *writer* has been controverted by Prof. Lightfoot in the Journal of Classical and Sacred Philology for March, 1856, p. 95. But see note in loc.

[6] That the two places of that name would thus be confounded, is nothing surprising to those who are familiar with tradition. The usual ground assigned for this idea, viz. the mention of Lucius (of Cyrene) as being at Antioch, ch. xiii. 1, is certainly far from satisfactory.

SECTION II.

ITS SOURCES.

1. The principal enquiry respecting the sources of the narrative in the Acts relates to the first part as far as ch. xiii. After that, the history follows the Apostle Paul, of whom its writer was subsequently the constant companion. From *him* therefore the incidents might be derived, where the writer himself was not present. I shall before the end of this section enquire how far the appearances warrant our supposing that his testimony *has* furnished such portions.

2. I proceed to enquire into the probable sources of the first part of our history. And here something will depend on our answer to another question,—*When* is it probable that Luke was engaged in drawing up the book? I shall endeavour to support in another section my firm conviction that its *publication* took place at the end of the two years mentioned in ch. xxviii. 30, 31. It may be convenient for me at present to assume that to have been the case, but my argument does not altogether depend on that assumption. I proceed on the hardly deniable inference, that of the last voyage and shipwreck a *regular journal* was kept by Luke—probably set down during the winter months at Malta. It must then be evident, that *at this time* the purpose of writing a δεύτερος λόγος was ripened in his mind. But *how long* had this purpose been in his mind? Am I altogether beside the mark in supposing, that it was with this purpose among others that he became one of Paul's company on the return to Asia in ch. xx. 4, 5? Whether (see Prolegg. to Luke, § iv. 2, 3) the Gospel was written for the most part during the interval between Luke being left at Philippi in ch. xvi. and his being taken up at the same place in ch. xx., or afterwards in Palestine,—on either supposition it is not improbable that the writing of the Acts was at this time already designed,—either as a sequel to the Gospel already finished, or simultaneously with the Gospel, as its future sequel.

3. It is very possible that the design may have grown under his hands, or more properly speaking have been by little and little suggested by the direction of the Spirit of God. He may have intended, on leaving Philippi with Paul (ch. xx. 4, 5), only to draw up a διήγησις of his own travels in company with that Apostle, to serve as a record of *his* acts and sayings in founding the churches in Europe and Asia. However this may have been, we find him recording minutely every circumstance of this voyage, which I take to have been the first written portion of the book. At any time during that or subsequent travels, or during the two years at Rome, he may have filled in those parts of the narrative

which occurred during his absence from Paul,—by the oral dictation of the Apostle.

4. Let us now suppose Paul already in custody at Cæsarea. The narrative has been brought down to that time. The circumstances of his apprehension,—his defence before the Jews,—their conspiracy,—his rescue from them and transmission to Felix,—all this has been duly and minutely recorded,—even the letter of Claudius Lysias having been obtained, probably by acquaintance with some one about Felix. An intention similar to that announced in παρηκολουθηκότι πᾶσιν ἀκριβῶς (Luke i. 3) is here evidently shewn.

5. But now Providence interposes, and lays aside the great Apostle for two years. During all this time Luke appears to have been not far from his neighbourhood, watching the turn of events, ready to accompany him to Rome, according to the divine announcement of ch. xxiii. 11. But "they also serve, who only stand and wait." What so natural, as that he should avail himself of this important interval to obtain, from Cæsarea and Jerusalem, and perhaps from other parts of Palestine, information by which he might complete his hitherto fragmentary notices? That accurate following up of every thing, or rather tracing down of every thing from its source,—what time so appropriate for it as this, when among the brethren in Judæa he might find many eye-witnesses and ministers of the word, and might avail himself of the διηγήσεις which of all places would be most likely to abound there where the events themselves had happened? During this interval therefore I suppose Luke to have been employed in collecting materials, *perhaps* for his Gospel, but certainly for the first part of the Acts.

6. His main source of information would be the church at Jerusalem. There, from James, or from some apostolic men who had been on the spot from the first, he would learn the second and fuller account of the Ascension,—the weighty events of the day of Pentecost, the following acts and discourses. In the fulness of the outpouring of the Holy Ghost on the apostles and elders at this time, which raised them above ordinary men in power of spirit and utterance, it would be merely an inference from analogy, that their remembrance of the words uttered at remarkable crises of the apostolic history should be something surpassing mere human recollection: that these hallowed words of the Spirit's own prompting should have abode with the church for its comfort and instruction, and finally have been committed to writing for all subsequent ages.

7. But if analogy would *a priori* suggest this, the phænomena of our history confirm it. The references (which have been on that account a singularly interesting labour) will shew to the attentive student in those speeches, quite enough peculiarities to identify them as the sentiments and diction of the great Apostle of the circumcision, while at the same

time there is enough of Luke's own style and expression to shew that the whole material has been carefully worked over and *græcized* by his hand.

8. It has been much disputed whether Luke *used written documents* in constructing this part of the Acts [7]. It may have been so. Detailed memoirs of some of the most important events may have been drawn up. If so, ch. ii. would in all probability be such a memoir. The *letters*, ch. xv. 23—29 (xxiii. 26—30), must have been of this kind: some of the discourses, as that of Peter ch. xi. 5—17, containing expressions unknown to Luke's style (see reff.): more or less, the other speeches of Peter, containing many striking points of similarity to (*both*) his Epistles,—see reff. At the same time, from the similarity of ending of the earlier sections (compare ch. ii. 46, 47; iv. 32 ff.; v. 42; ix. 31; xii. 24), from the occurrence of words and phrases peculiar to Luke in the midst of such speeches as those noticed above (e. g. σταθέντα ch. xi. 13, and see Dr. Davidson p. 30 for a list, which I have incorporated in the reff.), the inference must be (as in the last paragraph) that such documents were not adopted until their language had been revised, where thought necessary, by the author himself. The very minute and careful detail of ch. xii., evidently intended to give the highest authority to the narrative of Peter's miraculous deliverance,—so that the house itself of Mary the mother of John Mark is specified, the name of the female servant who went to the door, her remarks and the answer made to her, are all given,—has apparently been the result of diligent enquiry on the spot, from the parties concerned. We can hardly resist the inference that the very same persons who fifteen years before had been witnesses of the deliverance, now gave the details of an occurrence which they could never forget, and described their own feelings on it.

9. Whether Luke at this time can have fallen in with Peter personally, is very questionable. That Apostle certainly does not appear to have been at Jerusalem when Paul visited it: and from the omission of all mention of him after ch. xv., the natural inference is, that he was not there during any part of Paul's imprisonment. (See note on Gal. ii. 11, and Prolegg. to 1 Pet. § ii. 6, 7.)

10. But one very important section of the first part of the Acts is concerned with events which happened at Cæsarea,—and derived from information obtained there. There dwelt Philip the Evangelist, one of the seven (ch. xxi. 8): a most important authority for the contents of ch. vi. and viii. [8], if not also for some events previous to ch. vi. There

[7] See the question discussed by Dr. Davidson, pp. 21 ff.

[8] De Wette (Exeget. Handb. Apostg. p. 6) objects that Philip could hardly have imparted ch. viii. 39 in its present form. At first sight, it seems so: but the next verse εὐηγγελίζετο τὰς πόλεις πάσας, κ.τ.λ. can on the other hand hardly have been imparted by any *but* Philip: and this leads us to think whether subsequent enquiry

too, we may well believe, still dwelt, if not Cornelius himself[9], yet some of the συνεληλυθότες πολλοί of ch. x. 27,—the persons perhaps who had gone to fetch Peter from Joppa,—at all events plenty who could narrate the occurrences of that memorable day, and the words which formed the great proœm of the Gentile Gospel.

11. Connected with the Cæsarean part of our history, is one minute touch of truth and accuracy, which is interesting as pointing to careful research and information of the most trustworthy kind. The awful death of Herod Agrippa I. had happened on a great public occasion. It appears that the celebration of a festival in honour of Cæsar had also been selected as the time of audience for an embassy of the inhabitants of Tyre and Sidon, and during this audience, after making an oration to the embassy, Herod was struck by the hand of God. Now of this latter particular, the Sidonian embassy, the Jewish historian knows nothing. (See the passage quoted, ad loc. ch. xii. 21.) But Luke, who had made careful enquiries on the spot, who had *spent a week at Tyre*, ch. xxi. 4—7, —and Paul, who *had friends at Sidon*, ch. xxvii. 3, were better acquainted with the facts of the occurrence than to overlook, as Josephus did, the minute details in the general character of the festival.

12. One or two sections in the former part of the Acts require separate consideration.

(α) The *apology of Stephen*, from its length and peculiar characteristics, naturally suggests an enquiry as to the source whence it may probably have been obtained by Luke. And here I should feel little hesitation in ascribing a principal share in the report to him who was so deeply implicated in Stephen's martyrdom,—who shews by his own reference (ch. xxii. 20) to the part taken by him on that occasion, how indelibly it was fixed in his memory,—and who in more than one place of his recorded speeches and writings, seems to reproduce the very thoughts and expressions of Stephen. At the same time, it would be improbable that the church at Jerusalem should have preserved no memorial of so important a speech as that of her first martyr before his judges. So that, however we may be inclined to attribute much of its particularity and copiousness to information derived from Paul, it must be classed, as to its general form, among those contributions to the history obtained by Luke at Jerusalem.

(β) The *narrative of the conversion of Saul* in ch. ix. can hardly fail

respecting the eunuch (who as he had before come to Jerusalem to worship at the feast, so would again) may not have enabled Philip to add this particular, ἐπορεύετο γὰρ τ. ὁδὸν αὐτοῦ χαίρων, over and above what he could know at the time.

[9] It seems probable that the Roman forces never left Cæsarea during the whole period from Augustus to Vespasian. The territory during that time (see chronological table) was alternately part of the province of Syria, and a dependent kingdom: but the garrisons do not appear to have been changed in such cases.

to have been derived from himself. I have shewn in the notes that there are no discrepancies between this and the two other relations of the same event, but such as may easily be accounted for by the peculiar circumstances under which each is given, and the necessarily varying expressions of narratives which were afterwards not reduced into harmony with each other, but written faithfully down as delivered.

13. Agreeable with the above suppositions is the fact, that the former part of the book presents more traces of Hebraistic idiom, not only in speeches, but in the form of the historical narrative [1].

14. I proceed now to an enquiry promised in par. 1 of this section: *How far we have indications of the lacunæ in the author's personal testimony in the latter part having been filled in by that of Paul.*

Perhaps one of the best sections for the purpose of this examination will be that from ch. xvii. 16—xviii. 5, which relates to a time when Paul was *left alone.* Do we discover in the narrative or speech the traces of *an unusual hand,* and if so, *whose is it?* That *some unusual hand* has been here employed, is evident: for in the six verses 16—21 inclusive, we have no fewer than nine expressions foreign to Luke's style [2], or no where else occurring: and in the speech itself, no fewer than nineteen [3]. Now of these twenty-eight expressions, five are either peculiar to, or employed principally by Paul [4]; besides that we find the phrase τὸ πνεῦμα αὐτοῦ, so frequently (see reff.) used by him of his own spirit or feelings. That the ἅπαξ λεγόμενα in the speech exceed in number the expressions indicative of his style, may fairly be accounted for by the peculiar nature of the occasion on which he spoke. Here I think we can hardly fail to trace the hand of the Apostle by quite as many indications as we might expect to find. That Luke should, as in every other case, have wrought in the section into his work, and given it the general form of his own narrative, would only be natural, and we find it has been so [5].

15. It may be instructive to carry on the examination of this part of

[1] See ch. i. 15, 23: the connexion by καί ch. ii. 1—4: ἀπὸ προσώπου τ. συνεδρ., v. 41: ἠκούσθη ὁ λόγος εἰς τὰ ὦτα τ. ἐκκλησίας, xi. 22: παῖς θεοῦ (of Christ), ch. iii. 13, 26; iv. 27, 30; (of David) iv. 25: διὰ στόματος Δαυείδ or τῶν προφ., i. 16,—iii. 18, 21,—iv. 25:—οἱ υἱοὶ Ἰσρ., v. 21:—ἡ γερουσία, ib., &c.

[2] ἐκδεχομένου, παρωξύνετο, κατείδωλον, παρατυγχάνοντας, σπερμολόγος, ξένων (bis), καταγγελεύς, ξενίζοντα, ηὐκαίρουν.

[3] δεισιδαιμονεστέρους, ἀναθεωρῶν, σεβάσματα, βωμόν, ἐπεγέγραπτο, (ἀγνώστῳ,) εὐσεβεῖτε, ἀνθρωπίνων, (θεραπεύεται,) προσδεόμενος, ὁροθεσίας, κατοικίας, (ζητεῖν χαράγματι, (τέχνης,) ἐνθυμήσεως, τὸ θεῖον, ὑπεριδών, ἔστησεν.

[4] ἐκδέχομαι, παροξύνω, εὐκαιρέω, σέβασμα, ἀνθρώπινος.—καταγγέλλω, ὁρίζω, εἷς ἕκαστος with gen. partitive, are peculiar to Luke and Paul: ἀγνοέω is a favourite word in the Epistles of Paul.

[5] We have the characteristic διελέγετο, ἐπιλαμβάνομαι, εἰς τὰς ἀκοάς (Luke viii. 1), σταθείς, διερχόμενος, καθότι.

the history somewhat further. At ch. xviii. 5, Silas and Timotheus joined Paul at Corinth. One at least of these, Timotheus, was afterwards for a considerable time in the company of Luke in the journey from Philippi to Jerusalem. But on his arrival at Corinth, no alteration in the style of the narrative is perceptible. It still remains the mixed diction of Paul and Luke: the ἅπ. λεγγ. are fewer, while we have some remarkable traces of Paul's hand [6]. Again, in vv. 24—28 of the same chapter, we have a description of what took place with regard to Apollos at Ephesus, when Paul himself was absent. This portion it would be natural to suppose might have been furnished by Apollos himself, were it not for the laudatory description of ver. 24. If not by Apollos, then by Aquila and Priscilla to Paul on his return to Ephesus. And so it seems to have been. The general form is Luke's: the peculiarities are mostly Paul's [7].

16. The examination of these sections may serve to shew that the great Apostle appears to have borne a principal part in informing Luke with regard to such parts of his history: the traces of this his share in the work being visible by the occurrence of words and phrases peculiar to *him* in the midst of the ordinary narrative from Luke's own pen. These he preserved, casting the *merely narrative* matter into the form in which he usually wrote.

17. It yet remains, before terminating this section, to say something of the *speeches* reported in the latter part of the Acts. Are they *Paul's own words*, or has Luke in this case also gone over the matter, and left the impression of his style on it?

These speeches are, (α) the discourse to the Ephesian elders in ch. xx. 18—35,—(β) the apology before the Jews, ch. xxii. 1—21,—(γ) the apology before Felix, ch. xxiv. 10—21,—(δ) the apology before Agrippa and Festus, ch. xxvi. 1—29.

(α) The *discourse to the Ephesian elders* is a rich storehouse of phrases and sentiments peculiar to Paul. These are so numerous, and so remarkable, that nothing short of a complete study of the passage, with the references, will put the reader in full possession of them. Very faint traces are found of the hand of Luke [8]. Of those mentioned in

[6] *συνείχετο*, ver. 5,—*καθαρὸς ἐγώ*, 6,—*παρὰ τὸν νόμον*, 13,—*ἀδίκημα*, 14 (see ch. xxiv. 20), *ῥᾳδιούργημα*, ib. (see ch. xiii. 10), *ἠνεσχόμην ὑμῶν*, ib., *λόγου*, 15,—&c.

[7] *κατηχημένος, ἀκριβῶς ἤρξατο παῤῥησιάζεσθαι, ἐξέθεντο, διελθεῖν, ἀποδέξασθαι, παραγενόμενος, εὐτόνως διακατηλέγχετο* (an ἅπ. λ., but in Luke's manner of using long compounds), belong to Luke's style: *ζέων τῷ πνεύματι, δημοσίᾳ* (ch. xvi. 37; xx. 20 only), to that of Paul.

[8] Among these may perhaps be counted the opening words *ὑμεῖς ἐπίστασθε* (compare ch. x. 28, 37)—*ἐπέβην εἰς τ. 'Ασ.* (ch. xxi. 4),—*διῆλθον* (ver. 25);—*προσέχετε ἑαυτοῖς* (ver. 28),—*ἀναστήσονται* (ver. 30),—*ὑπέδειξα* (ver. 35). But most of these are such that we can only say Paul *has not* used the expressions, or not in the same sense: that he *would not* have done so, if occasion had offered, we cannot affirm.

the note, scarcely any are decisive, whereas hardly a line of the whole is without unmistakable evidences that we have here the words of Paul. In the Prolegomena to the Pastoral Epistles, I hope to shew the importance of this discourse, as bearing on the very difficult question of the diction and date of those precious and to my mind indubitable relics of the great Apostle[9].

(β) The *apology before the Jews* (ch. xxii. 1—21) was *spoken in Hebrew* (Syro-Chaldaic). *Another* interesting question is therefore here involved, *Did Luke understand Hebrew?* The answer to the two questions will be one and the same. We may find the diction of this translation either so completely Luke's, as to render it probable that he was the translator;—or it may bear traces, as usual, of Paul's own phraseology set down and worked up by Luke. In the former case, we may confidently infer that he must have understood Hebrew: in the latter, we may (but not with equal confidence, for Paul may by preference have given *his own version* of his own speech) conclude that that language was unknown to him. If again the speech is full of Hebraisms, it may lead us to infer that Paul himself was not the translator into Greek, but one who felt himself more strictly bound to a literal rendering than the speaker himself, who would be likely to give his own thoughts and meaning a freer and more Grecian dress. Now we *do find*, (1) that the speech is *full of Hebraisms:* (2) that while it contains several expressions occurring *no where but in the writings of Luke*[1], *not one* is found in it peculiar to Paul, or even strikingly in his manner. Our inference then is that *Luke himself has rendered this speech, from having heard it delivered;*—and consequently, that he *was acquainted with Hebrew.*

(γ) The short *apology before Felix* (ch. xxiv. 10—21) contains some traces of Paul's manner[2], but still they are scanty, and the evidences of Luke's hand predominate, as may be seen from the reff. Its very compendious character makes it probable that it may have been drawn up by Luke from Paul's *own report of the substance of what he said.*

(δ) The important *apology before Agrippa and Festus* (ch. xxvi. 1—29) is full of Paul's peculiar expressions[3]. It was spoken in Greek, and

9 See Vol. III. Prolegg. ch. vii. § i. 33 note.

1 *σύνειμι, εὐλαβής, αὐτῇ τῇ ὥρᾳ, ἔκστασις,* are peculiar to Luke: *ἐπιστάς* is a favourite word with him: and very many other expressions, as may be seen by reff., are in the common manner of his writings.

2 *ἀπρόσκοπος,—συνείδησις,—δι' ἐτῶν,*—and perhaps *ἀδίκημα.*

3 *ἥγημαι* (in this sense never used by Luke, but by Paul 11 times), *ὄντα σε* (acc. pendens, see reff.),—*διό,—μακροθύμως* (only used here, but the cognate words are verv favourite ones with Paul),—*προγινώσκοντες,—θρησκεία,—ἐπ' ἐλπίδι κ.τ.λ.,—νύκτα κ. ἡμέραν* (see reff.),—*καταντῆσαι* (see reff.),—*κρίνεται παρ' ὑμῖν,—ἔδοξα,—ἐναντία* (compare ch. xxviii. 17),—*ἁγίων* (in Acts, only ch. ix. 13, *of Paul,*—and in the section ch. ix. 32—43, but in the Epistles passim),—*τιμωρῶν,—τὰς ἔξω πόλεις,—ὑπὲρ τ. λαμπ.,*—

taken down very nearly as spoken. Some phrases however occur in it which seem to belong to Luke[4]; just enough to shew the hand which has committed the speech to writing. We must remember however that several of these are expressive of meanings not elsewhere occurring in Paul's composition, which therefore he may well, in uttering, have thus expressed.

18. Our conclusion from this examination may be thus stated: (1) *That in all cases the diction of the speeches was more or less modified by Luke's hand.* (2) *That they are not in any case* (as some have supposed) *composed by him for the speaker, but were really in substance, and for the most part in very words, uttered as written.* (3) *That the differences apparent in the greater or less amount of editorial diction in different speeches, remarkably correspond to the alleged occasions and modes of their delivery:*—where Paul spoke Hebrew, hardly any traces of his own style being discernible,—as also where a short compendium only of his speech is given; while on the other hand speeches manifestly reported at length and which were spoken in Greek originally, are full of the characteristic peculiarities of Paul himself.

19. For many other interesting particulars connected with the sources of the narrative in the Acts, I refer the student to Dr. Davidson's Introduction to the N. T. vol. ii.

SECTION III.

FOR WHAT READERS AND WITH WHAT OBJECT IT WAS WRITTEN.

1. The *Gospel* of Luke commences with a preface, in which he declares his object with sufficient precision. Dedicating it to his friend Theophilus, he describes it as a record of τὰ πεπληροφορημένα ἐν ἡμῖν πράγματα,—and asserts his purpose in writing it to be, ἵνα ἐπιγνῷς περὶ ὧν κατηχήθης λόγων τὴν ἀσφάλειαν. Now there can be little question that both these descriptions apply to the Acts also. The book is introduced without preface, as a *second part* following on the former treatise: a δεύτερος λόγος to the Gospel.

2. I have stated with regard to the *Gospel*, that we can hardly suppose Luke's design to have confined itself to Theophilus, but must believe that he followed the common practice of dedicating his work to some one person of rank or influence, and describing it as written for him. The same applies also to the Acts: and the class of readers for

κλῆρον ἐν τοῖς ἡγιασμένοις,—μετανοεῖν (absol.),—ἐκτός,—πρῶτος ἐξ ἀναστ.,—σωφροσύνη,—ἐν ὀλίγῳ,—ὁποῖος,—παρεκτός.

[4] ἐν φυλακαῖς κατέκλεισα,—ἐξουσίαν λαβών,—ἀναιρουμένων (never used by Paul),—περιλάμψαν,—καταπεσόντων,—συλλαβόμενοι,—διαχειρίσασθαι,—ἀποφθέγγομαι.

whom Luke wrote is the same as before; viz. *Christians, whether Jews or Gentiles.*

3. If a further specification of his object in writing be required, it can only be furnished by an unprejudiced examination of the contents of the book. These are found to be, *The fulfilment of the promise of the Father by the descent of the Holy Spirit: the results of that outpouring, by the dispersion of the Gospel among Jews and Gentiles.* Under these leading heads, all the personal and subordinate details may be ranged. Immediately after the ascension, Peter, the first of the twelve, the Rock on whom the church was to be built, the holder of the keys of the Kingdom, becomes the great Actor under God in the founding of the Church. He is the centre of the first great group of sayings and doings. The opening of the door to Jews (ch. ii.) and Gentiles (ch. x) is his office,—and by him, in the Lord's own time, is accomplished. But none of the existing Twelve were (humanly speaking) fitted to preach the Gospel to the cultivated Gentile world. To be by divine grace the spiritual conqueror of Asia and Europe, God raised up another instrument, from among the highly educated and zealous Pharisees. The preparation of this instrument for the work to be done,—the progress in his hand of that work—his journeyings, preachings and perils, his stripes and imprisonments, his testifying in Jerusalem, and being brought to testify in Rome,—these are the subjects of the latter half of the book, of which the great central figure is the Apostle Paul.

4. Nor can we attribute this with any probability to a *set design of a comparison between the two great Apostles*, or of an apology for Paul by exhibiting him as acting in consonance with the principles which regulated Peter. All such hypothesis is in the highest degree unnatural and forced. The circumstances before the narrator's view would, without any such design, have led to the arrangement of the book as we now find it. The writer was the companion of Paul;—and in the land which had been the cradle of the Church he gathered materials for the portion which might join his Gospel to the narrative with which Paul's history began. In that interval, Peter was the chief actor: Peter was the acknowledged 'chosen vessel' in the first days of the Gospel. But Luke does not confine himself to Peter's acts. He gives at length the mission of Philip to the Gaza road and the conversion of the Ethiopian Eunuch, with which Peter had no connexion whatever. He gives at length the history of Stephen—the origin of the office which he held,—his apology,—his martyrdom,—how naturally, as leading to the narrative of the conversion of him who took so conspicuous a part in the transactions of that day [5].

[5] Schneckenburger, who (as well as Griesbach and Baur) holds the theory against which this paragraph is directed, is obliged to suppose that Stephen was *purposely* introduced to be exhibited as the prototype and forerunner of Paul. That Stephen

5. Any view which attributes *ulterior design* to the writer, beyond that of faithfully recording such facts as seemed important in the history of the Gospel, is, I am persuaded, mistaken. Many ends *are* answered by the book in the course of this narration, but they are the designs of Providence, not the studied purposes of the writer :—e. g., the sedulous offer of the Gospel to the Jewish people,—their continual rejection of it,—the as continual turning to the Gentiles :—how strikingly does this come out before the reader as we advance,—and how easily might this be alleged as the design,—supported as the view would be by the final interview of Paul with the Jews at Rome, and his solemn application of prophecy to their unbelief and hardness of heart. Again, in the course of the book, more and more strongly does it appear that God's purpose was to gather a people out of the Gentiles to His name: so that by Michaelis *this* is assigned as one of two great objects of the book. And so we might pass on through the whole cycle of progress of the faith of Christ, and hypotheses might be raised, as each great purpose of Providence is seen unfolding, that *to narrate it* was the object of the work.

SECTION IV.

AT WHAT TIME AND PLACE IT WAS WRITTEN.

1. I see no cause for departing from the opinion already expressed in the Prolegomena to Luke's Gospel (Vol. I., Prol., § iv. 1) that the Acts was *completed and published at the expiration of the two years described in the last verse of chap.* xxviii. No reason can be assigned, why, had any considerable change in the circumstances of Paul taken place, it should not have been mentioned by Luke. The same will hold still more strongly of the *death* of the Apostle.

2. The prevalent opinion of recent critics in Germany has been, that the book was written *much later than this*. But this opinion is for the most part to be traced to their subjective leanings on the prophetic announcement of Luke xxi. 24. For those who hold that there is *no such thing as prophecy* (and this unhappily is the case with many of the modern German critics), it becomes necessary to maintain that that verse was written *after the destruction of Jerusalem*. Hence, as the Acts is the *sequel to the Gospel*, much more must the Acts have been written after that event. To us in England, who receive the verse in question as a truthful account of the words spoken by our Lord, and

was so, in some sense, is true enough; but the assimilation of Paul to Stephen is a result springing naturally out of the narrative, not brought about by the writer of the history. Supposing the facts to have been as related, it was most natural that Paul should earnestly desire the whole particulars respecting Stephen to be minutely recorded: and so we find them.

see in them a weighty prophetic declaration which is even now not wholly fulfilled, this argument at least has no weight.

3. The last-mentioned view (which is that of De Wette) differs from that of Meyer (Edn. 1), who saw in ch. viii. 26 (αὕτη ἐστὶν ἔρημος) a *terminus a quo*, and in the omission of all mention of the destruction of Jerusalem, a *terminus ad quem*, for the publication of the history; which he was therefore inclined to place at the beginning of the Jewish war, after the destruction of Gaza by the revolutionary bands of the Jews, and before the destruction of Jerusalem. But the notice of ch. viii. 26 cannot be fairly thus taken: see note there, in which I have endeavoured to give the true meaning of ἔρημος as applying to ὁδός and not to Gaza, and as spoken by the angel, not added by the Evangelist. Meyer's latter terminus, and the argument by which he fixes it, I hold to be sound. It would be beside all probability, that so great, and for Christianity so important an event, as the overthrow of the Jewish city, temple, and nation, should have passed without even an allusion in a book in which that city, temple, and nation, bear so conspicuous a part.

4. Meyer also (Edn. 1, Einl. p. 7) endeavoured to render a reason why the subsequent proceedings of Paul in Rome should not have been noticed. They were, he imagines, well known to Theophilus, an Italian himself, if not a Roman. But this is the merest caprice of conjecture. What convincing evidence have we that Theophilus was a Roman, or an Italian? And this view would hardly (though Meyer laboured to make it do so) account for the narration of what *did* take place in Rome,—especially for the last verse of the book. It is fair to state that in subsequent editions Meyer has abandoned this view for that impugned at the beginning of par. 2.

5. De Wette attempts to account for the history ending where it does, because the words of our Lord in ch. i. 8 had been accomplished, and so the object of the history fulfilled. But how were they more accomplished at that particular time than before? Rome *had not been specified* in that command: and *he who now preached at Rome was not formally addressed in those words.* Rather, if the object of the writer had been merely to trace these words to their fulfilment, should he have followed *the actual Apostles to whom they were spoken*, many of whom we have reason to believe much more literally preached ἕως ἐσχάτου τῆς γῆς, than St. Paul. But no such design, or none such in so formal a shape, was in the mind of our Evangelist. That the Lord commanded and his Apostles obeyed, would be the obvious course of history; but that the mere bringing of one of those Apostles to the head of the civilized world should have been thought to exhaust that command, is inconceivable as a ground for breaking off the narration.

6. Still more futile is the view that it was broken off because the

promise of ch. xxiii. 11 was now fulfilled (οὕτως σε δεῖ καὶ εἰς Ῥώμην μαρτυρῆσαι). For on this view, the *being brought before Cæsar* ought to have been *expressly narrated*: another promise having been given to Paul, ch. xxvii. 24, μὴ φοβοῦ, Παῦλε, Καίσαρί σε δεῖ παραστῆναι. Indeed this very argument tells forcibly in favour of the date commonly assigned. Without attributing it as an object in the mind of the writer, to relate the fulfilment of every divine promise recorded by him, we may at least regard it as probable, that *had he been able* to chronicle the fulfilment of this promise, he *would have done so*, seeing that the apology before Cæsar was so weighty an event, and that three former apologies, those before the Jews, before Felix, and before Festus and Agrippa, had been inserted.

7. If we look at the probabilities of the matter, we shall find that the time commonly assigned was by very far the most likely for the publication of the book. The arrival at Rome was an important period in the Apostle's life: the quiet which succeeded it seemed to promise no immediate determination of his cause: a large amount of historic material was collected:—or perhaps, taking another view, Nero was beginning 'in pejus mutari:' none could tell how soon the whole outward repose of Roman society might be shaken, and the tacit toleration which now the Christians enjoyed be exchanged for bitter persecution. If such terrors loomed in the prospect of even those who judged from worldly probabilities, there would surely be in the church at Rome prophets and teachers, who might tell them by the Holy Ghost of the storm which was gathering, and might warn them that the words lying ready for publication must be given to the faithful before its outbreak, or never. It is true that such *a priori* considerations would weigh little *against* presumptive evidence furnished by the book itself: but when arrayed in aid of such evidence, they carry with them no small weight: when we find that the time naturally and fairly indicated in the book itself for its publication, is that one of all others when we should conceive that publication most likely.

8. We thus get A.D. 63 (see the following table) for the date of the publication.

9. The same arguments which establish the date, also fix the place. At Rome, among the Christians there, was this history first made public, which has since then in all parts and ages of the church formed a recognized and important part of the canon of Scripture.

10. As regards the *title* of the book, we may observe, that it appears to represent the estimate, not of one culling these out of more copious materials, but of an age when these were *all* the Acts of the Apostles *extant*: and probably therefore proceeded not from the author, but from the transcribers.

SECTION V.

GENUINENESS, AND STATE OF THE TEXT.

∴. Eusebius (H. E. iii. 25), recounting the *ὁμολογούμεναι θεῖαι γραφαί*, says, *τακτέον ἐν πρώτοις τὴν ἁγίαν τῶν εὐαγγελίων τετρακτὺν* οἷς ἕπεται ἡ τῶν πράξεων τῶν ἀποστόλων γραφή. And in iii. 4,—*Λουκᾶς τὸ μὲν γένος ὢν τῶν ἀπ᾽ Ἀντιοχείας, τὴν δὲ ἐπιστήμην ἰατρός, τὰ πλεῖστα συγγεγονὼς τῷ Παύλῳ, καὶ τοῖς λοιποῖς δὲ οὐ περιέργως τῶν ἀποστόλων ὡμιληκώς, ἧς ἀπὸ τούτων προσεκτήσατο ψυχῶν θεραπευτικῆς ἐν δυσὶν ἡμῖν ὑποδείγματα θεοπνεύστοις καταλέλοιπε βιβλίοις· τῷ τε εὐαγγελίῳ . . . . καὶ ταῖς τῶν ἀποστόλων πράξεσιν, ἃς οὐκέτι δι᾽ ἀκοῆς, ὀφθαλμοῖς δὲ αὐτοῖς παραλαβὼν συνετάξατο.* And many earlier fathers, either by citation or by allusion, have sufficiently shewn that the book was esteemed by them part of the canon of Scripture.

(α) Papias (see Euseb. H. E. iii. 39) does not mention nor refer to the Acts. He speaks indeed of Philip, and his daughters, but mistakes him (?) for Philip the Apostle: and of Justus surnamed Barsabas. Nor are there any references in Justin Martyr which, fairly considered, belong to this book. Such as are sometimes quoted may be seen in Lardner, vol. i. p. 122. The same may be said of Clement of Rome. Ignatius is supposed to allude to it (*μετὰ δὲ τὴν ἀνάστασιν συνέφαγεν αὐτοῖς καὶ συνέπιεν.* Smyrn. § 3, p. 709. Compare Acts x. 41): so also Polycarp (*ὃν ἔγειρεν ὁ θεός, λύσας τὰς ὠδῖνας τοῦ ᾅδου.* Phil. § 1, p. 1005. Compare Acts ii. 24).

(β) The first direct quotation occurs in the Epistle of the Churches of Lyons and Vienne to those of Asia and Phrygia (A.D. 177) given in Euseb. H. E. v. 2. Speaking of the martyrs, they say, *ὑπὲρ τῶν τὰ δεινὰ διατιθέντων ηὔχοντο, καθάπερ Στέφανος ὁ τέλειος μάρτυς· κύριε, μὴ στήσῃς αὐτοῖς τὴν ἁμαρτίαν ταύτην.*

(γ) Irenæus frequently and expressly quotes this book: and in book iii. ch. 14, p. 201 f., he gives a summary of the latter part of the Acts, attributing it to Luke as its writer.

(δ) Clement of Alexandria quotes it often, and as the work of Luke: e. g. *καθὸ καὶ ὁ Λουκᾶς ἐν ταῖς πράξεσι τῶν ἀποστόλων ἀπομνημονεύει τὸν Παῦλον λέγοντα· Ἄνδρες Ἀθηναῖοι, κ.τ.λ.* (see Acts xvii. 22, 23) Strom. v. 12 (83), p. 696 P.

(ε) Tertullian often quotes it expressly: e. g. 'Adeo postea in Actis apostolorum invenimus, quoniam qui Joannis baptismum habebant, non accepissent Spiritum Sanctum, quem ne auditu quidem noverant' (compare Acts xix. 1—3), De baptismo, c. 10, vol. i. p. 1211. And again: 'cum in eodem commentario Lucæ, et tertia hora orationis demonstretur, sub qua Spiritu Sancto initiati pro ebriis habebantur, et sexta, qua Petrus ascendit in superiora,' &c. De jejuniis, c. 10, vol. ii. p. 966.

2. (α) The Marcionites (cent. iii.) and the Manichæans (cent. iv.) rejected the Acts as contradicting some of their notions. "Cur Acta respuatis jam apparet, ut deum scilicet non alium prædicantia quam creatorem, nec Christum alterius quam creatoris, quando nec promissio Spiritus sancti aliunde probetur exhibita, quam de instrumento Actorum." Tertull. adv. Marcion. lib. v. § 2, vol. ii. p. 472. And of the Manichæans, Augustine says, "Manichæi canonicum librum cujus titulus est Actus Apostolorum repudiant. Timent enim evidentissimam veritatem, ubi apparet, Sanctum Spiritum missum qui est a Domino Jesu Christo evangelica virtute præditus." Epist. ccxxxvii. 2, vol. ii. p. 1035.

(β) Some modern critics in Germany, especially Baur, have made use of the hypothesis, that the Acts is an apology for Paul (see above, § iii. 4), to throw discredit on the book, and to bring down its publication to the second century. But with the hypothesis will also fall that which is built on it; and from the reasoning of the preceding sections it may be seen how utterly impracticable it would have been for an imitator to draw up narratives and speeches which should present the phænomena, in relation to the facts underlying them, which these do.

3. The text of the Acts, in D and E of the leading MSS., and their cognates in the mss. and versions, is varied by many interpolations of considerable length. It may suffice to point out a few of these, referring the student to the various readings to examine them in detail:

chap. x. 25; xi. 2, 17, 25, 26, 28; xii. 10; xiv. 2, 7, 18, 19; xv. 2, 12, 20; xvi. 10, 30, 35, 39, 40; xvii. 15; xviii. 4, 27; xix. 1; xx. 3; xxiii. 24; xxiv. 24; xxv. 24; xxvii. 1; xxviii. 31.

Of these, some are remarkable as bearing considerable appearance of genuineness, e. g. those in ch. xii. 10, xvi. 10: some are unmeaning and absurd, as those in ch. xiv. 19, xvi. 39. Considerable uncertainty hangs over the whole question respecting these insertions. A critic of eminence, Bornemann, believes that the text of the Acts originally contained them all, and has been abbreviated by the hand of correctors: and he has published an edition on this principle.

4. The great abundance of various readings in the Acts, and the extent of space consequently devoted to them, will be observed by every reader. In no book of the N. T., with the exception of the Apocalypse, is the text so full of variations as in this. To this result several reasons may have contributed. In the many backward references to the Gospel history, and anticipations of statements and expressions occurring in the Epistles, temptations were found inducing the corrector to try his hand at assimilating, and as he thought reconciling, the various accounts. In places where ecclesiastical order or usage was in question, insertions or omissions were made to suit the habits and views of the church in after times. Where the narrative simply related facts,—any act or word apparently unworthy of the apostolic agent was modified for the sake of

decorum. Where St. Paul relates over again to different audiences the details of his miraculous conversion, the one passage was pieced from the other, so as to produce verbal accordance. These circumstances render the critical arrangement of the text in this book a task more than usually difficult.

SECTION VI.

CHRONOLOGY.

1. The chronology of the Acts has been the subject of many learned disquisitions both in ancient and modern times. It must suffice here (1) to point out to the reader those recent works where he will find the whole matter thoroughly discussed, and the results of older enquiries stated and criticized: and (2) to furnish a table arranged according to years, in which the contemporary sacred and profane history may be placed side by side, according to the conclusions which I myself have been led to form.

(α) The treatise of Anger, de temporum in Actis Apostolorum ratione, Lips. 1833, was by far the best complete discussion of the chronology which had appeared up to that time: and the student who masters this not very voluminous work, will be in entire possession of the state of the enquiry when it was published.

(β) But the ground has since been again gone over, and Anger's results somewhat shaken, by Wieseler, Chronologie des apostolischen Zeitalters, Göttingen, 1848, which is now the best and most important work on the subject. I have been led in several places to differ from Wieseler, but I do not on that account underrate the value of his researches. His work, as well as that of Anger, should be in the hands of every student who wishes to master the chronology of the apostolic period.

(γ) A work often referred to in these Prolegomena, Dr. Davidson's Introduction to the New Testament, will be found by the English reader to contain a very useful résumé of the views and arguments of other writers as well as his own conclusions; and is accompanied with the table usual in the German writers, giving at one glance the various dates assigned by different chronologists for the events in the apostolic history.

2. I proceed to give the chronological table above promised. It will be observed that *the chronology of the Acts takes us only to the end of the second year of St. Paul's* (first) *imprisonment at Rome.* With the important and difficult question respecting a *second* imprisonment, *we are here in no way concerned.* It will come before us for full discussion in the Prolegômena to the Pastoral Epistles, Vol. III. (§ ii. 17 ff.)

A.D. YEARS, ETC. U.C.	HIGH PRIESTS.	GOVERNORS OF JUDÆA, ETC.	EVENTS RELATED IN THE ACTS.
(TIBERIUS) (sole) Emperor from Aug. 19, A.D. 14. **30**.......................... 783 TO 35.......................... 789	CAIAPHAS, appointed by Valerius Gratus procurator of Judæa, A.D. 25 (Jos. Antt. xviii. 2. 2)......................	PONTIUS PILATUS, from A.D. 26, or early in 27 (Jos. Antt. xviii. 4. 2: see below, A.D. 36). (*Vitellius*, Prefect of Syria, A.D. 34.) Pilate is sent to Rome (to answer for his conduct) by Vitellius, late in 36: for (Antt. xviii. 4. 2) Tiberius died before his arrival there.	THE ASCENSION (May 18, Wieseler). PENTECOST (May 27), **Effusion of the Holy Spirit.** A.D. 30—37, the events related Acts ii. 42—vi. 8. Prosperous progress of the faith in Jerusalem.
37.......................... 790 (CALIGULA Emperor from March 16 (Tacit. Ann. vi. 50).)	displaced by Vitellius at the Passover. JONATHAN, son of Ananus (Antt. xviii. 4. 3)............ displaced by Vitellius at Pentecost (Antt. xviii. 5. 3). THEOPHILUS, son of Ananus (Antt. ib.)......................	*Marcellus*, appointed by Vitellius ἐπιμελητής of Judæa (Antt. ib.). MARYLLUS sent by Caligula to Judæa as Hipparch (Antt. xviii. 6. 10). (*Herod Agrippa* I. appointed by Caligula, a few days after his accession, king of the tetrarchy of Philip, i. e. Batanæa, Trachonitis, and Auranitis (Antt. xviii. 6. 10).) (His brother Herod made king of Chalcis.)	**Martyrdom of Stephen** (vii. 59).—Dispersion of the disciples (viii. 4).—Philip, and afterwards Peter and John, at Samaria (viii. 5—25).—Philip converts the Æthiopian eunuch, and preaches from Azotus to Cæsarea (viii. 26, 40).—**Conversion of Saul** (late in the year) (ix. 1—19).
38.......................... 791 TO 40.......................... 793		(On Aretas being in possession of Damascus, see note, Acts ix. 24, 25.) (*P. Petronius Turpilianus*, Prefect of Syria, A.D. 39.) (Agrippa returns from Rome to his new kingdom, in the 2nd year of Caligula (Antt. xviii. 6. 11).) (Antipas goes to Rome to solicit the title of king, but is banished to Lyons, and his tetrarchy given to Agrippa (Antt. xviii. 7. 2) A.D. 39-40. See Antt. xix. 8. 2.)	Peace of the Churches (ix. 31).—Circuit of Peter (ix. 32—43).—He preaches to Cornelius and his Gentile friends at Cæsarea (x. 1—48).—Gives an account of the same to the Church at Jerusalem (xi. 1—18).—After spending three years in Arabia and Damascus (Gal. i. 15—18), SAUL goes up to Jerusalem (**First visit**) and meets Peter (ix. 26—29. Gal. i. 18): remains fifteen days, then being in danger of his life is sent by the brethren to Tarsus.
41.......................... 794 (CLAUDIUS Emperor from Jan. 24 (Suet. Calig. 58).) TO **43**.......................... 796	removed by Agrippa (Antt. xix. 6. 2). SIMON son of Boëthus, surnamed Canthēras: removed by Agrippa in the same year, A.D. 42. MATTHIAS son of Annas....... removed by Agrippa in 43. ELIONÆUS son of Cantheras...	(AGRIPPA appointed by Claudius king over the whole dominions of Herod the Great his grandfather (Antt. xix. 5. 1).) HEROD AGRIPPA, King of Judæa: comes to his kingdom in 42, in the 2nd consulship of Claudius (Antt. xix. 5. 3,—6. 1). (*Vibius Marsus*, Prefect of Syria, A.D. 42.)	Meantime the Gospel had been preached to Gentiles at Antioch (xi. 19, 20). Barnabas is sent thither by the Church at Jerusalem, rejoices at what had taken place, and fetches Saul from Tarsus. They remain a year at Antioch (xi. 26).—The disciples are first called Christians (ib.).—Agabus prophesies a famine (xi. 28): supplies sent to the brethren in Judæa by the hands of Barnabas and Saul (**Second visit**) (xi. 30),—perhaps after Herod's death.

A.D. YEARS, ETC. U.C.	HIGH PRIESTS.	GOVERNORS OF JUDÆA, ETC.	EVENTS RELATED IN THE ACTS.
44........................ 797		(Death of Herod Agrippa (Antt. xix. 8. 2).) CUSPIUS FADUS, Procurator of Judæa, the younger Agrippa being retained at Rome (Antt. xix. 11. 2). (*C. Cassius Longinus*, Prefect of Syria, Antt. xx. 1. 1.)	Martyrdom of James the brother of John (or perhaps late in the preceding year) (xii. 2).—Imprisonment (at the Passover) and miraculous escape of Peter (xii. 3—17). DEATH OF HEROD AGRIPPA, very soon after, at Cæsarea (xii. 23).
45........................ 798	removed by Herod King of Chalcis (Antt. xx. 1. 3). JOSEPH son of Cami, ib.	(Herod king of Chalcis obtains from Claudius the power of appointing the High Priests and the custody of the temple and the sacred treasure (Antt. xx. 1. 3).)	
46........................ 799	removed by Herod King of Chalcis, prob. in 47 (Antt. xx. 5. 2).	TIBERIUS ALEXANDER, Procurator of Judæa (Antt. xx. 5. 2). The great famine is raging in Judæa (ibid.).	**First missionary journey** of Barnabas and Saul (henceforward PAUL) (xiii. 1—xiv. 28), to Cyprus and Asia Minor (46 or 47).
47........................ 800	ANANIAS son of Nebedæus, ib.	VENTIDIUS CUMANUS, Procurator of Judæa. Antt. xx. 5. 2. (About the same time, "in the eighth year of Claudius" (Antt. ibid.), Herod, king of Chalcis, dies (See also Bell. Jud. ii. 12. 1).)	
48........................ 801			This journey hardly occupies more than a year: they consequently return to Antioch in 47 or 48.
49........................ 802		(*Agrippa* the younger appointed king of Chalcis (B. J. ii. 12. 1).) (*Titus Ummidius Quadratus*, Prefect of Syria, Antt. xx. 6. 2: B. J. ii. 12. 5.)	After their return they remain a long time at Antioch with the disciples (xiv. 28).
50........................ 803 TO 54........................ 807	sent to Rome in 52 by Quadratus, in consequence of a dispute with the Samaritans,—together with Cumanus the Procurator (Antt. xx. 6. 2): but appears not to have lost his office (see note, Acts xxiii. 2).	(Cumanus deposed at Rome, see preceding column.) FELIX Procurator of Judæa (A.D. 53) (Antt. xx. 7. 1). (Agrippa II. promoted from Chalcis to be king of Batanæa, Trachonitis, Gaulanitis, &c. (B. J. ii. 12. 8).)	Dispute respecting the obligation of circumcision, &c. (xv. 1.)—Paul and Barnabas go up to Jerusalem (**Third visit**) on the matter (xv. 2, 3: Gal. ii. 1 ff.: fourteen years inclusive from Paul's conversion).—They return, and *tarry in Antioch*, teaching and preaching (xv. 35). (Interview with Peter at Antioch (Gal. ii. 11 ff.).) Dispute and separation between Paul and Barnabas.—**Second missionary journey** of Paul, accompanied by Silas (xv. 40), and Timotheus (xvi. 3),—perhaps not before the autumn of 51,—through Asia Minor to Macedonia and Greece (xvi. xvii.).—He spends a year and a half (xviii. 11) at Corinth (**First**

NERO, Emperor from October 13. (Tac. Ann. xii. 69: Suet. Claud. 45: Dio lx. 34.)			and **Second Epistle to the Thessalonians**), sets sail for the Pentecost at Jerusalem in the spring of 54, and after it (**Fourth visit**) returns to Antioch (xviii. 22).—In the autumn, apparently, he travels through τὰ ἀνωτερικὰ μέρη to Ephesus. Meantime, Apollos is preaching at Corinth (xix. 1).
55 .... 808 56 809		(Nero presents Agrippa II. with parts of Galilee and Peræa (Antt. xx. 8. 4).) (The Egyptian, alluded to Acts xxi. 38, leads a multitude into the wilderness. His followers are routed by Felix, but himself escapes (Antt. xx. 8. 6: B. J. ii. 13. 5).)	Paul at Ephesus till Pentecost, 57 (τριετίαν xx. 31: compare 1 Cor. xvi. 8, 9 and note). Here he writes (Ep. to Galatians? and) the **First Ep. to the Corinthians** not long before his departure (1 Cor. xvi. 8). We must place in this interval an unrecorded journey to Corinth: see below, ch. iii. § v. About Pentecost (57), after the tumult of xix. 23—41,
57 .... 810 58 811		he journeys to Macedonia (Acts xx. 1; 2 Cor. ii. 12, 13), where he writes the **Second Ep. to the Corinthians** (2 Cor. ix. 2 al.),—and thence to Greece, where he winters (xx. 2) and writes (from Corinth, Rom. xvi. 1, 23) the **Epistle to the Romans** (in the beginning of 58) (and Ep. to Galatians?).—Soon after, he sets out by land for Jerusalem,—spends Easter at Philippi, whence he sails April 5,—touching at Troas, Miletus, Patara, Tyre, and Ptolemais, to Cæsarea,—arriving at Jerusalem (**Fifth visit**) a few days before Pentecost (xx. 1—xxi. 16. Cf. xx. 16). He is seized by the Asiatic Jews in the temple, brought before Ananias and the Sanhedrim, rescued by the tribune Lysias from the plots of the Jews, and sent to Cæsarea to Felix, where he is accused by Ananias and the Sanhedrim, and kept in prison by Felix (xxi. 27—xxiii. 35).	
59 .... 812 60 813	ISHMAEL son of Phabi appointed H. P. by Agrippa II. (Antt. xx. 8. 8)	About the middle of 60 Felix is superseded by PORCIUS FESTUS (xxiv. 27. Antt. xx. 8. 9).	Paul in prison at Cæsarea. Being accused before Festus by the Jews, and in danger of being taken to be tried at Jerusalem, he appeals to Cæsar (xxv. 1—12),—is heard before Agrippa and Festus (xxv. 13—xxvi. 32), and sent off by sea to Rome late in the autumn.—Is shipwrecked at Malta, where he winters (xxvii. 1—xxviii. 11).
61 .... 814 62 .... 815 63 816	having gone to Rome to petition against Agrippa is displaced by him (in 61), and JOSEPH CABI appointed (Antt. xx. 8. 11) .... displaced by Agr. (61 or 62), and ANANUS appointed (Antt. xx. 9. 1) .... displaced in three months by Agr. (62), and JESUS son of Damnæus appointed (Antt. ibid.).	Death of Festus, prob. in summer 62. On the news arriving at Rome, ALBINUS is sent as his successor (Antt. xx. 9. 1).	Paul arrives in Rome (in February): and being kept in *custodia militaris*, dwells and preaches two years in his own hired house (xxviii. 11—31). At the end of this time probably the publication of the Acts takes place, and all beyond is tradition or conjecture. During the two years (probably) he writes the Epp. to the **Ephesians, Colossians,** and **Philemon:** and perhaps that to the **Philippians** (but qu.?).

NOTES TO THE CHRONOLOGICAL TABLE.

I. *On the identity of the Journey to Jerusalem related in Acts* xv., *with that referred to Gal.* ii. 1 ff.

Five visits of St. Paul to Jerusalem are related in the Acts. Now the visit of Gal. ii. 1 ff. must be either (α) one *distinct from all these,* or (β) *identical with one or other of them.*

(α) This hypothesis should not be resorted to, till every attempt to identify the visit with one of those recorded can be shewn to fail. Then only may we endeavour, as in the case of the unrecorded visit to Corinth (see below, chap. iii. § v.), to imagine some probable place for the insertion of such a visit. So that the legitimacy of this hypothesis must be tried by the results arrived at in the discussion of the other. The maintainers of it are Beza, Paley (hesitatingly; Hor. Paul., p. 71, Birks' edn.), Schrader (der Apostel Paulus, i. 74 ff.), and Tate.

(β) The visit in question is identical with one or other of those recorded in the Acts.

1. *It is not* **the first visit.** The identity of the visits of Acts ix. 26—29 and Gal. i. 18 being assumed (and it is hardly possible to doubt it), this follows as a matter of course.

2. *It is not* **the second visit** (Acts xi. 29, 30). For we read, Gal. ii. 7, that Paul was already recognized as entrusted with the Gospel of the uncircumcision, and as having preached vv. 8, 9 together with Barnabas among the Gentiles. Now the commission of Paul and Barnabas to preach to the Gentiles dates from Acts xiii. 1, *after* **the second visit.**

Also, at the time of **the second visit,** it is wholly improbable that Paul should have held a place of such high estimation in comparison with Peter, as we find him filling in Gal. ii. 8 ff.

Again, on this hypothesis, either the first visit, or his conversion, was *fourteen years* inclusive *before this,* which took place certainly before 46 A.D.; for then the famine was raging, and this relief was sent up by prophetic anticipation. This would bring, either the first visit, or his conversion itself, to A.D. 32: a date wholly improbable, whichever way we take the fourteen years of Gal. ii. 1.

3. The question of identity with the third visit is discussed below.

4. It is not **the fourth visit.** For in Gal. ii. 1, we read that *Barnabas went up with Paul:* but in Acts xv. 39, we find Paul and Barnabas separated, nor do we ever read of their travelling together afterwards,—and evidently Barnabas was not with him when he visited Jerusalem Acts xviii. 18—22. Besides, the whole character of the fourth visit as there related, is against the idea that any weighty matters were then transacted. The expression merely is ἀναβὰς καὶ ἀσπασάμενος τὴν ἐκκλησίαν κατέβη εἰς Ἀντιόχειαν. Again, if we assume the identity of the visit in question with *the fourth visit,* the Apostle can hardly be acquitted of omitting, in his statement of his conferences with the principal Apostles in Gal. ii., an intermediate occasion when the matters arranged between them had been of the most solemn and important kind. This would be scarcely ingenuous, considering the object which he had in Gal. ii.

5. It is not **the fifth visit.** For after this visit Paul did not return to Antioch, which he did after that in question, Gal. ii. 11.

6. It remains therefore, that it can only, if identical with any of the five, be **the third visit.** Is this probable?

(a) The *dates* agree. See the Chronological Table, and notes on Gal. ii. 1.

(b) The *occasions* agree. Both times, the important question relative to the obligation of Christians to the Mosaic law was discussed: both times, the work of Paul and Barnabas among the Gentiles was recognized. What need was there for this to be *twice* done? It is of no import whatever to the matter, that in Acts, the result is a public decree,—whereas in Gal., no mention of such a decree is made: the *history* relates that which was important for the church,—the *Epistle*, that which cleared the Apostle personally from the charge of dependence on man: all mention of the decree would in Gal. have been irrelevant. Similarly we may deal with the objection, that in Acts, a public council is summoned, whereas in Gal., it is expressly said that Paul laid forth to them the Gospel which he preached to the Gentiles, but κατ' ἰδίαν τοῖς δοκοῦσιν. This entirely agrees with Acts xv. 12, where Paul and Barnabas related to the *multitude, not the nature of the doctrine which they preached*, but only the patent proofs of its being from God,—ὅσα ἐποίησεν ὁ θεὸς σημεῖα κ. τέρατα ἐν τοῖς ἔθνεσιν δι' αὐτῶν.

(c) Nor is it any objection to the identity, that in Gal. ii. 2, Paul went up κατ' ἀποκάλυψιν,—whereas in Acts xv. 2, the brethren ἔταξαν that P. and B. should go up, in consequence of the trouble given by the Judaizers. How do we know that this revelation was not made *to the church*, and so directed their appointment? Or if it be understood that the revelation was made to Paul himself, who can say whether the determination of the brethren was not a *consequence* of it? Who can say again, whether Paul may not have been *reluctant* to go up, rather willing not to confer with flesh and blood on such a matter, and may have been *commanded by a vision* to do so? We have here again only the public and the private side of the same occurrence: the one, suitable to the ecclesiastical narrative: the other, to the vindication of his office by the Apostle.

(d) The result is strikingly put by Mr. Conybeare, Life and Epistles of Paul, edn. 2, vol. i. p. 546,—"The *Galatian visit* could not have happened *before* **the third visit**: because, if so, the Apostles at Jerusalem had already granted to Paul and Barnabas (Gal. ii. 3—6) the liberty which was sought for the εὐαγγέλιον τῆς ἀκροβυστίας: therefore there would have been no need for the church to send them again to Jerusalem upon the same cause. Again, *the Galatian visit* could not have occurred *after* **the third visit**: because, almost immediately after that period, Paul and Barnabas ceased to work together as missionaries to the Gentiles: whereas, up to the time of *the Galatian visit*, they had been working together."

(γ) It seems then to follow, that the Galatian visit is identical with that recorded in Acts xv.

Those who wish to see the whole question dealt with more in detail, and the names and arguments of the champions of each view recounted, may refer to Mr. Conybeare's Appendix I. at the end of vol. i. of Conybeare and Howson's Life of St. Paul: or to Dr. Davidson's Introd. vol. ii. pp. 112 ff.

II. *On the discrepancy of Tacitus and Josephus regarding Felix.*

Tacitus, Ann. xii. 54, has generally been supposed to be in error in stating that Cumanus and Felix were joint procurators before the condemnation of the former. His account is very circumstantial, but seems to shew an imperfect acquaintance with Jewish matters: whereas it is probable that Josephus was best informed in the affairs of his own country. The discrepancy is a very wide one, and if Tacitus is wrong, he has the whole history of the outbreak in Judæa circumstantially misstated to correspond. See Wieseler, Chron. des Apost. Zeitalters, p. 67, note.

EXCURSUS I.

ON "THE CITY OF LASÆA," AND OTHER PARTICULARS MENTIONED IN ACTS xxvii. 7—17.

Since the publication of the second edition of this volume, much light has been thrown on the interesting questions connected with the topography of this passage, by letters written to Mr. Smith from the Rev. George Brown, who accompanied the yacht St. Ursula, Hugh Tennent, Esq., on a cruise in the Mediterranean, in the winter of 1855—6. I have to thank Mr. Smith for having kindly forwarded to me copies of these letters as they arrived. The substance of them is now printed as an extract from Mr. Brown's Journal, in the second edition of Mr. Smith's "Voyage and Shipwreck of St. Paul," Appendix, No. 3. I extract here such portions as regard immediately the geographical points in question, referring my readers to the volume itself for the whole account, which is most graphic and entertaining.

I. "We asked Nicephorus (the old Greek already mentioned) what was the ancient name of Lutro? He replied without hesitation, 'Phœniki,' but that the old city exists no longer. This of course proved at once the correctness of Mr. Smith's conclusion. We were told further that the anchorage is excellent, and that our schooner could enter the harbour without difficulty. We next enquired the ancient name of the island of Gozzo, and he said at once, 'Chlavda,' or 'Chlavdanesa' (*χλαύδα*, or *χλαύδα νῆσος*), a reply equally satisfactory. He told us also that there was a tradition in these parts that *ἅγιος Παῦλος ἀπόστολος* had visited Calolimounias (the fair havens), and had baptized many people there."

II. "Friday, Jan. 18th (Calolimounias).—Nothing now remained to be done but to ascertain the exact position of Lasæa, a city which Luke says is nigh to the Fair Havens. . . . I asked our friend the Guardiano, *ποῦ ἐστι Λασέα* (*Λάσαια*)? He said at once, that it was two hours' walk to the eastward, close under Cape Leonda: but that it is now a desert place (*τόπω ἐρήμω*). Mr. Tennent was eager to examine it: so getting under weigh, we ran along the coast before a S.W. wind. Cape Leonda is called by the Greeks *Λέωνα*, evidently from its resemblance to a lion couchant, which nobody could fail to observe either from the W. or the E. Its face is to the sea, forming a promontory 340 or 400 feet high. Just after we passed it, Miss Tennent's quick eye discovered two white pillars standing on an eminence near the shore. Down went the helm: and putting the vessel round, we stood in close, wore, and hove to. Mr. H. Tennent and I landed immediately, just inside the cape, to the eastward, and I found the beach lined with masses of masonry. These were formed of small stones, cemented together with mortar so firmly, that even where the sea had undermined them, huge fragments lay on the sand. This sea-wall extended a quarter of a mile along the beach from one rocky face to another, and was evidently intended for the defence of the city. Above we found the ruins of two temples. The steps which led up to the one remain, though in a shattered state: and the two white marble columns noticed by Miss Tennent, belonged to the other. Many shafts, and a few capitals of Grecian pillars, all of marble, lie scattered about, and a gully worn by a torrent lays bare the substructures down to the rock. To the E. a conical rocky hill is girdled by the foundations of a wall: and on a platform between this and the sea, the pillars of another edifice lie level with the ground. Some peasants came down to see us from the hills above, and I asked them the name of the place. They said at once, 'Lasea:' so there could be no doubt. Cape Leonda lies five miles E. of the Fair Havens: but there are no roads whatever in that part of Candia. We took away some specimens of marble, and boarded our vessel: at four P.M., sailed for Alexandria."

III. LUTRO. "The health-officer told me, that though the harbour is open to the E., yet the easterly gales never blow home, being *lifted* by the high land behind, and that even in storms, the sea rolls in gently ('piano piano'). He says *it is the only secure harbour, in all winds, on the south coast of Crete:* and that during the wars between the Venetians and the Turks (the latter took the island in 1688, I think), as many as twenty or twenty-four war-galleys had found shelter in its waters. He further shewed us an inscription on a large slab which he says was found among some ruins on the point, and took us up the hill to see the traces of the site of the ancient Phœniki.

The outline of its ramparts is clearly discernible, and some cisterns hollowed in the rock: but the ploughshare has been driven over its site, and it displays 'the line of confusion and the stones of emptiness.'"

The inscription here alluded to was afterwards made out accurately by Mr. Brown, and is given by Mr. Smith in his Preface. It is interesting and important:

JOVI . SOLI . OPTIMO . MAXIMO .
SERAPIDI . ET . OMNIBVS . DIIS . ET .
IMPERATORI . CAESARI . NERVAE .
TRAJANO . AVG . GERMANICO . DACICO .
EPICTETVS . LIBERTVS . TABVLARIVS .
CVRAM . AGENTE . OPERIS . DIONYSIO .
SOSTRATI . FILIO . ALEXANDRINO . GVBERNATORE .
NAVIS . PARASEMO . ISOPHARIA . CL . THEONIS .

i. e. "Epictetus, the freedman and tabularius, to Jupiter, only O. M., to Serapis and all the gods, and to the imperator Cæsar Nerva Trajanus Augustus Germanicus Dacicus: the superintendent of the work being Dionysius son of Sostratus of Alexandria, gubernator (κυβερνήτης) of the ship whose sign is Isopharia, of the fleet of Theon."

Now as Mr. Smith points out, we have here several points of union with the text of the Acts.

1. It appears that Alexandrian ships did anchor and make long stay, perhaps winter, at Phœnice: otherwise Epictetus, the master of one, could hardly have remained long enough to superintend this votive building, whatever it was.

2. We see the accuracy of the Alexandrian nautical language employed by St. Luke. We have here κυβερνήτης (ch. xxvii. 11) as the designation of the master of the ship; and παρασήμῳ as indicating the name or sign of it (ch. xxviii. 11).

The *tabularius* was the notary, or agent, of the fleet to which the Isopharia belonged. Mr. Smith quotes an inscription:

CINCIO . L . F . SABINIANO . TABVLARIO . CLASS . RAVENN.

EXCURSUS II.

ON THE READING Ἑλληνιστάς IN ACTS xi. 20.

My attention has been directed to a pamphlet by Dr. Kay, late Principal of Bishop's College, Calcutta, "On the word *Hellenist*, with especial reference to Acts xi. 19 (20)." Dr. Kay defends the received reading Ἑλληνιστάς against the modern critical editors with considerable earnestness: I wish I could say that he had himself shewn the humility and impartial investigation which he demands from them, or abstained from that assumption which substantiates nothing, and that vituperation of his opponents which shakes a reader's confidence in even the best cause. I shall deal here simply with the residuum of critical argument in his work.

1. The MS. evidence in his favour is B (now apparently ascertained) D^6EHL p 13, and apparently the great mass of cursives: strong, it must be admitted, but not decisive, with AD^1 against him, and the testimony of ℵ divided ($ℵ^1$ reading Εὐαγγελιστάς, and $ℵ^3$, Ἕλληνας).

2. He states that Ἕλληνας is the easier word, and therefore "more likely to have supplanted Ἑλληνιστάς in a few MSS., than this latter to have supplanted it in nearly all." But it is remarkable that he did not notice the bearing on such an assertion of a fact which he himself subsequently alleges: viz. that in ch. vi. 1, "there is *no* MS. variation at all." Does not this circumstance shew, that the alteration here has not

been to Ἕλληνας for the reason he supposes? Does it not further make it probable that Ἑλληνιστάς being unquestioned there,—Ἕλληνας, here so difficult to fit into the narrative, has been changed to that other form, which presented no such difficulty? But of this more below.

3. Dr. Kay has certainly succeeded in neutralizing the testimony of some of the versions, by noticing that the Peschito, Vulgate, and others, read the same word here and in ch. vi. 1. In this respect his pamphlet has done good service, and our future digests should be modified by this fact being stated,—the remaining versions being carefully examined and discriminated.

4. As to the testimony of Fathers, Dr. Kay's argument is one so exceedingly loose and fallacious, that I can only wonder at its having satisfied himself. Chrysostom says ἴσως, διὰ τὸ μὴ εἰδέναι Ἑβραϊστί, Ἕλληνας αὐτοὺς ἐκάλουν. Will it be credited, that Dr. K. here argues thus: "I will venture to say that if you were to strike out the word Ἕλληνας, and put *x* in its stead, simply asking a person to determine from the sentence itself, for which of the two, Ἑλληνιστάς or Ἕλληνας, *x* had been substituted, the answer would be Ἑλληνιστάς." *My* answer would be *the other way*, seeing that the latter word would require no such explanation: but setting this aside, was there ever such a critical principle laid down, or experiment proposed, and that by one who justly censures Doddridge for the very same proposal in our text? "Strike out,"—not a dubious reading, for there is no doubt about Ἕλληνας in the text of Chrysostom's homily, but—" a difficult reading,—put *x* for it, and then say, according to the measure of your own apprehension and private judgment, what the word ought to be!" Truly, we may be thankful that the text of the New Testament has hitherto escaped the application of such a process.

5. In noticing the Editions, Dr. Kay has shewn singular unfairness. He has quoted a rash and foolish sentence from Doddridge, which says that "*common sense* would require us to adopt Ἕλληνας, even if it were not supported by the authority of any MS. at all," —and then charged all the critical Editors with having acted in this spirit, administering to them a severe admonition about 'altering the Scriptures by conjectural criticisms,' from Scott, who however himself believes 'Greeks' to be the right reading. In this, of course, the whole question is begged;—and the very reverse of our practice is charged on us. It is by no conjecture, which source of emendation I altogether repudiate, but owing to conscientious belief that Ἕλληνας is the original Scripture text, that I have edited it; and consequently all Dr. Kay's charges, and admonition, are out of place here.

6. His section 'on the meaning of the term Ἑλληνισταί,' as 'designating those Jews and proselytes who used the LXX version of the Scriptures in their synagogues,' tells us no more than all knew before. But when he proceeds to 'the suitableness of this meaning to the context' in Acts xi. 20, I cannot but think that he has missed the whole point of the narrative; and in treating of the objectors to this view, selecting myself as representing them, he has exhibited, as before, remarkable unfairness, and want of logical apprehension. I might point out both these *seriatim*, as indeed any reader may trace them in his pamphlet: but it may suffice to deal with two or three instances. Against Ἑλληνιστάς, I have argued, that "the Hellenists were long ago a recognized part of the Christian Church:" my inference being, that, were they here referred to, there would be no case justifying the phænomena in the text, viz. a special notice like ἐλάλουν **καὶ** (καί is inserted by our three most ancient MSS., A, B, and ℵ) πρὸς τοὺς Ἑλληνιστάς, as distinguished from Ἰουδαίους preceding,—a special mission of an apostle, as (for this is also implied in the text, not an hypothesis of mine) on some unusual occurrence. Now observe how this is treated by Dr. Kay:

"If this be an argument, it must mean something of the following kind:

"Some Hellenists had been converted at Jerusalem: *therefore* St. Luke cannot be here narrating a wonderful extension of the Christian church among the Hellenist body at Antioch."

"'Why not?' we ask. 'Because *we* have made up our mind that at this precise period a further *development of the church's constitution took place.*' It is sufficient to reply: '*That* is a mere *arbitrary assumption:* we are content to say with Newton, Hypotheses non fingo.'" Kay, p. 16.

I may safely appeal to the student of Scripture, whether this be not the very height of unfairness. I have advanced no hypothesis, but have been led into my view simply by the phænomena of the sacred text itself: by that "patient, inductive criticism," which Dr. Kay himself desiderates. His form of stating my argument keeps out of sight the very point on which it really turns. Instead of "*therefore* St. Luke cannot be here describing," he should have written, "but, from the diction and character of this portion of St. Luke's narrative, it is not probable that he is here describing."

7. The only other matter which I feel it necessary to notice is, the way in which he has dealt with what he has pleased to call my 'hypothesis' as to Barnabas being sent "not with the intent to sympathize with the work at Antioch, but to *discourage* it." This last word, italicized by Dr. Kay as being mine, has neither place nor representative in my note, and is a pure misrepresentation. My words are, "probably from what follows, the intention was to *ascertain the fact,* and to *deter* these persons from the *admission of the uncircumcised* into the church; or, at all events, to use his discretion in a matter on which they were as yet doubtful. The choice of such a man, *one* by birth *with the agents,* and of a *liberal spirit,* shews sufficiently that they wished to deal, not harshly, but gently and cautiously, whatever their reason was." This he designates as "a strange, and not very reverent hypothesis." What Dr. Kay may understand by *reverent,* I am at a loss to imagine. I understand by reverence for Scripture, a patient, and at the same time fearless study of its text, irrespective of previously formed notions, but consistently with its own analogies. Now the analogy here is not with the mission of Peter and John to Samaria, as Dr. Kay represents it, nor was Barnabas sent from the Apostles and elders, as in that case: but our analogous incident is to be found in Gal. ii. 12, where, as here, the Church at Jerusalem sent down messengers to Antioch on an errand of supervision. Had any one ventured to infer the character of *that* mission, and its possible effect even on an Apostle, he would doubtless have incurred even more strongly from Dr. Kay the charge of irreverence. But the sacred record itself has set inference at rest in that instance, and thereby given us an important datum whereby to infer the probable character of another mission from the same Church to the same Church; and our inference is, that the Jerusalem believers, whom we find ever jealous for the Judaic purity of the church, acted on this occasion from that motive. The whole character of that which is related of Barnabas's proceeding at Antioch shews that he was acting, not in pursuance of his mission thither, but in accordance with the feelings of his own heart from seeing the work of God on his arrival.

It were very much to be wished that able men, like Dr. Kay, would study fairness in representing those who differ from them on critical points. The same motives which he assumes exclusively for his own side in this matter, have actuated also those who maintain the other reading. We deprecate as much as he can, 'a bold alteration of texts, and a supercilious disregard of authority:' had he dealt fairly with us, and attributed to us *our own* arguments, and not fictitious ones of his creation, he would have been the first to see this.

It is only waste of precious time to spend our strength in jostling one another, when we have such a glorious cause to serve, and only our short lives to serve it in. Let all our strength and earnestness be spent over the Sacred Word itself. For sifting, elucidating, enforcing it, rivalry, if our purpose be simple and our heart single, is the surest pledge of union.

CHAPTER II.

OF THE EPISTLE TO THE ROMANS.

SECTION I.

ITS AUTHORSHIP AND INTEGRITY.

1. THIS Epistle has been universally believed to be the genuine production of the Apostle Paul. Neither the Judaizing sects of old, who rejected the Pauline Epistles, nor the sceptical critics of modern Germany, have doubted this. Some of the earliest testimonies are:

(α) Irenæus, adv. Hær. iii. 16. 3, p. 205: Hoc ipsum interpretatus est Paulus scribens ad Romanos: "Paulus apostolus Jesu Christi, &c." (Rom. i. 1):—et iterum ad Romanos scribens de Israel dicit, "Quorum patres, et ex quibus Christus, &c." Rom. ix. 5[1].

(β) Clem. Alex., Pædag. i. 8 (70), p. 140 P.:—.δε οὖν, φησὶν ὁ Παῦλος, χρηστότητα κ. ἀποτομίαν θεοῦ· κ.τ.λ. (Rom. xi. 22.) See also ib. 5 (19), p. 109 P. And the same, Strom. iii. 11 (75), p. 544: ὁμοίως δὲ καὶ ὁ Παῦλος ἐν τῇ πρὸς Ῥωμαίους ἐπ. γράφει· οἵτινες ἀπεθάνομεν τῇ ἁμαρτίᾳ, κ.τ.λ. (Rom. vi. 2.) See also ib. (76), p. 545, and al. freq.

(γ) Tertullian, adv. Praxeam, § xiii. vol. ii. p. 170: Deos omnino nec dicam nec dominos, sed apostolum sequar, ut, si pariter nominandi fuerint Pater et Filius Deum Patrem appellem, et Jesum Christum Dominum nominem (Rom. i. 7). Solum autem Christum potero deum dicere, sicut idem apostolus: ex quibus Christus, qui est, inquit, Deus super omnia benedictus in ævum omne (Rom. ix. 5).

More instances need not be given: the stream of evidence is continuous and unanimous.

2. But critics have not been so well agreed as to the INTEGRITY of the present Epistle. The last two chapters have been rejected by some: by others, parts of these chapters. Marcion rejected them, but on doctrinal, not on critical grounds. Heumann imagined ch. xii.—xv. to be a later written Epistle, and ch. xvi. to be a conclusion to ch. xi. Semler views ch. xv. as a private memorandum, not addressed to the Romans, but written to be communicated by the bearers of the Epistle to those whom they visited on the way,—and ch. xvi., as a register of persons to be saluted, also on the way. Schulz imagines that ch. xvi. was written from Rome to the Ephesians, and Schott fancied it to be fragments

[1] See also the same chapter, § 9, where there are six express citations from the Epistle.

of a smaller Epistle written by Paul in Corinth to some Asiatic church. But these notions, as Tholuck remarks (from whom these particulars are for the most part taken), remain the exclusive property of their originators. He himself recognizes the genuineness of the portion, as also Neander, Credner, De Wette, and Olshausen. The more recent objections of Baur are mentioned and refuted, in part by De Wette, Comm. juxta finem,—Tholuck, Comm. pp. 2, 3,—Olsh. Comm. iii. 34, 35, and fully, by Kling, theol. Stud. u. Krit. 1837, p. 308 ff.

3. Still more discrepancy of opinion has existed respecting the doxology at the end of the Epistle. I have summarily stated and discussed the evidence, external and internal, in the var. readings and notes in loc.: and a fuller statement may be found in Dr. Davidson's Introd. ii. 188 ff.: Tholuck, Einleitung, pp. 4—6; De Wette in loc.

SECTION II.

FOR WHAT READERS IT WAS WRITTEN.

1. The Epistle itself plainly declares (ch. i. 7) that it was addressed *to the saints who were at Rome.* The omission of the words ἐν Ῥώμῃ by some MSS. is to be traced to a desire to *catholicize* the Epistles of Paul;—see Wieseler, Chron. des Apostol. Zeitalters, p. 438.

With regard to *the Church at Rome,* some interesting questions present themselves.

2. BY WHOM WAS IT FOUNDED? Here our enquiries are enwrapped in uncertainty. But some few landmarks stand forth to guide us, and may at least prevent us from adopting a wrong conclusion, however unable we may still be to find the right one.

(α) *It was certainly not founded by an Apostle.* For in that case, the fact of St. Paul addressing it by letter, and expressing his intention of visiting it personally, would be inconsistent with his own declared resolution in ch. xv. 20, of not working where another had previously laid the foundation.

(β) This same resolution may guide us to an approximation at least to the object of our search. Had the Roman church been founded by the individual exertions of any preacher of the word, or had it owed its existence to the confluence of the converts of any other preacher than Paul, he would hardly have expressed himself as he has done in this Epistle. We may fairly infer from ch. xv. 20, that *he* had, proximately, laid the foundation of the Roman church: that is to say, it was originated by those to whom he had preached, who had been attracted to the metropolis of the world by various causes,—who had there laboured in the ministry with success, and gathered round them an important Christian community.

Of this community, though not his own immediate offspring in the faith, Paul takes charge as being the Apostle of the Gentiles. He longs to impart to them some χάρισμα (ch. i. 11): he excuses his having written to them τολμηρότερον ἀπὸ μέρους, by the dignity of that office, in which, as a priest, he was to offer the Gentiles, an acceptable and sanctified offering to God.

(γ) The character given in ch. i. 8 of the Roman Christians, that *their faith was spoken of in all the world*, has been taken as pointing to a far earlier origin than the preaching of Paul. But, even granting that some among the Roman Jews may have carried the faith of Christ thither soon after the Ascension (see Acts ii. 10; and Rom. xvi. 7, where Andronicus and Junias are stated *to have been in Christ before the Apostle*),—such a concession is not necessary to explain Rom. i. 8. Whatever happened *at Rome* is likely to have been very soon announced in the provinces, and to have had *more reporters*, wherever the journeys of the Apostle led him, than events occurring elsewhere. He could hardly fail to meet, in every considerable city which he had visited for the second time, in Judæa, Asia, Macedonia, and Greece (see Acts xviii. 22, 23; xix. 1; xx. 1, 2), believers who had received tidings of the increase and flourishing state of the Roman church. This occurrence of good news respecting them in all the cities might well suggest the expression, ἡ πίστις ὑμῶν καταγγέλλεται ἐν ὅλῳ τῷ κόσμῳ.

3. The above considerations lead me to the conclusion, that the Roman Church owed its origin, partly perhaps to believing Jews, who had returned or been attracted thither in the first days of Christianity, but mainly to persons converted under Paul's own preaching. This conclusion is strengthened by the long list of salutations in ch. xvi. to Christian brethren and sisters with whose previous course in many cases he had been acquainted.

4. It is not within the province of these Prolegomena to discuss the question respecting the presence, preaching, and martyrdom of Peter at Rome. That he did not *found* the Roman church, is plain from the above considerations, and is conceded by many of the ablest among the modern Romanists [2]. Nor have we any ground to suppose that he *was at Rome* up to, or at the date of this Epistle. No mention is made of him,—no salutation sent to him. At present therefore we may dismiss the question as not pertinent. In the prolegg. to the Epistles of Peter, it will recur, and require full discussion.

5. That the Roman church was composed of *Jews and Gentiles*, is manifest from several passages in our Epistle. In ch. ii. 17, iv. 1, 12,

[2] Tholuck, Einl. § 2, mentions Valesius, Pagi, Baluz, Hug, Klee: and an article in the Tubingen Theological Quarterly for 1824 (written according to Dr. Davidson by Feilmoser) which concludes that though Peter taught and suffered martyrdom in Rome, his stay there could not have much exceeded one year.

Jews are addressed, or implied: in ch. i. 13,—in the similitude of engrafting in ch. xi., and in xv. 15, 16,—Gentiles are addressed. In what proportion these elements co-existed, can only be determined from indications furnished by the Epistle itself. And from it the general impression is, that *it is addressed to Gentiles*, as the greater and more important part of its readers. Among them would be mostly found the 'strong' of ch. xiv., to whom principally the precepts and cautions concerning forbearance are written. To them certainly the expression τὰ ἔθνη in ch. i. 5, 13, xv. 15, 16, is to be applied, in the strict sense; and in those places it represents the persons to whom the Epistle is mainly addressed. The same may be said of ch. xi. 13, 14, where ὑμεῖς τὰ ἔθνη are evidently the majority of the readers, as contrasted with the τινὲς ἐξ αὐτῶν, the Jewish believers.

6. It may be interesting to add testimonies from profane writers which are connected with the spread of Christianity at Rome.

That the *Jews* were found in great numbers there, is evident.

(α) Josephus, Antt. xvii. 11. 1, mentioning an embassy which came to Rome from Judæa under Varus, in the time of Augustus, says, καὶ ἦσαν οἱ μὲν πρέσβεις οἱ ἀποσταλέντες γνώμῃ τοῦ ἔθνους πεντήκοντα, συνίσταντο δὲ αὐτοῖς τῶν ἐπὶ Ῥώμης Ἰουδαίων ὑπὲρ ὀκτακισχιλίους.

(β) Philo, leg. ad Caium, § 23, vol. ii. p. 569, in a passage too long for citation, says that Augustus gave them the free exercise of their religion, and a quarter beyond the Tiber for their habitation.

(γ) Dio Cassius xxxvii. 17, καὶ ἔστι καὶ παρὰ τοῖς Ῥωμαίοις τὸ γένος τοῦτο, κολουσθὲν μὲν πολλάκις, αὐξηθὲν δὲ ἐπὶ πλεῖστον, ὥστε καὶ ἐς παρῥησίαν τῆς νομίσεως ἐκνικῆσαι.

(δ) So far relates to Judaism proper: in the following it is impossible to say how far Christianity may have been ignorantly confounded with it.

Augustine, de Civ. Dei vi. 11, vol. vii. p. 192, cites from Seneca, 'in eo libro quem contra superstitiones condidit,'—De illis sane Judæis cum loqueretur, ait:—'Cum interim usque eo sceleratissimæ gentis consuetudo convaluit, ut per omnes jam terras recepta sit: victi victoribus leges dederunt.'

(ε) Tacitus, in the same place where he relates the persecution of the Christians by Nero on occasion of the fire at Rome, adds, 'repressaque in præsens exitiabilis superstitio rursus erumpebat, non modo per Judæam, originem ejus mali, sed per urbem etiam' . . . .

(ζ) Juvenal describes the Judaizing Romans at a later period in a strain of bitter satire, Sat. xiv. 96 ff.

(η) On the passages in Sueton. Claud. 25, and Dio Cass. lx. 6, relating to the expulsion or coercion of the Jews at Rome, see note on Acts xviii. 2.

7. It yet remains to consider the supposed discrepancy between our

Epistle, and the state of the Christian church at Rome implied some years subsequent to it in Acts xxviii. This discrepancy has been made the most of by Dr. Baur, and by him pronounced irreconcileable. The flourishing state of the Roman church set forth in this Epistle seems to him to be inconsistent with the tone used by the Jews in their speech to Paul, Acts xxviii. 22 : ἀξιοῦμεν δὲ παρὰ σοῦ ἀκοῦσαι ἃ φρονεῖς· περὶ μὲν γὰρ τῆς αἱρέσεως ταύτης γνωστὸν ἡμῖν ἐστιν ὅτι πανταχοῦ ἀντιλέγεται. Olshausen and Tholuck have been at much pains to give a solution of the difficulty : the former referring the circumstance to the entire severance between Christians and Jews at Rome made necessary by Claudius's persecutions of the Jews,—the latter, following many other Commentators, to an affected ignorance of the Christian sect on the part of the Jews.

On this I will remark,—that the difficulty itself does not seem to me so serious as the German writers generally have regarded it. The answer of the Jews was to a speech of Paul in which he had given a remarkable instance of his becoming to the Jews as a Jew. He represents, that he had no real quarrel with his nation : that in fact he was a prisoner for the hope of Israel. This hope they certainly knew, either from previous acquaintance with his name and character, or from his own lips in words which have not been recorded, to be bound up with belief in Jesus as the Messiah. They had received (see note in loc.) no message respecting him from Judæa laying any thing πονηρόν to his charge : and they were anxious to have an account *from himself* of his opinions and their ground : for as for this sect, they were well aware that every where it was a thing ἀντιλεγόμενον : the very word, be it observed, used in ver. 19 (and ch. xiii. 45), respecting the opposition raised by the Jews to Paul. Now we may avail ourselves of both Olshausen's and Tholuck's suppositions. On the one hand it was very likely that the intercourse between Jews and Christians at Rome would be exceedingly small. The Christian church, consisting mostly of Gentiles, would absorb into itself the Jews who joined it, and who would, for the reason assigned by Olshausen, studiously separate themselves from their unbelieving countrymen. Again, it would not be likely that the Roman Jews, in their speech to Paul, would enter into any particulars respecting the sect,—only informing him, since he had professed himself in heart at peace with his nation and bound on behalf of their hope, that they were well aware of the general unpopularity among Jews of the sect to which he had attached himself, and wished from him an explanation on this head. Something also must be allowed for the restraint with which they spoke to one under the special custody, as a state prisoner, of the highest power in Rome, and in the presence of a representative of that power.

Thus the difficulty is much lessened : and it belongs indeed to that class, the occurrence of which in the sacred text is to be regarded far rather as a confirmation of our faith, by shewing us how simple and veracious is the narrative of things said and done, than as a hindrance to it by setting one statement against another.

With respect to that part of it which concerns the notoriety of the Roman church,—I may remark that its praise for faith in all the world, being a matter reported by Christians to Christians, and probably unknown to 'those without,' need not enter as a disturbing element into our consideration.

8. For a judicious and clear statement of the subsequent history of the early Roman church, I cannot do better than refer my readers to the former part of the work of Mr. Shepherd, "The History of the Church of Rome."

SECTION III.

WITH WHAT OBJECT IT WAS WRITTEN.

1. In answering this question, critics have been divided between the claims of the unquestionably most important doctrinal portion of the Epistle, and the particular matters treated in the parenthetical section (ch. ix.—xi.) and the conclusion (ch. xiv.—xvi.). It has not enough been borne in mind, that the *occasion of writing* an Epistle is *one thing*, —the *great object* of the Epistle itself, *another*. The ill-adjusted questions between the Jewish and Gentile believers, of which St. Paul had doubtless heard from Rome, may have prompted him originally to write to them: but when this resolve was once formed,—the importance of Rome as the centre of the Gentile world would naturally lead him to lay forth in this more than in any other Epistle the statement of the divine dealings with regard to Jew and Gentile, now one in Christ. I will therefore speak separately of the prompting occasion, and the main object, of the Epistle.

2. The eulogy of the faith of the Roman Christians which Paul met with in all his travels, could hardly fail to be accompanied with notices respecting their peculiar difficulties. These might soon have been set at rest by his presence and oral teaching: and he had accordingly resolved long since to visit them (ch. i. 10—13). Hindrances however had occurred: and that advice which he was not as yet permitted to give by word of mouth, he was prompted to send to them in a letter.

3. The contents of that letter plainly shew what their difficulties were. Mixed as the church was of Jew and Gentile, the relative position in God's favour of each of these would, in defect of solid and broad views of the universality of man's guilt and God's grace, furnish a subject of continual jealousy and irritation. And if we assume that the Gentile believers much preponderated in numbers, we shall readily infer

that the religious scruples of the Jews as to times and meats would be likely to be with too little consideration overborne.

4. From such circumstances we may well conceive that, under divine guidance, the present form of the Epistle was suggested to the Apostle. The main security for a proper estimate being formed of both Jew and Gentile, would be, the possession of right and adequate convictions of the universality of man's guilt and God's free justifying grace. This accordingly it was Paul's great object to furnish ; and on it he expends by far the greatest portion of his labour and space. But while so doing, we may trace his continued anxiety to steer his way cautiously among the strong feelings and prejudices which beset the path on either hand. If by a vivid description of the depravity of Heathendom he might be likely to minister to the pride of the Jew, he forthwith turns to him and abases him before God equally with the others. But when this is accomplished, lest he should seem to have lost sight of the pre-eminence of God's chosen people, and to have exposed the privileges of the Jew to the slight of the Gentile, he enumerates those privileges, and dwells on the true nature of that pre-eminence. Again when the great argument is brought to a close in ch. viii., by the completion of the bringing in of life by Christ Jesus, and the absolute union in time and after time of every believer with him,—for fear he should seem amidst the glories of redemption to have forgotten his own people, now as a nation rejected, he devotes three weighty chapters to an earnest and affectionate consideration of their case—to a deprecation of all triumph over them on the part of the Gentile, and a clear setting forth of the real mutual position of the two great classes of his readers. Then, after binding them all together again, in ch. xii. xiii., by precepts respecting Christian life, conduct towards their civil superiors, and mutual love, he proceeds in ch. xiv. to adjust those peculiar matters of doubt,—now rendered comparatively easy after the settlement of the great principle involving them,—respecting which they were divided. He recommends forbearance towards the weak and scrupulous,—at the same time classing himself among the strong, and manifestly implying on which side his own apostolic judgment lay. Having done this, he again places before them their mutual position as co-heirs of the divine promises and mercy (ch. xv. 1—13), and concludes the Epistle with matters of personal import to himself and them, and with salutations in the Lord. And probably on re-perusing his work, either at the time, or, as the altered style seems to import, in after years at Rome, he subjoins the fervid and characteristic doxology with which it closes.

5. There seems quite enough in the circumstances of the Roman Church to have led naturally to such an Epistle, without supposing with some critics, that an elaborate plan of written doctrinal teaching, to supply the want of oral, was present to the mind of the Apostle. We

must not forget to whom he was writing, nor fail to allow for the greater importance naturally attaching to an Epistle which would be the cherished possession and exemplar of the greatest of the Gentile churches. It was an Epistle to all Gentiles, from the Apostle of the Gentiles: ὑμῖν λέγω τοῖς ἔθνεσιν· ἐφ' ὅσον μὲν [οὖν] εἰμι ἐγὼ ἐθνῶν ἀπόστολος, τὴν διακονίαν μου δοξάζω. It had for its end the settlement, on the broad principles of God's truth and love, of the mutual relations, and union in Christ, of God's ancient people, and the recently engrafted world. What wonder then, if it be found to contain an exposition of man's unworthiness and God's redeeming love, such as not even Holy Scripture itself elsewhere furnishes?

SECTION IV.

AT WHAT TIME AND PLACE IT WAS WRITTEN.

1. This is more plainly pointed out in our Epistle than in most of the others. The Apostle was about to set out for Jerusalem with a contribution from the churches of Macedonia and Achaia (ch. xv. 25 ff.). To make this contribution he had exhorted the Corinthian church, 1 Cor. xvi. 1 ff., and hinted the possibility of his carrying it to Jerusalem in person, after wintering with them. And again in 2 Cor. viii. ix. he recurs to the subject, blames the tardiness of the Corinthians in preparing the contribution, and (ib. xiii. 1) describes himself as coming to them immediately. Comparing these notices with Acts xx. 1 ff., we find that Paul left Ephesus (after Pentecost, see notes there) for Macedonia, wintered at Corinth, and thence went to Jerusalem accompanied by several brethren, bearing (ib. xxiv. 17) alms to his nation and offerings.

2. Thus far it would appear that it was written close upon, or during his journey to bear alms to Jerusalem. But the very place is pointed out by evidence which can hardly be misapplied. We have a special commendation of Phœbe, a deaconess of the church at *Kenchrea*, to the kindness and attention of the Roman Christians: such a commendation as could hardly have been sent, had she not been, as generally believed, the bearer of the letter. Again, greetings are sent (ch. xvi. 23) from Gaius, evidently a *resident*, for he is called ὁ ξένος μου καὶ ὅλης τῆς ἐκκλησίας. But on comparing 1 Cor. i. 14, we find Paul telling the Corinthians that he baptized among them one Gaius. These persons can hardly but be one and the same. Again, Erastus is mentioned as steward of *the city*. Therefore, as Tholuck remarks, of some city well known to the Romans, and one in which he must have been some time resident, so to speak of it. I may add, that after the mention of

Kenchrea, ἡ πόλις can be no other than Corinth: just as, if the Peiræus had been mentioned, ἡ πόλις would necessarily mean Athens. (An Erastus is said to have remained at Corinth, 2 Tim. iv. 20, but the identity is too uncertain for the notice to be more than a *possible* corroboration.)

3. From the above evidence it is placed almost beyond question that the Epistle was written *from Corinth,* at the close of the three months' residence there of Acts xx. 3,—the παραχειμασία of 1 Cor. xvi. 6,—when Paul was just about to depart (νυνὶ δὲ πορεύομαι, ch. xv. 25) for Jerusalem on his errand of charity.

4. By consulting the chronological table appended to the Prolegg. to the Acts, it will be seen that I place this visit in the winter of A.D. 57—58. The Epistle accordingly was sent in the spring of A.D. 58, the fourth of the reign of Nero.

SECTION V.

LANGUAGE AND STYLE.

1. It might perhaps have been expected, that an Epistle to Romans would have been written in Latin. But Greek had become so far the general language of the world, that there is no ground for surprise in the Apostle having employed it. Not to cite at length the passages in the classics (Tacit. de Orator. c. 29: Martial, Epig. xiv. 56: Juvenal, Sat. vi. 184—189) which point to the universal adoption of Greek habits and language at Rome, we have the similar instances of Ignatius, Dionysius of Corinth, Irenæus, all of whom wrote to the Roman Christians in Greek. Clement, Bishop of Rome, wrote in Greek. Justin Martyr addressed his apologies to the Roman Emperors in Greek. And if it be objected, that the greater number of the Christian converts would belong to the lower classes, we may answer, that a great proportion of these were native Greeks: see Juvenal, Sat. iii. 60—80.

2. In speaking of the *style of the Epistle,* the following general remarks on the style of the Apostle Paul, taken from Tholuck's Introduction to his Commentary on the Epistle to the Romans, p. 26 ff., are of considerable interest: "As in general we can best apprehend and estimate the *style* of a writer in connexion with his *character,* so is it with the Apostle Paul. The attributes which especially characterize the originality of Paul as an Author, are *Power, Fulness,* and *Warmth.* If to these attributes is added *Perspicuity* of unfolding thought, we have all united, which ennobles an orator. But fulness of ideas and warmth of feelings often bring with them a certain informality of expression: the very wealth of the productive power does not always leave time to

educate (as Hamann expresses it) the thoughts which are born into the light,—to arrange and select the feelings. Together with the excellences above mentioned, something of this defect is found in the style of the great Apostle of the Gentiles. Something of that which Dionysius of Halicarnassus de Comp. Verb. c. 22 says of 'compositio austera,' is applicable to the Apostle's method of expression. οὔτε πάρισα βούλεται τὰ κῶλα ἀλλήλοις εἶναι, οὔτε παρόμοια, οὔτε ἀναγκαίᾳ δουλεύοντα ἀκολουθίᾳ, ἀλλ' εὐγενῆ κ. ἁπλᾶ κ. ἐλεύθερα· φύσει τ' ἐοικέναι μᾶλλον αὐτὰ βούλεται, ἢ τέχνῃ, κ. κατὰ πάθος λέγεσθαι μᾶλλον, ἢ κατ' ἦθος. περιόδους δὲ συντιθέναι συναρτιζούσας τὸν νοῦν τὰ πολλὰ μὲν οὔτε βούλεται· εἰ δέ ποτε αὐτομάτως ἐπὶ τοῦτο κατενεχθείη, τὸ ἐνεπιτήδευτον ἐμφαίνειν ἐθέλει καὶ ἀφελές, κ.τ.λ. The high claims of St. Paul to the reputation of eloquence were acknowledged by remote Christian antiquity. Nay, we have in all probability an honourable testimony to the same effect from one of the most celebrated critics of heathen Rome,—that namely of the fragment of Longinus, where he ranks Paul with the first orators of ancient times, adding however the remark, that he appears more to persuade than to demonstrate[3]. From Christian antiquity we will adduce the testimony of Jerome, Ep. 48, ad Pammachium, c. 13, vol. i. p. 223:—'Paulum Apostolum proferam, quem quotiescunque lego, videor mihi non verba audire, sed tonitrua . . . . videntur quidem verba simplicia et quasi innocentis hominis ac rusticani, et qui nec facere nec declinare noverit insidias, sed quocunque respexeris, fulmina sunt. Hæret in causa, capit omne quod tetigerit, tergum vertit, ut superet: fugam simulat, ut occidat.' Add to this the words of Chrysostom de Sacerdotio iv. 7, vol. i. p. 431: ὥσπερ γὰρ τεῖχος ἐξ ἀδάμαντος κατασκευασθέν, οὕτω τὰς πανταχοῦ τῆς οἰκουμένης ἐκκλησίας τὰ τούτου τειχίζει γράμματα· καὶ καθάπερ τις ἀριστεὺς γενναιότατος ἕστηκε καὶ νῦν μέσος, αἰχμαλωτίζων πᾶν νόημα εἰς τὴν ὑπακοὴν τοῦ χριστοῦ, καὶ καθαίρων λογισμοὺς καὶ πᾶν ὕψωμα ἐπαιρόμενον κατὰ τῆς γνώσεως τοῦ θεοῦ."

3. After having stated, and visited with severe and deserved censure, the disparaging estimate formed by Rückert in his Commentary, and criticized in a friendly spirit the other extreme, taken by Rothe and Glöckler, of regarding all ellipses, anacolutha, and defects of style, only as so many hidden but intended excellences, Tholuck proceeds:

"We have then this question to ask ourselves: *with what ideas as to the ability of the Apostle as a writer ought the believing Christian to*

[3] The genuineness of this fragment has been defended by Hug, Einl. ins N. T. ii. 334 (342 of Wait's transl.), on grounds well worthy of consideration. (The passage runs thus: κορωνὶς δ' ἔστω λόγου παντὸς καὶ φρονήματος Ἑλληνικοῦ Δημοσθένης, Λυσίας, Αἰσχίνης, Ὑπερίδης, Ἰσαῖος, Δείναρχος (Δημοσθένης ὁ Κρίθινος), Ἰσοκράτης, Ἀντίφων· πρὸς τούτοις Παῦλος ὁ Ταρσεύς, ὅντινα καὶ πρῶτόν φημι προιστάμενον δόγματος ἀναποδείκτου.)

approach his works? And what is the result, when we examine in detail the Epistles of Paul in this bearing? The Fathers themselves frequently confess, that the whole character of Christianity forbids us from seeking classical elegance in the outward style of the New Testament:—as the SON OF GOD appeared in His life on earth in a state of humiliation, so also the *word of God*. In this sense, to cite one example out of many, Calvin says (on Rom. v. 15):—'Quum autem multoties discriminis mentionem repetat, nulla tamen est repetitio, in qua non sit ἀνανταπόδοτον, vel saltem ellipsis aliqua: *Quæ sunt quidem orationis vitia, sed quibus nihil majestati decedit cœlestis sapientiæ, quæ nobis per apostolum traditur.* Quin potius singulari Dei providentia factum est, ut sub contemptibili verborum humilitate altissima hæc mysteria nobis traderentur; ut non humanæ eloquentiæ potentia, sed sola spiritus efficacia niteretur nostra fides.' But it must be borne in mind, that this our concession with regard to the formal perfection of the apostolic writings has its limits: for were we to concede that imperfection of form amounted to absolute *informality*, the *subject-matter itself* would be involved in the surrender. If the aim of the apostolic teaching is not to be altogether frustrated, we can hardly object to the assumption, that the divine ideas have been propounded in such a form, that by a correct use of the requisite means they may be discovered, and their full meaning recognized. Assuming this, it is impossible to form so low an estimate as Rückert's of the style of the Apostle: while at the same time we cannot see that the believing Christian is entitled to assume in him an academic correctness of syllogistic form, a conscious and perfect appreciation of adequacy of expression, reaching to the use of every particle. If we are to require these excellences from an apostolic writer, why not also entire conformity to classical idiom of expression? And if we besides take into account the peculiarity of the Apostle's character above pointed out, are we not obliged to confess, that so universal a *reflection*, such a *calculation*, as Rothe's theory supposes, is altogether inconsistent with that character,—that such a precisely measured style would be inexplicable from a spirit like that of the Apostle, except on the assumption of a *passive inspiration?* and as regards the point itself, I cannot see, that the writings of Paul, examined in detail, justify this prejudice in their favour, even according to the ingenious and minute exegesis of Rothe himself. (This he instances by examining Rothe's account of the defective constructions in Rom. v. 12 f.) * * * * That the great Apostle was no ordinary thinker,—that he did not, after the manner of enthusiasts, carried away by warmth of feeling, write down what he himself did not understand, is beyond question:—but that all which hitherto has been accounted in him negligence or inaccuracy of expression, proceeded from conscious intention of the writer,—can neither be justly assumed a priori, nor convincingly shown a posteriori."

4. To these general remarks of Tholuck I may add some notice of the peculiarities of the argumentative style of the Apostle, with which we are so much concerned in this Epistle.

(α) It is his constant habit to *insulate* the one matter which he is considering, and regard it irrespective of any qualifications of which it may admit, or objections to which it lies open,—up to a certain point. Much of the difficulty in ch. v. vi. vii. has arisen from not bearing this in mind.

(β) After thus treating the subject till the main result is gained, he *then* takes into account the qualifications and objections, but in a manner peculiar to himself; introducing them by putting the overstrained use, or the abuse, of the proposition just proved, in an interrogative form, and answering the question just asked. On a superficial view of these passages, they assume a sort of dramatic character, and have led many Commentators to suppose *an objector* to be present in the mind of the Apostle, to whom such questions are to be ascribed. But a further and deeper acquaintance with St. Paul's argumentative style removes this impression, and with it, much of the obscurity arising from supposing, or not knowing when to suppose, an interchange of speakers in the argument. We find that it is the Apostle himself speaking throughout, and in his vivid rhetorical manner proposing the fallacies which might be derived from his conclusions as matters of parenthetical enquiry.

(γ) Perhaps one of the most wonderful phænomena of St. Paul's arguments, is the manner in which all such parenthetical enquiries are interwoven into the great subject; in which while he pursues and annihilates the off-branching fallacy, at the same time he has been advancing in the main path,—whereas in most human arguments each digression must have its definite termination, and we must resume the thesis where we left it. A notable instance of this is seen in ch. vi. of our Epistle; in which while the mischievous fallacy of ver. 1 is discussed and annihilated, the great subject of the introduction of Life by Christ is carried on through another step—viz. the establishment of that life as one of *sanctification.*

Among the minor characteristics of the Apostle's style, may be enumerated,

(δ) *Frequent and complicated antitheses*, requiring great caution and discrimination in exegesis. For often the different members of the antithesis are not to be taken in the same extent of meaning; sometimes the literal and metaphorical significations are interchanged in a curious and intricate manner, so that perhaps in the first member of two antithetical clauses, the subject may be literal and the predicate metaphorical, and in the second, vice versa, the subject metaphorical and the predicate literal. Sometimes again, the terms of one member are to be amplified to their fullest possible, almost to an exaggerated meaning: whereas those of the second are to be reduced down to their least possible, almost to a depreciated meaning. To retain such antitheses in a version or exegesis is of course, generally speaking, impossible: the appropriateness of the terms depends very much on their conventional value in the original language. Then comes the difficult task of breaking up the sentence, and expressing neither more nor less than the real meaning under a different grammatical form: an attempt almost always sure to fail even in the ablest hands.

(ε) *Frequent plays upon words,* or rather perhaps, choice of words from their similarity of sound. Much of the terseness and force of the Apostle's expressions is necessarily lost in rendering them into another language, owing to the impossibility of expressing these paronomasiæ; and *without them,* it becomes exceedingly difficult to ascertain the real weight of the expression itself; to be sure that we do not give more than due importance in the context to a clause whose *aptness* was perhaps its chief characteristic, and on the other hand to take care that we do not overlook the real importance of clauses whose value is not their mere aptness, but a deep insight into the philosophy of the cognate words made use of, as exponents of lines of human thought ultimately convergent.

(ζ) *Accumulation of prepositions,* often with the same or very slightly different meanings. That this is a characteristic of St. Paul's style there can be no doubt: and the difficulty created by it is easily obviated if this be borne in mind. The temptation of an expositor is to endeavour to give precise meaning and separate force to each preposition, thereby exceeding the intention of the sentence, and distorting the context by elevating into importance clauses of comparative indifference.

(η) *The frequency and peculiarity of his parenthetical passages.* The difficulty presented by this characteristic is, in few words, that of disentangling with precision such clauses and passages. The danger is twofold: 1. lest we too hastily assume an irregular construction, not perceiving the parenthetical interruption: 2. lest we err on the other hand, which has more commonly been the case, in assuming the existence of parenthetical clauses where none exist. St. Paul's parentheses are generally well marked to the careful observer; and it must be remembered that the instances of anacoluthon and irregular construction are at least as frequent: so that we are not, for the sake of clearing up a construction, to throw in parentheses, as is often done, to the detriment of the sense.

The peculiarity of his parentheses consists in this, that owing to the fervency and rapidity of his composition he frequently deserts, in a clause apparently intended to be parenthetical, the construction of the main sentence, and instead of resuming it again, proceeds with the parenthesis as if it were the main sentence.

Instances of almost all these characteristic difficulties will be found in chap. v. of this Epistle, where, so to speak, they reach their culminating point.

5. Two cautions are necessary, on account of the lax renderings of our authorized version, by which the details of the argument of this and other Epistles have been so disguised, that it is almost impossible for the mere English student intelligently to apprehend them.

(*a*) *The emphatic position of words* is of the highest importance. Pages might be filled with an account of misrenderings of versions and Commentators from disregard to the rules of emphasis. The student will continually find such instances alleged and criticized in these notes; and will be surprised that so momentous a matter should have been generally overlooked.

(*b*) *The distinction between the aorist and perfect tenses* is in our authorized version very commonly disregarded, and thereby the point of the sentence altogether missed. Instances are continually occurring in the Epistles: and it has been my endeavour in the notes to draw the student's attention to them with a view to their correction.

6. For much interesting matter on this subject the student is referred to Tholuck, Römerbrief, Einleitung: and to Dr. Davidson, Introd. vol. ii. p. 144 ff.

CHAPTER III.

THE FIRST EPISTLE TO THE CORINTHIANS.

SECTION I.

ITS AUTHORSHIP AND INTEGRITY.

1. As far as I am aware, the first of these has never been doubted by any critic of note. Indeed he who would do so, must be prepared to dispute the historical truth of the character of St. Paul. For no more complete transcript of that character, as we find it set forth to us in the Acts, can be imagined, than that which we find in this and the second Epistle. Of this I shall speak further below (§ vii.).

2. But external testimonies to the Authorship are by no means wanting.

(α) Clement of Rome, in his Epistle to this very Church of Corinth, says, c. 47, p. 305 f.:—ἀναλάβετε τὴν ἐπιστολὴν τοῦ μακαρίου Παύλου τοῦ ἀποστόλου. τί πρῶτον ὑμῖν ἐν ἀρχῇ εὐαγγελίου ἔγραψεν; ἐπ' ἀληθείας πνευματικῶς ἐπέστειλεν ὑμῖν, περὶ αὐτοῦ τε καὶ Κηφᾶ καὶ Ἀπολλώ, διὰ τὸ καὶ τότε προσκλίσεις ὑμᾶς πεποιῆσθαι[1].

(β) Polycarp, ad Philippenses, c. 11, p. 1020:—"Qui autem ignorant judicium Domini? An nescimus, quia sancti mundum judicabunt[2]? sicut Paulus docet."

(γ) Irenæus adv. Hær. iv. 27 (45). 3, p. 264:—"Et hoc autem apostolum in epistola quæ est ad Corinthios manifestissime ostendisse, dicentem: Nolo enim vos ignorare, fratres, quoniam patres nostri omnes sub nube fuerunt[3] &c." And almost in the same words Cyprian, Testim. i. 4, citing the same passage.

(δ) Athenagoras, de resurrect. mort. 18, p. 331:—εὔδηλον παντὶ τὸ λειπόμενον, ὅτι δεῖ, κατὰ τὸν ἀπόστολον, τὸ φθαρτὸν τοῦτο καὶ διασκεδαστὸν ἐνδύσασθαι ἀφθαρσίαν[4], ἵνα κ.τ.λ.

(ε) Clement of Alexandria cites this epistle very frequently and explicitly: e. g. Pædag. i. 6 (33), p. 117 P.:—σαφέστατα γοῦν ὁ μακάριος Παῦλος ἀπήλλαξεν ἡμᾶς τῆς ζητήσεως ἐν τῇ προτέρᾳ πρὸς Κορινθίους ὧδέ πως γράφων· Ἀδελφοί, μὴ παιδία γίνεσθε ταῖς φρεσὶν κ.τ.λ.[5]—And he proceeds to quote also 1 Cor. xiii. 11, with πάλιν ὁ Παῦλος λέγει.

(ζ) Tertullian de Præscript. adv. Hær. c. 33, vol. ii. p. 46,—"Paulus in prima ad Corinthios notat negatores et dubitatores resurrectionis."

See Lardner: and Davidson's Introd. vol. ii. p. 253 f., where more testimonies are given.

3. The integrity of this Epistle has not been disputed. The whole of it springs naturally out of the circumstances, and there are no difficulties arising from discontinuousness or change of style, as in some passages of the Epistle to the Romans.

SECTION II.

FOR WHAT READERS IT WAS WRITTEN.

1. "CORINTH (formerly Ephyre, Apollod. i. 9,—which afterwards was its poetic name, Ovid, Met. ii. 240. Virg. Georg. ii. 264. Propert. ii. 5. 1 al.) was a renowned, wealthy (Il. β. 570. Hor. ii. 16. Dio Chrysost. xxxvii. p. 464), and beautiful commercial city (Thuc. i. 13. Cic. rep. i. 4), and in the Roman times the capital of Achaia propria (Apul. Met. x. p. 239, Bipont), situated on the isthmus of the Peloponnese between

[1] 1 Cor. i. 10 f. [2] 1 Cor. vi. 2. [3] 1 Cor. x. 1 f.
[4] 1 Cor. xv. 53. [5] 1 Cor. xiv. 20.

the Ionian and Ægean seas (hence *bimaris*, Ovid, Met. v. 407 ; Hor. Od. i. 7. 2,—ἀμφιθάλασσος, διθάλασσος) and at the foot of a rock which bore the fortress Acrocorinthus (Strabo, viii. 379 ; Plut. vit. Arat. 16; Liv. xlv. 28),—forty stadia in circumference. It had two ports, of which the western (twelve stadia distant) was called Lechæon (Λέχαιον, Lechæum, Lecheæ, Plin. iv. 5), the eastern (seventy stadia distant) Kenchreæ (Strabo, viii. 380 ; Paus. ii. 2, 3 ; Liv. xxxii. 17 ; al.). The former was for the Italian, the latter for the Oriental commerce : so Strabo, l. c. : Κεγχρεαὶ κώμη καὶ λιμὴν ἀπέχων τῆς πόλεως ὅσον ἑβδομήκοντα στάδια. τούτῳ μὲν χρῶνται πρὸς τοὺς ἐκ τῆς Ἀσίας, πρὸς δὲ τοὺς ἐκ τῆς Ἰταλίας τῷ Λεχαίῳ. Arts and sciences flourished notably in Corinth (Pindar, Ol. xiii. 21 ; Herod. ii. 167 ; Plin. xxxiv. 3. xxxv. 5 ; Cic. Verr. ii. 19 ; Suet. Tiber. 34). The Corinthian plate was especially celebrated. But these advantages were accompanied by much wantonness, luxury, and gross corruption of morals (Athenæus, vii. 281. xiii. 543 ; Alciphr. iii. 60 ; Strabo, viii. 378 ; Eustath. Iliad β. p. 220). (These vices were increased by the periodical influx of visitors owing to the Isthmian games, and by the abandoned and unclean worship of Aphrodite, to whose temple more than a thousand priestesses of loose character were attached. See testimonials in Wetst.) The city (lumen totius Græciæ, Cic. Manil. 5) was taken, pillaged, and destroyed by L. Mummius (Flor. ii. 16 ; Liv. Epitome lii.) in A.U.C. 608, 146 B.C. (cf. Plin. xxxiv. 3),—but re-established (as the colony *Julia Corinthus*) by Julius Cæsar, A.U.C. 710, B.C. 44,—and soon recovered its former splendour (Aristid. Or. 3, p. 23, ed. Jebb), and was accordingly in St. Paul's time the seat of the Roman proconsul of Achaia (Acts xviii. 18). See, on the whole, Strabo, viii. 378 ff.; Paus. ii. 1 ff." Winer, Realwörterbuch. An interesting description of the present remains of Corinth will be found in Leake's Morea, vol. iii. ch. xxviii.

2. The Christian church at Corinth was founded by St. Paul on his first visit, related in Acts xviii. (1—18). He spent there a year and a half, and his labours seem to have been rewarded with considerable success. His converts were for the most part Gentiles (1 Cor. xii. 2), but comprised also many Jews (Acts xviii. 8 : see too ver. 5, and note) ; both however, though the Christian body at Corinth was numerous (Acts ib. 4, 8, 10), were principally from the poorer classes (1 Cor. i. 26 ff.). To this Crispus the ruler of the synagogue (Acts xviii. 8 ; 1 Cor. i. 14) formed an exception, as also Erastus the chamberlain (οἰκονόμος) of the city (Rom. xvi. 23), and Gaius, whom the Apostle calls ὁ ξένος μου κ. ὅλης τῆς ἐκκλησίας. And we find traces of a considerable mixture of classes of society in the agapæ (1 Cor. xi. 22).

3. The method of the Apostle in preaching at Corinth is described by himself, 1 Cor. ii. 1 ff. He used great simplicity, declaring to them only the cross of Christ, without any adventitious helps of rhetoric or

worldly wisdom. The opposition of the Jews had been to him a source of no ordinary anxiety: see the remarkable expression Acts xviii. 5, and note there. The situation likewise of his Gentile converts was full of danger. Surrounded by habits of gross immorality and intellectual pride, they were liable to be corrupted in their conduct, or tempted to despise the simplicity of their first teacher.

4. Of this latter there was the more risk, since the Apostle had been followed by one whose teaching might make his appear in their eyes meagre and scanty. Apollos is described in Acts xviii. 24 ff. as a learned Hellenist of Alexandria, mighty in the Scriptures, and fervent in zeal. And though by the honourable testimony there given[6] to his work at Corinth, it is evident that his doctrine was essentially the same with that of Paul, yet there is reason to think that there was difference enough in the outward character and expression of the two[7] to provoke comparison to the Apostle's disadvantage, and attract the lovers of eloquence and philosophy rather to Apollos.

5. We discover very plain signs of an influence antagonistic to the Apostle having been at work in Corinth. Teachers had come, of Jewish extraction (2 Cor. xi. 22), bringing with them letters of recommendation from other churches (2 Cor. iii. 1), and had built on the foundation laid by Paul (1 Cor. iii. 10—18; 2 Cor. x. 13—18) a worthless building, on which they prided themselves. These teachers gave out themselves for Apostles (2 Cor. xi. 5, 13), rejecting the apostleship of Paul (1 Cor. ix. 2; 2 Cor. x. 7, 8), encouraging disobedience to his commands (2 Cor. x. 1,6), and disparaging in every way his character, and work for the Gospel (see for the former, 2 Cor. iv. 1, 2 ff.; v. 11 ff., and notes in both places: for the latter, 2 Cor. xi. 16—xii. 12). It is probable, as De Wette suggests, that these persons were excited to greater rage against Paul, by the contents of the first Epistle; for we find the plainest mention of them in the second. But their practices had commenced before, and traces of them are very evident in ch. ix. of this Epistle.

6. The ground taken by these persons, as regarded their Jewish position, is manifest from these Epistles. They did not, as the false teachers among the Galatians, insist on circumcision and keeping the law: for not a word occurs on that question, nor a hint which can be construed as pointing to it. Some think that they kept back this point in a church consisting principally of Gentiles, and contented themselves with first setting aside the authority and influence of Paul. But I should rather believe them to have looked on this question as closed,

[6] ὃς παραγενόμενος συνεβάλετο πολὺ τοῖς πεπιστευκόσιν διὰ τῆς χάριτος, ver. 27. See also 1 Cor. iii. 6.

[7] See especially 1 Cor. xvi. 12, and note.

and to have carried on more a negative than a positive warfare with the Apostle, upholding, as against him, the authority of the regularly constituted Twelve, and of Peter as the Apostle of the circumcision, and impugning Paul as an interloper and innovator, and no autoptic witness of the events of the Gospel history: as not daring to prove his apostleship by claiming sustenance from the Christian churches, or by leading about a wife, as the other Apostles, and the brethren of the Lord, and Cephas. What their positive teaching had been, it is difficult to decide, except that, although founded on a recognition of Jesus the Christ, it was of an inconsistent and unsubstantial kind, and such as would not stand in the coming day of fiery trial (1 Cor. iii. 11 ff.).

7. That some of these teachers may have described themselves as *peculiarly belonging to Christ*, is a priori very probable. St. Paul had had no connexion with our Lord while He lived and taught on earth. His Christian life and apostolic calling began at so late a period, that those who had seen the Lord on earth might claim a superiority over him. And this is all that seems to be meant by the ἐγὼ δὲ χριστοῦ of 1 Cor. i. 12, especially if we compare it with 2 Cor. x. 7 ff., the only other passage where the expression is alluded to. There certainly persons are pointed out, who boasted themselves in some peculiar connexion with Christ which, it was presumed, Paul had not; and were ignorant that the weapons of the apostolic warfare were not carnal, but spiritual.

8. It would also be natural that some should avow themselves *the followers of Paul himself*, and set perhaps an undue value on him as God's appointed minister among them, forgetting that all ministers were but God's servants for their benefit.

9. It will be seen from the foregoing remarks, as well as from the notes, that I do not believe these tendencies to have developed themselves into *distinctly marked parties*, either before the writing of our Epistle or at any other time. In the Epistle of Clement of Rome, written some years after, we find the same contentious spirit blamed (c. 47, p. 308), but it appears that by that time its ground was altogether different: we have no traces of the Paul-party, or Apollos-party, or Cephas-party, or Christ-party: ecclesiastical insubordination and ambition were then the faults of the Corinthian church.

10. Much ingenuity and labour has been spent in Germany on the four supposed distinct parties at Corinth, and the most eminent theologians have endeavoured, with very different results, to allot to each its definite place in tenets and practice. I refer the student for a complete account of the principal theories, to Dr. Davidson's Introduction, vol. ii. p. 224 ff., and Conybeare and Howson's Life of St. Paul, vol. i. chap. xiii.:—and for separate expositions, to Neander, Pfl. u. Leit., 4th edn. pp. 375—397: Olshausen, Bibl. Comm. iii. 475 ff.: Schaff, Gesch.

d. christlichen Kirche, § 64: Stanley, Epistle to the Corinthians, Introduction.

SECTION III.

WITH WHAT OBJECT IT WAS WRITTEN.

1. The object of writing this Epistle was twofold. The Apostle had been applied to by the Corinthians to advise them on matters connected with their *practice in the relations of life* (ch. vii. 1), and with their liberty of action as regarded *meats offered to idols* (ch. viii.—x.); they had apparently also referred to him the question whether their *women* should be *veiled in the public assemblies* of the church (ch. xi. 3—16): and had laid before him some difficulties respecting the *exercise of spiritual gifts* (ch. xii.—xiv.). He had enjoined them to make a *collection for the poor saints at Jerusalem:* and they had requested directions, how this might best be done (ch. xvi. 1 ff.).

2. These enquiries would have elicited at all events an answer from St. Paul. But there were other and even more weighty reasons why an Epistle should be sent to them just now from their father in the faith. Intelligence had been brought him by the family of Chloe (ch. i. 11) of their *contentious spirit*. From the same, or from other sources, he had learned the occurrence among them of a *gross case of incest*, in which the delinquent was upheld in impunity by the church (ch. v. 1 ff.). He had further understood that the Christian brethren were in the habit of carrying their disputes before heathen tribunals (ch. vi. 1 ff.). And it had been represented to him that there were *irregularities* requiring reprehension *in their manner of celebrating the Agapæ*, which indeed they had so abused, that they could now be no longer called the Supper of the Lord. Such were their weighty errors in practice: and among these it would have been hardly possible that Christian doctrine should remain sound. So far was this from being the case, that some among them had even gone to the length of denying the Resurrection itself. Against these he triumphantly argues in ch. xv.

3. It has been questioned whether St. Paul had the *defence of his own apostolic authority* in view in this Epistle. The answer must certainly be in the affirmative. We cannot read chapters iv. and ix. without perceiving this. At the same time, it is most probable that the hostility of the false teachers had not yet assumed the definite force of personal slander and disparagement,—or not so prominently and notoriously as afterwards. That which is the primary subject of the 2nd Epistle, is but incidentally touched on here. But we plainly see that his authority had been already impugned (see especially ch. iv. 17—21), and his apostleship questioned (ch. ix. 1, 2).

SECTION IV.

OF THE NUMBER OF EPISTLES WRITTEN BY PAUL TO THE CORINTHIANS.

1. If we were left to infer a priori, it would be exceedingly probable that an Epistle had been sent to the Corinthians before this, which we call the first. It appears from ch. xvi. 1 that they wanted some directions as to the method of making "*the collection for the saints.*" We may ask,—*when enjoined and how?* If by the Apostle in person, the directions would doubtless have been asked for and given at the time. It would seem then to follow, that a command to make the collection had been sent them either by some messenger, or in an epistle.

2. The uncertainty, however, which would rest upon this inference, is removed by the express words of the Apostle himself. In ch. v. 9 he says, ἔγραψα ὑμῖν ἐν τῇ ἐπιστολῇ, μὴ συναναμίγνυσθαι πόρνοις. In my note on those words, I have endeavoured to shew that the only meaning which in their context they will legitimately bear, is, that this command, *not to associate with fornicators*, was contained in a previous Epistle to them, which has not been preserved to us. Those who maintain that the reference is to the present Epistle, have never been able to produce a passage bearing the slightest resemblance to the command mentioned[8].

3. The opinions of Commentators on this point have been strangely warped by a notion conceived a priori, that it would be wrong to suppose any apostolic Epistle to have been lost. Those who regard, not preconceived theories, but the facts and analogies of the case, will rather come to the conclusion that *very many* have been lost. The Epistle to Philemon, for example, is the only one remaining to us of a class, which if we take into account the affectionate disposition of St. Paul, and the frequency of intercourse between the metropolis and the provinces, must have been numerous during his captivity in Rome. We find him also declaring, 1 Cor. xvi. 3 (see note there), his intention of giving recommendatory letters, if necessary, to the bearers of the collection from Corinth to Jerusalem: from which proposal we may safely infer that on other occasions, he was in the habit of writing such Epistles to individuals or to churches. To imagine that *every writing* of an inspired Apostle *must necessarily have been preserved to us*, is as absurd as

[8] Perhaps the most extraordinary theory ever propounded by one who has evidently spent some pains on his subject, is that of Mr. Paget, in his "Unity and Order of the Epistles of St. Paul," in which, on account of a fancied resemblance of this command to that in Heb. xii. 16 (which if examined proves to be *no* resemblance), he maintains ἡ ἐπιστολή here to be the *Epistle to the Hebrews*, which he imagines to have been a sort of general circular epistle to all the churches, written previously to those addressed to particular congregations. I need hardly remind the student, how entirely all the data of every kind furnished by that Epistle are against such a supposition.

it would be to imagine that all his *sayings* must necessarily have been recorded. The Providence of God, which has preserved so many precious portions both of one and the other, has also allowed many, perhaps equally precious, of both, to pass into oblivion.

4. The time of writing this lost Epistle is fixed, by the history, between Paul's leaving Corinth Acts xviii. 18, and the sending of our present Epistle. But we shall be able to approximate nearer, when we have discussed the question of the Apostle's visits to Corinth[9].

5. Its contents may be in some measure surmised from the data furnished in our two canonical Epistles.

He had in it given them a command, *μὴ συναναμίγνυσθαι πόρνοις*, which being taken by them in too strict and literal a sense, and on that account perhaps overlooked, as impossible to be observed, is explained in its true sense by him, 1 Cor. v. 9—12.

It also contained, in all probability, an announcement of a plan of visiting them on his way to Macedonia, and again on his return from Macedonia (2 Cor. i. 15, 16), which he changed in consequence of the news heard from Chloe's household (1 Cor. xvi. 5—7), for which alteration he was accused of lightness of purpose (*ἐλαφρία*, 2 Cor. i. 17).

We may safely say also (see above) that it contained a command to make a collection for the poor saints at Jerusalem. Further than this we cannot with any safety surmise.

It was evidently a short letter, containing perhaps little or nothing more than the above announcement and injunctions, given probably in the pithy and sententious manner so common with the Apostle[1].

SECTION V.

OF THE NUMBER OF VISITS MADE BY PAUL TO THE CORINTHIANS.

1. The controversy on this point will be cut very short, if the interpretation given in the notes of 2 Cor. xii. 14, xiii. 1, be assumed as correct:—and, as I have there maintained, I believe that neither the words nor the context will admit any other. The Apostle had paid *two visits* to Corinth before the sending of *that*, and consequently of *this* Epistle.

2. The difficulty in this inference, which has led Commentators to adopt an unnatural rendering of the above passages, is, that *but one visit* is *recorded*, viz. that in Acts xviii. 1 ff. For both Epistles were written before the second visit in Acts xx. 2, 3. (Compare Acts xix. with 1 Cor. xvi. 8, and 2 Cor. ix. 2 with Acts xx. 1, 2.)

3. But manifestly, the history of St. Paul's apostolic career in the

[9] See below, § v.

[1] See Rom. xii. 9 ff.; 1 Thess. v. 16 ff.

Acts is very fragmentary and imperfect. Long and important journeys are dismissed in a few words[2]: some, e. g. that to Arabia, and the missionary tour in Syria and Cilicia, Gal. i. 21 ff., not being even mentioned. No notice is taken of the foundation of the churches of Galatia, unless the cursory mention of Acts xvi. 6, be taken as such :—and of the copious catalogue of perils undergone by him in 2 Cor. xi. 24 ff., but few can be identified in the history. That a journey to Corinth should have escaped mention, where more extensive journeys and more important events have been omitted or slightly touched on, would not be at all improbable.

4. Such a journey must of course be inserted between Acts xviii. 18, when his first visit to Corinth ended, and xx. 2, when the second Epistle was sent from Macedonia. But these limits are further narrowed by the history itself. From xviii. 18 to xix. 9, when we find the Apostle established at Ephesus, is evidently a continuous narrative. And as plainly, no visit took place between the sending of the first and second Epistle, as is decisively proved by 2 Cor. i. 15—23. Now the first Epistle was sent from Ephesus, in the early part of the year in which he left that city, 1 Cor. xvi. 8. So that our *terminus a quo* is the settling at Ephesus, Acts xix. 10, and our *terminus ad quem* the spring preceding the departure from Ephesus, Acts xx. 1. During this time, a visit to Corinth took place.

5. Let us see whether any hints of his own throw light on this necessary inference. In 2 Cor. xi. 25 we read τρὶς ἐναυάγησα, and this in a description of his *apostolic* labours : so that we must not go back beyond his conversion for any of these shipwrecks. Now his recorded voyages are these : (1) From Cæsarea to Tarsus, Acts ix. 30. (2) Possibly, from Tarsus to Antioch, xi. 25 : but more probably this was a land-journey. (3) From Seleucia to Cyprus, xiii. 4. (4) From Paphos to Perga, xiii. 13. (5) From Attalia to Antioch, xiv. 26. (6) From Troas to Philippi, xvi. 11, 12. (7) From Macedonia to Athens, xvii. 14, 15. (8) From Kenchreæ to Ephesus, xviii. 18, 19. (9) From Ephesus to Cæsarea, ib. 21, 22. (10) From Ephesus to Macedonia, xx. 1. Of these, it is certain that no shipwreck took place during (6), for it is minutely detailed : it is extremely improbable that any took place during (3), (4), and (5), as the account of the first missionary tour is circumstantial and precise. The same may be said of (7), in which the words οἱ δὲ καθιστάνοντες τὸν Παῦλον ἤγαγον ἕως Ἀθηνῶν will scarcely admit of such an interruption. It is hardly probable that any shipwreck took place in those voyages the purpose of which is described as being at once attained, to which class belong (8) and (9), and, if it is to be counted as a voyage, (2). The two left, of which

[2] E. g., ch. xv. 41, xvi. 6, xviii. 23, xix. 1, xx. 2, 3.

we have absolutely *no* account given, are (1) and (10). It is quite possible that he may have been shipwrecked on both these occasions, and such an assumption with regard to (10) would suggest another interpretation of the difficult allusion, 2 Cor. i. 8—10. But even assuming this, more voyages seem to be required to account for three shipwrecks. It is true that the evidence thus acquired is very slight—but however trifling, it is at least in favour of, and not against, the hypothesis of an unrecorded visit to Corinth.

6. The nature of the visit may be gathered in some measure from extant hints. It was one made ἐν λύπῃ, 2 Cor. ii. 1, where see note: why, we might well suppose, but are not left to conjecture: for he tells them (2 Cor. xiii. 2 and note) that during it he warned them, that *if he came again, he would not spare* (the sinners among them); and 2 Cor. xii. 21, there is a hint given that God had, on this occasion, *humbled him among them*. It was a visit unpleasant in the process and in recollection: perhaps very short, and as sad as short: in which he seems merely to have thrown out solemn warnings of the consequences of a future visit of apostolic severity if the abuses were persisted in,—and possibly to have received insult from some among them on account of such warnings.

7. If we enquire what *sort* of sin had occasioned the visit, the answer seems to be furnished by 2 Cor. xii. 21, μὴ πάλιν ἐλθόντος μου ταπεινώσει με ὁ θεός μου πρὸς ὑμᾶς, καὶ πενθήσω πολλοὺς τῶν προημαρτηκότων καὶ μὴ μετανοησάντων ἐπὶ τῇ ἀκαθαρσίᾳ καὶ πορνείᾳ καὶ ἀσελγείᾳ ᾗ ἔπραξαν. It was probably on account of these, the besetting sins of the place, that his second visit had been made in grief; it was to abstain from these sins and the company of those who committed them, that he had enjoined them in his lost Epistle: and accordingly, while we find in our first Epistle detailed notice of the special case of sin which he had recently heard of as occurring among them, the subject of πορνεία is alluded to (vi. 12—20) only in a summary way, and in one which shews that he is rather replying to an excuse set up after rebuke in the matter, than introducing it for the first time.

SECTION VI.

AT WHAT PLACE AND TIME THIS EPISTLE WAS WRITTEN.

1. The place of writing it is pointed out in ch. xvi. 8,—ἐπιμενῶ δὲ ἐν Ἐφέσῳ ἕως τῆς πεντηκοστῆς, to have been EPHESUS.

A mistaken rendering of the words (ib. ver. 5) Μακεδονίαν γὰρ διέρχομαι, as if they signified 'for I *am passing through* Macedonia,'—led probably to the subscription in the rec. and our English Bibles, ἐγράφη ἀπὸ Φιλίππων. But the idea has never been seriously entertained.

2. The above notice from ch. xvi. 8 also shews, that at the time of writing, the Apostle intended to quit Ephesus after Pentecost of that year. And on connecting this with Acts xix., xx., it appears (see notes, and chronological table in Prolegg. to Acts) that he really did leave Ephesus about Pentecost in the year 57. We may assume therefore (as we have no ground for supposing that he referred to a previous year and afterwards changed his purpose) that *the Epistle was written in the former part of the year* 57.

3. It will be seen by my notes on 1 Cor. v. 7, that I cannot see in the words καθώς ἐστε ἄζυμοι any allusion to the fact of the days of unleavened bread being then present. I have endeavoured to shew that external probability, as well as spiritual analogy, is against the idea that St. Paul would have so expressed himself. But *there still is no reason, why the nearness or presence of that season may not have suggested to him the whole train of thought* there occurring,—especially when we know independently that he was writing during the *former part of the year.*

4. It is almost certain then that the Epistle was written *before Pentecost,* A.D. 57 : and probable, that *somewhat about Easter* was the exact time.

5. The Apostle had at this time already sent off Timotheus and Erastus to Macedonia (cf. Acts xix. 22, and 1 Cor. iv. 17), the former (1 Cor. ib.) with the intention of his proceeding on to Corinth, if possible (1 Cor. xvi. 10), and preparing the way for his own apostolic visit (iv. 17). Possibly also his mission had reference to the collection for the saints at Jerusalem (see 2 Cor. viii., and xii. 18); but the language used is ambiguous, and we cannot pronounce positively that Timotheus reached Corinth on this journey. (See below, ch. iv. § ii. 4.)

6. The Epistle is addressed in the name of Sosthenes ὁ ἀδελφός, as well as in that of the Apostle. It is hardly possible that this Sosthenes should be the same as the person of that name mentioned Acts xviii. 17 [3]: see note there. The conjectures respecting him I have given on 1 Cor. i. 1. He bears no part in the Epistle itself, any more than Timotheus in 2 Cor.: the Apostle, after mentioning him, immediately proceeds εὐχαριστῶ τῷ θεῷ μου.

7. It is uncertain, who were the *bearers* of the Epistle : but perhaps the common subscription is right in assigning that office to Stephanas, Fortunatus, and Achaicus. For they are mentioned as being present with the Apostle (1 Cor. xvi. 17) from Corinth: and as an injunction is given (ib. 18) that they should be honourably regarded by the Corinthians, it is highly probable that they were intending to return.

[3] Unless indeed, as Mr. Birks supposes, Horæ Apostolicæ, p. 215 f., he was converted subsequently to that occurrence.

SECTION VII.

MATTER AND STYLE.

1. As might have been expected from the occasion of writing, the matter of this epistle is very various. It is admirably characterized by Mr. Conybeare, in Conybeare and Howson's Life and Epistles of St. Paul, vol. ii. p. 28 (2nd edn.):—

"This letter is, in its contents, the most diversified of all St. Paul's Epistles: and in proportion to the variety of its topics, is the depth of its interest for ourselves. For by it we are introduced as it were behind the scenes of the apostolic Church, and its minutest features are revealed to us under the light of daily life. We see the picture of a Christian congregation as it met for worship in some upper chamber, such as the house of Aquila or of Gaius could furnish. We see that these seasons of pure devotion were not unalloyed by human vanity and excitement: yet, on the other hand, we behold the heathen auditor pierced to the heart by the inspired eloquence of the Christian prophets, the secrets of his conscience laid bare to him, and himself constrained to fall down on his face and worship God: we hear the fervent thanksgiving echoed by the unanimous Amen: we see the administration of the Holy Communion terminating the feast of love. Again, we become familiar with the perplexities of domestic life, the corrupting proximity of heathen immorality, the lingering superstition, the rash speculation, the lawless perversion of Christian liberty: we witness the strife of theological factions, the party names, the sectarian animosities. We perceive the difficulty of the task imposed upon the Apostle, who must guard from so many perils, and guide through so many difficulties, his children in the faith, whom else he had begotten in vain: and we learn to appreciate more fully the magnitude of that laborious responsibility under which he describes himself as almost ready to sink, 'the care of all the churches.'

"But while we rejoice that so many details of the deepest historical interest have been preserved to us by this Epistle, let us not forget to thank God, who so inspired His Apostle, that in his answers to questions of transitory interest he has laid down principles of eternal obligation. Let us trace with gratitude the providence of Him, who 'out of darkness calls up light;' by whose mercy it was provided, that the unchastity of the Corinthians should occasion the sacred laws of moral purity to be established for ever through the Christian world;—that their denial of the resurrection should cause those words to be recorded whereon reposes, as upon a rock that cannot be shaken, our sure and certain hope of immortality."

2. In style, this Epistle ranks perhaps the foremost of all as to sublimity, and earnest and impassioned eloquence. Of the former, the

description of the simplicity of the Gospel in ch. ii.,—the concluding apostrophe of ch. iii. (ver. 16—end),—the same in ch. vi. (ver. 9—end),—the reminiscence of the shortness of the time, ch. vii. 29—31,—the whole argument in ch. xv.,—are examples unsurpassed in Scripture itself: and of the latter, ch. iv. 8—15, and the whole of ch. ix.; while the panegyric of Love, in ch. xiii., stands, a pure and perfect gem, perhaps the noblest assemblage of beautiful thoughts in beautiful language extant in this our world. About the whole Epistle there is a character of lofty and sustained solemnity,—an absence of tortuousness of construction, and an apologetic plainness, which contrast remarkably with the personal portions of the second Epistle.

3. No Epistle raises in us a higher estimate of the varied and wonderful gifts with which God was pleased to endow the man whom He selected for the Apostle of the Gentile world: or shews us how large a portion of the Spirit, who worketh in each man severally as He will, was given to him for our edification. The depths of the spiritual, the moral, the intellectual, the physical world are open to him. He summons to his aid the analogies of nature. He enters minutely into the varieties of human infirmity and prejudice. He draws warning from the history of the chosen people: example, from the Isthmian foot-race. He refers an apparently trifling question of costume to the first great proprieties and relations of Creation and Redemption. He praises, reproves, exhorts, and teaches. Where he strikes, he heals. His large heart holding all, where he has grieved any, he grieves likewise; where it is in his power to give joy, he first overflows with joy himself. We may form some idea from this Epistle better perhaps than from any one other,—because this embraces the widest range of topics,—what marvellous power such a man must have had to persuade, to rebuke, to attract and fasten the affections of men.

CHAPTER IV.

THE SECOND EPISTLE TO THE CORINTHIANS.

SECTION I.

ITS AUTHORSHIP AND INTEGRITY.

1. THE former of these is undoubted. No Epistle more clearly marks itself out as the work of the Author whose name it bears. It is inseparably connected with the First, following it up, and only differing from it as circumstances since occurring had affected the mind of the

writer. See this more dwelt on, when I speak of its style and matter, below, § iii.

2. The external testimonies are,

(α) Irenæus, Hær. iii. 7. 1, p. 182 :

Quod autem dicunt, aperte Paulum in secunda ad Corinthios dixisse : In quibus Deus sæculi hujus excæcavit mentes infidelium.

(β) Athenagoras, de resurr. mort. xviii. p. 331 :

εὔδηλον παντὶ τὸ λειπόμενον . . . . ἕκαστος κομίσηται δικαίως ἃ διὰ τοῦ σώματος ἔπραξεν, εἴτε ἀγαθὰ εἴτε κακά.

(γ) Clement of Alexandria very frequently cites our epistle : e. g., Strom. iii. 14 (94), p. 553, P. :

αὐτίκα βιάζεται τὸν Παῦλον ἐκ τῆς ἀπάτης τὴν γένεσιν συνιστάναι. λέγειν διὰ τούτων· φοβοῦμαι δὲ μή, ὡς ὁ ὄφις Εὔαν ἐξηπάτησεν, κ.τ.λ. (2 Cor. xi. 3.)

And again, Strom. iv. 16 (102), p. 607, P. :

ὁ ἀπόστολος (specified as Παῦλος previously) . . . . ειρηκεν ἐν τῇ δευτέρᾳ πρὸς τοὺς Κορινθίους· ἄχρι γὰρ τῆς σήμερον ἡμέρας τὸ αὐτὸ κάλυμμα τοῖς πολλοῖς ἐπὶ τῇ ἀναγνώσει τῆς παλαιᾶς διαθήκης μένει.

(δ) Tertullian, de Pudicitia, ch. 13 init. vol. ii. p. 1003:

Novimus plane et hic suspiciones eorum. Revera enim suspicantur apostolum Paulum in secunda ad Corinthios eidem fornicatori veniam dedisse, quem in prima dedendum Satanæ in interitum carnis pronuntiarit, &c. He then cites 2 Cor. ii. 5—11.

See more testimonies in Davidson, vol. ii. p. 279.

3. The *integrity* of this Epistle has not however been unquestioned. Semler (in 1767) imagined it to consist of three separate epistles,—(1) chapters i. to viii. + Rom. xvi. 1 to 20 + ch. xiii. 11 to 13. This he supposes to have been the letter which Titus bore on his second mission to Corinth. (2) On receiving intelligence of the effect produced at Corinth, the Apostle writes a second Epistle in justification of himself, chap. x. 1 to xiii. 10. (3) An Epistle sent to the other churches in Achaia on the subject of the collection for the saints at Jerusalem, ch. ix. To this curious theory a convincing refutation was furnished by Gabler (De capp. ult. ix.—xiii. poster. ep. P. ad Corr. ab eadem haud separandis, Gotting. 1782). Weber again (de numero Epp. P. ad Corr. rectius constituendo, 1798) thought it had been originally *two* Epistles, (1) chapters i. to ix. + xiii. 11 to 13,—(2) ch. x. 1 to xiii. 10. But Meyer (from whom the foregoing particulars are taken) quotes respecting all such fanciful discussions a good remark of Hug (Einl. ii. p. 376), that it would be just as reasonable to suppose the περὶ στεφάνου of Demosthenes to be two orations, because in the former part the orator defends himself calmly and in detail, and in the latter breaks out into fierce and bitter invective. Certainly, on the principle which these critics have adopted, the first Epistle to the Corinthians might be divided into at least eight separate epistles, marked off by the successive changes of subject.

SECTION II.

CIRCUMSTANCES, PLACE, AND TIME OF WRITING.

1. At the time of writing this Epistle, Paul had recently left Asia (2 Cor. i. 8): in doing so had come by Troas (ii. 12): and thence had sailed to Macedonia (ibid.; cf. Acts xx. 1, 2), where he still was (ch. viii. 1; ix. 2, where notice especially the *present* καυχῶμαι,—ix. 4). In Asia, he had undergone some great peril of his life (2 Cor. i. 8, 9), which (see note there) can hardly be referred to the tumult at Ephesus (Acts xix. 23—41 [1],—but from the nature of his expressions was probably a grievous sickness, not unaccompanied with deep and wearing anxiety. At Troas, he had expected to meet Titus (2 Cor. ii. 13), with intelligence respecting the effect produced at Corinth by the first Epistle. In this he was disappointed (ii. 13), but the meeting took place in Macedonia (vii. 5, 6), where the expected tidings were announced to him (vii. 7—16). They were for the most part favourable, but not altogether. All who were well disposed had been humbled by his reproofs: but evidently his adversaries had been further embittered. He wished to express to them the comfort which the news of their submission had brought to him, and at the same time to defend his apostolic efficiency and personal character against the impugners of both. Under these circumstances, and with these objects, he wrote this Epistle, and sent it before him to break the severity with which he contemplated having to act against the rebellious (ch. xiii. 10), by winning them over if possible before his arrival.

2. The *place* of writing is no where clearly pointed out. There is no ground for supposing it to have been Philippi, as commonly imagined [2]. Nay such a supposition is of itself improbable. In ch. viii. 1 Paul announces to the Corinthians the generosity which had been the result of God's grace given ἐν ταῖς ἐκκλησίαις τῆς Μακεδονίας. It is hardly likely that he would make such announcement, if he had hitherto been stationary at Philippi, the *first* of those churches on his way from Asia. All that we can say is, that the Epistle was written at one of the Macedonian churches; more probably at the last which he visited than at the first. The principal of those churches were at Philippi, Thessalonica, and Berœa. We know from 1 Thess. ii. 17, 18, how anxious the Apostle was again to visit the Thessalonian church: and in the absence of all detail

[1] I cannot help being surprised that any one who has studied the character and history of the Apostle should still refer this passage to that tumult. The supposition lays to his charge a meanness of spirit and cowardice, which certainly never characterized him, and to avow which would have been in the highest degree out of place in an Epistle, one object of which was to vindicate his apostolic efficiency.

[2] The common subscription assigns Philippi: but whether from tradition, or mere hasty inference, is quite uncertain.

respecting this journey in Acts xx. 1, 2, we may well believe that he would have spent some time at Thessalonica. If then Philippi from its situation is improbable, it would seem likely that Thessalonica was the place. But all is conjecture, beyond the fact that it was written from Macedonia.

3. The *time* of writing is fixed within very narrow limits. About Pentecost A.D. 57 (see chronological table in Prolegg. to Acts) Paul left Ephesus for Troas : there he stayed some little time : thence went to Macedonia ; and sufficient time had elapsed for him to have ascertained the mind of the Macedonian churches and to have made the collection. Here falls in our Epistle : after which (Acts xx. 2) he came into Greece (Corinth) and abode there three months : and then is found, after travelling by land through Macedonia, at Philippi on his return at Easter, 58. So that the Epistle was written in the summer or autumn of 57.

4. Two questions belong to this part of our subject, which it is not very easy to answer. From 1 Cor. iv. 17, we learn that Timotheus had been sent to Corinth by Paul (see also Acts xix. 22, where he is said to have been sent with Erastus to Macedonia) to prepare the Corinthians for his own coming by reminding them of his ways and teaching. And in 1 Cor. xvi. 10, 11, we find directions given to them for their reception of Timotheus and speeding his return : "for," adds the Apostle, "I expect him with the brethren." Here, however, some little uncertainty is expressed as to his visiting them, the words being ἐὰν δὲ ἔλθῃ Τιμόθεος. Now at the time of writing this second Epistle, we find Timotheus with Paul in Macedonia (2 Cor. i. 1), without any hint given of his having been at Corinth, or of any tidings respecting the church there having come through him. Nay there is an apparent presumption that he had not been at Corinth : for in 2 Cor. xii. 18 where speaking of those whom he had sent to Corinth he mentions Titus by name, no allusion is made to Timotheus. Had he been at Corinth, or not ?

I believe, in spite of these apparent obstacles to the view, that he *had been* there. The purpose of his mission, as stated in 1 Cor. iv. 17, is too plain and precise to have been lightly given up. And, as Meyer suggests, the relinquishing of the intended journey of Timotheus as well as that of the Apostle, would have furnished to the adversaries another ground for the charge of fickleness of purpose, which they would not fail to use against him. Had therefore the journey been abandoned, some notice and apology would probably have been found in this Epistle. That Timotheus is not mentioned in this Epistle as having gone to them, is easily accounted for by the circumstance that he is associated with the Apostle in the writing of the Epistle.

Meyer believes that tidings had been brought by him from Corinth of an unfavourable kind respecting the effect of the first Epistle ; and that the state of the Apostle's mind described in 2 Cor. ii. 12, vii. 5, is to be traced to the reception of these tidings, not merely to the anxiety of suspense.

5. The second question regards the *mission of Titus* to Corinth, which took place subsequently to our first Epistle, and on the return from which he brought to the Apostle the further tidings of the effect of that letter, referred to 2 Cor. vii. 6. The most natural supposition is that he was sent to ascertain this matter: and this is the view of De Wette and others. Bleek however, with whom agree Credner, Olshausen, and Neander, makes a totally different hypothesis, which is thus expressed by the latter, Pfl. u. Leit. p. 437: "Timotheus had brought to the Apostle painful tidings which excited his anxiety, especially respecting the agitation caused by one individual, who insolently set himself against Paul and endeavoured to oppose his apostolic authority. (This latter view he defends by explaining 2 Cor. ii. 5, vii. 12, not of the incestuous person of 1 Cor. v. but of some adversary of the Apostle.) On this account Paul sent Titus to Corinth with a letter (now lost), in which he expressed himself very strongly on these circumstances; so that after Titus had set out, his heart, full as it was of paternal love towards the Corinthian church, was distressed with fear lest he had written somewhat too harshly, and been too severe upon them." This ingenious conjecture, while it might serve to clear up some expressions in 2 Cor. ii. 1—4, which seem too strong for the first Epistle, can perhaps hardly be admitted in the absence of any allusion whatever of a clearer character. All we can say is, it *may* have been so: and after all that has been written on the visits of Timotheus and Titus, we shall hardly arrive nearer the truth than a happy conjecture.

SECTION III.

MATTER AND STYLE.

1. In no other Epistle are these so various, and so rapidly shifting from one character to another. Consolation and rebuke, gentleness and severity, earnestness and irony, succeed one another at very short intervals and without notice. Meyer remarks: "The excitement and interchange of the affections, and probably also the haste under which Paul wrote this Epistle, certainly render the expressions often obscure and the constructions difficult, but serve only to exalt our admiration of the great oratorical delicacy, art, and power, with which this outpouring of Paul's spirit, especially interesting as a self-defensive apology, flows and streams onward, till at length in the sequel its billows completely overflow the opposition of the adversaries. Erasmus strikingly says, Paraphr. Dedicat.,—'Sudatur ab eruditissimis viris in explicandis poetarum ac rhetorum consiliis, at in hoc rhetore longe plus sudoris est, ut depre-

hendas quid agat, quo tendat, quid vetet : adeo stropharum plenus est undique, absit invidia verbis. Tanta vafrities est, non credas eundem hominem loqui. Nunc ut limpidus quidam fons sensim ebullit, mox torrentis in morem ingenti fragore devolvitur, multa obiter secum rapiens, nunc placide leniterque fluit, nunc late, velut in lacum diffusus, exspatiatur. Rursum alicubi se condit, ac diverso loco subitus emicat, cum visum est, miris mæandris nunc has nunc illas lambit ripas, aliquoties procul digressus, reciprocato flexu in sese redit.' We may also apply to our Epistle the words in which Dionys. Hal., de admiranda vi dicendi in Demosthene, c. 8, designates the style of that orator,—μεγαλοπρεπῆ, λιτήν· περιττήν, ἀπέριττον· ἐξηλλαγμένην, συνήθη· πανηγυρικήν, ἀληθινήν· αὐστηρήν, ἱλαράν· σύντονον, ἀνειμένην· ἡδεῖαν, πικράν· ἠθικήν, παθητικήν."

2. The matter of the Epistle divides itself naturally into three parts :

1. ch. i. to vii. 16. Here he *sets forth to them his apostolic walk and character*, not only with regard to *them*, though he frequently refers to this, but *in general*.

2. viii. 1 to ix. 15. He *reminds them of their duty to complete the collection for the poor saints at Jerusalem*.

3. x. 1 to xiii. 10. *Polemical justification of his apostolic dignity and efficiency* against his disparagers.

CHAPTER V.

APPARATUS CRITICUS.

SECTION I.

1. *Manuscripts written in uncial letters.*

A. The CODEX ALEXANDRINUS, Cent. V. (*See Vol. I.*)

B. The CODEX VATICANUS, Cent. IV. (*See Vol. I.*)

C. The CODEX EPHRÆMI, Cent. V. (*See Vol. I.*)

D. (*Of the Acts.*) The CODEX BEZÆ, Cent. V. or VI. (*See Vol. I.*)

D. (*Of St. Paul's Epistles.*) The CODEX CLAROMONTANUS in the Imperial library at Paris, No. 107 : a græco-latin MS., of, as Tischendorf believes, the *sixth century*. It contains all the Epistles of Paul, except Rom. i. 1 παυλος . . . . to αγαπητοις θεου, ver. 7. Another hand, but an ancient one, has supplied 1 Cor. xiv. 13 διο ο λαλων . . . to σημειον εισιν, ver. 22. Similarly Rom. i. 27—30. Tischendorf remarks : "It is very difficult to distinguish the correctors who have at different times touched this codex. The second corrector (D^{3}, about the eighth century), whom I have oftenest cited, found most of the passages which he touched already corrected : hence D^{3} denotes generally two persons, of whom the former (D^{3a}) seldom differs from the latter (D^{3b}), so that the difference can be noted. D^2 touched a few places, and correctors subsequent to D^3 about as many. Sometimes when it is hard to say which has corrected, I have marked it D^{corr}." This codex was published by Tischendorf in 1852. "It is one of the most valuable MSS. extant: none of the texts published by Tischendorf is so important, with the single exception of the palimpsest Codex Ephræmi."—Tregelles. Horne's Introd. iv. p. 193[1].

E. (*Of the Acts.*) The CODEX LAUDIANUS (græco-latin: the latin being in the left hand column, the greek in the right hand) in the Bodleian library at Oxford. It is written without accents, in rather clumsy uncial letters, by a Greek scholar, but probably among the Latins. Its place of writing has been imagined to have been Sardinia, from the preamble of an edict, which is written at the end: *Φλαύιος Παγκράτιος σὺν θεῷ ἀποεπάρχων δοὺξ Σαρδινίας δῆλα ποιῶ τὰ ὑποτεταγμένα*: but this, as Dr. Tregelles remarks, only shews it to have been in that island during the period of the *duces.* Now the Duces of Sardinia were first constituted by Justinian in 534 (Wetst.): and if, as Michaelis infers from the writing (see also Marsh's note), the MS. is more ancient than this Dux Sardiniæ, its date might be at the earliest the end of the fifth or beginning of the sixth century. But Bp. Marsh (note, as above) has shewn by the writing that it is more recent than the Codex Bezæ: which circumstance, if the date now usually assigned to the Codex Bezæ be correct (the middle of the sixth century), would bring it down about a century later. It was brought to England from Sardinia, became, it is supposed by Wetstein, the property of the Venerable Bede, as it, and no other Greek MS., contains the various readings which he has noted in his commentary in the Acts. It was lost sight of for a long time, till Abp. Laud became its possessor, and gave it to the Bodleian library. Michaelis characterizes it as a MS. of the utmost importance, and ascribes to it the merit of having decided him against the notion that the græco-latin MSS. have been corrupted from the latin. See Michaelis, Marsh's ed. vol. ii. pt. i. pp. 269—274; Horne's Introd. vol. iv. pp. 187—189, where there is a facsimile of the greek and latin of this MS. It was published by Hearne in 1715, but the edn. is very scarce, only 120 copies having been printed. Tischendorf has re-examined the MS. and is going to republish it[2].

(E. (*Of St. Paul's Epistles.*) The CODEX SANGERMANENSIS, now Petropolitanus (having been rescued from the fire of the abbey of

[[1] The text of this MS. as well as those of the preceding is exhibited in "Novum Testamentum Græce, Oxonii 1864," referred to in the foot-note on ℵ in Proleg. to Vol. I. ch. vii. § i. p. 116.]

[[2] The MS. was published by Tischendorf in 1870 in Monumenta Sacra inedita, Nova Collectio, Vol. IX.]

St. Germain near Paris and taken to St. Petersburg), appears to be only a copy, and that a faulty one, of D, the Codex Claromontanus, with its occasional corrections. It abounds with mistakes, and has some monstrous readings made up of the various corrections of D: Tischendorf instances *δικαιωσινην*, Rom. iv. 25; *μετα ταυειτα τοις δωενδεκα*, 1 Cor. xv. 5; *νιδιζομενο θεατριζομενοι*, Heb. x. 38. "Probably not older than the *ninth* or *tenth century*." (Tregelles.) Only quoted in the lacunæ of D.)

F. The CODEX AUGIENSIS, now in the library of Trinity College, Cambridge. It is a græco-latin MS., which formerly belonged to the Monastery of Augia Major in Switzerland, and was probably written in the latter half of the *ninth century* (Tregelles thinks, the *eighth*). Published by Scrivener in 1859.

[G. (*Of the Acts.*) FRAGMENTUM PETROPOLITANUM, brought from the East by Tischendorf in 1859: contains Acts ii. 45—iii. 8. Of the *seventh century*.]

G. [*Of St. Paul's Epistles.*] The CODEX BOERNERIANUS, also a græco-latin MS., now in the Royal library at Dresden. This MS., which was also written in the *ninth century*, has a singular affinity with the Codex Augiensis, without being a copy of it. "It may be deemed certain that the Greek of each of these MSS. was a copy (mediate or immediate) of a more ancient codex; from which the copyist of each of these departed at times by mere error. The general description of the Codex Sangallensis (Δ of the Gospels) applies equally to this MS., to which it was once joined: and whatever shews the history of the one will apply equally to that of the other. . . . . This MS. of course is not a distinct authority from F as to the readings of St. Paul's Epistles: *together*, however, they are valuable as a united testimony to the readings of the ancient and valuable codex from which they must have alike sprung." (Tregelles.) In this edition we have only quoted this MS. when it differs from F, or when F is defective.

H. (*Of the Acts.*) "The Codex Mutinensis 196 [ii. G 3[3]]: of the ninth century. It begins ch. v. 28, *και βουλεσθαι*: is deficient from *αι χηραι*, ch. ix. 39, to *ιδου*, ch. x. 19: from *ιδια*, xiii. 36, to *τερατα*, xiv. 3. From *κακειθεν*, xxvii. 4, to the end, is supplied in uncial letters by some hand of about the eleventh century. The other omissions have been supplied by a more recent hand, in the fifteenth or sixteenth century." It was collated by Scholz, and since then more completely by Tischendorf and by Tregelles.

H. (*Of St. Paul's Epistles.*) The CODEX COISLINIANUS No. 202 in the Royal library at Paris, apparently (Tischdf.) of the *sixth century*.

[[3] This correction, with several in the list of cursive mss., is taken from Dean Burgon's letters on "Manuscript Evangelia in Foreign Libraries," published in the Guardian Newspaper, 1873, 4.]

It once contained 14 leaves, but, as is noted in the codex itself,—"post incendium librorum impressorum et subitaneam translationem manuscriptorum non inventa sunt nisi xii folia." The two missing leaves are in the Imperial library at St. Petersburg. [Four more were found in the collection of Porphyrius Antonius by Tischdf., who identifies as a portion of this MS., Matthæi's Frag. Mosq. (Heb. x. 1—7, 32—38).] Edited by Montfaucon and accurately transcribed by Tischendorf.

I. Fragmenta Palimpsesta Tischendorfiana, Cent. V. to VII. (*See Vol. I.*)

K. Codex Mosquensis, Library of the Holy Synod No. xcviii. Cent. IX. (Matthæi's g). Formerly belonged to the monastery of St. Dionysius on Mount Athos. Contains the Catholic Epistles with a catena and the Epistles of Paul with scholia by Damascene. It is on parchment and in folio. Each page is divided into two columns; the text being written in large square uncials ; the commentary, in round letters joined to one another. Collated by Matthæi, who gives a facsimile of part of the text in the volume of his Gr. Test. which contains the Cath. Epistles, and describes it in that containing the Ep. to Rom. pp. 265-7. Scholz inserted this MS. by mistake in his list of *Cursives*, as Acts 102, Epp. Paul 117.

L. Codex Angelicus Romanus, a MS. in the Angelican library of Augustinian monks at Rome, formerly the property of Cardinal Passionei. It contains the Acts, beginning viii. 10, *μις του θεου*,—the Catholic Epistles, and the Epistles of Paul to Heb. xiii. 10. "It cannot have been written," says Tischendorf, "before the middle of the *ninth century*." Formerly called G of the Acts—J of St. Paul's Epistles.

M. The Codex Uffenbachianus, Cent. X. Consists of fragments at Hamburg and in the British Museum. The former contains the beginning and end of the *Epistle to the Hebrews*. Published by Tischendorf in his "Anecdota Sacra et Profana."

[O. Fragmentum Petropolitanum. Contains 2 Cor. i. 20—ii. 12. Cited from Tischdf. N. T. ed. 8.]

P. Codex Porphyrianus, Cent. IX. Published by Tischendorf, who found it in the possession of the Russian Archimandrite Porfiri, Monumenta Sacra inedita, Voll. V. VI. It contains the Acts, Epistles, and Apocalypse. The Acts has been collated for this edition, and the readings in 1 and 2 Cor. taken from Tregelles.

[Q. Fragmenta quædam. Cent. V. Only cited on 1 Cor. vi. 14; vii. 3, 13.

R. A fragment cited by Tischdf. on 2 Cor. xi. 14—18.]

א The Codex Sinaiticus, Cent. IV. (See Vol. I.)

Frag. Coisl. In the scholia of a MS. of part of the O. T. in the Benedictine library at St. Germain, Wetstein found Acts ix. 24, 25, written by the transcriber of the MS., i. e. in the beginning of the seventh century. To this discovery Tischendorf has added several more passages; ch. iv. 33, 34: x. 13, 15: xxii. 22, and some from the Gospels. The MS. itself is called the Codex Coislinianus 1, from Coislin, Bp. of Metz, its earliest known possessor. See Wetstein, Michaelis, and Tischendorf.

Frag. Tischdf. (*See* "I." *above.*)

2. *Manuscripts written in cursive letters.*

NOTE.—It is intended to include in this Table mention of those MSS. only which contain, and of those particulars which concern, the portion of the N. T. comprehended in this Volume. The missing numbers will be found in the Prolegomena to Vol. IV., pt. ii.; those in the Acts column being designated Cath., and those in the Paul column Heb.

a. Lambeth No. 1182. "Dates from the *twelfth century* at the earliest[4]."

b. Lambeth No. 1183. Written A.D. 1358.

c. A manuscript once in the possession of Professor Carlyle; returned to the Patriarch of Jerusalem in 1817. It was numbered 1184 in the Lambeth Catalogue. Mr. Scrivener gives its readings from "a scholarlike and seemingly accurate collation of it with the Greek text of Mill, made by the Rev. W. Sanderson of Morpeth, in or about the year 1804." Ascribed to the *fifteenth century.*

d. Lambeth No. 1185. "Might also be considered a series of fragments in several different hands[4]." Assigned to the *fifteenth century* or somewhat earlier.

e. in Acts, Lambeth 1255. Contains Acts and Past. Epp.—in Paul, (= a. of the Apocalypse,) Lambeth No. 1186. Contains the Pauline Epistles and the Apocalypse. *Eleventh century.*

f. Codex Theodori. Bears date A.D. 1295

g. Codex Wordsworthianus. *Thirteenth century.*

h. (= b. of the Apocalypse.) Codex Butler 2. British Museum, Additional MS. No. 11837. It bears date A.D. 1157[5].

k. Trin. Coll. Cantab. B. x. 16. Written A.D. 1316.

l. (Scholz's Act. 24, Paul. 29.) Chr. Coll. Cantab. F. i. 13. Written about the end of the *twelfth century.*

[4] Scrivener. The readings of mss. "a" to "o" are cited from the Appendix to Mr. Scrivener's edn. of the "Codex Augiensis." It has not been thought worth while to encumber the page with every various reading found in these manuscripts; but whenever any variation of the uncials is mentioned, the testimony of these accurately collated documents is added.

[5] Formerly Cod. Prædicatorum S. Marci 701.

m. Scholz's Act. 31, Paul. 37.) CODEX LEICESTRENSIS. Cited as "69" in the Gospels, and as "f" in the Apocalypse. (*See Vol. I.*)

n. (Scholz's Act. 53, Paul. 30.) Emm. Coll. Cantab. i. 4. 35. Of about the *twelfth century*.

o. (Scholz's Act. 61 and 111, Paul. 61 and 221.) University Library, Cambridge, Mm. 6. 9. Of the *twelfth* or *thirteenth century*.

p. (Tischendorf's "lo[ti]" [(edn. 7), Tregelles' and Tischdf.'s (edn. 8) 61].) CODEX LONDINENSIS TISCHENDORFIANUS. British Museum, Additional MS. 20,003. "Unquestionably the most valuable cursive MS. of the Acts yet known." (Scriv.) "Can hardly be estimated too highly." (Treg.) "Haud dubie antiquissimi codicis uncialis, qui ipse periit, exemplum est." (Tischdf.)

Acts.	Epp. Paul.	Designation.	Cent.	Collator, &c.	Gosp.	Apoc.
1	1	Reuchlini. Basle K. iii. 3 (late B. vi. 27).	X.	Wetstein "bis atque accurate."	1	—
2	2	Basle (late B. ix. ult.) [A. N. iv. 4. Burgon].	XV.	Mill (*B.* 2).	—	—
3	3	Corsendoncensis. Vienna, Theol. 5. (Kol.)	XII.	Walker and Alter.	3	—
4	4	Basle (late B. x. 20) [A. N. iv 5].	XV.	Mill (*B.* 3). Wetstein throughout Epp. [Written by several hands.]	—	—
5	5	Paris 106 (formerly 2871).	XII.	Stephens (δ′) Wetst. Scholz.	5	—
6	6	Paris 112 (formerly 3425).	XIII.	Steph. (ϵ′) Wetst.	6	—
..	7	Basle (late B. vi. 17) [A. N. iii. 11].	X ?	Readings given in Wetstein. Text surrounded by various Scholia from Gennad., Œc., Sevrn., &c. On parchment.	—	—
..	[8]	. . . .	—	Steph. (ζ′) = Acts 50. *Identified by some with* 132 (Paul) *below*.	—	—
7	9	Paris 102 (formerly 2870).	X.	Steph. (ι′) Wetst.	—	—
(8)	(10)	*Not identified.*	—	Stephens (ια′).	—	—
9	11	Cambridge Univ. Lib. MS. Kk. 6. 4 (also numbered Acts 112, Paul 225).	XI.	Steph. (ιγ′) Wetst. (Def. Acts iii. 6—17.)	—	—
10	12	Paris 237 (formerly 2869).	X.	Steph. (ιϵ′) Wetst. "de integro."	—	2
11	..	Paris 103 (formerly 2872).	X.	Wetstein (Acts). Reiche (Paul). (Def. Acts ii. 20—31; 1 Cor. xii. 17—xiii. 2.) = Paul 140.	—	—
—	(13)	*See Vol. III.*	—			
..	(14)	*See Vol. III.* (= Acts 47.)	XVI.		90	—
—	(15)	*See Vol. III.*	—			
12	16	Paris 219 (formerly 1886).	XI.	Wetstein.	—	4
13	17	Paris 14 (COLBERTINUS 2844).	XI.	Tregelles.	33	—
14	18	Paris, Coislinianus 199.	XI.	Wetstein.	35	17
15	—	Paris, Coislinianus 25.	XI.	Wetstein.		
16	19	Paris, Coislinianus 26.	XI.	Wetstein.		
—	20	Paris, Coisl. 27 (formerly 247).	X.	Wetstein. (mutilated.)		
17	21	Paris, Coislinianus 205.	XI.	Wetstein. (1 Cor. xvi. 17—2 Cor. i. 7, &c., supplied in a later hand.)	—	19
18	22	Paris, Coislinianus 202 A.	XIII.	Wetstein.	—	18
19	23	Paris, Coislinianus 200.	XIII.	Steph. (θ′) Wetst.	38	—
..	24	Bodleian, Misc. 136. Ebnerianus.	XII.	Described by Schœnleben, occasionally quoted by Wetstein. = Acts 48.	105	—

Acts.	Epp. Paul.	Designation.	Cent.	Collator, &c.	Gosp.	Apoc.
20	25	Westmonasteriensis (935). British Museum. King's Library i. B. 1.	XIV.	Wetstein.		
21	26	Cambridge Univ. Lib. MS. Dd. 11. 90.	XIII.	(Def. Acts i.—xii. 1; xiv. 23—xv. 10; Rom. xv. 14—16, 24—26; xvi. 4—20; 1 Cor. i. 15—iii. 12, &c.)	—	—
22	..	British Museum Additional MSS. 5115-7.	1326?	(Epp., Cent. xii., Scrivener) "Obiter inspectus a Wetstenio. Lectiones cap. xx. Act. mecum communicavit Rev. Paulus." (Griesbach.) = Paul 75.	109	—
23	28	Bodleian, Baroccianus 3.	XIII.	Mill (*Baroc.*). (Def. up to Acts xi. 13.) 1 Cor. xv. collated by Griesb.	—	6
24	29	*See above*, "l."				
..	30	*See above*, "n."				
25	31	Brit. Mus. Harleian 5537.	1087	Mill. (*Cov.* 2.) Acts xiv.—xviii. Rom. i.—iv. collated by Griesb.	—	7
26	32	Brit. Mus. Harl. 5557.	XII.	Mill. (*Cov.* 3) Readings of Acts i.—iii. in Griesb. (Def. Acts i. 1—11; 1 Cor. xi. 7—xv. 56.)	—	—
27	33	Brit. Mus. Harl. 5620.	XV.	Mill. (*Cov.* 4.) Perhaps a copy of 29.		
28	34	Brit. Mus. Harl. 5778.	XII.	Mill. (*Sin.*) (Def. Acts i. 1—20.)	—	d
29	35	Geneva 20.	XII.	Mill. (*Genev.*)		
30	36	Bodleian, Misc. 74.	XII	Mill. (*Hunt.* 1.) Begins Acts xv. 19. "Perlegi Rom. v., viii.; 1 Cor. xv. . . ." (Griesbach).	—	9
31	37	*See above*, "m."				
32	38	Bodleian, Laud. 31.	XIII.	Mill. (*Laud.* 2.) Rom. i.—v. reexamined by Griesb.	51	—
33	39	Lincoln Coll. Oxford, 82.	XI.	Mill. (*Lin.* 2.) Acts collated by Dobbin. (Def. Rom. i. 1—20.)	—	—
34	40	Trin. Coll. Dublin. Montfortianus.	XVI.	Barrett and Dobbin.	61	92
35	41	Magdalen Coll. Oxford, 9.	XI.	Mill. (*Magd.* 1.)	57	—
36	—	New Coll. Oxford, 58.	XIII.	Mill. (*N.* 1.) Apparently the MS. from which Cramer's Catena is printed.		
—	(42)	Magdalen Coll. Oxford. *Has been ascertained to be part of the same MS. as* Paul 27. *See Vol. III.*	XI.	Mill. (*Magd.* 2.) Contains only Rom. Corr.		
37	43	New Coll. Oxford, 59.	XIII.	Mill. (*N.* 2.)	—	—
38	44	Leyden 77, Voss.	XIII.	Sarrau. Mill's *Pet.* 1. Wetstein.		
(39)	(45)	*Situation unknown.*	—	Sarrau. Mill's *Pet.* 2. Belonged (with *Pet.* 1 and 3) to Paul Petavius. (Def. Acts i. 1—xviii. 22; 1 Cor. iii. 16—x. 13.)	—	11
40	46	Vatican Alex. 179.	XI.	Zacagni and Birch. Mill's *Pet.* 3.	—	12
41	..	Vatican 2080.	XII.	Inspected by Birch and Scholz. = Paul 194.	175	20
—	47	Bodleian, Roe. [16[6], not] 2.	XII.	Mill. Treg. Rom. and 1 Cor. xiv., collated by Griesbach.		

[[6] This correction is due to the Rev. W. D. Macray, of the Bodleian Library, who states that the ms. was brought from Turkey by Sir Thomas Roe, and given by him to the Library in 1628. Several readings have been verified for this edition, some by Mr. Macray, others by Mr. E. D. Hake of Ch. Ch.]

Acts.	Epp. Paul.	Designation.	Cent.	Collator, &c.	Gosp.	Apoc.
42	48	Frankfort on the Oder. Seidelianus.	XI.	Middeldorpf, in Rosenmüller's Comm. Theol. (Def. Acts ii. 3–34.)	—	13
43	49	Vienna. Theol. 300 (Nessel.).	XII.	Mill. (*Vien.*) and Alter.	76	—
..	(50)	*See Vol. III.*				
(44)	(51)	*See Vol. III.*				
45	52	Hamburg. Uffenbachianus.	XV.	Wetstein and Bengel.	—	16
(46)	..	Munich 375 (= Paul 55).	XI.	Bengel (Aug. 6). Œc.'s comm. (Does not contain the Acts.)	—	—
—	53	*See above,* "M."				
—	54	Munich 412 (formerly Augsburg 5).	XII.	Bengel. (Contains only Rom. vii. 7—xvi. 24.)		
(47)	..	*The same MS. as* Paul 14 *above.*				
48	..	*The same MS. as* Paul 24 *above.*				
..	55	*The same MS. as* Acts 46 *above.*				
—	(56)	*See Vol. III.*				
..	57	Vienna. Theol. 23 (Nessel.).	XIII.	Edited by Alter. = Acts 65.	218	33
(50)	..	*The same MS. as* Paul 8 *above.*				
—	58	Vatican 165.	XII.	Edited by Zacagni. Called Cryptoferratensis.	—	—
—	59	Paris Coisl. 204.	XI.	Inspected. Catena.	—	—
—	(60)	*See Vol. III.*				
..	61	*See above,* "o."		Mill's *Hal.*		
51	..	Paris 56.	XII.	Inspected by Scholz. = Paul 133.	—	52
(52)	..	*The same MS. as* Paul 50 *above.*				
53	..	*See above,* "n."				
54	..	Paris, Arsenal 4.	XI.	Inspected by Simon and Scholz. = Paul 130.	43	—
56	..	Bodleian, Clark 4.	XII.	Inspected by Scholz. = Paul 227.		
57	..	Copenhagen 1.	1278	Hensler in Birch. = Paul 72.	234	—
58	..	Bodleian, Clark 9.	XIII.	Inspected by Scholz. = Paul 224.	—	—
59	62	Brit. Mus. Harl. 5588.	XIII.	Acts xi. xii. xiii., Rom. and 1 Cor. i.—vii., collated by Griesbach.		
60	63	Brit. Mus. Harl. 5613.	1407	Acts i.—viii., Rom., 1 Cor., 2 Cor. iii.,—collated by Griesbach.	—	e
61[7]	..	*See above,* "o."				
..	(64)	*See above,* "M."				
62	65	Paris 60.	XIV.	Inspected by Griesbach and Scholz.		
—	(66)	*See Vol. III.*				
..	67	Vienna. Theol. 302 (Nessel.).	XII.	Alter and Birch. = Acts 66.	—	34
63	68	Vienna. Theol. 313 (Nessel.).	XIII.	Alter and Birch.		
64	69	Vienna. Theol. 303 (Nessel.).	XIII.	Alter and Birch.		
65	..	*The same MS. as* Paul 57 *above.*				
66	..	*The same MS. as* Paul 67 *above.*				
67	70	Vienna. Theol. 221 (Nessel.).	1331	Alter and Birch.		
—	71	Vienna. Theol. 10 (Kollar).	XII.	Alter and Birch. [Def. Rom. i. 1—9, &c.]		
..	72	*The same MS. as* Acts 57 *above.*				
68	73	Upsala, Sparwenfeld 42.	XII.	(2 Cor. XIth cent.) Aurivillius. (Def. up to Acts viii. 14. 1 Cor. xiii. 6—xv. 38 twice over.)	—	—
69	74	Wolfenbüttel xvi. 7.	XII.	Knittel. in Matthæi.	—	30
..	75	*The same MS. as* Acts 22 *above.*				

[7 This number is assigned by Tischendorf (edn. 8) and Tregelles to Scr.'s "p." See above.]

Acts.	Epp. Paul.	Designation.	Cent.	Collator, &c.	Gosp.	Apoc.
—	76	Leipsic.	XIII.	Matthæi. Contains Rom., 1 Cor. up to v. 3, . . with Thl.'s comm.		
70	77	Vatican 360.	XI.	"Rom., 1 Cor. i.—iv. accurate examinavi; reliqua cursim modo perlustravi." Birch.	131	66
71	78	Vatican 363.	XI.	Birch (cursorily inspected).	133	—
72	79	Vatican 366.	XIII.	Birch (cursorily inspected).	—	37
73	80	Vatican 367.	XI.	Birch ("Per omnia contuli")	—	—
74	—	Vatican 760.	XII.	A MS. of the Acts inspected by Birch and Scholz. Catena.	—	—
—	81	Vatican 761.	XII.	Inspected by Birch. Œc.'s comm.	—	—
—	82	Vatican 762.	XII.	Inspected by Birch. Contains Rom., Corr., with Catena.	—	—
—	83	Vatican 765.	XI.	Inspected by Birch. Comm. on marg.	—	—
—	84	Vatican 766.	XII.	Inspected by Birch. Comm. on marg.	—	—
—	85	Vatican 1136.	XIII.	Epp. inspected by Birch.	—	39
75	86	Vatican 1160.	XIII.	Inspected by Birch and Scholz.	141	40
76	87	Vatican 1210.	XI.	Birch (Acts, Rom., al. "exacte").	142	—
77	88	Vatican, Palat. 171.	XIV.	Examined in select places by Birch. Zacagni.	149	25
78	89	Vatican, Alex. 29.	XII.	Birch ("Per omnia accurate examinavi"). (Def. 2 Cor. xi. 15—xii. 1.)		
79	90	Vatican, Urb. 3.	XI.	Inspected by Birch.	—	—
80	91	Vatican, Pio 50.	XII.	Birch ("Per omnia diligenter bis collatus").	—	42
81	—	Barberinus 377.	XI.	Inspected by Birch.	—	—
82	92	Rome, Propaganda 250.	1274	Zoega in Birch.	180	44
83	93	Naples 1. B. 12. (*See below* Acts 173, Paul 211.)	XI.	Inspected by Birch.		
84	94	Florence, Laur. Lib. iv. 1.	X.	Inspected by Birch.	—	—
85	95	Florence, Laur. Lib. iv. 5.	XIII.	Inspected by Birch.	—	—
86	96	Florence, Laur. Lib. iv. 20.	XI.	Inspected by Birch.	—	75
87	97	Florence, Laur. Lib. iv. 29.	X.	Inspected by Birch.	—	—
88	98	Florence, Laur. Lib. iv. 31.	XI.	Inspected by Birch.	—	—
89	99	Florence, Laur. Lib. iv. 32.	1093	Inspected by Birch.	—	45
—	100	Florence, Laur. Lib. x. 4.	XII.	Inspected by Birch. Comm.	—	—
—	101	Florence, Laur. Lib. x. 6.	XI.	Inspected by Birch. Comm.	—	—
—	102	Florence, Laur. Lib. x. 7.	XI.	Inspected by Birch. Var. comm.	—	—
—	103	Florence, Laur. Lib. x. 19.	XII.	Inspected by Birch. Catena.	—	—
91	104	*See above*, "h."				
92	105[8]	Bologna, Can. Reg. 640.	XI.	Inspected by Scholz.	204	—
93	106	Venice 5.	XV.	Rinck.	205	88
94	107	Venice 6.	XV.	Rinck.	206	omd.
95	108	Venice 10.	XV.	Rinck.	209	46
96	109	Venice 11.	XI.	Rinck. (Def. Acts i. 1—12; xxv. 21—xxvi. 18.)		
97	—	Wolfenbüttel. Gud. Gr. 104 A.	XII.	(Scholz ?) (Def. Acts xvi. 39—xviii. 18.) = Paul 241.		
98	113	(Moscow ?) (Cod. Stauronicet.)	XI.	Matthæi (a).		
99	114	Moscow 5.	1445	Matthæi (c).		
100	115	Moscow 334.	XI.	Matthæi (d).		
101	116	Moscow 333.	XIII.	Matthæi (f).		

[8 Burgon's memorandum, letter 3, to Rev. F. H. Scrivener, implies that this MS. does not contain any portion of St. Paul's Epistles.]

Acts.	Epp. Paul.	Designation.	Cent.	Collator, &c.	Gosp.	Apoc.
102	117	*The MS. called "K" above.*				
103	118	Moscow 193.	XII.	Matthæi (h). Scholia, but Acts i. 1—ix. 12 given continuously.		
—	119	Moscow 292.	XI.	Matthæi (i). Contains 1 and 2 Cor., with Thl.'s comm.	—	—
104	120	Dresden. (Cod. Matth.)	XI.	Matthæi (k).	241	47
105	121	Moscow 380.	XII.	Matthæi (l).	242	48
106	122	Moscow 328.	XI.	Matthæi (m).		
—	123	Moscow 99.	XI.	Matthæi (n). Scholia.	—	—
—	124	Moscow 250.	XIV.	Matthæi (q). Contains Rom. i.—xiii. with Thl.'s comm.		
(108)	..	Escurial χ. iv. 17.	XI.	Moldenhauer. See Birch, Gospels. = Paul 228.	226	—
(109)	..	Escurial χ. iv. 12.	XIV.	Moldenhauer. See Birch, Gospels. = Paul 229.	228	—
(110)	..	Camb. Univ. Lib. MS. Nn. 5. 27.	—	A folio copy of the Greek Bible printed "Basileæ per Joan. Hervagium 1545." A few notes are written on the margin. = Paul 222.	441	—
(111)	..	*The same MS. as* "o" *and* 61 *above.*				
(112)	..	*The MS. numbered* Acts 9 *above.*				
—	125	Munich 504.	1387	Inspected by Scholz.	—	—
—	126	Munich 455.	XIV.	Inspected by Scholz. Prob. copied from the same MS. as preceding.	—	—
—	(127)	Munich 110.	XVI.	A transcript of Rom. vii. 7—ix. 1, as written in MS. Paul 54.	—	—
..	128	Munich 211.	XI.	Inspected by Scholz. = Acts 179.	—	82
—	129	Munich 35.	XVI.	Inspected by Scholz. Thl.'s comm. (So Hardt.)	—	—
..	130	*The same MS. as* Acts 54 *above.*				
..	131	Paris, Coisl. 196.	XI.	Inspected by Scholz. = Acts 132.	330	—
113	132	Paris 47.	1364	Reiche.	18	51
..	133	*The same MS. as* Acts 51 *above.*				
114	134	Paris 57.	XIII.	Reiche.		
115	135	Paris 58.	XIII.	Inspected by Scholz. (Def. Acts i. 1—xiv. 27.)	—	53
116	136	Paris 59.	XVI.	Inspected by Scholz.	263	—
117	137	Paris 61.	XIII.	Reiche.		
118	138	Paris 101.	XIII.	Parts collated by Scholz. (Def. Acts xix. 8—xxii. 17.)	—	55
119	139	Paris 102 A.	X.	Inspected by Scholz. (Def. 2 Cor. i. 8—ii. 4.)	—	56
..	140	*The same MS. as* Acts 11 *above.*				
120	141	Paris 103 A.	XI.	Scholz. (Def. Acts xxviii. 23—Rom. ii. 26.)	—	—
121	142	Paris 104.	XIII.	Inspected by Scholz.	—	—
122	143	Paris 105.	XI.	Scholz. Contains only (in this vol.) Acts xiii. 48—xv. 22; xv. 29—xvi. 36; xvii. 4—xviii. 26; xx. 16—xxviii. 17; Rom. i. 1—iv. 16.	—	—
123	144	Paris 106 A.	XIV.	Inspected by Scholz.	—	—
—	146	Paris 109.	XVI.	Inspected by Scholz. Contains Rom., 1 Cor.	—	—
—	147	Paris 110.	1511	Inspected by Scholz. Contains 1 and 2 Cor.	—	—

Acts.	Epp. Paul.	Designation.	Cent.	Collator, &c.	Gosp.	Apoc.
124	149	Paris 124.	XVI.	Inspected by Scholz.	—	57
125	150	Paris 125.	XIV.	Inspected by Scholz.		
—	151	Paris 126.	XVI.	Inspected by Scholz.	—	—
126	153	Paris 216.	X.	Inspected by Scholz.		
127	154	Paris 217.	XI.	Inspected by Scholz. Reiche. Thdrt.'s comm. on Epp. Paul.		
128	155	Paris 218.	XI.	Inspected by Scholz. Catena.	—	—
129	156	Paris 220.	XIII.	Inspected by Scholz. Comm., txt often omitted.	—	—
130	—	Paris 221.	XII.	Inspected by Scholz. (Def. Acts xx. 38—xxii. 3.)	—	—
—	157	Paris 222.	XI.	"Coll. magna codicis pars," Scholz. (Def. Rom. i. 1—11, 21—29, iii. 26—iv. 8, ix. 11—22; 1 Cor. xv. 22—43.)	—	—
131	158	Paris 223.	XII.	Inspected by Scholz. (Epistles A.D. 1045.)	—	—
—	159	Paris 224.	XI.	Inspected by Scholz. Catena.	—	64
—	160	Paris 225.	XVI.	Inspected by Scholz. Fragments with Thl.'s comm.	—	—
—	161	Paris 226.	XVI.	Inspected by Scholz. Contains Rom., with comm.	—	—
—	162	Paris 227	XVI.	Inspected by Scholz. Contains 1 Cor. xvi., with Cat.	—	—
—	164	Paris 849.	XVI.	Inspected by Scholz. Thdrt.'s comm., with text on marg.		
132	..	*The same MS. as* Paul 131 *above.*				
133	166	Turin C. i. 40 (285).	XIII.	Scholz, "accurate coll."	—	—
134	167	Turin C. ii. 17 (19).	XI.	Colld. Acts iii.—viii.; Rom. x., seq., by Scholz. (Def. Acts i., ii.)	—	—
—	168	Turin C. ii. 38 (325).	XII.	Inspected by Scholz. Comm. (Def. Rom. i. 1—iii. 19.)	—	—
135	..	Turin C. ii. 5 (302).	XII.	Inspected by Scholz. = Paul 170.	339	83
136	169	Turin C. ii. 31 (1).	XII.	Inspected by Scholz.	—	—
..	170	*The same MS. as* Acts 135 *above.*				
—	171	Ambros. Lib. Milan 6. [B. 6 inf.]	XIII.	Inspected by Scholz. Rom., 1 Cor., 2 Cor. i. 1—v. 19, written by a later hand.	—	—
—	172	Milan 15. [A. 51 sup.?]	XII.	Inspected by Scholz. Comm. after Chr.	—	—
137	..	Milan 97. [E. 97 sup.]	XI.	Inspected by Scholz. = Paul 176.		
138	173	Milan 102. [E. 102 sup.]	XIV.	Inspected by Scholz.	—	—
139	174	Milan 104. [H. 104 sup.]	1434	Inspected by Scholz.	—	—
—	175	Milan 125. [F. 125 sup.]	XV.	Inspected by Scholz. Continuous comm.	—	—
..	176	*The same MS. as* Acts 137 *above.*				
140	..	Venice 546.	XI.	(Part Cent. xiii.) Inspected by Scholz. Catena. = Paul 215.	—	74
141	..	Florence, Laur. Lib. vi. 27.	XII.	Inspected by Scholz. = Paul 239.	189	—
	177	Modena 14. (MS. II. A. 14.)	XV.	Inspected by Scholz.		
142	178	Modena 243. (MS. III. B. 17.)	XII.	Inspected by Scholz.		
	179	Part (written in cursive letters) of the MS. called "H of the Acts."				
144	180	Florence, Laur. Lib. vi. 13.	XIII.	Inspected by Scholz.	363	—
145	181	Florence, Laur. Lib. vi. 36.	XIII.	Inspected by Scholz. [Does not exist. Burgon.]	365	—
146	182	Florence, Laur. Lib. 2708 (?).	1332	Inspected by Scholz.	367	—
147	183	Florence, Laur. Lib. iv. 30.	XII.	Inspected by Scholz.	—	76

Acts.	Epp. Paul.	Designation.	Cent.	Collator, &c.	Gosp.	Apoc.
148	184	Florence, Laur. Lib. 2574 (?).	984	Inspected by Scholz.	—	—
150	..	Florence, Riccardi Lib. 84.	XV.	Inspected by Scholz. = Paul 230 = lect. 37.	368	84
151	..	Vatican, Ottob. 66.	XV.	Inspected by Scholz. = Paul 199.	386	70
(152)	..	Camb. Univ. Lib. MS. Nn. 3. 20, 21.		A copy of the printed Greek Test. 8vo. London, 1728, interleaved and bound up in two volumes; contains MS. notes by John Taylor. = Paul 223.	442	—
153	..	Brit. Mus. Harl. 5796.	XV.	Inspected by Scholz. = Paul 240.	444	—
..	185	Rome, Vallicella Lib. E. 22.	XVI.	Inspected by Scholz. = Acts 167.	393	—
..	186	Rome, Vallicella Lib. F. 17	1330	Inspected by Scholz. = Acts 170.	394	—
154	187	Vatican 1270.	XV.	Inspected by Scholz. Comm. contains (of St. Paul) only Rom., 1 Cor.	—	—
155	188	Vatican 1430.	XII.	Inspected by Scholz.	—	—
—	189	Vatican 1649.	XIII.	Inspected by Scholz. Thdrt.'s comm.	—	—
156	190	Vatican 1650.	1073	Inspected by Scholz. (Def. Acts i. 1—v. 4. Comm. on Epp. Paul.)		
157	191	Vatican 1714.	XII.	Inspected by Scholz. Contains fragments of Acts, Rom., and 1 Cor.	—	—
158	192	Vatican 1761.	XI.	Inspected by Scholz.	—	—
159	—	Vatican 1968.	XI.	"Cursim coll. Cod. integer," Scholz. (Def. Acts i. 1—v. 28, vi. 14—vii. 11.)	—	—
160	193	Vatican 2062.	XI.	Inspected by Scholz. Scholia. Begins Acts xxviii. 19.	—	—
..	194	*The same MS. as* Acts 41 *above.*				
—	195	Vatican, Ottob. 31.	X.	Inspected by Scholz. Comm. (Def. Rom. and greater part of 1 Cor.)	—	—
—	196	Vatican, Ottob. 61.	XV.	Inspected by Scholz.	—	—
—	197	Vatican, Ottob. 176.	XV.	Inspected by Scholz.	—	78
161	198	Vatican, Ottob. 258.	XIII.	Inspected by Scholz. Latin Version. Begins Acts ii. 27.	—	69
..	199	*The same MS. as* Acts 151 *above.*				
162	200	Vatican, Ottob. 298.	XV.	Inspected by Scholz. Latin Version.	—	—
163	201	Vatican, Ottob. 325.	XIV.	Inspected by Scholz. (Def. Acts iv. 19—v. 1.)		
—	202	Vatican, Ottob. 356.	XV.	Inspected by Scholz. Contains Rom. with Catena.	—	—
164	203	Vatican, Ottob. 381.	1252	Inspected by Scholz.	390	71
166	204	Rome, Vallicella Lib. B. 86.	XIII.	Inspected by Scholz.	—	22
167	..	*The same MS. as* Paul 185 *above.*				
168	205	Rome, Vallicella Lib. F. 13.	XIV.	Inspected by Scholz.	—	—
169	206	Rome, Ghigi Lib. R. v. 29.	1394	Inspected by Scholz.	—	—
—	207	Rome, Ghigi Lib. R. v. 32.	XV.	Inspected by Scholz. Comm.	—	—
—	208	Rome, Ghigi Lib. R. viii. 55.	XI.	Inspected by Scholz. Thdrt.'s comm.	—	—
170	..	*The same MS. as* Paul 186 *above.*				
171	209	Two MSS. in the Library of the Collegio Romano.	XVI.	Inspected by Scholz.	—	—
172	210		XVI.	Inspected by Scholz.	—	—
(173)	(211)	Naples (no number). *Apparently the same MS. as* Acts 83, Paul 93 *above.*	—	Inspected by Scholz.	—	—
174	212	Naples 1, C. 26.	XV.	Inspected by Scholz.	—	—

Acts.	Epp. Paul.	Designation.	Cent.	Collator, &c.	Gosp.	Apoc.
—	213	Rome, Barberini Lib. 29.	1338	Inspected by Scholz. Scholia.	—	—
—	214	Vienna 167 (Lambec 46).	XV.	Inspected by Scholz. Contains Rom., 1 Cor., with comm.	—	—
..	215	*The same MS. as* Acts 140 *above.*				
175	216	Mon. of S. Bas. Messana, 2.	XII.	Inspected by Munter.	—	—
—	217	Palermo.	XII.	Inspected by Scholz. Begins 2 Cor. v. 1.	—	—
176	218	Syracuse.	XII.	Inspected by Munter.	421	—
177	219	Leyden. Meermann 116.	XII.	Dermout. (Def. Acts i. 1—14, xxi. 14—xxii. 28; Rom. i. 1—vii. 13.)	122	—
178	..	Middlehill, Worcestershire 1461. *See* "Apoc. m," *Vol. IV.*	XI.	(Inspected by Scholz?) Once Meermann 118. = Paul 242.	—	87
179	..	*The same MS. as* Paul 128 *above.*				
180	..	Strasburg. Molsheimensis.	XII.	Readings of Acts and Epp. communicated to Scholz. = Paul 238.	431	—
181	220	Berlin, Diez. 10.	XV.	(Def. Acts i. 11—ii. 11; Rom. i. 1—27; 1 Cor. xiv. 12—xv. 46; 2 Cor. i. 1—viii. 5.)	400	—
..	(221)	*The same MS. as* "o" *and* 61 *above.*				
..	(222)	*See* Acts [110] *above.*				
..	(223)	*See* Acts [152] *above.*				
..	224	*The same MS. as* Acts 58 *above.*				
..	(225)	*The same MS. as* Acts 9, Paul 11 *above.*				
..	227	*The same MS. as* Acts 56 *above.*				
..	228	*The same MS. as* Acts 108 *above.*				
..	229	*The same MS. as* Acts 109 *above.*				
..	230	*The same MS. as* Acts 150 *above.*				
182	..	} Two MSS. in a Monastery on	XII.	} Inspected by Scholz. = Paul 243.	—	—
182A	..	} the Island of Patmos.	XIII.			
183	231	Gr. Mon. Jerusalem 8.	XIV.	Inspected by Scholz.	—	—
184	232	Gr. Mon. Jerusalem 9.	XIII.	Inspected by Scholz. Comm.	—	85
185	233	Mon. S. Saba, nr. Jerusalem 1.	XI.	Inspected by Scholz.	—	—
186	234	Mon. S. Saba, nr. Jerusalem 2.	XIII.	Inspected by Scholz.	457	—
187	235	Mon. S. Saba, nr. Jerusalem 10.	XIII.	Inspected by Scholz.	462	86
188	236	Mon. S. Saba, nr. Jerusalem 15.	XII.	Inspected by Scholz.	—	—
189	237	Mon. S. Saba, nr. Jerusalem 20.	XIII.	Inspected by Scholz.	466	89
..	238	*The same MS. as* Acts 180 *above.*				
..	239	*The same MS. as* Acts 141 *above.*				
..	240	*The same MS. as* Acts 153 *above.*				
..	241	*The same MS. as* Acts 97 *above.*				
..	242	*The same MS. as* Acts 178 *above.*				
..	243	} *The same MSS. as* Acts 182 *above.*				
..	243A	}				
190	244	Christ Church, Oxford, Wake 34 (2 Scholz).	XI.	Acts xviii.—xx. collated by Scholz.	—	27
191	245	Christ Church, Oxford, Wake 38 (3 Scholz).	XI.	Def. Acts i. 1—11.		
192	246	Christ Church, Oxford, Wake 37 (4 Scholz).	XI.	Def. Acts xii. 4—xxiii. 32.		
8-pe	8-pe	St. Petersburg xi. 1. 2. 230.	XII.	Muralt.	8-pe	

[Other manuscripts recently discovered[9] :—

i. Monasterium Παντοκρατορος, Mt. Athos (not numbered). Contains the (Acts ? and) Epistles with a Catena, chiefly from Œcumenius, except on 1 and 2 Cor. Early half of tenth century.

ii. Monastery of St. Catherine, Mt. Sinai. Catena on St. Paul's Epistles, apparently differing little from Œcumenius. Probably eleventh or twelfth century.

iii. Ferrara 187. N.A. 7 (Vol. III.). A well-written Codex, containing the whole of the N. T. (Vols. I. and II. containing the O. T.), apparently of the fourteenth century.

iv. Milan Ambros. Z. 34 sup. A small 4to paper ms. Contains the Cath. Epp., St. Paul's Epp., and a Synaxarium; followed by the four Gospels. Of the thirteenth or fourteenth century.

v. Milan Ambros. N. 272 sup. S. Pauli Epp. cum notis marginalibus.

vi. Florence Riccardi 85. Small 8vo. St. Paul's Epistles.

vii. Modena (xiii.) ii. A. 13. Contains the Acts and Catholic Epistles.

viii. Modena (lxxi.) ii. C. 4. Contains the Acts and Catholic Epistles.

ix. Modena (ccxliii.) iii. B. 17. Contains the Acts and Epistles (Catholic and Pauline).

x. Modena (cii.) ii. D. 3. Contains the Acts and Epistles (Catholic and Pauline).

xi. Modena (xiv.) ii. A. 14. Contains St. Paul's Epistles.]

The following is a List of Lectionaries.

	Designation.	Date.	Name of Collator, and other information.
lect-1	Leyden 243. Scaligeri.	XI.	Wetstein and Dermout. Contains (of this Vol.) Acts i. 15—26; ii. 22—47; iii. 12, 13, 18; iv. 1—21; id. 23—31; x. 34—43; xiii. 34—42; xxviii. 11—31; Rom. v. 6—19; 1 Cor. xi. 25—32; xv. (= ev-6)
lect-2	Brit. Mus., Cotton Vesp. B. 18.	XI.	"Contains the portions of Acts and Epp. appointed to be read throughout the whole year. Casley collated it in 1735, and Wetstein inserted his extracts." (Michaelis.) Mutilated at beg. and end.
lect-3	Bodleian, Baroc. 202?	995	
lect-4	Brit. Mus., Harl. 5731.	XIV.	Griesbach. Contains the following fragments:—Acts vi. 8—vii. 5; vii. 47—60; 1 Cor. i. 18—24; iv. 9—16; xii. 27—xiii. 8. (= Gosp. 117)
lect-5	Bodleian, Cromwell. 11. (Olim 296.) A liturgy book, containing 5thly (pp. 149—290), εὐαγγελοαποστόλων τῶν μεγάλων ἑορτῶν.	1225	Griesbach, who says "Variantes lectiones collegi e Rom. vi. 3—11; xiii. 11—xiv. 4; xiv. 19—23; xvi. 25—27; 1 Cor. i. 18—24; ix. 19—x. 4; xi. 23—32, &c."

[9] The notice of the first two mss. has been furnished by Mr. P. E. Pusey, that of the others has been derived from Dean Burgon's letters on Manuscript "Evangelia" in the *Guardian*, 1873-4.

	Designation.	Date.	Name of Collator, and other information.
lect-6	Göttingen (C. de Missy).	XV.	Matthæi (v). See his appendix to Thess. Contains a large number of the usual lections.
lect-7	Copenhagen 3.	XV.	Hensler in Birch. (= ev-44)
lect-9	Paris 32.	XII.	Inspected by Scholz. (= ev-84)
lect-10	Paris 33.	XII.	Inspected by Scholz. (= ev-85)
lect-11	Paris 34.	XII.	Inspected by Scholz.
lect-12	Paris 375.	1022	Scholz. An important MS. (= ev-60)
lect-13	Moscow Synod, 4.	X.	Matthæi (b).
lect-14	Moscow Synod, 291.	XII.	Matthæi (e).
lect-16	Moscow Synod, 266.	XV.	Matthæi (ξ). Contains Acts xiii. 25—32; xix. 1—8; Rom. v. 6—9; vi. 18—23; 1 Cor. iv. 9—16; x. 1—4; xii. 27—xiii. 7. (= ev-52)
lect-17	Moscow Synod, 267.	XV.	Matthæi (χ) } Contain several lections in Acts, and some in Rom.; 1 Cor.; in 2 Cor. only xi. 21—xii. 9. (=ev-53)
lect-18	Moscow Synod, 268.	1470	Matthæi (ψ) (=ev-54)
lect-19	Moscow, Typogr. 47.	1602	Matthæi (ω). Contains Acts xii. 1—11; xiii. 25—32; xxvi. 1—20; Rom. xiii. 11—xiv. 4; xv. 1—7; 1 Cor. i. 18—ii. 1; iv. 9—16; ix. 2—12; x. 1—4; xii. 27—xiii. 7; xv. 1—11; 2 Cor. i. 8—11; xi. 21—xii. 9. (= ev-55)
lect-20	Moscow, Typogr. 9.	XVI.	Matthæi (16). Contains Acts ii. 1—11. (= ev-56)
lect-21	Paris 294.	XI.	Inspected by Scholz. (= ev-83)
lect-22	Paris 304.	XIII.	Inspected by Scholz.
lect-23	Paris 306.	XII.	Inspected by Scholz.
lect-24	Paris 308.	XIII.	Mostly O. T. lections; only a few from N. T.
lect-25	Paris 319.	XI.	Inspected by Scholz.
lect-26	Paris 320.	XII.	Inspected by Scholz. Mutilated.
lect-27	Paris 321.	XIII.	Inspected by Scholz. Defective.
lect-28	Bodleian, Selden 2.	XV.	Griesbach. (= ev-26)
lect-29	Paris 370.	XII.	Some lections from Gospp. and Epp. (= ev-94)
lect-30	Paris 373.	XIII.	
lect-31	Paris 276.	XV.	Inspected by Scholz. (= ev-82)
lect-32	Paris 376.	XIII.	Entered in list of MSS. of Gospels as 324.
lect-33	Paris 382.	XIII.	"Cursim coll. magna codicis pars," Scholz.
lect-34	Paris 383.	XV.	Inspected by Scholz.
lect-35	Paris 324.	XIII.	Inspected by Scholz. (= ev-92)
lect-36	Paris 326.	XIV.	Inspected by Scholz. (= ev-93)
lect-37	Riccardi Lib. Florence 84.	XV.	*See* Acts 150, Paul 230 *above*.
lect-38	Vatican 1528.	XV.	
lect-39	Vatican, Ottob. 416.	XIV.	(= ev-133)
lect-40	Barberini Lib. Rome 18.	XIV.	Some parts of Cent. X.
lect-41	Barberini Lib. Rome (no number).	XI.	The first 114 leaves are lost.
lect-42	Vallicella Lib. Rome, C. 46.	XVI.	
lect-43	Riccardi Lib. Florence 2742.	?	(Inspected by Scholz ?)

	Designation.	Date.	Name of Collator, and other information.
lect-44	Glasgow (Missy BB).	?	Manuscript collations by Missy were once in Michaelis' possession.
lect-45	Glasgow (Missy CC).	1199	
lect-46	Ambros. Lib. Milan 63.	XIV.	Inspected by Scholz.
lect-47	Ambros. Lib. Milan 72.	XII.	Inspected by Scholz. (= ev-104)
lect-48	Laur.Lib. Florence 2742(?).	XIII.	Inspected by Scholz. (= ev-112)
lect-49	Mon. St. Saba, nr. Jerus., 16.	XIV.	(Inspected by Scholz ?)
lect-50	St. Saba 18.	XV.	Inspected by Scholz.
lect-51	St. Saba 26.	XIV.	Inspected by Scholz.
lect-52	St. Saba (no number).	1059	Inspected by Scholz.
lect-53	St. Saba (no number).	XIV.	Inspected by Scholz. (= ev-160)
lect-54	St. Saba (no number).	XIII.	
lect-56	Frankfort on Oder, Seideli.		A leaf of a lectionary bound up with ms. Acts 42, Paul 48. Contains 1 Cor. ix. 2—12.
lect-57	Ch. Ch. Oxf., Wake 12 (1 Scholz).	XI.	(= ms. 26 Apoc.)
lect-58	Ch. Ch. Oxf., Wake 33 (5 Scholz).	1172	

SECTION II.

ANCIENT VERSIONS REFERRED TO IN THIS VOLUME. (VSS.)

The LATIN Versions (latt).

vulg. The vulgate, usually quoted from the Clementine edition (vulg-ed.). The Sixtine edition (vulg-sixt.) is occasionally cited when it differs from the others ; as also are the following mss.:—

am. amiatinus, written about A.D. 541. Tischendorf has edited it, and considers it the oldest and most valuable extant.

demid. demidovianus. Published by Matthæi. Written in the XIIth century.

fuld. fuldensis. Readings given in Lachmann's N. T. Written in the VIth century.

flor. floriacensis.

harl. harleianus, No. 1772. Collation given by Griesbach Symb. Crit.

lux. luxoviensis. A lectionary cited by Mabillon and Sabatier.

[reg. Cited from Tischdf. on Acts iii. 3.]

tol. toletanus. A collation was published by Blanchini in his "Vindiciæ Can. Script."

F-lat. The Latin column of the Codex Augiensis. Cent. IX.

old-lat. The Old Latin Version in use before Jerome's revision is cited from the following manuscripts :—

D-lat. (*Acts.*) The Latin of the Codex Bezæ. Cent. VI.

D-lat. (*Paul.*) The Latin of the Codex Claromontanus. Cent. VI.

E-lat. (*Acts.*) The Latin of the Codex Laudianus. Cent. VI.

G-lat. The Latin written word by word over the corresponding Greek words in the Codex Boernerianus.

fri. Fragments of St. Paul's Epistles in the covers of certain Codices Frisingenses at Munich. Written Cent. V. or VI. Deciphered by Tischendorf.

guelph. Fragmenta guelpherbytana. Fragments of the Ep. to Rom. in Knittel's Wolfenbüttel Gothic palimpsests. Edited by Tischdf. in his "Anecdota sacra."

spec. Mai's Speculum.

The Syriac Versions (syrr).

Syr. The Peschito. Supposed to have been made as early as the second century.

syr. The later or Philoxenian. Cent. V. Revised by Thomas of Harkell, A.D. 616, who probably introduced the asterisks and obeli [1], and the notes in the margin.

The Egyptian or COPTIC Versions (coptt).

copt. The Coptic or Memphitic.

copt-dz. Codex Diez. Written about the tenth century.

copt-schw. Schwartze's edition.

copt-wilk. Wilkins' edition.

[copt-boett. Boetticher's edition.]

sah. The Thebaic or Sahidic.

sah-ming. Mingarel's edition.

sah-mnt. Munter's edition.

sah-woide. Woide's MS. Published in the Appendix to Cod. Alex.

basm. The Bashmuric so closely follows sah as to be of no critical value except where sah is deficient.

The GOTHIC version (goth): made from the Greek by Uphilas about the middle of the *fourth century*.

The ÆTHIOPIC version (æth): assigned to the *fourth century*.

æth-rom. The edition given in the Roman polyglott.

æth-pl. Pell Platt's edition.

The ARMENIAN version (arm): made in the *fifth century*.

arm-usc. Uscan's edition.

arm-zoh. Zohrab's edition.

[arm-rieu. Cited on Acts xx. 25.]

[1] It is Mr. Pusey's impression that many of the readings thus marked correspond to the words in Italic characters in our English version, indicating a necessity of the idiom. The same remark applies to certain of the readings of the Syriac versions which we have enclosed in brackets.

SECTION III.

FATHERS AND ANCIENT WRITERS CITED IN THE DIGEST OF THIS VOLUME [2].

(N.B.—The abbreviation is designated by the thick type. In the remainder of the word or sentence *Latin* writers are described in Italics.)

Acacius, Cent^{y}. IV. or V. (from Catenæ.)
Acta Concilii **Chalcedon**ensis, A.D. 451
Alcimus *Ecdicius Avitus.* (See **Avit**.)
Ambr*ose*, *Bp. of Milan*, A.D. 374—397
Ambr*osia***st***er*, **i. e.** *Hilary the Deacon*, fl. 384
Ammonius of Alexandria, 220
Amphilochius, Bp. of Iconium, 374
Anastasius Sinaita, Cent^{y}. VI.
Andreas of Crete, 635
Antiochus of Ptolemais, 614
Antonius Monachus, b. 251, d. 356
Apollinarius, Bp. of Laodicea, 362
Archelaus of Mesopotamia, 278
Arnob*ius of Africa*, 306
Athanasius, Bp. of Alexandria, 326—373
Athenagoras of Athens, 177
Aug*ustine*, *Bp. of Hippo*, 395—430
Avit*us*, *Bp. of Vienne*, 490—523
Barnabas, Cent^{y}. I. or II.
Basil, Bp. of Cæsarea, 370—379
Basil of **Sel**eucia, fl. 440
Bede, *the Venerable*, 731 ; **Bede-gr**, a Greek MS. cited by Bede, nearly identical with Cod. "E," mentioned in this edn only when it differs from E.
Cæsarius of Constantinople, 368
Cæs*arius*, *Episc.* **Arel***atensis*, 502—544
Canons Apostolic, Cent^{y}. III.
Cassiod*orus*, b. 479, d. 575
Chrom*atius*, *Bp. of Aquileia*, 402
Chronicon Paschale, Cent^{y}. VII.
Chrysol*ogus*, *Peter*, *Bp. of Ravenna*, 433—450
Chrysostom, Bp. of Constantinople, 397—407 ; **Chr-mss** as cited by Tischdf. from Matthæi ; **-montf**, from Montfaucon ; **Chr-wlf**, Wolfenbüttel ms. of Chr written in Cent^{y}. VI.
Clement of Alexandria, fl. 194
Clement, Bp. of **Rome**, 91—101
Cosmas Indicopleustes, 535
Constitutions, Apostolic, Cent^{y}. III.
Cypr*ian*, *Bp. of Carthage*, 248—258
Cyril, Bp. of Alexandria, 412—444. **Cyr-p** denotes readings supplied by Mr. Pusey [*Cyr* is used when the citation is *apparently* uniform]
Cyril, Bp. of **Jer**usalem, 348—386
Damascenus, Johannes, 730
Dialogue against the Marcionites printed amongst the works of Origen
"**Dialogi** de **Trin**itate," variously ascribed to Ath Thdrt Max
Didymus of Alexandria, 370
Diodorus, Bp. of Tarsus, 378—394

[2] Orig-c or Chr-cat means Orig or Chr as given in Cramer's Catena. Orig-schol, scholium ascribed to Origen. Chr$_{h.l.}$, Chr *hoc loco*. Hippolytus is cited sometimes as Hip, sometimes as Hippol; Gregory of Nyssa, as Nys, Nyss, and Nyssen: in all cases the abbreviation marked in the above list is the shortest used in this volume.

Dionysius, Bp. of Alexandria, 247—265
Dionysius Areopagita, Cent^y. V.
Ennodius, *Bp. of Pavia*, d. 521
Ephrem Syrus, b. 299, d. 378
Epiphanius, Bp. of Salamis in Cyprus, 368—403
[Epistle of the Church of Lyons, 171]
Eucherius, *Bp. of Lyons*, 434—454
Eulogius, Bp. of Alexandria, 581—608
Eusebius, Bp. of Cæsarea, 315—320
Eustathius, Bp. of Antioch, 323
Euthalius, Bp. of Sulci, 458
Eutherius, Bp. of Tyana, 431
Euthymius Zigabenus, 1116
Faustinus, 383
Fulgentius, *Bp. of Africa*, 508—533
Gaudentius, *Bp. of Brescia*, 387
Gennadius, Bp. of Constantinople, 458—471
Gildas, fl. 581
Helvidius (cited by Jer.), 383
Hesychius of Jerusalem, Cent^y. IV. or VI.
Hilary, *Bp. of Poictiers*, 354—368
Hippolytus, disciple of Irenæus, 220
Homilies ascribed to Clement, Cent^y. III.
Idacius, *the name under which* [*was*] *published* [*the*] *work* "de Trinitate" [*formerly ascribed to*] *Vig.* [*now to Ath.*]
Ignatius, Bp. of Antioch, d. 107
Irenæus, Bp. of Lyons, 178
Isidore of Pelusium, 412
Jacobus, Bp. of Nisibis, cir. 320—340
Jerome, fl. 378—420
Julian, Emperor, 331—363
Julian (*cited by Aug.*), *Pelagian Bp. in Italy*, 416
Justin Martyr, fl. 140—164

Leo, *Bp. of Rome*, 440—461
Leontius Scholasticus, 580
Lucifer, *Bp. of Cagliari*, 354—367
Macarius of Egypt, 301—391
Manes, cited by Epiphanius
Marcellus, cited by Eus.
Marcion, 130; fragments in Epiph. (Mcion-e) and Tert. (Mcion-t)
Marcosii, cited by Iren.
Marcus Monachus, 390
Marius Mercator, 418
Martyrium Clementis
Maximus Taurinensis, 430—466
Maximus Confessor, fl. 630—662
Maximin, *the Arian, cited by Aug.*
Meletius, Bp. of Antioch, 381
Methodius, fl. 290—312
Michael Psellus of Constantinople, d. 1078
Nazianzum, Gregory, Bp. of, fl. 370—389
Nestorius, Bp. of Constantinople, 428—431
Nonnus of Panopolis, Cent^y. V.
Novatian, 251
Nyssa, Gregory, Bp. of, 371
Œcumenius of Tricca in Thrace, Cent^y. XI.?
Origen, b. 185, d. 254
"Quæstiones et Responsiones ad Orthodoxos" ascribed to Justin M.
Orosius, 416
Orsiesius the Egyptian, 345
Pacianus, *Bp. of Barcelona*, 370
Palladius, Bp. of Hellenopolis, 368—401
Pamphilus of Palestine, fl. 294
Paulinus, *Bp. of Aquileia*, 776—804
Pelagii *Ep. ad Demetr.* 417 ?
Peter, Bp. of Alexandria, 300—311
Philastrius, *Bp. of Brescia*, fl. 380
Philo Carpasius, 400
Photius, Bp. of Constantinople, 858—891

Photinus, Bp. of Sirmium (cited by Epiphanius), d. 379
Polycarp, Bp. of Smyrna, d. 169
Porphyry, d. 304
"**Prædest***inatus*." *A work ascribed to Vincent of Lerins* (434)
Primas*ius*, Cent^y. VI.
Proclus, Bp. of Constantinople, 434
Procopius of Gaza, 520
"*De* **Promiss***ionibus dimid. temp.*"
"**Quæst***iones ex vet. et nov. Testt.*" *Printed among the works of Aug.*
"*De* **Rebap***tismate.*" *Among Cypr's works*
Ruf*inus of Aquileia*, 397
Salv*ianus*, 440
Sedul*ius*, 430
Seniores, quoted by Iren., Cent^y. I. or II.
Serapion of Egypt, 345
Severus of Antioch, Cent^y. VI.
Severianus, Bp. in Syria, 400
"*De* **Sing***ularitate* **Cler***icorum.*" *Among Cypr's works*
Smyrnæorum **Ep**istola de Martyrio Polycarpi, 167
Synopsis ascribed to Athanasius
Tarasius, Bp. of Constantinople, 786
Tatian of Syria, 172
Tert*ullian*, 200
Thaumaturgus, Gregory, Bp. of Neocæsarea, 243
Theodore, Bp. of **Heracl**ea, 394
Theodore, Bp. of **Mops**uestia, 399—428
Theodore of the **Stud**ium, 795—826
Thdrt, Bp. of Cyrus, 420—458
Theodotus the Gnostic. Extracts made by Clement of Alexandria
Theodotus of **Ancyr**a, 433
Pseudo **Theodul**us, Cent^y. XII.
Theophy**l**act, Abp. of Bulgaria, 1071; **Thl-sif**, as edited by Sifanius; **Thl-fin**, by Finettius, from a Vatican MS.
Tich*onius*, 390
Timothy, Bp. of Alexandria, 380
Titus, Bp. of Bostra, cir. 360—377
Vict*or* **Vit***ensis, an African Bp., Cent^y. V.*
Victor of Antioch, 401
Victorin*us*, 380
Vict*or, Episc.* **Tun***unensis*, 565
Vig*ilius of Thapsus*, 484 [3]
Zeno, *Bp. of Verona*, 362—380
Zonaras of Constantinople, 1118

To this list may be added the following ABBREVIATIONS USED IN THE DIGEST :—

aft, after.
al, alii.
appy, apparently.
bef, before.
beg, beginning.
comm, commentary—when appended to the name of a Father, denotes that the reading referred to is found in the body of his commentary, and not in the text (txt) printed at the head of the commentary. This last is often very much tampered with.
corr, corrector. corrd, corrected.
ctra, contra.

[[3] A work on the Trinity formerly ascribed to Vigilius is now assigned to Athanasius.]

def, defective.
ed or edn, edition.
elsw, elsewhere.
elz, elzevir edition of the Greek Test.
e sil, e silentio collatorum.
exc, except.
expr, expressly.
follg or flg, the following words.
gr, Greek. gr-lat-ff, Greek and Latin Fathers.
ins, insert—"ins και AB" means that the MSS. A and B insert και.
int, interpreter or interpretation—appended to the name of a Father means that the citation is made from a translation, not from the original.
marg, margin.
om, omit—"om και AB" means that the MSS. A and B omit the και given in the text or inserted by other MSS.
Ps, Pseudo—used in citing the spurious works ascribed to Ath. and other Fathers.
pref, prefix.
rec, the *textus receptus*, or received text of the Greek Testament. This is used when Steph and elz agree.
rel, reliqui—means that all the other manuscripts named on the margin have the reading to which it is appended.
simly, similarly.
Steph, Stephens' Greek Testament.
transp, transpose.
txt, text—when followed by a list of MSS., versions, &c., means that the reading adopted in this edition is supported by those MSS., versions, &c. (See also under comm above.)
ver, verse.
vss, versions.
vv, verses.

The figures 2, 3, &c., inserted *above* the line to the right hand, imply a second, third, &c., hand in a MS. Thus B^1 means the original scribe of B; C^2, the first corrector of C; C^3, the second; D^r, a recent scribe in D, by whom corrections were made or parts not originally in the MS. supplied.

The same figures *below* the line, imply *recurrence* of the reading 2, 3, &c. times in the author mentioned; e. g. Aug_1, $Orig_5$, Bas_3: similarly are used the words sæpe, aliq, or alic (aliquoties or alicubi), ubique [4].

Words printed in the digest in the larger type used for the text

[4] -2-mss appended to the name of a Father means that the reading cited is contained in two mss. of that Father.

Chr-5-mss_3 means that in 5 mss. of Chrysostom the reading cited occurs 3 times.

itself are to be taken as of equal authority with the reading printed in the text : the place in the text where such readings occur being indicated by an asterisk.

Notice referred to on pp. 15, &c.

ἁπας would seem to be the true reading in 56 passages of the N. T., in only 14 however of these is it found without any variation in the uncial MSS. In the 42 remaining cases some one or more uncials have substituted πας. On the other hand πας occurs upwards of 1100 times, and in no more than 4, or at the most 10 cases have uncial mss. put ἁπας in its stead—so that the tendency of the transcribers has clearly been to alter ἁπας into πας ; on examination it also appears that this tendency has been alike yielded to by the scribes of the recent and of the ancient MSS. In cases, therefore, where the rarer word is supported by *any* trustworthy MSS., however few in number and however great the array in favour of πας, ἁπας has been accepted as the true reading.

SECTION IV.

LIST, AND SPECIFICATION OF EDITIONS OF OTHER BOOKS QUOTED, REFERRED TO, OR MADE USE OF IN THIS VOLUME.

N.B. Works mentioned in the list given in the Prolegg. to Vol. I. are not here again noticed.

A. V. R. The Authorized Version revised by five Clergymen. Rom., 1 and 2 Cor. London 1858-60.

Biscoe, History of the Acts of the Holy Apostles confirmed &c., Oxf. 1840.

Bisping, Erklärung des Briefes an die Römer, Münster 1854. Rom. Catholic.

Börnemann, Acta Apostolorum ad fidem codicis Cantabrigiensis &c., Grossenhain et Lond. 1848.

Catena in Acta Apostolorum, ed. Cramer, Oxf. 1838.

Chrysostom, Opera, cited by Benedictine pages in Migne's Patrologia Græca, voll. xlvii.—lxiv. The homilies on the Acts and Rom. are in vol. ix. (lx.), those on 1 and 2 Cor. in vol. x. (lxi.).

Conybeare and Howson, Life and Epistles of St. Paul, with maps, plates, coins, &c., 2 voll. 4to. London 1850-52 : 2nd edn., 2 voll. 8vo., Lond. 1856.

Davidson, Dr. S., Introduction to the New Testament, vol. ii., Acts—2 Thess.; Lond. 1849.

De Wette, Exegetisches Handbuch u.s.w.—Apostelgeschichte, 2nd edn., Leipzig 1841 : Römer, 4th edn., Leipzig 1847 : Corinther, 2nd edn., Leipzig 1845.

ESTIUS, Comment. in omnes Pauli Epistolas, 2 voll. folio, Douay 1614.
EWBANK, W. W., Commentary on the Ep. to the Romans, Lond. 1850.
FRITZSCHE, Pauli ad Romanos Epistola, 3 voll., Hal. Sax. 1836.
HACKETT, PROF., Commentary on the Acts, Boston, U.S. 1852.
HEMSEN, Der Apostel Paulus u.s.w., Göttingen 1850.
HODGE, PROF. C., Commentary on the Epistle to the Romans, 3rd edn., London : The Religious Tract Society.
HUMPHRY, W. G., Commentary on the Acts, Lond. 1847.
JOWETT, PROF., The Epistles of St. Paul to the Thessalonians, Galatians, Romans : with critical Notes and Illustrations : Lond. 1856. (See Vol. III. Prolegg. ch. v. § i. par. 1, note.)
LACHMANN AND BUTTMANN, Novum Testamentum græce et latine &c., vol. ii., Berlin 1850.
LEWIN, T., Life and Epistles of St. Paul, 2 vols., London 1851.
MEYER, H. A. W., Kritisch-exegetischer Commentar über das Neue Testament :—Apostg., Göttingen 1835 : 1 Corinth., 2nd edn., do. 1849 : 2 Cor., 2nd edn., do. 1850.
NEANDER, AUG., Geschichte der Pflanzung u. Leitung der christlichen Kirche durch die Apostel, 4th edn., Hamburg 1847.
ŒCUMENIUS, Commentaria, &c., in Migne's Patrologia Græca, voll. cxviii. cxix.
PALEY, Horæ Paulinæ : ed. Birks, Lond. 1850.
PEILE, DR., Annotations on the Apostolic Epistles, vol. i. Rom.—Corr. Lond. 1848.
PHILIPPI, DR. F. A., Commentar über den Brief Pauli an die Römer, vol. i., Frankf. 1855.
SCHRADER, Der Apostel Paulus, u.s.w., 5 voll. Leipzig 1829-36.
SMITH, JAMES, ESQ., On the Voyage and Shipwreck of St. Paul, Lond. 1848 : 2nd edn., Lond. 1856.
STANLEY, DEAN, The Epistles of St. Paul to the Corinthians : with Critical Notes and Illustrations [5].
STIER, DR. RUDOLF, Die Reden der Apostel, Leipzig 1829.—Andeutungen für gläubiges Schriftverständniss : zweite Sammlung, Leipzig 1828.
STUART, MOSES, Commentary on the Epistle to the Romans, Lond. 1838.
TERTULLIANUS, in Migne's Patrologia Latina, voll. i.—iii.
THEODORET, Opera, in Migne's Patrologia Græca, voll. lxxx.—lxxxiv.
THEOPHYLACT, in Migne's Patrologia Græca, voll. cxxiii.—cxxvi.
THOLUCK, Römerbrief, u.s.w., Halle 1842 : 5th edn., 1856.

[5] The reader will observe that I have worked with Dean Stanley's book, and have often extracted from, and referred to it. It is a valuable contribution to the literature of these important Epistles : not so much in its scholarship, as in the power of illustration, and graphic description of usage and circumstance, which pervade the notes. The second edition is referred to in this present volume.

TREGELLES, DR., An Account of the printed Text of the Greek New Testament, London 1854; Greek Testament, Part iv., Rom.—2 Thess., 1869.

UMBREIT, DR., Der Brief an die Römer auf dem Grunde des Alten Testamentes ausgelegt, Gotha 1856.

WINER, G. B., A Treatise on the Grammar of N. Test. Greek. Translated with additions, &c., by Rev. W. F. Moulton, M.A., Edinburgh.

WORDSWORTH, BISHOP, The Greek Testament, &c. Part ii., Lond. 1857.

Readings of the Codex Vaticanus (B) in the text of this volume, which have been ascertained by the Editor's personal inspection of the MS. at Rome, February, 1861.

Acts i. 11. *ουτος*, not *ουτως* as Bentley.
ii. 7. in *απαντες*, the first *α* is written over the line by 1. m.
34. *ο* bef *κυριος* is added by 1. and 2. m.
38. aft *αμαρτιων* ins **υμων**, not *ημων* as Bch.
iii. 2. the *το* after *εβασταζε* is superadded by 1. m.
21. the *των* before *απ αιωνος* is written in the margin by 2. m.
iv. 4. **ως**, not *ωσει*, as in Mai.
6. **ο αρχιερευς** is the reading of the codex [not as Tischdf.].
14 *τεθαραπ.* and *τεθεραπ.* are *both* from the 1. m.
18. *του* before *ιησου* is added by 1. m. and 2. m.
20. **ειδαμεν**: over the *ει* is written *ο* by 1. m., over the *α* is written *ο* by 2. m. (not both by Tischdf.'s B^3).
v. 2. *συνιδυιης*, but *ε* is written over by 1. m. and 2. m.
21. The codex has **παραγενομενον** *a prima manu*, not *-νοι* as Tischdf.
25. *prima manus* has *εθεσθαι*.
38. *τα* is added by 1. m. and 2. m.
vii. 10. 2. m. has *εξελ.*, not *εξιλ.* as Bentley and Tischdf.
11. *ηυρισκον* is in codex.
17. *ηγγι***ζεν**, not *-ισεν* as Birch.
22. **λογ. κ. εργ.**, not *εργ. κ. λογ.* as Bentley.

Acts vii. 39. **αλλα**, not *αλλ'* as Mai. This was wrongly extracted from my notes of B in my last [fifth] edition.
47. **οικοδ.** *a prima manu*.
51. *καρδι***ας**, not *-αν* as Bentley.
viii. 25. **ευηγγελιζοντο**, not *ευεγγελη.* as Birch.
28. **τον προφ.** *ησ.*, not *ησ. τον προφ.* as Birch.
34. *τουτο* is *a prima manu*.
ix. 6. **αλλα**.
13. **σου** is in codex, not omitted, as in Bentley.
25. after *καθηκεν*, **αυτον**, not *-ου* as Bentley.
26. **εις** *ιερουσ.*, not *εν* as Birch.
36. *τις ην μαθ.*, not *τις μαθ.* as Bentley.
x. 45. *πν.* **του** *αγ.*, not *πν. αγ.* as Bentley.
xi. 3. *εισηλθ***εν**, not *-θες* as Bentley.
12. **διακρειναντα** not *-νοντα* as Bentley.
13. **απηγγ.**, not *ανηγγ.* as Bentley.
18. *αρα και*, not *αρα γε και* as Mai.
24. *τω κυριω* is in margin a 2. m. (sic).
xiii. 1. **συ***μεων*, not *σιμ.* as Bentley.
11. **επεσεν**, not *επεπεσεν* as Mai.
13. *αν***ε***χθ.* is 1. m., not *αναχθ.* as Mai.
26. **ημιν**, as in Mai ed. 1, not *υμιν*, as in ed. 2.
29. *παντα* **τα** *γεγρ.*, not *παντα γεγρ.* as Bentley.

Acts xiii. 39. εν νομω, not τω νομω as Birch.
xiv. 10. the 2nd και is written over by 1. m.
12. μεν βαρν., not βαρν. as Bentley.
xv. 1. περιθμητε is 1. m., but the addition is 1. m. also. (Tischdf. wrongly assigns it to his B³.)
xvi. 12. κακειθεν εις, as in Mai ed. 1, not κ. τε εις, as in ed. 2 [6].
xvii. 7. λεγοντες ειναι, not ειν. λεγ. as Bentley.
20. θελει, not θελοι as Mai ed. 1.
34. αρεοπ. is 1. m., -ωπ. is 2. m.
xix. 2. ουδ', not ουδε as Mai.
13. υμας, not μεν υμας as Bentley.
29. της συγχ., not συγχ. as Bentley.
40. ου ου δυνησ. as Mai ed. 2, not ου δυνησ. as ed. 1.
xx. 4. βεροιαιος, not -ροαι- as Birch.
16. κεκρει 1. m., κεκρικει 2. m.
23. λεγον as Mai ed. 1, not -ων as ed. 2.
26. διοτι as Mai ed. 2, not διο as ed. 1.
32. την κληρονομιαν, not κληρ. as Muralto.
xxi. 3. αναφαναντες is 2. m. So in my collation: but Tischdf., who has examined this place with care, says that B¹ wrote ΝᾹ; then his B³ wrote Ē upon the Ā, and afterwards placed an A over the line. So that it would now appear as if B¹ had read -εντες.
4. 1. m. repeats ελεγαν after πνευματος.
5. (6 ed. Verc.) προσευξ., not -ηυξ. as Bentley.
id. αλληλους και, not και as Bentley.
13. ο before παυλος is added by 1. m.
24. ξυρησονται is 1. m. as Rulotta and Vercellone.
xxii. 5. 1. m. has πρεσβυτερειον: 2. m., -ριον.

Acts xxii. 24. ανεταζεσθαι, not -ταξ- as Bentley.
28. 1. m. has πολειτειαν.
xxiii. 7. λαλουντος as Bentley, not -ησαντος as Mai. This was wrongly extracted from my notes of B in my last [fifth] edition.
18. σοι is written over by 1. m.
28. κατηγαγον to αυτων is in marg. a 1. m.
35. κελευσας, not κελευσας τε as Bentley.
xxv. 25. in αυτου δε του παυλου, παυλου has dots over it a 1. m.
xxvii. 14. 1. m. decidedly wrote ευρακυλων: 2. m. placed υ over the α, and λ between the κ and υ, and altered the Λ to Δ, but in so doing, he has left the right foot of the Λ of 1. m. visible beyond the corner of his own Δ.
28. ευρον οργυιας εικοσι, not ευρον εικοσι as Bentley.
xxviii. 11. αλεξανδρινω has η written over the ι, but *not by* 1. m. as Rulotta, and Mai ed. 1.
16. επετραπη, not -πει as Birch.
Rom. i. 1. χ̄υ ῑυ, not ῑυ χ̄υ as Mai.
12. 2. m. has συμπ., not συνπ.
v. 1. εχωμεν is 1. m.: εχομεν 2. m.
vii. 22. τω νομ., not τι νομ. as misprinted in Mai ed. 2.
viii. 2. σε απο, not απο.
5. τα του πν. as Mai ed. 1, not του πν. as ed. 2.
24. τι is added by 1. m.
ix. (3. συγγενων is in the original text, there has been no erasure: the words αδελφων μου των are in the margin by the 2nd hand) [7].
8. τουτεστιν οτι a 1. m. (οτι over the line).
xiii. 2. ανθεστ., not αθεστ. as misprinted in Mai ed. 2.
11. υμας, not ημας as Bentley.
xiv. 6. και ο εσθ., not ο εσθ. as Bentley.

[6] Tischdf.'s " male M. in utraque ed. repetiit receptam " is altogether wrong. Mai has not printed the rec. in either edn.

[7] Supplied by the Rev. C. Cure.

Rom. xv. 26. ποιησασθε 1. and 2. m.: no correction.
xvi. 7. **γεγοναν**, not -ασιν as Mai.
1 Cor. i. 2. **τη** εκκλ., not εκκλ. as Bentley.
11. μοι is 1. m.: μου 2. m., not as Verc.
ii. 13. διδα**κτοις**, not -τω.
iii. 2. **δυνασθε**, not εδυν.
9. συνεργοι 1. m.
iv. 11. 1. m. γυμνειτ.: 2. m. -**νιτ**. This was wrongly extracted from my notes of B in my last [fifth] edition.
15. εγεννησα, not -ενη- as Bentley.
vii. 5. There is no writing in the margin, as asserted by Woide from Mico.
17. μεμερικεν **ο κυριος**, not ο θεος.
id. ουτως περιπατειτω και, not omitted, as Bentley.
viii. 11. **ο** αδελφος, not αδελφος as Bentley.
x. 9. απ**ω**λλ., not απολλ. as Bentley.
xii. 21. **τι** περισσοτερον, not περισσοτερον as Bentley.
xiv. 16. ευλογης **εν** πνευματι, not ευλογης τω πνευματι as Mai.
1 Cor. xiv. 39. μου is not expunged as Mai, but left faint (as 1. m. wrote it) by 2. m., with a dot over each letter.
xv. 19. ηλ**πικοτες** εσμεν **μονον**, not as Bentley.
2 Cor. i. 4. επι πασ**η τη** θλιψει, not επι πασῃ θλιψει as Bentley.
iii. 15. αναγειν**ωσκηται**, not -εται as Mai.
iv. 6. **οτι θεος**, not οτι ο θεος as Mai.
v. 15. **οτι εις**, not οτι ει εις as Mai.
vii. 4. **εν** τη χαρα, not τη χαρα as Mai.
ix. 2. πε**ρυσι**, not περισι as Mai. It was stated in my former table that 2. m. had corrected it to περησι. But this was wrongly copied from my MS. notes upon the codex, and refers to the next item.
3. **υμων** is 1. m. η is written above the line by 2. m.
x. 12. ενκρειναι and συνκρειναι, without any erasures of the ε by 1. m. as stated by Rulotta.
xii. 1. δει ου, with no punctuation as in Mai.

ΠΡΑΞΕΙΣ ΑΠΟΣΤΟΛΩΝ.

I. 1 Τὸν [a] μὲν [b] πρῶτον [c] λόγον [d] ἐποιησάμην περὶ πάντων,
ὦ Θεόφιλε, [e] ὧν [f] ἤρξατο Ἰησοῦς ποιεῖν τε καὶ διδάσκειν
2 [g] ἄχρι [g] ἧς [g] ἡμέρας [h] ἐντειλάμενος τοῖς ἀποστόλοις
[i] διὰ πνεύματος ἁγίου, οὓς ἐξελέξατο, [k] ἀνελήμφθη.

C πνευματος... ABCD Eℵ a b c d f g h k m o p 13

a (μέν solitarium) Rom. vii. 12 reff. b of two, Matt. xxi. 28, 31. Heb. viii. 7. ix. 6. x. 9. 2 Kings xviii. 27. c = here only. 2 Macc. xv. 37. ὁ μὲν πρότ. λόγος ἦν ἡμῖν, ὦ Θεόδοτε, περὶ κ.τ.λ. Philo. Q. om. prob. liber, § 1, vol. ii. p. 444. See 1 Chron. xxix. 29. d = here only. Xen. Cyr. i. 6. 13. ἐποίησε δημόσια γράμματα, Herodian vii. 6. 6. e attr., Matt. xviii. 19. ver. 22. ch. ii. 22. iii. 25. vii. 16. 2 Cor. i. 6. 1 John iii. 24. Gen. ii. 3. Zeph. iii. 11. Winer, § 24. 1. f = Matt. iv. 17. Mark i. 45. Luke xiii. 25. see Gen. ii. 3. g Luke i. 20. xvii. 27. h constr., ch. xiii. 47. John xiv. 31. i traject., see ch. xix. 4 al. k = vv. 11, 22. Mark xvi. 19. 4 Kings ii. 9. (-λημψις, Luke ix. 51.)

TITLE: rec ins *των αγιων* bef *αποστ.*, with a b d g h k 13 and the subscriptions of A^2EGH; *των* m p Orig Chr Synop: om B D(-ξις): om *αποστολων* also ℵ and the margins of B(Tischdf).—pref *λουκα ο, λουκα ευαγγελιστου* b 13. 40, *πραξαποστολος συν θω̄ των αγιων αποστολων· λουκα του ευαγγελιστου* d, *αι* g h.—*αρχη συν θεω πραξαποστολος* f.

CHAP. I. 1. rec ins *ο* bef *ιησ.* (*the ο of ηρξατο was probably mistaken for the article*), with AEℵ p 13. 36 rel Constt [$Orig_1$ Did_3 Bas_1 Chr_1 $Euthal_1$ $Antch_1$]: om BD. 2. *ανελημφθη* bef *εντειλαμενος . . . εξελεξατο* D [Syr syr-mg sah]. at end add *και εκελευσε κηρυσσειν το ευαγγελιον* D syr-mg Aug_3, simly sah [Vig_1].

On the title, see Prolegomena. **1—3.** INTRODUCTION.] **1. τὸν μὲν πρ. λ.**] The latter member of this sentence, *ταννῦν δέ, . . .* is wanting (see Winer, § 63, I. 2, e. γ), and the author proceeds at once to his narration, binding this second history to the first by recapitulating and enlarging the account given in the conclusion of the Gospel. **πάντων**] Whatever latitude may be given to this word, it must at all events exclude the notion that Luke had at this time seen the Gospels of Matt. or Mark, in which many things which Jesus did and taught are contained, which he had *not* related in his *πρῶτος λόγος*. On Theophilus, see notes, Luke i. 3. **ὧν ἤρξατο Ἰησ.**] I cannot think *ἤρξατο* here to be merely pleonastic. Its position here shews that it is *emphatic*, and the parallel cases (see reff.) all point to a distinct and appropriate meaning for the word. That meaning here seems to be, that the Gospel contained the *ἀρχάς*, the *outset*, of all the doings and teachings of our Lord, as distinguished from this second treatise, which was to relate their sequel and results. Meyer understands it—*which Jesus first of all men did*, &c. But this introduces a meaning irrelevant to the context, besides *not giving* the emphasis to *ἤρξατο*, but to *Ἰησοῦς*. The position of emphasis given to the verb shews, that the *beginning* of the doing and teaching of Jesus must be contrasted with the *continuance* of the *same*, now about to be related. **2. ἐντειλ. τ. ἀπ.**] See Luke xxiv. 48 ff., and ver. 4 below. **διὰ πν. ἁγ.** may be joined either with *ἐντειλάμενος* (as in vulg copt Chr Thl); or with *ἐξελέξατο* (as in syrr æth Cyr Aug Vig). In the *former* case, our Lord is said to have given His commands to the Apostles **through**, or **in the power of**, the Holy Ghost. Similarly He is said, Heb. ix. 14, **διὰ πνεύματος αἰωνίου** *ἑαυτὸν προσενέγκαι ἄμωμον τῷ θεῷ*. In the *latter*, He is said to have chosen the Apostles by the power of the Holy Ghost. Similarly, in ch. xx. 28, Paul tells the Ephesian elders, that the Holy Ghost had made them overseers in the Church of God. The former construction however appears much the best, as expressing not, as might at first seem, a mere common-place, but the propriety of the fact,—that His last commands were given **in the power of** (see John xx. 22) **the**

3 οἷς καὶ [l] παρέστησεν ἑαυτὸν ζῶντα μετὰ τὸ [m] παθεῖν αὐτὸν
[n] ἐν πολλοῖς [o] τεκμηρίοις [p] δι' ἡμερῶν τεσσεράκοντα
[q] ὀπτανόμενος αὐτοῖς καὶ λέγων τὰ περὶ τῆς [r] βασιλείας
τοῦ θεοῦ. 4 καὶ [s] συναλιζόμενος αὐτοῖς [t] παρήγγειλεν ἀπὸ
Ἱεροσολύμων μὴ [u] χωρίζεσθαι, ἀλλὰ [v] περιμένειν τὴν
[w] ἐπαγγελίαν τοῦ πατρὸς [x] ἣν ἠκούσατέ [x] μου, 5 ὅτι Ἰωάν-

ABCD ℵE a b c d f g h k m o p 13

l = ch. ix. 41. Rom. vi. 13, 16, 19. xii. 2. 2 Cor. xi. 2. Gen. xlvii. 2 (Ald.).
m abs., Luke xxii. 15. (xxiv. 46.) ch. iii. 18. Heb. ix. 26 al.
n = Matt. vi. 7. 1 Cor. iv. 4.
o here only †. Wisd. v. 11. xix. 13. 3 Macc. iii. 24. Xen. Mem. i. 1. 2.
p = Heb. ii. 15. (ch. v. 19. xvi. 9. xvii. 10 ?)
q here only. 3 Kings viii. 8. Tobit xii. 19 [ℵ def.] only.
r Luke ix. 11. ch. viii. 12. xix. 8.
s here only †. (Ps. cxl. 5 alius in Hexapl.) Herod. i. 62. Xen. Anab. vii. 3. 48. συναυλιζ., Prov. xxii. 24.
t = Luke viii. 56. ch. iv. 18. v. 28, 40. 1 Kings xxiii. 8.
u = ch. xviii. 1, 2. 1 Chron. xii. 8.
v here only. Gen. xlix. 18. Wisd. viii. 12 only.
w = Luke xxiv. 49. ch. ii. 33. Gal. iii. 14, 22. Eph. iii. 6. Heb. iv. 1 et passim. Amos ix. 6.
x constr., Matt. vii. 24, 26. τάδε μου ἄκουσον, Lucian Dial. Deor. xx. 13. Winer, § 30. 7. d.

3. [for οις, ο ις C.] τεσσ. bef ημερ., omg δια, D(δι is written over the line by D-corr[1]). οπτανομενοις D[1]. τας D[1].

4. συναλισκομενος D[1]: συναλισγομενος D[8]: συναυλιζομενος b^2 c d^1 e m 36^1. 40, the Greek fathers are confused between this reading and txt (*see Tischdf*): *convescens* vulg E-lat[2] [Syr coptt arm] Bede: *convivens* D-lat [*salem sumens* syr]. aft συναλ. ins μετ αυτων D [*illis* lux syrr coptt æth arm]. rec παρηγγ. bef αυτοις, with B D(see above) ℵ rel 36 vulg coptt [syrr arm Eus_1 $Euthal_1$] Œc Thl Aug: txt ACE Chr_2.—παρηγγελλεν E-gr b d [Eus_1 $Euthal_1$]. ην ηκουσατε(so D[3] [ηκουσα D[1]]) φησιν δια του στοματος μου D vulg[with lux] æth Hil Aug; am [fuld] D-lat om φησιν; and in D-gr φησιν δια του στοματος are marked for erasure by a later hand.

Holy Ghost. To take διὰ πν. ἁγ. with ἀνελήμφθη (see Olsh. i. 629) seems to me inadmissible; as also is Dr. Burton's rendering, "having told His Apostles that His commands would be more fully made known to them by the Holy Ghost."

ἀνελήμφ.] = ἀνεφέρετο εἰς τὸν οὐρ., Luke xxiv. 51. The use of the verb in this abbreviated form, without the εἰς τ. οὐρ., testifies to the familiarity of the apostolic church with the Ascension as a formal and recognized event in our Lord's course.

3. ἐν π. τεκμ.] See Luke xxiv. 31, 39, 43. The ἐν is in its signification of *investiture*, in which it introduces the element or condition in which, and thus the means by which, an agent operates.

ὀπτανόμενος] οὐ γὰρ ὥσπερ πρὸ τῆς ἀναστάσεως ὡς ἀεὶ μετ' αὐτῶν ἦν, οὕτω καὶ τότε· οὐ γὰρ εἶπε **τεσσεράκοντα ἡμέρας**, ἀλλὰ **δι' ἡμερῶν τεσσεράκοντα**· ἐφίστατο γὰρ καὶ ἀφίστατο πάλιν, Chrysostom. This is the only place where the interval between the Resurrection and the Ascension is specified.

τὰ περ. τ. β. τ. θ.] **τά**, in the widest sense; not ῥήματα merely:—**the matters.** The article has been taken to imply (and so in some of my earlier editions), that during this period they received from our Lord the whole substance of the doctrine of 'the Kingdom of God.' But this remark seems to lose its propriety owing to the *present* participle λέγων. Both the participles, ὀπτανόμενος and λέγων, carry with them a ratiocinative force, in dependence on τεκμηρίοις: "proofs, consisting in this, that He" &c. And thus the art. τά gives the sentence the meaning, "and inasmuch as the things which he said were those pertaining to the Kingdom of God;" thus serving only to define λεγόμενα. [What things these were, we are not told. Certainly, not future events in their detail,—as the next portion of the narrative shews us. I should rather believe them to have concerned the future founding and government of the Church: though even here the greatest Apostles were apparently left to the unfolding of the teaching of the Holy Spirit as years went on.]

4—14.] THE LAST DISCOURSES AND ASCENSION OF THE LORD. RETURN OF THE APOSTLES TO JERUSALEM; RECAPITULATION OF THEIR NAMES.

4. συναλιζ.] not middle, '*assembling them*,' as Calv. (*congregans eos*), Grot., Olsh., and others, which is without example; but passive, = συναλισθείς, Hesych., as E. V. Chrys., the Vulg., &c., interpret it '*eating and drinking*;' so E. V. marg., Thl., Œc., &c., κοινωνῶν ἁλῶν, mistaking the etymology. The conjecture of Hemsterhuis, συναλιζομένοις (which however is found in Didymus), is quite unnecessary.

ἀπὸ Ἱερ. μὴ χωρ.] See Luke xxiv. 49. 'Simul manere jussi sunt, quoniam uno omnes Spiritu donandi erant. Si fuissent dispersi, unitas minus cognita fuisset.' Calvin.

περιμ.] **to await**, i. e. wait till the completion of: the περι implies this. The ancient idea mentioned by Wordsw. that our Lord commanded the Apostles to remain at Jerusalem for *twelve years* after the Ascension, is sufficiently refuted by His own words here, and by

νης μὲν ἐβάπτισεν ὕδατι, ὑμεῖς δὲ [y] ἐν πνεύματι [y] βαπτισθήσεσθε ἁγίῳ οὐ μετὰ πολλὰς [z] ταύτας ἡμέρας. 6 οἱ
μὲν οὖν [a] συνελθόντες [b] ἠρώτων αὐτὸν λέγοντες Κύριε,
[c] εἰ ἐν τῷ [d] χρόνῳ τούτῳ [e] ἀποκαθιστάνεις τὴν βασιλείαν
τῷ Ἰσραήλ; 7 εἶπεν δὲ πρὸς αὐτοὺς Οὐχ [f] ὑμῶν ἐστιν

y Matt. iii. 11 ‖ Mk. L. John i. 33.
z constr., here only. see note, and Exod. ii. 23.
a — ch. ii. 6. v. 16. x. 27. xvi. 13. xix. 32. 1 Cor. xi. 17 al. Ezek. xxxiii. 30.
b Matt. xv. 23 al. fr.
c = Matt. xii. 10. ch. vii. 1. xix. 2. xxi. 37 al. 3 Kings i. 27.
d = Matt. ii. 7 al.
e Mark iii. 5 ‖. viii. 25. ix. 12 ‖ Mt. Heb. xiii. 19 only. Lev. xiii. 16. pres., Matt. xi. 3.
f gen., 2 Thess. iii. 2. see Matt. xx. 23.

5. rec *βαπτισθ.* bef *εν πνευμ.*, with ACEℵ[3] 13. 36 rel [vss] Orig$_1$[int$_1$ Did$_1$ Cyr-jer$_1$ Chr$_1$ Cyr-p$_1$ Euthal$_1$] Œc Thl Ambr Rebapt$_1$ Gaud: *πν. αγ. βαπτ.* D Did$_1$ Hil$_1$ Victorin$_1$ Aug$_{[sæpe]}$: txt Bℵ[1] p.—add *και ο μελλετε λαμβανειν* D[1](and lat) tol Hil$_1$ Aug$_3$ [Max-taur$_1$]. aft *ημερας* add *εως της πεντηκοστης* D[1](and lat) sah Aug$_{[aliq]}$.

6. for *συνελθ.*, *ελθοντες* ℵ[1]. rec *επηρωτων*, with DE rel 36 [Chr-txt Euthal$_1$] Œc, *-τουν* C[3], *-τον* d 13: txt ABC[1]ℵ Chr-comm$_1$. *αποκαταστανεις εις την β. του ισρ.* D: om *εις* D[8](and lat); for *του*, *τω* D[8](appy): Aug has sometimes *representaberis? et quando regnum Israel?* sometimes *præsentabis regnum Israel.*

7. *ειπεν*, omg *δε*, B[1] Syr sah [arm-zoh]: *ειπεν ουν* B-corr: *ο δε ειπεν* C [arm-mss Orig-int$_1$] Aug$_2$: *και ειπεν* D, *ο δε αποκριθεις ειπ.* E æth: txt Aℵ rel vulg syr copt Thl. for *πρ. αυτους*, *αυτοις* E vulg coptt.

the subsequent history: cf. ch. viii. &c. That, in the main, they confined themselves to circuits in Palestine for some years, appears to be true; but surely would not be in compliance with such a command. **τ. ἐπαγγ. τ. πατρός**] See note on Luke xxiv. 49. **5.**] The Lord cites these words from the mouth of John himself, reff. Matt.;—and thus announces to them that, as John's mission was accomplished in baptizing *with water*, so now the great end of His own mission, the *Baptism with the Holy Ghost*, was on the point of being accomplished. Calvin remarks, that He speaks of the Pentecostal effusion as *being* the Baptism with the Holy Ghost, because it was a great representation on the whole Church of the subsequent continued work of regeneration on individuals: 'Quasi totius Ecclesiæ communis baptismus.' I may add, also because it was the *beginning* of a new period of spiritual influence, totally unlike any which had preceded. See ch. ii. 17. *ὕδατι* and **ἐν** *πν. ἁγ.* are slightly distinguished. The insertion of the preposition bef. *πν. ἁγ.* seems to give a dignity which the mere instrumental dative, *ὕδατι*, wants. **ταύτας** serves to bind on the *οὐ πολλ. ἡμ.* to the day then current; as we say, 'one of these days.' See Winer, § 23. 5, who instances 'ante *hos* quinque dies' in Lat, and quotes *πρὸ πολλῶν τῶνδε ἡμερῶν*, from Heliod. ii. 22. 97. 'Numerus dierum non definitus exercebat fidem discipulorum,' Bengel. **6.**] This *συνελθόντες* does not belong to another assembling, different from the former; but takes up again the *συναλιζόμενος* of ver. 4. Olsh. has mistaken the sense of the *μὲν οὖν*, which refers, not to another *incident*, but to other actors; *they*, as distinguished from Him who had been speaking. **Κύριε, εἰ . . .**] The stress of this question is in the words, prefixed for emphasis, **ἐν τῷ χρόνῳ τούτῳ.** That the Kingdom was, *in some sense*, and *at some time*, to be restored to Israel, was plain; nor does the Lord deny this implication (see on ver. 8). Their fault was, a too curious enquiry on a point reserved among the arcana of God. Lightfoot's idea, that the disciples wondered at the Kingdom being about to be restored to the ungrateful Jews, *at this time*, now that they had crucified Him, &c., would make our Lord's answer irrelevant. See Micah iv. 8, LXX. Meyer would refer *ἐν τῷ χρ. τού.* to the interval designated by *οὐ μετὰ πολλ. ταύ. ἡμ.*, 'during this time.' But this does not seem natural: I should rather understand it, **at this present period,—now.** The pres. **ἀποκαθιστάνεις**, is that so often used in speaking with reference to matters of prophecy, importing fixed determination: as in *ὁ ἐρχόμενος* (ref. Mt.) and the like. So that we must not render, "Art thou restoring?" but "*wilt*" or "*dost* thou restore?" As to the word itself, *καθιστάνω* (= *στημι*) is to establish or set up, and *ἀπό* gives the sense of completeness, or the cognate one of entire restitution. See Wordsw.'s note. **7.**] This is a *general* reproof and assertion, spoken with reference to *men*, as forbidden to search curiously into a point which Omniscience has reserved — the times and seasons of the future divine dealings. But it is remarkable that not *θεός*, but *ὁ πατήρ*, is here used; and this cannot fail to remind us of that saying (Mark xiii. 32), *περὶ δὲ τῆς ἡμέρας ἐκείνης*

γνῶναι [g] χρόνους ἢ [gh] καιροὺς οὓς ὁ πατὴρ [i] ἔθετο [l] ἐν τῇ
ἰδίᾳ ἐξουσίᾳ· 8 ἀλλὰ λήμψεσθε [k] δύναμιν [l] ἐπελθόντος τοῦ
ἁγίου πνεύματος ἐφ' ὑμᾶς, καὶ ἔσεσθέ μου [m] μάρτυρες ἔν
τε Ἱερουσαλὴμ καὶ [ἐν] πάσῃ Ἰουδαίᾳ καὶ Σαμαρείᾳ καὶ
[n] ἕως [no] ἐσχάτου τῆς [no] γῆς. 9 καὶ ταῦτα εἰπὼν βλεπόντων

ABCD Eℵ a b c d f g h k m o p 13

g 1 Thess. v. 1. Dan. ii. 21. h = Matt. xvi. 3. 2 Tim. iii. 1. see ch. xiv. 17. i = ch. v. 4. Hag. ii. 19, see Luke ix. 44. xxi. 14. ch. v. 4. xix. 21. k = Luke iv. 36. ix 1 al. Ps. lxvii. 35. l Luke i. 35. 1 Kings xi. 7. m = Luke xxiv. 48. ver. 22 and Acts passim. 1 Pet. v. 1. Isa. xliii. 10. n ch. xiii. 47 only, from Isa. xlix. 6. o constr., see Heb. i. 2. 1 Pet. i. 20. Jude 18.

8. rec μοι (*corr to the common constr* εσεσθε μοι), with E rel 36 [vss (æth has both)] Orig$_1$[int$_1$] Epiph Chr$_1$ [Cyr$_1$] Thl: txt ABCDℵ Orig$_1$ [Cyr-p$_1$]. om εν AC^{1}D a h p 40 coptt Orig$_1$ Hil: ins BC^{3}Eℵ rel 36 vulg syrr [arm] Orig$_1$ Chr$_3$ [Euthal$_1$] Did-int$_1$ Thl.

9. ειποντων ℵ^1 m. καυτα ειποντος αυτου νεφελη υπεβαλεν αυτον και απηρθη απο (ins των D^2) οφθ. αυτ. D, simly sah Aug$_{aliq}$; *et cum hæc* D-lat. αυτων bef βλεποντων B.

ἢ τῆς ὥρας οὐδεὶς οἶδεν, οὐδὲ ἄγγελος ἐν οὐρανῷ, οὐδὲ ὁ υἱός, **εἰ μὴ ὁ πατήρ.** It may be observed however, that the same assertion *is not made here:* only the times and seasons said to be in the *power* of the Almighty Father, Who ordereth all things κατὰ τὴν βουλὴν τοῦ θελήματος αὐτοῦ. The *Knowledge of the Son* is not here in question, only *that of the disciples.* It is an enquiry intimately connected with the interpretation of the two passages, but one beyond our power to resolve, how far, among the things not yet put under His feet, may be this very thing, the *knowledge of that day and hour.* Bengel attempts to evade the generality of the οὐχ ὑμῶν ἐστιν:—'quæ apostolorum *nondum* erat nosse, per Apocalypsin postea sunt significata.' But signified *to whom?* What individual, or portion of the Church, has ever read plainly these χρόνους ἢ καιρούς in that mysterious book? There is truth in Olsh.'s remark, that the Apostles were to be less prophets of the future, than witnesses of the past; but we must not so limit the ὑμῶν, nor forget that the γνῶναι χρόνους ἢ καιρ. has very seldom been imparted by prophecy, which generally has formed a testimony to this very fact, that God has them in His foreknowledge, and, while He announces the events, conceals for the most part in obscurity the *times.* **χρ. ἢ καιρ.**] not synonymous; as Meyer observes, καιρός is always a definite limited space of time, and involves the idea of transitoriness. See also Tittmann, N. T. Synonymes, pp. 39—45. **ἔθ. ἐν τῇ ἰδ. ἐξ.**] Some (De Wette, al.) render 'hath appointed *by* His own power;' I should rather take ἐν ἐξ. as in ch. v. 4, **in His own power,** and understand by ἔθετο **kept,** '(hath) placed,' as E. V. But the aor. sense should be preserved: the period referred to being that of the arrangement of the divine counsels of Redemption.

8.] 'Quod optimum frænandæ curiositati remedium erat, Christus eos revocat tam ad Dei promissionem, quam ad mandatum.' Calvin. **ἀλλά,** 'antitheton inter id quod discipulorum erat, vel non erat; tum inter id quod illo tempore futurum erat, et inter id quod in ulteriora reservatum erat.' Bengel. **δύναμιν,** *that* power, *especially,* spoken of ch. iv. 33, connected with their office of witnessing to the resurrection; but also all other spiritual power. See Luke xxiv. 49. μου, not emphatic, as Wordsw here and often elsewhere: see note on Matt. xvi. 18. The emphasis would be extremely out of place here: it was not their subordination to Him, but their office as witnesses, which was the contrast to their ambitious aspirings. **μάρτυρες**] This was the peculiar work of the Apostles[: so they say of themselves, ch. v. 32, ἡμεῖς ἐσμὲν αὐτοῦ μάρτυρες τῶν ῥημάτων τούτων]. See on vv. 21, 22, and Prolegg. Vol. I. ch. i. § iii. 5. **ἔν τε Ἱερ. . . . . .**] By the extension of their testimony, from Jerusalem to Samaria, and then indefinitely over the world, He reproves, by implication, their carnal anticipation of the restoration of the Kingdom to *Israel* thus understood. The Kingdom was to be one founded on μαρτυρία, and therefore reigning in the convictions of men's hearts; and not confined to Judæa, but coextensive with the world.

They understood this command only of *Jews* scattered through the world, see ch. xi. 19. De Wette observes, that these words contain *the whole plan of the Acts:* λήμψεσθε δύναμιν κ.τ.λ., ch. ii. 1—end; ἐν Ἱερουσαλήμ, ch. iii. 1—vi. 7; then the martyrdom of Stephen dispersed them *through Judæa,* vi. 8—viii. 3; they preach *in Samaria,* viii. 4—40; and, from that point, the conversion of the Apostle of the *Gentiles,* the vision of Peter, the preaching and journeys of Paul. In their former mission, Matt. x. 5, 6, they had been expressly forbidden from preaching either to Samaritans or Gentiles. **9.**] This appears (see Prolegg. Vol. I. ch. iv. § iv. 2) to be an account of the Ascension given to Luke *subsequently to the publication of his*

1 εμβλεποντες
ABCD Eℵ a b c d f g h k l m o p 13

αὐτῶν [p] ἐπήρθη, καὶ νεφέλη [q] ὑπέλαβεν αὐτὸν [r] ἀπὸ τῶν
ὀφθαλμῶν αὐτῶν. 10 καὶ ὡς [s] ἀτενίζοντες ἦσαν εἰς τὸν
οὐρανὸν [t] πορευομένου αὐτοῦ, [u] καὶ ἰδοὺ ἄνδρες δύο [v] παρειστήκεισαν αὐτοῖς ἐν [w] ἐσθήσεσιν [x] λευκαῖς, 11 οἳ καὶ εἶπαν
"Ἄνδρες Γαλιλαῖοι, τί ἑστήκατε [y] ἐμβλέποντες εἰς τὸν
οὐρανόν; οὗτος ὁ Ἰησοῦς ὁ [z] ἀναλημφθεὶς ἀφ' ὑμῶν εἰς
τὸν οὐρανὸν οὕτως ἐλεύσεται [a] ὃν τρόπον ἐθεάσασθε
αὐτὸν [b] πορευόμενον εἰς τὸν [b] οὐρανόν. 12 τότε [c] ὑπέστρεψαν

p Luke xxiv. 50. John xiii. 18 al. met., 2 Cor. x. 5. Prov. iii. 5.
q = here (ch. ii. 15 reff.) only. Ps. xxix. 1.
r = Luke xxiv. 31.
s w. εἰς, ch. iii. 4. vi. 15. vii. 55. xi. 6. xiii. 9. 2 Cor. iii. 7, 13. w. dat., ch. iii. 12 reff.
t abs., Matt. ii. 9 al. fr. see esp. John xvi. 7.
u red., Luke ii. 21. vii. 12 [ch. x. 17].
v ver. 3 reff. ch. xxvii. 23.
w here (Luke xxiv. 4 rec.) only. 2 Macc. iii. 33 only.
x = Matt. xvii. 2 ||. John xx. 12. Eccl. ix. 8. 2 Macc. xi. 8.
y w. εἰς, Matt. vi. 26. Isa. li. 1, 2.
z = ver. 2 reff.
a Matt. xxiii. 37 ||. ch. vii. 28. 2 Tim. iii. 8 only. Gen. xxvi. 29. see ch. xv. 11.
b 1 Pet. iii. 22.
c ch. viii. 25 reff.

10. rec εσθητι λευκη, with C^3DE rel 36 syr [æth $Euthal_1$] Chr_1 $Cosm_1$ Orig-int Aug_1: txt ABC^1ℵ p vulg Syr coptt arm (Eus_1) [$Epiph_2$ Promiss $Bede_1$].

11. (ειπαν, so ABC^1Dℵ p.) βλεποντες B E[-gr] $ℵ^1$ d g k o p 13 Eus_1 [$Cyr\text{-}p_2$] $Thdrt_1$ Thl-sif: Chr-mss vary: txt ACD$ℵ^3$ rel 36(sic) $Thdrt_2$ [Cyr_1 $Cosm_1$] Thl-fin, *aspicientes* vulg E-lat Aug_{aliq}. om 2nd εις τον ουρ. D 33^1-4. 105 tol Aug_1 Vig Avit.

Gospel, more particular in detail than that found in it. He has not repeated here details found there; see Luke xxiv. 50—52. On the Ascension in general, see note on Luke, l. c. **ἐπήρθη**] "**was taken up**,—we may understand of the commencing ascent . . . **ὑπέλαβεν** by a pregn. constr. involves the idea of *away* as well as *up*, and hence takes after it **ἀπό**. This verb describes the close of the scene, as far as it was visible to the spectators." Hackett. **νεφέλη**] There was a manifest propriety in the last withdrawal of the Lord, while ascending, not consisting in a *disappearance* of His Body, as on former occasions since the Resurrection; for thus might His abiding Humanity have been called in question. As it was, He went up, past the visible boundary of Heaven, the cloud,—*in human form*, and so we think of and pray to Him.

10. ἀτενίζ. ἦσαν] **they were gazing**, *stood gazing*. **εἰς τ. οὐρ.** belongs to ἀτενίζ., not to πορευομ., see reff. **πορευομένου**, not πορευθέντος: implying that the cloud remained visible for some time, probably ascending with Him. **παρειστήκεισαν**, *imperf.* in sense, as the perf. is *present*: **were standing by them. ἄνδρες**] evidently angels. See Luke xxiv. 4; John xx. 12. **11. οἳ καὶ εἶπαν**] **who** (not only appeared but) **also said.** There is a propriety in the address, ἄνδρ. Γαλιλαῖοι. It served to remind them of their origin, their call to be His disciples, and the duty of obedience to Him resting on them in consequence. **ὃν τρόπον**] **in the same manner as**;—to be taken in all cases literally, not as implying mere certainty: see reff. **οὕτως**, i. e. ἐν νεφέλῃ, Luke xxi. 27 [in the clouds of heaven: and in the same human form]. His corporeal identity is implied in οὗτος ὁ Ἰησοῦς. **ἐλεύσεται**] 'Non ii, qui ascendentem viderunt, dicuntur venturum *visuri*. Inter ascensionem et inter adventum gloriosum nullus interponitur eventus eorum utrique par: ideo hi duo conjunguntur. Merito igitur Apostoli ante datam Apocalypsin diem Christi ut valde propinquum proposuerunt. Et congruit majestati Christi, ut toto inter ascensionem et inter adventum tempore sine intermissione expectetur.' Bengel.

12.] In so careful a writer (see Luke i. 3) there must be some reason why this minute specification of distance should be here inserted, when no such appears in the Gospel. And I believe this will be found, by combining the hint dropped by Chrysostom,—δοκεῖ δέ μοι καὶ σαββάτῳ γεγονέναι ταῦτα· οὐ γὰρ ἂν οὕτω τὸ διάστημα ἐδήλωσεν . . . . . εἰ μὴ ὡρισμένον τι μῆκος ἐβάδιζον ἐν τῇ ἡμέρᾳ τοῦ σαββάτου,—with the declaration in the Gospel (xxiv. 50) that he led them out *as far as to Bethany*. This latter was (John xi. 18) *fifteen stadia* from Jerusalem, which is more than twice the Sabbath-day's journey (2000 cubits = about six furlongs). Now if the Ascension happened on the Sabbath, it is very possible that offence may have arisen at the statement in the Gospel: and that therefore the Evangelist gives here the more exact notice, that the spot, although forming part of the district of Bethany, was yet on that part of the Mount of Olives which fell within the limits of the Sabbath-day's journey. This of course must be a mere conjecture; but it will not be impugned by the fact of the Ascension being kept by the Church in after ages on a Thursday. This formed no hindrance to Chrysostom in making the above supposition: although the festival was certainly

εἰς Ἱερουσαλὴμ ἀπὸ ὄρους τοῦ καλουμένου [d] ἐλαιῶνος, ὅ ABCD
ἐστιν ἐγγὺς Ἱερουσαλήμ, σαββάτου [e] ἔχον [f] ὁδόν. 13 καὶ Eℵ a b c d f g h k
ὅτε [g] εἰςῆλθον, εἰς τὸ [h] ὑπερῷον ἀνέβησαν οὗ [i] ἦσαν [k] κατα- l m o p 13
μένοντες, ὅ τε Πέτρος καὶ Ἰωάννης καὶ Ἰάκωβος καὶ
Ἀνδρέας, Φίλιππος καὶ Θωμᾶς, Βαρθολομαῖος καὶ Μαθθαῖος, Ἰάκωβος Ἀλφαίου καὶ Σίμων ὁ ζηλωτής, καὶ
Ἰούδας Ἰακώβου. 14 οὗτοι πάντες [i] ἦσαν [l] προσκαρτεροῦντες [m] ὁμοθυμαδὸν τῇ [n] προσευχῇ σὺν γυναιξὶν καὶ
Μαρίᾳ τῇ μητρὶ τοῦ Ἰησοῦ καὶ τοῖς ἀδελφοῖς αὐτοῦ.

d Luke xix. 29. xxi. 37 only. Jos. Antt. vii. 9. 2. = τὸ ὄρ. τῶν ἐλαιῶν, Luke xix. 37 al.
e see John viii. 57. ix. 21, 23.
f = Luke ii. 44. 3 Kings xix. 4.
g = ch. ix. 6. Matt. viii. 5 al. ellips., here only.
h ch. ix. 37, 39. xx. 8 only. 2 Kings xviii. 33. Ezek. xli. 7.
i constr., ch. ii. 5 reff.
k here only. Num. xx. 1 al.
l = ch. vi. 4 al4. Rom. xii. 12. xiii. 6. Col. iv. 2 (Mark iii. 9) only. Num. xiii. 21 only. Sus. 6 Theod.
m ch. ii. 46 al8. Rom. xv. 6 only. L.P. Num. xxiv. 24 al.
n abs., Matt. xxi. 13 ||, from Isa. lvi. 7. Ps. iv. 2 al.

13. εισηλθεν D-gr. rec ανεβησαν bef εις τ. υπ. (*corrn to avoid the ambiguity of* εισηλθ. εις το υπ.), with DEℵ[3] rel 36 tol syrr coptt [arm-zoh Aug$_1$]: om ανεβ. ℵ[1]: txt ABC[1.3] p vulg [æth arm-usc] (Orig$_1$) Chr$_1$ Thl-fin-comm$_1$ Bede-gr. rec transp ιωαν. and ιακ., with (E) rel 36 syr [arm-zoh Chr$_1$ Thl]: txt ABCDℵ p vulg Syr [coptt æth arm-usc] Aug.—κ. ανδρ. bef κ. ιωαν. E Bede-gr: *petr. et joh. et andr. et jac.* Bede-lat. om 3rd και D. ins ο του bef αλφαιου D d. om 7th και D. om ο (bef ζηλωτης) ℵ[1].

14. ℵ has ομοθυμαδον both before and after προσκαρτ., ℵ[3] disapproving the 2nd. rec (aft προσευχη) ins και τη δεησει (*Phil* iv. 6), with C[3] rel 36 (Orig$_1$) [Chr$_1$]; και δεησει, omg τη, m: om ABC[1]DEℵ p H[r] vulg syrr coptt æth arm Chr$_1$ Thl-fin-comm Cypr$_2$ Aug Jer Bede. ins ταις bef γυν. D. aft γυν. ins και τεκνοις D. μαριαμ BE p 40 sah [æth]: txt ACDℵ rel 36 [copt]. om τη D[1] (ins D[2]). om του B. rec ins συν bef τοις αδ. αυτ. (*corrn, to avoid connecting the brethren of our Lord with His mother*), with BC[3]E rel syrr Chr$_1$: om AC[1]Dℵ vulg copt æth arm Cypr$_2$ Aug$_2$.

observed in his time (see Bingham, Orig. Eccl. xx. 6. 5. There is no mention of it in the Fathers of the first three centuries). *Forty days* from the Resurrection is an expression which would suit as well the Saturday of the seventh week as the Thursday. The distance of the Mount of Olives from Jerusalem is stated by Josephus at five stadia, Antt. xx. 8. 6,—at six stadia, B. J. v. 2. 3; different points being taken as the limit. The present church of the Ascension rather exceeds the distance of six stadia from the city. The use of **ἐλαιών, -ῶνος**, here (and in reff.) by Luke only is remarkable, especially as the whole passage is so much in his own distinctive style as to preclude the idea of his having transferred a written document. ἔχον is not for ἀπέχον, but as in τριάκ. κ. ὀκτ. ἔτη ἔχων, John v. 5, and in reff.; the space or time mentioned being regarded as an *attribute* of the subject. **13. εἰςῆλθ.**] 'into the city;' see reff. **τὸ ὑπερῷ.**] The idea that this was a chamber in *the Temple* has originated in low literal-harmonistic views, Luke having stated (Luke xxiv. 53) that they were διὰ παντὸς ἐν τῷ ἱερῷ. As if such an expression could be literally understood, or taken to mean more than that they were there at all appointed times (see ch. iii. 1). It is in the highest degree improbable that the disciples would be found *assembled* in *any public* place at this time. The upper chamber was *perhaps* that in which the last Supper had been taken; *probably* that in which they had been since then assembled (John xx. 19, 26), but *certainly* one in a *private house*. Lightf. shews that it was the practice of the Jews to retire into a large chamber under the flat roof for purposes of deliberation or prayer. See Neander, Pfl. u. Leit., p. 13, note. Epiphanius, de ponderibus, c. 14 (vol. iii. p. 170), relates that when Hadrian came to Jerusalem, εὗρε τὴν πόλιν πᾶσαν ἠδαφισμένην καὶ τὸ ἱερὸν τοῦ θεοῦ καταπεπατημένον, παρεκτὸς ὀλίγων οἰκημάτων καὶ τῆς τοῦ θεοῦ ἐκκλησίας μικρᾶς οὔσης, ἔνθα ὑποστρέψαντες οἱ μαθηταί, ὅτε ὁ σωτὴρ ἀνελήφθη ἀπὸ τοῦ Ἐλαιῶνος, ἀνέβησαν εἰς τὸ ὑπερῷον. ἐκεῖ γὰρ ᾠκοδόμητο, τουτέστιν ἐν τῷ μέρει Σιών· ἥτις ἀπὸ τῆς ἐρημώσεως περιελήφθη, ... ἕως χρόνου Μαξίμου τοῦ ἐπισκόπου καὶ Κωνσταντίνου τοῦ βασιλέως, ὡς σκηνὴ ἐν ἀμπελῶνι, κατὰ τὸ γεγραμμένον. And Nicephorus viii. 30 (see Wordsw.) says that the Empress Helena enclosed in her larger church the chamber where took place ἡ τοῦ ἁγίου πνεύματος κάθοδος ἐν τῷ ὑπερῴῳ. **οὗ ἦσαν κατ.**] not to be taken as in E. V. '*where abode both Peter,*' &c.; which gives the idea that Peter, &c. were *already in the chamber*, and the rest *joined them there*:—but, on entering the city, they went up into the upper chamber,

15 Καὶ ° ἐν ταῖς ἡμέραις ταύταις ᵖ ἀναστὰς Πέτρος ἐν
μέσῳ ᑫ τῶν ᑫ ἀδελφῶν εἶπεν (ἦν τε ʳ ὄχλος ˢ ὀνομάτων ᵗ ἐπὶ
τὸ αὐτὸ * ὡς ἑκατὸν εἴκοσι) 16 ᵘ Ἄνδρες ἀδελφοί, ᵛ ἔδει ʷ πληρωθῆναι τὴν ˣ γραφὴν [ταύτην] ἣν ʸ προεῖπεν τὸ ᶻ πνεῦμα

o ch. vi. 1. Luke i. 39. vi. 12 al. p = ch. xv. 7 reff. q = ch. ix. 30 reff. r ch. vi. 7 reff. s = Rev iii. 4. xi. 13. Num. xxvi. 53. t ch. ii. 1, 44, 47 (iii. 1). iv. 26 (from Ps. ii. 3). 1 Cor. xi. 20. Ps. xxxvi. 38. u ch. vii. 2 al. fr. v = ch. iv. 12 reff. w = ch. iii. 18 reff. x = Mark xii. 10. Luke iv. 21. John xix. 24. 2 Tim. iii. 16. y Gal. v. 21. 1 Thess. iv. 6 only †. προείρ., Rom. ix. 29 al. z Heb. iii 7. ix. 8. x. 15. see 2 Pet. i. 21.

15. for και εν, εν δε DE sah syr-mg Aug_1. ins ο bef πετρ. D. εμμεσω ACE. rec for αδελφων, μαθητων (*corrn, to avoid the triple recurrence of* αδελφ. *in vv.* 14, 15, 16. *Meyer and De W. take* αδ. *to have been a corrn to suit* ανδρ. ἀδελφοι *in ver.* 16, *but the other is much more prob*), with C^3DE rel 36 syrr Chr Thl $Cypr_1$ Aug_2: txt ABC^1ℵ 13 vulg coptt æth arm Aug. for τε, δε CD^7 vulg D^7-lat E-lat syrr copt $Cypr_1$ Aug_2: γαρ *præterea* D^1 : om sah æth. ins ο bef οχλος D. for ονοματων, ανδρων E : *hominum* vulg(not fuld) Syr æth [$Cypr\text{-}ms_1$]. *ὡσεὶ ACℵ 40 Thl-fin : ως BDE rel [Chr_1]. rec εικοσιν, with rel : txt ABCEℵ f m p 13. 36 : ρκ' D.
16. δει D(txt D-$corr^1$) vulg [copt arm-ms] $Iren\text{-}int_1$(principal-mss : given nominatim by Stieren) Aug_1 Vig_1 Gild. (Iren-int has *oportebat* apud Harvey.) om ταυτην

where they (usually) **sojourned** (not '*dwelt*:' they did not all dwell in one house; see John xix. 27, note), **namely, Peter,** &c. On the catalogue of the Apostles, see Matt. x. 2, note. **14.**] **σὺν γυναιξίν** has been rendered '*with their wives*,' to which sense Bp. Middleton inclines, justifying it by σὺν γυναιξὶν καὶ τέκνοις, ch. xxi. 5. But the omission of the articles there may be accounted for on the same principle as in Matt. xix. 29, viz. that which Bp. M. calls *enumeration*, ch. vi. § 2. Here I think we must take σὺν γυν. not as meaning '*with women*,' as Hackett, but, the art. not being expressed after the preposition σύν, as = σὺν ταῖς γυν. (see Middl. ch. vi. § 1), and interpret γυν., **the women**, viz. those spoken of by Luke himself, Luke viii. 2, 3,—where, besides those named, he mentions ἕτεραι πολλαί. Many of these were certainly not wives of the Apostles; and that those women who were 'last at the Cross and earliest at the tomb' should not have been assembled with the company now, is very improbable. **καὶ Μαρίᾳ**] The καί gives eminence to *one* among those previously mentioned. So τῶνδε εἵνεκα, καὶ γῆς ἱμέρῳ, Herod. i. 73. See Hartung, Partikellehre, i. 145. This is the last mention of her in the N. T. The traditions, which describe her as (1) dying at the age of fifty-nine, in the fifth year of Claudius (Niceph. H. E. ii. 21), or (2) accompanying John to Ephesus, and being buried there (see Winer, Realwörterb. art. Maria), are untrustworthy. Other accounts, with the authorities, may be seen in Butler's Lives of the Saints, Aug. 15. The fable of the Assumption has *no foundation even in tradition.* **τοῖς ἀδελφ. αὐτ.**] This clearly shews, as does John vii. 5 compared with vi. 69, 70, that *none of the brethren of our Lord were of the number of the Twelve.* When they were converted, is quite uncertain. See the whole subject discussed in note on Matt. xiii. 55, and in the Prolegomena to the Epistle of James. In both cases of *one* being distinguished from a number, cited here by Wordsw. to shew that James the Less may have been one of these brethren, viz. that of Μαρία, as distinguished among the women here, and that of Joseph, ch. vii. 9, he does not observe that the *general statement precedes* the individual distinction, as indeed it naturally must.

15—26.] Election of a Twelfth Apostle to fill the room of Judas Iscariot. **15. ἐν τ. ἡμ. τ.**] In the days between the Ascension and Pentecost; during which it appears that the number of the assembly had increased, not probably by fresh conversions, but by the gathering round the Apostles of those who had previously been disciples. **ἦν τε**] The very frequent use of τε is a peculiarity of the Acts, and should have its weight in determining the reading, even where, as here, δέ seems more appropriate. It occurs in the Gospel 5 times: in the Acts, 121. **ὀνομάτων**] [that is, of persons: but the term would hardly be used except where the number is small.] See note on Rev. iii. 4. **ἑκατὸν εἴκοσι**] De Wette asks, 'where were the 500 brethren of 1 Cor. xv. 6?' We surely may answer, 'not in Jerusalem.' See Neander, Pfl. u. Leit., p. 72, note. **16.**] We may enquire, by what change in mind and power Peter was able, *before the descent of the Spirit*, thus authoritatively to speak of Scripture and the divine purposes? The answer will be found in the peculiar gift of the Spirit to the Apostles, John xx. 21, 23; where see note. The pre-eminency of Peter here is the

τὸ [z] ἅγιον διὰ [a] στόματος Δαυεὶδ περὶ Ἰούδα τοῦ γενομένου
[b] ὁδηγοῦ τοῖς [c] συλλαβοῦσιν Ἰησοῦν, 17 ὅτι [d] κατηριθμη-
μένος [e] ἦν ἐν ἡμῖν καὶ [f] ἔλαχεν τὸν [g] κλῆρον τῆς [h] διακονίας ταύτης. 18 οὗτος μὲν οὖν [i] ἐκτήσατο [k] χωρίον [l] ἐκ
[mn] μισθοῦ τῆς [no] ἀδικίας, καὶ [p] πρηνὴς [q] γενόμενος [r] ἐλάκησεν

ABCD Eא a b c d f g h k l m o p 13

a = Luke i. 70. ch. iii. 18, 21. iv. 25. xv. 7. 2 Chron. xxxvi. 21, 22.
b Matt. xv. 14. xxiii. 16, 24. Rom. ii. 19 only. Ezra viii. 1 only. 1 Macc. iv. 2 al.
c = Matt. xxvi. 55 ‖. ch. xii. 3 al. Judg. vii. 25.
d here only. Gen. l. 3. 2 Chron. xxxi. 19.
e w. perf. part., ch. xxii. 29 reff.
f = 2 Pet. i. 1 (Luke i. 9. John xix. 24) only. (1 Kings xiv. 47. Wisd. viii. 19 only.) 3 Macc. vi. 1.
g ch. viii. 21 reff.
h = ch. xx. 14 reff.
i ch. xxii. 28 reff.
k = John iv. 5. ch. iv. 34. v. 3, 8. xxviii. 7. 1 Chron. xxvii. 27.
l = Matt. xx. 2. xxvii. 7.
m = Rom. iv. 4 reff.
n 2 Pet. ii. 13, 15. see 2 Macc. viii. 33.
o = Luke xiii. 27. 1 Kings iii. 13, 14.
p here only †. Wisd. iv. 19 only.
q = ch. xvi. 27 al.
r here only †.

ABC^{1}א p H^r vulg coptt æth arm Orig$_2$ Eus$_1$ Ath$_1$ Did$_1$[int$_1$] Vig$_1$ Gild (*omitted by homœotel:* or *erased as unnecessary with* ην, *and perhaps, as Mey. and De W., because no citation immediately follows*): ins C^{3}DE rel 36 syrr Chr$_1$ Iren-int$_1$ Aug$_1$. rec ins *τον* bef *ιησουν*, with C^{3}DE rel 36 Chr Thl: om ABC^{1}א Eus$_1$ Did$_1$.

17. om *ην* א^1. rec for *εν*, *συν* (*corrn to better Greek; see ref* 2 *Chron*), with rel syrr [æth arm] Chr: txt ABCDEא p 13 H^r vulg coptt Eus$_1$ Iren-int$_1$ Aug$_2$. for *και*, *ος* D^1-gr(txt D^4). ins *υπερβα* (*but in reference to eccl lection: see Tischdf* [N. T. Vat. proleg. p. xxxii]) bef *τ. διακ.* B^r-marg.

18. rec ins *του* bef *μισθ.* (*corrn in ignorance of the usage which omits the art aft a preposition; see Middleton, ch.* vi. 1), with o [13(e sil, Treg)] Thl-fin: om ABCDEא rel H^r Eus$_1$ Chr$_1$. aft **αδικ.** ins *αυτου* D [syr-w-ast sah æth Eus$_1$ Aug$_1$].

commencement of the fulfilment of Matt. xvi. 18, 19 (see note there). **17.**] **ὅτι**, not *'although'* (Kuinoel), but **because**: it gives the reason of the previous assertion, viz. that Judas held, and had betrayed, that place of high trust of which the prophecy spoke. Thus the **ὅτι** has reference to the *substance of the prophecy*, already in Peter's mind, and serves to explain ἡ ἔπαυλις αὐτοῦ and ἡ ἐπισκοπὴ αὐτοῦ. **ἔλαχεν τὸν κλῆρον**] not literally, but inasmuch as the *lot* of every man is regarded as being cast and appointed by God. κλῆρος, first, the *lot* itself; then, *that apportioned by lot;* then, *any species of apportionment*, whether *possession*, or *office*, as here. **18.**] This verse *cannot be regarded as inserted by Luke;* for, **1.** the place of its insertion would be most unnatural for an historical notice; **2.** the *μὲν οὖν* forbids the supposition: **3.** the whole style of the verse is rhetorical, and not narrative, e.g. *οὗτος*, *μισθοῦ τῆς ἀδικίας*. The **ἐκτήσατο χωρίον** does not appear to agree with the account in Matt. xxvii. 6—8; nor, consistently with common honesty, can they be reconciled, *unless we knew more of the facts than we do.* If we compare the two, that of Matthew is the more particular, and more likely to give rise to this one, *as a general inference from the buying of the field*, than *vice versâ*. Whether Judas, as Bengel supposes, 'initio emtionis facto, occasionem dederat ut Sacerdotes eam consummarent,' we cannot say: such a thing is of course possible[, but is certainly not contemplated by St. Matthew's account, where the priests settle to buy the field, on deliberation, what they should do with the money]. At all events we hence clearly see that *Luke could not have been acquainted with the Gospel of Matthew at this time*, or surely (not, he would have *repeated* St. Matt.'s account, as Wordsw. unfairly represents me to say, but) this apparent discrepancy would not have been found. The various attempts to reconcile the two narratives, which may be seen in most of our English commentaries, are among the saddest examples of the shifts to which otherwise high-minded men are driven by an unworthy system. See as a notable example, Wordsw.'s note, written since the above. I need hardly say to any intelligent and ingenuous reader, that his way of harmonizing,—viz. that as the *Jews* are said to have crucified our Lord when they were only the occasion of his being crucified, so Judas may be said to have bought the field when he only gave occasion to its being bought by the Chief Priests,—is entirely precluded here by the words ἐκ μισθοῦ τῆς ἀδικίας, 'out of the wages of his iniquity,' which plainly bind on the purchase to Judas as his personal act. **καὶ πρ. γεν.**] The connexion of this with the former clause would seem to point to the death of Judas having taken place *in* the field which he bought. See also ver. 19. **πρηνὴς γενόμενος** will hardly bear the meaning assigned to it by those who wish to harmonize the two accounts,—viz. that, having hanged himself, he fell by the breaking of the rope. πρηνής· ἐπὶ πρόσωπον πεπτωκώς, Hesych. ὅλον μὲν τὸ σῶμα κεῖσθαι πρηνὲς λέγομεν, ὅταν ἡ μὲν γαστὴρ κάτωθεν, ἄνωθεν δὲ ᾖ τὸ νῶτον, Galen, cited by Wetstein. πρηνής, εἰς τοὺμ-

[s] μέσος καὶ [t] ἐξεχύθη πάντα τὰ [u] σπλάγχνα αὐτοῦ, 19 καὶ
[v] γνωστὸν ἐγένετο πᾶσιν τοῖς [w] κατοικοῦσιν Ἱερουσαλήμ,
ὥστε κληθῆναι τὸ [x] χωρίον ἐκεῖνο τῇ [[y] ἰδίᾳ] [z] διαλέκτῳ
[y] αὐτῶν Ἀκελδαμάχ, [a] τουτέστιν [x] χωρίον αἵματος. 20 γέ-

s constr., Luke xxiii. 45. Gen. xv. 10. t = (-χεῖν, Matt. ix. 17.) 2 Kings xx. 10. u lit., here only. (2 Cor. vi. 12 reff.) 2 Macc. ix. 5 (6 ?) only. v = John xviii. 15, 16. ch. ix. 42. xv. 18. xix. 17. Ps. lxxv. 1. w constr., ch. ii. 9, 14 al5. Matt. xxiii. 21. Luke xiii. 4. Rev. (xii. 12, v. r.) xvii. 2 only. Hos. x. 5. 1 Macc. iii. 31. x ver. 18. y so John x. 12. 2 Pet. iii. 16. z ch. ii. 6, 8 al3. Acts only. Esth. ix. 26. a ch. xix. 4 reff.

om παντα A Thl-sif$_1$ Gaud$_1$.

19. ins ο bef και D-gr ℵ(but erased) 18 Aug$_1$: και τουτο sah. om ιδια B^{1}Dℵ arm: ins AB^{2}CE rel [Eus$_1$ Chr]. αυτων bef διαλ. E 163 Aug$_1$. rec ακελδαμα, with C 13 rel vulg syrr copt[-wilk arm] Chr: æth-mss are appy divided: txt(-αχ) ABD E(-ακ) ℵ p 40 am demid fuld tol lux sah Eus$_1$ Aug$_1$ Bede.—αχελδ. Aℵ p 40, *haceldamach* tol, *acheldamac* am fuld lux Bede, *akyldamach* sah[-ed], *-demach* æth-pl.—ακελδαιμαχ D.

προσθεν, ἐπὶ στόματος, Etymol. Nor again is it at all probable that the Apostle would recount what was a *mere accident accompanying his death*, when that death itself was the accursed one of *hanging*. What then are we to decide respecting the two accounts? That there should have been a double account actually current of the death of Judas at this early period is *in the highest degree improbable*, and will only be assumed by those (De Wette, &c.) who take a very low view of the accuracy of the Evangelists. Dismissing then this solution, let us compare the accounts themselves. In this case, *that* in Matt. xxvii. is *general*,—ours *particular*. *That* depends entirely on the exact sense to be assigned to **ἀπήγξατο** (וַיֵּחָנַק, καὶ ἀπήγξατο, 2 Sam. xvii. 23): whereas *this distinctly assigns the manner* of his death, without stating any cause for the falling on his face. It is obvious that, while the general term used by Matthew points mainly at *self-murder*, the account given here does not preclude the catastrophe related having happened, in some way, as a divine judgment, *during the suicidal attempt.* Further than this, with our present knowledge, we cannot go. *An accurate acquaintance with the actual circumstances* would account for the discrepancy, but *nothing else.* Another kind of death is assigned to Judas by Œcumenius, quoting from Papias: ἱστορεῖ Παπίας ὁ τοῦ Ἰωάννου τοῦ ἀποστ. μαθητὴς λέγων· μέγα τῆς ἀσεβείας ὑπόδειγμα ἐν τούτῳ τῷ κόσμῳ περιεπάτησεν Ἰούδας· πρησθεὶς γὰρ ἐπὶ τὴν σάρκα, ὥστε μὴ δύνασθαι διελθεῖν, ἁμάξης ῥαδίως διερχομένης, ὑπὸ τῆς ἁμάξης ἐπιέσθη, ὥστε τὰ ἔγκατα αὐτοῦ ἐκκενωθῆναι. Theophylact quotes the same on Matt. xxvii., but without the last words, ὑπὸ τῆς ἁμ. κ.τ.λ., which De Wette supposes to have been inserted from Œcumenius having misunderstood Papias. If so, the tradition is in accordance with, and has arisen from an exaggerated amplification of, our text. See the whole passage from Theophylact cited, and a discussion whether it is rightly ascribed to Papias, in Routh, Reliquiæ Sacræ, vol. i. p. 9, and notes.

ἐλάκησεν] **cracked asunder**: it implies bursting with a noise. It is quite possible that this catastrophe happening in the field, as our narrative implies, may have suggested its employment as a burial-place for strangers, as being defiled. So Stier, Reden der Apostel, i. 10. **19.**] It is principally from this verse that it has been inferred that the two vv. 18, 19 are *inserted by Luke.* But it is impossible to separate it from ver. 18; and I am disposed to regard both as belonging to Peter's speech, but freely Græcized by Luke, inserting *into the speech itself* the explanations τῇ [ἰδίᾳ] διαλ. αὐτ., and τουτέστιν χ. αἵμ., as if the speech had been spoken in Greek originally. This is much more natural, than to parenthesize these clauses; it is, in fact, what must be more or less done by all who report in a language different from that actually used by the speaker. The words and idioms of another tongue contain allusions and national peculiarities which never could have been in the mind of one speaking in a different language; but the ear tolerates these, or easily separates them, if critically exercised. **γνωστὸν . . .**] See Luke xxiv. 18. **ὥστε**] in Matt. xxvii. 8, the name 'the field of blood' is referred to the fact of its having been *bought with the price of blood:* here, to the fact of *Judas* having there *met with a signal and bloody death.* On the whole, I believe the result to which I have above inclined will be found the best to suit the phænomena of the two passages,—viz. that, with regard to the *purchase of the field*, the more circumstantial account in Matthew is to be adopted; with regard to the *death of Judas*, the more circumstantial account of Luke. The *clue which joins these has been lost to us:* and in this, only those will find any stumbling-block, whose faith in the veracity of the Evangelists is very

b Luke xx. 42.
c here only. Psa. lxviii. 25.
d art., Matt. iv. 3 al.
e = 1 Tim. iii. 1 (Luke xix. 44. 1 Pet. ii. 12) only. Psa. cviii. 8.
f = ch. ix. 39. x. 23 al. L. (Mark xiv. 53.)
g Eurip. Phœn. 534, 5. see ch. ix. 28. Ps. cxx. 8. Deut. xxxi. 2.
h = Luke ii. 8. xii. 14. Heb. x. 21.
i w. ἀπό, Matt. xx. 8. ch. viii. 35. x. 37. 1 Pet. iv. 17. Ezek. ix. 6.
k attr., ver. 1 reff.
l = ver. 2 reff.
m = ver. 9.
n ver. 8 reff.
o = ch. ii. 31. iv. 33. Rom. vi. 5. Phil. iii. 10. 1 Pet. i. 3. iii. 21 ‡.
p ch. vi. 6. xvii. 31.

ABCD Eℵ a b c d f g h k l m o p 13

γραπται γὰρ ἐν [b] βίβλῳ [b] ψαλμῶν Γενηθήτω ἡ [c] ἔπαυλις
αὐτοῦ ἔρημος, καὶ μὴ ἔστω [d] ὁ κατοικῶν ἐν αὐτῇ. καὶ
Τὴν [e] ἐπισκοπὴν αὐτοῦ λαβέτω ἕτερος. 21 δεῖ οὖν τῶν
[f] συνελθόντων ἡμῖν ἀνδρῶν ἐν παντὶ χρόνῳ ᾧ [g] εἰσῆλθεν
καὶ [g] ἐξῆλθεν [h] ἐφ' ἡμᾶς ὁ κύριος Ἰησοῦς, 22 [i] ἀρξάμενος
ἀπὸ τοῦ βαπτίσματος Ἰωάννου ἕως τῆς ἡμέρας [k] ἧς
[l] ἀνελήμφθη [m] ἀφ' ἡμῶν, [n] μάρτυρα τῆς [o] ἀναστάσεως
αὐτοῦ σὺν ἡμῖν γενέσθαι ἕνα τούτων. 23 καὶ [p] ἔστησαν

20. for 1st αυτου, αυτων m^1 o p vulg(not am demid &c) D^1-lat æth-rom arm [Chr_1]. for εστω, η D^1(txt D^3). rec for λαβετω, λαβοι (*corrn to suit* LXX), with E rel [Eus_1]: txt ABCDℵ p [arm] Eus_1 Chr_1.

21. ins τω bef χρονω D. rec ins εν bef ω, with C^3(and appy C^2) $Eℵ^3$ rel Chr: om ABC^1 D-corr $ℵ^1$ p vulg Aug_1.—ως D^1; *quoniam* D^1-lat. at end add χριστος D syr æth Aug_1.

22. for εως, αχρι Aℵ p. rec γενεσθαι bef συν ημ., with E 13 rel [syrr æth] Thl_2: txt ABCDℵ k m p 40 vulg arm Chr_2 Aug_1.

23. aft και ins τουτων λεχθεντων E. εστησεν D^1(and lat: txt D-$corr^1$) æth-rom

weak indeed. **Ἀκελδαμάχ**] חֲקֵל דְּמָא. The field originally belonged to a potter, and was probably a piece of land which had been exhausted of its clay fit for his purposes, and so was useless. Jerome relates that it was still shewn on the S. side of Mount Sion (ἐν βορείοις τοῦ Σιὼν ὄρους, but by mistake, Eusebius), in which neighbourhood there is even now a bed of white clay (see Winer, Realw., art. 'Blutacker').

20.] **γάρ**, the connexion being, 'all this happened and became known,' &c., '*in accordance with* the prophecy,' &c. Ps. lxix. is eminently a Messianic psalm,—spoken in the first place of David and his kingdom and its enemies, and so, according to the universal canon of O. T. interpretation, of Him in whom that kingdom found its true fulfilment, and of His enemies. And Judas being the first and most notable of these, the Apostle applies eminently to him the words which in the Psalm are spoken in the plural of all such enemies. The same is true of Ps. cix., and there *one* adversary is even more pointedly marked out. See also Ps. lv. **ἐπισκοπήν** = פְּקֻדָּה, office, or charge. The citations are freely from the LXX.

21.] **οὖν**, since all this has happened to Judas, and since it is the divine will that another should take the charge which was his. **ἐν παντὶ χρόνῳ**] This definition of the necessary qualification of an apostle exactly agrees with our Lord's saying in John xv. 27: καὶ ὑμεῖς δὲ μαρτυρεῖτε, ὅτι ἀπ' ἀρχῆς μετ' ἐμοῦ ἐστε. See Prolegg. Vol. I. ch. i. § iii. 5. **εἰσῆλθ. κ. ἐξῆλθ. ἐφ' ἡμᾶς**] An abridged construction for εἰσῆλθ. ἐφ' ἡμᾶς κ. ἐξῆλθ. ἀφ' ἡμῶν.

22. βαπτ. Ἰωάν.] Not '*His being baptized by John*' (as Wolf, Kuin., &c.); but **the baptism of John**, as a well-known date, including of course the opening event of our Lord's ministry, *His own* baptism. That John continued to baptize for some time after that, can be no possible objection to the assignment of 'John's baptism' generally, as the date of the commencement of the apostolic testimony (against De Wette). We may notice, that from this point the testimony of the Evangelists themselves in their Gospels properly begins, Matt. iii. 1, Mark i. 1, Luke iii. 1, John i. 6. **μάρτ. τῆς ἀναστ.**] This one event was the passage-point between the Lord's life of humiliation and His life of glory,—the completion of His work below and beginning of His work above. And to 'give witness with power' of the Resurrection (ch. iv. 33), would be to discourse of it *as being all this;* in order to which, the whole ministry of Jesus must be within the cycle of the Apostle's experience. It is remarkable that Peter here lays down *experience of matters of fact*, not eminence in any subjective grace or quality, as the condition of Apostleship. Still, the testimony was not to be *mere* ordinary allegation of matters of fact: any who had seen the Lord since His resurrection were equal to this;—but belonged to *a distinct office* (see John xiv. 26: also ch. v. 31, note), *requiring the especial selection and grace of God.*

23.] **ἔστησαν**, viz. the *whole company, to whom the words had been spoken;* not the eleven Apostles. **Ἰωσήφ . . . .**] The names **Ἰωσήφ** and

δύο, Ἰωσὴφ τὸν καλούμενον Βαρσαββᾶν, ὃς [q] ἐπεκλήθη
Ἰοῦστος, καὶ Μαθθίαν. 24 καὶ προσευξάμενοι εἶπαν Σὺ
κύριε [r] καρδιογνῶστα πάντων, [s] ἀνάδειξον ὃν ἐξελέξω ἐκ
τούτων τῶν δύο ἕνα 25 λαβεῖν τὸν τόπον τῆς [t] διακονίας
ταύτης καὶ [u] ἀποστολῆς, ἀφ' ἧς [v] παρέβη Ἰούδας πο-

q = ch. iv. 36. x. 5 al. Dan. x. 1.
r ch. xv. 8 only +. Herm. Past. ii. 4. 3 (see Nov. Test. Sinait., fol. 148*).
s Luke x. 1 only. Hab. iii. 2. = 2 Macc. ix. 23. see Luke i. 80.
t ver. 17.
u Rom. i. 5. 1 Cor. ix. 2. Gal. ii. 8 only. Deut. xxii. 7.
v = here (Matt. xv. 2, 3. 2 John 9) only. Exod. xxxii. 8. (Sir. xxiii. 18.)

Aug$_1$. for *ιωσηφ*, *ιωσην* B(Blc) 5 lect-1 syr sah. rec *βαρσαβαν*, with C rel vulg syrr Eus[-edd$_3$ Bas$_1$] Chr: txt ABEℵ b f g p am fuld coptt Eus-mss$_3$.—*βαρναβαν* D tol æth. (13 def.)

24. [*ειπαν*, so ABCDℵ p.] om *συ* D o. rec *εκ τ. τ. δυο ενα* bef *ον εξελ.*: txt ABCDEℵ rel [vulg] syr copt Eus Bas$_1$ Chr$_2$ Dion-areop Thl Procop: *ενα ον εξελ. εκ τ. τ. δ.* Syr arm. for *ενα*, *ανα*, making *αναλαβειν*, D[1](txt D[4]).

25. *τοπον* bef *τον* D. rec (for *τοπον*) *κληρον*, with C[3]Eℵ rel syrr [arm Eus$_1$(appy) Bas$_1$ Chr$_1$]: om æth (*την διακονιαν ταυτης τ. αποστ.*): txt ABC[1]D vulg coptt Procop$_1$ Aug$_1$. rec (for *αφ'*) *εξ*, with E rel Chr; *de* vulg E-lat: txt ABCDℵ p copt Bas$_1$, *a*

Ἰωσῆς, different forms of the same, are confused in the MSS., both here and in ch. iv. 36. But *Barsabbas* (or Barsabas) and *Barnabas* are not to be confounded: they are different names (Barsabbas = son of Sabba or Saba: on Barnabas, see ch. iv. 36, note); and Barnabas is evidently introduced in iv. 36 as a person who had not been mentioned before. Of Barsabas, nothing further is known. Euseb., iii. 39, states, on the authority of Papias, that he drank a cup of poison without being hurt. [There is a Judas Barsabbas mentioned in ch. xv. 22, whom some take to be his brother.] In all probability both the selected persons (see Eus. i. 12) belonged to the number of the Seventy, as it would be natural that the candidates for apostleship should be chosen from among those who had been already distinguished by Christ Himself among the brethren.
Justus is a Roman cognomen, assumed according to a custom then prevalent. The name Justus seems to have been common: Schöttgen, Hor. Hebr., on this place, gives two instances of Jews bearing it.
Μαθθίαν] Nothing historical is known of him. Traditionally, according to Nicephorus (H. E. ii. 40, Winer), he suffered martyrdom in Æthiopia; according to others, in Colchis (Menolog. Græc. iii. 198, Winer): another account (Perionii Vitæ Apost. p. 178 sqq., Winer) makes him preach in Judæa and be stoned by the Jews. Clem. Alex., Strom. ii. 9 [45], p. 452 P., vii. 13 [82], p. 882 P., mentions the *παραδόσεις* of Matthias, which perhaps were the same as an apocryphal gospel once current under his name, mentioned by Eus., H. E. iii. 25. See Winer, Realw.

24.] It is a question, *to Whom this prayer was directed.* I think all probability is in favour of the Apostle (for Peter certainly was the spokesman) having addressed *his glorified Lord.* And with this the language of the prayer agrees. No stress can, it is true, be laid on **κύριε**: see ch. iv. 29, where unquestionably *the Father* is so addressed: but the **ἐξελέξω**, compared with *οὐκ ἐγὼ ὑμᾶς τοὺς δώδεκα* **ἐξελεξάμην**, John vi. 70, seems to me almost decisive. See also ver. 2; Luke vi. 13; John xiii. 18, xv. 16, 19. The instance cited on the other side by Meyer, *ἐξελέξατο ὁ θεὸς διὰ τοῦ στόματός μου ἀκοῦσαι τὰ ἔθνη κ.τ.λ.*, is not to the point, as not relating to the matter here in hand; nor are the passages cited by De Wette, 2 Cor. i. 1; Eph. i. 1; 2 Tim. i. 1, where Paul refers his apostleship to *God,* since obviously all such appointment must be referred ultimately to *God:*—but the question for us is,—In these words, *did the disciples pray as they would have prayed before the Ascension,* or *had they Christ in their view?* The expression **καρδιογνῶστα** (used by Peter himself of *God,* ch. xv. 8) forms no objection: see John xxi. 17, also in the mouth of Peter himself. We are sure, from the *προσκυνήσαντες αὐτόν* of Luke xxiv. 52, that even at this time, before the descent of the Spirit, the *highest kind of worship was paid to the ascended Redeemer.* Still, I do not regard it as by any means *certain* that they addressed Christ, nor can the passage be alleged as convincing in controversy with the Socinian. **ἀνάδειξ.** *κ.τ.λ.*] Not, as in E. V., '*shew whether of these two Thou hast chosen,*' but appoint (see reff.) **one of these two (him) whom Thou hast chosen.** The difference is of some import: they did not pray for a sign merely, to shew whether of the two was chosen, but that the Lord would, by means of their lot, *Himself appoint* the one of His choice. **25.**] **τόπον** is from internal evidence, as well as manuscript authority,

w = Matt. xxvi. 52. Job xviii. 21. Prov. xxvii. 8.
x = here only. see Luke xv. 22. = βαλλ., Matt. xxvii. 35 ||.

ρευθῆναι εἰς τὸν [w] τόπον τὸν ἴδιον. 26 καὶ [x] ἔδωκαν [y] κλήρους αὐτοῖς, καὶ [z] ἔπεσεν ὁ [y] κλῆρος [z] ἐπὶ Μαθθίαν, καὶ
[a] συγκατεψηφίσθη μετὰ τῶν ἕνδεκα ἀποστόλων.
II. 1 Καὶ ἐν τῷ [b] συνπληροῦσθαι τὴν ἡμέραν τῆς

ABCD E ℵ a b c d f g h k l m o p 13

y = Matt. xxvii. 35 || only. Neh. x. 34. see ver. 17. z Jonah i. 7. a here only †.
b = Luke ix. 51 (viii. 23) only †. (-ρωσις, 1 Chron. xxxvi. 21.)

D-lat Aug$_1$. ιδιον τοπ. C: τοπ. τ. δικαιον A.

26. rec (for *αυτοις*) *αυτων* (*see note*), with D[1]E rel syr [arm] Chr$_1$ Aug-mss: om Syr Aug-ed$_1$: txt ABCD[2]ℵ p 13 vulg coptt æth Chr$_1$. om ὁ D[1](ins D[2]) m. *συψηφ.* D[1](but corrd): *κατεψ.* ℵ[1]. for *ενδεκα*, *ιβ′* *xii* D, so also Eus$_1$.

Chap. II. 1. for *και εν τω*, *και εγενετο εν ταις ημεραις εκειναις του* D. *τας*

the preferable reading. It has been altered to *κλῆρον* to suit ver. 17. **διακονίας**, implying the active duties; **ἀποστολῆς**, the official dignity of the office:—no figure of ἓν διὰ δυοῖν. **τὸν τόπον τὸν ἴδιον**] With the reading *τόπον* before, I think these words may be interpreted two ways: 1. that Judas *deserted this our τόπος*, our office and ministry, *to go to his own τόπος*, that part which he had chosen for himself, viz. the office and character of a traitor and enemy of God; 2. regarding the former word *τόπος* as being selected to correspond to the more proper and dreadful use of the word *here*, that Judas *deserted his τόπος*, his appointed place, here among us, that he might go to *his own appointed τόπος elsewhere*, viz. *among the dead in the place of torment*. Of these two interpretations, I very much prefer the second, on all accounts; as being more according to the likely usage of the word, and as more befitting the solemnity of such a prayer. At the same time, no *absolute sentence* is pronounced on the traitor, but that dark surmise expressed by the euphemism *τὸν τόπον τ. ἴδ.*, which none can help feeling with regard to him. To refer the words *πορ. εἰς τ. τόπ. τ. ἴδ.*, to the *successor* of Judas (Knatchbull, Hammond, al.), '*ut occupet locum ipsi a Deo destinatum*,' (1) is contrary to the form of the sentence, which would require *καὶ πορευθῆναι*; (2) is inconsistent with the words *πορ. κ.τ.λ.*, which are unexampled in this sense; (3) would divest a sentence, evidently solemn and pregnant, of all point and meaning, and reduce it to a mere tautology. It appears to have been very early understood as above; for Clement of Rome says of Peter (1 Cor. v.), *οὕτω μαρτυρήσας ἐπορεύθη εἰς τὸν ὀφειλόμενον τόπον τῆς δόξης*, an expression evidently borrowed from our text. Lightf., Hor. Hebr. in loc., quotes from the Rabbinical work Baal turim on Num. xxiv. 25,—'Balaam ivit in locum suum, i. e. in Gehennam.'

26. **ἔδωκ. κλήρους αὐτοῖς**] **They cast lots for them**, *αὐτοῖς* being a *dativus commodi*. The ordinary reading, whether *αὐτῶν* is referred to the Apostles or to the candidates, would require *τοὺς κλήρους*. *Αὐτῶν* has been an alteration, to avoid the rendering 'they gave lots *to* them.' These lots were probably tablets, with the names of the persons written on them, and shaken in a vessel, or in the lap of a robe (Prov. xvi. 33); he whose lot first leaped out being the person designated. **συγκατ.**] The *lot* being regarded as the divine choice, the suffrages of the assembly were unanimously given (not in *form*, but by cheerful acquiescence) to the candidate thus chosen, and he was 'voted in' among the eleven Apostles, i. e. as a *twelfth*. That Luke does not absolutely *say so*, and never afterwards speaks of the *twelve* Apostles, is surely no safe ground on which to doubt this. Stier seems disposed to question (in his Reden der Apostel, i. 18 ff., which however was a work of his youth) whether this step of electing a twelfth Apostle was altogether suitable to the then waiting position of the Church, and whether Paul was not in reality the twelfth, chosen by the Lord Himself. But I do not see that any of his seven queries touch the matter. We have the precedent, of all others most applicable, of the twelve tribes, to shew that the number, though ever *nominally kept*, was *really exceeded*. And this incident would not occupy a prominent place in a book where Paul himself has so conspicuous a part, unless it were by himself considered as being what it professed to be, the filling up of the vacant Apostleship.

Chap. II. 1—4.] The Outpouring of the Holy Spirit on the disciples.

1. **ἐν τῷ συνπληροῦσθαι . . . .**] **While the day of P. was being fulfilled**: 'during the progress of that particular day:' this is necessitated by the pres. tense. In *sense*, it amounts to '*when the day of P. was fully come*,' as E. V.: but not in grammar. Professor Hitzig, in a letter to Ideler, "Ostern und Pfingsten, u.s.w.," maintains that the meaning is, '*As the day of P.*

[c] πεντηκοστῆς ἦσαν πάντες [d] ὁμοῦ [e] ἐπὶ τὸ αὐτό. 2 καὶ

c ch. xx. 16. 1 Cor. xvi. 8 only †. Tobit ii. 1. 2 Macc. xii. 32. d (ch. xx. 18, v. r.) John iv. 36. xx. 4. xxi. 2. Ezra ii. 64. Job iii. 18 Symm. e ch. i. 15 reff.

ημερας vulg D-lat E-lat Syr æth arm [Ath-int$_1$] Aug$_1$ Vig. rec απαντες, with m rel Thl-sif: om Eא[1] Chr$_1$: txt ABC[1]א[3] c d p [Ath$_1$].—οντων αυτων παντων D Syr æth. —add οι αποστολοι c d k m H[r] Thl-fin. rec (for ομου) ομοθυμαδον, with C[3] E[-gr] rel [Ath-4-mss] Chr$_1$ Thl-sif: om D (syrr ?) copt sah(*inter se* for ομ. ε. το αυ.): txt ABC[1]א p Ath$_1$, *pariter* vulg, *simul* E-lat [Aug$_2$, *eadem animatione simul* Aug$_1$ Promiss$_1$].

drew on,'—'*was approaching its fulfilment :'* but this view is refuted by Neander, "Pflanzung u. Leitung, u.s.w.," p. 10, note. Hitzig supports his view by ver. 5, taking κατοικοῦντες to imply *constant residence,* not merely *sojourning on account of the feast,* which latter he says would have been specified if it were so. Neander replies, 1. that ἐν τ. συνπλ. τ. ἡ. τ. π. must necessarily mean that the day itself *had arrived ;* compare πλήρωμα τοῦ χρόνου or τῶν καιρῶν, Gal. iv. 4 and Eph. i. 10. In Luke ix. 51, it is not said of *the day,* but of the *days* of His being received up, including the whole period introductory to that event: and, by the very same interpretation, *the day of* P. must in this case *have arrived,* (and was *being accomplished,* i. e. in process of passing.) And again, if only the *approach* of that day were indicated, why should the *day itself* have been mentioned, seeing that it would then be no way concerned in the narrative ? On the propriety of the day itself as belonging to the narrative, see below. 2. It is true that in ver. 5, if we had that verse only before us, we should interpret κατοικ. of *dwelling,* permanently (no real difference being traceable between κατοικεῖν with an accus., and κατοικεῖν ἐν) ; but if we compare it with ver. 9, we shall see, that the *same persons* would thus be κατοικοῦντες in Jerusalem and *several other localities,*—which necessarily restricts the meaning, in ver. 5, to a *temporary sojourn.* And, granting that there may have been some *residents* in Jerusalem among these foreign Jews, the ἐπιδημοῦντες Ῥωμαῖοι certainly point to persons who were for some especial reason at Jerusalem at the time, as also the *proselytes.* And in ver. 14 Peter distinguishes the ἄνδρες Ἰουδαῖοι,—the residents, from οἱ κατοικοῦντες Ἱερουσ. ἅπαντες,—the sojourners. **τ. ἡμ. τῆς π.**] The *fiftieth day* (inclusive) after the sixteenth of Nisan, the second day of the Passover (Levit. xxiii. 16),—called in Exodus xxiii. 16, '*the feast of harvest,*'—in Deut. xvi. 10, '*the feast of weeks ;*'—one of the three great feasts, when all the males were required to appear at Jerusalem, Deut. xvi. 16. No supplying of ἡμέρας, or ἑορτῆς, is required after πεντηκοστῆς : the word had passed into a proper name, see ref. Tobit, where it is in appos. with ἑορτῇ, and ref. 2 Macc. At this time, it was simply regarded as the feast of harvest : among the later Jews, it was considered as the anniversary of the giving of the law from Sinai. This inference was apparently grounded on a comparison of Exod. xii. 2 and xix. 1. Josephus and Philo know nothing of it, and it is at the best very uncertain. Chrysostom's reason for the event happening when it did is probably the true one : ἔδει γὰρ ἑορτῆς οὔσης πάλιν ταῦτα γενέσθαι· ἵνα οἱ παρόντες τῷ σταυρῷ τοῦ χριστοῦ, οὗτοι καὶ ταῦτα ἴδωσιν (in Catena). See a number of other reasons given by Wordsw., more suo. The question, *on what day of the week* this day of Pentecost was, is beset with the difficulties attending the question of our Lord's last passover ; see notes on Matt. xxvi. 17, and John xviii. 28. It appears probable however that it was on the Sabbath,—i. e. if we reckon from *Saturday, the 16th of Nisan.* Wieseler (Chron. des Apostol. Zeitalters, p. 20) supposes that the Western Church altered the celebration of it to the first day of the week in conformity with her observance of Easter on that day. If we take the second day of the Passover as *Sunday, the 17th of Nisan,* which some have inferred from John xviii. 28, the day of Pentecost will fall on the *first day* of the week. The custom of the Karaites was, to keep Pentecost always *on the first day* of the week, reckoning not from the day after the great Passover-Sabbath, but from that *following the Sabbath* in Passover week—understanding הַשַּׁבָּת in Levit. xxiii. 15 of the *ordinary* Sabbath ;—but this cannot be brought to bear on our enquiry, as it probably arose later. **πάντες**] Not the Apostles only, nor the hundred and twenty mentioned ch. i. 15 ; but *all the believers in Christ,* then congregated at the time of the feast in Jerusalem. The former is manifest from ver. 14, when Peter and the eleven stand forward and allude to the rest as οὗτοι : and the latter follows on the former being granted. Both are confirmed by the universality of the promise cited by Peter, vv. 17 ff. See Chrys. below, on ver. 4. **ὁμοῦ**] **together** : the rec. ὁμοθυμαδόν implies more, viz. that their *purpose,* as well as their locality, was the same. **ἐπὶ τὸ**

ἐγένετο [d] ἄφνω ἐκ τοῦ οὐρανοῦ [e] ἦχος ὥςπερ [f] φερομένης
[g] πνοῆς [h] βιαίας καὶ [i] ἐπλήρωσεν ὅλον τὸν οἶκον οὗ
ἦσαν [k] καθήμενοι, 3 καὶ [l] ὤφθησαν αὐτοῖς [m] διαμεριζόμεναι
γλῶσσαι [n] ὡςεὶ πυρός, [o] ἐκαθισέν τε [o] ἐφ᾽ ἕνα ἕκαστον αὐτῶν,
4 καὶ [p] ἐπλήσθησαν ἅπαντες πνεύματος ἁγίου, καὶ ἤρξαντο

ABCD Eℵ a b c d f g h k l m o p 13

d ch. xvi. 26. xxviii. 6 only. Josh. x. 9. e = Luke (iv. 37) xxi. 25. Heb. xii. 19 only. Ps. cl. 3. f = here only. Isa. xxviii. 15, 18. g = here (ch. xvii. 25) only. Job xxxvii. 10. see Thucyd. iv. 100. h here only. = Exod. xiv. 21. Isa. lix. 19. i = John xii. 3. Hag. ii. 8. see Isa. vi. 4. k = Matt. iv. 16. Luke xxi. 35. Rev. xiv. 6. xvii. 15. Jer. xxxi. (xlviii.) 43. l Matt. xvii. 3. Luke i. 11. ch. vii. 2, 26 al. Exod. iii. 2, 16. m = Luke xii. 52 al. Gen. x. 25. n = Luke xxii. 44. Rev. i. 14. o constr., Mark xi. 2, 7. Rev. xx. 4. Gen. viii. 3 (4). p = Luke i. 15. ch. iv. 8, 31. ix. 17. xiii. 9. see Eph. v. 18.

2. aft και ins ειδου (*i. e.* ιδου) D [so Cyr$_2$]. for εκ, απο [*de*] E. βιαι. bef πνο. D 93-5². for ολον, παντα D[-gr], *omnem* E-lat Vig$_2$: *totam* vulg D-lat : *totum* Cypr. καθεζομενοι CD : txt ABEℵ rel [Dion$_1$ Ath$_1$ Cyr$_1$] Cyr-jer$_2$ Thdrt$_2$.

3. for γλωσσαι ωςει, γλωσσει ℵ¹. for εκαθ. τε, και εκαθ. B(Mai Btly Tischdf) ℵ p D-corr(and lat) [syrr(?) arm Dion] Ath$_1$ Cyr-jer$_2$ Did$_1$ Chr *Cyr*[-p] : και εκαθ. τε D¹[-gr] : εκαθ. (*alone*) B(Bch) : εκαθ. δε C¹ E-lat Did$_1$ Aug$_1$: txt AC³D² E[-gr] rel [vulg] syrr[?] copt Eus$_1$ Ath$_1$ Thdrt$_1$ Thl.—εκαθισαν (*corrn to suit* γλωσσαι) D-gr ℵ¹ syrr coptt Ath$_1$ Did$_2$ Cyr$_1$[-p].

αὐτό] *Where?* evidently *not in the temple, or any part of it.* The improbability of such an assemblage, separate and yet so great, in any of the rooms attached to the temple,—the words ὅλον τὸν οἶκον in ver. 2 (where see note),—the συνῆλθεν τὸ πλῆθος, ver. 6,—the absence of any mention of the temple,—all these are against such a supposition. Obviously no *à priori* consideration such as Olshausen alleges (in loc.), that "thus the solemn inauguration of the Church of Christ becomes more imposing by happening in the holy place of the Old Covenant," can apply to the enquiry. Nor can the statement that they were διὰ παντὸς ἐν τῷ ἱερῷ, Luke xxiv. 53, apply here (see above on ch. i. 13); for even if it be assumed that the hour of prayer was come (which it hardly could have been, seeing that some time must have elapsed between the event and Peter's speech), the disciples would not have been assembled separately, but would, as Peter and John, in ch. iii. 1, have gone up, mingled with the people. See more below. **2. ἦχ. ὥςπ. φερ. πνοῆς βιαίας**] could not be better rendered than in E. V., **a sound as of a rushing mighty wind.** The distinction between πνοῆς and πνεύματος, on which De Wette insists, can hardly be expressed in our language. It is possible that Luke may have used πνοῆς to avoid the concurrence of πνεύματος βιαίου and πνεύματος ἁγίου. It doubtless has its especial propriety;—it is the *breathing* or *blowing* which we hear: it was the sound as of a violent blowing, borne onward, which accompanied the descent of the Holy Spirit. To treat this as a natural phænomenon,—even supposing that phænomenon *miraculously produced*, as the earthquake at the crucifixion,—is contrary to the text, which does not describe it as ἦχος φερομένης πν. βι., but ἦχος **ὥςπερ** φ. πν. βι. It was the *chosen vehicle* by which the Holy Spirit was *manifested to their sense of hearing, as by the tongues of fire to their sense of seeing.* '**φέρεσθαι** ad violentum quo venti moventur impetum notandum adhiberi solet. Ӕl. Hist. An. vii. 24, ἐπειδὰν τὸ πνεῦμα βίαιον ἐκφέρηται: Diog. Laërt. x. 25. 104, διὰ τοῦ πνεύματος πολλοῦ φερομένου.' Kypke. **οἶκον**] Certainly Luke would not have used this word of a *chamber in the Temple,* or of *the Temple itself,* without further explanation. Our Lord, it is true, calls the Temple ὁ οἶκος ὑμῶν, Matt. xxiii. 38,—and Josephus informs us that Solomon's Temple was furnished τριάκοντα βραχέσιν οἴκοις, and again ἐπῳκοδόμηντο δὲ τούτοις ἄνωθεν ἕτεροι οἶκοι: but to suppose either usage here, seems to me very far-fetched and unnatural. **3. ὤφθ. αὐτοῖς**]—not, '*there were seen on them,*' as Luther; but as E. V., **there appeared unto them. διαμεριζόμεναι**] not, '*distributed,*' as μερισμοῖς in Heb. ii. 4: from the construction, διαμ. must refer to something characteristic, not of the *manner of apportionment,* but of the *appearance itself.* **ὡςεὶ πυρός**] see reff. They were *not* πυρός, as not possessing the burning power of fire, but only **ὡςεὶ** πυρός, *in appearance like that element.* **ἐκάθισεν**] viz. τὸ φαινόμενον: not τὸ πνεῦμα, nor ἡ γλῶσσα, but the *appearance* described in the preceding clause. I understand ἐκάθ. as usually interpreted, **lighted on their heads.** This also was no effect of natural cause, either ordinarily or extraordinarily employed: see on ver. 2. **4.**] On **ἅπαντες**, Chrys. says, οὐκ ἂν εἶπε πάντες, καὶ ἀποστόλων ὄντων ἐκεῖ, εἰ μὴ καὶ οἱ ἄλλοι μετέσχον. **ἤρξαντο λαλεῖν ἑτέραις γλώσσαις**] There can be no ques-

λαλεῖν [q] ἑτέραις [r] γλώσσαις [s] καθὼς τὸ πνεῦμα [t] ἐδίδου

q = 1 Cor. xiv. 21. Exod. xxx. 9. r = Matt. xvi. 17. ch. x. 46. xix. 6. 1 Cor. xii. 10, &c. xiv. 2, &c. Gen. x. 5. s = ch. xi. 29 reff. t = Matt. xiii. 11. Luke i. 74. John v. 26. ver. 27 and ch. xiii. 35 (from Ps. xv. 10). ch. x. 40. xiv. 3.

4. παντες AB[1]DEℵ p : txt (*see prolegomena*, ch. v. § 3, ad fin.) [B-corr[1·2]] C rel [Did_1 Ath_2 Cyr-jer_2 Chr_1 Cyr_2] Cosm. ηρξατο D[1][-gr](txt D-corr[1]). aft το πν. ins το

tion in any unprejudiced mind, that the fact which this narrative sets before us is, that the disciples began to *speak in* VARIOUS LANGUAGES, viz. *the languages of the nations below enumerated, and perhaps others.* All attempts to evade this are connected with some forcing of the text, or some far-fetched and indefensible exegesis. This then being laid down, several important questions arise, and we are surrounded by various difficulties. (1) Was this speaking in various languages a *gift bestowed* on the disciples *for their use afterwards*, or was it a *mere sign*, their utterance being only as they were mouth-pieces of the Holy Spirit? *The latter seems certainly to have been the case.* It appears on our narrative, καθὼς τὸ πνεῦμα ἐδίδου ἀποφθέγγεσθαι αὐτοῖς, **as the Spirit gave them utterance.** But, it may be objected, in that case they would not themselves understand what they said. I answer, that we infer *this very fact* from 1 Cor. xiv.; that the speaking with tongues was often found, *where none could interpret what was said.* And besides, it would appear from Peter's speech, that such, or something approaching to it, was the case in this instance. He makes no allusion to the *things said* by those who spoke with tongues; the *hearers alone* speak of their declaring τὰ μεγαλεῖα τοῦ θεοῦ. So that it would seem that here, as on other occasions (1 Cor. xiv. 22), tongues were for a sign, not to those that believe, but to those that believe not. If the first supposition be made, that the gift of speaking in various languages was bestowed on the disciples *for their after use in preaching the Gospel*, we are, I think, running counter to the whole course of Scripture and early patristic evidence on the subject. There is *no trace whatever* of such a power being possessed or exercised by the Apostles, or by those who followed them. (Compare ch. xiv. 11, 14; Euseb. iii. 39; Iren. iii. 1, p. 174.) The passage cited triumphantly by Wordsw. from Iren. iii. 17, p. 208, to shew that *Irenæus* understood the gift to be that of permanent preaching in many languages, entirely fails of its point:—"Quem et descendisse Lucas ait post ascensum Domini super discipulos in Pentecoste, habentem potestatem omnium gentium ad introitum vitæ (which Wordsw. renders "in order that all nations might be enabled to enter into life," suitably to his purpose, but not to the original) et ad assertionem novi Testamenti: unde et omnibus linguis conspirantes hymnum dicebant Deo, Spiritu ad unitatem redigente distantes tribus, et primitias omnium gentium offerente Patri." Here it will be observed is not a word about future preaching; but simply this event itself is treated of, as a symbolic one, a first fruit of the future Gentile harvest. The other passage, id. v. 6, p. 299, shews nothing but that the *gift of tongues* was not extinct in Irenæus's time: there is in it not a word of preaching in various languages. I believe, therefore, the event related in our text to have been a *sudden and powerful inspiration of the Holy Spirit, by which the disciples uttered, not of their own minds, but as mouth-pieces of the Spirit, the praises of God in various languages, hitherto, and possibly at the time itself, unknown to them.* (2) How is this ἑτέραις γλώσσαις λαλεῖν related to the γλώσσῃ λαλεῖν afterwards spoken of by St. Paul? I answer, that they are *one and the same thing.* γλώσσῃ λαλ. is to speak in *a* language, as above explained; γλώσσαις (ἑτέραις, or καιναῖς, Mark xvi. 17) λαλ., to speak in *languages*, under the same circumstances. See this further proved in notes on 1 Cor. xiv. Meantime I may remark, that the two are inseparably connected by the following links,—ch. x. 46, xi. 15,—xix. 6,—in which last we have the same juxtaposition of γλώσσαις λαλεῖν and προφητεύειν, as afterwards in 1 Cor. xiv. 1—5 ff. (3) *Who were those that partook of this gift?* I answer, the *whole assembly* of believers, from Peter's application of the prophecy, vv. 16 ff. It was precisely the case supposed in 1 Cor. xiv. 23, ἐὰν οὖν συνέλθῃ ἡ ἐκκλησία ὅλη ἐπὶ τὸ αὐτὸ καὶ πάντες λαλῶσιν γλώσσαις, εἰσέλθωσιν δὲ ἰδιῶται ἢ ἄπιστοι, οὐκ ἐροῦσιν ὅτι μαίνεσθε; These ἰδιῶται and ἄπιστοι were represented by the ἕτεροι of our ver. 13, who pronounced them to be drunken. (4) I would not conceal the difficulty which our minds find in conceiving a person supernaturally endowed with the power of speaking, *ordinarily and consciously*, a language which he has never learned. I believe that difficulty to be insuperable. Such an endowment would not only be contrary to the analogy of God's dealings, but, as far as I can see into the matter, self-contradictory, and therefore

u ver. 14. ch. xxvi. 25 only. 1 Chron. xxv. 1. Ps. lviii. 7. Ezek. xiii. 9, 19. Mic. v. 12. Zech. x. 2 only.

v constr., ch. i. 13, 14. viii. 1, 13. Luke i. 10, 20. Jer. xxxiii. (xxvi.) 20.

[u] ἀποφθέγγεσθαι αὐτοῖς. 5 [v] ἦσαν δὲ ἐν Ἱερουσαλὴμ κατοι-

ABCD Fℵabc dfghk lmop 13

αγιον E vulg æth. rec αυτοις bef αποφθεγγ. (*corrn for the sake of perspicuous order; but these trajections and insertions between a governing and a governed word are characteristic of Luke, and esp in Acts*), with C^3E rel [tol] syr Cyr-jer$_2$ [Chr$_1$ Cyr$_1$ Thdrt$_1$]: txt ABC^1Dℵ p vulg (sah ?) arm Ath$_2$ Cyr$_4$ Did$_2$ [Bas$_1$] Ambr Vig. (36 def.)

5. for εν, εις Aℵ[1]. εν ιερ. bef ησαν, omg δε, D. κατοικ. bef εν ιερ. C Syr

impossible. But there is *no such contradiction*, and to my mind *no such difficulty*, in conceiving a man to be moved to utterance of sounds *dictated by the Holy Spirit*. And the fact is clearly laid down by Paul, that the gift of *speaking* in tongues, and that of *interpreting*, were *wholly distinct*. So that the above difficulty finds no place here, nor even in the case of a person *both speaking and interpreting*: see 1 Cor. xiv. 13. On the question whether the speaking was necessarily *always* in a foreign tongue, we have no data to guide us: it would seem that it *was*; but the conditions would not *absolutely* exclude rhapsodical and unintelligible utterance. Only there is this objection to it: clearly, languages *were spoken* on *this* occasion,—and we have no reason to believe that there were two distinct kinds of the gift. (5) It would be quite beyond the limits of a note to give any adequate history of the exegesis of the passage. A very short summary must suffice. (α) The idea of a gift of *speaking in various languages* having been conferred *for the dissemination of the Gospel*, appears not to have originated until the *gift of tongues* itself had some time disappeared from the Church. Chrysostom adopts it, and the great majority of the Fathers and expositors. (β) Gregory Nyss. (see Suicer. Thes., γλῶσσα), Cyprian, and in modern times Erasmus and Schneckenburger, suppose that the miracle consisted in the multitude *hearing in various languages* that which the believers spoke in their native tongue: μίαν μὲν ἐξηχεῖσθαι φωνήν, πολλὰς δὲ ἀκούεσθαι. This view Greg. Naz. mentions, but not as his own, and refutes it (Orat. xli. 15, p. 743), saying, ἐκείνως μὲν γὰρ τῶν ἀκουόντων ἂν εἴη μᾶλλον ἢ τῶν λεγόντων τὸ θαῦμα. This view, besides, would make a distinction between this instance of the gift and those subsequently related, which we have seen does not exist. (γ) The course of the *modern German expositors* has been, (1) to *explain the facts related, by some assumption inconsistent with the text*, as e. g. Olshausen, by a magnetic 'rapport' between the speakers and hearers,—whereas the speaking took place *first*, independently of the hearers;—Eichhorn, Wieseler, and others, by supposing γλώσσῃ λαλεῖν to mean speaking *with the tongue only*, i. e. inarticulately in ejaculations of praise, which will not suit γλώσσαις λαλ.;—Bleek, by interpreting γλῶσσα = glossema, and supposing that they spoke in unusual, enthusiastic, or poetical phraseology,—which will not suit γλώσσῃ λαλ.;—Meyer (and De Wette nearly the same), by supposing that they spoke in an entirely new spiritual language (of which the γλῶσσαι were merely the individual varieties), as was the case during the Irvingite delusion in this country,—*contrary to the plain assertion of* vv. 6—8, that *they spoke*, and the *hearers heard*, in the *dialects* or *tongues of the various peoples* specified;—Paulus, Schulthess, Kuinoel, &c. by supposing that the assembly of believers was composed of Jews of various nations, who spoke as moved by the Spirit, but *in their own mother tongues*,—which is clearly inconsistent with ver. 4 and the other passages, ch. x. and xix., and 1 Cor. xiv., above cited:—(2) to take the whole of this narrative in its literal sense, but *cast doubts on its historical accuracy*, and on Luke's proper understanding of what really did take place. This is more or less done by several of the above mentioned, as a means of escape from the inconsistency of their hypotheses with Luke's narrative. But, *to set aside*, argumenti gratiâ, *higher considerations*,—is it at all probable that Luke, who must have *conversed with many eye and ear-witnesses of this day's events*, would have been misinformed about them in so vital a point as the very nature of the gift by which the descent of the Spirit was accompanied? There is every mark, as I hope I have shewn abundantly in the prolegomena, of the Acts having been written in the company and with the co-operation of *St. Paul*: can we suppose that he, who treats so largely of *this very gift* elsewhere, would have allowed such an inaccuracy to remain uncorrected, if it had existed? On the contrary, I believe this narrative to furnish *the key* to the right understanding of 1 Cor. xiv. and other such passages, as I there hope more fully to prove. **καθὼς** κ.τ.λ.] **according as** (i. e. '*in such measure and manner in each case as*') **the Spirit granted to them to speak** (be-

I ii. 6... ABCDE Iℵabc dfghk lmop 13

κοῦντες Ἰουδαῖοι ἄνδρες [w] εὐλαβεῖς [x] ἀπὸ παντὸς ἔθνους
τῶν [y] ὑπὸ τὸν οὐρανόν. 6 [z] γενομένης δὲ τῆς [z] φωνῆς ταύτης [a] συνῆλθεν τὸ [b] πλῆθος καὶ [c] συνεχύθη· ὅτι ἤκουον
[d] εἷς [d] ἕκαστος τῇ ἰδίᾳ [e] διαλέκτῳ λαλούντων αὐτῶν. 7 [f] ἐξ-

w Luke ii. 25. ch. viii. 2. xxii. 12 only. Lev. xv. 31. Micah vii. 2 AB2 Ald. compl. only. x = Luke xxiii. 51. John xi. 1. ch. xvii. 13, xxiii. 34 al. y ch. iv. 12. Col. i. 23. Deut. xxv. 19. z Luke ix. 35. ch. xix. 34. Rev. xi. 15. 2 Chron. v. 13. a = ch. i. 6 reff. b abs., ch. vi. 5. xv. 12, 30. xix. 9. xxiii. 7. c ch. ix. 22. xix. 32. xxi. 27, 31 only. Gen. xi. 9. Jonah iv. 1. 1 Macc. iv. 27. d Luke iv. 40. ch. xx. 31. Eph. iv. 16. Col. iv. 6. 1 Kings xiii. 20 Ald. e ch. i. 19 reff. f = ch. viii. 13 reff.

copt Aug_1 : *ιουδαιοι* bef *κατοικ.* E. *ανδρ.* bef *ιουδ.* C[1] : om *ιουδ.* ℵ. *ευλ.* bef *ανδρ.* D.

6. for *οτι*, *και* D[-gr] : *qui* D[1]-lat. *ηκουσεν* Bℵ syr : *ηκουεν* C p, *audiebat* vulg syrr sah Aug_3 $Bede_2$: *ηκουσαν* 40. 96. om *εἷς* Eℵ e 36. for *τη ιδ. διαλ. λαλ. αυτ.*, *λαλουντας ταις γλωσσαις αυτων* D Syr : *ταις γλωσσαις αυτων λαλ.* syr-mg Aug_2 : *lingua sua* vulg D-lat E-lat, *linguam suam* Bede.

stowed on them utterance). There is no emphasis, as Wordsw., on *αὐτοῖς*, but rather the contrary: placed thus behind the verb, it becomes insignificant in comparison with the fact announced, and with the subject of the sentence. The word *ἀποφθέγγεσθαι* has been supposed here to imply that they uttered short ejaculatory sentences of praise: so Chrys., *ἀποφθέγματα γὰρ ἦν τὰ παρ' αὐτῶν λεγόμενα*: Œc., Bloomf., and Wordsw. But in neither of the two other places in St. Luke (see reff.) will it bear this meaning, nor in any of the six where it occurs in the LXX: though in two of those (Mic. and Zech.) it has the peculiar sense of speaking oracularly, and in Ezek. xiii. 19 it represents כָּזַב, *mentior*. Our word to *utter*, to *speak out*, seems exactly to render it. It is never desirable to press a specific sense, where the more general one seems to have become the accepted meaning of a word. And this is especially so here, where, had any peculiar sense been intended, the verb would surely have held a more prominent position. Their utterance was none of their own, but the simple gift and inspiration of the Holy Spirit: see above. 5—13.] Effect on the Multitude. 5.] De Wette * maintains that these *κατοικοῦντες* cannot have been persons sojourning for the sake of the feast, but *residents*: but see above on ver. 1. I see no objection, with Meyer, to including *both residents and sojourners* in the term, which only specifies their *then* residence. **εὐλαβεῖς**] Not in reference to their having come up to the feast, nor to their dwelling from religious motives at Jerusalem (*τὸ κατοικεῖν εὐλαβείας ἦν σημεῖον, ἀπὸ τοσούτων ἐθνῶν πατρίδας ἀφέντας καὶ οἰκίαν καὶ συγγενεῖς, ἐκεῖ οἰκεῖν*, Chrys.), but stated as imparting a character and interest to what follows. They were not merely vain and curious listeners, but men of piety and weight. **ἀπὸ παντὸς ἔθν. . . . .**] Not perhaps used so much *hyperbolically*, as with reference to the significance of the whole event. As they were samples each of their different people, so collectively they represented all the nations of the world, who should hear afterwards in their own tongues the wonderful works of God. 6.] Whatever **τῆς φωνῆς ταύτης** may mean, one thing is clear,—that it *cannot* mean, '*this rumour*' ('*when this was noised abroad*,' E. V.: so also Erasm., Calv., Beza, Grotius, &c.), which would be unexampled (the two passages cited for this sense from the LXX are no examples; Gen. xlv. 16; Jer. xxvii. (l.) 46). We have then to choose between two things to which *φωνή* might refer: —(1) the *ἦχος* of ver. 2, to which it seems bound by the *past* part. **γενομένης** (compare ver. 2, *ἐγένετο . . . ἦχος*), which would hardly be used of a speaking which was *still going on* when the multitude assembled: compare also John iii. 8;—and (2) *the speaking with tongues* of ver. 4. To *this* reference, besides the objection just stated, there is also another, that the voices of a number of men, especially when diverse as in this case, would not be indicated by *φωνή*, but by *φωναί*: compare Luke's own usage, even when the voices cried out the same thing, Luke xxiii. 23, *οἱ δὲ ἐπέκειντο* **φωναῖς μεγάλαις** *αἰτούμενοι αὐτὸν σταυρωθῆναι, καὶ κατίσχυον* **αἱ φωναὶ** *αὐτῶν*. And when he uses the sing., he explains it, as in ch. xix. 34, *φωνὴ ἐγένετο μία ἐκ πάντων*. So that we may safely decide for the *former reference*. The *noise of the rushing mighty wind* was heard over all the neighbourhood, probably over all Jerusalem. **τὸ πλῆθος**] including the scoffers of ver. 13, as well as the pious strangers: but these latter only are here regarded in the *συνεχύθη* and in the *ἤκ. εἷς ἕκαστος*. On these latter words see above on ver. 4. Each one heard *λαλούντων αὐτῶν*,— i. e. either *various disciples speaking various tongues, each in some one only*: or *the same persons speaking now one now*

g = Matt. xxiii. 34. Luke xiii. 16. ch. xiii. 11, 46. xx. 22, 25. Judg. iv. 14 A compl.
h see ch. i. 19 reff.
i constr., ch. i. 19 reff.

ἵσταντο δὲ καὶ ἐθαύμαζον λέγοντες Οὐχὶ [g] ἰδοὺ ἅπαντες
οὗτοί εἰσιν οἱ λαλοῦντες Γαλιλαῖοι; 8 καὶ πῶς ἡμεῖς
ἀκούομεν ἕκαστος τῇ [h] ἰδίᾳ [e] διαλέκτῳ [h] ἡμῶν ἐν ᾗ ἐγεννήθημεν, 9 Πάρθοι καὶ Μῆδοι καὶ Ἐλαμῖται, καὶ οἱ [i] κατοικοῦντες τὴν Μεσοποταμίαν, Ἰουδαίαν τε καὶ Καππα-

ABCDE Iℵabc dfghk lmop 13

7. rec aft εξιστ. δε ins παντες (*from ver* 12), with ACEIℵ[1] rel 36 vulg syrr coptt [arm]; απαντες ℵ[3] 27-9. 69: om BD a e f h l m o H[r] æth Chr_1 Aug_3. rec aft λεγοντες ins προς αλληλους (*explanatory gloss; and hence became a var read also in some inferior mss in ver* 12: *not, as Mey., genuine here, and thence insd in ver* 12), with [C[2]]DEI rel syrr [arm Aug_3]: om ABC[1]ℵ p vulg coptt æth [Chr_1]. rec ουκ, with AC[I] rel [Chr_1]: ουχ DEℵ p: txt B (*the ι became absorbed by the follg ι, thence* ουχ (*as in* LXX-A *Judg* iv. 14; xv. 2), *and was* corrd *into* ουκ). rec παντες, with E rel: txt A B(see table) CDIℵ 36. οι λαλ. bef εισιν C[1] lect-12: εισιν bef ουτοι p: *qui loq. Gal. sunt* vulg.

8. [εκαστος bef ακουομεν E.] την διαλεκτον D[1]-gr(txt D[2]) vulg(not am but (Lachm) fuld) Aug_2(once τ. ιδιαν δ.) Jer. ημ. bef διαλ. E. εγενηθημεν AC[2 or 3] E[1] [f[1] k] p 1. 13 syr-mg Thl-fin.

9. om και ελαμιται ℵ[1]. om 3rd και D[1]-gr(ins D[2]). om τε D[1](and lat: ins D[5]) vulg (not am[1] fuld [tol]) [Aug_2].

another tongue. The former is more probable, although the latter seems to agree with some expressions in 1 Cor. xiv., e. g. ver. 18 (in the rec. and perhaps even in the present text). **συνεχύθη**] Observe ref. Genesis. **7.**] They were not, literally, *all* Galilæans; but certainly the greater part were so, and all the Apostles and leading persons, who would probably be the prominent speakers. **8—11.**] This question is broken, in construction, by the enumeration of vv. 9, 10, and then ver. 11 takes up the construction again from ver. 8. As regards the *catalogue itself*, —of course it cannot have been thus delivered as *part of a speech by any hearer on the occasion*, but is inserted into a speech expressing the general sense of what was said, and put, according to the usage of all narrative, into the mouths of all. The words **τῇ ἰδίᾳ διαλ. ἡμ. ἐν ᾗ ἐγεννήθημεν** are very decisive as to the nature of the miracle. The hearers could not have thus spoken, had *they* been *spiritually uplifted* into the comprehension of some *ecstatic language* spoken by the disciples. *They* were not spiritually acted on at all, but *spoke the matter of fact:* they were surprised at each recognizing, so far from his country, and in the mouths of Galilæans, his own native tongue. **9.**] **Πάρθοι**] The catalogue proceeds from the N.E. to the W. and S. See Mede, Book i. Disc. xx., who notices that it follows the order of the three great dispersions of the Jews, the Chaldean, Assyrian, and Egyptian. So also Wordsw. 'Habet (Parthia) ab ortu Arios, a meridie Carmaniam et Arianos, ab occasu Protitas Medos, a septentrione Hyrcanos,—undique desertis cincta,' Plin. vi. 29. See also Strabo, xi. 9, and Winer, Realw. **Μῆδοι**] Media, W. of Parthia and Hyrcania, S. of the Caspian sea, E. of Armenia, N. of Persia. **Ἐλαμῖται**] in pure Greek Ἐλυμαῖοι, inhabitants of Elam or Elymais, a Semitic people (Gen. x. 22). Elam is mentioned in connexion with Babylon, Gen. xiv. 1; with Media, Isa. xxi. 2; Jer. xxv. (xxxii. in LXX) 25; with, or as part of, Assyria, Ezek. xxxii. 24; Isa. xxii. 6; as a province of Persia, Ezra iv. 9; as the province in which Susan was situated, Dan. viii. 2 (but then Susiana must be taken in the wide sense, Ἐλυμαῖοι προσεχεῖς ἦσαν Σουσίοις, Strabo, xi. 13; xvi. 1). According to Josephus, Antt. i. 6. 4, the Elamæans were the progenitors of the Persians. We find scattered hordes under this name far to the north, and even on the Orontes near the Caspian (Strabo, xi. 13; xv. 3; xvi. 1). Pliny's description, the most applicable to the times of our text, is, 'Infra Eulæum (Susianen ab Elymaide disterminat amnis Eulæus, *paulo supra*) Elymais est, in ora juncta Persidi, a flumine Oronti ad Characem ccxl m. pass. Oppida ejus Seleucia et Sosirate, apposita monti Casyro,' vi. 27. **Μεσοποταμίαν**] the well-known district between the Euphrates and Tigris, so called merely as distinguishing its geographical position (Strabo, xvi. 1): it never formed a state. The name does not appear to be older than the Macedonian conquests. The word is used by the LXX, Vulg., and E. V. in Gen. xxiv. 10 to express אֲרַם נַהֲרַיִם, Aram of the two rivers. Similarly the Peschito renders it here, and ch. vii. 2. See Winer, Realw. **Ἰουδαίαν**] I can see no difficulty in Judæa

δοκίαν, Πόντον καὶ τὴν Ἀσίαν, 10 Φρυγίαν τε καὶ
Παμφυλίαν, Αἴγυπτον καὶ τὰ μέρη τῆς Λιβύης τῆς
κατὰ Κυρήνην, καὶ οἱ [k] ἐπιδημοῦντες Ῥωμαῖοι, Ἰουδαῖοί
τε καὶ [l] προσήλυτοι, 11 Κρῆτες καὶ Ἄραβες, ἀκούομεν
λαλούντων αὐτῶν ταῖς ἡμετέραις γλώσσαις τὰ [m] μεγαλεῖα
τοῦ θεοῦ; 12 [f] ἐξίσταντο δὲ πάντες καὶ [n] διηπόρουντο
ἄλλος πρὸς ἄλλον λέγοντες Τί ἂν [o] θέλοι τοῦτο εἶναι;

k ch. xvii. 21 only +.
l Matt. xxiii. 15. ch. vi. 5. xiii. 43 only. Exod. xii. 48, 49 al.
m Luke i. 49 only. Ps. lxx. 19.
n mid., here only. Dan. ii. 3 Symm. act. Luke ix. 7. ch. v. 24. x. 17 only. L.P.+
o = ch. xvii. 20 only. Herod. i. 78 al.

10. om τε D vulg [coptt arm]. aft αιγ. ins τε D-gr.
11. αραβοι D[1], *arabi* D-lat(txt D[4]).
12. rec διηπορουν, with CDEI rel 36 [Bas_1 Chr_1]: txt ABℵ. aft αλλον ins επι τω γεγονοτι D syr-mg Aug_1. ins και bef λεγ. D. for αν θελοι, θελει (*corrn to suit the direct form of speech after* λεγοντες) ABCD I(appy) p 36 Chr_2: θελοι ℵ [Bas_1]: txt E rel Thl.—τι τουτο θελει A 36(sic) 113.

being here mentioned. The catalogue does not proceed by *languages*, but by territorial division; and Judæa lies immediately S. of its path from Mesopotamia to Cappadocia. It is not Ἰουδαῖοι by birth and domicile, but οἱ κατοικοῦντες τὴν Ἰουδαίαν who are spoken of: the ἄνδρες εὐλαβεῖς settled in Judæa. And even if born Jews were meant, doubtless they also would find a place among those who heard in their mother-tongue the wonderful works of God. **Καππαδοκίαν**] At this time (since U.C. 770) a Roman province (see Tacit. Ann. ii. 42), embracing Cappadocia proper and Armenia minor. **Πόντον**] The former kingdom of Mithridates, lying along the S. coast of the Euxine (whence its name) from the river Halys to Colchis and Armenia, and separated by mountains from Cappadocia on the S. It was at this time divided into petty principalities under Roman protection, but subsequently (Suet. Nero 18) became a province under Nero. **τὴν Ἀσίαν**] i. e. here *Asia propria*, or rather the W. division of it, as described by Pliny, v. 27, as bounded on the E. by Phrygia and Lycaonia, on the W. by the Ægean, on the S. by the Egyptian sea, on the N. by Paphlagonia. Winer, Realw., cites from Solinus, 43: 'Sequitur Asia, sed non eam Asiam loquor quæ in tertio orbis divortio terminos omnes habet, . . . verum eam quæ a Telmesso Lyciæ incipit. Eam igitur Asiam ab Oriente Lycia includit et Phrygia, ab occid. Ægæa littora, a meridie mare Ægyptium, Paphlagonia a septentrione. Ephesus in ea urbs clarissima est.' See ch. xvi. 6, where the same appears to be intended. **10. Φρυγίαν**] ἡ μεγάλη Φρυγία of Strabo, xii. 8: Jos. Antt. xvi. 2. 2. It was at this time part of the Roman province of Asia. **Παμφυλίαν**] A small district, extending along the coast from Olbia (Strabo, xiv. 4), or Phaselis (Plin. v. 27), to Ptolemais (Strabo, l. c.). It was a separate tributary district (χωρὶς ὅπλων φορολογεῖται, Jos. B. J. ii. 16. 4): we find it classed with Galatia and ruled by the same person, Tac. Hist. ii. 9. **Αἴγυπτον**] Having enumerated the principal districts of Asia Minor, the catalogue passes (see above on the arrangement, ver. 9) to Egypt, a well-known habitation of Jews. Two-fifths of the population of Alexandria consisted of them, see Philo, in Flacc. 8, vol. ii. p. 525, and they had an Ethnarch of their own, Jos. Antt. xiv. 7. 2; xix. 5. 2. **τὰ μ. τ. Λιβύης τ. κ. Κυρήνην**] By this expression is probably meant Pentapolis, where Josephus (Antt. xiv. 7. 2), quoting from Strabo, testifies to the existence of very many Jews,—amounting in Cyrene to a fourth part of the whole population. The Cyrenian Jews were so numerous in Jerusalem, that they had a special synagogue (see ch. vi. 9). Several were Christian converts: see ch. xi. 20; xiii. 1. **οἱ ἐπιδημοῦντες Ῥωμαῖοι**] 'The Roman Jews dwelling (or then being) in Jerusalem,' see ref. The comma after Ῥωμαῖοι is better retained (against Wordsw.). **Ἰουδ. τ. κ. προσήλ.**] This refers more naturally to the whole of the past catalogue, than merely to the Roman Jews. The τε καί shews that it does not take up a new designation, but expresses the classes or divisions of those which have gone before. See a similar construction in John ii. 15, where τά τε πρόβατα κ. τοὺς βόας is epexegetic of πάντας preceding.
11. Κρῆτες κ. Ἄραβες] These words would seem as if they should precede the last. **μεγαλεῖα**] גְּדֹלוֹת, ref. Ps., see also ref. Luke. **13. ἕτεροι**] Probably native Jews, who did not understand the foreign languages. Meyer supposes,—persons pre-

p here only +. χλ., ch. xvii. 32 only +.
q here only. Job xxxii. 19 only.
r here only +. 3 Macc. v. 10.
s ch. xi. 13 reff.
t Luke xi. 27. ch. xiv. 11. xxii. 22. L. Judg. ix. 7.
u ver. 4 reff.
v constr., ch. i. 19 reff.
w ch. xiii. 38 reff.

13 ἕτεροι δὲ ᵖ διαχλευάζοντες ἔλεγον ὅτι ᑫ γλεύκους ʳ με-
μεστωμένοι εἰσίν. 14 ˢ σταθεὶς δὲ ὁ Πέτρος σὺν τοῖς ἕνδεκα
ᵗ ἐπῆρεν τὴν ᵗ φωνὴν αὐτοῦ καὶ ᵘ ἀπεφθέγξατο αὐτοῖς
Ἄνδρες Ἰουδαῖοι καὶ οἱ ᵛ κατοικοῦντες Ἱερουσαλὴμ ἅπαντες, τοῦτο ὑμῖν ʷ γνωστὸν ἔστω, καὶ ˣ ἐνωτίσασθε τὰ
ῥήματά μου. 15 οὐ γὰρ ὡς ὑμεῖς ʸ ὑπολαμβάνετε οὗτοι
ᶻ μεθύουσιν· ἔστιν γὰρ ὥρα τρίτη τῆς ἡμέρας· 16 ἀλλὰ

P κους μεμεσ-τωμενοι ... ABCDE IPℵ a b c d f g h k l m o p 13

x here only. Gen. iv. 23. Ps. v. 1 al. y = Luke vii. 43 (x. 30. ch. i. 9. 3 John 8) only. Jer. xliv. (xxxvii.) 9.
z Matt. xxiv. 49. John ii. 10. 1 Cor. xi. 21. 1 Thess. v. 7. Rev. xvii. 2, 6 only. 1 Kings xxv. 36. trans., Deut. xxxii. 42.

13. rec *χλευαζ.*, with EI^1 rel: txt $ABCD^6I^2$ℵ a c h k p 13. 36. 40.—*διεχλευαζον λεγοντες* D^1(and lat). aft *γλ.* ins *ουτοι* D: also, variously placed, vulg coptt.
14. ins *τοτε* bef *σταθ. δε* D^1-gr [simly Syr]. rec om *ὁ*, with CEP 13. 36 rel: ins ABDIℵ p 40 [Bas_1 Chr_1]. for *ενδεκα*, *δεκα* D^1(and lat^1: txt D^5), and add *αποστολοις* D lect-12 Syr Aug_1. aft *επηρ.* ins *πρωτος* D^1(and lat): aft *τ. φω. αυτου* ins *προτερον* E. aft *απεφθ.* ins *λεγων* C [arm] Aug. for *απεφθ. αυτ.*, *ειπεν* D [syrr]. *παντες* ABC(D)[I^1]ℵ p: txt (*see proleg*) EI^2P rel 36 vulg [Bas_1 Chr_1].—*παντες* bef *οι κατ. ιερ.* D [Aug_1]. *ημειν* D^1(txt D^4). om *και* bef *ενωτ.* D. *ενωτισατε* D^1: *-σαθε* D^4(sic).
15. *ουσης ωρας της ημ. γ'* D^1-gr(txt D-$corr^1$) vulg E-lat [Iren-int_1] Aug_1 $Gaud_1$.

viously hostile to Jesus and his disciples, and thus judging as in Luke vii. 34 they judged of Himself. **γλεύκους**] יַיִן, see ref. Job. *Sweet wine*, not necessarily *new* wine (nor is the "spiritual sense of the passage" any reason why a meaning should be given to the word which it need not bear. That sense in fact remains without the meaning in question): perhaps made of a remarkably sweet small grape, which is understood by the Jewish expositors to be meant by שֹׂרֵק or שֹׂרֵקָה, Gen. xlix. 11; Isa. v. 2; Jer. ii. 21,—and still found in Syria and Arabia (Winer, Realw.). Suidas interprets it, *τὸ ἀποστάλαγμα τῆς σταφυλῆς πρὶν πατηθῇ.*

14—36.] The speech of Peter. "Luke gives us here the first sample of the preaching of the Gospel by the Apostles, with which the foundation of Christian preaching, as well as of the Church itself, appears to be closely connected. We discover already, in this first sermon, all the peculiarities of apostolic preaching. It contains no reflections nor deductions concerning the doctrine of Christ,—no proposition of new and unknown doctrines, but simply and entirely consists of the proclamation of *historical facts*. The Apostles appear here as the witnesses of that which they had seen: the Resurrection of Jesus forming the central point of their testimony. It is true, that in the after-development of the Church it was impossible to confine preaching to this historical announcement only: it gradually became invested with the additional office of building up believers in knowledge. But nevertheless, the simple testimony to the great works of God, as Peter here delivers it, should never be wanting in preaching to those whose hearts are not yet penetrated by the Word of Truth." Olshausen, in loc. The discourse divides itself into two parts: 1. (vv. 14—21) '*This which you hear is not the effect of drunkenness, but is the promised outpouring of the Spirit on all flesh*,'—2. (vv. 22—36) '*which Spirit has been shed forth by Jesus, whom you crucified, but whom God hath exalted to be Lord and Christ.*' **14. σὺν τοῖς ἕνδεκα**] Peter and the eleven come forward from the great body of believers. And he distinguishes (by the *οὗτοι* in ver. 15) not *himself* from the *eleven*, but *himself and the eleven* from the rest. De Wette concludes from this, that the Apostles *had not themselves spoken with tongues*, as being an inferior gift (1 Cor. xiv. 18 ff.); perhaps too rashly, for this view hardly accords with **ἅπαντες**, which is the subject of the whole of ver. 4. **ἄνδρες Ἰουδ.**] the Jews, properly so called: native dwellers in Jerus. **οἱ κατ. Ἱερ. ἅπ.**, the sojourners (ver. 5) from other parts. **ἐνωτίσασθε** is a word unknown to good Greek, and belonging apparently to the Alexandrine dialect. Stier quotes 'inaurire' from Lactantius (R. der Ap. p. 32, not.). **15.] οὗτοι**, see above. **ὥρα τρίτη**] the *first hour of prayer:* before which no pious Jew might eat or drink: "Non licet homini gustare quidquam, antequam oraverit orationem suam." Berachoth. f. 28. 2; Lightf., Wetst.

But perhaps we need not look further than the ordinary intent of such a defence—the improbability of intoxication at that hour of the morning. See Eccl. x. 16; Isa. v. 11; 1 Thess. v. 7. **16.**] This prophecy is from the LXX, with very slight

...ii.17 I. ABCDE Pℵ a b c d f g h k l m o p 13

τοῦτό ἐστιν τὸ [a] εἰρημένον διὰ τοῦ προφήτου 17 [b] Ἔσται
ἐν ταῖς [c] ἐσχάταις [c] ἡμέραις, λέγει ὁ θεός, [d] ἐκχεῶ [e] ἀπὸ
τοῦ πνεύματός μου ἐπὶ [f] πᾶσαν [f] σάρκα, καὶ προφητεύσουσιν οἱ υἱοὶ ὑμῶν καὶ αἱ θυγατέρες ὑμῶν, καὶ οἱ [g] νεανίσκοι ὑμῶν [h] ὁράσεις ὄψονται, καὶ οἱ πρεσβύτεροι ὑμῶν
[i] ἐνυπνίοις [j] ἐνυπνιασθήσονται. 18 [k] καί [k] γε ἐπὶ τοὺς
δούλους μου καὶ ἐπὶ τὰς δούλας μου ἐν ταῖς ἡμέραις
ἐκείναις [d] ἐκχεῶ [e] ἀπὸ τοῦ πνεύματός μου, καὶ προφητεύσουσιν. 19 καὶ [l] δώσω [m] τέρατα ἐν τῷ οὐρανῷ [n] ἄνω καὶ
σημεῖα ἐπὶ τῆς γῆς [o] κάτω, αἷμα καὶ πῦρ καὶ [p] ἀτμίδα
καπνοῦ. 20 ὁ ἥλιος [q] μεταστραφήσεται εἰς σκότος καὶ ἡ
[r] σελήνη εἰς αἷμα, [s] πρὶν [s] ἢ ἐλθεῖν [t] ἡμέραν [t] κυρίου τὴν

a ch. xiii. 40 reff.
b ver. 21 reff. Joel ii. 28.
c 2 Tim. iii. 1. James v. 3. Isa. ii. 2 al.
d = ver. 33. ch. x. 45. Tit. iii. 6. Zech. xii. 10.
e = Mark vi. 43. Luke xx. 10 al.
f Matt. xxiv. 22. John xvii. 2. Rom. iii. 20. 1 Cor. i. 29 al. Ezek. xx. 48 al.
g ch. v. 10 reff.
h = Rev. (iv. 3 bis.) ix. 17 only. Zech. x. 2.
i here only. 1 Kings xxviii. 6, 15.
j Jude 8 only. Jud. vii. 13.
k ch. xvii. 27 [Luke xix. 42] only. (1 Cor. iv. 8.) Joel l. c. Aℵ$^{3a\cdot b}$ compl.
l = Matt. xxiv. 24. (|| Mk. v. r.) 3 Kings xiii. 3, 5.
m ch. vii. 36 reff.
n John xi. 41. Deut. iv. 39.
o Matt. xxvii. 51 || Mk. Mark xiv. 66. John viii. 23. Deut. iv. 39.
p James iv. 14 only. Lev. xvi. 13.
q Gal. i. 7. James iv. 9 only. Deut. xxiii. 5.
r Matt. xxiv. 29 || Mk. Rev. vi. 12 al. Isa. xiii. 10.
s Matt. i. 18. Mark xiv. 30. ch. vii. 2. Isa. vii. 15.
t 1 Thess. v. 2. 2 Pet. iii. 10 (1 Cor. i. 8. v. 5. 2 Cor. i. 14. 2 Thess. ii. 2) only. Isa. ii. 12.

16, 17. rec aft προφ. ins ιωηλ· και, with ABCEIPℵ rel 36 vulg E-lat syr [Cyr-jer$_1$ Bas$_1$ Chr$_1$] and, but placing ιωηλ bef προφ., æth Gaud (*corrns: 1st, the name of the prophet supplied; and 2ndly, the και inserted to suit the* LXX): ιωηλ, omg και, Syr copt [and after προφ, sah]: om D Iren-int(iii. 12, p. 193) Rebapt$_1$ Hil$_1$ Aug$_1$. for εν τ. εσχ. ημ., μετα ταυτα (*corrn to* LXX) B sah æth-pl Cyr-jer$_1$: μετα ταυτα εν τ. ε. ημ. C 103 arm. for ο θεος, κυριος DE vulg Iren-int Rebapt Hil. πασας σαρκας D^1-gr(txt D-corr^1). for υμων (1st and 2nd), αυτων D Rebapt Hil [1st Dion$_1$] (*corrn to suit* πασας σαρκας ?): om 2nd υμ. C [Dion$_1$]. om 3rd υμ. D Rebapt. om 4th υμ. (C^1[appy]) DE [Rebapt]. om αι (bef θυγ.) (C^1 ?) D. ορασει D^1. rec ενυπνια (*so* LXX-Bℵ$^{1\cdot 3a}$), with EP rel 36 vulg D-lat Chr$_1$ Sevrn$_1$: om D^1-gr: txt (*so* LXX-Aℵ^{3b}) ABC D^2[-gr] ℵ f k p 13.

18. for γε, εγω D^1(and lat: txt D^4). transpose τους δουλους and τας δουλας ℵ. om εν τ. ημ. εκ. and (*as* LXX) και προφητευσ. D Rebapt$_1$.

19. om (*as* LXX-ABℵ^1) ανω A m 37^1 Syr sah (of these Syr omits κατω: so also LXX). om αιμα to καπνου D.

20. μεταστρεφεται D^1-gr(txt D^2(and lat): -τραφισται D^{10}). om ἡ (*as* LXX) ACDEℵ p 13: ins BP rel 36 Chr$_1$. rec ins την bef ημεραν (*conform to* LXX-AB

variations. Where the copies differ, it agrees with the Alexandrine. The variations, &c., are noticed below. **τοῦτό ἐστιν**, '**this** *is*,' i.e. 'this is the fact, at which those words pointed.' See a somewhat similar expression, Luke xxiv. 44. **17.**] **ἐν ταῖς ἐσχ. ἡμ.** is an *exposition* of the *μετὰ ταῦτα* of the LXX and Hebrew, referring it to the days of the Messiah, as Isa. ii. 2; Micah iv. 1, al. See also 2 Tim. iii. 1; Heb. i. 1. **λέγει ὁ θεός** does not occur in the verse of Joel, but at the beginning of the whole passage, ver. 12, and is supplied by Peter here. **ἐκχεῶ**] LXX-Aℵ^{3b}: *καὶ ἐκχ.*, Bℵ^1. It is a later form of the future; see Winer, edn. 6, § 15. **ἀπὸ τοῦ πν.**] In the Heb. simply "My Spirit,"—אֶת־רוּחִי. The two clauses, *κ. οἱ νεαν.* and *κ. οἱ πρεσβ.*, are transposed in the LXX. **18. καί γε**] LXX-Aℵ$^{3a\cdot b}$: *καί*, Bℵ^1. Aft. *δούλας* om *μου* Bℵ^1. The Hebrew does not express it either time, but has, as in E. V., '*the servants and handmaids.*' *καὶ προφητεύσουσιν* is not in LXX nor Heb. **19.**] *καὶ δώσω τέρατα ἐν οὐρανῷ* Ed-vat.: txt ABℵ. *ἄνω, σημεῖα,* and *κάτω* are not in LXX nor Heb. **αἷμα κ. πῦρ . . . .**] Not, '*bloodshed and wasting by fire,*' as commonly interpreted: —not *devastations*, but **prodigies**, are foretold:—bloody and fiery appearances: —*pillars* of smoke, Heb. **20.**] See Matt. xxiv. 29. **ἡμ. κυρ.**] Not *the first coming of Christ*,—which interpretation would run counter to the whole tenor of the Apostle's application of the prophecy:—but clearly, *His second coming*; regarded in prophetic language as following close upon the outpouring of the Spirit, because it is the *next great event* in the divine arrangements. The Apostles probably expected this coming very soon (see note on Rom. xiii. 11); but this did not at all affect the accuracy of their expressions respecting it. Their days wit-

u μεγάλην καὶ v ἐπιφανῆ. 21 καὶ w ἔσται, πᾶς ὃς ἐὰν
x ἐπικαλέσηται τὸ ὄνομα κυρίου y σωθήσεται. 22 ἄνδρες
Ἰσραηλῖται, ἀκουσατε τοὺς λόγους τούτους. Ἰησοῦν
τὸν Ναζωραῖον, ἄνδρα z ἀπὸ τοῦ θεοῦ a ἀποδεδειγμένον
b εἰς ὑμᾶς c δυνάμεσιν καὶ m τέρασιν καὶ σημείοις d οἷς
ἐποίησεν δι' αὐτοῦ ὁ θεὸς e ἐν μέσῳ ὑμῶν, καθὼς αὐτοὶ

ABCDE
Pℵ a b c
d f g h k
l m o p
13

u = John vii. 37. xix. 31. Jude ver. 6. Rev. vi. 17. Mal. iv. 5.
v here only. Joel l. c. Mal. i. 14.
w constr., ver. 17. ch. iii. 23. Joel l. c. see Luke i. 34.
x ch. ix. 14, 21. xxii. 16. Rom. x. 13. 1 Cor. i. 2. Zech. xiii. 9.
y = Matt. x. 22 al. fr.
z = Matt. xi. 19. ch. x. 33. 2 Cor. vii. 13. Rev. ix. 18. Isa. xlv. 26.
a ch. xxv. 7. 1 Cor. iv. 9. 2 Thess. ii. 4 only. Esth. ii. 9 AB(not ℵ Ed-vat). 1 Macc. x. 34. Xen. Hell. iv. 4. 8.
b = Luke ix. 13. ch. xxiv. 17 al.
c = ch. viii. 13 reff.
d attr., ch. i. 1 reff.
e Luke ii. 46. ch. i. 15 al. Ps. cxxxiv. 9.

and gramml corrn), with ACEPℵ[3] rel 36: om (*so* LXX-א) BDℵ[1]. om και επιφ. Dℵ[1][ins ℵ-corr[1 or 3]].

21. om ver ℵ[1](ins in very small letters ℵ-corr[1]). rec *ος αν* (LXX), with ACDP ℵ-corr[1] rel Chr$_1$: txt BE 36. ins *του* bef *κυρ.* D[1].

22. *ισδραηλιται* (so ch. iii. 12 al) ℵ, *ιστρ.* B[1][E]. *ναζοραιον* (so ch. iii. 6 al) D[1]ℵ[1]. *αποδεδ.* bef *απο τ. θ.* (*corrn to avoid ambiguity of ανδρ. απο τ. θ.*) BC D-corr ℵ m p vulg [sah æth] arm Ath$_1$ Chr$_1$ [Thdot-anc$_1$ Thdrt] Iren-int$_1$ Fulg$_1$: txt AD[1]EP rel 36 D-lat [syr copt Ath$_1$ Cosm$_1$ Tert$_2$].—*δεδοκιμασμενον* D[1](appy: txt D[2]: *probatum* D-lat): *designatum* E-lat: *approbatum* vulg Iren-int Ambr Fulg.—*qui a Deo videri factus est apud vos* Syr. for *υμ.*, *ημας* D[1](and lat: txt D[2]) c k 100-27 lect-5 [Eus$_1$] (of these 100-27 have **ημων** below). for *οις*, *οσα* D[1](txt D[2]). om *ο* (bef *θεος*) C. *ο θ.* bef *δι' αυτου* E d l vulg (not am demid [fuld tol]) [Ath$_1$ Thdrt$_1$]. rec aft *καθως* ins *και* (*καθως και being a very common expr*), with C[3]P 13 rel [vulg-ed] syr Chr [Thdot-anc$_1$ Cosm$_1$]: om ABC[1]DEℵ m p 36. 40 Syr [coptt arm] æth [Eus$_1$] Ath$_2$ Iren-int$_1$. for *αυτοι, υμεις παντες* E; *υμεις* 117 vulg arm.

nessed the Pentecostal effusion, which was *the beginning of the signs of the end*: then follows the period, KNOWN TO THE FATHER ONLY, of waiting—the Church for her Lord,—the Lord Himself till all things shall have been put under His feet,—and then *the signs shall be renewed*, and *the day of the Lord shall come*. Meantime, and in the midst of these signs, the covenant of the spiritual dispensation is, ver. 21—'*Whosoever* shall call on the name of the Lord, shall be saved.' The gates of God's mercy are thrown open in Christ to all people:—no barrier is placed,—*no union with any external association or succession required*: the promise is to *individuals*, AS *individuals*: **πᾶς ὃς ἐάν**: which individual universality, though here by the nature of the circumstances spoken within the limits of the outward Israel, is afterwards as expressly asserted of Jew and Gentile, Rom. i. 17, where see note.

22.] **ἄνδρ. Ἰσρ.** binds all the hearers in *one term*, and that one reminds them of their covenant relation with God: compare πᾶς οἶκος Ἰσραήλ, ver. 36. **τὸν Ναζωραῖον**] Not emphatically used by way of contrast to what follows, as Beza, Wetst., &c.; but only as the ordinary appellation of Jesus by the Jews, see John xviii. 5, 7; ch. xxii. 8; xxvi. 9. **ἀπό**, not *for* ὑπό, here or any where else (see Winer, edn. 6, § 47, b): but signifying the *source whence*, not merely the *agency by which*, the deed has place. See reff., and especially James i. 13. **ἀποδεδειγμένον**] 'demonstratum,' more than '*approved*' (E. V.):—**shewn to be** that which He claimed to be. ἀποδεδ. must be taken with ἀπὸ τ. θεοῦ: not, as some have divided the words, ἄνδρ. ἀπὸ τ. θεοῦ, ἀποδ. κ.τ.λ.: Gal. i. 1 is no justification of this, for there ἀπό refers to ἀπόστολος,—and certainly Peter would never have barely thus named our Lord 'a man from God.' The whole connexion of the passage would besides be broken by this rendering: that connexion being, that the Man Jesus of Nazareth was *by God* demonstrated, *by God* wrought in among you, *by God's counsel* delivered to death, *by God* raised up (which raising up is argued on till ver. 32, then taken up again), *by God* (ver. 36), finally, made Lord and Christ. This was the process of argument then with the Jews,—proceeding on the identity of a man whom they had seen and known,—and then mounting up from His works and His death and His resurrection, to *His glorification*,—all THE PURPOSE AND DOING OF GOD. But if His *divine origin*, or even His divine *mission*, be stated at the outset, we *break this climacterical sequence*, and lose the power of the argument. The ἀποδεδειγμένον (εἶναι) ἀπὸ θεοῦ of Dr. Bloomfield is of course worse still. **οἷς** (ἃ) **ἐποίησεν δι' αὐτ. ὁ θ.**] not, as De Wette, *a low view of the miracles wrought by Jesus*, nor inconsistent with John ii. 11; but in strict accordance with the progress

οἴδατε 23 τοῦτον τῇ [f] ὡρισμένῃ [g] βουλῇ καὶ [h] προγνώσει
τοῦ θεοῦ [i] ἔκδοτον [k] διὰ χειρὸς [l] ἀνόμων [m] προσπήξαντες
[n] ἀνείλατε, 24 ὃν ὁ θεὸς [o] ἀνέστησεν [pq] λύσας τὰς [qr] ὠδῖνας
τοῦ θανάτου, [s] καθότι οὐκ ἦν δυνατὸν [t] κρατεῖσθαι αὐτὸν
ὑπ᾽ αὐτοῦ. 25 Δαυεὶδ γὰρ λέγει [u] εἰς αὐτὸν [v] Προορώμην
τὸν κύριον [w] ἐνώπιόν μου [x] διὰ παντός, ὅτι [y] ἐκ δεξιῶν μου

f ch. xvii. reff. g = Luke vii. 30. ch. iv. 28. Eph. i. 11. Heb. vi. 17. h 1 Pet. i. 2 only †. Judith ix. 6. xi. 19 only. see ch. xxvi. 5. i here only †. Bel & Dr. 22 Theod. = Herod. vi. 85. k = ch. xi. 30 reff. l = 1 Cor. ix. 21 3ce only. Wisd. xvii. 2. (Luke xxii. 37.) m here only †. n = ch. v. 33 reff. o = trans., of Christ, ver. 32. ch. xiii. 32, 34. xvii. 31 only. of others, John vi. 39, 40, 44, 54 only. p = Mark vii. 35. q Job xxxix. 2. τῶν ὠδ. λῦσαι δεσμούς, Æl. H. An. xii. 5. r = here (Matt. xxiv. 8 ‖ Mk. 1 Thess. v. 3) only. Ps. xvii. 5. s = Luke i. 7. xix. 9. (ver. 45.) ch. (iv. 35.) xvii. 31 only. L. t = here only. Josh. xviii. 1. Xen. Mem. iii. 2. 1. u = Eph. v. 32. Heb. vii. 14. 1 Pet. i. 11 only. v = here (ch. xxi. 29) only. Psa. xv. 8. w = Luke i. 19. ch. iv. 10 al. Gen. xxiv. 51. x Matt. xviii. 10. ch. x. 2. Rom. xi. 10. Isa. xlix. 16. y Matt. xx. 21, 23. Luke i. 11. ver. 34. ch. vii. 55, 56. Heb. i. 13. 1 Kings xxiii. 19.

23. rec aft εκδ. ins λαβοντες (*corrn to fill up the constr*), with DEPℵ^3 rel 36 syr [Eus$_1$ Cyr$_1$ Thdot-anc$_1$] Chr$_1$ [Cyr-p$_1$] Cosm$_1$: om ABC^{1}ℵ^1 p 40 vulg Syr coptt æth arm Ath$_1$ Iren-int$_1$ Victorin$_1$. rec χειρων (*corrn*), with C^{3}EP rel 36 vulg [Syr arm-zoh] coptt Chr$_1$ [Cosm$_1$] Iren-int$_1$: txt ABC^{1}Dℵ p 13 [syr æth Eus$_1$] Ath$_1$ Cyr[-p$_1$]. (ανειλατε, so ABCDEPℵ d p [13] 36 [Eus$_1$] Ath$_1$.)

24. aft λυσας ins δι αυτου E. for θανατου, αδου (*corrn from vv.* 27, 31 : *see also Ps.* xvii. 5) D vulg E-lat Syr copt Polyc$_1$ Epiph$_1$ Ps-Ath$_1$ Iren-int$_1$ [Thdrt-int$_1$].

25. ins μεν bef γαρ E 36. (προορωμην, so AB^{1}CDEℵ (not 36).) aft κυριον ins μου Dℵ : om ενωπιον Syr.

of our Lord through humiliation to glory, and with His own words in that very Gospel (v. 19), which is devoted to the great subject, *the manifestation, by the Father, of the glory of the Son*. This side of the subject is here especially dwelt on in argument with these Jews, to exhibit (see above) the whole course of Jesus of Nazareth, as the *ordinance and doing of* THE GOD OF ISRAEL. **23.**] **βουλή** and **πρόγνωσις** are not the same: the former designates the **counsel** of God—His Eternal Plan, by which He has arranged (cf. ὡρισμένῃ) all things; the latter, the **omniscience**, by which every part of this plan is foreseen and unforgotten by Him. **ἔκδοτον**] *by whom*, is not said, but was supplied by the hearers. τῇ ὡρισμ. &c. are not to be joined to ἔκδοτον as agents —the dative is that of *accordance* and *appointment*, not of agency:—see Winer, edn. 6, § 31. 6, b, and ch. xv. 1; 2 Pet. i. 21. **δ. χειρὸς ἀνόμων**] viz. of the Roman soldiers, see reff. **προσπήξαντες**] The harshness and unworthiness of the deed are strongly set forth by a word expressing the mechanical act merely, **having nailed up**, as in contrast with the former clause, from Ἰησοῦν to ὑμῶν. Peter lays the charge on the multitude, because they *abetted their rulers*,—see ch. iii. 17, where this is fully expressed: not for the far-fetched reason given by Olshausen, that 'all mankind were in fact guilty of the death of Jesus:' in which case, as Meyer well observes (and the note in Olsh.'s last edn. ii. p. 666, does not answer this), Peter must have said '*we*,' not '*you*.' **24.**] There is some difficulty in explaining the expression **ὠδῖνας** in the connexion in which it is here found. The difficulty lies, not in the connexion of λύειν with ὠδῖνας, which is amply justified, see reff., but in the interpretation of ὠδῖνας *here*. For ὠδῖνας θαν. must mean *the pains of death*, i. e. the pains which precede and end in death; a meaning here inapplicable. (The explanation of Chrys., Theophyl., Œc., ὁ θάνατος ὤδινε κατέχων αὐτόν, κ. τὰ δεινὰ ἔπασχε, will not be generally maintained at the present day. Stier does maintain it, Reden der Apostel, vol. i. p. 43 ff., but to me not convincingly: and, characteristically, Wordsw. also.) The fact may be, that Peter used the Hebrew word חֶבְלֵי, ref. Psa. '*nets*, or *bands*,' i. e. the nets in which death held the Lord captive; and that, in rendering the words into Greek, the LXX rendering of the word in that place and Ps. cxiv. 3, viz. ὠδῖνες, has been adopted. (But see Prolegg. to Vol. I. ch. ii. § ii. pp. 28, 29.) It has been attempted in vain by Olshausen and others to shew that ὠδῖνες sometimes in Hellenistic Greek signifies *bands*. No one instance cited by Schleusner (Lex. V. T.) of that meaning is to the point. See Simonis Lex., חבל.
οὐκ ἦν δυν. depends for its proof on the **γάρ** which follows. **25.**] **εἰς αὐτόν**, not '*of Him*,' but **in allusion to Him.** The 16th Psalm was not by the Rabbis applied to the Messiah: but Peter here proves to them that, if it is to be true in its highest and proper meaning of any one, it must be of Him. We are met at every

z = ch. xvii. 13. 2 Thess. ii. 2. see Heb. xii. 26, 27. Ps. xvi. 5.
a ch. vii. 41 reff.
b ch. xvi. 34. Matt. v. 12. Luke x. 21. 1 Pet. i. 6 al. Ps. ii. 11.
c here only. see ch. xxi. 28.
d Matt. xiii. 32 || only. Ps. xiv. 1.
e Rom. iv. 18 reff.

ABCDE Pℵ a b c d f g h k l m o p 13

ἐστὶν ἵνα μὴ [z] σαλευθῶ· 26 διὰ τοῦτο [a] ηὐφράνθη μου
ἡ καρδία καὶ [b] ἠγαλλιάσατο ἡ γλῶσσά μου, [c] ἔτι δὲ καὶ ἡ
σάρξ μου [d] κατασκηνώσει [c] ἐπ' [e] ἐλπίδι, 27 ὅτι οὐκ [f] ἐγκατα-
λείψεις τὴν [g] ψυχήν μου [h] εἰς [i] ᾅδην οὐδὲ [k] δώσεις τὸν
[l] ὅσιόν σου [m] ἰδεῖν [n] διαφθοράν. 28 [o] ἐγνώρισάς μοι [p] ὁδοὺς
ζωῆς, [q] πληρώσεις με [r] εὐφροσύνης [s] μετὰ τοῦ προσώπου
σου. 29 ἄνδρες ἀδελφοί, [t] ἐξὸν εἰπεῖν [u] μετὰ [u] παῤῥησίας
πρὸς ὑμᾶς περὶ τοῦ [v] πατριάρχου Δαυείδ, ὅτι καὶ [w] ἐτε-

f 2 Cor. iv. 9 reff. g = Rev. vi. 9. xx. 4 only. Wisd. iii. 1. Jos. Antt. vi. 14. 2. h constr., ch. viii. 40 reff. i Matt. xi. 23. Rev. i. 18 al. Hos. xiii. 14. k = ver. 4 reff. l = Heb. vii. 26. Ps. lxxxv. 2. m = Luke ii. 26. ch. xiii. 35 (from l. c.) &c. Heb. xi. 5. see Ps. lxxxviii. 48. n ver. 31. ch. xiii. 34, &c. only. Job xxxiii. 28. o 1 Cor. xii. 3 reff. p = Matt. xxi. 32. Prov. v. 6. q = ch. xiii. 52 reff. r ch. xiv. 17 only. Esth. ix. 18, 19. s constr., here only. l. c. t Matt. xii. 4. 2 Cor. xii. 4 only. Esth. iv. 2. w. aor., ch. xxi. 37 reff. u ch. iv. 29, 31. xxviii. 31 only. Lev. xxvi. 13. see John vii. 13. Eph. vi. 19. v ch. vii. 8, 9. Heb. vii. 4 only. 1 Chron. xxvii. 22. w Matt. ii. 19 al. gospp. only, exc. ch. vii. 15. Heb. xi. 22. 1 Chron. xix. 28.

26. (ηυφρανθη, so ABCDEPℵ m p 40 Clem_1.) rec η καρδ. bef μου (*corrn from LXX*), with ACDEPℵ[3] rel 36 : txt Bℵ[1] Clem_1. εφ' [C]Dℵ.
27. rec **αδου** (so *LXX-A*), with EP rel Orig_1 : txt (so *LXX-Bℵ*) ABCDℵ b c f (k ?) o p 40 Clem_1 Thl [Epiph_1].
28. γνωρισας D[1]-gr(txt D[2]). ευφροσυνην A[1](appy) [m] 96(sic Scholz), so A in *LXX* (Field is wrong).

turn by the shallow objections of the Rationalists, who seem incapable of comprehending the principle on which the sayings of David respecting himself are referred to Christ. To say, with De Wette, that Peter's proof lies not in any historical but only in an *ideal* meaning of the Psalm, is *entirely beside the subject.* To interpret the sayings of David (or indeed those of any one else) 'historically,' i. e. *solely as referring to the occasion which gave rise to them,* and having *no wider reference,* would be to establish a canon of interpretation wholly counter to the common sense of mankind. Every one, placed in any given position, when speaking of himself as in that position, speaks what will refer to others similarly situated, and most pointedly to any one who shall in any especial and pre-eminent way stand in that position. Applying even this *common rule* to David's sayings, the applicability of them to Christ will be legitimized:—but how much more, when we take into account *the whole circumstances of David's theocratic position, as the prophetic representative and type of Christ!* Whether the Messiah was *present or not to the mind of the Psalmist,* is of very little import: in some cases He plainly *was:* in others, as here, David's words, spoken of himself and his circumstances, could only be in their highest and literal sense true of the *great Son of David* who was to come. David often spoke *concerning himself;* but THE SPIRIT WHO SPOKE IN DAVID, **εἰς** τὸν χριστόν. The citation is verbatim from the LXX (except in the order of μου ἡ καρ.: see var. readd.): the Vatican, Sinaitic, and Alexandrine copies agree throughout, except in ᾄδην Bℵ (τον αδ. ℵ[1]) and ᾄδου (A), and εὐφροσύνης (Bℵ) and -νην (A), between which our MSS. also vary. **ἵνα μὴ σαλευθῶ**] Heb. *'I shall not be moved.'* **26. ἡ γλῶσσά μου**] Heb. כְּבוֹדִי, *'my glory:'* so in Ps. cviii. 1, where our prayer-book version renders "I will give praise with the best member that I have." Cf. also Ps. lvii. 8.
27. διαφθοράν] Heb. שַׁחַת, *'corruption,'* from שָׁחַת, corrupit,—or *'the pit,'* from שׁוּחַ, subsidere. De Wette maintains the last to be the only right rendering: but the Lexicons give both, as above, and Meyer and Stier defend the other.
28.] ἐγνώρισας κ.τ.λ.: Heb. *'Thou wilt make known.'* **πληρώσεις** κ.τ.λ.: Heb. *'Fulness of joys* (is) *with thy presence.'* These two last clauses refer to the Resurrection and the Ascension respectively. **29. ἄνδρες ἀδελφοί**] *q. d.,* 'I am your brother, an Israelite, and therefore would not speak with disrespect of David.' He prepares the way for the apologetic sentence which follows. **ἐξόν**] supply, not ἔστω, but ἐστίν, **I may,** &c.
The title 'Patriarch' is *only here* applied to *David,* as the progenitor of the kingly race:—Abraham and the sons of Jacob are so called in the N. T. reff. In the LXX, the word is used of chief men, and heads of families, with the exception of 2 Chron. xxiii. 20, where it represents "captains of hundreds." **ὅτι**] not, *because;* but **that,**—contains the subject of εἰπεῖν, and is that for which the apology is made. We learn from 1 Kings ii. 10, and Neh. iii. 16, that David was buried

λεύτησεν καὶ [x] ἐτάφη, καὶ τὸ [y] μνῆμα αὐτοῦ ἐστιν [z] ἐν ἡμῖν
ἄχρι τῆς ἡμέρας ταύτης. 30 προφήτης οὖν [a] ὑπάρχων καὶ
εἰδὼς ὅτι [b] ὅρκῳ [bc] ὤμοσεν αὐτῷ ὁ θεὸς ἐκ [d] καρποῦ τῆς
[e] ὀσφύος αὐτοῦ [f] καθίσαι ἐπὶ τὸν θρόνον αὐτοῦ, 31 [g] προ-
ϊδὼν ἐλάλησεν περὶ τῆς [h] ἀναστάσεως τοῦ χριστοῦ, ὅτι
οὔτε [i] ἐγκατελείφθη [ik] εἰς [k] ᾅδου οὔτε ἡ σὰρξ αὐτοῦ [i] εἶδεν
[i] διαφθοράν. 32 τοῦτον τὸν Ἰησοῦν [l] ἀνέστησεν ὁ θεός,
οὗ πάντες ἡμεῖς ἐσμὲν [m] μάρτυρες. 33 τῇ δεξιᾷ οὖν τοῦ

x 1 Cor. xv. 4 reff.
y ch. vii. 16 reff
z = Luke iv. 25, 27. Col. iii. 3. Num. xxiii. 21.
a = Luke viii. 41. ch. vii. 55 al. ‡ see Ps. liv. 19. Sir. xx. 16.
b see James v. 12. Gen. xxvi. 3.
c constr., here only. Isa. xix. 18.
d Psa. cxxxi. 11. = Luke i. 42. Gen. xxx. 2.
e = Heb. vii. 5, 10 only. Gen. xxxv. 11.
f trans., Matt. xix. 28. 1 Cor. vi. 4. Eph. i. 20 only. 1 Kings xxx. 21.
g Gal. iii. 8 only. = Ps. cxxxix. 3. Wisd. xix. 1. see Gen. xxxvii. 18.
h ch. i. 22 reff.
i ver. 27.
k here only. Isa. xiv. 19 al.
l = ver. 24 reff.
m ch. i. 8 reff.

29. το μνημιον D. for εν, παρ D vulg E-lat.

30. ειδων D^1[-gr](txt D^4). for οσφυος, καρδιας D^1(txt D$^{7\cdot 8}$: *præcordia* D-lat). rec aft οσφ. αυτου ins το κατα σαρκα αναστησειν τον χριστον (*explanatory gloss, taken into the text from margin*), with (D^{1}E)P rel syr Eus$_1$ (Chr$_1$) Thdrt Thl—but om το D^1, om το κ. σαρ. E. 4. 27-9 : αναστησαι D^{1}E 13 : aft τον χρ. ins και D-gr E 69. 96. 105 : om ABCD^{2}א p H^r vulg Syr coptt æth arm [Eus$_1$] Cyr$_1$ Iren-int$_1$ Victorin$_1$ [Fulg$_1$]. rec **του θρονου**, with EP^2 rel Chr [Cyr$_1$], θρονου (only) P^1 : txt ABCDא p Orig Eus$_2$ (LXX-B^r(B^1 def) א^{3a} *have* -νου, LXX-Aא^1 -νον : *Meyer thinks* -νον *a gramml alteration to suit better the transitive* καθισαι : *but qu ?*).

31. προειδως D^6 1. 60-9. 100-4-27-63 : προειδων (= προιδ.) ACE c e 13.—om προιδ. ελ. π. τ. D^1(and lat). rec for ουτε and ουτε, ου and ουδε (*corrn from ver* 27), with E-gr(ουκ) P rel syrr coptt Thdor-mops [Thdrt$_1$] : ουκ and ουτε 13 : ουτε and ουδε B : txt ACDא p 36 vulg E-lat Eus$_2$ Chr$_1$ Cyr$_1$ Iren-int Victorin Fulg Bede-gr. rec κατελειφθη, with P rel : txt ABCDEא d f h 13. 36 Eus$_2$ Thaum$_1$ Chr$_1$ [Cyr$_1$] Thdrt Thdor-mops. rec adds η ψυχη αυτου (*from ver* 27), with C^{3}EP rel syr(aft αδ.) [arm Thaum(bef εγκατ.)] Chr$_1$(bef εγκατ.) Thdrt(aft αδ.) Fulg$_1$ Philast$_1$: om ABC^{1}Dא p vulg Syr coptt æth Did-int Iren-int Victorin. αδην Bא b (k ?) o p 36 Eus$_2$ Thaum$_1$.

32. aft τουτον ins ουν D^1(and lat) E Ambr$_1$ Victorin$_1$.—om τον D^1-gr(txt D^8). εσμεν bef ημεις א : μαρτ. bef εσμεν D vulg [Did-int] : om εσμεν P^1 : txt ABCEP^2 rel.

at Jerusalem, in the city of David, i. e. the stronghold of Zion, 2 Sam. v. 7. Josephus, Antt. vii. 15. 3, gives an account of the high priest Hyrcanus, when besieged by Antiochus Eusebes,—and afterwards King Herod, opening the tomb and taking treasure from it. See also xiii. 8. 4; xvi. 7. 1; B. J. i. 2. 5. Dio Cassius (lxix. 14) mentions, among the prodigies which preceded Hadrian's war, that the tomb of Solomon (the same with that of David, see Jos. Antt. xvi. 7. 1) fell down. Jerome mentions (Epist. xlvi. (xvii.) ad Marcellam, vol. i. p. 209) that the tomb of David was visited in his time (the end of the fourth century). **30.**] **προφήτης**, in the stricter sense, *a foreteller of future events* by the inspiration of the Holy Spirit. **εἰδώς**] See 2 Sam. vii. 12. The words are not cited from the LXX, but rendered from the Hebrew. On the principle of interpretation of this prophecy, see above on ver. 25. **31.**] The word προϊδών distinctly asserts the prophetic consciousness of David in the composition of this Psalm. But of what sort that prophetic consciousness was, may be gathered from this same Apostle, 1 Pet. i. 10—12: that it was not a *distinct knowledge* of the events which they foretold, but only a conscious reference in their minds to the great promises of the covenant, in the expression of which they were guided by the Holy Spirit of prophecy to say things pregnant with meaning not patent to themselves but to us. **32.**] From ver. 25 has been employed in substantiating the Resurrection as the *act of God announced by prophecy* in old time: now the *historical fact* of its accomplishment is affirmed, and the vouchers for it produced. **οὗ**] either masc., see ch. i. 8; xiii. 31,—or neut. The former seems most probable as including the latter. 'We are His witnesses,' would imply, 'We testify to this His work,' which work implied the Resurrection. **πάντες**, first and most properly *the Twelve*: but, secondarily, the whole body of believers, all of whom, at this time, had probably seen the Lord since His Resurrection; see 1 Cor. xv. 6. **33.**] Peter now comes to the *Ascension*—the exaltation of Jesus to be, in the fullest sense, Lord and Christ. **τῇ δεξιᾷ**] **by the right hand**, not *'to the right hand.'* The great end of this

θεοῦ [n] ὑψωθεὶς τήν τε [o] ἐπαγγελίαν τοῦ πνεύματος τοῦ
ἁγίου [p] λαβὼν [p] παρὰ τοῦ πατρὸς [q] ἐξέχεεν τοῦτο ὃ ὑμεῖς
[καὶ] βλέπετε καὶ ἀκούετε. 34 οὐ γὰρ Δαυεὶδ [r] ἀνέβη [r] εἰς
τοὺς [r] οὐρανούς, λέγει δὲ αὐτὸς Εἶπεν κύριος τῷ κυρίῳ
μου Κάθου [s] ἐκ δεξιῶν μου 35 ἕως ἂν θῶ τοὺς ἐχθρούς
σου [t] ὑποπόδιον τῶν ποδῶν σου. 36 [u] ἀσφαλῶς οὖν
γινωσκέτω πᾶς [v] οἶκος Ἰσραὴλ ὅτι καὶ κύριον αὐτὸν

ABCDE PℵN a b c d f g h k l m o p 13

...οτι και d.

n Matt. xxiii. 12. ch. v. 31. xiii. 17. 2 Cor. xi. 7. 1 Pet. v. 6 al. Sir. xv. 5.
o = ch. i. 4 reff.
p John v. 34 &c. ch. iii. 5. xvii. 9. xx. 24. xxvi. 10. James i. 7. Rev. ii. 27. Num. xvii. 2.
q vv. 17, 18 reff.
r John iii. 13. Rom. x. 6 (from Deut. xxx. 12). Rev. xi. 12.
s ver. 25 reff. Psa. cix. 1.
t Matt. v. 35. Luke xx. 43. ch. vii. 49. Heb. i. 13. x. 13. James ii. 3 only. Isa. lxvi. 1. Ps. xcviii. 5.
u = here (Mark xiv. 44. ch. xvi. 23) only. Wisd. xviii. 6. see Gen. xxxiv. 25.
v = Matt. x. 6. ch. vii. 42. Heb. viii. 8, 10 (from Jer. xxxviii. [xxxi.] 31).

33. for *την τε, και την* D. rec *τ. αγ. πνευμ.*, with DP rel Thdrt$_1$ Cosm$_1$ Iren-int$_1$: txt ABCEℵ c p 13 Chr$_1$ [Cyr-p$_1$], *spiritus sancti* vss(appy). for *τουτο ο υμεις, υμειν ο* D¹(and lat: txt D⁶): aft *τουτο* ins *το δωρον* E [demid tol syrr] Iren-int [Did-int$_1$] Ambr. rec ins *νυν* bef *υμεις*, with C³EP rel syr Cosm$_1$ [aft, Iren-int$_1$]: om ABC¹Dℵ l p vulg Syr coptt [æth] arm Did[-int$_1$]. rec om 1st *και* (*as unnecessary*), with ACEPℵ rel [vss Did-int$_1$] Thdrt$_1$: ins BD 13 [arm-zoh].

34. for *λεγει δε, ειρηκεν γαρ* D [simly Syr]; *dixit autem* vulg(not am fuld &c). for *ειπεν, λεγει* D am lat-mss-in-Bede. ins *ο* bef *κυριος* (*as* LXX; *see also Matt* xxii. 44 ||) [A] B¹·²(sic, see table) [CE]Pℵ³.

35. om *αν* D¹(ins D²).

36. ins *ο* bef *οικ.* CD c. elz om 1st *και*, with Syr coptt [æth(Treg) Bas$_1$] Eustath-

speech is to shew forth (see above) the God of Israel as the *doer* of all these things. However well the sense '*to*' might seem to agree with the ἐκ δεξιῶν of ver. 34, we must not set aside a very suitable sense, nor violate syntax (for the construction is entirely unexampled in Hellenistic as well as prose classical Greek) in order to suit an apparent adaptation. The reference is carried on by the word **δεξιᾷ**, though it be not in exactly the same position in the two cases. And the ἀνέβη εἰς τοὺς οὐρ. of ver. 34 prepares the way for the ἐκ δεξιῶν following without any harshness. On the *poetic* dative after verbs of approach, see Musgr., Phœnissæ, 310 (303, Matth.), and Hermann, Antig. 234. See also ch. v. 31, and Winer (who defends the construction), edn. 6, § 31. 5. Wordsw. denies that the δεξιὰ θεοῦ is ever specified in the N. T. as the instrument by which He works. But he has omitted to state that this and the similarly ambiguous place, ch. v. 31, are *the only real instances of the expression being used*, all the rest being local, ἐκ δεξιῶν or ἐν δεξιᾷ: so that his dictum goes for nothing. And in the LXX the use of God's right hand as the instrument is very frequent: cf. Exod. xv. 6, 12; Ps. xvii. 36; lix. 5 (where the dat. is used as here), and about 20 other places; Isa. xlviii. 13; lxiii. 12, &c. After this, the objection, when applied to a speech so full of O. T. spirit and diction as this, would, even if valid as regards the N. T., be irrelevant. **ἐπαγγελίαν**] Christ is said to have received from the Father the promise above cited from Joel, which is spoken of *His days*. This, and not of course the declarations made by Himself to the same effect, is here *referred to*, though doubtless those were in Peter's mind. The very word, ἐξέχεεν, refers to ἐκχεῶ above, ver. 17. **τοῦτο**, 'this influence,' this merely; leaving to his hearers the inference, that *this*, which they saw and heard, must be none other than the effusion of the Spirit. **βλέπετε** need not imply, as Dr. Burton thinks, that "there was some visible appearance, which the people saw as well as the apostles:"—very much of the *effect* of the descent of the Spirit would be *visible*,—the enthusiasm and gestures of the speakers, for instance; not, however, the tongues of flame,—for then none could have spoken as in ver. 13. **34.**] This *exaltation* of Christ is also proved from prophecy—and from the same passage with which Jesus Himself had silenced His enemies. See notes, Matt. xxii. 41 ff. **δέ** is not '*for*,' which would destroy the whole force of the sentence: the Apostle says, **For David himself is not ascended into the heavens,**—*as he would be if the former prophecy applied to him*: but **he himself says**, removing all doubt on the subject, &c. The rendering δέ, *for*, makes it appear as if the ἀνέβη εἰς τ. οὐρ. were a mistaken inference from Psalm cx. 1, whereas that passage is adduced to preclude its being made from the other. **36.**] The conclusion from all that has been said. **πᾶς οἶκος Ἰσρ.** = πᾶς ὁ οἶκ. Ἰσρ., οἶκος being a familiar noun

καὶ χριστὸν ὁ θεὸς [w] ἐποίησεν, τοῦτον τὸν Ἰησοῦν ὃν
ὑμεῖς ἐσταυρώσατε.
37 Ἀκούσαντες δὲ [x] κατενύγησαν τὴν καρδίαν, εἶπόν
τε πρὸς τὸν Πέτρον καὶ τοὺς λοιποὺς ἀποστόλους Τί
ποιήσωμεν, ἄνδρες ἀδελφοί; 38 Πέτρος δὲ πρὸς αὐτοὺς
[y] Μετανοήσατε, καὶ [z] βαπτισθήτω ἕκαστος ὑμῶν [z] ἐπὶ τῷ

w = Matt. iv. 19. John vi. 15. Rev. i. 6 al. Gen. xlv. 9.
x here only. Gen. xxxiv. 7. Ps. cviii. 16. (-νυξις, Rom. xi. 8.)
y Matt. iii. 2. ch. iii. 19. viii. 22 al. Jer. viii. 6.
z constr., here only.

ap-Thdrt$_1$: ins ABCDEPℵ rel vulg syr [arm-zoh] æth-pl[Tischdf] Epiph$_2$ Nyss$_1$ [Bas$_1$ Ath$_1$ Chr$_1$] Iren-int$_1$ [Tert$_1$]. rec *και χριστον* bef *αυτον*, with EP rel Ath$_1$ Epiph$_3$ [Nyss$_2$ Cæs$_1$]: *και χριστον ο θεος* bef *αυτον* c m 4. 100: *αυτον* bef *κυριον* coptt (*all transpositions for perspicuity*): om *αυτον* D^1(and lat): txt ABCD^{2}ℵ 36 vulg arm Eustath$_1$ Ath$_1$ Bas$_2$ Chr$_1$ Iren-int$_1$. *εποι.* bef *ο θεος* (*corrn*) Bℵ p vulg[-ed] syrr copt æth [Bas$_1$] Ath$_2$ Leont$_1$ Tert$_1$ Amb$_1$: om *ο θ.* lect-12: txt ACDEP rel am fuld [demid Eustath$_1$ Bas$_1$ Chr$_1$] Epiph$_2$ Iren-int$_1$. (13 def.) om *τον* D^1(ins D^2).

37. for *δε*, *ουν* E-gr Aug$_1$.—*τοτε παντες οι συνελθοντες κ. ακουσαντες* D syr-mg. *κατηνυγησαν* E p. rec *τη καρδια* (*see Ps* cviii. 16), with DEP rel vulg: txt ABCℵ p [Bas$_1$ Epiph$_1$] Chr$_1$. (13 def.) for *ειπον τε*, *και ειπ.* E: *ειπ. δε* p: *ειποντες* D^{2}ℵ 1 18. 73. 103 Aug$_1$.—*και τινες εξ αυτων ειπαν* D^1[-gr]. om *λοιπους* D 104 [Aug$_1$]. rec *ποιησομεν*, with D rel Cyr-jer$_1$: txt ABCEPℵ a h k p Bas Epiph$_1$ Chr$_1$. (13 def.)—ins *ουν* bef *ποι.* (*see Lu* iii. 10) D Iren-int Aug$_2$. at end, add *υποδειξατε ημιν* DE tol syr-mg Aug$_4$[om$_1$].

38. rec ins *εφη* bef *προς αυτους*, with EP rel [syr coptt Thdrt$_1$]; *φησιν* bef *και βαπτ.* ACℵ p vulg Cyr-jer$_1$: *φησιν* bef *μεταν.* D: for *πετρ. δε*, *ειπε δε πετρος* a h 38. 67. 113 lect-12 Syr æth arm (*all these varr shew that originally the verb was not expressed*): om B 65. 127-63 demid. (13 def.) for *επι*, *εν* BCD [Cyr-jer$_1$] Epiph$_1$ [Cyr$_1$ Thdrt$_1$]: txt AEPℵ rel Bas$_1$ Chr$_1$.

used anarthrously: see Eph. ii. 21, note, and Winer, edn. 6, § 19, who however does not give *οἶκος* in his list: **the whole house of Israel**—for all hitherto said has gone upon proofs and sayings belonging to *Israel*, and to *all* Israel. **ὁ θεὸς ἐποίησεν**, as before, is the ground-tone of the discourse. **κύριον**, from ver. 34. **χριστόν**, in the full and glorious sense in which that term was prophetically known. The same is expressed ch. v. 31 by *ἀρχηγὸν κ. σωτῆρα ὕψωσεν.* The final clause sets in the strongest and plainest light the fact to which the discourse testifies—ending with **ὃν ὑμεῖς ἐσταυρώσατε,**—the remembrance most likely to carry compunction to their hearts. 'In clausula orationis iterum illis exprobrat quod Eum crucifixerint, ut majori conscientiæ dolore tacti ad remedium aspirent.' Calvin in loc. 'Aculeus in fine.' Bengel. **37—41.**] Effect of the discourse. **37. κατενύγ.**] *κατανύσσω* is exactly 'compungo.' The compunction arose from the thought that they had rejected and crucified Him who was now so powerful, and under whose feet they, as enemies, would be crushed. 'Concionis fructum Lucas refert, ut sciamus non modo in linguarum varietate exsertam fuisse Spiritus Sancti virtutem, sed in eorum etiam cordibus qui audiebant.' Calvin. **ποιήσωμεν**, the deliberative subjunctive,—cf. Winer, edn. 6, § 41, a. 4, *b.*—**What must we do?** **38.**] **μετανοήσατε**, not, as in Matt. iii. 2; iv. 17, *μετανοεῖτε*. The aorist denotes *speed*, a definite, sudden act: the present, a habit, more gradual, as that first moral and legal change would necessarily be. The word imports *change of mind;* here, change from thinking Jesus an impostor, and scorning Him as one crucified, to being baptized in His name, and looking to Him for remission of sins, and the gift of the Spirit. The miserable absurdity of rendering *μεταν.*, or 'pœnitentiam agite,' by '*do penance*,' or understanding it as referring to a *course of external rites*, is well exposed by this passage—in which the *internal change of heart and purpose* is insisted on, to be testified by admission into the number of Christ's followers. See Calvin's note. **βαπτισθήτω**] Here, on the day of Pentecost, we have the first mention and administration of Christian baptism. Before, there had been the *baptism of repentance* for the remission of sins, by John, Luke iii. 3; but now we have the important addition *ἐπὶ τῷ ὀνόμ. Ἰησοῦ χριστοῦ*,—**on the Name**—i. e. *on the confession* of that which the Name implies, and *into the benefits and blessings* which the Name implies. The Apostles and first believers were *not thus baptized*, because, ch. i. 5, they had received the

ὀνόματι Ἰησοῦ χριστοῦ [a] εἰς [a] ἄφεσιν [a] ἁμαρτιῶν, καὶ λήμ- ABCDE
ψεσθε τὴν [b] δωρεὰν τοῦ ἁγίου πνεύματος. 39 ὑμῖν γάρ Pℵabc
ἐστιν ἡ [c] ἐπαγγελία καὶ τοῖς τέκνοις ὑμῶν, καὶ πᾶσιν τοῖς fghkl
[d] εἰς [de] μακράν, ὅσους ἂν [f] προςκαλέσηται κύριος ὁ θεὸς mop13
ἡμῶν. 40 Ἑτέροις τε λόγοις [g] πλείοσιν [h] διεμαρτύρατο καὶ
παρεκάλει αὐτοὺς λέγων [i] Σώθητε ἀπὸ τῆς [k] γενεᾶς τῆς
[l] σκολιᾶς ταύτης. 41 Οἱ μὲν οὖν [m] ἀποδεξάμενοι τὸν λόγον
αὐτοῦ ἐβαπτίσθησαν, καὶ [n] προςετέθησαν [ἐν] τῇ ἡμέρᾳ

a Matt. xxvi. 28. Luke iii. 3 ‖ Mk. b = ch. viii. 20. x. 45. xi. 17. John iv. 10. c ch. i. 4 reff. d here only. 2 Kings vii. 19. e ch. xxii. 21 reff. f = ch. xiii. 2 reff. g = Luke xi. 53. ch. xiii. 31. xxiv. 17. xxv. 14. xxvii. 20. xxviii. 23. Luke only, exc. Heb. vii. 23. Num. ix. 19. h ch. viii. 25 reff. i = Matt. i. 21. Rom. v. 9. Ezek. xxxvi. 29. k = Matt. xxiv. 34 al. Ps. xi. 7. l = Phil. ii. 15. 1 Pet. ii. 18 (Luke iii. 5) only. Deut. xxxii. 5. m Luke viii. 40. ch. xviii. 27. xxi. 17. xxiv. 3. xxviii. 30+. 2 Macc. iii. 9 al. (-δεκτός, 1 Tim. ii. 3. v. 4 only.) n ver. 47. ch. v. 14. xi. 24. Num. xviii. 2. 1 Macc. ii. 43.

ins *του κυριου* bef *ιησ. χρ.* DE [am] syrr sah arm Cyr-jer$_1$ Bas$_1$ (Epiph$_1$) Thdrt$_3$ Cypr$_1$ Hil Lucif$_1$ Ambr Aug Vig. (Syr copt Iren-int om *χριστου.*) **των** *αμαρτ.* **υμων** A B(sic; see table) ℵ p vulg coptt æth Aug$_{alic}$; *των αμ.* **ημων** C: txt DEP 13 rel syrr [arm] Cyr-jer$_1$ Bas$_1$ Chr$_1$ [Cyr$_1$] Iren-int$_1$ Cypr$_1$ Lucif Ambr Aug$_{alic}$.

39. **ημιν** and **ημων** D Aug$_1$[txt$_1$]. for *οσους, ους* (*mistake in copying?*) AC 104 [coptt].

40. for *τε, δε* D-gr k: om c. (*διεμαρτυρατο*, so ABCDEℵ a h p Chr$_1$.) rec om *αυτους*, with EP rel Chr$_2$ 36-comm: ins ABCDℵ p 36-txt vulg [Syr coptt æth arm] Lucif$_1$, and, bef *παρεκαλει*, syr-w-ast. *ταυτ.* bef *της σκολιας* D lect-1 vulg Lucif [Aug$_1$].

41. for *αποδεξ.*, *πιστευσαντες* D (syr-mg Aug ins *και πιστευσαντες* bef *εβαπτισθησαν*). rec ins *ασμενως* bef *αποδεξ.* (*explanatory gloss on αποδεξ. from margin: or from ch* xxi. 17), with EP rel syrr Chr$_1$ Aug$_1$: om ABCDℵ p vulg coptt æth Clem$_1$ Aug$_1$. rec om *εν*, with EP rel (coptt?) Chr$_1$: ins (*possibly as a corrn to avoid the apparent connexion of τη ημ. εκ.* with *προσετεθησαν*) ABCDℵ p vulg.

BAPTISM BY THE HOLY GHOST, the *thing signified*, which superseded that by water, the *outward and visible sign*. The *result* of the baptism to which he here exhorts them, preceded by repentance and accompanied by faith in the forgiveness of sins in Christ, would be, the *receiving the gift of the Holy Spirit*. **39.**] **τοῖς τέκνοις ὑμ.**, viz. as included in the prophecy cited ver. 17, **your little ones**: not, as in ch. xiii. 32, '*your descendants*,' which would be understood by any Jew to be *necessarily implied*. [Thus we have a providential recognition of Infant Baptism at the very founding of the Christian Church.] **πᾶσιν τοῖς εἰς μακράν**, **the Gentiles**; see Eph. ii. 13. There is no difficulty whatever in this interpretation. The Apostles *always expected* the conversion of the Gentiles, as did every pious Jew who believed in the Scriptures. It was their conversion *as Gentiles*, which was yet to be revealed to Peter. It is surprising to see such Commentators as Dr. Burton and Meyer finding a difficulty where all is so plain. The very expression, *ὅσους ἂν προσκαλέσηται ὁ θεὸς ἡμ.*, shews in what sense Peter understood *τοῖς εἰς μακρ.*; not *all*, but as many as the Lord our God **προςκαλ.**, shall summon to *approach to Him*,—*bring near*,—which, *in his present understanding of the words*, must import—*by becoming one of the chosen people, and conforming to their legal observances*. **40.**] The words cited appear to be the concluding and inclusive summary of Peter's many exhortations, not only their general sense: just as if ver. 36 had been given as the representative of his whole speech above. **σώθητε** is improperly rendered in E. V. '*save yourselves*:' it is not (see Stier, R. A. i. 62) *σώζετε ἑαυτούς*, as in Luke xxiii. 35, 37, 39: **be saved**, Lasset euch retten, is the true sense. **σκολιᾶς**—see reff. Peter alludes to ref. Deut. **41.**] This *first baptism of regeneration* is important on many accounts in the history of the Christian Church. It presents us with two remarkable features: (1) It was conferred, *on the profession of repentance, and faith in Jesus as the Christ*. There was *no instruction in doctrine* as yet. The infancy of the Church in this respect corresponded to the infancy of the individual mind; the simplicity of faith came first,—the ripeness of knowledge followed. Neander well observes (Leit. u. Pflanz. p. 34) that among such a multitude, admitted by a confession which allowed of so wide an interpretation, were probably many persons who brought into the church the seeds of that Judaizing form of Christianity which afterwards proved so hostile to the true faith; while others, more deeply touched by the Holy Spirit, followed humbly the unfolding of

ἐκείνῃ [o] ψυχαὶ ὡσεὶ τρισχίλιαι. 42 [p] ἦσαν δὲ [q] προσκαρτεροῦντες τῇ [r] διδαχῇ τῶν ἀποστόλων καὶ τῇ [s] κοινωνίᾳ, τῇ [t] κλάσει τοῦ ἄρτου καὶ ταῖς προσευχαῖς. 43 [u] ἐγίνετο δὲ

o = ch. vii. 14. xxvii. 37. 1 Pet. iii. 20. Gen. xlvi. 15 al.
p constr., ver. 5 reff.
q ch. i. 14 reff. r Matt. vii. 28. ch. v. 28. xiii. 12. Rom. vi. 17 al. Ps. lix. tit. only. s = Gal. ii. 9. Lev. vi. 2. t Luke xxiv. 35 only †. u = but w. ἐπί, ch. v. 5 reff.

εκεινη bef τη ημερα D [am fuld demid]. ως ℵ[1] [1].

42. for ησαν δε, και ησαν D Syr. ins εν bef τη διδ. A 98 vulg D-lat. aft αποστ. add εν ιερουσαλημ D. rec ins και bef τη κλασει, with D[2]EPℵ[3] 13 rel [syr arm Chr$_1$]: om ABC D[1][and lat] ℵ[1] p [Syr coptt æth].

43. rec εγενετο (*corrn as more usual*), with EP rel Chr$_1$: txt A[B[2]]ℵ vulg syrr,

that teaching by which He perfected the apostolic age in the doctrine of Christ. (2) Almost without doubt, this first baptism must have been administered, as that of the first Gentile converts was (see ch. x. 47, and note), by *effusion or sprinkling, not by immersion.* The immersion of 3000 persons, in a city so sparingly furnished with water as Jerusalem, is equally inconceivable with a procession beyond the walls to the Kedron, or to Siloam, for that purpose.

42—47.] DESCRIPTION OF THE LIFE AND HABITS OF THE FIRST BELIEVERS. This description *anticipates;* embracing a period extending beyond the next chapter. This is plain from ver. 43: for the miracle related in the next chapter was evidently the first which attracted any public attention: vv. 44, 45, again, are taken up anew at the end of chap. iv., where we have a very similar description, evidently applying to the same period. **42.] τῇ διδαχῇ τῶν ἀποστ.**, compare Matt. xxviii. 20. **τῇ κοινωνίᾳ] community**: the living together as one family, and having things in common. It is no objection to this meaning, that the fact is *repeated* below, in ver. 45: for so is the κλάσις τοῦ ἄρτου in ver. 46, and the προσκ. ταῖς προσευχ.

The Vulg. interpretation of τῇ κοινωνίᾳ (καὶ) τῇ κλάσει τ. ἄρτ. by 'communicatione fractionis panis,' *per Hendiadyn*, is curious enough. If suggested by 1 Cor. x. 16, it should have been 'communicatione et fractione panis.' The adoption of the right reading renders this interpretation untenable. The supplying τῶν ἀποστ. after κοινωνίᾳ, as in E. V., is better than the last, but still I conceive bears no meaning defensible in construction. Very different is the κοινωνία τ. ἁγ. πνεύματος of 2 Cor. xiii. 13, because there the Holy Ghost is *imparted,* is that *of which* all partake, are κοινωνοί: whereas the κοιν. τῶν ἀποστ. must signify fellowship *with* the Apostles, or fellowship *with that Society* of which the Apostles were the chief; neither of which meanings I conceive κοιν. will bear. The special sense in which κοινωνία occurs, Rom. xv. 26, could not be here meant, or the word would have been qualified in some way, τῇ κοιν. (τῇ) εἰς τοὺς πτωχούς, or the like. **τῇ κλάσει τ. ἄρτου]** This has been very variously explained. Chrysostom (in Act. Homil. vii. p. 57) says, τὸν ἄρτον μοι δοκεῖ λέγων, καὶ τὴν νηστείαν ἐνταῦθα σημαίνειν, καὶ τὸν σκληρὸν βίον· τροφῆς γάρ, οὐ τρυφῆς μετελάμβανον. And similarly Œcumenius, and of the moderns Bengel: 'fractione panis, id est, victu frugali, communi inter ipsos.' But on ver. 46 he recognizes a covert allusion to the Eucharist.

The interpretation of ἡ κλ. τ. ἄρτ. [here] as *the celebration of the Lord's Supper* has been, both in ancient and modern times, the prevalent one. Chrysostom himself, in his 27th Hom. on 1 Cor., p. 422, interprets it, or at all events τῇ κοινωνίᾳ and it together, of the Holy Communion. And the Romanist interpreters have gone so far as to ground an argument on the passage for the administration *in one kind only.* But,—referring for a fuller discussion of the whole matter to the notes on 1 Cor. x. xi.,—barely to render ἡ κλάσις τοῦ ἄρτου the breaking of bread in the Eucharist, *as now understood,* would be to violate historical truth. The Holy Communion was at first, and for some time, till abuses put an end to the practice, *inseparably connected with the* ἀγάπαι, or *love-feasts,* of the Christians, and *unknown as a separate ordinance.* To these ἀγάπαι, accompanied as they were at this time by the celebration of the Lord's Supper, the κλάσις τοῦ ἄρτου refers,—from the custom of the master of the feast breaking bread in asking a blessing; see ch. xxvii. 35, where the Eucharist is out of the question.

No stress must be laid, for any doctrinal purpose, upon the article before ἄρτου: the construction here requires it, and below, ver. 46, where not required by the construction, it is omitted. I need hardly add that the sense inferred by Kypke and Heinrichs from Isa. lviii. 7, διάθρυπτε πεινῶντι τὸν ἄρτον σου,—that of giving bread to the poor, is in the highest degree improbable here, and inconsistent with the Christian use of ἡ κλάσις τοῦ ἄρτου else-

πάσῃ [v] ψυχῇ φόβος, πολλά τε [w] τέρατα καὶ σημεῖα [x] διὰ
τῶν ἀποστόλων ἐγίνετο. 44 πάντες δὲ οἱ πιστεύοντες
ἦσαν [y] ἐπὶ τὸ αὐτὸ καὶ [z] εἶχον ἅπαντα [a] κοινά, 45 καὶ τὰ
[b] κτήματα καὶ τὰς [c] ὑπάρξεις [d] ἐπίπρασκον καὶ [e] διεμέριζον
αὐτὰ πᾶσιν [f] καθότι ἄν τις [g] χρείαν [g] εἶχεν, 46 [h] καθ' ἡμέραν

[G ii. 45 ...] ABCDE GPℵ a b c f g h k l m o p 13

v = ch. iii. 23. Rom. ii. 9. xiii. 1. Gen. xvii. 14. w ch. vii. 36 reff. x = ch. iv. 16, 30 al. y ch. i. 15 reff. z = 1 Pet. ii. 12, 16. a = ch. iv. 32. Tit. i. 4. Jude 3 only (ch. x. 14 reff.) ‡. Wisd. vii. 3. b ch. v. 1. Matt. xix. 22 ‖ Mk. only. Prov. xxxi. (xxix.) 16. c Heb. x. 34 only. 2 Chron. xxxv. 7 al. d ch. iv. 34 reff. e Luke xxii. 17. John xix. 24, from Ps. xxi. 18. f = ch. iv. 35 only. Exod. i. 12, 17. Thucyd. iv. 118 fin. see ver. 24 reff. g abs., Mark ii. 25. ch. iv. 35. 1 Cor. xii. 24. 1 John iii. 17. h Matt. xxvi. 55. ch. iii. 2. xvi. 5. Heb. vii. 27 al. Num. iv. 16.

εγεινετο B¹CD. for *τε*, *δε* Bℵ p copt : *γαρ* sah : om D¹-gr(ins D³) m. aft *σημ.* ins *ου μικρα* E 25. aft *δια* ins *των χειρων* E 40 syr æth. *εγιν.* bef *δια τ. αποστ.* AC Syr copt æth.—*εγενετο* c e : *εγινοντο* E l 25. 64.—aft *αποστ.* add *εν ιερουσαλημ* ACEℵ vulg[(bef *εγιν.*) am] Syr copt : of these ACℵ vulg [am] copt further add *φοβος τε ην μεγας επι παντας* (*see ch* v. 5 al) : om BDP rel [sah æth arm].

44. ins *και* bef *παντες δε* ACℵ p. for *δε*, *τε* D. *πιστευσαντες* (*corrn*) Bℵ f Hʳ [æth arm] Orig₁ Thl-fin. om *ησαν* and *και* B 57 Orig₁ Salv₁. *παντα* D.

45. *κ. οσοι κτηματα ειχον η υπαρξεις* D [Syr].—om *τα* p. *εμεριζον* A. ins *καθ ημεραν* bef *πασι* D. for *καθοτι*, *τοις* D¹-gr(txt D⁶) : *καθως* 13.

46. for *καθ ημεραν, παντες* D¹[and lat] : *καθ ημ. παντες τε* D⁶.

where. **ταῖς προσευχ.**] **The appointed times of prayer** : see ver. 46. But it need not altogether exclude *prayer among themselves* as well, provided we do not assume any set times or forms of *Christian worship*, which certainly did not exist as yet. See notes on Rom. xiv. 5; Gal. iv. 10. **43.**] **πάσῃ ψυχῇ**, designating generally *the multitude*,—those who were not joined to the infant church. This is evident by the *πάντες δὲ οἱ πιστεύοντες* when the church is again the subject, ver. 44. **φόβος**, **dread**, reverential astonishment, at the effect produced by the outpouring of the Spirit. On the [anticipatory character of the] latter part of the verse see general remarks at the beginning * of this section. **44.**] If it surprise us that so large a number should be continually assembled together (for such is certainly the sense, not 'fraterno amore conjunctos,' as Calvin)—we must remember that a large portion of the *three thousand* were persons who had come up to Jerusalem for the feast, and would by this time have returned to their homes. **εἶχον ἅπαντα κοινά**] **they had all things** (in) **common**, i. e. *no individual property, but one common stock* : see ch. iv. 32. That this was *literally the case* with the infant church at Jerusalem, is too plainly asserted in these passages to admit of a doubt. Some have supposed the expressions to indicate merely a partial community of goods : 'non omnia vendiderunt, sed partem bonorum, quæ sine magno incommodo carere poterant,' Wetstein ; contrary to the express assertion of ch. iv. 32. In order, however, rightly to understand this *community*, we may remark : (1) *It is only found in the Church at Jerusalem.* No trace of its existence is discoverable any where else : on the contrary, St. Paul speaks [constantly] of the rich and the poor, see 1 Tim. vi. 17 ; 1 Cor. xvi. 2 [Gal. ii. 10 ; 2 Cor. viii. 13—15 ; ix. 6, 7] : also St. James, ii. 1—5 ; iv. 13. And from the practice having at first prevailed at Jerusalem, we may [partly] perhaps explain the great and constant poverty of that church, Rom. xv. 25, 26 ; 1 Cor. xvi. 1—3 : 2 Cor. viii. ix. : also ch. xi. 30 ; xxiv. 17. The non-establishment of this *community* elsewhere may have arisen from the inconveniences which were found to attend it in Jerusalem : see ch. vi. 1. (2) This community of goods was not, even in Jerusalem, enforced by *rule*, as is evident from ch. v. 4 [xii. 12], but, originating in free-will, became perhaps an understood custom, still however in the power of any individual not to comply with. (3) It was not (as Grotius and Heinrichs thought) *borrowed from the Essenes* (see Jos. B. J. ii. 8. 3), with whom the Apostles, who certainly must have sanctioned this community, do not appear historically to have had any connexion. But (4) it is much more probabl that it arose from a *continuation*, and application to the now increased number of disciples, *of the community in which our Lord and His Apostles had lived* (see John xii. 6 ; xiii. 29) *before.* (The substance of this note is derived from Meyer, in loc.) The practice probably did not long continue even at Jerusalem : see Rom. xv. 26, note. **45.**] **κτήματα,** * [probably] *landed property*, ch. v. 1—see reff. : *ὑπάρξεις*, any other possession ; *moveables*, as distinguished from land. **αὐτά**, **their price** ; see a similar construc-

τε [i] προσκαρτεροῦντες [i] ὁμοθυμαδὸν ἐν τῷ ἱερῷ, [k] κλῶντές
τε [l] κατ' οἶκον ἄρτον, [m] μετελάμβανον [n] τροφῆς ἐν [o] ἀγαλλιάσει καὶ [p] ἀφελότητι καρδίας, 47 [q] αἰνοῦντες τὸν θεὸν καὶ
ἔχοντες [r] χάριν [s] πρὸς ὅλον τὸν λαόν. ὁ δὲ κύριος [t] προς-
ετίθει τοὺς [u] σωζομένους [v] καθ' ἡμέραν [w] ἐπὶ τὸ αὐτό.

III. 1 Πέτρος δὲ καὶ Ἰωάννης [x] ἀνέβαινον εἰς τὸ ἱερὸν

i ch. i. 14 (reff.). k Matt. xiv. 19. ch. xx. 7, 11. xxvii. 35. 1 Cor. x. 16. xi. 24. Jer. xvi. 7. l ch. v. 42. Rom. xvi. 5. 1 Cor. xvi. 19. Col. iv. 15. Philem. 2. see ch. viii. 3. xx. 20.

m constr., ch. (xxiv. 25.) xxvii. 33, 34. 2 Tim. ii. 6. Heb. vi. 7. xii. 10 only †. Wisd. xviii. 9. n ch. ix. 19 reff. o Luke i. 14, 44. Heb. i. 9 (from Ps. xliv. 7). Jude 24 only. LXX, Psalms only. p here only †. q ch. iii. 8, 9. Luke ii. 13. Luke only, exc. Rom. xv. 11. Rev. xix. 5. Ps. cl. 1. r = Luke ii. 52. ch. vii. 10. Prov. iii. 4. s = Rom. v. 1 reff. t ver. 41. u 1 Cor. xv. 2 reff. v ver. 46. w = ch. i. 15 reff. x Luke xviii. 10. John vii. 14. Isa. ii. 3.

προσεκαρτερουν D. εν τω ιερω bef ομοθ. C [Syr] : om ομοθ D 3. 103. και κατ οικους αν (om αν D-corr) επι το αυτο κλωντες τε αρτον D.

47. for λαον, κοσμον D. rec aft καθ ημεραν ins τη εκκλησια (*explanatory gloss : see note*), with EP 13 rel syrr [Bas-sel$_1$] Chr$_1$, aft επι το αυτο D (D k 19. 40 syrr prefix εν) : om ABC[G]ℵ vulg coptt æth arm Cyr$_1$ [Lucif$_1$].

Chap. III. 1. rec δε bef πετρος, with EP rel 36 syr Chr$_2$:—επι το αυτο is omd at end of ch. ii. and insd aft ἀνεβαινον in Syr : D ends ch. ii. with εκκλησια, but begins ch. iii. εν δε ταις ημεραις ταυταις πετρος και : txt ABC(D)[G]ℵ m² p vulg coptt æth arm

tion Matt. xxvi. 9; and Winer, edn. 6, § 22. 3. 4. **καθότι ἂν . . .**] The ἄν with imperf. indic. in this connexion implies 'accidisse aliquid non certo quodam tempore, sed quotiescunque occasio ita ferret,' Herm. ad Viger., p. 818. See ch. iv. 35; Mark vi. 56; xi. 24; Soph. Philoct. 290 ff.; Aristoph. Lys. 510 ff. **46.**] **καθ' ἡμ. . . . ἐν τῷ ἱερῷ**—see Luke xxiv. 53. The words need not mean, though they *may* mean, that they were assembled in Solomon's porch, as in ch. v. 12—but most probably, that they regularly kept the hours of prayer, ch. iii. 1. **κατ' οἶκον**] *domi*, 'privatim' (Beng.), as contrasted with ἐν τῷ ἱερῷ. So also Wolf, Scal., Heinr., Olsh., Meyer, De Wette :—not, *domatim*, 'from house to house,' as Erasm., Salmasius, Kuinoel, al. :—the words *may* bear that meaning (see Luke viii. 1), but we have no trace of such a practice, of holding the ἀγάπαι successively at different houses. The κλάσις τ. ἄρτου took place at their *house of meeting*, wherever that was: cf. ch. xii. 12; and see ver. 42 note. **μετ. τροφ.**] **they partake of food** :—see reff. ;—viz. in these agapæ or breakings of bread. **ἀφελότητι**] In good Greek, ἀφέλεια: the adj. ἀφελής (see Palm and Rost) originally implying "free from stones or rocks" (ἀ, φελλεύς, stony or rocky land), and thus
* *simple, even, pure.* **47.**] **αἰνοῦντες τ. θ.** does not seem only to refer to *giving thanks at their partaking of food*, but to their general manner of conversation, including the recurrence of special ejaculations and songs of praise by the influence of the Spirit. **τοὺς σωζομένους**] **those who were in the way of salvation** : compare σώθητε, ver. 40 : **those who were being saved.** Nothing is implied by this word, to answer one way or the other the question, whether all these *were finally saved.* It is only asserted, that they were *in the way of salvation* when they were added to the Christian assembly. Doubtless, some of them might have been of the class alluded to Heb. x. 26–29 : at least there is nothing in this word to preclude it. Correct criticism, as well as external evidence, requires that the words ἐν τῇ ἐκκλησίᾳ or τῇ ἐκκλησίᾳ should be rejected, as having been an explanatory gloss, ('est hæc Chrysostomi, ut videtur, glossa, per Syrum et alios propagata ;' Bengel,) and ἐπὶ τὸ αὐτό brought back to its place and the meaning which it bears in this passage (see ver. 44), viz. **together,** in the sense of making up *one sum*, one body assembled in one place. Meyer attributes the separation of ἐπὶ τὸ αὐτό from Πέτρος to an ecclesiastical portion having begun ἐν ταῖς ἡμέραις ταύταις Π. κ. Ἰω. as D. De Wette asks, *why should those words have been inserted* at the beginning of a portion? Perhaps in accordance with a not uncommon practice of opening an ecclesiastical lection with such a phrase. Or possibly, I might suggest, as a *mistaken interpretation* of ἐπὶ τὸ αὐτό, which was not understood. Then when ἐπ. τ. αὐ. became joined to Πέτρος, τῇ ἐκκλ. would naturally be supplied after προσετίθει.

Chap. III. 1—10.] Healing of a lame man by Peter at the gate of the Temple. **1.**] **ἀνέβαινον, were going up.**

[y] ἐπὶ τὴν ὥραν τῆς προσευχῆς τὴν ἐνάτην. 2 καί τις ABCDE
ἀνὴρ χωλὸς [z] ἐκ κοιλίας μητρὸς αὐτοῦ [a] ὑπάρχων [b] ἐβα- GPℵ a b c f g h k
στάζετο, ὃν ἐτίθουν [c] καθ' ἡμέραν πρὸς τὴν θύραν τοῦ l m o p 13
ἱεροῦ τὴν λεγομένην [d] ὡραίαν, [e] τοῦ αἰτεῖν [f] ἐλεημοσύνην
παρὰ τῶν [g] εἰςπορευομένων εἰς τὸ ἱερόν· 3 ὃς ἰδὼν
Πέτρον καὶ Ἰωάννην μέλλοντας [h] εἰςιέναι εἰς τὸ ἱερὸν
[i] ἠρώτα [f] ἐλεημοσύνην λαβεῖν. 4 [k] ἀτενίσας δὲ Πέτρος [k] εἰς

y = Mark xv. 1. Luke x. 35. ch. iv. 5. Esth. v. 8 F (notA[appy]). Ald. compl.
z ch. xiv. 8 reff.
a = ch. ii. 30 reff.
b = ch. xxi. 35 (Rom. xi. 18 reff.).
c ch. ii. 46 reff.
d ver. 10. Matt. xxiii. 27. Rom. x. 15 only. 3 Kings i. 6.
e constr., 1 Cor. x. 13 reff.
f = Luke xi. 41. xii. 43. ch. ix. 36 al. Luke only, exc. Matt. vi. 2, &c. Tobit xii. 9.
g Mark i. 21 al.
h ch. xxi. 18, 26. Heb. ix. 6 only. Exod. xxviii. 23, 31 (29, 35). 1 Kings xvi. 6. 2 Macc. iii. 14 only.
i constr., see ch. xvi. 39 reff.
k ch. i. 10 reff.

Cyr_1 [$Lucif_1$]. aft *ιερον* ins *το δειλεινον ad vesperum* D. for *της προς. τ. εν.*, *ενατη τη προσευχη* D[1] : *την ενατην της προσευχης* D[3](and lat) arm. rec *εννατην*, with p rel : *νεατην* B(Bch) : txt A B(Mai Tischdf) CDE[G]Pℵ a b[2] g h l m.

2. ins *ιδου* bef *τις* D[1][and lat] Syr. om *υπαρχων* D [copt(appy)] Lucif : *constitutus* E-lat. the *το* in *εβασταζετο* is superadded, but by B[1](not as Tischdf). for *θυρ.*, *πυλην* (*see ver* 10 : *cf Eng Version*) E b o $Bas\text{-}sel_1$. *παρ αυτων εισπορ. αυτων* D[1][-gr].

3. for *ος ιδων*, *ουτος ατενισας τοις οφθαλμοις αυτου και ιδων* D [reg]. for *εισιεναι*, *ειναι* D[1]-gr(txt D[3]). aft *ηρ.* ins *αυτους* D [Syr æth] coptt. om *λαβειν* DP rel H[r] [reg syr] $Lucif_1$: *ut darent* Syr sah æth : ins ABCE[G]ℵ b o p 13 copt [arm Chr_1]. aft *λαβ.* ins *παρ' αυτων* E [(copt)].

4. *εμβλεψας δε ο π.* D. [*εις αυτον* bef *πετρος* G arm :] for *εις*, *προς* ℵ.

τὴν ἐνάτην] See ch. x. 3, 30. **τὴν ὥραν τῆς πρ.** generic;—**τὴν ἐν.**, specific. There were three hours of prayer; those of the morning and evening sacrifice, i. e. the *third* and *ninth* hours, and *noon*. See Lightfoot and Wetst. in loc. **2.**] **ἐβαστ.**, **was being carried.** They took him at the hours of prayer, and carried him back between times. **τὴν θύραν . . τ. λ. ὡραίαν**] The arrangement of the gates of the Temple is, from the notices which we now possess, very uncertain. Three entrances have been fixed on for the *θύρα ὡραία*: (1) The gate mentioned Jos. B. J. v. 5. 3: *τῶν δὲ πυλῶν αἱ μὲν ἐννέα χρυσῷ καὶ ἀργύρῳ κεκαλυμμέναι πανταχόθεν ἦσαν, ὁμοίως τε παραστάδες καὶ τὰ ὑπέρθυρα. μία δὲ ἡ ἔξωθεν τοῦ νεὼ Κορινθίου χαλκοῦ, πολὺ τῇ τιμῇ τὰς καταργύρους καὶ τὰς περιχρύσους ὑπεράγουσα.* This gate was also called *Nicanor's gate* (see the Rabbinical citations in Wetstein),—and lay on the eastern side of the Temple, towards the valley of Kedron. Jos. mentions it again, as *ἡ ἀνατολικὴ πύλη τοῦ ἐνδοτέρου, χαλκῆ οὖσα*, and gives a remarkable account of its size and weight: adding, that when, before the siege, it was discovered supernaturally opened in the night, *τοῦτο τοῖς ἰδιώταις κάλλιστον ἐδόκει τέρας· ἀνοῖξαι γὰρ τὸν θεὸν αὐτοῖς* **τὴν τῶν ἀγαθῶν πύλην.** But some find a difficulty in this. The lame man, they say, would not be likely to have been admitted so far into the Temple (but see Wetst. as above, where it appears that lepers used to stand at Nicanor's gate): and besides, he would have taken up his station naturally at an *outer* gate, where he might ask alms of *all* who entered. These conditions suit better (2) the gate *Susan;* as does also the circumstance mentioned ver. 11, that the people ran together to *Solomon's porch;* for this gate was on the east side of the court of the Gentiles, and close to Solomon's porch. Only the name *ὡραία* cannot be derived from the town Susan (from which the gate was named, having a picture of the town over it), that word signifying 'a lily;' the town being named, it is true, *διὰ τὴν ὡραιότητα τοῦ τόπου* (Athen. xii. 1, p. 573): but the derivation being too far-fetched to be at all probable. Another suitable circumstance was, that by this gate the market was held for sheep and cattle and other offerings, and therefore a greater crowd would be attracted. (3) Others again (Lightf. favours this) attempt to derive *ὡραία* from חֶלֶד, 'tempus,' and refer the epithet to two gates opening towards the city on the western side. But it is very unlikely that Luke should have used *ὡρ.* in so unusual a meaning:—not to say (see Lightf. Descr. Templi) that the meaning of חוּלְדָּה itself is very doubtful. So that the matter must remain in uncertainty. **3.**] **ἠρώτα . . . . . λαβεῖν,**—so Soph. Aj. 836, *αἰτήσομαι δέ σ' οὐ μακρὸν γέρας λαβεῖν*, and Aristoph. Plut. 240, *αἰτῶν λαβεῖν τι μικρὸν ἀργυρίδιον.* **ἐλεημ**, as in ref. Matt. The Jewish forms of asking alms are given in Vajicra Rabb. f. 20. 3. 4 (cited by Meyer),—'Merere in me:' 'In me benefac tibi,' and the like. **4. βλέψον εἰς ἡμᾶς**] Calvin's note is important: 'Non ita lo-

αὐτὸν σὺν τῷ Ἰωάννῃ εἶπεν [l] Βλέψον [l] εἰς ἡμᾶς. 5 ὁ δὲ
[m] ἐπεῖχεν αὐτοῖς [n] προσδοκῶν τὶ παρ' αὐτῶν [o] λαβεῖν.
6 εἶπεν δὲ Πέτρος Ἀργύριον καὶ χρυσίον οὐχ [p] ὑπάρχει
μοι· ὃ δὲ ἔχω, τοῦτό σοι δίδωμι. ἐν τῷ ὀνόματι Ἰησοῦ
χριστοῦ τοῦ Ναζωραίου [ἔγειραι καὶ] περιπάτει. 7 καὶ
[q] πιάσας αὐτὸν τῆς δεξιᾶς χειρὸς ἤγειρεν αὐτόν· [r] παραχρῆμα δὲ [s] ἐστερεώθησαν αἱ [t] βάσεις αὐτοῦ καὶ τὰ [u] σφυρά,
8 καὶ [v] ἐξαλλόμενος ἔστη καὶ περιεπάτει, καὶ εἰςῆλθεν σὺν
αὐτοῖς εἰς τὸ ἱερὸν περιπατῶν καὶ [w] ἁλλόμενος καὶ

l Matt. xxii. 16 ‖ Mk. Luke ix. 62. John xiii. 22. Sir. xl. 29.
m — 1 Tim. iv. 16. Luke xiv. 7 (ch. xix. 22. Phil. ii. 6) only. L.P. Job xxx. 26 BN (w. εν, A). Sir. xxxi. (xxxiv.) 2.
n constr., ch. xxviii. 6 only. 2 Macc. xii. 44. absol., Matt. xxiv. 50 al.
o = ch. ii. 33 reff. p ch. iv. 37. xxviii. 7. 2 Pet. i. 8. Sir. xx. 16. q = here only. (ch. xii. 4 reff.) r Luke i. 64 al9. ch. v. 10 al4. Luke only, exc. Matt. xxi. 19, 20. Num. vi. 9 al. s = ver. 16 only. Ps. xxxii. 6. lxxiv. 3. met., ch. xvi. 5 only. 1 Kings ii. 1. t here only. Exod. xxvi. 19, &c. u here only †. v here only. Joel ii. 5. w John iv. 14. ch. xiv. 10 only. Isa. xxxv. 6.

[...iii. 8 G]. d και εξαλλομ.... ABCDE PN a b c d f g h k l m o p 13

συν ιωαννην κ. ειπεν D^1. for βλεψον, ατενεισον (sic) D.

5. for επειχεν, ατενεισας D-gr. λαβ. bef παρ αυτ. DE vulg [(Syr) coptt] Lucif.—λαβ. bef τι E [coptt].—αυτου C.

6. πετρ. δε ειπ. AC[G] vulg coptt: txt B D(ο πετρ.) EPℵ syrr æth [arm Bas$_1$] Chr$_1$ Thl [Cypr$_1$] Lucif$_1$. ουκ Cℵ. rec ins εγειραι και (*addn from such passages as Luke* v. 23, vi. 8 *al?*), with C rel 36; εγειρε και AE[G]P m p: αναστα Epiph: om BDℵ sah. (*The authorities being divided,* εγειρε *and* -ραι *being no real variation, I have left it as doubtful.*)

7. πιασασας (sic) P. rec om 2nd αυτον, with DEP rel Chr$_2$: ins ABC[G]ℵ p 36 vulg syrr coptt æth arm Eus Bas$_1$ Bas-sel$_1$ Cypr$_1$ Lucif$_1$. και παραχρ. εσταθη και εστ. D. rec αυτου bef αι βασεις, with [D]EP rel: txt ABC[G]ℵ p [vulg Bas-sel$_1$ Sevrn$_1$ Lucif]. και στα σφυδρα (sic: but δ erased) ℵ, [A] B^1(Tischdf) also have σφυδρα [φυδρα C^1].

8. aft περιεπ. ins χαιρων E; χαιρομενος D. περιπ. bef ε. το ιερ. k 13. om last και (*see note*) A sah Lucif: ins BCEPℵ rel Iren-int.—om περιπ. κ. αλλ. κ. D æth.

quitur Petrus quin de consilio Dei certus sit: et certe his verbis singulare aliquod et insolitum beneficium sperare jubet. Quæri tamen potest, an facultatem habuerint edendi miracula quoties liberet. Respondeo, sic ministros fuisse divinæ virtutis, ut nihil suo arbitrio vel proprio motu tentarint, sed Dominus per ipsos egerit quum ita expedire noverat. Hinc factum est ut unum sanarint, non autem promiscue omnes. Ergo, quemadmodum in aliis rebus ducem et directorem habebant Dei Spiritum, ita etiam in hac parte. Ideo priusquam claudum surgere jubeat Petrus, conjecit in eum et defixit oculos. Talis intuitus non carebat peculiari Spiritus motu. Hinc fit ut tam secure de miraculo pronuntiet. Porro, excitare hoc verbo claudum voluit ad recipiendam Dei gratiam: ille tamen nihil quam eleemosynam exspectat.' **5. ἐπεῖχεν**] not τοὺς ὀφθαλμούς (as Bos and Kuinoel), which is *implied:*—but (see reff.) τὸν νοῦν, **fixed his attention on them.**

6.] 'Non dubium est, quin etiam iis qui non erant de communitate fidelium, datæ fuerint eleemosynæ: sed Petrus tum vel nil habebat secum, in via ad templum, vel non tantum dare poterat quantum ad sublevandum pauperem opus esset. Vide abstinentiam Apostoli in tanta administratione, cf. ii. 45, coll. iv. 35.' Bengel. But perhaps it is more simple to conclude that Peter spoke here of *his own station and means* in life—'I am no rich man, nor have I silver or gold to give thee.' **ἐν τῷ ὀνόμ.**] There is no ellipsis (as Heinr. and Kuinoel) of λέγω σοι, which weakens the force of the sentence: the name of Jesus is that in which, *by the power of which,* the "rise up and walk" is to be accomplished.

7. πιάσας . . . . ἤγειρεν] οὕτω καὶ ὁ χριστὸς ἐποίησε· πολλάκις λόγῳ ἐθεράπευσε, πολλάκις ἔργῳ, πολλάκις καὶ τὴν χεῖρα προήγαγεν, ὅπου ἦσαν ἀσθενέστεροι κατὰ τὴν πίστιν· ἵνα μὴ δόξῃ ἀπὸ ταυτομάτου γενέσθαι. Chrys. in Act. Hom. viii. p. 63. See Mark ix. 27. **βάσεις** are the **soles** of the feet,—**σφυρά,** the **ankles.** Luke, the physician, had made himself acquainted with the peculiar kind of weakness, and described it accordingly.

8.] **ἐξαλλ.** describes his first joyous liberation from his weakness: as soon as he felt himself strengthened, he leapt up, for joy. No suppositions need be made, such as πειράζων ἴσως ἑαυτόν (Chrys.): or that it was from ignorance how to walk (Bloomf.). His joy is quite sufficient to explain the gesture, and it is better to leave the narrative in its simplicity. If καί before αἰνῶν is omitted (see digest), the present participle has its ratiocinative

x ch. ii. 47 reff. y constr., 1 Cor. xiv. 37 reff. z = 2 Cor. viii. 19 reff. see Matt. xix. 8. a vv. 2, 3. b ch. v. 9. Matt. xxiv. 23 ||. John v. 2. c ver. 2. d = Luke iv. 28. v. 26. ch. v. 17. xiii. 45. Gen. vi. 11, 13. e Luke iv. 36. v. 9 only. Cant. iii. 8 (-βεῖν, Mark i. 27). f = Mark v. 42. xvi. 8. Luke v. 26 (ch. x. 10 reff.) only. Deut. xxviii. 28.

ABCDE Pℵ a b c d f g h k l m o p 13

ˣ αἰνῶν τὸν θεόν. 9 καὶ εἶδεν πᾶς ὁ λαὸς αὐτὸν περιπατοῦντα καὶ ˣ αἰνοῦντα τὸν θεόν· 10 ʸ ἐπεγίνωσκον δὲ αὐτὸν
ὅτι οὗτος ἦν ὁ ᶻ πρὸς τὴν ᵃ ἐλεημοσύνην καθήμενος ᵇ ἐπὶ τῇ
ᶜ ὡραίᾳ πύλῃ τοῦ ἱεροῦ· καὶ ᵈ ἐπλήσθησαν ᵉ θάμβους καὶ
ᶠ ἐκστάσεως ᵍ ἐπὶ τῷ ʰ συμβεβηκότι αὐτῷ. 11 ⁱ κρατοῦντος δὲ αὐτοῦ τὸν Πέτρον καὶ Ἰωάννην, ᵏ συνέδραμεν πᾶς
ὁ λαὸς πρὸς αὐτοὺς ᵇ ἐπὶ τῇ ˡ στοᾷ τῇ καλουμένῃ Σολο-
μῶντος ᵐ ἔκθαμβοι. 12 ἰδὼν δὲ ὁ Πέτρος ⁿ ἀπεκρίνατο
πρὸς τὸν λαὸν Ἄνδρες Ἰσραηλῖται, τί ᵒ θαυμάζετε ᵒ ἐπὶ
τούτῳ, ἢ ἡμῖν τί ᵖ ἀτενίζετε ὡς ἰδίᾳ δυνάμει ἢ ᑫ εὐσεβείᾳ

g Rom. vi. 21 reff. h Mark x. 32. Luke xxiv. 14. ch. xx. 19. xxi. 35. 1 Cor. x. 11. 1 Pet. iv. 12. 2 Pet. ii. 22 only. Gen. xlii. 4. i = Jud. xvi. 26 B. see Matt. ix. 25 al. k = Mark vi. 33 only. Judith vi. 16. met., 1 Pet. iv. 4 only. Ps. xlix. 18. l John v. 2. x. 23. ch. v. 12 only. Ezek. xlii. 3. m here only +. objectively, Dan. vii. 7 Theod. (-βεῖσθαι. Mark ix. 5.) plur., ch. v. 16. n = ch. v. 8 reff. o Luke iv. 22. xx. 26 al. Isa. lii. 15. p w. dat., Luke iv. 20. xxii. 56. ch. x. 4. xiv. 9. xxiii. 1 only. Job vii. 8 F[ἀτενοι (?) A] (Esdr. vi. 28) only. with εἰς, ch. i. 10 reff. q here only, exc. past. epp. (1 Tim. ii. 2 al.) & 2 Pet. (i. 3 al.) Isa. xi. 2. Wisd. x. 12.

9. rec *αυτον* bef *πας ο λ.*, with EP rel Chr_1 $Lucif_1$: txt ABCDℵ p vulg. for *θεον*, *κυριον* C.

10. rec (for *δε*) *τε*, with D E-gr P rel syr [arm Chr_1] $Lucif_1$: [om Syr sah :] txt ABCℵ p vulg E-lat copt $Bas\text{-}sel_1$. om *αυτον* ℵ¹(written above the line by ℵ-corr¹). for *ουτος*, *αυτος* (*corrn as more usual*) ACℵ g p 36 vulg [Syr] $Bas\text{-}sel_1$ $Lucif_1$: txt BDEP rel [syr coptt] Chr Thl. *καθεζομενος* D. *την ωραιαν πυλην* ℵ¹(ℵ³ correcting *τη ωραια* but not *πυλην*). for *συμβ.*, *γεγενημενω* D.

11. for ver, *εκπορευομενου δε του πετρου και ιωανου συνεξεπορευετο κρατων αυτους· οι δε θαμβηθεντες εστησαν εν τη στ. η* (*τη* D³) *κ. σ. εκθ.* D. for *δε*, *τε* A Syr. rec for *αυτου*, *του ιαθεντος χωλου* (*beginning of an ecclesiastical lection*), with P rel Thl: txt ABCDEℵ c p 36 [vulg] syrr coptt (æth) arm. om *τον* (bef *πετρ.*) c.—ins *τον* bef *ιωαν.* ABℵ m p Chr_1. rec *προς αυτους* bef *πας ο λαος*, with EP rel copt : txt ABCℵ p vulg syrr sah æth arm.

12. *αποκριθεις δε ο πετρ. ειπεν πρ. αυτους* D. rec om *ο*, with EP rel [Chr_1] : ins ABCDℵ k o p 13. for 1st *ἤ*, *ει* (*itacism*) ℵ. *ως ημων τη ιδια δυν. η ευσ.*

force, alleging the cause of the walking and leaping: and would best be rendered in English, **in his praising of God.**

11—26.] THE DISCOURSE OF PETER THEREUPON. **11. κρατοῦντος**] *holding*, physically: not spoken of mental adhesion, but of actual holding by the hand or arm, that he might not be separated from them in the crowd, but might testify to all, *who* his benefactors were. **στοᾷ τῇ κ. Σολομ.**] See John x. 23, note. **12. ἀπεκρίνατο**] viz. to their expressions of astonishment implied in *ἔκθαμβοι*. See Matt. xi. 25. **ἀπεκρίνατο** never signifies '*made an address*,' as Bloomf.; but always '*answered*:' cf. ch. v. 8, note. This second discourse of Peter may be thus divided: *This is no work of ours, but of God, for the glorifying of Jesus*, vv. 12, 13:—*whom ye denied and killed, but God hath raised up*, vv. 13—15:—*through whose name this man is made whole*, ver. 16:—*ye did it in ignorance, but God thereby fulfilled His counsel*, vv. 17, 18. *Exhortation to repent, that ye may be forgiven, and saved by this Jesus Christ at His coming*, vv. 19—21: *whose times have been the subject of prophecy from the first*, ver. 21. *Citations to prove this*, vv. 22—24: *its immediate application to the hearers, as Jews*, vv. 25, 26. There the discourse seems to be broken off, as ch. iv. 1 relates.

ἐπὶ τούτῳ] not, *at this* (event): but **at this man**, compare *αὐτόν* below, which would not be used at the *first* mention of one *then present*. Their error was not the *wonder* itself,—though even that would shew ignorance and weakness of faith, for it was truly no wonderful thing that had happened, viewed by a believer in Jesus,—but their wondering *at the Apostles*, as if they had done it by their own power. 'Ergo,' says Calvin, 'hoc est perperam obstupescere, quum in hominibus mentes nostræ subsistunt.' **δυνάμει, power,**—such as *magical craft*, or any other supposed means of working miracles: **εὐσεβείᾳ meritorious efficacy** with God, so as to have obtained this from Him *on our own account*. The distinction is important:—'*holiness*,' of the E. V., is not expressive of *εὐσεβ.*, which bears in it the

[r] πεποιηκόσιν [s] τοῦ περιπατεῖν αὐτόν; 13 ὁ θεὸς Ἀβραὰμ
καὶ Ἰσαὰκ καὶ Ἰακώβ, ὁ θεὸς τῶν [t] πατέρων [t] ἡμῶν,
ἐδόξασεν τὸν [u] παῖδα αὐτοῦ Ἰησοῦν, ὃν ὑμεῖς [v] μὲν
[w] παρεδώκατε, καὶ [x] ἠρνήσασθε [αὐτὸν] [y] κατὰ πρόσωπον
Πιλάτου, [z] κρίναντος ἐκείνου [a] ἀπολύειν. 14 ὑμεῖς δὲ
[b] τὸν ἅγιον καὶ [c] δίκαιον [x] ἠρνήσασθε, καὶ [d] ᾐτήσασθε
[e] ἄνδρα [f] φονέα [g] χαρισθῆναι ὑμῖν, 15 τὸν δὲ [h] ἀρχηγὸν
τῆς ζωῆς ἀπεκτείνατε· ὃν ὁ θεὸς [i] ἤγειρεν ἐκ [i] νεκρῶν, οὗ

r = Mark i. 17. vii. 37 al.
s constr., ch. vii. 19. xv. 20. xxvii. 1 al. Josh. xxii. 26. 3 Kings xiii. 16 B. Winer, edn. 6, § 44. 4.
t ch. v. 30 reff.
u = ver. 26 reff.
v μέν solitarium. Rom. vii. 12 reff.
w = Matt. xxvii. 18 || Mk. Jer. xxxiii. (xxvi.) 24.
x = ch. vii. 35 reff.
y = 2 Cor. x. 1 reff.
z constr., ch. xv. 19 reff.
a ch. xxvi. 32 reff.
b = John vi. 69. 1 John ii. 20.
c abs., ch. vii. 52 reff.
d constr., Luke xxiii. 23. ch. xiii. 28. 3 Kings xix. 4.
e Luke xxiv. 19. Judg. vi. 8.
f ch. vii. 52 reff.
g = 1 Cor. ii. 12 reff.
h ch. v. 31. Heb. ii. 10. xii. 2 only. 1 Macc. ix. 61. x. 47.
i 1 Cor. xv. 12 reff.

τουτο πεποιηκοτων τουτο (**του** D-corr) **περιπ. αυτ.** D [simly $Sevrn_1$]. **τουτον** E vulg Iren-int Cassiod.

13. ins θεος bef ισαακ and bef ιακ. AD vulg copt æth [arm] Iren-int, ins ο θεος Cℵ Chr_1 (*corrns to suit* LXX *Exod* iii. 6, *and Matt* xxii. 32 ||): om BEP rel syrr sah [$Sevrn_1$] $Thdot\text{-}ancyr_1$. for των, τω ℵ. for παιδα, πατερα ℵ^1(corrected by ℵ^5 (12th cent)). aft ιησ. ins χρ. D æth-pl. ημεις D[-gr]. rec om μεν (*erased because no correspondg* δε *follows*), with D m [13]: ins ABCEPℵ rel 36 vulg [syr Did_1] Chr Iren-int Jer_1. aft παρεδ. add εις κρισιν D syr-mg Iren-int; εις κριτηριον E. **απηρνησασθαι** D. om αυτον (*as needless*) ABCℵ p 36 vulg copt arm [æth Thdot-ancyr] Did_1 Iren-int Jer_1: ins DEP rel syr sah Chr. πειλατου του κρειναντος εκεινου απολυειν αυτον θελοντος D; *cum judicasset ille dismittere eum voluit* D-lat (*a curious instance of combination of readings*); του, θελοντος, and *voluit* are marked for erasure. κρινοντος C 13. απολλυειν ℵ.

14. δικαιον εβαρυνατε και ητησατε D: so for ηρνησ., *aggravastis* Iren-int. ins μαλλον bef ητησασθε E, aft ητησ. syr-mg. ins ζην και bef χαρισθηναι υμ. E Aug_1.

idea of *operative, cultive* piety, rather than of *inherent character*. **13. ὁ θ. Ἀβρ. κ.τ.λ.**] ‘Appellatio frequens in Actis, præ cæteris libris N. T., et illi periodo temporum conveniens.’ Bengel. ὅρα πῶς αὐτὸν (τὸν θεὸν) εἰσωθεῖ συνεχῶς εἰς τοὺς προγόνους· ἵνα μὴ δόξῃ καινόν τι εἰσάγειν δόγμα· καὶ ἐκεῖ (ch. ii.) τοῦ πατριάρχου Δαβὶδ ἐμνημόνευσε, καὶ ἐνταῦθα τῶν περὶ τοῦ Ἀβραὰμ . . . (Chrys.). **ἐδόξασεν**] not, as E. V., ‘*hath glorified*,’ implying, by *thus honouring His Name*: it is the historic aor., **glorified**, viz. by His exaltation through death—see John xii. 23; xvii. 10. **παῖδα**] not ‘*Son*,’ but **Servant**: *servant*, however, in that distinct and Messianic sense which the same expression bears in Isa. xl.—lxvi. in the LXX. **υἱός** is the word always used to designate Jesus as the SON of God. The above meaning is adopted by all the best modern Commentators, Pisc., Bengel, Olsh., Meyer, De W., Stier, some of whom refer to a paper of Nitzsch's in the Stud. u. Krit. for 1828, Heft 2, p. 331 ff. Olsh. says, ‘After N.'s remarks on the subject, no one hereafter can suppose this expression equivalent to υἱὸς τ. θ.’ “In the next age,” says Wordsw., “the term παῖς θεοῦ was applied to Christ as a *Son*. See Polycarp, Mart. § 14, p. 1040 (Migne); and S. Hippolyt. Philosoph. x. 33 (in Migne's Origen, tom. vi. p. 540), and contra Noëtum, § 5, 7, 11, pp. 809 ff. (Migne), and the note of Fabricius, ii. p. 10.”

κατὰ πρόσωπον Π. as E. V., ‘*in the presence of P.*,’ or better perhaps, **to the face of Pilate.** The expression is no Hebraism. Polybius often uses it. κατὰ πρόσωπον λεγομένων τῶν λόγων, xxv. 5. 2: κ. πρ. ἀπαντᾷν τοῖς πολεμίοις, xvii. 3. 3, &c. See Schweigh., Lexicon Polybianum. **κρίναντος ἐκ. ἀπολ.**, see Luke xxiii. 20; John xix. 4, 12. **14. ἅγιον κ. δίκαιον**] not only in the higher and divine sense present to Peter's mind, but also by Pilate's *own verdict*, and the testimony of the Jews' consciences. The sentence is full of antitheses; ἅγιον κ. δίκ. contrasts with the *moral impurity* of ἄνδρα φονέα,—ἀρχηγ. τ. ζωῆς, with the *destruction of life* implied in φονέα,—while ἀπεκτείνατε again stands in remarkable opposition to ἀρχ. τ. ζ. This last title given to our Lord implies (as Vulg.) ‘Auctorem vitæ:’ see reff.; so ἀρχηγὸν κ. καθηγεμόνα τῆς ὅλης ἐπιβολῆς Ἄρατον, Polyb. ii. 40. 2: ὅπερ (scil. want of occupation in mercenary soldiers) σχεδόν, ὡς εἰπεῖν, ἀρχηγὸν κ. μόνον αἴτιον γίνεται στάσεως, i. 66. 10 al. It is *possible*, that the words ἀρχ. τ. ζ. may contain an allusion to the great miracle which was the immediate cause of the enmity of their rulers to Jesus. But of course

j ch. i. 8 reff.
k = Luke v. 5. Phil. iii. 9 al. Job xxix. 22.
l constr., Rom. iii. 22 reff.
m ver. 7 reff.
n 1 Pet. i. 21.
o = here only. χρόνος μάθησιν δίδωσι, Eurip. Suppl. 419.
p here only. Isa. i. 6 Ed-vat. F (not ABℵ) only. (-ρος, 1 Thess. v. 23. James i. 4.)
q = Matt. xxvii. 24. Rom. iii. 18 (reff.).
r = Matt. xix. 3. Rom. x. 2. Phil. ii. 3. iv. 11.
s ch. xvii. 30 reff.
t ch. vii. 52 only †.
u ch. i. 16 reff.

ABCDE Pℵ a b c d f g h k l m o p 13

ἡμεῖς [j] μάρτυρές ἐσμεν.
16 καὶ [k] ἐπὶ τῇ [l] πίστει τοῦ [l] ὀνόματος αὐτοῦ τοῦτον ὃν θεωρεῖτε καὶ οἴδατε [m] ἐστερέωσεν τὸ ὄνομα αὐτοῦ· καὶ ἡ πίστις ἡ [n] δι' αὐτοῦ [o] ἔδωκεν αὐτῷ τὴν [p] ὁλοκληρίαν ταύτην [q] ἀπέναντι πάντων ὑμῶν.
17 καὶ νῦν, ἀδελφοί, οἶδα ὅτι [r] κατὰ [s] ἄγνοιαν ἐπράξατε, ὥςπερ καὶ οἱ ἄρχοντες ὑμῶν·
18 ὁ δὲ θεὸς ἃ [t] προκατήγγειλεν διὰ [u] στόματος πάντων τῶν προφητῶν

15. υμεις D^1(txt D^4).

16. om επι B$ℵ^1$ p [arm]: εν 119 [*in*] vulg D-lat E-lat coptt æth Iren-int. om ον D^1-gr(ins D^3). aft οιδατε ins οτι D^1-gr.

17. ins ανδρες bef αδελφοι DE. [for οιδα] επισταμεθα [D arm-mss. aft] οτι [ins] υμεις μεν D. aft επραξ. add πονηρον D^1, το πονηρον D^3 34 syr-mg Iren-int$_1$ Ambrst$_2$ [Aug$_1$].

18. for α, ο D-gr [Syr]: *qui* bodl demid hal Vig$_1$.

Peter had a higher view in the title than *merely* this. **16.]** **ἐπὶ τ. πίστει . . .**—The E. V. is right; through, or better, **on account of faith in His name.** The meaning, *for the sake of* (i.e. of awakening, in you, and in the lame man himself) *faith in his name* (Rosenm., Heinrichs, Olsh., Stier), though grammatically justified, seems against the connexion with the μάρτυρές ἐσμεν just before. It is evident to my mind that the πίστις τοῦ ὀν. αὐτ. is the faith of these μάρτυρες. **His name** (the efficient cause), **by means of**, or on account of (our) **faith in His name** (the medium operandi), &c. **ἐστερ.** and **ἔδωκ.** again are historic aorists,—**confirmed** and **gave**; better than '*hath confirmed*' and '*hath given*.' **κ. ἡ πίστις ἡ δι' αὐτοῦ**—**and that faith which is wrought by Him**—not 'faith in Him;' which is an inadmissible rendering. Peter's own words (ref. 1 Pet.) are remarkably parallel with, and the best interpreters of, this expression: ὑμᾶς τοὺς **δι' αὐτοῦ πιστοὺς εἰς θεόν,** τὸν ἐγείραντα αὐτὸν ἐκ νεκρῶν καὶ δόξαν αὐτῷ δόντα, ὥστε τὴν πίστιν ὑμῶν καὶ ἐλπίδα εἶναι εἰς θεόν. Some of the Commentators are anxious to bring in *the faith of the lame man himself* in this verse. Certainly it is according to analogy to suppose that *he had such faith*, from and after the words of Peter:—but, as certainly, there is *no allusion to it in this verse*, and the thread of Peter's discourse would be broken by any such. It is the firm belief in His name *on the part of us His witnesses*, of which he is here speaking, as the medium whereby His name (= the Power of the great dignity to which He has been exalted, the ἀρχηγία τῆς ζωῆς) had in this case worked. **17.]** **νῦν** introducing a new consideration: see 2 Thess. ii. 6. Here it softens the severer charge of ver. 14: sometimes it intensifies, as ch. xxii. 16; 1 John ii. 28: especially with **ἰδού**, ch. xiii. 11; xx. 22. No meaning such as '*now* that the real Messiahship of Him whom ye have slain is come to light' (Meyer) is admissible. **ἀδελφοί,** still softening his tone, and reminding them of their oneness of blood and covenant with the speaker. **κατὰ ἄγνοιαν]** There need be no difficulty in the application of the ἄγνοια to even the rulers of the Jews. It admits of all degrees—from the unlearned, who were implicitly led by others, and hated Him because others did,—up to the most learned of the scribes, who knew and rightly interpreted the Messianic prophecies, but from moral blindness, or perverted expectations, did not recognize them in our Lord. Even Caiaphas himself, of whom apparently this could least be said, may be brought under it in some measure: *even he* could hardly have delivered over Jesus to Pilate with the *full* consciousness that He was the Messiah, and that he himself was accomplishing prophecy by so doing. *Some degree* of ἄγνοια there must have been in them all.

The interpretation (Wolf) '*ye did, as your rulers* (*did*),' is of course inadmissible, being contrary to the usage of the words: πράσσειν ὥςπερ καί can never mean to imitate, but ἐπράξατε must refer to a definite act (understood), and ὥςπερ καί must take up another subject of ἐπράξατε.

18.] **πάντων,** see Luke xxiv. 27 and note. There is no hyperbole (Kuinoel) nor adaptation (Meyer) to Jewish exegetical views. 'Omnes prophetæ in universum non prophetarunt nisi de diebus Messiæ' (Sanhedr. 99. 1), was *not merely a Jewish view, but the real truth.* The prophets are here regarded as *one body*, actuated by *one Spirit;* and the sum of God's pur-

[v] παθεῖν τὸν χριστὸν αὐτοῦ [w] ἐπλήρωσεν οὕτως. 19 [x] μετανοήσατε οὖν καὶ [y] ἐπιστρέψατε [z] εἰς τὸ [a] ἐξαλειφθῆναι
ὑμῶν τὰς ἁμαρτίας, [b] ὅπως [b] ἂν ἔλθωσιν [c] καιροὶ [d] ἀναψύξεως [e] ἀπὸ προσώπου τοῦ κυρίου, 20 καὶ ἀποστείλῃ

v abs., ch. i. 3 reff. w ch. i. 16. xiii. 27. Matt. i. 22 al. fr. 2 Chron. xxxvi. 22. x ch. ii. 38 reff. y Matt. xiii. 15 & ch. xxviii. 27 (from Isa. vi. 10). Mark iv. 12. Luke xxii. 32. z ch. vii. 19. Rom. i. 11, 20 al. a Col. ii. 14. Rev. iii. 7. vii. 17. xxi. 4 only. Ps. l. 9. Isa. xliii. 25. 2 Macc. xii. 42. b Luke ii. 35. ch. xv. 17 (from Amos ix. 12 A). Rom. iii. 4 (from Ps. l. 4 [6]) only. c and constr., Luke xix. 44. Heb. ix. 10. Ps. lxviii. 13. d here only. Exod. viii. 15 only. (-ψυχεῖν, 2 Tim. i. 16.) e = here only. see 2 Thess. i. 9. Rev. xx. 11. Ps. xcvi. 5.

rec αυτου bef παθειν (*alteration to suit αυτου προφ. ver* 21), with P rel: txt BCDEℵ p vulg syrr arm Chr_1 $Iren\text{-}int_1$.—aft προφ. ins αυτου, retaining αυτου of txt, A(prob) c 66^2 æth-pl Vig_1.—om παθ. τ. χρ. (*homœotel* αυτου *to* αυτου ?) A.

19. for εις, προς Bℵ. τας αμ. bef υμων D [vulg(and demid) spec Iren-int $Tert_1$]. επελθωσιν D-gr $Tert_1$. aft αναψυξ. add υμιν E tol lat-mss-in-Bede, and aft ελθ. Bede-gr Syr syr-w-ast copt Iren-int (Tert). om του E k m 36.

pose, shewn by their testimony, is, *that* HIS CHRIST *should suffer*. Notice the inf. aor. **παθεῖν**, as in ch. i. 3, of a *definite single act*. 19.] **οὖν**, *quæ cum ita sint*. **εἰς τὸ ἐξαλ.**] The faith implied in ἐπιστρέψατε has for its aim, is necessarily (by God's covenant, see John iii. 15, 18) accompanied by, the wiping out of sin. **ὅπως ἂν ἔλθ. κ.τ.λ.**] This passage has been variously rendered and explained. To deal first with the *rendering*:—**ὅπως ἂν** *cannot mean 'when,'* as in E. V.—ὅπως never occurs in that sense in the N. T., nor indeed with an indic. at all; —and if it did, the addition of ἄν, and the use of a subjunctive, would preclude it here. It can have but one sense,—**in order that**. This being so, *what are* **καιροὶ ἀναψύξεως**? From the omission of the article, some have insisted (e. g. Stier, R. d. Apost. i. 89) on rendering it '*times, seasons*, of ἀναψ.' But this cannot be maintained. καιρός and καιροί are occasionally anarthrous when they manifestly must have the article in English. Cf. especially Luke xxi. 24, καιροὶ ἐθνῶν, where none would think of rendering, 'seasons of (the) Gentiles.' See for καιρός Matt. viii. 29; Mark xi. 13; 1 Pet. i. 5. And, since philologically we have to choose between 'seasons' and 'the seasons,' ἔλθωσιν must I think determine in favour of the latter. For by that word we must understand a definite *arrival*, one and the same for all, not a mere *occurrence*, as the other sense of καιροί would render necessary. This is also implied by the aorist, used, in a conditional sentence, of a *single fact*, whereas a recurrence or enduring of a state is expressed by the *present*. **In order that the times of** ἀνάψυξις **may come.** *What is* **ἀνάψ.**? Clearly, from the above rendering, *some refreshment, future*, and which *their conversion was to bring about*. But hardly, from what has been said, refreshment *in their own hearts*, arising from their conversion: besides the above objections, the following words, ἀπὸ προσώπου τοῦ κυρίου, are not likely to have been used in that case. No other meaning, it seems to me, will suit the words, but that of **the times of refreshment**, the great season of joy and rest, which it was understood the coming of the Messiah in His glory was to bring with it. That this should be connected by the Apostle with the conversion of the Jewish people, was not only according to the plain inference from prophecy, but doubtless was one of those *things concerning the kingdom of God* which he had been taught by his risen Master. The same connexion holds *even now*. If it be objected to this, that thus we have the conversion of the Jews regarded as *bringing about* the great times of refreshment, and those times consequently as *delayed by their non-conversion* ('neque enim est Mutate vos in melius, ut Deus mittat Christum: non esse potest: hoc non pendet a nostra μετανοίᾳ.' Morus in Stier R. A. i. 91), I answer, that, however true this may be in fact, the other is fully borne out by the manner of speaking in Scripture: the same objection might lie against the efficacy of *prayer*. See Gen. xix. 22; xxxii. 26; Mark vi. 5; 2 Thess. ii. 3; 2 Pet. iii. 12. **ἀπὸ προσώπ. τ. κυρ.**] **From the presence of God** (*the Father*), who has reserved these καιροί in His own power. When they arrive, it is by His decree, which goes forth from His presence. Cf. ἐξῆλθεν δόγμα παρὰ Καίσ. Αὐγ., Luke ii. 1. 20.] **ἀποστείλῃ** (see above), *literally*,—not figuratively, by the Spirit: —even if the word **send** be no where else applied to the second coming of the Lord, there is no reason why it should not be here: the whole ground and standing-point of these two orations of Peter are *peculiar*, and the very mention of the 'times of refreshment' *proceeding forth from the presence of the Father* would naturally lead to the position here assigned to the Son, as

τὸν [f] προκεχειρισμένον ὑμῖν χριστὸν Ἰησοῦν, 21 ὃν [g] δεῖ οὐρανὸν μὲν [h] δέξασθαι ἄχρι [i] χρόνων [j] ἀποκαταστάσεως πάντων, [k] ὧν [l] ἐλάλησεν ὁ θεὸς [m] διὰ στόματος τῶν [n] ἁγίων

ABCDE PℵA a b c d f g h k l m o p 13

f ch. xxii. 14. xxvi. 16 only. Exod. iv. 13. Josh. iii. 12. 2 Macc. iii. 7. viii. 9 only. g = ch. iv. 12 reff. h = Luke ix. 53. xvi. 4, 9. i and constr., ch. xvii. 30. Matt. ii. 7. Luke i. 57. j here only †. see note. k attr., ch. i. 1 reff. l = Luke xxiv. 25. ch. xxviii. 25. 2 Pet. i. 21. Ps. lxi. 11. m ch. i. 16 reff. n Luke i. 70. 2 Pet. iii. 2.

20. rec προκεκηρυγμενον (*either a mistake, or a gloss agreeable to the sense of vv.* 18, 21), with Orig [$Cosm_1$], *qui prædicatus est* vulg, *prius annunciatum* copt-wilk : txt ABCDEPℵ rel 36 syr-mg-gr Chr_2 : *præparatum* Iren-int_1 : *destinatum* and *prædesignatum* Tert : *prædestinatum* D-lat E-lat syrr sah [arm] : προκεχρισμενον æth. rec ιησ. bef χρ. (*corrn to more usual appelln, the connexion of* χρ. *not being perceived, see note*), with AC m p rel vss Chr_2 $Cosm_1$ Iren-int_1 : txt B D-gr EPℵ a c g h l syr sah.

21. χρονον D^1(txt D-$corr^1$) [m]. rec for των αγ., παντων αγ, with Cosm : παντων των αγ. EP 13 rel [syr] Chr_1 (*corrn to suit ver* 24, *and* των *omd in rec by mistake, owing to* -των *preceding*) : txt ABCDℵ (c ?) o p H^r [vss] $Orig_2$ Chr_1 Iren-int_1 $Tert_1$.—aft αγ.

one *sent* by the Father. See below, on ver. 26. Besides which, the aor. will not allow of the figurative interpretation, confining, as it does, the '*sending*' to one definite event. **προκεχειρισμένον**] **before appointed,** as apparently in the first ref.: or perhaps *προ-* merely gives the idea of *forth,* before the rest, as in the two others, and perhaps even in the first also. *ὑμῖν,* **to you,**—as your Messiah. According to the right reading, **χριστ. Ἰησοῦν,** *χριστόν* may be connected with *τὸν προκεχ. ὑμ.,* **Him who was predestined your Messiah, namely, Jesus.** **21. ὃν δεῖ οὐρ. μ. δέξασθαι**] These words admit of a double rendering : (1) '*Whom the heaven must receive.*' (2) '*Who must possess* (capessere) *the heaven.*' Of these the former is in my view *decidedly preferable,* both as best suiting the sense, and as being the natural rendering, whereas the other is forced. Only two or three instances of *δέχομαι* used in this sense are produced, and in these it gets the meaning by signifying 'to take to one's self,' as property or inheritance : which would surely never be said of *οὐρανόν,* thus barely expressed. Besides, *the* emphatic *position of* **οὐρανόν,** with **μέν** attached to it, is almost decisive against this rendering. I apprehend that this particle in a sentence of the present form is always found appended to the *subject,* never to the *object;* and that, if *οὐρ.* had been the object, the form of the sentence would necessarily have been **ὃν** *μὲν δεῖ κ.τ.λ.* The reason given by Bengel for rejecting the right rendering, '*Cœlo capi, i. e. cohiberi, concludi,* violenta est interpretatio, quasi cœlum Christo majus sit ; et inimica celsitudini Christi super omnes cœlos,' is best answered by himself 'Non tamen nullo sensu dici potuit, *cœlum suscipit Christum : admittit* scil. ut thronus Regem legitimum ;' only I would rather understand it *locally,* and recognize a parallel expression with that in ch. i., also *local, νεφέλη ὑπέλαβεν αὐτόν.* And so far from seeing in it any derogation from the Majesty of Christ, it seems to me admirably to set it forth : it behoves the *heaven* (which is *his,* obeying his will) to *receive Him* till the time appointed. The omission of the article cannot be adduced either way here : for *οὐρανός* 'the heaven,' is frequently anarthrous, as *ἥλιος* and other similar nouns : see (besides very numerous instances of *οὐρ. after a preposition,* which are hardly to the point) 2 Pet. iii. 12, and *τὰν πρὸς ἕσπερον κέλευθον οὐρανοῦ,* Eur. Orest. 1003. *Ζεύς ἐστιν αἰθήρ, Ζεὺς δὲ γῆ, Ζεὺς δ' οὐρανός,* Æsch. Frag. i. 96. The tragedians never prefix the article to *οὐρανός, γῆ* (meaning 'the earth'), *αἰθήρ,* or *ἥλιος,* except when qualified by an adjective, as *ὦ τὸν αἰπὺν οὐρ. διφρηλατῶν,* Soph. Aj. 832, and even then very seldom. Middleton has but very slightly noticed this, ch. iii. 1, § 5, note. **ἄχρι**] Not *during,* as the advocates of the *present spiritual sense* of the passage wish to render it, but **until**; see below. **χρόνων ἀποκαταστ. πάντων κ.τ.λ.**] The key both to the construction and meaning here, is our Lord's saying, Matt. xvii. 11, *Ἡλίας μὲν ἔρχεται καὶ* **ἀποκαταστήσει πάντα.** From this we see that **ἀποκατ. πάντων** stands alone, as the *ἀποκατ.* of *all things :* and that *ὧν does not belong to πάντων.* Next, what is **ἀποκατάστασις** ? We must be guided by the usage of the kindred verb *ἀποκαθίστημι* (or *-άνω*). Certainly, **to restore** is its usual import, and most strikingly so, accompanied however with the notion of a *glorious* and *complete* restoration, in ch. i. 6. To render our word *fulfilment,* and apply it to *πάντων ὧν ἐλάλ. κ.τ.λ.,* is against all precedent. And, in the sense of **restoration,** I cannot see how it can be applied to the work of the Spirit, as proceeding, during this the interim-state, in the hearts of men. This would be contrary to all Scripture analogy. I under-

[o] ἀπ' αἰῶνος αὐτοῦ [n] προφητῶν. 22 Μωυσῆς μὲν εἶπεν ὅτι
προφήτην ὑμῖν [p] ἀναστήσει κύριος ὁ θεὸς *ὑμῶν ἐκ τῶν
ἀδελφῶν ὑμῶν [q] ὡς ἐμέ· αὐτοῦ ἀκούσεσθε [r] κατὰ πάντα
ὅσα ἂν λαλήσῃ πρὸς ὑμᾶς. 23 [s] ἔσται δέ, [t] πᾶσα [u] ψυχὴ
[t] ἥτις ἐὰν μὴ ἀκούσῃ τοῦ προφήτου ἐκείνου [v] ἐξολεθρευθή-
σεται ἐκ τοῦ λαοῦ. 24 [w] καὶ πάντες [w] δὲ οἱ προφῆται ἀπὸ
Σαμουὴλ καὶ τῶν [x] καθεξῆς ὅσοι ἐλάλησαν καὶ [y] κατήγ-

o = Luke i. 70. ch. xv. 18. Ps. cxviii. 52.
p = Matt. xxii. 24. ch. vii. 37, from Deut. xviii. 15, 18.
q = Matt. vii. 29 al.
r = ch. xvii. 22. Col. iii. 20, 22. Heb. iv. 15.
s = and constr., ch. ii. 17, 21.
t Matt. vii. 24. x. 32. Col. iii. 17.
u = ch. ii. 43 reff.
v here only. Deut. vii. 10 al. Jos. Antt. viii. 11. 1.
w Matt. x. 18. John vi. 51. viii. 16, 17 al.
x Luke i. 3. viii. 1. ch. xi. 4. xviii. 23 only †. L.
y ch. xiii. 5 reff.

ins των B²-marg(sic: see table) Eℵ³ c k 13. rec αυτου προφ. bef απ αιωνος, with P rel 36: om απ. αιων. D 19 arm Cosm$_1$ Iren-int Tert$_1$: 13 has it thus, αγ. αυτου των απ' αι. προφ.: alii aliter (*prob the expr was found difficult, as Mey suggests, because strictly* απ' αιωνος *there were no prophets. Hence it was ejected to the marg and found its place variously when reinserted*): txt (*a very usual collocation in the Acts*) ABCEℵ (k) p. ins των bef προφ. D¹.—om αυτου k.

22. rec aft μεν ins γαρ (*to connect the prophecy of Moses, as an example, with ver 21*), with P rel Syr Chr$_1$: om ABCDEℵ b¹ o p 36 vulg syr coptt æth [arm] Chr$_1$ Iren-int$_1$. rec ins προς τους πατερας bef ειπεν, with P rel Thl: aft ειπεν DE sah æth arm Chr$_2$ Iren-int: om ABCℵ p vulg Syr copt.—(D d e f sah æth Iren-int add ημων aft the above insn; E 24. 43 add υμων.) *ἡμῶν CEPℵ¹ a^r b c e f h l o 13 syr sah æth Just$_1$ [Orig$_1$]: om B 60 Syr copt Chr$_1$ [Chron$_1$ Cosm$_1$]: υμων ADℵ³ p rel vulg [Orig$_1$] Chr$_1$ Iren[-int$_1$]. for 2nd υμων, ημων D-gr a 5. 14. 57. 95 lect-12. εμου D¹-gr(txt D²).

23. rec αν, with BDE rel [Orig$_1$ Eus$_1$ Chr]: txt ACPℵ b c d e f g l m o p. (εξολεθρ., so AB¹CD.)

24. om δε D. for οσοι, οι C²D²ℵ vulg: ο D¹: txt AB C¹(appy) C³E rel D-lat Chr [Cosm$_1$] Iren-int. ελαλησεν D¹: επροφητευσαν C² arm[-ed]. rec προκατηγγειλαν (*gloss*), with C² rel Cosm: txt AB C¹(appy) DEPℵ c d e f g k l m p 36 vulg syrr coptt æth arm Chr Thl Iren-int.

stand it then of the *glorious restoration of all things*, the παλιγγενεσία [Matt. xix. 28], which as Peter here says, is the theme of all the prophets from the beginning. No objection can be raised to this from the meaning of χρόνοι: see ch. vii. 17, and Peter's own language, 1 Pet. i. 20, ἐπ' ἐσχάτου τῶν χρόνων. If the distinction be true between χρόνοι and καιροί, as denoting a longer and a shorter period respectively, which I much doubt,—it does not affect this passage: for, either way, the χρόνοι ἀποκατ. will imply the time or period of the ἀποκατ., not the moment only when it begins or is completed, as καιρός (not καιροί) ἀποκατ. might. De Wette is hardly right in saying that the unexpressed δέ to answer to μέν is contained in the sense of ἀποκατάστασις: it is rather contained in the previous clause, καὶ ἀποστείλῃ, κ.τ.λ. In order to fill up the ellipsis, this clause would have to be repeated after προφητῶν—τότε δὲ αὐτὸν ἀποστελεῖ. **ὧν,** i. e. οὕς, agreeing with χρόνους, or perhaps περὶ ὧν, i. e. χρόνων. *It does not refer to* **πάντων,**—see above. On the testimony of the prophets, see ver. 18, note.

22.] This citation is a free but faithful paraphrase of the text in Deut. See LXX. That the words, as spoken by Moses, seem to point to the whole line of prophets sent by God, is not any objection to their being applied to Christ, but rather necessitates, and entirely harmonizes with, that application. See the parable Matt. xxi. 33—41. And *none* of the whole prophetic body entirely answered to the ὡς ἐμέ, *but Christ*. The Jews therefore rightly understood it (though not always consistent in this, compare John i. 21 with vi. 14) of the Messiah. **23. ἐξολεθρ.**] LXX ἐγὼ ἐκδικήσω ἐξ αὐτοῦ. This word, only known to later Greek, is often found in the LXX. See besides reff., Gen. xvii. 14; Deut. ix. 3; Ps. xvii. 40; lxxii. 27. In most places where it occurs, the readings vary between -ολοθρ- and -ολεθρ-; see var. readd. **24.**] See ver. 18, note. The construction of the Vulg., defended by Casaubon and adopted by Valcknaer and Kuinoel, τῶν καθεξῆς ὅσοι ἐλάλ., 'et omnes prophetæ a Samuel, et deinceps qui locuti sunt,' is not so good as the ordinary one in E. V. Cf. ἀρξάμενος ἀπὸ Μωυσέως καὶ ἀπὸ πάντων τῶν προφ., Luke xxiv. 27. Still less admissible is the rendering given in Dr. Burton's note, as perhaps the literal one, 'And to the same effect spoke) all

z = Matt. viii. 12. Luke xx. 34, 36. 2 Thess. ii. 3. Ezek. xxx. 5. see 4 Kings ii. 3, 5.
a = Luke i. 72. Rom. xi. 27. Ps. xxiv. 14.
b Heb. viii. 18 & x. 16, from Jer. xxxviii. (xxxi.) 33. Gen. xv. 18.

ABCDE Pℵ a b c d f g h k l m o p 13

γειλαν τὰς ἡμέρας ταύτας. 25 ὑμεῖς ἐστε οἱ [z] υἱοὶ τῶν
προφητῶν καὶ τῆς [ab] διαθήκης [c] ἧς [bd] διέθετο ὁ θεὸς [be] πρὸς
τοὺς [f] πατέρας [f] ὑμῶν, λέγων πρὸς Ἀβραὰμ Καὶ ἐν τῷ
[g] σπέρματί σου [h] ἐνευλογηθήσονται πᾶσαι αἱ [i] πατριαὶ τῆς
γῆς. 26 ὑμῖν πρῶτον [k] ἀναστήσας ὁ θεὸς τὸν [l] παῖδα αὐτοῦ
ἀπέστειλεν αὐτὸν [m] εὐλογοῦντα ὑμᾶς [n] ἐν τῷ [o] ἀποστρέφειν

c attr., ch. i. 1 reff. d as above (b). Luke xxii. 29 bis. Heb. ix. 16, 17 only. e = Heb. x. 16. Exod. xxiv. 8. Jer. xi. 10. f ch. vii. 51, 52. xxviii. 25. Matt. xxiii. 32. John vi. 49, 58. Heb. iii. 9 (from Ps. xciv. 9) only. Num. xxxii. 8, 14. g Rom. ix. 7 reff. Gen. xxii. 18. h Gal. iii. 8 only, from Gen. xii. 3 Ed-vat. (εὐλογ., A. B def.). i Luke ii. 4. Eph. iii. 15 only. Num. i. 18. k = ver. 22 reff. l = ver. 13. ch. iv. 27, 30. Matt. xii. 18 only. Isa. xlix. 6. m = Gal. iii. 9. Eph. i. 3 al. Gen. xii. 3 A compl. n = ch. iv. 30 reff. o = Luke xxiii. 14. 2 Tim. iv. 4. Job xxxiii. 17.

25. rec om οι (*as unnecessary, or perhaps in the way, as according to the common notion an art with the predicate* distributes *it*), with DP rel Chr$_2$ [Cosm$_1$]: ins ABCEℵ b^2 c e k p [coptt]. for ης, ην D^1(txt D^2). ο θ. bef διεθ. BD coptt Iren-int$_1$. rec ημων (*corrn, as οι πατ. ημων is the more usual; see ver* 13, *ch* vii. 12, 15), with CDPℵ^1 rel vulg syrr copt sah-ms æth [arm-ed Chr Cosm] Iren-int: txt ABEℵ^3 k m^1 p sah-woide arm[-mss] Chr$_1$ Thl Iren-int-ms. rec om εν, with E-lat [Cosm]: ins ABCD E[-gr] Pℵ rel. επευλογηθ. C: ευλογηθ. B e 3. 15. 27. 100-27-63 Chr Thl$_2$ Œc: txt (except the initial ε) is written over an erasure by A^1 [but θη above the line].

26. rec ο θεος bef αναστ. (*rearrangement for perspicuity*), with ADEP rel vulg syr coptt [æth arm, Treg] Chr$_1$ Iren-int$_1$: txt BCℵ Syr æth [arm(Tischdf) Chr$_1$]. rec aft τ. παιδ. αυτ. ins ιησουν (*marginal gloss. All such additions, if at all the subject of variations, are spurious*), with AP rel Cosm$_1$: om BCDEℵ p [vulg] Syr coptt æth arm Chr Thl$_3$ Iren-int$_1$. **εξαπεστειλεν** D Chron. om αυτον D Chr$_1$ Thl$_1$ Iren-int. ευλογουντας D-gr.

the prophets from S. downwards, as many as spoke and predicted these days.' *To what effect?* And would not the sentence thus amount to little more than saying, 'As many prophets as predicted these days, predicted these days?' Peter's aim is to shew the unanimity of *all the prophets* in *speaking of these times.* Samuel is named, more as being the *first great prophet after Moses,* than as bearing any part in this testimony. The prophetic period of which David was the chief prophet, *began in Samuel* (Stier). **τὰς ἡμ. ταύτ.]** **These days,** *now present,* not *the times of restoration,* as De Wette and others understand: which would require ἐκείνας. '*These days*' are, in fact, *connected with* the times of restoration, as belonging to the same dispensation and leading on to them; and thus the Apostle identifies the *then time* with this preparation for (ὅπως ἂν ἔλθ.) and expectation of (ἄχρι) those glories: but to make τὰς ἡμ. ταύτ. *identical* with the καιροὶ ἀναψ. and the χρόν. ἀποκατ., is to make him contradict himself. **25.]** He applies this to *them,* as being inheritors of the promises. They were descendants, according to the flesh, and fellow-partakers, according to the spirit. For a full comment on this promise made to Abraham, see Gal. iii. 16. This is cited freely from the LXX, which for οἱ πατριαί has τὰ ἔθνη. **26.]** **πρῶτον, first;** implying the offer to the Gentiles (but as yet, in Peter's mind, only *by embracing Judaism*) afterwards: see ch. xiii. 46; Rom. i. 16. It is strange how Olshausen can suppose that the Spirit in Peter overleapt the bounds of his subsequent prejudice with regard to the admission of the Gentiles:—*he never had any such prejudice,* but only against their admission *uncircumcised,* and *as Gentiles.*

It is still stranger how a scholar like Dr. Burton can propose the ungrammatical and unmeaning rendering, "πρῶτον is perhaps used with reference to Christ's first coming, as opposed to his second." This would require τὸ πρῶτον,—and would certainly imply in the mind of the speaker an *absolute exclusion of all but Jews till the second coming.* **ἀναστήσας,** not '*from the dead:*' but as in ver. 22. **παῖδα, His Servant;** see note, ver. 13. **ἀπέστειλεν,** indefinite, of the sending in the flesh; **sent,** not '*hath sent;*' it does not apply to the *present time,* but to God's procedure in raising up His Servant Jesus, and His mission and ministry: and is distinct from the ἀποστείλῃ of ver. 20. This is also shewn by the pres. part. εὐλογοῦντα, * ingeniously, but not quite accurately rendered in E. V. '*to bless you.*' He came **blessing you** (his coming was an act of blessing—it consisted in the εὐλογεῖν: an anarthrous present participle in such a connexion carries necessarily a slightly ratiocinative sense), **in** (as the conditional

ἕκαστον ἀπὸ τῶν [p] πονηριῶν ὑμῶν. IV. 1 Λαλούντων δὲ
αὐτῶν πρὸς τὸν λαὸν [q] ἐπέστησαν αὐτοῖς οἱ ἱερεῖς καὶ
ὁ [rs] στρατηγὸς τοῦ [r] ἱεροῦ καὶ οἱ Σαδδουκαῖοι, 2 [t] διαπονού-
μενοι διὰ τὸ διδάσκειν αὐτοὺς τὸν λαὸν καὶ [u] καταγγέλλειν
[v] ἐν τῷ Ἰησοῦ τὴν [w] ἀνάστασιν τὴν [w] ἐκ [w] νεκρῶν· 3 καὶ [x] ἐπέβαλον [x] αὐτοῖς τὰς [x] χεῖρας καὶ ἔθεντο εἰς [y] τήρησιν [z] εἰς
τὴν [z] αὔριον, ἦν γὰρ [a] ἑσπέρα ἤδη. 4 πολλοὶ δὲ τῶν ἀκουσάντων τὸν λόγον ἐπίστευσαν, καὶ ἐγενήθη ἀριθμὸς τῶν

...εις την C. ABDE Pℵ a b c d f g h k l m o p 13

p Matt. xxii. 18. Mark vii. 22. Luke xi. 39. Rom. i. 29. 1 Cor. v. 8. Eph. vi. 12 only. Isa. i. 16.
q = Luke ii. 9. xx. 1. xxiv. 4. ch. vi. 12 al. Luke only, exc. 1 Thess. v. 3. 2 Tim. iv. 2, 6‡. Wisd. vi. 5.
r ch. v. 24 Luke xxii. 52 only. s = as above (r), Luke xxii. 4. ch. v. 26 (xvi. 20, &c.) only‡. L. (Neh. ii. 16.) t ch. xvi. 18 only. Eccl. x. 9. 2 Macc. ii. 28 Ed-vat. F(not AB) only. u = ch. xiii. 5 reff. v = 1 Cor. xv. 22 reff. w Luke xx. 35. 1 Pet. i. 3 only. without ἐκ, 1 Cor. xv. 12 reff. x constr., Mark xiv. 46. Isa. xix. 16. see ch. xxi. 27. y = ch. v. 18 (1 Cor. vii. 19) only +. L.P. 1 Macc. v. 18. Thucyd. vii. 86. z Matt. vi. 34 only. Jos. iii. 5, a Luke xxiv. 29. ch. xxviii. 23 only. Gen. i. 5, &c.

εκαστος D¹(txt D²), *unus quisque* vulg D-lat Iren-int: om Syr. for απο, εκ D. for υμων, αυτων C¹ 13. 66² vulg D-lat copt Iren-int: αυτου 5. 27-9. 69. 100-4-27-63: om B Chr₂ Thl-ms (*corrections and omission to suit* εκαστον *which did not seem to tally with* υμων): txt A[C³]DE[P]ℵ rel syrr æth [arm] Cosm₁.

Chap. IV. 1. aft λαον ins τα ρηματα ταυτα D c Syr syr-mg Thl-sif₁ [ταυτα τα ρημ.] E Lucif₁. οι ιερ. bef αυτοις 13: om αυτ. D vulg Lucif. οι αρχιερεις (*alteration to more usual word: cf. Lu* xx. 1) BC æth [arm]. om κ. ο στρ. τ. ιερου D: ins aft σαδδ. Syr.
2. ins και bef διαπ. C¹(appy) [æth-pl]: καταπ. D⁷: καιαπ. D¹: om διαπ. æth[-rom]. αναγγειλλειν τον ιησουν εν τη αναστασει D. for την εκ, των DP a c d f g h l m o² Hʳ E-lat sah æth [arm] Chr₁ Thl₁ Lucif₁.
3. επειβαλοντες D-gr: om και (bef εθεντο) D-corr-gr. aft εθεντο ins αυτους (*to complete sense*) ACE k 36 vss Chr₁ Thl-fin; αυτοις m: om BDPℵ p rel Thl₁ Lucif₁. (The page in C ends εθεντο αυτους εις την, either adding την bef τηρησιν, or omg εις τηρησιν.) επαυριον D 40 [γαυριον ℵ¹].
4. om του λογον A. και αριθμ. τε εγεν. ανδρ. D¹[om τε D²]. rec ins ο bef αριθμος (*from supposed necessity of art*), with AEP p rel 36 Chr₁: om BDℵ.

element of the blessing) **turning every one from your iniquities**: thus conferring on you the best of blessings. εὐλογ., in allusion to ἐνευλογ., ver. 25. ἐν τῷ in this sense, see Luke viii. 5. The application to the *present time* is made by inference:—'*as that was His object then, so now:*'—but (see below) the discourse is unfinished. The *intransitive* sense of ἀποστρέφειν,—'*which blessing is to be gained by* (*in*) *every one of you turning from your iniquities,*'—given in the Vulg., 'ut convertat se unusquisque,' and maintained by Theophyl., Œc., Beza, Kuinoel, Meyer, &c., on the strength of ver. 19, is inadmissible,—as ἀποστρέφω is not found thus used in the N. T., and we have the precedent of ref. Luke and Rom. xi. 26 for the transitive sense. The argument from ver. 19 tells just as well for *it:* 'Repent and be converted, ... for this was the object of Jesus being raised up, to confer on you this very blessing, the *turning away* each of you from your iniquities.' This discourse does not come to a final conclusion as in ch. ii. 36, because it was *interrupted by the apprehension of the Apostles.*

Chap. IV. 1—4.] Apprehension and Imprisonment of the two Apostles. 1.] **ἐπέστ.**, see reff. **οἱ ἱερεῖς,** *the officiating priests,* as soon as they were released from their duties. The **στρατηγὸς τ. ἱεροῦ** was the captain of the Levitical guard of the temple, mentioned by Jos. B. J. vi. 5. 3, δραμόντες δὲ οἱ τοῦ ἱεροῦ φύλακες ἤγγειλαν τῷ στρατηγῷ. We hear in Jos. Antt. xx. 6. 2, of ὁ στρατηγὸς Ἄνανος: and in B. J. ii. 12. 6, he is said to be son of the high priest Ananias. In 2 Macc. iii. 4, we hear of the προστάτης τοῦ ἱεροῦ, who appears to have been the same officer. See Winer, Realw., art. Temple, end. **Σαδδουκ.**] See note on Matt. iii. 7. Perhaps *they* on this occasion had moved the guard and the priests to notice the matter: for **διαπον.** seems only to refer to *them.* Cf. also ch. v. 17. 2.] **ἐν τ. Ἰησ,**—not, as E. V., '*through* Jesus,' but in **the person** (or example) **of Jesus,** alleging Him as an example of that which the Sadducees denied: preaching by implication, inasmuch as one resurrection would imply that of all, the resurrection of the dead. The ἐν in reff. carries this somewhat further, but the usage is philologically the same. 'The resurrection *through* Jesus'

b constr., ch. ix. 3, 32, 37. xiv. 1. xxi. 1, 5. Matt. xviii. 13. Luke iii. 21. vi. 1, 6, 12 al.
c = ch. iii. 1 reff.
d here only. Esth. v. 8 A Ald. compl.
e Matt. xxii. 34. vv. 26, 27, 31. ch. xi. 26 al. Neh. vi. 2.

ABDE Pℵ a b c d f g h k l m o p 13

ἀνδρῶν [ὡς] χιλιάδες πέντε. 5 [b] ἐγένετο δὲ [cd] ἐπὶ τὴν
[d] αὔριον [e] συναχθῆναι αὐτῶν τοὺς [f] ἄρχοντας καὶ τοὺς
πρεσβυτέρους καὶ τοὺς γραμματεῖς ἐν Ἱερουσαλήμ, 6 καὶ
Ἄννας ὁ ἀρχιερεὺς καὶ Καϊάφας καὶ Ἰωάννης καὶ
Ἀλέξανδρος [g] καὶ ὅσοι ἦσαν ἐκ [h] γένους [i] ἀρχιερατικοῦ,
7 καὶ [k] στήσαντες αὐτοὺς [k] ἐν [τῷ] μέσῳ [l] ἐπυνθάνοντο Ἐν
[m] ποίᾳ [n] δυνάμει ἢ [o] ἐν ποίῳ [o] ὀνόματι ἐποιήσατε τοῦτο ὑμεῖς;

f = ch. xiii. 27 reff. g Col. ii. 1. Herod. i. 57. vii. 185. h = ch. vii. 13. xiii. 26. Rev. xxii. 16. Jer. xlviii. (xli.) 1. i here only +. Jos. Antt. xv. 3. 1. k Matt. xviii. 2 || Mk. [John viii. 3.] l constr., ch. x. 29. xxiii. 19. m = Luke vi. 32, 34. ch. xxiii. 34. Rom. iii. 27 al. 2 Kings xv. 2. n = ch. iii. 12 al. o = Luke x. 17. ver. 10. ch. xvi. 18 al.

rec ωσει, with EP rel Chr: ως B(sic, see table) D: om Aℵ p vulg copt æth Hil_1.

5. aft αυριον ins ημεραν D[1]. συνηχθησαν οι αρχ. κ. οι πρεσβ. κ. γρ. and αννας &c D [simly copt]. om αυτων D 3. 95[1] Syr copt æth. rec om 2nd and 3rd τους (*supposed unnecessary*), with EP rel: ins ABℵ b c o p. rec (for εν) εις (*corrn to suit* συναχθῆναι, *cf Matt* vi. 26, xiii. 30; *and esp* xxvi. 3), with Pℵ rel: txt ABDE b h k o p 36 Chr_2.—om εν ιερ. Syr.

6. rec ανναν τον αρχιερεα κ. καιαφαν κ. ιωαννην κ. αλεξανδρον, with EP rel 36 [Chr_1]: txt AB D(see last verse) ℵ p [vulg coptt].—om ο (bef αρχ.) B(sic; see table).—for ιωαννης, ιωναθας D.

7. om τω DEP rel Chr_1: ins ABℵ p 36. τουτο bef εποιησατε (so corrected a prima manu from εποιειτε) ℵ.

does not appear on the present occasion to have formed part of their preaching.

3.] **ἑσπέρα**, perhaps, from their adjourning the case till the next day, the second evening, beginning with the twelfth hour: see Matt. xiv. 15, and note. **4.] ἐγενήθη**—This form is unknown in good Greek: but common in Hellenistic,—see Col. iv. 11; 1 Thess. ii. 14; Winer, § 15. It appears to have been originally a Doric form: and is commonly, though this cannot always be pressed (1 Thess. i. 5, 6; ii. 5, and notes there), used where a passive sense is admissible, and an agent understood: cf. e. g. Matt. vi. 10; viii. 13; xxi. 42. Here the agent would be God: see ch. ii. 47. **τῶν ἀνδρῶν**] It does not appear whether we are to take this strictly as masculine, or more loosely as if it were ἀνθρώπων: Meyer thinks the former: Olshausen, that as yet only *men* attached themselves to the church (but see ch. i. 14): De Wette objects to the stricter view, that Luke does not so reckon, ch. ii. 41 (see however Luke ix. 14, and cf. || Mt.): but leaves it undecided. The laxer use of ἀνδρῶν occurs Luke xi. 31, and James i. 20. In ch. v. 14, *men and women both* are mentioned as being added to the Lord. Wordsw. sees in the 5000 ἄνδρες a fulfilment of the prophecy contained in the miracle of feeding the 5000. But how will the circumstances tally, seeing that these were but new converts, babes in grace, not yet fed to the full as were those others? And again, it is not quite certain whether this number was that of new converts on this occasion, or of the whole Church: but most probably the latter.

5—12.] The Apostles examined before the Sanhedrim. Peter's speech. **5.] αὐτῶν**, *of the Jews;* a construction frequently used where there can be little chance of mistaking to whom or what the pronoun refers, see John viii. 44, note; Rom. ii. 26; Winer, edn. 6, § 22. 3. 3 b. In this place, however, it *has been* mistaken: for Meyer refers αὐτῶν to the believers just mentioned, inasmuch as they were Jews: absurdly enough. **ἄρχ. κ. πρεσβ. κ. γρ.**] *The Sanhedrim:* see Matt. ii. 4; xxvi. 59; ch. v. 21. **ἐν Ἱερουσαλήμ**] Why is this specified? The difficulty of accounting for it has led in some MSS. to ἐν being altered to **εἰς**, so as to imply that certain of them who dwelt out of town (Lightf. &c.) were summoned *to Jerusalem.* I believe it merely implies that the meeting was not held *in the temple*, but *in the city*. **6.**] On Annas and Caiaphas, both called high priests, Luke iii. 2,—see note there. Of John and Alexander nothing is known. Lightfoot supposes John to be identical with the Jochanan ben Zacchai of the Talmud, who however (De W.) was not of the *high*-priestly, but only of the priestly race:—and Pearson, Wolf, Krebs, and Mangey suppose Alexander to have been the brother of Philo Judæus, mentioned by Jos. Antt. xviii. 8. 1. But this is very improbable; for he was Alabarch of the Jews at Alexan-

...αρχοντες p. ABDE Pℵ a b c d f g h k l m o 13

8 τότε Πέτρος [p] πλησθεὶς πνεύματος ἁγίου εἶπεν πρὸς
αὐτοὺς [q] Ἄρχοντες τοῦ λαοῦ καὶ [rs] πρεσβύτεροι [τοῦ [s] Ἰσ-
ραήλ], 9 εἰ ἡμεῖς σήμερον [t] ἀνακρινόμεθα [u] ἐπὶ [v] εὐεργεσίᾳ
[w] ἀνθρώπου ἀσθενοῦς, [x] ἐν τίνι οὗτος [y] σέσωσται, 10 [z] γνωστὸν ἔστω πᾶσιν ὑμῖν καὶ παντὶ τῷ λαῷ Ἰσραὴλ ὅτι [a] ἐν
τῷ [a] ὀνόματι Ἰησοῦ χριστοῦ τοῦ Ναζωραίου, ὃν ὑμεῖς
ἐσταυρώσατε, ὃν ὁ θεὸς [b] ἤγειρεν ἐκ [b] νεκρῶν, [x] ἐν τούτῳ
οὗτος [c] παρέστηκεν [d] ἐνώπιον ὑμῶν [e] ὑγιής. 11 οὗτός ἐστιν
ὁ λίθος ὁ [f] ἐξουθενηθεὶς ὑφ' ὑμῶν τῶν [g] οἰκοδόμων, ὁ
[h] γενόμενος εἰς [i] κεφαλὴν [ik] γωνίας. 12 καὶ οὐκ ἔστιν ἐν
ἄλλῳ οὐδενὶ [l] ἡ [l] σωτηρία· *οὔτε γὰρ [m] ὄνομά ἐστιν [n] ἕτερον
[o] ὑπὸ τὸν οὐρανὸν τὸ δεδομένον ἐν ἀνθρώποις, [x] ἐν ᾧ
[p] δεῖ [q] σωθῆναι ἡμᾶς. 13 θεωροῦντες δὲ τὴν τοῦ Πέτρου

p = ch. ii. 4 reff.
q ver. 5.
r = Matt. xxi. 23. Luke vii. 3. ch. xxv. 15.
s here only. Exod. xxiv. 1.
t Luke xxiii. 14. ch. xii. 19 al3. 1 Cor. ii. 14, 15 (bis) al7. only. L.P. 1 Kings xx. 12.
u = Rom. vi. 21 reff.
v 1 Tim. vi. 2 only. Ps. lxxvii. 11.
w constr., Rom. iii. 22. ix. 12 reff.
x = ch. xi. 14 reff.
y = ch. xiv. 9 reff.
z ch. xiii. 38 reff.
a ver. 7.
b 1 Cor. xv. 12 reff.
c ver. 26 (from Ps. ii. 3). Mark xiv. 47 al. 1 Kings xvi. 21, 22.
d = ch. ii. 25 reff.
e Matt. xii. 13 al. (chiefly John) in gospp. Tit. ii. 8 only. Isa. xxxviii. 21.
f Rom. xiv. 3 reff.
g here only. 4 Kings xxii. 6. Herod. ii. 121. Xen. Symp. iv. 4.
h constr., ch. v. 36 reff. Psa. cxvii. 22.
i Matt. xxi. 42 ‖ & 1 Pet. ii. 7 (from l. c.) only.
k ch. xxvi 26 reff.
l absol., John iv. 22 (ch. xiii. 26). Rom. xi. 11. Rev. vii. 10. xii. 10. xix. 1. Obad. 17 Aℵ[3b], Ald. compl. (om ἡ Bℵ[1]).
m = Phil. ii. 9 al.
n = ch. ii. 40 al.
o ch. ii. 5 reff. Job ii. 2.
p = Luke xxiv. 7. ch. iii. 21. xiv. 22. Dan. ii. 28.
q = ch. xvi. 30, 31 al. fr.

8. om του ισρ. (*as unnecessary aft* του λαου ?) ABℵ vulg coptt æth Cyr_2 Fulg : ins DEP rel 36 syrr Chr_2 $Iren\text{-}int_1$ $Cypr_1$. at end ins ακουσατε E 15-8. 36-7 vulg[-ed (not am fuld demid)] Syr æth Cypr.

9. aft ανακρινομ. ins αφ υμων DE syrr æth-pl $Iren\text{-}int_1$ $Cypr_1$. επ' D m. σεσωται ℵ.

10. for παντι, παν ℵ[1]. ins του κυριου bef ιησ. χρ. E vulg-ed(not am fuld demid). ins σημερον bef υγιης E : aft υγ. Bede-gr. add και εν αλλω ουδενι E syr-mg $Cypr_1$.

11. ημων D-gr. rec οικοδομουντων (*corrn to suit* LXX *and Matt* xxi. 42), with EP rel Chr [$Thdrt_1$ $Cypr_1$] : txt ABDℵ c 36 $Orig_1$ Did_2.

12. om η σωτ. D. *οὐδὲ (*philological correction? so Meyer*) ABℵ a b h k o 13. 36 [syr] coptt Did_1 Thdrt Bas_1 : ου D [Syr] : ουτε EP rel Chr_1. ετερον bef εστιν AE a c h m 13 demid fuld [tol Chr_1] : εσ. ετ. ον. D-gr [syr æth] Bas_1 $Iren\text{-}int_1$ [Orig-int] : ετ. ον. εσ. ℵ [vulg-ed] : txt B[P] rel. om υπο τον ουρανον P b c g l m o Hr Thl. ο δεδομενον D[1], *quod datum est* D-lat, *q. d. sit* Iren-int : txt D[3]. om εν D 117-63 vulg Iren-int Cypr. υμας B [$Ambrst_1$].

dria, Jos. ibid. 7.] **ἐν ποίᾳ δυνάμει**—not = ἐν π. ἐξουσίᾳ, 'in what *authority*,'—but **in what** (manner of) **power**; of what kind was the enabling cause, the element in which, as its condition, the deed was wrought?—**ἐν ποίῳ ὀνόματι**—not '*in what name*,'—i. e. '*by whose authority*,' but **by** ('*in*,' see above) **what** (manner of) **name**, spoken as a word of power: see ch. iii. 6, 16; Jos. Antt. viii. 2. 5. **τοῦτο**, not the *teaching* (Olshaus., &c.),—nor *both the miracle and the teaching* (Heinr.), but the *miracle*: and that only. 8.] **πλησθ. πν. ἁγ.**, i. e. specially, for the occasion. 9.] **εἰ**, **if**, with an implication of the fact being so: see ch. xi. 17. **ἐν τίνι**, not 'by (in) *whom*,'—this is not yet brought forward: but **wherein**, in what, as the conditional element. No *person* had been mentioned in the question, ver. 7,—nor does Peter afterwards say ἐν Ἰησοῦ χρ., but ἐν τῷ ὀνόμ. Ἰ. χρ. On the other hand, **ἐν τούτῳ**, ver. 10, may very well be masculine, as referring to Ἰησοῦς χρ. Himself, included in the previous words τῷ ὀν. Ἰ. χρ.:—it may also be neuter, 'in this Name:' but the masc. is preferable, on account of οὗτος following so soon in ver. 11. 10.] **ὃν . . . . ὃν**: the copula is omitted to make the contrast more striking. **παρέστηκεν, stands**, as in E. V. He was there present. 11.] See Matt. xxi. 42, note. 12.] In Jos. Antt. iii. 1. 5, Moses, praying to God for Israel, says, ἐν αὐτῷ γὰρ εἶναι τὴν σωτηρίαν αὐτοῦ, καὶ οὐκ ἐν ἄλλῳ. **σωτηρία** is used here in the higher sense of **salvation**, not with reference to the healing of the lame man. See reff. The article implies, 'the salvation for which we all look;' **our salvation**: ἐστὶν ἡ σωτ. is paraphrased in the next clause by δεῖ σωθῆναι

ABDE Pℵ a b c d f g h k l m o 13

r = ch. ii. 29. xxviii. 31. 1 Tim. iii. 13. Wisd. v. 1.
s = ch. x. 34. xxv. 25. Eph. iii. 18. see John i. 5.
t here only †.
u 1 Cor. xiv. 16, 23, 24. 2 Cor. xi. 6 only. Prov. vi. 8 (only ?).
v constr., 1 Cor. xiv. 37 reff.
w = Luke vii. 42. xii. 4 (ch. xxv. 26). Heb. vi. 14. Prov. iii. 27.
x Luke xxi. 15 only. Esth. viii. 8.
y Matt. xxvi. 59. ch. v. 27, 34. xxiii. 1 al. Jer. xv. 17.

[r] παῤῥησίαν καὶ Ἰωάννου, καὶ [s] καταλαβόμενοι ὅτι ἄνθρωποι [t] ἀγράμματοί εἰσιν καὶ [u] ἰδιῶται, ἐθαύμαζον, [v] ἐπεγίνω-
σκόν τε αὐτοὺς ὅτι σὺν τῷ Ἰησοῦ ἦσαν· 14 τόν τε ἄνθρωπον βλέποντες σὺν αὐτοῖς ἑστῶτα τὸν τεθεραπευμένον,
οὐδὲν [w] εἶχον [x] ἀντειπεῖν. 15 κελεύσαντες δὲ αὐτοὺς ἔξω τοῦ
[y] συνεδρίου ἀπελθεῖν, [z] συνέβαλλον πρὸς ἀλλήλους λέγοντες 16 Τί [a] ποιήσωμεν τοῖς ἀνθρώποις τούτοις; ὅτι
μὲν γὰρ [b] γνωστὸν σημεῖον γέγονεν [c] δι' αὐτῶν, πᾶσιν τοῖς
[d] κατοικοῦσιν Ἱερουσαλὴμ φανερόν, καὶ οὐ δυνάμεθα ἀρ-
νεῖσθαι· 17 ἀλλ' ἵνα μὴ [e] ἐπὶ πλεῖον [f] διανεμηθῇ [g] εἰς
τὸν λαόν, [[h] ἀπειλῇ] [i] ἀπειλησώμεθα αὐτοῖς μηκέτι λαλεῖν

xx. 32. Gen. xx. 9. z = here (ch. xvii. 18 reff.) only ‡. see Josh. xi. 5 Ald. compl. a constr., Matt. b = here only. (ch. i. 19 reff.) c = ver. 30. ch. ii. 43 al. d constr., ch. i. 19 reff. e ch. xx. 9. xxiv. 4. 2 Tim. ii. 16. iii. 9 only. Jer. ii. 12. f here only ‡. Deut. xxix. 26 only. g = John xxi. 23. ch. xx. 29. h ch. ix. 1 reff. i 1 Pet. ii. 23 only. Gen. xxvii. 42. [constr., ch. v. 28 reff.]

13. om και ιδιωτ. D. for τε, δε D 36 E-lat copt.

14. rec δε, with P rel 36 copt [arm] Thl-sif : om D[1] : txt ABD[3]Eℵ c [13] vulg syrr sah æth Chr_1 Thl-fin $Lucif_1$. αυτων D^1-gr(txt D^2). ειχον ποιησαι η αντειπειν D-gr.

15. κελευσαντος ℵ[1](txt ℵ-corr[1](?)). om δε D-gr c [Syr] æth. for απελθειν, απαχθηναι D-gr. rec συνεβαλον (*corrn to more usual tense*), with D c 36 syr sah æth [arm] Thl-fin : txt ABEPℵ rel vulg Syr copt Chr_1 Thl-sif Lucif.

16. rec ποιησομεν, with D-gr P rel E-lat vulg [$Bas\text{-}sel_1$] Chr Thl-fin $Lucif_1$: txt AB E-gr ℵ k m 13. 36 D-lat Thl-sif. γεγονεναι D^1-gr. φανεροτερον εστιν D-gr. rec αρνησασθαι (*the more common N. T. word*), with EP rel Chr : txt ABDℵ c $Bas\text{-}sel_1$.

17. om αλλ D-gr. for μη, δε A^2. πλεον τι D. aft λαον ins τα ρηματα ταυτα E syr-mg $Lucif_1$. om απειλη (*prob mistake in copying; perhaps omd as unnecessary*) ABDℵ vss $Bas\text{-}sel_1$ $Lucif_1$: ins EP rel 36 syr Chr_1 Thl. επιλησομεθα ουν αυτοις D^1-gr(απ. D^3 : -σωμεθα, adding *ergo*, D-lat).—(-σομεθα P b d e k^2 o [Thl-fin].) for μηκετι, μη A 142 [$Bas\text{-}sel_1$].

ἡμᾶς. **οὔτε γὰρ . . . .**] lit. **for neither is there another name under heaven (which is) given (by God) among men** (not '*to men*,' Vulg., Beza, Kuinoel), **whereby we must be saved**: i. e., as E. V. Dr. Burton's rendering, 'For neither is the name which is given among men, whereby we are to be saved, any other than this,' is ungrammatical.

13—18.] CONSULTATION AND SENTENCE OF THE SANHEDRIM. **13.**] **καταλαβόμενοι, having had previous knowledge**; not as E. V., which would be the partic. pres.; see the past, ch. xxv. 25. **ἰδιῶται,**—the word of contrast to those professionally acquainted with any matter: here therefore, **laics**, men of no knowledge on such a subject as this. **ἐπεγίνωσκον,—they recognized them**; (so Od. ω. 215, αὐτὰρ ἐγὼν πατρὸς πειρήσομαι ἡμετέροιο, αἴ κ' ἐμ' ἐπιγνοίη κ. φράσσεται ὀφθαλμοῖσιν: Plato, Euthyd. 301 E, ἆρα μοί ποτε αὕτη (ἡ σοφία) παραγενήσεται ὥστε μοι οἰκεία γενέσθαι; Ἐπιγνοίης ἂν αὐτήν, ὦ Σώκρατες, ἔφη, οἰκείαν γενομένην;) their astonishment setting them to think, and reminding them that they had seen these men with Jesus:—not *for a pluperfect*, here or any where else: nor is ἦσαν;—**that they (once) were with Jesus. 14.**] This, according to De W., is the only place in Luke where τε couples two sentences. He therefore objects to the reading; and also as destroying the contrast; but clearly the former is no sound critical reason, nor is it correct: see ch. i. 15 al. fr.:—and I cannot see that any contrast is intended: the two circumstances which the Sanhedrim found it difficult to gainsay were, the boldness of these illiterate men, conferred by their companionship with Jesus, *and* the presence of the healed man standing with them. **17. διανεμηθῇ] be scattered** or **spread**: lit., be distributed: so Plato, Minos, 317 D, τίς ἐπιστήμων διανεῖμαι ἐπὶ γῇ τὰ σπέρματα; and afterwards, τίς δὲ τὴν τροφὴν ἐπὶ τὰ τῶν ἀνθρώπων σώματα διανεῖμαι ἄριστος; **[ἀπειλῇ] ἀπειλ.]** for idiom, see reff. The construction of ἀπειλέω with an infin., stated by Dr. Bloomf. to be 'so rare that even the best lexx. scarcely adduce an example,' is its

[k] ἐπὶ τῷ ὀνόματι τούτῳ [l] μηδενὶ [l] ἀνθρώπων. 18 καὶ καλέ-
σαντες αὐτοὺς [m] παρήγγειλαν τὸ [n] καθόλου μὴ [o] φθέγγεσθαι μηδὲ διδάσκειν [k] ἐπὶ τῷ ὀνόματι τοῦ Ἰησοῦ. 19 ὁ δὲ
Πέτρος καὶ Ἰωάννης ἀποκριθέντες εἶπον πρὸς αὐτοὺς
[p] Εἰ δίκαιόν ἐστιν [q] ἐνώπιον τοῦ θεοῦ ὑμῶν [r] ἀκούειν
μᾶλλον ἢ τοῦ θεοῦ, [s] κρίνατε· 20 οὐ δυνάμεθα γὰρ ἡμεῖς ἃ
εἴδαμεν καὶ ἠκούσαμεν μὴ λαλεῖν. 21 οἱ δὲ [t] προσαπειλη-
σάμενοι [u] ἀπέλυσαν αὐτούς, μηδὲν [v] εὑρίσκοντες [w] τὸ πῶς
[x] κολάσωνται αὐτούς, διὰ τὸν λαόν, ὅτι πάντες ἐδόξαζον
τὸν θεὸν [y] ἐπὶ τῷ γεγονότι. 22 [z] ἐτῶν γὰρ ἦν πλειόνων
τεσσεράκοντα ὁ ἄνθρωπος [a] ἐφ᾽ ὃν γεγόνει τὸ σημεῖον
τοῦτο τῆς [b] ἰάσεως. 23 [u] ἀπολυθέντες δὲ ἦλθον πρὸς τοὺς
[c] ἰδίους καὶ ἀπήγγειλαν ὅσα πρὸς αὐτοὺς οἱ ἀρχιερεῖς καὶ

k Luke ix. 48, 49. xxi. 8 ||. xxiv. 47. ch. v. 28, 40.
l constr., Mark xi. 2. Luke xiv. 24. ch. xxiv. 23. James iii. 8. Exod. xvi. 29 A Ald. compl. Num. xvi. 15.
m = ch. i. 4 reff.
n here only. Ezek. xiii. 3, 22.
o 2 Pet. ii. 16, 18 only. Job xiii. 7 al.
p = Matt. xxvii. 49. Luke xiv. 28 31. Gen. xlii. 16.
q = Luke xvi. 15. 1 Tim. ii. 3. v. 4. 1 John iii. 22. 3 Kings iii. 10.
r = Matt. xvii. 5 al. Isa. xlii. 24.
s = Luke vii. 43. 1 Cor. xi. 13. Ps. lvii. 1.
t here only +.
u = ch. xxvi. 32 reff.
v – Luke v. 19. (and constr.) xix. 48.
w Luke i. 62. ix. 46.
x 2 Pet. ii. (4 v. r.) 9 only +. Wisd. xi. 16.
y Rom. vi. 21 reff.
z constr., Mark v. 42. Luke ii. 42 al. Exod. vii. 7.
a constr., see Mark xv. 33. Luke i. 65, 32 only. Prov. iii. 8.
b ver. 30 and Luke xiii.
c = ch. xxiv. 23 reff.

for *ανθρωπων*, *ανθρωπω* P a h l 13.

18. for *και καλ. αυτ.*, *συνκατατιθεμενων δε αυτων τη γνωμη φωνησαντες αυτους* D syr-mg(exc *φων. αυτ.*) Lucif; D goes on *παρηγγειλαντο κατα το μη φθ.* rec aft *παρηγγ.* ins *αυτοις* (*a common filling up*), with P rel vss Thl Lucif: om AB D-gr Eℵ k 36 vulg syr arm Chr_1. om *το* [B¹]ℵ¹.

19. *αποκρειθεις δε π. κ. ι.* D Syr æth. ins *ο* bef *ιωαν.* A. rec *πρ. αυτ.* bef *ειπον*, with P rel Thl: txt ABDEℵ c k 13 vulg syrr coptt [æth] arm Chr_1.—*ειπαν* B. *τουτο υμ. δικαιον φαινεται* E.

20. *δυνομεθα* B. rec *ειδομεν*, with B²(see table) EP rel (-*ω*- P a f): *οιδαμεν* B¹-corr: txt AB¹Dℵ $Chr\text{-}wlf_1$. om *μη* D¹(ins D⁵).

21. for *μηδεν*, *μη* D k vulg Syr coptt $Lucif_1$. aft *ευρισκ.* ins *αιτιαν* D Syr copt. om *το* E 18. *κολασωσιν* B¹: -*σονται* P Scr's mss [Chr Thl]. *φοβουμενοι τον λαον παντες γαρ* E.

22. ins *ην* bef *ο ανθ.*, retaining *ην* above, D-gr. rec *εγεγονει*, with AEPℵ rel: *εγενετο* k: txt BD. om *τουτο* D-gr $Iren\text{-}int_1$ $Lucif_1$.

23. *εκεινοι δε απολ.* E. [*ανηγγειλαν* ℵ(-*γιλ*-) a h Thl-sif.] transp *αρχ.*

ordinary construction: see Palm and Rost sub voce, and cf. Il. α'. 161; ν'. 143; ο'. 179, al. freq.: Od. λ'. 313; Xen. Mem. iii. 5. 4; Hell. v. 4. 7; Eur. Med. 287. The use of the middle in the active sense is confined to later Greek. **18.**] **ἐπί**, so as to make *that Name* the *subject* (basis) of their discoursing.

19—22.] The Apostles' answer and dismissal. **21.**] **προςαπειλ.**, **having threatened them in addition**;—with threats superadded to the inhibition of ver. 18. **μηδέν, no means**: not *μηδὲν αἴτιον*, see John xiv. 30. The difficulty with the Sanhedrim was, to find any means of punishing them which should not stir up the people; *διὰ τὸν λαόν* belongs to this clause, not to *ἀπέλυσαν αὐτ.*

22.] **πλ. τεσσ.** for *πλ. ἢ τεσσ.*, as sometimes in classical Greek; so *οὐκ ἔλασσον πέντε καὶ εἴκοσι*, Thucyd. vi. 95. See Winer, edn. 6, § 37, 5. The constr. **ἐφ' ὃν γεγόνει** (see as in reff.) is accounted for by the sense involved in it being the *access*, so to speak, of the event *to* the person mentioned. In the note on Rev. iv. 2, I have noticed that *καθῆσθαι ἐπί* is commonly used when the fact is announced for the *first time*, with an accus.: but afterwards when the same fact is again referred to, with a gen. or dat. **τὸ σημ. τῆς ἰάσ.**—the genitive of apposition; so *τὸν ἀρραβῶνα τοῦ πνεύματος*, 2 Cor. v. 5: *σημεῖον περιτομῆς*, Rom. iv. 11, &c. The circumstance of his being more than forty years old both gave notoriety to his person as having long resorted there, and made the miracle more notable, his malady being more confirmed.

23—31.] Prayer of the church thereupon. **23.**] **τοὺς ἰδίους**, the other Apostles, and possibly some others assembled with them. There is nothing in ver. 31 to mark that only the Apostles were

d ch. i. 14 reff. e = Luke xvii. 13. 1 Kings xxx. 4. f = Luke ii. 29. Rev. vi. 10. 2 Pet. ii. 2. Jude 4 only. (1 Tim. vi. 1, 2 al.) Isa. i. 24. iii. 1. g ch. xiv. 15. Rev. xiv. 7. Exod. xx. 11. (Gen. i. 1. Isa. xlii. 5.) h ch. i. 16 reff. i = Luke i. 69. Isa. xliv. 26. k 1 Cor. x. 29 reff. Psa. ii. 1. l here only. l c.

ABDE Pℵ a b c d f g h k l m o 13

οἱ πρεσβύτεροι εἶπαν. 24 οἱ δὲ ἀκούσαντες [d] ὁμοθυμαδὸν
[e] ἦραν φωνὴν πρὸς τὸν θεὸν καὶ εἶπαν [f] Δέσποτα, σὺ
[ὁ θεὸς] [g] ὁ ποιήσας τὸν [g] οὐρανὸν καὶ τὴν [g] γῆν καὶ τὴν
[g] θάλασσαν καὶ πάντα τὰ ἐν αὐτοῖς, 25 ὁ τοῦ πατρὸς ἡμῶν
διὰ πνεύματος ἁγίου [h] στόματος Δαυεὶδ [i] παιδός σου
εἰπὼν [k] Ἵνα τί [l] ἐφρύαξαν ἔθνη καὶ λαοὶ [m] ἐμελέτησαν
[n] κενά; 26 [o] παρέστησαν οἱ βασιλεῖς τῆς γῆς καὶ οἱ [p] ἄρχον-
τες [pq] συνήχθησαν [qr] ἐπὶ τὸ αὐτὸ [s] κατὰ τοῦ κυρίου καὶ [s] κατὰ
τοῦ [t] χριστοῦ [t] αὐτοῦ. 27 [p] συνήχθησαν γὰρ [u] ἐπ' ἀληθείας
ἐν τῇ πόλει ταύτῃ [v] ἐπὶ τὸν ἅγιον [w] παῖδά σου Ἰησοῦν, ὃν

2 Macc. vii. 34 only. m Mark xiii. 11. 1 Tim. iv. 15 only. Prov. viii. 7. n = 1 Cor. xv. 10 reff. φόβος κενός, Xen. Anab. ii. 2. 21. o ver. 10 reff. p ver. 5. q = Matt. xxii. 34. Neh. vi 2. r ch. i. 15 reff. s = Matt. xxvii. 1 al. t Rev. xi. 15. xii. 10 u ch. x. 34 reff. Deut. xxii. 20. v = Matt. xxvii. 27. w = ch. iii. 26 reff.

and πρεσβ. E. (ειπαν, so BDℵ.)

24. aft ακουσαντες ins και επιγνοντες την του θεου ενεργειαν D. την φων. αυτων E coptt æth: την φων. c. (ειπαν, so ABDPℵ.) om ο θεος ABℵ am demid fuld copt Ath_2 Did_2 [Hil_1]: ins DEP rel 36 æth [arm] Thl-fin $Lucif_1$.—κυριε ο θεος, omg συ, 13. 40. 96: συ ει ο θεος 32. 42. 69 lect-1 syrr sah Thl-sif $Iren\text{-}int_1$. (*The variations may be explained by the difficulty found in the position of* ο θεος, *some treating it as voc, others as nom, and glossing accordy.*)

25. rec ο δια στοματος Δαβιδ του παιδος σου (*see below*), with (P) rel 40 (om του P a c d g h k m 40) Chr_1 Thl-fin Hil: ος δια πνευματος αγιου δια του στομ. λαλησας δαυειδ παιδος σου D: alii aliter, see Scholz: txt ABEℵ 13. 36. (*It seems to me that every testimony tends to confirm the more difficult and complicated readg of the text. Meyer dismisses it as a congeries of various glosses. But glosses on what? Had the rec been the original, no reason can be assigned why it should have been glossed on at all,—nor, if it had been, why the glosses should have been inserted into the text in so unusual an order of constr. See note.*) for ειπων, λαλησας D.

27. rec om εν τη πολει ταυτη (*as unnecessary, see note*), with P rel Thl: ins ABDEℵ b c d e g k o 13 vss Chr_1 Cyr_2 $Iren\text{-}int_1$ $Tert_2$ $Lucif_1$ Hil_2.—aft πολει ins σου A. σου bef παιδα D 137 Hil_2.

present on this occasion. 24] **ὁμοθ. ἦραν φων.**, not, as Meyer supposes, literally all speaking together in a known formula of prayer, but led by some *one*, and all assenting; not τὰς φωνάς, but φωνήν: see note on ch. ii. 6. **σὺ [ὁ θεὸς] ὁ ποι.: Thou art God** (or, if ὁ θεός be omitted, **He**) **who hast made**:—not *Thou O God who hast made*:—in this latter case, the first sentence would go on to the end of ver. 26, and there abruptly end, without any prayer being expressed: whereas now it is an acknowledgment that it was the *same God*, who was now *doing* these things, that had beforetime prophesied them of Christ. 25.] The text of this verse (see var. readd.) is in a very confused state. I have kept to that of the oldest MSS., adopted also by Lachmann. Though harsh in construction, their words are not *senseless*, as De Wette styles them,—στόματος Δαυεὶδ . . . being in apposition with πνεύματος ἁγίου. The rec. has been an emendation and simplification of the text, which bears, in this its original form, the solemn and stately character, in the accumulation of parallel clauses, of the rest of the prayer; cf. ver. 27. **ἵνα τί κ.τ.λ.**] cited verbatim from the LXX. The Messianic import of this Psalm has been acknowledged even by those who usually deny all such reference, e. g. De Wette. Meyer endeavours to refer it to some circumstances then present, but is not bold enough to enter into any vindication of his view. **φρυάσσω** is only found in the middle in good Greek (see Kypke, Observ. ii. p. 30 f. Meyer). φρύαγμά ἐστι τὸ ἀλόγιστον κίνημα, Athanas. in Catena. 27.] The **γάρ** implies an acknowledgment of the truth of God in the fulfilment of the prophecy: *Thou art the God who hast, &c., for* these events have happened accordingly. **ἐν τῇ πόλει ταύτῃ**, which has been excluded from the text on account of its apparent redundance, answers to ἐπὶ Σιὼν ὄρος τὸ ἅγιον αὐτοῦ, Ps. ii. 6. See also Matt. xxiii. 37; Luke xiii. 33. The parts of this verse correspond accurately to those of the prophecy just quoted. **παῖδα, servant**, as before, ch. iii. 26. Jesus, *the Servant* of

ˣἔχρισας, Ἡρώδης τε καὶ Πόντιος Πιλάτος σὺν ἔθνεσιν
καὶ ʸλαοῖς Ἰσραήλ, 28 ποιῆσαι ὅσα ἡ ᶻχείρ σου καὶ ἡ
ᵃβουλή σου ᵇπροώρισεν γενέσθαι. 29 καὶ ᶜτὰ ᶜνῦν, κύριε,
ᵈἔπιδε ἐπὶ τὰς ᵉἀπειλὰς αὐτῶν, καὶ ᶠδὸς τοῖς δούλοις σου
ᵍμετὰ ᵍπαῤῥησίας ʰπάσης ⁱλαλεῖν τὸν ⁱλόγον σου 30 ʲἐν
τῷ τὴν ᵏχεῖρά σου ᵏἐκτείνειν [σε] εἰς ˡἴασιν, καὶ σημεῖα
καὶ ᵐτέρατα γίνεσθαι ⁿδιὰ τοῦ ⁿᵒὀνόματος τοῦ ἁγίου
ᵖπαιδός σου Ἰησοῦ. 31 Καὶ ᵠδεηθέντων αὐτῶν ʳἐσαλεύθη ὁ
ˢτόπος ἐν ᾧ ᵗἦσαν ᵗσυνηγμένοι, καὶ ᵘἐπλήσθησαν ἅπαντες
τοῦ ἁγίου πνεύματος, καὶ ⁱἐλάλουν τὸν ⁱλόγον τοῦ θεοῦ
ᵍμετὰ ᵍπαῤῥησίας.

x Luke iv. 18, from Isa. lxi. 1. ch. x. 38. 2 Cor. i. 21. Heb. i. 9 (from Ps. xliv. 7) only. L.P.H.
y plur., Rom. xv. 11 reff.
z see ch. xi. 21 reff. Ps. lxxvii. 42.
a ch. ii. 23 reff.
b 1 Cor. ii. 7 reff.
c ch. v. 38. xvii. 30. xx. 32. xxvii. 22 Acts only Gen. xi. 6 Ald. Matthiæ, § 282.
d Luke i. 25 only. Ps. cxi. 8.
e ch. ix. 1 reff. f ch. ii. 4 reff. g ch. ii. 29 reff. h = ch. xx. 19 reff. i ch. xi. 19 reff. j = ch. iii. 26. Rom. xv. 13. 4 Kings v. 18. k of God, here only. Exod. vii. 5. see Matt. viii. 3. ch. xxvi. 1. l ver. 22 reff. m ch. vii. 36 reff. n ch. x. 43. 1 Cor. i. 10 only. o ch. iii. 16. viii. 12 al. p ver. 27. q absol., here only. 3 Kings viii. 33 B. Sir. xxviii. 2. r Matt. xi. 7. ch. xvi. 26. Ps. xvii. 7. s = ch. vii. 49, from Isa. lxvi. 1. t = Matt. xxii. 41. Neh. vi. 2. u ch. ii. 4 reff.

λαος E 3. 33 Thl-sif Hil$_1$ Aug$_1$.
28. om 2nd *σου* A^{1}B am^1 E-lat^1 [arm] Hil$_1$ Lucif$_1$ Aug$_1$.
29. εφιδε D [εφειδε AE]. for *απειλας*, *αγιας* D^1-gr(txt D-corr^1). **πασ.** bef *παρρ.* D-gr E vulg copt Hil$_1$ Lucif$_1$: om *πασ.* g 26. 36. 57. 137 lect-1 Syr æth [Cyr-p$_2$].
30. for *χειρα σου εκτεινειν σε*, *χ. σε εκτ.* A; *χ. εκτ. σε* B: om *σε* DE ℵ^r(see Tischdf's note) e f 13 Chr$_2$: txt Pℵ^1 rel 36 Thl (*both pronouns here and σου in ver 27 agree better with the character of the diction of the prayer*). *γενεσθαι* D^1 (txt D^3) 133 Thl-sif. syr-mg has a note that "some copies have not the word *name*."
31. *παντες* ℵ^1. rec *πν. αγιου*, om *του* (*see ch* ii. 4), with EP 13. 36 re vulg Chr$_1$: txt ABD[ℵ] am [Iren-gr]. aft *παρρ.* ins *παντι τω θελοντι π.στευειν* DE Iren$_1$[-gr and]-int (Aug$_3$).

Jehovah, is the antitype and completion of David, and of all other servants of the Lord: what is said of them only partially and hyperbolically, is said literally and entirely of Him. **28.**] There is an ellipsis in the thought between ποιῆσαι and ὅσα: ποιῆσαι, (ὡς μὲν ἐδόκει, τὴν ἰδίαν βουλήν, ὄντως δὲ) ὅσα . . . As De Wette well remarks, συνήχθησαν ποιῆσαι is used *subjectively*, 'they were collected, to do,' and then the speaker changes his ground to an *objective* one in ὅσα—(as they believed—but *really*) as many things as *Thy* hand, &c. ποιῆσαι must not be rendered, with Kuinoel, 'ita ut facerent.' It does not express the *result*, but the *intention*, of their assembling. Still worse is it to take ποιῆσαι with ἔχρισας, 'Whom Thou hast anointed, ... to do,' &c., as some have proposed: the parenthesis, as well as the whole train of thought, forbidding it. **ἡ χείρ σ. κ. ἡ βουλή**] not a ἓν διὰ δυοῖν (Kuinoel): χείρ indicates the *Power*, βουλή the *Wisdom* of God. The Wisdom decreed, the Hand performed: but the same word προώρισεν is used of both by what grammarians call *zeugma*—as in γάλα ὑμᾶς ἐπότισα, οὐ βρῶμα, 1 Cor. iii. 2. See Winer, edn. 6, § 66. 2, e. **30.**] **ἐν τῷ**, see ref. ch. iii. and note there: **In Thy stretching forth** (while Thou stretchest forth) **Thine hand for** (εἰς, of the purpose) **healing, and that signs and wonders may come to pass by means of the Name of Thy Holy Servant Jesus.** **31.**] As the first outpouring of the Spirit, so this special one in answer to prayer, was testified by an outward and visible sign: but not by the *same* sign,—for that first baptism by the Holy Ghost, the great fulfilment of the promise, was not to be repeated. The rationalist Commentators have done good service by pointing out parallel cases, in profane writers, of *supposed* tokens of the divine presence. Virg. Æn. iii. 89. Ovid, Met. xv. 672. Schöttgen, Hor. Hebr. in loc., produces similar notices from the Rabbinical writings.

It was on every ground probable that the token of the especial presence of God would be some phænomenon which would be *recognized by those present as such.* Besides which, the idea was not derived from profane sources, but from the Scriptures: see Ps. xxix. 8; Isa. ii. 19, 21; xiii. 13; Ezek. xxxviii. 19 (especially); Joel iii. 16; Hagg. ii. 6, 7. **ἐπλήσθησαν**, with a fresh and renewed outpouring. **τοῦ ἁγ. πν.** is *personal:* **they were all filled with** ***the Holy Spirit:***

v here only. 2 Chron. xxx. 12.
w Phil. i. 27 only. 1 Chron. xii. 38.
x Matt. xxvii. 14. John i. 3. Rom. iii. 10 (2 Cor. vi. 5 v. r.). 2 Kings xiii. 30.
y neut. plu. part. w. dat., Luke viii. 3. xii. 15 only. Gen. xxxi. 18 Ed-vat(B def.) Ald. Job xx. 29 Bℵ Ald. compl. only. see ch. iii. 6 reff.

ABDE Pℵ a b c d f g h k l m o 13

32 Τοῦ δὲ πλήθους τῶν πιστευσάντων ἦν [v] καρδία
καὶ [w] ψυχὴ [vw] μία, καὶ [x] οὐδὲ εἷς τὶ τῶν [y] ὑπαρχόντων
αὐτῷ ἔλεγεν [z] ἴδιον εἶναι, ἀλλ' ἦν αὐτοῖς ἅπαντα [a] κοινά.
33 καὶ [b] δυνάμει μεγάλῃ [c] ἀπεδίδουν τὸ [d] μαρτύριον οἱ ἀπόστολοι τῆς [e] ἀναστάσεως τοῦ κυρίου Ἰησοῦ, [f] χάρις τε
μεγάλη ἦν [g] ἐπὶ πάντας αὐτούς. 34 οὐδὲ γὰρ [h] ἐνδεής τις
ὑπῆρχεν ἐν αὐτοῖς· ὅσοι γὰρ [i] κτήτορες [j] χωρίων ἢ οἰ-
κιῶν ὑπῆρχον, πωλοῦντες ἔφερον τὰς [k] τιμὰς τῶν [l] πιπρα-

z = John x. 3, 4, 12. a = ch. ii. 44 reff. b = ch. i. 8 reff. c = here only. d = 1 Cor. i. 6 reff. see 1 Cor. ii. 1. = μαρτυρία, John i. 7 and passim. e ch. i. 22 reff. f = Luke ii. 40 al. see note, and ch. ii. 47. g = Luke x. 6. [Rom. iii. 22.] 1 Pet. iv. 14. h here only. Deut. xv. 4, 7. i here only †. j ch. i. 18 reff. k = ch. v. 2, 3. vii. 16. Matt. xxvii. 6, 9 al. Isa. lv. 1. l Matt. xiii. 46. xviii. 25. xxvi. 9 ||. ch. ii. 45. v. 4. Rom. vii. 14 only. Exod. xxii. 3.

32. rec ins η bef καρδια, with D^3EP rel [coptt] $Orig_2$ Chr_3 Bas_2 [Cyr-p_4] $Leont_1$ Thl: om ABD^1ℵ [arm] $Orig_2$ (Ath Thdrt) Euthal Bas_3 [Cyr_1]. rec ins η bef ψυχη, with EP rel 36 $Orig_2$ Chr_3 Bas_2 [Cyr-p_4]: om ABDℵ [coptt arm] $Orig_2$ Euthal Bas_3 [Cyr_1]. aft μια ins και ουκ ην διακρισις εν αυτοις ουδεμια D(E) $Cypr_2$ $Zeno_1$ $Ambr_1$.—for διακ., χωρισμος, and for ουδ., τις E. om [2nd] και E. ουδεις D e l. om τι D[-gr]. **αυτου** D: αυτων P b^2 f g k l^1 m 40: om H^r 18. 36. 133. [ελεγον B^1.] **αλλα** D. παντα BD: txt AE[P]ℵ 13 rel 36.

33. rec μεγ. bef δυν., with EP rel Thl: txt ABDℵ a c h vulg Chr_1 Iren-int_1 Ors_1 Aug_1. οι αποστ. bef το μαρτ. AE a g h k o Thl-sif Ors_1 Aug_1. ins (aft ιησου) χριστου (A)DE(ℵ) Syr copt æth-rom arm Chr_1: [bef, copt:] om BP [rel] syr.—ιῡ χῡ bef του κῡ Aℵ 36 [aft κυρ. ins ημων 36 vulg(not am fuld demid) copt].—for κῡ ιῡ, ιῡ χῡ e Syr.—(*Very usual varr where the name ιησ. or χρ. occurs: the canon being in such cases, that* the simplest well-supported form of expression *was the genuine text.*)—τ. κ. ι. bef τ. αναστ. B.

34. for υπηρχεν, ην (*corrn to avoid tautology*) A(B)ℵ Fr-coisl a h Cyr_1: txt DEP rel.—ην bef τις B. οσοι γαρ κτητ. ησαν χωρ. η οικων υπηρχον (*combination*) D^1: om υπηρχ. D-corr (and lat) $ℵ^1$. D has πωλουντες. αι φεροντες (αιφερον (εφ. D^8) τας D^2 and lat, prefg και) τιμας των πιπρασκο . . των (-σκομενων D^2 and lat).

the *meaning* being the same with πν. ἁγ., the *influence of the Holy Spirit*,—but the form of expression varied. See ch. i. 8; ii. 33, 38; ix. 31; x. 45.

32—37.] THE STATE OF THE CHURCH AT THIS TIME. This passage forms the conclusion of this division of the history and the transition to ch. v. **32. τῶν πιστευσάντων**] Much the same meaning as τῶν πιστευόντων, but with reference to their having *become converts*, and specially to those mentioned in ver. 4,—though the description is general. 'Ubi regnum habet fides, animos ita conciliat ut omnes idem velint et nolint. Hinc enim discordiæ, quod non regimur eodem Christi Spiritu.' Calvin. On the community of goods, see note at ch. ii. 45. We have the view there taken strikingly confirmed here by the expressions used. **No one called** (reckoned) **any thing of his goods** (which were still τὰ ὑπάρχοντα αὐτῷ, not alienated) **(to be) his own.** (**ἔλεγεν**, *dicebat*: hoc ipso præsupponitur *proprietatem* possessionis non plane fuisse deletam. Bengel.) **33.**] The Apostles were the specially appointed witnesses of the Resurrection, ch. i. 22: and this their testimony they gave *with power*, i. e. with a special gift of the Holy Spirit to enforce and illustrate, to persuade and dispute on, those facts of which their own experience (see ver. 20) informed them. That the Spirit did not inspire them with unbroken uniformity in *matters of fact*, our present Gospels, the remnants to us of this very testimony, sufficiently witness. Nor was this necessary: each man reported what he had heard and seen;—and it was in the *manner* of delivering this report that the great power of the Spirit was shewn. See, on the whole subject, Prolegg. Vol. I. i. § iii. 5 ff. **χάρις**, better **grace**, i. e. from God, than *favour*, i. e. from the people, which would hardly be so absolutely designated. **34.**] **γάρ** gives a proof of God's grace working in them, in that they imparted their goods to the poor: see especially 2 Cor. viii. 7. **πιπρασκομένων, the things which were being sold**:—the process of selling, as regarded the whole church, yet going on, though completed in individual cases; in the places cited by Wetst. from Demosth. and Appian the pres. retains its proper force, as here. In Appian, B. Civ. v. p. 1088, the expression is, τιμὰς τῶν ἔτι

σκομένων 35 καὶ ἐτίθουν [m] παρὰ τοὺς πόδας τῶν ἀποστόλων, [n] διεδίδετο δὲ ἑκάστῳ [o] καθότι ἄν τις [o] χρείαν
εἶχεν. 36 Ἰωσὴφ δὲ ὁ [p] ἐπικληθεὶς Βαρνάβας [q] ἀπὸ τῶν
ἀποστόλων, ὅ ἐστιν [r] μεθερμηνευόμενον [s] υἱὸς [t] παρακλήσεως, Λευείτης, Κύπριος τῷ [u] γένει, 37 [v] ὑπάρχοντος αὐτῷ
[w] ἀγροῦ [x] πωλήσας ἤνεγκεν τὸ [y] χρῆμα καὶ ἔθηκεν [m] παρὰ
τοὺς πόδας τῶν ἀποστόλων. V. 1 Ἀνὴρ δέ τις Ἀνανίας
ὀνόματι σὺν Σαπφείρῃ τῇ γυναικὶ αὐτοῦ [x] ἐπώλησεν
[z] κτῆμα, 2 καὶ [a] ἐνοσφίσατο ἀπὸ τῆς [b] τιμῆς, [c] συνειδυίης
καὶ τῆς γυναικός, καὶ ἐνέγκας [d] μέρος τὶ [e] παρὰ τοὺς
πόδας τῶν ἀποστόλων ἔθηκεν. 3 εἶπεν δὲ ὁ Πέτρος

m Matt. xv. 30. ch. v. 2. vii. 58. 4 Kings iv. 37 Ald.
n Luke xi. 22. xviii. 22. John vi. 11 only. Josh. xiii. 6.
o ch. ii. 45 (reff.).
p ch. i. 23 reff.
q ch. ii. 22 reff.
r Matt. i. 23. Mark v. 41. xv. 22, 34. John i. (39 v. r.) 42. ch. xiii. 8 only +. Sir. prol. fin.
s = Mark iii. 17. Luke x. 6. xvi. 8. 1 Thess. v. 5 al. 2 Kings xiii. 28.
t = ch. xiii. 15. xv. 31. 2 Macc. xv. 11.
u = ch. xviii. 2 reff.
v = ch. iii. 6 reff.
w here only, exc. gospp. Mt. Mk. L. = Matt. xiii. 24, 44 al. Gen. xxiii. 9.
x 1 Cor. x. 25 reff.
y sing., here only. plur. Mark x. 23, 24 ‖ L. ch. viii. 18, 20. xxiv. 26 only. 2 Chron. i. 11, 12.
z ch. ii. 45 reff.
a Titus ii. 10 only. Josh. vii. 1. 2 Macc. iv. 32 only.
b = ch. iv. 34 reff.
c = 1 Cor. iv. 4 (reff.) only. Job xxvii. 6.
d = John xix. 23 al. Gen. xlvii. 24.
e ch. iv. 35, 37.

35. (διεδιδετο, so AB[1]DEℵ.) ins ενι bef εκαστω D. καθο (for καθοτι) and om αν P m 73.

36. rec ιωσης (*see note, ch* i. 23), with P 13 rel syr sah Chr_1 Thl : txt ABDEℵ 36. 40 vulg copt Syr æth arm Chr_1 $Epiph_1$. rec **υπο**, with D rel 36 Chr : txt ABEPℵ a d g h l m 40 H^r Thl. ερμηνευομενον B : om c^2. κυπρ. bef λευειτης D.

37. for αγρου, χωριον D^2(-ιον D^1). for παρα, προς Eℵ 36 Thl-sif.

CHAP. V. 1. εν αυτω δε τω καιρω ανηρ (*beginning of ecclesiastical portion*) E. ονομ. bef αναν. AD b c m vulg : txt BEPℵ [rel arm] Chr. σαπφειρα (*corrn*) BD a b^2 g h l o Chr_1 : σαφφυρα D^1(-ιρα D-corr) : σαμπφιρι 13 : σαμφιρη $ℵ^3$(παμφιρη $ℵ^1$) : txt A E(-φφιρη) P k m.

2. om και $ℵ^1$(eadem manu suppletum videtur). for απο, εκ D. rec συνειδυιας (*corrn*), with DP rel : txt ABEℵ. rec aft γυν. ins αυτου, with EP rel Thl : om AB D-gr ℵ 13 arm Chr_1. εθετο D.

3. aft ειπεν δε ins προς αυτον E; aft πετρος c; simly vulg-ms(Matthäi) syr-w-ast

πιπρασκομένων. 35.] **παρὰ τοὺς πόδας,**—not a Hebraism for the whole person—but *literal.* So Cicero pro Flacco, c. 28, 'Ante pedes Prætoris in foro expensum estauri pondo centum.' (Rosenm.) Wetstein gives several other examples. The Apostles, like the Prætor, probably sat upon a raised seat, on the step of which, at their feet, the money was laid, in token of reverence. 36.] Barnabas, בַּר נְבוּאָה, is υἱὸς προφητείας—and the interpretation has been generally made good by taking παράκλησις as included in προφητεία, and as in the sense of exhortation: see ch. xi. 23. Λευείτης] The Levites might possess land at all times within the precincts of the Levitical cities: such was the case, e. g., in Jer. xxxii. 7. At the division of the kingdoms, the priests and Levites all resorted to Rehoboam in Judah (and Benjamin), 2 Chron. xi. 13; from that time probably, but certainly after the captivity, when the Mosaic division of the land was no longer accurately observed, the possession of land by Levites seems to have been allowed. The whole subject is involved in some uncertainty: cf. Levit. xxv. 32 ff.; Num. xxxv. 1—8; Deut. xii. 12; xviii. 8, al.

Κύπριος] For the state of Cyprus at this time, see notes on ch. xi. 19; xiii. 4—7. 37. **χρῆμα**] Very unusual in this sense. See Herod. iii. 38, ἐπὶ πόσῳ ἂν χρήματι βουλοίατο τοὺς πατέρας ἀποθνήσκοντας ἀποσιτέεσθαι, and other examples in Wetstein.

CHAP. V. 1—11.] THE HISTORY OF ANANIAS AND SAPPHIRA. This incident, though naturally connected with the end of the last chapter, forms an important independent narrative. 1.] **Ἀνανίας**, עֲנָנְיָה, Neh. iii. 23, or חֲנַנְיָה, Dan. i. 6, in LXX: also 1 Chron. iii. 21, al. = *The cloud of God,* or *The mercy of God.* **Σαπφείρῃ**, perhaps from the Greek σάπφειρος, sapphire, or from the Syriac שפירא, beautiful (Grot.).

The crime of these two is well described by Meyer: 'By the sale of their field, and the bringing in of the money they in fact professed to give the *whole price* as a gift of brotherly love to the common stock: but their aim was to get for themselves the credit of holy love and zeal by *one portion* of the price, whereas they had selfishly kept back the other portion for themselves. They wished to serve *two* masters, but to appear to serve only *One.*' 3.] The

f John xvi. 6. see Eccles. ix. 3.
g Matt. v. 11 al. constr., here only. Deut. xxxiii. 29.
h = ch. i. 18 reff.
i = here only. 1 Macc. xv. 7.
k ch. iv. 34 reff.
l ch. i. 7.
m = ver. 9. Luke ii. 49 only. 2 Kings xix. 22. see John xiv. 22.

ABDE Pℵ a b c d f g h k l m o 13

Ἀνανία, διὰ τί [f] ἐπλήρωσεν ὁ Σατανᾶς τὴν καρδίαν σου
[g] ψεύσασθαί σε τὸ πνεῦμα τὸ ἅγιον καὶ [a] νοσφίσασθαί [σε]
ἀπὸ τῆς [b] τιμῆς τοῦ [h] χωρίου; 4 οὐχὶ [i] μένον σοὶ ἔμενεν, καὶ
[k] πραθὲν [l] ἐν τῇ σῇ [l] ἐξουσίᾳ ὑπῆρχεν; [m] τί ὅτι [n] ἔθου ἐν τῇ
καρδίᾳ σου τὸ πρᾶγμα τοῦτο; οὐκ [o] ἐψεύσω ἀνθρώποις,
ἀλλὰ τῷ θεῷ. 5 ἀκούων δὲ ὁ Ἀνανίας τοὺς λόγους
τούτους πεσὼν [p] ἐξέψυξεν. καὶ [q] ἐγένετο φόβος μέγας
ἐπὶ πάντας τοὺς ἀκούοντας. 6 [r] ἀναστάντες δὲ οἱ [s] νεώ-

n Luke ix. 44. xxi. 14. Hag. ii. 19. see ch. i. 7. o constr., here only. Josh. xxiv. 27. 2 Kings xxii. 45. Ps. lxxvii. 36. p ver. 10. ch. xii. 23 only. Judg. iv. 21 A Ald. compl. Ezek. xxi. 7 only. q = ver. 11. Luke i. 65. Gen. xxxv. 5. see ch. ii. 43. r = ch. viii. 26, 27 reff. s = John xxi. 18. 1 Tim. v. 1, 2 al. οἱ ν., Tit. ii. 6. Jer. xiv. 3.

[Syr coptt æth] Thl. rec om *ο*, with DP rel: ins ABEℵ b m 13 Chr$_1$. for *ανανια*, *προς ανανιαν* D vulg-mss(Lachmann). for *επληρ.*, *επηρωσεν* ℵ^1. *το αγ. πν.* D-gr. rec om 2nd *σε*, with ABEℵ c k l o 36: ins DP rel 38. 42. 95-6. 113-77 sah Leont$_1$. (*I have inserted it doubtfully, as more in character, and very likely to have been omitted as unnecessary.*)

4. *εμενον* (but corrd) ℵ^1: *μεσον* D^1-gr(txt D^2). om *εν* (*confounded with last syllable of* *πραθεν*) P. om *ση* D[-gr]. for *το πρ. τουτο*, *ποιησαι* (ins *το* D^2) *πονηρον τουτο* D sah: *facere dolose rem istam* D-lat. *εψευσου* D^1(txt D^2).

5. *ακουσας δε* D-gr: *και ευθεως ακουων* E. rec om *ο*, with D rel 36 Orig Bas$_1$: ins ABEPℵ a b d f g h k m o Chr$_1$ Thl. ins *παραχρημα* bef *πεσων* D. rec aft *ακουοντας* ins *ταυτα* (*see ver* 11), with EPℵ^3 rel syr [(æth-rom) arm Bas$_1$] Chr$_1$ Thl: om ABDℵ^1 vulg Syr coptt æth-pl Orig$_1$ Lucif$_1$.

6. aft *αναστ. δε* ins *παραχρημα* E.

διὰ τί implies the power of resistance to Satan—**Why hast thou allowed Satan to fill, &c.?** **4.**] **While it remained, did it not remain thine own?** i. e. was it not in thine absolute power? **and when sold, was it not** (i. e. the price of it) **in thine own power,** to do with it what seemed good to thee? **τί ὅτι,** i. e. *τί ἐστιν ὅτι*: see reff. **ἔθου ἐν τ. καρδ.,** = שׂוּם עַל־לֵב, Dan. i. 8; Mal. ii. 2. Satan suggested the lie, which Ananias ought to have repelled: instead of that, *he put it in his heart,*—placed it there where the springs of action are, and it passed out into an act. **οὐκ ἐψ. ἀνθ., ἀλλὰ τ. θ.**] This *οὐκ, ἀλλά*, is not always an absolute and exclusive negation and assertion, see Mark ix. 37; John xii. 44. But here it seems to be so, and to imply, 'Thine attempt to deceive was not to deceive *us,* men; but to deceive the Holy Ghost,—God, abiding in His church, and in us its appointed superintendents.' This verse is of weighty doctrinal import, as proving the Deity of the Holy Spirit; unless it be held, that the Holy Spirit whom (ver. 3) Ananias attempted to deceive, and God to whom he lied, are *different.* 'Hæc est sententia: Ananias mentitus est Deo et ejus Spiritui, non hominibus et Petro. Aude si potes, Sociniane, ita dicere: mentitus est non Spiritui Sancto et Petro, sed Deo.' Bengel. **5.**] The deaths of Ananias and Sapphira were beyond question *supernaturally inflicted* by Peter, speaking in the power of the Holy Spirit. This is the only honest interpretation of the incident. Many, however, and among them even Neander, attempt to account for them on natural grounds,—from their *horror at detection, and at the solemn words of Peter.* But, in addition to all other objections against this (see on *ἐξοίσουσιν*, ver. 9),—it would make man and wife *of the same temperament,* which would be very unlikely. We surely need not require any *justification* for this judicial sentence of the Apostle, filling as he did at this time the highest place in the church, and acting under the immediate prompting of the Holy Spirit. If such, however, be sought, we may remember that this was the first attempt made by Satan to obtain, by hypocrisy, a footing among Christ's flock: and that however, for wise reasons, this may since then have been permitted, it was absolutely necessary in the infancy of the church, that such attempt should be at once, and with severity, defeated. Bengel remarks: 'Quod gravitati pœnæ in corpore accessit, in anima *potuit* decedere.' **κ. ἐγέν. φόβ.** *κ.τ.λ.*] The *ἀκούοντες* can hardly be (Meyer) those *present,* who (De W.) not only *heard,* but saw: the remark is proleptical, and = that in ver. 11. **6.**] Were **οἱ νεώτεροι** *a class in the congregation* accustomed to perform such services,—or merely the younger men, from whom they would na-

τεροι [t] συνεστειλαν αὐτὸν καὶ [u] ἐξενέγκαντες [v] ἔθαψαν.
7 ἐγένετο δε, [w] ὡς ὡρῶν τριῶν [x] διάστημα, καὶ ἡ γυνὴ
αὐτοῦ μὴ εἰδυῖα το γεγονὸς εἰςῆλθεν. 8 [y] ἀπεκρίθη δὲ πρὸς
αὐτὴν Πέτρος Εἰπέ μοι [z] εἰ [a] τοσούτου τὸ [b] χωρίον
[c] ἀπέδοσθε; ἡ δὲ εἶπεν Ναὶ [a] τοσούτου. 9 ὁ δὲ Πέτρος
πρὸς αὐτὴν [d] Τί ὅτι [e] συνεφωνήθη [f] ὑμῖν [g] πειράσαι τὸ
[h] πνεῦμα [h] κυρίου; ἰδοὺ οἱ πόδες τῶν [v] θαψάντων τὸν
ἄνδρα σου [i] ἐπὶ τῇ θύρᾳ, καὶ [j] ἐξοίσουσίν σε. 10 [k] ἔπεσεν δὲ

t — here only +. Eur. Troad. 376. (1 Cor vii. 29 only. Sir. iv. 31.)
u = vv. 9, 10 (15. Mark viii. 23. Luke xv. 22. 1 Tim. vi. 7. Heb. vi. 8) only. see Luke vii. 12.
v 1 Cor. xv. 4 reff.
w = ver. 36 al.
x here only ‡. of space, Gen. xxxii. 16 al.
y = ch. iii. 12. Matt. xi. 25 al. Deut. xxvi. 5.
z = Matt. xxvi. 63. Mark xv. 44.
a gen. of price, Matt. x. 29. xxvi. 9. Rev. vi. 6. 4 Kings vii. 1.
b ver. 3.
c = ch. vii. 9. Heb. xii. 16 only. Gen. xxv. 33.
d ver. 4 reff.
e Matt. xviii. 19. xx. 2, 13. Luke v. 36. ch. xv. 15 only. 4 Kings xii. 8. impers., here only.
f dat., Matt. v. 21? James iii. 18. Winer, edn. 6, § 31. 10.
g 1 Cor. x. 9 reff. (= ἐκπ. ib.)
h 2 Cor. iii. 17. see Luke iv. 18, from Isa. lxi. 1.
i = ch. iii. 10, 11 reff.
j ver. 6 reff.
k Mark v. 22. John xi. 32. Rev. i. 17 only.

7. εως ℵ[1]. διαστεμα D.

8. for απεκρ., ειπεν D vulg[(not am &c) coptt æth Lucif$_1$].—προς ην ο πετρος εφη E. rec (for προς αυτην) αυτη, with P rel vulg Chr$_1$ Thl: om b[1]: txt ABDℵ d e m 36. 40 (syr-w-ast) Orig Lucif. rec ins ο bef πετρος, with DEP rel Orig$_1$ Chr: om ABℵ d 36. for ειπε μοι ει, επερωτησω σε ει αρα D-gr. το χωριον bef 1st τοσουτου D-gr sah. for 2nd δε, δη D[1](txt D-corr[1]).

9. rec aft πετρ. ins ειπε, with AP rel 36 [vss]: ειπεν δε πετρ. E: txt BDℵ vulg. om προς D[1]-gr(ins D[3]). aft τι ins ουν ℵ[1](ℵ[3] disapproving). συνεφωνησεν D. ins του bef κυρ. D. εισταντι επι τη θ. E. ταις θυραις A.

10. και επ. D Syr [æth] Lucif$_1$.

turally be expected? Meyer and Olshausen (also Mosh. and Kuin.) maintain the former; Neander and De W. the latter. We can hardly assume, as yet, any such official distinctions in the congregation as would mark off οἱ νεώτεροι from οἱ πρεσβύτεροι, which latter are first officially mentioned ch. xi. 30. Besides which, we have no such ecclesiastical class as οἱ νεώτεροι. And the use of **οἱ νεανίσκοι** in ver. 10, as applying to these same persons, seems to decide that they were *merely the younger members* of the church, acting perhaps in accordance with Jewish custom,—perhaps also on some hint given by Peter. **συνέστειλαν**] So περιστέλλω, Ezek. xxix. 5; Tobit xii. 13; Sir. xxxviii. 16, **wrapped the body up**,—probably in their own mantles, taken off in preparing to carry him out. The context will not permit any more careful enfolding of the body to be understood. The speedy burial of the dead, practised among the later Jews, was unknown in earlier times, see Gen. xxiii. It was grounded on Num. xix. 11 ff. The practice was to bury before sunset of the same day. The *immediate* burial in this case adds to the probability that the young men obeyed an intimation from the Apostle. **7.**] The construction is, ἐγένετο δέ, . . . καί, **It happened, that**: and ὡς ὡ. τ. διάστ. is parenthetical, not the nom. to ἐγένετο. See a precisely similar construction, Luke ix. 28: and Winer, edn. 6, § 62. 2. **8.**] **ἀπεκρ.**, perhaps *to her salutation*: or, it may be, to her manner, challenging a reply. The word must at any rate be taken as implying *some* previous communication, to which an answer was to be given. **τοσούτ.**, naming the sum: or perhaps pointing to the money lying at his feet. The sense *tantilli* (Born.) is *implied* of course, but not expressed by τοσούτου. No stress on ἀπέδοσθε as referring to the smallness of price: it is the ordinary word for selling, see reff.

9.] To *try the omniscience* of the Spirit then visibly dwelling in the Apostles and the church, was, in the highest sense, *to tempt the Spirit of God*. It was a saying in their hearts 'There is no Holy Spirit:' and certainly approached very closely to a sin against the Holy Ghost. Peter characterizes the sin more solemnly this second time, because by the wife's answer it was now proved to be no *individual lie* of a bad and covetous man, but a *preconcerted scheme* to deceive God. **οἱ πόδες**] Not that Peter heard (Olsh.) the tread of the young men outside (they were probably barefooted), but it is an expression common in the poetical or lively description of the Hebrews, and indeed of all nations (see Isa. lii. 7; Nah. i. 15; Rom. x. 15; Eurip. Hippol. 656; Soph. Œd. Col. 890, al. freq.), making the member whereby the person acts, the actor. I take the words to mean, that the time was just at hand for their return: see James v. 9. The space of three hours was not too long: they would have to carry the corpse to the burying-ground, at a considerable distance from the city (Lightf.),

[l] παραχρῆμα [k] πρὸς τοὺς [k] πόδας αὐτοῦ καὶ [m] ἐξέψυχεν· εἰςελθόντες δὲ οἱ [n] νεανίσκοι εὗρον αὐτὴν νεκρὰν καὶ [j] ἐξενέγκαντες [v] ἔθαψαν [o] πρὸς τὸν ἄνδρα αὐτῆς. 11 καὶ [p] ἐγέ-
νετο φόβος μέγας ἐφ᾽ ὅλην τὴν ἐκκλησίαν καὶ ἐπὶ πάντας
τοὺς ἀκούοντας ταῦτα.
12 [q] Διὰ δὲ τῶν χειρῶν τῶν ἀποστόλων ἐγίνετο σημεῖα
καὶ [r] τέρατα πολλὰ ἐν τῷ λαῷ. καὶ ἦσαν [s] ὁμοθυμαδὸν
ἅπαντες ἐν τῇ [t] στοᾷ Σολομῶνος· 13 τῶν δὲ [u] λοιπῶν
οὐδεὶς ἐτόλμα [v] κολλᾶσθαι αὐτοῖς, ἀλλ᾽ [w] ἐμεγάλυνεν αὐτοὺς ὁ λαός· 14 [x] μᾶλλον δὲ [y] προςετίθεντο [z] πιστεύοντες
τῷ κυρίῳ, [a] πλήθη ἀνδρῶν τε καὶ γυναικῶν· 15 ὥςτε [b] κατὰ
τὰς [c] πλατείας [d] ἐκφέρειν τοὺς ἀσθενεῖς καὶ [d] τιθέναι [e] ἐπὶ
[f] κλιναρίων καὶ [g] κραβάττων, ἵνα ἐρχομένου Πέτρου [h] κἂν

ABDE Pℵabc dfgh klmo 13

l ch. iii. 7 reff.
m ver. 5 reff.
n Matt. xix. 20, 22. Mark xiv. 51 (bis). xvi. 5. Luke vii. 14. ch. ii. 17. 1 John ii. 13, 14 only. Gen. xiv. 24.
o = Matt. iii. 16. Gal. i. 18.
p ver. 5.
q ch. xi. 30 reff.
r ch. vii. 36 reff.
s ch. i. 14 reff.
t ch. iii. 11 reff.
u Eph. ii. 3. 1 Thess. iv. 13. v. 6.
v = ch. ix. 26. x. 28. xvii. 34. 1 Cor. vi. 16, 17. Ruth ii. 8.
w = ch. x. 46 reff.
x = Luke v. 15. John xix. 8. ch. ix. 22 al.
y = ch. ii. 41 reff.
z absol., ch. iv. 32 al. fr.
a plur., here only. Ps. cxlvi. 4.
b = Luke x. 32 al.
c Luke xiv. 21. Rev. xxi. 21 al. Ezek. xxviii. 23.
d ver. 6 reff.
e = Rev. x. 2. Luke viii. 16.
f here only †. see Luke v. 19, 24.
g Mark ii. 4, &c. vi. 55. John v. 8, &c. ch. ix. 33 only †.
h = Mark v. 28. vi. 56. 2 Cor. xi. 16.

rec (for προς) παρα (*see ch* iv. 35, 37, v. 2), with EP rel [Chr_1] $Lucif_1$: επι 26. 37 : υπο 2: txt ABDℵ $Orig_1$, πρ. τ. π. αποστολου syr.—for πρ. τ. π., ενωπιον 15-8. 36. ευραν A : ηυραν E : txt BDPℵ rel [Chr]. συνστειλαντες εξηνεγκαν και D-gr.

11. om επι A sah. ακουοντες D, κατοικουντας P.

12. for δε, τε B Syr æth. Steph εγενετο, with h 4. 13-4-5. 78. 127-80 lect-12 $Cyr\text{-}jer_3$ Thl : txt ABDE[P]ℵ rel 36 Chr $Lucif_1$. rec εν τω λαω bef πολλα, with P rel 36 Chr Thl : om πολλα k 133 lect-12 : txt ABDEℵ m o 13 vulg Syr Lucif. for απαντες, παντες ABE 1 : txt DPℵ rel Chr : add συνηγμενοι Syr copt ; εν τω ιερω D 42 sah æth ; εν τω ναω συνηγμενοι E. aft εν τη στ. ins τη D 42. rec σολομωντος, with A k o [(13)] 36 Chr Thl : σαλομωντος ℵ : txt BDEP rel.

13. και ουδεις των λοιπων D æth. ουθεις B.

14. ins οι bef πιστ. A 13.

15. for κατα, και εις ABD^5ℵ k 13. 36. 40 ; και εν ταις πλατιες E : om æth : txt D^1P, none of the vss have και. om τας D^1. aft ασθεν. ins αυτων D. aft τιθ. ins ενπροσθεν αυτων E. rec κλινων (*corrn to more usual word*), with E[P] rel Chr Thdrt : txt ABDℵ rel Cyr-jer.—pref των A. (κραβαττων, so AB^1Dℵ.)

and when there, to dig a grave, and bury it.
ἐξοίσουσιν] This word, spoken *before her death, decisively proves* that death to have been not a *result* merely of her detection, but a judicial infliction. **10.**] **εἰςελθόντες, when they came in**: not implying that they immediately entered, but leaving room for some interval of time : see above.

12—16.] Progress of the Faith; miraculous power and dignity of the Apostles. **12.**] **δέ** is merely *transitional*, and does not imply any contrast to the φόβος just mentioned, q. d. 'notwithstanding this fear, the Apostles went on working, &c.' See ch. ii. 43.
ἅπαντες, the Apostles only, not *all the Christians*. It does not follow, from πάντες referring to *all the believers* in ch. ii. 1 (see note there), that ἅπαντες necessarily refers to the same here also. The Apostles are *the subject of the paragraph* : and it is to set forth *their* unanimity and dignity that the description is given. They are represented as distinct from all others, believers and unbelievers (both which I take to be included under the term οἱ λοιποί) : and the Jewish people itself magnified them. The further connexion see on ver. 14.
στ. Σολ.] See ch. iii. 11; John x. 23, note. **13.**] **τῶν λοιπῶν, all else**, whether believers or not : none dared to *join himself to* (see reff.), as being one of, or equal to, them : **but** (so far was this from being the case that) **the very people** (multitude) **magnified them.** **14.**] **And** (not parenthetical, but continuing the description of the dignity of the Apostles) the result of this was **that believers were the more added to the Lord** (not πιστ. τῷ κυρίῳ, but προσετ. τῷ κυρ., as decided by ch. xi. 24), **multitudes of men and women.** **15.**] **ὥςτε** now takes up afresh the main subject of vv. 12 and 13, the glorification of the apostolic office, **insomuch, that . . . . .** It is connected not only with ἐμεγάλυνεν αὐτ. ὁ λ., but also

ἡ [i] σκιὰ [k] ἐπισκιάσῃ τινὶ αὐτῶν.
16 [l] συνήρχετο δὲ καὶ τὸ
πλῆθος τῶν [m] πέριξ πόλεων Ἱερουσαλήμ, φέροντες ἀσθενεῖς
καὶ [n] ὀχλουμένους ὑπὸ [o] πνευμάτων [op] ἀκαθάρτων, [q] οἵτινες
ἐθεραπεύοντο ἅπαντες.
17 [r] Ἀναστὰς δὲ ὁ ἀρχιερεὺς καὶ πάντες οἱ σὺν αὐτῷ,
ἡ οὖσα [s] αἵρεσις τῶν Σαδδουκαίων, [tu] ἐπλήσθησαν [u] ζήλου

i Matt. iv. 16. Mark iv. 32. Luke i. 79. Col. ii. 17. Heb. viii. 5. x. 1 only. Judg. ix. 36.
k and constr., Mark ix. 7 (acc., ‖ Mt. L.). Luke i. 35 only. Ps. xc. 4.
l ch. i. 6 reff.

m here only †. Jos. B. J. ii. 19. 1. n here (Luke vi. 18 rec.) only †. Tobit vi. 7 (not ℵ). o Matt. x. 1 al. fr. in gospp. Rev. xvi. 13. xviii. 2. Zech. xiii. 2. p ch. x. 14 reff. q = ch. x. 41 reff. r ch. viii. 26, 27 reff. s ch. xv. 5. xxiv. 5, 14. xxvi. 5. xxviii. 22. 1 Cor. xi. 19. Gal. v. 20. 2 Pet. ii. 1 only ‡. Jos. Antt. xiii. 5. 9. see Lev. xxii. 18. t = ch. iii. 10 reff. u ch. xiii. 45 (reff.).

aft *σκ.* ins *αυτου* E 33 vulg [arm] Thdrt₁ Thl-fin. *επισκιασει* B [m] 13. 58. 133 Thl-fin. *αυτω* ℵ[1]. aft *αυτων* add *απηλλασσοντο γαρ απο πασης ασθενιας ως ειχεν εκαστος αυτων* D; *και ρυσθωσιν απο πασης ασθενιας ης ειχον* E; *et liberarentur ab infirmitatibus suis* vulg(not fuld) Lucif.—*liberabantur* am Lucif; *ab infirmitate* [Lucif, and] (omg *s.*) am demid.

16. *διο συνηρ.* E. om *και*(ins D[2]) *το* D[1]. for *περιξ*, *περι* D[1](txt D[5](?)). rec ins *εις* bef *ιερουσ.*, with DEP rel 36 demid [arm] Chr: *circa* syr coptt [æth]: om ABℵ k vulg Lucif.—"from the other cities round about Jer" Syr (Etheridge). for *υπο*, *απο* D. for *οιτινες*, *και* D-gr 38. 113 sah Lucif₁. *ειωντο παντες* D.

17. for *αναστ. δε*, *και ταυτα βλεπων αναστ.* E: om Syr. *ζηλους* B[1].

with ver. 12. **κατὰ τὰς πλ.**] **down the streets,** i. e. *in the line of the streets,*—see Winer, edn. 6, § 49, d. **κλιν. κ. κραβ.**] Kuinoel's distinction, that the latter is a poor and humble bed, the former a couch of richer character, appears to be unfounded. (So also Bengel.) **Πέτρου**] As the greatest, in pre-eminence and spiritual energizing, of the Apostles. Now especially was fulfilled to him the promise of Matt. xvi. 18 (see note there):—and even the shadow of the *Rock* (Isa. xxxii. 2, Heb., and E.V., spoken primarily of His divine Master) was sought for. We need find no stumbling-block in the fact of Peter's *shadow* having been believed to be the medium (or, as is surely implied, *having been* the medium) of working miracles. Cannot the 'Creator Spirit' work with any instruments, or with none, as pleases Him? And what is a hand or a voice, more than a shadow, except that the analogy of the ordinary instrument is a greater help to faith in the recipient? Where faith, as apparently here, did not need this help, the less likely medium was adopted. See, on the whole, ch. xix. 12, and note: and remark that only in the case of our Lord (Luke viii. 46 ‖) and His two great Apostles in the N. T.,—and of Elisha in the O. T., have we instances of this *healing virtue in the mere contact with or accessories of the person.* But what a fertile harvest of superstition and imposture has been made to spring out of these scanty examples! **16.**] Keep, in both verbs, *συνήρχετο* and *ἐθεραπεύοντο*, the imperfect sense; 'the multitude, &c., was coming together, bearing, &c.,—for all such (quippe qui) were being healed:' viz. when the next incident, *ἀναστὰς δὲ κ.τ.λ.*, happened [which forms a contrast to this waxing prosperity of the Church].

17—42.] Imprisonment, miraculous liberation, examination before the Sanhedrim, and scourging of the Apostles. **17.**] **ἀναστάς** is not redundant, but implies *being excited* by the popularity of the Apostles, and on that account commencing a course of action hostile to them: see reff. ('Non sibi quiescendum ratus est.' Beng. *διηγέρθη κινηθεὶς ἐπὶ τοῖς γενομένοις*, Chrys.) To suppose that the H. P. 'rose up' *after a council held* (Meyer) is far-fetched, and against the **ἐπλήσθησαν ζήλου**, which points to the kindling zeal of men first stirred up to action. **ὁ ἀρχ.**] Annas,—ch. iv. 6, and note on Luke iii. 2. **οἱ σὺν αὐτῷ**] **those who were with him** (see ch. iv. 13; xix. 38; xxii. 9). Not *the members of the Sanhedrim:* but *the friends and kindred* (ch. iv. 6) *of the H. P.:* see ver. 21: Kuinoel's 'qui a partibus ejus stabant' is too definite (De W.): it *was so*, but this meaning is not in the words. **ἡ οὖσα**] attr., but implying more than *οἱ ὄντες ἐξ αἱρέσεως τ. Σ.*:—the movement extended through *the whole sect.* On **αἵρ. τ. Σ.**, see Matt. iii. 7, note. The passage of Josephus, Antiq. xx. 9. 1, is worth transcribing: *πέμπει δὲ Καῖσαρ* (Nero) *Ἀλβῖνον εἰς τὴν Ἰουδαίαν ἔπαρχον, Φήστου τὴν τελευτὴν πυθόμενος. ὁ δὲ βασιλεὺς ἀφείλετο μὲν τὸν Ἰώσηπον τὴν ἀρχιερωσύνην, τῷ δὲ Ἀνάνου* **παιδί, καὶ**

18 καὶ [v] ἐπέβαλον τὰς [v] χεῖρας [v] ἐπὶ τοὺς ἀποστόλους καὶ ABDE
ἔθεντο αὐτοὺς ἐν [w] τηρήσει [x] δημοσίᾳ. 19 ἄγγελος δὲ Pℵabc dfgh
κυρίου [y] διὰ νυκτὸς ἤνοιξεν τὰς θύρας τῆς [z] φυλακῆς, klmo 13
ἐξαγαγών τε αὐτοὺς εἶπεν 20 Πορεύεσθε καὶ σταθέντες
λαλεῖτε ἐν τῷ ἱερῷ τῷ λαῷ πάντα τὰ ῥήματα τῆς [a] ζωῆς
ταύτης. 21 ἀκούσαντες δὲ εἰσῆλθον [b] ὑπὸ τὸν [c] ὄρθρον
εἰς τὸ ἱερὸν καὶ ἐδίδασκον. [d] παραγενόμενος δὲ ὁ ἀρχιερεὺς καὶ οἱ σὺν αὐτῷ [e] συνεκάλεσαν τὸ [f] συνέδριον καὶ
πᾶσαν τὴν [g] γερουσίαν τῶν υἱῶν Ἰσραήλ, καὶ [h] ἀπέστειλαν εἰς τὸ [i] δεσμωτήριον ἀχθῆναι αὐτούς. 22 οἱ δὲ

v ch. xxi. 27 reff.
w ch. iv. 3 reff.
x = here only +. see ch. xvi. 37 reff.
y ch. [xvi. 9.] xvii. 10. xxiii. 31. Herod. i. 62 init. & fin.
z = Matt. xiv. 10. Acts, ch. viii. 3 & passim. Heb. xi. 36. Neh. iii. 25.
a = here only (see note).
b = here only. Jonah iv. 10. so ὑπὸ τὴν ἑωθινήν, Polyb. i. 53. 4. ὑπὸ τὴν ὡραίαν (prima æstate), iii. 16. 7.
c Luke xxiv. 1 [John viii. 2] only. Joel ii. 2.
d Luke xii. 51. John iii. 23. Acts, ch. ix. 26. xvii. 10 & passim. Gen. xiv. 13.
e act., Mark xv. 16. Luke xv. 6 only. Josh. xxiii. 2. mid., ch. x. 24 al.
f ch. iv. 15 reff.
g here only. Exod. iii. 16 al. fr. (there also w. υἱ. Ἰσρ.)
h constr., w. pass., here only (?). see ch. xiii. 42 note. act., ch. xxvi. 17 reff.
i here bis. Matt. xi. 2. ch. xvi. 26 only. Gen. xxxix. 22 bis. xl. 3, 5 only.

18. επεβαλλον A [c]. rec aft χειρας ins αυτων, with EP rel (syr) coptt [Bas_1] Chr_1 : om ABDℵ 36. 40 vulg Syr arm Thl $Lucif_1$. εις τηρησειν E-gr Lucif(omg δημ.). aft δημ. ins και επορευθη εις εκαστος εις τα ιδια D.

19. τοτε δια ν. bef αγ. κ. D. rec ins της bef νυκτος, with EPℵ³ rel 36 [Bas_1] Chr_1 : om ABDℵ¹. ανοιξας Aℵ 36 vulg sah : ανεωξαν D¹-gr, ανεωξεν D⁸ Chr_1. for τε, δε B 73.—και εξ. E.

21. for ακουσ. δε, εξελθοντες δε E Syr. add εκ της φυλακης E. παραγενομενον B¹(sic, see table). aft συν αυτω ins εγερθεντες το πρωι D. συνκαλεσαμενοι D, retaining the και bef απεστειλαν.

αυτῷ Ἀνάνῳ λεγομένῳ, τὴν διαδοχὴν τῆς ἀρχῆς ἔδωκε. τοῦτον δέ φασι τὸν πρεσβύτατον Ἄνανον εὐτυχέστατον γενέσθαι· πέντε γὰρ ἔσχε παῖδας, καὶ τούτους πάντας συνέβη ἀρχιερατεῦσαι τῷ θεῷ, αὐτὸς καὶ πρότερον τῆς τιμῆς ἐπὶ πλεῖστον ἀπολαύσας, ὅπερ οὐδενὶ συνέβη τῶν παρ' ἡμῖν ἀρχιερέων. ὁ δὲ νεώτερος Ἄνανος . . . . θρασὺς ἦν τὸν τρόπον, καὶ τολμητὴς διαφερόντως· **αἵρεσιν δὲ μετῄει τῶν Σαδδουκαίων,** οἵπερ εἰσὶ περὶ τὰς κρίσεις ὠμοὶ παρὰ πάντας τοὺς Ἰουδαίους, καθὼς ἤδη δεδηλώκαμεν. This shews that the family of Annas, if not he himself, were connected with the sect of the Sadducees. They (see ch. iv. 1, note) were the chief enemies of the Apostles, for teaching *the resurrection*.

18. τηρ.] see ch. iv. 3. **20.] τῆς ζωῆς ταύτης,** an unusual expression, seems to refer to the peculiar nature of the enmity shewn towards them by the Sadducees, for preaching the ἀνάστασις ζωῆς—'of *this* LIFE, which they call in question.' Or perhaps τ. ζ. τ. may import the religion of Jesus having its issue in *life*. A similar expression, ὁ λόγος τῆς σωτηρίας ταύτης, occurs ch. xiii. 26. See also Rom. vii. 24. But beware of assuming in either of these passages the use of the figure called by the grammarians hypallage, so that τὰ ῥ. τῆς ζ. ταύτης = τὰ ῥήματα ταῦτα τῆς ζωῆς: for thus the sense is enervated, and the peculiar reference in each case lost. The indiscriminate application of these supposed figures of speech has been, and continues to be, one of the worst foes of sound exegesis. The deliverance, here granted to all the Apostles, was again vouchsafed to Peter in ch. xii., and is there related more in detail. It is there a minute touch of truth, that he should *mistake for a dream* (ver. 9) what he saw: having lain so long in prison, and his mind naturally dwelling on *this his former* miraculous liberation. **21.] ὑπὸ τ. ὄρθρ., at daybreak**: see reff. **παραγενόμενος**] to the ordinary session chamber in the Temple, on the south side of it (Winer, Realw.): and therefore, if the Apostles were teaching *in Solomon's porch* (ver. 12), not in their immediate vicinity. Perhaps the παραγενόμενος . . . . συνεκάλεσαν . . . . , implying that the summons was not issued till *after the arrival of the H. P. and his friends,* may point to a meeting of the Sanhedrim hurriedly and insufficiently called, for the purpose of 'packing' it against the Apostles. If so, they did not succeed, see ver. 40: perhaps on account of the arrival of some who had been listeners to the Apostles' preaching. **πᾶσαν τ. γερουσίαν**] Probably the πρεσβύτεροι, including perhaps some who were not members of the Sanhedrim; the well-known foes of Jesus and his doctrine. The expression π. τ. γερουσ. τῶν υἱ.

[d] παραγενόμενοι ὑπηρέται οὐχ εὗρον αὐτοὺς ἐν τῇ [z] φυ-
λακῇ· 23 [j] ἀναστρέψαντες δὲ ἀπήγγειλαν λέγοντες ὅτι
τὸ [i] δεσμωτήριον εὕρομεν [k] κεκλεισμένον ἐν πάσῃ [l] ἀσφα-
λείᾳ καὶ τοὺς φύλακας ἑστῶτας [m] ἐπὶ τῶν θυρῶν, ἀνοίξαντες δὲ [n] ἔσω οὐδένα εὕρομεν. 24 ὡς δὲ ἤκουσαν τοὺς
λόγους τούτους ὅ τε [o] στρατηγὸς τοῦ [o] ἱεροῦ καὶ οἱ
ἀρχιερεῖς, [p] διηπόρουν περὶ αὐτῶν τί ἂν γένοιτο τοῦτο.
25 [d] παραγενόμενος δέ τις ἀπήγγειλεν αὐτοῖς ὅτι ἰδοὺ οἱ
ἄνδρες οὓς ἔθεσθε ἐν τῇ [z] φυλακῇ εἰσὶν ἐν τῷ ἱερῷ ἑστῶτες
καὶ διδάσκοντες τὸν λαόν. 26 τότε [q] ἀπελθὼν ὁ [o] στρατηγὸς σὺν τοῖς ὑπηρέταις ἤγαγεν αὐτοὺς οὐ [r] μετὰ [r] βίας,
ἐφοβοῦντο γὰρ τὸν λαόν, [[s] ἵνα] μὴ [t] λιθασθῶσιν.

j = ch. xv. 16 only. Gen. viii. 9. see John ii. 15. 2 Cor. i. 12 al.
k Matt. vi. 6. xxv. 10. ch. xxi. 30. Rev. xxi. 25. Ezek. xliv. 1, 2.
l = 1 Thess. v. 3 (Luke i. 4) only. Lev. xxvi. 5. (-ῶς, Mark xiv. 44.)
m = Matt. xxi. 19. Gen. xviii. 1. (πρό, James v. 9. ch. xii. 6.)
n = John xx. 26. Gen. xxxix. 11.
o ch. iv. 1 reff.
p ch. ii. 12 reff.
q = Matt. ii. 22. ch. ix. 17. xxiii. 32. Gen. xix. 2.
r ch. xxiv. 7 (xxi. 35. xxvii. 41) only. Exod. i. 14. xiv. 25.
s = John xviii. 28 xix. 31. see Winer, edn. 6, § 56. 2, Remark.
t John [viii. 5.] x. 31, 32, 33. xi. 8. ch. xiv. 19. 2 Cor. xi. 25. Heb. xi. 37 only. 2 Kings xvi. 6, 13 only.

22. rec *υπηρ.* bef *παραγ.*, with DEP rel 36 sah: txt ABℵ a h vulg Syr copt æth Lucif$_1$. add *και ανυξαντες την φυλακην* D vulg syr-w-ast. *ουκ* D. *ηυρον* E. for *εν τη φυλ.*, *εσω* D.

23. for *δε*, *και* D^1(*δε και* D-corr^1). *απηγγειλον* ℵ. om *οτι* E-gr vulg Syr. rec aft *το* ins *μεν* (*to answer to δε follg*), with E-gr P rel 36 vulg coptt Chr$_1$ [Lucif$_1$]: om ABDℵ H^r E-lat syrr æth. *ηυραμεν* (twice) E [*ευραμεν* (1st) 13]. *ενκεκλειτμενον* D^1. rec ins *εξω* bef *εστ.* (*gloss to particularize, and to answer to εσω follg*), with Chr-txt: om ABDEPℵ rel vss Chr-comm$_2$ Lucif. rec for *επι*, *προ* (*more usual*), with E[-gr] P rel vulg-ed syr copt [arm] Chr: *προς* c: txt ABDℵ m 36, *ad* am fuld demid D-lat E-lat Syr sah.

24. rec ins *ιερευς και ο* bef *στρατηγος*, with P rel syr: *οι ιερεις και ο*, omg the preceding *ο τε*, E: *αρχιερευς και ο* 67. 98. 104 Chr: for *ο τε* to *αρχιερεις*, *ο τε στρατηγος κ. ο ιερευς του ιερου* 96; *οι αρχιερεις κ. οι στρατηγοι τ. ιε.* Syr æth: txt ABDℵ e 36 vulg coptt arm Lucif. *εθαυμαζον μεν τε και διηπ. π. αυτ. τι αν θελοι ειναι τ.* E. aft *αυτων* ins *το* ℵ^1(ℵ^3 disapproving). *γενηται* D^1(txt D^4).

25. rec aft *αυτοις* ins *λεγων*, with 36 [(æth) arm-mss] (Lucif$_1$): om ABDEPℵ rel vulg syrr coptt æth arm[-ed] Chr$_1$. om *οι* ℵ^1. om *εστωτες*(ins ℵ-corr^1) *και* ℵ^1.

26. [aft *στρατ.* ins *εν τω ιερω* E.] for *ηγαγ.*, *ηγεν* BD^{1}ℵ: *deducebant* D-lat: *απαγαγοντες* 13: *ηγαγον* [D^1] l: txt AEP rel 36 vulg Chr$_1$ Lucif. om *ου* D^1(and lat: ins D^3 or ^{5}). *φοβουμενοι γαρ* D-gr. om *ινα* (*to connect μη with εφοβ.*) BDEℵ 13: ins AP rel 36 Chr.

Ἰσραήλ, common in the LXX, is perhaps translated from the form of words in which they were summoned. γερουσία, being the ordinary word for the πρεσβύτεροι, would be the Hellenistic formal expression.

23. ἐν πάσ. ἀσφ.] Not, as Vulg., 'cum omni diligentia' (so Luth.), nor as E. V. '*with all safety*' (?); but **in all security**—'in a state of perfect safety.'

24.] If the ἱερεύς of the rec. be genuine, it must designate the *High* Priest; not that the word itself can bear the meaning (compare 1 Macc. xv. 1 and 2), but that the *context* points out *the priest* thus designated *to be* the H. P. (Meyer.) On **ὁ στρατ. τ. ἱερ.**, see note, ch. iv. 1. He appears to have been summoned to meet the Sanhedrim, perhaps as the offence had taken place within his jurisdiction. But he was probably one of the ἀρχιερεῖς (see Winer, Realw., Tempel, end). These latter were the *titular High Priests*, partly those who had served the office, partly the presidents of the twenty-four courses, partly the kindred of the H. P. (see Matt. ii. 4.) **αὐτῶν**] '*The Apostles*,' the αὐτούς of ver. 22: not '*these words*,' as would appear at first sight. **τί ἂν γέν. τοῦτο**] **To what this would come**; 'whereunto this would *grow*,' E. V.:—not 'quomodo factum sit,' as Kuin.,—nor 'quid hoc esset rei' (τί ὂν εἴη, as ch. x. 17), as Grot. and others. **26.**] [**ἵνα**] **μὴ λιθ.** depends upon οὐ μετὰ βίας, not upon ἐφοβ. If, however, ἵνα be *omitted*, then this latter is

27 ἀγαγόντες δὲ αὐτοὺς [u] ἔστησαν ἐν τῷ [v] συνεδρίῳ. καὶ
ἐπηρώτησεν αὐτοὺς ὁ ἀρχιερεὺς 28 λέγων [wx] Παραγγελίᾳ
[x] παρηγγείλαμεν ὑμῖν μὴ διδάσκειν [y] ἐπὶ τῷ ὀνόματι
τούτῳ, καὶ ἰδοὺ [z] πεπληρώκατε τὴν Ἱερουσαλὴμ τῆς
[a] διδαχῆς ὑμῶν, καὶ βούλεσθε [b] ἐπαγαγεῖν ἐφ' ἡμᾶς τὸ
[c] αἷμα τοῦ ἀνθρώπου τούτου. 29 Ἀποκριθεὶς δὲ Πέτρος
καὶ οἱ ἀπόστολοι εἶπαν [d] Πειθαρχεῖν δεῖ θεῷ μᾶλλον ἢ
ἀνθρώποις. 30 ὁ [e] θεὸς τῶν [f] πατέρων [f] ἡμῶν [g] ἤγειρεν
Ἰησοῦν, ὃν ὑμεῖς [h] διεχειρίσασθε [ik] κρεμάσαντες ἐπὶ [il] ξύλου.

H και βουλεσθαι... ABDE HP‎א a b c d f g h k l m o 13

u ch. iv. 7 reff. v = ch. iv. 15 reff. w ch. xvi. 24. 1 Thess. iv. 2. 1 Tim. i. 5, 18 only +. x constr., ch. [iv. 17.] xxiii. 14. Luke xxii. 15. John iii. 29. Gen. xxxi. 30 al. y ch. iv. 17 reff. z John xii. 3. ch. ii. 2 al. Hag. ii. 8. a = ch. ii. 42 reff. b 2 Pet. ii. 2, 5 only. Gen. vi. 17. c = Matt. xxiii. 35. xxvii. 25. 2 Kings i. 16. d ver. 32. ch. xxvii. 21. Titus iii. 1 only +. Sir. xxx. 28 (xxxiii. 37). Esdr. viii. 94 (90) only. e ch. iii. 13. xxii. 14. 1 Chron. xii. 17 al. f = John iv. 20. vi. 31. ch. iii. 13. vii. 11, &c. xiii. 17. xv. 10. xxii. 14. 1 Cor. x. 1. see ch. iii. 25. g = Matt. x. 8. ch. iii. 15 ? ‡. h ch. xxvi. 21 only +. i ch. x. 39. Gal. iii. 13, from Deut. xxi. 23. k = as above (i). Luke xxiii. 39 (Matt. xviii. 6. xxii. 40. ch. xxviii. 4) only. Gen. xl. 19. l = as above (i). 1 Pet. ii. 24.

27. ο ιερευς D¹-gr([and lat]: txt D⁵) Lucif₁.
28. rec ins ου bef παραγγ. (*making it a question, which has evidently been occasioned by* επερωτησεν), with D[-gr] EP‎א³ rel 36 syrr sah æth [arm Ath₁ Bas₁ Chr₁ Cyr₁] Thdrt: om AB‎א¹ vulg D-lat copt Ath₁ Cyr₁ Lucif₁. for διδασκ., λαλειν A lect-17 [Chr₁] Cyr₂ Thdrt. om 1st και D¹(and lat: ins D²). επληρωσατε A‎א Chr₁ Cyr₁. εφαγαγειν D¹(txt D⁸). εκεινου D¹-gr(txt D⁸) sah.
29. rec ins ο bef πετρ., with 13. 36 Thl: om ABEHP‎א rel [Bas₁] Chr₁.—D¹ omits αποκρ. to ειπαν, adding at end of ver ο δε πετρος ειπεν προς αυτους. [for δει, δε D¹-gr.] (ειπαν, so ABE‎א.)
30. ins δε bef θεος A‎א copt[-wilk]. ins τον παιδα αυτου bef ιησ. E.

the case. **28.**] δέον ἐρωτῆσαι πρῶτον, πῶς ἐξήλθετε; ὡς οὐδενὸς γενομένου, ἐρωτῶσι λέγοντες· κ.τ.λ. Chrys. The same shyness of open allusion to the names or facts connected with Jesus and the spread of his doctrine may be traced in the **ὀνόματι τούτῳ**, and the **ἀνθρώπου τούτου**, and is a strong mark of truth and circumstantiality. 'Fugit appellare Jesum: Petrus appellat et celebrat, vv. 30, 31.' Bengel. **ἐπαγ. ἐφ' ἡμᾶς**] not meaning, that *divine vengeance* would come on them for the murder of Jesus: but with a stress on ἡμᾶς—that the *people* would be incited to take vengeance on *them*, the Sanhedrim, for that murder. The preceding clause (πεπληρ. κ.τ.λ.) shews this to be their thought. Compare the pointed address of Peter to the Sanhedrim, ch. iv. 8—12, and the distinction between them and the people in iv. 21. This being so, the resemblance between this expression and the imprecation of the people in Matt. xxvii. 25 must not be too closely pressed, though the coincidence is too striking to escape notice. **29.**] Peter, by word of mouth; the Apostles, as a body, by *assent*, implied in *his own utterance* and *their silence*. There is no ellipse of ἄλλοι before ἀπόστ. This defence of Peter divides itself into the propositions of an ordinary syllogism—(1) *The statement of the general truth that we must obey God rather than men*: (2) *The reduction of the present circumstances under that general truth*, as being the work of the God of their Fathers—shewn in his having raised and glorified Jesus, for a definite purpose, to give, &c. (3) *The identification of themselves with the course of action marked out by the* **πειθαρχεῖν δεῖ** . . . in that they were bearing witness to God's work, under the inspiration of the Holy Spirit given them as men obedient to God. The whole is a *perfect model of concise and ready eloquence, and of unanswerable logical coherence*; and a notable fulfilment of the promise, δοθήσεται ὑμῖν ἐν ἐκείνῃ τῇ ὥρᾳ τί λαλήσητε (Matt. x. 19). **πειθαρχεῖν**] much stronger than ἀκούειν, ch. iv. 19,—as their conduct, in *persisting after prohibition*, had been more marked and determined. That was a mere '*listening to*' the proposition then made to them: this, a course of deliberate action, chosen and entered on. **θεῷ**—opposed to τῆς διδ. **ὑμῶν** of the H. P.; and to **ἀνθρώπου τούτου**. In the background, there would be the command of the angel, ver. 20: but it is not alleged: the great duty of preaching the Gospel of Christ is kept on its highest grounds. **30. τῶν πατ. ἡμ.**] thus binding on Christ and his work, to the *covenant* whereof all present were partakers. **ἤγειρεν**] both from the emphatic position of the verb, and from the context, it must refer to the resurrection, not merely, as in Matt. xi. 11, Luke i. 69, Judg. iii. 9, to *raising up* in the ordinary sense. **ὑμεῖς**, answering to the ἐφ' **ἡμᾶς** of the H. P. **ἐπὶ ξύλου**]

31 τοῦτον ὁ θεὸς [m] ἀρχηγὸν καὶ σωτῆρα [n] ὕψωσεν τῇ
δεξιᾷ αὐτοῦ, [o] δοῦναι [o] μετάνοιαν τῷ Ἰσραὴλ καὶ [pq] ἄφεσιν
[q] ἁμαρτιῶν. 32 καὶ ἡμεῖς ἐσμὲν αὐτοῦ [r] μάρτυρες τῶν
[s] ῥημάτων τούτων, [t] καὶ τὸ πνεῦμα [[t] δὲ] τὸ ἅγιον, ὃ ἔδωκεν
ὁ θεὸς τοῖς [u] πειθαρχοῦσιν αὐτῷ. 33 Οἱ δὲ ἀκούσαντες

m = ch. iii. 15 reff. n = ch. ii. 33 reff. o ch. xi. 18. 2 Tim. ii. 25. Wisd. xii. 19. Jos. Antt. xx. 8. 7. p Mark iii. 29. Eph. i. 7. Heb. ix. 22‡. q Matt. xxvi. 28. Luke i. 77. iii. 3. ch. ii. 38. Col. i. 14 al. r = ch. i. 8 and Acts passim. constr., ch. xiii. 31. Job xvi. 20. s double gen., Phil. i. 25. ii. 30. Heb. xiii. 7. t ch. iii. 24 reff. u ver. 29 reff.

31. for δεξια, δοξη D^1(*caritate* D-lat : txt D^2) sah Iren-int$_1$. ins του bef δουναι B ℵ^1(ℵ^3 disapproving) Chr$_2$; επι τω Chr$_1$. ins των bef αμαρτ. D^5.—add εν αυτω D^1(and lat) sah æth-rom.

32. for εσμεν αυτου, εν αυτω B 69^1. 100-5 Iren-int$_1$: αυτω m: om εσμεν æth: μαρτ. bef εσμεν A am D-lat Syr Iren-int$_1$: om αυτου AD^{1}ℵ g h vulg Syr [coptt] Chr$_1$ Did: syr places αυτου aft ρηματων: txt (αυτου *was prob omd from not being understood, and transposed from being thought to belong to* τ. ρηματων τουτων) D^{5}EHP 36 (æth) [arm] Chr$_1$. ins παντων bef των ρ. τ. D^1(and lat). om δε (*corrn ?*) ABD^{1}ℵ m vulg [Syr] sah arm Did$_1$ [Chr$_1$] Thl-fin Iren-int$_1$: ins D^{3}E (H ?) P rel 36 Chr$_1$ Thl-sif. for ὅ, ον D^{1}E : om B 17. 73 coptt : txt A D-corr H[P]ℵ rel 36.

33. ακουοντες P c h 104-5 [*audientes* D-lat E-lat Lucif$_1$]. aft ακου. ins ταυτα E

compare reff. and the similar contrast in ch. iii. 14, 15. The manner of death is described thus barely and ignominiously, to waken compunction in the hearers, to whom the expression was well known as entailing curse and disgrace on the victim.

31, 32.] **ἀρχηγ. κ. σωτ.**, not, '*to be* a Prince and a Saviour:' but the words are the predicate of τοῦτον—**as a P. and a S. ἀρχηγόν**, as ch. iii. 15, which see. **κ. σωτ.** not = τῆς σωτηρίας. Jesus was to be King and Captain of Israel, and *also their Saviour*. The two offices, though inseparably connected in fact, had each its separate meaning in Peter's speech: *a Prince*, to whom you owe obedience—*a Saviour*, by whom you must be saved from your sins. **τῇ δεξιᾷ, by** (not *to*) **His right hand**, as in ch. ii. 33, where see note. The great aim here, as there, is to set forth God as the DOER of all this. **δοῦναι**, in his *Kingly* prerogative; **μετ. κ. ἄφ. ἁμ.**, to lead to salvation (**εἰς** σωτηρίαν, as 2 Cor. vii. 10 : **εἰς** ζωήν, as ch. xi. 18) by him as a *Saviour*. Somewhat similarly Bengel: '**μετ.**, qua Jesus accipitur ut *Princeps:* ἄφεσ. qua accipitur ut *Salvator*.'

The key to this part of the speech is Luke xxiv. 47—49, where we have, in our Lord's command to them, the same conjunction of μετ. κ. ἄφεσ. ἁμ.—and immediately follows, as here, ὑμεῖς μάρτυρες τούτων, appointing them to that office which they were now discharging,—and, corresponding to **τὸ πνεῦμα τὸ ἅγ.** of our text, ἰδοὺ ἐγὼ ἐξαποστέλλω τὴν ἐπαγγελίαν τοῦ πατρός μου ἐφ' ὑμᾶς. By conjoining the Holy Ghost, as a witness, with themselves,—they claim and assert the promise of John xv. 26, 27 : see also the apostolic letter of ch. xv. 28. When we remember, how much of the apostolic testimony was given in *writing*, as well as by word of mouth, this declaration of Peter becomes an important datum for judging of the nature of that testimony also. See a very similar conjunction, 1 John v. 9.

They were God's witnesses, in the things which they had seen and heard as men: the *Holy Ghost in them* was God's Witness, in purifying and enlarging by His inspiration that their testimony to facts, and in unfolding, from (and as inseparable from) these witnessed facts,—*the things which eye hath not seen, nor ear heard.* And *in the Scripture* THESE SAME TESTIMONIES are conjoined; *that of the Apostles*, holy men under the guidance and reminding of the Holy Spirit, faithfully and honestly reporting those things which fall under human observation: and *that of God the Spirit Himself*, testifying, through them, those loftier things which no human experience can assure, nor human imagination compass. **ῥημάτων**] **histories, things expressed in words:** see note on Luke i. 4. **τοῖς πειθ.**] Not ἡμῖν, which might make an unreal distinction between the Apostles and the then believers, and an implied exclusion of the hearers from this gift,—but generally, to *all* the **πειθαρχοῦσιν** αὐτῷ, by this word recalling the opening of the speech and binding all together. So that the sense of the whole is, 'We are acting in obedience to God, and for the everlasting good of our common Israel: and otherwise we cannot do.' And a solemn invitation is implied. '*Be ye obedient likewise*.' It is remarkable that a similar word, **ὑπήκουον** τῇ πίστει, is used of the multitude of converted priests, ch. vi. 7.

v ch. vii. 54 only ‡. 1 Chron. xx. 3 only. w = Luke xiv. 31. John (xi. 53 v. r.) xii. 10. ch. xxvii. 39. 2 Cor. i. 17. Esth. iii. 6. x Luke xxii. 2. xxiii. 32. ch. ii. 23. vii. 21 al. Luke only, exc. Matt. ii. 16. Heb. x. 9. Ezek. xxvi. 8. y = ver. 27. z Luke v. 17. 1 Tim. i. 7 only +. see Neh. viii. 7 Ald. a 1 Cor. iii. 12. Heb. xiii. 4. Prov. iii. 15. b dat., ch. vii. 20 reff. Hom. Od. α'. 38. c = here only. see Job xi. 14. xxii. 23. Xen. Anab. vi. 6. 5. 25. d ch. xxvii. 28 reff. e Luke xii. 1. xvii. 3. xxi. 34. ch. xx. 28. (Deut. iv. 9.) f 2nd pers., 2 Cor. vii. 11 reff. g = Mark vi. 52. τώϋτὸ ἐποίησε τὸ καὶ ἐπὶ τῃ θυγατρί, Herod. iii. 14.

[v] διεπρίοντο καὶ [w] ἐβουλεύοντο [x] ἀνελεῖν αὐτούς. 34 ἀναστὰς δέ τις ἐν τῷ [y] συνεδρίῳ Φαρισαῖος ὀνόματι Γαμαλιήλ,
[z] νομοδιδάσκαλος [a] τίμιος [b] παντὶ τῷ λαῷ, ἐκέλευσεν [c] ἔξω
[d] βραχὺ τοὺς ἀνθρώπους [c] ποιῆσαι, 35 εἶπέν τε πρὸς
αὐτοὺς Ἄνδρες Ἰσραηλῖται, [e] προσέχετε [ef] ἑαυτοῖς [g] ἐπὶ
τοῖς ἀνθρώποις τούτοις τί μέλλετε πράσσειν. 36 πρὸ γὰρ

C ειπ... ABCDE HPℵ a b c d f g h k l m o 13

28 syr-w-ast sah. εβουλοντο (*corrn, εβουλευ. not being understood*) AB E[-gr] e l coptt æth [arm] Chr_2: επεβουλευσαντο b: εβουλευσαντο k Thl-fin: txt DHPℵ rel vulg [E-lat] syrr Lucif.

34. εκ του συνεδριου D-gr E(addg αυτων) copt: om ε. τ. συνεδρ. Syr. rec aft βραχυ ins τι, with (H)P rel [arm] Thl-sif: βραχυτητι o: txt ABDEℵ Chr_3.—τ. απ. βρ. τι H d e o [Thl-sif]: τ. απ. εξω βρ. ποιησαι D. rec (for ανθρωπους) αποστολους, with DEHP rel 36 [am² tol] syrr sah æth Chr_1: txt ABℵ vulg copt arm Chr_2.

35. for τε, δε C k [13] 58 [E-lat syr] copt. for αυτους, τους αρχοντας και τους συνεδριους D sah. εαυτους D¹. απο των ανθρωπων τουτων E tol [copt]. πραττειν ℵ.

33. διεπρίοντο] sc. *ταῖς καρδίαις* as ch. vii. 54. From its conjunction there with *ἔβρυχον τ. ὀδόντας*, it does not appear to have any connexion with the phrase *πρίειν* or *διαπρίειν τ. ὀδ.* with which Hesych. and Wetst. identify it. **They were cut asunder** (in heart). So Persius, iii. 8, 'turgescit vitrea bilis: *Findor*, ut Arcadiæ pecuaria rudere credas.' And Plautus, Bacch. ii. 3. 17, 'Cor meum et cerebrum, Nicobule, *finditur*, Istius hominis ubi fit quaque mentio.' And Euseb. H. E. v. 1 (in Suicer, sub voce, where he cites other authorities also), *ἐχαλέπαινον κ. διεπρίοντο καθ' ἡμῶν.* **ἐβουλεύοντο**] **they were purposing**, 'taking counsel with the intent,' see reff. **34.**] **Γαμαλιήλ** = גַּמְלִיאֵל, (see Numb. i. 10; ii. 20,) is generally, and not without probability, assumed to be identical with the celebrated Rabban Gamaliel, הַזָּקֵן (the old man), one of the seven, to whom, among their Rabbis, the Jews give this title Rabban (= ῥαββουνί, John xx. 16), a wise and enlightened Pharisee, the son of Rabban Symeon (traditionally the Symeon of Luke ii. 25) and grandson of the famous Hillel. His name often appears in the Mischna, as an utterer of sayings quoted as authorities. He died eighteen years before the destruction of the city. (See Lightf. Centuria Chorogr. Matth. præmissa, ch. xv.) He was the preceptor of St. Paul (ch. xxii. 3). Ecclesiastical tradition makes him become a Christian and be baptized by Peter and John (Phot. cod. 171, vol. iii. p. 118 b. Winer, Realw.), and in the Clementine Recognn. (i. 65, p. 1242), he is stated to have been at this time a Christian, but secretly. The Jewish accounts do not agree, which make him die a Pharisee, with much more probability. Nor is the least trace of a Christian leaning to be found in his speech: see below [on ver. 39]. And considering that he was a Pharisee, opposing the prevalent faction of Sadducæism in a matter where the Resurrection was called in question,—and a wise and enlightened man opposing furious and unreasoning zealots,—considering also, that when the *anti-pharisaical* element of Christianity was brought out in the acts and sayings of Stephen, his pupil Saul was found the foremost persecutor,—we should, I think, be slow to suspect him of any favouring of the Apostles *as followers of Jesus.* (See particulars respecting Gamaliel collected in Conybeare and Howson's St. Paul, edn. 2, vol. i. p. 69, f.) He does not here appear as the president of the Sanhedrim, but only as a member. **ἔξω ποιῆσαι**] see reff. **to put out**—'cause to withdraw.' They are recalled in ver. 40. **35.**] The words *ἐπὶ τ. ἀνθρ. τούτ.* may be joined either with *προσέχ. ἑαυτ.*, or with *τί μέλ. πράσσ.* The latter would give the more usual construction: and the transposition of words is not unexampled in the Acts, see ch. i. 2; xix. 4.

36.] A great chronological difficulty arises here. Josephus relates, Antt. xx. 5. 1, *Φάδου δὲ τῆς Ἰουδαίας ἐπιτροπεύοντος γόης τις ἀνὴρ Θευδᾶς ὀνόματι πείθει τὸν πλεῖστον ὄχλον ἀναλαβόντα τὰς κτήσεις ἕπεσθαι πρὸς τὸν Ἰορδάνην ποταμὸν αὐτῷ· προφήτης γὰρ ἔλεγεν εἶναι, καὶ προστάγματι τὸν ποταμὸν σχίσας, δίοδον ἔφη παρέξειν αὐτοῖς ῥᾳδίαν. καὶ ταῦτα λέγων πολλοὺς ἠπάτησεν. οὐ μὴν εἴασεν αὐτοὺς τῆς ἀφροσύνης ὄνασθαι Φάδος, ἀλλ' ἐξέπεμψεν ἴλην ἱππέων ἐπ' αὐτούς, ἥτις*

τούτων τῶν ἡμερῶν [h] ἀνέστη Θευδᾶς λέγων εἶναί [i] τινα ἑαυτόν, ᾧ [k] προσεκλίθη ἀνδρῶν ἀριθμὸς [l] ὡς τετρακοσίων· ὃς [m] ἀνῃρέθη, καὶ πάντες ὅσοι [n] ἐπείθοντο αὐτῷ [o] διελύθησαν καὶ [p] ἐγένοντο [p] εἰς οὐδέν.
37 [q] μετὰ τοῦτον [h] ἀνέστη Ἰούδας ὁ Γαλιλαῖος ἐν ταῖς ἡμέραις τῆς [r] ἀπογραφῆς, καὶ [s] ἀπέστησεν [t] λαὸν [u] ὀπίσω αὐτοῦ· κἀκεῖνος

h = ch. vii. 18, from Exod. i. 8. see ch. vi. 9. i = 1 Cor. iii. 7 reff. k here only †. Hom. Od. φ'. 138. προσκλίνων τοῖς Ῥοδίοις ὁ Πτολ. κατ. τ. ὅλην αἵρεσιν, Polyb. iv. 51. 5. l = ver. 7 al. m = ver. 33. n = ch. xxiii. 21. xxvii. 11. Gal. v. 7. James iii. 3. Prov. xxvi. 25. o here only ‡. διαλ. τὴν στρατιάν, Xen. Cyr. v. 5. 43. p Matt. xxi. 42, ch. iv. 11 and 1 Pet. ii. 7, from Ps. cxvii. 22. Luke xiii. 19. Rom. xi. 9. q ch. xiii. 25 reff. r Luke ii. 2 only †. 2 Macc. ii. 1 only. s = here only. (ver. 38.) Deut. xiii. 10. Herod. i. 154, and classics passim. t = Luke xxiii. 5 al. u = ch. xx. 30. 1 Tim. v. 15. Rev. xiii. 3, constr. prægn., see ch. xiii. 8. Luke iv. 38. Rom. xvi. 20.

36. ins μεγαν bef εαυτον D : aft, A²E k o 13. 36 tol Syr Cyr_1 Jer_1 : om A¹BCH[P]ℵ rel vulg syr coptt Eus_1 Chr_2. aft ω ins και D-gr. rec προσεκολληθη, with [c(-κολη-)] f k o [13, e sil] Chr_1 : προσεκληθησαν C¹(appy) : προσεκλειθησαν D-corr : προσετεθη 36 : *appositi sunt* Jer_1 : *inclinaverunt* syr : *adhæserunt* copt : *secuti sunt* Syr sah æth : *accesserunt* arm : txt AB[C³]ℵ a² b d h m, προσεκληθη (*itacism*) CD¹[EH]P a¹ g l, *consensit* vulg E-lat, *adsensum est* D-lat (*the varr have been interpretations of or substitutions for the* απαξ λεγ. *in N T*, προσεκλιθη). rec αριθ. bef ανδρ., with DHP rel vulg Chr_1 : txt ABCEℵ m demid [fuld Cyr_2]. rec ωσει, with HPℵ¹ rel 36 [Cyr_2] : txt ABCDEℵ³ h. τετρακοσιοι ℵ¹ [Cyr_1]. ος διελυθη(ανηρεθη D⁴) αυτος δι' αυτου D. om διελυθησαν D¹(ins D⁴). ουθεν D 33.

37. rec aft λαον ins ικανον, with [A²]HP rel 36 syrr sah [æth arm Cyr_1] : pref E k 40 copt [$Eus\text{-}mss_1$] : λα. πολυν C D-gr [Eus(edd Steph and Val)] : txt A¹Bℵ vulg

ἀπροσδόκητος ἐπιπεσοῦσα πολλοὺς μὲν ἀνεῖλε, πολλοὺς δὲ ζῶντας ἔλαβεν· αὐτόν τε τὸν Θευδᾶν ζωγρήσαντες ἀποτέμνουσι τὴν κεφαλήν, καὶ κομίζουσιν εἰς Ἱεροσόλυμα. But this was in the reign of Claudius, not before the year A.D. 44; and consequently at least twelve years after this speech of Gamaliel's. On this difficulty I will remark, that we are plainly *in no position* (setting all other considerations aside) to charge St. Luke with having put into the mouth of Gamaliel words which he could not have uttered. For Josephus himself, speaking of a time which would accord very well with that referred to by Gamaliel, viz. the time when Archelaus went to Rome to be confirmed in the kingdom, says, *ἐν τούτῳ δὲ καὶ ἕτερα μυρία θορύβων ἐχόμενα τὴν Ἰουδαίαν κατελάμβανε, πολλῶν πολλαχόσε κατ' οἰκείων ἐλπίδας κερδῶν καὶ Ἰουδαίων ἔχθρας ἐπὶ τὸ πολεμεῖν ὡρμημένων*. And among these there may well have been an impostor of this name. But all attempts to identify Theudas with any other leader of outbreaks mentioned by Josephus have failed to convince any one except their propounders: e. g. that cited in Biscoe from Usher, Ann., p. 797, who supposes him the same as Judas the robber, son of Ezechias, Jos. Antt. xvii. 10. 5,—of Sonntag, who tries to identify him with Simon, mentioned Jos. Antt. xvii. 10. 6; B. J. ii. 4. 2,—and of Wieseler, who would have us believe him the same with Matthias ὁ Μαργαλώθου, Antt. xxvii. 6. 2, 4. The assumption of Josephus having *misplaced his Theudas* is perhaps improbable; but *by no means impossible*, in a historian *teeming with inaccuracies*. (See this abundantly demonstrated in an article on 'the Bible and Josephus,' in the Journal of Sacred Literature for Oct. 1850.) All we can say is, that such impostors were too frequent, for any one to be able to say that there was not one of this name (a name by no means uncommon, see Cicero ad divers. vi. 10, and Grot. h. l.) at the time specified. It is exceedingly improbable, considering the time and circumstances of the writing of the Acts, and the evident supervision of them by St. Paul, the pupil of Gamaliel, that a gross historical mistake should have been here put into his mouth.

The λέγων εἶναι of our text is curiously related to the ἔλεγεν εἶναι of Josephus. **ὡς τετρακοσίων** hardly agrees with the τὸν πλεῖστον ὄχλον of Josephus above, and confirms the idea that different events are pointed at in the two accounts. But the Jewish historian speaks very widely about such matters: see note on ch. xxi. 38.

37.] The decided **μετὰ τοῦτον** fixes beyond doubt the place here assigned to Theudas. This Judas, and the occasion of his revolt, are related by Josephus, Antt. xviii. 1. 1, Κυρήνιος δὲ . . . . ἐπὶ Συρίας παρῆν, ὑπὸ Καίσαρος δικαιοδότης τοῦ ἔθνους ἀπεσταλμένος, κ. τιμητὴς τῶν οὐσιῶν γενησόμενος . . . . παρῆν δὲ καὶ Κυρ. εἰς τὴν Ἰουδαίων προσθήκην τῆς Συρίας γενομένην ἀποτιμησόμενός τε αὐτῶν τὰς οὐσίας, κ. ἀποδωσόμενος τὰ Ἀρχελάου χρήματα. Οἱ δέ, καίπερ τὸ κατ' ἀρχὰς ἐν δεινῷ φέροντες τὴν ἐπὶ

v ver. 36 reff. w Matt. xxvi. 31 (from Zech. xiii. 7 A$\aleph^3$). Luke i. 51. John xi. 52. Num. x. 35. x ch. iv. 29 reff. y = Luke iv. 13. ch. xxii. 29. 2 Cor. xii. 8. Sir. vii. 2. z = Matt. xv. 14. Mark xiv. 6. 4 Kings iv. 27. a see Matt. xxi. 25.

ABCDE HP$\aleph$ a b c d f g h k l m o 13

ἀπώλετο, καὶ πάντες ὅσοι [v] ἐπείθοντο αὐτῷ [w] διεσκορπίσθησαν. 38 καὶ [x] τὰ [x] νῦν λέγω ὑμῖν, [y] ἀπόστητε ἀπὸ τῶν
ἀνθρώπων τούτων καὶ [z] ἄφετε αὐτούς: ὅτι ἐὰν ᾖ [a] ἐξ
ἀνθρώπων ἡ [b] βουλὴ αὕτη ἢ τὸ [c] ἔργον τοῦτο, [d] καταλυθή-
σεται· 39 εἰ δὲ [a] ἐκ θεοῦ ἐστίν, οὐ *δύνασθε [d] καταλῦσαι
αὐτούς, [e] μήποτε καὶ [f] θεομάχοι [g] εὑρεθῆτε. 40 [v] ἐπείσθησαν
δὲ αὐτῷ, καὶ προσκαλεσάμενοι τοὺς ἀποστόλους [h] δείραντες [i] παρήγγειλαν μὴ λαλεῖν [k] ἐπὶ τῷ ὀνόματι τοῦ

b = Luke xxiii. 51. ch. xxvii. 12, 42. c John vii. 21. d = Rom. xiv. 20. 2 Macc. ii. 22. e constr., here only. see note. f here only †. Symm. only, Job xxvi. 5. Prov. ix. 18. xxi. 16. (χεῖν, 2 Macc. vii. 19. Eur. Iph. in Aul. 1409.) g = 2 Cor. iv. 2 reff. h Matt. xxi. 35. ch. xvi. 37. xxii. 19 al.‡ 2 Chron. xxix. 34 A (ἐκδ. B) only i = ch. i. 4 reff. k ch. iv. 17 reff.

D-lat Eus[ed Hein and Burt] Cyr_1. om *παντες* D 95. for *οσοι*, *οι* $C^{1\cdot3}$.

38. om *τα* (not B^1: corrd eadem manu: see table) E. aft *νυν* ins *εισιν αδελφοι* D (*εισιν* is marked for erasure). om *υμιν* $\aleph^1$(ins $\aleph$-$corr^1$). rec (for *αφετε*) *εασατε*, with DEHP rel 36 Chr_1: txt ABC$\aleph$. aft *αυτους* ins *μη μιαναντες τας χειρας* D 34: *μη μολυνοντες τας χ. υμων* E. om *αυτη* HP a b c f g h l [arm-mss] Thl-fin.

39. for *ει*, *εαν* E. *δυνήσεσθε BCDE$\aleph$ a h k 13(appy) 36 vulg Syr sah $Orig_1$ Chr_3 Thl-fin (*alteration to agree with the foregoing future, and the conditional* ει? *see note*): *δυνασθε* AHP rel fuld syr copt [æth] Thl-sif. rec *αυτο* (*alteration to suit* ἐργον), with C^1HP rel [vulg-ed] demid Syr coptt Chr_2 Thl Œc: *αυτον* 180: *τουτου διδασκαλιαν* $Orig_1$: txt ABC^2DE$\aleph$ am fuld syr æth arm. aft *αυτους* add *ουτε υμεις ουτε οι αρχοντες υμων* E; *ουτε υμεις ουτε βασιλεις ουτε τυραννοι· απεχεσθαι ουν απο των ανθρωπων τουτων* D: simly 33-marg 180 demid syr-w-ast. om *και* D^1(and lat: ins D^2) 163 [syrr] coptt.

40. for *επεισθησαν*, *επειστ . . . . ες* ("una litera ante *επ.* et quatuor fere ante *ες* deletis") D^1(txt D^2(?)). aft *δειρ.* ins *αυτους* E: *cæsis eis* D-lat. aft *λαλειν* ins

ταῖς ἀπογραφαῖς ἀκρόασιν, ὑποκατέβησαν τοῦ εἰς πλέον ἐναντιοῦσθαι . . . . Ἰούδας δὲ Γαυλανίτης ἀνὴρ ἐκ πόλεως ὄνομα Γάμαλα . . . ἠπείγετο ἐπὶ ἀποστάσει. And, in returning to the mention of him as the founder of the fourth sect among the Jews (xviii. 1. 6), he calls him *ὁ Γαλιλαῖος Ἰούδας*. From the above citation it is plain that this *ἀπογραφή* was that so called *κατ' ἐξοχήν*, under Quirinus: see Luke ii. 2 and note. His revolt took a theocratic character, his followers maintaining *μόνον ἡγεμόνα καὶ δεσπότην τὸν θεόν* (Jos. as above). **ἀπώλετο**] Not related by Josephus. **διεσκορπίσθησαν**] Strictly accurate—for they still existed, and at last became active and notorious again, under Menahem, son of Judas *τοῦ καλουμένου Γαλιλαίου, ὃς ἦν σοφιστὴς δεινότατος, καὶ ἐπὶ Κυρηνίου ποτὲ Ἰουδαίους ὀνειδίσας.* (B. Jud. ii. 17. 7; see also Antt. xx. 5. 2.) **38.**] **ἐὰν ᾖ, εἰ . . . ἐστίν**: implying by the first, perhaps, the manifold devices of human imposture and wickedness, any of which it might be, (q. d. *ὅτι ἂν ᾖ ἐξ ἀνθρώπ.*,) and all of which would equally come to nought,—and, on the other hand, the solemnity and fixedness of the divine purpose, by the *indicative*, which are also intimated, in our text, by the *pres. οὐ δύνασθε*.
Or perhaps the indicative is used in the second place, because that is the *case assumed*, and on which the advice is founded [at all events the distinction ought to be preserved, which is not done in E. V.]. **ἡ βουλή**] The whole plan—the **scheme**, of which this **ἔργον**, the fact under your present cognizance, forms a part. **39.**] The somewhat difficult connexion of **μήποτε κ. θ. εὑρ.** may be explained,—not by parenthesizing *ὅτι . . . . . αὐτούς*, but by understanding *'and ye will be obliged to give up your attempt'* (which thought is contained in *οὐ δύνασ. κατ. αὐτ.*), **lest ye be**, &c. **καί**] Opponents not only to them, but *also* to God:—'*even*,' in E. V., does not give the sense. As regards Gamaliel's advice, we may remark that it was founded on a view of the issues of events, agreeing with the fatalism of the Pharisees: that it betokens *no leaning towards Christianity*, nor indeed very much even of worldly wisdom;—but serves to shew how low the supreme council of the Jews had sunk both in their theology and their political sagacity, if such a fallacious *laissez-aller* view of matters was the counsel of the wisest among them. It seems certainly, on a closer view, as if they accepted, from fear of the people (see ver. 26), this opportunity of compromising the matter, which Gamaliel had designedly afforded

Ἰησοῦ, καὶ [l] ἀπέλυσαν. 41 Οἱ μὲν οὖν ἐπορεύοντο χαίροντες [m] ἀπὸ προσώπου τοῦ [n] συνεδρίου, ὅτι [o] κατηξιώθησαν
[p] ὑπὲρ τοῦ [p] ὀνόματος [q] ἀτιμασθῆναι, 42 [r] πᾶσάν τε [r] ἡμέραν
ἐν τῷ ἱερῷ καὶ [s] κατ' οἶκον οὐκ [t] ἐπαύοντο διδάσκοντες
καὶ [u] εὐαγγελιζόμενοι τὸν χριστὸν Ἰησοῦν.

VI. 1 Ἐν δὲ ταῖς ἡμέραις ταύταις [v] πληθυνόντων τῶν
μαθητῶν ἐγένετο [w] γογγυσμὸς τῶν [x] Ἑλληνιστῶν πρὸς
τοὺς [y] Ἑβραίους, ὅτι [z] παρεθεωροῦντο ἐν τῇ [a] διακονίᾳ τῇ
[b] καθημερινῇ αἱ [c] χῆραι αὐτῶν. 2 προσκαλεσάμενοι δὲ οἱ

l = ch. xxvi. 32 reff. m ch. vii. 45 reff. n ch. iv. 15 reff. o Luke xx. 35. (xxi. 36 v. r.) 2 Thess. i. 5 only. Gen. xxxi. 28 compl. 2 Macc. xiii. 12. 3 Macc. iii. 21 (only ?). p ch. ix. 16 reff. ellips., 3 John 7 only. q Mark xii. 4. Luke xx. 11. John viii. 49. Rom. i. 24. ii. 23. James ii. 6 only. Prov. xxii. 22. r Jer. xx. 7, 8. see Matt. xxviii. 20. 2 Pet. ii. 8. s ch. ii. 46 reff. t ch. xiii. 10 reff. u constr., ch. xi. 20 reff. v intrans., here only. Exod. i. 20. see ver. 7 reff. w John vii. 12. Phil. ii. 14. 1 Pet. iv. 9 only. Exod. xvi. 7, 9. x ch. ix. 29 (xi. 20 rec.) only †. see 2 Macc. iv. 13. y 2 Cor. xi. 22. Phil. iii. 5 only. Gen. xxxix. 14. xli. 12. z here only †. Xen. Mem. iv. 8. 7, but not =. a = ch. xi. 29. 2 Cor. ix. 1, 12, 13 ‡ (Esth. vi. 3 A [not Bℵ]. 1 Macc. xi. 58 only). b here only †. Judith xii. 15 only. c ch. ix. 39, 41 reff.

τινι E: *αυτους* A. rec aft *απελ.* ins *αυτους*, with DEHP rel 36 vulg [syrr æth arm Bas$_1$] Chr$_1$ [Lucif$_1$]: om ABCℵ [coptt].

41. aft *ουν* add *αποστολοι* D 180 syr. rec *υπ. τ. ον.* bef *κατηξ.*, with DEHP rel syr [arm] Chr$_1$ Thl Lucif: txt ABCℵ a d h m vulg Syr (coptt) Orig$_2$ [Bas$_1$] Thdrt$_2$ Ambrst$_2$ Quæst. rec aft *ονομ.* ins *αυτου*, with c d æth Orig$_2$; *του κυριου ιησου* E b f g l^2 syr; *ιησου* k o 13 vulg Thdrt$_1$; *τ. ιησ.* 36; *τ. χριστου* a e h m fuld tol [Eus$_1$] Chr$_1$ Thdrt$_1$ (*all plainly shewing the additions to be spurious*): om ABCDHPℵ Syr coptt [arm] Ammon-c.

42. for *τε*, *δε* D vulg E-lat coptt Lucif$_1$. rec *ιησ.* bef *τ. χρ.*, with HP rel am Syr copt æth-rom: *ιησ. χρ.* E 65 Chr$_1$: *τ. κυριον ιησ.*, omg *χρ.*, C k 13: *τ. κυρ. ιησ. χρ.* D [tol Syr] sah æth-pl[Tischdf (Lucif$_1$)]: txt ABℵ 36 [vulg-ed] fuld syr Bas$_1$ Cyr-jer$_1$ (Iren-int$_1$).—(om ver c.)

CHAP. VI. **1.** *ταυταις* bef *τ. ημ.* D-gr: for *ταυτ.*, *εκειναις* C^3 73 vulg sah. om 2nd *τη* D^1(ins D^6). *χειραι* P. at end ins *εν τη διακονια των εβραιων* D^1(and lat).

them. **40. δείραντες**] See Deut. xxv. 2,—for disobedience to their command. **41. τοῦ ὀν.**] Not '*this Name*' (as Beng. and Kuin. [nor, '*his Name*' (as E. V.)]), but **the Name**, *κατ' ἐξοχήν*, viz. of Christ. So the Heb. שֵׁם is used Levit. xxiv. 11, 16: see reff. and compare *τῆς ὁδοῦ*, ch. ix. 2, and Euseb. H. E. v. 18, *κέκριται* (sc. Alexander) . . . . *οὐ διὰ τὸ ὄνομα, ἀλλὰ δι' ἃς ἐτόλμησε λῃστείας.* **42. πᾶσαν ἡμ.**] **every day**, not '*all day long*,' which would be *πᾶσ. τὴν ἡμ.* On **κατ' οἶκον** see note on ref. **τὸν χρισ. Ἰησ.**] According to the true reading even more pointedly than in the rec., *τὸν χριστ.* is the predicate, and *Ἰησ.* the subject: **preaching** (that) **Jesus** (is) **the Christ.**

CHAP. VI. 1—7.] ELECTION OF SEVEN PERSONS TO SUPERINTEND THE DISTRIBUTION OF ALMS. **1.**] **δέ**, in contrast to the former entire unity of the church: introducing that great and important chapter in her history of *Judaizing divisions*, which from this time onward disquieted her. **ἐν τ. ἡμ. τ.**] See ch. i. 15:—but not necessarily as there, '*within a very few days*:' the expression is quite indefinite. Some time must have elapsed since ch. iv. 32. **Ἑλληνιστῶν—Ἑβραίους**] The *Hellenists* (from *ἑλληνίζειν*) were the *Grecian Jews:* not only those who were *themselves* proselytes, nor only those who *came of families* once proselytized,—but all who, on account of origin or habitation, *spoke Greek* as their ordinary language, and used ordinarily the LXX version. The *Hebrews* were the *pure Jews*, not necessarily *resident in Palestine* (e. g. Paul, who was Ἑβραῖος ἐξ Ἑβραίων, Phil. iii. 5. See also 2 Cor. xi. 22),—nor necessarily of *unmixed Jewish descent*, else the ἐξ Ἑβρ. would hardly have been an additional distinction,—but rather distinguished by *language*, as speaking the Syro-Chaldaic and using the Hebrew Scriptures. **παρεθεωροῦντο**] The use of this appropriate word shews, I think, that Olsh.'s supposition, that *χῆραι* implies *all their poor*, is not correct. Those poor who could attend for themselves and represent their case were served: but the *widows*, who required more searching out at their own houses, were overlooked. And this because the Apostles, who certainly before this had the charge of the duty of distribution, being already too much occupied in the ministry of the Word to attend personally to it, had entrusted it apparently to some deputies among the *Hebrews*, who had committed this oversight. For the low estimation in which the Hellenistic Jews were held by

δώδεκα τὸ [d] πλῆθος τῶν μαθητῶν εἶπαν Οὐκ [e] ἀρεστόν
ἐστιν ἡμᾶς [f] καταλείψαντας τὸν [g] λόγον τοῦ [g] θεοῦ [h] διακονεῖν [i] τραπέζαις. 3 [k] ἐπισκέψασθε οὖν, ἀδελφοί, ἄνδρας
ἐξ ὑμῶν [l] μαρτυρουμένους ἑπτά, [m] πλήρεις [m] πνεύματος καὶ
[n] σοφίας, οὓς [o] καταστήσομεν ἐπὶ τῆς [p] χρείας ταύτης·
4 ἡμεῖς δὲ τῇ προσευχῇ καὶ τῇ [q] διακονίᾳ τοῦ λόγου

ABCDE HPℵ a b c d f g h k l m o 13

d = ch. iv. 32. xvii. 4. Luke i. 10. xix. 37 al. absol., ver. 5. e John viii. 29. ch. xii. 3. 1 John iii. 22 only. Lev. x. 19. constr., here only. f = Matt. xix. 5 ‖ Mk., from Gen. ii. 24. 2 Pet. ii. 15. g ch. xi. 1 reff. h = here only. see Matt. iv. 11. Luke x. 40. John xii. 2. i = Matt. xv. 27. Luke xvi. 21. ch. xvi. 34. 2 Kings ix. 7. (see Matt. xxi. 12 ‖.) k = here only. Ezek. xxxiv. 11. — σκ., Gen. xli. 33. l = ch. x. 22 reff. 1 Tim. v. 10. Heb. xi. 2, 39 ‡. (Num. xxxv. 30.) m ch. vii. 55 reff. n = Col. iv. 5. o Matt. xxiv. 45, 47. Luke xii. 42. Gen. xli. 33, 41, 43. p = here only. 1 Macc. x. 37. 2 Macc. viii. 9. q = ch. xii. 25 reff. see ver. 1 reff.

2. om δε D[1]-gr(ins D-corr[1]) sah. (**ειπαν**, so ABC.) aft ειπ. ins *προς αυτους* D, *eis* Syr sah [æth(Tischdf)] Cypr$_1$. *ημιν* CD Thl-fin : txt ABEHP[ℵ] rel 36 [Clem$_1$] Bas$_1$ Mac$_1$ Marc$_1$ Chr$_1$ Thl-sif.—*καταλ.* bef *ημ.* E 13. 180. *καταλιποντας* E [k] 5. 13. 40. 180 lect-12 [Bas$_1$ Mac$_1$ Marc$_1$ Chr].

3. *επισκεψωμεθα* B. for *ουν*, *δη* A : *δε* Bℵ : om sah æth [arm Bas$_1$] : om *αδελφ.* A 13 æth Marc Orig-int : *τι ουν εστιν αδελφοι επισκεψασθαι* D : txt CEH[P] rel [vulg syrr copt Chr$_1$ Did-int$_1$]. *εξ υμ. αυτων* bef *ανδρ.* D. *πληρης* AEHP k.
rec aft *πνευμ.* ins *αγιου*, with A C[1·3](appy) EHP rel 36 [vulg-ed] demid sah Bas$_1$, *κυριου* Syr : om B C[2](appy) D(ℵ) am fuld lux (syr) copt Chr$_1$. (*The omission may have been made to suit ver* 10 : *at the same time the insertion of αγιου from ver* 5 *was very obvious, and is the more probable of the two.*)—ℵ[1] syr omit *και* also. rec *καταστησωμεν* (*corrn*), with HP e 13 vulg D-lat E-lat Marc$_1$: txt ABCDEℵ rel Bas$_1$ Chr$_1$. *αυτης* D[1][-gr](txt D[3](?)).

4. *ημ. δε εσομεθα . . . . προσκαρτερουντες* D(*sumus* and *perseveramus* D-lat [*perseveramus* also syr-mg]) : *προσκαρτερησωμεν* EH 1 m [13] Bas$_1$ Chr$_1$ Marc$_1$.

the *Hebrews*, see Biscoe, History of the Acts, pp. 60, 61. **ἐν τῇ διακ. τ. καθ.**] Some have argued from this that there must have been 'deacons' before: and that those now elected (see below on their names) were only for the service of the Hellenistic Jews. But I should rather believe, with De Wette and Röthe, that the Apostles had as yet, by themselves or by non-official deputies, performed the duty. The *διακονία* was the daily distribution of food: see on ver. 2. **2.**] **τὸ πλῆθος τ. μ.,**—'the *whole number* of disciples in Jerusalem:' summoning a general meeting of the church. How many they were in number at the time, is not said. Clearly the 120 names of ch. i. 15, cannot (Lightf.) be meant. **οὐκ ἀρεστόν ἐστιν**] 'non placet:' **it is not our pleasure**: not 'non æquum est,' as Beza, Calv., Kuin., and others (and E. V.), defending this rendering by *ἀρεστόν* being used in the LXX for the Heb. טוֹב : but even there it never signifies *good* or *right* absolutely, but is used subjectively, with בְּעֵינֶיךָ, 'in thine eyes:' see Gen. xvi. 6, *ὡς ἄν σοι ἀρεστὸν ᾖ* : also Deut. xii. 28, *τὸ ἀρεστὸν . . . . ἐναντίον κυρίου τ. θεοῦ σου.* **καταλείψαντας**] For to this it would come, if the Apostles were to enquire into, and do justice in, every case of asserted neglect. **διακονεῖν τραπέζαις**] It is a question whether this expression import the service of distributing money (see reff. and Luke xix. 23 al.) —or that of apportioning the daily public meals. The latter seems to me most probable, both on account of the *καθημερινή* above, and of the usage of *διακονεῖν* (see reff.). That both kinds of tables may be meant, is possible: but hardly probable.
3. ἐπισκ. οὖν] The similarity to ref. Gen. seems to shew that the **look ye out** of the E. V. is the right rendering. **μαρτυρουμένους**] For this use of the pass. not found in the Gospp., compare besides reff., Jos. Antt. iii. 2. 5, *τὸν στρατηγὸν Ἰησοῦν ἐνεγκωμίαζε, μαρτυρούμενον ἐφ᾽ οἷς ἔπραξεν ὑπὸ παντὸς τοῦ στρατοῦ*—and Marc. Antonin. vii. 62, *συνεχῶς ἐφιστάναι, τίνες εἰσὶν οὗτοι, ὑφ᾽ ὧν μαρτυρεῖσθαι θέλεις.* **ἑπτά**] Some have supposed a reference to the number of nations of which the Hellenistic Jews would perhaps be composed: some, to 7000, to which number the believers would by this time amount (Bengel): some, to the mystic number seven, so common in Jewish writings (Meyer, De Wette):—but the best remark is Lightfoot's:—'quare septem eligendi, dicat cui est audacia.' Some present consideration of convenience probably regulated the number. **ἐπὶ τ. χρείας τ.**] 'super hoc opus,' Vulg.:—'ad hunc usum,' Grot.:—'over this requirement (desideratum),' Meyer:—but the occurrence of the very same expression 1 Macc. x. 37, *ἐκ τούτων κατασταθήσεται ἐπὶ χρειῶν τῆς βασιλείας τῶν οὐσῶν εἰς πίστιν*, seems to make the sense **business** (as E. V.), **duty**, more probable. The *duty* (see above) was,

[r] προσκαρτερήσομεν. 5 καὶ [st] ἤρεσεν ὁ λόγος [tu] ἐνώπιον r = ch. i. 14 reff.
παντὸς τοῦ [v] πλήθους, καὶ [w] ἐξελέξαντο Στέφανον ἄνδρα s Matt. xiv. 6 || Mk. elsw.
[x] πλήρη πίστεως καὶ πνεύματος ἁγίου, καὶ Φίλιππον καὶ Paul (Rom. viii. 8 reff.).
Πρόχορον καὶ Νικανορα καὶ Τίμωνα καὶ Παρμενᾶν καὶ t Jer. xviii. 4. 1 Macc. viii. 21.
Νικόλαον [y] προσήλυτον Ἀντιοχέα, 6 οὓς [z] ἔστησαν [a] ἐν- u = Luke xiv. 10 al. Num. xiii. 34.
ώπιον τῶν ἀποστόλων· καὶ προσευξάμενοι [b] ἐπέθηκαν v absol., ch. ii. 6 reff.

w ch. xv. 7 reff. x ch. xix. 28 reff. y ch. ii. 10. xiii. 43. Matt. xxiii. 15 only. Exod. xxi. 48, 49 al z ch. i. 23. iv. 7. xxii. 30. Num. xxvii. 19, 22. a = ch. ii. 25 reff. b ch. viii. 17, 19 reff.

5. aft λογ. ins *ουτος* D Syr sah æth. *εναντιον* C. aft πληθ. ins *των μαθητων* D. *εξελεξαν τον* (sic) ℵ. *πληρης* [AC¹]D[EH] P(-*ρις*) ℵ. transpose *πιστεως* and *πνευματος* ℵ¹. *προχωρον* E 1 [-*χωρος* syr-mg-gr]. *νικανωρα* B²E [13] : *νικορα* D-gr : *νικαρινον* syr-mg-gr. *τειμωνα* B¹D [13] : *τιμονα* C² [*τιμων* syr-mg-gr]. *παρμενα* D¹(txt D-corr² (?)). *αντιοχεαν* C.
6. *ουτοι εσταθησαν* D-gr Syr sah. for *και*, *οιτινες* D-gr.

not that of ministering to the Hellenistic Jews only, but that of superintending the whole distribution. **4.] τ. διακονίᾳ τ. λόγου,** in opposition to the *διακονία τραπεζῶν*. 'Hæ partes sunt nobilissimæ, quas nemo episcopus alteri, quasi ipse majoribus rebus intentus, delegare potest.' Bengel. 'Hinc apparet non frustra precandi studium commendari verbi ministris.' Calvin. **5.] πίστεως,**—not in the lower sense (Kuin.) of 'truthfulness,'—but in the higher of **faith**, the root of all Christian virtues: see ch. xi. 24 (De W.).

Of these seven, Stephen and Philip (ch. viii. 5, 26, 40; xxi. 8) only are elsewhere mentioned. On the idea of Nicolas having founded the heretical sect of the Nicolaitanes, Rev. ii. 6, 15 (Lightf. and Grot. from Iren. adv. Hær. i. 26, p. 105, and Epiph. Hær. 25, p. 76), see note ad loc. From his being called *προσήλυτον Ἀντιοχέα*, some have argued (Heins.) that *he only* was a proselyte, and none of the rest: some (Salmasius), that *all* were proselytes,—but the rest, of Jerusalem. But neither inference seems justified: rather I should say that the addition simply imports that he became better known than the rest, from the very circumstance perhaps of Antioch having been afterwards so important a spot in the Christian history (ch. xi. 19, note). These names are *all Greek*: but we cannot thence infer that the seven were all Hellenists: the Apostles Philip and Andrew bore Greek names, but were certainly not Hellenists. There does appear however, in the case of these two Apostles, to have been a connexion with Greeks of some sort, see John xii. 20—22. Possibly, though Ἑβραῖοι, they may not have been ἐξ Ἑβραίων (see above on ver. 1), but sprung from intermarriage with Hellenists. And so these seven may have been partly Ἑβραῖοι, though their names seem to indicate, and their office would appear to require, that they were connected with Hellenists, and not likely to overlook or disparage them. The title of '*deacons*' is no where applied to these seven in Scripture, nor does the word occur in the Acts at all. In 1 Tim. iii. 8 ff. there is no absolute identification of the duties of deacons with those allotted to the seven, but at the same time nothing to imply that they were different. And *ἀνέγκλητοι*, ib. ver. 10, at all events is parallel with our *μαρτυρουμένους*, ver. 3. The universal consent of all Christian writers in regarding this as the institution of the office of deacons should not be overlooked: but at the same time we must be careful not to imagine that we have here the institution of the *ecclesiastical order* so named. The distinctness of the two is stated by Chrysostom, Hom. xiv. p. 115, *ὁποῖον δὲ ἆρα ἀξίωμα εἶχον οὗτοι, καὶ ποίαν ἐδέξαντο χειροτονίαν, ἀναγκαῖον μαθεῖν. ἆρα τὴν τῶν διακόνων; καὶ μὴν τοῦτο ἐν ταῖς ἐκκλησίαις οὐκ ἔστιν· ἀλλὰ τῶν πρεσβυτέρων ἐστὶν ἡ οἰκονομία. ὅθεν οὔτε διακόνων, οὔτε πρεσβυτέρων οἶμαι τὸ ὄνομα εἶναι δῆλον καὶ φανερόν. ἀλλὰ τέως εἰς τοῦτο ἐχειροτονήθησαν.* So also Œcumenius in loc.: *τοὺς ἐκλεγέντας εἰς διακόνους ἐχειροτόνησαν, οὐ κατὰ τὸν νῦν ἐν ταῖς ἐκκλησίαις βαθμόν, ἀλλὰ τοῦ διανέμειν μετὰ ἀκριβείας καὶ ὀρφανοῖς καὶ χήραις τὰ πρὸς διατροφήν.* See Suicer sub voce. But that the subsequent office of deacon was founded upon this appointment is very probable. The only one of these seven who appears in the subsequent history (ch. xxi. 8), is called *Φίλιππος ὁ εὐαγγελιστής*, probably from the success granted him as recorded in ch. viii. 12. In these early days titles sprung out of realities, and were not yet mere hierarchical classifications. **6.] ἐπέθηκαν,** viz. the Apostles. Their office of giving themselves to *prayer* is here specially exercised.

The *laying on of hands*, the earliest mention of which is connected with *blessing only* (Gen. xlviii. 14), was prescribed to

αὐτοῖς τὰς [b] χεῖρας. 7 Καὶ ὁ [c] λόγος τοῦ [c] θεοῦ [de] ηὔξανεν,
καὶ [df] ἐπληθύνετο ὁ ἀριθμὸς τῶν μαθητῶν ἐν Ἱερουσαλὴμ
σφόδρα, πολύς τε [g] ὄχλος τῶν ἱερέων [h] ὑπήκουον [i] τῇ ...σφο C.
πίστει.
8 Στέφανος δὲ [j] πλήρης χάριτος καὶ δυνάμεως ἐποίει
[k] τέρατα καὶ σημεῖα μεγάλα ἐν τῷ λαῷ. 9 [l] ἀνέστησαν δέ
τινες τῶν ἐκ τῆς συναγωγῆς τῆς λεγομένης Λιβερτίνων C νες...

ABCDE HPℵ a b c d f g h k l m o 13

c = ch. xi. 1. d = ch. vii. 17. xii. 24 al. Exod. i. 7. e as above (d). ch. xix. 20. Matt. vi. 28. Luke i. 80 al.‡ trans., 1 Cor. iii. 6. f as above (d). ch. ix. 31. 1 Pet. i. 2. see ver. 1. g ch. i. 15. Luke v. 29. vi. 17. Ezek. xxiii. 24. h = Rom. vi. 16, 17. x. 16 al. Deut. xx. 12. see Rom. i. 5. xvi. 26. i Luke xviii. 8. ch. xiii. 8. 1 Tim. v. 8. j ver. 5. k ch. vii. 36 reff. l — Luke x. 25. Mark xiv. 57, 60. 2 Chron. xiii. 4, 6.

7. for *θεου*, *κυριου* DE vulg[with fuld tol] syr Chr[-txt$_1$ Orig-int$_1$] : txt ABCHP rel [am demid Syr coptt arm Chr-comm$_1$]. *μανθανοντων* E. for *ιερεων*, *ιουδαιων* ℵ[1] e o [Syr Thl-fin]. *υπηκουον αν* (or rather *αυ*, Scriv) D[1] : *-ουεν* AE g vulg [syrr] Chr$_1$. at end ins *του ευαγγελιου* syr-mg.

8. rec (for *χαριτος*) *πιστεως* (*corrn from ver* 5), with HP rel [Chr$_1$]: *χαριτος κ. πιστ.* E : *χαριτος θεου* æth : txt ABDℵ k 36 vulg Syr coptt arm Bas$_1$ Did[-int$_1$ Procl$_1$]. transp *τερ.* and *σημ.* E 40. 96. aft *λαω* add *δια του ονοματος κυριου ιησου χρ.* D sah Aug; *δια του ονοματος του κυρ. ιησ. χρ.* k 13; *εν* [*τω*] *ονοματι του κυριου* E; *δ. τ. ον. κυρ.* syr-w-ast.

9. *καθ ο ανεστ. τινες* E : *adversus quem* &c E-lat. om 1st *των* ℵ. *των*

Moses as the form of conferring office on Joshua, Num. xxvii. 18, and from that time was used on such occasions by the Jews. From its adoption by the Apostles, it has ever been the practice of the Christian church in *ordaining*, or *setting apart* her ministers. It was also used by the Apostles on those who, having been baptized, were to be fully endowed with the gifts of the Holy Spirit: see ch. viii. 17; xix. 6, and Heb. vi. 2. 7.] **καί** (not 'therefore,' as Kuin.), **and**, i. e., on this measure being completed; as would be the case, seeing that these seven were not only servants of tables, but men full of the Holy Ghost and of wisdom:—and we soon hear of the part which Stephen bore in the work. **πολὺς ὄχλ. τ. ἱερέων**] The number of priests who returned from Babylon, Ezra ii. 36—39, was 4289: and the number would probably have much increased since then. No evasion of the historian's assertion is to be attempted. Casaubon, approved by Beza and Valcknaer, would read, *πολύς τε ὄχλος, καὶ τῶν ἱερέων* (sc. *τινὲς*) *ὑπ.*; and Heinsius, Wolf, Kuinoel, and Elsner attempt a distinction between *ὄχλος τῶν ἱερ.*, 'sacerdotes ex plebe,' and the 'sacerdotes docti.' But, besides that the words will not bear this meaning, the distinction is one wholly unknown in the N. T. At this time was probably the *culminating point of popularity of the church at Jerusalem.* As yet, all seemed going on prosperously for the conversion of Israel. The multitude honoured the Apostles: the advice of Gamaliel had moderated the opposition of the Sanhedrim: the priests were gradually being won over. But God's designs were far different. At this period another great element in the testimony of the church is brought out, in the person of Stephen,—its *protest against Pharisaism.* This arrays against it that powerful and zealous sect, and henceforward it finds neither favour nor tolerance with either of the parties among the Jews, but increasing and bitter enmity from them both.

8—Ch. VII. 60.] The accusation, defence, and martyrdom of Stephen.

8.] This is the first instance of any, *not an Apostle*, working signs and wonders. The power was perhaps conferred by the laying on of the Apostles' hands; though, that having been for a special purpose merely, and the working miracles being a fulfilment of the promise, Mark xvi. 17, 18, to *all believers*, I should rather refer the power to the *eminence of Stephen's faith.* **χάριτος**, **divine grace** (not 'favour with the people'): the effects of which, the miracles, were called **χαρίσματα.**

9.] **Λιβερτίνων** is rightly explained by Chrysostom: *οἱ Ῥωμαίων ἀπελεύθεροι.* Philo, Legat. ad Caium, § 23, vol. ii. p. 568, speaks of *τὴν πέραν τοῦ Τιβέρεως ποταμοῦ μεγάλην τῆς Ῥώμης ἀποτομὴν .... κατεχομένην κα οἰκουμένην πρὸς Ἰουδαίων*, and adds, *Ῥωμαῖοι δὲ ἦσαν οἱ πλείους ἀπελευθερωθέντες· αἰχμάλωτοι γὰρ ἀχθέντες εἰς Ἰταλίαν, ὑπὸ τῶν κτησαμένων ἠλευθερώθησαν, οὐδὲν τῶν πατρίων παραχαράξαι βιασθέντες* (p. 1014, Potter). Tacitus, Ann. ii. 85 (A.D. 19), relates, 'Actum et de sacris Ægyptiis Judaicisque pellendis: factumque Patrum consultum, ut quatuor millia libertini generis, ea superstitione infecta, queis idonea ætas, in insulam Sardiniam veherentur .... cæteri cederent Italia, nisi certam ante diem profanos ritus exuissent.' In this Josephus agrees, Antt. xviii. 3. 5,

καὶ Κυρηναίων καὶ Ἀλεξανδρέων καὶ τῶν [m] ἀπὸ Κιλικίας
καὶ Ἀσίας [n] συνζητοῦντες τῷ Στεφάνῳ, 10 καὶ οὐκ [o] ἴσχυον
[p] ἀντιστῆναι τῇ σοφίᾳ καὶ τῷ [q] πνεύματι ᾧ ἐλάλει. 11 τότε
[r] ὑπέβαλον ἄνδρας [s] λέγοντας ὅτι ἀκηκόαμεν αὐτοῦ [t] λαλοῦντος [t] ῥήματα [u] βλάσφημα [v] εἰς Μωυσῆν καὶ τὸν θεόν.
12 [w] συνεκίνησάν τε τὸν λαὸν καὶ τοὺς πρεσβυτέρους καὶ

m - ch. ii. 5 reff. n and constr., Mark viii. 11. ix. 14 †. w. πρός, ch. ix. 29. o = Matt. viii. 28. ch. xv. 10. xxv. 7 al. Isa. l. 2. p Matt. v. 39. ch. xiii. 8. Rom. ix. 19. xiii. 2. Lev. xxvi. 37. Job xli. 2. q = Luke i. 17 al. Dan. vi. 3. r here only †. Josh. xxiii. 4 Symm. so ὑπόβλητος, Jos. B. J. v. 10. 4. s constr., ch. xv. 27. 2 Pet. ii. 4. Winer, edn. 6, § 45. 1. t ch. xi. 14 reff. u = 2 Pet. ii. 11. Rev. xiii. 5 only ‡. (1 Tim. i. 13. 2 Tim. iii. 2 only. Isa. lxvi. 3 only. Wisd. i. 6 al.) v constr., Mark iii. 29. 2 Macc. viii. 4. Bel and Dr. 9 Theod. w here only †.

λεγομενων Aℵ k [13] coptt Chr-mss$_1$. om και ασιας AD[1](and lat: ins D[2]). (συνζητ., so AB[1]CDEℵ.)

10. for και, οιτινες D: om και sah. τη σοφ. τη ουση εν αυτω κ. τω πν. τω αγιω ω ελαλει, δια το ελεγχεσθαι αυτους (διοτι ελεγχοντο E) υπ (επ D[1]: υπ D[2]) αυτου μετα πασης παρρησιας· μη δυναμενοι ουν (ου D[1]) αντοφθαλμειν (so syr-mg, επιδη ουκ ηδυναντο αντιλεγιν E) τη αληθεια DE: simly from δια το ελεγχ. am[2] syr-mg.

11. λεγοντες Aℵ, so probably D[1]. [λαλουντας E[1]] λεγοντος ℵ[1] [om A[1](appy)]. βλασφημιας D-gr ℵ[1](but corrd) 137 vulg [arm].

12. ins και ταυτα ειποντες bef συνεκ. τε E.

relating a story as one of its causes, in which Ida, a freedwoman, was the agent of the mischief. Here then we have abundant reason for numbers of these Jews 'libertini generis' having come to Jerusalem, being among the *cæteri* who were ordered to quit Italy: and what place so likely a refuge for Jews as Jerusalem? Those who find a difficulty in this interpretation suppose them to have been inhabitants of Libertum, a town in Africa propria, or proconsularis, from which we find an episcopus Libertinensis sitting in the synod of Carthage in 411 (so Suidas, Λιβερτῖνοι, ὄνομα ἔθνους,—Schleusn., al.); or conjecture Λιβυστίνων to have been the true reading (so the Arm. version, *Libyorum*, Œcum., Lyra, Beza, Le Clerc, al.),—or even Λιβύων τῶν κατὰ Κυρήνην (Schulthess);—or suppose them (Lightf.) to have been freedmen from Jewish servitude,—or Italian freedmen, who had become proselytes. (The Arabic version given in the Paris polyglott curiously renders it *Corinthiorum*.) But none of these suppositions will bear examination, and the best interpretation is the usual one—that they were the descendants of Jewish freedmen at Rome, who had been expelled by Tiberius. There is no difficulty in their having had a synagogue of their own: for there were 460 or 480 synagogues at Jerusalem (Vitringa, Synag. p. 256. Lightf., Meyer). **Κυρηναίων**] See ch. ii. 10, note. **Ἀλεξανδρέων**] Two of the five regions of Alexandria were inhabited by Jews (see Jos. Antt. xiv. 7. 2, 10. 1; xix. 5. 2 al.). It was also the seat of the learning and philosophy of the Grecian Jews, which was now at its height. This metropolis of the Hellenists would certainly have a synagogue in Jerusalem. I understand *three* distinct synagogues to be meant, notwithstanding the somewhat equivocal construction,—and λεγομένης only to apply to the unusual term Λιβερτίνων. **τῶν ἀπὸ Κ.**] It seems doubtful whether this genitive also depends on συναγωγῆς. At first sight it would seem not, from the repetition of τῶν, answering to the τῶν before. But then we must remember, that as Κυρηναίων and Ἀλεξανδρέων both belong to *towns*, and towns well known as the residences of Jews, a change of designation would be necessary when the Jews of whole provinces came to be mentioned, and the synagogue would not be called that of the Κίλικες or Ἀσιανοί (ch. xx. 4), but that of **οἱ ἀπὸ Κ. κ. Ἀ.**:—and, this being the case, the article could not but be repeated, without any reference to the τῶν before. *Cilicia* was at this time a Roman province, the capital being the free city of Tarsus, see note on ch. ix. 11. *Asia*,—not exactly as in ch. ii. 9, where it is distinguished from Phrygia,—here and usually in the Acts implies Asia proconsularis, a large and important Roman province, including Mysia, Lydia, Caria, and Phrygia—known also as Asia cis Taurum. **11.**] Neander well remarks (Pfl. u. Leit., p. 81 ff.) that this false charge, coupled with the character of Stephen's apologetic speech, shews the *real character of his arguments with his opponents*:—that he seems to have been the first who plainly set forth the transitory nature of the law and temple, as compared with the permanence of the latter and better covenant, thus being in a remarkable manner the forerunner of St. Paul. **12.**] **τὸν λαόν**, *first*,—that by means of the popular feeling they might act upon the **πρεσβ. κ. γρ.**, the members of the Sanhedrim.

τοὺς γραμματεῖς, καὶ [x] ἐπιστάντες [y] συνήρπασαν αὐτὸν
καὶ ἤγαγον εἰς τὸ [z] συνέδριον, 13 [a] ἔστησάν τε μάρτυρας
[b] ψευδεῖς λέγοντας Ὁ ἄνθρωπος οὗτος οὐ [c] παύεται
[t] ῥήματα [t] λαλῶν [d] κατὰ τοῦ [e] τόπου τοῦ [e] ἁγίου καὶ τοῦ
νόμου. 14 ἀκηκόαμεν γὰρ αὐτοῦ λέγοντος ὅτι Ἰησοῦς ὁ
Ναζωραῖος οὗτος [f] καταλύσει τὸν τόπον τοῦτον καὶ
[g] ἀλλάξει τὰ [h] ἔθη ἃ [i] παρέδωκεν ἡμῖν Μωυσῆς. 15 καὶ
[k] ἀτενίσαντες εἰς αὐτὸν ἅπαντες οἱ [l] καθεζόμενοι ἐν τῷ
[z] συνεδρίῳ εἶδον τὸ πρόσωπον αὐτοῦ ὡσεὶ πρόσωπον ἀγγέλου. VII. 1 εἶπεν δὲ ὁ ἀρχιερεὺς [m] Εἰ [[m] ἄρα] ταῦτα [n] οὕτως

ABCDE HPℵab cdfgh klmo 13

x absol., Luke xx. 1. Zech. . 10, 11.
y ch. xix. 29. xxvii. 15. Luke viii. 29 only. Prov. vi. 25. 2 Macc. iii. 27. iv. 41 only.
z ch. iv. 15 reff.
a ch. i. 23. ver. 6.
b Rev. ii. 2. xxi. 8 only. Prov. xxiv. 32 (xxx. 9). see 1 Cor. xv. 15.
c and constr., ch. xiii. 10 reff.
d = Matt. v. 11. xii. 32.
e Matt. xxiv. 15. ch. xxi. 28 only. Ps. lxvii. 5.
f = Matt. xxvi. 61 ||. 2 Cor. v. 1. Ezra v. 12.
g 1 Cor. xv. 51, 52 reff.
h = Luke i. 9. ii. 42. ch. xv. 1. xxi. 21 al. Luke only, exc. John xix. 40. Heb. x. 25 †. 2 Macc. xi. 25.
i = 1 Cor. xi. 2, 23. 2 Pet. ii. 21. Jude 3.
k ch. i. 10 reff.
l Matt. xxvi 55. Luke ii. 46. John iv. 6. xi. 20. xx. 12. ch. xx. 9 only. Lev. xii. 5. Job xxxix. 27. Ezek. xxvi. 16 only.
m ch. viii. 22 reff.
n ch. xii. 15. xvii. 11. xxiv. 9.

om 2nd τους C[1] k. om επισταντες ℵ. aft ηγαγον ins αυτον A e (Syr syr-w-ob) coptt [æth(Tischdf)].

13. εστ. δε H 13. 40. 96 E-lat copt: και εστ. D. aft ψευδ. ins κατα(κατ D-corr) αυτου D [(æth)]. λεγοντες ℵ. ουτ. bef ο ανθρ. C [om ουτ. 13]. rec aft ρημ. ins βλασφημα (*insertion from ver* 11), with EHP (k) 36 lux æth arm [Chr_1] $Procl_1$ Thl: om ABCDℵ rel vulg syrr coptt [Chr_2 $Procl_1$] —κατα τ. τοπ. τ. αγιου κ. τ. νομου λαλων ρημ. βλασφ. k 13 Chr_2 $Procl_1$. λαλ. bef ρημ. BCℵ (k) vulg syrr coptt [(æth) arm(Tischdf) $Nyss_1$ Chr_1] $Procl_1$: txt ADEH[P] rel [arm(Treg)] Chr_2 Thl. rec aft αγ. ins τουτου (*to agree with ver* 14: *or perhaps because the meeting of the Sanhedrim seemed to have been in a part of the temple*), with BC 13 rel 36 tol syrr [copt] sah Chr_2 [$Nyss_1$ $Procl_1$]: bef, k: om ADEHPℵ a b c e f h l o vulg æth arm Nyss-ms Chr-comm $Damasc_1$.

14. εθνη B[1](corrd appy eadem manu). for α παρεδ., απερ εδωκεν P d 78[1]. 116-23.

15. ητενιζον δε αυτω D[1]-gr(txt D[2](and lat)): om εις ℵ[1](ins ℵ-corr[1]). for απαντες, παντες ABCD[[1]]Eℵ[1] c Thl-sif: om 13: txt (*see proleg*) D[[2]]HP rel Chr_1. καθημενοι D c 137-80. aft αγγ. ins εστωτος εν μεσω αυτων D: του θεου sah æth.

Chap. VII. 1. aft αρχ. ins τω στεφανω DE tol [*illi* coptt]. om αρα (*as unnecessary*) ABCℵ 36: ins D-gr EHP rel syr [(arm)] Chr_1: *enim* E-lat: not expressed in vulg D-lat [Syr(appy) æth]. τουτο D.

ἐπιστάντες] The same persons,—acting now by the authority of the Sanhedrim; Saul, among *οἱ ἀπὸ Κιλικίας*, being, as is afterwards (ch. vii. 58) implied, among the foremost,—**came upon him** (see reff.), **and seized him.** **13. ψευδεῖς**] The *falsehood* of their witness consisted, as in the similar case of our Lord, in taking Stephen's words out of their context, and *misrepresenting* what perhaps, totidem verbis, he *had actually said.* **τοῦ τόπ. τ. ἁγ.**] The *temple*, see reff. **14.**] We may either take the words thus, ὅτι Ἰησοῦς ὁ Ναζωραῖος, οὗτος κατ., "*that Jesus of N., he it is who shall destroy*' . . . . (see ch. vii. 35; 1 Cor. vi. 4), or ὅτι Ἰησοῦς, ὁ Ναζωραῖος οὗτος, κατ., '*that Jesus, this Nazarene, shall destroy* . . . .,'—or, which seems by far the best, take the whole together, **that this Jesus of N. shall destroy,** as in E. V. Compare ὁ Παῦλος οὗτος, ch. xix. 26. **15.**] It is a question with regard to this verse, Does it relate any *supernatural appearance, glorifying the face of Stephen,*—or merely describe the calm and holy aspect with which he stood before the council? The majority of Commentators suppose the latter: and certainly the foregoing description of Stephen would lead us to infer, that there was something remarkably striking in his appearance and demeanour, which overawed his adversaries. But both from the plain language of our text, well understood among the Jews to signify supernatural brightness (see examples in Wetstein), and from the fact that in Luke's own narrative we have supernatural brightness associated with angelic appearances more than once (see Luke ii. 9; ch. xii. 7), I should be inclined to think that the face of the martyr was *lighted up with a divine radiance.* That the effect on those present was not such as to prevent the examination proceeding, is no argument against this view: in the very mildness of the question of the H. P. which follows, I see the trace of some unusual incident exercising an influence over him. Chrysostom (who does not, however, seem to adopt the above interpretation, his τοῦτο καὶ ἡ δόξα Μωυσέως

[n] ἔχει; [2] ὁ δὲ ἔφη Ἄνδρες ἀδελφοὶ καὶ πατέρες, ἀκούσατε. ὁ [o] θεὸς τῆς [o] δόξης [p] ὤφθη τῷ [q] πατρὶ ἡμῶν [q] Ἀβραὰμ

o here only. Ps. xxviii. 3. see 1 Cor. ii. 8. Heb. ix. 5. Ps. xxiii. 7, 9.
p ch. ii. 3 reff.
q Luke i. 73. (xvi. 24, 30.) John viii. 39, 53 (56). Rom. iv. (1) 12, 16. James ii. 21 only.

2. αδελφη (sic) D^1-gr(txt D^2).

being apparently only rhetorical) explains well the effect on the council: *ἐπίχαριν δὲ αὐτὸν δοκεῖ μοι ποιῆσαι τὸν θεόν, τάχα ἐπεὶ ἔμελλε τινὰ ἐρεῖν, καὶ ἵνα εὐθέως τῇ προσόψει καταπλήξῃ αὐτούς. ἔστι γάρ, ἔστι καὶ πρόσωπα χάριτος γέμοντα πνευματικῆς ἐπέραστα τοῖς ποθοῦσιν εἶναι, καὶ αἰδέσιμα τοῖς μισοῦσι καὶ φοβερά. ἢ καὶ ὡς αἰτίαν τοῦτο εἶπεν, δι' ἣν ἠνέσχοντο τῆς δημηγορίας αὐτοῦ. τί δαὶ ὁ ἀρχιερεύς; . . . ὁρᾷς πῶς μετὰ ἐπιεικείας ἡ ἐρώτησις καὶ οὐδὲν τέως φορτικὸν ἔχουσα;* In Act. Homil. xv. p. 120. CHAP. VII. 1.] On the H. P.'s question, see Chrys. just quoted. It is parallel with Matt. xxvi. 62, but singularly distinguished from that question by its mildness: see above. **2—53.**] STEPHEN'S DEFENCE. In order to understand this wonderful and somewhat difficult speech, it will be well to bear in mind, (1) that the *general character* of it is *apologetic*, referring to the charge made against him: but (2) that in this apology, forgetting himself in the vast subject which he is vindicating, he every where mixes in the polemic and didactic element. A general synopsis of it may be thus given: (1) He shews (*apologetically*) that, so far from dishonouring Moses or God, he believes and holds in mind God's dealings with Abraham and Moses, and grounds upon them his preaching; that, so far from *dishonouring* the temple, he bears in mind its history and the sayings of the prophets respecting it; and he is proceeding,—when (interrupted by their murmurs or inattention? but see note, ver. 51) he bursts forth into a holy vehemence of invective against their rejection of God, which provokes his tumultuary expulsion from the council, and execution. (2) But simultaneously and parallel with this *apologetic* procedure, he also proceeds *didactically*, shewing them that a future Prophet was pointed out by Moses as the final Lawgiver of God's people,—that the Most High had revealed His spiritual and heavenly nature by the prophets, and did not dwell in temples made with hands. And (3) even more remarkably still does the *polemic* element run through the speech. "*It is not I, but* YOU, *who from the first times till now have rejected and spoken against God.*" And this element, just appearing ver. 9, and again more plainly vv. 25—28, and again more pointedly still in ver. 35, becomes dominant in vv. 39—44, and finally prevails, to the exclusion of the apologetic and didactic, in vv. 51—53. That other connected purposes have been discovered in the speech, as e. g. that so ably followed out by Chrys. Hom. xv.—xvii. (similarly Grot. and Calv.), of shewing that the covenant and promises were *before the law*, and sacrifice and the law *before the temple*,—is to be attributed to the wonderful depth of words uttered like these under the immediate inspiration of the Holy Spirit, presenting to us, from whichever side they are viewed, new and inimitable hues of heavenly wisdom. Many of these will be brought out as we advance.

The question, *from what probable source Luke derived his report of this speech*, so peculiar in its character and citations as to bear, even to the most prejudiced, decisive evidence of authenticity, can be only conjecturally answered: but in this case the conjecture can hardly be wrong. I have discussed the point in the Prolegg. to this vol. ch. i. § ii. 12 (a). Another question has been, in *what language* the speech was delivered. (1) It is a hardly disputable inference from ch. vi. 9, that Stephen was a Hellenist: (2) his citations and quasi-citations for the most part agree with the LXX version. Hence it seems most probable that he spoke *in Greek*, which was almost universally understood in Jerusalem. If he spoke in Hebrew (Syro-Chaldaic), then either those passages where the LXX varies from the Hebrew text (see below) must owe their insertion in that shape to some *Greek narrator* or to *Luke himself*,—or Stephen must have, in speaking, *translated them, thus varying*, into Hebrew: either supposition being in the highest degree improbable. **2. ἄνδρ. ἀδ. κ. πατ.**] So Paul, ch. xxii. 1, before a mixed assembly of Jews. The **ἄνδρ. ἀδ.** would embrace all: the **πατ.** would be a title of respect to the members of the Sanhedrim, in *this case*, but hardly in ch. xxii. 1. **ὁ θεὸς τ. δόξης**] Not = *θεὸς ἔνδοξος*, **but the God of** (i. e. who possesses and manifests Himself by) **Glory**, viz. the Shechinah, see Exod. xxiv. 16, 17, and ver. 55. The words **τῷ πατρὶ ἡμῶν** decide nothing as to Stephen's genuine Hebrew extraction. Any Jew would thus speak.

ὤφθη . . . . πρὶν ἢ κατ. αὐτ. ἐν Χαρ.] This was the Jewish tradition, though not asserted in Genesis. Thus Philo (de Abrah.

ὄντι ἐν τῇ Μεσοποταμίᾳ [r] πρὶν ἢ κατοικῆσαι αὐτὸν ἐν
Χαῤῥάν, 3 καὶ εἶπεν πρὸς αὐτὸν [s] Ἔξελθε ἐκ τῆς γῆς σου
καὶ [ἐκ] τῆς [t] συγγενειας σου, καὶ [u] δεῦρο εἰς τὴν γῆν ἣν
ἄν σοι δείξω. 4 Τότε ἐξελθὼν ἐκ γῆς Χαλδαίων κατῴκησεν ἐν Χαῤῥάν. κἀκεῖθεν [v] μετὰ τὸ ἀποθανεῖν τὸν πατέρα

...προς αυτον d. ABCDE HPℵ a b c f g h k l m o 13

r Matt. i. 18. Mark xiv. 30. ch. ii. 20. Isa. vii. 15.
s Gen. xii. 1.
t Luke i. 61. ver. 14 only. Exod. xii. 21. Job xxxii. 2.
u ver. 34 (from Exod. iii. 10). Matt. xix. 21 ||. John xi. 43. Rom. i. 13. Rev. xvii. 1. xxi. 9 only.
v ch. xix. 21 reff.

χαρρα E[so ver 4] m²: χαρα m¹: χαραν D-gr vulg(not am demid fuld &c).
3. for 1st εκ, απο D¹(txt D⁸, *de* D-lat [vulg E-lat]). om 2nd εκ B D-gr sah Thl[-fin]: ins (*so* LXX) ACEHPℵ rel 36 vss [Orig₁] Iren-int₁. aft συγγ. σου ins (*from* LXX) και εκ του οικου του πατρος σου E 65-7 Aug₂. aft δευρο ins ει D¹[-gr]. rec om την (*perhaps an error owing to similarity of endings: perhaps an attempt to render* γην *more indefinite*), with [C³(appy, Tischdf)] HP rel 36 Chr Thl: ins ABC¹DEℵ. εαν ℵ¹.
4. aft τοτε ins αβρααμ D Syr. και κατωκησεν D¹(and lat). for εν, εις H e f m o Thl: om 65-7: επι 13. for κακειθεν, κακει ην, insg και bef μετωκ., D¹

§ 15 end, vol. ii. p. 12), having paraphrased the divine command, says, διὰ τοῦτο τὴν πρώτην ἀποικίαν ἀπὸ τῆς Χαλδαίων γῆς εἰς τὴν Χαῤῥαίων λέγεται ποιεῖσθαι. But he accurately distinguishes between the λόγιον which he obeyed in leaving Chaldæa, and the θεὸς ὤφθη afterwards, adding a reason after his manner, why God could not be seen nor apprehended by him while he was yet χαλδαΐζων and an astrologer. The fact of his having left Ur by *some divine intimation* is plainly stated in Gen. xv. 7, and referred to in Neh. ix. 7. It was surely both natural and allowable to express this first command in the well-known words of the second. But we can hardly suppose that Stephen adopted the pluperfect rendering of וַיֹּאמֶר in Gen. xii. 1, as the LXX has εἶπεν. (Josephus, ordinarily cited as relating the same tradition, throws, as he often does, the whole history into confusion, saying, it is true, Antt. i. 7. 1, καταλείπει τ. Χαλδαίαν . . . τοῦ θεοῦ κελεύσαντος εἰς τὴν Χαναναίαν μετελθεῖν, but omitting entirely the sojourn in Haran, and connecting the migration with an outbreak of the Chaldæans against him for teaching the worship of the true God.) **Χαῤῥάν**] So the LXX for חָרָן, Gen. xi. 31, &c.; 4 Kings xix. 12; Ezek. xxvii. 23,—Κάῤῥαι τῆς Μεσοποταμίας, Herodian iv. 13 (Ptol. v. 18. 12. Strabo, xvi. p. 747),—'Carras cæde Crassi nobiles,' Plin. v. 24,—'Miserando funere Crassus Assyrias Latio maculavit sanguine Carras,' Lucan i. 104. It lay on an ancient road, in a large plain surrounded by mountains; it was still a great city in the days of the Arabian caliphs. See Winer, Realw. **4. μετὰ τὸ ἀποθανεῖν τὸν πατ. αὐτ.**] In Gen. xi. 26, we read that Terah lived 70 years and begot Abram, Nahor, and Haran; in xi. 32, that Terah lived 205 years, and died in Haran; and in xii. 4, that Abram was 75 years old when he left Haran. Since then cir. 70 + 75 = cir. 145, Terah must have lived cir. 60 years in Haran after Abram's departure. It seems evident, that the Jewish chronology, which Stephen follows, was at fault here, owing to the circumstance of Terah's death *being mentioned* Gen. xi. 32, *before* the command of Abram to leave Haran;—it not having been observed that the mention is *anticipatory*. And this is confirmed by Philo having fallen into the same mistake, de Migr. Abrah. § 32, vol. i. p. 464, πρότερον μὲν ἐκ τῆς Χαλδαϊκῆς ἀναστὰς γῆς Ἀβραὰμ ᾤκησεν εἰς Χαῤῥάν· **τελευτήσαντος δὲ αὐτοῦ τοῦ πατρὸς** ἐκεῖθε καὶ ἐκ ταύτης μετανίσταται. It is observable that the Samaritan Pentateuch in Gen. xi. 32, for 205, reads 145, which has most probably been an alteration to remove the apparent inconsistency. The subterfuge of understanding the *spiritual death* of Terah, who is, as a further hypothesis, supposed to have *relapsed into idolatry* at Haran, appears to have originated with the Rabbis (see Kuinoel ad loc. and Lightf. Hor. Heb.) on discovering that their tradition was at variance with the sacred chronology. They have not been without followers in modern Christendom. It is truly lamentable to see the great Bengel, warped by the unworthy effort of squaring at all hazards, the letter of God's word in such matters, write thus: 'Abram, dum Thara vixit in Haran, domum quodammodo paternam habuit in Haran, in terra Canaan duntaxat peregrinum agens; mortuo autem patre, plane in terra Canaan domum unice habere cœpit.' (This alteration of relation *in* the land being expressed by μετῴκισεν αὐτὸν εἰς!) The way in which the difficulty has been met by Wordsworth and others, viz. that we have no right to assume that Abram was born when Terah was 70, but may regard him as the *youngest son*, would leave us in this equally unsatisfactory posi-

αὐτοῦ [w] μετῴκισεν αὐτὸν εἰς τὴν γῆν ταύτην [x] εἰς ἣν ὑμεῖς
νῦν [x] κατοικεῖτε, 5 καὶ οὐκ ἔδωκεν αὐτῷ [y] κληρονομίαν
ἐν αὐτῇ, οὐδὲ [z] βῆμα ποδός· καὶ [a] ἐπηγγείλατο [a] δοῦναι
αὐτῷ [b] εἰς [c] κατάσχεσιν αὐτὴν καὶ τῷ [d] σπέρματι αὐτοῦ
[e] μετ᾽ αὐτόν, οὐκ ὄντος αὐτῷ τέκνου. 6 ἐλάλησεν δὲ
οὕτως ὁ θεός, ὅτι ἔσται τὸ [d] σπέρμα αὐτοῦ [f] πάροικον ἐν
γῇ [g] ἀλλοτρίᾳ, καὶ [h] δουλώσουσιν αὐτὸ καὶ [i] κακώσουσιν
ἔτη τετρακόσια. 7 καὶ τὸ ἔθνος ᾧ ἐὰν δουλεύσουσιν
[k] κρινῶ ἐγώ, ὁ θεὸς εἶπεν, καὶ μετὰ ταῦτα ἐξελεύσονται
καὶ [l] λατρεύσουσίν μοι ἐν τῷ τόπῳ τούτῳ. 8 καὶ ἔδωκεν

w ver. 43 only. 1 Chron. viii. 6. (-κεσία, see Matt. i. 11.)
x Matt. ii. 23. v. 13. 2 Chron. xix. 4 Ed-vat. (not AB.)
y = Heb. xi. 8. Josh. xiii. 14.
z = here only. Deut. ii. 5. (ch. xii. 21 reff.)
a Gen. xiii. 15. constr., Mark xiv. 11.
b = Mark xiii. 9. xiv. 9 al. Gen. xvii. 8.
c ver. 45 only. Num. xxxii. 5.
d Rom. ix. 7 reff. e ch. xiii. 25 reff. f ver. 29. Eph. ii. 19. 1 Pet. ii. 11 only. Gen. xv. 13.
g Rom. xiv. 4 reff. h Rom vi. 18, 22. 1 Cor. vii. 15. ix. 19. Gal. iv. 3. Tit. ii. 3. 2 Pet. ii. 19 only. Gen. l. c. Wisd. xix. 14. 1 Macc. viii. 11 only. i ver. 19. ch. xii. 1. xiv. 2. xviii. 10. 1 Pet. iii. 13 only. Exod. v. 22 al. k = 1 Cor. xi. 31, 32. Rev. xviii. 8. xix. 2. Gen. l. c.
l Matt. iv. 10 (from Deut. vi. 13). ver. 42. ch. xxiv. 14. Rom. i. 9 al. Exod. iii. 12. (-ρεία, Rom. ix. 4.)

(and lat: κακειθε D²). μετωικησεν D¹[-οικ-](txt D²)[EHP]. aft αυτ. ins ο θεος E Syr. aft κατοικ. ins και οι πατερες υμων DE syr-w-ast Aug, but for υμων, ημων D; D adds further οι προ ημων, syr-w-ast οι προ υμ.

5. for 2nd και, αλλ D [vulg] am &c sah Iren-int: txt ABCEHPℵ rel fuld syrr copt Chr Thl. rec αυτω bef δουναι: txt ABCDEHP b c e f g l m o [vulg arm].—δουναι αυτην εις κατασχ. αυτω AEℵ a h k 13. for last αυτω, αυτου C.

6. for ουτως, αυτω H¹ℵ k [vulg-ed Syr: om am fuld]: αυτω ουτως b 49. 96 [sah]. aft ο θ. ins προς αυτον D Iren-int₁: λεγων πρ. αυτον Syr. for αυτου, σου ℵ [vulg-sixt Syr coptt æth]. for αυτο, αυτους D vulg coptt æth: αυτω e 13. aft κακωσ. ins αυτο C [Syr syr-w-ob; αυτους vulg coptt æth]; αυτω 13.—κακ. αυτο κ. δουλ. E.

7. το δε C e 120 sah æth-pl. αν BD: txt ACEH[P]ℵ rel Chr₁. rec δουλευσωσιν (*corrn to suit* LXX), with BEHPℵ rel vulg [D-lat] Chr₁: txt AC D-gr [sah] Iren-int₁. rec ειπεν bef ο θ., with DEHP rel 36 vss Iren-int: txt ABCℵ. aft εξελ. ins εκειθεν E. λατρευσωσιν C¹[appy] E-gr.

tion:—Terah, *in the course of nature*, begets his son Abram at 130 (205—75): yet this very son Abram regards it as incredible that he himself should beget a son at 99 (Gen. xvii. 1, 17); and on the fact of the birth of Isaac being *out of the course of nature*, most important Scriptural arguments and consequences are founded, cf. Rom. iv. 17—21, Heb. xi. 11, 12. We may fairly leave these Commentators with their new difficulty: only remarking for our instruction, how sure those are to plunge into hopeless confusion, who, from motives however good, once begin to handle the word of God deceitfully. **μετ. αὐτ. εἰς**] In these words Stephen clearly recognizes the *second command*, to migrate from Haran to Canaan; and as clearly therefore made no *mistake* in ver. 2, but applied the expressed words of the second command to the first injunction, the λόγιον of Philo. **5. οὐκ ἔδωκεν**] There is no occasion here to wrest our text in order to produce accordance with the history. The field which Abraham bought for the burial of his dead surely did not come under the description of κληρονομία, nor give him any standing as a possessor in the land. To avoid this seeming inconsistency, Schöttgen and Bengel lay a stress on ἔδωκεν, 'agrum illum . . . non ex donatione divina accepit Abraham, sed emit, ipsa emtione peregrinum eum esse docente' (Bengel). Kuinoel and Olshausen take οὐκ for οὔπω. **καί** before ἐπηγγ. is not '*yet*' (Beza), nor is ἐπηγγ. to be construed *pluperfect* (id.); and **he promised** is the simple rendering of the words, and the right one. The following καί is by Kuin. rendered '*nimirum*:' but again it is only the simple copula, וּלְזַרְעֲךָ. **6, 7.**] A free citation from the LXX, with the words καὶ λατρ. μοι ἐν τ. τόπ. τούτῳ adapted and added from Exod. iii. 12. The shifts of some Commentators to avoid this plain fact are not worth recounting: but again, the student who would not handle the word of God deceitfully should be here and every where on his guard against them. The round number, 400 years, given here and Gen. l. c., is *further specified* Exod. xii. 40 as 430. (See Gal. iii. 17, and note.) **7.**] **ὁ θεὸς εἶπεν** is inserted by Stephen in passing from the narrative form (τὸ σπ. αὐτοῦ) into the direct (κρ. ἐγώ). **8.**] On the institution of circumcision, it is called a διαθήκη, Gen. xvii. 10, and the immediate promise of

αὐτῷ [m] διαθήκην [n] περιτομῆς· καὶ [o] οὕτως ἐγέννησεν τὸν
Ἰσαὰκ καὶ [p] περιέτεμεν αὐτὸν τῇ ἡμέρᾳ τῇ ὀγδόῃ, καὶ
Ἰσαὰκ τὸν Ἰακώβ, καὶ Ἰακὼβ τοὺς δώδεκα [q] πατρι-
άρχας. 9 καὶ οἱ [q] πατριάρχαι [r] ζηλώσαντες τὸν Ἰωσὴφ
[s] ἀπέδοντο εἰς Αἴγυπτον· καὶ [t] ἦν ὁ θεὸς [t] μετ' αὐτοῦ
10 καὶ [u] ἐξείλατο αὐτὸν ἐκ πασῶν τῶν [v] θλίψεων αὐτοῦ,
καὶ ἔδωκεν αὐτῷ [w] χάριν καὶ σοφίαν [x] ἐναντίον Φαραὼ
βασιλέως Αἰγύπτου, καὶ [y] κατέστησεν αὐτὸν [z] ἡγούμενον
[y] ἐπ' Αἴγυπτον καὶ ὅλον τὸν [a] οἶκον αὐτοῦ. 11 ἦλθεν
δὲ [b] λιμὸς ἐφ' ὅλην τὴν Αἴγυπτον καὶ Χαναὰν καὶ
[v] θλίψις μεγάλη, καὶ οὐχ [c] ηὕρισκον [d] χορτάσματα οἱ
[e] πατέρες [e] ἡμῶν. 12 ἀκούσας δὲ Ἰακὼβ [f] ὄντα [g] σιτία [h] εἰς
Αἴγυπτον [i] ἐξαπέστειλεν τοὺς [e] πατέρας [e] ἡμῶν πρῶτον,
13 καὶ [k] ἐν τῷ [k] δευτέρῳ [l] ἀνεγνωρίσθη Ἰωσὴφ τοῖς ἀδελφοῖς
αὐτοῦ, καὶ [m] φανερὸν [m] ἐγένετο τῷ Φαραὼ τὸ [n] γένος
Ἰωσήφ. 14 ἀποστείλας δὲ Ἰωσὴφ [o] μετεκαλέσατο Ἰακὼβ τὸν πατέρα αὐτοῦ, καὶ πᾶσαν τὴν [p] συγγένειαν

ABCDE HPℵab cfgh klmo 13

m = ch. iii. 25. Heb. ix. 4. Exod. xix. 5.
n 1 Cor. vii. 19 reff.
o = Rom. v. 12 reff.
p 1 Cor. vii. 18 reff. Gen. xxi. 4.
q here bis. ch. ii. 29. Heb. vii. 4 only. 1 Chron. xxiv. 31 B. xxvii. 22.
r = ch. xvii. 5. 1 Cor. xiii. 4. James iv. 2. Gen. xxxvii. 11.
s = ch. v. 8. Heb. xii. 16 only. Gen. xxxvii. 28, 36.
t ch. x. 38 reff. Gen. xxxix. 21, 23.
u = ver. 34. ch. xii. 11. xxiii. 27. xxvi. 17. Gal. i. 4. (Matt. v. 29. xviii. 9) only. Exod. iii. 8.
v Rom. v. 3 reff.
w = ch. ii. 47 reff. Gen. xxxix. 21.
x Mark ii. 12. Luke i. 6. xx. 26. xxiv. 19. ch. viii. 32 only. Ger. vi. 8.
y Luke xii. 14. vv. 27, 35. Heb. vii. 28. Gen. xli. 41.
z = Matt. ii. 6. Luke xxii. 26. Heb. xiii. 7, 17, 24. Deut. i. 15.
a = ch. x. 2 reff.
b Luke iv. 25. xv. 14. Gen. xli. 54.
c = Luke ix. 12. [Rom. iv. 1.] 2 Tim. i. 18. Lam. i. 6.
d here only ‡. Gen. xlii. 27. Deut. xi. 15 al.
e ch. v. 30 reff.
f constr., ch. xxiv. 10 reff.
g here only. Prov. xxx. 22. σῖτος. Gen. xlii. 2. σῖτα, Job xii. 11 al.
h = ch. xix. 22 reff.
i ch. ix. 30. xi. 22 al^4. Gal. iv. 4, 6. Luke i. 53. xx. 10, 11 only. L.P. Gen. xlv. 1.
k = here only.
l here only. Gen. xlv. 1.
m 1 Cor. iii. 13 reff.
n = ch. iv. 6 reff.
o ch. x. 32. xx. 17. xxiv. 25 only. Hos. xi. 2.
p ver. 3 reff.

8. for *ογδοη*, *εβδομη* ℵ^1. rec ins *ο* bef 2nd *ισαακ*, with DHP rel 36 Chr_1 Thl-fin: om ABCEℵ [k] Thl-sif. aft *ισ*. ins *εγεννησε* E [Syr copt, which have it after *ιακ*. also]. rec ins *ο* bef 2nd *ιακωβ*, with D^{2}HP rel 36 Chr Thl: om ABCD^{1}Eℵ [k].

10. (*εξειλατο*, so ABCDEPℵ m 36 Thl-fin.) *χαριν* bef *αυτ*. D-gr: om *αυτω* A. *εναντι* ℵ k [Chr_1]. ins *εφ* bef *ολον* AC E-gr ℵ g vulg syrr coptt[Tischdf]: om BDHP rel 36 E-lat Chr_1. for *αυτου*, *τουτον* B^1[txt B-corr^1(= B^2, Tischdf)].

11. rec *την γην αιγυπτου*, with EHP rel 36 syr æth [arm] Chr_1: *εφ ολης της αιγυπτου* D, *super omnem terram ægypti* D-lat (*see* LXX): txt ABCℵ vulg Syr coptt. (*ηυρισκον*, so B(sic: see table) EP k.)

12. rec *σιτα*, with HP rel Chr_1: *σιτον* 18 Thl-sif: *σιτεια* 15. 40. 100: txt ABCDEℵ. rec *εν αιγυπτω* (*corrn, as more usual: Meyer thinks* *εις αιγ*. *to have been a gloss to* *εξαπεστειλεν*, *and then to have found its way into the txt to the exclusion of the original* *εν αιγ*., *but this is far-fetched*), with DHP Chr Thl: txt ABCEℵ 40. *εξαπεστειλαν* ℵ^1.

13. for *εν*, *επι* D 18. *εγνωρισθη* AB: *εγνωσθη* 25: *agnitus est* E-lat: *recognitus est* D-lat: *cognitus est* vulg: txt CDEH[P]ℵ rel 36 Chr_1. om *αδελφοις* P. *εγενηθη* D. om *τω* (bef *φαραω*) ℵ. rec ins *του* bef *ιωσηφ* (*added for clearness*), with DHP rel Chr: om BC.—for *ιωσ*., *αυτου* AEℵ 40 vulg arm.

14. rec *τον πατ. αυ.* bef *ιακωβ*, with HP rel syrr Chr_1: om *ιακωβ* 15-8. 47^1. 163 æth: txt ABCDEℵ a h m vulg coptt arm. rec aft *συγγ*. ins *αυτου* (*for explicitness*), with DE rel [vulg-ed tol Syr coptt æth]: om ABCHPℵ b f g m o 36 am demid fuld

that covenant was δώσω σοι κ. τῷ σπέρματί σου μετά σε τὴν γῆν ἣν παροικεῖς, πᾶσαν τὴν γῆν Χαναὰν εἰς κατάσχεσιν αἰώνιον· καὶ ἔσομαι αὐτοῖς εἰς θεόν, id. ver. 8. **οὕτως**, **thus**, 'in this new covenant state;'—or, 'in fulfilment of the promise of *seed* implied in the above words.' In this word **οὕτως** lies hid the germ of the subsequent teaching of the Holy Spirit by St. Paul, Gal. iii. **9.**] Here we have the first hint of the rebellious spirit in Israel, which the progress of the history brings out.

10.] Observe (Mey.) the simple coupling of the clauses by καί, as characteristic of this speech. **χάριν κ. σοφ.**] No Hendiadys: **favour**, so that he was *acceptable* to Pharaoh (see reff.): and **wisdom**, so that Ph. consulted him and followed his suggestion, especially in the important case recorded Gen. xli. 38. **κατ-**

[q] ἐν [r] ψυχαῖς ἑβδομηκονταπέντε. 15 καὶ [s] κατέβη Ἰακὼβ
εἰς Αἴγυπτον, καὶ [t] ἐτελεύτησεν αὐτὸς καὶ οἱ [u] πατέρες
[u] ἡμῶν, 16 καὶ [v] μετετέθησαν εἰς Συχὲμ καὶ [w] ἐτέθησαν ἐν
τῷ [x] μνήματι [y] ᾧ [z] ὠνήσατο Ἀβραὰμ [a] τιμῆς [b] ἀργυρίου

q — Luke xiv. 31. Jude 14. Deut. x. 22. r = ch. ii. 41 reff. s = ch. xviii. 22 al. Gen. xii. 10. t ch. ii. 29 reff. u ch. v. 30 reff. v Gal. i. 6. Heb. vii. 12. xi. 5 bis. Jude 4 only. Sir. xliv. 16. Deut. xxvii. 17. w — John xix. 41, 42 al. 3 Kings xiii. 31. x Luke viii. 27, Mk. xxiii. 53. xxiv. 1. ch. ii. 29. Rev. xi. 9 only. Exod. xiv. 11. y attr., ch. i. 1 reff. z here only †. a = ch. iv. 34 reff. b ch. iii. 6. xx. 33. Exod. xxi. 32.

[syr] arm Chr. εβδ. bef ψυχ. (*see LXX*) DH a (c) f h m: ὁ και ε ψ D [(c)]: D syr Chr seem to join εν ε. π. ψ. with κατεβη follg (*see LXX Deut* x. 22).

15. rec κατεβη δε, with BH rel coptt [arm] Chr_1: κατεβη (alone) D 40. 73. 96 syr: txt ACEPℵ 36 vulg Syr æth. (*From similarity of* και κατ., και *dropped out as in* D, *and then* δε *was supplied.*) om εις αιγυπτον B. (*Omitted as superfluous? or perhaps it was a gloss from the marg. Tischendorf* (ed 7) *excludes it from the txt: but the authority is too weak.* [He has restored it in edn 8.]) aft αυτος ins εκει E Syr: τε D.

16. μετηχθησαν D. συχεν (1st) D-gr. rec (for ᾧ) ὃ, with HP rel Chr_1.

ἑστησεν] viz. Pharaoh: a change of subject: see reff. Gen. **14. ἐν ψυχαῖς ἑβδομηκονταπέντε**] In the Hebrew text, Gen. xlvi. 27; Exod. i. 5; Deut. x. 22, *seventy* souls are reckoned, viz. sixty-six born of Jacob, Jacob himself, Joseph, and his two sons born in Egypt. So also Josephus, Antt. ii. 7. 4; vi. 5, 6. But the LXX, whom Stephen follows, insert in Gen. xlvi. 20 an account of the children and grandchildren of Manasseh and Ephraim, five in number: and in ver. 27 read υἱοὶ δὲ Ἰωσὴφ οἱ γενόμενοι αὐτῷ ἐν γῇ Αἰγ., ψυχαὶ ἐννέα. πᾶσαι ψυχαὶ οἴκου Ἰακὼβ αἱ εἰσελθοῦσαι μετὰ Ἰακὼβ (om μετὰ Ἰακώβ, and ψυχαί below, A, but obviously without any effect on the general statement) εἰς Αἴγυπτον, **ψυχαὶ ἑβδομηκονταπέντε**:—reckoning, as it appears, curiously enough, among the sons of Joseph, Joseph himself, and his wife Asenath; for these are required to make up the nine, according to their ver. 20. And similarly in Exod. i. 5, and in Deut. x. 22 A. (Wordsw., who is careful to note that A omits μετὰ Ἰακώβ in Gen. xlvi. 27, omits the fact that it reads πέντε here, by stating "seventy" as the LXX testimony.) With regard to the various attempts to solve the difficulty (66 + 12 wives, minus (Joseph and his wife, and Judah's wife who died in Canaan) = 75, Seb. Schmid and Wolf:—that Stephen spoke of those who were *invited*,—Moses of those who *went*, Krebs and Loesner:—that πάντες should be read for πέντε, Beza:—&c.), see above on vv. 6, 7. The remarks of Jerome are curious:—he is arguing, on Gen. l. c., that the number *really was seventy*,—and adds, 'Quod si e contrario nobis id opponitur, quomodo in Actibus Apostolorum in concione Stephani dicatur ad populum, septuaginta quinque animas ingressas esse Ægyptum, facilis excusatio est. Non enim debuit sanctus Lucas, qui ipsius (istius?) historiæ scriptor est, in gentes Actuum Apostolorum volumen emittens, contrarium aliquid scribere adversus eam scripturam, quæ jam fuerat gentibus divulgata.' Philo, de Migr. Abr. § 36, vol. i. pp. 467 f., mentions both numbers (reading 75 in Gen. and 70 in Deut., see above), and gives allegorical reasons for both: and really Wordsworth's solution, that Stephen includes those born of Jacob's line in Egypt to shew that they "were equally children of the promise with those born in Canaan," is hardly better. When we come to understand **μετεκαλέσατο** . . . πᾶσαν τὴν συγγένειαν ἐν ψυχαῖς ἑβδομηκονταπέντε, as represented by *including, for a purpose, those already in Egypt*, it seems to me that a stigma is cast on St. Stephen far more serious than that of mere numeral inaccuracy. **16.**] **μετετέθησαν**, viz. αὐτὸς καὶ οἱ πατέρες ἡμῶν, not the latter only,—as Kuin., Olsh., and Wordsw., to evade part of the difficulty of the verse. The facts, as related in the O. T., were these: Jacob, dying in Egypt, was (Gen. l. 13) taken into the land of Canaan, and buried in the cave of Machpelah, before Mamre (on the rest of the verse see below): Joseph, dying also in Egypt, was taken in a coffin (Gen. l. 26) at the Exodus (Exod. xiii. 19), and finally buried (Josh. xxiv. 32) at Shechem. Of the burial of the other patriarchs the sacred text says nothing, but rather by the specification in Exod. xiii. 19, leaves it to be inferred that they were buried in Egypt. Josephus, Antt. ii. 8. 2, relates that they were taken and buried in *Hebron*, and adds, B. J. iv. 9. 7, ὧν καὶ τὰ μνημεῖα μέχρι τοῦ νῦν ἐν τῇδε τῇ πολίχνῃ (*Hebron*) δείκνυται, πάνυ καλῆς μαρμάρου καὶ φιλοτίμως εἰργασμένα:—the Rabbinical traditions mentioned by Wetst. and Lightf. report them to have been buried in *Sychem:* and Jerome (Ep. ad

c = Rev. iii. 18. 2 Kings xxiv. 21.
d = (here only?) 2 Macc. i. 31.
e = Luke xxi. 28. xxii. 1 al. Deut. xxxi. 14.
f = ch. iii. 21 reff.
g ch. i. 4 reff.
h = Matt. xiv. 7. Jer. li. (xliv.) 25.

[c] παρὰ τῶν υἱῶν Ἐμμὼρ τοῦ Συχέμ. 17 [d] καθὼς δὲ
[e] ἤγγιζεν ὁ [f] χρόνος τῆς [g] ἐπαγγελίας [y] ἧς [h] ὡμολόγησεν p ο χρονος... ABCDE HPℵa b c f g h k l m o p 13
ὁ θεὸς τῷ Ἀβραάμ, [i] ηὔξησεν ὁ λαὸς καὶ [i] ἐπληθύνθη
ἐν Αἰγύπτῳ, 18 [k] ἄχρι οὗ [l] ἀνέστη βασιλεὺς [m] ἕτερος ὃς
οὐκ ᾔδει τὸν Ἰωσήφ. 19 οὗτος [n] κατασοφισάμενος τὸ
[o] γένος ἡμῶν [p] ἐκάκωσεν τοὺς [q] πατέρας [r] τοῦ [s] ποιεῖν

ἐδέοντο δὲ . . ὁ δὲ ὡμολόγει, Xen. Anab. vii. 4. 13. i ch. vi. 7 (reff.). Exod. i. 7. k w. indic., ch. xxvii. 33. Rev. xvii. 17. see Heb. iii. 13. l = ch. v. 36, 37. Exod. i. 8. m = ch. ii. 40 al. n here only. Exod. i. 10. Judith v. 11. x. 19 only. o = ch. xviii. 2 reff. p ver. 6 reff. q absol., John vi. 58. vii. 22. ch. xiii. 32. xxvi. 6. Rom. ix. 5. xi. 28. xv. 8. Heb. i. 1. 2 Pet. iii. 4 only. r = ch. iii. 12 reff. s = Matt. iii. 3 ||. v. 36. Rev. xxi. 5.

txt ABCDEℵ c g l m. aft αβρ. ins ο πατηρ ημων E(sic). rec εμμορ, with EP rel: txt ABCDHℵ a c h copt Chr_1. for του, εν BCℵ[1] [copt] sah arm: του εν AEℵ[3] tol: του εκ syr: *et Sychem* D-lat: txt D-gr H(P) rel vulg æth Chr. (*The varr arise from this συχεμ having been mistaken for a* place, *as above.*) —του χεμ (passing from υ to υ) P.

17. for καθως, ως A. [for χρον., καιρος A.] rec ωμοσεν, with HP p rel syr-txt: επηγγειλατο DE tol syr-mg: txt ABC ℵ(ομολογ.), *confessus erat* vulg. [13 def.] (*The varr have arisen from the unusual sense of ωμολ.*)

18. rec αχρις (*corrn*), with AB[2]EHPℵ 36 Chr_1: txt B[1]CD Thl-sif_1. aft ετερος ins επ αιγυπτον ABCℵ o 36 Syr syr-mg coptt [æth arm]: om DEHP p [13(appy)] rel syr-txt Chr. for ηδει τον, εμνησθη του DE.

19. for ουτος, και D-gr(om D-lat). rec aft πατερας ins ημων, with ACEHP rel

Eustochium: Epitaph. Paulæ, 108 (27) 13, vol. i., p. 703) relating the pilgrimages of Paula to the sacred places, says: "transivit Sichem, ... atque inde divertens vidit duodecim Patriarcharum sepulchra." These traditions probably Stephen followed; and, in haste or inadvertence, classed *Jacob* with the rest. **ᾧ ὠνήσατο Ἀβραάμ**] The burying-place which Abraham bought was not at *Sychem*, but (Gen. xxiii. 3—20) at *Hebron*, and was bought of *Ephron the Hittite*. It was *Jacob* who (Gen. xxxiii. 19) bought a field where he had pitched his tent, near *Sychem*, of the *children of Hamor*, Shechem's father: and no mention is made of its being *for a burying-place*. The two incidents are certainly here *confused:* and no ingenuity of the Commentators has ever devised an escape from the inference. The mention of a few such attempts may suffice.—(1) The omission of Ἀβραάμ (Beza, Valck., Kuin., Schött., al.) against all manuscript evidence (not excepting E, the reading of which, variously stated by Meyer and Tischendorf, has been ascertained by inspection),—and against the construction also; for after μετετέθησαν, Ἰακώβ could hardly be the subject to ὠνήσατο:—(2) rendering, against all grammar, while omitting Ἀβραάμ, ὠνήσατο 'emptum erat' (Kuin.):—(3) construing Ἀβραάμ, *Abrahamides*, i. e. *Jacob* (Surenhus. al.):—(4) that of Wordsworth, made up of—omitting Jacob from the grammatical construction (see above);—*proving, from Jerome* and *Bede* (without any allusion to the passage of Josephus above cited!), that the other patriarchs were buried at Shechem:—a priori reasons why Stephen should have chosen to bring forward Shechem and not Hebron; reasons (see Wordsw.'s note) not very creditable, if they existed: &c. &c. The fact of the mistake occurring where it does, will be far more instructive to the Christian student than the most ingenious solution of the difficulty could be, if it teaches him fearlessly and honestly to recognize the phænomena presented by the text of Scripture, instead of wresting them to suit a preconceived theory. I entirely agree with Wordsworth, that "there is nothing in these difficulties which invalidates the claims of St. Stephen to Inspiration," any more than those expressions in Scripture "invalidate its inspiration," which imply that the sun revolves round the earth. But as Wordsw. lives in days when men are no longer burnt for asserting that the earth moves, he surely might abstain from railing in such unmeasured terms (see his Acts, p. 35, col. i.) at those who in contending for common fairness and honesty find it necessary to carry somewhat further the same canon of reasonable interpretation. Humble searchers after divine truth will not be terrified by being charged with "assumption and conceit," or being told that their exegesis can produce no result but "degeneracy, degradation, disbelief, and demoralization." But they will deeply feel it to be their duty, to caution the student against all crooked and disingenuous ways of handling the word of God. "Non tali auxilio, nec defensoribus istis." **17.**] **καθώς**, not '*when*' (as

τὰ [t] βρέφη [u] ἔκθετα αὐτῶν [v] εἰς τὸ μὴ [w] ζωογονεῖσθαι.
20 [x] ἐν [x] ᾧ [x] καιρῷ ἐγεννήθη Μωυσῆς καὶ ἦν [y] ἀστεῖος
[z] τῷ θεῷ. ὃς [a] ἀνετράφη μῆνας τρεῖς ἐν τῷ οἴκῳ τοῦ
πατρός. 21 [b] ἐκτεθέντος δὲ [c] αὐτοῦ [d] ἀνείλατο αὐτὸν ἡ θυγάτηρ Φαραὼ καὶ [a] ἀνεθρέψατο [c] αὐτὸν ἑαυτῇ [e] εἰς υἱόν.
22 καὶ [f] ἐπαιδεύθη Μωυσῆς ἐν πάσῃ σοφίᾳ Αἰγυπτίων, ἦν
δὲ [g] δυνατὸς ἐν λόγοις καὶ ἔργοις αὐτοῦ. 23 ὡς δὲ [h] ἐπλη-
ροῦτο αὐτῷ [i] τεσσερακονταετὴς χρόνος, [k] ἀνέβη ἐπὶ τὴν

t Luke i. 41, 44. ii. 12, 16. xviii. 15. 2 Tim. iii. 15. 1 Pet. ii. 2 only +. 1 Macc. i. 61. Ps. viii. 3 Aq.
u here only +. Ezek. xlii. 3 Alius in Hexap. (ἐκτιθέναι, ver. 21. Eur. Phœn. 25. Æl. Var. Hist. ii. 7. Philo, Vit. Moys. § 3, vol. ii. p. 83. ἔκθεσις, Wisd. xi. 14.)
v ch. iii. 19. Rom. i. 11, 20 al.
w Luke xvii. 33. 1 Tim. vi. 13 only. Exod. i. 17, 18, 22 al.
x here only. ἐν αὐτ. τ. κ., Luke xiii. 1. ἐν ἐκείν. τ. κ., Matt. xi. 25. ἐν τῷ κ. τούτ., Mark x. 30.
y Heb. xi. 23 only. Exod. ii. 2.
z dat., Jonah iii. 3. 2 Cor. x. 4. James ii. 5. (1 Cor. ix. 2.) Winer, edn. 6, § 31. 4 *a*. see Gen. x. 9. xxiii. 6. xxx. 8 (Heb.). Luke i. 15. 2 Cor. i. 12.
a here bis, ch. xxii. 3 only +. Wisd. vii. 4 BℵF(not A) &c. only.
b -- here only ‡. Wisd. xviii. 5. (ch. xi. 4 reff.) see ver. 19 reff.
c constr., John viii. 30. xii. 37.
d = here only. Exod. ii. 10. see ch. v. 33 reff.
e = ver. 5. ch. xiii. 22. Isa. xlix. 6.
f = ch. xxii. 3. 2 Tim. ii. 25 (1 Cor. xi. 32 reff.). Prov. xxix. 17.
g ch. xviii. 24 reff.
h — Luke xxi. 24. ver. 30. ch. ix. 23. xxiv. 27. Gen. xxv. 24.
i ch. xiii. 18 only.
k w. ἐπί, 1 Cor. ii. 9 only. Isa. lxv. 16, Jer. iii. 16. w. ἐν, Luke xxiv. 38 only.

36 am-corr[1] vss Chr$_1$: om BDℵ am[1] fuld. rec εκθετα bef τα βρεφη, with DEHP rel 36 Chr: τα βρεφη αυτων εκθετα m p: txt ABCℵ. aft ζωογον. ins τα αρρενα E.

20. rec aft πατρος ins αυτου, with DE g m o 13 Thl: om ABCHP rel Chr.—ℵ[1] has μου, but marked for erasure by the same hand.

21. rec εκτεθεντα δε αυτον, with EHP rel: txt ABCDℵ p 36. (ανειλατο, so ABCDE f[1] p [-λετο H(Treg, expr)].)—add εις (παρα D) τον ποταμον DE syr-w-ast. om αυτον (aft ανειλατο) a c e h k o Chr$_1$ Thl. om και D[1]-gr(ins D[2] or [4]). om αυτον (aft ανεθρ.) D[1](and lat) c, ins syr-w-ob; for εαυτη, αυτη D[1] 180: txt D[3]. om εις B.

22. rec om 1st εν, with B D-corr HP rel 36 vulg Orig-ms$_1$ [Eus$_1$ Did$_1$] Chr$_1$: ins ACEℵ vulg-ms coptt Orig$_5$ Ps-Just$_1$ Bas$_1$ Thdrt$_1$.—πασαν την σοφιαν D[1] [Clem$_1$(om την) Chr$_1$]. for δε, τε D E-gr l [vulg Syr sah]: txt ABCHPℵ rel 36 E-lat copt [arm] Chr$_1$. rec ins εν bef εργ., with E-gr P g l m 13 vulg: om A B(sic: see table) CDHℵ a b f h o p 36 E-lat Chr$_1$.—εργοις κ. εν λογοις c.—εν λογω κ. εν εργω k. rec om αυτου (*as unnecessary*), with HP rel syr Ps-Just Chr$_1$: ins ABCDEℵ p 36 vulg Syr coptt [æth arm].

23. μ' ετης (sic) bef αυτω D. for επι, εις H.

E. V., Beza, Kuin.), but as, 'in proportion as.' See ref. **19. τοῦ ποιεῖν] so that they exposed**, see ref. Meyer maintains that the inf. of the *purpose* is not to be departed from,—'in order that they might expose:' but I do not see that this meaning would express the fact. The purpose is afterwards expressed, **εἰς τὸ κ.τ.λ.**

20. ἀστ. τῷ θεῷ] add to reff. (Meyer), Hesiod, Op. 825, ἀναίτιος ἀθανάτοισιν,—and Æsch. Agam. 352, θεοῖς ἀναμπλάκητος. The expression here seems borrowed from tradition: Josephus calls the infant Moses παιδα **μορφῇ θεῖον**. Philo de vita Mos. § 3, vol. ii. p. 83, says, γεννηθεὶς οὖν ὁ παῖς εὐθὺς ὄψιν ἐνέφηνεν ἀστειοτέραν ἢ κατ' ἰδιώτην. **22.]** That Moses was instructed in the wisdom of the Egyptians, is not found in the O. T., but derived from tradition, and following as a matter of course from his adopted station as the son of Pharaoh's daughter. This *wisdom of the Egyptians*, celebrated by so many ancient writers (see Wetst. ad loc.), consisted mainly in natural philosophy, medicine, and mathematics, and its teachers were the priests. Philo de vita Mos. § 5, p. 84, enters into minute detail: ἀριθμοὺς μὲν οὖν κ. γεωμετρίαν, κ. τήν τε ῥυθμικὴν κ. ἁρμονικὴν κ. μετρικὴν θεωρίαν, κ. μουσικὴν τὴν σύμπασαν, διά τε χρήσεως ὀργάνων, κ. λόγων τῶν ἐν ταῖς τέχναις, κ. διεξόδοις τοπικωτέραις, Αἰγυπτίων οἱ λόγιοι παρέδοσαν. κ. προσέτι τὴν διὰ συμβόλων φιλοσοφίαν, ἣν ἐν τοῖς λεγομένοις ἱεροῖς γράμμασιν ἐπιδείκνυνται, κ. διὰ τῆς τῶν ζώων ἀποδοχῆς, ἃ καὶ θεῶν τιμαῖς γεραίρουσι. τὴν δὲ ἄλλην ἐγκύκλιον παιδείαν Ἕλληνες ἐδίδασκον· οἱ δ' ἐκ τῶν πλησιοχώρων, τά τε Ἀσσυρίων γράμματα, κ. τὴν τῶν οὐρανίων Χαλδαϊκὴν ἐπιστήμην. **δυνατὸς ἐν λόγοις]** So Josephus calls Moses πλήθεσιν ὁμιλεῖν πιθανώτατος, but *late in his course*, during the journey through the wilderness;—when the divine Spirit, as the book of Deuteronomy abundantly testifies, had turned his 'slowness of speech' into the most fervid eloquence. That he was so thus early, during his Egyptian course, was probably reported by tradition, but hardly seems to agree with Exod. iv. 10—16. **23. τεσσερα-**

[k] καρδίαν αὐτοῦ [l] ἐπισκέψασθαι τοὺς ἀδελφοὺς αὐτοῦ τοὺς ABCDE
[m] υἱοὺς Ἰσραήλ. 24 καὶ ἰδών τινα [n] ἀδικούμενον [o] ἠμύνατο HPℵ a b c f g h k
καὶ [p] ἐποίησεν [pq] ἐκδίκησιν τῷ [r] καταπονουμένῳ [s] πατάξας l m o p 13
τὸν Αἰγύπτιον. 25 ἐνόμιζεν δὲ [t] συνιέναι τοὺς ἀδελφοὺς
[αὐτοῦ] ὅτι ὁ θεὸς [u] διὰ χειρὸς αὐτοῦ [v] δίδωσιν [w] σωτηρίαν
αὐτοῖς· οἱ δὲ οὐ [t] συνῆκαν. 26 τῇ τε [x] ἐπιούσῃ ἡμέρᾳ [y] ὤφθη
αὐτοῖς [z] μαχομένοις, καὶ [a] συνήλασεν αὐτοὺς εἰς εἰρήνην
εἰπὼν Ἄνδρες ἀδελφοί ἐστε [ὑμεῖς]· [b] ἵνα τί ἀδικεῖτε
ἀλλήλους; 27 ὁ δὲ ἀδικῶν τὸν [c] πλησίον [d] ἀπώσατο αὐτὸν
εἰπὼν Τίς σε [e] κατέστησεν ἄρχοντα καὶ [f] δικαστὴν ἐφ'
ἡμᾶς; 28 μὴ [g] ἀνελεῖν με σὺ θέλεις [h] ὃν τρόπον [g] ἀνεῖλες
[i] ἐχθὲς τὸν Αἰγύπτιον; 29 ἔφυγεν δὲ Μωυσῆς [k] ἐν τῷ
[l] λόγῳ τούτῳ, καὶ ἐγένετο [m] πάροικος ἐν γῇ Μαδιάμ, οὗ

l = ch. xv. 36. Matt. xxv. 36, 43. James i. 27. Judg. xv. 1. m ch. x. 36 reff. Exod. ii. 11. n 1 Cor. vi. 7. 2 Cor. vii. 12. Isa. i. 17. o here only. Isa. lix. 16. p Luke xviii. 7, 8 only. Micah v. 15. q Rom. xii. 19 reff. r 2 Pet. ii. 7 only. 2 Macc. viii. 2 AB compl. Ald. (not Ed-vat F) only. s = Matt. xxvi. 31 ||, from Zech. xiii. 7. Exod. ii. 12. t w. ὅτι, Matt. xvi. 12. xvii. 13. Isa xliii. 10. abs., Matt. xiii. 13, 15 || (from Isa. vi. 9, 10). u ch. xi. 30 reff. v pres., ch. xvi. 38 reff. w = Luke i. 71. 1 Kings xiv. 45. Jos. Antt. ii. 9. 7. x ch. xxiii. 11. xvi. 11 reff. 1 Chron. xx. 1. see Matt. vi. 11 and note. y ch. ii. 3 reff. z John vi. 52. 2 Tim. ii. 24. James iv. 1 only. Exod. xxi. 22. a here only †. 2 Macc. iv. 26, 42. v. 5 only. συνελάσας τὰ θηρία, Xen. Cyr. i. 4. 14. συνελαυνόμενος ἄκων εἰς μάχην, Plut. Cæs. p. 728 (Wetst.). b 1 Cor. x. 29 reff. c Rom. xiii. 9, 10 reff. Exod. ii. 13. d Rom. xi. 1, 2 reff. e ver. 10 reff. Exod. ii. 14. f ver. 35. Luke xii. 14 only. Exod. l. c. g = ch. v. 33 reff. h ch. i. 11 reff. i John iv. 52. Heb. xiii. 8 only. 4 Kings ix. 26. k = Matt. vi. 7. John xvi. 30. 1 Pet. ii. 12. l = Luke i. 29. ch. v. 5 al. m ver. 6 reff. Exod. ii. 22.

ins του bef επισκ. E 180. om 2nd τους B.

24. aft αδικ. ins εκ του γενους αυτου DE Syr syr-w-ast æth.—om αυτ. D-gr. aft αιγ. add (*from Exod* ii. 12, LXX) και εκρυψεν αυτον εν τη αμμω D æth.

25. ενομιζον D-gr 13. om 1st αυτου BCℵ vulg(am demid, not tol): ins ADEHP rel. rec αυτ. bef σωτ., with EHP rel syrr sah [(æth) arm] Chr: txt ABCDℵ m p vulg copt. for οι, ου ℵ^{1}(but corrd). om ου D^{1}-gr(ins D-corr^{1}).

26. elz (for τε) δε, with EP vulg coptt [arm]: txt ABCD^{2}Hℵ rel 36 syrr æth Chr$_1$ Thl Œc.—for τη τε, τοτε D^{1}. aft μαχ. (-νος D^{1}-gr: txt D^{2}) ins και ειδεν αυτους αδικουντας D^{1}. συνηλλασσεν BCDℵ o sah æth, *reconciliabit* vulg, *reconciliavit* D-lat: συνηλλασεν H p: txt AEP rel [copt æth arm, appy] Chr. (*The varr appear to be occasioned by explanations of the origl* συνηλασεν.) αυτοις C^{1}H. om υμεις (*as unnecessary*) ABCEℵ p vulg sah arm Chr$_1$: ins HP rel 36 (syr copt) [æth].—τι ποιειτε ανδρες αδελφοι ινα τι αδικειται εις(om εις D^{2}) αλληλους D.

27. ειπας D. for και, η E [demid copt]. ημων (*from* LXX, *Exod* ii. 14) ABCHPℵ m^{2} p 13: txt DE rel Chr.

28. (εχθες, so B^{1}CDℵ.)

29. ουτως και εφυγαδευσεν Μωυσης D^{1}(txt D^{3}): εφυγαδευσεν δε Μωυσην E.

κονταετὴς χρ.] μέγας γενόμενος M., Exod. ii. 11, LXX. The exact age was traditional, see Lightf. **ἀνέβη**] No nominative (as διαλογισμός, Kuin.) must be supplied: it is impersonal; see reff. **24.**] **τὸν Αἰγύπτιον,** from the history being so universally known, that the agent in the ἀδικία would be readily supplied: see Winer, edn. 6, § 67. 1, d. **25.**] The present, **δίδωσιν,** sets forth the work of liberation as already begun by the act just related, see reff. Here we have again the *resistance to the Holy Spirit* hinted: see ver. 51, and note on ver. 2. **26.**] **αὐτοῖς,** to them, *two of them,* taken as representing his brethren the children of Israel. **συνήλασεν,** not imperf., '*he endeavoured to unite*:' the aorist will not bear this sense: nor is it needed:—the act, *on Moses' part,* was complete;—not '*he would have set them at one*' (E. V.), but, **he set them at one.** If the explanatory reading συνήλλασσεν be taken, we then have the imperfect force—"*he was reconciling,*" or "*attempted to reconcile,*" them. **ἄνδρες ἀδελφοί** should be taken together, as in Gen. xiii. 8, ἄνθρωποι ἀδελφοί ἐσμεν ἡμεῖς. See also ch. ii. 14 (De W.). **27.**] The *further progress of resistance to the Spirit* on the part of Israel. **29. Μαδιάμ**] So LXX, Exod. ii. 15, for מִדְיָן. Winer (Realw. 'Midian') supposes *this Madian* to have been a *nomad* detachment of the more settled Midianites,—which at that time was encamped in the neighbourhood of Sinai and Horeb. For Jethro, Moses' father-in-law, is not found there, in Exod. xviii. 1 ff., but comes to

ἐγέννησεν υἱοὺς δύο. 30 καὶ [n] πληρωθέντων ἐτῶν τεσσεράκοντα [o] ὤφθη αὐτῷ ἐν τῇ ἐρήμῳ τοῦ ὄρους Σινᾶ ἄγγελος
ἐν [pq] φλογὶ [p] πυρὸς [r] βάτου. 31 ὁ δὲ Μωυσῆς ἰδὼν [s] ἐθαύμαζεν τὸ [t] ὅραμα· προσερχομένου δὲ αὐτοῦ [u] κατανοῆσαι
[v] ἐγένετο φωνὴ κυρίου 32 Ἐγὼ ὁ θεὸς τῶν πατέρων
σου, ὁ θεὸς Ἀβραὰμ καὶ Ἰσαὰκ καὶ Ἰακώβ. [w] ἔντρομος
δὲ γενόμενος Μωυσῆς οὐκ ἐτόλμα [n] κατανοῆσαι. 33 εἶπεν
δὲ αὐτῷ ὁ κύριος [x] Λῦσον τὸ [xy] ὑπόδημα τῶν ποδῶν σου·
ὁ γὰρ τόπος ἐφ' ᾧ ἕστηκας γῆ ἁγία ἐστίν. 34 [z] ἰδὼν

n — ver. 23. o ver. 26. Exod. iii. 2. p Rev. i. 14. ii. 18. xix. 12. Ps. xxviii. 7. π. φ., 2 Thess. i. 8. Heb. i. 7. Sir. viii. 10. q as above (p). Luke xvi. 24 only. Judg. iii. 22. r Luke vi. 44 ∥ Mk. xx. 37. ver. 35 only. Exod. iii. 2 &c. Deut. xxxiii. 16. Job xxxi. 40 only.

s constr., Luke vii. 9. Jude 16. Job xxxii. 22. Xen. Cyr. iii. 1. 38. t ch. ix. 10 al8. Acts only, exc. Matt. xvii. 9. Gen. xlvi. 2. u Luke xii. 24, 27. ch. xi. 6. Heb. iii. 1. Gen. xlii. 9. v — John x. 35. ch. x. 13. xiii. 32. Gen. xv. 1, 4. w ch. xvi. 29. Heb. xii. 21 only. Ps. xvii. 7. Dan. x. 11 Theod. x — Luke iii. 16 | Mk. J. ch. xiii. 25. Exod. iii. 5. y as above (x). Matt. iii. 11. Luke xv. 22. Gen. xiv. 23. z here only. Exod. iii. 7 al. fr. constr., Heb. vi. 14, from Gen. xxii. 17.

δυω D^1(txt D^3).

30. aft *και* ins *μετα ταυτα* D. **πλησθεντων αυτω ετη** D^1(txt D^2(and lat)). rec aft *αγγελος* ins *κυριου* (*natural addn, and here occasioned by Exod* iii. 2, *LXX*), with DEHP rel Syr [æth arm] : om ABCℵ p vulg coptt. *πυρι φλογος* (*see note*) ACE 36 vulg Syr : txt BDHPℵ p rel syr coptt [æth arm] Chr Thl.

31. rec *εθαυμασε* (*corrn to historical tense*), with ABC rel vulg [syrr coptt æth arm] Chr : txt DEHPℵ b f g l m p 36 Aug_1. om *το οραμα* A. *και προσερ. αυτ.* (*κ*)*αι κατ.* D^1. *ο κυριος ειπεν αυτω λεγων* D Syr æth. for *κυρ.*, *εκ του ουρανου λεγουσα* E. rec aft *κυρ.* ins *προς αυτον*, with CEHP rel vulg-[clem] sah Chr : om ABℵ p am demid syr copt arm [Aug_1].

32. om *ο* (bef 1st *θεος*) CH^1 : *εγω ειμι θ.* E vulg(not am fuld) D-lat. om *ο* (bef 2nd *θ.*) C. rec ins *ο θεος* bef *ισ.* and bef *ιακ.*, with (D)EHP rel [vulg(with am demid tol) copt] æth Chr Thl : (om *ο*, twice, D :) om ABCℵ p [fuld] syrr [sah] arm. (*The insertion has prob been to suit LXX, which* D *does still more closely by omg the artt.*) *μωυσης* bef *γενομενος* ℵ. *ετολμησεν* ℵ.

33. om *ο* (bef *κυρ.*) A. for *κυρ.*, *θεος* E. for 1st clause, *και εγενετο φωνη προς αυτον* D. **λυσαι** D^4(?) 142. aft *υποδ.* ins *σου εκ* C^1 [syrr æth] : *εκ* C^2E k.—*σου* bef *τ. π.* B. rec for *εφ*, *εν* (*corrn to suit LXX*), with EHP rel 36 Chr_1 : txt $ABCD^2$ℵ p.—for *εφ ω*, *ου* D^1 : add *συ* C(*συν* C^1) lect-13 arm.

visit Moses from a distance. See also Numb. x. 29 ff. **υἱοὺς δύο**] Exod. ii. 22; iv. 20; xviii. 3. **30. ἐτ. τεσσ.**] This follows from the tradition of ver. 23, combined with Exod. vii. 7, 'Moses in palatio Pharaonis degit XL annos, in Midiane XL annos, et ministravit Israel XL annos.' Bereshith Rabba, f. 115. 3. (Mey.) **Σινᾶ**] *Horeb*, Exod. iii. 1. But both were points of the same mountain range, and the names were convertibly used. In Exod., Levit., and Numb., the law is said to have been given from *Sinai;* in Deut. from *Horeb.* 'The desert of Mount Sina' is the desert in which Mt. S. is situated. So 'the Peak of Derbyshire,' originally no doubt some single hill, has come to mean the whole district in which that hill is situated. **ἄγγελος**] Here, as continually in the O. T., the angel bears the authority and presence of God Himself: which angel, since God *giveth not his glory to another*, must have been the *great Angel of the covenant*, the מַלְאַךְ פָּנָיו of Isa. lxiii. 9, '*the Angel of His Presence,*'—the SON OF GOD. See below on εἰς διαταγὰς ἀγγέλων, ver. 53. Stier remarks, that this *second* appearance of God, *to Moses* (see ver. 2), introduces the *legal* dispensation, as the *first, to Abraham*, the *patriarchal.* The readings of the LXX, as well as of our text, vary between πυρὶ φλογός (B) and φλογὶ πυρός (A). The Heb. is בְּלַבַּת־אֵשׁ. The construction is, **in the fiery flame** (or, **the flaming fire) of a bush.** **32.**] The order of Exod. iii. 6, is here somewhat varied. The command to put off the shoe was given *on the approach* of Moses, and before these words were spoken. **οὐκ ἐτόλμ. καταν.** = εὐλαβεῖτο κατεμβλέψαι, LXX. **33.**] See Josh. v. 15. Putting off the sandals was a *mark of reverence.* The priests performed all their ministrations *barefooted.* The Arabs to this day continue the practice: they always enter their mosques barefooted. Among the Pythagoreans it was a maxim, ἀνυπόδητος θῦε κ. προσκύνει, Iamblich. vita Pythag 105 (Mey.). So Juvenal, Sat. vi. 158, 'Observant ubi festa mero pede sabbata

[z] εἶδον τὴν [a] κάκωσιν τοῦ λαοῦ μου τοῦ ἐν Αἰγύπτῳ, καὶ
τοῦ [b] στεναγμοῦ αὐτῶν ἤκουσα, και [c] κατέβην [d] ἐξελέσθαι
αὐτούς· καὶ νῦν [e] δεῦρο ἀποστείλω σε εἰς Αἴγυπτον.
35 τοῦτον τὸν Μωυσῆν ὃν [f] ἠρνήσαντο εἴποντες Τίς σὲ
[g] κατέστησεν ἄρχοντα καὶ [h] δικαστήν; τοῦτον ὁ θεὸς καὶ
ἄρχοντα καὶ [i] λυτρωτὴν ἀπέσταλκεν [k] σὺν χειρὶ ἀγγέλου
τοῦ [l] ὀφθέντος αὐτῷ ἐν τῇ [m] βάτῳ. 36 οὗτος [n] ἐξήγαγεν
αὐτοὺς [o] ποιήσας [p] τέρατα καὶ σημεῖα ἐν γῇ Αἰγύπτῳ καὶ
ἐν [q] ἐρυθρᾷ θαλάσσῃ καὶ ἐν τῇ ἐρήμῳ ἔτη τεσσεράκοντα.
37 οὗτός ἐστιν ὁ Μωυσῆς ὁ εἴπας τοῖς υἱοῖς Ἰσραὴλ
Προφήτην ὑμῖν [r] ἀναστήσει ὁ θεὸς ἐκ τῶν ἀδελφῶν ὑμῶν

ABCDE HPℵa b c f g h k l m o p 13

a here only. Exod. 1. c. Thucyd. vii. 82 init.
b Rom. viii. 26 only. Exod. ii. 24.
c = Gen. xi. 5. Exod. iii. 8.
d = ver. 10 reff.
e = Rev. xvii. 1. xxi. 9. Gen. xxxi. 44.
f = Matt. x. 33. ch. iii. 13, 14. 2 Pet. ii. 1 al.‡
g ver. 10 reff.
h ver. 27 reff.
i here only. Lev. xxv. 31, 32 Ps. xviii. 14. lxxvii. 35 only.
k σύν, = 1 Cor. xv. 10.
l ch. ii. 3 reff.
m ver. 30 reff.
n absol., Mark xv. 20. ch. v. 19.
o = ch. ii. 22. John xii. 37 al.
p in N. T. alw. w. σημ., ch. ii. 19, 22, 43 al5. Matt. xxiv. 24 ‖ Mk. John iv. 18. Rom. xv. 19. 2 Cor. xii. 12. 2 Thess. ii. 9. Heb. ii. 4 only. Exod. xi. 10.
q Heb. xi. 29 only. Exod. x. 19.
r = Matt. xxii. 24. ch. iii. 22, from Deut. xviii. 15, 18.

34. και ιδων γαρ D[1]. om μου D[1][and lat] (ins D[5]). for αυτων, αυτου BD [Syr]. ακηκοα D 9. νυνι C[2]. rec αποστελω, with HP rel (*here, though αποστειλω is accordg to LXX, the corrn to -ελω was so very obvious, that I have retained the more unusual form, esp as the authorities in its favour are so strong*): αποστελλῶ a: txt ABCDEℵ c p Chr.

35. aft δικαστ. ins εφ ημων CDℵ p 36; εφ ημας E k o Chr Thl-fin: so, tol Syr syr-w-ast coptt æth arm (*corrn to suit LXX and ver* 27): om ABHP rel vulg Thl-sif. rec om 2nd και, with ACHP rel vulg [Syr coptt arm] Chr: ins BDE p syr: it is supplied by ℵ[1] or ℵ-corr[1]. αρχηγον A a h Chr$_2$. for λυτρωτην, δικαστην ℵ[1]: λυτρωτην δικαστην ℵ[3]. rec απεστειλεν, with CHP rel Chr: txt ABDEℵ c p. rec (for συν) εν, with HPℵ rel 36 D-lat [Syr copt æth arm] Chr [?]: *per manum* vss: txt ABC D[-gr] E c p 13 vulg syr sah Chr$_2$ (*εν has appy arisen from a confusion with the last syll of απεσταλκεν. I cannot see the force of Meyer's reasoning, that συν is a corrn setting forth more strikingly the superhuman powers of Moses*).

36. ins ο bef ποιησας D[1][-gr]. for γη, τη BC m D-lat sah: om b[1]: txt A D-gr EHPℵ Chr$_1$. rec αιγυπτου, with D rel [vulg E[2]-lat syrr copt æth arm] Thl-fin: txt ABCEHPℵ h k l m o p 36 sah Chr$_1$.

37. om 1st ο DH a b[2] c e f h o [Chr$_2$]. rec ειπων (*corrn to more usual form*), with EHP rel 36 Chr: txt ABCDℵ p. rec ins κυριος bef ο θεος, with CEHP rel [Syr copt arm Chr$_1$]: om ABDℵ p vulg sah æth: for θεος, κυριος syr [Chr$_1$]. rec aft θεος ins υμων, with [P] b m 13: ημων EH rel Thl: om ABDℵ p vulg syrr coptt æth [arm]. om υμων ℵ[1].

reges.' On the sanctity of the place, Chrys. remarks,—οὐδαμοῦ ναός, κ. ὁ τόπος ἅγιος τῇ ἐπιφανείᾳ κ. ἐνεργείᾳ τοῦ χριστοῦ.

34.] ἰδὼν εἶδον, LXX. Emphatic, to express the רָאֹה רָאִיתִי of the Heb., as often elsewhere. The instances commonly cited from the classics, of the phrase φεύγων ἐκφεύγειν, Herod. v. 95; Aristoph. Acharn. 177; Nub. 168; Eur. Phœn. 1231, &c., do not apply: for, as Porson observes, 'in his locis simplici verbo conatus, composito effectus indicatur.' **ἀποστείλω]** aorist subjunctive, as LXX, Exod. iii. 10. See Winer, edn. 6, § 41. *a*. 4. *a*.

35.] The second τοῦτον is repeated emphatically. So οὗτος again, vv. 36, 37, 38 [to impress on them God's choice of one whom they rejected]. **ἠρνήσαντο**, ver. 27. The rejecter of Moses there is regarded as the *representative of the nation*: see note on αὐτοῖς, ver. 26. In this express mention of the rejection of Moses by the Jews and his election and mission by God, the parallel of Jesus Christ is no doubt in Stephen's mind, and the inference intended to be drawn, that *it does not follow that* God rejects *those whom* they rejected. The difficulty of **ἀπέσταλκεν** has caused it to be altered into the historic tense, ἀπέστειλεν. But the perf. sets forth not only the fact of God's sending Moses *then*, but the endurance of his mission till now —**him hath God sent**: with a closer reference than before, to Him whom God had *now* exalted as the true ἄρχοντα κ. λυτρωτήν. See ch. v. 31.

37.] See ch. iii. 22, notes. Our text has probably been altered to agree verbally with the former citation.

38.] γίνομαι μετά is not a Hebraism, as Kuin.: see reff. That Moses conversed with both the Angel

[s] ὡς ἐμέ. 38 οὗτός ἐστιν ὁ [t] γενόμενος ἐν τῇ [u] ἐκκλησίᾳ
ἐν τῇ ἐρήμῳ [t] μετὰ τοῦ ἀγγέλου τοῦ λαλοῦντος αὐτῷ ἐν
τῷ ὄρει Σινᾶ καὶ τῶν [v] πατέρων [v] ἡμῶν, ὃς [w] ἐδέξατο [x] λόγια [y] ζῶντα [z] δοῦναι ἡμῖν, 39 ᾧ οὐκ ἠθέλησαν [a] ὑπήκοοι
γενέσθαι οἱ [v] πατέρες [v] ἡμῶν, ἀλλὰ [b] ἀπώσαντο καὶ [c] ἐστράφησαν ἐν ταῖς καρδίαις αὐτῶν εἰς Αἴγυπτον, 40 εἰπόντες τῷ
Ἀαρὼν [d] Ποίησον ἡμῖν θεοὺς οἳ [e] προπορεύσονται ἡμῶν· ὁ
γὰρ [f] Μωυσῆς οὗτος, ὃς [g] ἐξήγαγεν ἡμᾶς ἐκ γῆς Αἰγύπτου, οὐκ οἴδαμεν τί [h] ἐγένετο [f] αὐτῷ. 41 καὶ [i] ἐμοσχοποίησαν ἐν ταῖς ἡμέραις ἐκείναις καὶ [j] ἀνήγαγον [k] θυσίαν τῷ
[l] εἰδώλῳ, καὶ [m] εὐφραίνοντο ἐν τοῖς [n] ἔργοις τῶν [n] χειρῶν

s —: ch. iii. 22. Matt. vii. 29.
t ch. ix. 19. xx. 18. Mark xvi. 10.
u = ch. xix. 32, 39, 41. see notes. Deut. xxxii. 1 (xxxi. 30).
v ch. v. 30 reff.
w = 2 Cor. vi. 1.
x Rom. iii. 2. Heb. v. 12. 1 Pet. iv. 11 only. Num. xxiv. 4, 16 al.
y = John vi. 51. Heb. iv. 12. x. 20. 1 Pet. i. 23. see Ps. cxviii. 50.
z = ver. 8. ch. xiii. 21 al. Ezek. xx. 11 and pass.

a 2 Cor. ii. 9. Phil. ii. 8 only. Prov. iv. 3. b ver. 27. Jer. ii. 37. c Matt. xviii. 3. 1 Kings x. 6. Lam. i. 20. see ver. 42. d Exod. xxxii. 1. e Luke i. 76 only. Exod. xiv. 19. Josh. x. 13. f constr., Rev. ii. 26. iii. 12. g see ver. 36. h Matt. viii. 13. 1 Macc. iv. 27. i here only +. Exod. xxxii. 8. j = here only. 3 Kings iii. 15 al. k abs., Matt. ix. 13. Heb. viii. 3 al. Gen. xlvi. 1. l 1 Cor. x. 19 reff. m ch. ii. 36. Luke xii. 19. Rom. xv. 10. 2 Cor. ii. 2. Gal. iv. 27. w. ἐν, Rev. xviii. 20. 1 Kings ii. 1. n Rev. ix. 20 (Heb. i. 10, from Ps. ci. 25) only. Ps. cxxxiv. 15. Isa. xxxvii. 19.

ωσει D[1]. rec aft εμε ins αυτου ακουσεσθε (*from* LXX), with CDE (ακουεσθε D[1][?], *quem audistis* E-lat[1]) rel 36 vulg syrr copt [æth arm]: om ABHPא a f g h l m p sah Chr$_2$ Thl-sif.

38. om 2nd του D[1](ins D[6]). **υμων** א: om e. for εδεξ., εξελεξατο B. **υμιν** [B] א.

39. for ω, οτι D-gr. (αλλα, so ABCDEHא k o.) **απεστρ.** D m. aft εστρ. ins και א[1](but corrd). rec om εν, with DEHP rel vulg Chr$_2$ Thl Iren-int$_1$: ins ABCא 36. 40 [coptt Cyr-p] Did-c. τη καρδια HP rel syr copt æth-pl Chr$_2$ Thl Iren-int$_1$: txt ABCDE p 36. 40 vulg Syr æth-rom [arm]. om αυτων D.

40. ειπαντες D. aft ουτος ins ο ανθρωπος א. ο εξαγαγων E. rec γεγονεν (*corrn to* LXX, *Exod* xxxii. 1), with DEHP p rel Chr$_1$: txt ABCא 36.

41. for ανηγαγον, απηγοντο D[1](ανηγοντο D-corr[1]: txt D-corr).

of the covenant and our fathers, implies that he was the *mediator between them*, as indeed ὃς ἐδέξατ. λόγ. ζ. more plainly declares. **ἐκκλησίᾳ** probably, the assembly held (Exod. xix.) for the promulgation of the law at Mt. Sinai, not '*the Church*' generally: but the article does not determine this: it would be expressed, whichever meaning we take. Wordsw. observes on the meaning which the words ἡ ἐκκλησία ἐν τῇ ἐρήμῳ carry for the student of Christian prophecy, Rev. xii. 1—6. **λόγια ζῶντα**] **living**, see reff., not = ζωοποιοῦντα (Grot., Kuin.), '*life-giving:*' still less to be understood '*given vivâ voce*' (Pisc. Alberti). So Soph. Œd. Tyr. 482, τὰ μεσόμφαλα γᾶς ἀπονοσφίζων | μαντεῖα· τὰ δ' αἰεὶ | ζῶντα περιποτᾶται.

39.] Another instance, brought home again by the words **οἱ πατέρες ἡμῶν**, of *rejection of God's appointed messenger and servant.* **ἐστράφησαν**] **they turned back in their heart to Egypt:** not, '*they wished to return to Egypt,*' of which in Exod. xxxii. there is no trace (but later, in Num. xiv. 4), and which would hardly suit **προπορεύσονται**; but 'they apostatized in heart to the Egyptian idolatries.' The very title by which Aaron proclaims his idol, is, 'These be thy gods, O Israel, which *brought thee up out of* the land of Egypt,' Exod. xxxii. 4. See also Neh. ix. 18. **40. προπορ.**] As God had done in the pillar of the cloud and fire. The plural is not (as Kuin.) put for θεόν, but is used categorically: not perhaps without implying also, that the only two religions were, the worship of Jehovah, and that of *idols*, a multitude. The plural is used by Aaron, see above. In the οὗτος may be implied, as Meyer suggests, 'who was the strong opponent of idolatry.' **41. ἐμοσχοποίησαν**] apparently in imitation of Apis, a bull worshipped at Memphis as the living symbol of Osiris. Herod. iii. 28. Diod. Sic. i. 21. Strabo, xvii. 805 (Winer, Realw. 'Kalb'). The *ox* was a common symbolic form of idols in the East; it was one of the cherubic forms, Ezek. i. 10; and the most recent discoveries at Nineveh have brought to light colossal bulls. Sir Gardiner Wilkinson (second series, ii. 97, Winer) thinks the golden calves of Israel to have been imitations of Mnevis, a bull kept at Heliopolis (Diod. Sic. i. 21. Strabo, xvii. 803) as a living symbol of the sun. Jeroboam afterwards set up golden calves at Bethel

o intrans. (appy), here only ‡. trans., Matt. v. 39. Rev. xi. 6 only. see ver. 39.
p — Rom. i. 24, 26, 28. Job xvi. 12. constr., here only. see ch. xvi. 4.
q ver. 7.
r Luke ii. 13 only.
s 3 Kings xxii. 19. Jer. vii. 18.

αὐτῶν. 42 [o] ἔστρεψεν δὲ ὁ θεὸς καὶ [p] παρέδωκεν αὐτοὺς ABCDE
[q] λατρεύειν τῇ [rs] στρατιᾷ τοῦ [s] οὐρανοῦ, καθὼς γέγραπται HPℵa b
ἐν βίβλῳ τῶν προφητῶν Μὴ [t] σφάγια καὶ θυσίας [u] προς- c f g h k
ηνέγκατέ μοι ἔτη τεσσεράκοντα ἐν τῇ ἐρήμῳ, [v] οἶκος Ἰσραήλ, l m o p
43 καὶ [w] ἀνελάβετε τὴν σκηνὴν τοῦ Μολόχ, καὶ τὸ [x] ἄστρον 13
τοῦ θεοῦ Ῥεφάν, τοὺς [y] τύπους οὓς ἐποιήσατε προςκυνεῖν
αὐτοῖς; καὶ [z] μετοικιῶ ὑμᾶς [a] ἐπέκεινα Βαβυλῶνος.

t here only. Amos v. 25. u = ch. xxi. 26. Heb. xi. 4. John xvi. 2. Num. xxxi. 50. v ch. ii. 36 reff. w = here only. (ch. xx. 13, 14. xxiii. 31. Eph. vi. 13, 16. 2 Tim. iv. 11.) x Luke xxi. 25. ch. xxvii. 20. Luke only, exc. Heb. xi. 12 (from Exod. xxxii. 13). y = here only. (ver. 4 al.) l. c. only. Jos. Antt. i. 19. 8, 10. z ver. 4 reff. a here only. = Isa. xviii. 1. of time, Lev. xxii. 27. Hag. ii. 19.

42. aft εστρ. δε ins αυτους C sah. om των D. εν τη ερ. οικ. ισ. bef ετη τεσ. (*see* LXX-*A*) A: εν τη ερημω is in the margin of B: εν ερ. bef ετη τεσ. a h. at end ins λεγει κυριος C [Cyr-p_1].

43. rec aft θεου ins υμων (*corrn to suit* LXX), with ACE[H]Pℵ rel vulg syr copt [æth Chr_1]; ημων a[1] l: om BD Syr sah arm $Orig_1$ $Iren\text{-}int_1$ $Philas_1$. rec ρεμφαν, with rel [$Orig_1$] Chr_1 Thl-fin: ρεμφαμ D [vulg $Iren\text{-}int_1$]: ρομφα B [Orig-ms]: ρομφαν ℵ[1] [Chr-ms]: ρεμφα p vulg-mss(Lachm) [arm]: ρεφα H: ρεφφα o: ρεφφαν h k l Œc: [ρεφραν P:] ραφαν 180 Just: txt (A)CE(ℵ[3]) g 13. 36 Syr syr-mg-gr coptt Orig-ms Thdrt Thl-sif Jer.—ραιφαν Aℵ[3] [Cyr-p_1]. for επεκ., επι (τα με)ρη D[1](txt D[4]); *in i... partes* D-lat, *in partem* E-lat.

and Dan, and with the same proclamation: see 1 Kings xii. 28. **42. ἔστρεψεν**] neuter, **changed,—turned**, as ἀναστρέψω, ch. xv. 16. No word, as ἑαυτόν, or τὴν γνώμην, or τὸ πρόσωπον αὐτοῦ, need be supplied: nor must ἔστρ. κ. παρ. be rendered '*again delivered them*' (Vitring., De Dieu, al.), a Hebraism which has no place in the N. T. (Mey.): nor must we understand αὐτούς (as C in var. readd.),—God turned *them*; for, though philologically there is no objection to this, the sense requires that ἔστρεψεν should form an introduction to παρέδωκεν—God, who had hitherto watched over them for good, *now provoked by their rebellion, turned*, and delivered them up to their own ways.

παρέδωκεν—not '*suffered them to fall into*:' all these explainings away of the strong expressions of Scripture belong to the rationalistic school of interpreters (which is not modern merely: even Chrysostom has here εἴασε): it was a *judicial delivering up*, not a mere letting alone, see reff. **τῇ στρ. τ. οὐρ.**] This fact is not mentioned in the Pentateuch, but may refer to the worship of Baal. In aftertimes we have frequent traces of star-worship: see 2 Kings xvii. 16; xxi. 3, 5; xxiii. 4, 5; Jer. xix. 13; Zeph. i. 5. See also Deut. iv. 19; xvii. 3; Job xxxi. 26. **βίβλ. τ. προφ.**] The book of the prophets, regarded as a whole. The citation (ref.) is from the LXX. **μὴ σφάγ. κ. θ.**] A question usually preceding a *negative* answer, see Matt. vii. 9; Rom. xi. 1; 1 Cor. ix. 8 al.: but not always: see Matt. xii. 23 (xxvi. 22); John iv. 29; viii. 22. Winer, edn. 6, § 57. 3, b. There is no stress on μοί ('Is it to *Me* that ye offered, &c. (i. e. to me only?') as Rosenm., Heinr., Olsh., Kuin., Stier: the position of μοί in the sentence will not allow of this). I should take the question here according to the usual construction, and understand it as a reproach, implying that God does not receive as offered to Him, sacrifices in which He has been made to share with idols:—**it is not true that ye offered to Me** (but no stress on Me) **sacrifices, &c.**; 'I regard it as never having happened.'

43.] The answer, by God Himself: **Yea, ἀνελάβετε, ye** [**took up, i. e.**] **carried about with you**, (not *My* tabernacle as your sole or chief holy place, but) **the tabernacle** (סִכּוּת, the portable tent for the image: Diod. Sic. xx. 65, mentions the ἱερὰ σκηνή in the Carthaginian camp) **of M.**, &c. Stephen was *not the sole* dishonourer, *if a dishonourer*, of the holy place—their fathers had done it before. **Μολόχ**] So the LXX: the Heb. has מַלְכְּכֶם, '*of your king*;'—the LXX probably followed another reading (מלכם is actually found in 577 Kennicot and 440[1] De Rossi), or perhaps explained the expression by the cognate name of this god. Moloch (Winer, Realw.) was the Phœnician Saturn: his image was of brass with the head of an ox, and outstretched arms of a man, hollow; and human sacrifices (of children) were offered, by laying them in these arms and heating the image by a fire kindled within. The rigid prohibitions of the worship of Moloch (Lev. xviii. 21; xx. 2—5) were openly

44 ἡ [b] σκηνὴ τοῦ [b] μαρτυρίου ἦν τοῖς [c] πατράσιν [c] ἡμῶν ἐν
τῇ ἐρήμῳ, καθὼς [d] διετάξατο ὁ λαλῶν τῷ Μωυσῇ ποιῆσαι
αὐτὴν κατὰ τὸν [e] τύπον ὃν ἑωράκει, 45 ἣν καὶ [f] εἰσήγαγον [g] διαδεξάμενοι οἱ [c] πατέρες [c] ἡμῶν μετὰ Ἰησοῦ ἐν τῇ
[h] κατασχέσει τῶν ἐθνῶν [i] ὧν [k] ἐξῶσεν ὁ θεὸς ἀπὸ [l] προς-

b Rev. xv. 5 only. Exod. xxvii. 21 al. fr.
c ch. v. 30 reff.
d mid., ch. xxiv. 23. 1 Cor. vii. 17. xi. 34. Tit. i. 5 only †.
e = Heb. viii. 5, from Exod. xxv. 40. Phil. iii. 17 al.
f = here only. Xen. Rep. Ath. ii. 3.
g here only. 2 Chron. xxxi. 12.
h ver. 5 only. Num. xxxii. 5.
i attr., ch. i. 1 reff.
k = here (ch. xxvii. 39) only. Jer. xxiv. 9.
l ch. v. 41. Rev. xx. 11. Num. xx. 6. Deut. xi. 23.

44. rec ins *εν* bef *τοις*, with D[1] E-gr k[2] 36 syr Thl-fin : [*cum* vulg-clem am[2], *apud* æth :] om ABCD[2]Pא p rel am[1] fuld lux E-lat copt Chr_1 Thl-sif. *υμων* A g o: om k m 13. *εταξατο* א[1]. om *ὁ* D. *αυτη* (sic) א. *κατα το πα(. . .)υπον* (? *παρατυπον*) D[1](txt D[4]). *εορακεν* DH, *εωρακεν* E 36.
45. *μ. ιησουν* D[1], *cum jesum* D-lat. *εξεωσεν* E א(but corrd) 5. 13. 180.

transgressed by Ahaz, 2 Kings xvi. 3; by Manasseh, ib. xxi. 6; see also xxiii. 10; Jer. vii. 31; xxxii. 35. In the kingdom of Israel this abomination had been long practised, see 2 Kings xvii. 17; Ezek. xxiii. 37. We find traces of it at Carthage (Diod. Sic. xx. 14), among the Phœnicians (Q. Curt. iv. 3. 23. Euseb. laud. Const. xiii. 4. Porphyr. de Abstin. ii. 56),—among the Cretans and Rhodians (Porphyr. ibid.), and the Assyrian colonists at Sepharvaim, 2 Kings xvii. 31. **τὸ ἄστρον τοῦ θ. Ῥεφάν**] Heb. כִּיּוּן, Chiún; but what the meaning of either this or Ῥαιφάν (LXX) is, we have nothing but conjecture to inform us. The principal opinions have been (1) that of Kircher, who maintains Ῥεφάν (Ῥηφάν) to be a Coptic word, signifying *the planet Saturn*, and answering to the Arabic 'Kewan:' (2) that of Hengstenberg, Authentie des Pentat. 110 ff., who entirely repudiates Kircher's interpretation, and supposes Ῥηφάν to have arisen from a misreading of ריון for כיון. But Winer (Realw.) prefers the former opinion, and supports it by the authority of eminent modern Coptic and Arabic scholars. De Wette and Hengstenberg believe כִּיּוּן to be an appellative noun, and would render it, Gestell, the *carriage* or *frame*, on which the star or image was carried: '*imaginem idolorum vestrorum*,' Vulg. Amos. l. c. Wordsw. after Cyr. alex. in Catena, supposes *ῥεφάν* to signify *σκότισμα*, or blindness, and suggests that the name may have been one given by the Jews in contempt, like Beelzebub, to the god of the Ekronites. See Smith, Bibl. Dict., art. Remphan. **Βαβυλῶνος**] *Δαμασκοῦ*, LXX and Heb. The fulfilment of the prophecy would make it very natural to substitute that name which had become inseparably associated with the captivity.

44. ἡ σκ. τ. μαρτ.] In opposition to the *σκ.* just mentioned: but also in pursuance of one of the great aims of the speech, *to shew that holiness is not confined to locality or building*. This part of his subject Stephen now enters on more particularly. The words *ἡ σκ. τ. μαρτ.* are the LXX rendering of אֹהֶל מוֹעֵד (Num. xvi. 18, 19 al.) 'the tabernacle of the assembly' (or 'congregation,' E. V.). They apparently derived the latter word from עוּד, 'testatus est,' instead of יָעַד, 'constituit.' **τύπον**] (ref.): another contrast, cf. *τύπους οὓς ἐποιήσατε*, ver. 43.

45. εἰσήγ.] absolute: **introduced**, viz. *εἰς τὴν γῆν*:—not connected with *ἐν τῇ κατασχ.*,—see below. **διαδεξ.**] **Having inherited it**, i. e. succeeded to its custody and privileges. The sense of 'successores,' 'qui majores exceperunt,' is ungrammatical; as also is that of 'postea,' 'deinceps.' **ἐν τῇ κατασχέσει**] **at** (or 'in') **their taking possession**. The Vulg. rendering, 'in possessionem gentium,' is philologically inadmissible; 'in terram a gentibus occupatam' (Calvin, De Dieu, Grot., Kuin.) is still worse. The passage of the LXX, Num. xxxii. 5, *δοθήτω ἡ γῆ αὕτη τοῖς οἰκέταις σου ἐν κατασχέσει*, brought forward to justify these renderings, is directly against them. The word is one of those examples of verbal nouns in *-σις* where the meaning hovers uncertainly between the act of doing and the thing done. Such is often the case with *καύχησις* in St. Paul. Cf. for a very near approach to the concrete meaning of this word, Num. xxvii. 4, 7. But, abstract or concrete, it always, as might be expected from the very composition of the word, is used of that final and settled possession which Israel took of the land, not of that transitory possession from which the gentes were driven out. So that Wordsw.'s rendering, "the portion, or possession of the Gentiles," is out of the question.

The martyr combines rapidly a considerable period, during which this *κατάσχεσις* and this expulsion was taking place (for it was not complete till the time of David) in order to arrive at the next great event of his history, *the substitution*

ABCDE HPℵ a b c f g h k l m o p 13

ώπου τῶν [e] πατέρων [e] ἡμῶν, 46 ἕως τῶν ἡμερῶν Δαυείδ, ὃς
[mn] εὗρεν [n] χάριν ἐνώπιον τοῦ θεοῦ καὶ [o] ᾐτήσατο [p] εὑρεῖν
[q] σκήνωμα τῷ * θεῷ Ἰακώβ· 47 Σολομῶν δὲ [r] ᾠκοδόμησεν αὐτῷ [r] οἶκον. 48 ἀλλ᾽ οὐχ ὁ [s] ὕψιστος ἐν [t] χειροποιήτοις [u] κατοικεῖ, καθὼς ὁ προφήτης λέγει, 49 [v] Ὁ οὐρανός
μοι θρόνος, ἡ δὲ γῆ [w] ὑποπόδιον τῶν ποδῶν μου· [x] ποῖον
[r] οἶκον [r] οἰκοδομήσετέ μοι, λέγει κύριος, ἢ τίς [y] τόπος
τῆς [z] καταπαυσεώς μου; 50 οὐχὶ ἡ [a] χείρ μου ἐποίησεν ταῦτα
πάντα; 51 [b] σκληροτράχηλοι καὶ [cde] ἀπερίτμητοι τῇ [d] καρδίᾳ
καὶ τοῖς [e] ὠσίν, ὑμεῖς ἀεὶ τῷ πνεύματι τῷ ἁγίῳ [f] ἀντιπί-

m = 2 Tim. i. 18. n Luke i. 30. Heb. iv. 16 only. Gen. xxxiii. 10. o constr. (but not ellips.), ch. iii. 14 reff. see Eccl. ii. 10. p Psa. cxxxi. 5. = Heb. xii. 17. see Hos. xii. 8. q 2 Pet. i. 13, 14 only. Ps. xxv. 8. r 1 Chron. xxviii. 6. Matt. vii. 24, 26. Luke vi. 48, 49 (but οἰκίαν). s abs., Luke i. 32, 35, 76. vi. 35 only. Deut. xxxii. 8 al. t ch. xvii. 24. Mark xiv. 58. Eph. ii. 11. Heb. ix. 11, 24 only. Isa. ii. 18. u of God, ch. xvii. 24. Matt. xxiii. 21. Eph. iii. 17 only. (see Eph. ii. 22.) Ps. ii. 8. Isa. lvii. 15. v Isa. lxvi. 1. w ch. ii. 35 reff. x ch. iv. 7 reff. y = ch. iv. 31. z Heb. iii. 11, 18. iv 1, 3, &c., only. Deut. xii. 9. = Ps. cxxxi. 14. a see ch. xi. 21 reff. b here only. Exod. xxxiii. 3, 5 al. c here only. d Ezek. xliv. 7. Jer. ix. 26. e Jer. vi. 10. f here only. Num. xxvii. 14. Herodian vi. 3.

46. om *ητησατο* ℵ[1]. *σκηνωμα* bef *ευρ.* D. * *οἴκῳ* BDHℵ[1]: *θεω* ACEPℵ[3] rel 36 vulg syrr [coptt æth arm] Chr_1.

47. *σαλωμων* AC: *σαλομων* ℵ. **οικοδ.** B[1](sic: see table) D. *εαυτω* CH Thl-sif.

48. *ο δε υψ. ου*(om *ου* D-lat) *κατοικ. εν χειρ.* D. rec aft *χειροπ.* ins *ναοις* (*explanatory gloss: or from ch* xvii. 4), with HP rel 36 [arm] Chr_1 Aug_1: om ABCDEℵ p vulg syrr coptt æth $Pamph\text{-}int_1$. for *καθως*, *ως* D: *καθως και* E-gr(and lat[2]) 76.

49. for *μοι*, *μου* D[1](txt D[3]): add *εστιν* D. *και η γη* (*as* LXX-B) B vss(not vulg syr [arm]). *οικοδομησατε* B 42. for *τις*, *ποιος* (*as* LXX) D. at end add *εστιν* D [k] 13 $Thdrt_1$.

50. *παντα* bef *ταυτα* (*cf* LXX) ACDEP l m: txt BHℵ p rel [vulg syrr $Cyr\text{-}p_1$].

51. for *τη καρδια*, *καρδιαις* (*corrd to plur to suit the plur subject*) ACD [$Cyr\text{-}p_1$]: *ταις καρδιαις* ℵ c Chr_1 [*cordibus* vulg syr æth arm]: *καρδιας* B(sic: see table): txt EHP

of the temple of Solomon for the tabernacle. **46. ᾐτήσατο]** asked permission, see 2 Sam. vii. 2 ff., in which this request is made through Nathan the prophet, and at first conceded by Nathan, though afterwards, on a revelation made from God, denied:—not *'wished'* (Grot., Kuin.: *'desired,'* E. V.). The vow (a species of prayer) here referred to, is defined by the words **εὑρεῖν σκήνωμα**, to be that mentioned Ps. cxxxi. 1—5 (LXX). **48.]** But, though Solomon built Him an house, *we are not to suppose, for all that, that He is confined to earthly spots.* **καθὼς ὁ πρ. λ.]** We have in substance the same declaration by Solomon himself at the dedication of his temple, 1 Kings viii. 27; see also the beautiful prayer of David, 1 Chron. xxix. 10—19. The citation is freely from the LXX. The student will not fail to be interested in observing the apparent reference to this declaration in Stephen's apology, by St. Paul, ch. xvii. 24. **51.]** I do not think there is any occasion to suppose an *interruption from the audience* to have occasioned this outbreak of holy indignation. At each separate recital (vv. 9, 25, 35, 39 ff.) he has dwelt, with continually increasing fervour, on the *rebellions against and rejections of God by His people.* He has now brought down the history to the establishment of the temple worship. From Solomon's time to his own, he saw but a succession of apostasies, idolatries, rejection of God's prophets:—a dark and loathsome catalogue, terminated by the betrayal and murder of the Just One Himself. It is not at all beyond probability, to believe that the zeal of his fervent spirit was by the view of this, the filling up of the measure of their iniquities, kindled into a flame of inspired invective. I find that this is also Neander's view, in opposition to the generality of Commentators (P. u. L., p. 92), as also that of Prof. Hackett, in his commentary on the Acts: and I cannot but think it far the most probable. ἐνταῦθα λοιπὸν καταφορικῶς τῷ λόγῳ κέχρηται. πολλὴ ἦν παρρησία μέλλοντος αὐτοῦ ἀποθνήσκειν· καὶ γὰρ καὶ τοῦτο οἶμαι αὐτὸν εἰδέναι, Chrysost. **σκληρ. κ. ἀπερ.]** Words and figures familiar to the prophets in speaking of the rebellious Israel: see, besides reff., Deut. ix. 6, 13; Neh. ix. 16:—Deut. x. 16; xxx. 6 Heb. See also Rom. ii. 29. **ὠσίν]** I should hardly think of any allusion to Ps. xl. (xxxix.) 6,—because

πτετε, [g] ὡς οἱ [h] πατέρες [h] ὑμῶν καὶ ὑμεῖς. 52 τίνα τῶν προφητῶν οὐκ [i] ἐδίωξαν οἱ [h] πατέρες [h] ὑμῶν; καὶ ἀπέκτειναν
τοὺς [k] προκαταγγείλαντας περὶ τῆς [l] ἐλεύσεως τοῦ [m] δικαίου,
οὗ νῦν ὑμεῖς [n] προδόται καὶ [o] φονεῖς ἐγένεσθε, 53 [p] οἵτινες
[q] ἐλάβετε τὸν νόμον [r] εἰς [s] διαταγὰς ἀγγέλων καὶ οὐκ
[t] ἐφυλάξατε. 54 Ἀκούοντες δὲ ταῦτα [u] διεπρίοντο ταῖς

...υμων c. ABCDEHP ℵ a b f g h k l m o p 13

g Matt. vi. 10. Thucyd. viii. 1.
h ch. iii. 25 reff.
i Matt. v. 10, 11. ch. ix. 4, 5. xxii. 4, 7, 8 al. Ps. vii. 1.
k ch. iii. 18 only †.
l here only †.
m abs., = ch. iii. 14. xxii. 14. 1 Pet. iii. 18. see James v. 6.
n Luke vi. 16. 2 Tim. iii. 4 only †. 2 Macc. v. 15. x. 13, 22 only.
o Matt. xxii. 7. ch. iii. 14. xxviii. 4. 1 Pet. iv. 15. Rev. xxi. 8. xxii. 15 only. 4 Kings ix. 31 compl. Wisd. xii. 5 only.
p – ch. x. 41 reff.
q = John vii. 39. Rom. iv. 11 al. Hos. xiii. 1.
r – ch. ii. 39. viii. 20.
s Rom. xiii. 2 only. Ezra iv. 11 only. see Gal. iii. 19.
t = ch. xvi. 4 reff.
u ch. v. 33 only ‡. 1 Chron. xx. 3 only.

p rel [tol] spec Syr coptt [Eus$_1$] Ath$_1$ Cyr-jer$_1$ [Orig-int$_2$].—add *υμων* ℵ o [Syr sah]. for *ως*, *καθως* D. ins *και* bef *υμων* D[1][-gr]. om *και υμεις* D [Orig-int$_1$].

52. for *οι πατ. υμ.*, *εκεινοι* D[1](txt D[6]). *απεκτ. αυτους τους προκαταγγελλοντας π.* (ins *της* D[3]) *ελ.* D[1]. rec **γεγενησθε** (*corrn to appy more suitable tense, see note*), with HP rel Chr$_1$ Thl: txt ABCDEℵ k p Orig$_1$ [Cyr-p$_1$].

53. *εφυλαξεσθε* A.

the LXX have rendered 'mine ears hast thou opened' by *σῶμα κατηρτίσω μοι.* **τῷ πν. τ. ἁγ. ἀντ.**] Apparently a reference to Isa. lxiii. 10. The instances as yet had been confined to *οἱ πατ. ὑμ.*: now he has arrived at their own times. The *two* are taken up again in the next verse.

52. τίνα τ. προφ.] See Matt. xxiii. 31 ff.: 2 Chron. xxxvi. 16: where the same general expressions are used of their persecuting the prophets. Such sayings are not to be pressed to the letter, but represent the uniform attitude of disobedience and hostility which they assumed to the messengers of God. See also the parable, Matt. xxi. 35. **τοὺς προκ.**] *The office of all the prophets,* see ch. iii. 18. The assertion is repeated, to connect them, by this title, with Him, whom they announced.

τοῦ δικαίου] Schöttg. vol. ii. p. 18, has shewn from the Rabbinical writings that this name was used by the Jews to designate the Messiah. See reff. and note on James v. 6. **προδόται**] By Judas's treachery, of which the Sanhedrists had been the accomplices; Matt. xxvi. 14—16: —**φονεῖς**, by the hands of the Romans; ch. ii. 23, note. **ἐγένεσθε** is preferable not only on account of its manuscript authority, but as being the *historical tense,* like the rest. It was probably altered to the perfect, as suiting the *time then present,* better than the aorist. **53.**] The use of **οἵτινες**, instead of *οἱ*, so very frequent in the Acts and Epistles, occurs when the clause introduced by it contains a *further explanation* of the position or classification of the person or persons alluded to, and not when the relative serves for simple identification. See Rom. i. 25, 32.

εἰς διαταγὰς ἀγγέλων] Many explanations have been given. Chrys. *διαταχθέντα νόμον λέγει, τὸν ἐγχειρισθέντα αὐτῷ δι' ἄγγελον τὸν ὀφθέντα αὐτῷ ἐν τῷ βάτῳ:* and Œc. *νόμον λαβόντας διατάξεις ἔχοντα, αἵτινες ἰσάγγελον ἐποίουν πολιτείαν ἔχειν τοὺς τελοῦντας αὐτόν.* Heinsius and Lightfoot understand by *ἀγγέλ.* *the prophets:* Grot., Calov., and Krebs, '*præsentibus angelorum ordinibus,*' taking *διαταγάς* = *διατάξεις* in the sense of divisions of an army (Judith viii. 36), in which it never occurs,—not to say that *εἰς* will not bear this: Beza, Calv., Pisc., Elsn., Hamm., Kuin., &c., '*ab angelis promulgatum,*' which *εἰς* will not bear (*ἐν*): Winer, Gr., edn. 6, § 32. 4, b, '*as commands of angels*' (but see below), which, however, was not the fact (Mey., who refers to Jos. Antt. xv. 5. 3, *ἡμῶν τὰ κάλλιστα τῶν δογμάτων καὶ τὰ ὁσιώτατα τῶν ἐν τοῖς νόμοις* **δι' ἀγγέλων παρὰ τοῦ θεοῦ** *μαθόντων*):—the Syriac version, '*per mandatum angelorum:*'—Vulg. and Calv., '*in dispositione* (or *-onibus*) *angelorum:*' Schöttg., '*per ministerium angelorum.*' These three last are precluded by the foregoing remarks. The key to the right rendering seems to be the similar expression in ref. Gal., *ὁ νόμος* **διαταγεὶς δι' ἀγγέλων.** The law was *given* by God, but *announced* by angels. The people received God's law then, **εἰς διαταγὰς ἀγγέλων, at the injunction** (a sense of *διατ.* amply justified, see Palm and Rost's lex. *διάταξις,* and Polyb. iv. 19. 10; 87. 5: and preferred by Winer in his last edn., ut supra) **of angels.** So Matt. xii. 41, *μετενόησαν* **εἰς τὸ κήρυγμα** *Ἰωνᾶ,* 'they repented *at the preaching* of Jonas.' The only other legitimate rendering, 'as the injunctions of angels,' comes under the objections made to Winer's former view, above. **54—60.**] Effect of the speech: stoning of Stephen. **54.**] **διεπρ.**, see note on ref.

55.] Certainly, in so far as the vision

v here only. Ps. xxxiv. 16 al. see Matt. viii. 12 al.
w = Matt. xv. 32. Luke xxiii. 28. Rev. i. 7.
x ch. ii. 30 reff.
y Luke iv. 1. ch. vi. 5. xi. 24 only.
z ch. i. 10 reff.
a ch. ii. 25 reff.
b = Mark v. 15. John ix. 8 al.
c Luke ii. 23 (from Exod. xiii. 12). xxiv. 31 &c. ch. xvi. 14. xvii. 3. L.-only, exc. Mark xii. 34.

καρδίαις αὐτῶν καὶ [v] ἔβρυχον τοὺς ὀδόντας [w] ἐπ' αὐτον. ABCDE HPℵ a b f g h k l m o p 13
55 [x] ὑπάρχων δὲ [y] πλήρης [y] πνεύματος [y] ἁγίου, [z] ἀτενίσας
εἰς τὸν οὐρανὸν εἶδεν δόξαν θεοῦ καὶ Ἰησοῦν ἑστῶτα [a] ἐκ
δεξιῶν τοῦ θεοῦ, 56 καὶ εἶπεν Ἰδοὺ [b] θεωρῶ τοὺς οὐρανοὺς
[c] διηνοιγμένους, καὶ τὸν υἱὸν τοῦ ἀνθρώπου [a] ἐκ δεξιῶν
ἑστῶτα τοῦ θεοῦ. 57 [d] κράξαντες δὲ [d] φωνῇ [d] μεγάλῃ [e] συν-
έσχον τὰ ὦτα αὐτῶν καὶ [f] ὥρμησαν [g] ὁμοθυμαδὸν ἐπ' αὐτόν,
58 καὶ [h] ἐκβαλόντες ἔξω τῆς πόλεως [i] ἐλιθοβόλουν. καὶ οἱ

d Matt. xxvii. 50. ver. 60. Rev. vi. 10 al. 2 Kings xix. 4.
e = here only. Isa. lii. 15.
f Matt. viii. 32 ||. ch. xix. 29 only. 1 Kings xv. 19. 2 Macc. x. 16. (-μή, ch. xiv. 5. -μημα, Rev. xviii. 21.)
g ch. i. 14 reff.
h = Matt. xxi. 39 ||. Luke iv. 29. Lev. xiv. 40.
i here bis. Matt. xxi. 35. xxiii. 37 ||. (John viii. 5, v. r.) ch. xiv. 5. Heb. xii. 20 only. Exod. viii. 26 al.

54. ακουσαντες δε αυτου D. om ταυτα ℵ[1]. και εβρ. τε D[1]. aft οδ. ins αυτων E k Syr sah æth.

55. aft πληρης ins πιστεως και ℵ o [Syr copt(Tischdf)]. ιησ. τον κυριον εκ δε. του θ. εστ. D. for τ. θεου, αυτου C 1 Thl-fin.

56. rec ανεωγμενους (*corrn to more usual word*), with D-corr[1] HP rel 36 $Epiph_2$ Chr_1 [$Nyss_1$ $Antch_1$] $Thdrt_2$: ηνεωγμ. D[1] : txt ABCℵ p Ath_1 $Cyr\text{-}jer_1$. εστ. bef εκ δεξ. ACEℵ[1] m [vulg-ed demid syrr copt arm æth-pl] $Epiph_1$ Chr_1 [$Antch_1$].

58. aft εκβ. ins αυτον A k 13 [Syr syr-w-ob] sah Thl-fin. aft ελιθ. ins αυτον D

of Stephen was *supernatural*, it was not *necessary* that the *material heavens should have been visible* to him; but from the words ἀτενίσας **εἰς τὸν οὐρανόν** it would seem that they *were*. We are not told *where* the Sanhedrim were assembled. It does not seem as if they were convened in the ordinary session room: it may have been in one of the courts of the temple, which would give room for more than the members of the Sanhedrim to be present, as seems to have been the case. **ἑστῶτα**] A reason why the glorified Saviour was seen *standing*, and not *sitting*, has been pleasingly given by Chrysostom (in Cramer's Catena): τί οὖν ἑστῶτα καὶ οὐχὶ καθήμενον; ἵνα δείξῃ τὴν ἀντίληψιν τὴν εἰς τὸν μάρτυρα· καὶ γὰρ περὶ τοῦ πατρὸς λέγεται "ἀνάστα ὁ θεός." Similarly Gregory the Great, Hom. ii. 29, vol. i. p 1572, 'Stephanus stantem vidit, quem adjutorem habuit.' So also Arator, i. 611 ff. p. 124, ed. Migne, 'pro martyre surgit, Quem tunc stare videt; confessio nostra sedentem Cum soleat celebrare magis.' (See also the collect for St. Stephen's day.) But not perhaps correctly: for 'help' does not seem here to be the applicable idea, but the *confirmation of his faith* by the ecstatic vision of the Saviour's glory at God's right hand. I should be rather disposed to think that there was reference in the vision to that in Zech. iii. 1, where Zech. sees Ἰησοῦν τὸν ἱερέα τὸν μέγαν, ἑστῶτα πρὸ προσώπου ἀγγέλου κυρίου. Stephen, under accusation of blaspheming the *earthly temple*, is granted a sight of the *heavenly temple*; being cited before the *Sadducee High Priest* who believed neither angel nor spirit, he is vouchsafed a vision of the *heavenly* HIGH PRIEST, standing and ministering at the throne amidst the angels and just men made perfect.

56.] This is the only time that our Lord is by human lips called the SON OF MAN * after His ascension (Rev. i. 13; xiv. 14, are not instances). And *why here?* I believe, for this reason. Stephen, full of the Holy Ghost, speaking *now* not of himself at all (ver. 55), but entirely by the utterance of the Spirit, repeats the *very words*, Matt. xxvi. 64, in which Jesus Himself, *before this council*, had foretold His glorification;—and assures them that that exaltation of the SON of MAN, which they should hereafter witness to their dismay, was *already begun and actual*.

58. ἔξω τ. πόλ.] See Levit. xxiv. 14. 'Locus lapidationis erat extra urbem: omnes enim civitates muris cinctæ paritatem habent ad castra Israelis.' Babyl. Sanhedr. ad loc. (Meyer.) Cf. also Heb. xiii. 12, 13. *

ἐλιθοβόλουν] **they stoned him**: an anticipation of the fact, the details of which follow: not, '*they prepared to stone him*:' nor 'jam in itinere ad supplicii locum petulanter eum lapidibus lacessebant' (Heinr.): nor need we conjecture ἐλιθολόγουν with Markland. Stoning was the punishment of blaspheming, Levit. xxiv. 16. The question whether this was a legal proceeding on sentence, or a tumultuary one, is not easy to answer. It would appear from John xviii. 31, that the Jews had not legally the power of putting any man to death (see note there). Certainly, from the narrative

[k] μάρτυρες [l] ἀπέθεντο τὰ ἱμάτια αὐτῶν [m] παρὰ τοὺς πόδας
[n] νεανίου καλουμένου Σαύλου, 59 καὶ [i] ἐλιθοβόλουν τὸν
Στέφανον [o] ἐπικαλούμενον καὶ λέγοντα Κύριε Ἰησοῦ δέξαι
τὸ [p] πνεῦμά μου. 60 [q] θεὶς δὲ τὰ [qr] γόνατα [s] ἔκραξεν [s] φωνῇ
[s] μεγάλῃ Κύριε, μὴ [t] στήσῃς αὐτοῖς ταύτην τὴν ἁμαρτίαν,
καὶ τοῦτο εἰπὼν [u] ἐκοιμήθη. VIII. 1 Σαῦλος δὲ ἦν
[v] συνευδοκῶν τῇ [w] ἀναιρέσει αὐτοῦ. ἐγένετο δὲ ἐν ἐκείνῃ τῇ

d επικαλουμενον... ABCDE HPℵ a b d f g h k l m o p 13

k = Deut xvii. 7. l Matt. xii. 14. Rom. xiii. 12. Eph. iv. 22, 25. Col. iii. 8. Heb. xii. 1. James i. 21. 1 Pet. ii. 1 only. = 2 Macc. viii. 35. m ch. iv. 35 reff. n ch. xx. 9 reff. Acts only. o ch. ii. 21 reff. p = Luke xxiii. 46 || Mt. J. Eccl. xii. 7. q ch. ix. 40. xx. 36. xxi. 5. Mark xv. 19. Luke xxii. 41 only +. see 3 Kings viii. 54. r as above (q). Rom. xi. 4 reff. Luke v. 8. Heb. xii. 12. s ver. 57. t met., here only. propr., Matt. xxvi. 15? 2 Kings xiv. 26. Zech. xi. 12. u = 1 Cor. vii. 39 reff. v 1 Cor. vii. 12, 13 reff. w here only. Num. xi. 15.

Syr syr-w-ast coptt [æth]. om αυτων HP a b[1] f g h l m Thl-sif: ins A(B)CDEℵ p rel 36 vss Chr_2.—εαυτ. B. aft νεαν. ins τινος D [tol] Syr arm: του f h 13.

59. aft ιησ. ins χριστε C d 40 Chr_1 [$Euther_1$].

60. om δε D[1][-gr](ins D-corr[1]): τε e. φωνην μεγαλην D[1]: φωνην μεγαλη C[1] p: om ℵ[1]. add λεγων D [vulg-ed] am [demid(not fuld lux)] spec [Syr] copt. **στησεις** D[1](txt D[8]) d 180 [στησας C]. rec την αμ. bef ταυτ., with EHPℵ rel [D-lat Ep-of-ch-Lyons $Orig_1$ $Bas_1$$Nys_1$] Chr_3 $Thdrt_1$: txt ABCD vulg spec $Petr_1$ Iren-int_1 $Cypr_1$.

before us, and from the fact of a bloody persecution having taken place soon after it, it seems that the Jews did, by connivance of, or in the absence of the Procurator, administer summary punishments of this kind. But here no sentence is recorded: and perhaps the very violence and zelotic character of the execution might constitute it, not an encroachment on the power of the Procurator, as it would have been if strictly in form of law, but a mere outbreak, and as such it might be allowed to pass unnoticed. That they observed the forms of *their own law*, in the place and manner of the stoning, is no objection to this view. **οἱ μάρτυρες**] See ref. [where it is enacted that the hands of the witnesses were to be first on the criminal to put him to death, and afterward the hands of all the people]. They disencumbered themselves of their loose outer garments, ὥστε εἶναι κοῦφοι καὶ ἀπαραπόδιστοι εἰς τὸ λιθοβολεῖν. Theophyl. **ἀπέθεντο**] to keep them. Such notices are deeply interesting, when we recollect by *whom* they were in all probability carefully inserted. See ch. xxii. 19, 20, and note on ch. xxvi. 10:—from which it appears that Saul can certainly not have been less than *thirty* at this time. He was a member of the Sanhedrim, and soon after was despatched on an important mission with their authority. **59.**] The attempt to escape from this direct prayer to the Saviour by making Ἰησοῦ the genitive, and supposing it addressed to the Father,—in the face of the ever-recurring words κύριος Ἰησοῦς (see Rev. xxii. 20 especially), and the utter absence of any instance or analogy to justify it,—is only characteristic of the school to which it belongs. Yet in this case it has been favoured even by Bentley and Valcknaer, who supposed θεόν to have been omitted in the text, being absorbed by the preceding -ον. But if any such accus. had been used, it would certainly have been τὸν θεόν. **δέξαι τὸ πν. μ.**] The same prayer in substance had been made by our Lord on the cross (ref. Luke) to His Father. To *Him* was now committed the key of David. Similarly, the young man Saul, in after years: πέπεισμαι ὅτι δυνατός ἐστιν τὴν παραθήκην μου φυλάξαι εἰς ἐκείνην τὴν ἡμέραν, 2 Tim. i. 12. **60.**] The more accurate philological Commentators, De Wette and Meyer, deny that στήσῃς here can, as ordinarily explained, refer to *weighing* (reff. Matt.; Jer. xxxix. (xxxii.) 10), since not the *sin*, but the *punishment*, would be the thing weighed out,—and it would be harsh to take the one for the other, in a sentence of this kind. Meyer would understand ἱστάναι as opposed to ἀφιέναι, τὴν ἁμαρτίαν, '*Fix not this sin upon them*:' but De Wette, as seems to me more probably, renders it **Reckon not this sin to them** ('lay not this sin to their charge,' E. V.), supporting this by Rom. x. 3. This again was somewhat similar (though not exactly, see note there) to our Lord's prayer, Luke xxiii. 34. **ἐκοιμήθη**] Not a Christian expression only: Wetstein, on Matt. xxvii. 52, cites Jewish examples: and we have in the Anthology, iii. 1. 10, τῇδε Σάων ὁ Δίωνος Ἀκάνθιος ἱερὸν ὕπνον | κοιμᾶται· θνήσκειν μὴ λέγε τοὺς ἀγαθούς. But it became *the usual* Christian *term* for death. Its use here, when the circumstances, and the actors in them, are remembered, is singularly touching, from the contrast.

CHAP. VIII. 1—3.] PERSECUTION OF THE CHURCH BY SAUL, CONSEQUENT ON *

x 2 Cor. xii. 10 reff.
y ch. xiii. 50.
z ver. 4. ch. xi. 19 only. Ezek. xxii. 15.
a plur., Luke xxi. 21. John iv. 35. James v. 4 only. Ezek. xii. 15.
b here only ‡. Job v. 26 only. Soph. Ajax, 1047.
c ch. ii. 5 reff.

ABCDE HPℵa b d f g h k l m o p 13

ἡμέρᾳ [x] διωγμὸς μέγας [y] ἐπὶ τὴν ἐκκλησιαν τὴν ἐν Ἱερο-
σολύμοις· πάντες δὲ [z] διεσπάρησαν κατὰ τὰς [a] χώρας τῆς
Ἰουδαίας καὶ Σαμαρείας πλὴν τῶν ἀποστόλων. 2 [b] συν-
εκόμισαν δὲ τὸν Στέφανον ἄνδρες [c] εὐλαβεῖς καὶ ἐποίησαν
[d] κοπετὸν μέγαν ἐπ' αὐτῷ. 3 Σαῦλος δὲ [e] ἐλυμαίνετο τὴν
ἐκκλησίαν [f] κατὰ τοὺς οἴκους [g] εἰςπορευόμενος [h] σύρων
τε ἄνδρας καὶ γυναῖκας [i] παρεδίδου εἰς [k] φυλακήν.

c ch. ii. 5 reff. Ps. lxxix. 13. d here only. Gen. l. 10. Micah i. 8. e here only. = 2 Chron. xvi. 10. and constr., f = Luke xiii. 22. ix. 6. viii. 1. g ch. iii. 2. Mark i. 21 al. h John xxi. 8. ch. xiv. 19. xvii. 6. Rev. xii. 4 only. 2 Kings xvii. 13. i constr., Luke xxi. 12. xxiv. 7. ch. xxii. 4. 2 Cor. iv. 11 al. Isa. xxxiv. 2 al. fr. k ch. v. 19 reff. 2 Kings xx. 3.

CHAP. VIII. 1. ℵ o join *σαυλος . . . αυτου* to ch vii. aft *μεγας* ins *και θλειψεις* D sah. rec *παντες τε*, with A k o: om *δε* ℵ[1] 13. 47: *και παντες* ℵ[3] [*et omnes* vulg Syr æth]: txt BCDEHP p rel syr coptt Ps-Eus $Isid_1$ Chr_1. om *της* D[1](ins D[2]). aft *αποσ.* add *οι εμειναν εν ιερουσαλημ* D[1] sah Aug_1.
2. *συνκομισαντες* [omg *δε*] D[1]-gr(txt D[5]): *συνεκομισαντο* b o. for *δε*, *τε* D[5](and lat) E-gr æth. rec *εποιησαντο*, with EHP rel Chr_1: txt ABCDℵ k p Chr_1 $Thdrt_1$.
3. *ο δε σ.* D. *ελυμηνατο* E-gr. ins *τους* bef *ανδρας* ℵ[1](ℵ[3] disapproving). *παρεδιδους*(sic) D[1].

THE DEATH OF STEPHEN. 1. **συνευδ.**] See reff.: and compare his own confession, ch. xxvi. 9—11. From this time, the narrative takes up Saul, and, at first with considerable interruptions (ch. viii. x. xi. xii.), but after ch. xiii. 1 entirely, follows his history. **ἐν ἐκ. τῇ ἡμ.** can hardly mean, as some (Dr. Burton, De Wette, Meyer, Stier) would render it, on *that very day*, viz. when Stephen was stoned. For what follows, *πάντες δὲ διεσπάρησαν* . . cannot have happened on the same day, but would take some little time: and it is hardly allowable to render *ἐγένετο* '*broke out*.' We have *ἐν ἐκ. τῇ ἡμέρᾳ* used indefinitely, Luke vi. 23; John xiv. 20; xvi. 23, 26. In Luke xvii. 31 it has direct reference to a *ἡμέρα* just mentioned. **πάντες**] Not perhaps *literally*,—or some of them soon returned: see ch. ix. 26—30. It may describe the *general* dispersion, without meaning that every individual fled. **Σαμαρείας**] Connected with ver. 4: this word is not without importance, as introducing the *next step in the dissemination of the Gospel*, according to our Lord's command in ch. i. 8. **πλὴν τῶν ἀποστόλων**] Perhaps, from their exalted position of veneration by the people, the persecution did not extend to them: perhaps they remained, as possessed of superior firmness and devotion. But this latter reason is hardly applicable, after the command of our Lord, 'When they persecute you in one city, flee to another.' Matt. x. 23. Stier (Reden d. Apostel, i. 253) refers their remaining to an intimation of the Spirit, to stay and strengthen those who were left (*ἑτέρους γενέσθαι θράσους αἴτιοι*, Chrys.). Mr. Humphry (Comm. on Acts) cites an ancient tradition, mentioned by Clem. Alex., Strom. vi. 5 [43], end, p. 762 P, from the Prædicatio Petri (and by Euseb. H. E. v. 18), that the Apostles were ordered by our Lord to remain at Jerusalem twelve years: *φησὶν ὁ Πέτρος εἰρηκέναι τὸν κύριον τοῖς ἀποστόλοις Ἐὰν μὲν οὖν τις θελήσῃ τοῦ Ἰσραὴλ μετανοῆσαι διὰ τοῦ ὀνόματός μου πιστεύειν ἐπὶ τὸν θεόν, ἀφεθήσονται αὐτῷ αἱ ἁμαρτίαι· μετὰ δώδεκα ἔτη ἐξέλθετε εἰς τὸν κόσμον, μή τις εἴπῃ Οὐκ ἀκηκόαμεν.* But this could not be the case, as we have Peter and John going down, to Samaria, ver. 14.
2. **ἄνδρ. εὐλαβεῖς**] Whether Jews or Christians is not certain. Ananias is so called, ch. xxii. 12 (not in rec.), and he was a Christian. At all events, there is no contrast implied in the *δέ* (as Mey.), 'Yet, notwithstanding the persecution and dispersion, pious men were found who, &c.:' the *δέ* is merely the transitional particle,—and, so far from its being any unusual thing to bury an executed person, it was commanded among the Jews. Olshausen thinks that, if they had been Christians, the term *ἀδελφοί* would have been used: but this does not seem by any means certain: we can hardly reason so minutely from the diction of one section in the narrative to that of another, especially in the case of a section so distinct and peculiar as this one. (Besides, *ἀδελφοί* in this sense does not occur till ch. ix. 30: see reff. there.) Probably they were pious Jews, not yet converts, but hearers and admirers of Stephen. 3. **ἐλυμαίνετο**] Properly used of wild beasts, or of hostile armies, devastating and ravaging. (See examples in Kuin.) **κατὰ τοὺς οἴκους, entering** (the houses) **from house to house,**—a pregnant construction. **σύρων**] So

4 Οἱ μὲν οὖν [l] διασπαρέντες [m] διῆλθον [n] εὐαγγελιζόμενοι
τὸν [n] λόγον. 5 Φίλιππος δὲ [o] κατελθὼν εἰς πόλιν τῆς
Σαμαρείας [p] ἐκήρυσσεν [q] αὐτοῖς τὸν χριστόν. 6 [r] προσεῖχον
δὲ οἱ ὄχλοι τοῖς λεγομένοις ὑπὸ τοῦ Φιλίππου [s] ὁμοθυμαδόν, [t] ἐν τῷ ἀκούειν αὐτοὺς καὶ βλέπειν τὰ σημεῖα ἃ
ἐποίει· 7 πολλοὶ γὰρ τῶν [u] ἐχόντων [uv] πνεύματα [uv] ἀκάθαρτα [w] βοῶντα φωνῇ μεγάλῃ [x] ἐξήρχοντο, πολλοὶ δὲ

l ver. 1. m abs., ver. 40. ch. x. 38. xiii. 14. xvii. 23. xx. 25. Luke v. 15 only. 1 Kings xxvi. 22. n ch. xv. 35 only. o = Luke iv. 31. ix. 37. ch. ix. 32 al. (Luke only, exc. James iii. 15.) 2 Macc. xi. 29 (Wisd. xi. 22) only. p = with acc. of person, 1 Cor. i. 23. Phil. i. 15. κ. τ. χρ., L.P. κ. τ. ἰησ., ch. ix. 20 reff. κ. χρ. ἰησ., 2 Cor. iv. 5. see 2 Cor. i. 19. q so ch. xx. 2. Matt. iv. 23. Luke iv. 15. 2 Cor. ii. 13. r = and constr., vv. 10, 11. ch. xvi. 14. 1 Tim. i. 4. iii. 8. iv. 1, 13. Tit. i. 14. Heb. ii. 1. vii. 13. 2 Pet. i. 19 only. Ps. v. 2. s ch. i. 14 reff. t ch. ix. 3 reff. u Mark iii. 30 only. v ch. v. 16 reff. w Luke xviii. 7, 38. ch. xvii. 6 al. Gen. xxxix. 14. x = Matt. xii. 43. xvii. 18. ch. xvi. 8 al.

4. ηλθον $\aleph^1$ [sah(Tischdf)]. at end add του θεου E vulg(with am tol, not fuld demid) Syr æth].
5. καλελθων D^1-gr(txt D^8). ins την bef πολ. (*exegetical addition. The art is not needed, see note*) ABℵ m. **καισαριας** $\aleph^1$.
6. rec for δε, τε, with E-gr HP rel (æth-pl) [Chr$_1$]: txt ABCD^{2}ℵ a h p 36 vulg E-lat syr coptt.—ως δε ηκουον παν οι οχλοι προσειχ. τοις λεγ. D^1(corrd to txt by D^3 and-corr). om του D^1(ins D^3) f. for ομοθ., (. . . . .) οντο or -τε D^1(txt D^3). αυτου $\aleph^1$(perhaps: ς added or renewed by $\aleph^3$).
7. rec πολλων (*alteration to avoid the difficulty: see note. Meyer's account, that* εξηρχετο *was first altered to* -οντο *to suit* πνευματα [*the converse is much more probable*], *and then* πολλων *to* -οι *to furnish a plur nom to* εξηρχοντο, *seems to me very unlikely*), with HP rel copt [arm] Chr$_1$: (. . .)(π(αρ)α)? (απο D^8) πολλοις D^1: txt ABCEℵ p 36 vulg syrr sah [æth-pl(Tischdf)]. rec μεγ. bef φωνη: txt ABCDEHPℵ rel vulg Chr. rec εξηρχετο (*see above*), with HP rel Chr: txt ABCDEℵ k p [sah(Tischdf) arm]. aft πολλ. δε

Philo, in Flacc. 9, vol. ii. p. 526, συρόμενοι κ. πατούμενοι διὰ τῆς πόλεως ἁπάσης ἐξαναλώθησαν. **παρεδίδου**] viz. to the gaolers—so παραδιδοὺς εἰς φυλακάς, ch. xxii. 4.

4—13.] Preaching of the Gospel in Samaria by Philip. **4.**] **μὲν οὖν** resumes the subject dropped at the end of ver. 1, and determines this verse to be the opening of a new section, not the close of the former. **διῆλθ.**] See reff. **εὐαγγ. τ. λόγ.**] Here first we become acquainted with the missionary language so frequent in the rest of the book: and we have **τὸν λόγον**, an expression very familiar among Christians when the book was written, for [the fuller one which must have prevailed at first] τ. λ. τοῦ θεοῦ. **5. Φίλιππος**] *The deacon;* not, as apparently implied in the citation from Polycrates in Eus. H. E. iii. 31, v. 24, *one of the twelve:* this is precluded by vv. 1 and 14. And it is probable, that the persecution should have been directed especially against the colleagues of Stephen. Philip is mentioned again as ὁ εὐαγγελιστής,—probably from his having been the first recorded who εὐηγγελίσατο τὸν λόγον,—in ch. xxi. 8,—as married and having four daughters, virgins, who prophesied. **πόλιν τ. Σαμ.**] Verbatim as John iv. 5, in which case it is specified as being Sychar (Sichem). As the words stand here (πόλιν = τὴν πόλιν, after εἰς, compare also 2 Pet. ii. 6), seeing that Σαμάρεια (vv. 9, 14; ch. ix. 31; xv. 3) signifies the *district*, I should be inclined to believe that Sychem is here also intended. It was a place of rising importance, and in after-times eclipsed the fame of its neighbour Samaria, which latter had been, on its presentation by Augustus to Herod the Great, re-fortified and called Sebaste, Jos. Antt. xv. 7. 3, and 8. 5. It still, however, bore the name of Samaria, Jos. xx. 6. 2,—where, from the context, the *district* can hardly be intended. **αὐτοῖς**] The inhabitants, implied in πόλις.

6. προσεῖχον . . .] If this place was Sychem, the narrative in John iv. will fully account for the readiness with which these people received the κήρυγμα τοῦ χριστοῦ—'*the proclamation of the Christ.*'

7.] According to the reading in the text, which is too strongly upheld by manuscript authority to be rejected for the easier ordinary one, πολλοί is a 'nominativus pendens' (compare ch. vii. 40; Rev. iii. 12. Winer, edn. 6, § 29. 1), **For in the case of many who had unclean spirits, they crying out with a loud voice, came out: ἐξήρχοντο** being plur., as often when the neuter plural betokens living agents; see Winer, edn. 6, § 58. 3, a. β. **πολλοί** has probably been altered to πολλῶν, to agree with τῶν ἐχόντων, on the difficulty being perceived.

[y] παραλελυμένοι καὶ [z] χωλοὶ [a] ἐθεραπεύθησαν· 8 ἐγένετο δὲ
πολλὴ χαρὰ ἐν τῇ πόλει ἐκείνῃ. 9 ἀνὴρ δέ τις ὀνόματι
Σίμων [b] προϋπῆρχεν ἐν τῇ πόλει [c] μαγεύων καὶ [d] ἐξιστά-

ABCDE HPℵ a b d f g h k l m o p 13

y Luke v. 18, 24. ch. ix. 33. Luke only, exc. Heb. xii. 12. 1 Macc. ix. 55.
z Matt. xi. 5. ch. iii. 2. Lev. xxi. 18.
a Matt. iv. 23. xvii. 18‡. (Sir. xviii. 19.)
b Luke xxiii. 12 only. Job xlii. 17 (only?).
c here only+. (-γος, ch. xiii. 6. -γεια, ver. 11.)
d -άνων here only. trans. Luke xxiv. 22 only. see Job xii. 17. Eur. Frag. Αὐγή 1, νῦν δ' οἶνος ἐξέστησέ με.

ins και E 13 syr Chr$_1$. om και D[1](ins D[2]) m. εθεραπευοντο D 13.

8. rec και εγ., with EHP rel syr: χαρα τ. μεγ. εγ. D-gr [Syr (sah)]: txt ABCℵ p copt. rec χ. μεγαλη, with DEHP rel [vulg-ed syr arm]: txt ABCℵ p am demid fuld [sah] æth.

9. προυπαρχων D-gr. om και D[1](ins D[2]). rec εξιστων, with D[2]EH rel Chr$_1$ Thl: *seducens* vulg Iren-int: *suadens* E-lat: *mentem auferens* D-lat: εξε(. . . .) (εξεσταvεν Wetst) D[1]: txt ABCPℵ p.

9. Σίμων] Neander, in the course of some excellent remarks on this whole history (see further on ver. 14), identifies, and I believe with reason, this Simon with one mentioned as living from ten to twenty years after this by Josephus, Antt. xx. 7. 2, καθ' ὃν καιρὸν τῆς Ἰουδαίας ἐπετρόπευσε Φῆλιξ, θεασάμενος ταύτην (Drusilla) . . . λαμβάνει τῆς γυναικὸς ἐπιθυμίαν, καὶ Σίμωνα ὀνόματι, τῶν ἑαυτῷ φίλων, Ἰουδαῖον, Κύπριον δὲ γένος, μάγον εἶναι σκηπτόμενον, πέμπων πρὸς αὐτὴν ἔπειθε τὸν ἄνδρα καταλιποῦσαν αὐτῷ γήμασθαι. The only difficulty seems to be, that Simon is stated by Justin Martyr, himself a Samaritan, to have been Σαμαρέα, ἀπὸ κώμης λεγομένης Γίττων. But it has struck me that either Justin, or perhaps more probably Josephus, may have confounded Ghittim with Chittim, i. e. Citium in Cyprus. This conjecture I also find mentioned in the Dict. of Biography and Mythology, sub voce. The account in Josephus is quite in character with what we here read of Simon: not inconsistent (Meyer) with ver. 24, which appears to have been uttered under terror occasioned by the solemn denunciation of Peter. Justin goes on to relate that he was worshipped as a God at Rome in the time of Claudius Cæsar, on account of his magical powers, and had a statue on the island in the Tiber, inscribed 'Simoni Deo Sancto.' Singularly enough, in the year 1574, a stone was found in the Tiber (or *standing on the island in the year* 1662, according to the Dict. of Biogr. and Myth.), with the inscription SEMONI SANCO DEO FIDIO SACRVM, i. e. to the God Semo Sancus, the Sabine Hercules, which makes it probable that Justin may have been misled. The history of Simon is full of legend and fable. The chief sources of it are the Recognitiones and Clementina of the pseudo-Clemens. He is there said to have studied at Alexandria, and to have been, with the heresiarch Dositheus, a disciple of John the Baptist. Of Dositheus he became first the disciple, and then the successor. Origen (in Matt. Comm. § 33, vol. iii. p. 851) makes Dositheus also a Samaritan: so also contra Cels. i. 57, vol. i. p. 372, and Hom. xxv. in Luc. vol. iii. p. 962. His own especial followers (Simoniani) had dwindled so much in the time of Origen, that he says νυνὶ δὲ τοὺς πάντας ἐν τῇ οἰκουμένῃ οὐκ ἔστι Σιμωνιανοὺς εὑρεῖν τὸν ἀριθμὸν οἶμαι τριάκοντα. καὶ τάχα πλείονας εἶπον τῶν ὄντων, contra Cels. ubi supra; see also ib. vi. 11, p. 638, and περὶ ἀρχῶν, iv. 17, p. 176. In the Recognitiones and the Clementina are long reports of subsequent controversies between Simon Magus and Peter, of which the scene is laid at Cæsarea. According to Arnobius (adv. Gentes, ii. 12, p. 828 ed. Migne), the Constt. Apostol. (ii. 14, p. 620; vi. 9, p. 932 ed. Migne), and Cyril of Jerusalem, he met with his death at Rome, having, during an encounter with Peter, raised himself into the air by the aid of evil spirits, and being precipitated thence at the prayer of Peter and Paul. [I saw in the church of S. Francesca Romana in the forum, a stone with two dents in it and this inscription, "On this stone rested the knees of S. Peter when the dæmons carried Simon Magus through the air."] The fathers generally regard him as the founder of Gnosticism: this may be in some sense true: but, from the very little authentic information we possess, it is impossible to ascertain how far he was identified with their tenets. Origen (contra Cels. v. 62, p. 625) distinctly denies that his followers were Christians in any sense: λανθάνει τὸν Κέλσον, ὅτι οὐδαμῶς τὸν Ἰησοῦν ὁμολογοῦσιν υἱὸν θεοῦ Σιμωνιανοί, ἀλλὰ δύναμιν θεοῦ λέγουσι τὸν Σίμωνα. **μαγεύων]** Not to be joined with προϋπῆρχεν (as in E. V. and Kuin.), which belongs to ἐν πόλει: **exercising magic arts**, such as then were very common in the East and found wide acceptance; impostors taking advantage of the very general expectation of a Deliverer at this time, to set them-

νων τὸ [e] ἔθνος τῆς Σαμαρείας, λέγων εἶναί [f] τινα ἑαυτὸν
[g] μέγαν· 10 ᾧ [h] προςεῖχον πάντες [i] ἀπὸ μικροῦ ἕως
[i] μεγάλου λέγοντες Οὗτός ἐστιν ἡ [k] δύναμις τοῦ θεοῦ ἡ
καλουμένη μεγάλη. 11 [h] προςεῖχον δὲ αὐτῷ διὰ τὸ [l] ἱκανῷ
[l] χρόνῳ ταῖς [m] μαγείαις [n] ἐξεστακέναι αὐτούς· 12 ὅτε δὲ
[o] ἐπίστευσαν τῷ Φιλίππῳ [p] εὐαγγελιζομένῳ περὶ τῆς [q] βασιλείας τοῦ [q] θεοῦ καὶ τοῦ ὀνόματος Ἰησοῦ χριστοῦ, ἐβαπτίζοντο ἄνδρες τε καὶ γυναῖκες. 13 ὁ δὲ Σίμων καὶ αὐτὸς
ἐπίστευσεν, καὶ βαπτισθεὶς [r] ἦν [s] προςκαρτερῶν τῷ Φιλίππῳ, [t] θεωρῶν τε σημεῖα καὶ [u] δυνάμεις μεγάλας γινο-

L μις του... ABCDE HLPℵ a b d f g h k l m o p 13

e = Matt. xxi. 43. ch. vii. 7. x. 22.
f with adj., Heb. x. 27. φοβερόν τι θέαμα, Lucian, Philopat. 8.
g = Luke i. 15, 32. vii. 16. ix. 48. ch. xix. 27. Heb. iv. 14. x. 21. xiii. 20. Ezra iv. 10.
h ver. 6 reff.
i Heb. viii. 11, from Jer. xxxviii. (xxxi.) 34.
k = Rom. i. 16. 1 Cor. i. 18, 24.
l Luke viii. 27. xx. 9. ch. xiv. 3. xxvii. 9 only. see ch. ix. 23, 43. dat. of duration, Luke viii. 29. Rom. xvi. 25.
m here only †. see ver. 9.
n 2 Cor. v. 13 reff. perf., here only.
o = Matt. xxi. 25 ||. John v. 24. 1 John v. 10 al. Gen. xv. 6.
p w. περί, here only. see ch. vii. 52.
q ch. xix. 8 reff.
r constr., ch. ii. 5 reff.
s = ch. i. 14 reff.
t ch. vii. 56 reff.
u = Matt. xi. 20, 21, 23 and ||. Mark vi. 2. ch. ii. 22. 1 Cor. xii. 10. Gal. iii. 5 ‡.

om το E. εθος B².

10. προσειχαν ℵ. om παντες HP rel æth-pl Iren-int$_1$: ins ABCDEℵ k p 13 vss Chr$_1$. rec om καλουμενη (*as appearing unnecessary, and being difficult, see note*), with HLP rel Syr sah æth-pl Chr: ins ABCDEℵ p 13 vulg syr copt æth-rom arm Orig$_2$ Iren-int$_1$.

11. μαγιαις ACDEHℵ f 13. εξιστακεναι ACEH k m o: txt BDLPℵ rel.

12. **του φιλιππου** ευαγγελιζομεν**ου** ℵ¹. rec ins τα bef περι, with HLP rel Chr$_1$: om ABCDEℵ p 36 vulg syrr [coptt] æth. for θεου, κῦ ℵ¹. rec ins του bef ιησ. (with 13): om ABCDEHLPℵ rel Chr Thl.—om ιησ. 13. om τε A lect-12 vss(some).

13. ins και bef προσκ. D¹. θεορων(sic) ℵ. for τε, τα B. transp. σημ. and δυν. EHLP rel syr Chr: txt ABCDℵ k m p 13. 36 vulg Syr coptt æth [arm].—μεγαλα E o syr-w-ast æth-pl: om HLP rel: txt ABCDEℵ k m p 13 vulg Syr coptt æth-rom Chr.

selves up by means of such trickeries as 'some great ones.' We have other examples in Elymas (ch. xiii.): Apollonius of Tyana; and somewhat later, Alexander of Abonoteichos: see these latter in Dict. of Biogr. and Myth. **τινὰ μέγαν**] Probably not in such definite terms as his followers later are represented as putting into his mouth: 'Ego sum sermo Dei . . . ego paracletus, ego omnipotens, ego omnia Dei.' Jerome on Matt. xxiv. 5, vol. vii. p. 193. **10. ἡ δύν. τ. θ. ἡ καλουμένη μεγάλη**] Neander (l. c.) and Meyer think that they must have referred to the λόγος, the creating and governing manifestation of God so much spoken of in the Alexandrine philosophy (see extracts from Philo in note on John i. 1. The term, but by no means with the same idea, was adopted by the Spirit, speaking by John, as belonging to the Son of God: see the same note, end), and must have regarded Simon as an incarnation of the λόγος (the μητρόπολις πασῶν τῶν δυνάμεων τοῦ θεοῦ, Philo), so that their erroneous belief would form some preparation for the great truth of an incarnate Messiah, preached by Philip. But to this De W. well replies, that we can hardly suppose the Alexandrine philosophy to have been so familiar to the mass of the people, and refers the expression to their popular belief of a *great angel* (Chron. Sam. 10), who might, as the angels were called by the Samaritans *the powers of God* (for which he refers to Reland, de Samar. § 7. Gesen. Theol. Samar. p. 21 ff.), be designated as ἡ δύν. τ. θ. ἡ καλουμένη μεγάλη. **καλουμένη** rests on such strong manuscript authority, and is so unlikely to have been inserted (the idea of a scholium to indicate the force of the art. (Bloomf.) is quite out of the question, no such scholium being here needed), that both on external and internal grounds it must form part of the text. The lit. rendering will be, **This man is the power of God which is called great**: the sense, 'This man is that power of God (see above) which we know as *the great one*.' λεγομένη, found in a few later mss., is an explanation of καλ. by a more usual word. **11.**] **ἐξεστακέναι** can hardly be as E. V., transitive, "*he had bewitched them:*" there appears to be no example of the perfect being thus used. **13.**] 'Simon saw his followers dropping off, and was himself astounded at the miracles wrought by Philip: he therefore thought it best himself also to acknowledge this superior power. He attached himself to Philip, and was baptized like the rest: but we are not, as the sequel shews, to understand that the preaching of the Gospel had made any impression on his heart, but that he accounted for what

μένας [v] ἐξίστατο. 14 Ἀκούσαντες δὲ οἱ ἐν Ἱεροσολύμοις ἀπόστολοι ὅτι [wx] δέδεκται ἡ Σαμάρεια τὸν [xy] λόγον τοῦ

ABCDE HLPℵ a b d f g h k l m o p 13

v mid., Matt. xii. 23. Mark ii. 12. vi. 51. Luke ii. 47. ch. ii. 7, 12. ix. 21 only. Gen. xliii. 33. w Luke ix. 53. 2 Cor. xi. 4. x Luke viii. 13. ch. xi. 1. xvii. 11. 1 Thess. i. 6. ii. 13. Prov. iv. 10. y ch. xi. 1 reff.

γινομενα EHLP rel : om C 126-80 lect-25 : txt ABDℵ k m p 13. εξισταντο C[1]D[1]ℵ[1]. 14. ιερουσαλημ D.

he saw in his own fashion. He was convinced, from the works which Philip did, that he was *in league with some powerful spirit:* he viewed baptism as the initiation into communion with that spirit, and expected that he should be able to make use of the higher power thus gained for his own purposes, and unite this new magical power to his own. All were baptized who professed belief in Jesus as the Messiah: there was therefore no reason for rejecting Simon, considering besides, that from the nature of the case he would for the time have given up his magical practices.' Neander, Pfl. u. Leit. p. 102. 'Hoc Simonis exemplo clare patet, non conferri omnibus indifferenter in Baptismo gratiam, quæ illic figuratur. Papistarum dogma est, Nisi quis ponat obicem peccati mortalis, omnes cum signis recipere veritatem et effectum. Ita magicam vim tribuunt Sacramentis, quasi absque fide prosint. Nos autem sciamus offerri nobis a Domino per Sacramenta quicquid sonant annexæ promissiones, et non frustra nec inaniter offerri, modo fide ad Christum directi ab ipso petamus quicquid Sacramenta promittunt. Quamvis autem nihil illi tunc profuerit Baptismi receptio, si tamen conversio postea secuta est, ut nonnulli conjiciunt, non extincta fuit nec abolita utilitas. Sæpe enim fit, ut post longum tempus demum operetur Spiritus Dei, quo efficaciam suam Sacramenta proferre incipiant.' Calvin in loc.

14—24.] Mission of Peter and John to Samaria. A question arises on this procedure of the Apostles:—whether it was as a matter of course, that the newly baptized should, by the laying on of hands subsequently, receive the Holy Ghost, —or whether there was in the case of these Samaritans any thing peculiar, which caused the Apostles to go down to them and perform this act. (1) The only analogous case is ch. xix. 5, 6: in using which we must observe that there it is distinctly asserted that the *miraculous* gifts of the Spirit followed the laying on of Paul's hands; and that by the expression ἰδών in ver. 18, which must be taken literally, the same is implied here. And on this point the remarks of Calvin are too important to be omitted: 'Hic occurrit quæstio. Dicit enim tantum *fuisse baptizatos* in nomine Christi, atque ideo nondum fuisse Spiritus participes. Atqui vel inanem et omni virtute et gratia carere Baptismum oportet, aut a Spiritu sancto habere quicquid efficaciæ habet. In Baptismo abluimur a peccatis: atqui lavacrum nostrum Spiritus sancti opus esse docet Paulus (Tit. iii. 5). Aqua Baptismi sanguinis Christi symbolum est: atqui Petrus Spiritum esse prædicat, a quo irrigamur Christi sanguine (1 Pet. i. 2). In Baptismo crucifigitur vetus noster homo, ut suscitemur in vitæ novitatem (Rom. vi. 6): unde autem hoc totum, nisi ex sanctificatione Spiritus? Denique Baptismo nihil reliquum fiet, si a Spiritu separetur. Ergo Samaritanos, qui vere Christum in Baptismo induerant, Spiritu quoque vestitos fuisse negandum non est (Gal. iii. 27). Et sane Lucas hic non de communi Spiritus gratia loquitur, qua nos sibi Deus in filios regenerat, sed de singularibus illis donis, quibus Dominus initio Evangelii quosdam esse præditos voluit ad ornandum Christi regnum.' And a little after: . . . 'Papistæ, dum ficticiam suam confirmationem extollere volunt, in hanc sacrilegam vocem prorumpere non dubitant, semichristianos esse, quibus manus nondum fuerunt impositæ. (See this asserted by Wordsworth, in loc. p. 40, col. 2, bottom.) Hoc jam tolerabile non est, quod quum symbolum hoc temporale esset, ipsi perpetuam legem finxerunt in Ecclesia. . . . . Atqui fateri coguntur ipsi quoque, Ecclesiam nonnisi ad tempus donis istis fuisse ornatam. Unde sequitur, impositionem manuum, qua usi sunt Apostoli, finem habuisse, quum effectus cessavit' (in loc.). And yet after this, Wordsw. refers to "Calvin here," "in whose opinion," says R. Nelson, "this passage in the Acts *shews that Confirmation was instituted by the Apostles.*" This example may serve to suggest extreme caution in trusting to Wordsw.'s reports of the opinions of the Fathers and ecclesiastical writers. The English church, in retaining the rite of confirmation, *has not grounded it on any institution by the Apostles,* but merely declared the laying on of hands on the candidates, to certify them (by this sign) of God's favour and goodness towards them, to be, '*after the example* of the holy Apostles.' Nor is there any trace in the office, of the *conferring of the Holy Ghost* by confirmation;—but a distinct recognition of the *former reception* of the Holy Spirit (at Baptism), and a prayer for the increase of His influence, proportioned to the

[z] θεοῦ, ἀπέστειλαν πρὸς αὐτοὺς Πέτρον καὶ Ἰωάννην, 15 οἵτινες [z] καταβάντες [a] προσηύξαντο [a] περὶ αὐτῶν ὅπως [bc] λάβωσιν [bc] πνεῦμα [c] ἅγιον· 16 οὐδέπω γὰρ ἦν ἐπ' οὐδενὶ αὐτῶν
[d] ἐπιπεπτωκός, [e] μόνον δὲ [fg] βεβαπτισμένοι [h] ὑπῆρχον [fg] εἰς
τὸ [f] ὄνομα τοῦ κυρίου Ἰησοῦ. 17 τότε [i] ἐπετίθεσαν τὰς
[i] χεῖρας ἐπ' αὐτούς, καὶ [bc] ἐλάμβανον [bc] πνεῦμα [b] ἅγιον.
18 ἰδὼν δὲ ὁ Σίμων ὅτι διὰ τῆς [k] ἐπιθέσεως τῶν χειρῶν τῶν

z ch. xxiv. 1, 22. Gen. xlii. 3.
a Luke vi. 28. Col. i. 3. iv. 3. 1 Thess. v. 25. 2 Thess. i. 11. iii. 1. Heb. xiii. 18 only. Ps. lxxi. 15.
b John vii. 39. Rom. viii. 15 bis. 1 Cor. ii. 12. 2 Cor. xi. 4. Gal. iii. 2.
c here 3ce. ch. (ii. 38) x. 47. xix. 2. John xx. 22.
d of the Spirit, ch. x. 44. xi. 15 only. = Luke i. 12. ch. xiii. 11. xix. 17. Rev. xi. 11 only. Gen. xv. 12. see Rom. xv. 3.
e Matt. viii. 8. Mark v. 36 al.
f Matt. xxviii. 19. ch. xix. 5. (Rom. vi. 3.) 1 Cor. i. 13, 15. w. ἐπί, ch. ii. 38. ἐν, ch. x. 48.
g 1 Cor. x. 2. Gal. iii. 27.
h Luke xi. 13. xvi. 14. ch. ii. 30. Rom. iv. 19 al. James ii. 15. 2 Pet. i. 8. ii. 19. iii. 11. w. part., ch. xix. 36 only.
i Num. xxvii. 18. Matt. ix. 18. ch. vi. 6. ix. 12, 17. xiii. 3 al.
k 1 Tim. iv. 14. 2 Tim. i. 6. Heb. vi. 2 only ‡. see 2 Chron. xxv. 27.

for θεου, χῡ ℵ^1. rec ins τον bef πετρ., with HLP rel [Did$_1$]: om ABCDEℵ o p 13 Eus$_1$ [Did$_1$] Chr$_1$. **15.** προσευξ. B.

16. om vv. 16, 17 (*similarity of endgs*) 13. rec (for ουδεπω) ουπω, with HL[P] rel: txt ABCDEℵ p 36 Did$_2$ Chr$_1$. for επ, επι D^1(txt D-corr^1): εν E^1. ουδενα D^1(txt D^4(?)). εβαπτισμ. ℵ^1. for κυρ., χριστου HLP a d e f g h l: aft κῡ ιῡ ins χρῡ D.

17. rec επετιθουν, with D^{1}EHLP rel Chr$_1$ Thl: txt A B(-θοσαν) C(-θεισαν) D-corr$^{1 \text{ or } 2}$ ℵ o p 36 Eus$_1$ Did$_2$ Cyr-jer$_1$.

18. rec (for ιδων) θεασαμενος, with HLP rel [Chr$_1$] Thl: txt ABCDEℵ b^1 d k o p

maturer life now opening on the newly confirmed. (2) If then we have here *no institution of a perpetual ordinance*, something peculiar to the case before us must have prompted this journey. And here again we have a question: Was that moving cause in the Samaritans, or in Philip? I believe the true answer to the question will be found by combining both. Our Lord's command (ch. i. 8) had removed all doubt as to Samaria being a legitimate field for preaching, and Samaritan converts being admissible. (So also with regard to Gentile converts,—see ch. x., notes: but, as the church at this time believed, they must be *circumcised*, which the Samaritans already were,—and *keep the law*, which after their manner the Samaritans did.) The sudden appearance, however, of a body of baptized believers in Samaria, by the agency of one who was *not one of the Apostles*,—while it would excite in them every feeling of thankfulness and joy, would require their presence and power, as Apostles, to perform their especial part as the divinely appointed Founders of the Church. Add to this, that the Samaritans appear to have been credulous, and easily moved to attach themselves to individuals, whether it were Simon, or Philip; which might make the Apostles desirous to be present in person, and examine, and strengthen their faith. Another reason may have been not without its influence: the Jewish church at Jerusalem would naturally for the most part be alienated in mind from this new body of believers. The hatred between Jews and Samaritans was excessive and unrelenting. It would therefore be in the highest degree important that it should be shewn to the church at Jerusalem, that these Samaritans, by the agency of the same Apostles, were partakers of the same visibly testified gifts of the one Spirit. The use of this argument, which was afterwards applied by Peter in the case of the Gentiles, unexpected even by himself, ch. xi. 17,—was probably no small part of the purpose of this journey to Samaria.

14. Πέτ. κ. Ἰωάν.] Perhaps *two*, in accordance with the δύο δύο of their first missionary journey (Mark vi. 7): so Paul and Barnabas afterwards (ch. xiii. 2): and the same principle seems to have been adhered to even when these last separated: Paul chose Silas, Barnabas took Mark. PETER,—because to him belonged, in this early part of the Gospel, in a remarkable manner, the first establishing of the church; it was the fulfilment of the promise ἐπὶ ταύτῃ τῇ πέτρᾳ οἰκοδομήσω μου τὴν ἐκκλησίαν. It was he who had (in common with all the Apostles, it is true, but in this early period more especially committed to him) τὰς κλεῖδας τῆς βασιλείας τῶν οὐρανῶν,—who opened the door to the 3000 on the day of Pentecost, now (as a formal and ratifying act) to the Samaritans, and in ch. x. to the Gentiles. So far, is plain truth of Scripture history. The monstrous fiction begins, when to Peter is attributed a fixed diocese and successors, and to those successors a delegated power more like that ascribed to Simon Magus than that promised to Peter. This is the last time that JOHN appears in the Acts. He is only once more mentioned in the N. T. (except in the Revelation), viz. as having been present in Jerusalem at Paul's visit, Gal. ii. 9. **15. προσηύξ.**] So laying

ἀποστόλων lm δίδοται τὸ m πνεῦμα, n προςήνεγκεν αὐτοῖς
o χρήματα 19 λέγων Δότε κἀμοὶ τὴν p ἐξουσίαν ταύτην,
ἵνα ᾧ ἐὰν i ἐπιθῶ τὰς i χεῖρας bc λαμβάνῃ bc πνεῦμα b ἅγιον.
20 Πέτρος δὲ εἶπεν πρὸς αὐτὸν Τὸ ἀργύριόν σου σὺν σοὶ
εἴη qr εἰς rs ἀπώλειαν, ὅτι τὴν t δωρεὰν τοῦ θεοῦ uv ἐνόμισας
διὰ o χρημάτων vw κτᾶσθαι. 21 οὐκ ἔστιν σοι xy μερὶς οὐδὲ
yz κλῆρος ἐν τῷ a λόγῳ τούτῳ· ἡ γὰρ b καρδία σου οὐκ
ἔστιν bc εὐθεῖα d ἔναντι τοῦ θεοῦ. 22 e μετανόησον οὖν e ἀπὸ
τῆς f κακίας σου ταύτης, καὶ δεήθητι τοῦ κυρίου, g εἰ g ἄρα

ABCDE HLPא a b d f g h k l m o p 13

l pres., ch. xvi. 38 reff. m Luke xi. 13. John iii. 34. ch. v. 32. xv. 8. 1 Thess. iv. 8 (1 John iv. 13). n = Matt. xxv. 20. 2 Kings xvii. 29. o ch. iv. 37 reff. p = Matt. x. 1 al. fr. 1 Macc. i. 15. q = ch. ii. 39. r Matt. vii. 13. Rom. ix. 22. 1 Tim. vi. 9. Heb. x. 39. Rev. xvii. 8, 11. Isa. xxxii. 2. s 2 Pet. ii. 1 &c. iii. 7, 16. t = ch. ii. 38 reff. u Matt. x. 34 al.+ Wisd. xiii. 2 al. v constr., 1 Cor. vii. 36. 2 Macc. vii. 19. Ps. xlix. 13 Symm. w ch. xxii. 28 reff. x Luke x. 42. ch. xvi. 12. 2 Cor. vi. 15. Col. i. 12 only. L.P. y Deut. xii. 12. xiv. 27. xviii. 1. Isa. lvii. 6. see Col. i. 12. z = ch. i. 17, 26. xxvi. 18. a = Luke iv. 36. ch. xv. 6. b here only. Ps. lxxvii. 37. c Luke iii. 4 ||, 5 (from Isa. xl. 3, 4). ch. ix. 11. xiii. 10. 2 Pet. ii. 15 only. d Luke i. 8 only. Exod. xxviii. 34 (38) al. fr. e here only. Jer. viii. 6 only. see Heb. vi. 1. (= μ. ἐκ, Rev. ii. 21 al4. ἐπί, 2 Cor. xii. 21.) f = 1 Cor. xiv. 20 reff. g ch. [vii. 1] xvii. 27. Mark xi. 13 only. Xen. Mem. ii. 2. 2. Anab. iii. 2. 22.

13. 36 Constt$_1$ Bas$_1$ Chr$_2$ Damasc[-ms$_1$] Taras$_1$. rec aft *πν.* ins *το αγιον* (*common addition, and suspicious wherever there is any variation in MSS*), with ACDEHLP rel 36 vss [Bas$_1$] Chr : om Bא sah Constt$_1$. *προσηνεγκαν* D^1[-gr](txt D^4).
19. ins *παρακαλων και* bef *λεγ.* D. Steph (for *εαν*) *αν*, with DH a b^2 g h l m o 36 Constt$_1$ Cyr-jer$_1$ Chr$_1$ [Bas$_1$ Damasc-ms$_1$] Taras$_1$: txt ABCELPא rel. aft *επιθω* ins *καγω* D.
20. *αυτους* א^1. om *το* and *σου* D^1(ins D^4). (*N.B.* D-lat is wanting from *το αργυριον σου* to ch x. 4.)
21. *μερος* E l. om *γαρ* D^1(txt D^3) 177^1. rec *ενωπιον* (*corrn to more usual word*), with EHLP rel Constt Taras : *εναντιον* C h p 13 Bas$_1$ Chr$_1$: txt ABDא 36.
22. rec for *κυρ.*, *θεου* (*corrn from ver* 21 : *or doctrinal ?*), with HLP rel vulg Syr Taras$_1$ [Iren-int$_1$] : txt ABCDEא k o p 13 syr coptt arm Constt$_1$ Bas$_1$ Chr$_1$ Ambr$_1$. *αφηθησεται σου* D^1(txt D^2) l^1.

on of hands is preceded by prayer, ch. vi. 6; xiii. 3. **18. ἰδών**] Its effects were therefore *visible* (see above), and consequently the effect of the laying on of the Apostles' hands was not the *inward* but the *outward miraculous* gifts of the Spirit. **προσήν. αὐτ. χρήματα**] De W. excellently remarks, 'He regarded the capability of imparting the Holy Spirit,—*rightly*, as *something conferred*, as a *derived power* (see ref. Matt.), but *wrongly*, as one to be obtained by an *external method*, without an *inward disposition:* and, since in external commerce every thing may be had for gold, *he wanted to buy it*. This is the essence of the sin of *Simony*, which is intimately connected with unbelief in the power and signification of the Spirit, and with materialism.' Clearly, from the narrative, Simon himself *did not receive the Spirit by the laying on of hands*. His nefarious attempt to treat with the Apostles was *before he himself had been presented to them for this purpose*. **20.**] The solemn denunciation of Peter, like the declaration of Paul, 1 Cor. vi. 13, has reference to the perishableness of all worldly good, and of those with it, whose chief end is the use of it (see Col. ii. 22), 'Thy gold and thou are equally on the way to corruption :' *thy gold*, as its nature is : *thou with it*, as having no higher life than thy natural corrupt one: as being bound in the σύνδεσμος τῆς ἀδικίας. The *expression of Peter*, 1 Pet. i. 7, χρυσίου τοῦ ἀπολλυμένου, is remarkably parallel with this (see too 1 Pet. i. 18). **ἐνόμισας**] aor. **thou thoughtest**: not '*thou hast thought*,' as E. V. The historic force of the tense is to be kept here : the Apostle uses it as looking forward to the day of ἀπώλεια, 'Let thy lot be ἀπ., and that because thou thoughtest,' &c. **κτᾶσθ.**] **to acquire**, not pass. as E. V., ungrammatically. **21. μερὶς . . . κλῆρος**] synonymous : the first lit., the second fig. (see ref.), but not without reference perhaps to the κληρονομία of the kingdom of God, the κλ. ἄφθαρτος, 1 Pet. i. 4. **τῷ λόγ. τούτ.**] **The matter now spoken of**,—'to which I now allude.' **εὐθεῖα**] Hardly, '*right before God*,' E. V., but **thy heart is not right**,—sincere, single-meaning,—**in God's presence**, 'as God sees it :' i. e., 'seen as it really is, by God, is not in earnest in its seeking after the gospel, but seeks it with unworthy ends in view.' **22.**] **εἰ ἄρα**, **if perhaps** (not '*ut sane*,' which it will not bear : see on its meaning, "*if, which none can say*," Hartung, Partikellehre, i. 440) : and the uncertainty refers, not to the doubt whether Simon would repent

[h] ἀφεθήσεταί σοι ἡ [i] ἐπίνοια τῆς καρδίας σου· 23 [k] εἰς γὰρ
[lm] χολὴν [mn] πικρίας καὶ [op] σύνδεσμον [p] ἀδικίας ὁρῶ σε ὄντα.
24 ἀποκριθεὶς δὲ ὁ Σίμων εἶπεν Δεήθητε ὑμεῖς ὑπὲρ ἐμοῦ
πρὸς τὸν κύριον, ὅπως μηδὲν [r] ἐπέλθῃ ἐπ' ἐμὲ ὧν εἰρήκατε.
25 Οἱ μὲν οὖν [s] διαμαρτυράμενοι καὶ [t] λαλήσαντες τὸν
[t] λόγον τοῦ κυρίου, [u] ὑπέστρεφον εἰς Ἱεροσόλυμα, πολλάς
τε [v] κώμας τῶν Σαμαρειτῶν [w] εὐηγγελίζοντο· 26 ἄγγελος

c εις... ABCDE HLPא a b c d f g h k l m o p 13

h — Rom. iv. 7 reff. i (—) here only. (Jer. xx. 10 only.) Sir. xl. 2 al. k = ver. 20. l Matt. xxvii. 34 only. m Deut. xxix. 18 Ed-vat., F &c. (not AB). Lam. iii. 15. n Rom. iii. 14, from Ps. ix. 7 (27). Eph. iv. 31. Heb. xii. 15 only. o Eph. iv. 3. Col. ii. 19. iii. 14 only. L.P. p here only. Isa. lviii. 6. r ch. xiii. 40 reff. s Luke xvi. 28. ch. ii. 40 al7. 1 Thess. iv. 6. Heb. ii. 6. L.P.H. Jer. vi. 10. t = ch. xi. 19 reff. u Luke i. 56 al. fr. Luke only, exc. (Mark xiv. 40 rec.) Gal. i. 17. Heb. vii. 1. 2 Pet. ii. 21. Gen. xliii. 10. v Matt. ix. 35. Luke ix. 52 al. fr. Josh. xiii. 30. w constr., Luke iii. 18. ch. xiv. 15, 21. xvi. 10. Isa. xl. 9 (?).

23. ηυ (= εν ? εις D²) γαρ πικριας χολη(χολης D²) κ. συνδεσμω(συνδεσμον D²) D¹. for ορω, θεωρω DE Constt$_1$ Chr$_2$.

24. om ο EH. aft ειπεν ins προς αυτους D (æth). ins παρακαλω bef δεηθ. D 137-80 syr-w-ast Constt$_1$. D¹ has altered δεηθητε to δεηθητι. for υπερ, περι D¹(txt D²) 96. for κυρ., θεον (*see above, ver* 22) D k m o 13 demid fuld syrr (but κυριον syr-mg) æth. for επ' εμε, μοι D : εμοι e : om επ' C. ins τουτων των κακων bef ων D. for ων, ον D¹(txt D²) : ως L. aft ειρ. ins κακων E : μοι D, D¹ syr-mg add also ος[om syr-mg] πολλα κλαιων ου διελυμπανεν.

25. διαμαρτυρομενοι LPא d f l o Thl-sif$_1$. for κυρ., θεου A 68 demid Syr copt [arm] : om τ. κ. 3. 4¹. 65. rec υπεστρεψαν (*alteration to historic tense*), with CEHLP rel vss Thl : txt ABDא p 36 vulg. rec ιερουσαλημ (*corrn to common form, see ver* 26. *It has been suggested that* -σολυμα *occurs here as belonging to a narrative in which this form has been the one used, see* vv. 1, 14 ; *whereas in the* follg *narrative,* -σαλημ *is used, vv* 26, 27), with HL[P] rel : txt ABCDEא c k o p 13. 36 [vulg] Chr [Aug$_1$]. for τε, δε D. rec ευηγγελισαντο (*see above, on* υπεστρ.), with HLP rel E-lat syr copt [æth] Chr Thl : txt ABCD E-gr א p 36 vulg [syr arm] sah Aug$_1$.

or not (see below on γάρ) : but as to whether or not his sin may not have come under the awful category of those unpardonable ones specified by our Lord, Matt. xii. 31, to which words the form ἀφεθήσεται seems to have a tacit reference. Peter does not *pronounce* his sin *to have been such,* but throws in this doubt, to increase the motive to repent, and the earnestness of his repentance. This verse is important, taken in connexion with John xx. 23, as shewing *how completely the Apostles themselves referred the forgiveness of sins to, and left it in, the sovereign power of God, and not to their own delegated power of absolution.*

23.] **γάρ** gives the reasons, not why it would be *difficult for forgiveness to take place,* but why *he had such extreme need of repentance and prayer,* as being tied and bound by the chain of sin. **ὄντα εἰς**] a pregnant construction—**having fallen into and abiding in** : not to be taken (as Kuin., &c.) as '*amounting to,*'—'totus quantus es, nil nisi venenum amarum es et colligatio iniquitatis,' which is very harsh, and improbable : nor (as Stier) is it prophetic, as to what *would be* the consequence, if he did not repent : '*I see that thou wilt come to,*' &c. Least of all must it be said, here or any where else, that εἰς is *put for* ἐν. I cannot too often remind my younger readers, that it is a fundamental maxim of all sound scholarship, that *no word is ever put for another.* **χολ. πικρ.**] see reff. 'the gall which is the very seat and essence of bitterness'—**a very gall of bitterness.** The poison of serpents was considered to be seated in their gall : so χολὴ ἀσπίδος ἐν γαστρὶ αὐτοῦ, Job xx. 14. See Plin. H. N. xi. 37.

24.] Simon speaks here much as Pharaoh, Exod. (viii. 28 ; ix. 28) x. 17,—who yet hardened his heart afterwards (Stier). It is observable also that he wishes merely for the *averting of the punishment.* The words ὅπως μηδὲν ἐπέλθῃ ἐπ' ἐμὲ ὧν εἰρήκατε seem remarkably to set forth the mere terror of the carnal man, without any idea of the ἐμέ becoming *another man* in thoughts and aims.

25—40.] Conversion of the Æthiopian eunuch by Philip's teaching.

25.] **μὲν οὖν** indicates (see note on ver. 4) that the paragraph should begin here, not at ver. 26 as commonly. **κώμας τ. Σαμ.**] It is interesting to recall Luke ix. 52, where on their entering into a κώμην Σαμ., *the same John* wishes to call down fire from heaven, καὶ ἀναλῶσαι αὐτούς. On constr. (εὐαγγ. w. accus.), see reff. The gradual sowing of the seed further and further from Jerusalem is advancing : not only is this eunuch to carry it to a far distant land, but Philip is sent

δὲ κυρίου ἐλάλησεν πρὸς Φίλιππον λέγων [x] Ἀνάστηθι καὶ πορεύου [y] κατὰ [z] μεσημβρίαν ἐπὶ τὴν [a] ὁδὸν τὴν [a] καταβαίνουσαν ἀπὸ Ἱερουσαλὴμ εἰς Γάζαν· αὕτη ἐστὶν [b] ἔρη-

ABCDE HLPℵ a b c d f g h k l m o p 13

x = Matt. ix. 9. Luke i. 39. iv. 29. ch. v. 6, 17. Jonah iii. 2.
y = ver. 36. ch. xxv. 6. (xxvii. 12.) Phil. iii. 14. Josh. v. 7.
z ch. xxii. 6 only. Gen. xviii. 1.
a here only. see Matt. vii. 13, 14. Prov. vii. 27.
b = here only?

26. πορευθητι CD.—αναστας πορ. D 40. for κατα, προς E 130-80 Chr_1. for επι, εις H : om p. B[1] repeats την οδον. aft 2nd την ins καλουμενην ℵ[1] (ℵ disapproving). om εστιν p.

to a desert road, away from town or village, to seek him. The imperfects (altered in the rec., see var. readd., into aorists) are significant. They were on their way back to Jerusalem, and were evangelizing the Samaritan villages, when the angel spake (aor.) to Philip. **26.**] An angel, *visibly appearing:* not in a dream,—which is not, as some suppose, implied by ἀνάστηθι, see reff. The ministration of angels introduces and brings about several occurrences in the beginning of the church, see ch. v. 19; x. 3; xii. 7 (xxvii. 23). The appearance seems to have taken place in Samaria, after the departure of Peter and John; see above, on the imperfects. He would reach the place appointed by a shorter way than through Jerusalem: he would probably follow the high road (of the itineraries, see map in Conybeare and Howson's St. Paul) as far as Gophna, and thence strike across the country southwestward, to join, at some point to which he would be guided, the road leading from Jerusalem to Gaza. **Γάζαν**] The southernmost city of Canaan (Gen. x. 19), in the portion of Judah (Josh. xv. 47), but soon taken from that tribe by the Philistines, and always spoken of as a Philistian city (1 Sam. vi. 17; 2 Kings xviii. 8; Amos i. 6—8; Zeph. ii. 4; Zech. ix. 5). In Jer. xlvii. 1, we have 'before Pharaoh (Necho?) smote Gaza,'—implying that at one time it was under Egypt. Alexander the Great took it after a siege of five months (Q. Curt. iv. 6, 7. Arrian, Alex. ii. 26), but did not destroy it (as Strabo relates in error, xvi. 759, see below in this note), for we find it a strong place in the subsequent Syrian wars, see 1 Macc. (ix. 52) xi. 61, f.; xiii. 43 (xiv. 7; xv. 28; xvi. 1); Jos. Antt. xiii. 5. 5; 13. 3 al. It was destroyed by the Jewish king Alexander Jannæus (96 A.C.), Jos. Antt. xiii. 13. 3, after a siege of a year, but rebuilt again by the Roman general Gabinius (Antt. xiv. 5. 3),—afterwards given by Augustus to Herod (xv. 7. 3), and finally after his death attached to the province of Syria (xvii. 11. 4). Mela, in the time of Claudius, calls it 'ingens urbs et munita admodum,' with which agree Eusebius and Jerome. At present it is a large town by the same name, with from 15,000 to 16,000 inhabitants (Robinson, ii. 640). The above chronological notices shew that it cannot have been ἔρημος at this time: see below. **αὕτη ἐστὶν ἔρημος**] The words, I believe, of the *angel*, not of Luke. There appear to have been two (if not more) ways from Jerusalem to Gaza. The Antonine itinerary passes from Jerus. to Eleutheropolis—Askalon—Gaza. The Peutinger Table, Jerus.—Ceperaria—Eleutheropolis—Askalon—Gaza. But Robinson (ii. 748. Winer, Realw.) found an ancient road leading *direct* from Jerusalem to Gaza, through the *Wadi Musurr*, and over the Beit Jiibrin, which certainly *at present* is ἔρημος, without towns or villages. Thus the words will refer to *the way:* and denote **the way of which I speak to thee is desert** (Schöttg. cites from Arrian, iii. p. 211, ἐρήμην δὲ εἶναι τὴν ὁδὸν δι' ἀνυδρίαν). Besides the above objection to applying ἔρημος to *Gaza*, there could be no possible reason for adding such a specification here, seeing that Gaza had nothing to do with the object of the journey, and the *road* would be designated *the road from Jerusalem to Gaza*, whether the latter city was inhabited, or in ruins. Those who apply ἔρημος to Gaza, have various ways of reconciling the apparent discrepancy with history: most of them follow Bede's explanation, that the *ancient* city was ἔρημος, and that the Gaza of this day was another town nearer the sea. But how this helps the matter I cannot perceive, unless we are to suppose that the deserted Gaza and the inhabited Gaza were so far apart that it was necessary to specify which was meant, because there would be from Jerusalem two different roads,—of which no trace is found, nor could it well be. Some again suppose (Hug, al.) that the Acts were written after the *second Gaza* was destroyed (Jos. B. J. ii. 18. 1), just before the destruction of Jerusalem, and that Luke inserts this notice: but to what purpose? and why *no more* such notices? In the passage of Strabo, commonly cited to support the application of ἔρημος to Gaza, ἔνδοξός ποτε γενομένη, κατεσπασμένη δ' ὑπὸ Ἀλεξάνδρου (the Great, according to Strabo, which it *was not*) καὶ μένουσα ἔρημος, the last three words are wanting in

μος. 27 καὶ [x] ἀναστὰς ἐπορεύθη. καὶ ἰδοὺ ἀνὴρ Αἰθίοψ
[c] εὐνοῦχος [d] δυνάστης Κανδάκης [e] βασιλίσσης Αἰθιόπων,
ὃς ἦν [f] ἐπὶ πάσης τῆς [g] γάζης αὐτῆς, ὃς ἐληλύθει [h] προς-
κυνήσων εἰς Ἱερουσαλήμ, 28 ἦν τε [i] ὑποστρέφων καὶ καθήμενος [k] ἐπὶ τοῦ [l] ἅρματος αὐτοῦ καὶ [m] ἀνεγίνωσκεν τὸν

c here &c., 5 times and Matt. xix. 12(3ce) only. Esth. ii. 14 al.
d Luke i. 52. 1 Tim. vi. 15 only. = Levit. xix. 15. Sir. viii. 1.
e Matt. xii. 42 ‖ L. Rev. xviii. 7 only. Jer. xxxvi. (xxix.) 2.
f = ch. xii. 20. Rom. ix. 5. Eph. iv. 6. 4 Kings x. 5.
g here only. Ezra vii. 21. Esth. iv. 7. see Luke xxi. 1 ‖. John viii. 20.
h abs., John iv. 20. xii. 20. ch. xxiv. 11. Jer. xxxiii. (xxvi.) 2.
i ver. 25 reff.
k = Matt. xix. 28. xxiii. 2 al.
l here &c., 3ce. Rev. ix. 9 only. 4 Kings x. 15.
m ch. xv. 21. 2 Cor. iii. 2, 15. 4 Kings xix. 14.

27. rec ins της bef βασ. (*corrn*), with HL[P] rel Chr_1 Thl: om ABCDEℵ p.—D[1] adds τινος. αυτου D[1](txt D[2]). om 2nd ος AC[1]D[1]ℵ[1] vulg sah Œc[-txt] (*corrn for constr sake, to prevent* ανηρ *being pendent, and make it the nom to* εληλυθει): ins BC[2]D[2]EHLPℵ[3] rel syr [arm] Chr [*et* Syr æth, *hic* copt]: ὡς 13. om εις D[1]: εν D[2]L.

28. for τε, δε BC E-lat syr coptt Chr_1. om 1st και (*as unnecessary to the constr*) D[1](ins D[2]) 40 vulg copt. om του C. om αυτου D[1](ins D[2]). om 2nd και Dℵ[1] a c e f 13(not 1st κ. as Sz) [sah arm Thl-sif] (*adopted by Lachm and Tischdf* 1849. *The omissions in this case seem to me very like attempts to escape from the repetitions of* και, *which however are characteristic of this section, see v* 27, *vv* 36, 38, 39. *The* τε *in* A *may have the same source*).—**αναγινωσκων** D vulg[*legensque*] sah.—for κ. ανεγ.,

some edd. and are supposed to have been *a gloss from the Acts.* Others suppose ἔρημος to signify '*unfortified,*' which standing alone it cannot. Besides, this notice would be wholly irrelevant;—and would probably not have been true,—see Mela above. The objection of Meyer to the interpretation given above, that if ἔρημ. referred to ἡ ὁδός, the article would be expressed, is not valid: the emphasis is on αὕτη; '*that way,* of which I speak, is desert:' not, 'is the desert one:' no reference is made to the other.

27. εὐνοῦχος] The very general use of eunuchs in the East for filling offices of confidence, and the fact that this man was minister to a female sovereign, makes it probable that he was literally an eunuch. If not so, the word would hardly have been expressed. No difficulty arises from Deut. xxiii. 1, for no inference can be drawn from the history further than that he may have been a proselyte of the gate, in whose case the prohibition would not apply. Nay, the whole occurrence seems to have had one design, connected with this fact. The walls of partition were one after another being thrown down: the Samaritans were already in full possession of the Gospel: it was next to be shewn that none of those physical incapacities which excluded from the congregation of the Lord under the old covenant, formed any bar to Christian baptism and the inheritance among believers; and thus the way gradually paved for the great and as yet incomprehensible truth of Gal. iii. 28. **Κανδάκης**] As Pharaoh among the Egyptians was the customary name of kings, so Candăce of the Queens among the Æthiopians in upper Egypt (Αἰθίοπες ὑπὲρ Αἰγύπτου οἰκοῦντες, Dio Cass. liv. 5),—in the island of Meroe, Plin. vi. 29, where he says, 'Ipsum oppidum Meroen ab introitu insulæ abesse LXX m. pass. . . . Regnare fœminam Candacen, quod nomen multis jam annis ad reginas transiit. . . . Cæterum cum potirentur rerum Æthiopes, insula ea magnæ claritatis fuit.' **γάζης**] A Persian term. Q. Curt. iii. 13. 5, 'pecuniam regiam, quam *gazam* Persæ vocant.' See Virg. Æn. i. 119. **ὃς ἐληλύθει . . .**] This did not only Jews and proselytes, but also those pious Gentiles who adhered to Judaism,—the proselytes of the gate, see John xii. 20. Euseb. ii. 1, prope fin., speaking of this eunuch says, ὃν **πρῶτον ἐξ ἐθνῶν** πρὸς τοῦ Φιλίππου δι' ἐπιφανείας τὰ τοῦ θείου λόγου ὄργια μετασχόντα, τῶν τε ἀνὰ τὴν οἰκουμένην πιστῶν **ἀπαρχὴν** γενόμενον κ.τ.λ., taking for granted that he was a Gentile. There were (see below, ch. xi. 21) cases of Gentile conversion before that of Cornelius; and the stress of the narrative in ch. x. consists in the miscellaneous admission of all the Gentile company of Cornelius, and their official reception into the church by that Apostle to whom was especially given the power. We may remark, that if even the plain revelation by which the reception of Cornelius and his company was commanded failed finally to convince Peter, so that long after this he vacillated (Gal. ii. 11, 12), it is no argument for the eunuch not being a Gentile, that his conversion and baptism did not remove the prejudices of the Jewish Christians. **28. ἀνεγίνωσκεν**] aloud, see ver. 30. Schöttg. quotes from the Rabbis: 'Qui in itinere constitutus est, neque comitem habet, is studeat in Lege.'

He probably read in the LXX, the use of which was almost universal in Egypt. The word περιοχή below (see on ver. 32)

προφήτην Ἡσαΐαν. 29 εἶπεν δὲ τὸ ⁿ πνεῦμα τῷ Φιλίππῳ
Πρόσελθε καὶ ᵒ κολλήθητι τῷ ˡ ἅρματι τούτῳ. 30 ᵖ προσδραμὼν δὲ ὁ Φίλιππος ἤκουσεν αὐτοῦ ᵐ ἀναγινώσκοντος
Ἡσαΐαν τὸν προφήτην, καὶ εἶπεν ᵠ Ἆρά ᵠ γε ʳ γινώσκεις ἃ
ᵐ ἀναγινώσκεις; 31 ὁ δὲ εἶπεν Πῶς γὰρ ἂν δυναίμην, ἐὰν
μή τις ˢ ὁδηγήσῃ με; ᵗ παρεκάλεσέν τε τὸν Φίλιππον ᵘ ἀναβάντα καθίσαι σὺν αὐτῷ. 32 ἡ δὲ ᵛ περιοχὴ τῆς ʷ γραφῆς
ἣν ᵐ ἀνεγίνωσκεν ἦν αὕτη· Ὡς ˣ πρόβατον ἐπὶ ʸ σφαγὴν
ᶻ ἤχθη, καὶ ὡς ᵃ ἀμνὸς ᵇ ἐναντίον τοῦ ᶜ κείραντος αὐτὸν
ᵈ ἄφωνος, οὕτως οὐκ ᵉ ἀνοίγει τὸ ᵉ στόμα αὐτοῦ. 33 ἐν τῇ
ᶠ ταπεινώσει αὐτοῦ ἡ ᵍ κρίσις αὐτοῦ ʰ ἤρθη, τὴν [δὲ] ⁱ γενεὰν

...φιλιππω D. ABCEH LPℵ a b c d f g h k l m o p 13

n absol., ch. x. 19 reff. o = Luke xv. 15. 2 Kings xx. 2. (ch. v. 13 reff. L.P., exc. Matt. xix. 5. Rev. xviii. 5.) p Mark ix. 15. x. 17 only. Gen. xviii. 2 al. q interrog. here only. see Luke xviii. 8. r = Mark iv. 13. Luke xviii. 34 al. Dan. ix. 25. s Matt. xv. 14. Luke vi. 39. John xvi. 13. Rev. vii. 7 only. Ps. xxiv. 5. t constr., Mark v. 17. Luke viii. 41. u = Luke v. 19. xix. 4 al. 3 Kings xii. 18. v here only‡. 4 Kings xix. 24. Ps. xxx. 21. (-έχειν, ch. xxiii. 25.) w = Rom. ix. 17 reff. x Matt. x. 16. Mark vi. 34. Isa. liii. 7. y Rom. viii. 36 reff. z ch. v. 21. xxv. 6, 23. Dan. iii. 13. a John i. 29, 36. 1 Pet. i. 19 only. Exod. xxix. 38 al. fr. b ch. vii. 10 reff. c ch. xviii. 18. 1 Cor. xi. 6 bis only. Gen. xxxi. 19. d = 1 Cor. xii. 2. (xiv. 10.) 2 Pet. ii. 16 only. Isa. l. c. Wisd. iv. 19. 2 Macc. iii. 29 only. e = here only. (ver. 35.) Ps. xxxviii. 9. f Luke i. 48. Phil. iii. 21. James i. 10 only. Gen. xvi. 11. g = James ii. 13. 2 Pet. ii. 11. h = ch. xxii. 22. John i. 29 al. i = Matt. xi. 16 al.

ανεγ. τε A; ανεγ. δε 40. ησ. bef τ. προφ. C m vulg(not am fuld demid).

30. rec τον πρ. bef ησ. (*corrn to same order as previously*), with EHLP p rel syr copt [arm(Treg)] Thl: txt ABCℵ 13 vulg sah [Syr æth arm(Tischdf)] Chr_1.

31. om γαρ E o 105 sah [Syr copt æth arm]. om αν A. με bef οδ. C. (οδηγησει B[1][οδαγ.] C[E]ℵ [13].) for τε, δε E coptt.

32. rec κειροντος (*so* LXX-Bℵ[1·3b]), with BP p rel $Orig_1$: txt (*so* LXX-Aℵ[3a]) ACEHLℵ f k l[1] m o[1] 36 [Ps-]Ign_1 $Chron_1$. ουτος HL f m[2] o 13.

33. om 1st αυτου (*corrn to* LXX) ABℵ vulg. om δε (*corrn to* LXX?) ABCℵ vulg syr sah: ins EHLP p 13 rel tol copt [arm] Chr Thl $Iren\text{-}int_1$ [mss and edd vary].

is not decisive (Olsh.) against this (as if there were περιοχαί only in the Hebrew, not in the LXX), as it would naturally be used as well of one as the other by those cognizant of the term. Besides, must there not have been περιοχαί in the copies of the LXX read in the synagogues?

29.] This is the first mention of that *inner prompting* of the Spirit referred to again, probably ch. xiii. 2, but certainly ch. x. 19; xvi. 6, 7. Chrysostom understands the words of *the appearance of an angel*, but the text hardly allows it. **κολλ.**] no stress—**attach thyself to.** **30.**] **ἆρά γε = Yea, but ....;** q. d. It is well, thou art well employed: but ...? On the force of ἆρα, used "ubi responsio expectatur negans id de quo erat interrogatum," see Hermann on Viger, p. 821. The γε strengthens the ἆρα, implying the passing over of all other considerations, and selecting this as the most important: see Hartung, Partikellehre, i. 376 f. It assumes, modestly, that he *did not* understand what he was reading. **γινώσκ. ἃ ἀναγ.**] So 2 Cor. iii. 2. So too Cato (Wetst.), 'Legere et non intelligere nec legere est.' "Valck. compares the celebrated paronomasia of Julian the Apostate, ἀνέγνων, ἔγνων, κατέγνων, and the courageous reply of the Christian Bishop to him, ἀνέγνως, ἀλλ' οὐκ ἔγνως· εἰ γὰρ ἔγνως, οὐκ ἂν κατέγνως." Wordsw. **31.**] γάρ gives the reason of the negative which is understood. The answer expresses at once humility and docility. **32.**] Perhaps it is best to render, **The contents of the** (passage of) **Scripture which he was reading were as follows:** see περιέχει, 1 Pet. ii. 6. Cicero indeed appears to use περιοχή in the sense of a 'paragraph,' or 'chapter;' ad Attic. iii. 25, 'At ego ne Tironi quidem dictavi, qui totas περιοχάς persequi solet, sed Spintharo syllabatim.' The citation is from the LXX-A, with only the variation of αὐτοῦ inserted after ταπεινώσει (and [δέ] before γενεάν).

33. ἐν τῇ ταπεινώσει αὐτοῦ ἡ κρίσις αὐτ. ἤρθη] Heb. 'He was taken away by distress and judgment' [so in the margin of E. V.]: i. e. as Lowth, 'by an oppressive judgment.' **γενεὰν αὐτοῦ**] i. e., **the age in which He shall live**—'the wickedness of his contemporaries.' The fathers, and Bede (and so Wordsworth), explain '*His generation*' of His eternal Sonship and His miraculous Incarnation. But the Heb. does not seem to bear this out. See the meaning discussed at length, and another interpretation defended in Stier,

αὐτοῦ τις [k] διηγήσεται ; ὅτι [h] αἴρεται ἀπὸ τῆς γῆς ἡ ζωὴ
αὐτοῦ. 34 ἀποκριθεὶς δὲ ὁ [l] εὐνοῦχος τῷ Φιλίππῳ εἶπεν
[m] Δέομαί [m] σου, περὶ τίνος ὁ προφήτης λέγει τοῦτο ; περὶ
ἑαυτοῦ ἢ περὶ ἑτέρου τινός ; 35 [n] ἀνοίξας δὲ ὁ Φίλιππος
τὸ [n] στόμα αὐτοῦ καὶ [o] ἀρξάμενος ἀπὸ τῆς [p] γραφῆς ταύτης
[q] εὐηγγελίσατο αὐτῷ τὸν Ἰησοῦν. 36 ὡς δὲ ἐπορεύοντο
[r] κατὰ τὴν ὁδόν, ἦλθον ἐπί τι [s] ὕδωρ, και φησιν ὁ [l] εὐνοῦχος Ἰδοὺ ὕδωρ· τί κωλύει με βαπτισθῆναι ; 38 καὶ ἐκέ-

k constr., here only. (Mark ix. 9. Luke viii. 39. ix. 10.) 1 Chron. xvi. 9. see ch. ix. 27 reff. Joel i. 3.
l ver. 27 reff.
m absol., Luke viii. 28. ch. xxi. 39. Gal. iv. 12 only.
n = Matt. v. 2. xiii. 35, from Ps. lxxvii. 2. ch. x. 34. xviii. 14. Job iii. 1. see Eph. vi. 19.
o ch. i. 22 reff.
p ch. i. 16 reff.
q constr., ch. xi. 20 reff.
r ver. 26 reff.
s = John iii. 23.

34. om *τουτο* B-txt : ins B¹-marg. for *εαυ.*, *αυτου* H. *τινος* bef *ετερου* E.
35. om *ο* E[H] c 137. aft *ταυτης* ins *και* א¹(א³ disapproving).
36. *ιδωρ* (2nd) א¹.
[37. rec inserts *ειπε δε ο Φιλιππος ει πιστευεις εξ ολης της καρδιας εξεστιν αποκριθεις δε ειπε πιστευω τον υιον του θεου ειναι τον ιησουν χριστον*, with (E) and 10 others specified by Scholz(addg "alii permulti") [vulg-ed tol] am² demid syr-w-ast arm Iren-gr(and int) Thl-fin-txt Cypr$_1$ Jer Aug Prædest Pacian—aft *δε* ins *αυτω* E [e arm]—om *ο φιλ.* [e] 36 syr [arm]—for *ει*, *εαν* E—aft *καρδ.* ins *σου* E [tol syr-w-ast arm] Cypr—for *εξεστιν*, *σωθησει* E ; alii aliter—aft *πιστ.* E has *εις τον χρ. τον υιον τ. θ.*—spec reads the whole thus *et respondens spado ait Credo filium dei esse Chr Jes.*—— : om ABCHLPא 13(sic) rel and 44 others specified by Scholz(addg "alii plurimi") am¹ fuld syrr coptt æth Chr$_2$ Thl-sif. (*The insertion appears to have been made to suit the formularies of the baptismal liturgies, it being considered strange that the eunuch should have been baptized without some such confession.*)]

Jesaias, &c., pp. 466—470. Cf. also Gesenius' Thesaurus under צוּר.
34. ἀποκριθείς] *to the passage of Scripture*, considered as the question proposed : not, to the question in ver. 30. We can hardly suppose any immediate reference in *ἑτέρου τινός* to Christ.
36. τὶ ὕδωρ] In the scholia to Jerome's Epitaph of Paula (not in Jerome himself) on the words, 'A Bethsur venit,' we have, 'hæc ætate Hieronymi vocabatur Bethsura : vicus est in tribu Juda, obvius vigesimo lapide euntibus ab Hierosolyma Chebron. Juxta hunc fons est ad radices montis ebulliens, qui ab eadem in qua gignitur humo sorbetur. In hoc fonte putant eunuchum Candacis Reginæ baptizatum fuisse.' Jerome's own words (Ep. 108 (27) ad Eustochium, 11, p. 700) are : 'cœpit per viam veterem pergere quæ ducit Gazam . . . . et tacita secum volvere, quomodo Eunuchus Æthiops, gentium populos præfigurans, mutaverit pellem suam, et dum vetus relegit instrumentum fontem reperit Evangelii. Atque inde ad dexteram transit. A Bethsur venit Escol' . . . where no reference is made to the tradition, save what may be inferred from the mention of Bethsur. Eusebius also (*περὶ τόπων*) states it to be twenty miles south of Jerusalem in the direction of Hebron : and so it is set down in the Jerus. Itin. and the Peutinger Tab. (Howson's map.) Pocock found there a fountain built over, and a village called Betur on the left. Fabri describes the fountain as the head of a considerable brook, and found near it the ruins of a Christian church. There is no improbability in the tradition except that, even supposing a way going across from Hebron straight to Gaza to be called *ἔρημος*, this would not be on that portion of it, but on the high road (Winer, Realw.). **τί κωλ. μ. βαπ.**] There is no reason for supposing Philip to have preached to him the necessity of baptism : his own acquaintance with Jewish practices, and perhaps his knowledge of the progress of the new faith in Jerusalem, would account for the proposition. [**37.**] The authorities against this verse are too strong to permit its insertion. It appears to have been one of those remarkable additions to the text of the Acts, common in D (which is here deficient) and its cognates : few of which, however, have found their way into the received text. This was made very early, as Irenæus has it. The manuscripts which contain it vary exceedingly : another strong mark of spuriousness in a disputed passage. See var. readd. Wordsw. retains it, citing Bornemann as doing the same ; but it is Bornemann's principle that all these insertions of D and its cognates formed part of the original text : so that his authority goes for nothing. Wordsw. also

t = Matt. xx. 32. Luke vii. 14. Josh. x. 12, 13. 4 Kings xiii. 18.
u vv. 28, 29.
v = John v. 7.
w Matt. iii. 16 ||. Gen. xli. 2.
x Luke iv. 18. ch. v. 9. 2 Cor. iii. 17. 3 Kings xviii. 12.

λευσεν [t] στῆναι τὸ [u] ἅρμα, καὶ [v] κατέβησαν ἀμφότεροι εἰς ABCEH LPℵ a b c d f g h k l m o p 13
τὸ ὕδωρ, ὅ τε Φίλιππος καὶ ὁ [l] εὐνοῦχος, καὶ ἐβάπτισεν
αὐτόν. 39 ὅτε δὲ [w] ἀνέβησαν ἐκ τοῦ ὕδατος, [x] πνεῦμα
[x] κυρίου [y] ἥρπασεν τὸν Φίλιππον, καὶ οὐκ εἶδεν αὐτὸν
οὐκέτι ὁ [l] εὐνοῦχος, [z] ἐπορεύετο γὰρ τὴν [z] ὁδὸν αὐτοῦ
χαίρων. 40 Φίλιππος δὲ εὑρέθη [a] εἰς Ἄζωτον, καὶ [b] διερ-

y — John vi. 15. 2 Cor. xii. 2, 4. Rev. xii. 5. ἥρπαζεν ὁ ποταμός, Xen. Anab. iv. 3. 6. Judg. xxi. 21.
z here only. Josh. iii. 4.
a = ch. ii. 27. xx. 14. Matt. ii. 23. Luke xi. 7 al. see ver. 20 reff.
b absol., ver. 4 reff.

38. *εις το υδωρ* bef *αμφοτεροι* E c k 137-80 syr copt Chr_1.

39. [*ανεβη* (for *-βησαν*) C 137. (13 def.)] for *εκ*, *απο* E c f o 137-77-80. *αγγελος κυριου ηρπασεν τον φιλιππον αγγελος δε κυριου* A[1]: *πνευμα αγιον επεπεσεν επι τον ευνουχον αγγελος δε* (*see note*) A-corr[1] 15-8. 27-9. 36. 60. 100 arm, syr stands thus *πνευμα κυριου* (*αγιον* syr-mg) **επεπεσεν επι τον ευνουχον αγγελος δε κυριου*: Jerome's testimony is doubtful. On Isa lxiii. 14, vol. iv. p. 754 [vol. iii. p. 470, ed Bened.], "*Spiritus Domini ductor ejus fuit,*" he says, *id est, gregis Domini, Spiritum autem hic Angelum debemus intelligere, qui ductor fuit populi Israel, juxta illud quod scriptum est* (*Ps* civ. 4, *Heb* i. 14). *Consideremus illud quod in Act. Ap. scribitur,* "*Spiritus Domini rapuit Philippum, et non vidit eum ultra eunuchus,*" an super Angelo debeamus accipere. Sunt qui Angelum in Spiritu sancto hæc fecisse testentur. But in Dial. adv. Lucif. 9, vol. ii. p. 182 [vol. iv. pt ii. p. 295], he says *Inde venit ut sine chrismate et episcopi jussione, neque presbyter, neque diaconus jus habeant baptizandi. . . Ut enim accipit quis, ita et dare potest:* nisi forte eunuchus a Philippo diacono baptizatus sine Spiritu sancto fuisse credendus est, *de quo scriptura ita loquitur* "*Et descenderunt ambo . . et quum abscederent ab aqua, Spiritus sanctus venit in Eunuchum.*" *Si autem illud objiciendum putas quia* "*Cum audivissent* . . . (vv 14—17)"—: txt is supported by Chr (who says οὐκέτι ἄγγελος ἀλλὰ τὸ πνεῦμα αὐτὸν ἁρπάζει) and by Did(who explains *spiritus domini* by *angelus domini*). *αυτου* bef *την οδον* B. [13 def.]

states that it is found in the codex amiatinus of the vulgate, which *it is not*, except as a correction a secunda manu.]

38. ἐκέλ.] viz. the eunuch. **39. πν. κυρ. ἥρπ. τ. Φ.**] The reading, '*the Spirit fell on the Eunuch, and an angel of the Lord caught away Philip,*' is curious, and has probably arisen from a desire to conform the results of the eunuch's baptism to the usual method of the divine procedure, and the snatching away of Philip to his commission, ver. 26. But the Spirit did not fall on the Samaritans after baptism by Philip.

The text clearly relates a supernatural disappearance of Philip: compare μήποτε ἦρεν αὐτὸν πνεῦμα κυρίου, 4 Kings ii. 16; no interpretation (as Eichhorn, Kuin., Olsh., Meyer) of his being suddenly hurried away by the prompting of the Spirit, will satisfy the analogy of the above-cited passage, and of (see below) a parallel one in Luke's own Gospel. The ἁρπάζειν of ref. John, which Meyer cites to justify his view, tells in my mind the other way; the fear was lest the multitude should come and *carry Him off* to make Him a King: and in the reff. I have therefore marked the two as bearing the same meaning.

οὐκ εἶδεν αὐτὸν οὐκέτι] Not 'never saw him from that day,' though (see below) that meaning may be indirectly included:—but as Luke xxiv. 31, αὐτὸς ἄφαντος ἐγένετο ἀπ' αὐτῶν, and as in the strictly parallel words of 4 Kings ii. 12, οὐκ εἶδεν αὐτὸν ἔτι,—after the going up of Elijah. These last words in my view decide the question, that the departure of Philip was miraculous. **γάρ**] refers to *what follows* (Φ. **δὲ** εὑρ.). Philip was found at Azotus: if the eunuch had gone *that way*, he might have met with him again: but he did not, for he went from the fountain *on his own way*, which did not lead through Azotus. **40. εὑρ. εἰς Ἄζ.**] A constr. prægnans,—**was borne to, and found at.** The word εὑρέθη again appears to refer to 4 Kings ii. 17. AZOTUS or ASHDOD (Josh. xiii. 3; 1 Sam. v. 5 al.) was one of the five principal cities of the Philistines, never, though nominally in Judah, thoroughly subjugated by the Jews:—it was taken by Tartan the Assyrian general (Isa. xx. 1),—again by Psammetichus, Herod. ii. 157; Jer. xxv. 20,—again by Judas Maccabæus (1 Macc. v. 68) and Jonathan (ib. x. 84), and by the latter destroyed;—rebuilt by Gabinius (Jos. Antt. xiv. 5. 3. B. J. i. 7. 7), and belonged to the kingdom of Herod, who left it in his will to his sister Salome (Antt. xvii. 8. 1; 11. 5). At present, it is a small village, retaining the name Esdud, but no remains. (Robinson, ii. 629;

χόμενος [c] εὐηγγελίζετο τὰς πόλεις πάσας, [d] ἕως τοῦ
ἐλθεῖν αὐτὸν εἰς Καισάρειαν.
IX. 1 Ὁ δὲ Σαῦλος ἔτι [e] ἐμπνέων [f] ἀπειλῆς καὶ φόνου
[g] εἰς τοὺς μαθητὰς τοῦ κυρίου, [h] προςελθὼν τῷ ἀρχιερεῖ
2 [i] ᾐτήσατο [i] παρ' αὐτοῦ [k] ἐπιστολὰς [l] εἰς Δαμασκὸν πρὸς

c constr., ver. 25 reff. d constr. w. inf here only. 1 Kings xvi. 11. 3 Kings xxii. 27 B, F (not A) &c. gen., ch. vii. 45 al. fr. e here only. and constr., Josh. x. 40 B (om gen., A Ald.). (-νευσις, Ps. xvii. 15.) f ch. iv. [17] 29. Eph. vi. 9 only. Job xxiii. 6. g ch. xxiii. 30. Rom. viii. 7 al. h = Matt. xxvii. 58 ‖ L. John xii. 21. ch. xxiii. 14 al. 3 Kings xxi. (xx.) 13. i ch. iii. 2. John iv. 9. James i. 5. 1 John v. 15 only. Deut. x. 12. k = ch. xv. 30. xxiii. 25, 33. Rom. xvi. 22 al. L.P., exc. 2 Pet. iii. 1, 16. Neh. ii. 7. l constr., here only. see 2 Cor. iii. 1.

40. *τας πολ. πα.* bef *ευ.* A. (ms 13 is very much defaced from viii. 30 to ix. 1, but the words *κωλυει με βαπτισθηναι και* can be read, thus shewing the omn of ver 37; again, in ver. 39, almost the only syllables legible are *πνευμα κυριου ηρπ*, thus shewing that cod. colb. does not here, as frequently elsw, agree with A's peculiar reading. Such are the results in two verses alone of Dr. Tregelles' painstaking collation of the mutilated parts of this important ms.)

Chap. IX. **1.** for *ετι*, *οτι* B[1]: om ℵ[1] 1 24-6. 78. 126 sah.
2. *επιστολας* bef *παρ αυτου* ℵ.

iii. 1, 232. Winer, Realw.) **τὰς πόλεις πάσας**] viz. Ekron, Jamnia, Joppa, Apollonia, on the direct road: or, if he deviated somewhat for the purpose, Lydda also (which seems implied ch. ix. 32). **Καισάρειαν**] See note, ch. x. 1.

Chap. IX. 1—30.] Conversion of Saul. **1.**] The narrative is taken up from ch. viii. 3, but probably with some interval, sufficient perhaps to cover the events of ch. viii. **ἐμπνέων**] Meyer charges the ordinary interpretation, '*breathing*,' i. e. as in E. V., '*breathing out*,' with an arbitrary neglect of the composition of the word. He would render it '*in*haling,' with the partitive genitives signifying the element. But the sense would thus be flat; and there seems to be no need for pressing the sense of the compound verb. We should perhaps hardly render it breathing *out*,—but **breathing**; his 'spiritus,' inhaled or exhaled, being *ἀπειλὴ κ. φόνος*. So *ἔθ' αἱματόεντος ἀναπνείων ὀρυμαγδοῦ*, Q. Calaber, xiv. 72, and *πνέων θυμοῦ*, Aristæn. I. ep. 5 (Kuin.). **ἐμπνέων, προςελθών**] As *σοὶ πιστεύσας, μεταναστάς*, Œd. Col. 172, where Hermann remarks, 'Si recte observavi, ea est hujus constructionis ratio, ut præcedat illud participium, quod, separatim enunciata sententia, indicativus esse verbi debet: ut hoc loco sensus sit, *ὅτι σοὶ ἐπίστευσα, μεταναστάς*.' **τῷ ἀρχιερεῖ**] See table in Prolegg. to Acts;—it would be Theophilus,—brother and successor to Jonathan, who succeeded Caiaphas, Jos. Antt. xviii. 5. 3. **2. ἐπιστολάς**] of authorization; written by the high priest (in this case, but not always, president of the Sanhedrim) in the name of *πᾶν τὸ πρεσβυτέριον*, ch. xxii. 5. **εἰς Δαμασκόν**] Damascus is probably the oldest existing city in the world. We read of it in Abraham's time (Gen. xiv. 15; xv. 2): then no more till David subdued it (2 Sam. viii. 6): it became independent again under Solomon (1 Kings xi. 24 ff.), and from that time was the residence of the kings of Syria (1 Kings xv. 18; xx. 1 ff.), who were long at war with Israel and Judah, and at last were permitted to prevail considerably over Israel (2 Kings x. 32; Amos i. 3, 4) and to exact tribute from Judah (2 Kings xii. 17, 18, see also 2 Kings xiii. 3, 22, 25). Damascus was recovered to Israel by Jeroboam II. (cir. 825 A.C. 2 Kings xiv. 28). Not long after we find Rezin, king of Syria, in league with Pekah, king of Israel, against Ahaz (2 Kings xv. 37). Ahaz invited to his assistance Tiglath-pileser, king of Assyria, who took Damascus and slew Rezin, and led the people captive (2 Kings xvi. 5—9; Isa. viii. 4). From this time we find it subject to Assyria (Isa. ix. 11; x. 9; xvii. 1), then to Babylon (2 Kings xxiv. 2; Jer. xxxv. 11),—Persia (Arrian. Alex. ii. 11, Δαρεῖος τῶν χρημ. τὰ πολλὰ . . . . . πεπόμφει εἰς Δαμασκόν, Strabo, xvi. 756; Q. Curt. iii. 12. 27),—the Syrian Seleucidæ (1 Macc. xi. 62; xii. 32),—and from the time of Pompey (64 A.C.), to the Romans, and attached to the province of Syria (Jos. Antt. xiv. 4. 5; 9. 5). Many Jews were settled there, and the majority of the wives of the citizens were proselytes, Jos. B. J. ii. 20. 2. On its subjection to Aretas, see below, ver. 24, note. It was later the residence of the Ommiad Caliphs, and the metropolis of the Mahommedan world. (Conybeare and Howson, edn. 2, vol. i. p. 106.) At present it is a large city, with (Burckhardt) 250,000 inhabitants, nearly 70,000 of whom are Christians. It is situated most beautifully, in a large and well-watered plain, on the river

τὰς συναγωγάς, ὅπως ἐάν τινας εὕρῃ τῆς ᵐ ὁδοῦ ὄντας
ἄνδρας τε καὶ γυναῖκας, δεδεμένους ἀγάγῃ εἰς Ἱερουσαλήμ.
3 ⁿ ἐν δὲ τῷ πορεύεσθαι ᵒ ἐγένετο αὐτὸν ᵖ ἐγγίζειν τῇ Δαμασκῷ, ᑫ ἐξαίφνης τε αὐτὸν ʳ περιήστραψεν φῶς * ἀπὸ
τοῦ οὐρανοῦ, 4 καὶ πεσὼν ἐπὶ τὴν γῆν ˢ ἤκουσεν φωνὴν
λέγουσαν αὐτῷ Σαοὺλ Σαούλ, τί με ᵗ διώκεις; 5 εἶπεν δὲ
Τίς εἶ [σύ], κύριε; ὁ δὲ Ἐγώ εἰμι Ἰησοῦς, ὃν σὺ ᵗ διώκεις.

ABCEH LPℵa b c d f g h k l m o p 13

m = ch. xviii. 26. xix. 9, 23. xxii. 4. xxiv. 14, 22.
n Matt. xiii. 4, 25. ch. iii. 26. viii. 6 al. Ezek. ix. 8.
o constr., ch. iv. 5 reff.
p dat., Luke vii. 12. xv. 25. ch. x. 9. xxii. 6. Exod. xxxii. 19.
q Mark xiii. 36. Luke ii. 13. ix. 39. ch. xxii. 6 only. Prov. xxiv. 22.
r ch. xxii. 6 only +.
s w. acc., ch. xxii. 9. xxvi. 14. John iii. 8. Rev. v. 11 al. Exod. xxxii. 18.
t = ch. vii. 52 reff.

for *τας*, *τα* B^1. for *εαν*, *αν* ℵ[E Chr_1]. *οντ.* bef *της οδ.* Aℵ p [syrr æth]: om *οντ.* 13 [vulg E-lat coptt].

3. rec *και εξαιφν.*, with EHLP rel Chr_1: txt ABCℵ p. rec *περιηστραψεν* bef *αυτον*, with EHLP 13 rel [vulg syrr arm] Chr: txt (A)BCℵ m p.—*αυτ. φως π.* A.—[elz] *περιεστρ.* [with] C^3; so, appy, but perh *περιαστρ.* A^1: *περιστρ.* C^1. *ἐκ (*corrn from ch* xxii. 6 ?) ABCLℵ d p Thl-fin, *de* vulg E-lat: *απο* EHP 13 rel Thl-sif. add *σκληρον σοι προς κεντρα λακτιζειν* (*from ch* xxvi. 14) E 180 am^2 Syr syr-w-ast (adding a note that these words are not here in the text, but where Paul gives the account of himself).

5. rec om (*as* ||) *συ*, with ABEHLPℵ rel: ins C. rec aft *ο δε* ins *κυριος ειπεν* (*κυριος appears to have been an insertion to avoid the apparent insufficiency of ο δε*;—*ειπεν*, *from ch* xxvi. 15), with HLP 13 rel syrr [sah] Chr_1 Thl; *κυριος προς αυτον* E o 11. 27-9. 66^2; *κυριος* 100 Hil; *ειπεν* ℵ k $p^{1\cdot 3}$ 43. 105-37 copt æth arm: om ABC p^2 36 vulg. aft *ιησ.* add *ο Ναζωραιος* (*from ch* xxii. 8) ACE [demid] Syr syr-w-ast copt æth Hil_1 Aug_2.

5, 6. rec aft *διωκ.* (omg *αλλα*) adds *σκληρον σοι προς κεντρα λακτιζειν τρεμων τε και*

Chrysorrhoas (Barrada), which divides into many streams (see 2 Kings v. 12), and fertilizes the plain (Strabo, xvi. 756, ἡ Δαμασκηνὴ χώρα διαφερόντως ἐπαινουμένη),—bounded on all sides by the desert. See Winer, Realw., from which the above is mainly taken: Vitringa in Jesaiam, p. 650 ff. (Notitia Damasci et Regni Damasceni), and a vivid description in C. and H., pp. 104—108. **πρὸς τ. συν.**] i. e. to the *presidents* of the synagogues, who would acknowledge the orders of the Sanhedrim, and could, under the authority of the Ethnarch, carry them out. **τῆς ὁδοῦ**] Not '*this way*,' E. V., which rendering should be kept for the places where the pronoun is *expressed*, as ch. xxii. 4,—but **the way**, viz. of 'salvation,' ch. xvi. 17, or 'of the Lord,' ch. xviii. 25. (The genitive, as *τῆς γνώμης εἶναι*, see 1 Cor. i. 12.) The expression 'THE WAY' had evidently become a well-known one among Christians (see reff.); and it only was necessary to prefix the pronoun when *strangers* were addressed.

The special journey to Damascus presupposes the existence of Christians there, and in some numbers. This would be accounted for by the return of many who may have been converted at the Pentecostal effusion of the Spirit, and perhaps also by some of the fugitives from the persecution having settled there. This latter is rendered probable by Ananias's ἤκουσα ἀπὸ πολλῶν περὶ τοῦ ἀνδρὸς τούτου, ver. 13.

3.] The journey from Jerusalem was probably made on the Roman road, i. e. that of the Itineraries, by Neapolis (Sichem) and Scythopolis, crossing the Jordan S. of the lake Tiberias,—Gadara, and so to Damascus. Or he might have joined,—either the Petra road, by Jericho and Heshbon, and so by Botsrah to D.,—or the Egyptian caravan-track, which passes to the north of the lake of Tiberias, and near Cæsarea Philippi. In either case the journey would occupy from five to six days, the distance being 130 to 150 miles. **περιήστρ. κ.τ.λ.**] It was (ch. xxii. 6) *περὶ μεσημβρίαν*,—and from ch. xxvi. 13, the light was *ὑπὲρ τὴν λαμπρότητα τοῦ ἡλίου*. These details at once cut away all ground from the absurd rationalistic attempt to explain away the appearance as having been *lightning*. Unquestionably, the inference is, that it was a bright noon, and the full splendour of the oriental sun was shining.

His companions saw the light, and were also cast to the ground, ch. xxvi. 13, 14; xxii. 9, see below on ver. 7. **4. λεγουσαν αὐτ.**] *τῇ Ἑβραΐδι διαλέκτῳ*, ch. xxvi. 14. And it is a remarkable undesigned coincidence, that the form **Σαούλ** should have been preserved in this account, and rendered in Greek in the translation of Paul's speech in ch. xxii. In ch. xxvi., where he was speaking in Greek before

6 ἀλλὰ [u] ἀνάστηθι καὶ εἴςελθε εἰς τὴν πόλιν, και
[v] λαληθήσεταί σοι ὅ τι σε δεῖ ποιεῖν. 7 οἱ δὲ ἄνδρες οἱ
[w] συνοδεύοντες αὐτῷ εἱστήκεισαν [x] ἐνεοί, ἀκούοντες μὲν

u Mark ix. 27. Luke iv. 39. v. 25. ver. 34. ch. xii. 7 al. 3 Kings xx. (xxi.) 7.
v = ch. [x. 32] xxii. 10. 1 Cor. xiv. 3. Ezek. iii. 22.
w here only +. Wisd. vi. 23 (25) only. (-δία, Luke ii. 44.)
x here only. Prov. xvii. 28. Isa. lvi. 10. Ep. Jer. 41 only.

θαμβων ειπε κυριε τι με θελεις ποιησαι και ο κυριος προς αυτον (*from ch* xxvi. 14, *and* xxii. 10. *Inserted by Erasmus from the Latin: in his annotations on* "Durum est tibi" *he says* "In græcis codicibus id non additur hoc loco, cum mox sequatur, *Surge;* sed aliquanto inferius, cum narratur hæc res." *See Treg on the Printed Txt p* 23), with no Greek manuscript as far as Griesbach ("codices græci, quantum scimus, nulli"), Scholz (repeating Gb's words), and Tischdf are aware—vulg(demid fuld) syr-w-ast(but varies, and syr ins αλλα) æth(but varies) arm(ed-usc: but addg αλλα) Thl-ed-fin-txt Hil_1(τρεμ. to ποι., omg the former part): αλλα is inserted and the rec omitted by all our manuscripts, by 23 others which Scholz specifies, by am[1] tol(Tischdf) Syr coptt [arm-zoh] Chr.

6. εισιθι B. rec om ὅ, with EHLP 13. 36 rel: ins ABCℵ p. δει bef σε E-gr: om σε k.

7. rec εννεοι, with L rel [$Chr-ed_1$]: txt ABCEHPℵ a b[1] h m p 13 syr-mg-gr. for μεν, δε (omg δε follg) p.

Festus, he inserts the words τῇ Ἑβρ. διαλ., to account for the use of the form Σαούλ: or perhaps he spoke the solemn words, ineffaceable from his memory, *as they were uttered, in Hebrew,* for King Agrippa. (See note on Σαούλ, ver. 17.) **τί με διώκεις;**] A remarkable illustration of Matt. xxv. 45. The με is not emphatic (agst Wordsw.); but the very lack of emphasis, assuming the awful fact, gives more solemnity to the question.

5. ὁ δέ] That Saul *saw,* as well as heard, Him who spoke with him, is certain from Ananias's speech, ver. 17, and ch. xxii. 14,—that of Barnabas, ver. 27,—from ch. xxvi. 16 (ὤφθην σοι), and from the references by Paul himself to his having seen the Lord, 1 Cor. ix. 1; xv. 8. These last I unhesitatingly refer to this occasion, and not to any subsequent one, when he saw the Lord ἐν ἐκστάσει, ch. xxii. 17. Such appearances could hardly form the subject of autoptic testimony which should rank with that of the other apostles: this, on the contrary, was no ἔκστασις, but the *real bodily appearance of the risen Jesus:* so that it might be adduced as the ground of testimony to His Resurrection. On the words excluded from our text, as having been interpolated from ch. xxvi. 14, and xxii. 10, see note at xxvi. 14. It is natural that the account of the *historian* should be less precise than that of the *person concerned, relating his own history.* In ch. xxvi. 15—18, very much more is related to have been said by the Lord: but perhaps he there, as he omits the subsequent particulars, includes the revelations made to him during the three days, and in the message of Ananias. **7.**] In ch. xxii. 9, οἱ δὲ σὺν ἐμοὶ ὄντες τὸ μὲν φῶς ἐθεάσαντο [κ. ἔμφοβοι ἐγένοντο], τὴν δὲ φωνὴν οὐκ ἤκουσαν τοῦ λαλοῦντός μοι. Two accounts seemingly (and certainly, in the *letter*) discrepant; but exceedingly instructive when their *spirit* is compared,—the *fact* being this: that the companions of Saul saw and were struck to the ground by the light, but saw οὐδένα, *no person:*—that they stood (or 'were fixed:' but I should acknowledge the discrepancy here, and recognize the more accurate detail of ch. xxvi. 14, that they *fell to the ground*) mute, hearing τῆς φωνῆς, the sound of the voice, but not τὴν φωνὴν τοῦ λαλοῦντός μοι, the words spoken and their meaning. Compare John xii. 29, note. (Only no stress must be laid on the difference between the gen. and acc. government of φωνή, nor indeed on the mere *verbal* difference of the two expressions;—but their spirit considered, in the possible reference which they might have to one and the same fact.) Two classes of readers only will stumble at this difference of the forms of narration; those who from enmity to the faith are striving to create or magnify discrepancies,—and those who, by the suicidal theory of verbal inspiration, are effectually doing the work of the former. * The devout and intelligent student of Scripture will see in such examples a convincing proof of the simple truth of the narrative,—the absence of all endeavour to pare away apparent inconsistencies or revise them into conformity,—the *bonâ fide* work of holy truthful men, bearing each his testimony to things seen and heard under the guidance, not of the spirit of bondage, but of that Spirit of whom it is said, οὗ τὸ πνεῦμα κυρίου, ἐλευθερία. I should not too hastily determine that this account *has not come from Saul himself,* on account of the above differences: they are

y ch. vii. 56 reff. z ch. xxii. 11 only. Judg. xvi. 26 A compl. only. a ch. xxiii. 12. Esth. iv. 16. b ch. vii. 31 reff. c = Heb. ii. 13 only. 1 Kings iii. 4. d ch. viii. 26 reff. e Matt. vi. 2. Luke xiv. 21. ch. xii. 10 only. Prov. xxxi. 23 ℵ. Isa. xv. 3. Tobit xiii. 18 (not ℵ). Sir. ix. 7 only.

ABCEH LPℵa b c d f g h k l m o p 13

τῆς φωνῆς, μηδένα δὲ [y] θεωροῦντες. 8 ἠγέρθη δὲ Σαῦλος
ἀπὸ τῆς γῆς, ἠνεῳγμένων δὲ τῶν ὀφθαλμῶν αὐτοῦ οὐδένα
ἔβλεπεν· [z] χειραγωγοῦντες δὲ αὐτὸν εἰσήγαγον εἰς Δαμασκόν. 9 καὶ ἦν ἡμέρας τρεῖς μὴ βλέπων, καὶ οὐκ [a] ἔφαγεν
οὐδὲ [a] ἔπιεν. 10 Ἦν δέ τις μαθητὴς ἐν Δαμασκῷ ὀνόματι
Ἀνανίας. καὶ εἶπεν πρὸς αὐτὸν ἐν [b] ὁράματι ὁ κύριος
Ἀνανία. ὁ δὲ εἶπεν [c] Ἰδοὺ ἐγώ, κύριε. 11 ὁ δὲ κύριος πρὸς
αὐτὸν [d] Ἀναστὰς πορεύθητι ἐπὶ τὴν [e] ῥύμην τὴν καλουμένην εὐθεῖαν, καὶ ζήτησον ἐν οἰκίᾳ Ἰούδα Σαῦλον ὀνό-

θεορουντες ℵ[3] : *ορωντες* ℵ[1].

8. rec ins *ο* bef *σαυλος*, with HLP rel: om ABCEℵ b[1] p. rec *ανεωγ.*, with BHLP rel: txt (A)CE(ℵ) p.—*ηνοιγ.* A: *ηνυγ.* ℵ[1]. for 2nd *δε*, *τε* HLP a b (c ?) d g h k l o æth arm[appy] Chr Thl. *ουδεν* (*cf ch* xxii.) A[1]Bℵ vulg E-lat syrr sah æth[-rom]: txt A[2]C E-gr HLP rel c*r* Chr Thl.—in ℵ *α* seems to have been begun above the line, but is left unfinished.

9. for *ουδε*, *και ουκ* C.

10. rec *ο κυρ.* bef *εν ορ.*, with HLP p rel vss [Chr_1]: txt ABCEℵ vulg æth-rom.

11. *αναστα* B fuld syrr(but so also ch x. 13, 20) coptt; and, adding *και*, vulg(not am) æth(but so also elsw when there is no varn in the Greek).

no more than might arise in narrations at different times by the same person.

εἱστήκεισαν] It will be well to warn younger readers against an error often found in English Commentators (e. g. Dr. Burton here),—that *ἕστηκα* is *past*, and *εἱστήκειν pluperfect* in signification,—*ἕστηκα*, 'I have been standing,' and *εἱστήκεισαν*, 'had been standing.' This error arises from forgetting the peculiar character of the verb *ἵστημι* with regard to transitive and intransitive meanings. *ἕστηκα* is *strictly present*,—*εἱστήκειν imperfect*: as much so as *sto* and *stabam*. See Matthiæ, § 206. And this accuracy is important here: they had *not* 'been standing,' but had fallen. See ch. xxvi. 14, *πάντων τε καταπεσόντων ἡμῶν εἰς τὴν γῆν*. Wordsw.'s explanation, that *εἱστήκεισαν* refers to the *standing still* of the cavalcade, not to the *standing* of Saul's companions, is untenable: for 1) the *ἐνεοί*, which qualifies the *εἱστήκεισαν*, forbids it: and 2) his justifying instances are all aorists, Luke vii. 14; viii. 44; ch. viii. 38, not perfect, which surely will not bear this sense of mere arrestation in a course.

8.] **On his eyes being opened** (it would seem that he had closed them on the first disappearance of the vision), **he saw no one.** He explains it, ch. xxii. 11, *ὡς δὲ οὐκ ἐνέβλεπον ἀπὸ τῆς δόξης τοῦ φωτὸς ἐκείνου*. He had seen, what those with him had not seen, the glorious Person of the Lord Jesus. See below on ver. 18.

9.] Obs. **μὴ** *βλέπων*, his personal subjective state: **οὐκ** *ἔφ.*, the historical fact.

οὐκ ἔφ. οὐδὲ ἔπ.] There is no occasion to soften these words: the effect produced on him by the *οὐράνιος ὀπτασία* (ch. xxvi. 19), aided by his own deeply penitent and remorseful state of mind, rendered him indifferent to all sustenance whatever.

10.] Paul adds, ch. xxii. 12, with particularity, as defending himself before the *Jews*, that Ananias was *ἀνὴρ εὐλαβὴς κατὰ τὸν νόμον μαρτυρούμενος ὑπὸ πάντων τῶν κατοικούντων Ἰουδαίων*: saying nothing of the command received by him, *nor that he was a disciple*. In ch. xxvi., speaking before the Roman governor, he *does not mention him.* Mr. Howson (edn. 2, vol. i. p. 114) remarks on the close analogy between the divine procedure by visions here, and in ch. x. Here, Ananias is prepared for his work, and Saul for the reception of him as a messenger, each by a vision: and similarly Peter and Cornelius in ch. x. I may add, that in ch. viii., where the preparation of heart was already found in the eunuch, *Philip only* was supernaturally prepared for the interview.

11.] "We are allowed to bear in mind that the thoroughfares of Eastern cities do not change, and to believe that the 'straight street,' which still extends through Damascus in long perspective from the eastern gate, is the street where Ananias spoke to Saul." (C. and H., p. 115.)

οἰκίᾳ Ἰούδα] The houses of Ananias and Judas are still shewn to travellers. Doubtless they (or at least the former) would long be remembered and pointed out by Christians; but, in the long degradation of Christianity in the East, most such identities must have

ματι Ταρσέα. 12 ἰδοὺ γὰρ [f] προςεύχεται, καὶ εἶδεν ἄνδρα
Ἀνανίαν ὀνόματι εἰςελθόντα καὶ [g] ἐπιθέντα αὐτῷ [g] χεῖρα
ὅπως [h] ἀναβλέψῃ. 13 ἀπεκρίθη δὲ Ἀνανίας Κύριε, [i] ἤκουσα
[i] ἀπὸ πολλῶν περὶ τοῦ ἀνδρὸς τούτου, ὅσα [k] κακὰ τοῖς
[l] ἁγίοις σου ἐποίησεν ἐν Ἱερουσαλήμ· 14 καὶ ὧδε [m] ἔχει
[m] ἐξουσίαν παρὰ τῶν ἀρχιερέων δῆσαι πάντας τοὺς [n] ἐπικαλουμένους τὸ ὄνομά σου. 15 εἶπεν δὲ πρὸς αὐτὸν ὁ κύριος
[o] Πορεύου, ὅτι [p] σκεῦος [q] ἐκλογῆς ἐστίν μοι οὗτος [r] τοῦ
[s] βαστάσαι τὸ ὄνομά μου [t] ἐνώπιον ἐθνῶν τε καὶ βασιλέων

f absol., ch. x. 9 reff. g ch. viii. 17 reff. h = Matt. xi. 5 al. in gospp. Acts, here 3ce, and ch. xxii. 13 bis only. Isa. xlii. 18. (-ψις, Isa. lxi. 1.) i Luke xxii. 71. 1 John i. 5. k and constr., 4 Kings viii. 12. w. πράττειν, ch. xvi. 28. w. ἐνδείκνυσθαι, 2 Tim. iv. 14. l = here first. Acts, vv. 32, 41, and ch. xxvi. 10 only. Epp. passim. (Matt. xxvii. 52. Ps. xv. 3 and freq.) m 1 Cor. vii. 37 reff. n ch. ii. 21 and Rom. x. 13 reff. o absol., Matt. ii. 8. ch. xxii. 21 al. fr. Jer. iii. 12. p = Rom. ix. (21) 22, 23. 2 Cor. iv. 7. (1 Thess. iv. 4.) 2 Tim. ii. (20) 21. (1 Pet. iii. 7. Ps. xxx. 12.) q Rom. ix. 11 reff. r constr., 1 Cor. x. 13 reff. s = here only ‡. t = ch. ii. 25 reff.

12. rec aft ειδεν ins εν οραματι (*addition to complete sense, as is shewn by its various position*), with EHLP 13. 36 rel; aft ανδρα BC: om Aℵ p vulg coptt æth. rec ονοματι bef ανανιαν, with HLP 13 rel [syrr]: om ον. sah æth-rom Chr_1: txt ABCEℵ a h m p vulg arm. τας χειρας BEℵ[3]: χειρας ACℵ[1] p(appy): txt HLP 13 rel syrr(but Syr(Etheridge) has the sing in ver 17) sah æth-pl.

13. rec ins ο bef ανανιας: om ABCEH[L]Pℵ. [ins και ειπεν bef κυρ. E æth.] rec ακηκοα (*corrn to seemingly more appropriate tense*), with HLP 13 rel Chr_1: ακηκοαμεν lect-14: txt ABCEℵ p. rec εποι. bef τ. αγιοις σου (*alteration of characteristic arrangement to more usual one*), with HLP 13 rel [syrr coptt æth arm] Chr Œc Thl: εν ιερ. bef εποι. A: txt BCEℵ m p [vulg] am demid fuld.—om σου p.

15. rec μοι bef εστ., with EHLP 13 rel coptt Archel Thdrt Thl Iren-int: txt ABCℵ c m p vulg syrr Did-c [Sev-c]. ins των bef εθνων BC[1](Cyr_2). rec om 1st τε, with HLP rel Chr [Sev-c] $Thdrt_2$ Thl-sif: ins ABCEℵ p 13. 36 Thl-fin.

been lost; and imposture is so easy, that it is hardly possible to cherish the thought that the spots now pointed out can be the true ones. And so of all cases, where we have not unalterable or unaltered data to go on. Still, true as this is, we have sometimes proofs and illustrations unexpectedly appearing, as research goes on, which identify as authentic, sites long pointed out by tradition. So that our way seems to be, to seek for all such elucidations, and meantime to suspend our judgment: but never to lose sight of, nor to treat contemptuously a priori, a local belief.

Ταρσέα] The first place where he is so specified. TARSUS was the capital of the province of Cilicia, a large and populous city (τῆς Κιλ. πόλιν μεγάλην κ. εὐδαίμονα, Xen. Anab. i. 2. 23) in a fruitful plain on the river Cydnus, which flowed through the midst of it ('Cydnos, Tarsum liberam urbem procul a mari secans.' Plin. v. 27. Strabo, xiv. 673. Q. Curt. iii. 5. 1), with a swift stream of remarkably cold water. Strabo speaks most highly of its eminence in schools of philosophy: τοσαύτη τοῖς ἐνθάδε ἀνθρώποις σπουδὴ πρός τε φιλοσοφίαν καὶ τὴν ἄλλην ἐγκύκλιον ἅπασαν παιδείαν γέγονεν, ὥσθ' ὑπερβέβληνται καὶ Ἀθήνας καὶ Ἀλεξάνδρειαν καὶ εἴ τινα ἄλλον τόπον δυνατὸν εἰπεῖν, ἐν ᾧ σχολαὶ καὶ διατριβαὶ τῶν φιλοσόφων καὶ τῶν λόγων γεγόνασι. διαφέρει δὲ τοσοῦτον, ὅτι ἐνταῦθα μὲν οἱ φιλομαθοῦντες ἐπιχώριοι πάντες εἰσί, xiv. 674. He enumerates many learned men who had sprung from it. It was (see Plin. above) an "urbs libera," i. e. one which, though under Rome, lived under its own laws and chose its own magistrates. This 'libertas' was granted to it by Antony (Appian. Civ. v. 7): and much later we find it a Roman *colony*. As a *free city*, it had neither the 'jus coloniarum,' nor the 'jus civitatis:' see ch. xxi. 39, also xxii. 28, and note. It is now a town with about 20,000 inhabitants, and is described as being a den of poverty, filth, and ruins. There are many remains of the old town (Winer, Realw.).

12. προςεύχεται] This word would set before Ananias more powerfully than any other, the state of Saul. **ἄνδρα Ἀν. ὀν.**] A man, whose name in the same vision he knew to be Ananias. The sight of the man and the knowledge of his name were both granted him in his vision.

13. τοῖς ἁγίοις σου] This is the first time that this afterwards well-known appellation occurs as applied to the believers in Christ. **14.**] It could hardly fail to have been notified to the Christians at Damascus by their brethren at Jerusalem, that Saul was on his way to persecute them. **15. σκ. ἐκλογῆς**] A genit. of

[u] υἱῶν τε Ἰσραήλ· 16 ἐγὼ γὰρ [v] ὑποδείξω αὐτῷ ὅσα δεῖ
αὐτὸν [w] ὑπὲρ τοῦ [w] ὀνόματός μου παθεῖν. 17 [x] ἀπῆλθεν δὲ
Ἀνανίας καὶ εἰςῆλθεν εἰς τὴν οἰκίαν, καὶ [y] ἐπιθεὶς ἐπ' αὐτὸν
τὰς [y] χεῖρας εἶπεν Σαοὺλ ἀδελφέ, ὁ κύριος ἀπέσταλκέν με,
Ἰησοῦς ὁ [z] ὀφθείς σοι ἐν τῇ ὁδῷ ᾗ ἤρχου, ὅπως [a] ἀνα-
βλέψῃς καὶ [b] πλησθῇς πνεύματος ἁγίου. 18 καὶ εὐθέως
[c] ἀπέπεσαν αὐτοῦ ἀπὸ τῶν ὀφθαλμῶν [d] ὡςεὶ [e] λεπίδες,
[a] ἀνέβλεψέν τε καὶ [f] ἀναστὰς ἐβαπτίσθη, 19 καὶ [gh] λαβὼν
[h] τροφὴν [i] ἐνίσχυσεν. ἐγένετο δὲ μετὰ τῶν ἐν Δαμασκῷ
μαθητῶν [j] ἡμέρας [j] τινάς, 20 καὶ εὐθέως ἐν ταῖς συναγωγαῖς

ABCEH LPℵab cdfgh klmo p13

u ch. x. 36 reff. v and constr., Luke (iii. 7 || Mt.) vi. 47. xii. 5. ch. xx. 35 only. Esth. v. 11. w ch. v. 41. xv. 26. xxi. 13. Rom. i. 5. 3 John 7 only. x — ch. v. 26 reff. y ch. viii. 17 reff. z ch. ii. 3 reff. a ver. 12. b ch. ii. 4 reff. c here only. Job xxix. 24. d = ch. ii. 3. Matt. iii. 16. e here only. Levit. xi. 9, 12. (-πίζειν, Tobit xi. 13 [ἀπολεπ. ℵ].) f ch. viii. 26 reff. g = John xix. 30. Mark xv. 23. 1 Tim. iv. 4. h here only. μεταλ. τρ., ch. ii. 46. xxvii. 33, 34. προςλ. τρ., xxvii. 36 i = here only. Gen. xlviii. 2. trans., Luke xxii. 43 only. 2 Kings xxii. 40. j ch. x. 48 reff.

17. for δε, τε A. τας χ. bef επ αυτ. C [coptt æth]. om ιησ. HLP b d g h k l m [sah] æth-rom Thl. om η ηρχου ℵ[1](ins ℵ-corr[1]).
18. (απεπεσαν, so ABCEHℵ p [13] Thl-sif.) rec απ. τ. οφθ. bef αυτ. (*more usual instead of more characteristic arrangement*), with CEHLPℵ rel: txt AB m. ως (*more usual word*) ABℵ[1] p [om copt æth]. for τε, δε C[2]ℵ copt. [C[1] doubtful.] rec aft τε ins παραχρημα (*addition for precision*), with [C[2]]EL rel syr [sah æth arm-ms]: om ABC[1]HPℵ d g l[1] m p 36 vulg Syr copt arm[-ed].
19. ενισχυθη BC[1]. rec aft εγ. δε ins ο σαυλος (*commencement of an ecclesiastical portion*: so lect-12 has εγεν. ειναι τον παυλον), with HLP rel: txt ABCEℵ c p [13] vulg syrr coptt æth arm Chr$_1$. ins οντων bef εν δαμασκω HLP b d g k m o Chr$_1$ Thl-fin.

quality: as we say, 'the man of his choice.' See Winer, edn. 6, § 34. 3, b. Paul often uses this word σκεῦος in a similar meaning, see reff., especially Rom. ix., &c., where it is in illustrating God's sovereign power in election. **βαστάσαι**, perhaps in reference to the metaphor in σκεῦος. **ἐθνῶν**] This would hardly be understood at the time: it was afterwards on a remarkable occasion repeated to Paul by the Lord in a vision (see ch. xxii. 21), and was regarded by him as the specific command which gave the direction to his ministry, see Gal. ii. 7, 8. **βασιλ.**] Agrippa, and probably Nero. **16. ὑποδείξω**] The fulfilment of this is testified by Paul himself, ch. xx. 23, 25: see also xxi. 11. **17. Σαούλ**] The Hebrew form of Saul's name is only found here, and in the report of our Lord's previous address to him. **κ. πλησθῇς πν. ἁγ.**] I can hardly think, with De W. and Meyer, that these words imply that the Lord had said to Ananias more than is above related: I would rather view them as a natural inference from what was said in ver. 15. In ch. xxii. 14, where the command to Ananias is omitted, *his* speech contains much of the reason given in the command here. It is remarkable again how Paul, speaking there to an infuriated Jewish mob, gives the words spoken just that form which would best gain him a favourable hearing with them—e. g. ὁ θεὸς τῶν πατέρων ἡμῶν,—ἰδεῖν **τὸν δίκαιον**,—πάντας ἀνθρώπους, avoiding as yet the hateful word ἔθνη. He there too gives ἀναστὰς βάπτισαι καὶ ἀπόλουσαι τὰς ἁμαρτίας σου, ἐπικαλεσάμενος τὸ ὄνομα αὐτοῦ as part of the exhortation of Ananias.

18. ὡςεὶ λεπίδες] The recovery of sight is plainly related as miraculous, the consequence of the divinely appointed laying on of the hands of Ananias. And this scaly substance which fell from his eyes was thrown off in the process of the instantaneous healing. **ἐβαπτίσθη**] It has been well remarked (Olsh.) that great honour was here placed upon the sacrament of baptism, inasmuch as not even Saul, who had seen the Lord in special revelation and was an elect vessel, was permitted to dispense with this, the Lord's appointed way of admission into His Church. **19. ἐνίσχ.**] intrans. see reff.

ἡμ. τινάς] A few days; of quiet, and becoming acquainted with those as brethren, whom he came to persecute as infidels: but not to learn from them the gospel (οὐδὲ γὰρ ἐγὼ παρὰ ἀνθρώπου παρέλαβον αὐτό, οὔτε ἐδιδάχθην, Gal. i. 12), nor was the time longer than to admit of εὐθέως being used, ver. 20,—and indeed the same εὐθέως of the whole space (including his *preaching* in our vv. 20, 21) preceding the journey to Arabia, in Gal. i. 16. Pearson places that journey *before* our ἐγένετο δέ,—which however is mani-

[k] ἐκήρυσσεν τὸν Ἰησοῦν, ὅτι [l] οὗτός ἐστιν ὁ υἱὸς τοῦ θεοῦ.
21 [m] ἐξίσταντο δὲ πάντες οἱ ἀκούοντες καὶ ἔλεγον Οὐχ
οὗτός ἐστιν ὁ [n] πορθήσας ἐν Ἱερουσαλὴμ τοὺς [o] ἐπικαλουμένους τὸ [p] ὄνομα τοῦτο; καὶ ὧδε [q] εἰς τοῦτο [q] ἐληλύθει,
ἵνα δεδεμενους αὐτοὺς ἀγάγῃ [r] ἐπὶ τοὺς ἀρχιερεῖς.
22 Σαῦλος δὲ μᾶλλον [s] ἐνεδυναμοῦτο, καὶ [t] συνέχυννεν τοὺς
Ἰουδαίους τοὺς κατοικοῦντας ἐν Δαμασκῷ, [u] συμβιβάζων
ὅτι [v] οὗτός ἐστιν ὁ χριστός. 23 ὡς δὲ [w] ἐπληροῦντο [x] ἡμέραι
[x] ἱκαναί, [y] συνεβουλεύσαντο οἱ Ἰουδαῖοι [z] ἀνελεῖν αὐτόν·

Fr.Coisl. contains vv. 23, 24.

k κη. τ. ἰησ., ch. xix. 13. 2 Cor. xi. 4, L.P. κη. τ. χρ., see ch. viii. 5 reff.
l ver. 22. Luke i. 32. ch. x. 36, 40. 1 John v. 20 al. fr.
m ch. viii. 13 reff.
n Gal. i. 13, 23 only +.
o ver. 14.
p ch. v. 28 (iv. 12. James ii 7).
q John xviii. 37 only. see Mark i. 38.
r = Matt. x. 18 al.
s Rom. iv. 20 al5. Paul only, exc. here, which is of Paul, and Heb. xi. 34. Ps. li. 7 (9). Judg. vi. 34 AB (not Ed-vat. F) only.
t ch. ii. 6 reff.
u 1 Cor. ii. 16 reff. Exod. xviii. 16.
v ver. 20 reff.
w ch. vii. 23 reff.
x ver. 43. ch. xviii. 18. xxvii. 7 L. see ch. viii. 11.
y constr., Rev. iii. 18 only. 1 Macc. ix. 69. see Dan. vi. 7 Theod. w. ἵνα, Matt. xxvi. 4. John xi. 53 only. w. ὅτι, John xviii. 14 only.
z ch. v. 33 reff.

20. rec for ιησ., χριστον (*doctrinal alteration? see note*), with HLP rel [arm-mss] Chr_1: alii aliter: txt ABCEא a c h p 13 vulg syrr [copt æth-rom arm-ed] $Iren_1$[-gr and]-int.

21. εξιστατο א[1](but corrd). for εν, εις Aא. εληλυθεν (*alteration, not observing the force of the pluperf?*) E-gr HLP p rel Chr_1: txt ABCא o (13) 36 E-lat. **αναγαγη** P [Chr_1].

22. aft ενεδ. ins τω λογω C, εν τω λ. E. rec συνεχυνεν, with A[B²]HLP rel: συνεχεεν E 57. 66². 137-80 Thl-fin: εσυνεχυνεν 13: txt B¹Cא. om 1st τους Bא¹.

23. ins αι bef ημεραι H.

festly against the sense of the text:—Michaelis and Heinrichs, between vv. 19 and 20,—to which there is the same objection: Kuinoel and Olsh., after ver. 25,—which the εὐθέως of Gal. i. 16 will not allow: Neander and Meyer, in the ἡμέραι ἱκαναί of ver. 23, which time however in our text is certainly allotted to the progress of his preaching in Damascus, and the increase of the hostility of the Jews in consequence. See below. **20. Ἰησοῦν**] The alteration to χριστόν has probably, as Meyer suggests, been made from doctrinal considerations, to fix on ὁ υἱὸς τοῦ θεοῦ the theological sense,—*that Christ is the Son of God*—instead of that which it now bears,—that *Jesus is the Son of God*, i. e. that Jesus of Nazareth *as a matter of fact*, is the Son of God, i. e. the Messiah expected under that appellation. Be this as it may, the following **τὸ ὄνομα τοῦτο** (ver. 21) is decisive for the reading Ἰησοῦν, and οὗτός ἐστιν ὁ χριστός ver. 22 still more so. **21. πορθήσας**] 'Militari verbo usus est,' Erasm. So Æsch. Choeph. 680, οἳ 'γώ, κατ' ἄκρας ἐνθάδ' ὡς πορθούμεθα. See also Sept. c. Theb. 176 (194 Dind.). **ἐληλύθει**] **had come** here, implying the abandonment of the purpose. **22.**] I regard the **μᾶλλον ἐνεδυναμοῦτο**, as the *only words beneath which can lie concealed the journey to Arabia*. Paul mentions this journey (Gal. i. 17) with no obscure hint that to it was to be assigned the reception by him, in full measure, of the Gospel which he preached. And such a reception would certainly give rise to the great accession of power here recorded. I am the more disposed to allot that journey this place, from the following considerations. The omission of any mention of it here can arise only from one of two causes: (1) whether Paul himself were the source of the narrative, or some other narrator,—*the intentional passing over of it, as belonging more to his personal history* (which it was his express purpose to relate in Gal. i.) *than to that of his ministry:* (2) on the supposition of Paul not having been the source of the narrative,—*the narrator having not been aware of it*. In either case, this expression seems to me one very likely to have been used:—(1) if the omission was *intentional*,—to record a remarkable accession of power to Saul's ministry, without particularizing whence or how it came: (2) if it was *unintentional*,—as a simple record of that which was observed in him, but of which the source was to the narrator unknown. **συνέχυννεν**] Chrysostom strikingly says, ἅτε νομομαθὴς ὢν ἐπεστόμιζεν αὐτοὺς καὶ οὐκ εἶα φθέγγεσθαι· ἐνόμισαν ἀπηλλάχθαι τῆς ἐν τοῖς τοιούτοις διαλέξεως ἀπαλλαγέντες Στεφάνου, καὶ Στεφάνου σφοδρότερον εὗρον ἕτερον. (Cramer's Catena.) **23. ἡμέραι ἱκαναί**] *In* Damascus, see above on ver. 19. The whole time, from his conversion to his journey to Jerusalem, was three years, Gal. i. 18. **ἀνελεῖν αὐτ.**] ἐπὶ τὸν ἰσχυρὸν συλλογισμὸν ἔρχονται

a constr., Phil iv. 5. Lev. iv. 14.
b ch. xx. 3, 19. xxiii. 30 only. Esth. ii. 22.

24 [a] ἐγνώσθη δὲ τῷ Σαύλῳ ἡ [b] ἐπιβουλὴ αὐτῶν. [c] παρετη- ABCEH
ροῦντο δὲ καὶ τὰς πύλας [d] ἡμέρας τε καὶ [d] νυκτὸς ὅπως LPℵ a b c d f g h
αὐτὸν [z] ἀνέλωσιν· 25 [e] λαβόντες δὲ οἱ μαθηταὶ αὐτοῦ k l m o p 13

c mid., Luke vi. 7. xiv. 1. Gal. iv. 10. Ps. xxxvi. 12. act., Mark iii. 2. Luke xx. 20 only. d gen., Luke xviii. 7. Rev. iv. 8 al4. Ps. i. 2. ν. κ. ἡμέρας, Mark v. 5. 1 Thess. ii. 9 al. Isa. xxxiv. 10. acc., ch. xx. 31 reff.
e Matt. xxi. 35, 39 Gen. xii. 5

24. [παυλω H.] rec παρετηρουν (*mistake: see below*), with HLP 13 rel: txt ABCEℵ Fr-coisl p 36 Orig$_1$. rec for δε και, τε (*the* -το *of* παρετηρουντο *being mistaken for* τε, *no other copula was wanted: and thus* δε και *was struck out: thus also the* και *in* L *&c as unnecessary aft* δε), with HP 13 rel Syr [æth] Chr: δε L 137-80 syr coptt arm[Gb]: txt ABCEℵ Fr-coisl p 36 vulg Orig. om τε A d f k Orig. for ημ. to ανελ., οπως πιασωσιν αυτον ημ. και νυκτ. A. ανελ. bef αυτον ℵ^3.

25. rec αυτον οι μαθηται, with EHLP 13 rel [vulg] syrr coptt æth-pl [arm] Chr-txt$_1$ Œc Thl: αυτον οι μαθ. αυτου b: οι μαθηται αυτον m p^2(or p-corr^1 ?): οι μαθηται 36. 69 lect-12: txt ABCℵ Fr-coisl p^1(perhaps) am demid Orig(vol. ii. p. 394) Chr(ἐπέτρεψε πάλιν οἱ Ἰουδαῖοι. ουκετι γὰρ συκοφάντας κ. κατηγόρους κ. ψευδομάρτυρας ἐπιζητοῦσιν, Chrys. Hom. xx.

24.] In 2 Cor. xi. 32, Paul writes, ἐν Δαμασκῷ ὁ ἐθνάρχης Ἀρέτα τοῦ βασιλέως ἐφρούρει τὴν πόλιν Δαμασκηνῶν, πιάσαι με [θέλων]. A somewhat difficult chronological question arises respecting the subordination of Damascus to this Aretas. The city, under Augustus and Tiberius, was attached to the province of Syria: and we have coins of Damascus of both these emperors, and again of Nero and his successors. But we have none of Caligula and Claudius; and the following circumstances seem to point to a change in the rulership of Damascus at the death of Tiberius. There had been for some time war between Aretas, king of Arabia Nabatæa (whose capital was Petra), and Herod Antipas, on account of the divorce by Herod of Aretas' daughter at the instance of Herodias, and on account of some disputes about their frontiers. A battle was fought, and Herod's army entirely destroyed (Jos. Antt. xviii. 5. 1). On this Antipas, who was a favourite with Tiberius, sent to Rome for help: and Vitellius, the governor of Syria, was commissioned to march against Aretas, and take him, dead or alive. While on his march, he heard at Jerusalem of the death of Tiberius (March 16, A.D. 37), and πόλεμον ἐκφέρειν οὐκέθ' ὁμοίως δυνάμενος διὰ τὸ εἰς Γάϊον μεταπεπτωκέναι τὰ πράγματα (Antt. xviii. 5. 3), abandoned his march, and sent his army into their winter quarters, himself returning to Antioch: Antt. ibid. This μεταπεπτωκέναι τὰ πρ. brought about a great change in the situation of Antipas and his enemy. Antipas was soon (A.D. 39) banished to Lyons, and his kingdom given to Agrippa, his foe (Antt. xviii. 7. 2), who had been living in habits of intimacy with the new emperor (xviii. 6. 5). It would be natural that Aretas, who had been grossly injured by Antipas, should, by this change of affairs, be received into favour; and the more so, as there was an old grudge between Vitellius and Antipas, of which Jos. says (Antt. xviii. 4. 5), ἔκρυπτεν ὀργήν, μέχρι δὴ καὶ μετῆλθε, Γαΐου τὴν ἀρχὴν παρειληφότος.

Now in the year 38 Caligula made several changes in the East, granting Ituræa to Soæmus, Lesser Armenia and parts of Arabia to Cotys, the territory of Cotys to Rhæmetalces,—and to Polemon, the son of Polemon, his father's government. These facts, coupled with that of no Damascene coins of Caligula and Claudius existing (which might be fortuitous, but acquires force when thus combined), make it probable that about this time Damascus, which belonged to the predecessors of Aretas (Jos. Antt. xiii. 5. 2), was granted to Aretas by Caligula. This would at once solve the difficulty. The other suppositions,—that the Ethnarch (see on 2 Cor. xi. 32) was only visiting the city (as if he could then have guarded the city to prevent Paul's escape),—or that Aretas had seized Damascus on Vitellius giving up the expedition against him (as if a Roman governor of a province would, while waiting for orders from a new emperor, quietly allow one of its chief cities to be taken from him), are in the highest degree improbable. The above is taken in substance from Wieseler, Chron. des Apost. Zeitalters, pp. 167—175. His further argument from a coin βασιλέως Ἀρέτα φιλέλληνος does not seem conclusive, as it leaves the latter title altogether unaccounted for. It probably (C. and H. i. pp. 101 and 132) belongs to a former Aretas.

25.] The reading in the text, **λαβ. οἱ μαθηταὶ αὐτοῦ**, is ambiguous. Chrys. (see in var. readd.), al. take it as if Saul had disciples of his own who did this. The only escape from this inference is by supposing an unusual government of a gen. by λαβόντες, such as we sometimes find in Ho-

νυκτος [f] διὰ τοῦ [g] τειχους [h] καθῆκαν αὐτὸν [i] χαλάσαντες
ἐν [k] σπυρίδι. 26 [l] παραγενόμενος δὲ [l] εἰς Ἱερουσαλὴμ
[m] ἐπειρᾶτο [n] κολλᾶσθαι τοῖς μαθηταῖς· καὶ πάντες ἐφοβοῦντο
αὐτόν, μὴ [o] πιστεύοντες [o] ὅτι [p] ἔστιν μαθητής. 27 Βαρνάβας
δὲ [q] ἐπιλαβομενος αὐτὸν ἤγαγεν πρὸς τοὺς ἀποστόλους,
καὶ [rs] διηγήσατο αὐτοῖς [r] πῶς ἐν τῇ ὁδῷ [t] εἶδεν τὸν [t] κύριον,
καὶ ὅτι ἐλάλησεν αὐτῷ, καὶ [r] πῶς ἐν Δαμασκῷ [u] ἐπαῤ-
ῥησιάσατο ἐν τῷ ὀνόματι Ἰησοῦ. 28 καὶ ἦν μετ' αὐτῶν
[v] εἰςπορευόμενος καὶ [v] ἐκπορευόμενος εἰς Ἱερουσαλήμ,
[u] παῤῥησιαζόμενος ἐν τῷ ὀνόματι τοῦ κυρίου, 29 ἐλάλει τε

f — 2 Cor. xi. 33 only.
g 2 Cor. xi. 33. Heb. xi. 30. Rev. xxi. 12 &c. (6 times) only. Exod xiv. 22.
h Luke v. 19. ch. x. 11. xi. 5 only. Exod. xvii. 11.
i Mark ii. 4. Luke v. 4, 5. ch. xxvii. 17, 30. 2 Cor. xi. 33 only. Jer. xlv. (xxxviii.) 6.
k Matt. xv. 37 ‖. xvi. 10 ‖ only †.
l Matt. ii. 1. [John viii. 2.] ch. xiii. 14. xv. 4 only. Josh xxiv. 11.
m ch. xxvi. 21 only. Prov. xxvi. 18 ℵ[3a], F(not A) Ald. only.
n ch. v. 13 reff.
o John xiv. 10. Rom. x. 9 1 Thess. iv. 14 al. Job xv. 31.
p pres., ch. xvi. 38 reff.
q constr., ch. xvi. 19. xviii. 17. Luke ix. 47. (xiv. 4.) xxiii. 27 only. (Prov. vii. 13.) gen., ch. xvii. 19 reff.
r constr., Mark v. 16. ch. xii. 17 only.
s as above (r). Mark ix. 9. Luke viii. 39. ix. 10. ch. viii. 33. Heb. xi. 32 only. Josh. ii. 23.
t John xx. 20. (ch. xxii. 18.) ὁρᾶν τ. κ., 1 Cor. ix. 1 reff.
u ch. xiii. 46. xiv. 3 al3. Eph. vi. 20. 1 Thess. ii. 2 only. L.P. Prov. xx. 9 al.
v here only. Zech. viii. 10. see ch. i. 21.

τοῖς μαθηταῖς αὐτοῦ· καὶ γὰρ μαθητὰς εἶχεν εὐθέως). rec καθηκαν bef δια τ. τειχ., omg αυτον (*correction apparently, for the sake of perspicuity, to prevent* λαβοντες *and* δια του τειχους *being connected together*), with HLP (13) rel Chr: txt ABC(E m) ℵ Fr-coisl p Orig.—om αυτον EHLP m rel: ins ABCℵ Fr-coisl p 13. σφυριδι [C]ℵ.

26. rec aft παρ. δε ins ο σαυλος (*insertion as in ver* 19: *further shewn by* ο παυλος *in* E *&c*), with HLP 13 rel syr æth-pl [arm] Chr-txt$_1$ Thl: ο παυλος E 33-4. 105: om ABCℵ p vulg coptt æth Chr-comm$_1$. for εις, εν EHLP rel Thl-sif: txt A B(sic: see table) Cℵ a d f g o p(Treg expr, so also Scriv) 36. επειραζεν (*corrn to more usual form, see reff*) ABCℵ p: txt EHLP 13. 36 rel Chr.

27. om 3rd και ℵ[1](ins ℵ-corr[1·3]). rec ins του bef ιησ., with EHLPℵ p 13 rel; κυριου, A 98-mg; του κῡ a h k lect-12: om BC m o.

28. om και εκπ. (*homœotel*) HLP b d f l m o Chr$_1$ Thl-sif. rec (for εις) εν, with H a h [vulg syrr æth arm] Chr$_1$: txt ABCELPℵ [m] p 13. 36 rel Chr$_1$. (*Meyer holds that* εις *is owing to a wish to have a prep that may apply to one or other of the participles: but surely no corrector would have left* εκπορ. εις *together, and* H *which omits* κ. εκπ. *reads* εν.) rec ins και bef παρρ., with EHLP rel vss Chr$_2$ Thl: om ABCℵ p 13. 40 fuld æth-rom arm. rec aft τ. κυρ. ins ιησου, with HLℵ[3] [m(omg του)] 13 rel æth-pl Chr$_1$: for τ. κῡ, ιῡ C 3. 10-4. 38. 67[2]. 80[1] Syr Chr$_1$: om κυρ. a h: txt ABEPℵ[1] p 40 vulg syr coptt æth-rom arm.

mer, e. g. ἀγκὰς λαβέτην ἀλλήλων, Il. ψ. 711; Ὀδυσῆος λάβε γούνων, Od. χ. 310: see also Il. γ. 369, θ. 371; Od. ε. 428, τ. 480. So we have κρατήσας τῆς χειρὸς αὐτῆς, Luke viii. 54. But whether this is justified in a case where the whole person is concerned, as here, may be a question. If it is, it must be because not the taking and bringing him to the spot, but the act of laying hold of him to put him into the basket, is intended. **διὰ τ. τείχους**] Further particularized by the addition of διὰ θυρίδος, 2 Cor. xi. 33. Such windows in the walls of cities are common in the East: see Josh. ii. 15, 1 Sam. xix. 12: and an engraving of part of the present wall of Damascus in C. and H. i. p. 124. **σπυρίδι**] σαργάνῃ, 2 Cor. xi. 33. See note there, and on Matt. xv. 37.

26. παραγ.] Immediately: the purpose of this journey was to become acquainted with Peter, Gal. i. 18: a resolution probably taken during the conspiracy of the Jews against him at Damascus, and in furtherance of his announced mission to the Gentiles: that, by conference with the Apostles, his sphere of work might be agreed on. And this purpose his escape enabled him to effect. **καί**] Not *but:* the δέ follows. **27.**] It is very probable that Barnabas and Saul may have been personally known to each other in youth. 'Cyprus is only a few hours' sail from Cilicia. The schools of Tarsus may naturally have attracted one who, though a Levite, was a Hellenist: and there the friendship may have begun, which lasted through many vicissitudes, till it was rudely interrupted in the dispute at Antioch (ch. xv. 39).' (C. and H., edn. 2, i. p. 127.) **τοὺς ἀποστ.**] Only Peter, and James the Lord's brother, Gal. i. 18, 19. Probably there were no other Apostles there at the time: if there were, it is hardly conceivable that Saul should not have seen them. On his second visit, he

καὶ [w] συνεζήτει [w] πρὸς τοὺς [x] Ἑλληνιστάς. οἱ δὲ [y] ἐπεχείρουν
[z] ἀνελεῖν αὐτόν. 30 [a] ἐπιγνόντες δὲ [b] οἱ [b] ἀδελφοὶ [c] κατήγαγον αὐτὸν εἰς Καισάρειαν καὶ [d] ἐξαπέστειλαν αὐτὸν εἰς
Ταρσόν.
31 Ἡ μὲν οὖν [e] ἐκκλησία [f] καθ' [f] ὅλης τῆς Ἰουδαίας καὶ
Γαλιλαίας καὶ Σαμαρείας [g] εἶχεν [g] εἰρήνην, [h] οἰκοδομουμένη καὶ [i] πορευομένη τῷ [k] φόβῳ τοῦ [k] κυρίου, καὶ τῇ
[l] παρακλήσει τοῦ ἁγίου πνεύματος [m] ἐπληθύνετο· 32 ἐγέ-

ABCEH LPℵ a b c d f g h k l m o p 13

w Mark i. 27. ix. 16. Luke xxii. 23 only +. see ch. vi. 9.
x ch. vi. 1 (reff.) only.
y Luke i. 1. ch. xix. 13 only. Esth. ix. 25.
z vv. 23, 24.
a absol., 1 Cor. xiii. 12 only.
b = John xxi. 23 only in Gospp. Acts and Epp. passim.
c ch. xxiii. 15 reff.
d ch. vii. 12 reff. L.P.
e sing. w. two or more places adjoined, here only.
f Luke iv. 14. xxiii. 5. ver. 42. ch. x. 37.
g John xvi. 33. Rom. v. 1 only.
h = ch. xx. 32. 1 Cor. viii. 1. x. 23. xiv. 4, 17. 1 Thess. v. 11.
i constr., ch. xiv. 16. Jude 11 only. Prov. xxviii. 26. see ch. xxi. 21. w. ἐν, Luke i. 6. 1 Pet. iv. 3. 2 Pet. ii. 10. Josh. xxii. 5 A Ald. compl.
k 2 Cor. v. 11 (reff.) only.
l = Rom. xii. 8 reff.
m ch. vi. 7 reff.

29. aft συνεζ. ins τε (but corrd) ℵ[1]. ελληνας A many vss(*Græcos*): vulg has *loquebatur quoque gentibus, et disputabat cum Græcis*, but am demid &c omit *gentibus* (*corrn from ch* xi. 20). rec αυτον bef ανελ., with HLP 13 rel: txt ABCEℵ a h m p [vulg] Chr$_1$.

30. for καισ., ιεροσολυμα A. add δια νυκτος E, νυκτος c 180 Syr syr-w-ast sah. om 2nd αυτον (*as unnecessary*) AE a[2] h: ins BCHLPℵ p rel.

31. rec **αι** μεν ουν εκκλησι**αι** [add πασαι E] &c ειχ**ον** . . οικοδομουμεν**αι**[-μενοι E] κ. πορευομεν**αι**[-μενοι E] &c επληθυν**ο**ντο (*see note*), with EHLP rel syr Chr$_1$ [Aug$_1$]: txt ABCℵ p 13 vulg Syr coptt æth arm Dion$_1$ Thl-fin.

saw John also (Gal. ii. 9). Perhaps he never saw in the flesh any other of the Apostles after his conversion. **διηγήσατο**] viz. Barnabas, not Saul. **29. Ἑλληνιστάς**] See ch. vi. 1 and note. This he did, partly, we may infer, to avoid the extreme and violent opposition which he would immediately encounter from the Jews themselves,—but partly also, it may well be believed, because he himself in the synagogues of the Hellenists had opposed Stephen formerly. **30. ἐπιγνόντες δὲ . . . .**] There was also another reason. He was praying in the temple, and saw the Lord in a vision, who commanded him to depart, for they would not receive his testimony:—and sent him from thence to the Gentiles: see ch. xxii. 17—21 and notes. His stay in Jerusalem at this visit was fifteen days, Gal. i. 18. **εἰς Καισάρειαν**] From the whole cast of the sentence, the κατήγαγον and ἐξαπέστειλαν, we should infer this to be Cæsarea Stratonis [see on ch. x. 1], even if this were not determined by the word Καισάρεια used absolutely, which always applies to this city, and not to Cæsarea Philippi (which De Dieu, Olsh., and others believe to be meant [see Matt. xvi. 13 and note]). From Gal. i. 21, it would appear that Saul about this time *traversed Syria* (on his way to Tarsus?). If so, he probably went by sea to Seleucia, and thence to Antioch. The ἐξαπέστειλαν looks more like a 'sending off' by sea, than a mere 'sending forward' by land. **εἰς Ταρσόν**] **towards**, 'for,' Tarsus. He was not idle there, but certainly preached the Gospel, and in all probability was the founder of the churches alluded to ch. xv. 23 and 41.

31.] Flourishing state of the church in Palestine at this time. Commencement of new section: compare μὲν οὖν, and note, ch. xi. 19. The reading **ἐκκλησία** can hardly (as Meyer) be an alteration to suit the idea of *the unity of the church*,—as in that case we should have similar alterations in ch. xv. 41; xvi. 5, where *no variations are found in the chief* mss. More probably, it has been altered here to conform it to those places. This description probably embraces most of the time since the conversion of Saul. De Wette observes, that the attention of the Jews was, during much of this time, distracted from the Christians, by the attempt of Caligula to set up his image in the temple at Jerusalem, Jos. Antt. xviii. 8. 2—9. **οἰκοδομουμένη**] See Matt. xvi. 18. It probably refers to both external and internal strength and accession of grace. Paul commonly uses it of *spiritual* building up: see reff. **πορ. τῷ φόβ.**] **walking in the fear**: for construction see reff.:—not '*following after the fear*' (Winer, edn. 2, § 31. 1; not in edn. 6, see § 31. 9),—nor 'walking *according to* the fear' as their *rule* (Meyer),—nor '*advancing* in the fear' (Beza, Wolf). **κ. τ. παρακλ. τ. ἁγ. πν. ἐπληθ.**] **And was multiplied** (reff.) **by the exhortation of** (i. e. inspired by) **the Holy Spirit**. This is the only rendering which suits the usage of the words. Those of the Vulg. 'consolatione replebantur,'—of Kuin., 'adjumento abundabant,' are un-

νετο δὲ Πέτρον [n] διερχόμενον διὰ πάντων [o] κατελθεῖν
καὶ πρὸς τοὺς [p] ἁγίους τοὺς [q] κατοικοῦντας Λύδδα.
33 εὗρεν δὲ ἐκεῖ ἄνθρωπόν τινα ὀνόματι Αἰνέαν [r] ἐξ ἐτῶν
ὀκτὼ [s] κατακείμενον ἐπὶ [t] κραβάττου, ὃς ἦν [u] παραλελυμένος. 34 καὶ εἶπεν αὐτῷ ὁ Πέτρος Αἰνέα, ἰᾶταί σε [v] Ἰησοῦς
ὁ χριστός· [w] ἀνάστηθι καὶ [x] στρῶσον σεαυτῷ. 35 καὶ
εὐθέως [w] ἀνέστη, καὶ εἶδαν αὐτὸν πάντες οἱ [q] κατοικοῦντες

n w. διά, Matt. xii. 43. 1 Cor. x. 1. 2 Cor. i. 16. Lev. xxvi. 5. (with acc., ch. xiii. 6 reff.)
o ch. viii. 5 reff.
p ver. 13.
q constr., ch. i. 19 reff.
r = Luke viii. 27 al. (3 Kings xviii. 12.)
s = Mark i. 30. ch. xxviii. 8. Prov. vi. 9.
t ch. v. 15 reff.
u ch. viii. 7 reff.
v ἰησ. ὁ χρ., here (ch. v. 42 v. r.) only. (ch. xviii. 5.)
w = ver. 6 reff.
x Mark xi. 8 bis || Mt. xiv. 15 || L. only. Job xvii. 13. Ezek. xxiii. 41. constr., here only. Esth. iv. 3.

32. rec λυδδαν (here and in ver 35 *alteration to an inflected form from the original* λυδδα: cf εις λυδδα παρελθων *Jos. B J* ii. 19. 1), with CEHL rel 36 Chr_1 : λυδαν P m 57 : txt ABℵ 13. 40. (13 def here.)—ℵ has εν λυδδα, but εν is marked for erasure by ℵ[1] or corr[1].

33. rec αιν. bef ονομ., with HLP rel 36 Chr_1 Thl-sif: om ονομ. 13 : txt ABCEℵ k m p vulg syrr arm (coptt æth) Thl-fin. rec κραββατω, with (EHL[P]) 13 rel Thl : txt ABCℵ p.—κραββατ. B[2] ; κραβαττ. AB[1]CEHLPℵ[3] : κραβακτ. ℵ[1].

34. ins ο κυρ. bef ιησ. A 15-8. 36. 40. 68 vulg[not fuld demid] sah æth arm $Thl\text{-}fin_1$ $Ambr_1$. om 2nd ο (*alteration to the Name* ιησ. χρ.) B[1](but "superadditur") Cℵ o 13 [Thl-fin] : ins AEHLP p rel Chr_1 [Thl-sif].

exampled, see reff. Neither must τῇ παρακλ. be coupled with τῷ φόβῳ, as in E. V., and by Beza and Rosenmüller, which would leave οἰκοδομ. standing by itself, and render the sentence totally unlike Luke's usual manner of writing.

32—35.] Healing of Æneas at Lydda by Peter. This and the following miracle form the introduction to the very important portion of Peter's history which follows in ch. x.,—by bringing him and his work before us again. **32. διερχόμ. δ. π.**] These words are aptly introduced by the notice in ver. 31, which shews that Peter's journey was not an escape from persecution, but undertaken at a time of peace, and for the purpose of visiting the churches. **πάντων** may be neuter, 'all parts:' but it is probably masc. and ἁγίων understood. Wieseler (p. 145, note) doubts whether we can say διέρχεσθαι διὰ πάντων τ. ἁγίων, —but see reff. The καί makes the masc. more likely, as it presupposes some ἅγιοι in the mind of the writer before. As I have implied on ver. 31, this journey of Peter's is not necessarily consecutive on the events of vv. 1—30. But an alternative presents itself here; either it took place *before the arrival* of Saul in Jerusalem, or *after his departure:* for Peter *was there during his visit* (Gal. i. 18). It seems most likely that it was *before his arrival.* For (1) it is Luke's manner in this first part of the Acts, where he is carrying on several histories together, to follow the one in hand as far as some resting-point, and then go back and take up another: see ch. viii. 2 thus taken up from ἀναιρέσει αὐτοῦ, ver. 1: ver. 4 going back to the διασπαρέντες:—ch. ix. 1 taken up from viii. 3:—xi. 19, from viii. 4 again:—and (2) the journey of Peter to visit the churches which were now resting after the persecution would hardly be delayed so long as three whole years. So that it is most natural to place this section, viz. ch. ix. 32—xi. 18 (for all this is continuous), *before the visit of Saul to Jerusalem,* and during his stay at Damascus or in Arabia. See further on xi. 19. **Λύδδα**] Lod, Neh. vii. 37. A large village near Joppa (ver. 38), on the Mediterranean (Jos. Antt. xx. 6. 2, κώμην τινὰ Λύδδαν λεγομ., πόλεως τὸ μέγεθος οὐκ ἀποδέουσαν), just one day's journey from Jerusalem (Lightf., Cent. Chor. Matth. præm. cxvi.). It afterwards became the important town of Diospolis. **33. Αἰνέαν**] Whether a believer or not, does not appear; from Peter's visit being to the *saints,* it would seem that he was: but perhaps the indefinite ἄνθρωπόν τινα may imply the contrary, as also Peter's words, announcing a free and unexpected gift from One whom he knew not. **34. στρῶσ. σεαυτ.**] Not '*for the future:*' but '*immediately,*' as a proof of his soundness. **35. πάντες . . . . οἵτινες**] Not '*all, who had turned to the Lord,*' as Kuin.: this would make the mention of the fact unmeaning,—and surely more would see him than the believers merely. The similar use of οἵτινες in the ref. shews its meaning to be *commensurate with the preceding* **πάντες**, and to gather them into a class, of which that which follows is predicated. **All that dwelt in L. and S. saw him;—which also (i. e. and they) turned to the Lord.** A general conversion of the inhabitants to

y so ch. xxiv. 1.
z ch. xxvi. 20 reff.
a here only +. Diog. Laert. iv. 2 (Att. -τρις).
b 1 Cor. xii. 30 reff.
c = Matt. x. 2. xxvi. 3. Col. iv. 11.
d = ch. xix. 28 reff.
e Paul only (Rom. ii. 7. xiii. 3 all.), exc. here and Heb. xiii. 21.
f plur., ch. x. 2, 4, 31. xxiv. 17 only. Dan. iv. 24 (27). see ch. iii. 2 reff.
g attr., ch. i. 1 reff.
h = Matt. x. 8 al. 2 Kings xiii. 4 A Ald. (-νῆς, B, F). (Ps. xxx. 10.)
i John xiii. 10. ch. xvi. 33. Heb. x. 22. 2 Pet. ii. 22. Rev. i. 5 only. Exod. ii. 5.
k ch. i. 13 reff. Acts only. 3 Kings xvii. 19.
l pres., ch. xvi. 38 reff.
m = ch. xi. 23 al. fr.
n here only. Num. xxii. 16.
o w. ἕως, Luke ii. 15. ch. xi. 19, 22 only. Gen. xxii. 5.

Λύδδα καὶ τὸν Σάρωνα, [y] οἵτινες [z] ἐπέστρεψαν [z] ἐπὶ τὸν ABCEH
[z] κύριον. 36 Ἐν Ἰόππῃ δέ τις ἦν [a] μαθήτρια ὀνόματι LPℵ a b
Ταβιθά, ἣ [b] διερμηνευομένη [c] λέγεται Δορκάς· αὕτη ἦν c d f g h
[d] πλήρης [e] ἀγαθῶν [e] ἔργων καὶ [f] ἐλεημοσυνῶν [g] ὧν ἐποίει. k l m o
37 ἐγένετο δὲ ἐν ταῖς ἡμέραις ἐκείναις [h] ἀσθενήσασαν αὐτὴν p 13
ἀποθανεῖν· [i] λούσαντες δὲ αὐτὴν ἔθηκαν ἐν [k] ὑπερῴῳ.
38 ἐγγὺς δὲ οὔσης Λύδδας τῇ Ἰόππῃ οἱ μαθηταὶ ἀκούσαντες ὅτι Πέτρος [l] ἐστὶν ἐν αὐτῇ ἀπέστειλαν δύο ἄνδρας
πρὸς αὐτὸν [m] παρακαλοῦντες Μὴ [n] ὀκνήσῃς [o] διελθεῖν

35. (ειδαν, so AB : ειδα C.) om τον ℵ[1]. Steph σαρωνᾶν (*corrn with the same view as* λυδδαν ; *but seeing* τον *before it, the transcriber could not make it an accus. fem., and has therefore made it a masc from* σαρωνας, *not seeing that it was already an accus from* σαρων), with b[1] c k p 36 : ασσαρωναν f : ασσαρωνα HL a b[2] g h l o 13 Chr_1, ασαρωνα P e 106[1] : txt BCE d m (coptt) Thl-fin : σαρρωνα [A(over an erasure)] ℵ.

36. εργ. bef αγ. BCE m 13 vulg spec [Bas_1] : txt AHL[P]ℵ rel Chr_2 Thl.

37. εθηκ. bef αυτ. Aℵ[1] p 40 : om αυτ. B : txt CEHL[P]ℵ[3] 13 rel Chr. ins τω bef υπερ. ACE a h o $Orig_1$: om BHLPℵ p rel Chr_1.

38. rec λυδδης, with B[2]EHLP rel 36 [Bas_1 Chr_1] : λυδδας Aℵ[1] (*possibly the original as* ABℵ *agree in* λυδδα *vv* 32, 35) : txt B[1]C[ℵ[3]] p. (13 def.) [aft οι ins δε H.] om δυο ανδρ. HLP a b d f g h l o Chr_1 Thl-sif. rec οκνησαι δ. ε. αυτων (*alteration to avoid the harshness of the direct constr with* παρακ. *Meyer thinks the direct constr has been written in the marg and found its way into the text*), with C[3](appy) HLP 13. 36 rel syrr [æth arm Bas_1] Chr : txt ABC[1]Eℵ p vulg spec [coptt]. (οκνησ(. .) p.)

the faith followed. **τὸν Σάρωνα**] Perhaps not a village, but (and the art. makes this probable) the celebrated *plain* of that name, extending along the coast from Cæsarea to Joppa, see Isa. xxxiii. 9; xxxv. 2; lxv. 10; Cant. ii. 1; 1 Chron. xxvii. 29; and Jerome on Isa. xxxiii. and lxv., vol. iv., pp. 436, 780. Mariti (Travels, p. 350) mentions a village Saren between Lydda and Arsuf (see Josh. xii. 18, marg. E. V.): but more recent travellers do not notice it. See Winer, Realw., where other places of the same name are mentioned.

36—43.] Raising of Tabitha from the dead. **36. ἐν Ἰόππῃ**] Joppa was a very ancient Philistian city, on the frontier of Dan, but not belonging to that tribe, Josh. xix. 46; on the coast (ch. x. 6), with a celebrated but not very secure harbour (Jos. B. J. iii. 9. 3: see 2 Chron. ii. 16; Ezra iii. 7; Jonah i. 3; 1 Macc. xiv. 5; 2 Macc. xii. 3),—situated in a plain (1 Macc. x. 75—77) near Lydda (ver. 38), at the end of the mountain road connecting Jerusalem with the sea. The Maccabean generals, Jonathan and Simon, took it from the Syrians and fortified it (1 Macc. x. 74—76; xiv. 5, 34. Jos. Antt. xiii. 9. 2). Pompey joined it to the province of Syria (Antt. xiv. 4. 4), but Cæsar restored it to Hyrcanus (xiv. 10. 6), and it afterwards formed part of the kingdom of Herod (xv. 7. 3) and of Archelaus (xvii. 11. 4), after whose deposition it reverted to the province of Syria, to which it belonged at the time of our narrative. It was destroyed by C. Cestius (Jos. B. J. ii. 18. 10); but rebuilt, and became a nest of Jewish pirates (Strabo, xvi. 759), in consequence of which Vespasian levelled it with the ground, and built a fort there (B. J. iii. 9. 3, 4), which soon became the nucleus of a new town. It is now called Jaffa (Ἰάφα, Anna Comnena, Alex. ii. p. 328), and has about 7000 inhabitants, half of whom are Christians. (Winer, Realw.)

Ταβιθά] טְבִיתָא, in Aramaic, answering to צְבִי Heb., δορκάς (Æl. Hist. An. xiv. 14), a gazelle. It appears also in the Rabbinical books as a female name (Lightf.): the gazelle being in the East a favourite type of beauty. See Cant. ii. 9, 17; iv. 5; vii. 3. Lightf. remarks, that she was probably a Hellenist, and thus was known by both names. **37. ἐν ὑπερῴῳ**] No art., as in the expressions εἰς οἶκον, 'on deck,' &c., which usually occur after prepositions, cf. Middl. ch. vi. § 1. See 1 Kings xvii. 19.

...αι χηραι H.
ABCEL Pℵ a b c d f g h k l m o p 13

ἕως ἡμῶν. 39 p ἀναστὰς δὲ Πέτρος q συνῆλθεν αὐτοῖς· ὃν
r παραγενόμενον s ἀνήγαγον εἰς τὸ k ὑπερῷον, καὶ t παρέστησαν αὐτῷ πᾶσαι αἱ u χῆραι κλαίουσαι καὶ v ἐπιδεικ-
νύμεναι w χιτῶνας καὶ ἱμάτια ὅσα ἐποίει x μετ᾽ αὐτῶν οὖσα
ἡ Δορκάς. 40 y ἐκβαλὼν δὲ ἔξω πάντας ὁ Πέτρος καὶ
z θεὶς τὰ z γόνατα a προσηύξατο, καὶ b ἐπιστρέψας πρὸς τὸ
c σῶμα εἶπεν Ταβιθά, d ἀνάστηθι. ἡ δὲ e ἤνοιξεν τοὺς
e ὀφθαλμοὺς αὐτῆς, καὶ ἰδοῦσα τὸν Πέτρον f ἀνεκάθισεν.
41 g δοὺς δὲ αὐτῇ g χεῖρα h ἀνέστησεν αὐτήν· i φωνήσας δὲ
τοὺς j ἁγίους καὶ τὰς u χήρας k παρέστησεν αὐτὴν ζῶσαν.
42 l γνωστὸν δὲ ἐγένετο m καθ᾽ m ὅλης τῆς Ἰόππης, καὶ n ἐπίστευσαν πολλοὶ n ἐπὶ τὸν κύριον. 43 ἐγένετο δὲ o ἡμέρας
o ἱκανὰς pq μεῖναι αὐτὸν ἐν Ἰόππῃ p παρά τινι Σίμωνι r βυρσεῖ.
X. 1 Ἀνὴρ δέ τις ἐν Καισαρείᾳ ὀνόματι Κορνήλιος, s ἑκα-

p ch. viii. 26 reff. q = ch. i. 21 reff. r absol., ch. xvii. 10 reff. s = Luke iv. 5. ch. xvi. 34. (Luke only, exc. Matt. iv. 1. Rom. x. 7. Heb. xiii. 20.) t = ch. iv. 10 reff. u Mark xii. 40. ch. v. 1. 1 Cor. vii. 8. 1 Tim. v. 3, &c. Ps. lxxvii. 64. v mid., here only. 2 Macc. xv. 32. (ch. xviii. 28.) w Matt. v. 40 al. Gen. xxxvii. 3. x = Matt. xvii. 17. John xiv. 9 al. y Mark v. 40. John vi. 37. Rev. xi. 2. 2 Chron. xxiii. 14. z ch. vii. 60 reff. a abs., ver. 12. b = ch. xvi. 18. w. πρός, Luke xvii. 4. 2 Cor. iii. 16. 1 Thess. i. 9. Ezek. xlii. 18. c Acts, here only. = Matt. xxvii. 52, &c. ‖. Jude 9. Josh. viii. 29. d = ver. 34. e ver. 8. Matt. ix. 30. 4 Kings iv. 35. f Luke vii. 15 only †. g here only. 4 Kings x. 15. h trans., = here only. see ch. ii. 24 reff. i = ch. x. 7. John i. 49. ii. 9 al. Tobit v. 8 (not ℵ). j ver. 13. k ch. i. 3 reff. l ch. i. 19 reff. m ver. 31 reff. n ch. xi. 17 al2. Rom. iv. 5, 24. L.P. Wisd. xii. 2. see Heb. vi. 1. o ver. 23 reff. p = John i. 39. ch. xvi. 15. Gen. xxiv. 55. q = ch. xxi. 7, 8 reff. r ch. x. 6, 32 only †. (-σα, Job xvi. 16.) s -χης, Matt. viii. 13. ch. xxiv. 23 al. -χος, Matt. viii. 5, &c. ch. xxvii. 6 al. Matt. Luke only. = κεντυρίων, Mark xv. 39, &c.

39. ins ο bef πετρος C c o 130 [Bas$_1$]. περιεστησαν [so Bas$_1$] αυτον c vulg E-lat spec Chr$_1$.

40. παντας bef εξω C m vulg spec [syrr] : om εξω e. rec om 1st και, with LP 13 rel vss Chr Thl-sif : ins ABCEℵ p [Syr] copt Thl-fin. ins παραχρημα bef ηνοιξεν E sah, bef ιδουσα æth-pl.

41. for 1st δε, τε A c [spec] Syr æth.

42. om της BC¹ : ins AC³ELPℵ rel Chr$_1$. rec πολλ. bef επιστ., with LP 13. 36 rel [syrr] Chr$_1$: txt ABCEℵ m p 40 vulg spec [coptt æth] arm.

43. for ικανας, τινας C 36. αυτον bef ημερας ικ. μ. AEℵ³ a h p 40 : om αυτ. Bℵ¹ b : txt CLP 13. 36 rel Chr$_1$. [om εν ιοππη L.]

CHAP. X. 1. rec aft τις ins ην (*corrn, see ch* ix. 36 ; *not observing that the constr is carried on to* ειδεν, *ver* 3), with P rel vss Thl : om ABCELℵ p 13. 36 E-lat Chr$_1$.

39. **πᾶσαι αἱ χ.**] The widows of the place, for whom she made these garments. **ἐποίει**] '*was making,*' i. e. used to make (i. e. weave) : not '*had made.*' 40. **ἐκβαλών**] After the example of his divine Master, see ref. Mark. 43. **βυρσεῖ**] From the extracts in Wetstein and Schöttgen, it appears that the Jews regarded the occupation of a tanner as a half-unclean one. In this case it would shew, as De W. observes, that the *stricter* Jewish practices were already disregarded by the Apostle. It also would shew, in how little honour he and his office were held by the Jews at Cæsarea.

CHAP. X. 1—48.] CONVERSION (BY SPECIAL DIVINE PREARRANGEMENT) AND BAPTISM OF THE GENTILE CORNELIUS AND HIS PARTY. We may remark, that the conversion of the Gentiles was *no new idea* to Jews or Christians, but that it had been universally regarded as to take place *by their reception into Judaism.* Of late, however, since the Ascension, we see the truth that the Gospel was to be a Gospel of the *uncircumcision*, beginning to be recognized by some. Stephen, carrying out the principles of his own apology, could hardly have failed to recognize it: and the Cyprian and Cyrenæan missionaries of ch. xi. 20 preached the word πρὸς τοὺς Ἕλληνας (not -ιστάς), *certainly before the conversion of Cornelius.* This state of things might have given rise to a permanent schism in the infant church. The Hellenists, and perhaps Saul, with his definite mission to the Gentiles, might have formed one party, and the Hebrews, with Peter at their head, the other. But, as Neander admirably observes (Pfl. u. Leit. p. 111), 'The pernicious influence with which, from the first, the self-seeking and one-sided prejudices of human nature threatened the divine work, was counter-

τοντάρχης ἐκ [t] σπείρης τῆς καλουμένης Ἰταλικῆς, 2 [u] εὐσεβὴς καὶ [v] φοβούμενος τὸν θεὸν σὺν παντὶ τῷ [w] οἴκῳ αὐτοῦ, [x] ποιῶν [y] ἐλεημοσύνας πολλὰς τῷ λαῷ καὶ [z] δεό-

ABCEL Pℵ a b c d f g h k l m o p 13

t Matt. xxvii. 27 ‖ Mk. John xviii. 3, 12. ch. xxi. 31. xxvii. 1 only †. Judith xiv. 11. 2 Macc. viii. 23. xii. 20, 22 only. u ver. 7. 2 Pet. ii. 9 only. Isa. xxiv. 16. (see ch. iii. 12 reff.) v = vv. 22, 35. ch. xiii. 16, 26 al. Prov. iii. 7. w = ch. vii. 10. xi. 14. xvi. 15, 31 al. Gen. vii. 1. x = Matt. vi. 1, 2. ch. ix. 36. xxiv. 17. Tobit xii. 9. y ch. ix. 36 reff. z absol. w. gen., here only. Job v. 8. see ch. iv. 31. 1 Thess. iii. 10.

om εκατονταρχ. L. σπειρας BP a b² g h¹ l o Chr.

2. rec aft ποιων ins τε, with LP 13 rel [syr] æth-pl Thl [Iren-int$_1$]: om ABCEℵ p 40 vulg Syr [coptt arm] æth-rom Chr$_1$ [Damasc-ms$_1$].

acted by the superior influence of the Holy Spirit, which did not allow the differences of men to reach such a point of antagonism, but enabled them to retain unity in variety. We recognize the preventing wisdom of God,—which, while giving scope to the free agency of man, knows how to interpose His immediate revelation just at the moment when it is requisite for the success of the divine work,—by noticing, that when the Apostles needed this wider development of their Christian knowledge for the exercise of their vocation, and when the lack of it would have been exceedingly detrimental,—*at that very moment*, by a remarkable coincidence of inward revelation with a chain of outward circumstances, the illumination hitherto wanting was imparted to them.'

1. **Καισαρείᾳ**] As this town bears an important part in early Christian history, it will be well to give here a full account of it. CÆSAREA (Palestinæ, Καισάρεια τῆς Παλαιστίνης, called παράλιος, Jos. B. J. iii. 9. 1; vii. 2. 2; Antt. xiii. 11. 2, or ἡ ἐπὶ θαλάττῃ K., Jos. B. J. vii. 1. 3; 2. 1, or Stratonis (see below),—distinguished from Cæsarea Philippi, see note Matt. xvi. 13) is between Joppa and Dora, 68 Rom. miles from Jerusalem according to the Jerus. Itinerary, 75 according to Josephus (i. e. 600 stadia, Antt. xiii. 11. 2. B. J. i. 3. 5),—36 miles (Abulfeda) from Ptolemais (a day's journey, ch. xxi. 8),—30 from Joppa (Edrisi);—one of the largest towns in Palestine (Jos. B. J. iii. 9. 1), with an excellent haven (Jos. Antt. xvii. 5. 1, Σεβαστὸς λιμήν,—ὃν κατασκευάσας Ἡρώδης πολλῶν χρημάτων ἐπὶ τιμῇ τῇ Καίσαρος καλεῖ Σεβαστόν). It was, even before the destruction of Jerusalem, the seat of the Roman Procurators (see ch. xxiii. 23 ff.; xxiv. 27; xxv. 1), and called by Tacitus (Hist. ii. 79) 'Judææ caput.' It was chiefly inhabited by Gentiles (Jos. B. J. iii. 9. 1; ii. 14. 4), but there were also many thousand Jewish inhabitants (Jos. B. J. ii. 18. 1; Antt. xx. 8. 7; Life, 11). It was built by Herod the Great (Amm. Marcell. xiv. 8, p. 29, Bipont. Beforetime there was only a fort there, called Στράτωνος πύργος, Jos. Antt. xv. 9. 6 al.; Strabo, xvi. 758; Plin. v. 14)—fortified, provided with a haven (see ch. ix. 30; xviii. 22; Joseph. above), and in honour of Cæsar Augustus named Cæsarea (at length Καισάρεια Σεβαστή, Jos. Antt. xvi. 5. 1). Vespasian made it a Roman colony (Plin. v. 13). Abulfeda (Syr. p. 80) speaks of it as in ruins in his time (A.D. 1300). At present there are a few ruins only, and some fishers' huts. (From Winer, Realw.) **ἑκατοντάρχης**] The subordinate officer commanding the sixth part of a cohort = half a maniple. See Dict. of Gr. and Roman Antt. **σπ. τ. καλ. Ἰταλ.**] *A cohort* (σπ.) *levied in Italy, not in Syria.* Mr. Humphry quotes from Gruter, Inscr. i. p. 434, 'Cohors militum Italicorum voluntaria, quæ est in Syria.' Biscoe (Hist. of the Acts, pp. 217—221) maintains that this was an independent cohort, not one attached to a legion. The *legio Italica* (Tacit. Hist. i. 59, 64; ii. 100; iii. 22) was not raised till Nero's time.

2. **εὐσ. κ. φοβ. τ. θ.**] i. e. he had abandoned polytheism, and was a worshipper of the true God: whether a proselyte of the gate, or not, seems uncertain. * That he *may* have been such, there is nothing in the narrative to preclude: nor does Meyer's objection apply, that it is not probable that, among the many thousand converts, no Greek proselyte had yet been admitted by baptism into the church. Many such cases may have occurred, and some no doubt had: but the object of this providential interference seems to have been, to give *solemn sanction* to such reception, by the agency of him who was both the chief of the Apostles, and the strong upholder of pure Judaism. It is hardly possible that μαρτυρούμενος ὑπὸ ὅλου τοῦ ἔθνους τῶν Ἰουδαίων (ver. 22) should have been said of a Gentile not in any way conformed to the Jewish faith and worship. The great point (ch. xi. 3) which made the present event so important, was, that Cornelius was ἀνὴρ **ἀκροβυστίαν ἔχων**. Doubtless also among his *company* (ver. 24) there must have been many who were *not proselytes.* **τῷ λαῷ**] The Jewish inhabitants, see ch. xxvi. 17, 23; xxviii. 17; John xi. 50; xviii. 14 al.

μενος τοῦ θεοῦ [a] διὰ παντός, 3 εἶδεν ἐν [b] ὁράματι [c] φανερῶς,
[d] ὡσεὶ περὶ [ef] ὥραν ἐνάτην τῆς [f] ἡμέρας, ἄγγελον τοῦ θεοῦ
εἰσελθόντα πρὸς αὐτὸν καὶ εἰπόντα αὐτῷ Κορνήλιε. 4 ὁ δὲ
[g] ἀτενίσας αὐτῷ καὶ [h] ἔμφοβος γενόμενος εἶπεν Τί ἐστιν,
κύριε; εἶπεν δὲ αὐτῷ Αἱ [i] προσευχαί σου καὶ αἱ [y] ἐλεημοσύναι σου [k] ἀνέβησαν [l] εἰς [m] μνημόσυνον [n] ἔμπροσθεν τοῦ
θεοῦ. 5 καὶ νῦν πέμψον ἄνδρας εἰς Ἰόππην καὶ [o] μετάπεμψαι Σίμωνά τινα ὃς [p] ἐπικαλεῖται Πέτρος· 6 οὗτος
[q] ξενίζεται [r] παρά τινι Σίμωνι [s] βυρσεῖ, ᾧ ἐστιν οἰκία [t] παρὰ
θάλασσαν. 7 ὡς δὲ ἀπῆλθεν ὁ ἄγγελος ὁ λαλῶν αὐτῷ,

a ch. ii. 25 reff. b ch. vii. 31 reff. c = here (Mark i. 45. John vii. 10) only †. d = Luke xxiii. 44. Judg. iii. 29. e acc. (w. περί), Matt. xx. 3, 5, 6, 9. xxvii. 46 only †. (without περί) John iv. 52. Rev. iii. 3 al. Josh. xi. 6. f ch. ii. 15 only †. ὥ. νυκτός, ch. xvi. 33. xxiii. 23 only †. g ch. iii. 12 reff. h Luke xxiv. 5, 37. ch. [xxii. 9] xxiv. 25. Rev. xi. 13 only. 1 Macc. xiii. 2 B Ald. (ἔκφ., Aℵ compl.) Sir. xix. 24 only. i plur., ch. ii. 42 al.† k — here only. Exod. ii. 23. 1 Macc. v. 31. see ch. xxi. 31. l = ch. xix. 27. Rom. iv. 3, &c. (from Gen. xv. 6) al. m Matt. xxvi. 13 ‖ Mk. only. Exod. xii. 14. Tobit xii. 12. n = Luke x. 21. 1 Thess. i. 3 al. (1 Kings xviii. 13.) o vv. 22, 29 bis. ch. xi. 13. xxiv. 24, 26. xxv. 3 only. Gen. xxvii. 45. Num. xxiii. 7. 2 Macc. xv. 31 only. p ch. i. 23 reff. q pass. = vv. 18, 32. ch. xxi. 16 (1 Pet. iv. 4, 12) only †. act., ver. 23 reff. r = Luke xi. 37. John i. 40. ch. xxi. 7, 16. s ch. ix. 43 reff. t Matt. xiii. 1. Mark v. 21. Heb. xi. 12 al. Num. xiii. 30. 3 Kings iv. 29.

3. for ειδεν, ωεδεν (but ω marked for erasure) ℵ[1]. om εν ℵ. rec om περι (*as unnecessary; this is much more probable than Meyer's suppn that* περι *was a gloss on* ωσει: *comp* περι ωρ. εκτ., *ver* 9), with LP rel [vulg æth] (Chr$_2$): ins ABCEℵ k o [p] 13. 36. 40 [syrr copt] Damasc[-ms$_1$ Iren-int$_1$].—περι, omg ωσει, c d 3. 65-7 (sah arm?).—ως ℵ[1] [p] 36. 40 Damasc[-ms$_1$]. rec εννατην, with L 13 rel: txt ABCEPℵ a b g h k l m p.

4. om 2nd αι C a d[1] m p [Damasc-ms$_1$]. om εις μνημοσυνον ℵ[1] [Damasc-ms$_1$]. rec ενωπιον (*substitution for the less usual* εμπροσθεν), with CELP 13 rel Sevrn$_1$ Chr$_1$: txt ABℵ p 36. 40.

5. rec εις ιοπ. bef ανδρ., with LP 13. 36 rel Chr$_1$: txt ABCEℵ m p vulg D-lat syrr coptt [æth] arm. rec om τινα (*corrn from* respect *to the Apostle. This is much more prob than Meyer's supposn, that* τινα *was inserted to conform the first* σιμ. *to the other. The same considerations have led to the var read in ver* 32), with ELPℵ 13 rel demid D-lat Syr sah [æth] (Orig$_1$) Chr$_1$ Iren-int$_1$: ins ABC p 36 vulg syr-mg copt arm. τον επικαλουμενον πετρον (*corrn from ch* xi. 13? *or or.gl, and* ος επικαλειται *a corrn from ver* 32? *the manuscript authority must decide*) ELP 13 rel Thl: txt ABCℵ a h p 36 Chr$_1$.

6. σιμωνι bef τινι C m [vulg arm]: om τινι D-lat [æth-pl]. ins η bef οικια C lect-12. rec aft θαλ. adds ουτος λαλησει σοι τι σε δει ποιειν (*interpolation from ver* 32, *and ch* ix. 6, *combined: see also ch* xi. 14), with [m-marg-recent] (36?) [vulg-ed] demid æth-rom Thl-fin; ος λαλησει ρημ. προς σε . . . to οικος σου from ch xi. 14 4-marg 8. 26-7. 73. 81 copt[-wilk]; ος λαλησει σοι 133: om ABCELPℵ p rel vss Chr$_1$ Thl-sif.

7. om 2nd ο LP g m lect-26. rec τω κορνηλιω (*explanatory corrn for* αυτω),

δεόμενος τ. θεοῦ διὰ π.] From Cornelius's own narrative, ver. 31, as well as from the analogy of God's dealings, we are certainly justified in inferring, with Neander, that the subject of his prayers was that he might be guided into truth, and if so, hardly without reference to that faith which was now spreading so widely over Judæa. This is not matter of conjecture, but is implied by Peter's οἴδατε τὸ γενόμ. ῥῆμα καθ' ὅλης τῆς Ἰουδαίας. Further than this, we cannot infer with certainty; but, if *the particular difficulty present in his mind* be sought, we can hardly avoid the conclusion that it was connected with the apparent necessity of embracing Judaism and circumcision in order to become a believer on Christ. **3. ἐν ὁράμ. φανερῶς**] not in a *trance*, as ver. 10, and ch. xxii. 17, —but *with his bodily eyes*: thus asserting the objective truth of the appearance. **ὡσεὶ περὶ ὥρ. ἐν.**] It here appears that C. observed the Jewish hours of prayer. **4. εἰς μνημ.**] Not *instar sacrificii* (Ps. cxli. 2) as Grot.: but, as E. V., **for a memorial**, '*so as to be a memorial.*' There has been found a difficulty by some in the fact that Cornelius's works were received as well pleasing to God, before he had justifying faith in Christ. But it is surely easy to answer, with Calvin and Augustine, 'non potuisse orare Cornelium, nisi fidelis esset.' His faith was all that he could then attain to, and brought forth its fruits abundantly in his life: one of which fruits, and the best of them, was, the earnest seeking by prayer for a better and more perfect faith. **7. ἀπῆλθεν**] So in

u ch. ix. 41 reff. v Luke xvi. 13. Rom. xiv. 4. 1 Pet. ii. 18 only. Gen. xliv. 33. w ver. 2 reff. x ch. i. 14 reff. y ch. xv. 12, 14 reff. z John i. 29, &c. ch. xiv. 20 al. Exod. xxxii. 6. a here only †. (-ρία, 2 Cor. xi. 26. -ρος, Gen. xxxvii. 24.) b dat., ch. ix. 3 reff.

ABCEL Pℵ a b c d f g h k l m o p 13

[u] φωνήσας δύο τῶν [v] οἰκετῶν καὶ στρατιώτην [w] εὐσεβῆ τῶν
[x] προςκαρτερούντων αὐτῷ, 8 καὶ [y] ἐξηγησάμενος ἅπαντα
αὐτοῖς, ἀπέστειλεν αὐτοὺς εἰς τὴν Ἰόππην. 9 τῇ δὲ
[z] ἐπαύριον [a] ὁδοιπορούντων ἐκείνων καὶ τῇ πόλει [b] ἐγγι-
ζόντων [c] ἀνέβη Πέτρος ἐπὶ τὸ [d] δῶμα [e] προσεύξασθαι περὶ
ὥραν ἕκτην. 10 ἐγένετο δὲ [f] πρόςπεινος, καὶ ἤθελεν [g] γεύσασθαι. [h] παρασκευαζόντων δὲ αὐτῶν [i] ἐγένετο ἐπ᾽ αὐτὸν
[k] ἔκστασις, 11 καὶ [l] θεωρεῖ τὸν [m] οὐρανὸν [n] ἀνεῳγμένον καὶ
[n] καταβαῖνον [o] σκεῦός τι ὡς [p] ὀθόνην μεγάλην, τέσσαρσιν

c = Luke v. 19. Josh. ii. 8. 4 Kings ix. 17. d Matt. x. 27 ||. xxiv. 17 ||. Luke v. 19 only. 2 Kings xi. 2. e absol., ch. ix. 12. xx. 36. f here only †. g = ch. xx. 11. Jonah iii. 7. Jos. Antt. vi. 14. 3. h 1 Cor. xiv. 8. 2 Cor. ix. 2, 3 only. 2 Macc. ii. 27. i = ch. v. 5 reff. 2 Chron. xiv. 14. xx. 29. k = ch. xi. 5. xxii. 17 only. (ch. iii. 10 reff.) Gen. ii. 21. xv. 12. l ch. vii. 56 reff. m Matt. iii. 10 || L. Rev. xix. 11. Ezek. i. 1. see ch. vii. 56. n = Matt. iii. 16. John i. 52. vi. 33 al. Gen. xxviii. 12. o Mark xi. 16. John xix. 29. Exod. iii. 22. p ch. xi. 5 only †. (-νιον, John xix. 40. Hos. ii. 9.)

with LP 13 rel syr Chr: [om copt:] txt ABCEℵ p vulg Syr [sah] æth arm. rec aft οικ. ins αυτου (*explanatory*), with LP 13. 36 rel vss Chr: om ABCEℵ p 40 arm.

8. rec αυτοις bef απαντα, with CLP 13. 36 rel [syrr æth] Chr_1: *illis visum* D-lat: txt ABEℵ p coptt.

9. for εκειν., αυτων (*corrn to correspond with* αυτοις *above*) AELℵ d k o p 13. 36: αυ. εκ. c: txt BCP rel Chr_1. for εκτην, ενατην $ℵ^3$ [36]. aft εκτ. ins της ημερας A tol.

10. rec (for αυτων) εκεινων (*probably from* εκεινων *having been in the margin in some* MSS *at ver* 9, *and thus inserted here by mistake, or as in note*), with LP rel Chr_1: txt ABCEℵ p 13. 36 $Orig_1$. rec επεπεσεν (*corrn to avoid the repetition of* εγενετο, *and to the more usual word, see ch* viii. 16 *reff. Meyer holds* επεπ. *to have been origl: but being usually said of* πνευμα, *and thus seeming inappropriate to* εκστασις, *to have been altered in conformity with ch* xxii. 17, γενεσθαι με εν εκστασει. *But this is very careless: for, Luke* i. 12, *we have* φοβος επεπ. επ αυτ., *and so ch* xix. 17: *and* xiii. 11, επεπ. επ αυτον αχλυς), with EL 13 rel vss Chr: (επεσεν 19. 78. 96 Clem:) txt ABCPℵ d p 36 copt $Orig_1$. [εκστ. bef επ αυτ. C coptt $Orig_1$.]

11. rec aft καταβαιν. ins επ αυτον (al αυτω) (*inserted to correspond with* αχρις εμου, *ch* xi. 5), with LP rel D-lat Chr_1 Thl: om $ABC^2Eℵ$ c p 13 vulg syrr coptt æth [arm] $Orig_2[int_1]$. (C^1 has perished.) om μεγαλην C^2.

Luke i. 38:—another token of the objective reality of the vision: εἰςελθόντα (ver. 3) and ἀπῆλθ. denoting the *real acts* of the angel, not the mere deemings of Cornelius. **λαλῶν** must be regarded as the imperfect participle, as in John ix. 8.

9.] By **δῶμα**, Jerome, Luther, Erasm., al., understand an upper chamber. But why not then ὑπερῷον, a word which Luke so frequently uses? It was the flat roof, much frequented in the East for purposes of exercise (2 Sam. xi. 2; Dan. iv. 29, marg.),—of sleeping in summer (1 Sam. ix. 26, by inference, and as expressed in LXX),—of conversation (ib. ver. 25),—of mourning (Isa. xv. 3; Jer. xlviii. 38),—of erecting booths at the feast of tabernacles (Neh. viii. 16),—of other religious celebrations (2 Kings xxiii. 12; Jer. xix. 13; Zeph. i. 5),—of publicity (2 Sam. xvi. 22; Matt. x. 27; Luke xii. 3. Jos. B. J. ii. 21. 5),—of observation (Judg. xvi. 27; Isa. xxii. 1),—and for any process requiring fresh air and sun (Josh. ii. 6). (Winer, Realw., art. Dach.) **ἕκτην**] The *second hour of prayer:* also of the mid-day meal. The distance was thirty Roman miles, part of which they performed on the preceding evening, perhaps to Apollonia,—and the rest that morning. **10. γεύσ.**] see reff. ἐκείνων is more likely to have been a correction of αὐτῶν as applying better to the people of the house, than the converse. **ἔκστασις**] The distinction of this appearance from the ὅραμα above (though the usage is not always strictly observed) is, that in this case that which was seen was a revelation *shewn* to the eye of the beholder when rapt into a supernatural state, having, as is the case in a dream, *no objective reality:* whereas, in the other case, the thing seen *actually happened*, and was beheld by the person as an ordinary spectator, in the possession of his natural senses. **11. τέσσ. ἀρχ.**] not, '*by the four corners,*' which would certainly require the article, as in reff.,—but **by four rope-ends.** This meaning of ἀρχή is justified by Diod. Sic. i. p. 104, who, speaking of harpooning the hippopotamus, says, εἶθ᾽

[q] ἀρχαῖς [δεδεμένον καὶ] [r] καθιέμενον ἐπὶ τῆς γῆς, 12 ἐν
ᾧ [s] ὑπῆρχεν πάντα τὰ [tu] τετράποδα καὶ [tvw] ἑρπετὰ τῆς γῆς
καὶ [tvx] πετεινὰ τοῦ [x] οὐρανοῦ. 13 καὶ [y] ἐγένετο φωνὴ
πρὸς αὐτόν, [z] Ἀναστὰς Πέτρε [a] θῦσον καὶ φάγε. 14 ὁ δὲ
D παν … Πέτρος εἶπεν [b] Μηδαμῶς κύριε· ὅτι [c] οὐδέποτε ἔφαγον [c] πᾶν
ABCDE LPℵ a b c d f g h k l m o p 13 [d] κοινὸν καὶ [e] ἀκάθαρτον. 15 καὶ φωνὴ [f] πάλιν [fg] ἐκ δευτέρου
πρὸς αὐτόν, Ἃ ὁ θεὸς [h] ἐκαθάρισεν σὺ μὴ [i] κοίνου.

q = ch. xi. 5 only. (Exod. xxviii. 23 compl. F (not AB). Ezek. xlviii. 1.) see note.
r ch. ix. 25 reff.
s ch. viii. 16 reff.
t ch. xi. 6. Rom. i. 23.
u as above (t) only. Gen. i. 24.
v as above (t). James iii. 7. Gen. vi. 7.
w as above (t u) only.
x Matt. vi. 26. viii. 20 ||. xiii. 32 ||. Luke viii. 5. xiii. 19. ch. xi. 6. Gen. i. 26.
y ch. viii. 31 reff.
z ch. viii. 26 reff. Dan. vii. 5.
a = Matt. xxii. 4. Luke xv. 23, 27, 30. John x. 10. ch. xi. 7 only. Deut. xii. 15. (ch. xiv. 13 reff.)
b ch. xi. 8 only. Ezek. iv. 14.
c constr., Rom. iii. 20 reff.
d = Mark vii. 2, 5. ver. 28. ch. xi. 8. Rom. xiv. 14 (3ce). Heb. x. 29. Rev. xxi. 27 only ‡. 1 Macc. i. 62.
e = ver. 28. ch. xi. 8. 1 Cor. vii. 14. 2 Cor. vi. 17. Rev. xviii. 2. (elsewh. always with πνεῦμα [ch. v. 16 reff.], exc. Eph. v. 5.) Judg. xiii. 14.
f Matt. xxvi. 42 only †.
g as above (f). Mark xiv. 72. John ix. 24. ch. xi. 9. Heb. ix. 28 only. Jer. i. 13.
h = ch. xi. 9. Heb. ix. 22, 23. see ch. xv. 8.
i = ch. xi. 9 (xxi. 28 reff.) only †.

om δεδεμενον και ABC²Eℵ 40 vulg æth arm $Orig_4$ Cyr_1 $Thdrt_1$: ins (C¹ perhaps) LP p rel 36 (D-lat syrr coptt) Chr_1.—transp καταβαινον and δεδεμενον c 13 [(syrr)].—also c has τεσσαρσιν αρχαις immediately aft ανεωγ. και ; 13, at end of ver.—καταβαινον is omd by lect-12 D-lat syrr sah ; these vss have other varns, e. g. *cœlum apertum ex quattuor principiis ligatum vas quodam et*(sic) *linteum splendidum quod differebatur de cœlo in terram* D-lat.

12. rec της γης bef 1st και (τετραποδα της γης : *see ch* xi. 6), with LP rel Chr : om τ. γ. 34². 66². 163 D-lat sah [$Orig\text{-}int_1$] : txt ABCEℵ p [13] (36) [vulg æth-pl(Tischdf)] Syr copt arm $Clem_1$ $Orig_2$ $Constt_1$.—ins τα επι bef τ. γης 36. rec ins τα θηρια και bef (τα) ερπ. (*from ch* xi. 6), with LP 13. 36 rel syr(θηρια syr-mg-gr) Chr_1, [κ. τ. θηρ.] aft ερπ. [m, aft γης] E : om ABC²ℵ p 40 vulg D-lat Syr coptt arm $Clem_1$ $Orig_2$[int_1] $Constt_1$ $Thdrt_1$ Aug_1.—rec ins τα bef ερπ., with LP 13. 36 rel $Clem_1$ Chr : om ABC²Eℵ p $Orig_2$ Constt.—(C¹ is illegible.) rec ins τα bef πετ. (*conformn to ch* xi. 6), with C¹ELP 13. 36 rel Clem Constt [$Orig_1$-int_2 Bas_1] Chr : om ABC²ℵ p $Orig_2$.

14. rec for και, η (*conformn to ch* xi. 8), with C D-gr ELP p rel copt Chr [$Cyr\text{-}p_3$] : txt ABℵ 13. 36 vulg D-lat syrr sah [arm] $Clem_1$ $Orig_1$ $Constt_1$ $Cyr\text{-}c_1$.

15. φωνησας δε D-gr. εκαθεριστεν ACLP m p [13] : txt BDEℵ [Fr-coisl] rel. for συ, σοι (*itacism?* as E p κυνου for κοιν.) D 13.

ἑνὶ τῶν ἐμπαγέντων ἐνάπτοντες ἀρχὰς στυπίνας ἀφίασι μέχρις ἂν παραλυθῇ. The *ends of the ropes* were attached to the sheet, and, in the vision, *they only were seen.* At all events, as Neander observes (Pfl. u. L. p. 126, note), these four ἀρχαί (whether ends of ropes attached to the corners, or those corners themselves) are not without meaning, directed as they are to the four parts of heaven, and intimating that men from the North, South, East, and West, now were accounted clean before God, and were called to a share in his kingdom : see Luke xiii. 29. The symbolism is, as usual, fancifully exaggerated by Wordsw. in his note. The four ἀρχαί are the four gospels, because the word ἀρχή occurs somewhere near the beginning of each, &c., &c. Who can wonder, after this, at the distrust of all Scripture symbolism by intelligent, but unspiritual minds? I have retained the words δεδ. καί, doubtfully, because it seems difficult to account for their insertion, but they may have been omitted to assimilate our text to ch. xi. 5.

12. πάντα τὰ τετ.] literally : not 'many of each kind,' nor 'some of all kinds,' in which case the art., the sense of which is carried on from τὰ τετρ. to the subsequent words (see ch. xi. 6), would be omitted :—in the vision it seemed to Peter to be an assemblage of *all creation.* **τετρ., ἑρπ., πετ.**] In ch. xi. 6, from which our text has been corrected, Peter follows the more strictly Jewish division : see there.

14.] Peter rightly understands the command as giving him free choice of *all* the creatures shewn to him. We cannot infer hence that the sheet contained *unclean animals only.* It was a mixture of clean and unclean,—the aggregate, therefore, being *unclean.* **κύριε**] So Cornelius to the angel, ver. 4. It is here addressed to the unknown heavenly speaker. On the clean and unclean beasts, &c., see Levit. xi. **15.**] These weighty words have more than one application. They reveal what was needed for the occasion, in a figure : God letting down from heaven clean and unclean alike, Jew and Gentile,—represented that He had made of one blood all nations to dwell on the face of all the earth : God having *purified* these, signified that the distinction was now

j ch. xi. 10 only †. k = ch. i. 2, 22. l Mark xvi. 19. ch. i. 11 only. 4 Kings ii. 11. m ver. 11 reff. n ch. ii. 12 reff. o = Luke viii. 9. xv. 26 al. p ver. 3. q here only †. r ch. xi. 11 only. 1 Kings xvii. 51. see ch. iv. 1 reff. s Matt. xxvi. 71. Luke xvi. 20. ch. xii. 13, 14 bis. xiv. 13. Rev. xxi. 12, &c. xxii. 14. Gen. xliii. 19. t absol., = Luke viii. 8, 54. xvi. 24. Dan. iv. 11 (14). u here only †.

16 τοῦτο δὲ ἐγένετο [j] ἐπὶ [j] τρίς, καὶ εὐθὺς [kl] ἀνελήμφθη τὸ ABCDE LPℵ a b c d f g h k l m o p 13
[m] σκεῦος εἰς τὸν [l] οὐρανόν. 17 ὡς δὲ ἐν ἑαυτῷ [n] διηπόρει ὁ
Πέτρος τί ἂν [o] εἴη τὸ [p] ὅραμα ὃ εἶδεν, [καὶ] ἰδοὺ οἱ ἄνδρες
οἱ ἀπεσταλμένοι * ἀπὸ τοῦ Κορνηλίου [q] διερωτήσαντες
τὴν οἰκίαν τοῦ Σίμωνος [r] ἐπέστησαν [r] ἐπὶ τὸν [s] πυλῶνα.
18 καὶ [t] φωνήσαντες [u] ἐπυνθάνοντο [u] εἰ Σίμων ὁ [v] ἐπικαλούμενος Πέτρος ἐνθάδε [w] ξενίζεται. 19 τοῦ δὲ Πέτρου
[x] διενθυμουμένου περὶ τοῦ [p] ὁράματος εἶπεν τὸ [y] πνεῦμα
αὐτῷ Ἰδοὺ ἄνδρες ζητοῦντές σε. 20 ἀλλὰ [z] ἀναστὰς H ιδου... ABCDE HLPℵ a b c d f g h k l m o p 13
[a] κατάβηθι, καὶ πορεύου σὺν αὐτοῖς μηδὲν [b] διακρινόμενος,
ὅτι ἐγὼ ἀπέσταλκα αὐτούς. 21 [a] καταβὰς δὲ Πέτρος
πρὸς τοὺς ἄνδρας εἶπεν Ἰδοὺ ἐγώ εἰμι ὃν ζητεῖτε·

v ch. i. 23 reff. w ver. 6 reff. x here only †. y absol., Matt iv. 1. ch. ii. 4. viii. 29. xi. 12, 28. xxi. 4. Rom. viii. 16, &c. z ch. viii. 26 reff. Gen. xxxv. 1 (Jer. xv. 10.) a = ch. xx. 10 reff. b = Matt. xxi. 21. Rom. iv. 20. xiv. 23. James i. 6 ‡.

16. rec (for ευθυς) παλιν (*from ch* xi. 10), with D-gr LP 13 rel E-lat syr Chr_1 (ανελημφθη bef παλιν D-gr): om 15. 36 D-lat Syr sah æth-pl arm $Constt_1$ [$Orig\text{-}int_1$] $Ambr_1$: txt ABC E[-gr] ℵ p vulg syr-mg copt æth-rom.

17. αυτω B k. D adds εγενετο. for ειη, ει D¹(txt D³). om και (*corrn of Hebraism?*) ABℵ p 36. 40 vulg [Syr coptt] arm: ins CDELP 13 rel fuld [syr] æth-rom Chr_1. * ὑπό BEℵ a b² c g h o p: απο ACDLP rel Chr_1. om του (bef κορν.) D $Thl\text{-}fin_1$. επερωτησαντες D. rec om του (bef σιμ.), with ELP 13 rel Thl-sif: ins ABCDℵ c p 40 Chr_1 Thl-fin.

18. επυθοντο BC.

19. rec ενθυμ. (*prob negligence of the significant compounded verb*), with b: διανοουμενου 15-8. 36 Did_2: add και διανοουμενου syr[-w-ast]: txt ABCDELP(ℵ) rel [Did_1] Chr.—διενθυμενου ℵ. rec αυτω bef το πνευμα, with DELP 13 rel [syrr æth Did_3] Chr: om αυτ. B copt: txt ACℵ m p vulg sah. rec aft ανδρες ins τρεις (*conformn to ch* xi. 11 *and ver* 7), with ACEℵ f p 13. 36 vulg Syr syr-mg [sah æth Did_3] Thl-fin; bef ανδ., copt; τινες arm; δυο B: om DHL[P] rel spec syr $Constt_1$ Cyr-jer[$-ms_1$] Chr_1 Thl-sif Aug_1 $Ambr_1$. rec ζητουσι, with ACDE[H]LP rel [Constt Did Cyr-jer Chr]: txt Bℵ p.

20. αναστα D¹(txt D³) vulg [syrr] coptt. rec διοτι, with LP 13 rel Constt Bas_1 [Did_2 Chr_1]: txt ABCDEHℵ h p 36. 40 Cyr-jer Did_1 [$Chr\text{-}c_1$].

21. τοτε κατ. DE Syr. ins ο bef πετρος DEL b d o Chr_1 Thl-fin: om ABCHPℵ p. 13. 36 rel Thl-sif. for τ. ανδ., αυτους C arm. rec aft ανδρας ins τους απεσταλμενους απο του κορν. προς αυτον (*explanatory interpolation, ver 21 beginning an ecclesiastical portion*), with H(but om του) (f) Thl-sif; τ. απεστ. υπο κορν. (alone)

abolished which was 'added because of transgressions' (Gal. iii. 19),—and all *regarded in his eyes as pure for the sake of His dear Son.* But the *literal truth of the representation* was also implied;—that the same distinctions between the animals intended for use as food were now done away, and free range allowed to men, as their lawful wants and desires invite them, over the whole creation of God: that creation itself having been *purified and rendered clean for use by the satisfaction of Christ.* The same truth which is asserted by the heavenly voice in Peter's vision, is declared Eph. i. 10; Col. i. 20; 1 Tim. iv. 4, 5. Only we must be careful not to confound this restitution with the ἀποκατάστασις πάντων of ch. iii. 21; see notes there. **16. ἐπὶ τρίς**] denoting the *certainty* of the thing revealed: see Gen. xli. 32. **17.**] Valcknaer and Stier understand ἐν ἑαυτῷ, as ch. xii. 11, where γενόμενος is expressed (see D in var. readd. here),—'when he came to himself,' but without γενόμενος this is very harsh, and it surely is better not to force from its obvious meaning so natural a conjunction of words as ἐν ἑαυτῷ διηπόρει. **18. φωνήσαντες**] **having called out (some one), they were enquiring.** The *present,* **ξενίζεται,** is a common mixed construction between the direct and the indirect interrogation. **19.**] See ch. viii. 29, note. **20. ἀλλά**] '*make no question as to who or what they are,—but:*'—so also ch. ix. 6. **ἐγώ**] The Holy Spirit, shed

τίς ἡ [c] αἰτία δι' ἣν πάρεστε; 22 οἱ δὲ εἶπαν Κορνήλιος
ἑκατοντάρχης, ἀνὴρ δίκαιος καὶ [d] φοβούμενος τὸν [d] θεόν,
[e] μαρτυρούμενός τε [e] ὑπὸ ὅλου τοῦ ἔθνους τῶν Ἰουδαίων,
[f] ἐχρηματίσθη ὑπὸ [g] ἀγγέλου [g] ἁγίου [h] μεταπέμψασθαί σε
εἰς τὸν οἶκον αὐτοῦ καὶ [i] ἀκοῦσαι [i] ῥήματα παρὰ σοῦ.
23 [k] εἰςκαλεσάμενος οὖν αὐτοὺς [l] ἐξένισεν. [m] τῇ δὲ ἐπαύριον
[n] ἀναστὰς [o] ἐξῆλθεν σὺν αὐτοῖς, καί τινες τῶν [p] ἀδελφῶν
τῶν ἀπὸ Ἰόππης [q] συνῆλθον αὐτῷ. 24 [m] τῇ δὲ ἐπαύριον
[r] εἰςῆλθον εἰς τὴν Καισάρειαν. ὁ δὲ Κορνήλιος [s] ἦν [t] προςδοκῶν αὐτούς, [u] συγκαλεσάμενος τοὺς [v] συγγενεῖς αὐτοῦ
καὶ τοὺς [w] ἀναγκαίους φίλους. 25 ὡς δὲ ἐγένετο [x] τοῦ [y] εἰςελθεῖν τὸν Πέτρον, [z] συναντήσας αὐτῷ ὁ Κορνήλιος
[a] πεσὼν [a] ἐπὶ τοὺς [a] πόδας [b] προσεκύνησεν. 26 ὁ δὲ Πέτρος

c = Luke viii. 47. ch. xxii. 24. 2 Macc. iv. 28, 35.
d ver. 2 reff.
e ch. xvi. 2. xxii. 12. Rom. iii. 21. 3 John 12. see ch. vi. 3 reff.
f = Matt. ii. 12, 22. Luke ii. 26. Heb. xi. 7. (ch. xi. 26. Rom. vii. 3.) act., Jer. xxxii. (xxv.) 17 al. ἐχρ. αὐτῷ κατὰ τ. ὕπνους ὁ θ., Jos. Antt. xi. 8. 4.
g Mark viii. 38 || L. Rev. xiv. 10 only.
h ver. 5 reff.
i John viii. 47. xii. 47. Deut. xxxii. 1.
k here only †.
l act., = ch. (xvii. 20.) xxviii. 7. Heb. xiii. 2 only †. Sir. xxix. 25. pass., ver. 6 reff.
m ver. 9 reff. Num. xi. 32.
n ch. viii. 26 reff.
o absol., ch. vii. 7 al. Gen. xix. 14.
p = ch. ix. 30 reff.
q ch. i. 21 reff.
r = Matt. viii. 5 al. fr. Ruth ii. 18.
s ch. ii. 5 reff.
t = Luke i. 21. 2 Pet. iii. 12 al. Ps. cxviii. 166.
u mid., Luke ix. 1. xv. 9. xxiii. 13. ch. xxviii. 17 only †. act., ch. v. 15 reff. Exod. vii. 11.
v Luke i. 58. L.P., exc. Mark vi. 4. John xviii. 26. Lev. xxv. 45.
w = here only (ch. xiii. 46 reff.) †. Jos. Antt. x. 1. 2, τρεῖς τοὺς ἀναγκαιοτάτους φ. αὐτῳ.
x ch. iii. 12 reff. Luke xvii. 1. Rev. xii. 7.
y Matt. x. 12. Mark vi. 22.
z Luke ix. 37. xxii. 10. ch. xx. 22. Heb. vii. 1, 10 only. Gen. xxxii. 1. (-τησις, Matt. viii. 34.)
a here only. 4 Kings iv. 37. (εἰς, John xi. 32 v. r.) πρός, Mark v. 22. παρά, Luke viii. 41. ἔμπροσθεν, Rev. xix. 10.
b = Matt. ii. 11. viii. 2 al. Job i. 20.

´m: om ABCDELPℵ p 13 rel vulg syrr coptt æth arm Chr Thl-fin. ins τι θελετε (-ται D) η bef τις η D syr (om 1st η D-lat syr). for τις η, τι η m: om η B.

22. (ειπαν, so ABCEℵ p.) add προς αυτον D Syr sah. aft κορν. ins τις D-gr Syr. for υπο, υφ D.

23. for εισκ. ουν, τοτε προσκαλ. E[-gr]: τοτε εισαγαγων ο πετρος D 40 sah, *introducens* vulg E-lat Syr(addg *Simon*); *ingressus* D-lat. εξεν. bef αυτ. D 40 vss. rec for αναστας, ο πετρος (αναστ. *being erased as unnecessary, the vacant space thus left in some copies has been filled up with* ο πετρ. *the subject of the verb*), with HLP rel Thl-sif: αναστ. ο π. [C]E c k m 13(omg ὁ) 36 syr Chr_1 Thl-fin: txt ABDℵ d p vulg Syr coptt æth. om 2nd των D. rec ins της bef ιοπ.: om ABCDEHLPℵ rel Chr. ιοππην D[1](txt D-corr[1]). συνελθαν D.

24. rec και τη (*corrn appy to avoid the recurrence of* τη δε, τη δε, ο δε), with HLP 13 rel Syr æth [arm] Chr_1 Thl-fin: txt ABCDEℵ p 40 vulg [syr] copt Thl-sif. εισηλθεν (*corrn to suit* εξηλθεν *above*) BD p [vulg] syr-txt æth Thl-sif: συνηλθον m: txt AEHLP 13. 36 rel [Syr] syr-mg [coptt arm], -θαν Cℵ. om την D m 133 [Thl]. ην προσδεχομενος αυτους και συνκ. D. for αυτου, αυτους B[1](Tischdf) [om p]. aft φιλους add περιεμεινεν D syr-mg.

25. rec om του, with H k 36: ins ABCELPℵ p 13 rel Bas_1 Chr_1 Thl. aft ποδας ins αυτου g o vulg Syr sah æth arm Thl-fin. for ver, προσεγγιζοντος δε του πετρου εις την καισαριαν, προδραμων εις των δουλων διεσαφησεν παραγεγονεναι αυτον. ο δε κορνηλιος εκπηδησας και συναντησας αυτω πεσων προς τους ποδας προσεκυνησεν αυτον (αυτω D-corr[1]) D syr-mg(but αυτου for προσεκ. αυτον).

down upon the Church to lead it into all the truth, had in His divine arrangements brought about, by the angel sent to Cornelius, their coming. **23. ἐξένισεν**] This was his first consorting with men uncircumcised and eating with them (ch. xi. 3): though perhaps this latter is not necessarily implied. **τινες τῶν ἀδ.**] *Six*, ch. xi. 12: in expectation of some weighty event to which hereafter their testimony might be required, as indeed it was, ib. **24. ἀναγκαίους**] **his intimate friends.** So Jos. Antt. xi. 6. 4, φίλος ἀναγκαιότατος τῷ βασιλεῖ, and Xen. Mem. ii. 1. 14, φίλους πρὸς τοῖς ἀναγκαίοις καλουμένοις ἄλλους κτῶνται βοηθούς. These, like himself, must have been fearers of the true God, or at all events must have been influenced by his vision to wait for the teaching of Peter. **25.** * **τοῦ εἰςελθ.**] This, the most difficult and best supported reading, is a harshness of construction hardly explicable (see Winer, edn. 6, § 44. 4) on any principles. It

c = Mark i. 31. ch. iii. 7. Dan. x. 10. d = ch. ix. 6 reff. e here only †. (-λος, Job xix. 19 Symm.) f = ch. i. 6 reff. g = ver. 38. ch. xi. 16. Luke vi. 4. h 1 Pet. iv. 3 only †. 2 Macc. vii. 1 al2. Jos. B. J. iv. 9. 10. Xen. Mem. i. 1. 9 (-ιστα). i = ch. v. 13 reff. k = ch. ix. 1 reff. Levit. xix. 33. l here only. 1 Kings vi. 10. xiii. 3, 5. 1 Macc. iv. 12. m constr., here only. = w. ὅτι, Matt. xvi. 21. Wisd. xiv. 4. w. acc., 1 Cor. xii. 31. 1 Kings xii. 23. n ver. 14 (reff.). o = Mark x. 18. xii. 37 al.

[c] ἤγειρεν αὐτὸν λέγων [d] Ἀνάστηθι· καὶ ἐγὼ αὐτὸς ἄνθρωπός εἰμι. 27 καὶ [e] συνομιλῶν αὐτῷ [y] εἰςῆλθεν, καὶ
εὑρίσκει [f] συνεληλυθότας πολλούς, 28 ἔφη τε πρὸς αὐτοὺς
Ὑμεῖς ἐπίστασθε [g] ὡς [h] ἀθέμιτόν ἐστιν ἀνδρὶ Ἰουδαίῳ
[i] κολλᾶσθαι ἢ [k] προςέρχεσθαι [l] ἀλλοφύλῳ· κἀμοὶ ὁ
θεὸς [m] ἔδειξεν μηδένα [n] κοινὸν ἢ [n] ἀκάθαρτον [o] λέγειν

ABCDE HLPℵ a b c d f g h k l m o p 13

26. rec αυτ. bef ηγ., with HLP rel Thl-sif: txt ABCDEℵ a c d f h k m [p] 13 [vulg arm Bas_1] Chr_1 Thl-fin. for αναστ., τι ποιεις D; syr-mg has both. κ. αυτ. εγ. C $Thdrt_1$: και γαρ εγω, omg αυτος, E Chr_1: om αυτος D sah: κ. γαρ εγ. αυτ. [c k 13] 137: txt ABHLPℵ p rel 36 $Marc_1$ Thl-sif.—rec for και εγω, καγω, with ADHLP a b d f g h l m o 13 [$Marc_1$ Thl-sif]: txt Bℵ p lect-12. aft ειμι ins ως και συ D^1(and lat) E(om και E-lat) copt æth.

27. for κ. συνομ. to ευρ., και εισελθων τε και ευρεν D^1(and lat).

28. bef επισ. ins βελτιον D Aug_1[om_2]. αθεμιστον D^1. ins ανδρι bef αλλοφ. D-gr lect-12 Syr sah. rec και εμοι, with HLP 13 rel [Chr_1]: και μοι p: txt ABCDEℵ o. εδειξ. bef ο θ. AEℵ vulg æth [$Orig\text{-}int_1$]. επεδειξ. D.

probably arose from taking the so frequent τοῦ with the infin. almost as *one word*, and equivalent to the infin. itself. **τοὺς πόδας**] viz. those of Peter. Kuinoel's rendering '*in genua* provolutus' is clearly inadmissible. **προσεκύν.**] "Adoravit; non addidit Lucas, '*eum*.' Euphemia." (Bengel.) May not the same reason have occasioned the omission of αὐτοῦ after πόδας? the one αὐτ. would almost require the other. It was natural for Cornelius to think that one so pointed out by an angel must be deserving of the highest respect; and this respect he shewed in a way which proves him not to have altogether lost the heathen training of his childhood. He must have witnessed the rise of the custom of paying divine honours first to those who were clothed with the delegated power of the senate (Suet., Octav. 52, mentions, "templa etiam proconsulibus decerni solere"), and then κατ' ἐξοχήν to him in whom the imperial majesty centered. **26. καὶ ἐγὼ αὐτ. ἄνθρ. εἰμι**] This was the lesson which Peter's vision had taught him, and he now begins to practise it:—the *common honour and equality of all mankind in God's sight.* Those who claim to have succeeded Peter, have not imitated this part of his conduct. See Rev. xix. 10; xxii. 8, in both which cases it is ἔμπροσθ. **τῶν ποδῶν** τοῦ ἀγγ., supporting the above rendering of ἐπὶ τ. πόδας. (See the gloss in D, ver. 25, digest.) **27.**] The second **εἰςῆλθεν** [see ver. 25] betokens the *completion* of his entering in; or (as De W. and Meyer) the former, his entering the *house*,—this latter, the *chamber*. **28.**] **ὑμεῖς, you, of all men, (best) know**: being those immediately concerned in the obstruction to intercourse which the rule occasioned. **ὡς ἀθέμιτον . . .] that it is unlawful, . . .** or 'how unlawful it is:' better the former, because in the order of the words, ἀθέμιτον has the stress on it: the other rendering would more naturally represent ὡς ἔστιν ἀθέμιτον. In both the reff. the ambiguity is the same. There is some difficulty about this unlawfulness of consorting with those ἀλλόφυλοι who, like Cornelius, worshipped the true God. It rests upon no legal prohibition, and seems, at first sight, hardly consistent with the zeal to gain proselytes predicated of the Pharisees, Matt. xxiii. 15,—with Jos. Antt. xx. 2. 3 (Ἰουδαῖός τις ἔμπορος, Ἀνανίας ὄνομα, πρὸς τὰς γυναῖκας εἰσιὼν τοῦ βασιλέως (Monobazus, of Adiabene) ἐδίδασκεν αὐτὰς τὸν θεὸν εὐσεβεῖν), and with the Rabbinical comment Schemoth Rabba on Exod. xii. 4, "Hoc idem est quod scriptum dicit Jes. lvi. 3. Et non dicet filius advenæ qui adhæsit Domino, dicendo: separando separavit me Dominus a populo suo." But whatever *exceptions* there may have been, it was unquestionably the *general practice* of the Jews to separate themselves in common life from uncircumcised persons. We have Juvenal testifying to this at Rome, Sat. xiv. 103, 'non monstrare vias, eadem nisi sacra colenti: Quæsitum ad fontem solos deducere verpos.' And Tacitus, Hist. v. 5, 'adversus omnes alios hostile odium, separati epulis, discreti cubilibus,' &c. . . . . **κἀμοί**] not, '*but* God hath shewed me,' as E. V.: **καί** can never have this meaning, and in all cases where it is so rendered we may trace the significance of the simple copula if we

ἄνθρωπον, 29 διὸ καὶ [p] ἀναντιῤῥήτως ἦλθον [q] μεταπεμφθείς.
[r] πυνθάνομαι οὖν, [s] τίνι [t] λόγῳ [q] μετεπέμψασθέ με; 30 καὶ
ὁ Κορνήλιος ἔφη [u] Ἀπὸ τετάρτης ἡμέρας [v] μέχρι ταύτης
τῆς ὥρας [w] ἤμην [[x] νηστεύων καὶ] [y] τὴν ἐνάτην [z] προσευχόμενος ἐν τῷ οἴκῳ μου, καὶ ἰδοὺ ἀνὴρ ἔστη [a] ἐνώπιόν μου
ἐν [bc] ἐσθῆτι [bd] λαμπρᾷ, 31 καί φησιν Κορνήλιε, [e] εἰσηκούσθη
σου ἡ προσευχὴ καὶ αἱ [f] ἐλεημοσύναι σου [g] ἐμνήσθησαν [a] ἐνώπιον τοῦ θεοῦ. 32 πέμψον οὖν εἰς Ἰόππην καὶ [h] μετακά-
λεσαι Σίμωνα ὃς [i] ἐπικαλεῖται Πέτρος· οὗτος [k] ξενίζεται
ἐν οἰκίᾳ Σίμωνος [l] βυρσέως [m] παρὰ θάλασσαν [· ὃς [n] παραγενόμενος λαλήσει σοι]. 33 [o] ἐξ αὐτῆς οὖν ἔπεμψα πρός σε,
σύ τε [p] καλῶς ἐποίησας [n] παραγενόμενος, [q] νῦν [q] οὖν πάντες

p here only †. Polyb. xxiii. 8. 11. (-τος, ch. xix. 36.)
q ver. 5 reff.
r constr., ch. iv. 7. xxiii. 19.
s constr., Rom. xi. 20, 30.
t = Matt. v. 32.
u = (1) Matt. xxii. 46. John xi. 53. ch. xx. 18 al. (but see note), or (2) ch. xv. 7. 2 Cor. viii. 10. ix. 2.
v ch. xx. 7 reff.
w ch. xi. 5 reff.
x Matt. vi. 16. ix. 14 &c. ‖ ch. xiii. 2, 3. Judg. xx. 26.
y acc., John iv. 52. Rev. iii. 3.
z absol., ver. 9 reff.
a = ch. ii. 25 reff.
b Luke xxiii. 11. James ii. 2, 3 only.
c as above (b). Luke xxiv. 4. ch. (i. 10 v. r.) xii. 21. James ii. 2 only †. 2 Macc. xi. 8.
d Rev. xv. 6. xviii. 14. xix. 8. xxii. 1, 16 only †. Wisd. vi. 12 al. Cant. v. 10 Symm.
e 1 Cor. xiv. 21 reff. Ps. iv. 3.
f plur., ch. ix. 36 reff.
g pass., Rev. xvi. 19 only. Ezek. xviii. 22. mid., ch. xi. 16 al. fr.
h ch. vii. 14 reff.
i ver. 5.
k ver. 6 reff.
l ch. ix. 43 reff.
m ver. 6 reff.
n absol., ch. xvii. 10.
o Mark vi. 25. ch. xi. 11. xxi. 32. xxiii. 30. Phil. ii. 23 only.
p = 1 Cor. vii. 37, 38 reff. 1 Macc. xii. 18, 22.
q ch. xv. 10. xvi. 36. xxiii. 15 only. Gen. xlv. 5.

29. *αναντιρητως* B^1D p. aft *μεταπεμφ.* ins *υφ υμων* DE.

30. for *τεταρτ.*, *της τριτης* D^1(txt D^2(appy): *nustertiana* D-lat). for *ταυτ. της*, *της αρτι* D. om *νηστ. και* (*erased perhaps, as nothing is said of fasting above, ver* 3) A^1BCℵ p vulg copt æth arm: ins A^2DEH(L)P 13. 36 rel syrr sah.—om *και . . . μου* L. for *και τ. εν.*, *την ενατην τε* D^1[-gr]. rec aft *εν.* ins *ωραν*, with HP 13. 36 rel Chr_1: om ABCDℵ p 40. *και προσευχ. απο εκτ. ωρ. εως ενατης* E. for 2nd *μου*, *εμου* ℵ.

31. *η προσευχ. σου* E 96. 142 lect-12 vulg D-lat: *η δεησις σου* e 80.

32. for *εν οικ. σ. β.*, *παρα τινα σ. β.* (*corrn from ch* ix. 43) C 36. 180. om *ος παρ. λαλ. σοι* (*to suit ver* 6?) ABℵ p vulg copt æth-rom: ins CDEHLP 13 rel vss Chr_1.

33. aft *προς σε* add *παρακαλων ελθειν προς ημας* D(D^3 and lat ins *σε* aft *ελθ.*) syr-w-ast. for *τε*, *δε* D E-lat coptt. ins *εν ταχει* bef *παραγ.* D. for *ουν*, *δου* D^1-gr(*ιδου* D-corr^1: txt D^3(and lat)).

examine. Here, for instance:—the two parties concerned are *ὑμεῖς, κἀγώ*. '*Ye*, though ye see me here, know, how strong the prejudice is which would have kept me away: *and I*, though entertaining fully this prejudice myself, yet have been taught &c.' **29. τίνι λόγῳ] on what account**: the dative of the *cause*: see reff.: and cf. Hes. Theog. 626: *γαίης φραδμοσύνῃσιν ἀνήγαγεν*,—Winer, edn. 6, § 31. 6. c, and Bernhardy, Syntax, ch. iii. 14. **30. ἀπὸ τετ. ἡμ.]** The rendering of Meyer and others, 'From the fourth day (reckoned back) down to this hour have I been fasting,' is ungrammatical; for (1) this would require **τῆσδε** *τῆς ὥρας*, and (2) *ἤμην* cannot possibly reach to the *present time*, but is the historical past: **I was fasting**. This being so, *ἀπὸ τετάρτης ἡμέρας* must indicate the time denoted by *ἤμην*—'quarto abhinc die'—**four days ago**; see reff. (2), which fully justify this rendering. De Wette's and Neander's rendering, 'For four (whole) days was I (i. e. had I been) fasting up to this hour (i. e. the hour in which he saw the vision),' does not satisfy **ταύτης** *τῆς ὥρας*, which must in that case be *ἐκείνης*, if indeed such an expression could be at all used of 'the time when the following incident took place.' The only legitimate meaning of *ταύτ. τ. ὥρ.* I take to be **this hour of the day**: and this meaning is further established by the omission of *ὥραν* after *ἐνάτην*. The hour alluded to is probably the *sixth*, the hour of the mid-day meal, which was the only one partaken by the Jews on their solemn days. (Lightf.) **λαμπρᾷ] bright.** In Luke (ref.) the brightness was in the colour: here, probably, in some supernatural splendour. The garment might have been white (as in ch. i. 10), or not,—but at all events, it was radiant with brightness. **31.]** The two are separated here, which were placed together in ver. 4, and each has its proper verb: *εἰσηκ. . . . ἡ προσευχὴ κ. αἱ ἐλ. . . . ἐμνήσθ.* **33.]** The reading *ἐνώπ. σου*, for *ἐνώπ. τοῦ θεοῦ*, is remarkable, and had it more manuscript authority, would seem as if it might have been genuine. It was much more likely to have been altered into *τ. θεοῦ* (as making the expression more solemn), than the con-

r here only. s ver. 48. ch xvii. 26. Matt. i. 24. viii. 4 || only. constr., here only. Jonah ii. 11 Bℵ3b Alex.(not A) Ald. t = ch. ii. 22 reff. u = ch. viii. 35 reff.

ABCDE HLPℵ a b c d f g h k l m o p 13

ἡμεῖς [r] ἐνώπιον τοῦ θεοῦ [r] πάρεσμεν ἀκοῦσαι παντα τὰ
[s] προστεταγμένα σοι [t] ἀπὸ τοῦ * θεοῦ. 34 [u] Ἀνοίξας δὲ
Πέτρος τὸ [u] στόμα εἶπεν [v] Ἐπ' ἀληθείας [w] καταλαμβάνομαι
ὅτι οὐκ ἔστιν [x] προσωπολήμπτης ὁ θεός, 35 ἀλλ' ἐν παντὶ
ἔθνει ὁ [y] φοβούμενος αὐτὸν καὶ [z] ἐργαζόμενος [a] δικαιοσύνην [b] δεκτὸς αὐτῷ ἐστιν, 36 τὸν [c] λόγον ὃν [c] ἀπέστειλεν

v Luke iv. 25. ch. iv. 27 al. Job ix. 2. w = ch. iv. 13 reff. x here only †. see James ii. 9. Rom. ii. 11. Luke xx. 21. y ver. 2 reff. z = Matt. vii. 23. Heb. xi. 33. James i. 20. Ps. xiv. 2. a = 1 John ii. 29. iii. 7, 10. Rev. xxii. 11. Isa. lviii. 2. b Luke iv. 19, 24. 2 Cor. vi. 2. Phil. iv. 18 only. Levit. i. 4. c Ps. cvi. 20.

for 1st τ. θεου, σου D[1](and lat) vulg Syr sah æth arm[-usc]. (*See note.*) om παρεσμεν D[1] sah. aft ακουσαι ins βουλομενοι παρα σου D[1]; *volumus* D-lat: βουλομ.(alone) Syr: παρα σου(alone) D[3]. om παντα D 96. 142 sah: τα προστ. σοι bef παντα A. rec υπο, with BHLPℵ[1] p 13. 36 rel Chr: παρα E: txt ACDℵ[3].
*κυρίου (*corrn to avoid repetition of* θεου?) ABCEℵ c [p[1](Treg)] 13. 36. 40 vulg syr copt arm: θεου DHLP p rel Syr sah Chr.[—om του p 13.]
34. το στομα bef πετρος D [am copt æth]. aft το στομα ins αυτου ACEℵ[3] d k o 36 [vulg-ed demid syrr coptt] æth arm: om BDHLPℵ[1] p am fuld [tol] Chr_2. καταλαμβανομενος D[1](txt D[2]?).
35. αλλα A. εσται A Constt.
36. ins γαρ bef λογ. C[1][appy] D-gr c 137 [spec] Syr syr-w-ast sah. om ον (*corrn to simplify the constr*) AB c p vulg [D-lat] coptt æth [arm]: ins C D[-gr] EHLP(ℵ[1]) rel 36 syrr $Cyr\text{-}jer_1$ Chr_2. (13 def.)—ον is marked for erasure by ℵ[1], or more probably by ℵ-corr[1].

verse: and the sense, 'We are all here present before *thee*,' follows better on the two preceding verses. **τὰ προστ.**] Not doubting that God, who had directed him to Peter, had also directed Peter what to speak to him. **34. ἀνοίξας τὸ στ.**] Used (see reff.) on occasions of more than ordinary solemnity. **ἐπ' ἀληθείας κατ.**] 'For the first time I now clearly, *in its fulness and as a living fact*, apprehend (grasp by experience the truth of) what I read in the Scripture (Deut. x. 17; 2 Chron. xix. 7; Job xxxiv. 19).'
35.] **ἀλλά** gives the explanation,—what it is that Peter now fully apprehends: **but** as opposed to προσωπολήμπτης in its now apparent sense. **ἐν παντὶ ἔθνει** κ.τ.λ.] It is very important that we should hold the right clue to guide us in understanding this saying. The question which recent events had solved in Peter's mind, was that of the admissibility of men of all nations into the church of Christ. *In this sense only*, had he received any information as to the *acceptableness* of men of all nations before God. He saw, that in every nation, men who seek after God, who receive His witness of Himself without which He has left no man, and humbly follow His will as far as they know it,—these have no *extraneous hindrance*, such as uncircumcision, *placed in their way* to Christ, but are capable of being admitted into God's church *though* Gentiles, and *as* Gentiles. That only *such* are spoken of, is agreeable to the nature of the case; for men who do not fear God, and work unrighteousness, are out of the question, not being likely to seek such admission. It is clearly unreasonable to suppose Peter to have meant, that *each heathen's natural light and moral purity would render him acceptable in the sight of God*:—for, if so, why should he have proceeded to preach Christ to Cornelius, or indeed *any more at all?* And it is equally unreasonable to find any verbal or doctrinal difficulty in ἐργ. δικαιοσύνην, or to suppose that δικ. must be taken in its forensic sense, and therefore that he alludes to the state of men *after becoming* believers. He speaks *popularly*, and certainly not without reference to the *character he had heard* of Cornelius, which consisted of these very two parts, that he *feared God*, and *abounded in good works*. The deeper truth, that the preparation of the heart itself in such men *comes from God's preventing grace*, is not in question here, nor touched upon.
36. τὸν λόγον] The construction is very difficult. Several ways have been proposed of connecting and rendering this accusative. (1) Erasm., Wolf, Heinrichs, Kuin., &c., take τὸν λόγον with οἴδατε, and understand τὸ γεν. ῥῆμ. κ.τ.λ. as in apposition with it. "*The word which, &c., ye know, viz. the* γεν. ῥ." But this immediate connexion of λόγ. and οἶδ. is hardly consistent with the interruption of the sense by οὗτος ... κύριος. (2) Meyer, and Winer, edn. 6, § 62. 3 end, adopt virtually the same construction, but understand ὑμ. οἶδ. to be a taking up

τοῖς [d] υἱοῖς Ἰσραὴλ [ef] εὐαγγελιζόμενος [f] εἰρήνην διὰ Ἰησοῦ
χριστοῦ· [g] οὗτός ἐστιν [h] πάντων [h] κύριος. 37 ὑμεῖς οἴδατε
τὸ [i] γενόμενον ῥῆμα [k] καθ' [k] ὅλης τῆς Ἰουδαίας, [lm] ἀρξάμενος
[m] ἀπὸ τῆς Γαλιλαίας μετὰ τὸ βάπτισμα ὃ [n] ἐκήρυξεν
Ἰωάννης, 38 Ἰησοῦν τὸν [o] ἀπὸ Ναζαρέθ, [p] ὡς [q] ἔχρισεν

d ch. v. 21. vi 23 (from Exod. ii. 11), 37. ix. 15. 2 Cor. iii. 7, 13. Rev. ii. 14. vii. 4.
e = Luke i. 19. 3 Kings i. 42. Ps. xxxix. 9.
f = [Rom. x. 15, from Isa. lii. 7.] Eph. ii. 17 only. Nah. i. 5.
g ch. ix. 20 reff.
h = Rom. x. 12 (Gal. iv. 1) only.
i = Luke ii. 15. iii. 2. John x. 35. ch. vii. 31 al. Gen. xv. 1. Jer. i. 1.
k ch. ix. 31 reff. L.
l constr., see note.
m ch. i. 22 reff.
n Luke iii. 3 ‖. Exod. xxxii. 5.
o = ch. xxiii. 34. Matt. xxi. 11. John i. 46. xi. 1. xii. 21 al.
p = ver. 28 reff.
q ch. iv. 27 reff.

37. om υμεις B æth-rom. γεναμενον E: γεγονος C c. om ρημα D. om 1st της D[1](ins D[3]). rec αρξαμενον, with LP [m] p 13. 36 rel [$Dial_1$] Chr_2 $Thdrt_1$; *quod factum est . . . incipiens* vulg E-lat $Iren\text{-}int_1$ Hil_1 $Ambr_1$, *q.f. . . . cum cœpisset* D-lat: txt ABC D-gr E-gr H 40. aft αρξ. ins γαρ AD vulg E-lat [$Dial_1$] Iren-int.
38. rec ναζαρετ, with AHL a b d f g h l o p 13 [Bas_1 $Thdrt_1$ $Cosm_1$]: txt BCDEPℵ

of the sense which was broken by (in this case) the *two* parentheses εὐαγγ. . . . . . χριστοῦ, and οὗτος . . . . κύριος. This also is the rendering of E. V. But it does not sufficiently account for the two clauses parenthesized. Besides, it is an objection to both these, that the hearers *did not know* the λόγος—'noverant auditores historiam de qua mox, non item rationes interiores, de quibus hoc versu.' Bengel. (3) Rosenm. and others *understand* **κατά**, 'secundum eam doctrinam quam Deus tradi jussit Israelitis,' or (4) take it as an accusativus pendens, 'ad sermonem filiis Israel missum quod attinet' . . . . But an accusative is never found thus standing alone, unless there be an anacoluthon, which (3) precludes, and which would, if assumed in (4), give us a construction of unexampled harshness. (5) Grot. and Beza take τὸν λόγον ὅν, for ὃν λόγον, 'quem nuncium,' justifying it by Matt. xxi. 42, and so nearly (6) Kypke, 'verbum quod misit . . . . illud in omnes habet potestatem,' a rendering altogether out of all N. T. analogy, as is also (7) that of Heinsius, who understands λόγος as personal, 'Verbum quod misit Deus, omnium est Dominus,' a usage confined in the N. T. to the writings of St. John, and, even if admissible, most harsh and improbable here. (8) I agree in the main with De Wette, who joins τὸν λόγον with καταλαμβάνομαι,—and regards ver. 36 as exegetic of ὅτι . . . . δεκτὸς αὐτῷ ἐστι. **Of a truth I perceive,** &c. . . . . . (and recognize this as) **the word which God sent to the children of Israel, preaching peace** (see reff.) **through Jesus Christ:** (then, for the first time, ἐπ' ἀληθείας καταλαμβανόμενος *this also,* on the mention of Jesus Christ, he adds οὗτός ἐστιν **πάντων** κύριος,) **He is Lord of** ALL MEN; with a strong emphasis on πάντων. I the more incline to this, the simplest and most forcible rendering, from observing that so far from ὑμεῖς οἴδατε being (Meyer's objection) a harsh beginning to a new sentence, it is the *very form* in which Peter began his address to them ver. 28, ὑμεῖς ἐπίστασθε, &c.: and, as there it answers to κἀμοί, so here also (ver. 39) to καὶ ἡμεῖς. **διὰ Ἰησ. χρ.** belongs to εὐαγγελ., not to εἰρήνην. **37. τὸ ῥῆμα**] **the matter:** not the *thing,* here or any where else: but the *thing said,* the 'materies' of the proclamation, in this case perhaps best *'the history.'* **γενόμενον**] Not '*which took place,*' but, **which was spoken,** 'published,' as E. V. See reff. This meaning, which ῥῆμα itself renders necessary, is further supported by καθ' ὅλης τ. Ἰουδ., which can only be properly said, and is used by Luke (only, see reff.) of a *publication,* or spreading of a rumour, not of the happening of an event or series of events relating to one person. **ἀρξ. ἀπ. τ. Γαλ.**] It was from Galilee first that the fame of Jesus went abroad, as Luke himself relates, Luke iv. 14, 37 (44 v. r.); vii. 17; ix. 6 (xxiii. 5). Galilee also was the nearest to Cæsarea, and may have been for this reason expressly mentioned. **ἀρξάμενος** is an unexpected transference of the case and gender into that of the prime agent, a construction common enough in the Apocalypse (iv. 1 reff.), but surprising in St. Luke. **μετὰ τὸ βάπτ.**] So also Peter dates the ministry of our Lord in ch. i. 22. (See note there.)
38. Ἰησοῦν τ. ἀπὸ Ναζ.] The *personal subject* of the γενόμενον ῥῆμα, q. d. 'Ye know the subject which was preached . . . . . viz. Jesus of Nazareth.'
ὡς ἔχρ. αὐτ.] **how that God anointed him . . . ,** not as Kuin. and Kypke, 'how that God anointed Jesus of N.,' taking αὐτόν as redundant by a Hebraism. See a construction very similar in Luke xxiv. 19, 20. The fact of the anointing with the Holy Spirit, in His baptism by John, was the historical opening of the ministry of Jesus: this anointing

r = Luke i. 17. vi. 19 al. s absol., ch. viii. 4 reff. t here only. Ps. xii. 6. (-της, Luke xxii. 25.) u James ii. 6 only. Ezek. xviii. 12. v Luke i. 66. John iii. 2. ch. vii. 9. xviii. 10. Isa. lviii. 11. w constr., Luke xxiv. 48. ch. i. 22. ii. 32. iii 15. xxvi. 16. x attr., ch. i. 1 reff. y = ch. v. 23 reff. z ch. v. 30 (reff.) a Matt. x. 8. xi. 5. xxviii. 6 ||. Rom. iv. 25. 1 Cor. xv. 4, &c. Isa. xxvi. 19. b = ch. ii. 4 reff. c Rom. x. 20 only, from Isa. lxv. 1. d here only †. see ch. iii. 20.

ABCDE HLPℵ a b c d f g h k l m o p 13

αὐτὸν ὁ θεὸς πνεύματι ἁγίῳ καὶ ʳ δυνάμει, ὃς ˢ διῆλθεν
ᵗ εὐεργετῶν καὶ ἰώμενος πάντας τοὺς ᵘ καταδυναστευομένους
ὑπὸ τοῦ διαβόλου, ὅτι ὁ θεὸς ᵛ ἦν μετ᾽ αὐτοῦ· 39 καὶ
ἡμεῖς ʷ μάρτυρες πάντων ˣ ὧν ἐποίησεν ἔν τε τῇ χώρᾳ
τῶν Ἰουδαίων καὶ ἐν Ἱερουσαλήμ· ὃν καὶ ʸ ἀνεῖλαν ᶻ κρεμάσαντες ἐπὶ ᶻ ξύλου. 40 τοῦτον ὁ θεὸς ᵃ ἤγειρεν τῇ τρίτῃ
ἡμέρᾳ καὶ ᵇ ἔδωκεν αὐτὸν ᶜ ἐμφανῆ γενέσθαι 41 οὐ παντὶ
τῷ λαῷ, ἀλλὰ μάρτυσιν τοῖς ᵈ προκεχειροτονημένοις ὑπὸ

k m vulg coptt Chr$_2$ Did [Bas$_1$ Iren-int$_1$]. for ως εχρ. αυτ., ον εχρ. D^1(and lat: D^3 adding αυτον) syrr arm Bas$_2$ Faustin$_1$. ins εν bef πν. αγ. EL b m. αγ. bef πνευμ. D. for ος, ουτος D tol Syr sah Iren-int Faustin: ως ℵ^1 13 lect-12 Thl[-fin$_1$]. καταδυναστευθεντας D. for διαβ., σατανα E-gr.

39. υμεις A D-gr. rec aft ημ. ins εσμεν, with HLP 13 rel [vulg] Cosm$_1$: om ABCDEℵ p 36 syrr æth [arm] Chr$_1$ Iren-int-mss$_1$[-ed-Stieren]. for παντων, αυτου D. om εν (bef ιερ.) BD p [vulg-ed] demid fuld: ins ACEHLPℵ 13. 36 rel am [arm] Chr Cosm Iren-int. rec om 3rd και (*its force not being seen*), with 13 rel [vulg] fuld [Syr(appy)] coptt Cosm Iren-int: ins ABCDEHLPℵ rel 36 am demid tol syr arm Chr$_2$. (ανειλαν, so ABCDEℵ p 13.)

40. ins εν bef τη τρ. ημ. C ℵ^1(ℵ^3 disapproving) m: μετα την τριτην ημεραν D^1(and lat). for αυτον, αυτω D^1[αυτω μεν D^3(Scriv)] o 45.

however was not His *first* unction with the Spirit, but only symbolic of that which He had in His incarnation: so Cyril in Johan. lib. xi. vol. vii. p. 993, οὐ δήπου πάλιν ἐκεῖνό φαμεν ὅτι τότε γέγονεν ἅγιος ὁ κατὰ σάρκα χριστός, ὅτε τὸ πνεῦμα τεθέαται καταβαῖνον ὁ βαπτιστής· ἅγιος γὰρ ἦν καὶ ἐν ἐμβρύῳ καὶ μήτρᾳ . . . ἀλλὰ δέδοται μὲν εἰς σημεῖον τῷ βαπτιστῇ τὸ θέαμα:—which unction abode upon Him, John i. 32, 33, and is alleged here as the continuing anointing which was upon Him from God. Stier well remarks, how entirely all personal address to the hearers and all doctrinal announcements are thrown into the background in this speech, and the *Person and Work and Office of Christ* put forward as the sole subject of apostolic preaching. **καταδυναστ.**] Subdued, so that he is their δυνάστης,—and this power used for their oppression. Here, it alludes to physical oppression by disease (see Luke xiii. 16) and possession: in 2 Tim. ii. 26, a very similar description is given of those who are *spiritually* bound by the devil. **ὁ θεὸς ἦν μετ᾽ αὐτ.**] So Nicodemus had spoken, John iii. 2; and probably Peter here used the words as well known and indicative of the presence of divine power and co-operation (see Judg. vi. 16): beginning as he does with the outer and lower circle of the things regarding Christ, as they would be matter of observation and inference to his *hearers*, and gradually ascending to those higher truths regarding His Person and Office, which were matter of *apostolic testimony* and demonstration from Scripture,—His resurrection (ver. 40), His being appointed Judge of living and dead (ver. 42), and the predestined Author of salvation to all who believe on Him (ver. 43). **39. καὶ ἡμεῖς**] Answering to ὑμεῖς οἴδατε, ver. 37. '*You* know the history as matter of universal rumour: and *we* are witnesses of the facts.' By this ἡμεῖς Peter at once takes away the ground from the exaggerated reverence for himself individually, shewn by Cornelius, ver. 25 (Stier): and puts himself and the rest of the Apostles in the strictly subordinate place of *witnesses* for Another. **ὃν καὶ ἀνεῖλ.**] **Whom also they killed.** καί is not '*yet*,' as Kuinoel, but merely introduces, in this case passing over it without emphasis, a new fact in this history. He even omits all mention of the *actors* in the murder, speaking as he did to Gentiles: a striking contrast to ch. ii. 23; iii. 14; iv. 10; v. 30,—when he was working conviction in the minds of *those actors themselves*. **κρεμ. ἐπὶ ξ.**] So also ch. v. 30, where see note. **41.**] Bengel would understand συνεφ. κ. συνεπ. of *previous intercourse during His ministry*, and parenthesize οὐ παντὶ . . . . αὐτῷ,—finding a difficulty in their having eaten and drunk with Him *after His Resurrection*. But this would make the significant οἵτινες ("people who") . . . . αὐτῷ very flat and unmeaning, especially after ver. 39: whereas the fact of their having eaten and drunk with

τοῦ θεοῦ ἡμῖν, [e] οἵτινες [f] συνεφάγομεν καὶ [g] συνεπίομεν αὐτῷ
[h] μετὰ τὸ [i] ἀναστῆναι αὐτὸν [i] ἐκ νεκρῶν. 42 καὶ [k] παρήγγειλεν ἡμῖν κηρύξαι τῷ λαῷ καὶ [l] διαμαρτύρασθαι ὅτι
[m] αὐτός ἐστιν ὁ [n] ὡρισμένος ὑπὸ τοῦ θεοῦ [o] κριτὴς ζώντων
καὶ νεκρῶν. 43 [p] τούτῳ πάντες οἱ προφῆται [q] μαρτυροῦσιν,
[r] ἄφεσιν [r] ἁμαρτιῶν λαβεῖν [s] διὰ τοῦ [s] ὀνόματος αὐτοῦ πάντα
τὸν [t] πιστεύοντα [t] εἰς αὐτόν. 44 Ἔτι λαλοῦντος τοῦ

...νεκρων C.
ABDE HLPא a b c d f g h k l m o p 13

e Matt. xvi. 28. ch. v. 16. vii. 53 (note). xiii. 31. Heb. vii. 5.
f Luke xv. 2. ch. xi. 3. 1 Cor. v. 11. Gal. ii. 21 only. Gen. xliii. 32. Ps. c. 5 only.
g here only. Esth. vii. 1 only. Judg. v. 11 Symm.
h ch. xix. 21 reff. 1 Chron. ii. 24.
i Mark vi. 14. ix. 9, 10. xii. 25. Luke xvi. 31. xxiv. 46. John xx. 9. ch. xvii. 3. Eph. v. 14. see ch. iv. 2.
k dat. and aor., ch. xvi. 18 reff.
l ch. viii. 25 reff.
m Matt. viii. 17. Luke xxiv. 21 al.
n = ch. xvii. (26 reff.) 31 ‡. σὲ...θεὸν ὥρισε δαίμων, Anthol. xii. 158. 7.
o = 2 Tim. iv. 8. James v. 9. Ps. vii. 11.
p ch. ix. 20 reff.
q = Luke iv. 22. John iii. 26. ch. xiii. 22. xv. 8 al.
r ch. v. 31 reff.
s = ch. iv. 30 reff.
t John ii. 11 and passim. ch. xiv. 23. xix. 4. Rom. x. 14 al.

41. ημιν bef υπο τ. θ. C syrr sah [Iren-int$_1$ Vig$_1$]. aft συνεφ. ins αυτω C syr. aft συνεπ. αυτω ins και συναναστραφημεν D^2 syr : συνεστρ. D^1, *conversi* D-lat : add further αυτω ημερας μ syr-w-ast. om αυτον D [E-corr]. aft νεκρων add ημερας μ D sah æth; δι ημερων τεσσαρακοντα E.

42. for παρηγγ., ενετειλατο D. for αυτος, ουτος (*corrn, but unnecessary*) BC D-gr E-gr L[e sil, Tischdf] k 13 syrr coptt : txt AHPא p rel vulg D-lat E-lat æth Chr$_2$ Cosm$_1$ Iren-int$_1$

43. τουτον HL : τουτο m^1 [o] 19. 66^2. 78 lect-2.

Him *after* His Resurrection gives most important testimony to the reality and identity of His risen Body. And there is no real difficulty in it: Luke xxiv. 41, 43 and John xxi. 12 give us instances; and, even if συνεπίομεν is to be pressed, it is no contradiction to Luke xxii. 18, which only refers to one particular kind of drinking. **προκεχ. ὑπ. τ. θεοῦ**] Had not Peter in his mind the Lord's own solemn words,—οὓς δέδωκάς μοι ἐκ τοῦ κόσμου, John xvii. 6? **42. τῷ λαῷ**] Here as elsewhere (ver. 2; John xi. 50 al. fr.), the *Jewish people:* that was all which, in the apostolic mind, up to this time, the command had absolutely enjoined. The further unfolding of the Gospel had all been brought about over and above this first injunction. Ch. i. 8 is no obstacle to this interpretation; for although literally fulfilled by the leadings of Providence, as related in this book, they did not so understand it when spoken. **κριτ. ζ. κ. νεκρ.**] So also Paul, ch. xvii. 31, preaching to Gentiles, brings forward the appointment of a Judge over all men as the central point of his teaching. This expression gives at once a universality to the office and mission of Christ, which prepares the way for the great truth declared in the next verse. It is impossible that the *living and dead* here can mean (as the Augsburg Catechism, and Olshausen) the *righteous and sinners:*—a canon of interpretation which should constantly be borne in mind is, *that a figurative sense of words is never admissible,* EXCEPT WHEN REQUIRED BY THE CONTEXT. Thus, in the passage of John v. 25 (where see notes), the sense of νεκροί is determined to be figurative by the addition of καὶ νῦν ἐστιν after ὥρα, no such addition occurring in ver. 28, where the literally dead, οἱ ἐν τοῖς μνημείοις, are mentioned. **43. πάντες οἱ προφ.**] All the prophets, generically: not that *every one* positively asserted this, but that the whole bulk of prophetic testimony announced it. To press such expressions to literal exactness is mere trifling. See ch. iii. 21, 24. **ἄφ. ἁμ. λαβ.** κ.τ.λ.] The *legal sacrifices,* as well as the declarations of the prophets, all pointed to the remission of sins by faith in Him. And the *universality* of this proclamation, πάντα τὸν πιστ., is set forth by the prophets in many places, and was recognized even by the Jews themselves, in their expositions of Scripture, though not in their practice.

44.] Peter had spoken up to this point: and was probably proceeding (cf. ἐν τῷ **ἄρξασθαί** με λαλεῖν, ch. xi. 15) to include his present hearers and all nations in the number to whom this blessing was laid open,—or perhaps *beyond this point* his own mind may as yet have been not sufficiently enlightened to set forth the *full* liberty of the Gospel of Christ,—when the fire of the Lord fell, approving the sacrifice of the Gentiles (see Rom. xv. 16): conferring on them the *substance before the symbol,*—the baptism with the Holy Ghost before the baptism with water: and teaching us, that as the Holy Spirit dispensed once and for all with the necessity of circumcision in the flesh, so can He also, when it pleases him, with the necessity of water baptism: and warning the Christian church not to put baptism itself in the

u ch. viii. 16 reff. v 2 Cor. v. 13 reff. w ch. xi. 2. Rom. iv. 12. Gal. ii. 12. Col. iv. 11. Tit. i. 10 only. x = ch. xvi. 1. 2 Cor. vi. 15. Eph. i. 1. Col. i. 2 al. y ver. 23. z = ch. ii. 38 reff. a -χεῖν, ch. ii. 17 reff. b ch. ii. 4 reff. c = Luke i. 46. ch. v. 13. xix. 17. Phil. i. 20. (L.P., exc. Matt. xxiii. 5.) 2 Kings vii. 26.

Πέτρου τὰ ῥήματα ταῦτα [u] ἐπέπεσεν τὸ [u] πνεῦμα τὸ ἅγιον
ἐπὶ πάντας τοὺς ἀκούοντας τὸν λόγον. 45 καὶ [v] ἐξέστησαν
οἱ [w] ἐκ [w] περιτομῆς [x] πιστοὶ ὅσοι [y] συνῆλθον τῷ Πέτρῳ, ...πιστοι m.
ὅτι καὶ ἐπὶ τὰ ἔθνη ἡ [z] δωρεὰ τοῦ ἁγίου πνεύματος ABDE
[a] ἐκκέχυται. 46 ἤκουον γὰρ αὐτῶν λαλούντων [b] γλώσσαις HLPℵ a b c d f g
καὶ [c] μεγαλυνόντων τὸν θεόν. τότε ἀπεκρίθη Πέτρος h k l o p 13
47 [d] Μήτι τὸ ὕδωρ δύναται [ef] κωλῦσαί τις [fg] τοῦ μὴ βαπτισθῆναι τούτους, οἵτινες τὸ [h] πνεῦμα τὸ [h] ἅγιον [h] ἔλαβον
ὡς καὶ ἡμεῖς; 48 [i] Προςέταξέν τε αὐτοὺς [k] ἐν τῷ [k] ὀνόματι
τοῦ κυρίου [k] βαπτισθῆναι. τότε [l] ἠρώτησαν αὐτὸν [m] ἐπιμεῖναι [n] ἡμέρας [n] τινάς.

d Matt. vii. 16. John iv. 29. Mal. iii. 8 B. e = Luke vi. 29. f Gen. xxiii. 6 g 1 Cor. x. 13 reff. h ch. viii. 15, 19 reff i constr., here only. (see ver. 33 reff.) Isa. xxxvi. 21 k see ch. viii. 16 reff. l constr., ch. xvi. 39 reff. m ch. xxi. 4, 10. xxviii. 12, 14. 1 Cor. xvi. 7, 8 al. L.P. [exc. John viii. 7.] Exod. xii. 39 B. n ch. ix. 19. xv. 36. xvi. 12. xxiv. 24. xxv. 13 only.

44. aft ετι ins δε P^2 b e f g o (syrr) sah [(æth)]. επεσεν (*mistake? or simple word for compound*) AD 13. 36 [rel]: txt BEHLPℵ [m] o p.

45. for οσοι, οι B vulg D-lat coptt: txt A D-gr EHL[P]ℵ 13. 36 rel Chr$_1$ Rebapt$_1$. συνηλθαν Bℵ. του πν. τ. αγ. B(sic: see table) D^3 40 [vulg Rebapt]: του πν. αγ. D^1: txt AEHLPℵ p 13. 36 rel Chr.

46. from λαλουντων to . . ν τον θεον is obliterated in D^1 (seeing (1) that D^4 fills up the space with txt written "laxius," (2) that Wetstein reports D^1 to have read μεγαλυνειν (omg και?), and (3) that D-lat has *prævaricatis linguis:* we may conjecture that D^1 possibly may have read γλωσσαις διαμεριζομεναις). for τοτε απεκρ., ειπεν δε D. rec ins ο bef πετρ., with DEHLP rel: om ABℵ p Chr$_1$.

47. rec κωλ. bef δυν., with D-corr HLP 13 rel Chr: κωλαι(corrd by D^5) τ. δυν. D^1: δυν. τ. κωλ. E^2 40: [om κωλ. E^1:] txt ABℵ p. for τουτους, αυτους D-gr. rec καθως (*corrn to more usual expr: or to suit ch* xv. 8), with EHLP rel: ωσπερ D: txt ABℵ a c h k p 13. 40 Epiph$_1$ Chr-comm$_1$ [Iren-c$_1$].

48. for τε, δε BEℵ d p 13 syr coptt: txt AHLP rel vulg æth [arm] Chr$_1$ Rebapt$_1$.—τοτε προσετ. D Syr. αυτοις Aℵ 33. rec βαπτισθ. bef εν τω ον. τ. κ., with DEHLP rel vss Chr Rebapt: txt ABℵ p 40 am demid [fuld tol arm] Cyr-jer$_1$. for του κυρ., ιησου χριστου (*corrn, as giving more precision to the baptismal formula*) ABEℵ c d k p^2 13. 36 am [tol demid] syr coptt [arm] Cyr-jer$_1$ Chr$_1$ Jer Rebapt$_1$: τ. κυρ. ιησ. χρ. D p^1 fuld [vulg-clem Syr]: τ. κυρ. ιησ. a h 38. 42. 57: txt HLP rel. for ηρωτ., παρεκαλεσαν D. ins προς αυτους bef επιμειναι D-corr vulg-ed Syr [coptt(Tischdf)] æth, so but διαμει. D^1.

place which circumcision once held. See further in note on Peter's important words, ch. xi. 16. The outpouring of the Spirit on the Gentiles was strictly analogous to that in the day of Pentecost; Peter himself describes it by adding (ch. xi. 15), **ὥςπερ καὶ ἐφ' ἡμᾶς ἐν ἀρχῇ.** Whether there was any visible *appearance* in this case, cannot be determined: perhaps from ver. 46 it would appear *not*. **45.**] We do not read that Peter himself was astonished. He had been specially prepared by the vision: *they had not.* The **λαλεῖν γλώσσαις** here is identified with the λ. **ἑτέραις** γλ. of ch. ii. 4, by the assertion of ch. xi. 15, just cited;—and this again with the ἐλάλουν γλώσσαις of ch. xix. 6:—so that the gift was *one and the same throughout.* On the whole subject, see note, ch. ii. 4.

47.] One great end of the unexpected effusion of the Holy Spirit was entirely to preclude the question which otherwise could not but have arisen, 'Must not these men be *circumcised before baptism?*'

τὸ ὕδωρ . . . τὸ πνεῦμα] The TWO *great* PARTS *of full and complete baptism:* the latter infinitely greater than, but not superseding the necessity of, the former. The article should here certainly be expressed: **Can any forbid** THE WATER **to these who have received** THE SPIRIT?

The expression κωλῦσαι, used with τὸ ὕδ., is interesting, as shewing that the practice was to *bring the water to the candidates, not the candidates to the water.* This, which would be implied by the word under any circumstances, is rendered certain, when we remember that they were assembled *in the house.*

48. προςέταξεν] As the Lord Himself when on earth *did not baptize* (John iv. 2), so did not ordinarily the Apostles

XI. 1 Ἤκουσαν δὲ οἱ ἀπόστολοι καὶ οἱ ἀδελφοὶ οἱ
ὄντες [o] κατὰ τὴν Ἰουδαίαν ὅτι καὶ τὰ ἔθνη [p] ἐδέξαντο τὸν
[q] λόγον τοῦ θεοῦ. 2 ὅτε δὲ [r] ἀνέβη Πέτρος εἰς Ἱερουσαλήμ, [s] διεκρίνοντο πρὸς αὐτὸν [t] οἱ [t] ἐκ [t] περιτομῆς 3 λέγοντες ὅτι [u] εἰσῆλθες [u] πρὸς ἄνδρας [vw] ἀκροβυστίαν [v] ἔχοντας
καὶ [x] συνέφαγες αὐτοῖς. 4 [y] ἀρξάμενος δὲ Πέτρος [z] ἐξετίθετο αὐτοῖς [a] καθεξῆς λέγων 5 Ἐγὼ [b] ἤμην ἐν πόλει
Ἰόππῃ [c] προσευχόμενος, καὶ εἶδον ἐν [d] ἐκστάσει [e] ὅραμα,
[f] καταβαῖνον [f] σκεῦός τι ὡς [f] ὀθόνην μεγάλην τέσσαρσιν
[f] ἀρχαῖς [g] καθιεμένην ἐκ τοῦ οὐρανοῦ, καὶ ἦλθεν [h] ἄχρι
ἐμοῦ. 6 [t] εἰς ἣν [i] ἀτενίσας [k] κατενόουν καὶ εἶδον τὰ [l] τετράποδα τῆς γῆς καὶ τὰ θηρία καὶ τὰ [l] ἑρπετὰ καὶ τὰ

o = ch. ii. 46. xiii. 1. xv. 23. 2 Macc i. 1.
p ch. viii. 14 reff.
q ch. vi. 7. viii. 14. xiii. 44, &c. 1 Cor. xiv. 36 al.
r Matt. xx. 17, 18. ch. xv. 2. xxv. 1, 9 al. Ezra ii. 1.
s constr., here only. Ezek. xx. 35, 36. w. dat., Jude 9. Jer. xv. 10.
t ch. x. 45 (reff.).
u ch. x. 3. xvi. 40. xvii. 2. Luke i. 28. Mark xv. 43. Judg. iii. 20.
v here only. Gen. xxxiv. 14.
w here and Paul (Rom. iii. 30 al18.) only.
x ch. x. 41 reff.
y ver. 15.
z = ch. (vii. 21.) xviii. 26. xxviii. 23 only. (Job xxxvi. 15.) λόγον ἐκθήσομαι, Jos. Antt. i. 12. 2.
a ch. iii. 24 reff. †
b constr., ch. x. 30. xxii. 19, 20 (Paul). Mark xiv. 49. Gal. i. 22. see ch. ii. 5 reff.
c absol., ch. x. 9 reff.
d ch. x. 10 reff.
e ch. vii. 31 reff.
f ch. x. 11 (reff.).
g ch. ix. 25 reff.
h = ch. xiii. 6. xx. 4. xxviii. 15. 2 Cor. x. 13, 14. Rev. xiv. 20. xviii. 5 ‡.
i ch. i. 10 reff.
k ch. vii. 31, 32 reff.
l ch. x. 12 (reff.).

CHAP. XI. 1. *ακουστον δε εγενετο τοις απ. κ. τοις αδ. οι εν τη ιουδ.* D Syr (*audito vero apostoli* &c D-lat, *τοις εν τ. ιουδ.* D[r]). *εδεξατο* D[1](txt D[5]).

2. rec *και οτε* (*alteration because the fact related seems a consequence of, rather than opposed to, ver* 1 ?), with HLP 13 syrr æth Chr[1]: txt ABEℵ p 36 vulg coptt [arm]. rec *ιεροσολυμα*, with (D)EHLP 13. 36 rel Chr: txt ABℵ p. D reads the verse thus: *ο μεν ουν πετρος δια ικανου χρονου ηθελησαι(-σεν* D[5]) *πορευθηναι εις ιεροσολυμα· και προσφωνησας τους αδελφους και επιστηριξας αυτους* (thus far also syr-w-ast, prefixing *et benedicebant Deo*, and adding *exiit* [and w-ob] *et docuit eos, και οτε ανεβη κ.τ.λ.*, as in rec) *πολυν λογον ποιουμενος δια των χωρων* (*civitates* D-lat) *διδασκων αυτους· ος και* (*quia et*) *κατηντησεν αυτοις και απηγγιλεν αυτοις την χαριν του θεου· οι δε* (*quia erant*) *εκ περιτομης αδελφοι διεκρινοντο προς αυτον* (*judicantes ad eum*).

3. rec *πρ. αν. ακ. εχ.* bef *εισηλθες*, with EHLP 13 rel syrr Chr[1] Thl-sif: txt ABDℵ a h p vulg coptt æth arm Thl-fin. *εισηλθεν* and *συνεφαγεν* B(sic: see table) L c p 13. 36 Syr syr[-txt(ctra mg) arm-zoh]. ins *συν* bef *αυτοις* D[1].

4. rec ins *ο* bef *πετρος*, with HLP rel: om ABDEℵ p 13. 40 Chr[1]. ins *τα* bef *καθεξης* D. om *καθεξης* [L][1] 4[1] copt.

5. *ιοπ.* bef *πολ.* D copt. om *προσευχομενος* ℵ[1]. om 2nd *εν* D[1]-gr(ins D-corr[1]) 96. *καταβαινων* (*error?*) A a p. *τετρασιν* D Epiph[1]. rec *αχρις*, with B[2]EH[L]P 13. 36 rel: *εως* D: txt AB[1][ℵ].

6. om *τα* (1st and 3rd) D[1](ins D[3]). om *της γης* P 3. 73. 80[1]: ins aft *θηρια* d g, aft *ερπετα* H Syr. in *ερπετα*, *ερ* is written above the line by ℵ[1]. om 4th *τα* D.

(see 1 Cor. i. 13—17, and note). Perhaps the same reason may have operated in both cases,—lest those baptized by our Lord, or by the chief Apostles, should arrogate to themselves pre-eminence on that account. Also, which is implied in 1 Cor. i. 17, as compared with Acts vi. 2, the ministry of the Word was esteemed by them their higher and paramount duty and office, whereas the subordinate ministration of the ordinances was committed to those who διηκόνουν τραπέζαις. **ἐν τῷ ὀν.**] = ἐπὶ τῷ ὀν., ch. ii. 38, where see note. Wahl compares ἀποκτείνειν ἐν τῇ προφάσει ταύτῃ, Lysias, p. 452.

CHAP. XI. 1—18.] PETER JUSTIFIES BEFORE THE CHURCH IN JERUSALEM, HIS HAVING CONSORTED WITH MEN UNCIRCUMCISED. **1. κατὰ τ. Ἰουδ.**] in Judæa, or perhaps more strictly, **throughout Judæa.** (See reff.) **ὅτι κ. τ. ἔθν.**] They seem to have heard the fact, without any circumstantial detail (but see on τὸν ἄγγελον below, ver. 13); and, from the charge in ver. 3,—from some reporter who gave the objectionable part of it, as is not uncommon in such cases, all prominence.

2.] **οἱ ἐκ περιτομῆς** must have come into use later as designating the circumcised generally: in this case *all* those spoken of would belong to the circumcision. Luke uses it in the sense of the *time when he wrote* the account.

4.] 'Having begun, set forth to them:' i. e. **began and set forth**: not for ἤρξατο ἐκτιθέναι, as Kuinoel. **5.**] **ἦλθ. ἄχρι**

1 πετεινὰ τοῦ οὐρανοῦ. 7 ἤκουσα δὲ καὶ φωνῆς λεγούσης
μοι [m] Ἀναστὰς Πέτρε [m] θῦσον καὶ φάγε. 8 εἶπον δὲ [m] Μηδαμῶς κύριε, ὅτι [m] κοινὸν ἢ [m] ἀκάθαρτον οὐδέποτε [n] εἰςῆλθεν [n] εἰς τὸ [n] στόμα μου. 9 ἀπεκρίθη δὲ φωνὴ [o] ἐκ δευτέρου
ἐκ τοῦ οὐρανοῦ Ἃ ὁ θεὸς [o] ἐκαθάρισεν σὺ μὴ [o] κοίνου.
10 τοῦτο δὲ ἐγένετο [p] ἐπὶ τρίς, καὶ [q] ἀνεσπάσθη πάλιν
ἅπαντα εἰς τὸν οὐρανόν. 11 καὶ ἰδοὺ [r] ἐξ αὐτῆς τρεῖς
ἄνδρες [s] ἐπέστησαν ἐπὶ τὴν οἰκίαν ἐν ᾗ *ἤμην, ἀπεσταλμένοι ἀπὸ Καισαρείας πρός με. 12 εἶπεν δὲ τὸ [t] πνεῦμά
μοι [u] συνελθεῖν αὐτοῖς. ἦλθον δὲ σὺν ἐμοὶ καὶ οἱ ἓξ ἀδελφοὶ οὗτοι, καὶ [v] εἰσήλθομεν εἰς τὸν οἶκον τοῦ ἀνδρός,
13 [w] ἀπήγγειλέν *τε ἡμῖν πῶς εἶδεν τὸν ἄγγελον ἐν τῷ
οἴκῳ αὐτοῦ [x] σταθέντα καὶ εἰπόντα αὐτῷ Ἀπόστειλον εἰς
Ἰόππην καὶ [y] μετάπεμψαι Σίμωνα τὸν [y] ἐπικαλούμενον
Πέτρον, 14 ὃς [z] λαλήσει [z] ῥήματα πρός σε [a] ἐν οἷς [ab] σωθήσῃ
σὺ καὶ πᾶς ὁ [c] οἶκός σου. 15 [d] ἐν δὲ τῷ [e] ἄρξασθαί με
λαλεῖν [f] ἐπέπεσεν τὸ πνεῦμα τὸ ἅγιον ἐπ' αὐτούς, [g] ὥσπερ

ABDE HLPℵ a b c d f g h k l o p 13

m ch. x. 13, 14 reff. n Matt. xv. 11 only. Dan. x. 3. o ch. x. 15 (reff.). p ch. x. 16 only. q Luke xiv. 5 only. Isa. xxi. 5 Ald. compl. Amo. ix. 2. Hab. i. 15 only. Bel and Dr. 42 Theod. r ch. x. 33 reff. s ch. x. 17 reff. t ch. x. 19 reff. u = ch. i. 21 reff. v Matt. viii. 5 al. fr. 3 Kings xiii. 7. w Matt. viii. 33. Luke viii. 20. ch. xv. 27. Gen. xiv. 13. x σταθείς, Luke xviii. 11, 40. xix. 8. ch. ii. 14. v. 20. xvii. 22. xxv. 18. xxvii. 21. L.+ y ch. x. 5. z Luke ii. 17, 50. John iii. 34. ch. vi. 11, 13. Deut. xviii. 20. a ch. iv. 9, 12. Rom. v. 10 only. Hos. i. 7. b = Matt. i. 21. ch. ii. 40. c = ch. x. 2 reff. d ch. ix. 3 reff. e ver. 4. ch. i. 1 reff. f ch. viii. 16 reff. g ch. iii. 17 only.

7. rec om 1st και, with HLP rel syr Chr_1 Thl-sif : for ηκ. δε και, και ηκ. D 15-8. 36 Syr æth : txt ABEℵ o p 13 coptt. φωνην λεγουσαν D. αναστα D-gr[1](txt D[5]) [vulg].
8. ειπα D. rec ins παν bef κοινον (*insertion from ch* x. 14), with HLP rel : om ABDEℵ c o p 13. 36 vulg syrr sah arm Chr_1 $Epiph_1$ Damasc. of ακαθαρτον, ℵ[1] wrote only ακα, ℵ-corr[1] supplied -θαρ, ℵ[3] -τον.
9. rec ins μοι bef φωνη (*from ch* x. 15), with EHLP rel syrr æth [arm-zoh] (Epiph ?) Chr_1 : om ABℵ p 36. 40 vulg coptt arm[-usc].—εγενετο (add δε D[2] and lat) φωνη εκ του ουρ. προς με D. εκ δευτ. bef φω. BE a h syr [æth-pl(Tischdf) arm] Chr_1 : om εκ δ. D 4.
10. rec παλιν bef ανεσπ. (*see ch* x. 16, *where* παλιν *was introduced in this order*), with EHLP rel Chr_1 : txt ABDℵ p [13] 40 vulg [syr] copt æth arm.
11. *ἦμεν AB D-gr ℵ 40 : *erant* D-lat : ημην EHLP p 13. 36 rel vss [arm ?] Chr_1. εμε ℵ[1].
12. rec μοι bef το πν. (*corrn of arrangement*), with EHLP 13. 36 rel syrr [æth arm] Chr_1 : txt ABDℵ p vulg coptt. rec aft αυτοις ins μηδεν διακρινομενον (*interpolation from ch* x. 20, *as is shewn by the number of variations : some inserting it accurately, some from memory*), with HLP rel Chr_1 ; μηδεν διακριναντα A B(sic : see table) ℵ[3] p 13 : μηδεν διακρινοντα Eℵ[1] 36 : om D syr. om 2nd δε D [arm].
13. *δὲ ABDℵ a h p 36 vulg syr copt Chr_1 Thl-fin : om sah : τε EHLP 13 rel Syr æth [arm] Thl-sif. om 1st τον D. om αυτω ABℵ p copt : ins DEHLP 13 rel vss Chr. for αποστ., πεμψον (*from ch* x. 5) B. rec aft ιοππ. ins ανδρας (*from ch* x. 5), with EHLP 13 rel syr Chr : om ABDℵ a h p 36 [vulg] Syr coptt æth arm.
15. aft λαλ. ins αυτοις D æth. επεσεν D a. επ αυτοις D[1](txt D[2]). ως D.

ἐμοῦ is a fresh detail. **12. οὗτοι**] They had accompanied him to Jerusalem, and were there to substantiate the facts, as far as they had witnessed them.

13. τὸν ἄγγελον] The art. almost looks as if the history of Cornelius's vision were known to the hearers. The difference between the vision of Cornelius and that of Peter is here again strikingly marked : while the latter is merely 'praying in the city of Joppa,' no place nor circumstance being named, the former sees the angel '*standing in his house*.'

Notice also that Peter never names Cornelius in his speech—because he, his character and person, was absorbed in the category to which he belonged,—that of men uncircumcised. **14. ἐν οἷς σωθ. κ.τ.λ.**] This is implied in the angel's speech: especially if the prayer of Cornelius had been for such a boon, of which there can be little doubt. **15. ἐν δὲ τῷ ἄρξασθαι . . .**] See note on ch. x. 44, as also for the rest of the verse.

[g] *καὶ ἐφ' ἡμᾶς* [h] *ἐν ἀρχῇ.* 16 *ἐμνήσθην δὲ τοῦ ῥήματος*
τοῦ κυρίου, [i] *ὡς ἔλεγεν Ἰωάννης μὲν ἐβάπτισεν ὕδατι,*
ὑμεῖς δὲ [k] *βαπτισθήσεσθε* [k] *ἐν πνεύματι ἁγίῳ.* 17 *εἰ οὖν*
[l] *τὴν* [lm] *ἴσην* [n] *δωρεὰν ἔδωκεν αὐτοῖς ὁ θεὸς ὡς καὶ ἡμῖν,*
[o] *πιστεύσασιν* [o] *ἐπὶ τὸν κύριον Ἰησοῦν χριστόν, ἐγὼ* [*δὲ*]
[p] *τίς ἤμην δυνατὸς* [q] *κωλῦσαι τὸν θεόν;* 18 *Ἀκούσαντες*
δὲ ταῦτα [r] *ἡσύχασαν καὶ* [s] *ἐδόξαζον τὸν θεὸν λέγοντες*
[t] *Ἄρα* [[t] *γε*] *καὶ τοῖς ἔθνεσιν ὁ θεὸς τὴν* [u] *μετάνοιαν* [v] *εἰς*
ζωὴν ἔδωκεν.

19 *Οἱ μὲν οὖν* [w] *διασπαρέντες* [x] *ἀπὸ τῆς* [y] *θλίψεως τῆς*

h John i. 1. Gen. i. 1.
i = ch. x. 28, 38.
k ch. i. 5 reff. 1 Cor. xii. 13.
l Luke vi. 34 only. Lev. vi. 40 (vii. 10).
m as above (l). Matt. xx. 12. Mark xiv. 56, 59. John v. 18. Phil. ii. 6. Rev. xxi. 16 only.
n ch. ii. 38 reff.
o ch. ix. 42 reff.
p = Rom. xiv. 4. Exod. iii. 11 constr., see note.
q Luke ix. 49 || Mk. ch. x. 47. Num. xi. 28.
r Luke xiv. 3. xxiii. 56. ch. xxi. 14. 1 Thess. iv. 11 only. L.P. Neh. v. 8.
s ch. xxi. 20 reff.
t Matt. vii. 20. xvii. 26. Gen. xxvi. 9.
u = ch. xx. 21. 2 Tim. ii. 25 ‡. (Prov. xiv. 15.) Wisd. xi. 24. xii. 10, 19. Sir. xliv. 16 only.
v = Rom. vi. 22. x. 1. 2 Cor. vii. 10. Jude 21.
w ch. viii. 1, 4 only. Ezek. xxii. 15.
x = Matt. xxviii. 4. Ezek. xxxi. 16. Exod. vi. 9.
y = ch. xx. 23. 2 Thess. i. 4 al. 2 Chron. xx. 9.

16. εμνησθημεν A. rec om *του* (bef *κυριου*), with HLP b d g [Did$_1$] Chr$_1$ Thl-fin: ins ABDEℵ p rel Thl-sif. aft ελεγεν ins *οτι* ℵ^3 a e h [Thl-sif].
17. δεδωκεν ℵ o [Did$_2$]. om *ο θεος* D Aug$_1$ Rebapt$_1$. om *δε* ABDℵ a h k o p 13. 36 vulg Syr [copt] æth arm Chr Did$_2$[int$_1$] Thl-fin Rebapt$_1$: ins EHLP rel syr sah Thl-sif.—om *τις* p. aft *τον θεον* ins *του μη δουναι αυτοις πνευμα αγιον πιστευσασιν επ αυτω* D, simly 8 syr-w-ast(*επι κυρ. ιησ. χρ.*) Aug$_1$.
18. εδοξασαν BD^{2}ℵ c h p vulg syrr coptt æth Chr$_1$ Thl-fin: *εδοξαν* D^1: txt AEHL[P] 13[e sil] 36 rel [arm] Thl-sif. *αρα* (*γε omd, its force not being seen: cf. note*) A B(sic: see table) D-gr ℵ k p 40: *forsitan* D-lat Syr: *utique* E-lat: *αραγε* E-gr HLP 13[e sil] 36 rel syr-mg-gr Chr. om *την* D. rec *εδωκ.* bef *εις ζ.*, with EHLP 13 rel vss Chr$_1$: [om *εις ζ.* arm:] txt ABDℵ p 40 am demid fuld tol.

16.] ch. i. 5. This prophecy of the Lord was spoken to his assembled followers, and promised to them that baptism which was the completion and aim of the inferior baptism by water administered to them by John. Now, God had Himself, by pouring out on the Gentiles the Holy Spirit, included *them* in the number of these *ὑμεῖς*, and pronounced them to be members of the church of believers in Christ, and partakers of the Holy Ghost, the end of baptism. This (in all its blessed consequences, = the gift of *μετάνοια, εἰς ζωήν*, see on ver. 18) was (ver. 17) the *ἴση δωρεά* bestowed on them: and, this having been bestowed,—to refuse the symbolic and subordinate ordinance,—or to regard them any longer as strangers from the covenant of promise, would have been, so far as in him lay, *κωλῦσαι τὸν θεόν.* **17.**] **πιστεύσασιν** belongs to both *αὐτοῖς* and *ἡμῖν*; setting forth the strict analogy between the cases, and the *community* of the faith to both.

[**δέ** (omitted in some MSS., the transcribers perhaps not being aware of the construction) brings out the contrast after *εἰ οὖν*, as frequently after *ἐπεί*, e. g. Od. ξ. 178, *τὸν ἐπεὶ θρέψαν θεοί, ἔρνεϊ ἶσον . . . τοῦ δέ τις ἀθανάτων βλάψε φρένας ἔνδον ἐΐσας*: Herod. iii. 68, *εἰ μὴ αὐτὴ Σμέρδιν . . . . γινώσκεις, σὺ δὲ παρὰ Ἀτόσσης πύθου.* See more examples in Hartung, Partikellehre, i. p. 184.] **τίς ἤμην δυν.**] A junction of two questions: (1) *Who was I that I should . . . .*, as ref. Exod.,—and (2) *Was I able to . . . .* We have a similar instance in *τίς τί ἄρῃ*, Mark xv. 24. See Winer, edn. 6, § 66. 5. 3.

18.] [**ἄρα γε** is more than *ἄρα*. *γε* has the effect of insulating the sentence, q.d. *whatever may be the consequences, or however mysterious the proceeding to us, this at least is plain, that God &c.* Compare Matt. vii. 20, 'therefore, *whatever they profess*, from their fruits,' &c.: and the other reff.: and see Hartung's chap. on *γε* in his Partikellehre, vol. i. p. 344, ff.] **εἰς ζωήν**] to be taken with *τὴν μετάνοιαν ἔδωκεν*, not with *τὴν μετάνοιαν* alone, which would be more probably *τὴν εἰς ζωήν*, **hath given unto the G. also repentance,—that they may attain unto life.** The involved position of the words in the present text is quite in St. Luke's manner.

19—30.] THE GOSPEL PREACHED ALSO IN ANTIOCH TO GENTILES. BARNABAS, BEING THEREUPON SENT BY THE APOSTLES FROM JERUSALEM, FETCHES SAUL FROM TARSUS TO ANTIOCH. THEY CONTINUE THERE A YEAR, AND, ON OCCASION OF A FAMINE, CARRY UP ALMS TO THE BRETHREN AT JERUSALEM. Our present section takes up the narrative at ch. viii. 2, 4. In vv. 19—21 it traverses rapidly the time occupied by ch. ix. 1—30, and that (undefined) of Saul's stay at Tarsus, and brings it down to the famine under Clau-

z = ch. iii. 16. viii. 2 al.
a ch. ix. 38 reff.
b ch. iv. 29, 31. viii. 25. xiii. 46. xvi. 6, 32. Phil. i. 14.
c constr., acc. Luke i. 19. ch. v. 42. viii. 35. xvii. 18. Gal. i. 16.

γενομενης [z] ἐπὶ Στεφάνῳ [a] διῆλθον [a] ἕως Φοινίκης καὶ
Κύπρου καὶ Ἀντιοχείας, μηδενὶ [b] λαλοῦντες τὸν [b] λόγον
εἰ μὴ μόνον Ἰουδαίοις. 20 ἦσαν δέ τινες ἐξ αὐτῶν ἄνδρες
Κύπριοι καὶ Κυρηναῖοι, οἵτινες ἐλθόντες εἰς Ἀντιόχειαν
ἐλάλουν καὶ πρὸς τοὺς Ἕλληνας [c] εὐαγγελιζόμενοι τὸν

ABDE HLPℵ a b c d f g h k l o p 13

19. επι στεφανου AE 13. 40 vulg D-lat Thl-sif: απο του στεφανου D-gr[om του D²]: txt BHLPℵ p 36 [Bas₁] Chr₁ Thl-fin. τον λογ. bef λαλ. D. **μονοις** D c vulg. ιουδαιοι (sic) ℵ.

20. rec **εισ**ελθ. (*perhaps from ver* 3), with HP 13 rel vulg Syr [arm] Thl: συνελθ. a: txt ABDE L[e sil, Tischdf] ℵ o p 36 syr coptt [æth] Chr₁. rec om 2nd και (*as not being understood, the whole sense having been confused by the reading* ελληνιστας *below*), with DEHLP 13[e sil] 36 rel fuld [syrr æth arm] coptt Chr: ins ABℵ(marks for erasure were added, but rubbed out by ℵ³) p [vulg] am demid.—και συνεζητουν 40. rec **ελληνιστας** (*apparently a correction, induced by the difficulty of preaching to Greeks as distinguished from Jews, having preceded the conversion of Cornelius: see note*), with BD⁶EHLP p 13. 36 rel (vulg and many versions do not seem to observe the distinction) Chr-txt₂: ευαγγελιστας ℵ¹: txt AD¹ℵ³ c [arm] Eus₁ Chr-comm₂ Œcdius.

19. μὲν οὖν] A resumption of what had been dropt before, see ch. viii. 4, continued from ver. 2: not however without reference to some narrative about to follow which is brought out by a δέ, answering to the μέν,—see ch. viii. 5, also ch. ix. 31, 32; xxviii. 5, 6,—and implying, whether by way of *distinction* or *exception*, a contrast to that μέν. **ἐπὶ Στ.**] **on account of Stephen**; see reff. Wolf, Kuin., Olsh., &c. render it '*after St.*:' the Vulg. *sub Stephano*, reading ἐπὶ **Στεφάνου**. **διῆλθον**] so ch. viii. 4, 40; ix. 32. **Φοινίκης**] properly, the strip of coast, about 120 miles long, extending from the river Eleutherus (near Aradus), to a little south of Tyre, and belonging at this time to the province of Syria: see ch. xv. 3; xxi. 2. Its principal cities were Tripolis, Byblos, Sidon, Tyre, and Berytos. It is a fertile territory, beginning with the uplands at the foot of Lebanon, and sloping to the sea, and held a distinguished position for commerce from the very earliest times. See Winer, Realw. **Κύπρου**] Cyprus was intimately connected by commerce with Phœnice, and contained many Jews (οὐ μόνον αἱ ἤπειροι μεσταὶ τῶν Ἰουδαϊκῶν ἀποικιῶν εἰσιν, ἀλλὰ καὶ νῆσων αἱ δοκιμώταται, Εὔβοια, **Κύπρος**, Κρήτη. Philo, Leg. ad Caium, § 36, vol. ii. p. 587. See also Jos. Antt. xiii. 10. 4). See on its state at this time, note on ch. xiii. 7. **Ἀντιοχείας**] A city in the history of Christianity only second in importance to Jerusalem. It was situated on the river Orontes, in a large, fruitful, and well-watered plain, 120 stadia from the sea and its port Seleucia. It was founded by Seleucus Nicator, who called it after his father Antiochus. It soon became a great and populous city (Ἀντ. ἡ μεγάλη, Philostr. Apoll. i. 16), and was the residence of the Seleucid kings of Syria (1 Macc. iii. 37; vii. 2; xi. 13, 44; 2 Macc. v. 21), and (as an 'urbs libera,' Pliny, v. 18) of the Roman proconsuls of Syria. Josephus (B. J. iii. 2. 4) calls it μεγέθους τε ἕνεκα καὶ τῆς ἄλλης εὐδαιμονίας τρίτον ἀδηρίτως ἐπὶ τῆς ὑπὸ Ῥωμαίοις οἰκουμένης ἔχουσα τόπον. Seleucus the founder had settled there many Jews (Jos. Antt. xii. 3. 1. See also xiv. 12. 6; B. J. ii. 18. 5; vii. 3. 3—and contra Apion. ii. 4, αὐτῶν γὰρ ἡμῶν οἱ τὴν Ἀντιόχειαν κατοικοῦντες, Ἀντιοχεῖς ὀνομάζονται· τὴν γὰρ πολιτείαν αὐτοῖς ἔδωκεν ὁ κτίστης Σέλευκος), who had their own Ethnarch. The intimate connexion of Antioch with the history of the church will be seen as we proceed. A reference to the principal passages will here be enough: see vv. 22, 26, 27; ch. xiii. 1; xv. 23, 35 ff.; xviii. 22. It became afterwards one of the five great centres of the Christian church, with Jerusalem, Rome, Alexandria, and Constantinople. Of its present state (Antakia, a town not one-third of its ancient size) a view is given in C. and H., where also, edn. 2, vol. i. pp. 149 ff., is a minute and interesting description of the city and its history, ancient and modern. See also Mr. Lewin's Life and Epistles of St. Paul, vol. i. p. 108 ff. (Principally from Winer, Realw.) **20. ἐξ αὐτῶν**] not, of these, *last mentioned Jews*: but, *of the* **διασπαρέντες**. This both the sense and the form of the sentence (μὲν οὖν . . . . δέ) require. **Κυρηναῖοι**] of whom Lucius mentioned ch. xiii. 1, as being in the church at Antioch, must have been one. Symeon called *Niger*, also mentioned there, may have been a Cyrenean proselyte. **Ἕλληνας**] The retaining and advocacy of the reading Ἑλληνιστάς has mainly arisen from a mistaken view that the baptism of Cornelius must necessarily

κύριον Ἰησοῦν. 21 καὶ ἦν [d] χεὶρ [d] κυρίου μετ᾽ αὐτῶν,
[e] πολύς τε [e] ἀριθμὸς ὁ πιστεύσας [f] ἐπέστρεψεν ἐπὶ τὸν
κύριον. 22 [g] ἠκούσθη δὲ ὁ [h] λόγος [i] εἰς τὰ ὦτα τῆς [j] ἐκκλησίας τῆς ἐν Ἱερουσαλὴμ [h] περὶ αὐτῶν, καὶ [k] ἐξαπέστειλαν
Βαρνάβαν [a] διελθεῖν [a] ἕως Ἀντιοχείας· 23 ὃς [l] παραγενόμενος καὶ ἰδὼν τὴν [m] χάριν τὴν τοῦ θεοῦ ἐχάρη, καὶ

d Luke i. 66. ch. xiii. 11 only. (ch. iv. 28, 30. vii. 50. Heb. i 10. x. 31. 1 Pet. v. 6.) Num. xi. 23.
e here only. Job xxxviii. 21.
f ch. xxvi. 20 reff.
g pass., Matt. xxviii. 14. Mark ii. 1. John ix. 32. 1 Cor. v. 1. 2 Chron. xxvi. 15.
h Luke v. 15. vii. 17 only. 2 Chron. ix. 5. ὁ λ. περὶ ἡμῶν, Xen. Anab. vi. 6. 13.
i Matt. x. 27. Luke i. 44. ix. 44. Isa. v. 9.
j ch. viii. 1. Rom. xvi. 1 al.
k ch. vii. 12 reff.
l absol., ch. xvii. 10 reff.
m = John i. 14, &c. 1 Cor. i. 4. 2 Cor. ix. 8. Col. i. 6.

comm$_2$ Thl-fin-ms. aft ιησ. ins χριστον D 96 æth-pl.

21. ην δε D-gr. rec om ὁ (*as unnecessary, not perceiving its force*), with DEHLP 13 rel Chr$_1$: ins ABℵ p 36.

22. aft 2nd της ins ουσης BEℵ c k p 13 Chr$_1$. rec ιεροσολυμοις (*corrn : cf ver* 2), with EHLP rel [vulg] Chr : txt ABDℵ p 36. (13 def.) ins τα bef περι αυτων E[-gr] k Chr. om διελθειν (*as unnecessary ; to simplify the constr : διελθ. εως is in Luke's manner*) ABℵ p vulg Syr copt æth arm : ins DEHLP 13. 36 rel syr Chr$_1$; ελθειν sah. ins της bef αντ. D[1].

23. ins και bef παραγ. D-gr. rec (aft την χαριν) om την (*as unnecessary : no reason can be given for its insertion in so unusual a connexion. It has peculiar force,*

have preceded the conversion of all other Gentiles. But that reading gives, in this place, no assignable sense whatever : for (1) the *Hellenists* were *long ago a recognized part* of the Christian church,—(2) among these διασπαρέντες themselves in all probability there were many Hellenists,—and (3) the term Ἰουδαῖοι *includes* the Hellenists,—the distinctive appellation of pure Jews being not Ἰουδαῖοι, but Ἑβραῖοι, ch. vi. 1. Nothing to my mind can be plainer, from what follows respecting Barnabas, than that these Ἕλληνες were Gentiles, *uncircumcised ;* and that their conversion took place *before any tidings had reached Jerusalem of the divine sanction given in the case of Cornelius.* See below : and Excursus ii. at the end of Prolegg. to Acts. **21. ἦν χεὶρ κυρ. μ. α.**] By *visible manifestations not to be doubted,* the Lord shewed it to be His pleasure that they should go on with such preaching ; αὐτῶν being, *the preachers to the Gentiles,* whose work the narrative now follows. **22.] ἠκ. εἰς τὰ ὦτα**, a Hebraism, see reff. **Βαρνάβαν**] himself a Cyprian, ch. iv. 36.

His mission does not seem exactly to have been correspondent to that of Peter and John to Samaria (nor can he in any distinctive sense, be said to have been *an Apostle, as they were :* see ch. xiv. 4, and note) : but more probably, from what follows, the intention was to *ascertain the fact,* and to *deter* these persons from the admission of the uncircumcised into the church : or, at all events, to use his discretion in a matter on which they were as yet doubtful. The choice of such a man, *one* by birth *with the agents,* and of a *liberal spirit,* shews sufficiently that they wished to deal, not harshly, but gently and cautiously,—whatever their reason was.

23, 24.] It is on these verses principally that I depend as determining the character of the whole narrative. It certainly is implied in them that the effect produced on Barnabas was *something different from what might have been expected :* that to sympathize with the work was *not the intent* of his mission, but a result brought about in the heart of a good man, full of the Holy Ghost and of faith, by witnessing the effects of Divine grace (**τ. χάρ. τὴν τοῦ θεοῦ**, not merely, '*the grace of God,*' but **the grace which (evidently) was that of God** [which he recognized as that of God] : the expression is deliberately used). And this is further confirmed to my mind by finding that he immediately *went and sought Saul.* He had been Saul's friend at Jerusalem : he had doubtless heard of the commission which had been given to him to preach to the *Gentiles :* but the church was waiting the will of God, to know *how* this was to be accomplished. *Here* was an evident door open for the ministry of Saul, and, in consequence, as soon as Barnabas perceives it, he goes to fetch him to begin his work in Antioch. And it was *here,* more properly, and not in Cæsarea, that the real commencement of the *Gentile church* took place, —although simultaneously, for the convincing of the Jewish believers at Jerusalem, and of Peter, and for the more solemn and authorized standing of the Gentile church, the important events at Cæsarea and Joppa were brought about. Wordsw.'s argument, that, as even Ἕλληνας may include Jews, we need not suppose this to have been a preaching to Gentiles,

[n] παρεκάλει πάντας τῇ [o] προθέσει τῆς καρδίας [p] προσμένειν
τῷ κυρίῳ, 24 ὅτι ἦν ἀνὴρ ἀγαθὸς καὶ [q] πλήρης πνεύματος
ἁγίου καὶ πίστεως. καὶ [r] προσετέθη [s] ὄχλος [st] ἱκανὸς
τῷ κυρίῳ. 25 [u] ἐξῆλθεν δὲ [u] εἰς Ταρσὸν [v] ἀναζητῆσαι
Σαῦλον, καὶ εὑρὼν ἤγαγεν εἰς Ἀντιόχειαν. 26 [w] ἐγένετο
δὲ [w] αὐτοῖς καὶ ἐνιαυτὸν ὅλον [wx] συναχθῆναι ἐν τῇ ἐκκλησίᾳ καὶ διδάξαι [s] ὄχλον [st] ἱκανόν, [y] χρηματίσαι τε
[z] πρώτως ἐν Ἀντιοχείᾳ τοὺς μαθητὰς [a] Χριστιανούς.

ABDE HLPℵ a b c d f g h k l o p 13

n ch. x. 38. xiv. 22 al. fr.
o = 2 Tim. iii. 10. (ch. xxvii. 13 reff.)
p = Wisd. iii. 9. see ch. xiii. 43. (ch. xviii. 18 reff.)
q ch. vii. 55 reff.
r ch. ii. 41 reff.
s here bis. Mark x. 46. Luke vii. 12. ch. xix. 26. (1 Macc. xiii. 11.)
t = as above (s). ch. xx. 37. xxii. 6.
u John i. 44. Matt. xi. 7. ch. xiv. 20. xvi. 10. 2 Cor. ii. 13.
v Luke ii. 44, 45 only. Job iii. 4. x. 6. 2 Macc. xiii. 21 only.
w constr., here only. see ch. xxii. 6, 17.
x ch. iv. 5 reff.
y = Rom. vii. 3 only (ch. x. 22 reff.) ‡. χρηματίσας Φιλέλλην, Jos. Antt. xiii. 11. 3 al.
z here only +. Polyb. mss. x. 11. 6.
a ch. xxvi. 28. 1 Pet. iv. 16 only.

see note), with DEHLP 13 rel Chr_1 : ins ABℵ. ins εν bef τω κυρ. B 40 vulg [*permanere in domino*] coptt.

24. ανηρ bef ην ℵ. om τω κυριω B[1](ins B[2]-marg (see table)).

25. for ver, ακουσας δε οτι σαυλος εστιν εις θαρσον(ταρσ. D[8]) εξηλθεν αναζητων αυτον· και ως(om ως D-corr) συντυχων παρεκαλεσεν (add αυτον D[6]) ελθειν εις αντιοχειαν D syr-mg. rec aft ταρσ. ins ο βαρναβας, with EHL[P] p 13 rel syr Chr_1: [pref vulg-ed(and am[2]):] om AB(D)ℵ am[1] fuld [demid] Syr (syr-mg) coptt arm. for αναζητ., αναστησαι B[1]. rec aft ευρ. ins αυτον, with HLP rel vss(most, but syr-w-ob): om ABEℵ a c h p 36 Chr $Chron_1$. rec aft ηγαγ. ins αυτον (*supplementary*), with EHLP rel [syrr æth] coptt Chr Thl-fin: om ABℵ a d f h k o p 36 [vulg] arm Chron Thl-sif.

26. for ver, οιτινες παραγενομενοι ενιαυτον ολον συνεχυθησαν (συναναχυθηναι τη εκκλησια και διδαξαι D[5], which conforms the follg to txt) οχλον ικανον· και τοτε πρωτον εχρηματισεν εν αντ. οι μαθ. χρ. D: syr-mg has the former part. rec αυτους (*corrn of constr*), with HLP Did_1 Chr_1: txt ABEℵ c p 13. 36. 40. rec om 1st και (*as unnecessary*), with EHLP rel 36 vss Chr: ins ABℵ [13] syr Ath[-int_1 Did_1]. om ολον E sah Chr_1. om 1st εν HLP a b c d e g h l Thl-sif. rec πρωτον, with AD[1]EHLP rel [Did_1 Cyr-jer_1 Chr_1]: txt BD[5]ℵ 36. εις αντ. A. χρηστιανους ℵ[1](but corrd) p.

is best answered by the context, in which the μηδενὶ εἰ μὴ μόνον Ἰουδαίοις is clearly contrasted with ἦσαν δὲ . . . καὶ πρὸς τοὺς Ἕλληνας, which contrast cannot be maintained without excluding Jews from this latter term.

23. παρεκάλει] in accordance with his name, which (ch. iv. 36) was interpreted υἱὸς παρακλήσεως. **25.**] This therefore took place after ch. ix. 30: *how long after*, we have no hint in the narrative, and the question will be determined by various persons according to the requirements of their chronological system. Wieseler and Schrader make it not more than from half a year to a year: Dr. Burton, who places the conversion of Saul in A.D. 31,—nine years. Speaking *à priori*, it seems very improbable that any considerable portion of time should have been spent by him before the great work of his ministry began. Even supposing him during this retirement to have preached in Syria and Cilicia,—judging by the analogy of his subsequent journeys, *a few months* at the most would have sufficed for this. For my own view, see Prolegg. to Acts, § vi. **26.**] The unusual word **πρώτως** seems to imply priority not only in time, but also in usage: at Antioch first and principally. So we have in Aristot. Eth. Nic. viii. 5, πρώτως καὶ κυρίως. **Χριστιανούς**] This name is never used by Christians *of themselves* in the N. T. (but οἱ μαθηταί, οἱ πιστοί, or οἱ πιστεύοντες, οἱ ἀδελφοί, οἱ ἅγιοι, οἱ τῆς ὁδοῦ), only (see reff.) as *spoken by*, or *coming from*, those without the church. And *of* those, it cannot have arisen with the Jews, who would never have given a name derived from the Messiah to a hated and despised sect. By the Jews they were called Ναζωραῖοι, ch. xxiv. 5, and *Galilæans*: and Julian, who wished to deprive them of a name in which they gloried (see below), and to favour the Jews, ordered that they should not be called Christiani; but Galilæi, Greg. Naz. Orat. iv. (in Jul. i.) 86, vol. i. p. 114. That it has a Latin form is no decided proof of a Latin origin: Latin forms had become naturalized among the Greeks, and in this case there would be no Greek adjective so ready to hand as the Latin possessive, sanctioned as it was by such forms as Pompeiani, Cæsariani, Herodiani (Christus being regarded as a proper name, see Tacit. Ann. xv. 44, '. . . quos vulgus . . . Christianos appellabat. Auctor ejus nominis Christus,

27 Ἐν ταύταις δὲ ταῖς ἡμέραις [b] κατῆλθον ἀπὸ Ἱεροσολύμων [c] προφῆται εἰς Ἀντιόχειαν. 28 [d] ἀναστὰς δὲ εἷς ἐξ
αὐτῶν ὀνόματι Ἄγαβος [e] ἐσήμανεν [f] διὰ [g] τοῦ [fg] πνεύματος
[h] λιμὸν μεγάλην [i] μέλλειν [i] ἔσεσθαι [k] ἐφ᾽ [k] ὅλην τὴν [l] οἰκουμένην, ἥτις [καὶ] ἐγένετο [m] ἐπὶ Κλαυδίου. 29 τῶν δὲ μαθ-

b ch. viii. 5 reff. c = ch. xiii. 1. xv. 32. xxi. 10. 1 Cor. xii. 28, 29. xiv. 29, &c. Eph. ii. 20. iii. 5. iv. 11 only. L.P. d = Mark xiv. 57, 60. ch. i. 15. vi. 9 al. Ezra x. 5. e John xii. 33. xviii. 32. xxi. 19. ch. xxv. 27. Rev. i. 1 only. Esth. ii. 22. constr., here only. f ch. i. 2. xxi. 4. Rom. v. 5. Eph. iii. 16. 2 Thess. ii. 2 al. L.P.H. g abs., ch. x. 19 reff. h fem., Luke xv. 14. 1 Macc. ix. 24 A. i ch. xxiv. 15. xxvii. 10. (fut., Acts only.) Eccl. i. 9 Symm. Xen. Anab. iii. 1. 2. See Winer, edn. 6, § 44. 7. k Mark xv. 33 || L. ch. v. 11. vii. 11 only. l = Luke ii. 1. xxi. 26. Isa. xxiv. 4 al. fr. m = Mark ii. 26. Luke iii. 2. iv. 27. Isa. liv. 9.

27. αυταις B c.

28. for αναστ. δε εις, ην δε πολλη αγγαλλιασις· συνεστραμμενων δε ημων εφη εις D Aug. εσημαινεν B vulg D-lat $Chron_1$: σημενων D-gr. rec μεγαν (*see note*), with D^1EHLP rel 36 Chr_1 $Chron_1$: om e: txt ABD^3ℵ p 40 ($Epiph_1$ [Did_1]). (13 def.) rec **οστις** (*see above*), with HLP rel 36 Chr : txt ABDEℵ p 13. 40 $Epiph_1$ [Did_1] $Chron_1$. om και ABDℵ p 13. 40 vss $Epiph_1$ $Chron_1$: ins EHLP rel 36 Syr Chr_1. rec aft κλαυδιου ins καισαρος, with EHLP rel 36 syrr $Epiph_1$ Chr : om ABDℵ p 13. 40 vulg coptt æth arm Chron [Did_1].

Tiberio imperitante, per procuratorem Pontium Pilatum supplicio affectus erat'). The name soon became matter of glorying among its bearers: ref. 1 Pet., Eus. H. E. v. 1, in the epistle of the churches of Lyons and Vienne, τοῦ ἡγεμόνος . . . . μόνον τοῦτο πυθομένου εἰ καὶ αὐτὸς εἴη Χριστιανός, τοῦ δὲ (Epagathus) λαμπροτάτῃ φωνῇ ὁμολογήσαντος, . . . and again, πρὸς πάντα τὰ ἐπηρωτημένα ἀπεκρίνατο (Sanctus) τῇ Ῥωμαικῇ φωνῇ, Χριστιανός εἰμι. And in the Clementine Liturgy (Humphry, Comm. on Acts, p. 84),—εὐχαριστοῦμέν σοι, ὅτι τὸ ὄνομα τοῦ χριστοῦ σου ἐπικέκληται ἐφ᾽ ἡμᾶς, καὶ σοὶ προσῳκειώμεθα. Before this, while the believers had been *included among Jews*, no distinctive name for them was needed: but now that a body of men, compounded of *Jews and Gentiles*, arose, distinct in belief and habits from both, some new appellation was required.

It may be observed, that the inhabitants of Antioch were famous for their propensity to jeer and call names; see instances in C. and H. i. p. 148, note 2. See several interesting particulars respecting the name collected in Wordsw.'s note: who however maintains that it was given by the Church herself. **27. ἐν τ. τ. ἡμ.**] It was during this *year*, ver. 26. **προφῆται**] Inspired teachers in the early Christian church, referred to in the Acts, and in the Epistles of Paul (see reff. and ch. xix. 6; xxi. 9; Rom. xii. 6; 1 Cor. xii. 10; xiii. 2, 8; xiv. 6; 1 Thess. v. 20). They might be of either sex (ch. xxi. 9). The foretelling of future events was not the usual form which their inspiration took, but that of an *exalted and superhuman teaching*, ranked by St. Paul above 'speaking with tongues,' in being the *utterance of their own conscious intelligence informed by the Holy Spirit*. This inspiration was however, occasionally, as here, and ch. xxi. 10, made the vehicle of *prophecy*, properly so called. **28. Ἄγαβος**] The same who prophesied Paul's imprisonment in Jerusalem, ch. xxi. 10, ff. From the form of his announcement *there*, we may infer the manner in which he ἐσήμανεν διὰ τοῦ πνεύματος *here*. It was **τάδε λέγει τὸ πν. τὸ ἅγιον.**

The fem. usage of **λιμός** prevailed among the Dorians (cf. Aristoph. Acharn. 708) and later Greeks: see Meyer, edn. 2, and Lobeck on Phryn. p. 188. We find it sometimes also in Ionic poets, e. g. in Hom. Hymn to Demeter, 311, λιμοῦ ὑπ᾽ ἀργαλέης: see other examples in Palm and Rost, sub voce. **ὅλην τ. οἰκουμένην**] not, '*all Judæa*,' though in fact it was so: the expression is a hyperbolical one in ordinary use, and not to be pressed as strictly implying that to which its literal meaning would extend. That it occurs in a *prophecy* (Meyer) is no objection to this: the scope and not the wording of the prophecy is given. But see below. **ἐπὶ Κλαυδίου**] In the *fourth* year of Claudius, A.D. 44, there was a famine in Judæa and the neighbouring countries (Jos. Antt. xx. 2. 5). And three others are mentioned during his reign: one in Greece (Eus. Chron. i. 79), and two in Rome (Dio Cassius, lx. 11. Tacitus, Ann. xii. 43), so that *scarcity* ἐπὶ Κλαυδίου *did extend through the greater part of the 'orbis terrarum,'* if it be thought necessary to press the words of the prophecy. The queen Helena of Adiabene and her son Izates helped the Jews with subsidies on the occasion (Jos. ibid., see also xx. 5. 2, where he calls it τὸν μέγαν λιμόν), both of corn and money. I do not believe that the words ἐπὶ Κλ. imply that the *events just related were not also in the reign of Claudius:*

n — ch. ii. 4. Mark iv. 33. Num. xxvi. 54.
o here only. Lev. xxv. 26, 28, 49. Wisd. x. 10 only. (-ρία, ch. xix. 25.)
p ch. xvii. 26 reff. constr., here only.
q = ch. vi. 1 reff.

ητῶν [n] καθὼς [o] εὐπορεῖτό τις, [p] ὥρισαν ἕκαστος αὐτῶν ABDE HLP**א** a b c d f g h k l o p 13
εἰς [q] διακονίαν [r] πέμψαι τοῖς [s] κατοικοῦσιν [s] ἐν τῇ Ἰουδαίᾳ
ἀδελφοῖς, 30 ὃ καὶ ἐποίησαν ἀποστείλαντες πρὸς τοὺς
[t] πρεσβυτέρους [u] διὰ χειρὸς Βαρνάβα καὶ Σαύλου.
XII. 1 [v] Κατ' [v] ἐκεῖνον δὲ τὸν [v] καιρὸν [w] ἐπέβαλεν Ἡρώδης ὁ βασιλεὺς τὰς χεῖρας [x] κακῶσαί τινας τῶν [y] ἀπὸ

r = Phil. iv. 16. s ch. i. 20 al. t — here for first time. ch. xiv. 23. xv. 2, &c. 1 Tim. v. 17, 19. James v. 14 al. Acts, past. and cath. epp. only. u ch. ii. 23. vii. 25. xiv. 3. xix. 11. 2 Chron. xxxiv. 14. v ch. xix. 23 only. Num. xxii. 4. see Rom. ix. 9. w Matt. xxvi. 50. Luke xx. 19. ch. iv. 3. v. 18 al. Gen. xxii. 12. constr., here only. x ch. vii. 6 reff. y = ch. xv. 5 (xxvii. 44).

29. (ευπορειτο, so AB(D)EHP[1](but altered eadem manu)**א** 13 a b e g k l [Eus-ms$_1$] Thl-sif.) *οι δε μαθ. καθως ευπορουντο* D. *ωρισεν* A 95[1].
30. for *ο*, *οι* L. aft *και* ins *ο* **א**[1](marked for erasure by **א**-corr[1]).

CHAP. XII. **1.** *ο βασ.* bef *ηρ.* **א** c[1] p [syr Eus-5-mss$_1$ Chr$_1$(txt$_1$)]. *τας χ.* bef *ηρ. ο β.* D.

but they are inserted to particularize the famine as being that well-known one, and only imply that the author was not *writing* under Claudius. **29.**] There is no need to suppose that the prophecy of Agabus preceded by any long time the outbreak of the famine: nor would it be any derogation from its prophetic character to suppose it even coincident with its first beginnings; it was the *greatness* and *extent* of the famine which was particularly revealed, and which determined the Christians of Antioch to send the relief. Baumgarten (vol. ii. p. 5), in tracing the gradual transition of the apostolic narrative from Jewish to Gentile Christianity, calls this contribution, sent from Antioch to Jerusalem, the first stretching out of the hand by the Gentile world across the ancient gulf which separated it from Israel. **τῶν δὲ μαθ.** κ.τ.λ. is a mixture of two constructions, οἱ δὲ μαθηταὶ καθὼς εὐπορεῖτό τις αὐτῶν. The church at Jerusalem was poor, probably in connexion with the community of goods, which would soon have this effect; see ch. ii. 44, note. **30. πρεσβυτέρους**] These were the *overseers* or *presidents* of the congregation,—an office borrowed from the synagogues, and established by the Apostles in the churches generally, see ch. xiv. 23. They are in the N. T. identical with ἐπίσκοποι, see ch. xx. 17, 28; Titus i. 5, 7; 1 Pet. v. 1, 2. So Theodoret on Phil. i. 1, ἐπισκόπους τοὺς πρεσβυτέρους καλεῖ· ἀμφότερα γὰρ εἶχον κατ' ἐκεῖνον τὸν καιρὸν τὰ ὀνόματα. The title ἐπίσκοπος, as applied to one person superior to the πρεσβύτεροι, and answering to our 'bishop,' appears to have been unknown in the apostolic times. Respecting the chronology of this journey to Jerusalem, see note on ch. xii. 25, and the table in the Prolegomena.

CHAP. XII. 1—25.] PERSECUTION OF THE CHURCH AT JERUSALEM BY HEROD AGRIPPA. MARTYRDOM OF JAMES THE BROTHER OF JOHN. IMPRISONMENT AND MIRACULOUS DELIVERANCE OF PETER. DEATH OF HEROD AT CÆSAREA. RETURN OF BARNABAS AND SAUL FROM JERUSALEM TO ANTIOCH. **1. κατ' ἐκ. τ. καιρ.**] *Before* the arrival of Barnabas and Saul in Jerusalem. The famine in Judæa broke out under Cuspius Fadus, and continued under Tiberius Alexander, procurators of Judæa. Now Cuspius Fadus was sent to Judæa by Claudius *on the death of Agrippa* (i. e. after Aug. 6, A.D. 44). The visit of Barnabas and Saul must have taken place about the time of, or shortly after, Agrippa's death. **Ἡρώδης ὁ βασιλεύς**] HEROD AGRIPPA I., grandson of Herod the Great,—son of Aristobulus and Berenice (Jos. Antt. xvii. 1. 2; B. J. i. 28. 1). Having gone to Rome, to accuse Herod the Tetrarch (Antipas), and fallen under the displeasure of Tiberius for paying open court to Caius Cæsar (Caligula), he was imprisoned and cruelly treated; but, on the accession of Caligula, released, and at once presented with the tetrarchy of Philip (Trachonitis),—who had lately died,—and the title of king. On this, Antipas, by persuasion of his wife Herodias, went to Rome, to try to obtain the royal title also, but was followed by his enemy Agrippa, who managed to get Antipas banished to Spain, and to obtain his tetrarchy (Galilee and Peræa) for himself. (Jos. Antt. xix. 8. 2.) Finally, Claudius, in return for services rendered to him by Agrippa, at the time of Caligula's death, presented him with Samaria and Judæa (about 41 A.D., Jos. Antt. xix. 5. 1), so that he now ruled (Jos. ibid.) all the kingdom of Herod the Great. His character, as given by Josephus, Antt. xix. 7. 3, is important as illustrating the pre-

τῆς [z] ἐκκλησίας. 2 [a] ἀνεῖλεν δὲ Ἰάκωβον τὸν ἀδελφὸν
Ἰωάννου [b] μαχαίρῃ. 3 ἰδὼν δὲ ὅτι [c] ἀρεστόν [d] ἐστιν τοῖς
Ἰουδαίοις, [e] προσέθετο [f] συλλαβεῖν καὶ Πέτρον· ἦσαν δὲ
[αἱ] [g] ἡμέραι τῶν [gh] ἀζύμων. 4 ὃν καὶ [i] πιάσας [k] ἔθετο [k] εἰς

z absol., Matt. xviii. 17 al. Judg. xxi. 5.
a = ch. v. 33 reff.
b Matt. xxvi. 47, &c. ch. xvi. 27. Rom. viii. 35 al. Exod. xv. 9.
c ch vi. 2 reff.
d pres., ch. xvi. 38 reff.
e = Luke xix. 11, xx. 11, 12 only. Gen. iv. 2. viii. 12. xviii. 29.
f ch. i. 16 reff.
g Mark xiv. 12. Luke xxii. 7. ch. xx. 6 (Matt. xxvi. 17) only +.
h as above (g). Mark xiv. 1 || L. 1 Cor. v. 7, 8 only. Lev. xxiii. 6.
i John vii. 30 al7. ch. iii. 7. 2 Cor. xi. 32. Rev. xix. 20 only. Cant. ii. 15. Sir. xxiii. 21 BℵF(not A) only.
k = ch. iv. 3. xiii. 29. Jer. xxxix. (xxxii.) 14. see ch. v. 18, 25. Gen. xli. 10.

aft εκκλ. add εν τη ιουδαια D syr-w-ast.

2. om δε 96 sah : και ανειλεν D Syr æth : ανειλ. δε και g 76. 177^2 [Thl-sif$_1$]. (μαχαιρη, so AB^{1}D^4(?) ℵ p.)

3. rec και ιδ. (*appy corrn to avoid recurrence of* δε : *or perhaps as agreeing better with the continuation of the same line of conduct*), with DHLP rel [syrr æth] Chr-txt$_1$: txt ABEℵ p 13. 36 vulg coptt Chr-comm$_1$. om εστιν ℵ^1. aft ιουδαιοις ins η επιχειρησεις αυτου επι τους πιστους D syr-mg. ins του bef συλλ. E. rec om αι, with BHLPℵ b^1 c l^1 o [arm] : ins ADE p rel 36 Chr$_1$[-txt]

sent chapter: ἐπεφύκει δὲ ὁ βασιλεὺς οὗτος εὐεργετικὸς εἶναι ἐν δωρεαῖς, καὶ μεγαλοφρονῆσαι ἔθνη φιλότιμος, καὶ πολλοῖς ἀθρόως δαπανήμασιν ἀνιστὰς αὑτὸν εἰς ἐπιφάνειαν, ἡδόμενος τῷ χαρίζεσθαι, καὶ τῷ βιοῦν ἐν εὐφημίᾳ χαίρων .... (see ver. 3) .... πραῢς δὲ ὁ τρόπος Ἀγρίππᾳ, καὶ πρὸς πάντας τὸ εὐεργετικὸν ὅμοιον. ἡδεῖα γοῦν αὐτῷ δίαιτα καὶ συνεχὴς ἐν τοῖς Ἱεροσολύμοις ἦν, καὶ τὰ πάτρια καθαρῶς ἐτήρει. διὰ πάσης γοῦν αὑτὸν ἦγεν ἁγνείας, οὐδὲ ἡμέρα τὶς παρώδευεν αὐτῷ τῆς νομίμης χηρεύουσα θυσίας. This character will abundantly account for his persecuting the Christians, who were so odious to the Jews, and for his vain-glorious acceptance of the impious homage of the people, ver. 23. **ἐπέβ. τ. χεῖρ.**] A pregnant construction. In full, it would be ἐπέβ. τὰς χ. ἐπί τινας τῶν ἀπὸ τ. ἐκκ., τοῦ κακῶσαι αὐτούς. Some expositors (Heinr., Kuin.), not seeing this, have endeavoured to give to ἐπέβ. τ. χ. the unexampled meaning, not justified by Deut. xii. 7, xv. 10, of '*took in hand*,' '*attempted*.' The E. V. '*stretched forth his hands*' (or, marg. '*began*') is equally inadmissible. It should be, **H. the K. laid his hands on certain of the church, to vex them.** **τῶν ἀπό**] See reff., and compare ch. vi. 9. **2. Ἰάκωβον**] Of him we know nothing besides what is related in the Gospels. He was the son of Zebedee, called (Matt. iv. 21) together with John his brother: was one of the favoured Three admitted to the death-chamber of Jairus's daughter (Mark v. 37), to the mount of transfiguration (Matt. xvii. 1), and to the agony in the garden (Matt. xxvi. 37). He, together with John his brother (named by our Lord 'Boanerges,' 'sons of thunder'), wished to call down fire on the inhospitable Samaritans (Luke ix. 54),—and prayed that his brother and himself might sit, one on the right hand and the other on the left, in the Lord's kingdom (Matt. xx. 20—24). It was then that He foretold to them their drinking of the cup of suffering and being baptized with the baptism which He was baptized with: a prophecy which James was the first to fulfil. *This is the only Apostle of whose death we have any certain record.* With regard to all the rest, tradition varies, more or less, as to the place, or the manner, or the time of their deaths. Eusebius, H. E. ii. 9, relates, from the Hypotyposes of Clemens, who had received it ἐκ παραδόσεως τῶν πρὸ αὐτοῦ, that the accuser of James, struck by his confession, became a Christian, and was led away with him to martyrdom, συναπήχθησαν οὖν ἄμφω, φησί, καὶ κατὰ τὴν ὁδὸν ἠξίωσεν ἀφεθῆναι αὐτῷ ὑπὸ τοῦ Ἰακώβου. ὁ δὲ ὀλίγον σκεψάμενος, εἰρήνη σοι, εἶπε, καὶ κατεφίλησεν αὐτόν. καὶ οὕτως ἀμφότεροι ὁμοῦ ἐκαρατομήθησαν. **μαχαίρῃ**] Probably according to the Roman method of beheading, which became common among the later Jews. It was a punishment accounted extremely disgraceful by the Jews: see Lightf. in loc. **3.**] See the character of Agrippa above. **προς. συλλ.**] A Hebraism: see reff. **αἱ ἡμ. τ. ἀζ.**] Wieseler (Chronol. der Apost. Zeit. pp. 215—220) regards the whole of the following narrative as having happened on one and the same day and night, viz. that of the 14th of Nisan (April 1), A.D. 44. He takes τὸ πάσχα in the strict meaning, '*the passover*,' i. e. the eating of the passover on the evening of the 14th of Nisan, and thinks that Herod was intending to bring Peter forth on the next morning. He finds support for this in the four quaternions of soldiers, the guard for one night (see below), and maintains that the expression τὸ πάσχα cannot apply to the whole festal period, which would have been τὴν ἑορτήν, or ταύτας τὰς ἡμέρας. But Bleek (Beiträge zur Ev.-kritik, p. 144) calls this view most arbitrary and even un-

l = Matt. v. 25. xviii. 34. Luke xii. 58. see ch. xvi. 4.
m here only †. τινὰ τῶν ἐν τοῖς τετραδίοις φυλάκων, Philo in Flacc. § 13, vol. ii. p. 533.
n = Luke viii. 29. ch. xxiii. 35. xxviii. 16.
o Matt. xxvi. 2, &c. ‖. 4 Kings xxiii. 22.
p here (Luke xxii. 66 v. r.) only. 2 Macc. vi. 10 A compl.

ABDE HLPℵ a b c d f g h k l o p 13

φυλακήν, [l] παραδοὺς τέσσαρσιν [m] τετραδίοις στρατιωτῶν [n] φυλάσσειν αὐτόν, βουλόμενος μετὰ τὸ [o] πάσχα [p] ἀναγαγεῖν αὐτὸν τῷ λαῷ.
5 ὁ μὲν οὖν Πέτρος [q] ἐτηρεῖτο ἐν τῇ φυλακῇ· [r] προσευχὴ δὲ [s] ἦν [t] ἐκτενῶς [u] γινομένη [u] ὑπὸ τῆς ἐκκλησίας [r] πρὸς τὸν θεὸν *[v] ὑπὲρ αὐτοῦ.
6 ὅτε δὲ ἤμελλεν [w] προαγαγεῖν αὐτὸν ὁ Ἡρώδης, τῇ νυκτὶ ἐκείνῃ [s] ἦν ὁ Πέτρος [x] κοιμώμενος [y] μεταξὺ δύο στρατιωτῶν δεδεμένος [z] ἁλύσεσιν δυσίν, [a] φύλακές τε πρὸ τῆς θύρας [q] ἐτήρουν

q = Matt. xxvii. 36. ch. xvi. 23. xxv. 4, 21. Prov. xix. 16.
r Rom. xv. 30. 2 Chron. xxxiii. 18. see Luke vi. 12.
s constr., ch. ii. 5 reff.
t 1 Pet. i. 22 only. Jonah iii. 8. (-νέστερον προσηύχετο, Luke xxii. 44 only. -νεια, ch. xxvi. 7. -νής, 1 Pet. iv. 8.)
u Luke ix. 7. xiii. 17. xxiii. 8. Eph. v. 12.
v = Matt. v. 44. περί, Col. i. 9. Luke vi. 28. xxii. 32. Col. i. 3 al.
w = ch. (xvi. 30.) xvii. 5. xxv. 26 †. 2 Macc. v. 18. Jos. Antt. xvi. 11. 6, προαγαγὼν (ὁ Ἡρώδης) εἰς ἐκκλησίαν τριακοσίους τῶν ἡγεμόνων.
x = Matt. xxviii. 13. Luke xxii. 45. (1 Cor. vii. 39 reff.) Prov. iv. 16.
y = Luke xi. 51 ‖. xvi. 26 †. (ch. xv. 9 reff.)
z here bis. Mark v. 3, &c. ‖. ch. xxi. 33. xxviii. 20. Eph. vi. 20. 2 Tim. i. 16. Rev. xx. 1 only †. Wisd. xvii. 17 only. Exod. xxviii. 22 Aq. Symm. (Theod.?). see LXX ib.
a ch. v. 23. ver. 19 only. Cant. v. 7.

4. for ον και, τουτον D [Lucif$_1$]. εν φυλακη E-gr. παραδιδους A, *tradens* vulg E-lat. om τεσσαρσιν H[^{1} : insd in marg eadem manu]. om 1st αυτον D vulg(not am [fuld]). αγαγειν A e.

5. rec εκτενης, with A^{2}EHLP p rel 36 [Bas$_1$] Chr$_1$ Sev-c$_1$: txt A^1(appy) Bℵ 13. 40 vulg E-lat Lucif$_1$.—πολλη δε προσευχη ην εν εκτενεια περι αυτου απο της εκκλ. πρ. τ. θ. περι αυτ.(sic) D(om 1st περι αυτου D-corr). γενομενη P e p. om πρ. τον θεον B. *περὶ A-corr BDℵ o p 13. 40 (*probably a corrn, see ch.* viii. 15 : *the two are indifferently used in this connexion, see Lexx and reff: but* περι *is the more usual*) : υπερ (A^1 ?)EHLP rel 36 [Bas$_1$] Chr Sev-c.

6. (ημελλ., so BELPℵ c l p 13.) rec προαγειν (*corrn*), with DEHLP rel Chr : προσαγειν ℵ o : txt A a p 36, προσαγαγειν B 13. rec αυτ. bef προ., with HLP rel Thl : txt ABDEℵ a h k o p 13. 36 Chr. om 1st ο D lect-12. κοιμουμενος D^1(txt D^s). for τε, δε D E-lat copt : om e 133. προς τη θυρα A.

natural; and I own, with all respect for Wieseler's general acumen, I am disposed to agree with this criticism. The whole cast of the narrative,—the ἦσαν **αἱ** ἡμέραι, not ἦν ἡ ἡμέρα τῶν ἀζ., Luke's own expression in his Gospel, xxii. 7,—the intimation of *enduring custody* in the παραδοὺς . . . . φυλάσσειν αὐτ.,—the delay implied in the βουλόμενος,—in the imperfects ἐτηρεῖτο,—ἦν γινομένη (not ἐγένετο),—the specification of τῇ νυκτὶ ἐκείνῃ as presupposing (notwithstanding what Wieseler says to the contrary) more nights preceding,—all this would be unaccountable in the precise historical diction of Luke, unless he had intended to convey an impression that *some days elapsed.* But still more decisive is his own definition of πάσχα, Luke xxii. 1, **ἡ ἑορτὴ τῶν ἀζύμων, ἡ λεγομένη πάσχα.** So that μετὰ τὸ πάσχα may well = μετὰ τὴν ἑορτὴν τῶν ἀζύμων. The argument from the four quaternions of soldiers proves nothing: the same sixteen (see below) may have had him in *permanent* charge, that number being appointed as adequate to the duties required. **4. τέσσαρσιν τετραδίοις**] In military arrangements, Herod seems to have retained the Roman habits, according to which the night was divided into four watches, and each committed to four soldiers (διδόασι φυλάκεια δύο· τὸ δὲ φυλάκειόν ἐστιν ἐκ τεσσάρων ἀνδρῶν, Polyb. vi. 33. 7), to two of whom the prisoner was chained, the other two keeping watch before the doors of the prison, forming the *first* and *second guards* of ver. 10. It is plain that this number being mentioned is no sign that the custody was only for *one night.* **μετὰ τὸ πάσχα**] (see above) **after the days of the feast,** i. e. after the 21st of Nisan. Herod, who (ver. 1, note) observed rigorously the Jewish customs, would not execute a prisoner during the feast: 'Non judicant die festo' (Moed Katon v. 2, Meyer). **ἀναγ. αὐτ. τῷ λαῷ**] See ref.: **to bring him out and sentence him in sight of the people.**

5.] On the *duration* implied by this verse, see above. **6. ἐκείνῃ**] emphatic: **that very night,** viz. which preceded the day of trial. The practice of attaching a prisoner to one keeper or more by a chain is alluded to by several ancient authors: e. g. Seneca, de Tranquill. 10, 'Eadem custodia universos circumdedit, alligatique sunt etiam qui alligaverunt, nisi tu forte leviorem in sinistra catenam putas:' and Epist. 5: 'Quemadmodum eadem catena et militem et custodiam copulat.' In the

τὴν φυλακήν. 7 καὶ ἰδοὺ ἄγγελος κυρίου [b] ἐπέστη, καὶ
[c] φῶς [cd] ἔλαμψεν ἐν τῷ [e] οἰκήματι· [f] πατάξας δὲ τὴν
...λεγων ανα d. [g] πλευρὰν τοῦ Πέτρου [h] ἤγειρεν αὐτὸν λέγων [i] Ἀνάστα
ABDE HLPℵ a bcfgh klop 13 [j] ἐν τάχει. καὶ [k] ἐξέπεσαν αὐτοῦ αἱ [z] ἁλύσεις ἐκ τῶν
χειρῶν. 8 εἶπέν τε ὁ ἄγγελος πρὸς αὐτὸν [l] Ζῶσαι καὶ
[m] ὑπόδησαι τὰ [n] σανδάλιά σου. ἐποίησεν δὲ οὕτως. καὶ
λέγει αὐτῷ [o] Περιβαλοῦ τὸ ἱμάτιόν σου καὶ ἀκολούθει
μοι. 9 καὶ ἐξελθὼν ἠκολούθει, καὶ οὐκ ᾔδει ὅτι ἀληθές
[p] ἐστιν τὸ γινόμενον [q] διὰ τοῦ ἀγγέλου, ἐδόκει δὲ [r] ὅραμα
βλέπειν. 10 [s] διελθόντες δὲ πρώτην [t] φυλακὴν καὶ δευτέραν ἦλθαν ἐπὶ τὴν πύλην τὴν [u] σιδηρᾶν τὴν [v] φέρουσαν
εἰς τὴν πόλιν, [w] ἥτις [x] αὐτομάτη ἠνοίγη αὐτοῖς· καὶ ἐξελθόντες [y] προῆλθον [z] ῥύμην μίαν, καὶ εὐθέως [a] ἀπέστη ὁ

b = ch. iv. 1 reff.
c Matt. v. 16. 2 Cor. iv. 6 only. (Prov. iv. 18.) see ch. xxvi. 13.
d as above (c). Matt. v. 15. xvii. 2. Luke xvii. 24. 2 Cor. iv. 6 only.
e here only ‡. = Wisd. xiii. 15. Thucyd. iv. 48 init. (Ezek. xvi. 24.)
f = here only. (see ver. 23.) = ἥψατο, 3 Kings xix. 5, 7.
g John xix. 34. xx. 20, 25, 27 only. Num xxxiii. 55. 2 Kings ii. 16 B Ald. compl.
h = Mark iv. 27. Luke viii. 24 al. Gen. xli. 4. i ch. ix. 6 reff. j Rom. xvi. 20 reff.
k ch. xxvii. 32. James i. 11 al. Isa. xxviii. 1, 4. l John xxi. 18 bis only. Neh. iv 18.
m Mark vi. 9. Eph. vi. 15 only. 2 Chron. xxviii. 15. Ezek. xvi. 10 only. n Mark vi. 6 only. Isa. xx. 2. Judith x. 4. xvi. 9 only. o Acts, here only. Luke xii. 27 ‖. Rev. iii. 5 al. Esth. v. 1. Ezek. xviii. 7, 16. p pres., ch. xvi. 38 reff. q ch. ii. 43. iv. 16 al.
r ch. vii. 31 reff. s constr., ch. xiii. 6 reff. t = here only. Xen. Cyr. i. 6. 43.
u Rev. ii. 27. ix. 9. xii. 5. xix. 15 only. Deut. iii. 11. v = here only. Xen. Cyr. v. 4. 41.
w ch. xi. 28 al. fr. x Mark iv. 28 only. Lev. xxv. 5, 11. 4 Kings xix. 29. Wisd. xvii. 6 only. = Jos. B. J. vi. 5. 3, ἡ πύλη . . . ὤφθη αὐτομάτως ἠνεῳγμένη. y constr., here only. Xen. Cyr. ii. 4. 18. (Matt. xxvi. 39 ‖. Gen. xxxiii. 14.) z ch. ix. 11 reff. a = ch. xv. 38 reff. 1 Kings xvi. 14.

7. aft επεστη ins τω πετρω D syr-w-ast sah æth. **επελαμψεν**, omg εν follg, D. for παταξας, νυξας D syrr, *compungens* Lucif$_1$. (εξεπεσαν, so ABDEℵ p.) [αι αλ. εκ τ. χ. bef] αυτου D-gr vulg [syrr] arm [Lucif$_1$].

8. for τε, δε (*alteration, as often, to more usual copula, but* τε *is characteristic of the Acts*) BDEH a c 36 [vulg syr] sah Thl-sif: txt ALPℵ p 13 rel Syr æth [arm] Chr$_1$ Thl-fin. πρ. αυτ. bef ο αγ. L b [Syr æth]. rec **περιζωσαι** (*alteration for more precision, and perhaps, as Meyer, to agree better with* υποδησαι, *also a compound*), with EHLP rel: txt ABDℵ a p 13. 36 Bas$_1$ Chr-comm$_1$. υποδυσαι B^1.

9. om και εξελθων ηκολουθει (και *to* και) P. rec aft ηκολ. ins αυτω (*supplementary, to corresp to* μοι *above*), with EHLℵ^3 rel am [syrr coptt æth] Chr$_1$: om ABD [P(see above)] ℵ^1 p 13. 40 tol arm. γενομ. L b c p 180. for δια, υπο (*corrn, not observing the peculiar force of* δια *here, said of the secondary agent. This is much more probable than the converse. Both exprr are used by Luke: cf for* δια, *reff: for* υπο, *Luke* ix. 7; xiii. 17; xxiii. 8. *But this latter he uses always of* our Lord, *the prime Agent in the miracle. See also Eph* v. 12) AH e l syr-mg [arm] Chr$_1$ Thl-fin: παρα c: txt BDELPℵ 13. 36 rel [vulg syrr copt] Chr$_1$ Thl-sif. for δε, γαρ D 3. 15-8. 36. 95. 180 tol Syr sah arm: om ℵ^1.

10. κ. δευτ. bef φυλ. D vulg Lucif. (**ηλθαν**. so ABℵ 13.) om την φερ. εις τ. π. L Syr: [for εις] επι p 13. 96. 142. rec ηνοιχθη, with EHLP Chr$_1$: txt ABDℵ p 13. 36. (ηνυγη B^{1}Dℵ: ηνοιγε 13.) aft εξελθ. ins κατεβησαν τους ζ' βαθμους και D. προσηλθ. D[L(-θαν)]. **απηλθεν** A.

account of the imprisonment of Herod Agrippa himself by Tiberius, Jos. Antt. xviii. 6. 7, we read of the συνδεδεμένος αὐτῷ στρατιώτης. And we have an edict of Constantius, commanding, for binding prisoners, 'prolixiores catenas, si criminis qualitas etiam catenarum acerbitatem postulaverit, ut et cruciatio desit, et permaneat sub fida custodia.' (Wieseler, p. 414.) See note on ch. xxiv. 23; see also ch. xxviii. 16, 20. **ἐτήρουν τὴν φυλ.**] not, *kept the watch* (Raphel, Wolf, al.),—but **guarded the prison.** **7.**] **οἰκήματι, the chamber.** It is in St. Luke's manner **to** relate simultaneously the angelic appearance and the shining of a light around: cf. Luke ii. 9; xxiv. 4; ch. x. 30. The light accompanied, or perhaps, as suggested here in syr-marg, *shone from*, the angel.

9.] **ἐξελθών**, viz. from the οἴκημα.

10.] The *first* and *second* watch or guard cannot mean the two soldiers to whom he was chained, on account of ἐξελθών above: but are probably the other two, one at the door of the chamber, the other at the outer door of the building. Then 'the iron gate leading into the city' was that outside the prison buildings, forming the exit from the premises. The situation of the prison is uncertain, but

ἄγγελος ἀπ᾽ αὐτοῦ. 11 καὶ ὁ Πέτρος ᵇ ἐν ἑαυτῷ ᵇ γενόμενος
εἶπεν Νῦν οἶδα ᶜ ἀληθῶς ὅτι ᵈ ἐξαπέστειλεν κύριος τὸν
ἄγγελον αὐτοῦ καὶ ᵉ ἐξείλατό με ἐκ ᶠ χειρὸς Ἡρώδου καὶ
πάσης τῆς ᵍ προςδοκίας τοῦ λαοῦ τῶν Ἰουδαίων. 12 ʰ συν-
ιδών τε ἦλθεν ⁱ ἐπὶ τὴν οἰκίαν τῆς Μαρίας τῆς μητρὸς
Ἰωάννου τοῦ ᵏ ἐπικαλουμένου Μάρκου, οὗ ἦσαν ˡ ἱκανοὶ
ᵐ συνηθροισμένοι καὶ ⁿ προσευχόμενοι. 13 ᵒᵖ κρούσαντος δὲ
αὐτοῦ τὴν ᵒ θύραν τοῦ ᑫ πυλῶνος ʳ προςῆλθεν ˢ παιδίσκη
ᵗ ὑπακοῦσαι, ὀνόματι Ῥόδη· 14 καὶ ᵘ ἐπιγνοῦσα τὴν ᵘ φωνὴν
τοῦ Πέτρου ᵛ ἀπὸ τῆς χαρᾶς οὐκ ἤνοιξεν τὸν ᑫ πυλῶνα,
ʷ εἰςδραμοῦσα δὲ ˣ ἀπήγγειλεν ˣ ἑστάναι τὸν Πέτρον πρὸ
τοῦ ᑫ πυλῶνος. 15 οἱ δὲ πρὸς αὐτὴν εἶπαν ʸ Μαίνῃ. ἡ δὲ
ᶻ διισχυρίζετο ᵃ οὕτως ᵃ ἔχειν. οἱ δὲ ἔλεγον Ὁ ᵇ ἄγγελός

ABDE HLPℵ a b c f g h k l o p 13

b here only. (see Luke xv. 17.) Xen. Anab. i. 5. 17.
c = John vii. 26. xvii. 8 only. Exod. xxxiii. 16.
d ch. vii. 12 reff.
e ch. vii. 10 reff.
f [ch. xxiv. 7.] John x. 28, 29 al. Mic. iv. 10.
g Luke xxi. 26 only. Gen. xlix. 10.
h = ch. xiv. 6 (v. 2. 1 Cor. iv. 4) only‡. (Lev. v. 1.) 1 Macc. iv. 21 al.
i = Matt. xxi. 19. Luke xxiv. 1 al. Gen. xxii. 9.
k ch. i. 23 reff.
l ch. xiv. 21. xix. 19 al. 1 Macc. xiii. 49.
m ch. xix. 25 only. Deut. i. 41.
n absol., ch. x. 9 reff.
o and constr., Luke xiii. 25 (Rev. iii. 20). Judg. xix. 22 A (Cant. v. 2). Judith xiv. 14 only.
p as above (o). ver. 16. Matt. vii. 7, 8. Luke xi. 9, 10. xii. 36 only.
q ch. x. 17 reff.
r constr., ch. vii. 31 al. Lev. xxi. 21.
s = Matt. xxvi. 69 al. Gen. xx. 17.
t = here only. Xen. Symp. i. 11.
u here only. 1 Kings xxvi. 17.
v = Matt. xiii. 44. xviii. 7. John xxi. 6 al. 2 Chron. v. 6.
w here only †. 2 Macc. v. 26 only.
x constr., here only (ch. xxvi. 20).
y John x. 20. ch. xxvi. 24, 25. 1 Cor. xiv. 23 only. Jer. xxxvi. (xxix.) 26. Wisd. xiv. 28 only.
z Luke xxii. 59 only †.
a ch. vii. 1 reff.
b = Matt. xviii. 10.

11. rec γενομ. bef εν εαυτω, with EHLP rel [syr coptt arm] Chr: txt ABDℵ a c p 13 vulg Lucif.—αυτω B¹. οτι bef αληθως DE æth Chr₁ Lucif₁. ins ο bef κυριος B c 180 [Chr]: ο θεος a 27-9. 36. 105-63. (εξειλατο, so ABDEH[L]ℵ p 13. 36.) ins εκ bef πασης E 73 vulg Lucif. om του λαου A Syr.
12. συν. δε A a k o p 13. 36 [E-lat] coptt: om τε 59¹: και συν. D: txt B E[-gr] HLPℵ rel [vulg syrr arm] Chr. add ο πετρος P f. rec om 1st της (*as unnecessary?*), with EHLP rel 36(sic) Chr₁: ins ABDℵ p. (13 def.)
13. [κρουσαντες D-gr p¹.] rec for αυτου, του πετρου (*explanatory*, συνιδων *beginning an ecclesiastical portion*), with EH rel 36 syr Chr [Thl-sif]: txt ABD[L]Pℵ p 13 vulg Syr coptt [æth] arm Thl-fin. πυλωνος is written by D⁶(?), the former reading which occupied more space having been obliterated: *foris* D-lat. προηλθε B²(Mai: "B³ et fortasse jam B²," Tischdf) ℵ 3 [*processit* vulg]. υπακουουσα ℵ¹(txt ℵ-corr¹). ον. ροδ. bef υπακ. D.
14. aft ηνοιξεν ins αυτω E c Syr syr-w-ast. for τον πυλωνα, την θυραν E. ins και bef εισδρ. δε D¹(and lat). om 2nd τον D¹(ins D³).
15. ο(sic) δε ε(λε)γον αυτη D¹: οι δε προς αυτην (without ειπ.) D¹.—ειπ. bef πρ. αυτ. 13. (ειπαν, so ABℵ [p].) for ελεγον, ειπαν B lect-12 [Chr₁]. aft ελεγον

seems to have been *in* the city. The additional clause in D (see var. readd.) is remarkable, and can hardly be other than genuine. **11.] ἐν ἑαυτῷ γ.**, as E. V. **coming to himself**: having recovered his self-consciousness. He was before in the half consciousness of one who is dreaming and knows that it is a dream: except that in his case the dream was *the truth*, and his supposition the unreality. **12. συνιδών]** Not, *considerans* (as Vulg., Beza, Grot.): nor, '*being aware of the place of meeting*,' with reference to what follows (Meyer), against which the aorist is decisive, importing some single act and not a state: but, as reff., referring to what *went before* (οἶδα ἀληθῶς κ.τ.λ.), **having become aware of it.** **Ἰωάννου]** It is uncertain whether this John Mark was the same as the Evangelist Mark: but they have been generally believed to be the same. For a full account of him, see Prolegomena to Mark (Vol. I. § i.). His mother Mary was not sister, but aunt of Barnabas: see Col. iv. 10, note. **15. ἄγγελός ἐστ. αὐτοῦ]** No other rendering but **his angel** will suit the sense: and with a few exceptions (Camero, Basnage, Hammond, and one or two more) all Commentators, ancient and modern, have recognized this meaning. Our Lord *plainly asserts the doctrine of guardian angels* in ref. Matt. (see note there): and from this we further learn in what sense His words were understood by the early church. From His words taken with the context (μὴ καταφρονήσητε **ἑνὸς** τῶν μικρῶν τούτων) we infer that *each one* has his guardian angel: from this passage we find not only that such was believed to be the case, but that it was supposed

ἐστιν αὐτοῦ. 16 ὁ δὲ Πέτρος [c] ἐπέμενεν [d] κρούων· [e] ἀνοίξαντες δὲ εἶδαν αὐτὸν καὶ [f] ἐξέστησαν. 17 [g] κατασείσας δὲ
αὐτοῖς τῇ χειρὶ [h] σιγᾷν, [i] διηγήσατο αὐτοῖς [i] πῶς ὁ κύριος
αὐτὸν [k] ἐξήγαγεν [k] ἐκ τῆς [l] φυλακῆς. εἶπέν τε Ἀπαγγείλατε
Ἰακώβῳ καὶ τοῖς ἀδελφοῖς ταῦτα. καὶ [m] ἐξελθὼν ἐπορεύθη
εἰς [n] ἕτερον τόπον. 18 [o] γενομένης δὲ [o] ἡμέρας ἦν [p] τάραχος
[q] οὐκ [q] ὀλίγος [r] ἐν τοῖς στρατιώταις [s] τί ἄρα ὁ Πέτρος
[s] ἐγένετο. 19 Ἡρώδης δὲ [t] ἐπιζητήσας αὐτὸν καὶ μὴ εὑρών,
[u] ἀνακρίνας τοὺς [v] φύλακας ἐκέλευσεν [w] ἀπαχθῆναι· καὶ
[x] κατελθὼν ἀπὸ τῆς Ἰουδαίας εἰς Καισάρειαν [y] διέτριβεν.

c [constr., John viii. 7.] ἀπειθῶν ἐπιμένει, Philo de Agricult. § 15, vol. i. p. 271.
d ver. 13.
e absol., Matt. xxv. 11. Luke xiii. 25. ch. v. 23 al. Isa. xxii. 22.
f = 2 Cor. v. 13 reff.
g w. dat., ch. xiii. 16. xxi. 40 only. Jos. Antt. viii. 11. 2. w. acc., ch. xix. 33 †. (1 Macc. vi. 38 only.)
h Luke ix. 36. xviii. 39. xx. 26. ch. xv. 12, 13. Rom. xvi. 25. 1 Cor. xiv. 28, 30, 34 only. L.P. Eccl. iii. 7. Sir. xiii. 23.
i ch. ix. 27 reff.
k ch. vii. 40. xiii. 17. Heb. viii. 9. Exod. xx. 2.
l = ver. 5 al.
m absol., vv. 9, 10. ch. xvi. 36. Exod. xvi. 4.
n = ch. xvii. 7 reff.
o = Luke iv. 42. vi. 13. ch. xvi. 35 al. L.
p ch. xix. 23 only. 1 Kings v. 9. Wisd. xiv. 25 ABCℵ Ald. compl. (-χή, Ed-vat.) only. [-χή, Mark xiii. 8.]
q ch. xiv. 28 al6. Acts only. Isa. x. 7.
r = Mark vi. 4 al.
s here only. see John xxi. 21. Luke i. 66.
t Luke iv. 42. 1 Kings xx. 1.
u ch. iv. 9 reff.
v ver. 6.
w = absol., here only. (see Gen. xlii. 16.) Matt. xxvii. 31 ‖. Ep. Jer. 18. constr., ch. xxi. 33.
x ch. viii. 5 reff.
y ch. xv. 35 al6.. Acts only, exc. John iii. 22. Jer. xlii. (xxxv.) 7.

add *προς αυτην τυχον* D Syr. om *ὁ* ℵ1 [Chr-comm$_1$]. rec *αυτου* bef *εστ.*, with DEHLPℵ3 13 rel Orig$_1$ [Eus$_1$ Chr$_1$]: txt ABℵ1.

16. om *πετρ.* D. *εξανοιξ. δε και ιδοντες αυτ. και εξ.* D1. (*ειδαν*, so AB.)

17. *κατασισαντος δε αυτου σιγ.* A. for *σιγαν*, *ινα σειγα . . σιν* D1. ins *εισηλθεν και* bef *διηγ.* D Syr syr-w-ast. om 2nd *αυτοις* Aℵ a p 13. 33. 69. 100-5 lect-12 vulg arm: ins BDEHLP rel 36 Chr. *αυτον* bef *ο κυρ.* A: *εξηγαγεν* bef *αυτον* p 13. 40. 73 [Thl-fin$_1$]. rec for *τε*, *δε* (*see above, ver* 3), with DHLP rel 36 syr copt Chr$_1$: txt ABEℵ p vulg Syr sah æth.

18. om *ουκ ολιγ.* D 76 Lucif$_1$: *μεγας* 15-8. 36. 180 Syr sah arm.

19. for *δε*, *τε* A a æth. *αποκτανθηναι* D1-gr(txt D-corr1·2) Syr copt [arm. (Tischdf gives also syr æth-pl)]. rec ins *την* bef *καισ.* (*insertion to answer to της ιουδ.*), with HLP rel Chr: om ABDEℵ a e p 13. 40. *διετριψεν* A [copt].

that such angel *occasionally appeared in the semblance* (seeing that he spoke with the voice) *of the person himself.* We do not, it is true, know who the speakers were: nor is the peculiar form in which they viewed the doctrine binding upon us: it may have been erroneous, and savouring of superstition. But of the *doctrine itself* this may not be said, *as the Lord Himself has asserted it.* See Wordsw.'s interesting note here. For what *purpose* they supposed this angel to have come, does not appear in the narrative.

17. κατασείσας] see reff. His motive was *haste:* he tells briefly the particulars of his deliverance, and, while it was yet night, hastily departs.

Ἰακώβῳ] James, *the brother of the Lord,* whom we find presiding over the church at Jerusalem, ch. xv. 13; xxi. 18; Gal. ii. 12. See Gal. i. 19; ii. 9. He appears also to be mentioned in 1 Cor. xv. 7. I believe him to have been one of those ἀδελφοὶ τοῦ κυρίου mentioned Matt. xiii. 55; John vii. 5; ch. i. 14; 1 Cor. ix. 5, of whom I have in the note on the first of these passages maintained, that they were His real maternal brethren, sons of Joseph and Mary:—to have been an *Apostle,* as Paul and Barnabas, but not of the number of the twelve (see note on ch. xiv. 4):—and to have been therefore of course distinct from James the son of Alphæus, enumerated (Matt. x. 3 ‖) *among* the twelve. The reasons for this belief I reserve for the Prolegomena to the Epistle of James.

εἰς ἕτερον τόπον] I see in these words a minute mark of truth in our narrative. Under the circumstances, the place of Peter's retreat would very naturally at the time be kept secret. It probably was unknown to the person from whom the narrative came, or designedly left indefinite. And so it has remained, the narrative not following Peter's history any longer. We find him again at Jerusalem in ch. xv. Whether he left it or not on this occasion is uncertain. It is not asserted in ἐξελθών,—which only implies that he left the *house.*

18. γενομένης ἡμέρας] Wieseler argues from this, and I think rightly, that the deliverance of Peter must have taken place in the *last* watch of the night (3—6 A.M. in April), for otherwise his escape would have been perceived *before* the break of day, viz. at the next change of the watch.

τί . . . . ἐγένετο] So Theocr. Id. xiv. 51, ἀδίστα Γοργοῖ, τί

20 ἦν δὲ [z] θυμομαχῶν Τυρίοις καὶ Σιδωνίοις· [a] ὁμοθυμαδὸν
δὲ [b] παρῆσαν [b] πρὸς αὐτόν, καὶ [c] πείσαντες Βλάστον τὸν
[d] ἐπὶ τοῦ [e] κοιτῶνος τοῦ βασιλέως [f] ᾐτοῦντο εἰρήνην, διὰ
τὸ [g] τρέφεσθαι αὐτῶν τὴν χώραν [h] ἀπὸ τῆς [i] βασιλικῆς,
21 [k] τακτῇ δὲ ἡμέρᾳ ὁ Ἡρώδης [l] ἐνδυσάμενος [m] ἐσθῆτα [i] βασιλικὴν καὶ [n] καθίσας ἐπὶ τοῦ [o] βήματος [p] ἐδημηγόρει πρὸς

ABDE HLPℵ a b c f g h k l o p 13

z here only †. Polyb. ix. 40. 4. μέχρι τῆς ἐσχάτης ἀναπνοῆς θυμομαχοῦντες, Diod. Sic. xvii. 33 end.
a ch. i. 14 reff.
b 2 Cor. xi. 8. Gal. iv. 18, 20 only.
c = Matt. xxviii 14. Gal. i. 10. 2 Macc. iv. 45. d ch. viii. 27 reff. e here only. Exod. viii. 3. f = ch. xvi. 29 reff. g = Matt. vi. 26 al. 3 Kings xviii. 13. h = Jude 23 al. i here bis. John iv. 46, 49. James ii. 8 only. *Num. xx. 17. k here only. Job xii. 5 only. l constr., Matt. vi. 25 al. Gen. xxxviii. 19. m ch. x. 30 reff. n constr., ch. xxv. 6 reff. o = Matt. xxvii. 19 || J. ch. (vii. 5.) xviii. 12, 16, 17. xxv. 6, 10, 17. Rom. xiv. 10. 2 Cor. v. 10 only. Neh. viii. 4. 2 Macc. xiii. 26. p here only. Prov. xxx. (see xxiv.) 31. (Neh. viii. 4 [6] Ald.) only. ἐδημηγόρει ἐν αὐτοῖς, Jos. Antt. ix. 13. 1.

20. for δε, γαρ D æth. rec aft δε ins ο ηρωδης (*as being the commencement of a new history,—that of the death of Herod*), with HLP rel 36 syr [arm] Chr_1, ηρωδης E a b¹ k o Thl-sif: om ABDℵ p 13. 40 vulg Syr coptt æth Lucif. D reads οι δε ομοθ. εξ αμφοτερων των πολεων παρησαν προς τον βασιλεα [simly syr-w-ast]. for του βασ., αυτου D-gr(om D-lat) o. ητησαντο A sah. τας χωρας αυτων D vulg Lucif: αυτους a: αυτ. την πολιν E-gr[and lat¹] 13. 33-4: *civitates* E-lat². for απο, εκ D 40. 105.

21. om ο B a. om και Bℵ p 40 [Bas-3-mss_1].

γενοίμεθα; **19. κατ. . . . . εἰς Καισ.**] These words are to be taken together, and ἐκεῖ or ἐν K. to be supplied with διέτριβεν. Kuin. takes εἰς K. as = ἐν K. with διέτρ., and κατελθών alone, which is not so natural on account of the position of the words. **20. θυμομαχῶν**] It is impossible that Herod should have been at *war* with the Tyrians and Sidonians, belonging as they did to a Roman province, and he himself being in high favour at Rome:—nor is this implied in our text. The quarrel, however it originated, appears to have been carried out on Herod's part by some commercial regulation opposed to their interest, dependent as they were on supplies from his territory. ἦν θυμ. is therefore best rendered as in E. V., **was highly displeased**. **ὁμ. παρῆσ.** viz. by a deputation. Blastus is a Roman name (Wetst. from an inscription), and, from Herod's frequent visits to Rome, it is likely that he would have Romans as his confidential servants. Blastus was his *cubicularius*, or *præfectus cubiculo* (Suet. Dom. 16): see ch. viii. 27. **εἰρήνην**] not (see above) *peace*, in its strict sense, but **reconciliation**. **διὰ τὸ τρέφεσθαι**] We learn from 1 Kings v. 11 that Solomon made presents of wheat and oil to Hiram in return for the cedar and fir-trees for the Lord's house: and from Ezek. xxvii. 17, that Judah and Israel exported wheat, honey, oil, and balm (or resin) to Tyre. In Ezra iii. 7 also, we find Zerubbabel giving meat, drink, and oil to them of Sidon and Tyre, to bring cedar-trees to Joppa. Mr. Humphry quotes from Bede, 'Tyrii necessariam habebant vicini regis amicitiam, eo quod eorum regio valde angusta et Galilææ Damascique pressa finibus esset.' An additional reason for their request at this particular time may have been, the prevalence of famine. **21.**] The account in Josephus is remarkably illustrative of the sacred text: τρίτον δὲ ἔτος αὐτῷ βασιλεύοντι τῆς ὅλης Ἰουδαίας πεπλήρωτο, καὶ παρῆν εἰς πόλιν Καισάρειαν . . . . συνετέλει δὲ ἐνταῦθα θεωρίας εἰς τὴν Καίσαρος τιμήν, ὑπὲρ τῆς ἐκείνου σωτηρίας ἑορτήν τινα ταύτην ἐπιστάμενος (probably the 'quinquennalia,' B. J. i. 21. 8. Wieseler, p. 133). καὶ παρ' αὐτὴν ἤθροιστο τῶν κατὰ τὴν ἐπαρχίαν ἐν τέλει καὶ προβεβηκότων εἰς ἀξίαν πλῆθος. δευτέρᾳ δὲ τῶν θεωριῶν ἡμέρᾳ στολὴν ἐνδυσάμενος ἐξ ἀργύρου πεποιημένην πᾶσαν, ὡς θαυμάσιον ὑφὴν εἶναι, παρῆλθεν εἰς τὸ θέατρον ἀρχομένης ἡμέρας. ἔνθα ταῖς πρώταις τῶν ἡλιακῶν ἀκτίνων ἐπιβολαῖς ὁ ἄργυρος καταυγασθεὶς θαυμασίως ἀπέστιλβε, μαρμαίρων τι φοβερὸν καὶ τοῖς εἰς αὐτὸν ἀτενίζουσι φρικῶδες. εὐθὺς δὲ οἱ κόλακες τὰς οὐδὲ ἐκείνῳ πρὸς ἀγαθοῦ ἄλλος ἄλλοθεν φωνὰς ἀνεβόων θεὸν προσαγορεύοντες, Εὐμενὴς τε εἴης, ἐπιλέγοντες, εἰ καὶ μέχρι νῦν ὡς ἄνθρωπον ἐφοβήθημεν, ἀλλὰ τοὐντεῦθεν κρείττονά σε θνητῆς φύσεως ὁμολογοῦμεν. οὐκ ἐπέπληξε τούτοις ὁ βασιλεὺς οὐδὲ τὴν κολακείαν ἀσεβοῦσαν ἀπετρίψατο. ἀνακύψας δ' οὖν μετ' ὀλίγον τὸν βουβῶνα τῆς ἑαυτοῦ κεφαλῆς ὑπερκαθεζόμενον εἶδεν ἐπὶ σχοινίου τινός· ἄγγελον δὲ τοῦτον εὐθὺς ἐνόησεν κακῶν εἶναι, ... καὶ διακάρδιον ἔσχεν ὀδύνην. (This owl, Eusebius, H. E. ii. 10, *professing to quote Josephus*, makes into an angel. Having prefaced his quotation, αὐτοῖς γράμμασιν ὧδέ πως τὸ θαῦμα διηγεῖται, he cites thus: . . . . ἀνακύψας δὲ μετ' ὀλίγον, τῆς ἑαυτοῦ κεφαλῆς ὑπερκαθεζόμενον εἶδεν ἄγγελον.

αὐτούς. 22 ὁ δὲ q δῆμος r ἐπεφώνει Θεοῦ φωνὴ καὶ οὐκ
ἀνθρώπου. 23 s παραχρῆμα δὲ t ἐπάταξεν αὐτὸν ἄγγελος
κυρίου u ἀνθ' ὧν οὐκ v ἔδωκεν τὴν v δόξαν τῷ θεῷ, καὶ
γενόμενος w σκωληκόβρωτος x ἐξέψυξεν. 24 ὁ δὲ y λόγος
τοῦ θεοῦ y ηὔξανεν καὶ y ἐπληθύνετο. 25 Βαρνάβας δὲ καὶ
Σαῦλος z ὑπέστρεψαν z ἐξ Ἱερουσαλὴμ ab πληρώσαντες τὴν

q Acts only. ch. xvii. 5. xix. 30, 33 ‡. Num. i. 20 al. fr.
r Luke xxiii. 21. ch. xxi. 34. xxii. 24 only +. 2 Macc. i. 23. Esdr. ix. 47 only.
s ch. iii. 7 reff.
t = Rev. xi. 6. xix. 15. Gen. viii. 21. 2 Macc. ix. 5.
u Luke i. 20. xii. 3. xix. 44. 2 Thess. ii. 10 only. L.P. Deut. viii. 20.
v = Luke xvii. 18. John ix. 24. Rom. iv. 20. Rev. iv. 9. xi. 13. xiv. 7. xvi. 9. xix. 7 only. Josh. vii. 19.
w here only +. σκώληξ, Mark ix. 44, &c. (from Isa. lxvi. 24) only.
x ch. v. 5 reff.
y ch. vi. 7 reff.
z ἐκ, here only. Ruth i. 6 Ald. ἀπό, Luke iv. 1. xxiv. 9.
a = Matt. iii. 15. ch. xiii. 25. xiv. 26 al. Ps. xix. 4.
b Col. iv. 17.

22. at beg, ins καταλλαγεντος δε αυτου τοις τυριοις D : *reconciliatus est iis autem* syr-w-ast. φωνη bef θεου HLP²(P¹ has επεφωνη θῦ και (sic)) b e f g l o vss[not latt] : φωνη κυριου c : φωναι D¹[and lat](txt D³) vulg Syr Lucif₁. ανθρωπων ℵ¹ [Syr].

23. αυτ. bef επατ. D c 180 Thl-fin. om την (*alteration to more usual expr*) DEHLP rel: ins ABℵ d h k p 13. 36 [Bas₁]. και καταβας απο του βηματος γενομ. κωληκοβρωτος(sic D¹ : σκωλ. D²) ετι ζων και ουτως εξεψυξεν D.

24. for θεου, κυριου B vulg. ηυξανετο A : ευξανε D¹(txt D³) : ηξανεν (sic) P.

25. απεστρεψεν D¹(txt D³). for εξ, απο B¹(appy, Tischdf) D(E) b c o 36 vulg Chr-ms : εις B¹-corr HLPℵ k l p syr-mg [æth-rom] Chr-mss Thl : txt A 13(sic) rel coptt [syrr æth-pl(Tischdf) arm] Chr₁.—aft ιερ. add εις αντιοχειαν E a b e o Syr sah. (*The variations have apparently arisen from a confusion of marginal glosses.* εις αντ. *may have been an explanatory gloss, afterwards* substituted *for* εξ ιερ.; *then* αντ. *may have again been corrected to* ιερ., *leaving the* εις *standing.*)

τοῦτον εὐθὺς ἐνόησε κακῶν εἶναι αἴτιον κ.τ.λ. On the impossibility of acquitting the ecclesiastical historian of the charge of wilful fraud, see Heinichen's second Excursus in his edition of Eusebius. It may be a caution to us as to how much we may believe of his quotations of authors which *do not remain to us.*) ἀθρόον δὲ αὐτῷ τῆς κοιλίας προσέφυσεν ἄλγημα μετὰ σφοδρότητος ἀρξάμενον. ἀναθεωρῶν οὖν πρὸς τοὺς φίλους Ὁ θεὸς ὑμῖν ἐγώ, φησίν, ἤδη καταστρέφειν ἐπιτάττομαι τὸν βίον, παραχρῆμα τῆς εἱμαρμένης τὰς ἄρτι μου κατεψευσμένας φωνὰς ἐλεγχούσης· καὶ ὁ κληθεὶς ἀθάνατος ὑφ' ὑμῶν ἤδη θανὼν ἀπάγομαι. . . . . συνεχῶς δὲ ἐφ' ἡμέρας πέντε τῷ τῆς γαστρὸς ἀλγήματι διεργασθεὶς τὸν βίον κατέστρεψεν. Antt. xix. 8. 2.

The circumstance related in our text, of the *answer to the Sidonian embassy,* of which Josephus seems not to have been aware, *having been one object* of Herod on the occasion, shews an accuracy of detail which well accords with the view of the material of this part of the Acts having been collected at Cæsarea, where the event happened (see Prolegg. to Acts, § ii. 11). **23.**] The *fact* may be correctly related by Josephus (see above): but our narrative alleges the *cause* of what happened to have been the *displeasure of God,* and the stroke to have been inflicted *by His angel.* Compare 2 Kings xix. 35; 1 Chron. xxi. 15, 16. But no *appearance* of an angel is implied: nor was I aware that such had ever been inferred; but I see in Valesius's note on Euseb. ii. 10, "Quasi vero non utrumque fieri potuerit, ut et bubo supra caput Agrippæ, et ex alia parte angelus eidem appareret." **σκωληκόβρωτος**] Another additional particular: and one to be expected from a physician. In several cases of deaths by divine judgment we have accounts of this loathsome termination of the disease. So Herodotus, iv. 205, ἡ Φερετίμη . . . . ζῶσα εὐλέων ἐξέζεσε: which he alleges as an instance that excessive indulgence of revenge, such as Pheretima had shewn against the Barcæans, is looked on with anger by the gods. See too the very similar account of the death of Antiochus Epiphanes, 2 Macc. ix. 5—9. So also Jos. Antt. xvii. 6. 5, describing the disease of which Herod the Great died, mentions σῆψις σκώληκας ἐμποιοῦσα. So also Euseb. (viii. 16) of the death of Galerius. So also Tertullian, ad Scapulam, c. 3, vol. i. p. 702, Migne, "Claudius Lucius Herminianus in Cappadocia, cum indigne ferens uxorem suam ad hanc sectam transiisse, solusque in prætorio suo vastatus peste vivus vermibus ebullisset, Nemo sciat, aiebat, ne gaudeant Christiani. Postea cognito errore suo, quod tormentis quosdam a proposito suo excidere fecisset, pæne Christianus decessit." **24.**] Similarly, ch. v. 12 ff.; vi. 7; ix. 31, a general statement of the progress and prosperity of the church of God forms the transition from one portion of the history to another. **25.**] The

c = ch. vi. 1 reff.† d ch. xv. 37, 38. Gal. ii. 1 only. Gen. xix. 17. Job i. 4 only. e ver. 12. f ch. xi. 1 reff. g ellips. of ἐκεῖ, Mark viii. 1. ch. xxii. 12. h ch. xi. 27 reff.

[bc] διακονίαν, [d] συμπαραλαβόντες [καὶ] Ἰωάννην τὸν [e] ἐπικληθέντα Μάρκον.

XIII. 1 Ἦσαν δὲ ἐν Ἀντιοχείᾳ [f] κατὰ τὴν [g] οὖσαν
ἐκκλησίαν [hi] προφῆται καὶ [ik] διδάσκαλοι, ὅ τε Βαρνάβας
καὶ Συμεὼν ὁ καλούμενος Νίγερ καὶ Λούκιος ὁ Κυρηναῖος,
Μαναήν τε Ἡρώδου τοῦ [l] τετράρχου [m] σύντροφος καὶ

d παραλαβόντες...

C ος Μαναην ...

ABCDE HLPℵa bcdfg hklop 13

i 1 Cor. xii. 28, 29. Eph. iv. 11. k Rom. ii. 20. 1 Tim. ii. 7. 2 Tim. i. 11†. 2 Macc. i. 10 only. l Luke iii. 19. ix. 7 || Mt. only. (-χεῖν, Luke iii. 1.) m here only†. = 2 Macc. ix. 29 only. Thuc. ii. 50 (of diseases). Xen. Mem. ii. 3, 4.

for 2nd και, τον D[1]: om ABℵ 36 vulg Syr [sah]: txt D[8]EHLP p rel syr copt [æth] Chr. (13 def.) επικαλουμενον Aℵ k p 13. 36 Thl-fin.

Chap. XIII. 1. rec aft ησαν δε ins τινες (*see note*), with EHLP 13. 36 rel syr [arm] Chr$_1$: om ABDℵ a p 40 vulg Syr [copt] sah æth. for ο τε, εν οις D[1] vulg [Ath-int$_1$]: add ην και D[3]-gr [Ath-int$_1$]. επικαλουμ. D o 180 lect-12. om ο (bef κυρηναιος) D. ηρ. και τετρ. D[1](and lat: txt D[8]). τετρααρχ. ℵ(but α erased) [copt sah-2-mss], τραρχ. B[1].

journey (ch. xi. 30) took place after the death, or about the time of the death, of Herod; see on ver. 1. The purpose of the mission would be very soon accomplished: Saul would naturally not remain longer in Jerusalem than was unavoidable, and would court no publicity: and hence there seems an additional reason for placing the visit *after* Herod's death: for, of all the persons whose execution would be pleasing to the Jews, Saul would hold the foremost place. Our verse is probably inserted as a note of passage from the last recorded fact of Barnabas and Saul (ch. xi. 30), to their being found at Antioch (xiii. 1). **Ἰωάνν.**] See above on ver. 12.

Chap. XIII. 1—XIV. 28.] First missionary journey of Paul and Barnabas. *Henceforward the history follows Saul* (or Paul, as he is now (ver. 9) and from this time denominated), *his ministry, and the events of his life, to the exclusion* (with the sole exception of the council in ch. xv.) *of all the other Apostles.*

XIII. 1.] The **τινες** of the rec. has been interpolated, to make it appear that the persons mentioned were not the *only* prophets and teachers at Antioch. The enumeration is probably inserted on account of the solemnity of the incident about to be related, that it might be known *who they were*, to whom the Holy Spirit entrusted so weighty a commission. That those enumerated were *all* then present, is implied by the τε . . . καί: see ch. i. 13. **προφῆται**] See on ch. xi. 27. **διδάσκ.**] Those who had the χάρισμα διδασκαλίας, see 1 Cor. xii. 28; Eph. iv. 11. They were probably less immediately the organs of the Holy Spirit than the προφῆται, but under His continual guidance in the gradual and progressive work of *teaching* the Word (see Neander, Pfl. u. L. p. 58).

Συμεὼν ὁ καλ. Νίγερ] Nothing is known of him. From his appellation of Niger, he may have been an African proselyte. **Λούκιος**] A Lucius, probably the same person, is mentioned Rom. xvi. 21 as a συγγενής of Paul. There is no reason to suppose him the same with Λουκᾶς (Lucanus),—but the contrary; for why should Paul in this case use *two different names?* See Col. iv. 14; 2 Tim. iv. 11; Philem. 24. Wetstein, believing them to be the same, quotes Herodotus, iii. 131, πρῶτοι μὲν Κροτωνιῆται ἰητροὶ ἐλέγοντο ἀνὰ τὴν Ἑλλάδα εἶναι, δεύτεροι δὲ **Κυρηναῖοι**, which certainly is curious enough. **Μαναήν**] The same name with Menahem (Μαναήμ or -ην LXX) the king of Israel, 2 Kings xv. 14. A certain Essene, of this name, foretold to Herod the Great, when a boy going to school, that he should be king of the Jews (Jos. Antt. xv. 10. 5). And in consequence, when he came to the throne, he honoured Manaen, and πάντας ἀπ' ἐκείνου τοὺς Ἐσσηνοὺς τιμῶν διετέλει. It is then not improbable that this Manaen may have been a son of that one: but see below. The Herod here meant was Antipas, who with his brother Archelaus (both sons of Herod the Great by Malthace a Samaritan woman, see Matt. xiv. 1, note) παρά τινι ἰδιώτῃ τροφὰς εἶχον ἐπὶ Ῥώμης, Antt. xvii. 1. 3. Both were at this time exiles, Antipas at Lyons, Archelaus at Vienne. **σύντροφος**] Probably '*collactaneus*' (Vulg.), foster-brother; not, '*brought up with*,' for, if he had been *brought up* with Antipas, he would *also have been with Archelaus*: see above. In this case, his mother may have called her infant by the name of the person who had brought the Essenes into favour with Herod, and no *relationship* with that person need have existed. **Σαῦλος**] *

Σαῦλος. 2 [n] λειτουργούντων δὲ αὐτῶν τῷ κυρίῳ καὶ
[o] νηστευόντων εἶπεν τὸ πνεῦμα τὸ ἅγιον [p] Ἀφορίσατε
[q] δή μοι τὸν Βαρνάβαν καὶ Σαῦλον εἰς τὸ ἔργον [r] ὃ
[s] προςκέκλημαι αὐτούς. 3 τότε [o] νηστεύσαντες καὶ [t] προς-
ευξάμενοι καὶ [u] ἐπιθέντες τὰς χεῖρας αὐτοῖς [v] ἀπέλυσαν.

n = here only ‡. (Heb. x. 11. Rom. xv. 27 only. Num. xviii. 2 al. fr.)
o ch. x. 30 reff.
p = Rom. i. 1. Gal. i. 15. Lev. xx. 26.
q = ch. xv. 36. Luke ii. 15. 1 Cor. vi. 20. Gen. xviii. 4.
r constr., ver. 39 (Luke i. 25?) only. *παρὰ πόλεσιν, αἷς* (i. e. *παρ' αἷς*) *ἀμφότεροι ξυμβῶσιν*, Thuc. i. 28. see Matthiæ, 595. 4.
s = ch. ii. 39. perf. pass., ch. xvi. 10. Joel ii. 32. so ch. xxv. 12. [John ix. 22.] 1 Pet. iv. 3. 4 Kings v. 25 al.
t absol., ch. x. 9 reff.
u ch. viii. 17 reff.
v = Matt. xiv. 15. xv. 23, 32. ch. xv. 30, 33 al. 1 Macc. x. 43. (Gen. xv. 2.)

2. aft *ειπ.* ins *αυτοις* E vulg[-ed(with demid, not am fuld] syrr sah[?] æth. rec aft *τον* ins *τε*, with a k o p 13: om ABCDEHLPℵ rel vss[appy] Ath_1 $Cyr\text{-}jer_1$ Bas_3 Chr_1 [$Thdrt_2$]. rec ins *τον* bef *σαυλ.*, with HLPℵ[1] rel [Bas_1] $Thdrt_2$ Thl: om ABCDE ℵ-corr[1] p 13 $Epiph_1$ $Cyr\text{-}jer_1$ Chr_1 [$Damasc_1$].

3. aft *προσευξ.* ins *παντες* D. *αυτ.* bef *τας χειρ.* E b k o 38 [(vulg Syr $Lucif_1$)]. om *απελυσαν* D: add *αυτους* E vulg syr-w-ob [Syr coptt] $Lucif_1$.

mentioned last, perhaps because the *prophets* are placed first, and he was *not one*, but a teacher: or it may be, that he himself furnished the account. This circumstance, which has been objected to by some as invalidating the accuracy of the account, is in fact an interesting confirmation of it, as being eminently characteristic of him who spoke as in 1 Cor. xv. 9; 2 Cor. xii. 6; Eph. iii. 8. See Baumgarten's striking remarks on this, vol. ii. p. 7 ff. From the arrangement of the copulæ, it would seem as if Barnabas, Symeon, and Lucius were prophets,—Manaen and Saul, teachers.

2. λειτουργούντων] The general word for the priestly service among the Jews, to which now had succeeded that of *προφῆται* and *διδάσκαλοι* in the Christian church: **ministering** is therefore the only word adequate to render it, as E.V. after the Vulg. '*ministrantibus Domino*:'—more closely to define it is not only impracticable, but is narrowing an expression purposely left general. Chrys. explains it by *κηρυττόντων*,—alii aliter: and the Romanist expositors understand the *sacrifice of the mass* to be meant; but in early times the word had no such reference (see reff., and Suicer sub voce). **εἶπεν τὸ πν. τὸ ἅγ.]** viz. by one of the prophets present, probably Symeon or Lucius: see above. The announcement being *to the church*, and several persons being mentioned, we can hardly, with Meyer, suppose it to have been an inner command merely to some one person, as in the case of Philip, ch. viii. 29. **δή** gives precision and force to the command, implying that it was for a special purpose, and to be obeyed at the time: see reff. **τὸ ἔργον]** Certainly, by ver. 4, we may infer that there had been, or was simultaneously with this command, a divine intimation made to Barnabas and Saul of the nature and direction of this work. *In general*, it had already been pointed out in the case of Saul, ch. ix. 15; xxii. 21; xxvi. 17. It consisted in preaching to the Gentiles the unsearchable riches of Christ, Eph. iii. 8. In virtue of the foundation of the Gentile churches being entrusted to them, Saul and Barnabas become after this Apostles, not vice versa; nor is there the least ground for the inference that this was a formal extension of the apostolic office, the pledge of its continuance through the episcopacy to the end of time. The apostolic office terminated with the apostolic times, and by its very nature, admitted not of continuance: the episcopal office, in its ordinary sense, sprung up after the apostolic times (see the remarkable testimonies cited by Gieseler, I. i. p. 115 f. note, from Jerome on Tit. i. 5, vol. vii. p. 694 f., and Aug. Epist. lxxxii. ad Hieron. 33, vol. ii. p. 290): and the two are entirely distinct. The confusion of the two belongs to that unsafe and slippery ground in church matters, the only logical refuge from which is in the traditional system of Rome. See the curious and characteristic note in Wordsw., in which he attempts to prove the identity of the two offices: and compare with it the words of Jerome, on Tit. i. 5, p. 695 f., "Episcopi noverint se magis consuetudine quam dispositionis dominicæ veritate presbyteris esse majores, et in commune debere ecclesiam regere." **3. νηστ. κ. προσευξ.]** not, '*jejunio et precibus* (viz. of ver. 2) *peractis*,' Kuin.: this was a *new* fasting and *special* prayer for Barnabas and Saul. Fasting and prayer have ever been connected with the solemn times of ordination by the Christian church; but the 'jejunia quatuor temporum,' or 'ember days at the four seasons,' for the special purpose of ordinations, were probably not introduced till the fourth or even fifth century. See Bingham, iv. 6. 6. **ἐπιθ. τ. χ. αὐτ.]** See on ch.

w ch. xvii. 10 only. Gen. xxiv. 54, 56, 59.
x ch. viii. 5 reff.
y ch. xiv. 26. xx. 15. xxvii. 1 only +.
z ch. iii. 24. iv. 2. 1 Cor. ii. 1. xi. 26. Phil. i. 17, 18 al.+ L.P. (-λεύς, ch. xvii. 13.)

4 αὐτοὶ μὲν οὖν [w] ἐκπεμφθέντες ὑπὸ τοῦ ἁγίου πνεύματος
[x] κατῆλθον ἰς Σελεύκειαν, ἐκεῖθέν τε [y] ἀπέπλευσαν εἰς
Κύπρον, 5 καὶ γενόμενοι ἐν Σαλαμῖνι [za] κατήγγελλον τὸν
[ab] λόγον τοῦ [b] θεοῦ ἐν ταῖς συναγωγαῖς τῶν Ἰουδαίων·
εἶχον δὲ καὶ Ἰωάννην [c] ὑπηρέτην. 6 [d] διελθόντες δὲ ὅλην
τὴν νῆσον [e] ἄχρι Πάφου εὗρον ἄνδρα τινὰ [f] μάγον

ABCDE HLP‌א a b c d f g h k l o p 13

a ch. xv. 36. xvii. 13. b ch. xi. 1 reff. c = Luke i. 2. ch. xxvi. 16. 1 Cor. iv. 1. (Prov. xiv. 35.) d constr., Luke ii. 35. ch. xii. 10. xiv. 24. xv. 3, 41 al. L. only, exc. 1 Cor. xvi. 5. Heb. iv. 14. Deut. ii. 7. e ch. xi. 5 reff. f here bis. Matt. ii. 1, &c., only. Dan. ii. 2

4. rec ουτοι (*corrn to more usual exprn*), with E-gr HLP copt(appy) Chr_1 [Did_1 $Lucif_1$] : οι D-gr lect-12 Ath[-int_1 Ps-Ath_1] : txt ABא a p 36 vulg D-lat E-lat syrr $Ambr_1$. (C illegible.) (B(Mai Tischdf expr) has εκπεμφθεντες not εκπεμψαντες as Bch.) rec του πν. του αγ., with EHLP rel [Did_1] : τ. πν. αγ. D^1 : txt ABC^2 D-corr א a p 13 [Ps-]Ath_1. (C^1 illegible.) απηλθ. A : καταβαντες δε D-gr. rec ins την bef σελ. and bef κυπρ., with EHLP rel : ins 1st but om 2nd την 13 Thl : om ABC^2Dא a o p Chron. for τε, δε HLP b d f g o p D-lat syr-mg sah Thl : om D-gr 64.

5. γεν. δε D. εν τη σαλαμεινι D-gr : εν σαλαμινη A E-gr L$א^3$ p : εις σαλαμινη $א^1$: *Salaminam* vulg[-ed] $Lucif_1$: *Salamina* am fuld D-lat E-lat : txt BC [H, e sil] P rel. κατηγγελον L c e g^1 k p : κατηγγειλαν D 73. 96. 142. for θεου, κυριου D-gr Syr Lucif. υπηρετουντα αυτοις D syr-mg : *in ministerio* vulg : εχοντες μεθ εαυτων και ιω. εις διακονιαν E. (*The corrections have appy been made for perspicuity.*)

6. και (πε)ριελθ. (διελθοντων, omg και, D^8) δε αυτων D. rec om ολην (*ολην and αχρι παφου being supposed to be inconsistent?*), with HLP rel [sah-woide] Thl : ins ABCDEא k p 36 vss $Lucif_1$. (13 def.) ηυρον E : ευραν A. add εκει C [o æth-pl(Tischdf) arm Thl-fin]. rec om ανδρα (*as superfluous*), with HLP rel : ins vi. 6.

4. ἐκπεμφ.] Under the guidance of the Spirit, who directed their course. **Σελεύκειαν**] A very strong fortified city (supposed impregnable, Strabo, xvi. p. 751), fifteen miles from Antioch,—on the Orontes, and five miles from its mouth. It was founded and fortified by Seleucus Nicator (Strabo, xvi. 749), who was buried there (Appian, Syr. 63). It was called *Seleucia ad mare*,—and *Pieria*, or ἡ ἐν Πιερίᾳ, from Mount Pierius, on which it was built, to distinguish it from other Syrian towns of the same name. This mountain is called Coryphæus, Polyb. v. 59, where is a minute description of the town and its site. Among other particulars he mentions, πρόσβασιν δὲ μίαν ἔχει κατὰ τὴν ἀπὸ θαλάττης πλευρὰν κλιμακωτὴν καὶ χειροποίητον, ἐγκλίμασι καὶ σκαλώμασι πυκνοῖς καὶ συνεχέσι διειλημμένην. This excavated way is to this day conspicuous amongst the ruins of the city. It was under the Seleucid kings the capital of a district Seleucis,—and, since Pompey's time, a *free city*. Strabo, xvi. 751. Plin. v. 21 (Winer, Realw.; and Mr. Lewin, Life of St. Paul, from an art. by Col. Chesney in the Geogr. Society's Transactions.) **εἰς Κύπρον**] The lofty outline of Cyprus is visible from the mouth of the Orontes (C. and H., edn. 2, i. p. 164). See below, ver. 7. It was the native country of Barnabas,—and, as John Mark was his kinsman, they were likely to find more acceptance there than in other parts. **5.**] Salamis was the nearest port to Seleucia on the eastern side of the island. It had a good harbour (λιμένα ἔχουσα κλαυστὸν χειμερινόν, Scylax, Peripl. p. 41). It was the residence of a king anciently (Herod. iv. 162), and always one of the chief cities of the island. There were very many Jews there, as appears by there being more than one synagogue. Their numbers may have been increased by the farming of the copper-mines by Augustus to Herod. On the insurrection of the Jews in the reign of Trajan, Salamis was nearly destroyed, and they were expelled from the island. Its demolition was completed by an earthquake in the reign of Constantine, who (or his immediate successors) rebuilt it and gave it the name of Constantia. The ruins of this latter place are visible near the modern Famagosta, the Venetian capital of the island (Winer, Realw., and C. and H. pp. 171, f.). **ὑπηρέτην**] Probably for the administration of baptism: see also 1 Cor. i. 14—17. **6.**] Paphos is on the western shore, with the length of the island between it and Salamis. It is Nea Paphos which is meant, about eight miles north of the Paphos more celebrated in classic poets for the temple and worship of Venus. It was destroyed by an earthquake in Augustus's reign, but rebuilt by him, Dio Cass. liv. 23. It is now called Baffa, and contains some important ruins. (Winer, Realw.) **τινὰ μάγον, κ.τ.λ.**] On the prevalence of such persons at this time, see ch.

[g] ψευδοπροφήτην Ἰουδαῖον, ᾧ ὄνομα Βαριησοῦς, 7 ὃς ἦν
σὺν τῷ [h] ἀνθυπάτῳ Σεργίῳ Παύλῳ, ἀνδρὶ [i] συνετῷ.
οὗτος [k] προσκαλεσάμενος Βαρνάβαν καὶ Σαῦλον [l] ἐπ-
εζήτησεν ἀκοῦσαι τὸν [b] λόγον τοῦ [b] θεοῦ. 8 [m] ἀνθίστατο
δὲ αὐτοῖς Ἐλύμας ὁ [f] μάγος ([n] οὕτως γὰρ [o] μεθερμηνεύεται
τὸ ὄνομα αὐτοῦ), [p] ζητῶν [q] διαστρέψαι τὸν [h] ἀνθύπατον
ἀπὸ τῆς [r] πίστεως. 9 Σαῦλος δὲ ὁ καὶ Παῦλος, [s] πλη-

g Matt. vii. 15. xxiv. 11. 2 Pet. ii. 1. Jer. vi. 13. Zech. xiii. 2.
h here &c. 3ce. ch. xviii. 12. xix. 38 only (see notes).
i Matt. xi. 25. Luke x. 21. 1 Cor. i. 19 (from Isa. xxix. 14) only. Prov. xvi. 21.
k = ch. v. 40 al. Gen. xxviii. 1.
l Rom. xi. 7 reff. constr., here only.
m mid., 2 Tim. iii. 8 only. Ps. lxxv. 7. (ch. vi. 10 reff.)
n = Matt. vi. 9. Mark ii. 12 al.
o ch. iv. 36 reff.
p = Luke vi. 19. ix. 9. xix. 47 al. fr. Exod. ii. 15.
q here bis. ch. xx. 30. Luke ix. 41 ‖ Mt. xxiii. 2. Phil. ii. 15 only. Exod. v. 4.
r = ch. vi. 7. xiv. 22. xvi. 5.
s ch. ii. 4 reff.

ABCD**א** k o p [am] syrr [arm] Chr_1 Thl ; so, but aft *τινα*, E 36 vulg[-ed fuld demid] sah Lucif [and, omg *τινα*, coptt æth(Tischdf)]. *ονοματι καλουμενον* D. *βαριησουα(ν* or *-μ)* D[1] : *Barjesuban* $Lucif_4$: *Barsuma* Syr : *βαριησουν* AD[s]HLP p rel syr-mg-gr Thl-sif : *βαριησου* **א** 40. 96. 105 vulg copt arm : txt BCE 13 sah Chr_1 Thl-fin.
add *ο μεθερμηνευεται ελυμας* E ; so, but *paratus*, i. e. *ετοιμας*, see on ver 8, demid Lucif.
7. **συνκαλεσαμενος** D. *και εζητησεν* D[1](*και* is marked for erasure by D corr).
8. for *ελυμ.*, *ετ(ο* or *α)ιμας* D[1], *etoemas* D-lat : *ελυιμας* D[4]. [for *μεθ.*, *ερμηνευεται* E, *μερμην.*(sic) p.] aft *πιστεως* ins *επειδη ηδιστα ηκουεν αυτων* D[1](and lat) : *οτι ηδεως αυτων ηκουεν* E syr-w-ast.

viii. 9, note. The Roman aristocracy were peculiarly under the influence of astrologers and magicians, some of whom were Jews. We read of such in connexion with Marius, Pompey, Crassus, Cæsar,—and later with Tiberius: and the complaints of Horace and Juvenal shew how completely, and for how long a time, Rome was inundated with Oriental impostors of every description. See Hor. Sat. i. 2. 1 ; Juv. Sat. iii. 13—16 ; vi. 542—546 ; x. 93, and C. and H. pp. 177 ff. **Βαριησοῦς**] He had given himself the Arabic title of Elymas, '*the wise man*' (from the same root as the Turkish 'Ulemah'), interpreted *ὁ μάγος* in our text. 7. **τῷ ἀνθυπάτῳ**] The Greek term for the Latin '*proconsul*,' the title of the governor of those provinces which were (semblably) left by the emperors to the government of the senate and people. The proconsul was appointed by lot, as in the times of the republic ; carried with him the lictors and fasces as a consul: but had no military power, and held office only for a year (Dio Cass. liii. 13). This last restriction was soon relaxed under the emperors, and they were retained five or even more years. The imperial provinces, on the other hand, were governed by a military officer, a Proprætor (*ἀντιστράτηγος*) or Legatus (*πρεσβευτής*) of the Emperor who was girded with the sword, and not revocable unless by the pleasure of the Emperor. The minor districts of the imperial provinces were governed by Procurators (*ἐπίτροποι*). (C. and H. pp. 173 ff. : Dio Cassius, liii. 13, 15 : Merivale, Hist. of the Romans under the Empire, ch. xxxii.) The title *ἡγεμών*, used in the N. T. of the procurator of Judæa, of the legatus of Syria, and of the emperor himself, is a general term for any governor. But we never find the more definite title of *ἀνθύπατος* assigned in the N. T. to a legatus. Cyprus, as Dio Cassius informs us, liii. 12, was originally an *imperial* province, and consequently was governed by a *proprætor* or *legatus* (so also Strabo, xiv. 685, *γέγονε στρατηγικὴ ἐπαρχία καθ' αὐτὴν . . . . . ἐγένετο ἐπαρχία ἡ νῆσος, καθάπερ καὶ νῦν ἐστι, στρατηγική*) : but immediately after he relates that Augustus *ὕστερον τὴν Κύπρον κ. τὴν Γαλατίαν τὴν περὶ Νάρβωνα* **τῷ δήμῳ ἀπέδωκεν**, *αὐτὸς δὲ τὴν Δαλματίαν ἀντέλαβε*. And in liv. 4, repeating the same, he adds, *καὶ οὕτως ἀνθύπατοι καὶ ἐς ἐκεῖνα τὰ ἔθνη πέμπεσθαι ἤρξαντο*. The title of Proconsul is found on Cyprian coins, both in Greek and Latin. (See C. and H. p. 187, who give an inscription (Boeckh, No. 2632) of the reign of Claudius, A.D. 52, mentioning the *ἀνθύπατοι*, a former and a present one, Julius Cordus and L. Annius Bassus.) Nothing more is known of this Sergius Paulus. Another person of the same name is mentioned by Galen, more than a century after this, as a great proficient in philosophy. He was of consular rank, and is probably the Sergius Paulus who was consul with L. Venuleius Apronianus, A.D. 168, in the reign of M. Aurelius. Another S. P. was one of the consules suffecti in A.D. 94 : but this could hardly have been the same.

8. **Ἐλύμας**] See above on ver. 6. **διαστρέψαι . . . . ἀπό**] A pregnant construction, as *ἀπέστησεν ὀπίσω*, ch. v. 37.

9. **ὁ καὶ Παῦλος**] This notice marks the transition from the former part of his history, where he is uniformly called

t ch. i. 10 reff. u ch. xix. 28 reff. v Jer. v. 27. Sir. xix. 26. w Matt. xxvi. 4. Rom. i. 29. 1 Thess. ii. 3. Job xiii. 7. x here only †. Xen. Rep. Lac. xiv. 4. (-γημα, ch. xviii. 14.)

σθεὶς πνεύματος ἁγίου, [t] ἀτενίσας εἰς αὐτὸν 10 εἶπεν Ὦ
[uv] πλήρης παντὸς [vw] δόλου καὶ πάσης [x] ῥᾳδιουργίας, [y] υἱὲ

ABCDE HLPℵ a b c d f g h k l o p 13

9. πληθεις DP. rec ins και bef ατεν., with DEHP rel [syrr æth arm] Thl: om ABCLℵ c f p 13.'36. 40 [vulg sah] Chr_1 $Lucif_1$.
10. om 1st πασης D^1(ins D^2) arm $Orig\text{-}int_1$ $Lucif_2$. υιοι D^1[-gr](txt D^2).

Saul, to the latter and larger portion, where he is without exception known as Paul. I do not regard it as indicative of any change of name at the time of this incident, or *from* that time: the evidence which I deduce from it is of a different kind, and not without interest to enquirers into the character and authorship of our history. Hitherto, our Evangelist has been describing events, the truth of which he had ascertained by research and from the narratives of others. But henceforward there is reason to think that the joint memoirs of himself and the great Apostle furnish the material of the book. In those memoirs the Apostle is universally known by the name PAUL, which superseded the other. If this was the first incident at which Luke was present, or the first memoir derived from Paul himself, or, which is plain, however doubtful may be the other alternatives, the commencement of that part of the history which is to narrate the teaching and travels of the Apostle Paul,—it would be natural that a note should be made, identifying the two names as belonging to the same person. The καί must not be understood as having any reference to *Sergius Paulus*, 'who *also* (as well as Sergius) was called Paul.' Galen (see above) uses the same expression in speaking of his Sergius Paulus: Σέργιός τε, ὁ καὶ Παῦλος . . . ., and then, a few lines down, calls him ὁ Παῦλος. It signifies that Paulus was a *second name* borne by Saul, in conformity with a Jewish practice as old as the captivity (or even as Joseph, see Gen. xli. 45), of adopting a Gentile name. Mr. Howson traces it through the Persian period (see Dan. i. 7; Esth. ii. 7), the Greek (1 Macc. xii. 16; xvi. 11; 2 Macc. iv. 29), and the Roman (ver. 1; ch. i. 23; xviii. 8, &c.), and the middle ages, down to modern times. Jerome has conjectured that the name was adopted by Saul *in memory of this event*: 'Diligenter attende, quod hic primum Pauli nomen inceperit. Ut enim Scipio, subjecta Africa, Africani sibi nomen assumpsit, et Metellus, Creta insula subjugata, insigne Cretici suæ familiæ reportavit;—et imperatores nunc usque Romani ex subjectis gentibus Adiabenici, Parthici, Sarmatici nuncupantur: ita et Saulus ad prædicationem gentium missus, a primo ecclesiæ spolio Proconsule Sergio Paulo victoriæ suæ tropæa retulit, erexitque vexillum ut Paulus diceretur e Saulo.' (In Ep. ad Philem. 1, vol. vii. pp. 746 f.) It is strange that any one could be found capable of so utterly mistaking the character of St. Paul, or of producing so unfortunate an analogy to justify the mistake. (I may observe that Wordsw.'s apology, that Jerome does not say that the Apostle *gave himself* this name on this account, is distinctly precluded by Jerome's language, "erexitque vexillum ut Paulus diceretur e Saulo." This Wordsw., translating the final words "and instead of Saul was called Paul," has missed seeing. Notice too Augustine's "*amavit*," below.) It is yet stranger that Augustine should, in his Confessions (viii. 4, vol. i. p. 753), adopt the same view: 'Ipse minimus Apostolorum tuorum . . . . ex priore Saulo Paulus vocari amavit, ob tam magnæ insigne victoriæ.' (Elsewhere Augustine gives another, but not much better reason: 'Paulus Apostolus, cum Saulus prius vocaretur, non ob aliud, quantum mihi videtur, hoc nomen elegit, nisi ut se ostenderet *parvum*, tanquam minimum Apostolorum.' De Spir. et Lit. c. 7, vol. x. p. 207.) So also Olshausen. A more probable way of accounting for the additional name is pointed out by observing that such names were often alliterative of or allusive to the original Jewish name:—as Grotius in his note: '*Saulus qui et Paulus*: id est, qui, ex quo cum Romanis conversari cœpit, hoc nomine, a suo non abludente, cœpit a Romanis appellari. Sic qui Jesus Judæis, Græcis *Jason* (or *Justus*, Col. iv. 11): Hillel, *Pollio*: Onias, *Menelaus* (Jos. Antt. xii. 5. 1): Jakim (= Eliakim), *Alcimus*. Apud Romanos, Silas, *Silvanus*, ut notavit Hieronymus: Pasides, *Pansa*, ut Suetonius in Crassitio: Diocles, *Diocletianus*: Biglinitza, soror Justiniani, Romane *Vigilantia*.' **ἀτενίσας εἰς αὐτόν**] It seems probable that Paul never entirely recovered his sight as before, after the δόξα τοῦ φωτὸς ἐκείνου. We have several apparent allusions to weakness in his sight, or to something which rendered his bodily presence contemptible. In ch. xxiii. 1, the same expression, **ἀτενίσας** τῷ συνεδρίῳ, occurs, and may have some bearing (see note there) on his not recognizing the high priest. See also Gal. iv. 13, 15; vi. 11, and 2 Cor. xii. 7, 9, and notes. The traditional notices of

[y] διαβόλου, [z] ἐχθρὲ πάσης [a] δικαιοσύνης, οὐ [b] παύσῃ
[q] διαστρέφων τὰς [c] ὁδοὺς κυρίου τὰς [d] εὐθείας; 11 καὶ νῦν
[e] ἰδοὺ [f] χεὶρ [f] κυρίου [g] ἐπὶ σέ, καὶ ἔσῃ τυφλὸς μὴ [h] βλέπων
τὸν [h] ἥλιον [ik] ἄχρι [k] καιροῦ. [l] παραχρῆμα δὲ [m] ἐπέπεσεν
ἐπ' αὐτὸν [n] ἀχλὺς καὶ [o] σκότος, καὶ [p] περιάγων ἐζήτει
[q] χειραγωγούς. 12 τότε ἰδὼν ὁ [r] ἀνθύπατος τὸ γεγονὸς
[s] ἐπίστευσεν [tu] ἐκπλησσόμενος ἐπὶ τῇ [tv] διδαχῇ τοῦ κυρίου.
13 [w] Ἀναχθέντες δὲ ἀπὸ τῆς Πάφου [x] οἱ περὶ Παῦλον

y see Matt. xiii. 38. John viii. 44. Eph. ii. 2. 1 John iii. 10 al.
z w. gen. of thing, Phil. iii. 18 only. κοινὸν ἐχθρὸν τῆς φύσεως ὅλης τῆς ἀνθρωπίνης, Demosth. κατ. Στεφα. 79.
a = Matt. v. 6 al. Ps. cxi. 9.
b constr., Luke v. 4. ch. v. 42. vi. 13. xx. 31. xxi. 32. Eph. i. 16. Heb. x. 2. Isa. xxxviii. 20.
c = Rom. xi. 33. Heb. iii. 10. Rev. xv. 3. Ps. xvii. 21.
d ch. viii. 21 reff.
e ch. ii. 7 reff.
f ch. xi. 21 reff. Ezek. xl. 1.
g = Matt. xxvii. 25. ch. xviii. 6. Rom. i. 18. ii. 2, 9. 2 Kings i. 16.
h Eccl. xi. 7.
i ch. xx. 6 reff.
k Luke iv. 13 only.
l ch. iii. 7 reff.
m ch. viii. 16 reff.
n here only †. Job iii. 5 Symm. Hom Il. υ. 321.
o = here only. Deut. xxviii. 29. σκότον δεδορκώς, Eur. Phœn. 377.
p absol., here only. intrans. w. acc., Matt. ix. 35. xxiii. 15. Mark vi. 6. w. ἐν, Matt. iv. 23. trans., 1 Cor. ix. 5 only.
q here only †. (-νεῖν, ch. ix. 8.)
r ver. 7.
s absol., John iv. 53. ch. iv. 4 al. fr.
t Matt. vii. 28. xxii. 33. Mark i. 22. xi. 18. Luke iv. 32.
u Mark vi. 2 al. Eccl. vii. 17. Wisd. xiii. 4. 2 Macc. vii. 12 only.
v = ch. ii. 42 reff.
w = Luke viii. 22. ch. xvi. 11 all. L. ‡. 2 Macc. v. 9.
x = here (John xi. 19 v. r.) only. see Mark iv. 10. Luke xxii. 49.

ins του bef κυριου B$\aleph^1$($\aleph^3$ disapproving). ins ουσας bef ευθειας D^1.

11. ins η bef χειρ (but marked for erasure) D^1. rec ins του bef κυρ.: om ABCDEHLP$\aleph$ rel. aft τυφλος ins και P o (syr). for αχρι, εως D. for δε, τε C$\aleph$ p vulg Syr copt æth Lucif$_1$ Jer$_1$: for παραχρημα δε, και ευθεως D (*corrns, the copulative conj seeming more appropriate*). επεσεν (*corrn to more simple exprn than* επεπεσεν επ) A B(sic: see table) D$\aleph$ [p] Thl-sif: txt CEHLP 13. 36 rel Chr Thl-fin. om επ' αυτον B [om επ A(appy)].

12. ιδων δε D-gr [(Syr æth)] Lucif$_1$. ins εθαυμασεν και bef επιστ. DE æth Lucif$_1$: εκπλ. bef επιστ. A [syr]: aft επιστ. ins τω θεω D; τω κυρ., omitting the rest, æth. εκπληττομ. B a b^2 g h k 13. for τ. κυρ., τ. θεου C Vig$_1$: του χριστου 63: των αποστολων 4.

13. ανεχθεντες(sic) B^1. rec ins τον bef παυλον, with HLP rel [Dion-6-mss] Thl:

his personal appearance (see C. and H. p. 181, note) represent him as having contracted and overhanging eyebrows. Whatever the word may imply, it appears like the graphic description of an eye-witness, who was *not* Paul himself. So also περιάγων ἐζήτει χειραγωγούς, below.

10. υἱὲ διαβ.] Meyer supposes an indignant allusion to the name Bar-jesus. This is possible, though hardly probable (see below). **διαβ.**, which usually has the article, is elsewhere found without it only in (1 Pet. v. 8) Rev. xii. 9, 22. See Moulton's Winer, p. 155, note 1. **πάσ. δικ.**, **of all that is right.** **διαστρ. κ.τ.λ.**] The οὐ παύσῃ evidently makes this apply, not to Elymas's conduct on this occasion merely, but to his whole life of imposture and perversion of others. The especial sin was, that of laying hold of the nascent enquiry after God in the minds of men, and wresting it to a wrong direction. **κυρίου**, here and ver. 11, is Jehovah. If, as some suppose, the reading of the name Bar-jesus is Bar-jehu, the repetition may be allusive: as in the other case might the ἐχθρὲ πάσ. δικαιοσύνης to the name Jesus. But Meyer supposes the various readings in the forms of the name (Barsuma, Barjesuban) to have arisen from a desire to reverence the Name *Jesus*. **τυφλὸς μὴ βλέπων**] so μνήσθητι μὴ ἐπιλάθῃ, Deut. ix. 7. **11. ἄχρι καιροῦ**] The punishment was only temporary, being accompanied with a gracious purpose to the man himself, to awaken repentance in him. The sense given to ἄχρι κ. by Tittmann and Meyer here and at ref. Luke, of ἕως τέλους, is one of which it seems to me incapable. **ἀχλὺς κ. σκότος**] In the same precise and gradual manner is the healing of the lame man, ch. iii. 8, described: ἔστη (first), κ. περιεπάτει. So here, first a dimness came on him,—then total darkness. And we may conceive this to have been evinced by his gestures and manner under the infliction. **12. ἐπὶ τῇ διδ. τ. κυρ.**] Hesitating as he had been before between the *teaching* of the sorcerer and that of the Apostle, he is amazed at the divine power accompanying the latter, and gives himself up to it. It is not said that he was *baptized*: but the supposition is not thereby excluded: see ver. 48; ch. xvii. 12, 34; xviii. 8, first part. **13. οἱ περὶ Π.**] Is there not a trace of the narrator being among them, in this expression? Henceforward *Paul is the principal person*, and Barnabas is thrown into the background. **Πέργην τ. Παμφ.**] Perga lies on the Cestrus, which flows into the bay of Attaleia. It is sixty stadia from

ἦλθον εἰς Πέργην τῆς Παμφυλίας· Ἰωάννης δὲ [y] ἀπο-
χωρήσας ἀπ᾽ αὐτῶν [z] ὑπέστρεψεν εἰς Ἱεροσόλυμα. 14 αὐτοὶ
δὲ [a] διελθόντες ἀπὸ τῆς Πέργης [b] παρεγένοντο [b] εἰς Ἀντιόχειαν τὴν Πισιδίαν, καὶ εἰςελθόντες εἰς τὴν συναγωγὴν τῇ [c] ἡμέρᾳ τῶν [c] σαββάτων [d] ἐκάθισαν. 15 Μετὰ
δὲ τὴν [e] ἀνάγνωσιν τοῦ [f] νόμου καὶ τῶν [f] προφητῶν [g] ἀπέστειλαν οἱ [h] ἀρχισυνάγωγοι [g] πρὸς αὐτοὺς [g] λέγοντες
Ἄνδρες ἀδελφοί, εἴ τις ἔστιν [i] λόγος [k] ἐν ὑμῖν [i] παρακλή-

ABCDE HLPℵ a b c d f g h k l o p 13

y Matt. vii. 23. Luke ix. 39 only. Jer. xxvi. (xlvi.) 5. 2 Macc. iv. 33 only.
z ch. viii. 25 reff.
a absol., ch. viii. 4 reff.
b ch. ix. 26 reff. Exod. xvi. 35.
c Luke iv. 16. ch. xvi. 13 only. Exod. xx. 8. see Luke xiii. 14, 16. ch. xx. 7 reff.
d abs., ch. xvi. 13 reff.
e 2 Cor. iii. 14. 1 Tim. iv. 13 only. Neh. viii. 8.
f Matt. v. 17. Luke xvi. 16. ch. xxvi. 14. xxviii. 23. Rom. iii. 21.
g Matt. xxvii. 19. Mark iii. 31 al. 2 Kings xix. 11.
h = Mark v. 22, &c. Luke viii. 49. xiii. 14. ch. xviii. 8, 17 only †.
i Heb. xiii. 22 only. 1 Macc. x. 24.
k = 2 Cor. xi. 10. 1 Cor. viii. 7 al.

om ABCDEℵ c p 13 Dion$_1$[-in-]Eus Chr$_1$. **αναχωρ.** E 180. *υπεστρεψαν* ℵ[1].

14. for *αυτοι δε*, *παυλος δε και βαρναβας* E. *εγενοντο* A. rec *της πισιδιας*, with DEHLP p 13 rel [vulg syrr arm]: *quæ est Pisidiæ* tol: txt ABCℵ. for *εισελθ.*, *ελθοντες* BCℵ[1] p copt. *την*(sic D[1] : *τη* D-corr) *ημετερα τω σαββατω* D.

15. rec om *τις*, with D-corr EHLP rel [syr sah æth arm] Chr$_1$ Thl : ins ABCD[1]ℵ a p 13. 36 vulg Syr copt. *εν υμιν* bef *λογος* (*alteration to connect* *λογος* *with* *παρακλ.*) ABC(H)ℵ a c p 13 vulg [syrr sah arm]: txt (D)EL(P) rel [(copt)] Thl.—om *εν* H.—aft *λογ.* ins *σοφιας* D : *sermo et intellectus in vobis exhortationis* D-lat.—*υμιν* is written above the line appy by P[1].

the mouth (εἶθ᾽ ὁ Κέστρος ποταμός, ὃν ἀναπλεύσαντι σταδίους ἑξήκοντα Πέργη πόλις, Strabo, xiv. p. 667), "between and upon the sides of two hills, with an extensive valley in front, watered by the river Cestrus, and backed by the mountains of the Taurus." (C. and H. vol. i. p. 195, from Sir C. Fellows's Asia Minor.) The remains are almost entirely Greek, with few traces of later inhabitants (p. 194 and note).

The inhabitants of Pamphylia were nearly allied in character to those of Cilicia (οἱ Πάμφυλοι, πολὺ τοῦ Κιλικίου φύλου μετέχοντες, Strabo, xii. § 7): and it may have been Paul's design, having already preached in his own province, to extend the Gospel of Christ to this neighbouring people. John probably took the opportunity of some ship sailing from Perga. His reason for returning does not appear, but may be presumed from ch. xv. 38 to have been, unsteadiness of character, and unwillingness to face the dangers abounding in this rough district (see below). He afterwards, having been the subject of dissension between Paul and Barnabas, ch. xv. 37—40, accompanied the latter again to Cyprus; and we find him at a much later period spoken of by Paul, together with Aristarchus and Jesus called Justus, as *having been a comfort to him* (Col. iv. 10, 11): and again in 2 Tim. iv. 11, *as profitable to him for the ministry*. **14. διελθόντες**] It is not improbable that during this journey Paul may have encountered some of the 'perils by robbers' of which he speaks, 2 Cor. xi. 26. The tribes inhabiting the mountains which separate the table-land of Asia Minor from the coast, were notorious for their lawless and marauding habits. Strabo says of Isauria, ληστῶν ἅπασαι κατοικίαι (xii. 6), and of the Pisidians, καθάπερ οἱ Κίλικες, λῃστρικῶς ἤσκηνται, xii. 7. He gives a similar character of the Pamphylians. **Ἀντιόχεια ἡ Πισιδία** or πρὸς Πισιδίᾳ, Strabo, xii. 8, was founded originally (Strabo, ib.) by the Magnetes on the Meander, and subsequently by Seleucus Nicator, and became, under Augustus, a Roman colony (ἔχουσα ἐποικίαν Ῥωμαίων, Strabo, ib.:—'Pisidarum colonia Cæsarea, eadem Antiocheia.' Plin. v. 24. 'In Pisidia juris Italici est colonia Antiochensium,' Paulus, Digest. i. 15). Its position is described by Strabo as being on a hill, and was unknown or wrongly placed till Mr. Arundell found its ruins at a place now called Yalobatch, answering to Strabo's description: where since an inscription has been found with the letters ANTIOCHEAE CAESARE (C. and H. pp. 205, 207 note). **15.**] The divisions of the law and prophets at present in use among the Jews were probably not yet arranged. Before the time of Antiochus Epiphanes, the *Law only* was read in the synagogues: but, this having been forbidden by him, the Prophets were substituted:—and, when the Maccabees restored the reading of the Law, that of the prophets continued as well. **ἀπέστειλαν**] Then they were not sitting in the πρωτοκαθεδρίαι, Matt. xxiii. 6, but somewhere among the congregation. The message was probably sent to them as having previously to this taught in the city, and thus being known to have come for that purpose. See, as illustrating our narrative,

σεως πρὸς τὸν λαόν, λέγετε. 16 ˡ ἀναστὰς δὲ Παῦλος καὶ
ᵐ κατασείσας τῇ χειρὶ εἶπεν Ἄνδρες Ἰσραηλῖται καὶ οἱ
ⁿ φοβούμενοι τὸν ⁿ θεόν, ἀκούσατε. 17 ὁ θεὸς τοῦ λαοῦ
τούτου Ἰσραὴλ ᵒ ἐξελέξατο τοὺς ᵖ πατέρας ᵖ ἡμῶν, καὶ
τὸν λαὸν ᑫ ὕψωσεν ἐν τῇ ʳ παροικίᾳ ἐν γῇ Αἰγύπτῳ, καὶ
ˢ μετὰ ᵗᵘ βραχίονος ᵗᵛ ὑψηλοῦ ʷ ἐξήγαγεν αὐτοὺς ἐξ αὐτῆς.
18 καὶ ὡς ˣ τεσσερακονταετῆ χρόνον ʸ ἐτροφοφόρησεν αὐτοὺς
ἐν τῇ ᶻ ἐρήμῳ· 19 καὶ ᵃ καθελὼν ἔθνη ἑπτὰ ἐν γῇ Χαναὰν

l = ch. vi. 9 reff.
m ch. xii. 17 reff.
n = ch. x. 2 reff.
o John vi. 70. xiii. 18. xv. 16, 19. Deut. iv. 37. Neh. ix. 7.
p ch. v. 30 reff.
q = Isa. i. 2. Luke i. 52. 2 Cor. xi. 7. Gen. xlviii. 19. 1 Chron. xvii. 17. Sir. l. 22.

1 Pet. i. 17 only. Ezra viii. 35. s = ch. v. 26. xxiv. 7. t here only. Exod. vi. 1, 6 al. (but w. ἐν). u Luke i. 51. John xii. 38 (from Isa. liii. 1) only. v = here only. (Rom. xii. 16 al.) w ch. xii. 17 reff. x ch. vii. 23 only. y here only. Deut. i. 31 bis (τροπ. compl. Orig. in Caten.). 2 Macc. vii. 27 only. z = Matt. iv. 1 ||. ch. vii. 30, &c. Deut. i. 31. a = ch. xix. 27. 2 Cor. x. 5. Ps. li. 5 (7).

16. ins ο bef παυλος D. aft οι ins εν υμιν H lect-11 Chr_1[-txt(om comm)].

17. for τουτου, του B: om 40 vulg æth. om ισραηλ (*as unnecessary*) EHLP rel syrr Chr_1 Thl: ins ABCDℵ a g p 13 vulg copt sah(omg λαου τουτ.) [æth arm]. for 1st και, δια D¹(txt D⁵[-gr]). ins τη bef γη D¹. αιγυπτου ABℵ a b c² d p 13 vulg: txt CDEHLP rel 36 Chr Thl.

18. om ως DE vulg Syr [coptt]. ετη μ̄ (omg χρονον) D. rec ετροποφορησεν (*alteration to what seemed a more appropriate word; see notes*), with BC²DHLPℵ p rel 36 vulg(*mores eorum sustinuit*) syr-mg-gr Orig Chr Œc Thl-fin (ετροφοπορ. Thl-sif): txt AC¹E [l¹(appy)] 13 syrr coptt æth arm Constt(*see Tischdf*) Cyr Hesych.

19. om και B p sah. εν γη χαναaν bef επτα E: om εν γ. χ. 13.

Luke iv. 17 ff. and notes. **16. κατασείσας τ. χειρί**] As was his practice; see ch. xxi. 40. See also ἐκτείνας τὴν χεῖρα, ch. xxvi. 1. On the character, &c. of Paul's speeches reported in the Acts, see Prolegg. § i. 13; ii. 17. The contents of this speech (vv. 16—41) may be thus arranged: I. *Recapitulation of God's ancient deliverances of His people and mercies towards them, ending with His crowning mercy, the sending of the Deliverer and promised Son of David* (vv. 16—25). II. *The history of the rejection of Jesus by the Jews, and of God's fulfilment of His promise by raising Him from the dead* (vv. 26—37). III. *The personal application of this to all present,—the announcement to them of justification by faith in Jesus, and solemn warning against the rejection of Him* (vv. 38—41). It is in the last degree unsafe to argue, as Wordsworth has done, that, because Strabo asserts the language of the Pisidians to have been neither Greek nor Lydian, St. Paul must have spoken to them by virtue of his miraculous gift of tongues. To the question put by Wordsw., "In what language did St. Paul preach in Pisidia?" we may reply, seeing that he preached in the synagogue after the reading of the law and prophets, "In the same language as that in which the law and prophets had just been read." **οἱ φοβ. τ. θ.**] The (uncircumcised) proselytes of the gate; not excluding even such pious Gentiles, not proselytes in any sense, who might be present. The speech, from the beginning and throughout, is *universal* in its application, embracing Jews and Gentiles.

17. τοῦ λαοῦ τούτου] 'Hoc dicit Pisidis, Judæos digito monstrans' (Grot.). Or rather, perhaps by the τούτου indicating, *without gesture*, the people *in whose synagogue they were assembled.* **τ. πατ. ἡμῶν**] It is evident that the doctrine so much insisted on afterwards by Paul, that all believers in Christ were the true children of Abraham, was fully matured already: by the τοῦ λαοῦ τούτου he alludes to the time when God was the God of the Jews only: by this ἡμῶν he unites all present in the now extended inheritance of the promises made to the fathers. **ὕψωσεν**] Evidently an allusion to Isa. i. 2, where the word is also used in the sense of 'bringing up,' nourishing to manhood. This was done by increasing them in Egypt so that they became a great nation: see ref. Gen. There is no reference to any *exaltation* of the people during their stay in Egypt: whether by their deliverance (Calv., Heinr., Elsner), or by the miracles of Moses (Meyer), or by Joseph's preferment to honour (Beza, Grot.). **18. ἐτροφοφόρησεν**] That this is the right reading, is rendered highly probable by manuscript authority here and still more in the LXX of ref. Deut., and, I conceive, *decided* by the Heb. of that passage, and by the expansion of the same image in Num. xi. 12. The compound verb (from ὁ, not ἡ, τροφός, as the similitude is that of a *man* (אִישׁ) bearing his son) implies carrying and caring for, as a nurse: see ref.

[b] κατεκληρονόμησεν [αὐτοῖς] τὴν γῆν αὐτῶν.
20 καὶ μετὰ ταῦτα ὡς ἔτεσιν τετρακοσίοις καὶ πεντήκοντα [c] ἔδωκεν

ABCDE HLPℵ a b c d f g h k l o p 13

b here only. trans., Deut. iii. 28. (i. 38, xxi. 16, B. 1 Macc. iii. 36 A.)

c constr., Eph. iv. 11. 3 Kings ii. 35.

rec κατεκληροδοτησεν (*corrn to fix the active sense on the verb: as also in* LXX, *see reff*), with a h o: txt ABCDEHLPℵ rel 36 Chr_1 Thl. om αυτοις BD^1ℵ p 13. 40 coptt: ins ACD^5EHLP rel [vulg syrr arm Chr]. for αυτων, των αλλοφυλων D^1: αυτων αλλοφ. D^5 syr-w-ast.

20. ως ετ. τετ. κ. πεντ. bef και μετα ταυτα (*see notes*) ABCℵ p 13. 36. 40 vulg (coptt) arm: om μ. τ. D^1 syrr: txt D^1EHLP rel æth.—for ως, εως D^1-gr: om AC [Syr copt]: *et quasi annis* D-lat: *quasi post annos* vulg: *et post annos* æth-rom. aft εδωκ. ins αυτοις E [syrr arm] sah Chr_1.

Macc. **19.** ἑπτά] See Deut. vii. 1; Josh. iii. 10; xxiv. 11. The unusual transitive sense of κατεκληρονόμησεν, justified by reff. LXX, has not been understood by the copyists, and has led to the rec. reading. From the occurrence of manifest references, in these opening verses of the speech, to Deut. i. and Isa. i., combined with the fact that these two chapters form the present lessons in the synagogues on one and the same sabbath, Bengel and Stier conclude that they had been then read. It may have been so: but see on ver. 15. **20.**] Treating the reading of ABCℵ (see var. readd.) as an attempt at correcting the difficult chronology of our verse, and taking the words as they stand, *no other sense* can be given to them, than that the time of the judges lasted 450 years. The dative ἔτεσιν (see ch. viii. 11) implies the duration of the period between ταῦτα (the division of the land), and Samuel the prophet, inclusive. And we have *exactly the same chronological arrangement* in Josephus; who reckons (Antt. viii. 3. 1) 592 years from the Exodus to the building of Solomon's temple,—arranging the period thus: (1) forty years in the wilderness: (2) twenty-five years under Joshua (στρατηγὸς δὲ μετὰ τὴν Μωυσέως τελευτὴν πέντε κ. εἴκοσι, Antt. v. 1. 29): (3) Judges (below): (4) forty years under Saul, see on ver. 21: (5) forty years under David, 1 Kings ii. 11: (6) four years of Solomon's own reign. This gives 592 — 149 = 443 years (about, ὡς, 450) for the Judges, including Samuel. That this chronology differs widely from 1 Kings vi. 1, is most evident,—where we read that Solomon began his temple in the four hundred and eightieth (LXX, four hundred and fortieth) year after the Exodus. All attempts to reconcile the two are arbitrary and forced. I subjoin the principal. (1) Perizonius and others assume that the years during which the Israelites were subject to foreign tyrants in the time of the Judges are *not reckoned* in 1 Kings vi. 1, and attempt, by adding them, to make out the period—in direct *contradiction* to the account there, which is, not that the *Judges lasted* a certain number of years, but that Solomon began to build his temple in the *four hundred and eightieth year after* the Exodus. (2) Calovius, Mill, &c. supply γενόμενα after πεντήκοντα, and construe, these things 'which happened in the space of 450 years,' viz. from the *birth of Isaac* to the division of the land. But why the *birth of Isaac?* The words too will not bear this construction. (3) Olshausen conceives the 450 years may include all from the Exodus, as far as the building of the temple. But to this the objection which he himself mentions is fatal, viz. that μετὰ ταῦτα and ἐκεῖθεν must beyond dispute give the termini *a quo* and *ad quem* of the period. (4) Others suppose various corruptions, here or at 1 Kings vi. 1, and by arbitrary conjecture emend so as to produce accordance.

It seems then that Paul followed a chronology current among the Jews, and agreeing with the book of Judges itself (the spaces of time in which, added together = exactly 450), and that adopted by Josephus, but not with that of our present Hebrew text of 1 Kings vi. 1. The objection to this view, that Josephus is not consistent with himself (Olsh.),—but in Antt. xx. 10. 1, contra Apion. ii. 2 gives *another* chronology, has arisen from not observing that in the latter places, where he states 612 years to have elapsed from the Exodus to Solomon's temple, he reckons *in* the twenty years occupied in building the temple and the king's house, 1 Kings vi. 38; vii. 1. His words are, Antt. xx. 10. 1, ἀφ' ἧς ἡμέρας οἱ πατέρες ἡμῶν ἐξέλιπον Αἴγυπτον Μωυσέως ἄγοντος, μέχρι τῆς τοῦ ναοῦ κατασκευῆς, ὃν Σολομῶν ὁ βασιλεὺς ἐν Ἱεροσολύμοις ἀνήγειρεν, ἔτη δυοκαίδεκα πρὸς τοῖς ἑξακοσίοις. To reckon in the thirteen years during which he was building his own house may be an *inaccuracy*, but there is no *inconsistency*.

Wordsworth, contrary to his usual practice, takes refuge in the amended text of ABC, and then characterizes in the severest language those who have had the moral courage to abide by the more diffi-

[d] κριτὰς ἕως Σαμουὴλ [τοῦ] προφήτου· 21 [e] κἀκεῖθεν [f] ᾐτήσαντο βασιλέα, καὶ [g] ἔδωκεν αὐτοῖς ὁ θεὸς τὸν Σαοὺλ
υἱὸν Κείς, ἄνδρα ἐκ φυλῆς Βενιαμείν, ἔτη τεσσεράκοντα·
22 καὶ [h] μεταστήσας αὐτὸν [i] ἤγειρεν τὸν Δαυεὶδ αὐτοῖς
[k] εἰς βασιλέα, ᾧ καὶ εἶπεν [l] μαρτυρήσας Εὗρον Δαυεὶδ τὸν
τοῦ Ἰεσσαί, ἄνδρα [m] κατὰ τὴν [m] καρδίαν μου, ὃς [n] ποιήσει
πάντα τὰ [no] θελήματά μου. 23 [p] τούτου ὁ θεὸς ἀπὸ τοῦ
[q] σπέρματος [r] κατ' [rs] ἐπαγγελίαν [t] ἤγαγεν τῷ Ἰσραὴλ
[u] σωτῆρα Ἰησοῦν, 24 [v] προκηρύξαντος Ἰωάννου [w] πρὸ

d = here only. Judg. ii. 16. e of time, here only. f ch. xvi. 29 reff. 1 Kings xii. 17. g Luke vii. 15 al. 1 Kings xii. 13. h = Luke xvi. 4 (ch. xix. 26. 1 Cor. xiii. 2. Col. i. 13) only. 3 Kings xv. 13. Dan. ii. 21. i = Luke i. 69. Judg. ii. 18. k = Luke ii. 34. ch. vii. 21. ver. 47. 1 Kings xv. 11. l = ch. x. 43 reff. m = here only. 1 Kings xiii. 14. n Isa. xliv. 28 (of Cyrus). Matt. vii. 21. xii. 50. John vii. 17 al. o plur., Eph. ii. 3 only. Jer. xxiii. 26. p ch. ix. 20 reff. q Rom. i. 3 reff. r Gal. iii. 29. 2 Tim. i. 1 only. s ch. i. 4 reff. t = Zech. iii. 9 (8). Isa. xlviii. 15. u ch. v. 31. Isa. xlv. 15. v here only †. w Matt. xi. 10, from Mal. iii. 1.

om του A(appy) Bℵ p.

21. (κεις, so ABCDℵ.) (βενιαμειν, so ABCℵ: -μειμ p.)

22. rec αυτοις bef τον δ. (*alteration of arrangement, to connect αυτοις with the verb*), with CEHLP 13. 36 rel [vulg syrr æth arm] Chr_1: txt ABDℵ coptt.—om τον D. ηυρον E. for του, υιον D 34. om ανδρα B^1E [Ath-3-mss $Hil\text{-}mss_2$]: om also κατ. τ. κ. μου ος E.

23. ο θ. ουν απο τ. σπ. αυτου D: om απο τ. σπερματος $ℵ^1$. rec for ηγαγ., ηγειρεν (*explanatory alteration, see ver* 22), with CD 13. 36 rel tol syrr sah [arm] $Thdrt_1$ Thl-fin: txt ABEHLPℵ b g l p vulg copt æth Ath_1 $Chr\text{-}comm_1$ Thl-sif. for σωτ. ιησ., σωτηριαν (*see note*), H(σρι αν) L b d f g h l 13 æth Chr_1 Thl-sif: σ. τον ιην. D: om ιησ. o 4^2. 14^1-6. 23. 37. 46. 56. 66. 76: txt ABCE[P]ℵ rel 36 vulg syrr copt arm.

cult reading, charging them with "arbitrary caprice," "gratifying a sceptical appetite," &c. I cite this as an example of that elastic criticism, which by any means within reach, and at any price, smooths away every difficulty from the sacred text. **Σαμουὴλ]** mentioned as the terminus of the period of the Judges, also as having been so nearly concerned in the setting up over them of Saul and David.

21. Σαοὺλ . . . . . ἄνδρα ἐκ φ. Β.] It may be not altogether irrelevant to notice that a *Saul, a man of the tribe of Benjamin,* was speaking; and to trace in this minute specification something characteristic and natural. **ἔτη τεσσεράκοντα]** So also Josephus: ἐβασίλευσε Σαοὺλ Σαμουήλου ζῶντος ἔτη ὀκτὼ πρὸς τοῖς δέκα· τελευτήσαντος δὲ δύο καὶ εἴκοσι, Antt. vi. 14. 9. In the O. T. the length of Saul's reign is not specified; 1 Sam. vii. 2 gives no reason, as Bengel thinks, why Saul's reign should have been *less than twenty years,* as the twenty years there mentioned do not extend to the bringing up of the ark by David, but only to the circumstances mentioned in the following verses. Biscoe has well shewn (p. 399), that as Saul was a young man when anointed king, and Ishbosheth his *youngest* son (1 Chron. viii. 33) was forty years old at his death (2 Sam. ii. 10), his reign cannot have been much short of that period. It is clearly against the construction to suppose Samuel's time as well as Saul's included in the forty years, following as they do upon the ἔδωκεν. Yet this has been done by the majority of Commentators. **22. μεταστήσας] having deposed him** (reff.): in this case, by his *death,* for David was not made king till then. Or perhaps μεταστ. may refer to the sentence pronounced against Saul, 1 Sam. xiii. 14, or xv. 23, 28, and ἤγειρεν to the whole process of the exaltation of David to be king. But I prefer the former. **ᾧ κ. εἶπεν μ.]** The two passages, Ps. lxxxix. (lxxxviii. LXX) 20, and 1 Sam. xiii. 14, are interwoven together: both were spoken of David, and both by prophetic inspiration. They are cited from memory, neither τὸν τοῦ Ἰεσσαί nor ὃς . . . . μου being found in them. These latter words are spoken of *Cyrus,* see reff. That such citations are left in their present shape in our text, forms a strong presumption that we have the speeches of Paul verbatim as delivered by him, and no subsequent general statement of what he said, in which case the citations would have been *corrected by the sacred text.* **23. κατ' ἐπαγγ. ἤγαγεν]** viz. the promise in ref. Zech. (LXX), where the very word ἄγω is used; not however excluding the many other promises to the same effect. The reading σωτηρίαν has probably arisen from the contracted way of writing Ἰησοῦν, thus: σωτηραῖν; and then from ver. 26 σωτηρίαν was adopted. **24. εἰσόδου]** referring

x 1 Thess. i. 9. ii. 1. Heb. x. 19. 2 Pet. i. 11 only. Mal. iii. 2.
y Mark i. 4. Luke iii. 3. ch. xix. 4 only.
z = ch. xii. 25 reff.
a Paul (ch. xx. 24. 2 Tim. iv. 7) only. Jer. viii. 6.
b ch. xxv. 18. xxvii. 27 only. L.P. Tobit viii. 16. Judith xiv. 14. Sir. xxiii. 21 only. Dan. vii. 25 Theod. (-νοια, 1 Tim. vi. 4.)
c ellips., Matt. xiv. 27. John iv. 26. viii. 24. xviii. 5.

ABCDE HLPℵ a b c d f g h k l o p 13

προσωπου τῆς [x] εἰσόδου αὐτοῦ [y] βάπτισμα [y] μετανοίας
παντὶ τῷ λαῷ Ἰσραήλ. 25 ὡς δὲ [z] ἐπλήρου Ἰωάννης τὸν
[a] δρόμον, ἔλεγεν Τί ἐμὲ [b] ὑπονοεῖτε εἶναι; οὐκ [c] εἰμὶ ἐγώ,
ἀλλ' ἰδοὺ ἔρχεται [d] μετ' ἐμὲ οὗ οὐκ εἰμὶ ἄξιος τὸ
[e] ὑπόδημα τῶν ποδῶν [e] λῦσαι. 26 Ἄνδρες ἀδελφοί, υἱοὶ
[f] γένους Ἀβραὰμ καὶ οἱ ἐν ὑμῖν [g] φοβούμενοι τὸν θεόν,
ἡμῖν ὁ [h] λόγος τῆς [i] σωτηρίας [i] ταύτης [k] ἐξαπεστάλη.
27 οἱ γὰρ [l] κατοικοῦντες [l] ἐν Ἱερουσαλὴμ καὶ οἱ [m] ἄρχοντες
αὐτῶν τοῦτον [n] ἀγνοήσαντες καὶ τὰς [o] φωνὰς τῶν προφητῶν τὰς [p] κατὰ [p] πᾶν σάββατον [q] ἀναγινωσκομένας [r] κρί-
ναντες [s] ἐπλήρωσαν, 28 καὶ μηδεμίαν [t] αἰτίαν θανάτου
εὑρόντες [u] ᾐτήσαντο Πιλάτον [v] ἀναιρεθῆναι αὐτόν. 29 ὡς

d = w. person, Acts only. ch. xix. 4 (Paul). v. 37. vii. 5. e ch. vii. 33 reff. f = ch. iv. 6 reff. g = ch. x. 2 reff. h constr., ch. xiv. 3 (of Paul). xx. 32 (Paul). 1 Cor. xii. 8. 2 Cor. v. 19. vi. 7. Eph. i. 13. Phil. ii. 16 al2. (Paul). Heb. v. 13. James i. 18. i here only. k ch. vii. 12 reff. l ch. xi. 29 reff. m = ch. iii. 17. iv. 5, &c. 1 Cor. ii. 6, 8. Josh. ix. 15 al. fr. n ch. xvii. 23 (Paul). Rom. x. 3. xi. 25. 1 Cor. xiv. 38. 2 Cor. ii. 11. 1 Kings xxvi. 21. o = ch. xxiv. 21 (Paul). vii. 31 (Steph.). p ch. xv. 21, 36. xviii. 4 al. q = Luke iv. 16. ch. xv. 21. 2 Cor. iii. 15 al. Neh. viii. 8. r = 1 Cor. xi. 31. 1 Pet. iv. 6. s = ch. iii. 18 reff. and passim. t = John xviii. 38. xix. 4, 6. ch. xxviii. 18. Prov. xxviii. 17. u constr., ch. iii. 14 reff. v ch. v. 33 reff.

24. om παντι HL Thl, παντι and λαω P d e f g h l o Chr-comm: om λαω only A: om ισρ. 68. 104 sah: txt BCDEℵ p 13. 36 vss. (*The variations have perhaps been occasioned by those in ver* 17 *above.*)—ℵ[1] began to write ιηλ. bef λαω, but marked the letters for erasure.

25. επληρουν D[1]. rec ins ο bef ιωαννης, with LP 13[e sil] rel Chr Thl-fin: om ABCDEHℵ a l p Thl-sif. rec (for τι εμε) τινα με, with CDEHLP 13 rel [vulg syrr copt arm] Chr: txt ABℵ sah [æth], τι μαι (= τι με) p. aft εγω ins ο χριστος E 68 lect-12 tol Thl-fin. αλλα, and μεθ D[1](μετ D[s]).

26. om και B. εν ημιν AD p. aft θεον ins ακουσατε E. rec (for ημιν) υμιν, with CEHLP rel [vulg syrr copt æth arm]: txt A B(sic: see table) Dℵ c p 13 syr-mg sah. aft ο λογος ins ουτος C d 6. 36. 65. 133-80 arm [om ταυτης C 133-80 Syr æth(*hic sermo vitæ*) arm]. rec απεσταλη, with EHLP rel Thl: txt ABCDℵ a h p 13. 36. 40 Chr_1.

27. om εν CE b d h k p 13 vulg Chr_2. for αυτ. τουτ. αγν., αυτ . s D[1](αυτον τ. αγνουντες D[6]). for κ. τ. φωνας, ... ταις τας γρ . . ας (μη συνιεντες τ. γραφας ?) D[1](txt D[8]): αγν. τ. γρ. E [simly Syr]. ins και bef κριν. D.

28. aft ευροντες ins εν αυτω D vulg syr-w-ast coptt æth. for ητησ. &c, κρειναντες αυτον παρεδωκαν πιλατω ινα εις αναιρεσιν D[1](*ut interficeretur* lat): D[8] reads ητησαντο π. ανερεθ., without erasing any portion of D[1]: for ητησαντο, ητησαν τον(sic) ℵ[1].

to ἤγαγεν above—his **coming forward publicly.** **25.]** **As John was fulfilling his course** (the expression is peculiar to Paul, see reff.) **he said** (not once but habitually). **τί ἐμὲ ὑπ. εἶν.]** Not, '*I am not that which ye suppose me to be,*' as Vulg. (reading τίνα,—quem me arbitramini esse, non sum ego); Luth., Grot., Kuin.,—making τί (or τίνα) relative, which it will not bear (see note on 1 Cor. xv. 2); but **What suppose ye me to be? I am not He.** See Luke iii. 15 ff. **26.** [The same two classes (see on ver. 16), Jews and God-fearing gentiles, are here again addressed.] **τ. σωτηρίας ταύτης]** viz. the salvation implied in Jesus being a σωτήρ—salvation *by Him.* **27.]** The position of ἡμῖν at the commencement of its clause in the last verse shews the emphasis to be on it, and now the reason is given—*for* the Jews in Jerusalem have rejected it. See ch. xxii. 18—21. **τὰς φωνάς** is not governed by ἀγνοήσαντες, which makes the sentence an unusually harsh one in construction, requiring αὐτόν to be supplied after κριν., and αὐτάς after ἐπλήρωσαν. The **καί**, as often, merely introduces, without the emphasis implied by our 'even,' a new element into the sentence. It is perhaps hardly possible to find in our language or the Latin any one word which may give exactly this slight shade of meaning, and no more: paraphrased, the sense might be (but imperfectly and clumsily) thus represented: **in their ignorance of Him** (not only rejected His salvation, but) **by judging Him, fulfilled the voices of the prophets,** &c. **28.]** Not, '*though,*' but rather **because** they found no cause: **when they found no cause of death in**

δὲ [wx] ἐτέλεσαν πάντα τὰ περὶ αὐτοῦ [x] γεγραμμένα, [y] καθ-
ελόντες ἀπὸ τοῦ [z] ξύλου [a] ἔθηκαν [a] εἰς μνημεῖον.
30 ὁ δὲ
θεὸς [b] ἤγειρεν αὐτὸν ἐκ [b] νεκρῶν,
31 ὃς [c] ὤφθη [d] ἐπὶ ἡμέρας
[e] πλείους τοῖς [f] συναναβᾶσιν αὐτῷ ἀπὸ τῆς Γαλιλαίας εἰς
Ἱερουσαλήμ, [g] οἵτινες νῦν εἰσιν [h] μάρτυρες αὐτοῦ πρὸς
τὸν λαόν.
32 καὶ ἡμεῖς ὑμᾶς [i] εὐαγγελιζόμεθα τὴν πρὸς
[k] τοὺς [k] πατέρας [l] ἐπαγγελίαν [m] γενομένην, ὅτι [n] ταύτην
ὁ θεὸς [o] ἐκπεπλήρωκεν τοῖς τέκνοις *αὐτῶν ἡμῖν [p] ἀναστήσας Ἰησοῦν,
33 ὡς καὶ ἐν *τῷ ψαλμῷ γέγραπται τῷ

w = Luke ii. 39. Ezra i. 1.
x = Luke xviii. 31. xxii. 37.
y = Luke xxiii. 53 || Mk. Josh. viii. 29.
z = ch. v. 30 reff.
a ch. iv. 3. xii. 4. Ruth iv. 16.
b 1 Cor. xv. 12 reff. L.P. principally.
c 1 Cor. xv. 5, &c.
d constr., ch. xvi. 18. xvii. 2. xix. 8, &c. xxvii. 20. Heb. xi.
30. (see Rom. vii. 1 al.)
e ch. ii. 40 reff.
f Mark xv. 41 only. 2 Chron. xviii. 2.
g = ch. x. 41 reff.
h ch. i. 8 reff.
i double acc., here only. acc., ch. viii. 25 reff.
k absol., ch. vii. 19 reff.
l ch. i. 4 reff.
m = ch. vii. 31 reff.
n ch. ix. 20 reff.
o here only. Exod. xxxii. 29 Ald. 2 Macc. viii. 10 only, but not =. τὰς ἐπαγγελίας ἐκπληροῦν, Polyb i. 67. 1. (-ρωσις, ch. xxi. 26.)
p = ch. ii. 24 reff.

29. ετελησαν A[Woide]: ετελουν D'(-εσεν D-corr¹). rec απαντα (*error? or alteration for more completeness?*) [with 13]: txt ABCDEHLPℵ rel. γεγρ. bef περι αυτου B [Syr æth]. aft γεγραμμενα add εισιν ητουντο τον πειλατον τουτον μεν σταυρωσαι, και επιτυχοντες παλιν και D¹, syr-mg has *postquam crucifixus esset* ητουντο τον πιλατον *ut de ligno detraherent eum*: συνετυχον *et detrahentes eum posuerunt in sepulchro*. for ξυλου, σταυρου E Syr. ins και bef εθηκαν D¹(and lat).

30. for ver, ον ο θεος (add *vero* D-lat) ηγειρεν D: add *tertia die* vulg(not tol). αυτον bef ηγειρεν E Chr_1.

31. ουτος ωφθη τοις συναναβαινουσιν αυτω απ. τ. γ. εις ιερ. εφ ημερ. πλειονας D (-αναβασιν D-corr, πλειους D⁸). rec om νυν (*as unnecessary? hardly for Meyer's reason, that they had been* now for some time *His witnesses*), with BEHLP rel æth-pl Chr_1: εισι bef νυν ℵ [æth-rom]: txt AC a k p 13. 36 Syr coptt [arm].—αχρι νυν D c 137 vulg syr. om αυτου H.

32. την προς τους is written over an erasure by ℵ¹ or ℵ-corr¹. aft πατερας ins ημων DE [vulg Syr æth]. γενομ. bef επαγγ. D Hil_2. *ἡμῶν (*to avoid the difficulty of* οι φοβουμενοι τον θεον *being present, ver* 16, *besides the* ανδρες ισραηλιται) ABC¹Dℵ vulg(υμων tol) æth $Ambr_1$: om ημιν sah Bede-gr: αυτων ημιν C³EHLP p 13. 36 rel syrr Chr_1 Thl-fin. for ιησουν, τον κυριον ιησ. χρ. D sah $Ambr_1$; so, insg ημων aft κυρ. 137 Hil_2; τον κυρ. ημων [bef ιησ.] syr-w-ast: αυτον εκ νεκρων A².

33. for ως και, ουτως γαρ D. *rec τῷ ψ. τῷ δευτ. γέγραπται, with ELP rel vulg [syr] Chr_1 [$Cosm_1$] $Ambr_1$ [simly Syr coptt æth]: τ. πρωτω ψ. γεγ.

him, they besought, &c.: see Luke xxiii. 22, 23. **29.**] The two verbs ἐτέλεσαν and ἔθηκαν have still the same subject, viz. οἱ κατοικοῦντες κ.τ.λ. De Wette rightly remarks, that Paul, in this compendious narrative, makes no distinction between friend and foe in what was done to our Lord, but regards both as fulfilling God's purpose regarding him. I may add, that there is also a contrast between what *men* did to Him, and **ὁ δὲ θεὸς** ἤγειρεν αὐτόν. Joseph and Nicodemus, be it observed, were both ἄρχοντες. Paul touches but lightly on the cross of Christ, and hastens on to the great point, the Resurrection, as the fulfilment of prophecy and seal of the Messiahship of Jesus. **31.**] The νῦν gives peculiar force to the sentence. **Who are at this moment witnesses,**—*living* witnesses; q. d. 'I am not telling you a matter of the *past* merely, but one made present to the people of the Jews (τῷ λαῷ) by living and autoptic testimony.'

32. ἡμεῖς ὑμᾶς] He and Barnabas were not of the number of the συναναβάντες, ver. 31, nor was their mission to the Jewish people. '*They* are at this moment witnessing to the people, *we*, preaching to you.' Stier observes (Red. d. Apost. p. 367) how entirely Paul sinks *himself*, his history and commission from Christ, in the great object of his preaching. **ἀναστήσας**] The * meaning **having raised Him from the dead** is absolutely required by the context: both because the word is repeated with ἐκ νεκρῶν (ver. 34), and because the Apostle's emphasis throughout the passage is on the *Resurrection* (ver. 30) as the *final fulfilment* (ἐκπεπλήρωκεν) *of God's promises regarding Jesus*. This is maintained by Luther, Hammond, Le Clerc, Meyer, &c.: the other meaning, '*having raised up*,' as in ch. vii. 37, προφήτην ὑμῖν ἀναστήσει ὁ κύριος,—by Calvin, Beza, Calov., Wolf, Michaelis, Rosenm., Heinrichs, Kuinoel, Olsh., and by Mr. Humphry. Meyer well

q Heb. i. 5. v. 5. Psa. ii. 7.
r trans., ch. xvii. 31 only.
s = ch. xxiii. 3. xxvi. 22, 23 al. 2 Macc. iii. 18.
t of a *state*, here only. see ch. viii. 25 reff.
u = ch. ii. 27 reff.
v = Isa. lv. 3 only.
w = 1 Tim. i. 15. iii. 1. iv. 9. Tit. iii. 8. Rev. xxi. 5. xxii. 6. Ps. lxxxviii. 28.

δευτέρῳ [q] Υἱός μου εἶ σύ, ἐγὼ σήμερον γεγέννηκά σε.
34 ὅτι δὲ [pr] ἀνέστησεν αὐτὸν [r] ἐκ νεκρῶν μηκέτι [s] μέλλοντα
[t] ὑποστρέφειν εἰς [u] διαφθοράν, οὕτως εἴρηκεν, ὅτι δώσω
ὑμῖν τὰ [v] ὅσια Δαυεὶδ τὰ [w] πιστά. 35 διότι καὶ ἐν [x] ἑτέρῳ
λέγει Οὐ [y] δώσεις τὸν [y] ὅσιόν σου [y] ἰδεῖν [y] διαφθοράν.
36 Δαυεὶδ μὲν γὰρ ἰδίᾳ [z] γενεᾷ [a] ὑπηρετήσας τῇ τοῦ θεοῦ
[b] βουλῇ [c] ἐκοιμήθη καὶ [d] προσετέθη πρὸς τοὺς πατέρας
αὐτοῦ καὶ [y] εἶδεν [y] διαφθοράν· 37 ὃν δὲ ὁ θεὸς [e] ἤγειρεν
οὐκ [y] εἶδεν [y] διαφθοράν. 38 [fg] γνωστὸν οὖν [g] ἔστω ὑμῖν,

...ιδιαH. ABCDE LPℵ a b c d f g h k l o p 13

x = ch. xvii. 7 reff. y Psa. xv. 10. see ch. ii. 27 reff. z = ch. xiv. 16. Eph. iii. 5. Judg. ii. 10. a ch. xx. 34. xxiv. 23 only +. Wisd. xvi. 24 al. Gen. xlix. 15 Aq. Symm. [?] b ch. ii. 23 reff. c = 1 Cor. vii. 39 reff. 3 Kings ii. 10. d (ch. ii. 41.) = Gen. xlix. 29. Judg. ii. 10. e ver. 30. ch. x. 40 reff. f ch. i. 19 reff. g ch. ii. 14. iv. 10. xxviii. 22, 28. Ezra iv. 12, 13.

D (no vss) Orig-schol$_{expr}$ Cypr-mss$_1$ Hil$_{2expr}$: τω δευτ. ψ. γεγρ. H o 4. 66. 76. 100 : txt ABCℵ a c p 13. 40 arm. at end, D syr-mg add (*from Ps* ii. 8) αιτησαι παρ εμου και δωσω σοι εθνη την κληρονομιαν σου και την κατασχεσιν σου τα περατα της γης.

34. οτε D 137 Hil$_2$. aft αυτον add ο θεος E 68 Syr Thl-fin. aft μελλ. ins αυτον E k 32. 66 Chr$_1$.

35. rec (for διοτι) διο, with CEHLP p^2 13. 36 rel Chr$_1$: *propter nos* E-lat : txt ABℵ p^1 : om D[-gr] Syr æth. ετερως D[-gr] : *alias* vulg : *alia* D-lat : εν τω ετ. 13.

36. om μεν D 26 vulg. [om τους C^2(πρους, for π. τ. C^1).]

37. for ον, ο D^1-gr(txt D-corr^1).

remarks, that this meaning would hardly in our passage have been thought of or defended, had it not been that the subjoined citation from Ps. ii. has been thought necessarily to apply to our Lord's *mission upon earth*. **33.**] The reading ἐν τῷ πρώτῳ ψαλμῷ is explained thus: "hic psalmus qui nobis secundus est olim primus fuit, quod is qui præcedit, tanquam prooemium, numeratus non esset." Rosenm. Arg. Ps. ii. St. Paul refers the prophecy in its full completion to the *Resurrection* of our Lord: similarly in Rom. i. 4, ὁρισθέντος υἱοῦ θεοῦ ἐν δυνάμει . . . . . ἐξ ἀναστάσεως νεκρῶν. **34. μηκέτι μέλλ.**] Compare Rom. vi. 9, χριστὸς ἐγερθεὶς ἐκ νεκρῶν οὐκέτι ἀποθνήσκει· θάνατος αὐτοῦ οὐκέτι κυριεύει. It is interesting to trace the same shades of thought in the speeches and epistles of Paul; and abundant opportunity of doing so will occur as we proceed. But here the ὑποστρ. εἰς διαφθ. does not merely imply *death*, so that Jesus should have once undergone it, and no more hereafter, as the E. V. seems to imply: but we must supply 'to die, and in consequence to' before the words, understanding them as the *result of death, if it had dominion over him:* thus the clause answers even more remarkably to Rom. vi. 9. **τὰ ὅσια** is the LXX rendering of חַסְדֵי, ref. Isa., which in 2 Chron. vi. 42, they have translated τὰ ἐλέη. The word 'holy' should have been preserved in the E. V., as answering to τὸν ὅσιόν σου below; **the mercies of David, holy and sure**: or **my holy promises which I made sure unto David.**

35. διότι καί] **wherefore also,**—correspondent to which purpose, of His Christ not seeing corruption. **ἑτέρῳ**] viz. ψαλμῷ, referring to ver. 33. **λέγει**] viz. ὁ θεός, not David: the *subject* is continued from vv. 32 and 34, and fixed by εἴρηκεν and δώσω just preceding. δώσεις and ὅσιον accurately correspond to δώσω and ὅσια before. See on ch. ii. 27. **36.**] The psalm, though spoken by David, cannot have its fulfilment *in David*. **ἰδίᾳ γενεᾷ**] The dative *commodi*, not 'sua generatione,' which is flat in the extreme. David ministered only to *the generation in which he lived:* but διὰ τούτου, remission of sins is preached ὑμῖν, and to *all who believe on Him*. **τῇ τοῦ θ. βουλῇ** is best taken with ὑπηρετήσας, not with ἐκοιμήθη:—as E. V., **after he had served his own generation by the will** (i. e. according to the appointment) **of God.** His whole course was marked out and fixed by God—he fulfilled it, and fell asleep. I prefer this, because joining τῇ τοῦ θ. β. with ἐκοιμήθη seems to diminish the importance of that verb in the sentence. (See, on the whole, 2 Sam. vii. 12; 1 Kings ii. 10.) **προσετ. κ.τ.λ.**] An expression arising from the practice of burying families together: see reff. and passim in O. T. **38.**] Paul speaks here of justification only in its *lowest* sense, as negative, and synonymous with remission of sins; he does not unfold here that higher sense of δικαιόω, the *accounting righteous*, which those who have from God are δίκαιοι ἐκ πίστεως. It is the first office of the

ἄνδρες ἀδελφοί, ὅτι διὰ [h] τούτου ὑμῖν [i] ἄφεσις [i] ἁμαρτιῶν
[k] καταγγέλλεται, 39 [καὶ] [l] ἀπὸ πάντων [m] ὧν οὐκ ἠδυνή-
θητε [n] ἐν νόμῳ Μωυσέως [ln] δικαιωθῆναι, [n] ἐν [h] τούτῳ πᾶς ὁ
πιστεύων [ln] δικαιοῦται. 40 [o] βλέπετε οὖν μὴ [p] ἐπέλθῃ [ἐφ'
ὑμᾶς] τὸ [q] εἰρημένον ἐν τοῖς προφήταις 41 Ἴδετε οἱ [r] κατα-
φρονηταί, καὶ θαυμάσατε καὶ [s] ἀφανίσθητε, ὅτι [t] ἔργον
[t] ἐργάζομαι ἐγὼ ἐν ταῖς ἡμέραις ὑμῶν, ἔργον ὃ οὐ μὴ

I πας ... ABCDE ILPℵ a b c d f g h k l o p 13

h ch. ix. 20 reff. i ch. v. 31 reff. k ver. 5 reff. l Rom. vi. 7 only. Sir. xxvi. 29. m constr., ver. 2 reff. n Rom. v. 9. 1 Cor. iv. 4. vi. 11. Gal. ii. 17. iii. 11. v. 4. more usually w. ἐκ. o = Matt. xxiv. 4 ||. 1 Cor. viii. 9. x. 12. Gal. v. 15 al.‡ p ch. viii. 24. Luke xxi. 26. James v. 1. Micah iii. 11. q pass., Luke ii. 24. iv. 12. ch. ii. 16. Rom. iv. 18. (act., ver. 34. Heb. i. 13. iv. 3, 4, 7.) r here only. Hab. i. 5. ii. 5. s = James iv. 14 (Matt. vi. 16, 19, 20) only. Job iv. 9. Hab. l. c. (not in Heb.) t Matt. xxvi. 10 || Mk. John iii. 21. vi. 28. ix. 4. 1 Cor. xvi. 10. Ps. xliii. 1. Hab. l. c.

38. *υμ.* bef *εσ.* Aℵ. *δι αυτου* E d 65-7. 133 æth : *δια τουτο* B[1] 15-8. 34. 73. 101-80.
39. om *και* AC[1]ℵ am(with fuld demid) æth-pl : ins BC[3]DELP rel [vulg-ed tol syrr coptt æth-rom arm] Chr₁. aft *και* add *μετανοια* D (syr-w-ast has it aft *αμαρτιων* ver 38). *εδυνηθητε* A : *ηδυνηθημεν* D-corr[1]-gr. rec ins *τω* bef *νομ.* (*corrn: but the art is not needed aft a preposition*), with ELP rel Thl : om A B(sic : see table) CDℵ h p 13. 40 Chr₁. aft *εν τουτω* ins *ουν* D syr-mg. [aft *πιστ.* ins *επ αυτω* I sah.] for *δικαιουται*, *δικαιωθηναι* (but corrd) ℵ[1]. at end ins *παρα θεω* D 137 syr-mg.
40. *απελθη* ℵ[1]. om *εφ υμας* (*as unnecessary? or because a difficulty was found in identifying* *υμεις* *with the* *καταφρονηται* *of the citation?*) BDℵ 13. 36 am tol : ins ACEILP rel [vulg-ed fuld demid syrr coptt æth arm].
41. for *ιδ.*, *ακουσατε* E. *καταφρονησατε* ℵ[1]. ins *και επιβλεψατε* (*from* LXX) bef *και θαυμασατε* I o syr Chr₁; aft *κ. θ.* E(but om *και*) a 27-9. 57. 69. 105-6. *θαυμασετε* ℵ l : *-ζετε* c. aft 1st *εργον* ins *ο* ℵ[1]. rec *εγω* bef *εργαζ.* (*corrn to* LXX), with CEILP rel 36 demid [æth] Chr₂ : *εγω εργαζομε εγω* ℵ : txt ABD k p 13 vulg [syrr] sah arm. om 2nd *εργον* DELP b c d f g h k l o tol syrr æth-pl Chr₂ Thl-sif : ins ABC I[from the space] ℵ p rel vulg coptt æth-rom [arm] Thl-fin. rec *ᾧ*, with c d h l 36 : txt ABCDEILPℵ rel Chr Thl.

Spirit by which he spoke, ἐλέγχειν περὶ ἁμαρτίας, before He ἐλέγχει περὶ δικαιοσύνης: therefore he dwells on the ἄφεσις ἁμαρτιῶν, merely just giving a glimpse of the great doctrine of justification, of which he had such wonderful things to write and to say. **39.] [And] from all things, from which ye could not in** (under) **the law of Moses be justified, in Him** (as ἐν χριστῷ, ἐν κυρίῳ passim) **every believer is** (habitual pres.) **justified.** **ἀπὸ πάντων** (ἀφ') **ὧν, from all things** (sins), **from which ....** but not implying that in the law of Moses there might be justification from *some* sins;—under the law there is *no* justification (ἐν νόμῳ οὐδεὶς δικαιοῦται παρὰ τῷ θεῷ, Gal. iii. 11):—but = **Christ shall do for you all that the law could not do:** leaving it for inference, or for further teaching, that this was absolutely ALL: that the law could do *nothing*. The same thought is expanded Rom. viii. 3, 4, τὸ γὰρ ἀδύνατον τοῦ νόμου, ἐν ᾧ ἠσθένει διὰ τῆς σαρκός, ὁ θεὸς κ.τ.λ. .... ἵνα τὸ δικαίωμα τ. νόμου πληρωθῇ ἐν ἡμῖν. This interpretation will be the more clearly established, when we remember that δικαιοῦν ἀπὸ ἁμαρτίας was not in any sense, and could not be, the office of the law, by which came the knowledge of sin. The expression δικαιοῦν ἀπὸ is only once used again by Paul (ref.), and that where he is arguing against the continuing in sin.

ὁ πιστεύων is not to be joined with ἐν τούτῳ, which (see above) is contrasted with ἐν νόμῳ M. It is quite in Paul's manner to use πᾶς ὁ πιστεύων thus absolutely: see Rom. i. 16; iii. 22; x. 4 (Gal. iii. 22). Still less, with Luther, can we take as far as δικαιωθῆναι with ver. 38, and make ἐν τούτῳ .... δικαιοῦται a separate sentence.

40.] The object of preaching the Gospel to the Jews *first* was for a testimony to them: its reception was almost uniformly unfavourable: and against such anticipated rejection he now warns them. **τοῖς προφ.]** The book of the prophets: see ch. iii. 18, note. **41. καταφρονηταί]** So the LXX for בַּגּוֹיִם, '*among the heathen,*' for which they seem to have read בּוֹגְדִים. So the Arabic, 'videte arrogantes:' and the Syriac, 'videte transgressores.' (Kuinoel.)

The prophecy was spoken of the judgment to be inflicted by means of the Chaldæans: but neither this nor any other prophecy is confined in its application to the occasion of which it was once spoken, but gathers up under it all analogous procedures of God's providence: such repeated fulfilments increasing in weight, and approaching nearer and nearer to that last and great fulfilment of all the promises of grace and all the threats of wrath, by which every prophetic word shall be exhausted.

u acc., John xi. 26. 1 Cor. xiii. 7. 1 John iv. 16. Hab. l. c.
v ch. xv. 3 only. Hab. l. c.
w ch. xvii. 15. xx. 7. xxvii. 43 only. Exod. xxviii. 31 (35).
x constr., 1 Thess. v. 27 al. see note.
y = Luke i. 20.
z = here only. (ch. xv. 9 reff.) Δαβίδου τε καὶ Σολομῶνος, ἔτι δὲ καὶ μεταξὺ τούτων βασιλέων, Jos. B. J. v. 4. 2, also Apion, i. 21. Φίλιππον . . . καὶ μεταξὺ δ' Ἀλέξανδρον τὸν υἱὸν . . ., Plutarch. Inst. Lac. 42.

[u] πιστεύσητε ἐάν τις [v] ἐκδιηγῆται ὑμῖν.
42 [w] Ἐξιόντων δὲ αὐτῶν [x] παρεκάλουν [y] εἰς τὸ [z] μεταξὺ σάββατον [x] λαληθῆναι αὐτοῖς τὰ ῥήματα ταῦτα.
43 [a] λυθείσης δὲ τῆς συναγωγῆς ἠκολούθησαν πολλοὶ τῶν Ἰουδαίων καὶ τῶν [b] σεβομένων [c] προσηλύτων τῷ Παύλῳ καὶ τῷ Βαρνάβᾳ, [d] οἵτινες [e] προσλαλοῦντες αὐτοῖς ἔπειθον αὐτοὺς [f] προσμένειν τῇ [g] χάριτι τοῦ θεοῦ.
44 Τῷ τε [h] ἐχομένῳ σαββάτῳ [i] σχεδὸν πᾶσα ἡ πόλις [kl] συνήχθη [l] ἀκοῦσαι τὸν [m] λόγον τοῦ [m] θεοῦ.
45 ἰδόντες δὲ οἱ Ἰουδαῖοι τοὺς ὄχλους [no] ἐπλήσθησαν [op] ζήλου, καὶ [q] ἀντέλεγον τοῖς ὑπὸ

ABCDE ILPℵ a bcdfg hklop 13

a = here only ‡. Diod. Sic. xix. 25, ἔλυσε τὴν ἐκκλησίαν. Polyb. v. 15. 3, λύειν τ. συνουσίαν. b Acts (ver. 50. ch. xvi. 14. xvii. 4, 17. xviii. 7, 13. xix. 27) only, exc. Matt. xv. 9 || Mk. (from Isa. xxix. 13.) Josh. iv. 24. c ch. ii. 10 reff. d ch. x. 41 reff. e ch. xxviii. 20 only. Exod. iv. 16 AB2 Ald. Wisd. xiii. 17 only. f = 1 Tim. v. 5 only. see ch. xi. 23 reff. g ch. xiv. 3. xv. 11. xviii. 27. xx. 24, 32. h = ch. xx. 15 reff. i ch. xix. 26. Heb. ix. 22 only †. 2 Macc. v. 2 only. k = ch. iv. 5 reff. l constr., ch. xv. 6. xx. 7. see 2 Kings iii. 34. m ch. xi. 1 reff. n ch. iii. 10 reff. o ch. v. 17. p = Rom. xiii. 13. 1 Cor. iii. 3. James iii. 14, 16. 1 Macc. viii. 16. q Luke xx. 27. L.P., exc. John xix. 12. Hos. iv. 4.

εκδιηγειται AL: -γησεται D^1. at end ins και εσειγησαν D, κ. εσιγησεν syr-w-ast.

42. rec om αυτων, addg instead δε εκ της συναγωγης των ιουδαιων (*supplementary, at beginning of an ecclesiastical portion; 98 has* των αποστολων εκ της συν. κ.τ.λ.), with P rel: αυτων εκ τ. συν. τ. ιουδ. L Thl-fin: txt ABCDEIℵ a p 13. 36 vulg syrr coptt arm Chr$_1$. om παρεκαλουν E; so B 81, insg ηξιουν bef λαληθηναι. rec aft παρεκ. ins τα εθνη (*added because it was considered necessary that this request should be ascribed to the Gentiles, on acct of the hostility of the Jews, ver* 45), with LP rel: om ABCDEIℵ a c k o p 13. 36 vulg syrr coptt æth arm Chr Thl Cassiod. for μεταξυ, εξης D. om τα D^1(ins D^5). om ταυτα P e l [H 36 Thl-sif].

43. aft δε ins αυτοις ℵ^1(ℵ^3 disapproving). aft σεβ. ins τον θεον E (syrr?) [copt]. om τω (bef βαρν.) DL [b]. om αυτοις (*as unnecessary?*) ELP rel vulg Œc Thl-sif: ins ABCD I[from the space] ℵ a k p 36 (vss) Chr$_1$ Thl-fin. (13 def.) επιθοντ. (επιθοντε or -θοντο?) D. [for αυτους, αυτον A^1, αυτοις p.] rec επιμενειν (*perhaps corrn to avoid* προσλαλουντες . . προσμενειν), with LP 13 rel Thl-sif: txt ABCDEℵ c d k o p 36 Chr Thl-fin. (I?) [for θυ̅, κυ̅ B^3(Tischdf).] at end ins εγενετο δε καθ ολης της πολεως διελθειν τον λογον του θεου D, so syr-mg, omg τ. θ. and putting an asterisk at διελθειν; εγ. δε κατα πασαν πολιν φημισθηναι τον λογ. E.

44. rec for τε, δε, with ACDℵ a b o p 13: om æth-rom: txt BE(L)P rel 36 syrr æth-pl Chr$_1$ Thl: τοτε for τω τε L 59. (I?) rec ερχομενω (*alteration* (*so* D (which every where alters εχομαι in this sense) Λℵ 69 *in Lu* xiii. 33), *the sense of* εχομενω *not being perceived*), with BC^{1}DE^{2}ILPℵ p rel 36 Chr: επερχομενω 3. 95: txt AC^{2}E^1 13. 40 Syr. for πασα, ολη D. for θεου, κυριου AB^{2}ℵ a p 13. 36. 40 am fuld tol sah: txt B^{1}CELP rel [vulg-ed] demid copt [syrr arm] Chr. (I def.)—D has ακουσαι παυλου πολυν τε λογον ποιησαμενου περι του κυριου.

45. for ιδοντες δε, και ιδοντες D. for τους οχλ., το πληθος D (sah) [arm]: om æth-rom. aft τοις ins λογοις D^1(and lat): λογοις τοις D^6 E Syr: om 1st τοις D^{10}.

42.] The insertions in the rec. have been made (see var. readd.) partly perhaps to remove the ambiguity in αὐτῶν, and to supply a subject to παρεκάλουν. But they confuse the sense. **ἐξιόντων αὐτ., As they (the congregation) were going out, they (the same) besought.** On the N.T. construction, **παρεκάλουν λαληθῆναι,** i.e. the passive inf. after verbs of commanding, exhorting, &c., see Buttmann, Grammatik des N. T.-lichen Sprachgebrauchs, § 141. 5, p. 236. He traces it to the influence of the Latin *jubere* and the like. See, among his many examples, Mark v. 43; vi. 27; ch. v. 21; xxii. 24; xxv. 21. **τὸ μεταξὺ σάβ.** appears, by the usage of Luke, to mean **the next sabbath-day,** not '*the following week.*' This last rendering would hardly suit εἰς, which fixes a definite occasion,—nor ver. 44, which gives the result. The ref. to Josephus abundantly justifies this use of μεταξύ. **43. λυθ. δὲ τ. σ.] After the breaking up of the synagogue.** **οἵτινες**] *Paul and Barnabas;* and αὐτοῖς, *to the Jews and proselytes:* not *vice versâ,* as Calvin inclines to believe: see a similar expression ch. xi. 23. There too, we have ἡ χάρις τοῦ θεοῦ similarly used of the *work of the Gospel begun in the hearts of the converts.* See also reff. **44.**] Whether ἐρχ. or ἐχ. be read, the sense will be **on the following**

[τοῦ] Παύλου λεγομένοις [[q] ἀντιλέγοντες καὶ] [r] βλασφημοῦντες. 46 [s] παῤῥησιασάμενοί τε ὁ Παῦλος καὶ ὁ
Βαρνάβας εἶπαν Ὑμῖν ἦν [t] ἀναγκαῖον πρῶτον λαληθῆναι
τὸν [m] λόγον τοῦ [m] θεοῦ· [u] ἐπειδὴ δὲ [v] ἀπωθεῖσθε αὐτὸν καὶ
οὐκ ἀξίους [w] κρίνετε ἑαυτοὺς [x] τῆς [x] αἰωνίου [x] ζωῆς, [y] ἰδοὺ
[z] στρεφόμεθα [z] εἰς τὰ ἔθνη. 47 οὕτως γὰρ [a] ἐντέταλται
ἡμῖν ὁ κύριος [b] Τέθεικά σε [b] εἰς [c] φῶς [c] ἐθνῶν, [d] τοῦ εἶναί
σε [e] εἰς σωτηρίαν [f] ἕως [f] ἐσχάτου τῆς γῆς. 48 ἀκούοντα
δὲ τὰ ἔθνη ἔχαιρον καὶ [g] ἐδόξαζον τὸν [g] λόγον τοῦ κυρίου,
καὶ ἐπίστευσαν ὅσοι ἦσαν [h] τεταγμένοι [i] εἰς ζωὴν αἰώνιον·

...τον I. ABCDE LPℵ a b c d f g h k l o p 13

r absol., ch. xviii. 6. 1 Pet. iv. 4. 2 Macc. x. 34.
s ch. ix. 27, 28 reff.
t = 2 Cor. ix. 5. Phil. i. 24. ii. 25. Heb. viii. 3 (ch. x. 24. 1 Cor. xii. 22. Tit. iii. 14) only +. 2 Macc. ix. 21.
u ch. xv. 24 reff.
v Rom. xi. 1, 2 reff.
w = ch. xvi. 15. xxvi. 8. Rom. xiv. 5. Prov. xvii. 15.
x John xvii. 3. 1 Tim. vi. 12 only. (see 1 John i. 2. ii. 25.)
y ch. ii. 7 reff.
z = here only. see ch. vii. 39.
a ch. i. 2. John xiv. 31. perf., here only. = 1 Kings xxi. 2.
b Isa. xlix. 6 Aℵ compl. 1 Thess. v. 9. 1 Tim. i. 12. 1 Pet. ii. 8.
c Luke ii. 32.
d 1 Cor. x. 13 reff.
e = ver. 22 reff.
f ch. i. 8 reff.
g 2 Thess. iii. 1 only.
h = ch. xv. 2. Rom. xiii. 1. 1 Cor. xvi. 15. (w. πρός and a dat., 2 Macc. vi. 21.)
i = Rev. xiii. 10.

om του (*as unnecessary: but it has force here*) ABℵ c: ins CDEILP 13. 36 rel Chr_1. λαλουμενοις ABEℵ p 13: ειρημενοις 64. 97 (*the varr have perhaps been introduced from other similar exprr, such as ch* xvi. 14, *and ver* 40): txt CDILP rel 36 Chr. om αντιλ. και ABCLℵ a d e p 13. 36 [vulg] Syr coptt æth arm: ins DIP rel syr Chr Thl: εναντιομενοι και E (*both the omission and the clumsy attempt in* E *seem to be emendations of the apparent tautology* αντελεγον . . αντιλεγοντες).

46. παρρησιασαμενος D[-σιαμ- D[1]] 105. rec δε (*as bringing out the contrast*), with EILP [syrr copt] Chr_1: om sah [arm]: *tunc* vulg: txt ABCDℵ o p 36. 40 æth. om 2nd ο D c 68 Thl-sif. (ειπαν, so ABDℵ p.) aft ειπ. ins προς αυτους D. om ην C o 177: it is aft πρωτ. in D. om αναγκ. D-gr. for επειδη, επει C p $Orig_4$ [Chr_1].—om δε (*from the two syll.*, -δηδε, *occurring together*) BD[1]ℵ[1] syr coptt Thl-sif: ins ACD[2]ELPℵ[3] p 13 rel [vulg(*sed quoniam*) Syr æth arm] $Orig_5$ $Thdrt_3$ Chr_2 [Bas_1 Cyr_1] Thl_2[-fin]. κρινατε D[1]: κρινεται D[2]: *judicastis* D-lat. εαυτοις B[1](Tischdf: txt B-corr[1·2]). εαυτ. bef κριν. E vulg $Thdrt_3$. [aft] στρεφ. [ins] ημεις E.

47. εντεταλκεν D[1] e 47-marg Cyr_1 $Thdrt_1$: εντελλεται p. om ημιν D[1]-gr(txt D[4]) 57[1][appy]: ημ. bef εντ. [c] 76. 95-7. 137. om ὁ ℵ[1]. aft ο κυρ. ins (*from* LXX) ιδου DE $Cypr_1$. φως (omg εις) τεθ. σε D[1] Cypr. τοις εθνεσιν D am demid [fuld tol Jer_1] Aug.

48. και ακουοντ. τα D Syr æth. εχαιρεν (sic) P e f g h l o. for εδοξαζ., εδεξαντο (*corrn: see ch* xi. 1) D Aug_2: εδοξαζεν P(appy) e g 97. 177[2]. for κυριου, θεου B D-gr E-gr copt [arm] Aug_1: om 105 Chr_1: [c] 68 syrr æth have τον θεον for τον λ. του κυ. [but c syr ins τ. λ. τ. κ. aft επιστ.], and 34, τον θεον και τον λ. του κυ. (*all corrns, or misunderstanding of corrns, from ch* xi. 1): txt ACLPℵ p vulg D-lat E-lat [sah Chr_1]. αιωνιαν B.

sabbath-day: not, as Heinrichs, '*on the following week-day.*' **συνήχθη**] '*In the synagogue;*' it was the sight of the Gentile crowds in *their* house of prayer which stirred up the jealousy of the Jews.

45. ἀντιλ. καί] These words (see var. readd.) form a graphic repetition, passing from the *particular thing which they did*, viz. contradict the words spoken by Paul, to *the spirit in which they did it*, viz. a contradictious and blaspheming one. It is no Hebraism. **46. πρῶτον**] See ch. iii. 26; Rom. i. 16. **47.**] Agreeing with LXX-Aℵ, B reading δέδωκα for τέθεικα. They refer the σε not to *themselves as teachers* (as Meyer seems to think), but to *Christ*. **48. τεταγμένοι**] The meaning of this word must be determined by the context. The Jews had *judged themselves unworthy of eternal life*: the Gentiles, as many as were disposed to eternal life, believed. *By whom* so disposed, is not *here* declared: nor need the word be in this place further particularized. *We know, that it is* God *who worketh in us the will to believe*, and that the preparation of the heart is of Him: but to find *in this text* pre-ordination to life asserted, is to force both the word and the context to a meaning which they do not contain. The key to the word here is the comparison of ref. 1 Cor. **εἰς** διακονίαν τοῖς ἁγίοις **ἔταξαν ἑαυτούς**, with ref. Rom. αἱ οὖσαι (ἐξουσίαι) ὑπὸ τοῦ θεοῦ **τεταγμέναι εἰσίν**: in both of which places the *agents* are expressed, whereas here the word is absolute. See also ch. xx. 13. The principal interpretations are: (1) Calvin, &c., who find here *predestination in the strongest sense*: 'ordinatio ista nonnisi ad

49 [x] διεφέρετο δὲ ὁ [y] λόγος τοῦ [y] κυρίου δι' ὅλης τῆς χώρας.
50 οἱ δὲ Ἰουδαῖοι [z] παρώτρυναν τὰς [a] σεβομένας γυναῖκας
τὰς [b] εὐσχήμονας καὶ τοὺς [c] πρώτους τῆς πόλεως, καὶ
[d] ἐπήγειραν [e] διωγμὸν [f] ἐπὶ τὸν Παῦλον καὶ Βαρνάβαν,
καὶ [g] ἐξέβαλον αὐτοὺς [g] ἀπὸ τῶν [h] ὁρίων αὐτῶν. 51 οἱ δὲ
[i] ἐκτιναξάμενοι τὸν [k] κονιορτὸν τῶν ποδῶν [l] ἐπ' αὐτοὺς
ἦλθον εἰς Ἰκόνιον. 52 οἵ τε μαθηταὶ [m] ἐπληροῦντο χαρᾶς

ABCDE LPℵ a b c d f g h k l o p 13

x here only. Wisd. xviii. 10. see ch. xxvii. 27. y ch. viii. 25. xv. 35, 36. 1 Thess. iv. 15 al. z here only +. a ver. 43 reff. b = Mark xv. 43. ch. xvii. 12 (1 Cor. vii. 35. xii. 24) only. Prov. xi. 25. (-μόνως, 1 Cor. xiv. 40. -μοσύνη, ch. xii. 23.) c = and constr., Mark vi. 21. Luke xix. 47. ch. (xvii. 4) xxv. 2. xxviii. 7, 17. d ch. xiv. 2 only. 1 Kings iii. 12 al. e 2 Cor. xii. 10 reff. f ch. viii. 1. g Matt. vii. 4. Mark xvi. 9 only. 2 Chron. xi. 16. h elsw., Matt. (ii. 16 al5.) and Mark (v. 17 al4.) only. Exod. viii. 2. i Matt. x. 14 ‖ Mk. ch. xviii. 6 only. Neh. v. 13. k Luke ix. 5 ‖ Mt. x. 11. ch. xxii. 23 only. Exod. ix. 9. l Luke ix. 5. m = Luke ii. 40. ch. ii. 28 (from Ps. xv. 11). Rom. xv. 13, 14. 2 Tim. i. 4. L.P. Ps. lxxxii. 16.

49. *και διεφ.* D a [Syr] æth. **καθ** *ολης* Aℵ a k 13. 73.

50. *παρωτρυνον* D^1-gr(txt D^5) : *παρωξυναν* p $Œc_1$. rec ins *και* bef *τας ευσχ.* (*attempt at corrn, from misunderstanding*), with ELP$ℵ^1$ rel [vulg æth] Chr_1 : om ABCD$ℵ^3$ p 13. 36 [syrr coptt] arm. ins *θλειψειν μεγαλην και* bef *διωγ.* D; *θλ. κ.* E. om *τον* D. rec ins *τον* bef *βαρν.* (*for uniformity*), with P rel Thl-sif: om ABCDELℵ a c k p 13 Chr Thl-fin. om *αυτων* B.

51. ins *απο* bef *των ποδ.* E c d g 133-7 syr Thl-fin. rec aft *ποδ.* ins *αυτων*, with DELP [Syr coptt æth] Chr : om ABCℵ a k p 13. 36 vulg syr arm. for *επ*, *εις* E. for *ηλθ.*, *κατηνησαν* D-gr : *ηλθεν* 133. ins *το* bef *ικ.* E.

52. rec for *τε*, *δε* (*corrn*), with CDELPℵ p rel syr coptt [arm] Chr : txt AB 13. 36 vulg Syr æth.

æternum Dei consilium potest referri'... 'ridiculum autem cavillum est referre hoc ad credentium affectum, quasi Evangelium receperint qui animis rite dispositi erant.' So the Vulgate, '*præordinati*:' and Aug. '*destinati*.' (2) 'Qui juxta ordinem a Deo institutum dispositi erant' (Franz, Calov.: but not Bengel (as De W.), who explains it as I have done above) : (3) 'Quibus, dum fidem doctrinæ habebant, certa erat vita beata' (Morus, Kuinoel): (4) 'Qui ad vitam æternam se ordinarant' (Grot., Limborch, Wolf, al.): (5) 'Quotquot erant dispositi, applicati, i. e. apti facti oratione Pauli ad vitam æt. adipiscendam' (Bretschneider) : (6) taking *τετ.* militari sensu, 'Qui de agmine et classe erant sperantium vel contendentium ad v. æ.' (Mede, and similarly Schöttg.) There are several other renderings, but so forced as to be mere caricatures of exegesis : see Meyer. It may be worth while to protest against all attempts to join *ἐπίστευσαν* with *εἰς ζωὴν αἰώνιον*, which usage will not bear. Wordsworth well observes that it would be interesting to enquire what influence such renderings as this of *præordinati* in the Vulgate version had on the minds of men like St. Augustine and his followers in the Western Church in treating the great questions of free will, election, reprobation, and final perseverance : and on some writers in the reformed churches who, though rejecting the authority of that version, were yet swayed by it away from the sense of the original here and in ch. ii. 47. The tendency of the Eastern Fathers, who read the original Greek, was, he remarks, in a different direction from that of the Western School. **50. τὰς σεβ. γυν.**] Women had a strong religious influence both for and against Christianity : see for the former ch. xvi. 14; xvii. 4; Phil. iv. 3; 1 Cor. vii. 16 : for the latter, compare Josephus's statement (B. J. ii. 20. 2), that the majority of the wives of the Damascenes were proselytes, with ch. ix. 22—25. Strabo (vii. 3 : C. and H. i. p. 219) says, *ἅπαντες τῆς δεισιδαιμονίας ἀρχηγοὺς οἴονται τὰς γυναῖκας· αὗται δὲ καὶ τοὺς ἄνδρας προκαλοῦνται πρὸς τὰς ἐπὶ πλέον θεραπείας τῶν θεῶν καὶ ἑορτὰς καὶ ποτνιασμούς.* These were proselytes of the gate, or at least inclined to Judaism. **ἐξέβαλον**] Though the *πρῶτοι τῆς πόλεως*, at the instigation, probably, of their wives, were concerned, this seems to have been no *legal* expulsion : for we find them revisiting Antioch on their return, ch. xiv. 21;—but only a compulsory retirement for peace, and their own safety's sake. **51.**] As commanded by our Lord, Matt. x. 14, where see note. **Ἰκόνιον**] A populous city, east of Antioch in Pisidia, lying in a fertile plain at the foot of, and almost surrounded by, Mount Taurus. It is reckoned by Xenophon (Anab. i. 2. 19) as belonging to Phrygia,—by Strabo (xii. 568) and Cicero (ad Famil. xv. 4) to Lycaonia, of which it was practically the capital, —by Ammianus Marcellinus (xiv. 2) to Pisidia. At this time, it was the capital of a distinct territory, ruled by a tetrarch (Plin. N. H. v. 27), and probably on that

καὶ πνεύματος ἁγίου. XIV. 1 ⁿ Ἐγένετο δὲ ἐν Ἰκονίῳ
ᵒ κατὰ τὸ αὐτὸ εἰςελθεῖν αὐτοὺς εἰς τὴν συναγωγὴν τῶν
Ἰουδαίων καὶ λαλῆσαι ᵖ οὕτως ᵖ ὥςτε πιστεῦσαι Ἰουδαίων
τε καὶ Ἑλλήνων πολὺ πλῆθος. 2 οἱ δὲ ᑫ ἀπειθήσαντες
Ἰουδαῖοι ʳ ἐπήγειραν καὶ ˢ ἐκάκωσαν τὰς ψυχὰς τῶν ἐθνῶν
κατὰ τῶν ἀδελφῶν. 3 ᵗ ἱκανὸν μὲν οὖν ᵗ χρόνον ᵘ δι-
έτριψαν ᵛ παῤῥησιαζόμενοι ʷ ἐπὶ τῷ κυρίῳ τῷ ˣ μαρτυροῦντι τῷ ʸᶻ λόγῳ τῆς ᶻᵃ χάριτος αὐτοῦ, ᵇ δίδοντι σημεῖα
καὶ ᶜ τέρατα γίνεσθαι ᵈ διὰ τῶν χειρῶν αὐτῶν. 4 ᵉ ἐσχίσθη
δὲ τὸ πλῆθος τῆς πόλεως, καὶ οἱ μὲν ᶠ ἦσαν ᶠ σὺν τοῖς
Ἰουδαίοις, οἱ δὲ ᶠ σὺν τοῖς ᵍ ἀποστόλοις. 5 Ὡς δὲ

H τερατα... ABCDE HLPℵ a b c d f g h k l o p 13

n constr., ch. iv. 5 reff. o here only. Exod. xxvi. 24. 3 Kings iii. 18. p John iii. 16 only. q John iii. 36. ch. xix. 9. Rom. xv. 31 al. Exod. xxiii. 21. r ch. xiii. 50. s ch. vii. 6 reff. t ch. viii. 11 reff. u ch. xii. 19 reff. v ch. ix. 27, 28 reff. w — Luke xviii. 9. 2 Cor. i. 9. vii. 13 al. x = ch. x. 43 reff.

y ch. xx. 32. z constr., ch. xiii. 26 reff. a = ch. xiii. 43 reff. b ch. ii. 4 reff. c ch. vii. 36 reff. d ch. v. 12. xix. 11, 26. Mark vi. 2 al. 2 Chron. xxxiv. 14. e = ch. xxiii. 7. 1 Macc. vi. 45. f 1 Cor. xv. 10. see 2 Kings ii. 10. g = ver. 14. see note.

CHAP. XIV. 1. for *αυτους, αυτον* (*see* xiii. 46) D-gr: om a. om *των ιουδαιων* ℵ¹. aft *ουτως* ins *προς αυτους* D: pref E, simly Syr. for *πιστευσαι, πιστευειν* D: *θαυμασαι* E, addg at end *και πιστευσαι*. [transp 2nd *ιουδ.* and *ελλην.* L.]

2. rec *απειθουντες* (*appy a corrn to the simpler and more usual pres part. Meyer believes that the pres has been altered to the aor to give the plup sense, but this is hardly likely*), with ELP rel Chr [Thl-sif]: txt ABCℵ a o p 13. 36. 40 Thl-fin.—for *οι δε* to *επηγειραν, οι δε αρχισυναγωγοι των ιουδ. και οι αρχοντες της συναγωγης επηγαγον αυτοις διωγμον κατα των δικαιων* D, simly syr-mg [E also aft *επηγ.* ins *διωγμον*]. at end ins *ο δε κυριος εδωκεν ταχυ ειρηνην* D demid syr-mg; *ο δε κυρ. ειρηνην εποιησεν* E.

3. *διετριβον* A. aft *διετρ.* ins *εκει* E Syr syr-w-ob [coptt]. *διατρειψαντες παρησιασαμενοι* D[-*σιαμ-* D¹]. ins *επι* bef *τω λογω* A ℵ¹(ℵ³ disapproving). rec ins *και* bef *διδ.*, with CL a b p æth [arm] Thl: om ABDEP(ℵ) 13. 36 rel vulg Syr coptt Chr.—*διδοντος* ℵ [p]. for *αυτων, αυτου* D¹(but corrd).

4. *ην δε εσχισμενον* D. for *οι δε, αλλοι δε* D. at end ins *κολλωμενοι δια τον λογον του θεου* D syr-mg; *κολλωμενοι*(alone) Syr.

account is not reckoned to any of the above-mentioned districts. It became famous in the middle ages as the capital of the Seljukian Sultans, and had a great part in the growth of the Ottoman empire. It is now Konía, a town of 30,000 inhabitants. (Winer, Realw.; C. and H. i. pp. 220, f.) 52.] See, for similar "joyful perorations," as Wordsworth well designates them, Luke xxiv. 52; ch. v. 41; xii. 24.

CHAP. XIV. 1.] **κατὰ τὸ αὐτό, together** (reff.): *ὁμοῦ*, Hesych.: not, '*in the same manner*,' as Wolf and others. **οὕτως ὥςτε**, as in E. V.; not *ἐγένετο . . . . ὥςτε . . .*, as Vater. **Ἑλλήνων**] Probably here these are the *σεβόμενοι τὸν θεόν* [see ch. xiii. 43, 50; xvi. 14; xvii. 4, 17; xviii. 7 and ch. x. 2 reff.], those of the uncircumcised who were more or less attached to the Jewish religion. 2.] The past part. indicates **who believed not**, viz. when Paul preached. **ἐκάκωσαν**, 'male affecerunt,'—*κακούργως διέθηκαν*, Chrys. So Jos. Antt. xvi. 1. 2, *κακοῦν, . . . καὶ τῆς εὐνοίας ἧς εἶχεν εἰς τοὺς παῖδας ἀφαιρεῖν*. Ver. 3 gives the sequel of ver. 1,—ver. 4, of ver. 2. The *μὲν οὖν*, as usual (see ch. xi. 19), takes up the narrative which had been interrupted.

3. **παῤῥ. ἐπὶ τ. κυρ.**] A pregnant construction:—'speaking with boldness, which boldness was grounded on confidence in the Lord.' **τῷ κυρίῳ** is GOD: see ch. iv. 29, 30, and ch. xx. 32, *τῷ θεῷ κ. τῷ λόγῳ τῆς χάριτος αὐτοῦ*. **διδόντι**, without *καί*, defines *μαρτυροῦντι*: viz. by **giving**, &c. 4.] So Virg. Æn. ii. 39, 'Scinditur incertum studia in contraria vulgus.' Such a split into two factions was a common occurrence, on far less important occasions, in these cities of Oriental Greeks. (C. and H. i. p. 223.) **τοῖς ἀποστόλοις**] This is the first place where Paul and Barnabas are so called. St. Paul constantly vindicates the title in his Epistles: cf. Rom. i. 1; 1 Cor. i. 1; ix. 1; xv. 9; 2 Cor. i. 1; Gal. i. 1; Col. i. 1; 1 Tim. i. 1; 2 Tim. i. 1; Tit. i. 1. It seems to have been borne in this higher sense also by James the Lord's brother: see Gal. i. 19, and note, and the prolegg. to the Epistle of James: and by Barnabas, here and in 1 Cor. ix. 5, 6: see also Gal. ii. 9. So that there were, widening the word beyond the Twelve, fifteen Apostles, usually so called. The word was also used in a still wider sense: see Rom. xvi. 7; 2 Cor. viii. 23; 1 Thess. ii. 6: in which

ἐγένετο [h] ὁρμὴ τῶν ἐθνῶν τε καὶ Ἰουδαίων σὺν τοῖς
ἄρχουσιν αὐτῶν, [i] ὑβρίσαι καὶ [k] λιθοβολῆσαι αὐτούς,
6 [l] συνιδόντες [m] κατέφυγον εἰς τὰς πόλεις τῆς Λυκαονίας
Λύστραν καὶ Δέρβην καὶ τὴν [n] περίχωρον, 7 κἀκεῖ [o] εὐαγγελιζόμενοι [p] ἦσαν.
8 Καί τις ἀνὴρ ἐν Λύστροις [q] ἀδύνατος τοῖς ποσὶν
[r] ἐκάθητο χωλὸς [s] ἐκ κοιλίας μητρὸς αὐτοῦ, ὃς οὐδέποτε
περιεπάτησεν. 9 οὗτος ἤκουεν τοῦ Παύλου λαλοῦντος·
ὃς [t] ἀτενίσας αὐτῷ καὶ ἰδὼν ὅτι [uv] ἔχει [v] πίστιν [w] τοῦ

ABCDE HLPℵ a b c d f g h k l o p 1

...ουδεποτε περι d.

ABCDE HLPℵ a b c f g h k l o p 13

h James iii. 4 only. Prov. iii. 25. (-μᾶν, ch. vii. 57.)
i Matt. xxii. 6. Luke xi. 45. xviii. 32. 1 Thess. ii. 2 only. 2 Kings xix. 43.
k ch. vii. 58 reff.
l ch. xii. 12 reff.
m Heb. vi. 18 only. Gen. xix. 20.
n Matt. iii. 5 al. Gen. xiii. 10.
o abs., Rom. xv. 20 reff.
p constr., ch. xxii. 29 reff.
q = Rom. (viii. 3 ?) xv. 1 only. (Luke xviii. 27 al.) Joel iii. 10.
r absol., Matt. xxvii. 36. Mark v. 15. Luke v. 17. John ix. 8.
s Matt. xix. 12. Luke i. 15. ch. iii. 2. Gal. i. 15. Ps. xxi. 10. lxx. 6.
t constr., ch. iii. 12 reff.
u pres., ch. xvi. 38 reff.
v Matt. xxi. 21. Mark iv. 40. xi. 22. Rom. xiv. 22. 1 Cor. viii. 2. 1 Tim. i. 19. James ii. 1, &c.
w constr., Luke xxii. 6. ch. xx. 3. Rom. xv. 23. 1 Cor. ix. [6,] 10. 1 Pet. iv. 17. Winer, § 44. 4. a.

5. om τε D 133 [vulg] Chr.. ins των bef ιουδ. D. αυτους bef κ. λιθ. E.
6. ins και bef κατεφ. D[1]. aft κατεφ. ins οι αποστολοι C[3] 40 Thl[-sif-ms]. λυκαωνιας D[1], simly ver 11. ins εις bef λυστ. C[1]D : και d. aft περιχ. ins ολη DE : pref vulg.
7. rec ησαν bef ευαγ., with CEHLP rel Chr : txt AB D-gr ℵ 13. 36 c p. at end ins *και εκεινηθη ολον το πληθος επι τη διδαχη· ο δε π. και β. διετριβον εν λυστροις* D ; *τον λογον του θεου· και εξεπλησσετο πασα η πολυπληθια επι τη διδ. αυτων· ο δε π. κ. β. διετρ. εν λ.* E[, simly] vulg-sixt.
8. αδυν. bef εν λ. Bℵ[1] : εκαθ. bef αδυν. D 137 : om εν λ. DE. om χωλ. D. ins της bef μητρ. D[1]. rec aft αυτου ins υπαρχων (*interpolated from ch* iii. 2), with HLP rel [copt] Chr_1 : om ABCDEℵ c p 13. 36 [vulg syrr æth arm]. elz περιεπεπατηκει (*see note*), with 57. 73-6-8. 80. 95-6 : Steph περιπεπατηκει, with DEHLP rel Chr : πεπατηκει 137 : txt ABCℵ a p 13. 36.
9. [at beg ins και E (c) syr æth.] aft ουτος ins ουκ ℵ. ηκουσεν (*alteration to suit the other aorists, the force of the imperf being overlooked : see note*) ADEHLℵ b c e p 13. 36 [vulg Syr copt æth arm Chr_1] : txt BCP rel [syr] sah. for λαλ., λεγοντος ℵ[1]. aft λαλ. ins υπαρχων εν φοβω D. ατενισας δε αυτω ο π. D: προς ον ατ. ο π. E. rec πιστ. bef εχ., with EHLP rel [vulg-clem arm] Chr : txt ABCDℵ a k p 13 am demid fuld [tol syrr æth] sah.

latter place Silvanus and Timotheus seem to be included in it. **5.**] **ὁρμή** is not a *rush* ('impetus,' Vulg. : 'assault,' E. V.), but as Hesych. βουλή, ἐπιθυμία,—as is manifest from συνιδόντες, rightly rendered in E. V. **they were ware of it**; which it would be strange if they were not, if an *assault* had been made on them. **6. Λύστραν**] τὰ Λ. also, ver. 8. This, as well as Derbe (of both which very little further is known), was probably a small town at the foot of the singular mountain-mass known as the Kara-dagh, or black mountain, Lystra being S., and Derbe S.E. from Iconium. The sites are very uncertain. There are the ruins of about forty Christian churches on the north side of the Kara-dagh, at a place called by the Turks Bin-bir-Kilisseh (the 1001 churches), which the most recent travellers believe may be Lystra (C. and H. i. pp. 225 ff.). In one of these places (probably at Lystra, see note, ch. xvi. 1) Paul found and took up Timothy on his second journey; and from τέκνον, 1 Cor. iv. 17, compared with πατήρ, as defined ib. ver. 15, we are justified in concluding that he had been converted *by the Apostle*; and, if so, during *this visit*. There appear to have been few Jews in the district: we hear of no synagogue. **Λυκαονίας**] Strabo describes Lycaonia (xii. 6) as a hilly plain among the mountain-spurs of Taurus, very ill watered, cold and bare, but exceedingly adapted for sheep-pasture and the growth of wool. **8. ἐκάθητο**] Not '*dwelt*,' as Kuin., but sat, probably in the forum or some place of resort. **περιεπάτησεν** is the historic past: **who never walked**. The pluperfect seeming more apt, it has been altered in the later MSS. accordingly. Meyer supposes the alteration to have been the other way, from "the constant preference which the Greeks gave in narration to the aorist over the plusq. perf.:" but qu.? **9.**] The imperfect **ἤκουεν** is important. He **was listening** to Paul's preaching, and, while listening, his countenance, read by the Apostle's gift of spiritual discernment, gave token of **faith to be healed** **ἀτεν. αὐτ.**] See note on

[x] σωθῆναι, 10 εἶπεν [y] μεγάλῃ [y] τῇ [y] φωνῇ Ἀνάστηθι ἐπὶ τοὺς
πόδας σου [z] ὀρθός. καὶ [a] ἥλατο καὶ περιεπάτει. 11 οἵ τε
ὄχλοι ἰδόντες ὃ ἐποίησεν Παῦλος [b] ἐπῆραν τὴν [b] φωνὴν
αὐτῶν Λυκαονιστὶ λέγοντες Οἱ θεοὶ [c] ὁμοιωθέντες ἀνθρώποις [d] κατέβησαν πρὸς ἡμᾶς. 12 ἐκάλουν τε τὸν Βαρνάβαν Δία, τὸν δὲ Παῦλον Ἑρμῆν, [e] ἐπειδὴ αὐτὸς ἦν
ὁ [f] ἡγούμενος τοῦ λόγου. 13 ὅ τε [g] ἱερεὺς τοῦ Διὸς τοῦ
ὄντος [h] πρὸ τῆς πόλεως ταύρους καὶ [i] στέμματα ἐπὶ

x = ch. iv. 9 al. y ch. xxvi. 24 only. Prov. xxvi. 25. z = here (Heb. xii. 13, from Prov. iv. 26) only. Mark v. 28. 3 Kings xxi. (xx.) 11. a ch. iii. 8 John iv. 14 only. Isa. xxxv. 6. b ch. ii. 14 reff. c = Rom. ix. 29 (from Isa. i. 9). d Matt. xxviii. 2. e ch. xv. 24 reff. f = here only. Dan. xi. 22 Theod. ὁ τῶν λόγων ἡγεμών, Iamblich. de Myster. init. g of false gods, here only. 4 Kings xi. 18. h ch. xii. 6, 14. ἄνασσ' Ογκα πρὸ πόλεως, Æsch. Theb. 162 (Dind.). i here only †. Zech. vi. 11 alii (Tromm.).

10. om τη (*as unnecessary, its force being overlooked*) BCD^{1}ℵ k p: ins AD^{3}EHLP rel. aft φωνη ins σοι λεγω εν τω ονοματι του κυριου ιησ. χρ. (*interpolation from ch* iii. 6) CDE a [e] o 13 [Syr syr-mg sah arm] Thl-fin (om τω, and aft κυρ. ins ημων E [om τ. κυρ. e 13]): om ABHLPℵ p rel vulg syr-txt copt æth Chr$_1$ Thl-sif. [ορθρος A:] ορθως E-gr HP [syr-mg] Thl-sif: add και περιπατει D syr-mg. aft 1st και ins παραχρημα E [tol]; ευθεως παραχρημα D syr-mg. rec ηλλετο (*alteration to suit the imperf* περιεπατει), with LP 13 rel syrr [arm] Thl, ηλετο H: ανηλατο D^1, ανηλλατο D^3: εξηλλατο E: txt ABCℵ [p] vulg(*exilivit et ambulabat*) [coptt] Chr$_1$. om 2nd και B^1(ins B^1-corr, see table) [copt].

11. rec δε (*alteration from the characteristic* τε), with CDEHLP p rel 13 [vulg syr sah arm] Chr: txt ABℵ 36. 40 Syr æth. [ιδοτες C.] rec ins ο bef παυλος, with HLP p rel: om ABCDEℵ c 13 Chr$_1$. om την D. om αυτων ℵ^1. ins τοις bef ανθρ. D l. ανθρωποι(sic) ℵ^1.

12. for τε, δε D a b g 40 [E-lat Cyr-c$_1$] Chr$_1$. rec aft 1st τον ins μεν (*to answer to the follg* δε), with B(sic: see table) C^{3}EHLP 13 rel syr copt Cyr-c$_1$ Chr: om AC^1(D)ℵ p 36 vulg [sah arm].—om τον also D. διαν DEHL P-corr o p 40. for επειδη, επει ℵ^1 k. om ο C^{1}D [c].

13. rec for τε, δε, with DEHLP rel syr coptt Thl: txt ABCℵ [a c] 36. 40 vulg [Syr] æth Chr—τοτε o p lect-12: τοτε C^1, but τ is erased.—οι δε ιερεις . . ενεγκαντες . . ηθελον D 96. του οντος δ. D c 137. [προς C^1: πρωτων πυλων p.] om της D^1: ins D^3. rec aft πολ. ins αυτων, with C^{3}EHLP rel syr Chr: om ABC^{1}Dℵ a p 13. 36 vulg coptt [Syr (æth) arm]. aft ταυρ. ins αυτοις D: aft στεμ., ch. xiii. 9.

10. μεγ. τῇ φ.] Raising his voice above the tone in which he was before speaking. The article is important.

11. Λυκαονιστί] The nature of this dialect is uncertain: its existence is further mentioned by Steph. Byzant., cf. τῇ τῶν Λυκαόνων φωνῇ, in note on ver. 20. The notice is inserted to shew that the Apostles *had no knowledge of the inference drawn by the crowd*, till they saw the bulls being brought to their doors, ver. 13. So Chrysostom: οὐκ ἦν τοῦτο οὐδέπω δῆλον· τῇ γὰρ οἰκείᾳ φωνῇ ἐφθέγγοντο, λέγοντες κ.τ.λ. διὰ τοῦτο οὐδὲν αὐτοῖς ἔλεγον (meaning, "for this reason they, the Lycaonians, spoke unintelligibly to the Apostles:" ἔλεγον taking up the λέγοντες. Wordsw. has, in his ardour to vindicate Chrysostom from heterodoxy, fallen into the mistake of rendering, "therefore the Apostles said nothing to them")· ἐπειδὴ δὲ εἶδον τὰ στέμματα, τότε ἐξελθόντες κ.τ.λ. Hom. xxx., p. 235 f. See, on the real nature of the gift of tongues, and the bearing of notices of this kind on its consideration, the note on ch. ii. 4. These ἐπιφάνειαι of the gods are frequent subjects of heathen poetry and mythology. Hom. Od. ρ. 484, says, καί τε θεοὶ ξείνοισιν ἐοικότες ἀλλοδαποῖσι Παντοῖοι τελέθοντες ἐπιστρωφῶσι πόληας. It was in the neighbouring country of Phrygia that Jupiter and Mercury were said to have wandered, and to have been entertained by Baucis and Philemon: 'Jupiter huc, specie mortali, cumque parente Venit Atlantiades positis caducifer alis.' (Ov. Met. viii. 626, f.) Dio Chrysostom (Orat. xxxiii. p. 408) says, φασὶ τοὺς οἰκιστὰς ἥρωας ἢ θεοὺς πολλάκις ἐπιστρέφεσθαι τὰς αὑτῶν πόλεις. (From Mr. Humphry's note.)

12.] This distinction is (besides the reason given) in accordance with what Paul himself cites (as the saying of his adversaries, it is true, but not therefore without some physical foundation), ἡ παρουσία τοῦ σώματος ἀσθενής. So Chrysostom, ἐμοὶ δοκεῖ καὶ ἀπὸ τῆς ὄψεως ἀξιοπρεπὴς εἶναι ὁ Βαρνάβας, Hom. xxx., p. 237.

ἡγούμενος τοῦ λόγου] So Iamblichus, of Hermes, in reff.: 'vocis et sermonis potens,' Macrob. Saturn. I. 8: λόγου προφήτης, Orph. H. xxvii. 4: λαλίστατος κ. λογιώτατος θεῶν ἁπάντων, Lucian, Gal-

k = ch. x. 17 reff.
l = and constr. w. inf. pres., John xvi. 19. Luke x. 29. ch. xvii. 18.
m = Mark xiv. 12 ‖ L. 1 Cor. v. 7. x. 20 only. (ch. x. 13 reff.) Exod. xxiii. 18 B.
n ver. 4.
o Matt. xxvi. 65. Josh. vii. 6.
p as above (o). Mark xiv. 63. Luke v. 6. viii. 29 only.
q here only. Deut. xxxiii. 22.
r Judith xiv. 17 B.
s Matt. viii. 29. ch. xvi. 17. xix. 28 al. Exod. v. 8.

τοὺς [k]πυλῶνας ἐνέγκας σὺν τοῖς ὄχλοις [l]ἤθελεν [m]θύειν. ABCDE
14 Ἀκούσαντες δὲ οἱ [n]ἀπόστολοι Βαρνάβας καὶ Παῦλος HLPא a b c f g h
[op]διαῤῥήξαντες τὰ [o]ἱμάτια αὐτῶν [qr]ἐξεπήδησαν εἰς τὸν k l o p 13
ὄχλον [rs]κράζοντες 15 καὶ [s]λέγοντες Ἄνδρες, τί ταῦτα
ποιεῖτε; καὶ ἡμεῖς [u]ὁμοιοπαθεῖς ἐσμεν ὑμῖν ἄνθρωποι,
[v]εὐαγγελιζόμενοι ὑμᾶς [w]ἀπὸ τούτων τῶν [x]ματαίων [wy]ἐπι-
στρέφειν [y]ἐπὶ [z]θεὸν [z]ζῶντα, ὃς [a]ἐποίησεν τὸν [a]οὐρανὸν
καὶ τὴν [a]γῆν καὶ τὴν [a]θάλασσαν καὶ πάντα τὰ ἐν αὐτοῖς,
16 ὃς ἐν ταῖς [b]παρῳχημέναις [c]γενεαῖς εἴασεν πάντα τὰ
ἔθνη [d]πορεύεσθαι ταῖς [e]ὁδοῖς αὐτῶν, 17 [f]καίτοιγε οὐκ
[g]ἀμάρτυρον ἑαυτὸν [h]ἀφῆκεν [i]ἀγαθουργῶν, [k]οὐρανόθεν ὑμῖν m ουρανοθεν...
[l]ὑετοὺς διδοὺς καὶ [m]καιροὺς [n]καρποφόρους, [o]ἐμπιπλῶν ABCDE
[p]τροφῆς καὶ [q]εὐφροσύνης τὰς καρδίας ὑμῶν. 18 Καὶ HLPא a b c f g h k l m o p 13

u James v. 17 only †. Wisd. vii. 3 only. v constr., ch. xvi. 10. Gal. i. 9. 1 Pet. i. 12. w ch. xxvi. 18. 1 Thess. i. 9. x = here only. (1 Cor. iii. 20 reff.) Levit. xvii. 7. Isa. ii. 20 al. y ch. xxvi. 20 reff. z see note. 1 Kings xvii. 36 (16). a ch. iv. 24 reff. b here only †. Xen. Anab. ii. 4. 1, end. c = ch. xiii. 36 reff. d constr., ch. ix. 31 reff. e = Luke i. 79. ch. ii. 28. Prov. i. 31. f John iv. 2 (ch. xvii. 27 v. r.) only. Xen. Mem. i. 2. 3. g here only †. οὐκ ἔστιν δὲ ἀμάρτυρον τὸ μέγεθος τ. προειρημένων χρημάτων, Jos. Antt. xiv. 7. 2. h = Matt. iii. 15. Heb. ii. 8. Ezek. xvi. 39. i 1 Tim. vi. 18 only †. k ch. xxvi. 13 only †. Æschin. p. 73. 5, from Hesiod. l ch. xxviii. 2. Heb. vi. 7. James v. 18. Rev. xi. 6 only. Deut. xi. 14. Job v. 10. Ep. Jer. 53. m = here only. τοῖς καιροῖς εἴκων, Polyb. iii. 9. 7. n here only. Ps. cvi. 34. cxlviii. 9. Jer. ii. 21 only. (-ρεῖν, Rom. vii. 4, 5.) o here only. Ps. cii. 5. cxliv. 16. see Rom. xv. 24. p ch. ix. 19 al. fr. Ps. cxxxv. 25. q ch. ii. 28 only. Isa. xxix. 19.

E [c] 137. ηθελον H l p tol Thl-sif, so also D (see above). επιθυειν D.

14. *ακουσας δε* omg (so Syr) *οι απ.* D. (In א the *ας* of *βαρναβας* is supplied perhaps by corr[1].) *εαυτων* ABא[3] 13. 36: txt CDEHLPא[1] p rel Chr_1. aft *αυτ.* ins *και* D[1]. rec *εισεπηδησαν* (*corrn to suit εις τ. οχλον*), with C[3]HLP rel Thl-fin: txt ABC[1]DEא a c p 13. 36 vulg syrr sah [copt æth] arm Chr Thl-sif-comm. for *εις*, *επι* C[1].

15. for *λεγοντες*, *φωνουντες* D[1]. ins *ει* (*εις*?) bef *τι* A[1]. om 2nd *και* D. *υμιν* bef *εσμ.* C [f h o] 38. 93. 113 Chr_2 [$Thdrt_1$ Thl-fin]; om *υμ.* H c 137: aft *ανθρ.* 13. for *υμας*, *υμιν τον θεον* D flor [spec] Iren-int. *επιστρεψητε*, insg *οπως* bef *απο*, D flor [spec] Iren-int: *επιστρεφητε*, insg *ινα* bef *απο*, E. rec **τον θ. τον ζ.** (*alteration for more precision: see note*), with HLP rel Chr_1: *τον θ. ζ.* D[1] [$Thdrt_1$]: *θ. τον ζ.* א[1]: txt ABC D-corr Eא[3] a k p 13. 40 Ath_1. *τον ποιησαντα* D.

16. for *ος*, *ο* D. for *παντα*, *κατα* D[1]. [for 2nd *ταις*, *τοις* L(Treg).]

17. *καιτοι* ABCא[3] a p[1] 13 Ath_1: *καιγε* DE (*probably corrections: the γε or the τοι being deemed unnecessary*): txt C[3]HLPא[1] p[2] rel 36 [Ath(ed Bened)] Chr_1 $Thdrt_1$. for *εαυτ.*, *αυτον* ABEא[1] c: txt CDHLPא[3] 13 rel Ath Chr Thdrt.—*αφηκ.* bef *εαυτ.* D. rec *αγαθοποιων* (*altern to more usual word*), with DELP rel Chr Thdrt: *αγαθοπων* H: txt ABCא [a p 13] Ath_1. rec **ημιν**, with a: om Aא[3] p 13 vulg æth Iren[-int_1]-2-mss: *αυτοις* Syr sah: txt BCDEHLPא[1] rel flor spec syr [arm] Ath Thdrt Thl Iren[-int_1]. *διδ.* bef *υετ.* Aא [a k] p 13. 73 lect-12 vulg [copt]. *εμπιμπλων* DE[P]. om *τας* D[1](ins aft *καρδιας* D[6]). rec *ημων* (*corrn, the assertion seeming to be of general application to the speaker as well as his hearers*), with AHLPא[3] 13 rel [vulg-ed] copt æth Chr_1: *αυτων* Syr sah [Ath-3-mss]: txt BCDEא[1] b c f k l o p am(and demid flor fuld tol) spec syr [arm] Ath Thdrt Thl-sif Iren[-int].

lus, 2. **13.**] **πρὸ τ. π.** (see reff.); i. e. of Ζεὺς πρόπυλος: no ellipsis of ἱεροῦ or any thing else. **ταύρους κ. στέμματα**] Not for ταύρους ἐστεμμένους: the garlands may have been to hang on the doors of the house where the Apostles were: or for manifold purposes connected with the sacrifice. 'Ipsæ denique fores, ipsæ hostiæ, ipsæ aræ, ipsi ministri et sacerdotes eorum coronantur.' Wetst. **τοὺς πυλῶνας** are not the gates of the city, but the *doors of the outer court of the house*: see ch. xii. 13. **14. οἱ ἀπόστολοι**] See note on ver. 4. The Apostles were *within*: on being told, they ἐξεπήδησαν—rushed forth, into the crowd. **15. ματαίων**] viz. θεῶν [contrasted with θεὸν ζῶντα]: the words of ref. 1 Thess. ἐπεστρέψατε πρὸς τὸν θεὸν ἀπὸ τῶν εἰδώλων, are remarkably like these. **θεὸν ζῶντα**, without the articles, is characteristic of Paul: see Rom. ix. 26; 2 Cor. iii. 3; vi. 16; 1 Thess. i. 9; 1 Tim. iii. 15; iv. 10 al. It also occurs Heb. iii. 12; ix. 14; x. 31; xii. 22; Rev. vii. 2. **16.**] Compare Rom. iii. 25, 26,

ταῦτα λέγοντες [r] μόλις [s] κατέπαυσαν τοὺς ὄχλους [t] τοῦ
μὴ [u] θύειν αὐτοῖς. 19 [v] Ἐπῆλθαν δὲ ἀπὸ Ἀντιοχείας καὶ
Ἰκονίου Ἰουδαῖοι, καὶ πείσαντες τοὺς ὄχλους καὶ [w] λι-
θάσαντες τὸν Παῦλον [x] ἔσυρον [y] ἔξω τῆς πόλεως, νομί-
ζοντες αὐτὸν τεθνηκέναι. 20 [z] κυκλωσάντων δὲ τῶν μαθητῶν αὐτὸν [a] ἀναστὰς εἰςῆλθεν εἰς τὴν πόλιν, καὶ
[b] τῇ ἐπαύριον [c] ἐξῆλθεν σὺν τῷ Βαρνάβᾳ [c] εἰς Δέρβην.

r ch. xxvii. 7, 8, 16. Rom. v. 7. 1 Pet. iv. 18 (from Prov. xi. 31) only.
s = here only. trans., Heb. iv. 8. Ps. lxxxiv. 3. intrans., Heb. iv. 4 (from Gen. ii. 2), 10 only.
t ch. xx. 20, 27. Rom. xv. 22.
u dat., 1 Cor. x. 20 only. Gen. xlvi. 1 al. fr.
v absol., Luke xi. 22. Eph. ii. 7. James v. 1. Prov. iv. 15. Josh. xxiv. 20.
w ch. v. 26 reff.
x ch. viii. 3 reff.
y Luke xiii. 33. ch. xxi. 5, 30. Neh. xiii. 20.
z = John x. 24 (Luke xxi. 20. Heb. xi. 30. Rev. xx. 9) only. 2 Chron. xxiii. 7.
a = ch. ix. 6 reff.
b ch. x. 9 reff.
c ch. xi. 25 reff.

18. μογις D coptt. κατεπαυσαντο C[1]. at end ins αλλα πορευεσθαι εκαστον εις τα ιδια C k m p 13. 36 syr-mg arm.

19. at beg ins διατριβοντων δε (so D[2] : om δε D[1]) αυτων και διδασκοντων, omg δε follg, DE a b f k m o p 13. 36. 40 syr-mg; so, but om και, C; and, but om διδασκοντων, arm Cassiod. (επηλθαν, so ABℵ p.) τινες ιουδ. απ. ικον. κ. αντ. D, τιν. απ. α. κ. ι. ιουδ. E vulg: οι απ. αντ. κ. ικ. και ιουδαιοι 15-8. 180. for πεισαντες, επισεισαντες D Syr: om 2nd και D-corr. και διαλεγομενων αυτων παρρησια επεισαν [ανεπεισαν m p] τ. οχλ. αποστηναι απ(om al) αυτων λεγοντες οτι ουδεν αληθες λεγουσιν αλλα παντα ψευδονται C a k m p syr-mg(adding και επισεισαντες τους οχλους) arm. λιθοβολησαντες A 15-8. 36. 180. [εσυραν DEL Chr_1.] om εξω ℵ[1]. rec νομισαντες, with CEHLP rel 36 Chr Œc Thl: txt ABDℵ p 13. 40. rec τεθναναι (*corrn: the contracted form was the more common: so Meyer*), with DEHLP rel Chr: txt ABCℵ a k p 13. 36.—τεθν. bef αυτ. D.

20. κυκλωσαντες D[1](txt D[2]). rec αυτ. bef τ. μαθ., with EHLP: τ. μαθ. αυτου (*see ch* ix. 25) D[1](and lat): txt ABCD[s]ℵ c h k m[2] p 13 Chr.—αυτων L [m[1]].—E adds αυτου. ins λυστραν bef πολιν D. om πολιν to πολιν next ver (*homœotel*) ℵ[1]. for τη, την D[1]. [εισηλθ. H.] συν is written by D[s], D[1] has perished.

and ch. xvii. 30. **17.**] Compare Rom. i. 19, 20. The words **οὐρανόθεν** ὑετοὺς διδούς had a remarkable applicability in a country where we have seen from Strabo (on ver. 6) that there was *great scarcity of water*. He relates that in one city of Lycaonia, where water was reached by digging the wells very deep, it was sold for money. The idea of Mr. Humphry, that the conclusion of this speech is a *citation from some lyric poet*, seems improbable on other accounts, and is rendered more so by the above-noticed propriety. **19. πείσαντες τοὺς ὄχλ.**] ἄπιστοι γὰρ Λυκάονες, ὡς καὶ Ἀριστοτέλης μαρτυρεῖ. Schol. on Homer, Il. δ. 88, 92. They stoned him, not in the Jewish method, but tumultuously and in the streets, dragging him out of the city afterwards. He refers to this stoning, 2 Cor. xi. 25, ἅπαξ ἐλιθάσθην. **20.**] **κυκλ.**, not to *bury him*, but, as would naturally be the case, *in mournful anxiety and regret.* **ἀναστάς**] The *prima facie*, and I think the right impression is, that this recovery was *supernatural.* It is not indeed so strongly implied, as to leave no doubt: especially as a blow from a stone would be likely to stun and occasion the appearance of death. **Δέρβην**] See above, on ver. 6. Strabo, xii. 6, says of it, τῆς δ' Ἰσαυρικῆς ἐστιν ἐν πλευραῖς ἡ Δέρβη, μάλιστα τῇ Καππαδοκίᾳ ἐπιπεφυκός, τὸ τοῦ Ἀντιπάτρου τυραννεῖον τοῦ Δερβήτου (cf. Cicero, Epp. xiii. 73, 'Cum Antipatro Derbete mihi non solum hospitium verum etiam summa familiaritas intercedit') . . . ἐφ' ἡμῶν δὲ καὶ τὰ Ἴσαυρα κ. τὴν Δέρβην Ἀμύντας εἶχεν, ἐπιθέμενος τῷ Δερβήτῃ, κ. ἀνελὼν αὐτόν. And Stephanus Byzantinus, Δέρβη φρούριον Ἰσαυρίας καὶ λιμήν (for this, evidently an error, the French translators of Strabo propose to read λίμνη. There is a large lake, now called Ak Göl, near the presumed site of Derbe, see C. and H. i. 239) . . . . τινὲς δὲ Δέλβειαν, ὅ ἐστι τῇ τῶν Λυκαόνων φωνῇ ἄρκευθος. (Wetst.) From this variety of the name, Δέλβεια, Mr. Hamilton thought the modern Divlé might be Derbe. Mr. Lewin (i. 167) objects, that there is no lake near Divlé: but this objection only affects the conjectural emendation mentioned above. From Derbe not being enumerated, 2 Tim. iii. 11, with Antioch, Iconium, and Lystra, as the scene of any of Paul's sufferings, we may perhaps infer that none befell him there. They may have fled to Derbe, as being in a different jurisdiction from Lystra; the latter being comprised in the Roman province of Galatia, whereas Derbe seems to have belonged at this time to Antiochus, king of Commagene. See Lewin, i. p. 168; Strabo, xiv. 5; Dio, lix. 8; lx. 8; Jos. Antt. xix. 5. 1.

21 [d] εὐαγγελισάμενοί τε τὴν πόλιν ἐκείνην καὶ [e] μαθητεύ-
σαντες [f] ἱκανοὺς [g] ὑπέστρεψαν εἰς τὴν Λύστραν καὶ εἰς
Ἰκόνιον καὶ εἰς Ἀντιόχειαν,
22 [h] ἐπιστηρίζοντες τὰς
ψυχὰς τῶν μαθητῶν, [i] παρακαλοῦντες [k] ἐμμένειν [l] τῇ
πίστει, καὶ ὅτι [m] διὰ πολλῶν θλίψεων [n] δεῖ ἡμᾶς [mo] εἰσελθεῖν εἰς τὴν [op] βασιλείαν τοῦ [p] θεοῦ.
23 [q] Χειροτονήσαντες
δὲ αὐτοῖς [r] κατ᾽ ἐκκλησίαν [s] πρεσβυτέρους, [t] προσευξάμενοι
[u] μετὰ [v] νηστειῶν [w] παρέθεντο αὐτοὺς τῷ κυρίῳ [x] εἰς ὃν
[x] πεπιστεύκεισαν.
24 καὶ [y] διελθόντες τὴν Πισιδίαν ἦλθον
εἰς Παμφυλίαν,
25 καὶ [z] λαλήσαντες ἐν Πέργῃ τὸν [z] λόγον
[a] κατέβησαν [a] εἰς Ἀττάλιαν,
26 κἀκεῖθεν [b] ἀπέπλευσαν εἰς

ABCDE HLPℵ a b c f g h k l m o p 13

d constr., ch. viii. 25 reff. e trans., Matt. xiii. 52. (xxvii. 57 intr.) xxviii. 19 only +. f — ch. xii. 12 reff. g ch. viii. 25 reff. h (—) ch. xv. 32, 41 only ‡. (2 Kings i. 6.) i = ch. xi. 23. xiii. 42 al. fr. k constr., here only. Jer. li. (xliv.) 25. Sir. xxviii. 6. τοῖς νόμοις ἐμμένων, Xen. Mem. iv. 4. 4. -- (but with ἐν) Gal. iii. 10, from Deut. xxvii. 26. Heb. viii. 9 (ch. xxviii. 30) only. l ch. xiii. 8 reff. m Matt. vii. 13 ||. Luke xviii. 25. John x. 2, 9. Rom. v. 12. Heb. ix. 12 only. Jer. xvii. 25. n ch. iv. 12 reff. o Matt. v. 20. Mark x. 23. John iii. 5 al. Paul, never. p ch. xix. 8 reff. q 2 Cor. viii. 19 only +. r = ch. xv. 21 reff. s = ch. xi. 30 reff. t absol., ch. x. 9 reff. u = 1 Tim. iv. 14 al. v 2 Cor. vi. 5 reff. w Luke xxiii. 46. ch. xx. 32. Ps. xxx. 5. x ch. x. 43 reff. y ch. xiii. 6 reff. Josh. xviii. 4. z ch. xi. 19 reff. a ch. xvi. 11, 22 reff. b ch. xiii. 4 reff.

21. ευαγγελιζομενοι (*corrn aft ver* 7 : *see also ch* xi. 20) ADEHP a : txt BCLℵ[3] p rel 36 vulg [Bas_1] Chr_1. for τε, δε D 40. 96 coptt. for την πολ. εκ., τους εν τη πολει D-gr. μαθητευσαν B[1](Tischd[1]). for ικ. υπεστρ., πολλους υπεστρεφον D[-gr]. om την (bef λυστρ.) D [h] 93. 113 Chr_1 Thl-fin. rec om εις (bef ικ. and bef αντ.) (*as unnecessary: the circumstantial repetition of* εις *is original*), with DHLP (vulg) E-lat [Bas_1] Chr : ins bef ικ. but om bef αντ. B : om bef ικ. but ins bef αντ. m : txt AC E-gr ℵ a p 13. 36. 40.

22. ins και bef παρακ. C a c 69. 100-5-37 syrr [æth] arm Thl-fin : παρακ. τε D-gr ℵ[3] vulg(not fuld tol). (for εμμενειν, ε̄ ενμενειν(sic) ℵ.) ελθειν D[1]-gr.

23. rec πρεσβ. bef κατ εκκλ., with EHLP rel [syr coptt æth] Chr : txt ABCDℵ a k m p 13 vulg Syr arm. κατα D. προσευξ. δε D : και πρ. c f vss [simly]. αυτοις L. πεπιστευκασιν D c e 78. 137.

24. διελθ. δε D copt. aft διελθ. ins εις ℵ. ηλθαν D. ins την bef παμφ. (*to correspond with* την πισ.) BCEℵ p 13. 40 : om ADHLP rel Chr.

25. εις περγην A am demid : εις την περγην ℵ[1](and [3] ?) [p]. aft τ. λογον ins του κυριου ACℵ (k) p 13. 40 vulg Syr syr-w-ast arm ; του θεου E. (ατταλιαν, so AB[1]CDEℵ.) at end, D 137 syr-w-ast add ευαγγελιζομενοι αυτους.

26. om απεπλευσαν B[1]-txt (insd in marg).

21. ὑπέστρ.] They were not far from the famous pass, called the 'Cilician gates,' which leads direct into that province : but, notwithstanding all that had befallen him, Paul prefers returning by the churches which he had founded, to a short and easy journey to the coast by his own home.

22. ἡμᾶς] Is not this a token of the presence of the narrator again ? My own conjecture would be, that he remained in Antioch during the journey to Iconium, &c., and back. The events between those two limits are much more summarily related than those before or after. In an art. in the Journal of classical and sacred philology, Camb., March, 1856, where the justice of the above conjecture is called in question, the writer says, 'here δεῖ ἡμᾶς εἰσελθ. &c. is the language of the preachers themselves, as the word ὅτι shews :' and proceeds to remark justly on the transition from the oblique to the direct narrative, as especially characteristic of St. Luke's style, and corroborative of the unity of authorship between different parts of the Acts, and between the Acts and the Gospel. But if so, should we not rather look for ὑμᾶς than ἡμᾶς ? The writer, I am glad to see, joins with me in rejecting the 'common' explanation (see Prolegg. § i. 13) that ἡμᾶς is used by the writer 'as a Christian, and of all Christians :' to what then would he have it referred ? I would rather, regarding the ὅτι as marking a transition to the direct narrative, take ἡμᾶς as an insensible translation into the first person on the part of the narrator, speaking of an exhortation which he heard and felt.

23. χειροτ.] '*cum suffragiis creassent*,' Erasm. : not necessarily as the meaning of the *word* conventionally,—which had passed to any kind of appointment, see ch. x. 41 : but by the analogy of ch. vi. 2—6. See ref. 2 Cor. The word will not bear Jerome's and Chrys.'s sense of '*laying on* of hands,' adopted by Roman Catholic expositors. Nor is there any reason here for departing from the usual meaning of electing by show

Ἀντιόχειαν, ὅθεν ἦσαν [c] παραδεδομένοι τῇ χάριτι τοῦ
θεοῦ εἰς τὸ [d] ἔργον ὃ [e] ἐπλήρωσαν. 27 [f] παραγενόμενοι
δὲ καὶ [g] συναγαγόντες τὴν ἐκκλησίαν [h] ἀνήγγελλον ὅσα
[i] ἐποίησεν ὁ θεὸς [i] μετ' αὐτῶν, καὶ ὅτι [k] ἤνοιξεν τοῖς ἔθνεσιν
[k] θύραν πίστεως. 28 [l] διέτριβον δὲ χρόνον [m] οὐκ [mn] ὀλίγον
σὺν τοῖς μαθηταῖς.

XV. 1 Καί τινες [o] κατελθόντες ἀπὸ τῆς Ἰουδαίας ἐδίδασκον τοὺς ἀδελφοὺς ὅτι ἐὰν μὴ [p] περιτμηθῆτε τῷ
[q] ἔθει τῷ Μωυσέως, οὐ δύνασθε σωθῆναι. 2 γενομένης οὖν
[r] στάσεως καὶ [s] ζητήσεως [m] οὐκ [m] ὀλίγης τῷ Παύλῳ καὶ

d μετ αυτων... ABCDE HLPℵ a b c d f g h k l m o p 13

c = ch. xv. 40. 1 Pet. ii. 23. John xix. 30 ‡. (Deut. i. 8.)
d = ch. xv. 38 reff.
e = ch. xii. 25 reff.
f absol., ch. xvii. 10 reff.
g = Matt. ii. 4. ch. xv. 30. Ps. xlix. 5.
h = ch. xv. 4. xix. 18. Rom. xv. 21. 2 Cor. vii. 7. Deut. xxvi. 3.
i Luke i. 72. x. 37. ch. xv. 4. Luke only. Gen. xxiv. 12.
k = 2 Cor. ii. 12 reff. l ch. xii. 19 reff. m ch. xii. 18 reff. n = Rev. xii. 12. o ch. viii. 5 reff. p 1 Cor. vii. 18 reff. q = ch. vi. 14 reff. constr., Tobit iii. 3. 2 Macc. vi. 1. r = ch. xxiii. 7, 10. (xxiv. 5 al. Prov. xvii. 14.) s John iii. 25. ch. xxv. 20. 1 Tim. i. 4. vi. 4. 2 Tim. ii. 23. Tit. iii. 9 only †.

27. συναξαντες D: συναγοντες p. rec ανηγγειλαν (*corrn to aorist as more usual*), with HLP rel vulg [syr æth arm]: ανηγγελον p: ανηγγελαν m: απηγγειλαν E k Bas_1 Chr_1: ανηγγειλον D: txt A B[ανηγελ. B[1]] Cℵ 13 copt. ο θεος bef εποι. Dℵ [a] c 96. 133-80 sah [Bas_1]. for μετ' αυτων, αυτοις(partly erased by D-corr) μετα των ψυχων αυτων D.

28. rec aft διετρ. δε ins εκει, with EHLP rel [syrr coptt] Chr: om ABCDℵ p 13. 36. 40 vulg æth arm.

Chap. XV. **1.** aft ιουδαιας ins των πεπιστευκοτων απο της αιρεσεως των φαρισαιων 8. 137 syr-mg (*see note*). [for εαν, αν A[1].] rec περιτεμνησθε (*Meyer thinks the aor, in the sense of the* futurum exactum, *may be an emendation. I shd rather think the* present *to have been the corrn, as being the simpler, and* not *therefore* '*the more genuine*,' as Bloomf.), with EHLP rel [Amm-c] Chr_1: txt ABCDℵ p 13. 36. 40 $Constt_1$ $Epiph_1$ (περιθμητε B[1]: but corrd eadem manu: see table). rec om 2nd τω, with C[2 or 3] DEHLP rel Constt [Amm-c] Chr: ins ABC[1]ℵ p: του 170. και τω εθει μω. περιπατητε D syr-mg [simly sah]. εθνι (but ν erased) ℵ. δυνησησθαι C: -σεσθε 36. 180.

2. for ουν, δε BC D-gr L[ℵ] a b h k p 36 Syr coptt: txt AEHP rel vulg D-lat syr [arm $Constt_1$] Chr. [13 def.] εκτασεως D-gr: ενστασεως l. rec συζητησεως, with Thl-fin: om και ζητ. E 68 vulg copt: txt ABCDHLPℵ p rel 36 Constt Chr Thl-

of hands. The Apostles may have admitted by ordination those *presbyters whom the churches elected.* **προσευξ. μ. νηστ.** belongs to παρέθ., not to χειροτον.

25. Ἀττάλειαν] A maritime town at the mouth of the river Catarrhactes, in Pamphylia, not far from the border of Lycia, built by Attalus Philadelphus, king of Pergamus, in a convenient position to command the trade of Syria or Egypt. It is still an important place, called Satalia. (Winer, Realw. C. and H. i. p. 242.) To reach it they had to cross the plain from Perga. **26.**] **ὅθεν**, as being the centre whence their apostolic commission had spread. **27.**] **μετ' αὐτῶν**, *with* (i. e. in dealing with) *them*, see reff.: not *to them*, as usually: nor *per ipsos*, as Beza, &c. **θύραν πίστ.**] The same metaphor is used in the reff. by Paul, and shews, perhaps, his hand in the narrative. On **χρόν. οὐκ ὀλίγ.**, see chronol. table in Prolegg.

Chap. XV. 1—35.] Differences respecting the necessity of circumcision for the Gentile converts. Council of the Apostles and elders at Jerusalem. **1. τινες**] Called in Gal. ii. 4, παρείσακτοι ψευδάδελφοι, οἵτινες παρεισῆλθον κατασκοπῆσαι τὴν ἐλευθερίαν ἡμῶν ἣν ἔχομεν ἐν χριστῷ Ἰησοῦ. See the addition in var. readd. probably from ver. 5. Doubtless it represents the fact. In spite of the special revelations which had accompanied the reception of the first Gentiles into the church, the strong Judaizing party adhered to their old prejudices respecting the necessity of conformity to the law of Moses. With this party Paul was in conflict all his life; and even long after, we find it raising its head again in the sects of the Ebionites and the Nazarenes. Neander (Pfl. u. L. p. 185, note) notices the account in Josephus (Antt. xx. 2. 4), where Izates, king of Adiabene, is converted to Judaism by a certain Ananias, who, for fear of a commotion among his people, allows him to remain uncircumcised—when a certain Eleazar, πάνυ περὶ τὰ πάτρια δοκῶν ἀκριβὴς εἶναι, pre-

τῷ Βαρνάβᾳ πρὸς αὐτούς, [t] ἔταξαν [u] ἀναβαίνειν Παῦλον
καὶ Βαρνάβαν καί τινας ἄλλους ἐξ αὐτῶν πρὸς τοὺς
ἀποστόλους καὶ πρεσβυτέρους εἰς Ἱερουσαλὴμ περὶ τοῦ
[v] ζητήματος τούτου. 3 οἱ μὲν οὖν [w] προπεμφθέντες ὑπὸ
τῆς ἐκκλησίας [x] διήρχοντο τήν τε Φοινίκην καὶ Σαμάρειαν,
[y] ἐκδιηγούμενοι τὴν [z] ἐπιστροφὴν τῶν ἐθνῶν· καὶ [a] ἐποίουν
χαρὰν μεγάλην πᾶσιν τοῖς ἀδελφοῖς. 4 [b] παραγενόμενοι
δὲ [b] εἰς Ἱερουσαλὴμ [c] παρεδέχθησαν ὑπὸ τῆς ἐκκλησίας καὶ
τῶν ἀποστόλων καὶ τῶν πρεσβυτέρων, [d] ἀνήγγειλάν τε

ABCDE HLPℵ a b c d f g h k l m o p 13

t act. absol., here (1 Cor. xvi. 15) only. 1 Chron. xvi. 7.
u ch. xi. 2 reff. Ezra vii. 6, 7.
v ch. xviii. 15. xxiii. 29. xxv. 19. xxvi. 3 only. Ezek. xxxvi. 37 A (not F.) Ald. only.
w ch. xx. 38. xxi. 5. Rom. xv. 24 al. L.P., exc. 3 John 6+. 1 Macc. xii. 4 al. Jos. Antt. xx. 2. 5.
x ch. xiii. 6 reff.
y ch. xiii. 41 (from Hab. i. 5) only.
z here only. Cant. vii. 10. Ezek. xlvii. 11.
a = Luke i. 68. Job xl. 15 (20). φόβον ποιοῦντες τοῖς ἵπποις, Xen. Anab. i. 8. 18.
b ch. ix. 26 reff.
c Mark iv. 20. ch. xvi. 21. xxii. 18. 1 Tim. v. 19. Heb. xii. 6 (from Prov. iii. 12) only. Exod. xxiii. 1.
d ch. xiv. 27 (reff.).

sif. [13 def.] om τω (bef βαρ.) DE. for προς αυτ., συν αυτοις D-gr: αυτοις 97. for εταξαν to προς D syr-mg have ελεγεν γαρ [*autem* D-lat] ο παυλος μενειν ουτως καθως επιστευσαν διισχυριζομενος (om D-lat) οι δε εληλυθοτες απο ιερουσαλημ παρηγγειλαν αυτοις (for αυτ., ουν syr-mg) τω παυλω κ. τω βαρν. και τισιν αλλοις αναβαινειν προς . . . om προς D-lat, and in conseq has *alios ascendere apostolos* &c. εξ αυτων bef αλλους ℵ. ins τους bef πρεσβ. C 180. for εις, εν E: om b^{1} c. ins οπως κριθωσιν επ αυτοις (επ αυτων D^{3} 137) bef περι D 137, syr-w-ast at end of ver.

3. **εκπευφθ.** E. rec om τε (*as unnecessary*), with AEHLP rel Chr: ins BCDℵ p 36. ins την bef σαμ. DH b d f m o Thl[-sif]. διηγουμενοι ℵ^{1}(txt ℵ-corr$^{1\cdot3}$).

4. ιεροσολυμα AB k p [vulg]: txt CDEHLPℵ rel 36 Chr. (13 def.) rec **απεδεχθησαν** (*appy a corrn, as being the usual word, cf Luke* viii. 40, *ch* xviii. 27, xxviii. 30,—*and see reff*), with CEHLP Chr: παρεδοθησαν D^{1}; υπεδ. 36. 180; προσεδ. k: txt ABD^{2}ℵ p. add μεγαλως CD^{2} (μεγως D^{1}, *mire* D-lat) 137 syr-w-ast sah Ambr$_{1}$. for υπο, απο (*perhaps originally, as in* C, *a corrn to suit* απεδεχθ., *and thence adopted even in copies which read* παρεδ.) BC 36. 180. om 1st και ℵ^{1}(ins ℵ-corr$^{1\cdot3}$). **απηγγειλαντες** D^{1}: απηγγειλαν τε D-corr b. om τε ℵ^{1}.

vails on him to perform the rite, for that without it he could not be a Jew. On the idea that Cerinthus and Ebion were the τινές here spoken of, see the patristic reff. in Wordsw.'s note. **2.**] Compare Gal. ii. 5. **ἔταξαν ἀναβ.**] I assume here what seems to me to be almost beyond the possibility of question (see note to chronological table in Prolegg., where I have given the reasons), that this journey was the same as that mentioned Gal. ii. 1—10. In that case, Paul there (ver. 2) says that he went up κατὰ ἀποκάλυψιν. In this expression I cannot see it necessarily implied that the revelation was made *to himself*, but that there was *some intimation* of the Holy Ghost, similar perhaps to that in ch. xiii. 2, in accordance with which the church at Antioch sent him and Barnabas;—there being προφῆται there, by whom the Spirit spoke His will. **τινας ἄλλους**] Titus was one, Gal. ii. 1, 3, and that, in all probability, in order to *give an example* of a *Gentile convert of the uncircumcision endowed with gifts of the Holy Spirit.* Titus is *not mentioned in the Acts:* but only in 2 Cor., Gal., 2 Tim., and the epistle addressed to him. **3. προπεμφ.**] This seems to have been something of an official escorting of them on the way, and perhaps parting from them with solemn commendation to God: not, as Morus and Heinrichs, 'rebus ad iter suscipiendum instructis,' which would hardly be thus specified, being a matter of course. At all events, it shews that the mind of the church was with them, not with the Judaizers. This was also the case in Phœnicia and Samaria, as is shewn by πᾶσιν below. **4.**] On their arrival at Jerusalem, there seems to have taken place an official reception of them and their message, *in public.* There they *related*—as a most important datum for the determination of the question—*God's dealings with them* (see on ch. xiv. 27), and recounted the places where churches of believing Gentiles had been founded. This having taken place, a *protest* was entered on the part of the Pharisee believers,—in no way doubting the truth of these conversions, nor in any way disparaging the ministry of Paul and Barnabas,—that it was necessary to circumcise αὐτούς, *those of whom they had spoken*, and to command them to keep the law of Moses.

It may be objected, that this view would not be consistent with Paul's statement, Gal. ii. 2, ἀνεθέμην αὐτοῖς τὸ εὐαγγέλιον ὃ κηρύσσω ἐν τοῖς ἔθνεσιν, **κατ' ἰδίαν δὲ τοῖς**

ὅσα ὁ θεὸς [d] ἐποιησεν μετ' αὐτῶν. 5 [e] ἐξανέστησαν δέ τινες
τῶν [f] ἀπὸ τῆς [g] αἱρέσεως τῶν Φαρισαιων [h] πεπιστευκοτες,
λέγοντες ὅτι δεῖ [i] περιτέμνειν αὐτους, [k] παραγγέλλειν τε
[l] τηρεῖν τὸν νόμον Μωυσέως. 6 [m] συνήχθησάν τε οἱ
ἀπόστολοι καὶ οἱ πρεσβυτεροι [n] ἰδεῖν περὶ τοῦ [o] λόγου
τούτου. 7 πολλῆς δὲ [p] συνζητήσεως γενομένης [q] ἀναστὰς
Πέτρος εἶπεν πρὸς αὐτοὺς Ανδρες ἀδελφοί, ὑμεῖς ἐπίστασθε ὅτι [rs] ἀφ' [s] ἡμερῶν [st] ἀρχαίων [u] ἐν ὑμῖν [v] ἐξελέξατο

e Mark xii. 19 ‖ L. only. Gen. xviii. 16. xix. 32, 34.
f ch. xii. 1 reff.
g ch. v. 17 reff.
h absol., ch. xvii. 12, 34. xviii. 8, 27. xxi. 20, 25 al.
i ver. 1.
k ch. i. 4 reff.
l = Matt. xix. 17. xxiii. 3. 1 John ii. 3, 4. Prov. iii. 21.
m = ch. iv. 5 reff. constr., ch. xiii. 44 reff.
n = here only. Wisd. ii. 17.
o = ch. viii. 21 reff.
p ch. xxviii. 29 v. r. only †. (-τεῖν, ch. vi. 9. -τητής, 1 Cor. i. 20.)
q = ch. i. 15. v. 34 al. 2 Chron. xx. 5.
r = ch. x. 30 reff. (2). Ezek. xxxviii. 8.
s see Isa. xxxvii. 26.
t Matt. v. 21, &c. Luke ix. 8, 19. ver. 21. ch. xxi. 16. 2 Cor. v. 17. 2 Pet. ii. 5. Rev. xii. 9. xx. 2 only. Ps. xliii. 1.
u = Mark vi. 4 al. constr., 3 Kings viii. 16 compared with 2 Chron. vi. 5, not as 1 Chron. xxviii. 4, 5.
v with inf., ch. i. 24 (Pet.). 2 Chron. vi. 6.

εποι. bef ο θ. D 38. 96. 137-42 [Thl-fin· επ. μ. αυτ. bef ο θ. p]. at end ins (*from ch* xiv. 27) και οτι ηνοιξεν τοις εθνεσι θυραν πιστεως C^3HL a b d f g Thl-fin.

5. for εξαν. to απο, D syr-mg have οι δε παραγγειλαντες αυτοις αναβαινειν προς τους πρεσβυτερους εξανεστησαν λεγοντες τινες απο (εξ. κατα των αποστ. οντες [πιστευοντες] απο syr-mg: D om λεγ. follg). aft τινες ins ανδρες A. πεπιστευκοτων L b l^2 o 27-9. 99 Jer. for οτι, ως E. for τε, δε D^1[-gr](txt D^3(?)).

6. rec for τε, δε (*alteration of the characteristic* τε *to more usual copula*), with ADEHLPℵ rel 36 coptt [syrr arm] Chr_1: txt BC d p 13 vulg æth. om 2nd οι D. for λογου, ζητηματος E [c] 137 syr: ρηματος 65.

7. rec συζητ., with HLP rel [Chr_1]: ζητησ. ABℵ a c p 13. 36. 40: txt CDE. ανεστησεν εν π͞νι πετρ. και ειπεν D^1(αναστας D^8; om εν π͞νι and και D-corr): aft αυτους ins εν πν. αγιω 137: aft πετρος syr-mg. om οτι $ℵ^1$. rec ο θ. εν ημιν εξελ.

δοκοῦσιν, μήπως εἰς κενὸν τρεχω ἢ ἔδραμον. But I cannot see any inconsistency, if the words used in both cases be accurately weighed. To the ἐκκλησία, ἀπόστολοι, and πρεσβύτεροι Paul and Barnabas gave a simple *recital* of how God had dealt with them among the Gentiles: but Paul did not lay before the whole assembly the *Gospel which he preached among the Gentiles*, viz. the indifference of the Mosaic law to their salvation (Gal. i. 7—9), for fear of its being hastily disparaged or repudiated, and so his work being hindered (μήπως κ.τ.λ.). But, *in private interviews* with the chief Apostles, James, Peter, and John (Gal. ii. 9), he *did unfold the whole freeness of this Gospel*, and so effectually, as to prepare the way for their full and public accordance with him at the council. **6.**] *The Apostles and elders only* are mentioned as having assembled: in which case πᾶν τὸ πλῆθος (ver. 12) must mean τῶν πρεσβυτέρων, and the decision of ver. 22 must have been arrived at *in a larger assembly*. But most probably the deliberation of the Apostles and elders implied the presence of the brethren also, who are intended by πᾶν τὸ πλ.,—and there was *but one assembly*. The objection, *that no one place could have held them*, is nugatory: the *official presence of all* is assumed continually in such cases, where the assembly is *open to all*.
λόγου] matter (in this case) of dispute: see reff. **7.**] A promiscuous debate, not perhaps without some angry feeling, ensued on their first coming together,—and among the *multitude*, as is implied in ver. 12,—man disputing with man. **Πέτρος**] Partly on account of the universal deference paid to him, but principally because of his peculiar fitness to open the apostolic decisions on the subject, from having been made the instrument of the *first public and approved reception of the Gentiles*.
ὑμεῖς ἐπίστ.] In Peter's speeches in ch. x., this phrase occurs at the beginning of a sentence, ver. 28, and ὑμεῖς οἴδατε, ver. 37: and we have traces of the same way of expressing the personal pronoun in his speeches, ch. ii. 15; iii. 14, 25. Such notices are important, as shewing that these reports are not only according to the *sense* of what was said, but the words spoken, *verbatim*. **ἀφ' ἡμ. ἀρχ.**] In regard to the whole time of the Gospel up to that day (about 20 years), the date of the conversion of Cornelius, *at least fifteen years before* this (cf. Gal. ii. 1, and notes to chron. table in Prolegg.), would very properly be so specified. The length of time elapsed is placed by Peter *in the strongest light*, to shew that the question had in fact been settled by divine interference *long since*. Notice (in reff.) the idioms, &c., *peculiar* to Peter:—ἐξελέξ. with inf.,—διὰ τ. στόμ.,—καρδιογν. (most probably);—or *characteristic* of him, πει-

ABCDE HLPℵ a b c d f g h k l m o p 13

ὁ θεὸς [w] διὰ τοῦ [w] στόματός μου ἀκοῦσαι τὰ ἔθνη τὸν
[x] λόγον τοῦ [x] εὐαγγελίου καὶ πιστεῦσαι. 8 καὶ ὁ [y] καρδιο-
γνώστης θεὸς [z] ἐμαρτύρησεν αὐτοῖς, δοὺς τὸ πνεῦμα τὸ
ἅγιον καθὼς καὶ ἡμῖν· 9 καὶ οὐθὲν [a] διέκρινεν [b] μεταξὺ
ἡμῶν τε καὶ αὐτῶν, [c] τῇ πίστει [d] καθαρίσας τὰς καρδίας
αὐτῶν. 10 [e] νῦν [e] οὖν τί [f] πειράζετε τὸν θεόν, [g] ἐπιθεῖναι
[hi] ζυγὸν ἐπὶ τὸν [ik] τράχηλον τῶν μαθητῶν, ὃν οὔτε οἱ
[l] πατέρες [l] ἡμῶν οὔτε ἡμεῖς [m] ἰσχύσαμεν [n] βαστάσαι; 11 ἀλλὰ
διὰ τῆς [o] χάριτος τοῦ κυρίου Ἰησοῦ [p] πιστεύομεν [q] σωθῆναι
[r] καθ' [r] ὃν [r] τρόπον κἀκεῖνοι. 12 [s] ἐσίγησεν δὲ πᾶν τὸ [t] πλῆθος,

w ch. i. 16 (Pet. reff.
x here only. see Col. i. 5.
y ch. i. 24 (Pet.) only +. Herm. Past. ii. 4. 3.
z constr., ch. x. 43 reff.
a 1 Cor. xi. 29. James ii. 4. Ezek. xxxiv. 17, 20.
b = Matt. xviii. 15. Rom. ii. 15 +. Wisd. iv. 10. xvi. 10. xviii. 23 only.
c ch. xiii. 8 reff.
d = Eph. v. 26. Tit. ii. 14. James iv. 8. Sir. xxxviii. 10.
e ch. x. 33 reff.
f 2 Cor. x. 9 reff.
g ver. 28. Matt. xxiii. 4. Luke xv. 5. xxiii. 26. 4 Kings xviii. 14.
h = Gal. v. 1. Matt. xi. 29, 30. 1 Tim. vi. 1 (Rev. vi. 5) only.
i Jer. xxxiv. (xxvii.) 8, 11. xxxv. (xxviii.) 14.
k ch. xx. 37. Mark ix. 42 || Mt. Luke xv. 20. xvii. 2. Rom. xvi. 4 only.
l ch. v. 30 reff.
m = ch. vi. 10 reff.
n Matt. xx. 12. Luke xiv. 27. John xix. 17. Gal. vi. 2, 5. 4 Kings xviii. 14.
o ch. xiii. 43 reff.
p with inf. (absol.), Rom. xiv. 2 only. Job xv. 22. πιστεύω τον χρόνον διδάξειν σε, Xen. Anab. vii. 7. 47. with ὅτι, Rom. vi. 8 al.
q inf. pass. absol., Matt. xviii. 25. Mark v. 43.
r ch. xxvii. 25 only. see ch. i. 11 reff. Rom. iii. 2.
s ch. xii. 17 reff. L.P. Exod. xiv. 14.
t = ch. ii. 6 reff.

(*corrn of order :—and ημ. corrn for υμ. as it seemed more according to ecclesiastical propriety for Peter to describe the selection as made* "from us apostles," *than* "from you the whole church"), with EHLP rel (h o υμ.) [vulg-ed syr: *in nobis elegit deus* am fuld demid]: ημειν ο θ. εξ. D^1 (εν ημ. ο θ. εξ. D-corr^1 c [Rebapt$_1$]) 137 : om εν υμ. m 99 Syr sah æth : txt ABCℵ a(ημιν) k p 13 [(copt Iren-int$_1$)] Constt. om του (bef στομ.) D^1(ins D^3) E [m^1] 96.

8. ο δε καρδ. ο θ. D. διεμαρτυρησεν C. om αυτοις E vulg sah Ambr$_1$ Rebapt.—rec aft δους ins αυτοις (*supplementary addn*), with CEHLP 36 [vulg syrr coptt æth arm] Constt Chr Iren-int$_1$ [Rebapt$_1$]: επ αυτους D: txt ABℵ p 13 Did.

9. om και A^1. rec ουδεν, with ACDEℵ rel 36 Chr$_1$: txt BHLP b g k l m. om τε D.

10. at beg ins και E æth. om ουν(appy) C^1. om ζυγον ℵ^1(ins corr^1?).

11. rec om του (with c?) : ins ABCDEHLPℵ rel Chr$_1$ Thdrt$_1$. rec aft ιησ. ins χριστου, with CD a m 13. 36 [vulg-ed] Syr copt[-ed arm] æth-pl Thl-fin [Iren-int$_1$]: om ABEHLPℵ p rel am demid fuld [tol] syr [copt-ms] sah æth-rom Chr Thdrt Tert$_1$. πιστευσομεν D^1-gr ℵ.

12. συνκατατεθεμενων δε των πρεσβυτερων τοις υπο του πετρου ειρημενοις εσειγησεν παν κ.τ.λ. D syr-w-ast. εσιγησαν C c. απαν E a^1 f m 13 Thl-fin.

ράζ. τ. θεόν,—(καθ)ὼς καὶ ἡμῖν (ch. x. 47: so ὥσπερ καί, ch. iii. 17; xi. 15),—ἀρχαίων *now*, compared with ἐν ἀρχῇ ch. xi. 15. Compare also with πειράζ τ. θεόν,—κωλῦσαι τ. θεόν, ch. xi. 17. **ἐν ὑμῖν] among you.** If ἡμῖν be read, then '*among us* (*Apostles*) :' see var. read. There is no ellipsis of 'me' after ἐξελ.: the E. V. expresses the construction rightly.

8, 9.] The allusion is throughout to *spiritual circumcision*, as the purification of the *heart*. God, who saw deeper than the mere fleshly distinction between Jew and Gentile, who knows that the hearts of *all* are unclean, and that the same all-sufficient sacrifice can cleanse them *all*, if applied by faith (compare the remarkable parallel, 1 Pet. i. 18—22 incl.), put no difference between us and them, but has been pleased to render them spiritually clean. **τῇ πίστει**, not simply '*by faith* :' but **by their faith, or by the faith in Christ.** **10.**] **πειρ.** (as κωλῦσαι, ch. xi. 17), **tempt**, *by putting obstacles in the way of* His evidently determined course. **ἐπιθεῖναι**, infin., marking the intended result of πειράζετε: cf. βῆ δὲ θέειν, βῆ δ' ἰέναι, μάστιξεν δ' ἐλάαν, &c. See Bernhardy, Syntax, p. 365. **ζυγόν**] See ref. Gal. Peter could not be so much referring to the mere outward observance of ceremonies, which he himself and the Jewish converts thought it expedient to retain,—but to the imposition of the law, as a condition of salvation, on the consciences of the disciples. So Neander (Pfl. u. L. p. 214). This being so, οὔτε . . . βαστάσαι will refer, not to the *burdensomeness* of ceremonies, but to the far more grievous burden of legal death, of which Paul cries out so bitterly in Rom. vii. 24,—and says, Gal. v. 3, μαρτύρομαι . . . παντὶ ἀνθρώπῳ περιτεμνομένῳ, ὅτι **ὀφειλέτης ἐστὶν ὅλον τὸν νόμον ποιῆσαι.**

11. Seeing that we *all in common* * believe that the grace of Christ is the sufficient, and only cause of our salvation, it can neither be reasonable nor according to

καὶ ἤκουον Βαρνάβα καὶ Παύλου [u] ἐξηγουμένων ὅσα
ἐποίησεν ὁ θεὸς σημεῖα καὶ [v] τέρατα ἐν τοῖς ἔθνεσιν δι'
αὐτῶν. 13 μετὰ δὲ τὸ [s] σιγῆσαι αὐτοὺς ἀπεκρίθη Ἰάκωβος
λέγων Ἄνδρες ἀδελφοί, ἀκούσατέ μου. 14 Συμεὼν [u] ἐξηγήσατο [w] καθὼς πρῶτον ὁ θεὸς [x] ἐπεσκέψατο λαβεῖν ἐξ
ἐθνῶν λαὸν [y] τῷ ὀνόματι αὐτοῦ. 15 καὶ τούτῳ [z] συμφω-
νοῦσιν οἱ [a] λόγοι τῶν [a] προφητῶν, καθὼς γέγραπται
16 Μετὰ ταῦτα [b] ἀναστρέψω καὶ [c] ἀνοικοδομήσω τὴν [d] σκη-

u here bis. Luke xxiv 35. John i. 18. ch. x. 8. xxi. 19 only. Judg vii. 13.
v ch vii. 36 reff.
w = 3 John 3 only.
x = Luke i. 68, 78. vii. 16. constr. ellipt., here only. Jer. xxxix. (xxxii.) 41 v. r. see Luke i. 25.
y Ps. vii. 17. Isa. xxv. 1.
z ch. v. 9 reff.
a Luke iii. 4. Deut. xiii. 3.
b ch. v. 23 reff.
c here bis only. Amos ix. 11.
d = here only, and Amos l. c.

βαρναβαν και παυλον εξηγουμενοι D¹(txt D³).

13. αναστας ιακ. ειπεν D Syr.

14. for επεσκ., επελεξατο E : εξελεξ. c¹ 137¹ : εξελεξ. και 13. εξ εθνων bef λαβ. C. rec ins επι bef τω ονομ., with HLP rel copt : om ABCDEℵ p 13. 36. 40 vulg syrr sah [arm] Constt₁ Chr₁ Procop₁ Iren-int₁ Jer Rebapt₁.[—om τω ον. αυ. also æth.]

15. for τουτω, τουτο HL o 13 : ουτως D¹(and lat : txt D³) sah Iren-int₁. συνφωνησουσιν D¹[-gr](txt D³ [*consonat* D lat]).

16. μετα δε D¹(and lat). [αναστρεψει A¹, but corrd eadem manu :] επιστρεψω D.

God's will, to fetter that grace with superfluous and vexatious conditions. See nearly the same argument retorted on Peter himself, Gal. ii. 14 ff. **κἀκεῖνοι** are *the Gentile Christians*, not *our fathers;*—*their* ground of trust is the same as ours : *ours*, no more than theirs. **12.**] The multitude (see above) then,—and not before, on account of their mutual disputes, —being tranquillized by Peter's speech, quietly received from Paul and Barnabas an account of the seals of *signs and wonders* by which God had stamped the approval of their ministry among the Gentiles. The miracles at Paphos and Lystra would be among the principal of these. **13.**] **αὐτούς**, viz. Paul and Barnabas. *Both had spoken :* doubtless wonders, unrecorded, had been wrought by the hand of Barnabas, which he had recounted. **Ἰάκωβος**] See note, ch. xii. 17, and the prolegg. to the epistle of James. I assume here, that this is James the Just, the brother of the Lord, the author of the Epistle : and though an ἀπόστολος (Gal. i. 19 : see also note on ch. xiv. 4), not one of the twelve. If we may presume to judge from the character of his Epistle, to say nothing of the particulars which tradition has handed down concerning him, his decision would come with remarkable weight on this occasion. For he is, among all the sacred writers of the N. T., the representative of the strictest adherence to and loftiest appreciation of the *pure standard of legal morality*. All that the law was, from its intrinsic holiness, justice, and goodness (Rom. vii. 12), capable of being to Christians, *he* would be sure to attribute to it. And therefore when *his judgment*, as well as that of Peter, is given in favour of the freedom of the Gentiles, the disputers, even of the Pharisaic party, are silenced. There does not seem to be in the following speech any decision *ex cathedra*, either in the ἀκούσατέ μου, or in the ἐγὼ κρίνω (ver. 19) : the decision lay in the weightiness, partly no doubt of the person speaking, but principally of the matter spoken by him.

14. Συμεών] James characteristically uses this Jewish form of the name: so also Peter himself, 2 Pet. i. 1. The name occurs Gen. xxix. 33, LXX; Luke ii. 25; iii. 30; ch xiii. 1; Rev. vii. 7 : the name Simon, elsewhere used in the N. T. for Peter, is found in 1 Chron. iv. 20 (Heb. Σεμών, LXX-ed.-vat., but Σεμιών B(Mai), Σεμειών, A). **τῷ ὀν.**] **for His name**: dat. commodi [for the service, or the making known, of His name]. On ἐπεσκ. λαβ., see reff. : the infin., as ἐπιθεῖναι, ver. 10, note. **λαόν**, answering to the λαός, so well known as His by covenant before. **15. τούτῳ**] Neuter, **to this** : not, '*to Him*,' in which case we should expect not οἱ λόγοι τῶν πρ., but οἱ προφῆται (Meyer). **16—18.**] The citation from Amos is made freely from the LXX : differing widely in the latter part from our present Hebrew text, which see in loc. E. V. In all probability the LXX had another reading before them, substituting perhaps יִדְרְשׁוּ אֹתִי for יִירְשׁוּ אֶת־ and אָדָם for אֱדוֹם. The existing Hebrew MSS. contain several minor variations, for which see Kennicott and De Rossi in loc. Of this we may at least be sure, that James, even if (as I believe) he *spoke in Greek*, and quoted as here given, would not himself (nor would the Pharisees present have

νὴν Δαυεὶδ τὴν πεπτωκυῖαν, καὶ τὰ [e]κατεσκαμμένα αὐτῆς
[c]ἀνοικοδομήσω, καὶ [f]ἀνορθώσω αὐτήν· 17 [g]ὅπως [g]ἂν [h]ἐκ-
ζητήσωσιν οἱ [i]κατάλοιποι τῶν ἀνθρώπων τὸν κύριον,
καὶ πάντα τὰ ἔθνη, [jk]ἐφ' οὓς [j]ἐπικέκληται τὸ [k]ὄνομά
μου [j]ἐπ' αὐτούς, λέγει κύριος ὁ ποιῶν ταῦτα 18 [l]γνωστὰ
[m]ἀπ' αἰῶνος. 19 διὸ ἐγὼ [n]κρίνω μὴ [o]παρενοχλεῖν τοῖς
[p]ἀπὸ τῶν ἐθνῶν [q]ἐπιστρέφουσιν [q]ἐπὶ τὸν θεόν, 20 ἀλλὰ
[r]ἐπιστεῖλαι αὐτοῖς [s]τοῦ [t]ἀπέχεσθαι [ἀπὸ] τῶν [u]ἀλισγη-

ABCDE HLPℵ a b c d f g h k l m o p 13

e Rom. xi. 3 only, from 3 Kings xix. 10. f Luke xiii. 13. Heb. xii. 12 only. Ps. xvii. 35. g ch. iii. 19 reff. h = Rom. iii. 11, from Ps. xiii. 2. Heb. xi. 6 (Luke x. 50, 51. Heb. xii. 17. 1 Pet. i. 10) only. i here only. Ezra iii. 8. j constr., Mark vii. 25. Rev. vii. 2. Levit. xv. 4. k James ii. 7 only. l ch. i. 19 reff. m ch. iii. 21. Luke i. 70. Gen. vi. 4. n w. inf., ch. iii. 13. xx. 16. xxv. 25 (xxvii. 1). 1 Cor. ii. 2. v. 3 (vii. 37). Tit. iii. 12. 2 Macc. xi. 25. o here only. w. dat., Job xvi. 3. 1 Macc. xii. 14. Diod. Sic. xiv. 27. w. acc., Jer. xxvi. (xlvi.) 27. 1 Macc. x. 35. Demosth. p. 242. 16. p ch. xii. 1. (xxvii. 44). q ch. xxvi. 20 reff. r ch. xxi. 25. Heb. xiii. 22 only. 3 Kings v. 8 A(not F.) only. s constr., ch. iii. 12 reff. t = with ἀπό, 1 Thess. iv. 3. v. 22 only. (Luke vii. 6 al.) Job i. 1 al. without, ver. 29 reff. u here only †. (-γεῖν, Mal. i. 7, 12. Dan. i. 8. Sir. xl. 29.)

κατεστρεμμενα B: *-στραμμενα* (*so LXX-A*) ℵ 13 Procop$_1$: **ανεσκαμμενα** E [*σκαμμενα* (the *σ* above the line) H]. *οικοδομησω* (2nd time) C[1](appy) 68.

17. om *αν* E a k Chr$_2$. for *κυρ.*, *θεον* D æth. for *ο ποιων*, *ποιησει* D[1][-gr] (txt D[3]): om *ο* Bℵ[1]. rec aft *ταυ.* ins *παντα*, with H 36 Syr [arm] Chr: pref., ELP e f g l syr Thl-sif: om ABCDℵ m p 13 vulg copt æth Constt Iren-int Rebapt.

18. rec at end adds *εστι τω θεω παντα τα εργα αυτου*, with EHLP rel syr Constt$_1$ Chr$_1$: *γνωστον απ' αι.* (add *εστιν* D vulg syr-mg Iren) *τω κυριω* (om syr-mg) *το εργον αυτου* AD vulg syr-mg [arm-usc] Iren-int$_1$: txt BCℵ a p 13. 29. 36. 63-5. 100-5-33-80 coptt arm[-zoh æth]. (*In the presence of so many apocryphal insertions as we find in the Acts, taking into account also the great variety, and seeing in it* (cf many more variations in Scholz ad loc) *an argument against the genuineness of the words,—seeing also that no possible reason can be given for their omission, if originally genuine, I have followed the authority of* BCℵ, *as also have Scholz and Tischdf* (ed 7 [and 8]). *Lachmann has adopted the reading of* AD al (see above), *which, as Meyer observes, is evidently an emendation of still later date than the rec.*)

20. [*αλλ* BCH c d m o p.] om 1st *του* [E]H. om *απο* (*as unnecessary ?*) B D-gr ℵ p 180 E-lat Œc$_1$: ins AC E-gr HLP 13 rel vulg [D-lat] Constt Chr Iren-int.

allowed it) have quoted any rendering, especially where the stress of his argument lay in it, *at variance with the original Hebrew.*

The prophecy regards that glorious restitution of the kingdom to (the Son of) David, which should be begun by the incarnation of the Lord, and perfected by His reign over all nations. During the process of this restitution those nations, as the effect of the rebuilding, should seek the Lord,—to whomsoever the gospel should be preached. There is here neither assertion nor negation of the national restoration of the Jews. Be this as it may (and I firmly believe in the literal accomplishment of all the prophecies respecting them as a nation), it is obvious, on any deep view of prophetic interpretation, that the glorious things which shall have *a* fulfilment in the literal Israel, must have *their complete and more worthy fulfilment* in the spiritual theocracy, of which the Son of David is the Head. **17. ἐφ' οὓς ἐπικέκλ.**] Notice the same expression in the Epistle of James (ref.). **18.**] The variation of reading here is remarkable. The text which I have given is in all probability the original, and the words inserted in the rec. have been intended as a help out of their difficulty. Not only are they wanting in several ancient MSS., but they bear the sure mark of spuriousness,—manifold variations in the MSS. where they do occur. The sense, and account of the text seem to be this: the Apostle paraphrases the *ὁ ποιῶν* (*πάντα*) *ταῦτα* of the LXX, adding *γνωστὰ ἀπ' αἰῶνος*, and intending to express 'saith the Lord, who from the beginning revealed these things,' viz. by the prophet (of old, see reff.) just cited. The addition in the rec. has been made to fill up the apparently elliptical *γνωστὰ ἀπ' αἰῶνος*, which not being found in the passage of Amos, was regarded as a sentence by itself. These last words, *κύρ. ὁ ποι. ταῦ. γν. ἀπ' αἰ.*, may perhaps be an allusion to the mystery of the admission of the Gentiles into the church, which was now being revealed practically, and had been from of old announced by the prophets: cf. Rom. xvi. 25, 26; Eph. iii. 5, 6, &c. **19.**] **ἐπιστρέφουσιν**, not as E. V. '*are turned*,' but **are turning**:—the converts daily gathered into the church. In **παρενοχλ.** there is no meaning of '*præter*, . . . *insuper*, molestiam creare:' but simply 'molestiam creare:' see reff.

μάτων τῶν [v] εἰδώλων καὶ τῆς [w] πορνείας καὶ τοῦ [x] πνικτοῦ
καὶ τοῦ αἵματος. 21 Μωυσῆς γὰρ [y] ἐκ γενεῶν [y] ἀρχαίων
[z] κατὰ πόλιν τοὺς [a] κηρύσσοντας αὐτὸν ἔχει ἐν ταῖς συναγωγαῖς [b] κατὰ πᾶν σάββατον [b] ἀναγινωσκόμενος. 22 Τότε
[c] ἔδοξεν τοῖς ἀποστόλοις καὶ τοῖς πρεσβυτέροις σὺν [d] ὅλῃ

v Rom. ii. 22. 1 Cor. x. 19 reff. w = Matt. xv. 19. 1 Cor. vi. 18 al. Hos. ii. 2. x ver. 29. ch. xxi. 25 only †. see 1 Kings xvi. 14, 15. Sir. li. 4. y see ver. 7 reff. z Luke viii. 4. ch. xiv. 23. Tit. i. 5. a — and constr., ch. viii. 5 reff. b ch. xiii. 27 (reff.). c = vv. 25, 28. Luke i. 3. Esth. i. 19. d ch. v. 11. Rom. xvi. 23. 1 Cor. xiv. 23. 2 Chron. xxx. 24 Ald.

om και του πνικτου (*appy, as Meyer, because in Levit no such command is formally expressed*) D Iren-int$_1$ Cypr Tert Jer(who says it was in some mss) Ambrst (who ascribes it to Greek interpolators): om του AB p 13. at end ins και οσα (add αν al) μη θελουσιν (-ωσιν al) εαυτοις (αυτ. al) γινεσθαι ετεροις μη ποιειτε D a b e o 7. 27-9. 60-9. 98-marg 106 sah æth Iren-int Cypr.

21. τους κηρ. [αυ. bef κ. πολ.] C m: εχει τ. κ. αυτον ε(χει) D(three letters lost, erased by D-corr).—for αυτον, αυτο͂υ (ν written over) (sic) ℵ[1].

20.] **ἐπιστεῖλαι**, to send an ἐπιστολή: then τοῦ ἀπ., of the purpose of such epistle,—**to the end that they may abstain**, &c. **ἀλισγ.** belongs to εἰδώλων only. Meyer understands it to refer to the four genitives, the pollutions of (1) idols, (2) fornication, (3) things strangled, (4) blood. This he rests on the non-repetition of ἀπό before τῆς πορν. But in this case the members do not correspond. The Gentile converts needed no command to abstain from the pollution of *idolatry:* and the use of the Alexandrine verb ἀλισγεῖν in reff. shews it to apply most naturally to pollution by *eating.* The ἀλ. τ. εἰδ. are the things polluted by being offered to idols, about which there was much doubt and contention in the early church:—see Exod. xxxiv. 15, and 1 Cor. viii. and x. 19. **τῆς πορνείας**] It may seem strange that a *positive sin* should be made the subject of these enactments which mostly regard things in themselves indifferent, but rendered otherwise by expediency and charity to others. In consequence we have the following attempts to evade the simple rendering of the word: (1) Beza, Selden, Schleusner, explain it of *spiritual fornication* in eating things offered to idols: (2) Morus and Heinrichs, of the committal of actual fornication at the *rites in idol temples:* (3) Salmasius, of the sin of the whore-*master:* (4) Calovius, of *concubinage:* (5) Lightfoot, of *marriage within the forbidden degrees:* (6) Teller, of *marriage with heathens:* (7) Bentley would read χοιρείας, '*swine's flesh:*' (8) πορκείας has also been conjectured (probably not by Bentley, as stated in Meyer, De W., and this work, edn. 1):—see other renderings in Meyer and De Wette. But the solution will best be found in the fact, that πορνεία was universally in the Gentile world regarded on the same footing with the other things mentioned, as an ἀδιάφορον, and is classed here as Gentiles would be accustomed to hear of it, among those things which they allowed themselves, but which the Jews regarded as forbidden. The moral abomination of the practice is not here in question, but is abundantly set forth by our Lord and his Apostles in other places. **πνικτοῦ**] as *containing the blood,*—see Levit. xvii. 13, 14. **αἵματος**] **blood,** in any shape: see Gen. ix. 4; Levit. xvii. 13, 14; Deut. xii. 23, 24. Cypr., Tertull., and others interpret the word of *homicide,* which is refuted by the context. **21.**] Living as the Gentile converts would be in the presence of Jewish Christians, who heard these Mosaic prohibitions read, as they had been from generations past, in their synagogues, it would be well for them to avoid all such conduct and habits as would give unnecessary offence. Other meanings have been proposed: as 'that it was superfluous to command these things to the Jews, for they would hear them in the synagogues' (so an ancient Schol., Lyra, and Neander),—whereas no question whatever was raised about Jewish converts:—'neque est metuendum, ut Moses propterea antiquetur,' Erasmus, al.: 'Pudori vobis foret et ignominiæ, si vos, homines Christiani . . . . hac in re inferiores a Judæis deprehenderemini, quod vos communione cum epulis sacrificialibus polytheismo favere videremini, quum illi Judæi . . . . monotheismo adhæreant tenacissime, eumque quavis septimana sibi inculcatum audiant,' Heinrichs. 'Nam quod ad Mosen attinet, non possunt, qui ex Judæis sunt, queri, eum sperni ab alienigenis nostri gregis, quando in nostris (?) non minus quam in Judaicis conventibus Moses, ita ut ab antiquo factum est, legitur, et quidem sabbatis,' Grot., Hammond. On the reading of the law, &c., in the synagogues, see

e John vi. 70. xv. 16, 19. ch. vi. 5. 1 Chron. xix. 10.
f Luke xxii 26. Heb. xiii. 7, 17, 24. 3 Kings ix. 5. Sir. xxxv. (xxxii.) 1.
g ch. ix. 30 reff.
h constr., ch. xxvi. 3 reff.
i ch. xi. 30 reff.
k ch. xi. 1 reff.

ABCDE HLPℵ a b c d f g h k l m o p 13

τῇ [d] ἐκκλησίᾳ [e] ἐκλεξαμένους ἄνδρας ἐξ αὐτῶν πέμψαι εἰς
Ἀντιόχειαν σὺν τῷ Παύλῳ καὶ Βαρνάβᾳ, Ἰούδαν τὸν
καλούμενον Βαρσαββᾶν καὶ Σίλαν, ἄνδρας [f] ἡγουμένους
ἐν τοῖς [g] ἀδελφοῖς,
23 [h] γράψαντες [i] διὰ χειρὸς αὐτῶν Οἱ
ἀπόστολοι καὶ οἱ πρεσβύτεροι [g] ἀδελφοὶ τοῖς [k] κατὰ τὴν
Ἀντιόχειαν καὶ Συρίαν καὶ Κιλικίαν [g] ἀδελφοῖς τοῖς ἐξ

22. εδοξασεν D[1]. om εξ αυτων A. om τω (*for uniformity*) DHLP rel Chr_1 : ins ABCEℵ a c p 13. ins τω bef βαρν. a c 13. rec επικαλουμενον (*explanatory corrn*), with HP rel Chr : txt ABCDELℵ p 13. 36 $Constt_1$. rec βαρσαβαν, with a 36 rel [vulg-ed demid arm] Chr : βαραββαν D : βαρναβαν fuld æth[-rom] : txt ABCEHLPℵ b e m p 13 am coptt Constt. ηγουμενοις ℵ[1].

23. rec aft αυτων ins ταδε (*addition as the variations shew*), with EHLPℵ[3] p 13. 36 syr [arm] $Constt_1$ Chr_1 ; επιστολην περιεχουσαν ταδε C D(but επιστ. bef δ. χ. α.) æth-pl ; επιστολην και πεμψαντες περιεχουσαν 137 syr-mg ; ουτως Syr ; επιστ. ουτως sah : om ABℵ[1] vulg copt æth-rom. rec ins και οι bef αδελφ. (*see note*), with EHLPℵ[3] rel 36 syrr copt æth [arm-zoh] $Constt_1$ Chr_1 : om ABCDℵ[1] p 13 vulg arm[-usc] $Iren\text{-}int_1$ Ath[$-int_1$] Pac_1 [om αδ. also 34 sah $Orig\text{-}int_1$]. om 1st τοις C[1](appy) 13. for κιλικιαν, κιλιαν A, κιλειαν D. τοις εξ εθ. bef αδ. D [om εξ H].

ch. xiii. 15, note. **22.] ἐκλεξαμένους** must not (with Kuin., al.) be taken for ἐκλεχθέντας; the 1 aor. middle can *never* have a passive signification: see Lobeck's note on Phrynichus, p. 319: where he gives a collection of seeming instances of such usage and explains them. Such irregularities of *case* in words in apposition as we have here (ἀποστόλοις . . . ἐκλεξαμένους . . . . γράψαντες . . . .) will not surprise any one versed in Hellenistic Greek. See e. g. Luke i. 73, 74; ch. xxv. 27; Heb. ii. 10; also ch. xxii. 17, ἐγένετο δέ μοι ὑποστρέψαντι . . . . . . κ. προσευχομένου μου . . . . γενέσθαι με ἐν ἐκστάσει . . . . and ref. (h). **Βαρσαββᾶν**] Of this Judas nothing further is known than that (ver. 32) he was a 'prophet' (see ch. xiii. 1). Wolf and Grotius hold him to have been the brother of Joseph Barsabas, ch. i. 23. **Σίλαν**] otherwise Silvanus (Σιλουανός): the former name [is found] in the Acts, the latter in the Epistles of Paul. He also was a 'prophet' (ver. 32). He accompanied Paul on his second missionary journey through Asia Minor and Macedonia (ver. 40—ch. xvii. 10),—remained behind in Berœa (xvii. 14), and joined Paul again in Corinth (xviii. 5; 1 Thess. i. 1; 2 Thess. i. 1), where he preached with Paul and Timotheus (2 Cor. i. 19). The Silvanus (1 Pet. v. 12), by whom the first Epistle of Peter was carried to the churches of Asia Minor, seems to be the same person. Tradition however distinguishes Silas from Silvanus, making the former bishop of Corinth, the latter of Thessalonica. On the hypothesis which identifies Silas with Luke and makes him the author of the Acts, see Prolegg. to Acts, § i. 11. β, γ. I may repeat here, that in my mind the description of Silas here as one of the ἡγούμενοι ἐν τοῖς ἀδελφοῖς, of itself, especially when contrasted with the preface to Luke's gospel, would suffice to refute the notion. It has been also supposed (by Burmann) that Silas (שְׁלִישִׁי) [*third*] is the same name with Tertius, who wrote the Epistle to the Romans, Rom. xvi. 22: but without reason: see Winer, Realw., "Tertius," and Michaelis, Introd. vol. iv. p. 89, Marsh's transl. **23.]** The omission of καὶ οἱ before ἀδελφοί, found (see var. read.) in all the first MSS., can (as Neander observes against De Wette) hardly have been occasioned by hierarchical considerations, seeing that it occurs as early as Irenæus, and that it would be equally against the strong hierarchical view to call the presbyters πρεσβ. ἀδελφοί, writing, as they were, to the ἀδελφοῖς. It seems very much more probable to me that the words καὶ οἱ were inserted to bring the decree into exact harmony with the beginning of ver. 22. In this, the first *official* mention of πρεσβύτεροι, it is very natural that the import of the term should be thus given by attaching ἀδελφοί to it. See, on the whole, Bp. Wordsw.'s note. **Κιλικίαν**] This mention of *churches in Cilicia*, coupled with the fact of Paul's stay at Tarsus (ch. ix. 30—xi. 25: see also Gal. i. 21), makes it probable that Paul preached the gospel there, *and to Gentiles*, in accordance with the vision which he had in the temple (ch. xxii. 21).

χαίρειν] Not a rendering by Luke of the Hebrew שלום, as Grotius; for the Epistle was certainly written in *Greek*,

ἐθνῶν [l] χαίρειν. 24 [m] ἐπειδὴ ἠκούσαμεν ὅτι τινὲς [n] ἐξ ἡμῶν
[n] ἐξελθόντες [o] ἐτάραξαν ὑμᾶς λόγοις [p] ἀνασκευάζοντες τὰς
ψυχὰς ὑμῶν, οἷς οὐ [q] διεστειλάμεθα, 25 [r] ἔδοξεν ἡμῖν γενομένοις [s] ὁμοθυμαδὸν [r] ἐκλεξαμένους ἄνδρας πέμψαι πρὸς
ὑμᾶς σὺν τοῖς [t] ἀγαπητοῖς ἡμῶν Βαρνάβᾳ καὶ Παύλῳ,
26 [u] ἀνθρώποις [v] παραδεδωκόσιν τὰς [w] ψυχὰς αὐτῶν [x] ὑπὲρ

l = ch. xxiii. 26. James i. 1 only (2 John 10, 11. Isa. xlviii. 22) ‡. Esdr. viii. 9. 2 Macc. ix. 19.
m Luke xi. 6. ch. xiii. 46. xiv. 12. 1 Cor. i. 21, 22 al. L.P. (Matt. xxi. 46 v. r.) 1 Macc. xv. 3.
n Matt. ii. 6. 1 John ii. 19. Deut. xiii. 13.
o = ch. xvii. 8, 13. Gal. i. 7. v. 10. Prov. xii. 25. ἢ ταράττει σε, . . . ὅτι . . . Xen. Mem. ii. 6. 17.
p here only †. (see ch. xvii. 6.) τὴν Λήκυθον καθελὼν κ. ἀνασκευάσας, Thuc. iv. 116.
q Mark vii. 36 al. Ezek. iii. 19.
r ver. 22 (reff.).
s ch. i. 14 reff.
t w. gen. (Matt. xii. 18). Rom. i. 7. xvi. 5, 8, 9. 1 Cor. x. 14. Phil. ii. 12 only. Ps. cxxvi. 2.
u = Matt. xiii. 45. Gen. ix. 20 al.
v = 1 Cor. xiii. 3. Dan. iii. 28 (95).
w = Matt. ii. 20. John x. 11. ch. xx. 24. Rom. xvi. 4. Rev. xii. 11 al. Exod. xxi. 23.
x ch. ix. 16 reff.

24. for επειδη, επι δε ℵ[1]. for ημων, υμων ℵ[1] [m[1] Thl-sif]. om εξελθ. Bℵ[1] a[1] [æth-rom] arm $Constt_1$ [Chr_1 Ath-int_1]: ελθοντες [H]L. εξεταραξαν D[1] a[1]. [ανασκευγαζοντες L.] rec aft υμων ins λεγοντες περιτεμνεσθαι (add δει E) και τηρειν τον νομον (*gloss from vv* 1, 5), with CEHLP syrr æth-pl [arm Thl] Iren[-int](aft διεστειλ.), περιτεμνειν αυτους τα τεκνα [κ. τ. τ. ν.] Chr-edd_1: om ABDℵ p 13 vulg coptt æth-rom $Constt_1$ $Epiph_1$ Ath[-int_1 Orig-int_1]. [διαστ. p:] διεστειλομεθα D[1](txt D[4]).
25. εκλεξαμενοις (*grammatical correction*) ABL p 13 rel: txt CDEHPℵ b f g l 36 $Constt_1$ Chr_1. for ημ., υμων D-gr [k m[1](?)].
26. παραδεδωκασιν D. την ψυχην D Iren-int_1.

as intended for Gentiles. The only other place where this Greek form of salutation occurs in an apostolic document (we have it in the letter of the chief captain Lysias, ch. xxiii. 26) is in James i. 1, which Bleek has remarked as a coincidence serving to shew his hand in the drawing up of this Epistle. **24.**] Neander remarks (Pfl. u. L. p. 223, note) that ἐξ **ἡμῶν** ἐξ. is a presumption in favour of the reading καὶ οἱ ἀδελφοί above: for that these men could hardly have gone out from among the Apostles and elders. But such a supposition is not necessary: ἡμῶν implies the church, the ἀδελφοί of whom they were the πρεσβύτεροι, whether καὶ οἱ be inserted or not. **ἀνασκ.**] See ref. Thucyd., where it will be seen that it implies *turning up the foundations*:—for Brasidas cleared the ground and consecrated it. Cf. Passow, sub voc. The words λέγοντες περιτέμνεσθαι κ. τηρεῖν τὸν νόμον, inserted in rec. after ὑμῶν, are *manifestly*, in my view, an interpolation, from the desire to specify in what particulars these persons had sought to unsettle the souls of the Gentile brethren. The defence of the clause set up by Meyer and De Wette,—that if interpolated it must be from ver. 5, not from ver. 1, and that this is improbable,—is best answered by observing that in E, one of the principal authorities for the insertion, the **δεῖ** after περιτέμνεσθαι betrays in very fact that the interpolation *was* from ver. 5, as also, but in a less degree, does the λέγοντες. The reasons given by Meyer and De W. why the words should have been *omitted*,—the similarity of ending in ὑ-ΜΩΝ and νό-MON,—or to square it with ver. 1, seem to me nugatory. The former is very improbable,—and the latter would have required the preservation of λέγ. περιτέμνεσθαι. The *variations* also in the clause are strong presumptions against it. The persons to whom the epistle was addressed would very well know *what* it was that had disturbed their minds, and the omission of formal mention of it would be natural, to avoid prominent cause of offence to the Jewish converts by an apparent depreciation of circumcision and the observance of the law. **25.**] **γεν. ὁμοθυμ.** may mean either '*assembled with one accord*,' as (perhaps) ch. i. 14; or '*having agreed with one consent*' as Meyer. I prefer the former meaning. So we have adverbs as predicates after verbs substantive, e. g., εἶναι διαφερόντως, Plato Legg. x. p. 892 c, κατύπερθε γίνεσθαι, Herod., &c. See Bernhardy, Syntax, p. 337. **Βαρν. κ. Παύλ.**] Paul has generally been mentioned first since ch. xiii. 43. (The exception, ch. xiv. 14, appears to arise from the people calling Barnabas Jupiter, and thus giving him the precedence in ver. 12, after which the next mention of them follows the same order.) But here, as at ver. 12, we have naturally the old order of precedence in the Jerusalem congregation preserved. **26. παραδ. τ. ψ.**] See reff. The sacrifice of their lives was made *by them*: they were martyrs *in will*, though their lives had not as yet been laid down in point of fact.
This is mentioned to shew that Paul and Barnabas could have no other motive than that of serving the Lord Jesus Christ,

y = Matt. xxvii. 57. ch. xxi. 24. z ver. 32. 2 Thess. ii. 2, 15. a ch. xi. 13 reff. constr., ch. vi. 11 reff. b ver. 10 reff. c = Rev. ii. 24 (Matt. xx. 12. 2 Cor. iv. 17. Gal. vi. 2. 1 Thess. ii. 6) only +. Sir. xiii. 2 (2 Macc. ix. 10) only. d here only +. Jos. Antt. xvi. 11. 2. Demosth. κατὰ Τιμοκρ. p. 706. 22. (ἐπαναγκαστής, Job iii. 18 Symm.) e gen., 1 Tim. iv. 3. 1 Pet. ii. 11 only. Jer. vii. 10. [w. ἀπό, ver. 20 reff.] f 1 Cor. viii. 1 reff. g ver. 20 (reff.). h Luke ii. 51 only. = Ps. xi. 7. Isa. lvi. 2. i = 2 Cor. vii. 11 reff. j see note. not as Eph. vi. 21. 2 Macc. ix. 19. k here (ch. xxiii. 30 rec.) only. 2 Macc. xi. 33.

ABCDE HLPℵ a b c d f g h k l m o p 13

τοῦ [x] ὀνόματος τοῦ κυρίου ἡμῶν Ἰησοῦ χριστοῦ. 27 ἀπεστάλκαμεν οὖν Ἰούδαν καὶ Σίλαν, [y] καὶ [y] αὐτοὺς [z] διὰ
λόγου [a] ἀπαγγέλλοντας τὰ αὐτά. 28 [r] ἔδοξεν γὰρ τῷ
ἁγίῳ πνεύματι καὶ ἡμῖν μηδὲν πλέον [b] ἐπιτίθεσθαι ὑμῖν
[c] βάρος, πλὴν τῶν [d] ἐπάναγκες, 29 [e] ἀπέχεσθαι [f] εἰδωλοθύτων καὶ αἵματος καὶ [g] πνικτῶν καὶ [g] πορνείας· ἐξ ὧν
[h] διατηροῦντες [i] ἑαυτοὺς εὖ [j] πράξετε. [k] ἔρρωσθε. 30 Οἱ

at end ins εις παντα πειρασμον DE 137 syr-mg.

27. aft λογ. ins πολλου E. απαγγελουντας D-gr [-γελοντες a m p]. ταυτα D¹(and lat: txt D²) sah æth-pl: και ταυτα syr: om æth-rom [om τα m].

28. τω πν. τω αγ. ABℵ k p 13 $Clem_1$: txt CDEHLP rel 36 $Constt_1$ Cyr-jer Chr_1 Bas_1 [$Cyr\text{-}p_1$] Œc Thl [$Iren\text{-}int_1$] $Cypr_1$ Pac_1. (after ημιν $ℵ^1$ has written κ, but marked it for erasure.) πλειον D [a] 105. for υμιν, ημειν D^1[-gr](txt D^8(?)). rec aft των επαναγ. ins τουτων, with ELP rel [arm] Chr: pref BCDHℵ a m p 13 vulg [syrr coptt] Constt [Did_1] Thl $Iren\text{-}int_1$ [$Cypr_1$]: om A 15-8. 36. 43. 180 $Clem_1$ $Epiph_2$ Cyr_1 Orig-int Pac-mss (τουτων *seems to have been a marginal supplementary gloss, which some inserted before, some after* των επαναγκες).—om των D^1(ins D^2(?)) $ℵ^1$ 13.[—επ αναγκαις (*itacism?*) ACℵ $Constt\text{-}edd_1$ $Cyr\text{-}edd_1$.]

29. rec κ. πνικτου (*alteration for uniformity with ver* 21), with A^2EHLP$ℵ^3$ 13. 36 vulg [syrr (æth) arm(Tischdf)] $Constt_1$ Chr_1 Œc Thl [Did_1 $Ath\text{-}int_1$]: om D $Iren\text{-}int_1$ $Cypr_1$ $Tert_1$ $Ambrst_1$ Pac_1 Jer_1 (*see on ver* 21): txt A^1BC$ℵ^1$ p coptt $Clem_2$ $Orig_1$. [aft πορν.] ins και οσα μη θελετε εαυτοις γενεσθαι ετερω [-ροις al] μη ποιειτε (*cf ver* 20) D(ποιειν D^1 : -ειν ται(sic) D^5) a e 25-9. 32. 42. 57. 69. 105-6-37 syr-w-ast æth Iren-int Cypr. for εξ, αφ D. πραξατε C D[-gr, *agitis* D-lat] HL æth-rom: πραξητε E. D adds φερομενοι εν τω αγιω πνευματι: also Iren(*ambulantes in sp. s.*) Tert (*vectante* or *rectante vos sp. s.*).

and to awaken trust in the minds of the churches. But, although this was so, the Apostles and Elders did not think proper to send only Paul and Barnabas, who were already so deeply committed by their acts to the same side of the question as the letter which they bore,—but as direct authorities from themselves, Judas and Silas also, who might by word confirm the contents of the Epistle. On the present part. (ἀπαγγ.) see reff. and Winer, edn. 6, § 45. 1. One account of it is, that during the mission implied in ἀπεστάλκαμεν they would be ἀπαγγέλλοντες. But a far more probable one, that the pres. part. here, as so often, *designates* merely, carrying rather a logical than a chronological force: "as announcers of." **27.**] **τὰ αὐτά**, as above, **the contents of the Epistle** (and any explanation required): not, as Neander, '*the same things as P. and B. have preached*:' **διὰ λόγου**, **by word of mouth**, as opposed to '*by letter*,' decides against this interpretation. **28. τῷ ἁγ. πν. καὶ ἡμ.**] Not = τῷ ἁγ. πν. ἐν ἡμ. (as Olsh.),—but as, in ch. v. 32, the Holy Spirit, given to the Apostles and testifying by His divine power, is *coupled with* their own human testimony,—so here the *decision of the Holy Spirit*, given them as leaders of the Church, is laid down as the *primary and decisive determination* on the matter,—and *their own formal ecclesiastical decision* follows, as giving utterance and scope to His will and command. The other interpretation weakens this accuracy of expression, and destroys the propriety of the sentence. Neander, in his last edn. of the Pfl. u. L. (p. 224, note), has given up the rendering of his former ones, ἔδοξεν γὰρ (τῷ ἁγίῳ πνεύματι) καὶ ἡμῖν, '*It seemed good* (*by the Holy Ghost*) *to us also*,' i. e. as well as to Paul and Barnabas. It was plausible, but quite untenable. Such ambiguity, in such a document, would surely be out of the question. The judgment as to what things were ἐπάναγκες is implied in ἔδοξεν, &c. **ἐπιτίθ.** had been used by Peter, ver. 10. **29.**] On the construction of **ἀπέχεσθαι** with ἀπό in ver. 20, and with a simple gen. here, Tittm., de Syn. N. T. p. 225, says well that the difference arises 'non quoad rem ipsam, sed modo cogitandi, ita ut in priori formula sejunctionis cogitatio ad rem, in posteriori vero ad nos ipsos referatur.' His following remarks are worth reading. **ἐξ ὧν, from which things**; not, as Meyer, '*according to which precepts*;' see John xvii. 15. **εὖ πράξ.**] Not, '*ye shall pros-*

μὲν οὖν [l] ἀπολυθέντες [m] κατῆλθον εἰς Ἀντιόχειαν, καὶ
[n] συναγαγόντες τὸ [o] πλῆθος [p] ἐπέδωκαν τὴν [q] ἐπιστολήν.
31 ἀναγνόντες δὲ [r] ἐχάρησαν [r] ἐπὶ τῇ [s] παρακλήσει.
32 Ἰούδας τε καὶ Σίλας, [t] καὶ [t] αὐτοὶ [u] προφῆται ὄντες, [t] διὰ
λόγου πολλοῦ [v] παρεκάλεσαν τοὺς ἀδελφοὺς καὶ [w] ἐπ-
εστήριξαν. 33 [xy] ποιήσαντες δὲ [x] χρόνον [l] ἀπελύθησαν
[z] μετ' [z] εἰρήνης ἀπὸ τῶν ἀδελφῶν πρὸς τοὺς ἀποστείλαντας
αὐτούς. 35 Παῦλος δὲ καὶ Βαρνάβας [a] διέτριβον ἐν
Ἀντιοχείᾳ διδάσκοντες καὶ [b] εὐαγγελιζόμενοι μετὰ καὶ
[c] ἑτέρων πολλῶν τὸν [b] λόγον τοῦ κυρίου.

l ch. xiii. 3 reff. m ch. viii. 5 reff. n ch. xiv. 27 reff. o ver. 12. p = Luke iv. 17. xi. 11, 12 || Mt. xxiv. 30, 42 (ch. xxvii. 15) only. Esth. ix. 11. q ch. ix. 2 reff. r 1 Cor. xiii. 6 reff. Jonah iv. 6. s Rom. xv. 4, 5 reff. Isa. lvii. 18. t ver. 27 (reff.). u ch. xi. 27 reff. v ch. xvi. 40. xx. 2 al. fr. Deut. xiii. 6. w ch. xiv. 22 reff. x ch. xviii. 23. Demosth. p. 392, οὐδ' ἐποίησαν χρόνον οὐδένα. y = ch. xx. 3. 2 Cor. xi. 25. James iv. 13. Prov. xiii. 23. z Heb. xi. 31 only. Gen. xxvi. 29. see ch. xvi. 36 reff. a ch. xii. 19 reff. b ch. viii. 4 only. see 1 Cor. xv. 2. c = ch. xvii. 7 reff.

30. aft απολυθ. ins εν ημεραις ολιγαις D¹[and lat]. rec (for κατηλθ.) ηλθον, with EHLP rel [syrr coptt] Chr₁ Thl-sif : txt ABCDא a p 13. 36. 40 vulg æth [arm] Thl-fin. συναγοντες D¹(txt D²). επιδεδωκαν E.

32. elz (for τε) δε, with D-gr vulg E-lat syr copt Thl-fin : om sah æth-rom [arm (Tischdf)] : txt ABC E-gr HLPא p 13 rel D-lat (Syr) æth-pl Chr₁ Thl-sif. for οντες, υπαρχοντες E : aft οντες ins πληρεις πνευματος αγιου D. om πολλου D 18. επεστηρισαν CE 73 : txt ABDHLP א-corr¹ p 13. 36 rel Chr : om και επεστ. א¹.

33. rec for αποστ. αυτους, αποστολους (*perhaps an explanatory gloss, substituted for the genuine text ;—but more probably a* mistake, *owing to* αποστ. *being common to the two words*), with EHLP rel syrr copt[-wilk] Chr₁ : txt ABCDא a p 13. 36. 40 vulg [copt-boett] sah æth-rom Thl-fin.—א had εαυτους, but the ε has been marked and then erased.

[**34.** rec εδοξε δε τω σιλα επιμειναι αυτου (*explanatory anticipation of ver* 40), with CD 13 rel [vulg-ed] syr-w-ast sah [copt-wilk æth] arm Œc Thl-fin (σειλεα D : παυλω æth : for επιμειναι, *sustinere eos* D-lat : for αυτου, αυτους CD¹, προς αυτους D-corr¹ : om ABEHLPא c d g h l m p am(and demid fuld) Syr copt[-boett] Chr Thl-sif). add further μονος δε ιουδας επορευθη D vulg-ed [tol] arm(not ed-1805).]

35. ο δε π. D. και μετα ετ. D¹(txt D⁵). at end κυ., which has perished in D¹, is supplied by D⁶(?).

per:' but as καλῶς ἐποίησας, ch. x. 33; 3 John 6,—**ye shall do well.** See the curious additions in var. readd. **ἔρρωσθε**] The customary 'valete' of the conclusion of epistles. **31. παρακλήσει**] It does not appear, because παρεκάλεσαν follows in the sense of 'exhorted,' that this word need mean '*exhortation.*' There was (De W.) very little *exhortation* in the letter: and it is much more natural to render it **consolation** here: it was the *matter of their joy*, which surely could not be said of the *orders to abstain* given in the letter. It has been observed by Mr. Pusey that syr. renders παρεκάλεσαν v. 32, by *comforted.* **32.**] **προφ. ὄντ.** gives the reason for their superadding to the appointed business of their mission the work of exhorting and edifying. On προφ., see ch. xi. 27; xiii. 1; Eph. ii. 20, and notes. **33.**] **ποι. χρ., having continued some time**: see reff. [**34.**] On every account it is probable that the words forming this verse in rec. (see var. readd.) are an interpolation. For, (1) manuscript evidence against them is weighty, especially as D, in the case of *insertions* in the Acts, is of very low authority. (2) The αὐτοῦ is **αὐτούς** in C and D, and αὐτοῖς and αὐτόθι in some cursives; and D and the Vulg. add μόνος δὲ Ἰούδ. ἐπορεύθη; the former shewing the copying of an indistinct marginal gloss which was not understood, and the latter betraying the secret of the whole, viz. that the notice was interpolated to account for Silas being found again at Antioch in ver. 40. (3) Internally considered, the insertion is very improbable: coming after ἀπελύθησαν unexplained (which from its voice and tense implies that the dismissal actually took place and they departed) and followed by Παῦλος **δέ** after ἔδοξε δὲ τῷ Σίλᾳ. On Silas's subsequent presence at Antioch, see note, ver. 40. We learn from Gal. ii. 10, that *a condition* was attached to the cordiality with which the Gentile mission of Paul and Barnabas was recognized by the chief Apostles: that they should *remember the poor*, i. e. the poor *at Jerusalem*:—that the wants of the mother church should not be forgotten by those converts, whose

36 Μετὰ δέ [d] τινας [d] ἡμέρας εἶπεν πρὸς Βαρνάβαν Παῦ- ABCDE
λος [e] Ἐπιστρέψαντες [f] δὴ [g] ἐπισκεψώμεθα τοὺς ἀδελφοὺς HLPℵ a
[h] κατὰ πόλιν πᾶσαν ἐν αἷς [i] κατηγγείλαμεν τὸν [i] λόγον bcdfg
τοῦ κυρίου, [k] πῶς [k] ἔχουσιν. 37 Βαρνάβας δὲ ἐβούλετο hklm
[l] συνπαραλαβεῖν καὶ Ἰωάννην τὸν καλούμενον Μάρκον· op 13
38 Παῦλος δὲ [m] ἠξίου τὸν [n] ἀποστάντα ἀπ' αὐτῶν ἀπὸ
Παμφυλίας καὶ μὴ [o] συνελθόντα αὐτοῖς εἰς τὸ [p] ἔργον, μὴ
[l] συνπαραλαμβάνειν [q] τοῦτον. 39 ἐγένετο δὲ [r] παροξυσ-
μός, ὥςτε [s] ἀποχωρισθῆναι αὐτοὺς ἀπ' ἀλλήλων, τόν
τε Βαρνάβαν [t] παραλαβόντα τὸν Μάρκον [u] ἐκπλεῦσαι εἰς

d ch. x. 48 reff. e see Luke xxii. 32 (and note). f = Luke ii. 15. ch. xiii. 2. 1 Cor. vi. 20. Gen. xviii. 4. g ch. vii. 23 reff. h ch. xiii. 27 reff. i ch. xiii. 5 reff. k Gen. xliii. 27. see Matt. iv. 24. Mark xvi. 18. l ch. xii. 25 reff. m = ch. xxviii. 22 (Luke vii. 7. 2 Thess. i. 11. 1 Tim. v. 17. Heb. iii. 3. x. 29) only. 1 Macc. xi. 28. n Luke ii. 37. iv. 13. ch. xii. 10. xix. 9 al. Ps. lxxix. 18. o = ch. i. 21 reff. p = ch. xiii. 2. xiv. 26. Phil. i. 22 al. q ch. xiii. 7 al. r Heb. x. 24 only. Deut. xxix. 28. Jer. xxxix. (xxxii.) 37 only. (-ύνεσθαι, ch. xvii. 16.) s Rev. vi. 14 only. (διαχ., Luke ix. 33.) Ezek. xliii. 21 only, but not =. t = Matt. xvii. 1. Num. xxii. 41. u ch. xviii. 18 xx. 6 only †. Xen. Anab. v. 6. 21, 23.

36. rec παυλ. bef πρ. βαρν., with DEHLP rel [syrr coptt æth arm(?) Bas_1]: txt ABCℵ m p 13 vulg Thl-fin.—ins ο bef παυλ. D. for δη, δε ℵ[1]. rec aft τους αδ. ins ημων (*not perceiving the sense of* τ. αδελφ.), with HLP rel æth [Bas_1] Thl: τους D c 36. 137-80: om ABCEℵ a p 13. 40 vulg [syrr] coptt arm Chr. rec πασ bef πολ., with DEHLP 13. 36 rel [vulg Bas_1] Chr: txt ABCℵ k m. οις D. for κατηγγ., εκηρυξαμεν C 15-8. 36. 180 [arm ?]. ins το bef πως E.

37. rec εβουλευσατο, with HLP rel Chr_1 Thl-sif: εβουλευετο D[-gr]: txt ABCEℵ a c e p 13. 36. 40 vulg [D-lat] syrr copt æth Thl-fin. συνπαραλαμβανειν A (13). rec (for και) τον, with HLP 13 rel Syr sah æth Thl-sif: om D a c: και τον Bℵ p: txt ACE h k 36 vulg syr copt arm Chr Thl-fin. επικαλουμενον CD [ℵ[3](but corrd)] c d k p 13. 40.

38. for ηξιου, ουκ εβουλετο λεγων D. αποστατησαντα(sic) A: αποστησαντα D. om απο παμφ. C? [C[1] doubtful]. συνελθοτα B[1](but corrd). om αυτοις D. aft εργ. add εις ο επεμφθησαν D tol. rec συμπαραλαβειν (*corrn for conformity to ver* 37), with EHLP rel Chr_1: txt ABCℵ a c p 36,—(συνπ., so AB[1]CEℵ.)—for μη συνπ. τ., D has τουτον μη ειναι συν αυτοις.

39. rec for δε, ουν (*corrn to suit the sequence of the* παροξ. *on the last verse*), with CEHLP rel 36 syrr [arm] Chr_1: txt ABDℵ p vulg coptt. αποχωρησαι E. τοτε βαρν. παραλαβων τ. μ. επλευσεν D: τον γε(or ο γε) syr [om τον A].

Judaical bond to her was thus cast loose. This was an object which Paul was ever most anxious to subserve. See Gal. l. c. and note.] **35.**] **διδάσκοντες**, to those who had received it,—**εὐαγγελιζόμενοι**, to those who had not.

36—CH. XVIII. 22.] PAUL'S SECOND MISSIONARY JOURNEY (unaccompanied by Barnabas, on account of a difference between them) THROUGH ASIA MINOR TO MACEDONIA AND GREECE, AND THENCE BY SEA, TOUCHING AT EPHESUS, TO JERUSALEM AND BACK TO ANTIOCH.

36. μετὰ δέ τινας ἡμ.] *How long*, we are not informed: but perhaps (?) during this time took place that visit of Peter to Antioch mentioned Gal. ii. 11 ff. when he sacrificed his Christian consistency and better persuasions to please some Judaizers, and even Barnabas was led away with the dissimulation. On this occasion Paul boldly rebuked him. See, on the whole occurrence, notes to Gal. l. c. **δή**, see above, ch. xiii. 2. **ἐν αἷς**, because πᾶσαν πόλιν involves a plurality: so Xen. Mem. i. 2. 62, ἐάν τις φανερὸς γένηται . . . τούτοις θάνατός ἐστιν ἡ ζημία: cf. Herm. ad Viger. p. 40. **38. ἠξίου**] Not as Vulg. 'rogabat:' but 'æquum censebat,' as Beza. It gives Paul's refusal in the strongest manner. The position of the accusatives also forcibly expresses his decided rejection of one who had not dared to face the dangers of the untried country before. **But Paul thought proper (as to) one who had fallen off from them from Pamphylia, and had not gone with them to the work, not to take with them that man.** We may well believe that Paul's own mouth gave originally the character to the sentence. **τὸν ἀποστ.**] See ch. xiii. 13. It hence is evident that his departure was not by the authority of the Apostles (as Benson). **39.**] ὁ Παῦλος ἐζήτει τὸ δίκαιον, ὁ Βαρνάβας τὸ φιλάνθρωπον, Chrysostom: who also remarks on their separate journeys,—ἐμοὶ δοκεῖ καὶ κατὰ σύνεσιν γεγενῆσθαι τὸν χωρισμόν, καὶ πρὸς ἀλλήλους εἰπεῖν ὅτι ἐπειδὴ ἐγὼ οὐ βούλομαι, σὺ δὲ βούλει, ἵνα μὴ μαχώ-

Κύπρον· 40 Παῦλος δὲ [v] ἐπιλεξάμενος Σίλαν [w] ἐξῆλθεν
[x] παραδοθεὶς τῇ χάριτι τοῦ κυρίου ὑπὸ τῶν ἀδελφῶν.
41 [y] διήρχετο δὲ τὴν Συρίαν καὶ Κιλικίαν, [z] ἐπιστηρίζων
τὰς [a] ἐκκλησίας. XVI. 1 [b] κατήντησεν δὲ εἰς Δέρβην
καὶ Λύστραν. [c] καὶ ἰδοὺ μαθητής τις ἦν ἐκεῖ ὀνόματι
Τιμόθεος, υἱὸς γυναικὸς Ἰουδαίας [d] πιστῆς, πατρὸς δὲ
Ἕλληνος, 2 ὃς [e] ἐμαρτυρεῖτο [e] ὑπὸ τῶν ἐν Λύστροις καὶ
Ἰκονίῳ ἀδελφῶν. 3 τοῦτον ἠθέλησεν ὁ Παῦλος σὺν αὐτῷ
[f] ἐξελθεῖν, καὶ [g] λαβὼν [h] περιέτεμεν αὐτὸν [i] διὰ τοὺς

v = here (John v. 2) only. Exod. xvii. 9. 2 Kings x. 9.
w = ch. xvi. 3, 40. xx. 1 al.
x ch. xiv. 26 reff.
y ch. xiii. 6 reff. Gen. xli. 46.
z ch. xiv. 22 reff.
a plur., Rom. xvi. 16 reff.
b w. εἰς, ch. xviii. 19, 24 al5. 1 Cor. x. 11. xiv. 36. Eph. iv. 13. Phil. iii. 11 only. 2 Macc. iv. 44. w. ἀντικρύς, ch. xx. 15 only L.P. (w. ἐπί, 2 Kings iii. 29 only.)
c ch. xi. 11. xii. 7. xxvii. 24 al.
d ch. x. 45 reff.
e ch. x. 22 reff.
f ch. xv. 40 reff.
g red., Matt. xiii. 31 al. of persons, here only. Num. iii. 6.
h 1 Cor. vii. 18 reff.
i = ch. iv. 21. x. 21.

40. σαυλος E-gr. επιδεξαμενος D. om του D1(ins D5). rec (for κυρ.) θεου, with CEHLP rel 36 [vulg-clem arm] syrr copt Chr1 [Thl-sif] : txt ABDℵ p 13. 40 am(and demid fuld tol) sah Thl-fin. απο D.

41. ins την bef κιλ. BD Thl-fin. at end ins παραδιδους τας εντολας των πρεσβυτερων D [vulg] demid fuld(not am tol) arm(not ed-1805) [*tradebantque iis ad custodiendum mandata apostolorum presbyterorumque* syr·mg].

Chap. XVI. **1.** διελθων δε τα εθνη ταυτα κατηντ. D syr-mg. ins και bef εις δερβ. AB a m 13. 36. 40 syr copt. ins εις bef λυστ. ABℵ c p. εκει bef ην D : om εκει 32-7. 57 æth. rec aft γυν. ins τινος, with HLP rel Syr sah Thl : om ABCDEℵ a k p 36. 40 vulg syr copt æth arm Chr. (13 def.) om ιουδαιας E.

2. ικονιου [E]ℵ.

μεθα, διανειμώμεθα τοὺς τόπους. ὥστε πάνυ εἴκοντες ἀλλήλοις τοῦτο ἐποίουν. Hom. xxxiv., p. 262. Yet it seems as if there were a considerable difference in the *character of their setting out.* Barnabas appears to have gone with his cousin [see Col. iv. 10, note] without any special sympathy or approval; whereas Paul was commended to the grace of God by the assembled church. We find Mark afterwards received into favour by Paul, see Col. iv. 10; 2 Tim. iv. 11; and in the former of those places it would seem as if he was dependent for his reception on Paul's special commendation. **40. Σίλαν**] He may perhaps have come down again to Antioch (see ver. 33) *in Peter's company.* We find (see above on ver. 22) a Silvanus in 1 Pet. v. 12, the bearer of that epistle to the congregations of Asia Minor. **41. Συρίαν κ. Κιλικ.**] See note, ver. 23. Here we finally lose sight of Barnabas in the sacred record.

Chap. XVI. 1.] We have Derbe first, as lying nearest to the pass from Cilicia into Lycaonia and Cappadocia. Paul probably travelled by the ordinary road through the 'Cilician gates,' a rent or fissure in the mountain-chain of Taurus, extending from north to south through a distance of eighty miles. See various interesting particulars in C. and H. i. p. 301 ff. and notes. **ἐκεῖ**] At *Lystra :* which, and not Derbe, was in all probability the birth-place of Timotheus : see on ch. xx. 4. This view is confirmed by ver. 2. He had probably been converted by Paul during his former visit, as he calls him his *son in the Lord,* 1 Cor. iv. 17 ; 1 Tim. i. 2 ; 2 Tim. i. 2 ; perhaps at Antioch in Pisidia, see 2 Tim. iii. 10, 11. His mother was Eunice, his grandmother Lois,—both women of well-known piety, 2 Tim. i. 5. Whether his father was a proselyte of the gate or not, is uncertain : he certainly was *uncircumcised.* He would be, besides his personal aptness for the work, singularly fitted to be the coadjutor to Paul, by his *mixed extraction* forming a link between Jews and Greeks.

2.] Some of these testimonies were probably *intimations of the Spirit respecting his fitness for the work ;* for Paul speaks, 1 Tim. i. 18, of τὰς προαγούσας ἐπὶ σὲ **προφητείας** (see ch. xiii. 1, 3). He was set apart for the work by the laying on of the hands of Paul and of the presbytery, 1 Tim. iv. 14 ; 2 Tim. i. 6, after he had made a good confession before many witnesses, 1 Tim. vi. 12. **3. λαβὼν περιέτ.**] As E. V. took and circumcised him. Every Israelite might perform the rite ; see Winer, Realw., art. 'Beschneidung.' **διὰ τ. Ἰουδ.**] That he might not at once, wherever he preached, throw a stumbling-block before the Jews, by having with him one by birth a Jew, but uncircumcised. There was here no concession in doctrine at all, and no reference whatever to the duty of Timotheus himself in the matter. In the case of Titus, a *Greek,* he dealt

Ἰουδαίους τοὺς ὄντας ἐν τοῖς [k] τόποις ἐκείνοις· [l] ᾔδεισαν
γὰρ ἅπαντες τὸν πατέρα αὐτοῦ, ὅτι Ἕλλην [m] ὑπῆρχεν.
4 ὡς δὲ [n] διεπορεύοντο τὰς πόλεις, [o] παρεδίδοσαν αὐτοῖς
[p] φυλάσσειν τὰ [q] δόγματα τὰ [r] κεκριμένα ὑπὸ τῶν ἀποστόλων καὶ πρεσβυτέρων τῶν ἐν Ἱεροσολύμοις.
5 Αἱ μὲν οὖν [s] ἐκκλησίαι [t] ἐστερεοῦντο τῇ [u] πίστει, καὶ
[v] ἐπερίσσευον τῷ ἀριθμῷ [w] καθ' ἡμέραν· 6 [x] διῆλθον δὲ τὴν
Φρυγίαν καὶ Γαλατικὴν χῶραν, [y] κωλυθέντες ὑπὸ τοῦ

ABCDE HLPℵ a b c d f g h k l m o p 13

k plur., Mark i. 45. Luke xi. 24 ‖. xxi. 11 ‖. ch. xxvii. 2, 29 only. 2 Chron. xxxiv. 6.
l constr., 2 Cor. xii. 3, 4. Job xxi. 27.
m ch. ii. 30 reff.
n acc., here (Luke vi. 1. xiii. 22. xviii. 36. Rom. xv. 24) only. Ps. viii. 8. 1 Macc. iii. 37.
o = 1 Cor. xi. 2 reff. (ch. xii. 4.)
p = Luke xi. 28. ch. vii. 53. xxi. 24. 1 Tim. v. 21 al. Eccles. xii. 13.
q Luke ii. 1. ch. xvii. 7. Eph. ii. 15. Col. ii. 14 only. Ezek. xx. 26 B Ald. &c. (but appy error) only. Dan. vi. 9 Theod.
r = ch. xx. 16. 1 Cor. v. 3. vii. 37. Tit. iii. 12. 2 Macc. xi. 25.
s plur., Rom. xvi. 16 reff.
t ch. iii. 7 reff.
u ch. xiii. 8 reff.
v 2 Cor. ix. 12. Phil. i. 9. Eccl. iii. 19.
w ch. ii. 46 reff.
x ch. xiii. 6 reff.
y = Matt. xix 14. ch. viii. 36 al. 1 Kings xxv. 26. pass., Rom. i. 13. Heb. vii. 23 only. Exod. xxxvi. 6.

3. παντες CD m: txt ABEHLPℵ p rel Chr_1. οτι ελλην ο πατηρ αυτου (*corrn for simplicity*) ABCℵ a m 13. 36. 40 [copt] sah Thl-fin: txt DEHLP rel Chr Thl-sif.
4. for ver, διερχομενοι δε τας πολεις εκηρυσσον και παρεδιδοσαν αυτοις μετα πασης παρρησιας τον κν ιην χρν αμα παραδιδοντες και τας εντολας αποστ. (των απ. D^5) κ. πρεσβ. τ. εν ιερ. D: aft τας πολ. ins εκηρυσσον μετα πασ. παρ. τ. κυρ. ιησ. χρ. syr-mg. [for διεπ., επορευοντο H Thl-sif.] rec παρεδιδουν, with HLP rel 36 [Bas_1] Chr: παρεδιδουσαν C: txt ABDEℵ p 13 [Thl-fin]. rec ins των bef πρεσβ. (*corrn for uniformity*), with EHLP rel Chr [Thl-sif]: om ABCDℵ a p 13 Bas Thl-fin. rec ιερουσαλημ, with EHLP [rel Bas] Chr [Thl-sif]: txt ABCDℵ a p 13 vulg Thl-fin.
5. om τη πιστ. D. περιεσσευον E 3. 65. 95^1 $Chr\text{-}mss_1$.
6. rec διελθοντες, with [H]LP rel vulg(*transeuntes . . vetati sunt*) Chr_1 Thl: txt ABCDEℵ a c d e k m p 13. 36. 40 syrr coptt [æth] arm $Epiph_1$ Did_1 [$Cæs_1$]. rec ins την bef γαλ. (*corrn for uniformity*), with EHLP 36 $Epiph_1$ Did_1 [Chr]: om ABCDℵ p 13 $Cæs_1$.

otherwise, no such reason existing: Gal. ii. 3. **4. τὰς πόλ.**] Iconium, and perhaps Antioch in Pisidia. He might at Iconium see the elders of the church of Antioch, as he did afterwards those of Ephesus at Miletus. If he went to Antioch, he might regain his route into Phrygia and Galatia by crossing the hills east of that city. **5.**] This general notice, with μὲν οὖν, like those at ch. ix. 31, xii. 24, marks the opening of a new section.
* **6—9.**] This very cursory notice of a journey in which we have reason to think so much happened,—the founding of the Galatian and Phrygian churches (see ch. xviii. 23, where we find him, on his second visit, στηρίζων πάντας τοὺς μαθητάς); the sickness of the Apostle alluded to Gal. iv. 13; the working of miracles and imparting of the Spirit mentioned Gal. iii. 5; the warmth and kindness of feeling shewn to Paul in his weakness, Gal. iv. 13—15,—seems to shew that the narrator was not with him during this part of the route; an inference which is remarkably confirmed by the sudden resumption of circumstantial detail with the use of the first person, at ver. 10. **6. Φρυγίαν**] There were two tracts of country called by this name: 'Phrygiam utramque (alteram ad Hellespontum, *majorem* alteram vocant) . . . . . Eumeni restituerunt.' Livy, xxxviii. 39. It is with 'Phrygia Major' that we are here concerned, which was the great central space of Asia Minor, yet retaining the name of its earliest inhabitants, and on account of its being politically subdivided among the contiguous provinces, impossible to define accurately (see C. and H. i. p. 280, note 1). The Apostle's route must remain very uncertain. It is probable that he may have followed the great road (according to his usual practice and the natural course of a missionary journey) from Iconium to Philomelium and perhaps as far as Synnada, and thence struck off to the N.E. towards Pessinus in Galatia. That he visited Colossæ, in the extreme S.W. of Phrygia, on this journey, as supposed by some, and maintained with some ingenuity by Mr. Lewin (Life and Epistles of St. Paul i. 191 ff.), is very improbable (see Wieseler, Chron. d. Apostgsch. pp. 28 ff.).
Γαλατικὴν χ.] The midland district, known as Galatia, or Gallo-græcia, was inhabited by the descendants of those Gauls who invaded Greece and Asia in the third century B.C., and after various incursions and wars, settled and became mixed with the Greeks in the centre of Asia Minor. They were known as a brave and freedom-loving people, fond of war, and either on their own or others' account, almost always in arms, and generally as cavalry. Jerome (in

ἁγίου πνεύματος ᶻλαλῆσαι τὸν ᶻλόγον ἐν τῇ Ἀσίᾳ,
7 ᵃἐλθόντες δὲ ᵃκατὰ τὴν Μυσίαν ᵇἐπείραζον εἰς τὴν
Βιθυνίαν πορευθῆναι, καὶ οὐκ ᶜεἴασεν αὐτοὺς τὸ πνεῦμα
Ἰησοῦ· 8 ᵈπαρελθόντες δὲ τὴν Μυσίαν ᵉκατέβησαν εἰς
Τρῳάδα. 9 καὶ ᶠὅραμα ᵍδιὰ [τῆς] νυκτὸς τῷ Παύλῳ

z ch. xi. 19 reff. a of place, here only. of person, Luke x. 33. b = & constr., ch. xxiv. 6 only‡. c ch. xiv. 16 al. Job ix. 18. d constr., Mark vi. 48 only. (ch. xxiv. 7 al.) Deut. ii. 14. e ch. xviii. 22 reff. f ch. vii. 31 reff. g see ch. v. 19 reff.

ins μηδενι bef λαλησαι D. aft τον λ. ins του θεου D vulg-ed spec Syr copt [æth-pl].
7. for ελθοντες, γενομενην D¹(-νοι D⁸). rec om δε, with HLP rel Chr Œc Thl: ins ABCDEℵ a b¹ d k m p 13. 36. 40 syr [(Syr)] coptt [(æth) arm Ps-]Ath₁ Epiph₁ Did₁. for επειρ., ηθελαν D Syr. rec (for εις) κατα (*perhaps merely a mistake, occasioned by κατα τ. μυσ. before: if an intentional alteration, the reason is not clear*), with HLP rel Thl-sif: txt ABCDEℵ c k m p 13. 40 Epiph₁ Chr Cyr₁ Thl-fin. om 2nd την D. rec πορευεσθαι (*corrn for the less usual inf. aor.*), with CDHLP 13 rel [Epiph₁] Chr Thl-sif: txt ABEℵ m p 36 Did₁ Thl-fin. rec om ιησου (*see note*), with HLP [p²] rel sah [arm-3-mss] Chr Thl; κυριου C¹ demid: txt ABC²DEℵ m p¹ 13. 36. 40 vulg syrr copt æth arm[-3-mss Did₁ Cyr-p] Orig-int₁.
8. διελθοντες D [syr arm-mss]. κατηντησαν D-gr.
9. εν οραματι D-gr E-lat Syr. om δια C. rec ins της, with CEHLPℵ p 13

the introduction to book ii. of his comm. on Galatians, vol. vii. p. 429) says that their speech was like that of the Germans in the neighbourhood of Treves: and perhaps Λυκαονιστί, ch. xiv. 11, spoken of the neighbouring district, may refer to this peculiar dialect. But Greek was extensively spoken. They were conquered by the consul Cn. Manlius Vulso, 189 B.C. (Livy xxxviii. 12, see 1 Macc. viii. 2), but retained their own governors, called as before tetrarchs, and afterwards kings (for one of whom, Deiotarus, a protégé of Pompey's, Cicero pleaded before Cæsar); their last king, Amyntas, passed over from Antony to Augustus in the battle of Actium. Galatia, after his murder, A.D. 26, became a Roman province. The principal cities were Ancyra,—which was made the metropolis of the province by Augustus,—Tavium, and Pessinus: in all, or some of which, the Apostle certainly preached. He was detained here on account of sickness (δι' ἀσθένειαν τῆς σαρκός, Gal. iv. 13). See further in Prolegg. to Gal. § ii. **κωλυθέντες**] By some special intimation, like that in ch. xiii. 2. **Ἀσίᾳ**] This name, applied at first to the district near the river Cayster in Lydia (Ἀσίῳ ἐν λειμῶνι, Καϋστρίου ἀμφὶ ῥέεθρα, Hom. Il. β. 461), came to have a meaning more and more widely extended, till at last it embraced, as at present, the whole vast continent, forming one of the quarters of the globe. But we never find this meaning in Scripture. The Asia of the Acts is not even our Asia Minor,—which name is not used till Orosius (i. 2, p. 16) in the fourth century A.D.,—but only a portion of the western coast of that great peninsula. (A full account of the history of the territory and its changes of extent will be found in C. and H., i. pp. 275 ff., and in Wieseler, pp. 32—35. I confine myself to its import in the Acts.) This, which was *the Roman province of Asia*,—Asia Propria, Plin. v. 28,—as spoken of in the Acts, includes only Mysia, Lydia, and Caria,—*excluding* Phrygia (ch. ii. 9 and here: 1 Pet. i. 1 it must be *included*) as in Pliny l. c.,—Galatia, Bithynia, Cilicia, Pamphylia, Lycia. See ch. xix. 26, &c.

7. **Βιθυνίαν**] At this time a Roman province (senatorial: Hadrian, whose favourite province it was, took it from the senate). **When they were come to** (i. e. to the borders of) **Mysia, they attempted to go into B.** The expression πν. Ἰησοῦ is remarkable, as occurring in all the great MSS., and from its peculiarity bearing almost unquestionable trace of genuineness,—the idea being quite untenable that the word Ἰησοῦ has been inserted here, *and no where else*, on doctrinal grounds. If the report of this journey came from an *unusual source*, an unusual expression would be accountable. 8.] **παρελθόντες** must from the context mean '*having passed by*,' i. e. as *regarded their work of preaching* (cf. ch. xx. 16),—and not 'having passed by' as *avoiding* it; for they could not get to the coast *without entering Mysia*. I adhere to this interpretation, notwithstanding what has been said against it by Dr. Bloomfield (Gr. Test. edn. 9). For this sense of παρέρχομαι, which is not figurative at all, but involved in the literal, cf. Hom. Il. θ. 239: Aristoph. Vesp. 636, 7: Plato, Phædr. p. 278 fin. **Τρῳάδα**] Troas (Alexandria Troas, in honour of Alex. the Great: now Eski Stamboul) was a colony *juris Italici* (see on ver.

[h] ὤφθη, ἀνὴρ Μακεδών τις ἑστὼς [i] παρακαλῶν αὐτὸν καὶ
[i] λέγων [k] Διαβὰς εἰς Μακεδονίαν [l] βοήθησον ἡμῖν.
10 ὡς δὲ τὸ [f] ὅραμα εἶδεν, εὐθέως [m] ἐζητήσαμεν [n] ἐξελθεῖν [n] εἰς
τὴν Μακεδονίαν, [o] συμβιβάζοντες ὅτι [p] προσκέκληται ἡμᾶς

ABCDE HLPℵ a b c d f g h k l m o p 13

h ch. ii. 3 reff. i ver. 15 reff. k Luke xvi. 26. Heb. xi. 29 only. 1 Kings xiii. 7. l Matt. xv. 25. Mark ix. 22, 24. ch. xxi. 28. 2 Cor. vi. 2, from Isa. xlix. 8. Heb. ii. 18. Rev. xii. 16 only. m = ch. xiii. 8 reff. n ch. xi. 25 reff o 1 Cor. ii. 16 reff. p ch. xiii. 2 reff.

rel Chr: om A^2(and appy A^1) BD 40. rec ωφθη bef τω παυλω, with ACD^1HLP rel 36 syrr [coptt æth arm] Chr_1: txt B D-corr Eℵ m p 13. 40 vulg. ins ωσει bef ανηρ D Syr sah. rec τις bef μακεδων, with HLP rel Chr: [om τις copt æth:] txt ABCDEℵ m p 13 Thl-fin.—rec aft ανηρ τις ins ην, with HLP rel Chr Thl-sif: aft μακεδων τις $ABCD^5$ℵ a m p 13 Thl-fin (*these variations of position shew the word to be spurious, inserted to fill up the imagined constr, it not being observed that* ανηρ &c *is in apposn with* οραμα): om D^1E 3. 47. 95^1. 103 Syr copt æth arm. aft εστως ins κατα το προσωπον αυτου D syr-w-ast[: simly] sah. ins και bef παρακαλων (*supplementary corrn*) ABCEℵ a p 13 vulg (syrr) æth: om DHLP rel coptt [arm] Chr_2. om αυτον D.

10. for ως to οτι, διεγερθεις ουν διηγησατο το οραμα ημιν και ενοησαμεν οτι D, simly sah. εξητησαμεν(sic) ℵ [m^1]. om την (*for uniformity with* εις μακ. *above: but that was the* first *this the* second *mention*) BCELPℵ a k p 13 Thl-sif: ins AH rel Thl-fin. om ημας $ℵ^1$.

12), and a free city, and was not reckoned as belonging to either of the provinces Asia or Bithynia. Whether it was for this reason that Paul and his companions visited it, is uncertain. He may have had the design of crossing to Europe, if permitted, which the subsequent vision confirmed. See ch. xx. 5; 2 Cor. ii. 12; 2 Tim. iv. 13.

9.] The vision seems to have appeared in the same way as that sent to Peter in ch. x. It was an *unreal* apparition, designed to convey a practical meaning. The context precludes our understanding it as a *dream*. **Μακεδών**] known probably by the affecting words spoken by him. There would hardly be any peculiarity of dress by which a Macedonian could be recognized. **10. ἐζητήσαμεν**] by immediate enquiry for a ship. This word is remarkable as the introduction of the *first person* in the narrative: which however is dropped at ver. 40, on Paul's leaving Philippi, and resumed again, ch. xx. 5, on occasion of sailing from Philippi. Thence it continues (in all places where we have reason to expect it: see below) to the end of the book. On the question, what is implied by this, we may remark, (1) That while we safely conclude from it that the writer was in company with Paul when he thus speaks, we cannot with like safety infer that he was not, where the third person is used. This latter must be determined by other features of the history. For it is conceivable that a narrative, even where it concerns all present, might be, in its earlier parts, written as of others in the *third* person, but might, when more intimacy had been established, or even by preference only, be at any point changed to the *first*. And again, the episodes where the chief person alone, or with his principal companion or companions, is concerned, would be many, in which the narrator would use the third person, not because he was not *present*, but because he was not concerned. This has not been enough attended to. If it be thought fanciful, I may refer to an undoubted instance in the episode, ch. xxi. 17, γενομένων ἡμῶν εἰς Ἱερ., to ch. xxvii. 1, ὡς δὲ ἐκρίθη τ. ἀποπλεῖν ἡμᾶς, . . .; during the whole of which time the writer was with or in the neighbourhood of Paul, and drops the *we*, merely because he is speaking of Paul alone. (2) One objection raised by De Wette to the common view, that *Luke* accompanied Paul from this time (except as above), is, that several times Paul's companions are mentioned, but Luke is never among them. On examining however one of the passages where this is done, we find that *after* the enumeration of Sopater, Aristarchus, Secundus, Gaius, Timotheus, Tychicus, and Trophimus, we are told, οὗτοι προελθόντες ἔμενον **ἡμᾶς** ἐν Τρῳάδι: so that the writer evidently regards himself as being closely associated with Paul, and does not think it requisite to enumerate himself among the companions of the Apostle. This may serve as a key to his practice on other occasions. On the whole, and after careful consideration of the subject, I see no reason to doubt the common view, that Luke *here joined the Apostle* (whether, as Wieseler suggests, as a *physician, on account of his broken health*, must of course be matter of conjecture, but is not improbable), and from this time (except from ch. xvii. 1—

ὁ θεὸς [q] εὐαγγελίσασθαι αὐτούς. 11 [r] ἀναχθέντες δὲ
ἀπὸ Τρῳάδος [s] εὐθυδρομήσαμεν εἰς Σαμοθρᾴκην, τῇ δὲ
[t] ἐπιούσῃ εἰς Νεάπολιν, 12 κἀκεῖθεν εἰς Φιλίππους, [u] ἥτις
ἐστὶν πρώτη τῆς [v] μερίδος τῆς Μακεδονίας πόλις, [w] κο-

q constr., ch. viii. 25 reff. r ch. xiii. 13 reff. s ch. xxi. 1 only †. t abs., ch. xx. 15. xxi. 18 (vii. 26. xxiii. 11) only. Prov. xxvii. 1. u ch. x. 41 reff. v ch. viii. 21 reff. Ezek. xlv. 7. w here only †.

rec (for θεος) κυριος, with DHLP rel syrr sah [arm] Chr_1 Thl-sif $Iren\text{-}int_1$: txt ABCEℵ a l p 13. 36 vulg copt æth Thl-fin. αυτοις A [d k] 13 Thl-sif: τους εν τη μακεδ. D.

11. rec for δε, ουν (*corrn to suit the sequence on the foregoing ver*), with BCHL P(appy) rel 36 syr-txt sah [arm $Iren\text{-}int_1$] Thl-sif: txt A(D)Eℵ m p 13 vulg syr-mg copt Chr Thl-fin.—τη δε επαυριον αχθ. (αναχθ. D[5]) απο D 137 [syr-mg]. rec ins της bef τρωαδος, with HL P(appy) rel Thdrt Thl: om ABCDEℵ c m p 13. 40 Chr_1. rec (for τη δε) τη τε, with H rel vulg æth [arm] Chr Thl: και τη D: txt A B(δ') CELℵ a b c k m o p 13 syr coptt. (P uncert.) aft επιουσ. ins ημερα D. νεαν πολιν ABD[5]ℵ.

12. rec εκειθεν τε, with HP rel Chr Œc Thl-sif[, *et inde*] vulg Syr copt æth: εκ. δε L [c] 137 syr sah: txt A B(sic: see table) CDEℵ a m p 13. 36 Thl-fin. for πρωτ., κεφαλη D Syr. om 1st της B: om της μερ. D c 14[1]. 96. 105-37-42 syrr æth Chr_1: μερις E-gr [arm]. om 2nd της (*to make the sense clearer*: μακεδονιας πολ. *expressing* 'Macedonian city' *better than* της μακεδονιας πολ.) ACEℵ a m p 40: ins BDHLP Chr. (13 def.)

xx. 5) accompanies him to the end of the history. See the question of the authorship of the Acts further discussed in the Prolegg. § i. 12—14. **11.**] They had a fair wind on this occasion: in ch. xx. 6, the voyage in the opposite direction took *five* days. This is also implied by εὐθυδρομήσαμεν: see ref., where it has the same sense, viz., **ran before the wind.** The coincidence of their *going to Samothrace* also shews it: determining the wind to have been from the S. or S.S.E. It is only a strong southerly breeze which will overcome the current southwards which runs from the Dardanelles by Tenedos (C. and H. i. p. 336): and this, combined with the short passage, is another mark of the veracity of our narrative. They seem to have anchored N. of the lofty island of Samothrace, under its lee. **εἰς Νεάπολιν**] In an E. by N. direction, past the island of Thasos. It was not properly in Macedonia, but in Thrace, and twelve (ten, C. and H. i. 339, from the Jerusalem Itinerary) Roman miles from Philippi, which was the frontier town of Macedonia strictly speaking: see below. It was by Vespasian, together with the whole of Thrace, attached to the province of Macedonia (Winer, Realw.). Some Roman ruins and inscriptions serve to point out the Turkish village of Cavallo as its site. **12. Φιλίππους**] Philippi was built as a military position on the site of the village Krenides (also called Datos, Appian, Bell. Civ. iv. 105, *οἱ δὲ Φίλιπποι πόλις ἐστίν, ἣ Δάτος ὠνομάζετο πάλαι, καὶ Κρηνίδες ἔτι πρὸ Δάτου· κρῆναι γάρ εἰσι περὶ τῷ λόφῳ ναμάτων πολλαί*), by Philip the Great of Macedon. The plain between the Gangites, on which the town is situate, and the Strymon, was the field of the celebrated battle of Antony and Octavius against Brutus and Cassius (cf. Dio Cassius, xlvii. 41 ff.: Appian, ubi supra): see more below. There is now an insignificant place on its site retaining the name Filiba (or Philippigi?). Winer, Realw. **πρώτη τῆς μερίδος τῆς Μακεδονίας πόλις**] * **The first Macedonian city of the district.** It was the first Macedonian city to which Paul and his companions came in that district,—Neapolis properly belonging to Thrace. And this epithet of πρώτη would belong to it not only as regarded the journey of Paul and Silas, but as Wieseler remarks (Chron. d. Apgsch. p. 37, note) as lying *furthest eastward*, for which reason also the *district* was called Macedonia *prima*, though furthest from Rome. The other explanations are, (1) '*chief city*,' as E. V. But this it was not: Thessalonica being the chief city of the whole province, and Amphipolis of the division (if it then subsisted) of *Macedonia prima*:—(2) πρώτη is taken as a title of honour (Hug, Kuin., De Wette), as we find in the coins of Pergamus and Smyrna (but not in the case of any city out of Asia Minor): (3) πόλις κολων. are united (Grot.),—'*the first city which was a colony*.' But there could be no reason for stating this: whereas there would be every reason to particularize the fact that they tarried and preached in the very first city to which they came, in the territory to which they were sent. **μερίδος** would seem to import that the division into Macedonia prima, secunda, &c., made long before this by Æmilius Paulus (Livy, xlv. 29), still

λωνία. ἦμεν δὲ ἐν ταύτῃ τῇ πόλει [x] διατρίβοντες [y] ἡμέρας
[y] τινάς, 13 τῇ τε [z] ἡμέρᾳ τῶν [z] σαββάτων [a] ἐξήλθομεν [a] ἔξω
τῆς [b] πύλης παρὰ ποταμόν, οὗ [c] ἐνομίζετο [d] προσευχὴ εἶναι,

ABCDE HLPℵa b c d f g h k l m o p 13

x ch. xii. 19 reff. y ch. x. 48 reff. z Luke iv. 16. ch. xiii. 14 only. Exod. xx. 8. see ch. xx. 7 reff. Luke xiv. 5 al. a Matt. xxi. 17. Heb. xiii. 13. b Luke vii. 12. Heb. xiii. 12. Ruth iv. 1. c = here only †. 2 Macc. xiv. 4. d ver. 16 only ‡. Jos. Antt. xiv. 10. 23 (see note).

ημην D[1][-gr](txt D[8]). for ταυτη, αυτη D-corr HLP rel Chr_1 Thl: txt ABCD[1]Eℵ a k p 13. 36 Syr.—τη bef αυτη b o.

13. for τε, δε D a c o 13 vulg E-lat syr coptt Thl. rec for πυλης, πολεως (*perhaps a margl expl of της πυλης: perhaps an error*), with EHLP rel 36 syr [copt-ms arm] æth-rom Chr: txt ABCDℵ a p 13. 40 vulg coptt. ins του bef ποταμ. D l 142 Thl-sif. ενομιζομεν ABC 13. 40 copt æth-rom (-αμεν C): ενομιζεν ℵ: εδοκει D Epiph (*alterations from misunderstanding: see note*): *putabant* arm: *videbatur* vulg: txt A[1](appy) EHLP rel 36 Chr Thl. προσευχην A[2]Cℵ p 13. 40 copt æth: ευχη

subsisted; this however is not necessary: μερίς might be merely a geographical subdivision. Wordsworth finds his solution of the difficulty in "the Hellenistic sense of the word μερίς, viz. a *frontier* or strip of *border land*, that by which it (?) is divided from some other adjacent territory: see Ezek. xlv. 7." But this supposed sense may be questioned. Certainly in the place cited μερίς has no such meaning. It there represents חֵלֶק, which is merely a *part* or *portion*. **κολωνία**] Philippi was made a *colonia* by Augustus, as a memorial of his victory over Brutus and Cassius, and as a frontier garrison against Thrace. Its full name on the coins of the city was Colonia Augusta Julia Philippensis. A Roman *colony* was in fact a portion of Rome itself transplanted to the provinces (Aulus Gellius, xvi. 13, calls them 'ex civitate quasi propagatæ—populi Romani quasi effigies parvæ simulacraque'). The colonists consisted of veteran soldiers and freedmen, who went forth, and determined and marked out their situation, with all religious and military ceremonies. The inhabitants of the coloniæ were *Roman citizens*, and were still *enrolled in one or other of the tribes*, and possessed the privilege of voting at Rome. In them the Roman law was strictly observed, and the Latin language was used on their coins and inscriptions. They were governed by their own senate and magistrates (Duumviri, as the consuls at Rome: see on στρατηγοί below, ver. 20), and not by the governor of the province. The land on which they stood was tributary, as being provincial, unless liberated from tribute by the special favour of the *jus Italicum*, or Quiritarian ownership of the soil. This Philippi possessed, in common with many other coloniæ and favoured provincial towns. The population of such places came in process of time to be of a mixed character: but only the descendants of the original colonists by Roman wives, or women of a people possessing the civitas, were Roman citizens. Hence new supplies of colonists were often necessary. See article 'Colonia' in Smith's Dict. of Antt., and C. and H. i. pp. 341, f. **ἐν ταύτῃ τῇ πόλει**] **In this city**,—as distinguished from the suburban place of prayer to which they afterwards, on the Sabbath, ἐξῆλθον ἔξω τῆς πύλης. Perhaps ταύτῃ may have been changed to αὐτῇ, to make the contrast stronger. ἐν αὐτῇ τῇ πόλει, as distinguished from ἔξω τῆς πύλης, would be too strong an expression for the calm simplicity of St. Luke's narrative style. **13. ποταμόν**] **a (or, the) river**; viz. the small stream Gangites, or Gangas: Leake, p. 217, cited by C. and H. i. 341; not, as Meyer and De Wette, the Strymon, the nearest point of which was many miles distant. The name Krenides, formerly borne by the city, was derived from the fountains of this stream. From many sources we learn, that it was the practice of the Jews to hold their assemblies for prayer *near water*, whether of the sea, or of rivers: probably on account of the frequent washings customary among them. Thus a decree of the Halicarnasseans in Joseph. Antt. xiv. 10. 23, allows the Jews τὰς προσευχὰς ποιεῖσθαι πρὸς τῇ θαλάσσῃ κατὰ τὸ πάτριον ἔθος. Thus Juvenal, speaking of the 'madida Capena' at Rome, adds, 'Nunc sacri fontis nemus, et delubra locantur Judæis,' iii. 13. And Tertullian, de Jejuniis, ch. 16, vol. ii. p. 976, 'Judaicum certe jejunium ubique celebratur, quum omissis templis per omne litus quocumque in aperto aliquando jam precem ad cœlum mittunt.' And ad Nationes, i. 13, vol. i. p. 579, he speaks of the 'orationes litorales' of the Jews. See also Philo in Flacc. § 14, vol. ii. p. 535. **οὗ ἐνομ. προσ. εἶναι**] **Where a meeting for prayer was accustomed to be**: i. e. '*where prayer was wont to be made*,' as E. V. That this is the meaning here, is plain from the use of **ἐνομίζετο εἶναι**, which *

καὶ [e] καθίσαντες ἐλαλοῦμεν ταῖς [f] συνελθούσαις γυναιξίν.
14 καί τις γυνὴ ὀνόματι Λυδία, [g] πορφυρόπωλις πόλεως
Θυατείρων, [hi] σεβομένη τὸν [i] θεόν, ἤκουεν, ἧς ὁ κύριος
[k] διήνοιξεν τὴν καρδίαν [l] προσέχειν τοῖς λαλουμένοις ὑπὸ
τοῦ Παύλου. 15 ὡς δὲ ἐβαπτίσθη, καὶ ὁ [m] οἶκος αὐτῆς,
[n] παρεκάλεσεν [n] λέγουσα Εἰ [o] κεκρίκατέ με [p] πιστὴν τῷ
[p] κυρίῳ εἶναι, εἰςελθόντες εἰς τὸν οἶκόν μου * [q] μείνατε·

e abs., Matt. v. 1. xiii. 48. ch. xiii. 14. 1 Cor. x. 7. Isa. xxx. 8.
f ch. i. 6 reff.
g here only +.
h ch. xiii. 43 reff.
i ch. xviii. 7, 13 only. Job i. 9 A Ald.
k = Luke xxiv. 45. (ch. vii. 56 reff.) 2 Macc. i. 4.
l = ch. viii. 6 reff.
m = ch. x. 2 reff.
n Matt. viii. 5. xviii. 29. Mark v. 12 al.
o = ch. xiii. 46 reff.
p here only. see 1 Cor. iv. 17.
q = ch. xxi. 7, 8 reff.

m 99 : txt A[1](appy) BEHLP rel 36. συνεληλυθυιαις D. aft συνελθ. add ημιν CE ℵ[1](ℵ[3] disapproving) æth.
14. ins της bef πολεως D. [for θεον, κυριον D[1](and lat, but -gr corrd eadem manu).] ins ητις bef ηκ. E. ηκουσεν D[1]-gr L a c k 13 vulg Chr Thl-fin. om του BD.
15. ins αυτη bef κ. ο οικ. Eℵ[3] d h 36-8. 93-7. 106-marg 113-77-80 demid fuld [syrr] sah arm Chr_1. ins πας bef ο οικ. D a 43. 69 æth. for κυριω, θεω D-gr æth * μένετε (*corrn to more usual?*) ABDEℵ p 13 : μεινατε CHLP rel 36 Chr [Bas_1].

could certainly not be said if the προσευχή were in this case a *building dedicated to prayer*. Were there no such qualification, we should understand the word of a προσευκτήριον or *synagogue*, as frequently used: τινὰς δὲ οἴκους ἑαυτοῖς κατασκευάσαντες ἢ τόπους πλατεῖς φόρων δίκην, **προσευχὰς** ταύτας ἐκάλουν· καὶ ἦσαν μὲν τὸ παλαιὸν προσευχῶν τόποι ἔν τε τοῖς Ἰουδαίοις ἔξω πόλεως, καὶ ἐν τοῖς Σαμαρείταις. Epiphanius, Hær. 80, § 1, p. 1067: and again, soon after, ἀλλὰ καὶ προσευχῆς τόπος ἐν Σικίμοις, ἐν τῇ νυνὶ καλουμένῃ Νεαπόλει, ἔξω τῆς πόλεως, ἐν τῇ πεδιάδι, ὡς ἀπὸ σημείων δύο, **θεατροειδής, οὕτως ἐν ἀέρι κ. αἰθρίῳ τόπῳ ἐστὶ κατασκευασθείς**, ὑπὸ τῶν Σαμαρειτῶν πάντα τὰ τῶν Ἰουδαίων μιμουμένων. Josephus, Vita p. 54, says, συνάγονται πάντες εἰς τὴν προσευχήν, μέγιστον οἴκημα πολὺν ὄχλον ἐπιδέξασθαι δυνάμενον. The προσευχή here was probably one of the open places spoken of in the above extracts from Epiph. The close of the verse also agrees best with an open place of resort. There seem to have been few, if any, *Jews* in Philippi: this assembly consisting merely of women attached to the Jewish faith. We hear of no opposition arising from Jews. There appears (ch. xvii. 1) to have been no synagogue.

14. πορφυρόπωλις] The guild of dyers (οἱ βαφεῖς) at Thyatira have left inscriptions, still existing, shewing the accuracy of our narrative. The celebrity of the purple dyeing of the neighbourhood is as old as Homer: ὡς δ' ὅτε τίς τ' ἐλέφαντα γυνὴ φοίνικι μιήνῃ Μῃονὶς ἠὲ Κάειρα, παρήϊον ἔμμεναι ἵππων, Il. δ. 141. So also Claudian, de Raptu Proserp. i. 270: 'non sic decus ardet eburnum *Lydia* Sidonio quod *fœmina* tinxerit ostro' (Lewin, i. 242). Thyatira was a city of the province of Asia. Thus, although forbidden to preach the word in *Asia*, their first convert at Philippi is an *Asiatic*. Lydia is a *proper name*, not 'ita dicta a solo natali,' as Grot.: though its origin may have been that. It was a common female name. See Hor. Od. i. 8; iii. 9. **σεβ. τ. θ.**] A proselyte; see reff. N. T. **ἤκουεν, was listening**,—when διήνοιξεν, the act of God, took place. **διήνοιξεν**] 'cor clausum per se: sed Dei est id aperire.' Bengel. **τ. λαλουμένοις**] It appears rather to have been a *conversation* (ἐλαλοῦμεν, *we* spoke—and not τὸν λόγον) than a set discourse: **the things which Paul was saying.** **15. ἐβαπτ., κ. ὁ οἶκος αὐτ.**] It *may be* (as Meyer maintains) that no inference for infant-baptism is hence deducible. The practice, however, does not rest on *inference*, but on the *continuity and identity of the covenant of grace to Jew and Christian*, the *sign only* of admission being altered. The Apostles, *as Jews*, would have proposed to administer baptism to the children, and Jewish or proselyte converts would, *as matter of course*, have acceded to the proposal; and that the practice thus by universal consent, tacitly (because at first unquestioned) pervaded the universal church, can hardly with any reason be doubted. See note on 1 Cor. vii. 14.

εἰ κεκρίκατε] **If ye have judged me**; modestly alluding to the decision respecting her faithfulness implied by their baptizing her, and assuming that such a judgment *had been passed*. Similarly εἰ ἡμεῖς ἀνακρινόμεθα, ch. iv. 9. **16.**] This happened on other occasions; not on the

καὶ [r] παρεβιάσατο ἡμᾶς. 16 ἐγένετο δὲ πορευομενων [s] ἡμῶν A ¹ C D E
εἰς τὴν [t] προσευχὴν [u] παιδίσκην τινὰ [v] ἔχουσαν πνεῦμα H L P ℵ a b c d f g
[w] πύθωνα [x] ὑπαντῆσαι [s] ἡμῖν, ἥτις [yz] ἐργασίαν πολλὴν h k l m o p 13
[ya] παρεῖχεν τοῖς [b] κυρίοις αὐτῆς [c] μαντευομένη. 17 αὕτη
[d] κατακολουθήσασα τῷ Παύλῳ καὶ ἡμῖν, [e] ἔκραζεν [e] λέγουσα
Οὗτοι οἱ ἄνθρωποι [f] δοῦλοι τοῦ [g] θεοῦ τοῦ [g] ὑψίστου εἰσίν,
οἵτινες [h] καταγγέλλουσιν ἡμῖν [i] ὁδὸν [i] σωτηρίας. 18 τοῦτο
δὲ ἐποίει [k] ἐπὶ πολλὰς ἡμέρας. [l] διαπονηθεὶς δὲ ὁ Παῦλος

r Luke xxiv. 29 only. Gen. xix. 9. 1 Kings xxviii. 23.
s constr., ch. xxi. 17 reff.
t ver. 13.
u ch. xii. 13 al. Gen. xx. 17.
v = John vii. 20. viii. 48, &c. ch. xix. 13.
w here only †.
x Luke viii. 27 ‖ Mt. (Mk. v. r.) xiv. 31. John iv. 51. xi. 20, 30. xii. 18 only †. Tobit vii. 1 (not ℵ).
y ch. xix. 24.
z = here bis. ch. xix. 24 (25. Luke xii. 58. Eph. iv. 19) only. L.P. (Gen. xxix. 27.) Xen. Mem. iii. 10. 1.
a = ch. xvii. 31. xxviii. 2 al. Ps. xxix. 7.
b = Matt. x. 24. Luke xvi. 8. Judg. xix. 11.
c here only. Deut. xviii. 10.
d Luke xxiii. 55 only. Jer. xvii. 16. 1 Macc. vi. 23 only.
e ch. xiv. 14 reff.
f ch. iv. 29. Tit. i. 1. Rev. vii. 3. Dan. iii. 26 Theod. 4 Kings x. 23.
g Mark v. 7 ‖ L. Heb. vii. 1. Gen. xiv. 18. see ch. vii. 48.
h ch. xiii. 5 reff.
i here only. see Matt. xxi. 32. Luke xx. 21. ch. ii. 28 al.
k ch. xiii. 31 reff.
l ch. iv. 2 (reff.) only.

υμας ℵ[1].

16. rec om *την*, with DHLP rel Chr_1 : ins ABCEℵ p 13. 40 $Orig_1$ Thl-fin. οχουσαν ℵ[1]. rec **πυθωνος** (*see note*), with D-corr[1] EHL P(*ποιθ.*) 13. 36 rel tol syr-mg-gr Chr : txt ABC[1]D[1]ℵ p vulg Orig. rec **απαντησαι**, with ADHLP rel Chr : txt BCEℵ p 13. 36 $Orig_1$. **υμιν** ℵ[1]. **παρειχετο** C. for *αυτης*, *δια τουτου* D[1][-gr(but marked for erasure); *per hoc* D-lat].

17. *κατακολουθουσα* B D-gr ℵ 36. 180. om *τω* B Orig. **εκραζον** and pref. *και* D[1]-gr(txt D[8]). om *ανθρωποι* D[1](and lat[1] : ins D[5]) $Lucif_1$. for *καταγγ.*, *ευαγγελιζοντε* D(-*τες* D[1]). elz **υμιν** (*alteration, as better suiting the person speaking*), with BD E-gr ℵ a b o 36 vulg syrr æth-pl [arm] $Thdrt_3$: txt AC[2]HLP p(sic) 13 rel E-lat coptt æth-rom Orig Chr Thdrt[-ed-rom_1] Eustath $Lucif_1$. [C[1] uncert.]

18. om 1st *δε* H sah. om *ο* ABℵ : ins CDEHLP rel 36 Chr_1.—*επιστρ. δε ο π. τω*

same day, as Heinrichs and Kuinoel fancy. In that case (besides other objections), if they had gone back from the house of Lydia to the place of prayer, the word would certainly have been *ἐξελθόντων*, and not *πορευομένων*. In ver. 15 is implied their taking up their abode with Lydia:—in this verse that they *habitually resorted* to this place of prayer to teach, and that what follows happened on such occasions.

It may be remarked that the E. V. of *πορευομένων εἰς* (*τὴν*) *προσευχήν*, '*as we went to prayer,*' has given rise to a curious abuse of the expression '*going to prayer,*' in the sense of '*beginning to pray,*' among the lower classes in England. **ἔχουσαν πνεῦμα πύθωνα**] On the whole subject of dæmoniacal possession, see note on Matt. viii. 32. This was a case in which the presence of the spirit was a *patent fact*, recognized by the heathen possessors and consulters of this female slave, and by them turned to account; and recognized also by the Christian teachers, as an instance of one of those works of the devil which their Lord came, and commissioned them, to destroy. All attempt to explain away such a narrative as this by the subterfuges of rationalism (as e. g. in Meyer, and even Lewin, i. 243, and apparently Hackett, p. 222), is more than ever futile. The fact of the *spirit leaving* the girl, and the masters *finding the hope of their gains gone*, is *fatal:* and we may see, notwithstanding all his attempts to account for it psychologically, that Meyer feels it to be so. **πύθωνα**] Plut. de Defectu Oracul. p. 414, says *ὥσπερ τοὺς ἐγγαστριμύθους Εὐρυκλέας* (from a prophet, Eurycles), *πάλαι, νυνὶ Πύθωνας προσαγορευομένους.* It is difficult to decide internally between the probabilities of *πύθωνα* and *πύθωνος*: I have retained the ancient reading, both from its external authority, and because I find so many Commentators explaining *πύθων* to be a *name of Apollo*, or *the serpent Python*, that the alteration into the gen. may thus be easily accounted for. Bp. Wordsworth has an interesting note on the probable reason for this new term appearing in the narrative, now that St. Paul is brought directly into contact with Greek and Roman divination.

17.] ἔκραζεν, used to cry out: several occasions are referred to. The recognition of Paul and his company here by the spirit is strictly analogous to that of our Lord by the dæmons, Matt. viii. 29; Luke iv. 34: and the same account to be given of both: viz. that the *evil spirit knew and confessed* the power of God and His Christ, whether in His own Person or that of His servants. **18. διαπονηθείς**] Not *mere* annoyance is expressed by this word, but rather holy indignation and sorrow at what he saw and heard; the Christian soldier

καὶ [m] ἐπιστρέψας τῷ πνεύματι εἶπεν [n] Παραγγέλλω σοι [o] ἐν
ὀνόματι Ἰησοῦ χριστοῦ [p] ἐξελθεῖν ἀπ᾽ αὐτῆς. καὶ [p] ἐξῆλθεν
[q] αὐτῇ τῇ [q] ὥρᾳ. 19 ἰδόντες δὲ οἱ [b] κύριοι αὐτῆς ὅτι ἐξῆλθεν ἡ [r] ἐλπὶς τῆς [z] ἐργασίας αὐτῶν, [s] ἐπιλαβόμενοι τὸν
Παῦλον καὶ Σίλαν [t] εἵλκυσαν εἰς τὴν [u] ἀγορὰν ἐπὶ τοὺς
ἄρχοντας, 20 καὶ [v] προσαγαγόντες αὐτοὺς τοῖς [w] στρατηγοῖς
εἶπαν Οὗτοι οἱ ἄνθρωποι [x] ἐκταράσσουσιν ἡμῶν τὴν πόλιν
Ἰουδαῖοι [y] ὑπάρχοντες, 21 καὶ [z] καταγγέλλουσιν [a] ἔθη ἃ

m = ch. ix. 40. constr., see note.
n inf. aor., Mark viii. 6. ch. x. 42. 1 Cor. vii. 10. 1 Tim. vi. 13. Josh. vi. 6.
o ch. iv. 7 reff.
p ch. viii. 7 reff.
q Luke ii. 38. xxiv. 33. ch. xxii. 13 only. Dan. iii. 6 (15. iv. 30 [33] Theod.) only. w. ἐν, Luke vii. 21. x. 21. xii. 12. xiii. 31. xx. 19 only. L. Dan. v. 5 only.
r constr., Gal. v. 5. Eph. i. 18. iv. 4. Col. i. 23.
s acc., ch. ix. 27 reff.
t = here (John vi. 44. xii. 32. xviii. 10. xxi. 6, 11) only. Jer. xlv. (xxxviii.) 13. see ch. xxi. 30.
u ch. xvii. 17. Ezek. xxvii. 12.
v Matt. xviii. 24. Luke ix. 41. ch. xxvii. 27. 1 Pet. iii. 18 only. Gen. xlviii. 9.
w = here, &c. 5 times only. (ch. iv. 1 reff.)
x here only. Ps. lxxxvii. 16.
y ch. ii. 30 reff.
z ch. xiii. 5 reff.
a ch. vi. 14 reff.

πν. και διαπον. D. *παραγγελω* C a [syr-mg-gr] : *παραγγέλω* p. rec ins *τω* bef *ον.*, with DHLP 13 rel Œc Thl : om ABCEא c h p Eustath$_1$ [Ps-]Ath Chr$_1$ [Eucher$_1$]. *ινα εξελθης* D : *εξελθε* 13. for *εξηλθ. αυτ. τ. ω.*, *ευθεως εξηλθ.* D æth-rom.

19. *και ιδοντ.* B Syr æth : om *δε* A^1 D-lat.—*ως δε ειδαν οι κυρ. της πεδισκης οτι απεστερησθαι της εργ. αυτ. ης ειχαν δι αυτης* D. rec ins *τον* bef *σιλ.* (*corrn for uniformity*), with ABEHLPא p 13. 36 rel Eustath Chr : om CD l. *ηλκυσαν* C : *εσυραν* E.

20. *προσαγαγοντας* D^1[-gr](txt D-corr^1). (*ειπαν*, so ABE H[e sil] א p.)

21. [*καταγγελουσιν* H b^1 m o p.] *τα εθνη* D^1(and lat^1) 15^1 : *ηθη* L : *sectam* tol

was goaded to the attack, but the mere satisfaction of anger was not the object, any more than the result, of the stroke. It is doubtful here, in mere grammar, whether the dat. **τῷ πνεύματι** is to be constructed with *ἐπιστρέψας* or with *εἶπεν*. But considering 1) that the *spirit* could hardly be the object of a bodily movement on the part of the Apostle, except as represented by the possessed damsel, and 2) that *ἐπιστρέφω* is never elsewhere found with a dative, but always with a preposition, *εἰς* or *πρός* or *ἐπί*, it is much the best to take *τῷ πνεύματι* with *εἶπεν*, and believe it to be thrown forward before its verb for the sake of emphasis.

19.] Her masters (a partnership of persons, not plur. for sing. They may have been the hæredes of some one to whom she had belonged) perceived that the hope of their gain had gone out (*with the dæmon*). **ἐπιλ. . . . εἵλκ.** gives the idea of force having been used. So we have 'obtorto collo ad prætorem trahor,' Plaut. Pœn. iii. 5. 45. Paul and Silas only are apprehended as having been the principal persons in the company. When De Wette says that, if Luke here were the narrator, he must say something of Timotheus, as he mentions him ch. xvii. 14, xviii. 5,—and yet holds (on ver. 10) that Timotheus himself is the narrator, he forgets that the same reasoning will apply to *him also*, if it applies at all, which I much doubt. When two persons of a company are described as being apprehended, we do not need an express assertion to assure us that the rest were not. **ἐπὶ τ. ἄρχοντας** said *generally :* they dragged them to the forum to the authorities,—afterwards specified as *στρατηγοί*.

20. **στρατηγοῖς**] The Duumviri of the colony, of whom at Capua Cicero says, 'cum in cæteris coloniis *Duumviri* appellentur, hi se Prætores (*στρατηγούς*) appellari volebant.' De Leg. Agr. c. 34. 'Messinenses,' says Wetstein, 'etiam nunc (cir. 1750) Prætorem sive Præfectum urbis *Stradigo* appellant.' The name, as a rendering of Prætor, had come from the Greek title of similar magistrates : so Aristotle, Politic. vii. 3, *ἐν ταῖς μικραῖς πόλεσι μία περὶ πάντων (ἀρχή)· καλοῦσι δὲ στρατηγοὺς καὶ πολεμάρχους.* **Ἰουδ. ὑπάρχοντες . . . . Ῥωμ. οὖσιν**] The distinction between *ὑπάρχων* and *ὤν* seems to be, that the former is used of something which the speaker or narrator wishes to put forward into notice, either as unknown to his reader or hearer, or in some way to be marked by him for praise or blame: whereas the latter refers to facts known and recognized, and taken for granted by both. Thus, we may notice that, when the fact of *Paul and Silas* being Romans is announced to the jailor, it is not *ἀνθ. Ῥωμαίους* **ὄντας**, but **ὑπάρχοντας** ; whereas here, both parties, the speakers and the addressed, being indisputably Romans, we have *Ῥωμαίοις* **οὖσιν**. The account of this may be, that *ὑπάρχω* is predicated of something of which the speaker informs the hearer, some *prior* knowledge which he possessed and now imparts,—*εἰμί* being

b w. pres., ch. (xxi. 27) xxii. 25. Matt. xiv. 4 al.
c ch. xv. 4. xxii. 18. Mark iv. 20. 1 Tim. v. 19. Heb. xii. 6 (from Prov. iii. 12) only. Exod. xxiii. 1.
d here only †. Num. xvi. 3 compl.
e here only †. 2 Macc. iv. 38 only.
f 2 Cor. xi. 25 only ‡. Judg. vi. 11.
g Luke x. 30. Rev. xxii. 18.

οὐκ [b] ἔξεστιν ἡμῖν [c] παραδέχεσθαι οὐδὲ ποιεῖν Ῥωμαίοις ABCDE
οὖσιν. 22 καὶ [d] συνεπέστη ὁ ὄχλος κατ' αὐτῶν, καὶ οἱ HLPℵa bcdfg
[w] στρατηγοὶ [e] περιρήξαντες αὐτῶν τὰ ἱμάτια ἐκέλευον hklm op13
[f] ῥαβδίζειν, 23 πολλάς τε [g] ἐπιθέντες αὐτοῖς [g] πληγὰς
[h] ἔβαλον εἰς [h] φυλακήν, [i] παραγγείλαντες τῷ [k] δεσμοφύλακι
[l] ἀσφαλῶς [m] τηρεῖν αὐτούς· 24 ὃς [n] παραγγελίαν τοιαύτην
λαβὼν [h] ἔβαλεν αὐτοὺς εἰς τὴν [o] ἐσωτέραν [h] φυλακὴν καὶ
τοὺς πόδας [p] ἠσφαλίσατο αὐτῶν εἰς τὸ [q] ξύλον. 25 [r] κατὰ δὲ
τὸ [s] μεσονύκτιον Παῦλος καὶ Σίλας [t] προσευχόμενοι [u] ὕμνουν
τὸν θεόν· [v] ἐπηκροῶντο δὲ αὐτῶν οἱ [w] δέσμιοι. 26 [x] ἄφνω

h Matt. v. 25. xviii. 30. Luke xii. 58. xxiii. 19, 25. Rev. ii. 10. (see Jer. xliv. [xxxvii.] 21.) i w. inf. pres., ch. i. 4 reff. k here, &c. 3ce only †. (see Gen. xxxix. 21, &c.) l = Mark xiv. 44 (ch. ii. 36) only ‡. (Gen. xxxiv. 25 only.) Tobit vi. 4 (5) [not ℵ]. m = ch. xii. 5, 6 reff. n ch. v. 28 reff. † o Heb. vi. 19 only. Levit. xvi. 2 (15). p Matt. xxvii. 64, 65, 66 only. Isa. xli. 10. Wisd. xiii. 15. q = here only. Job xxxiii. 11 Bℵ F &c. (not A). r = ch. xxvii. 27. Heb. iii. 8, from Ps. xciv. 8. s Mark xiii. 35. Luke xi. 5. ch. xx. 7 only. Ps. cxviii. 62. t absol., ch. x. 9 reff. u w. acc., Heb. ii. 12 only. Isa. xii. 4. Dan. iii. 23 Theod. absol., Matt. xxvi. 30 ‖ Mk. only. 1 Macc. xiii. 47. v here only †. (-ρόασις, 1 Kings xv. 22.) w Acts, here bis, ch. xxviii. 16 v. r., 17 al3. Matt. xxvii. 15, 16 ‖ Mk. Paul, Eph. iii. 1 al4. Heb. x. 34. xiii. 3 only. Lam. iii. 34. x ch. ii. 2. xxviii. 6 only. Josh. x. 9.

$Lucif_1$. α ουκ εξ. ημας παραδεξασθαι ουτε ποι. ρω. υπαρχουσιν D.

22. και πολυς οχλ. συνεπεστησαν κατ αυτ. κραζοντες τοτε (και D^8) οι D. (περιρηξ., so AB^1CDEHLℵ p 13.)

23. for τε, δε B p 40 E-lat copt. for παραγγειλαντες, παραγγιλας τε $ℵ^1$. τηρεισθαι D.

24. for ος, ο δε D[-gr, *qui* D-lat]. rec (for λαβων) ειληφως, with HLP rel Chr: txt ABCDEℵ a m p 13. 36. 40. for εβαλεν, ελαβεν A. rec αυτων bef ησφ. (*corrn of order*), with C^2DEHLP rel 36 Chr_1 : txt ABC^1ℵ p 13. ησφαλισαντο D^1. εν τω ξυλω D a^1.

25. om το ℵ.—κατα δε μεσον της νυκτος D^1(txt D^3). ins ο bef παυλος D b o. ins ο bef σιλας C. ins και bef οι δεσμ. C Orig. δεσμοι D^1(txt D^3).

predicated of the bare matter of fact. See ch. xvii. 27, 29; xxi. 20 (for both); xxii. 3; Gal. ii. 14 al., for ὑπάρχων: and for ὤν, John iii. 4; iv. 9 bis; Rom. v. 10 al. 'Versute composita fuit hæc criminatio ad gravandos Christi servos: nam ab una parte obtendunt Romanum nomen, quo nihil erat magis favorabile; rursum ex nomine Judaico, quod tunc infame erat (especially if the decree of Claudius, expelling them from Rome, ch. xviii. 2, had at this time been enacted) conflant illis invidiam: nam, quantum ad religionem, plus habebant Romani affinitatis cum aliis quibuslibet, quam cum gente Judaica.' Calvin.

21. ἔθη . . .] "Dio Cassius tells us that Mæcenas gave the following advice to Augustus:—*τὸ μὲν θεῖον πάντη πάντως αὐτός τε σέβου κατὰ τὰ πάτρια, καὶ τοὺς ἄλλους τιμᾷν ἀνάγκαζε· τοὺς δὲ ξενίζοντάς τι περὶ αὐτὸ καὶ μίσει καὶ κόλαζε·* and the reason is alleged, viz. that such innovations lead to secret associations, conspiracies, and cabals, *ἅπερ ἥκιστα μοναρχίᾳ συμφέρει.*" (C. and H. i. p. 356.) So Julius Paulus, Sentent. v. 21. 2, cited by Wetst., 'Qui novas et usu vel ratione incognitas religiones inducunt, ex quibus animi hominum moveantur, honestiores deportantur, humiliores capite premuntur.'

22. The multitude probably cried out tumultuously, as on other occasions (see Luke xxiii. 18; ch. xix. 28, 34; xxi. 30; xxii. 22, 23),—and the duumviri, without giving them a trial (*ἀκατακρίτους*, ver. 37), rent off their clothes, scil. by the lictors (*τοῖς ῥαβδούχοις ἐκέλευσαν τὴν ἐσθῆτά τε περικαταῤῥῆξαι καὶ ταῖς ῥάβδοις τὸ σῶμα ξαίνειν*, Dion. Hal. ix. 39). The form was, 'Summove, lictor, despolia, verbera,' Seneca (C. and H. i. 357). See also Livy, ii. 8; Valer. Max. ii. 28, in Wetst. Erasmus fancied that the duumviri rent *their own* clothes from indignation: but, to say nothing of the improbability of such a proceeding on the part of a Roman magistrate, a man could not very well **περιῤῥῆξαι** his own garments

24. τὸ ξύλον] Also called *κᾶλον, ποδοκάκη*, and *ποδοστράβη*, and in Latin, *nervus*: so 'noctu nervo vinctus custodibitur,' Plaut. Cap. iii. 5. 71. Eusebius (v. 1, vol. ii. p. 16, ed. Heinichen) mentions, speaking of the martyrs in Gaul, *τὰς ἐν τῷ ξύλῳ διατάσεις τῶν ποδῶν ἐπὶ πέμπτον διατεινομένων τρύπημα.*

25. προσευχ. ὕμν.] Not as E. V., '*prayed and sang praises*,'—but, praying, sang praises, or in their prayers, were singing praises. The distinction of modern times

δὲ [y] σεισμος εγενετο μέγας, ὥςτε [za] σαλευθῆναι τὰ [ab] θεμέλια
τοῦ [c] δεσμωτηρίου· ἠνεῴχθησαν δὲ [d] παραχρῆμα αἱ θύραι
πᾶσαι, καὶ πάντων τὰ [e] δεσμὰ [f] ἀνέθη. 27 [g] ἔξυπνος δὲ
[h] γενόμενος ὁ [i] δεσμοφύλαξ καὶ ἰδὼν ἀνεῳγμένας τὰς
θύρας τῆς φυλακῆς, [kl] σπασάμενος τὴν [km] μάχαιραν ἤμελλεν
ἑαυτὸν [n] ἀναιρεῖν, νομίζων [o] ἐκπεφευγέναι τοὺς [w] δεσμίους.
28 [p] ἐφώνησεν δὲ φωνῇ μεγάλῃ ὁ Παῦλος λέγων Μηδὲν
πράξῃς σεαυτῷ [q] κακόν· ἅπαντες γάρ ἐσμεν [r] ἐνθάδε.
29 [s] αἰτήσας δὲ [t] φῶτα [u] εἰςεπήδησεν, καὶ [v] ἔντρομος γενόμενος [w] προςέπεσεν τῷ Παύλῳ καὶ Σίλᾳ, 30 καὶ [x] προαγαγὼν αὐτοὺς ἔξω ἔφη Κύριοι, τί με δεῖ ποιεῖν ἵνα σωθῶ;

y = Matt. viii. 24. xxiv. 7. Rev. vi. 12 al. Ezek. xxxviii. 19.
z ch. iv. 31 reff.
a Ps. lxxxi. 5.
b neut. plur., here only. masc., Heb. xi. 10. Rev. xxi. 14, 19.
c Matt. xi. 2. ch. v. 21. 23 only. Gen. xxxix. 22 bis. xl. 3, 5 only.
d ch. iii. 7 reff.
e neut. pl., Luke viii. 29. ch. xx. 23 only †. δεσμοι, (Paul) Phil. i. 13. Ezek. iii. 25.
f = ch. xxvii. 40 (Eph. vi. 9. Heb. xiii. 5, from Deut. xxxi. 6) only ‡. (Ezek. i. 25 [26] A Ald. compl.)
g here only †. Esdr. iii. 3 only.
h ch. i. 18 al.
i ver. 23.
k Mark xiv. 47. Num. xxii. 31.
l as above (k) only. Josh. v. 13.
m ch. xii. 2 reff.
n = ch. v. 33 reff.
o absol., Heb. ii. 3. xii. 25 only. Isa. lxvi. 7. (Rom. ii. 3 reff. Judg. vi. 11.)
p Luke xxiii. 46. Rev. xiv. 18.
q = and constr., w. ποιέω, ch. ix. 13.
r Luke xxiv. 41. John iv. 15, 16. ch. x. 18. xvii. 6. xxv. 17 24 only †.
s Matt. vii. 10. Luke i. 63. ch. xii. 20. xiii. 21. 3 Kings xix. 4.
t = here only. 1 Macc. xii. 29. νυκτὸς ἐπιγενομενης φῶς ἔχων ὥςπερ νομίζεται . . . , Xen. Hellen. v. 1. 8.
u here only. Amos v. 19 only. Sus 26 Theod.
v = ch. vii. 32 reff.
w = Mark iii. 11. vii. 25. Luke v. 8. viii. 28, 47 ∥ Mk. (Matt. vii. 25) only. Ps. xciv. 6.
x ch. xii. 6 reff.

26. rec ανεωχθ., with HLP rel Chr_1 : ηνοιχθ. AEℵ p 13 $Orig_1$: txt BCD m Thl-fin. rec for 2nd δε, τε (*perhaps to avoid the recurrence of* δε,—*perhaps because the copulative is more natural*), with CHLP rel [vulg Syr æth arm] Chr : txt ABDEℵ a c[1] h k m p 13 syr coptt Thl-fin. om παραχρημα B $Lucif_1$. ανελυθη D[1] [*relaxata sunt* D-lat] ℵ[1].

27. for εξ. δε, και εξ. D Syr æth. δεσμοφυλας(sic) ℵ. τ. θυρ. bef ανεωγ. C vulg(not am demid fuld [tol]). ins και bef σπασ. D-gr[1]. rec om την, with AEHLPℵ p[2] 13. 36 rel Chr_2 : ins BCD p[1]. (ημελλ., so ABCELPℵ p.) ανελειν C[1]. εκπεφυγεναι A.

28. μεγ. bef φωνη AB D-lat am [fuld tol] coptt.—παυλος bef μεγ. φων. B [vulg Syr (copt) Lucif].—om ο BC[1]ℵ 13 Thl-sif. ποιησης E. ins τι bef κακον D-gr.

29. φωτα δε ετησας D. for γεν., υπαρχων C[1] D-gr c k[2] 40. aft προσεπ. ins προς τους ποδας D[1][and lat] vulg (syr-w-ob) [copt] sah $Lucif_1$. rec ins τω bef σιλα (*corrn for uniformity*), with AC[2]EHLPℵ p 13[e sil] 36 rel : om BC[1]D.

30. κ. προηγαγεν αυτ. εξω D : add τους λοιπους ασφαλισαμενος και D(om και D-corr) syr-w-ast(adding further *appropinquavit*).—προαγων ℵ[1]. for εφη, ειπεν αυτοις D coptt [Syr æth].

between prayer and praise, arising from our attention being directed to the *shape* rather than to the essence of devotion, was unknown in these days: see Col. iv. 2. 'Nihil crus sentit in nervo, quum animus in cœlo est.' Tertullian ad Martyres, c. 2, vol. i. p. 623. The imperfects shew that they *were singing*, and the prisoners (in the outer prison) *listening*, when the earthquake happened. **26. πάντων τὰ δεσμὰ ἀνέθη**] i. e. of *all the prisoners* in the prison: see below (ver. 28), ἅπαντες γάρ ἐσμεν ἐνθάδε. Doubtless there were gracious purposes in this for those prisoners, who before were listening to the praises of Paul and Silas; and the very form of the narrative, mentioning this listening, shews *subsequent communication* between some one of these and the narrator. Their chains were loosed, not by the earthquake, but by miraculous interference over and above it. It is some satisfaction to find, that neither Meyer, De Wette, nor Kuinoel have attempted to rationalize this wonderful example of the triumph of prayer. See some excellent remarks on Baur's attempt to do so, in Neander, Pfl. u. L. p. 302, note 3. **27. ἤμελ. ἑαυτ. ἀναιρ.**] The law de Custodia Reorum (Wetst.) says, 'Ad commentariensem receptarum personarum custodia observatioque pertineat, nec putet, hominem abjectum atque vilem objiciendum esse judici, si reus modo aliquo fuerit elapsus. Nam ipsum volumus hujusmodi pœnæ consumi, cui obnoxius docebitur fuisse, qui fugerit.' Dean Howson notices, by the examples of Cassius, Brutus, Titinius, and many of the proscribed, after the battle,—that Philippi is famous in the annals of suicide (p. 361). **29. φῶτα**] Not as E. V., '*a light*,' but **lights**, neut. plur.

30. προαγ. αὐτ. ἔξω] Into the outer prison: not perhaps yet *outside* the prison, which (from **ἀναγαγών**, ver. 34, when he takes

y ch. ix. 42 reff.
z ch. x. 2 reff.
a ch. xi. 19 reff.
b = John xix. 16. ch. xxi. 24. xxiii. 18.
c ch. xxiii. 23.
d ch. ix. 37 reff.
e = Heb. x. 22. Sir. xxx. (xxxiv.) 25.
f ch. iii. 7 reff.
g ch. ix. 39 reff.
h = Mark viii. 6, 7. 4 Kings vi. 22.
i = Matt. xv. 27. ch. vi. 2. Ps. lxxvii. 20.
k ch. ii. 26 reff.
l here only. Exod. i. 1 B compl. only. Jos. Antt. iv. 4. 4.
m dat., = ch. xviii. 8. John v. 24. viii. 31. Rom. iv. 3, from Gen. xv. 6. Tit. iii. 8. 1 John v. 10.
n ch. xii. 18 reff.

ABCDE HLPℵ a b c d f g h k l m o p 13

31 οἱ δὲ εἶπαν ʸ Πίστευσον ʸ ἐπὶ τὸν κύριον Ἰησοῦν, καὶ
σωθήσῃ σὺ καὶ ὁ ᶻ οἶκός σου. 32 καὶ ᵃ ἐλάλησαν αὐτῷ
τὸν ᵃ λόγον τοῦ κυρίου, σὺν πᾶσιν τοῖς ἐν τῇ οἰκίᾳ αὐτοῦ.
33 καὶ ᵇ παραλαβὼν αὐτοὺς ἐν ἐκείνῃ τῇ ᶜ ὥρᾳ τῆς ᶜ νυκτὸς
ᵈ ἔλουσεν ᵉ ἀπὸ τῶν πληγῶν, καὶ ἐβαπτίσθη αὐτὸς καὶ οἱ
αὐτοῦ πάντες ᶠ παραχρῆμα, 34 ᵍ ἀναγαγών τε αὐτοὺς εἰς
τὸν οἶκον ʰ παρέθηκεν ⁱ τράπεζαν καὶ ᵏ ἠγαλλιᾶτο ˡ παν-
οικεὶ ᵐ πεπιστευκὼς τῷ θεῷ. 35 ἡμέρας δὲ ⁿ γενομένης

31. (ειπαν, so AB C(appy) DEℵ p.) πιστευσαν ℵ[1]. for επι, εις E lect-12. rec aft ιησουν ins χριστον, with CDEHLP rel 36 [syrr sah æth arm] Thdrt₁ Chr₂: om ABℵ p 13 vulg copt Lucif₁. ins πας bef ο οικος E a g 13 æth arm.
32. om του D. for κυρ., θεου Bℵ[1]. rec (for συν) και (*alteration for simplicity, and to suit συ και ο οικ. above*), with EHL syrr [copt æth arm] Chr: txt ABCDPℵ p 13. 36. 40 vulg Lucif₁ (συμ ℵ p).
33. ελυσεν D[1](and lat: txt D[2]). αυτος bef εβ. D. ins οικειοι bef αυτου A; υιοι m lect-17: μετ Thl-fin.—ο οικος αυτου 40 vulg. (*These exx may serve to illustrate the practice of insertion to fill up any ellipsis.*) απαντες Bℵ [c].
34. και αναγ. τε D[1][-gr]: αν. δε C 13. 36 copt syr. rec aft οικ. ins αυτου, with ADEHLℵ 13 rel vss Chr: om BCP c p 36. 40 [Chr₁] Lucif₁. ins και bef παρεθηκεν D[1]. [aft παρεθ. ins αυτοις E vulg Syr coptt arm.] rec ηγαλλιασατο (*alteration to more usual historic tense*), with ABC[2] E-gr HLℵ p 13. 36 rel vulg copt [æth arm Lucif₁] Thl-fin: txt C[1](appy) DP b g h m o E-lat syrr sah Chr Thl-sif. rec πανοικι, with B[2]HLP rel: συν τω οικω αυτου D: om E: txt AB[1]Cℵ 13. for τω θεω, επι τον θεον [*in domino*] D.

them to his own house) seems to have been *underground*, or at all events on a lower level in the same building. In this same space they seem to have been joined by the jailor's family,—to have converted and baptized them, and to have been taken (to the well?) and washed from their stripes; and afterwards to have been led up (by stairs? see ref.) to his house, and hospitably entertained. The circumstantiality of the account shews that *some eye-witness* related it. His question, connected with the ὁδὸν **σωτηρίας** of the dæmoniac in ver. 17, makes it necessary to infer, as De Wette well observes, that he had previously become acquainted with the subject of their preaching. He wanted no means of escape from any danger but that which was *spiritual:* the earthquake was past, and his prisoners were all safe. Bengel admirably remarks: 'Non audierat hymnos Pauli, nam dormierat, sed tamen vel antea vel postea senserat, quis esset Paulus.' **31. ἐπὶ τ. κύριον**] Not without allusion to the **κύριοι**, by which name he had just addressed them. So Bengel: 'non agnoscunt se dominos.' Considering *who the person was* that asked the question,—a heathen in the depths of ignorance and sin,—and how indisputably therefore the answer embraces *all sinners whatever*,—there perhaps does not stand on record in the whole book a more important answer than this of Paul:—or, I may add, one *more strikingly characteristic of the Apostle himself and his teaching*. We may remark also, in the face of all attempts to establish a development of St. Paul's doctrine according to mere external circumstances,—that this reply was given before any one of his extant epistles was written. **καὶ ὁ οἶκός σου** does not mean that *his* faith would save his household,—but that the same way was open to them as to him; 'Believe, and thou shalt be saved: and the same of thy household.' **33. ἔλουσεν ἀπό**] A pregnant construction: 'washed them, so that they were purified from the blood occasioned by their stripes:' see reff. This is much more natural than to take ἀπό (as in ἀπὸ τῆς χαρᾶς (ch. xii. 14) and the like) as signifying 'on account of' (see Bernhardy, Syntax, p. 225). **34.**] ἀναγ., see reff. and note on ver. 30, **πεπιστευκώς**] Winer renders 'as one who has placed his trust in God:' but, as De W. observes, πεπιστευκώς must give the *ground* of his rejoicing (see 1 Cor. xiv. 18 (rec.), εὐχαριστῶ . . . λαλῶν, 'I give thanks . . . that I speak'). Thus the meaning will be, **rejoiced that he with all his house had been led to believe** (and thus as a necessary consequence to believe *in*) God. The expression πεπιστ. τῷ θεῷ could only be used of a converted *heathen*, not of a *Jew:* in ch. xviii. 8, of a Jew,

ἀπέστειλαν οἱ [o] στρατηγοὶ τοὺς [p] ῥαβδούχους, λέγοντες
[q] Ἀπόλυσον τοὺς ἀνθρώπους ἐκείνους. 36 ἀπήγγειλεν δὲ
ὁ [r] δεσμοφύλαξ τοὺς λόγους τούτους πρὸς τὸν Παῦλον,
ὅτι [s] ἀπέσταλκαν οἱ [o] στρατηγοὶ ἵνα [q] ἀπολυθῆτε· [t] νῦν
οὖν ἐξελθόντες πορεύεσθε ἐν [u] εἰρήνῃ. 37 ὁ δὲ Παῦλος ἔφη
πρὸς αὐτοὺς [v] Δείραντες ἡμᾶς [w] δημοσίᾳ [x] ἀκατακρίτους,
[y] ἀνθρώπους [y] Ῥωμαίους [z] ὑπάρχοντας, [a] ἔβαλαν εἰς [a] φυλακήν, καὶ νῦν [b] λάθρα ἡμᾶς [c] ἐκβάλλουσιν; [d] οὐ γὰρ
ἀλλὰ ἐλθόντες αὐτοὶ ἡμᾶς [e] ἐξαγαγέτωσαν. 38 ἀπήγγειλαν

...ειρηνη C.
ABDE HLPℵ a b c d f g h k l m o p 13

o vv. 20, 22 reff. p ver. 38 only +. q = ch. xxvi. 32 reff. r ver. 23. s constr., John iii. 17. 1 John iv. 9. t ch. x. 33 reff. u w. ἐν, 1 Cor. xvi. 11 reff. 2 Kings iii. 21. εἰς, Mark v. 34. Luke vii. 50 al. 1 Kings i. 17. μετ', ch. xv. 33 reff. v ch. v. 40 reff.
w ch. xviii. 28. xx. 20 only +. 2 Macc. vi. 10 only. (-ιος, ch. v. 18.) x ch. xxii. 25 only +.
y ch. xxii. 25. (Matt. xxvii. 32. ch. xxi. 39. Exod. ii. 11.) z ch. ii. 30 reff. a vv. 23, 24.
b Matt. i. 19. ii. 7. John xi. 28 only. Ps. c. 5. c Matt. ix. 25. ch. ix. 40. Gal. iv. 30, from Gen. xxi. 10. d here only. see note. e = ch. v. 19. vii. 36. Gen. xl. 14.

35. ημ. δε γεν. συνηλθον οι σστρατηγοι(sic) επι το αυτο εις την αγοραν και αναμνησθεντες τον σεισμον τον γεγονοτα εφοβηθησαν και απεστειλαν τους D syr-mg. λεγοντας D 68. at end ins ους εχθες παρελαβες D syr.

36. και εισελθων ο δεσμοφυλαξ απηγγ. D[, *et cum audivisset custos carceris ingressus dixit*] Syr. for δε, τε E-gr sah æth. om τουτους (*from similarity of endings*) BC D-gr a 36(sic) [arm(appy)]: ins AEHLPℵ p 13 rel vulg D-lat [(Syr) syr coptt] Chr_1. rec απεσταλκασιν (*grammatical corrn*), with DEHLP rel 36 Chr: απεστειλαν C p [Thl-fin]: txt ABℵ. (13 def.) for εν ειρ., εις ιρηνην ℵ: om D.

37. om πρ. αυτους E æth. ins αναιτειους bef δειρ. D. (βαλαν, so BDℵ.) αυτ. ημας bef ελθοντ. E: om ημ. HP.

38. rec ανηγγ., with HLP rel [Thl-sif]: txt ABDEℵ a m o p 36 Thl-fin. (13 def.)

we have ἐπίστευσεν τῷ κυρίῳ. **35.**] What had influenced the magistrates is not recorded. We can hardly suppose that the earthquake alone (as suggested by the addition in D; see digest) would have done so, as they would not have connected it with their prisoners; they may have heard what had taken place: but that, again, is hardly probable. I should rather set it down to calmer thought, repudiating the tumultuary proceeding of the evening before. **ῥαβδούχους**] **The lictors,**—'bearers of the rods,' *bacilli;* which, and *not fasces,* were carried before the colonial duumviri: see Cicero, de Leg. Agr. ubi supra, on ver. 20.

36.] Paul and Silas had returned to the prison: whither the jailor goes, accompanied by the lictors (ὁ δὲ Π. ἔφη πρ. **αὐτούς**, ver. 37), to announce the order.

37.] **δημοσίᾳ** and **λάθρα** are opposed: the *injury* had been *public:* the *reparation,* not to Paul and Silas merely, but to the Gospel of which they were the heralds, must be *public also.* **ἀνθρ. Ῥωμ. ὑπάρχ.**] By the Lex Valeria, passed A.U.C. 254, and the Lex Porcia, A.U.C. 506, Roman citizens were exempted from stripes and torture: by the former, till an appeal to the people was decided,—by the latter, absolutely. The following passages of Cicero illustrate our text: 'Porcia lex virgas ab omnium civium Romanorum corpore amovit.' Pro Rabirio, c. 3. 'Cædebatur virgis in medio foro Messanæ civis Romanus, judices: cum interea nullus gemitus, nulla vox alia istius miseri, inter dolorem crepitumque virgarum audiebatur, nisi hæc: Civis Romanus sum.' In Verrem, lib. v. 62, 63. 'Facinus est vinciri civem Romanum; scelus verberari; prope parricidium, necari.' Ibid. 66. Many others are given by Kuinoel, Biscoe, &c. On the question, *how Paul came to be born a Roman citizen,* see note on ch. xxii. 28: and on ὑπάρχ., note, ver. 20. Another irregularity had been committed by the duumviri, in scourging them *uncondemned:* 'causa cognita multi possunt absolvi: incognita quidem condemnari nemo potest.' Cic. in Verr. i. 9. 'Inauditi et indefensi tanquam innocenter perierant.' Tac. Hist. ii. 10. **ἐκβάλλ.**] **are they thrusting us out?** It does not follow, because ἐκβάλλω has no such sense in ch. ix. 40, &c., that therefore it has not here. The circumstances must determine; which here seem to require this sense: the **ἐκβάλλειν λάθρα** having a tinge of degradation in it, as if said of casting out that of which one is ashamed. **οὐ γάρ**] An elliptical answer to a question or position, the negative of which is self-evident: see Hartung, Partikellehre, ii. p. 48: Kühner, Gramm. § 741. 6: Hermann on Viger, p. 462. When it occurs with ἀλλά, it is best written without a stop between: cf. Aristoph. Ran, 58: μὴ σκῶπτέ μ', ὦ 'δέλφ'· οὐ γὰρ ἀλλ' ἔχω κακῶς:—ib. 193: μὰ τὸν Δί' οὐ γὰρ (scil. νεναυμάχηκα) ἀλλ' ἔτυχον ὀφθαλμιῶν, and 499, φέρε δὴ ταχέως αὔτ'· οὐ γὰρ ἀλλὰ πειστέον. Mr. Humphry re-

δὲ τοῖς [f] στρατηγοῖς οἱ [f] ῥαβδοῦχοι τὰ ῥήματα ταῦτα·
ἐφοβήθησαν δὲ ἀκούσαντες ὅτι Ῥωμαῖοί [g] εἰσιν, 39 καὶ
ἐλθόντες [h] παρεκάλεσαν αὐτούς, καὶ [e] ἐξαγαγόντες [i] ἠρώτων [k] ἀπελθεῖν [k] ἀπὸ τῆς πόλεως. 40 ἐξελθόντες δὲ
ἐκ τῆς φυλακῆς [l] εἰςῆλθον πρὸς τὴν Λυδίαν, καὶ
[m] ἰδόντες [n] παρεκάλεσαν τοὺς ἀδελφούς, καὶ [o] ἐξῆλθον.
XVII. 1 [p] Διοδεύσαντες δὲ τὴν Ἀμφίπολιν καὶ Ἀπολ-

ABDEHLPℵ a b c d f g h k l m o p 13

f ver. 35. g pres., Mark v. 14. John i. 40. ii. 9. ch. iv. 13. ix. 26. Heb. xi. 8, 13 al. Winer, edn. 6, § 40, 2. c. h = ch. xvii. 9 al. i constr., Luke v. 3. viii. 37. John iv. 40. ch. (iii. 3.) x. 48. xviii. 20. xxiii. 18. 1 Thess. v. 12 only. w. ἵνα, Mark vii. 26. Luke vii. 36. w. ὅπως, ch. xxiii. 20. k = Mark v. 17. l w. πρός, ch. xi. 3 reff. m = Luke viii. 20. ch. xxviii. 20 al. 4 Kings viii. 29. n = ch. xv. 32 reff. o = ch. xv. 40 reff. p Luke viii. 1 only. Gen. xiii. 17. Isa. lix. 8.

for 1st δε, τε E-gr ℵ Syr æth. for τοις, αυτοις οι D[1]. aft ταυτα ins τα ρηθεντα προς τους στρατηγους D[, simly] Syr. rec και εφοβ. (*corrn to more natural copula*), with EHLP rel vulg [syrr sah æth] Chr: txt ABℵ p 36. 40 copt.—οι δε ακουσαντες οτ. ρω. εισ. εφοβηθ. D[, simly Syr].

39. for κ. ελθοντ., και παραγενομενοι μετα φιλων πολλων εις την φυλακην D [137 syr also add εις τ. φυλ.]. ηρωτουν A Thl-fin: -τησαν E. rec (for απελθειν απο) εξελθειν, with HLP rel Chr: εξελθ. εκ (D)E: εξελθ. απο a: txt ABℵ p 13. 36. 40.—παρεκαλεσαν αυτους εξελθειν ειποντες ηγνοησαμεν τα καθ υμας, οτι εσται ανδρες δικαιοι (syr thus far w-ast) και εξαγαγοντες παρεκαλεσαν αυτους λεγοντες εκ της πολεως ταυτης εξελθατε μηποτε παλιν συντραφωσιν ημειν επικραζοντες καθ υμων D, simly 137 [syr].

40. for εκ, απο Bℵ a h 38 Thl-fin. ηλθον D E-lat. rec for προς, εις (*see note: and cf Mark* v. 12, 13): txt ABDEHLPℵ rel vulg sah arm Chr Thl. rec ιδοντ. τ. αδελφ. παρεκ. **αυτους**, with EHLP rel 36 vulg syrr sah æth [arm] Chr: txt ABℵ p 13. 40 copt.—ιδ. τ. αδ. διηγησαντο οσα εποιησεν κυριος αυτοις παρεκαλεσαντες (παρακαλεσαν(sic) τε D-corr) αυτους και D. εξηλθαν Dℵ.

Chap. XVII. 1. διελθοντες E. for αμφιπ., πολιν ℵ[1](txt ℵ-corr[1]). ins την bef απολλ. (*for uniformity*) ABEℵ a p 13: om (D)HL[P] rel.—την απ. κ. την αμφ. E. και κατηλθον (om και D-corr: κατηλθ. και D[3]) εις απολλωνιδα κακειθεν εις D.

marks, 'St. Paul submitted to be scourged by his own countrymen (five times, 2 Cor. xi. 24): for, though he might have pleaded his privilege as a Roman, to the Jews he "became as a Jew," observing their ceremonies, and submitting to their law.'
38. ἐφοβ.] For the account which they might have to give at Rome, as in Verres' case, or even for their popularity with the very mob of Roman citizens who had demanded the punishment. **39. παρεκάλεσαν**] Not '*comforted:*' but, as E. V., **besought them**: viz. not to make their treatment matter of legal complaint. In the request to depart from the city, the prætors seem to shew fear of a change in the temper of the mob. See the curious addition in the var. readd. **40.**] They do not depart hastily, or as though forced, but wait to reassure the brethren. πρός has probably been altered to εἰς, on account of the verb, not because Λυδίαν was mistaken (Meyer) for the country of that name. **παρεκ.**] exhorted, is better than '*comforted,*' E. V. The one in this case would imply the other. Chap. XVII. **1.**] Here (or rather perhaps at ἐξῆλθον, in the preceding verse) we have the first person again dropped,—implying apparently that the narrator did not accompany Paul and Silas. I should be inclined to think that Timotheus *went with them* from Philippi,—not, as is usually supposed, joined them at Berœa: see below on ver. 10. **διοδεύσαντες**] The ὁδός, on which they travelled from Philippi to Thessalonica, was the Via Egnatia, the Macedonian continuation of the Via Appia, and so named from Egnatia ('Gnatia lymphis iratis exstructa,' Hor. Sat. i. 5), in the neighbourhood of which the latter meets the Adriatic. It extended from Dyrrhachium in Epirus to the Hebrus in Thrace, a distance of 500 miles. The stages here mentioned are thus particularized in the itineraries: Philippi to Amphipolis, 33 miles: Amphipolis to Apollonia, 30 miles: Apollonia to Thessalonica, 37 miles. See more particulars in C. and H., i. pp. 368 ff.
Ἀμφίπολιν] Anciently called ἐννέα ὁδοί, Thucyd. i. 100. Herod. vii. 114, lying in a most important position, at the end of the lake Cercinitis, formed by the Strymon, commanding the only easy pass from the coast of the Strymonic gulf into Macedonia. ('Amphipoleos, quæ objecta claudit omnes ab oriente sole in Macedoniam aditus,' Liv. xlv. 30.) In consequence of this, the Athenians colonized the place, calling it Amphipolis, ἐπ' ἀμφότερα περιῤῥέοντος τοῦ Στρυμόνος, Thuc. iv. 102. It was the spot where Brasidas was killed, and for

λωνίαν ἦλθον εἰς Θεσσαλονίκην, ὅπου ἦν [ἡ] συναγωγὴ
τῶν Ἰουδαίων. 2 [q] κατὰ δὲ τὸ [qr] εἰωθὸς τῷ Παύλῳ εἰςῆλθεν
πρὸς αὐτοὺς καὶ [s] ἐπὶ σάββατα τρία [t] διελέγετο αὐτοῖς
[u] ἀπὸ τῶν [v] γραφῶν 3 [w] διανοίγων καὶ [x] παρατιθέμενος
ὅτι τὸν χριστὸν [y] ἔδει παθεῖν καὶ [z] ἀναστῆναι [z] ἐκ νεκρῶν,
καὶ ὅτι [a] οὗτός ἐστιν ὁ χριστὸς ὁ Ἰησοῦς ὃν ἐγὼ [b] καταγγέλλω ὑμῖν. 4 καί τινες ἐξ αὐτῶν [c] ἐπείσθησαν καὶ [d] προς-

Luke iv. 16. Num. xxiv. 1
r as above (q). Matt. xxvii. 15. Mark x. 1 only. Sir. xxxvii. 14.
s ch. xiii. 31 reff.
t = ver. 17. ch. xviii. 19. xx. 7 al. Acts only, exc. Mark ix. 34. Heb. xii. 5. Jude 9. Exod. vi. 27. 2 Macc. xi. 20.
u = ch. xxviii. 23.
v = plur. absol., John v. 39. ver. 11. ch. xviii. 24, 28 al. Paul, Rom. xv. 4. 1 Cor. xv. 3, 4 only.
w = Luke xxiv. 32. (ch. vii. 56 reff.)
x Matt. xiii. 24, 31. Exod. xix. 7. w. ὅτι, here only.
y = ch. iv. 12 reff.
z = ch. x. 41 reff.
a ch. ix. 20 reff.
b ch. xiii. 5 reff.
c absol., ch. xxi. 14 reff.
d here only †. τῷ . . . πατρὶ τῶν ὅλων προςκεκληρωμένοι, Philo de Fortit. § 7, vol. ii. p. 381.

ins την bef θεσσαλ. B 104. om ἡ (*see note*) ABDℵ p 13. 40 [copt]: ins EHLP rel [arm-ms] Chr Thl.

2. και κατα D¹(and lat) [Syr] æth. εισωθος(sic) [D¹-gr]. ο παυλος D vulg [E-lat arm] Syr æth. om και D [sah]. διελεξατο (*alteration to historic aorist*) ABℵ p 13 [syrr copt]: διελεχθη D E-gr c 36. 40 Chr-comm$_1$: txt HLP rel vulg E-lat [sah æth arm] Chr$_4$. for απο, εκ D.

3. om τον D¹(ins D⁵) [τ. χρ. aft εδει m 40 Syr arm(Tischdf) Thl-fin]. rec ο χρ. ιησ., omg 2nd ὁ, with HLP 13 rel Thl: χρ. ιησ. AD p Chr$_1$: ιησ. ο χρ. E c f h Chr$_1$: ιησ. χρ. ℵ: [*Chr. Jes.* am demid tol syr sah æth arm-ed: *Jes. Chr.* vulg-ed Syr copt arm-mss:] txt B.

previously failing to succour which Thucydides was exiled: see Thucyd. iv. and v., and Grote's Hist. of Greece, vol. vi. p. 625 ff., where there is a plan of Amphipolis. After this it was a point of contention between the Athenians and Philip, and subsequently became the capital of Macedonia Prima,—see Livy, xlv. 30, where Paulus Æmilius proclaims, at Amphipolis, the freedom and territorial arrangements of Macedonia. It is now called Emboli.

Ἀπολλωνίαν] Its situation is unknown, but was evidently (see the distances above given) inland, not quite half-way from Amphipolis to Thessalonica, where the road crosses from the Strymonic to the Thermaic gulf. Leake saw some ruins at about the right spot, but did not visit them: and Cousinéry mentions seeing, on an opposite hill, the village of Polina. Pliny mentions it (N. H. iv. 10), 'regio Mygdoniæ subjacens, in qua recedentes a mare Apollonia, Arethusa.' It must not be confounded with a better known Apollonia near Dyrrhachium, on the western coast, also on the Via Egnatia. See C. and H. i. pp. 376 f.

Θεσσαλονίκην] At this time the capital of the province Macedonia, and the residence of the proconsul (Macedonia had been an *imperial*, but was now a *senatorial province*). Its former names were Emathia, Halia, and Therma: it received its name of Thessalonica from Cassander, on his rebuilding and embellishing it, in honour of his wife Thessalonica, sister of Alexander the Great. So Strabo, lib. vii. excerpt. 10: who, ib. excerpt. 3, calls it Θεσσαλονικεία. It was made a *free city* after the battle of Philippi: and every thing in this narrative is consistent with the privileges and state of an *urbs libera*. We read of its δῆμος ver. 5, and its πολιτάρχαι ver. 6: not, as at the Roman colony of Philippi, of ῥαβδοῦχοι (lictors), and στρατηγοί (duumviri), ch. xvi. 20, 35. It has ever been an important and populous city, and still continues such (pop. 70,000), being the second city in European Turkey, under the slightly corrupted name of Saloniki. For a notice of the church there, see Prolegg. to first Ep. to the Thessalonians, § ii. **[ἡ] συναγ.**] The article is in all probability genuine: implying that there was no other synagogue for the towns lately traversed: and shewing the same minute acquaintance with the peculiarities of this district as our narrative has shewn since the arrival at Neapolis. **2. κατὰ τ. εἰωθ.**] See marg. reff. in E. V Paul was most probably suffering still from his 'shameful treatment' at Philippi, 1 Thess. ii. 2 **διελέγ.**] **argued**, see reff. **ἀπὸ τ. γραφ.** is best taken with **διελέγ.**, not with **διανοίγων**: see reff. **3. ὅτι οὗτος . . . .**] See examples of the change of construction, ch. i. 4; xxiii. 22; Luke v. 14. The rendering is nearly as E. V., literally, **that this is the Christ, namely, Jesus, whom I preach unto you.** So Meyer. The ὁ χριστός takes up τὸν χριστόν above, and attaches to ὁ Ἰησοῦς the office concerning which this necessity of suffering, &c., was predicated.

Even the particularity of this παθεῖν (ἀπέθανεν) κ. ἀναστῆναι is reproduced in 1 Thess. iv. 14. **4. προςεκληρώθ.**] **were added** (as if by lot, that being deter-

εκληρώθησαν τῷ Παύλῳ καὶ τῷ Σίλᾳ, τῶν τε [e] σεβομένων ABDE
ʿΕλλήνων πλῆθος πολύ, γυναικῶν τε τῶν [f] πρώτων [g] οὐκ HLPℵ a b c d f g
[g] ὀλίγαι. 5 [h] ζηλώσαντες δὲ οἱ Ἰουδαῖοι καὶ [i] προςλαβό- h k l m o p 13
μενοι τῶν [k] ἀγοραίων ἄνδρας τινὰς πονηροὺς καὶ [l] ὀχλο-
ποιήσαντες [m] ἐθορύβουν τὴν πόλιν, καὶ [n] ἐπιστάντες τῇ
οἰκίᾳ Ἰάσονος [o] ἐζήτουν αὐτοὺς [p] προαγαγεῖν εἰς τὸν [q] δῆμον·
6 μὴ εὑρόντες δὲ αὐτοὺς [r] ἔσυρον [τὸν] Ἰάσονα καί τινας
[s] ἀδελφοὺς ἐπὶ τοὺς [t] πολιτάρχας, [u] βοῶντες ὅτι οἱ τὴν
[v] οἰκουμένην [w] ἀναστατώσαντες [x] οὗτοι καὶ [y] ἐνθάδε πάρεισιν,

e ch. xiii. 43 reff. f = Matt. xxii. 38. Luke xv. 22. ch. xiii. 50 reff. Dan. x. 13. g ch. xii. 18 reff. h = ch. vii. 9 reff. i = ch. xviii. 26. Matt. xvi. 22 ‖ Mk.‡ 2 Macc. viii. 1. k = here (ch. xix. 38) only †. Herod. ii. 141 al. (see Wetstein.) l here only †. m Matt. ix. 23 ‖ Mk. ch. xx. 10 only. Judg. iii. 26. Nahum ii. 3. Wisd. xviii. 19. Sir. xl. 6 only. (-βος, ch. xxi. 34.) n ch. vi. 12. (absol.) Jer. xxi. 2. o = ch. xiii. 8 reff. p = ch. xii. 6 reff. q ch. xii. 22 reff. r ch. viii. 3 reff. s = ch. ix. 30 reff. t here bis only †. u ch. viii. 7 al. v = ch. xxiv. 5. w ch. xxi. 38. Gal. v. 12 L.P. Dan. vii. 23 LXX. Ps. x. 1 Aq. x ch. ix. 20 reff. y ch. xvi. 28 reff.

4. επιστευσαν E c 13. 40. om 2nd τω B. aft τω σιλαια(sic) ins τη διδαχη πολλοι, omg τε, D. ins και bef ελληνων AD 13. 40 vulg copt. rec πολ. bef πλ., with HLP rel Chr_1 Thl-sif: txt ABDEℵ a c h k m p 13 vulg arm Chr_1 Thl-fin. for γυν. τε, και γυναικες D.

5. rec ins απειθουντες bef ιουδαιοι, with D b k o; ins οι απειθ. aft ιουδ. HLP a d f g h m, and aft και προςλαβ. c 137: om AB [E(but see below)] ℵ p 13. 36. 40. 142 vulg syrr coptt [æth-pl] arm.—om ζηλωσαντες and και, transposing προςλαβ. to beg of ver, HLP b d f g h l o 142: txt ABEℵ p 13. 36. 40 vulg syrr coptt arm.—οι δε απειθ. ιουδ. συνστρεψαντες, omg κ. προςλ., D.—ζηλωσαντες προςλαβομενοι, omg all the rest, 66 æth[-rom]. rec τινας bef ανδρας, with DHLPℵ rel [Thl-sif]: txt ABE a h k p 13 vulg Thl-fin.—(τιν. αν. bef των αγ. D [arm].) aft πονηρ. ins απειθησαντες E. om και οχλοπ. D. εθορυβουσαν D. rec επισταντες τε (for κ. επ.), with HLP rel Chr_1: και επιστευσαν(sic) 13: txt ABDEℵ a k m p 13[Treg] Thl-fin. ιασωνος ADE d h k l m Thl-fin, so (exc A) in vv 6, 9. [αυτον A^1(appy).] rec αγαγειν, with HP rel Thl: προςαγαγ. E[-gr] c 137: αναγαγ. L 11: εξαγαγ. D-gr 104 coptt æth-pl: txt ABℵ a b k o p 13. 36. 40, *producere* vulg D-lat E-lat.

6. εσυραν DE a b Chr_1: ευρον $ℵ^1$: txt ABHLP$ℵ^3$ [m] p 36 Thl. om τον (*as unnecessary: or from similarity of endings, -ρον τον*) ABDℵ p [13]: ins EHLP rel 36 Chr. ιασωναν D^1. τινες D^1(txt D^2). aft τινας ins αλλους E. βοωντας A lect-2. aft βοων. ins και λεγοντες D. aft ουτοι ins εισιν D^1.

mined by God, who gave them the Holy Spirit of adoption: ὃς καὶ ἐνεργεῖται ἐν ὑμῖν τοῖς πιστεύουσιν, 1 Thess. ii. 13) to the great family of which Paul and Silas were members. The sense is passive, not middle. The word is not uncommon in Philo. **σεβ. ʿΕλλ.**] See reff. The aptitude of *women* for the reception of the Gospel several times appears in this book,—see above, ch. xvi. 13 ff., and below, vv. 12, 34. **5. προςλαβ.**] **Having taken to them,** as their accomplices, to assist them in the ὀχλοποιῆσαι which follows. **ἀγοραίων**] Such men as Aristophanes calls πονηρὸς κἀξ ἀγορᾶς, —Demosthenes, περίτριμμα ἀγορᾶς,—Xenophon, τὸν ἀγοραῖον ὄχλον,—Plutarch, ἀγοραίους καὶ δυναμένους ὄχλον συναγαγεῖν: see many other instances in Wetstein, who mentions the modern 'canaille' (*canalicolæ*). Cicero calls them 'subrostrani:' Plautus, 'subbasilicani.' These may be alluded to in οἱ ἴδιοι συμφυλέται, 1 Thess. ii. 14. (See note on ἀγοραῖοι, ch. xix. 38.) **ἐπιστ., having fallen upon,—beset.** **Ἰάσονος**] With whom (ver. 7) Paul and Silas lodged. He appears, perhaps (?), again with Paul at Corinth, Rom. xvi. 21, but did not accompany him into Asia, ch. xx. 4. **6. πολιτάρχας**] The following inscription, found on an arch *at Thessalonica*, is given from Boeckh, No. 1967, in C. and H. i. 395: πολειταρχουντων Σωσιπατρου του Κλεοπατρας και Λουκιου Ποντιου Σεκουνδου Πουβλιου Φλαουιου Σαβεινου Δημητριου του Φαυστου Δημητριου του Νικοπολεως Ζωιλου του Παρμενιωνος του και Μενισκου Γαιου Αγιλληιου Ποτειτου . . . . Here we have this very title applied to the Thessalonian magistrates, shewing the exact accuracy of our narrative; and, curiously enough, we have three of the *names* which occur here, or in the Epistles, as companions of Paul: viz. Sosipater (*of Berœa*, ch. xx. 4: see Rom. xvi. 21, and note); Secundus (*of Thessalonica*, ch. xx. 4); and Gaius (*the Macedonian*, note, ch. xix. 29). **τὴν οἰκ. ἀναστ.**] The words presuppose some rumour of Christianity and its spread

7 οὓς [z] ὑποδέδεκται Ἰάσων· καὶ οὗτοι πάντες [a] ἀπέναντι
τῶν [b] δογμάτων Καίσαρος πράσσουσιν, βασιλέα λέγοντες
[c] ἕτερον εἶναι Ἰησοῦν. 8 [de] ἐτάραξαν δὲ τὸν [d] ὄχλον καὶ
τοὺς [t] πολιτάρχας ἀκούοντας ταῦτα, 9 καὶ [f] λαβόντες τὸ
[g] ἱκανὸν [f] παρὰ τοῦ Ἰάσονος καὶ τῶν λοιπῶν [h] ἀπέλυσαν
αὐτούς. 10 οἱ δὲ ἀδελφοὶ εὐθέως [i] διὰ νυκτὸς [k] ἐξέπεμψαν
-όν τε Παῦλον καὶ τὸν Σίλαν εἰς Βέροιαν, οἵτινες [l] παρα-

z Luke x. 38. xix. 6. James ii. 25 only †. Tobit vii. 8. 1 Macc. xvi. 15 only.
a = here only. (Rom. iii. 18 reff.) 2 Kings x. 17 B Ald.
b ch. xvi. 4 reff.
c = ch. i. 20. xii. 17. xiii. 35. xv. 35 al.
d ver. 13.
e ch. xv. 24 reff.
f ch. ii. 33 reff.
g = here only. see Lev. xxv. 26.
h = ch. xxvi. 32 reff.
i ch. v. 19 reff.
k ch. xiii. 4 only. Gen. xxiv. 54, 56, 59.
l absol., Luke xii. 51. xix. 16. John iii. 23. ch. v. 21, 22. ix. 39. x. [32] 33. 1 Cor. xvi. 3 al. fr. Gen. xiv. 13.

7. (πρασσουσιν, so ABDEHLPℵ a b c d f g h k l o p 13 Chr_1 Thl-sif.) ετερον bef λεγοντες ειναι A B(sic: see table) ℵ a c f h k [p] 13 vulg syr [arm Chr_1]: λεγ. ειν. ετ. E: txt DHLP rel [Syr coptt] Chr_1.
8. for τον οχλ., την πολιν E. και εταραξεν τους πολ. και τον οχλ. ακουσαντες (τα D^2) ταυ. D.—[Syr also transp οχλ. and πολιτ.]
10. om ευθ. δια νυκτ. A [om δια ν. p]. εξεπεμψαν bef δια νυκτος ℵ. rec ins της bef νυκτος, with EHLP rel Chr_1 Thl-sif: om BDℵ a m 13. 40 $Petr_1$ Thl-fin. om τε D 3. 32. 42. 57. 95^1 sah [arm]: δε p^1.

having before reached the inhabitants of Thessalonica. **7. οὗτοι πάντες**] All these people, i. e. *Christians, wherever found.* A wider acquaintance is shewn, or at least assumed, with the belief of Christians, than extended merely to Jason and his friends. **ἀπέναντι . . πράσσ.**] Not '*do this in the face of the decrees,*' which would require τοῦτο with πράσσ., but as E. V. The δόγματα in this case would be the Julian 'leges majestatis.' **βασιλέα κ.τ.λ.**] This false charge seems to have been founded on Paul's preaching much at Thessalonica concerning the triumphant παρουσία of Christ. This appears again and again in his two Epistles: see 1 Thess. i. 10; ii. 19; iii. 13; iv. 13—18; v. 1, 2; 2 Thess. i. 5, 7—10; ii. 1—12: and particularly 2 Thess. ii. 5, where he refers to his having often told them of *these things*, viz. the course, and destruction of Antichrist, by whom these Jews might perhaps misrepresent Paul as designating Cæsar. **9. λαβόντες τὸ ἱκανόν**] 'Satisdatione accepta;' either by *sureties*, or by a *sum of money*, or both. They bound over Jason and the rest (τινας ἀδελφούς, ver. 6) to take care that no more trouble was given by these men: in accordance with which security they sent them away; and by night, to avoid the notice of the ὄχλος. **10.**] It does not follow, because Timotheus is not mentioned here, that therefore he did not accompany, or at all events follow, Paul and Silas to Berœa. He has never been mentioned since he joined Paul's company at Lystra. The very intermitted and occasional notices of Paul's companions in this journey should be a caution against rash hypotheses. The general character of the narrative seems to be, that where Paul, or Paul and Silas, are alone or principally concerned, all mention of the rest is suspended, and sometimes so completely as to make it appear as if they were absent: then, at some turn of events they appear again, having in some cases been really present all the time. I believe Timotheus to have been with them at Thessalonica the first time, because it does not seem probable that Paul would have sent to them one to confirm and exhort them concerning their faith (1 Thess. iii. 2) who had not known them before, especially as he then had Silas with him. And this is confirmed by both the Epistles to the Thessalonians, which are from Paul, Silvanus, and Timotheus. From these Epistles we learn that, during his residence among them, Paul worked with his own hands (1 Thess. ii. 9; 2 Thess. iii. 8) to maintain himself: and from Phil. iv. 15, 16, that the Philippians sent supplies more than once towards his maintenance. Both these facts, especially the last, seeing that the distance from Philippi was 100 Roman miles, make it very improbable that his stay was so short as from three to four weeks: nor is this implied in the text: much time may have elapsed while the πλῆθος πολύ of ver. 4 were joining Paul and Silas. See further in Prolegg. to 1 Thess., Vol. III. § ii. 2 ff. **Βέροιαν**] According to the Antonine Itinerary 61, according to the Peutinger Table 57 Roman miles (S.W.) from Thessalonica. Berœa was not far from Pella, in Macedonia Tertia, Liv. xlv. 30, at the foot of Mt. Bermius. It was afterwards called Irenopolis, and now Kara Ferla, or Verria, and is a city of the second rank in European Turkey, containing from 15,000

m here only. Exod. xxxiii. 8.
n ch. ix. 20 reff.
o — here (Luke xix. 12. 1 Cor. i. 26) only. (Job i. 3. 2 Macc. x. 13 only.)
p ch. x. 41 reff.
q ch. viii. 14 reff.
r — Mark iii. 5. ch. ii. 29. v. 26 al. 1 Chron. xxix. 22.
s 2 Cor. viii. 11, 12, 19. ix. 2 only†. Sir. xlv. 23 only. (-μος, Rom. i. 15.)
t Luke xi. 3. xix. 47 only. see ch. ii. 46 reff.

γενομενοι εἰς τὴν συναγωγὴν [m] ἀπῄεσαν τῶν Ἰουδαίων. ABDE HLPℵ a
11 [n] οὗτοι δὲ ἦσαν [o] εὐγενέστεροι τῶν ἐν Θεσσαλονίκῃ, bcdfg
[p] οἵτινες [q] ἐδέξαντο τὸν λόγον [r] μετὰ πάσης [s] προθυμίας, hklm op 13
[t] τὸ καθ' ἡμέραν [u] ἀνακρίνοντες τὰς [v] γραφάς, εἰ [w] ἔχοι
ταῦτα [w] οὕτως. 12 πολλοὶ μὲν οὖν ἐξ αὐτῶν ἐπίστευσαν,
καὶ τῶν Ἑλληνίδων γυναικῶν τῶν [x] εὐσχημόνων καὶ
ἀνδρῶν [y] οὐκ [y] ὀλίγοι. 13 ὡς δὲ ἔγνωσαν οἱ [z] ἀπὸ τῆς
Θεσσαλονίκης Ἰουδαῖοι ὅτι καὶ ἐν τῇ Βεροίᾳ [a] κατηγγέλη
ὑπὸ τοῦ Παύλου ὁ [ab] λόγος τοῦ [b] θεοῦ, ἦλθον κἀκεῖ [c] σαλεύ-
οντες καὶ [d] ταράσσοντες τοὺς [d] ὄχλους. 14 εὐθέως δὲ τότε
τὸν Παῦλον [e] ἐξαπέστειλαν οἱ ἀδελφοὶ πορεύεσθαι *[f] ὡς

u = ch. iv. 9 reff. v ver. 2 reff. w ch. vii. 1 reff. x ch. xiii. 50 reff. y ch. xii. 18 reff. z = ch. ii. 5 reff. a ch. xiii. 5 reff. b ch. xi. 1 reff. c = ch. ii. 25 (from Ps. xv. 8). 2 Thess. ii. 2 only. (ch. xvi. 26 al.) 1 Macc. vi. 8. d ver. 8. e ch. vii. 12 reff. f see note. 4 Kings ii. 11 B Ald. (ἕως, A compl.).

rec των ιουδαιων bef απηεσαν (*correction of order*), with ABDℵ a k m p 13. 36 vulg Thl-fin : txt EHLP rel Chr_1 Thl-sif.—εισηεσαν E vulg [Syr sah].

11. ευγενεις D-gr. ins τη bef θεσσ. D. aft λογον ins του θεου E. for πασης προθυμιας, παρρησιας E-gr. om το (*as unnecessary*) ADEℵ a h p 13 36 [Chr-3-mss_1] : ins BHLP rel Chr_2 Thl. εχει D^1(txt $D^{2\ or\ 3}$) E c l Thl-sif.

12. τινες μεν ουν αυτων D. om ουν E a^1 Thl-sif. aft επιστ. add τινες δε ηπιστησαν D 137. for ελλην. to ολιγοι D^1 has ελληνων και των ευσχημονων ανδρες κ. γυναικες ικανοι επιστευσαν (*Græcorum et non placentium et viri et mulieres pleres*[sic] *crediderunt* D-lat : ελληνιδων, and ins και bef ανδρες, D^2-gr : for 1st και, γυναικων D^5 : for ανδρ. κ. γυν., ανδρων ουκ ολιγοι D^3 : ικ. επιστ. are omd by D-corr).

13. om της DE. οτι (ο) λογ. (του) θεου κατηγγ. εις βεροιαν (και) επιστευσαν και ηλθον (εις αυτην) D(ο του are insd by D^5, και and εις αυτην omd by D-corr). rec om και ταρασσοντες, with EHLP rel æth Chr_1 : ins AB D^2(τασσοντες D^1) ℵ a c m p 13. 40 vulg syrr coptt arm. at end ins ου διελιμπανον D Syr.

14. for ευθ. δε τοτε τον, τον μεν ουν D Syr : *statimque* D-lat : om τοτε c 40. 137 syr sah [æth]. οι αδ. εξαπ. απελθειν D. *ἕως (*see note*) ABEℵ p 13. 40 [vulg Syr copt] : om D b^1 e o sah [æth] : ως HLP rel 36 [syr arm] Chr_1 Œc Thl.

to 20,000 souls. (Winer, Realw. C. and H. i. 399 f.) Wetstein quotes a remarkable illustration from Cicero in Pisonem, c. 26:—'Thessalonicam omnibus inscientibus noctuque venisti, qui cum concentum plorantium et tempestatem querelarum ferre non posses, in oppidum devium Berœam profugisti.' **11. εὐγενέστεροι**] Theophyl. and Œc. explain it by ἐπιεικέστεροι, but this is rather its *result*, than its meaning:—**more noble** is our best word for it;—of nobler disposition;—stirred up, not to envy, but to enquiry. **ταῦτα**] viz. the doctrine of ver. 3, which Paul and Silas preached here also. **12.**] The designation conveyed in Ἑλληνίδων is to be supplied before ἀνδρῶν also. So εἰς πᾶσαν πόλιν κ. τόπον, Luke x. 1. See Winer, edn. 6, § 59. 5. **13.**] **οἱ ἀπὸ τ. Θ.**, as E. V., **of Thessalonica**. No inference that they came *from* Thess. can be drawn from this expression: but it is asserted below. See Heb. xiii. 24. **ἦλθον κἀκεῖ σαλ.**] Not, as E. V., '*they came thither also, and stirred up . . . .*,' which destroys the force of the sentence: but **they came, and stirred up there also . . . .**: no *journey* having been related of them *before*, but a precisely similar act of exciting the people. From the distance, some time must have elapsed before this could take place: and that some time *did* elapse, we may gather from 1 Thess. ii. 18, where Paul relates that he made several attempts to revisit the Thessalonians (which could be only during his stay at Berœa, as he left the neighbourhood altogether when he left that town), but was hindered. **14. ὡς ἐπὶ τ. θ.**] The various readings seem to have arisen from not understanding **ὡς**,—which cannot, here or any where else, be redundant (as De Dieu, Raphel, Wolf, Heinrichs, &c.): nor can it well here signify that his going, '*as if to the sea*,' was only a *feint*, to deceive his enemies (as Beza, Piscator, Grot., Olsh., Neander, &c.): for, as there is no mention of any land journey, or places passed through on his way to Athens, there can be little doubt that he *did really go by sea*. But

ἐπὶ τὴν θάλασσαν, [g] ὑπέμεινέν τε ὅ τε Σίλας καὶ ὁ Τιμόθεος ἐκεῖ.
15 Οἱ δὲ [h] καθιστάνοντες τὸν Παῦλον ἤγαγον [i] ἕως
Ἀθηνῶν, καὶ [k] λαβόντες [k] ἐντολὴν πρὸς τὸν Σίλαν καὶ
Τιμόθεον, ἵνα ὡς τάχιστα ἔλθωσιν πρὸς αὐτόν, [l] ἐξῄεσαν.
16 ἐν δὲ ταῖς Ἀθήναις [m] ἐκδεχομένου αὐτοὺς τοῦ Παύλου,
[n] παρωξύνετο τὸ [o] πνεῦμα αὐτοῦ ἐι αὐτῷ [p] θεωροῦντος

g = Luke ii. 43 only. Num. xxii. 19. Jos. Antt. vi. 5. 2.
h (-άνειν) here only. = 2 Chron. xxviii. 15. Josh. vi. 23.
l = Luke ii. 15. ch. xxiii. 23.
k John x. 18. Col. iv. 10. 2 John 4 only.
l ch. xiii. 42 reff.
m 1 Cor. xi. 33. xvi. 11. Heb. x. 13. xi. 10. James v. 7 only ‡. Gen. xliii. 9 al.
n 1 Cor. xiii. 5 only. Deut. ix. 18. (-υσμός, ch. xv. 39, of Paul.)
o = Luke i. 47. John xiii. 21. ch. xix. 21 (of Paul). Rom. i. 9. viii. 16 xii. 11. 1 Cor. ii. 11. v. 3, 4. xiv. 14, &c. Paul principally.
p w. particip., = ch. viii. 13. xxviii. 6.

rec *υπεμενον*, with HLP rel 36 Chr_1 Thl-sif: *υπεμειναν* Bℵ a e p: *απεμειναν* E 13: *επεμειναν* m $Thdrt_1$ Thl-fin (*corrections to suit constr*): txt AD [c] Syr sah. rec for *τε*, *δε* (*correction of characteristic τε, and to avoid recurrence*), with DHLP rel vulg coptt [arm] Chr_1 $Thdrt_1$ [Thl-sif]: txt ABEℵ c m p 13 syrr æth Thl-fin. *εκει* bef *ο τε σιλας* H. om 2nd *τε* D.

15. rec *καθιστωντες* (*corrn of unusual form*), with D^8EHLPℵ^3 13 rel: *αποκαθιστωντες* 36 [*αποκαθιστανοντες* p]: *καταστανοντες* D^1: *καθισπαντες*(sic) ℵ^1: txt AB. rec aft *ηγ.* ins *αυτον*, with EHLP rel 36 [vulg-ed am syrr coptt arm] Chr: om ABDℵ c m p 13 fuld tol Thl-fin. ins *των* bef *αθ.* E. *παρηλθεν δε την θεσσαλιαν· εκωλυθη γαρ εις αυτους κηρυξαι τον λογον· λαβ. δε* D. for *εντολ.*, *επιστολην* E-gr Syr: add *παρα παυλου* D: *απ αυτου* E [vulg] Syr arm[-usc]. ins *τον* bef *τιμ.* B[E]ℵ p 13 [Chr_1(om_1)]. for *ινα ως ταχ.*, *οπως εν ταχει* D.

16. for *αυτους*, *αυτου* D^1(txt D^3) ℵ^1 96 Syr.—om *του παυλου* ℵ^1. om *το* D^1 (ins $D^{3 \text{ or } 4}$). rec *θεωρουντι* (*corrn to agree with αυτω. This is much more prob than that, as Meyer suspects, αυτω should have been altered to the gen to svit the gen absol before*), with DHLP rel Chr_1 Thl-sif: txt ABEℵ a k p 13. 40 Thl-fin.

ὡς ἐπὶ τ. θ. I believe simply to indicate the *direction in which* the Berœan brethren sent him forth [implying probably that all that was known at Berœa of his intended route was, that it was in the direction of the sea]. ὡς is used thus before participles and prepositions, without any assignable reference to its (more usual) subjective reference in such a connexion. Thus Hermann on Soph. Philoct. 58, says 'cogitationem significat particula ὡς. Sed multo usu factum est, ut aliquando etiam ibi usurparetur, ubi non opus esset respici id, quod quis in mente haberet.' We have the same expression in Pausan. ii. 25, καταβάντων δὲ (the walls of Tyrius) ὡς ἐπὶ θάλασσαν, ἐνταῦθα οἱ θάλαμοι τῶν Προίτου θυγατέρων εἰσίν,—and Diod. Sic. xiv. 49, κελεύσας κατὰ τάχος λάθρα πλεῖν ὡς ἐπὶ Συρακοσίους,—and Polyb. passim in Wetst.,—e.g. καθήκουσαν (τὴν Σελουκείαν) ὡς ἐπὶ θάλασσαν, v. 59,—and with the same signification. *Where* he embarked for Athens, is not said: probably (C. and H. i. 403) at Dium, near the base of Mt. Olympus, to which two roads from Berœa are marked in the ancient tables. **15. καθιστ.**] So Odyss. ν. 274, τούς μ' ἐκέλευσα Πύλονδε καταστῆσαι καὶ ἐφέσσαι,—and Arrian, Ind. xxvii. 1, καταστήσειν αὐτοὺς μέχρι Καρμανίας. *Who these were* is not said.

The course of *Timotheus* appears to have been, as far as we can follow it from the slight notices given, as follows:—when Paul departed from Berœa, not having been able to revisit Thessalonica as he wished (1 Thess. ii. 18), he sent Timotheus (from Berœa, not from Athens) to exhort and confirm the Thessalonians, and determined to be left at Athens *alone* (1 Thess. iii. 1), Silas meanwhile remaining to carry on the work at Berœa. Paul, on his arrival at Athens, sends (by his conductors, who returned) this message to both, to come to him as soon as possible. They did so, and found him (ch. xviii. 5) at Corinth. See Prolegg. to 1 Thess., Vol. III.

Ἀθηνῶν] See a long and interesting description of the then state of Athens, its buildings, &c., in C. and H. chap. x. vol. i. pp. 407 ff.; and Lewin, i. pp. 268 ff. It was a *free city*. Strabo (ix. 1) gives an epitome of its fortunes from the Roman conquest nearly to this time: Ῥωμαῖοι δ' οὖν παραλαβόντες αὐτοὺς δημοκρατουμένους ἐφύλαξαν τὴν αὐτονομίαν αὐτοῖς κ. τὴν ἐλευθερίαν. ἐπιπεσὼν δ' ὁ Μιθριδατικὸς πόλεμος τυράννους αὐτοῖς κατέστησεν οὓς ὁ βασιλεὺς ἐβούλετο, τὸν δ' ἰσχύσαντα μάλιστα τὸν Ἀριστίωνα κ. ταύτην βιασάμενον τὴν πόλιν. ἐκ πολιορκίας ἑλὼν Σύλλας ὁ τῶν Ῥωμαίων ἡγεμὼν ἐκόλασε· τῇ πόλει δὲ συγγνώμην ἔνειμε, καὶ μέχρι νῦν ἐν ἐλευθερίᾳ τε ἐστὶ

q κατείδωλον οὖσαν τὴν πόλιν. 17 r διελέγετο μὲν οὖν ἐν
τῇ συναγωγῇ τοῖς Ἰουδαίοις καὶ τοῖς s σεβομένοις, καὶ
ἐν τῇ ἀγορᾷ tu κατὰ u πᾶσαν u ἡμέραν πρὸς τοὺς v παρατυγ-
χάνοντας· 18 τινὲς δὲ καὶ τῶν Ἐπικουρείων καὶ Στοϊκῶν
φιλοσόφων w συνέβαλλον αὐτῷ. καί τινες ἔλεγον Τί ἂν
x θέλοι ὁ y σπερμολόγος οὗτος λέγειν; οἱ δὲ z Ξένων

ABDE HLPℵ a b c d f g h k l m o p 13

q here only †. ἐλαία κατάκαρπος, Ps. li. 8 (10). Hos. xiv. 7. κατώδυνος, 1 Kings i. 10. xxx. 6. διὰ τόπων καταδένδρων, Diod. Sic. xvi. 31. νεανίας καταβόστρυχος, Eur. Phœn. 146. r ver. 2 reff. s = ch. xiii. 43 reff. t ch. xiii. 27 reff. u here only. see Heb. iii. 13. v here only †. w. dat., Jos. Antt. ii. 9. 5. absol., Xen. Apol. Socr. 11. w Luke xiv. 31. ii. 19. ch. iv. 15. xviii. 27. xx. 14 only. 1 Macc. iv. 34. γυναιξὶ σ. λόγους, Eur. Iph. Aul. 830. x = ch. xiv. 13 reff. y here only †. Demosth. 269. 19. z = Matt. xxv. 35 al. Luke, here and ver. 21 only. Ruth ii. 10.

17. ins τοις bef εν τη αγ. D 137 syr-mg sah. παρατυχοντας D^1(txt D^3).

18. rec om 1st και (*as unnecessary*), with E c f k 36 [vulg syr coptt (æth) arm] Thl: ins ABDHLPℵ p 13 rel Syr Chr_1. επικουριων A[B^1]DEℵ c k p. rec ins των bef στοικων, with DHL P(perhaps) rel Chr: om ABEℵ a c d l p 13. 40. rec στωικων, with B p rel Chr [Thl-sif]: txt ADEHL P(perhaps) ℵ a c f k 13. 36 coptt Thl-fin. συνεβαλον L a b c d^1 f g h m 36 Chr_1 Thl-sif: συνελαβον D^1[-gr](txt D-corr¹). θελη D(txt D^8): θελει c 13. 40.

κ. τιμῇ παρὰ τοῖς Ῥωμαίοις. See also Tacit. Ann. ii. 53. **16. κατείδωλον**] This ἅπαξ λεγόμενον is formed after the analogy of κατάμπελος, κάθυδρος, &c. See reff. The multitude of statues and temples to the gods in Athens is celebrated with honour by classic writers of other nations, and with pride by their own. A long list of passages is given in Wetstein. The strongest perhaps is from Xen. de Repub. Ath., who calls Athens ὅλη βωμός, ὅλη θῦμα θεοῖς καὶ ἀνάθημα. **17.**] The οὖν (as De W. remarks against Meyer and Schneckenburger) does not necessarily give the *consequence* of what has been stated in ver. 16, but only continues the narration. See above on ch. xi. 19. **ἐν τῇ ἀγορᾷ**] Strabo (x. 1) speaking of the Eretrians in Eubœa says that some suppose them to have been named ἀπὸ τῆς Ἀθήνησιν Ἐρετρίας, ἣ νῦν ἐστιν ἀγορά (as distinguished from the Ceramicus, which was the *old* forum). It was the space before the στοὰ ποικίλη, where the Stoics held their διαλέξεις. **18. Ἐπικουρείων**] The Epicurean philosophy was antagonistic to the gospel, as holding the atomic theory in opposition to the creation of matter,—the disconnexion of the Divinity from the world and its affairs, in opposition to the idea of a ruling Providence,—and the indissoluble union, and annihilation together, of soul and body, as opposed to the hope of eternal life, and indeed to all spiritual religion whatever. The Epicureans were the materialists of the ancient world. The common idea attached to Epicureanism must be discarded in our estimate of the persons mentioned in our text. The summum bonum of the real Epicureans, far from being a degraded and sensual pleasure, was ἀταραξία of mind, based upon φρόνησις,—perhaps the best estimate of the highest good formed in the heathen world;—and their ethics were exceedingly strict. But the abuse to which such a doctrine was evidently liable, gave rise to a pseudo-Epicureanism, which has generally passed current for the real, and which amply illustrated the truth, that 'corruptio optimi est pessima.' For their chimerical ἀταραξία, Paul offered them τὴν εἰρήνην τὴν ὑπερέχουσαν πάντα νοῦν, Phil. iv. 7. **Στοϊκῶν**] So named from the στοὰ ποικίλη (see above), founded by Zeno of Cittium in the fourth century B.C., but perhaps more properly by Cleanthes and Chrysippus in the third century B.C. Their philosophy, while it approached the truth in holding one supreme Governor of all, compromised it, in allowing of any and all ways of conceiving and worshipping Him (see below, vv. 24, 25),—and contravened it, in its pantheistic belief that all souls were emanations of Him. In *spirit* it was directly opposed to the gospel,—holding the independence of man on any being but himself, together with the subjection of God and man alike to the stern laws of an inevitable fate. On the existence of the soul after death their ideas were various: some holding that all souls endure to the conflagration of all things,—others confining this to the souls of good men,—and others believing all souls to be reabsorbed into the Divinity. By these tenets they would obviously be placed in antagonism to the doctrines of a Saviour of the world and the resurrection,—and to placing the summum bonum of man in abundance of that grace which ἐν ἀσθενείᾳ τελεῖται, 2 Cor. xii. 9. **τινες ἔλεγον . . . . οἱ δέ**] These are not to be taken as belonging the one to the Epicureans, the other to the Stoics,—but rather as describing two classes, common

[a] δαιμονίων δοκεῖ [b] καταγγελεὺς εἶναι· ὅτι τὸν Ἰησοῦν
καὶ τὴν [c] ἀνάστασιν [d] εὐηγγελίζετο [αὐτοῖς].
19 [e] ἐπιλαβόμενοί τε αὐτοῦ ἐπὶ τὸν Ἄρειον πάγον ἤγαγον

a = here only. Xen. Mem. i. 1. 1.
b here only +. (-λλειν, ver. 23.)
c absol., Matt. xxii. 22, 23, 30 || L. John xi. 24, 25. ch. xxiii. 8.
d constr., ch. xi. 20 reff.
e = and constr., Matt. xiv. 31. Luke ix. 47. ch. xxi. 30, 33. Isa. iv. 1. (acc. ch. ix. 27 reff.)

for οι δε, οιδεν D[1]. καταγγελλευς [A-corr[1] E] ℵ. om last clause D. rec αυτοις bef ευηγγελιζετο, with 36: om αυτοις BLPℵ[1] rel syr sah arm Chr: αυτου ευηγγ. αυτοις a 14. 27-9. 68-9. 105-6 Syr copt æth-pl[?]: txt AEHℵ[3] c f k m p 13 vulg Thl. (*The varr have principally been produced by* αυτου *being inserted after* αναστασιν, *it being imagined that the resurr of* Jesus *was intended. Hence the origl* αυτοις *was transposed and altered, and, from* αυτου *and* αυτοις *being alternately erased, finally disappeared altogether. So Meyer.*)

19. μετα δε ημερας τινας επιλαβ. αυτου ηγαγον αυτον επι τον αριον παγ. πυνθανομενοι και λεγ. D 137 syr. (om τον D[1]: ins D[2]: μ. δε ημ. τιν. are marked with ast in syr.) for τε, δε B p 13. 36 coptt. αριον ADEℵ, so ver 22.

perhaps to both schools,—the one of which despised him and his sayings, and the other were disposed to take a more serious view of the matter, and charge him with bringing in new deities. **σπερμολόγος**] *σπερμολόγος εἶδος ἐστὶν ὀρνέου λωβωμένου τὰ σπέρματα· ἐξ οὗ οἱ Ἀθηναῖοι σπερμολόγους ἐκάλουν τοὺς περὶ ἐμπόρια καὶ ἀγορὰς διατρίβοντας, διὰ τὸ ἀναλέγεσθαι τὰ ἐκ τῶν φορτίων ἀποῤῥέοντα, καὶ διαζῆν ἐκ τούτων.* Eustath. ad Odyss. ε. 490, where Damm observes, *σπερμολογεῖν*, 'verbum recentiorum; dicitur *ἐπὶ τῶν ἀλαζονευομένων ἀμεθόδως ἐπὶ μαθήμασιν ἐκ τινῶν παρακουσμάτων*, si quis quid arripuit forte ex disciplinis, eoque se imperite jactat:' **babbler** is the very best English word: as both signifying *one who talks fluently to no purpose*, and hinting also that his talk is *not his own*. **ξένων δαιμ.**] *ἀδικεῖ Σωκράτης . . . . καινὰ δαιμόνια εἰσφέρων*, was one of the charges on which Athens put to death her wisest son.

δαιμόνια is not plural for singular, as Kuin.: nor merely, though this is somewhat more probable, marks the category, as Meyer: nor can it refer (Chrys., Theophyl., Œcum., Hammond, Heinrichs) to Jesus *and the ἀνάστασις*, mistaken for a goddess (a sufficient answer to which strange idea is, that **ἡ ἀνάστασις** is merely a *statement in the mouths of others*, of the doctrine taught by Paul, which he would hardly ever, if ever, specify by *this word*,—compare vv. 31 and 32): but alludes (as De Wette) to *the true God*, the God of the Jews, *and Jesus Christ* His Son: the Creator of the world (ver. 24), and the Man whom He hath appointed to judge it, ver. 31. **καταγγελεύς**] Compare ver. 23, end; which is an express answer to this charge. **19. ἐπιλαβ.**] * No violence is implied: see reff. **ἐπὶ τὸν Ἄρειον πάγον**] There is no allusion here to the *court* of Areiopagus, nor should the words have been so rendered in E. V.—especially as the same Ἀρείου πάγου below (ver. 22) is translated '*Mars' Hill*.' We have in the narrative *no trace of any judicial proceeding*, but every thing to contradict such a supposition. Paul merely makes his speech, and, having satisfied the curiosity of the multitude who came together on Mars' Hill, departs unhindered:—**they brought him up to the hill of Mars.** Wordsworth believes he finds a trace of a judicial proceeding in Ἄνδρες Ἀθηναῖοι, denoting rather a public apology than a private discussion: and in the conversion of Dionysius *the Areopagite*. But what words other than those would St. Paul have been likely to use in making a speech to a concourse of Athenians? for no one supposes it to have been a *private* discussion. And why should not Dionysius have been present? As a convert of note, he would naturally have his title attached. The following note is borrowed from Mr. Humphry's Commentary:—'It might be expected that on the hill of Mars the mind of the stranger would be impressed with the magnificence of the religion which he sought to overthrow. The temple of the Eumenides was immediately below him: opposite, at the distance of 200 yards, was the Acropolis, which, being entirely occupied with statues and temples, was, to use the phrase of an ancient writer (Aristides), ἀντ' ἀναθήματος, as one great offering to the gods. The Persians encamped on the Areiopagus when they besieged the Acropolis (Herod. viii. 52): from the same place the Apostle makes his first public attack on Paganism, of which the Acropolis was the stronghold. Xerxes in his fanaticism burnt the temples of Greece (Æschyl. Pers.: Cic. de Leg. ii. 10). Christianity advanced more meekly and surely: and though the immediate effect of the Apostle's sermon was not great, the Parthenon in time became a Christian church (Leake, Athens, p. 277). Athens

λέγοντες Δυνάμεθα γνῶναι τίς ἡ [f] καινὴ αὕτη ἡ ὑπὸ σοῦ ABDE
λαλουμένη [f] διδαχή; 20 [g] ξενίζοντα γάρ τινα [h] εἰςφέρεις HLP‎א a b c d f g
εἰς τὰς [i] ἀκοὰς ἡμῶν· βουλόμεθα οὖν γνῶναι *τί ἂν [k] θέλοι h k l m o p 13
ταῦτα εἶναι. 21 Ἀθηναῖοι δὲ πάντες καὶ οἱ [l] ἐπιδημοῦντες
[m] ξένοι [n] εἰς οὐδὲν ἕτερον [o] ηὐκαίρουν ἢ λέγειν τι ἢ ἀκούειν
[p] καινότερον. 22 [q] σταθεὶς δὲ ὁ Παῦλος ἐν μέσῳ τοῦ
Ἀρείου πάγου ἔφη Ἄνδρες Ἀθηναῖοι, [r] κατὰ πάντα [s] ὡς

f Mark i. 27. g = 1 Pet. iv. 4, 12 only +. (ch. x. 6, 23 reff.) 2 Macc. ix. 6. Diod. Sic. xii. 53, of Gorgias, τῷ ξενίζοντι τῆς λέξεως ἐξέπληξε τοὺς Ἀθηναίους. h = here (Matt. vi. 13. Luke v. 18, 19. xi. 4. xii. 11. 1 Tim. vi. 7. Heb. xiii. 11) only. (Soph. Aj. 149.) i Luke vii. 1. Heb. v. 11. 1 Cor. xii. 17. Mark vii. 35. Ps. xvii. 44. k = ch. ii. 12 only. l ch. ii. 10 only +. m ver. 18. n = Matt. v. 13. ch. xix. 27 al. o Mark vi. 31. 1 Cor. xvi. 12 only +. Polyb. xx. 9. 4. (-ρία, Luke xxii. 6. -ρος, Mark vi. 21. -ρως, 2 Tim. iv. 2.) p = Matt. xiii. 52. Isa. xlii. 9. compar., see ver. 22. Winer, edn. 6, § 35. 4. q ch. xi. 13 reff. r = ch. iii. 22 reff. s = 1 Cor. x. 15. 2 Cor. vi. 13.

om 2nd η BD. απο [for υπο] D¹(Wtst) [διδ (Scr)]. λεγομενη E p: καταγγελλομενη D-gr: *narratio doctrinæ* D-lat.

20. φερεις D: εισφερει א¹: add ρηματα DE. (P has lost a few words in vv 20, 21.) *τίνα θέλει (*mistake in writing* τι αν; *which was the easier on acct of the plural* ταυτα) A B(sic: see table) א p 13[θελη] 40, *quæ hæc sint* [copt] sah: τινα θελοι a 69: [*quinam hi sint* syrr: *quænam sit* æth:] τι αν θελει P: τι αν θελοι DEHL rel vulg (*quidnam velint hæc esse*) Chr Thl[-fin(θελη)]. ταυτα bef θελ. c 137: om ταυτα E.

21. aft επιδ. ins εις αυτους D-gr sah. (ηυκαιρουν, so ABDEא c p 13. 40 Thl-fin.) rec for 2nd η, και (*corrn to avoid the awkwardness of the recurrence of* η *with different meanings*), with EHLP p rel 36 [Syr copt æth] Bas Chr: txt ABDא vulg syr sah [arm]. aft ακουειν ins τι ABא, so [vulg syrr coptt] but om the τι aft λεγ. (*The* repetition *has originated in the transposition for elegance.*)

22. om ο ABא Thl-sif. for εφη, ειπεν [E]א 180.

ceased to be a *κατείδωλος πόλις*,—and the repugnance of the Greeks to images became so great, as to be a principal cause of the schism between the churches of the east and west in the eighth century.' The hill of Mars was so called according to Paus. i. 28. 5, *ὅτι πρῶτος Ἄρης ἐνταῦθα ἐκρίθη*. It was on the west of the Acropolis. The Areiopagus, the highest criminal court of Athens, held its sittings there. To give any account of it is beside the purpose, there being no allusion to it in the text. Full particulars may be found sub voce in Smith's Dict. of Gr. and Rom. Antt.

δυνάμ. γνῶν.] A courteous method of address (not ironical, as Kuin. and Stier). **21.**] A remark of the narrator (as I believe, *Paul himself*, see Prolegg. to Acts, § ii. 14) as a comment on the *καινή* and *ξενίζοντα* of the verse before. **εὐκαιρῶ**, *vaco*, Gloss. Vet. It is not a classic Attic word: *εὐκαιρεῖν οὐδεὶς εἴρηκε τῶν παλαιῶν, Ἕλληνες δέ*, Mœris. "*σχολὴν ἄγω*," *καὶ* "*εὖ σχολῆς ἔχω*," *οὐ* "*σχολάζω·*" *τὸ δὲ* "*εὐκαιρεῖν*" *πάντη ἀδόκιμον*, Thom. Mag. On this character of the Athenians, compare that given of them, Thucyd. iii. 38, *μετὰ καινότητος μὲν λόγου ἀπατᾶσθαι ἄριστοι*, where the scholiast evidently has our text in his mind; *ταῦτα πρὸς τοὺς Ἀθηναίους αἰνίττεται, οὐδέν τι μελετῶντας πλὴν λέγειν τι καὶ ἀκούειν καινόν*:—Demosth. (Philippic. i. p. 43), *ἢ βούλεσθε, εἰπέ μοι, περϊιόντες αὐτῶν πυθέσθαι κατὰ τὴν ἀγορὰν Λέγεταί τι καινόν; γένοιτο γὰρ ἄν τι καινότερον ἢ Μακεδὼν ἀνὴρ κ.τ.λ.* (so also in Philipp. Epist. pp. 156, 157.) The comparative, *καινότερον*, is used as here by Theophr. in giving the character of a loquacious person: *οἷος ἐρωτῆσαι Ἔχεις περὶ τοῦδε εἰπεῖν καινόν; καὶ ἐπιβαλὼν ἐρωτᾷν Μὴ λέγεταί τι καινότερον;* It implies, as we should say, **the very last news.** **22.**] The Commentators vie with each other in admiration of this truly wonderful speech of the great Apostle. Chrysostom: *τοῦτό ἐστι τὸ εἰρημένον τῷ ἀποστόλῳ, ἐγενόμην τοῖς ἀνόμοις ὡς ἄνομος, ἵνα κερδήσω ἀνόμους· Ἀθηναίοις γὰρ δημηγορῶν, οὐκ ἀπὸ προφητῶν οὐδὲ ἀπὸ τοῦ νόμου διελέχθη, ἀλλ' ἀπὸ βωμοῦ τὴν παραίνεσιν ἐποιήσατο· ἀπὸ τῶν οἰκείων αὐτοὺς ἐχειρώσατο δογμάτων· διὸ οὐκ εἶπεν* "*ἄνομος,*" *ἀλλ'* "*ὡς ἄνομος.*" 'The oration of Paul before this assembly is a living proof of his apostolic wisdom and eloquence: we see here how he, according to his own words, could become a Gentile to the Gentiles, to win the Gentiles to the Gospel.' Neander, Pfl. u. L., p. 317. And Stier very properly remarks (Reden der Apostel, ii. 131), 'It was given to the Apostle in this hour, what he should speak; this is plainly to be seen in the following discourse, which we might weary ourselves with praising and admiring in various ways; but far better than all so-called praise from our poor tongues is the

t δεισιδαιμονεστέρους ὑμᾶς θεωρῶ· 23 u διερχόμενος γὰρ καὶ v ἀναθεωρῶν τὰ w σεβάσματα ὑμῶν εὗρον καὶ x βωμὸν ἐν ᾧ y ἐπεγέγραπτο z Ἀγνώστῳ θεῷ. a ὃ οὖν b ἀγνοοῦντες

t here only †. = Xen. Cyr. iii. 3. 58. Jos Antt. xiv. 10. 13, 14. (-μονία, ch. xxv. 19 only.) compar., ver. 21. u absol., ch. viii. 4 reff. v Heb. xiii. 7 only †. ἀ. τὴν κακίαν τῶν ποιημάτων, Diod. Sic. xiv. 109. w 2 Thess. ii. 4 only. Wisd. xiv. 20. xv. 17 Bℵ, F(not A) &c. Bel and Dr. 27 Theod. only. x here only. Jer. vii. 31 al. y Mark xv. 26. Rev. xxi. 12. Heb. viii. 10. x. 16 only. Num. xvii. 2, 3. z here only †. Wisd. xi. 18. xviii. 3. 2 Macc. i. 19. ii. 7 only. a 1 Cor. vii. 24. b ch. xiii. 27 reff.

23. for αναθεωρων, διιστορων D¹(txt D⁵, *perspiciens* D-lat); ιστορων $Clem_1$[txt_1]. σεβαστα ℵ. η (ην D²) γεγραμμενον D rec ον and τουτον

humble recognition, that the Holy Ghost, the spirit of Jesus, has here spoken by the Apostle, and therefore it is that we have in his discourse a masterpiece of apostolic wisdom.' The same Commentator gives the substance of the speech thus: '*He who is* (by your own involuntary confession) *unknown to you Athenians* (religious though you are),—*and yet* (again, by your own confession) *able to be known,—the all-sufficing Creator of the world, Preserver of all creatures, and Governor of mankind, —now commandeth all men* (by me His minister) *to repent, that they may know Him, and to believe in the Man whom He hath raised from the dead, that they may stand in the judgment, which He hath committed to Him.'* **ἄνδρες Ἀθ.**] The regular and dignified appellation familiar to them as used by all their orators,—of whose works Paul could hardly be altogether ignorant. **κατὰ π.**, **in every point of view**: see reff. **δεισιδαιμονεστέρους**] **carrying your religious reverence very far**: an instance of which follows, in that they, not content with worshipping *named* and *known* gods, worshipped even an *unknown* one. *Blame* is neither expressed, nor even implied: but their *exceeding veneration* for religion laid hold of as a *fact*, on which Paul, with exquisite skill, engrafts his proof that he is introducing *no new* gods, but enlightening them with regard to an object of worship on which they were confessedly in the dark. So Chrysost.: **δεισ.**, τουτέστιν εὐλαβεστέρους . . . . . ὥσπερ ἐγκωμιάζειν αὐτοὺς δοκεῖ, οὐδὲν βαρὺ λέγων. To understand this word as E. V. '*too superstitious*' ('superstitiosiores,' Vulg., so Luther, Calov., Wolf), is to miss the fine and delicate tact of the speech, by which he at once parries the charge against him, and in doing so introduces the great Truth which he came to preach. The word itself has both senses: δεισιδαίμων, ὁ εὐσεβής, Hesych.:—ἐν τῷ τοιούτῳ (in battle) γὰρ δὴ οἱ δεισιδαίμονες ἧττον τοὺς ἀνθρώπους φοβοῦνται, Xen. Cyrop. iii. 3. 58: and on the other hand, Theophrast. Char. 16, explains δεισιδαιμονία by δειλία πρὸς τὸ δαιμόνιον: and Pollux, εὐσεβής, θεῶν ἐπιμελής, ὁ δὲ ὑπερτιμῶν, δεισιδαίμων καὶ δεισίθεος. The character thus given of the Athenians is confirmed by Greek writers: thus, Pausan. i. 24. 3, Ἀθηναίοις περισσότερόν τι ἢ τοῖς ἄλλοις ἐς τὰ θεῖά ἐστι σπουδῆς. See other instances in Wetstein. Josephus, c. Apion. ii. 11, calls them εὐσεβεστάτους τῶν Ἑλλήνων. 23.] **ἀναθ.**, **looking over**, 'reconnoitring.' **σεβάσμ.**] not, as E. V., '*devotions*:' but **objects of religious worship**, temples, altars, statues, &c.: see reff. **καί**] over and above the many altars to your own and foreign deities. πολλὰ γὰρ τῶν ξενικῶν ἱερῶν παρεδέξαντο, . . . καὶ δὴ καὶ τὰ Θρᾴκια καὶ τὰ Φρύγια, Strabo, x. p. 472. **ἀγνώστῳ θεῷ**] **To an** (not, *the*) **unknown God.** That this was the veritable inscription on the altars (not as Jerome on Tit. i. 12, vol. vii. p. 707, 'Inscriptio aræ non ita erat ut Paulus asseruit: *ignoto Deo:* sed ita: Diis Asiæ et Europæ et Africæ, Diis ignotis et peregrinis. Verum quia Paulus non pluribus Diis ignotis indigebat sed uno tantum ignoto Deo, singulari verbo usus est'), the words ᾧ ἐπεγέγραπτο, **on which had been inscribed**, are decisive. Meyer well remarks, that the historical fact would be abundantly established from this passage, being Paul's testimony of what he *himself had seen*,—and spoken *to* the Athenian people. But we have our narrative confirmed by the following: Paus. i. 1. 4, ἐνταῦθαι καὶ βωμοὶ θεῶν τε ὀνομαζομένων ἀγνώστων, καὶ ἡρώων καὶ παίδων τῶν Θήσεως καὶ Φαλήρου:—Philostratus, Vita Apollon. vi. 3, σωφρονέστερον τὸ περὶ πάντων θεῶν εὖ λέγειν, καὶ ταῦτα Ἀθήνῃσιν, οὗ καὶ ἀγνώστων δαιμόνων βωμοὶ ἵδρυνται. On which Winer well says, that it by no means follows that each altar had the inscription in the plural, θεοῖς ἀγνώστοις, but more naturally that the plural has been used to suit βωμοί, and that the inscription on each was as here. The commonly cited passage of (Pseudo-) Lucian, Philopatr. 9, and 29, νὴ τὸν ἄγνωστον ἐν Ἀθήναις, is no testimony, the dialogue being spurious, and the reference to our text evident. The origin of such altars has been variously explained: Diog. Laert. (vita Epimenid.) says, that Epime-

[c] εὐσεβεῖτε, [a] τοῦτο ἐγὼ [d] καταγγέλλω ὑμῖν. 24 ὁ θεὸς ὁ
[e] ποιήσας τὸν [e] κόσμον καὶ πάντα τὰ ἐν αὐτῷ, [f] οὗτος [g] οὐρανοῦ καὶ [gh] γῆς [i] ὑπάρχων [gh] κύριος οὐκ ἐν [k] χειροποιήτοις
ναοῖς [k] κατοικεῖ, 25 οὐδὲ ὑπὸ χειρῶν [l] ἀνθρωπίνων [m] θεραπεύεται [n] προσδεόμενος τινός, αὐτὸς διδοὺς πᾶσι ζωὴν καὶ

ABDE HLPℵ a b c d f g h k l m o p 13

c 1 Tim. v. 4 only †. Eur. Phœn. 1331. (see ch. iii. 12 reff.)
d ch. xiii. 5 reff.
e here only †.
f ch. ix. 20 reff.
g Matt. xi. 25. (Gen. xxiv. 7.)
h Josh. iii. 11, 13.
i ch. viii. 16 reff.
k ch. vii. 48 (reff.).
l Rom. vi. 19. 1 Cor. ii. 13. iv. 3. x. 13. James iii. 7. 1 Pet. ii. 13 only. Num. v. 6.
m = here only. Prov. xxix. 26. Isa. liv. 17.
n here only. Prov. xii. 9. Sir. iv. 3 al4.

(*see note*), with A^{2}EHLPℵ^3 13[e sil] 36 rel [coptt(appy) arm] Clem [Ps-]Ath Chr$_1$ Cosm$_1$ Aug: *ο* and *τουτον* p: txt A^{1}BDℵ^1 vulg Orig$_1$ Jer. *υμων* B^1(Tischdf).

24. rec *κυρ.* bef *υπαρχ.*, with DHLP rel Clem$_1$ Chr$_1$ [Thdrt$_1$ Thl-sif] Iren-int$_1$: txt ABEℵ a k m p 13. 40 vulg(*cum sit dom.*) [syrr coptt æth arm] Clem$_1$ Thdrt$_1$ Thl-fin. *κατοικοι* D^1(txt D^8).

25. for *ουδε*, *οδε* D^1(txt D^5). rec *ανθρωπων* (*probably an error*), with E[-gr] HL 13 rel [vulg syrr coptt arm] Chr$_1$ Thdrt$_1$ Cosm$_1$: txt ABDℵ a p vulg [E-lat] Clem$_2$ Thdrt$_1$ Iren-int$_1$.—*ανθρ.* bef *χειρων* ℵ. (P def.) ins *ως* bef *προσδεομενος* ℵ^1(ℵ^3 disapproving) 25 D-lat E-lat [arm] Thdrt(twice, but once in only one ms) Iren-int. for *τινος*, [*τι*] *αυτος* D^8: om D^1 lectt-12-3. om *αυτος* H 16. 37. 56. 100 Chr$_1$. *οτι ουτος ο δους* D^1 ([*οτι ουτος*] *διδους* D-corr$^{1 \text{ or } 2}$): *δους* H Clem$_1$ Chr$_1$.

nides, on occasion of a plague, advised the Athenians to let go white and black sheep from the Areiopagus, and on the spots where they lay down to erect altars **τῷ προσήκοντι θεῷ**: *ὅθεν*, he adds, *ἔτι καὶ νῦν ἔστιν εὑρεῖν κατὰ τοὺς δήμους τῶν Ἀθηναίων βωμοὺς ἀνωνύμους.* Eichhorn conjectures that they may have been ancient altars erected before the use of writing, and thus inscribed in after-times. But I should rather suppose that the above anecdote furnishes the key to the practice: that on the occurrence of any remarkable calamity or deliverance not assignable to the conventionally-received agency of any of the recognized deities, *an unknown God* was reverenced as their author. That the *God of the Jews* was meant (as supposed by Calov., Wolf, al.) is very improbable. 'Quod ignotis Diis altare erexerant, signum erat nihil ipsos tenere certi: habebant quidem ingentem Deorum turbam . . . . . sed dum illis permiscent ignotos Deos, hoc ipso fatentur nihil de vera Divinitate se habere compertum. . . . . Inde apparet inquietudo, quod se nondum defunctos fatentur, ubi popularibus Diis litarunt,' &c. Calvin. **ὃ . . . . τοῦτο**] The *ὅν* and *τοῦτον* of the rec. have probably been alterations from reverential motives. The neuters give surely the deeper, and the more appropriate sense. For Paul does not *identify* the true God with the dedication of, or worship at, the altar mentioned: but speaks of *the Divinity* (*τὸ θεῖον*) of whom they, by this inscription, confessed themselves ignorant. (It may however be a warning of the uncertainty of *à priori* internal evidence for readings, that De Wette and Meyer suppose the masculines to have been altered *to produce this very sense*, and *to avoid the inference that Paul identified the unknown God with the Creator.*) But even a more serious objection lies against the masculines. The sentiment would thus be in direct contradiction to the assertion of Paul himself, 1 Cor. x. 20, **ἃ θύουσιν, δαιμονίοις καὶ οὐ θεῷ θύουσιν.** Compare also our Lord's words, John iv. 22, *ὑμεῖς προσκυνεῖτε* **ὃ** *οὐκ οἴδατε.* In **εὐσεβεῖτε**, we have another confirmation of the sense above insisted on for *δεισιδαιμονεστέρους*. He wishes to commend their reverential spirit, while he shews its misdirection. An important lesson for all who have controversies with Paganism and Romanism. **καταγγ.**] (See above, *καταγγελεύς* ver. 18.) **I am declaring,—making manifest,** to you. *ὑμεῖς με προελάβετε, φησίν· ἔφθασε ὑμῶν ἡ θεραπεία τὸ ἐμὸν κήρυγμα.* Chrys. **24.**] 'No wonder, that the devil, in order to diffuse idolatry, has blotted out among all heathen nations the recognition of *Creation*. The true doctrine of Creation is the proper refutation of all idolatry.' Roos. Einl. in die bibl. Geschicht., cited by Stier, Red. der Apost. ii. 140, who remarks, 'Only on the firm foundation of the Old Testament doctrine of Creation can we rightly build the New Testament doctrine of redemption: and only he, who scripturally believes and apprehends by faith the earliest words of Revelation, concerning a Creator of all things, can also apprehend, know, and scripturally worship, THE MAN, in whom God's word, down to its latest canonical Revelation, gathers together all things.' **οὐκ ἐν χειρ.**] A remarkable reminiscence of the dying speech of Stephen: see ch. vii. 48. Mr. Humphry notices the similarity, but difference in its conclusion, of the argument attributed to Xerxes in Cicero, Leg. ii. 10: 'Xerxes inflammasse

[o] πνοὴν καὶ τὰ πάντα, 26 ἐποίησέν τε ἐξ ἑνὸς [[p] αἵματος]
πᾶν ἔθνος ἀνθρώπων [q] κατοικεῖν [q] ἐπὶ παντὸς [r] προσώπου
τῆς [r] γῆς [s] ὁρίσας [t] προστεταγμένους [u] καιροὺς καὶ τὰς
[v] ὁροθεσίας τῆς [w] κατοικίας αὐτῶν, 27 [xy] ζητεῖν τὸν [y] θεόν,

o — here (ch. ii. 2) only. Gen. ii. 7. p = John i. 13. Hom. Il. ζ. 211. q w. gen., Rev. iii. 10 al8. only. w. acc., Ezek. xxxviii. 12. r = Luke xxi. 35. (xii. 56.) Gen. xi. 8. s Luke xxii. 22. ch. ii. 23. x. 42. xi. 29. ver. 31. Rom. i. 4. Heb. iv. 7 only. L.P.H. Num. xxxiv. 6. t = here only. (ch. x. 33 reff.) u absol., Gal. iv. 10. Gen. i. 14. v here only †. (-θετεῖν, Exod. xix. 12 Alius [Symm. &c.(Field)] in Hexapl.) w here only. Exod. xxxv. 3. Dan. ii. 11 Theod. x = Rom. x. 20 only. Exod. xxxiii. 7. y here only. 1 Chron. xxi. 30.

Steph (for και τα) κατα, with HL P(" certe videtur," Tischdf) rel Thdrt$_1$ Thl-fin. (*Meyer thinks* κατα παντα *ver* 22 *was still in the copyist's mind. At all events, it seems to be an error*) : και κατα 40 : txt ABDE(ℵ) p 36 vulg syr æth arm Clem$_2$ Chr$_2$ Thdrt$_1$ Cosm$_1$ Thl-sif.—om τα ℵ[1][E p].—om και τα παντα 13 Syr.

26. om τε DE syr [arm] : δε m. om αιματος ABℵ p 13. 40 vulg coptt æth[-pl (æth-rom om εξ ενος also)] Clem$_1$ Bede : ins DEHLP rel 36 syrr Thdrt$_2$ Chr$_{sæpe}$ Cosm Thl Iren-int. (*Meyer well remarks on the omission, that* it *is more likely to have happened owing to* **ενος αιματος**, *than that* αιματος *should be a gloss on* ενος,*—for that this would be rather given by* ανθρωπου.) for εθνος, γενος a c 23. 69. 96. 104-37-42 vulg [E-lat] syr-mg Clem Thl-fin Iren-int. ανθρωπου D-gr. rec παν το προσωπον (*corrn for ease of constr*), with HL rel Chr Thdrt$_1$ Cosm : παν προσωπον EP Thdrt$_1$: txt ABDℵ p 13. 36 Clem$_1$. rec προτεταγ., with D[1] 13 b f k [Cosm$_1$], *præfiniens* Iren-int$_1$: τεταγμ. a 14[1]. 69 : txt AB D-corr[1 or 2] EHLPℵ rel [vulg] Clem$_1$ Chr Thl. κατα οροθεσιαν D[1]-gr(txt D[5]) Iren-int.

27. ins μαλιστα bef ζητειν D-gr. rec for θεον, κυριον (*in this case we can hardly suppose* κυρ. *to be genuine, as De W. and Meyer, simply from the* à priori *difficulty of Paul having used the expression when speaking to heathens : the copyists are uniformly so careless where these two words are concerned, as to leave such considerations very uncertain*), with EP rel Cosm$_1$ Thl-sif : το (for τι, or τι το?) θειον εστιν D Iren-int : txt ABHLℵ a d p 13. 36. 40 vulg syrr coptt [arm] Chr$_2$ Thl-fin.

templa Græciæ dicitur, quod parietibus includerent deos, quibus omnia deberent esse patentia et libera, quorumque hic mundus omnis templum esset et domus.'

Where Paul stood, he might see the celebrated colossal statue of Athena Polias, known by the Athenians as ἡ Θεά, standing and keeping guard with spear and shield in the enclosure of the Acropolis.

25.] **θεραπεύεται, is (really and truly) served.** So θεὸς οὐ μυκτηρίζεται, Gal. vi. 7. **προσδ.**] ἐνδεῖσθαι μέν ἐστι τὸ παντελῶς μὴ ἔχειν· προσδεῖσθαι δὲ τὸ ἔχειν μὲν μέρος, ἔτι δὲ δεῖσθαι πρὸς τὸ τέλειον. Ulpian (in Wetst.). As the assertion of Creation contradicted the Epicurean *error*, so this laid hold of that portion of truth, which, however disguised, that school had apprehended: 'Omnis enim per se divûm natura necesse est | Immortali ævo summa cum pace fruatur. | . . . . . | Ipsa suis pollens opibus, *nihil indiga nostri*,' Lucret. i. 57. There is a verse in 2 Macc. xiv. 35, remarkable, as compared with the thoughts and words of Paul here: σύ, κύριε, τῶν ὅλων ἀπροσδεὴς ὑπάρχων, εὐδοκήσας ναὸν τῆς σῆς κατασκηνώσεως ἐν ἡμῖν γενέσθαι. **τινός**] neuter, as referring to the temples and statues offered by the Athenians. **ζωὴν κ. πνοήν**] He is the *Preserver*, as well as the Creator, of all; and all things come to us *from Him*. Compare, on **τὰ πάντα**, David's words, 1 Chron. xxix. 14, σὰ **τὰ πάντα**, καὶ ἐκ τῶν σῶν δεδώκαμέν σοι. **26.] ἐξ ἑνὸς [αἵμ.]** was said, be it remembered, to a people who gave themselves out for αὐτόχθονες : but we must not imagine that to refute this was the *object* of the words: they aim far higher than this, and controvert the whole genius of polytheism, which attributed to the various nations *differing mythical origins*, and *separate guardian gods*. It is remarkable, that though of all people the Jews were the most distinguished in their covenant state from other nations of the earth, yet to them only was given the revelation of the true history of mankind, as all created of *one blood*: a doctrine kept as it were in store for the gospel to proclaim. Not, 'hath made of one blood,' &c., as E. V., but **caused every nation of men (sprung) of one [blood] to dwell,** &c. See Matt. v. 32; Mark vii. 37. **παντὸς προσώπου**] The omission of the art. may be accounted for by the words following ἐπί (see Middleton, vi. 1): or, perhaps, by the parallelism of πᾶν ἔθνος, παντὸς προσώπου: or perhaps, as πᾶς οἶκος Ἰσραήλ, ch. ii. 36, because πρόσωπον τῆς γῆς is regarded as one appellative. See note on πᾶσα οἰκοδομή, Eph. ii. 21. **καιρ. . . . ὁροθ.**] He who was before (ver. 24) the *Creator*, then (ver. 25) the *Preserver*, is now the *Governor* of all men: prescribing to each nation

εἰ ἄρα γε [z] ψηλαφήσειαν αὐτὸν καὶ εὕροιεν, [a] καί [a] γε οὐ
[b] μακρὰν [b] ἀπὸ [c] ἑνὸς ἑκάστου ἡμῶν [d] ὑπάρχοντα· 28 [e] ἐν
αὐτῷ γὰρ ζῶμεν καὶ [f] κινούμεθα καὶ [g] ἐσμέν, ὡς καί τινες ...τινες
τῶν [h] καθ' ὑμᾶς [i] ποιητῶν εἰρήκασιν Τοῦ γὰρ καὶ [k] γένος p.
ἐσμέν. 29 [k] γένος οὖν [d] ὑπάρχοντες τοῦ θεοῦ οὐκ [l] ὀφείλομεν νομίζειν χρυσῷ ἢ ἀργύρῳ ἢ λίθῳ [m] χαράγματι
[n] τέχνης καὶ [o] ἐνθυμήσεως ἀνθρώπου, [p] τὸ [p] θεῖον εἶναι

ABDE HLPℵ a b c d f g h k l m o 13

z = here (Luke xxiv. 39. Heb. xii. 18. 1 John i. 1) only. Isa. lix. 10. opt., ch. xxiv. 19 reff. a ch. ii. 18 reff. b Matt. viii. 30. Mark xii. 34. Luke vii. 6. xv. 20. John xxi. 8. Eph. ii. 13, 17. (ch. xxii. 21 reff.) Deut. xxx. 11. c w. gen. partit., Luke iv. 40. xvi. 5. ch. ii. 3. xxi. 26. 1 Thess. ii. 11 al. L.P. d ch. ii. 30. viii. 16 reff. e cf. 1 Pet. i. 5, 22. f = here (Matt. xxiii. 4. xxvii. 39 ‖ Mk. ch. xxi. 30. xxiv. 5. Rev. ii. 5. vi. 14) only. Gen. vii. 14, 21 al. Xen. Mem. i. 1. 14. g emphat., Matt. ii. 18. xxiii. 30 al. h ch. xviii. 15 reff. i = here only. (Rom. ii. 13 reff.) k = ch. iv. 6 reff. l = 1 Cor. xi. 7, 10. Rom. xv. 1. m = here (Rev. xiii. 16, 17 al5.) only †. n = here only. (ch. xviii. 3 reff.) 3 Kings vii. 14. o = here (Matt. ix. 4. xii. 25. Heb. iv. 12) only †. (Job xxi. 27 Symm.) p here only †. Xen. Mem. i. 4. 18. (2 Pet. i. 3, 4. Exod. xxxi. 3.)

ψηλαφησαισαν D : -σαιεν a 3. 64. 95[1]. 105 : -σειεν Eℵ 40 Œc. αυτο D[1] (txt D[4]) [Iren-int$_1$]. for και (bef ευρ.), η AD 36. 40 vulg(not tol) sah [Clem$_1$] Iren-int$_1$. ευροισαν D[1]. rec καιτοιγε (*alteration to more usual word; the readg* και τοι *is not, as Meyer thinks, any sign that rec is genuine, but merely that* τοι *in the marg had been sometimes prefixed to the* γε, *sometimes substituted for it*), with P[2]ℵ a Chr$_1$ Cosm$_1$ Thl-fin : καιτοι AE Clem : και τε D[1] : txt B [D-corr] HLP[1] p 13. 36 rel Did Thl-sif. ου μακραν ου(ων D[3]) αφ D. υμων A[1]L k m. υπαρχοντος E lect-12 Clem : απεχοντα [a] 69. 98-marg 105 : om D[1](txt D[5]).

28. αυτη D[1](txt D[3](?)). aft εσμεν ins το καθ ημεραν D. ωσπερ D. ημας B 33. 68. 95-6. 105-37 copt. των κ. υμ. bef τινες D. om ποιητων D [æth-rom] Iren-int Ambr$_{[sæpe]}$. for του, τουτου D[1] e l[2] 19[2]. 21. 96 Iren-int : αυτου E[2] 35. 68 : *ipsius* E-lat vulg Hil$_1$: τουτων 3 : τουτο 137.

29. ins ουτε bef χρυσω D[1][and lat]. χρυσιω η αργυριω AE 40 Damasc$_3$ Thl-fin : χρυσιω η αργυρω ℵ [Thdrt-ed$_1$]. for και, η D-gr Iren-int$_r$: om coptt æth-rom. ανθρωπων E-gr æth.

its space to dwell in, and its time of endurance. **προςτετ.**, not **προτ.**, appointed, 'ordered by Him.' **27.**] **ζητεῖν** does not depend on ἐποίησεν, but gives the intent of the above-mentioned providential arrangement: **that they might seek God.** τὸν κύριον (as rec. and two uncial MSS. have) has probably been a careless mistake of a transcriber: τί τὸ θεῖόν ἐστιν, which appears to have been the reading of D, is one of its own strange glosses. **εἰ ἄρα**] **if by any chance,** denoting a contingency apparently not very likely to happen, see Hartung, Partikellehre, i. 440. **ψηλαφήσειαν**] Originally an Æolic form, but frequent in Attic Greek, for ψηλαφήσαιεν, see Luke vi. 11. On the word itself, compare Aristoph. (Pax, 691): προτοῦ μὲν οὖν | ἐψηλαφῶμεν ἐν σκότῳ τὰ πράγματα, | νυνὶ δ' ἅπαντα πρὸς λύχνον βουλεύσομεν. These lines, as Mr. Humphry observes, 'seem at once to illustrate the figurative use of the verb, and to express the condition of man prior and subsequent to revelation.' **καί γε . . . .**] 'Not that HE *is distant from us*, but that we are ignorant of Him.' See Rom. x. 6, 8; Jer. xxiii. 23, 24. **καί γε**, 'et quidem:' see Hartung, Partikellehre, i. 398 f.
28.] There is no justification for *the pantheist* in this. It is properly said only of the race of *men*, as being His offspring, bound to Him: proceeding from, and upheld by, and therefore living, moving, and being *in* Him:—but even in a wider sense *His Being*, though a separate objective Personality, involves and contains that of His creatures. See Eph. i. 10, where the same is said of Christ. **ἐν αὐτῷ** must not be taken for '*by* Him:' the subsequent citation would in that case be irrelevant.
ζῶμ. κιν. ἐσμ.] 'A climax: *out of* God we should have no *Life*, nor even *movement* (which some things without life have, plants, water, &c.), nay, not any *existence* at all (we should not have *been*).' Meyer. Storr's explanation of ζῶμεν by 'vivimus beate ac hilare,' and Kuinoel and Olshausen's of ἐσμέν by '*real being*,' i.e. '*the spiritual life*,' are evidently beside the purpose; the intent being to shew the *absolute dependence for every thing* of man on God,—and thence the *absurdity of supposing the Godhead like to the works of his* (man's) *hands.* **τοῦ γὰρ κ. γ. ἐσμ.**] Aratus, in the opening lines of the Phænomena . . . . πάντη δὲ Διὸς κεχρήμεθα πάντες· τοῦ γὰρ καὶ γένος ἐσμέν. Kleanthes also, Hymn. in Jov. 5, has ἐκ σοῦ γὰρ γένος ἐσμέν. Aratus was a *native of Tarsus*, about 270 B.C., and wrote astronomical poems, of which two, the φαινόμενα and διοσημεία, remain. Kleanthes was born at Assos, in Troas, about 300 B.C. The Apostle, by the plural, seems to have both poets in his

ὅμοιον. 30 τοὺς μὲν οὖν [q] χρόνους τῆς [r] ἀγνοίας [s] ὑπεριδὼν
ὁ θεὸς [t] τὰ [t] νῦν [u] παραγγέλλει τοῖς ἀνθρώποις πάντας
[v] πανταχοῦ [w] μετανοεῖν, 31 [x] καθότι [y] ἔστησεν ἡμέραν ἐν
ᾗ μέλλει [z] κρίνειν τὴν [a] οἰκουμένην ἐν [b] δικαιοσύνῃ, [c] ἐν
ἀνδρὶ [d] ᾧ [e] ὥρισεν, [f] πίστιν [fg] παρασχὼν πᾶσιν, [h] ἀναστήσας
αὐτὸν [h] ἐκ νεκρῶν. 32 ἀκούσαντες δὲ [i] ἀνάστασιν [i] νεκρῶν
οἱ μὲν [k] ἐχλεύαζον, οἱ δὲ εἶπαν Ἀκουσόμεθά σου περὶ
τούτου καὶ πάλιν· 33 [l] οὕτως ὁ Παῦλος [m] ἐξῆλθεν ἐκ

q constr., ch. iii. 21 reff. r ch. iii. 17. Eph. iv. 18. 1 Pet. i. 14 only. Levit. xxii. 14. s here only. Levit. xx. 4. Deut. xxii. 3. ὑπεριδὼν τῆς ἰδίας ἀσφαλείας, Dion. Hal. Antt. ii. 66. t ch. iv. 29 reff. u ch. i. 4 reff. v Mark i. 28. xvi. 20. Luke ix. 6. ch. xxiv. 3. xxviii. 22. 1 Cor. iv. 17 only. Isa. xlii. 22. (-χῇ, ch. xxi. 28.) w absol., ch. ii. 38. iii. 19. xxvi. 20 al. x = ch. ii. 24 reff. y = here only. z = Rom. iii. 6 (κόσμον). Psa. ix. 8. xcv. 13. xcvii. 10. a = ch. xix. 27 reff. b absol., ch. xxiv. 25. Rom. ix. 28. xlv. 17 al. Ps. as above (z). Sir. xiv. 26. c = Matt. xii. 24. Luke xi. 15. 1 Cor. vi. 2. d attr., ch. i. 1 reff. e = ch. x. 42. (ver. 26 reff.) f here only. Jos. Antt. xv. 7. 10, πίστ. παρεῖχε τ. λόγου τ. Βάβα παῖδας. g = ch. xvi. 16 reff. h ch. ii. 24 reff. i 1 Cor. xv. 12 reff. k here only †. Wisd. xi. 15. 2 Macc. vii. 27 only. Prov. xiv. 9 Aquil. (ἐκχλ. ib. Symm. διαχλ., ch. ii. 13.) l Rom. v. 12 reff. m 2 Cor. vi. 17, from Isa. lii. 11.

30. aft της αγνοιας ins ταυτης D¹[and lat] vulg. και τους χρον. μεν ουν E: *et tempora quidem* vulg. παριδων D¹(txt D-corr): [υ]περιδων D⁴ 103: *despiciens* vulg. απαγγελλει BN¹ [Ath-ms$_1$]. rec πασι (*alteration, to agree with* ανθρωποις. *Meyer and De Wette's idea, that* πασι *was altered to* παντας *to soften the assertion that God commanded* ανθ. πασι πανταχου,—*is in the highest degree improbable*), with HLP rel æth Ps-Ath$_1$ Chr Thdrt Cosm Thl Iren-int: ινα παντες D¹: *omnibus ut omnes* Syr: txt ABD⁴EN 13. 36. 40 [spec] Ath$_1$ Cyr$_1$: *ut omnes ubique pœnitentiam agant* vulg D-lat.

31. rec διοτι (*explan of* καθοτι), with HL rel Chr$_1$ Thl-sif: καθο 18. 36. 180: txt ABDEPN a c 13 Ath$_1$ [Ps-Ath$_1$ Bas$_1$] Thdrt$_3$ Cyr$_1$ Chron Thl-fin. [εστησαν D-gr.] for εν η μ. κρ., κρειναι D: *judicari* Iren-int$_1$; *judicare* Aug$_1$. om 2nd εν D-gr. aft ανδρι ins ιησου D Iren-int. παρεσχειν(sic) *exibere* D, παρασχειν 32. 57.

32. (ειπαν, so BEN.) rec παλιν περι τουτου. **33** και ουτως, with HLP rel 36 [syrr copt] Chr$_1$ Thl-sif: [περι τ. παλ. κ. ουτ. E:] txt AB(D)N 13. 40 [(vulg] arm) Thl-fin.—om και D [vulg arm].

mind. The τοῦ refers to *Zeus* in both cases, the admission being taken as a portion of truth regarding the Supreme God, which even heathen poets confessed. The καί has no connexion *here*, but is (see above) part of the verse in Aratus.

30. ὑπεριδών] In this word lie treasures of mercy for those who lived in the times of ignorance. God **overlooked** them [the rendering of the E. V. bears the same meaning, but is to our ears in these days objectionable]: i. e. corrected not this *ignorance itself* as a sin, but *the abuses even of this*, by which the heathen sunk into deeper degradation. The same argument is treated more at length in Rom. i. ii. The πᾶσι of the rec. and ἵνα πάντες of D¹ have both been corrections occasioned by the apparent difficulty of τοῖς ἀνθρώποις πάντας. The genuine reading gives the emphatic πάντας πανταχοῦ, following on the foregoing assertion of vv. 25, 26, its proper place. **31. καθότι**] See var. read. and reff.:—used by Luke and him only: *'seeing that,'* **inasmuch as. ἐν δικαιοσ.**] δικαιοσ. is the character of the judgment,—the element, of which it shall consist. **ἐν ἀνδρί**] Not, 'in (by) *a* man,' but **by** (i. e. in the person of) *the* **man**: the art. is omitted after the preposition: see Midd. vi. 1. The **ἐν** is not instrumental, properly speaking, here or any where else. Its judicial use is only a particular case of its usage of *investiture* or *elementary condition*: *in* the judge the judgment consists, is constituted; he is its vehicle and expression. See ref. 1 Cor. and note for examples of this use. **πίστ. κ.τ.λ.**] 'Quia res erat vix credibilis, argumentum adfert eximium.' Grotius.

32. ἀνάστ. νεκρ.] Perhaps here, *'when they heard of a resurrection of dead men,'* viz. of that of Christ, νεκρῶν being generic. But the same words are used in ref. 1 Cor. πῶς λέγουσιν ἐν ὑμῖν τινες ὅτι **ἀνάστασις νεκρῶν** οὐκ ἔστιν; so that I would rather take them here to mean that they inferred the general possibility of the resurrection of the dead, as a tenet of Paul's, from the one case which he mentioned. **οἱ . . . . οἱ δέ**] We must not allot these two parties as some have done, the former to the Epicureans, the latter to the Stoics: the description is general. The words **ἀκουσόμεθα . . . .** need not be taken as ironical. The hearing not having taken place is no proof that it was not intended at the time: and the distinction between these and the mockers seems to imply that they were in earnest.

33. οὕτως] 'In this state of the popular mind:' (with an expectation of

[mn] μέσου αὐτῶν· 34 τινὲς δὲ ἄνδρες [o] κολληθέντες αὐτῷ
[p] ἐπίστευσαν, ἐν οἷς καὶ Διονύσιος ὁ Ἀρεοπαγίτης καὶ γυνὴ
ὀνόματι Δάμαρις καὶ [q] ἕτεροι σὺν αὐτοῖς. XVIII. 1 Μετὰ
[δὲ] ταῦτα [r] χωρισθεὶς ἐκ τῶν Ἀθηνῶν ἦλθεν εἰς Κόρινθον,
2 καὶ εὑρών τινα Ἰουδαῖον ὀνόματι Ἀκύλαν, Ποντικὸν
[s] τῷ [st] γένει, [u] προσφάτως ἐληλυθότα ἀπὸ τῆς Ἰταλίας, καὶ
Πρίσκιλλαν γυναῖκα αὐτοῦ, διὰ τὸ [v] διατεταχέναι Κλαύ-
διον [r] χωρίζεσθαι πάντας τοὺς Ἰουδαίους ἀπὸ τῆς Ῥώμης,

ABDE HLP‭א a b c d f g h k l m o 13

n as above (m). Matt. xiii. 49. ch. xxiii. 10. 1 Cor. v. 2. Col. ii. 14. 2 Thess. ii. 7 only. Gen. xxxv. 2.
o ch. v. 13 reff.
p absol., ch. xv. 5 reff.
q = ch. xix. 39.
r w. ἐκ, here only †. w. ἀπό, ch. i. 4. 1 Chron. xii. 8.
s Mark vii. 26. ch. iv. 36. ver. 24.
t = ch. vii. 19. 2 Cor. xi. 26. Esth. ii. 10.
u here only. Deut. xxiv. 5. (-τος, Heb. x. 20.)
v Luke viii. 55. 1 Cor. vii. 17 al. L.P., exc. Matt. xi. 1. Ezek. xxi. 19. (-ταγή, ch. vii. 53.)

34. εκολληθησαν D[1][-gr](txt D[4]). for ο (bef αρεοπ.), τις D*: om B. aft αρεοπ. ins ευσχημων *complacens* D. om και γυν. ον. δ. D: aft γυν. ins τιμια E.

Chap. XVIII. **1.** om δε A B[μεταυτα B[1]] ‭א a 13 vulg copt [arm]: ins (D)EHLP rel 36 [syr sah Orig-int$_1$] Chr$_1$.—και μετα ταυτα Syr æth.—αναχωρησας δε, omg μετα ταυτα, D. rec aft χωρισθεις ins ο παυλος (*inserted just as δε was omitted, at beginning of an ecclesiastical portion*), with AEHLP rel 36 [syrr æth arm Orig-int] Chr: om BD‭א 13 vulg [copt] sah. for εκ, απο D.

2. [ευρον P e g[1]. εισεληλ. 13:] εληλυθα D[1](txt D[2]). τεταχεναι DELP f k m 13: τεχεναι(sic) ‭א[1]: προστεταχ. a d: διατεταχθεναι 137-73. κλαυδιος D[1] (txt D-corr[1]): om B. om τους D. rec (for 2nd απο) εκ (*prob corrn to suit χωρισθ. εκ in ver 1. So De Wette: Meyer thinks the απο to have been a corrn to suit απο της ιταλ., but the other suppn is much more likely, the same verb occurring in both*), with HP c f h l Chr$_1$: om 13: txt ABDEL‭א rel. aft ρωμης ins οι κε

being heard again?) [The "so" of the E. V. does not give this forcibly enough, but looks like a mere particle of transition.]

34. Διονύσιος ὁ Ἀρ.] Nothing more is known of him. Euseb. H. E. iii. 4; iv. 23, relates that he was bishop of Athens, and Niceph. iii. 11, that he died a martyr. The writings which go by his name are undoubtedly spurious.

γυνή] Not, as Chrys., de Sacerd. iv. 7, vol. i. p. 412, seems to infer from the form of the expression,—ἠκολούθησεν αὐτῷ μετὰ τῆς γυναικός, *the wife* of Dionysius: this would have been ἡ γυνὴ αὐτοῦ.

Chap. XVIII. **1.]** Corinth was at this time a *colony* (see note, ch. xvi. 12), the *capital of the Roman province of Achaia*, and *the residence of the proconsul*. For further particulars, see Prolegg. to 1 Cor. § ii.

2. Ἰουδαῖον] It appears that Aquila and Priscilla were *not Christians* at this time: it is the similarity of employment only which draws them to Paul, and their conversion is left to be inferred as taking place in consequence: see ver. 26.

Ποντικὸν τ. γ.] It is remarkable, that *Pontius Aquila* is a name found in the Pontian gens at Rome more than once in the days of the Republic (see Cicero, ad Fam. x. 33; Suet., Jul. Cæs. 78; Smith's Dict. of Biogr., art. Aquila, Pontius); whence some have supposed that this may have been a freedman of a Pontius Aquila, and that **Ποντ. τῷ γένει** may have been an inference from his name. But besides that Luke's acquaintance with the real origin of Aquila could hardly but have been accurate,—*Aquila*, the translator of the O. T. into Greek, was *also a native of Pontus*.

From the notices of Aquila and Priscilla in the Epistles, they appear to have travelled, fixing their abode by turns in different principal cities, for the sake of their business. In ver. 19, we have them left at Ephesus (see also ver. 26); in 1 Cor. xvi. 19, still there; in Rom. xvi. 3 ff., again at Rome; in 2 Tim. iv. 19, again at Ephesus.

διὰ τὸ διατεταχέναι . . .] Suet. Claud. 25, says, 'Judæos impulsore Chresto assidue tumultuantes Roma expulit:' but as he gives this without any fixed note of time,—as the words 'impulsore Chresto' may be taken in three ways (as indicative either (1) of an actual leader of that name, or (2) of some tumult connected with the expectations of a Messiah, or (3) of some dispute about Christianity),—Neander well observes, that after all which has been said on it, no secure historical inference respecting the date of the event, or its connexion with any Christian church at Rome, can be drawn. It was *as a Jew* that Aquila was driven from Rome: and there is not a word of Christians here. If one could identify this expulsion of the Jews with that of the 'mathematici' in Tacitus (Ann. xii. 52), which took place Fausto Sulla, Salv. Othone Coss. (A.D. 52), we might be on surer ground,—but this is very uncertain, and even improbable. The two

[w] προςῆλθεν αὐτοῖς, 3 καὶ διὰ τὸ [x] ὁμότεχνον εἶναι [y] ἔμενεν
[y] παρ' αὐτοῖς καὶ [z] ἠργάζετο, ἦσαν γὰρ [a] σκηνοποιοὶ τῇ
[b] τέχνῃ· 4 [c] διελέγετο δὲ ἐν τῇ συναγωγῇ [d] κατὰ πᾶν
σάββατον, [e] ἔπειθέν τε Ἰουδαίους καὶ Ἕλληνας. 5 ὡς δὲ
[f] κατῆλθον ἀπὸ τῆς Μακεδονίας ὅ τε Σίλας καὶ ὁ Τιμόθεος, [g] συνείχετο τῷ λόγῳ ὁ Παῦλος, [h] διαμαρτυρόμενος

w = here only. see ch. x. 28. x here only +. y ch. ix. 43 reff. z absol., Matt. xxi. 28. xxv. 16. Luke xiii. 14. John ix. 4. 1 Cor. ix. 6. 1 Thess. ii. 9 al. Exod. v. 18. a here only +. (-ποιεῖν, Isa. xxii. 15 Symm. -ποιΐα, Deut. xxxi. 10 LXX-mss. & Alius in Hexapl.) b = Rev. xviii. 22 (ch. xvii. 29) only. Sir. xxxviii. 34. (-νίτης, ch. xix. 24.) c = ch. xvii. 2 reff. absol., ch. xix. 8, 9. xx. 9. Sir. xiv. 20, BℵF(not A) Ald. d ch. xiii. 27 reff. e = ch. xix. 26. 2 Cor. v. 11. Wisd. xvi. 8. f = ch. viii. 5 reff. w. ἀπό, ch. xi. 27. xii. 19. xv. 1. g 2 Cor. v. 14 reff. Wisd. xvii. 20. h ch. viii. 25 reff.

κατωκησεν(-σαν D-corr[1]) εις την αχαιαν D, simly syr-mg. αυτω D[1]-gr(txt D[2]). add ο παυλος D.

3. om ειναι D. εμεινεν E[-gr] HL [a c(?) d m syr] Chr_1 Thl: *manebat* E-lat. προς αυτους D. (ηργαζ., so AB[1]DE[ℵ] k 13: -ζοντο ℵ[1][B copt(Tischdf) Orig-int]). om last clause D. rec την τεχνην, with H rel 36 Thl: txt ABELPℵ c g l 13. 40 Chr_2.

4. om ver am[1] fuld lat-mss-in-Bede: εισπορευομενος δε εις την συναγωγην κατα παν σαββατον διελεγετο και εντιθεις [*interponens*] το ονομα του κυριου ιησου και (om και D-corr) επιθεν δε [om D-lat] ου μονον ιουδαιους αλλα και ελληνας D; simly vulg-ed syr-mg aft σαββατον ins εντιθεις το ονομα του κυριου ιησου. for παν, μιαν H: παντα 13.

5. for ως δε κατηλθον, παρεγενοντο δε D. om της L h k. for ο τε, τοτε D[1]-gr: οτι ο. om ο bef τιμ. D 42, 173. rec for τω λογω, τω πνευματι (*substitution from misunderstanding; or perhaps, as Meyer, originally a scholium on συνειχετο, and thence has usurped the place of the origl* τω λογω), with H [L(sic, Treg)] P rel 36 syr-mg arm Chr_1: txt ABDEℵ c 13. 40 vulg syrr coptt æth Bas_2 $Thdrt_1$. om ὁ (bef παυ.) D. διαμαρτυρουμενος D[1] 40. 65 Thl-fin.

could hardly have been *united*. The circumstance related by Dio Cassius, lx. 6, which seems to contradict Suetonius and our text,—τοὺς Ἰουδαίους πλεονάσαντας αὖθις, ὥστε χαλεπῶς ἂν ἄνευ ταραχῆς ὑπὸ τοῦ ὄχλου σφῶν τῆς πόλεως εἰρχθῆναι, οὐκ ἐξήλασε μέν, τῷ δὲ πατρίῳ νόμῳ βίῳ χρωμένους ἐκέλευσε μὴ συναθροίζεσθαι,—probably describes a step taken by Claudius *previously* to this expulsion, which not improbably occasioned the tumults which made the expulsion necessary. The edict soon became invalid, or the prohibition was taken off: we find Aquila at Rome, Rom. xvi. 3, and many Jews resident there, ch. xxviii. 17 ff. 3. **ἠργάζετο**] "The Jewish Rabbis having no state pay, it was their practice to teach their children a trade. 'What is commanded of a father towards his son?' asks a Talmudic writer. 'To circumcise him, to teach him the law, to teach him a trade.' Rabbi Judah saith, 'He that teacheth not his son a trade, doth the same as if he taught him to be a thief:' and Rabban Gamaliel saith, 'He that hath a trade in his hand, to what is he like? He is like a vineyard that is fenced.'" C. and H. i. p. 58.

The places where Paul refers to his supporting himself by his own manual labour are,—ch. xx. 34 (Ephesus):—1 Cor. ix. 12 ff.; 2 Cor. vii. 2 (Corinth):—1 Thess. ii. 9; 2 Thess. iii. 8 (Thessalonica). In 2 Cor. xi. 9, we learn that supplies were also brought to him at Corinth from Macedonia, i. e. Philippi, see Phil. iv. 15. **σκηνοποιοί**] The general opinion now is, that Paul was a maker of tents from the 'cilicium,' or hair-cloth of Cilician goats. Thus Kuinoel, citing from Hug and Eichhorn, says of the former, "Ad hanc sententiam comprobandam monuit, Ciliciam, Pauli patriam, refertam fuisse hircis et capris villosis, eorumque villis Cilices usos esse ad conficiendum pannum, *Cilicium* inde dictum. Suidas: Κίλικος τράγος· ὁ δασύς· τοιοῦτοι γὰρ ἐν Κιλικίᾳ γίνονται τράγοι, ὅθεν καὶ τὰ ἐκ τῶν τριχῶν συντιθέμενα Κιλίκια καλοῦνται. Hoc panno usos esse milites, nautas, Nomadas, ad tentoria conficienda, v. Vegetius, de Re Mil. iv. 6. Plin. N. H. vi. 28, 'Nomades, infestatoresque Chaldæorum scenitæ . . . . et ipsi vagi, sed a tabernaculis cognominati, quæ *ciliciis* metantur, ubi libuit.' Solin. 33, 'Scenitæ caussam nominis inde ducunt, quod tentoriis succedunt, nec alias domos habent, ipsa autem tentoria *cilicina* sunt; ita nuncupantur velamenta caprarum pilis texta.'" If it be objected, that Paul would hardly find the raw material for this work in cities far from Cilicia, it may be answered, that this would not be required in the fabrication of *tents* from the *hair-cloth,* which doubtless itself would be an article of commerce in the markets of Greece. Chrysost. calls Paul sometimes

τοῖς Ἰουδαίοις τὸν χριστὸν Ἰησοῦν. 6 [i] ἀντιτασσομένων
δὲ αὐτῶν καὶ [k] βλασφημούντων [l] ἐκτιναξάμενος τὰ ἱμάτια
εἶπεν πρὸς αὐτοὺς Τὸ αἷμα ὑμῶν [m] ἐπὶ τὴν κεφαλὴν ὑμῶν·
[n] καθαρὸς ἐγὼ [o] ἀπὸ τοῦ [o] νῦν εἰς τὰ ἔθνη πορεύσομαι.
7 καὶ [p] μεταβὰς ἐκεῖθεν ἦλθεν εἰς οἰκίαν τινὸς ὀνόματι
Ἰούστου [qr] σεβομένου τὸν [r] θεόν, οὗ ἡ οἰκία ἦν [s] συνομοροῦσα
τῇ συναγωγῇ. 8 Κρίσπος δὲ ὁ [t] ἀρχισυνάγωγος [u] ἐπίστευσεν τῷ κυρίῳ σὺν ὅλῳ τῷ [v] οἴκῳ αὐτοῦ, καὶ πολλοὶ
τῶν Κορινθίων ἀκούοντες [w] ἐπίστευον καὶ ἐβαπτίζοντο.

ABDE HLPℵ a b c d f g h k l m o 13

i Rom. xiii. 2. James iv. 6. v. 6. 1 Pet. v. 5 (from Prov. iii. 34) only. 3 Kings xi. 34. Hos. i. 6 only.
k = ch. xiii. 45 reff.
l ch. xiii. 51 reff.
m = ch. xiii. 11. Matt. xxvii. 25. Rom. i. 18. ii. 2, 9. 2 Kings i. 16.
n = ch. xx. 26. Gen. xxiv. 8.
o Luke i. 48 al3. 2 Cor. v. 16. L.P. [exc. John viii. 11.] Ps. cxii. 2.
p Matt. xi. 1 al.† Wisd. vii. 27. xix. 19. 2 Macc. vi. 1, 9, 24 only.
q ch. xiii. 43 reff.
r = ch. xvi. 14. ver. 13 only.
s here only †.
t Mark v. 22, &c. Luke viii. 49. xiii. 14. ch. xiii. 15. ver. 17 only †.
u = w. dat., ch. xvi. 34 reff.
v ch. x. 2 reff.
w absol., ch. xv. 5 reff.

om τοις ιουδ. AH 177[1]. ins ειναι bef τ. χριστ. (*see ver* 28) ABDℵ a b d k o 13. 36 vulg Syr syr-w-ast [coptt æth] arm Bas_2 Thl-fin: om EHLP rel Chr Thdrt Thl-sif. ins κυριον bef ιησ. D. om ιησ. P.

6. at beg ins πολλου δε[*que*] λογου γεινομενου και γραφων διερμηνευομενων D syr-mg. for αντιτασσ., (ε)τι τασσ. D[1]-gr(txt D[4]): ανθισταμενων 15-8. 36. (D[1]-gr is very imperf in vv 6, 7.) aft εκτιναξ. ins ο παυλος D tol. aft τα ιματια ins αυτου D b k o [vulg-ed tol syrr copt] sah [æth] Thl-sif; pref, 40. 69. εγω α(φ υμω)ν νυν D[1](?) (and lat). πορευομαι D[1]H[1]L Chr(some mss).

7. om και D[1](? ins D[2]). for εκειθεν, (απο του ακυ)λα D[1](? [δε απο ακ., Scr]) 137. εισηλθεν A D[1](?) ℵ a 13 vulg Syr syr-mg sah æth[(appy) arm] Thl-fin: txt BD[2]E HL[P] rel 36 syr-txt copt Chr_1 Thl-sif. [for οικιαν, τον οικον D[1].] ονοματ(ο)ς D[1](txt D[2]): om A 2. 30. 104 æth. ins τιτιου bef ιουστου B[1] D[2]-gr syr; τιτου EPℵ 7. 15. 36. 81 vulg copt arm [Thl-fin] Jer, and (omg ιουστου) 2. 30 Syr sah (*originally prob a mistake arising from* ονοματιιουστ., *the* τι. *being taken for the abbreviated form of* τιτου *or* τιτιου): om AB[2] D[1][and lat] HL æth Chr Thl-sif. συνομοροουσα AD.

8. ο δε αρχισ. κρισπ. D. εις τον κυριον [*in domino*] D. for συν, εν H[1][corrd eadem manu?]. ακουσαντες HL c m Thl. at end add πιστευοντες τω θεω δια τ. ονοματος του κυριου ημων ιησου χριστου D, somewhat simly [from δια] syr-w-ast.

σκηνοῤῥάφος, sometimes σκυτοτόμος, a leather-cutter, imagining that the tents were made of leather; ἐπὶ σκηνοῤῥαφείου ἑστὼς δέρματα ἔῤῥαπτε (in Catena).

5.] See ch. xvii. 15; 1 Thess. iii. 6.

* **συνείχετο τῷ λόγῳ**] '*When Silas and Timotheus arrived* [see ch. xvii. 15 note] *from Macedonia, they found Paul anxiously occupied in discoursing to the Jews.*' This I believe to be the meaning: that they found him in a state of more than ordinary anxiety,—more than usually absorbed in the work of testifying to the Jews (see reff.):—a crisis in the work being imminent, which resulted in their rejection of the word of life. (On the whole character of his early preaching at Corinth, see notes, 1 Cor. ii. 1—5.) Thus only, the δέ in ver. 5 and that in ver. 6 will both be satisfied: **he discoursed in the synagogue, &c. . . . . but when Silas and Timotheus arrived, he was earnestly occupied in discoursing, &c. But, as they opposed themselves and blasphemed, &c.** Wordsworth adopts the view that after the arrival of Silas and Timotheus with supplies from Macedonia, Paul gave up his tent-making and gave himself up (συνείχετο) to preaching. But surely this is ungrammatical. The aor. (ὡς κατῆλθον) and imperf. (συνείχετο) require the rendering 'when they arrived, they found him συνεχόμενον.'

6.] **αἷμα** as in ch. xx. 26. The image and nearly the words, are from Ezek. xxxiii. 4. De Wette should have known better than to call a citation from the LXX an 'unpaulinischer Sprachgebrauch.' **ἀπὸ τοῦ νῦν**] Not *absolutely*, only *at Corinth*: for ver. 19 we find him arguing with the Jews again in the synagogue at Ephesus. I have adopted the punctuation of Lachmann, erasing the colon after ἐγώ: **I shall henceforth with a pure conscience go to the Gentiles.**

7.] In order to shew that he henceforth separated himself from the Jews, he, on leaving the synagogue, went no longer to the house of the Jew Aquila (who appears *afterwards* to have been converted), but to the house of a Gentile proselyte of the gate, close to the synagogue: q. d. 'in the sight of all the congregation in the synagogue:' for this seems to be the object in mentioning the circumstance.

8.] On this, a schism took place among the Jews. The ruler of the synagogue attached himself to Paul, and was, together with Gaius, baptized by the Apostle himself (1 Cor. i.

9 εἶπεν δὲ ὁ κύριος [x] ἐν [x] νυκτὶ δι' [y] ὁράματος τῷ Παύλῳ
Μὴ φοβοῦ, ἀλλὰ λάλει καὶ μὴ [z] σιωπήσῃς, 10 [a] διότι ἐγώ
[b] εἰμι μετὰ σοῦ, καὶ οὐδεὶς [c] ἐπιθήσεταί σοι [d] τοῦ [e] κακῶσαί
σε, [a] διότι λαός ἐστί μοι πολὺς ἐν τῇ πόλει ταύτῃ.
11 [f] ἐκάθισεν δὲ ἐνιαυτὸν καὶ μῆνας ἓξ [g] διδάσκων ἐν αὐτοῖς
τὸν [g] λόγον τοῦ θεοῦ. 12 Γαλλιωνος δὲ [h] ἀνθυπάτου ὄντος
τῆς Ἀχαΐας [i] κατεπέστησαν [k] ὁμοθυμαδὸν οἱ Ἰουδαῖοι τῷ

x 1 Thess. v. 2 only. Ps. lxxxvii. 1.
y ch. vii. 31 reff.
z Luke i. 20 al. Acts, her e only. Paul, never. Isa. xlii. 14.
a Luke i. 13 al. L.P. principally. Isa. xii. 2.
b ch. x. 38 reff.
c = here only. Gen. xliii. 18.
d constr., 1 Cor. x. 13 reff.
e ch. vii. 6 reff.
f = Luke xxiv. 49. Judg. xi. 17.
g ch. xi. 1 reff.
h ch. xiii. 7 reff.
i here only †.
k ch. i. 14 reff.

9. om ο D. rec δι οραματος bef εν νυκτι, with E H[της νυκτος] LP rel syr copt [sah] æth Chr_1: δι ορ. τω παυλω εν νυκτι D Thl-sif: εν οραματι της νυκτος c: εν οραματι (omg εν νυκ.) A, as also Syr: txt Bℵ a m 13. 40 vulg arm Thl-fin. σειωσης (sic) D^1(txt D^4).

10. at beg ins αλλα (but marked for erasure) $ℵ^1$. om σοι D-gr E. (εστι, so ABDℵ.) [μοι bef εστι L.]

11. rec τε (for δε), with E-gr HLP rel æth Chr_1 Thl: txt ABℵ a c m 13 vulg E-lat [Syr] syr coptt.—και εκαθ. D. add εν κορινθω D Syr syr-w-ast: εκει 40 [vulg-ed tol] demid sah arm. aft ενιαυτ. ins κ ενα ℵ (but κ is marked for erasure by $ℵ^1$). for εν αυτ., αυτους D-gr 4 [arm]; αυτοις 37. 56. 100.

12. [for δε, τε D Syr.] rec ανθυπατευοντος, with EHLP rel Chr: txt ABDℵ 36. 40. οι ιουδαιοι bef ομοθυμαδον B g coptt. for τω παυλω και, συνλαλησαντες μεθ εαυτων επι τον παυλον και επιθεντες τας χειρας D; ins επιθ. τ. χ. αυτω syr-w-ast sah.

14): and with him many of the Corinthians (Jews and Gentiles, it being the house of a proselyte), probably Aquila and Priscilla also, believed and were baptized.

9. λάλ. κ. μὴ σιωπ.] So, for solemnity's sake, we have an affirmation and negation combined, John i. 3. See also Isa. lviii. 1. **10. ἐπιθ. σοι**] See ref. and examples of this usage in Wetst.:—shall set on thee, as E. V. **λαός ἐστί μοι πολύς**] See John x. 16. As our Lord *forewarned* Paul in Jerusalem that *they would not* receive his testimony concerning Him, so here He *encourages* him, by a promise of much success in Corinth. The word λαός, the express title beforetime *of the Jews,* is still used now, notwithstanding *their secession.* **11.**] The year and a half may extend either to his *departure,* or to the incident in vv. 12 ff. Meyer would confine it to the latter, taking ἐκάθισεν in the sense of '*remained in quiet:*' but (see reff.) it will hardly bear such emphasis: and seeing that the incident in vv. 12 ff. was a notable fulfilment of the promise,—for though they set on him, *they could not hurt him,*—I should be disposed to take the other view, and regard ver. 12 to ἱκανάς, ver. 18, to have happened during this time. **12. Γαλλίωνος**] His original name was Marcus Annæus Novatus: but, having been adopted into the family of the rhetorician Lucius Junius Gallio, he took the name of Junius Annæus Gallio. He was brother of Lucius Annæus Seneca, the philosopher, whose character of him is in exact accordance with that which we may infer from this narrative: 'Nemo mortalium mihi tam dulcis est, quam hic omnibus:' 'Gallionem fratrem meum, quem nemo non parum amat, etiam qui amare plus non potest.' He is called 'dulcis Gallio' by Statius, Silv. ii. 7. 32. He appears to have given up the province of Achaia from ill health: 'Illud mihi in ore erat domini mei Gallionis qui cum in Achaia febrem habere cœpisset, protinus navem ascendit, clamitans non corporis esse sed loci morbum.' Senec. Ep. 104. He was spared after the execution of his brother (Tacit. Ann. xv. 73): but Dio Cassius, lxii. 25, adds, οἱ ἀδελφοὶ ὕστερον ἐπαπώλοντο, and Euseb. Chron. ad ann. 818 (A.D. 66), says that he put an end to himself after his brother's death. **ἀνθυπάτου**] See note on ch. xiii. 7. Achaia was originally a senatorial province (Dio Cass. liii. 12), but was temporarily made an imperial one by Tiberius. Tacit. Ann. i. 76, 'Achaiam ac Macedoniam, onera deprecantes, levari *in præsens* proconsulari imperio, tradique Cæsari placuit.' Claudius (Suet. Claud. 25) 'Provincias Achaiam et Macedoniam quas Tiberius ad curam suam transtulerat, senatui reddidit.' **τ. Ἀχαΐας**] The Roman province of Achaia contained Hellas and the Peloponnesus, and, with Macedonia, embraced all their Grecian dominions. It was so called, according to Pausanias (vii. 16. 7), because the Romans ἐχειρώσαντο Ἕλληνας δι' Ἀχαιῶν τότε τοῦ Ἑλληνικοῦ προεστηκότων (the Achaian league). "The **βῆμα** is mentioned three times in the course of this narrative (see vv. 16, 17). It was of two kinds: (1) fixed in some public and

l ch. xii. 21 reff. m = Rom. i. 26. xi. 24. Gal. i. 8, 9 al. n here only. Jer. xxxvi. (xxix.) 8. 1 Macc. i. 11 only. Xen. Mem. iii. 11. 10. o ver. 7. Jonah i. 9. p = ch. viii. 35 reff. q ch. xxiv. 20. Rev. xviii. 5 only. 1 Kings xxvi. 18. r here only †. (-γία, ch. xiii. 10.) s here only.

ABDE HLPℵ a b c d f g h k l m o 13

Παύλῳ καὶ ἤγαγον αὐτὸν ἐπὶ τὸ [l] βῆμα 13 λέγοντες ὅτι [m] παρὰ τὸν νόμον [n] ἀναπείθει οὗτος τοὺς ἀνθρώπους [o] σέβεσθαι τὸν θεόν. 14 μέλλοντος δὲ τοῦ Παύλου [p] ἀνοίγειν τὸ στόμα εἶπεν ὁ Γαλλίων πρὸς τοὺς Ἰουδαίους Εἰ μὲν [οὖν] ἦν [q] ἀδίκημά τι ἢ [r] ῥᾳδιούργημα πονηρόν, ὦ Ἰουδαῖοι, [s] κατὰ [s] λόγον ἂν [t] ἠνεσχόμην ὑμῶν. 15 εἰ δὲ [u] ζητήματά ἐστιν περὶ [v] λόγου καὶ ὀνομάτων καὶ νόμου τοῦ [w] καθ' ὑμᾶς, [x] ὄψεσθε αὐτοί· κριτὴς ἐγὼ τούτων οὐ βούλομαι εἶναι. 16 καὶ [y] ἀπήλασεν αὐτοὺς ἀπὸ τοῦ [l] βήματος. 17 [z] ἐπιλαβόμενοι δὲ πάντες Σωσθένην τὸν

3 Macc. iii. 14. δι' ἣν αἰτίαν ἀήττητος ὑπάρχειν διείληπτο, καὶ κατὰ λόγον, Diod. Sic. iv. 11. t = 2 Cor. xi. 1, &c. 2 Tim. iv. 3. Heb. xiii. 22. Job vi. 26. u ch. xv. 2 reff. v = 2 Tim. i. 13. Tit. i. 9. ii. 8. Heb. ii. 2. 1 John ii. 7. w ch. xvii. 28. xxvi. 3. Eph. i. 15. ἕκαστος τῶν καθ' ἑαυτὸν ἐρᾷ, Xen. Cyr. v. 1. 11. x = Matt. xxvii. 4, 24. (Exod. vi. 1.) y here only. Ezek. xxxiv. 12. Wisd. xvii. 8 only. = Xen. Mem. ii. 6. 12. z w. acc., ch. ix. 27 reff.

for επι, παρα ℵ, syr has προ του βηματος, prefixing, w-ast, προς ανθυπατον.

13. ins καταβοωντες και bef λεγοντες D. rec ουτος bef αναπ. (*corrn of characteristic order*), with DEHLP rel 36 vulg [(syrr) coptt] Chr_1 [Thl-sif]: txt ABℵ a h k 13 arm Thl-fin. πειθει H 40: ανατρεπει 1. 65. 133.

14. om ουν (*see note*) ABDEℵ a b c o 13. 36. 40 vulg syrr [copt] sah æth arm Chr_1: ins HLP rel.—om ην L d m 25: η A[1]. ins ανδρες bef ιουδαιοι D vulg. ανεσχομην Bℵ[1] 13; so, omg αν, A 33-4-6 (*confusion arising from ανηνεσχ.*).

15. rec ζητημα (*corrn to suit αδικημα and ραδιουργημα above: the plur has a meaning, see note*), with D[1][and lat] HLP rel 13 [E-lat] Chr Thl-fin: txt AB D[4]-gr E-gr ℵ a c 40 vulg syrr coptt arm Thl-sif. for εστιν, εχετε D-gr. rec aft κριτης ins γαρ, with EHLP rel 36 syrr sah [arm] Chr: om ABDℵ 13 vulg copt æth. for βουλομαι, θελω D.

16. απελυσεν D[1](txt D[4], *abjecit* D-lat) 133.

17. [α]πολαβομενοι D[1]-gr(txt D[4]). rec aft παντες ins οι ελληνες (*see note*), with DEHLP 13 rel syrr sah æth [arm Chr-txt_1]; οι ιουδαιοι 36. 180; ιουδ. 15-8: om ABℵ e[1] vulg copt Chr-comm(but om παντες too). ins μετα (? there is a space, but the writing has perished) bef σωσθενην D: *adprehendentes eum . . . cum Sosthenen*

open place: (2) moveable, and taken by the Roman magistrates to be placed wherever they might sit in a judicial character. Probably here and in the case of Pilate (John xix. 13), the former kind of seat is intended. See Smith's Dict. of Antiquities, under 'Sella.' See also some remarks on the tribunal—'the indispensable symbol of the Roman judgment-seat,' in the Edinburgh Review for Jan. 1847, p. 151." C. and H. vol. i. 494. **13. παρὰ τ. νόμον**] Against the Mosaic law:—the exercise of which, as a 'religio licita,' was allowed to the Jews. **14.**] Though manuscript authority is so strong against the *οὖν*, I have retained it, as also has Tischdf. (ed. 7 [not ed. 8]). Its *omission* may be easily accounted for, from the copyists finding it unnecessary and seemingly out of place: but on no supposition can its *insertion* be rendered probable. It stands very appropriately here, referring to the complaint of the Jews, either as uttered by them, or perhaps recapitulated by Gallio:—'*Ye have charged this man with lawless conduct.* **If now this had really been so . . . .**' **κατὰ λόγον**] See reff. We have the opposite παρὰ λόγον in 2 Macc. iv. 36. **ἂν ἠνεσχ. ὑμ.**] **I should have borne with** (patiently heard) **you.** **15.**] ζητήματα has apparently been altered to ζήτημα to suit the sense, there being but *one* question before Gallio. But the plural expresses contempt: **If it is questions, &c.**: as we should say, 'a parcel of questions.' See ch. xxiii. 29. **ὀνομάτων**] e. g. Paul asserted Jesus to be the Christ, which the Jews denied. This to a Roman would be a question of *names.* **τ. καθ' ὑμᾶς,** with emphasis: see reff. So Lysias (ch. xxiii. 29) declined to decide Paul's case; and Festus (ch. xxv. 20), though he did not altogether put the enquiry by, wished to judge it *at Jerusalem,* where he might have the counsel of those learned in the Jewish law. **17. πάντες**] Apparently, all the *mob,* i. e. the Gentile population present. Sosthenes, as the ruler of the synagogue (ἀρχ. = either the ruler, or *one* of the rulers; perhaps he had succeeded Crispus), had been the chief of the complainant Jews, and therefore, on their cause being rejected, and themselves ignominiously dismissed,

[a] ἀρχισυνάγωγον ἔτυπτον [b] ἔμπροσθεν τοῦ [1] βήματος· καὶ
οὐδὲν τούτων τῷ Γαλλίωνι [c] ἔμελεν. 18 Ὁ δὲ Παῦλος
ἔτι [d] προσμείνας [e] ἡμέρας [e] ἱκανάς, τοῖς ἀδελφοῖς [f] ἀποταξάμενος [g] ἐξέπλει εἰς τὴν Συρίαν, καὶ σὺν αὐτῷ Πρίσκιλλα
καὶ Ἀκύλας, [h] κειράμενος ἐν Κεγχρεαῖς τὴν κεφαλήν·

a ver. 8 reff. b = Matt. v. 24. vii. 6. 2 Cor. v. 10. c constr., here only. (1 Cor. ix. 9 reff.) Job xxii. 3. d absol., here only. Matt. xv. 32 ‖ Mk. ch. xi. 23. xiii. 43. 1 Tim. i. 3. v. 5 only. Judg. iii. 25 A Ald. Wisd. iii. 9 only. e ch. ix. 23 reff. f — ver. 21. Mark vi. 46. Luke ix. 61. xiv. 33. 2 Cor. ii. 13 only ‡. (Jer. xx. 2. 1 Macc. xi. 3 only.) Jos. Antt. viii. 13. 7. g ch. xv. 39 reff. h ch. viii. 32. 1 Cor. xi. 6 bis only. 2 Kings xiv. 26.

D-lat. εμελλεν EHLPℵ. *tunc Gallio fingebat eum non videre* D-lat(txt D⁴-gr, D[1] has τ . . . . . . ω γαλλιω . . . . εν, but the rest is illegible). aft τουτων ins των B[1].

18. aft παυλος ins εφη ℵ[1](erased by ℵ[3]). επλευσεν, *navigavit* D vulg: εξεπλευσεν E[2], *enavigavit* E-lat. rec την κεφαλην bef εν κεγχρεαις, with DEHLP rel [syrr sah æth-pl arm] Chr_1: om εν κεγχ. æth-rom: txt (*characteristic order*) ABℵ

was roughly treated by the mob. From this, certainly the right explanation, has arisen the gloss οἱ Ἕλληνες. The other gloss, οἱ Ἰουδαῖοι, has sprung from the notion that this Sosthenes was the same person with the Sosthenes of 1 Cor. i. 1, a Christian and a companion of Paul. But, not to insist on the improbability of the party driven from the tribunal having beaten one of their antagonists in front of the tribunal,—*why did they not beat Paul himself?* There is no ground for supposing the two persons to be the same, Sosthenes being no uncommon name. If they were, this man must have been converted afterwards; but he is not among those who accompanied Paul into Asia, either in ver. 18, or ch. xx. 4. The carelessness of Gallio about the matter clearly seems to be a further instance of his contempt for the Jews, and indisposition to favour them or their persecution of Paul. Had this been otherwise meant, certainly καί would not have been the copula. 'So little did the information against Paul prosper, that the informers themselves were beaten without interference of the judge.' Meyer.

18.] It has been considered doubtful whether the words κειρ. τ. κεφ. κ.τ.λ. apply to *Paul*, the subject of the sentence, or to *Aquila*, the last subject. The *former* is held by Chrys., Theoph., Aug., Jer., Isid., Bede, Calv., Beza, Calov., Wolf, Olsh., Neand., De Wette, Baumgarten, Hackett, Wordsworth (whose note may be profitably consulted), al.:—the *latter* by (Vulg.), Grot., Alberti, Kuinoel, Meyer, al., and more recently Dean Howson, vol. i. p. 498. But I quite agree with Neander (Pfl. u. Leit. p. 348, note), that if we consider the matter carefully, there can be no doubt that they *can only apply to Paul*. For, although this vow differed from that of the Nazarite, who shaved his hair at the *end* of his votive period, in the temple at Jerusalem, and burnt it with his peace-offering (Num. vi. 1—21), Josephus gives us a description of a somewhat similar one, B. J. ii. 15. 1, τοὺς γὰρ ἢ νόσῳ καταπονουμένους ἢ τισιν ἄλλαις ἀνάγκαις, ἔθος εὔχεσθαι πρὸ τριάκοντα ἡμερῶν ἧς ἀποδώσειν μέλλοιεν θυσίας, οἴνου τε ἀφέξεσθαι καὶ ξυρήσασθαι τὰς κόμας,—where it appears from ξυρήσασθαι (which, as Neander observes, if it applied to the *end* of the time, would be ξυρήσεσθαι (or perhaps rather θρέψειν)), that the hair was shaved thirty days before the sacrifice. At all events, *no sacrifice could be offered any where but at Jerusalem:* and every such vow would conclude with a sacrifice. Now we find, on comparing the subsequent course of Aquila with that of Paul,—that the former *did not go up to Jerusalem*, but remained at Ephesus (ver. 26): but that Paul *hastened by* Ephesus, and did go up to Jerusalem: see ver. 22. Again, it would be quite irrelevant to the purpose of Luke, to relate such a fact of *one of Paul's companions*. That he should do so apologetically, to shew that the Apostle still countenanced conformity with the law, is a view which I cannot find justified by any features of this book: and it surely would be a very far-fetched apology, and one likely to escape the notice of many readers, seeing that Aquila would not appear as being under Paul's influence, and even his conversion to the Gospel has not been related, but is left to be implied from ver. 26. Again, Meyer's ground for referring κειράμ. to Aquila,—that his name is here placed after that of his wife,—is untenable, seeing that, for some reason, probably the superior character or office in the church, of Priscilla, the same arrangement is found (in the best MSS. at ver. 26, and) at Rom. xvi. 3; 2 Tim. iv. 19. Lastly, the very form of the sentence is against a change of subject at κειράμενος. There are, from ver. 18 to 23 incl., a section forming a distinct narration, and complete in itself,—no less than *nine aorist participles, eight of which in-*

[ik] εἶχεν γὰρ [il] εὐχήν. 19 [m] κατήντησαν δὲ εἰς Ἔφεσον· κἀκείνους [n] κατέλιπεν [o] αὐτοῦ, αὐτὸς δὲ εἰςελθὼν εἰς τὴν συναγωγὴν [p] διελέχθη τοῖς Ἰουδαίοις. 20 [q] ἐρωτώντων δὲ αὐτῶν [r] ἐπὶ πλείονα χρόνον μεῖναι οὐκ [s] ἐπένευσεν, 21 ἀλλὰ [t] ἀποταξάμενος καὶ εἰπὼν πάλιν [u] ἀνακάμψω

...χρο l. ...ου d. ABDE HLPℵ a b c f g h k m o 13

i ch. xxi. 23 only. k = Luke xii. 50. 2 Cor. iv. 1. Phil. i. 30. l = as above [i] (James v. 15) only. Gen. xxxi. 13. m ch. xvi. 1 reff. n = Luke xv. 4. ch. xxiv. 27. xxv. 14. 1 Thess. iii. 1. Dan. x. 13. o ch. (xv. 34 v. r.) xxi. 4. Matt. xxvi. 36 only. 2 Kings xx. 4. p ch. xvii. 2 reff. q constr., ch. xvi. 39 reff. r = ch. xiii. 31 reff. s here only. Prov. xxvi. 24. 2 Macc. iv. 10. xi. 15. xiv. 20 only. t ver. 18. u Matt. ii. 12. Luke x. 6. Heb. xi. 15 only. Exod. xxxii. 27. Judg. xi. 39 A Ald. compl.

a m 13 vulg Thl-fin. πρ(ο)ςευχην D[1], *orationem* D-lat.

19. rec κατηντησε (*alteration to singular to suit* κατελιπεν *below*), with HLP rel 36(sic) vulg syr copt [æth-rom] Chr$_1$: καταντησας D-gr [arm]: txt ABEℵ k 13. 40 tol D-lat Syr sah æth-pl. και εκεινους EHP b d e f g l m o Chr Thl-sif: και τω επιοντι σαββατω εκεινους D: aft εφεσον ins τω επ. σαβ. 137 syr-w-ast. κατελειπεν AHLP 13. for αυτου, εκει (*more usual word*) ADEℵ 13 rel 40: txt BHLP 36 Chr. διελεξατο (*corrn to more usual form*) ABℵ a 13 Thl-fin: διελεγετο D k vulg(but am *disputavit*): txt EHLP rel 36 Chr (Thdrt$_1$).

20. for δε, τε D[1]([and lat:] txt D[8]) Syr æth. om αυτων 137: αυτον D[-gr[8]] (txt D[1]) L b d g[2] k m[2] o [arm] Thl-fin. πλιον D. επιμειναι ℵ[3]. rec aft μειναι ins παρ αυτοις (*explanatory addn*), with DEHLP rel Syr syr-w-ob copt Chr$_1$; εκει tol sah arm: παραμειναι αυτοις 25: txt ABℵ c 13. 36. 40 vulg æth.

21. (*On the whole verse, see note.*) (αλλα, so ABDEPℵ b c f g k o 13 Thl-sif.) rec απεταξατο, omg και, with HLP rel syr copt Chr Thl-sif: txt ABDEℵ a 13-5. 36. 40. 105-80 vulg æth Thl-fin.—om αλλα αποταξ. και Syr. rec (aft απεταξ.) ins αυτοις, with EHLP rel 36 Thl: om ABDℵ. rec aft ειπων ins δει με παντως την εορτην την ερχομενην ποιησαι εις ιεροσολυμα, with (D)HLP rel 36. 40 demid syrr Chr$_1$ Thl, but D has την εορτην ημεραν *solemnem diem*, and omits the second την, D[1] (corrd by D[8]) has also δε for με: aft θελοντος ins *sed nunc volo agere festum venturum in Jerusalem* æth-pl: om ABEℵ a 13-5. 105-80 vulg coptt æth-rom arm. rec aft παλιν ins δε, with HLP rel 15. 103-80 syr Chr Thl-sif: om AB D(omits παλιν also) Eℵ a 13. 36. 40 vulg coptt æth [arm].—Syr demid Thl-fin have και παλιν. καμψ of ανακαμψω has perished in D[1](supplied by D[8]).

disputably apply to Paul as the subject of the section: leaving it hardly open to question that κειράμενος also must be referred to him. There need be no enquiry *what danger* can have prompted such a vow on his part, when we recollect the catalogue given by him in 2 Cor. xi. Besides, he had, since his last visit to Jerusalem, been νόσῳ καταπονούμενος (see Jos. above, note on ch. xvi. 6, and Prolegg. to Gal. § ii. 3): it is true, a considerable time ago, but this need not prevent our supposing that the vow may have been then made, to be paid on his next visit to Jerusalem. That he had not sooner paid it, is accounted for by his having been since that time under continual pressure of preaching and founding churches, and having finally been detained by special command at Corinth. That he was now so anxious to pay it (ver. 21), consists well with the supposition of its having been long delayed. **ἐν Κεγχρεαῖς**] Κεγχρεαὶ κώμη κ. λιμὴν ἀπέχων τῆς πόλεως ὅσον ἑβδομήκοντα στάδια. τούτῳ μὲν χρῶνται πρὸς τοὺς ἐκ τῆς Ἀσίας, πρὸς δὲ τοὺς ἐκ τῆς Ἰταλίας τῷ Λεχαίῳ. Strabo, viii. 380. There was soon after a Christian church there: see Rom. xvi. 1. **19.** **Ἔφεσον**] Ephesus was the ancient capital of Ionia (Ptol. v. 2. 8), and at this time, of the Roman proconsular province of Asia,—on the Caÿster, near the coast, between Symrna and Miletus. It was famed for its commerce, but even more for its magnificent temple of Artemis (see ch. xix. 24, 27, and notes). See a full account of its situation and history, secular and Christian, in the Prolegg. to Eph. § ii. 2—6; and an interesting description, with plan, in Mr. Lewin's Life and Epistles of St. Paul, i. 344 ff. **αὐτοῦ**] Perhaps this may be said proleptically, referring to his journey to Palestine (De Wette): but on account of the δέ which follows, I should rather understand it to mean that the Jewish synagogue was (as sometimes the case, see Winer, Realw., 'Synagogen') *outside the town*, and that Priscilla and Aquila were left *in the town*. **διελέχθη**, aor., referring to one, and a transient occasion: διελέγετο, imperf., ver. 4, of his long stay, and continual discourses in the Corinthian synagogue. **21.**] The omission of the words here inserted in rec., δεῖ με πάντως τὴν ἑορτὴν τὴν ἐρχομένην ποιῆσαι εἰς Ἱεροσόλυμα, seems necessitated on the principle of being guided in doubtful cases by the

πρὸς ὑμᾶς τοῦ [v] θεοῦ [v] θέλοντος, [w] ἀνήχθη ἀπὸ τῆς
Ἐφέσου, 22 καὶ [x] κατελθὼν εἰς Καισάρειαν, [y] ἀναβὰς καὶ
[z] ἀσπασάμενος τὴν ἐκκλησίαν [a] κατέβη [a] εἰς Ἀντιόχειαν.
23 καὶ [b] ποιήσας [b] χρόνον τινὰ [c] ἐξῆλθεν, [d] διερχόμενος
[e] καθεξῆς τὴν Γαλατικὴν χώραν καὶ Φρυγίαν, [f] στηρίζων
πάντας τοὺς μαθητάς.

v see 1 Cor. iv. 19. (Heb. vi. 3.) James iv. 15. Sir. xxxix. 6.
w ch. xiii. 13 reff.
x ch. viii. 5 reff.
y absol., = Luke, here only. = John vii. 8, 10. xii. 20. Ezra vii. 6. Neh. viii. 8. Jonah i. 3.
z = ch. xxi. 7. xxv. 13. Exod. xviii. 7.
a John ii. 12. ch. vii. 15. xiv. 25. xvi. 8.
b = ch. xv. 33 reff.
c absol., ch. xv. 40 reff.
d ch. xiii. 6 reff.
e ch. iii. 24 reff.†
f = Rom. i. 11. xvi. 25 al. Ps. l. 12 (14).

ins και bef ανηχθη EHLP 13[απηχ.] rel 40 æth-pl Chr_1 : om ABD a 15. 36. 105-80 vulg sah æth-rom arm : aft ανηχθη ins δε ℵ[1](ℵ[3] disapproving). for ανηχθη to αναβας, ακυλαν δε κατελιπεν εν εφεσω αυτος γαρ εν πλοιω αχθεις ηλθεν εις καισαρειαν αναβ. δε syr-mg; simly 97. 137 : *Et Aquilam et Priscillam reliquit Ephesi, et ipse iter fecit per mare ac venit Cæsaream* Syr. for της, του D[1](txt D[8]).

22. ins και bef αναβας D [syrr sah æth]. (*This και was perhaps intended to be placed bef ανηχθη, but insd here by mistake.*)

23. ins και bef καθεξης ℵ[1](ℵ[3] disapproving). κατεξης D[1](txt D[4]). rec **επιστηριζων**, with DEHLP rel 36 Chr_1 : txt ABℵ 13.—pref και D 38.

testimony of our most ancient mss. The text thus produced is the shortest and simplest, and the facts, of other glosses having been attempted on this verse, and of ms. 36 inserting the words without altering the construction to suit them, and D omitting the καί before ἀνήχθη, and the δέ before ἀνακάμψω, tend perhaps to throw discredit on the insertion. The gloss, if such it be, has probably been owing to an endeavour to conform the circumstances to those related in ch. xx. 16. If they stand, and for those who read them, it may still be interesting to enquire at *what feast* they may be supposed to point. (1) *Not at the Passover:* for the ordinary duration of the 'mare clausum' was (Livy xxxvii. 9) till the vernal equinox. According to Vegetius de Re Milit. iv. 39, 'ex die iii. Id. Novembr. usque in diem vi. Id. Martii, maria claudebantur.' And we are not at liberty to assume an exceptional case, such as sometimes occurred (Philo, Leg. ad Caium, § 29, vol. ii. p. 573; Tacit. Ann. xii. 43; Plin. ii. 47). Hence, if the voyage from Corinth at all approached the length of that from Philippi to Jerusalem in ch. xx., xxi., he would have set sail at a time when it would have been hardly possible. (2) *Not at the feast of Tabernacles.* For if it were, he must have sailed from Corinth in August or September. Now, as he stayed there something more than a year and a half, his sea-voyage from Berœa to Athens would in this case have been made in the depth of winter; which (especially as a choice of land or water was open to him) is impossible. (3) It remains, then, that the feast should have been *Pentecost;* at which Paul also visited Jerusalem, ch. xx. 16. (The above is the argument of Wieseler, Chron. d. Apostelgesch. pp. 48—50, who however allows too long for the voyage from Corinth, forgetting that from the seven weeks' voyage of ch. xx. xxi. are to be taken seven days at Troas (xx. 6), seven at Tyre (xxi. 4), one at Ptolemais (xxi. 7), ἡμέραι πλείους at Cæsarea (xxi. 10),—in all certainly not less than three weeks.) The Apostle's promise of return was fulfilled ch. xix. 1 ff. **22. ἀναβάς**] *To Jerusalem:* for (1) it would be out of the question to suppose that Paul made the long detour by Cæsarea *only to go up into the town from the beach,* as supposed by most of those who omit δεῖ . . . . Ἱεροσ. in ver. 21, and *salute the disciples,*—and (2) the expression κατέβη εἰς Ἀντ., which suits a journey from Jerusalem (ch. xi. 27), would not apply to one from Cæsarea. **ἀσπ. τ. ἐκκλ.**] The payment of his vow is not mentioned, partly because it is understood from the mere mention of the vow itself, ver. 18,—partly, perhaps, because it was privately done, and with no view to attract notice as in ch. xxi.

23.] Paul's visit to the churches in Galatia and Phrygia. Either (1) Galatia is here a general term including Lycaonia, and Paul went by Derbe, Lystra, Iconium, &c. as before in ch. xvi., or (2) he did not visit Lycaonia this time, but went through Cappadocia: to which also the words διελθόντα τὰ ἀνωτερικὰ μέρη (ch. xix. 1) seem to point, ἡ ἄνω Ἀσία being the country east of the Halys. We find Christian churches in Cappadocia, 1 Pet. i. 1. On this journey, as connected with the state of the Galatian churches, see Prolegg. to Gal. § iii. 1. **καθεξῆς** implies taking the churches in order; regularly visiting them, each as they lay in his

24 Ἰουδαῖος δέ τις Ἀπολλὼς ὀνόματι, Ἀλεξανδρεὺς
g τῷ g γένει, ἀνὴρ h λόγιος, i κατήντησεν εἰς Ἔφεσον,
k δυνατὸς ὢν ἐν ταῖς l γραφαῖς. 25 m οὗτος ἦν n κατηχημένος τὴν op ὁδὸν τοῦ o κυρίου, καὶ qr ζέων s τῷ qs πνεύματι
ἐλάλει καὶ ἐδίδασκεν t ἀκριβῶς τὰ περὶ τοῦ Ἰησοῦ,
u ἐπιστάμενος μόνον τὸ βάπτισμα Ἰωάννου· 26 v οὗτός τε

ABDE HLPℵa bcfgh kmo13

g ver. 2 reff. h here only +. Herod. ii. 77. i ch. xvi. 1 reff. k = Luke xxiv. 19. ch. vii. 22. Jer. xxxix. (xxxii.) 19. l ch. xvii. 2 reff. m ch. ix. 20 reff. n Luke i. 4. ch. xxi. 21, 24. Rom. ii. 18. 1 Cor. xiv. 19. Gal. vi. 6 only +. Jos. vita § 65. o = here only. see Luke xx. 21. ch. xiii. 10. Ps. xvii. 21. p = ch. ix. 2 reff. (Matt. iii. 3 ||.) q Rom. xii. 11 only. r Job xxxii. 19 B ℵ &c. Philo, vita Mos. iii. § 38, vol. ii. p. 178. s = ch. xvii. 16 reff. t Matt. ii. 8. Luke i. 3. Eph. v. 15. 1 Thess. v. 2 (ver. 26 reff.) only. Deut. xix. 18. Wisd. xix. 17 only. Dan. vii. 19 Theod. (-βής, ch. xxvi. 5. -βεια, xxii. 3. -βοῦν, Matt. ii. 7.) u ch. xix. 15 reff. v ch. ix. 20 reff.

24. απολλωνιος D: απελλης ℵ[1] 15. 180 scholl copt arm: *Apollon* æth-rom: *Apollo* vulg E-lat Syr [syr].—ονοματι bef απ. D 13. γενει bef αλεξανδρευς, omg τω, D [(Syr)].

25. *ος ην κατηχημενος εν τη πατριδι τον λογον του κυριου* D. for την οδον, τον λογον D(as above) a b o 36. 66[2]. 76. om του (bef κυρ.) B k Thl-sif. ins ω bef ελαλει ℵ[1](erased by ℵ[3]). απελαλει D[1], *eloquebatur* D-lat: ελαλει δε B. om 2nd του D 13. 40. 68-9. 137. rec (for ιησ.) κυριου (*see notes. The varn in the art is no argument* (*as De Wette*) *agst the genuineness of the readg: the constant omn of artt aft prepp might easily lead to this: thus we have it omitted also bef* κυριου), with HP rel Chr_1 Thl-sif: txt ABDE [L(sic, Treg)] ℵ a c h 13. 36. 40 vulg syrr coptt æth arm Thl-fin.

route. One work accomplished by him in this journey was the ordaining (but apparently not collecting) a contribution for the poor saints at Jerusalem: see 1 Cor. xvi. 1. Timotheus and Erastus probably accompanied him, see ch. xix. 22; 2 Cor. i. 1; and Gaius and Aristarchus, ch. xix. 29; and perhaps Titus, 2 Cor. xii. 18 al. (and Sosthenes? (1 Cor. i. 1), but see on ver. 17.)

24—28.] Apollos at Ephesus, and in Achaia. **Ἀπολλώς**] abbreviated from Ἀπολλώνιος [as Lucas from Lucanus, &c.]: see var. read. **Ἀλεξανδρεύς**] Alexandria was the great seat of the Hellenistic [or later Greek] language, learning, and philosophy (see ch. vi. 9). A large number of Jews had been planted there by its founder, Alexander the Great. The celebrated LXX version of the O. T. was made there under the Ptolemies. There took place that remarkable fusion of Greek, Oriental, and Judaic elements of thought and belief, which was destined to enter so widely, for good and for evil, into the minds and writings of Christians. We see in the providential calling of Apollos to the ministry, an instance of adaptation of the workman to the work. A masterly exposition of the Scriptures by a learned Hellenist of Alexandria formed the most appropriate watering (1 Cor. iii. 6) for those who had been planted by the pupil of Gamaliel. **λόγιος**] either (1) *learned*, as Philo, Vita Mos. i. 5, vol. ii. p. 84, Αἰγυπτίων οἱ λόγιοι, and Jos. B. J. vi. 5. 3, who distinguishes, in the interpretation of the omens preceding the siege, οἱ ἰδιῶται from οἱ λόγιοι,—or (2) *eloquent:* so Jos. Antt. xvii. 6. 2 calls Judas and Matthias, Ἰουδαίων λογιώτατοι and πατρίων ἐξηγηταὶ νόμων. The etymologists make the former the ancient,—the latter a subsequent meaning. So Thom. Mag.: λογίους τοὺς πολυΐστορας οἱ ἀρχαῖοι Ἀττικίζοντες, ὡς καὶ Ἡρόδοτος· λογίους δὲ τοὺς διαλεκτικοὺς οἱ ὕστερον. The latter meaning is most appropriate here, both because the peculiar kind of learning implied by λόγιος [acquaintance with stories and legends] would not be likely to be predicated of Apollos,—and because the subsequent words, δυνατὸς ἐν τ. γραφαῖς, sufficiently indicate his *learning*, and in what it lay.

See on λόγιος as applied to Papias by Eusebius, prolegg. to Matt. § ii. 1 (α) note.

25.] Apollos had received (from his youth?) the true doctrine of the Messiahship of Jesus, as pointed out by John the Baptist: doubtless from some disciple of John: but more than this he knew not. The *doctrines* of the Cross,—the Resurrection,—the outpouring of the Spirit,—these were unknown to him: but more particularly (from the words ἐπιστ. μόνον τὸ βάπτ. Ἰωάν.) the *latter*, as connected with Christian baptism: see further on ch. xix. 2, 3. The mistake of supposing that he *did not know Jesus to be the Messiah*, has arisen from the description of his subsequent work at Corinth, ver. 28, but by no means follows from it: *this he did before*, but not so completely. The same mistake has led to the alteration of Ἰησοῦ into the κυρίου of the rec., it having been well imagined

ἤρξατο [w] παῤῥησιάζεσθαι ἐν τῇ συναγωγῇ. ἀκούσαντες
δὲ αὐτοῦ Πρίσκιλλα καὶ Ἀκύλας [x] προσελάβοντο αὐτόν,
καὶ [y] ἀκριβέστερον αὐτῷ [z] ἐξέθεντο τὴν [a] ὁδόν. 27 βουλομένου δὲ αὐτοῦ [b] διελθεῖν [b] εἰς τὴν Ἀχαΐαν [c] προτρεψάμενοι
οἱ ἀδελφοὶ ἔγραψαν τοῖς μαθηταῖς [d] ἀποδέξασθαι αὐτόν.
ὃς [e] παραγενόμενος [f] συνεβάλετο πολὺ τοῖς [g] πεπιστευκόσιν [h] διὰ τῆς [hi] χάριτος· 28 [k] εὐτόνως γὰρ τοῖς Ἰουδαίοις
[l] διακατηλέγχετο [m] δημοσίᾳ [n] ἐπιδεικνὺς διὰ τῶν [o] γραφῶν
εἶναι τὸν χριστὸν Ἰησοῦν.

w ch. ix. 27 reff. x = ch. xvii. 5 reff. y ch. xxiii. 15, 20. xxiv. 22 (ver. 25 reff.) only. z ch. xi. 4 reff. a absol., = ch. ix. 2 reff. b 2 Cor. i. 16 reff. Josh. xix. 27. c here only †. Wisd. xiv. 18. 2 Macc. xi. 7 only. d ch. ii. 41 reff. e absol., ch. xvii. 10 reff. f = here only. (ch. xvii. 18 reff.) Job xxxv. 3 F(not A). Wisd. v. 8. μέγα συμβάλλεται εἰς τὸ μανθάνειν, Xen. Cyr. i. 2. 8. g ch. xv. 5 reff. h absol., Gal. i. 15. Heb. xii. 28 only. i ch. xiii. 43 reff. k Luke xxiii. 10 only. Josh. vi. 7 (8) only. (-νος, 2 Macc. xii. 23 only. -νία, Eccl. vii. 8 Aℵ only.) l here only †. m ch. xvi. 37 reff. n = Heb. vi. 17 only ‡. (ch. ix. 39 al. Isa. xxxvii. 26.) o ch. xvii. 2 reff.

26. for *ουτος*, *ητος* D[1](txt D[4]) : *ουτως* m. om *τε* D-gr H sah æth-pl [arm]. om *τη* D[1](ins D[4]). *και ακουσαντος* D[1](*et quum audivissent* D-lat : txt D-corr[1]) Syr. rec *ακυλας και πρισκιλλα* (*alteration of characteristic order, cf Rom* xvi. 3, 2 *Tim* iv. 19), with DHLP rel 36 syrr sah [arm] Chr$_1$: txt ABEℵ 13 vulg copt æth.—*ακυλα* ℵ. *εξεθοντο* D : *-θετο* H. rec ins *του θεου* bef *οδον*, with HLP rel Chr : *την οδ. του θεου* ABℵ c k m 13. 40 am fuld tol syr [copt] sah arm Thl-fin : *τ. οδ. τ. κυριου* E g 36. 177 [vulg-clem] demid Syr : *τον λογον του κυρ.* 66[2]. 98-marg 105 lect-58 : [*τ. λ. τ. θεου* a :] *scripturas domini* Cassiod (*all these, as shewn by the varr, are supplementary emendations of the simple την οδον*) : txt D.
27. for ver, *εν δε τη εφεσω επιδημουντες*[*exeuntes*] *τινες κορινθιοι και ακουσαντες αυτου παρεκαλουν διελθειν συν αυτοις εις την πατριδα αυτων συνκατανευσαντος*[*redeunte*] *δε αυτου οι εφεσιοι*(*αδελφοι* syr-mg) *εγραψαν τοις εν κορινθω μαθηταις οπως αποδεξωνται τον ανδρα* D syr-mg : D adding *ος επιδημησας εις την αχαιαν πολυ*(*πολυν* D[1]) *συνεβαλλετο* [*contulit*] *εν ταις εκκλησιαις*. *εις την αχαιαν* bef *διελθειν* E. *συνεβαλλετο* A D-gr 57. 99 Thl-sif: *συνελαβετο* 30. 133. om *δια της χαριτος* (D) c 137 vulg(not tol) syr.
28. aft *δημοσια* ins *και κατ οικον* E. ins *διαλεγομενος και* bef *επιδεικνυς* D 137. *τον ιησ. ειναι χριστον* D [(syrr)] sah : om *τον* E.

that he could not teach ἀκριβῶς τὰ π. τοῦ Ἰησοῦ if he did not know him to be the Messiah : whereas by these words is imported that he knew and taught accurately the *facts* respecting Jesus, but of the *consequences* of that which he taught, of all which may be summed up in the doctrine of Christian baptism, he had no idea. **ἐπιστ. μόνον**] Meyer well remarks, that it is not meant that he was absolutely ignorant of the fact of there *being such a thing* as Christian baptism, but ignorant of its being any thing different from that of John : he knew, or recognized in baptism only that which the baptism of John was : a sign of repentance. **26. ἀκριβέστερον**] The former accuracy was only in *facts* : this is the still more expanded accuracy of *doctrine*. That was merely τὰ περὶ τοῦ Ἰησοῦ, as He lived and ministered on earth : this included also the promise of the Spirit, and its performance.

27. προτρεψάμενοι] probably Priscilla and Aquila principally. It may have been from their account of the Corinthian church, that he was desirous to go to Achaia. After προτρεψ. not Apollos, but *the disciples* (at Corinth) must be understood as an *object*. Otherwise αὐτόν would have been expressed. So the remarkable reading of D. **συνεβ.**] *contulit*, Vulg. **contributed**, to their help. **διὰ τῆς χάριτος**] Bengel, Olsh., Meyer, and others join these words with συνεβάλετο, and understand them '*by the Grace of God which was in him*.' But this, from their position, is very unnatural; and hardly less so from the διά, whereas such a sense would rather require τῇ χάριτι. In the only other two places where the expression occurs (reff.), it refers (1) to the electing grace of God, ref. Gal., (2) to the grace assisting believers to His service, ref. Heb. So that I adopt the more natural rendering of the E. V., **those who had believed through grace.** "The γάρ should be noticed. His coming was a valuable assistance to the Christians against the Jews, in the controversies which had doubtless been going on since Paul's departure." C. and H., edn. 2, ii. p. 10. **28.**] **διακατηλέγχετο, argued down**, as we say,—'*proved it in their teeth* :' and then the διά gives the sense of *continuity*,—that this was not done once or twice, but continuously.

m constr., ch. iv. 5 reff.
n ch. ix. 3 reff.
o ch. xiii. 6 reff.
p here only †. see 1 Macc. iii. 37. 2 Macc. ix. 23. ἡ ἄνω Ἀσίη, Herod. i. 95 and al. see Wetst.

ABDE HLP‭א a b c f g h k m o 13

XIX. 1 ᵐἘγένετο δὲ ⁿἐν τῷ τὸν Ἀπολλὼ εἶναι ἐν
Κορίνθῳ, Παῦλον ᵒδιελθόντα τὰ ᵖἀνωτερικὰ μέρη ἐλθεῖν
εἰς Ἔφεσον καὶ εὑρεῖν τινας μαθητάς, 2 εἶπέν τε πρὸς
αὐτοὺς ᑫΕἰ ʳπνεῦμα ʳἅγιον ʳἐλάβετε ˢπιστεύσαντες; ᵗοἱ δὲ
πρὸς αὐτὸν ᵘἈλλ' ᵘοὐδ' ᵛεἰ πνεῦμα ἅγιόν ʷἐστιν ἠκούσαμεν. 3 εἶπέν τε ˣΕἰς τί οὖν ˣἐβαπτίσθητε; οἱ δὲ εἶπαν

q ch. i. 6 reff. r ch. viii. 15 reff. s = Rom. xiii. 11. 1 Cor. iii. 5. xv. 2. Eph. i. 13. t ellips., ch. v. 9. ix. 5 al. u Luke xxiii. 15. 1 Cor. iii. 2. iv. 3. Gal. ii. 3. v = ch. x. 18. John ix. 25. 1 Cor. vii. 16. Jer. xxxvii. (xxx.) 6. w pres., ch. xvi. 38 reff. x ch. viii. 16 reff.

CHAP. XIX. 1. for εγενετο to ελθειν, D syr-mg have θελοντος δε του παυλου κατα την ιδιαν βουλην πορευεσθαι εις ιεροσολυμα ειπεν αυτω το πνευμα υποστρεφειν [revertere D-lat syr-mg] εις την ασιαν διελθων δε τα αν. μ. ερχεται. απολλων A²L 40: απελλην א¹ 180. for ελθ., διελθειν P: κατελθειν AEא a b o 13. 40 [arm] Jer₁. rec ευρων, omg τε in ver 2 (*alteration to simplify constr and get rid of the cha acteristic* τε), with (D)EHLP rel sah Chr: txt ABא 13 vulg copt [arm].

2. τε see above. rec aft οι δε ins ειπον, with HL rel [vulg-ed demid Syr coptt æth arm], ειπαν P Chr: om ABDE 13. 40 am tol syr. αλλ ουδε πν. αγ. λαμβανουσιν τινες ηκουσαμεν D¹(and lat: txt D⁴) syr-mg, simly sah. rec ουδε, with (D¹)EHLP rel 36 Chr Marc: txt A B(sic: see table) D².

3. ειπ. δε D a 133 lect-58: ο δε ειπ. AEא [k(οι δε ειπεν)] 13 vulg copt Jer: ειπεν ουν c syr Marc₁: txt BHLP rel 36 æth [arm] Chr₁. rec adds προς αυτους, with HLP rel [Syr coptt æth] Chr Marc: om ABDEא a c h 13. 36 vulg syr arm αυτοις [k] 40 lect-12 Thl-fin. (ειπαν, so ABEא 13: ελεγον D.)

CHAP. XIX. 1—41.] ARRIVAL, RESIDENCE, AND ACTS OF PAUL AT EPHESUS. 1. **τὰ ἀνωτερικὰ μέρη**] By this name were known the eastern parts of Asia Minor, beyond the river Halys, or in comparison with Ephesus, in the direction of that river. So Herodotus, speaking as a Halicarnassian, calls even the neighbourhood of Sardis τὰ ἄνω τῆς Ἀσίας, i. 177; including in the term, however, many of the inland districts, Assyria, Babylonia, &c. So that the reading ἀνατολικά, which is found in three cursives and Theophyl-sif., is a good gloss. **τινας μαθητάς**] These seem to have been in the same situation as Apollos, see on ch. xviii. 25. They cannot have been mere disciples of John, on account of πιστεύσαντες, which can bear no meaning but that of believing *on the Lord Jesus:* but they had received only John's baptism, and had had no proof of the descent of the Holy Spirit, nor knowledge of His gifts. 2. **ἐλάβ. πιστεύσ.**] The aorist should be faithfully rendered: not as E. V. '*Have ye received the Holy Ghost since ye believed?*' but **Did ye receive the Holy Ghost when ye became** (not, *when ye had become:* cf. προσευξάμενοι εἶπαν, ch. i. 24, and Winer, edn. 6, § 45. 6. b, also note on ver. 29) **believers?** i.e. '*on your becoming believers, had ye the gifts of the Spirit conferred on you?*' —as in ch. viii. 16, 17. This is both grammatically necessary (see also Rom. xiii. 11, ἐγγύτερον ἡμῶν ἡ σωτηρία ἢ ὅτε ἐπιστεύσαμεν), and absolutely demanded by the sense; the enquiry being, not as to any reception of the Holy Ghost during the period *since* their baptism, but as to one simultaneous with their first reception into the church: and their *not* having *then* received Him is accounted for by the *deficiency of their baptism.* **ἀλλ' οὐδέ**] **On the contrary, not even . . . ἠκούσαμεν**] Here again, not, 'we *have not* heard,' which would involve an absurdity: 'nam neque Mosen neque Johannem Baptistam sequi potuissent, quin de Spiritu Sancto ipso audissent' (Bengel); —but **we did not hear,** at the time of our conversion:—Our reception into the faith was unaccompanied by any preaching of the office or the gifts of the Spirit,—our baptism was not followed by any imparting of His gifts: **we did not so much as hear Him mentioned. ἐστιν** cannot, from its position, be emphatic, nor does it mean "were to be had" (Wordsw.), as John vii. 39. The stress of the sentence is on ἠκούσαμεν: so far from *receiving* the Holy Ghost, they did not even *hear* of His existence. Tiros only will find an objection to this rendering in ἐστίν (expecting ἦν): the present is commonly used after the aorist of declarative verbs or verbs of sense, in the clause which contains the matter declared, seen, or heard: the action being transferred *pro tempore* to the time spoken of. See reff. 3.] Paul's question establishes the above rendering, **to what then** (οὖν, if ye did not so much as hear of the Holy Ghost at your first believing) **were ye baptized?** If the question and answer in ver. 2 regarded, as in E. V., the *whole in-*

[x] Εἰς τὸ Ἰωάννου βάπτισμα. 4 εἶπεν δὲ Παῦλος Ἰωαννης
[y] ἐβάπτισεν [yz] βάπτισμα [z] μετανοίας, τῷ λαῷ [a] λέγων [b] εἰς
τὸν ἐρχόμενον [c] μετ' αὐτὸν [ad] ἵνα [b] πιστεύσωσιν, [e] τουτέστιν
εἰς τὸν Ἰησοῦν. 5 ἀκούσαντες δὲ [x] ἐβαπτίσθησαν [x] εἰς τὸ

y constr., Luke vii. 29. z Mark i. 4. Luke iii. 3. ch. xiii. 24 only. a = here only. (see note.) see Matt. iv. 3. xii. 16. Mark iii. 0. b w. εἰς, ch. x. 43 reff. c w. person, ch. xiii. 25 (Paul) reff. d arrangemt of words, John xiii. 29. Rom. xi. 31. 1 Cor. ix. 15. 2 Cor. ii. 4. Gal. ii. 10. e Matt. xxvii. 46. Mark vii. 2. ch. i. 19. Rom. (i. 12.) vii. 18 al4. Philem. 12. Heb. ii. 14 al5. 1 Pet. iii. 20.

4. for δε, τε H 192 Thl-sif [om Syr sah]. ins ο bef παυλος D a 180 lect-58. rec aft ιωαννης ins μεν (*see ch* i. 5), with EHLP rel syr copt Chr_1 $Marc_1$: om ABDℵ a 13. 40 vulg sah [arm]. rec ins χριστον bef ιησ., with HLP rel 36 Chr : for τον ιησ., χριστον D : add χρ. 105 lect-12 [Syr] sah æth-pl arm : om ABEℵ a 13[from the space] 40 vulg syr copt æth-rom.

5. aft ακουσ. δε ins τουτο D ([Syr]).

terval since their conversion, this enquiry would have been more naturally expressed in the perfect. See Gal. iii. 27, where there is the same necessity of preserving the historical sense of the aorists.

εἰς τί] **unto** (with a view to, as introductory to) **what profession?** They answer, **unto** (that indicated by) **the baptism of John,** viz.: *repentance,* and *the believing on Jesus, then to come,* but *now* (see ch. xviii. 25, note) *the object of our faith.* **4. εἰς τ. ἐρχ. . . . ἵνα π.]** This peculiar inversion of words, see reff., seems to mark the hand of Paul. **ἵνα** does not give (as Meyer) the mere purpose of his baptism (saying that *he baptized* in order that . . . .), but combines, as in similar uses of προσεύχομαι ἵνα and the like, the purport and purpose together: 'He commanded them that they *should* (purport)—and he spoke to them, that they *might* (purpose).' See this discussed in note on 1 Cor. xiv. 13. **5.]** Two singular perversions of this verse have occurred: (1) the Anabaptists use it to authorize the repetition of Christian baptism, whereas it is not *Christian baptism* which was repeated, seeing that John's baptism was *not such,* but only the baptism which they now for the first time received; and (2) Beza, Calixtus, Calov., Suicer, Glass., Buddeus, Wolf, and al., wishing to wrest this weapon out of the hands of the Anabaptists, oddly enough suppose this verse to belong still to Paul's discourse, and to mean, '*and the people when they heard him* (John), *were baptized into the name of the Lord Jesus.*' This obviously is contrary to fact, historically: and would leave our present narrative in a singular state: for Paul, having treated their baptism as *insufficient,* would thus proceed on it to impose his hands, as if it were *sufficient.* **εἰς τὸ ὄν. τ. κυρ. Ἰησοῦ]** Two questions arise here: (1) Was it the ordinary practice to rebaptize those who had been baptized either by John or by the disciples (John iv. 1 f.) *before baptism became, by the effusion of the Holy Spirit,* λουτρὸν παλιγγενεσίας? This we cannot definitely answer. That it was *sometimes* done, this incident shews: but in all probability, in the cases of the majority of the original disciples, the greater baptism by the Holy Ghost and fire on the day of Pentecost superseded the outward form or sign. The Apostles themselves received only this baptism (besides probably that of John): and most likely the same was the case with the original believers. But of the three thousand who were added on the day of Pentecost, very many must have been already baptized by John; and all were *rebaptized without enquiry.* (2) What conclusion can we deduce from this verse respecting the use or otherwise of baptism *in the name of the Father, and the Son, and the Holy Ghost,* in the apostolic period? The only answer must be, that at that early time we have no indication of set formulæ in the administration of either sacrament. Such formulæ arose of necessity, when precision in formal statement of doctrine became an absolute necessity in the church: and the materials for them were found ready in the word of God, who has graciously provided for all necessities of His church in all time. But, in matter of *fact,* such a baptism as this *was* a baptism into the name of the Father, Son, and Holy Ghost. As Jews, these men were already servants of the living God—and by putting on the Son, they received in a new and more gracious sense the Father also. And in the sequel of their baptism, the imposition of hands, they sensibly became recipients of God the Holy Ghost. Where such manifestations were present, the form of words might be wanting; but with us, who have them not, it is necessary and imperative. Dean Howson regards (i. 517; ii. 13) St. Paul's question in our ver. 3 as indicative that the name of the Holy Ghost was used in the baptismal formula. But

f ch. viii. 17 reff.
g here only. Ezek. ii. 2.
h ch. ii. 4 reff.
i ch. ii. 17, 18, from Joel ii. 28. of historical fact, here first.
k = ch. ii. 41 al. fr.
l ch. vi. 2 al. fr. δεκαδύο, ch. xxiv. 11 v. r. only. 1 Chron. xv. 10. Esth. ii. 12 only.
m ch. ix. 27 reff.
n ch. xiii. 31 reff.
o ch. xvii. 2 reff. absol., ch. xviii. 4 reff.

[x] ὄνομα τοῦ κυρίου Ἰησοῦ. 6 καὶ [f] ἐπιθέντος αὐτοῖς τοῦ
Παύλου [f] χεῖρας [g] ἦλθεν τὸ [g] πνεῦμα τὸ ἅγιον [g] ἐπ᾿ αὐτούς,
[v] ἐλάλουν τε [h] γλώσσαις καὶ [i] ἐπροφήτευον. 7 ἦσαν δὲ οἱ
πάντες ἄνδρες [k] ὡςεὶ *[l] δώδεκα. 8 εἰςελθὼν δὲ εἰς τὴν
συναγωγὴν [m] ἐπαῤῥησιάζετο [n] ἐπὶ μῆνας τρεῖς [o] διαλεγόμενος καὶ [p] πείθων τὰ περὶ τῆς [q] βασιλείας τοῦ [q] θεοῦ.
9 ὡς δέ τινες [r] ἐσκληρύνοντο καὶ [s] ἠπείθουν [t] κακολο-
γοῦντες τὴν [u] ὁδὸν [v] ἐνώπιον [w] τοῦ πλήθους, [x] ἀποστὰς ἀπ᾿
αὐτῶν [y] ἀφώρισεν τοὺς μαθητάς, [z] καθ᾿ ἡμέραν [o] διαλεγόμενος ἐν τῇ [a] σχολῇ Τυράννου. 10 τοῦτο δὲ ἐγένετο
[n] ἐπὶ ἔτη δύο, ὥστε πάντας τοὺς [b] κατοικοῦντας τὴν

ABDE HLPℵa bcfgh kmo13

p ch. xviii. 4. constr., here (ch. xxviii. 23 rec.) only. q Acts, ch. i. 3. viii. 12. xiv. 22 (xx. 25 v. r.). xxviii. 23, 31 only. Luke and Mark passim. r Rom. ix. 18 reff. s ch. xiv. 2 reff. t Matt. xv. 4 ‖ Mk. (from Exod. xxi. 16). Mark ix. 39 only. u = ch. ix. 2 reff. v = 1 Cor. i. 29. 3 John 6. w absol., ch. ii. 6 reff. x ch. xv. 38 reff. y = Matt. xiii. 49. xxv. 32. Luke vi. 22. 2 Cor. vi. 17. Gal. ii. 12 only. (ch. xiii. 2 reff.) Gen. ii. 10. z ch. ii. 46 reff. a here only ‡. (Gen. xxxiii. 14. Prov. xxviii. 19 only.) b constr., ch. i. 19 reff.

om του D¹(ins D³) lect-58. aft ιησ. ins χριστου D 64. 137 syr-w-ast [Syr sah æth-pl] Jer₁ Ambr₁: add further εις αφεσιν αμαρτιων D syr-w-ast (and Jer in ver 4).
6. επιθεντο(sic) D¹(txt D²). rec ins τας bef χειρας, with EL rel 36 Chr₁ Marc₁: om ABHPℵ c m. (13 def.)—χειρα D am demid Syr æth, D also places χειρα bef του παυλου. for ηλθ., ευθεως επεπεσεν D Jer₁: *continuo venit* tol. επ αυτοις D¹(txt D⁴) lect-58. for τε, δε D-gr o 25 E-lat coptt: om m D-lat arm. aft γλωσσαις ins ετεραις [so sah] *et senserunt illi in seipsis quod et interpretarentur ipsi.* τινες δε syr-mg. rec προεφητ., with EHLP rel Chr: εφητευον a¹: txt ABDℵ 36. (13 def.)
7. *rec δεκαδυο, with HLP rel Chr₁ Thl-sif: δωδεκα (*see ch* xxiv. 11) ABDEℵ a k m 13. 36. 40 Thl-fin.
8. aft εισελθων δε ins ο παυλος D Syr æth. ins εν δυναμει μεγαλη bef επαρρησιαζετο D syr-mg. om τα BD lect-12 vss: ins AEHLPℵ 13. 36 Chr₁. for θεου, κυριου 36 (so c in ver 10; and for κυριου, θεου k in ver 20).
9. τινες μεν ουν αυτων D[-gr]. aft την οδον ins του κυριου E [vulg-ed tol] am² demid: του θεου 5. 8. 73 Syr. aft του πληθους ins των εθνων DE Syr syr-w-ast. [ins] τοτε [bef αποστας] D Syr syr-w-ast. [aft] αποστας [ins] ο παυλος D Syr [syr-w-ast æth]. ins το bef καθ᾿ ημεραν D c. om εν ℵ¹: but afterwards supplied *eadem manu.* τυραννιου D-gr 3. 95¹. rec aft τυραννου ins τινος (*see ch* x. 22, xiii. 15, xvii. 34, *where also* D *inserts* τις), with DEHLP rel 36 [vulg-clem am syr arm] Chr₁, add further απο ωρας ε′ εως δεκατης D 137 syr[-mg]: om ABℵ [13 from the space] 27-9. 81 fuld tol [Syr] coptt.
10. for ωστε to ελλ., ε(ω)ς[*ita ut*] παντες οι κατοικουντες την ασιαν (η)κουσαν τους

the inference seems to me insecure.

6.] See ch. viii. 17; x. 46, and note on ch. ii. 4: and on ἐπροφ., ch. xi. 27, note.

7.] **οἱ πάντ.**, in all: so Herod. vii. 4, βασιλεύσαντα τὰ πάντα ἔτεα ἕξ τε κ. τριήκοντα: Thuc. v. 120, πεσόντων δὲ τῶν πάντων πολλῶν. See Kühner, § 489 c.

9.] Probably the school of Tyrannus was a private synagogue (called Beth Midrasch by the Jews), where he might assemble the believing Jews quietly, and also invite the attendance of Gentiles to hear the word. But it is also possible that, as commonly supposed, Tyrannus may have been a Gentile sophist. The name occurs as a proper name, 2 Macc. iv. 40 Ed-vat. (Αυρανου AB), —and with τινος (see var. readd.).

10. **ἔτη δύο**] We cannot derive any certain estimate of the length of Paul's stay in Ephesus from these words,—even if we add the three months of ver. 8,—for vv. 21, 22 admit of an *interval after the expiration of the two years and three months.* And his own expression, ch. xx. 31, τριετίαν, implies that it was longer than from this chapter would at first sight appear. He probably (compare his announced intention, 1 Cor. xvi. 8, with his expectation of meeting Titus at Troas, 2 Cor. ii. 12, 13, which shews that he was not far off the time previously arranged) left Ephesus about or soon after the third Pentecost after that which he kept in Jerusalem. See Prolegg. to 1 Cor. § vi.

πάντας τ. κατ.] Hyperbolical:—*all had the opportunity,* and probably some of every considerable town availed themselves of it. To this long teaching of Paul the seven

Ασίαν ἀκοῦσαι τὸν [c]λόγον τοῦ [c]κυρίου, Ἰουδαίους τε
καὶ Ἕλληνας. 11 [d]δυνάμεις τε οὐ τὰς [e]τυχούσας ὁ
θεὸς ἐποίει [f]διὰ τῶν χειρῶν Παύλου, 12 ὥστε καὶ ἐπὶ
τοὺς ἀσθενοῦντας [g]ἀποφέρεσθαι ἀπὸ τοῦ [h]χρωτὸς
αὐτοῦ [i]σουδάρια ἢ [k]σιμικίνθια καὶ [l]ἀπαλλάσσεσθαι ἀπ'
αὐτῶν τὰς νόσους τά τε [m]πνεύματα τὰ [m]πονηρὰ [n]ἐκ-
πορεύεσθαι. 13 [o]ἐπεχείρησαν δέ τινες καὶ τῶν [p]περιερχο-

d σουδαρια... ABDE HLPℵ a b c d f g h k m o 13

c ch. xiii. 49 reff.
d = Matt. vii. 22. ch. ii. 22. Gal. iii. 5 ‡.
e = ch. xxviii. 2 only ‡. 3 Macc. iii. 7. μικρὰς καὶ τὰς τυχούσας πράξεις, Polyb. i. 25. 6. οὐ τ. τυχοῦσαν ἀπορίαν, id. i. 42. 12. οὐχ ὁ τυχὼν ἀνήρ (said of Moses), Longin. de Subl. § 9.
f ch. xiv. 3 reff.
g w. ἐπί, Rev. xxi. 10. εἰς, Luke xvi. 22. 1 Cor. xvi. 3. Rev. xvii. 3. 2 Chron. xxxvi. 7. absol., Mark xv. 1 only.
h here only. Exod. xxviii. 38 (42).
i Luke xix. 20. John xi. 44. xx. 7 only †.
k here only †.
l = here (Luke xii. 58. Heb. ii. 15) only. Job ix. 34. constr., Xen. Anab. vii. 1. 4.
m = Luke vii. 21. viii. 2. Acts, here, &c., 4 times only. Luke only, exc. Matt. xii. 45. 1 Kings xix. 9.
n = here [and Matt. xvii. 21] only.
o ch. ix. 29 reff.
p = here only. Xen. Œcon. x. 10. (ch. xxviii. 13 reff.)

λογους του κυριου ιουδαιοι και ελληνες D[1]-gr(txt (but απαντας) D[4]). rec aft κυρ. ins ιησου, with [H(sic, Treg)] LP rel: om ABDEℵ a c k 13. 36. 40 vulg syrr coptt [æth] arm.

11. for τε, δε D[1]-gr(txt D[4]) a h 38 syr copt Thl-sif. rec εποιει bef ο θεος, with HLP rel [vulg-clem] syrr copt æth Chr_1 Thl-sif: txt ABDEℵ m 13 am(and demid fuld tol) sah arm Thl-fin.

12. rec επιφερεσθαι (*prob corrn to suit* επι τ. ασθ.: *see note*), with DHLP rel [æth (appy)] Chr_1: περιφ. 96. 142: txt ABEℵ a 13. 36. 40 [syrr(appy) arm], *deferrentur* vulg [L[1] repeats επιφ. aft αυτου]. for ἤ, και 7. 68. 104-5 vulg-ed(and tol) Thl-fin: η και D-gr arm. απαλλασεσθαι B[1] h[1] o. [for πνευματα τα, πνα] τα D[E]. rec εξερχεσθαι (*more usual word for the going out of evil spirits, see Luke* iv. 35, 36, 41, viii. 2, 29, 33 *al*, *ch* viii. 7, xvi. 18), with HLP rel Chr: txt ABDEℵ a c d k 13. 36. 40. rec adds απ αυτων (*supplementary insertion*), with HLP rel Chr: εξ αυτων sah: om ABDEℵ a c d k 13. 36. 40 vulg syrr copt [æth] arm.

13. rec (for και) απο, with LP 13 rel copt Chr: και απο H 25. 73. 95[1]-8-9 (syr) arm: *et de* vulg: εκ D 43 (*the* και *has been omd either as unnecessary, or perhaps, as Meyer, because it seemed unworthy of St. Paul to couple him with these: then the* απο *or* εκ *inserted, to define the gen more exactly*): txt ABEℵ a c m Syr.

churches of Asia owe their establishment.

11. **οὐ τὰς τυχ.**] See reff. **miracles of no ordinary kind.** *In what* they differed from the usual displays of power by the Apostles, is presently related: viz. that even garments taken from him were endued with miraculous power. **12.**] The rec. reading, ἐπιφέρεσθαι, may have been occasioned by the ἐπί preceding: the other, again, by the ἀπό following: in such uncertainty the reading of the ancient MSS. must prevail. **σουδ.**] **handkerchiefs**: see ref. Luke, and notes there. **σιμικ.**] not *napkins*, but *semicinctia*, **aprons**, such as servants and artisans use. ἀμφότερα λινοειδῆ εἰσι, Schol. *Diseases*, and *possession by evil spirits*, are here plainly *distinguished* from each other. The rationalists, and semi-rationalists, are much troubled to reconcile the fact related, that such handkerchiefs and aprons *were instrumental in working the cures*, with what they are pleased to call a popular notion founded in superstition and error. But in this and similar narratives (see ch. v. 15, note) Christian faith finds no difficulty whatever. All miraculous working is an exertion of the direct power of the All-powerful; a suspension *by Him* of His ordinary laws: and whether He will use *any* instrument in doing this, or *what* instrument, must depend altogether on His own purpose in the miracle—the effect to be produced on the recipients, beholders, or hearers. Without His special selection and enabling, *all instruments were vain;* with these, *all are capable.* In the present case, as before in ch. v. 15, it was His purpose to exalt His Apostle as the Herald of His gospel, and to lay in Ephesus the strong foundation of His church. And He therefore endues him with this extraordinary power. (Wordsw. sees an especial fitness in this having occurred at *Ephesus* (see on ver. 19), and refers to God having shewed in Egypt that His power was greater than that of Satan working by magicians: and it may well have been so.) But to argue by analogy from such a case,—to suppose that because our Lord was able, and Peter, and Paul, and in O. T. times Elisha, were enabled, to exert this peculiar power, therefore the same will be possessed by the body or relics of every real or supposed saint, is the height of folly and fanaticism. The true analogy tends directly the other way. In *no cases but these* do we find the power, even in the apostolic days: and the general cessation of all extraordinary gifts of the Spirit would lead us to the inference that

q here only †. τρόπους ἐξορκώσεων κατέλιπεν, Jos. Antt. viii. 2. 5 (of Solomon). (see below [u].)
r here only.
s 2 Tim. ii. 19. Isa. xxvi. 13.
t = ch. xvi. 16 reff.
u (and constr.) Mark v. 7 only. (2 Chron. xxxvi. 13. Neh. xiii. 25 B‎א &c.) ἐνορκίζω, 1 Thess. v. 27. Neh. as above, A. ἐξορκίζω, Matt. xxvi. 63 only. Gen. xxiv. 3. Judg. xvii. 2 A Ald. compl. only.
v ch. ix. 20 reff.
w = here only.
x constr. (without οἱ), ch. ii. 5 reff.
y w. acc., ch. xviii. 25. James iv. 14. Jude 10. Deut. xxxi. 27.
z here only. 1 Kings x. 6. xi. 6. xvi. 13 only.
a = here (Matt. xx. 25 ‖ Mk. 1 Pet. v. 3) only. Num. xxi. 24. xxxii. 22, 29. Ps. ix. 25.
b = Rev. xii. 8 only. Exod. i. 9. Ps. xii. 4.

ABDE HLP‎א a b c d f g h k m o 13

μένων Ἰουδαίων [q] ἐξορκιστῶν [rs] ὀνομάζειν [r] ἐπὶ τοὺς
[t] ἔχοντας τὰ [m] πνεύματα τὰ [m] πονηρὰ τὸ [s] ὄνομα τοῦ [s] κυρίου
Ἰησοῦ, λέγοντες [u] Ὁρκίζω ὑμᾶς τὸν Ἰησοῦν [v] ὃν Παῦλος
[v] κηρύσσει. 14 *ἦσαν δέ τινες Σκευᾶ Ἰουδαίου [w] ἀρχ-*
ιερέως ἑπτὰ υἱοὶ [οἱ] τοῦτο [x] ποιοῦντες. 15 *ἀποκριθὲν δὲ τὸ*
[m] πνεῦμα τὸ [m] πονηρὸν εἶπεν αὐτοῖς Τὸν Ἰησοῦν γινώσκω
καὶ τὸν Παῦλον [y] ἐπίσταμαι· ὑμεῖς δὲ τίνες ἐστέ; 16 *Καὶ*
[z] ἐφαλόμενος ὁ ἄνθρωπος ἐπ᾽ αὐτοὺς ἐν ᾧ ἦν τὸ [m] πνεῦμα τὸ
[m] πονηρόν, [a] κατακυριεύσας ἀμφοτέρων [b] ἴσχυσεν κατ᾽ αὐτῶν,

περιερχομενω D^1[-gr]. om του D^1(ins D^3). rec ορκιζομεν (*alteration to suit the plurals preceding*), with HLP rel [syrr sah æth arm-mss] Chr: εξορκιζομεν a o 36: txt ABDE‎א 13. 40 vulg copt [arm]. ins κυριον bef ιησ. ‎א^1. rec ins ο bef παυλος, with L rel Thl: om ABDE H[e sil] P‎א c m 13. 40 Chr$_1$.

14. for ver, εν οις[*in quo*] και[om syr-mg] υιοι (add επτα syr-mg) σκευα τινος ιερεως ηθελησαν το αυτο ποιησαι εθος ειχαν τους τοιουτους εξορκιζειν και εισελθοντες προς τον δαιμονιζομενον [*introierunt adimplentes*] ηρξαντο επικαλεισθαι το ονομα λεγοντες παραγγελλομεν σοι εν ιησου ον παυλος κηρυσσει εξελθειν (εξ. bef κηρ. D^1) D syr-mg. τινος B(D) E-gr 36 demid Syr copt [arm] (*alteration,* τινες *not appearing to the copyist to agree with the definite* επτα): τινας m: txt AHLP‎א 13 rel vulg E-lat syr Chr$_1$. rec υιοι bef σκευα (omg it after επτα), with (D)HLP rel 36 (Syr copt) syr Chr: om m 180: txt ABE‎א a 13(sic) 14^1-5-8. 40 vulg arm (sah). σκευια A. ιουδαιοι L. om οι (*originally perhaps owing to* οι *of* υιοι *preceding*) AB‎א a 13.

15. τοτε απεκριθη το πν. το πον. (και) ειπεν D, και insd by D^4. rec om αυτοις, with EHLP rel Thl-sif: ins ABD‎א a c m 13. 36 vulg syrr coptt æth arm Chr$_1$ Thl-fin. ins μεν bef ιησουν B E-gr ‎א^3 c 40. 137 syr [Cassiod$_1$].

16. rec εφαλλομενος, with (D)EHLP‎א^3 rel Chr$_1$: εναλλομ. D: txt AB‎א^1. rec επ' αυτους bef ο ανθρωπος (*alteration of characteristic order*), with (D)HLP [vulg-clem Syr coptt æth] Chr$_1$ Thl-sif: om επ αυτους a 69. 105 arm: E places it aft το πονηρον: txt AB‎א c m 13. 40 am(and demid fuld) syr Chr-comm$_1$ Thl-fin.—εις αυτους D vulg. rec ins και bef κατακυριευσας, with HLP‎א^1 rel 36 vulg [arm, Treg] Chr: om ABDE‎א^3 a c 13. 40 copt [sah] arm. κυριευσας D: κρατησας 15-8. 36. 180: κατακυριευσαν AEHLP rel: -σεν a: txt B‎א c o 13. rec for αμφοτερων, αυτων (*corrn to suit* επτα above: *see note*), with HLP rel Syr: αυτου d: [*eorum septem* sah: *eorum*] *omnium* æth-rom: om E: txt ABD‎א a 13. 36. 40 vulg syr-mg-gr [copt arm] Thl-fin. ενισχυσεν ‎א^1 e: κατισχυσε c.

à fortiori these, which were even then the rarest (οὐχ αἱ τυχοῦσαι), have ceased also.

13.] See note on Matt. xii. 27, respecting the Jewish exorcists. These men, seeing the success of Paul's agency in casting out devils, adopt the Name of Jesus in their own exorcisms.

14. ἀρχιερέως] The word must be used in a wide sense. He may have been chief of the priests resident at Ephesus: or perhaps chief of one of the twenty-four courses.

τινες does not belong to ἑπτά, see ch. xxiii. 23, but stands alone, recalling the τινες of the preceding verse. Without the οἱ it would be, '*certain men, &c. were attempting this,*' ἦσαν and ποιοῦντες being taken together. With it, **They were** (it was) **certain men, seven sons, &c. who attempted this.**

15.] The narrative, from describing the nature of the attempt, passes to a single case in which it was tried, and in which (see below) two only of the brothers were apparently concerned. No difference between γινώσκω and ἐπίσταμαι must be pressed:—the two verbs are apparently used as separating Jesus and Paul, so that they do not stand together in the same category:—as in E. V., **Jesus I know, and Paul I know**: the One being God in heaven, the other man on earth.

16. ἀμφοτέρων] The weight of manuscript evidence for this reading is even surpassed by its internal probability. There would be every reason, as *seven* have been before mentioned, for altering it into αὐτῶν: but no imaginable one for substituting it for αὐτῶν. *Two only*, it would seem, were thus employed on this particular occasion:

ὥςτε γυμνοὺς καὶ [c] τετραυματισμένους [d] ἐκφυγεῖν ἐκ τοῦ
οἴκου ἐκείνου. 17 τοῦτο δὲ ἐγένετο [e] γνωστὸν πᾶσιν Ἰουδαίοις τε καὶ Ἕλλησιν τοῖς [f] κατοικοῦσιν τὴν Ἔφεσον,
καὶ [g] ἐπέπεσεν φόβος ἐπὶ πάντας αὐτούς, καὶ [h] ἐμεγαλύνετο
τὸ ὄνομα τοῦ κυρίου Ἰησοῦ. 18 πολλοί τε τῶν [i] πεπιστευκότων ἤρχοντο [k] ἐξομολογούμενοι καὶ [l] ἀναγγέλλον-
τες τὰς [m] πράξεις αὐτῶν. 19 [n] ἱκανοὶ δὲ τῶν τὰ [o] περίεργα πραξάντων [p] συνενέγκαντες τὰς [q] βίβλους [r] κατ-
έκαιον [s] ἐνώπιον πάντων· καὶ [t] συνεψήφισαν τὰς [u] τιμὰς
αὐτῶν καὶ [v] εὗρον [w] ἀργυρίου [x] μυριάδας πέντε. 20 οὕτως
[y] κατὰ [y] κράτος τοῦ [z] κυρίου ὁ [z] λόγος [a] ηὔξανεν καὶ [b] ἴσχυεν.

c Luke xx. 12 only. Ezek xxviii. 16.
d ch. xvi. 27 al. Judg. vi. 11.
e = ch. i. 19 reff.
f constr., ch. i. 19 reff.
g ch. viii. 16 reff.
h = ch. x. 46 reff.
i absol., ch. xv. 5 reff.
k = Matt. iii. 6. Mark i. 5. James v. 16‡.
l ch. xiv. 27 reff.
m = Matt. xvi. 27. Luke xxiii. 51. Rom. viii. 13. (xii. 4.) Col. iii. 8 only. 2 Chron. xii. 15.
n = ch. xii. 12 reff.
o = here (1 Tim. v. 13) only†. (-γάζεσθαι, 2 Thess. iii. 11. Sir. iii. 23. -γεία, Sir. xli. 22.)
p = here only‡. Xen. Anab. vi. 4. 9.
q Matt. i. 1 al. Dan. ix. 2.
r Matt. xiii. 30. Luke iii. 17 al. Gen. xxxviii. 24.
s = ch. ii. 25 reff.
t here only†.
u = Matt. xxvii. 9. 1 Cor. vi. 20. vii. 23. Ps. xlviii. 8.
v = ch. xxvii. 28. 1 Chron. xx. 2.
w sing., = here only. 3 Kings x. 29. see Matt. xxvii. 9.
x Luke xii. 1. ch. xxi. 20. Heb. xii. 22. Jude 14. Rev. v. 11. ix. 16 only. Deut. xxxiii. 17.
y here only†. Jos. Antt. viii. 11. 3.
z ch. xiii. 49 reff.
a intr., ch. vi. 7 reff.
b = here only. Exod. i. 20. Xen. Cyr. vi. 1. 24. see ver. 16.

aft εκφυγειν ins αυτους A.

17. ins τοις bef ιουδ. EP 192. om τε DE sah. om την A¹E c 137. επεσεν (*mistake: or prep omd as unnecessary*) AD 13, επεεν E.—φοβος bef επ. D. ins ο bef φοβος ℵ¹. om του DP (o¹?) 101-33.

18. for τε, δε D[-gr] 36 coptt. πιστευοντων D [vulg E-lat]: -σαντων E[-gr] 28. (Mai Tischdf state expr agst Bch that there is in B no insn aft εξομ.)

19. om δε D¹-gr: τε E syr Bas₁ Chr₁. των περι τα εργα D¹[-gr](txt D²). aft συνενεγκαντες ins και D κατεκαυσαν E vulg. συνκατεψηφισαν E. om last και D¹(ins D²).

20. rec ο λογος bef του κυριου (*corrn of characteristic order*), with HLPℵ³ 13. 36 rel [am sah-marg arm] copt Chr₁: [ο λ. τ.] θεου E [k] 21. 73. 106² vulg[-clem(with fuld &c.)] sah[-txt] arm: txt ABℵ¹. ουτως κατα κρατος ενισχυσεν και η πιστις του θεου ηυξανε και επληθυνετο(επληθυνε D¹) D: Syr also has η πιστις του θεου. ισχυσεν ℵ.

and Luke has retained the word as it stood in the record furnished to him. Whether any similar occurrence happened to the rest, we are not informed: this one is selected as most notorious. **γυμνούς**] With their clothes torn off them. **18.**] The natural effect of such an occurrence was to induce a horror of magical arts, &c., which some were still continuing to countenance or practise secretly, together with a profession of Christianity. Such persons now came forward and confessed their error. The πράξεις of this verse denotes the *association with* such practices: the next verse treats of the *magicians themselves*. **19. περίεργα**] '*male sedula*' ('*curiosa*,' Hor. Epod. xviii. 25). τὶς τῶν περιέργων in Aristænet. Ep. ii. 18, is '*a magician*' (Kuin.). **τὰς βίβλους**] Magical *formulæ*, or *receipt-books*, or *written amulets*. These last were celebrated by the name of Ἐφέσια γράμματα. So Eustath. ad Hom. Od. τ. p. 694 (Kuin.): Ἐφέσια γράμματα—ἐπῳδαὶ γάρ τινες φασὶν ἐκεῖναι ἦσαν, ἃς καὶ Κροῖσος ἐπὶ τῆς πυρᾶς εἰπὼν ὠφελήθη· καὶ ἐν Ὀλυμπίᾳ δὲ φασί, Μιλησίου καὶ Ἐφεσίου παλαιόντων τὸν Μιλήσιον μὴ δύνασθαι παλαίειν διὰ τὸ τὸν ἕτερον περὶ τῷ ἀστραγάλῳ ἔχειν τὰ Ἐφέσια γράμματα· ὧν γνωσθέντων καὶ λυθέντων αὐτῷ, τριακοντάκις τὸ ἑξῆς πεσεῖν τὸν Ἐφέσιον. See more illustrations in Wetst. They were copies of the mystic words engraved on the image of the Ephesian Artemis. Eustath. in C. and H. ii. 16. **ἀργ. μυρ. πέν.**] 50,000 drachmæ, i. e. denarii: for the drachma of the Augustan and following ages was not the real Attic drachma, but the Roman denarius—about 8½*d*. of our money: which makes the entire value about £1770. That drachmæ and not shekels (Grot., Hamm.) are meant, is plain: for Luke is writing of a Grecian town, and to a Greek. **20. κατὰ κράτος**] "Eo modo dicitur urbs αἱρεῖσθαι κατὰ κράτος, *quæ vi expugnatur*, apud Plut. Apophth. p. 176. Hinc lucem mutuatur locus, Act. xix. 20, ubi dicitur verbum Domini κατὰ κράτος ἰσχύειν, *per vim invalescere*, quasi oppugnans et vi expugnans corda hominum." Hermann on Viger, p. 632. So κατὰ μικρόν, κατ' ὀλίγον, καθ' ὑπερβολήν, κατὰ κόσμον. See Bernhardy, Syntax, p. 241, f.

c = Luke vii. 1. d = Luke ix. 44. xxi. 14. ch. v. 4. Hagg. ii. 19. see ch. i. 7. e ch. xvii. 16 reff. f ver. 1. g ch. i. 3. xx. 1. Heb. x. 15, 26 al. Gen. xiv. 17. h = ch. iv. 12 reff. i of place, = here only. k Matt. xxv. 44. Rom. xv. 25 al.+ l = here (ch. iii. 5 reff.) only. Gen. viii. 10, 12. Xen. Cyr. v. 4. 38.

21 Ὡς δὲ [c] ἐπληρώθη ταῦτα, [d] ἔθετο ὁ Παῦλος ἐν τῷ
[e] πνεύματι [f] διελθὼν τὴν Μακεδονίαν καὶ Ἀχαΐαν πορεύεσθαι εἰς Ἱεροσόλυμα, εἰπὼν ὅτι [g] μετὰ τὸ γενέσθαι
με ἐκεῖ [h] δεῖ με καὶ Ῥώμην [i] ἰδεῖν. 22 ἀποστείλας δὲ εἰς
τὴν Μακεδονίαν δύο τῶν [k] διακονούντων αὐτῷ, Τιμόθεον
καὶ Ἔραστον, αὐτὸς [l] ἐπέσχεν χρόνον [m] εἰς τὴν Ἀσίαν.
23 ἐγένετο δὲ [n] κατὰ τὸν [n] καιρὸν [n] ἐκεῖνον [o] τάραχος [o] οὐκ
[o] ὀλίγος περὶ [p] τῆς ὁδοῦ. 24 Δημήτριος γάρ τις ὀνόματι
[q] ἀργυροκόπος [r] ποιῶν [s] ναοὺς [t] ἀργυροῦς Ἀρτέμιδος
[uv] παρείχετο τοῖς [w] τεχνίταις [o] οὐκ [o] ὀλίγην [u] ἐργασίαν,

ABDE HLPℵ a b c d f g h k m o 13

m = Mark i. 39. ch. viii. 40. xxi. 13. xxiii. 11. xxv. 4 al. n ch. xii. 1 only. Num. xxii. 4. o ch. xii. 18 (reff.). p ch. ix. 2 reff. q here only. Judg. xvii. 4 B. Jer. vi. 29 only. (-πεῖν, Jer. ib.) r partic., = ch. xv. 29. xvi. 34. 2 Pet. i. 19. Winer, edn. 6, § 45. 4. s = here only. ἔπεμψαν δὲ . . . χρυσοῦς ναούς, Diod. Sic. xx. 14. t 2 Tim. ii. 20. Rev. ix. 20 only. Isa. ii. 20. u ch. xvi. 16 (reff.). v mid., = Col. iv. 1. Tit. ii. 7. see Winer, edn. 6, § 38. 6. w ver. 38. Rev. xviii. 22. Heb. xi. 10 only. Deut. xxvii. 15. (-νη, ch. xviii. 3.)

21. for ως to ταυτα, τοτε D. (ο) παυλος bef εθετο DE 137.—om ο D 137. om εν E-gr 40. 68. διελθειν ADEP k. ins την bef αχαιαν (*corrn for uniformity*) ADE a b d o 13: om BHLPℵ rel 36 Chr_1. ins και bef πορευεσθαι DP^2. rec ιερουσαλημ, with HLP rel 36 Thl-sif: txt ABEℵ c k [13] 40 vulg $Chr\text{-}comm_1$ Thl-fin [$Orig\text{-}int_1$], ιεροσολυσολυμα D.

22. for αποστ. δε, και αποστ. D Syr æth. om την Eℵ b k m o. for διακονουντων αυτω, διακονουν (= -ων?) αυτων A: for αυτω, αυτων [H] e. aft αυτω $ℵ^1$ has written ειπ, but marked it for erasure. aft χρονον ins ολιγον D-gr 25: τινα χρ. 40 arm. εν τη ασια[*in Asiam*] D sah.

24. for ονοματι, ην D-gr: om D-lat sah. ναον αργυρουν $ℵ^1$. om αργυρους B. ins ος bef παρειχε (*repeating the termination of* Αρτεμιδος) D. παρειχε (*confusion from* τοις *follg*) A^1DE: txt A^2BHLPℵ rel 36 Chr. rec εργασιαν bef ουκ ολιγην, with EHLP rel syr Chr Thl-sif: txt ABDℵ k m 13 vulg [arm(Tischdf)] Thl-fin.

21. ταῦτα] The occurrences of vv. 19, 20. **ἐν τῷ πν.**] An expression mostly used by Paul, see ref. **δεῖ**] As he was sent to the Gentiles, he saw that the great metropolis of the Gentile world was the legitimate centre of his apostolic working. Or perhaps he speaks under some divine intimation that *ultimately* he should be brought to Rome. If so, his words were literally fulfilled. He *did* see Rome after he had been at Jerusalem this next time: but after considerable delay, and as a prisoner. Cf. the same design expressed by him, Rom. i. 15; xv. 23—28; and Paley's remarks in the Horæ Paulinæ. **22.**] He intended *himself to follow* after Pentecost, 1 Cor. xvi. 8. This mission of Timothy is alluded to 1 Cor. iv. 17 (see ib. i. 1); xvi. 10. The object of it was to bring these churches in Macedonia and Achaia into remembrance of the ways and teaching of Paul. It occurred shortly before the writing of 1 Cor. He was (1 Cor. xvi. 11) soon to return:—but considerable uncertainty hangs over this journey. We find him again with Paul in Macedonia, 2 Cor. i. 1: but apparently he had not reached Corinth. See 1 Cor. xvi. l. c.; and 2 Cor. xii. 18, where he would probably have been mentioned, had he done so. On the difficult question respecting a journey of Paul himself to Corinth during this period, see notes, 2 Cor. xii. 14; xiii. 1,—and Prolegg. to 1 Cor. § v. **Ἔραστον**] This Erastus can hardly be identical with the Erastus of Rom. xvi. 23, who must have been resident at Corinth: see there: and therefore hardly either with the Erastus of 2 Tim. iv. 20; see note there. **εἰς τ. Ἀσίαν**] i. e. in (but beware of imagining εἰς to be '*put for*' ἐν, here or any where. It gives the *direction* of the tarrying, as in the expressions ἐς δόμους μένειν, Soph. Ag. 80, and διεκαρτέρουν εἰς τὴν πατρίδα, Lycurg. cont. Leocr., p. 158. It is far better to take it thus, with Meyer, than with Winer, Gr., edn. 6, § 50. 4. b, as importing 'in favour of,' 'for the benefit of') Ephesus: Asia is named by way of contrast with Macedonia, just before mentioned. This is evident by the following event taking place at Ephesus.

24. ναοὺς ἀργ.] These were small models (ἀφιδρύματα) of the celebrated temple of the Ephesian Artemis, with her statue, which it was the custom to carry on journeys, and place in houses, as a charm. Chrys. καὶ πῶς ἔνι ναοὺς ἀργυροῦς γενέσθαι; ἴσως ὡς κιβώρια μικρά. Ammian. Marcellin. xxii. 13: 'Asclepiades philosophus . . . . deæ cœlestis argenteum breve figmentum quocunque ibat secum solitus efferre . . . .' Diod. Sic. i. 15: ναοὺς χρυ-

25 οὓς [x] συναθροισας, καὶ τοὺς [y] περὶ τὰ τοιαῦτα ἐργάτας,
εἶπεν Ἄνδρες, ἐπίστασθε ὅτι [z] ἐκ ταύτης τῆς [u] ἐργασίας ἡ
[a] εὐπορία ἡμῖν [z] ἐστιν, 26 καὶ [b] θεωρεῖτε καὶ ἀκούετε [b] ὅτι οὐ
μόνον Ἐφέσου ἀλλὰ [c] σχεδὸν πάσης τῆς Ἀσίας ὁ Παῦλος
οὗτος [d] πείσας [e] μετέστησεν [f] ἱκανὸν [f] ὄχλον, λέγων ὅτι
οὐκ εἰσὶν θεοὶ οἱ [g] διὰ χειρῶν [h] γινόμενοι. 27 οὐ μόνον δὲ
τοῦτο [i] κινδυνεύει ἡμῖν τὸ [k] μέρος εἰς [l] ἀπελεγμὸν [m] ἐλθεῖν,
ἀλλὰ καὶ τὸ τῆς [n] μεγάλης [o] θεᾶς ἱερὸν Ἀρτέμιδος [pq] εἰς
οὐθὲν [q] λογισθῆναι, [r] μέλλειν τε καὶ [s] καθαιρεῖσθαι

x ch. xii. 12 only. Deut. i. 41.
y = Luke x. 40, 41. περὶ τὴν ἐργασίαν ὄντες τῆς χώρας, Diod. Sic. i. 74.
z = Luke xii. 15. John xviii. 36.
a here only †. Judg. vi. 12 Aquil. Prov. xii. 4 Symm. (-εῖσθαι, ch. xi. 29.)
b Mark xvi. 4. John iv. 19. xii. 19. ch. xxvii. 10. (Dan. iii. 27 [94].)
c ch. xiii. 44 reff.
d ch. xviii. 4 reff.
e = here only. (ch. xiii. 22 reff.) Josh. xiv. 8. τὰ ἐκεῖ πάντα πρὸς Λακεδαιμονίους μετέστησεν, Xen. Hell. ii. 2. 5.
f ch. xi. 24 (reff.).
g ch. xiv. 3.
h = John i. 3. Heb. xi. 3. Gen. ii. 4.
i ver. 40. absol., Luke viii. 23. 1 Cor. xv. 30 only. Isa. xxviii. 13. w. τοῦ and inf., Jonah i. 4.
k = here only. 3 Macc. v. 17.
l here only †. (ἐλεγμός, 4 Kings xix. 3 ‖ Isa.)
m = John v. 24. Job xxxiii. 28 Bℵ F(not A) &c.
n ch. viii. 9 reff.
o here (vv. 35, 37 v. r.) only †.
p = ch. x. 4 reff.
q Rom. ii. 26. iv. 3. ix. 8. Wisd. ix. 6.
r = ch. xx. 38 al.
s = 2 Cor. x. 5. Jer. xxix. 16. (xlix. 17.) constr. here only. καθαιρεῖν τι τῆς τοῦ θεοῦ δόξης, Diod. Sic. iv. 8.

25. for ους, ουτος (omg και) D 137 tol [Syr] sah: c has ουτος but retains και. τοιαυτας(sic) ℵ. for εργατας, τεχνετας D-gr-corr(-ταις D¹): *artifices* E-lat. for ειπεν, εφη D. add προς αυτους D [Syr sah æth]. aft ανδρες ins συντεχνειται D syr-w-ast sah. επιστασται(sic) D. rec ημων (*corrn, as more usual constr*), with HLP rel syrr æth Chr₁ Thl-sif: txt ABDEℵ c d 13. 40 vulg coptt [arm] Thl-fin.
26. ακουετε και θεωρειτε D Syr. om οτι D[-gr]. ins εως bef εφεσ. D-gr 14¹: της a m Thl-fin.—*ipsius Ephesi* D-lat. εφεσιου D. aft αλλα ins και A D-gr L 13. 36. 40. 106-80 demid Syr Chr₁ Thl-sif: om BEHPℵ rel vulg D-lat coptt [syr æth arm] Thl-fin. om της D¹(ins D²) m. aft ουτος ins τις τοτε D¹: *hic quidam tunc* D-lat. om πεισας ℵ. απεστησεν E. aft οτι ins ουτοι D-gr. om οι ℵ¹ 57. γενομενοι D¹(γεινομ. [B¹]D²) 68.
27. om δε E-gr. ημιν bef κινδυνευει D m (-νευσει D²ℵ [vulg]). το μερος bef κινδ. ημ. A c 137. om αλλα ℵ¹. rec αρτεμιδος bef ιερον (*corrn of characteristic order*), with ABLℵ 13. 36 rel Thl-fin: txt DEHP b f g o Chr₁ Thl-sif Jer₁. rec ουδεν, with DEL 13. 36 rel Chr: txt ABHPℵ d f. λογισθησεται (*emendation of constr*) ADE vulg Syr: txt BHLPℵ rel 36 Chr Thl. μελλει A¹(D¹) a e vss Thl [Jer₁]: txt BD²EHLPℵ 13 rel Chr Œc.—αλλα καθερισθαι μελλει(ν) D. Steph (for τε) δε, with HL rel vulg Chr₁ Thl: om a e: txt ABEPℵ o 13 [(Syr) syr coptt (æth) arm] Jer₁. om και E c.

σοῦς δύο. Dio Cass. xxxix. 20: νεὼς Ἥρας βραχὺς ἐπὶ τραπέζης τινὸς πρὸς ἀνατολῶν ἱδρυμένος. We may find an exact parallel in the usages of that corrupt form of Christianity, which, whatever it may pretend to teach, in practice honours similarly the "great goddess" of its imagination. **25. τὰ τοιαῦτα**] All sorts of memorials or amulets connected with the worship of Artemis. Dean Howson (ii. p. 98) suggests that possibly *Alexander the coppersmith* may have been one of these craftsmen: see 2 Tim. iv. 14. **26.**] The people believed that the images themselves were gods: τὰ χαλκᾶ καὶ τὰ γραπτὰ καὶ λίθινα μὴ μαθόντες, μηδὲ ἐθισθέντες ἀγάλματα καὶ τιμὰς θεῶν, ἀλλὰ **θεοὺς** καλεῖν. Plutarch de Isid. p. 379, c (Wetst.): see ch. xvii. 29. And so it is invariably, wherever images are employed *professedly as media* of worship. The genitives Ἐφ. and Ἀσ. are governed by ὄχλον. **27.**] **ἡμῖν** is best taken as the *dativus incommodi*, not for ἡμῶν, nor with τὸ μέρος, but with κινδυνεύει. **μέρος**, as we say, **department. ἀλλὰ καί**] **but that eventually even the temple itself of the great goddess Artemis will be counted for nothing.** μεγάλη was the usual epithet of the Ephesian Artemis: Xen. Ephes. i. p. 15: ὀμνύω τε τὴν πάτριον ἡμῖν θεόν, τὴν μεγάλην Ἐφεσίων Ἄρτεμιν. There is an inscription in Boeckh, 2963 c, containing the words της μεγαλης θεας αρτεμιδος προ πολεως. The same inscription also mentions γραμματεύς and ἀνθυπατος. C. and H. ii. 98. The temple of Artemis at Ephesus, having been burnt to the ground by Herostratus on the night of the birth of Alexander the Great (B.C. 355), was restored with increased magnificence, and accounted one of the wonders of the ancient world. Its dimensions were 425 × 220 feet, and it was surrounded by 127 columns, 60 feet high. It was standing in all its grandeur at this time. See C. and

Luke ix. 43. t 2 Pet. i. 16 only. Jer. xl. (xxxiii.) 9. Dan. vii. 27 LXX. Esdr. i. 5 only. u = ch. xvii. 31. Rev. iii. 10. xii. 9. Ps. ix. 8. v ch. xiii. 43 reff. Bel and Dr. 22. w = John i. 14. ch. vi. 3, 5, 8. ix. 36. xiii. 10. Isa. i. 4. x = Luke iv. 28. Eph. iv. 31. Rev. xii. 12 al. Gen. xlix. 6.

ABDE HLPℵ a b c d f g h k m o 13

τῆς [t] μεγαλειότητος αὐτῆς ἣν ὅλη ἡ Ἀσία καὶ ἡ [u] οἰκουμένη [v] σέβεται. 28 ἀκούσαντες δὲ καὶ γενόμενοι [w] πλήρεις
[x] θυμοῦ ἔκραζον λέγοντες [y] Μεγάλη ἡ Ἄρτεμις Ἐφεσίων.
29 καὶ [z] ἐπλήσθη ἡ πόλις τῆς [a] συγχύσεως, [b] ὥρμησάν τε
[b] ὁμοθυμαδὸν εἰς τὸ [c] θέατρον [d] συναρπάσαντες Γάϊον καὶ
Ἀρίσταρχον Μακεδόνας, [e] συνεκδήμους Παύλου· 30 Παύλου δὲ βουλομένου εἰσελθεῖν εἰς τὸν [f] δῆμον, οὐκ εἴων
αὐτὸν οἱ μαθηταί. 31 τινὲς δὲ καὶ τῶν Ἀσιαρχῶν, ὄντες
αὐτῷ φίλοι, πέμψαντες πρὸς αὐτὸν [g] παρεκάλουν, μὴ

y ver. 27 al. see notes. z = Luke iv. 28. v. 26. ch. v. 17. xiii. 45. Gen. vi. 11. a here only. Gen. xi. 9. 1 Kings v. 12. xiv. 20 only. (-χύνειν, ver. 32.) b ch. vii. 57 (reff.). c here bis. 1 Cor. iv. 9 only †. (-τρίζεσθαι, Heb. x. 33.) d ch. vi. 12 reff. e 2 Cor. viii. 19 only †. f ch. xii. 22 reff. g constr., ch. viii. 31 reff.

rec την μεγαλειοτητα (*see note*), with HLP rel vulg Chr Thl: txt ABEℵ a c 13. 36. 40 syr sah.—om τ. μεγ. αυτης D. (Mai Tischdf note expr agst Bch that B does not om αυτης ην.) for ην, η D[1]. om 1st η BD [Thl-sif: η ασια ολη m]. om 2nd η B k m.

28. ταυτα δε ακουσ. D [arm]. aft θυμου ins δραμοντες εις το αμφοδον D 137, simly syr-mg. om η D[1](ins D[4]).

29. rec aft η πολις ins ολη (*see ch* xxi. 30), with EHLP rel syr sah Chr_1: pref ολη, D 36(sic) Syr æth: om ABℵ 13. 40 vulg copt arm. rec om της, with (D[1])Eℵ[3] k 13: ins A B(sic: see table) D[6]HLPℵ[1] rel Chr_1.—συνεχυθη ολ. η π. αισχυνης D[1]-gr. for τε, δε D-gr m copt: om sah arm. ins και bef συναρπασαντες D. μακεδονες D[1](txt D[4 or 8]): μακεδονα 15. 180: μακεδονιας d 56. 117-77[1]: om 100. rec ins του bef παυλου (with e?): om ABDEHLPℵ rel.

30. rec του δε παυλου (*possibly from the concurrence of* παυλου παυλου), with EHLP rel 36 Chr: βουλομενου δε του παυλου D: του παυλου δε ℵ[3] k: txt ABℵ[1] m 13. for ουκ ειων αυτον οι μαθηται, οι μαθ. εκωλυον D(*non sinebant* D-lat) Syr æth.

31. for οντες, υπαρχοντες D. αυτου E-gr: *amici ejus* vulg. for εαυτον, αυτον ℵ[1] [c] 100.

H. ch. xvi. vol. ii. pp. 84 ff. **τῆς μεγαλειότητος** is the more difficult and probably original reading: **and that she should be deposed from her greatness, whom** &c. **29. εἰς τὸ θέατρον**] The resort of the populace on occasions of excitement, as Wetst. shews by many instances. So Tacit. Hist. ii. 80, 'Tum Antiochensium theatrum ingressus, *ubi illis consultare mos* * *est*.' 'Of the site of the theatre, the scene of the tumult raised by Demetrius, there can be no doubt, its ruins being a wreck of immense grandeur. I think it must have been larger than the one at Miletus; and that exceeds any I have elsewhere seen. . . . . Its form alone can now be spoken of, for every seat is removed, and the proscenium is a heap of ruins.' Fellows, Asia Minor, p. 274. 'The theatre of Ephesus is said to be the largest known of any that have remained to us from antiquity.' C. and H. ii. p. 83, note 3. **συναρπ.**] It is not implied that they seized Gaius and Aristarchus *before* they rushed into the theatre: compare προσευξάμενοι εἶπαν, ch. i. 24, also ch. xviii. 27, and Winer, edn. 6, § 45. 6. b. **Γάϊον**] A different person from the Gaius of ch. xx. 4, who was of Derbe, and from the Gaius of Rom. xvi. 23, and 1 Cor. i. 14, who was evidently a Corinthian. Aristarchus is mentioned ch. xx. 4; xxvii. 2; Col. iv. 10; Philem. 24. He was a native of Thessalonica. **31. Ἀσιαρχῶν**] The Asiarchæ were officers elected by the cities of the province of Asia to preside over their games and religious festivals. Of these it would be natural that the one who for the time presided would bear the title of ὁ Ἀσιάρχος: cf. Eus. H. E. iv. 15: but no more is known of such presidency. Wetst. quotes several inscriptions and coins in which the name occurs, and cites many analogous names of like officers elsewhere: Ciliciarcha, Syriarcha, Phœniciarcha, Helladarcha, &c. The Asiarch Philip at Smyrna is mentioned by Eusebius (H. E. iv. 15) as presiding in the amphitheatre at the martyrdom of Polycarp. These Ephesian games in honour of Artemis took place in May, which whole month (another singular coincidence with the practices of idolatrous Christendom) was sacred to, and named Artemisian after, the goddess. In Boeckh, Inscr. 2954, we have the decree ὅλον τὸν μῆνα τὸν ἐπώνυμον τοῦ θείου ὀνόματος εἶναι ἱερὸν καὶ ἀνακεῖσθαι τῇ θεῷ, ἄγεσθαι δὲ ἐπ' αὐταῖς (scil. τοῦ μηνὸς

[h] δοῦναι ἑαυτὸν εἰς τὸ [c] θέατρον. 32 [i] ἄλλοι μὲν οὖν [i] ἄλλο
τι ἔκραζον· ἦν γὰρ ἡ [k] ἐκκλησία [l] συγκεχυμένη, καὶ [m] οἱ
[m] πλείους οὐκ ᾔδεισαν τίνος ἕνεκα [n] συνεληλύθεισαν. 33 ἐκ
δὲ τοῦ ὄχλου *[o] προεβίβασαν Ἀλέξανδρον, [p] προβαλόντων
αὐτὸν τῶν Ἰουδαίων· ὁ δὲ Ἀλέξανδρος [q] κατασείσας τὴν
χεῖρα ἤθελεν [r] ἀπολογεῖσθαι τῷ [f] δήμῳ. 34 [s] ἐπιγνόντες δὲ
ὅτι Ἰουδαῖός [t] ἐστιν, φωνὴ ἐγένετο μία [u] ἐκ πάντων ὡς
[v] ἐπὶ ὥρας δύο κραζόντων Μεγάλη ἡ Ἄρτεμις Ἐφεσίων.
35 [w] καταστείλας δὲ ὁ [x] γραμματεὺς τὸν ὄχλον φησὶν
Ἄνδρες Ἐφέσιοι, τις [y] γάρ ἐστιν ἀνθρώπων ὃς οὐ γινώσκει τὴν Ἐφεσίων πόλιν [z] νεωκόρον [a] οὖσαν τῆς [b] μεγάλης

h = here only. εἰς τὰς ἐρημίας αὑτὸν διδούς, Jos. Antt. xv. 7. 7, and Diod. Sic. v. 59.
i ch. xxi. 34. (Wisd. xviii. 8.)
k = vv. 39, 41. ch. vii. 38 only. Sir. xxvi. 5.
l ch. ii. 6 reff.
m 1 Cor. ix. 19 reff.
n = ch. i. 6 reff.
o Matt. xiv. 8 only. Exod. xxxv. 34. Deut. vi. 7 only. προβιβάσας τὸ μειράκιον εἰς λόγους ἀποῤῥήτους, Polyb. xxiv. 3. 7. συμβ., 1 Cor. ii. 16 reff.
p = here (Luke xxi. 30) only. Jer. xxvi. (xlvi.) 4 Aℵ Ald. compl.
q ch. xii. 17 reff.
r Luke xii. 11. xxi. 14. Acts, ch. xxiv. 10. xxvi. 24 al3. Rom. ii. 15. 2 Cor. xii. 19 only. L.P. Jer. xii. 1. xxxviii. (xxxi.) 6. 2 Macc. xiii. 26 only.
s Luke xxiii. 7. ch. xxii. 29. xxviii. 1. Jer. v. 5.
t pres., ch. xvi. 38 reff.
u = ch. v. 38, 39. John iii. 25 al.
v ch. xiii. 31 reff.
w here bis only †. 2 Macc. iv. 31 only.
x = here only. (Ezra vii. 6, &c.)
y Matt. ix. 5. Job xix. 23.
z here only †. ἡ λευιτικὴ φυλὴ νεωκόρων κ. ἱερέων ἐστίν, Philo de Prof. § 17, vol. i. p. 560.
a constr., ch. xxiv. 10 reff.
b = ch. vv. 27, 28, 34.

32. om τι D 42 vulg. η γαρ εκκλησια ην D[-gr]. πλειστοι D-gr. rec ενεκεν, with DEHLP rel: txt ABℵ 13. 36 Thl-fin. νεληλυθασιν H: -λυθησαν L [g¹] Thl-sif.

33. * συνεβίβασαν ABEℵ a (*corrn, perhaps on acct of the unusual word, perhaps to avoid the repetition of* προ): συν εβιβασαν 13(appy): κατεβιβ. D¹, *distraxerunt* D-lat, *detrax.* vulg [E-lat: *produx.* tol]: προεβιβασαν D⁴ or ⁸ HLP rel 36 Chr₁. elz προβαλλοντων, with DLP b² c g m[Scriv] o 13. 36 Thl: txt ABEHℵ [m(Treg)] rel 40 Chr. αυτων L¹ 40 Thl-sif. **ο ουν** A k [am] demid fuld tol: ο δ' ουν ℵ¹. τη χειρι Dℵ³ 40 Chr Thl-fin. for ηλθεν, ηθελεν ℵ¹. for δημω, λαω E.

34. rec επιγνοντων (*corrn, to avoid the pendent nominative*), with a b o 36 Œc: txt ABDEHLPℵ 13 rel Chr₁ Thl-sif. om εκ D, so vulg coptt. ωσει B 13. κραζοντες Aℵ. om η D¹(ins D⁴). μεγ. η αρτ. εφ. is repeated in B.

35. κατασεισας DE c 137 Thl-sif: *compescuisset* D-lat, *sedasset* vulg E-lat. τον οχλον bef ο γραμματευς B m 130 copt. εφη *dixit* E vulg. for εφεσιοι, αδελφοι ℵ¹ [arm]. rec ανθρωπος (*corrn*), with D(pref ὁ D¹) HLP rel syr æth Chr₁ Thl-sif: txt ABEℵ a c k m 13. 36. 40[των αν.] vulg Syr copt (sah) arm Thl-fin. for εφεσ., ημετεραν *vestram* D. πολιν bef εφεσ. E coptt. ναοκορον D¹(txt D²) [νεοκ. ELP a c(?) 13]. for ουσαν, ειναι D: add και ℵ¹(ℵ³ disapproving). rec aft μεγαλης ins θεας, with HLP rel æth [arm] Chr: om ABDEℵ c 13. 36. 40 vulg syrr coptt Isid₁.

ἡμέραις) τὰς ἑορτὰς καὶ τὴν τῶν Ἀρτεμισίων πανήγυριν. C. and H. ii. 95. **δοῦναι**] Kypke remarks: 'latet in phrasi, quod periculum Paulo in theatro immineat.' E. V. **adventure himself**; an excellent translation. **33.**] **ἐκ τ. ὄχλ. some of the multitude.** **προεβ.** **urged forward**, through the crowd; the Jews pushing him on from behind, 'propellentibus.'

It is uncertain whether this Alexander is mentioned elsewhere (but see on 2 Tim. iv. 14). He appears to have been a Christian convert from Judaism, whom the Jews were willing to expose as a victim to the fury of the mob: or perhaps one of themselves, put forward to clear them of blame on the occasion. **34. ἐπιγνόντες**] The nom. is an anacoluthon, as in ch. xxiv. 5 al. See Winer, edn. 6, § 63, i. 1.

They would hear nothing from a Jew, as being an enemy of image-worship.

35. καταστ.] When he had quieted, lulled, the crowd. **ὁ γραμματεύς**] **the town-clerk** is the nearest English office corresponding to it. He was the keeper of the archives and public reader of decrees, &c., in the assemblies. Thucyd. vii. 10, τὴν ἐπιστολὴν ἐπέδοσαν· ὁ δὲ γραμματεὺς τῆς πόλεως παρελθὼν ἀνέγνω τοῖς Ἀθηναίοις. 'Among the Ephesian inscriptions in Boeckh, we find the following: M. I. Αυρ. Διονυσιον τον ιεροκηρυκα και β ασιαρχον εκ των ιδιων Τ. Φλ. Μουνατιος φιλοσεβαστος ο γραμματευς καὶ ασιαρχησας. No. 2990.' C. and H. ii. 96. **γάρ** gives a reason for the *καταστείλας*. See Herm. on Viger, p. 829. **νεωκόρον**] Probably a **virger** or adorner (Suidas says, *not a sweeper:* ὁ τὸν νεὼν κοσμῶν κ. εὐτρεπίζων, ἀλλ' οὐχ ὁ σαρῶν) of the temple: here used as implying that Ephesus had the charge and keeping of the temple. The

c here only +. αὐτὸ μὲν τὸ ἄγαλμα διοπετές, ὡς λέγουσιν, Herodian i. 11.
d here only +. Symm., Job xi. 2. xxxiii. 13. (-τως, ch. x. 29.)
e 1 Pet. i. 6 only. 1 Macc. xii. 11. (see 1 Tim. v. 13.)

Ἀρτέμιδος καὶ τοῦ [c] διοπετοῦς; 36 [d] ἀναντιῤῥήτων οὖν ABDE
ὄντων τούτων [e] δέον ἐστὶν ὑμᾶς [w] κατεσταλμένους [f] ὑπ- HLPℵ a b c d f g
άρχειν καὶ μηδὲν [g] προπετὲς πράσσειν. 37 [h] ἠγάγετε γὰρ h k m o 13
τοὺς ἄνδρας τούτους οὔτε [i] ἱεροσύλους οὔτε [k] βλασφη-
μοῦντας τὴν [l] θεὸν ἡμῶν. 38 εἰ μὲν οὖν Δημήτριος καὶ οἱ
σὺν αὐτῷ [m] τεχνῖται ἔχουσιν πρός τινα [n] λόγον, [o] ἀγόραιοι
[p] ἄγονται καὶ [q] ἀνθύπατοί εἰσιν· [r] ἐγκαλείτωσαν ἀλλήλοις.

f ch. ii. 30 reff. g 2 Tim. iii. 4 only. Prov. x. 14. xiii. 3. Sir. ix. 18 only. h absol., Matt. xxi. 7. John vii. 45 al. Dan. iii. 13. i here only +. 2 Macc. iv. 42 only. (-εῖν, Rom. ii. 22. -ία, 2 Macc. xiii. 6.) k constr., Matt. xxvii. 39. 4 Kings xix. 22. (Rom. ii. 24 al.) l fem., here only. m ver. 24 reff. n = here only. ἐμοὶ . . . πρὸς τούτους ὁ λόγος, Demosth. πρὸς Λακρ., p. 942. 17. see Heb. iv. 13. o = here (ch. xvii. 5) only +. τὰς διοικήσεις, ἐν αἷς τὰς ἀγοραίους ποιοῦνται, Strabo xiii. p. 932 (Wahl). μοι ἄγοντι τὸν ἀγοραῖον, Jos. Antt. xiv. 10. 21. p = Luke xxiv. 21. 2 Macc. ii. 16. q ch. xiii. 7, 8, 12. xviii. 12 only. see notes. r constr., ch. xxiii. 28. Sir. xlvi. 19. w. κατά and gen., Rom. viii. 33, pass. ver. 40. ch. xxiii. 29. xxvi. 2, 7 only. L.P.

διοςπετους D[-gr] 68: *hujus jovis* D-lat: *joviseprolis* E-lat: *jovisque prolis* vulg.
36. αναντιρητων B¹L. [om ουν E¹-gr: E-lat has an empty space for αναντ. ουν οντ. τουτ.] τουτων bef οντων A b o: om τουτων ℵ¹ 13. aft προπετες ins τι ℵ³ (πρασσειν, so ABDEHL[P]ℵ 13 rel(not m) Chr.)
37. from ηγαγετε to τουτους is inserted in the margin of P by a later hand. aft τουτους ins ενθαδε D syr-mg [arm: *in hunc locum* sah]. for ουτε (twice), μητε D. rec την θεαν (*corrn*), with D¹E²P a b¹ [c, e sil] o 13 Thl-fin: txt ABD³E¹HLℵ rel 36 Chr-c₁ Thl-sif. rec υμων, with E¹-gr HLP rel vulg syr copt æth-rom Chr₁ Thl-fin: txt ABDE²ℵ b f o 13 E-lat Syr sah æth-pl [arm] Chr-c₁ Thl-sif.
38. aft δημητριος ins ουτος D Syr: pref ὁ c 137. οι bef και D¹[-gr](txt D⁴). rec προς τινα λογον bef εχουσιν (*alteration of characteristic order*), with 13(appy): txt AB(D)EHLPℵ rel vulg [syr (coptt) arm] Chr Thl.—ins αυτους bef τινα D, *cum aliquos quendam* D-lat.

title is found (Wetst.) on inscriptions as belonging to Ephesus: η φιλοσεβαστος Ἐφεσιων βουλη και ο νεωκορος δημος καθιερωσαν επι ανθυπατου Πεδουκαιου Πρεισκεινου ψηφισαμενου Τιβ. Κλ. Ιταλικου του γραμματεως του δημου (Boeckh, No. 2966); and seems to have been specially granted by the emperors to particular cities: thus we have ὅσα ἐπετύχομεν παρὰ τοῦ κυρίου Καίσαρος Ἀδριανοῦ δι' Ἀντωνίου Πολέμωνος δεύτερον δόγμα συγκλήτου, καθ' ὃ **δὶς** νεωκόροι γεγόναμεν: and on coins of Hadrian, Ἐφεσίων **δὶς** νεωκόρων, &c.: and similarly of Elagabalus, Νικομηδέων **τρὶς** νεωκόρων: of Maximin, Μαγνήτων νεωκόρων Ἀρτέμιδος. See also C. and H. ii. p. 89, where will be found an engraving of a coin exhibiting both the words νεωκόρος and ἀνθύπατος (ver. 38). **τ. διοπετοῦς**] To give peculiar sanctity to various images, it was given out that they had fallen from heaven; so Euripides of the statue of Artemis at Tauris, ἔνθ' Ἄρτεμις σὴ σύγγονος βωμοὺς ἔχει, | λαβεῖν τ' ἄγαλμα θεᾶς ὃ φασὶν ἐνθάδε | εἰς τούσδε ναοὺς οὐρανοῦ πεσεῖν ἄπο. Iph. Taur. 86, and 977, he calls it διοπετὲς ἄγαλμα, οὐρανοῦ πέσημα. So also Pausan. Att. 26, τὸ δὲ ἁγιώτατον . . . ἐστὶν Ἀθηνᾶς ἄγαλμα ἐν τῇ νῦν ἀκροπόλει . . . φήμη δ' ἐς αὐτὸ ἔχει, πεσεῖν ἐκ τοῦ οὐρανοῦ. The image is described by Pliny, xvi. 72: 'de ipso simulacro Deæ ambigitur. Cæteri ex ebeno esse tradunt: Mucianus ter consul ex his qui, proxime viso eo, scripsere, vitigineum, et nunquam mutatum, septies restituto templo.' **37.**] From this verse it appears that Paul had proceeded at Ephesus with the same caution as at Athens, and had not held up to contempt the worship of Artemis, any further than unavoidably the truths which he preached would render it contemptible. This is also manifest from his having friends among the Asiarchs, ver. 31. Chrysostom, however, treats this assertion of the town-clerk merely as a device to appease the people: τοῦτο ψεῦδος· ταῦτα μὲν πρὸς τὸν δῆμον. **γάρ** refers to the προπετές with which he had charged them: 'and this caution is not unneeded, — for &c.' see Meyer; and Herm. as above, on ver. 35. **38. ἀγόραιοι**] **court-days** (the grammarians distinguish ἀγοραῖος, 'circumforaneus,' an idler in the market, and ἀγόραιος, as in our text: so Suidas: but Ammonius *vice versâ*: and the distinction is now believed to be mere pedantry): and **ἄγονται** implies that they were then actually going on. They were the periodical *assizes* of the district, held by the proconsul and his *assessors* (see below). The Latin phrase for ἀγοραίους ἄγειν was *conventus agere*, or *peragere*, or *convocare*; cf. Cæs. B. G. i. 54; v. 1; viii. 46. Hence the district itself was called *conventus*. See Smith's

39 εἰ δέ τι περὶ [s] ἑτέρων [t] ἐπιζητεῖτε, ἐν τῇ [u] ἐννόμῳ [v] ἐκκλησίᾳ
[w] ἐπιλυθήσεται. 40 καὶ γὰρ [x] κινδυνεύομεν [y] ἐγκαλεῖσθαι
[z] στάσεως περὶ τῆς [a] σήμερον, μηδενὸς [b] αἰτίου [c] ὑπάρχοντος
περὶ οὗ [οὐ] δυνησόμεθα [d] ἀποδοῦναι λόγον τῆς [e] συστροφῆς
ταύτης. 41 καὶ ταῦτα εἰπὼν [f] ἀπέλυσεν τὴν [v] ἐκκλησίαν.
XX. 1 [g] Μετὰ δὲ τὸ [h] παύσασθαι τὸν [hi] θόρυβον προςκαλεσάμενος ὁ Παῦλος τοὺς μαθητὰς καὶ [k] παρακαλέσας,
[l] ἀσπασάμενος [m] ἐξῆλθεν πορευθῆναι εἰς [τὴν] Μακεδονίαν.
2 [n] διελθὼν δὲ τὰ [o] μέρη ἐκεῖνα καὶ [k] παρακαλέσας [p] αὐτοὺς

s = ch. xvii. 34. t Rom. xi. 7 reff. u = here (1 Cor. ix. 21) only +. Prol. Sir. only. εἰθισμένα κ. ἔννομα, Xen. Cyr. viii. 7. 10. v = ver. 32. Judith xiv. 6. w = here only ‡. (Mark iv. 34 only. Gen. xli. 12 only. -σις, 2 Pet. i. 20.) x ver. 27 reff. y ver. 38 reff.

z = Mark xv. 7. Luke xxiii. 19, 25. ch. xxiv. 5. Prov. xvii. 14. a constr., here only. (ch. xx. 26.) b Luke xxiii. 4, 14, 22 only +. (-ος, Heb. v. 9.) c ch. viii. 16 reff. d Matt. xii. 36. Luke xvi. 2. [Rom. xiv. 12.] 1 Pet. iv. 5. Dan. vi. 2 Theod. e ch. xxiii. 12 only. Amos vii. 10. f = ch. xiii. 3 reff. g ch. xix. 21 reff. h Judith vi. 1. i ch. xxi. 34 reff. k ch. xv. 32 reff. l = here only. (ch. xviii. 22 reff.) Xen. Anab. vii. 1. 40. m = ch. xv. 40 reff. n ch. xiii. 6 reff. o ch. xix. 1. p ch. viii. 5 reff.

39. for περι ετερων, περαιτερων (*seems like a mistake from itacism*) d 36: περαιτέρω B(Tischdf) [13(περετ.): *ulterius* D-lat]: περ ετερον E. επιζητειται (*itacism?*) ℵ c d o [ζητειτε E]. εν τω νομω εκκλησια D^1(so, but εκκλησιας D^2 and lat: txt D^4).
40. σημερον ενκαλεισθαι στασεως μηδενος αιτιου οντος D. περι ου **ου** δυνησομεθα (*perhaps, as Meyer, from a careless repetition of* ου: *more likely, as Bornemann in loc, inserted by those who placed a colon at* υπαρχοντος *and regarded* περι . . . ταυτης *as a new member of the sentence*) A B(sic: see table) H L(for οὗ, ουν L^1) Pℵ b c e f g h m o syrr [æth(appy)] arm: om οὐ DE 13[e sil] 36 rel vulg coptt Chr-comm$_1$ Thl-fin. δουναι (*prob the simple verb was substituted for the compd rather than* vice versâ: *both exprr are in ordinary use*) HL[P] b d e g [Chr$_1$] Thl-sif: txt ABDEℵ 13. 36 rel Chr$_1$ Œc-ms Thl-fin. ins περι bef της συστρ. (*consequent on regarding* συστρ. *as in apposn with the preceding gen:—q. d.* viz. concerning this συστρ.) ABEℵ d k m 36. 40 D-lat arm Thl-fin: om D[-gr] HLP rel [vulg] Chr Thl-sif. (13 def.)

Chap. XX. 1. for προσκαλ., μεταπεμψαμενος BEℵ m 13. 36. 40 coptt æth-rom Thl-fin: μεταστειλαμενος a 69. 98-marg 105: txt ADHLP rel Chr$_1$ Thl-sif. om ὁ D. ins πολλα bef παρακ. D. rec om παρακαλεσας (*see note*), with HLP rel Chr$_1$ Thl-sif: ins AB(D)Eℵ a c m 13. 36 [vulg syrr] copt [sah æth arm] Thl-fin.—παρακελε(υ)σας D^1? for ασπ., αποσπασαμενος D^1: και ασπ. Eℵ: ασπασαμενος τε D^4 a c m 36 Thl-fin. πορευεσθαι (*corrn*) ABEℵ 36 Thl-fin: om D 27. 66^2. 105: txt HLP 13(sic) rel Chr Thl-sif. om την BDE L[e sil] ℵ a b c k m o Thl-fin: ins AHP 13[e sil] rel Chr$_1$ Thl-sif.
2. ins παντα bef τα μερη D. εκεινη D^1(txt D^4). for παρακαλεσας αυτους, χρησ(αμενο)ς(?) D^1-gr(txt D^2).

Dict. of Antiquities, art. Conventus. Pliny, H. N. v. 29 fin., mentions Ephesus as one of these assize towns. **ἀνθύπατοι]** **there are** (such things as) **proconsuls:** the fit officers before whom to bring these causes: a categoric plural. So the Commentators generally. But may not the 'consiliarii' of the proconsul who were his assessors at the 'conventus,' held in the provinces, have themselves popularly borne the name? We find in Jos. B. J. ii. 16. 1, that Cestius, the ἡγεμών of Syria, on receiving an application respecting Florus's conduct at Jerusalem, μετὰ ἡγεμόνων ἐβουλεύετο,—which ἡγεμόνες were his *assessors*, or *consiliarii*. (See on ch. xxv. 12, and Smith's Dict. of Antt., ut supra.)

ἐγκαλ. ἀλλ.] **let them** (the plaintiffs and defendants) **plead against one another.** **39.]** 'Legitimus cœtus est, qui a magistratu civitatis convocatur et regitur.' Grot. The art. points out the regularly recurring assembly, of which they all knew. **40.]** **γάρ** assumes that this assembly was an *unlawful* one. **μηδενὸς** κ.τ.λ.] **There being no ground why** (i. e. in consequence of which) **we shall be able to give an account,** i. e. 'no ground whereon to build the possibility of our giving an account.' The reading περὶ οὗ οὐ (see digest) seems to involve the sentence in almost inextricable confusion. To read περὶ τῆς συστ. τ. and take it in apposit. with περὶ οὗ, 'hujus rei, videlicet conventus hujus' (Bornemann), is very harsh.

Chap. XX. 1—XXI. 16.] Journey of Paul to Macedonia and Greece, and thence to Jerusalem. **1.]** παρακαλέσας has probably been omitted on account of the two participles coming together: or perhaps on account of the same

q ch. xv. 32. r ch. xv. 33 reff. s ch. ix. 24 reff. t ch. xiii. 13 reff. u = Philem. 14. 2 Macc. iv. 39. constr., Luke ix. 55 v. r. 2 Macc. xi. 37. v constr., ch. iii. 12 reff. w = ch. viii. 25 reff. x here only +. 2 Macc. xv. 2 only. y = ch. xi. 5 reff.

[q] λόγῳ πολλῷ ἦλθεν εἰς τὴν Ἑλλάδα, 3 [r] ποιήσας τε ABDE HLPℵ a b c d f g h k m o 13
μῆνας τρεῖς, γενομένης αὐτῷ [s] ἐπιβουλῆς ὑπὸ τῶν Ἰου-
δαίων μέλλοντι [t] ἀνάγεσθαι εἰς τὴν Συρίαν ἐγένετο
[u] γνώμης [v] τοῦ [w] ὑποστρέφειν διὰ Μακεδονίας. 4 [x] συνείπετο δὲ αὐτῷ [y] ἄχρι τῆς Ἀσίας Σώπατρος Πύῤῥου
Βεροιαῖος, Θεσσαλονικέων δὲ Ἀρίσταρχος καὶ Σεκοῦνδος,
καὶ Γάϊος Δερβαῖος καὶ Τιμόθεος, Ἀσιανοὶ δὲ Τυχικὸς
καὶ Τρόφιμος. 5 [z] οὗτοι [δὲ] [a] προελθόντες [b] ἔμενον ἡμᾶς

z ch. ix. 20 reff. a = ver. 13. 2 Cor. ix. 5. (ch. xii. 10 al.) Gen. xxxiii. 14. b = here only. Job xxxvi. 2. (see ver. 23.)

3. for τε, δε D 38 E-lat copt. for γενομ., και γενηθεισης D^2 : κ. γενηθεις D^1-gr. επιβουλης bef αυτω ABEℵ a h 13 : txt DHLP rel vulg Chr_1. μελλων E. αγεσθαι E. rec γνωμη, with B^2HLP rel syr-mg-gr [Chr_1] : txt AB^1Eℵ 13. 36.—ηθελησεν αναχθηναι εις συριαν ειπεν δε το πνευμα αυτω υποστρεφειν δια της μακεδονιας D syr-mg(proceeding as D below as far as εξιεναι).

4. for συνειπετο δε αυτω αχρι, μελλοντος ουν[*autem* D-lat syr-mg] εξειεναι αυτου μεχρι D (*comitari eum* D-lat). om αχρι της ασιας (*to conform to follg ; cf note*) Bℵ 13 vulg [coptt] æth Bede. rec om πυρρου (*see note*), with HLP rel syrr æth Chr Thl-sif: ins ABDEℵ a b m o 13. 36. 40 vulg syr-mg coptt arm Thl-fin $Orig\text{-}int_1$. βεροιος $ℵ^1$: βερυιαιος $D\text{-}gr^1$(txt D^4). ins ο bef δερβαιος A [13] : δουβ(ε)ριος *doverius* D^1(and lat: txt D^4). for ασιανοι, εφεσιοι D (syr-mg) sah. for τυχικος, ευτυχος D.

5. rec om δε, with DHLP rel 36 vulg Syr [arm] Chr_1 Thl-sif: ins ABEℵ a c 13. 40 syr copt Thl-fin. προςελθοντες (*see ver* 13) A(?) B^1 E-gr HLPℵ f g k m. εμεινον (but ι erased) ℵ. for ημας, αυτον D-gr.

word occurring again in ver. 2. **2.**] Notices of this journey may be found 2 Cor. ii. 12, 13; vii. 5, 6. He delayed on the way some time at Troas, waiting for Titus,—broke off his preaching there, though prosperous, in distress of mind at his non-arrival, 2 Cor. ii. 12, 13,—and sailed for Macedonia, where Titus met him, 2 Cor. vii. 6. That Epistle was written during it, from Macedonia (see 2 Cor. ix. 2, καυχῶμαι, 'I am boasting'). He seems to have gone to the confines at least of Illyria, Rom. xv. 19. **αὐτούς**] The Macedonian brethren: so ch. xvi. 10 al., see reff., and Winer, edn. 6, § 22. 3. **Ἑλλάδα**] Achaia, see ch. xix. 21. **3. ποιήσας**] This stay was made at Corinth, most probably: see 1 Cor. xvi. 6, 7: and was during the winter, see below on ver. 5. During it the Epistle to the Romans was written: see Prolegg. to Rom. § iv. **μέλλοντι ἀνάγεσθαι**] This purpose, of going from Corinth to Palestine by sea, is implied ch. xix. 21, and 1 Cor. xvi. 3—7. **τοῦ ὑποστρ.**] The genit. is not (as Meyer) governed directly by γνώμης, which would be more naturally followed by εἰς τὸ ὑπ.: but denotes the purpose, as in reff. **4. ἄχρι τ. Ἀσίας**] It is not hereby implied that they went *no further* than to Asia: Trophimus (ch. xxi. 29) and Aristarchus (ch. xxvii. 2), and probably others, as the bearers of the alms from Macedonia and Corinth (1 Cor. xvi. 3, 4), accompanied him to Jerusalem. **Σώπατρος Πύῤῥου Βεροιαῖος**] This mention of his father is perhaps made to distinguish him (?) from Sosipater, who was with Paul at Corinth (Rom. xvi. 21). The name Πύῤῥου has been erased as that of an unknown person, and because the mention of the father is unusual in the N. T.:—no possible reason can be given for its *insertion* by copyists. **Ἀρίσταρχος**] See ch. xix. 29; xxvii. 2; Col. iv. 10; Philem. 24. Secundus is altogether unknown. The Gaius here is not the Gaius of ch. xix. 29, who was a *Macedonian.* The epithet Δερβαῖος is inserted for distinction's sake. Timotheus was from *Lystra,* which probably gives occasion to his being mentioned here in close company with Gaius of Derbe. All attempts to join Δερβαῖος with Τιμόθεος in the construction are futile. Timotheus was *not of Derbe,* see ch. xvi. 1, 2: and the name Caius (Γάϊος, Gr.) was far too common to create any difficulty in there being two, or three (see note, ch. xix. 29) companions of Paul so called. With conjectural emendations of the text (Δερβ. δὲ Τιμοθ., Kuin., Valck.) we have no concern. **Ἀσιανοὶ Τ. κ. Τ.**] Tychicus is mentioned Eph. vi. 21, as sent (to Ephesus from Rome) with that Epistle. He bore also that to the Colossians, Col. iv. 7, at the same time. See also 2 Tim. iv. 12; Tit. iii. 12. Trophimus, an Ephesian, was in Jerusalem with Paul,

ἐν Τρωάδι· 6 ἡμεῖς δὲ [c] ἐξεπλεύσαμεν μετὰ τὰς [d] ἡμέρας τῶν
[d] ἀζύμων ἀπὸ Φιλίππων, καὶ ἤλθομεν πρὸς αὐτοὺς εἰς
τὴν Τρωάδα [e] ἄχρι ἡμερῶν πέντε, οὗ [f] διετρίψαμεν ἡμέρας
ἑπτά. 7 Ἐν δὲ [g] τῇ μιᾷ τῶν [g] σαββάτων [h] συνηγμένων
ἡμῶν [i] κλάσαι ἄρτον, ὁ Παῦλος [k] διελέγετο αὐτοῖς μέλ-

c ch. xv. 39 reff. d ch. xii. 3 reff. e = ch. xiii. 11. Luke iv. 13. Rom. i. 13 al. 2 Macc. xiv. 15. f ch. xii. 19 reff. g Luke xxiv. 1. John xx. 1 (19. Mark xvi. 2. 1 Cor. xvi. 2). see ch. xiii. 14 reff. h ch. iv. 5 reff. constr., ch. xiii. 44 reff. i ch. ii. 46 reff. k ch. xvii. 2 reff.

6. om *την* D. rec *αχρις*, with H rel: *απο* Eℵ 13: *infra* E-lat: txt ABLP d Thl-sif.—for *αχρι ημερων πεντε*, *πεμπταιοι* D. for *ου*, *οπου* AEℵ 13: *ου και* 40. 137: *και* c: *εν η και* D: txt BHLP rel 36 Chr. [for *επτα*, *πεντε* L[1](but corrd).]

7. for *δε*, *τε* D Syr æth. om *τη* E k. aft *μια* ins *πρωτη* D-gr. rec for *ημων*, *των μαθητων* (*alteration to suit αυτοις—see note*), with HLP rel Bas_1 Thl-sif: txt ABDEℵ a[1] c 13. 36. 40 vulg syrr (copt) [sah] æth arm Chr_2 Thl-fin. rec ins *του* bef *κλασαι*, with D Thl-fin: om ABEHLPℵ 13 rel [Bas_1] Chr_2 Thl-sif.

ch. xxi. 29: and had been, shortly before 2 Tim. was written, left sick at Miletus. (See Prolegg. to 2 Tim. § i. 5.) **5. οὗτοι**] The persons mentioned in ver. 4: not only Tychicus and Trophimus. The mention of Timotheus in this list, distinguished from ἡμᾶς, has created an insuperable difficulty to those who suppose Timotheus himself to be the narrator of what follows: which certainly cannot be got over (as De Wette) by supposing that Timotheus might have inserted himself in the list, and then tacitly excepted himself by the ἡμᾶς afterwards. The truth is apparent here, as well as before, ch. xvi. 10 (where see note), that the anonymous narrator was in very intimate connexion with Paul; and on this occasion we find him remaining with him when the rest went forward. **προελθ. κ.τ.λ.**] For what reason, is not said: but we may well conceive, that if they bore the contributions of the churches, a better opportunity, or safer ship, may have determined Paul to send them on, he himself having work to do at Philippi: or perhaps, again, as Meyer suggests, Paul may have remained behind to keep the days of unleavened bread. But then why should not they have remained too? The same *motive* may not have operated with them; but in that case no reason can be given why they should have been *sent on*, except as above. It is not impossible that both may have been combined:—before the end of the days of unleavened bread, a favourable opportunity occurs of sailing to Troas, of which they, with their charge, avail themselves: Paul and Luke waiting till the end of the feast, and taking the risk of a less desirable conveyance. That the feast had *something* to do with it, the mention of μετὰ τ. ἡ. τ. ἀζ. seems to imply: such notices being not inserted ordinarily by Luke for the sake of *dates*. The assumption made by some (see, e. g. Mr. Lewin, p. 587), that the rest of the company sailed at once for Troas from Corinth, while Paul and Luke went by land to Philippi, is inconsistent with συνείπετο, ver. 4. From the notice here, we learn that Paul's stay in Europe on this occasion was about three-quarters of a year: viz. from shortly after Pentecost, when he left Ephesus (see on ch. xix. 10), to the next Easter. **6. ἄχρ. ἡμ. πέντε**] **in five days**, see reff. The wind must have been adverse: for the voyage *from* Troas *to* Philippi (Neapolis) in ch. xvi. 11, seems to have been made in *two* days. It appears that they arrived on a Monday. Compare notes, 2 Cor. ii. 12, ff. **7. ἐν τῇ μιᾷ τ. σαββ.**] We have here an intimation of the continuance of the practice, which seems to have begun immediately after the Resurrection (see John xx. 26), of assembling on the first day of the week for religious purposes. (Justin Martyr, Apol. i. 67, p. 83, says, τῇ τοῦ ἡλίου λεγομένῃ ἡμέρᾳ πάντων κατὰ πόλεις ἢ ἀγροὺς μενόντων ἐπὶ τὸ αὐτὸ συνέλευσις γίνεται.) Perhaps the greatest proof of all, that this day was thus observed, may be found in the early (see 1 Cor. xvi. 2) and at length general prevalence, *in the Gentile world*, of the *Jewish seven-day period* as a *division of time*,—which was entirely foreign to Gentile habits. It can only have been introduced as following on the practice of especial honour paid to this day. But we find in the Christian Scriptures no trace of any *sabbatical* observance of this or any day: nay, in Rom. xiv. 5 (where see note), Paul shews the untenableness of any such view under the Christian dispensation. The idea of the *transference of the Jewish sabbath from the seventh day to the first* was an invention of later times. **κλάσαι ἄρτον**] See note on ch. ii. 42. The breaking of bread in the Holy Communion was at this time inseparable from the ἀγάπαι. It took place apparently in the evening (after the day's work was ended), and at the end of the assembly, after the preaching of the word (ver. 11). **αὐτοῖς**, in the third person, the dis-

λων [l] ἐξιέναι [m] τῇ ἐπαύριον, [n] παρέτεινέν τε τὸν λόγον
[o] μέχρι [p] μεσονυκτίου· 8 ἦσαν δὲ [q] λαμπάδες [r] ἱκαναὶ ἐν τῷ
[s] ὑπερῴῳ οὗ ἦμεν [t] συνηγμένοι. 9 [u] καθεζόμενος δέ τις
[v] νεανίας ὀνόματι Εὔτυχος ἐπὶ τῆς [w] θυρίδος, [x] καταφερόμενος ὕπνῳ [y] βαθεῖ, [z] διαλεγομένου τοῦ Παύλου
[a] ἐπὶ πλεῖον, [x] κατενεχθεὶς [b] ἀπὸ τοῦ ὕπνου ἔπεσεν ἀπὸ
τοῦ [c] τριστέγου κάτω καὶ [d] ἤρθη νεκρός. 10 [e] καταβὰς

ABDE HLPℵ a b c d f g h k m o 13

l ch. xiii. 42 reff. m ch. x. 9 reff. n here only. Gen. xlix. 13. Num. xxiii. 28. Ps. xxxv. 10 only. τοσοῦτον παρατείνειν χρόνον, Jos. Antt. i. 3. 9. o of time, Matt. xi. 23. ch. x. 30. 1 Tim. vi. 14 al. Ps. civ. 19. p Mark xiii. 35. Luke xi. 5. ch. xvi. 25 only. Judg. xvi. 3. q Matt. xxv. 1, &c. John xviii. 3. Rev. iv. 4. viii. 10 only. Gen. xv. 17. r Luke xxiii. 9 al. 1 Macc. xv. 26. s ch. i. 13 reff. Acts only. t ver. 7 al. u ch. vi. 15 reff. v ch. vii. 58. xxiii. 17 only. L. Zech. ii. 4. w 2 Cor. xi. 33 only. Josh. ii. 15, 18. x = here bis (ch. xxv. 7. xxvi. 10) only ‡. Ps. lxxv. 7 Aq. Dan. v. 20 Theod. Herodian i. 11, of the ἄγαλμα διοπετές,—ἐξ οὐρανοῦ κατενεχθῆναι λόγος. (καταφορά Aq., Gen. ii. 21. xv. 12.) y Luke xxiv. 1 (John iv. 11. Rev. ii. 24) only. Sir. xxii. 7. z ver. 7. absol., ch. xviii. 4 reff. a ch. iv. 17 reff. b = ch. xii. 14 reff. c here only †. Symm., Gen. vi. 16 [17]. Ezek. xlii. 6. στοαὶ τρίστεγοι, Dion. Hal. Antt. iii. 68. d = Mark vi. 29. 1 Macc. ix. 19. e = Matt. xxiv. 17. ch. x. 20, 21. 1 Kings ix. 27. Xen. Cyr. i. 4. 8.

om τε D-gr. μεχρις P.

8. **υπολαμπαδες** *faculæ* D. rec for ημεν, ησαν (*see above on* ημων, *ver* 7), with c k [copt æth-rom Thl-sif]: txt ABDEHLPℵ 13. 36 rel vulg syrr sah [æth-pl] arm Chr_1 Thl-fin. om συνηγμενοι E.

9. rec καθημενος (*corrn to more usual form*), with HLP rel Chr_1: txt ABDEℵ a 13. 36. om νεανιας E. επι τη θυριδι κατεχομενος υπνω βαρει D. om του (bef παυλου) D. for απο, υπο DH b o 40 Chr. πεσων, omg και follg, E. και ος ηρθη D¹-gr.

course being addressed to the disciples at Troas: but the first person is used before and after, because all were assembled, and partook of the breaking of bread together. Not observing this, the copyists have altered ἡμῶν above into τῶν μαθητῶν, and ἦμεν into ἦσαν, to suit αὐτοῖς. **8. λαμπάδ. ἱκ.**] This may be noticed, as Meyer observes, to shew that the fall of the young man could be well observed: or, perhaps, because many lights are apt to increase drowsiness at such times. Calvin and Bengel suppose,—in order that all suspicion might be removed from the assembly ('ut omnis abesset suspicio scandali,' Beng.); Kuin. and partly Meyer,—that the lights were used for solemnity's sake,—for that both Jews and Gentiles celebrated their festal days by abundance of lights. But surely the adoption of either Jewish or Gentile practices of this kind in the Christian assemblies was very improbable. **9.**] Who Eutychus was, is quite uncertain. The occurrence of the name as belonging to slaves and freedmen (Rosenm. and Heinrichs, from inscriptions), determines nothing. **ἐπὶ τῆς θυρίδος**] **On the window-seat.** The windows in the East were (and are) without glass, and with or without shutters. **καταφερόμενος ὕπν.**] Wetstein gives many instances of the use of καταφέρομαι, either absolute, or with εἰς ὕπνον, signifying '*to be oppressed with, borne down towards, sleep.*' Thus Aristotle, de somn. et vig. iii. p. 456. b. 31, ed. Bekk.: τὰ ὑπνωτικὰ . . . πάντα . . . καρηβαρίαν . . . ποιεῖ . . . καὶ **καταφερόμενοι** καὶ νυστάζοντες τοῦτο δοκοῦσιν πάσχειν, καὶ ἀδυνατοῦσιν αἴρειν τὴν κεφαλὴν καὶ τὰ βλέφαρα: and Diod. Sic. iii. 57, **κατενεχθεῖσαν** εἰς ὕπνον ἰδεῖν ὄψιν. I believe the word is used here and below *in the same sense,* not, as usually interpreted, here of the effect of sleep, and below of *the fall* caused by the sleep. It implies that relaxation of the system, and collapse of the muscular power, which is more or less indicated by our expressions '*falling* asleep,' '*dropping* asleep.' This effect is *being produced* when the first participle is used, which is therefore *imperfect,*—but as Paul was going on long discoursing, took *complete possession of him,* and, having been **overpowered,—entirely relaxed in consequence of the sleep,** he *fell.* In the **ἤρθη νεκρός** here, there is a *direct assertion,* which can hardly be evaded by explaining it, '*was taken up for dead,*' as De Wette, Olsh.;—or by saying that it expresses the *judgment of those who took him up,* as Meyer. It seems to me, that the supposition of a mere suspended animation is as absurd here as in the miracle of Jairus's daughter, Luke viii. 41—56. Let us take the narrative as it stands. The youth falls, and is taken up dead: so much is plainly asserted. (First, let it be remembered that Luke, a physician, was present, who could have at once pronounced on the fact.) Paul, not a physician, but an Apostle,—gifted, not with medical discernment, but with miraculous power, goes down to him, falls on him and embraces

C λων αυτου... (see var. read.) ABCDE HLPℵ a b c d f g h k m o 13

δὲ ὁ Παῦλος [f] ἐπέπεσεν αὐτῷ καὶ [g] συμπεριλαβὼν εἶπεν
Μὴ [h] θορυβεῖσθε· ἡ γὰρ [i] ψυχὴ αὐτοῦ ἐν αὐτῷ ἐστιν.
11 [j] ἀναβὰς δὲ καὶ [k] κλάσας τὸν ἄρτον καὶ [l] γευσάμενος,
[m] ἐφ᾿ ἱκανόν τε [n] ὁμιλήσας ἄχρι [o] αὐγῆς, [p] οὕτως [q] ἐξῆλθεν.
12 [r] ἤγαγον δὲ τὸν παῖδα ζῶντα, καὶ [s] παρεκλήθησαν [t] οὐ
[tu] μετρίως. 13 ἡμεῖς δὲ [v] προελθόντες ἐπὶ τὸ πλοῖον
[w] ἀνήχθημεν ἐπὶ τὴν Ἄσσον, ἐκεῖθεν [x] μέλλοντες [y] ἀνα-
λαμβάνειν τὸν Παῦλον· οὕτως γὰρ [z] διατεταγμένος ἦν,
[x] μέλλων αὐτὸς [a] πεζεύειν. 14 ὡς δὲ [b] συνέβαλλεν ἡμῖν

f = ver. 37. (ch. viii. 16 reff.) Esth. vii. 8.
g here only. Ezek. v. 3 only.
h ch. xvii. 5 reff.
i = ch. xv. 26 reff.
j ch. viii. 31.
k ch. ii. 46 reff.
l = ch. x. 10 reff.
m here only. 2 Macc. viii. 25. see Luke xxiii. 8.
n Luke xxiv. 14, 15 ch. xxiv. 26 only. Prov. xxiii. 30.
o here only. Isa. lix. 9. 2 Macc. xii. 9 only.
p = John iv. 6. ch. xxvii. 17. see Heb. vi. 15.
q = ch. xv. 40 reff.
r Luke x. 34 al. 1 Kings xv. 20.
s = Matt. ii. 18. v. 4. Luke xvi. 25. Gen. xxiv. 67.
t here only.
u 2 Macc. xv. 38 only. (-ος, Sir. xxxiv. [xxxi.] 20. Xen. Mem. iv. 1. 1.)
v ver. 5.
w ch. xiii. 13 reff.
x = vv. 3, 7.
y = here bis. ch. xxiii. 31. 2 Tim. iv. 11 only. (ch. i. 2. vii. 43.)
z 1 Cor. vii. 17. xi. 34. L.P., exc. Matt. xi. 1. 1 Chron. ix. 33.
a here only +. μέχρις ἐνταῦθα ἐπέζευσεν ἡ στρατιά, Xen. Anab. v. 5. 4. (-ζῃ, Mark vi. 33.)
b = here only. (ch. xvii. 18 reff.)

10. aft επεπεσεν ins επ᾿ c 106 : επεσεν επ D. συμπεριβαλων C[1], and add αυτου C [(syrr coptt arm)] : συμπαραλαβων c k 40. 105 : add αυτον a 36. ins και bef ειπεν D[1]-gr.

11. [om 1st και B (sah).] rec om τον (*the force of the art being overlooked,—see note*), with D[2]EHLPℵ[3] rel Chr, Thl-sif : ins ABCD[1]ℵ[1] 13 Thl-fin. for τε, δε D-gr E-gr Thl-sif. (αχρι, so AB[1]C[2]Eℵ Thl-sif.) αυτης ℵ[1].

12. for ηγαγον δε τον παιδα, D has ασπαζομενων δε αυτων ηγαγεν[*adduxerunt*] τον νεανισκον.

13. προσελθ. (*see ver* 5) AB[1]EHP f g h k m o Chr, Thl-sif : κατελθ. D[-gr] Syr [*ascendimus* D-lat] for 1st επι, εις D d 133. rec (for 2nd επι) εις, with DHLP rel 36 Chr Thl-sif : txt ABCEℵ [a] 13. 40 Thl-fin. for ασσον, θασον, or θασσον L(but not in ver 14) P o 73-6-8. 99. 100-1 syrr sah : ασον b[1] f k 13. 106 æth : νασον 15-8. 36, and so in ver. 14. rec ην bef διατεταγμενος (*ἦν διατ. is St. Luke's habit almost uniformly, but it is not the habit of the great* MSS *to alter this order*), with DHLP rel Chr : εντεταλμενος ην C 15. 36. 180 : txt A B[-νον B[1]] Eℵ a m 13. ins ως bef μελλων D 36. αυτος [bef μελ.] E.

14. om δε C[1](appy). rec συνεβαλεν (*alteration to historic aorist as so freq*), with CDHL rel 36 vulg E-lat Chr : συνεβαλλον ℵ[1] : txt AB E-gr Pℵ[3] 40. for 1st εις, επι ℵ[1].

him,—a strange proceeding for one bent on discovering suspended animation, but not so for one who bore in mind the action of Elijah (1 Kings xvii. 21) and Elisha (2 Kings iv. 34), each time over a *dead body*,—and *having done this, not before*, bids them not to be troubled, for *his life was in him.* I would ask any unbiassed reader, taking these details into consideration, which of the two is the natural interpretation,—and whether there can be any reasonable doubt that *the intent of Luke is to relate a miracle of raising the dead*, and that he mentions the falling on and embracing him as the outward significant means taken by the Apostle to that end? **11.**] The intended breaking of bread had been put off by the accident. **τὸν ἄρτ.**, as ch. ii. 42. Were it not for that usage, the article here might import, 'the bread which it was intended to break,' alluding to ἄρτ. above. **γευσάμενος**] having made a meal, see reff. The agape was a veritable meal. Not '*having tasted it*,' viz. the bread which he had broken;—though that is implied, usage decides for the other meaning. **οὕτως**] '*After so doing*:' see reff. **12.**] As in the raising of Jairus's daughter, our Lord commanded that something should be given her to eat, that nature might be recruited, so doubtless here rest and treatment were necessary, in order that the restored life might be confirmed, and the shock recovered. The time indicated by αὐγή must have been before or about 5 A.M.: which would allow about four hours since the miracle. We have here a minute but interesting touch of truth in the narrative. Paul, we learn afterwards, ver. 13, intended to go afoot. And accordingly here we have it simply related that he started away from Troas before his companions, not remaining for the reintroduction of the now recovered Eutychus in ver. 12.

13. Ἄσσον] A sea-port (also called Apollonia, Plin. v. 32) in Mysia or Troas, oppo-

[c] εἰς τὴν Ἄσσον, [y] ἀναλαβόντες αὐτὸν ἤλθομεν εἰς Μιτυλήνην, 15 κἀκεῖθεν [d] ἀποπλεύσαντες τῇ [e] ἐπιούσῃ [f] κατηντήσαμεν [g] ἀντικρὺς Χίου. τῇ δὲ [h] ἑτέρᾳ [i] παρεβάλομεν
εἰς Σάμον, καὶ μείναντες ἐν Τρωγυλίῳ τῇ [k] ἐχομένῃ
ἤλθομεν εἰς Μίλητον. 16 [l] κεκρίκει γὰρ ὁ Παῦλος [m] παρα-
πλεῦσαι τὴν Ἔφεσον, ὅπως μὴ [n] γένηται αὐτῷ [o] χρονο-
τριβῆσαι ἐν τῇ Ἀσίᾳ· [p] ἔσπευδεν γάρ, εἰ δυνατὸν εἴη
αὐτῷ, τὴν ἡμέραν τῆς [q] πεντηκοστῆς [rs] γενέσθαι [s] εἰς
Ἱεροσόλυμα. 17 Ἀπὸ δὲ τῆς Μιλήτου πέμψας εἰς Ἔφεσον [t] μετεκαλέσατο τοὺς [uv] πρεσβυτέρους τῆς [u] ἐκκλησίας.

l ηλθομεν... ABCDE HLPℵ a b c d f g h k l m o 13

c ch. viii. 40 reff. d ch. xiii. 4 reff. e ch. xvi. 11 reff. f ch. xvi. 1 reff. g here only †. Exod. xxviii. 26 Symm. Theod. h = ch. xxvii. 3. Xen. Cyr. iv. 6. 10. i = here (Mark iv. 30 rec.) only ‡. ες Ἰωνίαν παραβαλεῖν, Thucyd. iii. 32. (Prov. ii. 2 al.) k = Mark i. 38. Luke xiii. 33. ch. xiii. 44. xxi. 26. Heb. vi. 9 only. 2 Macc. xii. 39. l = ch. xv. 19 reff. m here only †. Xen. Anab. vi. 2. 1. n Matt. xviii. 13. Gal. vi. 14. Gen. xliv. 7, 17. o here only †. οἱ δ' ἄνθρωποι τοῖς διπλοῖς χρῶνται ὅταν ἀνώνυμον ᾖ κ. ὁ λόγος εὐσύνθετος, οἷον τὸ χρονοτριβεῖν, Aristot. Rhet. iii. 3. p Luke ii. 16. xix. 5, 6. ch. xxii. 18. 2 Pet. iii. 12 only. 2 Chron. x. 18. q ch. ii. 1 reff. r = Matt. xxvi. 6. Luke x. 32. xxii. 40 al. s Luke iv. 23. ch. xxi. 17. xxv. 15. t ch. vii. 14 reff. u James v. 14 only. (see ch. xiv. 23.) v ch. xi. 30 reff.

15. και εκειθεν E. rec αντικρυ (*corrn*), with B²HP rel [Thl-fin] : txt AB¹CDELℵ 13. 36. 40 Thl-fin. for ετερα, εσπερα B 15-9. 73. παρελαβομεν D¹-gr(txt D⁴). om και μειναντες εν τρωγυλιω, and aft τη ins δε ABCEℵ [a] 13 vulg [copt æth-pl arm] : txt (*the occasion of the omn has probably been, that Trogylium is not in Samos, which at first sight the text appeared to imply*) DHLP rel 36 syrr sah Chr_1 Thl.—rec τρωγυλλιω, with HP rel 36: txt (D)L h m o (c f g k) Chr_1, τρωγυλια D-gr, *Trogylio* D-lat. ερχομενη D¹ a m 95¹-6. 142.

16. rec εκρινε (*an ecclesiastical portion begins at ver* 16, *which has occasioned the alteration of the pluperf into the independent historic aor*), with C³HLP rel Chr, Thl-sif: txt ABC¹DEℵ a 13. 36 vulg. for οπως μη γενηται αυτω [αυτον H] χρονοτριβησαι, μηποτε γενηθη αυτω κατασχεσις τις *ut non contingeret ei morandi quis* D. rec (for ειη) ην, with LP rel 40 Chr Thl : txt (*but looks like a somml corrn*) ABCEℵ a 13. 36.—om ει δυνατον ειη DH æth-rom. εις την ημεραν D : τη ημερα H. for εις, εν D¹(txt D⁴). ιεδουσαλημ AEℵ a c 13. 40 : txt BCDHLP rel 36 Chr.

17. μετεπεμψατο D. om τους E.

site to Lesbos, twenty-four Roman miles (Peutinger Table) from Troas, built on a high cliff above the sea, with a descent so precipitous as to have prompted a pun of Stratonicus, the musician (see Athen. viii., p. 352), on a line of Homer, Il. ζ. 143, Ἄσσον ἴθ', ὥς κεν θᾶσσον ὀλέθρου πείραθ' ἵκηαι. Strab. xiii. 1, p. 126, Tauchn. Paul's *reason* is not given for wishing to be alone: probably he had some apostolic visit to make. **14. Μιτυλήνην**] The capital of Lesbos, on the E. coast of the island, famed (Hor. Od. i. 7. 1: Epist. i. 11. 17) for its beautiful situation. It had two harbours: the northern, into which their ship would sail, was μέγας κ. βαθύς, χώματι σκεπαζόμενος, Strabo, xiii. 2, p. 137. **15. παρεβάλ.**] **we put in**: so Charon, in the Frogs, to his boatman, ὠόπ, παραβαλοῦ, 180; and 271, παραβαλοῦ τῷ κωπίῳ: see many examples in Wetst. Then they made a short run in the evening to Trogylium, a cape and town on the Ionian coast, only forty stadia distant, where they spent the night. He had passed in front of the bay of Ephesus, and was now but a short distance from it. **Μίλητον**] The ancient capital of Ionia (Herod. i. 142). See 2 Tim. iv. 20, and note.

16. κεκρίκει] We see here that the ship was at Paul's disposal, and probably hired at Philippi, or rather at Neapolis, for the voyage to Patara (ch. xxi. 1), where he and his company embark in a merchant vessel, going to Tyre. The separation of Paul and Luke from the rest at the beginning of the voyage may have been in some way connected with the hiring or outfit of this vessel. The expression **κεκρίκει** (or ἔκρινε, which will amount to the same thing, only it must not be taken '*for the pluperfect*,' here or any where else) is too subjectively strong to allow of our supposing that the Apostle merely followed the previously determined course of a ship in which he took a passage. **παραπλ. τ. Ἐφ.**] He may have been afraid of detention there, owing to the machinations of those who had caused the uproar in ch. xix. F. M., in his notes, gives another reason: "He seems to have feared that, had he run up the long gulf to Ephesus, he might be detained in it by the westerly winds, which blow long, especially in the spring." But these would affect him nearly as much at Miletus. **17.**] The distance from

18 ὡς δὲ [w] παρεγένοντο [w] πρὸς αὐτόν, εἶπεν αὐτοῖς Ὑμεῖς
ἐπίστασθε, [xy] ἀπὸ πρώτης ἡμέρας [y] ἀφ' ἧς [z] ἐπέβην εἰς
τὴν Ἀσίαν, [a] πῶς μεθ' ὑμῶν τὸν πάντα χρόνον [r] ἐγενόμην,
19 [b] δουλεύων τῷ κυρίῳ [c] μετὰ [d] πάσης [e] ταπεινοφροσύνης
καὶ δακρύων καὶ [f] πειρασμῶν τῶν [g] συμβάντων μοι ἐν
ταῖς [h] ἐπιβουλαῖς τῶν Ἰουδαίων, 20 ὡς οὐδὲν [i] ὑπεστει-

w Matt. iii. 13. Luke vii. 20. viii. 19. xi. 6 only. Josh. xviii. 8.
x ch. x. 30 reff. constr., see ch. i. 2.
y attr., here only? see ch. xxiv. 11.
z = and constr. ch. xxi. 4. see ch. xxi. 2. xxv. 1. (xxvii. 2 reff.) Josh. xiv. 9.
a = Mark v. 16. ch. ix. 27.
b = (see note) Paul (Rom. vii. (6) 25 al5.) only, exc. Matt. vi. 24. Luke xvi. 13. Ps. ii. 11.
c ch. xvii. 11 reff.
d ('all possible') ch. iv. 29. xxiii. 1. Rom. i. 29. Eph. i. 3. 2 Pet. i. 5. Jude 3 al.
e Eph. iv. 2. Phil. ii. 3. Col. ii. 18, 23. iii. 12. Paul only, exc. 1 Pet. v. 5+. (-φρων, 1 Pet. iii. 8. -φρονεῖν, Ps. cxxx. 2.)
f = Luke xxii. 28. Gal. iv. 14 al. Deut. iv. 34.
g ch. iii. 10 reff.
h ch. ix. 24 reff.
i ver. 27. Gal. ii. 12. Heb. x. 38 only‡. Diod. Sic. xiii. 70, εἰς τὸ λοιπὸν ὁ Κῦρος ἐκέλευσεν αἰτεῖν, μηδὲν ὑποστελλόμενον. So Jos. B. J. i. 20. 1.

18. for παρεγενοντο, εσκληρυνοντο E-gr. aft αυτον ins ομου οντων αυτων A: ομοσε οντ. αυτ. D4(ομωσ εοντων D1) 40-marg: ομοθυμαδον E 73: *et simul essent* vulg (*interpolations for particularity*): om BCHLPℵ rel 36 [syrr coptt æth arm] Chr. for αυτοις, προς αυτους D1(πρ. αυτοις D4). aft επιστασθε ins αδελφοι D: pref. 5. 8. 73 sah. for αφ, εφ D1(txt D4): om h 38. 93. for εις, επι E. for πως to εγενομην, D has ως τριετιαν η και πλειον ποταπως μεθ υμων ην παντος χρονου: D-corr has πως for ποταπως, D4(?) τον παντα χρονον, and D5 adds εγενομην: *fui per omne tempore* D-lat.

19. aft κυριω add μεθ υμων C c 15-8, 36 [syr] Chr-txt1. rec ins πολλων bef δακρ. (*prob interpolation: see 2 Cor* ii. 4), with CHLP rel 36 æth-rom arm [Bas2] Chr: aft syr: om ABDEℵ 13. 40 vulg Syr coptt æth-pl Lucif1. συμβαινοντων C.

Miletus to Ephesus is about thirty miles. He probably, therefore, stayed three or four days altogether at Miletus. **τοὺς πρεσβ.**] called, ver. 28, ἐπισκόπους. This circumstance began very early to contradict the growing views of the apostolic institution and necessity of prelatical episcopacy. Thus Irenæus, iii. 14. 2, p. 201: 'In Mileto convocatis *episcopis et presbyteris*, qui erant ab Epheso *et a reliquis proximis civitatibus*.' Here we see (1) the two, bishops and presbyters, distinguished, as if *both* were sent for, in order that the titles might not seem to belong to the same persons,—and (2) other neighbouring churches also brought in, in order that there might not seem to be ἐπίσκοποι in one church only. That neither of these was the case, is clearly shewn by the plain words of this verse: he sent *to Ephesus*, and summoned *the elders of the church* (see below on διῆλθον, ver. 25). So early did interested and disingenuous interpretations begin to cloud the light which Scripture might have thrown on ecclesiastical questions. The E. V. has hardly dealt fairly in this case with the sacred text, in rendering ἐπισκόπους, ver. 28, '*overseers*;' whereas it ought there as in all other places to have been **bishops**, that the fact of *elders and bishops having been originally and apostolically synonymous* might be apparent to the ordinary English reader, which now it is not. **18.**] The evidence furnished by this speech as to the literal report in the Acts of the words spoken by Paul, is most important. It is a treasure-house of words, idioms, and sentiments, peculiarly belonging to the Apostle himself. Many of these appear in the reff., but many more lie beneath the surface, and can only be discovered by a continuous and verbal study of his Epistles. I shall point out such instances of parallelism as I have observed, in the notes. The contents of the speech may be thus given: *He reminds the elders of his conduct among them* (vv. 18—21): *announces to them his final separation from them* (vv. 22—25): *and commends earnestly to them the flock committed to their charge, for which he himself had by word and work disinterestedly laboured* (vv. 26—35). **ἀπὸ πρ. ἡμ.**] These words hold a middle place, partly with ἐπίστασθε, partly with ἐγενόμην. The knowledge on their part was coextensive with his whole stay among them: so that we may take the words with ἐπίστασθε, at the same time carrying on their sense to what follows. **μεθ' ὑμ. ἐγεν.**] So 1 Thess. i. 5, οἴδατε οἷοι ἐγενήθημεν ἐν ὑμῖν,—ii. 10, ὑμ. μάρτυρες . . . ὡς ὁσίως . . . ὑμῖν τοῖς πιστεύουσιν ἐγενήθημεν. See 1 Cor. ix. 20, 22. **19. δουλεύων τῷ κυρ.**] With the sole exception of the assertion of our Lord, 'Ye cannot serve God and mammon,' reff. Matt., Luke, the verb δουλεύω for 'serving God' is used by *Paul only*, and by him seven times, viz. besides reff., Rom. xii. 11; xiv. 18; xvi. 18; [Phil. ii. 22(?)] Col. iii. 24; 1 Thess. i. 9. **μετ. π. ταπ.**] Also a Pauline expression, 2 Cor. viii. 7; xii. 12. **πειρασμῶν**] See especially Gal. iv. 14. **20. ὑπε-**

λάμην τῶν [k] συμφερόντων [l] τοῦ μὴ [m] ἀναγγεῖλαι ὑμῖν καὶ
διδάξαι ὑμᾶς [n] δημοσίᾳ καὶ [o] κατ᾽ οἴκους, 21 [p] διαμαρτυρόμενος Ἰουδαίοις τε καὶ Ἕλλησιν τὴν εἰς θεὸν [q] μετάνοιαν καὶ [r] πίστιν [r] εἰς τὸν κύριον ἡμῶν Ἰησοῦν.
22 [s] καὶ νῦν [s] ἰδοὺ [t] δεδεμένος ἐγὼ τῷ [u] πνεύματι πορεύομαι
εἰς Ἱερουσαλήμ, τὰ ἐν αὐτῇ [v] συναντήσοντά μοι μὴ
εἰδώς, 23 [w] πλὴν ὅτι τὸ πνεῦμα τὸ ἅγιον [x] κατὰ [x] πόλιν
[p] διαμαρτύρεταί μοι [y] λέγων ὅτι [z] δεσμὰ καὶ [a] θλίψεις με
[b] μένουσιν. 24 ἀλλ᾽ οὐδενὸς [c] λόγου [c] ποιοῦμαι τὴν [d] ψυχὴν

ABCDE HLPℵ a b c d f g h k l m o 13

k part., 1 Cor. xii. 7. Heb. (vii. 35. x. 33 v. r.) xii. 10 only. Deut. xxiii. 6.
l constr., ch. xiv. 18 reff.
m = John iv. 25. xvi. 13, &c. ver. 27. 1 Pet. i. 12. Deut. xxiv. 8.
n ch. xvi. 37 reff.
o — Matt. xxiv. 7 ||. (ch. xiv. 23. ii. 46 reff.)
p ch. viii. 25 reff.
q ch. xi. 18 reff.
r = ch. xxiv. 24 reff.
s ch. xiii. 11.
t = here only. δεδεμ. ἰσχυροτέρᾳ ἀνάγκῃ, Xen. Cyr. viii. 1. 12.
u = ch. xvii. 16 reff.
v = here only. Eccl. ii. 14. ix. 11. (ch. x. 25 reff.)
w = here only. Amos ix. 8.
x ch. xv. 21 (36). Tit. i. 5.
y masc., Mark ix. 26. 1 Cor. xii. 2. Eph. iv. 17, 18. Rev. iv. 8. xix. 14 al. Winer, edn. 6, § 59. 4.
z ch. xvi. 26 reff.
a ch. xi. 19 reff.
b see ver. 5.
c = and constr., here only. see Job xiv. 3. xxii. 4.
d ch. xv. 26 reff.

20. των συμφεροντων bef υπεστειλαμην C. om μη D Lucif$_1$. om υμας D Thl-sif Lucif$_1$ Jer$_1$. κατ οικους και δημοσια D.

21. διαμαρτυραμενος H m Bas-ms$_1$ Thl-sif: -ρουμενος D[1]. rec ins τον bef θεον (*corrn for uniformity*), with ADHLP 13. 36 rel Bas-ms Thl-fin: om BCEℵ d h k Bas$_1$ Chr$_1$ Thl-sif. aft πιστιν ins την EHLP rel Bas Chr Thl: om ABCℵ a 13. 36; also D, which reads δια του κυριου ημ. ιησ. χρ. om ημων E. rec aft ιησ. ins χριστον (*common addn*), with ACDEℵ 13. 36 rel Syr copt æth-pl [arm] Chr$_1$ Thl-fin: om BHLP b c g h syr sah æth-rom Bas$_1$ Thl-sif Lucif$_1$.

22. rec εγω bef δεδεμενος, with DHLP rel am [tol syrr Did$_1$ Thl-sif] Chr$_1$ Epiph$_1$: txt (*characteristic order*) ABCEℵ a k 13 vulg Ath-[4-]mss$_1$ Thl-fin. ιεροσολυμα D. συναντησαντα (*prob originally a mistake*) A D-gr E-gr H [l[1]] m 13: συμβησομενα (*gloss*) C a 15. 36 .68-9. 180 lect-12: txt BLPℵ rel vss Ath Chr [Thl-fin]. εμοι Bℵ[1]. for ειδως, γεινωσκων D.

23. το αγ. πν. D-gr: το πν. μοι το αγ. c 47. 137 Epiph Chr. om κατα πολιν E. ins πασαν bef πολιν D vulg syrr æth Lucif$_1$. διεμαρτυρατο AEℵ[3] 13. 40 Ath-[2-]mss$_1$. rec om μοι (*as unnecessary?*), with HLP rel æth-rom Thl-sif: ins ABCDEℵ a b d e k m 13. 36. 40 vulg syrr copt [sah] æth-pl arm Ath$_2$ Bas$_1$ [Epiph$_1$ Thdrt-ms$_1$] Thl-fin Lucif$_1$ Jer. rec λεγον, with A B(sic: see table) Cℵ rel: txt DEHLP 13 f (k?) l[1] m[1] 36. rec με bef και θλιψεις (*alteration perhaps to avoid* μεμενουσιν), with LP rel Thdrt Thl-fin: μοι aft μενουσιν D: txt ABCEHℵ a c k 13. 40 vulg arm Cyr-jer Bas$_1$ Did$_1$ Chr Thl-sif. at end add εν ιεροσολυμοις D vulg[-ed(aft θλ.) am[1](but marked for erasure)](not demid) syr-w-ast sah [Orig-int$_1$] Lucif$_1$.

24. rec λογον, with AD[1]EHLPℵ[3] 13 rel 40: txt BCD[4]ℵ[1] sah æth arm. rec aft ποιουμαι ins ουδε εχω, with EHLP rel 36: ins εχω ουδε bef ποιουμαι Aℵ[3] 13. 40, εχω μοι ουδε D[1]: om BCD[4]ℵ[1] Syr sah æth arm. rec aft την ψυχην ins μου, with

στειλάμην] So again ver. 27. The sense in Gal. ii. 12 is similar, though not exactly identical—'*reserved* himself,' withdrew himself from any open declaration of sentiments. In Heb. x. 38 it is different. **τῶν συμφερ.**] See reff. **21. εἰς θ. . . . εἰς τ. κύρ. Ἰ.**] This use of εἰς is mostly Pauline: and in ch. xxiv. 24 it seems to be taken from his own expression. **22. δεδεμένος τῷ πνεύματι**] **bound in my spirit.** This interpretation is most probable, both from the construction, and from the usage of the expression τὸ πνεῦμα repeatedly by and of Paul in the sense of *his own spirit.* See ch. reff., where the principal instances are given. The dative, as here, is found Rom. xii. 11, τῷ πν. ζέοντες,—1 Cor. v. 3, παρὼν τῷ πνεύμ. (1 Cor. xiv. 15, 16?),—2 Cor. ii. 13, οὐκ ἔσχηκα ἄνεσιν τῷ πν. μου, and al., see also ch. xix. 21. *How* he was bound *in the spirit* is manifest, by comparing other passages, where the Holy Spirit of God is related to have shaped his apostolic course. He was bound, by the Spirit of God leading captive, constraining, his own spirit. As he went up to Jerusalem **δεδεμένος τῷ πνεύματι**, so he left Judæa again **δεδεμένος τῇ σαρκί**,—*a prisoner according to the flesh.* He had no detailed knowledge of futurity—nothing but what the Holy Spirit, in general forewarnings, repeated at every point of his journey (κατὰ πόλιν; see ch. xxi. 4, 11, for two such instances), announced, viz., imprisonment and tribulations. That *here* no *inner voice* of the Spirit is meant, is evident from the words **κατὰ πόλιν.** (Two of

[e] τιμίαν ἐμαυτῷ ὡς [f] τελειῶσαι τὸν [g] δρόμον μου καὶ τὴν
[h] διακονίαν ἣν [i] ἔλαβον [i] παρὰ τοῦ κυρίου Ἰησοῦ, [k] διαμαρτύρασθαι τὸ εὐαγγέλιον τῆς [k] χάριτος τοῦ θεοῦ.
25 [l] καὶ νῦν [l] ἰδοὺ ἐγὼ οἶδα ὅτι οὐκέτι [t] ὄψεσθε τὸ [t] πρόσωπόν
μου ὑμεῖς πάντες, ἐν οἷς [u] διῆλθον [v] κηρύσσων τὴν [vw] βασι-

e = James v. 7. 1 Pet. i. 19 al. Prov. iii. 15. viii. 11.
f = John iv. 34 al. Sir. l. 19. see Phil. iii. 12. Wisd. iv. 13.
g Paul (ch. xiii. 25. 2 Tim. iv. 7) only. Jer. viii. 6.
h = ch. i. 17, 25. vi. 4. Rom. xi. 13 †. (ch. vi. 1 al. L.P., exc. Heb. i. 14. Rev. ii. 19.)
i ch. ii. 33 reff.
k = ch. xiii. 43 reff.
l ver. 22.
t = here (Rev. xxii. 4) only. θεωρεῖν, ver. 38. ὁρᾶν, Col. ii. 1. ἰδεῖν, 1 Thess. ii. 17. iii. 10.
u = ch. viii. 4 reff. 1 Chron. xxi. 4.
v here only. κ. τὸ εὐαγγ. τῆς β., Matt. ix. 35. κ. τ. β. τ. θεοῦ, ch. xxviii. 31 only.
w absol., Matt. viii. 12. xiii. 19, 38 al.

D¹EH vulg: om ABC D⁴(and lat) LP א c 13[for ψ., ευχην] 36. 40. εμαυτου D¹[-gr](txt D²). for ως, εως א³: ωστε E b c d o 13. 40. 137: ως το C 104: του [*quam*] D. τελειωσω Bא. rec aft τον δρομον μου ins μετα χαρας (*interpolation appy: see Phil* i. 4, *Col* i. 11, *Heb* x. 34 *&c: the* finishing *his course appearing not emphatic enough*), with CEHLP rel 36 syr [arm] Chr$_1$: om ABDא 13. 40 vulg Syr coptt æth Lucif$_1$. aft διακονιαν ins του λογου D vulg[with demid tol(not am fuld)] Lucif Ambr.—for ην, ον D¹-gr(txt D⁴). παρελαβον D b c k o 137. aft διαμαρτυρασθαι ins ιουδαιοις και ελλησιν D sah Lucif. om του (bef θεου) D¹(ins D⁶).

25. om ιδου E l 13. 40. 73 Lucif$_1$. οιδα bef εγω C m: om εγω 180 Iren-int$_1$. for ουκετι, ουκ א [D-lat]. rec aft την βασιλειαν ins του θεου (*supple-*

the three other places where this phrase occurs are from the mouth or pen of Paul.)

23. τὸ πν. διαμαρτύρ.] Compare Rom. viii. 16, τὸ πνεῦμα συμμαρτυρεῖ τῷ πν. ἡμῶν. **24.**] The reading in the text, amidst all the varieties, seems to be that out of which the others have all arisen, and whose difficulties they more or less explain. The first clause is a combination of two constructions, οὐδενὸς λόγου ποιοῦμαι τὴν ψυχὴν ἐμαυτοῦ, and οὐ ποιοῦμαι (ἡγοῦμαι, Phil. iii. 7, 8) τὴν ψυχὴν τιμίαν ἐμαυτῷ. The best rendering in English would be, **I hold my life of no account, nor precious to me.** Then again the confused construction of the former clause shews itself in the ὡς of the latter, which is not '*so that*,' but '*as*,' q. d. before, '*so* precious.' '*I do not value my life, in comparison with the finishing my course.*' Render then the whole verse: **But I hold my life of no account, nor is it so precious to me, as the finishing of my course.** **τελειῶσαι**] See the same image, with the same word, remarkably expanded, Phil. iii. 12—14. There in ver. 12 he has used τετελείωμαι,—and,—as is constantly the case when we are in the habit of connecting certain words together, —the δρόμος immediately occurs to him, which he works into a sublime comparison in ver. 14. **δρόμον**] A similitude peculiar to Paul: occurring, remarkably enough, in his speech at ch. xiii. 25. He uses it without the word δρ., at 1 Cor. ix. 24—27, and Phil. iii. 14. **καὶ τ. δ.**] **and** (i. e. even) **the ministry,** &c. **καί** in this sense gives that which, in matter of fact, runs parallel with the metaphorical expression just used,—stands beside it as its antitype. **ἔλαβον**] Compare Rom. i. 5, δι' οὗ **ἐλάβομεν** χάριν κ. ἀποστολήν. **25.**] It has been argued from ἐν οἷς διῆλθον, that the elders of other churches besides that of Ephesus must have been present. But it might just as well have been argued, that *every one* to whom Paul had there preached must have been present, on account of the word πάντες. If he could regard the elders as the representatives of the various churches, of which there can be no doubt, why may not he similarly have regarded the *Ephesian* elders as representatives of the churches of proconsular Asia, and have addressed all in addressing them? Or may not these words have even a wider application, viz., to *all* who had been the subjects of his former personal ministry, in Asia and Europe, now addressed through the Ephesian elders? See the question, whether Paul *ever did see the Asiatic churches again,* discussed in the Prolegg. to the Pastoral Epistles, § ii. 18 ff. I may remark here, that the word οἶδα, in the mouth of Paul, does not necessarily imply that he spoke from divine and unerring knowledge, but expresses his own conviction of the certainty of what he is saying: see ch. xxvi. 27, which is much to our point, as expressing his firm persuasion that king Agrippa *was* a believer in the prophets: but certainly no infallible knowledge of his heart:—Rom. xv. 29, where also a firm persuasion is expressed:—Phil. i. 19, 20, where οἶδα, ver. 19, is explained to rest on ἀποκαραδοκία καὶ ἐλπίς in ver. 20. So that he may here ground his expectation of never seeing them again, on the plan of making a journey into the west

λείαν. 26 διότι [x] μαρτύρομαι ὑμῖν ἐν τῇ [y] σήμερον [y] ἡμέρᾳ,
ὅτι [z] καθαρός εἰμι [a] ἀπὸ τοῦ [b] αἵματος πάντων· 27 οὐ γὰρ
[c] ὑπεστειλάμην [c] τοῦ μὴ [c] ἀναγγεῖλαι πᾶσαν τὴν [d] βουλὴν τοῦ
θεοῦ ὑμῖν. 28 [e] προσέχετε οὖν [e] ἑαυτοῖς καὶ παντὶ τῷ [f] ποιμνίῳ ἐν ᾧ ὑμᾶς τὸ πνεῦμα τὸ ἅγιον [g] ἔθετο [h] ἐπισκόπους,

ABCDE HLPℵ a bcdfg hklm o 13

x ch. xxvi. 22. Gal. v. 3. Eph. iv. 17. 1 Thess. ii. 12 only †. P. w. ὡς, Jos. B. J. iii. 8. 3 end.
y Matt. xxviii. 15. Rom. xi. 8. 2 Cor. iii. 14 only. Josh. v. 9. Jer. i. 18.
z ch. xviii. 6. Gen. xxiv. 8.
a = Matt. xxvii. 24. 2 Kings iii. 28.
b ch. xviii. 6.
c ver. 20 (reff.).
d ch. ii. 23 reff. Wisd. vi. 4.
e Luke xii. 1. xvii. 3. xxi. 34. ch. v. 35 only. Deut. iv. 9.
f here bis. Luke xii. 32. 1 Pet. v. 2, 3 only. Jer. xiii. 17.
g = 1 Cor. xii. 18, 28. Gen. xvii. 5.
h (here first.) Phil. i. 1. 1 Tim. iii. 2. Tit. i. 7. 1 Pet. ii. 25 only. 2 Chron. xxxiv. 12. Isa. lx. 17. (-πή, 1 Tim. iii. 1. -πεῖν, 1 Pet. v. 2.)

mentary addn, as shewn by the variations), with EHLP rel vulg Syr [copt-wilk arm-rien] æth Thdrt Thl: του ιησου D sah; τ. κυρ. ιησ. Lucif: om ABCℵ c 13. 36 syr copt arm Chr_1.

26. rec (for διοτι) διο, with C[D⁶]HL 13. 36 rel [Bas_1] Thl: txt A B(sic: see table) EPℵ g: διο και f 32. 57. 104.—for διοτι to οτι, αχρι ουν της σημερον ημερας D^1(*propter quod hodierno die* D-lat: txt D^6). rec (for ειμι) εγω (*see ch* xviii. 6, *where there is no varn*), with AHLP rel [Syr] copt Bas_1 Chr_6 Thl-sif: εγω ειμι a 69. 105 arm: ειμι εγω sah Jer: txt BCDEℵ c 13. 36. 40 vulg syr [sah] Amm_1 Bas_3 [Iren-int_1 $Lucif_1$]. aft παντων add υμων E a d e l syrr copt æth [arm-mss].

27. om μη D^1-gr(ins D^5(?)) 66^2. 73. 81. 177^1 [arm(Treg)] $Lucif_1$. rec υμιν bef πασαν τ. βουλ. τ. θ., with AEHLP$ℵ^3$ rel syrr coptt [æth arm] Bas_4 Chr_1 Iren-int_1: txt BC(D)$ℵ^1$ m 13 vulg [Iren-int_1].—ημιν D^1[-gr](txt D^4) [om $Lucif_1$].

28. om ουν (προσεχετε *is the beginning of an ecclesiastical portion*) ABDℵ o 13. 36 lectt vulg copt [æth arm] Did_1 Thdrt $Lucif_1$: ins CEHLP rel spec syrr Chr_1 [Bas_1] Iren-int_1. [αυτοις (for εαυτ.) D^1 l^1.] το αγ. πν. D-gr [spec].

after seeing Rome, which he mentions Rom. xv. 24, 28, and from which, with bonds and imprisonment and other dangers awaiting him, he might well expect never to return. So that what he here says need not fetter our judgment on the above question. **26.**] The use of μαρτύρομαι is peculiar to Paul, see reff. **28. προσέχ. ἑαυτοῖς**] If we might venture to trace the hand of *Luke* in the speech, it would be perhaps in this phrase: which occurs only as in reff. **τ. ποιμνίῳ**] This similitude does not elsewhere occur in Paul's writings. We find it (reff.) where we should naturally expect it, used by him to whom it was said, 'Feed my sheep.' But it is common in the O. T. and sanctioned by the example of our Lord Himself. **τὸ πν. τ. ἅγ.**] See ch. xiii. 2. **ἔθετο**] So Paul, reff. 1 Cor. **ἐπισκόπους**] See on ver. 17, and Theodoret on Phil. i. 1, ἐπισκόπους τοὺς πρεσβυτέρους καλεῖ· ἀμφότερα γὰρ εἶχον κατ' ἐκεῖνον τὸν καιρὸν τὰ ὀνόματα (Olsh.). The question between θεοῦ and κυρίου rests principally on internal evidence—which of the two is likely to have been the original reading. The manuscript authority, now that it is certain that B has θεοῦ *a prima manu*, as also ℵ, is weighty on both sides. The early patristic authority for the expression αἷμα θεοῦ is considerable. Ignat. Ephes. i., p. 644, has ἀναζωπυρήσαντες ἐν αἵματι θεοῦ. Tertull. ad Uxor. ii. 3, vol. i., p. 1293, "pretio empti, et quali pretio? sanguine Dei." Clem. Alex., 'Quis dives salvus,' c. 34, vol. ii., p. 344, has δυνάμει θεοῦ πατρός, κ. αἵματι θεοῦ παιδός, κ. δρόσῳ πνεύματος ἁγίου. On the other hand Athanasius (contra Apol. ii. 14, vol. ii., p. 758) says, οὐδαμοῦ δὲ αἷμα θεοῦ δίχα σαρκὸς παραδεδώκασιν αἱ γραφαί, ἢ θεὸν δίχα σαρκὸς παθόντα ἢ ἀναστάντα. In attempting to decide between the two readings, the following alternatives and considerations may be put: (I.) IF κυρίου WAS THE ORIGINAL, it is very possible (1) *that some busy scribe may have written at the side, as so often occurs*, θεοῦ. This having been once done, the interests of orthodoxy would perpetuate the gloss, and by degrees it would be *adopted into the text and supersede the original word*, or become combined with it, as is actually the case in HL and a vast body of mss. Or, continuing supposition I., it may have been (2) *that the expression* ἐκκλησίαν τοῦ κυρίου, *not found any where else, may have been corrected into the very usual one*, ἐκκλ. (τοῦ) θεοῦ, which occurs eleven times in the Epistles of Paul. Or (3), which I consider exceedingly improbable (see below), *the alteration may have been made solely in the interest of orthodoxy*. Such are possible, and the two former not improbable, contingencies.
On the other hand (II.) IF θεοῦ WAS THE ORIGINAL, *but one reason* can be given why it should have been altered to κυρίου, and *that one* was *sure to have operated*. It would stand as a bulwark against Arianism, an assertion which no skill could evade, which *must therefore be modified*. If θεοῦ stood in the text originally, *it was sure to be altered to* κυρίου. The converse was

[i] ποιμαίνειν τὴν ἐκκλησίαν τοῦ *θεοῦ, ἣν [k] περιεποιήσατο
διὰ τοῦ αἵματος τοῦ ἰδίου. 29 ἐγὼ οἶδα ὅτι [l] εἰςελεύσονται
μετὰ τὴν [m] ἄφιξίν μου [n] λύκοι [o] βαρεῖς εἰς ὑμᾶς μὴ

i = John xxi. 16. 1 Pet. v. 2. 2 Kings v. 2. k Luke xvii. 33. 1 Tim. iii. 13 only. Gen. xxxi. 18. Isa. xxxi. 5. l John x. 1. ch. xix. 30. m here only †. 3 Macc. vii. 18. Herodot. ix. 77. n = Matt. vii. 15 (x. 16. Luke x. 3. John x. 12 bis) only. (Ezek. xxii. 27.) o = here only. (ch. xxv. 7 reff.)

*κυρίου AC^{1}DE a 13. 36. 40 syr-mg coptt arm (Eus$_1$) Ath-ms$_1$ (Constt$_1$) Did$_2$ Chr(on Eph iv. 12) (Thdor-stud$_1$) Thl-fl-ms Iren-int$_1$ Lucif$_1$ (Aug) Jer$_1$ Sedul: χριστου Syr(ed and 2-mss[7th cent and later]) æth-pl [Ps-Ign$_1$] Ath-4-mss Thdrt$_2$ (cf συντρέχετε εἰς τὴν ἐκκλησίαν τοῦ κυρίου ἣν περιεποιήσατο τῷ αἵματι τοῦ χριστοῦ Constt): κυριου και θεου C^{3}HLP rel: κυριου θεου 3. 95^2: θεου Bℵ c vulg Syr-5-mss[6th and 7th cent] syr syr-lect Ign$_1$ Ps-Ath$_1$ Epiph$_2$ Bas$_1$ [Chr$_3$ Cyr$_2$] Antch$_2$ Thl-fin Ambr$_1$ Ors$_1$ Primas$_1$. aft περιεποιησατο ins εαυτω D sah, *sibi constituit* Iren[-int$_1$]. rec του ιδιου αιματος (*alteration, says Meyer, owing to* θεου, *because* του ιδιου *might be referred to* Christ (*as a gen*): *but surely this is carrying subtlety somewhat too far. It has been evidently a corrn for simplicity, not observing the emphasis*), with HLP rel Ath$_1$ Chr$_1$ [Antch$_1$] Thl: txt ABCDEℵ a c m 13. 36. 40 [vulg syr-mg-gr] arm Did$_1$ Iren-int$_1$ Lucif$_1$.

29. rec aft εγω ins γαρ (*to connect and strengthen the sentence*), with C^{3}EHLP rel syrr sah [arm] Chr$_1$: οτι εγω B: εγω δε ℵ^3 copt: και εγω æth: txt AC^{1}Dℵ^1 13. 36 vulg Iren-int$_1$ Lucif$_1$. rec aft οιδα ins τουτο (*like preceding*), with C^{3}EHLP rel syr Chr: om ABC^{1}Dℵ a 13. 36 [vulg Syr coptt æth arm] Iren-int$_1$ Lucif. αφεξιν D[E: αφηξιν L].

not sure, nor indeed likely, from similar reasons, the passage offering no stumbling-block to orthodoxy. (III.) Pauline usage must be allowed its fair weight in the enquiry. It must be remembered that we are in the midst of a speech, which is (as observed in the Prolegg. to Acts, § ii. 17 a) a complete storehouse of Pauline words and expressions. Is it *per se* probable, that he should use an expression which *no where else occurs in his writings, nor indeed in those of his contemporaries?* Is it *more* probable, that the early scribes should have altered an unusual expression for an usual one, or that a writer so constant to his own phrases should here have remained so? Besides,—in most of the places where Paul uses ἐκκλησία τοῦ θεοῦ, it is in a manner *precisely similar to this,*—as the *consummation of a climax*, or in a position of peculiar solemnity, cf. 1 Cor. x. 32; xv. 9; Gal. i. 13; 1 Tim. iii. 5, 15: and, cæteris paribus, I submit that the present passage loses by the substitution of κυρίου the peculiar emphasis which its structure and context seem to require in the genitive, introduced as it is by προσέχετε . . . . . ποιμαίνειν, and followed by the intensifying clause ἣν περιεποιήσατο διὰ τοῦ αἵματος τοῦ ἰδίου. (IV.) On the whole then, weighing the evidence on both sides,—seeing that it is more likely that the alteration should have been to κυρίου than to θεοῦ,—more likely that the speaker should have used θεοῦ than κυρίου, and more consonant to the evidently emphatic position of the word, I have decided for the rec. reading, which in Edd. 1, 2 I had rejected. And this decision is confirmed by observing the habits of the great mss. respecting the sacred names. It appears that B has *no bias* for θεός where the others have κύριος: we find it thus reading in Luke ii. 38 (so DLX^{1}Ξℵ); ch. xvi. 10 (so ACEℵ); xvii. 27 (so AHLℵ); xxi. 20 (so ACELℵ); Col. iii. 16 (so AC^{1}D^{1}Fℵ); while on the other hand it has κυ ιυ in Rom. xv. 32, where the others have θυ or χυ ιυ; χυ in Eph. v. 21, where rec. has θυ; κυ in ch. viii. 22, with ACDEℵ, where rec. and the mss. have θυ: similarly in ch. x. 33, and xv. 40: in Rom. x. 17 χυ, with CD^{1}ℵ^1, for θυ: xiv. 4, κς, with AC^{1}ℵ, for θς. This evidence seems to remove further off the chance of deliberate alteration here to θεοῦ, and leaves the above considerations their full weight. (V.) Of course any reading which *combines* the two, κυρίου and θεοῦ, is by the very first principles of textual criticism inadmissible. (VI.) The principal names on either side are—for the rec. θεοῦ, Mill, Wolf, Bengel, Matthäi, Scholz: for κυρίου, Grotius, Le Clerc, Wetst., Griesb., Kuin., De Wette, Meyer, Lachmann, Tischendorf, Tregelles. **περιεπ.**] Luke and Paul (in pastoral Epp. only), see reff. **29.**] **ἄφιξις** is here used in an unusual sense. An instance is found, Jos. Antt. iv. 8. 47, where Moses says, ἐπεὶ πρὸς τοὺς ἡμετέρους ἄπειμι προγόνους, καὶ θεὸς τήνδε μοι τὴν ἡμέραν τῆς πρὸς ἐκείνους ἀφίξεως ὥρισε . . . . . which is somewhat analogous, but more easily explained. That in Herod. ix. 77 (init.) also seems analogous. In Demosth. de Pace, p. 58 (fin.), we have τὴν τότε ἄφιξιν εἰς τοὺς πολεμίους ἐποιήσατο, which is most like the usage here. Perhaps, absolutely put, it must signify '*my*

p Rom. xi. 21 reff. Deut. xxxiii. 3. 2 Kings xii. 4, 6.
q = ch. v. 36, 37. vii. 18, from Exod. i. 8.
r Matt. xvii. 17 ‖ L. Luke xxiii. 2. ch. xiii. 8, 10. Phil. ii. 15 only. Deut. xxxii. 5.
s constr., 1 Cor. x. 13 reff.
t = here [Matt. xxvi. 51. Luke xxii. 41. ch. xxi. 1) only. Jer. xii. 14.

ABCDE HLP‭א a b c d f g h k l m o 13

[p] φειδόμενοι τοῦ [f] ποιμνίου, 30 καὶ ἐξ ὑμῶν αὐτῶν [q] ἀναστήσονται ἄνδρες λαλοῦντες [r] διεστραμμένα, [s] τοῦ [t] ἀποσπᾷν
τοὺς μαθητὰς [u] ὀπίσω ἑαυτῶν. 31 διὸ [v] γρηγορεῖτε, [w] μνη-
μονεύοντες [w] ὅτι [x] τριετίαν [y] νύκτα καὶ [y] ἡμέραν οὐκ
[z] ἐπαυσάμην [a] μετὰ δακρύων [b] νουθετῶν [c] ἕνα ἕκαστον.
32 καὶ [d] τὰ νῦν [e] παρατίθεμαι ὑμᾶς τῷ θεῷ καὶ τῷ [fg] λόγῳ
τῆς [gh] χάριτος αὐτοῦ, τῷ δυναμένῳ [i] οἰκοδομῆσαι καὶ δοῦναι
τὴν [k] κληρονομίαν [k] ἐν τοῖς [k] ἡγιασμένοις πᾶσιν. 33 ἀργυρίου ἢ χρυσίου ἢ [l] ἱματισμοῦ οὐδενὸς [m] ἐπεθύμησα· 34 αὐτοὶ

u ch. v. 37 reff. v = Matt. xxiv. 42. 1 Cor. xvi. 13 al. (Jer. v. 6.) w Paul only. Eph. ii. 11. 2 Thess. ii. 5. (ὡς, 2 Macc. x. 6.) x here only †. (-τής, 2 Chron. xxxi. 16. -τίζω, Gen. xv. 9. see ch. xxviii. 30.) y ch. xxvi. 7. 2 Thess. iii. 8. Paul only, exc. Mark iv. 27. Esth. iv. 16. elsew. gen., as ch. ix. 24 reff. z constr., ch. xiii. 10 reff. a Heb. v. 7. xii. 17. 2 Macc. xi. 6. b Rom. xv. 14. 1 Cor. iv. 14. Col. i. 28. iii. 16. 1 Thess. v. 12, 14. 2 Thess. iii. 15 only. P. Job iv. 3. (-θεσία, 1 Cor. x. 11.) c ch. ii. 6 reff. d ch. iv. 29 reff. e Luke xxiii. 46. ch. xiv. 23. Ps. xxx. 5. f ch. xiv. 3. g constr., ch. xiii. 26 reff. h ch. xiii. 43 reff. i = ch. ix. 31 reff. k = an constr., Eph. i. 18. (see ch. xxvi. 18.) l Luke vii. 25. ix. 29. John xix. 24. 1 Tim. ii. 9 only. Ps. xliv. 9. m constr., 1 Tim. iii. 1 only. (Rom. vii. 7 al.) Prov. xxiii. 3, 6.

30. om 1st *αυτων* B e sah æth. for *αποσπαν*, *αποστρεφειν* D-gr Syr. rec (for *εαυτων*) *αυτων*, with CDEHLP rel Bas$_1$ Chr$_1$: txt ABא.

31. *νυκταν* A. for *και*, *δε* D^1[-gr](txt D^4). at end ins *υμων* DE a b c d k o vulg (syrr) coptt æth [Antch$_1$] Thl-fin Lucif$_1$ Jer$_1$ Ors$_1$. (D-lat is deficient from ver 31 to ch xxi. 2.)

32. *υμιν*(sic) א[H]. rec aft *υμας* ins *αδελφοι* (*for solemnity ; were it genuine, as Meyer observes, there would be no possible reason for* omitting *it*), with CEHLP rel 36 æth-rom Chr$_1$: aft *τω θεω*, c 137 lect-58 : om ABDא 13 vulg syrr coptt æth-pl [arm] Jer$_1$ Ors$_1$. for *θεω*, *κυριω* B 33. 68 coptt. rec *εποικοδομησαι*, with HLP rel Chr$_{expr}$(*ουκ ειπεν οικοδομησαι αλλ εποικοδομησαι, δεικνυς οτι ηδη ωκοδομηθησαν. But may not this have been the history of its alteration, to render the word more strictly appropriate?*) : txt ABCDEא 13. 36 [*ædificare* vulg E-lat Jer]. add *υμας* DE 29. 76 lect-58 Syr sah æth : pref, a b o 14^1. 66^2-9. 76. 81. 105^1 Chr$_1$. rec aft *δουν.* ins *υμιν*, with CHLP 13. 36 rel vss : om ABDEא vulg copt. rec om *την*, with DHLP rel [Chr] : ins A B(sic : see table) CEא. add *αυτου* A. aft *εν* ins *αυ*(. .)*ς* (? *αυτοις*) D^1. for *πασιν*, *των παντων* D.

33. for 1st *η*, *και* D vulg ([demid]not am &c) spec [Antch$_1$]. *ουθενος* AEא [Antch$_1$] : txt BCDHLP rel 36. add *υμων* DE spec arm.

34. rec aft *αυτοι* ins *δε*, with 13[(e sil) copt Thl-fin] : *γαρ* 106 : [*et vos* Syr æth-rom :] om ABCDEHLPא rel vulg syr [sah] æth[-pl] arm Bas$_1$ (Chr$_1$).

death ;' see the above passage of Josephus. **λύκοι βαρεῖς**] not *persecutors*, but *false teachers*, from the words **εἰσελ. εἰς ὑμᾶς**, by which it appears that they were to *come in among the flock*, i. e. to be baptized Christians. In fact ver. 30 is explanatory of the metaphoric meaning of ver. 29. **φείδομαι** is only used by Paul, except 2 Pet. ii. 4, 5. **30.**] **ὑμῶν αὐτ.** does not necessarily signify the *presbyters:* he speaks to them as being the whole flock. **31.**] **μνημ. ὅτι** is only (reff.) used by Paul. **νύκτα κ. ἡμέραν**] This expression is remarkable: we have it (see reff.) in Mark, but Luke always uses the genitive, except in the speeches of Paul: and so Paul himself, except as in reff. **νουθετῶν** (reff.) is used only by Paul. On the *three years* spoken of in this verse, see note, ch. xix. 10. We may just remark here (1) that this passage being precise and definite, must be the master key to those others (as in ch. xix.) which give wide and indefinite notes of time: and (2) that it seems at first sight to preclude the idea of a journey (as some think) to Crete and Corinth having taken place during this period. But this apparent inference may require modifying by other circumstances: cf. Prolegg. to 1 Cor. § v. 4. **32. τ. λόγ. τῆς χάρ. αὐτ.**] I should be inclined to attribute the occurrence of this expression in ch. xiv. 3, to the narrative having come from Paul himself, or from one imbued with his words and habits of thought. See ver. 24. **τῷ δυν.**] Clearly spoken of *God*, not of the *word of His grace*, which cannot be said *δοῦναι κληρον.*, however it might *οἰκοδομῆσαι.* The expression *κληρον. ἐν τ. ἡγ. πᾶσ.* is strikingly similar to *τῆς κληρονομίας αὐτοῦ ἐν τοῖς ἁγίοις*, Eph. i. 18, addressed to this same church. See also ch. xxvi. 18. **33.**] See 1 Sam. xii. 3; and for similar avowals by Paul himself, 1 Cor. ix. 11, 12; 2 Cor. xi. 8, 9; xii. 13. **34.**] See 1 Cor. iv. 12, which

γινωσκετε ὅτι ταῖς [n] χρείαις μου καὶ τοῖς οὖσιν μετ' ἐμοῦ
[o] ὑπηρέτησαν αἱ χεῖρες αὗται· 35 [p] πάντα [q] ὑπέδειξα ὑμῖν
ὅτι οὕτως [r] κοπιῶντας δεῖ [s] ἀντιλαμβάνεσθαι τῶν [t] ἀσθενούντων, [u] μνημονεύειν τε τῶν [v] λόγων τοῦ [v] κυρίου Ἰησοῦ,
ὅτι αὐτὸς εἶπεν [w] Μακάριόν ἐστιν [w] μᾶλλον διδόναι ἢ
λαμβάνειν. 36 καὶ ταῦτα εἰπὼν [x] θεὶς τὰ [x] γόνατα αὐτοῦ
σὺν πᾶσιν αὐτοῖς προσηύξατο. 37 [y] ἱκανὸς δὲ [z] κλαυθμὸς
ἐγένετο πάντων, καὶ [ab] ἐπιπεσόντες ἐπὶ τὸν [bc] τράχηλον τοῦ
Παύλου [d] κατεφίλουν αὐτόν, 38 [e] ὀδυνώμενοι μάλιστα [f] ἐπὶ
τῷ λόγῳ [g] ᾧ εἰρήκει, ὅτι οὐκέτι [h] μέλλουσιν τὸ [i] πρόσωπον
αὐτοῦ [i] θεωρεῖν. [k] προέπεμπον δὲ αὐτὸν εἰς τὸ πλοῖον.

n = ch. xxviii. 10. Rom. xii. 13. Phil. ii. 25. iv. 16, 19. Tit. iii. 14. Sir. xxxix. 33.
o ch. xiii. 36 (reff.). xxiv. 23 only +.
p constr., 1 Cor. ix. 25. x. 33. Eph. iv. 15. P.
q = Luke (iii. 7 ‖ Mt.) vi. 47. xii. 5. ch. ix. 16 only. Esth. iv. 6.
r 1 Cor. xv. 10 reff.
s Luke i. 54. 1 Tim. vi. 2 only. L.P. Isa. xli. 9. (συναντιλ., Rom. viii. 26.)
t = here only. (2 Cor. xii. 10. Job iv. 4.) see 1 Thess. v. 14.
u w. gen., Luke xvii. 32 al. 1 Chron. xvi. 15.
v 1 Tim. vi. 3.
w constr., Mark ix. 42. 1 Cor. ix. 15. see Matthiæ, § 458.
x ch. vii. 60 reff.
y ch. xi. 24 reff.
z Matt. ii. 18. viii. 12 al5. Luke xiii. 28 only. Gen. xlvi. 29.
a ver. 10.
b Luke xv. 20 only. Gen. xlvi. 29.
c ch. xv. 10 reff.
d Matt. xxvi. 49 ‖ Mk. Luke vii. 38, 45. xv. 20 only. Exod. iv. 27. Ruth i. 9, 14.
e = Luke ii. 48 (xvi. 24, 25) only. Isa. xl. 29.
f = James v. 1 al. Zech. xii. 10.
g attr., ch. i. 1 reff.
h = ch. xix. 27 al.
i see ver. 25 reff.
k ch. xv. 3 reff.

[for γιν.] οιδατε A. τας χρειας(sic) D¹(txt D²). aft χρ. μου ins πασιν D¹. aft αυται ins μου D sah : μου αυται Syr copt æth.

35. ins και bef παντα CD² b o 36. 40 Syr [arm]. for παντα, πασι D¹(txt D²). των ασθενουντων bef αντιλαμβανεσθαι A. om τε (A¹?) D¹ coptt: ins D². τον λογον LP a d² e f k 4. 14². 22. 42. 57. 65-9. 73. 96-9. 126-56-63-91-2 lect-58 sah æth arm Chr Thl-sif. του λογου h 26. 38. 40. 93 lect-18 vulg (*both corrns, because but* one *saying is cited*). om ιησου A[²(?)] 2. 30. 68. 96. 142 Epiph₁ Chr₁ Bas₁. ουτος and μακαριος D¹(txt D²). rec διδοναι bef μαλλον, with a m [o Syr Bas₁] : txt ABCDEHLPℵ 13 rel vulg spec syr arm [Bas₁] Chr.

36. ειπας D¹(txt D-corr¹). om αυτου D¹(ins D⁶) [f arm]. συμπασιν L[P]. om αυτοις C¹ 36 arm. προσευξατο B¹D.

37. for δε, τε ℵ [(Syr)]. rec εγενετο bef κλαυθμος (*corrn of order to bring* κλαυθμος *and* παντων *together*), with HLP rel [syrr copt arm] Thl-sif: txt ABCDEℵ a [(c)] h k m 13. 40 vulg [sah] Thl-fin. om του D-corr c 180 Thl-sif. κατεφιλων ℵ¹.

38. μαλιστα επι τω λογω bef οδυνωμενοι, omg ω ειρηκει (ins D-corr¹) and adding (aft οδυν.) οτι ειπεν, D¹(om ειπεν D-corr). for ουκετι μελλουσιν, μελλει (σο)ι D¹ (txt D⁴). om αυτου D¹(ins D⁵). for εις, επι D. om το (bef πλοιον) P.

he wrote when at Ephesus. χρεία, with a gen. of the *person in want*, is an expression of Paul only; see among reff. ὑπηρετεῖν is used only twice more; once *by* Paul, ch. xiii. 36, once *of* Paul, ch. xxiv. 23.

The construction is varied in this sentence. **ταῖς χρ.** μου, καὶ (not τῶν ὄντων, but) τοῖς οὖσιν μετ' ἐμοῦ. This is not without meaning—his friends were among his χρεῖαι—he supplied by his labour, not his and their wants, but *his wants* and *them*. **αἱ χ. αὗται**] also [strikingly] in Paul's manner: compare τῶν δεσμῶν τούτων, ch. xxvi. 29,—and ch. xxviii. 20.

35. πάντα] In all things: so Paul (only), see reff. **κοπιῶντας**] A word used by Paul fourteen times, by Luke once only (Luke v. 5 (xii. 27 v. r.)). **τῶν ἀσθενούντων**] Not here *the weak in faith* (Rom. xiv. 1. 1 Cor. viii. 9), as Calvin, Beza, Grot., Bengel, Neander, Meyer, Tholuck, —which the context both before and after will not allow:—but the poor (τοὺς πένητας ἀσθενοῦντας, Aristoph. Pac. 636. ὅ τε γὰρ ἀσθενέστερος ὁ πλούσιός τε τὴν δίκην ἴσην ἔχει, Eurip. ap. Stob. cxv. (Wetst.)), as Chrys., Theoph., Heinrichs, Kuin., Olsh., De Wette. **Μακ. ἐστιν κ.τ.λ.**] This saying of our Lord is one of very few not recorded in the Gospels, which have come down to us. Many such must have been current in the apostolic times, and are possibly preserved, unknown to us, in such epistles as those of James, Peter, and John. Bengel remarks, 'alia mundi sententia est:' and cites from an old poet in Athenæus, viii. 5, ἀνόητος ὁ διδούς, εὐτυχὴς δ' ὁ λαμβάνων. But we have some sayings the other way: not to quote authors who wrote after this date, and might have imbibed some of the spirit of Christianity, we find in Aristotle, Eth. Nicom. iv. 1, μᾶλλόν ἐστιν τοῦ ἐλευθερίου τὸ διδόναι οἷς δεῖ ἢ λαμβάνειν ὅθεν δεῖ, καὶ μὴ λαμβάνειν ὅθεν οὐ δεῖ. τῆς ἀρετῆς γὰρ μᾶλλον τὸ εὖ ποιεῖν ἢ τὸ εὖ πάσχειν.

l constr., ch. iv. 5 reff.
m ch. xiii. 13 reff.
n = Luke xxii. 41. (ch. xx. 30 reff.) 2 Macc. xii. 10.
o ch. xvi. 11 only +.
p ch. xxv. 17. xxvii. 18. Luke vii. 11 (w. ἡμέρα, ix. 37) only. L.

XXI. 1 ὡς δὲ [l] ἐγένετο [m] ἀναχθῆναι ἡμᾶς [n] ἀποσπασθέντας
ἀπ' αὐτῶν, [o] εὐθυδρομήσαντες ἤλθομεν εἰς τὴν Κῶ, [p] τῇ
δὲ [p] ἑξῆς εἰς τὴν Ῥόδον, κἀκεῖθεν εἰς Πάταρα. 2 καὶ
εὑρόντες πλοῖον [q] διαπερῶν εἰς Φοινίκην, [r] ἐπιβάντες
[m] ἀνήχθημεν. 3 [s] ἀναφανέντες δὲ τὴν Κύπρον καὶ [t] κατα-
λιπόντες αὐτὴν [t] εὐώνυμον ἐπλέομεν εἰς Συρίαν, καὶ
[u] κατήλθομεν εἰς Τύρον· [v] ἐκεῖσε γὰρ τὸ πλοῖον [w] ἦν

...φ(.)-νεικην D.
ABCEH LPℵ a b c d f g h k l m o 13

q Matt. ix. 1. xiv. 34 ‖ Mk. Mark v. 21. Luke xvi. 26 only. Deut. xxx. 13. r absol., here only. = ch. xxvii. 2.
s Luke xix. 11 only. Cant. vi. 4 (only?). constr. pass., Rom. vi. 17. Gal. ii. 7. Heb. xi. 2 al. t constr., here only. u = ch. xxvii. 5. (ch. viii. 5 reff.) v ch. xxii. 5 only. Job xxxix. 29.
w constr. (see note), ch. ii. 5 reff. Winer, edn. 6, § 45. 5.

CHAP. XXI. 1. om αναχθ. A^1(appy) : ins aft ημας A^2 : αναχθεντας ℵ^1 : αχθηναι P d 3. 100. αποσπασθεντες BE^2 [L a b. (13 uncert.)] (κα)ι επι(β)αντ(ε)ς ανηχθημεν αποσπασθεντων δε (ημω)ν D^1(txt D^4). for ηλθομεν, ηκομεν D. om την D. rec κων, with HLP l m : *Coum* vulg : *Chio* tol : txt ABCDEℵ rel 36 syrr coptt arm Œc Thl-fin Cassiod$_1$, *Cho* am. (13 def.) for εξης, επιουση D om την (bef ροδον) CD 40 Chr$_2$. πατερα AC. at end ins κ μυρα D vulg-ms, [κ.] μυρρα sah.

2. διαπερουν E 73. 105 : διαπερον Lℵ^3 a k Thl-fin : διαπορευομενον 137.

3. Steph αναφαναντες (*corrn, not perceiving the force of the passive*), with B^1(see table) ℵ a^2 b c o Chr(some mss) : txt AB^2(see table) CEHL[P] 13. 36 rel [Chr$_1$]. aft δε ins εις την P [40]. om την E. om και A k m [vulg-clem tol] demid(not am fuld). καταλειποντες AHL h^1 13 (but -πόντες HL). om επλεομεν A[^{1}(appy)] : επλευσαμεν E^2[-gr] : *navigavimus* vulg E-lat : *collavimus* D-lat. rec (for κατηλθομεν) κατηχθημεν, with CHLP rel Chr$_1$: *deposti sumus* E-lat : *venimus* vulg : *enavigavimus* D-lat : txt AB E-gr ℵ 13 [syr] coptt æth. εκει H d 133 vulg. rec ην bef το πλοιον, with HLP rel 36 [syrr arm Chr$_1$]. txt ABCEℵ c 13. 137 [vulg].

XXI. 1.] The E. V., '*After we had gotten from them,*' does not come up to the original: δείκνυσι τὴν βίαν τῷ εἰπεῖν ἀποσπασθέντας ἀπ' αὐτῶν, Chrys. **εὐθυδρομ.**] See ref., **having run before the wind.** *Cos,* opposite Cnidus and Halicarnassus, celebrated for its wines (εὔκαρπος πᾶσα, οἴνῳ δὲ καὶ ἀρίστη, καθάπερ Χίος κ. Λέσβος, Strab. xiv. 2), rich stuffs ('nec Coæ referunt jam tibi purpuræ,' Hor. iv. 13. 13), and ointments (γίνεται δὲ μύρα κάλλιστα κατὰ τόπους . . . . ἀμαράκινον δὲ Κῷον καὶ μήλινον, Athen. xv. p. 688). The chief town was of the same name (Hom. Il. β. 677), and had a famous temple of Æsculapius (Strabo, ibid.). It was the birth-place of Hippocrates. The modern name, Stanchio, is a corruption of ἐς τὰν Κῶ [as Stamboul for Constantinople is of ἐς τὰν πόλιν]. See Winer, Realw. *Rhodes* was at this time free, cf. Strabo, xiv. 2; Tac. Ann. xii. 58: 'Redditur Rhodiis libertas, adempta sæpe aut firmata, prout bellis externis meruerant, aut domi seditione deliquerant.' See also Suet. Claud. 25, 'Rhodiis (libertatem) ob pœnitentiam veterum delictorum reddidit.' It was reduced to a Roman province under Vespasian, Suet. Vesp. 8. The situation of its chief town is praised by Strabo, l. c. The celebrated Colossus was at this time broken and lying in ruins, ib. *Patara,* in Lycia ('caput gentis,' Liv. xxxvii. 15), a large maritime town, a short distance E. of the mouth of the Xanthus. It had a temple and oracle of Apollo, Herod. i. 182. 'Delius et Patareus Apollo,' Hor. iii. 4. There are considerable ruins remaining, Fellows, Asia Minor, p. 219 ff. Lycia, p. 115 ff. Winer, Realw. Here they leave their ship hired at Troas, or perhaps at Neapolis (see note on xx. 16), and avail themselves of a merchant ship bound for Tyre. **3. ἀναφανέντες**] for the construction, see reff. and Winer, edn. 6, § 39. 1: **having been shewn Cyprus,** literally. Wetst. cites from Theophanes, p. 392, περιεφέροντο ἐν τῷ πελάγει, ἀναφανέντων δὲ αὐτῶν τὴν γῆν, εἶδον αὐτοὺς οἱ στρατηγοί. 'The graphic language of an eye-witness, and of one familiar with the phraseology of seamen, who, in their own language, appear to *raise* the land in approaching it.' Smith, Voyage and Shipwreck of St. Paul. But would not this remark rather apply to the *active* participle? Compare 'aerias Phæacum abscondimus arces,' Æn. iii. 291. **εὐώνυμον**] sc. αὐτήν, i. e. to the E. This would be the straight course from Patara to Tyre. **ἐπλ. εἰς Σ.,—we held our course,** steered, **for Syria. κατήλθ.**] **we came down to,** the result of having borne

[x] ἀποφορτιζόμενον τὸν [y] γόμον. 4 [z] ἀνευρόντες δὲ τοὺς
μαθητὰς [a] ἐπεμείναμεν [b] αὐτοῦ ἡμέρας ἑπτά, [c] οἵτινες τῷ
Παύλῳ ἔλεγον [d] διὰ τοῦ πνεύματος μὴ [e] ἐπιβαίνειν εἰς
Ἱεροσόλυμα. 5 ὅτε δὲ [f] ἐγένετο [g] ἐξαρτίσαι ἡμᾶς [h] τὰς

x here only †. κυβερνήτης χειμώνων ἐπ. γινομένων ἀποφορτίζεται, Philo de Præm. 5, vol. ii. p. 413.
y Rev. xviii. 11, 12 only. Exod. xxiii. 5 only.
z Luke ii. 16 only †.
a = ch. x. 48 reff.
b ch. xviii. 19 reff.
c ch. x. 41 reff.
d ch. xi. 28 reff.
e = and constr., ch. xx. 18. (xxvii. 2 reff.)
f constr., ver. 1 al.
g = here (2 Tim. iii. 17) only †. Jos. Antt. iii. 2. 2.
h = Luke ii. 6, 22, 43.

4. rec και ανευροντες (*corrn of copula, as frequently*), with C^3HLP rel D-lat syrr æth [arm] Chr_1 Thl[-sif]: txt ABC^1E a m 13. 36. 40 vulg copt [sah] Thl-fin. om τους (*corrn, the art not seeming in place*) HLP b c d e f g h k l o 137 Chr Thl[-sif]. αυτοις (*alteration to suit οιτινες which follows*) AEL k Thl-fin: προς αυτους Chr_2, *apud eos* D-lat E-lat [syrr coptt æth]: txt BCHPא 13 rel. ελεγαν B: repeated by B^1 after πνευματος (see table). rec **αναβαινειν** (*substitution of more usual word*), with EHLP rel vulg Chr Did_1 [$Epiph_1$] Thl-sif: txt ABCא 13(appy) 36. 40 Thl-fin. rec ιερουσαλημ, with HLP rel $Epiph_1$ Chr Did_1: txt ABCEא a k 13. 36. 40 vulg D-lat Thl-fin.

5. rec ημας bef εξαρτισαι (*alteration of order to avoid* ημας τας ημερας), with B(see below) CHL (P[οτι . . . εξαρτησαι]) א rel 36 Chr: txt A B(but marking the words for transposition) E: οτε δε εγενετο εξελθειν ημας ημερας εξαρτησαι επ. (9. 100) 13: *sequenti autem die exeuntes ambulamus viam nostram* D-lat: *post hos autem dies amb.*

down upon. **Τύρον**] This city, so well known for its commercial importance and pride, and so often mentioned in the O. T. prophets, was now a free town (Jos. Ant. xv. 41. Strabo, xvi. 2, οὐχ ὑπὸ τῶν βασιλέων δ' ἐκρίθησαν αὐτόνομοι μόνον, ἀλλὰ καὶ ὑπὸ τῶν Ῥωμαίων) of the province of Syria. **ἐκεῖσε**] If this is an adv. of motion as generally, the reference may be to the carrying and depositing the cargo in the town (De Wette), or to the thitherward direction of the voyage (Meyer): but in the only other place where ἐκεῖσε occurs (ref. [see also ref. Job]) it simply = ἐκεῖ, so that perhaps no *motion* is included. **ἀποφορτ.**] The pres. part. indicates the intention, as διαπερῶν before. 4. **δέ**] Implying, 'the crew indeed were busied with unlading the ship: but we, **having sought out** (by enquiry) **the disciples.**' . . . . . '*Finding disciples*' (E.V.) is quite wrong. It is not improbable that Paul may have preached at Tyre before, when he visited Syria and Cilicia (Gal. i. 21) after his conversion,—and again when he confirmed the churches (ch. xv. 41): **τοὺς** μαθ. seems to imply this. **ἡμ. ἑπτ.**] The time taken in unlading:—they apparently proceeded in the same ship, see ver. 6. The notice here is very important, that these Tyrian disciples said to Paul *by the Spirit*, that he should not go to Jerusalem,—and *yet he went thither*, and, as he himself declares, δεδεμένος τῷ πνεύματι, *bound in spirit by the leading of God.* We thus have an instance of that which Paul asserts 1 Cor. xiv. 32, that the spirits of prophets are *subject to prophets*, i. e., that the revelation made by the Holy Spirit to each man's spirit was under the influence of that man's will and temperament, moulded by and taking the form of his own capacities and resolves. So here: these Tyrian *prophets* knew by the Spirit, which testified this in every city (ch. xx. 23), that bonds and imprisonment awaited Paul. This appears to have been announced by them, shaped and intensified by their own intense love and anxiety for him who was probably their father in the faith (see [**τοὺς** μαθ. above, and] ver. 5). But he paid no regard to the prohibition, being himself under a leading of the same Spirit too plain for him to mistake it. See below, vv. 10 ff. 5. **ἐξαρτίσαι**] This * is ordinarily a naval word, signifying to *fit out* or *refit* a ship (with or without πλοῖον, Passow). But this can hardly be the meaning here. Meyer would render '*when we had spent these days in refitting,*' so that τ. ἡμ. would be the accusative of duration,—'*when we had refitted during the days.*' But not to mention that τὰς ἡμ., without ταύτας, would be harsh in such a connexion,—is not the *aorist* ἐξαρτίσαι fatal to the rendering? Would it not in this case be *present*, if implying the continued action during the days,—*perfect*, if implying that that action was over (in which latter case ἡμ. would be dative)? The aorist, as almost invariably in dependent clauses, must refer to some *one act* occurring at one time. So that if the meaning given by Theoph., Œc. πληρῶσαι (Hesych. τελειῶσαι) be found no where else, it is almost necessary so to understand the word here. And it is doing no violence to its import: the same verb which indicates the completion of a ship's readiness for a voyage, might well be applied to the completion of

ἡμέρας, [i] ἐξελθόντες ἐπορευόμεθα, [k] προπεμπόντων ἡμᾶς ABCEH
πάντων σὺν γυναιξὶ καὶ τέκνοις [l] ἕως [m] ἔξω τῆς πόλεως, LPℵ a b c d f g h
καὶ [n] θέντες τὰ [n] γόνατα ἐπὶ τὸν [o] αἰγιαλὸν [p] προσευξάμενοι k l m o 13
6 [q] ἀπησπασάμεθα ἀλλήλους, καὶ [r] ἀνέβημεν εἰς τὸ πλοῖον,
ἐκεῖνοι δὲ [s] ὑπέστρεψαν εἰς [t] τὰ ἴδια. 7 ἡμεῖς δὲ τὸν
[u] πλοῦν [v] διανύσαντες ἀπὸ Τύρου [w] κατηντήσαμεν εἰς
Πτολεμαΐδα, καὶ [x] ἀσπασάμενοι τοὺς ἀδελφοὺς [y] ἐμείναμεν
ἡμέραν μίαν [y] παρ' αὐτοῖς. 8 [z] τῇ δὲ ἐπαύριον [a] ἐξελθόντες
ἤλθομεν εἰς Καισάρειαν, καὶ εἰσελθόντες εἰς τὸν οἶκον
Φιλίππου τοῦ [a] εὐαγγελιστοῦ, ὄντος [b] ἐκ [c] τῶν ἑπτά,

i = ch. xv. 40 reff. k ch. xv. 3 reff. l w. prepos., ch. xxvi. 11. Luke xxiv. 50. Levit. xxiii. 14. m Luke xiii. 33. ch. xiv. 19. Neh. xiii. 20. n ch. vii. 60 reff. o Matt. xiii. 2, 48. John xi. 4. ch. xxvii. 39, 40 only. Judg. v. 17 A Ald. compl. Sir. xxiv. 14 A(not F) Bℵ Ald. only. p absol., ch. x. 9 reff. Ezra x. 1. q here only †. r = Matt. xiv. 32 || Mk. xv. 39. John xxi. 11. Jonah i. 3 Ed-vat.(not B) Ald. s ch. viii. 25 reff. t John xvi. 32. xix. 27. Esth. v. 10. u ch. xxvii. 9, 10 only †. Wisd. xiv. 1 only. v here only †. 2 Macc. xii. 17 only. πολλὴν ὁδὸν διήνυσαν, Xen. Cyr. iv. 2. 15. w ch. xvi. 1 reff. x ch. xviii. 22 reff. y John i. 40. iv. 40. ch. ix. 43. xviii. 3. z ch. x. 9 reff. a Eph. iv. 11. 2 Tim. iv. 5 only. b Luke xxii. 58 al. c see ch. ii. 14 al.

v. n. Syr. om εξελθοντες A 105. γυναιξιν CE[H]P: txt AB[L]ℵ rel. om εως ℵ D-lat. in ℵ προσευξαμενοι is written before επι τ. αιγ., but marked for erasure by ℵ[1 or 3], and repeated in its proper place.

5, 6. rec for προσευξαμενοι απησπασαμεθα αλληλους και, προσηυξαμεθα και ασπασαμενοι αλληλους, with HLP rel vulg Chr_1 Thl: txt A B(sic: see table) CEℵ a d 13. 36. 40 Syr.—προσευξ. LP 4. 100-6 Chr_1.—απεσπασαμεθα C: απησπασαμενοι 40: απησπασμεθα A [13[1]].

6. rec επεβημεν (*corrn to more usual term*), with HLP 13[e sil] rel Thl-sif: ενεβημεν (*more usual*) BEℵ[3] k 73 Chr_1: txt ACℵ[1] a c d 36. 40. 137 Thl-fin.

7. κατεβημεν (*corrn to more usual word*) AEℵ[3]. πτολεμαιδαν ℵ[1]. επεμειναμεν A k 40.

8. rec aft εξελθοντες ins οι περι τον παυλον (εξελθ. *begins an ecclesiastical portion*), with HLP rel æth-rom Thl-sif; οι αποστολοι 47 lectt-13-4: om ABC [D(Wetst)] E(ℵ) c e h k 13. 36. 40 vulg D-lat syrr copt [sah æth-pl] arm Chr_1 Thl-fin.—ℵ has σ written, but marked for erasure 'prima manu.' Steph ηλθον (*to suit* οι περι τ. παυλον), with HLP rel Thl-sif: txt A(B)C [D(Mill)] Eℵ k 13. 36 vulg [D-lat] syrr coptt æth [arm(Tischdf)] Eus_1 Chr_1 [Thl-fin].—ηλθαμεν B [εισελθ. D(Mill)]. rec ins του bef οντος (*for precision*), with a 13[e sil]: om ABCEHLPℵ rel Eus_1 Chr. (D-lat is deficient in vv 8—10; but readings are preserved in Scriv's notes.)

a period of time. Our own word 'fulfil' has undergone a similar change of meaning since its first composition: and πληρῶσαι is used both of manning a ship and of fulfilling a period of time. **ἐξελθ.**] from the house where they were lodged. **ἕως ἔξω τ. π.**] "We passed through the city to the western shore of the ancient island, now the peninsula, hoping to find there a fitting spot for the tent, in the open space between the houses and the sea." Robinson, iii. 392. **ἐπὶ τὸν αἰγιαλόν**] "Yet had we looked a few rods further, we should have found a very tolerable spot by a threshing-floor, where we might have pitched close upon the bank, and enjoyed, in all its luxury, the cool sea-breeze, and the dashing of the surge upon the rocky shore." id. ibid. **7. τὸν πλοῦν διανύσ.**] **Having ended our voyage,** viz. *the whole voyage,* from Neapolis to Syria. The E. V., '*when we had finished our course from Tyre,*' is allowable, but this would more probably have been τὸν ἀπὸ Τύρου. 'With their landing at Ptolemais their voyage ended: the rest of the journey was made by land.' (De Wette.) ἀπὸ Τύρου will thus be taken with κατηντήσαμεν. **Πτολεμαΐδα**] Anciently Accho (Ἀκχώ, LXX, Judg. i. 31,—in Gr. and Rom. writers Ἄκη, Ace), called Ptolemais from (probably) Ptolemy Lathurus (Jos. Antt. xiii. 12. 2 ff., see 1 Macc. x. 56 ff.; xi. 22, 24; xii. 45, 48; 2 Macc. xiii. 24). It was a large town with a harbour (Jos. Antt. xviii. 6. 3). It was never (Judg. i. 31) fully possessed by the Jews, but belonged to the Phœnicians, who in after times were mixed with Greeks. But after the captivity a colony of Jews is found there (Jos. B. J. ii. 18. 5). The emperor Claudius gave it the 'civitas,' whence it is called by Pliny, v. 17; xxxvi. 65, 'Colonia Claudii Cæsaris.' It is now called St. Jean d'Acre, and is the best harbour on the Syrian coast, though small. It lies at the end of the great road from Damascus to the sea. Population now about 10,000. The distance from Ptolemais to Cæsarea is forty-four miles. For Cæsarea, see on ch. x. 1. **8. Φιλ. τ. εὐαγγ.**] It is possible that he may have had this appellation from his having been the first to travel about preaching the gospel: see ch. viii. 5 ff.

[y] ἐμείναμεν [y] παρ' αὐτῷ. 9 τούτῳ δὲ ἦσαν θυγατέρες τέσ- d ch. xix. 6 reff.
σαρες παρθένοι [d] προφητεύουσαι. 10 [e] ἐπιμενόντων δὲ e ch. x. 48 reff. f = ch. ii. 40 reff.
ἡμέρας [f] πλείους, [g] κατῆλθέν τις ἀπὸ τῆς Ἰουδαίας g = ch. viii. 5 reff.
D προφητης... [h] προφήτης ὀνόματι Ἄγαβος, 11 καὶ ἐλθὼν πρὸς ἡμᾶς h ch. xi. 27 reff. i = Mark xv. 24 al.
ABCDE HLPℵ a καὶ [i] ἄρας τὴν [k] ζώνην τοῦ Παύλου, δήσας ἑαυτοῦ τοὺς k here bis. Matt. iii. 4
bcdfg πόδας καὶ τὰς χεῖρας εἶπεν Τάδε λέγει τὸ πνεῦμα τὸ || Mk. x. 9 || Mk. Rev. i. 13. xv. 6 only.
hklm o13 ἅγιον, τὸν ἄνδρα οὗ ἐστιν ἡ [k] ζώνη αὕτη οὕτως δήσουσιν 3 Kings ii. 5.
ἐν Ἱερουσαλὴμ οἱ Ἰουδαῖοι καὶ [l] παραδώσουσιν εἰς χεῖρας l = Matt. xvii. 22 al. fr. Job xvi. 12.

9. rec παρθενοι bef τεσσαρες, with EHLP rel [syrr] Thl: παρθενοι bef θυγατερες C Eus_1: txt AB [D(Wtst)] ℵ a k m 13 D-lat [am fuld demid tol arm(Tischdf)].

10. rec aft επιμενοντων δε ins ημων (*addn for precision*), with ELPℵ[3] rel syr-mg [arm] Chr_1: αυτων ℵ[1]: txt ABCH k 13. 36 syr[-txt] Bas_1. προφητης bef απο της ιουδαιας L.

11. om και D-lat: ανελθων δε D[1]-gr: txt D[2]. rec for εαυτου, τε αύτου (*in some late mss* αὐτου *probably from misunderstanding, supposing that it was* Paul's *hands and feet that he bound*), with HLP rel [Syr] Chr_1: txt ABCDEℵ a b c (m) o 13. 36 [syr coptt arm] $Cyr\text{-}jer_1$ Bas_1, also Orig(δησ. εαυτον χειρων κ. ποδων) Aug Cassiod. rec τας χειρας και τους ποδας (*corrn from Luke* xxiv. 39, 40? *see var read John* xi. 14: *so De W. Meyer thinks* ποδ. κ. χ. *arose from its being the* natural order of binding: *but surely this would be more likely to be the* origl order of narrating, *than to strike a copyist as necessary to be observed*), with A a[1] c d m coptt æth Chr_1(omg τας and τους) Orig(above): txt BCDEHLPℵ 13 rel 40 vulg syrr arm Cyr-jer Bas_1. for εν, εις D 26. 63. 97-8. 106 Chr_1 $Epiph_1$ and (prefixg απελθοντα) $Orig_1$. om οι D[1](ins D[2]) Chr Thl-sif. aft εις ins τας ℵ[1](ℵ[3] disapproving).

The office of Evangelist, see reff., seems to have answered very much to our *missionary*: Theodoret, on Eph. iv. 11, says, ἐκεῖνοι περιϊόντες ἐκήρυττον: and Euseb. H. E. iii. 37, ἔργον ἐπετέλουν εὐαγγελιστῶν, τοῖς ἔτι πάμπαν ἀνηκόοις τοῦ τῆς πίστεως λόγου κηρύττειν τὸν χριστὸν φιλοτιμούμενοι, καὶ τὴν τῶν θείων εὐαγγελίων παραδιδόναι γραφήν. The latter could hardly have been part of their employment so early as this; nor had εὐαγγέλιον in these times the peculiar meaning of a *narrative of the life of Christ*, but rather embraced the *whole good tidings of salvation by Him*, as preached to the Jews and Heathens. See Neander, Pfl. u. L., pp. 258, 264. Euseb., iii. 31, apparently mistakes this Philip for *the Apostle*: as did also (see Valesius's note, Euseb. l. c.) Clement of Alexandria and Papias.

ὄντος ἐκ τ. ἑπτά] See ch. vi. 5, and note. Meyer and Winer (edn. 6, § 20. l. c.) well remark (see De Wette also), that the participle without the article implies that the reason why they abode with him was that he was one of the seven: 'ut qui esset,' &c. and in English **being** (one) **of the seven.** The fact of Philip being settled at Cæsarea, and known as ὁ εὐαγγελιστής, seems decisive against regarding the occurrence of ch. vi. 3 ff. as the establishment of any permanent order in the church.

9.] This notice is inserted apparently without any immediate reference to the history, but to bring so remarkable a circumstance to the knowledge of the readers. The four daughters had the gift of προφητεία: see on ch. xi. 27. Eusebius (see, however, his mistake above) gives from Polycrates traditional accounts of them,—that two were buried at Hierapolis, and one at Ephesus. From that passage, and one cited from Clement of Alex. (δύο θυγατέρες αὐτοῦ γεγηρακυῖαι παρθένοι, Polycr., Euseb. iii. 31. . . . . Φίλιππος τὰς θυγατέρας ἀνδράσιν ἐξέδωκε, Clem., Eus. iii. 30), it would appear that two were afterwards married, according to tradition. To find an argument for the so-called 'honour of virginity' in this verse, only shews to what resources those will stoop who have failed to apprehend the whole spirit and rule of the gospel in the matter. They are met however on their own ground by an argument built on another misapprehension (that of Philip being a deacon in the ecclesiastical sense): ὥστε οὖν καὶ τῷ κοινωνήσαντι γάμων διακονεῖν ἔξεστι.

10.] This Agabus in all probability is identical with the Agabus of ch. xi. 28. That there is no reference to that former mention of him, might be occasioned by different sources of information having furnished the two narratives.

11.] Similar symbolical actions accompanying prophecy are found 1 Kings xxii. 11; Isa. xx. 2; Jer. xiii. 1 ff.; Ezek. iv. 1 ff., 9 ff.; v. 1, &c. De Wette remarks that τάδε λέγει τὸ

ἐθνῶν. 12 ὡς δὲ ἠκούσαμεν ταῦτα, [m] παρεκαλοῦμεν ἡμεῖς
τε καὶ οἱ [n] ἐντόπιοι [o] τοῦ μὴ [p] ἀναβαίνειν αὐτὸν εἰς Ἱερουσαλήμ. 13 τότε ἀπεκρίθη ὁ Παῦλος Τί [q] ποιεῖτε κλαίοντες
καὶ [r] συνθρύπτοντές μου τὴν καρδίαν; ἐγὼ γὰρ οὐ μόνον
δεθῆναι ἀλλὰ καὶ ἀποθανεῖν [s] εἰς Ἱερουσαλὴμ [t] ἑτοίμως
[u] ἔχω [v] ὑπὲρ τοῦ [v] ὀνόματος τοῦ κυρίου Ἰησοῦ. 14 μὴ
[w] πειθομένου δὲ αὐτοῦ [x] ἡσυχάσαμεν εἰπόντες Τοῦ κυρίου
τὸ [y] θέλημα [y] γινέσθω. 15 [z] Μετὰ δὲ τὰς [z] ἡμέρας [z] ταύτας
[a] ἐπισκευασάμενοι [p] ἀνεβαίνομεν εἰς Ἱεροσόλυμα· 16 [b] συνῆλθον δὲ καὶ τῶν μαθητῶν ἀπὸ Καισαρείας σὺν ἡμῖν,

ABCDE HLPℵ a b c d f g h k l m o 13

...εκ κεσα D.

ABCEH LPℵ a b c d f g h k l m o 13

m = Matt. xiv. 36 al. fr. 2 Macc. ix. 26. constr., here only. n here only +. see Gen. xxvi. 7. o ch. iii. 12 reff. p ch. xi. 2 reff. q 1 Cor. xv. 29 reff. r here only +. s = ch. xix. 22 reff. t 2 Cor. xii. 14. 1 Pet. iv. 5 only. Dan. iii. 15 only. (all w. ἔχειν) see 2 Cor. x. 6. u = as above (t). ch. vii. 1 reff. Mark v. 23 al. v ch. ix. 16 reff. w absol., ch. xvii. 4. Luke xvi. 31. Esth. iv. 4 B &c. Xen. Cyr. v. 1. 8. x = Luke xiv. 4. ch. xi. 18 (Luke xxiii. 56. 1 Thess. iv. 11) only. Neh. v. 8. y Matt. vi. 10. xxvi. 42 only. z here (ch. i. 5) only. see ch. xv. 36. xxiv. 24. Heb. viii. 10. a here only ‡. 2 Chron. xxxiv. 10. ἐπ. ὅσα ἐδύναντο ὑποζύγια, Xen. Hell. vii. 2. 18. b = ch. i. 21 reff.

12. *παρακαλουμεν* D¹[-gr](txt D⁴). om *τε* D Thl-sif. aft *οι εντοπιοι* ins *τον παυλον* D æth. *επιβαινειν* D. om *αυτον* E 93-5 Bas. at end add *τοτε* (*see next ver*) C m 13. 40.

13. rec *απεκριθη δε*, with C¹ 13 syr Chr₁ [Bas₁]: *απεκριθη τε* HLP d f g h k l m æth Thl: *ειπεν*[*respondit*] *δε προς ημας* D (*from the various assignment of τοτε to ver 12 or ver 13, it was omitted altogether, and then some copula became necessary*): txt ABC²Eℵ 13 rel 36. 40 vulg Syr coptt arm. om *ο* B¹(ins B¹-corr: see table). aft *παυλος* ins *και ειπεν* AEℵ a b d k o 13 vulg Syr [sah(Tischdf)] æth arm. om *κλαιοντες και* ℵ¹. *συνθριπτοντες* P c: *θορυβουντες* D¹(txt D⁵) Tert Jer. for *γαρ*, *δε* E-gr 95¹ vulg-ms Tert₁. aft *δεθηναι* ins *βουλομαι* D. for *εις*, *εν* ℵ(but *εις* is written over the line 'prima ut videtur manu'). *ετοιμως εχω* bef *εις ιερουσαλημ* A [f] æth. aft *ιησου* ins *χριστου* CD Syr arm (Cyr₂ Thdrt₂ Tert₂) Jer₁ Ambrst Aug₁.

14. ins *οι* bef *ειποντες* D¹[-gr]. aft *ειπ.* ins *προς αλληλους* D. rec *το θελημα* bef *του κυριου* (*alteration of characteristic order*), with DHLP rel vss Chr₁ [Bas₁ Tert₂]: txt ABCEℵ m 13 vulg arm.—for *κυρ.*, *θεου* D-gr 32. 73 æth [Tert₁]. rec *γενεσθω* (*corrn to more usual*), with HLP 13 rel Chr [Bas₁]: txt ABCDEℵ f g m o 36. (*γειν.* AB¹DEℵ.)

15. *τινας ημερας* [omg *ταυτ.*] D-gr. rec *αποσκευασαμενοι*, with c 13: *παρασκευασ.* C a 7. 69. 73. 105: *αποταξαμενοι* D-gr: *επισκεψαμενοι* H 68. 106: *præparati* vulg syrr copt æth: *præparantes* E-lat: *refecimus nos* D-lat: txt AB E-gr LP(ℵ) rel 36. 40 Pamph Chr₁ Thl-sif Thl-fin-comm.—*επισκευασαμενον* (but corrd) ℵ¹. *αναβαινομεν* CDL-ℵ³(om ℵ¹). rec *ιερουσαλημ*, with HLP 13 rel vulg Thl: txt ABC D[Wtst Mill] Eℵ a 36 Euthal₁ Chr₁.

16. om *συνηλθον δε και των μαθητων* D¹[Wtst Mill](and lat). ins *εκ* bef *των μαθ.* E vulg. for *απο*, *εκ* D¹[Wtst](txt D²).

πνεῦμα τὸ ἅγιον is the N. T. prophetic formula, instead of *τάδε λέγει ὁ κύριος* of the O. T. **12. τοῦ μή**] A similar gen. after exhortation, is found ch. xv. 20. **13.**] The *τότε*, which has been changed in the rec. for the ordinary copula, gives solemnity to the answer about to be related: q. d. **It was then that Paul said.** **συνθρύπτοντες**] The present part. does not imply the *endeavour* merely, here or any where else, but as Meyer quotes from Schaefer, Eurip. Phœn. 79, 'Vere incipit actus, sed ob impedimenta caret eventu.' **γάρ**] Either, '*your proceeding is in vain, for . . . .*'—or '*cease to do so, for . . . .*' **εἰς Ἱερ.] on my arrival at**: the motion to, which was the subject in question, is combined with that which might result on it: see reff. and ch. ii. 39. **14. τ. κ. τὸ θέλ. γιν.**] One of the passages from which we may not unfairly infer, that the Lord's prayer was used by the Christians of the apostolic age. See note on 2 Tim. iv. 18. **15. ἐπισκευασάμενοι**] The remarkable variety of reading in this word shews that much difficulty has been found in it. The rec. *ἀποσκευασάμενοι* (which may perhaps have arisen from the mixture of *ἀποταξάμενοι* (D) with *ἐπισκευασάμενοι*), would mean, not, '*having deposited our* (useless) *baggage,*' —but, '*having discharged our baggage,*' 'unpacked the matters necessary for our journey to Jerusalem, from our coffers.' But *ἐπισκ.* is the better supported reading, and suits the passage better: **having packed up**, made ourselves ready for the journey. '*Carriages*' in the E. V. is used,

[c] ἄγοντες [d] παρ' ᾧ [e] ξενισθῶμεν Μνάσωνί τινι Κυπρίῳ
[f] ἀρχαίῳ μαθητῇ. 17 [gh] γενομένων δὲ ἡμῶν [g] εἰς Ἱεροσόλυμα [i] ἀσμένως [k] ἀπεδέξαντο [h] ἡμᾶς οἱ ἀδελφοί. 18 τῇ
δὲ [l] ἐπιούσῃ [m] εἰσῄει ὁ Παῦλος σὺν ἡμῖν [e] πρὸς Ἰάκωβον,
πάντες τε [n] παρεγένοντο οἱ [o] πρεσβύτεροι. 19 καὶ [p] ἀσπασάμενος αὐτοὺς [q] ἐξηγεῖτο καθ' ἓν [r] ἕκαστον [s] ὧν ἐποίησεν
ὁ θεὸς ἐν τοῖς ἔθνεσιν διὰ τῆς [t] διακονίας αὐτοῦ. 20 οἱ δὲ
ἀκούσαντες [u] ἐδόξαζον τὸν θεόν, εἶπόν τε αὐτῷ [v] Θεωρεῖς,

Dησαν... ABCDE HLPℵ a b c d f g h k l m o 13

c = ch. xvii. 15 al.
d attr., here only? see note.
e ch. x. 6 reff.
f ch. xv. 7 reff.
g ch. xx. 16 reff.
h constr., ch. iv. 1. xvi. 16. 2 Cor. xii. 21 al. see 2 Cor. iv. 18.
Winer, § 30. 11 remark.
i here (ch. ii. 41 rec.) only†. 2 Macc. iv. 12. x. 33 A (-νος, B &c.) only.
k ch. ii. 41 reff.
l ch. xvi. 11 reff.
m ch. iii. 3 reff.
n absol., ch. xvii. 10 reff.
o ch. xi. 30 reff.
p = ch. xviii. 22 reff.
q ch. x. 8. xv. 12, 14. Luke xxiv. 35. Luke only, exc. John i. 18. Judg. vii. 13.
r ch. xvii. 27 reff.
s attr., Rom. xv. 18 reff.
t ch. xx. 24 reff.
u Matt. xv. 31. Luke v. 25, 26. ch. xi. 18 al. Exod. xv. 2.
v = John iv. 19. xii. 19. ch. xxvii. 10. Heb. vii. 4. 2 Macc. ix. 23.

for *αγοντες, ουτοι δε ηγαγον* D[Wtst Mill]: *simulque adducerunt* D-lat. add *ημας* DE sah arm. for *παρ ω, προς ους* D¹-gr(Wtst: txt Ussher). aft *ξενισθ.* add *και παραγενομενοι εις τινα (την* syr-mg) *κωμην εγενομεθα παρα* D syr-mg. *νασωνι* D¹(and lat) fuld tol: *ιασωνι* ℵ demid copt: *μνασω* B g 1. 18. om *τινι* A¹. *μαθητη* bef. *αρχαιω* D(Wtst). D-lat has the passage thus: *et cum venerunt in quendam civitatem fuimus ad nasonem quendam cyprium discipulum antiquum et inde exeuntes venimus hierosolyma* (thus far, nearly, syr-mg also) *susceperunt autem nos cum lætitia fratres.* (readings of D-gr [vv 16—18] are in Scriv's notes, see above on ver 8.)

17. rec *εδεξαντο* (*substitution of simpler word*), with HLP rel: *υπεδεξ.* D(Mill &c) [*υπεδεξαν τε* D(Wtst), *υπεδεξαν δε* D(Ussher)]: txt ABCEℵ a k 13. 36 40 Chr-comm.

18. for *δε, τε* A E-gr ℵ 40 syrr æth: txt BCHLP 13. 36 rel vulg D-lat E-lat coptt Chr_1. for *παρεγ., ησαν δε παρ αυτω* D¹[and lat](txt D⁶). aft *οι πρεσβυτεροι* ins *συνηγμενοι* D 34.

19. *ους ασπαμενος*(sic) *διηγειτο ενα εκαστον ως εποιησεν* D¹-gr(txt D²). om *εν* D¹(ins D-corr¹). om *δια* ℵ 1.

20. *ακουοντες* HL k. *εδοξασαν* Dℵ Thl-fin. rec (for *θεον*) *κυριον*, with DHP rel syr sah: txt ABCELℵ a d f g k o 13. 36. 40 vulg Syr copt arm Chr. for *ειπον τε, ειποντες* CD c g h m syr Chr. (*ειπαν* Eℵ: *ειπεν* 13.) om *αυτω* D.

as at Judg. xviii. 21 (where it answers to τὸ βάρος, LXX-B), for *baggage, things carried.* **16.**] Two renderings are given to the latter clause of this verse: (1) making Μνάσωνι, &c. depend on ἄγοντες, and agreeing by attr. with ᾧ, as E. V., '*and brought with them one Mnason, ... with whom we should lodge*' (so Beza, Calvin, Wolf, Schött., &c.): and (2) resolving the attraction into ἄγοντες παρὰ Μνάσωνα, παρ' ᾧ ξ. '*bringing us to Mnason,*' *&c.* (So Grot., Valcknaer, Bengel, De Wette, Meyer, al.) Both are legitimate: and it is difficult to choose between them. The probability of Mnason being a resident at Jerusalem, and of the Cæsarean brethren going to introduce the company to him, seems to favour the *latter:* as also does the fact that Luke much more frequently uses ἄγω with a person *followed by a preposition* than absolutely. Of Mnason nothing further is known. **ἀρχαίῳ** probably implies that he had been a disciple ἐξ ἀρχῆς, and had accompanied our Lord during His ministry. See ch. xi. 15, where the term ἐξ ἀρχῆς is applied to the time of the Pentecostal effusion of the Spirit.

17—XXIII. 35.] PAUL AT JERUSALEM: MADE PRISONER, AND SENT TO CÆSAREA. **17. οἱ ἀδελφοί**] The Christians generally: not the Apostles and elders, as Kuin., who imagines from vv. 20, 21, that 'cœtus non favebat Paulo.' But (1) this is by no means implied: and (2) James and the elders are not mentioned till ver. 18. **18. Ἰάκωβον**] James, 'the brother of the Lord:' the president of the church at Jerusalem: see ch. xii. 17; xv. 13; Gal. ii. 12, and notes,—and Prolegg. to the Epistle of James, vol. iv. pt. 1, § i. 24—37. **19.**] On the particular kind of attraction (reff.), in a gen. plur. after a partitive adjective, see Winer, edn. 6, § 24. 2. b. **20.**] While they praised God for, and fully recognized, the work wrought by him among the *Gentiles*, they found it requisite to advise him respecting the suspicion under which he laboured among the believing Jews. They,—led, naturally perhaps, but incorrectly (see 1 Cor. vii. 18), by some passages of Paul's life (and of his already written Epistles?), in which he had depreciated legal observances in comparison with faith in Christ, and spoken strongly against their adoption by Gentile converts,—apprehended that he advised on the part of the *Hellenistic* believers, an entire

ἀδελφέ, πόσαι [w] μυριάδες εἰσὶν ἐν τοῖς Ἰουδαίοις τῶν [x] πεπιστευκότων, καὶ πάντες [y] ζηλωταὶ τοῦ νόμου [z] ὑπάρχουσιν· 21 [a] κατηχήθησαν δὲ περὶ σοῦ ὅτι [b] ἀποστασίαν [c] διδάσκεις ἀπὸ Μωυσέως [c] τοὺς [d] κατὰ τὰ [d] ἔθνη πάντας Ἰουδαίους, λέγων μὴ [e] περιτέμνειν αὐτοὺς τὰ τέκνα μηδὲ τοῖς [f] ἔθεσιν [g] περιπατεῖν. 22 [h] τί οὖν ἐστιν; [i] πάντως δεῖ [k] συνελθεῖν [l] πλῆθος, ἀκούσονται γὰρ ὅτι ἐλήλυθας. 23 τοῦτο οὖν ποίησον ὅ σοι λέγομεν· εἰσὶν ἡμῖν ἄνδρες τέσσαρες [m] εὐχὴν [m] ἔχοντες [n] ἐφ᾽ ἑαυτῶν· 24 [o] τούτους [p] παραλαβὼν [q] ἁγνίσθητι σὺν αὐτοῖς, καὶ [r] δαπάνησον ἐπ᾽ αὐτοῖς ἵνα [s] ξυρήσονται τὴν κεφαλήν, καὶ γνώσονται πάν-

ABCDE HLPℵ a b c d f g h k l m o 13

w = Luke xii. 1. (ch. xix. 19 reff.) x = ch. xv. 5 reff. y = ch. xxii. 3. 1 Cor. xiv. 12. Gal. i. 14. Tit. ii. 4. 1 Pet. iii. 13 (Luke vi. 15. ch. i. 13) only. 2 Macc. iv. 2. (Exod. xx. 5 al.) z ch. ii. 30 reff. a ch. xviii. 25 reff. b 2 Thess. ii. 3 only. 3 Kings xx. (xxi.) 13 A Ald. compl. 2 Chron. xxix. 19. Jer. ii. 19 (xxxvi.(xxix.) 32 compl.). 1 Macc. ii. 15 only. c constr., Mark vi. 34. John xiv. 26. Heb. v. 12. Prov. xxii. 21. d here only. e 1 Cor. vii. 18 reff. f ch. vi. 14 reff. g constr., Gal. v. 16. 2 Cor. xii. 18. (see ch. ix. 31.) h 1 Cor. xiv. 15, 26. i = Luke iv. 23. ch. xxviii. 4. (Rom. iii. 9.) 1 Cor. (v. 10.) ix. 10, 22. xvi. 12 only †. L.P. Tobit xiv. 8 (not ℵ). 2 Macc. iii. 13 only. k = ch. i. 6 reff. l absol., see ch. ii. 6 reff. m ch. xviii. 18 (reff.) only. n = here only. o ch. ix. 20 reff. p = ch. xvi. 33 reff. q = here bis. ch. xxiv. 18. John xi. 55 (James iv. 8. 1 Pet. i. 22. 1 John iii. 3) only. Exod. xix. 10. r w. ἐπί, here only. w. ὑπέρ, 2 Cor. xii. 15. w. ἐν, James iv. 3. absol., Mark v. 26. Luke xv. 14 only †. 1 Macc. xiv. 32. s 1 Cor. xi. 5, 6 only. Numb. vi. 18, 19.

rec (for εν τοις ιουδαιοις) ιουδαιων, with HLP rel syr Chr [and, after πεπιστ., arm] Thdrt$_2$ Thl : εν τη ιουδαια D Syr sah Aug$_1$: om εν τ. ιουδ. ℵ : txt ABCE a 13. 36. 40 vulg copt æth Ambrst$_1$. aft παντες ins ουτοι(τουτοι D[1]) D 38 tol Syr Ambrst$_1$ Aug$_1$ [ζητουσιν και 13].

21. κατηχησαν 25. 40 : κατηκησαν D[1](*diffamaverunt* D-lat : txt D[2]). om δε ℵ[1]. om τα D[1]. for παντας, εισιν D[1](and lat) : om AE 13 vulg copt : txt BCD[4]HL[P]ℵ rel 36 [syrr sah æth arm] Chr$_1$. ιουδαιοις D[1](txt D[4]). om λεγων D : λεγω ℵ[1]. [ins] οφιλειν [bef] περιτεμνειν E vulg. μητε[μηδε D[4]] εν τοις εθνεσιν D[1], *neque gentes ejus ambulant* D-lat.—ins αυτου(αυτους D[4]) bef περιπ. D[1].

22. om δει συνελθειν πληθος and γαρ (*expunged as not understood*) BC[1] 15. 73. 137-80 syrr coptt æth arm : ins AC[2]DEHLPℵ rel vulg Chr$_1$.—ins το bef πληθος D[4].—rec πληθος bef συνελθειν, with DHLP rel Chr : txt AC[2]Eℵ a d h 13. 40 vulg.—om γαρ C[2] : om γαρ οτι ℵ[1]. εληλυθες B.

23. for ὅ, οπερ E. for εφ᾽, αφ(sic) B(Tischdf) ℵ.

24. επ αυτους A a 13 : εις αυτους D. rec ξυρησωνται, with AB[2]CH L[ξυρισων (sic)] rel 36 Chr; ξυρωνται D[1]: txt B[1](sic) D[2]EPℵ c k l o 13. rec γνωσι (*grammatical corrn aft* ινα), with HLP rel Chr$_1$ Thl-sif, *cognoscant* D-lat: txt ABC D-gr Eℵ a d m 13 (36) 40 vulg (Thl-fin).—(-σωνται 36 Thl-fin.)

apostasy from Moses and the ordinances of the law. **θεωρεῖς**] This can hardly be a reference (as Olsh.) to the elders present, as representatives of the μυριάδες of believing Jews; for only those of Jerusalem were there:—but refers to Paul's own experience, and knowledge of the vast numbers of the Jews who believed at Jerusalem, and elsewhere in Judæa. **πόσαι μυριάδες** is perhaps not to be strictly taken: see reff. Baur suspects, on account of this expression, that the words τῶν πεπιστ. are spurious; but quite without reason. Eusebius quotes from Hegesippus (H. E. ii. 23), πολλῶν καὶ τῶν ἀρχόντων πιστευόντων ἦν θόρυβος τῶν Ἰουδαίων καὶ γραμματέων καὶ Φαρισαίων λεγόντων ὅτι κινδυνεύει πᾶς ὁ λαὸς Ἰησοῦν τὸν χριστὸν προσδοκᾶν. On the other hand, Origen (tom. i. in Joann. § 2, vol. iv. p. 3) says, that probably the whole number of believing Jews at no time had amounted to 144,000. On εἰσὶν . . . ὑπάρχουσι, see note, ch. xvi. 20, 21. **21.** **κατηχήθησαν**] **they were sedulously informed** (at some time in the mind of the speaker. The sense of the aor. must be preserved. Below, ver. 24, it is the perfect): viz., by the anti-Pauline judaizers. * **τοῖς ἔθεσιν**] The dat. of the *rule*, or *form, after which*: see reff. **22. πάντως δ. συνελθ. πλ.**] Not, as E. V., Calv., Grot., Calov., '*the multitude must needs come together*,' i. e. there must be a meeting of the whole church (τὸ πλῆθος, ch. ii. 6): but **a multitude** (of these Judaizers) **will certainly come together**: '*they will meet and discuss your proceeding in a hostile manner.*' **23. εὐχήν**] A vow of Nazarites. This vow must not be confounded, historically or analogically, with that of ch. xviii. 18: see note there, and Num. vi. 2–21. **24. παραλαβών**] **having taken to thyself**, as comrades. **ἁγν. σὺν αὐτ.**] **become a Nazarite with them.** The same expression occurs in the LXX, Num. vi. 3, in describing the Nazarite's duties. **δαπάν. ἐπ᾽ αὐτ.**] "More

τες ὅτι [t] ὧν [a] κατήχηνται περὶ σοῦ [u] οὐδέν ἐστιν, ἀλλὰ
[v] στοιχεῖς [w] καὶ [w] αὐτὸς [x] φυλάσσων τὸν νόμον. 25 περὶ
δὲ τῶν [y] πεπιστευκότων ἐθνῶν ἡμεῖς [z] ἐπεστείλαμεν, [a] κρί-
ναντες μηδὲν τοιοῦτον [b] τηρεῖν αὐτούς, εἰ μὴ [c] φυλάσσεσθαι
αὐτοὺς τό τε [d] εἰδωλόθυτον καὶ [τὸ] αἷμα καὶ [e] πνικτὸν
καὶ [e] πορνείαν. 26 τότε ὁ Παῦλος [f] παραλαβὼν τοὺς
ἄνδρας τῇ [g] ἐχομένῃ ἡμέρᾳ σὺν αὐτοῖς [f] ἁγνισθεὶς [h] εἰςῄει
εἰς τὸ ἱερόν, [i] διαγγέλλων τὴν [j] ἐκπλήρωσιν τῶν ἡμερῶν
τοῦ [k] ἁγνισμοῦ, ἕως οὗ [lm] προςηνέχθη ὑπὲρ [n] ἑνὸς ἑκάστου
αὐτῶν ἡ [mo] προςφορά. 27 ὡς δὲ [p] ἔμελλον αἱ ἑπτὰ ἡμέραι

t attr., Luke ix. 36 al. u = ch. xxv. 11. v ellips., here only. στ., Rom. iv. 12. Gal. v. 25. vi. 16. Phil. iii. 16 only. Eccles. xi. 6 only, but not =. w ch. xv. 27, 32. Matt. xxvii. 57. x = ch. xvi. 4 reff. y = ch. xv. 5 reff. z ch. xv. 20 reff. a = ch. xv. 19 reff. b = ch. xv. 5 reff. c w. acc., = 2 Tim. iv. 15. 2 Kings xx. 10. d 1 Cor. viii. 1 reff. e ch. xv. 20 (reff.). f ver. 24. g = ch. xx. 15 reff. h ch. iii. 3 reff. i Luke ix. 60. Rom. ix. 17 (from Exod. ix. 16) only. j here only +. 2 Macc. vi. 14 only. (-ροῦν, ch. xiii. 33.) k here only. Num. vi. 5. l ch. vii. 42 reff. Heb. v. 1, 3. ix. 7. Levit. i. 2, 3 al. m Heb. x. 8. n ch. xvii. 27 reff. o = ch. xxiv. 17. Heb. x. 5, 10, 14, 18. Ps. xxxix. 6. p = Luke vii. 2. John iv. 47. ch. xxvii. 33. Jer. xxxvi. (xxix.) 10.

ins *περι* bef *ων* C a e 36. 40. ins *και* bef *στοιχεις* A: *οτι πορευου* D¹-gr(*ambulans* D-lat: txt D² or ⁴). om *και* D¹(and lat: txt D² or ⁴). rec *τον νομον* bef *φυλασσων*, with HLP rel Syr Thl-sif: txt ABCD E[*φυλασσιν*] ℵ a c m 13 vulg [syr] Chr₁ Thl-fin.

25. for *εθνων*, *ανθρωπων* E. aft *εθνων* ins *ουδεν εχουσι λεγειν προς σε*, and (aft *ημεις*) *γαρ* D sah. *απεστειλαμεν* (*more usual word*) B D[-gr] l 40 syr copt [arm]: txt ACEHLPℵ 13. 36 rel vulg D-lat Syr sah [æth(appy)] Chr₁. *κρινοντες* D¹(txt D² or ⁴) 100. om *μηδεν τοιουτον τηρειν αυτους ει μη* ABℵ 13. 40 vulg Syr copt [sah] æth[?] (*prob because no such clause is found in the apostolic decree ch* xv. 28. *It can hardly have been interpolated*): ins CDEHLP rel 36 syr arm Chr Aug.—*τοιουτο* CE. om *τε* D c 137 [Chr₁]. om *το* (bef *αιμα*) ABCDℵ a c 13: *απο ιδωλοθυτων και αιματος και πνικτου και πορνιας* E [syr]: txt HLP rel Chr. om *και πνικτον* D sah Jer Aug: om *και* 15. 36. ins *τε* bef *πνικτον* l m 40. 99 Chr Thl-fin. Syr æth-pl invert the order, *πορν. κ. πνικτ. κ. αιμα.*

26. om *ο* DE. [for *εχομ.*,] *επιουση* D. *εισηλθεν* D. for *εως ου*, *οπως donec* D. om *η* D [g].

27. *συντελουμενης δε της εβδομης ημερας* D: *cum advenisset dies septimus* Syr. *ημελλον* ELP c h m. [om *αι* E.]

apud Judæos receptum erat, et pro insigni pietatis officio habebatur, ut in pauperum Nasiræorum gratiam ditiores sumptus erogarent ad sacrificia (see Num. vi. 14 ff.) quæ dum illi tonderentur, offerre necesse erat." Kypke. Jos. Antt. xix. 6. 1, relating Agrippa's thank-offerings at Jerusalem, says, *διὸ καὶ Ναζιραίων ξυρᾶσθαι διέταξε μάλα συχνούς.* On the shaving the head, see Num. vi. 18. De Wette remarks: 'James and the elders made this proposal, assuming that Paul could comply with it *salvâ conscientiâ*,—perhaps also as a proof, to assure themselves and others of his sentiments: and Paul accepted it *salvâ conscientiâ*. But this he could only have done on one condition, that he was sure by it not to contribute in these four Nazarites to the error of *justification by the works of the law*. He might keep, and encourage the keeping of the law,—but not with the purpose of thereby deserving the approbation of God.' **25.**] See ch. xv. 28, 29. **26.**] Paul himself entered into the vow with them (**σὺν αὐτοῖς ἁγν.**), and the time settled (perhaps the least that could be assigned: the Mischna requires thirty days) for the completion of the vow, i. e. the offering and shaving of their heads, was seven days. No definite time is prescribed in Num. vi., but there seven days is the time of purification *in case of uncleanness during the period of the vow.* **διαγγέλλων**] **making known** to the ministers of the temple. **τὴν ἐκπλήρωσιν**] **the fulfilment**, i. e. *that he and the men had come to fulfil*: **announcing their intention of fulfilling.** **ἕως οὗ προςηνέχθη**] '*donec offerretur*,' Vulg. The aor. indic. is unusual in an indirect construction, where the aor. subj. is almost always found (ch. xxiii. 12, 21; xxv. 21). But we have Plato, Gorg. p. 506, *ἡδέως . . . ἂν . . . διελεγόμην,* **ἕως** *αὐτῷ τὴν τοῦ 'Αμφίονος* **ἀπέδωκα** *ῥῆσιν*,—and Cratyl. 396, *οὐκ ἂν ἐπαυόμην διεξιὼν . . . . ἕως ἀπεπειράθην τῆς σοφίας ταυτησὶ τί ποιήσει.* (De W.) **ἡ προςφορά**] See Num. vi. 13—17. **27. αἱ ἑπτ. ἡμ.**] Of the votive period: not (as Chrys. and Bede) since Paul's arrival in Jerusalem. Five days of the seven had passed: see

[q] συντελεῖσθαι, οἱ ἀπὸ τῆς Ἀσίας Ἰουδαῖοι θεασάμενοι
αὐτὸν ἐν τῷ ἱερῷ [r] συνέχεον πάντα τὸν ὄχλον, καὶ
[s] ἐπέβαλον [s] ἐπ' αὐτὸν τὰς [s] χεῖρας 28 κράζοντες Ἄνδρες
Ἰσραηλῖται, [t] βοηθεῖτε. οὗτός ἐστιν ὁ ἄνθρωπος ὁ κατὰ
τοῦ λαοῦ καὶ τοῦ νόμου καὶ τοῦ [u] τόπου τούτου πάντας
[v] πανταχῇ διδάσκων, [w] ἔτι τε καὶ Ἕλληνας [x] εἰσήγαγεν
εἰς τὸ ἱερὸν καὶ [y] κεκοίνωκεν τὸν [u] ἅγιον [u] τόπον τοῦτον.
29 [z] ἦσαν γὰρ [za] προεωρακότες Τρόφιμον τὸν Ἐφέσιον ἐν τῇ
πόλει σὺν αὐτῷ, ὃν ἐνόμιζον ὅτι εἰς τὸ ἱερὸν [x] εἰσήγαγεν
ὁ Παῦλος. 30 [b] ἐκινήθη τε ἡ πόλις ὅλη, καὶ ἐγένετο
[c] συνδρομὴ τοῦ λαοῦ, καὶ [d] ἐπιλαβόμενοι τοῦ Παύλου
[e] εἷλκον αὐτὸν [f] ἔξω τοῦ ἱεροῦ, καὶ εὐθέως [g] ἐκλείσθησαν
αἱ θύραι. 31 [h] ζητούντων· τε αὐτὸν ἀποκτεῖναι, [i] ἀνέβη
[k] φάσις τῷ [l] χιλιάρχῳ τῆς [m] σπείρης ὅτι ὅλη [n] συγχύννεται

ABCDE HLPℵa bcdfg hklm o13

...αι θυραι C.
ABDE HLPℵa bcdfg hklm o13

q Mark xiii. 4. Luke iv. 2, 13. Rom. ix. 28. Heb. viii. 8 only. Job i. 5.
r ch. ii. 6 reff.
s Matt. xxvi. 50. Luke xx. 19. xxi. 12. John vii. 30. ch. v. 18. Gen. xxii. 12. see ch. iv. 3.
t ch. xvi. 9 reff.
u Matt. xxiv. 15. ch. vi. 13. Ps. lxvii. 5. 2 Macc. ii. 18.
v here only. Isa. xxiv. 11. Wisd. ii. 9. 2 Macc. viii. 7 only. (-χοῦ, ch. xvii. 30.)
w Luke xiv. 26 only. see ch. ii. 26.
x = ch. ix. 8. Luke xxii. 54. Jer. xlii. (xxxv.) 4.
y Matt. xv. 11, &c. ||. Heb. ix. 13 (ch. x. 15. xi. 9) only †.
z constr., ch. xxii. 29 reff.
a = here (ch. ii. 25 from Ps. xv. 8) only ‡.
b = ch. xxiv. 5 (xvii. 28 reff.). see 1 Macc. xiii. 44.
c here only †. Judith x. 18. 3 Macc. iii. 8 only. (-τρέχειν, ch. iii. 11.)
d ch. xvii. 19 reff.
e James ii. 6 only. Eccl. i. 5. see ch. xvi. 19.
f ver. 5.
g ch. v. 23 reff.
h = ch. xiii. 8 reff.
i see ch. x. 4.
k here only †. Susan. 55 Theod.
l = John xviii. 12. vv. 33, 37, &c. 1 Kings xviii. 13.
m ch. x. 1 reff.
n ver. 27.

aft οι ins δε D-gr. α only of απο is written by D^1, the rest supplied by D^2.
aft ιουδαιοι ins εληλυθοτες D. θεασαμενοι αυτον εν τω ιερω bef οι α. τ. α. ιουδαιοι C 180: θεασ. αυτον bef οι α. τ. α. ιουδ. c 137. συνεχεαν C 180: συνεσχον 20. 41: συνεκεινησαν τε E: *concitaverunt* vulg E-lat: *confuderunt* D-lat. om παντα E 2. 41. επεβαλαν A$ℵ^1$: επιβαλλουσιν D: επεβαλλον b^1 o Thl-sif. rec τας χειρας bef επ αυτον (*corrn of arrangement*), with HLP rel coptt Thl-sif: txt ABCDEℵ a c h (k) m 13. 40 vulg syrr arm Chr Thl-fin.

28. aft τοπου ins του αγιου AC^2 73 lectt-13-4. τουτους (but *s* marked and then erased) $ℵ^1$. rec πανταχου (*alteration to more usual word*), with HLP rel Chr: txt ABCDEℵ b c o 13. 36. om τε D m. εισηγεν D^1(txt D^3) 95^1. om το D^1(ins D^2). κεκοινωνηκε B^2E o 36. 137: εκοινωνησεν D^1: εκοινωσεν D-corr: κεκοινωνκεν (but ν marked and erased) $ℵ^1$.

29. for προεωρ., εορακοτες HL, εωρακοτες P d f g h k l m vulg(not tol) sah æth Chr_1 Thl-sif. om τον ℵ. ενομισαμεν (but *putaverunt*) D. om ο D.

30. τον παυλον E d. om αυτον D fuld. for και to θυραι, εκλισθησαν ευθεως (σαν being written above the line) $ℵ^1$.

31. rec (for τε) δε, with D^2[-gr] HL[P] rel 36 vulg syr coptt Chr: txt ABEℵ a Syr æth. (13 def.)—(και) ζητ. D^1[and lat]. rec συγκεχυται, with EHLP$ℵ^3$ rel Chr, *confusa est* D-lat E-lat: txt AB^1 D-gr $ℵ^1$, συγχυνεται B^2 13, *confunditur* vulg.

on ch. xxiv. 11. Cf. on the whole, Bp. Wordsworth's note. **ἀπὸ τ. Ἀσ.**] From Ephesus and the neighbourhood, where Paul had so long taught. 'Paulus, dum fidelibus placandis intentus est (viz. the believing Jews), in hostium furorem incurrit (viz. of the unbelieving Asiatic Jews).' Calv., in Meyer, who adds, 'In how many ways had those who were at Jerusalem this Pentecost, already persecuted Paul in Asia?' Notice the similarity of the charge against him to that against Stephen, ch. vi. 13. **28. Ἕλληνας**] The generic plural: *only one* is intended, see next verse. They meant, into the inner court, which was forbidden to Gentiles. **29. Τρόφ.**] See ch. xx. 4, note. We here learn that he was an Ephesian. **30.**] The Levites shut the doors to prevent profanation by a riot, and possibly bloodshed, in the temple: hardly, as Bengel, 'ne templi tutela uteretur Paulus:'—the right of asylum was only (Exod. xxi. 13, 14) for murder unawares (Meyer). But by ver. 14 there, and by Joab's fleeing to the altar, 1 Kings ii. 28 ff., we see that it was resorted to on other occasions. **31. ζητούντων κ.τ.λ.**] By *beating him*: see ver. 32. **ἀνέβη**] **went** (was carried) **up**; *up*, either because of his *high station*, as commanding officer, or because he was *locally* stationed in the tower Antonia, overlooking (from the N.W.) the temple, where the riot was. **τῷ χιλιάρχῳ τ. σπ.**] Claudius Lysias (ch. xxiii. 26), the tribune of the cohort (whose proper complement was 1000 men). **33. ἁλύσ. δυσί**] See ch. xii. 6. He would

Ἱερουσαλήμ· 32 ὃς [o] ἐξ αὐτῆς [p] παραλαβὼν στρατιώτας
καὶ [q] ἑκατοντάρχας [r] κατέδραμεν ἐπ' αὐτούς. οἱ δὲ ἰδόντες
τὸν [l] χιλίαρχον καὶ τοὺς στρατιώτας [s] ἐπαύσαντο τύπτοντες τὸν Παῦλον. 33 τότε [t] ἐγγίσας ὁ χιλίαρχος
[u] ἐπελάβετο αὐτοῦ καὶ [v] ἐκέλευσεν δεθῆναι [w] ἁλύσεσι δυσί,
καὶ ἐπυνθάνετο τις [ἂν] εἴη καὶ τί ἐστιν πεποιηκώς.
34 [x] ἄλλοι δὲ [x] ἄλλο τι [y] ἐπεφώνουν ἐν τῷ ὄχλῳ· μὴ
δυναμένου δὲ αὐτοῦ γνῶναι τὸ [z] ἀσφαλὲς διὰ τὸν [a] θόρυβον, [v] ἐκέλευσεν ἄγεσθαι αὐτὸν εἰς τὴν [b] παρεμβολήν.
35 ὅτε δὲ ἐγένετο ἐπὶ τοὺς [c] ἀναβαθμούς, [d] συνέβη [e] βα-
στάζεσθαι αὐτὸν ὑπὸ τῶν στρατιωτῶν διὰ τὴν [f] βίαν τοῦ
ὄχλου· 36 ἠκολούθει γὰρ τὸ πλῆθος τοῦ λαοῦ κράζοντες
[g] Αἶρε αὐτόν. 37 μέλλων τε εἰσάγεσθαι εἰς τὴν [b] παρεμβολὴν ὁ Παῦλος λέγει τῷ χιλιάρχῳ [h] Εἰ [i] ἔξεστίν μοι
εἰπεῖν τι πρός σε; ὁ δὲ ἔφη [k] Ἑλληνιστὶ γινώσκεις;

o ch. x. 33 reff. p ch. xvi. 33 reff. q ch. x. 1 reff. r here only. 3 Kings xix. 20 B. Job xvi. 11. Xen. Anab. vii. 1. 20. (-δρομή, 2 Macc. v. 3.) s constr., ch. xiii. 10 reff. t Luke xii. 33. xviii. 40. xxiv. 15. ch. xxiii. 15. Gen. xxvii. 27. u ch. xvii. 19 reff. v constr., ch. xii. 19. w ch. xii. 6 reff. x ch. xix. 32 (ref.) only. y ch. xii. 22 reff. z = ch. xxii. 30. xxv. 26 (Phil. iii. 1. Heb. vi. 19) only ‡. Xen. Mem. iv. 6. 15. a Matt. xxvi. 5 ‖ Mk. xxvii. 24. Mark v. 38. ch. xx. 1. xxiv. 18 only. Jer. xxx. (xlix.) 2. (-βεῖν, ch. xvii. 5.) b = here bis. ch. xxii. 24. xxiii. 10, &c. Heb. (xi. 34.) xiii. 11, 13. Rev. xx. 9 only. Isa. xxi. 8. c ver. 40 only. 3 Kings x. 19, 20. d impers. and constr., here only. (ch. iii. 10 reff.) 2 Macc. iii. 2. e ch. iii. 2 reff. f ch. v. 26 reff. g = Luke xxiii. 18. Isa. lvii. 1. see ch. xxii. 22. h ch. i. 6 reff. i w. aor., ch. ii. 29. Matt. xix. 3. 2 Cor. xii. 4. Esth. iv. 2. Ezra iv. 14. 1 Macc. xiv. 44 (only). k John xix. 20 only. ξυνίει Ἑλληνιστί, Xen. An. vii. 6. 8. 'Græcè scire,' Cic. de Fin. ii. 5.

32. for παραλ., λαβων B, *sumptis* D-lat. rec εκατονταρχους, with D²HLP rel 36 Chr: txt ABD¹Eℵ 13.

33. εγγισας δε HLP rel Syr[και εγγ.] Œc Thl[-sif]: txt ABDEℵ a c m 13. 36 vulg syr [coptt] æth Chr₁ Thl-fin. αλυσεσιν δυσιν DEHP: αλυσεσι δυσιν m: txt ABLℵ 13 rel. rec ins αν bef ειη, with EHLP rel Chr: om ABDℵ a 36. (13 def.) τις εστιν πεποικως(sic) D¹.

34. for αλλο τι, αλλα D syr Chr₁. rec (for επεφωνουν) εβοων, with HLP rel Chr Thl-sif: επεβοων c (m) 25. 40: txt ABDEℵ 13. 36 Thl-fin. rec μη δυναμενος δε and om αυτου (*emendation of style*), with HLP rel 36 Chr [Thl-sif]: txt AB(D)Eℵ m 13 Thl-fin.—και μη δυν. αυτ. D.

35. for επι, εις D. for βαστ. αυτον, τον παυλον βαστ. D. for οχλου, λαου D.

36. om του λαου D. rec κραζον (*grammatical emendation*), with DHLP rel [vulg(with am fuld demid tol) E-lat syr] Chr: txt AB E-gr ℵ a b d k o 13. 36. 40 Syr copt Thl. αναιρεισθαι *tollite* D.

37. om ο παυλος D: ο π. bef εις arm [simly sah]. τω χειλιαρχ. αποκριθεις ειπεν D. for ειπειν, λαλησαι D [arm; *loqui* latt]. om τι DHLP d f g h l tol Syr æth[?] arm Thl-sif: ins ABEℵ 13. 36 rel vulg syr copt Chr Thl-fin [τις m].

thus be in the custody of two soldiers. **τίς [ἂν] εἴη, who he might be** (subjective possibility): and **τί ἐστιν πεπ., what he had done** (assuming that he must have done *something*). **34. παρεμβ.]** The camp or barracks attached to the tower Antonia;—or perhaps 'into the tower' itself: but the other is the more usual meaning of παρεμβ. "For a full history and description of the fortress of Antonia, see Robinson, i. pp. 431, 435; Williams, Holy City, i. 99; ii. 403—411; Howson, ii. 311." Wordsworth. **35. ἀναβαθμ.]** The steps leading up into the tower. The description of the tower or fort Antonia in Jos. B. J. v. 5. 8, sets the scene vividly before us:—πυργοειδὴς δὲ οὖσα τὸ πᾶν σχῆμα, κατὰ γωνίαν τέσσαρσιν ἑτέροις διείληπτο πύργοις· ὧν οἱ μὲν ἄλλοι πεντήκοντα τὸ ὕψος, ὁ δὲ ἐπὶ τῇ μεσημβρινῇ καὶ κατ' ἀνατολὴν γωνίᾳ κείμενος ἑβδομήκοντα πηχῶν ἦν, ὡς καθορᾶν ὅλον ἀπ' αὐτοῦ τὸ ἱερόν. καθὰ δὲ συνῆπτο ταῖς τοῦ ἱεροῦ στοαῖς, εἰς ἀμφοτέρας εἶχε **καταβάσεις**· δι' ὧν κατιόντες οἱ φρουροί, καθῆστο γὰρ ἀεὶ ἐπ' αὐτῆς τάγμα Ῥωμαίων, καὶ διϊστάμενοι περὶ τὰς στοὰς μετὰ τῶν ὅπλων, ἐν ταῖς ἑορταῖς τὸν δῆμον, ὡς μή τι νεωτερισθείη, παρεφύλαττον· φρούριον γὰρ ἐπέκειτο τῇ πόλει μὲν τὸ ἱερόν, τῷ ἱερῷ δὲ ἡ Ἀντωνία. **37. Ἑλληνιστὶ γιγ.]** as 'Græce nescire,' Cic. pro Flacc. 4,—τοὺς Συριστὶ ἐπισταμένους, Xen. Cyr. vii. 5. 31: and reff. There is no ellipsis of

l ch. xvii. 6 reff. m here only †. Jos. B. J. ii. 13. 3. n ch. xvi. 37 reff. o here only ‡. Gen. xxx. 42. Job xlii. 11 only. p Luke xv. 15. xix. 14. Heb. viii. 11 only. Prov. xi. 9. q Matt. xix. 8. Luke ix. 61. ch. xxvii. 3 al. Job xxxii. 14.

38 οὐκ ἄρα σὺ εἶ ὁ Αἰγύπτιος ὁ πρὸ τούτων τῶν ἡμερῶν ABDE
[l] ἀναστατώσας καὶ ἐξαγαγὼν εἰς τὴν ἔρημον τοὺς τετρα- HLPℵ a
κισχιλίους ἄνδρας τῶν [m] σικαρίων; 39 εἶπεν δὲ ὁ Παῦλος b c d f g
Ἐγὼ [n] ἄνθρωπος μέν εἰμι Ἰουδαῖος Ταρσεύς, τῆς Κιλικίας h k l m
οὐκ [o] ἀσήμου πόλεως [p] πολίτης, δέομαι δέ σου [q] ἐπίτρεψόν o 13
μοι λαλῆσαι πρὸς τὸν λαόν. 40 [q] ἐπιτρέψαντος δὲ αὐτοῦ
ὁ Παῦλος ἑστὼς ἐπὶ τῶν [r] ἀναβαθμῶν [s] κατέσεισεν τῇ χειρὶ
τῷ λαῷ, πολλῆς δὲ [t] σιγῆς γενομένης [u] προσεφώνησεν τῇ

r ver. 35. s ch. xii. 17 reff. t Rev. viii. 1 only. Wisd. xviii. 14 only. ἦν πολλὴ πανταχόθεν σιγή, Xen. Cyr. vii. 1. 25. u absol., Luke xiii. 12. xxiii. 20 only. 2 Chron. xxix. 28 Ald. 2 Macc. xv. 15 only. dat., ch. xxii. 2.

38. for *ουκ αρα*, *ου* D. *εξαναστατωσας* E. *σιρικαριων* E.
39. om *ειμι* ℵ[1]. for *ταρσευς* to *πολιτης*, *εν ταρσω δε της κιλικιας γεγεννημενος* D-gr. for *επιτρ.*, *συνχωρησαι* D(*cujus rogo obsegro autem mihi* D-lat). ins *λογον* bef *λαλ.* ℵ[1](ℵ[3] disapproving).
40. ins *και* bef *επιτρεψαντος δε* D[1]-gr: *και επιτ.*, omg *δε*, D-lat Syr: om *δε* L 96. for *αυτου*, *του χιλιαρχου* D sah. *εστως ο π. επ. τ. αν. και σεισας* D. for *τω λαω*, *τον λαον* H c k Chr(some mss): *προς αυτους* D Syr. for *δε σιγης*, *τε ησυχειας* D. *γενομενης* bef *σιγης* B. *γεναμενης* A.

λαλεῖν. **38. οὐκ ἄρα σὺ εἶ]** **Thou art not then, as I believed . . . . .** The E. V., after the Vulg., '*art not thou*' . . . ('nonne tu es . . .') would require ἆρ' οὐ or οὔκουν, Winer, edn. 6, § 57. 3. See also Luke xvii. 17; John xviii. 37. **Αἰγύπτιος]** The inference of the tribune was not, as in Bengel, 'Græce loquitur: ergo est Ægyptius;' but the very contrary to this. His being able to speak Greek is a proof to Lysias that he is *not* that Egyptian. This Egyptian is mentioned by Josephus, Antt. xx. 8. 6, ἀφικνεῖται δέ τις ἐξ Αἰγύπτου κατὰ τοῦτον τὸν καιρὸν εἰς τὰ Ἱεροσόλυμα, προφήτης εἶναι λέγων, καὶ συμβουλεύων τῷ δημοτικῷ πλήθει σὺν αὐτῷ πρὸς ὄρος τὸ προσαγορευόμενον Ἐλαιῶν ἔρχεσθαι, ὃ καὶ τῆς πόλεως ἄντικρυς κείμενον ἀπέχει στάδια πέντε· θέλειν γάρ, ἔφασκεν, αὐτοῖς ἐκεῖθεν ἐπιδεῖξαι, ὡς κελεύσαντος αὐτοῦ πίπτοι τὰ τῶν Ἱεροσολύμων τείχη, δι' ὧν τὴν εἴσοδον αὐτοῖς παρέξειν ἐπηγγέλλετο. Φῆλιξ δὲ ὡς ἐπύθετο ταῦτα, κελεύει τοὺς στρατιώτας ἀναλαβεῖν τὰ ὅπλα, καὶ . . . . προσβάλλει τοῖς περὶ τὸν Αἰγύπτιον· καὶ τετρακοσίους μὲν αὐτῶν ἀνεῖλε, διακοσίους δὲ ζῶντας ἔλαβεν. ὁ δὲ Αἰγύπτιος αὐτὸς διαδράσας ἐκ τῆς μάχης ἀφανὴς ἐγένετο. But in B. J. ii. 13. 5, he says of the same person, περὶ **τρισμυρίους** ἀθροίζει τῶν ἠπατημένων, περιαγαγὼν δὲ αὐτοὺς ἐκ τῆς ἐρημίας εἰς τὸ Ἐλαιῶν καλ. ὄρ. κ.τ.λ. . . . . . . ὥστε συμβολῆς γενομένης . . . . . διαφθαρῆναι κ. ζωγρηθῆναι **πλείστους** τῶν σὺν αὐτῷ. It is obvious that the *numerical* accounts in Jos. are inconsistent with our text, and with *one another*. This latter being the case, we may well leave them out of the question. At different times of his rebellion, his number of followers would be variously estimated; and the tribune would naturally take it as he himself or his informant had known it, at some one period. That this is so, we may see by noticing that our narrative speaks of his *leading out*,—whereas Josephus's numbers are those whom he *brought back from* the wilderness against Jerusalem, by which time his band would have augmented considerably. **τοὺς τετρ.]** **the four thousand,**—the matter being one of notoriety. **σικαρίων]** From *sica*, a dagger; they are described by Jos. B. J. ii. 13. 3, ἕτερον εἶδος λῃστῶν ἐν Ἱεροσολύμοις ὑπεφύετο, οἱ καλούμενοι **σικάριοι**, μεθ' ἡμέραν καὶ ἐν μέσῃ τῇ πόλει φονεύοντες ἀνθρώπους· μάλιστα δὲ ἐν ταῖς ἑορταῖς μισγόμενοι τῷ πλήθει, καὶ ταῖς ἐσθήσεσιν ὑποκρύπτοντες μικρὰ ξιφίδια, τούτοις ἔνυττον τοὺς διαφόρους. . . . . πρῶτος μὲν οὖν ὑπ' αὐτῶν Ἰωνάθης ὁ ἀρχιερεὺς ἀποσφάζεται· μετὰ δὲ αὐτὸν καθ' ἡμέραν ἀνῃροῦντο πολλοί . . . The art. is generic. **39. μέν]** Our **indeed,**—implying 'not the Egyptian, but,'—exactly renders it: **I indeed am:** so Aristoph. Plut. 355, μὰ Δί' ἐγὼ μὲν οὔ. See Hartung, Partikellehre, ii. 413. **οὐκ ἀσήμου πόλ.]** See note, ch. ix. 11. The expression is an elegant one, and very common. Wetst. gives many examples, and among them one from Eurip. Ion 8, ἔστιν γὰρ οὐκ ἄσημος Ἑλλήνων πόλις. There was distinction in his being a πολίτης of an *urbs libera*. "Many of the coins of Tarsus bear the epigraphs μητρόπολις and αὐτόνομος." Wordsw. from Akermann, p. 56. **40. τῇ Ἑβρ. διαλ.]** The Syro-Chaldaic, the mother-tongue of the Jews in Judæa at this time:

[v] Ἑβραΐδι [w] διαλέκτῳ λέγων [XXII.] 1 Ἄνδρες ἀδελφοὶ
καὶ πατέρες, [x] ἀκούσατέ [x] μου [x] τῆς πρὸς ὑμᾶς νυνὶ [y] ἀπολογίας. 2 ἀκούσαντες δὲ ὅτι τῇ [z] Ἑβραΐδι [z] διαλέκτῳ
[a] προσεφώνει αὐτοῖς, μᾶλλον [bc] παρέσχον [cd] ἡσυχίαν. καί
φησιν 3 Ἐγώ εἰμι ἀνὴρ Ἰουδαῖος, γεγεννημένος ἐν Ταρσῷ
τῆς Κιλικίας, [e] ἀνατεθραμμένος δὲ ἐν τῇ πόλει ταύτῃ
[f] παρὰ τοὺς πόδας Γαμαλιήλ, [g] πεπαιδευμένος κατὰ
[h] ἀκρίβειαν τοῦ [i] πατρῴου νόμου, [j] ζηλωτὴς ὑπάρχων
τοῦ θεοῦ καθὼς πάντες ὑμεῖς ἐστε σήμερον· 4 ὃς ταύτην
τὴν [k] ὁδὸν [l] ἐδίωξα [m] ἄχρι [m] θανάτου, [n] δεσμεύων καὶ [o] παραδιδοὺς εἰς φυλακὰς ἄνδρας τε καὶ γυναῖκας, 5 ὡς καὶ
ὁ ἀρχιερεὺς [p] μαρτυρεῖ μοι καὶ πᾶν τὸ [q] πρεσβυτέριον

v ch. xxii. 2. xxvi. 14 only †.
w ch. i. 19 reff. Acts only.
x constr., John xii. 47.
y w. πρός, here only. Xen. Mem. iv. 8. 5. w. dat., 1 Cor. ix. 3. 1 Pet. iii. 15. (ch. xxv. 16 reff.)
z ch. xxi. 40.
a = w. dat., Luke vii. 32 || Mt. Esdr. ii. 21 (18). vi. 22 only. see Luke vi. 13. abs., ch. xxi. 40.
b = ch. xvi. 16 reff.

c Job xxxiv. 29. d = 1 Tim. ii. 11, 12 (2 Thess. iii. 12) only. Prov. vii. 9. (-ιος, 1 Tim. ii. 2. 1 Pet. iii. 4.) e ch. vii. 20, 21 only †. Wisd. vii. 4, BℵF(not A) &c. only. f Luke viii. 35. ch. iv. 35, 37. v. 2 al. 4 Kings iv. 37 Ald. g = ch. vii. 22 reff. h here only. Dan. vii. 16 (see note and ch. xviii. 25 reff.). i ch. xxiv. 14. xxviii. 17 only. Prov xxvii. 10. 2 Macc. vi. 1 Ed-vat. Ald. compl. &c.(not AB). j ch. xxl. 20 reff. (-λοῦν, Num. xxv. 13.) k ch. ix. 2 reff. l = ch. vii. 52 reff. m Rev. ii. 10. xii. 11 only. μέχρι θαν., 2 Macc. xiii. 14. n = here (Matt. xxiii. 4) only. Gen. xlix. 11. o constr., ch. viii. 3 reff. p Rom. x. 2. Gal. iv. 15. Col. iv. 13. q = Luke xxii. 66 (1 Tim. iv. 14) only †. (Susan. 50 Theod. A Ald. compl.)

for εβραιδι, ιδια A.

Chap. XXII. 1. rec νυν, with a f 13[e sil] Chr: txt ABDEHLPℵ rel 36 Thl.

2. προsφωνει D E[-gr] H am fuld tol Œc Thl-sif: προσεφωνησεν L a b c k o 36. 40, *adlocutus est* E-lat: txt ABPℵ rel [Syr coptt æth] Chr_1 Thl-fin, *loquebatur* demid [*loqueretur* vulg-clem. (13 uncert.)] (D-lat is deficient from this point to ver 10.) om αυτοις D: αυτων A¹(perhaps). for παρεσχον ησυχιαν, ησυχασαν D.

3. rec aft εγω ins μεν, with HLP rel syr copt æth Chr_2: om ABDEℵ a 13. 36 vulg sah [arm]. ανηρ bef ειμι ℵ¹: ιουδαιος bef ανηρ D. εν ταρσω τ. κιλ. bef γεγεννημενος D: γεγενημενος A o. γαμαλιηλου B 36 Chr_1. παιδευομενοs D. aft πεπαιδευμενος ins δε H k m [syr] Chr_1. om υπαρχων D vulg. εσται υμει ςπαντες D.

4. for os, και D Syr æth. μεχρι D c: εως k [Chr_1]. φυλακην D 96. 142. 80 am.

5. om o D¹(ins D-corr¹) 56. 180. aft αρχιερευς ins ανανιας 137 syr-w-ast. μαρτυρησει D: εμαρτυρει B: επιμαρτυρει 137. for παν, ολον D [απαν k 40].

his motive is implied (ch. xxii. 2) to be, that they might be the more disposed to listen to him. Chap. XXII. 1.] This speech of Paul repeats the narrative of his conversion to Christianity, but this time most skilfully arranged and adapted (within legitimate limits) to avoid offence and conciliate his hearers. Proofs of this will appear as we go on. See an enquiry into its diction and rendering into Greek, in the Prolegg. § ii. 17 β. 3.] De Wette and others would place the comma after *ταύτῃ*, so to make the two clauses, beginning with *γέγ.* and *ἀνατ.*, exactly correspond. But (not to insist, with Meyer, on the reason that a new circumstance is introduced with each participle) it is surely better, as the rule of the sentence seems to be to place the participles *before* the words which qualify them, to take ἐν τῇ πόλει ταύτῃ παρὰ τ. π. Γ., *all* as the qualification of ἀνατεθραμμένος, and punctuate, as commonly done, after Γαμαλιήλ. On *Gamaliel*, see note, ch. v. 34. The expression παρὰ τ. πόδ. (see ch. iv. 35, note) indicates that the rabbi sat on an elevated seat and the scholars on the ground or on benches, literally *at his feet*.

κατὰ ἀκρ.] (The art. omitted aft. a prep.) **According to the strict acceptation of the law of my fathers**; = κατὰ τὴν ἀκριβεστάτην αἵρεσιν τῆς ἡμετέρας θρησκείας, ch. xxvi. 5;—i. e. as a Pharisee. So Jos. B. J. ii. 8. 18, Φαρισαῖοι . . . οἱ δοκοῦντες μετὰ ἀκριβείας ἐξηγεῖσθαι τὰ νόμιμα. Some of the older Commentators make τοῦ πατρῴου νόμου governed by πεπαιδ., and take κατὰ ἀκρίβ. adverbially: which would give a very vapid sense, the accuracy and carefulness of his education having been already implied in παρὰ τ. π. Γαμαλιήλ.

καθὼς . . .] Not meaning *'in the same way as* YE *are all this day'* (but *now* in *another* way): but **as ye all are this day**: 'I had the same zealous character (not excluding his still retaining it) which you all shew to-day.' A conciliatory comparison.

5. ὁ ἀρχ.] '**The High Priest** *of that*

r = ch. ix. 2 reff.
s ch. xxi. 3 only. Job xxxix. 29. τῶν ἐκεῖσε ἐθνῶν, Jos. Antt. iii. 2. 1.
t ch. xxvi. 11 only. Ezek. v. 17. (-ία, Heb. x. 29.)
u constr. w. inf., Matt. xviii. 13. ch. iv. 5. xi. 26 al. fr.
v ch. ix. 3 (reff.).
w = ch. x. 9. Matt. xx. 3. 2 Macc. v. 1.
x ch. viii. 26 only. Gen. xviii. 1.
y ch. ix. 3 only †.
z = ch. xi. 24 reff.
a here only. Ps. cxviii. 25.
b ver. 4.
c ch. x. 4 reff.
d ch. ix. 4 reff.
e ch. ix. 6 (reff.).

παρ ὧν καὶ [r] ἐπιστολὰς δεξάμενος πρὸς τοὺς ἀδελφοὺς ABDE
εἰς Δαμασκὸν ἐπορευόμην, ἄξων καὶ τοὺς [s] ἐκεῖσε ὄντας HLPℵ a
δεδεμένους εἰς Ἱερουσαλήμ, ἵνα [t] τιμωρηθῶσιν. 6 [u] ἐγένετο b c d f g h k l m o 13
δέ μοι πορευομένῳ καὶ [v] ἐγγίζοντι τῇ Δαμασκῷ [w] περὶ
[x] μεσημβρίαν [y] ἐξαίφνης ἐκ τοῦ οὐρανοῦ [y] περιαστράψαι φῶς
[z] ἱκανὸν περὶ ἐμέ, 7 ἔπεσά τε εἰς τὸ [a] ἔδαφος καὶ ἤκουσα
φωνῆς λεγούσης μοι Σαοὺλ Σαούλ, τί με [b] διώκεις ; 8 ἐγὼ ...μοι d.
δὲ ἀπεκρίθην Τίς εἶ, κύριε ; εἶπέν τε πρός με Ἐγώ ABDE HLPℵ a b c f g h
εἰμι Ἰησοῦς ὁ Ναζωραῖος ὃν σὺ [b] διώκεις. 9 οἱ δὲ σὺν k l m o 13
ἐμοὶ ὄντες τὸ μὲν φῶς ἐθεάσαντο [καὶ [c] ἔμφοβοι ἐγένοντο],
τὴν δὲ φωνὴν οὐκ [d] ἤκουσαν τοῦ λαλοῦντός μοι. 10 εἶπον
δὲ Τί ποιήσω, κύριε ; ὁ δὲ κύριος εἶπεν πρός με [e] Ἀναστὰς πορεύου εἰς Δαμασκόν, κἀκεῖ σοι [e] λαληθήσεται περὶ
πάντων ὧν [f] τέτακταί σοι ποιῆσαι. 11 ὡς δὲ οὐκ [g] ἐν- ...παν-
έβλεπον [h] ἀπὸ τῆς [i] δόξης τοῦ φωτὸς ἐκείνου, [k] χειραγω- των D. ABEHL
γούμενος ὑπὸ τῶν [l] συνόντων μοι ἦλθον εἰς Δαμασκόν. Pℵ a b c f g h k l m o 13

f = ch. xiii. 48. xv. 2 al. 1 Macc. xii. 26. constr., here only. Xen. de Rep. Lac. xi. 6, τοῖς δὲ ἕπεσθαι τέτακται.
g = Mark viii. 25 only ‡. h = ch. xii. 14 reff. Exod. vi. 9. i = Luke ix. 31, 32. 1 Cor. xv. 40, 41. 2 Cor. iii. 7, 18. Exod. xvi. 10. k ch. ix. 8 only. Judg. xvi. 26 A compl. only. (-γός, ch. xiii. 11.)
l Luke ix. 18 only. Jer. iii. 20. Esdr. vi. 2. 2 Macc. ix. 4 only.

om και (bef επιστ.) D 3 fuld coptt [Syr æth]. for προς τους αδ., παρα των αδελφων D. αξαι E [ἐξ ὧν(sic) 13] : om αξων to δεδεμενους H. εκει D : *ut adducerem inde vinctos* vulg. for εις (bef ιερουσ.), εν D.

6. for εγεν. to μεσημβρ. D[1] has ενγιζοντι δ(ε μ)οι μεσημβριας (ins τη D[2]) δαμασκω (txt D[6]). for εκ, α(πο) D[1](txt D[2]). περιεστραψεν E 137 : -ψα μ(ε) D[1] (-ψαι D-corr) : περιαστραψαν P.

7. for επ. τε, και επ. D [επ. δε coptt]. (επεσα, so ABEHPℵ d f m 36. 40 Ath₁ Thl.) σαυλε σαυλε (*as lat, ver* 13) D l 25. for ειμι, ει D[1](txt D[2 or 3]). at end ins σκληρον σοι προς κεντρα λακτιζειν E demid syr-mg Ath₁.

8. aft απεκριθην ins και ειπα ℵ [Syr]. for τε, δε D. εμε [A]Bℵ[1]. ναζοραιος [D[1](txt D[2])] ℵ[1].

9. ℵ[1] has omitted σαν in εθεασαντο. om και εμφοβοι εγενοντο ABHℵ 13 vulg Syr copt arm : ins DELP rel (36) syr sah æth Chr₁. (*On the one hand we may place the possibility of omn from similarity of endings (so Meyer) ; on the other, interpolation from the* ειστηκεισαν εννεοι *of ch* ix. 7 : *the fact noticed by Tischdf* (N. T. ed 7 [not ed 8]) *that* εμφ. γεν. *is a phrase almost peculiar to St. Luke does not tell distinctly either way :* εννεοι *could not be used in this connexion.*) ηκουον E-gr ℵ[3] [Thl-sif].

10. ειπα D. om κυριος D k, simly sah æth. εντετακται B[1] : εντεταλται B[2]. for περι to σοι, τι σε δει (*see ch* ix. 6) H 4[1]. 34. 95[1]-8-marg 100 Chr: *de omnibus quæ te oporteat facere* vulg (E-lat). om σοι E.

11. ουδενεβλεπον (i. e. either ουδεν εβλεπον or ουδ' ενεβλεπον) B : εβλεπον E 18, ανεβλ. 68. 100 Thl-fin : *ut autem surrexi(surrexit* D[1]) *non videbam* D-lat. for υπο, απο A.

day, who is still living :' i. e. Theophilus, see on ch. ix. 1. Similarly, the whole Sanhedrim = '*those who were then members, and now survive.*' **παρ' ὧν καί**] from whom, moreover. **πρὸς τοὺς ἀδελφ.**] to the Jewish (*their*) brethren (see ch. xxviii. 21). Bornemann's rendering, '*against the* (Christian) *brethren,*' is altogether inadmissible. If ever Paul spoke to the Jews *as a Jew*, it was on this occasion. **καὶ τοὺς ἐκ.**] even those who were there. **ἐκεῖσε**] if resolved, would be εἰς Δαμασκόν,—a similar construction to εἰς οἶκόν ἐστιν, Mark ii. 1, '*those who had settled at Damascus and were then there.*' **6.**] On Paul's conversion and the comparison of the accounts in chapp. ix., xxii., and xxvi., see notes on ch. ix. I have there treated of the discrepancies, real or apparent. **11.**] See notes, ch. ix. 8, 18. **12.**] That Ananias was a *Christian*, is not *here* mentioned,—

12 Ἀνανίας δέ τις ἀνὴρ [m] εὐλαβὴς [n] κατὰ τὸν [n] νόμον
[o] μαρτυρούμενος [o] ὑπὸ πάντων τῶν [p] κατοικούντων Ἰουδαίων,
13 ἐλθὼν πρός με καὶ [q] ἐπιστὰς εἶπέν μοι Σαοὺλ ἀδελφέ,
[r] ἀνάβλεψον. κἀγὼ [s] αὐτῇ τῇ ὥρᾳ [rt] ἀνέβλεψα [t] εἰς αὐτόν.
14 ὁ δὲ εἶπεν Ὁ [u] θεὸς τῶν [v] πατέρων [v] ἡμῶν [w] προεχειρί-
σατό σε [x] γνῶναι τὸ [x] θέλημα αὐτοῦ καὶ ἰδεῖν τὸν [y] δίκαιον
καὶ ἀκοῦσαι [z] φωνὴν [z] ἐκ τοῦ στόματος αὐτοῦ, 15 ὅτι ἔσῃ
[a] μάρτυς αὐτῷ πρὸς πάντας ἀνθρώπους [b] ὧν ἑώρακας καὶ
ἤκουσας. 16 καὶ νῦν τί [c] μέλλεις; [d] ἀναστὰς βάπτισαι
καὶ [e] ἀπόλουσαι τὰς ἁμαρτίας σου, [f] ἐπικαλεσάμενος τὸ
ὄνομα αὐτοῦ. 17 ἐγένετο δέ μοι [g] ὑποστρέψαντι εἰς Ἱερουσαλὴμ καὶ [h] προσευχομένου μου ἐν τῷ ἱερῷ γενέσθαι με
ἐν [i] ἐκστάσει 18 καὶ ἰδεῖν [k] αὐτὸν λέγοντά μοι [l] Σπεῦσον
καὶ ἔξελθε [m] ἐν τάχει ἐξ Ἱερουσαλήμ, διότι οὐ [n] παρα-
δέξονταί σου [τὴν] [op] μαρτυρίαν [p] περὶ ἐμοῦ. 19 κἀγὼ εἶπον

m ch. ii. 5 reff. n ch. xxiv. 14. Phil. iii. 5. Heb. viii. 5 al. Deut. xvii. 11. o = ch. x. 22 reff. p ellips., ch. xiii. 1 reff. q absol., Luke ii. 38. x. 40. xx. 1. ver. 20. r = ch. ix. 12 reff. s ch. xvi. 18 reff. t = Matt. xiv. 19 al. Gen. xv. 5. u ch. vii. 32. Deut. i. 11 al. fr. v ch. v. 30 reff. w ch. iii. 20. xxvi. 16 only. Exod. iv. 13. Josh. iii. 12. 2 Macc. iii. 7. viii. 9 only. x (Luke xii. 47.) Rom. ii. 18. see Eph. v. 17. Col. i. 9. Ps. cii. 7. y absol., ch. vii. 52 reff. z ch. xi. 9 al. Isa. lxvi. 6. a = ch. i. 8 reff. b attr., ch. i. 1 reff. see ver. 10. c = here only. Xen. Cyr. i. 3. 15. d ver. 10. e 1 Cor. vi. 11 only. Job ix. 30 only. f ch. ii. 21 reff. g ch. viii. 25 reff. h absol., ch. x. 9 reff. i ch. x. 10 reff. k = Mark iv. 38 al. l ch. xx. 16 reff. constr., Gen. xviii. 6. xxiv. 18, 20. m Rom. xvi. 20 reff. n = Mark iv. 20. ch. xvi. 21 (reff.). Exod. xxiii. 1. o = John i. 19. iii. 11, &c. 1 John v. 9. Rev. i. 2, 9. xi. 7 al. p here only. see John i. 7.

12. rec (for ευλαβης) ευσεβης, with E rel: om A vulg (*the omn has prob been because the sentence is complete without the epithet: ευσεβης, a gloss on ευλαβης*): txt BHLPℵ a b c g k o 13. 36. 40. μαρτυρομενος A¹. aft κατοικουντων ins εν δαμασκω (*supplementary gloss*) HL 13 rel demid tol syr [sah] æth arm Chr_1: aft ιουδ., 73: om ABEPℵ f g vulg Syr copt.

13. εμε ABℵ. εβλεψα A.

14. προεχειρησατο AL k: προsεχειρησατο ℵ(but s marked and erased) P. om 1st και A¹. om του A k l 95¹.

15. μαρτ. αυ. πρ. π. ανθρ. bef εση B. aft ων ins τε E-gr b*c o 36 [Thl-sif-comm].

16. the second λ of μελλεις was appy added by P-corr. rec (for αυτου) του κυριου, with HL rel Thl-sif: add ιησου k 43. 99 (*explanatory corrections*): txt ABEPℵ a c 13. 36 vulg D-lat syrr coptt æth arm Chr_1 Thl-fin.

17. προsευχομενω, omg μου, E e 93·5. for με, μοι L a²-marg 99. 106-37: om 25. 40. 96. 105. in ℵ σθαι of γενεσθαι is written twice.

18. for ιδειν, ιδον ℵ [36] 180. rec ins την, with EHLP rel 36 Chr: *testimonium meum* D-lat: om (*as unnecessary* ?) ABℵ a 13.

and ἀνὴρ . . . Ἰουδαίων is added: both, as addressed to a *Jewish audience.* Before the *Roman governor* in ch. xxvi., he *does not mention him at all,* but compresses the whole substance of the command given to Ananias into the words spoken by the Lord to himself. A heathen moralist could teach,—'Quid de quoque viro, et cui dicas, sæpe videto' (Hor. Ep. i. 18. 68): and a Christian Apostle was not unmindful of the necessary caution. Such features in his speeches are highly instructive and valuable to those who would gather from Scripture itself its own real character: and be, not slaves to its letter, but disciples of its spirit.

13. ἀνέβλ. εἰς αὐτόν] De W. remarks, that the two meanings of ἀναβλέπω here unite in the word: **I looked, with recovered sight, upon him.** **14—16** is not related, but included, in ch. ix. 15—19.

14. ὁ θ. τ. πατ. ἡμ.] So Peter, ch. iii. 13; v. 30. In ch. ix. 17, ὁ **κύριος** is the word: this title is given *for the Jews.*

τὸν δίκαιον] So Stephen, ch. vii. 52. How forcibly must the whole scene have recalled *him,* whom presently (ver. 20) he mentions *by name.*

16. ἀπόλουσαι . . .] This was the Jewish as well as the Christian doctrine of baptism. See ref. 1 Cor. and note.

αὐτοῦ] of Jesus, **τοῦ δικαίου.** Paul carefully avoids mentioning to the Jews *this Name,* except where it is *unavoidable,* in ver. 8: so αὐτόν again, ver. 18.

17.] viz. as related ch. ix. 26—30, where nothing of this vision, or its having been the cause of his leaving Jerusalem, is hinted.

18.] **περὶ ἐμοῦ** is to be taken with μαρτυρίαν,

Κύριε, αὐτοὶ ἐπίστανται ὅτι ἐγὼ [q] ἤμην [r] φυλακίζων καὶ
[s] δέρων [t] κατὰ τὰς συναγωγὰς τοὺς [u] πιστεύοντας [u] ἐπὶ
σέ. 20 καὶ ὅτε [v] ἐξεχύννετο τὸ αἷμα Στεφάνου τοῦ [w] μάρ-
τυρός σου, καὶ αὐτὸς [q] ἤμην [x] ἐφεστὼς καὶ [y] συνευδοκῶν
καὶ [z] φυλάσσων τὰ ἱμάτια τῶν [a] ἀναιρούντων αὐτόν. 21 καὶ

ABEH LPℵ a b c f g h k l m o 13

D και φυλασσων.

q constr., ch. xi. 5 reff. r here only †. Wisd. xviii. 4 only. s ch. v. 40 reff. t Luke ix. 6. ch. viii. 3. xx. 20. xxvi. 11. u ch. ix. 42 reff. v -χυν., Matt. xxiii. 35. xxvi. 28. Luke xi. 50 al. w see note. x ver. 13. perf., ch. xxviii. 2. 2 Tim. iv. 6 only. Zech. i. 10. y 1 Cor. vii. 12, 13 reff. z = Luke xi. 21. Exod. xxii. 7. a = ch. v. 33 reff.

19. πεπιστευκοτας E-gr: *qui credebant* vulg D-lat E-lat.
20. rec εξεχειτο (*corrn to more usual form*), with HLP rel Chr_1 [Thl-sif]: txt ABEℵ 13. 36 Thl-fin. (εξεχυνετο B²E 13. 36: txt AB¹ℵ.) om στεφανου A 68: τ. μαρτ. bef στεφ. 38. 73 (*the omn is hardly accountable, if it was originally in the text: at the same time, the manuscript authority is too light to allow of its being* now *omitted. Meyer suggests the similarity of ending,* στεφανου του: *but this would occasion the omn of* του, *not of* στεφανου): txt BEHLPℵ [vulg &c] Chr. **πρωτο**μαρτυρος L a c k m: πρωτου μαρτ. 7 syr. εστως A 37. rec aft συνευδοκων ins τη αναιρεσει αυτου (*interpolated from ch* viii. 1), with HLP rel (13) 36 syr [arm] Chr_1: τη βουλη των αναιρουντων αυτον (and λιθαζοντων for αναιρ. below) Syr: om AB D(appy: D-lat ends with *consentiens*) Eℵ 40 vulg coptt æth. om και (bef φυλασσων) HLP b c f l o syr Chr_1 Thl-sif: ins ABDEℵ rel 36 vulg coptt.—φυλ. τε c 137.

not with the verb, as Meyer and Winer maintain. Their objection, that then it must be τὴν μαρτ. **τὴν** περὶ ἐμοῦ is answered by remarking, (1) that Paul does not always observe accuracy in this usage of the article: e. g. Eph. vi. 5, ὑπακούετε τοῖς κυρίοις κατὰ σάρκα, for τ. κυρ. τοῖς κατα σάρκα, or τοῖς κατὰ σάρκα κυρίοις, which he has written in the ||, Col. iii. 22,—1 Thess. iv. 16, οἱ νεκροὶ ἐν χριστῷ ἀναστήσονται πρῶτον. See also Rom. vi. 4; Col. ii. 14, and notes:—and (2) that there may have been a reason for the irregularity here, inasmuch as, if either the article had been expressed after μαρτ., or τὴν π. ἐμ. μαρτ. had been used, σου would have appeared to be governed by παραδέξονται—'they will not receive *from thee* thy testimony concerning me,'—which is not precisely the meaning intended to be conveyed. (See Mr. Green's Gram. of N. T. p. 163.) **19.**] The probable account of this answer is, that Paul thought his former great zeal *against* Christ, contrasted with his present zeal *for* Him, would make a deep impression on the Jews in Jerusalem: or, perhaps, he wishes by his earnest preaching of Jesus as the Christ among them, to *undo the mischief of which he before was the agent*, and therefore alleges his former zeal and his consenting to Stephen's death as reasons why he should remain in Jerusalem. **αὐτοί** can only refer to the same persons as the subjects of παραδέξονται above: not (as Heinrichs) to the foreign Jews;—"Idcirco iter apostolicum extra urbem detrectat, quod undique odio petitum se iri prævidet, Hierosolymis autem in apostolorum collegio delitescere se posse opinatur:"—a motive totally unworthy of Paul, and an interpretation which happily the sentence will not bear. **20. μάρτυρός σου**] * "E. V. '*thy martyr*,' following Beza: Vulg., and Erasm, *testis tui*. The Apostle may have here used the (Hebrew, עֵד, as Wordsworth) word in its strict primary sense; for a view of Christ in His glory was vouchsafed to Stephen, and it was by *bearing witness* of that manifestation that he hastened his death (ch. vii. 55 ff.). The present meaning of the word *martyr* did, however, become attached to it at a very early period, and is apparently of apostolic authority: e. g. Rev. xvii. 6, and Clem. Rom. 1 Cor. v., p. 217 (cited in note on ch. i. 25). . . . The transition from the first to the secondary sense may be easily accounted for. Many who had only seen with the eye of faith, suffered persecution and death as a proof of their sincerity. For such constancy the Greek had no adequate term. It was necessary for the Christians to provide one. None was more appropriate than μάρτυρ, seeing what had been the fate of those whom Christ had appointed to be His *witnesses* (ch. i. 8). *They* almost all suffered: hence *to witness* became a synonym for *to suffer*; while the suffering was in itself a kind of testimony." (Mr. Humphry.) Bp. Wordsworth well designates this introduction of the name of Stephen "A noble endeavour to make public reparation for a public sin, by public confession in the same place where the sin was committed." **καὶ αὐτός**] I myself also. **21.**] The object of Paul in relating this vision appears to have been to shew

C και ειπεν... ABCDE HLPℵ a b c f g h k l m o 13

εἶπεν πρός με Πορεύου, ὅτι ἐγὼ εἰς ἔθνη [b] μακρὰν [c] ἐξ-
αποστελῶ σε. 22 ἤκουον δὲ αὐτοῦ ἄχρι τούτου τοῦ
λόγου, καὶ [d] ἐπῆραν τὴν [d] φωνὴν αὐτῶν λέγοντες [e] Αἶρε
ἀπὸ τῆς γῆς τὸν [f] τοιοῦτον, οὐ γὰρ [g] καθῆκεν αὐτὸν ζῆν.
23 [h] κραυγαζόντων τε αὐτῶν καὶ [i] ῥιπτούντων τὰ ἱμάτια
καὶ [k] κονιορτὸν βαλλόντων εἰς τὸν ἀέρα, 24 ἐκέλευσεν ὁ
χιλίαρχος εἰσάγεσθαι αὐτὸν εἰς τὴν [l] παρεμβολήν, [m] εἴπας
[n] μάστιξιν [o] ἀνετάζεσθαι αὐτόν, ἵνα [p] ἐπιγνῷ δι' ἣν [q] αἰτίαν
οὕτως [r] ἐπεφώνουν αὐτῷ. 25 ὡς δὲ [s] προέτειναν αὐτὸν
τοῖς [t] ἱμᾶσιν, εἶπεν πρὸς τὸν [u] ἑστῶτα ἑκατόνταρχον [ὁ

b absol., Luke xv. 20. ch. ii. 39. (xvii. 28 reff.) Eph. ii. 13, 17 only. Zech. x. 9. c ch. vii. 12 reff. d ch. ii. 14 reff. e = ch. viii. 33 reff. f = 1 Cor. v. 5, 11. 2 Cor. ii. 6, 7. x. 11. (xii. 2, &c.) g Rom. i. 28 only. Deut. xxi. 17. Sir. x. 23. constr. imperf., see ch. xxv. 22 reff. h absol., Matt. xii. 19. Ezra iii. 13. i = (see note) here only. Herodot. iv. 94, 188. k ch. xiii. 51 reff. l ch. xxi. 34, 37 reff. m = Mark v. 43. x. 49. Luke xix. 15. Exod. xxxv. 1. n = Heb. xi. 36 (Mark iii. 10. v. 29, 34. Luke vii. 21) only. Prov. xxvi. 3. o ver. 29 only. Judg. vi. 29 A Ald. compl. only. Susan. 14 Theod. p = ch. xxiii. 28 reff. Gen. xxxi. 32. q ch. x. 21 reff. r ch. xii. 22 reff. dat., here only. s here only †. 2 Macc. xv. 15. t Mark i. 7 | L.J. only. Job xxxix. 10. Isa. v. 18, 27. Sir. xxx. (xxxiii.) 26 only. Demosth. περὶ παραπρ. p. 402, end. u absol., ch. xvi. 9. Matt. xx. 6. xxvi. 73. John xii. 29 al.

21. εμε C. εθνος E-gr 25. εξαποστελλω D e Ath$_1$: αποστελω [B Chr$_1$, αποστελλω(but *mittam*)] E.

22. ηκουσαν D syrr. rec καθηκον (*the meaning of the imperf not being apprehended, as the varr shew*), with [D-corr] a Thl-fin : καθηκει 68-9. 98^2. 105 : καθηκαν 18. 43 : txt ABCD^{1}EHLPℵ rel 36 Hip$_1$ Ath$_1$ Chr$_2$ Thl-sif.

23. κραζοντων C c g l o Chr$_1$ Thl-sif. rec δε (*alteration of characteristic* τε), with DEHLPℵ rel 36 vulg [syr arm] copt Chr : txt ABC Syr æth. om αυτων D? ριπτοντων DEHL a b o 40 Thl. for αερα, ουρανον D Syr Cassiod$_1$: αεραν ℵ^1.

24. rec αυτον bef ο χιλιαρχος, with HLP rel 36 Thl-sif : om c 137-42 : txt ABCDEℵ a h k m 13. 40 vulg Chr$_1$ Thl-fin. rec αγεσθαι, with HLP h [13(sic)] rel æth-rom : txt ABCDEℵ a m 36. 40 vulg Chr$_1$ Thl-fin. (*The* εισ- *seems to have been dropped out when the order was altered.*) rec ειπων (*more usual form*), with HLP (13) rel 36 Chr : ειπε δε k : txt ABCDEℵ. ανεταζειν D^1(txt D^2) : εταζεσθαι E m 40 : εξετ. 4. γνω A 13. 36 Chr$_1$. κατεφωνουν D c 137. for αυτω, περι αυτου D : αυτου 137 [Chr].

25. rec προετεινεν (*to suit the subject* ο χιλ., *no more persons having been mentd: this the varr shew*), with P k l m o : προσετεινεν H Thl-sif : προετεινον AE Thl-fin : txt BLℵ a b c g h 13. 36 Chr(some mss have προσετεινον), προσετειναν CD 40. 137 [*adstrinxissent* vulg, *extendissent* E-lat, simly syrr copt æth arm]. (f doubtful [sah def].) εκατονταρχην D 73. om ο παυλος D syr Chr$_1$: ins ABCEHLPℵ

that his own inclination and prayer had been, *that he might preach the Gospel to his own people:* but that it was by the imperative command of the Lord Himself that he went to the Gentiles. **22. τούτου τ. λόγου**] viz. the announcement that he was to be *sent to the Gentiles.* 'Populi terrarum non vivunt,' was the maxim of the children of Abraham. Chetubb. fol. iii. 2 (Meyer). **καθῆκεν**] 'decuerat:' implying, *he ought to have been put to death long ago* (when we endeavoured to do it, but he escaped). **23. ῥιπτούντων**] Not '*flinging off* their garments,' as preparing to stone him, or even as *representing* the action of such preparation: the former would be futile, as he was in the custody of the tribune,—the latter absurd, and not borne out by any known habit of the Jews: but **shaking,** *jactitantes,* **their garments,** as shaking off the dust, abominating such an expression and him who uttered it. The casting dust into the air was part of the same gesture. Chrys. explains it, ῥιπτάζοντες, ἐκτινάσσοντες. **24.**] The tribune, not understanding the language in which Paul spoke, wished to extract from him by the scourge the reason which so exasperated the Jews against him. In this he was acting illegally: 'Non esse a tormentis incipiendum, Div. Augustus constituit.' Digest. Leg. 48, tit. 18, c. 1 (De W.). **ἐπεφών.**] they were thus crying out against him. **25.**] **And while they were binding him down with the thongs.** Dr. Bloomfield quotes from Dio Cassius, xi. 49, 'Αντίγονον ἐμαστίγωσε σταυρῷ προσδήσαντες, and explains rightly, I think, the προ in both verbs to allude to the *position* of the prisoner, which was, bent forward, and tied with a sort of gear made of leather to an inclined post. De W. and others render τοῖς ἱμᾶσιν, '*for the scourge*' (dat. commodi); but why should

Παῦλος] [v] Εἰ [w] ἄνθρωπον Ῥωμαῖον καὶ [x] ἀκατάκριτον [y] ἔξεστιν ὑμῖν [z] μαστίζειν; 26 ἀκούσας δὲ ὁ ἑκατόνταρχος
προσελθὼν τῷ χιλιάρχῳ ἀπήγγειλεν λέγων Τί μέλλεις
ποιεῖν; ὁ γὰρ ἄνθρωπος οὗτος Ῥωμαῖός ἐστιν. 27 προσελθὼν δὲ ὁ χιλίαρχος εἶπεν αὐτῷ Λέγε μοι, σὺ Ῥωμαῖος
εἶ; ὁ δὲ ἔφη Ναί. 28 ἀπεκρίθη ὁ χιλίαρχος Ἐγὼ πολλοῦ [a] κεφαλαίου τὴν [b] πολιτείαν ταύτην [c] ἐκτησάμην. ὁ
δὲ Παῦλος ἔφη Ἐγὼ δὲ καὶ γεγέννημαι. 29 εὐθέως οὖν
[d] ἀπέστησαν ἀπ' αὐτοῦ οἱ μέλλοντες αὐτὸν [e] ἀνετάζειν.
[f] καὶ ὁ χιλίαρχος [f] δὲ ἐφοβήθη [g] ἐπιγνοὺς ὅτι Ῥωμαῖός

ABCDE HLPℵ a b c f g h k l m o 13

...απ' αυτου D.

ABCE HLPℵ a b c f g h k l m o 13

v = ch. i. 6 reff. w ch. xvi. 37 reff. x ch. xvi. 37 only †. y w. pres., ch. xvi. 21 reff. z here only. Num. xxii. 25. Wisd. v. 11 only. (-γοῦν, Matt. x. 17 al.) a = here (Heb. viii. 1) only. Levit. vi. 4. b - - here (Eph. ii. 12) only †. 3 Macc. iii. 21. c = and constr., Josh. xxiv. 32. w. ἐκ, ch. i. 18. w. διά, ch. viii. 20. Matt. x. 9. (Luke xxi. 19. 1 Thess. iv. 4 only.) d ch. v. 38 reff. e ver. 24. f Matt. x. 18. John vi. 51. viii. 16, 17. ch. iii. 24. g ch. xix. 34 reff.

13. 36 rel vss Thl Œc, but copt arm put it after ειπεν. (*If the words originally formed part of the text, it is very unlikely that they should have been omitted, while insertions of this kind are very common: but the manuscript evidence being so very strong, it seems best to insert the words in brackets.*) εξεστιν υμιν bef ανθρωπον . . . D [Syr æth : μαστ. bef υμ. H :] for εξεστιν, εστιν ℵ¹.

26. for ακουσας δε, τουτο ακ. D. εκατονταρχης ACDℵ¹ : txt BEHLPℵ³ 13. 36 rel Chr. add οτι ρωμαιον εαυτον λεγει D 137. rec απηγγειλεν bef τω χιλιαρχω (*alteration of order to avoid the ambiguity,* προσελθ. τω χ. *or* τω χ. απηγγ.), with HLP rel Thl-sif: txt ABCDEℵ a (c) h k m 13. 40 vulg [syrr æth] copt arm Chr_1 Thl-fin.—(ε)πηγ. D¹(Wtst, Kipl : txt D² [ανηγ. c]). om λεγων D c 137 syr : D syr-w-ast ins αυτω in place of λεγων. rec ins ορα bef τι (*interpolated appy to give precision, and break the abruptness of the text*), with DHLP rel æth Chr_1 : om ABCEℵ 13. 36. 40 vulg syrr copt arm. om γαρ D¹(ins D²(?)) æth.

27. τοτε προσελθ. ο χ. επηρωτησεν αυτον D. from ελθων δε to ευθεως ο ver 29 has been re-written by B¹. for αυτω, τω παυλω L. om μοι ℵ¹. rec ins ει bef συ (*interpolated, to make the interrogation plainer*), with LP rel [vulg-clem] demid Chr_1 : om ABCDEHℵ a c f m 13. 36 am fuld tol syrr copt arm Amm-c. for εφη ναι, ειπεν ειμι D.

28. rec aft απεκ. ins τε, with HP rel vulg [Syr (æth)] Thl : δε BCEℵ a c k 13. 36 syr copt : om AL 40 arm Chr_1 : και αποκριθεις ο χ. (και) ειπεν (αυτω) D(και erased, αυτω added by D²(?)). for πολλου, οιδα ποσου D and "alia editio" mentd by Bede. (*Remarkable, and possibly original,* πολλου *being a gloss : but if so, the genuine reading has been now overborne by the intruder.*) om την C. παυλος δε εφη D : om H. om 2nd δε Cℵ¹ 42. 96. 142 Thl-sif : om δε και copt. γεγενημαι A D-corr e m¹ 13.

29. for ευθεως ουν, τοτε D [(æth)]. om δε ℵ¹. ins πολιτης bef ρωμαιος E vulg.

μάστιξιν be varied? and can it be shewn (as Dr. B. asks) that the word in the plural will bear this meaning? **ἑκατόνταρχον**] The 'centurio supplicio præpositus' of Tacitus and Seneca,—standing by to superintend the punishment. **εἰ ἄνθ. κ.τ.λ.**] See ch. xvi. 37, note.

28.] Dio Cassius, lx. 17, mentions that, in the reign of Claudius, Messalina used to sell the freedom of the city, and at very various prices at different times: ἡ πολιτεία μεγάλων τὸ πρῶτον χρημάτων πραθεῖσα, ἔπειθ' οὕτως ὑπὸ τῆς εὐχερείας ἐπευωνήθη, ὥστε καὶ λογοποιηθῆναι ὅτι κἂν ὑάλινά τις σκεύη συντετριμμένα δῷ τινί, πολίτης ἔσται. **ἐγὼ δὲ καὶ γεγ.**] **But I** (besides having the privilege like thee of being a Roman citizen) **was also born one.** *How was Paul a Roman citizen by birth?* Certainly not because he was of Tarsus: for (1) that city had no such privilege, but was only an 'urbs libera,' not a Colonia nor a Municipium: and (2) if this had been so, the mention of his being a man of Tarsus (ch. xxi. 39) would have of itself prevented his being scourged. It remains, therefore, that his father or some ancestor must have obtained the civitas, either as a reward for service ('urbes, merita erga P. R. allegantes, ... civitate donavit,' Suet. Aug. 47) or by purchase. It has been suggested that the father of Saul may have been sold into slavery at Rome, when Cassius laid a heavy fine on the city [of Tarsus] for having espoused the cause of Octavius and Antony, Appian, B. C. iv. 64, and very many of the Tarsians were sold to pay it. He may have acquired his freedom and the citizenship afterwards. See Mr. Lewin, i. p. 4. But

[h] ἔστιν καὶ ὅτι αὐτὸν [i] ἦν [i] δεδεκώς. 30 [j] τῇ δὲ [j] ἐπαύριον
βουλόμενος γνῶναι τὸ [k] ἀσφαλές, [l] τὸ τί [m] κατηγορεῖται
ὑπὸ τῶν Ἰουδαίων, ἔλυσεν αὐτὸν καὶ ἐκέλευσεν [n] συνελθεῖν τοὺς ἀρχιερεῖς καὶ πᾶν τὸ [o] συνέδριον, καὶ [p] κατ-
αγαγὼν τὸν Παῦλον [q] ἔστησεν εἰς αὐτούς. XXIII. 1 [r] ἀτενίσας δὲ ὁ Παῦλος τῷ [o] συνεδρίῳ εἶπεν Ἄνδρες ἀδελφοί,

h pres., ch. xvi. 38 reff. i ver. 19. constr., ch. i. 17. viii. 16. ix. 33. xii. 6. xviii. 25. (xxi. 33.) Gal. ii. 11. j ch. x. 9 reff. k = ch. xxi. 34 reff. l Luke i. 62. ix. 46. ch. iv. 21. Rom. viii. 26. m pass., Matt. xxvii. 12. ch. xxv. 16 only †. n = ch. i. 6 reff. o ch. iv. 15 reff. p ch. xxiii. 15 reff. q constr., here only. (see ch. vi. 6.) r w. dat., ch. iii. 12 reff. L.P. 2 Macc. x. 13.

rec ην bef αυτον, with HLP rel Chr$_1$ Thl-sif: txt ABCEℵ 13 Thl-fin. δεδωκως A^1 36-8. 73. 99. 101-6 Thl-sif: δεδηκως A^{2}C: δεδοικως 96^2. 105. add και παραχρημα ελυσεν αυτον 137 syr-w-ast. (*Henceforth in Acts*, D *being deficient, its readings may be approximated to by noticing those of its nearest cognates*, 137 and syr-w-ast.)

30. επιουση c 137. om το E. κατηγορειτο c 137. rec (for υπο) παρα, with HLP g [l] m Thl-sif: txt ABCEℵ 13. 36 rel 137 Chr$_1$ Thl-fin. ins πεμψας bef ελυσεν 137 syr-w-ast. rec aft αυτον ins απο των δεσμων (*supplementary gloss*), with HLP rel æth-pl Thl: om ABCEℵ a 13. 40 vulg syrr coptt æth[-rom] arm Chr. rec ελθειν (*see note:* or *the preceding* -σεν *perhaps, as Meyer, caused the omn of* συν-), with HLP rel Syr copt æth Thl-sif: εισελθειν 99. 137: συνεισελθειν c: txt ABCEℵ a b k m o 36. 40 vulg syr sah Chr Thl-fin. (13 def.) rec for παν, ολον (*see Mk* xiv. 55), with HLP rel Thl-sif: txt ABCEℵ a c h k m 13. 36. 137 Chr Thl-fin, απαν 40. (*omne* vulg, but so also in Mk xiv. 55 and Matt xxvi. 59.) rec aft συνεδριον ins αυτων (*gloss, referring to* ιουδαιων *above*), with HLP rel (Syr) Thl: om ABCEℵ a c k 13. 36. 40. 137 vulg syr coptt æth arm Chr. [om τον E.]

Chap. XXIII. 1. τω συνεδριω bef ο παυλος ACEℵ a 13 vulg Lucif$_1$: txt (B) HLP

this is mere conjecture. **29. καὶ . . . δέ]** moreover, 'more than that.' **ἐφοβ.]** There is no inconsistency (as De W.) in the tribune's being afraid because he had bound him, and then letting him remain thus bound. Meyer rightly explains it, that the tribune, having committed this error, is afraid of the possible consequences of it ('facinus est vinciri civem R., scelus verberari,' Cic. Verr. v. 66), and shews this by taking the first opportunity of either *undoing it*, or *justifying his further detention*, by *loosing him*, and *bringing him before the Sanhedrim.* His fear was on account of his *first false step;* but it was now too late to reverse it: and the same reason which leads him to continue it now, operates afterwards (ὁ δέσμιος Π., ch. xxiii. 18) when the hearing was delayed. That ἦν δεδεκώς cannot, as Bloomfield and Wordsworth suppose, refer only to the *binding before scourging*, its immediate juxtaposition with ἔλυσεν in the next verse sufficiently shews. Besides, the mere circumstance of a preparation for scourging having been begun in ignorance, and *left off as soon as the knowledge was received*, would rather have relieved, than occasioned, the fear of the tribune. A more cogent reason still is, that ἦν δεδεκώς can properly only apply to an action *still continuing* when the fear was felt: **that he had put him into custody.** 'The centurion believed Paul's word, because a false claim of this nature, being easily exposed, and punishable with death (Suet. Claud. 25), was almost an unprecedented thing.' Hackett. **30. τὸ τί]** The art. is epexegetical: see reff. It seems remarkable that the tribune in command should have had the power to summon the Sanhedrim: and I have not seen this remarked on by any Commentator. Some of the ancient correctors of the text, however, seem to have detected the difficulty, and to have altered συνελθεῖν into the vapid ἐλθεῖν in consequence. **καταγ.]** From Antonia to the council-room. According to tradition (see Biscoe, p. 147, notes), the Sanhedrim ceased to hold their sessions in the temple about twenty-six years before this period. Had they done so now, Lysias and his soldiers could not have been present, as no heathen was permitted to pass the sacred limits. Their present council-room was in the upper city, near the foot of the bridge leading across the ravine from the western cloister of the temple. Lewin, p. 672.

XXIII. 1.] **ἀτενίσας** seems to describe * that peculiar look, connected probably with infirmity of sight, with which Paul has already been described as regarding those before him: and may perhaps account for his not knowing that the person who spoke to him was the high priest, ver. 5. See ch. xiii. 9, note. The purport of Paul's asser-

s — (all possible) ch. xx. 19 reff.
t 1 Tim. i. 5, 19. 1 Pet. iii. 16, 21. (Heb. xiii. 18.)
u 2 Cor. i. 12 reff.
v Phil. i. 27 only +. μετὰ πάσης . . . ἀρετῆς ἐνθάδε πεπολίτευμαι, Jos. Life, § 49 and § 2. τοῖς νόμοις πολιτεύεσθαι, 2 Macc. vi. 1. (-τευμα, Phil. iii. 20.)
x w. inf. pres., here only. Xen. Anab. ii. 3. 6. w. inf. aor., Mark vi. 39. Luke viii. 31 al. Esth. i. 8.
y = Mark xiv. 47, 69, 70. Luke xix. 24. John xviii. 22. xix. 26.
z = ch. xiii. 34 reff.
a here only. Exod. xxx. 3 al. (see Eph. ii. 14.)
b Matt. xxiii. 27 only. Deut. xxvii. 2, 4. Prov. xxi. 9 only.
c = Matt. xxii. 44 (from Ps. cix. 1). xxvii. 19. Rev. iv. 2, &c.
d here only. Ps. cxviii. 51. Xen. Mem. iv. 4, 21. (-ία, 2 Pet. ii. 16. -ος, Prov. ii. 22.)
e w. acc., John ix. 28 only. Deut. xxxiii. 8. pass., 1 Cor. iv. 12. 1 Pet. ii. 23 only. (-ία, 1 Tim. v. 14. 1 Pet. iii. 9. -ος, 1 Cor. v. 11. vi. 10.)

ἐγὼ [s] πάσῃ [tu] συνειδήσει [t] ἀγαθῇ [v] πεπολίτευμαι τῷ θεῷ ἄχρι
ταύτης τῆς ἡμέρας. 2 ὁ δὲ ἀρχιερεὺς Ἀνανίας [x] ἐπέταξεν
τοῖς [y] παρεστῶσιν αὐτῷ τύπτειν αὐτοῦ τὸ στόμα. 3 τότε
ὁ Παῦλος πρὸς αὐτὸν εἶπεν Τύπτειν σε [z] μέλλει ὁ θεός,
[a] τοῖχε [b] κεκονιαμένε· καὶ σὺ [c] κάθῃ κρίνων με κατὰ τὸν
νόμον, καὶ [d] παρανομῶν κελεύεις με τύπτεσθαι; 4 οἱ δὲ
[y] παρεστῶτες εἶπον Τὸν ἀρχιερέα τοῦ θεοῦ [e] λοιδορεῖς;

ABCE HLPℵ a b c f g h k l m o 13

rel 36 [syrr coptt æth arm] Chr_2.—om ὁ B c 40. 137 Chr_2. της ημερας bef ταυτης c m 13. 137 [syr].

2. for επεταξεν, εκελευσεν C a 36. τ. παρεστ. αυτω bef επεταξεν c 137: om αυτω ℵ[1].

3. προς αυτον bef ο παυλος ℵ: ειπεν bef προς αυτον C vulg(not am fuld tol) [Syr coptt æth]: om πρ. αυτ. 100. [13 def.] κεκονιασμενε C[1] $Orig_1$. for παρανομων, παρα τον νομον E vulg [arm] Lucif.

4. ειπαν Bℵ [13].

tion seems to be this: being charged with neglecting, and teaching others to neglect the law of Moses, he at once endeavours to disarm those who thus accused him, by asserting that up to that day *he had lived a true and loyal Jew*,—obeying, according to his conscience, the law of that divine πολιτεία of which he was a covenant member. Thus πεπολίτευμαι τῷ θεῷ will have its full and proper meaning: and the words are no vain-glorious ones, but an important assertion of his innocence. **2. Ἀνανίας**] He was at this time the *actual high priest* (ver. 4). He was the son of Nebedæus (Jos. Antt. xx. 5. 2),—succeeded Joseph son of Camydus, Antt. xx. 1. 3; 5. 2,—and preceded Ismael, son of Phabi (Antt. xx. 8. 8, 11). He was nominated to the office by Herod, king of Chalcis, in A.D. 48 (Antt. xx. 5. 2); and sent to Rome by Quadratus, the prefect of Syria, to give an account to the emperor Claudius (Antt. xx. 6. 2): he appears, however, not to have lost his office, but to have resumed it on his return. This has been regarded as not certain,—and the uncertainty has produced much confusion in the Pauline chronology. But as Wieseler has shewn (Chronol. d. Apostelgeschichte, p. 76, note), there can be no reasonable doubt that it was so, especially as Ananias came off victorious in the cause for which he went to Rome, viz. a quarrel with the Jewish procurator Cumanus,—who went with him, and was condemned to banishment (Antt. xx. 6. 3). He was deposed from his office not long before the departure of Felix (Antt. xx. 8. 8), but still had great power, which he used violently and lawlessly (ib. 9. 2): he was assassinated by the sicarii [see ch. xxi. 38, note] at last (B. J. ii. 17, 9). **3.**] It is perfectly allowable (even if the fervid rebuke of Paul be considered exempt from blame) to contrast with his conduct and reply that of Him Who, when similarly smitten, answered with perfect and superhuman meekness, John xviii. 22, 23. Our blessed Saviour is to us, in all His words and acts, the *perfect pattern for all under all circumstances:* by aiming at whatever He did in each case, we shall do best: but even the greatest of his Apostles are *so far* our patterns only, as they *followed Him*, which certainly in this case Paul *did not.* That Paul thus answered, might go far to *excuse* a like fervent reply in a Christian or a minister of the gospel,—but must never be used to *justify* it: it may serve for an *apology*, but never for an *example.* **τύπτειν σε μέλλει κ.τ.λ.**] Some have seen a prophetic import in these words;—see above on the death of Ananias. But I would rather take them as an expression founded on a conviction that God's just retribution would come on unjust and brutal acts. **τοῖχε κεκον.**] Lightfoot's interpretation, "quod (Ananias) colorem tantum gestaret pontificatus, cum res ipsa evanuerit," is founded on the hypothesis (*for it is none other*) that the high priesthood was vacant at this time, and Ananias had thrust himself into it. The meaning is as in ref. Matt.; and in all probability Paul referred in thought to our Lord's saying. **κάθῃ κρίνων με**] This must not be taken as favouring the common interpretation of ver. 5 (see below): for the *whole*

5 ἔφη τε ὁ Παῦλος Οὐκ ᾔδειν, ἀδελφοί, ὅτι [f] ἐστὶν ἀρχ-
ιερεύς· γέγραπται γὰρ [ὅτι] [g] Ἄρχοντα τοῦ λαοῦ σου οὐκ
[h] ἐρεῖς [h] κακῶς. 6 γνοὺς δὲ ὁ Παῦλος ὅτι τὸ ἓν μέρος [f] ἐστὶν

f pres., ch. xvi. 38 reff.
g Exod. xxii. 28.
h here only. Exod. l. c. Lev. xix. 14. Isa. viii. 21 only. so καλῶς εἰπεῖν, w. acc., Luke vi. 26.

5. rec om 2nd *οτι*, with CEHLP rel 36 Chr_1 Thl-sif Œc : ins ABℵ k 13 Thl-fin.

Sanhedrim were the judges, and sitting to judge him according to the law. **4.**] Hence we see that not only by the Jews, but by the tribune, who was present, Ananias was regarded as the veritable high * priest. **5.**] (1) The ordinary interpretation of these words since Lightfoot, adopted by Michaelis, Eichhorn, Kuinoel, and others, is, that Ananias *had usurped the office during a vacancy*, and therefore was not recognized by Paul. They regard his being sent to Rome as a virtual setting aside from being high priest, and suppose that Jonathan, who was murdered by order of Felix (Antt. xx. 8. 5), was appointed high priest in his absence. But (α) there is no ground whatever for believing that his office was vacated. He won the cause for which he went to Rome, and returned to Jerusalem: it was only when a high priest was detained as hostage in Rome, that we read of another being appointed in his room (Antt. xx. 8. 11): and (β) which is fatal to the hypothesis, *Jonathan himself* (ὁ ἀρχιερεύς) *was sent to Rome with Ananias* (B. J. ii. 12. 6, τοὺς ἀρχιερεῖς Ἰωνάθην καὶ Ἀνανίαν . . . . ἀνέπεμψεν ἐπὶ Καίσαρα). Jonathan was called by the title merely as having been previously high priest. He succeeded Caiaphas, Antt. xviii. 4. 3: and he was not high priest again afterwards, having expressly declined to resume the office, Antt. xix. 6. 4. Nor can *any other Jonathan* have been elevated to it,—for Josephus gives, *in every case*, the elevation of a new high priest, and his whole number of twenty-eight from Herod the Great to the destruction of Jerusalem (Antt. xx. 10. 5) agrees with the notices thus given. (See Wieseler, Chron. Synops. der 4 Evv. p. 187, note: and Biscoe, pp. 48 ff.) So that this interpretation is untenable. (2) Chrys. and most of the ancient Commentators supposed that Paul, having been long absent, was really *unacquainted with the person* of the high priest. But this can hardly have been: and even if it were, the position and official seat would have pointed out to one, who had been himself a member of the Sanhedrim, the president of the council. (3) Calvin, Camerar., al., take the words *ironically*: '*I could not be supposed to know that one who conducted himself so cruelly and illegally, could be the high priest.*' This surely needs no refutation, as being altogether out of place and character. (4) Bengel, Wetst., Kuinoel, Olsh., Neander, al., understand the words as an acknowledgment of rash and insubordinate language, and render οὐκ ᾔδειν, '*I did not give it a thought*,' '*I forgot*:' and so Wordsworth. But as Meyer remarks, '*reputare*' is never the meaning of εἰδέναι; and were any pregnant or unusual sense intended, the context (as at 1 Thess. v. 12) would suggest it. (5) On the whole then, I believe that the only rendering open to us, consistently with the simple meaning of the words, and the facts of history is, **I did not know that it** (or **he**) **was the high priest**: and that it is probable that the solution of his ignorance lies in the fact of his *imperfect sight*—he heard the insolent order given, but knew not from whom it proceeded. I own that I am not entirely satisfied with this, as being founded perhaps on too slight premises: but as far as I can see there is no *positive* objection to it, which there is to every other. The objection stated by Wordsworth, "If St. Paul could not discern that Ananias was high priest, how could he see that he sat there as his judge?" would of course be easily answered by supposing that Paul who had himself been a member of the Sanhedrim may have known Ananias by his voice: or indeed may not (as above) have known him at all personally. It is hardly worth while to notice the rendering given by some, 'I knew not that *there was a high priest*.' Had any such meaning been intended, it would have been further specified by the construction. Besides which, it renders Paul's apology irrelevant, by eliminating from it the person who is necessarily its subject. **γέγραπται γάρ**] Implying in this, '*and the law is the rule of my life*.' Even in this we see the consummate skill of Paul. **6.**] Surely no defence of Paul for adopting this course is required, but all admiration is due to his skill and presence of mind. Nor need we hesitate to regard such skill as the fulfilment of the promise, that in such an hour, the Spirit of wisdom should suggest words to the accused, which the accuser should not be able to gainsay. All prospect of a fair trial was hopeless: he well knew from past and present experience, that personal odium would bias his judges, and violence prevail over justice: he therefore (Neand.)

Σαδδουκαίων, τὸ δὲ ἕτερον Φαρισαίων, ἔκραζεν ἐν τῷ ⁱ συνεδρίῳ Ἄνδρες ἀδελφοί, ἐγὼ Φαρισαῖός εἰμι, υἱὸς Φαρισαίων·
περὶ ᵏ ἐλπίδος καὶ ˡ ἀναστάσεως ˡ νεκρῶν ἐγὼ ᵐ κρίνομαι.
7 τοῦτο δὲ αὐτοῦ λαλήσαντος ἐγένετο ⁿ στάσις τῶν Φαρισαίων καὶ Σαδδουκαίων, καὶ ᵒ ἐσχίσθη τὸ ᵖ πλῆθος· 8 Σαδδουκαῖοι μὲν γὰρ λέγουσιν μὴ εἶναι ᵠ ἀνάστασιν μήτε ἄγγελον μήτε ʳ πνεῦμα, Φαρισαῖοι δὲ ˢ ὁμολογοῦσιν τὰ ἀμφό-
τερα· 9 ἐγένετο δὲ ᵗᵘ κραυγὴ ᵗ μεγάλη. καὶ ᵛ ἀναστάντες
τινὲς τῶν γραμματέων τοῦ ʷ μέρους τῶν Φαρισαίων ˣ διεμά-
χοντο λέγοντες Οὐδὲν κακὸν ʸ εὑρίσκομεν ἐν τῷ ἀνθρώπῳ
τούτῳ· ᶻ εἰ δὲ ʳ πνεῦμα ἐλάλησεν αὐτῷ ἢ ἄγγελος;

ABCE HLPℵ a b c f g h k l m o 13

p ουδεν.. ... ABCE HLPℵ a b c f g h k l m o p 13

i ch. xxii. 30. k = here only. see Ps. xv. 9. l 1 Cor. xv. 12 reff. m = ch. xxiv. 21. xxvi. 6. Ps. cviii. 7. n = ch. xv. 2 (reff.). o ch. xiv. 4. 1 Macc. vi. 45. p absol., ch. ii. 6 reff. q absol., ch. xvii. 18 reff. r = Luke xxiv. 37, 39. Heb. i. 14. 3 Kings xxii. 21. s = John xii. 42. Rom. x. 9, 10. 1 Tim. vi. 12.
t Luke i. 42. Rev. xiv. 18 only. Neh. v. 1. u as above (t). Matt. xxv. 6. Eph. iv. 31. Heb. v. 7. Rev. xxi. 4 only. v = ch. i. 15. xv. 7 al. 2 Chron. xx. 5. w ver. 6. x here only. 2 Kings xiv. 6 (compl.). Sir. viii. 1, 3. xxxviii. 28. li. 19 Ed-vat. &c. (not ABℵ) only. y = Luke xxiii. 14. Mal. i. 6. z = Rom. ix. 22.

6. [aft ετερον ins των L.] rec εκραξεν, with AEHLP rel vulg [syr coptt æth arm] Chr$_1$: txt BCℵ 36 [Syr]. rec (for 2nd φαρισαιων) φαρισαιου (*corrn, the relation being conceived to be that of a son to his father* only), with EHLP rel [coptt æth arm] Chr: txt ABCℵ 13. 36. 40 vulg Syr syr(sic) Tert$_1$. om 2nd εγω B copt [sah Tert$_1$. (C^1 doubtful.)]

7. for λαλησαντος, ειποντος AEℵ^3 a b k o 13. 40 Thl-fin: ειπαντος ℵ^1: λαλουντος B(sic: see table) 66^1. 100: txt CHL[P] rel 36 Chr$_1$ Thl-sif. for εγενετο, επεπεσεν B^1; επεσεν B-corr$^{1\cdot2}$(appy) [c] syr. rec ins των bef σαδ. (*insn for uniformity*), with HL rel 36: om ABC b k m o Thl-sif.—των σαδδ. και φαρ. Eℵ c g m [13] syr Chr Thl-fin.—om και σαδδ. (*homœotel*) P 78. 101-4. **διεσχισθη** E.

8. σαδδουκαι(sic) ℵ^1. om μεν B o vulg E-lat sah: ins AC E-gr HLPℵ rel 36 syr copt [arm] Chr. rec for 1st μητε, μηδε (*corrn, see note*), with HLP rel Chr Thl-sif: txt ABCEℵ a c h k l 13. 36. 40 Thl-fin.

9. rec (for τινες των γραμματεων) οι γραμματεις, with rel Thl-sif: γραμματεις HLP f æth: τινες (and om του μερους) AE 13 vulg copt: τινες γραμματεις k 21^2 Syr: τινες των (φαρισαιων) γραμματεων m: txt B(C)ℵ a c 13. 36. 40 syr sah arm Chr$_1$ Thl-fin.—*quidam scribarum et pars pharisæorum* sah: *scribæ et pharisæi* æth: for μερους, γενους 99. 105: ins εκ bef τ. γραμμ. C. aft διεμαχοντο ins προς αλληλους ℵ. om εν ℵ^1 137. rec aft αγγελος ins μη θεομαχωμεν (*interpoln from ch* v.

uses, in the cause of Truth, the maxim so often perverted to the cause of falsehood, 'divide et impera.' In *one tenet* above all others, did the religion of Jesus Christ and the belief of the Pharisees coincide that of *the resurrection of the dead*. That *they* looked for this resurrection by right of being the seed of Abraham, and denied it to all others,—whereas *he* looked for it through Jesus whom they hated, in whom *all* should be made alive who had died in Adam,—this was *nothing to the present point:* the belief was common—in the truest sense it was the *hope of Israel*—in the truest sense does Paul use and bring it forward to confound the adversaries of Christ. At the same time (De W.) by this strong assertion of his Pharisaic standing and extraction, he was further still vindicating himself from the charge against him. So also ch. xxvi. 7. **υἱ. Φαρισαίων**] **A son of Pharisees**, i. e. *A Pharisee of Pharisees*,'—'by descent from father, grandfather, and upwards, a pure Pharisee.' This meaning not having been apprehended, the -ων was altered into -ου. **ἐλπ. κ. ἀναστ.**] **the hope and the resurrection of the dead.** The art. is omitted after the prep., see Midd. ch. vi. § 1. **8.**] See note, Matt. iii. 7, for both Pharisees and Sadducees: and for an account of the doctrine of the latter, Jos. Antt. xviii. 1. 4; B. J. ii. 8. 14. In the latter place he says, ψυχῆς τὴν διαμονήν, καὶ τὰς καθ' ᾅδου τιμωρίας καὶ τιμὰς ἀναιροῦσι. The former μήτε has been altered to μηδέ to suit τὰ ἀμφότερα, because with ἀναστ. **μήτε ἄγγ.** μήτε πν. *three* things are mentioned (and thus we have *hæc omnia* as a var.): whereas, if μηδέ is read, the two last are coupled, and form *only one*. But τὰ ἀμφ. is used of *both things*, the one being the *resurrection*, the other the *doctrine of spiritual existences:* the two specified classes of the latter being combined generically.—τὰ ἀμφ., **them both,—both of them,—the two. 9.**] The sentence is an apo-

d ο κυ-ριος... ABCE HLPℵ a b c d f g h k l m o p 13

10 πολλῆς δὲ γενομένης [a] στάσεως, * φοβηθεὶς ὁ χιλίαρχος
μὴ [b] διασπασθῇ ὁ Παῦλος ὑπ᾽ αὐτῶν, ἐκέλευσεν τὸ [c] στράτευμα [d] καταβὰν [e] ἁρπάσαι αὐτὸν [f] ἐκ μέσου αὐτῶν ἄγειν
τε εἰς τὴν [g] παρεμβολήν. 11 τῇ δὲ [h] ἐπιούσῃ νυκτὶ
[i] ἐπιστὰς αὐτῷ ὁ κύριος εἶπεν Θάρσει· ὡς γὰρ [k] διεμαρ-
τύρω [l] τὰ [l] περὶ ἐμοῦ [m] εἰς Ἱερουσαλήμ, οὕτως σε [n] δεῖ καὶ
[m] εἰς Ῥώμην μαρτυρῆσαι. 12 [o] γενομένης δὲ [o] ἡμέρας ποιήσαντες [p] συστροφὴν οἱ Ἰουδαῖοι [q] ἀνεθεμάτισαν ἑαυτούς,
λέγοντες μήτε [r] φαγεῖν μήτε [r] πιεῖν ἕως οὗ ἀποκτείνωσιν τὸν
Παῦλον. 13 ἦσαν δὲ πλειους τεσσεράκοντα οἱ ταύτην τὴν

a ver. 7.
b Mark v. 4 only. Jer. ii. 20.
c = Luke xxiii. 11. ver. 27 (Matt. xxii. 7. Rev. ix. 16. xix. 14, 19 bis) only †. 1 Macc. ix. 34.
d = ch. xx. 10 reff.
e = John vi. 15. ch. viii. 39. Judg. xxi. 21.
f ch. xvii. 33 reff.
g ch. xxi. 34, 37 reff.
h ch. vii. 26 (xvi. 11 reff.).
i = ch. iv. 1 reff.
k ch. viii. 25 reff. w. acc. ch. xviii. 5. xx. 21, 24. xxviii. 23. Exod. xviii. 20.
l ver. 15. ch. xxviii. 31. Sir. xix. 30.
m = ch. xix. 22 reff.
n ch. iv. 12 reff.
o ch. xii. 18 reff.
p ch. xix. 40 reff. 4 Kings xv. 15.
q here, &c. 3ce. Mark xiv. 71 only. Num. xxi. 2.
r ch. ix. 9. Tobit vii. 11 ℵ.

39), with C[3]HLP rel 36 sah; *quid est in hoc?* Syr: om ABC[1]Eℵ 13. 40 vulg syr copt æth arm, also (from their explanations) Amm$_1$ Chr$_1$ Isid$_1$.

10. στασεως bef γενομενης AC vulg: txt BEHLPℵ p 13. 36 rel Chr$_1$.—[γινομ. B(γειν.) ℵ,] -μενος (but η is written above ο) ℵ[1]. * rec εὐλαβηθείς, with HLP rel Thl-sif: φοβηθεις ABCEℵ a c p 13. 36. 40. 137 arm Chr$_1$ Thl-fin Lucif. απ αυτων CE. καταβηναι και H[L]P rel 137 vulg syr sah Thl: txt ABCEℵ a f p 13. 36 Syr Chr. om εκ μεσου αυτων ℵ[1]. απαγειν (*corrn for particularity*) AE, *deducere* vulg: txt BCHLPℵ p 13. 36 rel. om τε B m copt.

11. rec aft θαρσει ins παυλε, with C[3]HLP p rel arm-zoh(1805) Thl Ambrst$_1$; aft ειπεν ins *Paulo* Syr æth, αυτω b o: om ABC[1]Eℵ [a] 13. 36. 40 vulg syr coptt arm[-mss] Chr$_1$ Lucif$_1$. διεμαρτυρου C.

12. for δε, τε B c syrr æth. rec τινες των ιουδαιων συστροφην (*corrn to suit ver* 13), with HLP rel vulg Syr sah Thl-sif Lucif: txt ABCEℵ (a) p 13. 36. 40. 137 syr copt æth arm Chr Thl-fin.—(L k m have συστροφην bef τινες; c 137 syr Chr Thl-fin, aft οι ιουδ.: a omits οι.) om λεγοντες Cℵ[3] a b c h o 40 syrr(ins syr-mg) arm Chr$_1$. πειν B(so ver 21). for αποκτεινωσιν, ανελωσιν A h 14. 38. 113 Chr.

siopesis, not requiring any filling up: answering to our Engl. **But what if a spirit** (genus) **or an angel** (species) **have spoken to him?** Perhaps in this they referred to the history of his conversion as told to the people, ch. xxii. On the recent criticism which sees in all this a purpose in the writer to compare Paul with Peter, see Prolegg. to Acts, § iii. 4. **10.**] The fact of all our best MSS. reading φοβηθεὶς here, and not the unusual word εὐλαβηθείς, must carry it into the text. It is one of those cases where, notwithstanding our strong suspicion that the later MSS. contain the true reading, we are bound to follow our existing authorities: no sufficient subjective reason being assigned for the correction either way. **διασπασθῇ**] to be taken *literally*, not as merely = '*should be killed*.' The Pharisees would strive to lay hold of him to rescue him: the Sadducees, to destroy him, or at all events to secure him. Between them both, there was danger of his being **pulled asunder by them.** **11.**] By these few words, the Lord assured him (1) of a *safe issue from his present troubles*; (2) of an *accomplishment of his intention of visiting Rome*; (3) of the certainty that however he might be sent thither, he should *preach the gospel, and bear testimony there.* So that they upheld and comforted him (1) in the *uncertainty of his life from the Jews*: (2) in the *uncertainty of his liberation from prison at Cæsarea*: (3) in the *uncertainty of his surviving the storm in the Mediterranean*: (4) in the *uncertainty of his fate on arriving at Rome.* So may one crumb of divine grace and help be multiplied to feed five thousand wants and anxieties. **εἰς**, see reff. and ch. ii. 39, —pregnant. **12.**] **οἱ Ἰουδ.** as opposed to Paul, the subject of the former verse. The copyists thought it unlikely that *all* the Jews were engaged in it, and so altered it to τινες τῶν Ἰουδ., and then transposed it for euphony. Wetstein and Lightf. adduce instances of similar conspiracies,—not to eat or drink till some object be gained. See 1 Sam. xiv. 24 ff.; and Jos. Antt. xv. 8.

[s] συνωμοσίαν ποιησάμενοι, 14 [t] οἵτινες [u] προσελθόντες τοῖς ABCE
ἀρχιερεῦσιν καὶ τοῖς πρεσβυτέροις εἶπαν [vw] Ἀναθέματι HLPℵ a bcdfg
[qw] ἀνεθεματίσαμεν [x] ἑαυτοὺς μηθενὸς [y] γεύσασθαι ἕως οὗ ἀπο- hklm op 13
κτείνωμεν τὸν Παῦλον. 15 [z] νῦν [z] οὖν ὑμεῖς [a] ἐμφανισατε
τῷ χιλιάρχῳ [b] σὺν τῷ [c] συνεδρίῳ, ὅπως [d] καταγάγῃ αὐτὸν
εἰς ὑμᾶς [e] ὡς μέλλοντας [f] διαγινώσκειν [g] ἀκριβέστερον
[h] τὰ περὶ αὐτοῦ· ἡμεῖς δὲ [i] πρὸ τοῦ [k] ἐγγίσαι αὐτὸν [l] ἕτοιμοί ἐσμεν τοῦ [m] ἀνελεῖν αὐτόν. 16 [n] ἀκούσας δὲ ὁ υἱὸς τῆς
ἀδελφῆς Παύλου τὴν [o] ἐνέδραν, [p] παραγενόμενος καὶ εἰςελθὼν εἰς τὴν [q] παρεμβολὴν ἀπήγγειλεν τῷ Παύλῳ.
17 προσκαλεσάμενος δὲ ὁ Παῦλος ἕνα τῶν ἑκατοντάρχων
ἔφη Τὸν [r] νεανίαν τοῦτον [s] ἀπάγαγε πρὸς τὸν χιλίαρχον·
[t] ἔχει γὰρ ἀπαγγεῖλαί τι αὐτῷ. 18 ὁ μὲν οὖν [u] παραλαβὼν
αὐτὸν ἤγαγεν πρὸς τὸν χιλίαρχον, και φησιν Ὁ [v] δέσμιος ...χι-λιαρ C.
Παῦλος προσκαλεσάμενός με [w] ἠρώτησεν τοῦτον τὸν ABEH
νεανίσκον ἀγαγεῖν πρός σε, [t] ἔχοντα τι λαλῆσαί σοι. LPℵ ab cdfgh klmo p 13

s here only. (-ότης, Gen. xiv. 13.) t = ch. x. 41 reff. u = ch. ix. 1 reff. v Rom. ix. 3 reff. w Deut. xiii. 15. x 2 Cor. iii. 1 reff. y = and constr., Luke xiv. 24. 1 Kings xiv. 24. z ch. x. 33 reff. a = ver. 22. ch. xxiv. 1. xxv. 2, 15. (Matt. xxvii. 53. John xiv. 21, 22.) Heb. (ix. 24.) xi. 14 only. Esth. ii. 22. b = 1 Cor. i. 2. 2 Cor. i. 1. Phil. i. 1. c ch. iv. 15 reff. d act., = Luke v. 11. ch. ix. 30. xxii. 30. vv. 20, 28. Rom. x. 6, L.P. 3 Kings i. 33. pass., ch. xxvii. 3. xxviii. 12. e = Luke xxiii. 14. ver. 20. ch. xxvii. 30. xxviii. 19. f ch. xxiv. 22 only. Num. xxxiii. 56. 2 Macc. ix. 15. (-γνωσις, ch. xxv. 21. -γνωρίζειν, Luke ii. 17.) g = ch. xviii. 26 reff. h ver. 11. i Luke xxii. 15. Gal. ii. 12 al. Gen. xiii. 10. k ch. xxi. 33 reff. l constr., here only. (Luke xxii. 33.) 1 Kings xiii. 21. m = ch. v. 33 reff. n constr., Matt. xi. 2. Luke xxi. 9 al. 3 Kings x. 1. o ch. xxv. 3 only. Josh. viii. 7. (-δρον, Josh. viii. 2. Wisd. xiv. 12 al. fr. in LXX. -δρεύειν, ver. 21.) p absol., ch. xvii. 10 reff. q ch. xxi. 34, 37 reff. r ch. xx. 9 reff. s = Luke xiii. 15. [ch. xxiv. 7.] 4 Kings xi. 4. t = Luke vii. 40, 42. ch. xxv. 26 al. u ch. xvi. 33 reff. v ch. xvi. 25, 27 reff. w ch. xvi. 39 reff.

13. rec πεποιηκοτες (*corrn appy to connect πεπ. ησαν as pluperf*), with HP rel Chr_1 Thl : ποιησαντες L e g 11. 27-9. 80. 126 : om o : txt ABCEℵ a [p] 13. 36. 40 Thl-fin.
14. (ειπαν, so ABCEP p.) rec μηδενος (*corrn to more usual form*), with BCEHPℵ rel 36 : txt AL k. (13 def.)
15. syr-mg (and simly sah $Lucif_1$) after *nunc igitur* has *rogamus vos ut hoc nobis faciatis, ut quum congregaveritis consessum, indicetis chiliarcho ut deducat eum ad nos.* rec aft οπως ins αυριον (*interpoln from ver* 20), with HLP rel Thl : om ABCEℵ a p 13. 36 vulg syrr copt æth arm Chr_1 $Lucif_1$. rec αυτον bef καταγαγη, with HP rel Chr_1 : txt ABCELℵ a g h k m p 13. 40 vulg arm Chr-c_1 $Lucif_1$. rec (for εις) προς (*corrn to more usual*), with CHLP rel 36 Chr : txt ABEℵ p sah. ακριβεστερον bef διαγινωσκειν (C) c l m 40. 137 vulg [arm] $Lucif_1$. (γινωσκ. C.) om τα 137. om 2nd του Eℵ[1] a g. at end ins εαν δεη και αποθανειν 137 syr-mg.
16. elz το ενεδρον, with HLP rel Chr_1 Thl-sif : txt ABCEℵ a c k p 13. 36.—B[2] has τὴν ἔνεδραν(sic). παραγεναμενος B[1]. [for παρεμβ., συναγωγην A.]
17. for εφη, ειπεν [C] p 36. 180. απαγε Bℵ p. rec τι bef απαγγειλαι, with CHLPℵ rel 36 vulg [syrr æth arm] Chr : txt ABE k p 13.
18. rec νεανιαν (*from preceding verse*), with BHLP rel 36 : txt AEℵ a g p 13. 40. σοι is written over the line by B[1].

3, 4. 14.] It is understood from the narrative that it was to the *Sadducees*, among the chief priests and elders, that the murderers went. That the high priest belonged to this sect, cannot be inferred with any accuracy. 15.] **σὺν τῷ συνεδρ.** belongs to ὑμεῖς, or perhaps better to ἐμφανίσατε—**do you give official intimation** (intimation conveyed by the whole Sanhedrim). **ὅπως** expresses the *purpose* of ἐμφαν.,—**τοῦ ἀν. αὐτ.**, that of ἕτοιμοί ἐσμ. (Meyer). **διαγιν. ἀκρ.**] not as E. V. '*enquire something more perfectly*:'—but (see reff.) **to determine with greater accuracy**, or perhaps, neglecting the comparative sense, **to determine accurately.** 16.] It is quite uncertain whether Paul's sister's son lived in Jerusalem, or had accompanied him thither. The ἡμᾶς of ch. xx. 5, will include more than merely Luke. But from this knowledge of the plot, which presupposes other acquaintances than he would have been likely to make if he had come with Paul, I should suppose him to have been domiciled at Jerusalem, possibly under instruction, as was formerly Paul himself, and thus likely, in the schools, to have heard

19 ˣ ἐπιλαβόμενος δὲ τῆς ˣ χειρὸς αὐτοῦ ὁ χιλίαρχος καὶ
ʸ ἀναχωρήσας ᶻ κατ' ἰδίαν ᵃ ἐπυνθάνετο Τί ἐστιν ὃ ᵗ ἔχεις
ἀπαγγεῖλαί μοι; 20 εἶπεν δὲ ὅτι οἱ Ἰουδαῖοι ᵇ συνέθεντο
ᶜ τοῦ ᵈ ἐρωτῆσαί σε ᵈ ὅπως ᵉ αὔριον τὸν Παῦλον ᶠ κατ-
αγάγῃς εἰς τὸ ᵍ συνέδριον ʰ ὡς μέλλων τι ⁱ ἀκριβέστερον
ᵏ πυνθάνεσθαι περὶ αὐτοῦ. 21 σὺ οὖν μὴ ˡ πεισθῇς αὐτοῖς·
ᵐ ἐνεδρεύουσιν γὰρ αὐτὸν ἐξ αὐτῶν ἄνδρες πλείους τεσσεράκοντα, ⁿ οἵτινες ⁿ ἀνεθεμάτισαν ἑαυτοὺς μήτε ⁿ φαγεῖν
μήτε ⁿ πιεῖν ἕως οὗ ⁿ ἀνέλωσιν αὐτόν· καὶ νῦν εἰσιν ἕτοιμοι,
ᵒ προσδεχόμενοι τὴν ἀπὸ σοῦ ᵖ ἐπαγγελίαν. 22 ὁ μὲν οὖν
χιλίαρχος ᑫ ἀπέλυσεν τὸν νεανίσκον, ʳ παραγγείλας μηδενὶ
ˢ ἐκλαλῆσαι ὅτι ταῦτα ᵗ ἐνεφάνισας πρός ᵘ με. 23 καὶ
προσκαλεσάμενος δύο ᵛ τινὰς τῶν ἑκατοντάρχων εἶπεν
ʷ Ἑτοιμάσατε στρατιώτας διακοσίους, ὅπως πορευθῶσιν
ˣ ἕως Καισαρείας, καὶ ʸ ἱππεῖς ἑβδομήκοντα καὶ ᶻ δεξιολάβους διακοσίους, ᵃ ἀπὸ τρίτης ᵇ ὥρας τῆς ᵇ νυκτός, 24 ᶜ κτήνη
τε ᵈ παραστῆσαι, ἵνα ᵉ ἐπιβιβάσαντες τὸν Παῦλον ᶠ διασώ-

x Mark viii. 23. Zech. xiv. 13.
y Matt. ii. 12 al9. Mark iii. 7. John vi. 15. ch. xxvi. 31 only. 1 Kings xix. 10.
z Matt. xiv. 13, 23. xvii. 1 al. fr. 2 Macc. iv. 5 only.
a = ch. iv. 7. x. 29.
b Luke xxii. 5. John ix. 22 only. 1 Kings xxii. 13. Dan. ii. 9 Theod.
c constr., ch. iii. 12 reff.
d Luke vii. 3. xi. 37. see ver. 18.
e 1 Cor. xv. 32 reff.
f ver. 15 reff.
g ch. iv. 15 reff.
h = ver. 15 reff.
i = ch. xviii. 26 reff.
k w. περί, here only.
l = ch. v. 36, 37 reff.
m (trans.) Luke xi. 54 only. Deut. xix. 11. (-δρα, ver. 16. ch. xxv. 3.)
n see vv. 12—15.
o ch. xxiv. 15 reff.
p ch. i. 4 reff.
q = ch. xiii. 3 reff.
r ch. xvi. 18 reff.
s here only †. Judith xi. 9 only. τίς ὁ ἐκλαλήσας; Demosth. περὶ τ. παραπρ., p. 354. 23.
t ver. 15 reff.
w. πρός, here only. Wisd. xvi. 21.
u constr., ch. i. 4. xvii. 3 al.
v = Luke vii. 19 L.
w and constr., Rev. viii. 6. (ix. 15.)
x ch. xvii. 15.
y ver. 32 only. Gen. l. 9.
z here only †.
a = Matt. xxvii. 45.
b ch. xvi. 33.
c 1 Cor. xv. 39 reff.
d constr., here only. see Col. i. 22.
e Luke x. 34. xix. 35 only. 2 Kings vi. 3. see Matt. xxi. 5.
f = ch. xxvii. (43)-44. xxviii. 1, 4 (Matt. xiv. 36. Luke vii. 3. 1 Pet. iii. 20). w. εἰς, Gen. xix. 19. Jos. Antt. xii. 4. 9, end.

19. επιλαβομενου(sic) ℵ¹. επυνθανετο bef κατ ιδιαν A.
20. συνεθοντο H¹. rec εις το συνεδριον καταγ. τον παυλον, with HP rel Thl-fin Œc: καταγαγης bef τον παυλον L c [(k)] 137 [vulg-clem] syrr coptt [(æth)] (*perhaps transpositions to avoid* αυριον τον παυλον): om τον παυλον (*homœotel*) 40: txt ABEℵ a m p 13 am(and demid fuld tol) [arm] Chr. rec μελλοντες (*corrn to suit ver* 15), with b² c d l [vulg syrr sah arm] Thl-fin: μελλοντα HLP a m Thl-sif: μελλοντων ℵ³ f g k 36. 137 Chr: txt ABE o p 40 copt æth, μελλον ℵ¹ b¹ 13. ins τι bef περι H¹(τα H²).
21. rec ετοιμοι bef εισιν, with HLP rel 36 vulg Chr₁: txt ABEℵ a m p 13. 40 Thl-fin.
22. rec νεανιαν (*ver* 17), with HLP p rel 36 Chr₁: txt ABEℵ a 13. 40. εμε Bℵ.
23. τινας bef δυο Bℵ p 13: om τινας 73 [not exprd in vulg Syr (coptt ?) arm]. for εβδομηκοντα, εκατον 137 syr-mg sah æth-rom. δεξιοβολους A (ms mentd by Erasm): *jaculantes dextra* Syr: *lancearios* vulg sah æth: *jaculatores* copt.
24. [om τε H(Treg, expr).] aft παυλον ins νυκτος 137 syr-mg. διασωσι B¹[H]

the scheme spoken of. **21. (τὴν) ἐπαγγελίαν]** not, '*an order*' (as Rosenm., al.), nor '*a message*' (as Grot., Beza, Wolf, al.): but the [not *a*, as E. V.] **promise** (to that effect): as constantly in N. T.

22.] ὅτι . . . με, a variation of person, as in reff. **23. δύο τινάς] some two:** see reff., and Winer, edn. 6, § 25. 2. *b*.

στρατιώτας, the ordinary heavy-armed legionary soldiers: distinguished below from the ἱππεῖς and δεξιολάβοι.

* **δεξιολάβους]** This word has never been satisfactorily explained. Suidas, Phavorinus, Beza, Kuin., al., explain it παραφύλακες:—Meursius, in his Glossarium Græcobarbarum,—a kind of *military lictors*, παρὰ τὸ λαβεῖν τὴν τοῦ δεσμίου δεξιάν;—the Vulgate, *lancearios* (*spearmen*, E. V.):—Meyer, a sort of light-armed troops, *rorarii* or *velites*,—either *jaculatores* or *funditores*. He quotes a passage from Constantine Porphyrogenitus (οἱ δὲ λεγόμενοι τουρμάρχαι εἰς ὑπουργίαν τῶν στρατηγῶν ἐτάχθησαν. σημαίνει δὲ τοιοῦτον ἀξίωμα τὸν ἔχοντα ὑφ' ἑαυτὸν στρατιώτας τοξοφόρους πεντακοσίους, καὶ πελταστὰς τριακοσίους, καὶ δεξιολάβους ἑκατόν) where they are distinguished from bowmen and peltastæ,—and derives the name from *grasping the weapon with the right hand*, which the peltastæ and bowmen could not be said to do. The reading of A, δεξιοβόλους (*jaculantes dextrâ* Syr.), is apparently a correction. **24. δια-**

g = here &c., 3ce. ch. xxiv. 1, 10. xxvi. 30. Matt. xxvii. 2, &c. Luke xx. 20. (Gen. xxxvi. 15 al.) Jos. Antt. xviii. 3. 1.
h ch. ix. 2 reff.
i = 1 Pet. ii. 6 (Luke v. 9) only. 2 Macc. xi. 16. ἡ μὲν ἐπιστολὴ τοῦτον περιεῖχε τὸν τρόπον, Jos. Antt. xii. 4. 11, beg.
k = (Rom. vi. 17). 3 Macc. iii. 30.

σωσιν πρὸς Φήλικα τὸν [g] ἡγεμόνα, 25 γράψας [h] ἐπιστολὴν
[[i] περι]έχουσαν τὸν [k] τύπον τοῦτον· 26 Κλαύδιος Λυσίας
τῷ [l] κρατίστῳ [g] ἡγεμόνι Φήλικι [m] χαίρειν. 27 τὸν ἄνδρα
τοῦτον [n] συλλημφθέντα ὑπὸ τῶν Ἰουδαίων καὶ μέλλοντα
[o] ἀναιρεῖσθαι ὑπ' αὐτῶν [p] ἐπιστὰς σὺν τῷ [q] στρατεύματι
[r] ἐξειλάμην [αὐτὸν] μαθὼν ὅτι Ῥωμαῖός ἐστιν. 28 βουλό-
μενός τε [s] ἐπιγνῶναι τὴν αἰτίαν δι' ἣν [t] ἐνεκάλουν
αὐτῷ, [u] κατήγαγον αὐτὸν εἰς τὸ [v] συνέδριον αὐτῶν· 29 ὃν
εὗρον [t] ἐγκαλούμενον περὶ [w] ζητημάτων τοῦ νόμου αὐτῶν,
μηδὲν δὲ [xy] ἄξιον [x] θανάτου ἢ [z] δεσμῶν [a] ἔχοντα [b] ἔγκλημα.

ABEH LPℵ a b c d f g h k l m o p13

l Luke i. 3. ch. xxiv. 3. xxvi. 25 only ‡. m ch. xv. 23 reff. n ch. i. 16 reff. o ver. 15. p = ch. iv. 1 reff. q ver. 10. r = ch. vii. 10 reff. s = Luke i. 4. ch. xxii. 24. 1 Cor. xiii. 12. Jer. v. 5. t ch. xix. 38 reff. u ver. 15 reff. v ch. iv. 15 reff. w ch. xv. 2 reff. plu., ch. xviii. 15. x Luke xxiii. 15. ch. xxv. 11, 25. xxvi. 31. Rom. i. 32 only. y = as above (x). Luke xii. 48. ch. xiii. 46 al. Deut. xxv. 2. z ch. xvi. 26 reff. xxvi. 29, 31 al. Ps. ii. 3. a = 1 Tim. v. 12. John ix. 41. xv. 22, 24. xix. 11. 1 John i. 8. b ch. xxv. 16 only †.

o: *διασωσουσιν* E m: *διασωσονται* 40. aft *ηγεμονα* add *εις καισαρειαν* 95^1. 137, so (aft *διασωσωσιν*) syr-w-ast. at end ins *εφοβηθη γαρ μηποτε αρπασαντες αυτον οι ιουδαιοι αποκτενωσι και αυτος μεταξυ εγκλημα εχη ως αργυριον ειληφως* 137 syr-w-ast, so also vulg-ed(not am demid fuld tol &c) and (aft *διασωσιν*) arm-usc(rejected by Zohrab).

25. rec *περιεχουσαν*, with AHLP rel 36 Chr_1, *περιεχουσα* f: om sah: *εχουσαν* BEℵ a c p 13. 137.

27. (*εξειλαμην*, so ABEℵ p 13.) om *αυτον* (*as superfluous in the constr*) ABEℵ a d p 13. 36 vulg [arm] Chr: ins HLP rel Thl.

28. rec (for *τε*) *δε*, with HLP rel E-lat syr copt [arm] Chr_1: *ουν* sah: txt AB E-gr ℵ 36 vulg Syr æth Thl. rec *γνωναι*, with EHLP rel Chr_1: txt A B(sic) ℵ a c k p 13. 36. 137 Chr-ms. om (*passing from αυτω to αυτων*) *κατηγαγον αυτον εις το συνεδριον αυτων* B^1(ins B^1-marg(see table)) p [om *εις το συν. αυτ.* ath-rom]. om *αυτον* Aℵ k 13. 137.

29. aft *αυτων* ins *μωυσεως και ιησου τινος* 137 syr-mg. om *δε* LP b g h o p 40. 137 Chr_1. rec *εγκλημα* bef *εχοντα*, with ELP rel [(Syr)] Chr: txt AB [H(Treg expr)] ℵ a b k l m o p 13. 40 vulg [syr arm] Thl-fin. at end ins *εξηγαγον αυτον μολις τη βια* 137 syr-w-ast(but *απηγ.*).

σώσωσιν] **escort safe the whole way.** **Φήλικα**] FELIX was a freedman of the Emperor Claudius: Suidas and Zonaras gave him the prænomen of *Claudius*, but Tacit. (Ann. xii. 54) calls him *Antonius* Felix, perhaps from Antonia, the mother of Claudius, as he was brother of Pallas, who was a freedman of Antonia (Tacit. ib. and Jos. Antt. xx. 7. 1). He was made sole procurator of Judæa after the deposition of Cumanus (having before been three years joint procurator with him, Tacit. ib.) principally by the influence of the high priest Jonathan (Antt. xx. 8. 5), whom he afterwards procured to be murdered (ibid.). Of his character Tacitus says, 'Antonius Felix per omnem sævitiam et libidinem jus regium servili ingenio exercuit,' Hist. v. 9. His procuratorship was one series of disturbances, false messiahs, sicarii and robbers, and civil contests, see Jos. Antt. xx. 8. 5, 6, and 7. He was eventually (A.D. 60) recalled, and accused by the Cæsarean Jews, but acquitted at the instance of his brother Pallas (Antt. xx. 8. 10). On his wife Drusilla, see note, ch. xxiv. 24. **25.**] [**περι**]**έχ.**, **τύπ.**, see reff. **26. κρατίστῳ**] See ref. Luke. This letter seems to be given (translated from the Latin) *as written*, not merely according to its general import (see the false statement in ver. 27): *from what source*, is impossible to say, but it may be imagined that the contents transpired through some officers at Jerusalem or at Cæsarea friendly to Paul. Such letters were called *elogia*: so Modestin. Dig. lib. 49, tit. 16, leg. 3 (Facciolati): 'Desertorem auditum ad suum ducem cum elogio præses mittet,' 'with an abstract of the articles brought against him.' **27. σὺν τῷ στρ.**] **with the troop**; see above ver. 10, and note, ch. xxi. 32. **ἐξειλ. μαθὼν ὅτι Ῥ. ἐστιν**] This was *an attempt to conceal the fault that he had committed*, see ch. xxii. 29. For this assertion cannot refer

30 ᶜ μηνυθείσης δέ μοι ᵈ ἐπιβουλῆς ᵉ εἰς τὸν ἄνδρα ἔσεσθαι,
ᶠ ἐξ αὐτῆς ἔπεμψα πρός σε, ᵍ παραγγείλας καὶ τοῖς
ʰ κατηγόροις λέγειν ⁱ τὰ ⁱ πρὸς αὐτὸν ᵏ ἐπὶ σοῦ. 31 Οἱ μὲν
οὖν στρατιῶται κατὰ τὸ ˡ διατεταγμένον αὐτοῖς ᵐ ἀναλαβόντες τὸν Παῦλον ἤγαγον ⁿ διὰ νυκτὸς εἰς τὴν Ἀντι-
πατρίδα, 32 ᵒ τῇ δὲ ᵒ ἐπαύριον ᵖ ἐάσαντες τοὺς ᵠ ἱππεῖς
ʳ ἀπέρχεσθαι σὺν αὐτῷ, ˢ ὑπέστρεψαν εἰς τὴν ᵗ παρεμ-
βολήν· 33 ᵘ οἵτινες εἰσελθόντες εἰς τὴν Καισάρειαν καὶ
ᵛ ἀναδόντες τὴν ʷ ἐπιστολὴν τῷ ˣ ἡγεμόνι, ʸ παρέστησαν
καὶ τὸν Παῦλον αὐτῷ. 34 ἀναγνοὺς δὲ καὶ ᶻ ἐπερωτή-
σας ᵃ ἐκ ᵇ ποίας ᶜ ἐπαρχίας ᵈ ἐστίν, καὶ πυθόμενος ὅτι
ᵃ ἀπὸ Κιλικίας, 35 ᵉ Διακούσομαί σου, ἔφη, ὅταν καὶ οἱ

c Luke xx. 37. John xi. 57. 1 Cor. x. 28 only +. 2 Macc. iii. 7. vi. 11. xiv. 37 only.
d ch. ix. 24 reff.
e = ch. ix. 1 reff.
f ch. x. 33 reff.
g ch. i. 4 reff.
h [John viii. 10 rec.] ver. 35. ch. [xxiv. 8.] xxv. 16, 18 only. Prov. xviii. 17. 2 Macc. iv. 5 only. (-ήγωρ, Rev. xii. 10.)
i ch. xxviii. 10 reff. see ver. 15.
k = Matt. xxviii. 14. ch. xxiv. 19. xxv. 9. xxvi. 2.

l Luke xvii. 9, 10. 1 Cor. vii. 17. L.P., exc. Matt. xi. 1. Judg. v. 9. m = ch. xx. 13, 14. 2 Tim. iv. 11 only. (ch. i. 2. vii. 43.) n ch. v. 19 reff. o ch. x. 9 reff. p = here (ch. xvi. 7 al.) only. q ver. 23. r = ch. v. 26 reff. s ch. viii. 25 reff. t ch. xxi. 34, 37 reff. u = ch. x. 41 reff. v here only +. Sir. i. 22 only. ἀνέδωκε τοῖς ἐφόροις τὰς ἐπιστολάς, Diod. Sic. xi. 45. w ch. ix. 2 reff. x vv. 24, 26. y = Matt. xxvi. 53. ch. ix. 41. (2 Cor. iv. 14.) Gen. xlvii. 2 Ald. z Matt. xii. 10 al. 1 Kings xvii. 56 A Ed-vat. &c. (B def.) a ch. ii. 5 reff. b = ch. iv. 7 reff. c ch. xxv. 1 only +. (-ος, Ezra v. 3.) d pres., ch. xvi. 38 reff. e here only. Deut. i. 16. Job ix. 33 BℵF(not A) &c. only.

30. rec ins μελλειν bef εσεσθαι (*see ch* xi. 28; xxiv. 15; xxvii. 10), with HLP rel syr Chr_1: om ABEℵ a p 13. 36. 40. 137 vulg æth. rec aft εσεσθαι ins υπο των ιουδαιων (*explanatory gloss*), with HLP rel Syr sah: om ABEℵ a c p 13. 36. 40. 137 vulg syr copt arm.—for εξ αυτης, εξ αυτων AEℵ a c p 13. 40 syr arm [Chr_1]: txt BHLP rel 36 Syr copt [sah] Thl.—επιβ. εσεσθαι εις τον ανδρα εξ αυτων επεμψα κ.τ.λ. 13: *et quum mihi perlatum esset de insidiis, quas paraverant illi, misi &c* vulg: aft εξ αυτης ins ουν L. aft τ. κατηγοροις ins αυτου E Syr coptt. for τα προς αυτον, αυτους Aℵ 13 vulg[*ut dicant:* not represented in] coptt [æth]: αυτου 40: om τα B E-lat Syr [arm]. om επι σου p: for επι, περι 67. 137. rec at end adds ερρωσο, with ELℵ p rel 36 [vulg-clem] demid tol syrr æth-pl (Chr[-montf]) Thl Œc; ερρωσθε (*see ch* xv. 29) HP 26. 78. 100-1 Chr(mss and ed[-morel]): om AB 13 am fuld coptt æth-rom.

31. [aft αυτοις ins εποιουν L.] rec ins της bef νυκτος, with HLP rel Thl-sif: om (*cf ch* v. 19; xvi. 9; xvii. 10) ABEℵ p 13. 40. 137 Chr_1 Thl-fin.

32. rec [for απερχ.] πορευεσθαι (*corrn for less usual exprn*), with HLP rel 36 syr Cyr_1 Thl, *ire* E-lat, *ut irent* vulg: txt AB E-gr ℵ e p 13, *abire* copt. επεστρεψαν ℵ.

33. τω ηγεμονι bef την επιστολην L m 40 [arm]. om και τον παυλον E: om τον 137.

34. rec aft αναγνους δε ins ο ηγεμων (*supplementary*), with HLP rel sah Thl: om ABEℵ p 13. 36. 40 vulg syrr copt æth arm Chr_1. aft κιλικιας ins εστιν A ℵ[1](but marked for erasure) 68. αναγνους δε την επιστολην επηρωτησε τον παυλον εκ ποιας επαρχιας ει και ειπεν κιλικιας και πυθομενος ειπεν ακουσομαι οταν κ.τ.λ. syr-mg: simly 137 ins την επιστολην [και επερωτησας], has ει for εστιν, and continues εφη κιλιξ κ. πυθ. εφη ακουσ. σου οταν κ.τ.λ.

to the *second* rescue, see next verse.

30.] Two constructions are combined here: (1) μηνυθείσης ἐπιβουλῆς τῆς ἐσομένης, and (2) μηνυθέντος, ἐπιβουλὴν ἔσεσθαι.

31.] Antipatris, forty-two Roman miles from Jerusalem, and twenty-six from Cæsarea, was built by Herod the Great, and called in honour of his father. It was before called Kapharsaba (Jos. Antt. xiii. 15. 1; xvi. 5. 2). In Jerome's time (Epitaph. Paulæ, 8, vol. i. p. 696) it was a 'semirutum oppidum' (Winer, Realw.). They might have well made so much way during the night and the next day,—for the text will admit of that interpretation,—τῇ ἐπαύρ. being not necessarily the morrow *after they left Jerusalem,* but *after they arrived at Antipatris.*

32. τοὺς ἱππεῖς] As they had now the lesser half of their journey before them, and that furthest removed from Jerusalem. The δεξιολάβοι appear to have gone back with the soldiers. **35. διακούσ.**] 'The expression is in conformity

f ver. 30 reff. g absol., ch. xvii. 10 reff. h John xviii. 28 || Mt. Mk., 33. xix. 9. Phil. i. 13 only +. i — ch. xii. 4 reff. k absol., ch. viii. 15 reff. l here only. m so ch. ix. 35. n ch. xxiii. 15 reff.

[f] κατήγοροί σου [g] παραγένωνται, κελεύσας ἐν τῷ [h] πραι- ABEH
τωρίῳ τοῦ Ἡρώδου [i] φυλάσσεσθαι αὐτόν. LPℵ a b
XXIV. 1 Μετὰ δὲ πέντε ἡμέρας [k] κατέβη ὁ ἀρχιερεὺς c d f g h
Ἀνανίας μετὰ πρεσβυτέρων τινῶν καὶ [l] ῥήτορος Τερτύλ- k l m o
λου τινός, [m] οἵτινες [no] ἐνεφάνισαν τῷ [p] ἡγεμόνι [o] κατὰ τοῦ p 13
Παύλου. 2 [q] κληθέντος δὲ αὐτοῦ ἤρξατο [r] κατηγορεῖν ὁ

o and constr., ch. xxv. 2. p ch. xxiii. 24 &c. reff. q -: ch. iv. 18. 2 Kings ix. 9. r ver. 19. ch. xxv. 16. xxviii. 19‡. 1 Macc. vii. 6.

35. om και 37. 101-37 vulg(not am demid) syrr copt æth Thl-sif. παραγινονται P: -γενονται f p[Scr]: -γονται HL [p(Treg)]. rec εκελευσε τε (*emendation of style*), with HLP 13. 36 rel [vulg Syr copt æth] Chr_1: κελευσαντος ℵ[1]: txt A B(sic: see table) [E]ℵ[3] c k p 40. 137 syr Thl-fin. for του, τω B: om HLP rel 137 Chr_1: txt AEℵ c h m p 13. rec αυτον bef εν τω πραιτωριω, with HLP rel 36 Chr: txt ABEℵ c k p 13. 40. 137 vulg [coptt] arm Thl-fin.

Chap. XXIV. 1. for πεντε, τινας A. rec (for πρεσβ. τινων) των πρεσβυτερων, with HLP rel Syr copt æth: txt ABEℵ c k m [p] 13. 36. 40. 137 vulg syr sah arm Thl. [ανεφ. k:] επεφαν[ησαν] P. 2. om αυτου B.

with the Roman law; the rule was, "Qui cum elogio mittuntur, *ex integro audiendi sunt*."' Hackett. **ἐν τῷ πραιτ. τ. Ἡρ.**] The procurator resided in the former palace of Herod the Great. Here Paul was 'militi traditus' (Digest. cited by De W.), not in a prison, but in the buildings attached to the palace.

Chap. XXIV. 1—XXVI. 32.] Paul's imprisonment at Cæsarea. **1. μετὰ πέντε ἡμ.**] After five days—or on the fifth day—from Paul's *departure for Cæsarea.* This would be the natural *terminus a quo* from which to date the proceedings of the High Priest, &c., who were *left* in Jerusalem. That it is so, appears from ver. 11. See note there. **πρεσβ. τινῶν**] The more ancient mss. reading this, all we can say is that we have not sufficient authority to retain the reading of the rec. τῶν πρεσβυτέρων, though it appears more likely to be original, and to have given offence as seeming to import that the *whole* Sanhedrim went down. This is one of the cases where, in the present state of our evidence, we are obliged to adopt readings which are not according to subjective canons of criticism. **ῥήτορος**] An *orator forensis* or *causidicus,* persons who abounded in Rome and the provinces; sometimes called συνήγοροι, or δικολόγοι. Kuin. says: 'Multi adolescentes Romani qui se foro dederant, cum magistratibus in provincias se conferebant, ut caussis provincialium agendis se exercerent, et majoribus in urbe actionibus præpararent.' So Cælius (see Cic. pro Cælio, c. 30), in Africa. **Τερτύλλου**] A diminutive from Tertius, as Lucullus from Lucius,—Catullus from Catius. The name occurs Plin. Ep. v. 15; and *Tertulla,* Suet. Aug. 69 (Wetst.). **ἐνεφάνισαν**] (not, '*appeared,*' ἑαυτούς, sub.;—see reff.) laid information; and, as it seems, not by writing, but by word of mouth, since they appeared in person, and Paul was called to confront them. **2.**] 'Inter præcepta rhetorica est, judicem laudando sibi benevolum reddere.' (Grot.) Certainly Tertullus fulfils and overacts the precept, for his exordium is full of the basest flattery. Contrast with πολλῆς εἰρ. τυγχ., Tac. Ann. xii. 54: 'Interim Felix intempestivis remediis delicta accendebat, æmulo ad deterrima Ventid. Cumano, cui pars provinciæ habebatur: ita divisis, ut huic Galilæorum natio, Felici Samaritæ parerent, discordes olim, et tum, contemptu regentium, minus coercitis odiis. Igitur *raptare inter se, immittere latronum globos, componere insidias, et aliquando prœliis congredi, spoliaque et prædas ad Procuratores referre;*'—Hist. v. 9, quoted above, on ch. xxiii. 24;—and Jos. Antt. xx. 8. 9, οἱ πρωτεύοντες τῶν τὴν Καισάρειαν κατοικούντων Ἰουδαίων εἰς τὴν Ῥώμην ἀναβαίνουσι, Φήλικος κατηγοροῦντες· καὶ πάντως ἂν ἐδεδώκει τιμωρίαν τῶν εἰς Ἰουδαίους ἀδικημάτων, εἰ μὴ πολλὰ αὐτὸν ὁ Νέρων τῷ ἀδελφῷ Πάλλαντι παρακαλέσαντι συνεχώρησε . . . . There was just enough foundation for the flattery, to make the falsehood of its general application to Felix more glaring. He had put down some rebels (see ch. xxi. 38, note) and assassins (Antt. xx. 8. 4), 'ipse tamen his omnibus erat nocentior' (Wetst.). It has been remarked (by Dean Milman, Bampton Lectures, p. 185) that the character of this address is *peculiarly Latin* (but qu.?); and it has been inferred from a passage in Valerius Maximus (cited at length in C. and

Τέρτυλλος λέγων [3] Πολλῆς εἰρήνης [s] τυγχάνοντες [t] διὰ
σοῦ καὶ [u] διορθωμάτων [v] γινομένων τῷ ἔθνει τούτῳ διὰ
τῆς σῆς [w] προνοίας, [x] πάντῃ τε καὶ [y] πανταχοῦ [z] ἀπο-
δεχόμεθα, [a] κράτιστε Φῆλιξ, [b] μετὰ [c] πάσης [d] εὐχαριστίας.
[4] ἵνα δὲ μὴ [e] ἐπὶ πλεῖόν σε [f] ἐγκόπτω, [g] παρακαλῶ ἀκοῦσαί σε ἡμῶν [h] συντόμως τῇ σῇ [i] ἐπιεικείᾳ. [5] [k] εὑρόντες
γὰρ τὸν ἄνδρα τοῦτον [l] λοιμὸν καὶ [m] κινοῦντα [n] στάσιν
πᾶσιν τοῖς Ἰουδαίοις τοῖς [o] κατὰ τὴν [op] οἰκουμένην, [q] πρωτο-
στάτην τε τῆς τῶν Ναζωραίων [r] αἱρέσεως, [6] ὃς καὶ τὸ
ἱερὸν [s] ἐπείρασεν [t] βεβηλῶσαι, ὃν καὶ [u] ἐκρατήσαμεν [καὶ

s = Luke xx. 35. ch. xxvi. 22. xxvii. 3. 2 Tim. ii. 10. Heb. viii. 6. xi. 35. L.P.H. 1 Macc. xi. 42.
t = Matt. xviii. 7. Luke xxii. 22 ||. Rom. v. 12, &c.
u here only †.
v constr., ch. ii. 43 al. fr.
w Rom. xiii. 14 only. Josh. xx. 3 F(not A) compl. Wisd. xiv. 3. xvii. 2. 2 Macc. iv. 6 only. (-νοεῖσθαι, Rom. xii. 17.)
x here only †. Sir. l. 22 only.
y ch. xvii. 30 reff.
z ch. ii. 41 reff.
a ch. xxiii. 26 reff.
b ch. xvii. 11 reff.
c = ch. xx. 19 reff.
d = 1 Cor. xiv. 16. 2 Cor. iv. 15. ix. 11, 12 al. Paul only, exc. Rev. iv. 9. vii. 12 †. Wisd. xvi. 28. Sir. xxxvii. 11. 2 Macc. ii. 27 only.
e ch. iv. 17 reff.
f Rom. xv. 22. Gal. v. 7. 1 Thess. ii. 18. 1 Pet. iii. 7 only †. Dan. ix. 26 Theod. (Ald.)
g = Matt. xviii. 29. ch. xiii. 42. constr., ch. viii. 31 reff.
h here only. Prov. xxiii. 28 only. (-ος, 2 Macc. ii. 31.)
i 2 Cor. x. 1 only †. Wisd. ii. 19. (-κής, Phil. iv. 5. -κῶς, 1 Kings xii. 22.) constr. dat., Matthiæ, § 499.
k = Rom. vii. 10 al.
l = here (Luke xxiv. 11) only. 1 Kings xxx. 22. Ps. i. 1.
m = ch. xxi. 30 (xvii. 28 reff.).
n = ch. xix. 40 reff.
o here only.
p = ch. xvii. 6.
q here only. Job xv. 24 only.
r ch. v. 17 reff.
s = and constr., ch. xvi. 7 only ‡.
t Matt. xii. 5 only. Neh. xiii. 17, 18. Ezek. xxii. 26. (-λος, 1 Tim. i. 9.)
u = acc., Matt. xviii. 28 al. Ps. lv. tit.

3. rec **κατ**ορθωματων, with HLP rel Chr_1 Thl: txt ABEℵ p 13. 36. 137 Chr-ms. *γενομενων* L c 137 Thl-fin: *γιγνωμενων* m.
4. *εκκοπτω* L Thl-fin: *κοπτω* A^1(appy) m 13. (*ενκοπτω* A^2B^1Eℵ.) *σε* bef *ακουσαι* E: om *σε* L e m 36 Chr. [om *συντομως* A^1(appy: insd eadem manu).]
5. *στασεις* (*corrn as suiting better* *πασιν τ. ιουδ. κ.τ.λ.*) ABEℵ p 13. 36. 40 vulg copt Chr_1 Thl-fin: txt HLP rel syrr sah æth Thl-sif. [for *τε*, *δε* E 13.]
6—8. om from *και κατα* to *προς σε* ABHLPℵ d g^1 h l p am^1(and fuld tol) coptt: ins

H., vol. i. p. 3), that all pleadings, even in Greek provinces, were conducted before Roman magistrates *in Latin*. But Mr. Lewin has well observed (ii. 684), "under the emperors trials were permitted in Greek, even in Rome itself, as well in the senate as in the forum (Dio Cassius, lvii. 15, says of Tiberius, *πολλὰς μὲν δίκας ἐν τῇ διαλέκτῳ ταύτῃ* (viz. Greek) *καὶ ἐκεῖ* (in the senate) *λεγομένας ἀκούων, πολλὰς δὲ καὶ αὐτὸς ἐπερωτῶν*); and it is unlikely that greater strictness should have been observed in a distant province. The name Tertullus proves little, as the Greeks, and even the Jews, very commonly adopted Roman names." On this latter point, see note, ch. xiii. 9. **διόρθωμα** is 'an amelioration or reform:' *κατόρθωμα*, 'res præclare facta,' generally, whether military or civil ('quæ nos aut recta aut recte facta dicamus, si placet, illi autem appellant *κατορθώματα*.' Cic. de Fin. iii. 7). Phrynichus remarks, p. 250, *ἁμαρτάνουσιν οἱ ῥήτορες οὐκ εἰδότες ὅτι τὸ κατορθῶσαι, δόκιμον. τὸ δ' ἀπὸ τούτου ὄνομα ἀδόκιμον, τὸ κατόρθωμα*,—where see Lobeck's note. I have, as always where reason to the contrary is not *very clear*, followed the authority of the most ancient MSS. **προνοίας**] 'providentiæ.' 'Hoc vocabulum sæpe diis tribuerunt' (Beng.). 'Providentia Cæsaris' is a common phrase on the coins of the emperors (Mr. Humphry). **3. πάντῃ κ. πανταχοῦ**] belongs to *ἀποδεχ.*, not to *γινομένων*, in which case they would naturally precede the participle,—**We receive, &c., not only here in thy presence, but also at all times and in all places.** A refinement of flattery **4. ἐπὶ πλεῖον**] viz. than the matter demands: **too long. ἐγκόπτ.**] See reff. **συντόμως**] As Meyer observes, we need not supply *λεξόντων*, but take *συντ.* as the measure of the time implied in *ἀκοῦσαι*. **5. λοιμόν**] See reff. and Demosth. p. 794. 5, *οὗτος οὖν αὐτὸν ἐξαιτήσεται ὁ φαρμακός, ὁ λοιμὸς* . . . The construction here is an anacoluthon, there being nothing to follow up the part. *εὑρόντες*. The part. cannot be taken for the finite verb. See Winer, edn. 6, § 45. 6. b. **ἡ οἰκουμένη**] would here mean the Roman 'orbis terrarum.' **Ναζωρ.**] This is the only place in the N. T. where the Christians are so called. The *Jews* could not call them by any name answering to *Christians*, as the hope of *a Messiah* was professed by themselves. **[6.]** * Considerable difficulty rests on the omission of the words *καὶ κατά* to *πρὸς σέ*. Their absence from the principal MSS., their many variations in those which con-

κατὰ τὸν ἡμέτερον νόμον ἠθελήσαμεν κρῖναι. 7 [v] παρ- ABEH
ελθὼν δὲ Λυσίας ὁ χιλίαρχος [w] μετὰ πολλῆς [w] βίας ἐκ LPℵ a b
τῶν [x] χειρῶν ἡμῶν [y] ἀπήγαγεν, 8 κελεύσας τοὺς [z] κατ- c d f g h
ηγόρους αὐτοῦ ἔρχεσθαι πρὸς σέ]· παρ' οὗ δυνήσῃ αὐτὸς k l m o
[a] ἀνακρινας περὶ πάντων τούτων [b] ἐπιγνῶναι [c] ὧν ἡμεῖς p 13
[d] κατηγοροῦμεν αὐτοῦ. 9 [e] συνεπέθεντο δὲ καὶ οἱ Ἰουδαῖοι, [f] φάσκοντες ταῦτα [g] οὕτως [g] ἔχειν. 10 ἀπεκρίθη τε

v = Luke xii. 37. xvii. 7. Exod. iii. 3. w ch. v. 26 (reff.) only. x ch. xii. 11 reff. y ch. xxiii. 17 reff. z ch. xxiii. 30 reff. a ch. iv. 9 reff. b ch. xxiii. 28 reff. c attr., ch. i. 1 reff. d constr., ch. xxv. 11. Mark xv. 3, 4. 1 Macc. vii. 25. see Luke xxiii. 14. e here only. Deut. xxxii. 27. Ps. iii. 7 Aℵ Ald. compl. f ch. xxv. 19. Rom. i. 22 only. Gen. xxvi. 20. 2 Macc. xiv. 27, 32 only. g ch. vii. 1 reff.

(*with consid varr, see below*) E 13 rel 36. 40 syrr æth Chr_1 Thl Cassiod. (*See notes.*) for ηθελ., ηβουληθημεν (or εβ.) [f] m 40. 66². rec κρινειν, with rel Thl-fin: κριναι E a b g² k m o 13. 36 Chr Thl-sif. 7. for μετα πολλης to προς σε, ηρπασεν αυτον εκ των χειρων ημων πεμψας προς σε f. (*cf* m *below.*) βια πολλη g² 32. 46. 57. 66¹. for απηγαγεν, αφειλετο g² 32. 42[-λατο]-6. 57.—[add] και προς σε απεστειλεν 32. 42-6. 57. 66¹: [simly Syr:] κελευσασθαι επι σε παραγγειλας τοις κατηγοροις ερχεσθαι επι σοι 180. aft απηγαγεν ins αυτον [and transp bef] εκ των χειρων ημων m. 8. aft κελευσας ins και a g² 32. 42. 57. 69. 133 arm. om αυτου [a o] 69. rec επι, with rel: προς E a 46. 133.

8. for οὗ, ω E 36: ων b m¹ o 8. 15. 27-9. 66¹. 106-80: txt ABHLPℵ vulg copt Chr Thl Œc. om αυτος A: αυτους 40. at end ins ειποντος δε αυτου ταυτα 137 syr-w-ast.

9. rec συνεθεντο, with b o: απεκριναντο sah æth: *adjecerunt* vulg E-lat: *litigarunt* Syr: txt AB E-gr HLPℵ p rel 36. 40. 137 syr Chr_1: συνεπειθοντο 13. 180.

10. rec δε (*alteration of characteristic* τε), with HLP 13. 36 rel E-lat [vulg syr

tain them, are strongly against their genuineness; as also is the consideration that no probable reason for their omission can be suggested. On the other hand, as De Wette observes, it is hardly imaginable that so little should have been assigned to the speaker as would be if these words were omitted. Besides this, the historic aorist ἐκρατήσαμεν seems to require some sequel, some reason, after this seizure, why he was there present and freed from Jewish durance. The phænomena are common enough in the Acts, of unaccountable insertions, and almost always in D (here deficient). See a list of such in Prolegg. to Acts, § v. 3. But in this place it is the *omission* which is unaccountable, for no similarity of ending, no doctrinal consideration can have led to it. The two reasons cited from Matthæi by Bloomfield, ed. 9,—1) "that the critics believed the Jews hardly likely to have accused Lysias himself,"—2) "because the words παρ' οὗ, at ver. 8, must be referred to Paul: though by its (*sic*) position, it seems to refer to Lysias," are futile and childish enough (on the latter of them, see below); and I only refer to them, to shew by what sort of considerations English readers are still supposed to be influenced.

I still retain the words, in dark brackets, being as much at a loss as ever to decide respecting them, and being moved principally by the aorist ἐκρατήσαμεν, inexplicable without any sequel. It may of course be said that this very circumstance may have given rise to their insertion. But of the two it seems to me less likely that Tertullus should have ended with ἐκρατήσαμεν, than that an abridgment of his speech should have been attempted. It may be a question how far we can detect traces of deliberate abridgment, in our early MSS., of the text of the Acts.] **8.] παρ' οὗ**, if the disputed words be *inserted*, refers naturally enough to *Lysias;* but if they be omitted, to *Paul*, which would be very unlikely,—that the judge should be referred to the prisoner (for examination by *torture* (Grot. and al.) on one who had already claimed his rights as a Roman citizen can hardly be intended) for the particulars laid to his charge. Certainly it might, on the other hand, be said that Tertullus would hardly refer the governor to Lysias, whose interference he had just characterized in such terms of blame; but (which is a strong argument for the genuineness of the doubtful words) remarkably enough, we find Felix, ver. 22, putting off the trial *till the arrival of Lysias.* **9. συνεπέθ.] joined in setting upon him,** bore out Tertullus in his charges. **10. ἐκ πολλῶν ἐτῶν]** Felix was now in the seventh year of his procuratorship, which began in the twelfth year of Claudius, A.D. 52. The

ὁ Παῦλος, [h] νεύσαντος αὐτῷ τοῦ [i] ἡγεμόνος λέγειν, [k] Ἐκ
πολλῶν ἐτῶν [l] ὄντα σε κριτὴν τῷ ἔθνει τούτῳ ἐπιστάμενος
[m] εὐθύμως [n] τὰ [n] περὶ ἐμαυτοῦ [o] ἀπολογοῦμαι, 11 δυναμένου
σου [p] ἐπιγνῶναι ὅτι οὐ πλείους εἰσίν [p] μοι ἡμέραι * δώδεκα
ἀφ' [q] ἧς [r] ἀνέβην [s] προσκυνήσων εἰς Ἱερουσαλήμ, 12 καὶ
οὔτε ἐν τῷ ἱερῷ εὗρόν με [t] πρός τινα [tu] διαλεγόμενον ἢ
[v] ἐπίστασιν ποιοῦντα ὄχλου, οὔτε ἐν ταῖς συναγωγαῖς οὔτε

h John xiii. 24 only ‡. Prov. iv. 25 only.
i ch. xxiii. 24 &c. reff.
k = ch. ix. 33. xv. 21 al.
l constr., particip., Luke iv. 23. viii. 46. ch. vii. 12. xix. 35. xxvi. 3. 2 Tim. ii. 8.
m here only †. Polyb. iii. 34. 9. (-ος, ch. xxvii. 36. -εῖν, ch. xxvii. 22.)
n ch. xxiii. 15. xxviii. 15. Luke xxii. 37. Phil. ii. 19, 20, 23.
o ch. xix. 33 reff.
p constr., Matthiæ, § 388. Hom. Il. χ. 155. ω. 765.
q constr., 1 Cor. vii. 1. see ch. xx. 18.
= ch. xi. 2 reff. Ezra vii. 6, 7.
s = ch. viii. 27 reff.
t Mark ix. 34. ch. xvii. 17 only. Exod. vi. 27.
u = ch. xvii. 2 reff.
v 2 Cor. xi. 28 only †. 2 Macc. vi. 3 only.

coptt Cassiod$_1$] Chr$_1$: txt AB E-gr ℵ a^1 c p 40. 137 Syr æth Thl-sif. [for λεγειν to κριτην syr-mg has *defensionem habere pro se, statum autem assumens divinum dixit, Ex multis annis es judex.*] for ετων, ενιαυτων E. aft κριτην ins δικαιον E c e h k 36. 40. 137 syr Chr$_1$(οὐκ ἔστι ταῦτα κολακείας τὰ ῥήματα, τὸ μαρτυρῆσαι τῷ δικαστῇ δικαιοσύνην) Thl Avit. rec ευθυμοτερον, with HLP rel Chr Thl-sif : txt ABEℵ c d p 13. 36. 40. 137 [vulg coptt æth arm] Ath$_1$ Thl-fin.

11. om σου A. rec γνωναι, with HLP 13 rel Chr$_1$: txt ABEℵ b c k o p 36. 137 Thl. rec aft ημεραι ins η : om ABEHLPℵ rel. * rec δεκαδύο (*see ch* xix. 7 reff), with HLP rel 36 Chr: δωδεκα ABEℵ c m p 13. 40. 137 Thl. προσκυνησαι E 137 sah, *adorare* vulg [-νησω p]. rec (for εις) εν, with L[P] rel [syr] Chr : om 13 : txt ABEHℵ a^2 d p 13. 36. 40 [Syr æth] Thl.

12. τινας E-gr. rec επισυστασιν, with HLP rel : εποστασιαν p^1 : αποστασιαν p^2 [Scr] : txt ABEℵ 13. 40 vulg. (*There is the like varn in the* MSS *in the only other place where the word occurs.*) for 3rd ουτε, ουδε p.

contrast between Tertullus's and Paul's 'captatio benevolentiæ' is remarkable. The former I have characterized above. But the Apostle, using no flattery, yet alleges the one point which could really win attention to him from Felix, viz. his confidence arising from speaking before one *well skilled by experience in the manners and customs of the Jews.* **11. ἡμέραι δώδεκα**] The point of this seems to be, that Felix having been so long time a judge among the Jews, must be well able to search into and adjudicate on an offence whose whole course was comprised within so short a period. The twelve days may be thus made out : 1. his arrival in Jerusalem, ch. xxi. 15—17 ; 2. his interview with James, ib. 18 ff. ; 3. his taking on him the vow, ib. 26 ; 3—7. the time of the vow, interrupted by—7. his apprehension, ch. xxi. 27 ; 8. his appearance before the Sanhedrim, ch. xxii. 30 ff. ; 9. his departure from Jerusalem (at night) ; and so to the 13th, the day now current, which was the 5th inclusive from his leaving Jerusalem. This, which is also De Wette and Meyer's arrangement, is far more natural than that of Kuin., Olsh., Heinr., &c., who suppose that the days which he had already spent at Cæsarea are *not to be counted,* because his raising disturbances while in custody was out of the question. The view advocated by Wieseler (Chron. der Apost.-gesch. pp. 103 ff.), that Paul was *apprehended* on the *very day* of his appearance with the men in the temple, I cannot but regard, notwithstanding his arguments in its favour, as inconsistent with the text of ch. xxi. 26, 27 ; as also his idea that the Apostle *did not take the vow on himself :* the expression σὺν αὐτοῖς ἁγνισθείς clearly negativing the latter supposition ; and τῶν ἡμερῶν τοῦ ἁγνισμοῦ, ver. 26, being manifestly, unless to one warped by a hypothesis, identical with αἱ ἑπτὰ ἡμέραι of ver. 27. See note there. I mention this *here,* because these suppositions materially affect his arrangement of the twelve days, which he gives thus : 2nd, from Cæsarea to Jerusalem ; 3rd, interview with James; 4th, (Pentecost) visit to the temple with the Nazarites, *and apprehension ;* 5th, before the Sanhedrim ; 6th, departure from Jerusalem ; 7th, arrival in Cæsarea ; then, five days from *that* (but see note on ver. 1), Ananias, &c., *leave* Jerusalem (but how does this appear from ver. 1 ? κατέβη must surely denote their arrival at Cæsarea, where the narrator, or, at all events, the locus of the history is) ; 13th, arrival of Ananias, &c., at Cæsarea, *and* hearing (improbable) of Paul. So that the above hypotheses are not the *only* reasons for rejecting Wieseler's arrangement.

[w] κατὰ τὴν πόλιν· 13 οὔτε [x] παραστῆσαι δύνανταί σοι περὶ
[y] ὧν νυνὶ [z] κατηγοροῦσίν μου. 14 ὁμολογῶ δὲ τοῦτό σοι,
ὅτι κατὰ τὴν [a] ὁδὸν ἣν λέγουσιν [b] αἵρεσιν οὕτως [c] λατρεύω
τῷ [d] πατρῴῳ θεῷ, [e] πιστεύων πᾶσιν τοῖς [f] κατὰ τὸν [g] νόμον
καὶ [τοῖς ἐν] [h] τοῖς [g] προφήταις γεγραμμένοις, 15 [i] ἐλπίδα
ἔχων [i] εἰς τὸν θεὸν ἣν καὶ [k] αὐτοὶ [k] οὗτοι [l] προσδέχονται,
[m] ἀνάστασιν [n] μέλλειν [n] ἔσεσθαι δικαίων τε καὶ ἀδίκων.
16 [o] ἐν τούτῳ καὶ αὐτὸς [p] ἀσκῶ [q] ἀπρόσκοπον [r] συνείδησιν

ABEH LPℵ a b c d f g h k l m o p 13

C -πιδα εχων... ABCEH LPℵ a b c d f g h k l m o p 13

w Luke viii. 39. xv. 14.
x = here only. παραστῆσαι ὅτι ταύτην ἔχει ἰσχύν, Jos. Antt. viii. 2. 5. Xen. Œc. xiii. 1.
y constr., John xvii. 9. Heb. v. 8. 2 Pet. ii. 12.
z and constr., ver. 8.
a see ch. ix. 2 reff.
b ver. 5.
c ch. vii. 7 reff.
d ch. xxii. 3 reff.
e = dat., Luke i. 20 al. fr. 2 Chron. ix. 6.
f ch. xxii. 12 reff.
g ch. xiii. 15 reff.
h constr. (if dat. of agency), Matt. vi. 1. Luke xxiii. 15. xxiv. 35. Gen. xxxi. 15.
i 1 Pet. i. 21. (John v. 45. 2 Cor. i. 10.) see 1 John iii. 3. (ch. xxvi. 18.)
k ver. 20. ch. xxv. 25. Rom. xiii. 6. 2 Cor. ii. 3. vii. 11, &c.
l = ch. xxiii. 21. Tit. ii. 13. Jude 21. 2 Macc. viii. 11.
m ch. xvii. 18 reff. see Dan. xii. 2.
n ch. xi. 28 reff.
o = Matt. vi. 7. John xvi. 30 al.
p here only †. 2 Macc. xv. 4 only. ἄσκει τοιαύτη νοῦν δι' αἰῶνος μένειν, Soph. Electr. 1024.
q 1 Cor. x. 32. Phil. i. 10 only. P.† Sir. xxxv. (xxxii.) 21 only.
r 2 Cor. i. 12 reff.

13. *ουδε* Bℵ p. Steph aft *παραστησαι* (Tischdf (ed 7) is wrong) ins *με*, with c f g l m 66¹-9. 78. 96-7. 100-4-6-42 [copt æth(Treg)]; *μοι* 2. 18. 161; *σοι* 15. 133-80; *με νυν* HP 27-9. 98-9 Thl-sif; *μοι νυν* 177: [*νυν* b l o:] om ABELℵ p 13(sic) rel [vulg syrr sah arm]. rec om *σοι*, with HLP rel syr sah æth Chr: ins ABEℵ a² d g k m p 13. 40 vulg Syr copt arm. rec (for *νυνι*) *νυν*, with EHLP 13. 36 rel: om k 3. 30: txt ABℵ d m p 137 Thl-fin.

14. ins *μου* bef *θεω* 137: *patri deo meo* [am demid fuld, *p. et d. m.*] vulg[-clem]. om *πασιν* B. om *τον* B 56 Chr₁. Steph om *τοις εν*, with AHLP ℵ³(*εν τοις*) 13 rel vulg coptt æth [arm] Thl-sif: elz om *τοις*, with (syrr) Epiph₁ Chr₁: txt BEℵ¹ b c k m o p 36. 40. 137 Thl-fin.

15. for *εις*, *προς* Cℵ a 68-9 Thl-fin. om *τον* C 180. om *ουτοι* ℵ [arm?]. rec aft *εσεσθαι* ins *νεκρων* (*supplementary addition*), with EHLP rel 36 syrr æth Thl-sif: om ABCℵ k p 13. 40 vulg coptt arm Chr Thl-fin.

16. rec *δε* (*και not being understood*), with HP 13 rel copt: *δε και* c g 25. 80. 100-77 arm Chr₁ Thl-sif: *τε και* m: txt ABCELℵ b d k o p 40. 137 vulg syrr sah [æth] Thl-fin. *εχων* HLP rel 36. 137 Chr: txt ABCEℵ d p 13 vulg syrr coptt Thl Œc.

12. κατὰ τὴν πόλ.] **throughout the city**, 'any where in the city;' as we say, '*up and down the streets.*' **14.**] The **δέ** here has its peculiar force, of taking off the attention from what has immediately preceded, and raising a new point as more worthy of notice. **But** ('*if thou wouldst truly know the reason why they accuse me*'), 'hinc illæ lacrymæ.' **αἵρεσιν**, in allusion to *αἱρέσεως* used by Tertullus, ver. 5. The word is capable of an indifferent or of a bad sense. Tertullus had used it in the latter. Paul explains what it really was. **οὕτως** = *κατὰ ταύτην*. Notice in the words **πατρῴῳ θεῷ** the skill of Paul. The term was one well known to the Greeks and Romans, and which would carry with it its own justification. "Invisum quippe erat gentibus, nominatim etiam Romanis, si quis se peregrinis aut diis aut deorum cultibus addiceret; præterea Judæis per multa imperatorum et magistratuum decreta et senatus consulta sancita erat potestas, Deum patrium colendi, patriis ritibus et sacris utendi. Jos. Antt. xiv. 17; xvi. 4" (Kuinoel). In his address *to the Jews* (ch. xxii. 14) the similar expression *ὁ θ. τῶν πατέρων ἡμῶν*, brings out more clearly those *πατέρες*, in whom Felix had no interest further than the identification of *Paul's religion with that of his ancestors* required. **κατὰ τ. ν.**] See on *κατ. τ. πόλιν*, above. Then (if the words in brackets be omitted: and it is not easy to imagine that St. Luke wrote them) the dat. is used of the personal agents, the prophets. He avoids saying '*by Moses*,' because the mention of *the law* would carry more weight. **15. αὐτοὶ οὗτοι**] It would appear from this, that the High Priest and the deputation *were not of the Sadducees*. But perhaps this inference is too hasty; Paul might regard them as representing the whole Jewish people, and speak *generally*, as he does of the same hope ch. xxvi. 7, where he assigns it to *τὸ δωδεκάφυλον ἡμῶν*. **νεκρῶν**, inserted here in some mss. to fill up the meaning, is not likely to have been spoken by the Apostle. The juxtaposition of those words, which excited mockery even when the Gospel was being *directly preached*, would hardly have been hazarded in this defence, where every expression is so carefully weighed. **16. ἐν τούτῳ**] **Accordingly**, i. e. 'having and cherishing this

ἔχειν [s] πρὸς τὸν θεὸν καὶ τοὺς ἀνθρώπους [t] διὰ παντός.
17 [u] δι᾽ ἐτῶν δὲ [v] πλειόνων [w] ἐλεημοσύνας [x] ποιήσων [y] εἰς τὸ
ἔθνος μου [z] παρεγενόμην καὶ [a] προσφοράς, 18 [b] ἐν * αἷς εὗρόν
με [c] ἡγνισμένον ἐν τῷ ἱερῷ, οὐ [d] μετὰ [e] ὄχλου οὐδὲ [d] μετὰ
[f] θορύβου, τινὲς δὲ ἀπὸ τῆς Ἀσίας Ἰουδαῖοι, 19 οὓς ἔδει
[g] ἐπὶ σοῦ [h] παρεῖναι καὶ [i] κατηγορεῖν εἴ [k] τι [kl] ἔχοιεν [m] πρὸς
ἐμέ. 20 ἢ [n] αὐτοὶ [n] οὗτοι εἰπάτωσαν τί εὗρον [ἐν ἐμοὶ]

s = Rom. v. 1 reff. t ch. ii. 25 reff. u = Matt. xxvi. 61. Gal. ii. 1 al. Deut. xv. 1. v = ch. ii. 40 reff. w ch. ix. 36 reff. x = ch. x. 2 reff. y = ch. ii. 22. Luke ix. 13 al. z absol., ch. xvii. 10 reff. a ch. xxi. 26 reff. b = Mark vi. 48. Luke xvi. 10 al. c ch. xxi. 24, 26 reff. d = ch. v. 26 al. e Luke xxii. 6. Ezek. xxiii. 24. f ch. xxi. 34 reff. Ezek. vii. 11. g ch. xxiii. 30 reff. h see ch. x. 33. i ver. 2. k Matt. v. 23. Mark xi. 25 al. l opt. (subjective possibility), = ch. xvii. 27. Luke xxii. 23 al. Winer, edn. 6, § 41. *b*. 4. c. m = ch. xxv. 19. 1 Cor. vi. 1. Col. iii. 13. n ver. 15.

aft προς ins τε L b c d h l o 137 syr Chr Thl-fin. δια παντος bef προς E c: om δια παντος 32. 42. 57[1]. 137.

17. rec παρεγενομην bef ελεημοσυνας κ.τ.λ. (*transposn for perspicuity*), with HLP rel [syrr coptt æth] Chr_1; και προσφ. bef παρεγ. Eℵ[3] c 137: om παρεγ. A: txt BCℵ[1] m p 13. 40 vulg Thl-fin.

18. *rec οἷς, with HLP rel Chr_1 Thl-sif: αις (*corrn to suit* προσφορας ?) ABCEℵ b[1] c o [p] 13. 36. 40. 137 Thl-fin. aft θορυβου ins *et apprehenderunt me clamantes et dicentes tolle inimicum virum* demid. elz om δε, with HLP [æth arm] Thl-fin: ins ABCEℵ p 13 rel 36. 40. 137 vulg syr coptt Thl-sif. ins των bef απο CE b c f o 36. 40. 137 Thl. ιουδαιων E b c o 36 syr.

19. Steph δει, with HL b f g k l m o 137 sah æth Chr_1: txt ABCEPℵ p 13. 36 rel vulg syrr copt [arm] Chr_1 Thl. rec με, with HLP rel 36 Chr: txt ABCEℵ p 13.

20. for η, ει (*itacism?*) AC. rec ins ει bef τι (*corrn from ver* 19), with a c vulg syr [(æth)]: om ABCEHLPℵ p 13. 36 rel Syr copt arm Chr_1. om εν εμοι ABℵ p 13. 40: ins CEHLP rel 36 [vulg syrr copt arm] Chr.

hope;' see reff. **καί**] also, '*as well as they.*' **17.**] **δέ** refers back to the former δέ, ver. 14. 'But the matter of which they complain is this, that after an absence of many years,' &c. See 1 Cor. xvi. 3, 4; 2 Cor. viii. ix. notes, ch. xx. 4. **18.**] De W. observes, that ἡγνισμ. can only refer to προσφ., not to ἐλεημ.: thus **αἷς** may have been altered to οἷς, to give a general neuter sense, *amidst which occupations:* and the sense will be **among** or **engaged in which offerings**: it being in the temple. But this seems far-fetched and unlikely, and Meyer's supposition, that οἷς has been altered to αἷς to suit προσφοράς, certainly has an air of probability. The use of a verb referring to two substantives, to only one of which it is applicable, is too common to require illustration. But, as so often in this book, we must follow the best MSS., our only fixed evidence, as against any questionable subjective considerations. The construction is irregular. A subject to εὗρον has to be supplied by a reference to some nominative case implied in οὐ μετὰ ὄχ. οὐδ. μ. θορ., thus: **amidst which they found me purified in the temple, none who detected me in the act of raising a tumult . . . . but certain Asiatic Jews . . . .** This would leave it to be inferred that no legal officers had apprehended him, but certain private individuals, illegally; who besides had not come forward to substantiate any charge against him. Bornemann would supply οὐχ οὗτοι μέν before τινες δέ; but the objection to this is, that the negative οὐ μετὰ ὄχ. . . . . stands already as the proper opponent clause to τινες δέ, and we should thus have two negative clauses together. On this sense of δέ, see Viger, ed. Hermann, p. 16, note 24; and Hermann's note, p. 702. 19. The latter remarks, "intelligitur in hac formula, *quam malum, stultum est,* vel simile quid."

19.] **ἔχοιεν**, not ἔχουσιν, implying the subjective possibility merely, and disclaiming all knowledge of what the charge might be. The sentence is an anacoluthon: δεῖ is absolutely asserted in the present: then ἔχοιεν in the opt. follows, as if the hypothetical ἔδει had been used: and hence the correction to ἔδει. (So I wrote in former editions, and so I still believe: but the text must follow the evidence of the great MSS. [1870.]) On the opt. after the hypothetical indicative, see Bernhardy, Syntax, p. 386 ff. This also is a skilful argument on the part of the Apostle:—it being the custom of the Romans not to judge a prisoner without the accusers face to face, he deposes that *his real accusers were the Asiatic Jews* who first raised the cry against him in the

ᵒ ἀδίκημα στάντος μου ᵍ ἐπὶ τοῦ ᵖ συνεδρίου, 21 ἢ περὶ μίας
ταύτης ᑫ φωνῆς ʳ ἧς ˢ ἐκέκραξα ἐν αὐτοῖς ἑστώς, ὅτι περὶ
ᵗ ἀναστάσεως ᵗ νεκρῶν ἐγὼ ᵘ κρίνομαι σήμερον ᵍ ἐφ' ὑμῶν.
22 ᵛ ἀνεβάλετο δὲ αὐτοὺς ὁ Φῆλιξ, ʷ ἀκριβέστερον εἰδὼς τὰ
περὶ τῆς ˣ ὁδοῦ, εἴπας Ὅταν Λυσίας ὁ χιλίαρχος ʸ καταβῇ, ᶻ διαγνώσομαι ᵃ τὰ ᵃ καθ' ὑμᾶς, 23 ᵇ διαταξάμενος τῷ
ἑκατοντάρχῃ ᶜ τηρεῖσθαι αὐτόν, ἔχειν τε ᵈ ἄνεσιν, καὶ
μηδένα ᵉ κωλύειν τῶν ᶠ ἰδίων αὐτοῦ ᵍ ὑπηρετεῖν αὐτῷ.

ABCEH LPℵ a b c d f g h k l m o p 13

o ch. xviii. 14 reff. p ch. iv. 15 reff. q = ch. xiii. 27 al. r attr., ch. i. 1 reff. s aor. redupl., here only. Num. xi. 2. LXX almost always. t 1 Cor. xv. 12 reff. u ch. xxiii. 6 reff. v here only. (Ps. lxxvii. 21. See Schleusn. Lex. V. T. in voc.) τὸ πλουσιωτέραν τὴν πόλιν ποιεῖν ἀναβαλούμεθα, Xen. Mem. iii. 6. 6. (-βολή, ch. xxv. 17.) w ch. xviii. 26 reff. x = ch. ix. 2 reff. y absol., ver. 1. z ch. xxiii. 15 only (reff.). a ch. xxv. 14. Eph. vi. 21. Phil. i. 12. Col. iv. 7. b Luke viii. 55. ch. xviii. 2 al. c = ch. xii. 5, 6 reff. d = here (2 Cor. ii. 13. vii. 5. viii. 13. 2 Thess. i. 7) only. L.P. 2 Chron. xxiii. 15. e = ch. xvi. 6 reff. f = ch. iv. 23. 1 Tim. v. 8. see John i. 11. Titus i. 12. g = ch. xiii. 36 (reff.). xx. 34 only.

21. φωνης bef ταυτης E c k 137 syr Thl-sif. rec εκραξα, with EHLP rel 36 Thl-fin: txt ABCℵ a b d m o p 13. 40 Chr_2 Thl-sif. rec εστως bef εν αυτοις (*corrn to avoid ambig of reference of εν αυτ.?*), with HLP rel syrr [arm] Chr: txt ABCEℵ c k m p 13. 40. 137 vulg copt Thl. om εγω C. rec υφ (*corrn, the force of εφ not being perceived*), with EHLPℵ rel 36 vulg [copt] Chr: [αφ e:] txt ABC m p 13. 40 Syr (æth).

22. rec at beg ins ακουσας δε ταυτα (omitting the δε following), with [H]LP rel 36 Thl: om ABCEℵ c p 13. 40. 137 vulg syrr copt (æth) arm Chr.—ο φηλιξ ανεβαλετο αυτους L &c as above: ο φηλιξ bef αυτους c Chr: αυτοις p. rec ειπων (*corrn to more usual form*), with EHLP rel 36: txt ABCℵ p. for καθ, κατεσε (but corrd) ℵ[1].

23. aft διαταξαμενος ins τε, with H rel vulg[*jussitque* (so E-lat) æth] Syr Chr_1; δε L: om ABC E[-gr] Pℵ b[1] c o p 13. 36. 40. 137 syr copt arm Thl-fin. [εκατονταρχω E 13:] χιλιαρχη ℵ[1], but corrd by ℵ[1] or ℵ-corr[1]. rec (for αυτον) τον παυλον, with HLP rel Syr æth Chr [Thl-sif]: txt ABCEℵ c k p 13. 36. 40. 137 vulg syr copt arm Thl-fin. rec aft υπηρετειν adds η προσερχεσθαι, with HLP rel 36 Chr: om ABCEℵ p 13 vulg syrr copt arm.

temple,—*not the Sanhedrim,* who merely received him at the hands of others,—and that *these were not present.* **20.] Or let these persons themselves say, what fault they found in me while I stood before the Sanhedrim, other than in the matter of this one saying. . . . .** τί serves for τί ἄλλο. So in English: **What fault but this**: i. e. 'What *other* fault but this.'

21.] ἐφ' ὑμ., before you: less usual than ὑφ' ὑμ., which is probably a correction. **22. ἀνεβάλετο αὐτ.]** '*ampliavit eos*:' viz. both parties. **ἀκρ. εἰδὼς τὰ π. τ. ὁδ.]** These words will bear only one philologically correct interpretation, **having more accurate knowledge about the way**: not, '*till he should obtain* more accurate knowledge' (ungrammatical): nor, '*since he had now obtained*' (viz. by Paul's speech: but εἰδώς cannot be rendered 'certior factus'). But this, the only right rendering, is variously understood. Chrys. says: ἐπίτηδες ὑπερέθετο (he adjourned the case purposely), οὐ δεόμενος μαθεῖν, ἀλλὰ διακρούσασθαι βουλόμενος τοὺς Ἰουδαίους. ἀφεῖναι οὐκ ἤθελε δι' ἐκείνους. Luther and Wolf: "distulit, . . . non quod sectæ ignarus esset, aut pleniorem sibi notitiam ejus comparare vellet, sed quia, cum satis illam jam cognitam haberet, Judæos amplius sibi molestos esse nolebat." But these interpretations, as De W. observes, overlook the circumstance, that such a reason for adjournment would be as unfavourable to *Paul,* as to the *Jews.* Meyer explains it, that he adjourned the case, '*because*,' &c. But this (De W.) would imply that he was favourably disposed to *Paul.* The simplest explanation is that given by De W.: He put them off to another time, not as requiring any more information about 'the way,' *for that matter he knew before,*—but waiting for the arrival of Lysias. Whether Lysias was expected, or summoned, or ever came to be heard, is very doubtful. The *real* motive of the 'ampliatio' appears in ver. 26. The comparative implies, "more accurate than to need additional information." **διαγν. τὰ καθ' ὑμ.] I will adjudge your matters.** So in reff. also. **23.] διαταξάμενος** is in apposition with εἴπας, and both belong to ἀνεβάλετο. **ἄνεσιν]** De W. and Meyer explain this of '*custodia libera,*' φυλακὴ ἄδεσμος (Arrian, Exp. ii. 15). But this can hardly be. Lipsius (Excurs. II. on Tacit. Ann. iii. 22; vi. 3, cited by Wieseler, Chron. d. Apost.-g. p. 380) says, 'Præter *custodiam militarem* alia duplex, apud magistratus, et apud vades. Apud magistratus,

24 Μετὰ δὲ [h] ἡμέρας [h] τινὰς [i] παραγενόμενος ὁ Φῆλιξ
σὺν Δρουσίλλῃ τῇ γυναικί, οὔσῃ Ἰουδαίᾳ, [k] μετεπέμψατο
τὸν Παῦλον καὶ ἤκουσεν αὐτοῦ περὶ τῆς [l] εἰς χριστὸν
πίστεως. 25 [mn] διαλεγομένου δὲ αὐτοῦ περὶ [no] δικαιοσύνης
καὶ [p] ἐγκρατείας καὶ τοῦ [q] κρίματος τοῦ [r] μέλλοντος,
[s] ἔμφοβος γενόμενος ὁ Φῆλιξ ἀπεκρίθη [t] Τὸ [t] νῦν [t] ἔχον
πορεύου, [u] καιρὸν δὲ [v] μεταλαβὼν [w] μετακαλέσομαί σε·
26 ἅμα καὶ ἐλπίζων ὅτι [x] χρήματα δοθήσεται αὐτῷ ὑπὸ

h ch. x. 48 reff. i absol., ch. xvii. 10 reff. k ch. x. 5 reff. l ch. xx. 21. xxvi. 18. Col. ii. 5. Paul, or *of* Paul, only. m ch. xvii. 2 reff. n Isa. lxiii. 1. o absol., ch. xvii. 31 reff. p Gal. v. 23. 2 Pet. i. 6 (bis) only †. Sir. xviii. 30 (title) only. (-τής, Tit. i. 8. -τεύεσθαι, 1 Cor. vii. 9. ix. 25.) q = Heb. vi. 2. 1 Pet. iv. 17. Rev. xx. 4. (Prov. xxi. 15 al.) r = Matt. xii. 32. Rom. v. 14 al. s ch. x. 4 reff. t here only. Tobit vii. 11. u = Gal. vi. 10. Hagg. i. 2, 4. v = (and constr.) here (ch. ii. 46 reff.) only. μεταλ. καιρ. ἁρμόττοντα, Polyb. ii. 16. 15. w ch. vii. 14 reff. x ch. iv. 37 reff.

24. τινας bef ημερας AE c 137 vulg Syr [Chr_1] : txt BCHLPℵ 13. 36 rel [syr Thl]. rec aft γυναικι ins αυτου, with Eℵ[1.3] rel vulg [syrr copt arm] Thl-sif Œc : pref ιδια BC[2] [a b k m o] 36 [syr-mg(appy)] Amm-c_1 Thl-fin : ins both A [ℵ-corr[1]] p : om both C[1]HLP [c f g h l] Chr. (*Both* ιδια *and* αυτου *are additions to fix the sense of* γυναικι.) aft ιουδαια ins παρακαλουσῃ οπως ιδῃ τον παυλον και ακουσῃ τον λογον ως ουν εβουλετο ικανον ποιησαι εποιησεν τουτο syr-mg. ins και bef μετεπεμψατο ℵ[1](ℵ[3] disapproving). om αυτου C[1]. aft χριστον ins ιησουν ELℵ[1] d f g h l m p 36 vulg [demid] syr copt Chr Thl-fin; ῑυ(sic) B : pref, am(and fuld tol) æth [arm] : om A C[1.2](appy) HP ℵ-corr[1.3] 13 rel Syr Thl-sif.

25. εγκρατειας και δικαιοσυνης ℵ. μελλοντος bef κριματος (omg του) C m 40 arm Chr-$comm_1$. rec aft μελλοντος ins εσεσθαι (*appy a corrn aft ver* 15), with HLP rel Chr_2: om ABCEℵ p 13. 36. 40. 137 [not exprd in vulg syrr copt æth arm]. aft εμφοβος ins δε A[H copt(Treg)]. εχων L 13 : εχουν H. παραλαβων A : λαβων a b d k o p 13. 40 Thl-sif.

26. rec ins δε bef και, with copt Thl-fin : om ABCEHL[P]ℵ p 13. 36 rel 137 vulg syr [arm] Chr_1 Thl-sif. om 1st αυτω B : αυτω bef δοθησεται c.

quum reus Consuli, Prætori, Ædili, interdum et Senatori, etiam non e magistratu, committebatur : quod nonnisi in *reis illustrioribus* usurpatum, eaque *custodia libera* dicta : vid. Tacit. Ann. vi. 3; Sall. Cat. xlvii.; Liv. vi. 36; Cic. Brut. xcvi.; Dio lviii. 3. Custodia apud vades, quum eorum periculo fidejussoribus reus tradebatur : vid. Tacit. Ann. v. 8; Suet. Vitell. 2.' Now, Wieseler argues, as Paul *was not bailed*,—and was not 'e reis illustrioribus,' and besides was *delivered to a centurion to keep*, his cannot have been 'custodia *libera*,' but '*militaris*:' relaxed however as much as was consistent with safe custody. He cites Josephus, who says (Antt. xviii. 6. 10) of the custody of Agrippa, φυλακὴ μὲν γὰρ καὶ τήρησις ἦν, μετὰ μέντοι **ἀνέσεως** τῆς εἰς τὴν δίαιταν. **Remission**, or **relaxation**, would be a better rendering than '*liberty*.' **24. παραγεν.**] Into the hall or chamber where Paul was to speak. **Δρουσίλλῃ**] She was daughter of Herod Agrippa I. (see ch. xii.) and of Cypros,—and sister of Agrippa II. She was betrothed at six years old (Jos. Antt. xix. 9. 1) to Epiphanes, son of Antiochus, king of Commagene; but (Antt. xx. 7. 1) he declining the marriage, not wishing to be circumcised and become a Jew, she was married to the more obsequious **Azizus**, king of Emesa. Not long after, Felix, being enamoured of her beauty, persuaded her, by means of a certain Simon, a Cyprian magician (see note on ch. viii. 9), to leave her husband and live with him (Antt. xx. 7. 2). She bore him a son, Agrippa : and both mother and son perished in an eruption of Vesuvius, in the reign of Titus (ibid.). The Drusilla mentioned by Tacitus (Hist. v. 9), a granddaughter of Antony and Cleopatra, must have been *another wife* of Felix, who was *thrice* married, and each time to persons of royal birth; 'trium reginarum maritus,' Suet. Claud. 28. **25.**] It is remarkable that Tacitus uses of Felix (Ann. xii. 54) the expression 'cuncta malefacta sibi impune ratus.' The fear of Felix appears to have operated merely in his *sending away* Paul : no impression for *good* was made on him. **26.**] 'Lex Julia de repetundis præcipit, ne quis ob hominem in vincula publica conjiciendum, vinciendum, vincirive jubendum, exve vinculis dimittendum; neve quis ob hominem condemnandum absolvendumve . . . . aliquid acceperit.' Digest. xl. 11. 3. Cited by Mr. Humphry, who observes : Albinus, who succeeded Festus, so much encouraged this kind of bribery, that no malefactors remained in prison, except those who did

τοῦ Παύλου, διὸ καὶ [y] πυκνότερον αὐτὸν [k] μεταπεμπόμενος
[z] ὡμίλει αὐτῷ.
27 [a] Διετίας δὲ [b] πληρωθείσης ἔλαβεν
[c] διάδοχον ὁ Φῆλιξ Πόρκιον Φῆστον, θέλων τε [de] χάριτα
[ef] καταθέσθαι τοῖς Ἰουδαίοις ὁ Φῆλιξ [g] κατέλιπεν τὸν
Παῦλον [h] δεδεμένον.

XXV. 1 Φῆστος οὖν [i] ἐπιβὰς τῇ [k] ἐπαρχίᾳ μετὰ
τρεῖς ἡμέρας [l] ἀνέβη εἰς Ἱεροσόλυμα ἀπὸ Καισαρείας,
2 [mn] ἐνεφάνισάν τε αὐτῷ οἱ ἀρχιερεῖς καὶ οἱ [o] πρῶτοι τῶν
Ἰουδαίων [n] κατὰ τοῦ Παύλου, καὶ [pq] παρεκάλουν αὐτὸν

ABCEH LPℵ a b c d f g h k l m o p 13

y here only +. 2 Macc. viii. 8 only. (-νος, Luke v. 33. 1 Tim. v. 23, only. Ezek. xxxi. 3 A Ald. compl. only.)
z Luke xxiv. 14, 15. ch. xx. 11 only. w. dat., here only. Prov. xxiii. 30.
a ch. xxviii. 30 only +. (-τής, Matt. ii. 16. 2 Macc. x. 3.) see ch. xx. 31.
b = ch. vii. 23 reff. c here only. 1 Chron. xviii. 17. so *successorem accepit*, Plin. Epist. ix. 13 end. d = 2 Cor. viii. 4 reff. e ch. xxv. 9. f = as above [e] (Mark xv. 46) only. 1 Macc. x. 23 Ed-vat F (not ABℵ) &c. εὐεργεσίαν καταθέσθαι, Demosth. 193. 22. g = ch. xviii. 19 reff. h = Mark xv. 7. Isa. xlii. 7. i = here only. see ch. xx. 18. xxi. 4. k ch. xxiii. 34 only +. (-χος, Ezra v. 3.) l = ch. xv. 2. Matt. xx. 18. Ezra vii. 6, 7. m ch. xxiii. 15 reff. n ch. xxiv. 1. o ch. xiii. 50 reff. p = Matt. xviii. 29. q Matt. viii. 34 only. Plut. vit. Demetr. § 38.

rec aft παυλου ins οπως λυση αυτον (*a gloss from the marg*), with HLP rel 36 copt æth-pl Chr Thl: om ABCEℵ p [13] 40 vulg syrr [æth-rom] arm. for ωμιλει, διελεγετο C 15-8. 36. 180.

27. φαιστον P(so elsw). aft φηστον ins τον δε παυλον ειασεν εν τηρησει δια δρουσιλλαν 137 syr-mg. for τε, δε ℵ[3] b c d e g h k l^2 o p^2 13. 40. 137 vulg Syr [syr] copt Chr_1 Thl. rec χαριτας, with HP rel 36 [arm] Amm-c_1 Thl-sif: χαριν (*see ch* xxv. 9) ELℵ[3] c k 40. 137 vulg (syrr copt) Chr Thl-fin: txt ABCℵ[1] p 13.

Chap. XXV. 1. τη επαρχειω A ℵ[1](-χιω): την επαρχιαν p.

2. ενεφανησαν [L m(ανεφ.)] 25-6. 68. 105 Thl-fin (so also [some in] ch xxiv. 1; xxv. 15). rec δε (*alteration of characteristic* τε), with EHLP rel syr copt [arm] Thl-sif: txt ABCℵ k p 13. 40 vulg Syr æth Chr_1 Thl-fin. rec ο αρχιερευς, with HP rel Thl-sif: txt ABCELℵ c d p 36. 40. 137 vulg syrr copt æth arm [Chr_2 Thl-fin].

not offer money for their liberation (Jos. B. J. ii. 14. 1). St. Paul did not resort to this mode of shortening his tedious and unjust imprisonment, and Tertullian ('de Fuga in Persecutione,' 12, p. 116) quotes his conduct in this respect against those who were disposed to purchase escape from persecution: a practice which prevailed and became a great evil in the time of Cyprian. See his Epistles, lii. and lxviii., denouncing the Libellatici. **27. διετίας**] viz. of Paul's imprisonment. **Πόρκιον Φῆστον**] Festus appears to have succeeded Felix in the summer or autumn of the year 60 A.D.: but the question is one of much chronological difficulty. It is fully discussed in Wieseler, Chron. d. Apost.-g. pp. 91—99. He found the province (Jos. Antt. xx. 8. 10) wasted and harassed by bands of robbers and sicarii, and the people the prey of false prophets. He died, after being procurator a very short time,—from one to two years. Josephus (B. J. ii. 14. 1) contrasts him, as a putter down of robbers, favourably with his successor Albinus. On the deposition, &c., of Felix, see note, ch. xxiii. 24. **χάριτα καταθέσθαι**] See reff. 'Est locutio bene Græca, Demostheni quoque usitata et Xenophonti: quales locutiones non paucas habet Lucas, ubi non alios inducit loquentes, sed ipse loquitur, et quidem de rebus ad religionem non pertinentibus.' Grot. The reading χάριτα, brought into the text by the evidence of the best MSS., has apparently been a correction to suit the context, only *one* such act being spoken of. The plural would describe the *wish* of Felix to confer *obligations* on the Jews, who were sending to complain of him at Rome,—and so win their favour. **δεδεμένον**] There was no *change* in the method of custody, see note on ver. 23. He left him in the '*custodia militaris*' in which he was.

XXV. 1.] The term ἐπαρχία is properly used of a *province*, whether imperial or senatorial (see note on ch. xiii. 7),—but is here loosely applied to Judæa, which was only a procuratorship, attached to the *province* of Syria. So also Josephus calls Festus ἔπαρχος, Antt. xx. 8. 11; as also Albinus, ib. 9. 1. **2. οἱ ἀρχ.**] It has been imagined, that ὁ ἀρχ. of the rec. has been a correction to suit the former part of the narrative. But it may be that οἱ ἀρχιερεῖς has been substituted for it, to suit the assertion of Festus, ver. 15. So Meyer and De Wette. The High Priest now was Ishmael the son of Phabi, Jos. Antt. xx. 8. 11 [see chronological table in Prolegg.]. **πρῶτοι** is more general than πρεσβύτεροι, though most of the *first men* must have been members of the Sanhedrim.

3 ʳ αἰτούμενοι ˢ χάριν κατ' αὐτοῦ, ᑫ ὅπως ᵗ μεταπέμψηται
αὐτὸν εἰς Ἱερουσαλήμ, ᵘ ἐνέδραν ποιοῦντες ᵛ ἀνελεῖν αὐτὸν
ʷ κατὰ τὴν ὁδόν. 4 ὁ μὲν οὖν Φῆστος ἀπεκρίθη ˣ τηρεῖσθαι τὸν Παῦλον ʸ εἰς Καισάρειαν, ἑαυτὸν δὲ μέλλειν ᶻ ἐν
ᶻ τάχει ᵃ ἐκπορεύεσθαι· 5 Οἱ οὖν ἐν ὑμῖν, φησίν, ᵇ δυνατοὶ
ᶜ συγκαταβάντες, εἴ τι ἐστὶν ἐν τῷ ἀνδρὶ ᵈ ἄτοπον ᵉ κατ-
ηγορείτωσαν αὐτοῦ. 6 ᶠ διατρίψας δὲ ᵍ ἐν αὐτοῖς ἡμέρας
οὐ πλείους ὀκτὼ ἢ δέκα, ʰ καταβὰς ʰ εἰς Καισάρειαν, ⁱ τῇ
ⁱ ἐπαύριον ᵏ καθίσας ἐπὶ τοῦ ˡ βήματος ἐκέλευσεν τὸν Παῦλον ᵐ ἀχθῆναι. 7 ⁿ παραγενομένου δὲ αὐτοῦ ᵒ περιέστησαν
αὐτὸν οἱ ᵖ ἀπὸ Ἱεροσολύμων ᵖ καταβεβηκότες Ἰουδαῖοι,
πολλὰ καὶ ᑫ βαρέα ʳ αἰτιώματα ˢ καταφέροντες, ἃ οὐκ
ᵗ ἴσχυον ᵘ ἀποδεῖξαι, 8 τοῦ Παύλου ᵛ ἀπολογουμένου ὅτι

r = ch. xii. 20. Matt. vii. 9 ‖. 3 Kings xix. 4.
s = 2 Cor. viii. 4 reff.
t ch. x. 5 reff.
u ch. xxiii. 16 only (reff.).
v = ch. v. 33 reff.
w ch. viii. 36 reff.
x = ch. xii. 5, 6 reff.
y = ch. xix. 22 reff.
z Rom. xvi. 20 reff.
a absol., Luke iii. 7 (ch. ix. 28). Josh. xv. 18 B &c.
b = 1 Cor. i. 26. 2 Chron. viii. 9.
c here only. Ps. xlviii. 17. Cant. tr. pu. 25. Wisd. x. 13 only.
d ch. xxviii. 6 reff.
e and constr., ch. xxiv. 8 reff.
f ch. xii. 19 reff.
g = ch. xxiv. 21 al. fr.
h ch. xviii. 22 reff.
i ch. x. 9 reff.
k = ch. xii. 21. ver. 17. Matt. xxiii. 2. 3 Kings viii. 20.
l ch. xii. 21 reff.
m = ch. viii. 32 reff.
n = absol., ch. xvii. 10 reff.
o = John xi. 42 (2 Tim. ii. 16. Tit. iii. 9) only. 2 Kings xiii. 31.
p Mark iii. 22. Luke x. 30 al.
q Matt. xxiii. 4, 23. ch. xx. 29. 2 Cor. x. 10. 1 John v. 3 only. Exod. xviii. 18.
r here only +.
s = ch. xxvi. 10 (xx. 9 bis) only. Gen. xxxvii. 2.
t = ch. vi. 10 reff.
u ch. ii. 22 reff.
v ch. xix. 33 reff.

3. for *κατ*, *παρ* C e 18. 36. 105-80 tol Syr [arm] Chr-txt$_1$. *ιεροσολυμα* E k 96. *ενεδρον* c 137 Chr$_1$. at end ins *οι την ευχην πεποιηκοτες κατα το δυνατον ινα εν ταις χερσιν αυτων γενηται* syr-mg.

4. rec *εν καισαρεια*, with HLP rel 36 Chr$_1$: txt ABCEℵ p 13. 40. om *μελλειν* E. *εκπορευεσθαι* bef *εν ταχει* ℵ^3.

5. [for *οι*, *ει* L m o.] rec *δυνατοι* bef *εν υμιν φησι* (*transposition for perspicuity*), with HLP rel syr æth: txt ABCE ℵ(but *ημιν* for *υμιν*) m [p] 13[*δυνατος*] 40 vulg arm Chr-comm$_1$. *καταβαντες* ℵ. rec (for *ατοπον*) *τουτω*, with HLP rel [æth] Chr$_1$ Thl: *τουτω ατοπον* a c g^2 m 137 [(Syr)] syr [Thl-fin$_1$]: om 105-33: *ατοπον* bef *εν τω ανδρι* b e o: txt ABCEℵ d p 13. 40 vulg [copt] arm Lucif$_1$.

6. rec om *ου*, with E-gr HLP a^1 c f h k l syr(ins *πλειους* above the line) [copt] Thl-sif: om *ου πλειους* 137 Syr syr-txt sah: ins ABCℵ p 13. 36 rel vulg E-lat copt arm Thl-fin [Lucif$_1$].—*ου πλειους* bef *ημερας* ℵ. *πλειονας* B: *πλειονες* 38. rec om *οκτω*, with HLP rel Thl-sif: txt ABCEℵ a m p 13 vulg syrr coptt [æth] arm Thl-fin. ins *και* bef *τη επαυριον* A c, so (but *κατεβη* above) 180 vulg syr Lucif. *αχθηναι* bef *τον παυλον* L copt [arm(Tischdf)] Lucif$_1$. *προαχθηναι* ℵ^1(ℵ^3 disapproving).

7. rec om *αυτον*, with HP rel copt Chr$_1$ Thl-sif: ins ABCLℵ b o 36. 40 [vulg syrr arm] Lucif$_1$: *αυτω* E p 13 Thl-fin. rec *αιτιαματα*, with rel 36 Thl-sif: [*αιτηματα* h 13:] txt ABCEHLPℵ a^2 d f m p Chr Thl-fin. rec (for *καταφ.*) *φεροντες*, with HLP rel 36 coptt æth Chr$_1$ Thl: *επιφεροντες* E: txt ABCℵ p 13. 40 [arm-zoh, *objicientes* E-lat] vulg Lucif. rec adds *κατα του παυλου* (*omg του παυλου next ver*), with [H]P rel 36 syr Chr Thl Œc: *τω παυλω* E: *κατ' αυτου* L 17-8. 68 Syr copt (æth) [arm-mss]: om ABCℵ p vulg arm[-zoh] Lucif. *ισχυσαν* ℵ^1.

8. rec aft *απολογ.* ins *αυτου* (*corrn following on the insertion of κατα του παυλου*

Festus, relating this application, ver. 15, calls them *πρεσβύτεροι*. **3.] χάριν** = *καταδίκην*, ver. 15. **ποιοῦντες**, not for *ποιήσοντες*: they were *making*, *contriving*, the ambush already. The country was at this time, as may be seen abundantly in Jos. Antt. xx., full of sicarii; who were hired by the various parties to take off their adversaries. **5. οἱ δυνατοί]** not, as in E. V., those among you that are able (to go down?): but, **the powerful among you**: those who from their position and influence are best calculated to represent the public interests. See Meyer and Wordsworth. **6.]** The number of days is variously read: which has probably arisen from the later MSS., which have *η* for the *ὀκτώ* of the more ancient ones: thus *η* has been omitted on account of the *η* following. It is possible, as Meyer also observes, that a perverted notion of the necessity of an absolute precision in details in the inspired text, may have occasioned the erasure of one of the numbers. **7. περιέστησαν]** Without the *αὐτόν*, as in rec., this might mean round the *βῆμα*, or round Festus: and perhaps the insertion has been made to clear this up. **καταφέροντες, bringing against him**: see var. readd. and ref.

οὔτε [w] εἰς τὸν νόμον τῶν Ἰουδαίων οὔτε εἰς τὸ ἱερὸν οὔτε
εἰς Καίσαρα τὶ [w] ἥμαρτον. 9 ὁ Φῆστος δὲ θέλων τοῖς
Ἰουδαίοις [x] χαριν [x] καταθέσθαι, ἀποκριθεὶς τῷ Παύλῳ
εἶπεν Θέλεις [y] εἰς Ἱεροσόλυμα [y] ἀναβὰς ἐκεῖ περὶ τούτων
[z] κριθῆναι [a] ἐπ' ἐμοῦ; 10 εἶπεν δὲ ὁ Παῦλος [a] Ἐπὶ τοῦ [1] βήματος Καίσαρος ἑστώς [b] εἰμι, οὗ με δεῖ [z] κρίνεσθαι. Ἰουδαίους οὐδὲν ἠδίκησα, ὡς καὶ σὺ [c] κάλλιον [d] ἐπιγινώσκεις.
11 εἰ μὲν οὖν ἀδικῶ καὶ [e] ἄξιον [e] θανάτου πέπραχά τι, οὐ

ABCEH LPℵ a b c d f g h k l m o p 13

w 1 Cor. vi. 18 reff.
x ch. xxiv. 27 (reff.).
y ch. xi. 2 reff.
z = ver. 20. Rom. iii. 4, from Ps. l. 4 (6).
a ch. xxiii. 30 reff.
b constr., Matt. x. 26. Luke xii. 6. John iii. 21. ch. xxvi. 26. 1 Cor. i. 10. v. 2 al.
c compar. = ch. xxvii. 13. 2 Cor. vii. 7. viii. 17. 2 Tim. i. 17, 18 al. Winer, edn. 6, § 35. 4.
d ch. xxiii. 28 reff.
e ch. xxiii. 29 reff.

above), with HP rel 36 Chr_1 Thl-sif: του παυλου απολογουμενου αυτου L: txt ABCEℵ c m p 13. 40. 137 vulg syrr copt æth [arm] Thl-fin $Lucif_1$.—add δε (aft the first word) E 36 am(and demid fuld [tol]) Thl-sif $Lucif_1$, τε Syr. om τι 57. 80. 105: τινα 137.

9. for δε, ουν A (k 40[omg ο]). rec τοις ιουδαιοις bef θελων, with HLP rel Chr_1 Thl-sif: txt ABCEℵ c k m p 13. 40. 137 vulg[-clem(after καταθεσθαι) am fuld demid tol syrr copt] arm Thl-fin. χαριτα A. rec κρινεσθαι, with HLP rel 36 Chr [Thl-sif]: txt ABCEℵ d k p 13. 40 Thl-fin.

10. om ο A f. εστως bef επι του βηματος καισαρος ℵ[1] m [(copt)]: B has it in both places. ηδικηκα Bℵ (p). γινωσκεις C c d[1] 2. 30. 137.

11. rec (for ουν) γαρ (*corrn, as Meyer, because* ει μεν ουν *seemed contradictory to* ουδεν ηδικησα), with HLP rel [vulg syr æth] Thl-sif: om 40 E-lat: txt ABC E-gr ℵ d k p 36 copt [arm] $Chr\text{-}comm_1$ Thl-fin. (13 def.) for και, η E 29 vulg [Syr] $Chr\text{-}comm_1$.

8.] These were the three principal charges to which the πολ. κ. βαρ. αἰτ. of the Jews referred (Meyer). **9.**] **κριθῆναι**, the aor., refers to the *one act*, of *deciding finally* concerning these charges. This not having been seen, the later MSS. have substituted κρίνεσθαι, which is more '*going to law*,' '*being involved* in a trial.' The question is asked of Paul as a Roman citizen, having a right to be tried by Roman law: and more is contained in it, than at first meets the eye. It *seems* to propose only a change of *place;* but doubtless in the **ἐκεῖ** κριθῆναι was contained by implication a sentence pronounced by the Sanhedrim. **ἐπ' ἐμοῦ** may mean no more than ἐπὶ σοῦ, ch. xxvi. 2, viz., that the procurator would *be present* and sanction the trial: so Grot., "visne a synedrio judicari me præsente?" Otherwise, a journey to Jerusalem would be superfluous. Festus may very probably have anticipated the rejection of this proposal by Paul, and have wished to make it appear that the obstacle in the way of Paul being tried by the Sanhedrim arose not from *him*, but from the prisoner himself. **10.**] Paul's refusal has a positive and a negative ground —1. '*Cæsar's tribunal is my proper place of judgment: 2. To the Jews I have done no harm, and they have therefore no claim to judge me*' (De W.). **ἐπ. τ. β. Καίσ.**] Meyer quotes from Ulpian, "Quæ acta gestaque sunt a procuratore Cæsaris sic ab eo comprobantur, atque si a Cæsare ipso gesta sint." In **οὗ με δεῖ κρίνεσθαι**, Wordsworth has again fallen into the mistake of supposing **με** (and again in ver. 11) to be emphatic (see note, Matt. xvi. 18), which it cannot possibly be under any circumstances. The form of the sentence which would express the sense built by him on this error, would be, οὗ δεῖ ἐμὲ κριθῆναι, or οὗ ἐμὲ δεῖ κριθῆναι. But the sense, when thus given, surely is wholly alien from the person speaking and from the situation: as is also the understanding δεῖ as alluding to divine intimation made to him. The δεῖ is simply of his right as a Roman citizen: the με simply enclitic, and of no rhetorical force at all. **κάλλιον**] Not 'for the superlative,' here or any where else:—the comparative is elliptical, requiring 'than . . . .' to be supplied by the hearer: so also in reff. Here, the ellipsis would be readily supplied from Festus's own speech, which appeared to assume that there was some ground of trial before the Sanhedrim. κάλλιον will therefore mean, **better than thou choosest to confess.** We have an ellipsis of the same kind in our phrase '*to know better.*' Or it may be in this case as in 2 Tim. i. 18, '*better, than that I need say more on it:*' but I prefer the other interpretation. **11.**] Both readings, εἰ **μὲν γάρ**, and εἰ μὲν **οὖν**, will suit the sense. In the former case, it is, '*For if I am an offender,* . . . .:' in the latter, **If, now, I am an offender** . . . . ,—taking up the supposition *generally*, after having denied the *particular*

[f] παραιτοῦμαι τὸ ἀποθανεῖν· εἰ δὲ [g] οὐδέν ἐστιν [g] ὧν
οὗτοι [h] κατηγοροῦσίν μου, οὐδείς με δύναται αὐτοῖς [i] χαρίσασθαι. Καίσαρα [k] ἐπικαλοῦμαι. 12 τότε ὁ Φῆστος
[l] συλλαλήσας μετὰ τοῦ [m] συμβουλίου ἀπεκρίθη Καίσαρα
[k] ἐπικέκλησαι, [n] ἐπὶ Καίσαρα [n] πορεύσῃ.
13 [o] Ἡμερῶν δὲ [p] διαγενομένων [o] τινῶν Ἀγρίππας ὁ βα-

f Luke xiv. 18, 19. 1 Tim. iv. 7. Heb. xii. 25 (bis). L.P.H. Esth. iv. 8.
g ch. xxi. 24.
h and constr., ch. xxiv. 8 reff.
i = ver. 16 only. see ch. iii. 14 reff.
k = here, &c., 4 times. ch. xxvi. 32. xxviii. 19 only. see ch. ii. 21.
l w. μετά, Matt. xvii. 3. πρός, Luke iv. 36. dat., Luke ix. 30 ‖ Mk. xxii. 4 only. Exod. xxxiv. 35.
m = here only †. (Matt. xii. 14 al.) Prov. xv. 22 Theod.
n ch. ix. 11. xvii. 14.
o ch. x. 48 reff.
p Mark xvi. 1. ch. xxvii. 9 only †. 2 Macc. xi. 26 only.

for το, του H f l m o Thl. for μου, μοι L 78[1]. for αυτοις, τουτοις CL 36: txt ABEHPℵ p rel Chr.

12. συμβουλου L 18: συνεδριου C: συνεδ. κ. συμβ. 68.

13. om τινων c k 1. 36. 137 Chr: τριων 3. 95. 108.

case of his having *offended the Jews.* Meyer and De Wette are at issue about the internal probability of these readings: I am disposed to agree with Meyer that a difficulty was felt in the οὖν (no expression is more frequently misunderstood and altered than μὲν οὖν) and it was corrected into γάρ. This εἰ assumes the *conviction* after proof; as the following **εἰ** does the *acquittal.* **οὐ. με δύν.**] Said of *legal* possibility: 'non fas est aliquem . . . . .' The dilemma here put by Paul is, "*If I am guilty, it is not by them, but by Cæsar, that I must be* (*and am willing to be*) *tried, sentenced, and punished. If I am innocent, and Cæsar acquits me, then clearly none will be empowered to give me up to them: therefore, at all events, guilty or innocent, I am not to be made their victim.*" **Καίσ. ἐπικαλ.**] **I call upon,** i. e. *appeal to* (provoco ad) **Cæsar.** This power (of 'provocatio ad *populum*') having existed in very early times (e. g. the case of Horatius, Livy i. 26), was ensured to Roman citizens by the Lex Valeria (see Livy ii. 8, U.C. 245), suspended by the Decemviri, but solemnly re-established after their deposition (Liv. iii. 55, U.C. 305), when it was decreed that it should be unlawful to make any magistrate from whom there did not lie an appeal. When the emperors absorbed the power of the populus and the tribunitial veto in themselves, the 'provocatio ad populum' and 'appellatio ad tribunos' were both made to the *princeps.* See Smith's Dict. of Antt. art. Appellatio. In Pliny's celebrated Epistle respecting the Bithynian Christians (x. 97), we read, "Fuerunt alii similis amentiæ: quos, quia cives Romani erant, adnotavi in urbem remittendos." **12. συμβουλίου**] The '*conventus*,' or σύνοδος of citizens in the provinces, assembled to try causes on the ἀγοραῖοι (ἡμέραι), see ch. xix. 38. A certain number of these were chosen as judices, for the particular causes, by the proconsul, and these were called his '*consiliarii*' (Suet. Tib. 33), or '*assessores*' (πάρεδροι, Suet. Galba 19). So in Jos. (B. J. ii. 16. 1), Cestius, on receiving an application from Jerusalem respecting the conduct of Florus, μετὰ ἡγεμόνων ἐβουλεύετο, i. e. with his assessors, or συμβούλιον. He consulted them to decide whether the appeal was to be conceded, or if conceded, to be at once acted on. (Mr. Lewin cites from the Digests, xlix. 5. 7: 'Si res dilationem non recipiat, non permittitur appellare.') The sense is stronger and better without a question at ἐπικέκλησαι. Thus were the two—the design of Paul (ch. xix. 21), and the promise of our Lord to him (ch. xxiii. 11)—brought to their fulfilment, by a combination of providential circumstances. We can hardly say, with De W. and Meyer, that these must have *influenced* Paul in making his appeal; that step is naturally accounted for, and was rendered necessary by the difficulties which now beset him; but we may be sure that the prospect at length, after his long and tedious imprisonment, of *seeing Rome,* must at this time have cheered him, and caused him to hear the ἐπὶ Καίσαρα πορεύσῃ of Festus with no small emotion. **13.**] HEROD AGRIPPA II., son of the Herod of ch. xii. (see note on ver. 1 there), was at Rome, and seventeen only, when his father died (Jos. Antt. xix. 9. 1). Claudius (ib. 9. 2) was about to send him to succeed to the kingdom, but was dissuaded by his freedmen and favourites, and sent Cuspius Fadus as procurator instead. Soon after, Claudius gave him the principality of Chalcis, which had been held by his uncle Herod (Antt. xx. 5. 2),—the presidency of the temple at Jerusalem and its treasures (Antt. xx. 1. 3),—and the appointment of the High Priest. Some years after the same emperor added to his jurisdiction the former tetrarchy of Philip, and Batanæa, Trachonitis, and Abilene (Antt. xx. 7. 1), with the title of King

q ch. xvi. 1 reff. r ch. xviii. 22. xxi. 7. Exod. xviii. 7. s ch. ii. 40 reff. t ver. 6. u Gal. ii. 2 only. 2 Macc. iii. 9 ‡. v ch. xxiv. 22 reff. w ch. xxiv. 27. x ch. xvi. 25, 27 reff. y here only. 2 Macc. iii. 7. z = ch. xx. 16 reff. a ch. xxiii. 15 reff. b = ch. iv. 8 reff. c ch. xii. 20 reff. ver. 3.

σιλεὺς καὶ Βερνίκη [q] κατήντησαν εἰς Καισάρειαν [r] ἀσπασάμενοι τὸν Φῆστον. 14 ὡς δὲ [s] πλείους ἡμέρας [t] διέτριβον
ἐκεῖ ὁ Φῆστος τῷ βασιλεῖ [u] ἀνέθετο [v] τὰ [v] κατὰ τὸν Παῦλον,
λέγων Ἀνήρ τις ἐστὶν [w] καταλελειμμένος ὑπὸ Φήλικος
[x] δέσμιος, 15 [y] περὶ οὗ [z] γενομένου μου [z] εἰς Ἱεροσόλυμα
[a] ἐνεφάνισαν οἱ ἀρχιερεῖς καὶ οἱ [b] πρεσβύτεροι τῶν Ἰου-
δαιων, [c] αἰτούμενοι κατ᾽ αὐτοῦ [d] καταδίκην· 16 πρὸς οὓς
ἀπεκρίθην ὅτι οὐκ ἔστιν [e] ἔθος Ῥωμαίοις [f] χαρίζεσθαί τινα
ἄνθρωπον πρὶν ἢ ὁ [g] κατηγορούμενος [h] κατὰ [h] πρόσωπον
ἔχοι τοὺς [i] κατηγόρους, [k] τόπον τε [l] ἀπολογίας λάβοι

ABCEH LPא a b c d f g h k l m o p 13

d here only †. Wisd. xii. 27 only. Ælian, Var. Hist. v. 18. Herodian, vii. 4. e = John xix. 40. Heb. x. 25. (ch. vi. 14 reff.) f = ver. 11. g absol., ch. xxiv. 2 reff. pass., ch. xxii. 30 reff. h 2 Cor. x. 1 reff. i ch. xxiii. 30 reff. k = Rom. xv. 23. Heb. viii. 7. xii. 17. Wisd. xii. 10. l ch. xxii. 1. 1 Cor. ix. 3. 2 Cor. vii. 11. Phil. i. 7, 16. 2 Tim. iv. 16. 1 Pet. iii. 15 only †. Wisd. vi. 10 only.

βερενικη C^2 arm : βερηνικη (appy) C^1, but ver 23, C has βερονικης, and so here E-lat demid tol Cassiod$_1$. [κατηντησεν C.] rec ασπασομενοι, with p rel 36 vulg E-lat syrr [arm] Chr$_1$ Thl-fin : txt AB E-gr HLPא [k^1 l^1(appy) m(Scr)] copt æth Thl-sif. (C is uncertain.)

14. διετριβεν HP d f g k l æth-rom Thl-sif. [om τα A^1 k^1(appy).]

15. ενεφανισθησαν B^1(txt B$^{2\cdot3}$, Tischdf). aft ενεφανισαν ins μοι E-gr vulg arm. rec δικην (*see note*), with EHLP p rel 36 Chr$_1$: txt ABCא 13. 40 Bas$_1$, *damnationem* vulg.

16. ρωμαιους P m 101. τινι C o 27-9. 105. rec aft ανθρωπον ins εις απωλειαν, with HLP rel 36 Syr syr-w-ast Chr$_1$ Thl : om ABCEא c p 13. 40 am fuld coptt [æth] arm Ath$_1$ Thdrt$_1$ Bas$_1$; *damnare* (= χαριζ . . . εις απωλειαν) vulg-ed [demid tol] : *donare* am fuld. εχοι bef κατα προσωπον א. for τε, δε B E-gr.

(B. J. ii. 12. 8). Nero afterwards annexed Tiberias, Tarichea, Julias, and fourteen neighbouring villages to his kingdom (Antt. xx. 8. 4). He built a large palace at Jerusalem (ib. 8. 11); but offended the Jews by constructing it so as to overlook the temple (ib.), and by his capricious changes in the high priesthood,—and was not much esteemed by them (B. J. ii. 17. 1). When the last war broke out, he attached himself throughout to the Romans. He died in the third year of Trajan, and fifty-first of his reign, aged about seventy (Winer, Realw.). **Βερνίκη**] The Macedonian form (Βερενίκη or Βερονίκη) for Φερενίκη. She was the eldest daughter of Herod Agrippa I., and first married to her uncle Herod, prince of Chalcis (Antt. xix. 5. 1). After his death she lived with Agrippa her brother, but not without suspicion (φήμης ἐπισχυούσης, ὅτι τῷ ἀδελφῷ συνήει, Antt. xx. 7. 3; see also Juv. Sat. vi. 156 ff.); in consequence of which (οὕτως γὰρ ἐλέγξειν ᾤετο ψευδεῖς τὰς διαβολάς, Antt. ib.) she married Polemo, king of Cilicia. The marriage was, however, soon dissolved (ib.), and she returned to her brother. She was afterwards the mistress of Vespasian (Tac. Hist. ii. 81), and of Titus (Suet. Tit. 7); Winer, Realw.). **ἀσπασάμενοι**] on his accession to the procuratorship, to gain his favour. **14. ἀνέθετο**] laid before, so reff. He did this, not only because Agrippa was a Jew, but because he was (see above) *governor of the temple*.

15.] It seems more probable that the unusual word καταδίκη should have been changed to δίκην, especially as κατά precedes, than the converse. Luke never uses δίκη, except as *personified*, ch. xxviii. 4; and in the only two places besides where it occurs in the N. T. (2 Thess. i. 9; Jude 7), it has the sense of *condemnation* or *punishment;* and in neither place is there any various reading. **16. χαρίζεσθαι**] The words inserted in the rec., εἰς ἀπώλειαν, are a correct supplement of the sense; to give up, i. e. *to his enemies, and for destruction.* De W. remarks, that the construction of πρίν with an opt. without ἄν, is only found here in the N. T. (not that it occurs with ἄν). Hermann, on Viger, p. 442, restricts the opt. with πρὶν ἤ to cases where ' res narratur ut cogitatio alicujus :' so Paus., μὴ πρότερον φάναι ζητοῦντι μηνύσειν πρὶν ἢ οἱ καὶ ἐν Ἀκροκορίνθῳ γένοιτο ὕδωρ. On the practice of the Romans, here nobly and truly alleged, see citations in Grot. and Wetst. in loc. **τόπον**] This use of τόπος

περὶ τοῦ [m] ἐγκλήματος. 17 [n] συνελθόντων οὖν [αὐτῶν]
[o] ἐνθάδε [p] ἀναβολὴν μηδεμίαν ποιησάμενος, [q] τῇ [q] ἑξῆς
[r] καθίσας ἐπὶ τοῦ [r] βήματος ἐκέλευσα [r] ἀχθῆναι τὸν ἄνδρα·
18 περὶ οὗ [s] σταθέντες οἱ [t] κατήγοροι οὐδεμίαν [u] αἰτίαν [v] ἔφερον
ὧν ἐγὼ [w] ὑπενόουν [πονηράν], 19 [x] ζητήματα δέ τινα περὶ
τῆς ἰδίας [y] δεισιδαιμονίας εἶχον [z] πρὸς αὐτόν, καὶ περί τινος
Ἰησοῦ τεθνηκότος, ὃν [a] ἔφασκεν ὁ Παῦλος ζῆν. 20 [b] ἀπο-
ρούμενος δὲ ἐγὼ [[c] εἰς] τὴν περὶ τούτων [d] ζήτησιν, [e] ἔλεγον
[e] εἰ βούλοιτο πορεύεσθαι εἰς Ἱεροσόλυμα κἀκεῖ [f] κρίνεσθαι
περὶ τούτων. 21 τοῦ δὲ Παύλου [g] ἐπικαλεσαμένου [hi] τηρηθῆναι αὐτὸν [i] εἰς τὴν τοῦ [k] σεβαστοῦ [l] διάγνωσιν, ἐκέλευσα
[h] τηρεῖσθαι αὐτὸν ἕως οὗ [m] ἀναπέμψω αὐτὸν πρὸς Καίσαρα.

m ch. xxiii. 29 only †.
n = ch. i. 6 reff.
o ch. xvi. 28 reff.
p here only ‡. (Neh. v. 13.) ἀναβολὴν τοῦ δεινοῦ ἐποιήσατο, Thucyd. ii. 42. (-βάλλεσθαι, ch. xxiv. 22.)
q ch. xxi. 1 reff.
r ver. 6 (reff.).
s ch. xi. 13 reff.
t ver. 16.
u = Matt. xxvii. 37 al. Gen. iv. 13.
v John xviii. 29. 2 Pet. ii. 11 only. see ver. 7.
w ch. xiii. 25 reff.
x ch. xv. 2 reff.
y here only †. = Jos. Antt. xix. 5. 3. (-μων, ch. xvii. 22.) z = ch. xxiv. 19 reff. a ch. xxiv. 9 reff. b Mark vi. 20 v. r. Luke xxiv. 4. John xiii. 22. 2 Cor. iv. 8. Gal. iv. 20 only. Gen. xxxii. 7. w. εἰς, here only. see Matthiæ, § 578. (-ρία, Luke xxi. 25.) c = Rom. iv. 20. d = 1 Tim. vi. 4. 2 Tim. ii. 23. Tit. iii. 9 (John iii. 25. ch. xv. 2. 1 Tim. i. 4) only †. e constr., here only. f ver. 9. g ver. 11. h ch. xii 5, 6 reff. i 2 Pet. ii. 4. k = ver. 25 only †. see ch. xxvii. 1. l here only †. Wisd. iii. 18 only. (-γινώσκειν, ch. xxiii. 15. xxiv. 22.) m = Luke xxiii. 7 (11), 15 (Philem. 11) only †. Polyb. i. 7. 12.

17. rec ins *αυτων*, with AEHLPℵ p 13(sic) rel Chr_1 : om B 40-2. 57. 81. 95¹-7 : *ενθαδε* bef *αυτων* C c (137 [?]). *μηδεμιαν* bef *αναβολην* E k. *ποιησαμενοι* ℵ¹.
18. rec *επεφερον*, with HP rel Chr_1 : *υπεφερον* 80 lect-5 : txt ABCELℵ c p 13. 36. 40. 137. rec *υπενοουν* bef *εγω*, with EHLP rel 36 Chr Thl-sif: txt ABCℵ m p 13 vulg Thl-fin. rec om *πονηραν*, with HLP rel [copt] Chr Thl-sif: ins *πονηρων* BEℵ³ p; *malum* vulg; *πονηρα* C²ℵ¹; *πονηριας* arm; *πονηραν* AC¹ c k m 13(sic) 36. 40. 137 am(*malam*) syrr æth Thl-fin.
19. *αυτους* A. for *εφασκεν*, *ελεγεν* c 137.
20. rec ins *εις*, with CEL rel [Thl-fin]: om ABHPℵ b d f h k l o p Thl-sif.—om *περι* c m 137 : aft *περι* ins *την* h k. rec *τουτου* (*corrn to suit παυλος*, or *ιησου*?), with HP rel Chr_1[-txt Thl-sif] : txt ABCELℵ c h k m p 13. 36. 40 syrr copt æth [(arm)] Chr_2 Thl-fin. for *πορευεσθαι*, *κρινεσθαι* ℵ¹. rec *ιερουσαλημ*, with LP 13[e sil] rel [Thl-sif] : txt ABCEHℵ c k m p 36. 137 Thl-fin. *κριθηναι* L.
21. for *τηρηθηναι*, *τηρεισθαι* C. *αυτον* bef *τηρεισθαι* c 13. 68. 137 [Thl-sif]. rec *πεμψω* (*neglect of force of compound*), with HLP rel Chr_1 [Thl-sif] : txt ABCEℵ c k m p 13. 36. 40. 137 Thl-fin.

as the Lat. 'locus,' is not found in good Greek. **18. περὶ οὗ σταθ.]** See ver. 7: E. V., '*against whom*,' supposing περὶ οὗ to refer to (ἐπ)έφερον, is wrong. The word πονηράν or πονηρῶν, added in the best MSS. at the end of this verse, looks very like a gloss to explain ὧν or αἰτίαν, and this suspicion is strengthened by the variations in its form and place. 'Hinc iterum conjicere licet, imo aperte cognoscere, adeo futiles fuisse calumnias ut in judicii rationem venire non debuerint, perinde ac si quis convicium temere jactet.' Calv. **19.] δεισιδαιμ.** is used by Festus in a *middle* sense, certainly not as = '*superstition*,' E. V., speaking as he was to Agrippa, a Jew. **20.]** See the *real reason* why he proposed this, ver. 9. This he now conceals, and alleges his *modesty* in referring such matters to the judgment of the Jews themselves. This would be pleasing to his guest Agrippa. **ἀπορ. εἰς]** so σὺ δ' εἰς τὰ μητρὸς μὴ φοβοῦ νυμφεύματα, Soph. Œd. Tyr. 980; and ἀμφινοῶ ἐς τέρας, Antig. 372. **ἔλεγον]** There is a mixed construction between '*I said, wilt thou?*' as in ver. 9, and '*I asked him whether he would ....*' **21.] τηρηθῆναι** is not for εἰς τὸ τηρ. (as Grot. and De W.), but follows directly on ἐπικαλεσαμένου. The construction is again a mixed one between '*appealing so as to be kept*,' and '*demanding to be kept*.' **σεβαστοῦ]** This title, = Augustus, was first conferred by the senate on Octavianus (αὐτὸς γενόμενος ἀρχὴ σεβασμοῦ καὶ τοῖς ἔπειτα, Philo de Legat. ad Caium, 21, vol. ii. p. 566), and borne by all succeeding emperors. Dio Cassius (liii. 16) says: Αὔγουστος, ὡς καὶ πλεῖόν τι ἢ κατὰ ἀνθρώπους ὤν, ἐπεκλήθη. πάντα γὰρ τὰ ἐντιμότατα καὶ τὰ ἱερώτατα αὔγουστα προσαγορεύεται. ἐξ οὗπερ καὶ σεβαστὸν αὐτὸν καὶ ἑλληνίζοντές πως, ὥσπερ τινὰ σεπτόν, ἀπὸ τοῦ σεβά-

22 Ἀγρίππας δὲ πρὸς τὸν Φῆστον [n] Ἐβουλόμην καὶ αὐτὸς
τοῦ ἀνθρώπου ἀκοῦσαι. [o] Αὔριον φησὶν ἀκούσῃ αὐτοῦ.
23 [p] Τῇ οὖν [p] ἐπαύριον ἐλθόντος τοῦ Ἀγρίππα καὶ τῆς
Βερνίκης [q] μετὰ πολλῆς [r] φαντασίας καὶ εἰςελθόντων
εἰς τὸ [s] ἀκροατήριον σύν τε χιλιάρχοις καὶ ἀνδράσιν τοῖς
κατ' [t] ἐξοχὴν τῆς πόλεως, καὶ κελεύσαντος τοῦ Φηστου
[u] ἤχθη ὁ Παῦλος. 24 καί φησιν ὁ Φῆστος Ἀγρίππα
βασιλεῦ καὶ πάντες οἱ [v] συμπαρόντες ἡμῖν ἄνδρες, θεωρεῖτε
τοῦτον περὶ οὗ ἅπαν τὸ πλῆθος τῶν Ἰουδαίων [w] ἐνέτυχον
μοι ἔν τε Ἱεροσολύμοις καὶ [x] ἐνθάδε [[y] ἐπι]βοῶντες μὴ δεῖν

ABCEH LPℵ a b c d f g h k l m o p 13

n imperf., = Rom. ix. 3. (ch. xxii. 22) Gal. iv. 20. see Winer, edn. 6, § 41. a. 2.
o 1 Cor. xv. 32 reff.
p ch. x. 9 reff.
q = ch. v. 26. xxvii. 10 al. fr. 1 Macc. ix. 37.
r here only ‡. Hab. ii. 18, 19. Zech. x. 1. Wisd. xviii. 17 only. = Polyb. i. 37. 5 al.
s here only †. (-τής, Rom. ii. 13.)
t here only ‡. Job xxxix. 28 only.
u ver. 6.
v here only. Prov. viii. 27. Wisd. ix. 10 only.
w Rom. viii. 27, 34. xi. 2. Heb. vii. 25 only †. 2 Macc. iv. 36 al.
x ch. xvi. 28 reff.
y here only †. Wisd. xiv. 1 only. θεοὺς ἐπιβοώμενοι, Thucyd. iii. 59. Polyb. xviii. 8. 1. βοᾷν, ch. viii. 7 reff.

22. rec aft φηστον ins εφη, with CEHLP p rel 36 [demid : pref *dixit* vulg-ed:] ειπεν a : om ABℵ 13 am [fuld]. (ει was written and rubbed out by ℵ[3].) rec ins ο δε bet αυριον, with CEHLP p 13 rel (36) [(Syr) syr] : om ABℵ vulg copt. (*The account of both these insertions I take to have been, that as the words stood,* αγριππας *appeared to be the subj of* φησιν,—*and* εφη *and* ο δε *were inserted to distinguish the speakers.*)

23. εις ελθοντος E[-gr]. ακρωτηριον ℵ[1] [ακροτ. H]. rec ins τοις bef χιλιαρχοις (*the usage of omg art aft a preposition not being recognized*), with HLP rel 36 Chr_1 : om ABCEℵ c k p 13. 40. 137. [aft ανδρ. ins και E-gr : τοις e.] rec aft κατ' εξοχην ins ουσι (*supplementary interpoln*), with EHLP rel 36 : om ABCℵ p 13. 40 $Chr\text{-}comm_1$.

24. (απαν, so ABCEℵ [not L] c k p 13. 36. 40. 137 Thl-fin.) ενετυχεν B 25. 40 [vulg syrr. for και ενθαδε to ουκ εχω ver 26] syr-mg has *ut traderem eum iis ad tormentum sine defensione. Non potui autem tradere eum propter mandata quæ habemus ab Augusto. Si autem quis eum accusaturus esset, dicebam ut sequeretur me in Cæsaream, ubi custodiebatur. Qui quum venissent, clamaverunt ut tolleretur e vita. Quum autem hanc et alteram partem audivissem, comperi quod in nullo reus esset mortis. Quum autem dicerem : Vis judicari cum iis Hierosolymæ? Cæsarem appellavit. De quo nihil certum scribere domino meo habeo.* rec επιβοωντες, with CEHLP rel [Chr_1, *acclamantes* vulg-ed demid] : βοωντες ABℵ p [*clamantes* am fuld tol].

ζεσθαι, προσεῖπον. On ἀναπέμψω, Bornemann cites Lucian, Tox. § 17 : ὁ δὲ βασιλεῖ τῷ μεγάλῳ ἀναπέμπει αὐτόν. **22.**] **ἐβουλόμην** does not (as Calv.) imply any *former* wish of Agrippa to hear Paul. It is, as Meyer explains it, a modest way of expressing a wish, formed in this case while the procurator was speaking, but spoken of by Agrippa as if now past by, and therefore not pressed. We say somewhat similarly, '*I was wishing.*' See ref. Rom. and note there. Cf. Aristoph. Av. 1027 : ἐκκλησιάσαι δ' οὖν ἐδεόμην οἴκοι μένων : and see other examples in Bernhardy, Syntax, p. 373 ff. Agrippa, as a Jew, is anxious to hear Paul's defence, as a matter of national interest. The procurator's ready consent is explained, ver. 26. **23.**] **φαντασία** is of frequent use in this sense in Polybius and later Greek writers. Herodotus uses the verb φαντάζεσθαι for '*superbire,*' vii. 201 : ὁρᾷς ὡς τὰ ὑπερέχοντα ζῶα κεραυνοῖ ὁ θεός, οὐδ' ἐᾷ φαντάζεσθαι. See Wetst., who finely remarks on the words, 'In eadem urbe, in qua pater ipsorum a vermibus corrosus ob superbiam perierat.' **ἀκροατήριον**] after the Latin '*auditorium* :' perhaps no fixed hall of audience, but the chamber or saloon set apart for this occasion. **χιλιάρχοις**] Jos. (B. J. iii. 4. 2), speaking of Titus's army, says, προσεγένοντο δὲ καὶ ἀπὸ Καισαρείας πέντε (σπεῖραι). These, then, were the tribunes of the cohorts stationed at Cæsarea. Stier remarks (Red. der Apostel, ii. 397), "Yet more and more complete must the giving of the testimony in these parts be, before the witness departs for Rome. In Jerusalem, the long-suffering of the Lord towards the rejectors of the Gospel was now exhausted. In Antioch, the residence of the Præses of Syria, the new mother church of Jewish and Gentile Christians was flourishing; here, in Cæsarea, the residence of the procurator, the testimony which had begun in the house of Cornelius the centurion, had now risen upward, till it comes before this brilliant assembly of all the local authorities, in the presence of the last

αὐτὸν ζῆν μηκέτι.
25 ἐγὼ δὲ [z] κατελαβόμην μηδὲν [a] ἄξιον αὐτὸν [a] θανάτου πεπραχέναι, [b] αὐτοῦ δὲ [b] τούτου [c] ἐπικαλεσαμένου τὸν [d] σεβαστόν, [e] ἔκρινα πέμπειν.
26 περὶ οὗ [f] ἀσφαλές τι γράψαι τῷ [g] κυρίῳ οὐκ [h] ἔχω, διὸ [i] προήγαγον αὐτὸν [j] ἐφ' ὑμῶν καὶ μάλιστα [j] ἐπὶ σοῦ, βασιλεῦ Ἀγρίππα, ὅπως τῆς [k] ἀνακρίσεως γενομένης [l] σχῶ τί γράψω·
27 [m] ἄλογον γάρ μοι δοκεῖ πέμποντα [n] δέσμιον μὴ καὶ τὰς κατ' αὐτοῦ [o] αἰτίας [p] σημᾶναι.

XXVI. 1 Ἀγρίππας δὲ πρὸς τὸν Παῦλον ἔφη [q] Ἐπιτρέπεταί σοι περὶ σεαυτοῦ λέγειν. τότε ὁ Παῦλος [r] ἐκ-

z = ch. iv. 13 reff.
a = ch. xxiii. 29 reff.
b ch. xxiv. 15 reff.
c ver. 11.
d ver. 21.
e = ch. xv. 19 reff.
f = ch. xxi. 34 reff.
g = 1 Cor. viii. 5 al.
h ch. xxiii. 17 &c. reff.
i — ch. xii. 6 reff.
j ch. xxiii. 30 reff.
k here only †. 3 Macc. vii. 5. Polyb. viii. 19. 8. (-νειν, ch. xxiv. 8 al.)
l see ch. iv. 14 reff.
m = here (2 Pet. ii. 12. Jude 10) only ‡. (Exod. vi. 12. Numb. vi. 12. Wisd. xi. 15 only.)
n ch. xvi. 25, 27 reff.
o ver. 18.
p ch. xi. 28 reff.
q and constr., ch. xxviii. 16. 1 Cor. xiv. 34. 1 Tim. ii. 12. Xen. Cyr. viii. 4. 29. w. aor., ch. xxi. 39, 40 reff.
r Matt. viii. 3 al. Gen. xiv. 22. ἀνέτεινε τὴν δεξιὰν ὡς δημηγορήσων, Polyæn. iv. p. 317. (Wahl.)

rec *ζην* bef *αυτον*, with HLP rel Chr$_1$ Thl-sif: om *ζην* B^1(Tischdf): txt A B-corr^1 CEℵ a^1 b k m o p 13. 40 vulg [Syr] arm Chr-comm$_1$ Thl-fin.

25. rec *καταλαβομενος* and ins *και* aft *πεπραχεναι*, with HLP ℵ^1(but om *και*) rel 36 syr Thl (13 Thl-fin retain *και*): txt ABCEℵ^3 p 40 vulg syr copt [arm]. rec *θανατου* bef *αυτον* (*transp of characteristic order*), with HLPℵ rel 36 [vulg-ed] Chr$_1$: om *αυτον* p 73: *αυτον* bef *αξιον* g 68 Thl-fin: [*πεπρ. αυ.* bef *θ.* c:] *θ. πεπραχεναι* bef *αυτον* 105-37: txt ABCE 13. 40 am(and demid fuld tol). for *τουτου*, *του παυλου* B^1(but *παυλου* has dots placed over it by the original scribe, see table: txt B^2). rec aft *πεμπειν* ins *αυτον*, with EHLP rel [syr copt] Chr Thl: om ABCℵ p 13. 36. 40 vulg [Syr] arm.

26. *ασφαλως* C. *προςηγαγον* E-gr l 16-7: *επηγαγ.* A. om *σου* ℵ^1(ins ℵ-corr$^{1.3}$). *κρισεως* [for *ανακρ.*] E. for *σχω*, *εχω* AE p 137 Thl-fin. rec (for *γραψω*) *γραψαι*, with EHLP rel 36 Chr$_1$: txt ABCℵ p 13 (syrr).

27. *πεμποντι* L 37. 43. 133. E vulg place *μη* aft *αιτιας*.

CHAP. XXVI. **1.** *επιτετρεπται* L: *επιτετραπται* b c o p 137 Thl-fin. rec (for *περι*) *υπερ*, with BLP rel Chr$_1$: txt ACE H[*λεγ. π. σε.*] ℵ c p 13. 36.—*λαλειν περι σ.* c 137. aft *παυλος* ins *πεποιθως και εν πνευματι αγιω παρακληθεις* syr-mg.

king of the Jews." **24. ἅπαν τὸ πλ.]** At Jerusalem (ver. 1) literally, by the popular voice (probably) of some tumultuous outcry:—here, by their deputation.

25. αὐτοῦ δὲ τούτου] he himself moreover. These reasons did really coexist as influencing his determination. Mr. Lewin cites, on ver. 12, Dig. xlix. 1. 16: 'Constitutiones quæ de recipiendis, necnon, appellationibus loquuntur, ut nihil novi fiat, *locum non habent in eorum persona quos damnatos statim puniri publici interest, ut sunt insignes latrones, vel seditionum concitatores, vel duces factionum.*'

26. ἀσφαλές] fixed, definite. The whole matter had been hitherto obscured by the exaggerations and fictions of the Jews. **τῷ κυρίῳ]** viz. Nero. Augustus and Tiberius refused this title; Caligula and (apparently) all following bore it. "Thus Tertullian, Apol. xxxiv. vol. i. p. 430: 'Augustus imperii formator ne dominum quidem dici se volebat;' and Suet. Aug. 53: 'Dominum se appellari ne a liberis quidem aut nepotibus vel serio vel joco passus est;' and Tib. 27: 'Dominus appellatus a quodam denuntiavit ne se amplius contumeliæ causa nominaret.' *Caligula* accepted the title, according to Victor, ap. Eckhel, viii. 364. Herod Agrippa had applied it to *Claudius* (Philo ap. Spanheim. Numism. ii. 482); but it was not a *recognized* title of any emperor before *Domitian*. Suet. Dom. 13: 'Martial,—Edictum Domini Deique nostri.'" Mr. Humphry. **γράψω** has apparently been altered to *γράψαι* to suit the *τί γράψαι* above. Olsh. remarks, that now first was our Lord's prophecy Matt. x. 18, Mark xiii. 9 fulfilled. But Meyer answers well, that we do not know enough of the history of the other Apostles to be able to say this with any certainty. James the greater, and Peter, had in all probability stood before Agrippa I. See ch. xii. 2, 3. **XXVI. 1.]** The *stretching out of the hand* by a speaker was not, as Hammond supposes, the same as the *κατασείειν τῇ χειρί* of ch. xii. 17; xiii. 16. The latter was to ensure silence; but this, a formal attitude usual with orators. Apuleius, Met. ii. p. 54 (Meyer), describes it

τείνας τὴν [r] χεῖρα [s] ἀπελογεῖτο 2 Περὶ πάντων ὧν
[t] ἐγκαλοῦμαι ὑπὸ Ἰουδαίων, βασιλεῦ Ἀγρίππα, [u] ἥγημαι
ἐμαυτὸν μακάριον [v] ἐπὶ σοῦ μέλλων σήμερον [s] ἀπολογεῖσθαι, 3 μάλιστα [w] γνώστην [x] ὄντα σε πάντων τῶν [y] κατὰ
Ἰουδαίους [z] ἐθῶν τε καὶ [a] ζητημάτων. διὸ δέομαι [b] μακροθύμως ἀκοῦσαί μου. 4 τὴν μὲν οὖν [c] βίωσίν μου [τὴν]
[d] ἐκ [de] νεότητος, τὴν [f] ἀπ' ἀρχῆς γενομένην ἐν τῷ ἔθνει μου
ἔν τε Ἱεροσολύμοις, [g] ἴσασι πάντες Ἰουδαῖοι 5 [h] προγινώ-
σκοντές με [i] ἄνωθεν, ἐὰν θέλωσιν [j] μαρτυρεῖν, ὅτι κατὰ
τὴν [k] ἀκριβεστάτην [l] αἵρεσιν τῆς ἡμετέρας [m] θρησκείας
[n] ἔζησα [n] Φαρισαῖος. 6 καὶ νῦν [o] ἐπ' ἐλπίδι τῆς εἰς τοὺς

ABCEH LPℵ a b c d f g h k l m o p 13

s ch. xix. 33 reff.
t ch. xix. 38 reff.
u = 2 Cor. ix. 5. Phil. ii. 3. Heb. x. 29 al. Job xlii. 6.
v ch. xxiii. 30 reff.
w here only ‡. 1 Kings xxviii. 3. = Sus. 42 Theod.
x constr., ch. xxiv. 10 reff. see Eph. iv. 2. iii. 17, 18. Col. iii. 16 al. Paul chiefly. see Winer, edn. 6, § 63. i. 2. a.
y = ch. xviii. 15 reff.
z ch. vi. 14 reff.
a ch. xv. 2 reff.
b here only †. (-μος, Exod. xxxiv. 6. -μία, Rom. ii. 4. -μεῖν, 1 Cor. xiii. 4.)
c here only †. Prol. Sir. only. Ps. xxxviii. 6 Symm. (-οῦν, 1 Pet. iv. 2.)
d Mark x. 20 || L. Jer. xxii. 21.
e as above (d). 1 Tim. iv. 12 only.
f Matt. xix. 4, 8. Luke i. 2 al. Isa. lxiii. 19.
g Eph. v. 5. Heb. xii. 17. James i. 19 only †.
h = 2 Pet. iii. 17 only. (Rom. viii. 29 reff.)
i = Luke i. 3 ‡. (Wisd. xix. 6.)
j = ch. xxii. 5. John iii. 28.
k here only. Sir. xviii. 29. xix. 25. xxxiv. (xxxi.) 24. xxxv. (xxxii.) 3 only. (-βῶς, ch. xviii. 25.)
l ch. v. 17 reff.
m James i. 26, 27. Col. ii. 18 only †. Wisd. xiv. 18, 27 only. (-κος, James i. 26. -κεύειν, Wisd. xi. 15. xiv. 16.)
n constr., here only.
o = ch. iv. 9 only. ἐγκληθεῖσαν ἐπὶ φαρμακείᾳ, Diod. Sic. iv. 55. (so περί, ch. xxiii. 6. xxiv. 21.)

rec *απελογειτο* bef *εκτ. την χειρα*, with HLP rel syr Chr_1 Thl-sif: txt ABCEℵ k m p 13. 40 vulg Syr copt [æth] arm Thl-fin.—*τας χειρας* c 137.

2. for *περι παντων* to *ζητηματων*, 137 has *περι παντων των κατα ιουδαιους εθνη τε και ζητηματων επισταμενος*. rec *μελλων απολογεισθαι επι σου σημερον* (*simplifn of order*), with [(copt)]: *επι σ. μ. απολογ. σημερον* EHLP rel vulg syr Chr_1 Thl-sif: txt ABCℵ m (p) 13 [Syr (æth) arm] Thl-fin.—for *μελλων*, *μελλω* p.

3. *σε* bef *οντα* Cℵ[1] m[2] 73: om *σε* 180. om *παντων* A 17. 25 copt æth. *ιουδαιων* AE d f. *ηθων* HLP a d f g m Thl-fin: *εθνων* A 15. 27. 105. aft *ζητηματων* ins *επισταμενος* ACℵ[3] 13: aft *μαλιστα* (above), 15-8. 36 Syr: aft *σε*, 7: aft *σε* ins *ειδως* 6. 29 [aft *παντων* m[1], aft *οντα* m[2]]. rec aft *δεομαι* ins *σου*, with CHLP rel Syr copt Chr_1: om ABEℵ k p 13. 36. 40 vulg syrr æth arm.

4. rec ins *την*, with AC[2]ELPℵ p 13 [rel] Chr: om BC[1]H m.—*την απ' αρχης* bef *την εκ νεοτητος* E. rec om *τε* (*misapprehension*), with CHLP p 13. 36(sic) rel vulg [E-lat syr copt æth arm] Chr: ins AB E-gr ℵ 40 Syr. *ισασιν* CEP [p(Scr)]: txt AB[HL]ℵ rel. rec ins *οι* bef *ιουδ.* (*more usual exprn*), with AC[2]HLPℵ rel 36 [Chr_2 Thl]: om BC[1]E d k m p 13 Chr-$comm_1$.

5. *προςγινωσκοντες* C[1]. om *με* c 137 [arm].

6. rec (for *εις*) *προς* (*corrn, see note*), with CHLP rel 36 Chr: txt ABE[ℵ] d p

very precisely: 'Porrigit dextram et ad instar oratorum conformat articulum, duobusque infimis conclusis digitis ceteros eminentes porrigit.' The hand was *chained*—τούτων τ. δεσμ., ver. 29. **2.**] There is no force in Meyer's observation, that by the omission of the art. before Ἰουδαίων, Paul wishes to express that the charges were made by *some, not by all* of the Jews. That omission is the one so often overlooked by the German critics (e. g. Stier also here), *after a preposition*. See Middl. ch. vi. § 1, and compare κατὰ Ἰουδαίους in the next verse, of which the above cannot be said. **μέλλων** contains the ground of **ἥγημαι, in that I am to defend myself.**

3. γν. ὄντα σε] For the construction see reff.; and cf. Viger (ed. Hermann), p. 337, where many examples are given—e. g. Herod. vi. 109: ἐν σοὶ νῦν ἔστιν ἢ καταδουλῶσαι Ἀθήνας, ἢ ἐλευθέρας ποιήσαντα μνημόσυνον λιπέσθαι κ.τ.λ.

4.] The μὲν οὖν takes up ἀπολογεῖσθαι: q. d. 'well, then, to begin my apology.'

5. ἀκριβεστάτην] See ch. xxii. 3: κατὰ ἀκρίβειαν τοῦ πατρῴου νόμου. Jos. (B. J. i. 5. 2) calls the Pharisees σύνταγμά τι Ἰουδαίων δοκοῦν εὐσεβέστερον εἶναι τῶν ἄλλων, καὶ τοὺς νόμους ἀκριβέστερον ἀφηγεῖσθαι. The use of the term finds another example in Eph. v. 15, βλέπετε πῶς ἀκριβῶς περιπατεῖτε, which command it illustrates. **θρησκεία**] ἡ λατρεία· ὅθεν καὶ ἑτερόθρησκος, ἑτερόδοξος. Suidas. We have an instance here of αἵρεσις used in an indifferent sense. **6.**] The rec. text has apparently been corrected after ch. xiii. 32; for there we have πρός, and no ἡμῶν. The **εἰς** has its propriety here, combining the ideas of *address towards*, and of *ethical relation to*, its object: so ἐς δ' ὑμᾶς ἐρῶ μῦθον, Æsch. Pers. 159:

[p] πατέρας [p] ἡμῶν ἐπαγγελίας γενομένης ὑπὸ τοῦ θεοῦ
ἕστηκα [q] κρινόμενος, 7 εἰς ἣν τὸ [r] δωδεκάφυλον ἡμῶν ἐν
[s] ἐκτενείᾳ [t] νύκτα καὶ ἡμέραν [u] λατρεῦον ἐλπίζει [v] καταντῆσαι, περὶ ἧς ἐλπίδος [w] ἐγκαλοῦμαι ὑπὸ Ἰουδαίων, βασιλεῦ.
8 τί [x] ἄπιστον [y] κρίνεται [z] παρ᾽ ὑμῖν [a] εἰ ὁ θεὸς νεκροὺς

I εγκαλουμαι... ABCEH ILPℵ a b c d f g h k l m o p 13

p ch. v. 30 reff. q ch. xxiii. 6 reff. r here only †. s here only †. Judith iv. 9 bis. 2 Macc. xiv. 38 only. (-νής, 1 Pet. iv. 8. -νῶς, 1 Pet. i. 22.) t ch. xx. 31 reff (ch. xvi. 1 reff. u Acts vii. 7 reff. v = Paul (1 Cor. x. 11. xiv. 36. Eph. iv. 13. Phil. iii. 11) only. w ch. xix. 38 reff. see above (o). x = here only (1 Cor. vi. 6 al.) ‡. Demosth., p. 15, ult., καὶ μὸ Δί᾽ οὐδὲν ἄπιστον ἴσως. y = ch. xiii. 46 reff. z = Matt. vi. 1. Rom. ii. 13. Eph vi. 9. a Rom. viii. 13, 17. Col. iii. 1.

13. 40. rec om ημων, with HLP 13 [arm, Treg] Thl-sif: ins ABCEℵ b c d m o p 36. 40. 137 vulg syrr copt æth arm[Gb] Chr_1 Thl-fin. om του L 142.

7. λατρευων H [13] 73. καταντησειν B. rec ins των bef ιουδαιων [with arm-edd]: om ABCEHILPℵ rel [arm-mss Chr_1]. rec aft βασιλευ ins αγριππα, with HLP rel 40 syrr [æth Chr_1]: om BCEIℵ p 13 vulg [copt arm] $Chron_1$ Thl[-fin]. —rec βασ. αγρ. bef υπο (των) ιουδαιων, with HLP rel syr [arm] Chr: om βασιλευ (αγριππα) A 18. 36: βασιλευ (with or without αγρ.) aft υπο ιουδ. BCEIℵ a² d k m p 13. 40 vulg Syr æth $Chron_1$ Thl-fin.

ψόγος ἐς Ἕλληνας μέγας, Eur. Bacch. 778 (735): δημοκρατίας κατίστα εἰς τὰς πόλιας, Herod. vi. 43. See Bernhardy, Syntax, p. 217, where many more examples are given.

The promise spoken of is not that of the resurrection merely, but that of a Messiah and His kingdom, *involving* (ver. 8) *the resurrection*. This is evident from the way in which he brings in the mention of Jesus of Nazareth, and connects His exaltation (ver. 18) with the universal preaching of repentance and remission of sins. But he *hints* merely at this hope, and does not explain it fully; for Agrippa knew well what was intended, and *the mention of any king but Cæsar* would have misled and prejudiced the Roman procurator. There is great skill in binding on his former Pharisaic life of orthodoxy (in externals), to his now real and living defence of the hope of Israel. But though he thus far identifies them, he makes no concealment of the difference between them, ver. 9 ff. **7. τὸ δωδεκάφυλ.**] The Jews in Judæa and those of the dispersion also. See James i. 1. There was a difference between Paul and the Jews, which lies beneath the surface of this verse, but is yet not brought out: *he* had already arrived at the accomplishment of this hope, to which *they*, with all their sacrifices and zeal, were as yet only earnestly *tending*, having it yet in the future only (so Rom. x. 2: ζῆλον θεοῦ ἔχουσιν, ἀλλ᾽ οὐ κατ᾽ ἐπίγνωσιν). It was *concerning this hope* (in what sense appears not yet) that he was accused by the Jews. The adverb ἐκτενῶς and subst. ἐκτένεια are disapproved by the philologists, as belonging to later Greek. See Lobeck on Phrynichus, p. 311. We have the adj., Æsch. Suppl. 990: ἐκτενὴς φίλος. **8.**] Having impressed on his hearers the injustice of this charge from the Jews, with reference to his holding that hope which they themselves held, he now leaves much to be filled up, not giving a confession of his own faith, but proceeding as if it were well understood. 'You assume rightly, that I mean by *this hope*, in my own case, my believing it accomplished in the crucified and risen Jesus of Nazareth.' Then, this being acknowledged, he goes on to shew how his own view became so changed with regard to Jesus; drawing, by the μὲν οὖν (ver. 9), a contrast in some respects between *himself*, who was supernaturally brought to the faith, and *them*, who yet could not refuse to believe that God could and might raise the dead. All this he mainly addresses to Agrippa (ver. 26), as being the best acquainted with the circumstances, and, from his position, best qualified to judge of them. It may be, as Stier suggests, that if not open, *yet practical* Sadduceism had tainted the Herodian family. Paul knew, at all events, how generally the highly cultivated, and those in power and wealth, despised and thought ἄπιστον the doctrine of the resurrection.

εἰ . . . ἐγείρει] not, as commonly rendered, '*that God should raise the dead*' (E. V.): but the question is far stronger than this, if the conjunction be taken in its literal meaning: **why is it judged by you a thing past belief, if God raises the dead?** i. e. '*if God, in His exercise of power, sees fit to raise the dead* (the word implying that such a fact *has veritably taken place*), *is it for you to refuse to believe it?*' Compare the declaration of our Lord, Luke xvi. 31: οὐδ᾽ ἐάν τις ἐκ νεκρῶν ἀναστῇ πεισθήσονται. We have many instances of this use of εἰ:—Xen. Mem. i. 1. 13, ἐθαύμαζε δὲ εἰ μὴ φανερὸν αὐτοῖς ἐστίν: ib. 18, ὅσα δὲ πάντες ᾔδεσαν, θαυμαστὸν εἰ μὴ τούτων ἐνεθυμήθησαν: ib. i. 2. 13, ἐγὼ δ᾽ εἰ μέν τι κακὸν ἐκείνῳ τὴν πόλιν

b = ch. x. 40 reff. c w. dat., = here only. δοκῶ μοι, Xen. Hier. i. 6. see 1 Cor. iii. 18 reff. Herod. ii. 93, and exx. in Wetst. d = ch. xxiv. 19 reff. e = ch. (xxvii. 4) xxviii. 17. 1 Thess. ii. 15. Tit. ii. 8. (Ezek. xviii. 18.) f = ch. ix. 13 reff. g Luke iii. 20 only. Jer. xxxix. (xxxii.) 3. h ch. ix. 14. Bel & Dr. 26 [25, LXX].

[b] ἐγείρει; 9 ἐγὼ μὲν οὖν [c] ἔδοξα ἐμαυτῷ [d] πρὸς τὸ ὄνομα ABCEH
Ἰησοῦ τοῦ Ναζωραίου δεῖν πολλὰ [e] ἐναντία πρᾶξαι, ILPℵ a bcdfg
10 ὃ καὶ ἐποίησα ἐν Ἱεροσολύμοις, καὶ πολλούς τε τῶν hklm op13
[f] ἁγίων ἐγὼ ἐν φυλακαῖς [g] κατέκλεισα, τὴν παρὰ τῶν
ἀρχιερέων [h] ἐξουσίαν [i] λαβών, [j] ἀναιρουμένων τε αὐτῶν
[k] κατήνεγκα [l] ψῆφον, 11 καὶ [m] κατὰ πάσας τὰς συναγωγὰς
πολλάκις [n] τιμωρῶν αὐτοὺς [o] ἠνάγκαζον [p] βλασφημεῖν,
[q] περισσῶς τε [r] ἐμμαινόμενος αὐτοῖς [s] ἐδίωκον [t] ἕως καὶ
εἰς τὰς [u] ἔξω πόλεις. 12 [v] ἐν οἷς πορευόμενος εἰς τὴν
Δαμασκὸν [w] μετ᾽ ἐξουσίας καὶ [x] ἐπιτροπῆς τῆς παρὰ
τῶν ἀρχιερέων, 13 [y] ἡμέρας [y] μέσης [z] κατὰ τὴν ὁδὸν εἶδον,

i ch. ii. 33 reff. j ch. v. 33 reff. k = ch. xxv. 7 (xx. 9 bis) only. Gen. xxxvii. 2. l = here (Rev. ii. 17 bis) only ‡. (Exod. iv. 25.) m = ch. xxii. 19 reff. n ch. xxii. 5 only (Paul). Ezek. v. 17. (-ρία, Heb. x. 29.) o = ch. xxviii. 19. Gal. ii. 3, 14 ‡. (Prov. vi. 7 only.) 2 Macc. vi. 1 al. p = Luke xxii. 65. 4 Kings xix. 4, 6, 22. q Matt. xxvii. 23. Mark x. 26. xv. 14 only. Ps. xxx. 23. (Rom. iii. 1. 2 Cor. i. 12 reff.) r here only †. (-μανής, Wisd. xiv. 23.) s = Matt. xxiii. 34. 1 Macc. v. 22. t w. prep., ch. xxi. 5 reff. u = here only. 4 Kings xvi. 18. see 1 Cor. v. 12 reff. v ch. xxiv. 18 (v. r.). w = Luke xxi. 27. Isa. xxxiii. 17. Dan. vii. 13 Theod. x here only †. 2 Macc. xiii. 14 only. (-πος, Matt. xx. 8.) y here only. see Matt. xxv. 6. z ch. viii. 36 al. Ezek. xliii. 2.

9. om μεν B. ins του bef ιησ. ℵ[1](ℵ[3] disapproving) [o]. ναζοραιου ℵ.
10. for ο, διο B. εποιησαν ℵ[1](but corrd). rec om 1st τε, with BHLP rel: ins δε 36. 180: txt ACEIℵ p 13. rec om 2nd εν (*as unnecessary*), with HP rel Chr: ins ABCEILℵ b k m o p 13. 36. 40. 137 vulg. for 2nd τε, δε H a[2] c 137 E-lat syr copt Thl-fin. om αυτων E. κατηνεγκαν ℵ.
11. om τε B: δε E-gr copt [æth-pl].
12. rec ins και bef πορευομενος, with HLP rel Syr Chr[1] Thl-sif: om ABCEIℵ c p(Tischdf [Treg(expr)]) 13. 36. 40 vulg syr copt æth arm Thl-fin. om την [A]E a b c h k o 137. om της παρα (*as unnecessary*) AEI 40 vulg Syr [copt arm]: om παρα Bℵ c p 137: om της 80 Thl-fin: txt CHLP 13 rel syr [æth] Chr[1] Thl-sif.
13. om ημερας ℵ[1]. for κατα την, κατην(sic) ℵ.

ἐποιησάτην οὐκ ἀπολογήσομαι: on which examples Hermann remarks, ad Viger. p. 504, "in his locis omnibus rem non dubiam et incertam indicat εἰ, sed plane certam et perspicuam." **9.**] Henceforward he passes to *his own* history,—how he once refused, like them, to believe in Jesus: and shews them both the process of his conversion, and the ministry with which he was entrusted to others.

μὲν οὖν, well then, resuming the character described vv. 4, 5. **10, 11.**] This is the διωγμὸς μέγας of ch. viii. 1. We are surprised here by the unexpected word ἁγίων, which it might have been thought he would have rather in this presence avoided. But, as Stier remarks, it belongs to the more confident tone of this speech, which he delivers, not as a *prisoner defending himself*, but as one being heard before those who were his *audience, not his judges.*

* **κατήνεγκα ψῆφον** can hardly be taken *figuratively*, as many Commentators, trying to escape from the inference that the νεανίας Saul was a member of the Sanhedrim; but must be understood as testifying to *this very fact*, however strange it may seem. He can hardly have been *less than* thirty when sent on his errand of persecution to Damascus. The genitive is supposed by Elsner and Kypke to be dependent on κατήνεγκα; but this is harsh, and it is better to take (as most Commentators, and Meyer, and De W.) it as absolute, and κατήνεγκα as *local*, '*detuli sententiam*:' **when their deaths were being compassed, I gave in my vote** (scil. *against* them, as in ref.). On the fact, cf. συνευδοκῶν τῇ ἀναιρέσει αὐτοῦ, ch. viii. 1. **11. τιμωρῶν**] viz. *by scourging;* compare Matt. x. 17. **ἠνάγκαζον** does not imply that any *did* blaspheme (Christ: so Pliny, Ep. n. 97, speaks of ordering the Bithynian Christians '*maledicere Christo*,' and adds, 'quorum nihil cogi posse dicuntur qui sunt revera Christiani'): the imperf. only relates the *attempt*. The persecuting the Christians even to foreign cities, forms the transition to the narrative following. **12. ἐν οἷς**] **In which things (being engaged).** **13.**] See notes on ch. ix. 3—8, where I have treated of the discrepancies, real or only apparent,

βασιλεῦ, [a] οὐρανόθεν [b] ὑπὲρ τὴν [c] λαμπρότητα τοῦ ἡλίου
[d] περιλάμψαν με φῶς καὶ τοὺς σὺν ἐμοὶ πορευομένους,
14 πάντων τε [e] καταπεσόντων ἡμῶν εἰς τὴν γῆν [f] ἤκουσα
φωνὴν λέγουσαν πρός με τῇ [g] Ἑβραΐδι [h] διαλέκτῳ Σαοὺλ
Σαούλ, τί με [i] διώκεις; [k] σκληρόν σοι πρὸς [l] κέντρα
[m] λακτίζειν. 15 Ἐγὼ δὲ εἶπα Τίς εἶ, κύριε; ὁ δὲ κύριος
εἶπεν Ἐγώ εἰμι Ἰησοῦς ὃν σὺ [i] διώκεις. 16 ἀλλὰ [n] ἀνάστηθι καὶ [o] στῆθι [o] ἐπὶ τοὺς πόδας σου· [p] εἰς τοῦτο γὰρ
[q] ὤφθην σοι, [r] προχειρίσασθαί σε [s] ὑπηρέτην καὶ [t] μάρτυρα

a ch. xiv. 17 only +.
b = 2 Cor. i. 8 al.
c here only Ps. lxxxix. 17. Dan. xii. 3 Theod.
d Luke ii. 9 only +.
e Luke viii. 6. ch. xxviii. 6 only. Ps. cxliv. 14.
f constr., ch. ix. 4 reff.
g ch. xxi. 40. xxii. 2 only.
h ch. i. 19 reff.
i = ch. vii. 52 reff.
k = here (Matt. xxv. 24. John vi. 60. James iii. 4. Jude 15) only. Gen. xxi. 12.
l 1 Cor. xv. 55 (from Hos. xiii. 14), 56. Rev. ix. 10 only.
m here only +. (ἀπολακ., Deut. xxxii. 15.)
n ch. ix. 6 reff.
o Rev. xi. 11. Ezek. ii. 1.
p Mark i. 38. ch. ix. 21 al.
q ch. ii. 3 reff.
r ch. iii. 20. xxii. 14 (reff.) only.
s = ch. xiii. 5 reff.
t ch. x. 39 reff.

βασιλευς B[1](Tischdf).

14. rec δε (*altern of characteristic* τε), with [C]HLP rel copt Chr$_1$ [Thl-sif]: txt ABEIℵ c p 13. 36. 40. 137 vulg syrr Thl-fin. om ημων B d. aft γην ins δια τον φοβον εγω μονος 137, simly syr-mg. rec (for λεγουσαν προς με) λαλουσαν προς με και λεγουσαν, with LP rel [λαλουσης and λεγουσης a] æth Chr$_1$ Thl-sif: om 13: so also, omg και λεγουσαν, H b o [arm]: φωνης λεγουσης προς με E-gr m, *vocem loquentem ad me* E-lat, simly vulg: txt ABCIℵ p 36. 40 syrr. (*The shorter reading* λεγ. πρ. με *may perhaps have been adopted from ch* ix. 4, xxii. 7, *or, as also* λαλ. πρ. με, *to avoid what seemed, but is not, a tautology;* λαλ. *and* λεγ. *not being equivalent.*)

15. om δε I[1]. (ειπα, so ABCEH k l p [13] Thl-fin.) rec om κυριος, with HP rel æth-pl Chr Thl-sif: ins ABCEILℵ k m p 36 [137] vulg syrr copt arm Thl-fin. (13 def.) aft ειπεν ins προς με E Syr copt æth-pl. aft ιησ. ins ο ναζωραιος [m] 40. 137 [demid] Syr syr-w-ast.

16. om και στηθι B[1](ins B[2,3], Tischdf). προχειρασθαι A. for σε, σοι ℵ[1] [ες m].

between the three accounts of Saul's conversion. See also ch. xxii. 6—10.

14. τῇ Ἑβρ. διαλ.] These words are expressed here only. In ch. ix. (see note) we have the *fact* remarkably preserved by the Hebrew form Σαούλ; in ch. xxii. he was speaking in Hebrew (Syro-Chald.), and the notice was not required. (Beware again of the supposed emphatic με of Wordsworth.) **σκληρ. σοι πρ. κ. λ.]** This is found here only; in ch. ix. the words are spurious, having been inserted from this place. The metaphor is derived from oxen at plough or drawing a burden, who, on being pricked with the goad, kick against it, and so cause it to pierce deeper. (See Schol. on Pind. l. c. below.) It is a Greek, and not (apparently) a Hebrew proverb; but this is no reason why it should not be used in Hebrew, just as it is in Latin. Instances of its use are Pind. Pyth. ii. 173: χρὴ δὲ πρὸς θεὸν οὐκ ἐρίζειν . . . . φέρειν δ' ἐλαφρῶς ἐπαυχένιον λαβόντα ζυγὸν ἀρήγει. ποτὶ κέντρον δέ τοι λακτιζέμεν τελέθει ὀλισθηρὸς οἶμος. Æschyl. Agam. 1633: πρὸς κέντρα μὴ λάκτιζε, μὴ πήσας μογῇς. Eurip. Bacch. 791: θυμούμενος πρὸς κέντρα λακτίζοιμι, θνητὸς ὢν θεῷ. See also Æsch. Prom. 323, and other examples in Wetst.; Plautus (Truc. iv. 2. 59); and Terence, Phorm. i. 2. 27; 'Nam quæ inscitia est advorsum stimulum calces?' **15—18.]** There can be no question that Paul here *condenses into one, various sayings of our Lord to him at different times, in visions,* see ch. xxii. 18—21; and *by Ananias,* ch. ix. 15; see also ch. xxii. 15, 16. Nor can this, on the strictest view, be considered any deviation from truth. It is what all must more or less do who are abridging a narrative, or giving the general sense of things said at various times. There were reasons for its being minute and particular in the *details of his conversion;* that once related, the commission which he thereupon received is not followed into *its* details, but *summed up as committed to him by the Lord himself.* It would be not only irreverent, but false, to imagine that he put *his own thoughts* into the mouth of our Lord; but I do not see, with Stier, the necessity of maintaining that all these words were actually *spoken* to him *at some time* by the Lord. The message delivered by Ananias certainly furnished some of them; and the unmistakeable utterings of God's Spirit (τὸ πνεῦμα Ἰησοῦ, ch. xvi. 7) which supernaturally led him, may have furnished more, all within the limits of truth.

16.] εἰς τοῦτο refers to what follows,

ὧν τε εἶδες [u] ὧν τε [q] ὀφθήσομαί σοι, 17 [v] ἐξαιρούμενός
σε ἐκ τοῦ λαοῦ καὶ ἐκ τῶν ἐθνῶν, εἰς οὓς ἐγὼ [w] ἀποστέλλω σε 18 ἀνοῖξαι ὀφθαλμοὺς αὐτῶν, [x] τοῦ [yz] ἐπιστρέψαι
[y] ἀπὸ [a] σκότους εἰς [a] φῶς καὶ τῆς [b] ἐξουσίας τοῦ σατανᾶ
[z] ἐπὶ τὸν θεόν, [x] τοῦ λαβεῖν αὐτοὺς [c] ἄφεσιν [c] ἁμαρτιῶν καὶ
[de] κλῆρον ἐν τοῖς [e] ἡγιασμένοις [f] πίστει τῇ [f] εἰς ἐμέ.
19 [g] ὅθεν, βασιλεῦ Ἀγρίππα, οὐκ ἐγενόμην [h] ἀπειθὴς τῇ
[i] οὐρανίῳ [k] ὀπτασίᾳ, 20 ἀλλὰ τοῖς ἐν Δαμασκῷ πρῶτόν τε

...επιστρεψαι I.

...απειθης τη C.

ABEHLPℵ a b c d f g h k l m o p 13

u constr., see note. v = ch. vii. 10 reff. w constr., Mark iii. 14. 1 Cor. i. 17. 4 Kings xix. 16. see ch. v. 21. x 1 Cor. x. 13 reff. y ch. xiv. 15 reff. z ver. 20 reff. a 1 Pet. ii. 9. Eph. v. 8. b = Luke xx. 20. xxii. 53. Col. i. 13. c ch. v. 31 reff. d ch. i. 17 reff. e see ch. xx. 32. Eph. i. 18. f ch. xxiv. 24 reff. g = Mt. xiv. 7. Heb. ii. 17. iii. 1. vii. 25. viii. 3. ix. 18. xi. 19. Judith viii. 20. h Rom. i. 13 reff. i fem., Luke ii. 13. (Matt. v. 48. vi. 14, 26, 32. xv. 13. xxiii. 9 only. Esdr. vi. 15. 2 Macc. vii. 34 AB(not Ed vat.) &c. ix. 10 only.) Dan. iv. 23 (26) Theod. k 2 Cor. xii. 1 reff.

aft ειδες ins με BC^1(appy) 137 syr [Syr arm] $Ambr_1$ Aug_1.

17. rec om 2nd εκ, with CHLP rel 36 vulg E-lat Chr_1 Thl-sif: ins AB E-gr Iℵ k l p 13. 40 fuld Thl-fin. rec for εγω, νυν (*marginal gloss, which has overborne the* εγω): om c e: vulg Thl-fin have both: txt ABCEHILPℵ rel [Syr] syr copt æth-pl arm Chr_1 Thl-sif Aug_1. rec σε bef αποστελλω, with HLP rel Chr: txt ABCEIℵ c d f k m p 13 vulg [arm] Thl.—αποστελω HIP^1 a c d g k demid copt Thl-sif: εξαποστελλω C m p 13. 36 Thl-fin.

18. for αυτων, τυφλων EI tol Aug_1. αποστρεψαι AH b c m o p Chr_1 Thl-sif Aug_1: υποστρ. P 27. 78: txt BCEILℵ 13. 36 vulg [$Clem_1$ Thl-fin]. ins απο bef της εξουσιας CEL a c 36. 137 (vulg) Thl-fin: om ABHPℵ p 13 [$Clem_1$] Chr Thl-sif Œc, aft ηγιασμ. ins πασιν (*see ch* xx. 32) E.

προχειρ. &c.,—**γάρ** gives the reason for ἀνάστηθι, &c. (Meyer.) **προχειρ.**] See reff. **μάρτυρα ὧν τε εἶδες**] Stier remarks, that Paul was the witness of the *glory of Christ:* whereas Peter, the first of the former twelve, describes himself (1 Pet. v. 1) as 'a witness of the *sufferings* of Christ, and a partaker of the glory that shall be revealed.' So true it was that this ἔκτρωμα among the Apostles, became, by divine grace, *more than they all* (1 Cor. xv. 8—10). The expression ὑπηρέτην ὧν εἶδες may be compared with ὑπηρέται τοῦ λόγου, which Luke calls the αὐτόπται, Luke i. 2. **ὧν τε ὀφθήσομαί σοι**] (1) ὀφθ. must be *passive*, not (as Bornemann, Winer (not in edn. 6, § 39. 3, remark 1), Wahl, al.) causative ('videre faciam'),—but as E. V., **I will appear unto thee.** (2) the gen. is exactly paralleled (Meyer) by Soph. Œd. Tyr. 788, ὧν μὲν ἱκόμην = τούτων (rather ἐκείνων) δι' ἃ ἱκόμην. So here ὧν = τούτων (ἐκείνων) δι' ἃ ὀφθ., **the things in** (or on **account of) which I will appear to thee.** That such visions did take place, we know, from ch. xviii. 9; xxii. 18; xxiii. 11; 2 Cor. xii. 1; Gal. i. 12. **17. ἐξαιρούμενός σε**] *delivering thee from,* as E. V.: not, as Kuin., al., and Conyb., '*choosing thee out of:*' see reff. **τοῦ λαοῦ**] as elsewhere, **the Jewish people.** 'Hic armatur contra omnes metus qui eum manebant, et simul præparatur ad crucis tolerantiam.' Calvin. **εἰς οὕς**] to *both,* the people, and the Gentiles; not the Gentiles only. **18. τοῦ ἐπιστ.**] not, as Beza, and E. V., '*to turn them:*' but, **that they may turn;** see ἐπιστρέφειν, ver. 20. The general reference of οὕς becomes tacitly modified (not expressly, speaking as he was to the Jew Agrippa) by the expression σκότος and ἐξουσία τοῦ σατανᾶ, both, in the common language of the Jews, applicable only to the Gentiles. But in reality, and in Paul's mind, they had their sense as applied to Jews,—who were in spiritual darkness and under Satan's power, however little they thought it. See Col. i. 13. **τοῦ λαβ.**] A *third step:* first the *opening of the eyes*—next, *the turning to God*—next, the *receiving remission of sins* and *a place among the sanctified;* see ch. xx. 32. This last reference determines πίστει τῇ εἰς ἐμέ to belong not to ἡγιασμένοις but to λαβεῖν. Thus the great object of Paul's preaching was to awaken and shew the necessity and efficacy of πίστις ἡ εἰς ἐμέ. And fully, long ere this, had he recognized and acted on this his great mission. The epistles to the Galatians and Romans are two noble monuments of the Apostle of Faith. **19. ἀπειθής**] See Isa. l. 5 in LXX. **20. τοῖς ἐν Δαμ. πρ.**] See ch. ix. 20. **εἰς** belongs to ἀπήγγελ. (De W.), not to τοῖς (ἐν Δαμ.) as Meyer; see Luke viii. 34; and on this sense of εἰς,

καὶ Ἱεροσολύμοις, [[l] εἰς] πᾶσάν τε τὴν χώραν τῆς Ἰουδαίας
καὶ τοῖς ἔθνεσιν [l] ἀπήγγελλον [m] μετανοεῖν καὶ [n] ἐπιστρέφειν
[n] ἐπὶ τὸν θεόν, [op] ἄξια τῆς [o] μετανοίας ἔργα πράσσοντας.
21 ἕνεκα τούτων με οἱ Ἰουδαῖοι [q] συλλαβόμενοι ἐν τῷ ἱερῷ
[r] ἐπειρῶντο [s] διαχειρίσασθαι. 22 [t] ἐπικουρίας οὖν [u] τυχὼν
τῆς ἀπὸ τοῦ θεοῦ ἄχρι τῆς ἡμέρας ταύτης [v] ἕστηκα,
[w] μαρτυρόμενος [x] μικρῷ τε καὶ [x] μεγάλῳ, οὐδὲν [y] ἐκτὸς
λέγων [z] ὧν τε οἱ προφῆται ἐλάλησαν [a] μελλόντων
γίνεσθαι καὶ Μωυσῆς, 23 [b] εἰ [c] παθητὸς ὁ χριστός, [b] εἰ

l = and constr. here only. (ch. xii. 14.) w. εἰς, Luke viii. 34.
m absol., ch. xvii. 30 reff.
n Luke i. 16 (act.), ch. ix. 25. xi. 21. xiv. 15. xv. 19. ver. 18. 1 Pet. ii. 25. Deut. xxx. 2. see 2 Cor. iii. 16.
o Matt. iii. 8 ∥ L.
p = Luke xxiii. 41.
q = ch. i. 16 reff.
r ch. ix. 26 only. Prov. xxvi. 18 ℵ^{3a} F(not A) Ald. only.
s ch. v. 30 only †.
t here only †. Wisd. xiii. 18 only.
u = ch. xxiv. 2 reff.
v = here only.
w ch. xx. 26 reff.
x ch. viii. 10. Heb. viii. 11. Rev. xi. 18. xiii. 16 al. Isa. ix. 14.
y = 1 Cor. xv. 27. Isa. xxvi. 13.
z constr., ver. 16 a.
a ch. xiii. 34 reff. Isa. xlviii. 6.
b = ver. 8. 3 Kings i. 51 al.
c here only †.

20. rec om 1st *τε*, with EHLP 13. 36 rel Chr: ins ABℵ p. ins *εν* bef *ιερ.* AE k 36. 40 (Syr) Thl[-sif]: *τοις εν* c 137 lect-12: om BHLPℵ p rel Chr [Thl-fin]. om *εις* ABℵ [tol] (*on acct of -οις preceding?*). [om 2nd *τε* L.] om *την* H^1 96. 142. Steph *απαγγελλων*, with HLP g m: *απαγγελλω* [rel] 14. 38. 65. 76. 95-7-9. 104-13-33-77 Chr$_1$: *απηγελλω* 13: *παρηγελλον* 96: txt ABEℵ p 36 vulg [(syrr) copt æth arm]. ins *ζωντα* bef *θεον* m 36. 40 arm. aft *αξια* ins *τε* E.
21. *οι ιουδ. συλλαβ.* bef *με* A a^2 c 137 [copt arm(Tischdf)]: *οι ιουδ.* bef *με* EL m p Chr$_1$ Thl-fin: om *με* 180. om *οι* BLℵ^1 m p 13 Chron$_1$ Thl-fin. *συλλαβουμενοι* ℵ [*συλλαμβανομενοι* P]. ins *οντα* bef *εν τω* Eℵ^3 [c] m p 13. 36. 40. 137 vulg syr Chron: *οντα με* ℵ^1. *διαχερωσασθαι* ℵ^1.
22. rec for *απο*, *παρα* (*more usual*), with HLP rel Chr$_1$ [Thl-sif: *υπο* c]: txt ABEℵ p 13. 36. 40 Chron$_1$ Thl-fin. rec *μαρτυρουμενος* (*see notes*), with E a f g Thl-fin: *μαρτυρωμενος* 13: txt ABHLPℵ p rel 36. 40 vulg Chr Chron Thl-sif.

note on ver. 6 above. **22.**] The *οὖν* refers to the whole course of deliverances which he had had from God, not merely to the last. It serves to close the narrative, by shewing how it was that he was there that day,—after such repeated persecutions, crowned by this last attempt to destroy him. **μαρτυρόμενος**] The mere love of paradox and difficulty, as it seems to me, has led De Wette and Meyer to prefer the ordinary reading *-ρούμενος*, although very weakly supported by MSS., and yielding hardly any appropriate sense. *μαρτυρούμενος must be passive,* and signify (see reff. below) '*testified to,*' '*borne witness of:*' the datives *μικρῷ* and *μεγάλῳ* must be the agents, '*by small and great*' (to which there is no objection grammatically, but every objection analogically, see ch. x. 22; xvi. 2; xxii. 12, in all which *μαρτύρουμαι* is followed by *ὑπό*), and *λέγων* must be predicative, '*as saying:*' i. e., '*that I say.*' But this would be contrary to the fact: Paul was *not thus borne witness of by all,* but on the contrary accused of being a despiser of the law by a great majority of his own countrymen. There can, I think, be no question either critically or exegetically of the correctness of the other reading *μαρτυρόμενος*, **bearing witness**, as directly appropriate to the office to which Paul was appointed,—that of a *witness* (ver. 16); and then *μικρῷ τε καὶ μεγάλῳ*, **to small and great**, so flat and meaningless on the other interpretation, admirably suits the occasion,—standing as he was before an assembly of the greatest of the land. **23. εἰ**] not for *ὅτι*—but just as in ver. 8,—**if,—if at least:** meaning, that the things following were patent facts to those who knew the prophets. See Heb. vii. 15, where *εἰ* has the same sense. **παθητός**] not, as Beza, '*Christum fuisse passurum*' (so E. V., '*should suffer*'): but as Vulg., '*si passibilis Christus.*' Paul does not refer to the prophetic announcement, or the historical reality, of the *fact* of Christ's suffering, but to the *idea* of the Messiah as *passible* and suffering being in accordance with the testimony of the prophets. That the fact of His having suffered on the cross was in the Apostle's mind, can hardly be doubted: but that the words do not assert it, is evident from the change of construction in the next clause, where the fact of the bringing life and immortality to light by the resurrection is spoken of,—*εἰ παθητὸς ὁ χρ.,—εἰ . . . .* **μέλλει καταγγέλλειν.** In Justin Martyr, Trypho c. 89, p. 187, the follow-

d = Col. i. 18. e 1 Cor. xv. 12 reff. f ch. xiii. 5 reff. g and constr., Luke xii. 11. ch. xxiv. 10. (xix. 33 reff.) h ch. xiv. 10 only. Prov. xxvi. 25. i ch. xii. 15 reff. k = John vii. 15. Eur. Hippol. 951. l here only. Ps. xxxix. 4. Hos. ix. 7 B F(not A) &c., 8. Wisd. v. 4 only. Jos. Antt. ii. 14. 1.

πρῶτος [d] ἐξ [e] ἀναστάσεως [e] νεκρῶν φῶς [a] μέλλει [f] καταγγέλλειν τῷ τε λαῷ καὶ τοῖς ἔθνεσιν. 24 ταῦτα δὲ αὐτοῦ ABEH
[g] ἀπολογουμένου ὁ Φῆστος [h] μεγάλῃ [h] τῇ [h] φωνῇ φησιν LPℵ a b c d f g h
[i] Μαίνῃ, Παῦλε· τὰ πολλά σε [k] γράμματα εἰς [l] μανίαν k l m o p 13
[m] περιτρέπει. 25 ὁ δὲ Οὐ [i] μαίνομαί φησιν, [n] κράτιστε Φῆστε,
ἀλλὰ ἀληθείας καὶ [o] σωφροσύνης ῥήματα [p] ἀποφθέγγομαι.
26 ἐπίσταται γὰρ περὶ τούτων ὁ βασιλεύς, πρὸς ὃν καὶ
[q] παῤῥησιαζόμενος λαλῶ. [r] λανθάνειν γὰρ αὐτόν τι τού-

m here only †. Wisd. v. 24 only. τὸ θεῖον—εἰς ὀργὴν περιτραπέν, only †. 2 Macc. iv. 37 only. n = Luke i. 3. ch. xxiii. 26. xxiv. 3 only ‡. o 1 Tim. ii. 9, 15 p ch. ii. 4, 14 only. 1 Chron. xxv. 1. (-γμα, Deut. xxxii. 2.) q ch. ix. 27 reff. r and constr., 2 Pet. iii. 5, 8 (Mark vii. 24. Luke viii. 47. Heb. xiii. 2) only. Lev. v. 3.

23. μελλειν HPℵ[1] m[1] p 40. rec om τε (*as unnecessary*), with LP rel 36 $Chron_1$ Thl-sif: ins AB E-gr Hℵ b h k l o p 13. 40 Chr_1 Thl-fin.
24. λαλουντος αυτ. κ. απολ. E vulg æth-pl [αυτου απολ. H]. rec εφη (*corrn to historical tense*), with HLP rel: εφωνησε 35: ειπε c 64. 137: txt ABEℵ k p 13. 40 Thl.
25. aft ο δε ins παυλος ABEℵ d p 13 (36) 40 vulg [Syr copt æth-pl arm] Thl-fin: om HLP rel syr Thl-sif. (αλλα, so AELPℵ rel(not h) Chr_1.)
26. om και B 25 [copt arm. for λαλω, λεγω 13.] om τι B a 36. 137.

ing words are put into the mouth of Trypho the Jew: παθητὸν τὸν χριστόν, ὅτι αἱ γραφαὶ κηρύσσουσι, φανερόν ἐστι. See also the same, Trypho c. 36, p. 133, and c. 76, p. 173. **πρῶτος ἐξ ἀναστάσεως** = πρῶτος ἀναστάς, or πρωτότοκος ἐκ τῶν νεκρῶν, Col. i. 18, but implying that this light, to be preached to the Jews (ὁ λαός) and Gentiles, must arise *from the resurrection* of the dead, and that Christ, *the first* ἐξ ἀναστάσεως, was to announce it. See Isa. xlii. 6; xlix. 6; lx. 1, 2, 3; Luke ii. 32; ch. xiii. 47. **24.**] The words ταῦτα ἀπολογουμένου must refer, on account of the present part., to the last words spoken by Paul: but it is not necessary to suppose that *these only* produced the effect described on Festus. Mr. Humphry remarks, "Festus was probably not so well acquainted as his predecessor (ch. xxiv. 10) with the character of the nation over which he had recently been called to preside. Hence he avails himself of Agrippa's assistance (xxv. 26). Hence also he is unable to comprehend the earnestness of St. Paul, so unlike the indifference with which religious and moral subjects were regarded by the upper classes at Rome. His self-love suggests to him, that one who presents such a contrast to his own apathy, must be mad: the convenient hypothesis that much learning had produced this result, may have occurred to him on hearing Paul quote prophecies in proof of his assertions." **μαίνῃ**] **Thou art mad**, not merely, '*thou ravest*,' nor '*thou art an enthusiast*:' nor are the words spoken in jest (Olsh.),—but in earnest (θυμοῦ ἦν κ. ὀργῆς ἡ φωνή, Chrys.). Festus finds himself by this speech of Paul yet more bewildered than before (De W.). **τὰ πολλὰ γράμμ.**] Meyer understands Festus to allude to the many rolls which Paul had with him in his imprisonment (we might compare τὰ βιβλία, μάλιστα τὰς μεμβράνας of 2 Tim. iv. 13) and studied (so also Heinrichs and Kuinoel), —but the ordinary interpretation, **thy much learning**, seems more natural, and so De W. **εἰς μ. περιτρέπει**] **Is turning thy brain.** **25.**] **ἀλήθεια** may be spoken *warmly* and *enthusiastically*, but *cannot be predicated of a madman's words:* **σωφροσύνη** is directly opposed to μανία. So Xen. Mem. i. 16, recounting the subjects of Socrates' discourses, τί δίκαιον, τί ἄδικον· τί σωφροσύνη, τί μανία· τί ἀνδρία, τί δειλία. The expression ἀληθείας &c. ῥήματα, though of course in sense = ῥήματα ἀληθῆ, &c., yet has a distinctive force of its own, and is never to be confounded with, or supposed to be put by a Hebraism for the other. Such forms occur in classic as well as Hellenistic writers, and indeed in all languages: the idea expressed by them being, *the derivation of the quality predicated, from its source:*—so here, **words** (not merely true and sober, but) **of truth and soberness**,—springing from, and indicative of, subjective truth and soberness. **26.**] Agrippa is doubly his witness, (1) as *cognizant of the facts* respecting Jesus, (2) as *believing the prophets.* This latter he does not only assert, but appeals to the faith of the king as a Jew for its establish-

των οὐ [s] πείθομαι οὐθέν· οὐ γάρ [t] ἐστιν ἐν [u] γωνίᾳ πεπραγμένον τοῦτο. 27 πιστεύεις, βασιλεῦ Ἀγρίππα, τοῖς
προφήταις; οἶδα ὅτι πιστεύεις. 28 ὁ δὲ Ἀγρίππας πρὸς
τὸν Παῦλον [v] Ἐν ὀλίγῳ με πείθῃ [w] χριστιανὸν ποιῆσαι.

s = Luke x. 6. t constr., ch. xxv. 10 reff. u Matt. vi. 5. xxi. 42 ||. ch. iv. 11, and 1 Pet. ii. 7, from Ps. cxvii. 22. Rev. vii. 1. xx. 8 only. v here bis. Eph. iii. 3 only. see 1 Pet. v. 12. w ch. xi. 26. 1 Pet. iv. 16 only.

rec *ουδεν*, with HLP rel [*ουδεν πειθ.* m] Chr: om A E(but see below) 13. 40: txt B ℵ[1](ℵ[3] disapproving) p: om 1st *ου* a b c o p. for 2nd *ου*, *ουδε* E[2] m 36. 40: *ουδεν* E[1](and lat). om *εστιν* H[L]P f g h l [ins aft *γων.* m 40, aft *τουτο* a].

28. rec aft *προς τον παυλον* ins *εφη*, with EHLP rel 36 Chr [*ait* tol]: om ABℵ p 13. 40. 137 vulg. rec **πειθεις** *χρ.* **γενεσθαι**, with EHLP rel 36 [vulg Syr syr-txt] (*introire* æth-pl) Cyr-jer$_1$ Chr$_1$: *πειθεις χρ. ποιησαι* Bℵ p 13. 40 syr-mg copt: txt A. (*The reading of* Bℵ *has apparently been the result of some confusion. I have preferred therefore that of* A: *see note.*)—*χρ***η***στιανον* (but corrd) ℵ[1].

ment. **ἐν γωνίᾳ . . . . τοῦτο**] *This*, the act done to Jesus by the Jews, and its sequel, was not done in an obscure corner of Judæa, but in the metropolis, at a time of more than common publicity.

28. ἐν ὀλίγῳ] These words of Agrippa have been very variously explained. (1) The rendering *'propemodum,' 'parum abest, quin,'* (*'almost,'* E. V.,) adopted by Chrys., Beza, Grot., Valla, Luther, Piscator, Calov., &c. is inadmissible, for want of any example of *ἐν ὀλίγῳ* having this meaning, which would require *ὀλίγου* (*ὀλίγου μ' ἀπωλέσας*, Aristoph. Vesp. 829, and al.), or *ὀλίγου δεῖ*, or *παρ' ὀλίγον*. (2) Calvin, Kuinoel, Schöttg., Olsh., Neander, take it for *ἐν ὀλίγῳ χρόνῳ*, which certainly is allowable, but does not correspond to *μεγάλῳ* below, nor, as I believe, does it come up to the *general* sense of the expression. (3) The phrase *ἐν ὀλίγῳ* occurs in Greek writers with various nouns understood according to the nature of the case,—and sometimes it will bear any of several supplements with equal propriety. Thus in Demosth. p. 33. 18, *ῥᾴδιον εἰς ταὐτὸ πάνθ' ὅσα βούλεταί τις ἀθροίσαντα ἐν ὀλίγῳ*, where Schaefer in his Index Græcitatis says, scil. *χρόνῳ*, aut *χώρῳ*, aut *λόγῳ*, aut *πόνῳ*. So also here we may understand *λόγῳ* or *πόνῳ* (or *χρόνῳ*?)—or still better as it seems to me, *leave the ellipsis unsupplied* (see Eph. iii. 3). We have a word in English which exactly expresses it,—one which has fallen into disuse, but has no equivalent; **lightly**: i. e. with little pains, few words, small hesitation. Then next as to the *reading*, I have followed the * most ancient MSS., in editing **ποιῆσαι** and not *γενέσθαι*. This being so, we have to choose between *πείθεις* of Bℵ and *πείθῃ* of A. It is almost impossible to give any assignable meaning to the former; and I suspect it has come in by a confusion of the two readings. Whereas *πείθῃ* seems to take up the *πείθομαι* of ver. 26. The received reading has probably found its way in from first imagining that *πειθ-* had to do with *Paul's persuading Agrippa*, and then the *ποιῆσαι* having no sense, became conformed to the *γενέσθαι* in the Apostle's speech below. And now, as to the *sense of Agrippa's saying*. In determining this, enough attention has not been paid to two points: (1) the *present tense*, *πείθῃ*, **thou art persuading** thyself, art imagining; and (2) the use, *in the mouth of a Jew*, and *that Jew a king*, of the *Gentile and offensive appellation χριστιανός*. To my mind, the *first* of these considerations decides that Agrippa is characterizing *no effect on himself*, but *what Paul was* fancying in his mind, reckoning the *πείθομαι* which he had expressed above: the *second*, that he speaks of something *not* that he is *likely to become*, but that *contrasts strangely with his present worldly position and intentions*. I would therefore render the words thus: **Lightly** (with small trouble) **art thou persuading thyself that thou canst make me a Christian**: and understand them, in connexion with Paul's having attempted to make Agrippa a witness on his side,—*'I am not so easily to be made a Christian of, as thou supposest.'* Most of the ancient Commentators (especially as reading *πείθεις*) take the words as implying some effect on Agrippa's mind, and as spoken in earnest: but this I think is hardly possible, philologically or exegetically. I may add that the emphatic position of both **ἐν ὀλίγῳ** and **χριστιανόν**, before their respective verbs, strongly confirms the view taken above. I must again caution the reader against the mistake committed by Wordsworth, in supposing the enclitic *με* to be emphatic, which it cannot be, *ἐμέ* being required in such a case. Indeed, a more insignificant position than it here holds, next to the most emphatic word of the sentence, cannot be conceived.

29 ὁ δὲ Παῦλος [x] Εὐξαίμην [y] ἂν τῷ θεῷ καὶ [v] ἐν ὀλίγῳ
καὶ ἐν μεγάλῳ οὐ μόνον σὲ ἀλλὰ καὶ πάντας τοὺς
ἀκούοντάς μου σήμερον γενέσθαι τοιούτους [z] ὁποῖος
κἀγὼ εἰμὶ [a] παρεκτὸς τῶν [b] δεσμῶν τούτων. 30 ἀνέστη
τε ὁ βασιλεὺς καὶ ὁ [c] ἡγεμὼν ἥ τε Βερνίκη καὶ οἱ [d] συγ-
καθήμενοι αὐτοῖς, 31 καὶ [e] ἀναχωρήσαντες ἐλάλουν πρὸς
ἀλλήλους λέγοντες ὅτι οὐδὲν [f] θανάτου [f] ἄξιον ἢ [f] δεσμῶν
πράσσει ὁ ἄνθρωπος οὗτος. 32 Ἀγρίππας δὲ τῷ Φήστῳ
ἔφη [g] Ἀπολελύσθαι ἐδύνατο ὁ ἄνθρωπος οὗτος, εἰ μὴ
[h] ἐπεκέκλητο Καίσαρα.

XXVII. 1 Ὡς δὲ [i] ἐκρίθη [k] τοῦ [l] ἀποπλεῖν ἡμᾶς εἰς

...παυλος E. ABHL Pℵ a b c d f g h k l m o p 13

x dat. and constr., here only. see Xen. Mem. iii. 14. 3. constr., w. πρός, 2 Cor. xiii. 7. (ch. xxvii. 29 reff.)
y = here only. Xen. Mem. iii. 5. 1.
z 1 Cor. iii. 13. Gal. ii. 6. 1 Thess. i. 9. James i. 24 only †.
a Matt. v. 32. 2 Cor. xi. 28 only †. Deut. i. 36 Aq.
b ch. xxiii. 29 reff.
c ch. xxiii. 24, &c., reff.
d Mark xiv. 54 only. Exod. xxiii. 33 Ald. (Tromm) Ps. c. 6 only.
e ch. xxiii. 19 reff.
f ch. xxiii. 29 (reff.).
g = Matt. xxvii. 15, &c. ch. iii. 13. iv. 21, 23. v. 40. xvi. 35, 36. xxviii. 18. Heb. xiii. 23 2 Macc. xii. 25.
h ch. xxv. 11 reff.
i = ch. xv. 19 reff.
k constr., ch. iii. 12 reff.
l ch. xiii. 4. xiv. 26. xx. 15 only †.

29. rec aft ο δε παυλος ins ειπεν, with HLP rel [Syr copt æth arm] Chr, εφη 36: om ABℵ p 13. 40. 137 vulg syr. ευξαμην [H]Lℵ[1] c[1] l p [ηυξ. P f]. rec (for μεγαλω) πολλω (*see notes*), with HLP rel 36 æth Chr₁: [εν πολλω κ. εν ολ. m:] txt ABℵ k p 13. 40 vulg syr-mg-gr copt arm.

30. rec ins και ταυτα ειποντος αυτου bef ανεστη (*addn for perspicuity*), with HLP rel syr-w-ast Thl: και ταυτα ειποντος 137 æth-rom: om ABℵ c p 13 vulg Syr æth-pl arm.—rec om τε: txt as above, but c 13. 40 syr copt Chr₁ have δε.

31. αξιον bef θανατου A c copt: η δεσμων bef αξιον Bℵ k m p 13. 40 vulg[exc tol]. ins τι bef πρασσει Aℵ k m p 13 vulg[not demid (copt)].

32. επικεκλ. AL 40 Thl: txt BH[P]ℵ p 13. 36 rel Chr.

Chap. XXVII. 1. και ουτως εκρινεν ο ηγεμων αναπεμψαι καισαρα 64: και ουτως εκρινεν αυτον ο ηγ. αναπεμψαι καισαρι 97: ως ουν εκρινεν ο ηγ. του πεμπεσθαι αυτον προς καισαρα τη επιουση εκαλεσεν εκατονταρχον τινα ονοματι ιουλιανον σπειρης σεβαστης παρεδιδου αυτω τον παυλον συν ετεροις δεσμωταις syr-mg: και εκρινε περι αυτου ο φηστος πεμπεσθαι αυτον προς καισαρα εις την ιταλ. κ.τ.λ. Syr. for ημας, τους περι παυλου (ως *begins an eccl lection, see ch* xxi. 8 *rec*) P[π. τον παυλον] m lectt: *eum* vulg.

29.] I could wish to God, that whether with ease or with difficulty (on my part), not only thou, but all who hear me to-day, might become such as I am, except only these bonds. He understands ἐν ὀλίγῳ just as Agrippa had used it, **easily,** ‘*with little trouble,*’ ‘*with slight exertion:*’ and contrasts with it ἐν μεγάλῳ (πολλῷ has been an alteration to suit the imagined supplement χρόνῳ), **with difficulty,** ‘*with great trouble,*’ ‘*with much labour.*’ Those interpreters who understand χρόνῳ above, render this ‘seu tempore exiguo opus fuerit, seu multo’ (Schött.); those who take ἐν ὀλ. for ‘*almost,*’ ‘non propemodum tantum, sed plane’ (Grot.): ‘*not only almost, but altogether,*’ E. V. In **εὔχεσθαι θεῷ** the dative implies the *direction* of the wish or request to God: so Æsch. Agam. 852, θεοῖσι πρῶτα δεξιώσομαι: Il. γ. 318, θεοῖσι δὲ χεῖρας ἀνέσχον, and freq. See examples in Bernhardy, Syntax, p. 86.

δεσμῶν] He shews the chain, which being in ‘*custodia militaris,*’ he *bore on his arm,* to connect him with the soldier who had charge of him. [This exception may be regarded as a proof of the perfect courtesy of the great Apostle.] **31. πράσσει**] generally, of his life and habits. No *definite act* was alleged against him: and his apologetic speech was in fact a *sample* of the acts of which he was accused. **32.**] Agrippa in these words delivers his judgment as a Jew: ‘*For aught I see, as regards our belief and practices, he might have been set at liberty.*’ But now he could not: ‘nam appellatione potestas judicis, a quo appellatum est, cessare incipit ad absolvendum non minus quam ad condemnandum. Crimina enim integra servanda sunt cognitioni superioris.’ Grot.

Chap. XXVII. 1—XXVIII. 31.] Paul’s voyage to Rome and sojourn there. I cannot but express the benefit I have derived in my commentary on this section, from Mr. Smith’s now well-known treatise on the voyage and shipwreck of St. Paul: as also from various letters which he has from time to time put into my hands, tending further to elucidate the subject. The substance of these will be found embodied in an excursus following the chronological table in the prolegomena.

τὴν Ἰταλίαν, [m] παρεδίδουν τόν τε Παῦλον καί τινας ἑτέρους [n] δεσμώτας ἑκατοντάρχῃ ὀνόματι Ἰουλίῳ [o] σπείρης [p] σεβαστῆς. 2 [q] ἐπιβάντες δὲ πλοίῳ Ἀδραμυττηνῷ μέλλοντι [r] πλεῖν [εἰς] τοὺς κατὰ τὴν Ἀσίαν τόπους, [s] ἀνήχ-

m = ch. xii. 4. xxviii 16 v. r.
n ver. 42 only. Gen. xxxix. 20. (-τήριον, ch. v. 21, 23.)
o ch. x. 1 reff.
p = here only. see ch. xxv. 21, 25.
q = ch. xxi. 2 (Matt. xxi. 5, from Zech. ix. 9. ch. xx. 18. xxi. 4. xxv. 1) only. dat., here only.
r Luke viii. 23. ch. xxi. 3. vv. 6, 24. Luke only, exc. Rev. xviii. 17. constr. (accus.) here only. Isa. xlii. 10. πλ. τ. θάλασσαν, Sir. xliii. 24. 1 Macc. xiii. 29. πλ. τὰ πελαγη, Polyb. iii. 4. 10.
s ch. xiii. 13 reff.

παρεδιδου A a 40 demid Syr copt Thl-sif. om ετερους c p[1] 137 syr : δεσμ. bef ετ. L. ins ιουλιω bef as well as after ονοματι ℵ[1].

2. aft επιβ. ins εν c 137. αδραμυντηνω AB[1] (13 copt arm), al vary. rec μελλοντες (*corrn to suit* επιβαντες), with HLP rel vulg[with fuld demid tol] Chr: txt ABℵ a b c d o p 13. 36. 40. 137 am syrr copt æth-pl arm. rec om εις, with HLP rel Chr_1 Thl-sif [*circa* vulg] : ins επι c 36. 137 syr : ins εις ABℵ p 13. 40 Thl-fin.

1.] **τοῦ** (see reff.) contains the purpose of ἐκρίθη. The matter of the decision implied in ἐκρίθη is expressed in this form as if governed by the substantive κρίσις, as in ch. xx. 3, ἐγένετο γνώμης τοῦ ὑποστρέφειν. Meyer remarks that the expressions κελεύειν ἵνα, εἰπεῖν ἵνα, θέλειν ἵνα, &c. are analogous. **ἡμᾶς**] Here we have again the *first person*, the narrator having, in all probability, remained in Palestine, and in the neighbourhood of Paul, during the interval since ch. xxi. 18. **παρεδίδουν**] *Who?* perhaps the assessors with whom Festus took counsel on the appeal, ch. xxv. 12: but more likely the plural is used indefinitely, the subject being 'they,' = 'on' (Fr.), or '*man*' (Germ.). **ἑτέρους δ.**] This expression, says Meyer, is purposely chosen, to intimate, that they were prisoners *of another sort* (not also Christians under arrest). But De W. shews this to be a mistake, by ἕτεραι πολλαί, Luke viii. 3, = ἄλλαι πολλαί, Mark xv. 41, in both places meaning '*many others of the same sort.*' Here also they are of the *same class*, as far as δεσμῶται is concerned: further, nothing is implied in the narrative, one way or the other. **σπείρης σεβαστῆς**] There is some difficulty in determining what this cohort was. We must not fall into the mistake of several of the Commentators, that of confounding this σπ. σεβαστή with an ἴλη ἱππέων καλουμένη Σεβαστηνῶν, mentioned by Josephus, B. J. ii. 12. 5, and Antt. xx. 6. 1, this latter implying '*natives of Samaria*' (Σεβαστή),—whereas our word is the same adjective as that name itself, and cannot by any analogy have reference to it. More than one of the *legions* at different times bore the honorary title 'Augusta.' Wetst. quotes from Claudian de Bell. Gild. 'Dictaque ab Augusto legio:' from inscriptions in Mauritania, Legio III. Aug., II. Aug., VIII. Aug.: from Ptolemy, ii. 3, λεγεὼν δευτέρα σεβαστή (in Britain); iv. 3, λε-
* γεὼν γ. σεβαστή; but of a '*cohors* Augusta,' or 'Augustana,' we never hear. De Wette and Meyer suggest (but we have no historical proof of the supposition) that it was one among the five cohorts stationed at Cæsarea (see note, ch. xxv. 23) thus distinguished as the body-guard of the emperor (?), and therefore chosen for any services immediately concerning him, as in this case. Meyer thinks it may be the same (but then would the appellations be different?) with the σπεῖρα Ἰταλική of ch. x. 1. It is remarkable that almost all the Commentators have assumed, without any reason, that this σπ. σεβαστή must have been *stationed at Cæsarea*, whereas it may well have been a cohort, or body of men so called, at Rome. Wieseler is the only one that I have seen who has not fallen into this error. He controverts the other interpretations (Chron. d. Apost.-g. note, p. 391), and infers that Julius belonged to the *Augustani*, mentioned Tacitus xiv. 15, and Suet. Nero, 20 and 25 (see also Dio Cass. lxi. 20: ἦν μὲν γάρ τι καὶ ἴδιον αὐτῷ σύστημα ἐς πεντακισχιλίους στρατιώτας παρεσκευασμένον· Αὐγούστειοί τε ὠνομάζοντο· καὶ ἐξῆρχον τῶν ἐπαίνων, and lxiii. 8), who appear to have been identical with the *evocati* (veterans specially summoned to service by the emperors), and to have formed Nero's body-guard on his journey to Greece. The first levying of this band by Augustus, Dio relates, xlv. 12. To this Julius seems to have belonged,—to have been sent on some service into Asia, and now to have been returning to Rome.

We read of a Julius Priscus, Prefect of the Prætorian guards under Vitellius, who killed himself 'pudore magis quam necessitate,' after the military murder by Mucianus of Calpurnius Galerianus. This was ten years after the date of our narrative; but the identity of the two must be only conjectural. **2. Ἀδραμυττηνῷ**] Adramyttium (Ἀδραμύττιον, -ειον, or Ἀτραμύττιον, and in Plin. v. 32, Adramytteos) was a seaport with a harbour in Mysia, an Athenian colony. It is now a village called Endramit. Grotius, Drusius, and others

θημεν, ὄντος σὺν ἡμῖν Ἀριστάρχου Μακεδόνος Θεσσαλο-
νικέως, 3 τῇ τε [t] ἑτέρᾳ [u] κατήχθημεν εἰς Σιδῶνα, [v] φιλαν-
θρώπως τε ὁ Ἰούλιος τῷ Παύλῳ [w] χρησάμενος [x] ἐπέτρεψεν
πρὸς τοὺς [y] φίλους πορευθέντι [z] ἐπιμελείας [a] τυχεῖν. 4 κἀκεῖθεν [s] ἀναχθέντες [b] ὑπεπλεύσαμεν τὴν Κύπρον διὰ τὸ

...τυχειν H. ABLP‎א abcdf ghkl mop 13 [H is continued in an uncial writing of about the xith cent.]

t = ch. xx. 15. Xen. Cyr. iv. 6. 10. u pass., = ch. xxviii. 12 only. (act., ch. xxiii. 15 reff.) v here only †. 2 Macc. ix. 27 only. φιλ. διακεῖσθαι πρὸς . . . . . Polyb. i. 68. 13. (-πος, Wisd. i. 6. -πία, ch. xxviii. 2. -πεῖν, 2 Macc. xiii. 23.) w = (see 2 Cor. xiii. 10.) Gen. xxvi. 29. Xen. Mem. iv. 6. 5 (often). x inf. aor., ch. xxi. 39 reff. pres., ch. xxvi. 1 reff. y = 3 John 15. z here only. Prov. iii. 8. (-λής, Prov. xi. 2 Sym. -λῶς, Luke xv. 8. -λεῖσθαι, Luke x. 34.) a = ch. xxiv. 2 reff. b ver. 7 only †.

αρισταρχος א[1]. θεσσαλονικεων, adding δε [τε c] αρισταρχ. κ. σεκ. [c] 137 syr (*see ch* xx. 4).

3. for τε, δε Lא[3] k m p 40 vulg copt Chr$_1$. σιδονα א[1]. ιουλιανος A. Steph om τους, with c o: ins ABHLPא p 13 rel Chr Thl Œc. rec πορευθεντα, with HLP rel Chr$_1$ Thl-sif: txt ABא p 13. 36 Thl-fin.

erroneously suppose *Adrumetum* to be meant, on the north coast of Africa (Winer, Realw.). **πλεῖν [εἰς] τοὺς . . . .]** The bracketed εἰς is in all probability an insertion to help off the harshness of the construction. But the accusative is indicative of the direction. We have ἦλθε Πολυνείκης χθόνα, Eur. Phœniss. 110. See Winer, edn. 6, § 32. 1, on the accus. after neuter verbs, and Bernhardy, Syntax, pp. 114 ff., and other instances in Wetstein. **Ἀριστάρχ.]** See ch. xix. 29; xx. 4; Col. iv. 10; Philem. 24. In Col. iv. 10, Paul calls him his συναιχμάλωτος, but perhaps only figuratively: the same term is applied to Epaphras, Philem. 23, where follows Ἀρίσταρχος, Δημᾶς, Λουκᾶς, οἱ **συνεργοί** μου. **3. Σιδῶνα]** This celebrated city is generally joined in the N. T. with Tyre, from which it was distant 200 stadia (Strabo, xvi. 756 ff.), and of which it was probably the mother city. It was within the lot of the tribe of Asher (Josh. xix. 28), but never conquered by the Israelites (Judg. i. 31; iii. 3). From the earliest times the Sidonians were renowned for their manufactures of glass ('Sidon artifex vitri,' Plin. v. 19), linen (πέπλοι παμποίκιλοι ἔργα γυναικῶν Σιδονίων, Il. ζ. 290), silversmith's work (Il. ψ. 743, and Od. ο. 115, &c.), and for the hewing of timber (1 Kings v. 6; Ezra iii. 7). In ancient times, Sidon seems to have been under Tyre, and to have furnished her with mariners (see Ezek. xxvii. 8). It went over to Shalmaneser, king of Assyria (Jos. Antt. ix. 14. 2); but seems under him, and afterwards under the Chaldæans and Persians, to have had tributary kings of its own (Jer. xxv. 22; xxvii. 3; Herod. viii. 67). The Sidonians furnished the best ships in Xerxes' navy, Herod. vii. 96, 99. Under Artaxerxes Ochus Sidon freed itself, but was by him, after a severe siege, taken and destroyed (Diod. Sic. xvi. 43 ff.). It was rebuilt, and soon after went over to Alexander, keeping its own vassal kings. After his death it was alternately under Syrian and Egyptian rule, till it fell under the Romans. The present Saida is west of ancient Sidon, and is a port of some commerce, but insecure, from the sanding up of the harbour (Winer, Realw. See also Robinson, vol. iii. pp. 415 ff., who gives an account of the history of Sidon during the middle ages). **πορευθέντι]** This dat. looks very like a grammatical correction: the **πορευθέντα** of the rec. would be an instance of an acc. with inf. after a dat. preceding, as ch. xxvi. 20; xxii. 17. The φίλοι here mentioned were probably Christian brethren (see ch. xi. 19, where the Gospel is said to have been preached in Phœnicia; and ch. xxi. 3, where we find brethren at *Tyre*); but it is usual in that case for ἀδελφοί or μαθηταί to be specified: cf. ch. xxi. 4, 7. The ἐπιμελείας τυχεῖν was perhaps to obtain from them that outfit for the voyage which, on account of the official precision of his custody at Cæsarea, he could not there be provided with.

4. ὑπεπλεύσαμεν] sailed under, i. e. '*in the lee of,*' Cyprus. "Ubi navis vento contrario cogitur a recto cursu decedere, ita ut tunc insula sit interposita inter ventum et navem, dicitur ferri *infra* insulam." Wetst., who also says, "Si ventus favisset, alto se commisissent, et Cyprum ad dexteram partem reliquissent, ut Act. xxi. 3, nunc autem coguntur legere littus Ciliciæ, inter Cyprum et Asiam." With this explanation Mr. Smith agrees; and there can hardly be a doubt that it is the right one. The κατὰ τὴν Ἀσίαν τόποι of ver. 2 being to the *west* of Pamphylia (which was not in Asia, ch. ii. 10), the direct course thither would have been *S. of Cyprus;* but having the wind contrary, i. e. from the W. or N.W. ("the very wind which might have been expected in this part of the Mediterranean at this season (summer). Admiral de Saumarez writes, Aug. 19, 1798, 'We

τοὺς ἀνέμους εἶναι [c] ἐναντίους, 5 τό τε [d] πέλαγος τὸ [e] κατὰ
τὴν Κιλικίαν καὶ Παμφυλίαν [f] διαπλεύσαντες [g] κατήλθομεν
εἰς Μύῤῥα τῆς Λυκίας. 6 κἀκεῖ εὑρὼν ὁ ἑκατοντάρχης
πλοῖον Ἀλεξανδρῖνον [h] πλέον εἰς τὴν Ἰταλίαν, [i] ἐνεβί-
βασεν ἡμᾶς εἰς αὐτό. 7 ἐν [j] ἱκαναῖς δὲ [j] ἡμέραις [k] βραδυ-
πλοοῦντες καὶ [l] μόλις [m] γενόμενοι [d] κατὰ τὴν Κνίδον,

c = Mark vi. 48 || Mt. (xv. 39. ch. xxvi. 9 reff.) only.
d Matt. xviii. 6 only †. 2 Macc. v. 21 only.
e = ver. 2. Luke x. 32. Matt. xxiv. 7.
f here only †. Xen. Anab. vii. 8. 1.
g = ch. xxi. 3. (ch. ii. 5 reff.)
h ver. 2 reff.
i here only. Prov. iv. 11 only.
j = ch. ix. 23 reff.
k here only †.
l ch. xiv. 18 reff.
m = ch. xx. 16 al.

5. om την a 137. πλευσαντες Hr. add δι ημερων δεκαπεντε c 137 syr-w-ast. κατηλθαμεν Aℵ: κατηχθημεν b d h o 14. 38. 57. 66. 76. 93-7-8-marg 113 lect-5: ηλθομεν 25 vulg Syr. for μυρρα, λυστρα A vulg copt arm-mg Cassiod$_1$ Bede$_1$: λυστραν ℵ: μοιρων Hr: σμυρναν m Bede-gr [Jer$_1$]: σμυρα arm[-ed]: txt B [syr-mg-gr Jer], and μυρα LP 13 rel syrr Chr Thl.

6. κακειθεν A l 24: κακεισε m 15. 25. 36. 40. 180. om την Hr b c h k l o. aft αυτο ins τουτο ℵ^1(ℵ^3 disapproving).

have just gained sight of Cyprus, so invariably do the westerly winds prevail at this season.'" Smith, p. 27), they kept under shelter of Cyprus, i. e. between Cyprus and Cilicia; and so διαπλεύσαντες, **having sailed the whole length of** the sea off Cilicia and Pamphylia, they came to Myra. See the account of the reverse voyage, ch. xxi. 3, where, the wind being nearly in the same quarter (see ver. 1, εὐθυδρομήσαντες εἰς τ. Κῶ), the direct course was taken, and they left Cyprus at a distance (for so ἀναφ. seems to imply) on their left, in going to Tyre. On the διαπλεύσαντες, &c., it may be well to quote (from Smith) the testimony of M. de Pagés, a French navigator, who, on his voyage from Syria to Marseilles, informs us that after making Cyprus, "the winds from the west, and consequently contrary, which prevail in these places during the summer, *forced us to run to the north.* We made for the coast of Caramania (Cilicia), in order to meet the northerly winds, *which we found accordingly.*" **5. Μύῤῥα**] εἶτα Μύρα ἐν εἴκοσι σταδίοις ὑπὲρ τῆς θαλάττης ἐπὶ μετεώρου λόφου, Strabo xiv. 3,—Λέντλος ἐπιπεμφθεὶς Ἀνδριάκῃ Μυρέων ἐπινείῳ, τήν τε ἅλυσιν ἔῤῥηξε τοῦ λιμένος, καὶ εἰς Μύρα ἀνῄει. The neighbourhood is full of magnificent ruins; see Sir C. Fellows's Lycia, ch. ix. The name still remains. The various readings merely shew that the copyists were unacquainted with the place.

6.] The Alexandrian ship *may* have been laden with corn for Rome; but this cannot be inferred from ver. 38, for the ship had been *lightened before*, ver. 18. On her size, see below, ver. 37. Most probably this ship had been prevented taking the direct course to Italy, which was by the south of Crete, by the prevailing westerly winds. Under such circumstances, says Mr. Smith (p. 32), "ships, particularly those of the ancients, unprovided with a compass, and ill calculated to work to windward, would naturally stand to the N. till they made the land of Asia Minor, which is peculiarly favourable for such a mode of navigation, because the coast is bold and safe, and the elevation of the mountains makes it visible at a great distance; it abounds in harbours, while the sinuosities of its shores and the westerly current would enable them, if the wind was at all off the land, to work to windward, at least as far as Cnidus, where these advantages ceased. Myra lies due N. from Alexandria, and its bay is well calculated to shelter a windbound ship. The Alexandrian ship was not, therefore, out of her course at Myra, even if she had no call to touch there for the purposes of commerce." **πλέον**, the present, should be rendered **on her voyage.** **7. βραδυπλ.**] It is evident that the ship was encountering an adverse wind. The distance from Myra to Cnidus is only 130 geogr. miles, which, with a fair wind, would not take more than one day. Mr. Smith shews that the wind was N.W., or within a few points of it. "We learn from the sailing directions for the Mediterranean, that, throughout the whole of that sea, but mostly in the eastern half, including the Adriatic and Archipelago, N.W. winds prevail in the summer months; . . . the summer Etesiæ come from the N.W. (p. 197); which agrees with Aristotle's account of these winds,—οἱ ἐτησίαι λεγόμενοι μίξιν ἔχοντες τῶν τε ἀπὸ τῆς ἄρκτου φερομένων κ. ζεφύρου, de Mundo, ch. iv. According to Pliny (ii. 47), they begin in August, and blow for forty days." **μόλις**] **with difficulty**: not as E. V., '*scarce*,' which being also an adv. of *time*, gives the erroneous idea to the English reader that the ship had *scarcely reached* Cnidus when the wind became un-

m here only †. n ver. 4 only †. o ver. 13 only †. Diod. Sic. xiii. 3. p ch. viii. 11 reff.

μὴ [m] προσεῶντος ἡμᾶς τοῦ ἀνέμου, [n] ὑπεπλεύσαμεν τὴν
Κρήτην κατὰ Σαλμώνην, 8 [l] μόλις τε [o] παραλεγόμενοι
αὐτὴν ἤλθομεν εἰς τόπον τινὰ καλούμενον Καλοὺς
Λιμένας, ᾧ ἐγγὺς ἦν πόλις Λασέα. 9 [p] ἱκανοῦ δὲ

ABLPℵ abcdf ghkl mop13

7. προσεεωντος ℵ.

8. om τινα A 133 Syr [æth-pl]. πολις bef ην Aℵ a^2 13. for λασεα, αλασσα A 40. 96. 109 syr-mg (*Alasa*) : *Thalassa* vulg æth and mss mentd by Jer : *Thessala* al : λαισσα $ℵ^3$: txt BH^{r}LP p 13 rel syr copt æth-pl Chr Thl Œc Jer_1 (of these, H^{r}LP rel (exc m) Chr Thl have (*through common confusion of vowels*) λασαια), λασσαια $ℵ^1$.

favourable. **γεν. κατά**] **having come over against,** as E. V. **Κνίδον**] Cnidus is a peninsula at the entrance of the Ægean Sea, between the islands of Cos and Rhodes, having a lofty promontory and two harbours, Strabo, xiv. 2. "With N.W. winds the ship could work up from Myra to Cnidus; because, until she reached that point, she had the advantage of a weather shore, under the lee of which she would have smooth water, and, as formerly mentioned, a westerly current; but it would be slowly and with difficulty. At Cnidus that advantage ceased." Smith, p. 37. **μὴ προσεῶντ.**] The common idea has been that the prep. in composition implies that the wind would not suffer them to *put in at* Cnidus. But this would hardly be reconcileable with the fact; for when off Cnidus they would be in shelter under the high land, and there would be no difficulty in putting in. I should be rather inclined to regard this clause as explaining the μόλις above, and the πρός in composition as implying *contribution,* or *direction:* 'with difficulty, the wind not permitting us by favouring our course.' **ὑπεπλ.** [see above on ver. 4] **τ. Κρ. κ. Σαλμώνην**] "Unless she had put into that harbour (Cnidus), and waited for a fair wind, her only course was to run under the lee of Crete, in the direction of Salmone, which is the eastern extremity of that island." Salmone (Capo Salomon) is described by Strabo (x. 4) as ὀξὺ ἀκρωτήριον τὸ Σαμώνιον, ἐπὶ τὴν Αἴγυπτον νεῦον, καὶ τὰς Ῥοδίων νήσους. Pliny (iv. 12) calls it Sammonium. **8. μόλις παρ.**] "After passing this point (Salmone), the difficulty they experienced in navigating to the westward along the coasts of Asia, would recur; but as the south side of Crete is also a weather shore with N.W. winds, they would be able to work up as far as Cape Matala. Here the land trends suddenly to the N., and the advantages of a weather shore cease, and their only resource was to make for a harbour. Now Fair Havens is the harbour nearest to Cape Matala, the farthest point to which an ancient ship could have attained with N.W.-ly winds." Smith, ib. **παραλεγ.** does not, as Servius on Æn. iii. 127 supposes, imply that the ship was *towed* ("funem legendo, i. e. colligendo, aspera loca prætereunt"), but, as Meyer explains it, that, the places on the coast being touched (or perhaps, rather, *appearing*) one after another, are, as it were, *gathered up* by the navigators. Mr. Smith (p. 42) exposes the mistake of Eustathius (adopted by Valpy, from Dr. Falconer), by which the ship taking the *S. coast of Crete* is attempted to be explained: viz. δυσλίμενος ἡ Κρήτη πρὸς τὴν βόρραν: whereas there are, in fact, excellent harbours on the N. side of Crete,—Souda and Spina Longa. **Καλοὺς Λιμένας**] The situation of this anchorage was ascertained by Pococke, from the fact of the name still remaining. "In searching after Lebena farther to the west, I found out a place which I thought to be of greater consequence, because mentioned in Holy Scripture, and also honoured by the presence of St. Paul, that is, 'the Fair Havens, near unto the city of Lasea;' for there is another small bay about two leagues to the E. of Matala, which is now called by the Greeks good or fair havens (λιμέονες καλούς):" (Calolimounias of Mr. Brown's letter: see excursus as above.) Travels in the East, ii. p. 250: cited by Mr. Smith, who adds: "The most conclusive evidence that this is the Fair Havens of Scripture, is, that its position is precisely that where a ship circumstanced as St. Paul's was, must have put in. I have already shewn that the wind must have been about N.W.;—but with such a wind she could not pass Cape Matala: we must therefore look *near, but to the E. of* this promontory, for an anchorage well calculated to shelter a vessel in N.W. winds, but not *from all winds,* otherwise it would not have been, in the opinion of seamen (ver. 12), an unsafe winter harbour. Now here we have a harbour which not only fulfils every one of the conditions, but still retains the name given to it by St. Luke." Smith, p. 45. He also gives an engraving of the place from a sketch by Signr. Schranz, the artist who accompanied Mr. Pashley in his

p χρόνου q διαγενομένου καὶ ὄντος ἤδη r ἐπισφαλοῦς τοῦ
s πλοὸς διὰ τὸ καὶ τὴν t νηστείαν ἤδη u παρεληλυθέναι,
v παρῄνει ὁ Παῦλος 10 λέγων αὐτοῖς Ἄνδρες, w θεωρῶ
ὅτι x μετὰ y ὕβρεως καὶ πολλῆς z ζημίας οὐ μόνον τοῦ
a φορτίου καὶ τοῦ πλοίου ἀλλὰ καὶ τῶν b ψυχῶν ἡμῶν
c μέλλειν c ἔσεσθαι τὸν s πλοῦν. 11 ὁ δὲ ἑκατοντάρχης τῷ
d κυβερνήτῃ καὶ τῷ e ναυκλήρῳ μᾶλλον f ἐπείθετο ἢ τοῖς

q ch. xxv. 13. Mark xvi. 1 only †. 2 Macc. xi. 26 only. r here only †. Wisd. ix. 14 only. (-λῶς, Wisd. iv. 4.) s here bis. ch. xxi. 7 only †. Wisd. xiv. 1 only. t = here only. (2 Cor. vi. 5 reff.) u = Matt. xiv. 15. 1 Pet. iv. 3. Jer. viii. 20. Dan. ii. 9 Theod. v ver. 22 only †. 2 Macc. vii. 25, 26 only. (-νεσις, Wisd. viii. 9.) w ch. xix. 26 reff. x = ch. v. 26. xxv. 23 al. fr. 1 Macc. ix. 37. y = ver. 21 (2 Cor. xii. 10) only. τὴν ἀπὸ τῶν ὄμβρων ὕβριν, Jos. Antt. iii. 6. 4, end. (-ίζειν, ch. xiv. 5. -ιστής, Rom. i. 30.) z ver. 21. Phil. iii. 7, 8 only. Ezra vii. 26. (-οῦν, 1 Cor. iii. 15.) a = here (Matt. xi. 30. xxiii. 4. Luke xi. 46 bis. Gal. vi. 5) only ‡. (Sir. xxi. 16. -τίζειν, Matt. xi. 28.) b = ch. xv. 26 reff. c ch. xi. 28 reff. d Rev. xviii. 17 only. Prov. xxiii. 34. Ezek. xxvii. 8, 27, 28 only. (-νᾷν, Prov. xii. 5. -νησις, 1 Cor. xii. 28.) e here only †. f = ch. v. 36, &c. reff.

10. θεορω ℵ[1]. [μεθ m.] rec φορτου, with b c[1] o Thl-fin: txt ABH[r]LPℵ p 13 rel 36. 40. 137 Chr₁ Thl-sif. υμων L[2][Tischdf] ℵ[3] lect-12 [copt].
11. rec επειθετο bef μαλλον, with H[r]LP rel syrr [arm, Treg] Thl-sif: txt ABℵ k m

travels. There is no ground for identifying this anchorage with καλὴ ἀκτή mentioned as a *city* in Crete by Steph. Byzant. For *this* is clearly *not* the name of a city, by the subjoined notice, ᾧ ἐγγὺς ἦν πόλις Λασέα. Nor is there any reason to suppose, with Meyer, that the name **καλοὶ λιμ.** was euphemistically given,—because the harbour was not one to winter in: this (see above) it may not have been, and yet may have been an excellent refuge at particular times, as now, from prevailing westerly winds. **Λασέα**] This place was, until recently, altogether unknown; and from the variety of readings, the very name was uncertain. Pliny (iv. 12) mentions *Lasos* among the cities of Crete, but does not indicate its situation. It is singular, and tends to support the identity of Lasos with our Lasea, that as here Alassa, so there Alos, is a various reading. The reading Thalassa appears to have been an error of a transcriber from -αλασσα forming so considerable a part of a word of such common occurrence. There is a *Lisia* named in Crete in the Peutinger Table, which may be the same. On the very interesting discovery of *Lasea* by the Rev. G. Brown in the beginning of the year 1856, see the excursus at the end of Prolegg. to Acts. The ruins are on the beach, about two hours eastward of Fair Havens. **9. ἱκανοῦ χρ.**] Not '*since the beginning of our voyage*,' as Meyer:—the time was spent *at the anchorage*. **τοῦ πλοός**] Not '*sailing*,' but **the voyage**, viz. to Rome,—which henceforth was given up as hopeless for this autumn and winter. That this is the meaning of ὁ πλοῦς, see ch. xxi. 7. And by observing this, we avoid a difficulty which has been supposed to attend the words. *Sailing* was not unsafe so early as this (see below); but to undertake so long a voyage, was. **τὴν νηστείαν**] **The fast,** κατ' ἐξοχήν, is the solemn fast of the day of expiation, the 10th of Tisri, the seventh month of the Jewish ecclesiastical year, and the first of the civil year. See Levit. xvi. 29 ff.; xxiii. 26 ff. This would be about the time of the autumnal equinox. The *sailing season* did not close so early: 'Ex die igitur tertio iduum Novembris, usque in diem sextum iduum Martiarum, maria clauduntur.' Vegetius (Smith, p. 45, note) de Re Milit. iv. 39. **10.**] From the use of θεωρῶ here, and from the saying itself, it seems clear to me that Paul was not uttering *at present* any prophetic intimation, but simply his own sound judgment on the difficult question at issue. It is otherwise at vv. 22—24. As Smith remarks, "The event justified St. Paul's advice. At the same time it may be observed, that a bay, open to nearly one half the compass, could not have been a good winter harbour." (p. 47.) **μετὰ ὕβρεως** is interpreted by Meyer as subjective—'*accompanied with presumption on our part*:' but not to mention that this would be a very unusual sense, ver. 21, κερδῆσαι τὴν ὕβριν ταύτ. κ. τ. ζημίαν, is decisive (De W.) against it. **ὅτι . . . μέλλειν**] A mixing of two constructions, see Winer, edn. 6, § 44. 8, remark 2. This is most flagrant in later writers, as Pausanias and Arrian,—see Bernhardy, Syntax, p. 369; but is also found earlier, e. g. Plato, Charm., p. 165: οὐκ ἂν αἰσχυνθείην ὅτι μὴ οὐχὶ ὀρθῶς φάναι εἰρηκέναι. Isæus, περὶ τοῦ φιλοκτ. κληρ. p. 57: ἐπειδὴ δὲ προσδιαμεμαρτύρηκεν ὡς υἱὸν εἶναι γνήσιον Εὐκτήμονος τοῦτον . . . See other references in Winer, l. c. **11. τ. ναυκλήρῳ**]

ὑπὸ [τοῦ] Παύλου λεγομένοις. 12 [g]ἀνευθέτου δὲ τοῦ
[h]λιμένος [i]ὑπάρχοντος πρὸς [k]παραχειμασίαν [l]οἱ πλείονες
[m]ἔθεντο [mn]βουλὴν [o]ἀναχθῆναι ἐκεῖθεν, [p]εἴ [p]πως δύναιντο
[q]καταντήσαντες εἰς Φοίνικα [r]παραχειμάσαι [h]λιμένα τῆς
Κρήτης [s]βλέποντα [t]κατὰ [u]λίβα καὶ [t]κατὰ [v]χῶρον.

ABLPℵ abcdf ghkl mop 13

g here only †. (εὔθετος, Luke ix. 62.) h here bis. ver. 8 only. Ps. cvi. 30. i ch. ii. 30 reff. k here only †. Diod. Sic. xix. 68 (see below [r]). l 1 Cor. ix. 19 reff. m here only. Judg. xix. 30. n = ch. v. 38 reff. o ch. xiii. 13 reff. p Rom. i. 10. xi. 14. Phil. iii. 11 only. w. opt., here only. q ch. xvi. 1 reff. r ch. xxviii. 11. 1 Cor. xvi. 6. Tit. iii. 12 only †. (see above [k].) s = here only. Ezek. xi. 1 al. t see note. (ch. viii. 26, 36. Phil. iii. 14.) u here only. Gen. xiii. 14 al. v here only †.

p 13. 40 vulg arm Chr-comm$_1$ Thl-fin. rec ins του, with H^{r}LP 13. 36 rel Chr$_2$: om ABℵ p.

12. rec πλειους, with H^{r}LP 13. 36 rel Chr$_1$: txt ABℵ p 40. rec κακειθεν, with H^{r}P rel syr Thl: txt ABLℵ b c h k o p 13. 36. 40 vulg Syr [copt] arm Chr. δυνανται A.

the owner of the ship. Wetst. cites from Plutarch, *ναύτας μὲν ἐκλέγεται κυβερνήτης, καὶ κυβερνήτην ναύκληρος.* So Hesych.: *ναύκληρος, ὁ δεσπότης τ. πλοίου,*—and Xen. Œcon. viii. 12: *φορτίων, ὅσα ναυκλήροις κέρδους ἕνεκα ἄγεται.* (Kuin.)

12.] See above on ver. 8. The anchorage was sheltered from the N.W., but not from *nearly half the compass.* Grotius and Heinsius's rendering of *πρὸς παραχειμ.*, 'ad vitandam tempestatem,' is contrary to usage, besides being singularly inconsistent with the fact in more ways than one. For *this purpose* the anchorage *was* **εὔθετος**, and in it they had (see next verse) actually *ridden out the storm,* before they left it. **ἐκεῖθεν**] The **κἀκεῖθεν** of the rec. would be **thence also**, as from their former stopping-places. **Φοίνικα**] Ptolemy (iii. 17) calls the haven **Φοινικοῦς**, and the city (lying some way inland) **Φοῖνιξ**. Strabo (x. 4) says, *τὸ δὲ ἔνθεν ἰσθμός ἐστιν ὡς ἑκατὸν σταδίων, ἔχων κατοικίαν πρὸς μὲν τῇ βορείῳ θαλάττῃ Ἀμφιμάλλαν, πρὸς δὲ τῇ νοτίῳ Φοινικὴ τῶν Λαμπέων.* This description, and the other data belonging to Phœnice, Smith (p. 48) has shewn to fit the modern *Lutro,* which, though not known now as an anchorage, probably from the silting up of the harbour, is so marked in the French admiralty chart of 1738, and "if then able to shelter the smallest craft, must have been capable of receiving the largest ships seventeen centuries before." See an inscription making it highly probable that Alexandrian ships did winter at Lutro, in the excursus at the end of Prolegg. to Acts. **βλέποντα κατὰ λίβα κ. κατὰ χῶρον**] **looking** (literally) **down the S.W. and N.W. winds**; i. e. *in the direction* of these winds, viz. N.E. and S.E. For *λίψ* and *χῶρος* are *not quarters of the compass,* but *winds;* and *κατά*, used with a wind, denotes the direction of its blowing,—**down the wind.** This interpretation, which I was long ago persuaded was the right one, I find now confirmed by the opinion of Mr. Smith, who cites Herod. iv. 110, *ἐφέροντο κατὰ κῦμα καὶ ἄνεμον,* and Arrian, Periplus Euxini, p. 3, *ἄφνω νεφελὴ ἐπαναστᾶσα ἐξεῤῥάγη κατ' εὖρον.* So also *κατὰ ῥόον*, Herod. ii. 96. And in Jos. Antt. xv. 9. 6, the coasts near Cæsarea are said to be *δύσορμα διὰ τὰς κατὰ λίβα προσβολάς.* See also Thucyd. vi. 104. In the reff., the substantive is not one of motion like *λίψ, χῶρος,* or *ῥόος*, but of fixed location, as *μεσημβρία, σκόπος.* The *direction* then is towards the *spot* indicated, just as in the present case it is in that of the *motion* indicated. The harbour of Lutro satisfies these conditions; and is even more decisively pointed out as being the spot by a notice in the Synecdemus of Hierocles, **Φοινίκη ἤτοι Ἀράδενα· νῆσος Κλαῦδος.** Now Mr. Pashley found a village called Aradhena a short distance above Lutro, and another close by called Anopolis, of which Steph. Byz. says, *Ἀράδην πόλις Κρήτης· ἡ δὲ Ἀνωπόλις λέγεται, διὰ τὸ εἶναι ἄνω.* From these data it is almost demonstrated that the port of Phœnice is the present port of Lutro. Ptolemy's longitude for port Phœnice also agrees. See Smith, pp. 51 ff. Mr. Smith has kindly sent me the following extract from a letter containing additional confirmation of the view: 'Loutro is an excellent harbour; you open it unexpectedly, the rocks stand apart and the town appears within. During the Greek war, when cruising with Lord Cochrane, ... chased a pirate schooner, as they thought, right upon the rocks; suddenly he disappeared, and when rounding in after him,—like a change of scenery, the little basin, its shipping, and the town of Loutro, revealed themselves.' See Prof. Hackett's note, impugning the above view and interpreta-

13 [w] ὑποπνεύσαντος δὲ [x] νότου δόξαντες τῆς [y] προθέσεως [z] κεκρατηκέναι, [a] ἄραντες [b] ἆσσον [c] παρελέγοντο
τὴν Κρήτην. 14 μετ' οὐ πολὺ δὲ [d] ἔβαλεν κατ'

w here only †. x = ch. xxviii. 13. Luke xii. 55 (xi. 31 ‖ Mt. xiii. 29. Rev. xxi. 13) only. Exod. x. 13. Sir. xliii. 16 al. y = Rom. viii. 28. ix. 11. Eph. i. 11. iii. 11. 2 Tim. i. 9 ‡. 2 Macc. iii. 8. z = here only. (Heb. vi. 18.) κρ. τῆς προθ., Diod. Sic. xvi. 20. a = here only. So Thucyd. ii. 23 al. b here only. comparat., = ch. xxv. 10 reff. c ver. 8. d = here only. see note.

13. υποπνευσαντες(sic) ℵ.

tion; which however does not alter my opinion. Dean Howson gives his solution thus: "The difficulty is to be explained simply by remembering that sailors speak of every thing from their own point of view, and that the harbour (see chart in C. and H. ii. 397) does look—*from the water towards the land which encloses it*—in the direction of S.W. and N.W." But I cannot believe, till experience can be shewn to confirm the idea, that even sailors could speak of a harbour as '*looking*' in the direction in which *they* would look when entering it. **13. ὑποπνεύσαντος**] as E. V., **softly blowing**, compare ὑπομειδιάω. The S. wind was favourable for them in sailing from Fair Havens to Phœnice. **δόξ. τ. προθ. κεκρατ.**] **imagining that they had** (as good as) **accomplished their purpose**; i. e. that it would now be a very easy matter to reach Phœnice. **ἄραντες** "may be translated either '*weighed*,' or '*set sail*;' for ancient authors supply sometimes τὰς ἀγκύρας, and sometimes τὰ ἱστία . . . . . Julius Pollux, however, like St. Luke, supplies neither, which is certainly the most nautical way of expressing it: he says, αἴροντες ἀπὸ τῆς γῆς, lib. i. 103." Smith, p. 55. **ἆσσον παρ.**] They crept close along the land till they passed Cape Matala. "A ship which could not lie nearer to the wind than seven points, would just weather that point which bears W. by S. from the entrance of Fair Havens. We see therefore the propriety of the expression **ἆσσον** παρ., 'they sailed *close* by Crete,' which the author uses to describe the first part of their passage." Smith, p. 56. The Vulg. has: 'quum sustulissent de Asson,' connecting ἄραντες with Ἄσσον, and understanding the latter as the name of a Cretan town. There is an Asus mentioned by Pliny (iv. 12), but it is 'in Mediterraneo,' not on the coast,—and the construction would be inadmissible. Erasmus, Luther, &c., have taken Ἄσσον as the accusative of direction, 'when they had weighed for Assus.' But besides the *local* objection, this construction also would be most harsh, as ἄραντες does not indicate the progress of their voyage, but only the setting out. Heinsius took ἄραντες = ἀναφανέντες, ch. xxi. 3,—'postquam Asos attollere se visa est' (Meyer). But there can be little doubt that all of these are mistakes, and that ἆσσον is the adverb.

14. ἔβαλεν κατ' αὐτῆς] These difficult words have been taken in three ways: (1) (The common interpretation) referring αὐτῆς to τὴν Κρήτην just mentioned. Thus they might mean, (α) '*drove* (*us*) *against Crete*,' or (β) '*struck* (*blew*) *against Crete*,' i. e. in the direction of Crete. Now of these, (α) is contrary to the *expressed* fact:—they were *not driven against Crete*. And (β) is as inconsistent with the *implied* fact. Had the wind blown in the direction of Crete at all, they, who gave themselves up to it, and were driven before it (ἐπιδόντες ἐφερόμεθα, ver. 15), must have been *stranded on the Cretan coast, which they were not*. (2) referring αὐτῆς to *the ship*, understood. This is adopted by Dr. Bloomfield and Mr. Smith. (The latter, I find by a letter received since this note was written, now understands it as I have explained it below.) But not to mention the harshness occasioned by having to supply a subject for αὐτῆς which has never yet been mentioned,—a decisive objection against this rendering is, that the ship throughout the narrative is τὸ πλοῖον, not ἡ ναῦς, in every place except ver. 41,—and τὸ πλ. occurs in the very next clause, which, had *this* been meant of the ship, would certainly have been expressed συναρπασθείσης δέ, or συναρπασθείσης δὲ αὐτῆς. (3) referring αὐτῆς to προθέσεως. In that case ἔβαλεν κατ' αὐτῆς must either (α) = κατέβαλεν ἡμᾶς ἀπ' αὐτῆς, as Plato, Euthyph. 15 E, ἀπ' ἐλπίδος με καταβαλὼν μεγάλης ἀπέρχει, which is harsh, and hardly allowable; or (β) be understood, taking the neuter sense of βάλλω (ποταμὸς εἰς ἅλα βάλλων, Il. λ. 722), as meaning '*blew against it*,' so as to thwart their design. And so Luther: 'erhob sich wider ihr Vornehmen.' But this mixture of literal and figurative is also harsh, and hardly allowable. (4) A method has occurred to me of rendering the words, which seems to remove all harshness, whether of reference in αὐτῆς, or of construction. There can be no question that the *obvious* reference of αὐτῆς is to *Crete*. What

αὐτῆς ἄνεμος [e] *τυφωνικὸς ὁ καλούμενος* [f] *εὐρακύλων.* ABLPℵ abcdf ghkl mop13
15 [g] *συναρπασθέντος δὲ τοῦ πλοίου καὶ μὴ δυναμένου* [h] *ἀντ-*
οφθαλμεῖν τῷ ἀνέμῳ [i] *ἐπιδόντες* [k] *ἐφερόμεθα.*
16 [l] *νησίον*

e here only +. (-ών, Isa. xiii. 21 Aq. [so Montf. from Jer. but?]) f here only +. g ch. vi. 12 reff. h here only +. Wisd. xii. 14 only. i = here only ‡. (ch. xv. 30 reff.) k = (nautical) here bis only. Diod. Sic. xx. 16. (Lev. xxvi. 36. see ch. ii. 2.) l here only.

14. for *κατ' αυτης*, *κατα ταυτης* ℵ. om *ο καλ. ευρ.* and *συν* of *συναρπ.* P^1(ins P-corr). rec *ευροκλυδων*, with H^rL P-corr p(*ευρο κλυδω*) rel Syr Chr_1 : *ευρυκλυδων* B^2 40. 133 : *ευρακλυδων* syr-mg-gr : *ευρακυκλων* arm : *aquilo maris* (omg *τυφ. ο καλ.*) æth : *ευτρακηλων* copt[-wilk] : *ευρακηλων* sah : *ευρακοιδων* (*itacism*) 13 : txt (*see note*) A B^1(see table) ℵ [copt-boet], confirmed by *Euroaquilo* vulg $Cassiod_1$, by 13 sah and in some measure (*ευρακ.*) by syr arm copt[-wilk].

15. *δυνομενου* B^1. aft *επιδοντες* ins *τω πλεοντι κ. συστειλαντες τα ιστια* c 137 : *τη πνεουση κ. συναγοντες τα ιστια* syr-w-ast.

then is **ἔβαλεν κατ' αὐτῆς**? *ἔβαλεν* applied to wind may be understood as above, neuter, or reflective, '*blew*,' '*rushed*.' Assuming this, and that there is no object to be supplied between *ἔβαλεν* and the preposition, *κατ' αὐτῆς* may surely be rendered, as in *βῆ δὲ κατ' Οὐλύμποιο καρήνων*,—*κατ' Ἰδαίων ὀρέων*,—*κατὰ πέτρης*, &c., viz. **down** (from) **Crete**, '*down the high lands forming the coast*.' It is a common expression in lake and coasting navigation, that 'a gust came down the valleys.' And this would be exactly the direction of the wind in question. When they had doubled, or perhaps were now doubling, Cape Matala, the wind suddenly changed, and the typhoon *came down upon them from the high lands*;—at first, as long as they were sheltered, only by fits down the gullies, but as soon as they were in the open bay past the cape, with its full violence. This, the hurricane rushing down the high lands when first observed, and afterwards *συναρπάζων τὸ πλοῖον*, seems to me exactly to describe their changed circumstances in passing the cape. A confirmation of this interpretation may be found by Luke himself using *κατέβη* to express the descending of a squall from the hills on the lake of Gennesareth, Luke viii. 23, where Matt. and Mark have only *ἐγένετο* and *γίνεται*. Mr. Smith also suggests *κατὰ τοῦ κρημνοῦ*, Luke viii. 33, as confirmatory. The above is also Dean Howson's view. See, in the excursus appended to the Prolegg. to Acts, the confirmation of this view in what actually happened to the Rev. G. Brown's party. **τυφωνικός**] "The sudden change from a south wind to a violent northerly wind, is a common occurrence in these seas. (Captain J. Stewart, R.N., in his remarks on the Archipelago, observes, "It is always safe to anchor under the lee of an island with a northerly wind, as it dies gradually away; but it would be extremely dangerous *with southerly winds, as they almost invariably shift to a violent northerly wind*.") The term '*typhonic*' indicates that it was accompanied by some of the phænomena which might be expected in such a case, viz. the agitation and whirling motion of the clouds caused by the meeting of the opposite currents of air when the change took place, and probably also of the sea, raising it in columns of spray. Pliny (ii. 48), speaking of 'repentini flatus,' says, 'verticem faciunt qui Typhon vocatur:' Aul. Gell. xix. 1, 'Turbines etiam crebriores . . . et figuræ quædam nubium tremendæ quas *τυφῶνας* vocabant.'" Smith, p. 60. **εὐρακύλων**] I have adopted the reading of ABℵ, according to my principle of going, in all cases where there is no overpowering objection, by our most ancient MSS. It may be that *εὐρακύλων* had become in common parlance corrupted into *εὐροκλύδων*, an anomalous word, having no assignable derivation, but perhaps arising from the Greek sailors having changed the Latin termination into one having significance for themselves. Mr. Smith, in his appendix, 'On the Wind Euroclydon,' has satisfactorily answered the objections of Bryant to the compound *εὐρακύλων*,—by shewing that *εὖρος* properly, was not the S.E., but the E. wind; and that compounds of Greek and Latin in the names of winds are not unknown, e. g. Euro-Auster.

The direction of the wind is established by Mr. S., from what follows, to have been about *half a point N. of E.N.E.*; and the subsequent narrative shews that the wind *continued to blow from this point till they reached Malta*. **15. συναρπ.**] **being hurried away**, '*borne along*,' by it: see reff. **ἀντοφθαλμεῖν**] It is hardly likely that this term, which is used so naturally and constantly of men *facing an enemy* (Polyb. i. 17. 3, and eight times more), and also metaphorically of *resisting temptation* (*μὴ δύνασθαι τοῖς χρήμασιν ἀντοφθαλμεῖν*, Polyb. xxviii. 17. 18), should have been originally a naval term,

δέ τι [m] ὑποδραμόντες καλούμενον Κ[λ]αῦδα, [n] ἰσχύσαμεν
[o] μόλις [p] περικρατεῖς γενέσθαι τῆς [q] σκάφης, 17 ἣν ἄραντες
[r] βοηθείαις [s] ἐχρῶντο, [t] ὑποζωννύντες τὸ πλοῖον, φοβού-

C -φης ην αραντες... ABCLP ℵ a b c d f g h k l m o p 13

m here only †. n = ch. vi. 10 reff. o ch. xiv. 18 reff. p here only †. q vv. 30, 32 only †. Bel & Dr. 33 (32) only, but not =. (-ος, 2 Macc. xii. 3, 6.) r Heb. iv. 16 only. Ps. vii. 10. Sir. xl. 24 al. (-θεῖν, ch. xxi. 28. -θός, Heb. xiii. 6.) s ver. 3. 1 Cor. vii. 21 al. L.P. Wisd. ii. 6. t here only †. 2 Macc. iii. 19 only. Polyb. xxvii. 3. 3. Plato, Rep. x. 616. 3, εἶναι γὰρ τοῦτο τὸ φῶς σύνδεσμον τοῦ οὐρανοῦ, οἷον τὰ ὑποζώματα τ. τριηρῶν, οὕτω πᾶσαν ξυνέχον τὴν περιφοράν. see Thucyd. i. 29.

16. [υπεκδρ. a:] υποδραμουντες B[1] 93-5. rec κλαυ-, with AH[r]LP ℵ(but λ erased) p rel 13. 36. 40. 137 syr syr-mg-gr [copt arm] Chr Thl Œc: καυ- B vulg æth Jer$_1$, *Kyra* or *Keuda* Syr, *Gaudem* Cassiod$_1$.—rec -δην, with H[r]LP rel: -δαν c 25 lect-12, -*dam* fuld: -δα Bℵ p 13. 40. 137 vulg syr syr-mg-gr copt æth [arm]. (A has only ΚΛΑ, the remaining letters are gone at the end of a line.) rec μολις bef ισχυσαμεν (*corrn of order?*), with H[r]LP rel 36 syrr copt æth-pl Chr$_1$: txt ABℵ m p 13 (40) vulg.

17. βοηθειας H[r] c p 36. 96 lect-12: -θιαν ℵ[1].

derived from the practice of painting *eyes* on either side of the beaks of ships. More probably the expression was transferred to a ship from its usage in common life. **ἐπιδόντες**] So Plutarch de Fortun. Rom. cited in note on ver. 26. Either '*the ship*,' or '*ourselves*,' may be supplied: or better perhaps, *neither*, but the word taken generally—**giving up**. **ἐφερόμεθα**] passive: **we were driven along.**

16. ὑποδραμόντες] **running under the lee of.** "St. Luke exhibits here as on every other occasion, the most perfect command of nautical terms, and gives the utmost precision to his language by selecting the most appropriate: they ran before the wind *to leeward of Clauda*, hence it is ὑποδραμόντες: they sailed with a side wind *to leeward of Cyprus and Crete*: hence it is ὑπεπλεύσαμεν" (Smith, p. 61, note). **Κλαῦδα**] Here again, there can be little doubt that the name of the island was Καῦδα, or Γαῦδα, as we have in some MSS., or, as in Pliny and Mela, Gaudos: but Ptol. (iii. 7) has Κλαῦδος, and the corruption was very obvious. The island is the modern Gozzo. **ἰσχύσαμ. μόλ.** κ.τ.λ.] "Upon reaching Clauda, they availed themselves of the smooth water under its lee, to prepare the ship to resist the fury of the storm. Their first care was to secure the boat by hoisting it on board. This had not been done at first, because the weather was moderate, and the distance they had to go, short. Under such circumstances, it is not usual to hoist boats on board, but it had now become necessary. In running down upon Clauda, it could not be done, on account of the ship's way through the water. To enable them to do it, the ship must have been rounded to, with her head to the wind, and her sails, if she had any set at the time, trimmed, so that she had no head-way, or progressive movement. In this position she would drift, broadside to leeward. I conclude they passed round the *east* end of the island: not only because it was nearest, but because 'an extensive reef with numerous rocks extends from Gozzo to the N.W., which renders the passage between the two isles very dangerous' (Sailing Directions, p. 207). In this case the ship would be brought to on the starboard tack, i. e. with the right side to windward." . . . . "St. Luke tells us they had much difficulty in securing the boat. He does not say *why*: but independently of the gale which was raging at the time, the boat had been towed between twenty and thirty miles after the gale had sprung up, and could scarcely fail to be filled with water." Smith, pp. 64, 65.

17.] **ἄραντες, having taken on board.** **βοηθείαις**] **measures to strengthen the ship**, strained and weakened by labouring in the gale. Pliny (ii. 48) calls the typhoon 'præcipua navigantium pestis, non antennas modo, verum ipsa navigia contorta frangens.' Grot., Heinsius, &c., are clearly wrong in interpreting βοηθεί., '*the help of the passengers*.'

ὑποζωννύντες τ. πλ.] **undergirding**, or *frapping* the ship. "To frap a ship (*ceintrer un vaisseau*) is to pass four or five turns of a large cable-laid rope round the hull or frame of a ship, to support her in a great storm, or otherwise, when it is apprehended that she is not strong enough to resist the violent efforts of the sea: this expedient, however, is rarely put in practice." Falconer's Marine Dict.:—Smith, p. 60, who brings several instances of the practice, in our own times. See additional ones in C. and H. ii. 404, f. Horace seems to allude to it, Od. i. 14. 3, 'ac sine funibus Vix durare carinæ Possint imperiosius Æquor.' See reff. **τὴν σύρτιν**] **The Syrtis**, on the African coast; there were two, the greater and the lesser (αἱ φοβεραὶ καὶ τοῖς ἀκούουσι Σύρτεις, Jos.

μενοί τε μὴ εἰς τὴν [u] σύρτιν [v] ἐκπέσωσιν [w] χαλάσαντες τὸ ABCLP
[x] σκεῦος οὕτως [k] ἐφέροντο. 18 [y] σφοδρῶς δὲ [z] χειμαζομένων ℵabcd
ἡμῶν [a] τῇ [a] ἑξῆς [b] ἐκβολὴν ἐποιοῦντο, 19 καὶ τῇ [c] τρίτῃ fghkl
[d] αὐτόχειρες τὴν [e] σκευὴν τοῦ πλοίου [f] ἔῤῥιψαν· 20 μήτε mop13
δὲ ἡλίου μήτε [g] ἄστρων [h] ἐπιφαινόντων [i] ἐπὶ [k] πλείονας ἡμέρας, [l] χειμῶνός τε [m] οὐκ [m] ὀλίγου [n] ἐπικειμένου, [o] λοιπὸν

u here only +. v = vv. 26, 29 only. Diod. Sic. ii. 60, ἐκπεσεῖν εἰς ἄμμους, and al. w ch. ix. 25 reff. x here only. Jonah i. 5. Xen. Œc. viii. 12. y here only. Gen. vii. 19 A compl. Sir. xiii. 13 (only ?). (-ρός, Exod. x. 19.) z here only. Prov. xxvi. 10 only. a ch. xxi. 1 reff. b here only. Jonah i. 5. c alone, Luke xiii. 32 only. Exod. xxi. 29. w. ἡμέρα, Matt. xvi. 21 al. fr. d here only +. e here only. Gen. xxxi. 25 Ald. (Jonah i. 5 ?) only. σκευὴν ἑκατὸν τριήρεσι, Diod. Sic. xiv. 79. f ver. 29. Matt. ix. 36. xv. 30. xxvii. 5. Luke iv. 35. xvii. 2 only. Gen. xxi. 15. (-πτεῖν, ch. xxii. 23.) g ch. vii. 43 reff. h Luke i. 79. Tit. ii. 11. iii. 4 only. Deut. xxxiii. 2. (-νεια, 2 Thess. ii. 8. -νής, ch. ii. 20.) i ch. xiii. 31 reff. k = ch. ii. 40 reff. l = Matt. xvi. 3 (xxiv. 20 ‖ Mk. John x. 22. 2 Tim. iv. 21) only. Job xxxvii. 6. m ch. xii. 18 reff. n = here (Luke v. 1. xxiii. 23. John xi. 38. xxi. 9. 1 Cor. ix. 16. Heb. ix. 10) only. Job xix. 3. o = 2 Tim. iv. 8.

εκπλεσωσιν ℵ[1]. ins και bef χαλ. P [arm]. om το ℵ[1].

18. for δε, τε A 25 spec Syr æth-pl.

19. rec εῤῥιψαμεν (*corrn to first person to suit* αυτοχειρες : *so Meyer, which is much more probable than that, as De W.*, -αμεν *should have been altered to* -αν, *to suit* ·ποιουντο : *see note*), with HLP rel syrr copt æth-pl Chr_1: txt AB^2C a b o p 13. 36 40 vulg spec [arm], ερειψαν B[1], εριψαν ℵ.

20. πλειους ℵ[1] c[appy] g 101. om λοιπον B.

B. J. ii. 16. 4), of which the former was the nearer to them. **ἐκπέσωσιν**] See reff. and add φερόμενοι τῷ πνεύματι . . . . ἐξέπιπτον πρὸς τὰς πέτρας, Herodot. viii. 13. **χαλ. τ. σκεῦος**] "It is not easy to imagine a more erroneous translation than that of our authorized version: 'Fearing lest they should fall into the quicksands, they strake sail, and so were driven.' It is in fact equivalent to saying that, fearing a certain danger, they deprived themselves of the only possible means of avoiding it." Smith, p. 67. He goes on to explain, that *if they had struck sail*, they must have been driven *directly towards the Syrtis*. They therefore set what sail the violence of the gale would permit them to carry, turning the ship's head off shore, she having already been brought to on the starboard tack (right side to the wind). The adoption of this course would enable them to run before the gale, and yet keep wide of the African coast, which we know they did. But what is **χαλ. τὸ σκεῦος**? It is interpreted by Meyer, De W., and most Commentators, of *striking sail* (as E.V.): but this (see above) could not be: "In a storm with a contrary wind or on a lee-shore, a ship is obliged to lie-to under a very low sail: *some sail* is absolutely necessary to keep the ship steady, otherwise she would pitch about like a cork, and roll so deep as to strain and work herself to pieces." Encycl. Brit. art. 'Seamanship:' Smith, p. 72, who interprets the words, **lowering the gear**, i. e. sending down upon deck the gear connected with the fair-weather sails, such as the *suppara*, or top-sails. A modern ship sends down top-gallant masts and yards, a cutter strikes her topmast, when preparing for a gale. In this case it was perhaps the heavy yard which the ancient ships carried, with the sail attached to it, and the heavy ropes, which would by their top-weight produce uneasiness of motion as well as resistance to the wind. See a letter addressed to Mr. Smith by Capt. Spratt, R.N., quoted in C. and H. ii. p. 405, note 5. **οὕτως**] i. e. "not only with the ship undergirded, and made snug, but with storm-sails set, and on the starboard tack, which was the only course by which she could avoid falling into the Syrtis." Smith, ib. **18. ἐκβολ. ἐποι.**] "The technical terms for taking cargo out of a ship, given by Julius Pollux, are ἐκθέσθαι, ἀποφορτίσασθαι, κουφίσαι τὴν ναῦν, ἐπελάφρυναι, ἐκβολὴν ποιήσασθαι τῶν φορτίων. So that both here, and afterwards in ver. 38 (ἐκούφιζον τ. πλοῖον), St. Luke uses appropriate technical phrases." Smith, ib. *Of what the freight consisted*, we have no intimation. Perhaps *not of wheat*, on account of the separate statement of ver. 38. See ref. **19. τ. σκευὴν τ. πλ. ἐῤῥ.**] ἡ σκευή is the *furniture* of the ship—beds, moveables of all kinds, cooking utensils, and the spare rigging. **αὐτόχειρες** is used with ἔῤῥιψαν as shewing the urgency of the danger—when the seamen would with their own hands, cast away what otherwise was needful to the ship and themselves. This not being seen, αὐτόχ. has been supposed to imply the *first person*, and ἐῤῥίψαμεν has crept in: see var. readd. **20.**] The sun and stars were the only guides of

[p] περιῃρεῖτο ἐλπὶς πᾶσα [q] τοῦ σώζεσθαι ἡμᾶς. 21 πολλῆς
τε [r] ἀσιτίας [s] ὑπαρχούσης, τότε [t] σταθεὶς ὁ Παῦλος ἐν
μέσῳ αὐτῶν εἶπεν Ἔδει μέν, ὦ ἄνδρες, [u] πειθαρχήσαντάς
μοι μὴ [v] ἀνάγεσθαι ἀπὸ τῆς Κρήτης, [w] κερδῆσαί τε τὴν
[x] ὕβριν ταύτην καὶ τὴν [x] ζημίαν. 22 καὶ [y] τὰ [y] νῦν [z] παραινῶ
ὑμᾶς [a] εὐθυμεῖν· [b] ἀποβολὴ γὰρ [c] ψυχῆς οὐδεμία ἔσται ἐξ
ὑμῶν [d] πλὴν τοῦ πλοίου. 23 παρέστη γάρ μοι ταύτῃ τῇ
νυκτὶ τοῦ θεοῦ οὗ εἰμὶ [ἐγὼ] ᾧ καὶ [e] λατρεύω ἄγγελος,
24 λέγων Μὴ φοβοῦ, Παῦλε· Καίσαρί σε δεῖ [f] παραστῆναι καὶ ἰδοὺ [g] κεχάρισταί σοι ὁ θεὸς πάντας τοὺς
[h] πλέοντας μετὰ σοῦ. 25 διὸ [a] εὐθυμεῖτε, ἄνδρες· πιστεύω

p = 2 Cor. iii. 16. Heb. x. 11 (ver. 40) only. Zech. x. 11.
q constr., ch. xiv. 9 reff.
r here only +. (-τος, ver. 33. -τεῖν, 1 Macc. iii. 17 -τί, Job xxiv. 6.)
s ch. ii. 30 reff.
t ch. xi. 13 reff.
u ch. v. 29 reff.
v ch. xiii. 13 reff.
w = here only. (1 Cor. ix. 19 &c. reff.) τὸ μιανθῆναι τὰς χεῖρας κερδαίνειν, Jos. Antt. ii. 3. 2.
x ver. 10.
y ch. iv. 29 reff.
z ver. 9 only (reff.).
a here bis. James v. 13 only. Ps. lxvii. 18 (17) Ald. [Trom.] only. (see ver. 36 al.)
b Rom. xi. 15 only +. (-βάλλειν, Mark x. 50. Heb. x. 35.)
c = ch. xv. 26 reff.
d [John viii. 10.] ch. xv. 28. xx. 23. Deut. i. 36.
e ch. vii. 7 reff.
f = Rom. xiv. 10. Dan. vii. 10.
g 2 Cor. ii. 10 reff.
h ver. 2 reff.

rec πασα bef ελπις, with CH[r]Pℵ rel 36 Chr_1 : π. η ελ. L [a] : txt AB k m p 13 vulg spec.

21. rec δε, with H[r]LP rel syr copt Chr_1 : txt ABCℵ c p 13. 40. 137 vulg spec Syr æth-pl [arm] Thl-fin. om τοτε A 21. εμμεσω A. for αυτων, ημων c 137. om της H[r] [d]. ζημημιαν(sic) P.

22. αποβλη(sic) P. ουδεμια bef ψυχης ℵ[1] 80.

23. for ταυτη, τηδε ℵ[1]. rec τη νυκτι bef ταυτη : txt ABCH[r]LP(ℵ) rel 40. 137 vulg [spec] arm Chr_1 Thl-sif (Thl-fin om ταυτ.). rec αγγελος bef του θεου (*corrn of order*), with H[r]LP rel vulg spec; bef ω κ. λατρευω 13: txt ABCℵ m 40. 137. rec om εγω, with BC[1]H[r]LP p 13 rel spec Chr_1 : ins AC[2]ℵ 40 vulg copt æth[?] arm.

the ancients when out of sight of land. The expression, **all hope was taken away,** seems, as Mr. Smith has noticed, to betoken that a greater evil than the mere force of the storm (which perhaps had some little abated:—χ. οὐκ ὀλίγου seems to imply that it still indeed raged, but not as before) was afflicting them, viz., *the leaky state of the ship,* which increased upon them, as is shewn by their successive lightenings of her. **21. ἀσιτίας**] "What caused the abstinence? A ship with nearly 300 people on board, on a voyage of some length, must have had more than a fortnight's provisions (and see ver. 38): and it is not enough to say with Kuinoel, 'Continui labores et metus a periculis effecerant ut de cibo capiendo non cogitarent.' 'Much abstinence' is one of the most frequent concomitants of heavy gales. The impossibility of cooking, or the destruction of provisions from leakage, are the principal causes which produce it." Smith, p. 75: who quotes instances. But doubtless anxiety and mental distress had a considerable share in it. **τότε** brings vividly before us the consequence of the ἀσιτία when they were in that condition, languid and exhausted with fasting and fears. **κερδῆσαι**] '*lucrifecisse,*' **to have gained,** not = *to have incurred,*—but **to have turned to your own account,** i. e. 'to have spared or avoided.' So Jos. in ref. Aristotle, Magn. Mor. ii. 8, ᾧ κατὰ λόγον ζημίαν ἣν λαβεῖν, τὸν τοιοῦτον κερδάναντα εὐτυχῆ φάμεν ('if he escape it'). Plin. vii. 40, 'quam quidem injuriam lucrifecit ille.' Cicero, Verr. i. 12, 'lucretur indicia veteris infamiæ' ('may have them wiped out,' and so make gain of them by getting rid of them). **ὕβριν**] See on ver. 10. "The ὕβριν was to their persons, the ζημίαν to their property." C. and H. ii. 410, note 4. **22.**] The neglect of precision in ἀποβολὴ ψυχῆς οὐδεμία . . . . πλὴν τοῦ πλοίου is common enough. So Rev. xxi. 27, οὐ μὴ εἰσέλθῃ . . . πᾶν κοινὸν κ. ποιῶν βδέλυγμα . . . εἰ μὴ οἱ γεγραμμένοι ἐν τῷ β. τ. ζωῆς. See Winer, edn. 6, § 67. 1. e. **23.**] Paul characterizes himself as dedicated to and the servant of God, to give solemnity to and bespeak credit for his announcement. At such a time, the servants of God are highly esteemed. **24. κεχάρισται**] "Etiam centurio, subserviens providentiæ divinæ, Paulo condonavit captivos, ver. 43. . . . . Non erat tam periculoso alioqui tempore periculum, ne videretur Paulus, quæ necessario dicebat, gloriose dicere." Bengel. **μετὰ σοῦ**] "Paulus,

γὰρ τῷ θεῷ ὅτι οὕτως ἔσται [i] καθ' [i] ὃν [i] τρόπον λελάληταί ABCLP
μοι. 26 εἰς νῆσον δέ τινα δεῖ ἡμᾶς [k] ἐκπεσεῖν. 27 Ὡς δὲ ℵabcd fghkl
[l] τεσσαρεςκαιδεκάτη νὺξ ἐγένετο [m] διαφερομένων ἡμῶν ἐν mop13
τῷ Ἀδρίᾳ, [n] κατὰ [o] μέσον τῆς [o] νυκτὸς [p] ὑπενόουν οἱ [q] ναῦται
[r] προςάγειν τινὰ αὐτοῖς χώραν, 28 καὶ [s] βολίσαντες [t] εὗρον
[u] ὀργυιὰς εἴκοσι, [v] βραχὺ δὲ [w] διαστήσαντες καὶ πάλιν
[s] βολίσαντες [t] εὗρον [u] ὀργυιὰς δεκαπέντε, 29 φοβούμενοί

i ch. xv. 11 only. see ch. i. 11 reff. Rom. iii. 2. k = ver. 17. l ver. 33. Gen. xiv. 5. m ch. xiii. 49. n = ch. xvi. 25. Heb. iii. 8, from Ps. xciv. 8. o here only. see ch. xvi. 25. Matt. xxv. 6. p ch. xiii. 25 reff. q here bis. Rev. xviii. 17 only +. (-τικός, 3 Kings ix. 27. Jonah i. 5.) r = here only. (ch. xvi. 20 reff.) Josh. iii. 9. 1 Kings vii. 10 al. fr. s here bis only +. (-λή, Luke xxii. 41.) t - - ch. xix. 19. 1 Chron. xx. 2. u here bis only +. v = Luke xxii. 58. ch. v. 34 (John vi. 7. Heb. ii. 7 [from Ps. viii. 5], 9. xiii. 22) only. Isa. lvii. 17. w Luke xxii. 59. xxiv. 51 only. trans., Isa. lix. 2.

26. ημας bef δει B.

27. επεγενετο A p vulg: txt BCH[r]LPℵ rel 36 Chr$_1$. for προςαγειν, προςανεχειν B[2]: προςαχειν B[1]: προςεγγιζειν c 137: προςαγαγειν 40: προαγαγειν ℵ[1].

28. for 1st και, οιτινες ℵ[1]. οργυας (twice) b[1] p 13, so (once) H[r] o. for 2nd ευρον, ευρομεν C[1].

in conspectu Dei, princeps navis, et consiliis gubernator." Ib. **26. δεῖ**] Spoken prophetically, as also ver. 31: not perhaps from actual revelation imparted in the vision, but by a power imparted to Paul himself of penetrating the future at this crisis, and announcing the Divine counsel.

Mr. Humphry compares and contrasts the speech of Cæsar to the pilot under similar circumstances: τόλμα κ. δέδιθι μηθέν, ἀλλὰ ἐπιδίδου τῇ τύχῃ τὰ ἱστία καὶ δέχου τὸ πνεῦμα, τῷ πνέοντι πιστεύων, ὅτι Καίσαρα φέρεις καὶ τὴν Καίσαρος τύχην, Plut. de Fortun. Rom. p. 518. **27. διαφερ.**] **driven about,** or **up and down,** as E. V., not '*drifting through,*' as Dr. Bloomf., though this may have been the *fact;* see examples below. Plutarch speaking of the tumult during which Galba was murdered, τοῦ φορείου καθάπερ ἐν κλύδωνι δεῦρο κἀκεῖ διαφερομένου (probably from Tacitus, 'Agebatur huc illuc Galba, *vario turbæ fluctuantis impulsu,*' Hist. i. 40); Philo, de Migr. Abr. p. 454, ἐπαμφοτερισταὶ πρὸς ἑκάτερον τοῖχον, ὥσπερ σκάφος ὑπ' ἐναντίων πνευμάτων διαφερόμενον, ἀποκλίνοντες. The reckoning of days counts from their leaving Fair Havens: see vv. 18, 19. **ἐν τῷ Ἀδρίᾳ**] Adria, in the wider sense, embraces not only the Venetian Gulf, but the sea to the south of Greece:—so Ptolemy (iii. 16), ἡ δὲ Πελοπόννησος ὁρίζεται . . . ἀπὸ δυσμῶν καὶ μεσημβρίας τῷ Ἀδριατικῷ πελάγει. So also (iii. 4) ἡ δὲ Σικελία ὁρίζεται . . . . ἀπὸ δὲ ἀνατολῶν ὑπὸ τοῦ Ἀδρίου πελάγους. In fact, he bounds Italy on the S., Sicily on the E., Greece on the S. and W., and Crete on the W. by this sea, which notices sufficiently indicate its dimensions. So also Pausanias (v. 25), speaking of the straits of Messina, says that the sea there is θαλάσσης χειμεριωτάτη πάσης. οἵ τε γὰρ ἄνεμοι ταράσσουσιν αὐτὴν ἀμφοτέρωθεν τὸ κῦμα ἐπάγοντες, ἐκ τοῦ Ἀδρίου, καὶ ἐξ ἑτέρου πελάγους ὃ καλεῖται Τυρσηνόν. **ὑπενόουν**] What gave rise to this suspicion? Probably the sound (or even the apparent sight) of breakers. "If we assume that St. Paul's Bay, in Malta, is the actual scene of the shipwreck, we can have no difficulty in explaining what these indications must have been. No ship can enter it from the east without passing within a quarter of a mile of the point of Koura: but before reaching it, the land is too low and too far from the track of a ship driven from the eastward, to be seen in a dark night. When she does come within this distance, it is impossible to avoid observing the breakers: for with north-easterly gales, the sea breaks upon it with such violence, that Capt. Smyth, in his view of the headland, has made the breakers its distinctive character." Smith, p. 79.

I recommend the reader to study the reasonings and calculations by which Mr. Smith (pp. 79—86) has established, I think satisfactorily, that this χώραν could be no other than the point of Koura, east of St. Paul's Bay, in Malta. **προςάγειν**] **was approaching them.** The opposite is ἀναχωρεῖν, 'recedere.' 'Lucas optice loquitur, nautarum more.' Kuin. **28. βολίσαντες**] βολίζειν, ἤγουν βάθος θαλάσσης μετρεῖν μολυβδίνῃ καθέτῳ, ἢ τοιούτῳ τινί. Eustath. on Il. ε. p. 427 (Wetst.).

ὀργυιάς] ὀργυιὰ σημαίνει τὴν ἔκτασιν τῶν χειρῶν σὺν τῷ πλάτει τοῦ στήθους (Etymol. Magn.) = therefore very nearly one fathom. Every particular here corresponds with the actual state of things. At twenty-five fathoms depth (as given in evidence at the court-martial on the officers of the Lively, wrecked on this point in 1810), the curl of the sea was seen on the

τε μή που [x] κατὰ [y] τραχεῖς τόπους [k] ἐκπέσωμεν, ἐκ
[z] πρύμνης [a] ῥίψαντες [b] ἀγκύρας τέσσαρας [c] εὔχοντο
[d] ἡμέραν [d] γενέσθαι. 30 τῶν δὲ [q] ναυτῶν [e] ζητούντων
φυγεῖν ἐκ τοῦ πλοίου καὶ [f] χαλασάντων τὴν [g] σκάφην
εἰς τὴν θάλασσαν, [h] προφάσει [i] ὡς ἐκ [k] πρώρας
[b] ἀγκύρας μελλόντων [l] ἐκτείνειν, 31 εἶπεν ὁ Παῦλος
τῷ ἑκατοντάρχῃ καὶ τοῖς στρατιώταις Ἐὰν μὴ οὗτοι

x vv. 5, 7 reff.
y Luke iii. 5 (from Isa. xl. 4) only.
z ver. 41. Mark iv. 38 only †.
a ver. 19 reff.
b here bis. ver. 40. Heb. vi. 19 only †.
c ch. xxvi. 29. Rom. ix. 3. 2 Cor. xiii. 7, 9. James v. 16. 3 John 2 only. Num. xi. 2.
d ch. xii. 18 reff.
e = ch. xiii. 8 reff.
f ch. ix. 25 reff.
g ver. 16.
h Mark xii. 40 ‖ L. John xv. 22. Phil. i. 18. 1 Thess. ii. 5 only. Ps. cxl. 4.
i = ch. xxiii. 15 reff.
k ver. 41 only †. (-ρεύς, Ezek. xxvii. 29.)
l = here only. Ps. lix. 8 (10). elsw. w. χείρ, ch. xxvi. 1 al.

29. for τε, δε C‎א c p 13 vulg syr copt Thl-sif. rec μηπως (*corrn to simpler word*), with HʳLP rel 36 copt Chr: μηπω A: txt BC‎א c p 13. 40 Thl-sif. (που is written above the line by א[1] or corr[1].) rec (for κατα) εις, with HʳLP rel 36 Chr_1: txt ABC‎א c p 13. 40 Thl-sif. rec εκπεσωσιν, with c d f p sah [æth-pl arm Thl]: txt ABCHʳLP‎א 13 rel 137 vulg syrr copt Chr. (ευχοντο, so B[1]CHʳ.)

30. εκφυγειν A c 96. 137-42. πρωρης A[א[3]] d 13: πλωρης א[1]. rec μελλοντων bef αγκυρας (*corrn of order for euphony*), with HʳLP‎א rel am [demid tol] Chr: txt ABC m p 13. 40.

rocks in the night, but no land. The twenty fathoms would occur somewhat past this: the fifteen fathoms, in a direction W. by N. from the former, after a time sufficient to prepare for the unusual measure of anchoring by the stern. And just so are the soundings (see Capt. Smyth's chart, Smith, p. 88), and the shore is here full of τραχεῖς τόποι, mural precipices, upon which the sea must have been breaking with great violence. **29. ἐκ πρύμνης**] The usual way of anchoring in ancient, as well as in modern navigation, was *by the bow*: 'anchora de prora jacitur.' But under certain circumstances, they anchored *by the stern*; and Mr. Smith has shewn from the figure of a ship which he has copied from the "Antichità de Ercolano," that their ships had hawse-holes aft, to fit them for anchoring by the stern. "That a vessel *can* anchor by the stern is sufficiently proved (if proof were needed) by the history of some of our own naval engagements. So it was at the battle of the Nile. And when ships are about to attack batteries, it is customary for them to go into action prepared to anchor in this way. This was the case at Algiers. There is still greater interest in quoting the instance of the battle of Copenhagen, not only from the accounts we have of the precision with which each ship let go her anchors astern as she arrived nearly opposite her appointed station, but because it is said that Nelson stated after the battle that he had that morning been reading Acts xxvii." C. and H. ii. p. 414. The passage from Cæsar, Bell. Civ. i. 25, 'has quaternis ancoris ex quatuor angulis distinebat, ne fluctibus moverentur,' is not to the purpose, for it was in that case a platform composed of two vessels, and anchored by the four corners. "The anchorage in St. Paul's Bay is thus described in the Sailing Directions: 'The harbour of St. Paul is open to E. and N.E. winds. It is, notwithstanding, safe for small ships; the ground, generally, being very good: and while the cables hold, there is no danger, *as the anchors will never start*.'" Smith, p. 92. **εὔχοντο**] Uncertain, whether their ship might not *go down at her anchors*: and, even supposing her to ride out the night safely, uncertain whether the coast to leeward might not be iron-bound, affording no beach where they might land in safety. Hence also the ungenerous but natural attempt of the seamen to save their lives by taking to the boat. See Smith, p. 97. **30.**] "We hear of anchors being laid out from both ends of a ship (ἑκατέρωθεν), Appian, Bell. Civ. p. 723." ib. **ἐκτείνειν**] because in this case they would *carry out* the anchors to the *extent* of the cable which was loosened.

31. ἐὰν μὴ κ.τ.λ.] "Mirum est quod reliquos vectores salvos posse fieri negat, nisi retentis nautis: quasi vero Dei promissionem exinanire penes ipsos fuerit. Respondeo, Paulum hic de potentia Dei præcise non disputare, ut eam a voluntate et mediis sejungat: et certe non ideo fidelibus virtutem suam Deus commendat, ut contemptis mediis torpori et socordiæ indulgeant, vel temere se projiciant, ubi certa est cavendi ratio. . . . . Neque tamen propterea sequitur, mediis vel adminiculis alligatam esse Dei manum, sed quum Deus hunc vel illum agendi modum ordinat, hominum sensus continet, ne

m Mark ix. 43, 45. John xviii. 10, 26. Gal. v. 12 only. Deut. xxiii. 1.
n John ii. 15 only. 2 Kings viii. 2.
o = ch. xii. 7 reff.
p ch. vii. 18 reff.
q ver. 29.
r = ch. xxi. 27 reff.
s = and constr., ch. xxiv. 4.
t ch. ii. 46 reff.
u ch. ix. 19 reff.
v ver. 27. Gen. xiv. 5.
w absol., Matt. xxiv. 50. ch. (iii. 5. x. 24 reff.) xxviii. 6.
x here only +. (-τία, ver. 21.)
y here only.

μείνωσιν ἐν τῷ πλοίῳ, ὑμεῖς σωθῆναι οὐ δύνασθε. 32 τότε ABCLP
m ἀπέκοψαν οἱ στρατιῶται τὰ n σχοινία τῆς g σκάφης, ℵabcd fghkl
καὶ εἴασαν αὐτὴν o ἐκπεσεῖν. 33 p ἄχρι δὲ οὗ q ἡμέρα r ἤμελ- mop13
λεν q γίνεσθαι, s παρεκάλει ὁ Παῦλος ἅπαντας t μεταλαβεῖν u τροφῆς, λέγων v Τεσσαρεςκαιδεκάτην σήμερον ἡμέραν
w προςδοκῶντες, x ἄσιτοι y διατελεῖτε μηθὲν z προςλαβόμενοι.
34 διὸ s παρακαλῶ ὑμᾶς t μεταλαβεῖν u τροφῆς· τοῦτο γὰρ
a πρὸς τῆς ὑμετέρας σωτηρίας b ὑπάρχει· οὐδενὸς γὰρ
ὑμῶν cd θρὶξ ἀπὸ τῆς κεφαλῆς d ἀπολεῖται. 35 εἴπας δὲ
ταῦτα καὶ λαβὼν ἄρτον e εὐχαρίστησεν τῷ θεῷ f ἐνώπιον
πάντων, καὶ g κλάσας ἤρξατο ἐσθίειν. 36 h εὔθυμοι δὲ
γενόμενοι πάντες καὶ αὐτοὶ z προςελάβοντο ui τροφῆς.
37 j ἤμεθα δὲ k αἱ k πᾶσαι l ψυχαὶ ἐν τῷ πλοίῳ διακόσιαι

Deut. ix. 7. Jer. xx. 18. 2 Macc. v. 27 only. z = ver. 36 only. (ch. xxviii. 2 al.) a = here only. ἐπισκεψόμεθα ἐάν τι ἡμῖν πρὸς λόγου ᾖ, Plato, Gorg. 459. b ch. viii. 16 reff. c Matt. x. 30. 1 Kings xiv. 45. d Luke xxi. 18. e Rom. i. 21 reff. f = Luke i. 19. Gen. xxiv. 51. g ch. ii. 46 reff. h here only +. 2 Macc. xi. 26 only. (-μως, ch. xxiv. 10. -μεῖν, vv. 22, 25.) i gen., Rev. ii. 17. Winer, edn. 6, § 30. 7. c. j Matt. xxiii. 30 bis. Eph. ii. 3 only. k so ch. xix. 7. l = ch. ii. 41 reff.

31. εν τω πλοιω bef μεινωσιν ℵ1 c h [vulg syrr Thl-sif].

32. rec οι στρατιωται bef απεκοψαν (*corrn of order for perspicuity*), with HrLP rel coptt [arm Thl-fin] Chr_1 : txt ABCℵ c m 13. 40. 137 vulg syrr æth[Treg] Thl-sif.

33. rec εμελλεν bef ημερα, with HrLP rel [Syr] syr æth[(Treg) arm] Chr Thl: txt ABCℵ p 13 vulg. (ημελλεν, so BCLP c l p 13. 40 Thl-sif.) rec μηδεν, with CHrLP rel 36 Chr : txt ABℵ 40. προσλαμβανομενοι (*corrn to suit* προσδοκωντες) A 40 lect-12, -λαμβομ., but μ marked for erasure, P.

34. aft διο ins και B. παρακα(sic) ℵ. rec προςλαβειν (*from* προσλ. *above*), with HrLP rel Thl-sif : txt ABCℵ b d h k o p 13. 36. 137 Chr_1 Thl-fin. add τι ℵ1 : τινος c [137 Thl-sif]. for προς, προ B 101. ημετερας ALP a h syr Thl-fin : txt BCHrℵ p 13 rel [vulg Syr coptt æth-pl arm] Chr Thl-sif. ουθενος A. rec (for απο) εκ (*corrn from Luke* xxi. 18), with HrLPℵ rel Thl : txt ABC p 13. 36. 40. 137. rec πεσειται (*corrn to* LXX, *see* 3 *Kings* i. 52, 1 *Kings* xiv. 45, 2 *Kings* xiv. 11. *If, as Meyer supposes,* απολ. *were a corrn from Luke* xxi. 18, *we should not have had the future, but as there,* ου μη αποληται), with HrLP rel syr sah Chr_1 : txt ABCℵ m p 13. 40 vulg Syr copt æth arm Thl-fin.

35. rec ειπων (*corrn to more usual form*), with HrLP p 13 rel 36 [Bas_1 Chr_1] : txt ABCℵ 24. ηυχαρ. P [l m] p 137 : ευχαριστησας ℵ : και ευχαριστησας 40 [ευχαριστησας τε(appy) k].

36. απαντες ℵ1(but α erased). προσελαβον A 40 : προσελαμβανον c : μετελαμβανον 137 : μεταλαβαν(sic) ℵ.

37. rec ημεν (*corrn to more usual form*), with CHrLP 13. 36 rel Chr_1 : txt ABℵ p 40. rec εν τω πλοιω bef αι πασαι ψ. (*corrn of order to connect* ψυχαι *and* διακ.), with HrLP rel [(Syr)] syr Chr [Thl-fin] : txt (A)BCℵ (k m p) 13. 40. 137 vulg copt arm (Chr-$comm_1$) Thl-sif.—om αι A k m p, πασαι bef αι [13] Chr-$comm_1$ [απασαι m]. for διακοσιαι εβδομηκοντα εξ, Cος p(so Scriv ; [Tischdf also, ed 8.]) for διακοσιαι, ως (*mistake arising from* ω *of* πλοιω *and* C *of the numeral, so Tischdf*

præscriptas sibi metas transiliant." Calvin. 33.] This precaution on the part of Paul was another means taken of providing for their safety. All would, on the approaching day, have their strength fully taxed: which therefore needed recruiting by food. **ἄχρι . . . οὗ . . . until it began to be day**: i. e. in the interval between the last-mentioned occurrence and daybreak, Paul employed the time, &c. **προςδοκῶντες**] waiting the cessation of the storm. The following expressions, ἄσιτ. διατ., μηθ. προσλ., are spoken hyperbolically, and cannot mean literally that they had abstained entirely from food *during the whole fortnight*.

πρός with a gen. ('e salute vestra') is only found here in N. T.: compare ref., and ἐλπίσας πρὸς ἑωυτοῦ τὸν χρησμὸν εἶναι, Herodot. i. 75. 35.] "Paul neither *celebrates an* ἀγάπη (Olsh.), nor acts as the *father of a family* (Meyer), but simply

ἑβδομηκονταέξ. 38 [m] κορεσθέντες δὲ [u] τροφῆς [n] ἐκούφιζον
τὸ πλοῖον [o] ἐκβαλλόμενοι τὸν σῖτον εἰς τὴν θάλασσαν.
39 ὅτε δὲ [p] ἡμέρα [p] ἐγένετο, τὴν γῆν οὐκ [q] ἐπεγίνωσκον,
[r] κόλπον δέ τινα [s] κατενόουν ἔχοντα [t] αἰγιαλόν, εἰς ὃν
[u] ἐβουλεύοντο, εἰ δύναιντο, [v] ἐξῶσαι τὸ πλοῖον. 40 καὶ
τὰς [w] ἀγκύρας [x] περιελόντες [y] εἴων εἰς τὴν θάλασσαν, ἅμα
[z] ἀνέντες τὰς [a] ζευκτηρίας τῶν [b] πηδαλίων, καὶ [c] ἐπάραντες

m 1 Cor. iv. 8 only. Deut. xxxi. 20 only.
n here only. Jonah i. 5. 1 Kings vi. 5.
o = here only. (Matt. viii. 12 al.)
p vv. 29, 33.
q = and constr., Matt. xiv. 35. xvii. 12. see ch. xxviii. 1.
r = here (Luke vi. 38. xvi. 22, 23. John i. 18. xiii. 23) only‡. (Gen. xvi. 5.)
s Matt. vii. 3 ∥ L. 2 Macc. ix. 25.
t ch. xxi. 5 reff.
u = ch. v. 33 reff.
v = here (ch. vii. 45) only. Thucyd. ii. 90.
w vv. 29, 30 reff.
x = here only. (ver. 20 reff.)
y = Luke xxii. 51. Exod. xxxii. 10.
z = ch. xvi. 26 (reff.).
a here only †.
b James iii. 4 only †.
c = ch. i. 9.

[ed 7]) B sah. for εξ, πεντε A : om m.
38. ins της bef τροφης H^{r}LP d g l m Chr$_1$. εκβαλομενοι L a. om την א^1.
39. for επεγ., εγινωσκον B 25. for εις, προς A. rec εβουλευσαντο, with H^{r}LP rel Chr$_1$: εβουλοντο A p æth-pl : txt BCא [k] 13(sic) 36 vulg [syrr copt arm]. for δυναιντο, δυνατον CH^{r}LP rel 36 Syr æth[(?) arm] Chr$_1$: txt ABא [m^1] p 13 vulg [syr] Thl. εκσωσαι B^{1}C copt æth [arm].
40. προελοντες א^1.

as a *pious Jew*, who asks a blessing before he eats." De Wette. **36.**] When we reflect *who were included* in these πάντες,—the soldiers and their centurion, the sailors, and passengers of various nations and dispositions, it shews remarkably the influence acquired by Paul over all who sailed with him. **37.**] Explanatory of πάντες: q. d., '*and this was no small number; for we were*,' &c. **38.** **ἐκούφ. τ. πλοῖον**] See above on ver. 18. This wheat was either the remainder of the cargo, part of which had been disposed of in ver. 18—or was the *store for their sustenance*, the cargo having consisted of some other merchandise. And this latter is much the more likely, for two reasons: (1) that σῖτος is mentioned here and not in ver. 18, which it would have been in all probability, had the material cast out there been the same as here; and (2) that the fact is related *immediately after* we are assured that they were *satisfied with food*: from whence we may infer almost with certainty that **ὁ σῖτος** is the *ship's provision*, of part of which they had been partaking. It is a sufficient answer to Mr. Smith's objection to this ("to suppose that they had remaining such a quantity as would lighten the ship is quite inconsistent with the previous abstinence," p. 99), that the ship was provisioned for the voyage to Italy for 276 persons, and that *for the last fourteen days hardly any food had been touched*. This would leave surely enough to be of consequence in a ship ready to sink from hour to hour. **39.**] It may be and has been suggested, that *some of the Alexandrian seamen must have known Malta*;—but we may answer with Mr. Smith that "St. Paul's Bay is remote from the great harbour, and possesses no marked features by which it might be recognized." p. 100. **κόλπον . . . . ἔχοντ. αἰγιαλόν**] a **creek having a sandy beach.** Some Commentators suppose that it should be αἰγιαλὸν ἔχοντα κόλπον, since every creek must have a beach: but what is meant is, a creek with a *smooth, sandy beach*, as distinguished from a rocky inlet. **ἐξῶσαι**] Not, '*to thrust in*,' as E. V., but **to strand**, '*to run a-ground*:' so Thucyd., ref., and more in Wetst. **40.**] (1) They *cut away all four anchors* (the περι may allude to the cutting round each cable in order to sever it, or to the going round and cutting all four), and left them in the sea (εἰς τ. θάλ. 'in the sea, *into* which they had been cast'). This they did to save time, and not to encumber the water-logged ship with their additional weight. (2) They let loose the ropes which tied up the rudders. "Ancient ships were steered by two large paddles, one on each quarter. When anchored by the stern in a gale, it would be necessary to lift them out of the water, and secure them by lashings or rudder bands, and to loose these bands when the ship was again got under way." Smith, p. 101. (3) They raised (ἐπαίρειν, '*to raise up*,' contrary to κατέχειν, '*to haul down*,' a sail) their ἀρτέμων to the wind. It would be impossible in the limits of a note to give any abstract of the long and careful reasoning by which Mr. Smith has made it appear that the 'artemon' was the **foresail** of the ancient ships. I will only notice from him, that the rendering '*mainsail*' in our E. V. was probably a mistaken translation from Bayfius or De Baif, the earliest of the modern writers 'de re navali,' and perhaps the only one extant when the translation was made: he says, "est autem artemon velum majus navis, ut in Actis Apost. xxvii.

τὸν [d] ἀρτέμωνα τῇ [e] πνεούσῃ [f] κατεῖχον [f] εἰς τὸν [t] αἰγιαλόν. ABCLP
41 [g] περιπεσόντες δὲ εἰς τόπον [h] διθάλασσον, [i] ἐπέκειλαν ℵ a b c d
τὴν [k] ναῦν· καὶ ἡ μὲν [l] πρῶρα [m] ἐρείσασα ἔμεινεν [n] ἀσάλευ- f g h k l
τος, ἡ δὲ [o] πρύμνα [p] ἐλύετο ὑπὸ τῆς [q] βίας [τῶν [r] κυμάτων]. m o p 13
42 τῶν δὲ στρατιωτῶν [s] βουλὴ ἐγένετο ἵνα τοὺς [t] δεσμώ-
τας ἀποκτείνωσιν, μήτις [u] ἐκκολυμβήσας [v] διαφύγῃ· 43 ὁ

d here only †. e constr., here only. f = here only. Polyb. i. 25. 7. Thucyd. viii. 23. g Luke x. 30. James i. 2 only. 2 Kings i. 6. h here only †. οὐκ εἰκὸς διθάλαττον εἶναι τὸ πέλαγος τὸ Ἀτλαντικόν, Strabo, i. p. 11. i here only †. Hom. Od. ι. 148. k here only. 3 Kings ix. 26. l ver. 30. m here only. Prov. v. 5. Polyb. iii. 46. 1. n Heb. xii. 28 only. Exod. xiii. 16. Deut. vi. 8. xi. 18 only. o ver. 29 reff. p = Rev. v. 2. Esdr. i. 55 (52). q ch. v. 26 reff. Acts only. r Matt. viii. 24 ‖ Mk. xiv. 24. Jude 13 only. Ps. cvi. 25. s = ch. v. 38 reff. w. ἵνα, here only. t ver. 1 only. Gen. xxxix. 20. u here only †. Diod. Sic. xx. 88. (κολυμβ., ver. 43.) v here only. Josh. viii. 22.

rec αρτεμονα, with LP 13[e sil] rel: txt AB²CHʳℵ a b² c d f g l m² p syr-mg-gr, αρτομωνα B¹.

41. rec εποκειλαν, with B²Hʳ(εποκιλαν) LP rel 36: txt AB¹Cℵ p 13. 40. for πρωρα, πρωτη A. εμενεν A Hʳ[Tischdf; e contra, Treg] c h vulg: txt BCLPℵ 13 rel Chr_1. πριμνα B¹. διελυετο L m [b o] 137 lect-12: ελυτο ℵ. απο ℵ¹ k. om των κυματων (*possibly because the transcriber's eye passed from* των *to* των *in ver* 42) ABℵ¹ [syrr copt]: ins CHʳLPℵ³ 13. 36 rel [arm(Treg); but Griesb cites it as omg της βιας] Chr_1: *a vi maris* vulg: *a fluctibus maris* æth.

42. om δε C¹. ins ινα bef μητις ℵ³. εκκολυβησας(sic) ℵ: εγκολυμβ. g. rec διαφυγοι (*grammatical emendation, see note*), with k m: txt ABCHʳLPℵ p 13 rel 36. 137 Chr_1.

. . etenim etiam nunc nomen Veneti vulgo retinent et artemon vocant." These words, 'velum majus,' they rendered by *mainsail;* whereas the *largest sail* of the Venetian ships at the time was the *foresail.* The French 'artimon,' even now in use, means the sail at the *stern* (mizen). But this is no clue to the ancient meaning, any more than is our word *mizen* to the meaning of the French *misaine,* which is the foresail.

The usual technical name of the foresail was δόλων, that of the mizen, ἐπίδρομος. See on the whole question, Smith's Dissertation on the Ships of the Ancients, appended to his Voyage and Shipwreck of St. Paul. Mr. Pusey informs me that Syr. translates ἀρτέμωνα by '*armnon parvum*' (*armnon* being its word for σκεῦος, ver. 17), and syr. in a note says that ἀρτέμων is "a small *armnon* at the ship's head." **τῇ πνεούσῃ**] scil. αὔρᾳ. Dat. commodi;—**for the wind** (to fill);—or (according to Meyer and De Wette) of direction,—**to the wind.** (4) They made for the beach. The expression, **κατέχειν** (ναῦν or νῆτ) εἰς . . . for "to steer to land," is not uncommon in the classics: cf. examples in Wetst. It seems to get this meaning by a pregnant construction, "to keep the ship (or, to keep one's course in the ship) in hand (and direct it) towards . . . ."

41. **τόπον διθάλασσον**] At the west end of St. Paul's Bay is an *island,* Selmoon or Salmonetta, which *they could not have known to be such* from their place of anchorage. This island is separated from the mainland by a channel of about 100 yards wide, communicating with the outer sea. Just within this island, in all probability, was the place where the ship struck, **in a place where two seas met.** **ἐπέκειλαν**] ἐπικέλλειν is used by Homer (ref.) in the sense of 'adpellere navem.' Its commoner use is intransitive: see Hom. ib. ver. 138, and Apollon. Rhod. ii. 352, 382; iii. 575. In Od. ε. 114, it is said of the ship itself, ἠπείρῳ ἐπέκελσε. The ἐποκέλλειν of the rec. is used several times by Thucydides, and has the same twofold usage: cf. Thucyd. iii. 12; iv. 28; viii. 102: **they ran the ship a-ground.** "The circumstance which follows, would, but for the peculiar nature of the bottom of St. Paul's Bay, be difficult to account for. The rocks of Malta disintegrate into very minute particles of sand and clay, which when acted on by the currents, or by surface agitation, form a deposit of tenacious clay: but in still water, where these causes do not act, mud is found; but it is only in the creeks where there are no currents, and at such a depth as to be undisturbed by the waves, that mud occurs. . . . A ship therefore, impelled by the force of the gale into a creek with a bottom such as that laid down in the chart, would strike a bottom of mud, graduating into tenacious clay, into which the fore part would fix itself and be held fast, while the stern was exposed to the force of the waves." Smith, p. 103.

42.] ἵνα gives not only the *purpose,* but the substance of the βουλή. **Their counsel was,—to kill,** &c.: this it *was,* and *to this it tended.* διαφύγοι has probably been

δὲ ἑκατοντάρχης, βουλόμενος [w] διασῶσαι τὸν Παῦλον,
[x] ἐκώλυσεν αὐτοὺς τοῦ [y] βουλήματος, ἐκέλευσέν τε τοὺς
δυναμένους [z] κολυμβᾶν [a] ἀποῤῥίψαντας πρώτους ἐπὶ
τὴν γῆν [b] ἐξιέναι, 44 καὶ τοὺς λοιποὺς [c] οὓς μὲν ἐπὶ
[d] σανισιν [c] οὓς δὲ ἐπί τινων τῶν [e] ἀπὸ τοῦ πλοίου.
καὶ οὕτως [f] ἐγένετο πάντας [w] διασωθῆναι ἐπὶ τὴν γῆν.
XXVIII. 1 Καὶ [w] διασωθέντες τότε [g] ἐπέγνωμεν ὅτι
Μελίτη ἡ νῆσος καλεῖται. 2 οἵ τε [h] βάρβαροι [i] παρεῖχαν
οὐ τὴν [k] τυχοῦσαν [l] φιλανθρωπίαν ἡμῖν· [m] ἅψαντες γὰρ

w see ch. xxiii. 24 reff. x ch. x. 47 reff. constr., here only. Mic. ii. 4. Xen. Cyr. ii. 4. 23. Polyb. ii. 8. 8. y Rom. ix. 19. 1 Pet. iv. 3 only +. 2 Macc. xv. 5 only. ὅπερ ἦν τούτοις βούλημα, Demosth. 1109. 15. z here only +. Isa. xxv. 11 Symm. (-βήθρα, John v. 2.) a = and constr., here only. Lucian, Ver. Hist. i. 30, ἀποῤῥίψαντες ἐνηχόμεθα. pass., Mic. vii. 19 B &c. b ch. xiii. 42 reff. c 1 Cor. xi. 21 reff. d here only. 4 Kings xii. 9 Ed-vat. F(not AB) Ald. Cant. viii. 9. Ezek. xxvii. 5 only. e see ch. xii. 1. xv. 5. f constr., ch. iv. 5 reff. g constr., Luke vii. 37. ch. xix. 34. xxii. 29. Ezek. xvi. 62. see ch. xxvii. 39. h here bis. Rom. i. 14. 1 Cor. xiv. 11 (bis). Col. iii. 11 only. Ezek. xxi. 31. i = ch. xvi. 16 reff. xxii. 2. 1 Tim. vi. 17. k = ch. xix. 11 reff. l Tit. iii. 4 only +. 2 Macc. vi. 22. (-πως, ch. xxvii. 3.) m = Luke viii. 16. xi. 33. xv. 8 [xxii. 55 v. r.] only. Judith xiii. 13.

43. εκατονταρχος P[HL Chr_1 Thl-sif]. τον παυλον bef διασωσαι A 13. 68. 8-pe. for βουληματος, βηματος $ℵ^1$: βουλευματος a f. for τε, δε C c p 13. 40. 137 syr copt. εκκολυμβαν B. αποριψαντας Cℵ. της γης $ℵ^1$ c [137].

Chap. XXVIII. 1. aft διαθωσαντες ins οι περι (τον) παυλον εκ του πλοος (*beginning of an ecclesiastical portion*) C^3-marg L b g k m o Thl-sif : τον is omd by C^3 : alii aliter : οι περι τ. π. βαρβαροι 1-marg. rec επεγνωσαν (*corrn to suit ch* xxvii. 39 ?), with C^3-marg H^rLP rel 36 Chr_1 : txt $ABC^1ℵ$ c^1 p 13. 137 vulg syrr copt æth [arm]. μελιτηνη B^1 [syr-mg-gr arm].

2. rec δε (*altern of characteristic* τε), with $H^rLPℵ$ rel 36 [vulg arm] copt Chr_1 : txt ABC c p 13. 40 syrr æth Thl-sif. (παρειχαν, so ABℵ.) rec αναψαντες (*corrn to more precise word*), with H^rLP rel 36 Chr_3 : txt ABCℵ [c] p 13. 40.

a correction to suit ἐγένετο. But the subjunctive after the past is merely a mixture of construction of the historic past with the historic present, and is used where the scene is intended to be vividly set before the reader. 43.] ἀποῤῥίψαντας is reflective, sc. ἑαυτούς. 44. **τοὺς λοιπούς**] scil. ἐπὶ τὴν γῆν ἐξιέναι. **τινων τῶν ἀπὸ τ. π.**] probably, as E. V., **broken pieces of the ship** :—some of the parts of the ship : the σανίδες being **whole planks**, perhaps of the decks. **διασωθ. ἐπί**] may be = διασ. κ. ἀφικέσθαι ἐπί, —a constructio prægnans, but this need not be, as διασωθῆναι is *to get safe through*, and ἐπί is simply the direction in which the act is carried out. XXVIII. 1. **Μελίτη**] The whole course of the narrative has gone to shew that this *can be no other than* Malta. The idea that it is not Malta, but *Meleda*, an island off the Illyrian coast in the Gulf of Venice, seems to be first found in Constantine Porphyrogenitus, de Adminiculis Imperii, p. 36—νῆσος μεγάλη τὰ Μέλετα ἤτοι τὸ Μαλοζεᾶται, ἣν ἐν ταῖς πράξεσι τ. ἀποστ. ὁ ἅγιος Λουκᾶς μέμνηται, Μελίτην ταύτην προσαγορεύων. It has been adopted by our own countrymen, Bryant and Dr. Falconer, and abroad by Giorgi, Rhoer, and more recently Paulus. It rests principally on three mistakes :—1. the meaning of the name Adria (see above on ch. xxvii. 27),—2. the fancy that there are no poisonous serpents in Malta (ver. 3),—3. the notion that the Maltese would not have been called βάρβαροι. The idea itself, when compared with the facts, is preposterous enough. Its supporters are obliged to place Fair Havens on the *north side of Crete*,—and to suppose the wind to have been the hot *Sirocco* (compare ver. 2). Further notices of this question, and of the state of Malta at the time, will be found in the notes on the following verses. Observe, their previous *state* of ignorance of the island is expressed by the imperf. ἐπεγίνωσκον ;—the *act* of recognition by the aor. ἐπέγνωμεν [ch. xxvii. 30]. 2. **βάρβαροι**] A term implying very much what our word **natives** does, when speaking of any little-known or new place. They were not Greek colonists, therefore they were barbarians (Rom. i. 14). If it be necessary strictly to vindicate the term, the two following citations will do so : ἔστι δὲ ἡ νῆσος αὕτη (Malta) **Φοινίκων ἄποικος**, Diod. Sic. v. 12.—ἐν δὲ Σικελίᾳ ἔθνη **βάρβαρα** τάδε ἐστίν, Ἐλυμοί, Σικανοί, Σικελοί, **Φοίνικες**, Τρῶες, Scylax, Periplus,

n here bis only †. Judith vii. 5 al.
o = Rom. xiv. 1, 3. xv. 7. Philem. 17. Ps. xxvi. 10. lxxii. 24.
p ch. xiv. 17 reff.
q = here only. ὁ ἐφεστὼς ζόφος, Polyb. xviii. 3.7. see 2 Tim. iv. 6.

ⁿ πυρὰν ᵒ προσελάβοντο πάντας ἡμᾶς διὰ τὸν ᵖ ὑετὸν ABCLP
τὸν ᑫ ἐφεστῶτα καὶ διὰ τὸ ʳ ψῦχος. 3 ˢ συστρέψαντος δὲ ℵ a b c d f g h k l
τοῦ Παύλου ᵗ φρυγάνων τι ᵘ πλῆθος καὶ ἐπιθέντος ἐπὶ m o p 13
τὴν ⁿ πυρὰν ᵛ ἔχιδνα ʷ ἀπὸ τῆς ˣ θέρμης ʸ διεξελθοῦσα
ᶻ καθῆψεν τῆς χειρὸς αὐτοῦ. 4 ὡς δὲ εἶδον οἱ ʰ βάρβαροι
ᵃ κρεμάμενον τὸ θηρίον ἐκ τῆς χειρὸς αὐτοῦ, πρὸς ἀλλήλους ἔλεγον ᵇ Πάντως ᶜ φονεύς ἐστιν ὁ ἄνθρωπος οὗτος,

r John xviii. 18. 2 Cor. xi. 27 only. Gen. viii. 22. s here (Matt. xvii. 22 v. r.) only. Judg. xi. 3 B. 2 Macc. xiv. 30. (συστροφή, ch. xix. 40.) t here only. = Job xxx. 7. Isa. xl. 24. u = Luke ii. 13. John xxi. 6. v Matt. iii. 7 || L. xii. 34. xxiii. 33 only †. Isa. lix. 5 Aq. w = Matt. xiii. 1. Luke ix. 5 al. Sir. xxiv. 3. x here only. Job vi. 17. (-μαίνεσθαι, Mark xiv. 54.) y here only. Job xx. 25. z here only †. trans., Polyb. viii. 8. 3, τὰς πρώρας τῶν ὀργάνων εἰς ἀκίνητον καθῆπτε. So Xen. Cyneg. vi. 9. a ch. v. 30 reff. 1 Macc. i. 61. b ch. xxi. 22 reff. c ch. vii. 52 reff.

προσανελαμβανον ℵ¹ c [προσελαμβ. 137]. om παντας A copt æth[?] Chr-ms₁ : ημας bef παντας 13 lect-12 [vulg] : om ημας 40. υφεστωτα L 13. om 2nd δια ℵ¹ [vulg].

3. σφρυγανων (but σ marked for erasure) ℵ¹. rec om τι (*as unnecessary*), with HʳLP rel 36 syr [Syr arm Thl-sif] Chr₁ : ins ABCℵ(perhaps *prima manu : in small letters*) 13. 40 vulg(not am) Thl-fin, τε p. επιθεντες(sic) ℵ. [add του παυλου A.] rec (for απο) εκ (*see note*), with rel Chr Thl-sif : txt ABCHʳLPℵ b c k o p 13. 36. 40. 137 Thl-fin, *a calore* vulg. rec εξελθουσα (*corrn, the compound* διεξ. *not being elsw found in N T, and its force not being seen, vide note*), with [A]BCℵ p 13. 36 rel Chr-comm₁ Thl-fin : txt HʳLP a d f g k l o Thl-sif. καθηψατο C b h o 36. 40. 137 Chr.

4. ειδαν B. rec ελεγον bef προς αλληλους (*corrn of order for perspicuity*), with HʳLP rel copt [æth(Treg) arm] Chr : om προς αλληλους Syr : txt ABCℵ c m p 13. 40. 137 vulg syr Thl.

p. 4. **προσελάβ.**] **received us**, not *to their fire* (Meyer), but as in reff. **ὑετόν**] 'Post ingentes ventos solent imbres sequi.' Grot. **τὸν ἐφεστ.**] not, '*which came on suddenly*' (Meyer), but **which was on us**:—another instance of overlooking the *present* sense of ἕστηκα. **ψῦχος**] This is decisive against the Sirocco, which is a hot and sultry wind even so late as the month of November, and moreover (Smith, p. 109) seldom lasts more than three days.

3. **συστρέψαντος**] "vincti officium faciebat submisse, aliis quoque inserviens." Bengel. **φρυγάνων**] From the circumstance of the concealed viper, these were probably heaps of neglected wood gathered in the forest. **ἐπιθέντος κ.τ.λ.**] The difficulty here is, that there are *now no venomous serpents* in Malta. But as Mr. Smith observes, "no person who has studied the changes which the operations of man have produced on the animals of any country, will be surprised that a particular species of reptiles should have disappeared from Malta. My friend, the Rev. Mr. Landsborough, in his interesting excursions in Arran, has repeatedly noticed the gradual disappearance of the viper from the island since it has become more frequented. Perhaps there is no where a surface of equal extent in so artificial a state as that of Malta is at the present day,—and no where has the aboriginal forest been more completely cleared. We need not therefore be surprised that, with the disappearance of the woods, the noxious reptiles which infested them should also have disappeared." pp. 111, 112. The reading **ἐκ τ. θέρμ.** has been an explanation of ἀπό, which here signifies **from** *locally*, not '*on account of*.' To suppose the converse ("the ἀπό was adopted by those who thought the sense was '*on account of* the fire,'" Dr. Bloomf.),—is simply absurd; for 1) no man ever could suppose the sense of ἐκ in such a connexion to be this: and 2) even if any one did, he would not have substituted another ambiguous preposition, ἀπό. Paul had placed the faggot on the fire, and was settling or arranging it in its place, when the viper glided out of the heat and fixed on his hand. **διεξελθ.** gives the more precise sense, and is a less usual word than ἐξελθ. The serpent glided out *through* the sticks. **καθῆψεν**] **attached itself**: a usage unexampled in earlier Greek. The narrative leaves no doubt that the bite did veritably take place. 4.] The natives, who were sure to know, here positively declared it to have been a *venomous* serpent. I make these remarks to guard against the disingenuous shifts of rationalists and semi-rationalists, who will have us believe either that the viper *did not bite*, or that if it did, it was *not venomous*. **πάντως φον.**

...ουκ ειασεν C. ABLPℵ a b c d f g h k l m o p 13

ὃν [d] διασωθέντα ἐκ τῆς θαλάσσης ἡ [e] δίκη ζῆν οὐκ εἴασεν.
5 ὁ μὲν οὖν [f] ἀποτινάξας τὸ θηρίον εἰς τὸ πῦρ ἔπαθεν
οὐδὲν κακόν. 6 οἱ δὲ [g] προσεδόκων αὐτὸν [h] μέλλειν
[i] πίμπρασθαι ἢ [k] καταπίπτειν [l] ἄφνω νεκρόν. [m] ἐπὶ [m] πολὺ
δὲ αὐτῶν [n] προσδοκώντων καὶ [o] θεωρούντων μηδὲν [p] ἄτοπον
εἰς αὐτὸν γινόμενον, [q] μεταβαλόμενοι ἔλεγον αὐτὸν εἶναι
θεόν. 7 Ἐν δὲ [r] τοῖς [r] περὶ τὸν τόπον ἐκεῖνον [s] ὑπῆρχεν

d see ch. xxiii. 24 reff. e = here (2 Thess. i. 9. Jude 7) only. Demosth. 422, 11; 722, 25. f Luke ix. 5 only. Judg. xvi. 20 A Ald. compl. 1 Kings x. 2. Lam. ii. 7 only. (-αγμα, Isa. i. 31, Symm.)

g ch. iii. 5 reff. h = ch. xxi. 27 reff. i here only †. εὐθὺς διοιδεῖ καὶ πίμπραται τὸ σῶμα, Diod. Sic. ii. 12. k Luke viii. 6. ch. xxvi. 14 only. Ps. cxliv. 14. l ch. ii. 2. xvi. 26 only. Josh. x. 9. m here only. (see ch. xx. 9, 11.) 2 Kings iii. 1. μῖσος οὐκ ἐπὶ πολὺ ἀντέχει, Thuc. ii. 64. n absol., ch. xxvii. 33 reff. o w. particip., ch. xvii. 16. p Luke xxiii. 41. ch. xxv. 5. 2 Thess. iii. 2 only. Job iv. 8. q here only. Josh. viii. 21. Jos. B. J. v. 9. 3, καλὸν πρὸ ἀνηκέστου συμφορᾶς μεταβαλέσθαι: and freq. act. inter., Job x. 8. 2 Macc. vi. 29 Ed-vat. F(not AB) Ald. r = here only. ἤρξατο ταπεινοῦσθαι τὰ περὶ τὰς Θήβας, Diod. Sic. i. 50. see ch. xiii. 13. s ch. iii. 6 reff.

om 2nd της ℵ[1].

5. αποτιναξαμενος (*corrn from ch* xiii. 51, xviii. 6? *so De W.*) AH[r]L p rel 13. 36. 40. 137 [Amm-c] Chr[1] Thl-fin: txt BPℵ a f m Thl-sif. for κακον, πονηρον c: om ℵ[1].

6. προσεδοκουν H[r]L 13. 40 Thl-sif. [μελλων A.] πιπρασθαι A o[1] 1. 3. 4. 68: πεπρασθαι lect-12: εμπιμπρασθαι 27-9: εμπιπρασθαι ℵ[1] 40. 66[2]. 98-marg 105. προσδοκουντων A: -κοντων L f k p. θεωρωντων ℵ[1]: θεωρησαντων c: θεωμενων l. μηθεν B. rec μεταβαλλομενοι, with H[r]Lℵ 13 rel [Chr[1]]: txt ABP b c p 40. ελεγαν B. rec θεον bef αυτον ειναι, with H[r]LP rel [arm] Chr: ειναι αυτον θεον A: αυτον θεον ειναι a c k m 13 [syrr] Thl-sif: txt Bℵ p vulg Thl-fin.

ἐστ.] 'vincula videbant,' Beng. The idea of his being a murderer is not to be accounted for (as Elsner, Wolf, Kuin.) by the *member* which was bitten (for this would fit any crime which the hand could commit),—nor by supposing (Heinsius) the bite of a serpent to have been the Maltese punishment for murder; it is accounted for by the obviousness of the crime as belonging to the most notorious delinquents, and the aptness of the assumed punishment,—death for death. **ἡ δίκη**] **Justice,** or *Nemesis.* What the Phœnician islanders called her, does not appear; but the *idea* is common to all religions. **5.**] "Luke does not so much as hint, that any divine intervention took place." De Wette. True enough: but why? Because Luke believed that the very dullest of his readers would understand it without any such hint. According to these rationalists, a fortunate concurrence of accidents must have happened to the Apostles, totally unprecedented in history or probability. Besides, did not the natives themselves in this case testify to the fact? None were so well qualified to judge of the virulence of the serpent,—none so capable of knowing that the hanging on Paul's hand implied the communication of the venom:—yet they change him from a murderer into a god, on seeing what took place. Need we further evidence, that the divine power which they mistakenly attributed to Paul himself, was really exerted on his behalf, by Him who had said ὄφεις ἀροῦσιν? See below on ver. 8. The fact that St. Luke understood what the natives said, is adduced by Wordsworth as another proof (see his and my note on ch. xiv. 11) that the Apostles and Evangelists commonly understood unknown tongues. But such an inference here has absolutely nothing to rest on. Are we to suppose that these βάρβαροι had no means of intercourse with Greek sailors? **6.**] Both these, the inflammation of the body, and the falling down dead suddenly, are recorded as results of the bite of the African serpents. Mr. Humphry quotes from Lucan, ix. 790, 'Nasidium Marsi cultorem torridus agri Percussit Prester (*an African serpent named from this very verb* πίμπρασθαι): illi rubor igneus ora Succendit, tenditque cutem, pereunte figura:' and, of the bite of the asp, ix. 815: 'At tibi, Leve miser, fixus præcordia pressit Niliaca serpente cruor: nulloque dolore Testatus morsus, subita caligine mortem Accipis, et somno Stygias descendis ad umbras.' **προσδοκώντων**] not, as E. V., '*when they had looked,*' —but **when they were long looking.** **μεταβαλ.**] There is no need to supply τ. γνώμην, though it is sometimes expressed:—so οἱ πλεῖστοι τῶν ἀνθρώπων κ. μεταβάλλονται πρὸς τὰ παρόντα, κ. ταῖς τύχαις εἴκουσι, Lysias, pro Nicia fratre (Wetst.): μεταβάλλεσθαι δοκεῖ καὶ οὐδὲν ἔχειν πιστὸν ἡ πόλις, Demosth. pro Megalop. (id.),—in neither of which places can τ. γνώμην well be understood. **θεόν**] "Comparabant vel Herculi qui in ulnis adhuc jacens angues superavit: vel Æsculapio, qui cum serpente pingitur." Wetst. and so also Grot. But so much as

[t] χωρία τῷ [u] πρώτῳ τῆς νήσου, ὀνόματι Ποπλίῳ, ὃς
[v] ἀναδεξάμενος ἡμᾶς ἡμέρας τρεῖς [w] φιλοφρόνως [x] ἐξένισεν.
8 [y] ἐγένετο δὲ τὸν πατέρα τοῦ Ποπλίου [z] πυρετοῖς καὶ
[a] δυςεντερίῳ [b] συνεχόμενον [c] κατακεῖσθαι· πρὸς ὃν ὁ
Παῦλος [d] εἰςελθών, καὶ [e] προσευξάμενος, [f] ἐπιθεὶς τὰς
χεῖρας αὐτῷ, ἰάσατο αὐτόν. 9 τούτου δὲ γενομένου καὶ
οἱ λοιποὶ οἱ ἐν τῇ νήσῳ ἔχοντες [g] ἀσθενείας προςήρχοντο
καὶ [h] ἐθεραπεύοντο, 10 οἳ καὶ πολλαῖς [ij] τιμαῖς [j] ἐτίμησαν
ἡμᾶς, καὶ [k] ἀναγομένοις [l] ἐπέθεντο [m] τὰ [jm] πρὸς τὰς [jn] χρείας.

I επιθεις... ABILP ℵ a b c d f g h k l m o p 13

t ch. i. 18 reff. u and constr., ch. xiii. 50 reff. v Heb. xi. 17 only +. 2 Macc. vi. 19. viii. 36 only. w here only +. 2 Macc. iii. 9. Xen. Cyr. v. 5. 32. (-φρών, 1 Pet. iii. 8 rec. -φρονεῖν, 2 Macc. ii. 25.) x ch. x. 23 reff. y constr., ch. iv. 5 reff. z Matt. viii. 15 ‖. John iv. 52 only. Deut. xxviii. 22 only. (-έσσειν, Matt. viii. 14.) a here only +. b = Matt. iv. 24. Luke iv. 38. viii. 37, 45 al. Job iii. 24. see 2 Cor. v. 14 reff. (-οχή, 2 Cor. ii. 4.) c = Mark i. 30. John v. 3, 6. Prov. vi. 9. d w. πρός, ch. xi. 3 reff. e absol., ch. x. 9 reff. f ch. viii. 17 reff. g = Matt. viii. 17. Luke v. 15 al. fr. 2 Macc. ix. 21, 22. h ch. viii. 7 reff. i = Rom. xiii. 7 (see note). j Sir. xxxviii. 1. k ch. xiii. 13 reff. l = here only. Xen. Cyr. viii. 2. 4. m Luke xiv. 32. xix. 42. 2 Pet. i. 3. n ch. xx. 34 reff.

7. rec τρεις bef ημερας, with AH^{r}LPℵ p (13) rel 36 Chr$_1$: om a 69: txt B c k m 40. 137.

8. rec δυςεντερια, with p rel 36 [Synop$_1$] Chr$_1$: -τεριοις 13: -αις 25. 40: txt ABH^r LPℵ m. προσελθων P. aft προσευξ., ευξαμενος is repeated by B^1, but marked for erasure.

9. rec for δε, ουν (*seemingly more natural copula*), with H^{r}LP rel 36 Thl: txt ABIℵ c g k p 13. 40. 137 syr copt Chr$_1$. aft γενομ. ins υγιους H^r. om 1st και B [copt]. rec εχοντες ασθενειας bef εν τη νησω, with H^{r}LP rel 36 syr Chr$_1$ [Thl-sif]: txt ABIℵ k m p 13. 40 vulg (Syr) copt Thl-fin. προηρχον B.

10. om οι P 73 lect-13. for τα, τας A 137: om ℵ^1. rec την χρειαν (*Meyer thinks* τας χρειας *a gloss for* τα προς την χρειαν,—*De W., that the plur has crept in from ch* xx. 34. *But Bornemann rightly objects* (1) *that the* τας *preceding in* A 137 *shews the transcriber's eye to have passed on to* τας *of* τας χρειας *in earlier copies,* (2) *that the use of the plur is much rarer than of the singular: see also note*), with H^{r}LP p rel 36 Chr$_1$: txt ABIℵ 13. 40. 137 vulg syr.

this can hardly be inferred: nor are we sure of the theogony of these Phœnician barbarians. **7.**] **πρῶτος** Μελιταίων was probably an official title: the more so, as Publius can hardly have borne the appellation from his *estates*, during his father's lifetime. Two inscriptions have been found in Malta, at Citta Vecchia, which seem to establish this view: a Greek one, containing the words α(υλος) κ(αστρι)κιος κυρ. προυδινς ιππευς ρωμ πρωτος μελιταιων και πατρων αρξας και αμφιπολευς α σ (Αὐγούστῳ σεβαστῷ) θεω . . . . , and a Latin one, with the same title, 'Mel. primus.' If so (and his Roman name further confirms it), Publius was *legatus of the Prætor of Sicily*, to whose province Malta belonged; see Cic. in Ver. ii. 4. 18. **ἡμᾶς**] Hardly perhaps more than Paul and his companions, and, it may be, Julius. At ver. 10, a *special reason* had occurred for his honouring Paul and his company: at present, his hospitality must have been prompted by the courtesy of Julius, who could hardly fail himself to be included in it. The three days were probably till they could find a suitable lodging. **8. πυρετοῖς**] Hippocrates also uses the plural. It probably indicates the recurrence of fever fits. **δυςεντερίῳ**] δυςεντερία, Ἀττικῶς· -ριον, Ἕλληνες. Mœris;—**dysentery.** Dr. Falconer makes this an argument against 'Melita Africana' being meant. "Such a place, dry and rocky, and remarkably healthy, was not likely to produce a disease which is almost peculiar to moist situations." But Mr. Smith answers, that the changed circumstances of the island might produce this change also: and besides, that he is informed by a physician of Valetta, that the disease is by no means uncommon in Malta. **ἐπιθεὶς τ. χεῖρας αὐτῷ**] It is remarkable, that so soon after the '*taking up of serpents*,' we should read of Paul having '*laid his hands on the sick and they recovered*.' See the two in close connexion, Mark xvi. 18. **10. τιμαῖς**] The ordinary interpretation of this as *rewards, gifts*, may be right, but is not necessary. In all the passages quoted to support it, ref. Sir., Cicero, ad Diversos, xvi. 9 ('Curio misi ut medico honos haberetur'), the expression τιμή is *general*, and the *context* renders an inference probable as to *what sort of* τιμή is meant. See especially 1 Tim. v. 3, 17 and notes. Here there is no such unavoidable indication, whereas the other meaning

11 Μετὰ δὲ τρεῖς μῆνας [k] ἀνήχθημεν ἐν πλοίῳ [o] παρα-
κεχειμακότι ἐν τῇ νήσῳ, Ἀλεξανδρίνῳ, [p] παρασήμῳ
Διοσκούροις. 12 καὶ [q] καταχθέντες εἰς Συρακούσας [r] ἐπεμείναμεν ἡμέρας τρεῖς· 13 ὅθεν [s] περιελθόντες [t] κατηντήσαμεν εἰς Ῥήγιον καὶ μετὰ μίαν ἡμέραν [u] ἐπιγενομένου
[v] νότου [w] δευτεραῖοι ἤλθομεν εἰς Ποτιόλους, 14 οὗ εὑρόντες
ἀδελφοὺς [x] παρεκλήθημεν παρ᾽ αὐτοῖς [r] ἐπιμεῖναι ἡμέρας

o ch. xxvii. 12 reff.
p here only +. 3 Macc. ii. 29. see note.
q = ch. xxvii. 3 (xxiii. 15 reff.).
r ch. x. 48 reff.
s ch. xix. 13. 1 Tim. v. 13. Heb. xi. 37 only. Job i. 7.
t ch. xvi. 1 reff.
u here only +. Ep. Jer. 47 only, but not =. πνεύματος ἐπιγενομένου, Thucyd. iv. 30.
v ch. xxvii. 13 reff.
w here only. see John xi. 39. 1 Kings ix. 20. Xen. Cyr. v. 2. 2, beg.
x constr., ch. xiii. 42, but pass. here only.

11. ηχθημεν [for ανηχ.] H^r a b^1 k l m o. διοσκοροις P^1(corrd appy *eadem manu*) b p^2 40.
12. συρακουσσας B(Tischdf). ημεραις τρισιν B. **13.** περιελοντες $Bℵ^1$.
14. rec (for παρ) επ᾽, with H^rLP rel Chr_1 Thl-sif: txt ABIℵ d m^1 p 13. 36. 40 Thl-fin. επιμειναντες H^r c 137 syr(adding *apud eos* with ast) Thl : [μειναντες l:] επιμεινα(sic) A.

is rendered probable by the form of the sentence, which opposes to these τιμαί, bestowed on them during their whole stay, τὰ πρὸς τ. χρείας, with which they were loaded at their departure. Render it therefore **honoured us with many honours** (or '*distinctions*,' or '*attentions*'). τὴν χρείαν has perhaps been an alteration after St. Paul's ἅπαξ κ. δὶς εἰς τὴν χρείαν μοι ἐπέμψατε, Phil. iv. 16. **11.**] They probably set sail (see on ch. xxvii. 9) not earlier than the sixth of the ides of March (i. e. Mar. 10). **παρασήμῳ Διοσκούροις**] **with the sign (of) the Dioscuri**, as ὀνόματι Ποπλίῳ, ver. 7; not, '*with the Dioscuri as a sign.*' So in the inscription found by the Rev. G. Brown at Lutro (Phœnice) in Crete, given at length in the excursus at the end of the prolegg. to Acts, we have "gubernator navis parasemo Isopharia." The ancient ships carried at their prow a painted or carved representation of the sign which furnished their name, and at the stern a similar one of their tutelar deity. Sometimes these were one and the same, as appears to have been the case with this ship. Cyril, in Cat., says, ἔθος ἀεί πως ἐν ταῖς Ἀλεξανδρέων μάλιστα ναῦσι πρός γε τῇ πρώρῃ δεξιά τε καὶ εἰς εὐώνυμα γραφὰς εἶναι τοιαύτας. See Virg. Æn. x. 209; Ovid, Trist. i. 9. 1; Pers. Sat. vi. 30. Castor and Pollux, sons of Jupiter and Leda, were considered the tutelar deities of sailors. See Hor. Od. i. 3. 2; 12. 28. **12.**] Syracuse is about eighty miles, a day's sail, from Malta.
13.] **περιελθόντες** apparently denotes the roundabout course of a vessel tacking with an adverse wind. That the wind was not favourable, follows from ἐπιγενομένου below. Mr. Lewin's account is, "as the wind was westerly, and they were under shelter of the high mountainous range of Etna on their left, they were obliged to stand out to sea in order to fill their sails, and so came to Rhegium by a circuitous sweep." And he cites a case of a passage from Syracuse to Rhegium, in which a similar circuit was taken for a similar reason, p. 736. The day at Rhegium, as perhaps the three at Syracuse before, was spent probably in waiting for the wind. **ἐπιγ. νότ.**] **the South wind having sprung up,**—succeeded the one which blew before. **δευτεραῖοι**] viz. *after leaving Rhegium*: a distance of about 180 nautical miles. **Ποτιόλους**] Puteoli (anciently Dicæarchia, Strab. v. 4, now Puzzuoli) was the most sheltered part of the bay of Naples. It was the principal port of Southern Italy, and, in particular, formed the great emporium for the Alexandrian wheat ships. Strabo, xvii. 1. Seneca (Ep. 77) gives a graphic account (cited by Smith, p. 117) of the arrival of the Alexandrine fleet at Puteoli: "Subito nobis hodie Alexandrinæ naves apparuerunt, quæ præmitti solent et nuntiare secuturæ classis adventum; tabellarias vocant. Gratus illarum adspectus Campaniæ est. Omnis in pilis Puteolorum turba constitit, et ex ipso genere velorum, Alexandrinas quamvis in magna turba navium intelligit, solis enim licet supparum (*the topsail*) intendere quod in alto omnes habent naves. Nulla enim res æque adjuvat cursum, quam summa pars veli; illinc maxime navis urgetur. Itaque quoties ventus increbuit majorque est quam expedit, antenna submittitur, minus habet virium flatus ex humili: cum intrare capreas et promontorium ex quo 'Alta procellos speculatur vertice Pallas,' cæteræ velo jubentur esse contentæ, supparum Alexandrinarum insigne est."
14.] These Christians were perhaps Alexandrines, as the commerce was so con-

ἑπτά· καὶ [y] οὕτως εἰς τὴν Ῥώμην ἤλθαμεν. 15 κἀκεῖθεν
οἱ ἀδελφοὶ ἀκούσαντες [z] τὰ [z] περὶ ἡμῶν ἦλθαν εἰς
[a] ἀπάντησιν ἡμῖν [b] ἄχρι Ἀππίου Φόρου καὶ Τριῶν Ταβερνῶν, οὓς ἰδὼν ὁ Παῦλος [c] εὐχαριστήσας τῷ θεῷ ἔλαβεν
[d] θάρσος.
16 Ὅτε δὲ εἰσήλθομεν εἰς Ῥώμην, * [h] ἐπετράπη τῷ

ABILP ℵ a b c d f g h k l m o p 13

y = Rom. v. 12 reff. z ch. xxiv. 10 reff. a (in N. T. always w. εἰς.) Matt. xxv. 6. 1 Thess. iv. 17 only. 1 Kings ix. 14. (-τᾷν, Matt. xxviii. 9.) b ch. xi. 5 reff. c Rom. i. 8 reff. d here only. ἀναλ. θ., Job xvii. 9. (-σεῖν, ch. xxiii. 11.) e = ch. xxvii. 1 reff. f ch. xvi. 25, 27 reff. g here only †. h = and constr., ch. xxvi. 1 reff.

rec ηλθομεν, with H^rIP p rel 36 : εισηλθομεν L : txt ABℵ.—ηλθ. bef εις (την) ρωμην AI [b k o] p 13. 40 vulg [Syr copt æth(Treg)].—om την AI a b c k o 13. 40. 137 Thl-fin.

15. om οι B 96. rec εξηλθον, with H^rLP rel 36 Chr_1 : txt BIℵ, -θον A p 40. (13 def.) υπαντησιν $ℵ^1$ [40] : συναντησιν g. ημων I c d g k o p 13. 36. 40 [arm] Thl-sif: υμιν $ℵ^1$. rec αχρις, with H^rILP rel 36 : txt ABℵ p 13. aft αχρι, π was written by $ℵ^1$, but marked and erased.

16. rec ηλθομεν (*the force of the compound not being regarded*), with LP rel 36 vulg syr Chr_1 Thl Œc : ηλθον H^r : txt ABIℵ d m p 13. 40 Syr copt æth. (-θαμεν A, but not Bℵ rel. [I doubtful.]) ins την bef ρωμην L$ℵ^1$($ℵ^3$ disapproving) c 137 lect-12 3-pe. *rec aft ρωμην ins ὁ ἑκατόνταρχος [e] παρέδωκε τοὺς [f] δεσμίους τῷ [g] στρατοπεδάρχῃ(-χῳ H^rLP g^1 (k ?) 1 m), going on τῷ δὲ Παύλῳ ἐπετράπη, with H^rLP rel 36 syr-w-ast Thl : om ABIℵ p 40 vulg (Syr) arm Chr_1

siderable between the two places. **ουτως**] *after this stay with them :* implying that the request was complied with.

15.] The brethren at Rome had heard probably by special message sent by some of their fellow-voyagers. See a detailed account of the stages of the journey not here mentioned, in C. and H. ii., pp. 438 ff. **τὰ περὶ ἡμῶν**] **the news concerning us**, i. e. that we were coming. **Ἀππίου Φόρου κ. Τ. Ταβερνῶν**] Luke writes as one of the travellers *to* Rome, who would come on Appii Forum (forty-three miles from Rome) first. It was on the Via Appia (" Censura clara eo anno (U.C. 442) Appii Claudii, et C. Plautii fuit : memoriæ tamen felicioris ad posteros nomen Appii, quod viam munivit et aquam in urbem duxit, eaque unus perfecit." Liv. ix. 29), which leaving Rome by the Porta Capena, passed through the Pontine marshes, as far as Capua. Being not far from the coast (Strabo, v. 233), it was the resort of sailors (' Forum Appî differtum nautis, cauponibus atque malignis.' Hor. Sat. i. 5. 3. It has been suggested to me, that these may have been sailors belonging to the canal boats, as Appii Forum is too far inland to have been resorted to by sailors from the coast), and an unpleasant halting-place for travellers, having, besides, 'aqua deterrima' (ib. ver. 7). The 'Tres Tabernæ' was a 'taberna deversoria,' or way-side inn, ten miles nearer Rome. Cicero mentions both in the letters to Atticus, ii. 10, 'Ab Appii Foro hora quarta : dederam aliam paullo ante Tribus Tabernis.' The brethren were in two parties : some had come the longer, others the shorter distance, to meet the Apostle. We have in Jos. Antt. xvii. 12. 1, an account of the pretended Alexander, on his way to Rome, landing at Dicæarchia (Puteoli, see above), and it is added, προσελθόντος εἰς τὴν Ῥώμην λόγου τοῦ περὶ αὐτοῦ, πᾶν τὸ τῇδε Ἰουδαίων πλῆθος ὑπαντιάζοντες ἐξῄεσαν. Suet. relates, on Caligula's return from Germany, "populi R. sexum, ætatem, ordinem omnem usque ad vicesimum lapidem effudisse se." Cal. c. 4. And Tacit. Ann. iii. 5, speaking of the honours paid by Augustus to the body of Drusus, says, "ipsum quippe asperrimo hiemis Ticinum usque progressum, neque abscedentem a corpore simul urbem intravisse." **θάρσος**] Both encouragement as to his *own arrival*, as a prisoner, in the vast metropolis,—in seeing such affection, to which he was of all men most sensible ; and encouragement as to his *great work* so long contemplated, and now about to commence in Rome,—in seeing so promising a beginning for him to build on.

16.] [The omission of the words ὁ ἑκατ. . . . . to στρατοπεδάρχῳ(-χῃ) [though too strongly attested to allow us to retain them in the text] may have been originally caused by the transcriber's eye passing from -αρχος to -αρχω, as in Syr. ('permisit centurio Paulo') : this done, the emendation of the text so as to construe by ejecting ὁ ἑκατόνταρχος was obvious. It does not follow, *from the singular being used*, that there was *but one* præfectus prætorio at this time, and *that one* Burrus ;—though it may have been so. *The prefect* mentioned

Παύλῳ μένειν [i] καθ' ἑαυτὸν σὺν τῷ [k] φυλάσσοντι
αὐτὸν στρατιώτῃ. 17 [l] ἐγένετο δὲ μετὰ ἡμέρας τρεῖς
[m] συγκαλέσασθαι αὐτὸν τοὺς ὄντας τῶν Ἰουδαίων [n] πρώ-
τους· [o] συνελθόντων δὲ αὐτῶν ἔλεγεν πρὸς αὐτοὺς Ἐγώ,
ἄνδρες ἀδελφοί, οὐδὲν [p] ἐναντίον ποιήσας τῷ λαῷ ἢ τοῖς
[q] ἔθεσιν τοῖς [r] πατρῴοις, [s] δέσμιος ἐξ Ἱεροσολύμων [t] παρ-
εδόθην εἰς τὰς χεῖρας τῶν Ῥωμαίων, 18 οἵτινες [u] ἀνακρί-
ναντές με ἐβούλοντο [v] ἀπολῦσαι διὰ τὸ μηδεμίαν [w] αἰτίαν
[w] θανάτου [x] ὑπάρχειν ἐν ἐμοί. 19 [y] ἀντιλεγόντων δὲ τῶν
Ἰουδαίων [z] ἠναγκάσθην [a] ἐπικαλέσασθαι Καίσαρα, οὐχ
[b] ὡς τοῦ ἔθνους μου [c] ἔχων τι [d] κατηγορεῖν. 20 διὰ ταύτην

...ιεροσολυμων I. ABLPℵ abcdf ghkl mop 13

i James ii. 17 only. Gen. xliii. 32. see Rom. xiv. 22. k = ch. xii. 4 reff. l constr., ch. iv. 5 reff. m mid., ch. x. 24 reff. n ch. xiii. 50 reff. o = ch. i. 6 reff. p = ch. xxvi. 9 reff. q ch. vi. 14 reff. r ch. xxii. 3 reff. s ch. xvi. 25, 27 reff. t ch. xxi. 11. Matt. xvii. 22 al. Job xvi. 12. u ch. iv. 9 reff. v = ch. xxvi. 32 reff. w ch. xiii. 28 reff. x ch. viii. 16 reff. y Luke xx. 27. ch. xiii. 45. Rom. x. 21. L.P., exc. John xix. 12. Hos. iv. 4. z = ch. xxvi. 11. Gal. ii. 3, 14. 1 Macc. ii. 25. a ch. xxv. 11 reff. b = ch. xxiii. 15 reff. c constr., ch. xxi. 13. xxiii. 17, 18. Luke vii. 40. xii. 50. Winer, § 44. 3. d ch. xxiv. 2 reff.

[txt and comm]. (13 def, but has not space enough for the addition.) for εαυτ., αυτον B. add εξω της παρεμβολης 137 demid syr-w-ast.

17. rec for αυτον, τον παυλον, with H[r]LP rel Syr æth[-pl(Tischdf) Chr$_1$]: txt ABIℵ k p 13. 36. 40. 137 vulg syr copt [æth(Treg) arm]. δε aft συνελθ. is written twice by ℵ[1]. rec ανδρες αδελφοι bef εγω, with H[r]LP rel 36 Syr Chr$_1$ [Thl-sif]: txt ABI(ℵ) c p 13. 40. 137 vulg syr copt arm Thl-fin.—for εγω, λεγων ℵ[1] (but corrd).

18. ins πολλα bef ανακριναντες c 137 syr-w-ast. ανακρινοντες ℵ[1]. add με ℵ[1](ℵ[3] disapproving).

19. aft ιουδαιων ins και επικραζοντων αιρε τον εχθρον ημων c 137 syr-w-ast. aft μου ins ου (but marked and erased) ℵ[1]. rec κατηγορησαι, with H[r]LP rel 36 Chr$_1$: txt ABℵ p 13. 40. add αλλ ινα λυτρωσωμαι την ψυχην μου εκ θανατου c 137 syr-w-ast.

might be *one of the two* who preceded Burrus, or one of the two who followed him—so that no chronological datum is here contained (against Wieseler, who builds upon it: Chron. der Apostg. p. 86). He attempts to meet the above argument by accounting it improbable that the prisoners would be *consigned to either* of the prefects; this may have been so,—but they certainly would be delivered to *one, not to both;* and the fact might well be thus related. Luke is not so precise in Roman civil and military matters, as that he necessarily should in this case have written ἑνὶ τῶν στρατοπεδάρχων. The '*præfectus prætorio*' was the person officially put in charge with the prisoners sent from the provinces: so Plin. Epp. x. 65, "Vinctus mitti ad præfectos prætorii mei debet." The prætorian camp was outside the Porta Viminalis, where it had been fixed and fortified by Sejanus: see Tacit. Ann. iv. 2. [It was incorporated in Aurelian's walls, and now forms a square projection from their line.]] **ἐπετράπη τῷ Π.**] This permission probably resulted from the letters of Festus, expressing that no crime was laid to the charge of Paul; perhaps also partly from the favour of Julius, and his report of the character and bearing of Paul on the journey. **στρατιώτῃ**] a Prætorian, to whom he was chained; see below, ver. 20; and note on ch. xxiv. 23. **17.**] The banishment of Jews from Rome (ch. xviii. 2) had either tacitly or openly been abrogated some time before this. Priscilla and Aquila had returned when the Epistle to the Romans was written, Rom. xvi. 3. Paul was naturally anxious to set himself right with the Jews at Rome—to explain the cause of his being sent there, in case no message had been received by them concerning him from Judæa,—and to do away if possible with the unfavourable prejudice which such letters, if received, would have created respecting his character. The fact of his sending for them, and their coming to him, seems to shew (as in the gloss on ver. 16: see digest) that he was not imprisoned in the Prætorian camp, but was already in a private lodging. **18. ἐβούλ. ἀπολῦσαι**] This may have been at ch. xxv. 8. The possibility of such a release is asserted by Agrippa, ch. xxvi. 32. **19.**] 'My appeal was a defensive and necessary step—not an offensive one, to complain of my nation.' The inf.

οὖν τὴν αἰτίαν [e]παρεκάλεσα ὑμᾶς [f]ἰδεῖν καὶ [g]προςλαλῆσαι· ABLP‭א‬ abcdf ghkl mop 13
ἕνεκεν γὰρ τῆς [h]ἐλπίδος τοῦ Ἰσραὴλ τὴν [i]ἅλυσιν ταύτην
[k]περίκειμαι. 21 οἱ δὲ πρὸς αὐτὸν εἶπαν Ἡμεῖς οὔτε
[l]γράμματα περὶ σοῦ ἐδεξάμεθα ἀπὸ τῆς Ἰουδαίας, οὔτε
[m]παραγενόμενός τις τῶν [n]ἀδελφῶν ἀπήγγειλεν ἢ ἐλά-
λησέν τι περὶ σοῦ πονηρόν. 22 [o]ἀξιοῦμεν δὲ παρὰ σοῦ
ἀκοῦσαι ἃ [p]φρονεῖς· περὶ μὲν γὰρ τῆς [q]αἱρέσεως ταύτης [r]γνωστὸν ἡμῖν ἐστιν ὅτι [s]πανταχοῦ [t]ἀντιλέγεται.

e = here only. Xen. Cyr. i. 5. 7, ὑμᾶς παρεκάλεσα. f = ch. xvi. 40. Luke viii. 20 al. 4 Kings viii. 29. g ch. xiii. 43 only. Exod. iv. 16 AB2 Ald. Wisd. xiii. 17 only. h constr. w. gen. of pers., 2 Cor. i. 6. Phil. i. 20. Ps. lxiv. 6. i ch. xii. 6 reff. k Luke xvii. 2 || Mk. Heb. v. 2. xii. 1 only †. 4 Macc. xii. 3. l = here only. (Luke xvi. 6, 7. Gal. vi. 11.) 1 Macc. v. 10. m absol., ch. xvii. 10 reff. n = ch. xxii. 5. Deut. xv. 3. o = ch. xv. 38 (reff.) only. p = Rom. xii. 3 al. 2 Macc. xiv. 26. q ch. v. 17 reff. r = ch. xiii. 38 reff. s ch. xvii. 30 reff. t ver. 19.

20. παρεκαλεσαν (but ν erased) ‭א‬[1]. for προςλ., λαλησαι H[r]. εινεκεν A, so ‭א‬, but ι erased.

21. The greater part of this ver is def in P, and smaller portions of vv 22 and 23. (ειπαν, so ABH[r]‭א‬ p.) εδεξαμεθα bef περι σου A P[appy] 13 vulg æth-pl Thl-fin: txt BH[r]L‭א‬ p rel 36 syrr Chr_1 [$Euthal_1$] Thl-sif.—for περι, κατα ‭א‬.

22. ακουσαι bef παρα σου L‭א‬ b d o 40: om ακουσαι 13.—for παρα, περι H[r]. rec εστιν bef ημιν, with H[r]LP rel vulg spec Chr_1 Thl-sif: txt AB‭א‬ k m p 13. 40 [Ps-Ath_1] Thl-fin.—υμιν p.

aor. of the rec. would point to *some one definite charge:* **κατηγορεῖν** means 'to play the accuser against my nation in any thing:' indicating the habit. **20.**] **παρεκάλεσα** is here in its primary meaning, **I have called you to me.** **διὰ ταύτ. τ. αἰτ.,** for the reason just stated: because I have no hostile feeling to my nation. Then ἕνεκεν γὰρ . . . adds another motive; for not only so, but I may well wish to see and speak with you, being a prisoner *for the hope of Israel* (see ch. xxvi. 6, and notes). **21.**] It may seem strange that they had received no tidings concerning him. But, as Meyer well remarks, (1) *before* his appeal, the Jews in Judæa had no definite reason to communicate with the Jews in Rome respecting him, having no expectation that Paul, then a prisoner in Judæa, and the object of their conspiracies there, would ever go to Rome, or come into connexion with their brethren there. And (2) *since* his appeal, it would have been hardly possible for them to have sent messengers who should have arrived before him. For his voyage followed *soon after his appeal* (ch. xxv. 13; xxvii. 1), and was *so late in the year,* that for the former reason it is as unlikely that any deputation from them should have left *before* him, as for the latter, *after* him. Had any left within a few days, the same storm would have in all probability detained them over the winter, and they could not certainly have made a much quicker voyage than Paul's ship to Puteoli. Still, as casual, non-official tidings might have reached them, Paul shewed this anxiety. It appears, however, that *none had come.* Olshausen's view, that the banishment of the Jews from Rome under Claudius had interrupted the relations between the Roman and Judæan Jews, is hardly probable: see on ver. 17. **22.**] The δέ and μέν are inverted: "μέν si dicitur non sequente δέ, aut intelligi potest δέ, aut omittitur illa pars orationis in qua sequi debebat δέ, quæ aliquando præcedit." Herm. ad Viger., p. 839. It precedes, because it connects with the foregoing. **ἀξ. παρὰ σοῦ, we beg of thee:** see reff. **τῆς αἱρ. ταύτ.**] To which they perhaps inferred that Paul belonged, from ver. 20: or they might have heard thus much generally respecting him by rumour, though they had received no special message. Their short notice of Christianity is perhaps the result of caution, seeing as they did the favour shewn by the authorities towards Paul (see Hackett, p. 392): or perhaps of dissimulation. Many Commentators have noticed the omission of all mention of the *Christian Church at Rome,* and of Paul's connexion with or work among them. And some recently in Germany (e. g. Bauer) have called in question the credibility of the Acts on this account. But without any reason: for the work of the Apostle among *churches already founded* is not the subject of our history, and is seldom related by Luke, without a special reason. Of the three years at Ephesus (ch. xx. 31),—the year and a half (ch. xviii. 11), and three months (ch. xx. 3) at Corinth, we know from the narrative nothing that took place among the Christians themselves. Besides, one great object of this history is to shew forth Paul as

23 ᵘ ταξάμενοι δὲ αὐτῷ ἡμέραν * ἦλθον πρὸς αὐτὸν εἰς τὴν
ᵛ ξενίαν ʷ πλείονες, οἷς ˣ ἐξετίθετο ʸ διαμαρτυρόμενος τὴν
ᶻ βασιλείαν τοῦ ᶻ θεοῦ, ᵃ πείθων τε αὐτοὺς περὶ τοῦ Ἰησοῦ
ᵇ ἀπό τε τοῦ ᶜ νόμου Μωυσέως καὶ τῶν ᶜ προφητῶν, ᵈ ἀπὸ
ᵈᵉ πρωῒ ᵈ ἕως ᵈᶠ ἑσπέρας. 24 καὶ οἱ μὲν ᵍ ἐπείθοντο τοῖς λεγομένοις, οἱ δὲ ʰ ἠπίστουν. 25 ⁱ ἀσύμφωνοι δὲ ὄντες πρὸς
ἀλλήλους ᵏ ἀπελύοντο εἰπόντος τοῦ Παύλου ˡ ῥῆμα ˡ ἕν,
ὅτι ᵐ καλῶς τὸ πνεῦμα τὸ ἅγιον ⁿ ἐλάλησεν διὰ Ἡσαΐου
τοῦ προφήτου πρὸς τοὺς ᵒ πατέρας ᵒ ὑμῶν 26 ᵖ λέγων ᵍ Πορεύθητι πρὸς τὸν λαὸν τοῦτον καὶ εἰπὸν Ἀκοῇ ἀκούσετε καὶ
οὐ μὴ συνῆτε· καὶ βλέποντες βλέψετε καὶ οὐ μὴ ἴδητε.
27 ʳ ἐπαχύνθη γὰρ ἡ καρδία τοῦ λαοῦ τούτου, καὶ τοῖς
ὠσὶν ˢ βαρέως ἤκουσαν, καὶ τοὺς ὀφθαλμοὺς αὐτῶν
ᵗ ἐκάμμυσαν· μήποτε ἴδωσιν τοῖς ὀφθαλμοῖς καὶ τοῖς ὠσὶν
ἀκούσωσιν καὶ τῇ καρδίᾳ συνῶσιν καὶ ᵘ ἐπιστρέψωσιν καὶ
ἰάσομαι αὐτούς. 28 ᵛ γνωστὸν οὖν ὑμῖν ἔστω ὅτι τοῖς

E πορευθητι... ABELP ℵ a b c d f g h k l m o p 13

u = ch. xv. 2. Matt. xxviii. 6. constr., here only. Job xiv. 13. τοὺς φόρους τοῖς Ἕλλησι τάξας, Ælian, Var. Hist. xi. 9.
v Philem. 22 only †. Ælian, Var. Hist. iii. 37.
w ch. ii. 40 reff.
x ch. xi. 4 reff.
y ch. viii. 25 reff. constr., ch. xxiii. 11 reff.
z ch. xix. 8 reff.
a w. περί, here only.
b = ch. xvii. 2.
c ch. xiii. 15 reff.
d 3 Kings xxii. 35.
e Matt. [xvi. 3] xx. 1 al. Gen. xxxii. 24.
f Luke xxiv. 29. ch. iv. 3 only. Lev. xi. 24.
g = Luke xvi. 31. ch. xvii. 4.
h Mark xvi. 11, 16. Luke xxiv. 11, 41. Rom. iii. 3. 2 Tim. ii. 13 only †. Wisd. x. 7 al.
i here only †. Wisd. xviii. 10 only. ἀσ. πρ. ἀλλήλους, Diod. Sic. iv. 1.
k = ch. xiii. 3 reff.
l Matt. xxvii. 14. see Matt. xxi. 24.
m — Matt. xv. 7 al. Jer. i. 12.
n ch. iii. 21 reff.
o ch. iii. 25 reff.
p constr., Rev. iv. 7, 8 al. see ch. xxi. 23.
q Isa. vi. 9, 10.
r = Matt. xiii. 15 (from l. c.) only. Deut. xxxii. 15.
s Matt. xiii. 15 (from l. c.) only. Gen. xxxi. 35. 2 Macc. xi. 1. xiv. 27 only.
t Matt. xiii. 15 only. Isa. l. c. xxix. 10. Lam. iii. 44 only.
u = ch. iii. 19 reff.
v ch. xiii. 38 reff.

23. *rec ἧκον, with H^r LP rel Chr₁ : ηλθον A(-θαν) Bℵ k p 13. 36. 40. διαμαρτυρουμενος p 36 Thl-fin : διαμαρτυραμενοι ℵ¹ : -ραμενος ℵ³ : παρατειθεμενος A.[—add αυτοις L.] om 1st τε ℵ¹ : και πειθων d. rec ins τα bef περι (*as rec in ch* viii. 12, *and txt in ch* xix. 8), with L rel Chr₁ : om ABH^r ℵ a c p 13. 36. 40. 137 vulg spec [syrr copt æth(Treg) arm].
24. aft μεν ins ουν ℵ¹.
25. for 1st δε, τε ℵ¹ [36. 40 vulg Syr]. for δια, περι ℵ¹. π. τ. πατερας υμων bef δια ησ. τ. προφ. A.—rec ημων (*most prob altered to conform it to Paul's being a Jew, and to the tone of his other speeches: not as Meyer and Bornemann, altered to* υμ. *to distinguish him from the Jews, or because the speech was solely addressed to Jews. The* υμ. *here has an important and characteristic meaning*), with H^r LP rel 36 vulg spec copt [æth-pl arm] Chr₁ Ambr₁ : om syr : txt ABℵ k p 13. 40 Syr Ath[-int₁] Cyr-jer₁ Bas₂ Did₃ [Amm-c₁] Quæst₁.
26. rec λεγον, with AH^r rel 36 [Bas₁] Chr₁ : txt BLPℵ f 13 [Euthal₁] Thl. rec ειπε (*commoner form*), with c [Did₂] Thl : txt ABEH^r LPℵ p 13 rel [Bas₁] Chr₁. ακουσητε and βλεψητε AE [m] (p) 13 Thl-sif : -σετε and -ψητε H^r ℵ³ : txt BLPℵ¹ rel 36 [Bas₁] Chr Thl-fin.[—om κ. βλεπ. βλεψ. p.] συνειτε L p Thl-fin : συνιετε 13.
27. εβαρυνθη ℵ¹. aft 1st ωσιν ins αυτων Aℵ b d o 13 tol (Syr) æth-pl arm [Sev-c₁] Thl-fin Jer₂(om₂). om και τη καρδια συνωσιν ℵ¹. επιστρεψουσιν [so LXX-ℵ] AE p Thl[-sif]. rec ιασωμαι (*so in Matt* xiii. 15), with E p 13 Chr₁ : txt [so LXX] ABH^r LPℵ g¹ l 137 Sev Thl.
28. rec εστω bef υμιν, with AEH^r LPℵ rel : txt B m p.

working out the Lord's implied command (ch. i. 8), to preach the Gospel 'to the Jew first, and also to the Gentile,' and, having every where done this, it is but natural that he should open his commission in Rome by assembling and speaking to the *Jews*.

23. **τ. ξενίαν**] Probably the μίσθωμα of ver. 30: hardly, as Olsh., the house of Aquila. **πείθων**] **persuading**: not '*teaching*,' as Kuin., nor '*trying to persuade*.' Meyer well remarks,—Paul, on his part, subjectively, performed that indicated by πείθειν; that this did not produce its objective effect in all his hearers, does not alter the meaning of the word. 25. **εἰπόντος**] **they departed, but not before Paul had said one saying.** It is very remarkable, that the same prophetic quotation with which our Lord opened his teaching by parables [Matt. xiii. 14, 15], should form the solemn close of the historic Scriptures. **26.**] the πορεύθ. κ. εἰπόν

w see ch. xiii. 26.
x = Luke ii. 30. iii. 6. Eph. vi. 17 only. Ps. xcvii. 2. Isa. lx. 6.
y fut. mid., John v. 25, 28. otherwise, Acts (ch. iii. 22, 23. xvii. 32) only. Num. ix. 8.
z ch. xv. 7 (reff.) only †.
a ch. xiv. 22 reff.
b ch. xxiv. 27 only. (-τής, Matt. ii. 16. 2 Macc. x. 3.) see ch. xx. 31.

ἔθνεσιν [w] ἀπεστάλη τοῦτο τὸ [wx] σωτήριον τοῦ θεοῦ· αὐτοὶ ABELP
καὶ [y] ἀκούσονται *. ℵ a b c d f g h k l m o p 13
30 [a] Ἐνέμεινεν δὲ [b] διετίαν ὅλην ἐν ἰδίῳ [c] μισθώματι, καὶ
[d] ἀπεδέχετο πάντας τοὺς [e] εἰσπορευομένους πρὸς αὐτόν,
31 [f] κηρύσσων τὴν [fg] βασιλείαν τοῦ [g] θεοῦ καὶ διδάσκων [h] τὰ
περὶ τοῦ κυρίου Ἰησοῦ χριστοῦ [i] μετὰ πάσης [i] παῤῥησίας
[k] ἀκωλύτως.

ΠΡΑΞΕΙΣ ΑΠΟΣΤΟΛΩΝ.

c here only ‡. (Deut. xxiii. 18.) (-οῦσθαι, Matt. xx. 1, 7.) d ch. ii. 41 reff. e w. πρός, here only. Esth. ii. 14. f ch. xx. 25 (reff.). g ch. xix. 8 reff. h ch. xxiii. 11. Sir. xix. 30. i ch. ii. 29 reff. k here only †. Job xxxiv. 31 Symm. (-τος, Wisd. vii. 22.)

rec om τουτο (*as unnecessary ?*), with E[-gr] H^{r}LPℵ^3 tol æth[(Treg) copt(Treg) arm Euthal$_1$] Thl : ins ABℵ^1 c p 13. 36. 40 vulg E-lat syrr [æth-pl(Tischdf)] Chr$_1$.

[29. *rec ins καὶ ταῦτα αὐτοῦ εἰπόντος ἀπῆλθον οἱ Ἰουδαῖοι, πολλὴν ἔχοντες ἐν ἑαυτοῖς [z] συζήτησιν, with H^{r}LP rel 36 syr-w-ast æth[-rom(Treg) arm-usc] Chr$_1$ Thl : om ABEℵ c p 13. 40 am(with demid fuld &c) spec[from the space] Syr copt [æth-pl arm-zoh]. (*In the paucity of uncial* MSS, *and seeing that there are no considerable varr in the omitted passage, I have treated it as doubtful. It is perhaps one of those many additions which* D *alone of the first class* MSS *would have contained, had it been preserved to us, and was inserted on acct of the abrupt transition from ver* 28 *to ver* 30 : *but see notes.*)]

30. rec (for ενεμ.) εμεινεν, with AEH^{r}LPℵ^3 rel 36 Chr$_1$: επεμεινεν c 137-56 : txt B(ℵ^1) p 13.—ενεμιναν(sic) ℵ^1. rec aft δε ins ο παυλος, with H^{r}LP rel 36 tol Syr syr-w-ast æth Chr : om ABEℵ c p 13. 40 vulg copt arm. aft αυτον ins ιουδαιους 137 : ιουδαιους τε και ελληνας c tol syr-w-ast.

31. aft διδασκων, add *quoniam hic est Christus filius Dei, per quem omnis mundus judicabitur* tol : aft ακωλυτως, λεγων οτι ουτος εστιν χριστος ιησους ο υιος του θεου δι' ου κοσμος ολος μελλει κρινεσθαι syr demid. om ιησου ℵ^1. at end add αμην c 15-8. 36. 40-3. 96 am fuld harl syr Chr-ms.

SUBSCRIPTION. πραξεις των αγιων αποστολων AEH^{r}L : om d g l m [k 13] : επληρωθησαν αι πρ. τ. αγ. απ. P : τελος των πραξιων b o : τελ. συν θεω των πρ. τ. απ. 137 : τελος τ. πραξ. τ. αγιων αποστ. f : πραξεις των αποστολων p : txt Bℵ.

is referred to *himself*, in his application of the prophecy. These words are not cited by our Lord (Matt. xiii. 14). **28.**] **τοῦτο** was probably omitted as superfluous, and perhaps to suit Luke iii. 6. It adds greatly to the force : **this, the message of God's salvation,** q. d. '*there is no other for those who reject this.*' **αὐτοὶ καὶ ἀκ.**] **They will also** (besides having it sent to them) **hear it.** "Quod expertus erat Paulus in multis Asiæ et Europæ urbibus, ut apud gentes sermonis felicior esset seges, idem et nunc futurum prospiciebat." Grot. [**29.**] This verse has not the usual characteristic of spurious passages,—the variety of readings in those manuscripts which contain it. It *may* perhaps, after all, have been omitted as appearing superfluous after ver. 25.] **30, 31.**] It is evident that Paul was not *released from custody*, but continued with the soldier who kept him,—(1) from the expressions here ; *he received all who came in to him*, but we do not hear of his preaching in the synagogue or elsewhere : he preached and taught *with all boldness* and *unhindered*, both being mentioned as remarkable circumstances, and implying that there were reasons why this could hardly have been expected : and (2) from his constantly speaking of himself in the Epistles written during this period, as a *prisoner*, see Eph. vi. 19, 20 ; Col. iv. 3, 4 ; Philem. 9 ; Philipp. passim. On the whole question regarding the chronology of his imprisonment,—and the reason of this abrupt ending of the history, see Prolegg. to Acts, § iv. 4—7 :—and on its probable termination and the close of St. Paul's life, see the Prolegg. to the Pastoral Epistles, § ii. 17 ff.

ΠΡΟΣ ΡΩΜΑΙΟΥΣ.

I. 1 Παῦλος [a] δοῦλος Ἰησοῦ χριστοῦ, [b] κλητὸς ἀπό-

a Phil. i. 1. James i. 1. 2 Pet. i. 1.
b = vv. 6, 7. 1 Cor. i. [1] 2, 24. Jude 1 al. 2 Kings xv. 11.

...απο-στολος G. ABCEK L[P]א a b c d f g h k l m n o 17 [47]

TITLE.—rec παυλου του αποστολου η προς ρωμαιους επιστολη : επ. παυ. πρ. ρω. l: του αγιου και πανευφημου αποστ. παυ. επ. προς ρω. L 14. 44. 80 : παυλου [απ.] επ. πρ. ρω. m: πρ. ρω. παυ. επ. k: παυ. επ. πρ. ρω. 17 : [επ. τ. παναγιου π. τ. απ. πρ. ρωμ. P: πρ. ρ. επ. h:] txt ABCא n o [47] and D[F] at head of pages. (προς ρ(. .)α(.)υς is legible in C.)

CHAP. I. 1. χριστου bef ιησου B(sic : see table) am(with fuld tol &c) [arm] $Orig_2$ Aug_1 $Ambr_1$ $Ambrst_1$ [$Cassiod_1$] Bede.

CHAP. I. 1—7.] ADDRESS OF THE EPISTLE, WITH AN ANNOUNCEMENT OF PAUL'S CALLING, TO BE AN APOSTLE OF THE GOSPEL OF THE SON OF GOD. "Epistola tota sic methodica est, ut ipsum quoque exordium ad rationem artis compositum sit. Artificium quum in multis apparet, quæ suis locis observabantur, tum in eo maxime, quod inde argumentum principale deducitur. Nam Apostolatus sui approbationem exorsus, ex ea in Evangelii commendationem incidit: quæ quum necessario secum trahat disputationem de fide, ad eam, quasi verborum contextu manu ducente, delabitur. Atque ita ingreditur principalem totius Epistolæ quæstionem, fide nos justificari: in qua tractanda versatur usque ad finem quinti capitis." Calvin. Paul in the addresses of his Epistles never uses the common Greek formula χαίρειν (James i. 1), but always a *prayer for blessing* on those to whom he is writing. In all his Epistles (as in both those of Peter, and in the Apocalypse) this prayer is for χάρις and εἰρήνη, except in 1 and 2 Tim., where it is for χάρις, ἔλεος, and εἰρήνη, as in 2 John. In Jude only we find ἔλεος, εἰρήνη, and ἀγάπη. The address here differs from those of most of Paul's Epistles, in having *dogmatic clauses* parenthetically inserted:—such are found also in the Epistle to Titus, and (in much less degree) in that to the Galatians. These dogmatic clauses regard, 1. the *fore-announcement of the Gospel through the prophets*: 2. the *description and dignity of Him* who was the subject of that Gospel: 3. the *nature and aim of the apostolic office* to which Paul had been called,—including the *persons addressed* in the objects of its ministration. **1. δοῦλος Ἰ. χ.**] so also Phil. i. 1, and Tit. i. 1 (δοῦλος θεοῦ, ἀπόστ. δὲ χ. Ἰ.),—but usually ἀπ. χ. Ἰ. (2 Cor. Eph. Col. 1 Tim. 2 Tim.): [κλητὸς] ἀπ. χ. Ἰ. (1 Cor.),—simply ἀπόστολος (Gal.),—δέσμιος χ. Ἰ. (Philem.), but in almost all these places the reading varies between χριστοῦ Ἰησοῦ and Ἰησοῦ χριστοῦ. The expression answers to the Hebr. עֶבֶד יְהוָה, the especial O. T. title of Israel, and of individuals, as Moses, Joshua, David, Daniel, Job, and others, who as prophets, kings, &c., were raised up for the express work of God. See Umbreit's note, Der Brief an die Römer auf dem Grunde des alten Testaments ausgelegt, p. 153 f. It must not be rendered *slave* with Schrader, nor *pius cultor* with Fritzsche: because, as Mehring remarks, the former excludes the element of freewill, while the latter does not express the entire dedication to Christ.

κλητὸς ἀπόστ.] In naming himself *a servant of Jesus Christ*, he bespeaks their attention as *a Christian speaking to Christians*: he now further specifies the *place which he held by the special calling of God*: **called**, and that to the very highest office, of **an apostle**; and even more—among the Apostles, not one by original selection, but one *specially called*. "Ceteri

στολος, [c] ἀφωρισμένος εἰς [d] εὐαγγέλιον [d] θεοῦ, 2 ὃ [e] προ-
επηγγείλατο διὰ τῶν προφητῶν αὐτοῦ ἐν [fg] γραφαῖς
[g] ἁγίαις 3 περὶ τοῦ υἱοῦ αὐτοῦ, τοῦ [h] γενομένου ἐκ [i] σπέρ- C του γενομ...
ματος [i] Δαυεὶδ [k] κατὰ [k] σάρκα, 4 τοῦ [l] ὁρισθέντος υἱοῦ θεοῦ ABCEK L[P]ℵ a b c d f g h k l m n o 17 [47]

c Acts xiii. 2. Gal. i. 15. Lev. xx. 26.
d ch. xv. 16 reff.
e 2 Cor. ix. 5 only +.
f plur., Acts xvii. 2 reff.
g here only. see ch. xvi. 26. 2 Tim. iii. 16.
h = Gal. iv. 4. Phil. ii. 7. Acts xix. 26.
i Luke i. 55. John vii. 42. (Acts xiii. 23.) 2 Tim. ii. 8. Jer. xxii. 30.
k = ch. iv. 1. ix. 3, 5. 1 Cor. x. 18. Gal. iv. 23, 29 al. Paul only. see John viii. 15. 2 Cor. xi. 18.
l Acts xvii. 26 reff.

quidem apostoli per diutinam cum Jesu consuetudinem educati fuerunt, et primo ad sequelam et disciplinam vocati, deinde ad apostolatum producti. Paulus, persecutor antehac, de subito apostolus per vocationem factus est. Ita Judæi erant sancti ex promissione: Græci, sancti ex mera vocatione, ver. 6. Præcipuam ergo *vocatus apostolus* cum *vocatis sanctis* similitudinem et conjunctionem habebat." Bengel. **ἀπόστολος** must not be taken here in the wider sense, of a *missionary*, as in ch. xvi. 7, but in its higher and peculiar meaning, in which the Twelve bore the title (οὓς καὶ ἀποστόλους ὠνόμασεν, Luke vi. 13), and Paul (and perhaps Barnabas), and James the Lord's brother. This title was not conferred on Paul by the ἀφορίσατε δή μοι of the Holy Spirit, Acts xiii. 2, but *in virtue of his special call by the Lord in person*; compare σκεῦος ἐκλογῆς, Acts ix. 15, with ἐξελεξάμην, John vi. 70; xiii. 18; xv. 16; Acts i. 2. "Neque enim iis assentior, qui eam de qua loquitur vocationem ad æternam Dei electionem referant." Calvin. **ἀφωρισμένος**] not in Acts xiii. 2, merely, though that was a particular application of the general truth:—but (as in Gal. i. 15, ὁ ἀφορίσας με ἐκ κοιλίας μητρός μου) *from his birth*. "Idem *Pharisæi* etymon fuerat: hoc autem loco Paulus se non solum ex hominibus, ex Judæis, ex discipulis, sed etiam ex doctoribus segregatum a Deo significat." Bengel. **εἰς**] **for the purpose of announcing.** **εὐαγγέλιον θεοῦ** = τὸ εὐαγ. τοῦ θ., which (see reff.) is the usual form. Bp. Middleton (on ver. 17) remarks on the *anarthrousness* of Paul's style, and cites from Dion. Hal. de Comp. Verb. c. 22, as a character of the αὐστηρὰ ἁρμονία, that it is ὀλιγοσύνδεσμος, **ἄναρθρος**. See the passage cited at length in the Prolegomena, § v. 2, —**the good tidings sent by** (not concerning) **God**. The genitive is not, as in τὸ εὐαγγέλιον τῆς βασιλείας, Matt. iv. 23, one of apposition, but of *possession* or origin; **God's Gospel**. And so, whenever the expression '*the Gospel of Christ*' occurs, it is not 'the Gospel *about* Christ,' but *Christ's Gospel*; that Gospel which flows out of His grace, and is His gift to men. Thus in the very beginning of the Epistle, these two short words announce that the Gospel is *of God*,—in other words, that *salvation is of grace only*.

2.] This *good tidings* is no new invention, no after-thought,—but was *long ago announced* in what God's prophets wrote concerning His Son:—and announced by way of *promise*, so that God stood pledged to its realization. ἐπειδὴ δὲ καὶ καινοτομίαν ἐνεκάλουν τῷ πράγματι, δείκνυσιν αὐτὸ πρεσβύτερον Ἑλλήνων ὄν, καὶ ἐν τοῖς προφήταις προδιαγραφόμενον. Chrys. Hom. ii. p. 431. **γραφ. ἁγ.**] not, '*in sacred writings*,'—nor '*in passages of Holy Writ*:'—but **in the Holy Scriptures.** The expression used is defined enough by the adjective, to be well understood without the article;—so πνεῦμα ἁγιωσ. below,—πν. ἅγιον passim. See Winer, edn. 6, § 19. 2 (and for nouns in government, Middleton, ch. iii. § 6). *But one* set of writings being holy, it was not necessary to designate them more particularly. See also above on εὐαγγ. θεοῦ. This expression (**εὐαγγ. ὃ προεπηγγ.**) is used in the strictest sense. Moses gave the *Law*: the prophets proclaimed the *Gospel*. See Umbreit's note, p. 159.

3. περὶ τοῦ υἱοῦ αὐτοῦ] belongs to **ὃ** προεπ. above,—**which he promised beforehand, &c., concerning His Son,** i. e. 'which (good tidings) He promised beforehand, &c., *and indicated that it should be* concerning His Son.' This is more natural than to bind these words to εὐαγγ. θεοῦ which went before. Either meaning will suit ver. 9 equally well. Christ, the Son of God, is the *great subject* of the good news. **γενομένου**] not ὄντος, see John i. 1—3, and notes [nor as in E. V. '*was made*.' There is nothing in the word indicating *creation*, however true that may have been: see John i. 14]. **κατὰ σάρκα**] On the side of His humanity, our Lord ἐγένετο; *that* nature of His begins only then, when He was γενόμενος ἐκ γυναικός, Gal. iv. 4. **σάρξ** is here used exactly as in John i. 14, ὁ λόγος σὰρξ ἐγένετο, to signify *that whole nature, body and soul*, of which the outward visible tabernacle of the FLESH is the concrete representation to our senses.

The words **ἐκ σπέρματος Δαυείδ** cast a hint back at the *promise* just spoken of. At the same time, in so solemn an enuncia-

[m] ἐν [m] δυνάμει [n] κατὰ [no] πνεῦμα [op] ἁγιωσύνης [q] ἐξ [r] ἀναστάσεως
[r] νεκρῶν, Ἰησοῦ χριστοῦ τοῦ κυρίου ἡμῶν, 5 δι᾽ οὗ ἐλά-

m Mark ix. 1. ch. xv. 13, 19. 1 Cor. iv. 20. xv. 43. Col. i. 29 al. n Gal. iv. 29. o here only. see John xiv. 17. 2 Tim. i. 7. 1 John iv. 6. p 2 Cor. vii. 1. 1 Thess. iii. 13 only. Ps. xcv. 6. xcvi. 12. cxliv. 5. 2 Macc. iii. 12 only. q = James ii. 18 (bis). Rev. viii. 11 al. r 1 Cor. xv. 12 reff. L.P.H.

tion of the dignity of the Son of God, they serve to shew that even according to the human side, His descent had been fixed in the line of him who was Israel's anointed and greatest king. **4.**] The simple antithesis would have been, *τοῦ μὲν γενομένου . . . ὄντος δὲ υἱοῦ θεοῦ κατὰ πνεῦμα*, see 1 Tim. iii. 16. But (1) wonderful solemnity is given by dropping the particles, and taking up separately the human and divine nature of Christ, keeping *ὁ υἱὸς αὐτοῦ* as the great subject of both clauses, and thus making them, not contrasts to one another, but correlative parts of the same great whole. And (2) the Apostle, dwelling here on *patent facts*,—the announcements of prophecy,—the history of the Lord's Humanity,—does not deal with the *essential subsistent Godhead of Christ*, but with *that manifestation of it* which the great fact of the Resurrection had made to men. Also (3) by amplifying *πνεῦμα* into *πν.* **ἁγιωσύνης**, he characterizes the Spirit of Christ as one of absolute holiness, i. e. as *divine* and *partaking of the Godhead:* see below. **ὁρισθέντος**] "Multo plus dicit quam ἀφωρισμένος, ver. 1: nam *ἀφορίζεται unus e pluribus, ὁρίζεται unicus quispiam.*" Bengel. See reff. Nor does it = *προορισθέντος*, as vulg. *prædestinatus*, and as Irenæus (iii. 22. 1, p. 219) and Augustine de Prædest. Sanctorum, c. 15, vol. x. p. 982:—"Prædestinatus est ergo Jesus, ut qui futurus erat secundum carnem filius David, esset tamen in virtute Filius Dei secundum Spiritum Sanctificationis: quia natus est de Spiritu Sancto et Virgine Maria." But this is one of the places where Augustine has been misled by the Latin:—the text speaks, not of the *fact* of Christ's *being* the Son of God barely, but of the *proof* of that fact by His Resurrection. Chrysostom has given the right meaning: *τί οὖν ἔστιν* **ὁρισθέντος**; *τοῦ δειχθέντος, ἀποφανθέντος, κριθέντος, ὁμολογηθέντος παρὰ τῆς ἁπάντων γνώμης καὶ ψήφου* . . . . Hom. ii. p. 432. That an example is wanting of this exact use of the word, is, as Olsh. has shewn, no objection to such use; the *ὁρίζειν* here spoken of is not the objective '*fixing*,' '*appointing*' of Christ to be the Son of God, but the *subjective manifestation in men's minds that He is so*. Thus the objective words *ποιεῖν* (Acts ii. 36), *γεννᾷν* (Acts xiii. 33) are used of the same *proof* or *manifestation* of Christ's Sonship by His Resurrection. So again *ἐδικαιώθη*, 1 Tim. iii. 16. **ἐν δυνάμει** belongs to *ὁρισθέντος*,—not to *υἱοῦ θεοῦ*,—nor again is it a parallel clause to *κατ. πν. ἁγ.* and *ἐξ ἀναστ. νεκ.* (as Chrys., who interprets it *ἀπὸ τῶν θαυμάτων ἅπερ ἔπραττε*, Theophyl. &c.) **manifested with power (to be) the Son of God.** See reff. **κατὰ πνεῦμα ἁγιωσύνης**] *ἁγιωσ.* is not = *ἅγιον*; this epithet would be inapplicable here, for it would point out the *Third Person in the Blessed Trinity*, whereas it is *the Spirit of Christ Himself*, in distinction from His Flesh, which is spoken of. And this Spirit is designated by the gen. of quality, *ἁγιωσύνης*, to shew that it is not a human, but a divine Spirit which is attributed *here* to Christ,—a Spirit to which holiness belongs as its essence. The other interpretations certainly miss the mark, by overlooking the *κατὰ σάρκα* and *κατὰ πνεῦμα*, the two sides of the Person of Christ here intended to be brought out. Such are that of Theodoret (*διὰ τῆς ὑπὸ τοῦ παναγίου πνεύματος ἐνεργουμένης δυνάμεως*),—Chrys. (*ἀπὸ τοῦ πνεύματος, δι᾽ οὗ τὸν ἁγιασμὸν ἔδωκεν*), &c. Calvin and Olshausen seem to wish to include the notion of *sanctifying* (*ἁγιασμός*) in *ἁγιωσύνη*,—which however true, is more than strictly belongs to the words. See by all means, on the whole, Umbreit's important note, pp. 164—172. **ἐξ**] not '*from and after*' (as Theodoret, Luther, Grotius, al.), nor = *ἀπό*, which could not be used here, but **by**, as indicating the source, *out of* which the demonstration proceeds. **ἀναστάσεως νεκρῶν**] not = *ἀναστ.* **ἐκ** *νεκρῶν*,—which, besides the force done to the words, would be a weakening of the strong expression of the Apostle, who takes here summarily and by anticipation the Resurrection of Jesus as being, including, involving (*ἐγώ* **εἰμι** *ἡ ἀνάστασις*, John xi. 25) *the* (*whole*) *Resurrection of the dead.* So that we must not render as E. V. '*the resurrection from the dead*,' but **the resurrection of the dead,** regarded as accomplished in that of Christ. It was the full accomplishment of *this*, which more than any thing declared Him to be the Son of God: see John v. 25—29. Thus in these words lies wrapped up the argument of ch. vi. 4 ff. **Ἰησ. χρ. τ. κυρ. ἡμ.**] Having given this description of the Person and dignity of the Son of God, very Man and very God, he now identifies

βομεν [s] χάριν καὶ [t] ἀποστολὴν [uv] εἰς [uw] ὑπακοὴν [ux] πίστεως
ἐν πᾶσιν τοῖς ἔθνεσιν [y] ὑπὲρ τοῦ ὀνόματος αὐτοῦ, 6 ἐν οἷς
ἐστε καὶ ὑμεῖς [z] κλητοὶ Ἰησοῦ χριστοῦ, 7 πᾶσιν τοῖς
οὖσιν ἐν Ῥώμῃ [a] ἀγαπητοῖς θεοῦ, [z] κλητοῖς [b] ἁγίοις.

s = ch. xii. 3. xv. 15. 1 Cor. iii. 10. Gal. ii. 9. Eph. iii. 2.
t Acts i. 25. 1 Cor. ix. 2. Gal. ii. 8 only. Deut. xxii. 7.
u ch. xvi. 26.
v — vv. 16, 17. 1 Pet. i. 22.
w ch. v. 19. 2 Cor. vii. 15. Heb. v. 8. 1 Pet. i. 2 al. 2 Kings xxii. 36 only. constr., ch. xvi. 26. 2 Cor. x. 5. 1 Pet. i. 22.
x objective, = Acts vi. 7.
y Acts ix. 16 reff.
z ver. 1. w. gen., here only. (see note.)
a w. gen., Matt. xii. 18. Acts xv. 25 (of Paul). ch. xvi. 5, 8, 9. 1 Cor. x. 14. Phil. ii. 12 only. Ps. cxxvi. 2.
b = Acts ix. 13 reff.

G εν πασι... D κλητοις... ABCDG KL[P]א a b c d f g h k l m n o 17 [47] (*On the omission of E, see prolegomena.*)

7. om *εν ρωμη* G schol-in-47(*το εν ρωμη, ουτε εν τη εξηγησει, ουτε εν τω ρητω μνημονευει*). for *αγαπητ. θεου*, *εν αγαπη θεου* G am fuld[1] D[1]-lat Ambrst-ms$_1$: om E 82.

this divine Person with Jesus Christ, the Lord and Master of Christians,—the historical object of their faith, and (see words following) the Appointer of himself to the apostolic office. **5. δι' οὗ**] as in Gal. i. 1; 1 Cor. i. 9, designating the Lord Himself as the Agent in conferring the grace and Apostleship. **ἐλάβομεν**] not '*all Christians*,'—but **we**, the Apostle himself, as he not unfrequently speaks. No others need be here included in the word. *Those to whom he is writing* cannot be thus included, for they are specially contrasted with the subject of *ἐλάβομεν* by the following *ὑμεῖς*. Nor can the aor. **ἐλάβομεν** refer to any general bestowal of this kind, indicating, as it must, a definite past event, viz. the reception of the Apostleship by himself. To maintain (as Dr. Peile, Annotations on the Epistles, vol. i. Appendix) that the subject of *ἐλάβομεν* must be the same as the *ἡμῶν* which has preceded, is to overlook, not only the contrast just noticed, and the habit of Paul to use indiscriminately the singular or plural, when speaking of himself,—but also the *formulary* character of the expression, 'Jesus Christ our Lord,' in which the 'we' alluded to in 'our' is too faintly indicated to become the subject of a following verb. **χάριν**] Hardly, as Augustine, "*gratiam* cum omnibus fidelibus, *apostolatum* autem non cum omnibus communem habet" (Olsh.): for he is surely speaking of *that peculiar χάρις*, by which he wrought in his apostleship more than they all; see reff. **ἀποστολήν**] Strictly, **apostleship**, 'the office of an Apostle,' see reff.: not any *mission*, or *power of sending ministers*, resident in the *whole church*, which would be contrary to the usage of the word. The *existence* of such a power is not hereby denied, but *this place* refers *solely to the office of Paul* as an Apostle. Keep the **χάρ. κ. ἀποστ.** separate, and strictly consecutive, avoiding all nonsensical figures of Hendiadys, Hypallage, and the like. It was the general bestowal of *grace*, which conditioned and introduced the special bestowal (**καί**, as so often, coupling a specific portion to a whole) of *apostleship*: cf. 1 Cor. xv. 10. **εἰς**] **with a view to**,—'in order to bring about.' **ὑπακοὴν πίστεως**] The anarthrous character above remarked (on *εὐαγγ. θεοῦ*, ver. 1) must be here borne in mind, or we shall fall into the mistake of supposing *ὑ. π.* to mean '*obedience produced by faith*.' The key to the words is found in ref. Acts, *πολύς τε ὄχλος τῶν ἱερέων* **ὑπήκουον τῇ πίστει**, compared with Paul's own usage of joining an objective genitive with *ὑπακοή*, see 2 Cor. x. 5, *εἰς τὴν ὑπακοὴν τοῦ χριστοῦ*. So that *πίστεως* is **the faith**; not = 'the gospel which is to be believed' (as Fritzsche, citing ch. x. 16), but the *state of salvation, in which men stand by faith*. And so these words form an introduction to the great subject of the Epistle. **ἐν πᾶσιν τ. ἔθν.**] **in order to bring about obedience to the faith among all** (the) **nations**. The *Jews* do not here come into account. There is no inclusion, and at the same time no express exclusion of them: but Paul was commissioned as *the Apostle of the Gentiles*, and he here magnifies the great office entrusted to him. **ὑπὲρ τ. ὀν. αὐτ.**] **on behalf of His name**, i. e. 'for His glory:' see reff. "In the name of Christ is summed up what He had done and was, what the Christian ever bore in mind, the zeal which marked him, the name wherewith he was named." Jowett. See also Umbreit's note. The words are best taken as belonging to the whole, from *δι' οὗ* to *ἔθνεσιν* [as declaring the purpose for which the grace and apostleship had been received].

6. ἐν οἷς . . . .] The whole to *χριστοῦ* should be taken together: **among whom ye also are called of Jesus Christ**; otherwise, with a comma at *ὑμεῖς*, the assertion, '*among whom are ye*,' is flat and unmeaning. De Wette and Calvin would take *Ἰησοῦ χρ.* as a gen. of *possession*, because the call of believers is generally referred to the Father: but sometimes the Son is said to call likewise, see John v. 25;

[c] χάρις ὑμῖν καὶ [c] εἰρήνη ἀπὸ θεοῦ πατρὸς ἡμῶν καὶ κυρίου Ἰησοῦ χριστοῦ.
8 Πρῶτον μὲν [d] εὐχαριστῶ τῷ [e] θεῷ [e] μου διὰ Ἰησοῦ χριστοῦ περὶ πάντων ὑμῶν, ὅτι ἡ πίστις ὑμῶν [f] καταγ-

c see introductory note.
d w. dat., Luke xviii. 11. John xi. 41. Acts xxvii. 35. xxviii. 15. 1 Cor. i. 4 al. Judith viii. 25. (Wisd. xviii. 2.) 2 Macc. i. 11 only.
e Matt. xxvii. 46 bis || Mk. (from Ps. xxi. 1.) John xx. 17, 28. 1 Cor. i. 4. 2 Cor. xii. 21. Phil. i. 3. iv. 19. Philem. 4. Rev. ii. 7. iii. 12 (four times) only. Psalms and Prophets passim.
f Acts xiii. 5 reff.

8. om *δια ιησ. χρ.* א[1](ins corr[1]) c. rec (for *περι*) *υπερ* (*see note*), with D^3GL[P] rel Chr Thdrt: [*pro* latt syr arm Orig-int_1:] txt ABCD^1Kא o 17 [Syr] Damasc.

1 Tim. i. 12:—and with *ἀγαπητοὶ θεοῦ* following so close upon it, the expression can I think hardly be taken otherwise than as **called by Jesus Christ**. *ἐκλεκτοὶ αὐτοῦ*, Matt. xxiv. 31, cited by De W. is hardly parallel. **7.**] This verse follows, in the sense, close on ver. 1. **ἀγ. θ., κλητ. ἁγ.**] Both these clauses refer to *all the Christians addressed:* not (as Bengel) the first to Jewish, the second to Gentile believers. No such distinction would be in place in an exordium which anticipates the result of the Epistle—that Jew and Gentile are one in guilt, and one in Christ. **ἀπ. θ. πατ. ἡμ. κ. κυρ. Ἰ. χ.**] Not, as Erasmus, '*from God, the Father of us and of our Lord Jesus Christ,*'—but **from God our Father, and from the Lord Jesus Christ.** God is the *Giver* of Grace and Peace,—Christ the *Imparter*.

8—17.] Opening of the Epistle. *His thankfulness for the faith of the Romans: remembrance of them in his prayers: wish to visit them: hindrances hitherto, but still earnest intention of doing so, that he may further ground them in that Gospel, of which he is not ashamed, inasmuch as it is* THE POWER OF GOD TO ALL WHO BELIEVE. *This leads to the announcement (in a citation from the Scripture) of one great subject of the Epistle,—viz.:* JUSTIFICATION BY FAITH.

8.] This placing himself in intimate connexion with his readers by mention of and thankfulness for their faith or Christian graces, is the constant habit of Paul. The three Epistles, Gal., 1 Tim., and Titus, are the only exceptions: Olsh. adds 2 Cor., but in ch. i. 3—22 we have an equivalent: see especially vv. 6, 7, 11, 14. **μέν**] The corresponding *δέ* follows, ver. 13. 'Ye indeed are prospering in the faith: but I still am anxious *further* to advance that fruitfulness.' There is no *ἔπειτα* to follow to *πρῶτον*. **τῷ θεῷ μου**] *ὅρα μεθ' ὅσης διαθέσεως εὐχαριστεῖ. οὐ γὰρ εἶπε, τῷ θεῷ, ἀλλὰ* **τῷ θεῷ μου**· *ὃ καὶ οἱ προφῆται ποιοῦσι, τὸ κοινὸν ἰδιοποιούμενοι. καὶ τί θαυμαστὸν εἰ οἱ προφῆται; αὐτὸς γὰρ αὐτὸ συνεχῶς ὁ θεὸς φαίνεται ποιῶν ἐπὶ τῶν δούλων, θεὸν Ἀβραὰμ καὶ Ἰσαὰκ καὶ Ἰακὼβ ἰδιαζόντως λέγων ἑαυτόν.* Chrys. Hom. iii. p. 436. **διὰ Ἰ. χ.**] "Velut per Pontificem magnum: oportet enim scire eum qui vult offerre sacrificium Deo, quod per manus Pontificis debet offerre." Origen. So also Calvin, "Hic habemus exemplum, quomodo per Christum agendæ sunt gratiæ, secundum Apostoli præceptum ad Heb. xiii. 15." Olshausen says, "This is no mere phrase, but a true expression of the deepest conviction. For only by the Spirit of Christ dwelling in men's hearts are thanksgivings and prayer acceptable to God." But perhaps here it is better to take the words as expressing an acknowledgment that the faith of the Romans, for which thanks were given, *was due to, and rested on* the Lord Jesus Christ: see ch. vii. 25, and rendering there. **περί**] This prep. and *ὑπέρ* both occur in this connexion, see 1 Cor. i. 4; Col. i. 3; 1 Thess. i. 2; 2 Thess. i. 3; Eph. i. 16; Phil. i. 4:—and it is impossible to say, in cases of their confusion by the MSS., which may have been substituted for the other. The internal criticism which would adopt *ὑπέρ* as being the less usual, may be answered by the probability that *ὑπέρ*, being known to be sometimes used by Paul, may have been substituted as more in his manner for the more usual *περί*. So that manuscript authority in such cases must be our guide; and this authority is here decisive. The difference in meaning would be, that *ὑπέρ* would give more the idea that thanks were given by Paul *on their behalf*, as if he were *aiding them* in giving thanks, for such great mercies: whereas *περί* would imply only that they were the *subject* of his thanks,—that he gave thanks *concerning them.* **ἡ πίστις ὑμ.**] "In ejusmodi gratulationibus Paulus vel totum Christianismum describit, Col. i. 3, sqq.,—vel partem aliquam, 1 Cor. i. 5. Itaque hoc loco *fidem* commemorat, suo convenienter instituto, vv. 12, 17." Bengel. **καταγγέλλεται**] De Wette notices the other side of the report, as given by the Jews at Rome, Acts xxviii. 22, to Paul himself. This *praise* was in the *Christian churches,* and brought by

γέλλεται ἐν ὅλῳ τῷ κόσμῳ. 9 [g] μάρτυς γάρ μου ἐστὶν ὁ
θεός, ᾧ [h] λατρεύω ἐν τῷ [i] πνεύματί μου [j] ἐν τῷ εὐαγγελίῳ
τοῦ υἱοῦ αὐτοῦ, [k] ὡς [l] ἀδιαλείπτως [mn] μνείαν ὑμῶν [m] ποιοῦμαι πάντοτε [o] ἐπὶ τῶν [o] προσευχῶν μου 10 δεόμενος, [p] εἴ
πως [qr] ἤδη [r] ποτὲ [s] εὐοδωθήσομαι [t] ἐν τῷ [t] θελήματι τοῦ

ABCDG KL[P]ℵ a b c d f g h k l m n o 17 [47]

g 2 Cor. i. 23. Phil. i. 8. 1 Thess. ii. 5, 10. Gen. xxxi. 50. constr., Acts v. 32.
h Acts vii. 7 reff.
i Acts xvii. 16 reff.
j 2 Cor. viii. 18. x. 14 al.
k = Acts x. 28. Phil. i. 8.
l 1 Thess. i. 2. ii. 13. v. 17 only †. 2 Macc. xv. 7 al. (-τος, ch. ix. 2. 2 Tim. i. 3.)
m Eph. i. 16. 1 Thess. i. 2. Philem. 4. Ps. cx. 4.
n as above (m). Phil. i. 3. 1 Thess. iii. 6. 2 Tim. i. 3 only.
o Eph. i. 16. 1 Thess. i. 2. Philem. 4 only. ἐπὶ τῶν δείπνων, Diod. Sic. iv. 3.
p ch. xi. 14. Phil. iii. 11. Acts xxvii. 12 (w. opt.) only.
q ch. xiii. 11.
r Phil. iv. 10 only. Thuc. viii. 69.
s 1 Cor. xvi. 2. 3 John 2 bis, only. Gen. xxxix. 3, 23. 2 Chron. xiii. 12. (-δος, Num. xiv. 41. -δως, Prov. xxx. [see xxiv.] 29.)
t Heb. x. 10. (Col. iv. 12.)

9. *μαρτυρ* D[1]. for 1st *μου*, *μοι* D[1]G b[1] o vulg syrr arm lat-ff. for *ως*, *πως* *quomodo* G [Orig-int$_1$].
10. for *ει πως*, *οπως* L o 5. 71-7. 93 lect-12.

Christian brethren. **ἐν ὅλῳ τῷ κόσμῳ**] A popular hyperbole, common every where, and especially when speaking of general diffusion through the Roman empire, the 'orbis terrarum.' The praise would be heard in every city where there was a Christian church,—intercourse with the metropolis of the world being common to all. **9.**] "Asseveratio pia, de re necessaria, et hominibus, remotis præsertim et ignotis, occulta." Bengel. There could be no other witness to his practice in his secret prayers, but God: and as the assertion of a habit of incessantly praying for the Roman Christians, whom he had never seen, might seem to savour of an exaggerated expression of affection, he solemnly appeals to this only possible testimony. To the Eph., Phil. (see however Phil. i. 8), Col., Thess., he gives the same assurance, but without the asseveration. The thus calling God to witness is no uncommon practice with Paul: see reff. in E. V. **ᾧ λατρ.**] The *serving God in his spirit* was a guarantee that his profession was sincere, and that the oath just taken was no mere form, but a solemn and earnest appeal of his spirit. See also Phil. iii. 3 (present text), and John iv. 24. "The LXX use *λατρεύω* generally (not so, but only in a few places, e. g. Num. xvi. 9, Ezek. xx. 32; it is mostly rendered by *λειτουργεῖν*; *λατρεύειν* for the most part rendering עָבַד) for the Heb. שֵׁרֵת, which mostly implies the service of the priests in the temple: e. g. Num. iii. 31; iv. 12; xviii. 2, &c. The Apostle means then, that he is an intelligent, true priest of his God, not in the temple, but in his spirit,—not at the altar, but at the gospel of His Son." Umbreit. **ἐν τῷ εὐαγ.**] *ἡ τοῦ εὐαγγελίου προσθήκη τὸ εἶδος δηλοῖ τῆς διακονίας*, Chrys. Hom. iii. p. 438. His peculiar method of *λατρεία* was concerned with the gospel of the Son of God. "Quidam accipiunt hanc particulam, quasi voluerit Paulus cultum illum, quo se prosequi Deum dixerat, ex eo commendare, quod Evangelii præscripto respondeat: certum est autem, spiritualem Dei cultum in Evangelio nobis præcipi. Sed prior interpretatio longe melius quadrat, nempe quod suum Deo obsequium addicat in Evangelii prædicatione." Calvin. See *εὐαγγελίον*, Phil. iv. 15. [**ὡς ἀδιαλείπτως**] **how unceasingly**: the words may also mean '*that without ceasing*,' but the former rendering seems the better of the two.] **πάντοτε** belongs to the following, not to the preceding words. This latter construction would not be without example,—*ἐν παντὶ καιρῷ ἀδιαλείπτως*, 1 Macc. xii. 11, but this very example shews that if so, its natural place would be close to *ἀδιαλείπτως*. The whole phrase is a favourite one with Paul, see reff. "*πάντοτε* vice nominis accipio, ac si dictum foret, 'In omnibus meis orationibus, seu quoties precibus Deum appello, adjungo vestri mentionem.'" Calvin. **αἱ προσευχαί μου** must be understood of his *ordinary stated* prayers, just in our sense of **my prayers**: "quoties ex professo et quasi meditatus Deum orabat, illorum quoque habebat rationem inter alios." Calv.

10. εἴ πως] **if by any means.** No subject of *δεόμενος* is expressed, but it is left to be gathered from this clause, as in Simon's entreaty, Acts viii. 24, *δεήθητε ὑμεῖς ὑπὲρ ἐμοῦ . . . . ὅπως μηδὲν ἐπέλθῃ ἐπ' ἐμὲ ὧν εἰρήκατε*, where *ὅπως κ.τ.λ.* is not the *contents* of the prayer, but the *end aimed at* by it. **ἤδη ποτέ**] **before long**:—lit., '*at last, some day or other.*' **εὐοδωθήσομαι**] **I shall be allowed, prospered**: see reff., and Deut. xxviii. 29: and cf. Umbreit's note. The rendering, '*I might have a prosperous journey*' (Vulg. and E.V.), is etymologically incorrect; the passive of *ὁδόω*, '*to shew the way*,' '*to bring into the way*,' must be 'to *be shewn* the way,' or '*brought* into the *

θεοῦ ἐλθεῖν πρός ὑμᾶς· 11 [u] ἐπιποθῶ γὰρ ἰδεῖν ὑμᾶς, ἵνα
τὶ [v] μεταδῶ [w] χάρισμα ὑμῖν [x] πνευματικὸν [y] εἰς τὸ [z] στηριχθῆναι ὑμᾶς, 12 τοῦτο δέ ἐστιν [a] συνπαρακληθῆναι ἐν
ὑμῖν διὰ τῆς ἐν ἀλλήλοις πίστεως ὑμῶν τε καὶ ἐμοῦ.
13 οὐ [b] θέλω δὲ ὑμᾶς [bc] ἀγνοεῖν, ἀδελφοί, [c] ὅτι πολλάκις
[d] προεθέμην ἐλθεῖν πρὸς ὑμᾶς, καὶ [e] ἐκωλύθην [f] ἄχρι τοῦ
[g] δεῦρο, ἵνα τινὰ [h] καρπὸν σχῶ καὶ ἐν ὑμῖν καθὼς καὶ ἐν

u w. inf., 2 Cor. v. 2. 1 Thess. iii. 6. 2 Tim. i. 4. (Ps. cxviii. 20.) see 2 Cor. ix. 14 reff.
v ch. xii. 8 reff. constr., 1 Thess. ii. 8. 2 Macc. viii. 12. Xen. Anab. iv. 5. 5.
w = ch. v. 15, 16. vi. 23. xii. 6. 1 Cor. i. 7 al. Paul only, exc. 1 Pet. iv. 10 †.
x = Eph. i. 3. Col. iii. 16.
y Acts iii. 19. vii. 19. ver. 20 al.
z = Luke xxii. 32. ch. xvi. 25 al. Ps. l. 12 (14).
a here only †.
b ch. xi. 25. 1 Cor. x. 1. xii. 1. 2 Cor. i. 8. 1 Thess. iv. 13.
c ch. ii. 4. vi. 3. Wisd. xii. 10.
d = Eph. i. 9 (ch. iii. 25) only ‡. Exod. xl. 4.
e Acts xvi. 6 reff. see Acts xxviii. 31.
f Acts xx. 6 reff.
g = and w. art., here only. (Acts vii. 3 reff.)
h = John iv. 36. ch. vi. 21, 22. Phil. i. 22. iv. 17. James iii. 18. Jer. xvii. 10.

12. τουτ εστιν, omg δε, A latt(but G-lat has *id est aut hoc enim est*) [Orig-int$_1$: om Syr]. rec συμπαρακληθηναι, with B²(sic: see table) L[KP]: txt AB¹CDGℵ. om 2nd εν G [arm]. ins της [bef] πιστεως G.

13. for ου θελω, ουκ οιομαι D¹[and lat] G Ambrst$_1$. for δε, γαρ C 73 fuld: om k¹. rec καρπον bef τινα: om τινα L 42. 115 Syr copt [æth(appy)]: txt ABC(D)GK[P]ℵ rel vulg gr-ff lat-ff.—for τινα, τι D¹. for σχω, εχω G 77. om 2nd και G [l] o 48. 109-78 [fuld] æth.

way.' So Herod. vi. 73, ὡς τῷ Κλεομενεϊ εὐωδώθη τὸ ἐς τὸν Δημάρητον πρῆγμα. **ἐν τῷ θελ. τοῦ θεοῦ**] **In the course of,—by, the will of God.** **ἐλθεῖν** belongs to εὐοδωθήσομαι, not to δεόμενος. **11. ἐπιποθῶ**] not '*I vehemently desire*:' ἐπί does not *intensify*, but merely expresses the direction of the πόθος, see Herod. v. 93, and compare such expressions as μὴ προσεῶντος ἡμᾶς τοῦ ἀνέμου, Acts xxvii. 7. **ἵνα τὶ μεταδῶ χάρισμα πν.**] That the χάρισμα here spoken of was no mere supernatural power of working in the Spirit, the whole context shews, as well as the meaning of the word itself in reff. And even if χάρισμα, barely taken, could ever (1 Cor. xii. 4, 9 are no examples, see there) mean technically a *supernatural endowment of the Spirit*, yet the epithet πνευματικόν, and the object of imparting this χάρισμα, *confirmation in the faith*, would here preclude that meaning. Besides, Paul did not value the mere bestowal of these 'gifts' so highly, as to make it the subject of his earnest prayers incessantly. The gift alluded to was παράκλησις, as De Wette observes. **πνευμ., spiritual**:—springing from the Spirit of God, and imparted to the spirit of man. **εἰς τὸ στηρ. ὑμ.**] Knowing the trials to which they were exposed, and being conscious of the fulness of spiritual power for edification (2 Cor. xiii. 10) given to him, he longed to impart some of it to them, that they might be confirmed. "The Apostle does not say εἰς τὸ στηρίζειν ὑμ., for this belongs to God; see ch. xvi. 25. He is only the instrument: hence the passive." Philippi. **12.**] εἶτα ἐπειδὴ καὶ τοῦτο σφόδρα φορτικὸν ἦν, ὅρα πῶς αὐτὸ παραμυθεῖται διὰ τῆς ἐπαγωγῆς. ἵνα γὰρ μὴ λέγωσι, τί γάρ; σαλευόμεθα καὶ περιφερόμεθα, καὶ τῆς παρὰ σοῦ δεόμεθα γλώττης εἰς τὸ στῆναι βεβαίως, προλαβὼν ἀναιρεῖ τὴν τοιαύτην ἀντίῤῥησιν οὕτω λέγων (ver. 12). ὡς ἂν εἰ ἔλεγε, μὴ ὑποπτεύσητε ὅτι κατηγορῶν ὑμῶν εἶπον, οὐ ταύτῃ τῇ γνώμῃ ἐφθεγξάμην τὸ ῥῆμα· ἀλλὰ τί ποτέ ἐστιν, ὅπερ ἠβουλήθην εἰπεῖν; Πολλὰς ὑπομένετε θλίψεις ὑπὸ τῶν διωκόντων περιαντλούμενοι· ἐπεθύμησα τοίνυν ὑμᾶς ἰδεῖν, ἵνα παρακαλέσω, μᾶλλον δὲ οὐχ ἵνα παρακαλέσω μόνον, ἀλλ' ἵνα καὶ αὐτὸς παράκλησιν δέξωμαι. Chrys. Hom. ii. p. 440. The inf. συμπαρακληθῆναι is parallel with στηριχθῆναι, ἐμέ being understood: **that is, that I with you may be comforted among you, each by the faith which is in the other.** That the gift he wished to impart to them was παράκλησις, is implied in the **συνπαρακλ.** See the same wish expressed in different words ch. xv. 32, and the partial realization of it, Acts xxviii. 15. **ἐν ἀλλήλοις**, which might otherwise be ambiguous, is explained by ὑμῶν τε καὶ ἐμοῦ to mean *which we recognize in one another*: or as above and in A. V. R. The expression "*mutual faith*," of the E. V. should properly mean, *faith which each has in the other*. **πίστις** is used in the most general sense—*faith* as the necessary condition and working instrument of all Christian exhortation, comfort, and confirmation; producing these, and evidenced by them. **13. οὐ θέλω δὲ ὑμ. ἀγ.**] A Pauline formula: see reff. **καὶ ἐκωλ. ἄχρι τ. δεῦρο** is best as a parenthesis, as it is impossible that ἵνα can depend on

τοῖς λοιποῖς ἔθνεσιν. 14 ῞Ελλησίν τε καὶ [i] βαρβάροις,
σοφοῖς τε καὶ [k] ἀνοήτοις [l] ὀφειλέτης εἰμί· 15 [m] οὕτως [n] τὸ
[n] κατ' ἐμὲ [o] πρόθυμον καὶ ὑμῖν τοῖς ἐν Ῥώμῃ [p] εὐαγγελίσασθαι. 16 οὐ γὰρ [q] ἐπαισχύνομαι τὸ εὐαγγέλιον· [r] δύναμις

ABCDG KL[P]ℵ a b c d f g h k l m n o 17 [47]

i Acts xxviii. 2, 4 reff. k Luke xxiv. 25. Gal. iii. 1, 3. 1 Tim. vi. 9. Tit. iii. 3 only, L.P. Prov. xvii. 28. l ch. viii. 12. xv. 27. Matt. vi. 12. xviii. 24. Luke xiii. 4. Gal. v. 3 only †. Soph. Aj. 590. m = Rev. iii. 16. n ch. ix. 5. Eph. vi. 21. Polyb. x. 44. 1. see ch. xii. 18. o Matt. xxvi. 41 ‖ Mk. only. 2 Chron. xxix. 31. (-μως, 1 Pet. v. 2. -μία, Acts xvii. 11.) p constr., Gal. iv. 13. pass., 1 Pet. iv. 6. q Luke ix. 26 (bis) ‖ Mk. ch. vi. 21. 2 Tim. i. 8. Heb. ii. 11 al. Job xxxiv. 19 Bℵ. Isa. i. 29 Aℵ$^{1.3b}$ Ald. compl. only. r = Acts viii. 10 reff.

15. for το κατ εμε, ο επ εμε G-gr: *quod in me promptum est* vulg G-lat $Sedul_1$ Pel: *quod in me est promtus sum* D-lat Ambr Ambrst $Sedul_1$. ins εν bef υμιν D^1(and lat^1) b^1 o am $fuld^1$ G-lat: επ G-gr. om τοις εν ρωμη G.

16. for το, επι *super* G: *de* Aug_1 Vig. rec aft ευαγγελιον ins του χριστου, with D^3KL[P] rel Thl Œc: om $ABCD^1G$ℵ 17 vulg syrr copt arm $Orig_1$[-int_1] Eus_4 Bas_1 Cyr[-p] Chr Thdrt Procop Damasc Phot $Tert_1$ Arnob Hil_1.

ἐκωλύθην. So Demosth. p. 488. 7, ἐμοὶ δ', ὦ ἄνδρες Ἀθ., δοκεῖ Λεπτίνης (καί μοι πρὸς Διὸς μηδὲν ὀργισθῇς· οὐδὲν γὰρ φλαῦρον ἐρῶ σε) ἢ οὐκ ἀνεγνωκέναι τοὺς Σόλωνος νόμους ἢ οὐ συνιέναι. The *reason of the hindrance* is given in ch. xv. 20—22: it was, *his* φιλοτιμία *to preach the gospel where it had not been preached before, rather than on the foundation of others.* **καρπόν**] Not, 'wages,' or 'result of my apostolic labour,' for such is not the ordinary meaning of the word in the N. T., but *fruit borne by you* who have been planted to bring forth fruit to God. This fruit I should then gather and present to God; cf. the figure in ch. xv. 16: see also Phil. i. 22 and note. **14.**] The connexion seems to be this: He wishes to have some fruit, some produce of expended labour, among the Romans as among other Gentiles. Till this was the case, he himself was a *debtor* to every such people: which situation of *debtor* he wished to change, by paying the debt and conferring a benefit, into that of one having money out at interest there, and yielding a καρπός. The debt which he owed to all nations was (ver. 15) the obligation laid on him to preach the gospel to them; see 1 Cor. ix. 16. **῞Ελλ. — βαρβ. — σοφ. — ἀνοήτ.**] These words must not be pressed as applying to any particular churches, or as if any one of them designated the Romans themselves,—or even as if σοφοῖς belonged to ῞Ελλησιν, and ἀνοήτοις to βαρβάροις. They are used, apparently, merely as comprehending *all Gentiles,* whether considered in regard of race or of intellect; and are placed here certainly not without a prospective reference to the universality of guilt, and need of the gospel, which he is presently about to prove existed in the Gentile world. Notice that he does not call himself a debtor to the *Jews*—for they can hardly be included in βαρβάροις (see Col. iii. 11). Though he had earnest desires for them (ch. ix. 1—3; x. 1), and every where preached to them first, this was not his peculiar ὀφείλημα, see Gal. ii. 7, where he describes himself as πεπιστευμένος **τὸ εὐαγγέλιον τῆς ἀκροβυστίας,** καθὼς Πέτρος τῆς περιτομῆς. **15. οὕτως**] "Est quasi . . . . illatio a toto ad partem insignem." Bengel. '*As* to all Gentiles, *so* to you, who hold no mean place among them.' **16.**] The **οὐ γὰρ ἐπαισχύνομαι** seems to be suggested by the *position of the Romans in the world.* 'Yea, to you at Rome also: for, though your city is mistress of the world, though your emperors are worshipped as present deities, though you are elated by your pomps and luxuries and victories, yet I am not ashamed of the apparently mean origin of the gospel which I am to preach; for (and here is the transition to his great theme) it is,' &c. So for the most part, Chrysostom, Hom. iii. p. 444. **δύναμις γὰρ θ. ἐστίν**] The gospel, which is the greatest example of the Power of God, he strikingly calls *that Power itself.* (Not, as Jowett, '*a divine power,*' nor is δικαιοσ. θεοῦ below to be thus explained, as he alleges.) So in 1 Cor. i. 24 he calls Christ, *the Power of God.* But not only is the gospel the great example of divine Power; it is the *field of agency* of the power of God, working in it, and interpenetrating it throughout. The bare substantive δύναμις here (and 1 Cor. i. 24) carries a *superlative* sense: the *highest and holiest vehicle* of the divine Power, the δύναμις κατ' ἐξοχήν. "It is weighty for the difference between the Gospel and the Law, that the Law is never called God's power, כֹּחַ, but light, or teaching, in which a man must walk, Ps. xxxvi. 10; cxix. 105; Prov. vi. 23; Isa. ii. 5." Umbreit. And the *direction in which* this power acts in the gospel is **εἰς σωτηρίαν**—it is a

γὰρ θεοῦ ἐστιν [s] εἰς σωτηρίαν παντὶ τῷ πιστεύοντι, Ἰου- s = ver. 5 reff. t ch. iii. 5, 21,
δαίῳ τε πρῶτον καὶ Ἕλληνι. 17 [t] δικαιοσύνη γὰρ [t] θεοῦ ἐν 22. x. 3. 2 Cor. v. 21. James i. 20. 2 Pet. i. 1. (Micah vi. 5.)

om εις σωτηριαν G. for ιουδαιω τε, ιουδε(sic) ℵ[1](txt ℵ-corr[1]). om πρωτον BG Tert$_1$: ins ACDKL[P]ℵ 17 rel [vulg syrr copt æth arm] Orig[and -int$_1$ Eus$_5$ Did$_1$] Chr$_1$ Thdrt Damasc Thl Œc Bede.

healing, saving power: for as Chrysostom reminds us, there is a power of God εἰς κόλασιν, and εἰς ἀπώλειαν, see Matt. x. 28.

But *to whom* is this gospel the power of God to save? **παντὶ τῷ πιστεύοντι.** The *universality* implied in the παντί, the *condition* necessitated in the πιστεύοντι, and the δύναμις θεοῦ acting εἰς σωτηρίαν, are the great subjects treated of in the former part of this epistle. *All* are proved to be *under sin*, and so *needing God's righteousness* (ch. i. 18—iii. 20), and the *entrance* into this righteousness is shewn to be *by faith* (ch. iii. 21—v. 11). Then the δύναμις θεοῦ in freeing from the dominion of sin and death, and as issuing in salvation, is set forth (ch. v. 11—viii. 39). So that if the subject of the Epistle is to be stated in few words, these should be chosen: **τὸ εὐαγγέλιον, δύναμις θεοῦ εἰς σωτηρίαν παντὶ τῷ πιστεύοντι.** This expresses it better than merely '*justification by faith*,' which is in fact only a subordinate part of the great theme,—only the *condition necessitated by man's sinfulness for his entering the state of salvation:* whereas the argument extends *beyond this*, to the *death unto sin* and *life unto God* and *carrying forward of the sanctifying work of the Spirit*, from its first fruits even to its completion. **Ἰουδ. πρῶτον κ. Ἑλλ.**] This is the *Jewish* expression for all mankind, as Ἑλλ. κ. βαρβ. ver. 14 is the *Greek* one. Ἑλλ. here includes *all Gentiles.* **πρῶτον** is not *first* in order of time, but **principally** (compare ch. ii. 9), spoken of *national precedence*, in the sense in which the Jews were to our Lord οἱ ἴδιοι, John i. 11. Salvation was ἐκ τῶν Ἰουδαίων, John iv. 22. See ch. ix. 5; xi. 24. Not that the Jew has any *preference* under the gospel; only he *inherits*, and has a *precedence.* οὐδὲ γὰρ ἐπεὶ δὴ πρῶτός ἐστι, καὶ πλέον λαμβάνει τῆς χάριτος· ἡ γὰρ αὐτὴ δωρεὰ καὶ τούτῳ κἀκείνῳ δίδοται· ἀλλὰ τάξεώς ἐστι τιμὴ μόνον τὸ **πρῶτος.** Chrys. Hom. iii. p. 445. **17.**] An explanation, *how* the gospel is the *power of God to salvation*, and how it is so *to the believer:*—because in it **God's righteousness** (not His *attribute* of righteousness,—'the righteousness of God,' but righteousness *flowing from, and acceptable to Him*) is unfolded, and the more, the more we believe. I subjoin De Wette's note on δικ. θεοῦ. "The Greek δικ. and the Heb. צְדָקָה are taken sometimes for 'virtue' and 'piety' which men possess or strive after,—sometimes imputatively, for 'freedom from blame' or 'justification.' The latter meaning is most usual with Paul: δικ. is that which is so in the sight of God (ch. ii. 13), the result of His justifying forensic Judgment, or of '*Imputation*' (ch. iv. 5). It may certainly be imagined, that a man *might obtain* justification by *fulfilling the law:* in that case his righteousness is an ἰδία (δικαιοσύνη) (ch. x. 3), a δικ. ἐκ τοῦ νόμου (Phil. iii. 9). But it is impossible for him to obtain a 'righteousness of his own,' which at the same time shall avail before God (ch. iii. 20; Gal. ii. 16). The Jews not only *have* not fulfilled the law (ch. iii. 9—19), but *could* not fulfil it (vii. 7 ff.): the Gentiles likewise have rendered themselves obnoxious to the divine wrath (i. 24—32). God has ordained that the whole race should be included in disobedience. Now if man is to become righteous from being unrighteous,—this can only happen by God's grace,—because God *declares him righteous*, assumes him to be righteous, δικαιοῖ (iii. 24; Gal. iii. 8):—δικαιοῦν is not only negative, '*to acquit*,' as הִצְדִּיק Exod. xxiii. 7; Isa. v. 23; ch. ii. 13 (where however see my note), but also positive, '*to declare righteous:*' but never '*to make* righteous' by transformation, or imparting of moral strength by which moral perfection may be attained. *Justificatio* must be taken as the old protestant dogmatists rightly took it, *sensu forensi*, i. e. *imputatively.* God justifies for Christ's sake (ch. iii. 22 ff.) on condition of faith in Him as Mediator: the result of *His justification* is δικαιοσύνη ἐκ πίστεως, and as He imparts it freely, it is δικαιοσύνη θεοῦ (gen. subj.) or ἐκ θεοῦ, Phil. iii. 9: so Chrys. &c. (δικ. θεοῦ is ordinarily taken for δικ. παρὰ θεῷ, as Luth.: 'die Gerechtigkeit die vor Gott gilt:' compare ch. ii. 13; iii. 20; Gal. iii. 11; but that this is at least not necessary, see 2 Cor. v. 21). This justification is certainly an objective act of God: but it must also be subjectively apprehended, as its *condition* is subjective. It is *the acquittal from guilt, and cheerfulness of conscience, attained through*

u = Matt. xi. 25. xvi. 17 al. Isa. lvi. 1.
v Hab. ii. 4.
w = Luke xvii. 30. 1 Cor. iii. 13. 2 Thess. ii. 3.

αὐτῷ [u] ἀποκαλύπτεται ἐκ πίστεως [s] εἰς πίστιν, καθὼς γέγραπται [v] Ὁ δὲ δίκαιος ἐκ πίστεως ζήσεται.
18 [w] Ἀποκαλύπτεται γὰρ [x] ὀργὴ [x] θεοῦ ἀπ' οὐρανοῦ [y] ἐπὶ

ABCDG KL[P]ℵ abcdf ghkl mno17 [47]

x John iii. 36. (ch. iii. 5. ix. 22.) Eph. v. 6. Rev. xix. 15. y = Acts xiii. 11 reff

17. for γαρ, δε A Clem$_1$. aft δικαιος ins μου (*as* LXX-A) C[1]; aft εκ πιστεως (*as* LXX-Bℵ) syr Eus [Orig-int$_1$] Jer$_1$: txt ABDGKL[P]ℵ rel Clem$_1$ [Did$_1$] Chr Thdrt Iren-int$_1$ Ambr.

faith in God's grace in Christ,—the very frame of mind which would be proper to a perfectly righteous man,—if such there were,—the harmony of the spirit with God,—peace with God. All interpretations which overlook the fact of imputation (the R.-Cath., that of Grotius, Baumgarten-Crusius, &c.) are erroneous." To say, with Jowett, that all attempts to define δικαιοσ. θεοῦ are "the after-thoughts of theology, which have no real place in the interpretation of Scripture," is in fact to shut our eyes to the great doctrinal facts of Christianity, and float off at once into uncertainty about the very foundations of the Apostle's argument and our own faith: of which uncertainty his note here is an eminent example. **ἐν αὐτῷ**] **in it,** '*the gospel:*' not, in τῷ πιστεύοντι. **ἀποκαλύπτεται**] generally used of *making known* a thing hitherto concealed: but here of that gradually more complete realization of the state of justification before God by faith in Christ, which is the continuing and increasing gift of God to the believer in the Gospel. **ἐκ πίστεως**] "ἐκ points to the condition, or the subjective ground. πίστις is faith in the sense of *trust,* and that (a) *a trustful assumption of a truth* in reference to knowledge = *conviction:* (b) *a trustful surrender of the soul,* as regards the *feeling.* Here it is especially the latter of these: that trust reposed in God's grace in Christ, which tranquillizes the soul and frees it from all guilt,—and especially trust in the atoning death of Jesus. Bound up with this (not by the meaning of the words, but by the idea of unconditional trust, which excludes all reserve) is *humility,* consisting in the abandonment of all merits of a man's own, and recognition of his own unworthiness and need of redemption." De Wette. **εἰς πίστιν**] ἀπὸ πίστεως ἄρχεται κ. εἰς πιστεύοντα λήγει (Œcum.) seems the most probable interpretation, making πίστιν almost = τοὺς πιστεύοντας, see ch. iii. 22: but not entirely,—it is still the *aspect,* the *phase,* of the man, which is receptive of the δικαιοσύνη θεοῦ, and to this it is revealed. The other interpretations,—'*for the increase of faith*' (Meyer),—'*that faith may be given to it*' (Fritzsche, Tholuck, Krebs),—'*proceeding from faith, and leading to a higher degree of faith*' (Baumg.-Crus.),—do not seem so suitable or forcible. It will be observed that ἐκ π. εἰς π. is taken with ἀποκαλύπτεται, not with δικαιοσύνη. The latter connexion would do for ἐκ π., but not for εἰς π. * **καθὼς γέγρ.**] He shews that *righteousness by faith* is *no new idea,* but found in the prophets. The words (ref.) are cited again in Gal. iii. 11; Heb. x. 38, in the former place with the same purpose as here. They are used in Habakkuk with reference to credence given to the prophetic word: but properly speaking, *all faith is one,* in whatever word or act of God reposed: so that the Apostle is free from any charge of forcing the words to the present purpose. The two ways of arranging them, ὁ δίκαιος —ἐκ πίστεως ζήσεται, and ὁ δίκαιος ἐκ πίστεως—ζήσεται, in fact amount to the same: if the former, which is more agreeable to the Heb., be taken, ζήσεται must mean, 'shall live *on,*' *endure in his δικαιοσύνη, by means of faith,* which would assert that it was a δικαιοσύνη of faith, as strongly as does the latter. See by all means, on the quotation, Umbreit's note: and Delitzsch, der Proph. Habakuk, p. 51 ff. This latter remarks (I quote from Philippi), "The Apostle rests no more on our text than it will bear. He only places its assertion, that the life of the just springs from his faith, in the light of the N. T."

CHAP. I. 18—XI. 36.] THE DOCTRINAL EXPOSITION OF THE ABOVE TRUTH: THAT THE GOSPEL IS THE POWER OF GOD UNTO SALVATION TO EVERY ONE THAT BELIEVETH. And herein, ch. i. 18—iii. 20,—*inasmuch as this power of God consists in the revelation of God's righteousness in man by faith, and in order to faith the first requisite is the recognition of man's unworthiness, and incapability to work a righteousness for himself,—the Apostle begins by proving that all, Gentiles and Jews, are* GUILTY *before God, as holding back the truth in unrighteousness. And* FIRST, ch. i. 18—32, OF THE GENTILES. **18.**] He first states the general fact, of *all mankind;* but immediately passes off to the consideration of the *majority* of mankind, the Gen-

πᾶσαν [z] ἀσέβειαν καὶ ἀδικίαν ἀνθρώπων τῶν τὴν ἀλήθειαν
ἐν ἀδικίᾳ [a] κατεχόντων, 19 [b] διότι τὸ [c] γνωστὸν τοῦ θεοῦ

z h. xi. 26 (from Isa. lix. 20). 2 Tim. ii. 16. Tit. ii. 12. Jude 15, 18 only. Jer. v. 6. (-βης, ch. iv. 5. -βεῖν, 2 Pet. ii. 6.) a = 2 Thess. ii. 6 (see note). b = Acts xviii. 10, or 1 Cor. xv. 9. c = Acts i. 19 reff. (see note.) constr., see Winer, § 34. 2.

18. ins *των* bef *ανθρωπων* D[1]G.

tiles; reserving the Jews for exceptional consideration afterwards. **ἀποκ. γάρ**] The statement of ver. 17 was, that the RIGHTEOUSNESS *of* God is revealed. The necessary condition of this revelation is, *the* DESTRUCTION *of the righteousness of* MAN by the revelation of God's anger against sin. **ἀποκαλύπτεται**, not *in the Gospel* (as Grot.): not *in men's consciences* (as Tholuck, ed. 1, Reiche): not *in the miserable state of the then world* (as Köllner): but (as implied indeed by the adjunct ἀπ' οὐρανοῦ,—that it is a *providential, universally-to-be-seen* revelation) in the PUNISHMENTS which, ver. 24, God has made to follow upon sin, see also ch. ii. 2 (so De W., Meyer, Tholuck, ed. 5, &c.). So that ἀποκ. is of an *objective reality here,* not of an evangelic internal and subjective unfolding. **ὀργὴ θεοῦ** is anthropopathically, but with the deepest truth, put for *the righteousness of God in punishment* (see ch. ii. 8; v. 9; Eph. ii. 3; Matt. iii. 7; John iii. 36). It is the opposite, in the divine attributes, to *Love* (De W.). **ἀπ' οὐρ.** (see above) belongs to ἀποκαλύπτεται, not to θεοῦ, nor to ὀργὴ θεοῦ (ἡ ἀπ' οὐρ.). **ἀσέβειαν, godlessness; ἀδικίαν, iniquity**: but neither term is exclusive of the other, nor to be formally pressed to its limits. They overlap and include each other by a large margin: the specific difference being, that ἀσέβ. is more the *fountain* (but at the same time partially the result) of ἀδικία,—which ἀδικ. is more the *result* (but at the same time partially the fountain) of ἀσέβεια. ἀδικ. is the *state* of the thoughts and feelings and habits, induced originally by forgetfulness of God, and in its turn inducing impieties of all kinds. We may notice by the way, that the word ἀσέβεια forms an interesting link to the Pastoral Epistles [where it, and its opposite εὐσέβεια are the ordinary terms for an unholy and a holy life]. **ἀνθρ. τῶν τὴν ἀλ. ἐν ἀδικίᾳ κατεχόντων**] **of men who hold back the truth in iniquity**: who, possessing enough of the germs of religious and moral verity to preserve them from abandonment, have checked the development of this *truth* in their lives, in the love and practice of sin. That this is the meaning of κατεχόντων here is plain from this circumstance: that wherever κατέχω in the N. T. signifies 'to hold,' it is *emphatic,* 'to hold *fast,*' or 'to *keep to,*' or 'to take or have *complete possession of*:' see for the first, Luke viii. 15; 1 Cor. xi. 2; xv. 2; 1 Thess. v. 21; Heb. iii. 6, 14; x. 23: for the second, Luke xiv. 9 (every other place except the lowest being excluded): for the third, Matt. xxi. 38; 1 Cor. vii. 30. Now no such emphatic sense will apply here. If the word is to mean 'holding,' it must be only in the loosest and least emphatic sense: 'having a half and indistinct consciousness of,' which does not at all correspond to the κατά, indicating vehemence of purpose, as in καταφιλέω, &c. But the meaning '*keeping back,*' '*hindering the development of,*'—while it has a direct example in Paul's own usage in reff., and in Luke iv. 42, and indirect ones in (the spurious John v. 4) Acts xxvii. 40; ch. vii. 6; Philem. 13,—admirably suits the sense, that men had (see vv. 19 ff.) knowledge of God sufficient, if its legitimate work had been allowed, to have kept them from such excesses of enormity as they have committed, but that this ἀλήθεια they κατεῖχον ἐν ἀδικίᾳ, i. e. *crushed, quenched,* in (as the element, conditional medium in which) their state and practice of unrighteousness. It is plain that to take ἐν ἀδικίᾳ for ἀδίκως (as Theophyl. and Reiche) is to miss the force of the expression altogether—the pregnant **ἐν**, '*in and by,*' implying that it is their ἀδικία,—the very absence of δικαιοσύνη for which the argument contends,—which is the *status wherein,* and the *instrument whereby,* they hold back the truth lit up in their consciences. **19.**] **διότι, because,** may either give the reason why *the anger of God is revealed,* and thus apply to all that follows as far as ver. 32, being taken up again at vv. 21, 24, 26, 28 (so Meyer): or may explain τῶν . . . . κατεχ. (so Thol.): which latter seems most probable: the *subauditum* being, '(this charge I bring against them), because.' For he proves, first (ver. 20) that they *had* the ἀλήθεια; then (vv. 21 ff.) that they *held it back.* **τὸ γνωστόν, that which is known,** the objective knowledge patent and recognized in Creation:—so Chrys., Theodoret, Luther, Reiche, Meyer, De Wette, al.:—not '*that which may be known*' (as Orig., Theophyl., Œc., Erasm., Beza, Grot., al. [and E. V.]), which would assert what, as simple matter of fact, was not the case,

φανερόν ἐστιν [d] ἐν αὐτοῖς· ὁ θεὸς γὰρ αὐτοῖς [e] ἐφανέρωσεν.
20 τὰ γὰρ [f] ἀόρατα αὐτοῦ [g] ἀπὸ [h] κτίσεως κόσμου τοῖς
[i] ποιήμασιν [k] νοούμενα [l] καθορᾶται, ἥ τε [m] ἀΐδιος αὐτοῦ
δύναμις καὶ [n] θειότης, [o] εἰς τὸ εἶναι αὐτοὺς [p] ἀναπολογήτους, 21 [q] διότι [r] γνόντες τὸν [r] θεὸν οὐχ ὡς θεὸν [s] ἐδόξασαν

ABCDG KL[P]א a b c d f g h k l m n o 17 [47]

d = ch. ii. 15. e ch. iii. 21. xvi. 26. John i. 31 al. fr. Jer. xl. (xxxiii.) 6 only. f Col. i. 15, 16. 1 Tim. i. 17. Heb. xi. 27 only. Gen. i. 2. Isa. xlv. 3. 2 Macc. ix. 5 only. g = Matt. xxv. 34. h = Mark x. 6. xiii. 19. 2 Pet. iii. 4. i Eph. ii. 10 only. Isa. xxix. 16. k = Matt. xxiv. 15. 2 Tim. ii. 7. Heb. xi. 3. Prov. i. 2, 6. l here only. Num. xxiv. 2. Job x. 4 only. m Jude 6 only †. Wisd. vii. 26 only. (-ότης, Wisd. ii. 23 BF [not Aא].) n here only. Wisd. xviii. 9 only. (-ος, Acts xvii. 29.) o ch. iv. 11 reff. = 2 Cor. viii. 6. p ch. ii. 1 only †. q = 1 Cor. xv. 9. r 1 Cor. i. 21 reff. s = 1 Cor. vi. 29. Mal. i. 11. Dan. v. 23. xi. 38 Theod.

19. for διοτι, οτι D¹G Chr$_1$. rec γαρ bef θεος, with D³KL[P rel] Ath$_1$ Thl Œc: txt ABCD¹Gא m 17 Orig$_2$ Eus$_1$ Ath$_1$ Chr Thdrt.
20. for αορ., ορατα G-gr 115. om αιδιος L. [θεοτης P Did$_1$(txt$_{1expr}$).]

that *all which could be known of God* was φανερὸν ἐν αὐτοῖς. He speaks *now* not of what they *might have known* of God, but of what they *did know*. Thus τὸ γνωστ. τ. θεοῦ will mean, *that universal objective knowledge of God as the Creator* which we find more or less in every nation under heaven, and which, as matter of historical fact, was proved to be in possession of the great Gentile nations of antiquity. **φαν. ἐστ. ἐν αὐτοῖς**] **is evident in them**, i. e. *in their hearts*: not, *to them* (as Luth.),—nor, *among them* (as Erasm., Grot., &c.): for if it had been a thing acknowledged *among them*, it would not have been κατεχόμενον. Every man has in him this knowledge; his senses convey it to him (see next verse) with the phænomena of nature. **ὁ θ. γ. ἐφ.**] gives the reason why that which is known of God is manifest in them, viz. because God Himself so created the world as to leave impressed on it this testimony to Himself. Notice, and keep to, the ***historic aorist***, ἐφανέρωσεν, not '*hath* manifested it' (perf.), but **manifested it**, viz. at the Creation. This is important for the right understanding of ἀπὸ κτ. κόσμ. ver. 20.

20.] **For** (justifying the clause preceding) **His invisible attributes** (hence the plur. applying to δύναμις and θειότης which follow), **ἀπὸ κτίσεως κόσμ.**, **from the time of the creation**, when the manifestation was made by God: not = ἐκ κτίσεως κ. 'by the creation of the world;' which would be tautological, τοῖς ποιήμασι νοούμενα following, besides that κτίσις κόσμου cannot = ἡ κτίσις, in the sense of 'the creation,' i. e. 'the creatures.' Umbreit has here a long and important note on O. T. prophecy in general, which will be found well worth study. **τοῖς ποιήμ. νοούμ.**] **being understood** (apprehended by the mind, see reff.) **by means of His works** (of creation and sustenance, —not here of moral government), **καθορᾶται, are perceived**; not, 'are *plainly* seen,'—this is not the sense of κατά in καθοράω, but rather that of looking down on, taking a survey of, and so apprehending or perceiving. **ἥ τε ἀΐδ. αὐτ. δύν.**] **His eternal Power.** To this the evidence of Creation is plainest of all: Eternal, and Almighty, have always been recognized epithets of the Creator. **κ. θειότης**] **and Divinity** (not *Godhead*, which would be θεότης). The fact that the Creator is *divine*;—is of a *different nature* from ourselves, and accompanied by distinct attributes, and those of the highest order,—which we call *divine*. **εἰς τὸ εἶναι αὐτ. ἀναπολ.**] εἰς τό with an inf. never *properly* indicates only the *result*, 'so that;' but is often *used* where *the result*, and *the intention*, are bound together in the process of thought. This is done by a very natural habit in speaking and writing, of transferring one's self to the position of the argument, and regarding that which contributed to a result, as worked purposely for that result. And however true it is, that in the doings of the Allwise, *all results are purposed*,—to give the sense '*in order that they might be inexcusable*,' would be manifestly contrary to the whole spirit of the argument, which is bringing out, not at present *God's sovereignty in dealing with man*, but *man's inexcusableness in holding back the truth by unrighteousness*. **εἰς τό**, then, in this case, is most nearly expressed by **wherefore**, or **so that**. See Winer, edn. 6, § 44. 6. οὐ διὰ τοῦτο ταῦτα πεποίηκεν ὁ θεός, εἰ καὶ τοῦτο ἐξέβη. οὐ γὰρ ἵνα αὐτοὺς ἀπολογίας ἀποστερήσῃ, διδασκαλίαν τοσαύτην εἰς μέσον προύθηκεν, ἀλλ' ἵνα αὐτὸν ἐπιγνῶσιν· ἀγνωμονήσαντες δὲ πάσης ἑαυτοὺς ἀπεστέρησαν ἀπολογίας. Chrys. Hom. iv. p. 450.

21. διότι] expands ἀναπολογήτους—'*without excuse*, because . . .' **γνόντες**] '*with the knowledge above stated*.' This participle testifies plainly that matter of

ᾐ [t] ηὐχαρίστησαν, ἀλλ' [u] ἐματαιώθησαν ἐν τοῖς [v] διαλογισμοῖς αὐτῶν, καὶ [w] ἐσκοτίσθη ἡ [x] ἀσύνετος αὐτῶν καρδία.
22 [y] φάσκοντες εἶναι σοφοὶ [z] ἐμωράνθησαν 23 καὶ [a] ἤλλαξαν
τὴν δόξαν τοῦ [b] ἀφθάρτου θεοῦ [c] ἐν [d] ὁμοιώματι [e] εἰκόνος
[f] φθαρτοῦ ἀνθρώπου καὶ [g] πετεινῶν καὶ [h] τετραπόδων καὶ
[i] ἑρπετῶν. 24 [k] διὸ [[k] καὶ] [l] παρέδωκεν αὐτοὺς ὁ θεὸς ἐν

t 1 Cor. xi. 24 reff. u here only. 1 Kings xiii. 13. Jer. ii. 5. (-ότης, ch. viii. 20.) v = 1 Cor. iii. 20 (from Ps. xciii. 11). James ii. 4. w = ch. xi. 10, from Ps. lxviii. 23 (Matt. xxiv. 29 ‖ Mk. Luke xxiii. 45. Rev. viii. 12) only. x Matt. xv. 16 ‖ Mk. ver. 31. ch. x. 19 (from Deut. xxxii. 21) only. y Acts xxiv. 9. xxv. 19 only. Gen. xxvi. 20. 2 Macc. xiv. 27, 32 only. z = 1 Cor. i. 20 (Matt. v. 15. Luke xiv. 34) only. Jer. x. 13. 2 Kings xxiv. 10. a Psa. cv. 20. 1 Cor. xv. 51, 52 reff. b 1 Cor. ix. 25. xv. 52. 1 Tim. i. 17. 1 Pet. i. 4, 23. iii. 4 only +. Wisd. xii. 1. xviii. 4 only. (-σία, ch. ii. 7). c constr., Ps. l. c. d ch. v. 14. vi. 5. viii. 3. Phil. ii. 7. Rev. ix. 7 only. Deut. iv. 17, 18. e ch. viii. 29 reff. f 1 Cor. ix. 25. xv. 53, 54. 1 Pet. i. 18, 23 only +. Wisd. ix. 15 al2. 2 Macc. vii. 16 only. g Acts x. 12 reff. Deut. xiv. 19, 20. h Acts x. 12. xi. 6 only. Gen. xxxiv. 23. i Acts as above (h). James iii. 7 only. Gen. i. 24. k = [ch. iv. 22.] Phil. ii. 9. l = Acts vii. 42. constr., vv. 26, 28. ch. vi. 17. Eph. iv. 19. Isa. xxxiii. 23. Sir. iv. 19.

21. om η A. (**ηυχαριστησαν**, so ACDℵ c d k l m n 17 $Clem_1$ $Orig_2$ Eus_1 [$Meth_1$] Thdrt Thl.) **αλλα** B. *καρδια* bef *αυτων* D¹G vulg [Orig-int_2 Aug].
23. *ηλλαξαντο* K c g h k $Orig_1$[and mss_2] Eus_1.
24. om *και* ABCℵ 17 vulg [spec Syr copt arm] $Orig_1$[and int_2] Did_1 Damasc Aug Ambrst Pelag: ins DGKL[P] rel syr Ath_1 Chr Thdrt. om *ο θεος* C¹(appy) Did_1

fact, and not of *possibility,* has been the subject of the foregoing verses. From this point, we take up what they MIGHT HAVE DONE, *but* DID NOT. **οὐχ ὡς θεὸν ἐδόξ.**] **They did not give Him glory** (*δοξάζω* here principally of recognition by worship) AS GOD, i. e. as the great Creator of all, distinct from and infinitely superior to all His works. Bengel well divides **ἐδόξασαν** and **ηὐχαρίστησαν**—"*Gratias agere* debemus ob beneficia: *glorificare* ob ipsas virtutes divinas." They *did neither:* in their *religion,* they deposed God from His place as Creator,—in their *lives,* they were ungrateful by the abuse of His gifts. **ἐματαιώθησαν**] הָבַל, *vanus fuit,* is used of worshipping idols, 2 Kings xvii. 15; Jer. ii. 5, and הֶבֶל, *vanitas,* of an idol, Deut. xxxii. 21; 1 Kings xvi. 26 al.: and hence probably the word *ματαιόω* was here chosen. **διαλογισμοῖς**] **their thoughts:** but generally in N. T. in a *bad* sense: **they became vain** (idle, foolish) **in their speculations.** **ἐσκοτίσθη ἡ ἀσύν. αὐτ. καρδ.**] *ἀσύνετος* is not the *result of ἐσκοτ.,*—'*became darkened so as to lose its understanding,*'—but the converse,—**their heart** (*καρδία* of the whole inner man,—the seat of knowledge and feeling) **being foolish** (unintelligent, not retaining God in its knowledge) **became dark** (lost the little light it had, and wandered blindly in the mazes of folly). **22. φάσκοντες εἶν. σοφ.**] Not, '*because they professed themselves wise,*' but **while they professed themselves wise—professing themselves to be wise.** The words relate perhaps not so much to the schools of philosophy, as to the assumption of wisdom by the Greeks in general, see 1 Cor. i. 22, of which assumption their philosophers were indeed eminent, but not the only examples. **23. ἤλλαξαν κ.τ.λ.**] quoted from ref. Ps., only *τὴν δόξαν αὐτῶν,* '*their* glory,' of the Psalm, is changed to '*God's* glory,'—viz. His Power and Majesty visible in the Creation. **ἐν** represents the conditional element in which the change subsisted. **ἀφθάρτου** and **φθαρτοῦ** shew by contrast the folly of such a substitution: He who made and upholds all things must be *incorruptible,* and *no corruptible thing can express His likeness.* **ὁμοιώματι εἰκόνος**] **the similitude of the form**—*εἰκόνος* generalizes it to mean *the human form,* it not being any one particular man, but the *form of man* (examples being abundant) to which they degraded God,—and so of the other creatures. Deities of the *human* form prevailed in Greece—those of the *bestial* in Egypt. Both methods of worship were practised in Rome. **24—32.**] *Immorality, and indeed bestiality, were the sequel of idolatry.* **24.**] The **καί** after *διό* may import, *As they advanced in departure from God, so God also on His part gave them up,* &c.;—*His* dealings with *them* had a progression likewise. **παρέδωκεν**] not merely permissive, but judicial: **God delivered them over.** As sin begets sin, and darkness of mind deeper darkness, grace gives place to judgment, and the divine wrath hardens men, and hurries them on to more fearful degrees of depravity. **ἐν ταῖς ἐπιθ.**] **in the lusts**—not *by* nor *through* the lusts (as Erasmus and E. V.);—the lusts of the heart were the *field of action,* the department of their being, *in which* this dis-

ταῖς [mn] ἐπιθυμίαις τῶν [n] καρδιῶν αὐτῶν εἰς [o] ἀκαθαρσίαν
[p] τοῦ [q] ἀτιμάζεσθαι τὰ σώματα αὐτῶν ἐν αὐτοῖς, 25 [r] οἵτινες
[s] μετήλλαξαν τὴν [t] ἀλήθειαν τοῦ θεοῦ [u] ἐν τῷ [v] ψεύδει καὶ
[w] ἐσεβάσθησαν καὶ [x] ἐλάτρευσαν τῇ [y] κτίσει [z] παρὰ τὸν
[a] κτίσαντα, ὅς ἐστιν [b] εὐλογητὸς [bc] εἰς τοὺς αἰῶνας, ἀμήν.
26 διὰ τοῦτο [d] παρέδωκεν αὐτοὺς ὁ θεὸς εἰς [e] πάθη [f] ἀτιμίας·
αἵ τε γὰρ [g] θήλειαι αὐτῶν [r] μετήλλαξαν τὴν [h] φυσικὴν
[i] χρῆσιν [k] εἰς τὴν [l] παρὰ [m] φύσιν, 27 [n] ὁμοίως [n] τε [n] καὶ οἱ
[o] ἄρσενες [p] ἀφέντες τὴν [h] φυσικὴν [i] χρῆσιν τῆς [g] θηλείας

ABCDG KL[P]א abcdf ghkl mno17 [47]

m = 1 Thess. iv. 5. 2 Pet. ii. 18. Xen. Cyr. i. 6. 34.
n Sir. v. 2 Bא3c F Ald. (om. ACא1).
o Paul (ch. vi. 19. 2 Cor. xii. 21. Eph. iv. 19 al5.) only, exc. Matt. xxiii. 27. Prov. vi. 16.
p = 1 Cor. x. 13 reff.
q Acts v. 41 reff.
r = Acts x. 41 reff.
s here bis only. Esth. ii. 20 Bא &c.(not A). Esdr. i. 31 (29) al.
t = here only. see 1 Thess. i. 9.
u = Eph. iv. 14 al. fr.
v = 2 Thess. ii. 11. 1 John ii. 21. Isa. xliv. 20.
w here only +.
x ver. 9.
y = ch. viii. 39 reff.
z = ch. xiv. 5 reff.
a Mark xiii. 19. Eph. iii. 9. Col. iii. 10. 1 Tim. iv. 3 al. Deut. iv. 32.
b ch. ix. 5 reff.
c ch. xi. 36. Heb. xiii. 8.
d ver. 24.
e Col. iii. 5. 1 Thess. iv. 5 only +. Job xvi. 4 Symm. = Xen. Mem. iii. 10. 8.
f ch. ix. 21. 1 Cor. xi. 14. xv. 43. 2 Cor. vi. 8. xi. 21. 2 Tim. ii. 20 only. P. Jer. xx. 11.
g fem., here bis only. Lev. xxvii. 4. neut., Matt. xix. 4 ‖ Mk. Gal. iii. 28 only. Gen. i. 27. vii. 2.
h here bis. 2 Pet. ii. 12 only +. (-κῶς, Jude 10.)
i here bis only. 1 Kings i. 28. Wisd. xv. 7, 15. Sir. xviii. 8 only. Thuc. vii. 5.
k = James iv. 9. Rev. xi. 6.
l = Acts xviii. 13. ch. iv. 18. xi. 24. Gal. i. 8, 9 al.
m ch. ii. 14, 27. xi. 21, 24 (3ce). 1 Cor. xi. 14. Gal. ii. 15. iv. 8. Eph. ii. 3. James iii. 7 bis. 2 Pet. i. 4 only +. Wisd. vii. 20 only.
n here only. see 1 Cor. vii. 3, 4.
o here 3ce. Matt. xix. 4 ‖ Mk. Luke ii. 23. Gal. iii. 28. Rev. xii. 5, 13 only. Jer. xx. 15.
p = Matt. xxiii. 23. Rev. ii. 4. Judg. ix. 9, &c. A Ald. compl. propr., Matt. iv. 11, 22.

Ath-mss$_1$. [om *εις ακαθαρσιαν* A^1(insd eadem manu, appy).] rec **εαυτοις**, with D^3EGKL[P] 17 rel [Orig$_1$] Chr$_2$ Thdrt Damasc Thl Œc: txt ABCD^1**א**.

[25. *εσεβαστησαν* P. *την κτισιν* P.]

26. for *χρησιν*, *κτισιν* D^1: *sensum* D-lat. aft *παρα φυσιν*, add *χρησιν* D^1G vulg arm [Ambrst] Jer.

27. for *τε*, *δε* AD^1G[P] d l 17 [47] vulg syr Clem$_1$ [Eus$_1$] Ath$_2$ Chr$_2$ Thdrt Damasc Thl [Orig-int$_1$] Aug Ambrst: om C a^1 b h o copt Orig$_1$[and int$_1$] Jer$_2$: txt BD^3KL**א** Syr æth [Ephr$_1$] Œc. om *οι* L k [Euthal-ms]. [Steph] (1st) *αρρενες*, with ACD^3[K, e sil] L[P]**א** rel Ath$_2$ Chr Thdrt [Ephr$_1$ Damasc] Thl: txt BD^1G (c?)

honour took place. **ἀκαθαρσίαν**] more than mere profligacy in the satisfaction of natural lust (as Olsh.); for the Apostle uses cognate words ἀτιμάζεσθαι and ἀτιμία here and in ver. 26:—**bestiality**; impurity in the *physical*, not only in the social and religious sense. **τοῦ ἀτιμάζεσθαι**] the genitive may imply either (1) the *purpose* of God's delivering them over to impurity, '*that their bodies should be dishonoured*,' or (2) the result of that delivering over, '*so that their bodies were dishonoured*,' or (3) the nature of the ἀκαθαρσία, as πάθη ἀτιμίας below,—'*impurity, which consisted in their bodies being dishonoured*.' The second of these seems most accordant with the usage of the Apostle and with the argument. ἀτιμάζεσθαι is most likely *passive* (Beza, al. De Wette), as the middle of ἀτιμάζω is not found in use. And this is confirmed by the old and probably genuine reading *αὐτοῖς*, which has been altered to *ἑαυτοῖς* from imagining that '*they*' was the subject to *ἀτιμάζεσθαι*. **So that their bodies were dishonoured among them.** **25.**] This verse casts light on the *τὴν ἀλήθ. ἐν ἀδικίᾳ κατεχόντων* of ver. 18. The *truth of God* (the true notion of Him as the Creator) which they professed, they changed into (see on ἐν, ver. 23) *a lie* (ψεῦδος = שֶׁקֶר, used of idols, Jer. xvi. 19), thus counteracting its legitimate agency and depriving it of all power for good. **σεβάζομαι**, of the honour of *respect* and *observance* and *reverence*,—**λατρεύω**, of *formal worship with sacrifice and offering*. Both verbs belong to *τῇ κτίσει*; though *σεβάζομαι* would require an accusative, **λατρεύω**, the nearest, takes the government. **τῇ κτ.**] the *thing made*, the **creature**—a general term for all objects of idolatrous worship. **παρά, beyond**—which would amount to the exclusion of the Creator.

The doxology expresses the horror of the Apostle at this dishonour, and puts their sin in a more striking light. But we need not supply *εἰ καὶ οὗτοι ὕβρισαν*, as Chrys. **εὐλογητός** is **Blessed,** *κατ' ἐξοχήν*: the LXX put for it the perf. part., Ps. cxvii. 24. The adjective is usually of *God*: the participle, of man. **26.**] **πάθη ἀτιμ.**,—see above, ver. 24,—stronger than *ἄτιμα πάθη*, as setting forth the *status*, ἀτιμία, to which the *πάθη* belonged. Contrast 1 Thess. iv. 4, *τὸ ἑαυτοῦ σκεῦος κτᾶσθαι* **ἐν τιμῇ**. **χρῆσιν**] *usum venereum*; see examples in Wetstein. This abuse is spoken of first, as being the most revolting to nature. "In peccatis arguendis sæpe scapha debet scapha dici. Pu-

[q] ἐξεκαύθησαν ἐν τῇ [r] ὀρέξει αὐτῶν εἰς ἀλλήλους, [o] ἄρσενες
[s] ἐν [o] ἄρσεσιν τὴν [t] ἀσχημοσύνην [u] κατεργαζόμενοι καὶ τὴν
[v] ἀντιμισθίαν ἣν ἔδει τῆς [w] πλάνης αὐτῶν ἐν ἑαυτοῖς [x] ἀπο-
λαμβάνοντες. 28 καὶ καθὼς οὐκ [y] ἐδοκίμασαν τὸν θεὸν
[z] ἔχειν ἐν [a] ἐπιγνώσει, [b] παρέδωκεν αὐτοὺς ὁ θεὸς [b] εἰς
[c] ἀδόκιμον νοῦν, ποιεῖν τὰ μὴ [d] καθήκοντα, 29 [e] πεπληρω-
μένους [f] πάσῃ [g] ἀδικίᾳ, [hik] πονηρίᾳ, [il] πλεονεξίᾳ, [km] κακίᾳ,

q here only. Deut. xxix. 20. Diod. Sic. xiv. 108. Polyb. ix. 10. 10. r here only †. Sir. xxiii. 6 al. s = 1 Tim. i. 16. t = here (Rev. xvi. 15) only. (Exod. xx. 26.) Jos. Antt. xvi. 7. 6. (-μων, 1 Cor. xii. 23. -μονεῖν, 1 Cor. vii. 36.) u = ch. ii. 9 reff. v 2 Cor. vi. 13 only †. w = James v. 20. 2 Pet. ii. 18. Jude 11. Ezek. xxxiii. 10. x Luke vi. 34. xxiii. 41 al. Num. xxxiv. 14. 2 Macc. iv. 46. vi. 21. viii. 6 only. y = here only ‡. Jos. Antt. ii. 7. 4. see ch. xiv. 22 reff. 1 Cor. iii. 13 reff. z = 1 Tim. iii. 4. so ἔχειν ἐν αἰτίαις or δι' αἰτίας, Thuc. ii. 18. see Viger, p. 249. a ch. iii. 20 reff. Hos. iv. 1. b ver. 24. c 1 Cor. ix. 27. 2 Cor. xiii. 5, 6, 7. 2 Tim. iii. 8. Tit. i. 16. Heb. vi. 8 only. P.H. Prov. xxv. 4. Isa. i. 22 only. d Acts xxii. 22 only. Deut. xxi. 17. 2 Macc. vi. 4. e constr., Luke ii. 40. 2 Cor. vii. 4 only. 2 Macc. vii. 21. f = Acts xx. 19 reff. g Luke xiii. 27. Acts i. 18. Ps. xxvii. 3. h Acts iii. 26 reff. i Mark vii. 22. k 1 Cor. v. 8. l Eph. iv. 19. 2 Pet. ii. 3 al. Ezek. xxii. 27. m = 1 Cor. xiv. 20 reff.

Athen₁ Orig₁ Eus₁ Œc. αρρενες (2nd) ACא¹ b¹ 17 Clem Orig₁ Ath₅ [Ephr] Chr Thdrt: txt BDGL[KP] א-corr¹ [Eus₂ Damasc] Thl Œc. εν αρρεσι Aא¹ 5. 17 Clem Orig Ath₁ Thdrt: txt BCDGL[KP] א-corr¹ [Eus₂ Ephr₁ Damasc] Ath₁ Chr Thl Œc. for εαυτ., αυτοις BK 35.

28. om ο θεος A א¹(ins corr¹) 2 Nyss Damasc Hil-ms₁ Vict-tun: Chr₁ has it bef αυτους.

29. rec aft αδικια ins πορνεια, with L rel syrr [arm Bas₁ Nyss₁ (Ephr₁) Euthal-ms] Thdrt Thl Œc Ennod, and D¹EG vulg Lucif Ruf Ambrst aft κακια, omg πονηρια: [P ins και πορν. (omg πονηρ.), and m ακαθαρσια πορν.:] om ABCKא 17 copt æth Ephr₁ Bas₁[and mss₁] Chr₁ Isid Max Gennad Damasc [Orig-int₁] Aug. κακια bef πλεονεξ. Aא [Syr] Ephr₁ [Orig-int₄] Aug: κακ. πον. πλ. C 17 copt æth Damasc: κακ. πορνεια πλεον. D¹(aft πορν. ins πονηρ. D³ [d]) G [(d)] 2. 46. 71. 92: txt B(K[P] omg πονηρ.) L rel syr Bas₃ [Nyss₁] Chr Thdrt Thl Œc.

dorem præposterum ii fere postulant qui pudicitia carent . . . Gravitas et ardor stili judicialis, proprietate verborum non violat verecundiam." Bengel. 27.] **τὴν ἀσχημ.** perhaps, as De W., '*the* (well-known, too frequent) *indecency*,'—'cui ipsa corporis . . . conformatio reclamat,' Bengel: but more probably the article is only generic, as in 2 Pet. i. 5–8 repeatedly. **τὴν ἀντιμισθίαν**] The Apostle treats this ἀτιμία into which they fell, as a *consequence of*, a *retribution for*, their departure from God into idolatry,—with which *in fact* it was closely connected. *This shame*, and not its *consequences*, which are not *here* treated of, is the ἀντιμισθία of their πλάνη, their aberration from the knowledge of God, which they received. This is further shewn by ἣν ἔδει in the past tense. εἰ γὰρ καὶ μὴ γέεννα ἦν, μηδὲ κόλασις ἠπείλητο, τοῦτο πάσης κολάσεως χεῖρον ἦν. εἰ δὲ ἥδονται, τὴν προσθήκην μοι λέγεις τῆς τιμωρίας. Chrys. Hom. v. p. 457. **ἐν ἑαυτοῖς, in their own persons**, viz. by their degradation even below the beasts.

28.] The play on δοκιμάζω and ἀδόκιμος can hardly be expressed in any other language. 'Non probaverunt' and 'reprobum' of the Vulgate does not give it. **Because they reprobated the knowledge of God, God gave them over to a reprobate mind**, is indeed a very inadequate, but as far as the *form* of the two words is concerned, an *accurate* representation of it. (Mr. Conybeare gives it,—"As they thought fit to cast out the acknowledgment of God, God gave them over to an outcast mind.") For ἀδόκιμος is not 'judicii expers' (as Beza, Tholuck, &c.), but **reprobate**, *rejected by God*. God withdrew from them His preventing grace and left them to the evil which they had chosen. The *active* sense of ἀδόκιμος, besides being altogether unexampled, would, in the depth of its meaning, be inconsistent with the assertion of the passage. God did *not* give them up to a mind which had *lost the faculty of discerning*, but to a mind judicially abandoned to that depravity which, being well able to exercise the δοκιμασία required, not only does not do so, but in the headlong current of its abandonment to evil, sympathizes with and encourages (ver. 32) its practice in others. It is the '*video* meliora *proboque*,' which makes the 'deteriora sequor' so peculiarly criminal.

οὐκ ἐδοκίμασαν ἔχειν is not = ἐδοκίμ. οὐκ ἔχειν (as Dr. Burton): the latter would express more a *deliberate act of the judgment* ending in rejection of God, whereas the text charges them with *not having exercised* that judgment which would, if exercised, have led to the retention of God in their knowledge. **ἔχειν ἐν ἐπιγν.**]

[n] μεστοὺς [opqr] φθόνου, [o] φόνου, [opr] ἔριδος, δόλου, [s] κακοηθείας, ABCDG KL[P]ℵ abcdf ghkl mno17 [47]
[t] ψιθυριστάς, 30 [u] καταλάλους, [v] θεοστυγεῖς, [w] ὑβριστάς,
[xy] ὑπερηφάνους, [xz] ἀλαζόνας, [a] ἐφευρετὰς κακῶν, [x] γονεῦσιν

n = Matt. xxiii. 28. ch. xv. 14. James iii. 8, 17 al. Ezek. xxxvii. 1. Nah. i. 10 only.
o [Gal. v. 20, 21.] p Phil. i. 15. 1 Tim. vi. 4. q as above (op). Matt. xxvii. 18 ‖ Mk. Tit. iii. 3. James iv. 5. 1 Pet. ii. 1 only. Wisd. vi. 23 (25). 1 Macc. viii. 16 only. r 1 Cor. i. 11 reff.
s here only †. 3 Macc. iii. 22. vii. 3. κακοήθεια, τὸ ἐπὶ τὸ χεῖρον ὑπολαμβάνειν ἅπαντα, Aristot. Rhet. ii. 13.
t here only †. (-ίζειν, Ps. xl. 7. -ισμός, 2 Cor. xii. 20.) u here only †. (-λία, 2 Cor. xii. 20. -λεῖν, James iv. 11.) v here only †. w 1 Tim. i. 13 only. Prov. vi. 17 al. (-τρια, Jer. xxvii. [l.] 31. -τικός, Prov. xx. 1.) x 2 Tim. iii. 2. y as above (x). Luke i. 51. James iv. 6. 1 Pet. v. 5 only. Ps. cxviii. 21, 51. (-νία, Mark vii. 22.) z as above (x) only. Job xxviii. 8. Prov. xxi. 24. Hab. ii. 5 only. a here only †.

φονων G D¹-lat [tol] Lucif₁ : [φον. bef φθ. 17 :] εριδος bef φονου A. om δολου A.
30. κακολαλους D. (vv. 27—30 are in a difft hand from the rest of D.)

So Job xxi. 14,—"they say to God, Depart from us: for we desire not the knowledge of thy ways," and xxii. 15—17.

29—31.] **πεπληρωμένους** belongs to the subject of *ποιεῖν*, understood. The reading *πορνείᾳ* appears to have arisen out of *πονηρίᾳ*, and is placed by some MSS. after that word, by some after *κακίᾳ*, omitting *πον.* The Apostle can hardly have written it here, treating as he does all these immoralities of the heart and conscience as *results* of, and *flowing from*, the licentious practices of idolatry above specified. Accurate distinctions of ethical meaning can hardly be found for all these words. Without requiring such, or insisting on each excluding the rest, I have collected the most interesting notices respecting them. Umbreit has illustrated their LXX usage and Hebrew equivalents. **ἀδικίᾳ**] Perhaps a general term, comprehending all that follow: such would be according to the usage of the Epistle: but perhaps to be confined to the stricter import of **injustice**; of which on the part of the Romans, Wetst. gives abundant testimonies. **πονηρίᾳ**] Ammonius interprets *τὸ πονηρόν, τὸ δραστικὸν κακοῦ*,—used therefore more of the tempter and seducer to evil. **πλεονεξίᾳ**] **covetousness** (not as 1 Thess. iv. 6, see there), of which the whole provincial government and civil life of the Romans at the time was full. 'Quando | major avaritiæ patuit sinus?' exclaims Juvenal, soon after this. Sat. i. 87. **κακίᾳ**] more the *passive side of evil*—the capability of and proclivity to evil,—the opposite to *ἀρετή*:—so Arist. Eth. Nic. ii. 3. 6, *ὑπόκειται ἄρα ἡ ἀρετὴ εἶναι . . . . τῶν βελτίστων πρακτική· ἡ δὲ κακία, τοὐναντίον.* **φθόνου** and **φόνου** are probably put together from similarity of sound. So Eurip. Troad. 770 ff., *ὦ Τυνδάρειον ἔρνος, οὔποτ' εἶ Διὸς | πολλῶν δὲ πατέρων φημί σ' ἐκπεφυκέναι, | Ἀλάστορος μὲν πρῶτον, εἶτα δὲ φθόνου, | φόνου τε, θανάτου θ', ὅσα τε γῆ τρέφει κακά.* **κακοηθείας**] see reff. **ψιθυρ. secret maligners,—καταλ. open slanderers.** The distinction attempted to be set up by Suidas and others, between *θεομισής, ὑπὸ θεοῦ μισούμενος*, and *θεομίσης, ὁ μισῶν τὸν θεόν*, has been applied to *θεοστυγεῖς* also, which has therefore been written *θεοστύγεις*. But the distinction is untenable; all compound adjectives in *ης* being oxyton.

* **θεοστυγής** is never found in an active sense, '*hater of God*,' but always in a passive, **hated by God** (cf. Eur. Troad. 1205, *ἡ θεοστυγὴς Ἑλένη*: Cycl. 395, *τῷ θεοστυγεῖ ᾅδου μαγείρῳ*: ib. 598: so *θεοφιλής*, Demosth. 1486 ult.: *εὐτυχεστάτην πασῶν πόλεων τὴν ὑμετέραν νομίζω καὶ θεοφιλεστάτην*: and Æsch. Eum. 831); and such is apparently the sense here. The order of crimes enumerated would be broken, and one of a totally different kind inserted between *καταλάλους* and *ὑβριστάς*, if *θεοστ.* is to signify '*haters of God*.' But on the other supposition,—if any crime was known more than another as '*hated by the gods*,' it was that of '*delatores*,' abandoned persons who circumvented and ruined others by a system of malignant espionage and false information. And the crime was one which the readers of this part of Roman history know to have been the pest of the state; see Tacitus, Ann. vi. 7, where he calls the delatores 'Principi quidem grati, et *Deo exosi*.' So also Philo, ap. Damascen. (quoted by Wetst.) *διάβολοι καὶ θείας ἀποπέμπτοι χάριτος, οἱ τὴν αὐτὴν ἐκείνῳ διαβολικὴν νοσοῦντες κακοτεχνίαν, θεοστυγεῖς τε καὶ θεομισεῖς πάντη.* It does not follow that the *delatores only* are intended, but the expression may be used to include all those abandoned persons who were known as *Diis exosi*, who were employed in pursuits hateful and injurious to their kind. So Wetst., Meyer, Rückert, Fritzsche, De Wette:—the majority of Commentators incline to the *active* sense,—so Theodoret, Œc., Erasm., Luther, Calv., Beza, Estius, Grot., Tholuck, Reiche, &c. **ὑβριστάς**] opposed by Xenoph. Mem. i. and Apol. Socr. to *σώφρων*, 'a discreet and modest man:' but here perhaps, as said by Paul of himself, ref. 1 Tim., 'qui contumeliâ afficit,'

[x b] ἀπειθεῖς, 31 [c] ἀσυνέτους, [d] ἀσυνθέτους, [e] ἀστόργους,
[f] ἀνελεήμονας, 32 [g] οἵτινες τὸ [hi] δικαίωμα τοῦ θεοῦ [hk] ἐπιγνόντες, ὅτι οἱ τὰ τοιαῦτα πράσσοντες [mn] ἄξιοι [n] θανάτου
εἰσίν, οὐ μόνον αὐτὰ ποιοῦσιν, ἀλλὰ καὶ [o] συνευδοκοῦσιν
τοῖς πράσσουσιν.
II. 1 Διὸ [p] ἀναπολόγητος εἶ, ὦ ἄνθρωπε πᾶς ὁ [q] κρί-

b Luke i. 17. Acts xxvi. 19. 2 Tim. iii. 2. Tit. i. 6. iii. 3 only. L.P. Deut. xxi. 18. (-θεῖν, -θεια, ch. xi. 30.)
c ver. 21 reff.
d here only. Jer. iii. 8, 10, 11 only. Demosth. p. 383. 6.
e 2 Tim. iii. 3 only †. Æschin. p. 47, 29.
f here only. Prov. v. 9. xi. 17.
g = Acts x. 41 reff.
h Job xxxiv. 27.
i = Luke i. 6. ch. ii. 26. viii. 4. Heb. ix. 1, 10. Exod. xv. 25.
k = 1 Cor. xiii. 12 reff.
m = of persons, ch. xiii. 46. Matt. x. 10 al. Deut. xxv. 2.
n Acts xxiii. 29 reff.
o 1 Cor. vii. 12, 13 reff.
p ch. i. 20 only †.
q = ch. xiv. 3, 4 reff.

31. rec aft *αστοργους* ins *ασπονδους* (*gloss in marg to explain ασυνθετους*), with CD^3KL[P]$\aleph^3$ rel vulg syr [arm $Nyss_1$] Chr_1(omg *ασυνετους*) Thdrt; pref, 17. 76 Thl; bef *ασυνθετους* D^3: om $ABD^1G\aleph^1$ $fuld^1$ [Syr] copt $Ephr_2$ Damasc [$Orig\text{-}int_1$] $Lucif_1$.

32. *επιγνωντες* L 17 [$Ephr_1$(txt_1)]: *επιγινωσκοντες* B 80: *γνοντες* Thl: *ειδοτες* 116 Chr: add *ουκ ενοησαν* D Bas: *ουκ εγνωσαν* G 8-pe: *ου συνηκαν* 15: *non intellexerunt*, or the like, latt [$Orig\text{-}int_1$ $Cypr_1$ $Lucif_1$ Ambrst]. *ου μονον γαρ* (*see above*) D^1: *ου μ. δε* 46 Bas [Euthal-ms]: *και*[*et*] *ου μ.* vulg[-clem] Ambrst. **ποιουντες** and *συνευδοκουντες* B: *ου μον. οι ποιουντες αυτα αλ. και οι συνευδοκουντες* some mentd by Isid vulg(not am^1) D^2-lat G-lat [(syrr)] arm ($Clem\text{-}rom_1$) $Ephr_2$ [$Orig\text{-}int_1$ $Cypr_1$ $Lucif_1$].

'an insulting person.' **ὑπερηφάνους**] *ἔστι δὲ ὑπερηφανία καταφρόνησίς τις πλὴν αὑτοῦ τῶν ἄλλων*, Theophr. Char. 34. It may be observed that Aristotle, Rhet. ii. 16, mentions *ὑβρισταί* and *ὑπερήφανοι* as examples of *τῷ πλούτῳ ἃ ἕπεται ἤθη*. **ἀλαζόνας**] see reff. *δοκεῖ δὲ καὶ ἀλαζὼν εἶναι ὁ θρασὺς καὶ προσποιητικὸς ἀνδρείας*, Aristot. Eth. Nic. iii. 10. *δοκεῖ δὴ ὁ μὲν ἀλαζὼν προσποιητικὸς τῶν ἐνδόξων εἶναι, καὶ μὴ ὑπαρχόντων, καὶ μειζόνων ἢ ὑπάρχει* . . . . (*ἕνεκα δόξης καὶ τιμῆς*) . . . . *καὶ γὰρ ἡ ὑπερβολὴ καὶ ἡ λίαν ἔλλειψις ἀλαζονικόν*, Ibid. iv. 13. **ἐφευρ. κακ.**] 'Sejanus omnium facinorum repertor habebatur,' Tacit. Ann. iv. 11:—'scelerumque inventor Ulixes,' Virg. Æn. ii. 161: *στασιάρχαι, φιλοπράγμονες, κακῶν εὑρεταί, ταραξιπόλιδες*, Philo in Flacc. § 4, vol. ii. p. 520:—*πάσης κακίας εὑρετής* (of Antiochus Epiph.), 2 Macc. vii. 31. **ἀσυνέτους, destitute of** (moral) **understanding**, see Col. i. 9, and reff. Here perhaps suggested by the similarity of sound to **ἀσυνθέτους, without good faith,** *οὐκ ἐμμένοντας ταῖς συνθήκαις*, Suid. and Hesych. In the same sense, *εὐσυνθετεῖν* and *ἀσυνθετεῖν* are opposed by Chrysippus and Plutarch (see Wetst.). **ἀστόργους**] *μὴ ἀγαπῶντάς τινα*, Hesych. And Athenæus, speaking of *οἱ καλούμενοι ὄρνιθες μελεαγρίδες*,—*ἔστι δὲ ἄστοργον πρὸς τὰ ἔκγονα τὸ ὄρνεον, καὶ ὀλιγωρεῖ τῶν νεωτέρων*, xiv. p. 655 c. "In hac urbe nemo liberos tollit, quia, quisquis suos hæredes habet, nec ad cœnas nec ad spectacula admittitur." Petronius, 116. (Wetst.) **32.**] The Apostle advances to the *highest grade of moral abandonment*,—the knowledge of God's sentence against such crimes, united with the contented practice of them, and encouragement of them in others. **τὸ δικαίωμα τ. θ.**] **the sentence of God,** unmistakeably pronounced in the conscience. **ὅτι** κ.τ.λ.] viz. **that they who do such things are worthy of death**; this *is* the sentence, and must not be enclosed in a parenthesis, as in Wetstein, Griesbach, and Scholz. **θανάτου**, *what sort of death?* Probably a general term for the *fatal* consequence of sin; that such courses *lead to ruin*. The word can hardly be pressed to its exact meaning: for many of the crimes mentioned could never be visited with judicial capital punishment in this world (as Grot.): nor could the heathen have any definite idea of eternal, spiritual death, as the penalty attached to sin (Calov.),—nor again, any idea of the *connexion* between sin and natural death. "Life and Death," remarks Umbreit, "are ever set over against one another in the O. T. as well as in the N. T., the one as including all good that can befall us, the other, all evil." p. 246. The description here given by the Apostle of the moral state of the heathen world should by all means be compared with that in Thucyd. iii. 82—84, of the moral state of Greece in the Peloponnesian war: and a passage in Wisd. xiv. 22—31, the opening of which is remarkably similar to our text: *εἶτ' οὐκ ἤρκεσε τὸ πλανᾶσθαι περὶ τὴν τοῦ θεοῦ γνῶσιν, ἀλλὰ* . . . . , ver. 22, and again ver. 27, *ἡ γὰρ τῶν ἀνωνύμων εἰδώλων θρησκεία παντὸς ἀρχὴ κακοῦ καὶ αἰτία καὶ πέρας ἐστίν*.

II. 1—29.] *Secondly*, THE SAME, *that all are guilty before God*, IS PROVED OF THE JEWS ALSO. And first, vv. 1—11, *no man* (the practice of the Jews being hinted at) *must condemn another, for all alike are*

νων· [r] ἐν ᾧ γὰρ [q] κρίνεις τὸν [s] ἕτερον, σεαυτὸν [t] κατα- ABCDG KL[P]ℵ
κρίνεις· τὰ γὰρ αὐτὰ πράσσεις ὁ [q] κρίνων. 2 οἴδαμεν δὲ a b c d f
ὅτι τὸ [u] κρῖμα τοῦ θεοῦ ἐστὶν [v] κατὰ [v] ἀλήθειαν [w] ἐπὶ τοὺς g h k l m n o 17
τὰ τοιαῦτα πράσσοντας. 3 [x] λογίζῃ δὲ τοῦτο, ὦ ἄνθρωπε [47]
ὁ [q] κρίνων τοὺς τὰ τοιαῦτα πράσσοντας καὶ ποιῶν αὐτά,
[x] ὅτι σὺ [y] ἐκφεύξῃ τὸ [u] κρῖμα τοῦ θεοῦ; 4 ἢ τοῦ [z] πλούτου
τῆς [ab] χρηστότητος αὐτοῦ καὶ τῆς [cd] ἀνοχῆς καὶ τῆς
[ade] μακροθυμίας [f] καταφρονεῖς, [g] ἀγνοῶν [g] ὅτι τὸ [h] χρηστὸν
τοῦ θεοῦ εἰς μετάνοιάν σε [i] ἄγει, 5 κατὰ δὲ τὴν [k] σκλη- ...σε αγει κα. C.

r ch. xiv. 22. 1 Pet. ii. 12. s ch. xiii. 8. 1 Cor. iv. 6. vi. 1. x. 24, 29 al. Exod. xvi. 15. t = Matt. xxvii. 3. [John viii. 10.] ch. xiv. 23. Esth. ii. 1. u = Mark xii. 40. Luke xx. 47. ch. iii. 8. xiii. 2 al. Jer. xxviii. (li.) 10. v here only. w = Acts xiii. 11 reff. x constr., (ch. xiv. 14) 2 Cor. x. 7, 11. Heb. xi. 19. 1 Macc. vi. 9. y = Luke xxi. 36. 2 Cor. xi. 33. 1 Thess. v. 3 (Acts xvi. 27 reff. xix. 6) only. L.P.H. 2 Macc. vii. 35. z = ch. ix. 23. xi. 33. Eph. i. 7, 18. ii. 7 al. (Paul.) τρυφᾷς ὑπὸ πλούτου τῆς σοφίας, Plato, Euthyphr. p. 12 A. (= πλῆθος, LXX. Ps. lxviii. 16 al.) a 2 Cor. vi. 6. Gal. v. 22. b as above (a). ch. iii. 12. xi. 22 (3ce). Eph. ii. 7 al2. P. Ps. xxiv. 7. (-τεύεσθαι, 1 Cor. xiii. 4.) c (=) ch. iii. 25 only †. (1 Macc. xii. 25 only. Jos. Antt. vi. 5. 1.) d see Eph. iv. 2. ch. ix. 22. 1 Tim. i. 16 al. Prov. xxv. 15. (-μεῖν, 1 Cor. xiii. 4. -μως, Acts xxvi. 3.) f Matt. xviii. 10. 1 Cor. xi. 22 al. Prov. xiii. 13. g ch. i. 13 reff. h 1 Cor. xv. 33 reff. Ps. xxxiii. 8. constr., ch. i. 19, 20. i = ch. viii. 14. Gal. v. 18. 2 Tim. iii. 6. Polyb. i. 15. 13. k here only. = Deut. ix. 27. see Matt. xix. 8.

ABDG KL[P]ℵ a b c d f g h k l m n o 17 [47]

CHAP. II. 1. ins κριματι bef κρινεις C¹ m 73. 80. 93. 179 syr-w-ast copt.
2. for δε, γαρ Cℵ m 17. 80. 122-79 vulg D-lat copt arm Chr_1 Pelag: txt AB D-gr GKL[P] rel Thdrt Damasc Thl Œc [$Orig\text{-}int_1$ Ambrst] $Tert_1$: om 23 æth.
3. [for λογ. to πρασσοντας, νομιζεις ουν ο ταυτα πρασσων P.] τουτω A.

guilty. **1.**] The address passes gradually to the Jews. They were the people who *judged*—who pronounced all Gentiles to be born in sin and under condemnation:—doubtless there were also proud and censorious men among the Gentiles, to whom the rebuke might apply, but these are hardly in the Apostle's mind. This is evident by comparing τὰ γὰρ αὐτὰ πράσσεις ὁ κρίνων with vv. 21—23, where the same charge is implied in a direct address to the Jew. **διό**, on account of this δικαίωμα θεοῦ decreeing death against the doers of these things—FOR *thou doest them thyself*. Therefore thy setting thyself up as a judge, is unjustifiable. **πᾶς ὁ κρίνων**] The Jew is not yet named, but hinted at (see above): not in order to conciliate the Jews (Rückert), but on account of the as yet purposely general form of the argument. This verse is in fact the major of a syllogism, the minor of which follows, vv. 17—20, where the position here declared to be unjustifiable, is asserted to be assumed by *the Jew*. **ἐν ᾧ . . .**] **For wherein** (not *'in that'*), as E. V.—i. e. *'in the matter in which.'* **2.**] **οἶδ. δέ**, *'atqui scimus'*—**now we know. κατὰ ἀλ.**] **according to truth**, as E. V., De Wette:—not, *'truly,' 'revera'* (as Raphel, &c.)—for οἴδαμεν, on which the emphasis is, implies certain knowledge. Nor does κατὰ ἀλ. belong to κρῖμα, *'judgment according to truth'* (as Olsh.),—but to ἐστίν, **is**, (proceeds) **according to justice** (John viii. 16). **3.**] Here he approximates nearer to the Jews. They considered that because they were the children of Abraham they should be saved, see Matt. iii. 7, 9. **τοῦτο**, viz. ὅτι σὺ ἐκφ., following. **σύ** has the emphasis on it, **thou thyself**,—*'thou above all others.'* **4.**] **ἤ, or** (introducing a new error or objection, see ch. iii. 29; vi. 3; xi. 2), *'inasmuch as God spares thee day by day* (see Eccles. viii. 11), *dost thou set light by His long-suffering, ignorant that His intent in it is to lead thee to repentance?'* **πλούτου**,—a favourite word with the Apostle (see reff.),—the **fulness**, 'abundance.' **χρηστ.**, as shewn by His **ἀνοχή** and **μακροθ.** (reff.) **ἀγνοῶν, not knowing**,—being blind to the truth, **that . . .** Grot., Thol., al. would render it *'not considering:'* but as De Wette remarks, it is a *wilful and guilty ignorance*, not merely an inconsiderateness, which is blamed in the question. **ἄγει, is leading thee**: this is its intent and legitimate course, which thy blindness will frustrate. 'Malo *deducit* quam *invitat*; quia illud plus quiddam significat. Neque tamen pro adigere accipio, sed pro manu ducere.' Calvin. **5.**] I am inclined with Lachmann to regard the question as continued. If not, the responsive contrast to the question in ver. 4 would begin more emphatically than with κατὰ δὲ . . .; it would be σὺ δὲ κατὰ . . . . or θησαυρίζεις δὲ σεαυτῷ κατὰ . . . . But the enquiry loses itself in the digressive clauses following, and no where comes pointedly to an end. I have therefore not placed a mark of interrogation at ἄγει or at θεοῦ, as Lachm. does,—

ῥότητά σου καὶ [l] ἀμετανόητον καρδίαν [m] θησαυρίζεις σεαυτῷ
[n] ὀργὴν ἐν [o] ἡμέρᾳ [no] ὀργῆς καὶ [p] ἀποκαλύψεως [q] δικαιοκρισίας
τοῦ θεοῦ, 6 ὃς [r] ἀποδώσει [r] ἑκάστῳ [r] κατὰ τὰ ἔργα αὐτοῦ,
7 τοῖς μὲν καθ' [s] ὑπομονὴν [t] ἔργου [t] ἀγαθοῦ [u] δόξαν καὶ

l here only †.
m = Prov. i. 18. (Matt. vi. 19, 20 al.)
n abs., Luke xxi. 23. ch. iii. 5. iv. 15 al.
o Rev. vi. 17. Zeph. ii. 3.
p = 1 Cor. i. 7. 2 Thess. i. 7. al.
q here only †. Hos. vi. 5 (for מִשְׁפָּט) Incert. [Quinta?] in Hexapl. (-κρίτης, 2 Macc. xii. 41.)
r = Matt. xvi. 27. Rev. xxii. 12. Prov. xxiv. 12.
s = Luke xxi. 19. ch. v. 3, 4. Heb. xii. 1 al. Ezra x. 2. see James i. 4. constr., 1 Thess. i. 3.
t Acts ix. 36 reff. sing., ch. xiii. 3.
u = ch. v. 2. viii. 18. ix. 23 al.

5. for *αποκαλυψεως*, *ανταποδοσεως* A (æth[-rom]) Cæs-arel$_1$. ins *και* bef *δικαιοκρισιας* D³KL[P]ℵ³ 17 rel syr (æth[-rom]) Orig$_2$ Eus$_2$ Ephr$_2$ Bas$_1$ Chr$_1$ [Cyr$_2$-p Euthal-ms] Thdrt$_{sæpe}$: *της* 3. 33-5. 108-21: om ABD¹Gℵ¹ vulg Syr copt goth [arm] Orig$_3$[and int$_{sæpe}$ Eus$_1$] Damasc Œc Iren-int$_1$ Cypr Lucif.

but have left the construction to explain itself. **κατά**] not, '*in proportion to*' (Meyer), but as E. V. **after**, '*in consonance with*,' '*secundum*,'—describing the state out of which the action springs: see ver. 7, *καθ' ὑπομονήν*. **ἀμεταν.**] not admitting that *μετάνοια* to which God is leading thee. **ἐν ἡμέρᾳ**, not for, nor = *εἰς ἡμέραν*, nor should it be rendered '*against* the day,' as E. V. I need hardly remind any accurate scholar, that such an interpretation as '*ἐν* for *εἰς*' is *no where* to be tolerated. It belongs to *ὀργήν*,—**wrath in the day of wrath**, 'wrath which shall come upon thee in that day,'—not to *θησαυρίζεις*, imagining which has led to the mistake. The *ἡμέρα ὀργῆς* is the *day of judgment*, viewed in its relation to *sinners*: see reff. **ἀποκαλ. δικαιοκρ.**] **the manifestation** (public enforcement, it having been before latent though determined) **of God's righteous judgment.** The reading *ἀποκ.* **καὶ** *δικαιοκρ.* would mean, '*the appearance* (reff.) *of God, and his righteous judgment*,'—not referring merely to *the detection of men's hearts*, as Origen, Theophyl., Rückert. But the reading is not strongly upheld, nor is it according to the mode of speaking in the argument—see ch. i. 17, 18. **6, 7.**] This *retribution* must be carefully kept in its place in the argument. The Apostle is here speaking *generally*, of the general system of God in governing the world,—the judging according to each man's works—punishing the evil, and rewarding the righteous. No question *at present* arises, *how* this righteousness in God's sight *is to be obtained*—but the truth is only stated broadly at present, to be further specified by and by, when it is clearly shewn that by *ἔργα νόμου* no flesh can be justified before God. The neglect to observe this has occasioned two mistakes: (1) an idea that by this passage it is proved that not faith only, but works also in some measure, justify before God (so Toletus in Pool's Syn.), and (2) an idea (Tholuck 1st edn. and Köllner) that by *ἔργου ἀγαθοῦ* here is *meant* faith in Christ. However true it be, so much is certainly not *meant* here, but merely the fact, that *every where, and in all, God punishes evil, and rewards good.* **7, 8. τοῖς μὲν καθ' ὑπ. . . . . ὀργὴ κ. θυμός**] **To those who by endurance in good works seek for glory and honour and immortality** (will He render) **eternal life: but to those who are** (men) **of self-seeking, and disobey the truth, but obey iniquity** (shall accrue) **anger and wrath,** &c. The verb *ἀποδώσει*, ver. 6, should have two accusatives, representing the two sides of the final retribution,—*ζωὴν αἰών.* and *ὀργήν*, &c. But the second of these is changed to a nominative and connected with *ἔσται* understood, and made the first member of the following sentence, *δόξα δὲ κ.τ.λ.* being opposed to it. Thus also two datives belong to *ἀποδώσει*, viz. *τοῖς . . . . ζητοῦσιν*,—and *τοῖς . . . ἀδικίᾳ*. To *ζητοῦσιν* belong *δόξ. κ. τιμ. κ. ἀφθ.* as its accusatives, and *καθ' ὑπομ. ἔργ. ἀγ.* as its adverb. This, as De Wette remarks, is the only admissible construction: in opposition to (α) Œcum. and Beza, who divide *ἔργ. ἀγ.* from *καθ' ὑπομ.* (*iis quidem qui secundum patientem expectationem quærunt boni operis gloriam*),—(β) Bengel, Knapp, Fritzsche, Olsh., and Krehl, who take *τοῖς . . . . ἀγαθοῦ* as meaning '*those who endure in good works*' (as Œc. does *τοῖς καθ' ὑπομ.* *those who endure*, absol.), and *δόξαν . . . . ζητοῦσιν*, as in apposition with it,—(γ) Photius (in Œcum.), Luther, and Estius, who take it, *τοῖς . . . . . ζητοῦσιν ζωὴν αἰών.*,—*δόξαν κ.τ.λ.*,—(δ) Reiche, who takes *τοῖς μέν*,—'*to the one*,'—alone, and makes *καθ' ὑπομ.* parallel to *κατὰ τὰ ἔργα*, representing the *rule of judgment*, taking the rest as (γ). **ἔργου**, sing. of *moral habitude* in the whole, the *general course of life and action* (see reff.). **δόξαν**, *absolute* imparted *glory* like His own, see Matt. xiii. 43; John xvii. 22:—**τιμήν**, *recognition, relative precedence*, see Matt.

τιμὴν καὶ [v] ἀφθαρσίαν [w] ζητοῦσιν ζωὴν αἰώνιον· 8 τοῖς δὲ
[x] ἐξ [y] ἐριθείας καὶ [z] ἀπειθοῦσι μὲν τῇ [a] ἀληθείᾳ, [b] πειθομένοις
δὲ τῇ [c] ἀδικίᾳ, [def] ὀργὴ καὶ [efg] θυμός, 9 [fhi] θλῖψις καὶ [ij] στενοχωρία, [k] ἐπὶ πᾶσαν [l] ψυχὴν ἀνθρώπου τοῦ [m] κατεργα-
ζομένου [n] τὸ [n] κακόν, Ἰουδαίου τε πρῶτον καὶ Ἕλληνος·

ABDG KL[P]ℵ a b c d f g h k l m n o 17 [47]

v = 1 Cor. xv. 42, &c. 2 Tim. i. 10 (Eph. vi. 24) only +. (Wisd. ii. 23. vi. 18, 19 only.)
w = Matt. vi. 33. Col. iii. 1 al. Ps. xxxiii. 14.
x = John xviii. 37. ch. iii. 26. iv. 12, 14. Gal. iii. 7 al.
y 2 Cor. xii. 20. Gal. v. 20. Phil. i. 17. ii. 3. James iii. 14, 16 only +.
z = ch. x. 21. Deut. xxi. 20.
a = 1 John i. 6 al.
b = Acts v. 36 reff.
c ch. i. 18 al.
d ver. 6.
e Eph. iv. 21.
f Ps. lxxvii. 49.
g = Rev. xv. 1. Ezek. v. 15.
h = 2 Thess. i. 6.
i ch. viii. 35. 2 Cor. vi. 4. Isa. viii. 22. xxx. 6.
j as above (i). 2 Cor. xii. 10 only. (-ρεῖσθαι, 2 Cor. iv. 8.)
k = Acts xiii. 11 reff.
l Acts ii. 43 reff. Luke ix. 56 v. r. Num. xix. 11, 13.
m = ch. i. 27. vii. 13, 15, 17, 18. 1 Cor. v. 3. 1 Pet. iv. 3. Ps. lxvii. 31 (28) ℵ[3a] Ald. compl.
n John xviii. 23. ch. vii. 21. xii. 21 (bis). xiii. 4 (bis). xvi. 19. 1 Cor. xiii. 5. 3 John 11 only. Deut. xxx. 15.

8. ερηθειας A f: ερειθιας B[1]D[3]G: εριθιας D[1]. om μεν BD[1]Gℵ[1] Th[ph-ant$_1$]: ins AD[3]KL[P]ℵ[3] 17 rel syr Orig$_1$[and int$_2$] Ephr Chr Thdrt Damasc Thl Œc. rec θυμος και οργη, with D[3]KL[P] 17 rel syr [Eus$_1$ Euthal-ms] Thdrt Œc: txt ABD[1]Gℵ m vulg Syr [copt] arm Orig$_1$[and int$_2$] Ephr$_1$ Damasc Thl.

9. ιουδαιω and ελληνι G m 1. 109 D[1]-lat.

x. 32; xxv. 34:—**ἀφθαρσίαν, incorruptibility**: so the aim of the Christian athlete is described, 1 Cor. ix. 25, as being to obtain στέφανον ἄφθαρτον. **8. τοῖς δὲ ἐξ ἐριθείας**] as in reff., to be supplied by οὖσιν, those who live in, act from, are situated in and do their deeds from—ἐριθεία as a status, as οἱ ἐξ spoken of *place*. **ἐριθεία**,—not from ἔρις, from which it is distinguished 2 Cor. xii. 20; Gal. v. 20, but from ἔρῑθος, a hired workman, whence ἐριθεύω or -ομαι, properly 'to work for hire,' but met. and generally, '*ambitum exercere*,' used principally of official persons, who seek their own purposes in the exercise of their office, and (according to the analogy of παιδεία from παιδεύω, δουλεία from δουλεύω, ἀλαζονεία from ἀλαζονεύομαι) ἐριθεία, '*ambitus*,' '*self-seeking*,' '*greed*.' It stands opposed to ὑπομονὴ ἔργου ἀγαθοῦ, which requires self-denial and forbearance. There seems to be no reason why this, the proper meaning, should not here apply, without seeking for a more far-fetched one, as '*the party spirit of the Jews*,' Rückert. The mistake of rendering it '*contentiousness*,' and imagining a derivation from ἔρις prevailed universally (Orig., Chrys., Theodoret, Theophyl., Œcum., Hesych. (ἠριθεύετο, ἐφιλονείκει), Vulg., Erasm., Grot., &c., and even the more recent English Commentators, Bloomf., Slade, and Peile, τοῖς ἐξ ἐριθείας, i. e. τοῖς ἐρίζουσι) according to De Wette, *down to Rückert*, who first suggested the true derivation. It appears to have arisen from ἐρεθίζω being somewhat similar in sound. Aristotle uses it in the sense of 'ambitus,' canvassing for office, in Polit. v. 3,—μεταβάλλουσι δὲ αἱ πολιτεῖαι καὶ ἄνευ στάσεως διά τε τὰς ἐριθείας, ὥσπερ ἐν Ἡραίᾳ· ἐξ αἱρετῶν γὰρ διὰ τοῦτο ἐποίησαν κληρωτάς, ὅτι ᾑροῦντο τοὺς ἐριθευομένους. Fritzsche, who has an excursus on the word, renders οἱ ἐξ ἐριθ.,—'*malitiosi fraudum machinatores*.' Ignatius, ad Philad. § 8, p. 704, opposes ἐριθ. to χριστομαθία. On the whole, **self-seeking** seems best to lay hold of the idea of the word: see note on Phil. i. 16, 17. **ἀπειθ. μ. τῇ ἀλ.**] Hindering (see ch. i. 18) the truth which they possess from working, by self-abandonment to iniquity. **ὀργὴ κ. θυμός**] According to this arrangement (see var. readd.) the former word denotes the *abiding, settled mind of God towards them* (ἡ ὀργὴ τ. θεοῦ μένει ἐπ' αὐτόν, John iii. 36),—and the latter, the *outbreak* of that anger at the great day of retribution. So the grammarians: θυμὸς μέν ἐστι πρόσκαιρος (*excandescentia*, as Cicero)· ὀργὴ δὲ πολυχρόνιος μνησικακία, Ammon. See the same further brought out by Tittmann, Syn. i. p. 131. **9. θλῖψ. κ. στεν.**] An expression from the LXX (see reff.): the former signifying more the outward weight of objective infliction,—the latter the subjective feeling of the pressure. It is possible, in the case of the *suffering Christian*, for the former to exist without the latter: so 2 Cor. iv. 8, ἐν παντὶ θλιβόμενοι, ἀλλ' οὐ στενοχωρούμενοι. But here the objective weight of infliction and the subjective weight of anguish, are co-existent. **ἐπὶ πᾶσαν ψ. ἀνθ.**] probably a periphrasis for the sake of emphasis and solemnity. Had it been (as Fritzsche and Meyer) to indicate that the soul is the suffering part of the man (nearly so Olsh.), it should have been as De W. observes, ἐπὶ ψυχὴν παντὸς ἀνθρ., or ἐπὶ πᾶσαν ψυχὴν ἀνθρώπων (see reff.). **κατεργ.**] κατεργάζομαι and ἐργάζομαι seem to have but this slight difference,—that κατεργάζομαι, answering rather to our 'commit,' is more naturally used of *evil*, as manifested and judged of by *separate acts* among men, whereas ἐργάζομαι, answering to our 'work,' is used indifferently of both good

10 ᵒ δόξα δὲ καὶ τιμὴ καὶ ᵖ εἰρήνη παντὶ τῷ ᵠ ἐργαζομένῳ
ʳ τὸ ʳ ἀγαθόν, Ἰουδαίῳ τε πρῶτον καὶ Ἕλληνι. 11 οὐ γάρ
ἐστιν ˢ προσωποληψία παρὰ τῷ θεῷ· 12 ὅσοι γὰρ ᵗ ἀνόμως ἥμαρτον, ᵗ ἀνόμως καὶ ᵘ ἀπολοῦνται, καὶ ὅσοι ᵛ ἐν
ᵛ νόμῳ ἥμαρτον, διὰ νόμου ʷ κριθήσονται· 13 οὐ γὰρ οἱ

o = ver. 7. p = John xiv. 27. ch. v. 1. viii. 6 [x. 15 (from Isa. lii. 7)] al. q = Matt. vii. 23. xxvi. 10. Gal. vi. 10 al. Ps. xiv. 2. r Matt. xix. 17. Luke vi. 45. ch. vii. 13 bis. xii. 21. xiii. 3, 4. Philem. 14 al. 2 Kings xiv. 17. see John v. 29. 1 Pet. iii. 11. s Eph. vi. 9. Col. iii. 25. James ii. 1 only †. (-πτης, Acts x. 34. -πτεῖν, James ii. 9.) t here bis only †. 2 Macc. viii. 17 only; but not =. (-μος, 1 Cor. ix. 21.) u = Matt. xviii. 14. 1 Cor. i. 18. 2 Cor. ii. 15. iv. 3. 2 Thess. ii. 10. Lev. xxiii. 30. v — here only. (Gal. iii. 11. v. 4.) w = Acts xvii. 31. ver. 16. ch. iii. 6 al. Ps. xcv. 13.

10. τω εργαζ. το αγαθον bef παντι G. **11.** om τω D¹.

and evil. That this is not always kept to, see reff., especially ch. vii. 18, and Plato Legg. iii. p. 686, end, in both which places, however, *definite acts* are spoken of. The *pres. part.* denotes the status or habit of the man. **Ἰουδ. τε πρῶτον**] Because the Jew has so much greater advantages, and better opportunities of knowing the divine will: and, therefore, pre-eminent responsibility. **10. εἰρήνη**] Here in its highest and most glorious sense, see reff. **11.**] This remark serves as the transition to what follows, not merely as the confirmation of what went before. As to what *preceded*, it asserts that though the Jew has had great advantages, he shall be justly judged for his use of them, not treated as a favourite of Heaven: as to what *follows*, it introduces a comparison between him and the Gentile to shew *how fairly* he will be, for those greater advantages, regarded as *πρῶτος* in responsibility. And thus we gradually (see note on ver. 1) pass to the direct comparison between him and the Gentile, and consideration of his state.

12—16.] *The justice of a* GENERAL *judgment of* ALL, *but according to the advantages of each.* **12. ὅσοι γ. ἀνόμως . . . .**] **For as many as have sinned without** (the) **law** (of Moses): **shall also perish without** (the) **law** (of Moses): i. e. *it shall not appear against them in judgment.* Whether that will *ameliorate* their case, is not even hinted,—but only the *fact*, as consonant with God's justice, stated. That this is the meaning of *ἀνόμως* is clear from 1 Cor. ix. 21. That even these have sinned against *a νόμος*, is presently (ver. 14) shewn. Chrys. says (Hom. vi. p. 466), ... *ὁ μὲν γὰρ Ἕλλην ἀνόμως κρίνεται· τὸ δὲ* **ἀνόμως** *ἐνταῦθα οὐ τὸ χαλεπώτερον, ἀλλὰ τὸ ἡμερώτερον λέγει·* (this is perhaps saying too much, see above) *τουτέστιν, οὐκ ἔχει κατηγοροῦντα τὸν νόμον. τὸ γὰρ ἀνόμως τοῦτ' ἔστι, χωρὶς τῆς ἐξ ἐκείνου κατακρίσεως, φησίν, ἀπὸ τῶν τῆς φύσεως λογισμῶν καταδικάζεται μόνων. ὁ δὲ Ἰουδαῖος, ἐννόμως, τουτέστι, μετὰ τῆς φύσεως καὶ τοῦ νόμου κατηγοροῦντος· ὅσῳ γὰρ πλείονος ἀπήλαυσεν ἐπιμελείας, τοσούτῳ μείζονα δώσει δίκην.* **καί** (De W.) serves to range *ἀπολ.*, as well as *ἥμαρτ.* under the common condition *ἀνόμως*: **As many as without the law have sinned, without the law shall also perish.** **ἀπολοῦνται**, the *result* of the judgment on them, rather than *κριθήσονται*, its *process*, because the absence of the law would thus seem as if it were the *rule by which they are to be judged*,—whereas it is only an *accident* of that judgment, which *depends on other considerations.* **ἐν νόμῳ**, **under** (*in*, as a status) **the** (Mosaic) **law**; not '*a* law,' which would make the sentence a truism: it is on *that very* undeniable assumption, '*that all who have had a law given shall be judged by that law*,' that the Apostle constructs his argument, asserting it with regard to the Mosaic law in the case of the Jews, and proving that the Gentiles have had a law given to them in the testimony of their consciences. As to the omission of the article, no inference can be drawn, as the word follows a preposition: see ver. 23, where *ἐν νόμῳ* unquestionably means '*in the law of Moses.*' Besides, these verses are no general assertions concerning men who have, and men who have not, a law revealed (for *all have one*), but a *statement of the case as concerning Jews and Gentiles.* **νόμος**, *throughout*, signifies *the law of Moses*, even though anarthrous, in every place, except where the absence of the article corresponds to a *logical* indefiniteness, as e. g. *ἑαυτοῖς εἰσιν νόμος*, ver. 14: and even there not '*a* law:' see note. And I hope to shew that it is never thus anarthrously used as = *ὁ νόμος*, except where usage will account for such omission of the article. **διὰ νόμ. κριθ.**] Now, **shall be judged by the law**: for that will furnish the *measure* and *rule* by which judgment will proceed. **13.**] This is to explain to the Jew the fact, that not his mere hearing of the law read in the synagogue (= his being by birth and privilege a Jew) will justify him before God, but (still keeping to general principles and not touching as yet on the *impossibility of being thus*

x ἀκροαταὶ νόμου δίκαιοι y παρὰ τῷ θεῷ, ἀλλ' οἱ z ποιηταὶ ABDG
νόμου a δικαιωθήσονται. 14 ὅταν γὰρ ἔθνη τὰ μὴ νόμον KL[P]א abcdf
ἔχοντα b φύσει c τὰ τοῦ νόμου ποιῶσιν, οὗτοι νόμον μὴ ghkl mno17
ἔχοντες ἑαυτοῖς εἰσιν νόμος, 15 d οἵτινες e ἐνδείκνυνται τὸ [47]
f ἔργον τοῦ νόμου g γραπτὸν ἐν ταῖς καρδίαις αὐτῶν,
h συμμαρτυρούσης αὐτῶν τῆς i συνειδήσεως καὶ k μεταξὺ

x James i. 22, 23, 25 only. Isa. iii. 3 only.
y 1 Cor. iii. 19. Gal. iii. 11 al.
z = James, as above (x), and iv. 11 (Acts xvii. 28) only †. 1 Macc. ii. 67 only.
a = Paul (Acts xiii. 39. ch. iii. 20 al23.) only, exc. Luke xviii. 14. James ii. 21, 24, 25. Ps. cxlii. 2.
b Gal. ii. 15. iv 8. Eph. ii. 3 only. (ch. i. 26 reff.)
c constr., ch. viii. 5. Matt. xvi. 23. Luke ii. 49. Thuc. viii. 31.
d = Acts x. 41 reff.
e = ch. ix. 17 (from Exod. ix. 16), 22. 2 Cor. viii. 24. Eph. ii. 7. 1 Tim. i. 16 (2 Tim. iv. 14 [see note there] al2. Heb. vi. 10, 11) only. P.H. (Gen. l. 15, 17.)
f see ver. 7 reff.
g here only. 2 Chron. xxxvi. 22. Esdr. ii. 2. 2 Macc. xi. 15 only.
h ch. viii. 16. ix. 1 only †.
i 2 Cor. i. 10 reff. (Eccles. x. 20.) Wisd. xvii. 11 only.
k Acts xv. 9 reff.

13. [om ver P.] rec ins *του* bef 1st *νομου*, with KL 17 rel [arm] Mcion-e Chr Thdrt Phot: om ABDGא [47[2] Orig(Tischdf) Euthal-ms] Damasc. om *τω* BD[1] k[1] [$Orig_1$]: ins AD[3]GKLא rel $Mcion\text{-}e_1$ [$Orig_1$] Chr Thdrt. for *αλλ' οι*, *αλλα* G. rec ins *του* bef 2nd *νομου*, with D[3]KL 17 rel $Mcion\text{-}e_1$ Chr Thdrt Phot: om ABD[1]Gא [$Orig_2$ Euthal-ms] Damasc. aft *δικαιωθησονται* ins *παρα θεω* G [spec].

14. for *γαρ*, *δε* G æth arm $Orig_1$[(txt_1 and int_2): om a]. ins *τα* bef *εθνη* G k. rec *ποιη* (*grammatical corrn*), with D[3] rel [Eus_1] Chr Thdrt: *ποιει* KL[P n] 17: *ποιουσιν* D[1]G [Cyr_2-p Euthal-ms]: txt ABא [47-marg] $Clem_1$ $Orig_3$ Damasc. for *ουτοι*, *οι τοιουτοι* G vulg D-lat $Orig_1$[and int_2] (Hil).

15. *ενδιγνυνται* A: *ενδικν.* Gא. *της συνειδησεως* bef *αυτων* DG [arm]: *αυτοις τ. συν.* tol[1] [Orig-int_2] Chr Jer: *αυτοις τ. σ. αυτων* vulg Pelag Ambrst: txt ABKL[P]א 17 rel [$Orig_3$-int_1 Chr_1].

justified) the doing of the law. *τοῦ* has been apparently inserted in both cases in the later MSS. from seeing that *νόμος* was indisputably the law of Moses, and stumbling at the unusual expression *οἱ ἀκροαταὶ νόμου*. But the *οἱ* in both cases is *generic*, and *ἀκροατὴς-νόμου*, *ποιητὴς-νόμου* (almost as *one word* in each case), 'a *hearer-of-the-law*,' a '*doer-of-the-law*.' So that the correct English for *οἱ ἀκροαταὶ νόμου* is **hearers of the law**, and for *οἱ ποιηταὶ νόμου*, **doers of the law**. It is obvious, that with the *omission* of the *τοῦ* in both places, the whole elaborate and ingenious criticism built by Bp. Middleton on its *use*, falls to the ground. (See Middleton, Gr. Art. in loc.) His dictum, that such an expression as *οἱ ἀκροαταὶ νόμου* is *inadmissible*, will hardly in our day be considered as deciding the matter.

14.] **ἔθνη, the Gentiles** [in general]; see ch. iii. 29; xi. 13; xv. 10, 12. In this place, *ἔθνη τὰ μὴ νόμ. ἔχοντα* is the only way in which the sense required could be expressed, for *τὰ ἔθνη τὰ μὴ ν. ἔχ.*, would mean '*those Gentiles who have not the law*,' as also would *ἔθνη μὴ νόμον ἔχ.*, whereas the meaning clearly is, **the Gentiles not having the law.** **νόμον**] Again, '*the* law,' viz. *of Moses*. *A* law, they have; see below. **φύσει, by nature,** *τοῖς φυσικοῖς ἑπόμενα λογισμοῖς*, Schol. in Matthaï. **τὰ τοῦ νόμου π.**] **do things pertaining to the law** [i. e. the things about which the law is concerned], e. g. abstain from stealing, or killing, or adultery. But it by no means follows that the Apostle means that the Gentiles could *fulfil* the law, do *the* things, i. e. *all* the things enjoined by the law (as De Wette): he argues that a conscientious Gentile, who knows not *the law*, does, when he acts in accordance with requirements of the law, so far set up the (see below on the art.) law to himself. *τὰ τοῦ νόμου* is interpreted by Beza, Wetst., and Elsner, '*that which the law does*,' i. e. make sanctions and prohibitions: but this can hardly be. The Apostle does not deny certain virtues to the Gentiles, but maintains the inefficiency of those, and all other virtues, towards man's salvation. **ἑαυτοῖς εἰσιν νόμος**] **are to themselves** (so far) **the law**, not '*a* law,' for *a law* may be just or unjust, God's law or man's law: there is *but one law of God*, partly written in men's consciences, more plainly manifested in the law of Moses, and fully revealed in Jesus Christ. The art. could not have been here used without stultifying the sentence by distributing the predicate, making the conscientious heathen to be to himself *the whole of the law*, instead of '*the law, so far as he did the works of the law*.' Cf. Aristot. Eth. iv. 14, *ὁ δὲ χαρίεις κ. ἐλευθέριος οὕτως ἕξει οἷον νόμος ὢν ἑαυτῷ.* **15.**] **ἐνδεικν., by their conduct shew forth,**—give an example of. **τὸ ἔργ. τοῦ νόμου** = *τὰ τοῦ νόμου* above: but sing. as applying to each of the particular cases supposed in the *ὅταν* .... *ποιῶσιν*. If it had here been *τὰ ἔργα τοῦ νόμου*, it might have been understood to mean *the whole works of the law*, which the indefinite *ὅταν* prevents above.

...απολογου P. ...ο θεος G.

ABDK LℵR abc dfghk lmno 17 [47]

ἀλλήλων τῶν [l]λογισμῶν [m]κατηγορούντων ἢ καὶ [n]ἀπο-
λογουμένων. 16 ἐν ἡμέρᾳ [o]ᾗ [p]κρινεῖ ὁ θεὸς τὰ [q]κρυπτὰ
τῶν ἀνθρώπων, κατὰ τὸ [r]εὐαγγέλιόν [r]μου διὰ Ἰησοῦ
χριστοῦ. 17 εἰ δὲ σὺ Ἰουδαῖος [s]ἐπονομάζῃ καὶ [t]ἐπαναπαύῃ

l 2 Cor. x. 5 only. Prov. vi. 18. Jer. xi. 19.
m = John v. 45 al. Paul, Acts xxiv. 13 al3. Epp., here only †. 1 Macc. vii. 6.
n abs., Luke xxi. 14. Acts xxvi. 1 (xix. 33 reff.). L.P. Jer. xii. 1.
o constr., 2 Cor. i. 4. Matt. xxiv. 50.
p ver. 12 reff.
q Matt. vi. 4 al. Deut. xxix. 29. constr., 1 Cor. iv. 5. xiv. 25. 2 Cor. iv. 2. Isa. xxii. 9.
r ch. xvi. 25. 2 Tim. ii. 8 only. see 2 Cor. iv. 3. 1 Thess. i. 5. 2 Thess. ii. 14.
s here only. Gen. iv. 17, 25.
t = here (Luke x. 6) only. (Num. xi. 25.) Micah iii. 11. w. dat., 1 Macc. viii. 12.

διαλογισμων G.

16. rec (for ᾗ) οτε, with DGKLℵ 17 rel vulg syr [arm spec Ps-]Ath$_1$ Chr Thdrt Œc [Orig-int$_3$]: [*cum* æth :] txt A B(η ημ.) tol Syr copt Cyr[-p$_1$] Damasc(ἐν ᾗ) [Orig-int$_1$] Ambr Aug Ambrst. χρ. bef ιησ. B(ℵ[1] ?): εν χριστω ιησ. Orig$_1$: om ιησ. [Mcion-in-]Tert : δια ιυ̅ χυ̅ is written by ℵ-corr[1] over an erasure. add του κυριου ημων D G-lat Ambr$_1$ [Ambrst].

17. rec for ει δε, ιδε (*see note*), with D[3]L rel syr Chr Thdrt Œc: txt ABD[1]Kℵ d[2] [47[2]] vulg G-lat Syr [copt æth arm] Clem$_1$ Damasc Thl [Euthal-ms Orig-int$_4$ Ambrst]. επαναπαυει K 17(sic) [Euthal-ms].

γραπτὸν ἐν τ. κ. αὐτ.] Alluding to the tables of stone on which the law was written: see a similar figure 2 Cor. iii. 3. **συμμαρτ. αὐτ. τ. συνειδ.**] This is a *new* argument, not a mere continuation of the ἔνδειξις above. Besides their giving this example by actions consonant with the law, their *own conscience,* reflecting on the thing done, *bears witness to it as good.* **συμμ.**, not merely = μαρτ., as Grot., Thol., nor = *una testatur*, viz. as well as their practice,—but **confirming by its testimony,** the συν signifying the agreement of the witness with the deed, as *con* in *contestari, confirmare* :—perhaps also the συν may be partly induced by the συν in συνειδήσεως,—referring to the reflective process, in which a man confers, so to speak, with himself. **καὶ μετ. ἀλλ. κ.τ.λ.**] **and their thoughts** (*judgments* or *reflections*, the self-judging voices of the conscience, which being corrupted by sinful desires are often *divided*) **among one another** (i. e. thought against thought in inner strife) **accusing, or perhaps excusing** (these two participles are *absolute*, describing the office of these judgments,—and nothing need be supplied, as '*them*,' or '*their deeds*'). Notice the similarity of this strife of conscience, and its testimony, as here described, to the higher and more detailed form of the same conflict in the Christian man, ch. vii. 16. **16.**] *To what has this verse reference?* Hardly to that just preceding, which surely speaks of a process going on *in this life* (so however Chrys. takes it. See also a fine passage in Bourdaloue's Sermons, Vol. i. Serm. ii. p. 27, ed. Paris, 1854): nor, as commonly assumed, to κριθήσονται (ver. 12), which only terminates one in a series of clauses connected by γάρ :—but to *the great affirmation of the passage, concluding with ver.* 10. To this it is bound, it appears to me, by the τὰ κρυπτὰ τῶν ἀνθρώπων, answering to πᾶσαν ψυχὴν ἀνθρώπου, ver. 9. This affirmation is the *last* sentence which has been in the dogmatic form :—after it we have a series of quasi-parenthetic clauses οὐ γάρ—ὅσοι γάρ—οὐ γάρ—ὅταν γάρ; i. e., the reasons, necessitated by the startling assertion, are one after another given, and, that having been done, *the time is specified when the great retribution shall take place.* **κατὰ τὸ εὐαγγ. μου**] See reff. **according to** (not belonging to κρινεῖ as the *rule of judgment*, but to the whole declaration, 'as taught in,' 'as forming part of') **the Gospel entrusted to me to teach.** **διὰ Ἰησ. χρ.**] **by Jesus Christ,** viz. as *the Judge*—see John v. 22 :—belongs to κρινεῖ. See also Acts xvii. 31. **17—24.**] *The pride of the Jews in their law and their God contrasted with their disobedience to God and the law.* **17. εἰ δέ**] This has been in the later MSS. changed into ἴδέ, apparently to avoid the anacoluthon, or perhaps merely by mistake originally. The anacoluthon, however, is more apparent than real. It is only produced by the resumption of the thread of the sentence with οὖν, ver. 21. Omit (in the sense) only that word, and all proceeds regularly—'*But if thou art denominated a Jew, and &c. . . ., thou that teachest thy neighbour, dost thou not teach thyself?*' &c. The **εἰ δὲ σύ** carries on the apostrophe from ver. 5, since when it has been broken off by reference to the great day of retribution and its rule of judgment; the **σύ** identifies the person addressed here as the same indicated by the **σου** and **σεαυτῷ** there, and by **ὦ ἄνθρωπε** in ver. 1. Thus the Apostle by degrees *sets in his place as a Jew* the somewhat indefinite object of his remonstrances hitherto,—and reasons with him as such. **ἐπον.**] No stress on ἐπ-,—**art named,** 'denomi-

u Paul (ver. 17. ch. v. 3, 11. 2 Cor. x. 15 al.) only, exc. James i. 9. iv. 16. Jer. ix. 23, 24.
v Acts xxii. 14 reff.
w ellips., here only. see ch. xii. 2.
x Phil. i. 10.
y = Luke xii. 56. Ps. xvi. 3.
z = 1 Cor. xv. 41. Dan. vii. 3.

νόμῳ καὶ [u]καυχᾶσαι [u]ἐν θεῷ 18 καὶ [v]γινώσκεις [vw]τὸ θέλημα ABDK
καὶ [xy]δοκιμάζεις τὰ [xz]διαφέροντα, [a]κατηχούμενος ἐκ τοῦ Lℵ a b c d f g h k
νόμου, 19 [b]πέποιθάς τε σεαυτὸν [c]ὁδηγὸν εἶναι τυφλῶν, l m n o 17 [47]
φῶς τῶν [d]ἐν [d]σκότει, 20 [e]παιδευτὴν [f]ἀφρόνων, διδάσκαλον
[g]νηπίων, ἔχοντα τὴν [h]μόρφωσιν τῆς [i]γνώσεως καὶ τῆς
ἀληθείας ἐν τῷ νόμῳ· 21 ὁ οὖν διδάσκων ἕτερον σεαυτὸν
οὐ διδάσκεις; ὁ κηρύσσων [k]μὴ κλέπτειν κλέπτεις; 22 ὁ
λέγων [k]μὴ μοιχεύειν μοιχεύεις; ὁ [l]βδελυσσόμενος τὰ

a Luke i. 4. Acts xviii. 25. xxi. 21, 24. 1 Cor. xiv. 19. Gal. vi. 6 only †. b constr. w. inf., 2 Cor. x. 7. c Acts i. 16 reff. d Luke i. 79. 1 Thess. v. 4. 1 John i. 6. see Matt. iv. 16. Isa. ix. 2. e Heb. xii. 9 only. Hos. v. 2. Sir. xxxvii. 19 only. f Luke xi. 40. xii. 20. 1 Cor. xv. 36. 2 Cor. xi. 16 bis, 19. xii. 6, 11. Eph. v. 17. 1 Pet. ii. 15 only. Job v. 3. g = 1 Cor. iii. 1 reff. h 2 Tim. iii. 5 only †. (-οῦσθαι, Gal. iv. 19.) i = Luke i. 77. xi. 52 al. Mal. ii. 7. k constr., Acts xxi. 4, 21. l = here (Rev. xxi. 8) only. Exod. v. 21.

rec ins *τω* bef *νομω*, with D^3KL 17 rel [arm Euthal-ms] Thdrt Thl Œc: om ABD^1ℵ $Clem_1$ Did_1 $Chr\text{-}comm_1$(and mss) Damasc.
20. om *διδασκ. νηπιων* A. **21.** ins *τον* bef *ετερον* L n 1. 30-8. 93.

nated,'—'hast the name put on thee;' see reff. **ἐπαναπ.**] Used of *false trust*, see reff. The *τῷ* of the rec. has been inserted in the later MSS. before *νόμῳ*, because it here clearly applied to the 'law of Moses,' and the absence of the article gave offence. It is omitted, because 'the law' is not here *distributed*—it is not *the law itself in its entirety*, which is meant, but *the fact of having or of knowing the law*:—the strict way of expressing it would perhaps be, 'in the fact of possessing a law,' which condensed into our less accurate English, would be in one word, **in the law**: viz. 'which thou possessest.' **καυχ. ἐν θ.**] viz. 'as thy *Covenant God*:' 'as being peculiarly thine.' **18. γιν. τὸ θέλ.**] *θεός* having been just mentioned, it is left to be inferred that *θέλημα* refers to Him. **δοκιμ. τ. διαφ.**] **provest** (in the sense of sifting and coming to a conclusion on) **things which differ**,—*ἐναντία ἀλλήλοις, δικαιοσύνην κ. ἀδικίαν, κ.τ.λ.* Theod. *κρίνεις τί δεῖ πρᾶξαι κ. τί μὴ δεῖ πρᾶξαι*, Theophylact. The Vulg. 'probas utiliora,' and E. V. '*approvest the things that are more excellent*,' is somewhat flat in meaning, and not so applicable. **κατηχ. ἐκ τοῦ νόμ.**] **being** (habitually, not in youth only,—force of pres.) **instructed** (not merely catechetically but didactically, in the synagogues, &c.) **out of the law** (**τοῦ** *νόμου*, though after a preposition—because the law is *distributed*—it is the book of the law, the *law itself*, out of which the *κατήχησις* takes place).

19.] **πέποιθας**, sometimes with *ἑαυτῷ* or *ἐφ' ἑαυτῷ* (see Luke xviii. 9), and sometimes with *ὅτι* (Luke, ib.; Gal. v. 10; Phil. ii. 24; Heb. xiii. 18),—**regardest thyself as**,—**art confident in thyself as being**. **ὁδηγὸν τυφλ.**] We can hardly say with Olsh., that the Apostle *undoubtedly* refers to the saying of our Lord, Matt. xv. 14,—but rather that both that saying and this were allusive to a title 'leaders of the blind' given to themselves by the Pharisees, with which Paul as a Pharisee would be familiar. Similarly, the following titles may have been well-known and formal expressions of Jewish pride with reference to those who were without the covenant.

20.] **μόρφωσιν**, not the mere apparent likeness (Theophylact, &c.), but the *real representation*. The law, as far as it went, was a reflexion of the holiness and character of God. Hardly so much is *here* meant (Olsh.), as that the law *contained a foreshadowing of Christ*,—for the Apostle is speaking now more of *moral* truth and knowledge, by which a rule of judgment is set up, sufficient to condemn the Jew as well as the Gentile. But after all, this clause (*ἔχοντα . . . νόμῳ*) is not to be pressed as *declaring a fact*, but taken subjectively with regard to the Jew, after *πέποιθας*, and understood of *his estimate* of the law. **ἐν τῷ νόμῳ**, because the *book of the law*, the whole law, is denoted.

[**21.**] "And now the righteous rebuke may no longer be restrained. Such advantages and such pretensions ought undoubtedly to be followed and justified by a corresponding course of holy conduct." Ewbank.] **22. ὁ βδελ. τὰ εἴδ. ἱεροσυλεῖς**] The contrast here must be maintained; which it will not be if we understand *ἱεροσυλεῖς* of robbing the temple of God of offerings destined for him (Jos. Antt. xviii. 3, 4). And *τὰ εἴδωλα* leads into the kind of robbery which is meant. **Thou who abhorrest idols, dost thou rob their temples?** That it was necessary to vindicate Jews from such a charge, appears from Acts xix. 37: and Jos. Antt. iv. 8. 10 gives as a law, *μὴ συλᾶν ἱερὰ ξενικά, μηδ' ἂν ἐπωνομασμένον ᾖ τινι θεῷ κειμήλιον λαμβάνειν*.

[m] εἴδωλα [n] ἱεροσυλεῖς; 23 ὃς [o] ἐν νόμῳ [o] καυχᾶσαι, διὰ τῆς
[p] παραβάσεως τοῦ νόμου τὸν θεὸν [q] ἀτιμάζεις; 24 τὸ γὰρ
ὄνομα τοῦ θεοῦ δι' ὑμᾶς [r] βλασφημεῖται ἐν τοῖς ἔθνεσιν,
καθὼς γέγραπται. 25 περιτομὴ μὲν γὰρ [s] ὠφελεῖ, ἐὰν
[t] νόμον [t] πράσσῃς· ἐὰν δὲ [u] παραβάτης νόμου ᾖς, ἡ
περιτομή σου [v] ἀκροβυστία [w] γέγονεν. 26 ἐὰν οὖν ἡ [v] ἀκροβυστία τὰ [x] δικαιώματα τοῦ νόμου [y] φυλάσσῃ, οὐχὶ ἡ
[v] ἀκροβυστία [z] αὐτοῦ [a] εἰς περιτομὴν [a] λογισθήσεται; 27 καὶ
[b] κρινεῖ ἡ [c] ἐκ [cd] φύσεως [v] ἀκροβυστία τὸν νόμον [e] τελοῦσα

G η περιτομη... ABDG KLℵ a b c d f g h k l m n o 17 [47]

m w. art., Acts xv. 20. 1 Cor. xii. 2. 1 Thess. i. 9. 1 John v. 21. 2 Chron. xvii. 3.
n here only +. (-λος, Acts xix. 37. -λία, 2 Macc. xiii. 6.)
o ver. 17.
p w. gen., here only. 2 Macc. xv. 10. abs., ch. iv. 15 reff. (-βάτης, ver. 25.)
q Acts v. 41 reff.

r Isa. lii. 5. Tit. ii. 5. s absol., = John vi. 63 only. Hab. ii. 18. Xen. Anab. v. 1. 12. t here only. see John vii. 19. u here bis. Gal. ii. 18. James ii. 9, 11 only +. Symm., Ps. xvi. 4; Ezek. xviii. 10 [Montf., not Field]. v ch. iv. 9—12 al. Paul only, exc. Acts xi. 3. Gen. xvii. 11. w = Matt. iv. 3 ‖ L. John ii. 9. x. 16. x ch. i. 32 reff. y act., = Acts xvi. 4 reff. Exod. xv. 26. z indef. pron., Luke xxiii. 51. John viii. 44. Eph. v. 12. 1 Pet. iii. 14. Jude 24 al. Winer, edn. 6, § 22. 3. 2). a = ch. ix. 8 reff. b see ch. xiv. 22. James iv. 11, 12. c here only. d = Gal. ii. 15. (ch. i. 26 reff.) e = James ii. 8. Gal. v. 16.

25. om *γαρ* d m vulg D-lat æth arm [Orig-int$_3$] lat-ff. for *πρασσης*, *φυλασσης* D^1-gr [arm]; *observes* vulg D-lat [Ambrst]; *custodias* [Orig-int] Aug$_2$. *ακροβιστια*(but corrd) ℵ^1.

26. for *τα δικαιωματα*, *δικαιωμα* G-gr G^2-lat harl^1 [Orig-int$_1$(txt$_2$)]. *φυλασσει* L. for *ουχι*, *ουχ* Bℵ 44 Damasc: txt DGKL 17 rel Chr [Cyr$_1$-p] Thdrt Thl Œc. (A uncert.)

27. om *η εκ φυσ. ακροβ.* G.

23.] **ἐν νόμῳ**, see above (ver. 17) for the omission of the art.—but it is not *διὰ παραβάσεως νόμου*, because a *παράβασις* is **τοῦ** *νόμου*, the law being broken *as a whole* (see James ii. 10: and on *παραβάτης νόμου* below, ver. 25). And *τῆς παρ. τ. νόμ.*, is **thy breaking of the law.**

This question comprehends the previous ones. **24.**] 'For what is written in the prophet Isaiah [also in Ezekiel, xxxvi. 20, 23], is no less true now of you:' 'the fact is so, as it is written.' **25—29.**] Inasmuch as CIRCUMCISION was the especial sign of the covenant, and as such, a distinction on which the Jewish mind dwelt with peculiar satisfaction: the Apostle sets forth, *that circumcision without the keeping of the law is of no avail, and that true circumcision and true Judaism are matters of the heart, not of the flesh only.* ἀλλ' ἡ περιτομὴ μέγα, φησίν. ὁμολογῶ κἀγώ, ἀλλὰ πότε; ὅταν ἔχῃ τὴν ἔνδον περιτομήν. καὶ σκόπει σύνεσιν, πῶς εὐκαίρως τὸν περὶ αὐτῆς εἰσήγαγε λόγον. οὐ γὰρ εὐθέως ἀπ' αὐτῆς ἤρξατο, ἐπειδὴ πολλὴ ἦν αὐτῆς ἡ ὑπόληψις· ἀλλ' ἡνίκα ἔνδειξεν αὐτοὺς ἀπὸ τοῦ μείζονος προσκεκρουκότας καὶ τῆς εἰς θεὸν βλασφημίας αἰτίους, τότε λοιπὸν λαβὼν τὸν ἀκροατὴν κατεγνωκότα αὐτῶν, καὶ γυμνώσας τῆς προεδρίας, εἰσάγει τὸν περὶ περιτομῆς λόγον, θαῤῥῶν ὅτι οὐδεὶς αὐτῇ ψηφιεῖται λοιπόν. Chrys. Hom. vii. 474. **25.**] **περιτομή**, chosen as an example in point, and as the most comprehensive and decisive example; and *μὲν γάρ* binds it on to the foregoing reasoning: q. d. '*in the same way circumcision, &c.*' **νόμον**, not *τὸν νόμον*, **πράσσῃς**,—because the latter would import *the perfect fulfilment of the whole law:* whereas the supposition is of acting according to the law, **doing the law.** *παραβάτης νόμου* here, not *τοῦ νόμου*, the *παραβάτης νόμου*, like *ἀκροατὴς-νόμου* and *ποιητὴς-νόμου*, ver. 13, being a designation generally of a *law-breaker*, as *those* of a *law-hearer* and *law-fulfiller.* **ἀκροβ. γέγ.**] *counts for nothing:* the Jewish transgressor is no better off than the Gentile transgressor. **26. ἡ ἀκροβ.**] i. e. *οἱ ἐν τῇ ἀκροβυστίᾳ.* **τὰ δικαίωμ.**] plainly, the *moral* requirements, not the ceremonial: for one of the very first of the latter was, *to be circumcised.* The case is an *impossible one:* nor does the Apostle put it as possible, only as shewing manifestly, that circumcision, the sign of the covenant of the Law, was *subordinate to the keeping of the Law* itself. The articles shew how completely hypothetical the case is—no less than entire fulfilment of all the moral precepts of the law being contemplated. **οὐχὶ ἡ . . .**] 'In such a case would not he be counted as a circumcised person?' **27.**] I prefer with De Wette (and Erasm.), Luth., Bengel, Wetst., Knapp, and Meyer, to regard this verse not as a continuation of the question, but as a separate emphatic assertion, and as leading the way to the next verse. **κρινεῖ**, 'shall rise up in judgment against,' **judge** indirectly by his example. See Matt. xii. 41, 42, where *κατακρίνω* is used in a sense precisely similar. **ἡ ἐκ φύσεως ἀκροβ.**] 'he, who remains in his natural state of uncircumcision.' *ἐκ*

σὲ τὸν [f] διὰ [g] γράμματος καὶ περιτομῆς [u] παραβάτην νόμου. ABDG
28 οὐ γὰρ ὁ [h] ἐν τῷ [h] φανερῷ Ἰουδαῖός ἐστιν, οὐδὲ ἡ [h] ἐν KLℵ a b c d f g h
τῷ [h] φανερῷ [i] ἐν [i] σαρκὶ περιτομή, 29 ἀλλ' ὁ [hk] ἐν τῷ k l m n o 17 [47]
[hk] κρυπτῷ Ἰουδαῖος, καὶ περιτομὴ [l] καρδίας ἐν [m] πνεύματι
οὐ [m] γράμματι· οὗ ὁ [n] ἔπαινος οὐκ [o] ἐξ ἀνθρώπων ἀλλ'
[o] ἐκ τοῦ θεοῦ.

f = ch. iv. 11. xiv. 20. 2 Cor. ii. 4. Heb. ix. 12. Winer, edn. 6, § 47 i.
g see note & ver. 29 reff.
h here [Matt. vi. 4, 6 rec.] only.
i ch. viii. 8, 9. 2 Cor. x. 3. Gal. ii. 20. vi. 12. Eph. ii. 11 (bis). Phil. i. 22. iii. 3, 4 (bis). Col. ii. 1. 1 Tim. iii. 16. Philem. 16. 1 Pet. iv. 1, 2. 1 John iv. 2. 2 John 7.
k Matt. as above (h). John vii. 4, 10. xviii. 20.
l = 1 Cor. iv. 5. Ezek. xliv. 7, 9.
m ch. vii. 6. 2 Cor. iii. 6.
n Paul (1 Cor. iv. 5. Eph. i. 6 al6.) only, exc. 1 Pet. i. 7. ii. 14.
o = Matt. i. 20. Acts v. 39. ch. v. 16.

29. αλλα (1st) D¹G. for 2nd εν, ος G D-lat. αλλα (2nd) B. om του (bef θε.) D²G a. aft θεου ins εστιν D¹ vulg lat-ff.

φύσ. is contrasted with διὰ γράμ. κ. περιτ. below. The position of ἐκ φύσεως decides for this rendering and against joining it with τελοῦσα, which would require ἡ ἀκροβυστία, ἐκ φύσεως τὸν νόμον τελοῦσα. **τὸν νόμ. τελ.**] such is the supposition—that an uncircumcised man could fully act up to the (moral) requirements of the law. It is not ἡ τὸν νόμ. τελ.; because ἀκροβ. is used in the widest abstract sense: no distinction is made between one and another uncircumcised person, but some one man is taken as an example of ἀκροβυστία. So that the omission of the art. does not give a new hypothetic sense, '*if it fulfil the law*,' but merely restates the hypothesis: **fulfilling** (as it does, as we have supposed) **the law.** **σὲ τὸν . . . . . παραβάτην νόμου**] Here again the position of διὰ γράμματος κ. περιτομῆς, between τὸν and παραβάτην, sufficiently shews that, as ἐκ φύσεως above, it is a qualification of σὲ τὸν παραβάτην νόμου. Bp. Middleton (it appears, Gr. Art. in loc. and compare his ref.) would take σὲ τὸν διὰ γράμματος κ. περιτομῆς (ὄντα), '*thee who art a professor of the law and a circumcised person*,' and understand εἶναι after παραβάτην, —*shall adjudge thee to be a transgressor of the law*. But this appears exceedingly forced, and inconsistent with the position of παραβ. νόμου, which if it had been thus emphatic, would certainly have been placed either before, or immediately after κρινεῖ. We may well imagine that such an interpretation would not have been thought of, except to serve the supposed canon, that, 'if τόν were immediately the article of παραβάτην, νόμου depending on it could not be anarthrous.' See above on παραβ. νόμ. ver. 25, and on ver. 13. **διὰ γρ. κ. περ.**] διά (see reff.) is here used of the *state in which the man is* when he does the act, *regarded as the medium* through which the act is done. It is rightly rendered **by** in E. V. [though this gives too much the idea of the state being the instrument by means of which] (not, '*in spite of*,' as Köllner and al.). **γράμματος**] 'litera scripta,' the *written word*: here in a more general sense than in ver. 29, where it is pressed to a contrast with πνεῦμα: **thee, who in a state of external conformity with the written law and of circumcision, art yet a transgressor of the law.** In vv. **28, 29**, supply the ellipses thus: in ver. 28, fill up the subjects from the predicates,—οὐ γὰρ ὁ ἐν τῷ φανερῷ ('Ιουδαῖος) 'Ιουδαῖός ἐστιν, οὐδὲ ἡ ἐν τῷ φανερῷ ἐν σαρκὶ (περιτομὴ) περιτομή (ἐστιν); in ver. 29, fill up the predicates from the subjects,—ἀλλ' ὁ ἐν τῷ κρυπτῷ 'Ιουδαῖος ('Ιουδαῖός ἐστιν), καὶ περιτομὴ καρδίας ἐν πνεύματι οὐ γράμματι (περιτομή ἐστιν). Thus the *real Jew only*, and the *real circumcision only*, are *expressed* in both verses. This is the arrangement of Beza, Estius, Rückert, De Wette: Erasm., Luther, Meyer, Fritzsche, take 'Ιουδαῖος, and ἐν πν. οὐ γράμ., as the predicates in ver. 29; but the latter gives a very vapid sense, besides that the opposition of ὁ ἐν τῷ φανερῷ, and ὁ ἐν τῷ κρυπτῷ is, as De W. observes, also vapid. **29.**] **ἐν τῷ κρ.** as belonging to 'Ιουδ. is parallel with καρδίας as belonging to περιτομή, both designating the inner and spiritual reality, of which the name of Jew and the carnal circumcision are only the signs. **περ. καρδ.** is no new expression:—we have it virtually in Deut. x. 16; Jer. iv. 4: see also Acts vii. 51. **ἐν πν. οὐ γρ.**] **in [the] spirit, not in [the] letter.** Not merely 'spiritually, not externally:' nor does πν. allude to the *necessitating cause* of circumcision (the uncleanness of the inner man) (Œc., Grot., Estius, Fritzsche): —nor signify the *material* ('quæ spiritu constat,' Erasm.): nor the *rule* (Meyer), —but as De Wette rightly, the *living power or element*, wherewith that inner sphere of being is filled—**ἐν** being [used] as in Acts xvii. 28, of that in which any thing lives and moves,—compare χαρὰ ἐν πν. ἁγίῳ, ch. xiv. 17,—ἀγάπη ἐν πν., Col. i. 8,—δουλεύειν ἐν καιν. πν., ch. vii. 6,—εἶναι

III. 1 Τί οὖν τὸ [p] περισσὸν τοῦ Ἰουδαίου, ἢ τίς ἡ
[q] ὠφέλεια τῆς περιτομῆς; 2 πολὺ [r] κατὰ [r] πάντα [r] τρόπον.
[s] πρῶτον [s] μὲν [[s] γὰρ] ὅτι [t] ἐπιστεύθησαν τὰ [u] λόγια τοῦ
θεοῦ. 3 [v] τί γάρ; εἰ [w] ἠπίστησάν τινες· μὴ ἡ [x] ἀπιστία

p — Matt. v. 37, 47. Eccles. vii. 1 Bℵ &c. Dan. v. 12, 14 Theod. (-σσεια, Eccles. i. 3.)
q Jude 16 only. Job xxii. 3. Ps. xxix. 9.
r = Num. xviii. 7. see Acts xv. 11.
s 1 Cor. xi. 18.
t = 1 Cor. ix. 17. constr., Acts xxi. 3. Gal. ii. 7. 1 Thess. ii. 4. πιστευθέντος τὴν ἐν Περγάμῳ βιβλιοθήκην, Diog. Laert. vii. 1. 29. Winer, edn. 6, § 39. 1. *a*.
u Acts vii. 38. Heb. v. 12. 1 Pet. iv. 11 only. Num. xxiv. 4, 16 al.
v Phil. i. 18.
w = 2 Tim. ii. 13. (Acts xxviii. 24 reff. -τος, Luke xii. 46.)
x = ch. xi. 20. Heb. iii. 19. see note.

Chap. III. 1. om ἡ Gℵ[1] [c 47(Tischdf)].
2. rec ins γαρ, with AD[3]KLℵ 17 rel syr [Chr$_1$ Euthal-ms] Thdrt Phot Thl Œc: om BD[1]G [copt æth arm] vulg Syr Chr$_1$ Orig[-int$_2$ Damasc Ambrst]. aft επιστευθησαν ins αυτοις G[2].
3. ηπειθησαν A, *deliquerunt* Pacian$_1$.

ἐν πν., ch. viii. 9. So that πνεῦμα *here* is not man's spirit, nor properly the Holy Spirit, but *the spirit*, as opposed to *the letter*, of the Jewish law and of all God's revelation of himself. **οὗ**] viz. Ἰουδαίου,—of the true Jew. περιτομὴ καρδ. as belonging to him, is subordinate. The ἔπαινος of such a character, (for ἔπαινος it must be,) can only come from him who sees ἐν τῷ κρυπτῷ (Matt. vi. 4, 6), and can discern the heart. III. 1—20.] Taking into all fair account the real advantages of the Jews, these cannot, by the testimony of Scripture itself concerning them, exempt them from this sentence of guiltiness before God, in which all flesh are involved. 1—4.] *The circumcised Jew did unquestionably possess great advantages, which were not annulled by the rebellion of some.* 1.] **οὖν**, 'quæ cum ita sint.' If true Judaism and true circumcision be merely spiritual, what is the profit of external Judaism and ceremonial circumcision? **περισσόν**] **advantage, profit, pre-eminence,**—see reff. It is best to take the question, not as *coming from an objector*, which supposition has obscured several parts of this Epistle, but as *asked by the Apostle himself*, anticipating the thoughts of his reader. 2.] **πολύ** answers the first question of ver. 1, but takes no account of the second, as it is virtually included in the first. Nor can it be properly regarded as answered in ch. iv. 1 ff. (see there). **κατὰ πάντα τρ.**] not merely *omnino*, but as E. V. (in) **every way**, i. e. in all departments of the spiritual life. **πρῶτον**] The Apostle begins as if intending to instance *several* of these advantages, but having mentioned the greatest, leaves it to his reader to fill in the rest, and turns to establish what he has just asserted. For πρῶτον can only be **first**,—'secondly,' &c., being to follow: —not, '*primarium illud*' (as Beza),—nor '*præcipue*' (as Calv.),—nor '*id quod præcipuum est*' (as Calov.), all of which are attempts to avoid the anacoluthon: compare a similar one at ch. i. 8. **ἐπιστ.**] see reff.—**they were entrusted with. τὰ λόγια τ. θεοῦ**] These words look very like a reminiscence of Stephen's apology, see Acts vii. 38. These oracles are not only the law of Moses, but all the revelations of God hitherto made of Himself *directly*, all of which had been entrusted to *Jews only*. By these they were received into a special covenant, which advantage is therefore included in their being entrusted with the divine oracles. 3.] And this advantage is not cancelled, nor the covenant annulled, by their disobedience. **τί γάρ;**] **For what?** ('quid enim?' Hor. Sat. i. 1. 7.) The γάρ confirms the preceding—the τί indicates some difficulty, or anticipated objection to it. **εἰ ἠπίστ. τινες**] If we place an interrogation at γάρ, we must render this, **suppose some were unfaithful**; if only a comma, as in E. V., '*For what if . . .*' The former seems preferable, as more according to usage. See Phil. i. 18. **ἠπίστησαν, did not believe.** If this seem out of place here, where he is not speaking of faith or want of faith as yet, but of ἀδικία (ver. 5) and moral guilt, we may meet the objection by remembering that unbelief is here taken more on its practical side, as involving *disobedience*, than on the other. They were ἄπιστοι, *unfaithful to the covenant*, the very condition of which was to walk in the ways of the Lord and observe his statutes. The word may have been chosen on account of ἐπιστεύθησαν above and τ. πίστιν τ. θεοῦ below. **μὴ ἡ ἀπ. κ.τ.λ.**] **shall their unfaithfulness** (to the covenant: see above, and Wisdom xiv. 25: in the root of the matter, their *unbelief*, as in reff.: and the substantive ἀπιστία is bound to the verb ἠπίστησαν, but its *rendering* must be ruled by the contrast to ἡ πίστις τοῦ θεοῦ, which *must* be "the *faithfulness* of God") **cancel (nullify) the faithfulness of God?** 'Because they have broken faith on their part, shall God break

αὐτῶν τὴν y πίστιν τοῦ θεοῦ z καταργήσει; 4 a μὴ γένοιτο·
b γινέσθω δὲ ὁ θεὸς c ἀληθής, πᾶς δὲ ἄνθρωπος d ψεύστης,
καθὼς γέγραπται e Ὅπως e ἂν f δικαιωθῇς ἐν τοῖς λόγοις
σου καὶ νικήσῃς ἐν τῷ g κρίνεσθαί σε. 5 εἰ δὲ ἡ h ἀδικία
ἡμῶν θεοῦ i δικαιοσύνην j συνίστησιν, k τί k ἐροῦμεν; μὴ
ἄδικος ὁ θεὸς ὁ l ἐπιφέρων τὴν m ὀργήν; n κατὰ ἄνθρωπον
λέγω. 6 o μὴ γένοιτο· ἐπεὶ p πῶς q κρινεῖ ὁ θεὸς τὸν
κόσμον; 7 εἰ γὰρ ἡ ἀλήθεια τοῦ θεοῦ r ἐν τῷ ἐμῷ s ψεύ-

y = Matt. xxiii. 23. Tit. ii. 10 al. Prov. xii. 22.
z Paul (ver. 31. 1 Cor. xiii. 8 al. fr.) only, exc. Luke xiii. 7. Heb. ii. 14. Ezra iv. 21, 23. v. 5. vi. 8 only.
a Paul (ver. 6 alll.) only, exc. Luke xx. 16. Josh. xxii. 29. Gen. xliv. 17.

[P ημων ...]

ABDG KL[P]ℵ a b c d f g h k l m n o 17 [47]

b = ch. xi. 6. 1 Cor. xiii. 1 al. c subj., Matt. xxii. 16. John iii. 33. vii. 18. viii. 26. 2 Cor. vi. 8 ‡. d John viii. 44, 55. 1 Tim. i. 10. Tit. i. 12. 1 John i. 10 al4. Psa. cxv. 11 (2). e Acts iii. 19 reff. Psa. l. 4 (6). f = Luke vii. 29, 35. 1 Tim. iii. 16. Ps. l. c. g = Acts xxv. 9, 10 al. h = ch. i. 18 al. i ch. i. 17 reff. j = ch. v. 8. 2 Cor. vi. 4. vii. 11. Gal. ii. 18. Paul only (exc. Luke ix. 32. 2 Pet. iii. 5). Wisd. vii. 14. Diod. Sic. xiv. 45. k ch. iv. 1. vi. 1. vii. 7. viii. 31. ix. 14, 30 only. P. Josh. vii. 8. l = Jude 9 (only). Gen. xxxvii. 22. ἐπιφ. τινὶ πόλεμον, Polyb. xv. 18. 4. m = ch. ii. 5, 8. n Gal. iii. 15. 1 Cor. ix. 8. (see ch. vi. 19. 2 Cor. iii. 3. xv. 32. Gal. i. 11. 1 Pet. iv. 6.) o ver. 4 reff. p = Luke xi. 18. ch. vi. 2 al. q = ch. ii. 12 reff. r = ch. v. 9. Matt. xvii. 21. Luke xxi. 34. s here only †. Job xxxiv. 6 Aq. Theod. [Symm.(Field, Auct. ad Hex.)].

καταργησῃ L b¹ o Chr-2-mss: *καταργει* 47. *κατεργασει* 5: *κατηργησε* 28. 76 syrr Cypr Pelag Vig.

4. for *γινεσθω*, *εστω* G-gr; *est* vulg D-lat Syr $Cypr_4$, *est* and *esto* G-lat, *sit* $Ambr_1$: *γενεσθω* L c Chr_1. for *δε*, *γαρ* G D-lat Syr Cypr Ambrst Sedul: *ουν* arm. for *καθως*, *καθαπερ* Bℵ Thdrt: *ως* 73: *καθο* 76. *νικησεις* ADℵ n: *νικησις* 17.

5. *δικαιοσυνην* bef *θεου* G vulg [$Orig\text{-}int_1$]. aft *οργην* ins *αυτου* ℵ¹(ℵ³ disapproving) [Syr copt $Philastr_1$].

7. [for *ει*, *η* P.] for *γαρ*, *δε* A[ℵ] d 5. 23. 57. 74. 124 harl copt Damasc.

faith also on His?' **4.] μὴ γέν., let it not be:** see reff. The Apostle uses this expression of pious horror, when he has supposed or mentioned any thing by which the honour, truth, or justice of God would be compromised, as here by His covenant-word being broken. It is often found in Polybius, Arrian, and the later Greek writers. **γινέσθω κ.τ.λ.]** 'rather let us believe all men on earth to have broken their word and truth, than God His. Whatever becomes of men and their truth, *His truth must stand fast.*' The citation which follows goes to the depth of the matter. It is the penitent confession of a sinner, that he is sensible how entirely *against God* his sin has been, and how clearly his own unworthiness sets God's judgment against sin vindicated before him. And to this meaning the objection in the next verses is addressed,—see below. **That thou mightest be justified** (shewn to be just) **in thy sayings** (sentences, words of judgment), **and mightest conquer when Thou art judged,**—בְּשָׁפְטֶךָ '*in thy judging,*' which cannot well be our rendering of *ἐν* **τῷ κρίνεσθαί** *σε*,—i. e. 'when thy dealings are called in question by men.' **5.]** In the citation, the penitent regarded his sin as having been the instrument of bringing out God's justice into clearer light. On the abuse which might be made of such a view, the Apostle founds another question:—It would almost seem as if God would be unjust in inflicting His wrath (the consequences of His wrath) on men whose very impiety has been the means whereby His own righteousness has been shewn forth, and established.' **ἡμῶν]** '*of the Jews*' (Grot., De Wette, &c.), not 'of all men' (Fritzsche), for only to the Jews can ver. 7 apply. **δικαιοσύνην]** viz. that established by the *δικαιοῦσθαι* of ver. 4; not *His goodness* (as Chrys., Theodoret, Grot., al.),—nor *His truth* (Beza, al.). **κατὰ ἄνθρωπον λέγω]** said, as elsewhere by Paul, to excuse a supposition bearing with it an aspect of inconsistency or impiety:—not implying that he speaks *in the person of another*, but that he puts himself into the place of the generality of men, and uses arguments such as they would use. **6.]** He does not enter into the objection and answer it in detail, but rejects at once the idea of God being *unjust*, alluding probably to Gen. xviii. 25, by recalling to mind, that *the Judge of all the earth must do right.* **ἐπεί, for** (i. e. 'if it were so,' 'alioquin'). **τὸν κόσμον** is not *the Gentiles* (Bengel, Reiche, Olsh., al.), nor is the respondent in ver. 7 a Gentile (Olsh., al., not Bengel), but one of the *ἡμῶν* in ver. 5, only individualized to bring out *one such case* of pretended injustice more strikingly.

7.] This follows (connected by **γάρ**) upon ver. 6, and shews that the supposition if carried out, would overthrow all God's judgment, and (ver. 8) the whole moral life of man. **How shall God judge the world? For, if the truth** (faithfulness) **of God abounded** (was manifested, more clearly established) **by means of my falsehood** (unfaithfulness), **to His glory** (so that the result has been the setting forth

σματι [t] ἐπερίσσευσεν [u] εἰς τὴν δόξαν αὐτοῦ, [v] τί ἔτι κἀγὼ
ὡς [w] ἁμαρτωλὸς [x] κρίνομαι ; 8 καὶ μὴ καθὼς [y] βλασφη-
μούμεθα καὶ καθώς φασίν τινες ἡμᾶς λέγειν ὅτι ποιήσωμεν
τὰ κακὰ ἵνα [z] ἔλθῃ τὰ ἀγαθά ; ὧν τὸ [a] κρῖμα [b] ἔνδικόν
ἐστιν. 9 [c] Τί οὖν ; [d] προεχόμεθα ; [e] οὐ [e] πάντως. [f] προ-

t Phil. i. 26. 1 Thess. iv. 1. Tobit iv. 16 [ℵ def.]. u — 1 Cor. ii. 7. x. 31. Eph. i. 6 al. v ch. ix. 19. Gal. v. 11. w Matt. ix. 10. xi. 19. ch. v. 8, 19. Ps. xlix. 16. x = John viii. 15. 1 Cor. v. 12 (bis). y = ch. xiv. 16. 1 Cor. x. 30. Tit. iii. 2. James ii. 7. z = Matt. xviii. 7. a — ch. ii. 2 reff. b Heb. ii. 2 only †. c ch. vi. 15. xi. 7. d here only. Eccl. x. 10 Symm. see note. e = here only. see 1 Cor. v. 10. xvi. 12. (Acts xxi. 22 reff.) Winer, edn. 6, § 61. 4 (5). f. here only †.

8. om 2nd και BK a 39. 74 [æth(appy, Treg)]. om οτι G 76. 120 vulg Epiph$_1$ [Orig-int] Aug Pelag Ambrst. om τα (bef κακα) D^1.

9. προεχωμεθα AL (k^1) : ερουμεν æth : προκατεχομεν περισσον D^1(and lat) G 31 Syr Chr-2-mss$_2$: κατεχομεν π. Thdrt Sev : *tenemus* D-lat G-lat [Orig-int$_2$] Ambrst-mss. [om ου παντως D^{1}GP syrr(ins syr-mg) æth Chr-2-mss$_1$ Thdrt Severn-c Orig-int.]

of His glory), **why any longer** (ἔτι, this being so,—assuming the premises) **am I also** (i. e. as well as others,—am I to be involved in a judgment from which I ought to be exempt) **judged** (to be judged,—the pres. expressing the rule or habit of God's proceeding) **as a sinner? And** (why should we) **not** (in this case rather say) **as we** (I Paul, or we Christians) **are slanderously reported, and as some give out that we** (do) **say** (ὅτι recitantis), **"Let us do evil that good may come?" whose condemnation** (not that of our slanderers (Grot., Tholuck), but that of those who so say and act) **is according to justice** (not only by the preceding argument, but by the common detestation of all men, for such a maxim as doing evil that good may come).

The way adopted generally (Calv., Beza, Grot., Bengel, Wolf, Rückert, Köllner, Tholuck) is to connect ver. 7 by γάρ with ver. 5, and to regard κατὰ ἄνθρ. . . . . κόσμον as a series of parentheses; but I very much prefer that given above, which, in the main, is De Wette's. Fritzsche and Schrader strangely enough regard κἀγώ as bona fide the individual Paul, and κρίνομαι as the judgment passed by his adversaries ("nam si Dei veracitas meo peccatoris mendacio abunde in Dei laudem cessit, cur adhuc ego quoque, Paulus, tanquam facinorosus ab hominibus reus agor," &c.): Reiche, Olsh., &c. put ver. 7 into the mouth of a *Gentile:* Bengel, into that of a *Jew.* Doubtless the main reference of this part of the argument is to Jews: but the reasoning from the introduction of the words τὸν κόσμον (see above) is *general,* applying both to Jew and Gentile, and shewing the untenableness of *any* such view as that of the Jewish objection of ver. 5.

9—20.] *The Jew has no preference, but is guilty as well as the Gentile, as shewn by Scripture; so that no man can by the* * *law be righteous before God.* **9.**] **τί οὖν** cannot be joined with προεχόμεθα (Œc., &c.), because οὐδέν would then have been the answer. There is considerable difficulty in **προεχόμεθα.** The meaning of προέχομαι every where else is *passive,* 'to be surpassed,' and προέχω, act., is to surpass, or have the pre-eminence. So Plut. p. 1038 D (Wetst.), κατ' οὐδὲν προεχομένοις ὑπὸ τοῦ Διός, 'cum Jove minores non sint:' and Herod. i. 32, ὁ μὲν δὴ μέγα πλούσιος ἀνόλβιος δέ, δυοῖσι προέχει τοῦ εὐτυχοῦς μόνον, &c. (see Wetst.) Those therefore who have wished to preserve the usage of the word, have variously interpreted it in that attempt: (α) Wetst. would render it passively, and understand it (as spoken by a Jew) '*Are we surpassed by the Gentiles?*' But (1) for this inference there is no ground in what went before, but the contrary (vv. 1 ff.),—and (2) the question if it mean this, is not dealt with in what follows. (β) Œcum. (2nd altern.) regards it as said by a Gentile, '*Are we surpassed by the Jews?*' but for this question there is no ground in the preceding, for all has tended to lower the Jews in comparison and reduce all to one level. (γ) Reiche and Olsh. take it passively, and render, '*Are we preferred* (*by God*)?' but no example of this meaning occurs, the above use in Plutarch not justifying it. (δ) Koppe and Wahl render, taking it as the middle voice, '*What can we then allege* (*as an excuse*)?' but this will not suit οὐ πάντως. (ε) Meyer, '*What then, have we an excuse?*' but προεχόμ. has not this meaning. (ζ) Fritzsche, '*What then? do we excuse ourselves* (i. e. shall we make any excuse)?' But (1) προεχ. *is put absolutely;* and (2) the answer would rather be μηδαμῶς than οὐ πάντως, which replies to a question on *matter of fact.* Besides (3) the argument would then go to shew, not that all are *sinners, as it does,* vv. 10—20, but that all are liable to God's wrath, *without excuse.* (η) The only way left seems (with Theophyl., Œc. (1st altern.), Schol. in Matthaï, Pelag., Vulg., Erasm., Luther, Calv., Beza, Grot.,

g = Matt. viii. 9. ch. vi. 14, 15. Gal. iii. 10. iv. 2 &c. Deut. xxxiii. 3.
h Psa. xiii. 1 ff. BN^1 (AN^{3a} &c. om our vv. 13—18) freely at beg.
i Acts iv. 32 reff.
k = ch. xv. 21 reff.
l Acts xv. 17 reff.
m ch. xvi. 17. 1 Pet. iii. 11 only. = Job xxxiv. 27. Mal. ii. 8. Psa. lii. 3 BN F &c. (A def.)
n here only. 4 Kings iii. 19. Jer. xi. 16. Polyb. i. 14. 6 al.

ητιασάμεθα γὰρ Ἰουδαίους τε καὶ Ἕλληνας πάντας [g] ὑφ' ABDG KL[P]א
ἁμαρτίαν [g] εἶναι, 10 καθὼς γέγραπται [h] ὅτι οὐκ ἔστιν abcdf
δίκαιος [i] οὐδὲ εἷς· 11 οὐκ ἔστιν ὁ [k] συνιών, οὐκ ἔστιν ὁ ghkl mno17
[l] ἐκζητῶν τὸν θεόν· 12 πάντες [m] ἐξέκλιναν, ἅμα [n] ἠχρειώ- [47]
θησαν· οὐκ ἔστιν ποιῶν [o] χρηστότητα, οὐκ ἔστιν ἕως
ἑνός. 13 [p] τάφος ἀνεῳγμένος ὁ [q] λάρυγξ αὐτῶν, ταῖς
γλώσσαις αὐτῶν [r] ἐδολιοῦσαν. [s] ἰὸς [t] ἀσπίδων ὑπὸ τὰ
[u] χείλη αὐτῶν. 14 [v] ὧν τὸ στόμα [w] ἀρᾶς καὶ [x] πικρίας [y] γέμει.
15 [z] ὀξεῖς οἱ πόδες αὐτῶν [a] ἐκχέαι [a] αἷμα. 16 [b] σύντριμμα καὶ
[c] ταλαιπωρία ἐν ταῖς ὁδοῖς αὐτῶν, 17 καὶ [d] ὁδὸν [d] εἰρήνης
οὐκ ἔγνωσαν. 18 [e] οὐκ ἔστιν [f] φόβος [f] θεοῦ [g] ἀπέναντι τῶν

o = here only. (ch. ii. 4 reff.) Ps. xxxvi. 3. p Matt. xxiii. 27, 29 al^4. only. Psa. v. 9. q here only. Ps. clix. 6. r here only. Num. xxv. 28. Ps. ll. cc. (v. xiii.) civ. 25 only. s James iii. 8. v. 3 only. Psa. (l. c. BN1) cxxxix. 3. Ezek. xxiv. 6, 11, 12, 13. Ep. Jer. 12, 24 only. t here only. Job xx. 14. u Matt. xv. 8 ‖ Mk. 1 Cor. xiv. 21. Heb. xi. 12. xiii. 15. 1 Pet. iii. 10 (from Ps. xxxiii. 13) only. v Psa. ix. 7 (27) (singular). w here only. Hos. iv. 2. x = Acts viii. 23 reff. y Matt. xxiii. 6, 7. Luke xi. 39. Rev. iv. 6, 8 al^5. only. z = here (Rev. i. 16. ii. 12. xiv. 14, &c. xix. 15) only. Amos ii. 15. a (-χύν., Acts xxii. 20.) Rev. xvi. 6 only. Gen. ix. 6. Isa. lix. 7, 8. Prov. i. 16 AN3 &c. (not BCN1). b here only. Prov. xx. 30 al. c James v. 1 only. Isa. xlvii. 11. (-ρος, ch. vii. 24.) d Luke i. 79 only. l. c. (Ps.) Isa. only. e Psa. xxxv. 1. f 2 Cor. vii. 1 only. (φ. τ. κυρίου, Acts ix. 31. 2 Cor. v. 11. φ. χριστοῦ, Eph. v. 21.) = Neh. v. 9. Isa. xi. 3. g Matt. xxi. 2. xxvii. 24, 61. Acts iii. 16. xvii. 7 only. Josh. xxiv. 26.

for προητ., ητιασαμεθα D^{1}G 31. 89^1 [syr-txt(προ w-ast, appy)] Chr-2-mss$_1$ Œc-comm, *causati sumus* latt. om γαρ D^1 [Syr æth(appy, Treg)]. aft ιουδ. τε ins πρωτον A. **απαντας** G: παντα n. **υπο** B.

10. ουδ D^1 l.

11. om 1st ο ABG [(vulg Orig-int Ambrst)]: ins DKL[P]א syrr arm Euthal-ms] Chr$_1$ Thdrt Damasc Thl Œc. om 2nd ο BG [latt, as before]. for εκζ., ζητων B.

12. ηχρεωθησαν AB^{1}D^{1}Gא. ins ο bef ποιων (*so Ps* xiii. 3 א^1) Dא [Orig-int$_1$ Ambrst]. om 2nd ουκ εστιν B 67^2 Syr.

13. λαρυξ A[P a] d k: -υνξ G.

14. aft στομα ins αυτων B(not Tischdf [N. T. Vat.]) 17.

Bengel, Tholuck, Köllner, Schrader, De Wette, al.) to take προεχόμεθα as middle, and understand it as προέχομεν—**Have we** (Jews) **the** (any) **preference?** We have an use of παρέχομαι as active, Acts xix. 24, Tit. ii. 7. See also Winer, edn. 6, § 38. 5. **οὐ πάντως**] **No, by no means.** This would more naturally be πάντως οὐ, see reff. But we have οὐδὲν πάντως for 'not at all,' Herod. v. 34. The meaning 'not in every way,' 'not altogether,'—as 1 Cor. v. 10 and Theophr. de Caus. Plant. vi. 24 (Wetst.), ποιεῖ γὰρ οὐ πάντως, ἀλλ' ἐὰν οὐλή τις ᾖ ὑπόκαυστος,—will not apply, for it does not agree with what follows, where the Apostle proves *absolute equality* in respect of his argument. **προητ. . . . . εἶναι**] **we have before proved** (chs. i. ii.) **both Jews and Gentiles all to be under sin**; the construction is not acc. and inf.,—*that* Jews and Gentiles *are* under sin,—but Ἰουδ. . . . πάντας is acc. after the verb, and ὑφ' ἁμ. εἶναι the matter of the charge,—q. d. 'we have before brought in guilty Jews and Gentiles all as sinners.' **10—18.**] *Proof of this universal sinfulness from the Scripture,* said directly (ver. 19) of the Jews, but a portion including, and taken for granted of, the Gentiles. Compare throughout the LXX (reff.). **11.**] In the Psalm,—Jehovah looked down from heaven on the children of men, to see εἰ ἔστι συνιὼν ἢ ἐκζητῶν τ. θ. He found *none.* This result is put barely by the Apostle as the testimony of Scripture, giving the sense, but departing from the letter. **13.**] **ἐδολιοῦσαν,** an Alexandrine form for ἐδολίουν; see Lobeck, Phrynichus, p. 349. The *open sepulchre* is an emblem of *perdition,* to which their throat, as the instrument of their speech, is compared. **15.**] The LXX (Isa. l. c.) have οἱ δὲ πόδες αὐτῶν ἐπὶ πονηρίαν τρέχουσι, ταχινοὶ ἐκχέαι αἷμα· καὶ οἱ διαλογισμοὶ αὐτῶν διαλογισμοὶ ἀπὸ φόνων (διαλ. ἀφρόνων Aא)· σύντριμμα καὶ ταλαιπωρία ἐν ταῖς ὁδοῖς αὐτῶν, καὶ ὁδὸν εἰρήνης οὐκ οἴδασιν (ἔγνωσαν, A). **19.**] He proves the applicability of these texts to the Jews by their being found in the *Jewish Scriptures:* not in any *Gentile representation,* which might exclude Jews, but spoken universally, in those very books which were the cherished possession of the Jews them-

ὀφθαλμῶν αὐτῶν. 19 οἴδαμεν δὲ ὅτι ὅσα ὁ νόμος λέγει,
τοῖς [h] ἐν τῷ νόμῳ λαλεῖ, ἵνα πᾶν στόμα [i] φραγῇ καὶ [k] ὑπόδικος γένηται πᾶς ὁ κόσμος τῷ θεῷ. 20 διότι [l] ἐξ [m] ἔργων
[m] νόμου [n] οὐ [lo] δικαιωθήσεται [np] πᾶσα [p] σὰρξ [q] ἐνώπιον αὐ-
τοῦ· διὰ γὰρ νόμου [r] ἐπίγνωσις ἁμαρτίας. 21 Νυνὶ δὲ

F μω λαλει... ABDF KL[P]ℵ a b c d f g h k l m n o 17 [47] (*On the omission of G see proleg.*)

h = Luke viii. 43. ch. iv. 10. Philem. 20 al. i 2 Cor. xi. 10. Heb. xi. 33 only. 2 Macc. xiv. 36 Ald. see Dan. vi. 22 Theod. k here only†. ἐάν τις τούτων τι παραβαίνῃ ὑπόδικος ἔστω τῷ παθόντι, Demosth. 518. 3. l ver. 30. ch. iv. 2. v. 1. Gal. ii. 16 (3ce). iii. 8, 24. James ii. 24 (bis), 25. m = ver. 28. Gal. ii. 16 (3ce). iii. 2, 5, 10 only. n Matt. xxiv. 22. Acts x. 14. Gal. ii. 16. Exod. xv. 26. Psa. cxlii. 2. o = ch. ii. 13 reff. p Acts ii. 17 reff. q = Luke xvi. 15. Ps. l. c. r Paul, ch. i. 28. x. 2. Eph. iv. 13 alll. elsw., Heb. x. 26. 2 Pet. i. 2, 3, 8. ii. 20 only. Prov. ii. 5.

19. for λεγει, λαλει ℵ[1] vulg D-lat Orig$_1$[int$_4$ Ambrst]. for λαλει, λεγει D[1]F[K Syr].
20. *ου δικ.* bef *εξ εργ. νομ.* D F(and lat) fuld [Orig-int$_1$(txt$_1$)] Ambrst. *επιγνωσεως* F.

selves. **ὁ νόμος**] Here, the whole O. T., the law, prophets, and Psalms: see John x. 34, where our Lord cites a Psalm as in '*the law.*' **τοῖς ἐν τῷ ν. λαλεῖ**] **it speaks** (not says,—λαλέω is not '*to say,*' see John viii. 25, note) **to** (or **for**, dat. commodi: i. e. its language belongs to, is true of, when not otherwise specified) **those who are in** (under) **the law.** So that the Jews cannot plead exemption from this description or its consequences. **ἵνα**] **in order that**—not '*so that:*' the bringing in all the world guilty before God is an especial and direct aim of the revelation of God's justice in the law,—that His grace by faith in Christ may come on all who abandon self-righteousness and believe the gospel. **πᾶν στόμα φραγῇ**] If the *Jew's* mouth is shut, and his vaunting in the law taken away, then much more the *Gentile's*, and the *whole world* (see above ver. 6) becomes (*subjective*, as γίνεσθω ver. 4) guilty before God. **20.**] *The solemn and important conclusion of all the foregoing argument.* But not only the *conclusion from it:* it is also the great truth, which when arrived at, is seen to have necessitated the subordinate conclusion of ver. 19, the stopping of every mouth, &c. And therefore it is introduced, not with an illative conjunction, '*wherefore*' (which διότι will not bear), but with '*because.*' **Because by the works of the law** (God's law: whether in the partial revelation of it written in the consciences of the Gentiles, or in the more complete one given by Moses to the Jews,—not, *by works of law:* no such general idea of *law* seems to have ever been before the mind of the Apostle, but always *the law*, emanating from God) **shall no flesh be justified before Him** (the future as implying possibility,—perhaps also as referring to the great day when πᾶσα σάρξ shall stand before God,—perhaps also as a citation from ref. Ps. LXX, οὐ δικαιωθήσεται ἐνώπιόν σου πᾶς ζῶν. οὐ . . . . πᾶσα, which we render by *nulla*, must be kept in the mind to its logical precision: *All flesh*—subject—*shall be*—copula—*not justified*—predicate). The Apostle does not *here* say either (1) that justification by legal works would be impossible if the law could be wholly kept, or (2) that those were not justified who observed the prescribed sacrifices and offerings of the *ceremonial* law (of which he has never once spoken, but wholly of the moral): but he infers from his argument on *matters of fact*, a result in *matter of fact: 'Mankind, Jew and Gentile, have all broken God's law, and are guilty before Him: Man keeps not God's law. By that law then he cannot arrive at God's righteousness.'* **διὰ γὰρ . . . .**] **For by** [**means of**] **the law** (as before, whether partially known to the Gentile or more fully to the Jew) **is the knowledge of sin** (whatever knowledge each has,—whether the accusing and excusing of the Gentile's conscience, or the clearer view of offence against Jehovah granted to the Jew). The reasoning is:—the law has no such office, in the present state of human nature manifested both in history and Scripture, as to *render righteous:* its office is altogether different, viz. to *detect and bring to light the sinfulness* of man. Compare Gal. ii. 16.

21—V. 11.] The entrance into God's righteousness (ch. i. 17) is shewn to be by faith. **21—26.**] *The Apostle resumes the declaration* of ch. i. 17 (having proved that man has no righteousness of his own resulting from the observance of God's law): viz. *that God's righteousness is revealed by Christ, whose atoning Death is, consistently with God's justice, sufficient for the pardon of sin to those who believe in Him.* **21. νυνί**] Is this of *time*, '*now*,' in contradistinction to ages past, = ἐν τῷ νῦν καιρῷ, ver. 26,—or is it merely = 'as things are,' '*now we find?*' The former is held by Grot., Bengel, Tholuck, Reiche, Olsh., Rückert, al.,—the latter by Fritzsche, Meyer, and De Wette. The *former* is *true* in sense, and applicable

[s] χωρὶς νόμου [t] δικαιοσύνη θεοῦ [u] πεφανέρωται, [vw] μαρτυρουμένη [w] ὑπὸ τοῦ [x] νόμου καὶ τῶν [x] προφητῶν, 22 [t] δικαιοσύνη
[y] δὲ θεοῦ διὰ [z] πίστεως Ἰησοῦ χριστοῦ, [b] εἰς πάντας [καὶ
[c] ἐπὶ πάντας] τοὺς πιστεύοντας. οὐ γάρ ἐστιν [d] διαστολή·
23 πάντες γὰρ ἥμαρτον καὶ [e] ὑστεροῦνται τῆς [f] δόξης [f] τοῦ
θεοῦ, 24 [g] δικαιούμενοι [h] δωρεὰν τῇ αὐτοῦ [i] χάριτι διὰ τῆς

C και των προφητων... ABCDF KL[P]א a b c d f g h k l m n o 17 [47]

s = ver. 28. ch. iv. 6. vii. 8, 9. 1 Cor. iv. 8 al.
t ch. i. 17 reff.
u ch. i. 19 reff.
v = John xviii. 37. 3 John 3. Heb. vii. 8.
w Acts x. 22 reff.
x Acts xiii. 15 reff.
y = Phil. ii. 8.
z constr., Mark xi. 22. Acts iii. 16. Gal. ii. 16, 20. James ii. 1 al.
b = Gal. iii. 14.
c Acts iv. 33 reff.
d ch. x. 12 reff.
e — (but act.) Luke xxii. 35 al. Ps. xxii. 1. w. ἐν, 1 Cor. i. 7. constr., 2 Cor. xi. 5.
f constr., John xii. 43.
g w. dat., ver. 28. Tit. iii. 7 only. (ch. ii. 13 reff.)
h Matt. x. 8. 2 Cor. xi. 7. Exod. xxi. 2. (John xv. 25, from Ps. xxxiv. 19.)
i = ch. v. 15 al.

21. [ins *του* bef *θεου* F.] *μαρτυρομενη* D[1].

22. for *ιησ. χρ.*, *εν χριστω ιησ.* A: om Chr_1: om *ιησου* B ($Tert_1$): txt CDFKL[P]א 17 rel vss $Clem_1$ $Orig_1$[(int_1) Damasc] Thdrt Thl Œc Pelag Ambrst Chrom Bede.

om *και επι παντας* (*possibly from homœotel: on the other hand, the longer text may be the junction of two readings*) ABCא[1][P 47[1]] copt (æth) arm $Clem_1$ ($Orig_1$[int_1]) Cyr[-p_1] Aug_3: ins DFKLא[3] 17 [rel] syrr vulg(but am demid [harl] al Damasc om *εις παντ. και*) Chr_1 [Euthal-ms] Thdrt Thl Œc Ambrst $Chrom_1$.

to the circumstances of the gospel: but the meaning is *too strong*, where no contrast of time is expressly in view. I therefore prefer the latter, especially as Paul's usage elsewhere justifies it; see ch. vii. 17; 1 Cor. xv. 20. **χωρὶς νόμου**] **without the** (help of the) **law**, 'independently of the law:' not 'without the *works* of the law;' for here it is not *the way to* the δικ. θεοῦ which is spoken of (which is *faith*), but that δικ. *itself*. **δικαιοσ. θεοῦ**] **God's righteousness:** in what sense, see ch. i. 17, and note. **πεφανέρωται**] viz. in the facts of the gospel. The perfect sets forth the manifestation of this righteousness in history as an *accomplished and still enduring fact*—the ἀποκαλύπτεται of ch. i. 17 denotes the continual unfolding of this righteousness in the hearts and lives of faithful believers. **μαρτυρουμένη** κ.τ.λ.] **being borne witness to** (pres. because the law and prophets remain on record as a revelation of God's will) **by the law and the prophets** (not merely the types and prophecies, but the *whole body* of the O. T., see Matt. xxii. 40). **22. δικαιοσ. δὲ θ.**] **but that** (so δέ in Herod. vii. 8, Ἀρισταγόρῃ τῷ Μιλησίῳ, δούλῳ δὲ ἡμετέρῳ,—and i. 114, ὑπὸ τοῦ σοῦ δούλου, βουκόλου δὲ παιδός: the contrast being between the general mention which has preceded, and the specific distinction now brought in. See Hartung, Partikellehre i. 168 ff.) **the righteousness of God** (i. e. 'I mean, the righteousness of God **διὰ πίστεως Ἰ. χρ.**') **which is** (ἡ is not necessary, the art. being often omitted in cases where the ear is reminded of a usage of the cognate verb with a preposition, such as δικαιοῦσθαι διὰ πίστεως. Compare Col. i. 4, ἀκούσαντες τὴν πίστιν ὑμ. ἐν χριστῷ Ἰησ., and Eph. iii. 4, δύνασθε νοῆσαι τὴν σύνεσίν μου ἐν τῷ μυστηρίῳ (συνιέντες ἐν πάσῃ σοφίᾳ occurs Dan. i. 4 Theod.). See Winer, edn. 6, § 20. 2. b) **by the faith in Jesus Christ** (gen.: see reff.). * **εἰς πάντ. [κ. ἐπὶ πάντ.]** depends on πεφανέρωται,—(is revealed) **unto** ('towards,' 'so as to penetrate to') **all[, and upon** ('over,' 'so as to be shed down on,' but in the theological meaning, no real difference of sense from **εἰς**; this repetition of prepositions to give force is peculiar to Paul, see ver. 30, and Gal. i. 1) **all] who believe.** Probably the repetition of πάντας was suggested by the two kinds of believers, Jew and Gentile, so as to prepare the way for *οὐ γάρ ἐστι διαστολή* (but still no essential difference in the interpretations of εἰς and ἐπί must be sought). **23.** * [**ὑστεροῦνται** should be rendered **fall short**, not, as E. V., "come short," since this latter may be taken for the past tense, after the auxiliary "*have*."] **τῆς δόξης τοῦ θεοῦ**] **Of the praise which comes from God,** see reff. (so Grot., Thol., Reiche, Fritz., Meyer, Rückert, De Wette): not, '*of praise in God's sight*' (Luther, Calv., Estius, Köllner): nor, '*of glory with God*,' as ch. v. 2 (Œc., Beza, al.),—for the Apostle is not speaking here of future reward, but of present worthiness: nor, *of the glorious image of God* which we have lost through sin (Calov., al., Rückert, Olsh.), which is against both the usage of the word, and the context of the passage. **24.**] δικαιούμενοι agrees with πάντες, without any ellipsis; nor need it be resolved into καὶ δικαιοῦνται: the participial sentence is subordinated to the great general statement of the insufficiency of all to attain to the glory of God. It is not necessary, in the interpretation, that the subjects of πάντες and δικαιούμενοι should be in matter of fact strictly commensurate:—'*all* have sinned—*all* are (must be, *if justified*) justified freely, &c.'

[k] ἀπολυτρώσεως τῆς [l] ἐν χριστῷ Ἰησοῦ, 25 ὃν [m] προέθετο
ὁ θεὸς [n] ἱλαστήριον διὰ πίστεως [o] ἐν τῷ αὐτοῦ αἵματι,
[p] εἰς [q] ἔνδειξιν τῆς δικαιοσύνης αὐτοῦ, διὰ τὴν [r] πάρεσιν

k Luke xxi. 28. ch. viii. 23. 1 Cor. i. 30. Eph. i. 7, 14. iv. 30. Col. i. 4. Heb. ix. 15. xi. 35 only. L.P.H. Dan. iv. 32 LXX only. (-οῦν, Exod. xxi. 8. Zeph. iii. 1.) l = ch. vi. 11. viii. 2 al. m = here (ch. i. 13. Eph. i. 9) only. Polyb. i. 33. 9, προθέμενοι τοὺς γροσφομάχους. n = here (Heb. ix. 5) only. see note. o = Matt. xii. 27, 28 al. p ch. i. 5 reff. q here bis. 2 Cor. viii. 24. Phil. i. 28 only +. r here only +. (-ιέναι, Sir. xxiii. 2.)

25. ιλαστηρειον F: om arm: *propitiatorem* D-lat vulg-sixt harl² Ambrst Oros₁ Jer Ambr: *propitiationem* vulg[-clem(with am &c) F]-lat syr: *placationem* Hil₁. rec ins της bef πιστεως, with BC³D³KL[P] 17 rel Chr-txt₁ [Bas₁ Euthal-ms] Thdrt Œc: om C¹D¹Fℵ Orig₃ Eus₃ Bas₁ Cyr[-p₂] Damasc Thl.—om δια πιστεως A Chr-comm(and 2-mss). for 1st αυτου, εαυτου B 47. for παρεσιν, πωρωσιν 46: παραινεσιν 69. 116: [παρεσνεσιν k:] *propositum* D¹-lat Aug₂ Ambrst Pelag-comm.

δωρεάν] see reff.: here 'without merit or desert as arising from earnings of our own;' '*gratis*.' **τῇ αὐτοῦ χάριτι**] **by His grace**, i. e. 'His free undeserved Love,' as the working cause (De W.).
διὰ τῆς ἀπολ. κ.τ.λ.] **By means of the propitiatory redemption which is in** (has been brought about by, and is now in the Person of) **Christ Jesus.** **ἀπολύτρωσις**, redemption by a λύτρον, **propitiation**,—and, as expressed by the preposition ἀπο, redemption *from* some state of danger or misery: here,—redemption *from the guilt of sin by the propitiatory sacrifice of Christ's death*, see reff. and Matt. xx. 28. In Eph. i. 7 this ἀπολύτρωσις is defined to = ἡ ἄφεσις τῶν παραπτωμάτων.
25.] **προέθετο**, not here '*decreed*,' as in reff. N. T.,—but **put forth, set forth**, manifested historically in His incarnation, sufferings, and exaltation. Wetst. quotes Thucyd. ii. 34, τὰ ὀστᾶ προτίθενται τῶν ἀπογενομένων, 'they expose the bones of the deceased to public view.'
ἱλαστήριον] **as a propitiatory offering.** So we have σωτήρια, Exod. xx. 24,—χαριστήριον (εὐχαριστήριον A), 2 Macc. xii. 45,—and καθάρσιον, Herod. i. 35, in the sense of thank-offerings and offerings of purification (no subst., as θῦμα, need be supplied,—the words being themselves substantives): and we have this very word in Dio Chrysos. Orat. ii. p. 184 (cited by Stuart), where he says that the Greeks offered an ἱλαστήριον τῇ Ἀθήνᾳ, a propitiatory sacrifice. The ordinary interpretation (Theodoret, Theophyl., Luth., Calv., Grot., Calov., Wolf, Olsh.) is founded on the sense in which the LXX use the word, as signifying the golden cover of the ark of the covenant, between the Cherubim, where Jehovah appeared and whence He gave His oracles. τὸ ἱλαστήριον πέταλον ἦν χρυσοῦν, ἐπέκειτο δὲ τῷ κιβωτῷ. ἑκατέρωθεν δὲ εἶχε τὰ τῶν χερουβὶμ ἐκτυπώματα. ἐκεῖθεν τῷ ἀρχιερεῖ λειτουργοῦντι ἐγίνετο δήλη τοῦ θεοῦ ἡ εὐμένεια .... τὸ ἀληθινὸν ἱλαστήριον ὁ δεσπότης ἐστὶ χριστός· ἐκεῖνο δὲ τὸ παλαιὸν τούτου τὸν τύπον ἐπλήρου. ἁρμόττει δὲ αὐτῷ ὡς ἀνθρώπῳ τὸ ὄνομα, οὐχ ὡς θεῷ· ὡς γὰρ θεός, αὐτὸς διὰ τοῦ ἱλαστηρίου χρηματίζει. Theodoret: on which Theophylact further,—ἐδήλου δὲ πάντως τὴν ἀνθρωπίνην φύσιν, ἥτις πῶμα ἦν τῆς θεότητος, ἐπικαλύπτουσα ταύτην. The expression occurs in full, ἱλαστήριον ἐπίθεμα, Exod. xxv. 17: elsewhere ἱλαστήριον only, as ref. Heb. See also Philo, Vita Mos. iii. 8, vol. ii. p. 150. But De Wette well shews the inapplicability of this interpretation, as not agreeing with εἰς ἔνδειξιν κ.τ.λ. (which requires a *victim*, see below), and as confusing the unity of the idea here, Christ being (according to it) one while a victim (ἐν τῷ αὐτοῦ αἵματι), and another, something else. The other interpretation (Vulg. *propitiationem*: so E. V.: Beza, Rückert, al.: adj.—Rosenmüller, Wahl), which makes ἱλαστήριον an adj. agreeing with ὅν, '*a propitiator*,' hardly agrees with προέθετο, implying an external demonstration of Christ as the ἱλαστήριον, not merely an appointment in the divine œconomy. **διὰ πίστεως**] **by faith**, as the subjective means of appropriation of this propitiation:—not to be joined with ἐν αὐτοῦ αἵματι (but the omission of τῆς is no objection to this, see above on ver. 22), as Luth., Calv. al., Olsh., Rückert,—for such an expression as πίστις or πιστεύω ἐν τῷ αἵμ. Ἰ. χρ. would be unexampled,—and (which is decisive) the clause ἐν τῷ αὐτοῦ αἵματι requires a primary, not a subordinate place in the sentence, because the next clause, εἰς ἔνδ. τ. δικ. αὐτ., directly refers to it. As διὰ πίστ. is the subjective means of appropriation, so ἐν τῷ αἵμ. αὐτοῦ is the objective means of manifestation, of Christ as a propitiatory sacrifice. **αἷμα** does not = θάνατος, but refers to propitiation *by blood*,—the well-known typical use of it in sacrifice.
εἰς ἔνδειξιν κ.τ.λ.] **in order to the manifestation of His righteousness**: this is the aim of the putting forth of Christ as an expiatory victim. **δικαιοσύνη**, not *truth* (Ambrst., al.),—not *goodness* (Theodoret, Grot., Hammond, Koppe,

τῶν [s] προγεγονότων [t] ἁμαρτημάτων ἐν τῇ [u] ἀνοχῇ τοῦ θεοῦ, 26 [v] πρὸς τὴν [q] ἔνδειξιν τῆς δικαιοσύνης αὐτοῦ ἐν [w] τῷ νῦν [w] καιρῷ, [x] εἰς τὸ εἶναι αὐτὸν δίκαιον καὶ [y] δικαιοῦντα [z] τὸν ἐκ [a] πίστεως [a] Ἰησοῦ. 27 [b] Ποῦ οὖν ἡ [c] καύ-

ABCDF KL[P]א a b c d f g h k l m n o 17 [47]

s here only +. 2 Macc. xiv. 3 only. t Mark iii. 28, 29. 1 Cor. vi. 18 only. Isa. lviii. 1. u ch. ii. 4 reff. v Acts iii. 10. 1 Cor. vi. 5 al. w ch. viii. 18. xi. 5. 2 Cor. viii. 14 only. Gen. xxx. 20. x Acts iii. 19. vii. 19. ch. i. 11, 20 al. y ch. ii. 13 reff. z constr., ch. ii. 8 reff. a constr., ver. 22. b = 1 Cor. i. 20. c Paul (ch. xv. 17. 1 Cor. xv. 31 al7.) only, exc. James iv. 16. Jer. xii. 13.

26. rec om *την*, with D³KL Chr Thdrt [Euthal-ms] Thl Œc: ins ABCD¹א[P 47] $Clem_1$ Cyr_1. (F 17 omit from *δικ. αυτου* ver 25 to *δικ. αυτου* ver 26.) om *και* F fuld Ambrst. for *δικαιουντα*, *δικαιουν* D¹. om *ιησου* F 52 E-lat: for *ιησ.*, *ιησ. χρ.* vulg[with demid harl tol] copt Thdrt [$Orig\text{-}int_1$] Ambrst Pelag[-comm]: *χρ. ιησ.* D¹-lat: *του κυρ. ημ. ιησ. χρ.* Syr: *ιησουν* D-gr L b d f g m o 17 $Clem_1$: txt ABCKא[P 47] am fuld D²-lat syr æth [arm Euthal-ms] Chr_1 Thl Œc Aug_2 $Oros_1$.

Rosenm., Reiche),—not both these combined with *justice* (Beza),—not *justifying* or *sin-forgiving* righteousness (Chrys., Aug., Estius, Krehl, B.-Crus.),—not the *righteousness which He gives* (Luther, Elsner, Wolf, al.), which last would repeat the idea already contained in ver. 21 and rob *εἰς τὸ εἶναι αὐτ. δίκαιον* of all meaning,—not *holiness*, which does not correspond to *δίκαιος* and *δικαιοῦν*,—but **judicial righteousness**, JUSTICE (as Orig., Calov., Tholuck, Meyer, Schrader, Rückert ed. 2, al.). This interpretation alone suits the requirements of the sense, and corresponds to the idea of *δικαιοῦν*, which is itself judicial. A *sin-offering* betokens on the one side the expiation of guilt, and on the other ensures pardon and reconciliation: and thus the Death of Christ is not only a proof of God's grace and love, but also of His judicial righteousness which requires punishment and expiation. (Mainly from De Wette.) **διὰ τ. πάρεσιν κ.τ.λ.**] = *διὰ τὸ παριέναι τὸν θεὸν τὰ προγ. ἁμαρτήματα ἐν τῇ ἀνοχῇ αὐτοῦ*, and contains the *reason why* God would manifest His judicial righteousness; **on account of the overlooking of the sins which had passed, in the forbearance of God**: i. e. to vindicate that character for justice, which might seem, owing to the suspension of God's righteous sentence on sin in former ages in His forbearance, to be placed in question:—to shew, that though He did not then fully punish for sin, and though He did then set forth inadequate means of (subjective) justification,—yet He did both, not because His justice was slumbering, nor because the nature of His righteousness was altered,—but because *He had provided a way* whereby sin might be forgiven, and He might be just. Observe, *πάρεσις is not forgiveness* [nor "*remission*," as E. V. erroneously renders it], but [**passing over**, or] **overlooking**, which is the work of *forbearance* (see Acts xvii. 30), whereas *forgiveness* is the work of *grace*,—see ch. ii. 4:—nor is *τῶν προγεγ. ἁμ.*, 'the sins of each man which precede his conversion' (Calov.), but *those of the whole world before the death of Christ*. See the very similar words Heb. ix. 15. The rendering *διά*, '*by means of*' (Origen, Luth., Calv., Calov., Le Clerc, Elsn., Koppe, Reiche, Schrader), is both ungrammatical and unmeaning. **26. πρὸς τὴν ἔνδ. κ.τ.λ.**] The art. distinguishes this *ἔνδειξις* from the former, as the *fuller and ultimate object*, of which that *ἔνδειξις* was a subordinate part:—**with a view to the** (or His) **manifestation of his righteousness in this present time.** The shewing forth that He was righteous throughout His dealings with the whole world, by means of setting forth an adequate and complete propitiation in the death of Christ, was *towards*, formed a subsidiary manifestation to, His *great manifestation of His righteousness* (same sense as before, *judicial* righteousness, *justice*) *under the Gospel*. The joining *πρὸς τὴν ἔνδειξ. κ.τ.λ.* with *ἐν τῇ ἀνοχῇ τ. θεοῦ* (Beza, Rückert ed. 2, Thol., al.) would draw off the attention from the leading thought of the sentence to a digression respecting the *ἀνοχή τ. θ.*, which is not probable. **εἰς τὸ εἶναι κ.τ.λ.**] **in order that He may be** (*shewn to be*:—the whole present concern is with *ἔνδειξις*, the *exhibition to men* of the righteousness of God) **just and** (yet, on the other side) **justifying him who is of** (the) **faith in Jesus** (*τὸν ἐκ πίστ. Ἰησ.*, him who belongs to, stands in, works from as his standing-point, faith in Jesus: see ch. ii. 8, note, and reff.).

27—IV. 25.] JEWISH BOASTING ALTOGETHER REMOVED *by this truth*, NOT *however* BY MAKING VOID THE LAW, *nor* BY DEGRADING ABRAHAM FROM HIS PRE-EMINENCE, *but* BY ESTABLISHING THE LAW, *and shewing that Abraham was really* JUSTIFIED BY FAITH, *and is the* FATHER OF THE FAITHFUL. **27.] ἡ καύχησις, the boasting**, viz. *of the Jews*, of which he had spoken before, ch. ii., not '*boasting*'

χησις; [d] ἐξεκλείσθη. διὰ [e] ποίου νόμου; τῶν [f] ἔργων;
οὐχί, ἀλλὰ διὰ νόμου πίστεως. 28 [g] λογιζόμεθα * γὰρ
[h] δικαιοῦσθαι πίστει ἄνθρωπον [i] χωρὶς [j] ἔργων [j] νόμου.
29 ἢ Ἰουδαίων ὁ θεὸς μόνον, οὐχὶ καὶ ἐθνῶν; ναὶ καὶ
ἐθνῶν, 30 [k] εἴπερ εἷς ὁ θεὸς ὃς [j] δικαιώσει περιτομὴν [k] ἐκ
πίστεως καὶ [l] ἀκροβυστίαν διὰ τῆς πίστεως. 31 νόμον

d Gal. iv. 17 only. Exod. xxiii. 2 B. 2 Macc. xiii. 21 (only ?). e = Acts iv. 7 reff. f = ch. iv. 2, 6 al. fr., Paul. James ii. 14—26. g = and constr., ch. xiv. 14. Phil. iii. 13. Wisd. xv. 12. h w. dat., ver. 24 reff. i ver. 21. j ver. 20 (reff.). k ch. viii. 9 reff. l Paul (ch. ii. 25. iv. 9, &c. 1 Cor. vii. 18, 19 al.) only, exc. Acts xi. 3. Gen. xvii. 11.

27. aft *καυχησις* ins *σου* F latt [Orig-int$_4$] Aug$_2$. for *ουχι*, *ουκ* D[1]: *ου* F. om 2nd *δια* D[1].

28. *λογιζωμεθαι* D[3]K[P]. * rec *οὖν* (*prob corrn from misunderstandg of λογιζομαι to convey a* conclusion : *see note*), with BCD[3]KL[P] 17 rel syrr Chr$_1$ Thdrt [Euthal-ms] Thl Œc: *γαρ* AD[1]F‎א [47] latt copt [(æth arm)] Cyr[-p$_1$] Damasc [Orig-int$_1$] Ambrst Aug$_1$ Ambr. rec *πιστει* bef *δικαιουσθαι* (*to throw emphasis on πιστει, supposing the ver to convey a solemn conclusion*), with KL[P]א[3] 17 rel syrr [arm] Chr Thdrt [Euthal-ms Thl Œc]: for *πιστει ανθρωπον*, *ανθρ. δια πιστεως* F vulg æth [Orig-int$_4$ Ambrst] Aug: txt ABCDא[1] [47] (copt). *αρθρωπον* B[1].

29. om *η* n 39[1] Thdrt: *μη* A[1](appy) 39[2] [Julian(in Cyr)]: *ει* 77: *an* latt [Orig-int]. *μονων* B a b [o] 23. 39. 47-8. 76 Clem$_2$ Ath$_1$ Chr$_1$(mss vary) Cyr Thl (but aft *ιουδ.* Clem$_2$ Ath$_1$): *μονος* D: txt ACFKL[P]א 17 rel Ath$_1$ [Eus$_1$ Chr$_1$ Cyr-p(with some variation of mss) Damasc] Thdrt Œc, *tantum* latt. rec aft *ουχι* ins *δε*, with L[P] 17 rel syr Chr Cyr$_1$[-p] Thdrt Thl Œc: om ABCDFKא k [47] latt Syr copt [æth arm] Clem$_2$ Ath$_2$ Chr-ms$_1$ Cyr[-p$_2$] Damasc [Orig-int$_1$ Hil$_1$ Ambrst].

30. rec *επειπερ* (*corrn*), with D[1.3]FKL[P]א[3] 17 [47-marg] rel Eus$_2$ Ath$_2$ Chr$_1$ Thdrt Thl Œc: *quoniam quidem* latt Ambr[st Orig-int$_1$]: txt ABCD[2]א[1] [47-txt] Clem$_1$ Orig$_1$ Cyr$_3$[mss vary] Did$_1$ Damasc: *siquidem* Jer$_1$ Pacian$_1$. om *ο* D[1] Orig$_1$.

in general, which will not suit ver. 29. (So Theodoret, *τὸ ὑψηλὸν τῶν Ἰουδαίων φρόνημα*,—Chrys., Theophyl., Œc.:—Vulg.: *gloriatio tua:* Bengel, Rückert, Meyer, De Wette, al.) **ἐξεκλ.**] *οὐκ ἔτι χώραν ἔχει*, Theodoret. **διὰ π. ν. κ.τ.λ.**] **By what law** (is it excluded)? (is it by that) **of works? No, but by the law** (*norma*, the rule) **of faith.** The contrast is not here between *the law* and *the Gospel* as two dispensations, but between the *law of works* and the *law of faith,* whether found under the law, or the Gospel, or (if the case admitted) any where else. This is evident by the Apostle proving below that *Abraham was justified*, not by works, so as to have whereof to boast, but by faith.

28.] **λογιζόμεθα,** not '*we conclude,*' but **we hold, we reckon,** see reff.: the former is against N. T. usage; and has probably caused the change of *γάρ* into *οὖν*, by some who imagined that this verse was a conclusion from the preceding argument. **For we hold** (as explanatory of the verse preceding,—on the other supposition the two verses are disjointed, and the conclusion comes in most strangely), **that a man is justified by faith [apart from]** (*without* [but more than without—so distinctly without as to be utterly and entirely separate from and independent of]) **the works of the law** (not *works of law*); and therefore boasting is excluded.

29.] In shewing how completely Jewish boasting is excluded, Paul purposes to take the ground of their own law, and demonstrate it from that. He will shew that God is not (the God) of Jews alone, but of Gentiles, and that *this very point was involved in the promise* made to Abraham, *by believing which he was justified* (ch. iv.), and therefore that it lies in the *very root and kernel of the law itself.* But, as often elsewhere, he passes off from this idea again and again, recurring to it however continually,—and eventually when he brings forward his proof-text (*πατέρα πολλῶν ἐθνῶν τέθεικά σε*, iv. 17), *Abraham's faith*, and *not this fact*, has become the leading subject.

30. εἴπερ] **if at least** (if we are to hold to what is manifest as a result of our former argument) **God is One, who shall justify the circumcision** (= the Jews, after the analogy of ch. ii. 26) **by** (*ἐκ*, as the preliminary condition,—the state *out of which* the justification arises) **faith, and the uncircumcision** (the Gentiles) **through** (by means of) **their faith.** Too much stress must not be laid on the difference of the two prepositions (see ver. 22 and note). The omission of the art. in *ἐκ πίστ.* and its expression in *διὰ τῆς πίστ.* are natural enough: the former expresses the *ground* of justification, generally taken, *ἐκ πίστεως, by faith:* the latter the *means*

m ver. 3 reff. n ver. 4 reff. o = Heb. x. 9. Num. xxx. 14. 1 Macc. xv. 5. -άνω, see ch. vi. 13. 1 Cor. iii. 1 reff. 8. xxvi. 12. p ch. iii. 5 reff. q = Luke ix. 12. Acts vii. 11. 2 Tim. i. 18. Gen. vi.

οὖν [m] καταργοῦμεν διὰ τῆς πίστεως; [n] μὴ γένοιτο, ἀλλὰ νόμον [o] ἱστάνομεν. ABCDF KL[P]ℵ a b c d f g h k l m n o 17 [47]

IV. 1 [p] Τί οὖν ἐροῦμεν [[q] εὑρηκέναι] Ἀβραὰμ τὸν

31. rec ιστωμεν, with D³KLℵ³[P 47-marg] rel Chr₁ Thdrt [Euthal-ms] Thl Œc: [ισταμεν 47-txt:] συνιστωμεν 17. 65. 93 lect-6: περιστανομεν D¹: txt ABCD²Fℵ¹ Orig₁ Cyr[-p₁] Damasc.

Chap. IV. 1. rec αβρααμ τον πατερα ημων bef ευρηκεναι, with KL[P] 17 rel syrr Chr[-txt Euthal-ms] Thdrt Thl Œc Gennad Phot: om ευρηκεναι B 47¹ [Chr-comm₁]: ins bef αβρααμ ACDFℵ latt [copt æth arm] Cyr[-p₁] Damasc [Orig-int₁] Ambrst [aft

whereby the man lays hold on justification, διὰ τῆς πίστεως, *by his faith*: the former is the objective ground, the latter the subjective medium. Jowett's rendering of περιτομὴν ἐκ πίστεως, '*the circumcision that is of faith*,' though ingenious, is hardly philologically allowable, nor would it correspond to the other member of the sentence, which he rightly renders '*and the uncircumcision through their faith*.' To understand τῆς πίστεως (as Mr. Green, Gr. p. 300) as referring to πίστεως just mentioned '*by the instrumentality of the identical faith which operates in the case of the circumcised*,' is to contradict the fact: the faith was not, strictly speaking, identical in this sense, or the two cases never need have been distinguished. See vv. 1, 2. **31.**] But again the Jew may object, if this is the case, if Faith be the *ground*, and Faith the *medium*, of justification for all, circumcised or uncircumcised, *surely the law is set aside and made void*. That this is not so, the Apostle both here asserts, and is prepared to shew by working out the proposition of ver. 29, that the law itself belonged to a covenant whose *original recipient was justified by faith*, and whose main promise was, the *reception and blessing of the Gentiles*. * **νόμον**, not '*law*,' but **the law**, as every where in the Epistle. We may safely say that the Apostle never argues of *law*, abstract, in the sense of *a system of precepts*,—its attributes or its effects,—but always of THE LAW, concrete,—*the law of God given by Moses*, when speaking of the Jews, as here: *the law of God*, in as far as written in their consciences, when speaking of the Gentiles: and when including both, *the law of God* generally, His written as well as His unwritten will. Many Commentators have taken this verse (being misled in some cases by its place at the end of the chapter) as standing by itself, and have gone into the abstract grounds why faith does not make void the law (or moral obedience); which, however true, *have no place here*: the design being to shew that the law itself *contained this very doctrine*, and was founded in the promise to Abraham on a covenant embracing Jews and Gentiles,—and therefore was not degraded from its dignity by the doctrine, but rather established as a part of God's dealings,—consistent with, explaining, and explained by, the Gospel.

IV. 1—5.] *Abraham himself was justified by faith*. The reading and punctuation of this verse present some difficulties. As to the first (see var. read.), the variation in the order of the words, and the reading προπάτορα seemed to me formerly, however strongly supported, to have sprung out of an idea that κατὰ σάρκα belonged to πατέρα. This being supposed, εὑρηκέναι appeared to have been transposed to throw πατέρα ἡμ. κατὰ σάρκα together,—and then, because Abraham is distinctly proved (ver. 11) to have been *in another sense* the father of the faithful, πατέρα to have been altered to the less ambiguous προπάτορα, *ancestor*, a word not found in the N. T., but frequent in the Fathers. I therefore in the 3rd edition of this vol., with De Wette, Tholuck, and Tischendorf (in his last [7th, not 8th] edn.), retained the rec. text. Being now however convinced that we are bound to follow the testimony of our best MSS., and to distrust such subjective considerations as unsafe, and generally able to be turned both ways, I have adopted the reading of A(B)CDFℵ &c., bracketing εὑρηκέναι as of doubtful authority, omitted as it is by B. Grot., Le Clerc, and Wetst. punctuate, τί οὖν ἐροῦμεν; εὑρηκ. . . . . σάρκα:—and Matthaï, τί οὖν; ἐροῦμ. . . . . σάρκα; supplying δικαιοσύνην (or more rightly an indefinite τι) after εὑρηκέναι. But as Thol. well remarks, both these methods of punctuating would presuppose that Paul had given some reason in the preceding verses for imagining that Abraham *had* gained some advantage according to the flesh: which is not the case. **1. οὖν**] The Apostle is here contending with those under the law *from their own standing-point*: and he follows up his νόμον

[r] προπάτορα ἡμῶν [s] κατὰ [s] σάρκα; 2 εἰ γὰρ Ἀβραὰμ [t] ἐξ
ἔργων [t] ἐδικαιώθη, [uv] ἔχει [vw] καύχημα. Ἀλλ' οὐ [x] πρὸς
θεόν· 3 τί γὰρ ἡ [y] γραφὴ λέγει; [z] Ἐπίστευσεν δὲ Ἀβραὰμ

r here only †. Ps. xxix. 8 Symm. s ch. i. 3 reff. t ch. iii. 20 reff. u = ch. xv. 17. 1 Cor. xv. 31. v Gal. vi. 4. w Paul (1 Cor. v. 6 al8.) only, exc. Heb. iii. 6. Deut. x. 21 al. x = Mark xii. 12, or John i. 1, 2. y ch. ix. 17 reff. z w. dat., Gen. xv. 6. Acts xvi. 34 reff.

σαρκα 47-marg]. rec (for προπατ.) πατερα, with C[3]DFKL[P] ℵ-corr[1] 17 rel latt syr Chr[txt and comm Euthal-ms] Thdrt Gennad Phot Thl Œc: *patriarcham* Syr: txt ABC[1]ℵ[1.3] copt æth arm Eus Cyr[-p$_1$] Damasc.

2. αλλα F. rec ins τον bef θεον, with D[3]KL[P] 17 rel Chr$_1$ Thdrt [Euthal-ms Damasc]: om ABCD[1]Fℵ.

3. in ℵ γαρ has been written twice, but the first erased. om δε (*as unnecessary*) D[1]F b o latt [Syr æth arm] Chr$_1$ [Euthal-ms Orig-int$_4$] Cypr$_1$.

ἱστάνομεν, by **what therefore** ('hoc concesso,' 'seeing that you and I are both upholders of the law') **shall we say,** &c. This verse, and the argument following, are not a *proof*, but a *consequence*, of νόμον ἱστ., and are therefore introduced, not with **γάρ**, but with **οὖν**. **εὑρηκέναι** [if read]] viz. *towards his justification*, or more strictly, *earned* as his own, to boast of. **κατὰ σάρκα** belongs to **εὑρ.**, not (as Chrys., Theophyl., Erasm.) to **προπάτορα ἡμ.** For the course and spirit of the argument is not to limit the paternity of Abraham to a mere fleshly one, but to shew that he was the spiritual father of all believers. And the question is not one which requires any such distinction between his fleshly and spiritual paternity (as in ch. ix. 3, 5). This being so, *what does* **κατὰ σάρκα** *mean?* It cannot allude to *circumcision;* for that is rendered improbable, not only by the parallel expression ἐξ ἔργων in the *plural*, but also by the consideration, that circumcision was no ἔργον at all, but a *seal of the righteousness which he had by faith* being yet uncircumcised (ver. 11),—and by the whole course of the argument in the present place, which is not to disprove the exclusive privilege of the Jew (that having been already done, chs. ii. iii.), but to shew that *the father and head of the race himself was justified not by works, but by faith.* Doubtless, in so far as circumcision was a mere *work of obedience*, it might be in a loose way considered as falling under that category: but it came *after* justification, and so is *chronologically* here excluded. **κατὰ σάρκα** then is in contrast to κατὰ πνεῦμα,—and refers to *that department of our being from which spring works*, in contrast with *that in which is the exercise of faith:* see ch. viii. 4, 5. **2.**] **For if Abraham was** [not '*were*' as E. V.] **justified** (assuming, as a fact known to all, that he *was justified* by some means) **by works, he hath matter of boasting** (not expressed here whether *in the sight of men*, or *of God*, but taken generally: the proposition being assumed, 'He that has earned justification by works, has whereof to *boast*'). Then, in disproof of this,—that Abraham has matter of boasting,—whatever *men* might think of him, or attribute to him (e. g. the perfect keeping of the law, as the Jews did), one thing at least is clear, that *he has none before God.* (**πρός**, probably as in the second ref., *with*, in the sense of *chez:* apud Deum.) This we can prove, (ver. 3) **for what saith the Scripture? Abraham believed God** (God's promise) **and it** (τὸ πιστεῦσαι) **was reckoned** (so LXX. Heb., 'He reckoned it') **to him as** (ch. ii. 26) **righteousness.** The whole question so much mooted between Protestants on the one hand, and Romanists, Arminians, and Socinians on the other, as to whether this righteousness was reckoned (1) '*per fidem*,' being *God's righteousness imputed* to the sinner; or (2) '*propter fidem*,' so that God made Abraham righteous *on account of the merit of his faith*, lies in fact in a small compass, if what has gone before be properly taken into account. The Apostle has proved Jews and Gentiles to be *all under sin:* utterly unable by works of their own to attain to righteousness. Now *faith*, in the second sense mentioned above, is strictly and entirely *a work*, and as such would be the *efficient cause* of man's justification,—which, by what has preceded, *it cannot be.* It will therefore follow, that it was not the *act of believing* which was reckoned to him as a righteous act, or on account of which perfect righteousness was laid to his charge, but that the *fact of his trusting God to perform His promise introduced him into the blessing promised.* God declared his purpose (Gen. xii. 3) of blessing all the families of the earth in Abraham, and again (Gen. xv. 5) that his seed should be as the stars of heaven, when as yet he had no son. Abraham *believed this promise, and became partaker of this blessing.* But this blessing was, *justification by faith in Christ.* Now Abraham could not, in the strict sense of the words, be justified by faith *in Christ*,—nor is it

τῷ θεῷ, καὶ [a] ἐλογίσθη αὐτῷ [a] εἰς δικαιοσύνην. 4 τῷ δὲ
[b] ἐργαζομένῳ ὁ [c] μισθὸς οὐ λογίζεται [d] κατὰ [d] χάριν, ἀλλὰ
κατὰ [e] ὀφείλημα· 5 τῷ δὲ μὴ [b] ἐργαζομένῳ, [f] πιστεύοντι δὲ
[f] ἐπὶ τὸν [g] δικαιοῦντα τὸν [h] ἀσεβῆ, [a] λογίζεται ἡ πίστις
αὐτοῦ [a] εἰς δικαιοσύνην. 6 [i] καθάπερ καὶ Δαυεὶδ [j] λέγει τὸν

ABCDF KL[P]ℵ a b c d f g h k l m n o 17 [47]

a = ch. ix. 8 reff. Prov. xvii. 28. 1 Macc. ii. 52. Ps. cv. 31.
b absol., Acts xviii. 3 reff.
c = Matt. xx. 8. Luke x. 7. 1 Cor. iii. 8 al. Gen. xxxi. 7.
d ver. 16.
e = here (Matt. vi. 12) only. Deut. xxiv. 10. Thuc. ii. 40. (-λή, ch. xiii. 7.)
f ver. 24. Acts ix. 42. xi. 17. see Matt. xxvii. 42 v. r.
g ch. ii. 13 reff.
h ch. v. 6. 1 Tim. i. 9. 1 Pet. iv. 18. 2 Pet. ii. 5. iii. 7. Jude 4, 15 (bis) only. Prov. xxi. 30. (-βεια, ch. i. 18.)
i Paul (ch. xii. 4. 1 Cor. xii. 12 al8.) only, exc. Heb. iv. 2. Lev. xxvii. 8 only (?). see Heb. v. 4.
j = John viii. 27. Phil. iii. 18.

4. rec ins το bef οφειλημα (*appy as agreeing better with the idea of a definite obligation incurred: i. e.* = τὸ ὀφειλόμενον, *'what is due from the employer,' as indeed Bloomf. explains it*): om ABCDFKL[P]ℵ rel [arm]. B[1] repeats from ο μισθος to εργαζομενω, ver 5, but the passage is marked for erasure, except the first ο.
5. ασεβην D[1]Fℵ.
6. for καθαπερ, καθως DF. ins ο bef δαυειδ DF [g].

necessary to suppose that he directed his faith forward to the promised Redeemer in Person; but in so far as God's gracious purpose was revealed to him, he grasped it by faith, and that righteousness which was implied, so far, in it, was imputed to him. Some have said (Tholuck, e. g.) that the parallel is incomplete—Abraham's *faith* having been reckoned to him for righteousness, whereas, in our case, *the righteousness of Christ* is reckoned to us as our righteousness, *by* faith. But the incompleteness lies in the nature of the respective cases. In his case, *the righteousness itself* was not yet manifested. He believed *implicitly*, taking the *promise, with all it involved and implied, as true.* This then was his way of entering into the promise, and by means of his faith was bestowed upon him that full justification which that faith never apprehended. Thus *his faith itself*, the mere fact of implicit trust in God, was counted to *him* for righteousness. But though *the same righteousness* is imputed to us who believe, and by means of faith also, it is no longer the mere fact of believing implicitly in God's truth, but the reception of *Christ Jesus the Lord* by faith, which justifies us (see vv. 23—25 and note). As it was then the realization of God's words by faith, so now: but *we* have *the Person of the Lord Jesus for the object of faith*, explicitly revealed: *he had not.* In both cases justification is *gratuitous*, and is *by faith:* and so far, which is as far as the argument here requires, the parallel is strict and complete. **4. τῷ ἐργαζομ.**] (q. d. τῷ ἐργάτῃ, but the part. is used because of the negative τῷ μὴ ἐργαζ. following)—**to the workman** (him that works for hire, that earns wages, compare προσηργάσατο, Luke xix. 16) **his wages are not reckoned according to** (as a matter of) **grace** (favour), **but according to** (as a matter of) **debt.** The stress is on κατὰ χάριν, not on λογίζεται, which in this first member of the sentence, is used hardly in the strict sense, of *imputing* or *reckoning*, but of *allotting* or *apportioning*:—its use being occasioned by the stricter λογίζεται below. And the sentence is a *general* one, not with any peculiar reference to Abraham,—except that after κατὰ χάριν we may supply ὡς τῷ Ἀβραάμ, if we will; for this is evidently assumed. **5.**] **But to him who works not** (for hire,—is not an ἐργάτης looking for his μισθός) **but believes on** (casts himself in simple trust and humility on) **Him who justifies** (accounts just, as in ver. 3) **the ungodly** ('*impious*:' stronger than 'unrighteous:'—no allusion to Abraham's having formerly been in idolatry,—for the sentence following on ver. 4, which is *general* and of universal application, *must also be general,—including* of course Abraham: ἀσέβεια is the state of all men by nature),—**his faith is reckoned as righteousness.** κατὰ χάριν is of course implied.

6—8.] *The same is confirmed by a passage from David.* This is not a fresh example, but a confirmation of the assertion involved in ver. 5, that a man may believe on Him who justifies the ungodly, and have his faith reckoned for righteousness. The applicability of the text depends on the persons alluded to *being sinners*, and *having sin not reckoned to them.* **ἀσεβεῖς** and **λογίζομαι** are the two words to be illustrated. The Psalm, strictly speaking, says nothing of the imputation of *righteousness*,—but it is implied by Paul, that the *remission of sin* is *equivalent* to the *imputation of righteousness*—that there is *no negative state of innocence*—none intermediate between acceptance for righteousness, and rejection for sin. *

6. λέγ. τὸν μακ.] **pronounces the blessedness,** 'the *congratulation*:' in allusion perhaps to the Heb. form, אַשְׁרֵי '(*O*) *the blessings of*,' .... It is

[k] μακαρισμὸν τοῦ ἀνθρώπου ᾧ ὁ θεὸς [l] λογίζεται δικαιοσύνην [m] χωρὶς ἔργων, 7 Μακάριοι ὧν [n] ἀφέθησαν αἱ [o] ἀνομίαι
καὶ ὧν [p] ἐπεκαλύφθησαν αἱ ἁμαρτίαι. 8 μακάριος ἀνὴρ ᾧ
οὐ μὴ [l] λογίσηται κύριος ἁμαρτίαν. 9 ὁ [k] μακαρισμὸς οὖν
οὗτος [q] ἐπὶ τὴν περιτομήν, [r] ἢ καὶ [q] ἐπὶ τὴν [s] ἀκροβυστίαν; λέγομεν γὰρ ὅτι [l] ἐλογίσθη τῷ Ἀβραὰμ ἡ πίστις
[l] εἰς δικαιοσύνην· 10 πῶς οὖν [l] ἐλογίσθη; [t] ἐν περιτομῇ
ὄντι, ἢ [t] ἐν [s] ἀκροβυστίᾳ; οὐκ [t] ἐν περιτομῇ, ἀλλ᾽ [t] ἐν
[s] ἀκροβυστίᾳ. 11 καὶ [u] σημεῖον ἔλαβεν [v] περιτομῆς, [w] σφραγῖδα τῆς δικαιοσύνης τῆς [v] πίστεως τῆς [t] ἐν τῇ [s] ἀκροβυστίᾳ,

k here bis. Gal. iv. 15 only †.
l ver. 3.
m ch. iii. 21 reff.
n = Matt. vi. 12. xii. 31. Acts viii. 22. Isa. xxii. 14. Psa. xxxi. 1.
o = Matt. vii. 23. xiii. 41. ch. vi. 19 al. Exod. xxxiv. 9.
p here only, l. c. Gen. vii. 19 A &c., 20 A Ed-vat. compl. (B def.) (-υμμα, 1 Pet. ii. 16.)
q = Acts iv. 33 reff. Mark ix. 12, 13. Heb. vii. 13.
r 1 Cor. ix. 8 reff.
s ch. iii. 30 reff.
t = ch. iii. 19 reff.
u = Matt. xxvi. 48. 1 Cor. xiv. 22. Gen. xvii. 11.
v constr., gen. of apposit., Acts iv. 22. 2 Cor. v. 5. Col. iii. 24. Winer, edn. 6, § 59. 8. a.
w = 1 Cor. ix. 2 (2 Tim. ii. 19. Rev. v. 1 all12.) only. (Hagg. ii. 24.)

7. for επεκ., εκαλυφθησαν B².

8. for ᾧ, οὗ (so *LXX*-ABℵ¹) BD¹Gℵ¹: txt (so *LXX-edd* ℵ³ᵃ) ACD³FKL[P]ℵ³ rel [Euthal-ms Thdrt Damasc]. λογισεται K[P] n 17 [Euthal-ms].

9. [αυτος F²(not G: -τους F¹).] aft περιτομην ins μονον D [vulg-clem] harl¹ (not am demid fuld) Ambrst. for 2nd επι, εις C: om 29. 33: om επι την a. om οτι BD¹ℵ [47]. om η πιστις K: ins aft δικαιοσ. 17. 62.

10. om οντι F vulg(not fuld¹) D³-lat [Syr] Cyr₂.

11. περιτομην AC¹ [m-marg-corr(sic Treg) 47 arm] syrr Orig-schol[and int₁] Chr₁ Procop₁ Damasc: txt BC²DFKL[P]ℵ 17 rel latt copt Orig-c Chr₁ Cyr₁[-p] Thdrt Thl Œc [Euthal-ms Ambrst]. aft σψραγιδα ins δια F: της περιτομης L. om της (bef δικ.) A. om τη DF b c o Procop Damasc.

very clear that this righteousness must be *χωρὶς ἔργων*, because its imputation consists in the remission and hiding of *offences*, whereas none can be legally righteous in whom there is any, even the smallest offence. **8.]** **οὐ μὴ λογίσηται**, as the same construction usually in the N. T., is *future* (Winer, edn. 6, § 56. 3), and must be referred to the great final judgment. Or we may say with Olsh. that the expression is an O. T. one, regarding sin as lying covered by the divine long-suffering till the completion of the work of Christ, at which time first real forgiveness of sins was imparted to the ancient believers; compare Matt. xxvii. 53; 1 Pet. iii. 18. In this last view the *future* will only refer to all such cases as should arise.

9—12.] *This declaration of blessedness applies to circumcised and uncircumcised alike. For Abraham himself was thus justified when in* UNCIRCUMCISION, *and was then pronounced the father of the faithful, uncircumcised as well as circumcised.* **μακαρισμός** of course includes the *fact, on account of which* the congratulation is pronounced,—the *justification itself.* **9. ἐπί]** sc. λέγεται, see reff. The form of the question, with ἢ καί, presupposes an affirmative answer to the latter clause; which affirmative answer is then made the ground of the argumentation in vv. 10, 11, 12:—**On the uncircumcision (-cised) also. For we say,** &c. The stress is on **τῷ Ἀβραάμ**, not on **ἡ πίστις**: **for we say that** TO ABRAHAM **faith was reckoned for righteousness.** **10.]** **πῶς, under what circumstances?** The interval between the recognition of his faith (Gen. xv. 6) and his circumcision, was perhaps as much as twenty-five, certainly not less (Gen. xvii. 25) than fourteen years. **11.]** **And he received** (from God) **the sign** (token, or symbol) **of circumcision** (gen. of apposition, see reff. The reading *περιτομήν* appears to have been an alteration on account of *σφραγῖδα* following), **a seal** (the Targum on Cant. iii. 8, cited by Tholuck, has the expression, 'the seal of circumcision,' and in Sohar, Levit. vi. 21, it is called 'a holy sign.' So also Baptism is called in the Acta Thomæ, § 26, ἡ σφραγὶς τοῦ λουτροῦ, and elsewhere in the Fathers simply ἡ σφραγίς. Grabe, Spicil. Patr. i. 333) **of the righteousness** (to stamp, and certify the righteousness) **of the faith** (gen. of apposition (but not *in* appos. with δικ. by *construction*),—'of the righteousness which consisted in his faith,'—not, 'of his justification by faith:' the present argument treats of faith *accounted* as righteousness) **which was** (or, '*which he had*:' τῆς may refer either to δικ. or to πίστ.,—but better to the former, because the object is to shew that the righteous-

x Acts iii. 19. vii. 19. ver. 18. ch. i. 11, 20 al.
a = ch. ii. 27 reff.
b = ch. ii. 8 reff.
c Acts x. 45 reff.
d Acts xxi. 24. Gal. v. 25. vi. 16. Phil. iii. 16 only.

ˣ εἰς τὸ εἶναι αὐτὸν πατέρα πάντων τῶν πιστευόντων ᵃ δι' ˢ ἀκροβυστίας, ˣ εἰς τὸ ˡ λογισθῆναι [καὶ] αὐτοῖς τὴν δικαιοσύνην,
12 καὶ πατέρα περιτομῆς τοῖς οὐκ ᵇᶜ ἐκ ᶜ περιτομῆς μόνον, ἀλλὰ καὶ τοῖς ᵈ στοιχοῦσιν τοῖς ᵉ ἴχνεσιν τῆς ᵗ ἐν ˢ ἀκροβυστίᾳ πίστεως τοῦ ᶠ πατρὸς ἡμῶν ᶠ Ἀβραάμ·
13 οὐ γὰρ διὰ νόμου ἡ ἐπαγγελία τῷ Ἀβραὰμ ἢ τῷ ᵍ σπέρ-

ABCDF KL[P]ℵ abcdf ghkl mno17 [47]

Eccles. xi. 5 only, but not =. 42. 7. (dat., ch. xiii. 13.) e 2 Cor. xii. 18. 1 Pet. ii. 21‡. Sir. xxi. 6. ἴχνη τῆς ἀληθείας, Polyb. iv. f Acts vii. 2 reff. g ch. i. 3 reff.

for δι, δια AD¹F L[e sil]: txt BCD²·³ [K(e sil) P]ℵ rel [Euthal-ms Thdrt Damasc]. om και ABℵ¹ [47] a demid tol [copt] Orig-schol Cyr[-p₁] Damasc: ins CDFK L[P]ℵ³ 17 rel latt syrr æth [arm Orig-int₂] Thdrt Thl Œc. om την C²D¹ℵ [arm Damasc]: for την, εις A d 32 [47] 114-24 Syr, *ad justitiam* vulg D³-lat G-lat[(*in j.*) Orig-int₁] Ambrst Pelag Aug.

12. om τοις ουκ εκ περιτομης (*homœot*) ℵ¹(ins ℵ-corr¹). [στοιλουσειν *qui sectantur* F: τυχουσι l m(m¹, Treg).] rec ins τη bef ακροβυστια, with D³KL[P] rel Chr₁ [Euthal-ms] Thdrt Thl: om ABCD¹Fℵ a¹ c f h l m n [47 Cyr-p] Procop₁ Damasc.—της πιστ. της εν (τη) ακροβ. DKL [P(τ. π. τοις)] a b c f (g) h k l n o 17 vulg(not am fuld harl¹) [Euthal-ms] Thdrt lat-ff: om πιστεως ℵ¹(ins ℵ-corr¹).

13. om η ℵ¹(ins ℵ-corr¹).

ness was imputed in uncircumcision) **during his uncircumcision.** In literal historical matter of fact, Abraham received circumcision as a seal of *the covenant* between God and him (Gen. xvii. 1—14). But this covenant was only a *renewal of that very one, on the promise of which Abraham's faith was exercised,* Gen. xv. 5, 6,—and each successive renewal of which was a fresh approval of that faith. The Apostle's point is,—that the righteousness was reckoned, and the promise made, to Abraham, *not in circumcision, but in uncircumcision.*

εἰς τὸ εἶναι . . . .] **In order that he might be** (not 'so that he is;' see Gal. iii. 7) **the father of all in uncircumcision** (διά, see reff.,—'conditionis') **that believe.** Abraham is *the father of the faithful.* But the triumph and recognition of that faith whereby he was constituted so, was not during his circumcision, but during his uncircumcision:—therefore *the faithful, his descendants, must not be confined to the circumcised, but must take in the uncircumcised also.* On πατέρα in this sense, Tholuck compares the expression Gen. iv. 20; 1 Macc. ii. 54 (Φινεὲς ὁ πατὴρ ἡμῶν ἐν τῷ ζηλῶσαι ζῆλον), and Maimonides, 'Moses is the father of all the prophets who succeeded him.' See also our Lord's saying, John viii. 37, 39. The Rabbinical book Michlal Jophi on Mal. ii. (Thol.) has a sentiment remarkably coincident with that in our text: "Abraham is the father of all those who follow his faith." **εἰς τὸ λογ. κ.τ.λ.]** (is in *fact* parenthetical, whether brackets are used or not; for otherwise the construction from the former to the latter πατέρα would not proceed) **in order that the righteousness** (which Abraham's faith was reckoned as being,—the righteousness of God, then hidden though imputed, but now revealed in Jesus Christ) **might be imputed to them also.**

12. καὶ (εἰς τὸ εἶναι αὐτὸν) **πατέρα περιτομῆς . . . .]** **And** (that he might be) **father of the circumcision** (the circumcised) **to those** (dat. commodi 'for those,' 'in the case of those') **who are not only** (physically) **of the circumcision, but also who walk** (the inversion of the article appears to be in order to bring out more markedly τοῖς ἐκ περιτ. and τοῖς στοιχ.,—who are not only οἱ ἐκ περιτ., but also οἱ στοιχοῦντες . . . .) **in the footsteps** (reff.) **of the faith of our father** (speaking here as a Jew) **Abraham** (which he had) **while he was in uncircumcision.** (The art. would make it 'during his uncircumcision,'—but the sense is better without it, the word being generalized.)

13—17.] *Not through the* LAW, *but through* THE RIGHTEOUSNESS OF FAITH, *was* THE INHERITANCE OF THE WORLD *promised to Abraham: so that not only they who are of the law, but they who follow Abraham's faith are* HEIRS OF THIS PROMISE.

13.] γάρ, strictly **for.** The argumentation is an expansion of πατέρα πάντ. τῶν πιστευόντων above. If these believers are Abraham's *seed,* then his promised inheritance is *theirs.*

διὰ νόμου] not, '*under the law,*'—nor, '*by works of the law:*'—nor, '*by the righteousness of the law:*' but, **through the law,** so that the law should be the *ground,* or *efficient cause,* or medium, of the promise. None of these it was, as matter of historical fact. **For not through the law was the promise** (made) **to Abraham, or** (ἤ in negative sentences answers to καί in affirm., see Matt. v. 17) **to his seed, viz. that he should be heir of the world, but by the righteousness of faith.** This specifica- *

ματι αὐτοῦ, [h] τὸ [i] κληρονόμον αὐτὸν εἶναι κόσμου, ἀλλὰ
διὰ δικαιοσύνης πίστεως, 14 εἰ γὰρ οἱ [b] ἐκ νόμου [i] κληρονόμοι, [j] κεκένωται ἡ πίστις καὶ [k] κατήργηται ἡ ἐπαγγελία.
15 ὁ γὰρ νόμος [l] ὀργὴν [m] κατεργάζεται. οὗ δὲ οὐκ ἔστιν
νόμος, οὐδὲ [n] παράβασις. 16 διὰ τοῦτο [o] ἐκ πίστεως, ἵνα

h τό w. inf., 1 Thess. iii. 3. i = Tit. iii. 7. Heb. i. 2. vi. 17. xi. 7. James ii. 5. Micah i. 15. j = 1 Cor. i. 17. ix. 15. 2 Cor. ix. 3 (Phil. ii. 7) only‡. (Jer. xiv. 2. xv. 9 only.) k ch. iii. 3 reff. l = ch. ii. 5, 8 reff. m — ch. v. 3. vii. 8, 13. 2 Cor. iv. 17. James i. 3 al. n absol., ch. v. 14. Gal. iii. 19. 1 Tim. ii. 14. Heb. ii. 2. ix. 15 only. Ps. c. 3. Wisd. xiv. 31 only. w. gen., ch. ii. 23. 2 Macc. xv. 10 only. o = ch. iii. 20, 30 al.

[*ειναι* bef *αυτον* K n 17.] rec ins *του* bef *κοσμου*, with KL[P] 17 rel [Euthal-ms] Thdrt Thl Œc: om ABCDFא d [47 arm] Damasc. for *δια δικαιοσυνης*, *δικαιοσυνην* F[-gr: om *δια* a² c]. (*διακαιοσυνης* G¹.)

15. for *ου*, *που* [F]G¹ [arm]. rec (for *δε*) *γαρ* (*see note*), with DFKL[P]א³ rel latt syrr Chr(*οτι ο νομ.* for *ο γαρ ν.* above) Œc [Euthal-ms Orig-int$_1$] Ambrst Aug$_3$: txt ABCא¹ syr-mg copt [arm Cyr-p$_1$] Thdrt Thl [Damasc Orig-int$_3$] Julian Ambr$_1$. *παραβασεις* (*itacism*) A F[-gr].

16. aft *πιστεως* ins *ιησου* D¹(and lat¹). aft *ινα* ins *η* A 45. 80 arm.

tion of the promise has perplexed most of the Commentators. The actual promise, Gen. (xii. 2, 3) xiii. 14—17; xv. 18; xvii. 8, was the possession of the *land of Canaan.* But the Rabbis already had seen, and Paul, who had been brought up in their learning, held fast the truth,—that much more was intended in the words which accompany this promise, 'In thee (or in thy seed) shall all families of the earth be blessed,' than the mere possession of Canaan. They distinctly trace the gift of the world to Abraham to *this promise,* not to the foregoing. So Bemidbar Rabb. xiv. 202. 3 (Wetst.),—'Hortus est mundus, quem Deus tradidit Abrahamo, cui dictum est, "et eris benedictio"' (see other citations in Wetst.). The *inheritance of the world* then is not the possession of Canaan merely (so that κόσμου should = γῆς) either *literally,* or as a *type* of a better possession,—but that *ultimate lordship over the whole world* which Abraham, as the father of the faithful in all peoples, and Christ, as the Seed of Promise, shall possess: the *former* figuratively indeed and only implicitly,—the *latter* personally and actually. See ch. viii. 17; Matt. v. 5; 2 Tim. ii. 12; 1 Cor. xv. 24. Another difficulty, that this promise was *made* chronologically *before* the reckoning of his faith for righteousness, is easily removed by remembering that the (indefinite) making of the promise is here treated of as the *whole process of its assertion,* during which Abraham's faith was shewn, and the promise continually confirmed. **αὐτόν** *includes* his seed.

14.] The supposition is now made which ver. 13 denied,—and its consequences shewn. **For if they who are of the law** (who belong to the law, see reff.: not, 'who keep the law,' nor is δίκαιοι to be supplied) **are inheritors** (i. e. inherit 'ejus rei causâ,' *by virtue of* the law: they may be inheritors by the righteousness of faith, but *not quoad their legal standing*), **faith is** (thereby) **made empty** (robbed of its virtue and rendered useless), **and the promise is annulled** (has no longer place). How and why so? The Apostle himself immediately gives the reason. **15.**] **For the law works** (brings about, gives occasion to) **wrath** (which from its very nature, excludes *promise,* which is an act of *grace,*—and *faith,* which is an attribute of *confidence*);—**but where** (or, *for where;* but I should regard **γάρ** as introduced to suit the idea of the second clause rendering a reason for the first) **there is no law** (lit. '*where the law is not*'), **neither** (is there) **transgression.** 'We should rather expect (says De W.) the affirmative clause, "And where the law is, there is transgression:" but the negative refers to the time before the Mosaic law, when there was no transgression and therefere also no wrath.' *Yes;* but not because there was *no* transgression then; the purpose of the Apostle here is not to deny the existence of the law of God written in the heart (which itself brings in the knowledge of sin) before Moses, but to shew that no promise of inheritance can be by the law, because the property of the law is, the more it is promulgated, to *reveal transgression* more,—*not to unfold grace.* So that *comparatively* (see notes on ch. vii.) there was no transgression before the law of Moses; and if we conceive a state in which the law whether written or unwritten should be *altogether absent* (as in the brute creation), there would be *no transgression whatever.*

But observe (see ch. v. 12—14) that this reasoning does not touch the doctrine of the original taint of our nature in Adam,—only referring to the discrimination of acts, words, and thoughts by the conscience *in the light of the law:* for **παράβασις** is not *natural corruption,* but *an act of transgression:* nor does the Apostle here

p ver. 4. ellips., Gal. ii. 9. v. 13.
q ver. 11 reff.
r 2 Cor. i. 7. Heb. ii. 2. iii. (6 v. r.) 14. vi. 19. ix. 17. 2 Pet. i. 10, 19 only †. Wisd. vii. 23 only.
s Acts i. 4 reff.
t = ver. 13.
u ch. ii. 8 reff.
v Gen. xvii. 5.

ABCDF KL[P]ℵ a b c d f g h k l m n o 17 [47]

[p] κατὰ χάριν, [q] εἰς τὸ εἶναι [r] βεβαίαν τὴν [s] ἐπαγγελίαν
παντὶ τῷ [t] σπέρματι, οὐ τῷ [u] ἐκ τοῦ νόμου μόνον, ἀλλὰ
καὶ τῷ [u] ἐκ πίστεως [f] Ἀβραάμ, ὅς ἐστιν [f] πατὴρ πάντων
[f] ἡμῶν
17 (καθὼς γέγραπται [v] ὅτι πατέρα πολλῶν ἐθνῶν
[w] τέθεικά σε) [x] κατέναντι [y] οὗ ἐπίστευσεν θεοῦ, τοῦ [z] ζωοποιοῦντος τοὺς νεκροὺς καὶ [a] καλοῦντος τὰ μὴ ὄντα ὡς

w = 1 Tim. ii. 7. 2 Tim. i. 11. Heb. i. 2. 2 Pet. ii. 6. Jer. i. 5. x = 2 Cor. ii. 17. xii. 19 (Mark xi. 2 ‖ L.[Mt. and Matt. xxvii. 24, v. r.] xii. 41. xiii. 3) only. Exod. xxxii. 11 A Ald. (Num. xxv. 4.) y attr., Luke i. 4. Winer, edn. 6, § 24. 2. b. z John v. 21. ch. viii. 11. 1 Cor. xv. 22 al. 4 Kings v. 7. a see note, and Isa. xli. 4. xlviii. 13. 4 Kings viii. 1 (?). τὰ μὴ ὄντα ἐκάλεσεν εἰς τὸ εἶναι, Philo de Creat. Princ. § 7, vol. ii. p. 367.

aft *νομου* ins *εστιν* D^4. om *μονον* and *και* F(and lat) 91 D-lat : om *και* fuld harl[1].
17. **επιστευσας** F, *credidisti* vulg-mss(demid flor fuld tol, besides F-lat) D-lat Syr Ambrst Vig Pelag ; *credent* æth : **επιστευσαν** D^1-gr. [θεω F.]

deny the former, even in the imaginable total absence of the law of God. **16.**] **For this** (viz. the following) **reason it** (the *inheritance*,—not the *promise;* the promise was not strictly speaking ἐκ πίστεως :—nor must we supply *they*, meaning the heirs, who although they might fairly be said to be ἐκ πίστεως (compare οἱ ἐκ νόμου above, and reff.) could hardly be without harshness described as being κατὰ χάριν) **was by faith that it might be** (strictly the *purpose*;—not, 'so that it was') **according to grace** (free unmerited favour. As the *law* bringing the *knowledge of guilt*, works *wrath*,—so the *promise*, awakening *faith*, manifests God's *free grace*,—the end for which it was given); **in order that the promise might be sure** (not, 'so that the promise was sure :' this was the *result*, but the Apostle states this as the aim and end of the inheritance being by faith,—quoad *the seed of Abraham*,—that they all might be inheritors,—as the manifestation of God's grace was the higher aim and end) **to all the seed, not only to that** (part of it) **which is of the law** (see ver. 14), **but to that which is of the faith** (walks in the steps of the faith, ver. 12) of **Abraham** (it is altogether wrong to make Ἀβραάμ depend on σπέρματι expressed or understood, as Œcum., Koppe, and Fritzsche). The part of the seed which is of the law *here* is of course confined to *believing* Jews; *the seed* being *believers only*. This has been sometimes lost sight of, and the whole argument of vv. 13—16 treated as if it applied to the doctrine of justification by faith without the works of the law, a point *already proved, and now presupposed*,—the present argument being an historical and metaphysical one, proceeding on the facts of Abraham's history, and the natures respectively of the law and grace, to prove him to be the father of all believers, uncircumcised as well as circumcised. **ὅς ἐστιν πατὴρ πάντων ἡμῶν**] By the last declaration, the *paternity* of Abraham, which is co-extensive with the *inheritance*, has been extended to *all who are of his faith ;* here therefore it is reasserted : ἡμῶν meaning τῶν πιστευόντων.

17. καθὼς γέγρ.] The words (ref.) are spoken of the numerous progeny of Abraham according to the flesh : but not without a reference to that covenant, according to the terms of which all nations were to be blessed in him. The Apostle *may* here cite it as comparing his natural paternity of many nations with his spiritual one of all believers : but it seems more probable that he regards the prophecy as *directly announcing* a paternity far more extensive than mere physical fact substantiated.

These words are parenthetical, being merely a confirmation by Scripture testimony of ὅς ἐστιν πατ. πάντ. ἡμ., with which (see below) the following words are immediately connected. **κατέναντι οὗ ἐπίστευσεν θεοῦ**] The meaning appears to be, 'Abraham was the father of us all,—though not physically, nor in actuality, seeing that we were not as yet,—yet *in the sight and estimation of God*,—in his relation with God, with whom no obstacles of nature or time have force.'

The resolution of the attraction must be κατέναντι θεοῦ, κατέναντι οὗ ἐπίστευσεν, as in ref. Luke, **before God, in whose sight he believed.** (Chrysostom's interpretation (and similarly Theodoret, al.),—ὥσπερ ὁ θεὸς οὐκ ἔστι μερικὸς θεός, ἀλλὰ πάντων πατήρ, οὕτω καὶ αὐτὸς . . . . τὸ γὰρ 'κατέναντι' **ὁμοίως** ἐστί,—does not fall in with the context, and is certainly a mistake.) **τοῦ ζωοπ. τ. νεκρ.**] **Who quickens the dead,**—a general description of God's almighty creative power (see 1 Tim. vi. 13), applied particularly to the matter in hand—the deadness of generative physical power in Abraham himself, which was quickened by God (but *νεκρούς* is a wider

ὄντα· 18 ὃς [b] παρ᾽ ἐλπίδα [c] ἐπ᾽ [c] ἐλπίδι [d] ἐπίστευσεν, [e] εἰς τὸ
γενέσθαι αὐτὸν πατέρα πολλῶν ἐθνῶν κατὰ τὸ [f] εἰρημένον
[g] Οὕτως ἔσται τὸ [t] σπέρμα σου, 19 καὶ μὴ [hi] ἀσθενήσας [i] τῇ
πίστει, [οὐ] [k] κατενόησεν τὸ ἑαυτοῦ σῶμα [ἤδη] [l] νενε-

b = Acts xviii. 13. ch. i. 26. xvi. 17 al.
c Acts ii. 26 (from Ps. xv. 9). ch. viii. 20. 1 Cor. ix. 10 al. L.P. Hos. ii. 18.
d w. dat. of thing, Luke xxiv. 26 only.
e ver. 11 reff.
f Acts xiii. 40 reff.
g Gen. xv. 5.
h = 2 Cor. xi. 21. xiii. 9. ch. xiv. 2, 21. 1 Macc. xi. 49.
i ch. xiv. 1 only.
k = Heb. x. 24. Isa. lvii. 1.
l Col. iii. 5. Heb. xi. 12 only†.

18. εφ. ελπιδι C[1]D[1]F. γενασθαι F(but not G). (in ℵ κατα seems to have been written twice, and the first erased.) [for ειρημ., γεγραμμενον K Syr.] at end add *ως αι αστερες του ουρανου και το αμμον της θαλασσης* F vulg-sixt(with flor F-lat al) some lat-ff, simly 106-8 marg Thl [demid]; *sicut stellæ cœli* harl[1] G-lat; *sicut arena maris* fuld mar, *sicut arena quæ est in litore maris* tol.

19. ins εν bef τη πιστει D[1]F vulg-sixt(with [fuld[1]] F-lat) D[1]-lat G-lat [Orig-int$_1$ (om$_4$)] Julian. om ου (*see notes*) ABCℵ am fuld-corr Syr copt Chr$_1$[and ms$_1$] Damasc Julian: ins DFKL[P] rel latt syr Chr$_1$[-montf Chron$_1$] Thl Œc Ambrst. om ηδη BF [47] am(and demid harl) old-lat Syr æth Chr$_2$ Epiph$_1$ [Orig-int$_1$]: ins ACDKL[P]ℵ rel syr-w-ast [copt arm] Thdrt [Euthal-ms Chron$_1$ Damasc Thl

term than νενεκρωμένον, the *genus*, of which that is a *species*). The peculiar excellence of Abraham's faith, that it overleaped the obstacles of physical incapacity, and nonentity, and believed implicitly God's promise. Compare 2 Cor. i. 9. **καὶ καλ. τὰ μὴ ὄντα ὡς ὄντα**] Much difficulty has been found here: and principally owing to an idea that this clause must minutely correspond with the former, and furnish another instance of God's creative Almightiness. Hence Commentators have given to καλεῖν the sense which it has in reff., '*to summon into being*,' and have understood ὡς ὄντα as if it were εἰς τὸ εἶναι. Thus, more or less, and with various attempts to escape from the violence done to the construction, Chrys., Grot., Elsn., Wolf, Fritzsche, Tholuck, Stuart, De Wette, al. I see however in this latter clause not a repetition or expansion of the former, but a new attribute of God's omnipotence and eternity, on which Abraham's faith was fixed, **Who calleth** (nameth, speaketh of) **the things that are not, as being** (as if they *were*). This He *did in the present case with regard to the seed of Abraham*, which *did not as yet exist:*—the two key-texts to this word and clause being, ἐν Ἰσαὰκ **κληθήσεταί** σοι σπέρμα ch. ix. 7 (see note there),—and Acts vii. 5, ἐπηγγείλατο δοῦναι αὐτῷ εἰς κατάσχεσιν αὐτὴν καὶ τῷ σπέρματι αὐτοῦ μετ᾽ αὐτόν, **οὐκ ὄντος αὐτῷ τέκνου.** These τέκνα, which were at present in the category of *τὰ μὴ ὄντα*, and the nations which should spring, physically or spiritually, from him, God ἐκάλει ὡς ὄντα, *spoke of as having an existence*, which word Abraham believed. And here, as in the other clause, the καλεῖν τὰ μὴ ὄντα ὡς ὄντα is not confined to the case in point, but is a general attribute of all God's words concerning things of time, past, present, and future, being to His Omnipotence and Omniscience, *all one*. His purposes, *when formed*, are *accomplished*, save in so far as that evolution of secondary causes and effects intervenes, which is also His purpose. This also Abraham apprehended by his faith, which rested on God's absolute power to do what He had promised (see below). **18—22.**] *A more detailed description of this* (Abraham's) *faith, as reposed on God's Omnipotence.* **18.**] **Who against hope** (where there was nothing to hope) **believed in** (ἐπί, with dat., in its literal import signifying close adherence, is accordingly used to connect an act with that to which it is immediately attached as its ground or accompaniment. Thus here, the hope existed as the necessary concomitant and in some sense the condition of the faith) **hope, in order to his becoming the father of many nations** (i. e. as a step in the process of his becoming, and one necessary to that process going forward. He would never have become, &c., had he not believed. To render εἰς τὸ γεν. 'that he should become,' and connect it with ἐπίστευσεν (Theophyl., Beza, all., De Wette) is against Paul's usage, who never connects πιστεύω with a neut. inf.,—and not justified by Phil. i. 23; 1 Thess. iii. 10.

The mere *consecutive* sense, 'so that he became,' here, as every where, is a weakening of the sense (see however note on ch. i. 20),—and besides, would introduce an objective clause in a passage which all refers subjectively to Abraham). **οὕτως**] viz. *as the stars of heaven:* see l. c.,—and compare Ps. cxlvii. 4. **19.**] The reading (with or without οὐ?) must first be considered. Reading οὐ, the sense will be, **And not being weak in faith, he paid no attention to,** &c. Omitting οὐ, '*And not being weak in* (his) *faith, he was well aware of*, &c.—*but did not*,' &c. Of these, the second agrees the better with εἰς δὲ

κρωμένον, [m] ἑκατονταέτης [n] που [o] ὑπάρχων, καὶ τὴν [p] νέκρωσιν τῆς [q] μήτρας Σάῤῥας, 20 [r] εἰς δὲ τὴν [s] ἐπαγγελίαν
τοῦ θεοῦ οὐ [t] διεκρίθη τῇ [u] ἀπιστίᾳ, ἀλλ' [v] ἐνεδυναμώθη τῇ
πίστει, [w] δοὺς [w] δόξαν τῷ θεῷ, 21 καὶ [x] πληροφορηθεὶς ὅτι ὃ
[y] ἐπήγγελται δυνατός ἐστιν καὶ ποιῆσαι. 22 [z] διὸ [[z] καὶ]
[a] ἐλογίσθη αὐτῷ [a] εἰς δικαιοσύνην. 23 οὐκ ἐγράφη δὲ δι'
αὐτὸν μόνον ὅτι [a] ἐλογίσθη αὐτῷ, 24 ἀλλὰ καὶ δι' ἡμᾶς,

ABCDF KL[P]א abcdf ghkl mno17 [47]

m here only. Gen. xvii. 17 only. n of time, here (Heb. ii. 6. iv. 4) only. o Acts viii. 16 reff. p 2 Cor. iv. 10 only †. q Luke ii. 23 (from Exod. xiii. 2) only. Gen. xx. 18. r constr. [Acts xxv. 20], Soph. Ant. 372. s Acts i. 4 reff. t = Acts x. 20 reff. u ch. iii. 3 reff. v Acts ix. 22 *of* Paul, otherwise Paul (Eph. vi. 10 al4.) only, exc. Heb. xi. 34. Ps. li. 7 (9). Judg. vi. 34 AB(not Ed-vat. F.) &c. only. w Luke xvii. 18. John ix. 24. Acts xii. 23. Josh. vii. 19. x = ch. xiv. 5 reff. only. y := sign. act., Heb. xii. 26 only. pass., Gal. iii. 19. 2 Macc. iv. 27. 1 aor., James i. 12 al. z = [ch. i. 24] Phil. ii. 9. a ver. 3.

Œc]. (vulg (with fuld) join it with εκατοντ.) υπαρχει D¹[-gr].

20. om δε F æth. αλλα B. for ενεδ., εδυναμωθη F [ενδυν. m].

21. om 1st και (*as unnecessary: but the repetitions of* και *are characteristic*) D⁴F latt [Ambrst].

22. om και BD¹F Syr copt [arm]: ins ACD³KL[P]א rel vulg syr Thdrt Thl Œc [Euthal-ms Chron₁ Damasc₁ Orig-int₂] Ambrst Julian Sedul.

23. μονον bef δι αυτον DF latt. at end ins εις δικαιοσυνην D⁴ vulg(not am [fuld]) Syr Chr Cyr[-p₁] Thdrt(prefixing η πιστις) Thl [Orig-int₁] Ambrst Sedul.

τὴν ἐπ. ver. 20,—but the first very much better suits the context; the object being, *to extol Abraham's faith*, not to introduce the new and somewhat vapid notice of his being well aware of those facts of which it may be assumed as a matter of course that he could not be ignorant. The Apostle does not want to prove that Abraham was in his sound senses when he believed the promise, but that he was so strong in faith as to be able to overleap all difficulties in its way. The erasure of οὐ seems to have been occasioned by the use of καί instead of οὐδέ before τὴν νέκρωσιν. And the following δέ, without being strongly adversative, falls well into its place—**He took no account of, &c. but . . . .**

The rendering, 'And he did not, being weak in faith, take account of, &c.' (omitting οὐ, and making μή the ruling neg. particle of the clause), is ungrammatical: οὐ would be required. Abraham did indeed feel and express the difficulty (Gen. xvii. 17), but his faith overcame it, and he ceased to regard it. But most probably Paul here refers only to Gen. xv. 5, 6, where his belief was implicit and unquestioning. **ἑκατοντ.**] Abraham's own expression in l. c., where he also describes Sarah as being 90. His exact age was 99. Gen. xvii. 1, 24. **20.**] On δέ, see above. **But with regard to** (ref.) **the promise of God he doubted not through unbelief**—(De Wette thinks from the analogy of πιστεύειν εἴς τι,—that εἰς τ. ἐπ. is perhaps the immediate object of διακρίνεσθαι: q. d. 'did not disbelieve in the promise of God'), **but was strong** (lit. 'was strengthened,' 'shewed himself strong') **in faith** (dat. of reference, 'with regard to faith.' **τῇ** ἀπ. and **τῇ** πίστ., because both are here strictly abstract, being set against one another as opposites). **δοὺς δόξ. τῷ θ.**] viz. by recognizing His Almighty power (see reff., especially Luke). **21.**] **πληρ.**, see ch. xiv. 5, **being fully persuaded. ἐπήγγελται** is not passive (nor ὅ nom.), but middle, and 'God' the subject; **that, what He has promised, He is able also to perform. 22.**] **διό**, on account of the nature of this faith, which the Apostle has now since ver. 18 been setting forth;—because it was a simple unconditional credence of God and His promise. If we read **καί**, it imports besides being thus great and admirable, it was reckoned to him for righteousness:—**ἐλογίσθη**, viz. τὸ πιστεῦσαι τῷ θεῷ. **23—25.**] *Application of that which is said of Abraham, to all believers on Christ.* **23.**] **ἐγράφη, was written,** not the more usual γέγραπται, '*is written:*' similarly in the parallel, 1 Cor. x. 11; and in our ch. xv. 4. The aorist asserts the design of God's Spirit *at the time* of penning the words: the perfect may *imply* that, but more directly *asserts* the intent of our Scriptures *as we now find them.* **Now it was not written for his sake alone** (merely to bear testimony to him and his faith) **that it was reckoned unto him,—but for our sake also** (for our benefit, to bear testimony to us of the efficacy of faith like his. Observe that διά in the two clauses has not exactly the same sense,—'for *his* sake' being = (1) *to celebrate his faith,*—and (2) for *our* sake =*for our profit;* see on ver. 25), **to whom it** (i. e. τὸ πιστεύειν τῷ θεῷ, as ver. 22) **shall be reckoned** (for righteousness:—

οἷς μέλλει [a] λογίζεσθαι, τοῖς [b] πιστεύουσιν [b] ἐπὶ τὸν
[c] ἐγείραντα Ἰησοῦν τὸν κύριον ἡμῶν [c] ἐκ νεκρῶν, 25 ὃς
[d] παρεδόθη διὰ τὰ [e] παραπτώματα ἡμῶν καὶ [f] ἠγέρθη διὰ
τὴν [g] δικαίωσιν ἡμῶν.
V. 1 [h] Δικαιωθέντες οὖν [h] ἐκ πίστεως [ik] εἰρήνην [k] ἔχωμεν

b ver. 5 reff. c 1 Cor. xv. 12 reff. d = ch. viii. 32. 1 Cor. xi. 23. Gal. ii. 20. Eph. v. 25. Isa. liii. 12. e ch. v. 15, &c Matt. vi. 14. Gal. vi. 1. Ps. xviii. 12. Ezek. xviii. 26. f = Acts x. 40 reff. g ch. v. 18 only ‡. Levit. xxiv. 22 only. h ch. iii. 20 reff. i = ch. ii. 10 reff. k John xvi. 33. Acts ix. 31 only.

24. [μελλεις F-gr(not G) : μελλη P m[1](? Scr).] εγειροντα A.
25. for δικαιωσιν, δικαιοσινην(sic) D[4], δικαιοσυνην a 17. 73-7. 89[1]. 93 lectt-13-14 Cyr$_1$ Chron$_1$.

Chap. V. 1. rec εχομεν, with B[2] F-gr [P] ℵ-corr[1] rel Syr(Etheridge: see also Mehring p 457 ff) syr Did$_1$ Epiph$_1$ Cyr$_2$[-p] Sedul : txt AB[1](sic: see table) CDKLℵ[1] f h[1] m 17 latt(including F-lat) Syr copt [æth arm] Chr$_3$ Thdrt Damasc Thl Œc [Tit$_1$ Orig-int$_3$ Ambrst] Pelag Oros Aug Cassiod.

μέλλει λογ. is a *future*, as ch. iii. 30; v. 19 (Thol.),—not, as Olsh. al., spoken as from the time and standing of Abraham), **who believe on** (this specifies the ἡμᾶς: and the belief is not a mere historical but a *fiducial* belief) **Him who raised Jesus our Lord from the dead** (the central fact in our redemption, as the procreation of the seed of promise was in the performance of the promise to Abraham, see ch. i. 4; 1 Cor. xv. 14 ff.; and resembling it in the ζωοποιῆσαι τοὺς νεκρούς).

24.] **ἐκ νεκρῶν** is almost (see Col. ii. 12; 1 Thess. i. 10) always anarthrous, as indeed νεκροί sometimes is (for 'the dead') in classic writers, e. g. Thucyd. iv. 14; v. 10, end: and see Winer, edn. 6, § 19. 1. The omission may in this phrase be accounted for by the preposition (Middleton, ch. vi. 1): but I suspect Winer is right in looking for the cause of the absence of the article after prepositions rather in the usage of the particular *substantive* than in any idiom of general application.

* **25.**] Here we have another example of the alliterative use of the same preposition where the meanings are clearly different (see above, vv. 23, 24). Our Lord was delivered up (to death) for or on account of our sins (i. e. *because we had sinned*):—He was also raised up (from the dead) for or on account of our justification (i. e. not *because we had been*, but *that we might be justified*). This separate statement of the great object of the death and resurrection of Christ must be rightly understood, and each member of it not unduly pressed to the exclusion of the other. The great complex event by which our justification (death unto sin and new birth unto righteousness) has been made possible, may be stated in one word as the GLORIFICATION of Christ. But this glorification consisted of two main parts,—His Death, and His Resurrection. In the former of these, He was made a sacrifice for sin; in the latter, He elevated our humanity into the participation of that Resurrection-life, which is also, by union with Him, the life of every justified believer. So that, when taking the two *apart*, the *Death* of Christ is more properly placed in close reference to *forgiveness of sins*,—His Resurrection, to *justification unto life* everlasting. And thus the Apostle treats these two great events, here and in the succeeding chapters. But he does not view them respectively as the causes, *exclusively of one another*, of forgiveness and justification: e. g. (1) ch. v. 9, we are said to be justified *by His blood*, and 2 Cor. v. 21 God made Him sin for us, *that we might become the righteousness of God* in Him: and (2) 1 Cor. xv. 17, if Christ is not raised, *we are yet in our sins*. So that, though these great events have their separate propriety of reference to the negative and positive sides of our justification, the one of them cannot be treated separately and exclusively of the other, any more than can the negative side of our justification, the non-imputation of our sin, without the positive, the imputation of God's righteousness. It will be seen from what I have said above that I cannot agree with Bp. Horsley's view, that as our transgressions were the *cause* of Jesus being delivered up, so our justification must be the *cause* of His being raised again. Such a pressing of the same sense on διά is not necessary, when Paul's manifold usages of the same preposition are considered: and the regarding our justification (in the sense here) as a fact past, is inconsistent with the very next words, δικαιωθέντες ἐκ πίστεως, which shew that *not the objective fact*, but its *subjective realization*, is here meant.—In these words (of ver. 25) the Apostle *introduces the great subject* of chaps. v.—

1 = Acts ii. 47. xxiv. 16. 2 Cor. vii. 4. 1 John iii. 21. v. 14.
m Eph. ii. 18. iii. 12 only (in both places, w. art.) †.
n = vv. 17, 20, 21. ch. vi. 1 al. fr.
o = John viii. 44. 1 Cor. xv. 1. 2 Cor. i. 24.
p ch. ii. 17 reff. w. ἐπί and dat. here only. Ps. xlviii. 6.

1 πρὸς τὸν θεὸν διὰ τοῦ κυρίου ἡμῶν Ἰησοῦ χριστοῦ, ABCDF
2 δι' οὗ καὶ τὴν m προσαγωγὴν ἐσχήκαμεν εἰς τὴν n χάριν KL[P]א abcdf
ταύτην ἐν ᾗ o ἑστήκαμεν, καὶ p καυχώμεθα ἐπ' ἐλπίδι τῆς ghkl mno17 [47]

2. rec aft εσχηκαμεν ins τη πιστει (*marginal gloss*), with CKL[P]א[1] rel vulg syr copt æth-pl [arm] Chr_1 Thdrt [$Cyr\text{-}p_1$ Euthal-ms Damasc $Orig\text{-}int_2$] lat-ff: εν τη πιστει A א-corr[1](but εν erased) 93. 124 fuld Syr Tit_1 Chr_1: om BDF old-lat æth-rom [$Orig\text{-}int_2$]. for χαριν, χαραν A d[1]: χαρν(sic) m. for επ, εφ D[1]F.

viii.,—DEATH, *as connected with* SIN, —*and* LIFE, *as connected with* RIGHTEOUSNESS. The various ramifications of this subject see in the headings below.

CHAP. V. 1—11.] *The blessed consequences of justification by faith.* 1.] It is impossible to resist the strong manu-
* script authority for the reading ἔχωμεν in this verse. For indeed this may well be cited as the crucial instance of overpowering diplomatic authority compelling us to adopt a reading against which our subjective feelings rebel. Every internal consideration tends to impugn it. If admitted, the sentence is *hortatory*. '*Being then justified by faith*, let us have *peace with God*.' (This is the only admissible sense of the first person subjunctive in an affirmative sentence like the present. The usage is an elliptical one: ἴωμεν, '*that we go*,' i. e. '*it is time*,' or in an address, '*permit*, &c. that we go.' Thus Od. χ. 77, ἔλθωμεν ἀνὰ ἄστυ: Il. χ. 450, ἴδωμ', ἅτιν' ἔργα τέτυκται. See other examples in Kühner, Gramm. § 463. The *deliberative* sense, attempted to be given by Dr. Tregelles (see Kitto's Journal of Bibl. Lit. No. xiv. p. 465 ff.) can only have place in an *interrogative* or *dubitative* clause, and every example given by Mr. Green, whom he cites for his supposed sense, as well as by Kühner (§ 464), is of this kind. Besides, to call the sense 'we ought to have,' *deliberative*, seems a misnomer.) But how can man be exhorted to *have* peace with God? To be *reconciled* to God, he may, 2 Cor. v. 20: but of this there is no mention here, and *having* (been allowed to believe in and enjoy) *peace with God*, depends on, not *our* reconciliation to Him, not any thing subjective in ourselves, but the objective fact of *His reconciliation to us*. If, as some say, ἔχωμεν = κατέχωμεν, Heb. x. 23, the article would be required before εἰρήνην, and (perhaps) before πρὸς or διά. Besides which there are two objections in the *form of the sentence* to this reading: (1) ἔχ. is coupled by καί (δι' οὗ καί) to ἐσχήκαμεν, and this connexion necessitates, in my view, that the first verb should *assert a fact*, as the second undoubtedly does. With the former verb in the subjunctive we should hardly have expected the καί where it is. (2) If ἔχωμεν be hortatory, καυχώμεθα, in verse 2, must be so likewise: (for if we were exhorted to the *lesser* degree of confidence, εἰρήνην ἔχειν, such exhortation can hardly be founded on the existence already of the *greater* degree, καυχᾶσθαι κ.τ.λ.) which, both as to sense and construction, is very improbable. I believe (but see below) an account of the reading may be sought, as in 1 Cor. xv. 49, in a tendency of those who transcribed some of our MSS. to give such assertions a *hortatory*, or, where interrogative, a *deliberative form*: thus we have σωθησώμεθα in some MSS., ver. 10,—ζήσωμεν, ch. vi. 2,—πιστεύωμεν or πιστεύσωμεν, and συνζήσωμεν, ch. vi. 8,—ὑπακούσατε, ch. vi. 17,—προσεύξωμαι (bis), 1 Cor. xiv. 15,—πείθωμεν, 2 Cor. v. 11,—πιστεύωμεν, John iv. 42,—συνζήσωμεν and συμβασιλεύσωμεν, 2 Tim. ii. 11, 12:—or perhaps the whole ground of the account to be given of the ω is better shifted to a more general habit of the MSS. (even the greatest and best, see instances in prolegg. to Vol. I. ch. vi. § i. 36, 37) to confound ο and ω: so that in very many cases, such variation can hardly be called a different reading at all.

The whole passage is *declaratory of the consequences flowing from justification by faith*, and *does not exhort, but assert*. Nor, would it seem, does the place for exhortation arrive, till these consequences have been in the fullest and freest manner set forth,—indeed so fully and freely, that the objection arising from their supposed abuse has first to be answered. **Being therefore justified** ('*having been justified*:' —it is an *act past* on the Christian, not like sanctification, an abiding and increasing work) **by** (as the ground) **faith, let us** (believers in Christ: I render the *existing text*) **have peace** ('reconcilement;' the opposite of ὀργή, see ver. 9) **with** ('in regard of,' see reff.) **God through** (by means of) **our Lord Jesus Christ.** With regard to the nature of this peace (= *state of reconciliation*, 'no more condemnation,' as ch. viii. 1) see above, on the reading ἔχωμεν. 2.] **Through whom we have also** (so διὸ [καί], ch. i. 24; iv. 22, where καί, if read, serves to

[q] δόξης τοῦ θεοῦ. 3 [r] οὐ μόνον δέ, [r] ἀλλὰ καὶ [p] καυχώμενοι
[p] ἐν ταῖς [s] θλίψεσιν, εἰδότες ὅτι ἡ [s] θλῖψις [t] ὑπομονὴν
[u] κατεργάζεται, 4 ἡ δὲ [t] ὑπομονὴ [v] δοκιμήν, ἡ δὲ [v] δοκιμὴ
ἐλπίδα· 5 ἡ δὲ ἐλπὶς οὐ [w] καταισχύνει, ὅτι ἡ [x] ἀγάπη τοῦ
θεοῦ [y] ἐκκέχυται ἐν ταῖς καρδίαις ἡμῶν [z] διὰ [z] πνεύματος
ἁγίου τοῦ δοθέντος ἡμῖν· 6 εἴ γε χριστὸς ὄντων ἡμῶν

q = ch. ii. 7 reff. r ch. viii. 23. 2 Cor. viii. 19 al. fr. s = Matt. xiii. 21. Acts vii. 10, 11 al. 2 Kings xxii. 19. Nah. i. 7. t ch. ii. 7 reff. u ch. iv. 15 reff. v here bis. 2 Cor. ii. 9. viii. 2. ix. 13. xiii. 3. Phil. ii. 22 only †. Ps. lxvii. 31 Symm. w ch. ix. 33 & x. 11 (from Isa. xxviii. 16). 2 Cor. vii. 14 al. x = ch. viii. 39. 2 Cor. xiii. 13. y = Acts ii. 17 (from Joel ii. 28) al. z Acts xi. 28 reff.

3. aft *ου μονον δε* ins *τουτο* D[1][-gr]. rec *καυχωμεθα* (*mechanical repetition from preceding ver*), with ADFK L(-*ο*-) [P]א rel [vulg copt æth arm spec] Tit$_1$ Chr Thdrt Thl Œc [Orig-int$_2$] Cypr$_2$: txt BC Orig$_2$ [Ephr$_1$] Tert$_1$.
5. for *ημων*, *υμων* א[1].
6. rec (for *ει γε*) *ετι γαρ*, with ACD[1.3]K[P]א rel [syr arm] Epiph$_2$ Chr$_1$ Thdrt Damasc [Orig-int$_2$]: *εις τι γαρ* D[2]F: *ut quid enim* latt Iren-int$_1$ Faustin: *ει γαρ* h [: *ει γαρ ετι*] fuld[1] Isid$_1$ Aug$_2$: *ει δε* L Syr: txt B.

shew the coherence and likelihood of that which is asserted,—answering almost to our 'as might be expected') **had our access** (the persons spoken of having come to the Father by Christ,—see Eph. ii. 18,
* —the access is treated of as a thing past. *τῇ πίστει* and *ἐν τῇ πίστει* appear to have been glosses, explanatory of the method of access. The access would *normally* take place in baptism) **into this grace** (namely, the grace of justification, apprehended and held fast subjectively (from what follows); not, *τὸ πάντων ἐπιτυχεῖν τῶν διὰ βαπτίσματος ἀγαθῶν* (Chrys. al.), which is inconsistent with *ἐν ᾗ ἑστήκ.*: not, '*the Gospel*' (Fritz.), for the same reason; not, '*hope of blessedness*' (Beza), for that *follows*: least of all '*the grace of the apostolic calling*' (Semler), which is quite beside the purpose) **wherein we stand** (see parallels in reff. 1 and 2 Cor.; i. e. *abide accepted and acquitted with God*; see also 1 Cor. x. 12, and ch. xi. 20); **and** (couple to *εἰρήν. ἔχωμεν*, not to *ἐν ᾗ ἑστήκ.*) **glory in the hope** (*καυχάομαι* is found with *ἐπί, ἐν, περί, ὑπέρ*, and (Thol.) with an acc. of the object. In Heb. iii. 6 we have *τὸ καύχημα τῆς ἐλπίδος*) **of the glory of God** (of sharing God's glory by being with Christ in His kingdom, John xvii. 24, see reff.). **3.**] **And not only so** (not only must we triumph in hope, which has regard to the future), **but glorying in** (not *amidst*; the *θλ.* is the *ground* of triumph) [**our**] **tribulations, knowing** (because we know) **that tribulation works endurance** (supposing, i. e. we remain firm under it), **and endurance, approval** (of our faith and trust, 2 Cor. ii. 9; ix. 13: not, '*proof*' (*δοκιμασία*), as Grot.; nor '*experience*,' as E. V.,—'*δοκιμή* est qualitas ejus, qui est *δόκιμος*.' Bengel,—the *result* of proof), **and approval** (fresh) **hope**; **and hope** (but for *αὕτη ἡ ἐλπ.* as Olsh.) **shames** (**us**) **not** (by disappointing us; 'mocks us not'); **because God's love** (not '*the love of God*,' i.e. *man's love for God*,—as Theodoret, and even Aug., misled by the Latin; see reff., and compare the explicit *τὴν ἑαυτοῦ ἀγάπην εἰς ἡμᾶς*, which answers to this in ver. 8) **is** (has been) **poured out** ('*effusa*,' not '*diffusa*' (Vulg.), which latter word perhaps misled Aug., owing to whose mistake the true interpretation was lost for some centuries, although held by Orig., Chrys., and Ambrose. See Trench on St. Augustine, ch. v. p. 89:—i. e. 'richly imparted') **in our hearts** (*ἐν may* be taken pregnantly, *ἐκκέχ. εἰς καὶ μένει ἐν*,—or better, denotes the locality where the outpouring takes place,—the heart being the seat of our love, and of appreciation and sympathy with *God's love*) **by means of the Holy Spirit** (who is the Outpourer, John xvi. 14; 1 Cor. ii. 9, 10) **which was given to us** (Olsh. rightly refers the aorist part. to the Pentecostal effusion of the Holy Spirit). 'Prima hæc est in hac tractatione Spiritus Sancti mentio. Nimirum ad hunc usque terminum quum perductus est homo, operationem Sp. Sancti notanter denique sentit.' Bengel.

6.] The text here is in some confusion,—see var. readd. The whole may perhaps have arisen from an ecclesiastical portion having begun *χριστὸς ὄντων ἡμῶν ἀσθενῶν ἔτι* . . . When this found its way into the text, *ἔτι* was repeated. This offended the transcribers: but the first *ἔτι* could not be *erased*, because *γάρ* followed; it may then have been conjecturally emended to *εἰ* (and *γάρ* to *γέ* as in B, or *δέ* as in L), or *εἰς τί*,—some retaining *ἔτι* in both places. The place of *ἔτι* is often, in the case of absolutes, at the beginning of a sentence, with the subject of the sentence between it and the word or words to which it applies; so *ἔτι αὐτοῦ λαλοῦντος*, Matt. xii. 46,—*ἔτι δὲ αὐτοῦ μακρὰν ἀπέχοντος*, Luke xv. 20, &c. On reconsidera-

[a] ἀσθενῶν ἔτι [b] κατὰ καιρὸν [c] ὑπὲρ [d] ἀσεβῶν ἀπέθανεν. ABCDF
7 [e] μόλις γὰρ [c] ὑπὲρ δικαίου τὶς ἀποθανεῖται. [c] ὑπὲρ γὰρ KL[P]א abcdf
τοῦ ἀγαθοῦ [f] τάχα τὶς καὶ [g] τολμᾷ ἀποθανεῖν· 8 [h] συν- ghkl mno17
ίστησιν δὲ τὴν ἑαυτοῦ ἀγάπην εἰς ἡμᾶς, ὅτι ἔτι [i] ἁμαρ- [47]
τωλῶν ὄντων ἡμῶν χριστὸς [e] ὑπὲρ ἡμῶν ἀπέθανεν.
9 [k] πολλῷ οὖν [k] μᾶλλον [l] δικαιωθέντες νῦν [l] ἐν τῷ αἵματι

a = 1 Cor. ix. 22. see 1 Cor. iv. 10. Prov. xxii. 22. Ps. cvi. 12. b = here only. Num. xxiii. 23. (John v. 4.) see Num. ix. 13. c = John vi. 51. x. 15. xi. 51, 52. Luke xxii. 19 al. fr. d = ch. iv. 5 reff. e Acts xiv. 18. xxvii. 7, 8, 16. 1 Pet. iv. 18 (from Prov. xi. 31) only. f Philem. 15 only +. Wisd. xiii. 6. xiv. 19 only. g = 1 Cor. vi. 1 reff. h ch. iii. 5 reff. i ch. iii. 7 reff. k Paul (here, &c., four times. 1 Cor. xii. 22. 2 Cor. iii. 9, 11. Phil. i. 23. ii. 12) only, exc. Matt. vi. 30. Mark x. 48 || L. see Heb. xii. 9, 25. l Acts xiii. 39. 1 Cor. iv. 4. vi. 11. Gal. ii. 17. iii. 11. v. 4.

rec (aft *ασθενων*) om *ετι*, with D³KL[P] rel [Orig-int$_2$]: ins ABCD¹Fא latt Damasc Iren-int [Orig-int$_1$].

7. *μογις* א¹(txt א-corr¹) [Orig$_1$]. om 2nd *γαρ* L 2. 32. 62. lect-18 : *δε* 238.

8. rec aft *ημας* ins *ο θεος* (*supplementary insertn, as is shewn by the variations in its position*), with ACK[P]א rel copt [Orig$_1$ Cyr$_1$ Euthal-ms Damasc] Chr$_1$ Œc: bef *εις ημας*, DFL latt syr Dial$_1$ Chr-ms$_1$ Thdrt Thl Iren-int$_1$ [Orig-int$_1$] Aug: [aft] *δε* arm: transp freely Syr [æth]: om B. om *ετι* 109 Dial$_1$: for *ετι*, *ει* Syr Chr$_1$: *ει ετι* D^2b(and lat¹) F tol [spec Orig-int$_1$] Cypr$_1$ Hil$_2$ Aug$_1$ Pelag Ambrst. *ημων* bef *οντων* L Chr$_1$.

9. om *ουν* D¹F fuld¹ [demid spec] copt arm Dial$_1$ Iren-int$_1$ [Orig-int$_1$ Hil$_2$ Ambrst] Cypr$_1$ aft *δικαιωθεντες* ins *εν* (but erased) א¹.

tion, however, seeing that if we follow the most ancient MSS., we must either *repeat* **ἔτι**, which seems very unlikely to have been originally written, or adopt the reading of B, I have taken the latter alternative. **If, that is** (on **εἴ γε**, see note, 2 Cor. v. 3, and Eph. iii. 2), **Christ when we were yet weak** ('powerless for good;'—or even stronger than that:—there seems in this verse to be a tacit reference to Ezek. xvi. See especially vv. 7, 8 of that chap. in the LXX,—*σὺ δὲ ἦσθα γυμνὴ καὶ ἀσχημονοῦσα καὶ διῆλθον διὰ σοῦ καὶ ἴδον σε, καὶ ἰδοὺ καιρός σου . . . καὶ διεπέτασα τὰς πτέρυγάς μου ἐπὶ σέ, καὶ ἐκάλυψα τὴν ἀσχημοσύνην σου, καὶ ὤμοσά σοι· καὶ εἰσῆλθον ἐν διαθήκῃ μετὰ σοῦ, λέγει κύριος*), **in due season** (i. e. at the appointed time; compare reff. and Gal. iv. 4, and *καιρός* in the quotation above) **Christ died for** ('on behalf of,' see reff.) **ungodly men** (not *ὑπὲρ* **ἡμῶν**, because the Apostle wishes to bring out fully by this strong antithesis, which he enlarges on in the next verses, the greatness of the divine Love to man). **7.**] The greatness of this Love, of Christ's death on behalf of the impious, is brought out by shewing that there is none such among *men*, nay that such a self-sacrifice,—not unexampled where a *good* man, one loving his fellow-men and loved by them, is to be rescued,—is hardly found to occur on behalf of the pious and just. **For hardly will any one die on behalf of a just man** (masc.,—not neuter, 'for justice' or 'righteousness sake,' as Jer., Erasm., Luth., al.: for the matter in hand is Christ's death on behalf of *persons*)—**for** (this second 'for' is exceptive, and answers to 'but I do not press this without exception,' understood) **on behalf of the good man** (the art. as pointing him out generally, as in the expression, 'the fool,' 'the wise man,' 'the righteous,' 'the wicked') **perhaps** (*τάχα* opens a possibility which *μόλις* closes) **one doth even dare** (i. e. is even found to venture; the pres. implies habituality—it may occur here and there) **to die.** The distinction here made between *δίκαιος* and *ἀγαθός*, is also found in Cicero, de Of. iii. 15, 'Si vir bonus is est qui prodest quibus potest, nocet nemini, recte *justum* virum, *bonum* non facile reperiemus.' (But some edd. read 'istum virum bonum.')

The interpretation which makes *δίκαιος* and *ἀγαθός* refer to the same man, and the second clause = 'I do not say that such a thing *may* not sometimes occur,' is very vapid, and loses sight of the antithesis between *δίκαιος*, and *ἄδικος* (= *ἀσεβής* = *ἁμαρτωλός*). **8.**] **But** (as distinguished from human examples) **He** (i. e. God. The omission of *ὁ θεός*, which critical principles render necessary, is in keeping with the perfectly general way in which the contrast is put, merely with *τίς*, not *ἀνθρώπων τίς*. The subject is supplied from *ἡ ἀγάπη τοῦ θεοῦ* ver. 5) **gives proof of** ('establishes' (reff.);—not 'commends') **His own love** (*own*, as distinguished from that of men in ver. 7) **towards us, in that while we were yet** (as opposed to *νῦν* in the next verse) **sinners** (= *ἀσθενῶν* = *ἀσεβῶν* [ver. 6], and opposed to *δίκαιος* and *ἀγαθός*, ver. 7) **Christ died for us.** **9—11.**] The Apostle further *shews the blessed fruits of justification*, viz. *salvation*, both *from wrath*, and *with life.* The *argument* proceeds from the beginning of the chapter: but the *connexion*, as so frequent with St. Paul, is

αὐτοῦ [m] σωθησόμεθα δι' αὐτοῦ ἀπὸ τῆς [n] ὀργῆς· 10 εἰ γὰρ
ἐχθροὶ ὄντες [o] κατηλλάγημεν τῷ θεῷ διὰ τοῦ θανάτου τοῦ
υἱοῦ αὐτοῦ, [k] πολλῷ [k] μᾶλλον [o] καταλλαγέντες [p] σωθησόμεθα [p] ἐν τῇ [q] ζωῇ αὐτοῦ· 11 [r] οὐ μόνον δέ, [r] ἀλλὰ καὶ
[s] καυχώμενοι [s] ἐν τῷ θεῷ διὰ τοῦ κυρίου ἡμῶν Ἰησοῦ
χριστοῦ, δι' οὗ νῦν τὴν [t] καταλλαγὴν ἐλάβομεν.
12 Διὰ τοῦτο ὥςπερ [u] δι' ἑνὸς ἀνθρώπου ἡ ἁμαρτία [v] εἰς

m = Matt. i. 21. Acts ii. 40. Jer. xxxvii. (xxx.) 7.
n Matt. iii. 7. ch. i. 18. iii. 5.
o (=) here bis. 1 Cor. vii. 11. 2 Cor. v. 18, 19, 20 only‡. (Jer. xxxi. [xlviii.] 39.) 2 Macc. i. 5. vii. 33. viii. 29 only.
p = Acts xi. 14 reff.
q = 2 Cor. iv. 10, 11, 12.
r ver. 3.
s ch. ii. 17 reff.
t (=) ch. xi. 15. 2 Cor. v. 18, 19 only‡. (Isa. ix. 5.) 2 Macc. v. 20 only.
u = Acts xxiv. 2 reff.
v = Wisd. xiv. 14 (?). see John i. 9.

10. A omits from *τω θεω* to *τω θεω* ver **11.** om 1st *του* F(but not G). *σωθησωμεθα* L g^1.]

11. aft *ου μονον δε* ins *τουτο* D^1F $fuld^1$ arm Ambrst. *καυχωμεθα* L b (c d *-ο-*) h m latt [(Syr) æth] arm Thl [$Orig\text{-}int_2$ Ambrst] : *καυχωμεν* F. om *χριστου* B.

immediately with the parenthetical sentences just preceding. **Much more then** (if He *died* for us when *sinners*, a fortiori will He *save* us now that we are *righteous* by virtue of that His death) **having been now justified by His blood** (see remarks on ch. iv. 25) **we shall be saved by Him from the wrath** (*to come*, or *of which we know:* force of the art.). **10.**] The same is substantiated in another form: 'we were enemies (see below) when He died and reconciled us: much more now that we have been reconciled, and He lives, shall we by His life be saved.' **For if, being enemies** (*ἐχθροί* may either be active, as Col. i. 21, '*haters of God;*' so *ἐχθρά*, ch. viii. 7; Eph. ii. 15: or passive, as ch. xi. 28,—'*hated by God.*' But here the latter meaning alone can apply, for the Apostle is speaking of the Death of Christ and its effects as applied to all time, not merely to those believers who then lived: and those unborn at the death of Christ could not have been *ἐχθροί* in the active sense), **we were reconciled** (*καταλλάσσεσθαί τινι* also may be taken of *giving up anger against any one,*—see ref. 1 Cor., and Jos. Antt. vi. 7. 4, *οὐ γὰρ ἑώρα τὸν θεὸν διαλλαττόμενον,*— or of *being received into favour by any one,*—see 1 Kings xxix. 4, *ἐν τίνι διαλλαγήσεται οὗτος τῷ κυρίῳ αὐτοῦ;* and Jos. Antt. v. 2. 8, *διαλυσάμενος τὰς μέμψεις, καταλλάττεται πρὸς αὐτήν,*—the latter of which meanings, *were received into favour with God,* must for the reason above given be here adopted) **to God by means of the death of His Son** (this great fact is further explained and insisted on, in the rest of the chapter), **much more, having been reconciled** (but here comes in the assumption that the corresponding subjective part of reconciliation has been accomplished, viz. justification by faith: compare 2 Cor. v. 19, 20, *θεὸς ἦν ἐν χριστῷ* **κόσμον καταλλάσσων ἑαυτῷ** . . . . *δεόμεθα ὑπὲρ χριστοῦ,* **καταλλάγητε τῷ θεῷ.** Both these, the objective reception into God's favour by the death of Christ, and the subjective appropriation, by faith, of that reception, are included), **we shall be saved by means of His Life** (not here *that which he now does* on our behalf, but simply *the fact of His Life,* so much enlarged on in ch. vi.: and our sharing in it). **11.**] A further step still—not only has the reconciled man confidence that he shall escape God's wrath, but *triumphant* confidence,—joyful hope in God. **But** (aber) **not only so, but** (sondern) **glorying in God** (particip. not as the finite verb, but in every case either the consequence of an anacoluthon, or finding its justification in the construction: so here "not only shall we be saved," but that in a triumphant manner and frame of mind. See Winer, edn. 6, § 45. 6 [a]) **through our Lord Jesus Christ, through whom we have now** (not in contrast with the future glory, '*even now,*' as Thol., for that would be more plainly expressed,—but as in ver. 9) **received (our) reconciliation** (to God [not as in E. V. "*the atonement,*" at least in the common theological acceptance of the term: for that is not here treated of, but our reconcilement to God]).

12—VIII. 39.] The Power of God (ch. i. 16) is set forth as freeing from the dominion of sin and death, and issuing in salvation. **12—19.**] *The bringing in of* reconciliation *and* life *by* Christ *in its analogy to the bringing in of* sin *and* death *by* Adam.

12.] This verse is one of acknowledged difficulty. The two questions meeting us directly are (1) To what does *διὰ τοῦτο* refer? (2) *ὥςπερ*, 'like as,' may introduce the first member of a comparison, the second being to be discovered; or may introduce the second, the first having to be discovered. I shall endeavour to answer

τὸν [v] κόσμον [v] εἰςῆλθεν, καὶ διὰ τῆς ἁμαρτίας ὁ θάνατος,
καὶ [w] οὕτως [x] εἰς πάντας ἀνθρώπους [ὁ θάνατος] [x] διῆλθεν
[y] ἐφ' ᾧ πάντες ἥμαρτον. 13 [z] ἄχρι γὰρ νόμου ἁμαρτία ἦν

w = Acts vii. 8. xvii. 33. xxviii. 14. ch. xi. 26. 1 Cor. xi. 28. xiv. 25.
x 2 Cor. i. 16 reff.
y 2 Cor. v. 4. see Matt. xix. 9. Acts iii. 16.
z = ch. i. 13 al.

ABCDF KL[P]ℵ a b c d f g h k l m n o 17 [47]

12. *εις τον κοσμον* bef *η αμαρτια* DF latt(am fuld &c though not vulg-ed) $Ambr_1$. rec aft *ανθρωπους* ins *ο θανατος* (*marginal gloss specifying the subj of διηλθεν, as is shewn by the varr*), with ABCKL[P]ℵ rel vulg [(Syr) $Orig_2(int_4)$ Euthal-ms Damasc] Thl Œc [Ambrst] Aug_{aliq}; aft *διηλθεν* arm Chr_1 $Thdrt_2$: bef *εις π. α.* syr-w-ast: om DF [fuld æth $Orig_1$] $Aug_{sæpe}$ $Ambr_1$ Pac_2 Leo_1 Bede.

both questions in connexion. (1) I conceive *διὰ τοῦτο* to refer to that blessed state of confidence and hope just described: 'on this account,' here meaning, 'quæ cum ita sint:' 'this state of things, thus brought about, will justify the following analogy.' Thus we must take *ὥσπερ*, either (α) as beginning the comparison, and then supply, 'so by Christ in His Resurrection came justification into the world, and by justification, life;' or (β) as concluding the comparison, and supply before it, 'it was,' or 'Christ wrought.' This latter method seems to me far the best. For none of the endeavours of Commentators to supply the second limb of the comparison from the following verses have succeeded: and we can hardly suppose such an ellipsis, when the next following comparison (ver. 16) is rather a *weakening* than a strengthening the analogy. We have example of this use of *ὥσπερ*, in Matt. xxv. 14, and of *καθώς*, Gal. iii. 6.

Consequently (the method of God's procedure in introducing life by righteousness resembled the introduction of death by sin: 'it was') **like as by one man** (the Apostle regards the *man* as involving generic succession and transmitting the corrupt seed of sin, *not the woman:* but when he speaks of the *personal* share which each had in the transgression, 1 Tim. ii. 14, he says, 'Adam was not deceived, but the woman being deceived was in the transgression') **sin** (as a POWER ruling over mankind, see ch. iii. 9, and ver. 21,—partly as a *principle* which exists in us all, and developes itself in our conduct, partly as a *state* in which we are involved; but the idea here must not be *confined* (Calv.) to *original sin,* as it reaches much wider, to sin both original and actual: nor to the *habit of sinning* (as Olsh.): nor is it merely the *propensity to sin* (as Röthe): nor is sin *personified* merely as in ch. vii. 8, 11) **entered into the world** (not 'esse cœpit,' 'primum commissa est,' as Reiche, Fritz., and Meyer: but *literally,*—'entered into,' 'gained access into,' the *moral world,*—for sin involves moral responsibility. So Gal. iii. 23, *πρὸ τοῦ δὲ ἐλθεῖν τὴν πίστιν,* 'before the faith *came in*'), **and by means of sin** (as the appointed penalty for sin, Gen. ii. 17; iii. 19) **death** (primarily, but not *only,* physical death: as *ἁμαρτία,* so *θάνατος,* is *general,* including the lesser in the greater, i. e. *spiritual and eternal death.* See ch. vi. 16, 21; vii. 10; viii. 6; 2 Cor. vii. 10), **and thus** (by this entering in of sin and death; i. e. in fact, by this *connexion of sin and death,* as appears by *ἐφ' ᾧ πάντες ἥμαρτον*) **death** (whether *ὁ θάν.* be genuine or not, death is the subject of *διῆλθεν*) **extended to all men** (see reff. De W. well says that *πάντ. ἀνθρ.* differs from *κόσμον,* as the concrete part from the abstract whole, and *διέρχ.* from *εἰςέρχεσθαι,* as the going from house to house differs from the entering a town. Obs., that although the subject of *διῆλθεν* is plainly only *death,* not *sin and death,* yet the spreading of *sin* over all men is *taken for granted,* partly in the *οὕτως,* partly in the following clause), **because** (*ἐφ' ᾧ,* lit. of close juxtaposition: and so '*on ground of,*' '*on condition that,*' which meaning, if rightly applied, suits the case in hand. *Life* depended on a certain condition, viz. obedience: *Death* on another, viz. disobedience. Mankind have disobeyed: the condition of Death's entrance and diffusion has been fulfilled: Death extended to all men, as a consequence of the fact, that,—posito, that, = *because,* all have sinned.

Orig., Aug., Beza, and Estius render it as Vulg., '*in quo*' (Adam): Chrys., Theophyl., Œc., Elsner, '*propter quem:*' Grot., '*per quem*') **all sinned** (see ch. iii. 23:—not '*were sinful,*' or '*were born in sin,*' as Calvin would restrict the meaning: *sin,* as above remarked, is here, throughout, both *original* and *actual:* in the *seed,* as planted in the nature by the sin of our forefather: and in the *fruit,* as developed by each conscious responsible individual in his own practice. So that Calvin's argument,—'hic non agi de actuali peccato, colligere promptum est: quia si reatum quisque sibi arcesseret, quorsum conferret Paulus Adam cum Christo?' does not apply, and the objection is answered by Paul himself, where he says, distinguishing between the *παράπτωμα* and the *χάρισμα*

ἐν κόσμῳ, ἁμαρτία δὲ οὐκ [a] ἐλλογεῖται μὴ ὄντος νόμου,
14 ἀλλὰ [bc] ἐβασίλευσεν ὁ θάνατος ἀπὸ Ἀδὰμ [d] μέχρι
Μωυσέως καὶ [c] ἐπὶ τοὺς μὴ ἁμαρτήσαντας [e] ἐπὶ τῷ

a here only. -γᾶν, Philem. 18 only +. b = vv. 17, 21. ch. vi. 12. c Luke i. 33 xix. 14, 27. Gen. xxxvii. 8. d of time, Matt. xi. 23. Acts x. 30. xx. 7. 1 Tim. vi. 14 al. Ps. civ. 19. e Luke i. 59. Ezra ii. 61. Neh. vii. 63.

13. ελλογατο A ℵ-corr[1]-marg[-ται]: ελλογειτω f, ενελογειτο (*imputabatur*) ℵ[1] ([ελογ.] 52. 108) vulg(but not am) G-lat syrr copt æth lat-ff: λελογισται lect-19: ευλογειται 71-7.
14. (αλλα, so BD.) for 2nd επι, εν B, *in similitudine* (or *-nem*) latt Iren-int [Orig-int] Jer.

below, vv. 15, 16, τὸ δὲ χάρισμα **ἐκ πολλῶν παραπτωμάτων** εἰς δικαίωμα. The παράπτωμα was not only that of one, the original cause of the entry of sin, but the often repeated sins of individual men:—nor, '*suffered the punishment of sin*,' as Grot. and Chrys., θνητοὶ γεγόνασι).

Observe how entirely this assertion of the Apostle contradicts the Pelagian or individualistic view of men, that each is a separate creation from God, existing solely on his own exclusive responsibility,—and affirms the Augustinian or traducian view, that all are evolved by God's appointment from an original stock, and though individually responsible, are generically involved in the corruption and condemnation of their original.

13.] How, consistently with ch. iv. 15, could all men sin, *before the law?* This is now explained. **For up to (the time of) the law** (= ἀπὸ Ἀδ. μέχρι Μωυσ. ver. 14: not '*during the time of the law*,' as Orig., Chrys.,—τοῦ νόμου δοθέντος, ... ἕως ὁ νόμος ἦν,—Theodoret,—an allowable rendering of the words, but manifestly inconsistent with the sense;—nor, '*as far as there was law, there was sin*,' as Dr. Burton,—which is both inadmissible from the μέχρι Μωυσέως following, and would not answer to the simple matter of fact, ἦν ἐν κόσμῳ) **there was sin in the world** ('men sinned,' see Gen. vi. 5—13; committed actual sin: not, men were *accounted* sinners because of Adam's sin; the Apostle reminds us of the *historical fact*, that *there was sin in the world* during this period): **but sin is not reckoned** (as transgression) **where the law is not.** **ἐλλογεῖται** has given rise to much dispute. Very many Commentators (Aug., Ambr., Luth., Melanc., Calv., Beza, Rückert, Tholuck, Stuart, al.) explain it of *consciousness of sin by the sinner himself*, as in ch. vii. 7: but (1) as De Wette observes, this is not the natural sense of the word, which implies TWO parties, one of whom sets down something to the account of the other (ref.): (2) this interpretation would bring in a new and irrelevant element,—for the Apostle is not speaking in this chapter at all of *subjective human consciousness*, but throughout of *objective truths with regard to the divine dealings:* and (3) it would be altogether inconsistent with the declarations of ch. ii. 15,—where in this sense the ἐλλογισμός of sin by the νόμον μὴ ἔχοντες is distinctly asserted. I am persuaded that the right sense of ἐλλ. is, reckoned, '*set down as transgression*,'—'put in formal account,' *by God*. In the case of those who had not the written law, ἁμαρτία is not formally reckoned as παράβασις, set over against the command: but in a certain sense, as distinctly proved ch. ii. 9—16, it *is reckoned* and they are condemned for it. Nor is there any inconsistency, as Tholuck complains, in this view. Other passages of Paul's writings support and elucidate it. He states the object of the law to be, ch. vii. 13, ἵνα γένηται καθ' ὑπερβολὴν ἁμαρτωλὸς ἡ ἁμαρτία διὰ τῆς ἐντολῆς. The revelation of the law *exaggerated*, brought into prominent and formal manifestation, the sinfulness of sin, which *was before culpable and punishable*, but in a less degree. With this view also agree Acts xvii. 30; ch. ii. 12, ὅσοι ἀνόμως ἥμαρτον, ἀνόμως καὶ ἀπολοῦνται,—and iii. 25, in so far as they state an analogous case. The objection to taking οὐκ ἐλλογεῖται *relatively*, '*is not fully reckoned*,' will hardly be urged by those who bear in mind the Apostle's habit of constantly *stating relative truths as positive*, omitting the qualifying particles: see e. g. ch. vii. 7, where with ἁμαρτίαν and with οὐκ ᾔδειν both, we must supply qualifications (see notes there).

14.] **But** (notwithstanding the last assertion that sin is not fully reckoned where the law is not) **death reigned** (was a power to which all succumbed) **from Adam to Moses** (μέχρι Μωυσ. = ἄχρι νόμου above): i. e. although the full ἐλλογισμός of sin did not take place between Adam and Moses, *the universality of death is a proof that all sinned*,—for death is the consequence of sin:—in confirmation of ver. 12. **καὶ ἐπὶ τ. μὴ ἁμ.**] **even** (notwithstanding the different degrees of sin and guilt out of, and under, the law) **over those who sinned not according to the similitude** (reff.) **of the** TRANSGRESSION **of Adam.** (1) ἐπὶ τῷ ὁμ. belongs to ἁμαρτ. and not to ἐβασι-

f = ch. vi. 5 (i. 23 reff.). g ch. iv. 15 reff. h = 1 Cor. x. 6‡. i = Matt. xii. 32. Acts xxiv. 25 al. Wisd. xix. 1. k ch. iv. 25 reff. l = ch. vi. 23. xi. 29.

[f] ὁμοιώματι τῆς [g] παραβάσεως Ἀδάμ, ὅς ἐστιν [h] τύπος
τοῦ [i] μέλλοντος, 15 ἀλλ᾽ οὐχ ὡς τὸ [k] παράπτωμα, οὕτως
καὶ τὸ [l] χάρισμα· εἰ γὰρ τῷ τοῦ ἑνὸς [k] παραπτώματι

ABCDF KL[P]א a b c d f g h k l m n o 17 [47]

15. om 1st *και* B [Syr copt]. aft *πολλω* ins *ουν* A Syr.

λευσεν (as Chrys., Theophyl., Bengel, Elsn., al.),—for that would bring in, in the words τοὺς μὴ ἁμαρτήσαντας, an absolute contradiction to ἐφ᾽ ᾧ πάντες ἥμαρτον, by asserting that there were some who *did not sin.* (2) The emphasis lies on **παράβασις**, as distinguished from **ἁμαρτία.** Photius (in De W.),—ὁ μὲν (Ἀδ.) ὡρισμένην κ. νομοθετηθεῖσαν ἐντολὴν παρέβη κ. ἥμαρτεν· οἱ δὲ ἡμάρτανον τὸν αὐτοδίδακτον τῆς φύσεως λόγον ἐνυβρίζοντες. They all *sinned:* but had not, like Adam, *transgressed* a positive revealed command. (3) There is no reference here, as some Commentators (Beza, al.) have supposed, to the case of *children* and *idiots,*—nor (as Grot., Wetst.) to *those who lived pious lives.* The aim is to prove, that the seed of sin planted in the race by the one man Adam, has sprung up and borne fruit in all, so as to bring them under death;—death temporal, and spiritual;—of these, some have sinned without the law, i. e. *not as Adam did, and as those after Moses did:* and though sin is not formally reckoned against them, death, the consequence of sin, reigned, as matter of historical fact, over them also. It is most important to the clear understanding of this weighty passage to bear in mind, that the first member of the comparison, *as far as* it extends, is this: 'As by Adam's transgression, of which we are by descent inheritors, we have become (not by imputation merely, but by propensity) *sinners,* and have thus incurred *death,* so &c.' ..... (see below). **ὅς ἐστιν τύπος τ. μέλλ.]** **who is a figure** (or type: not thus used by LXX, see Umbreit's note) **of the future** (**Adam** [the second Adam, viz. Christ]). This clause is inserted on the first mention of the name Adam, the *one man* of whom he has been speaking, to recall the purpose for which he is treating of him,—as *the figure* (ref.) *of Christ.* **τοῦ μέλλ.**, not 'qui futurus erat,' as Beza [and E. V.], Reiche; but spoken from the Apostle's *present* standing, '*who is to come.*' The fulfilment of the type will then take place completely, when, as 1 Cor. xv. 22, ἐν τῷ χριστῷ πάντες ζωοποιηθήσονται. Still less, with Koppe, can ὅς be taken by attr. for ὅ, and τοῦ μέλλοντος be interpreted '*of that which is to come,*' viz. life and salvation: see 1 Cor. xv. 45.

Many suppose these words ὅς ἐστ. τύπ. τ. μέλλ. to be the apodosis of ver. 12: but see there. **15—17.]** *Though Adam and Christ correspond as opposites, yet there is a remarkable difference, which makes the free gift of grace much more eminent than the transgression and its consequences, and enhances the certainty of its end being accomplished.* **But not** (in all points) **as the act of transgression** (of Adam, as the cause inducing sin and death on his race), **so also is the gift of grace** (i. e. justification: not a direct contrast, as ὑπακοή in ver. 19: the Apostle has more in mind here the *consequence* of the παραπτ., and to that opposes the χάρισμα. De W.). **15. εἰ γὰρ κ.τ.λ.]** *Distinction the first,* in Degree:—and in the form of a hypothetical inference 'a minori ad majus.' **For if by the transgression of the one** (man) **the many** (have) **died, much more did the grace of God, and the gift abound in** (by means of) **the grace of the one man Jesus Christ towards the many.** (1) The first question regards πολλῷ μᾶλλον. Is it the '*a fortiori*' of logical inference, or is it to be joined with ἐπερίσσευσεν as quantitative, describing the *degree of abounding?* Chrys. (πολλῷ γὰρ τοῦτο εὐλογώτερον), Grot., Fritz., Thol., adopt the former, and provided only *the same thing is said here as in ver.* 17, the usage there would decide it to be so: for there it cannot be quantitative. But I believe that not to be so. Here, the question is of *abounding,* a matter of *degree,* there, of *reigning,* a matter of *fact.* Here (ver. 16) the contrast is between the judgment, coming of *one* sinner, to condemnation, and the free gift, of (see note below) *many* offences, to justification. So that I think the quantitative sense the better, and join **πολλῷ μᾶλλον** with ἐπερίσσευσεν, in the sense of **much more abundant** (rich in diffusion) **was the gift,** &c. (2) **χάρις**, not the grace *working in men,* here, but the grace which *is in, and flows from, God.* (3) ἐν χάριτι τῇ τοῦ ...., not to be joined (Thol.) with ἡ δωρεά, as if it were ἡ ἐν χάρ. (which would be allowable), but with ἐπερίσσ. The *grace of our Lord Jesus Christ* (His self-offering love, see 2 Cor. viii. 9) is the medium by which the free gift is imparted to men. (4) The aorist ἐπερίσσ. should here be kept to its indefinite his-

[m] οἱ πολλοὶ ἀπέθανον, [n] πολλῷ [n] μᾶλλον ἡ χάρις τοῦ θεοῦ
καὶ ἡ [o] δωρεὰ ἐν χάριτι τῇ τοῦ ἑνὸς ἀνθρώπου Ἰησοῦ
χριστοῦ [p] εἰς [m] τοὺς πολλοὺς [q] ἐπερίσσευσεν. 16 καὶ οὐχ
ὡς δι' ἑνὸς ἁμαρτήσαντος τὸ [r] δώρημα· τὸ μὲν γὰρ
[s] κρῖμα [t] ἐξ ἑνὸς [u] εἰς [v] κατάκριμα, τὸ δὲ [l] χάρισμα [t] ἐκ
πολλῶν [k] παραπτωμάτων [u] εἰς [w] δικαίωμα. 17 εἰ γὰρ

m = ver. 19 bis. ch. xii. 5. 1 Cor. x. 17, 33.
n vv. 9, 10 reff.
o Acts ii. 38 reff. Wisd. xvi. 25.
p ch. viii. 18. 2 Cor. i. 5.
q ch. iii. 7 al. constr., Eph. i. 8. 2 Cor. ix. 8, but περ. transitive.
r James i. 17 only †.
s see 1 Pet. iv. 17. Rev. xx. 4.
t ch. ii. 29 reff.
u = ch. i. 5. xvi. 26. 1 Pet. i. 22.
v here bis. ch. viii. 1 only †. (-νειν, ch. ii. 1. -σις, 2 Cor. iii. 9. vii. 3.)
w = here only. see note and ch. i. 32 reff.

om εν F-gr.

16. for αμαρτησαντος, αμαρτηματος D(and lat[1]) F [vulg-clem demid] fuld[1](not am harl[1] al) Syr [æth Orig-int$_1$(txt Orig$_1$) Aug$_2$(txt$_{sæpe}$): αμαρτητος(sic) ℵ[1]. om γαρ F-gr 45 lect-19, syr has it w-ast. at end add ζωης D[1](and lat[1]) fuld[1] æth.

torical sense, and not rendered as a perfect, however true the fact expressed may be: *both* are treated of here as *events*, their time of happening and present reference not being regarded. **16.**] *Distinction the second,* in KIND. The former difference was quantitative: this is modal. **And not as** (that which took place) **by one that sinned, so is the gift.** It is a question whether any thing, and what, is to be supplied before δι' ἑνὸς ἁμαρτ. Röthe, Meyer, and Tholuck (and so E. V.), would supply nothing, and render, 'And not as by one having sinned, so is the gift.' But (De W.) this has against it, (1) that since the γάρ following *gives the reason* for this sentence, this must *contain implicitly all* that that next expands in detail; which is not merely the distinction between springing from *one man* and out of *many offences,* but much more: and (2) that thus διά would = ἐκ or *vice versa,* whereas διά characterizes the *bringer in,* and ἐκ the *occasion.* Others have supplied τὸ κρῖμα (Bengel, Köllner): τὸ κατάκριμα (Theophyl., Reiche): ὁ θάνατος εἰσῆλθεν (Grot., Estius, Koppe):—but inasmuch as it is purposely left indefinite, to be explained in the next verse, it is better to supply an indefinite phrase which may be thus explained: e. g. τὸ γενόμενον, '*that which took place by one,*' [or '(*it was*) *through one,*'] &c. **τὸ μὲν γὰρ κ.τ.λ.] For the judgment** (pronounced by God upon Adam) **came of** (was by occasion of) **one** (man having sinned,—supply ἁμαρτήσαντος: παραπτώματος would be hardly allowable, and would not help the sense, inasmuch as many *sinners,* as well as many sins, are implied in πολλ. παραπτ. below), **unto condemnation** (its result, in his own case and that of his posterity: supply, as in ver. 18 is expressed, (ἐγένετο) εἰς πάντας ἀνθρώπους); **but the gift of grace was by occasion of many transgressions** (where sin abounded, ver. 20, there grace much more abounded: the existence of *the law* being implied in παραπτ.) **unto justification.** The only difficulty here is *the sense of* **δικαίωμα.** The ordinary meaning of the word is τὸ ἐπανόρθωμα τοῦ ἀδικήματος, 'the amendment of an evil deed:' so Aristotle, Eth. Nicom. v. 10, διαφέρει δὲ τὸ ἀδίκημα καὶ τὸ ἄδικον, καὶ τὸ δικαίωμα καὶ τὸ δίκαιον· ἄδικον μὲν γάρ ἐστι τῇ φύσει ἢ τάξει· τὸ αὐτὸ δὲ τοῦτο ὅταν πραχθῇ, ἀδίκημά ἐστι· πρὶν δὲ πραχθῆναι οὔπω, ἀλλ' ἄδικον. ὁμοίως δὲ καὶ δικαίωμα· καλεῖται δὲ καὶ τὸ κοινὸν μᾶλλον δικαιοπράγημα, δικαίωμα δὲ τὸ ἐπανόρθωμα τοῦ ἀδικήματος. But this, which Aristot. insists on as the proper, but not perhaps usual sense of the word, is not to be pressed in the N. T., and does not, though upheld by Calv., Calov., Wolf, and Röthe, suit the context as contrasted with κατάκριμα. Other renderings are, '*an absolutory sentence*' (Meyer, Fritz., al.): '*a righteous act,*' as in ver. 18; Baruch ii. 19; '*righteousness,*' as in Rev. xix. 8 (where see note): '*a righteous cause,*' or *plea* (LXX, Jer. xi. 20): '*justification*' (E. V., Luth., De Wette, al.). The first seems to me to be right, as standing most exactly in contrast with κατάκριμα; the use of the -μα being partly perhaps accounted for by the alliteration of the ending marking more strongly the antithesis. Thus as κατάκριμα is a *sentence of condemnation,* so δικαίωμα will be a *sentence of acquittal.* This in fact amounts to *justification.* **17.**] *Distinction the third,* also in KIND; that which came in by the *one sinner,* was the *reign of* DEATH: that which shall come in by the *One, Jesus Christ,* will be *a reigning in* LIFE. **For** (carrying on the argument from ver. 15, but not so as to make parenthetical (Röthe) ver. 16—for δικαιοσύνης presupposes δικαίωμα) **if by the transgression of the one** (man; the reading ἐν (τῷ) ἑνὶ παραπτώματι goes with ἁμαρτήματος for ἁμαρτήσαντος in ver. 16: both have evidently been corrections) **death reigned by means of**

x ver. 14 reff. y 2 Cor. viii. 2. x. 15. James i. 21 only. Eccles. i. 3 al. z = Matt. xviii. 8, 9. John v. 29 al. fr. a = 1 Cor. iv. 8. Rev. v. 10. xx. 4, 6. xxii. 5. b ch. vii. 3, 25. viii. 12. ix. 16, 18. xiv. [12] 19. Gal vi. 10 al3. P. c = ver. 12. d = Rev. xv. 4 only. Baruch ii. 19. see note on ver. 16. e ch. iv. 25 only ‡. Levit. xxiv. 22 only. f 2 Cor. x. 6. Heb. ii. 2 only †. (-ούειν, Matt. xviii. 17.)

ABCDF KL[P]ℵ a b c d f g h k l m n o 17 [47]

τῷ τοῦ ἑνὸς [k] παραπτώματι ὁ θάνατος [x] ἐβασίλευσεν
διὰ τοῦ ἑνός, [n] πολλῷ [n] μᾶλλον οἱ τὴν [y] περισσείαν τῆς
χάριτος καὶ τῆς [o] δωρεᾶς τῆς δικαιοσύνης λαμβάνοντες
ἐν [z] ζωῇ [a] βασιλεύσουσιν διὰ τοῦ ἑνὸς Ἰησοῦ χριστοῦ.
18 [b] Ἄρα [b] οὖν ὡς δι' ἑνὸς [k] παραπτώματος [c] εἰς πάντας
ἀνθρώπους [u] εἰς [v] κατάκριμα, οὕτως καὶ δι' ἑνὸς [d] δικαι-
ώματος [c] εἰς πάντας ἀνθρώπους [u] εἰς [e] δικαίωσιν ζωῆς·
19 ὥσπερ γὰρ διὰ τῆς [f] παρακοῆς τοῦ ἑνὸς ἀνθρώπου

17. for *τω του ενος*, *εν ενι* AF; *εν τω ενι* D-gr: *εν ενος* 47[-txt] am(with demid al) $Orig_2$: *τω* 44: txt BCKLℵ[P 47[1]-marg rel] vulg[-clem fuld] D-lat Syr [syr copt æth arm] Chr_1 Thdrt Thl Œc [Euthal-ms Damasc $Orig\text{-}int_1$] Aug_2. om *της δωρεας* B 49 $Orig_2$ $Chr\text{-}comm_1$ $Iren\text{-}int_1$ $Aug_{sæpe}$: *την δωρεαν* 67[2] Thl: add *και* 63 vulg syrr $Chr\text{-}2\text{-}mss_1$ $Isid_1$ Thdrt Ambrst Pelag. om *της δικαιοσ.* C 70[1] $Orig_1$[ins_2 and int_5]. ins *τη* bef *ζωη* L k 17. 93. *βασιλευουσιν* [D[3](appy, Tischdf) P] o 17. 47. 77. 91 $Orig_1$ Chr_1[(txt_1) Damasc]. *χρ.* bef *ιησου* B $Orig_2$(agst $Orig_1$ [int_5] Iren-int).

18. aft *ενος* ins *ανθρωπου* ℵ[1](ℵ[3] disapproving) [æth]. *παραπτωμα* F(*per unius delictum*) m 46 [Syr (copt)]. for *δικαιωματος*, *το δικαιωμα* DG [m]; *και δικαιωμα* F(*per unius justitiam*).

the one (man), **much more** (logical—*a fortiori*) **shall they who receive the abundance of the grace and of the gift of righteousness** (ver. 15: beware of the shallow and weakening notion, that it is "for τῆς δικαιοσύνης δεδωρημένης") **reign in life** (eternal) **by means of the one** (Man) **Jesus Christ.** περισσεία answers to ἐπερίσσευσεν, ver. 15: τῆς χάριτος, to ἡ χ. τοῦ θεοῦ; only here, as at ch. i. 5, the word signifies not only the grace flowing from God, but the same grace implanted and working in man:—δωρεᾶς, to δωρεά there, but qualified by τῆς δικαιοσύνης, answering to δικαίωμα in ver. 16.

The present λαμβάνοντες, instead of λαβόντες, is not merely used in a substantive sense, *receptores* (as Fritz. and Meyer), but signifies that the reception is not *one act* merely, but a *continued process* by which the περισσεία is imparted. (So Röthe, De W., Thol.) **ἐν ζωῇ βασ.**] "Antithesis to ὁ θάνατος ἐβασ. We should expect ἡ ζωὴ βασιλεύσει, but Paul designedly changes the form of expression that he may bring more prominently forward the idea of free personality. ζωή is not only corporeal (the resurrection), but also spiritual and moral,—as also in θάνατος we must include διὰ τῆς ἁμαρτίας ver. 12. βασιλεύσουσιν is brought in by the antithesis: but it is elsewhere used (see reff.) to signify the state of blessedness, partly in an objective theocratic import (of the reign of the saints with Christ), partly in a subjective moral one,—because *reigning* is the highest development of freedom, and the highest satisfaction of all desires." De Wette. 18.] *Recapitulation and co-statement of the parallel and distinctions.* **Therefore** (ἄρα οὖν, see reff., is placed by Paul at the beginning of a sentence, contrary to classical usage) **as by means of one trespass** (not, '*the transgression of one*,' as Erasm., Luth., Calv., Koppe, Fritz., Thol. [similarly E. V.], which is contrary to usage, and to ver. 17, where that meaning is expressed by τῷ τοῦ ἑνὸς παραπτώματι. In this summing up, the Apostle puts the antithetical elements *as strongly and nakedly as possible in contrast*; and therefore abridges the 'trespass of one' and 'the righteous act of one' into 'one trespass' and 'one righteous act') **it came upon** (ἐγένετο, indefinite, being supplied) **all men unto condemnation,—so also by means of one righteous act** (the Death of Christ viewed as the acme of His Obedience, see Phil. ii. 8 = ἡ ὑπακοὴ τοῦ ἑνός below; not as in ver. 16,—nor *Righteousness*, as Thol., which would not contrast with παραπτ., a *single act*) **it came upon all men** (in extent of grace,—*in posse*, not *in esse* as the other) **unto justification of** (conferring, leading to) **life.** 19.] **For** (in explanation of ver. 18) **as by the disobedience of** (the) **one man the many** (= πάντες ἄνθρωποι above, but not so expressed here, because in the other limb of the comparison πάντ. ἄνθρ. could not be put, and this is conformed to it: see there) **were made** (not, '*were accounted as*' (Grot. al.): nor '*became by imputation*' (Beza, Bengel): nor '*were proved to be*' (Koppe, Reiche, Fritz.): see reff.) **sinners** (not ὑπεύθυνοι κολάσει, as Chrys., Theophyl.: '*actual sinners by practice*,' is

[g] ἁμαρτωλοὶ [h] κατεστάθησαν [i] οἱ πολλοί, οὕτως καὶ διὰ
τῆς [k] ὑπακοῆς τοῦ ἑνὸς δίκαιοι [h] κατασταθήσονται [i] οἱ
πολλοί. 20 νόμος δὲ [l] παρεισῆλθεν, ἵνα [m] πλεονασῃ τὸ
[n] παράπτωμα. οὗ δὲ [m] ἐπλεόνασεν ἡ ἁμαρτία, [o] ὑπερεπερίσ-

g ch. iii. 7 reff.
h = 2 Pet. i. 8. 3 Macc. iii. 5. Deut. xxviii. 13.
i ver. 15 reff.
k ch. i. 5 reff.
l Gal. ii. 4 only †. παρεισῆλθε λάθρα νυκτὸς ἐντὸς τῶν τειχῶν, Polyb. ii. 55. 8.
m Paul (here bis. ch. vi. 1. 2 Cor. iv. 15 al4.) only, exc. 2 Pet. i. 8. 2 Chron. xxiv. 11.
n ver. 15.
o 2 Cor. vii. 4 only †. (-ῶς, Mark vii. 37.)

19. aft 2nd ενος add ανθρωπου D'F Iren-gr$_1$ Cyr$_2$[-p(om$_1$)] Aug$_1$(om$_{aliq}$) Ambr$_1$ [om$_1$].—του ενος ανθρ. bef υπακοης F.
20. for 1st δε, γαρ L. for οὗ, οπου F.

meant, the disobedience of Adam having been the *inlet* to all this: compare ἐφ' ᾧ πάντες ἥμαρτον ver. 12 and the notes, on the *kind of sin* spoken of in this whole passage, as being both original and actual), **so also** (after the same manner or analogy likewise) **by means of the obedience** (unto death, see on last verse) **of (the) One** (man) **shall** (*future,* because, as in ch. iii. 30, justification, as regards the many, is *not yet completed.* De W.) **the many** (= πολλοί, compare Matt. xxvi. 28; Mark x. 45, but thus expressed because πολλοί would not have answered in the other limb of the comparison. *In order to make the comparison more strict,* the πάντες who have been made sinners are *weakened* to the indefinite οἱ πολλοί, the πολλοί who shall be made righteous are *enlarged* to the indefinite οἱ πολλοί. Thus *a common term of quantity* is found *for both,* the one *extending to its largest* numerical interpretation, the other *restricted to its smallest*) **be made** (see above) **righteous** (not by *imputation* merely, any more than in the other case: but 'shall be made really and actually righteous, as completely so as the others were made really and actually sinners.' When we say that man has no righteousness *of his own,* we speak of him as *out of Christ:* but *in Christ* and united to Him, he is *made righteous,* not by a fiction, or *imputation only* of Christ's righteousness, but by a real and living spiritual union with a righteous Head as a righteous member, righteous *by means of,* as an effect of, the righteousness of that Head, but not merely righteous by transference of the Righteousness of that Head; just as in his natural state he is united to a sinful head as a sinful member, sinful by means of, as an effect of, the sinfulness of that Head, but not merely *by transference* of the sinfulness of that Head). See the whole question respecting πάντες and οἱ πολλοί treated in Tholuck's Comm. in loc. **20.**] *How the law* (of Moses) *came in, in the divine economy.* **But** (i. e. the two things spoken of ver. 19 did not *simply* and *immediately* happen) **the law** (of Moses: not *law,* in the abstract, nor '*the law of nature,*' as Dr. Peile,—nor even *the law of God* in its *general* sense, as often in ch. i. ii.;—but here strictly THE LAW OF MOSES, as necessitated by vv. 13, 14 in this same argument) **came in besides** (besides the fact of the many being made sinners, and as a transition point to the other result: formed a *third term,* besides these two, in the summary of God's dealings with man: compare προσετέθη, Gal. iii. 19: not πρὸς καιρὸν ἐδόθη, Theophyl.: not, *came in between Christ and Adam* (the *fact,* but not the *interpretation*) as Theodoret and Calv.:—not = εἰσῆλθεν merely),—**in order that** (τελικῶς, its *design,*—not merely ἐκβατικῶς, its result, as Chrys., al.; here, and every where else. So of ver. 21) **the trespass** (*created* by the law; for where no law, no transgression, ch. iv. 15:—not merely the *knowledge of sin,* but *actual* transgression) **might be multiplied** (in *actual fact:* not 'be abundantly exhibited,' or any such evasive sense). No possible objection can be taken to this statement by those who view the Law as a preparation for Christ. If it was so, then the effect of the Law, the creating and multiplying transgression, was *an end in the divine purposes,* to bring out the necessity of One who should deliver from sin and bring in righteousness. "Those who weaken this telic ἵνα into 'so that,' in order to guard the Apostle from what seems to them a doctrine unworthy of God, overlook equally his firm standing on the acknowledged ground of historic fact and actuality, as the humility with which here, as ever (ch. xi. 33, 34), he bows before the mystery of the οἰκονομία τοῦ θεοῦ." Umbreit. **But** (this terrible end, the multiplying of transgression, was not, however, God's *ultimate* end: He had a further and gracious one) **where** ('*when,*' De Wette, after Grot., al.: but Tholuck justly remarks that instances of this meaning of οὗ in *prose* are wanting. In verse it seems to occur, Eur. Iph. Aul. 96, but even there may be rendered '*in the case where*') **sin** (the generic of the specific παράπτωμα) **was multiplied, (God's) grace did beyond**

σευσεν ἡ χάρις, 21 ἵνα ὥσπερ ᵖ ἐβασίλευσεν ἡ ἁμαρτία ἐν ABCDF
τῷ θανάτῳ, οὕτως καὶ ἡ χάρις ᵖ βασιλεύσῃ διὰ δικαιο- KL[P]ℵ abcdf
σύνης ᵠ εἰς ζωὴν αἰώνιον διὰ Ἰησοῦ χριστοῦ τοῦ κυρίου ghkl mno17
ἡμῶν. [47]

VI. 1 ʳ Τί οὖν ʳ ἐροῦμεν; ˢ ἐπιμένωμεν τῇ ἁμαρτίᾳ, ἵνα ἡ
χάρις ᵗ πλεονάσῃ; 2 ᵘ μὴ γένοιτο. ᵛ οἵτινες ʷ ἀπεθάνομεν
τῇ ἁμαρτίᾳ, ˣ πῶς ἔτι ʸ ζήσομεν ʸ ἐν αὐτῇ; 3 ᶻ ἢ ᵃ ἀγνοεῖτε

p ver. 14 reff. q ver. 16 reff. r ch. iii. 5 reff. s = ch. xi. 22, 23. Col. i. 23. 1 Tim. iv. 16. L.P. [exc. John viii. 7.] (Exod. xii. 39 B.) t ch. v. 20 reff. u ch. iii. 4 reff. v Acts x. 41 reff. w = and constr., Gal. ii. 19. (ver. 10. ch. xiv. 8.) w. ἀπό, Col. ii. 20. x = ch. iii. 6. 1 Cor. xv. 12. Gal. iv. 9. Gen. xxxix. 9. y = Col. (ii. 20.) iii. 7 only. z = ch. ii. 4. iii. 29. a ch. i. 13 reff.

21. om. τω F. for βασιλευσῃ, -σει KL c l¹ o [47] 77. 115-6-21-2. χρ. bef ιησ. B.

Chap. VI. 1. rec επιμενουμεν, with rel Chr_1 Thdrt Gennad-c Diod-c Thl Œc $Tert_1$ [*perseverabimus* (*perferemus* Tert-ms)], *permanebimus* vulg G-lat [F-lat $Orig\text{-}int_3$] $Aug_{s\text{æ}pe}$: επιμενομεν Kℵ[P d n 47] 1. 57. 68. 109 lect-13 copt [Euthal-ms]: επιμεινωμεν L [k] 93. 124: txt ABCD F[-gr] b¹ m o 17 Syr Damasc. ins εν bef τη A[Woide, e contra Cowper, expr], *in peccato* latt.

2. aft οιτινες ins γαρ F latt syrr (not Tert). ζησωμεν CFL 17 Diod $Chr\text{-}ms_1$.

measure abound (not '*did much more abound*,' as E. V.: for words compounded with ὑπέρ have a *superlative, not a comparative* signification, e. g. ref. ὑπερλίαν, ὑπερνικάω, ὑπερυψόω, κ.τ.λ.,—and Paul often uses these compounds. The E. V. has likewise destroyed the force of the comparison by rendering the different words πλεονάζω and περισσεύω both by one word '*abound*'). **21.**] *The purpose of this abounding of grace:—its ultimate prevalence and reign, by means of righteousness, unto life eternal.* **That, as sin reigned** (the historic indefinite past, because the standing-point of the sentence is, *the restitution of all things hereafter*) **in death** (ἐν, of that *in and by which* the reign was exercised and shewn: *death* was the central act of sin's reign. He does not here say, '*death reigned by sin*,' as in vv. 12—14, because *sin* and *grace* are the two points of comparison, and require to be the *subjects*), **so also grace may reign by means of** (not ἐν here, though it might be so, if δικαιοσ. applied to *our being made righteous*: but as it applies to the *Righteousness of Christ* making us righteous, it is διά) **righteousness, unto** (leading to) **life eternal through** (by means of) **Jesus Christ our Lord** ('Jam ne memoratur quidem Adamus, solius Christi mentio viget.' Bengel).

Chap. VI.—VIII.] The moral effects of justification. VI. 1—14.] *No encouragement given hereby* (see ch. v. 20) *to a life in sin: for the baptized are dead to sin, and walk in a new* (vv. 1—7) *life, and one* (vv. 8—11) *dedicated to God.* **1.**] **What then shall we say?** —the introduction of a difficulty or objection arising out of the preceding argument, and referring to ch. v. 20. See ch. iii. 5. **ἐπιμένωμεν**, '*must we think that we may persist*,'—the deliberative subjunctive. So εἴπωμεν ἢ σιγῶμεν, Eur. Ion 758: παρέλθω δόμους, Med. 1275. See Kühner, Gramm. § 464, and note on ch. v. 1. [**Are we to continue** ('*Must we think that we may persist*," in other words] "*May we persist*") **in** (our natural state and commission of) **sin, that** (God's) **grace may be multiplied** (ch. v. 20)? **2.**] **μὴ γέν.** (see reff.), used of some inference in itself abhorrent from reverence or piety, or precluded by some acknowledged fact inconsistent therewith. The latter is here the ground of rejection. An *acknowledged fact* in the Christian life follows, which *precludes* our persisting in our sin. **We who** (οἵτινες describing *quality*, not merely matter of fact) **died** (historic aorist, not perf. as in E. V. [the true reference is thus most unfortunately lost]: the time referred to being that of our *baptism*) **to sin** (reff. and examples in Wetst.:—became as separate from and apathetic towards sin as the dead corpse is separate from and apathetic towards the functions and stir of life: μένειν ἀκίνητον ὥσπερ τὸν νεκρόν, Chrys. '*Sin*,' τῇ ἁμ. = as above), **how shall we live any longer therein** (= περιπατεῖν ἐν—but not, as De W., ζῆν with a dative: ζῆν ἔν τινι is a further step than ζῆν τινι, implying *introition*, and not merely *sympathy*)? **3.**] **Or** (supposing you do not assent to the argument in the last verse, see reff.) **are ye ignorant** (the foregoing axiom is brought out into recognition by the further statement of a truth universally acknowledged) **that all we who were** (i. e. all of us, having been [not as E. V., again most unfortunately, "*so many of us as were*;" giving it to be understood that some of them had

ὅτι ὅσοι [b] ἐβαπτίσθημεν [b] εἰς χριστὸν Ἰησοῦν, [h] εἰς τὸν
θάνατον αὐτοῦ [b] ἐβαπτίσθημεν; 4 [c] συνετάφημεν οὖν αὐτῷ
διὰ τοῦ βαπτίσματος εἰς τὸν θάνατον, ἵνα ὥςπερ [d] ἠγέρθη
χριστὸς ἐκ [d] νεκρῶν διὰ τῆς [e] δόξης τοῦ πατρός, οὕτως
καὶ ἡμεῖς ἐν [f] καινότητι ζωῆς [g] περιπατήσωμεν. 5 εἰ γὰρ
[h] σύμφυτοι γεγόναμεν τῷ [i] ὁμοιώματι τοῦ θανάτου αὐτοῦ,

b Acts viii. 16 reff. 2 reff.
c Col. ii. 12 only †.
d 1 Cor. xv. 12 reff.
e see John xi. 40.
f ch. vii. 6 only. Ezek. xlvii. 12 only.
g = Acts xxi. 21. w. ἐν, 2 Cor. iv.
h here only ‡. Amos ix. 13. Zech. xi. 2 only.
i ch. i. 23 reff.

3. om *ιησουν* B [(a)] 31-9. 73. 109-18-20-24 lect-8 [Euthal-ms] Chr Thl [Orig-int$_3$ (ins$_4$)]: *ιησ.* bef *χριστ.* [o] 80 Syr æth.
4. om *τον* D[1]F k[1]. for *δια*, *υπο* D[1](appy).

not been thus baptized]) **baptized into Christ Jesus** (*'into participation of,' 'into union with,'* Christ, in His capacity of spiritual Mastership, Headship, and Pattern of conformity) **were baptized into** (introduced by our baptism into a state of conformity with and participation of) **His death?** The Apostle refers (1) to an acknowledged fact, in the signification, and perhaps also in the manner (see below) of baptism—that it put upon us (Gal. iii. 27) a state of conformity with and participation in Christ;—and (2) that this state involves a death *τῇ ἁμαρτίᾳ* even as He died *τῇ ἁμαρτίᾳ* (ver. 10);—the meaning being kept in the background, but all the while not lost sight of, that the *benefits of His Death* were likewise made ours by our introduction into the covenant.

4.] A further explanation of the assertion in the last verse proceeding (*οὖν*) on its concession by the reader. **We were then** (not the temporal but inferential 'then:' q. d. "You grant my last position: Well then," . . .) **buried with Him** (*καθάπερ ἔν τινι τάφῳ τῷ ὕδατι καταδυόντων ἡμῶν τὰς κεφαλὰς ὁ παλαιὸς ἄνθρωπος θάπτεται, καὶ καταδὺς κάτω κρύπτεται ὅλως καθάπαξ*, Chrys. on John iii. Hom. xxv. 2, vol. viii. p. 151) **by means of our baptism into** (His) **death** (*τοῦ βαπτ. εἰς τὸν θάνατον* belong together, not *συνετάφ. εἰς τ. θ.*, which would hardly bear any sense. The absence of the art. before *εἰς* is no objection to this;—it is unnecessary, because no distinction from any other baptism is brought out, and *τὸ βάπτ.-εἰς-τὸν-θάν.* is connected as one idea); **in order that, as Christ was raised from the dead by the glory** (*δόξα* and *δύναμις* are cognate ideas; compare the import of the Heb. עֹז and the LXX in Ps. lxviii. 35 (lxvii. 34 LXX), Isa. xii. 2: and *τὸ κράτος τῆς δόξης* in Col. i. 11. The divine *δόξα* includes all that manifests the Creator to the creature: and hence also his Almightiness. Tholuck.

The renderings '*in Dei gloriam*' (Beza, Bretschneider), and '*because He is the image of the Father*' (Dr. Burton, altern.), are inadmissible for *διά* with a gen.) **of the Father** (Theodoret makes *ἡ δόξα τοῦ πατρός* = *ἡ οἰκεία θεότης* of the Son, which is manifestly wrong), **thus we also should walk in newness of life** (not = '*a new life;*'—nor are such expressions ever to be diluted away thus: the abstract *καινότητι* is used to bring the quality of *newness*, which is the point insisted on, more into prominence, compare 2 Thess. ii. 11; 1 Tim. vi. 17 [and notes]; Winer, edn. 6, § 34. 3. The comparison is not only (as Stuart) between our Lord's *physical* death and resurrection, and our *spiritual*; but reaches far deeper: see notes on vv. 10, 11).

5.] * The Apostle confirms the last verse by a necessary sequence that *those who are united to Him in His Death, shall be also in His resurrection.* **For** (confirmatory) **if we have become united with the likeness of His Death** (*σύμφυτος* = either (1) '*congenital,*'—as *διὰ τὴν σύμφυτον δικαιοσύνην*, spoken of Samuel, Jos. Antt. vi. 3. 3,—or (2) '*cognate,*' of like nature,—or (3) '*arising simultaneously,*'—or (4) '*grown together,*'—or (5) '*planted with,*' 'consitus.' The rendering of Syr., Vulg., Luth., E. V., '*planted together,*' is inadmissible, *-φυτος* being not from *φυτεύω*, but from *φύω*: as also is that of Erasm. and Calv.,—'*insititii.*' The fourth meaning, '*grown together,*' 'intimately and progressively united,'—'coaluimus,' as Grot.,—seems here to apply best. Obs. *σύμφ.* is to be connected with *τῷ ὁμ.*, not with *τῷ χριστῷ* understood, as in ver. 6: in which case we should have to supply *τῷ ὁμοιώματι* again before *τῆς ἀναστάσεως*, which would be not only grammatically difficult, but would not correspond to the sense: for Christians, it is true, partake of the *likeness* only of Christ's *death*, but of His *actual Resurrection itself*, as the change of construction shews: see below), **so shall we be also** (*ἀλλά* after a hypothetical clause serves to strengthen the inference: see

[k] ἀλλὰ καὶ τῆς [l] ἀναστάσεως ἐσόμεθα, 6 τοῦτο γινώσκοντες, ὅτι ὁ [m] παλαιὸς ἡμῶν [m] ἄνθρωπος [n] συνεσταυρώθη,
ἵνα [o] καταργηθῇ τὸ [p] σῶμα τῆς [p] ἁμαρτίας, [q] τοῦ μηκέτι
[r] δουλεύειν ἡμᾶς τῇ ἁμαρτίᾳ· 7 ὁ γὰρ ἀποθανὼν [s] δεδι-

ABCDF KL[P]ℵ a b c d f g h k l m n o 17 [47]

k = 1 Cor. iv. 15 reff. Hom. Il. α. 81, f. l = Acts i. 22 reff. m Eph. iv. 22. Col. iii. 9. see 1 Cor. v. 7, 8. n Matt. xxvii. 44 ‖ Mk. J. Gal. ii. 20 only †. o ch. iii. 3 reff. p gen., = ch. vii. 23, 24. viii. 13. Col. ii. 11. q 1 Cor. x. 13 reff. r Matt. vi. 24. ch. vii. 6 al. Deut. xiii. 4 A Ald. s Acts xiii. 39 only. Sir. xxvi. 29.

5. for αλλα, αμα F latt. aft αναστ. ins αυτου F Syr [copt æth] arm.
6. ins και bef τουτο B : τουτο δε 179. καταργηση A æth.

reff., and Hartung, Partikellehre, ii. p. 40) **with His Resurrection** (a change of construction : because it could not well have been said σύμφυτοι τοῦ ὁμοιώματος τ. θ. above, the gen. after adjectives compounded with σύν denoting the thing actually partaken (cf. Kühner, § 519, and Bernhardy, Syntax, p. 171 : who cites examples in σύντροφος, Soph. Philoct. 203,—σύννομος, Eur. Hel. 1508,—σύμφωνος, Aristoph. Av. 658,—συμφυής, Plato Legg. iv. p. 721,—συνήθης, ib. v. p. 739,—σύμψηφος, Cratyl. p. 398), and hardly the mere figure or likeness of it,—and similarly it could not well here be said σύμφ. τῇ ἀναστάσει, because the dat. would not be strong enough to denote the state of which we shall be actual partakers. The future is used *perhaps* because of the *inference*, as a logical sequence,—'If, &c., ... A *shall* = B :'—but more probably with a deeper meaning, because the participation in His Resurrection, however partially and in the inner spiritual life, attained *here*, will only then be accomplished in our entire being, when we 'shall wake up after his likeness').

6.] **Knowing** (recollecting) **this, that our old man** (former self, personality before our new birth—opposed to καινός or νέος ἄνθρ., καινὴ κτίσις,—see Col. iii. 10; 2 Cor. v. 17; Eph. iv. 22—24,—not merely the guilt of sin, nor the power of sin, but the *man*. The idea is not Jewish, as Tholuck has shewn : the passage quoted from the Sohar-chadasch not bearing the meaning commonly given to it,—and if it did, that book itself being a production probably of the sixteenth century) **was** (at our baptism) **crucified with Him** (the great key to our text is ref. Gal. As the death of the Lord Jesus was by *crucifixion*, the Apostle uses the same expression of our death to our former sinful self, which is not only by virtue of, but also *in the likeness of*, Christ's death,—as signal, as entire, as much a death of cutting off and putting to shame and pain), **in order that** (the aim and end of the συσταυρωθῆναι) **the body of sin might be annulled** ("τὸ σῶμ. τῆς ἁμαρτ. belongs together, and τῆς ἁμαρτ. is not to be joined with καταργ. as being = ἀπὸ τῆς ἁμαρτ. (Theodoret, Wahl);—nor is τὸ σῶμ. τ. ἁμ., '*the totality of sin*' (Orig. 2, Theophyl. 1, Grot.); nor '*the substance or essence of sin*,' after the Heb. (Rabbinical) usage of עֶצֶם and גוּף (Schöttg.): nor, '*the mass of sin*' (Thol. 1);—nor a mere figure to carry out the idea of being crucified with Christ (Calov., Wolf, Reiche, Olsh., Stuart 2, al.);—nor = ἡ σάρξ τ. ἁμαρτ.; but '*the body, which belongs to or serves sin*,' in which sin rules or is manifested, = τὰ μέλη, ver. 13, in which is ὁ νόμος τῆς ἁμαρτίας, ch. vii. 23,—τὸ σῶμα τ. θανάτου, ch. vii. 24,—αἱ πράξεις τοῦ σώματος, ch. viii. 13,—τὸ σῶμα τῆς σαρκός, Col. ii. 11." De Wette: with whom agree Orig. 1, Theophyl. 2, Beza, Bengel, Meyer, Tholuck, Stuart 1, al. But as De W. further remarks, we must not understand that the body is the *seat of sin*, or at all events must not so understand those words as if the *principle of sin* lay in the *body*, which is not true, for it lies in the *will*). **καταργηθῇ, might be rendered powerless** (annulled as far as regards activity and energy. The word occurs twenty-five times in Paul's Epistles (elsewhere, Luke xiii. 7, Heb. ii. 14 only), and does not appear to signify absolute *annihilation*, but as above. Gregory of Nyssa has gone into the meaning in his discourse on 1 Cor. xv. 28, vol. i. p. 1325), **that we might no longer be in bondage** (be slaves to) **sin** (i. e. that the body should no longer be under the dominion of sin, see below, ver. 12).

7.] The difficulty of this verse arises from the Apostle having in a short and pregnant sentence expressed a whole similitude, joining, as he elsewhere does in such cases, the subject of the first limb of the comparison with the predicate of the second. Fully expressed, it would stand thus: 'For, as a man that is dead is acquitted and released from guilt and bondage (among *men* : no reference to *God's* judgment of him): so a man that has died to sin is acquitted from the guilt of sin and released from its bondage.' I express δεδικ. by this periphrasis in both cases, because I believe that all this is implied in it: 'is acquitted,' 'has his quittance,' from sin, so that Sin (personified) has no more claims on him, either as a creditor or as a master: cannot detain him for debt, nor sue him for service. A larger refer-

καίωται [s] ἀπὸ τῆς ἁμαρτίας. 8 εἰ δὲ [t] ἀπεθάνομεν σὺν
χριστῷ, [u] πιστεύομεν [u] ὅτι καὶ [v] συνζήσομεν αὐτῷ, 9 εἰδότες
ὅτι χριστὸς [w] ἐγερθεὶς ἐκ [w] νεκρῶν οὐκ ἔτι ἀποθνήσκει·
θάνατος αὐτοῦ οὐκ ἔτι [x] κυριεύει. 10 [y] ὃ γὰρ ἀπέθανεν,
τῇ [z] ἁμαρτίᾳ ἀπέθανεν [a] ἐφάπαξ· [y] ὃ δὲ ζῇ, [b] ζῇ τῷ θεῷ.
11 οὕτως καὶ ὑμεῖς [c] λογίζεσθε [d] ἑαυτοὺς [e] νεκροὺς μὲν τῇ
ἁμαρτίᾳ, [b] ζῶντας δὲ τῷ θεῷ ἐν χριστῷ Ἰησοῦ. 12 μὴ

t = 2 Cor. v. 15. u Matt. ix. 28. Mark xi. 23. Acts ix. 26 al. see Acts xv. 11 reff. v 2 Cor. vii. 3. 2 Tim. ii. 11 only †. w ver. 4. x here bis. Luke xxii. 25. ch. vii. 1. xiv. 9. 2 Cor. i. 24. 1 Tim. vi. 15 only. L.P. Gen. iii. 16. y acc. of object, Gal. ii. 20. Rev. xviii. 7. z dat., Col. iii. 23 al. a = Heb. vii. 27. ix. 12. x. 10 (1 Cor. xv. 6) only †. b = Gal. ii. 19. 1 Pet. ii. 24. c = and constr., ch. xiv. 14. Phil. iii. 13. Wisd. xv. 15. d 2nd pers., 2 Cor. vii. 11 reff. e constr., here only. see ch. vii. 8.

8. for δε, γαρ F[-gr] tol: ουν Syr. (G-lat has *autem* aut *enim*.) rec (for συνζ.) συζ., with B²CKL[P] rel: txt AB¹DFא n 17.—-ωμεν CK[P] k [Bas_1 Damasc] Thl: συνζησομεθα F. for αυτω, τω χριστω D¹F latt(not demid fuld tol [spec]) Syr Aug_1[(txt_2). 17 def.]

11. rec aft νεκρους μεν ins ειναι, with KL[P]א³ rel [vulg spec syr Orig-c(and int_2) $Chr\text{-}ed_2$ Euthal-ms] Did_1 Thdrt Hil_1 [Ambrst]: bef νεκρ. μεν, BCא¹ Damasc: om ADF 17 [Syr arm] copt æth $Chr\text{-}ms_1$ $Tert_1$. rec at end adds τω κυριω ημων, with CKL[P]א rel [vulg-clem arm] Syr(but pref to χρ. ιησ.) copt Chr_1 Thl [Did_1 $Orig\text{-}int_1$] Ambrst: om ABD F[(but a space is left) spec am fuld] demid flor harl tol æth syr Bas_2 Cyr[-p_1] Thdrt Thl-comm Œc-comm $Tert_2$ Hil_1 $Aug_{[sæpe]}$ Pelag Sedul Bede.

ence is thus given to δεδικ. than the purposes of the present argument, which is treating of the power, not the guilt of sin, required: but that it is so, lies in the nature of ἁμαρτία, the service of which *is guilt*, and the deliverance from whose service necessarily brings with it *acquittal*.

8—11.] *This new life must be one dedicated to God.* 8.] **Now** (continuing the train of argument) **if we died with Christ, we believe that we shall also** (the future as in ver. 5,—because the life with Him though here begun, is not here completed: and the πιστεύομεν used more of *dogmatic belief*, than of *trust*, though the latter meaning is not altogether absent) **live with Him.**

9.] This and the following verse explain what sort of a life with Christ is meant, by what we know of the Resurrection-life of Christ himself. The only difficulty here is in **οὐκ ἔτι κυριεύει**, as implying that Death *had* dominion over Christ, which we know it *had not:* see John x. 17, 18; ii. 19; Acts ii. 24. But this vanishes, when we remember that our Lord, by submitting to Death, virtually, and in the act of death, surrendered Himself into the power of Death. Death could not hold Him, and had no power over Him further than by his own sufferance: but power over Him it *had*, inasmuch as *He died.* 10.] **For** (the proof of the foregoing) **the death which He died** (not '*in that He died*,' as E. V., nor is ὅ for καθ' ὅ, either here or in ref. Gal., but the accus. objective, governed by the verb. So also of ὃ δὲ ζῇ below), **unto sin He died** (De Wette well remarks that we must in *expressing* this verse abide by the *indefinite* reference to sin in which the death of Christ is placed; if we attempt to make it more definite, '*for sin*,' or '*to that state, in which He suffered the punishment of sin*,' we shall lose the point of comparison, which lies in '*to sin*,' and '*to God*.' If we are to *expand* the words '*died to sin*,' we must say that our Lord at death passed into a state in which He had '*no more to do with sin*'—either as *tempting* Him (though in vain), or as *requiring to be atoned for* (this having been now effected), or as *met by Him* in daily contradiction which He endured from sinners) **once for all** (so that it is not to be repeated: see reff.); **but the life which He liveth** (see above) **He liveth unto God** (indefinite again, but easily filled up and explained: *to God*,—as being glorified by and with the Father, as entirely rid of conflict with sin and death, and having only God's (properly so called) work to do,—as waiting till, in the purposes of the Father, all things are put under Him:—and *to* (for) *God*, as being the manifestation and brightness of the Father's glory). 11.] *An exhortation to realize this state of death unto sin and life unto God with Christ.* **Thus** (after the same manner as Christ) **do ye also** (imperative: Meyer only holds it to be indic.) **account yourselves** (better than '*infer yourselves to be*,' as Chrys. and Beza,—see reff. and on ch. iii. 28) **dead** (indeed) **unto sin** (as ver. 2 and following), **but alive unto God in Christ Jesus** (i. e. '*by virtue of your union with Him:*' not *through* (διά) Christ Jesus; in this chapter it is not Christ's *Mediator-*

f = ch. v. 14 reff.
g ch. viii. 11. 1 Cor. xv. 53, 54. 2 Cor. iv. 11. v. 4 only. Job xxx. 23.
h ch. iv. 11 reff.
i ch. i. 24 reff.
k = here &c. (5 times). Luke ii. 22. ch. xii. 1. Ps. v. 3.
l Paul (here bis. ver. 19 bis. 1 Cor. vi. 15 [3ce] al22.) only, exc. Matt. v. 29, 30. James iii. 5, 6. iv. 1. Exod. xxix. 17 al.
m here bis. John xviii. 3. ch. xiii. 12. 2 Cor. vi. 7. x. 4 only. Jer. xxi. 4.
n ver. 11.
o 1 Cor. ix. 20 reff.

οὖν [f] βασιλευέτω ἡ ἁμαρτία ἐν τῷ [g] θνητῷ ὑμῶν σώματι, ABCDF
[h] εἰς τὸ ὑπακούειν ταῖς [i] ἐπιθυμίαις αὐτοῦ. 13 μηδὲ KL[P]ℵ
[k] παριστάνετε τὰ [l] μέλη ὑμῶν [m] ὅπλα ἀδικίας τῇ ἁμαρτίᾳ, a b c d f
ἀλλὰ [k] παραστήσατε [n] ἑαυτοὺς τῷ θεῷ ὡσεὶ ἐκ νεκρῶν g h k l
ζῶντας, καὶ τὰ [l] μέλη ὑμῶν [m] ὅπλα δικαιοσύνης τῷ θεῷ. m n o 17
14 ἁμαρτία γὰρ ὑμῶν οὐ [x] κυριεύσει· οὐ γάρ ἐστε [o] ὑπὸ [47]
νόμον, ἀλλὰ [o] ὑπὸ χάριν.

12. επακουειν F [Meth-ms$_1$]. rec αυτῃ εν ταις επιθ. αυτου (*appy a combination of the two readings*), with C^{3}KL[P] rel syr [Bas$_2$ Euthal-ms] Chr$_1$ Thdrt Thl Œc: αυτῃ, omg the rest, DF spec Iren-int$_1$ [Orig-int$_1$] Tert$_1$ Vict-tun$_1$: txt ABC^{1}ℵ [47] vulg (not F-lat) D^2-lat Syr coptt æth arm Orig$_2$[int$_3$] Epiph$_1$ Antch$_1$ Damasc Jer Aug$_{[sæpe]}$ Sedul Bede.

13. rec (for ωσει) ως, with DFKL[P] 17 rel [Bas$_2$] Chr$_1$ Thdrt Thl Œc: txt ABCℵ [47] Epiph$_1$ Damasc. ζωντες D^{1}F. om τα (bef 2nd μελη) B.

14. for 1st ου, ουκετι ℵ^1(marked for erasure by ℵ^3 but the marks erased) [K Orig-c$_1$ Thdrt]. (αλλα, so BCD^{1}Fℵ^1.)

ship, but His *Headship*, which is prominent.—ἐν χρ. Ἰησ., is not (Reiche, Meyer, Fritz.) to be joined with both νεκρ. τῇ ἁμ. and ζῶν. τ. θ., but only with the latter, next to which it stands, and of which it is literally and positively, whereas of the other it is only figuratively (τῷ ὁμοιώμ., ver. 5) and negatively true).

12, 13.] *Hortatory inferences from ver.* 11: *from* μή *to* τῇ ἁμαρτίᾳ, *negative, answering to* νεκροὺς τῇ ἁμ.,—*then positive, answering to* ζῶντας τῷ θεῷ.

12.] **βασιλευέτω** answers to the imagery throughout, in which Sin is a master or lord. It is hardly right to lay a stress on it, and say (as Chrys.) οὐκ εἶπε μὴ οὖν ζήτω ἡ σὰρξ μηδὲ ἐνεργείτω, ἀλλ', ἡ ἁμαρτία μὴ **βασιλευέτω.** οὐ γὰρ τὴν φύσιν ἦλθεν ἀνελεῖν, ἀλλὰ τὴν προαίρεσιν διορθῶσαι: it is no matter of comparison between *reigning* and *indwelling merely*, but between *reigning* and *being deposed*.

But why τῷ **θνητῷ** ὑμ. σώματι? Orig., al., explain it '*dead to sin*,' which it clearly cannot be. Chrys., Theodoret, Grot., and Reiche suppose the word inserted to remind us of *the other life*, and the shortness of the conflict, or (Theophyl.) of the shortness of sinful pleasures; Köllner,—to point out that it is dishonourable to us to serve Sin, whose reign is confined to the *mortal* body; Fritzsche, 'quoniam, qui peccato ministrum se præbet, adhuc in *mortali* corpore hærere nec nisi fragilis vitæ meminisse videtur;' De Wette, Tholuck, al., that the Apostle, wishes to keep in view the connexion between *sin and death* on the one hand, and *that* συνζῆν *which is freed from death* on the other. This last view seems the most probable. See 2 Cor. iv. 11 and note. There is considerable uncertainty in the reading of the latter part of this verse. That which I have adopted is supported by the primary MSS. and has the approval of Lachmann, Tischendorf, Meyer, and De Wette.

13.] **Nor render** (see reff.;—as a soldier renders his service to his sovereign, or a servant to his master) **your members** (more particular than 'your bodies;' the individual members being instruments of different lusts and sins) **as instruments** (or, '*weapons*,' as Vulg., most of the Greek expositors, and Luth., Calv., Beza, Tholuck, which latter defends this rendering by Paul's fondness for military similitudes, and by the occurrence of ὀψώνια below, ver. 23;—but as De W. observes, the comparison here is to *servitude* rather than *soldiership*) **of unrighteousness to sin; but render** (the *present* imperat. above denotes habit,—the exhortation guards against the recurrence of a devotion of the members to sin: this *aorist* imperat., on the other hand, as in ch. xii. 1, denotes an *act* of self-devotion to God once for all, not a mere recurrence of the habit) **yourselves** (not merely *your members*, but your whole selves, body, soul, and spirit) **to God, as alive from having been dead** (as in vv. 4 ff. and Eph. ii. 1—5), **and your members as instruments** (see above) **of righteousness to God** (dat. '*commodi*,' as indeed is τῇ ἁμαρτ. above, the dat. after παριστ. being there left to be supplied, because of τῇ ἁμ. following).

14.] An assurance, confirming (by the γάρ) the *possibility of the surrender to God* commanded in the last verse, *that sin shall not be able to assert and maintain its rule in those who are not under the law but under grace.* The future κυριεύσει cannot be taken as a

15 [p] Τί οὖν; ἁμαρτήσωμεν, ὅτι οὐκ ἐσμὲν [o] ὑπὸ νόμον p ch. iii. 9. xi. 7.
ἀλλὰ [o] ὑπὸ χάριν; [q] μὴ γένοιτο. 16 οὐκ οἴδατε ὅτι ᾧ q ch. iii. 4 reff.
[k] παριστάνετε [h] ἑαυτοὺς δούλους [r] εἰς [s] ὑπακοήν, δοῦλοί ἐστε r ch. v. 16 reff. s ch. i. 5 reff.
[t] ᾧ ὑπακούετε, ἤτοι ἁμαρτίας [r] εἰς θάνατον ἢ [s] ὑπακοῆς t constr., Matt. xix. 11. xx. 24.

15. rec *αμαρτησομεν*, with rel Chr$_1$ Thdrt$_1$ [Damasc] Thl Œc: *ημαρτησαμεν* F, *peccavimus* am [fuld] harl D^3-lat G-lat: txt ABCDKL[P]א c m n 17 [47 Euthal-ms] Clem$_1$. (*αλλα*, so BCFא^1 [Damasc].)
16. ins *η* bef *ουκ* D^{1}F demid flor harl^1 sah Sedul. om *εις θανατον* DE [am] Syr sah arm-zoh(1805) [Orig-int$_1$] Aug.

command or exhortation, which use of the future would if not always, yet certainly here, require the second person,—and would hardly suit a personification like *ἁμαρτία*. The second part of the verse refers back to ch. v. 20, 21, where the law is stated to be the multiplier of transgression,—and accords with 1 Cor. xv. 56, *ἡ δύναμις τῆς ἁμαρτίας, ὁ νόμος*. The stress is on **κυριεύσει**: q. d. 'Your efforts to live a life of freedom from the tyranny of sin shall not be frustrated by its after all tyrannizing over you and asserting its dominion: for ye are not under that law which is the strength of sin, but under that grace (here in the widest sense, justifying and sanctifying,—grace in all its attributes and workings) in which is no condemnation,' ch. viii. 1. It will be seen from the above, that I interpret *κυριεύσει* rather of the *eventual* triumph of sin by obtaining domination over us, than of its reducing us under its subjection as servants in this life. This is necessary, both to fit this verse into the context, and to suit the question which arises in the next. See Calvin's masterly note. So also Tholuck and De Wette.

The discussions (in Stuart and al.) as to whether *νόμ.* is the moral or ceremonial law, and as to whether we are bound by the former, are irrelevant here: the assertion being merely that of the general *matter of fact*, about which there can be no question, that we (Christians) are not *under the law*, placed in a covenant of legal obedience, but under grace,—placed in a covenant of justification by faith and under the promise of the indwelling Spirit—subjects of a *higher law*—even the *law of the spirit of life in Christ Jesus*, ch. viii. 2. Whether we are *bound* by the law, and how far, depends on how far the law itself spoke the immutable moral truth of God's government of the world, or was adapted to temporary observances and symbolic rites now abolished,—the whole of which subject is not under consideration here. I make these remarks to justify myself for not entering into those long and irrelevant discussions with which many of our commentaries are interrupted, and the sense of the Apostle's argument confounded. **15—23.**] *The being under grace* (free from the condemnation of sin) *and not under the law, is no encouragement to sin: for* (vv. 16—19) *we have renounced the service of sin, and have become the servants of righteousness: and* (vv. 20—23) *the consequences of the service of sin are terrible and fatal, whereas those of the service of righteousness are blessed and glorious.* **15.**] **τί οὖν** (sc. *ἐστίν*); = *τί οὖν ἐροῦμεν;* ver. 1. **ἁμαρτήσωμεν**] *Must we imagine that we may sin?* **may we sin?**—the aor. because he is speaking of *committing acts of sin* [not of a habit of living in sin, although that would be induced by such acts]: on the deliberative subjunctive, see ver. 1. This question is not, any more than that of ver. 1, put into the mouth of an objector, but is part of the Apostle's own discourse, arising out of what has preceded, and answered by him in the following verses. **16.**] 'You are the servants either of God or of sin,—there is no third course.' The former part of the verse as far as *ὑπακούετε* reminds them merely of an universal truth,—that the yielding ourselves servants for obedience to any one, implies the *serving*, being (in reality) the servants of such person. Then this is applied in the form of a dilemma, implying that there is no third service, q. d. 'Now this must be true of you *with regard either to sin or to God.*' **Know ye not, that to whom ye yield yourselves servants with a view to obedience, his servants ye are to whom ye obey,** (and in this case) **either** (*ἤτοι—ἤ* only occurs here in N. T. *ἤτοι* in alternatives is exclusive, cf. Herod. i. 11, *δίδωμι αἵρεσιν, ὁκοτέρην βούλεαι τραπέσθαι . . .* **ἤτοι** *κεῖνόν γε τὸν ταῦτα βουλεύσαντα δεῖ ἀπόλλυσθαι,* **ἢ** *σὲ τὸν ἐμὲ . . . .* Isocr. *ἀντιδ.* p. 317, *ἦλθεν ἂν ἤτοι κατηγορήσων ἢ καταμαρτυρήσων*, and see Hartung, Partikellehre, ii. 355 f.) (**servants**) **of sin, unto death** ('with death as the result,'—not physical death merely, nor eternal death merely, but DEATH (by sin) in its most general sense, as the contrast to (life by) RIGHTEOUSNESS,—the state of misery

[r] εἰς δικαιοσύνην; 17 [u] χάρις δὲ τῷ θεῷ, ὅτι ἦτε δοῦλοι
τῆς ἁμαρτίας, ὑπηκούσατε δὲ [v] ἐκ καρδίας [w] εἰς ὃν
[v] παρεδόθητε [x] τύπον [y] διδαχῆς, 18 [z] ἐλευθερωθέντες δὲ
ἀπὸ τῆς ἁμαρτίας [a] ἐδουλώθητε τῇ δικαιοσύνῃ. 19 [b] ἀνθρώπινον λέγω διὰ τὴν [c] ἀσθένειαν τῆς σαρκὸς ὑμῶν.
ὥσπερ γὰρ [d] παρεστήσατε τὰ [d] μέλη ὑμῶν [e] δοῦλα τῇ
[f] ἀκαθαρσίᾳ καὶ τῇ [g] ἀνομίᾳ [h] εἰς τὴν [g] ἀνομίαν, οὕτως

ABCDF KL[P]א abcdf ghkl mno 17 [47]

u = ch. vii. 25. 1 Cor. xv. 57. 2 Cor. ii. 14. viii. 16. ix. 15.
v Mark xii. 30, 33. Luke x. 27. 1 Tim. i. 5. 2 Tim. ii. 22. 1 Pet. i. 22. Deut. iv. 29.
w constr., ch. i. 24. see note.
x Acts xxiii. 25. 3 Macc. iii. 30.
y Acts ii. 42 reff.
z John viii. 32, 36. ver. 22. ch. viii. 2, 21. Gal. v. 1 only +. Sir. l. 21 Ald. 2 Macc. i. 27. ii. 22 only.
a Acts vii. 6 reff.
b Acts xvii. 25 reff. see ch. iii. 5.
c 1 Cor. ii. 3 reff.
d ver. 13.
e adj. here bis only. Wisd. xv. 7. Eur. Hec. 137.
f ch. i. 24 reff.
g ch. iv. 7 reff.
h ch. v. 16 reff. Acts xi. 18 reff.

17. ins καθαρας bef καρδιας A 13. 26 Chr_1-mss($txt_{h.\,l.}$), *ex toto corde* æth.
18. for δε, ουν Cא[1] [arm]: om m 39. 62 lect-12 tol (copt).
19. for δουλα (twice), δουλευειν F latt [$Orig\text{-}int_4$ Ambrst]. om εις την ανομιαν B Syr Sedul.

induced by sin, in all its awful aspects and consequences:—and so throughout this passage and ch. vii.), **or of obedience** (τοῦ θεοῦ, sc.—obedience to Him who alone ought to be obeyed) **unto righteousness** (with righteousness as its result; not imputed merely, nor implanted merely, but RIGHTEOUSNESS in its most general sense as the contrast to *death,*—the state of blessedness induced by holiness, and involving in it, as a less in a greater, *eternal life:* and so throughout this passage)? 17, 18.] The dilemma solved for them by reference to the matter of fact: *that they were once servants of sin, but on receiving the gospel, obeyed its teaching: and consequently were freed from the service of sin, and became the servants of righteousness:*—and this in the form of a thanksgiving to God (1 Cor. i. 14) whose work in them it was. There is a stress on **ἦτε** as referring to a state *past.* So Eph. v. 8: on account of which stress apparently the μέν, which would naturally follow it, is omitted. **17. ὑπ. . . . . διδαχῆς**] Attr.: the simple construction would be ὑπηκούσατε τῷ τύπῳ τῆς διδ. εἰς ὃν (or ὃν) παρεδόθητε, **ye obeyed** (ὑπ. on account of ὑπακοή above) **from the heart** (reff.) **that form of teaching** (so μόρφωσις ch. ii. 20: see examples in Fritzsche, vol. i. p. 418; most probably used of the practical *norma agendi* accompanying the doctrine of the gospel; so Calv., Luth., Beza, Reiche:—De W. thinks it is the Pauline form of teaching, of justification by faith, distinguished from the Judaistic) **to which ye were delivered** ([not as E. V., '*which was delivered you*'] this inversion to the passive agrees admirably with τύπος, as a mould, exemplar, or pattern after which they were to be fashioned: so κατὰ τὰ δόγματα τυποῦσθαι, Arrian. Enchir. ii. 19 (Thol.): and Beza,—'hoc dicendi genus magnam quandam emphasin videtur habere. Ita enim significatur evangelicam doctrinam quasi instar typi cujusdam esse, cui veluti immittamur, ut ejus figuræ conformemur, et totam istam transformationem aliunde provenire.' (Thol.) And Chrys. remarks, τὸ παραδοθῆναι, τὴν τοῦ θεοῦ βοηθείαν αἰνίττεται. See on the construction, Winer, edn. 6, § 24. 2. b).

18. ἐλευθ. . . . . δικαιοσ.] **And** (this verse is closely united with the foregoing; Rückert, Reiche, and Meyer think that it might be stated as a syllogistic conclusion, of which the dilemma is the major, and the *fact* of ver. 17 the minor) **being freed from sin, ye were enslaved** (see on next verse) **to righteousness.** **19.**] For the expression **ἐδουλώθητε** the Apostle apologizes: 'it is not literally so; the servant of righteousness is *no slave,* under no yoke of bondage; but in order to set the contrast between the former and the new state better before you, I have used this word:' **I speak as a man** (according to the requirements of rhetorical antithesis) **on account of the** (intellectual, as De W. and Thol.: not moral, as Meyer and Olsh.) **weakness of your flesh** (i. e. 'because you are σαρκικοί and not πνευματικοί, and want such figures to set the truth before you.' Orig., Chrys., Theodoret, Calv., Estius, Wetst., al., take these words in a totally different sense: '*I require of you nothing which your fleshly weakness will not bear*'): **for** (explanatory of ἐδουλώθ.) **like as ye** (once) **rendered up your members** (as) **servants to impurity and to lawlessness** (two divisions of ἁμαρτία—impurity, against a man's self,—lawlessness against God), **unto lawlessness** (both which, ἀκαθ. and ἀνομ., *lead to* ἀνομία, *result* in it: 'qui justitiæ serviunt, *proficiunt:* ἄνομοι, iniqui, sunt *iniqui, nihil amplius.*' Bengel: not '*from one* ἀνομία *to another,*' as Œcum., Theophyl., Luth., Grot., Erasm.,

νῦν [d] παραστήσατε τὰ [d] μέλη ὑμῶν [e] δοῦλα τῇ δικαιοσύνῃ
[h] εἰς [i] ἁγιασμόν. 20 ὅτε γὰρ δοῦλοι ἦτε τῆς ἁμαρτίας,
ἐλεύθεροι ἦτε τῇ [k] δικαιοσύνῃ. 21 τίνα οὖν [l] καρπὸν
[l] εἴχετε τότε; [m] ἐφ᾽ οἷς νῦν [n] ἐπαισχύνεσθε, τὸ μὲν γὰρ
[o] τέλος ἐκείνων θάνατος. 22 νυνὶ δὲ [p] ἐλευθερωθέντες [p] ἀπὸ
τῆς [p] ἁμαρτίας, [p] δουλωθέντες δὲ τῷ θεῷ, [l] ἔχετε τὸν
[l] καρπὸν ὑμῶν [h] εἰς [i] ἁγιασμόν, τὸ δὲ [o] τέλος ζωὴν αἰώνιον, 23 τὰ γὰρ [q] ὀψώνια τῆς ἁμαρτίας θάνατος, τὸ
δὲ [r] χάρισμα τοῦ θεοῦ ζωὴ αἰώνιος ἐν χριστῷ Ἰησοῦ

i Paul (here bis. ver. 22. 1 Cor. i. 30 al5.) only, exc. Heb. xii. 14. 1 Pet. i. 2. 2 Macc. xiv. 36.
k dat., ver. 2 reff. 1 Cor. xiv. 20.
l ch. i. 13 reff.
m = Luke ii. 47. Acts iii. 10, 12. iv. 21. Jer. ii. 12.
n ch. i. 16 reff.
o = 2 Cor. xi. 15. Phil. iii. 19. Heb. vi. 8. 1 Pet. iv. 17. Wisd. iii. 19.
p ver. 18.
q Luke iii. 14. 1 Cor. ix. 7. 2 Cor. xi. 8 only†. Esdr. iv. 56. 1 Macc. iii. 28. xiv. 32 only.
r = ch. v. 15, 16. xi. 29.

aft *ουτως* ins *και* K 7 tol Syr [coptt] arm $Tert_2$ Sedul. for 2nd *δουλα*, *οπλα* A.

21. [*ποτε* D¹-gr(appy).] rec om *μεν*, with ACD³KL[P]א¹ rel [vulg copt arm] $Clem_1$ Chr_1 Thl Œc [Damasc $Orig\text{-}int_2$ $Tert_1$ Ambrst]: ins BD¹Fא³ syr Chr-mss Thdrt. at end ins *εστιν* F latt(not fuld) [$Orig\text{-}int_2$].

22. for *δε*, *τε*(but corrd) א¹.

[**23.** om *τα γαρ* to *αιωνιος* (*passing from αιων. to αιων.*) P.]

al.: because (De W.) *ἀνομία* is not an *act*, but a principle), **so now render up your members** (as) **servants to righteousness** (see ver. 16) **unto** (leading to, having as its result, perfect) **sanctification** (contrast to *ἀνομία*, and both embracing their respective consequences). **20—23.**] As a *further urging of the above exhortations*, the Apostle *contrasts* the *end* of *their former life* with that of their *present*. **20.**] **γάρ** introduces a *motive* for the foregoing: but the verse [properly] belongs to the *following*: for ver. 22 is the contrast to it. Meyer and Fritz. think it to be an explanation of ver. 19, but are certainly mistaken. **For when ye were servants of sin, ye were free in relation to** (dat. of regard or reference, Winer, edn. 6, § 31. 1) **righteousness.** There is doubtless a latent irony in the use of **ἐλεύθεροι** here; but it must not be brought out too strongly: it does not appear, till the *end* of that freedom is declared.
21.] '*Well, then, ye were free: and what was the benefit?*' *οὖν* concedes and assumes.
There are two ways of pointing: (1) that of E. V., carrying on the question to *ἐπαισχύνεσθε*, and supplying *ἐπ᾽ ἐκείνοις* before *ἐφ᾽ οἷς*, adopted by Chrys., Œc., Vulg., Beza, Grot., Estius, Bengel, Reiche, Meyer, Fritz., Stuart, al. But this though good as far as construction is concerned, is inconsistent with the N. T. meaning of *καρπός*, which is '*actions,*' the *fruit of the man* considered as the tree, not '*wages,*' or '*reward,*' the *fruit of his actions*: see below, ver. 22, and ch. i. 13, note. So even Phil. i. 22 (see note).
So that I much prefer (2) the punctuation of Theod. Mops., Theodoret, Theophyl., Luth., Melancth., Koppe, Flatt, Tholuck, Rückert, Köllner, Olsh., Lachm., Griesb., De Wette, al., placing the interrogation at *τότε*, and making *ἐφ᾽ οἷς ν. ἐπαισχ.* the answer. **What fruit then had ye at that time? (Things, deeds) of which ye are now ashamed. τὸ μὲν γὰρ τέλ. ἐκ. θ.**] *the reason of their present shame.* **For the end** (= virtually *ὀψώνια*, ver. 23, and would be a mere repetition of *καρπός* on the first method of punctuation above) **of those things** (those *καρποί* consisting of sinful acts) **is death** (death in the widest sense, see note on ver. 16,—physical, which has been the end of sin, in which we are all involved,—and spiritual and eternal, which will be the end of actual sin if followed out). **22.**] Contrast of your present state to that former one: **freedom from sin as a master,—servitude** (compare *ἀνθρώπινον λέγω*, ver. 19) **to God** (a higher description than merely *δικαιοσύνη*, the actual antithesis to *ἁμαρτία*, ver. 18. *The devil* would be the corresponding antithetical power: and not unfrequently appears in the teaching of Paul: but usually in casual expressions, as Eph. iv. 27; vi. 11; 2 Tim. ii. 26, not as the principal figure in a course of argument),—**fruit** (see on *καρπός*, above, ver. 21,—and remark *τὸν καρπόν, your fruit,* fruit actually brought forth, q. d. *ἔχετε καρπόν, καὶ ὁ καρπὸς ὑμῶν ἁγιασμός*) **unto** (leading unto perfect) **sanctification,—and the end** (governed by *ἔχετε*) **life everlasting. 23.**] The *ends* of the two courses placed pointedly and antithetically, and the inherent difference, that whereas **death** (see above) is the **wages** (*ὀψ.* = pay, or ration, of soldiers; compare the similitude in ver. 13, and remarks there) **of sin, earned and paid**

m ch. vi. 3 (reff.). n ch. vi. 9, 14 reff. o generic sing., Matt. xix. 10. Mark ii. 27 al. p 1 Cor. vii. 39. Gal. iv. 1. see 2 Pet. i. 13. Deut. xii. 19. q here only. Num. v. 29. Prov. vi. 24, 29. Sir. ix. 9. xli. 21 only.

ABCDF KL[P]א a b c d f g h k l m n o 17 [47]

τῷ κυρίῳ ἡμῶν. VII. 1 m Ἢ m ἀγνοεῖτε, ἀδελφοί, γινώσκουσιν γὰρ νόμον λαλῶ, m ὅτι ὁ νόμος n κυριεύει o τοῦ
ἀνθρώπου p ἐφ' p ὅσον p χρόνον ζῇ; 2 ἡ γὰρ q ὕπανδρος
γυνὴ τῷ ζῶντι ἀνδρὶ r δέδεται νόμῳ· ἐὰν δὲ ἀποθάνῃ ὁ
ἀνήρ, st κατήργηται tu ἀπὸ τοῦ νόμου v τοῦ ἀνδρός. 3 w ἄρα
w οὖν ζῶντος τοῦ ἀνδρὸς x μοιχαλὶς y χρηματίσει, ἐὰν
za γένηται ἀνδρὶ ab ἑτέρῳ· ἐὰν δὲ ἀποθάνῃ ὁ ἀνήρ, ἐλευθέρα

r = 1 Cor. vii. 27, 39. s ch. iii. 3 reff. t ver. 6. Gal. v. 4. u = ch. vi. 18, 22. 2 Cor. xi. 3. v gen. of reference, Mark i. 4. John v. 29 bis. 2 Cor. ix. 13 al. Winer, edn. 6, § 30. 2. β. w ch. v. 18 reff. x here bis. Matt. xii. 39. xvi. 4 || Mk. James iv. 4. 2 Pet. ii. 14 only. Ezek. xvi. 38 al. y = Acts xi. 26 only. ἐχρημάτιζε βασιλεύς, Diod. Sic. xx. 53. z = here 3ce only. Levit. xxii. 12. a Deut. xxiv. 2 (4). Jer. iii. 1. b ver. 23 reff.

CHAP. VII. 1. γιγνωσκουσιν L. 2. om 2nd του F(but not G). 3. aft ζωντος, add $\overline{\chi\rho}$ G. χρημ. bef μοιχ. DF latt goth [copt Orig-int$_2$]. add η γυνη A copt Orig$_1$[om$_3$(and int$_1$)] Chr$_1$[om$_1$]. aft ο ανηρ ins αυτης DF [d] Syr.

down,—**eternal life is** no ὀψώνιον, nothing earned, but **the free gift of God** to His soldiers and servants;—and that **in** (not 'through,'—*true* enough, but not implied in ἐν, see above on ver. 11) **Christ Jesus our Lord.** VII. 1—6.] The explanation and proof of the assertion ch. vi. 14, οὐ γάρ ἐστε ὑπὸ νόμον, ἀλλὰ ὑπὸ χάριν: the answer to the question of vi. 15 having occupied vi. 16—23. 1—4.] *The Christian is dead to the law by being dead with Christ, and has become His.* 1.] Connect with ch. vi. 14, which is in fact the sentence immediately preceding. Reiche and Meyer connect with vi. 23; 'The gift of God is eternal life in Jesus Christ our Lord: this you can only doubt by being ignorant,' &c. Krehl believes ch. vii. to be the expansion of 'Death is the wages of sin,'—and ch. viii., of 'the free gift of God is eternal life.' But not only does this division not hold, for much of ch. viii. regards the conflict with sin and infirmity,—but the prominence of νόμος as the subject here forbids the connexion with ὀψώνια τῆς ἁμαρτ. θάνατος. The steps of the proof are these: *The law binds a man only so long as he lives* (ver. 1):—e. g. a married woman is only bound to her husband so long as he lives (vv. 2, 3):—so also the Christian *being dead* with Christ and alive to Him *is freed from the law* (ver. 4). **ἀδελφοί**] Not addressed particularly to *Jewish* Christians: see below: but generally to the Roman church. **γινώσκουσιν γ. νόμ. λαλ.**] **For I am speaking** (writing) **to men acquainted with the law**; i. e. the persons to whom I address this epistle are such as know the law: not 'I speak to *those who know* the law,' as if he were now addressing a different class of persons,—which would require τοῖς γὰρ γινώσκουσιν τὸν νόμον τοῦτό φημι, see Gal. iv. 21. Nor does the knowledge of the law here affirmed of the Romans prove that the majority of them were Jewish Christians: they may have been Gentile proselytes. **ὅτι ὁ νόμ. κυρ. τοῦ ἀνθρ. . . . .**] **that the** (Mosaic: for of that, and not of any other law, is the whole argument) **law hath power over a man** (not ὁ νόμ. τοῦ ἀνθρώπου, 'a man's law,' and κυριεύει absolute, 'has dominion,'—as Hamm. and Dr. Burton, which is very questionable Greek and still worse sense) **as long time as he** (the man, see vv. 4 and 6:—not *the law*, as Origen, Erasm., Grot., Estius, al., which would introduce the irrelevant question of the *abrogation of the law*, whereas the whole matter in argument is the *relation of the Christian* to the law) **lives.** 2.] **For** (not merely = e. g., but, as Thol., the example is itself the proof) **the married** (ref.) **woman is bound by the law to the living husband: but if the husband die, she is set free from** (lit. annulled from) **the law of** ('*regarding*,' compare reff. and ὁ νόμος τοῦ λεπροῦ, Levit. xiv. 2) **the husband** (no hypallage). 3.] **And accordingly** (ἄρα οὖν, '*from the same consideration, it follows that*') **while her husband lives she shall be called** (see ref.:—and on this use of the future, as declaring what shall follow on a condition being fulfilled, Winer, edn. 6, § 40. 6) **an adulteress, if she attach herself to** (become the wife of) **another man: but if her husband die, she is free from the law** (τοῦ ἀνδρός), so that (it matters little whether τοῦ μή is the *result* or the *purpose*: it is better always to keep the latter in view, and to regard the result in such sentences as for the moment spoken of as the purpose to which its constituents contributed) **she is not an adulteress,**

ἐστὶν [u] ἀπὸ τοῦ νόμου, [c] τοῦ μὴ εἶναι αὐτὴν [x] μοιχαλίδα
[za] γενομένην ἀνδρὶ [ab] ἑτέρῳ. 4 ὥςτε ἀδελφοί μου, καὶ ὑμεῖς
[d] ἐθανατώθητε [e] τῷ νόμῳ διὰ τοῦ σώματος τοῦ χριστοῦ, εἰς
τὸ [za] γενέσθαι ὑμᾶς [ab] ἑτέρῳ, τῷ [f] ἐκ νεκρῶν [f] ἐγερθέντι, ἵνα
[g] καρποφορήσωμεν τῷ θεῷ. 5 ὅτε γὰρ ἦμεν ἐν τῇ [h] σαρκί,

c 1 Cor. x. 13 reff.
d Matt. x. 21 al5. in Gospp. ch. viii. 13, 36 (from Ps. xliii. 22). 2 Cor. vi. 9. 1 Pet. iii. 18. 2 Chron. xxiii. 15.
e dat., ch. vi. 10, 11.
f 1 Cor. xv. 12 reff.
g here bis. Matt. xiii. 23 ||. Mark iv. 28. Col. i. 6, 10 only. Hab. iii. 17. Wisd. x. 7 only. (-ρος, Acts xiv. 17.)
h = ch. viii. 12 al. see note.

4. *και υμεις* bef *αδελφοι μου* ℵ [goth arm Damasc]. *μοι* F. *καρποφορεσωμεν* and -*φορεσαι* in ver 5 F.
5. *ημην* D[1][-gr]. om 1st *εν* F[-gr].

though she have attached herself to another man. So far all is clear. But when we come to the application of the example, *this* must carefully be borne in mind, as tending to clear up all the confusion which has here been found by Commentators:—that the Apostle is insisting on the fact, that DEATH DISSOLVES LEGAL OBLIGATION: but he is not drawing an exact parallel between the persons in his example, and the persons in his application. The comparison might be thus made in terms common to both: (1) *Death has dissolved the legal obligation between man and wife: therefore the wife is at liberty to be married to another:*—(2) *Death has dissolved the legal obligation between the law and us: therefore we are at liberty to be married to another.* So far the comparison is strict. Further it will not hold: for in the *example*, the *liberated person* is the *survivor*,—in the *thing treated*, the *liberated person* is the *dead person*. And so far from this being an oversight or an inaccuracy, it is no more than that to which, more or less, all comparisons are liable; and no more can be required of them than that they should fit, in the kernel and intent of the similitude. If it be required here to apply the example further, there is no difficulty nor inconsistency in saying (as Chrys. al.) that our first Husband was the Law, and our second is Christ; but then it must be carefully borne in mind, that we are freed, not by *the law having died to us*, (which matter here is not treated,) but by *our having died to the law*. It is not necessary with Calv. and Tholuck, to suppose that in ver. 4 there is an euphemistic inversion, 'we are dead to the law,' instead of 'the law is dead to us;' indeed such a supposition would, from what is said above, much weaken the argument, which rests on our *being slain with Christ*, and so *freed from the law*. 4.] **So then** (inference both from ver. 1, the general fact, and vv. 2, 3, the example), **my brethren, ye also** (as well as the woman in my example, who is dead to the law of her husband) **were slain to the law** (*crucified*, see Gal. ii. 19, 20. The *more violent word* is used instead of ἀπεθάνετε, to recall the violent death of Christ, in which, and after the manner of which, believers have been put to death to the law and sin,—and the *historic aorist* to remind them of the great Event by which this was brought about) **by means of the** (crucified) **Body** (compare διὰ τῆς προσφορᾶς τοῦ σώματος τοῦ Ἰησ. χρ., Heb. x. 10) **of Christ, that you should become attached to another,** (even) **to Him who was raised from the dead** (alluding both to the comparison in vv. 2, 3, γένηται ἀνδρὶ ἑτέρῳ, and to ch. vi. 4, 5, ἵνα ὥσπ. ἠγέρθη χριστὸς κ.τ.λ.), **that we should** (here strictly *final*, as Thol., Meyer, De W., &c. Not merely *ecbatic*, as Fritzsche) **bring forth fruit** (alluding to καρπόν, ch. iv. 22, and at the same time (Luke i. 42) carrying on the similitude of marriage. Not that this latter must be pressed, for there is only an allusion to it: nor on the other hand need the least objection be raised to such an understanding of the words, as any one conversant with St. Paul's way of speaking on this subject will at once feel: compare 2 Cor. xi. 2; Eph. v. 30—32) **to** (dat. commodi, '*to the honour of*') **God.**

5, 6.] *In the fleshly state* (before we died with Christ) *sinful passions which were by the Law worked in us and brought forth fruit to death: but now that we are dead to the law, we are no longer servants in the oldness of the letter, but in the newness of the spirit.* The Law (ch. v. 20, alluded to again vi. 14) was the *multiplier of sin* To this thought, and the inferences from it, the Apostle now recurs, and contrasts the state under the law in this respect, with that of the believer in Christ. **For when we were in the flesh** (= virtually, "under the law:" see the antithesis in ver. 6: so almost all Commentators, ancient and modern, except Beza, Bengel, Reiche, and Thol., who take it to mean the mere fleshly state, in which the Spirit is not yet energizing, and Ambrst., Calov., Olsh., al., who interpret it of the state of the unregenerate. But *how* does ἐν τῇ

τὰ [i] παθήματα τῶν [k] ἁμαρτιῶν τὰ [l] διὰ τοῦ νόμου [m] ἐνηρ-
γεῖτο ἐν τοῖς [n] μέλεσιν ἡμῶν [o] εἰς τὸ [g] καρποφορῆσαι
τῷ θανάτῳ· 6 νυνὶ δὲ [p] κατηργήθημεν ἀπὸ τοῦ νόμου,
ἀποθανόντες ἐν ᾧ [q] κατειχόμεθα, ὥστε [r] δουλεύειν ἡμᾶς
ἐν [s] καινότητι [t] πνεύματος καὶ οὐ [u] παλαιότητι [t] γράμματος.
7 [v] Τί οὖν [v] ἐροῦμεν; ὁ νόμος ἁμαρτία; [w] μὴ γένοιτο·

ABCDF KL[P]א a b c d f g h k l m n o 17 [47]

i Paul, ch. viii. 18 al7. Heb. ii. 9, 10. x. 32. 1 Pet. i. 11 al3. only †.
k gen. obj., ch. i. 26.
l Acts iii. 16. 1 Pet. i. 21.
m Matt. xiv. 2 ∥ Mk. Paul, 1 Cor. xii. 6 al15. James v. 16 only. Isa. xli. 4.
n ch. vi. 13 reff.
o ver. 12 reff.
p ver. 2.
q = [John v. 4.] ch. i. 18. 2 Thess. ii. 6.
r ch. vi. 6. Acts xx. 19 reff.
s ch. vi. 4 only. Ezek. xlvii. 12 only.
t ch. ii. 29. 2 Cor. iii. 6.
u here only †. Eurip. Hel. 1062. (-ος, ch. vi. 6.)
v ch. iii. 5 reff.
w ch. iii. 4 reff

6. [for *νυνι*, *νυν* F.] rec *αποθανοντος* (*see note*): *του θανατου* DF latt Jer: txt ABCKL[P]א rel am[1] syrr copt goth æth arm Bas$_1$ Chr$_1$ *Cyr*[-p Did$_1$ Euthal-ms] Thdrt Damasc [Orig-int$_2$] Tert$_1$. om *ημας* BF [Tert$_1$].

σαρκί denote 'under the law?' Some say, *on account of its carnality*, as more or less Theodoret, Œc., Hammond, Grot., al.: some, *on account of the power of sin under the law*,—as Chrys., Theophyl., Calv., al.: best of all is it to understand it, with Rückert, Köllner, Meyer, Fritz., De Wette, as pointing to the period *before death with Christ*, in which we were sensual and sinful: so that *ἐν τῇ σαρκὶ εἶναι* forms a contrast with *θανατωθῆναι*. But, as De W. observes, it must not with Fritz. be rendered 'quum viveremus,' as this is never the sense of *ἐν* (*τῇ*) *σαρκὶ* (*εἶναι*),—not even 2 Cor. x. 3: nor, I may add, Phil. i. 24) **the stirrings** (*'passions of sins,'* objective gen., which *led to sins*: not by hendiadys for *παθήμ. ἁμαρτωλά*, which, as always, destroys the force) **of sins, which were by means of the law** (the *incitements*,—not the *sins*, in this place, though ultimately it was so, the incitement *leading* to the sin. The full meaning of **διὰ τοῦ νόμου** must be kept, 'which were *by means of* the law:' i. e. the law *occasioned them*. Locke argues for the rendering, '*under the law*,' 'in the time of the law,' which would destroy the force of the argument connecting *the law* with *sin*, here put so strongly as to require the question of ver. 7) **wrought** ('energized:' not pass., but middle: see note on Gal. v. 6) **in our members** (the instruments of sin, ch. vi. 13) **to the bringing forth of fruit** (see on *τοῦ μή* ver. 3: the *καρποφ.* was the final object of their energizing, not the mere result. In *καρποφ.* *here*, the allusion to *progeny* is very distant, if it exists at all. Meyer makes it refer to an adulterous state, and personifies *θάνατος*; but this can hardly be) **unto death** (only a verbal antithesis to *τῷ θεῷ*: —'whose end was death'): **6.**] **But now** (opposed to *ὅτε*, ver. 5) **have we been delivered** (annulled) **from the law, having died** (**to that**) **wherein we were held** (the reading *ἀποθανόντος* cannot even be brought into discussion, as it appears to be only a conjecture of Beza's, arising from a misunderstanding of the text (and of Chrysostom's commentary, who did not read it),—see the analogy explained on ver. 1: the other reading, *τοῦ θανάτου*, is a correction to suit ver. 5. So that *ἐν ᾧ* either refers directly to *νόμου*, *ἀποθανόντες* being absolute and parenthetic, or we must understand *ἐκείνῳ* aft. *ἀποθ.* I prefer the latter, as suiting better the style of the Apostle and the whole connexion. The omission of the demonstrative pron. probably is occasioned by a desire to give especial prominence to the fact of *ἀποθανόντες*, or perhaps on account of the prepos. *ἀπό* in composition, as in ch. x. 14, *πῶς οὖν ἐπικαλέσωνται εἰς ὃν οὐκ ἐπίστευσαν*;), **so that we serve** (not '*should serve*,' as E. V.: the pres. describes the actual state: —understand '*God*' after serve) **in the newness of the Spirit** (i. e. of the Holy Spirit of God, who originates and penetrates the Christian life:—the *first mention* of the Spirit so much spoken of in ch. viii.) **and not in the oldness of the letter** (the law being only a collection of precepts and prohibitions, but the Gospel a service of freedom, ruled by the Spirit, whose presence is liberty). *καινότης* and *παλαιότης* are not as in ch. vi. 4, *καινότητι ζωῆς*, *attributes* of the genitives which follow them, but *states in which* those genitives are the *ruling elements*.

7—25.] *An explanation of the part which the law has in bringing out sin, by example of the Apostle's own case.* In this most important and difficult passage, it is of the first consequence to have a clear view of the *form* of illustration which the Apostle adopts, and of the *reason why he adopts it*. The former has been amply treated of by almost all Commentators: the latter, too generally, has escaped their enquiry. But it furnishes, if satisfactorily treated, a key to the other. I ask then first,

ἀλλὰ τὴν ἁμαρτίαν οὐκ [x] ἔγνων εἰ μὴ διὰ νόμου· τήν [y] τε

x ἄν omitted, John ix. 33. xv. 22. xix. 11. Gal. iv. 15. Winer, edn. 6, § 42. 2.
y = ch. i. 26. [2 Cor. x. 8.]

why St. Paul *suddenly changes here to the first person?* And the answer is, because he is about to draw a conclusion negativing the question (ὁ νόμος ἁμαρτία;) upon purely *subjective* grounds, proceeding on that which *passes within*, when the work of the law is carried on in the heart. And he is about to depict this work of the law by an example which shall set it forth in vivid colours, in detail, in its connexion with sin in a man. What example then so apposite, as *his own?* Introspective as his character was, and purified as his inner vision was by the Holy Spirit of God, what example would so forcibly bring out the inward struggles of the man which prove the holiness of the law, while they shew its inseparable connexion with the production of sin? If this be the reason why the first person is here assumed (and I can find no other which does not introduce into St. Paul's style an arbitrariness and caprice which it least of all styles exhibits), then we must *dismiss from our minds all exegesis which explains the passage of any other*, in the first instance, *than of Paul himself:* himself indeed, as an *exemplar*, wherein others may see themselves: but not himself *in the person* of others, be they the *Jews*, nationally or individually, or *all mankind*, or *individual men.* This being done, there arises now a question equally important,—Of *what self* is it that he speaks throughout this passage? Is it *always the same?* If so, is it always the *carnal, unregenerate* self? or always the *spiritual, regenerate?* Clearly *not the latter always;* for to that self the historical account of vv. 7—13 will not apply, and still less the assertion, in the *present*, of ver. 14. Clearly *not the former always:* for to that the assertion of ver. 22 will not apply, nor that of ver. 25. Is it always the *complex self*, made up of the prevailing spiritual-regenerate, with the remains of the carnal-unregenerate? *Not always this:* although this seems nearer to satisfying the conditions: for in the description ver. 9, ἐγὼ ἔζων χωρὶς νόμου ποτέ, and in ἐγὼ σάρκινός εἰμι κ.τ.λ. ver. 14, there is no complexity, but the ἐγώ is *clearly the carnal man.* Therefore not always the same. If not always the same, *where is the distinction?* If we look carefully, the Apostle himself will guide us to it. Having carried on the ἐγώ unqualified and unexplained till ver. 18, he there has occasion to say οὐκ οἰκεῖ ἐν ἐμοὶ ἀγαθόν. But he is conscious that, as he had written to the Cor. (1 Cor. iii. 16), τὸ πνεῦμα τοῦ θεοῦ οἰκεῖ ἐν ὑμῖν: he therefore finds it necessary to correct himself by an explanation, *what ἐγώ he meant*, and adds to ἐν ἐμοί,—**τουτέστιν ἐν τῇ σαρκί μου.** So that ἐγώ there is equivalent to ἡ σάρξ μου, i. e. 'myself in my state of *life to* the law and sin, and acting according to the motions of sin.' Again, when the *approval of the law of God* is affirmed (not the mere θέλω, which I will treat by and by), it is not barely ἐγώ, but to avoid confusion, in ver. 22 the Apostle adds **κατὰ τὸν ἔσω ἄνθρωπον**, and in ver. 25, prefixes **αὐτός**; in both cases shewing that (see notes below) he speaks of the *complex man*, himself made up of an ἔσω, and an ἔξω ἄνθρωπος, of ὁ νοῦς and ἡ σάρξ. Are we then justified in assuming, that up to ver. 22 the carnal-unregenerate self is spoken of, but after that the complex self? Such a supposition would not be consistent with the assertion of the θέλω from ver. 15 onwards: *no such will existing in the carnal unregenerate man.* I believe the true account will be nearly as follows:—from ver. 7—13 incl. is *historical*, and the ἐγώ *there* is the *historical self*, under the working of conviction of sin, and shewing the work of the law; in other words, *the carnal self in the transition state*, under the first motions towards God generated by the law, which the law could never have perfected. Then at ver. 14, Paul, according to a habit very common to him, keeps hold of the carnal self, and still having it in view, *transfers himself into his present position*,—altering the past tense into the present, still however meaning by ἐγώ (in ver. 14), *ἡ σάρξ μου.* But, having passed into the present tense, he immediately mingles with this mere action of the law upon the natural conscience, the motions of the will towards God which are in conflict with the motions towards sin in the members. And hence arises an apparent verbal confusion, because the ἐγώ e. g. in ver. 17, of whom it is said, οὐκ ἔτι ἐγὼ κατεργάζομαι αὐτό, being the entire personality, the *complex self*, is of far wider extent than the ἐγώ of whom it is said οὐκ οἰκεῖ ἐν ἐμοί, τουτέστιν ἐν τῇ σαρκί μου, ἀγαθόν. But the latter ἐγώ, in this part of the chapter, is shewn to be (vv. 17, 20) no longer properly ἐγώ, but ἡ οἰκοῦσα ἐν ἐμοὶ ἁμαρτία,—and so it *passes altogether out of sight* after ver. 20, and *its place is taken by the actual then existing complex self* of Paul, compounded of the regenerate spiritual man, sympathizing with God's law, serving God's law, in conflict with the still remaining though decadent carnal man, whose essence it is to serve the law of sin, to bring captive to the law

z ch. i. 24 reff. ^{y}γὰρ ^{z}ἐπιθυμίαν οὐκ ᾔδειν, εἰ μὴ ὁ νόμος ἔλεγεν Οὐκ ABCDF KL[P]א a b c d f g h k l m n o 17 [47]

of sin. This state of conflict and division against one's self would infallibly bring about utter ruin, and might well lead to despair (ver. 24), but for the rescue which God's grace has provided by Jesus Christ our Lord. And this rescue has been such, that I, the αὐτὸς ἐγώ of ver. 25, the *real self*, the nobler and better part of the man, serve, with the νοῦς (see there), the law of God: whereas it is only with the flesh, according to which (ch. viii. 4) *I do not walk*, but overcome and mortify it, that I serve (am still subject to) the law of sin. Then this subjection of the flesh to the law of sin, to the δουλεία τῆς φθορᾶς, is fully set out, in its *nature,—consequences to the carnal,*—and *uses to the spiritual,*—in ch. viii.

Any thing like a summary of the exegesis of this passage would be quite beyond my limits. I must refer the student to commentaries on *this epistle alone,*—and especially to that of Tholuck, where a complete and masterly history is given. It may suffice here to say, that most of the ancients suppose ἐγώ to represent *mankind*, or *the Jews generally*, and the whole to be taken chronologically,—to ver. 9 as *before* the law, after ver. 9 as *under* the law. This was once Augustine's view, Prop. 44 in Ep. ad Rom. vol. iii. p. 2071, but he afterwards changed it (Retract. i. 23, vol. i. p. 620) and adopted in the main that advocated above.

The default of a history of the exegesis will be found to be in some measure compensated by the account of opinions given under the separate verses below.

7.] **τί οὖν ἐρ.**, see note, ch. vi. 1.

ὁ ν. ἁμαρτία;] **Is the law** (not, as Jowett, '*conscience*,' but in our case, the revealed law of God, which awoke the conscience to action) **sin?**—not '*the cause of sin*,' which in one sense the Apostle would not have denied,—but *sin*, abstract for concrete, *sinful*, or, as Bengel, 'causa peccati peccaminosa.' ὁ νόμος itself being abstract, that which is predicated of it is abstract also. The contrast is, ὁ νόμος ἅγιος, ver. 12. The question itself refers back to ver. 5, τὰ παθήματα τῶν ἁμαρτιῶν τὰ διὰ τοῦ νόμου. It is asked, *not by an objector*, but by the Apostle himself, in anticipation of an objection. **ἀλλά**] Is but here in contrast to ὁ νόμ. ἁμαρτ., meaning, 'so far from that,'—or is it a qualification of μὴ γένοιτο, meaning 'but still it is true, that ....?' Neither explanation exactly suits the context, which is, by a proper elucidation of the law's working as regards sin, to prove it to be holy. I would rather understand ἀλλά, **but what I mean is ....,—I say not that, but ....** There surely is no *contrast* to ὁ νόμ. ἁμαρτία, see ver. 8.

οὐκ ἔγνων] 'non cognoscebam, ni ....,' —**I was living in a state of ignorance of sin, were it not ....** This construction comprehends in it οὐκ ἂν ἔγνων as a consequence, and is therefore often said to be put for it; but it has its propriety, as here, where a historical state is being described, and the unconditional indicative is more appropriate. Tholuck makes it = 'non cognoveram, ni ....,' in which case the indic. expresses more plainly than the conjunctive the absolute dependence of the fact on the condition. There is some difficulty in understanding the mutual relation of the clauses, τὴν ἁμ. οὐκ ἔγνων, and τήν τε γὰρ ἐπιθ. οὐκ ᾔδειν. It is well known that τε differs from καί, in not *coupling things co-ordinate*, but *attaching things subordinate*, to a former. Thus Thucyd. i. 9 begins Ἀγαμέμνων τέ μοι δοκεῖ ...., on which Poppo remarks (cited by Thol.), 'Sequitur *exemplum* auctæ Græcorum opulentiæ .... ductum ex rebus Agamemnonis et causis expeditionis Trojanæ;' an *example* being a subordinate verification of a general categorical statement. The γάρ also shews that the second clause is subordinated to, and alleged in substantiation of the first. Then *what is* **ἁμαρτία**? Is it sin in *act*, or sin in *principle*,—the principle of sin? Not *sin in act*, so that ἁμ. οὐκ ἔγν. should mean, '*I had not entered into contact with sin*,' i.e. '*had not sinned:*' as Fritz.: for then the law would have truly and actually been the cause of sin: nor, *sin in act*, so that the meaning were, '*I had not known the nature of a sinful act:*' for this would not agree with the subordination of ἐπιθυμία below: the ἐπιθ. being more general (πᾶσαν ἐπιθ.) than the particular acts which it induced. But the reference must be to *sin in principle*, the principle of sin: **I had not recognized such a thing as sin, but by means of the law.** So Calv., Melancth., Calov., Rückert, Kölln., Olsh., Thol., De Wette. **The law** here is in the full sense of *the Mosaic law* as regarded *himself*,—not excluding the wider sense on which I have insisted in the former part of the Epistle when applied to *others*.

τήν τε γὰρ ...] **For neither** ('neque enim') **had I known** (by experience: 'known any thing of') **coveting** (the motions of the flesh towards sin,—whether acted on or not,—whether consented to or not:—this *motion* he would not have *perceived*, because he was simply *moving with it*) **if the law had not said, Thou shalt**

[a] ἐπιθυμήσεις· 8 [b] ἀφορμὴν δὲ λαβοῦσα ἡ ἁμαρτία διὰ [c] τῆς
[c] ἐντολῆς [d] κατηργάσατο ἐν ἐμοὶ [e] πᾶσαν [z] ἐπιθυμίαν·
[f] χωρὶς γὰρ νόμου ἁμαρτία [g] νεκρά. 9 ἐγὼ δὲ [h] ἔζων [f] χωρὶς
νόμου [i] ποτέ. [k] ἐλθούσης δὲ [c] τῆς [c] ἐντολῆς ἡ ἁμαρτία

a Exod. xx. 17. Deut. v. 21. absol., ch. xiii. 9. 1 Cor. x. 6. James iv. 2. 2 Kings xxiii. 15.
b ver. 11. 2 Cor. v. 12. xi. 12 bis. Gal. v. 13. 1 Tim. v. 14 only. P. Ezek. v. 7 only.
c = Luke xxiii. 56. 1 Tim. vi. 14.
d ch. iv. 5 reff.
e = Acts xx. 19 reff.
f ch. iii. 21 reff.
g = James ii. 17 al.
h (subjective) here only.
i = John ix. 13. ch. xi. 30 al.
k = but objective, Gal. iii. 23, 25.

7. om τε F latt [copt Orig-int$_2$]. for 2nd νομος, λογος L. επιθυμησης K[P].
8. om δε D[1](and lat[1]). rec κατειργασατο, with AB[2]CFKLℵ rel: txt B[1]D[P] d. ins η bef αμαρτια ℵ[3] [Meth$_1$ Chr$_1$ Gennad-c$_1$ Isid-c$_1$]. aft νεκρα ins ην F latt Syr [copt arm Orig-int$_2$] Jer Aug Sedul Ambrst Pel [pref K goth].
9. εζην B : εζουν 17.

not covet (reff. Exod. Deut.). '*Covet,*' in the above sense. The Apostle omits all the objects there specified, and merely lays hold of the idea contained in ἐπιθυμήσεις. And it may well be said and strictly, that the 'coveting' there spoken of would lead to all kinds of sin—therefore murder, adultery, &c., if carried out: and that the prohibition of desire there serves as an example of what the law actually forbids elsewhere. 8.] **But** (proceeding with the development of sin by means of the law) **sin** (the sinful principle or propensity, but without any conscious personification on the part of the Apostle,—see some excellent remarks on personification in Tholuck) **having found occasion** (ἀφορμή, as its derivation shews, means more than mere opportunity,—it indicates the furnishing the material and ground of attack, the *wherewith* and *whence* to attack. The words here are not to be joined, as Luth., Olsh., Meyer, with διὰ τ. ἐντολῆς [which belongs to κατηργάσατο, see below]:—for (1) ἀφορμ. λαβεῖν διά would not express *whence* the ἀφορμή is taken, as παρά or ἐκ, but only *by what means* some ἀφ. is taken from some source,—which would not here suit the Apostle's meaning, seeing that the *source itself was* the commandment,—and (2) ver. 13, διὰ τοῦ ἀγ. κατεργ., decides the matter here,—but *absolutely*, as frequently, see Wetst.) **by means of the commandment** (not = τοῦ νόμου, but the *tenth commandment*, the prohibition in question) **wrought in me** (not '*wrought out,*' 'brought into action,' but '*originated*' [using this commandment as its instrument]) **all (manner) of coveting; for without the law sin is** (not 'was:' the omission of the verb substantive shews the sentence to be a *locus communis*,—and compare ch. iv. 15) **dead** (powerless and inactive: compare 1 Cor. xv. 56, ἡ δύναμις τ. ἁμαρτίας ὁ νόμος). This *deadness of sin without the law* must not be understood as meaning that sin was committed but not recognized, the conscience being not informed nor awakened: such a statement would be *true*, but would *not touch the matter argued here*. Erasmus (Thol.) well explains the νεκρά,—'Quum ante legem proditam (but see below) quædam peccata nescirem, quædam ita scirem, ut mihi tamen licere putarem, quod vetita non essent,—levius ac languidius sollicitabatur animus ad peccandum, ut frigidius amamus ea, quibus ubi libeat potiri fas sit. Cæterum legis indicio proditis tot peccati formis, universa cupiditatum cohors irritata prohibitione cœpit acrius ad peccandum sollicitare.' Compare also Prov. ix. 17, and (Wetst.) Ovid. Amor. ii. 19. 3, 'Quod licet ingratum est, quod non licet acrius urit:' and ib. iii. 4. 17, 'Nitimur in vetitum semper, cupimusque negata:' and Seneca, de Clem. i. 23 (Thol.), 'Parricidæ cum lege cœperunt, et illis facinus pœna monstravit:' and a remarkable passage from Cato's speech in Livy xxxiv. 4, 'Nolite eodem loco existimare, Quirites, futuram rem, quo fuit, antequam lex de hoc ferretur. Et hominem improbum non accusari tutius est, quam absolvi, et luxuria non mota tolerabilior esset, quam erit nunc, ipsis vinculis, sicut fera bestia, irritata, deinde emissa.' 9.] It is a great question with Interpreters, *of what period* Paul here speaks. Those who sink his own personality, and think that he speaks merely as one of mankind, or of the Jews, understand it of the period before the law was given: some, of Adam in Paradise before (?) the prohibition: those who see Paul himself throughout the whole think that he speaks,—some, of his state *as a Pharisee:* this however would necessitate the understanding the legal death which follows, of his *conversion*, which cannot well be: some, of his state as a *child*, before that freedom of the will is asserted which causes rebellion against the law as the will of another: so Meyer, Thol., al. Agreeing in some measure with the last view, I would extend the limits further, and say that he speaks of *all that time, be it mere childhood or much more, before the law began its work*

[l] ἀνέζησεν, 10 ἐγὼ δὲ [h] ἀπέθανον· καὶ [m] εὑρέθη μοι ἡ ἐντολὴ ABCDF
ἡ [n] εἰς [o] ζωήν, αὕτη [n] εἰς [p] θάνατον. 11 ἡ γὰρ ἁμαρτία KL[P]ℵ abcdf
[q] ἀφορμὴν λαβοῦσα διὰ τῆς ἐντολῆς [r] ἐξηπάτησέν με, καὶ ghkl mno17
δι' αὐτῆς [s] ἀπέκτεινεν. 12 ὥστε ὁ [t] μὲν νόμος ἅγιος, καὶ ἡ [47]
[u] ἐντολὴ [u] ἁγία καὶ δικαία καὶ ἀγαθή. 13 [v] Τὸ οὖν [v] ἀγαθὸν
ἐμοὶ ἐγένετο θάνατος; [w] μὴ γένοιτο· ἀλλ' ἡ ἁμαρτία, ἵνα

l Luke xv. 24 (32. ch. xiv. 9. Rev. xv. 5 v.r.) only +. m = 1 Cor. iv. 2 reff. n ellips., ver. 5. o = Matt. xix. 17. Deut. xxx. 15. p = ch. v. 12. q ver. 8 reff. r ch. xvi. 18. 1 Cor. iii. 18. 2 Cor. xi. 3. 2 Thess. ii. 3. 1 Tim. ii. 14 only. P. Exod. viii. 29 B &c. only. Susan. 56 Theod. s = 2 Cor. iii. 6. t μέν solitar., Acts i. 1 (and note). iii. 13. Col. ii. 23. Heb. xii. 9 al. Winer, § 63, i. 2. e. γ. u 2 Pet. ii. 12. v ch. ii. 10 reff. w ch. iii. 4 reff.

10. om 2nd η L m[1] 48. 77. 100 [Meth_1] Chr-ms.
13. [for το ουν, τι ουν το P Meth_1.] rec for εγενετο, γεγονε (*corrn, the historic aor not being understood*), with KL rel Chr Cyr-c Gennad-c Thdrt Œc Thl: om F: txt ABCDℵ[P 47(Tischdf)] Meth. Damasc. (αλλ, so BCF[P] a k m[(Scr, e contra

within him,—before the deeper energies of his moral nature were aroused (see on **ἐλθούσης** below). **But** (ἔζων opposed, but only formally, to νεκρά, and so having δέ: so Meyer and De W.) **I was alive** (not merely '*lived*,' 'went on,' but emphatic, '*vivus eram*,' as Aug., i. e. 'lived and flourished,'—contrasted with ἀπέθανον below) **without the law** (the law having no recognized place in my moral existence) **once; but when the commandment** (above, ver. 8) **came** (purely subjective; not '*was enacted*,' 'came in,'—but '*came to me*,' as we say, '*came home to me*,' 'was brought home to me'), **sin sprung into life** (not '*revived*:' however *true* it may be that sin was *merely dormant*, the idea insisted on here, is, that it was *dead* and *came to life*, began to live and flourish:—but this is not to be compared with ἀνέβλεψα in John ix. 11; see note there), **10.**] **but I died** (ceased to live-and-flourish as before,—fell into that state of unhappiness, which even afterwards under the gospel he calls θάνατος, ver. 24, ch. viii. 2): **and** (not an additional particular, but = 'and so,' merely changing the *subject* from 'I,' to 'the commandment') **the commandment which was for** (tending to) **life** (compare ch. x. 5, ὁ ποιήσας αὐτὰ **ἄνθρωπος ζήσεται** ἐν αὐτοῖς, and reff. there: the *life* is one of *prosperity* primarily, but capable of, and indeed requiring (x. 5) **a** higher interpretation), **this (very commandment)** (αὕτη directs attention in a marked way to the antecedent subject: so frequently αὐτός and ἐκεῖνος: see Matt. xxiv. 13: Winer, edn. 6, § 23. 4) **was found** (subjective—οὐκ εἶπεν ὅτι ἡ ἐντολὴ **γέγονέ** μοι θάνατος, ἀλλ' **εὑρέθη**, τὸ καινὸν καὶ παράδοξον τῆς ἀτοπίας οὕτως ἑρμηνεύων, Chrys.) **by me** (to be) **unto** (tending to) **death** (explained on ἀπέθ. above). **11.**] **For** (explanatory how ver. 10 happened) **sin** (the sinful principle within me) **having found occasion** (absol. as in ver. 8, where see note),—**by means of the commandment deceived me** (there is a plain reference to the Tempter deceiving Eve, which was accomplished by means of the commandment, exciting doubt of and objection to it, and lust after the forbidden thing: see reff. 2 Cor., 1 Tim.), **and by it slew me** (i. e. brought me into the state of misery and death, mentioned in ver. 10;—but there is an allusion again to the effect of the fall as the act of the Tempter). **12.**] **So that** (seeing it was not the law in general, nor this particular commandment, that wrought coveting in me, but the *sinful principle in me taking advantage of these*, which themselves were given εἰς ζωήν and not εἰς θάνατον) **the law (indeed) is holy** (μέν, as understanding a δέ to follow—'but it was sin,' &c.: which does follow in an expanded form, in ver. 13), **and the commandment** (οὐκ ἐπιθυμήσεις, ver. 8) **holy and just and good** (Theodoret thus accounts for the epithets: **ἁγίαν** προσηγόρευσεν ὡς τὸ δέον διδάξασαν· **δικαίαν** δέ, ὡς ὀρθῶς τοῖς παραβάταις τὴν ψῆφον ἐξενεγκοῦσαν· **ἀγαθὴν** δέ, ὡς ζωὴν τοῖς φυλάττουσιν εὐτρεπίζουσαν. See also 1 Tim. i. 8). **13.**] **Did then the good** (= 'that which was good,' i. e. ἡ ἐντολή, but made abstract for the sake of greater contrast) **become death** (so ὁ νόμ., **ἁμαρτία**, ver. 7) **to me?** Was it, after all, *the commandment itself* that became to me this death of which I speak? **Far from it: but** (it was) **sin** (that became death to me. The construction adopted by Vulg., Luth., al., ἀλλὰ ἡ ἁμαρτία, ἵνα φανῇ ἁμ., διὰ τ. ἀγ. μοι κατεργαζομένη [ἦν] θάνατον, is hardly admissible);—**that it might appear** (be shewn to be) **sin**, (by) **working death to me by means of the good** (that which was good: see above. The misuse and perversion of good is one of the tests whereby the energy of evil is detected; so that sin, by its perversion of the (good)

φανῇ ἁμαρτία, διὰ [v] τοῦ [v] ἀγαθοῦ μοι [x] κατεργαζομένη
θάνατον, ἵνα [y] γένηται [z] καθ᾽ [za] ὑπερβολὴν [b] ἁμαρτωλὸς ἡ
ἁμαρτία διὰ τῆς ἐντολῆς. 14 [c] οἴδαμεν γὰρ [c] ὅτι ὁ νόμος
[d] πνευματικός ἐστιν, ἐγὼ δὲ [e] σάρκινός εἰμι [f] πεπραμένος
ὑπὸ τὴν ἁμαρτίαν. 15 ὃ γὰρ [x] κατεργάζομαι οὐ γινώσκω·

x ch. ii. 9 reff.
y = ch. iii. 4. xi. 6. 1 Cor. xiii. 1 al.
z 1 Cor. xii. 31. 2 Cor. i. 8. iv. 17. Gal. i. 13 only.
a as above (z). 2 Cor. iv. 7, 17. xii. 7 only. P.† (-βάλλειν, 2 Cor. iii. 10. -λλόντως, 2 Cor. xi. 23.)
b = here only. (ch. iii. 7 reff.)
c ch. ii. 2. iii. 19. viii. 22, 28. 1 Cor. viii. 1, 4. 2 Cor. v. 1. 1 John iii. 2, 14 al.
d ch. i. 11. 1 Cor. xii. 1. xiv. 1 al.†
e 1 Cor. iii. 1. 2 Cor. iii. 3. Heb. vii. 16 only. 2 Chron. xxxii. 8. Ezek. xi. 19. xxxvi. 26 only. (-ικός, ch. xv. 27.)
f = here only. 4 Kings xvii. 17. 1 Macc. i. 15. (Acts iv. 34 reff.)

Treg) 47]. (A uncert.)) *η αμαρτια* bef *αμαρτωλος* DF tol [copt] arm Aug$_1$ Ambrst.
14. for *γαρ*, *δε* A D[-gr] L syr-mg Orig$_1$[int$_1$ Bas$_1$] Cyr[-p$_1$] Thdrt Aug$_1$: om æth arm Aug$_2$ Jer$_1$: txt BCFK[P]ℵ rel [latt syrr copt goth] Orig$_2$[int$_1$ Meth$_1$] Tit$_1$ Did$_1$ Chr$_1$ [Damasc Hil$_1$]. rec *σαρκικος* (*corrn to more usual and appy more appropriate word? but the two are constantly confused*), with K(e sil) L[P]ℵ^3 Orig$_1$ Chr$_1$ [Euthal-ms] Thdrt$_2$ Phot$_1$ Thl Œc : txt ABCDFℵ^1 b^1 o 17 Meth$_2$ Ephr$_1$ Nyss$_1$ Bas$_1$ [mss vary] Cyr[-p$_1$] Damasc.

commandment into a cause (evil) of death, was shewn in its real character *as sin.* That this is the rendering is evident by the following clause, which is parallel with it. Erasm., Valla, Elsner, Dr. Burton, al., make ἁμαρτία the *subject:* 'that sin might appear to be working death, &c.' ('so that sin *appears* to *have effected* my death,' &c. Dr. Burton, most ungrammatically): there is no objection to this on the ground of ἁμαρτ. being anarthrous, as even Bp. Middleton himself reluctantly acknowledges; —the objection lies in the context, as above), **that** (explains and runs parallel with the former ἵνα, as in 2 Cor. ix. 3, where he adds to the 2nd ἵνα, καθὼς ἔλεγον) **by means of the commandment sin might become exceeding** (above measure) **sinful**: i. e. that sin, which was before unknown as such, might, being vivified and brought into energy by (its opposition to) the commandment, be brought out as being (not merely '*shewn to be*') exceedingly sinful (sinful in an exaggerated degree—prominent in its true character as the opponent of God). **14.**] On the change into the present tense here, see above in the remarks on the whole section. Hitherto has been *historical:* now the Apostle passes to the *present time,* keeping hold yet of the carnal ἐγώ of former days, whose remnants are still energizing in the renewed man. **For** (by way of explaining and setting in still clearer light the relative positions of sin and the law, and the state of inner conflict brought about by their working) **we know** (it is an acknowledged principle amongst us, see reff.) **that the law is spiritual** (sprung from God, who is a Spirit, and requiring of men spiritual purity. These meanings, which have been separately held by different Commentators, may, as Thol. and De W. observe, well be united): **but I** (see beginning of section) **am carnal** ([subject to the law of the flesh, and in bondage to it, see below] σάρκινος, stronger than σαρκικός; *carneus* rather than *carnalis,* but it is doubtful whether the two endings were not used indiscriminately: see Tholuck), **sold** (into slavery, see reff.; but the similitude must not be exacted in *all particulars,* for it is only the fact of slavery, as far as its victim, *the man,* is concerned, which is here prominent) **under** (to, and so as to be under the power of) **sin.** Tholuck (who differs from the view of this section advocated above, yet) adds here: "The ἐγώ appears here in its totality as sinful, while in vv. 16, 20 it is distinguished from sin. That Paul does not here bear in mind this distinction, may be justified by the maxim, 'a potiori fit denominatio;' the ἐγώ is a slave, and has not his own will: as ver. 23 shews, the ἐγώ which is hostile to sin, the νόμος τοῦ νοός, is under coercion, and the man is a captive. So Arrian in Epict. ii. 22: ὅπου γὰρ τὸ ἐγὼ καὶ τὸ ἐμόν, ἐκεῖ ἀνάγκη ῥέπειν τὸ ζῶον, εἰ ἐν **σαρκί**, ἐκεῖ τὸ κυριεῦον εἶναι, εἰ ἐν προαιρέσει, ἐκεῖνο (qu. ἐκεῖ?) εἶναι." The latter clause of the verse is the very strongest assertion of man's subjection to the slavery of sin in his carnal nature. **15.**] **For** (a proof of this πεπρᾶσθαι under sin, viz. not being able to do what I would, vv. 15—17) **that which I perform** (am in the habit of doing) **I know not** (act blindly, at the dictates of another: which is proper to a slave. σκοτοῦμαι φησί, συναρπάζομαι, ἐπήρειαν ὑπομένω, οὐκ οἶδα πῶς ὑποσκελίζομαι, Chrys. The meaning, '*I approve not,*' introduced by Aug. and held by Erasm., Beza, Grot., Estius, Semler, al., is not sanctioned by usage,—see note on 1 Cor. viii. 3,—and would make the following clause almost a tautology): **for** (explanation of last assertion, shewing how such

οὐ γὰρ ὃ θέλω, τοῦτο πράσσω, ἀλλ' ὃ μισῶ, τοῦτο ποιῶ. ABCDF KL[P]א
16 εἰ δὲ ὃ οὐ θέλω, τοῦτο ποιῶ, [g] σύμφημι τῷ νόμῳ ὅτι a b c d f
[h] καλός. 17 νυνὶ δὲ [i] οὐκ ἔτι ἐγὼ [k] κατεργάζομαι αὐτό, g h k l m n o 17
ἀλλὰ ἡ [lm] οἰκοῦσα [l] ἐν ἐμοὶ ἁμαρτία. 18 οἶδα γὰρ ὅτι οὐκ [47]
[lm] οἰκεῖ [l] ἐν ἐμοί, [n] τουτέστιν ἐν τῇ σαρκί μου, ἀγαθόν. τὸ
γὰρ θέλειν [o] παράκειταί μοι, τὸ δὲ [k] κατεργάζεσθαι [p] τὸ
[p] καλὸν οὔ. 19 οὐ γὰρ ὃ θέλω ποιῶ ἀγαθόν, ἀλλὰ ὃ οὐ θέλω

g here only †. Xen. Anab. v. 8. 8.
h = 1 Tim. i. 18. iv. 4. see below (p).
i = ch. xi. 6.
k ver. 13.
l here 3ce. ch. viii. 9, 11. 1 Cor. iii. 16. Gen. iv. 16. xvi. 3.
m as above (l). 1 Cor. vii. 12, 13. 1 Tim. vi. 16 only.
n Acts xix. 4 reff.
o here only bis †. Sir. xxxiv. (xxxi.) 16. Hom. Od. χ. 65. Polyb. iv. 38. 7. iii. 57. 8. Xen. Anab. vii. 3. 22.
p here bis. 2 Cor. xiii. 7. Gal. vi. 9. 1 Thess. v. 21 only. Amos v. 14.

15. om 1st *τουτο* DF goth Meth$_1$ [Orig-int$_1$] Pelag (copt om both): ins ABCKL[P]א rel vulg [syrr æth arm] Orig$_1$[int$_2$] Meth$_1$ Chr$_1$ [Bas$_1$ Euthal-ms] Thdrt Aug$_1$ [Ambrst]. αλλα א.

16. *συνφημι* DFא. for *καλος*, *καλον εστιν* F.

17. (αλλα, so BDF L[e sil, Tischdf].) for *οικουσα*, *ενοικουσα* Bא [Meth$_1$(in Phot-ms)] Ambrst (*ενοικει* am Ambrst in follg ver).

18. ins *το* bef *αγαθον* F Meth$_3$ Cyr[-p$_1$ Thdrt-c$_1$]. for *δε*, *γαρ*, and for *καλον*, *αγαθον* F [Euthal-ms Damasc Orig-int Ambrst$_1$]. rec (for *ου*) *ουχ ευρισκω*, with DFKL[P] rel [vulg syrr goth (æth)] arm-mg Chr$_1$ Thdrt Jer Sedul : txt ABCא [47] copt arm Meth$_1$ Cyr[-p] gr-mss-mentd-by-Aug Aug$_{sæpe}$.

19. ins *τουτο* bef *ποιω* C c vulg [Orig-int$_1$] Jer$_{aliq}$. (αλλα, so BD¹א.) for *ου θελω*, *μισω* F vulg-sixt(with F-lat) Thdrt [Orig-int$_1$(txt$_1$)] : om G.

blind service comes to pass) **not what I desire, that do I** (this *θέλω* is not the *full determination of the will*, the standing with the bow drawn and the arrow aimed; but rather the *inclination* of the will,—the taking up the bow and pointing at the mark, but without power to draw it :—we have *θέλω* in the sense of *to wish*, 1 Cor. vii. 7, 32; xiv. 5; 2 Cor. xii. 20), **but what I hate** (= *οὐ θέλω*, ver. 19: no distinction in intensity between *θέλω* and *μισῶ*), **that I do** (no distinction here between *πράσσω* and *ποιῶ*, as apparently in John iii. 20, 21, where see note: for they are interchanged in vv. 19, 20). The Commentators cite several parallel passages from profane writers: e. g. Seneca, Hippol. 604, 'Vos testor omnes cœlites, hoc quod volo, me nolle;'—Epictetus, Enchiridion ii. 26, *ἐπεὶ γὰρ ὁ ἁμαρτάνων οὐ θέλει ἁμαρτάνειν, ἀλλὰ κατορθῶσαι, δῆλον ὅτι ὃ μὲν θέλει οὐ ποιεῖ, καὶ ὃ μὴ θέλει ποιεῖ*: —the well-known lines of Ovid, Met. vii. 19, 'aliudque cupido, Mens aliud suadet: video meliora proboque, Deteriora sequor:' —Plautus, Trinummus iii. 2. 31, 'Scibam ut esse me deceret, facere non quibam miser:'—&c. **16.**] **But if** (= '*now seeing that*;' takes up the foregoing and draws an inference from it) **what I wish not, that I do, I agree with** (bear witness to) **the law that it is good** (viz. 'in that the *law* prohibits what *I also* dislike,—the law and I are as one in proscribing the thing,—the *law*, and *my wish*, tend the same way'). **17.**] **Now however** ('quod autem quum ita sit,' *not* of time, as Grot., 'nunc post legem datam,'—or Koppe, 'ex quo Christianus factus sum') **it is no longer** (not a chronological, but a logical sequence, '*it can no more be said, that*;' see reff.) **I that perform it** (*κατεργ.* as recalling vv. 8—15), **but sin that dwelleth in me.** Here the *ἐγώ* is *not the complex responsible self*, by which the evil deed is wrought, and which incurs the guilt of working it: but the *self of the* WILL *in its higher sense*, the *ἔσω ἄνθρωπος* of ver. 22. The not bearing this in mind has led to error in interpretation and doctrine: e. g. when it is supposed that the Christian is not responsible for his sins committed against his spiritual will and higher judgment; whereas we are all responsible for the *ἔργα* of the sin that dwelleth in us, and it is in this very subjection to and involution with the law of sin in our members, that the misery consists, which leads to the cry in ver. 24.

18.] *An explanation of the οἰκοῦσα ἐν ἐμοὶ ἁμαρτία of the last verse.* **For I know** (by experience, detailed in the next verse) **that there dwells not in me, that is, in my flesh, (any) good (thing).** I said, *sin that dwelleth in me*, because I feel sure, from experience, that *in me* (meaning by 'me' not that higher spiritual self in which the Spirit of God dwells, but the lower carnal self: see on this important limitation the remarks at the beginning of the section) *dwells no good thing*. And what is my proof of this? How has experience led me to this knowledge? **For** (the proof from experience) **the wish** (to do good) **is present with me** (*παρ.*, not metaphorical, see reff., but, as *προκεῖμαι* in

κακόν, τοῦτο πράσσω. 20 εἰ δὲ ὃ οὐ θέλω [ἐγώ], τοῦτο
ποιῶ, [i] οὐκ ἔτι ἐγὼ [k] κατεργάζομαι αὐτό, ἀλλὰ ἡ [lm] οἰκοῦσα
[l] ἐν ἐμοὶ ἁμαρτία. 21 [q] εὑρίσκω ἄρα τὸν [r] νόμον τῷ θέλοντι
ἐμοὶ ποιεῖν [p] τὸ [p] καλόν, ὅτι ἐμοὶ [s] τὸ [s] κακὸν [o] παράκειται.
22 [t] συνήδομαι γὰρ τῷ νόμῳ τοῦ θεοῦ κατὰ τὸν [u] ἔσω
[u] ἄνθρωπον, 23 [v] βλέπω δὲ [w] ἕτερον νόμον ἐν τοῖς [x] μέλεσίν

q = Acts xix. 19. xxvii. 28. 1 Chron. xx. 2.
r = Heb. vii. 16.
s ch. ii. 9 reff.
t here only +. Xen. Mem. iii. 11. 10. Herod. iii. 36. Eurip. Med. 136.
u Eph. iii. 16. see 2 Cor. iv. 16. 1 Pet. iii. 4. ὁ ἐντὸς ἄνθρ., Plato Rep. ix. p. 589.
v = and constr., Heb. x. 25.
w = Matt. viii. 21. vv. 3, 4 al.
x ch. vi. 13 reff.

20. rec aft θελω ins εγω (*corrn for emphasis: or for conformity with εγω below?*), with AKL[P]א rel syr copt goth Thdrt [Damasc Orig-int$_1$] Aug$_{sæpe}$: om BCDF b o latt Syr[appy] æth arm [Meth$_1$] Chr-ms$_1$ Cyr Ambr Ambrst Pelag Aug$_1$. (**αλλα**, so BD[1]א.)

21. om οτι to παρακειται F. **22.** for θεου, κυριου 34: νοος B.

Homer, used commonly of meats served up to, lying before, any one); **but to perform that which is good, is not** (the absence of εὑρίσκω in ABCא, and the variations of γινώσκω and ἔχω in one or two mss. and versions,—and besides, the somewhat unusual termination of the sentence with οὔ,—are too strong presumptions of its being an interpolation, to allow of its retention) **(present with me).** **19.**] And this οὐ παρακεῖσθαι of the *doing* good is shewn *by my acts*, in that I *do not* the good that I wish (to do), but the evil which I do not wish, that *I do*. **20.**] The inference of ver. 17 restated, with the premiss of ver. 16 in the place of νυνὶ δέ:—but its meaning is now clearer and deeper than then; we know now that the ἐγώ which in the present verse does not the evil thing, is *the better* ἐγώ of the ἔσω ἄνθρωπος,—whereas the ἐμοί in which sin dwells and rules, though included in the complex self, is *the lower* ἐγώ, ἡ σάρξ μου. And so the way is now prepared for at once setting forth the *conflict* within us *between these two*. **21.**] **I find then** (i. e. as appears from what has been detailed) **the** (this) **law** (presently to be defined as *the law of sin in my members*, and exemplified in the following words: so τοῦ ῥήματος τοῦ κυρίου, ὡς ἔλεγεν, Acts xi. 16:—τῶν λόγων τοῦ κυρίου Ἰησοῦ, ὅτι αὐτὸς εἶπεν, Acts xx. 35 (De W.). This is the view of Calv., Beza, Grot., Estius, Wolf, Winer, Meyer (ed. 1, but in subsequent editions he has altered his view more than once), De Wette, al. It cannot well be referred to the *Mosaic law*, as, with various forced arrangements and constructions, Chrys., Theophyl., Theodoret, Tholuck, Olsh., Fritz., Köllner; the great objection being, that all these *do violence to the context*. Tholuck's remark, that had νόμον meant as above, it would have been anarthrous, or τοῦτον τὸν νόμον, is sufficiently answered by the above examples: and the dative after εὑρίσκω, to which he also objects as inadmissible in any language, is justified by Soph. Œd. Col. 966, οὐκ ἂν ἐξεύροις ἐμοὶ | ἁμαρτίας ὄνειδος οὐδέν,—and by Plato, Rep. iv. p. 421, ἕτερα . . τοῖς φύλαξιν εὑρήκαμεν, 'alia invenimus nostris custodibus observanda,' Ficin.) **to me** (for myself) **wishing to do good, that** (consisting in this, that) **evil is present with** (see above, ver. 18) **me.**

22, 23.] *Explanation of the conflict above alleged to exist.* **For I delight in** (σύν not signifying participation with others, but as perhaps in συνλυπούμενος, Mark iii. 5, and in the phrase σύνοιδά μοι; denoting 'apud animum meum.' Thol. συνήδομαι is a stronger expression than σύμφημι, ver. 16) **the law of God after the inner man** (= νοῦς, ver. 25,—see reff.—and compare Peter's ὁ κρυπτὸς τῆς καρδίας ἄνθρωπος, ref. 1 Pet. But not *merely* the *mental and reasoning part of man*:—for that surely *does not* delight in the law of God:—it is *absolutely necessary* to presuppose the *influence of the Holy Spirit*, and to place the man in *a state of grace before this assertion can be true*. And it is surprising to find Commentators like Tholuck and De Wette, while they acknowledge that συνήδομαι is stronger than σύμφημι, yet denying the gradual introduction of the *spiritual man* in the description of this conflict. True, THE SPIRIT is not yet introduced, because purposely kept back until treated of as the great deliverer from this state of death; the man is as yet described as compounded of the outer and inner man, of ἡ σάρξ and ὁ νοῦς, and the operations of the two are detailed *as if unassisted*,—even the term πνεῦμα for the human spirit being as yet avoided,—but all this is done, because *the object is to set the conflict and misery, as existing even in the spiritual man, in the strongest light*, so that the question in ver. 24 may lead the way to the *real uses* and *blessed results* of this conflict in ch. viii.); **but I see** (= *'find:'*—as if he were a spectator of that which is going on

y here only +. z Luke xxi. 24. 2 Cor. x. 5. 2 Tim. iii. 6 only. 3 Kings viii. 46. (-τος, Luke iv. 18 only. -τεύειν, Eph. iv. 8 only. -σία, ib. and Rev. xiii. 10 bis only.)

μου [y] ἀντιστρατευόμενον τῷ [r] νόμῳ τοῦ νοός μου, καὶ [z] αἰχ-
μαλωτίζοντά με [ἐν] τῷ νόμῳ [a] τῆς ἁμαρτίας τῷ ὄντι ἐν
τοῖς [x] μέλεσίν μου.
24 [b] ταλαίπωρος ἐγὼ ἄνθρωπος· τίς με
[c] ῥύσεται ἐκ τοῦ σώματος [a] τοῦ θανάτου τούτου;
25 [d] χάρις

ABCDF KL[P]ℵ a b c d f g h k l m n o 17 [47]

a genit., — ch. vi. 6 reff.
b Rev. iii. 17 only. Isa. xxxiii. 1. (-ρία, ch. iii. 16. -ρεῖν, James iv. 9.)
c — and constr., Luke i. 74. 2 Cor. i. 10 al. Exod. vi. 6. w. ἀπό, Matt. vi. 13. ch. xv. 31 al. Ps. cxxxix. 1.
d = ch. vi. 17 reff.

23. [for 1st *μου*, *μοι* F-gr.] *αντιστρατ. κ. αιχμαλ.* (omg *με*) *τω νομ. του νοος μου τω οντι* A. rec om 2nd *εν*, with (A)CL rel syrr [arm] $Meth_2$ $Cæs_1$ Chr_1 Cyr[-p_2 Damasc:] ins BDFK[P]ℵ b[1] c k m n o 17 latt coptt goth $Clem_1$ Thdrt [Euthal-ms Orig-int_3 Ambrst. [47(sic).]]

25. rec for *χαρις τω θεω*, *ευχαριστω τω θεω* (*see notes*), with AKLℵ[1] rel syrr goth $Orig_1$ Chr Œc Thl: *η χαρις του θεου* D vulg [Orig-int_2 Ambrst Jer_1], *η χαρις του κυριου* F: txt B 213 sah (æth) $Meth_1$ $Orig_1$, and *χ. δε τω θ.* C[2](C[1] uncert) ℵ-corr[1] 10-7. 31. 73.

within) **a different law** (differing in kind and aim, not = ἄλλος merely) **in my members** (= ἐν τῇ σαρκί μου, ver. 18), **warring against** ([in continual dissension and conflict with] ἀντιστρ. is not to be joined with βλέπω so as to = ἀντιστρατεύεσθαι, though that would be an allowable construction, see Acts viii. 23; 1 Cor. viii. 10,—but βλέπω—μου forms an independent sentence antithetic to συνήδομαι—ἄνθρωπον) **the law of my mind** (the consent viz., to the law of God, which my mind yields; not = the law of God, any more than the different law in my members = the law of sin,—but both meaning the standard or rule set up, which inclination follows:—the one in the νοῦς, *in harmony with the law of God*,—the other in the μέλη or σάρξ, *subservient*, and causing subservience, *to the principle or law of sin*), **and bringing me** (the whole complex self—the 'me' of personality and action) **into captivity with** (ἐν, not exactly '*by means of*,' but pointing out the department in which, the investiture with which, the taking captive has place. Nor would the simple dative be '*by means of*,' as Chrys., Theodoret, Theophyl.,—but merely '*to*:' the dat. commodi aft. αἰχμαλ.) **the law of sin** (the sinful principle, of resistance to God's law, ἡ ἁμαρτία as awakened and set energizing, ver. 9, by that law) **which is in my members.** Commentators have much disputed whether the ἕτερος νόμος, and the νόμος τῆς ἁμαρτ., both ἐν τοῖς μέλεσίν μου, are *different*, or the *same*. The former view is held by Calv., Beza, Köllner, Rückert, De W.: the latter by Reiche, Meyer, Fritz., Tholuck. It appears to me (see above) that the identity cannot be maintained without introducing great confusion into the sentence.

24.] *The division of the man against himself,—his inward conflict, and miserable state of captivity to sin in the flesh, while with the mind he loves and serves the law of God. From this wretched condition, which is a very death in life, who shall deliver him?* **σώματος** cannot well be figurative, '*universitas vitiorum*,' or '*mortifera peccati massa*,' but must, on account of the part which ἡ σάρξ and τὰ μέλη have hitherto borne, be *literal*. Then *how is* **τούτου** *to be taken?* Some (Syr., Erasm., Calv., Beza, Olsh., Winer) join it with σώματος, and (not Winer) justify the construction as a Hebraism: but Winer has refuted the notion (edn. 6, § 34. 3. b) of a Hebraism, and the arrangement has no Greek example. It can only be joined with θανάτου;—and that most fitly, as the *state which he has been describing* is referred to by **τοῦ θανάτου τούτου.** Then **the body of this death** will mean, 'the body whose subjection to the law of sin brings about this state of misery,' compare σῶμα τῆς ἁμαρτίας, ch. vi. 6. From this body, as the instrument whereby he is led captive to the law of sin and death, he cries out for deliverance: i.e to be *set free*, as ch. viii. 2, *from the law of sin and death*. Some Commentators, misled by the notion of a Hendiadys (σώματος τοῦ θ. = θνητοῦ σώματος), a most fruitful source of error in exegesis, have imagined that the verse implies a wish to be *delivered from the body* (by death), and expresses a *weariness of life*.

The cry is uttered, as De Wette well observes, in *full consciousness* of the *deliverance which Christ has effected*, and as *leading to the expression of thanks* which follows. And so, and no otherwise, is it to be taken.

25.] The rec. εὐχαριστῶ has but slender authority, and in the great variety of readings, it is not easy to determine. ἡ χάρις τοῦ θεοῦ is evidently a correction to answer to τίς above; so that our choice lies between χάρις τῷ θ. and χάρις δὲ τῷ θ. The sentence is (not, of course, constructionally, as the var. readg. ἡ χάρις τοῦ θεοῦ, but logically) an *answer* to the *preceding question*: **Thanks to God** (who hath accomplished this) **by means of Jesus Christ our Lord.** This exclamation and thanksgiving more than all convince me,

τῷ θεῷ διὰ Ἰησοῦ χριστοῦ τοῦ κυρίου ἡμῶν. [e] ἄρα [e] οὖν αὐτὸς ἐγὼ τῷ μὲν [f] νοῒ [g] δουλεύω νόμῳ θεοῦ, τῇ δὲ σαρκὶ νόμῳ ἁμαρτίας. VIII. 1 οὐδὲν ἄρα νῦν [h] κατάκριμα τοῖς ἐν χριστῷ Ἰησοῦ· 2 ὁ γὰρ νόμος τοῦ [i] πνεύματος τῆς

e ch. v. 18 reff.
f = ver. 23. see 2 Thess. ii. 2.
g = Acts xx. 19 reff.
h ch. v. 16, 18 only +.
i (ver. 10.) Rev. xi. 11. Ezek. xxxvii. 5.

80. 93 copt arm Cyr[-p_1]. εγω bef αυτος D[1](and lat) vulg [spec Orig-int_1 Ambrst]. om μεν Fℵ[1] latt [Orig-int_1] lat-ff.

Chap. VIII. 1. om νυν D[1][-gr 47-marg] Syr æth arm Cyr[-p_1] (Jer_1) $Victorin_1$ $Prædest_1$. rec at end ins μη κατα σαρκα περιπατουσιν (so far, with AD[2] vulg [spec F-lat] Syr goth arm Bas_1 Chr_1 lat-ff) αλλα κατα πνευμα (*supplied from ver 4, from a misunderstanding of the argument: see notes*), with D[3]KL[P]ℵ[3] rel [syr] Thdrt Thl Œc: om BCD[1] F[-gr(a space is left)] ℵ[1] [47-txt] coptt æth Orig-schol Ath_1 Dial Cyr[-p_1 Orig-int_1] Aug_2.

that Paul speaks of *none other than himself*, and *carries out as far as possible* the misery of the conflict with sin in his members, *on purpose to bring in the glorious deliverance which follows*. Compare 1 Cor. xv. 56, 57, where a very similar thanksgiving occurs. **ἄρα οὖν** κ.τ.λ.] These words are most important to the understanding of the whole passage. We must bear in mind that it had begun with the question, Is the law sin? The Apostle has proved that it is not, but is holy. He has shewn the *relation that it holds to sin*, viz. that of *vivifying it* by means of man's natural aversion to the commandment. He has further shewn, that in himself, even as delivered by Christ Jesus, a conflict between the law and sin is ever going on: the misery of which would be death itself, were not a glorious deliverance effected. He now sums up his vindication of the law as holy; and at the same time, sums up the other side of the evidence adduced in the passage, from which it appears that the flesh is still, even in the spiritual man, subject (*essentially*, not practically and energetically) to the law of sin, —which subjection, in its nature and consequences, is so nobly treated in ch. viii. **So then** (as appears from the foregoing), **I myself** (I, who have said all this against and in disparagement of the law; I, who write of justification by faith without the deeds of the law: not '*I alone*,' without Christ, as opposed to the foregoing,—as De Wette, Meyer: nor, '*ego idem*,' I, one and the same person, as Beza, Erasm., Calv., Olsh.: nor '*ille ego*,' as Grot., Thol. See, for the meaning given above, ch. viii. 26 (αὐτὸ τὸ πνεῦμα); ix. 3; xv. 14; 2 Cor. xii. 13, in all which places (see on ch. xv. 14) it has the same force) **with my mind (indeed)** (ὁ νοῦς = ὁ ἔσω ἄνθρ. as in ver. 23) **serve the law of God** (cf. συνήδομαι, ver. 22), **but with my flesh** (the ἐγώ of ver. 18; and the σάρξ throughout of ch. viii.) **the law of sin.** It remains to be seen how this latter subjection, which in the *natural man carries all with it*, is *neutralized*, and issues only in the death of the *body* on account of sin, *in those who do not walk after the flesh, but after the Spirit.* Chap. VIII. 1—39.] *In the case of those who are in Christ Jesus, this divided state ends in the glorious triumph of the Spirit over the flesh: and that* (vv. 1—17), *though incompletely, not inconsiderably, even here in this state,* —*and* (vv. 18—30) *completely and gloriously hereafter. And* (vv. 31—39) *the Christian has no reason to fear, but all reason to hope; for nothing can sever him from God's love in Christ.* 1—17.] *Although the flesh is still subject to the law of sin, the Christian, serving not the flesh, but walking according to the Spirit, shall not come into condemnation, but to glory with Christ.* 1.] **There is therefore** (an inference from ch. vii. 25, because *with their mind*, and that mind *dwelt in and led by the Spirit of Christ*, they serve, *delight in*, the *law of God*) **now** (this νῦν is emphatic, and follows upon the question and answer of vii. 24, 25, —*rebus sic stantibus*,—**now** that a deliverance has been effected from the body of this death, by Christ. This is certain from the γάρ which follows, setting forth the fact of the deliverance) **no condemnation** (reff.; = the penal consequence of sin original and actual) **to those** (who are) **in Christ Jesus.** The expression ἐν χρ. Ἰησ. refers particularly to the last place where *God's gift of life eternal in Christ Jesus our Lord* was spoken of, ch. vi. 23,—and generally to all that was said in that chapter of our incorporation into and union with Him. The words μὴ κατὰ σάρκα περιπατοῦσιν, ἀλλὰ κατὰ πνεῦμα, '*walking as they do not according to the flesh but according to the Spirit*,' are probably a gloss introduced from ver. 4, right enough

[i] ζωῆς ἐν χριστῷ Ἰησοῦ [k] ἠλευθέρωσέν * με ἀπὸ τοῦ νόμου
τῆς ἁμαρτίας καὶ τοῦ θανάτου. 3 τὸ γὰρ [l] ἀδύνατον τοῦ
νόμου, [m] ἐν ᾧ [n] ἠσθένει διὰ τῆς σαρκός, ὁ θεὸς τὸν ἑαυτοῦ

ABCDF KL[P]ℵ a b c d f g h k l m n o 17 [47]

k ch. vi. 18 reff.
l see Acts xiv. 8 reff. constr. nom., see Heb. viii. 1. acc., 2 Cor. xii. 17.
m = Heb. ii. 18.
n = 2 Cor. xiii. 3.

2. [om εν χρ. ιησ. K Chr_2 $Tert_1$.] * σε BFℵ spec Syr Chr_2(but mss vary) [$Tert_1$]; ημας copt æth $Dial_1$ $Meth_1$: με ACDKL[P] rel vulg syr sah goth æth [arm (but some mss om) $Clem_1$ Did_{alic} Ath_1] Chr_2 Thdrt [Cyr_1-p Damasc Orig-int_1] $Tert_1$ Ambr Jer.

in sense (see there), but out of place here, because this *moral* element of 'those in Christ' is *not yet brought in:* the present assertion is *general,* and is made good in detail by and by. See digest. **2.**] **For** (a reason why there is no condemnation) **the law** (*norma,* method = influence, as in ἕτερον νόμον, ch. vii. 23,—used here perhaps for sharper contrast to the νόμος ἁμαρτ. below) **of the Spirit of life** (the Lord and Giver of life—life used in an incipient higher sense than ἔζων in ch. vii. 9,—see below) **freed me** (aor., referring to the time of his conversion. There is no stronger proof to my mind of the identity of the speaker in the first person throughout with the Apostle himself, than this extension of that form of speaking into this chapter: nothing more clearly shews, that there he was describing a really existing state within himself, but insulating, and as it were *exaggerating* it (as so often), to bring out more clearly the glorious deliverance to follow. If σε be read, the address is a general one to the reader, leading on to the ἡμῖν below: and the foregoing argument does not apply) **in Jesus Christ** (I follow the more regular grammatical arrangement in taking ἐν χρ. Ἰησ. with the verb. Thus also Thol. and De Wette.

It may be taken (notwithstanding the absence of the art., at which indeed only tiros will stumble) with ζωῆς, as Luther, which seems to suit ch. vi. 23,—or with τοῦ πν. τ. ζ., as Piscator and Flatt,—or with ὁ νόμ. τ. π. τ. ζ., as Calv.) **from the law of sin** (vii. 25) **and death** (*death* again here bears a higher meaning than in ch. vii. *We are now on higher ground:*—**κατάκριμα** having been mentioned, which is the punishment of sin, death now *involves that,* and is not only temporal misery, but eternal ruin also. This '*law of the Spirit of life*' having freed him from the law of sin and death, so that he serves another master, *all claim of sin on him is at an end*—he is acquitted, and there is no condemnation for him).

3.] **For** (explanation of ver. 2, shewing the method of this liberation) **that which was not in the power of the law** (the construction is a nominativus pendens, as in ref. Heb., in apposition with the following sentence, ὁ θεὸς κ.τ.λ.: so Rückert, Meyer, Fritz., De W., Tholuck: Winer, § 32. 7, makes it an acc. governed by ἐποίησεν understood (stating however in edn. 6, the nom. pendens as an alternative; see also § 63. I. 2. d): Olsh. al., make it an acc. absol. or supply κατά: Camerarius and Beza, διά;—but the above seems the simplest. **τὸ ἀδύνατ. τοῦ νόμου** may mean either, '*that part of the law which was impossible,*'—'could not be obeyed,'—as τὸ γνωστὸν τοῦ θεοῦ, ch. i. 19;—or, '*the inability of the law*' = ἡ ἀδυναμία τ. ν., as τὸ χρηστὸν τοῦ θεοῦ, ch. ii. 4;—or, '*that which was unable to be done by the law.*' Of these, the first is out of the question, because νόμος must be the subject of ἐν ᾧ ἠσθ. κ.τ.λ.:—the second would give the first clause the meaning, '*that wherein the inability of the law shewed itself,*' viz. its powerlessness διὰ τ. σαρκός. The third yields by far the best meaning: see below on διὰ τ. σ.) **in that** (this clause gives a reason and explanation of the ἀδύνατον, see however the note on ref. Heb.) **it was weak** (the Apostle keeps in mind his defence of the holiness of the law undertaken in ch. vii., and as Chrys. observes, δοκεῖ μὲν διαβάλλειν τὸν νόμον, εἰ δέ τις ἀκριβῶς προσέχοι, καὶ σφόδρα αὐτὸν ἐπαινεῖ . . . οὐδὲ γὰρ εἶπε τὸ πονηρὸν τοῦ νόμου, ἀλλὰ **τὸ ἀδύνατον**· καὶ πάλιν **ἐν ᾧ ἠσθένει**, οὐκ, ἐν ᾧ ἐκακούργει, ἐν ᾧ ἐπεβούλευε. Hom. xiv. p. 563) **through the flesh** (i. e. in *having to act* through the flesh: not, 'on account of the flesh,' i. e. of the hostility, or weakness of the flesh, which would be διὰ τὴν σάρκα. The flesh was the *medium through which* the law,—being a νόμος ἐντολῆς σαρκίνης, Heb. vii. 16,—*wrought,* and οἱ ἐν σαρκί the *objects on which.* So the gen. here is similar to that in 2 Cor. ii. 4, ἔγραψα ὑμῖν διὰ πολλῶν δακρύων, and 1 Pet. v. 12, δι' ὀλίγων ἔγραψα, indicating the *state in* or *medium through which,* the action is carried on),—**God** (did) **sending His own Son** (the stress is on ἑαυτοῦ, and the word is pregnant with meaning:—His *own,* and therefore like Himself, holy and *sinless.* This implication should be borne in mind, as the suppressed antithesis to ἁμαρτ., three times repeated afterwards. Another antithesis may be implied—ἑαυτοῦ, and therefore *spiritual,* not acting merely through

υἱὸν πέμψας ἐν [o] ὁμοιώματι [p] σαρκὸς [p] ἁμαρτίας καὶ [q] περὶ
ἁμαρτίας [r] κατέκρινεν τὴν ἁμαρτίαν ἐν τῇ σαρκί, 4 ἵνα τὸ

o ch. i. 23 reff. p constr., Phil. iii. 21 bis. q = Heb. x. 6, 18. Num. viii. 8. Lev. v. 11. r ch. ii. 1 reff.

the flesh, though in its likeness, but bringing a higher spiritual life into the manhood) **in the likeness of the flesh of sin** (the flesh *whose attribute and character was* SIN. The gen. is not = ἁμαρτωλοῦ, but implies far more—[not merely the contamination by, but] the belonging to and being possessed by. De Wette observes, 'The words ἐν ὁμοιώμ. σαρκ. ἁμ. appear almost to border on Docetism; but in reality contain a perfectly true and consistent sentiment. σὰρξ ἁμαρτ. is *flesh* (human nature, John i. 14; 1 John iv. 2; Heb. ii. 14) *possessed with sin:* the Apostle could not then have said **ἐν σαρκὶ** ἁμ. without making Christ *partaker of sin:* nor could he have said merely ἐν σαρκί, for then the bond between the Manhood of Jesus, and sin, would have been wanting: he says then, ἐν ὁμοιώμ. σαρ. ἁμ.,—meaning by that, He had a nature *like sinful human nature,* but had not Himself a *sinful nature,*—compare Heb. iv. 15: οὐ γὰρ ἔχομεν ἀρχιερέα μὴ δυνάμενον συνπαθῆσαι ταῖς ἀσθενείαις ἡμῶν, πεπειρασμένον δὲ κατὰ πάντα καθ' ὁμοιότητα χωρὶς ἁμαρτίας. The *likeness* must be referred not only to σάρξ, but also to the epithet τῆς ἁμ.:—it did not however consist in this, that He took our sins (literally) on Himself, and became Himself sinful (as Reiche), which would not amount to likeness of *nature,*—but in this, that He was *able to be tempted,* i. e. subjected to sensuous incitements, e. g. of *pain,* which in other men break out into sin, but in Him did not.' See Phil. ii. 7, and note. σάρξ is not = σῶμα, but as in John i. 14, the *material,* of which man is in the body compounded),—**and on account of sin** (to be joined with πέμψας, not as Chrys. al. Vulg., with κατέκρινεν: least of all as Luther, "und verdammete die Sünde in Fleisch *durch Sünde.*" The '*for,*' or '*on account of,*' sin, is at present *indefinite,* and not to be restricted to Christ's death as a sin-offering, which is not just now the subject. 'On account of sin' then, = *to put away sin,* as reff. Heb.), **condemned sin in the flesh** (not 'the sin which was in the flesh,' which would probably (not certainly) have been τὴν ἐν τ. σ., and which is against the context, in which ἁμ. is throughout an *absolute principle.* **κατέκρινεν** is allusive to κατάκριμα ver. 1. Hence it has been taken to mean that God condemned, *punished,* sin in the flesh by the death of Christ: so Orig., Erasm., Calv., Melancthon, Calov., Olsh., al. But that can hardly be the meaning here, for several reasons. 1. The Apostle is not speaking of the removal of the *guilt,* but of the *practice* of sin, and of the real fulfilment of the law in those who are in Christ. It is this which even in ver. 1 is before him, grounding as he does the οὐδὲν κατάκριμα on the δουλεύω νόμῳ θεοῦ—on the *new and sanctifying power of the Spirit by Christ,* in spite of *the continued subjection of the flesh to the law of sin.* 2. The context shews that the weakness of the law was, its having no *sanctifying* power;—it could arouse sin, but it could not condemn and cast it out. This indeed is the burden of ch. vii. The absence of *justifying* power in the law has already been dealt with. 3. The following verse clearly makes the fulfilling the δικαίωμα of the law no matter of mere imputation, but of περιπατεῖν κατὰ πνεῦμα.

We must then look for the meaning of κατακρίνειν in the *effects* and accompaniments of condemnation,—*victory over,* and *casting out of* sin. See, for example, John xii. 31, where κρίσις τοῦ κόσμου τούτου is explained by ὁ ἄρχων τοῦ κόσμου τούτου ἐκβληθήσεται ἔξω, and ib. xvi. 11. As early as Irenæus (Hær. iii. 20. 2, p. 214) this was seen to be the sense: 'ut condemnaret peccatum, et jam quasi condemnatum projiceret illud extra carnem:'—so Chrys., ἐνίκησεν αὐτήν, τὴν δύναμιν αὐτῆς ἐξέλυσε,—Œcum. 2, πῶς ἐξῆρε; κατακρίνας αὐτὴν—καὶ δείξας ἁλοῦσαν. πῶς οὖν ἑάλω καὶ ἥττηται; ἐν τῇ σαρκὶ αὐτοῦ. προσιέναι γὰρ βουληθεῖσα κ. μὴ ἰσχύσασα ἑάλω κ. ἥττηται,—and Theophyl. (τὴν σάρκα) ἡγίασε κ. ἐστεφάνωσε, κατακρίνας τὴν ἁμαρτίαν ἐν τῇ σαρκὶ προσληφθείσῃ καὶ δείξας ὅτι οὐ φύσει ἁμαρτωλὸς ἡ σάρξ. And so, in modern times, Beza, Vitringa, Bengel, the Schmidts, Rosenm., Meyer, De Wette, Tholuck, Locke, Stuart, al., and mainly Grot., Reiche, and Fritz., who however render it 'interfecit' or 'supplicio affecit,' and understand the occasion to have been the *Death of Christ,*—though the condemnation of sin is owing to His sinlessness, not to His sacrifice. I have dwelt at length on this question, as being very important to the right apprehension of the whole chapter, in this part of which *not the justification,* but the *sanctification,* of Christians is the leading subject. It is a strong confirmation of the above view, that God's condemnation of sin in the flesh by Christ is stated in ver. 3 as the ground of

r = ch. i. 32 reff.
s = ch. xiii. 8 al.
t ch. i. 3, 4 (reff.).
u ch. vi. 4 reff.
v constr., Matt. xvi. 23. Luke ii. 49. ch. ii. 14. Thuc. viii. 31.
w = Matt. xvi. 23 ‖ Mk. ch. xii. 16. Phil. iii. 19. Col. iii. 2. 1 Macc. x. 20.
x here 3ce. ver. 27 only +. 2 Macc. vii. 21. xiii. 9 only.

[r] δικαίωμα τοῦ νόμου [s] πληρωθῇ ἐν ἡμῖν τοῖς μὴ [t] κατὰ
[t] σάρκα [u] περιπατοῦσιν, ἀλλὰ [t] κατὰ [t] πνεῦμα. 5 οἱ γὰρ
[t] κατὰ [t] σάρκα ὄντες [v] τὰ τῆς σαρκὸς [w] φρονοῦσιν, οἱ δὲ
[t] κατὰ [t] πνεῦμα [v] τὰ τοῦ πνεύματος. 6 τὸ γὰρ [x] φρόνημα
τῆς σαρκὸς θάνατος, τὸ δὲ [x] φρόνημα τοῦ πνεύματος ζωὴ
καὶ [y] εἰρήνη. 7 [z] διότι τὸ [x] φρόνημα τῆς σαρκὸς [a] ἔχθρα εἰς
θεόν· τῷ γὰρ νόμῳ τοῦ θεοῦ οὐχ [b] ὑποτάσσεται, οὐδὲ γὰρ
δύναται· 8 οἱ δὲ [c] ἐν [c] σαρκὶ ὄντες θεῷ [d] ἀρέσαι οὐ δύνανται.

ABCDF KL[P]ℵ abcdf ghkl mno17 [47]

y = ch. ii. 10 reff. z = ch. i. 21. 1 Cor. xv. 9. a Luke xxiii. 12. Gal. v. 20. Eph. ii. 15, 16. James iv. 4 only. Gen. iii. 15. w. εἰς, here only. b Luke ii. 51 al. Dan. vi. 13 Theod. 1 Chron. xxix. 24. c ch. ii. 28 reff. d Acts vi. 5 reff. ch. xv. 1, &c. 1 Cor. vii. 32, &c. 1 Thess. iv. 1. 2 Tim. ii. 4. Prov. xii. 21.

7. for διοτι, οτι F. for δυναται, ουναται ℵ[1]. 8. ins τω bef θεω D.

(ver. 2) my being freed from *the law of sin and death:* because, viz. *Christ's victory over sin is mine, by my union with Him and participation in His Spirit.* **ἐν τῇ σαρκί** is not '*in His flesh,*' or '*by means of His flesh,*' as Orig., Syr.(Peschito), Beza, Grot., Reiche, Olsh., al., but 'in *the flesh,*' which Christ and ourselves have in common), **4.]** **in order that** (the purpose of God's condemning sin in the flesh) **the righteous demand** (or, requirement) **of the law** (= all its requirements (statutes), but here *combined in one for the sake of more distinct objectivity.* The variations in interpretation of ver. 3 have given rise to corresponding ones here. But here the matter has been more complicated still by the Vulg. rendering δικαίωμα, 'justificatio,' which has thrown the weight of the Romanist interpreters on the side of 'justitia imputata.' The usage of the word itself would preclude any such reference here, besides the considerations urged in the note above) **might be fulfilled in us** (*find its full accomplishment;*—not merely = 'be performed *by* us,'—for the Apostle has a much deeper meaning, viz. that the *aim of God in giving the Law* might be *accomplished* in us, in our sanctification, which is the ultimate end of our redemption, Eph. ii. 10; Col. i. 22. The passive is used, to shew that the work is not ours, but that of God by His grace, Olsh., Thol., De Wette) **who walk** (not '*walking as we do,*' which would be anarthrous,—but a description of *all* those of whom the above is true) **not after the flesh but after the Spirit** (who, notwithstanding that we are bound up with a σὰρξ ἁμαρτίας, do not *walk in our daily life* according to, or led by, the νόμος τῆς ἁμαρτίας ὁ ἐν τοῖς μέλεσιν ἡμῶν, but according to and led by the νόμος τοῦ πνεύματος τῆς ζωῆς, in Christ Jesus—members of Him, and participating in that victory over sin which He obtained, by which the power of sin in our flesh is broken). **5.]** **For** (explanation of the last) **those who live according to the flesh** (ὄντες not quite = περιπατοῦντες, but nearly:—the latter is the *evidence* of the former, and a *consequence* of it: οἱ κατὰ σάρκα ὄντες = οἱ σάρκινοι) **mind** ('*think of,*' 'care for, and strive after,' see reff.) **the things belonging to the flesh** (its objects of desire): **but those (who live) according to the Spirit** (= οἱ πνευματικοί, see above), **(mind) the things belonging to the Spirit** (the higher aims and objects of desire of the spiritual life). **6.]** **For** (the spiritual man cannot seek the things of the flesh, because) **the mind** (*thoughts, cares,* and *aims* as above) **of the flesh is** (ends in—the copula (=), as when it joins the two signs of an algebraic operation;—'*amounts to, being worked out*') **death** (not merely *physical,* nor mere *unhappiness,* as sometimes in ch. vii., but as in ver. 2, in the largest sense, extending to eternity); **but the mind** (*thoughts, cares, and aims*) **of the Spirit, is** (see above) **life and peace** (in the largest sense, as above). In this argument there is a suppressed premiss, to be supplied from ver. 2; viz. 'The Spirit is the Spirit of *life.*' Hence it follows that the spiritual man cannot mind the things of the flesh, because such mind is *death.* The addition καὶ εἰρήνη seems to be made to enhance the unlikelihood of such a minding,—the peace of the Spirit being a blessed contrast to the tumult of the fleshly lusts, even in this life. **7.]** **Because** (reason why the mind of the flesh is death) **the mind of the flesh is enmity** (contrast to εἰρήνη above) **against God** (it being assumed that *God is the source of* **ζωή**, and that ἔχθρα against Him is the absence of all true peace): **for it does not submit itself** (better [than the passive of the E. V.]) **to the law of God,—for neither can it** (this was proved in ch. vii.): **8.]** **but** (takes up the other and inferential member of the proposition, answering to a suppressed μέν preceding,—τὸ μὲν φρόνημα κ.τ.λ. [bringing in a further consequence: if the mind of

9 ὑμεῖς δὲ οὐκ ἐστὲ [c] ἐν [c] σαρκὶ ἀλλὰ [e] ἐν πνεύματι, [f] εἴπερ
πνεῦμα θεοῦ [g] οἰκεῖ ἐν ὑμῖν. [h] εἰ δέ τις [i] πνεῦμα χριστοῦ
[h] οὐκ [i] ἔχει, οὗτος οὐκ ἔστιν αὐτοῦ. 10 εἰ δὲ χριστὸς ἐν
ὑμῖν, τὸ μὲν σῶμα νεκρὸν διὰ ἁμαρτίαν, τὸ δὲ πνεῦμα ζωὴ
διὰ δικαιοσύνην. 11 εἰ δὲ τὸ πνεῦμα τοῦ [k] ἐγείραντος [τὸν]
Ἰησοῦν [k] ἐκ νεκρῶν [g] οἰκεῖ ἐν ὑμῖν, ὁ [k] ἐγείρας χριστὸν [k] ἐκ
νεκρῶν [l] ζωοποιήσει καὶ τὰ [m] θνητὰ σώματα ὑμῶν, διὰ τὸ

e = John iv. 23. Eph. vi. 18. Col. i. 8. see Rev. i. 10. iv. 2 al.
f ch. iii. 30. ver. 17. 1 Cor. viii. 5. xv. 15. 2 Cor. v. 3 v. r. 2 Thess. i. 6. 1 Pet. ii. 3 only.
g ch. vii. 17 reff.
h Matt. xxvi. 42. 1 Cor. vii. 9.
i 1 Cor. vii. 40. Jude 19.
k 1 Cor. xv. 12 reff.
l ch. iv. 17 reff.
m ch. vi. 12 reff.

9. (αλλα, so BD[1]א [Meth$_1$].)

10. om ει δε χρ. εν υμ. F. aft σωμα ins εστιν F. (δια αμ., so ABCD[3]F L[e sil, Tischdf (δι Treg)] d g m.) for ζωη, ζη F vulg (not am fuld harl[1]) arm.

11. ins τον bef ιησ. ABא[1] o [47]: om CDFKL[P]א[3] rel (Clem$_1$) [Meth$_1$ Euthal-ms] Cyr-jer$_1$ Chr$_1$ Thdrt$_1$ Thl Œc. rec ins τον bef χριστον, with KL[P]א[3] rel Hipp$_1$ [Ps-Ath$_1$ Sevrn$_1$] Thdrt Thl Œc: om AB(C)D[1.3]Fא[1] [Valent$_1$ Meth$_2$ Epiph Bas$_4$ Dial-trin$_1$ (and, adding ιησ., Ath$_1$ Did$_1$ *Cyr*-p Damasc)].—for χριστον, χρ. ιησ. A(aft νεκρ.) D[1] א[1](aft νεκρ. [so Cyr$_1$-p]) [Ath$_1$ Did$_1$ Cyr$_2$-p Damasc]: ιησ. χρ. C(aft νεκρ.) vulg copt æth[-rom arm-usc Ath$_1$ Did$_1$ Cyr$_1$-p Orig-int$_2$ Aug$_1$]: τον ιησουν lect-13, τον κυριον 114-5, τ. κυρ. ημ. ιησ. χρ. Syr [Orthod$_1$]: txt BD[3]FKL[P] rel syr sah [æth-pl arm-zoh Valent$_1$ &c(as above) Orig-int$_1$ Ambrst] Iren-int$_3$ Tert$_2$ Hil$_1$. om και Aא 39. 47 [arm-edd Orig$_2$ Meth$_1$ Epiph$_1$]. elz δια του ενοικουντος αυτου πνευ-

the flesh cannot be subject to God's law, then they who are in the flesh, and are led by that mind, cannot please God]. Calv., Beza, al. render it '*therefore*,' and so E. V., '*so then*,' erroneously) **they who are in the flesh** (as their *element of life and thought:* nearly = κατὰ σάρκα ὄντες above, which however denotes the rule which they follow. In 2 Cor. x. 3, the two are distinguished: ἐν σαρκὶ γὰρ περιπατοῦντες οὐ κατὰ σάρκα στρατευόμεθα) **cannot please God.** Melancthon remarks (Thol.),—'Hic locus maxime refutat Pelagianos et omnes qui imaginantur homines sine Spiritu Sancto legi obedire.' **9.**] **But** (oppos. to οἱ κατ. σάρ. ὄντες) **ye are not in the flesh** (see above), **but in the Spirit, if so be that** ('*provided that;*' not '*since*,' as Chrys., Olsh., al., which would be ἐπείπερ: Chrys. tries to prove εἴπερ = ἐπείπερ here by adducing ref. 2 Thess., where, however, as here, the meaning is, '*if so be that*,' '*if at least*.' That this is the meaning here is evident by the exception which immediately follows). **But** (this must be rightly understood: for) **if any man has not** ([not '*have not*,' as E. V.; the case is put as an existent one] οὐκ, and not μή, because it belongs to the verb and not to εἰ. De W. See Winer, edn. 6, § 55. 2. d) **the Spirit of Christ** (= πν. θεοῦ above. Obs. here that πν. θεοῦ, πν. χριστοῦ, and χριστός, *are all used of the Holy Spirit indwelling in the Christian*), **he is not His** (belongs not to Him, in the higher and blessed sense of being united to Him as a member of Him).

10.] **Now** ([in slight] contrast to the last verse [he brings out one point, which might seem to be an exception to the blessed consequences of the life-giving power of Christ indwelling in us]) **if Christ is in you** (= πν. θεοῦ οἰκεῖ ἐν ὑμ., see 2 Cor. iii. 17), **the** (your) **body indeed is dead on account of sin** (still remains dead, see 2 Cor. iv. 11—14, under the power of death physical (and eternal?) because of sin which it, *per se*, stands in, and serves), **but the** (your) **spirit** (τὴν ψυχὴν λέγει, ὡς πνευματικὴν ἤδη γεγενημένην. Schol. ap. Matthæi (Thol.): or rather perhaps he [now] uses πνεῦμα, regarding our spirits as possessed and penetrated by God's Spirit) **is life** (this would hardly be said if *only our human spirits* were meant, but the description would be in the adjectival form) **on account of righteousness** (not *here* the imputed righteousness of justification, which is not now under treatment, but the *implanted righteousness of the sanctification of the Spirit.* This appears not only from the context, but also from the διὰ ἁμαρτίαν, which answers to it).

11.] **But** (δέ takes up and continues the supposition in the former verse, with which in fact this is nearly identical, but with the important additional particular (whence the contrast) τοῦ ἐγείραντ. κ.τ.λ.) **if the Spirit of Him who raised Jesus from the dead, dwells in you** (which Spirit is therefore *powerful over death*, and besides renders you *partakers of Christ's Resurrection*), **He who raised Christ from the dead** (the personal name, Jesus, reminds more of the historic fact of the resurrection of the one Person, Jesus: the official and mystical name,

*

n 2 Cor. vi. 16. Col. iii. 16. 2 Tim. i. 5, 14 only. Lev. xxvi. 32.
o ch. v. 13 reff.
p ch. i. 14 reff.
q constr., 1 Cor. x. 13 reff.
r ch. i. 3 reff.
v = Heb. x. 38. xii. 9.

[n] ἐνοικοῦν αὐτοῦ πνεῦμα ἐν ὑμῖν. 12 [o] ἄρα [o] οὖν, ἀδελφοί, ABCDF KL[P]א
[p] ὀφειλέται ἐσμὲν οὐ τῇ σαρκὶ [q] τοῦ [r] κατὰ [r] σάρκα ζῆν. a b c d f
13 εἰ γὰρ [r] κατὰ [r] σάρκα ζῆτε, [s] μέλλετε ἀποθνήσκειν· εἰ δὲ g h k l m n o 17
πνεύματι τὰς [t] πράξεις τοῦ σώματος [u] θανατοῦτε, [v] ζήσεσθε. [47]

s = Acts xxi. 27. xxviii. 6. t = Acts xix. 18 reff. u ch. vii. 4 reff.

ματος (*see notes*), with ACא[P² rel mss-in-]Dial-trin (*Dial* iii. 20, *Athanas. Opp. vol* iv. *p* 452 [1234, ed. Migne]. *The Maced. has previously said* οὕτως οὐ γέγραπται Διὰ τοῦ . . ἀλλὰ Διὰ τό . ., *and adds* ἐὰν οὖν που ἓν ᾗ δεύτερον ἀντίγραφον εὑρεθῇ ἐσφαλμένον παρ' ὑμῖν . . . . *to which the Orthodox replies,* ἔχομεν δεῖξαι ὅτι ἐν ὅλοις ἀρχαίοις ἀντιγράφοις οὕτω γέγραπται· ἐπεὶ δὲ νομίζεις τοῦτο ἀντιλεγόμενον εἶναι, πληροφορήθητι καὶ ἐξ ἄλλης γραφικῆς ἀποδείξεως. *Maced.* εἰπέ, τοῦτο γὰρ ἀντιλέγεται) syr copt æth [sah-woide arm] Clem$_1$ Hipp$_1$ Cyr-jer$_1$ Ath$_3$ Did$_3$[int$_1$ Meth$_1$(and ms$_1$)] Bas$_4$ Epiph$_2$ Chr$_2$ Cyr[-p Damasc] Mac$_1$ Ambr Aug$_{sæpe}$ Vig: txt BDFKL[P¹] b c f g h k l n o 17 [47] latt Syr sah Orig$_3$[int$_2$ Euthal-ms] Meth$_1$ Chr$_1$ Thdrt Sevrn$_1$ Iren-int$_1$ Tert$_1$ Hil$_1$ Ambrst Jer Ambr$_{alic}$ Aug$_1$ Pelag Sedul Fulg.

13. for του σωματος, της σαρκος DF latt [Ephr$_1$] Iren-int Orig$_1$[int$_3$] Did[-int$_1$] Tert$_1$ Cypr$_1$ Ambrst Ambr Jer Aug Pelag Sedul Bede: txt ABCKL[P]א rel [syrr copt æth] sah Orig$_5$ Chr$_2$ Thdrt [Did$_1$ Damasc].

Christ, of the body of which He is the Head and we the members,—all raised with Him by the one Spirit dwelling in all) **shall quicken** (not merely ἐγερεῖ, because it is not merely the resurrection of the body which is in the Apostle's view,—see below) **even your mortal bodies** (the higher phase of the ζωοποιεῖν takes place in the *spirit* of man: and even of that which takes place in the body, there are two branches—one, the quickening it from being a tool of unrighteousness unto death (eternal),—the other, the quickening it out of death (physical) to be a new and glorified body. And the καί joined with θνητά, here, signifies that the working of the πνεῦμα ζωοποιοῦν shall not stop at the purely spiritual resurrection, nor at that of the body from dead works to serve the living God, but shall extend *even to the building up the spiritual body in the future new and glorious life*), **on account of His Spirit which dwells in you.** Here the reading is much disputed, whether it be the acc. or gen.: see var. readd. The gen. can only mean, 'by means of,' 'through,' His Spirit, &c.: this the acc. may include, (it not being specified *for what reason* it is on the Spirit's account, and leaving it open to be His presence, or His agency,) but must be rendered 'on account of,' or 'because of,' His Spirit, &c. Thus *both may* imply that the Holy Spirit is the *agent* in the quickening; but the gen. cannot bear the other meaning, that God will quicken, &c. *because of* His Spirit, &c. Hence in dispute with the *Macedonians*, who denied the divinity of the Holy Spirit, the gen. reading was important to the orthodox, as expressing agency, and that alone. But it seems pretty clear that the variation was older than the time of this heresy, and, however it may then have been appealed to, its origin cannot be assigned to any falsification by either of the then disputant parties. As to how far the Holy Spirit is the *direct Agent* in the resurrection of the body, see note on πνεῦμα ζωοπ., 1 Cor. xv. 45, and on 2 Cor. v. 5. Here, His direct agency cannot be in any way surprising, for it is *the whole process of bringing from death to life, extending even to the mortal body*, which is here spoken of—and unquestionably, 'the Lord and Giver of Life' is the agent throughout in this quickening. 'Non de ultima resurrectione, quæ momento fiet, habetur sermo, sed de continua Spiritus operatione, quæ reliquias carnis paullatim mortificans, cœlestem vitam in nobis instaurat.' Calv.:—but perhaps 'non *solum* de ultima resurrectione,' would have been more correct: for it certainly is *one thing* spoken of.

12, 13.] **So then, brethren, we are** (inference from the assurance in the last verse) **debtors** (we owe fealty: to what or whom, he leaves the reader to supply from ver. 11), **not to the flesh, to live according to the flesh** (Chrysostom well explains the qualification, τοῦ κατὰ σ. ζ.,—καὶ γὰρ πολλὰ αὐτῇ ὀφείλομεν, τὸ τρέφειν αὐτήν, τὸ θάλπειν, τὸ ἀναπαύειν, τὸ θεραπεύειν νοσοῦσαν, τὸ περιβάλλειν, καὶ μυρία ἕτερα λειτουργεῖν. ἵν' οὖν μὴ νομίσῃς ὅτι ταύτην ἀναιρεῖ τὴν διακονίαν, εἰπὼν **οὐκ ἐσμ. ὀφ. τῇ σαρ.**, ἑρμηνεύει αὐτὸ λέγων **τοῦ κ. σ. ζῆν**· . . . τουτέστι μὴ ποιῶμεν αὐτὴν κυρίαν τῆς ζωῆς τῆς ἡμετέρας. Hom. xiv. p. 576): **for if ye live according to the flesh, ye** [**must** (or,] **will,** μέλλετε of the *certain* end of your present course) **die** (ζῆν and ἀποθν. here in their full and pregnant sense, involving body and soul here and hereafter: but not to be understood as excluding the carnal from *any*

14 ὅσοι γὰρ πνεύματι θεοῦ [w] ἄγονται, οὗτοι [x] υἱοί εἰσιν
θεοῦ. 15 οὐ γὰρ [y] ἐλάβετε [yz] πνεῦμα [za] δουλείας πάλιν [b] εἰς
φόβον, ἀλλὰ [y] ἐλάβετε [yz] πνεῦμα [zc] υἱοθεσίας, [d] ἐν ᾧ [ef] κρά-

w = and constr., Gal. v. 18. 2 Tim. iii. 6.
x ver. 19 reff.
y Acts viii. 15 reff.
z constr., 2 Cor. iv. 13. Eph. i. 17. 2 Tim. i. 7.
a ver. 21. Gal. iv. 24. v. 1. Heb. ii. 15 only. Exod. xx. 2 al.
b = ch. v. 16 reff.
c ver. 23. ch. ix. 4. Gal. iv. 5. Eph. i. 5 only †.
d = Gal. vi. 1.
e Gal. iv. 6.
f Mark x. 48 ∥ L. Ps. lxxvi. 1. cvi. 6, &c.

14. rec ειισιν υιοι θεου (*corrn of order, as is also υ. θ. ει.*), with KL[P] rel [vulg-clem(with harl tol) copt syr arm $Clem_1$] Chr_2 Thdrt [Cyr_2-p Euthal-ms Gennad-c Orig-int_1] Iren-int_1 : υι. θε. εισ. ACDא [47 spec] fuld æth $Orig_1$[int_1 Did_3] Damasc $Cypr_1$ [Ambrst] Cassiod Gaud: txt BF am(with demid al) Syr $Orig_1$[int_2] Did[-int_1] Hil_2 Aug Bede.

15. (αλλα, so ABCא [$Clem_1$ $Orig_1$].)

resurrection—only from that which is truly ζῆν,—any more than the spiritual are exempted from *all* death, but only from that which is truly θάνατος): **but if by the Spirit ye slay** (abolish, annul) **the deeds** (hardly as Thol. 'sensu obscœno,' but as Col. iii. 9, the whole course of habits and action which has the flesh for its prompter) **of the body** (= τῆς σαρκός, but here concrete to give more vivid reality: compare τὰ ἔργα τῆς σαρκός, Gal. v. 19), **ye shall live** (not μέλλετε ζῆν, this *Life* being no natural consequence of a course of mortifying the deeds of the body, but the gift of God through Christ: and coming therefore in the form of an assurance, '*ye shall live*,' from Christ's Apostle. On ζῆν, see above). **14.**] **For** (ground of the assurance contained in ζήσεσθε) **as many as are led by** (reff.;—the slaying the deeds of the body by the Spirit, implies the being under the Spirit's guidance) **the Spirit of God, these** (emphatic—'these and no others') **are sons of God.**
υἱὸς θ. differs from τέκνον θ. in implying the higher and more mature and conscious member of God's family, see Gal. iv. 1—6, and note on 6. Hence *our Lord is never called τέκνον but always* **υἱὸς θεοῦ**. This latter, applied to a Christian, signifies 'one born of God' in the deepest relation to him,—and hence a partaker of His nature, 1 John iii. 9; 1 Pet. i. 23 (Tholuck, similarly Olsh.). **15, 16.**] *Appeal to the* CONSCIOUSNESS *of the Christian to confirm the assertion* (assumed for the moment that he *is led* by God's Spirit) *that he is a son of God.* **For** (confirmantis) **ye did not receive** (at your becoming Christians) **the spirit of bondage** (= 'the Spirit which ye received was not a spirit of bondage.' πν. is not *merely a* spirit, *a disposition*, but evidently refers to the same πν. which afterwards is πν. υἱοθεσ., and αὐτὸ τὸ πν. The Apostle seems however in this form of expression, both here and elsewhere, see reff., to have combined the objective Πνεῦμα given to us by God with our own subjective πνεῦμα. In the next verse they are separated) [**leading back** (or,] **again**[; but the latter word is undesirable, as] it has been imagined here that the πάλιν must refer to a former bestowal of the πνεῦμα δουλείας, and consequently that the reference is to the O. T. dispensation. In this two different sets of Commentators have found difficulties; (1) those, as Chrys.,—who would hold from John vii. 39, that the Holy Spirit was *absolutely not given* under the O. T., and (2) those, as Cocceius, who holding Him to have been given, *deny that His character was* πν. δουλείας. But there seems to me to be no occasion to go back for the reference of πάλιν to the O. T. The state of the *natural man* is δουλεία: the Holy Spirit given to them, the agent of their birth into, and sustainer of, a new state, was not a πν. δουλείας πάλιν εἰς φ., a spirit merely to retain them in, or take them back into their old state, viz. a state of *slavery*:—to *whom*, or whether to *different masters*, is not here in question, but the *state* merely—the object of the gift of the Holy Spirit was not to lead them *back* into this) **towards fear** (*so as to bring about or result in* fear, see ch. vi. 19. πάλιν can hardly, as De W., be taken with εἰς φόβ.), **but ye received the Spirit of** (the Spirit *whose effect* was, see above) **adoption** (this stricter meaning, and not that of *mere sonship*, is plainly that intended by the Apostle, both here and in reff. So Fritz., Meyer, Olsh., Harless on Eph. i. 5, Tholuck: on the other hand Luther, Winer, Rückert, De Wette, al., see on ver. 23. Of course, the *adoption to be a son involves sonship*, but not the converse), **in whom** (compare ἐν πνεύματι ch. ii. 29, and ver. 9. Luth. and Tholuck, '*through*, by means of, whom:' but τὸ πνεῦμα = Him *in* whom, not merely Him *by* whom, not being merely an external agent, but an indwelling and pervading power) **we cry** (the earnest expression of supplicating prayer, see reff. LXX) **Abba, Father** (I have said, on ref. Mark, that ὁ πατ. does not appear to be a mere explanation of אַבָּא, but to have been joined to it in one phrase, as a form of address: expressing probably, a corresponding 'my father,' אָבִי, in the Heb. expression. Luther, to

ζομεν [eg] Ἀββᾶ [g] ὁ πατήρ. 16 αὐτὸ [h] τὸ πνεῦμα [i] συμμαρτυρεῖ
τῷ [k] πνεύματι ἡμῶν ὅτι ἐσμὲν [l] τέκνα [l] θεοῦ. 17 εἰ δὲ τέκνα,
καὶ [m] κληρονόμοι· [m] κληρονόμοι μὲν θεοῦ, [n] συγκληρονόμοι
δὲ χριστοῦ· [o] εἴπερ [p] συνπάσχομεν, ἵνα καὶ [q] συνδοξασθῶ-

ABCDF KL[P]ℵ a b c d f g h k l m n o 17 [47]

g Gal. as above (e). Mark xiv. 36 only. h absol., Acts x. 19 reff. i ch. ii. 15. ix. 1 only †. k = Acts xvii. 16 reff. l = ver. 21. ch. ix. 8. John i. 12. xi. 52. Phil. ii. 15. 1 John iii. 1, 2, 10. v. 2. (see Gal. iv. 28, 31. Eph. v. 8.) m ch. iv. 13 reff. n Eph. iii. 6. Heb. xi. 9. 1 Pet. iii. 7 only †. (-μεῖν, Sir. xxii. 23.) o ver. 9 reff. p 1 Cor. xii. 26 only †. 1 Kings xxii. 8 Symm. [or Anon.] q here only †.

16. at beg ins ωστε D[-gr] : aft αυτο ins γαρ 115-24 vulg(demid harl[1] mar[1] : not am [fuld tol]) Thdrt Thl [Orig-int$_1$ Did-int$_1$] Pel.

17. for 1st κληρον., συνκληρονομοι D[1][-gr]. (συνπασχ., so AB[1]CDFℵ.—χωμεν A[P b (m) 17. 47 Tert$_1$ Cypr$_2$].)

express the familiarity of Abba, renders 'lieber Vater,' '*dear Father*'). See on the whole, the strictly parallel place, ref. Gal. **16.**] *And this confidence is grounded on the testimony of the Spirit itself.* So Chrys.: οὐ γὰρ ἀπὸ τῆς φωνῆς ἰσχυρίζομαι μόνον, φησίν, ἀλλὰ καὶ ἀπὸ τῆς αἰτίας ἀφ' ἧς ἡ φωνὴ τίκτεται . . . . οὐ γὰρ τοῦ χαρίσματός ἐστιν ἡ φωνὴ μόνον, ἀλλὰ καὶ τοῦ δόντος τὴν δωρεὰν παρακλήτου· αὐτὸς γὰρ ἡμᾶς οὗτος ἐδίδαξε διὰ τοῦ χαρίσματος οὕτω φθέγγεσθαι. Hom. xiv. p. 579. This verse being without copula, is best understood to refer to the same as the preceding, and the assertion to concern the same fact as the last verb, κράζομεν,—as if it were αὐτοῦ τοῦ πν. συμμαρτυροῦντος κ.τ.λ., grounding that fact on an act of the indwelling Spirit Himself. See again Gal. iv. 6. **The Spirit itself** (not '*idem Spiritus*,' as Erasm. and similarly Luth., Reiche, al.: the αὐτό expresses the independence, and at the same time, as coming from God, the preciousness and importance of the testimony) **testifies to our spirit** (see ch. ii. 15, and note: not '*una testatur*:' the σύν in composition does not refer to τῷ πν. ἡμ., but to *agreement in the fact*, as in 'contestari,' 'confirmare') **that we are children of God.** What is this *witness of the Spirit itself?* All have agreed, and indeed this verse is decisive for it, that it is *something separate from, and higher than, all subjective inferences and conclusions.* But on the other hand it does *not consist in mere indefinite feeling*, but in a *certitude of the Spirit's presence and work continually asserted within us.* It is manifested, as Olsh. beautifully says, in His comforting us, His stirring us up to prayer, His reproof of our sins, His drawing us to works of love, to bear testimony before the world, &c. And he adds, with equal truth, "On this direct testimony of the Holy Ghost rests, *ultimately*, all the regenerate man's conviction respecting Christ and His work. For belief in Scripture itself (he means, in the highest sense of the term 'belief,' = '*conviction personally applied*') has its foundation in this experience of the divine nature of the (influencing) Principle which it promises, and which, while the believer is studying it, infuses itself into him." The same Commentator remarks, that this is one of the most decisive passages against the pantheistic view of the identity of the Spirit of God and the spirit of man. However the one may by renovating power be rendered like the other, there still is a specific difference. The spirit of man may *sin* (2 Cor. vii. 1), the Spirit of God *cannot*, but can only be grieved (Eph. iv. 30), or quenched (1 Thess. v. 19), and it is by the infusion of this highest Principle of Holiness, that man becomes ONE SPIRIT with the Lord Himself (1 Cor. vi. 17). **τέκνα θεοῦ**] Here, (not υἱοί) because the testimony respects the very ground and central point of sonship, *likeness to and desire for God*: the testimony of the Spirit shewing us by our yearnings after, our confidence in, our regard to God, that we are verily begotten of Him. **17.**] CONSEQUENCES *of our being children of God.* **But** (announcing a result, as in a mathematical proposition: 'but, if &c.') **if children, also heirs** (which is the universal rule of mankind: but κληρ. here must not be carried to the extent of the idea of *heir* in all directions: it is merely the *one side* of *inheriting by promise*, which is here brought out: the word referring back probably to ch. iv. 13, 14, the promise to Abraham); **heirs of God** (as our Father, giving the inheritance to us), **and joint-heirs with Christ** (whom God has made κληρονόμον πάντων, Heb. i. 2. Tholuck remarks: "It is by virtue of their substantial unity with the father, that the children come into participation of his possession. The Roman law regarded them as continuators of his personality. The *dignity* of the inheritance is shewn (1) by its being God's possession, (2) by its being the possession of the Firstborn of God. By the Roman law, the share of the firstborn was no greater than that of the other children,—and the N. T. sets forth this view, making the redeemed equal to Christ (ver. 29), and Christ's possessions, theirs; 1 Cor. iii. 21—

μεν· 18 [r] λογίζομαι γὰρ ὅτι οὐκ [st] ἄξια τὰ [u] παθήματα [v] τοῦ
νῦν [v] καιροῦ [sw] πρὸς τὴν [xy] μέλλουσαν [yz] δόξαν [ya] ἀποκα-
λυφθῆναι [b] εἰς ἡμᾶς. 19 ἡ γὰρ [c] ἀποκαραδοκία τῆς [d] κτίσεως

r = and constr., ch. ii. 3 reff. (iii. 28.) s here only. t = Gen. xxiii. 9. 1 Chron. xxi. 22, 24. Prov. iii. 15. viii. 11. Sir. xxvi. 15. (see note.) u ch. vii. 5 reff. v ch. iii. 26 reff. w = Jer. xxiii. 28. x = ver. 13. w. inf. aor., Gal. iii. 23. Rev. i. 19. iii. 2. xii. 4. transp. of words, Gal. iii. 23. 1 Cor. xii. 22. y 1 Pet. v. 1. z = ch. ii. 7 reff. a = Luke xvii. 30. ch. i. 18. b = here only. c Phil. i. 20 only +. (-κεῖν, Ps. xxxvi. 7 Aq. Jos. B. J. iii. 7. 26. Polyb. xvi. 2. 8.) d = Mark xvi. 15. (ver. 39.) Judith xvi. 14.

18. for γαρ, δε A[P] 9 æth: *ergo* Ambrst [om Lucif$_1$].

23; John xvii. 22. In the *joint-heirship* we must not bring out this point, that Christ is *the rightful Heir*, who shares His inheritance with the other children of God: it is as adoptive children that they get the inheritance, and Christ is so far only the means of it, as He gives them power to become sons of God, John i. 12"); **if at least** (see above on ver. 9) **we are suffering with Him, that we may also be glorified with Him**: i. e. 'if (provided that) we are found in that course of participation in Christ's sufferings, whose aim and end, as that of His sufferings, is to be glorified as He was, and with Him.' But the εἴπερ does not regard the *subjective* aim, q. d. 'If at least our aim in suffering is, to be glorified,'—but the *fact* of our being partakers of that course of sufferings with Him, *whose aim is, wherever it is found*, to be glorified with Him.
Thol. takes the ἵνα as dependent on συγκληρ. (= ὥστε), and εἴπερ συνπ. as quasi-parenthetical; but the above seems to me more satisfactory. The connexion of *suffering with Christ*, and *being glorified with Him* is elsewhere insisted on, see 2 Tim. ii. 11; 1 Pet. iv. 13; v. 1.
This last clause serves as a transition to vv. 18—30, in which the Apostle treats of *the complete and glorious triumph of God's elect, through sufferings and by hope, and the blessed renovation of all things in and by their glorification.*
18.] **For** (= this suffering with Him in order to being glorified with Him is no casting away of toil and self-denial, seeing that) **I reckon** (implying, 'I myself am one who have embraced this course, being convinced') **that the sufferings of this present period** (of trial and sorrow, contrasted with the period of triumph following the παρουσία of Christ) **are insignificant** (οὐκ ἄξια = ἀνάξια,—no gen. or verb understood. ἄξιος and ἀνάξιος are found in the sense of '*worthy* (or *unworthy*) *to be compared with*' in the classics: so Hom. Il. θ. 234, νῦν δ' οὔθ' ἑνὸς ἄξιοι ἐσμὲν Ἕκτορος, and Plato, Protag. (Wetst.), ἀνάξιά ἐστι τ' ἀγαθὰ τῶν κακῶν, and again τίς ἄλλη ἀναξία ἡδονὴ πρὸς λύπην ἐστίν;) **in comparison with the glory which is to be revealed** (μέλλ. put first, as in reff., but apparently not, as De W., for the sake of emphasis. Thol. cites Demosth., p. 486. 10, ἐν τοῖς οὖσι νόμοις κυρίοις, in which there is no emphasis, as neither in ref. 1 Cor. **ἀποκαλ.**, at the ἀποκάλυψις of Christ. On the sentiment, see 2 Cor. iv. 17) **with regard to us** (not merely ἡμῖν, as spectators, but εἰς ἡμᾶς, as the subjects of the revelation; the E. V. is not far wrong, '*in us*,' taking the εἰς in a pregnant sense as ἦν κηρύσσων **εἰς** τὰς συν., Luke iv. 44 [but it must not be understood as meaning *within us*, in our hearts]). Bernard amplifies this—de Convers. ad Cleric. c. xxi. 37 (30), vol. i. p. 494,—'non sunt condignæ passiones hujus temporis ad præteritam culpam quæ remittitur, non ad præsentem consolationis gratiam quæ immittitur, non ad futuram gloriam quæ promittitur nobis.'
19 ff.] *The greatness of this glory is shewn by the fact that* ALL CREATION, *now under the bondage of corruption, shall be set free from it by the glorification of the sons of God.* **For** (proof of this transcendent greatness of the glory, not, as De W., of the certainty of its manifestation, though this secondary thought is perhaps in the background) **the patient expectation** (hardly = ἡ σφόδρα προσδοκία, as Chrys., whom Luther and E. V. follow; but better προσδοκία εἰς τὸ τέλος,—the ἀπό denoting, as also in ἀπεκδέχεται, that the expectation continues till the time is exhausted, and the event arrives) **of the creation** (= *all this world except man*, both animate and inanimate: see an account of the exegesis below) **waits for** (see above) **the revelation of the sons of God** ('revelatur gloria: et tum revelantur etiam filii Dei.' Beng. υἱῶν, not τέκνων, because their sonship will be complete, and possessed of all its privileges and glories). **ἡ κτίσις** has been very variously understood. There is a full history of the exegesis in Tholuck. De Wette sums it up thus: "The Creation,—i. e. things created,—has by many been erroneously taken in an arbitrarily limited sense; e. g. as applying only, I. to *inanimate creation*, as Chrys., Theophyl., Calv., Beza, Aret., '*mundi machina*,' Luther, the Schmidts, al., Fritz., '*mundi machina, cœli sidera, aer, terra*:'—against this are the words οὐχ ἑκοῦσα and συνστενάζει κ. συνωδίνει, implying *life* in the κτίσις,—

τὴν [e] ἀποκάλυψιν τῶν [f] υἱῶν τοῦ θεοῦ [g] ἀπεκδέχεται. 20 τῇ
γὰρ [h] ματαιότητι ἡ [d] κτίσις [i] ὑπετάγη οὐχ [k] ἑκοῦσα ἀλλὰ
διὰ τὸν [l] ὑποτάξαντα, [m] ἐπ' ἐλπίδι, 21 ὅτι καὶ αὐτὴ ἡ

ABCDF KL[P]ℵ abcdf ghkl mno17 [47]

e ch. ii. 5. 1 Cor. i. 7. 2 Thess. i. 7 al. Sir. xi. 27. f Matt. v. 9. Luke vi. 35. xx. 36. ver. 14. Gal. iii. 26. Rev. xxi. 7. g here &c., 3ce. 1 Cor. i. 7. Gal. v. 5. Phil. iii. 20. Heb. ix. 28. 1 Pet. iii. 20 only †. h = here (Eph. iv. 17. 2 Pet. ii. 18) only. Eccles. i. 2. (-οῦσθαι, ch. i. 21.) i ver. 7 reff. k 1 Cor. ix. 17 only. Exod. xxi. 13 only. l act., 1 Cor. xv. 27 & Heb. ii. 8, from Ps. viii. 6. Eph. i. 22. Phil. iii. 21. m ch. iv. 18 reff.

19. om του F. **20.** for ουχ εκουσα, ου θελουσα F. εφ B¹D¹Fℵ. **21.** διοτι D¹Fℵ. om η F.

for to set these down to mere personification is surely arbitrary:—and one can imagine no reason why bestial creation should be excluded. II. to *living creation:* (1) to *mankind;* Aug., Turret., all., take it of *men not yet believers:* (2) Locke, Lightf., Hammond, Semler, of the *yet unconverted Gentiles:* (3) Cramer, Gersdorf, al., of the *yet unconverted Jews:* (4) Le Clerc, al., of the *converted Gentiles:* (5) al., of the *converted Jews;* (6) al., *of all Christians:*"—"but," as he proceeds, "against (II.) lies this objection, that if the Apostle had wished to speak of the *enslaving and freeing of mankind,* he hardly would have omitted reference to sin as the ground of the one and faith of the other, and the judgment on unbelievers. But on the other hand we must not extend the idea of κτίσις *too wide,* as Theodoret, who includes the *angels,* Köllner, who understands the *whole Creation,* animate and inanimate, rational and irrational, and Olsh., who includes the *unconverted Gentiles:* nor make it *too indefinite,* as Koppe and Rosenm.: '*tota rerum universitas.*' The right explanation is, *all animate and inanimate nature as distinguished from mankind:* so Irenæus, Grot., Calov., Wolf, Rückert, Reiche, al., Meyer, Neander, Schneckenburger, Thol." The idea of the renovation and glorification of all nature at the revelation of the glory of our returned Saviour, will need no apology nor seem strange to the readers of this commentary, nor to the students of the following, and many other passages of the prophetic word: Isa. xi. 6 ff.; lxv. 17 ff.; Rev. xxi.; 2 Pet. iii. 13; Acts iii. 21.

20.] *Explanation of the* REASON WHY *all creation waits, &c.* **For the creation was made subject to vanity** (= הֶבֶל, Ps. xxxix. 6,—where (xxxviii. 5) the LXX have τὰ σύμπαντα ματαιότης. So also Eccles. i. 2 and passim. It signifies the *instability, liability to change and decay,* of all created things) **not willingly** ('cum a corruptione naturâ res omnes abhorreant.' Bucer in Thol.) **but on account of** (διά is so far from losing its proper meaning by the reference of τὸν ὑποτάξαντα to God, as Jowett affirms, that it gains its strictest and most proper meaning by that reference: see ver. 11. He is the occasion, and His glory the end, of creation's corruptibility) **Him who made it subject** (i. e. God. Chrys., al., interpret it of *Adam,* who was the *occasion* of its being subjected; and at first sight the acc. with διά seems to favour this. But I very much doubt whether this view can be borne out. For (1) does not ὑποτάξαντα imply a *conscious act of intentional subjugation,* and not merely an *unconscious occasioning of the subjugation?* Thus we have it said of God, ref. 1 Cor., πάντα γὰρ **ὑπέταξεν** ὑπὸ τοὺς πόδας αὐτοῦ· ὅταν δὲ κ.τ.λ., δῆλον ὅτι ἐκτὸς **τοῦ ὑποτάξαντος** αὐτῷ τὰ πάντα. And (2) the acc. aft. διά is in reality no reason against this. He is speaking of the *originating cause* of this subjection, not of the efficient means of it. He says that creation was not subjected ἑκοῦσα, i. e. διὰ τὸ θέλημα ἑαυτῆς, but διὰ τὸν ὑποτάξαντα. At the same time such a way of putting it, removing as it were the supreme will of God to a wider distance from corruption and vanity, and making it not so much the worker as the occasion of it, as well as this indefinite mention of Him, is quite intelligible on the ground of that reverential awe which so entirely characterizes the mind and writings of the Apostle. If the *occasion pointed at* by ὑποτάξαι be required, I should hardly fix it at the Fall of man, but at his *creation,* in the eternal counsels,—when he was made *capable of falling, liable to change.* The explanation of **ὁ ὑποτάξας** as meaning '*the devil*' (Locke, al.), hardly needs refutation. See Matt. x. 28, and note),—**in** ('*on condition of,*' '*in a state of,*' see ch. iv. 18, and note on ἐφ' ᾧ, ch. v. 12) **hope** (ἐπ' ἐλπίδι must not be joined with ὑποτάξαντα, because then the ἐλπίς becomes *the hope of the* ὑποτάξας,—but with ὑπετάγη, being the hope of the ὑποταγεῖσα), **because** (not '*that,*' after ἐλπίς,—for then it is not likely that αὐτὴ ἡ κτίσις would be so emphatically repeated: the clause now announces a *new fact,* and thus the emphasis is accounted for. To suppose the whole clause *subjective to the* **ἐλπίς**, would be to attribute to the yearnings of creation, *intelligence* and *rationality,*—consciousness of itself and of

[d] κτίσις [n] ἐλευθερωθήσεται ἀπὸ τῆς [o] δουλείας τῆς [p] φθορᾶς n ch. vi. 18 reff. o ver. 15 reff.
εἰς τὴν [q] ἐλευθερίαν τῆς [r] δόξης τῶν [s] τέκνων τοῦ [s] θεοῦ. p = 1 Cor. xv. 42, 50. Gal. vi. 8. Col. ii.
22 οἴδαμεν γὰρ ὅτι πᾶσα ἡ [d] κτίσις [t] συνστενάζει καὶ [u] συν- 22. 2 Pet. i. 4. ii. (12, bis)
ωδίνει [vw] ἄχρι τοῦ [w] νῦν· 23 [x] οὐ μόνον δέ, [x] ἀλλὰ καὶ 19 only. Jonah ii. 7.
αὐτοὶ τὴν [y] ἀπαρχὴν τοῦ πνεύματος ἔχοντες ἡμεῖς καὶ q 2 Cor. iii. 17. James i. 25. ii. 12 al.
αὐτοὶ ἐν [z] ἑαυτοῖς [a] στενάζομεν, [b] υἱοθεσίαν [c] ἀπεκδεχόμενοι, Lev. xix. 20. r ver. 18.

s ver. 16 reff. t here only †. u here only †. v = ch. i. 13. 1 Cor. iv. 11. 2 Cor. iii. 14. Gal. iv. 2 al. w Phil. i. 5. x ch. v. 3. 2 Cor. viii. 19 al. fr. y ch. xi. 16. xvi. 5. 1 Cor. xv. 20, 23. xvi. 15. 2 Thess. ii. 13. James i. 18. Rev. xiv. 4 only. Exod. xxiii. 19 al. fr. z 1st pers., 2 Cor. iii. 1 reff. a Mark vii. 34. 2 Cor. v. 2, 4. Heb. xiii. 17. James v. 9 only. Isa. xxiv. 7. b ver. 15 reff. c ver. 19.

22. for *γαρ*, *δε* A: om æth. (*συνστεναζει*, so B[1]DF 17.) for *συνωδ.*, *ωδυνει* F.

23. rec 2nd *και* bef *ημεις*, with (DF)KL[P] 17 rel [syr] Chr_1 $Thdrt_1$(readg *κ. ημ. αυτ.* before) [Thl] Œc: txt ACℵ [47] Damasc.—DF transpose *και ημεις αυτοι* and *και αυτοι*: B [$Meth_1$ Orig-int_1 Aug_1] (omg *ημεις*) have *και αυτοι* both times: for other variations see Scholz. *συνστεναζομεν* (or *συστ.*) D f 38. 72. om *υιοθεσιαν* DF Ambrst.

God) **the creation itself also** (not only we, the sons of God, but even creation itself) **shall be delivered from the bondage of corruption** (its subjection to the law of decay, see Heb. ii. 15) **into** (pregnant: *shall be delivered from, &c., and admitted into*) **the freedom of the glory** (beware of the fatal *hendiadys*: 'the freedom of the glory' is not in any sense = 'the glorious freedom;' in the latter, 'glorious' is merely an epithet whereby the freedom is characterized, as in 'His rest shall be glorious:' in the former the freedom is described as consisting in, belonging to, being one component part of, the glorified state of the children of God: and thus the thought is carried up to the state to which the freedom belongs) **of the children** (*τέκνων* and not *υἱῶν* here, perhaps as embracing God's universal family of creation, admitted, each in their share, to a place in incorruptibility and glory). **22.**] **For we know** (said of an acknowledged and patent fact, see ch. ii. 2; iii. 19; vii. 14) **that the whole creation groans together and travails together** (not, groans and travails *with us* or *with mankind*, which would render the *οὐ μόνον δὲ ἀλλά* of the next verse superfluous. On the figure in *συνωδίνει* see John xvi. 21, note) [**until now** (i. e.] **up to this time** = *from the beginning till now*: no reference to time future, because *οἴδαμεν γάρ* expresses the results of *experience*). **23.**] The text here is in inextricable confusion (see var. read.), but the sense very little affected. **But** (moreover) **not only** (the creation), **but even ourselves, possessing** (not '*who possess*,' *οἱ ἔχοντες*, but '*though we possess*') **the firstfruit of the Spirit** (i. e. the indwelling and influences of the Holy Spirit *here*, as an earnest of the full harvest of His complete possession of us, *πνεῦμα* and *σάρξ* and *ψυχή*, hereafter. That this is the meaning, seems evident from the analogy of St. Paul's imagery regarding the Holy Spirit: he treats of Him as an *earnest* and *pledge* given to us, Eph. i. 14; 2 Cor. i. 22; v. 5, and of His full work in us as the efficient means of our glorification hereafter, ver. 11; 2 Cor. iii. 18. Various other renderings are,—(1) '*the first outpouring of the Spirit*,' in point of time,—Wetst., Reiche, Kölln., Mey., al.,—which would be irrelevant: (2) '*the highest gifts of the Spirit*,' as the Schmidts, al. The gen. *πν.* may be partitive or subjective:—the firstfruit of the Spirit,—which *Spirit is* the harvest,—or the firstfruit of the Spirit,—which the *Spirit gives*:—or even in apposition, the firstfruit of the Spirit, i. e. which *consists in* (the gift of) *the Spirit*. I prefer the first, from analogy—the Spirit being generally spoken of as *given*, not as *giving*,—and God as the Giver), **even we ourselves** (repeated for emphasis, and *ἡμεῖς* inserted to involve himself and his fellow-workers in the general description of the last clause. Some (Wolf, Kölln.) have imagined *the Apostles only* to be spoken of: some, that the Apostles are meant in one place, and all Christians in the other) **groan within ourselves, awaiting the fulness of** [**the** (or,] **our**) **adoption** (*ἀπεκδ.*, as above, ver. 19, but even more strongly here, '*wait out*,' 'wait for the end of.' Our adoption is *come already*, ver. 15, so that we do not wait for *it*, but for the *full manifestation of it*, in our bodies being rescued from the bondage of corruption and sin. This which in Gr. is expressed by the verb, in Eng. must be joined to the substantive. The omission of the art. before *υἱοθ.* is probably on account of its preceding its verb,—*υἱοθ. ἀπεκδ.* = *ἀπεκδ. τὴν υἱοθ.*, for emphasis' sake) **the redemption** (in apposition with *υἱοθ.*, or rather with the fulness

τὴν [d] ἀπολύτρωσιν τοῦ σώματος ἡμῶν. 24 τῇ γὰρ ἐλπίδι
ἐσώθημεν, ἐλπὶς δὲ [e] βλεπομένη οὐκ ἔστιν ἐλπίς· ὃ γὰρ
βλέπει τίς, [f] τί [[f] καὶ] ἐλπίζει; 25 εἰ δὲ ὃ οὐ βλέπομεν,
ἐλπίζομεν, [g] δι' [gh] ὑπομονῆς [c] ἀπεκδεχόμεθα. 26 [i] ὡσαύτως
δὲ καὶ τὸ πνεῦμα [k] συναντιλαμβάνεται τῇ [l] ἀσθενείᾳ ἡμῶν.
[m] τὸ γὰρ τί προσευξώμεθα [o] καθὸ δεῖ οὐκ οἴδαμεν, ἀλλ'
αὐτὸ τὸ πνεῦμα [p] ὑπερεντυγχάνει [q] στεναγμοῖς [r] ἀλαλήτοις·

ABCDF KL[P]ℵ a b c d f g h k l m n o 17 [47]

d ch. iii. 24 reff. e = 2 Cor. iv. 18 (4 times). f 1 Cor. xv. 29, 30. g Heb. xii. 1. h ch. ii. 7 reff. i 1 Cor. xi. 25 reff. k Luke x. 40 only. Gen. xxx. 8 Ed-vat.(B def.) Exod. xviii. 22. Num. xi. 17. Ps. lxxxviii. 21 only. (ἀντιλ., Acts xx. 35.) l Matt. viii. 17. 1 Cor. ii. 3 reff. m art., Mark ix. 23. Luke i. 62. Acts xxii. 30. 1 Thess. iv. 1. principally L.P. Winer, edn. 6, § 18. 3. o 2 Cor. viii. 12 (bis). 1 Pet. iv. 13 only. Levit. ix. 5 B. p here only †. q Acts vii. 34 only. Job iii. 24 al. r here only †. = ἀνεκλ., 1 Pet. i. 8.

24. ins η bef βλεπομενη F 55. om τι B¹(added by original scribe: see table) ℵ¹ [47 copt]. rec ins και, with ACKLℵ[P 47¹]: om BDF 47-marg(noting τὸ παλαιὸν οὕτως ἔχει [ο γαρ βλεπει τις ελπιζει]) latt. for ελπιζει, υπομενει Aℵ¹ 47-marg [but see above]: *exspectat* syrr $Ambr_1$.

26. rec ταις ασθενειαις (*see note*), with KL[P] 17 rel [syr copt] Chr_1 Thdrt Thl Œc: της δεησεως F: txt ABCDℵ m [47] vulg Syr [æth arm] $Cyr\text{-}jer_1$ Damasc [$Orig\text{-}int_2$] lat-ff. [om ημων D¹(and lat¹).] προσευξομεθα DKL[P] rel $Orig_1$ Naz $Cyr\text{-}jer_1$ Mac_1 Chr_2 [Cyr_4-p] Damasc Œc: προσευχομεθα F: txt ABCℵ Chr_2 $Thdrt_2$ Thl. rec aft υπερεντυγχανει ins υπερ ημων, with CKL[P]ℵ³ 17 rel vulg D³-lat [F-lat] Syr [syr copt arm-mss] $Cyr\text{-}jer_1$ [Eus_1] Did Epiph[-ms_1] Chr_1 Thdrt $Aug_{sæpe}$ Jer: [pref 47 Hil_2:] om ABDFℵ¹ arm[-zoh] $Orig_3$(always adds τω θεω) Epiph[-ed] Damasc Aug_1.

of sense implied in υἱοθ. ἀπεκδ., q. d. '*expecting that full and perfect adoption which shall consist in . . .*') of our body (not, '*rescue from our body*,' as Erasm., Le Clerc, Reiche, Fritz., al.,—which though allowable in grammar,—see Heb. ix. 15,—is inconsistent with the doctrine of the change of the vile and mortal into the glorious and immortal body,—Phil. iii. 21; 2 Cor. v. 2—4,—but the (entire) redemption,—rescue,—of the body from corruption and sin). **24, 25.**] **For** (confirmation of the last assertion, proving *hope to be* our present state of salvation)—**in hope were we** (not, '*are we*,' nor '*have we been*') **saved**: i. e. our first apprehension of, and appropriation to ourselves of, salvation which is by faith in Christ, was effected in the condition of *hope*: which hope (Thol.) is in fact *faith in its prospective attitude*,—that faith which is ὑπόστασις ἐλπιζομένων, Heb. xi. 1. The dat. ἐλπίδι is not a dat. of reference,—'*according to hope*,'—but of the form or condition. **Now hope that is seen** (the object or fulfilment of which is present and palpable) **is not hope: for that which any one sees, why does he** [**also** (or, at all)] **hope for?** If καί is to stand in the text, it conveys, after an interrogative word, a sense of the utter *superfluity* of the thing questioned about, as being irrelevant, and out of the question. 'Qui interrogat τί χρὴ προσδοκᾶν; exspectat aliquid, sed dubius est quid eveniat. Qui interrogat τί χρὴ καὶ προσδοκᾶν; desperat de salute, nec eam usquam exspectari posse existimat.' Bremi in Demosth. Phil. i. 46, cited in Hartung, Partikellehre, i. 137. **25.**] **But if that which we do not see, we hope for, with patience we wait for it.** Patience (endurance) is the state, in which,—through which *as a medium*,—our waiting takes place: hence **δι'** ὑπομονῆς, as ἔγραψα ὑμ. διὰ πολλῶν δακρύων, 2 Cor. ii. 4.

26.] **Likewise** (another help to our endurance, co-ordinate with the last—our patience is one help to it, but not the only one) **the Spirit also** (the Holy Spirit of God) **helps our weakness** (not, helps us *to bear* our weakness, as if the weakness were the burden, which the Spirit lifts for and with us,—but, helps *our weakness*,—*us who are weak*, to bear the burden of ver. 23. And this weakness is not only inability to pray aright, which is only an *example* of it, but *general weakness*. This has been seen, and the reading consequently altered to the plural, which was at first perhaps a marginal gloss). **For** (example of the help above mentioned;—the τό binding together the clause,—see reff.,—and here implying 'exempli gratiâ,'—'for *this viz.* what to &c.') **what we should pray as we ought** (two things;—*what we* should pray,—the *matter* of our prayer;—and *how* we should pray it,—the *form* and *manner* of our prayer) **we know not: but the Spirit itself** (Thol. remarks,—αὐτό brings into more prominence the idea of the πνεῦμα, so as to express of what dignity our Intercessor is,—an Intercessor who knows best what our wants are) **intercedes** (ὑπέρ here does not intensify the verb, as in ὑπερνικᾶν and the like, and as Œc., Erasm., Luth., Bengel, render it,—but implies

27 ὁ δὲ [s] ἐρευνῶν τὰς καρδίας οἶδεν τί τὸ [t] φρόνημα τοῦ
πνεύματος, ὅτι [u] κατὰ [u] θεὸν [v] ἐντυγχάνει ὑπὲρ [w] ἁγίων.
28 οἴδαμεν δὲ ὅτι τοῖς [x] ἀγαπῶσιν τὸν [x] θεὸν πάντα [y] συνεργεῖ

s John v. 39. vii. 52. 1 Cor. ii. 10. 1 Pet. i. 11. Rev. ii. 23 only. Prov. xx. 27.
t vv. 6, 7 reff.
u 2 Cor. vii. 9—11.
v Acts xxv. 24 reff.
w ch. i. 7 al. fr. Acts ix. 13 reff.
x 1 Cor. viii. 3 reff.
y Mark xvi. 20. 1 Cor. xvi. 16. 2 Cor. vi. 1. James ii. 22 only †. Esdr. vii. 2. 1 Macc. xii. 1 only. (-γος, ch. xvi. 3.)

27. (ερaυνων ℵ: txt B(Verc expr, Tischdf) [&c.: ευρενων m].) **υπερ**εντυγχανει L[Tischdf] 73: εννtυγχανι ℵ.

the *advocacy*,—'convenire aliquem super negotio alterius,' as Grot.,—to express which the ὑπὲρ ἡμῶν of the rec. has been inserted) **with groanings which cannot be expressed:**—i. e. the Holy Spirit of God dwelling in us, knowing our wants better than we, Himself pleads in our prayers, raising us to higher and holier desires than we can express in words, which can only find utterance in sighings and aspirations: see next verse. So De W., Thol., Olsh. Chrys. (Hom. xiv., p. 586) interprets it of the χάρισμα of prayer —and adds ὁ γὰρ τοιαύτης καταξιωθεὶς χάριτος, ἑστὼς μετὰ πολλῆς τῆς κατανύξεως, μετὰ πολλῶν τῶν στεναγμῶν τῶν κατὰ διάνοιαν τῷ θεῷ προσπίπτων, τὰ συμφέροντα πᾶσιν ᾔτει:—similarly Œc. and Theophyl. Calv. understands, that the Spirit suggests to us the proper words of acceptable prayer, which would *otherwise have been unutterable by us*: and similarly Beza, Grot. ἀλαλήτοις may bear three meanings—1, *unspoken*: 2, *that does not speak,—mute* (see LXX, Job xxxviii. 14; Sir. xviii. 33 compl.): 3, *that cannot be spoken*. The analogy of verbals in -τος in the N. T. favours the latter meaning: compare ἀνεκδιήγητος, 2 Cor. ix. 15,—ἄρρητος, 2 Cor. xii. 4,—ἀνεκλάλητος, 1 Pet. i. 8 (Thol.). Macedonius gathered from this verse that the Holy Spirit is *a creature*, and *inferior to God*, because He *prays to God for us*. But as Aug. Tract. vi. in Joan. 2, vol. iii. p. 1425, remarks, 'non Spiritus Sanctus in semetipso apud semetipsum in illa Trinitate gemit, sed *in nobis* gemit, quia gemere nos facit.' No *intercession in heaven* is here spoken of, but a *pleading in us* by the indwelling Spirit, of a nature above our comprehension and utterance. **27.**] **But** (opposed to ἀλαλήτοις—'though unutterable by us') **He who searcheth the hearts** (God) **knoweth what is the mind** (*intent*, or *bent*, as hidden in those sighs) **of the Spirit.** A difficulty presents itself in the rendering of the next clause. If ὅτι be *causal*, **because He** (the Spirit) **pleads for the saints according to the will of God**, it would seem that οἶδεν must bear the meaning '*approves*,' otherwise the connexion will not be apparent; and so Calv. and Rückert have rendered it. Hence Grot., Reiche, Meyer, Fritz. render ὅτι, '*that*,' and construe,—'*knows what is the mind of the Spirit*,'—*that He pleads with God* (so Reiche and Fritz., and Winer, edn. 6, § 49. d, for κατὰ θ.) *for the saints*: justifying the repetition of θεόν, implied before, by 1 John iv. 8, ὁ μὴ ἀγαπῶν οὐκ ἔγνω τὸν θεόν, ὅτι ὁ θεὸς ἀγάπη ἐστίν. But I must confess that the other rendering seems to me better to suit the context: and I do not see that the ordinary meaning of οἶδεν need be changed. The assurance which we have that God the Heart-Searcher interprets the inarticulate sighings of the Spirit in us, is,—not strictly speaking, His Omniscience,—but *the fact that the very Spirit who thus pleads, does it* κατὰ θεόν,—in pursuance of the divine purposes and in conformity with God's good pleasure. So that, as its place before the verb would suggest, κατὰ θεόν is emphatic, and furnishes the reason of the οἶδεν. A minor objection against the explicative ὅτι is, that we have οἴδαμεν ὅτι immediately following. All these pleadings of the Spirit are heard and answered, even when *inarticulately uttered*; we may extend the same comforting assurance to the *imperfect and mistaken verbal utterances* of our prayers, which are not themselves answered to our hurt, but the answer is given to the voice of the Spirit which speaks through them, which we *would* express, but *cannot*. Compare 2 Cor. xii. 7—10, for an instance in the Apostle's own case. **28.**] Having given an example, in *prayer*, how the Spirit *helps our weakness*, and out of our ignorance and discouragement brings from God an answer of peace, he now extends this to *all things*—all circumstances by which the Christian finds himself surrounded. These may seem calculated to dash down hope, and surpass patience; but *we know better concerning them*. **But** (the opposition seems most naturally to apply to ver. 22, the groaning and travailing of all creation) **we know** (as a point of the assurance of faith) **that to those who love God** (a stronger designation than any yet used for believers) **all things** (every event of life, but especially, as the context requires, those which are adverse. To include, with Aug. de Corrept. et Grat., c. ix. (24), vol. x. pt. i. p. 930, the *sins* of believers in this πάντα, as making them 'humiliores et doctiores,' is manifestly to introduce an element which did not enter

z = ch. xiii. 4 reff.
a Acts xxvii. 13 reff.
b ch. i. 7 al.
c ch. xi. 2. Acts xxvi. 5. 1 Pet. i. 20. 2 Pet. iii. 17 only †. Wisd. vi. 13. viii. 8. xviii. 6. (-γνωσις, Acts ii. 23.)
d 1 Cor. ii. 7 reff.
e Phil. iii. 21 only †. (-φίζεσθαι, Phil. iii. 10.)

* [z] εἰς [r] ἀγαθόν, τοῖς κατὰ [a] πρόθεσιν [b] κλητοῖς οὖσιν. ABCDF KL[P]ℵ a b c d f g h k l m n o 17 [47]
29 ὅτι οὓς [c] προέγνω, καὶ [d] προώρισεν [e] συμμόρφους τῆς

28. * aft συνεργει ins ὁ θεὸς AB ($Orig_2$ [æth]): om CDFKL[Pℵ] rel vulg [syrr copt arm] $Clem_1$ $Orig_4$[int_1 Eus_1 Cyr-c_1] (Cyr-jer_1) Chr_3 Thdrt Œc Thl $Lucif_1$ Ambr $Aug_{[sæpe]}$. ins το bef αγαθον L a f k 48. 57. 72-3-4. 109-77 lectt-8-13 $Clem_1$ $Orig_1$ Cyr-jer_1 Chr-ms [$Ephr_2$ Thdrt-txt $Antch_1$] Thl.

into the Apostle's consideration; for he is here already viewing the believer as *justified by faith, dwelt in by the Spirit, dead* to sin) **work together** (συνεργεῖ, absolute, or ἀλλήλοις implied: not, '*work together for good with those who love God*,'—'loving God' *being* a 'working for good:' which, though upheld by Thol., seems to me harsh, and inconsistent with the emphatic position of τοῖς ἀγ. τ. θ. Surely also in that case πάντα would have been τὰ πάντα, *all things*, as *one party working*, set over against οἱ ἀγαπῶντες τ. θ., the *other party working:* whereas πάντα συνεργεῖ gives rather the sense of all things *co-operating one with another*. If the reading of AB be adopted, we should understand either (1) that God causeth all things to work, &c.: taking συνέργει as from συνέργω, *concludo:* or (2) that, as Syr. renders it, "*in every thing He helpeth them for good.*" But in this last case, we should require τὰ πάντα) **for** (towards, to bring about) **good** (their eternal welfare;—the fulfilment of the purpose of the ἀγάπη τ. θεοῦ ἡ ἐν χριστῷ Ἰησοῦ τ. κυρ. ἡμῶν, ver. 39),—**to those who are called** (not only *invited*, but effectually called—see below) **according to (His) purpose.** In this further description the Apostle designates the believers as not merely *loving God*, but being *beloved by God*. The *divine side* of their security from harm is brought out, as combining with and ensuring the other. They are sure that all things work for their good, not only because *they love Him who worketh all things*, but also because *He who worketh all things hath loved and chosen them*, and carried them through the successive steps of their spiritual life. The *calling* here and elsewhere spoken of by the Apostle (compare especially ch. ix. 11) is the working, in men, of "the everlasting purpose of God whereby before the foundations of the world were laid, He hath decreed by His counsel secret to us, to deliver from curse and damnation those whom He hath chosen in Christ out of mankind, and to bring them by Christ to everlasting salvation." Art. X. of the Church of England. To specify the various ways in which this calling has been understood, would far exceed the limits of a general commentary. It may suffice to say, that on the one hand, Scripture bears constant testimony to the fact that all believers are chosen and called by God,—their whole spiritual life in its origin, progress, and completion, being *from Him:*—while on the other hand its testimony is no less precise that He willeth all to be saved, and that none shall perish except by *wilful rejection* of the truth. So that, on the one side, GOD'S SOVEREIGNTY,—on the other, MAN'S FREE WILL,—is plainly declared to us. *To receive, believe, and act on both these, is our duty, and our wisdom.* They belong, as truths, no less to *natural* than to revealed religion: and every one who believes in a God must acknowledge both. But all attempts to *bridge over the gulf between the two* are *futile* in the present imperfect condition of man. The very reasonings used for this purpose are clothed in language framed on the analogies of this lower world, and wholly inadequate to describe God regarded as He is in Himself. Hence arises confusion, misapprehension of God, and unbelief. I have therefore simply, in this commentary, endeavoured to enter into the full meaning of the sacred text, whenever one or other of these great truths is brought forward; not explaining either of them away on account of possible difficulties arising from the recognition of the other, but recognizing as fully the *elective and predestinating decree of God* where it is treated of, as I have done, in other places, *the free will of man.* If there be an inconsistency in this course, it is at least one in which the nature of things, the conditions of human thought, and Scripture itself, participate, and from which no Commentator that I have seen, however anxious to avoid it by extreme views one way or the other, has been able to escape. See, for a full treatment of the subject, Tholuck's Comm. in loc.

29, 30.] The Apostle now goes backward from κλητοῖς, to explain *how this* CALLING *came about.* It sprung from God's *foreknowledge*, co-ordinate with His *fore-determination* of certain persons (to be) conformed to the image of His Son, that Christ might be exalted as the Head of the great Family of God. These persons, thus foreknown and predetermined, He, in the course of His Providence actually, but

[f] εἰκόνος τοῦ υἱοῦ αὐτοῦ, [g] εἰς τὸ εἶναι αὐτὸν [h] πρωτότοκον ἐν [i] πολλοῖς ἀδελφοῖς.
30 οὓς δὲ [d] προώρισεν, τούτους καὶ [k] ἐκάλεσεν· καὶ οὓς [k] ἐκάλεσεν, τούτους καὶ
[l] ἐδικαίωσεν· οὓς δὲ [l] ἐδικαίωσεν, τούτους καὶ [m] ἐδόξασεν.
31 [n] Τί οὖν [n] ἐροῦμεν πρὸς ταῦτα; εἰ ὁ θεὸς ὑπὲρ ἡμῶν,
τίς [o] καθ' ἡμῶν;
32 ὅς γε τοῦ ἰδίου υἱοῦ οὐκ [p] ἐφείσατο,

f Matt. xxii. 20 ||. ch. i. 23. 1 Cor. xi. 7. xv. 49. 2 Cor. iv. 4 al. Gen. i. 26, 27.
g ch. iv. 11 reff.
h Luke ii. 7. Col. i. 15, 18. Heb. i. 6. xi. 28. xii. 23. Rev. i. 5 only. Gen. iv. 4 al.
i Matt. xx. 28. Heb. ii. 10. ix. 28.
k = ch. ix. 11. 1 Cor. vii. 15. Gal. v. 8. Eph. iv. 1. 2 Thess. ii. 14 al.
l ch. ii. 13 reff.
m = (of Christ), John vii. 39 and passim. Of *us*, here only. see Esther iii. 1. vi. 6, 7.
n ch. iii. 5 reff.
o = Matt. xii. 30. Gal. iii. 21. v. 23.
p ch. xi. 21 reff. Gen. xxii. 16.

30. for προωρισεν, προεγνω A [Orig-int$_1$]. και ους εδικ. A æth [Syr Orig-int$_2$].
32. ος ουδε υιου ιδιου εφεισ. F; ος (add γε D³) ουδε του ιδιου υιου εφεισ. D.

in His eternal decree implicitly, called, bringing them through justification to glory;—and all this is spoken of as *past*, because *to Him who sees the end from the beginning,—past, present, and future* ARE NOT, but ALL IS ACCOMPLISHED WHEN DETERMINED. **Because whom He foreknew** (but in what sense? This has been much disputed: the Pelagian view,—'*eos quos præsciverat credituros*,' is taken by Orig., Chrys., Œc., Theophyl., Augustine (prop. 55, in Ep. ad Rom. vol. iii. p. 2076), Ambr., Erasm. in paraphrase, Calov., Reiche, Meyer, Neander, and others; the sense of *fore-loved*, by Erasm. in commentary, Grotius, Estius, the Schmidts, &c.: that of *fore-decreed*, by Thol. edn. 1, and Stuart,—which however Thol. in subsequent editions suspects to be ungrammatical without some infinitive following, and prefers a sense combining foreknowledge and recognition-as-His:—that of *elected, adopted as His sons*, by Calvin,—'Dei autem præcognitio, cujus hic Paulus meminit, non nuda est præscientia, ut stulte fingunt quidam imperiti, sed adoptio qua filios suos ab improbis semper discrevit,'—Rückert, De Wette, al. That this latter is *implied*, is certain: but I prefer taking the word in the ordinary sense of **foreknew**, especially as it is guarded from being a 'nuda præscientia' by what follows: see below and Gal. iv. 9), **He also fore-ordained** (His foreknowledge was not a mere *being previously aware* how a series of events would happen: but was co-ordinate with, and inseparable from, His having *pre-ordained* all things) **conformed** (i.e. to be conformed) **to the image of His Son** (the dat. and gen. are both found after words like σύμμορφος; compare σύμφυτος, ch. vi. 5. The *image* of Christ here spoken of is not His moral purity, nor His sufferings, but as in 1 Cor. xv. 49, that entire form, of *glorification in body* and *sanctification in spirit*, of which Christ is the perfect pattern, and all His people shall be partakers. To accomplish this transformation in us is the end, *as regards us*, of our election by God; not merely to rescue us from wrath. Compare 1 John iii. 2, 3; Phil. iii. 21: and on the comprehensive meaning of μορφή, Phil. ii. 6, 7,—where it expresses both 'the form of *God*' in which Christ was, and '*the form of a servant*' in which He became incarnate), **that He might** (or *may*, as Calv., but the reference in the aorist is to the *past* decree of God) **be firstborn among many brethren** (i. e. that He might be shewn, acknowledged to be, and glorified as THE SON OF GOD, pre-eminent among those who are by adoption through Him the sons of God. This is the further end of our election, *as regards Christ*: His glorification in us, as our elder Brother and Head): **30.**] **but whom He fore-ordained, those he also called** (in making the decree, He left it not barren, but provided for those circumstances, all at His disposal, by which such decree should be made effectual in them. ἐκάλεσεν, supply, εἰς τὴν ἑαυτοῦ βασιλείαν καὶ δόξαν 1 Thess. ii. 12; other expressions are found in 1 Cor. i. 9; 2 Thess. ii. 14; 1 Tim. vi. 12; 1 Pet. v. 10): **and whom He called, these He also justified** (the Apostle, remember, is speaking entirely of *God's acts* on behalf of the believer: he says nothing *now* of that faith, through which this justification is, *on his part*, obtained): **but whom He justified, them He also glorified** (He did not merely, in His premundane decree, acquit them of sin, but also *clothe them with glory*: the aorist ἐδόξασεν being used, as the other aorists, to imply the completion in the divine counsel of all these, which are to us, in the state of time, so many successive steps,—simultaneously and irrevocably. So we have the perfect in John xvii. 10, 22).

31—39.] *The Christian has no reason to fear, but all reason to hope; for nothing can separate him from God's love in Christ.* **31.**] **What then shall we say to these things** (what answer can the hesitating or discouraged find to this array of the merciful acts of God's love on behalf of the believer)? **If God is for us** (and this He has been proved to be, vv. 28—30,—in having foreknown, predesti-

ἀλλὰ ὑπὲρ ἡμῶν πάντων [q] παρέδωκεν αὐτόν, πῶς οὐχ
καὶ σὺν αὐτῷ τὰ πάντα ἡμῖν [r] χαρίσεται; 33 τίς [s] ἐγκαλέσει κατὰ [tu] ἐκλεκτῶν [u] θεοῦ; θεὸς ὁ [v] δικαιῶν; 34 τίς
ὁ [w] κατακρίνων; χριστὸς ὁ ἀποθανών, [x] μᾶλλον δὲ [καὶ]
[y] ἐγερθείς, ὃς καὶ ἔστιν [z] ἐν [z] δεξιᾷ τοῦ θεοῦ, ὃς καὶ
[a] ἐντυγχάνει ὑπὲρ ἡμῶν; 35 τίς ἡμᾶς [b] χωρίσει ἀπὸ τῆς

[...θεου P.] ABCDF KLℵ a b c d f g h k l m n o 17 [47]

q ch. iv. 25 reff. r Acts xxv. 11, 16. 1 Cor. ii. 12. 2 Cor. ii. 7, 10 al.+ L.P. 2 Macc. iii. 33. s Acts xix. 38 reff. constr., here only. Soph. Philoct. 328. t Matt. xx. 16. xxiv. 22, &c. ch. xvi. 13 al. Isa. xxviii. 16. u Col. iii. 12. Tit. i. 1. gen., ch. i. 6, 7. v ver. 30. w Matt. xxvii. 3. [John viii. 10, 11.] ch. ii. 1 al. Esth. ii. 1. x = Gal. iv. 9. Eph. iv. 28. v. 11. y ver. 11. z = Eph. i. 20. Col. iii. 1. Heb. i. 3. viii. 1. x. 12. xii. 2. 1 Pet. iii. 22 only. Ps. xv. 11. a = and w. ὑπέρ, Heb. vii. 25. (Acts xxv. 24 reff.) b Matt. xix. 6. Ezek. xlvi. 19. w. ἀπό, ver. 39. Heb. vii. 26. Wisd. i. 3.

(αλλα, so BD¹Fℵ.) om τα D¹F [arm].

34. aft χριστος ins ιησους ACFLℵ 17 vulg copt æth arm Did$_1$ Cyr[-p] Damasc [Orig-int$_1$] Aug$_1$ Maximin$_1$: om BDK rel syrr Cyr-jer$_1$ Chr$_1$ Thdrt [Euthal-ms Iren-int$_1$ Hil$_1$]. rec ins 1st και, with DFKL rel latt(but not am¹) [Syr(omg μαλλον δε)] syr Cyr-jer$_1$ Chr$_1$ Thdrt$_1$ Iren-int Hil$_1$ Ambr Aug Maximin: om ABCℵ g k l 17 copt [æth arm] Did$_1$ Damasc [Orig-int$_1$]. (και is left out in B ed Mai, as in Tischdf and in the collations of Btly and Bch; but Mai has got into some confusion with regard to Bch's reading.) aft εγερθ. add εκ νεκρων ACℵ¹(om ℵ³?) 17 copt æth[("ut solet," Tischdf) Did$_1$] Chr$_1$ Damasc. om και (bef εστιν) ACℵ¹ b c o [47] vulg D¹-lat copt [goth] Cyr-jer Did$_1$ Chr$_2$ Cyr[-p$_1$ Damasc] Thdrt Iren-int$_1$ [Orig-int$_1$ Hil$_1$ Ambr$_1$ Aug$_1$]: ins B D[and lat³] FKLℵ³ am harl² syrr Œc Thl Maximin$_1$ Ambrst. om του B o.

35. aft τις ins ουν F latt(not am) [arm Orig-int$_1$)ins$_{sæpe}$). χωρση A c Orig$_1$ (txt$_{sæpe}$).]

nated, called, justified, glorified us), **who (is) against us?** 32.] (God) **Who even** (taking one act as a notable example out of all) **did not spare His own Son** (HIS OWN,—His υἱὸς μονογενής, the only one of God's sons who is One with Him in nature and essence, begotten of Him before all worlds. No other sense of ἰδίου will suit its position here, in a clause already made emphatic by γε, in consequence of which whatever epithet is fixed to υἱοῦ must partake of the emphasis), **but delivered Him up** (not necessarily εἰς θάνατον only, but generally, as ἔδωκεν, John iii. 16: 'largitus est, quem sibi retinere poterat,' as Tholuck, from Winer) **on behalf of us all** (so that every one of us believers, even the most afflicted, has an equal part in Him. Of others, nothing is said here), **how shall He not** (how can it be that He will not) **also with Him** (in consequence of and in analogy with this His greatest gift: it is a question 'a majori ad minus') **give freely to us all things** (all that we need or hope for; or even more largely, all created things for ours, to subserve our good, and work together for us: compare 1 Cor. iii. 22)? 33.] The punctuation of these verses is disputed. Many (Aug., Ambr., Reiche, Köllner, Olsh., Meyer, De Wette, and Griesb., Knapp, Lachmann) follow, in vv. 33, 34, the undoubted form of ver. 35, and place an interrogation after each clause, as in the text; while Luther, Beza, Grot., Wolf, Tholuck, al., make θεὸς ὁ δικ. and χριστὸς ὁ ἀποθ. κ.τ.λ. the *reply to* and *rejection of* the questions preceding them. The former method is preferable, as preserving the form of ver. 35, and involving no harshness of construction, which the other does, in the case of χριστός followed by the two participles.

Who shall lay (τι) **any charge against the elect of God** (ἐγκαλέω usually with a dat. see reff.)? **Shall God** (ἐγκαλέσει), **who justifies them** (Chrys. strikingly says, οὐκ εἶπε "θεὸς ὁ ἀφεὶς ἁμαρτήματα," ἀλλ' ὃ πολλῷ μεῖζον ἦν **θεὸς ὁ δικαιῶν.** ὅταν γὰρ ἡ τοῦ δικαστοῦ ψῆφος δίκαιον ἀποφήνῃ, καὶ δικαστοῦ τοιούτου, τίνος ἄξιος ὁ κατηγορῶν; Hom. xv. p. 597)? **Who is he that condemns them** (the pres. part. as expressing the official employment, 'is their accuser,' is better than the fut., as corresponding more closely with δικαιῶν)? **(Is it) Christ who died, yea who rather is also risen, who also is at the right hand of God, who also intercedes for us?** "All the great points of our redemption are ranged together, from the death of Christ to His still enduring intercession, as reasons for negativing the question above." De W.

35.] **Who** (i. e. *what:* but masc. for uniformity with vv. 33, 34) **shall separate us from the love of Christ?** Is this (1) *our love to Christ*, or (2) *Christ's love to us*, or (3) *our sense of Christ's love to us?* The first of these is held by Origen, Chrys., Theodoret, Ambr., Erasm., al. But the difficulty of it lies in consistently interpreting ver. 37, where not our *endurance in love to Him*, but our *victory by means of His love to us*, is alleged. And besides, it militates against the conclusion in ver. 39,

ἀγάπης τοῦ χριστοῦ; [c] θλῖψις ἢ [c] στενοχωρία ἢ [d] διωγμὸς
ἢ [e] λιμὸς ἢ [f] γυμνότης ἢ [g] κίνδυνος ἢ [h] μάχαιρα; 36 καθὼς
γέγραπται ὅτι ἕνεκεν σοῦ [i] θανατούμεθα ὅλην τὴν ἡμέραν,
[kl] ἐλογίσθημεν [l] ὡς πρόβατα [m] σφαγῆς. 37 ἀλλ' ἐν τούτοις πᾶσιν [n] ὑπερνικῶμεν διὰ τοῦ [o] ἀγαπήσαντος [o] ἡμᾶς.
38 [p] πέπεισμαι γὰρ ὅτι οὔτε [q] θάνατος οὔτε [q] ζωή, οὔτε
ἄγγελοι οὔτε [r] ἀρχαί, οὔτε [qs] ἐνεστῶτα οὔτε [qt] μέλλοντα,

c ch. ii. 9 (reff.).
d 2 Cor. xii. 10 reff.
e Paul, 2 Cor. xi. 27 only. Acts xi. 28 al.
f 2 Cor. xi. 27. Rev. iii. 18 only. Deut. xxviii. 48 only.
g 2 Cor. xi. 26 (8 times) only. Ps. cxiv. 3.
h = Matt. x. 34. Jer. ix. 16.
i ch. vii. 4 reff. Psa. xliii. 22.
k = ch. ix. 8 reff.
l 1 Cor. iv. 1. 2 Cor. x. 2. Job xli. 20.
m Acts viii. 32. James v. 5 only. l. c. Isa. xxxiv. 2, 6. gen., Zech. xi. 4.
n here only †.
o of Christ, Gal. v. 20. Eph. v. 2.
p constr., ch. xiv. 14. xv. 14. 2 Tim. i. 5, 12. acc. and inf., 2 Macc. ix. 27.
q so 1 Cor. iii. 22.
r = (see note) 1 Cor. xv. 24. Eph. i. 21 al. Dan. vii. 27 Theod.
s = 1 Cor. vii. 26 reff.
t Acts xxiv. 25 reff.

for *χριστου*, *θεου* B([adding] *της εν χριστου ιησου*) ℵ a[1] [Cyr-p$_1$(txt$_3$)]. om 2nd *η* D[1](and lat[1]) F-gr].

36. rec *ενεκα* (so LXX-B), with CK [Ephr$_1$ Bas$_1$] Thdrt Damasc Thl Œc: txt (so LXX-Aℵ) ABDFLℵ m n 17 [47] Clem$_1$ Orig$_1$ Meth$_1$ Chr$_1$.

37. *τον αγαπησαντα* DF latt [Tert$_1$ Cypr$_3$ Hil$_1$ Lucif$_1$].

38. *αγγελος* DF [copt] Aug$_3$ Ambrst: not Hil$_1$ Aug$_{sæpe}$. aft *ουτε αρχαι* add *ουτε εξουσιαι* (*see Col* ii. 15 *al*) C f n 46. 73. 80. 109-21 syr-w-ast [Bas$_1$ Antch$_1$]: pref, D[not D[1]-lat]. rec *ουτε δυναμεις* bef *ουτε ενεστωτα ο. μ.*, with KL rel vulg[-ed demid harl[2]] Syr goth Chr$_5$ Thdrt$_1$ Œc Thl Aug: txt ABCDFℵ m [47 am fuld harl[1]] tol syr copt [æth arm-zoh] Eus$_1$ Ephr$_1$ Cyr[-p$_1$] Damasc Orig[-int$_{sæpe}$] lat-ff (*ουτ. δυν. has been suspected as spurious* (*Fritz., Tholuck, in De Wette*): *but no mss omit it, unless* (*appy*) [116](*Mtt*) *and* [*Clem$_1$ Antch$_1$ Orig-int$_1$ and*] *one or two lat-ff who have ουτε εξουσιαι*).

which ought certainly to respond to this question. The third meaning is defended by Calvin. But the second, as maintained by Beza, Grot., Est., al., Thol., Reiche, Meyer, De Wette, appears to me the only tenable sense of the words. For, having shewn that God's great love to us is such that none can accuse nor harm us, the Apostle now *asserts the permanence of that love* under all adverse circumstances—that none such can affect it,—nay more, that it is by that love that we are enabled to obtain the victory over all such adversities. And finally he expresses his persuasion that no created thing shall ever separate us from that love, i. e. shall ever be able to pluck us out of the Father's hand. 36.] The quotation here expresses,—'all which things befall us, as they befell God's saints of old,—and it is no new trials to which we are subjected:—What, if we verify the ancient description?' 37.] **But** (negation of the question *θλῖψις . . . . μάχαιρα;*) **in all these things we are far the conquerors** (hardly, '*more than conquerors*:' the *ὑπέρ* intensifies the degree of *νικᾶν*, as in *ὑπερπερισσεύειν* and the like, but does not express a superiority over *νικᾶν*) **through Him who loved us** (i. e. so far from all these things separating us from His love, that very love has given us a glorious victory over them).
The reading *διὰ τὸν ἀγαπήσαντα ἡμᾶς* would amount to the same in meaning:—'*on account of Him who loved us*' implying, as in vv. 11, 20, that He is the efficient cause of the result. It is doubted whether '*He who loved us*' be the Father, or our Lord Jesus Christ. This is, I think, decided by *τῷ ἀγαπῶντι ἡμᾶς καὶ λούσαντι ἡμᾶς . . . . ἐν τῷ αἵματι αὐτοῦ*, Rev. i. 5. The use of such an expression as a title of our Lord in a doxology, makes it very probable that *where unexplained*, as here, it would also designate Him. 38.] **For I am persuaded** (a taking up and amplifying of the *ὑπερνικῶμεν*—our victory is not only over these things, but I dare assert it over greater and more awful than these) **that neither death, nor life** (well explained by De W. as the two principal possible states of man, and not as = 'any thing dead or living,' as Calvin and Koppe), **nor angels, nor principalities** (whether good or bad; *ἀρχή* is used of good, Col. i. 16; ii. 15 (see note); of bad (1 Cor. xv. 24 ?), Eph. vi. 12; here, as Eph. i. 21, *generally*. *ἄγγελοι*, absolutely, seems never to be used of *bad* angels: if it here means good angels, there is no objection, as Stuart alleges, to the rhetorical supposition that they might attempt this separation, any more than to that of *an angel from heaven preaching another gospel*, Gal. i. 8), **nor things present nor things to come** (no vicissitudes of *time*), **nor powers** (some confusion has evidently crept into the arrangement. Ephr. Syr. reads, *οὔτ. ἀρχαὶ οὔτ. ἐξουσίαι οὔτ. ἐνεστ. οὔτ. μέλλ. οὔτ. δυνάμεις οὔτ. ἄγγελοι;*

u = Matt. xxiv. 29 ‖. 1 Pet. iii. 22. Isa. xxxiv. 4.
v 2 Cor. x. 5 only. Job xxiv. 24. Judith x. 8. xiii. 4 only.

οὔτε [u] δυνάμεις, 39 οὔτε [v] ὕψωμα οὔτε [w] βάθος, οὔτε τὶς
[x] κτίσις [y] ἑτέρα δυνήσεται ἡμᾶς [z] χωρίσαι ἀπὸ τῆς [a] ἀγάπης τοῦ [a] θεοῦ τῆς ἐν χριστῷ Ἰησοῦ τῷ κυρίῳ ἡμῶν.
IX. 1 [b] Ἀλήθειαν λέγω [c] ἐν χριστῷ, οὐ [d] ψεύδομαι,

ABCDF KLℵ a b c d f g h k l m n o 17 [47]

w Eph. iii. 18 al. Isa. vii. 11. x = ch. i. 25. (vv. 19, &c.) Heb. iv. 13. Judith ix. 12. y = ch. xiii. 9. 1 Tim. i. 10. z ver. 35. a = ch. v. 5. 2 Cor. xiii. 13. b = 2 Cor. xii. 6. Eph. iv. 25. Ps. xiv. 2. c = 2 Cor. xii. 19. Eph. iv. 17. d 2 Cor. xi. 31. Gal. i. 20. 1 Tim. ii. 7.

39. om *τις* DF latt syrr [copt goth æth $Orig_1(txt_1)$-$int_1(txt_5)$ $Tert_1$ Hil_1 Ambrst $Aug_{sæpe}$]. **του κυριου** AC F[-gr].

Basil, οὔτε ἄγγ. οὔτ. ἀρχ. οὔτ. ἐξουσ. οὔτ. δυνάμεις οὔτ. ἐνεστ. οὔτ. μέλλ. I follow, with Griesb., Lachm., Tischdf., the very strong consent of the ancient MSS.), **nor height nor depth** (no extremes of *space*), **nor any other created thing** (*κτίσις* cannot here be the whole creation, as Chrys., —ὃ λέγει τοιοῦτόν ἐστιν· εἰ καὶ ἄλλη τοσαύτη κτίσις ἦν ὅση ἡ ὁρωμένη, ὅση ἡ νοητή, οὐδὲν ἄν με τῆς ἀγάπης ἐκείνης ἀπέστησε,—but any *creature*, such as are all the things named) **shall be able to sever us from the love of God which is in Christ Jesus our Lord** (here plainly enough *God's love to us in Christ*,—to us, as we are in Christ, to us, manifested in and by Christ).

CHAP. IX.—XI.] The Gospel being now established, in its fulness and freeness, as the power of God unto salvation to every one that believeth,—a question naturally arises, not unaccompanied with painful difficulty, respecting the exclusion of that people, as a people, to whom God's ancient promises were made. With this national rejection of Israel the Apostle now deals: first (ix. 1—5) *expressing his deep sympathy with his own people:* then (vv. 6—29) *justifying God, Who has not* (vv. 6—13) *broken His promise, but from the first chose a* portion *only of Abraham's seed, and that* (vv. 14—29) *by His undoubted elective right, not to be murmured at nor disputed by us His creatures: according to which election a remnant shall now also be saved.* Then, as to the rejection of so large a portion of Israel, *their own self-righteousness* (vv. 30—33) *has been the cause of it, and* (x. 1—12) *their ignorance of God's righteousness,—notwithstanding that* (vv. 13—21) *their Scriptures plainly declared to them the nature of the Gospel, and its results with regard to themselves and the Gentiles, with which declarations Paul's preaching was in perfect accordance. Has God then cast off his people* (xi. 1—10)? *No—for a remnant shall be saved according to the election of grace, but the rest hardened, not however for the purpose of their destruction, but* (xi. 11—24) *of mercy to the Gentiles: which purpose of mercy being fulfilled, Israel shall be brought in again to its proper place of blessing* (xi. 25—32). He concludes the whole with *a humble admiration of the unsearchable depth of God's ways, and the riches of His Wisdom* (xi. 33—36).

In no part of the Epistles of Paul is it more requisite than in this portion, to bear in mind his habit of INSULATING *the one view of the subject under consideration, with which he is at the time dealing.* The *divine side* of the history of Israel and the world is in the greater part of this portion thus *insulated:* the facts of the divine dealings and the divine decrees insisted on, and the *mundane* or *human side* of that history kept for the most part out of sight, and only so much shewn, as to make it manifest that the Jews, on their part, failed of attaining God's righteousness, and so lost their share in the Gospel.

It must also be remembered, that, whatever inferences, with regard to God's disposal of *individuals*, may justly lie from the Apostle's arguments, the assertions here made by him are universally spoken with a *national* reference. Of the eternal salvation or rejection of any individual Jew there is here no question: and however logically true of any individual the same conclusion may be shewn to be, we know as matter of fact, that in such cases *not the divine, but the human side,* is that ever held up by the Apostle—the universality of free grace for all—the riches of God's mercy to all who call on Him, and consequent exhortations to all, to look to Him and be saved. De Wette has well shewn, against Reiche and others, that the apparent inconsistencies of the Apostle, at one time speaking of absolute decrees of God, and at another of culpability in man,—at one time of the election of some, at another of a hope of the conversion of all,—resolve themselves into the necessary conditions of thought under which we all are placed, being compelled to acknowledge the divine Sovereignty on the one hand, and human free will on the other, and alternately appearing to lose sight of one of these, as often as for the time we confine our view to the other.

IX. 1—5.] *The Apostle's deep sympathy*

[e] συμμαρτυρούσης μοι τῆς [f] συνειδήσεώς μου ἐν πνεύματι e ch. ii. 15. 16 only †.
ἁγίῳ, 2 ὅτι λύπη μοί ἐστιν μεγάλη καὶ [g] ἀδιάλειπτος f 2 Cor. i. 12 reff.
[h] ὀδύνη τῇ καρδίᾳ μου. 3 [i] ηὐχόμην γὰρ [k] ἀνάθεμα εἶναι g 2 Tim. i. 3 only †. (-τως, ch. i. 9.)
αὐτὸς ἐγὼ [l] ἀπὸ τοῦ χριστοῦ ὑπὲρ τῶν ἀδελφῶν μου, h 1 Tim. vi. 10 only. Jer.

viii. 18. i Acts xxvii. 29 reff. imperf., = Acts xxv. 22 reff. k Acts xxiii. 14. 1 Cor. xii. 3. xvi. 22. Gal. i. 8, 9 only. Deut. vii. 26. = ch. vii. 2. 2 Cor. xi. 3. Col. ii. 20. 2 Thess. i. 9.

CHAP. IX. 1. aft χριστω add ιησου D[1][and lat] F [arm-mss Orig-int$_1$(om$_2$)] Ps-Ath$_1$ Ambrst. for 2nd εν, συν F[-gr].
2. της καρδιας K 17. 219[1].
3. ευχομην DKL c k l n 17 [Orig-c$_1$] Thdrt-ms: ευχομαι 41. ειναι bef αναθεμα ℵ. rec αυτος εγω bef αναθεμα ειναι, with CKL rel vss [Orig-c$_1$ -int$_1$] Ath$_1$ Thdrt [Damasc] Cypr$_1$: txt ABDF(ℵ) syr goth Chr$_1$ [Orig-int$_1$] Ambr$_1$ Pac$_1$. υπο DG.

with his own people Israel. The subject on which he is about to enter, so unwelcome to Jews in general, coupled with their hostility to himself, and designation of him as a πλάνος (2 Cor. vi. 8: compare also 2 Cor. i. 17; ii. 17; iv. 1, 2; vii. 2 al.), causes him to begin with a προπαραίτησις or deprecation, bespeaking credit for simplicity and earnestness in the assertion which is to follow. This deprecation and assertion of sympathy he puts in the forefront of the section, to take at once the ground from those who might charge him, in the conduct of his argument, with hostility to his own alienated people.

I say (the) **truth in Christ** (as a Christian,—as united to Christ; the ordinary sense of the expression ἐν χριστῷ, so frequent with the Apostle. It is not an oath, '*by* Christ,'—for though ἐν with ὄμνυμι bears this meaning, we have no instance of it where the verb is not expressed),—**I lie not** (confirmation of the preceding, by shewing that he was aware of what would be laid to his charge, and distinctly repudiating it),—**my conscience bearing me witness of the same** (the σύν in composition, as in reff., denoting *accordance with the fact*, not *joint testimony*) **in the Holy Spirit** (much as ἐν χριστῷ above:—a conscience not left to itself but informed and enlightened by the Spirit of God. Strangely enough, Griesb., Knapp, and Koppe take these words also for a formula jurandi, and connect them with οὐ ψεύδομαι), **that** (not *because*, or *for*, as Bengel: ὅτι, as in 2 Cor. xi. 10, introducing the *matter* to which the asseveration was directed,—I say the truth, when I say, that ....) **I have great sorrow and unceasing anguish in my heart.** The reason of this grief is reserved for a yet stronger description of his sympathy in the next verse.

3.] **For I could wish** (the imperf. is not *historical*, alluding to his days of Pharisaism, as Pelag. and others, but *quasi-optative*, as in reff. '*I was wishing,' had it been possible,*—ηὐχόμην εἰ ἐνεχώρει, εἰ ἐνεδέχετο, Phot. The sense of the imperf. in such expressions is the proper and strict one (and no new discovery, but common enough in every schoolboy's reading): the act is unfinished, an obstacle intervening. So in Latin, 'faciebam, ni ....,' the completed sentence being, 'faciebam, et perfecissem, ni ...') **that I myself** (on αὐτὸς ἐγώ see ch. vii. 25; it gives emphasis, as ἐγὼ Παῦλος, [2 Cor. x. 1] Gal. v. 2: 'I, the very person who write this and whom ye know') **were a curse** (a thing accursed, **ἀνάθεμα** in the LXX = חֵרֶם, an irrevocable devotion to God, or, a thing or person so devoted. All *persons* and *animals* thus devoted were put to death; none could be redeemed, Levit. xxvii. 28, 29. The subsequent scriptural usage of the word arose from this. It never denotes simply an exclusion or excommunication, but always devotion to perdition,—a curse. Attempts have been made to explain away the meaning here, by understanding *excommunication*, as Grot., Hammond, Le Clerc, &c.; or even *natural death* only, as Jerome, al.: but excommunication included cursing and delivering over to Satan:—and the mere wish for natural death would, as Chrys. eloquently remarks, be altogether beneath the dignity of the passage. Perhaps the strangest interpretation is that of Dr. Burton: "St. Paul had been set apart and consecrated by Christ to His service; and he had prayed that this devotion of himself might be for the good of his countrymen:"—it is however no unfair sample of a multitude of others, all more or less shrinking from the full meaning of the fervid words of the Apostle) **from Christ** (i. e. cut off and separated from Him for ever in eternal perdition. No other meaning will satisfy the plain sense of the words. ἀπό in the sense of ὑπό, making Christ the *agent* of the curse, would be hardly admissible: still less the joining,—as Carpzov and Elsner,—ἀπό with ηὐχόμην. On this wish, compare Exod. xxxii. 32) **in behalf**

m = ch. xvi. 7, &c. (?) Levit. xxv. 45.
n ch. i. 3 reff.
o = Acts x. 41 reff.
p ch. viii. 15 reff.
q = Heb. ix. 5. Exod. xl. 34. 3 Kings viii. 11.

τῶν [m] συγγενῶν μου [n] κατὰ [n] σάρκα, 4 [o] οἵτινές εἰσιν Ἰσραηλῖται, ὧν ἡ [p] υἱοθεσία καὶ ἡ [q] δόξα καὶ αἱ [r] διαθῆκαι καὶ
ἡ [s] νομοθεσία καὶ ἡ [t] λατρεία καὶ αἱ [u] ἐπαγγελίαι, 5 ὧν
οἱ [v] πατέρες, καὶ ἐξ ὧν ὁ χριστὸς τὸ [n] κατὰ [n] σάρκα, ὁ ὢν
[w] ἐπὶ πάντων θεὸς [xy] εὐλογητὸς [x] εἰς τοὺς [x] αἰῶνας, ἀμήν.

ABCDF KLℵ a b c d f g h k l m n o 17 [47]

...αμην C

r = Acts iii. 25. vii. 8. Heb. passim. (plur., Gal. iv. 24. Eph. ii. 12 only.) Gen. xvii. 2 al. s here only +. 2 Macc. vi. 23 only. (-θετεῖν, Heb. vii. 11. -της, James iv. 12.) t John xvi. 2. ch. xii. 1. Heb. ix. 1, 6 only. Exod. xii. 25, 26. u see ch. iv. 13. xv. 8. Gal. iii. 16. v absol., Acts vii. 19 reff. w = Eph. iv. 6 al. x ch. i. 25. 2 Cor. xi. 31. Ps. lxxxviii. 52. y (see note.) as above (x). Mark xiv. 61. Luke i. 68. 2 Cor. i. 3. Eph. i. 3. 1 Pet. i. 3 only.

ABDF KLℵ a b c d f g h k l m n o 17 [47]

om αδελφ. μ. των B[1](ins B[2]-marg(see table)). om 2nd μου D[1] F[-gr goth Chr$_1$ Ambr$_1$ Aug$_1$]: add των DF a[2] Syr Cyr[-p$_1$ Bas-2-mss$_1$] Thdrt.

4. om ων η υιοθ. to επαγγελιαι A: om και αι διαθ. κ. η νομοθ. L. η διαθηκη BD F[-gr vulg-clem] demid harl[2] [æth Ps-]Ath Chr-mss Cypr$_1$ Jer$_1$ Sedul: txt CKℵ rel latt (inclg am harl[1] tol) syrr copt goth [arm] Epiph$_1$ Chr$_1$ Thdrt Phot$_1$ [Euthal-ms Damasc Orig-int$_4$] Hil$_1$ [Ambrst Aug$_1$]. η επαγγελια D [copt] Chr-mss: επαγγελια F.

5. om οι F. om και F Hip$_2$ [Epiph$_1$ Hil$_2$] Cypr$_1$ Pelag (not Iren[-int$_1$ Hil$_1$] Aug). for το, τα C[1]: om το F Epiph$_1$ Thdrt$_1$.

of (in the place of; or, if thus I could benefit, deliver from perdition) **my brethren, my kinsmen according to the flesh.** The wish is evidently not to be pressed as entailing on the Apostle the charge of inconsistency in loving his nation more than his Saviour. It is the expression of an affectionate and self-denying heart, willing to surrender all things, even, if it might be so, eternal glory itself, if thereby he could obtain for his beloved people those blessings of the Gospel which he now enjoyed, but from which they were excluded. Nor does he describe the wish as ever actually formed; only as a conceivable limit to which, if admissible, his self-devotion for them would reach. Others express their love by professing themselves ready to give their life for their friends; he declares the intensity of his affection by reckoning even his *spiritual* life not too great a price, if it might purchase their salvation. 4.] Not only on their relationship to himself does he ground this sorrow and this self-devotion: but on the recollection of their ancient privileges and glories. **Who are Israelites** (a name of honour, see John i. 48; 2 Cor. xi. 22; Phil. iii. 5); **whose (is) the adoption** (see Exod. iv. 22; Deut. xiv. 1; xxxii. 6; Isa. i. 2 al.), **and the glory** (perhaps their general preference and exaltation, consequent on the υἱοθεσία,—but far more probably, as all the other substantives refer to separate matters of fact,—the Shechinah or visible manifestation of the divine Presence on the mercy-seat between the cherubims: see reff.), **and the covenants** (not, *the two tables of the law,*—as Beza, Grot., al.,—which formed but one covenant, and are included in νομοθεσία; nor, *the Old and New Testament Covenants,*—as Aug., Jer., Calov., Wolf,—see Gal. iv. 24 ff.: but *the several renewals of the covenant* with Abraham, Isaac, Jacob, and finally with the whole people at Sinai:—see Gen. xv. 9—21; xvii. 4, 7, 10; xxvi. 24; xxviii. 13; Exod. xxiv. 7, 8 al.), **and the law-giving** ('si alii Solonibus et Lycurgis gloriantur, quanto justior est gloriandi materia de Domino!' Calv. νομοθ. is both the act of giving the Law, and the Law thus given), **and the service** (ordinances of worship: see ref. Heb.), **and the promises** (probably only those to the patriarchs, of a Redeemer to come, are here thought of, as the next two clauses place the patriarchs and Christ together without any mention of the prophets. So Abraham is described, Heb. vii. 6, as τὸν ἔχοντα τὰς ἐπαγγελίας), —**whose are the fathers** (probably to be limited to Abraham, Isaac, and Jacob:—so De W., but Stephen gives οἱ πατ. a much wider meaning in Acts vii. 11, 12, 19, 39, 44, and so apparently Paul himself, Acts xiii. 17. In all those places, however, except Acts vii. 19, ἡμῶν follows, whereas here the word is absolute: so that the above limitation may be true),—**and of whom is Christ, as far as regards the flesh** (τό,—acc., as also in ch. xii. 18, —implies that He was not *entirely* sprung from them, but had another nature: q. d. '*on his human side,*'—'*duntaxat quod attinet ad corpus humanum,*' as Erasmus), **who is God over all** (prob. neuter; for τὰ πάντα, not οἱ πάντες, is the equivalent nominative in such sentences: see ch. xi. 36) **blessed for ever. Amen.** The punctuation and application of this doxology have been much disputed. By the early Church it was generally rendered as above, and applied to Christ,—so Iren., Tert., Orig. h. l., Athan., Epiph., Chrys., Theodoret, Theophyl., Œc. Wetstein has, it is true, collected passages from the fathers to shew that they applied the words ὁ ἐπὶ πάντων θεός to *the* FATHER

6 οὐχ [z] οἷον δὲ ὅτι [a] ἐκπέπτωκεν ὁ [b] λόγος τοῦ [b] θεοῦ· οὐ

z = here only. Winer, edn. 6, § 64. 6.
a = here only. see James i. 11. — πίπτειν, Luke xvi. 17. διαπ., Josh. xxi. 43 (45). Judith vi. 9. b Acts xi. 1 reff.

alone, and protested against their application to the SON; but these passages themselves protest only against the erroneous Noetian or Sabellian view of the *identity* of the Father and the Son, whereas in Eph. iv. 5, 6, εἷς κύριος, and εἷς **θεὸς** κ. πατὴρ πάντων, **ὁ ἐπὶ πάντων**, are plainly distinguished. That our Lord is not, in the strict exclusive sense, ὁ ἐπὶ πάντων θεός, every Christian will admit, that title being reserved for the Father: but that He *is* ἐπὶ πάντων θεός, none of the passages goes to deny. Had our text stood ἐξ ὧν ὁ χρ. τὸ κατὰ σάρκα, ὁ ἐπὶ πάντων θεὸς ὁ εὐλογητὸς εἰς τοὺς αἰῶνας, it would have appeared to countenance the above error, which as it now stands it cannot do. The first trace of a different interpretation, if it be one, is found in an assertion of the emperor Julian (Cyril, p. 321. Wetst.) τὸν γοῦν Ἰησοῦν οὔτε Παῦλος ἐτόλμησεν εἰπεῖν θεόν, οὔτε Ματθαῖος οὔτε Μάρκος, ἀλλ' ὁ χρηστὸς Ἰωάννης. The next is in the punctuation of two cursive mss. of the twelfth century (5 and 47), which place a period after σάρκα, thus insulating ὁ ὢν ἐπὶ πάντων . . . . ἀμήν, and regarding it as a doxology to God over all, blessed for ever. This is followed by Erasm., Wetst., Semler, Reiche, Köllner, Meyer, Fritzsche, Krehl, al. The objections to this rendering are, (1) ingenuously suggested by Socinus himself (Thol.), and never yet obviated,—that without one exception in Hebrew or Greek, wherever an ascription of blessing is found, the predicate εὐλογητός (בָּרוּךְ) *precedes* the name of God. (In the one place, Ps. lxvii. 19 LXX, κύρ. ὁ θ. εὐλογητός, εὐλογητὸς κυρ. ἡμέραν καθ' ἡμέραν, which seems to be an exception, the first εὐλ. has no corresponding word in the Heb. and perhaps may be interpolated. So Stuart, and even Eichhorn, Einleit. ins A. T. p. 320. In Yates's vindication of Unitarianism, p. 180, this is the only instance cited. Such cases as 3 Kings x. 9; 2 Chron. ix. 8; Job i. 21; Ps. cxii. 2, are no exceptions, as in all of them the verb εἴη or γένοιτο is expressed, requiring the substantive to follow it closely.) And this collocation of words depends, not upon the mere aim at perspicuity of arrangement (Yates, p. 180), but upon the circumstance that the stress is, in a peculiar manner, in such ascriptions of praise, on the predicate, which is used in a pregnant sense, the copula being omitted. (2) That the ὤν, on this rendering, would be superfluous altogether (see below). (3) That the doxology would be unmeaning and frigid in the extreme. It is not the habit of the Apostle to break out into irrelevant ascriptions of praise; and certainly there is here nothing in the immediate context requiring one. If it be said that the survey of all these privileges bestowed on his people prompts the doxology,—surely such a view is most unnatural: for the sad subject of the Apostle's sympathy, to which he immediately recurs again, is the apparent *inanity* of all these privileges in the exclusion from life of those who were dignified with them. If it be said that the *incarnation of Christ* is the exciting cause, the τὸ κατὰ σάρκα comes in most strangely, depreciating, as it would on that supposition, the greatness of the event, which then becomes a source of so lofty a thanksgiving. (4) That the expression εὐλογητὸς εἰς τοὺς αἰῶνας is twice besides used by Paul, and each time unquestionably not in an ascription of praise, but in *an assertion regarding the subject of the sentence.* The places are, ch. i. 25, ἐλάτρευσαν τῇ κτίσει παρὰ τὸν κτίσαντα, ὅς ἐστιν εὐλογητὸς εἰς τοὺς αἰῶνας. ἀμήν,—and 2 Cor. xi. 31, ὁ θεὸς κ. πατὴρ τ. κυρ. Ἰησοῦ οἶδεν, ὁ ὢν εὐλογητὸς εἰς τοὺς αἰῶνας, ὅτι οὐ ψεύδομαι: whereas he twice uses the phrase εὐλογητὸς ὁ θεός as an ascription of praise, without joining εἰς τοὺς αἰῶνας. (5) That in the latter of the above-cited passages (2 Cor. xi. 31), not only the same phrase as here, but the same construction, ὁ ὤν, occurs, and that there the whole refers to the subject of the sentence. I do not reckon among the objections the want of any contrast to τὸ κατὰ σάρκα, because that might have well been left to the readers to supply. Another mode of punctuation has been suggested (Locke, Clarke, al.), and indeed is found in one ms. of the same date as above (71): to set a period after πάντων and refer ὁ ὢν ἐπὶ πάντων to Christ, understanding by πάντων all the preceding glorious things, or the πατέρες only, or even 'all things.' This lies open to all the above objections except (5), and to this in addition, that as Bp. Middleton observes, we must in that case read **ὁ** θεός.

Variety of reading there is none worth notice: the very fathers [Ephr. Cypr-ed. Hil-ed. Leo] generally cited as omitting θεός, *having* it in the best manuscripts and editions. Crell (not Schlichting, see Thol. p. 484, note, edn. 1842) proposed (and is followed by Whiston, Whitby, and Taylor) to transpose ὁ ὢν into ὢν ὁ;—but besides the objection to the sense thus arising, εὐλογη-

γὰρ πάντες οἱ ἐξ Ἰσραήλ, οὗτοι Ἰσραήλ· 7 οὐδ᾽ ὅτι εἰσὶν ABDF
[c] σπέρμα [c] Ἀβραάμ, πάντες τέκνα, ἀλλ᾽ Ἐν Ἰσαὰκ [d] κλη- KLℵ a b c d f g h
θήσεταί σοι σπέρμα. 8 [e] τοῦτ᾽ ἔστιν, οὐ τὰ τέκνα τῆς k l m n o 17 [47]
[n] σαρκός, ταῦτα [f] τέκνα τοῦ [f] θεοῦ, ἀλλὰ τὰ [g] τέκνα τῆς
[g] ἐπαγγελίας [h] λογίζεται [h] εἰς σπέρμα. 9 ἐπαγγελίας γὰρ
ὁ λόγος οὗτος, [i] Κατὰ τὸν [i] καιρὸν [i] τοῦτον [j] ἐλεύσομαι
καὶ ἔσται τῇ Σάῤῥᾳ υἱός. 10 [k] οὐ μόνον δέ, ἀλλὰ καὶ

c John viii. 33, 37. (Acts iii. 25. vii. 5, 6.) ch. xi. 1. 2 Cor. xi. 22. Gal. iii. 29. Heb. ii. 16. Isa. xli. 8.
d Gen. xxi. 12. = Isa. xlviii. 1.
e Acts xix. 4 reff.
f ch. viii. 16 reff.
g Gal. iv. 28 only.
h ch. ii. 26 (reff.). v. 3, &c. viii. 36. Acts xix. 27. Wisd. ix. 6.
i Gen. xviii. 10 (see note). see Acts xii. 1. xix. 23.
j see John xiv. 23.
k ch. v. 3, 11. viii. 23. 2 Cor. viii. 19.

6. for 2nd ισραηλ, ισραηλειται DF latt(not tol) [arm] Chr-ms$_1$(and Mtt's mss$_2$) [Orig-int$_3$] Ambrst Aug$_1$: txt ABKLℵ rel Orig$_2$ Cæs$_1$ [Nys$_1$ Cyr-p Procop] Aug$_{\text{sæpe}}$ Tich.

7. ισακ ℵ^1[DG fuld (so D ver 10)].

8. aft τουτ εστιν add οτι B^1(sic : see table) ℵ^3 m 116 [arm] Orig$_1$. om του F m 67^2. 70. 114-20.

9. om ο D.

τός would probably in that case (not necessarily, as Bp. Middleton in loc.) have the art. : not to mention that no conjecture arising from doctrinal difficulty is ever to be admitted in the face of the consensus of MSS. and versions. The rendering given above is then not only that most agreeable to the usage of the Apostle, *but the only one admissible by the rules of grammar and arrangement.* It also admirably suits the context : for, having enumerated the historic advantages of the Jewish people, he concludes by stating one which ranks far higher than all,—that from them sprung, according to the flesh, He who is God over all, blessed for ever. ἀμήν implies no optative ascription of praise, but is the accustomed ending of such solemn declarations of the divine Majesty ; compare ch. i. 25. **6—13.**] *God has not broken His promise : for He chose from the first but a* portion *of the seed of Abraham* (6—9), *and again only* one *out of the two sons of Rebecca* (10—13).

6.] **Not however that** (οὐχ οἷον δέ, ὅτι = οὐ τοῖον δὲ λέγω, οἷον ὅτι . . . . , '*but I do not mean such a thing, as that* . . . . ,' or '*the matter however is not so, as that* . . . .' De W. cites from Athen. vi. p. 244, οὐχ οἷον βαδίζει, and from Phrynich. p. 332, οὐχ οἷον ὀργίζομαι, in a similar sense. The rendering, '*it is not possible that,*' would require ordinarily οἷόν τε with an infinitive,—and St. Paul is asserting, not the *impossibility*, however true, of God's word being broken, but the *fact*, that it *was not broken*) **the word** (i. e. the promise) **of God has come to nothing** (see reff., so Lat., *excidit*); viz. by many, the majority of the nominal Israel, missing the salvation which seemed to be their inheritance by promise. **For not all who are sprung from Israel** (= Jacob, according to Tholuck : but this does not seem necessary : Israel here as well as below may mean the *people*, but here in the popular sense, there in the divine idea), **(these) are Israel** (veritably, and in the sense of the promise).

7.] **Nor, because they are** (physically) **the seed of Abraham, are all children** (so as to inherit the promise), **but** (we read), "**In Isaac shall thy seed be called**" (i. e. those only shall be called truly and properly, for the purposes of the covenant, thy seed, who are descended from Isaac, not those from Ishmael or any other son. Thol. renders καλεῖν here by erwecken, 'to raise up') : **8.**] **that is** (that amounts, when the facts of the history are recollected, to saying) **not [they which are] the children of the flesh** (begotten by natural generation, compare John i. 13, and Gal. iv. 29) **are the children of God ; but the children of the promise** (begotten not naturally, but by virtue of the divine promise (Gal. iv. 23, 28), as Isaac) **are reckoned for seed. 9.**] **For this word was** (one) **of promise** (not, '*For this was the word of promise,*' i. e. οὗτος γὰρ ὁ λ. τῆς ἐπαγγ. The stress is on ἐπαγγελίας : the children of *promise* are reckoned for seed : for this word, in fulfilment of which Isaac was born, was a word of *promise*), **According to this time** (כָּעֵת חַיָּה, 'when the time (shall be) reviviscent,'—as De W., Thol., al. :—i. e. next year at this time. The citation is a free one ; the LXX has ἐπαναστρέφων ἥξω πρός σε κατὰ τὸν καιρὸν τοῦτον εἰς ὥρας, κ. ἕξει υἱὸν Σάῤῥα ἡ γυνή σου. The change into ἔσται τῇ Σάῤῥᾳ υἱός is probably made for the sake of emphasis—the promise was *to Sarah*) **I will come, and Sarah shall have a son. 10, 11.**] **And not only** (so) (i. e. not only have we an example of the election of a son of Abraham by one woman, and the rejection of a son by an-

Ῥεβέκκα ἐξ ἑνὸς [l] κοίτην ἔχουσα, Ἰσαὰκ τοῦ πατρὸς
ἡμῶν, 11 [m] μήπω γὰρ γεννηθέντων μηδὲ πραξάντων τὶ
ἀγαθὸν ἢ [n] φαῦλον, ἵνα ἡ κατ' [o] ἐκλογὴν [p] πρόθεσις τοῦ
θεοῦ [q] μένῃ, οὐκ ἐξ ἔργων ἀλλ' ἐκ τοῦ [r] καλοῦντος,
12 ἐῤῥέθη αὐτῇ ὅτι ὁ [s] μείζων [t] δουλεύσει τῷ [u] ἐλάσσονι,

[P τ εκλογην...]

l = here (Luke xi. 7. ch. xiii. 13. Heb. xiii. 4) only. Num. v. 20.
m Heb. ix. 8 only.
n Paul, Tit. ii. 8 only. John iii. 20. v. 29. James iii. 16 only. Prov. xxii. 8.
o Acts ix. 15. ch. xi. 5, 7, 28. 1 Thess. i. 4. 2 Pet. i. 10 only †. Isa. xxii. 7 Aq.
p Acts xxvii. 13 reff.
q = Matt. xi. 23. 1 Cor. iii. 14. 2 Cor. ix. 9. 1 Pet. i. 23, 25, from Isa. xl. 8.
r = ch. viii. 30 reff.
s = Heb. xi. 24. Gen. x. 21. xxix. 16. Gen. xxv. 23.
t = John viii. 33. Acts vii. 7, from Gen. xv. 14.
u = 1 Tim. v. 9 (John ii. 10. Heb. vii. 7) only. l. c. (Gen. i. 16.)

11. for μηδε, η F latt [Ambrst]. rec (for φαυλ.) κακον (*more usual word*), with DFKL rel Chr_1 [Euthal-ms] Thdrt Thl Œc: txt ABℵ m [47] $Orig_3$ Cyr[-p_1] Damasc. rec του θεου bef προθεσις, with Chr[-$montf_1$]: txt ABDFKL[P]ℵ rel latt $Orig_3$[int_3] Chr-2-mss Thdrt. μεινη F [μενει P 17].

12. rec ερρηθη, with B^2D^2L rel $Orig_2$ Chr_1: txt AB^1D^1FK[P]ℵ b d f h k n o [Chr_1 Damasc] Thdrt.[—add γαρ P]. om αυτη D^1(and lat) $harl^1$ $Orig_3$[int_2(ins int_1)] Ambrst Bede. μειζον $ℵ^1$.

other, but also of election and rejection of the *children of the same woman*, Rebecca, and that *before they were born.* οὐ μόνον δέ introduces an *à fortiori* consideration.

In the construction supply τοῦτο only), **but when Rebecca also had conceived** (see ref. Num. and ch. xiii. 13, where the meaning is not exactly the same though cognate) **by one man** (in the former case, the children were by *two wives;* the difference between that case and this being, that there, was diversity of parents, here, identity. The points of contrast being then this diversity and identity, the *identity of the father also* is brought into view. This is well put by Chrys.: ἡ γὰρ Ῥεβέκκα καὶ μόνη τῷ Ἰσαὰκ γέγονε γυνή, καὶ δύο τεκοῦσα παῖδας, ἐκ τοῦ Ἰσαὰκ ἔτεκεν ἀμφοτέρους· ἀλλ' ὅμως οἱ τεχθέντες τοῦ αὐτοῦ πατρὸς ὄντες, τῆς αὐτῆς μητρός, τὰς αὐτὰς λύσαντες ὠδῖνας, καὶ ὁμοπάτριοι ὄντες καὶ ὁμομήτριοι, καὶ πρὸς τούτοις καὶ δίδυμοι, οὐ τῶν αὐτῶν ἀπήλαυσαν. Hom. xvi. p. 610), **our father Isaac** (τ. πατ. ἡμ., probably said without any special reference, the Apostle speaking as a Jew. If with any design it might be, as Thol. remarks, to shew that even among the *Patriarchs'* children such distinction took place. Christians being τέκνα ἐπαγγελίας, the expression might apply to them: but, as the same Commentator observes, the argument here is to shew that *not all the children of promise* belonged to the ἐκλογή. See ch. iv. 1—12. As to the construction here, it is best to regard ἀλλὰ καὶ . . . ἔχουσα . . . ἡμῶν as a sentence begun but intercepted by the remark following, and resumed in another form at ἐῤῥ. αὐτῇ),—**for** (not answering to 'furnishes us an example' supplied after ἔχουσα, but elliptically put, answering to the apprehension in the Apostle's mind of the force of the example which he is about to adduce. For this use of γάρ see John iv. 44, note; Herod. i. 8, Γύγη, οὐ γὰρ . . . .; 30, ξεῖνε Ἀθ. παρ' ἡμέας γὰρ . . . . Thucyd. i. 72, τῶν δὲ Ἀθ. ἔτυχε γὰρ . . . .; and other examples in Hartung, Partikellehre, i. 467) **without their having been yet born** (the subject, the children, is to be supplied partly from the fact of her pregnancy just stated, partly from the history, well known to the readers. μή instead of οὐ is frequently used by later Greek writers in participial clauses: Winer, edn. 6, § 55. 5; so Acts ix. 9, ἦν . . . μὴ βλέπων κ. οὐκ ἔφαγεν . . ., and Luke xiii. 11, μὴ δυναμένη ἀνακύψαι. See Schäfer, Demosth. iii. 395, and Hartung, ii. 130—132) **or having done any thing good or ill** (φαῦλ. an unusual word with Paul = properly ἁπλοῦν, ῥᾴδιον, εὐτελές, as Timæus in Lex. to Plato, with whom it is a very common word in this sense. Ruhnken, on the word in Timæus, gives from the Lex. Rhetor. MS., τὸ φ. σημαίνει δέκα· ἐπί τε προσώπου καὶ πράγματος τὸ κακόν. τὸ μικρόν, κ. τὸ εὐκαταφρόνητον, κ. τὸ ἀσθενές. κ. τὸ ἄδοξον. κ. τὸ ἀνόητον, κ.τ.λ. This will shew the connexion of the strict and the wider meaning), **[to the end] that the purpose of God according to** (purposed in pursuance of, or in accordance with, or (Thol.) with reference to His) **election** (Thol. prefers taking κατ' ἐκλ. adjectively, as Bengel has rendered it, '*propositum electivum*,' and as in Polyb. vi. 34. 8, εἷς ἑκάστης ἀνὴρ λαμβάνεται κατ' ἐκλογήν, '*electively*') **may** (not *might;* the *purpose* is treated as *one* in all time, which would be nullified if once thwarted) **abide** (stand firm; the opposite of ἐκπίπτειν, see reff. 1 Pet., Isa.),—**not [depending on] works** (ch. iii. 20; iv. 2) **but on Him that calleth,**—(this clause does not seem to depend on any one word of the foregoing or following, as on ἐῤῥέθη, Calv., Luth.;—or μένῃ, Rückert, Meyer;—or κατ' ἐκλογήν, Fritz.;—but to be a general

v Mal. i. 2, 3. w ch. iii. 5 reff. x Luke xiii. 27. ch. i. 29 al. Ps. xci. 15. y ch. ii. 11. Demosth., p. 318. 13. z ch. iii. 4 reff. a Matt. ix. 27 al. Exod. xxxiii. 19.

13 καθὼς γέγραπται ᵛ Τὸν Ἰακὼβ ἠγάπησα, τὸν δὲ Ἠσαῦ
ἐμίσησα. 14 ʷ Τί οὖν ἐροῦμεν; μὴ ˣ ἀδικία ʸ παρὰ τῷ θεῷ;
ᶻ μὴ γένοιτο. 15 τῷ Μωσῇ γὰρ λέγει ᵃ Ἐλεήσω ὃν ἂν ᵃ ἐλεῶ,
καὶ ᵇ οἰκτειρήσω ὃν ἂν ᵇ οἰκτείρω. 16 ᶜ ἄρα ᶜ οὖν οὐ τοῦ
θέλοντος οὐδὲ τοῦ ᵈ τρέχοντος, ἀλλὰ τοῦ ᵃ ἐλεῶντος θεοῦ.

ABDF KL[P]ℵ a b c d . g h k l m n o 17 [47]

a -ᾶν (pres.) here bis. Jude 23 only. Prov. xxi. 26 A (not F &c.) B[1]ℵ. b here bis only. 4 Kings xiii. 23. c ch. v. 18 reff. d = 1 Cor. ix. 24. Gal. v. 7. Ps. cxviii. 32. gen., Acts i. 7. Heb. v. 14.

13. **καθαπερ** B $Orig_1$. **14.** om τω D^1F.
15. rec γαρ bef μωση, with AKL rel Chr Thdrt: txt BDF[P]ℵ Damasc. μωυσ. FKLℵ[P rel]: txt ABD [g].— -σει B^2F c d g Chr-2-mss [Damasc]: -ση AB^1DKLℵ [P rel] Thdrt.
16. rec ελε**ου**ντος, with B^2K [rel $Orig_4$ Eus_1 Chr Thdrt Damasc]; ευδοκουντος L: txt AB^1DF[P]ℵ.

characteristic of the whole transaction; see a similar ἐκ in ch. i. 17. Thol., De W. Thus viewed, or indeed however taken, it is decisive against the Pelagianism of the Romanists, who by making our faith as foreseen by God the cause of our election, affirm it to be ἐξ ἔργων. See the matter discussed in Thol.),—**it was said to her** (ὅτι is recitantis; the LXX have καί), **"The elder shall serve the younger"** (this prophecy is distinctly connected in Gen. xxv. with the prophetic description of the children as two *nations*,—λαὸς λαοῦ ὑπερέξει, καὶ ὁ μείζων κ.τ.λ. But the nations must be considered as spoken of in their progenitors, and the elder nation = that sprung from the elder brother. History records several subjugations of Edom by the kings of Judah; first by David (2 Sam. viii. 14);—under Joram they rebelled (2 Kings viii. 20), but were defeated by Amaziah (2 Kings xiv. 7), and Elath taken from them by Uzziah (2 Kings xiv. 22); under Ahaz they were again free, and troubled Judah (2 Chron. xxviii. 16, 17, compare 2 Kings xvi. 6, 7),—and continued free, as prophesied in Gen. xxvii. 40, till the time of John Hyrcanus, who (Jos. Antt. xiii. 9. 1) reduced them finally, so that thenceforward they were incorporated among the Jews): **as it is written, Jacob I loved, but Esau I hated** (there is no necessity here to soften the '*hated*' into '*loved less*:' the words in Malachi proceed on the fullest meaning of ἐμίσησα, see ver. 4 there, "The people against whom the Lord hath indignation for ever").

14–29.] *This election was made by the indubitable right of God, Who is not therefore unjust.* **14.**] **What then shall we say** (anticipation of a difficulty or objection, see reff.,—but not *put into the mouth of an objector*)? **Is there unrighteousness** (injustice) **with** (in) **God** (viz. in that He chooses as He will, without any reference to previous desert)? **Let it not be:** **15.**] **for He saith to Moses, "I will have mercy on whomsoever I have mercy, and [I] will have compassion on whomsoever I have compassion."** The citation is from the LXX, who insert the indefinite ἄν, the Heb. being . . . . חַנֹּתִי אֶת־אֲשֶׁר אָחֹן; the meaning apparently being, 'whenever I have mercy on any, it shall be *pure mercy*, no human desert contributing;' which agrees better with the next verse than the ordinary rendering, which lays the stress on the ὃν ἄν; and is not inconsistent with ver. 18, ὃν θέλει, ἐλεᾷ: because if God's mercy be *pure mercy* without any desert on man's part, it necessarily follows that he has mercy on whom He will, His will being the only assignable cause of the selection. **16.**] **So then** (inference from the citation) **it is not of** (God's mercy 'does not belong to,'—'is not in the power of,' see reff.) **him that willeth** (any man willing it) **nor of him that runneth** (any man contending for it, see reff. and Phil. iii. 14. There hardly can be any allusion to Abraham's wish for Ishmael, Gen. xvii. 18, and Esau's running to hunt for venison, as Stuart, Burton, al.), **but of God that hath mercy.** I must pause again here to remind the student, that I purposely do not enter on the disquisitions so abundant in some commentaries on this part of Scripture, by which it is endeavoured to reconcile the sovereign election of God with our free will. *We shall find that free will asserted strongly enough for all edifying purposes by this Apostle, when the time comes.* At present, he is employed wholly in asserting the divine Sovereignty, the glorious vision of which it ill becomes us to distract by continual downward looks on this earth. I must also protest against all endeavours to make it appear, that no inference lies from this passage as to the *salvation of individuals.* It is most true (see remarks at the beginning of this chapter) that the *immediate subject* is

17 λέγει γὰρ [e] ἡ γραφὴ τῷ Φαραὼ ὅτι [f] εἰς [g] αὐτὸ [g] τοῦτο
[h] ἐξήγειρά σε, ὅπως [i] ἐνδείξωμαι ἐν σοὶ τὴν δύναμίν μου
καὶ ὅπως [k] διαγγελῇ τὸ ὄνομά μου ἐν πάσῃ τῇ γῇ.
18 [c] ἄρα [c] οὖν ὃν θέλει *[a] ἐλεεῖ, ὃν δὲ θέλει [l] σκληρύνει.

e sing., Mark xii. 10. xv. 28. John ii. 22 and passim. ch. iv. 3 al.
f Mark i. 38. John xviii. 37. Acts ix. 21.
g Acts xxiv. 15 reff.
h = here (1 Cor. vi. 14) only. Judg. v. 12. Ps. vii. 6 al. Jos. Antt. viii. 11.
i and constr., 1 Tim. i. 16. (see ver. 22.) Exod. ix. 16.
k Luke ix. 60. Acts xxi. 26 only. l. c.
l Acts xix. 9. Heb. iii. 8, 13, 18. iv. 7 only. Exod. iv. 21 (הִזֵּק). vii. 3 (הִקְשָׁה), al.

17. ενδειξομαι F[not G] L[P 17] c l¹ Chr-ms. aft [2nd] οπως ins αν F. διαγγελει L[P] f o [-γειλη m].
18. In A, from ον δε θ. to η ουκ εχει ver. 21 is in a later hand. [aft 1st θελει ins ο θεος D.] *ἐλεᾷ D¹F.—aft ελ. ins ον δε θελει ελεει B¹(Tischdf: om B²).

the national rejection of the Jews : but we must consent to hold our reason in abeyance, if we do not recognize the inference, that the sovereign power and free election here proved to belong to God extend to *every exercise* of His mercy—whether temporal or spiritual—whether in Providence or in Grace—whether national or individual. It is in parts of Scripture like this, that we must be especially careful *not to fall short of what is written :* not to allow of any compromise of the plain and awful words of God's Spirit, for the sake of a caution which He Himself does not teach us. **17.**] The same great truth shewn on its *darker side :*—not only as regards God's *mercy*, but His *wrath* also. **For** (confirmation of the *universal* truth of the last inference) **the Scripture** (identified with God, its Author : the case, as Thol. remarks, is different when merely something *contained* in Scripture is introduced by ἡ γραφὴ λέγει : there ἡ γρ. is merely personified. The justice of Thol.'s remark will be apparent, if we reflect that this expression could not be used of the *mere ordinary words of any man* in the historical Scriptures, Ahab, or Hezekiah,—but only where *the text itself* speaks, or where *God spoke*, or, as here, *some man under inspiration of God*) **saith to Pharaoh, For this very purpose** (ὅτι recitantis; the LXX have καὶ ἕνεκεν τούτου) **did I raise thee up** (LXX διετηρήθης, '*thou wert preserved to this day :*' Heb. הֶעֱמַדְתִּיךָ from עָמַד, *stetit*, in Hiph. *stare fecit ;* hence taken to signify (1) '*constituit, muneri præfecit,*' as 1 Kings xii. 32; Isa. xxi. 6 (LXX σεαυτῷ στῆσον σκόπον); Esth. iv. 5,—(2) '*confirmavit,*' as 1 Kings xv. 4 al.,—and (3) '*prodire fecit, excitavit,*' Dan. xi. 11; Neh. vi. 7 : the meaning '*incolumem præstitit,*' given in the Lexicons, seems to be grounded on the following of the LXX in this passage, who apparently understood it of Pharaoh being kept safe through the plagues. This has been done by modern interpreters [perhaps] to avoid the strong assertion which the Apostle here gives, purposely deviating from the LXX, that Pharaoh was '*raised up,*' called into action in his office, to be an example of God's dealing with impenitent sinners. The word chosen by the Apostle, ἐξεγείρω, in its transitive sense, is often used by the LXX for 'to rouse into action :' see besides reff. Ps. lvi. 8; lxxix. 2; Cant. iv. 16 al. So that the meaning (3) given above for the Heb. verb—'prodire fecit, excitavit,' was evidently that intended by ἐξήγειρα), **that I may shew in thee** ('in thee as an example,'—'in thy case,'—'by thee') **my power** (τ. ἰσχύν μου LXX-B : δύν. (which is read in A) is perhaps chosen by the Apostle as more *general*, ἰσχύς applying rather to those deeds of miraculous power of which Egypt was then witness), **and that my Name may be proclaimed in all the earth** (compare as a comment, the words of the song of triumph, Exod. xv. 14—16). **18.**] **Therefore He hath mercy on whom He will** (ref. to ver. 15, where see note), **and whom He will, He hardeneth.** The frequent recurrence of the expression σκληρύνειν τὴν καρδίαν in the history of Pharaoh should have kept Commentators (Carpzov, Ernesti, al., and of Lexicographers, Wahl and Bretschneider) from attempting to give to σκληρύνω the sense of '*treating hardly,*' against which the next verse would be decisive, if there were no other reason for rejecting it. But it is very doubtful whether the word can ever bear the meaning. The only passage which appears to justify it (for in 2 Chron. x. 4 it clearly has the import of *hardening, making severe*) is Job xxxix. 16, where ἀπεσκλήρυνε τὰ τέκνα ἑαυτῆς (αὑτῆς Aא) the LXX version of the Heb. הִקְשִׁיחַ, is supposed to mean, '*treats her offspring hardly.*' But the LXX by this compound seem to have intended, '*casts off her offspring in her hardness ;*' the E. V. has, 'She is hardened against her young ones.' Whatever difficulty there lies in this assertion, that

19 ἐρεῖς μοι οὖν ^m Τί [οὖν] ἔτι ^n μέμφεται; τῷ γὰρ ^o βουλήματι αὐτοῦ τίς ^p ἀνθέστηκεν; 20 ὦ ἄνθρωπε, ^q μενοῦνγε
σὺ τίς εἶ ὁ ^r ἀνταποκρινόμενος τῷ θεῷ; μὴ ἐρεῖ τὸ

ABDF KL[P]א abcdf ghkl mno17 [47]

m ch. iii. 7. Gal. v. 11.
n Heb. viii. 8 (Mark vii. 2 rec.) only +. Sir. xi. 7. xli. 7. 2 Macc. ii. 7 only.
o Acts xxvii. 43. 1 Pet. iv. 3 only +. 2 Macc. xv. 5 only.
p Acts vi. 10 reff.
q ch. x. 18 (Luke xi. 28 v. r.) only.
r Luke xiv. 6 only. Judg. v. 29 A Ald. compl. Job xvi. 9. xxxii. 12 only.

19. rec 1st *ουν* bef *μοι*, with DFKL [rel] latt [copt] Orig$_2$[int$_2$] Chr$_1$ Thdrt: om *ουν* 73. 118 arm: txt ABא[P 47] m syr goth Orig$_1$ [Damasc]. rec om 2nd *ουν*, with AKL[P]א rel vulg [syrr copt æth arm] Orig$_4$ Chr$_1$ Thdrt Aug[$_{\text{sæpe}}$ Ambrst]: ins BDF Jer$_1$ Sedul. elz om *γαρ*, with G-lat: ins ABDFKL[P]א rel [vss] Orig$_4$[int$_3$] Ath$_1$ Chr$_1$ Thdrt Thdor-mops Damasc Aug.

20. rec *μενουνγε* bef *ω ανθρ.* (*to suit the arrangement in other places: see reff. Had the μενουνγε been transposed in* A &c *to avoid placing it first in the sentence* (see Phryn Lobeck, p. 342), *the same various reading would have occurred in the other places, which it does not*), with D³KLא³[P 47-marg(sic)] rel syrr copt [goth (arm)] Orig$_3$ Chr$_1$ Thdrt Thdor-mops$_1$ Œc Thl: om *μενουνγε* D¹F latt æth [(Meth) Orig-int$_3$ Aug$_{\text{sæpe}}$] Jer: txt A(B)א¹ m [47-txt Orig$_1$] Chr-ms$_1$ Damasc.—om *γε* B.

God *hardeneth* whom He will, lies also *in the daily course of His Providence,* in which we see this hardening process going on in the case of the prosperous ungodly man. The fact is patent, whether declared by revelation or read in history: but to the solution of it, and its reconciliation with the equally certain fact of human responsibility, we shall never attain in this imperfect state, however we may strive to do so by subtle refinements and distinctions. The following is the admirable advice of Augustine (ad Sixtum, Ep. cxciv. 6. 23, vol. ii. p. 882), from whom in this case it comes with double weight: "Satis sit interim Christiano ex fide adhuc viventi, et nondum cernenti quod perfectum est, sed ex parte scienti, nosse vel credere quod neminem Deus liberet nisi gratuitâ misericordiâ per Dominum nostrum Jesum Christum, et neminem damnet nisi æquissimâ veritate per eundem Dominum nostrum Jesum Christum. Cur autem illum potius quam illum liberet aut non liberet, scrutetur qui potest judiciorum ejus tam magnum profundum, — verumtamen caveat præcipitium." **19.**] **Thou wilt say then to me** (there seems no reason to suppose the objector a Jew, as Thol. after Grot., Calov., Koppe, al.:—the objection is a *general one,* applying to all mankind, and likely to arise in the mind of any reader. The expression ὦ ἄνθρωπε seems to confirm this), **Why then doth He yet find fault** (ἔτι as ch. iii. 7, assuming your premises,—'*if this be so:*' at the same time it expresses a certain irritation on the part of the objector: 'exprimit morosum fremitum,' Bengel. μέμφομαι has a stronger sense than mere *blame* here: Hesych. interprets it αἰτιᾶται, ἐξουθενεῖ, καταγινώσκει: see the apocryphal reff. Thol.)? **For who resists** (not, '*hath resisted:*' ἀνθέστηκεν, like ἕστηκεν, is *present,* see Winer, edn. 6, § 40. 4. b, and compare ἐφέστηκεν, 2 Tim. iv. 6) **His will** (i. e. if it be His will to harden the sinner, and the sinner goes on in his sin, he does not resist but goes with the will of God)? **Yea rather** (μενοῦνγε, see reff., takes the ground from under the previous assertion and supersedes it by another: implying that it has a certain show of truth, but that the proper view of the matter is yet to be stated. It thus conveys, as in ref. Luke, an intimation of rebuke; here, with severity: 'that which thou hast said, may be correct human reasoning—but as against God's sovereignty, thy reasoning is out of place and irrelevant'), **O man** (perhaps without emphasis implying the contrast between man and God,—for this is done by the emphatic σύ following, and we have ἄνθρωπε unemphatic in ch. ii. 1), **who art THOU that repliest against** (the ἀντί seems to imply contradiction, not merely dialogue: see besides reff., ἀνταπόκρισιν, Job xiii. 22, BCא) GOD?—implying, 'thou hast neither right nor power, to call God to account in this manner.' Notice, that the answer to the objector's question does not lie in these vv. 20, 21, but in the following (see there);—the present verses are a rebuke administered to the *spirit* of the objection, which forgets the immeasurable distance between us and God, and the relation of Creator and Disposer in which He stands to us. So Chrys.,—καὶ οὐδὲ τὴν λύσιν εὐθέως ἐπάγει, συμφερόντως καὶ τοῦτο ποιῶν· ἀλλ' ἐπιστομίζει πρῶτον τὸν ζητοῦντα, λέγων οὕτω **μενοῦνγε . . . . θεῷ;** ποιεῖ δὲ τοῦτο, τὴν ἄκαιρον αὐτοῦ περιεργίαν ἀναστέλλων, κ. τὴν πολλὴν πολυπραγμοσύνην, κ. χαλινὸν περιτιθείς, κ. παιδεύων εἰδέναι τί μὲν θεὸς τί δὲ ἄνθρωπος, κ. πῶς ἀκατάληπτος αὐτοῦ ἡ πρόνοια, κ. πῶς ὑπερβαίνουσα τὸν ἡμέτερον λογισμόν, κ. πῶς ἅπαντα αὐτῷ πείθεσθαι δεῖ· ἵνα ὅταν τοῦτο κατασκευάσῃ παρὰ τῷ ἀκροατῇ, κ. καταστείλῃ κ. λεάνῃ τὴν γνώμην, τότε μετὰ πολλῆς εὐκολίας ἐπ-

[s] πλάσμα τῷ [t] πλάσαντι Τί με ἐποίησας οὕτως; 21 ἢ
οὐκ ἔχει [u] ἐξουσίαν ὁ [v] κεραμεὺς τοῦ [w] πηλοῦ, ἐκ τοῦ
αὐτοῦ [x] φυράματος ποιῆσαι [y] ὃ μὲν [z] εἰς τιμὴν [a] σκεῦος,
[y] ὃ δὲ [z] εἰς [b] ἀτιμίαν; 22 [c] εἰ δὲ θέλων ὁ θεὸς [d] ἐνδείξασθαι τὴν ὀργὴν καὶ [e] γνωρίσαι τὸ [f] δυνατὸν αὐτοῦ
[g] ἤνεγκεν ἐν πολλῇ [h] μακροθυμίᾳ [i] σκεύη ὀργῆς [k] κατηρτισμένα εἰς [l] ἀπώλειαν, 23 καὶ [m] ἵνα [e] γνωρίσῃ τὸν [no] πλοῦτον
τῆς [o] δόξης αὐτοῦ ἐπὶ [i] σκεύη [p] ἐλέους, ἃ [q] προητοίμασεν

s here only. Job xl. 14 (19). Isa. xxix. 16. t 1 Tim. ii. 13 only. Gen. ii. 7, 8. u and constr., 1 Cor. ix. 12 reff. v Matt. xxvii. 7, 10 only. Ps. ii. 9. Isa. xlv. 9. (-μικός, Rev. ii. 27.) w John ix. 6, &c. (5 times) only. Gen. xi. 3.

x ch. xi. 16. 1 Cor. v. 6, 7. Gal. v. 9 only. Exod. xii. 34. y 1 Cor. xi. 21 reff. z = ch. i. 1, 5 al. fr. a = 2 Tim. ii. 20, 21. Heb. ix. 21 al. Exod. iii. 22. b ch. i. 26 reff. c Acts xxiii. 9. d constr., ch. ii. 15. Eph. ii. 7. Tit. ii. 10. iii. 2. Heb. vi. 10, 11. see ver. 17. P.H. Gen. l. 15, 17. e 1 Cor. xii. 3 reff. f = here only. constr., ch. i. 19, 20. viii. 3. g = Heb. xii. 20 only. (see Heb. xiii. 13.) φέρειν τὶ πράως, Xen. Cyr. ii. 2. 9. h ch. ii. 4 reff. i see ver. 21. Jer. xxvii. (l.) 25. constr., Acts ix. 15. k = Heb. x. 5 (from Ps. xxxix. 6). xi. 3. (Matt. iv. 21.) l = Acts viii. 20 reff. John xvii. 12. Jer. xxvi. (xlvi.) 2[1]. m constr., see Winer, edn. 6, § 63. I. 1. n ch. ii. 4 reff. o Eph. i. 18. iii. 16. (Phil. iv. 19.) Col. i. 27. p Luke i. 50 &c. Eph. ii. 4. Exod. xx. 6. q Eph. ii. 10 only. Isa. xxviii. 24. Wisd. ix. 8 only.

for εποιησας, επλασας D[-gr] Syr Thl-marg.
22. om ηνεγκεν F D^1-lat $Julian_1$. ins εις bef σκευη F [D^1-lat] Ambrst Julian.
23. om 1st και B m 39. 47-marg 67^2. 80. 116 vulg copt goth arm[Griesb, not Treg] (Orig[-int_5]) Jer Pel Sedul $Fulg_1$. for τον πλουτον, το πλουτος F. [for δοξης, χρηστοτητος P.]

ἄγων τὴν λύσιν, εὐπαράδεκτον αὐτῷ ποιήσῃ τὸ λεγόμενον. Hom. xvi. p. 614. Similarly Calvin: 'Hac priori responsione nihil aliud quam improbitatem illius blasphemiæ retundit, argumento ab hominis conditione sumpto. Alteram mox subjiciet, qua Dei justitiam ab omni criminatione vindicabit.' **Shall the thing formed** (properly of a production of *plastic* art, moulded of clay or wax) **say to him who formed it, "Why madest thou me thus?"**

These words are slightly altered from Isa. xxix. 16 LXX,—*μὴ ἐρεῖ τὸ πλάσμα τῷ πλάσαντι αὐτό*(om. *αὐτό* Aℵ), *Οὐ σύ με ἔπλασας; ἢ τὸ ποίημα τῷ ποιήσαντι, Οὐ συνετῶς με ἐποίησας;* **Or** (introduces a new objection, or fresh ground of rebuke, see ch. ii. 4; iii. 29; vi. 3; xi. 2) **hath not the potter power over the clay** (the similitude from ref. Isa. In Sir. xxxvi. (xxxiii.) 13, we have a very similar sentiment: *ὡς πηλὸς κεραμέως ἐν χειρὶ αὐτοῦ . . . . οὕτως ἄνθρωποι ἐν χειρὶ τοῦ ποιήσαντος αὐτούς.* And even more strikingly so, Wisd. xv. 7: *καὶ γὰρ κεραμεὺς ἁπαλὴν γῆν θλίβων ἐπίμοχθον πλάσσει πρὸς ὑπηρεσίαν ἡμῶν ἕκαστον*(*ἓν ἕκ.* ACℵ), *ἀλλ' ἐκ τοῦ αὐτοῦ πηλοῦ ἀνεπλάσατο τά τε τῶν καθαρῶν ἔργων δοῦλα σκεύη τά τε ἐναντία πάνθ'*(*πάντα* Aℵ) *ὁμοίως· τούτων δὲ ἑκατέρου*(*ἑτέρου* $Bℵ^{3a}$, *ἑτέρων* $ℵ^1$) *τίς ἑκάστου ἐστὶν ἡ*(om. *ἡ* ℵ) *χρῆσις, κριτὴς ὁ πηλουργός.* See also Jer. xviii. 6), **out of the same lump to make one vessel unto honour** (honourable uses) **and another unto dishonour** (dishonourable uses. See ref. 2 Tim. The honour and dishonour are not here the *moral purity or impurity* of the human vessels, but their *ultimate glorification* or *perdition*. The Apostle in asking this question, rather aims at striking dumb the objector by a statement of God's undoubted right, against which it does not become us men to murmur, than at unfolding to us the actual state of the case. This he does in the succeeding verses; see above, from Chrys. and Calv.)? **22.] But what if** (by the elliptical *εἰ δέ* the answer to the question of the objector, ver. 19, seems to be introduced; *ἐὰν οὖν* occurs in a similar connexion John vi. 62; and *ἀλλ' εἰ*, Soph. Œd. Col. 590,—*ἀλλ' εἰ θέλοντάς γ' οὐδὲ σοὶ φυγεῖν καλόν;* See Hartung, Partikellehre, ii. 212. 6) (1) **God, purposing to shew forth His wrath, and to make known His power** (that which He could do), **endured with much long-suffering vessels of wrath fitted** [prepared, made complete and ready] **for destruction; and** (what if this took place) (2) **that He might make known the riches of His glory on** (not *to*, as De Wette, who joins it with *γνωρίσῃ*,—but '*toward*,' **on**, 'with regard to,' dependent on *πλοῦτον*, as *πλουτῶν εἰς*, ch. x. 12) **the vessels of mercy, which He before prepared for glory?** I have given the whole, that my view of the construction might be evident: viz. that (1) and (2) are parallel clauses, both dependent on *εἰ δέ*; *θέλων* giving the purpose of the 1st, and *ἵνα γν.* that of the 2nd. They might be cast into one form by writing the 1st *ὁ θ., ἵνα ἐνδείξηται . . . . κ. γνωρίσῃ*,—or the 2nd, *καὶ θέλων γνωρίσαι.* Only I do not, as Calv., Beza, Grot., Bengel, De Wette, Meyer, and Winer, understand the same *ἤνεγκεν . . . . ἀπώλ.*, as belonging to both, but only to the 1st, and supply before the 2nd, 'What if this took place,' viz. this *ὃν θέλει, ἐλεεῖ.* Other constructions

r = ch. ii. 7 reff.
s = Mark i. 2. Heb. iv. 7. see ch. xi. 2.
t Hosea ii. 23 (B).
u Hosea i. 10.

εἰς [r] δόξαν; 24 οὓς καὶ ἐκάλεσεν ἡμᾶς οὐ μόνον ἐξ
Ἰουδαίων, ἀλλὰ καὶ ἐξ ἐθνῶν, 25 ὡς καὶ [s] ἐν τῷ Ὡσηὲ
λέγει Καλέσω τὸν οὐ λαόν μου λαόν μου, καὶ τὴν οὐκ
[t] ἠγαπημένην ἠγαπημένην· 26 [u] καὶ ἔσται ἐν τῷ τόπῳ
οὗ ἐῤῥέθη αὐτοῖς Οὐ λαός μου ὑμεῖς, ἐκεῖ κληθήσον-

ABDF KL[P]ℵ a b c d f g h k l m n o 17 [47]

25. om *εν* B.

26. for *οὗ*, *ω* ℵ[1](txt ℵ corr[1] ?) [Thdrt]. rec *ερρηθη*, with B[2]D[3]L rel Œc: txt AB[1] D[1]-gr K[P]ℵ d f h k l[2][*ευρ.* l[1]] n 17 [Euthal-ms Damasc] Thdrt Thl.—for *ερρ. αυτ.*, *αν κληθησονται* F[-gr] (D[1]-lat Ambrst): *in loco liberata* (*ερρυσθη?*) *in quo vocabatur* Iren-int.

have been,—to make *ἵνα* depend on *κατηρτισμένα*—'*prepared to destruction for this very purpose, that* &c.' So Fritz. and Rückert, ed. 2; but this seems to overlook *καί*, or to regard it as = *καὶ τοῦτο*:—to take ver. 23 as a new sentence, supplying *ἐκάλεσεν ἡμᾶς*, as Tholuck. Stuart supplies *θέλων* before *ἵνα γν.*, and *ἠλέησεν* before *οὓς ἐκάλεσεν ἡμᾶς*. This in fact amounts to nearly the same as my own view, but appears objectionable, inasmuch as it joins ver. 24 to ver. 23: see below.

The argument is, 'What if God, in the case of the vessels of wrath prepared for destruction, has, in willing to manifest His power and wrath, also exhibited towards them long-suffering (to lead them to repentance, ch. ii. 4,—a mystery which we cannot fathom), and in having mercy on the vessels of mercy prepared for glory, has also made manifest the riches of His glory?' Then in both these dispensations will appear, not the arbitrary power, but the rich goodness of God. The theological difficulties in *κατηρτισμένα* and *προητοίμασεν* (in both cases *God* is the agent; not they themselves, as Chrys., Theophyl., Olsh. Bengel, however, rightly remarks, "non dicit quæ *προκατήρτισε*, cum tamen ver. seq. dicat 'quæ præparavit.' Cf. Matt. xxv. 34 cum ver. 41, et Act. xiii. 46 cum ver. 48") are but such as have occurred repeatedly before, and, as Stuart has well observed, are inherent, not in the Apostle's argument, nor even in revelation, but in *any consistent belief of an omnipotent and omniscient God*. See remarks on ver. 18. *σκεύη ὀργῆς* and *σκεύη ἐλέους* are *vessels prepared to subserve*, as it were to *hold*, His *ὀργή* and *ἔλεος*: hardly, as Calvin, *instruments to shew forth*: that is *done*, over and above their being *σκεύη*, but is not necessary to it.

The *σκ. ὀργ.* and *σκ. ἐλ.* are not to be, with a view to evade the general application, confined to the instances of Pharaoh and the Jews: these instances give occasion to the argument, but the argument itself is general, extending to all the dealings of God. **24.**] **Of which kind** (*quales*, agreeing with *ἡμᾶς*—i. e. *σκεύη ἐλέους*) **He also called us, not only from among the Jews, but also from among the Gentiles.** It being entirely in the power of God to preordain and have mercy on whom He will, He has exercised this right by calling not only the remnant of His own people, but a people from among the Gentiles also. **25, 26.**] It is difficult to ascertain in what sense the Apostle cites these two passages from Hosea as applicable to the Gentiles being called to be the people of God. That he *does so*, is manifest from the words themselves, and from the transition to the Jews in ver. 27. In the prophet they are spoken of *Israel*; see ch. i. 6—11, and ch. ii. throughout: who after being rejected and put away, was to be again received into favour by God. Two ways are open, by which their citation by the Apostle may be understood. Either (1) he brings them forward to shew that it is consonant with what we know of God's dealings, to *receive as His people*, those who *were* formerly *not His people*—that this may now take place with regard to the Gentiles, as it was announced to happen with regard to Israel,—and even more,—that Israel in this as in so many other things was the prophetic mirror in which God foreshewed on a small scale His future dealings with mankind,—or (2) he adduces them from mere applicability to the subject in hand, implying, 'It has been with us Gentiles, as with Israel in the prophet Hosea.' I own I much prefer the former of these, as more consonant with the dignity of the argument, and as apparently justified by the *καί*,—as He saith *also* in Hosea, implying perhaps that the matter in hand was not that directly prophesied in the citation, but one analogous to it. Chrys. takes the same view: *εἰ γὰρ ἐπὶ τῶν ἀγνωμονησάντων μετὰ πολλὰς εὐεργεσίας, καὶ ἀλλοτριωθέντων, καὶ τὸ λαὸς εἶναι ἀπολωλεκότων, τοσαύτη γέγονεν ἡ μεταβολή, τί ἐκώλυε καὶ τοὺς οὐ μετὰ τὴν οἰκείωσιν ἀλλοτριωθέντας, ἀλλ' ἐξ ἀρχῆς*

ται υἱοὶ θεοῦ ζῶντος. 27 Ἡσαΐας δὲ [v] κράζει [w] ὑπὲρ
τοῦ Ἰσραὴλ [x] Ἐὰν ᾖ ὁ ἀριθμὸς τῶν υἱῶν Ἰσραὴλ
ὡς ἡ [yz] ἄμμος τῆς [y] θαλάσσης, τὸ [a] ὑπόλειμμα σωθήσεται.
28 λόγον γὰρ [bc] συντελῶν καὶ [cd] συντέμνων [ἐν [e] δικαιοσύνῃ·
ὅτι λόγον [d] συντετμημένον] ποιήσει κύριος ἐπὶ τῆς γῆς.
29 καὶ καθὼς [f] προείρηκεν Ἡσαΐας [g] Εἰ μὴ κύριος σαβαὼθ
[h] ἐγκατέλιπεν ἡμῖν σπέρμα, ὡς Σόδομα ἂν ἐγενήθημεν καὶ
ὡς Γόμοῤῥα ἂν [i] ὡμοιώθημεν. 30 [k] Τί οὖν [k] ἐροῦμεν; ὅτι

v John i. 15 al. w = 2 Cor. i. 6 vii. 4. Phil. i. 7. x Isa. x. 22, 23. y Rev. xii. 18. xx. 8 only. Gen. xxxii. 12. see Heb. xi. 12. z as above (y). Matt. vii. 26. a here only. Mic. v. 7, 8 al. b constr. part., ch. v. 3, 11. c Acts xxi. 27 reff. = Lam. ii. 17. Jer. vi. 11. Isa. xxviii. 22. d here only. l. c. e Acts xvii. 31 reff. f = 2 Pet. iii. 2. Jude 17 +. g Isa. i. 9. h 2 Cor. iv. 9 reff. i = Acts xiv. 11. Heb. ii. 17. elsw. Mt. Mk. L. only. Ps. xxvii. 1. k ch. iii. 5 reff.

[aft κληθ. ins ουτοι P : αυτοι 71-3 arm.]

27. rec **κατα**λειμμα (*corrn to* LXX *where no* MS *has* υπολ.), with DFKL[P] ℵ-corr[1] rel Thdrt : εγκαταλειμμα Chr : υποκαταλειμμα 47 : txt ABℵ[1] Eus_2.

28. om εν δικαιοσυνη οτι λογον συντετμημενον (*by mistake from similarity of* συντεμνων and συντετμημενον ?) ABℵ[1] [47[1]] Syr copt Eus_2 Damasc Aug_2 (æth has the ver thus : *quia consummatum et præcisum verbum enarret Deus in mundo* : om συντελ. to λογον Thdrt) : ins DFKL[P]ℵ[3] rel latt syr goth [arm(omg οτι) $Euthal_1$] Eus_1 Chr_1 Œc Thl Jer Ambrst Bede.

29. εγκατελειπεν AD[3]FKL[P n]. εγενηθεν B[1](Tischdf). **ο**μοιωθημεν AFL[P Euthal-ms].

ἀλλοτρίους ὄντας, κληθῆναι, κ. ὑπακούσαντας τῶν αὐτῶν ἀξιωθῆναι; Hom. xvi. p. 618. The fem. τήν is used because the Jewish people was typified by the *daughter* of the prophet, Hos. i. 6, who was called Lo-ruhamah, 'not having obtained mercy.' The sense, not the words of the LXX, is quoted. By ἐν τῷ τόπῳ . . . . ἐκεῖ must not I think be understood, in any particular place, as Judæa, nor among any peculiar people, as the Christian Church : but as a general assertion, that in every place where they were called 'not His people,' there they shall be called 'His people.'

27.] *A proof from Scripture of the fact, that a part of Israel are excluded.* Here again the *analogy* of God's dealings, in the partial deliverance of Israel from captivity, and their great final deliverance from death eternal, is the key to the interpretation of the prophecy cited. The words are spoken by Isaiah of the return from captivity of a remnant of Israel. 28.] The reference of this latter part of the citation is not very plain. It is almost verbatim from the LXX, the γάρ (which is found in Aℵ but not in B) being perhaps adopted by the Apostle as continuing the testimony, = 'for the prophet proceeds,'—and the LXX having κατάλειμμα for ὑπόλειμμα (see digest), and ἐν τῇ οἰκουμένῃ ὅλῃ for ἐπὶ τῆς γῆς. The literal rendering of the Heb. is, "The consummation (or consumption) decided, overfloweth with righteousness: for a decision (or consumption) and a decree shall the Lord Jehovah of Sabaoth make in the midst of all the land." As it stands in the LXX, the meaning seems to be, *the Lord will complete and soon fulfil His word in righteousness* (viz. his denunciation of consuming the Assyrian and liberating the remnant of His people): *for the Lord will make a rapidly accomplished word in the midst of all the land.* The E. V., Calv., and others, render λόγον, 'work,' a signification which it never has. If the above interpretation be correct, and the view which I have taken of the analogy of prophecy, it will follow that this verse is adduced by the Apostle as confirming the certainty of the salvation of the remnant of Israel, seeing that now, as then, He with whom a thousand years are as a day, will swiftly accomplish His prophetic word in righteousness. 29.] Another proof of a *remnant* to be saved, from a *preceding* part of the same prophecy. (Such seems to be the sense of προείρ. here,—and so Beza, Calv., Grot., al.; De W., Thol., al., prefer 'prophesied;' but surely there is no necessity for affixing an unusual sense to the word, where the ordinary one (see all the reff.) suits much better.) "**ὁμοιοῦσθαι ὡς** is a construction in which two ideas, 'to become as,' and 'to become like to,' are mingled, as in Heb. נִמְשַׁל כְּ, Ps. xlix. 13, 21; compare Mark iv. 30." Tholuck. On 'Jehovah Sabaoth,' Bengel remarks, "Pro Hebraico צְבָאוֹת in libro 1 Sam. et Jesaia σαβαώθ ponitur; in reliquis libris omnibus παντοκράτωρ." (This is not strictly the case : δυνάμεων is found in several places : and σαβαώθ occurs in Zech. xiii. 2 Bℵ.)

The citation is verbatim from the LXX, who have put σπέρμα for the Heb. שָׂרִיד, 'residuum,'—implying a remnant

ἔθνη τὰ μὴ [lm] διώκοντα [m] δικαιοσύνην, [n] κατέλαβεν δικαιοσύνην, δικαιοσύνην δὲ τὴν [o] ἐκ πίστεως·
31 Ἰσραὴλ δὲ [l] διώκων νόμον δικαιοσύνης, [p] εἰς νόμον οὐκ [pq] ἔφθασεν.

ABDF KL[P]ℵ abcdf ghkl mno17 [47]

l = ch. xii. 13. xiv. 19. Phil. iii. 12, 14. 1 Thess. v. 15. Isa. li. 1. Sir. xxvii. 8.
m 1 Tim. vi. 11. 2 Tim. ii. 22.
n = 1 Cor. ix. 24. Phil. iii. 12. Exod. xv. 9. Deut. xxviii. 45.
o = ch. x. 6. Gal. iii. 8.
p = Phil. iii. 16. Dan. xii. 12 Theod.
q as above (p). Thess. iv. 5. w. ἄχρι, 2 Cor. x. 14. w. ἐπί, Matt. xii. 28 || L. 1 Thess. ii. 16 only. Eccl. viii. 14. Dan. iv. 25 (28) Theod.

[**30.** for *την*, *της* F.]

31. [*δικαιοσ.* bef 1st *νομον* P: *δικαιοσυνην* omg *νομ.* k ?] rec aft 2nd *νομον* ins *δικαιοσυνης* (*corrn for clearness' sake? see notes*), with F(but with a mark inserted before it) KL[P]ℵ[3] rel D[3]-lat vulg syrr goth [arm Euthal-ms] Chr$_1$ Thdor-mops$_2$ Thdrt Œc Thl Jer$_3$ Aug$_4$: om ABDGℵ[1] [47] copt Procop$_1$ Damasc Orig-int$_4$ Ambrst-comm Sedul.[—om *εις νομ.* also o 17.] *εφθοχεν* F(and G).

for a fresh planting. **30—33.**] *The Apostle takes up again the fact of Israel's failure, and shews how their own pursuit of righteousness never attained to righteousness, being hindered by their self-righteousness and rejection of Christ.* These verses do not contain, as Chrys., Œc., Theophyl., the *τοῦ χωρίου παντὸς λύσις*—this *λύσις* is simply in the creative right of God, as declared ver. 18;—but they are a comment on ver. 16, that it is not of him that willeth, nor of him that *runneth:* the same similitude of running being here resumed, and it being shewn that, so far from man's running having decided the matter, the Jews *who pressed forward* to the goal attained not, whereas the Gentiles, *who never ran*, have attained. If this is lost sight of, the connexion of the whole is much impaired, and from doctrinal prejudice, a wholly wrong turn given to the Apostle's line of reasoning,—who resolves the awful fact of Israel's exclusion not into any causes arising from man, but into the supreme will of God,—which will is here again distinctly asserted in the citation from Isaiah (see below). **What then shall we say?** This question, when followed *by a question*, implies of course a *rejection* of the thought thus suggested—but when, as here, by an *assertion*, introduces a further unfolding of the argument from what has preceded. I cannot agree with Flatt, Olsh., al., that *ὅτι κ.τ.λ.* is to be regarded as a question: for, as Rückert has observed, (1) Paul could not put interrogatively, as a supposition in answer to *τί οὖν ἐροῦμεν*, a sentiment not intimated in nor following from the foregoing; (2) there would be no answer to the question thus asked, but the *διὰ τί*, ver. 32, would ask another question, proceeding on the assumption of that which had been before by implication negatived; and (3) the answer, *ὅτι κ.τ.λ.* ver. 32, would touch only the case of the Jews, and not that of the Gentiles, also involved, on this supposition, in the question. **That the Gentiles** (not, as Meyer and Fritz., 'some Gentiles'), **which pursue not after** (see especially reff. Phil.) **righteousness** (not *justification*, which is merely 'the being accounted righteous,' 'the way in which righteousness is ascribed:' not this, but *righteousness itself*, is the aim and end of the race) **attained to** (the whole transaction being regarded as a historical fact) **righteousness, even** (*δέ* brings in something new, different from the foregoing, but not strongly opposed to it, see Winer, edn. 6. § 53. 7. *b*:—the opposition here, though fine and delicate, is remarkable: righteousness—not however that arising from their own works, but the righteousness, &c.) **the righteousness which is of faith:** **31.**] —**but Israel, pursuing after the law of righteousness** (what is the *νόμος δικαιοσύνης*? Certainly not = *δικαιοσύνη νόμου*, as Chrys., Theodoret, Œcum., Calv., Beza, Bengel, by the so-called, but as Thol. observes, unlogical figure of Hypallage:—it may mean either (1) as Meyer, Fritz., Thol., an *ideal law of righteousness*, a *justifying law*,—or (2) as Chrys., al.,—see above,—*the law of Moses*, thus described: or (3) which I believe to be the true account of the words, **νόμος** *δικαιοσ.* is put regarding the Jews, rather than merely *δικαιοσ.*, because in their case there was a prescribed norm of apparent righteousness, viz. the law, in which rule and way they, as *matter of fact*, followed after it. The above, as I believe, mistaken interpretations arise from supposing *νόμον δικαιοσ.* to be = *δικαιοσ.*, which it is not. The Jews followed after, aimed at the fulfilment of '*the law of righteousness*,' thinking by the observance of that law to acquire righteousness. See ch. x. 3, 5, and note; and compare John's coming *ἐν ὁδῷ δικαιοσύνης*, Matt. xxi. 32), **arrived not at** [notice the change in the verb] **the law** (fell far short even of that law, which was given them. It is surprising, with ch. x. 3—5 before them, how De Wette and Tholuck can pronounce the reading *νόμον* without *δικαιοσύνης* to be without sense. The Jews followed after, thinking to perform it entirely, their *νόμος δικαιοσύνης*: which *δικαιοσ. ἐκ τοῦ νόμου* the Apostle defines, ch. x. 5, to

32 [r] *διὰ τί; ὅτι οὐκ ἐκ πίστεως, ἀλλ' [s] ὡς ἐξ ἔργων [νόμου]*
[t] *προσέκοψαν τῷ λίθῳ τοῦ [u] προσκόμματος,* 33 *καθὼς*
γέγραπται [v] Ἰδοὺ τίθημι ἐν Σιὼν λίθον [u] προσκόμματος
καὶ [w] πέτραν [wx] σκανδάλου, καὶ ὁ [y] πιστεύων [y] ἐπ' αὐτῷ οὐ
[z] *καταισχυνθήσεται.*

r Paul, 1 Cor. vi. 7 (bis). 2 Cor. xi. 11 only.
s = Philem. 14.
t Matt. iv. 6 ‖ L. vii. 27. John xi. 9, 10. ch. xiv. 21. 1 Pet. ii. 8 only. Prov. iii. 23.
u ch. xiv. 13, 20. 1 Cor. viii. 9. 1 Pet. ii. 8 only. Isa. xxix. 21.
v Isa. (viii. 14) xxviii. 16.
w 1 Pet. ii. 8.
x = Matt. xviii. 7. ch. xiv. 13 al. Ps. xlviii. 14.
y ch. x. 11. 1 Pet. ii. 6 (from l. c. Aℵ Ald. compl.).
z = ch. v. 5. x. 11 al. Ps. xxiv. 20.

32. om *νομου* (*see notes*) ABFℵ¹ [47-txt] vulg copt [Orig-int$_2$] Jer$_1$ Aug$_{sæpe}$ Ambrst: ins DKL[P]ℵ³ rel syrr goth [arm] Chr$_1$(*οὐκ εἶπεν Ἐξ ἔργων, ἀλλ' Ὡς ἐξ ἔργων νόμου δεικνὺς ὅτι οὐδὲ ταύτην εἶχον τὴν δικαιοσύνην*) Thdor-mops$_1$ Thdrt [Damasc] Œc Thl. [*προσεκοψεν* ℵ¹ l, *προεκ.* o.] rec aft *προσεκοψαν* ins *γαρ* (*see note*), with D³KL[P]ℵ³ rel vulg [fuld] syrr Chr$_1$ Thdor-mops$_1$ Thdrt Aug$_1$ Jer$_1$ Sedul: om AB D¹[and lat] Fℵ¹ a¹ [47-txt] am(with tol) copt goth [Damasc Orig-int$_2$] Ambrst.

33. rec ins *πας* bef *ο πιστευων* (*insd to conform this ver to ch* x. 11, *rather than omd to suit the* LXX: not one ms *omits it in ch* x. 11), with KL[P] rel D³-lat vulg syr [arm Euthal-ms] Chr$_1$ Thdor-mops$_1$ Thdrt Jer$_1$: om ABDFℵ [47] Syr copt goth æth Orig$_1$[int$_2$ Cyr-p$_1$] Damasc Aug$_1$ Ambrst. *ου μη καταισχυνθη* (*see* LXX) DF.

be *ὁ ποιήσας αὐτὰ ἄνθρωπος ζήσεται ἐν αὐτοῖς*, but they did not attain to—not in this case *κατέλαβεν*, but *ἔφθασεν εἰς*—the law—they therefore never attained *righteousness*. It is surely far more easy to imagine how a transcriber should have inserted *δικαιοσύνης*, than how he should have omitted it. It probably was a marginal gloss to explain the second *νόμον*, and thence found its way into the text (I may notice, that ch. x. 3 is not a case in point, the *νόμον* here having an independent and exceptional meaning of its own, which introduces an element not belonging to *ἰδίαν* there)). **Wherefore? because** (*pursuing it*) **not by faith, but as** (used subjectively, as 'if about to obtain their object by:' see Winer, edn. 6, § 65. 9, and compare 2 Pet. i. 3) **by [the] works [of the law** (the evidence for and against *νόμου* is about equally balanced. On the one side we have the Apostle's usage, see ch. iii. 28 reff.,—and the possibility of a transcriber omitting *νόμου*, either as having twice occurred already, or for more complete antithesis,—and on the other we have the temptation to correct *ἔργων* to *ἔργων νόμου* to suit that very usage. On the whole I incline to omit *νόμου*, but do not regard the evidence as sufficiently clear to justify its exclusion from the text)], **they stumbled at the stone of stumbling** (the similitude of a race is still kept up. The insertion of *γάρ* has arisen from a period being placed at *νόμου*. It confuses the sense, making it appear as if the stumbling was the cause of, or at all events coincident with, their pursuing *οὐκ ἐκ π. κ.τ.λ.*, whereas it was this mistaken method of pursuing which caused them to stumble against the stone of stumbling. Thus we have instances in the Greek chariot races, of competitors, by an error in judgment in driving, striking against the *στήλη* round which the chariots were to turn, see Soph. Elect. 730 f. There is a close analogy between our text and the exhortation in Heb. xii. 1 f. There, after the triumphs of faith have been related, we are exhorted to run with patience the race set before us, looking to Jesus, the Author and Finisher of *our faith*: where notice, that the sacred Writer seems to have had in his mind the same comparison of Him to the pillar or goal, to which the eyes of the runners would be exclusively directed). **33.**] *Appeal to the prophecy of Isaiah*, as justifying this comparison of Christ to a stone of stumbling. The citation is gathered from two places in Isaiah. The 'stone of stumbling and rock of offence,' mentioned ch. viii. 14, is substituted for the 'corner-stone elect, precious,' of ch. xxviii. 16. The solution of this is very simple. Isa. viii. 14 was evidently interpreted by the Jews themselves of the Messiah: for Simeon, Luke ii. 34, when speaking of the child Jesus as the Messiah, expressly adduces the prophecy as about to be fulfilled. Similarly Isa. xxviii. 16 was interpreted by the Chaldee Targum, the Babylonish Talmud (Tract Sanhedrin, fol. xxxviii. 1, Stuart), &c. What was there then to prevent the Apostle from giving to this Stone, plainly foretold as to be laid in Zion, that designation which prophecy also justifies, and which bears immediately on the matter here in hand? The translation of Isa. viii. 14 is after the Heb.,—the LXX having apparently read differently. See 1 Pet. ii. 6—8, where the same two texts are joined, and also Ps. cxviii. (cxvii.) 22. **οὐ καταισχυνθήσεται**, LXX (Isa. xxviii. 16),

X. 1 Ἀδελφοί, ἡ μὲν [a] εὐδοκία τῆς ἐμῆς καρδίας καὶ
ἡ δέησις πρὸς τὸν θεὸν ὑπὲρ αὐτῶν [b] εἰς σωτηρίαν.
2 [c] μαρτυρῶ γὰρ αὐτοῖς ὅτι [de] ζῆλον [e] θεοῦ ἔχουσιν, ἀλλ᾽
οὐ [f] κατ᾽ [g] ἐπίγνωσιν. 3 [h] ἀγνοοῦντες γὰρ τὴν τοῦ [i] θεοῦ
[i] δικαιοσύνην, καὶ τὴν ἰδίαν [δικαιοσύνην] [k] ζητοῦντες
[l] στῆσαι, τῇ [i] δικαιοσύνῃ τοῦ [i] θεοῦ οὐχ [m] ὑπετάγησαν.

ABDF KL[P]ℵ a b c d f g h k l m n o 17 [47]

a = here only. Sir. xviii. 31. (Matt. xi. 26 al.)
b Acts xi. 18. ch. vi. 22. Jude 21.
c Acts xxii. 5. Gal. iv. 15. Col. iv. 13.
d = John ii. 17, from Ps. lxviii. 9. 2 Cor. vii. 7, 11.
e 2 Cor. xi. 2. see Acts xxii. 3. f Acts iii. 17 reff. g ch. iii. 20 reff. h Acts xiii. 27 reff. i ch. i. 17 reff. k = Acts xiii 8 reff. l = ch. iii. 31. Heb. x. 9. Num. xxx. 14. m = 1 Cor. xv. 28. 2 Macc. xiii. 23. see ch. viii. 7 reff.

CHAP. X. 1. rec aft η δεησις ins η (*corrn: see note*), with KL rel Chr Thdrt [Euthal-ms Damasc: μου P]: om ABDFℵ [47 arm]. προς τον θν is written over an erasure by ℵ[1]. rec for αυτων, του ισραηλ (*explanatory gloss*), with KL rel Thdrt Œc Thl: txt ABDF[P]ℵ 17 [47-txt] latt syrr copt arm Chr$_1$ Cyr[-c] Damasc [Orig-int$_2$] Ambrst Aug$_{sæpe}$ Pel Sedul Bede. rec ins εστιν bef εις σωτηριαν, with KL[P]ℵ[3] rel syr Chr$_1$ Thdrt [Euthal-ms Thl Œc]: om ABDFℵ[1] [47-txt] Syr goth [(æth) arm] Cyr[-c Damasc] Aug$_1$.

3. for γαρ, δε A 57 Leo. om 2nd δικαιοσυνην ABD[P 47-txt] vulg copt arm Clem$_1$ Cyr[-p$_2$] Bas$_2$ Chr$_1$ Procop$_1$ Damasc [Ambrst] Aug$_{sæpe}$: ins FKLℵ rel [D-lat[1]] syrr goth æth Chr$_4$ Thdrt Œc Thl [Orig-int$_2$] Iren[-int$_1$]-mss Tert$_1$ Ambr$_1$ Aug$_2$, and aft ζητουντες m.

οὐ μὴ καταισχυνθῇ, gives a secondary meaning of the Heb. לֹא יָחִישׁ, 'shall not *make haste*:' i. e. shall not fly in terror, shall not be confounded.

CHAP. X. 1—13.] *The Jews, though zealous for God, are yet ignorant of God's righteousness* (1—3), *as revealed to them in their own Scriptures* (4—13).

1.] **Brethren** ('nunc quasi superata præcedentis tractationis severitate comiter appellat *fratres*.' Bengel), **the inclination of my heart** (εὐδοκία is seldom, if ever, used to signify the *motion of desire*, but imports the *rest of approving satisfaction*. Possibly there is here a mixture of constructions: the Apostle's εὐδοκία would be their *salvation itself*,—his δέησις πρὸς τὸν θ. ὑπὲρ αὐτ. was **εἰς** σωτ. The μέν requires a corresponding δέ, not expressed, but implied in the course of vv. 2, 3, where the obstacle to their σωτήρ. is brought out), **and my supplication to God on their behalf** (Israel, see ch. ix. 32, προσέκοψαν), **(is) for (their) salvation** (lit. 'towards salvation.' The insertion of the art. after δέησις has apparently been an over-careful grammatical correction: it is by no means universal in the N. T., even where the Greek writers insert it,—and here, seeing that there could be no δεήσεις to any other than God, the omission would be more natural. τοῦ Ἰσραήλ has been substituted by the adoption of a gloss: ἐστίν to complete the sense). The Apostle's meaning seems to be, to destroy any impression which his readers may have received unfavourable to his love of his own people, from the stern argument of the former chapter. 2.] **For** (reason why I thus sympathize with their efforts, though misdirected) **I bear witness to them that they have a zeal for God** (for this meaning of the gen. see reff., especially 2 Cor. xi. 2, and note there), **but not according to** (in accordance with, founded upon, and carried on with) **knowledge** (accurate apprehension of the way of righteousness as revealed to them). 3.] **For** (explanation of οὐ κατ᾽ ἐπίγν.) **not recognizing** ('*being ignorant of*' is liable to the objection, that it may represent to the reader a state of *excusable* ignorance, whereas they *had it before them*, and *overlooked* it) **the righteousness of God** (not, the *way of justification* appointed by God, as Stuart, al.: but that only *righteousness* which avails before God, which becomes ours in justification; see De Wette's note, quoted on ch. i. 17), **and seeking to set up their own righteousness** (again, not *justification*, but *righteousness*: that, namely, described ver. 5; not that it was ever theirs, but the Apostle speaks subjectively. Notwithstanding the MS. authority against δικαι. after ἰδίαν, it would seem as if it had been written for emphasis' sake by the Apostle, and omitted on account of the word occurring thrice in the sentence), **they were not subjected** (historical: *implying*, but not itself *bearing*, a perfect sense. The passage,—not in a middle sense, as De Wette and Thol.,—expresses the *result only*; it might be themselves, or it might be some other, that subjected them,—but the historical fact was, that they *were not subjected*) **to the righteousness of God** (the δικ. τ. θ. being considered as a *rule* or *method*, to which it was necessary to conform, but to which they were never subjected as they were to the law of Moses). *

4 [n] τέλος γὰρ νόμου χριστὸς [b] εἰς δικαιοσύνην παντὶ τῷ
πιστεύοντι. 5 Μωυσῆς γὰρ [o] γράφει τὴν [p] δικαιοσύνην
τὴν [p] ἐκ [p] νόμου, [q] ὅτι ὁ ποιήσας αὐτὰ ἄνθρωπος ζήσεται

n = 1 Pet. i. 9. see note and 2 Cor. iii. 13.
o constr., John i. 46. see Luke xviii. 31.
p Phil. iii. (6) 9. see Gal. iii. 21.
q Lev. xviii. 5. see Neh. ix. 29. Ezek. xx. 21.

5. rec ins *του* bef *νομου*, with DFKL[P] rel [arm Chr Thdrt Damasc]: om (A)Bℵ. —for *νομου*, *πιστεως* A. *οτι* bef *τ. δικ. τ. εκ ν.* AD^{1}ℵ^1 17^1 vulg Damasc [Orig-int$_4$ Ambrst Cassiod$_1$]. om *αυτα* (as LXX-AB(not Ed-vat [&c])) A D-gr ℵ^1 vulg Damasc [Orig-int$_4$]: *eam* D^2-lat copt[-wilk] goth Cassiod$_1$: *ταυτα* 17^1 m^1 æth. om *ανθρωπος* F Syr Chr$_1$ Hil.

4—13.] The *δικαιοσύνη τ. θ.* is now explained to be summed up in that Saviour who was *declared to them in their own Scriptures.* **For** (establishing what was last said, and at the same time unfolding the *δικ. τ. θ.* in a form which rendered them inexcusable for its non-recognition) **Christ is the end of the Law** (i. e. *the object at which the law aimed:* see the similar expression 1 Tim. i. 5, *τὸ τέλος τῆς παραγγελίας ἐστὶν ἀγάπη.* Various * meanings have been given to *τέλος.* (1) *End*, finis, *chronological:* 'Christ is the termination of the law.' So the latt., Augustine, Luther, al., Olsh., Meyer, Fritz., De Wette, al. But this meaning, unless understood in its pregnant sense, that Christ, who has succeeded to the law, was also the object and aim of the law, says too little. In this pregnant sense Tholuck takes the word 'end,' the *end in time and in aim.* It may be so; but I prefer simply to take in the idea of Christ being the end, i. e. *aim* of the law, as borne out by the following citations, in which nothing is said of the *transitoriness* of the law, but much of the notices which it contains of righteousness by faith in Christ. (2) Clem. Alex.,—*πλήρωμα γὰρ ν. χρ. εἰς δικ. π. τῷ πιστ.*, De Div. Serv. § 9, p. 940 P. Theodoret, Calv., Grot., al., take *τέλος* for '*accomplishment*,' a sense included in the general meaning, but not especially treated here,—the following quotations not having any reference to it. (3) The meaning, *end in the sense of object or aim*, above adopted, is that of the Syr., Chrys., Theophyl., Beza, Bengel, al. Chrys. observes: *εἰ γὰρ τοῦ νόμου τέλος ὁ χριστός, ὁ τὸν χριστὸν οὐκ ἔχων, κἂν ἐκείνην* (i. e. *δικαιοσύνην*) *δοκῇ ἔχειν, οὐκ ἔχει· ὁ δὲ τὸν χριστὸν ἔχων, κἂν μὴ ᾖ κατωρθωκὼς τὸν νόμον, τὸ πᾶν εἴληφε. καὶ γὰρ τέλος ἰατρικῆς ὑγιεία. ὥσπερ οὖν ὁ δυνάμενος ὑγιῆ ποιεῖν, κἂν μὴ τὴν ἰατρικὴν ἔχῃ, τὸ πᾶν ἔχει. ὁ δὲ μὴ εἰδὼς θεραπεύειν, κἂν μετιέναι δοκῇ τὴν τέχνην, τοῦ παντὸς ἐξέπεσεν· οὕτω ἐπὶ τοῦ νόμου καὶ τῆς πίστεως, ὁ μὲν ταύτην ἔχων, καὶ τὸ ἐκείνου τέλος ἔχει· ὁ δὲ ταύτης ἔξω ὤν, ἀμφοτέρων ἐστὶν ἀλλότριος.* Hom. xvii. p. 622. *νόμου* is here plainly *the law of Moses:* sec Middleton in loc.) **unto righteousness** (i. e. so as to bring about righteousness, which the law could not do) **to** (dat. commodi) **every one that believeth.** "Had they only used the law, instead of abusing it, it would have been their best preparation for the Saviour's advent. For indeed, by reason of man's natural weakness, it was always powerless to justify. It was never intended to make the sinner righteous before God; but rather to impart to him a knowledge of his sinfulness, and to awaken in his heart earnest longings for some powerful deliverer. Thus used, it would have ensured the reception of the Messiah by those who now reject Him. Striving to attain to real holiness, and increasingly conscious of the impossibility of becoming holy by an imperfect obedience to the law's requirements, they would gladly have recognized the Saviour as the end of the law for righteousness." Ewbank.

5.] **For** (proof of the impossibility of legal righteousness, as declared even in the law itself) **Moses describes** (reff.) **the righteousness which is of** (abstr.—not implying that it has ever been attained, but rather presupposing the contrary) **the law, that** (*ὅτι* recitantis, not *γράφ. ὅτι*, in which case we should have *αὐτήν*. The *eam* of some versions has apparently arisen from misunderstanding *ὅτι*) **the man who hath done them** (the ordinances of the law) **shall live in** (in the strength of, by means of, as his status) **it** (the righteousness accruing by such doing of them). As regards the *life* here promised, the Jewish interpreters themselves included in it more than mere earthly felicity in Canaan, and extended their view to a better life hereafter: see Wetst. in loc. Earthly felicity it doubtless *did* impart, compare Deut. xxx. 20; but even there, as Thol. observes, '*life*' seems to be a general promise, and length of days a particular species of felicity. "In the N. T.," he continues, "this idea (of life) is always exalted into that of life blessed and eternal:—see Matt. vii. 14; xviii. 8, 9; Luke x. 28."

6—8.] *The righteousness which is of faith* * *is described, in the words spoken in Scripture by Moses of the commandment given by him,—as not dependent on a long and*

r ch. ix. 30. Gal. iii. 8. s Deut. xxx. 12. t Acts ii. 34 reff. u = ch. ix. 8. v Acts xxiii. 15 reff.

ἐν αὐτῇ. 6 ἡ δὲ [r] ἐκ πίστεως δικαιοσύνη οὕτως λέγει,
[s] Μὴ εἴπῃς ἐν τῇ καρδίᾳ σου Τίς [t] ἀναβήσεται εἰς τὸν
οὐρανόν; [u] τοῦτ᾽ ἔστιν χριστὸν [v] καταγαγεῖν· 7 ἢ Τίς

ABDF KL[P]א abcdf ghkl mno17 [47]

rec (for αυτη) αυτοις (*from* LXX), with DFL[KP]א^3 rel [syrr arm(Treg) Chr$_1$ Thdrt Ambrst]: txt ABא^1 17 [47] vulg D^2-lat copt goth arm[-ed-ven(Sz) Orig-int$_4$] Damasc Pel Sedul Bede.

difficult process of search, but near to every man, and in every man's power to attain. I believe the account of the following citation will be best found by bearing in mind that the Apostle is speaking of Christ as the *end of the law* for righteousness to the believer. He takes as a confirmation of this, a passage occurring in a prophetic part of Deut., where Moses is foretelling to the Jews the consequences of rejecting God's law, and His mercy to them even when under chastisement, if they would return to Him. He then describes the law in nearly the words cited in this verse. Now the Apostle, regarding Christ as the *end* of the law, its great central aim and object, quotes these words not merely as suiting his purpose, but as bearing, where originally used, an *à fortiori* application to faith in Him who is the end of the law, and to the commandment to believe in Him, which (1 John iii. 23) is now '*God's commandment.*' If spoken of *the law* as a manifestation of God in man's heart and mouth, much more were they spoken of Him, who is *God manifest in the flesh*, the *end of the law and the prophets.* This view is, it is true, different from that of almost all eminent Commentators, ancient and modern,—who regard the words as merely *adapted* or *parodied* by the Apostle as suiting his present purpose. Thus, with minor shades of difference, Chrys., Beza, Grot., Vatabl., Luther, Wolf, Bengel, Koppe, Flatt, Rückert, De Wette, Thol., Stuart, Hodge, al. But we must remember that it is in this passage Paul's object not merely to *describe* the righteousness which is of faith in Christ, but to *shew it described already in the words of the law.* The Commentators who have taken more or less the view that the Apostle cites the words *as bearing the sense put on them*, are Calvin, Calovius, Reiche, Meyer, Fritz., Olsh.

But the righteousness which is of faith speaketh on this wise (personified, as Wisdom in the Prov.), **Say not in thine heart** (i. e. 'think not,' a Heb. idiom. The LXX has merely λέγων, לֵאמֹר. The Apostle cites freely, giving the explanation of λέγων, viz. *thinking*), **Who shall go up to heaven** (LXX, ἀναβ. ἡμῖν (ἡμῶν, A) εἰς τ. οὐρ., see Prov. xxx. 4)?—**that is** (see note above:—that imports in its full and unfolded meaning), **to bring down Christ:—or who shall go down into the abyss** (LXX, τίς διαπεράσει ἡμῖν εἰς τὸ πέραν τῆς θαλάσσης; The Apostle substitutes τίς κατ. εἰς τ. ἄβ. as the direct contrast to τίς ἀν. εἰς τ. οὐρ., as in ref. Ps.; see also Amos ix. 2:—and as better suiting the interpretation which follows)?—**that is, to bring up Christ from the dead.** There is some difficulty in assigning the precise view with which the Apostle introduces these questions. Tholuck remarks, "The different interpretations may be reduced to this, that the questions are regarded either (1) as questions of *unbelief*, or (2) as questions of *embarrassment*, or (3) as questions of *anxiety*." The first view is represented by De Wette, who says, "In what sense these questions, from which the righteousness which is of faith dissuades men, are to be taken, is plain from ver. 9, where the Resurrection of Christ is asserted as the one most weighty point of historical Christian belief:—they would be *questions* of unbelief, which regards this fact as not accomplished, or as now first to be accomplished. Thus also, probably, are we to understand the *first question*, as applying to the *Incarnation of Christ*." This is more or less also the view of Chrys., Theodoret, Theophyl., Œc., Erasm., Estius, Semler, Koppe, Meyer, al., Rückert (who refers the doubt or the unbelief to the *full accomplishment* of redemption by the Incarnation and Resurrection of Christ), Reiche, and Köllner (who refer καταγ. to the *ascended* Saviour, thereby destroying the symmetry of the whole,—because the latter question undoubtedly refers to bringing Christ not from a *present* but from a *past* state, from which He has historically come). (2) The second view, that they are questions of *embarrassment*, is taken by L. Capellus, Wolf, Rosenm., and Stuart, which last says, "The whole (of Moses's saying) may be summed up in one word, omitting all figurative expression: viz. *the commandment is plain and accessible.* You can have, therefore, no excuse for neglecting it. So in the case before us. *Justification by faith in Christ* is a plain and intelligible doctrine. It is not shut up in mysterious language . . . . It is like what Moses says of the statutes which he gave to Israel, plain, intelligible, accessible . . . .

[w] καταβήσεται εἰς τὴν [x] ἄβυσσον; [u] τοῦτ᾽ ἔστιν χριστὸν
ἐκ νεκρῶν [y] ἀναγαγεῖν. 8 ἀλλὰ τί λέγει; [z] Ἐγγύς σου
τὸ ῥῆμά ἐστιν, ἐν τῷ στόματί σου καὶ ἐν τῇ καρδίᾳ σου·
[u] τοῦτ᾽ ἔστιν τὸ [a] ῥῆμα τῆς πίστεως ὃ κηρύσσομεν· 9 ὅτι

w = Eph. iv. 9, 10. Ps. cxxxviii. 8.
x Luke viii. 31 only, exc. Rev. ix. 1, 2, 11 al4. Gen. i. 2.
y — Heb. xiii. 20. Ps. xxix. 3.
z Deut. xxx. 14. constr., John iii. 23. vi. 19, 23.
a = Acts x. 37. 1 Pet. i. 25. (John vi. 63. xiv. 10, plur.)

8. aft λεγει ins η γραφη D [17] vulg(not demid tol) [arm] $Orig_4$[-int_2] Cyr[-p_2(om_2)] Thdrt Hil_1 Ambrst Pel Sedul Bede: aft τι, F [copt æth]. 1st εστιν bef 1st το ρημα (*see* LXX) DF [vulg goth arm Orig-int_2 Hil_1 Ambrst].

It is brought before the mind and heart of every man: and thus he is without excuse for unbelief." (3) The third view, that they are questions of *anxiety*, is that of Calv., Beza, Pisc., Bengel, Knapp, Fritz., and Tholuck:—by none perhaps better expressed than by Ewbank, Comm. on the Ep. to the Rom., p. 74: "Personifying the great Christian doctrine of free justification through faith, he represents it as addressing every man who is anxious to obtain salvation, in the encouraging words of Moses: 'Say not in thine heart, (it says to such an one) &c. . . . .' In other words, 'Let not the man, who sighs for deliverance from his own sinfulness, suppose that the accomplishment of some impossible task is required of him, in order to enjoy the blessings of the Gospel. Let him not think that the personal presence of the Messiah is necessary to ensure his salvation. Christ needs not to be brought down from heaven, or up from the abyss, to impart to him forgiveness and holiness. No. Our Christian message contains no impossibilities. We do not mock the sinner by offering him happiness on conditions which we know that he is powerless to fulfil. We tell him that Christ's word is near to him: so near, that he may speak of it with his mouth, and meditate on it with his heart . . . . .' Is there any thing above human power in such a confession, and in such a belief? Surely not. It is graciously adapted to the necessity of the very weakest and most sinful of God's creatures." [I will now take up the three views afresh, and state the objections.] (1) The objection to this view, as alleged by Tholuck, is, that in it, the contrast with ver. 5 is lost sight of. And this is so far just, that it must be confessed we thus lose the ideas which the Apostle evidently intended us to grasp, those of insuperable difficulty in the acquisition of righteousness by the law, and of facility,—by the gospel. Also,—it puts *too forward* the allegation of the great matters of historical belief, which are not *here* the central point of the argument, but introduced as the objects which *faith, itself that central point*, apprehends. (2) The last objection has some force as against *this* view. The regarding the questions as mere questions of difficulty and intellectual bewilderment does not adequately represent the ζῆλος θεοῦ predicated of the Jews, on the assumption of which the whole passage proceeds. Here, however, it seems to me, we have more truth than in (1): for the plainness and simplicity of the truth to be believed is unquestionably one most important element in the righteousness which is of faith. (3) Here we have the important element just mentioned, not indeed made the prominent point of the questions, but, as it appears to me, properly and sufficiently kept in view. The anxious follower after righteousness is not disappointed by an impracticable code, nor mocked by an unintelligible revelation: the word is *near him*, therefore *accessible; plain and simple*, and therefore *apprehensible;* and, taking (1) into account, we may fairly add, —deals with *definite historical fact*, and therefore *certain:* so that his salvation is not contingent on an amount of performance which is *beyond him*, and therefore *inaccessible: irrational*, and therefore *inapprehensible: undefined*, and therefore *involved in uncertainty*. Thus, it seems to me, we satisfy all the conditions of the argument: and thus also it is clearly brought out, that *the words themselves* could never have been spoken by Moses of the righteousness which is of *the law*, but of that which is of *faith*. **8.**] **But what says it? The word is near thee, in thy mouth** (to confess), **and in thine heart** (to believe): **that is** (see above), **the word of faith** (which forms the substratum and object of faith, see Gal. iii. 2; 1 Tim. iv. 6) **which we** (ministers of Christ: or perhaps, I Paul) **preach.** This verse has been explained in dealing with vv. 6 and 7.

9.] **Because** (explanation of the word being near thee: so Thol., De Wette, Stuart, al. Others take ὅτι here as in ver. 5, merely recitantis, making ἐάν κ.τ.λ. the ῥῆμα preached. But as Thol. observes, (1) the duty of confessing the Lord Jesus can hardly be called part of the contents of the preaching of faith, but the prominence *

ἐὰν [b] ὁμολογήσῃς [c] ἐν τῷ [c] στόματί σου κύριον Ἰησοῦν,
καὶ [d] πιστεύσῃς ἐν τῇ καρδίᾳ σου [d] ὅτι ὁ θεὸς αὐτὸν
[e] ἤγειρεν ἐκ νεκρῶν, σωθήσῃ· 10 καρδίᾳ γὰρ πιστεύεται
[f] εἰς δικαιοσύνην, στόματι δὲ [b] ὁμολογεῖται [f] εἰς σωτηρίαν.
11 λέγει γὰρ ἡ [g] γραφὴ Πᾶς ὁ [h] πιστεύων ἐπ' αὐτῷ οὐ
[h] καταισχυνθήσεται. 12 οὐ γάρ ἐστιν [i] διαστολὴ Ἰουδαίου τε καὶ Ἕλληνος· ὁ γὰρ αὐτὸς κύριος πάντων
[k] πλουτῶν εἰς πάντας τοὺς [l] ἐπικαλουμένους αὐτόν.

ABDF KL[P]ℵ a b c d f g h k l m n o 17 [47]

b = John ix. 22. xii. 42. Acts xxiii. 8. 1 Tim. vi. 12.
c = ch. xv. 6 only. Ps. lxxxviii. 1.
d Acts ix. 26 reff.
e = 1 Cor. xv. 12 reff.
f vv. 1, 4.
g sing., ch. ix. 17 reff.
h ch. ix. 33, from Isa. xxviii. 16. see Sir. ii. 10.
i ch. iii. 22. 1 Cor. xiv. 7 only. = Exod. viii. 23.
k = Luke xii. 21. 1 Tim. vi. 18. Exod. xxx. 15.
l Acts ii. 21 reff. Joel ii. 32.

9. aft ομολογησης ins το ρημα B 71 $Clem_1$. for κυριον ιησουν, οτι κυριος ιησους B $Clem_1$ Cyr[-p(sometimes omg οτι)] : so, addg εστιν, copt Hil Aug. aft ιησουν ins χριστον A Bas[-ed(omg κυρ.). πιστευεις P : -σεις m, σις 17.] ηγειρεν bef αυτον A b k o [arm $Clem_1$] Cyr-jer_1 $Cyr_{sæpe}$[-p].
[10. for στοματι, στομα P m.]
11. ins μη bef καταισχυνθησεται (*see ch* ix. 23 *v. r.*) DF.
12. ιουδαιω και ελληνι D[-gr].

given to that duty shews a reference to the words of Moses: (2) the making ὅτι render a reason for ἐγγύς σου κ.τ.λ. suits much better the context and form of the passage: (3) the fact of the confession with the mouth standing *first*, also shews a reference to what has gone before: for when the Apostle brings his own arrangement in ver. 10, he puts, as natural, the belief of the heart first), **if thou shalt confess with thy mouth** (same order as ver. 8) **the Lord Jesus** (not, I think, 'Jesus as the Lord' (see the readg of B al.): this might very well be,—and κύριον might, as Thol., be the predicate placed first for emphasis, did not Paul frequently use κύριος Ἰησοῦς for '*the Lord Jesus*,'—see (ch. xiv. 14 after a prep.) 1 Cor. i. 3 al.; Phil. (ii. 19) iii. 20; Col. iii. 17 (1 Thess. i. 1; iv. 1). 1 Cor. xii. 3 is hardly an example on the other side: see note there, but 2 Cor. iv. 5 is, cf. note *there*), **and believe in thine heart that God raised Him from the dead** (here, as in 1 Cor. xv. 14, 16, 17, regarded as the great central fact of redemption), **thou shalt be saved** (inherit eternal life). Here we have the two parts of the above question again introduced: the *confession of the Lord Jesus* implying his having *come down* from heaven, and the *belief in His resurrection* implying His having been *brought up* from the dead. **10.**] **For** (refers back to ver. 6, where the above words were ascribed to ἡ ἐκ πίστεως δικαιοσύνη, and explains how πιστεύσ. ἐν τῇ καρδ. refer to the acquiring of righteousness) **with the heart faith is exercised** (**πιστεύεται**, men believe) **unto** (so as to be available to the acquisition of) **righteousness, but** (q. d. 'not only so: but there must be an outward confession, in order for justification to be carried forward to salvation') **with the mouth confession is made unto salvation.** Clearly the words δικ. and σωτ. are not used here, as De W., al., merely as different terms for the same thing, for the sake of the parallelism: but as Thol. quotes from Crell., σωτ. is the 'terminus ultimus et apex justificationis,' consequent not merely on the act of justifying faith as the other, but on a good confession before the world, maintained unto the end. **11.**] **For** (proof of the former part of ver. 10) **the Scripture saith, Every one who believeth on Him shall not be ashamed.** πᾶς is neither in the LXX nor the Heb., but is implied in the indefinite participle. The Apostle seems to use it here as taking up παντὶ τῷ πιστεύοντι, ver. 4. See ch. ix. 33. **12.**] **For** (an explanation of the strong expression **πᾶς** ὁ πιστεύων, as implying the *universal* offer of the riches of God's mercy in Christ) **there is no distinction of Jew and Greek** (Gentile. See ch. iii. 22); **for the same Lord of all** (viz. *Christ*, who is the subject here: vv. 9, 11, 13 cannot be separated. So Orig., Chrys., Œc., Calov., Wolf, Bengel, Rück., Meyer, Fritz., De Wette, Tholuck, al. So πάντων κύριος of Christ, Acts x. 36. Most modern Commentators make ὁ αὐτός the subject, and κύριος the predicate. But I prefer the usual rendering, both on account of the strangeness of ὁ αὐτός thus standing alone, and because this Apostle uses the expression ὁ αὐτὸς κύριος, 1 Cor. xii. 5, and even ὁ αὐτὸς θεός, ib. 6, for 'the same Lord,' and 'it is the same God.' Stuart supplies, '(there is) the same Lord:' but this is harsh,—and unnecessary, if the participle πλουτῶν be taken as συντελῶν κ. συντ. in ch. ix. 28) **is rich towards all** ('by **εἰς** is signified the direction in which the

13 πᾶς γὰρ ὃς ἂν [l] ἐπικαλέσηται τὸ ὄνομα κυρίου
σωθήσεται. 14 πῶς οὖν [l] ἐπικαλέσωνται [m] εἰς ὃν οὐκ
[n] ἐπίστευσαν; πῶς δὲ πιστεύσωσιν [m] οὗ οὐκ [o] ἤκουσαν;
πῶς δὲ ἀκούσωσιν χωρὶς κηρύσσοντος; 15 πῶς δὲ κηρύξ-
ωσιν ἐὰν μὴ ἀποσταλῶσιν; καθὼς γέγραπται Ὡς [p] ὡραῖοι
οἱ πόδες τῶν [[qr] εὐαγγελιζομένων [r] εἰρήνην, τῶν] [q] εὐαγγελιζομένων ἀγαθά. 16 Ἀλλ᾽ οὐ πάντες [s] ὑπήκουσαν τῷ

C μη αποσταλωσιν...

ABCDF KL[P]א a b c d f g h k l m n o 17 [47]

m constr., Eurip. Med. 751, ὄμνυμι ...ἐμμένειν ἅ σου κλύω. n w. εἰς, Acts x. 43 reff. o = w. gen., here only. Xen. Mem. iii. 5. 9. Hom. Od. α. 289. see Acts xxiii. 16. p Acts iii. 2 reff. (Isa. lii. 7.) q = Luke i. 19. ii. 10. r Acts x. 36 reff. s Acts vi. 7 reff.

14. rec επικαλεσονται (*see note*), with KL[P] rel Clem$_1$ [Ath$_1$ Euthal-ms] Thdor-mops$_1$ Chr$_1$ Thdrt Damasc Thl Œc: txt ABDFא a. ins η bef 1st πως δε F latt [Syr arm Ambrst]. rec πιστευσουσιν, with AKL rel Clem$_1$ [Ps-]Ath Chr[-montf Euthal-ms] Thdrt Damasc Thl Œc: txt BD F[-gr(επιστ.) P]א Chr-ms$_1$. rec ακουσουσιν, with L rel Clem$_1$ [Ath$_1$] Chr-montf$_1$ Thdrt Thl Œc: ακουσονται DFKא^1[P 47] d Damasc: txt A^{2}Bא^3 m 17 Chr-2-mss. (A^1 illegible.) [for χωρις, ανευ P.]

15. rec κηρυξουσιν, with rel Clem$_1$ Chr[-montf$_1$] Thdrt Damasc: [ε]κηρυσσουσιν F[-gr]: ακουσωσιν c: txt ABDKL[P]א a 17 Chr-2-mss$_1$ [Euthal-ms]. καθαπερ B: καθα Chr-ms. om ευαγγελιζομενων ειρηνην των (*homœotel*) ABCא^1 [47-txt] coptt æth Clem$_1$ Orig$_1$[-int$_4$ Euthal$_1$] Epiph$_1$ (Thdor-mops$_1$) Damasc: ins D(F)KL[P]א^3 rel latt syrr goth arm Chr$_1$ Thdrt Thl Œc Tert$_3$ Ambr$_2$ Jer$_2$ Hil$_2$.—om των F.—*evang. bona evang. pacem* Iren-int Tert$_1$ Hil$_1$.—om *evang. bona* Epiph$_1$ Hil$_1$. rec ins τα bef αγαθα, with D$^{2.3}$KLא^1 rel Clem$_1$ Chr$_1$ [Euthal$_1$(and ms] Thdrt: om [*as* LXX] ABCD^{1}Fא^3[P 47-txt Eus$_1$] Orig$_1$ Damasc.

16. aft υπηκουσαν ins εν (but marked for erasure) א^1.

stream of grace rushes forth.' Olsh.) **who call upon Him.** 13—21.] *Proof from Scripture of this assertion, and argument thereon.* 13.] **For every one, whosoever shall call upon the Name of the Lord** (Jehovah,—but used here of Christ beyond a doubt, as the next verse shews. There is hardly a stronger proof, or one more irrefragable by those who deny the Godhead of our Blessed Lord, of the unhesitating application to Him by the Apostle of the name and attributes of Jehovah) **shall be saved.** 14, 15.] It has been much doubted to whom these questions refer,—to Jews or to Gentiles? It must, I think, be answered, *To neither exclusively.* They are generalized by the πᾶς ὃς ἄν of the preceding verse, to mean *all,* both Jews and Gentiles. And the inference in what follows, though mainly concerning the rejection of the unbelieving Jews, has regard also to the reception of the Gentiles: see below on vv. 19, 20. At the same time, as Meyer remarks, "the necessity of the Gospel ἀποστολή must first be laid down, in order to bring out in strong contrast the disobedience of some." **How then** (i. e. *posito,* that the foregoing is so) **can they** (men, represented by the πᾶς ὃς ἄν of ver. 13) **call on** (I have followed the majority of the chief MSS. in reading the aor. subjunctive instead of the future indic. So also ch. vi. 1) **Him in whom they have not believed** (i. e. begun to believe: so ch. xiii. 11)? **But how can they believe (in Him) of whom they have not heard** (construction see reff.)? **But how can they hear without a preacher? But how can men preach unless they shall have been sent? As it is written, How beautiful are the feet of those who [publish glad tidings of peace, who] publish glad tidings of** (τά is excluded by the strong manuscript testimony against it) **good things.** The Apostle is shewing the *necessity* and *dignity* of the preachers of the word, which leads on to the *universality* of their preaching, leaving all who disobey it without excuse. He therefore cites this, as shewing that their instrumentality was one recognized in the prophetic word, where their office is described and glorified. The applicability of these words to the preachers of the Gospel is evident from the passage in Isaiah itself, which is spoken indeed of the return from captivity, but in that return has regard to a more glorious one under the future Redeemer. We need not therefore say that the Apostle uses Scripture words merely as expressing his own thoughts in a well-known garb;—he alleges the words as a prophetic description of the preachers of whom he is writing. 16.] In this preaching of the Gospel some have been found obedient, others disobedient: and this was before announced by Isaiah. The persons here meant are as yet kept indefinite,—but evidently the Apostle has in his mind the unbelieving Jews, about whom his main discourse is employed.

But not all hearkened to (historic: dur-

εὐαγγελίῳ. Ἡσαΐας γὰρ λέγει Κύριε, τίς ἐπίστευσεν τῇ
[t] ἀκοῇ ἡμῶν; 17 ἄρα ἡ πίστις [u] ἐξ ἀκοῆς, ἡ δὲ ἀκοὴ διὰ
[v] ῥήματος [v] χριστοῦ. 18 ἀλλὰ [w] λέγω, [x] μὴ [x] οὐκ ἤκουσαν; ...λεγω K.
[y] μενοῦνγε [z] εἰς πᾶσαν τὴν γῆν [r] ἐξῆλθεν ὁ [a] φθόγγος ABCD FL[P]ℵ
αὐτῶν, καὶ εἰς τὰ [b] πέρατα τῆς [c] οἰκουμένης τὰ ῥήματα a b c d f g h k l
αὐτῶν. 19 ἀλλὰ [w] λέγω, [x] μὴ Ἰσραὴλ [x] οὐκ ἔγνω; πρῶτος m n o 17 [47]

t = John xii. 38, from Isa. liii. 1. 1 Thess. ii. 13. Heb. iv. 2.
u Gal. iii. 2, 5.
v here only. see John v. 47. Acts xi. 16.
w ch. xi. 1, 11.
x here bis. 1 Cor. ix. 4, 5. xi. 22 only. P.
y (Luke xi. 28 v. r.) ch. ix. 20 only †.
z Matt. ix. 26. Mark i. 28. Psa. xviii. 4.
a 1 Cor. xiv. 7 only. Ps. l. c. Wisd. xix. 18 only.
b = Matt. xii. 42. Luke xi. 31 (Heb. vi. 16 only. Ps. ii. 8 al. fr.
c Paul here only. Matt. xxiv. 14. Luke ii. 1 al2. Acts xi. 28 al4. Heb. i. 6. ii. 5. Rev. iii. 10. xv. 9. xvi. 14 only. Ps. lxxi. 8.

17. [aft *αρα* ins *ουν* F m sah.] rec (for *χριστου*) *θεου*, with A D[2·3][-gr] KL[P] ℵ-corr[1·3] rel syrr æth-pl Clem₁ [Ps-]Ath₁ Thdor-mops₁ Chr₁ Thdrt Damasc Sedul: *Dei Christi* [Ps-]Bede: [om F Hil₁:] txt BCD[1]ℵ[1] [47-txt] vulg coptt goth æth-rom [arm Orig-int₂] Ambrst Aug₁ Pel.
18. om *μενουνγε* F D[1]-lat [Orig-int₂]. aft *πασαν* ins *γαρ* D[1](and lat[1]).
19. rec *ουκ εγνω* bef *ισραηλ* (*corrn for elegance?*), with D[2]L rel syrr Thdrt Thl: txt

ing the preaching) **the glad tidings** (οὐ πάντες, because πάντες, see vv. 11—13, were the objects of the preaching, and must hearken to it if they would be saved):—(and this too was no unlooked-for thing, but predetermined in the divine counsel) **for Esaias saith, Lord** (κύριε is not in the Heb.), **who believed the hearing of us** [(i.e. as in our Version,] **our report**)? **17.**] **Faith then** (conclusion from ver. 16, τίς ἐπίστ. τῇ ἀκοῇ) **is from hearing** (the *publication* of the Gospel produces belief in it), **and the hearing** (the effect of the publication of the Gospel) **is by means of** (not, 'in obedience to,' but 'by,' as its instrument and vehicle) **the word of Christ** (θεοῦ has probably been a rationalizing correction, to suit better the sense of the prophecy. ῥήματος is used possibly, as De Wette suggests, as a preparation for τὰ ῥήματα αὐτ. in ver. 18). **18.**] **But** (in anticipation of an objection that Israel, whom he has especially in view, *had not sufficiently heard* the good tidings) **I say, Did they not hear** (ἤκουσαν partly founded on the cognate ἀκοή of the last verse, partly recalling the ἤκουσαν of ver. 14)? **nay rather** (ch. ix. 20, note) **into all the earth went forth their voice, and to the ends of the world their words.** It is remarkable that so few of the Commentators have noticed (I have found it only in Bengel, and there but faintly hinted: Olsh., who defends the applicability of the text, does not even allude to it) that Psal. xix. is *a comparison of the sun, and glory of the heavens,* with the *word of God.* As far as ver. 6 the glories of nature are described: then the great subject is taken up, and the parallelism carried out to the end. So that the Apostle has not, as alleged in nearly all the Commentators, merely accommodated the text allegorically, but *taken it in its context*, and followed up the comparison of the Psalm. As to the assertion of the preaching of the Gospel having gone out into all the world, when as yet a small part of it only had been evangelized,—we must remember that it is not the *extent,* so much as the *universality in character,* of this preaching, which the Apostle is here asserting; that word of God, hitherto confined within the limits of Judæa, had now broken those bounds, and was preached in all parts of the earth. See Col. i. 6, 23.

19.] **But** (in anticipation of another objection, that this universal evangelizing and admission of all, had at any rate *taken the Jews by surprise,*—that they had not been forewarned of any such purpose of God) **I say, Did Israel** (no emphasis on Israel—they are not *first here introduced,* nor have the preceding verses been said only of the Gentiles; but they have been during those verses in the Apostle's mind, and are now *named for distinctness' sake,* because it is not now a question of their having *heard,* which they did in common with all, but of their having *been aware* from their Scriptures of God's intention with regard to themselves and the Gentiles) **not know** (supply, not 'the Gospel,' τὴν ἀκοήν, as Chrys., Estius, Rückert, Olsh., al.,—but, *the fact that such a general proclamation of the Gospel would be made* as has been mentioned in the last verse, raising up the Gentiles into equality and rivalry with themselves—so Meyer, Fritz., Thol., De Wette, Stuart, al.—Others supply variously:—Calv. and Beza, 'the truth of God,'—so as to have an advantage over the Gentiles:—Bengel, 'justitiam Dei:'—Bretschneider and Reiche take Ἰσραήλ for the *object* of ἔγνω, and understand ὁ θεός as its *subject:* 'Did not God know,—acknowledge, regard with love,—Israel?' But surely the context will not

Μωυσῆς λέγει Ἐγὼ [d] παραζηλώσω ὑμᾶς [e] ἐπ' [f] οὐκ ἔθνει,
[e] ἐπὶ ἔθνει [g] ἀσυνέτῳ [h] παροργιῶ ὑμᾶς. 20 Ἠσαΐας δὲ
[i] ἀποτολμᾷ καὶ λέγει [k] Εὑρέθην [[l] ἐν] τοῖς ἐμὲ μὴ [m] ζητοῦσιν, [n] ἐμφανὴς ἐγενόμην τοῖς ἐμὲ μὴ [o] ἐπερωτῶσιν.
21 [p] πρὸς δὲ τὸν Ἰσραὴλ λέγει Ὅλην τὴν ἡμέραν
[q] ἐξεπέτασα τὰς χεῖράς μου πρὸς λαὸν [r] ἀπειθοῦντα καὶ
[s] ἀντιλέγοντα.

d ch. xi. 11, 14. 1 Cor. x. 22 only. Deut. xxxii. 21.
e = Luke i. 29, 47 al.
f = 1 Pet. ii. 10. Lam. i. 6.
g ch. i. 21 reff.
h Eph. vi. 4 only. l. c. 3 Kings xv. 30 al. (-σμός, Eph. iv. 26.)
i here only +. Jos. Antt. xv. 10. 3.
k Isa. lxv. 1.
l = 1 Tim. i. 16.
m = Acts xvii. 27 (reff.) only.
n Acts x. 40 only. Exod. ii. 14.
o = here only. Isa. l. c. Ezek. xx. 3 (?).
p = Luke xviii. 9. xx. 19. Heb. i. 7, 8.
q here only. Isa. lxv. 2.
r ch. ii. 8 al. Deut. xxi. 20.
s Luke xx. 27. Acts xiii. 45. L.P., exc. John xix. 12. Hos. iv. 4.

ABCD[1·3]F[P]א d m [47] latt coptt goth [æth] arm Chr$_1$ Damasc [Orig-int$_2$] Hil$_1$.
for1st υμας, αυτους (*from* LXX) Cא[3] [æth]. for επι, επ' BC[2]D[Aא] m [Clem$_1$]. for 2nd υμας, αυτους א[3].

20. om αποτολμα και D[[1·3] and D-lat[1](not D[2], appy(Tischdf)]F. rec om εν (*corrn to suit* LXX?), with ACD[2·3]L[P]א rel vulg Clem$_1$ Chr$_1$ Thdrt [Euthal-ms Damasc] Hil$_1$: ins BD[1]F sah[appy] goth[appy] Ambrst. aft εγενομην ins εν BD[1] [Orig-int$_2$].

21. for 2nd προς, επι D Clem$_1$. om και αντιλεγοντα F Hil$_1$: for αντιλεγ., λεγ. D[1][and lat].

allow this)?—**First** (in the order of the prophetic roll; q. d. their very earliest prophet: compare Matt. x. 2, πρῶτος Σίμων κ.τ.λ. Thol., after Rückert, observes, "The Apostle has in his mind a whole series of prophetic sayings which he might adduce, but gives only a few instead of all, and would shew by the πρῶτος, that even in the earliest period the same complaint (of Israel's unbelief) is found") **Moses saith, I will provoke you** (Heb. and LXX, 'them') **to jealousy against** (those who are) **no nation** (the Gentiles, as opposed to *the people* of God), **against a nation that hath no understanding** (נָבָל, the spiritual fool of Ps. xiv. 1; liii. 1; Prov. xvii. 21) **will I anger you.** The original reference of these words, as addressed to Israel by Moses, is exactly apposite to the Apostle's argument. Moses prophetically assumes the departure of Israel from God, and his rejection of them, and denounces from God that as they had moved Him to jealousy with their 'no-gods' (idols) and provoked Him to anger by their vanities,—so He would, by receiving into his favour a 'no-nation,' make them jealous, and provoke them to anger by adopting instead of them a foolish nation. On the interpretation of De Wette, al., that the meaning is, God would deliver the children of Israel, as a prey to the idolatrous nations of Canaan, the parallels will not hold; nor do the following verses in Deut. (22—25) justify it. 20.] **But** (even more than this: there is stronger testimony yet) **Esaias is very bold and says** (i. e. as we say, 'dares to say,' '*ventures to speak thus plainly*.' Thol. compares Æschin. de Falsa Leg. c. 45: κἂν ἐθελήσῃ σχετλιάζειν κ. λέγειν), **I was found** (so LXX, the Heb. is נִדְרַשְׁתִּי, 'I was sought:' but apparently in the sense of Ezek. xiv. 3; xx. 3, 'enquired of:' which amounts to εὑρέθην. In Ezek. xiv. the LXX render it ἀποκρίνεσθαι—and so Stier here, Ich gebe Antwort . . .) **by** (or **among**) **those who sought me not, I became manifest to those who asked not after me.** The clauses are inverted in order from the LXX. De Wette and other modern Commentators have maintained that Isa. lxv. 1 is spoken of the Jews, and not of the Gentiles; their main argument for this view being the connexion of ch. lxiv. and lxv. But even granting this connexion, it does not follow that God is not speaking in reproach to Israel in ch. lxv. 1, and reminding them prophetically, that while they, His own rebellious people, provoke Him to anger, the Gentiles which never sought Him have found Him. The whole passage is thoroughly gone into and its true meaning satisfactorily shewn, in Stier's valuable work, "Jesaias, nicht Pseudo-Jesaias," pp. 797 ff., who remarks that '*the nation which was not called by my Name*,' in lxv. 1, can only primarily mean the Gentiles. 21.] **But of** (not '*to*,' but '*with regard to*:' see reff. The words are not an *address*) **Israel** (evidently emphatic;—the former words having been said of the Gentiles) **he saith** (ibid. ver. 2), **All the day** (after μου in LXX) **I stretched forth my hands** (the attitude of gracious invitation) **to a people disobedient and gainsaying**

t ch. x. 18, 19. ver. 11.
u Acts vii. 27, 39. xiii. 46. 1 Tim. i. 19 only. L.P. Psa. xciii. 14. Ezek. xliii. 9.
v ch. iii. 4 reff.

XI. 1 [t] Λέγω οὖν, μὴ [u] ἀπώσατο ὁ θεὸς τὸν λαὸν
αὐτοῦ; [v] μὴ γένοιτο· καὶ γὰρ ἐγὼ [w] Ἰσραηλίτης εἰμί, ἐκ
[x] σπέρματος Ἀβραάμ, φυλῆς Βενιαμείν. 2 οὐκ [u] ἀπώσατο

ABCD FL[P]ℵ a b c d f g h k l m n o 17 [47]

w John i. 48. Acts ii. 22. 2 Cor. xi. 22 al.† Jos. Antt. ii. 9. 1.
x ch. ix. 7 reff.

Chap. XI. 1. for *τον λαον*, *την κληρονομιαν* F $Ambr_4$ Ambrst. aft *αυτου* ins *ον προεγνω* $AD^1ℵ^3$ [Chr_1] Thl Ambrst-comm Aug_2. (*βενιαμειν*, so A B^2(Rl: Tischdf ascribes it to his $B^{2\cdot3}$[*βενιαμ* B^1(Tischdf N. T. Vat)]) Cℵ m 17.)

(rebellious; the same word סֹרֵר occurs Deut. xxi. 18). Chap. XI. 1—10.] *Yet God has not* cast off *His people, but there is a remnant according to the election of grace* (1—6),—*the rest being hardened* (7—10). **1.] I say then** (a false inference from ch. x. 19—21,—made in order to be refuted), **Did** (*μή*, it cannot surely be, that) **God cast off His people** (as would almost appear from the severe words just adduced)? **Be it not so: for I also am an Israelite** (*ἐκ γένους Ἰσρ.*, Phil. iii. 5), **of the seed of Abraham** (mentioned probably for solemnity's sake, as bringing to mind all the promises made to Abraham), **of the tribe of Benjamin** (so Phil. iii. 5). There is some question *with what intent* the Apostle here brings forward *himself*. Three ways are open to us: either (1) it is as *a case in point*, as an example of an Israelite who has *not been rejected* but *is still one of God's people:* so almost all the Commentators—but this is hardly probable,—for in this case (α) he would not surely bring one only example to prove his point, when thousands might have been alleged—(β) it would be hardly consistent with the humble mind of Paul to put himself alone in such a place,—and (γ) *μὴ γένοιτο* does not go simply to *deny* a hypothetical *fact*, but applies to *some deprecated consequence* of that which is hypothetically put:—or (2) as De Wette, al., he implies, '*How can I say such a thing, who am myself an Israelite*, &c.?' 'Does not my very nationality furnish a security against my entertaining such an idea?'—or (3) which I believe to be the right view, but which I have found only in the commentary of Mr. Ewbank,—as implying that if such a hypothesis were to be conceded, it would exclude from God's kingdom the *writer himself, as an Israelite*. This seems better to agree with *μὴ γένοιτο*, as deprecating the *consequence* of such an assertion.
But a question even more important arises, not unconnected with that just discussed: viz. *who are* **ὁ λαὸς αὐτοῦ**? In order for the sentence *καὶ γὰρ ἐγὼ κ.τ.λ.* to bear the meaning just assigned to it, it is obvious that *ὁ λαὸς αὐτ.* must mean the people of God *nationally* considered. If Paul deprecated such a proposition as the rejection of *God's people*, because he himself would thus be *as an Israelite* cut off from God's favour, the rejection assumed in the hypothesis must be *a national rejection.* It is against *this* that he puts in his strong protest. It is *this* which he disproves by a cogent historical parallel from Scripture, shewing that there is a remnant *καὶ ἐν τῷ νῦν καιρῷ* according to the election of grace: and not only so, but that that part of Israel (considered as having continuity of national existence) which is for a time hardened, shall ultimately come in, and so all Israel (nationally considered again, Israel *as a nation*) shall be saved. Thus the covenant of God with Israel, having been *national*, shall ultimately be fulfilled to them *as a nation:* not by the gathering in merely of *individual* Jews, or of *all* the Jews *individually*, into the Christian church,—but by the *national restoration* of the Jews, not in unbelief, but as a *Christian believing nation*, to *all that can, under the gospel, represent their ancient pre-eminence*, and to the *fulness of those promises which have never yet in their plain sense been accomplished to them.* I have entered on this matter here, because a clear understanding of it underlies all intelligent appreciation of the argument of the chapter. Those who hold *no national restoration of the Jews to pre-eminence*, must necessarily confound the *ἐν τῷ νῦν καιρῷ* remnant according to the election of grace, with the *οἱ λοιποί*, who nationally shall be grafted in again. See this more fully illustrated where that image occurs, ver. 17 ff. **2.] God did not cast off his people which he foreknew** (*προέγνω* as in reff.: '*which, in His own eternal decree before the world, He selected as the chosen nation, to be His own, the depositary of His law, the vehicle of the theocracy, from its first revelation to Moses, to its completion in Christ's future kingdom.*' It is plain that this must here be the sense, and that the words must not be limited, with Orig., Aug., Chrys., Calv., al., to the *elect Christian people of God from among* the Jews, with Paul as their representative: see on ver. 1. On this explanation, the question of ver. 1 would be *self-contradictory*, and this negation a

ὁ θεὸς τὸν λαὸν αὐτοῦ ὃν [y] προέγνω. ἢ οὐκ οἴδατε [z] ἐν
Ἠλίᾳ τί λέγει ἡ [a] γραφή; ὡς [bc] ἐντυγχάνει τῷ θεῷ [b] κατὰ
τοῦ Ἰσραήλ, 3 Κύριε, τοὺς προφήτας σου ἀπέκτειναν, τὰ
[d] θυσιαστήριά σου [e] κατέσκαψαν, κἀγὼ [f] ὑπελείφθην μόνος,
καὶ [g] ζητοῦσιν τὴν [g] ψυχήν μου. 4 ἀλλὰ τί λέγει αὐτῷ
ὁ [h] χρηματισμός; [i] Κατέλιπον ἐμαυτῷ ἑπτακισχιλίους
ἄνδρας, οἵτινες οὐκ [k] ἔκαμψαν [k] γόνυ [l] τῇ Βάαλ. 5 οὕτως
οὖν καὶ ἐν [m] τῷ νῦν [m] καιρῷ [n] λεῖμμα κατ' [o] ἐκλογὴν
[p] χάριτος γέγονεν. 6 εἰ δὲ χάριτι, [q] οὐκ ἔτι ἐξ ἔργων,

y = ch. viii. 29 (reff.).
z see ἐπί, Luke xx. 37.
a sing., ch. ix. 17 reff.
b here only. 1 Macc. viii. 32.
c Acts xxv. 24. ch. viii. 27, 34. Heb. vii. 25 only +. 2 Macc. iv. 36. (-τευξις, 1 Tim. ii. 1.)
d Matt. v. 23 al. 3 Kings xix. 10, 14.
e Acts xv. 16 only, from Amos ix. 11.
f here only. Gen. xxx. 36 al. (-λειμμα, ch. ix. 27.)
g = Matt. ii. 20 only. Exod. iv. 19.
h here only. Prov. xxxi. (see xxiv.) 1. 2 Macc. ii. 4. xi. 17 only.
i = Luke xx. 31. Heb. iv. 1 only. 3 Kings xix. 18.
k ch. xiv. 11. Eph. iii. 14. Phil. ii. 10. 1 Chron. xxix. 20. see Acts vii. 60 reff.
l fem. (not l. c.), Judg. ii. 13 & iii. 7 (A Ald. compl.). Zeph. i. 4. Hos. ii. 8 al.
m ch. iii. 26 reff.
n here only. Josh. xiii. 12 F(not A) compl. 4 Kings xix. 4 only. (ὑπόλ., ch. ix. 27.)
o ch. ix. 11 reff.
p gen. subject., Luke iv. 22.
q = ch. vii. 17, 20.

2. rec at end ins λεγων, with Lℵ[1] rel Syr [æth] Thl Œc: om ABCDF[P]ℵ[3] [47(sic)] latt [syr] coptt arm Eus$_1$ Chr$_1$ Thdrt Damasc [Orig-int$_2$] Ambr.
3. rec ins και bef τα θυσιαστηρια, with DLℵ[3] rel syrr [æth arm] Just Chr$_2$ Thdrt [Euthal-ms Damasc]: om ABCF[P]ℵ[1] 17 [47(sic)] latt coptt Eus$_2$ Chr$_1$ [Orig-int$_2$].
4. κατελειπον ACFL[P] n. for τη, το F: τω G.
5. λιμμα AB[1]CD[1]Fℵ: ληµμα B[2]. [17 uncert.] κατ' εκλογης D[1].

truism. It would be inconceivable, that God should cast off *His elect*). **Or** (see ch. ix. 21 al.:—introduces a new objection to the matter impugned) **know ye not what the Scripture saith in** (the history of) **Elias** (better thus than '*with regard to*,' as Luth., Erasm., Calv., Beza, al. Tholuck gives examples: from Pausan. viii. 37. 3,—ἔστιν ἐν Ἥρας ὅρκῳ τὰ ἔπη,—i. e. in that part of the Iliad (ξ. 278) where Hera swears by the Titans: from Thucyd. i. 9,—καὶ ἐν τοῦ σκήπτρου ἅμα τῇ παραδόσει εἴρηκεν αὐτὸν πολλῇσι νήσοισι κ. Ἄργεϊ παντὶ ἀνάσσειν, i. e. in that part of the Iliad (β. 108) where the transmission of the sceptre is related)? **how** (depends on οὐκ οἴδατε) **he pleads with** (see reff.—and note, ch. viii. 26) **God against Israel,** &c. The citation is a free one from the LXX. The clauses τοὺς προφ., and τὰ θυσιαστ. are inverted, ἐν ῥομφαίᾳ is omitted, and κἀγὼ ὑπελείφθ. μόνος is put for καὶ ὑπολέλειμμαι ἐγὼ μονώτατος. The altars, as De W. observes, were those on the high places, dedicated to God. **4.] But what saith the divine response to him** (χρηματισμός, see reff. and reff. to the verb, Acts x. 22)? **I have left to myself** (here the Apostle corrects a mistake of the LXX, who have for κατέλιπον—καταλείψεις,—in the Complut. ed. κατλείψω. He has added to the Heb. הִשְׁאַרְתִּי,—'*I have left*,' '*kept as a remainder*,'—**ἐμαυτῷ**, a simple and obvious filling up of the sense) **seven thousand men, who** (the sense of the saying, as far as regards the present purpose, viz. to shew that *all these were faithful men*; in the original text and LXX, it is implied that *these were all the* faithful men,—ἑπτὰ χιλιάδας ἀνδρῶν, πάντα γόνατα ἃ οὐκ ὤκλασαν γόνυ(om. γόνυ A) τῷ Β. κ. πᾶν στόμα ὃ οὐ προσεκύνησεν(προσκυνήσει A) αὐτῷ. But this was not necessary to be brought out here) **never bowed knee to Baal.** "Here the LXX, according to the present text, have τῷ, not τῇ Βάαλ: but elsewhere (see reff.) they write the fem.: and probably the Apostle read it so in his copy." Fritz. According to this Commentator, they wrote the fem., taking Baal for a female deity; according to Beyer, Addit. ad Seld. de diis Syr., Wetst., Koppe, Olsh., Meyer,—because Baal was an androgynous deity;—according to Gesenius, in Rosenmüller, Rep. i. 39, to designate *feebleness*, compare the Rabbinical אֱלוֹהוֹת, 'false gods,' and other analogous expressions in Tholuck. "The regarding τῇ Βάαλ as put for τῇ τοῦ Βάαλ, scil. εἰκόνι or στήλῃ, as Erasm., Beza, Grot., Estius, al., and Bretschneider, is perfectly arbitrary." De Wette. In Tobit i. 5 AB, we have, πᾶσαι αἱ φυλαὶ αἱ συναποστᾶσαι ἔθυον τῇ Βάαλ τῇ δαμάλει,—where the golden calves of the ten tribes seem to be identified with Baal, and where a curious addition in ℵ (in this part published by Tischdf. as Codex Friderico-Augustanus) refers expressly to their establishment by Jeroboam. **5.] Thus then** (analogical inference from the example just cited) **in the present time also** (or, *even in the present time*, scil.

ἐπεὶ ἡ χάρις q οὐκ ἔτι γινεται χάρις· [εἰ δὲ ἐξ ἔργων,
q οὐκ ἔτι χάρις, ἐπεὶ τὸ ἔργον q οὐκ ἔτι ἐστὶν ἔργον.]
7 r τί οὖν; ὃ s ἐπιζητεῖ Ἰσραήλ, t τοῦτο οὐκ u ἐπέτυχεν,
ἡ δὲ v ἐκλογὴ u ἐπέτυχεν· οἱ δὲ λοιποὶ w ἐπωρώθησαν,

ABCD FL[P]ℵ a b c d f g h k l m n o 17 [47]

r ch. iii. 9. vi. 15. s Matt. vi. 32. xii. 39 al. 1 Kings xx. 1. t Acts ix. 20 reff. u here bis. Heb. vi. 15. xi. 33. James iv. 2 only. Gen. xxxix. 2. Prov. xii. 27 only. v ch. ix. 11 reff. = here only. w Mark vi. 52. viii. 17. John xii. 40. 2 Cor. iii. 14 only. Job xvii. 7 Bℵ &c. only. (-ρωσις, ver. 25.)

6. for γινεται, εστ[α]ι C^2(appy) [F-lat: εστι] 54 syrr Chr_1 Thdrt: *est* vulg D-lat lat-ff. om last clause ACDFℵ[1] [P 47-txt] latt coptt (æth) arm Damasc [Orig-int_1] Ambr Ambrst Aug: [om ει δε to χαρις 17:] ins (with some variations) BLℵ[3] rel syrr Chr Thdrt ('both, in text: they do not expl it in comm; but that does not prove its omn:' Tischdf [ed. 7]) Gennad-c_1 Thl Œc. (*See notes.*)—(rec ins εστι bef 3rd χαρις: omd by B.—for εργον at end, χαρις (*by mistake?*) B.)

7. επεζητει F 73 latt syrr [Orig-int_1] lat-ff. rec **τουτου** (*grammatical corrn*), with d g h l^2 Chr_1-montf Thdor-mops[-c_1 Cyr-c_1 Damasc] Thdrt: txt ABCDFL[P]ℵ rel Chr_1 Chr_1-2-mss. επερωθησαν(sic) C (m? [sic, Tischdf]): επορευθησαν c: επηρωθησαν 66^2: *excæcati sunt* latt [arm Orig-int_1].

of Israel's national rejection) **there is a remnant** (a part has remained faithful, which thus has *become* a λεῖμμα) **according to** (in virtue of,—in pursuance of) **the election** (selection, choice of a few out of many) **of grace** (made not for their desert, nor their foreseen congruity, but of God's free unmerited favour). **6.**] 'And let us remember, when we say an election *of grace*, how much those words imply: viz. nothing short of the entire exclusion of all human *work* from the question. Let these two terms be regarded as, and kept, distinct from one another, and do not let us attempt to mix them and so destroy the meaning of each.' So that the meaning of the verse is to clear up and remove all doubt concerning the meaning of '*election of grace*,'—and to profess on the part of the Apostle perfect readiness to accept his own words in their full sense, and to abide by them. This casts some light on the question of the genuineness of the bracketed clause (see authorities in var. readd.). The object being *precision*, it is much more probable that the Apostle should have written both clauses in their present formal parallelism, and that the second should have been early omitted from its seeming superfluity, than that it should have been inserted from the margin. Besides which, as Fritz. has remarked, the words do not correspond sufficiently with those of the first clause to warrant the supposition of their having been constructed to tally with it: we have for χάριτι in the first, ἐξ ἔργων in the second,—for γίνεται χάρις, ἐστὶν ἔργον;—and the plur. ἔργα would probably have been retained in the inference of clause 2. **But** (directing attention to the *consequence* of the admission, ἐκλ. **χάριτος**) **if by grace** (the selection has been made), **it is no longer** (when we have conceded that, we have excluded its being) **of** (arising out of, as its source) **works: for** (*in that case*) **grace no longer becomes** (i. e. becomes no longer—loses its efficacy and character as) **grace** (the freedom and 'proprio motu' character, absolutely necessary to the idea of *grace*, are lost, the act having been prompted from without):—**but if of** (arising out of, as the cause and source of the selection) **works, no longer is it** (the act of selection) **grace; for** (in **that case**) **work no longer is work** (the essence of work, in our present argument, being '*that which earns reward*,' and the reward being, as supposed, the election *to be of the remnant*,—if so earned, there can be no admixture of divine favour in the matter; it must be *all earned, or none: none conferred by free grace, or all*). These cautions of the Apostle are decisive against all attempts at compromise between the two great antagonist hypotheses, of salvation by God's free grace, and salvation by man's meritorious works. The two *cannot be combined* without destroying the plain meaning of words. If now the Apostle's object in this verse be to guard carefully the doctrine of election by free grace from any attempt at an admixture of man's work, *why* is he anxious to do this *just at this point?* I conceive, because he is immediately about to enter on a course of exposition of the divine dealings, in which, more than ever before, he *rests all upon God's sovereign purpose*, while at the same time he shews that purpose, though apparently severe, to be one, *on the whole, of grace and love*.

7.] **What then** (what therefore must be our conclusion from what has been stated? We have seen that God hath not cast off his own chosen nation, but that even now there is a remnant. This being so, what aspect do matters present? This he asks to bring out an answer which may

8 καθὼς γέγραπται Ἔδωκεν αὐτοῖς ὁ θεὸς [x] πνεῦμα
[y] κατανύξεως, [z] ὀφθαλμοὺς [a] τοῦ μὴ βλέπειν, καὶ [b] ὦτα
[a] τοῦ μὴ ἀκούειν, ἕως τῆς [c] σήμερον [c] ἡμέρας. 9 καὶ
Δαυεὶδ λέγει [d] Γενηθήτω ἡ [e] τράπεζα αὐτῶν [d] εἰς [fgh] παγίδα
καὶ [d] εἰς [gi] θήραν καὶ [d] εἰς [hk] σκάνδαλον καὶ [d] εἰς [l] ἀνταπόδομα αὐτοῖς, 10 [m] σκοτισθήτωσαν οἱ ὀφθαλμοὶ αὐτῶν
[a] τοῦ μὴ βλέπειν, καὶ τὸν νῶτον αὐτῶν [n] διὰ παντὸς

x = ch. viii. 1 bis. 1 Cor. iv. 21. 2 Cor. iv. 13. Gal. vi. 1. Eph. i. 17 al. Isa. xxix. 10.
y here only. l. c. & Ps. lix. 3 (5) only. (-νύσσειν, Acts ii. 37. Sir. xx. 21.)
z Deut. xxix. 4.
a constr., 1 Cor. x. 13 reff.
b Paul, Acts xxviii. 27 bis (from Isa. vi. 10). 1 Cor. ii. 9. xii. 16 only. c Matt. xxviii. 15. Acts xx. 26. 2 Cor. iii. 14 only. Josh. v. 9. d constr., Acts v. 36 reff. Psa. lxviii. 22. e = 1 Cor. x. 21 bis. Ps. lxxvii. 20. f Luke xxi. 35. 1 Tim. iii. 7. vi. 9. 2 Tim. ii. 26 only. Prov. vii. 23. g Ps. xxxiv. 8. h Josh. xxiii. 13. Ps. cxl. 9. i here only. = Hos. v. 2. k = Matt. xvi. 23. ch. ix. 33 al. 1 Kings xviii. 21. l Luke xiv. 12 only. Ps. xxvii. 4. 2 Chron. xxxii. 25. (-δοσις, Col. iii. 24.) m = ch. i. 21 (reff.) only. l. c. n Acts ii. 25. x. 2 al. Isa. xlix. 16.

8. καθαπερ BΝ. ὁ is written twice in Ν.
[**8, 9.** ημερας και δαυιδ is supplied at the foot of the page in F-gr(not G).]
9. ins καθαπερ bef και δαυειδ C.

set in view the **οἱ λοιποί**)? **That which Israel is in search of** (viz. δικαιοσύνη, see ch. ix. 31; x. 1 ff.), **this it** (as a nation) **found not** (on ἐπιτυγχάνω w. an acc., see Matthiæ, Gr. Gr. § 363 obs.), **but the election** (the abstract, because Israel has been spoken of in the abstract, and to keep out of view for the present the mere individual cases of converted Jews in the idea of an *elected remnant*) **found it**:

8.] **but the rest were hardened** (not '*blinded*;' see note on Eph. iv. 18:—σκληροτέραν ἡ ἀπιστία τὴν καρδίαν αὐτῶν ἀπειργάσατο. Theodoret. It is passive, and implies *God as the agent*. This for the sake of the context, ἔδωκεν αὐτοῖς **ὁ θεὸς** κ.τ.λ., not necessarily for the meaning of the word itself, which might indicate 'became hard,' but certainly *does not here*),—**as it is written** (if we are to regard these passages as merely *analogous instances* of the divine dealings, we must remember that the *perspective of prophecy*, in stating such cases, *embraces all analogous ones*, the divine dealings being self-consistent,—and *especially that great one*, in which the words are most prominently fulfilled), **God gave to them** (LXX and Heb., πεπότικεν ὑμᾶς) **a spirit** (see reff.) **of stupor** (there is at the end of Fritzsche's commentary on this chapter an elaborate excursus on κατάνυξις, in which he has thoroughly investigated its derivation and meaning. He comes to the conclusion that it is derived from κατανύσσω, 'compungo,' and *might* signify any excitement of mind, pity, sadness, &c.,—but in the few places where it occurs, it *does* import *stupor* or *numbness*: so ref. Ps. ἐπότισας ἡμᾶς οἶνον κατανύξεως,—which Hammond explains to mean the stupifying wine given to them that were to be put to death. Hamm. also cites from Marcus Eremita, νουθεσ. ψυχ. p. 918, a passage where he describes πόνον τῆς κατανύξεως as the consequence of οἰνοποσίαι. Tholuck compares the similar meanings of 'frappé,' *struck*, betroffen),—**eyes that they should not see** (such eyes that they might not see: in the Heb. and LXX the negative is joined with the verb, καὶ οὐκ ἔδωκεν κύριος ὁ θ. ὑμῶν κ.τ.λ.) **and ears that they should not hear unto this present day.** These last words are not, as Beza, E. V., Griesb., Knapp, to be separated from the citation, and joined to ἐπωρώθησαν: they belong to the words in Deut. and are adduced by St. Paul as applying to the day then present, as they did to the day when Moses spoke them: see 2 Cor. iii. 15.

9.] **And David saith, Let their table be for a snare and for a net** (θήρα more usually 'a hunt,' or the act of taking or catching,—but here and in ref. *a net*, the instrument of capture. It is not in the Heb. nor in the LXX, and is perhaps inserted by the Apostle to give emphasis by the accumulation of synonymes), **and for a stumbling-block and for a recompense to them** (the LXX have εἰς παγίδα κ. εἰς ἀνταπόδοσιν κ. εἰς σκάνδαλον. The Heb. of εἰς ἀνταπόδοσιν, as at present pointed, is לִשְׁלוֹמִים, 'to the secure.' It has been supposed that the LXX pointed לַשְׁלוּמִים or לְשִׁלּוּמִים, 'for retributions.' See Ps. xci. 8: but qu.?):

10.] **let their eyes be darkened that they may not see, and their back bow thou down always.** "Instead of bending the back, the Heb. text speaks of making the loins to tremble, מָתְנֵיהֶם הַמְעַד. This elsewhere is a sign of *great terror*, Nah. ii. 10; Dan. v. 6: and the *darkening of the eyes* betokens in the Psalm, a weakened, humbled, servile condition, just as in

[o] σύγκαμψον. 11 [p] λέγω οὖν, μὴ [q] ἔπταισαν ἵνα [r] πέσω- ABCD
σιν; [s] μὴ γένοιτο· ἀλλὰ τῷ αὐτῶν [t] παραπτώματι ἡ FL[P]א abcdf
σωτηρία τοῖς ἔθνεσιν, [u] εἰς τὸ [v] παραζηλῶσαι αὐτούς. ghkl mno17
12 εἰ δὲ τὸ [t] παράπτωμα αὐτῶν [w] πλοῦτος κόσμου καὶ [47]
τὸ [x] ἥττημα αὐτῶν [w] πλοῦτος ἐθνῶν, [yz] πόσῳ [y] μᾶλλον

o here only. l. c. 4 Kings iv. 35 only.
p ver. 1 al.
q (=) James ii. 10. iii. 2 (bis). 2 Pet. i. 10 only. 1 Kings iv. 2.
r = ch. xiv. 4 reff.
s ch. iii. 4 reff.
t ch. iv. 25 reff.
u ch. iv. 11 reff. Isa. xxxi. 8 only.
v ch. x. 19 reff. (see 2 Cor. xii. 13 reff.)
w = Heb. xi. 26.
x 1 Cor. vi. 7 only.
y Matt. vii. 11. x. 25. Luke xi. 13. xii. 24, 28. ver. 24. Philem. 16. Heb. ix. 14 only.
z as above (y). Matt. xii. 12. Heb. x. 29 only.

12. om ver A.

Deut. xxviii. 65—67. It is plain from διὰ παντός, that we must not suppose the infirmities of *age* to be meant. The Apostle might well apply such a description to the servile condition of the bondmen of the law, see Gal. iv. 24." Tholuck.

11—24.] *Yet this exclusion and hardening has not been for their destruction, but for mercy to the Gentiles, and eventually for their own restoration.* **11.**] **I say then** (see on ver. 1), **Did they** (who? see below) **stumble in order that they should fall** (not '*sic, ut caderent*'—as Vulg.,—so Orig., Chrys., Grot., al., denoting the *result* merely: neither the grammar nor the context will bear this: the Apostle is arguing respecting *God's intent* in the παράπτωμα of the Jewish nation. He here calls it by this mild name to set forth that it is not final. The subject of ἔπταισαν is the αὐτοί of the following verses, i. e. the *Jews, as a people:* not the *unbelieving individuals,* who *are characterized as* **πεσόντες**, ver. 22. He regards the λοιποί as the representatives of the Jewish people, who have *nationally stumbled,* but not *in order to their final fall,* seeing that God has a gracious purpose towards the Gentiles even *in* this πταῖσμα of theirs, and intends to raise *them nationally from it* in the end. This distinction, between the πταίσαντες, *the whole nation as a nation,* and the πεσόντες, the *unbelieving branches who have been cut off,* is most important to the right understanding of the chapter, and to the keeping in mind the separate ideas, of the *restoration of individuals* here and there throughout time, and the *restoration of Israel* at the end. The stress is on **πέσωσιν**, and it is the *fall* which is denied: not on ἵνα πέσωσιν, so that the *purpose* merely should be denied, and the fall admitted)? **God forbid: but** (the truer account of the matter is) **by their trespass** (not *fall,* as E. V.) **salvation (has come) to the Gentiles, for to provoke them** (Israel) **to jealousy.** Two gracious purposes of God are here stated, the latter wrought out through the former. By this stumble of the Jews out of their national place in God's favour, and the admission of the Gentiles into it, the very people thus excluded are to be stirred up to set themselves in the end effectually to regain, as a nation, that pre-eminence from which they are now degraded. **12.**] Then the Apostle argues on this, as Meyer well says, 'a felici effectu causæ pejoris ad feliciorem effectum causæ melioris:'—**But** ('*posito,* that'—as in last verse—taking for granted the historical fact, that the stumble of the Jews has been coincident with the admission of the Gentiles) **if their trespass is the world's wealth** (the *occasion* of that wealth,—the wealth itself being the participation in the unsearchable riches of Christ), **and** (this latter clause parallel to and explanatory of the less plainly expressed one before it) **their loss, the wealth of the Gentiles, how much more (shall) their replenishment (be all this)?** On ἥττημα and πλήρωμα much question has been raised. I have taken both as answering strictly to the comparison here before the Apostle's mind, viz. that of impoverishing and enriching,—and the genitives αὐτῶν [&c.] as *subjective:* q. d. '*if their impoverishment be the wealth of the Gentiles, how much more shall their enrichment be!*' But several other interpretations are possible. (1) ἥττημα may mean as in ref. 1 Cor., *degradation,* and πλήρωμα would then be *fulness, re-exaltation* to the former measure of favour,—or perhaps, as where Herod. iii. 22 says ὀγδώκοντα ἔτεα ζόης πλήρωμα, 'their *completion,*' 'their highest degree of favour.' (2) If we regard the meaning of πλήρωμα in ver. 25, we shall be tempted here to render it, '*full number,*' and similarly ἥττημα, '*small number.*' So the majority of Commentators: Chrys., Theodoret, Erasmus, Beza, Bucer, Grot., Bengel, Reiche, De W. (but only as regards πλήρ.:—he renders ἥττ. with Luther, Schade) and Olsh. (see below). Thus the argument will stand: 'If their unbelief (i. e. of one part of them) is the world's wealth, and their small number (i. e. of believers, the other part of them), the wealth of the Gentiles, how much more their full (restored) number!' i. e. as Olsh. explains it, 'If so few Jews can do so much

τὸ [a] πλήρωμα αὐτῶν; 13 ὑμῖν δὲ λέγω τοῖς ἔθνεσιν.
[b] ἐφ᾽ [b] ὅσον μὲν οὖν εἰμι ἐγὼ ἐθνῶν ἀπόστολος, τὴν
[c] διακονίαν μου [d] δοξάζω, 14 [e] εἴ πως [v] παραζηλώσω μου
τὴν [f] σάρκα καὶ [g] σώσω τινὰς ἐξ αὐτῶν. 15 εἰ γὰρ ἡ

a = here only. see Eph. i. 23 notes. John i. 16. ver. 25.
b = Matt. (ix. 15) xxv. 40, 45 (2 Pet. i. 13) only.
c = Acts xx. 24 reff.
d = 2 Cor. iii. 10. Judg. ix. 9.
e ch. i. 10.
f Gen. xxxvii. 27.
g = 1 Cor. vii. 16 (bis). ix. 22. 1 Tim. iv. 16. James v. 20.

13. rec (for δε) γαρ, with DFL rel latt goth Chr_1 Thdrt[-ed] Thl Œc [$Orig\text{-}int_1$ Ambrst]: *ουν* C: om æth: txt ABℵ[P 47 arm] syrr copt Thdrt-ms Damasc. rec om *ουν* (*see notes*), with L rel vulg D^3-lat syr [copt(Treg) æth] Chr_1 Thdrt Thl Œc [$Orig\text{-}int_2$ Ambrst] Aug: om *μεν ουν* DF goth [arm]: ins ABC[P]ℵ copt[(Tischdf) Cyr_1 Damasc]. om *εγω* A n 73. 80. 108-16-8 arm $Thdrt\text{-}ms_1$: ins bef *ειμι* F [vulg goth] Cyr_1 [$Orig\text{-}int_2$ Ambrst]. *δοξασω* F [17] 46. 109 latt $Thdrt[\text{-}ed]_1(txt_2)$ [$Orig\text{-}int_2$] lat-ff(but not Aug_2).
14. *την σαρκα* bef *μου* DF.

for the Gentile world, what will not the whole number do?' But thus we shall lose the '*a minori ad majus*' argument—'if their *sin* has done so much, how much more their *conversion?*' unless indeed it be said that τὸ ἥττημα *implies* a national παράπτωμα. Besides, it can hardly be shewn that ἥττημα will bear this meaning of 'a small number.' (3) Tholuck, from whom mostly this note is taken, notices at length the view of Olsh., after Origen, that the idea of a *definite number of the elect* is here in the Apostle's mind,—that the falling off of the Jews produces a deficiency in the number, which is filled up by the elect from the Gentiles, as ver. 25: understanding by πλήρωμα both there and here, if I take his meaning aright, the *number required to fill up the roll of the elect,* whether of Jews, as here, or Gentiles, as there. Tholuck, while he concedes the legitimacy of the *idea* of a πλήρωμα τῶν σωζομένων, maintains, and rightly, that in this section *no such idea is brought forward:* and that it would not have been intended, without *some more definite expression of it than we now find.*

I have thought it best as above, considering the very various meanings and difficulty of the word πλήρωμα, to keep here to that which seems to be indicated by the immediate context, which is, besides, the primitive meaning of the word. It must be noticed, that the fact, of *Israel being the chosen people of God,* lies at the root of all this argument. Israel is *the nation,* the covenant people,—the vehicle of God's gracious purposes to mankind. Israel, nationally, is deposed from present favour. That very deposition is, however, accompanied by an outpouring of God's riches of mercy on the Gentiles; not as rivals to Israel, but *still considered as further from God, formally and nationally, than Israel.* If then the *disgrace of Israel* has had such a blessed accompaniment, how much more blessed a one shall *Israel's honour* bring with it, when His own people shall once more be set as a praise in the midst of the earth, and the glory of the nations.

13.] 'Why, in an argument concerning the *Jews,* dwell so much on the reference to the *Gentiles* discernible in the divine œconomy regarding Israel? Why make it appear as if the treatment of God's chosen people were regulated not by a consideration of *them,* but of the less favoured Gentiles?' The present verse gives an answer to this question. **But** (apology for the foregoing verse:—if γάρ be read, the sense will be much the same—**For** (i. e. let it be understood, that), &c.) **I am speaking to you the Gentiles. Inasmuch therefore** (**μὲν οὖν** is surely not to be rejected as yielding no sense,—as De Wette and Tholuck, who object to it as proceeding from those who hold a new sentence to begin at ἐφ᾽ ὅσον, and ὑμῖν . . . . ἔθνεσιν to refer to the foregoing:—but the usage of μὲν οὖν in 1 Cor. vi. 4 seems strictly analogous to that in our text, where no new sentence is begun in any sense which may not be true here. **ἐφ᾽ ὅσον,** not '*as long as,*' as Orig. and Vulg.) **as I am Apostle of the Gentiles, I honour mine office** (by striving for their conversion and edification at all times,—by introducing a reference to them and their part in the divine counsels, even when speaking of mine own people), **if by any means I may** (regarding it as a real service done on behalf of Israel, thus to honour mine office by mentioning the Gentiles, if this mention may) **provoke to jealousy mine own flesh** (the Jews) **and may save some of them.** **15.**] **For** (a reason for my anxiety for the salvation of Israel: not merely for the sake of mine own kinsmen, but because their recovery will bring about the blessed consummation of all believers. Vv. 13, 14 should not then be in a parenthesis) **if the rejection of them** (not '*their loss,*' as Luth.

[h] ἀποβολὴ αὐτῶν [i] καταλλαγὴ κόσμου, τίς ἡ [j] πρόσλημψις, εἰ μὴ ζωὴ ἐκ νεκρῶν; 16 εἰ δὲ ἡ [kl] ἀπαρχὴ ἁγία,
καὶ τὸ [lm] φύραμα· καὶ εἰ ἡ [n] ῥίζα ἁγία, καὶ οἱ [o] κλάδοι.

ABCD FL[P]א a b c d f g h k l m n o 17 [47]

h Acts xxvii. 22 only (reff.) †. i (=) ch. v. 11. 2 Cor. v. 18, 19 only ‡. (Isa. ix. 5.) 2 Macc. v. 20 only. j here only †. (-λαμβάνειν, ch. xiv. 3.) k ch. viii. 23 reff. l Num. xv. 21. m ch. ix. 21 reff. only in Epp. n Matt. iii. 10. xiii. 6 al. Job xiv. 8. Ezek. xxxi. 7. o Matt. xiii. 32 al. here &c. (5 times)

15. κοσμω F. for προσλ., προλ. CF k[1].
16. for δε, γαρ A: om C[2] goth [æth]. om 2nd ει F[P[1]] 70-1. 109 lect-13 arm Chr-ms$_1$.

and Beng., by which the antithesis to πρόσλημψις is weakened) **be** (the occasion of) **the reconciliation of the world** (of the Gentiles, viz. to God), **what** (‘*qualis*,’ ‘of what kind,’ in its effect) **(will be) their reception, but** (the occasion of) **life from the dead? ζωὴ ἐκ νεκρ.** may be variously taken. (1) it may be metaphorical, as in ch. vi. 13, and may import, that so general a conversion of the world would take place, as would be like life from the dead. So, more or less, Calv., Calov., Estius, Bengel, Stuart, Hodge, al., and Theophyl., Phot., who explain it of a joy like that of the resurrection. But against this interpretation lies the objection, that *this is already involved* in καταλλαγὴ κόσμ., and thus no new idea would be brought out by the words, which stand in the most emphatic position. (2) it may mean that ‘life from the dead’ *literally* should follow on the restoration of the Jewish people; i. e. that the Resurrection, the great consummation, is bound up with it. So Chrys., Orig. (“tunc enim erit assumptio Israel, quando jam et mortui vitam recipient, et mundus ex corruptibili incorruptibilis fiet, et mortales immortalitate donabuntur”), Theodoret, Reiche, Meyer, Fritzsche, Rückert ed. 2, Tholuck, al. The objection to this view seems to be, that the Apostle would hardly have used ζωὴ ἐκ νεκρῶν thus predicatively, if he had meant by it a fixed and predetermined *event*;—but that, standing as it does, it must be *qualitative*, implying *some further blessed state* of the reconciled world, over and above the mere reconciliation. This might well be designated ‘*life from the dead*,’ and in it may be *implied* the glories of the first resurrection, and deliverance from the bondage of corruption, without supposing the words ζωὴ ἐκ νεκρῶν = ἡ ἀνάστασις τῶν νεκ. Stuart well compares Ezek. xxxvii. 1—14, which was perhaps before the mind of the Apostle:—but he gives a mere ethical interpretation to it. 16—24.] *Such a restoration of Israel was to be expected from a consideration of their destination and history. This is set forth in similitudes, that of the root and branches being followed out at some length,—and their own position, as engrafted Gentiles, brought to the mind of the readers.* **But** (a further argument for their restoration following on ἀλλά, ver. 11) **if the firstfruit be holy, so also the lump** (not here the firstfruit of the *field*, as Grot., Rosenm. (nor is φύραμα the cake made by the priests out of the firstfruits which fell to them, Deut. xviii. 4, as Estius, Koppe, Köllner, Olsh., al.);—but the portion of the kneaded lump of dough (φύρω), which was offered as a heave-offering to the Lord, and so sanctified for use the rest: see ref. Num. where the same words occur);—**and if the root be holy, so also the branches.** *Who are the* **ἀπαρχή** *and the* **ῥίζα**? First of all, there is no impropriety in the two words applying to the *same thing*. For though, as Olsh. remarks, the branches being *evolved from the root*, it rather answers to the φύραμα than to the ἀπαρχή, and, as Rückert, the firstfruit succeeds the lump in time, while the root precedes the branches,—yet, as Thol. replies, *the* ἁγιότης *is the point of comparison*, and in ἁγιότης the ἀπαρχή precedes and gives existence to the φύραμα. This being so, (1) the ἀπαρχή and ῥίζα have generally been taken to represent *the patriarchs;* and I believe rightly (except that perhaps it would be more strictly correct to say, *Abraham himself*). The ἀγαπητοὶ διὰ τοὺς πατέρας of ver. 28 places this reference almost beyond doubt. Origen explains the ῥίζα to be *our Lord*. But He is Himself *a branch*, by descent from Abraham and David (Isa. xi. 1; Matt. i. 1), if genealogically considered; and if mystically, *the whole tree* (John xv. 1). De Wette prefers to take as the firstfruit and root, the *ideal theocracy* founded on the patriarchs,—the *true, faithful children* of the patriarchs, and as the branches, those united by mere external relationship to these others. This he does, because in the *common acceptation*, the κλάδοι who are cut off ought to be *severed from their physical connexion* with Abraham, &c., which they *are not*. This objection I do not conceive applicable here: because, as we see evidently from ver. 23, the severing and re-engrafting are types, not of *genealogical*

17 εἰ δέ τινες τῶν [o] κλάδων [p] ἐξεκλάσθησαν, σὺ δὲ [q] ἀγριέλαιος ὢν [r] ἐνεκεντρίσθης ἐν αὐτοῖς καὶ [s] συγκοινωνὸς
τῆς [n] ῥίζης τῆς [t] πιότητος τῆς [u] ἐλαίας ἐγένου, 18 μὴ

p here &c. 3ce only. Levit. i. 17 only. q ver. 24 only † see Isa. xliv. 14 F(not A) compl. Jer. xvii. 6. r here &c. (6 times) only †. Wisd. xvi. 11 only. s 1 Cor. ix. 23. Phil. i 7. Rev. i. 9 only †. (-εῖν, Eph. v. 11.) t here only. Judg. ix. 9. u ver. 24. Jame iii. 12. Rev. xi. 4 only, exc. (w. ὄρος) in Gospp. Gen. viii. 11.

17. for *ενεκ.*, *εκεντρισθης* L. om *εν* C^1(appy). rec ins *και* bef *της πιοτητος*, with AL[D$^{2\cdot3}$P]ℵ^3 rel [vulg syrr goth æth arm Chr$_1$ Thdrt Antch$_1$ Orig-int$_1$]: om BC(D^{1}F)ℵ^1 copt Damasc[-txt]. *εγενου της πι. της ελαιας* [omg *της ριζης*] D^{1}F k (Cyr-jer$_1$) Iren-int$_2$.

disunion and reunion, but of *spiritual*. Meanwhile, De W.'s view appears less simple than the ordinary one, which, as I hope to shew, is borne out by the whole passage. (2) Then, *who are indicated by the* **φύραμα** *and the* **κλάδοι**? Israel, considered as the people of God. The lump, which has received its *ἁγιότης* from the *ἀπαρχή*, = Israel, beloved for the fathers' sakes: the assemblage of branches, evolved from Abraham, and partaking of his holiness. But one thing must be especially borne in mind. As Abraham himself had an outer and an inner life, so have the branches. They have an *outer life*, derived from Abraham by *physical descent*. Of this, *no cutting off can deprive them*. It may be compared to the very organization of the wood itself, which subsists even after its separation from the tree. But they have, while they remain in the tree, an *inner life*, nourished by the circulating sap, by virtue of which they are constituted *living parts* of the tree: see our Lord's parable of the vine and the branches, John xv. 1 ff. It is of *this life*, that their severance from the tree deprives them: it is *this life*, which they will *re-acquire* if grafted in again. See a very ingenious but artificial explanation in Olsh., who agrees in the main with De W.:—and the whole question admirably discussed in Tholuck. The *ἁγιότης* then here spoken of, consists in their *dedication to God as a people*—in their being *physically evolved from a holy root*. This peculiar ἁγιότης (see 1 Cor. vii. 14, where the children of one Christian parent are similarly called *ἅγια*) renders their *restoration to their own stock* a matter, not of wonder and difficulty, but of reasonable hope and probability. I may notice in passing, that those expositors who do not hold a restoration of the Jewish people to national preeminence, find this passage exceedingly in their way, if we may judge by their explanations of this ἁγιότης. E. g. Mr. Ewbank remarks: 'Holy they are, inasmuch as there is *no decree against their restoration* to their place of life and fruitfulness.' Surely this is a new meaning of 'holy:' the same would be true of a Hottentot: in his case, too, there is no decree against his reception into a place (and in Mr. E.'s view, the restoration of the Jew is nothing more) of life and fruitfulness in the Church of God.

17.] **But** (introduces a hypothesis involving a seeming inconsistency with the *ἁγιότης* just mentioned) **if some of the branches** (the *τινες*, as Thol. remarks, depreciates the number, in order to check the Gentile pride) **were broken out** (from the tree), **and thou** (a Gentile believer) **being a wild olive** (*ἀγριέλαιος*, the tree, spoken of a sprout or branch of it. Better so than, as Fritz., Meyer, to make *ἀγρ.* an adj., 'of wild olive,' which can only be used of that which *is made out of the wood*, as *ἀγριέλαιος σκυτάλη*. Thol.) **wast grafted in** (Clem. Alex. Strom. vi. [15] § 119, p. 799 P., enumerates four different kinds of *ἐγκεντρισμός*, using it as a general term for grafting and budding. The difficulty here is, that the Apostle *reverses* the natural process. It is the *wilding*, in practice, which is the *stock*, and the graft inserted is a sprout of the *better tree*. I believe that he *does not here regard* what is the fact in nature: but makes a supposition perfectly legitimate,—that a wilding graft on being inserted into a good tree, thereby becomes partaker of its qualities. No allusion can be intended to a practice mentioned by Columella, de Re Rust. v. 9, of inserting a wilding graft into a good tree to increase the vigour and growth of the tree: for this would completely stultify the illustration—the point of which is, a *benefit* received by the wilding from the tree, not one *conferred* by the wilding on it) **among them** (i.e. among the branches,—*τοῖς κλάδοις*: or perhaps *αὐτοῖς* may imply the *remnants* of the branches broken off. The renderings, '*in their stead*,' '*in locum*,' as De W. after Chrys., Theophyl., Beza,—and '*in their place*,' '*in loco*,' Meyer, Olsh., are surely inadmissible), **and becamest a fellow-partaker** (with the branches: or perhaps simply 'a partaker,' *σύν* not implying *fellows in participation*, but merely the participation itself) **of the root of the fatness** (of that root, on union with which all the develop-

[v]κατακαυχῶ τῶν [o]κλάδων· εἰ δὲ [v]κατακαυχᾶσαι, οὐ
σὺ τὴν [n]ῥίζαν [w]βαστάζεις, ἀλλὰ ἡ [n]ῥίζα σέ. 19 ἐρεῖς
οὖν [p]Ἐξεκλάσθησαν [o]κλάδοι ἵνα ἐγὼ [r]ἐγκεντρισθῶ.
20 [x]καλῶς. τῇ [y]ἀπιστίᾳ [p]ἐξεκλάσθησαν, σὺ δὲ τῇ πίστει
ἕστηκας. μὴ * [z]ὑψηλοφρόνει, ἀλλὰ φοβοῦ· 21 εἰ γὰρ ὁ
θεὸς τῶν [ab]κατὰ [b]φύσιν [o]κλάδων οὐκ [c]ἐφείσατο, [[d]μή

ABCD FL[P]א a b c d f g h k l m n o 17 [47]

v (—) here bis. James ii. 13. iii. 14 only. Jer. xxvii. (l.) 11, 38 (Zech. x. 12) only.
w ch. xv. 1. Matt. xx. 12. John xvi. 12. 4 Kings xviii. 14. Sir. vi. 25 only. Bel & Dr. 36 Theod.
x Matt. xv. 7. John iv. 17 al. 2 Kings iii. 13.
y = ch. iii. 3. Heb. iii. 19. dat. of cause, see ver. 30.
z 1 Tim. vi. 17 only †. see ch. xii. 16 reff.
a = ch. ix. 11. Col. iii. 22.
b here &c. (3ce) only †. see below (l).
c Paul (Acts xx. 29. ch. viii. 32. 1 Cor. vii. 28 al.) only, exc. 2 Pet. ii. 4, 5. Ezek. xxxvi. 21.
d = 1 Cor. viii. 9. ellips., here only.

18. for κατακαυχασαι, συ καυχασαι D^{1}F Ambrst. (αλλα, so BD^{1}א.)

19. for εξεκλασθησαν, ει κλασθησαν[*si fracti sunt*] F [D-lat^1 Orig-int$_1$]. rec ins οι bef κλαδοι, with D^1 b c[e sil] o Thdrt [Antch$_1$] Thl : om A B(Tischdf, expr) CD^{3}FL[P]א rel Chr$_1$ [Antch$_1$] Damasc.

20. for εξεκλασθησαν, εκλασθησαν B(Tischdf, expr) D^{1}F : txt ACD^{3}L[P]א rel Chr$_1$ Thdrt [Antch$_1$ Damasc]. [for συ, συν D^1(appy ; but ν erased, as is also one letter before and one after πιστι : απιστια, Wetst).] *ὑψηλὰ φρόνει ABא.

21. ει γαρ is written over an erasure by א^1. rec ins μη πως, with DFL rel [vulg syrr goth arm] Chr$_1$(καὶ οὐκ εἶπεν Οὐδὲ σοῦ φείσεται, ἀλλὰ Μή πως οὐδὲ σοῦ

ment of life and its fertility depend: which is the source of the fatness. With καί, it will mean, of the source of life, and also of the development of that life itself in all richness of blessing) **of the olive-tree**, 18.] **do not boast against the branches** (which were broken off): **but if thou boastest against them** (know that . . . or let this consideration humble thee, that . . . Similarly 1 Cor. xi. 16, εἰ δέ τις δοκεῖ φιλόνεικος εἶναι, ἡμεῖς τοιαύτην συνήθειαν οὐκ ἔχομεν, κ.τ.λ. See Winer, edn. 6, § 66. 1 a) **it is not thou that bearest the root, but the root thee.** The ground of humiliation is—"Thou partakest of thy blessings solely by union with God's spiritual church, which church has for its root that Father of the faithful, from whom they are descended. Regard them not therefore with scorn." This is expanded further in ver. 20. 19.] **Thou wilt then** (*posito*, that thou boastest, and defendest it) **say, Branches** (it would look as if the art. had been erased, to square this sentence with ver. 17, where τινὲς τ. κλάδων only were broken off. Or we might think, as Matthäi has remarked (Thol.), that, 'Gentilis loquitur arrogantius,' using οἱ κλ. in his pride, to signify that the branches, generically, have now become subject to excision on his account. But the fact, now ascertained by Tischdf., that B omits the art., makes nearly the whole manuscript authority against it) **were broken off that I** (emphatic) **might be grafted in.** 20.] **Well** (the fact, involving even the *purpose*, assumed in ἵνα, is conceded. When Thol. denies this, he forgets that the *prompting cause* of their excision, their unbelief, is distinct from the *divine purpose* of their excision, the admission of the Gentiles, and belongs to a different side of the subject):—**through their unbelief** (or perhaps, '*through unbelief*,' abstract. There is often a difficulty in distinguishing the possessive from the abstract (i. e. generic) article. Thol. observes that the *instrumental* use of the dat. and that of διά with the gen. differ in this, that the latter expresses more the *immediate* cause, the former the mediate and more remote. The explanation of this would be, that the dative only acquires its *instrumental* use through another, more proper attribute of the case, that of *reference to, form or manner in which:* see Bernhardy, Syntax, ch. iii. 14, pp. 100—105) **they were broken off, but thou by thy faith** (see above:—'*through*' indicates better the *prompting cause of a definite act*,—'*by*,' the *sustaining condition of a continued state*. Thus we should always say that we are justified *through*, not *by*, faith, —but that we stand *by*, not *through*, faith) **standest** (in thy place, in the tree, opposed to ἐξεκλάσθησαν. Thol. prefers the sense in ch. xiv. 4, and certainly the adoption of πεσόντες ver. 22, seems to shew that the figurative diction is not strictly preserved). —**Be not high-minded, but fear:** 21.] **for if God did not spare the natural branches** (the branches which grew according to natural development, and were not engrafted),—(supply 'I fear,' or 'it is to be feared,' or simply 'fear,' or 'take heed,' as in ref.) **lest He shall also not spare** THEE. The fut. ind. with μή πως, the apparent incongruity of which has probably caused the variety of reading, implies, as Herm., Soph. Aj. 272, observes with regard to the ind. pres., 'μή ἐστὶ

[... χρηστοτητα P.]

[d] πως] οὐδὲ σοῦ [e] φείσεται. 22 ἴδε οὖν [e] χρηστότητα καὶ
[f] ἀποτομίαν θεοῦ· ἐπὶ μὲν τοὺς [g] πεσόντας [f] ἀποτομία,
ἐπὶ δὲ σὲ [e] χρηστότης θεοῦ, ἐὰν [h] ἐπιμείνῃς τῇ [e] χρη-
στότητι· ἐπεὶ καὶ σὺ [i] ἐκκοπήσῃ. 23 κἀκεῖνοι δέ, ἐὰν
μὴ [h] ἐπιμείνωσιν τῇ [y] ἀπιστίᾳ, [k] ἐγκεντρισθήσονται· δυνατὸς γάρ ἐστιν ὁ θεὸς πάλιν [k] ἐγκεντρίσαι αὐτούς·
24 εἰ γὰρ σὺ ἐκ τῆς [ab] κατὰ [b] φύσιν [i] ἐξεκόπης [k] ἀγρι-
ελαίου καὶ [l] παρὰ [l] φύσιν [k] ἐνεκεντρίσθης εἰς [m] καλλι-
έλαιον, [n] πόσῳ [n] μᾶλλον οὗτοι [o] οἱ [ab] κατὰ [b] φύσιν

e ch. ii. 4 reff.
f here bis only †. δεῖ . . . ἀποτομίαν τῇ πραότητι μιγνύναι, Plut. de Lib. Educ. p. 13, D. (-μος, Wisd. v. 20.)
g = ch. xiv. 4 reff.
h = ch. vi. 1 reff.
i here bis. Matt. iii. 10 || L. v. 30. vii. 19. xviii. 8. Luke xiii. 7, 9. 2 Cor. xi. 12 only. Deut. vii. 5.
k ver. 17.
l ch. i. 26 (reff.) only.
m here only †. Aristot. de Plant. i. 6.
n ver. 12.
o ellips., ch. iv. 14 al.

φείσηται, ὑποτεμνόμενος τοῦ λόγου τὸ φορτικὸν τῇ ἀμφιβολίᾳ) Thdrt [Antch$_1$] Thl Œc Iren-int$_1$ Cypr$_1$ Ambrst: om (*corrn to avoid fut. with μη πως?*) ABCℵ[P 47-txt] copt Damasc [Ors$_1$ Antch$_1$ Orig-int$_3$] Aug$_3$. rec φεισηται, with Chr-montf$_1$ Chr-c$_1$ Thl Œc: txt [A] B(sic) CDFL[P]ℵ rel Chr-2-mss$_1$ Thdrt Antch$_2$ Damasc.

22. ins του bef [1st] θεου B. rec αποτομιαν (*see note*), with DFL ℵ^3(but ν erased) rel [vulg] Clem$_1$ Eus$_1$ Chr$_1$ Thdrt Phot$_1$ [Cyr$_1$ Orig-int$_2$ Hil$_1$ Ambrst]: txt ABCℵ^1 (Orig$_1$) Damasc. rec χρηστοτητα, with D^3[and lat] FL rel [vulg] Clem Chr Cyr[-p$_1$] Thdrt Phot [Orig-int$_2$ Hil$_1$ Ambrst]: -τητος(sic) ℵ: txt ABC D^1[-gr arm] (Orig$_1$) Eus$_1$ Damasc. rec om θεου (*see note*), with D$^{2\cdot3}$FL rel demid Syr [syr goth æth] Clem$_1$ Orig$_1$[(-int$_2$) (Eus$_1$) Cyr$_1$] Chr$_1$ Thdrt [Hil$_1$ Ambrst Aug$_{sæpe}$]: ins ABCD^{1}ℵ vulg copt arm Damasc Pel. for επιμειν., επιμενης BD^{1}ℵ.

23. rec και εκεινοι, with L rel Chr$_1$ Thdrt: txt ABCDFℵ c d k [47] Damasc. for επιμειν., επιμενωσιν BD^{1}ℵ^1. ο θεος bef εστιν L a h k l 17.

(ἔσται) verentis quidem est ne quid nunc sit (*futurum sit*), sed indicantis simul, putare, se ita esse (*futurum esse*), ut veretur.' See Winer, edn. 6, § 56. 2. b. β, and 64. i. 7. a, also Col. ii. 8; Heb. iii. 12. **22.**] The caution of the preceding verse is unfolded into a setting before the Gentile of the true state of the matter. **Behold therefore** (*posito*, that thou enterest into the feeling prompted by the last verse) **the goodness and the severity** (no allusion to ἀποτέμνω in its literal sense) **of God:—towards those who fell** (see on ver. 11. Here the πεσόντες are opposed to σύ, the figure being for the moment dropped: for πίπτειν can hardly be used of the *branches*, but of *men*) **severity; but towards thee, the goodness of God** (the nominatives here, as involving a departure from the construction, are preferable: and the repetition of θεοῦ is quite in the manner of the Apostle: see 1 Cor. i. 24, 25. Rückert thinks that because Clem. Alex. Pædag. i. 8 [70], p. 140 P., understands χρηστότης, in ἐὰν ἐπιμείνῃς τῇ χρηστότητι, of the χρηστότης of *men* (τουτέστι τῇ εἰς χριστὸν πίστει), θεοῦ may have been a marginal gloss to guard against this mistake, and may have found its way into the text, misplaced. But this is hardly probable: θεοῦ is much more likely to have been erased as unnecessary), **if thou abide by** (reff.) **that goodness; for** ([supply **otherwise**:] assuming that thou dost *not* abide by that goodness) **thou also shalt be cut off** (ind. fut. The placing only a comma at ἐκκοπήσῃ, as Meyer,—not Lachm. (ed. 2) and Tischend. (ed. 7 [and 8]),—prevents the break evidently intended between the treatment of the case of the Gentile and that of the Jews).

23.] **And they moreover, if they continue not** (not exactly the same meaning as before: the χρηστότης before being external and objective, this, as in ch. vi. 1, a subjective state) **in their** (see on ver. 20) **unbelief, shall be grafted in: for God is able to graft them in again.** Some, e. g. Grot., represent this last clause as implying, that God's power to graft them in again has always been the same, but has waited for their change of mind, to act: 'Nihil est præter incredulitatem quod Deum impediat eos rursum pro suis assumere et paterne tractare:'—but surely De W.'s interpretation is far better:—'The Apostle obscurely includes in the ἐγκεντρ. the removal of their unbelief and the awakening of faith, and this last especially he looks for from above:'—for, as he observes, the *power* of God would not be put forward, if the other were the meaning. **24.**] **For** (proof that, besides God's undoubted power to re-engraft them, the idea of their being so re-engrafted is not an unreasonable one) **if** THOU **wast cut off from the olive-tree which is by**

ᵏ ἐγκεντρισθήσονται τῇ ἰδίᾳ ᵏ ἐλαίᾳ. 25 ᵖ Οὐ γὰρ θέλω
ὑμᾶς ᵖ ἀγνοεῖν, ἀδελφοί, τὸ ᑫ μυστήριον τοῦτο, ἵνα μὴ
ἦτε ἐν ἑαυτοῖς ʳ φρόνιμοι, ὅτι ˢ πώρωσις ᵗ ἀπὸ ᵗ μέρους τῷ
Ἰσραὴλ γέγονεν ᵘ ἄχρις οὗ τὸ ᵛ πλήρωμα τῶν ἐθνῶν

ABCD FLℵ a b c d f g h k l m n o 17 [47]

p ch. i. 13. 1 Cor. x. 1. xii. 1. 2 Cor. i. 8. 1 Thess. iv. 13. q = see note. ch. xvi. 25 al. Dan. ii. 18. r Matt. xxv. 2, &c. Gen. xli. 33. w. ἐν, 1 Cor. iv. 10. w. παρά, ch. xii. 16. Prov. iii. 7. s Mark iii. 5. Eph. iv. 18 only †. (-ροῦν, ver. 7.) t ch. xv. 15, 24. 2 Cor. i. 14. ii. 5 only. P. Josh. xviii. 20. see 1 Cor. xiii. 9, &c. xiv. 27. Heb. ix. 5. u constr., 1 Cor. xi. 26. Gal. iii. 19 al. v = here only ‡. (ver. 12.)

25. θελω bef γαρ ℵ: θελω δε (omg γαρ) m. [ημας F-gr(not G). om μη A¹.] rec (for εν) παρ (*see ch.* xii. 19), with CDLℵ rel Thdor-mops$_1$ Chr$_1$ Thdrt [Orig-int$_2$]: om F 47. 67² latt copt [Hil$_1$ Ambrst Aug$_{sæpe}$]: txt AB goth[?] Damasc. for αχρις, αχρι B¹.

nature wild, and wast grafted contrary to nature into a good olive-tree, how much more shall these, the natural branches, be engrafted in their own olive-tree? It is a question, as Tholuck remarks, whether κατὰ φύσιν and παρὰ φύσιν denote merely *growth in the natural manner and growth* (by engrafting) *in an unnatural* (i. e. artificial) *manner*,—or that the *wild* is the *nature of the Gentile*, and the *good olive that of the Jew*, so that the sense would be—'If thou wert cut out of the wild olive which is thine naturally, and wert engrafted contrary to (thy) nature into the good olive, how much more shall these, the natural branches,' &c. But then the latter part of the sentence does not correspond with the former. We either should expect the οἱ to be omitted (as is done in some mss.), or must, with Fritz., place a comma after οὗτοι, and, taking οἱ as the relative, construe, 'How much more these, who shall, agreeably to (their) nature, be grafted,' &c. Tholuck describes the question as being between a comparison of *engrafting* and *not engrafting*, and one of engrafting the *congruous* and the *incongruous*: and, on the above ground, decides in favour of the former,—κατὰ φύσιν signifying merely *natural growth*, παρὰ φ., *unnatural growth*, i.e. the growth of the *grafted scion*. But however this may fit the *former* part of the sentence, it surely cannot satisfy the requirements of the *latter*, where the κατὰ φύσιν (κλάδοι) are described as being *engrafted* (which would be παρὰ φύσιν) into *their own* olive-tree. We must at least assume a mixture of the two meanings, the antithesis of κατὰ and παρὰ φ. being rather verbal than logical,—as is so common in the writings of the Apostle. Thus in the former case, that of the Gentile, the fact of *natural growth* is set against that of *engrafted growth*: whereas in the latter, the fact of *congruity of nature* (τῇ ἰδίᾳ ἐλαίᾳ) is set against *incongruity*,—as making the re-engrafting more probable. **25—32.**] *Prophetic announcement that this re-engrafting* SHALL ACTUALLY TAKE PLACE (25—27), *and explanatory justification of this divine arrangement* (28—32). **25.**] **For** (I do not rest this on mere hope or probability, but have direct revelation of the Holy Spirit as to its certainty) **I would not have you ignorant, brethren** (see reff.,—used by the Apostle to announce, either as here some authoritative declaration of divine truth, or some facts in his own history not previously known to his readers), **of this mystery** (μυστ. Tholuck in his 4th edition classifies the meanings thus: (1) *such matters of fact, as are inaccessible to reason, and can only be known through revelation*: (2) *such matters as are patent facts, but the process of which cannot be entirely taken in by the reason.* He adds a third sense,—that, which is no mystery *in itself*, but *by its figurative import*. Of the first, he cites chap. xvi. 25; 1 Cor. ii. 7—10; Eph. i. 9; iii. 4; vi. 19; Col. i. 26, al., as examples: of the second, 1 Cor. xiv. 2; xiii. 2; Eph. v. 32; 1 Tim. iii. 9, 16: of the third, Matt. xiii. 11; Rev. i. 20; xvii. 5; 2 Thess. ii. 7. The first meaning is evidently that in our text:—'a prophetic event, unattainable by human knowledge, but revealed from the secrets of God') **that ye be not wise in your own conceits** (that ye do not take to yourselves the credit for wisdom superior to that of the Jews, in having acknowledged and accepted Jesus as the Son of God,—seeing that ye merely ἠλεήθητε τῇ τούτων ἀπειθείᾳ, ver. 30),—**that hardening** (not '*blindness*:' see above on ver. 7, and Eph. iv. 18 note) **has happened in part** (Calvin explains it '*quodammodo* .... qua particula voluisse mihi duntaxat videtur temperare verbum alioqui per se asperum,'—but there is no trace of such a desire above, ver. 7;—the τινες ver. 17 establishes the ordinary acceptation, that a *portion* of Israel have been hardened. **ἀπὸ μ.** may be joined with πώρωσις, or with γέγονεν: from the arrangement of the words, best with the former) **to Israel, until** (ἄχρις οὗ has been variously rendered by those who wish to escape from the prophetic assertion of the restoration of Israel.

εἰσέλθῃ, 26 καὶ w οὕτως πᾶς Ἰσραὴλ σωθήσεται, καθὼς w = ch. v. 12 reff.

So Calv.: "*donec* non infert temporis progressum vel ordinem, sed potius valet perinde ac si dictum foret, *ut* plenitudo gentium;"—al., "while .... shall come in:' but Thol. well observes that ἄχρ. οὗ with an ind., if any thing *actually happening* is spoken of, may have the meaning of '*while*,' even with an aor.: but with a subj. of the aorist, a *possible future event* is indicated, which *when it enters puts an end to the former*: see reff.) **the completion of the Gentiles shall have come in** (scil. to the Church or Kingdom of God, where we, the Apostle and those whom he addresses, are already: as we use the word 'come in' absolutely, with reference to the place in which we are. Or the word may be used absolutely, as it seems to be in Luke xi. 52, of *entering into the Kingdom of God*. In order to understand τὸ πλήρ. τ. ἐθν., we must bear in mind the character of the Apostle's present argument. He is dealing with *nations*: with the Gentile nations, and the Jewish nation. And thus dealing, he speaks of τὸ πλήρ. τ. ἐθν. coming in, and of πᾶς Ἰσραήλ being saved: having *no regard* for the time to the *individual destinies* of Gentiles or Jews, but regarding nations as each included under the common bond of consanguinity according to the flesh. The πλήρωμα τῶν ἐθνῶν I would regard then as signifying '*the full number*,' '*the totality*,' of the nations, i. e. *every nation under heaven*, the prophetic subjects (Matt. xxiv. 14) of the preaching of the gospel. Stuart denies that πλήρωμα will admit of this meaning. But the sense which he allows to it of "completion, i. q. πλήρωσις" (?), amounts in this case to the same thing: that completion not arriving till *all* have come in: the πλήρωμα τῶν ἐθνῶν importing that which πληροῖ τὰ ἔθνη. The idea of an elect number, however true in itself ('plenitudo gentium in his intrat, qui secundum propositum vocati,' Aug. cited by Tholuck), does not seem to belong to this passage).

* 26.] **And thus** (when this condition shall have been fulfilled) **all Israel shall be saved** (*Israel as a nation*, see above: not individuals,—nor is there the slightest ground for the notion of the ἀποκατάστασις). This prophecy has been very variously regarded. Origen, understanding by the 'omnis Israel qui salvus fiet,' the 'reliquiæ quæ electæ sunt,' yet afterwards appears to find in the passage his notion of the final purification of all men,—of the believing, by the word and doctrine: of the unbelieving, by purgatorial fire. Chrysostom gives no explanation: but on our Lord's words in Matt. xvii. 11, he says, ὅταν εἴπῃ ὅτι Ἠλίας μὲν ἔρχεται κ. ἀποκαταστήσει πάντα, αὐτὸν Ἠλίαν φησί, **κ. τὴν τότε ἐσομένην τῶν Ἰουδαίων ἐπιστροφήν**,—and shortly after calls him τῆς δευτέρας παρουσίας πρόδρομος. Similarly Theodoret and Gregory of Nyssa (in Thol.); so also Augustine, de Civ. Dei xx. 29, vol. vii. p. 704,—'ultimo tempore ante judicium (per Eliam, exposita sibi lege) Judæos in Christum verum esse credituros, celeberrimum est in sermonibus cordibusve fidelium.' Similarly most of the fathers (Estius), and schoolmen (Thol.);—Jerome, however, on Isa. xi. 11, vol. iv. p. 162, says, 'Nequaquam juxta nostros Judaizantes, in fine mundi quum intraverit plenitudo gentium, tunc omnis Israel salvus fiet: sed hæc omnia de primo intelligamus adventu.' Grotius and Wetst. believe it to have been fulfilled after the destruction of Jerusalem, when μυρίοι ἐκ περιτομῆς became believers in Christ (Eus. H. E. iii. 35). But Thol. has shewn that neither could the number of Gentiles received into the Church before that time have answered to the πλήρωμα τ. ἐθνῶν, nor those Jews to πᾶς Ἰσραήλ, which expression accordingly Grotius endeavours to explain by a Rabbinical formula, that "all Israel have a part in the Messiah;" which saying he supposes the Apostle to have used in a spiritual sense, meaning the Israel of God, as Gal. vi. 16. The Reformers for the most part, in their zeal to impugn the millenarian superstitions then current, denied the future general conversion of the Jews, and would not recognize it even in this passage:—Luther *did so* [recognize it], at one time, but towards the end of his life spoke most characteristically and strongly of what he conceived to be the impossibility of such national conversion (see extract in Tholuck's note, p. 616):—Calvin says: 'Multi accipiunt de populo Judaico, ac si Paulus diceret instaurandum adhuc in religionem ut prius: sed ego Israelis nomen ad totum Dei populum extendo, hoc sensu, Quum Gentes ingressæ fuerint, simul et Judæi ex defectione se ad fidei obedientiam recipient. Atque ita complebitur salus totius Israelis Dei, quem ex utrisque colligi oportet: sic tamen ut priorem locum Judæi obtineant, ceu in familia Dei primogeniti.' Calovius, Bengel, and Olshausen, interpret πᾶς Ἰσρ. of the *elect believers of Israel*: Beza, Estius, Koppe, Reiche, Köllner, Meyer, Tholuck, De Wette, al., hold that the words refer, as I have explained them above, to a national restoration of Israel to God's favour. I have not mixed with

γέγραπται "Ἥξει ἐκ Σιὼν ὁ [x] ῥυόμενος, [y] ἀποστρέψει
[z] ἀσεβείας ἀπὸ Ἰακώβ· 27 καὶ [a] αὕτη αὐτοῖς ἡ παρ' ἐμοῦ
[b] διαθήκη, [a] ὅταν [cd] ἀφέλωμαι τὰς [d] ἁμαρτίας αὐτῶν. 28 κατὰ
μὲν τὸ εὐαγγέλιον [e] ἐχθροὶ δι' ὑμᾶς, κατὰ δὲ τὴν [f] ἐκλογὴν
[g] ἀγαπητοὶ διὰ τοὺς [h] πατέρας. 29 [i] ἀμεταμέλητα γὰρ τὰ
[k] χαρίσματα καὶ ἡ [l] κλῆσις τοῦ θεοῦ. 30 ὥσπερ γὰρ ὑμεῖς

ABCD FLℵ a b c d f g h k l m n o 17 [47]

x ch. vii. 24 reff. Isa. lix. 20. pres. part., Matt. iv. 3. xxvi. 48. 1 Thess. iii. 5 al.
y Acts iii. 26 reff.
z ch. i. 18 reff.
a 1 John v. 2. w. ἐάν, 1 John ii. 3.
b = Luke i. 72. Acts iii. 25. Ps. xxiv. 14.
c mid., Luke xvi. 3 only. Hos. ii. 9.
d Heb. x. 4. Isa. xxvii. 9. Sir. xlvii. 11.
e = Gal. iv. 16.
f ch. ix. 11 reff.
g Matt. iii. 17. ch. i. 7 al. Ps. cvii. 6.
h absol., Acts vii. 19 reff.
i 2 Cor. vii. 10 only †.
k ch. v. 15, 16. vi. 23.
l Paul (1 Cor. i. 26. vii. 20. Eph. i. 18. Phil. iii. 14 al.) only, exc. Heb. iii. 1. 2 Pet. i. 10. Jer. xxxviii. (xxxi.) 6. Judith xii. 10 A Ald. compl. only.

26. rec ins και bef αποστρεψει (*as* LXX), with $D^{2\cdot3}$L rel [latt syrr copt arm] $Orig_1$ Chr_1 Thdrt: om ABC D^1[-gr] Fℵ [47 æth $Euthal\text{-}ms_1$ Damasc].—αποστρεψαι F goth.
30. om ver $ℵ^1$ [ins ℵ-$corr^1$]. rec ins και bef υμεις, with $D^{2\cdot3}Lℵ^3$ rel vulg syrr [arm] Chr(-montf and 2-mss): om ABC D^1[and lat] F ℵ-$corr^1$ [d 47] copt goth æth

the consideration of this prophecy the question of the restoration of the Jews *to Palestine*, as being clearly irrelevant to it: the matter here treated being, *their reception into the Church of God.* **καθὼς γέγρ.**] This quotation appears to have for its object to shew that the Redeemer was to come *for the behoof of God's own chosen* * *people.* For ἐκ Σιών, the LXX have ἕνεκεν Σιών (לְצִיּוֹן), the E. V. '*to Zion.*' The Apostle frequently varies from the LXX, and a sufficient reason can generally be assigned for the variation: here, though this reason is not apparent, we cannot doubt that such existed, for the LXX would surely have suited his purpose even better than ἐκ, had there been no objection to it. It may be that the whole citation is intended to express the sense of prophecy rather than the wording of any particular passage, and that the Apostle has, in ἐκ Σιών, summed up the prophecies which declare that the Redeemer should *spring out of Israel.* **ὁ ῥυόμ.** is in the Heb. 'a deliverer'—the Apostle adopts the LXX, probably as appropriating the expression to Christ. **ἀποστρ. κ.τ.λ.**] Heb. and E. V. '*and unto them that turn from transgression in Jacob.*' **ὅταν ἀφέλ.** from another place in Isa. (ref.),—hardly from Jer. xxxi. (LXX, xxxviii.) 34, as Stuart;—and also containing a general reference to the character of God's new covenant with them, rather than a strict reproduction of the original meaning of any particular words of the prophet. "How came the Apostle, if he wished only to express the general thought, that the Messiah was come for Israel, to choose just this citation, consisting of two combined passages, when the same is expressed more directly in other passages of the Old Testament? I believe that the ἥξει gave occasion for the quotation: if he did not refer this directly to the second coming of the Messiah, yet it allowed of being indirectly applied to it." Tholuck. **28.**] **With regard indeed to the gospel** (i. e. 'viewed from the gospel side,' looked on as we must look on them if we confine our view solely to the principles and character of the Gospel), **they** (the Jewish people considered as a whole) **are enemies** (θεοῦ: not μου, as Theodoret, Luther, Grot., al.—scil. in a state of exclusion from God's favour: not active, 'enemies to God,' as Grot., Bengel) **for your sakes; but with regard to the election** (viz. of Israel to be God's people, see vv. 1, 2—not that of Christians, as Aug. al.:—i. e. 'looked on as God's elect people'), **they are beloved for the fathers' sakes** (i. e. not *for the merits* of the fathers, but because of the covenant with Abraham, Isaac, and Jacob, so often referred to by God as a cause for His favourable remembrance of Israel). **29.**] **For** (explanation how God's favour regards them still, though for the present cast off) **the gifts** (generally) **and calling** (as the most excellent of those gifts. That calling seems to be intended 'qua posteros Abrahæ in fœdus adoptavit Deus,' Calv. A very similar sentiment is found ch. iii. 3, where the same is called ἡ πίστις τ. θεοῦ. But the words are true not only of this calling, but of every other. Bengel says, 'dona, erga Judæos: vocatio, erga gentes:' similarly of κλῆσις, De W., 'die Berufung durch das Ev.' But thus the point of the argument seems to be lost, which is, that the Jews being once chosen as God's people, will never be entirely cast off) [**of God cannot be repented of,** i. e.] **are irretractable** (do not admit of a change of purpose. The E. V., '*without repentance,*' is likely to mislead. Compare Hosea xiii. 14). **30**] **For** (illustration of the above position) **as ye** (manuscript evidence is too decided against the καί to allow of its being retained: but we

[m] ποτὲ [n] ἠπειθήσατε τῷ θεῷ, νῦν δὲ [o] ἠλεήθητε τῇ τούτων
[p] ἀπειθείᾳ, 31 οὕτως καὶ οὗτοι νῦν [n] ἠπείθησαν, τῷ [q] ὑμετέρῳ
[r] ἐλέει [s] ἵνα καὶ αὐτοὶ [o] ἐλεηθῶσιν. 32 [tu] συνέκλεισεν γὰρ ὁ
θεὸς [v] τοὺς [v] πάντας [u] εἰς [p] ἀπείθειαν, ἵνα [v] τοὺς [v] πάντας
[o] ἐλεήσῃ. 33 ὦ [w] βάθος [xy] πλούτου καὶ [yza] σοφίας καὶ [yab] γνώ-

...νυν ηπει. C.
ABDF Lℵ a b c d f g h k l m n o 17 ⌊47⌋

m = John ix. 13. ch. vii. 9 al.
n = ch. ii. 8. x. 21. Deut. xxi. 20.
o ch. ix. 15, &c. pass., Matt. v. 7. 1 Cor. vii. 25. 2 Cor. iv. 1. 1 Tim. i. 13, 16. 1 Pet. ii. 10. Prov. xxi. 10. Hos. ii. 23 (25) A.
p here bis. Eph. ii. 2. v. 6. Col. iii. 6. Heb. iv. 6, 11 only †. (-θής, ch. i. 30.) constr., ver. 20.
q = 1 Cor. xv. 31. see ch. xv. 4.
r Luke i. 50, &c. ch. ix. 23. Eph. ii. 4. Ps. cxliii. 2.
s inversion of words, 2 Cor. ii. 4 reff.
t Luke v. 6. Gal. iii. 22, 23 only. Josh. vi. 1 al.
u here only. Ps. lxxvii. 50, 62. εἰς τοιαύτην ἀμηχανίαν συγκλεισθείς, Diod. Sic. xix. 19. So Dion. Hal. viii. p. 520. Polyb. iii. 63. 3, and fr.
v 1 Cor. ix. 22. x. 17. 2 Cor. v. 10, 14. Eph. iv. 13. Phil. ii. 21. P.
w ch. viii. 39. Eph. iii. 18 al. Isa. vii. 11.
x ch. ii. 4 reff.
y Rev. v. 12 only.
z = 1 Cor. i. 21. Eph. iii. 10.
a 1 Cor. xii. 8.
b 1 Cor. xiii. 2.

[Chr-2-mss$_1$] Damasc Thl [Orig-int$_2$] Jer Aug$_{sæpe}$.—ποτε bef υμεις A: ποτε και υμεις b o. νυνι B Chr$_1$. ελεηθητε C (m ?) Thl.

31. for ουτοι, αυτοι D^{1}F [syr-marg Cyr-p$_1$: *isti* latt Orig-int$_2$ Ambrst]. aft αυτοι ins υστερον 5. 17. 93: παλιν Cyr[-p$_1$]; νυν (*possibly mechanical repetition*) BD^1(ℵ) [copt] Damasc.—om αυτοι ℵ^1.

32. for 1st τους παντας, τα παντα D^1, παντα F [Iren$_1$: *omnia*] latt Iren-int$_2$ [Ambr$_{sæpe}$].

may suspect that it has been struck out as superfluous, in ignorance (Thol.) of the Greek usage which often doubles καί in two parallel clauses) **in times past were disobedient to God** (nationally—as Gentiles, before the Gospel) **but now have** (lit. 'were compassionated,' historical) **received mercy** (scil. by admission into the church of God) **through** (as the occasion; the breaking off of the natural branches giving opportunity for the grafting in of you) **the disobedience of these** (i.e. unbelief, considered as an act of resistance to the divine will: see 1 John iii. 23), **so these also have now** (under the Gospel) **disobeyed** (are now in a state of unbelieving disobedience), **in order that through the mercy shewed to you** (viz. on occasion of the fulness of the Gentiles coming in) **they also may have mercy shewn them** ('the objective view corresponding to the subjective εἰς τὸ παραζηλῶσαι αὐτούς, ver 11.' De W.). Some place the comma after ἐλέει instead of ἠπείθησαν, and construe, either, as Erasm., Calv., al., '*they have disobeyed through* (upon occasion of) *the mercy shewn to you*,' or as Vulg., Luth., Estius, al., '*they have become disobedient to the mercy shewn to you*.' But thus the parallelism is weakened, and the μυστήριον of ver. 25 lost sight of. Examples of the emphatic word being placed before ἵνα are found in reff. **32.**] **For** (foundation of the last stated arrangement in the divine purposes) **God shut up** (not shut up *together*; σύν, as in so many cases, implying, not *co*-participation on the part of the subjects of the action, but the character of the action itself: so in 'concludere.' The sense is here as in the examples, which might be multiplied by consulting Schweighæuser's Index to Polyb., '*to involve in*,' '*to subject to*.' The aor., which should be kept in the rendering, refers to the time of the act in the divine procedure) **all** (the reading τὰ πάντα has probably been introduced from Gal. iii. 22) **men in** (into) **disobedience** (general here,—every form, unbelief included), **that He may have mercy on all.** No mere *permissive* act of God must here be understood. The Apostle is speaking of the divine arrangement by which the guilt of sin and the mercy of God were to be made manifest. He treats it, as elsewhere (see ch. ix. 18 and note), entirely with reference to the *act of God*, taking no account, for the time, of human agency; which however, when treating of us and our responsibilities, he brings out into as prominent a position: see as the most eminent example of this, the closely following ch. xii. 1, 2. But there remains some question, *who are the* **οἱ πάντες** *of both clauses?* Are they *the same?* And if so, *is any support given to the notion of an* ἀποκατάστασις *of all men?* Certainly they are identical: and signify *all men*, without limitation. But the ultimate difference between the *all men* who are shut up under disobedience, and the *all men* upon whom mercy is shewn is, that by all men *this mercy is not accepted*, and so men become *self-excluded* from the salvation of God. GOD'S ACT remains the same, equally gracious, equally universal, whether men accept His mercy or not. This contingency is *here not in view*: but simply *God's act* itself. We can hardly understand the οἱ πάντες *nationally*. The marked universality of the expression recalls the beginning of the Epistle, and makes it a solemn conclusion to the argumentative portion, after which the Apostle, overpowered with the view

c here only †. Prov. xxv. 3 Symm. (ἐξερευνᾶν, 1 Pet. i. 10.) d ch. v. 16. Ps. cxviii. 75. e Eph. iii. 8 only. Job v. 9. ix. 10. xxxiv. 24 only. f = Acts xiii. 10. Heb. iii. 10. Rev. xv. 3. Ps. xvii. 21. g 1 Cor. ii. 16, from Isa. xl. 13. h here only. 2 Kings xv. 12. i here only. Job xli. 3 Heb. = Isa. xl. 14 Aℵ Ald. (4 Kings vi. 11. 2 Macc. vii. 37 only.) k ch. xii. 19. (and Heb. x. 30, from Deut. xxxii. 35.) Luke xiv. 14 bis. 1 Thess. iii. 9. 2 Thess. i. 6 only. L.P.H. Isa. lxiii. 7. l 1 Cor. viii. 6.

σεως θεοῦ, ὡς [c] ἀνεξεραύνητα τὰ [d] κρίματα αὐτοῦ καὶ [e] ἀνεξ- ABDF
ιχνίαστοι αἱ [f] ὁδοὶ αὐτοῦ. 34 τίς γὰρ ἔγνω [g] νοῦν κυρίου; Lℵ a b c d f g h k
ἢ τίς [h] σύμβουλος αὐτοῦ ἐγένετο; 35 ἢ τίς [i] προέδωκεν l m n o 17 [47]
αὐτῷ καὶ [k] ἀνταποδοθήσεται αὐτῷ; 36 ὅτι [l] ἐξ αὐτοῦ καὶ

33. ins του bef θεου F 17. (ανεξεραυνητα, so AB¹ℵ)
34. for κυριου, θεου D¹(and lat¹) Zeno₁.

of the divine Mercy and Wisdom, breaks forth into the sublimest apostrophe existing even in the pages of Inspiration itself.

33—36.] *Admiration of the goodness and wisdom of God, and humble ascription of praise to Him.* 33.] There is some doubt whether σοφίας and γνώσεως are genitives *after* πλούτου, as in E. V., or *parallel with* it. The former view is adopted by Thom. Aquin., Luther, Beza, Calvin, Estius, Reiche, and al. The grounds on which Reiche supports it are thus given and refuted by Tholuck: (1) "If these three genitives are co-ordinate, καί must stand either before *all*, or before the last only." But in the case of three nouns placed co-ordinately in this manner, καί is prefixed to the two latter only, see ch. ii. 7; xii. 2; Luke v. 17. (2) "πλοῦτος is no *qualitative* idea, but only a quantitative idea." But *wherein* the riches *consist*, is ordinarily indicated by the context; and here there can be but little doubt on the matter, if we compare ch. x. 12; in Phil. iv. 19 we also read of the πλοῦτος of God. This also answers (3) "that πλοῦτος without an adjunct expresses no definite attribute of God." (4) "in the following citation, vv. 34, 35, two only of these, σοφία and γνῶσις, are mentioned." But this may be doubted. Chrys. says, on ver. 36, αὐτὸς εὗρεν, αὐτὸς ἐποίησεν, αὐτὸς συγκροτεῖ. καὶ γὰρ καὶ **πλούσιός** ἐστι, καὶ οὐ δεῖται παρ' ἑτέρου λαβεῖν· καὶ **σοφός** ἐστι, καὶ οὐ δεῖται συμβούλου. τί λέγω συμβούλου; οὐδὲ **εἰδέναι** τις δύναται τὰ αὐτοῦ, ἀλλ' ἢ μόνος αὐτὸς ὁ πλούσιος κ. σοφός. Hom. xix. p. 653. Perhaps this latter is altogether too finedrawn: but it is favoured by Bengel, Olsh., and Tholuck. I prefer therefore the view of Chrys., Theodoret, Grot., Bengel, Tholuck, Köllner, and Olsh.,—to take πλούτου, σοφίας, γνώσεως, as three co-ordinate genitives: **πλ.** denoting the **riches of the divine goodness**, in the whole, and in the result just arrived at, ver. 32: **σοφ.**, the divine **wisdom** of proceeding in the apparently intricate vicissitudes of nations and individuals: **γνώσ.** (if a distinction be necessary, which can hardly be doubted) the divine **knowledge** of all things from the beginning,—God's comprehension of the end and means together in one unfathomable depth of Omniscience.

How unsearchable are His judgments (the determinations of His wisdom, regarded as in the divine Mind; answering perhaps to γνῶσις. So Thol.: De W. however denies this meaning to κρίματα, and renders it *decrees*, referring it to the blinding of the Jews) **and His ways unable to be traced out** (His methods of proceeding, answering to σοφία, Thol. But this is perhaps too subtle). 34.] **For** (confirmation of ἀνεξερ. and ἀνεξιχν. by a citation from Scripture. It is made from two separate places in the LXX, more perhaps as a reminiscence than as a direct quotation) **who hath known the mind** (γνῶσις, but see above) **of the Lord? or who hath been His counsellor** (σοφία?)? 35.] **or who hath previously given to Him, and it shall be repaid to him?**—from Job xli. 3 (11 E. V.), where the LXX (xli. 2) have τίς (add ἐστιν ὃς A) ἀντιστήσεταί μοι, κ. ὑπομενεῖ; But the Heb. is מִי הִקְדִּימַנִי וַאֲשַׁלֵּם, '*who hath anticipated* (i. e. by the context, *conferred a benefit on*) *me, that I may repay him?*' And to this the Apostle alludes, using the third person.

We can hardly doubt that this question refers to the freeness and richness of God's mercy and love. 36.] **For** (ground of vv. 33—35. Well may all this be true of Him, for) **of Him** (in their origin:—'quod dicit, "ex ipso," hoc ipsum, *quod sumus* indicat:' Orig. Chrys. somewhat differently: see above on ver. 33), **and through Him** (in their subsistence and disposal:—'"per Ipsum," quod per ejus providentiam dispensamur in vita:" Orig.), **and unto Him** ('"in Ipso," (so Vulg. and some other vss.) quod perfectio omnium et finis in Ipso erit tunc, cum erit Deus omnia in omnibus:' Orig.) **are all things** (not only, though chiefly, *men*,—but the whole creation). Origen remarks, 'Vides, quomodo in ultimis ostendit, quod in omnibus quæ supra dixit signaverit, mysterium Tri-

[l] δι αὐτοῦ καὶ [l] εἰς αὐτὸν [m] τὰ πάντα· αὐτῷ ἡ [n] δόξα εἰς τοὺς αἰῶνας. ἀμήν.

XII. 1 [o] Παρακαλῶ οὖν ὑμᾶς, ἀδελφοί, [p] διὰ τῶν [q] οἰκτιρμῶν τοῦ θεοῦ, [r] παραστῆσαι τὰ σώματα ὑμῶν θυσίαν ζῶσαν, ἁγίαν, [s] εὐάρεστον τῷ θεῷ, τὴν [t] λογικὴν

[p ζω-σαν ...]

m = Col. i. 16. Rev. iv. 11. Job viii. 3. n = Luke ii. 14. xvii 18. John ix. 24. Acts xii. 23. Jude 25 al. Ps. xcv. 7. ellips., ch. xvi. 27. Gal. i. 5. Eph. iii. 21. o = and constr., Acts xxiv. 4. xxvii. 34 al. p = ch. xv. 30. 1 Cor. i. 10. 2 Cor. x. 1. 1 Thess. iv. 2. q 2 Cor. i. 3. Phil. ii. 1. Col. iii. 12. Heb. x. 28 only. Isa. lxiii. 15. r Luke ii. 22. ch. vi. 13, &c. Ps. v. 3. s here bis. ch. xiv. 18. 2 Cor. v. 9. Eph. v. 10. Phil. iv. 18. Col. iii. 20. Tit. ii. 9. Heb. xiii. 21 only +. Wisd. iv. 10. ix. 10 only. (-τως, Heb. xii. 28 only. -τεῖν, Heb. xi. 5.) t 1 Pet. ii. 2 only +. προςφέρουσιν (οἱ ἄγγελοι) κυρίῳ . . λογικὴν . . προςφοράν, Test. xii. Patrum, p. 547 b.

36. aft *αιωνας* ins *των αιωνων* FG² [fuld demid tol $spec_1(om_1)$ Syr $Orig\text{-}int_2$ $Cypr_1$ Hil_1].

Chap. XII. 1. *τω θεω* bef *ευαρεστον* A[P]ℵ¹ vulg [spec Damasc $Orig\text{-}int_2$ $Ambr_1$ Ambrst] $Aug_{sæpe}$.

nitatis. Sicut enim in præsenti loco quod ait, "quoniam ex Ipso, et per Ipsum, et in Ipso sunt omnia:" convenit illis dictis, quæ idem Apostolus in aliis memorat locis, cum dicit (1 Cor. viii. 6): "Unus Deus Pater ex quo omnia, et unus Dominus noster Jesus Christus, per quem omnia:" et item in Spiritu Dei dicit revelari omnia, et per hæc designat, in omnibus esse providentiam Trinitatis: ita et cum dicit "altitudo divitiarum," Patrem, ex quo omnia dicit esse, significat: et sapientiæ altitudinem, Christum, qui est sapientia ejus, ostendit: et scientiæ altitudinem, Spiritum Sanctum, qui etiam alta Dei novit, declarat.' And, if this be rightly understood,—not of a *formal allusion* to the Three Persons in the Holy Trinity, but of an *implicit reference* (as Thol.) to the *three attributes of Jehovah* respectively manifested to us by the three coequal and coeternal Persons,—there can hardly be a doubt of its correctness. The objection of De Wette, that not *εἰς*, but *ἐν*, would be the designation of the Holy Spirit and His relation to the Universe, applies to that part of Origen's Commentary which rests on the Vulg. *in ipso* and to the idea of a *formal recognition*: but not to Tholuck's remark, illustrated from *ὁ ἐπὶ πάντων κ. διὰ πάντων κ. ἐν πᾶσιν ἡμῖν*, Eph. iv. 6, as referring to *εἷς θεός, εἷς κύριος, ἓν πνεῦμα*. Only those who are dogmatically prejudiced can miss seeing that, though St. Paul has never *definitively expressed* the doctrine of the Holy Trinity in a definite formula, yet he was conscious of it as a living reality.

XII. 1—XV. 13.] Practical exhortations founded on the doctrines before stated. And first, ch. xii. *general exhortations to a Christian life.*

1.] **οὖν** may apply to the whole doctrinal portion of the Epistle which has preceded, which, see Eph. iv. 1; 1 Thess. iv. 1, seems the most natural connexion,—or to ch. xi. 35, 36 (so Olsh., Meyer), or to the whole close of ch. xi. (so Tholuck.) Theodoret remarks: *ὅπερ ἔστιν ὀφθαλμὸς ἐν σώματι, τοῦτο τῇ ψυχῇ πίστις, καὶ τῶν θείων ἡ γνῶσις. δεῖται δὲ ὅμως αὕτη τῆς πρακτικῆς ἀρετῆς, καθάπερ ὁ ὀφθαλμὸς χειρῶν καὶ ποδῶν καὶ τῶν ἄλλων μορίων τοῦ σώματος. τούτου δὲ χάριν ὁ θεῖος ἀπόστολος τοῖς δογματικοῖς λόγοις καὶ τὴν ἠθικὴν διδασκαλίαν προστέθεικε.* **διά**] introduces, as in reff., an idea which is to give force to the exhortation. **οἰκτιρμῶν**] viz. those detailed and proved throughout the former part of the Epistle. *δι' αὐτῶν οὖν τούτων, φησί, παρακαλῶ, δι' ὧν ἐσώθητε· ὥςπερ ἂν εἴ τις τὸν μεγάλα εὐεργετηθέντα ἐντρέψαι βουλόμενος, αὐτὸν τὸν εὐεργετήσαντα ἱκέτην ἀγάγοι.* Chrys. Hom. xx. p. 656. **παραστῆσαι**] the regular word for *bringing to offer in sacrifice* (reff.). **τ. σώματα ὑμ.**] Most Commentators say, merely for *ὑμᾶς αὐτούς*,—to suit the metaphor of a *sacrifice*, which consisted of a body: some * (Thol., al.), because the body is the *organ of practical activity*, which practical activity is to be dedicated to God: better with Olsh. and De Wette,—as an indication that the sanctification of Christian life is to extend to that part of man's nature which is most completely under the bondage of sin. **θυσίαν**] Chrys. strikingly says, *πῶς ἂν γένοιτο τὸ σῶμα, φησί, θυσία; μηδὲν ὀφθαλμὸς πονηρὸν βλεπέτω, καὶ γέγονε θυσία· μηδὲν ἡ γλῶσσα λαλείτω αἰσχρόν, καὶ γέγονε προςφορά· μηδὲν ἡ χεὶρ πραττέτω παράνομον, καὶ γέγονεν ὁλοκαύτωμα. μᾶλλον δὲ οὐκ ἀρκεῖ ταῦτα, ἀλλὰ καὶ τῆς τῶν ἀγαθῶν ἡμῖν ἐργασίας δεῖ, ἵνα ἡ μὲν χεὶρ ἐλεημοσύνην ποιῇ, τὸ δὲ στόμα εὐλογῇ τοὺς ἐπηρεάζοντας, ἡ δὲ ἀκοὴ θείαις σχολάζῃ διηνεκῶς ἀκροάσεσιν. ἡ γὰρ θυσία οὐδὲν ἔχει ἀκάθαρτον, ἡ θυσία*

u ch. ix. 4 reff. v 1 Pet. i. 14 only +. w Luke xvi. 8. xx. 34. 1 Cor. i. 20. ii. 6 (bis) al6. L.P. only, exc. Matt. xii. 32 [xiii. 40]. x Matt. xvii. 2

[u] λατρείαν ὑμῶν, 2 καὶ μὴ [v] συνσχηματίζεσθαι τῷ [w] αἰῶνι
[w] τούτῳ, ἀλλὰ [x] μεταμορφοῦσθαι τῇ [y] ἀνακαινώσει τοῦ
[z] νοός, [a] εἰς τὸ [b] δοκιμάζειν ὑμᾶς τί τὸ θέλημα τοῦ θεοῦ
τὸ ἀγαθὸν καὶ [s] εὐάρεστον· καὶ [c] τέλειον. 3 λέγω γὰρ [d] διὰ
τῆς [e] χάριτος τῆς [e] δοθείσης μοι παντὶ τῷ ὄντι ἐν ὑμῖν,

ABDF L[P]א a b c d f g h k l m n o 17 [47]

|| Mk. 2 Cor. iii. 18 only +. Ps. xxxiii. 1 Symm. y Tit. iii. 5 only +. z = ch. i. 28. Col. ii. 18. a ch. iv. 11 reff. b Luke xiv. 19. 1 Cor. iii. 13. Eph. v. 10. Phil. i. 10. Prov. xvii. 3. c = Matt. v. 48. xix. 21. Phil. iii. 15 al. Gen. vi. 9. d = Gal. i. 15. iii. 18. iv. 23. Philem. 22. e 1 Cor. i. 4 reff.

2. (*συνσχημ.*, so B[1]DFא.) rec *-σχηματιζεσθε* and *μεταμορφουσθε*, with B[1]L[P] rel latt syrr copt goth [(æth) arm] $Clem_1$ Chr_1 Thdrt Damasc [Phot-c_1 Orig-int_3 $Cypr_2$ Ambrst]: *-αι* and *-ε* [D[2.3]-gr] n 17; *-ε* and *-αι* א c o[1]: txt AB[2] D[1][-gr] F g k Thl. *αιωνιω* B. rec aft *νοος* ins *υμων*, with D[3]L[P]א rel [latt syrr goth (æth) arm Cyr_1] Thdrt [Damasc Orig-int_4 Ambrst] $Aug_{sæpe}$: om AB D[1][-gr] F [47] copt $Clem_1$ [$Orig_1$] $Cypr_2$. om 2nd *του* F.

ἀπαρχὴ τῶν ἄλλων ἐστί. καὶ ἡμεῖς τοίνυν καὶ χειρῶν καὶ ποδῶν καὶ στόματος καὶ τῶν ἄλλων ἁπάντων ἀπαρχώμεθα τῷ θεῷ. Hom. xx. p. 656 f. **ζῶσαν**] In opposition to the *Levitical* θυσίαι, which were *slain animals*. Our great sacrifice, the Lord Jesus, having been slain for us, and by the shedding of His Blood perfect remission having been obtained διὰ τῶν οἰκτιρμῶν τοῦ θεοῦ, we are now enabled to be offered to God no longer by the shedding of blood, but as *living sacrifices*. This application of the figure of a sacrifice occurs in Philo, who ('quod omnis probus liber,' § 12, vol. ii., p. 457) describes the Essenes as οὐ ζῷα καταθύοντες, ἀλλ' ἱεροπρεπεῖς τὰς ἑαυτῶν διανοίας κατασκευάζειν ἀξιοῦντες. See also Jos. Antt. xviii. 1. 5. τῷ θεῷ belongs to εὐάρεστον, not to παραστῆσαι. **τὴν λογικὴν λατρ. ὑμ.**] "This *may* certainly be in apposition with θυσίαν (Reiche, Meyer), the acc. denoting the result and intention;—θυσία however alone can hardly be called a λατρεία, but παραστῆσαι θυσίαν may: therefore it is preferable to take the acc. as in apposition with *the whole sentence,* and supply some verb of exhorting: see 1 Tim. ii. 6; 2 Thess. i. 5." Tholuck. **λογικήν** (reff.) is opposed to σαρκικήν, see Heb. vii. 16. So Chrys.,—οὐδὲν ἔχουσαν σωματικόν, οὐδὲν παχύ, οὐδὲν αἰσθητόν. Theodoret, Grot., al., take it as '*having reason,*' 'rational,' opposed to sacrifices of animals which have no reason: Photius, Basil, and Calvin, '*rational,*' as opposed to superstitious. But the former meaning is far the best, and answers to the πνευματικὰς θυσίας of 1 Pet. ii. 5. **2.**] **συνσχηματίζεσθαι** is not imperative in sense, but dependent on παρακαλῶ. (Of course, in all such questions betwen ε and αι, the confusing element of itacism comes in: but in no case where both forms are equally admissible in the text, can the mere suspicion of itacism be allowed to decide the question.) **ὁ αἰὼν οὗτος**, here, the *whole world of the ungodly*, as contrasted with the spiritual kingdom of Christ. The dat. ἀνακαινώσει is not the instrument by which, but the *manner in which* the metamorphosis takes place: that wherein it consists: compare περιετμήθητε περιτομῇ ἀχειροποιήτῳ, Col. ii. 11. **εἰς τὸ δοκιμάζειν, that ye may prove**, viz. in this process and the active Christian life accompanying it, compare reff. Eph., Phil.: not '*that ye may be able to prove,*' 'acquire the faculty of proving,' as Bucer, Olsh., Rückert: the Apostle is not speaking of acquiring wisdom here, but of practical proof by experience. **τὸ ἀγαθ. κ. εὐάρ. κ. τέλ.** are not epithets of τὸ θέλημα τ. θεοῦ as in E. V., for in that case they would be superfluous, and in part (τέλειον) inapplicable: but abstract neuters, see ver. 9, **that ye may prove what is the will of God** (viz. that which is) **good and acceptable** (to Him) **and perfect.** The non-repetition of the art. shews that the adjectives all apply to the same thing.

3—21.] *Particular exhortations grounded on and expanding the foregoing general ones.* This is expressed by the γάρ, which *resumes*, and binds to what has preceded. And first, *an exhortation to humility in respect of spiritual gifts,* vv. 3—8.

3.] **λέγω**, a mild expression for 'I command:' enforced *as* a command by διὰ τ. χ. . . . 'by means of my apostolic office,' 'of the grace conferred on me to guide and exhort the Church:' reff. **παντὶ τῷ ὄντι ἐν ὑμ.**,—a strong bringing out of the *individual* application of the precept. οὐχὶ τῷ δεῖνι καὶ τῷ δεῖνι μόνον, ἀλλὰ καὶ ἄρχοντι κ. ἀρχομένῳ, κ. δούλῳ κ. ἐλευθέρῳ, κ. ἰδιώτῃ κ. σοφῷ, κ. γυναικὶ κ. ἀνδρί, κ. νέῳ κ. γέροντι. Chrys. Hom. xx. p. 603.

μὴ [f] ὑπερφρονεῖν [g] παρ' ὃ δεῖ [h] φρονεῖν, ἀλλὰ [h] φρονεῖν [a] εἰς
τὸ [i] σωφρονεῖν, [k] ἑκάστῳ ὡς ὁ θεὸς [kl] ἐμέρισεν [m] μέτρον
πίστεως. 4 [n] καθάπερ γὰρ ἐν ἑνὶ σώματι πολλὰ [o] μέλη
ἔχομεν, τὰ δὲ [o] μέλη πάντα οὐ τὴν αὐτὴν ἔχει [p] πρᾶξιν,
5 οὕτως [q] οἱ [q] πολλοὶ ἓν σῶμά ἐσμεν ἐν χριστῷ, τὸ δὲ [r] καθ'
εἷς ἀλλήλων [o] μέλη. 6 ἔχοντες δὲ [s] χαρίσματα κατὰ τὴν
[t] χάριν τὴν [t] δοθεῖσαν ἡμῖν [u] διάφορα, [v] εἴτε [w] προφητείαν,

f here only †. Job xxxi. 13 [?] & xli. 6 [7] Symm. πλούτῳ ὑπερφρονέουσαι, Herod. i. 199. (See 2 Macc. ix. 12) constr. inf., Matt. v. 39. Acts xxi. 21. g = ch. xiv. 5 reff. h = Acts xxviii. 22 al. 2 Macc. xiv. 26. i Mark v. 15. Luke viii. 35. 2 Cor. v. 13. Tit. ii. 6. 1 Pet. iv. 7 only †. k and constr., 1 Cor. vii. 17. (iii. 5.) l = Mark vi. 41. Luke xii. 13. 2 Cor. x. 13. Heb. vii. 2. Prov. xxix. 24. m 2 Cor. x. 13. Eph. iv. 7, 13, 16. = Paul only. n ch. iv. 6 reff. o ch. vi. 13 reff. p = here only. (Acts xix. 18 reff.) Sir. xi. 10. Xen. Mem. ii. 1. 6. q = ch. v. 15 reff. r Mark xiv. 19. [John viii. 9.] Rev. iv. 8. 3 Macc. v. 34. s ch. v. 15. vi. 23. xi. 29. 1 Cor. xii. 4 al. P. only, exc. 1 Pet. iv. 10 †. t ver. 3. u = Heb. ix. 10 (i. 4. viii. 6) only. Deut. xxii. 9. v so 1 Cor. iii. 22. Col. i. 16. w = 1 Cor. xii. 10. xiii. 2 al. (Rev. i. 3.) see Sir. xxiv. 33.

3. aft *χαριτος* ins *του θεου* L d f m 5. 48². 67. 73. 113-4-5-20-4 fuld guelph [syr goth] æth arm Thl Aug$_{\text{sæpe}}$. for ὅ, α B²: om *παρ ο δει φρονειν* F 70. *εμερισεν* bef *ο θεος* (*see* 1 *Cor* vii. 17) A guelph [am tol] Syr [Orig-int$_2$ Ambrst].
4. for *καθαπερ*, *ωσπερ* D¹F. rec *μελη* bef *πολλα*, with AL[P] rel Chr$_1$ [Bas$_1$ Antch$_1$] Damasc Œc: txt BDFℵ latt Thdrt Thl [Orig-int$_2$ Ambrst Aug$_{\text{sæpe}}$]. *παντα* bef *μελη* F(not G), so also vulg Syr [Ambrst Aug$_{\text{sæpe}}$].
5. om *εσμεν* F. rec (for *το*) *ο* (*alteration to suit εἷς*), with D²·³[L] rel vulg (and F-lat) Syr Eus$_1$ Chr$_1$ Thdrt Thl Œc: txt ABD¹ F-gr ℵ[P 47-txt] Antch$_1$ Damasc.
[**6.** for *δε*, *ουν* P: *enim* Orig-int$_1$. *δαφοραν* D¹.]

μὴ ὑπερφρ. κ.τ.λ.] There is a play on the words *φρονεῖν*, *ὑπερφρονεῖν*, and *σωφρονεῖν*, which can only be clumsily conveyed in another language: 'not to be high-minded, above that which he ought to be minded, but to be so minded, as to be sober-minded.' Wetst. quotes from Charondas in Stobæus, Sentent. xlii., *προσποιείσθω δὲ ἕκαστος τῶν πολιτῶν σωφρονεῖν μᾶλλον ἢ φρονεῖν*,—and from Thucyd. ii. 62,—*ἰέναι δὲ τοῖς ἐχθροῖς ὁμόσε, μὴ φρονήματι μόνον, ἀλλὰ καὶ καταφρονήματι.* But *φρονεῖν* must not be taken, with Calvin, 'admonet ut ea tantum cogitemus et meditemur, quæ nos sobrios et modestos reddere potuerunt:'—the thoughts implied in it being, **thoughts of one's self.** **ἑκάστῳ ὡς**] = *ὡς ἑκάστῳ* (reff.), not (*λέγω*) *ἑκάστῳ, ὡς* .... **μέτρον πίστεως** is the *receptivity* of *χαρίσματα*, itself no inherent congruity, but the gift and apportionment of God. It is in fact the *subjective designation* of *ἡ χάρις ἡ δοθεῖσα ἡμῖν*, ver. 6. But we must not say, that (Ewb.) "faith, in this passage, means *those gifts or graces which the Christian can only receive through faith*:" this is to confound the receptive faculty with the thing received by it, and to pass by the great lesson of our verse, that *this faculty* is nothing to be proud of, but God's gift. **4.**] **γάρ**, elucidating the fact, that God apportions variously to various persons: because the Christian community is like a *body* with many members having various duties. See the same idea further worked out, 1 Cor. xii. 12 ff. **5. τὸ δὲ καθ' εἷς**] **But** [**severally,** i. e.] **as regards individuals.** A solœcism for *τὸ δὲ εἷς καθ' ἕνα*, as *ἓν καθ' ἕν* in ref. Rev. Wetst., on ref. Mark, gives many examples of it. **Members of one another** = fellow-members with one another,—members of the body of which we one with another are members. **6.**] The *δέ* = 'and not only so, but' .... **χάρις,** see above, ver. 3, on *μέτρ. πίστ.* These *χαρίσματα* are called, 1 Cor. xii. 7, *ἡ φανέρωσις τοῦ πνεύματος.* "These *χαρίσματα δάφορα* are next specified. The two first accusatives are grammatically dependent on *ἔχοντες*: by degrees the Apostle loses sight of the construction, and continues with the concrete *ὁ διδάσκων*, which still he binds on to the foregoing by *εἴτε*,—but at *ὁ μεταδιδούς*, omits this also, and, at ver. 9, introduces the abstract *ἡ ἀγάπη*." Thol. **εἴτε προφητείαν**] There is some dispute about the construction of these clauses. The ordinary rendering regards them as elliptical, and supplies before *κατὰ* and *ἐν*, *χρησάσθω αὐτῇ* or *ὥστε εἶναι αὐτήν* or the like. But Reiche, Meyer, De Wette, suppose *no ellipsis*, joining *κατὰ τὴν ἀναλ.*, &c. to the foregoing substantives, as *κατὰ τὴν χάριν* to *χαρίσματα*. This construction must however be dropped at *ἐν ἁπλότητι*, which is manifestly to be rendered with a verb supplied: and (2) it reduces the four first mentioned gifts to a bare catalogue, and deprives the passage of its aim, which is to keep each member of the body in its true place and work without any member boasting against

x here only †. (-γως, Wisd. xiii. 5.) y Acts xx. 24 reff. z = Luke iii. 18. Acts ii. 40 al. a = Acts ix. 31. 2 Cor. viii. 4.

κατὰ τὴν [x] ἀναλογίαν τῆς πίστεως· 7 [v] εἴτε [y] διακονίαν, ἐν ABDF L[P]ℵ
τῇ [y] διακονίᾳ· [v] εἴτε ὁ διδάσκων, ἐν τῇ διδασκαλίᾳ· 8 [v] εἴτε a b c d f
ὁ [z] παρακαλῶν, ἐν τῇ [a] παρακλήσει· ὁ [b] μεταδιδούς, ἐν g h k l m n o 17
[c] ἁπλότητι· ὁ [d] προϊστάμενος, ἐν [e] σπουδῇ· ὁ [f] ἐλεῶν, ἐν [47]

1 Tim. iv. 13. Heb. xii. 5. xiii. 22. L.P.H. b ch. i. 11. Luke iii. 11. Eph. iv. 28. 1 Thess. ii. 8 only. L P. Job xxxi. 17. Wisd. vii. 13. c 2 Cor. viii. 2. ix. 11, 13. xi. 3. Eph. vi. 5. Col. iii. 22 only. P. 1 Chron. xxix. 17. d 1 Thess. v. 12. 1 Tim. iii. 4, 5, 12. v. 17. Tit. iii. 8, 14 only. P. Prov. xxvi. 17. e = 2 Cor. vii. 11, 12. 2 Pet. i. 5. Jude 3. Exod. xii. 11. f ch. xi. 31 reff.

7. ειτ[ε (ειτ ℵ³,] appy) **ο** διακονων ℵ³ m [$Bas_1(txt_1)$ Thdrt-ms(omg *o*)]. for ο διδασκων, διδασκαλειαν A.
8. om ειτε D¹F latt [Bas_1 $Orig\text{-}int_1$] Pel. προιστανομενος ℵ.

another. Tholuck quotes a passage of very similar construction from Epictet. Dissert. iii. 23. 5. He is speaking of reading and philosophizing from ostentation, and says that every thing which we do, must have its aim, its ἀναφορά;—λοιπόν, ἡ μὲν τίς ἐστι κοινὴ ἀναφορά, ἡ δ' ἰδία. πρῶτον, ἵν' ὡς ἄνθρωπος. ἐν τούτῳ τί περιέχεται; . . . ἡ δ' ἰδία πρὸς τὸ ἐπιτήδευμα ἑκάστου καὶ τὴν προαίρεσιν· ὁ κιθαρῳδός, ὡς κιθαρῳδός· ὁ τέκτων, ὡς τέκτων· ὁ φιλόσοφος, ὡς φιλόσοφος· ὁ ῥήτωρ, ὡς ῥήτωρ. See also the same construction in 1 Pet. iv. 10, 11.

On προφητεία, the gift of the προφῆται, see note, Acts xi. 27. **κατ. τ. ἀναλ. τ. πίστ.**] **(let us prophesy) according to the proportion** (compare Justin Mart. Apol. i. 17, p. 54: "each will be punished πρὸς ἀναλογίαν ὧν ἔλαβε δυνάμεων παρὰ θεοῦ") **of faith.** But *what* faith? *Objective* ('fides *quæ* creditur'), or *subjective* ('fides *quâ* creditur')? *the* faith, or *our* faith? The comparison of μέτρον πιστεως above, and the whole context, determine it to be the latter; the measure of *our* faith: 'quisque se intra sortis suæ metas contineat, et revelationis suæ modum teneat, ne unus sibi omnia scire videatur.' To understand ἀναλογία τ. π. objectively, as 'the rule of faith,' as many R.-Cath. expositors, and some Protestant, e. g. Calvin, 'fidei nomine significat prima religionis axiomata,'—seems to do violence to the context, which aims at shewing that the measure of faith, itself the gift of God, is the receptive faculty for all spiritual gifts, which are therefore not to be boasted of, nor pushed beyond their provinces, but humbly exercised within their own limits.

7. διακονίαν] *any subordinate ministration in the Church.* In Acts vi. 1 and 4, we have the word applied both to the lower ministration, that of alms and food, and to the higher, the διακ. τοῦ λόγου, which belonged to the Apostles. But here it seems to be used in a more restricted sense, from its position as distinct from prophecy, teaching, exhortation, &c. **ἐν τῇ διακ.**] Let us confine ourselves humbly and orderly to that kind of ministration to which God's providence has appointed us, as profitable members of the body. **ὁ διδάσκων**] The *prophet* spoke under *immediate inspiration;* the διδάσκαλος under inspiration working by the secondary instruments of his will and reason and rhetorical powers. Paul himself seems ordinarily, in his personal ministrations, to have used διδασκαλία. He is nowhere called a *prophet*, but appears as distinguished from them in several places: e. g. Acts xi. 27; xxi. 10, and apparently xiii. 1. Of course this does not affect the appearance of *prophecies*, commonly so called, in his writings. The inspired διδάσκαλος would speak, though not technically προφητείας, yet the mind of the Spirit in all things: not to mention that the apostolic office was one in dignity and fulness of inspiration far surpassing any of the subordinate ones, and in fact including them all.

ἐν τῇ διδασκαλίᾳ] as before: he is to teach in the sphere, within the bounds, of the teaching allotted to him by God,—or for which God has given him the faculty.

8.] The **παρακαλῶν** was not necessarily distinct from the προφητεύων,—see 1 Cor. xiv. 31. **ὁ μεταδιδούς** appears to be the *giver of the alms to the poor,*—either the deacon himself, or some distributor subordinate to the deacon. This however has been doubted, and not without reason: for a transition certainly seems to be made, by the omission of the εἴτε, from *public* to *private* gifts. We cannot find any ecclesiastical meaning for ἐλεῶν (though indeed Calvin, al., understand by it "viduas et alios ministros qui curandis ægrotis, secundum veterem Ecclesiæ morem, præficiebantur"),—and the very fact of the three preceding being all limited to their respective official spheres, whereas these three are connected with qualitative descriptions, speaks strongly for their being *private acts*, to be always performed *in the spirit* described. Add to all, that, as Vitringa remarks, διαδιδόναι is more properly to *distribute* (Acts iv. 35), **μεταδιδόναι** to *impart of one's own to another.* I would therefore render it: **He that bestoweth.** **ἐν ἁπλότητι**] ordinarily, '*with simplicity.*' But seeing that ἁπλό-

[g] ἱλαρότητι. 9 ἡ ἀγάπη [h] ἀνυπόκριτος. [i] ἀποστυγοῦντες τὸ
πονηρόν, [k] κολλώμενοι [l] τῷ [l] ἀγαθῷ· 10 τῇ [m] φιλαδελφίᾳ εἰς
ἀλλήλους [n] φιλόστοργοι· τῇ [o] τιμῇ ἀλλήλους [p] προηγού-
μενοι· 11 τῇ [e] σπουδῇ μὴ [q] ὀκνηροί· [r] τῷ [rs] πνεύματι [s] ζέον-

g here only. Prov. xviii. 22 only. (-ρός, 2 Cor. ix. 7.) h 2 Cor. vi. 6. 1 Tim. i. 5. 2 Tim. i. 5. James iii. 17. 1 Pet. i. 22 only +. Wisd. v. 18. xviii. 16 only. constr., Heb. xiii. 5. i here only +. k = Luke xv. 15. Acts viii. 29. 2 Kings xx. 2. l ch. ii. 10 reff. m 1 Thess. iv. 9. Heb. xiii. 1. 1 Pet. i. 22. 2 Pet. i. 7 (bis) only +. (-φος, 1 Pet. iii. 8.) n here only +. (-γως, 2 Macc. ix. 21. -γία, 2 Macc. vi. 20.) o = John iv. 44. Acts xxviii. 10. ch. ii. 7 al. Ps. xlviii. 12, 20. p here only. Prov. xvii. 14 al. 2 Macc. iv. 40. q = Matt. xxv. 26 (Phil. iii. 1) only. Prov. vi. 6, 9. r = Acts xvii. 16 reff. s Acts xviii. 25 (reff.) only.

9. for αποστυγ., μεισουντες F.

της, referred to alms-giving, bears another and an objective meaning, this hardly satisfies me, because σπουδή and ἱλαρότης designate not so much the inward frame of mind, as the outward character of the superintendence and the compassion: as might be expected, when gifts to be exercised *for mutual benefit* are spoken of. In 2 Cor. viii. 2; ix. 11, 13, Jos. Antt. vii. 13. 4 (where David admires Araunah, τῆς ἁπλότητος καὶ τῆς μεγαλοψυχίας), the word signifies *'liberality:'* so perhaps ἁπλῶς also, James i. 5, but see note there. This meaning is not recognized by Wahl, Lex., but defended by Tholuck, who connects it with the phrase found in Stobæus, Eclog. Phys. i. p. 123, ἁπλοῦν τὰς χεῖρας, 'to open the hands wide:'—and I would thus render it here. **ὁ προϊστάμενος**] **He that presides**—but over what? If over *the Church* exclusively, we come back to *offices* again: and it is hardly likely that the rulers of the Church, as such, would be introduced so low down in the list, or by so very general a term, as this. In 1 Tim. iii. 4, 5, 12, we have the verb used of *presiding over a man's own household:* and in its absolute usage here, I do not see why that also should not be included. Meyer would understand it of *'patronage* of strangers' (ch. xvi. 2). Stuart in his Excursus on this place, appended to his Commentary, takes up and defends the same view. But, not insisting on the *general* usage of the word being preferable where it occurs *absolutely*, will ἐν σπουδῇ apply to this meaning? Of course so far as σπουδή is applicable to *every* employment, it might, but more than this is required, where words are connected in so marked a manner as here. Giving προϊστάμενος the ordinary meaning, these words fit admirably: implying that he who is by God set over others, be they members of the Church or of his own household, must not allow himself to forget his responsibility, and take his duty indolently and easily, but must προΐστασθαι σπουδαίως, making it a serious matter of * continual diligence. **ὁ ἐλεῶν**] See above: **He that sheweth mercy,** is the very best rendering: and I cannot conceive that any *officer of the Church* is intended, but every private Christian who exercises compassion. It is in exhibiting compassion, which is often the compulsory work of one obeying his conscience rather than the spontaneous effusion of love, that *cheerfulness* is so peculiarly required, and so frequently wanting. And yet in such an act it is even of more consequence towards the effect,—consoling the compassionated, than the act itself. κρείσσων λόγος ἢ δόσις, Sir. xviii. 16. **9—21.**] *Exhortations to various Christian principles and habits.* **9.**] Olsh., De Wette, al., would understand ἐστίν,—not ἔστω,—the ellipsis of the imperative being unusual. But I cannot see how this can be here. Clearly the three preceding clauses are *hortative;* as clearly, those which follow are so likewise. Why then depart from the prevalent character of the context, and make this *descriptive?* **ἀποστυγ.**] This very general exhortation is probably, as Bengel says, an explanation of ἀνυπόκριτος:—our love should arise from a genuine cleaving to that which is good, and aversion from evil: not from any by-ends. **10.**] **in brotherly love** (dat. of the respect or regard in which), **affectionate.** **φιλόστ.**] properly of love of *near relations;* agreeing therefore exactly with φιλαδελφία. **προηγούμενοι**] "invicem prævenientes," latt. μὴ μένε φιλεῖσθαι παρ' ἑτέρου, ἀλλ' αὐτὸς ἐπιπήδα τούτῳ καὶ κατάρχου, Chrys.: similarly Syr., Theophyl., Erasm., Luther: —or, = ἀλλήλους ἡγούμενοι ὑπερέχοντας ἑαυτῶν, Phil. ii. 3; so Origen, Theodoret, Grot.: or, as in ref. 2 Macc. *'setting an example to,' 'going before,'* which however does not seem to apply here, unless we render τῇ τιμῇ, *'in yielding honour:'* 'in giving honour, anticipating one another' (so Stuart). **11.**] **in zeal** (not *'business,'* as E. V., which seems to refer it to the affairs of this life, whereas it relates, as all these in vv. 11, 12, 13, to Christian duties *as such:* as 'fervency of spirit,' 'acting as God's servants,' 'rejoicing in hope,' &c.) **not slothful.** **ζέων τῷ πν.** is used of Apollos, in ref. The

t = Acts xx. 19 reff. see notes.
u = Matt. x. 22. xxiv. 13 ||. 2 Tim. ii. 12. James v. 11. 1 Pet. ii. 20. Job xiv. 14.
v Acts i. 14 (reff.).
w Acts xx. 34 reff.
x Acts ix. 13 reff.

ABDF L[P]ℵ a b c d f g h k l m n o 17 [47]

τες· τῷ κυρίῳ ᵗ δουλεύοντες. 12 τῇ ἐλπίδι χαίροντες· τῇ
θλίψει ᵘ ὑπομένοντες· τῇ ᵛ προσευχῇ ᵛ προσκαρτεροῦντες·
13 ταῖς ʷ χρείαις τῶν ˣ ἁγίων ʸ κοινωνοῦντες· τὴν ᶻ φιλο-
ξενίαν ᵃ διώκοντες. 14 ᵇᶜ εὐλογεῖτε τοὺς ᵈ διώκοντας ὑμᾶς·
ᵇᶜ εὐλογεῖτε, καὶ μὴ ᶜᵉ καταρᾶσθε. 15 χαίρειν μετὰ χαιρόν-
των, κλαίειν μετὰ κλαιόντων. 16 ᶠ τὸ ᶠ αὐτὸ εἰς ἀλλήλους

y ch. xv. 27. Gal. vi. 6. Phil. iv. 15. 1 Tim. v. 22. Heb. ii. 14. 1 Pet. iv. 13. 2 John 11 only. Wisd. vi. 25. Polyb. ii. 32. 8 al. z Heb. xiii. 2 only +. (-νος, 1 Pet. iv. 9.) a = ch. ix. 30, 31 reff. b = 1 Cor. iv. 12. 1 Pet. iii. 9 al. c Luke vi. 28. James iii. 9. Gen. xii. 3. d = Matt. v. 44. Acts vii. 52 reff. 2 Kings xxi. 5. e as above (c). Matt. xxv. 41. Mark xi. 21 only. Gen. v. 29. (-ρα, Gal. iii. 10.) f ch. xv. 5. 2 Cor. xiii. 11. Phil. ii. 2. iv. 2.

11. Steph (for κυριω) καιρω, with D¹ F[-gr] 5 G-lat lat-mss-mentd-by-[Orig-int]-Jer Cypr Ambrst$_{expr}$: txt ABD$^{2\cdot3}$L[P]ℵ rel gr-mss-mentd-by-[Orig-int]-Jer-Ambrst [vulg F-lat syrr copt goth æth arm] Clem$_1$ Ath$_1$ Bas$_1$ Chr$_1$ Thdrt Euthal[(Wetst: not in Zacagn. Euthal-ms om τ. κ. δ.) Antch$_3$ Damasc] Thl Œc [Orig-int$_1$] Jer Pel Aug Primas Sedul Bede. υπομενονντες ℵ [-μενος A¹].

13. for χρειαις, μνειαις D¹F mss-mentd-by-Thdor-mops(ἔνια τῶν ἀντιγράφων) am Hil$_1$ Ambrst Aug$_1$: txt ABD³[LP]ℵ rel [vulg-clem(with fuld demid harl tol) syrr(and syr-mg-gr) copt goth æth arm] Clem$_1$ Chr$_2$ Thdrt Thdor-mops$_2$ Damasc Thl Œc Aug$_1$ Bede : [Orig-int$_1$] Sedul Pel speak of both readings.

14. om υμας (*homœotel?*) B 47. 67² am Clem : τους εχθρους ημων Orig$_1$: om ευλ. τ. διωκ. υμ. (*passing from* 1*st* ευλογειτε *to* 2*nd*) F [spec Orig-int]-ms: these words are aft καταρασθε in D$^{1\cdot3}$[and lat] : txt AL[D²P]ℵ rel [vulg &c Clem] Chr Bas Thdrt. [ευλογεισθαι (2nd) D¹(appy).]

15. rec ins και bef κλαιειν, with AD³L[P 47(sic)] rel Syr copt [æth] (Orig$_1$) Chr$_1$ Thdrt [Damasc Tert$_1$ Ambr$_1$] : om BD¹Fℵ latt syr goth arm [Orig-int$_1$] Ambrst Pel Aug$_1$ Sedul Bede.

Holy Spirit lights this fire within: see Luke xii. 49; Matt. iii. 11. **τ. κυρίῳ δουλ.**] The external authorities, as will be seen in the var. read., are strongly in favour of this reading. The balance of internal probability, though not easy at once to settle, is I am persuaded on the same side. The main objection to κυρίῳ has ever been, that thus the Apostle would be inserting here, among particular precepts, one of the most general and comprehensive character. So Hilary (in Wetst.) and al. But this will be removed, if we remember, *of what he is speaking:* and if I mistake not, the other reading has been defended partly owing to forgetfulness of this. The *present* subject is, the *character of our zeal for God.* In it we are not to be ὀκνηροί, but fervent in spirit,—and that, *as servants of God.* A very similar reminiscence of this relation to God occurs Col. iii. 22—24: οἱ δοῦλοι, . . . ὃ ἐὰν ποιῆτε, ἐκ ψυχῆς ἐργάζεσθε ὡς τῷ κυρίῳ καὶ οὐκ ἀνθρώποις, εἰδότες ὅτι ἀπὸ κυρίου ἀπολήμψεσθε τὴν ἀνταπόδοσιν τῆς κληρονομίας. **τῷ κυρίῳ χριστῷ δουλεύετε.** The command, **τῷ καιρῷ** δουλεύειν, would surely come in very inopportunely in the midst of exhortations to the *zealous service of God.* At the same time, it is not easy to give an account of the origin of the reading. The ἐξαγοραζόμενοι τὸν καιρόν of Eph. v. 16 may have led to the filling up of the contracted κυρίῳ (κῷ) with this word: and the notion that σπουδῇ referred to *worldly business,* may have favoured the sense thus given. For examples of the phrase τῷ καιρῷ δουλεύειν and 'tempori inservire,' see Wetst. As to its applicability at all to Christians, De Wette well remarks, "The Christian may and should certainly *employ* (Eph. v. 16) τὸν καιρόν (time and opportunity), but not *serve* it." Athanas. (in Wetst.) ad Dracont. says, οὐ πρέπει τῷ καιρῷ δουλεύειν, ἀλλὰ κυρίῳ. **12.**] The datives here are not parallel. τῇ ἐλπίδι is the *ground of* the joy in χαίροντες,—but τῇ θλίψει *the state in which* the ὑπομονή is found. **13.**] The reading μνείαις is curious, as being a corruption introduced, hardly accidentally, in favour of the *honour of martyrs by commemoration.* **τ. φιλοξ διώκ.**] οὐκ εἶπεν **ἐργαζόμενοι**, ἀλλὰ **διώκοντες**, παιδεύων ἡμᾶς μὴ ἀναμένειν τοὺς δεομένους, πότε πρὸς ἡμᾶς ἔλθωσιν, ἀλλ' αὐτοὺς ἐπιτρέχειν κ. καταδιώκειν. Chrys. Hom. xxi. p. 676. **14.**] "The Sermon on the Mount must have been particularly well known; for among the few references in the N. T. Epistles to the direct words of Christ there occur several to it: e. g. 1 Cor. vii. 10. James iv. 9; v. 12 (we may add iv. 3; i. 2, 22; ii. 5, 13; v. 2, 3, 10). 1 Pet. iii. 9, 14; iv. 14." Tholuck. **15.**] Inf. for imperative: see Phil. iii. 16: and Winer, edn. 6, § 43. 5. d. **16.**] **Having** (the participial construction is resumed, as in ver. 9) **the same spirit towards one**

[fg] φρονοῦντες· μὴ τὰ [hi] ὑψηλὰ [gi] φρονοῦντες, ἀλλὰ τοῖς
[k] ταπεινοῖς [l] συναπαγόμενοι. μὴ γίνεσθε [m] φρόνιμοι παρ'
[n] ἑαυτοῖς. 17 μηδενὶ [o] κακὸν [o] ἀντὶ κακοῦ [op] ἀποδιδόντες·
[q] προνοούμενοι καλὰ [r] ἐνώπιον πάντων ἀνθρώπων· 18 [s] εἰ
δυνατόν, [t] τὸ [t] ἐξ ὑμῶν μετὰ πάντων ἀνθρώπων [u] εἰρηνεύον-
τες· 19 μὴ [n] ἑαυτοὺς [v] ἐκδικοῦντες, [w] ἀγαπητοί, ἀλλὰ [x] δότε
[x] τόπον τῇ ὀργῇ· γέγραπται γὰρ [y] Ἐμοὶ [za] ἐκδίκησις, ἐγὼ
[zb] ἀνταποδώσω, λέγει κύριος. 20 ἀλλὰ ἐὰν [c] πεινᾷ ὁ ἐχθρός

g = ch. viii. 5 reff. h = Luke xvi. 15. 1 Kings ii. 3. i ch. xi. 20 v. r. k = Luke i. 52. 2 Cor. (vii. 6 reff.) x. 1. James i. 9. Isa. xi. 4. l Gal. ii. 13. 2 Pet. iii. 17 only. Exod. xiv. 6 only. m w. παρά, here only (see ch. xi. 25 reff.). Prov. iii. 7. n 2nd pers., 2 Cor. vii. 11 reff. o 1 Thess. v. 15. 1 Pet. iii. 9. (Prov. xvii. 13.) p = Matt. vi. 4, 6. Luke x. 35 al. q 2 Cor. viii. 21. 1 Tim. v. 8 only. Prov. iii. 4. (-νοια, ch. xiii. 14.) r = Acts iv. 19 reff. Mal. ii. 17. s Matt. xxiv. 24. Gal. iv. 15. t = here only. Hom. Il. α. 525, ἐξ ἐμέθεν. see ch. i. 15. u Mark ix. 50. 2 Cor. xiii. 11. 1 Thess. v. 13 only. 3 Kings xxii. 45. Sir. vi. 6. v Luke xviii. 3, 5. 2 Cor. x. 6. Rev. vi. 10. xix. 2 only. 4 Kings ix. 7. (-κος, ch. xiii. 4.) w 2 Cor. vii. 1 reff. x Luke xiv. 9. Eph. iv. 27. Sir. iv. 5. xxxviii. 12. see Heb. xii. 17. y Deut. xxxii. 35. z Heb. x. 30. (Jer. xxviii. [l.] 6.) a as above (z). Luke xviii. 7, 8. xxi. 22. Acts vii. 24. 2 Cor. vii. 11. 2 Thess. i. 8. 1 Pet. ii. 14 only. Judg. xi. 36. b ch. xi. 35 reff. c Matt. iv. 2. v. 6 al. Prov. xxv. 21, 22.

[**16.** for μη τα υψ. φρον., αγαπητοι P^1. συναπαγαμενοι B^1.]

17. aft καλα ins ενωπιον του θεου και (*see* 2 *Cor* viii. 21; *Prov* iii. 4) A^2 ($Polyc_1$); ου μονον ενωπ. τ. θ. αλλα και F vulg goth arm[-usc spec Ambrst] $Lucif_1$: om A^1(appy) BDL[P]ℵ rel Syr [syr copt æth arm-zoh Chr_1 Thdrt Damasc $Orig\text{-}int_1$]. for παντων, των A^2 D^1[and lat] F guelph harl tol [spec] $Lucif_1$: txt (A^1 ?)BD^3L[P]ℵ rel [vulg-clem(with am fuld demid) syrr copt goth arm Bas_1] Chr_1 (Thdrt) Damasc Thl Œc Ambrst Sedul Bede.

19. [εκδικησεις A F-gr $Orig_1$(txt_1-int_3).] ανταποδω F.

20. rec (for αλλα εαν) εαν ουν, with D^3-gr L rel Chr_1 Thdrt Thl Œc: εαν (alone) D^1-gr F guelph D^3-lat [spec] goth: εαν γαρ Syr Did_1: [*etsi* syr, *etsi quoque* æth:] txt AB[P]ℵ m vulg D^1-lat [copt arm] Bas_1 Damasc [$Orig\text{-}int_1$.

another, i. e. actuated by a common and well-understood feeling of mutual allowance and kindness. **μὴ τὰ ὑψ.**] It is a question, whether τοῖς ταπεινοῖς is neuter or masc. Certainly not *necessarily neuter*, as De W.: the Apostle's antitheses do not require such minute correspondence as this. The sense then must decide. In τὰ ὑψηλὰ φρονοῦντες, the ὑψηλά are necessarily *subjective*, the *lofty thoughts of the man.* But in τοῖς ταπεινοῖς συναπαγόμενοι the adj. is necessarily *objective;* some outward objects with which the persons exhorted are συναπάγεσθαι. And those outward objects are defined, if I mistake not, by the τὸ αὐτὸ **εἰς ἀλλήλους** φρονοῦντες. This spirit towards one another is not to be a spirit of haughtiness, but one of community and sympathy, **condescending to men of low estate,** as E. V. admirably renders it. For **συναπ.**, see reff. and compare Zosimus, Hist. v. 6, cited by Tholuck, καὶ αὐτὴ ἡ Σπάρτη συναπήγετο τῇ κοινῇ τῆς Ἑλλάδος ἁλώσει. The insertion of the seemingly incongruous μὴ γίνεσθε . . ἑαυτοῖς is sufficiently accounted for by reference to ch. xi. 25, where he had stated this frame of mind as one to be avoided by those whose very place in God's church was owing to His free mercy. *Being uplifted one against another* would be a sign of this fault being present and operative. **17.**] The construction is resumed. The Apostle now proceeds to exhort respecting conduct *to those without.* **προνοούμ. καλὰ . . . .**] from ref. Prov., which has ἐνώπιον κυρίου καὶ ἀνθρώπων.

18.] The εἰ δυνατόν, as well remarked by Thol. and De Wette, is *objective only*—not '*if you can,*' but **if it be possible**—if *others will allow it.* And this is further defined by τὸ ἐξ ὑμῶν: all YOUR *part is to be peace:* whether you actually live peaceably or not, will depend then solely on how *others* behave towards *you.* **19.**] So Matt. v. 39, 40. **ἀγαπητοί**] 'The more difficult this duty, the more affectionately does the Apostle address his readers, with this word.' Thol. **δότε τόπον**] **allow space,** i. e. '*interpose delay,*' to **anger.** So Livy viii. 32, "Legati circumstantes sellam orabant, ut rem in posterum diem differret, et *iræ suæ spatium,* et consilio tempus, *daret.*" So that we must not understand τῇ ὀργῇ, '*your* anger,' nor [exactly, though it comes to that,] '*God's* anger,' but '*anger,*' generally;—'*give wrath room:*' 'proceed not to execute it hastily, but leave it for its legitimate time, when He whose it is to avenge, will execute it: make not the wrath your own, but leave it for God.' So in the main, but mostly understanding [exclusively] τ. ὀρ. τοῦ θεοῦ, Chrys., Aug., Theodoret, and the great body of Commentators. Some Fathers interpret it, '*yield to the anger*

d 1 Cor. xiii. 3 only. Num. xi. 4, 18 al. e Matt. xxv. 35, 37, 42. Job xxii. 7. f Matt. x. 42. 1 Cor. iii. 2, &c. xii. 13. Rev. xiv. 8. Judg. iv. 19. g here only. l. c. Ps. xvii. 8, 12. (-κία, John xviii. 18.) h 2 Tim. iii. 6 only. l. c. Judith. xv. 11 only.

σου, [d] ψώμιζε αὐτόν· ἐὰν [e] διψᾷ, [ef] πότιζε αὐτόν. τοῦτο ABDF L[P]א abcdf ghkl mno17 [47]
γὰρ ποιῶν [g] ἄνθρακας πυρὸς [h] σωρεύσεις ἐπὶ τὴν κεφαλὴν
αὐτοῦ. 21 μὴ νικῶ ὑπὸ [i] τοῦ [i] κακοῦ, ἀλλὰ νίκα [k] ἐν [i] τῷ
[i] ἀγαθῷ [i] τὸ [i] κακόν.

XIII. 1 Πᾶσα [l] ψυχὴ [m] ἐξουσίαις [n] ὑπερεχούσαις [o] ὑποτασσέσθω. οὐ γάρ ἐστιν [m] ἐξουσία εἰ μὴ * ἀπὸ θεοῦ, αἱ
δὲ οὖσαι ὑπὸ θεοῦ [p] τεταγμέναι εἰσίν. 2 ὥστε ὁ [q] ἀντι-

i ch. ii. 9, 10 (reff.). k = Matt. xii. 27, 28. Mark xiv. 1 al. l Acts ii. 43 reff. m = 1 Cor. xv. 24. Eph. iii. 10. vi. 12. Tit. iii. 1. n – 1 Pet. ii. 13 (Phil. ii. 3. iii. 8. iv. 7) only. Gen. xli. 40. (-οχή, 1 Cor. ii. 1.) o ch. viii. 7 reff. p Luke vii. 8. Acts xiii. 48. xv. 2. q Acts xviii. 6 reff.

ins και bef εαν διψα D^1(and lat, Tischdf; D^3, Treg): εαν δε διψα $D^{2\cdot 3}$(Tischdf) goth arm]. της κεφαλης B.
21. μη νικου A. for υπο, απο F.

Chap. XIII. 1. for πασα ψυχη . . υποτασσεσθω, πασαις . . . υποτασσεσθε D^1F harl [fuld spec] Iren-int$_1$ Ambrst. *ὑπὸ ABD^{3}L[P]א rel Bas$_1$ Isid$_1$ Chr$_1$ Thdrt-ms: απο D^1F Orig$_1$ Thdrt Damasc. rec aft ουσαι ins εξουσιαι, with D^{3}L[P] rel syrr [Orig$_1$] Chr$_1$ Thdrt Thl Œc: om ABD^{1}Fא latt copt goth æth arm Iren-int$_2$ Did-int$_1$[appy] Ambrst Aug. [for υπο, απο F.] rec ins του bef θεου, with Lא^3 rel Orig$_1$ Thdrt Chr-ms$_1$: om ADF[P]א^1 1 m Chr Damasc.

(*of your adversary*);' but this meaning for δότε τόπον is hardly borne out. The citation varies from the LXX, which has ἐν ἡμέρᾳ ἐκδικήσεως ἀνταποδώσω;—and is nearer the Heb.,—לִי נָקָם וְשִׁלֵּם, "mine is revenge and requital." It is very remarkable, that in Heb. x. 30 the citation is made in the same words. **20.**] The οὖν would mean 'quod cum ita sit;'—carrying on the sentence with the assumption of the last thing stated. This perhaps may not have been understood, and hence may have arisen the alteration or omission of οὖν in the MSS. But the evidence is very strong for its omission. *What is meant by* **ἄνθρακας πυρὸς σωρεύσεις**? The expression ἄνθρ. πυρ. occurs more than once in Ps. xviii., of the *divine punitive judgments.* Can those be meant here? Clearly not, in their bare literal sense. For however true it may be, that ingratitude will add to the enemy's list of crimes, and so subject him more to God's punitive judgment, it is impossible that to *bring this about* should be set as a precept, or a desirable thing among Christians. Again, can the expression be meant of the *glow and burn of shame* which would accompany, even in the case of a profane person, the receiving of benefits from an enemy? This *may* be meant; but is not probable, as not sufficing for the majesty of the subject. Merely to *make an enemy ashamed of himself*, can hardly be upheld as a motive for action. I understand the words, '*For in this doing, you will be taking the most effectual vengeance;*' as effectual as if you heaped coals of fire on his head. **21.**] If you suffered yourselves to be provoked to revenge, you would be yielding to the enemy,—overcome by that which is evil: do not thus,—but in this, and in all things, **overcome the evil** (in others) **by your good.**

Chap. XIII. 1—7.] *The duty of cheerful obedience to the powers of the state.* It has been well observed (Calv., Thol., De Wette. See Neander, Pflanzung u. Leitung, &c. 4th ed. p. 460 ff.) that *some special reason* must have given occasion to these exhortations. We can hardly attribute it to the seditious spirit of the *Jews at Rome*, as their influence in the Christian Church there would not be great; indeed, from Acts xxviii. the two seem to have been remarkably distinct. But disobedience to the civil authorities may have arisen from mistaken views among the Christians themselves as to the nature of Christ's kingdom and its relation to existing powers of this world. And such mistakes would naturally be rifest there, where the fountain of earthly power was situated: and there also best and most effectually met by these precepts coming from apostolic authority. The way for them is prepared by vv. 17 ff. of the foregoing chapter. 1 Pet. ii. 13 ff. is parallel: compare notes there.

1.] **ὑποτασσέσθω**, see 1 Cor. xvi. 16, is reflective, **subject himself**, i. e. 'be subject of his own free will and accord.' **For there is no authority** (in heaven or earth—no power at all) **except from God: and** (so δέ, 2 Cor. vi. 15, 16. It introduces a second clause as if μέν had stood in the first) **those that are** (the existing powers which we see about us), **have been ordained by God.** We may observe that the Apostle here pays no regard to the question of the duty of Christians in revolutionary move-

τασσόμενος τῇ [m] ἐξουσίᾳ τῇ τοῦ θεοῦ [r] διαταγῇ [s] ἀνθ-
έστηκεν· οἱ δὲ [s] ἀνθεστηκότες ἑαυτοῖς [t] κρίμα λήμψονται.
3 οἱ γὰρ [u] ἄρχοντες οὐκ εἰσὶν [v] φόβος τῷ [w] ἀγαθῷ [w] ἔργῳ,
ἀλλὰ τῷ κακῷ. θέλεις δὲ μὴ φοβεῖσθαι τὴν [m] ἐξουσίαν;
τὸ ἀγαθὸν ποίει, καὶ [x] ἕξεις [xy] ἔπαινον ἐξ αὐτῆς· 4 θεοῦ
γὰρ διάκονός ἐστιν σοὶ [z] εἰς [a] τὸ [za] ἀγαθόν. ἐὰν δὲ [b] τὸ
[b] κακὸν ποιῇς, φοβοῦ· οὐ γὰρ [c] εἰκῇ τὴν [d] μάχαιραν [e] φορεῖ·
θεοῦ γὰρ διάκονός ἐστιν, [f] ἔκδικος [g] εἰς [g] ὀργὴν τῷ [b] τὸ [b] κακὸν πράσσοντι. 5 διὸ [h] ἀνάγκη [o] ὑποτάσσεσθαι οὐ μόνον διὰ
τὴν ὀργήν, ἀλλὰ καὶ [i] διὰ τὴν [ik] συνείδησιν. 6 διὰ τοῦτο

r Acts vii. 53 only. Ezra iv. 11 only. see Gal. iii. 19.
s Acts vi. 10 reff.
t = ch. ii. 2 reff.
u = Matt. ix. 18. xx. 25 al. fr.
v = here only. Gen. xxxi. 42, 53. Isa. xxxiii. 3.
w sing., ch. ii. 7. plur., Acts ix. 36 reff.
x here only.
y ch. ii. 29 reff.
z ch. viii. 28. xv. 2. xvi. 19 only. see 1 Cor. xi. 17.
a ch. ii. 10 reff.
b ch. ii. 9 reff.
c [Matt. v. 22.] 1 Cor. xv. 2. Gal. iii. 4 (bis). iv. 11. Col. ii. 18 only. Prov. xxviii. 25 only.
d Acts xii. 2 reff.
e Matt. xi. 8. John xix. 5. 1 Cor. xv. 49 (bis). James ii. 3 only. Prov. xvi. 23, 27. Sir. xi. 5. xl. 4 only.
f 1 Thess. iv. 6 only †. Wisd. xii. 12. Sir. xxx. 6 only. (-κεῖν, -κησις, ch. xii. 19.)
g 1 Thess. v. 9.
h = Heb. ix. 16, 23.
i 1 Cor. x. 25, 27. 1 Pet. ii. 19.
k 2 Cor. i. 12 reff.

3. rec των αγαθων εργων α. των κακων, with D[3][-gr] L rel syrr [arm] Chr_1 Thdrt [Ambrst-ed]: txt ABD[1]F[P]ℵ latt copt goth ($Clem_1$) Damasc [($Orig\text{-}int_1$)] $Iren\text{-}int_1$ Cypr ($Tert_1$) Aug Pacian Sedul Bede.
4. om σοι F b[1] o 116. om 1st το B. om εις οργην D[1]F: εις οργην bef εκδικος D[3](and lat[3]) ℵ[1] b c f k n o 17 Chr_1 Thdrt.
5. om αναγκη (making υποτασσεσθαι = -σθε) DF [guelph spec] goth $Iren\text{-}int_1$ $Sedul_1$. om και F (but F-lat has *et*).

ments. His precepts regard an *established power*, be it what it may. *It*, in all matters lawful, *we are bound to obey*. But even the parental power does not extend to things unlawful. If the civil power commands us to violate the law of God, we must obey God before man. If it commands us to disobey the common laws of humanity, or the sacred institutions of our country, our obedience is due to the higher and more general law, rather than to the lower and particular. These distinctions must be drawn by the wisdom granted to Christians in the varying circumstances of human affairs: they are all only subordinate portions of the great duty of *obedience to* LAW. To obtain, by lawful means, the removal or alteration of an unjust or unreasonable law, is another part of this duty: for all authorities among men must be in accord with the highest authority, the moral sense. But even where law is hard and unreasonable, *not disobedience*, but *legitimate protest*, is the duty of the Christian. **2.] ἀντιτασσ.**, see above on ὑποτασσ. **ἑαυτοῖς κρίμα λ.] shall receive for themselves** (the dat. incommodi) **condemnation**, viz. *punishment from God*, through His minister, the civil power. **3.]** And the *tendency* of these powers is *salutary*: to encourage good works, and discourage evil. It is not *necessary* to set a note of interrogation after ἐξουσίαν: the clause may be treated as hypothetical,—see 1 Cor. vii. 18. Tholuck observes, that this verse is a token that the Apostle wrote the Epistle *before the commencement of the Neronian persecution*. Had this been *otherwise*, the *principle* stated by him would have been *the same*; but he could hardly have passed so apparent an exception to it without remark. **4.] τὴν μάχαιραν,** perhaps in allusion to the dagger worn by the Cæsars, which was regarded as a symbol of the power of life and death: so Tacitus, Hist. iii. 68, of Vitellius, "adsistenti Consuli exsolutum a latere pugionem, velut jus necis vitæque civium, reddebat." Dio Cassius also, xlii. 27, mentions the wearing of τὸ ξίφος on all occasions by Antony, as a sign that he τὴν μοναρχίαν ἐνεδείκνυτο. In ancient and modern times, the sword has been carried before sovereigns. It betokens the power of capital punishment: and the reference to it here is among the many testimonies borne by Scripture against the attempt to abolish the infliction of the penalty of death for crime in Christian states. **εἰς ὀργήν** seems to be inserted for the sake of parallelism with εἰς ἀγαθόν above: it betokens the *character* of the ἐκδίκησις,—that it *issues in wrath*. The ὀργή is referred to in τὴν ὀργήν, ver. 5. **5.] διό,** because of the divine appointment, and mission of the civil officer. **ἀνάγκη—ye must needs submit yourselves**—there is a moral necessity for subjection:—one not only of terror, but of conscience: compare διὰ τὸν κύριον, 1 Pet. ii. 13. **6.] διὰ τοῦτο . . καί** is *parallel with* διό, ver. 5,—giving *another* result of the divine appointment of the civil power;—not *dependent on*

γὰρ καὶ [l] φόρους [m] τελεῖτε· [n] λειτουργοὶ γὰρ θεοῦ εἰσιν εἰς ABDF
[o] αὐτὸ [o] τοῦτο [p] προσκαρτεροῦντες. 7 [q] ἀπόδοτε πᾶσιν τὰς L[P]א abcdf
[r] ὀφειλάς, τῷ [s] τὸν [l] φόρον τὸν [l] φόρον, τῷ τὸ [t] τέλος τὸ ghkl mno17
[t] τέλος, τῷ τὸν φόβον τὸν φόβον, τῷ τὴν τιμὴν τὴν [47]
τιμήν. 8 Μηδενὶ μηδὲν ὀφείλετε, εἰ μὴ τὸ ἀλλήλους
ἀγαπᾷν. ὁ γὰρ ἀγαπῶν [u] τὸν ἕτερον νόμον [v] πεπλήρωκεν·
9 τὸ γὰρ [w] οὐ μοιχεύσεις, οὐ φονεύσεις, οὐ κλέψεις, οὐκ
ἐπιθυμήσεις, καὶ [x] εἴ τις [x] ἑτέρα ἐντολή, ἐν τῷ λόγῳ
τούτῳ [y] ἀνακεφαλαιοῦται, [ἐν [z] τῷ] [a] ἀγαπήσεις [b] τὸν [b] πλησίον σου ὡς σεαυτόν. 10 ἡ ἀγάπη [b] τῷ [b] πλησίον κακὸν

l here 3ce. Luke xx. 22. xxiii. 2 only. Judg. i. 28.
m = Matt. xvii. 24 only ‡. (ch. ii. 27 al.)
n ch. xv. 16. Phil. ii. 25. Heb. i. 7 (from Ps. ciii. 4). viii. 2 only. Josh. i. 1 (A Ald.). 3 Kings x. 5.
o Acts xxiv. 15 reff.
p Acts i. 14 reff.
q ch. xii. 17 reff.
r Matt. xviii. 32. 1 Cor. vii. 3 only †. (-ημα, ch. iv. 4.)
s ellips., 2 Cor. viii. 15. Phil. iii. 14. Winer, edn. 6, § 64. i. 4.
t = here bis. Matt. xvii. 25 only. Num. xxxi. 28, &c. 1 Macc. x. 31.
u ch. ii. 1 reff.
v = ch. viii. 4 al.
w Exod. xx. 13, &c.
x 1 Tim. i. 10.
y Eph. i. 10 only †. Ps. lxxi. 20 Theod. [and Quinta Ed.]
z Gal. v. 14. see ch. viii. 26 reff.
a Levit. xix. 18.
b ch. xv. 2. Matt. v. 43. xix. 19 al. fr. Exod. ii. 13.

7. rec aft *αποδοτε* ins *ουν*, with D[3][and lat] FL[P]א[3] rel [47(sic) vulg-clem(with fuld harl) goth arm] syrr Chr$_1$ Thl Œc Ambrst: om AB D[1][-gr] א[1] am(with demid tol) coptt (Orig$_2$[-int$_4$]) Damasc Cypr$_1$) Aug$_{\text{sæpe}}$ Cassiod$_1$.

8. *οφιλοντες* א[1] c [Orig$_1$]: -*λητε* א[3]: -*λειτε* B[1](Tischdf). rec *αγαπαν* bef *αλληλους* (*corrn of order to agree with next clause?*), with L rel syr coptt [æth] Thl Œc: txt ABDF[P]א m latt Syr [goth] arm Orig$_2$[-int$_2$] Chr$_1$ Thdrt Damasc Cypr$_1$.

9. for *το γαρ*, *γεγραπται γαρ* F Ambr$_2$. [*μοιχευσης*, *κλεψης* &c P.] rec aft *κλεψεις* ins *ου ψευδομαρτυρησεις* (*corrn to the decalogue*), with [P]א rel [vulg-clem (with demid harl) syr æth arm] copt Chr$_1$ Œc [Orig-int$_1$]: var transp al: txt ABDFL c g l 17 [47] am(with fuld tol al) Syr sah [goth] Clem$_2$ Orig$_2$ [Thdrt Damasc Ambr$_2$ Aug$_{\text{sæpe}}$ Ambrst]. aft *ετερα* ins *εστιν* [A]א[1](א[3] disapproving) [17 vulg D-lat F-lat Damasc Orig-int$_1$]. rec *τουτω* bef *τω λογω*, with AL[P] rel Clem$_2$ Dial$_1$ Cyr[-p$_1$ Chr$_1$ Thdrt Damasc]: txt BDFא d m Orig$_2$. om 2nd *εν τω* BF latt [Orig-int$_1$ Ambrst]: om *εν* Clem$_1$ Orig$_1$: ins ADL[P]א rel vss Clem$_2$ Orig$_2$ Chr Thdrt [Damasc]. rec (for *σεαυ.*) *εαυτον*, with F[LP] rel Chr Cyr[-p$_1$] Thl Œc: mss of Clem Dial vary: *σαυτον* g[1]: txt ABDא b c d h o Orig$_2$ Thdrt Damasc.

ver. 5. **τελεῖτε** is indicative, not imperative: the command follows ver. 7. **For they** (the ἄρχοντες) **are ministers of God, attending upon this very duty,** viz. λειτουργεῖν,—hardly (as Koppe, Olsh., Meyer) φόρους τελεῖν, for in ver. 7 the Apostle has evidently in view the whole official character of these λειτουργοί. Reiche, al., construe, "For those who wait upon this very thing are ministers of God," which would require **οἱ** εἰς αὐτ. τ. προσκ.:—Koppe, 'For λειτουργοί are of God:'—but this again would require οἱ γὰρ λειτ.—Tertullian remarks, Apolog. xlii. vol. i. p. 494, that what the Romans lost by the Christians refusing to bestow gifts on their temples, they gained by their conscientious payment of taxes. 7.] Before the accusatives supply αἰτοῦντι, as the correlative of ἀπόδοτε. **φόρος** is **tax**, or **tribute**,—*direct* payment for state purposes: **τέλος**, **custom**, **toll**, *vectigal*. **φόβος**, to those set over us and having power: **τιμή**, to those, but likewise to all on whom the state has conferred distinction. 8—10.] *Exhortation to universal love of others.* 8.] **ὀφείλετε** is not indic. (as Koppe, Reiche, al.), which would require οὐδενὶ οὐδέν,—and would be inconsistent with the ὀφειλαί just mentioned,—but imperative: '*Pay* all other debts: *be indebted* in the matter of love *alone*.' This debt increases the more, the more it is paid: because the practice of love makes the principle of love deeper and more active. Aug., Ep. cxcii. (lxii.), ad Cœlest. vol. ii. p. 868, says: "Redditur enim (caritas), cum impenditur, debetur autem etiam si reddita fuerit; quia nullum est tempus quando impendenda jam non sit. Nec cum redditur amittitur, sed potius reddendo multiplicatur." **πεπλήρωκεν**, **hath** (in the act) **fulfilled**: compare the perfects, John iii. 18; ch. xiv. 23. **νόμον** is not the Christian law, but *the Mosaic law* of the decalogue. "This recommendation of Love has, as also the similar one, Gal. v. 23, κατὰ τῶν τοιούτων οὐκ ἔστιν νόμος,—an apologetic reference to the upholders of the law, and depends on this evident axiom,—'He who practises Love, *the higher duty*, has, even before he does this, fulfilled the law, *the lower*.'" De Wette. 9.] **ἀνακεφαλ.**, **brought under one head**,—'united in the one principle from which all flow.' 10.] All the commandments of the law above cited are *negative*: the formal fulfilment

C ουν νομου... ABCD FL[P]א a b c d f g h k l m n o 17 [47]

οὐκ [c] ἐργάζεται· [d] πλήρωμα οὖν νόμου ἡ ἀγάπη. 11 [e] καὶ
[e] τοῦτο εἰδότες τὸν καιρόν, ὅτι [f] ὥρα [g] ἤδη ὑμᾶς ἐξ ὕπνου
[h] ἐγερθῆναι· νῦν γὰρ [i] ἐγγύτερον ἡμῶν ἡ σωτηρία ἢ ὅτε
[k] ἐπιστεύσαμεν. 12 ἡ νὺξ [l] προέκοψεν, ἡ δὲ ἡμέρα [m] ἤγγικεν·
[n] ἀποθώμεθα οὖν τὰ [o] ἔργα τοῦ [o] σκότους, [p] ἐνδυσώμεθα

c = ch. ii. 10 reff. d = here only ‡. (ch. xi. 12, 25.) e 1 Cor. vi. 6, 8. Eph. ii. 8. Phil. i. 28. 3 John 5. f = John xii. 23. Rev. xiv. 15. and constr., Gen. xxix. 7. g = ch. i. 10. h = Eph. v. 14. Prov. vi. 9. i = Matt. xxiv. 32 al. Ezek. xxx. 3. comp., here only. k = Acts xix. 2. 1 Cor. iii. 5. xv. 2. Eph. i. 13. l Luke ii. 52. Gal. i. 14. 2 Tim. ii. 16. iii. 9, 13 only. L.P.† Ps. xliv. 5, Incert. in Hexapl. [? Symm.] (-κοπή, Phil. i. 12.) m = Matt. iii. 2. xxi. 34. Lam. iv. 18. n Acts vii. 58 reff. = Col. iii. 8. o Eph. v. 11 only. see John vi. 28, 29. viii. 39, 41. Gal. v. 19. 1 Thess. i. 3. p = 1 Cor. xv. 53, 54 reff.

10. om *η αγ.* to *εργαζ.* A [Cyr$_1$(appy)]. for *ουκ εργ.*, *ου κατεργ.* D^1 b f 17. for *ουν*, *δε* D^1[and lat] F spec Aug$_{sæpe}$(txt$_1$) : *γαρ* 115 [Ambrst] : *quia* Syr : om [P] 93 lect-12.

11. *ιδοντες* A^1 F[-gr] G^2[-gr]. rec *ημας* bef *ηδη* (*corrn for euphony ?*), with FL rel goth Clem$_1$ Chr$_1$ Thdrt Thl Œc : [*ηδη* bef *ωρα* P: om *ηδη* Syr æth arm :] txt ABCDא m vulg Damasc Jer$_1$ Ambrst.—rec **ημας**, with DFLא^3 rel [vulg Syr coptt goth arm Chr Thdrt Damasc] : om syr [æth Orig-int$_1$] : txt A B(sic : see table) C[P]א^1 d m [Clem$_1$. **υμων** P k.]

12. *ηγγισεν* A. for *αποθωμ.*, *αποβαλωμεθα* D$^{1\cdot3}$F [*abjiciamus* latt Orig-int$_1$ Cypr$_1$ Ambrst]. rec for *ενδυσ. δε*, *και ενδυσ.* (*corrn, no contrast seeming to be implied*), with C^{3}D$^{2\cdot3}$FLא^3 rel [vulg æth arm] Chr$_1$ Cyr$_1$[txt-p$_2$] Thdrt Cypr$_1$

of them is therefore attained, by *working no ill* to one's neighbour. What *greater things* Love works, he does not now say : it *fulfils the law*, by *abstaining from that which the law forbids*. 11—14.] *Enforcement of the foregoing, and occasion taken for fresh exhortations, by the consideration that* THE DAY OF THE LORD IS AT HAND. **11.] καὶ τοῦτο, and this**, i. e. '*and let us do this*,' viz., live in no debt but that of love (see reff.), for other reasons, and especially for this following one. **ὥρα ἤδη ἐγερθῆναι]** "The Inf. Aor. here, as after verbs of willing, ordering, &c., betokens the *completion* of the act in question. See Winer, § 45. 8 (edn. 6, § 44. 7)." De Wette. **ὕπνος** here = the state of worldly carelessness and indifference to sin, which allows and practises the ἔργα τοῦ σκότους. The imagery seems to be taken originally from our Lord's discourse concerning His coming : see Matt. xxiv. 42 : Mark xiii. 33, and Luke xxi. 28—36, where several points of similarity to our vv. 11—14 occur. **ἐγγύτ. ἡμ. ἡ σωτ. ἢ ὅτε ἐπιστ.]** σωτηρία, as ἀπολύτρωσις Luke xxi. 28, and ch. viii. 23, of the *accomplishment of salvation*. **ἡμῶν** [is best] taken with ἐγγύτερον, '*nearer to us*,' see ch. x. 8, [though] ἐγγίζει ἡ ἀπολύτρωσις ὑμῶν, Luke xxi. 28, seems [at first sight] to favour the usual connexion with σωτηρία. **ἐπιστ.] we first believed** ;—see reff. Without denying the legitimacy of an individual application of this truth, and the importance of its consideration for all Christians of all ages, a fair exegesis of this passage can hardly fail to recognize the fact, that the Apostle here as well as elsewhere (1 Thess. iv. 17 ; 1 Cor. xv. 51), speaks of the coming of the Lord as *rapidly approaching*. Prof. Stuart, Comm. p. 521, is shocked at the idea, as being inconsistent with the inspiration of his writings. How this can be, I am at a loss to imagine. "OF THAT DAY AND HOUR KNOWETH NO MAN, NO NOT THE ANGELS IN HEAVEN, NOR [EVEN] THE SON : BUT THE FATHER ONLY." Mark xiii. 32. And to reason, as Stuart does, that because Paul corrects in 2 Thess. ii. the mistake of imagining it to be *immediately at hand* (or even *actually come*, see note on ἐνέστηκεν there), therefore he did not himself expect it soon, is surely quite beside the purpose. The fact, that the nearness or distance of that day was *unknown to the Apostles*, in no way affects the prophetic announcements of God's Spirit by them, concerning its preceding and accompanying circumstances. The '*day and hour*' formed no part of their inspiration :—the *details of the event, did*. And this distinction has singularly and providentially turned out to the edification of all subsequent ages. While the prophetic declarations of the events of that time remain to instruct us, the *eager expectation* of the time, which *they expressed in their day*, has also remained, a token of the true frame of mind in which each succeeding age (and each succeeding age *a fortiori*) should contemplate the ever-approaching coming of the Lord. On the *certainty of the event*, our faith is grounded : by the *uncertainty of the time* our hope is stimulated, and our watchfulness aroused. See Prolegg. to Vol. III. ch. v. § iv. 5—10. **12.] ἡ νύξ**, the *lifetime of the world*,—the *power*

δὲ τὰ [q] ὅπλα τοῦ φωτός. 13 ὡς ἐν [r] ἡμέρᾳ [st] εὐσχημόνως ABCD
[s] περιπατήσωμεν, μὴ [uvw] κώμοις καὶ [uwx] μέθαις, μὴ [wy] κοί- FL[P]א abcdf
ταις καὶ [wz] ἀσελγείαις, μὴ [wab] ἔριδι καὶ [wbc] ζήλῳ· 14 ἀλλὰ ghkl mno17
[p] ἐνδύσασθε τὸν κύριον Ἰησοῦν χριστόν, καὶ τῆς σαρκὸς [47]
[d] πρόνοιαν μὴ ποιεῖσθε [e] εἰς [f] ἐπιθυμίας.

XIV. 1 Τὸν δὲ [g] ἀσθενοῦντα τῇ [g] πίστει [h] προςλαμβά-

q ch. vi. 13 reff. r = 1 Thess. v. 5, 8. 2 Pet. i. 19. s 1 Thess. iv. 12. t as above (s). 1 Cor. xiv. 40 only +. (-μων, -μοσύνη, 1 Cor. xii. 23, 24.) u Gal. v. 21. v as above (u). 1 Pet. iv. 8 only +. Wisd. xiv. 23. 2 Macc. vi. 4 only. w dat., ch. iv. 12. x as above (u). Luke xxi. 34 only. Isa. xxviii. 7. Hag. i. 6. Judith xiii. 15. y ch. ix. 10 reff. plur., here only. z Mark vii. 22. 2 Cor. xii. 21. 1 Pet. iv. 3 al.+ Wisd. xiv. 26 only. a 1 Cor. i. 11 reff. b 1 Cor. iii. 3. 2 Cor. xii. 20. Gal. v. 20. Sir. xl. 5. c = Acts xiii. 45 reff. d Acts xxiv. 2 only (reff.). e = ver. 4 al. f ch. i. 24 reff. g ch. iv. 19 (reff.). h = Acts xxviii. 2 reff.

[Ambrst]: ενδυσ. (only) א[1] [sah-ms]: txt ABC[1]D[1][P sah-woide] copt goth $Clem_1$ Damasc [$Orig\text{-}int_1$]. for υπλα, εργα A D[and lat[1]].

13. ερισι κ. ζηλοις B [sah ($Cypr_1$)] $Ambr_2$.

14. (αλλα, so ABD[3]א.) om κυριον B [$Clem_1$]: add ημων sah. χρ. bef ιησ. B goth: om χρ. c k Ambr. om και D[1]F. aft σαρκ. ins ημων sah. εν επιθυμιαις F latt [$Orig\text{-}int_3$(txt_1) Ambrst Aug_1]: εις επιθυμιαν AC Ath_1 Thdrt-ms-comm Damasc: εν επιθυμια $Ambr_1$: txt BD[LP]א rel $Ps\text{-}Ign_1$ $Clem_1$ Chr_1 [Bas_1 $Cyr\text{-}p_1$] Thdrt Thl Œc.

of darkness, see Eph. vi. 12: **ἡ ἡμέρα**, the *day of the resurrection*, 1 Thess. v. 4; Rev. xxi. 25; of which resurrection we are *already partakers* and are to *walk as such*, Col. iii. 1—4; 1 Thess. v. 5—8. **Therefore,—let us lay aside** (as it were a clothing) **the works of darkness** (see Eph. v. 11—14, where a similar strain of exhortation occurs), **and put on** (δέ corresponding to an understood μέν) **the armour of light** (described Eph. vi. 11 ff.—the arms *belonging to a soldier of light*—one who is of the υἱοὶ φωτός and υἱοὶ ἡμέρας, 1 Thess. v. 5,—not, as Grot. 'arma splendentia'). **13.**] **κοίταις**, in a bad sense: the act itself being a defilement, when unsanctified by God's ordinance of marriage. See reff. **ἀσελγείαις**, plural of *various kinds* of wantonness: so ὑποκρίσεις, φθόνους, καταλαλιάς, 1 Pet. ii. 1. **14.**] Chrys. says, on Eph. iv. 24, οὕτω καὶ ἐπὶ φίλων λέγομεν, ὁ δεῖνα τὸν δεῖνα ἐνεδύσατο, τὴν πολλὴν ἀγάπην λέγοντες, κ. τὴν ἀδιάλειπτον συνουσίαν. See examples in Wetst. The last clause is to be read, τῆς σαρκὸς πρόνοιαν μὴ ποιεῖσθε | εἰς ἐπιθυμίας,—not τῆς σαρκὸς πρόνοιαν | μὴ ποιεῖσθε εἰς ἐπιθυμίας,—and rendered, **Take not** (any) **forethought for the flesh, to fulfil its lusts**, not '*Take not your forethought for the flesh, so, as to fulfil its lusts*' (Wartet des Leibes, doch also, daß er nicht geil werde, Luth.). This latter would be τὴν πρόνοιαν τ. σαρκ. μὴ π. εἰς ἐπιθ.,—or τῆς σ. πρόν. ποιεῖσθε μὴ εἰς ἐπιθ.: see construction of the next verse. Chap. XIV. **1—XV. 13.**] On the conduct to be pursued towards weak and scrupulous brethren. There is some doubt who the ἀσθενοῦντες τῇ πίστει were, of whom the Apostle here treats; whether they were *ascetics*, or *Judaizers*. Some habits mentioned, as e. g. the abstinence from *all meats*, and from *wine*, seem to indicate the former: whereas the *observation of days*, and the use of such expressions as κοινόν [ver. 14], and again the argument of ch. xv. 7—13, as plainly point to the latter. The difficulty may be solved by a proper combination of the two views. The over-scrupulous Jew *became an ascetic by compulsion.* He was afraid of pollution by eating meats sacrificed or wine poured to idols: or even by being brought into contact, in foreign countries, with casual and undiscoverable uncleanness, which in his own land he knew the articles offered for food would be sure not to have incurred. He therefore abstained from *all prepared food*, and confined himself to that which he could trace from natural growth to his own use. We have examples of this in Daniel (Dan. i.), Tobit (Tob. i. 10, 11), [and in] some Jewish priests mentioned by Josephus, Life, § 3, who having been sent prisoners to Rome, οὐκ ἐξελάθοντο τῆς εἰς τὸ θεῖον εὐσεβείας, διετρέφοντο δὲ σύκοις καὶ καρύοις. And Tholuck refers to the Mishna as containing precepts to this effect. All difficulty then is removed, by supposing that of these over-scrupulous Jews some had become converts to the gospel, and with neither the obstinacy of legal Judaizers, nor the pride of ascetics (for these are not hinted at here), but in *weakness of faith*, and the scruples of an over-tender conscience, retained their habits of abstinence and observation of days. On this account the Apostle characterizes and treats them mildly: not with the severity which he employs towards the Colossian Judaizing ascetics and those mentioned in 1 Tim. iv. 1 ff. The question treated in

νεσθε μὴ εἰς [i] διακρίσεις [k] διαλογισμῶν.
2 [l] ὃς μὲν [m] πιστεύει φαγεῖν πάντα, [l] ὁ δὲ [g] ἀσθενῶν [n] λάχανα ἐσθίει.
3 ὁ ἐσθίων τὸν μὴ ἐσθίοντα μὴ [o] ἐξουθενείτω, ὁ δὲ μὴ ἐσθίων τὸν ἐσθίοντα μὴ [p] κρινέτω· ὁ θεὸς γὰρ αὐτὸν [h] προσελάβετο.
4 σὺ τίς εἶ ὁ [p] κρίνων [q] ἀλλότριον [r] οἰκέτην;

i 1 Cor. xii. 10. Heb. v. 14 only. Job xxxvii. 16 only.
k ch. i. 21. 1 Cor. iii. 20 (from Ps. xciii. 11). James ii. 4 al.
l here only. see Matt. xiii. 8. ch. ix. 21 al.
m = Acts xv. 11 reff.
n Matt. xiii. 32 ||. Luke xi. 42 only. Gen. ix. 3.
o = Luke xviii. 9. Acts iv. 11. ver. 10. 1 Cor. i. 28. vi. 4 al. Prov. i. 7.
p = Matt. vii. 1. ch. ii. 1 &c. Col. ii. 16. James iv. 11.
q Luke xvi. 12. John x. 5. Acts vii. 6. ch. xv. 20. 2 Cor. x. 15, 16. Ps. cviii. 11.
r Luke xvi. 13. Acts x. 7. 1 Pet. ii. 18 only. Gen. ix. 25.

Chap. XIV. 2. **ος** δε ασθ. F. εσθι**ετω** D^1F latt[(not D^1-lat) arm] Ambrst [$Aug_{sæpe}$].

3. for εξουθεν., κρινετω A 68 lect-5 [$Orig\text{-}int_1$]. rec (for ο δε μη) και ο μη, with D^3L[P]$\aleph^3$ rel vulg [syrr sah æth Bas_1] $Epiph_1$ Thdrt Thl Œc [$Orig\text{-}int_2$ Aug_1 Ambrst]: ουδε ο μη (omg μη aft) F: txt ABC$D^1\aleph^1$ goth $Clem_2$ Damasc. γαρ bef θεος L 77.

1 Cor. viii. was somewhat different: there it was, concerning meat *actually offered* to an idol. In 1 Cor. x. 25—27, he touches the same question as here, and decides against the stricter view. See the whole matter discussed in Tholuck's Comm. in loc., De Wette's Handbuch, and Stuart's Introd. to this chap. in his commentary. 1—12.] *Exhortation to mutual forbearances, enforced by the axiom, that every man must serve God according to his own sincere persuasion.* 1.] *The general duty of a reconciling and uncontroversial spirit towards the weak in faith.* The **δέ** binds this on to the *general* exhortations to mutual charity in ch. xiii.: q. d. 'in the particular case of the weak in faith,' &c.: but also implies a contrast, which seems to be, in allusion to the Christian perfection enjoined in the preceding verses,—'but do not let your own realization of your state as children of light make you intolerant of short-coming and infirmity in others.' **ἀσθ.**, see reff.: the particular weakness consisted in a want of broad and independent principle, and a consequent bondage to prejudices. **πίστις** therefore is used in a general sense, to indicate the moral soundness conferred by faith,—the whole character of the Christian's conscience and practice, resting on faith. **τῇ**, better **the faith,** than '*his* faith:' '*weak* in his (subj.) faith' would be opposed to '*strong* in his (subj.) faith, '*his faith*,' remaining in substance the same: whereas here the (subj.) *faith itself* is weak, and 'weak in the faith' = holding THE FAITH imperfectly, i. e. not being able to receive the faith in its strength, so as to be above such prejudices. **προσλαμβ.**] '*give him your hand*,' as Syr. (Thol.): 'count him one of you:' opposed to rejecting or discouraging him. **μὴ εἰς**] **but not with a view to**: 'do not adopt him as a brother, in order then to begin' . . . **διακρίσ. διαλ.**] **discernments of thoughts,** lit.: i. e. *disputes in order to settle the points on which he has scruples.*' In both the reff., διάκρισις has the meaning of '*discernment of*,' 'the power of distinguishing between.' And **διαλογισμοί** in the N. T. implies (ordinarily in a bad sense), '*thoughts*:' what kind of thoughts, the context must determine. Here, evidently, *those scruples in him*, in which his weakness consists,—and *those more enlightened views in you*, by which you would fain remove his scruples. Do not let your association of him among you be *with a view to settle these disputes*. The above ordinary meanings of the words seem to satisfy the sense, and to agree better with εἰς than 'ad altercationes disputationum,' as Beza, or 'ad certamina cogitationum,' as Estius:—and are adopted by most of the ancient and modern Commentators. 2.] The **ὃς μέν**, the strong in faith, so indicated by what follows, is opposed to ὁ δὲ ἀσθενῶν (not to be taken ὁ δὲ, ἀσθενῶν, κ.τ.λ.), by which τὸν ἀσθενοῦντα of ver. 1 is resumed. **πιστεύει φαγεῖν**, either **believes that he may** (ἐξεῖναι) **eat,**—or **ventures to eat.** The latter is favoured by ref. Acts, πιστεύομεν σωθῆναι, '*we trust to be saved*;' though that also may be expanded into 'we believe that we shall be saved,' as E. V. **λάχ. ἐσθ.**] See remarks introductory to this chapter. 3.] There is no need to supply πάντα after ἐσθ. and μὴ ἐσθ. I would rather take ὁ ἐσθ. as **the eater,** and ὁ μὴ ἐσθ. **the abstainer.** **ἐξουθ.**, for his weakness of faith,—**κρινέτω**, for his laxity of practice. **For God has accepted** (adopted into his family) **him** (i. e. the *eater*, who was *judged*,—his place in God's family doubted: *not the abstainer*, who was only despised, set at nought,—and to whom the words cannot, by the construction, apply. 4.] **Who art thou** (see ch. ix. 20) **that judgest the servant of another** (viz. as De W., of *Christ*,—for a κύριος in this passage is marked, vv. 8, 9.

τῷ ἰδίῳ κυρίῳ [s] στήκει ἢ [t] πίπτει. [u] σταθήσεται δέ, [v] δυνατεῖ γὰρ ὁ κύριος [w] στῆσαι αὐτόν. 5 [x] ὃς μὲν [y] κρίνει
ἡμέραν [z] παρ' ἡμέραν, [x] ὃς δὲ [y] κρίνει πᾶσαν ἡμέραν.
ἕκαστος ἐν τῷ ἰδίῳ νοῒ [a] πληροφορείσθω. 6 ὁ [b] φρονῶν

ABCD FL[P]א abcd ghkl mno17 [47]

s Paul (1 Cor. xvi. 13. Gal. v. 1. Phil. i. 27. iv. 1. 1 Thess. iii. 8. 2 Thess. ii. 15) only, exc. Mark iii. 31. xi. 25. Exod. xiv. 13 A compl. t = ch. xi. 11, 22. 1 Cor. x. 12. Prov. xi. 28. u 2 Cor. xiii. 1. 2 Cor. ix. 8. xiii. 3 only †. w = here only? see ch. iii. 31. Ps. cxviii. 38. x 1 Cor. xi. 21 reff. see ver. 2. y = Acts xiii. 46 reff. z = ch. i. 25. Luke xiii. 2. Ps. cxxxiv. 5. a = ch. iv. 21 (Col. iv. 12. 2 Tim. iv. 5, 17. Luke i. 1) only. Eccles. viii. 11 only. (-ρία, Col. ii. 2.) b see ch. viii. 5 reff.

4. rec *δυνατος γαρ εστιν* (*more usual expression*), with L rel Thdrt [Damasc: *δυνατι γαρ εστιν* D^3(appy)]: *δυνατος γαρ*, omg *εστιν*, D^2[P] syr(adding *εστιν* with ob) Bas_1 Chr_1: txt ABCD^1Fא. rec for *κυριος*, *θεος* (*corrn to suit ver* 3? *θεος there does not vary*), with DFL [rel] latt syr Chr_1 Thdrt [Bas-ed Damasc $Cypr_2$ Aug_{alic} Ambrst]: txt ABC[P]א Syr(addg *αυτου*) coptt goth arm [Bas-mss_1 $Orsies_1$] Aug_1 Opt.

5. aft *ος μεν* ins *γαρ* AC[P]$א^1$ latt goth [Bas_1 Damasc] Ambrst: om BDFL$א^3$ rel [syrr copt æth arm Chr_1 Orig-int_1] Dial Aug_2 Jer_2. om *εν* A 38. 54 fuld Chr_1 Thdrt.

as being Christ,—and the Master is the same throughout. *ὁ θεός* before is unconnected with this verse)? **to his own Master** (dat. commodi or incommodi according as *στ.* or *πίπτ.* befalls: 'it is his own master's matter, and his alone, that') **he stands** ('remains in the place and estimation of a Christian, from which thou wouldest eject him;' not, as Calv., Grot., Estius, Wolf, al., 'stands hereafter in the judgment,' which is not in question here: see 1 Cor. x. 12) **or falls** (from his place, see above): **but he shall be made to stand** (notwithstanding thy doubts of the correctness of his practice): **for the Lord** (or, *his Lord*, in allusion to *τῷ ἰδίῳ κυρίῳ* above) **is able to make him stand** (in faith and practice. These last words are inapplicable, if standing and falling at the great day are meant). Notice, this argument is entirely directed *to* the *weak*, who uncharitably judges the *strong*,—not vice versâ. The *weak* imagines that the *strong* cannot be a true servant of God, nor retain his steadfastness amidst such temptation. To this the Apostle answers, (1) that *such judgment belongs only to Christ, whose servant he is:* (2) that *the Lord's Almighty Power is able to keep him up, and will do so.*

* **5.**] **One man** (the weak) **esteems** (selects for honour,—*κρίνει ἀξίαν τιμῆς*) (one) **day above** (reff.) (another) **day**; **another** (the strong) **esteems** (*ἀξίαν τιμῆς*) **every day. Let each be fully satisfied in his own mind.** It is an interesting question, what indication is here found of the observance or non-observance of a day of obligation in the apostolic times. The Apostle *decides nothing;* leaving *every man's own mind* to guide him in the point. He classes the observance or non-observance of particular days, with the eating or abstaining from particular meats. In both cases, he is concerned with things which he evidently treats as of *absolute indifference in themselves.* Now the question is, supposing the divine obligation of one day in seven to have been recognized by him *in any form*, could he have thus spoken? The obvious inference from his strain of arguing is, that he *knew of no such obligation*, but believed *all times and days to be*, to the Christian strong in faith, ALIKE. I do not see how the passage can be otherwise understood. If any one day in the week were invested with the sacred character of the Sabbath, it would have been *wholly impossible* for the Apostle to commend or uphold the man who judged all days worthy of equal honour,—who as in ver. 6 paid *no regard* to the (any) day. He must have visited him with his strongest disapprobation, as violating a command of God. *I therefore infer, that sabbatical obligation to keep any day, whether seventh or first, was not recognized in apostolic times.* It must be carefully remembered, that this inference does not concern the question of the observance of *the Lord's Day* as *an institution of the Christian Church, analogous to* the ancient Sabbath, binding on us from considerations of *humanity* and *religious expediency*, and *by the rules of that branch of the Church in which Providence has placed us*, but not in any way inheriting the divinely-appointed obligation of the other, or the strict prohibitions by which its sanctity was defended. The reply commonly furnished to these considerations, viz. that the Apostle was speaking here only of *Jewish* festivals, and therefore cannot refer to Christian ones, is a quibble of the poorest kind: its assertors themselves distinctly maintaining the obligation of one such Jewish festival on Christians. What I maintain is, that had the Apostle believed as they do, he could not by any possibility have written thus. Besides, in the face of **πᾶσαν ἡμέραν**, the assertion is altogether unfounded.

6.] The words in brackets were probably omitted from the similar ending

τὴν ἡμέραν [c] κυρίῳ [b] φρονεῖ[, καὶ ὁ μὴ [b] φρονῶν τὴν
ἡμέραν, [c] κυρίῳ οὐ [b] φρονεῖ]. καὶ ὁ ἐσθίων [c] κυρίῳ ἐσθίει,
[d] εὐχαριστεῖ γὰρ τῷ θεῷ· καὶ ὁ μὴ ἐσθίων [c] κυρίῳ οὐκ
ἐσθίει καὶ [d] εὐχαριστεῖ τῷ θεῷ.
7 οὐδεὶς γὰρ ἡμῶν [c] ἑαυτῷ
ζῇ, καὶ οὐδεὶς [c] ἑαυτῷ ἀποθνήσκει·
8 ἐάν τε γὰρ ζῶμεν,
[c] τῷ κυρίῳ ζῶμεν, ἐάν τε ἀποθνήσκωμεν, [c] τῷ κυρίῳ
ἀποθνήσκομεν. ἐάν τε οὖν ζῶμεν ἐάν τε ἀποθνήσκωμεν,
[e] τοῦ κυρίου ἐσμέν.
9 [f] εἰς τοῦτο γὰρ χριστὸς ἀπέθανεν
καὶ [g] ἔζησεν, [f] ἵνα καὶ νεκρῶν καὶ ζώντων [h] κυριεύσῃ.
10 σὺ

c dat., ch. vi. 2, 10 al. Winer. edn. 6, § 31. 4. b. τῷ πατρὶ ζῶντες, Dion. Hal. iii. p. 153. θεοῖς τέθνηκεν οὗτος, Soph. Aj. 990.
d ch. i. 8 reff.
e = gen., 1 Cor. iii. 23 reff.
f (Mark i. 38.) John xviii. 37. Acts ix. 21. 1 John iii. 8 al.
g = Rev. ii. 8. xx. 4. 4 Kings xiii. 21. vi. 15 only. L.P. Gen. iii. 16.
h Luke xxii. 25. ch. vi. 9, 14, vii. 1. 2 Cor. i. 24. 2 Tim.

6. om *και ο μη φρ. την ημ. κ. ου φρ.* (*homœotel*) ABC^{1}DFℵ vulg copt æth [Orig-int$_1$] Ambrst Aug$_2$; om from *ημεραν* to *ημεραν* 66^1, from *εσθιει* to *εσθιει* 71-3 lect-19: from *τω θεω* to *τω θεω* L: ins C^{3}L[P] rel syrr [arm] Bas$_1$ Chr-txt$_1$ Thdrt-txt Damasc Phot$_1$ Thl Œc. rec om *και* (bef *ο εσθ.*) [with 47]: ins ABCDFL[P]ℵ rel [vulg syrr copt æth arm] Bas Chr Thdrt Damasc Thl Œc [Orig-int$_1$] Ambrst Pel. [for *ευχ. γαρ*, *και ευχ.* P c Syr arm(Tischdf) Clem$_1$ Isid$_1$ Damasc.] for 1st *θεω*, *κυριω* A 52: *Creatori* Ambrst.

8. for 1st *αποθνησκωμεν*, *αποθνησκομεν* ADF[P 47] a^1 Ephr$_1$ Damasc: *αποθανωμεν* CL l o 17: (*both appear to be corrns: the former for uniformity, imagining that ζωμεν, ζωμεν were both indic; the latter for the sense, as representing the state after death:*) *αποθανομεν* n: txt Bℵ rel Chr$_1$ *Cyr*[-p] Thdrt. om 2nd *τω* F. for *αποθνησκομεν*, *αποθνησκωμεν* [CL]ℵ d^1 k [Chr-ms]. aft last *εαν τε* ins *ουν* F. for 2nd *αποθνησκωμεν*, *αποθνησκομεν* ADF[P] f m^1 n [47 Ephr$_1$] Thl: *αποθανωμεν* 108-35. 219: txt BCLℵ 17 rel Chr$_1$ *Cyr*[-p Damasc] Thdrt.

9. rec ins *και* bef *απεθανεν*, with C^{3}D^{2}Lℵ^3 rel am [Syr] syr Chr$_2$ Thdrt Thl Œc [Iren-int$_1$ Orig-int$_1$ Fulg$_1$]: om A[appy] BC^{1}D$^{1.3}$F[P]ℵ^1 a c g 17 vulg copt [æth arm] Orig$_3$[-int$_1$] Cyr-jer$_1$ Chr$_1$ Cyr[-p] Anast$_1$ Damasc [Ambrst] Sedul. rec ins *και ανεστη* bef *κ. εζησεν* (*see notes*), with L[D^{2}P]ℵ^3 rel [syr Ephr$_1$ Chr$_1$] Thl Œc: aft, Syr: ins *και ανεστη*, putting *εζησ.* bef *κ. απεθ. κ. ανεστη* D$^{1.3}$ Iren-int$_1$ Gaud$_1$: om ABCFℵ^1 fuld-vict syr copt [æth] arm Dion Cyr-jer$_1$ Chr$_1$ Cyr$_{sæpe}$ Anast$_1$ Damasc [Orig-int$_2$].—rec **ανεζησεν**, with Thdrt: *ανεστη* F vulg Orig$_3$ Pel Fulg: txt ABCDL[P] ℵ rel.

φρονεῖ of both clauses having misled some early copyists; but perhaps it may have been intentionally done, after the observation of the Lord's Day came to be regarded as binding. **φρονῶν, taking account of**, 'regarding.' **εὐχαριστεῖ**, adduced as a practice of both parties, shews the universality among the early Christians of *thanking God at meals;* see 1 Tim. iv. 3, 4. The *εὐχαριστία* of the *μὴ ἐσθίων* was over his 'dinner of herbs.' **κυρίῳ** is CHRIST. **7.**] This verse illustrates the *κυρίῳ* of the former, and at the same time sets in a still plainer light than before, that *both parties*, the eater and the abstainer, are servants of another, even Christ. **ἑαυτῷ** and **κυρίῳ** are datives commodi: **ζῆν** and **ἀποθνήσκειν** represent the whole sum of our course on earth.

8.] The inference,—that we are, under all circumstances, living or dying (and a fortiori *eating or abstaining*, *observing days or not observing them*), CHRIST'S: His property. **9.**] And this lordship over all was the *great end* of the Death and Resurrection of Christ. By that Death and Resurrection, the crowning events of his work of Redemption, He was manifested as the righteous Head over the race of man, which now, and in consequence man's world also, belongs by right to Him alone. The rec. text here, *ἀπέθ. κ. ἀνέστη κ. ἀνέζησεν*, may have arisen by the insertion (1) of *ἀνέζησεν* as clearer than *ἔζησεν*, and (2) of *ἀνέστη* from the margin, where it was a gloss (1 Thess. iv. 14) explaining *ἀνέζησεν* or *ἔζησεν*. Or, on the other hand, supposing it to have been the original, *ἀνέζησεν* may have been altered to *ἔζησεν* and *κ. ἀνέστη* left out, to conform it to vv. 7 and 8. In such a case of doubt, the weight of early authority must decide. **ἔζησεν, lived**, viz. *after His death;* = *ἀνέζησεν*. The historical aorist points to a stated event as the commencement of the reviviscence, viz. the Resurrection. **κ. νεκρ. κ. ζώντων**] here, for uniformity with what has gone before: in sense comprehending *all created beings*.

10.] He returns to the duty of abstaining,—the *weak*, from *judging* his

i vv. 3, 4 reff. k = Matt. vii. 3 al. l ver. 3 reff. m = Acts xxvii. 24. Dan. vii. 10. n Acts xii. 21 reff. o = Num. xiv. 21, 28. Jer. xxii. 24. Ezek. v. 11. Zeph. ii. 9. p Isa. xlv. 23. constr. of oath, 2 Cor. i. 18. Judith xii. 4. q ch. xi. 4 reff. r = ch. xv. 9. Matt. xi. 25. Phil. ii. 11. 2 Kings xxii. 50. l. c. Aℵ[3b]. s ch. v. 18 reff. t Acts xix. 40 reff. u 2 Cor. ii. 1. see 1 Pet. ii. 19. v = Acts xvi. 4. xx. 16. 1 Cor. vii. 37. 2 Cor. ii. 1. w ch. ix. 33 (reff.). x = Matt. xvi. 23. 1 Cor. i. 23. Rev. ii. 14. Ps. xlix. 21. y constr., ch. viii. 38 reff. z = Acts x. 14 reff. a see ch. ii. 27. ver. 20. 2 Cor. ii. 4. v. 7. b = ch. vi. 11. Phil. iii. 13. Wisd. xv. 15. c dat., = 1 Cor. iv. 3.

δὲ τί [i] κρίνεις τὸν [k] ἀδελφόν σου ; ἢ καὶ σὺ τί [l] ἐξουθενεῖς ABCD
τὸν ἀδελφόν σου ; πάντες γὰρ [m] παραστησόμεθα τῷ FL[P]ℵ abcdf
[n] βήματι τοῦ θεοῦ. 11 γέγραπται γὰρ [o] Ζῶ ἐγώ, λέγει ghkl mno17
κύριος [p] ὅτι ἐμοὶ [q] κάμψει πᾶν [q] γόνυ, καὶ πᾶσα γλῶσσα [47]
[r] ἐξομολογήσεται τῷ θεῷ. 12 [s] ἄρα [[s] οὖν] ἕκαστος ἡμῶν περὶ
ἑαυτοῦ [t] λόγον [[t] ἀπο]δώσει τῷ θεῷ. 13 μηκέτι οὖν ἀλλήλους [i] κρίνωμεν, ἀλλὰ [u] τοῦτο [v] κρίνατε μᾶλλον, [u] τὸ μὴ
[w] τιθέναι [w] πρόσκομμα τῷ ἀδελφῷ ἢ [wx] σκάνδαλον. 14 οἶδα
καὶ [y] πέπεισμαι ἐν κυρίῳ Ἰησοῦ ὅτι οὐδὲν [z] κοινὸν [a] δι'
ἑαυτοῦ, εἰ μὴ τῷ [b] λογιζομένῳ τι [z] κοινὸν εἶναι, [c] ἐκείνῳ

10. aft τον αδελφ. σου (1st) add εν τω μη εσθιειν D^1F am^2 Ambrst : also [F-lat] am^2 Ambrst aft αδελφ. σου (2nd) add εν τω εσθ. rec for θεου, χριστου (*see note*), with C^2(appy) L[P]$ℵ^3$ rel [vulg-clem demid] syrr goth [æth arm-ed Did_2] $Orig_1$ Chr_2 $Thdor\text{-}mops_2$ Thdrt $Gennad_1$ [$Tert_1$] : txt $ABC^1DFℵ^1$ [47-marg] am(with fuld harl mar tol) copt [arm-mss] Damasc [$Orig\text{-}int_3$](*quod vero in præsenti quidem loco tribunal Dei, ad Cor. vero tribunal Christi posuit, ego quidem nullam puto [esse] differentiam*) Aug_1 [Fulg Sedul.—47^1 omits the last clause.]

11. for οτι, ει μη D^1[-gr(appy, Tischdf)] F[-gr] (G-lat has both). εξομολογησεται bef πασα γλωσσα (so *LXX*-A) B $D^{1\cdot3}$[and lat] F goth [(Syr æth) $Orig\text{-}int_1$] Ambrst Sedul : txt ACD^2L[P]ℵ rel vulg syr copt [arm Did_2] Chr_1 Thdrt Damasc Thl Œc $Aug_{sæpe}$.

12. om ουν BD^1F[P^1 Syr] : ins ACD^3L[P^2]ℵ rel [syr copt goth arm] Chr_1 Thdrt [$Antch_1$ Damasc]. **υμων** C 116. for εαυ., αυτου C. **αποδωσει** BD^1F Chr_1 : δωσει ACD^3L [P(bef λογον)] ℵ rel $Polyc_1$ $Chr\text{-}ms_1$ Thdrt [$Antch_1$ Damasc] Thl Œc. om τω θεω B [D^2(appy, Treg)] F (Polyc) $Cypr_1$ Aug_2 : ins ACDL[P]ℵ rel [vss] Chr_1 Thdrt [$Antch_1$ Damasc $Orig\text{-}int_2$] Ambrst.

13. κρινετε D^1F [-νομεν P(so P m^1 for -νωμεν above)]. om **προσκομμα** and ἤ B Syr [arm].—for ἤ, εις b^1 m n o [47^2] $Chr\text{-}ms_1$ Cyr_1 $Antch_1$.

14. for κυρ., χριστω L[P] b k m n o. for εαυτου, αυτου ADFL[P] rel Chr_1 $Thdrt_{expr}$ Œc : txt BCℵ d m Chr_1 Damasc Thl.

stronger brother; the *strong*, from *despising* the weaker. It seems probable that χριστοῦ has been substituted for θεοῦ in the later MSS. from 2 Cor. v. 10. The fact of Origen *once* citing it, decides nothing, in the presence of the expression βήματος τοῦ χριστοῦ in 2 Cor. **11.**] The citation is according to the present Alexandrine text, except that our ζῶ ἐγώ = κατ' ἐμαυτοῦ ὀμνύω. **ἐξομ.**] **shall praise**, see reff. LXX-B$ℵ^{1\cdot3a}$ following the Heb. has ὀμεῖται(ὀμνῖται $ℵ^1$) πᾶσα γλῶσσα τὸν θεόν(κύριον ℵ). **12.**] The stress is on **περὶ ἑαυτοῦ** : and the next verse refers back to it, laying the emphasis on ἀλλήλους. 'Seeing that our account to God will be of *each man's own self*, let us take heed lest by judging *one another* (**κρίνομεν** here in the general sense of 'pass judgment on,' including both the ἐξουθενεῖν of the strong and the κρίνειν of the weak) we *incur the guilt* of ἀπολλύειν one another.' **13—23.**] *Exhortation to the strong to have regard to the conscientious scruples of the weak, and follow peace, not having respect merely to his own conscience, but to that of the other, which is his rule, and being violated leads to his condemnation.* **13.**] See above. The second **κρίνατε** is used as corresponding to the first, and is in fact a play on it: 'pulchra mimesis ad id quod præcedit,' Bengel: see James ii. 4 for another instance:—**but determine this rather.** **πρόσκομμα** (see ver. 21), **an occasion of stumbling**, in *act* : **σκάνδαλον** (ib.), **an occasion of offence**, in *thought*. **14.**] *The general principle laid down*, that *nothing is by its own means*,—i. e. for any thing in itself (φύσει, Chrys.),—*unclean, but only in reference to him who reckons it to be so.* **πέπεισμ. ἐν κυρ. Ἰησ.**] These words give to the persuasion the weight, not merely of Paul's own λογίζομαι, but of apostolic authority. He is persuaded, in his capacity

[z] κοινόν. 15 εἰ γὰρ [d] διὰ [e] βρῶμα ὁ ἀδελφός σου [f] λυπεῖ-
ται, οὐκ ἔτι κατὰ ἀγάπην [g] περιπατεῖς. μὴ τῷ [e] βρώματί
σου ἐκεῖνον [h] ἀπόλλυε, ὑπὲρ οὗ χριστὸς ἀπέθανεν. 16 μὴ
[i] βλασφημείσθω οὖν ὑμῶν [k] τὸ ἀγαθόν. 17 οὐ γάρ [l] ἐστιν ἡ
[m] βασιλεία τοῦ [m] θεοῦ [n] βρῶσις καὶ [o] πόσις, ἀλλὰ [p] δικαιοσύνη καὶ εἰρήνη καὶ [q] χαρὰ ἐν [q] πνεύματι ἁγίῳ· 18 ὁ γὰρ
ἐν τούτῳ [r] δουλεύων τῷ χριστῷ [s] εὐάρεστος τῷ θεῷ καὶ

d = John xv. 3. ch. xv. 15. 1 Cor. vii. 5.
e Matt. xiv. 15 ‖. Luke iii. 11. 1 Cor. x. 3 al. Hag. ii. 13.
f Matt. xix. 22 ‖. 2 Cor. ii. 2, &c., al. Sir. xxvi. 28.
g = ch. xiii. 12. 1 Thess. iv. 12 al. fr.
h = 1 Cor. viii. 11. xv. 18. James iv. 12. 2 Pet. iii. 9.
i = ch. iii. 8 reff.
k = here only. (ch. ii. 10 reff.)
l = John xvii. 3.
m = 1 Cor. iv. 20. see Rev. i. 9.
n = John iv. 32. vi. 27 (bis), 55. 1 Cor. viii. 4. 2 Cor. ix. 10. Col. ii. 16. Heb. xii. 16 (Matt. vi. 19, 20) only. Gen. ii. 9 al.
o John vi. 55. Col. ii. 16 only. Dan. i 10 only.
p absol., Acts xvii. 31 reff.
q 1 Thess. i. 6.
r = Acts xx. 19 reff.
s ch. xii. 1, 2 reff.

15. rec for γαρ, δε (*see note*), with [L(sic, Treg)] 17 rel [syrr] goth Chr_1 Thdrt : txt ABCDF[P]א d m vulg syr-mg copt [arm $Antch_1$] $Damasc_1$ [$Orig\text{-}int_2$] Ambrst Jer. om ὁ F. απολυε D^3L a h^1 k m n-marg [o] : καταλυε n^1 : απολλυειν (and καταλυειν in ver 20) F (as latt).

16. om ουν F goth arm. ημων DF vulg [spec] Syr copt[has both] goth æth[?] $Clem_1$ Damasc [$Orig\text{-}int_1$] $Ath\text{-}int_1$ Ambrst Aug_1.

[17. βρωσεις AC F-gr. ποσεις A F-gr.]

18. rec τουτοις (*see note*), with D^3L$א^3$ rel syrr goth [arm] Chr_1 Thdrt [Thl Œc] $Tert_1$: txt ABC D^1[and lat] F[P]$א^1$ vulg [spec] coptt Orig Chr $Damasc_1$ [$Orig\text{-}int_3$]$_{expr}$ Ambrst Aug_2 Pel Bede. om τω (bef χριστ.) AD^1F : ins BCD^3L[P]א rel Chr Thdrt Damasc. for χρ., θεω B^1(Tischdf [N. T. Vat.]) 30. 115 [κυριω 47].

as connected with Christ Jesus,—*as having the mind of Christ.* **15.**] The reading γάρ, besides the overwhelming authority in its favour, is the more difficult and characteristic. It can hardly (as Meyer and Tholuck) depend on the εἰ μὴ κ.τ.λ., for thus an awkwardness would be introduced into the connexion of the clauses: but I believe it to be elliptical, depending on the suppressed restatement of the precept of ver. 13: q. d. 'But this knowledge is not to be your rule in practice, but rather, &c., as in ver. 13: '*for* if,' &c. **βρῶμα**, barely put, to make the contrast greater between the *slight occasion*, and the *great mischief done.* The mere λυπεῖν your brother, is an offence against *love:* how much greater an offence then, if this λυπεῖν end in ἀπολλύειν—in ruining (causing to act against his conscience, and so to commit sin and be in danger of quenching God's Spirit within him) by a MEAL of thine, a brother, for whom Christ died! "Ne pluris feceris tuum cibum, quam Christus vitam suam." Bengel. See an exact parallel in 1 Cor. viii. 10, 11. **16.**] *Your strength of faith* (Orig., Calv., Beza, Grot., Estius, Bengel, Olsh., al., interpret **τὸ ἀγ.** '*your freedom,*' as in 1 Cor. x. 29; but here the contrast is between the *weak* and the *strong:*—so De W. Chrys. leaves it doubtful: ἢ τὴν πίστιν φησίν, ἢ τὴν μέλλουσαν ἐλπίδα τῶν ἐπάθλων, ἢ τὴν ἀπηρτισμένην εὐσέβειαν) *is a good thing; let it not pass into bad repute:* use it so that it may be honoured, and encourage others. **17.**] For it is not worth while to let it be disgraced and become useless for such a trifle; for no part of the advance of Christ's gospel can be bound up in, or *consist in, meat and drink:* but in **righteousness** (ὁ ἐνάρετος βίος, Chrys., but of course to be taken in union with the doctrine of the former part of the Epistle—*righteousness by justification,—bringing forth the fruits of faith,* which would be hindered by faith itself being disturbed), **and peace** (ἡ πρὸς τὸν ἀδελφὸν εἰρήνη, ᾗ ἐναντιοῦται αὕτη ἡ φιλονεικία, id.) **and joy** (ἡ ἐκ τῆς ὁμονοίας χαρά, ἣν ἀναιρεῖ αὕτη ἡ ἐπίπληξις, id.) **in the Holy Ghost:** in connexion with, under the indwelling and influence of, as χαίρετε ἐν κυρίῳ (Phil. iv. 4) and the expressions ἐν κυρ., ἐν χριστῷ, generally:—not, as De W., '*joy which has its ground in the Holy Ghost,*' though this is *true.* So, on the other hand, a man under the influence of, possessed by an evil spirit, is called ἄνθρωπος ἐν πνεύματι ἀκαθάρτῳ, Mark i. 23. **18.**] The reading τούτῳ is too strongly supported to be rejected for the rec. τούτοις, as is done by Thol. and De Wette, because the latter is the *easier* reading, and might refer to δικ. εἰρ. and χαρ. I have therefore adopted it. But I do not understand it (as Orig., al.) of πνεύματι ἁγίῳ. It would be unnatural that a subordinate member of the former sentence, belonging only to χαρά, should be at once raised to be the emphatic one in this, and the three graces just emphatically mentioned, lost sight of. I believe τούτῳ to

[t] δόκιμος τοῖς ἀνθρώποις. 19 [u] ἄρα [u] οὖν [v] τὰ τῆς εἰρήνης
[w] διώκωμεν καὶ [v] τὰ τῆς [x] οἰκοδομῆς τῆς εἰς ἀλλήλους.
20 μὴ ἕνεκεν [y] βρώματος [z] κατάλυε τὸ [a] ἔργον τοῦ θεοῦ.
πάντα μὲν καθαρά, ἀλλὰ κακὸν τῷ ἀνθρώπῳ τῷ [b] διὰ
[c] προσκόμματος ἐσθίοντι. 21 [d] καλὸν τὸ μὴ φαγεῖν [e] κρέα
μηδὲ πιεῖν οἶνον μηδὲ [f] ἐν ᾧ ὁ ἀδελφός σου [g] προσκόπτει
ἢ [h] σκανδαλίζεται ἢ [i] ἀσθενεῖ. 22 σὺ [k] πίστιν [ἣν] [k] ἔχεις [;]

ABCD FL[P]א a b c d f g h k l m n o 17 [47]

t (=) ch. xvi. 10. 1 Cor. xi. 19. 2 Cor. x. 18. xiii. 7. 2 Tim. ii. 15. James i. 12 only. (1 Chron. xxviii. 18.)
u ch. v. 18 reff.
v ch. ii. 14 reff. see Luke xiv. 32.
w ch. ix. 30, 31 reff.
x = Paul only, ch. xv. 2. 1 Cor. (iii. 5) xiv. 3, &c. 2 Cor. (v. 1) x. 8. xii. 19. xiii. 10. Eph. iv. 29. (Matt. xxiv. 1 al. Ezek. xvii. 17.)
y ver. 15.
z = Matt. xxiv. 2. xxvi. 61. Acts v. 38. 2 Cor. v. 1. Gal. ii. 18. Ezra v. 12.
a = Phil. i. 6.
b = ch. ii. 27 reff.
c ver. 13.
d = Matt. xviii. 8. 1 Cor. vii. 1, &c. 1 Tim. ii. 3. Gen. ii. 18.
e 1 Cor. viii. 13 only. Gen. ix. 4 al. fr.
f ch. ii. 1. 1 Pet. ii. 12.
g ch. ix. 32 reff.
h = Matt. xv. 12. 1 Cor. viii. 13 (bis) al. fr. Sir. ix. 5. xxiii. 8. xxxv. (xxxii.) 15 only.
i vv. 1, 2. ch. iv. 19 reff.
k Acts xiv. 9 reff.

και δοκιμοις τοις ανθρωποις B G[1]-gr : *και τοις ανθρωποις δοκιμοις* 77.

19. *διωκομεν* ABFL[P]א a o Chr-ms$_1$: txt CD rel vss [Chr-edd Thdrt Damasc Orig-int$_1$ Ambrst]. at end add *φυλαξωμεν* D[1][and lat] F vulg(not demid) [spec Ambrst] (not Aug).

20. *απολλυε* א[1]. aft *καθαρα* ins *τοις καθαροις* א[3].

21. *κρεας* D[2] m. *πινειν* F Clem$_1$[txt$_1$] : *πειν* B[1]D[1]. for *προσκοπτει*, *λυπειται* [P] א[1](txt א-corr[1]). om *η σκανδαλιζ. η ασθενει* ACא[1] Syr copt æth Damasc [Orig-int$_2$] Aug$_1$: ins BDFL[P]א[3] rel vulg syr [sah (arm) spec] Bas$_2$ Chr$_2$ Thdrt Thl Ambrst Pel.

22. rec om *ην*, with DFL[P] rel vulg syrr [sah æth arm Damasc] Chr$_1$ Thdrt Ambrst Aug$_1$: ins ABCא tol [copt Orig-int$_1$] Aug$_2$ Pel.

express the aggregate of the three, and *ἐν τούτῳ* to be equivalent to *οὕτως*, as Baumg.-Crusius. **δόκ. τ. ἀνθρ.**, as a man of *peace* and *uprightness*: *οὐ γὰρ οὕτω σε θαυμάσονται τῆς τελειότητος, ὡς τῆς εἰρήνης κ. τῆς ὁμονοίας πάντες· τούτου μὲν γὰρ τοῦ καλοῦ πάντες ἀπολαύσονται, ἐκείνου δὲ οὐδὲ εἷς.* Chrys. Hom. xxvi. p. 713. 19.] Inference from the foregoing two verses—**οἰκοδ. τ. εἰς ἀλλ., edification towards one another, i. e.** the work of edification, finding its exercise in our mutual intercourse and allowances. So *τῇ ἀγάπῃ εἰς ἀλλ.*, 1 Thess. iii. 12.

20.] **τὸ ἔργον τ. θεοῦ** has been variously understood; by Fritz. and Baumg.-Crusius, as = *δικαιοσ. εἰρήνη, κ. χαρά*: by Meyer and Krehl, as = *the Christian status of the offended brother*, so as to be parallel to ver. 15: by Theodoret and Reiche, as = *the faith of thy fellow-Christian*: by Morus, Rosenm., al., as = *ἡ βασιλεία τοῦ θ.*, '*the spread of the Gospel.*' But I believe the expression *οἰκοδομή* having just preceded is the clue to the right meaning: and that *τὸ ἔργον* = *τὴν οἰκοδομήν* in the Apostle's mind. He calls Christians in 1 Cor. iii. 9, *θεοῦ γεώργιον, θεοῦ οἰκοδομή*. Thus it will mean, *thy fellow-Christian, as a plant of God's planting, a building of God's raising*. So, nearly, De Wette and Tholuck. **All things indeed are pure, but** (it is) **evil to the man** ('there is criminality in the man;' Meyer supplies *τὸ καθαρόν*, Grot. *τὸ βρῶμα*, Fritz. *τὸ πάντα φαγεῖν*: but nothing need be supplied, any more than to *καλόν*) **who eats with offence** (i. e. *giving* offence to his weak brother, as Theodoret, Calv., Beza, Grot., Estius, Bengel, Thol., De Wette, al. That this is the right interpretation is shewn by the sentence standing between two others *both addressed to the strong who is in danger of offending the weak*. But Chrys., Theophyl., Œc., Meyer, al., take the sense of '*receiving* offence,' and understand it of the *weak*). 21.] **It is good not to eat meats nor to drink wine, nor (to do any thing:** the ellipsis is a harsh one. Fritzsche says, "aut supple *φαγεῖν ἢ πιεῖν τοῦτο, ἐν ᾧ κ.τ.λ.*, as Thl., Beng., Flatt, al.,—or *ποιεῖν* (or *πράσσειν*) *τοῦτο ἐν ᾧ κ.τ.λ.*, as Grot. Meyer, &c. Præfero illud, quoniam per totum hunc locum de cibo potuque agitur." But why should not the Apostle, as so often, be deducing a general duty from the particular subject?) **in (by) which thy brother stumbles, or is offended** (see on ver. 13), **or is weak** (Thol. remarks that the three verbs form a climax *ad infra*). 22.] **The faith which thou hast** (this reading, which is the more probable on critical grounds, was perhaps changed into the *σὺ πίστιν ἔχεις* of the rec. on account of the position of the *σύ*. But this is quite in St. Paul's manner; cf. ver. 4; 1 Cor. xv. 36; 2 Cor. ii. 10. However, the other reading is very ancient, and it is impossible to decide positively between them. If it is taken, the interrogative rendering, "**Hast thou faith?**" better suits the lively cha-

l κατὰ σεαυτὸν ἔχε m ἐνώπιον τοῦ θεοῦ. μακάριος ὁ μὴ
n κρίνων ἑαυτὸν f ἐν ᾧ o δοκιμάζει. 23 ὁ δὲ p διακρινόμενος
ἐὰν φάγῃ q κατακέκριται, ὅτι οὐκ r ἐκ πίστεως· πᾶν δὲ ὃ
οὐκ r ἐκ πίστεως, ἁμαρτία ἐστίν. XV. 1 s ὀφείλομεν δὲ
ἡμεῖς οἱ t δυνατοὶ τὰ u ἀσθενήματα τῶν v ἀδυνάτων
w βαστάζειν καὶ μὴ x ἑαυτοῖς y ἀρέσκειν. 2 ἕκαστος ἡμῶν

l Heliodor. vii. 10. (De W.) ἐχεμύθει κ. κατὰ σαυτὸν ἔχε κ. μηδενὶ φράζε, Jos. Antt. ii. 11. 1. see Acts xxviii. 16 reff.
m = ch. xii. 17. Acts iv. 19 reff.
n = vv. 3, 4 reff.
o = 1 Cor. xvi. 3. 2 Cor. viii. 8. 1 Thess. ii. 4. Jos. Antt. iii. 4. 1. p = Matt. xxi. 21. Acts x. 20. ch. iv. 20. James i. 6 ‡. (Jer. xv. 10.) q ch. ii. 1 reff. (perf., ch. xiii. 8. John iii. 18.) r ellips., ch. ii. 8 reff. s = Luke xvii. 10. John xiii. 14. xix. 7. Acts xvii. 29 al. t = 2 Cor. xiii. 9. u here only +. v Acts xiv. 8 reff. w ch. xi. 18 reff. Matt. viii. 17. Gal. vi. 2. x 1st pers., 2 Cor. iii. 1 reff. y ch. viii. 8 reff.

rec (for σεαυ.) σαυτον, with rel [Chr_1]: σεαυτω F: txt ABCDL[P]ℵ c g k l [m(Treg)] n o 17 [47]. om ενωπιον του θεου ℵ·(ins ℵ-corr[1]) [Chr_1].

23. αν B. [κατακρινεται P.] for ὅ, το D[1][P] m 71.—om παν to πιστεως (*homœotel*) ℵ[1](ins ℵ-corr[1]). aft αμαρτια εστιν ins ch xvi. 25—27 AL[P] rel and most other mss(nearly 200 in number) syr goth[appy] arm-zoh [Chr $Cyr-p_1$ Thdrt Damasc mss-mentd-by-Orig-int], of these A[P] 5. 17. 109 have it in both places: om in both places [D[3](appy, Tischdf)] F(but in G there is a space left here and in F a space at xvi. 24) [Mcion-in-Orig-int mss-mentd-by-Jer]: txt BCD[1]ℵ 16. 80. 137-76 vulg Syr copt æth [$Orig-int_1$] Ambrst Pel Bede.

Chap. XV. 1. [om δε P[1] b[1] o.] αρεσκον F[-gr].

2. rec aft εκαστος ins γαρ: om ABCDFL[P]ℵ rel vulg syr copt [æth] Bas_1 Chr_1 Thdrt Damasc [$Orig-int_1$] Ambrst. υμων D[2]F[P] rel vulg [spec] Bas[-ed] Chr_1 Thdrt Damasc Thl [$Orig-int_2$] Pel Jer Leo: txt ABCD[1·3]Lℵ d h k n 17 [47(sic)] syrr copt [Bas-2-mss_1 Chr-c_2 Œc Aug Sing-cler].

racter of the address than the affirmative, "*Thou hast faith*") **have (it) to thyself** (reff.) **before God**. Chrys., who does not read the last words (ἐν. τ. θ.), says, πίστιν ἐνταῦθα οὐ τὴν περὶ δογμάτων, ἀλλὰ τὴν περὶ τῆς προκειμένης ὑποθέσεως λέγει: . . ., ἐκείνη μὲν γὰρ μὴ ὁμολογουμένη καταστρέφει, αὕτη δὲ ὁμολογουμένη ἀκαίρως. Hom. xxvi. p. 714. '*Before God*,'—because He is the object of faith: hardly, as Erasm., "comprimens inanem gloriam quæ solet esse comes scientiæ,"—for there is *no trace of a depreciation* of the strong in faith in the chapter,—only a *caution as to their conduct* in regard of their weaker brethren. With μακάριος begins the closing and general sentence of the Apostle with regard to *both:* it is a blessed thing to *have no scruples* (the *strong in faith* is in a situation to be envied) about things in which we allow ourselves (Olsh. refers to the addition in the Codex Bezæ at Luke vi. 4,—where our Lord is related to have seen a man tilling his land on the Sabbath, and to have said to him, εἰ μὲν οἶδας τί ποιεῖς, μακάριος εἶ, εἰ δὲ μὴ οἶδας, ἐπικατάρατος, καὶ παραβάτης εἶ τοῦ νόμου): 23.] **but he that doubteth** (the situation just described *not* being his), **incurs condemnation if he eat** (the case in point particularized), **because** (he eats) **not from faith** (i. e. as before,—see Chrys. above,—from a *persuasion of rectitude* grounded on and consonant with his life of faith. That '*faith in the Son of God*' by which the Apostle describes his own life in the flesh as being lived (Gal ii. 20), informing and penetrating the motives and the conscience, will not include, will not sanction, an act done against the testimony of the conscience): **but** (introducing an *axiom*, as Heb viii. 13) **all that is not from** (grounded in, and therefore consonant with) **faith** (the great element in which the Christian lives and moves and desires and hopes), **is sin.** Augustine, Thomas Aquinas, al., have taken this text as shewing that 'omnis infidelium vita peccatum est.' Whether that be the case or not, cannot be determined from this passage, any more than from Heb. xi. 6, because *neither here nor there is the* 'infidelis' *in question.* Here the Apostle has in view *two Christians*, both living by faith, and by faith doing acts pleasing to God: and he reminds them that whatever they do *out of harmony* with this great principle of their spiritual lives, belongs to the category of sin. In Heb. xi. the Writer is speaking of one who had the testimony of having (eminently) pleased God: this, he says, he did by faith; for *without faith* it is impossible to please Him. The question touching the 'infidelis,' must be settled by another enquiry: Can he whom we thus name *have faith*,—such a faith as may enable him to do acts which are not sinful? a question impossible for *us* to solve.

Chap. XV. 1—13.] *Further exhortations to forbearance towards the weak,*

z ch. xiii. 9, 10 reff. a ch. xiii. 4 reff. b = ch. xiv. 19 reff. c constr., 1 Cor. i. 31. see ch. ix. 7. d 1 Tim. iii. 7. Heb. x. 33. xi. 26. xiii. 13 only. Isa. xliii. 28. e Psa. lxviii. 9. Matt. v. 11 al. Prov. xxv. 10. f Acts xx. 37 reff. met., Acts viii. 16 reff. Exod. xv. 16. Ald. 1 Macc. x. 36 only. k = 2 Cor. i. 3, &c., al. Ps. xciii. 19. n ch. viii. 27. 2 Cor. vii. 9—11. g Gal. iii. 1. Eph. iii. 3. Jude 4 only†. Esdr. vi. 31 [32] F(προσγρ. A) h objective, here only. see ch. xi. 31. 1 Cor. xv. 31. i ch. ii. 7 reff. l plur., Acts xvii. 2 reff. m ch. xii. 16 reff.

ABCD FL[P]ℵ abcdf ghkl mno17 [47]

τῷ [z] πλησίον [y] ἀρεσκέτω [a] εἰς τὸ [a] ἀγαθὸν πρὸς [b] οἰκοδομήν.
3 καὶ γὰρ ὁ χριστὸς οὐχ ἑαυτῷ [y] ἤρεσεν, [c] ἀλλὰ καθὼς
γέγραπται Οἱ [d] ὀνειδισμοὶ τῶν [e] ὀνειδιζόντων σε [f] ἐπ-
έπεσαν ἐπ' ἐμέ. 4 ὅσα γὰρ [g] προεγράφη εἰς τὴν [h] ἡμετέραν διδασκαλίαν ἐγράφη, ἵνα διὰ τῆς [i] ὑπομονῆς καὶ
διὰ τῆς [k] παρακλήσεως τῶν [l] γραφῶν τὴν ἐλπίδα ἔχωμεν.
5 ὁ δὲ θεὸς τῆς [i] ὑπομονῆς καὶ τῆς [k] παρακλήσεως
δῴη ὑμῖν [m] τὸ αὐτὸ [m] φρονεῖν ἐν ἀλλήλοις [n] κατὰ χριστὸν

om εις το αγαθον ℵ[1](ins ℵ-corr[1]).

3. om ὁ D[1]F. rec επεπεσον (as LXX-Ed-vat), with L rel: txt (as LXX-Bℵ: A def) ABCDF[P]ℵ (g[1]?) l m n 17 [47] Damasc.

4. προεγραφη D[1]F: εγραφη B latt æth [arm Orig-int$_2$ Ambrst]: txt ACD[3]L[P]ℵ rel [-φει LP]. add παντα B[P] m 17 [47]. rec (for εγραφη) προεγραφη, with AL[P]ℵ[3] rel syr Chr$_1$ Thdrt Damasc: txt BCDFℵ[1] vulg Syr copt goth æth [arm spec] Clem$_1$ [Orig-int] Ambrst Aug$_3$ [-φει LP]. rec om 2nd δια, with [C-corr(appy) P]DF vulg syr copt goth [spec Clem$_1$] Chr Thdrt$_3$ [Orig-int$_1$] Ambrst Aug Oros: ins ABCLℵ b d f g n Thdrt$_1$. [εχομεν P a f n 17.] aft εχωμεν ins της παρακλησεως B.

5. ιησ. bef χρ. AC[1] F(not G-lat) [P]ℵ m vulg syrr [æth arm-ed] Did$_1$ Thdrt [Orig-int$_1$] Ambrst.

from the example of Christ (1—3),—*and unanimity* (4—7) *as between Jew and Gentile, seeing that Christ was prophetically announced as the common Saviour of both* (8—13). 1.] By ἡμεῖς οἱ δυν. the Apostle *includes himself among the strong*, as indeed he before indicated, ch. xiv. 14. **τὰ ἀσθ.** are *general*, not merely referring to the scruples before treated. **ἀρέσκειν** (reff.) to please or satisfy as a habit or motive of action. Tholuck quotes from the Schol. on Æsch. Prom. 156, παρ' ἑαυτῷ δίκαιον ἔχων Ζεύς,—πάντα δικαίως οἰόμενος ποιεῖν, **αὐτὸς ἑαυτῷ ἀρέσκων** καὶ δίκαιον νομίζων εἶναι ὅπερ ἂν βούληται πράττειν. 2.] The qualification, εἰς τὸ ἀγ. πρὸς οἰκ., excludes all *mere* pleasing of men from the Christian's motives of action. The Apostle repudiates it in his own case, Gal. i. 10. Bengel remarks, '*bonum*, genus, *ædificatio*, species:'—to a good end, and that good end his edification.

3.] ἐξῆν αὐτῷ μὴ ὀνειδισθῆναι, ἐξῆν μὴ παθεῖν ἅπερ ἔπαθεν, εἴγε ἤθελε τὸ ἑαυτοῦ σκοπεῖν· ἀλλ' ὅμως οὐκ ἠθέλησεν, ἀλλὰ τὸ ἡμέτερον σκοπήσας τὸ ἑαυτοῦ παρεῖδε, Chrys. Hom. xxvii. p. 721 The citation is made *directly*, without any thing to introduce the formula citandi, as in ch. ix. 7, where even the formula itself is wanting:—there is no ellipsis. The words in the Messianic Psalm are addressed to *the Father*, not to those *for whom* Christ suffered: but they prove all that is here required, that He did not please *Himself*; His sufferings were undertaken on account of the Father's good purpose—mere work which *He gave Him to do*. 4.] The Apostle both justifies the above citation, and prepares the way for the subject to be next introduced, viz. the *duty of unanimity*, grounded on the testimony of these Scriptures to Christ. The **ὅσα προεγρ.** applies to the *whole ancient Scriptures*, not to the prophetic parts only. **ἡμετ.** viz. of *us Christians*,—προεγρ. implying πρὸ ἡμῶν.

ἵνα διὰ τ. ὑπ. κ.τ.λ.] τουτέστιν, ἵνα μὴ ἐκπέσωμεν· ποικίλοι γὰρ οἱ ἀγῶνες ἔσωθεν, ἔξωθεν· ἵνα νευρούμενοι κ. παρακαλούμενοι παρὰ τῶν γραφῶν ὑπομονὴν ἐπιδειξώμεθα· ἵνα ἐν ὑπομονῇ ζῶντες μένωμεν ἐπὶ τῆς ἐλπίδος. ταῦτα γὰρ ἀλλήλων ἐστὶ κατασκευαστικά, ἡ ὑπομονὴ τῆς ἐλπίδος, ἡ ἐλπὶς τῆς ὑπομονῆς· ἅπερ ἀμφότερα ἀπὸ τῶν γραφῶν γίνεται, Chrys. ubi supra. As in this comment, ὑπομονῆς, as well as παρακλήσεως, is to be joined with τῶν γραφῶν,—otherwise it stands unconnected with the subject of the sentence. The genitives then mean, **the patience and the comfort arising from the Scriptures**,—produced by their study.

5, 6.] *Further introduction of the subject, by a prayer that God, who has given the Scriptures for these ends, might grant them unanimity, that they might with one accord shew forth His glory.* In the title given to God, the ὑπομονή and παράκλησις just mentioned are taken

Ἰησοῦν, 6 ἵνα [o] ὁμοθυμαδὸν [p] ἐν ἑνὶ [p] στόματι [q] δοξάζητε
τὸν [r] θεὸν καὶ [r] πατέρα τοῦ κυρίου ἡμῶν Ἰησοῦ χριστοῦ.
7 διὸ [s] προςλαμβάνεσθε ἀλλήλους, καθὼς καὶ ὁ χριστὸς
[s] προςελάβετο ὑμᾶς, [t] εἰς δόξαν τοῦ θεοῦ. 8 λέγω γὰρ
χριστὸν [u] διάκονον γεγενῆσθαι περιτομῆς [v] ὑπὲρ ἀληθείας
θεοῦ [w] εἰς τὸ [x] βεβαιῶσαι τὰς [y] ἐπαγγελίας τῶν [z] πατέρων,
9 τὰ δὲ ἔθνη ὑπὲρ [a] ἐλέους [q] δοξάσαι τὸν θεόν, καθὼς
γέγραπται Διὰ τοῦτο [b] ἐξομολογήσομαί σοι ἐν ἔθνεσιν,

o Acts i. 14 reff. p ch. x. 9 only. Ps. lxxxviii. 1. q = Acts xxi. 20 reff. r Paul (2 Cor. i. 3. xi. 31. Eph. i. 3. Col. i. 3) only, exc. 1 Pet. i. 3. Rev. i. 6. see 1 Cor. xv. 24. Gal. i. 4. s = Acts xxviii. 2 reff. ch. xiv. 1, 3. t ch. iii. 7 reff. u see Gal. ii. 17. v = Phil. ii. 13. w ch. iv. 11 reff. x Mark xvi. 20. 1 Cor. i. 6, 8. 2 Cor. i. 21. Col. ii. 7. Heb. ii. 3. xiii. 9. Ps. xl. 12. cxviii. 28 only. y ch. ix. 4. (iv. 13.) Gal. iii. 16. z absol., Acts vii. 19 reff. a ch. xi. 31 reff. b ch. xiv. 11 reff. Psa. xvii. 49.

7. [om ο F(not G).] rec ημας, with BD[1][P] rel Thdrt [Damasc]: txt ACD[2·3]FLℵ b c g l[2] m n o 17 [vulg spec] syrr copt goth arm [æth Orig-int$_4$] Chr$_1$ Ambrst. rec om του, with L rel Chr$_1$ Thdrt [Damasc]: ins ABCDF[P]ℵ m.

8. rec (for γαρ) δε (*see note*), with L rel syrr [arm] Chr$_1$ Thdrt [Thl Œc]: txt ABCDF[P]ℵ vulg copt goth Cyr[-p$_2$ Damasc Orig-int$_1$] Ambrst. rec ins ιησουν bef χριστον, with DF [b o] harl syrr; aft χρ. L rel vulg goth [Ath$_1$] Thdrt$_2$ Thl Œc [Ambrst]: om ABCℵ copt [æth arm Did$_1$] Epiph$_1$ Chr-comm$_1$ Cyr[-p$_1$] Damasc [Orig-int$_1$]. γενεσθαι (*corrn?*) BC[1]D[1]F c [arm] Ath$_1$: txt AC[2]D[3]L[P]ℵ rel [Did$_1$] Epiph$_1$ Chr$_2$ Cyr[-p$_2$] Thdrt Damasc.

9. for τουτο, του προφητου ℵ[1](txt ℵ·corr[1]). [aft εθνεσιν ins κυριε c h 17 vulg-clem(and harl tol guelph, not am fuld demid) syr copt Chr$_1$ Pel Sedul: και(? = κε̄) ℵ[3].]

up again: q. d. "The God who alone can give this patience and comfort." The later form of the opt., δῴη, is also found 2 Tim. i. 16, 18; Eph. i. 17 al., in LXX Gen. xxvii. 28; xxviii. 4 al. See Winer, edn. 6, § 14. 1. g. **κατὰ χρ. Ἰησοῦν, according to** (the spirit and precepts of) **Christ Jesus,**—see reff. **6. τὸν θεὸν κ. πατ.**] De Wette regards τὸν θεὸν as independent of Ἰησοῦ χρ.,—'*God, and the Father of our Lord Jesus Christ.*' The usage of the article will not decide the matter, because on either rendering, the accusatives both refer to the same Person: but the ordinary one, **the God and Father . . . .** is preferable on account of its simplicity. **7.] Wherefore** (on which account, viz. that the wish of the last verse may be accomplished) **receive** (see ch. xiv. 1) **one another, as Christ also received you,—with a view to God's glory** (that this is the meaning of εἰς δόξαν τοῦ θεοῦ, appears by ver. 9, τὰ δὲ ἔθνη ὑπὲρ ἐλέους **δοξάσαι τὸν θεόν**). The Apostle does not expressly name *Jewish and Gentile converts* as those to whom he addresses this exhortation, but it is evident from the next verse that it is so. **8.] For** (reason for the above exhortation. This not having been seen, it has been altered to δέ) **I say, that Christ hath been made** (has come as: the effects still enduring. It can hardly be that the usual historical aorist γενέσθαι (see var. readd.) was altered to the unusual perfect γεγενῆσθαι. The tendency of correction was entirely the other way) **a minister** (He came διακονῆσαι, Matt. xx. 28) **of the circumcision** (an expression no where else found, and doubtless here used by Paul to humble the pride of the *strong*, the Gentile Christians, by exalting God's covenant people to their true dignity) **on account of the truth of God** (i.e. for the fulfilment of the Divine pledges given under the covenant of circumcision) **to confirm the promises of** (*made to*, gen. obj.; cf. ἡ εὐλογία τοῦ Ἀβραάμ, Gal. iii. 14) **the fathers** (i.e. Christ came to the *Jews* in virtue of a *long-sealed compact, to the fulfilment of which God's truth was pledged*): **but** (I say) **that the Gentiles glorified God** (or 'should glorify God:' Winer, in his former editions, § 45. 8, took it as a perfect, and co-ordinate with γεγενῆσθαι: I would regard it (and so, apparently, Winer now, edn. 6, § 44. 7. c) as the historic aorist, and understand '*each man at his conversion.*' Least of all can it be subordinated to εἰς τό, as is done in E. V.) **on account of** (His) **mercy** (the emphasis is on ὑπὲρ ἐλέους: the Gentiles have no *covenant promise* to claim,—they have nothing but the pure mercy of God in grafting them in to allege—therefore the Jew has an advantage), &c. The citations are from the Law, the Prophets, and the Psalms. The first, originally spoken by David of his joy after his deliverances and triumphs, is prophetically said of Christ in His own Person. It is adduced to shew that among the Gentiles Christ's

καὶ τῷ ὀνόματί σου [c] ψαλῶ. 10 καὶ πάλιν [d] λέγει [e] Εὐ-
φράνθητε ἔθνη μετὰ τοῦ λαοῦ αὐτοῦ. 11 καὶ πάλιν
[[d] λέγει] [f] Αἰνεῖτε πάντα τὰ ἔθνη τὸν [f] κύριον, καὶ [g] ἐπαι-
νεσάτωσαν αὐτὸν πάντες οἱ [h] λαοί. 12 καὶ πάλιν Ἡσαΐας
λέγει Ἔσται ἡ [i] ῥίζα τοῦ Ἰεσσαί, καὶ ὁ [k] ἀνιστάμενος
[l] ἄρχειν ἐθνῶν, [m] ἐπ' αὐτῷ ἔθνη [m] ἐλπιοῦσιν. 13 ὁ δὲ
θεὸς τῆς ἐλπίδος [n] πληρώσαι ὑμᾶς [o] πάσης χαρᾶς καὶ
εἰρήνης [p] ἐν τῷ πιστεύειν, [q] εἰς τὸ [r] περισσεύειν ὑμᾶς ἐν τῇ
ἐλπίδι [s] ἐν δυνάμει πνεύματος ἁγίου.
14 [t] Πέπεισμαι δέ, ἀδελφοί μου, καὶ αὐτὸς ἐγὼ περὶ

ABCD FL[P]א abcdf ghkl mno17 [47]

c 1 Cor. xiv. 15 (bis). Eph. v. 19. James v. 13 only. 1 Kings xvi. 16.
d = Gal. iii. 16. see 1 Cor. vi. 16.
e Acts vii. 41 reff. Deut. xxxii. 43.
f here only. Psa. cxvi. 1. (elsw., θεόν, Acts ii. 47 reff.)
g Luke xvi. 8. 1 Cor. xi. 2, 17, 22 only. Ps. cxlvii. 12 (1).
h plur., Acts iv. 25 (from Ps. ii. 1), 27. Rev. vii. 9. x. 11. xi. 9. xvii. 15.
i Isa. xi. 1, 10. see Rev. v. 5. xxii. 16.
k = Heb. vii. 11, 15 and, but act., Acts iii. 22 (from Deut. xviii. 15), 26.
l = Mark x. 42 only. Gen. i. 26, 28 al.
m constr., 1 Tim. iv. 10. vi. 17. Ps. xxi. 5. dat. only, Matt. xii. 21. w. ἐπί and acc., 1 Tim. v. 5. 1 Pet. i. 13 (iii. 5 rec.). w. εἰς, John v. 45. 2 Cor. i. 10. 1 Pet. iii. 5.
n Acts xiii. 52 reff.
o = Acts xx. 19 reff.
p = Acts iv. 30 reff.
q ch. iv. 11 reff.
r ch. iii. 7 reff. Sir. xix. 24.
s ch. i 4 reff.
t constr., ch. viii. 38 reff.

ψαλω bef τω ον. σ. DG [copt].

11. ins λεγει BDF syrr copt goth æth[-rom arm-mss] : om ACL[P]א rel vulg [æth-pl arm-ed] (Chr_1) Thdrt Damasc Thl Œc [$Orig\text{-}int_1$] Ambrst. rec *τον κυρ.* bef *π. τα εθνη* (*corrn to* LXX, *where none read as in txt*), with CFL rel Syr [æth arm-mss] Thl Œc [$Orig\text{-}int_1$]: txt ABDא[P 47] vulg syr goth arm[-ed] Chr_1 Thdrt [Damasc Ambrst]. rec *επαινεσατε* (*so* LXX-Ed-vat(B *def*) א[3a] *&c*), with FL[P] rel Chr_1 Thdrt [Thl Œc] : txt (*so* LXX-Aא[1]) ABC[D]א $Chr\text{-}ms_1$ Damasc.

12. λεγει bef *ησαιας* א [copt]. *ανισταvομενος* א (*see digest ch* xii. 8).

13. πληροφορησαι υμας (add εν B) *παση χαρα κ. ειρηνη* BF: txt ACDL[P]א rel. [om *εν τω πιστ.* DF spec arm Vig_1.] om *εις το περισσευειν* (*homœotel*) B 57. om εν (bef *τη ελπιδι*) D[1] F[-gr] Chr-ms.

14. *κ. α. ε. π. υμ.* bef *αδελφοι μου* DF Syr Thdrt.—om *μου* D[1]F Thdrt Ambrst. for *περι*, *υπερ* B.

triumphs were to take place, as well as among the Jews. **10.] καὶ πάλ. λέγει,** viz. *ἡ γραφή*, or *ὁ θεός*, which is in substance the same: not impersonal: see ref. 1 Cor., note. The *present* Heb. text of Deut. xxxii. 43 will not bear this, which is the LXX rendering. But Tholuck remarks, "According to the present text the difficulty arises, that we must either take גּוֹיִם of the Jewish tribes, or construe הַרְנִין with an accus., instead of with לְ (Gesen.): the reading of the LXX may therefore be right." There is however a reading אֶת־עַמּוֹ found in one and perhaps another of Kennicott's mss. which will bear the rendering of our text. In several passages where the Gentiles are spoken of prophetically, the Hebrew text has apparently been tampered with by the Jews. See Kitto's Journal of Sacred Literature for January, 1852, pp. 275 ff. **11, 12.]** The *universality* of the praise to be given to God for His merciful kindness in sending His Son is prophetically indicated by the first citation. In the latter a more direct announcement is given of the *share which the Gentiles were to have* in the root of Jesse. The version is that of the LXX, which here differs considerably from the Heb. The latter is nearly literally rendered in E.V.: "And in that day there shall be a root (Heb. 'and it shall happen in that day, a branch') of Jesse, which shall stand for an ensign of the people: to it shall the Gentiles seek." **13.]** The hortatory part of the Epistle, as well as the preceding section of it (ver. 5), concludes with a solemn wish for the spiritual welfare of the Roman church. The words **τῆς ἐλπίδος** connect with *ἐλπιοῦσι* of the foregoing verse, as was the case with *τῆς ὑπομονῆς κ. τῆς παρακλήσεως* in ver. 5. **χαρᾶς κ. εἰρήνης,** as the happy result of faith in God, and unanimity with one another; see ch. xiv. 17.

XV. 14—XVI. 27.] CONCLUSION OF THE EPISTLE. Personal notices, respecting the Apostle himself (xv. 14—33),—respecting those greeted (xvi. 1—16), and greeting: together with warnings against those who made divisions among them (xvi. 16—23);—and concluding doxology (xvi. 24—27). **14—33.]** He first (14—16) *excuses the boldness of his writing*, by the allegation of his *office* as *Apostle of the Gentiles*. **14.] αὐτὸς ἐγω, I myself,** = 'idem,' Lat.,—' notwith-

ὑμῶν ὅτι καὶ αὐτοὶ [u] μεστοί ἐστε [v] ἀγαθωσύνης, [n] πε-
πληρωμένοι [o] πάσης [τῆς] [w] γνώσεως, δυνάμενοι καὶ
ἀλλήλους [x] νουθετεῖν· 15 [y] τολμηρότερον δὲ ἔγραψα
ὑμῖν[, ἀδελφοί,] [z] ἀπὸ [z] μέρους, ὡς [a] ἐπαναμιμνήσκων ὑμᾶς
[b] διὰ τὴν [c] χάριν τὴν [c] δοθεῖσάν μοι ὑπὸ τοῦ θεοῦ 16 [q] εἰς
τὸ εἶναί με [d] λειτουργὸν χριστοῦ Ἰησοῦ [e] εἰς τὰ ἔθνη,
[f] ἱερουργοῦντα τὸ [g] εὐαγγέλιον τοῦ [g] θεοῦ, ἵνα γένηται
ἡ [h] προσφορὰ τῶν ἐθνῶν [i] εὐπρόσδεκτος, [k] ἡγιασμένη
[k] ἐν πνεύματι ἁγίῳ. 17 [l] ἔχω οὖν τὴν [lm] καύχησιν ἐν

u ch. i. 29 reff. v Gal. v. 22. Eph. v. 9. 2 Thess. i. 11 only. Neh. ix. 35. w = 1 Cor. i. 5 al. fr. x Acts xx. 31 reff. y here only †. Polyb. i. 17. 7, τολμηρό-τερον ἐγχειρεῖν τοῖς πράγμασι. (-ρός, Sir. xix. 2, 3.) z ch. xi. 25 reff. a here only †. b = ch. xiv. 15 reff. c 1 Cor. i. 4 reff. d ch. xiii. 6 reff. e = Col. i. 25. f here only †. see notes. g Mark i. 14. (Acts xx. 24.) ch. i. 1. 2 Cor. xi. 7. 1 Thess. ii. 2, 8, 9. (1 Tim. i. 11.) 1 Pet. iv. 17 only. h Acts xxi. 26. xxiv. 17. Eph. v. 2. Heb. x. 5 (from Ps. xxxix. 6), &c., nly. i ver. 31. 2 Cor. vi. 2. viii. 12. 1 Pet. ii. 5 only †. k (and constr.) John xvii. 17, 19. 1 Cor. i. 2. Heb x. 10, 29. Isa. x. 17. l 1 Cor. xv. 31. m ch. iii. 27 reff.

om *και αυτοι* DF Chr-comm[not 1-ms]. for *αγαθωσυνης*, *αγαπης* F vulg Ambrst Pel. ins *και* bef *πεπληρωμενοι* DF Syr. ins *της* B[P]א k n $Clem_1$ [Damasc]: om ACDFL rel. *αλληλους* bef *δυναμενοι* and om *και* $D^{1.3}$[-gr] F. for *αλληλ.*, *αλλους* L rel vulg syrr Chr_2 Thdrt Thl Œc [$Orig\text{-}int_2$]: txt ABCDFא[P 47] (f?).

15. *τολμηροτερως* AB: txt CDFL[P]א rel. om *αδελφοι* ABCא[1] copt æth Chr_1 Cyr[-p_2 $Orig\text{-}int_2$] Aug_1: ins DFL[P]א[3] rel vulg Syr [syr arm Damasc] Thdrt Ambrst. for *επαναμ.*, *αναμιμνησκων* B: *υπαναμ.* o. for *υπο*, *απο* BFא[1] Damasc: txt ACDL[P]א[3] rel.

16. for *ειναι*, *γενεσθαι* D^1[-gr] F[-gr]. rec *ιησ.* bef *χρ.*, with DL rel Syr copt [æth arm] Chr_1 Thdrt: txt ABCF[P]א m vulg syr Cyr[-p_2 Damasc] Orig[-int_1 Ambrst] Aug_2. om *εις τα εθνη* B. *γενηθη* B. om *ευπροσδεκτος* F $Fulg_1$.

17. rec om *την* (*the art not being understood*), with AL[P]א rel [arm] Chr_1 [Cyr-p_1 Damasc] Thdrt: ins B C[appy] DF m.

standing what I have written:' see ch. vii. 25, note. Meyer understands it, '*without information from others*:' Bengel and Olsh., '*I myself, as well as others*:' Rückert, 'I not only wish it (ver. 13), but *am persuaded for myself* that it is so.' **καὶ αὐτοί, ye also yourselves,** i. e. without exhortation of mine. **15.] ἀπὸ μέρους** restricts the τολμηρότερον to certain parts of the Epistle, e. g. ch. xi. 17, ff. 25; chaps. xiii. and xiv. **ἔγραψα,** the *dabam* or *scribebam* of the Latins in epistolary writing. **ὡς ἐπαν. ὑμ., as putting you anew in remembrance. διὰ τ. χάριν . . . . , because of the grace, &c.;** i. e. 'my apostolic office was the ground and reason of my boldness:'—not = διὰ τῆς χάριτος ch. xii. 3. **16.] That I might be** (εἰς τό gives the *purpose of the grace being given*, not of the ἔγραψα) **a ministering priest of Christ Jesus for** (in reference to) **the Gentiles, ministering in the Gospel of God** (ἱερουργοῦντα, προσφέροντα θυσίαν, Hesych.: but the εὐαγγέλ. τ. θεοῦ is not the θυσία, but signifies *that wherein*, in behoof of which, the ἱερουργεῖν took place: so Josephus, de Macc. § 7, speaking of the martyrs for the law, says, τοιούτους δεῖ εἶναι τοὺς **ἱερουργοῦντας τὸν νόμον** ἰδίῳ αἵματι, καὶ γενναίῳ ἱδρῶτι τοῖς μέχρι θανάτου πάθεσιν ὑπερασπίζοντας), **that the offering [up] of the Gentiles** (gen. of apposition: *the Gentiles themselves are the offering*; so Theophyl. αὕτη μοι ἱερωσύνη, τὸ καταγγέλλειν εὐαγγέλιον. μάχαιραν ἔχω τὸν λόγον· θυσία ἐστὲ ὑμεῖς) **may be acceptable, sanctified by the Holy Ghost.** The language is evidently figurative, and can by no possibility be taken as a sanction for any view of the Christian minister as a *sacrificing priest*, otherwise than *according to that figure*—viz. that he offers to God *the acceptable sacrifice of those who by his means believe on Christ.* "Facit se antistitem vel sacerdotem in Evangelii ministerio, qui populum, quem Deo acquirit, in sacrificium offerat, atque hoc modo sacris Evangelii mysteriis operetur. Et sane hoc est Christiani pastoris sacerdotium, homines in Evangelii obedientiam subigendo veluti Deo immolare: non, quod superciliose hactenus Papistæ jactarunt, oblatione homines reconciliare Deo. Neque tamen ecclesiasticos pastores simpliciter hic vocat Sacerdotes, tanquam perpetuo titulo: sed quum dignitatem efficaciamque ministerii vellet commendare Paulus, hac metaphora per occasionem est usus. Hic ergo finis sit Evangelii præconibus in suo munere, animas fide purificatas Deo offerre." Calvin.

17—22.] *The Apostle boasts of the extent and result of his apostolic mission among the Gentiles, and that in places*

χριστῷ Ἰησοῦ [n] τὰ πρὸς τὸν θεόν· 18 οὐ γὰρ [o] τολμήσω
τι [o] λαλεῖν [p] ὧν οὐ [q] κατειργάσατο χριστὸς δι' ἐμοῦ [r] εἰς
[r] ὑπακοὴν ἐθνῶν, [s] λόγῳ καὶ [s] ἔργῳ, 19 [t] ἐν δυνάμει
σημείων καὶ [u] τεράτων, [t] ἐν δυνάμει πνεύματος [ἁγίου],
ὥςτε με ἀπὸ Ἱερουσαλὴμ καὶ [v] κύκλῳ [w] μέχρι τοῦ Ἰλ-
λυρικοῦ [x] πεπληρωκέναι τὸ εὐαγγέλιον τοῦ χριστοῦ.
20 οὕτω δὲ [y] φιλοτιμούμενον [z] εὐαγγελίζεσθαι, οὐχ ὅπου
[a] ὠνομάσθη χριστός, ἵνα μὴ ἐπ' [b] ἀλλότριον [c] θεμέλιον

ABCD FL[P]א a b c d f g h k l m n o 17 [47]

n Luke xiv. 32. Acts xxviii. 10. Heb. ii. 17. v. 1.
o Phil. i. 14. see 2 Macc. iv. 2.
p attr., Acts xxi. 19. 1 Cor. vii. 1. 2 Cor. xii. 17. Heb. v. 8. Winer, edn. 6, § 24. 2, end.
q ch. ii. 9 reff.
r ch. i. 5 (reff.).
s 2 Cor. x. 11. Col. iii. 17. 1 John iii. 18. (see 1 Cor. iv. 19, 20. 1 Thess. i. 5.)
t ver. 13.
u Acts vii. 36 reff.
v absol., Mark iii. 34. vi. 6, 36. Luke ix. 12 only. 2 Chron. xxxiv. 6. w. gen., Rev. iv. 6. v. 11. vii. 11 only. Gen. xxxv. 5 al.
w of place, here only. (ch. v. 14 reff.) Job xxxviii. 11.
x = Col. i. 25. see Acts xii. 25.
y 2 Cor. v. 9. 1 Thess. iv. 11 only †.
z absol., Luke ix. 6. xx. 1. Acts xiv. 7. 1 Cor. i. 17. ix. 16 bis, 18 only. Nah. i. 15.
a = 2 Tim. ii. 19 only. Isa. xxvi. 13.
b ch. xiv. 4 reff.
c = 1 Cor. iii. 10, 11, 12. Heb. vi. 1.

rec om *τον*, with b: ins ABCDFL[P]א rel Did$_2$ Chr Cyr$_1$ Damasc Thdrt Œc.

18. for *τολμησω*, *τολμω* Bא^3 latt Did$_2$ Dial-trin$_1$ Cyr[-p$_1$ Orig-int$_2$ Archel Ambrst]. rec *λαλειν* bef *τι*, with L rel copt [syrr æth arm] Œc: txt ABCDF[P]א m [vulg] Bas$_1$ Ath$_1$ Did$_3$ Archel Chr$_2$ *Cyr*[-p] Thdrt [Damasc Orig-int$_2$ Ambrst]—for *λαλειν*, *ειπειν* DF: *λεγειν* and *λαλησαι* gr-ff. *κατηργασατο* DFL. ins *ο* bef *χριστος* F. aft *δι εμου* add *λογων* B. for *υπακ.*, *ακοην* B.

19. aft 1st *δυναμ.* ins *αυτου* D^{1}F. (G^1 also ins *αυτου* aft 2nd *δυν.*) rec aft *πνευματος* ins *θεου*, with D^{2}L[P]א rel Syr [syr-txt Euthal-ms] Chr-txt$_2$ Cyr[-p$_1$ Damasc] Thdrt Thl Œc; *αγιου* AC D$^{1\cdot3}$[and lat] F c m 17 [47] vulg copt syr[-marg] arm Ath$_1$ Bas$_1$ Chr-comm Cyr[-p$_2$ Did$_2$] Dial$_1$: om B Pel-comm Vig$_1$. *ωστε πεπληρωσθαι απο ιερ. μεχρι του ιλλ. και κυκλω το* DF.

20. *φιλοτιμουμαι* (*corrn of constr*) B D^1[-gr] F[P]: *-μουμενος* 116-[29^2]: om vulg D-lat [Orig-int$_1$]: txt ACD$^{2\cdot3}$Lא rel Orig. [*ευαγγελισασθαι* P n Chr-mss$_1$.] for *ουχ οπου*, *οπου ουκ* D^1[-gr] F Chr$_1$. ins *ο* bef *χριστος* D^{1}F Chr$_2$. *επ' απολλοτριω θεμελιω* F.

where none had preached before him. **I have therefore** (consequent on the grace and ministry just mentioned) **my boasting** (i. e. 'I venture to boast:' not = ἔχω καύχημα, '*I have whereof I may glory,*' as E. V., but, as De W., = ἔχω καυχᾶσθαι, '*I can, or dare, boast*') **in Christ Jesus** (there is no stress on ἐν χρ. Ἰησ.,—it merely qualifies τὴν καύχησιν as no vain glorying, but grounded in, consistent with, springing from, his relation and subserviency to Christ) **of** (concerning) **matters relating to God** (my above-named sacerdotal office and ministry). **18.**] The connexion is: 'I have *real* ground for glorying (in a legitimate and Christian manner);' **for I will not** (as some false apostles do, see 2 Cor. x. 12—18) **allow myself to speak of any of those things which** (ὧν for ἐκείνων, ἅ, attr.) **Christ did** NOT **work by me** (but by some other) **in order to the obedience** (subjection to the Gospel) **of the Gentiles** (then, as if the sentence were in the affirmative form, 'I will only boast of what Christ has veritably done *by me* towards the obedience of the Gentiles,' he proceeds) **by word and deed,** **19.**] **in the power of signs and wonders, in the power of the [Holy] Spirit** (the signs and wonders (reff.) are not spiritual, but external miraculous acts,—see 2 Cor. xii. 12), **so that** (result of the κατειργάσατο) **from Jerusalem** (the eastern boundary of his preaching) **and the neighbourhood** (κύκλῳ is not to be joined with μέχρι τ. Ἰλλ. as Calov., al., but refers (reff.) to Jerusalem, meaning perhaps its immediate neighbourhood, perhaps Arabia (?), Gal. i. 17,—but hardly Damascus and Cilicia, as De W. suggests, seeing that they would come into the route afterwards specified, from Jerusalem to Illyricum), **as far as Illyricum** (Illyricum bordered on Macedonia to the S. It is possible that Paul may literally have advanced to its frontiers during his preaching in Macedonia; but I think it more probable, that he uses it broadly as the '*terminus ad quem*,' the next province to that in which he had preached), **I have fulfilled** (ref.:—'*executed my office of preaching,*' so that εὐαγγέλιον τοῦ χρ. = τὸ εὐαγγελίζεσθαι τὸν χρ.) **the Gospel of Christ.**

20.] **But** (limits the foregoing assertion) **thus** (after the following rule) **being careful** (reff.: the word in the Apostle's usage seems to lose its primary meaning of '*making a point of honour.*' The particip. agrees with με, ver. 19) **to preach the Gospel, not where Christ was** (previously) **named, that I might not build on the foundation of another, but according as it is written** (i. e. according to the following

[d] οἰκοδομῶ, 21 [e] ἀλλὰ καθὼς γέγραπται Οἷς οὐκ [f] ἀνηγγέλη περὶ αὐτοῦ, ὄψονται, καὶ οἳ οὐκ ἀκηκόασιν [g] συν-
ήσουσιν. 22 διὸ καὶ [h] ἐνεκοπτόμην [i] τὰ [i] πολλὰ [k] τοῦ ἐλθεῖν
πρὸς ὑμᾶς· 23 νυνὶ δὲ μηκέτι [l] τόπον ἔχων ἐν τοῖς
[m] κλίμασιν τούτοις, [n] ἐπιποθίαν δὲ ἔχων [o] τοῦ ἐλθεῖν
πρὸς ὑμᾶς [p] ἀπὸ [qr] ἱκανῶν [r] ἐτῶν, 24 [s] ὡς ἂν πορεύωμαι
εἰς τὴν Σπανίαν, (ἐλπίζω γὰρ [t] διαπορευόμενος θεάσασθαι ὑμᾶς καὶ ἀφ' ὑμῶν [u] προπεμφθῆναι [v] ἐκεῖ, ἐὰν ὑμῶν
πρῶτον [w] ἀπὸ [w] μέρους [x] ἐμπλησθῶ.) 25 νυνὶ δὲ πορεύ-

d = Gal. ii. 18. (ἐποικ., 1 Cor. iii. 12.)
e ver. 3.
f Acts xiv. 27 reff. Isa. lii 15.
g ch. iii. 11. Matt. xiii. 13, &c. Eph v. 17. Ps. ii. 10. Prov. ii. 5.
h Acts xxiv. 4 reff.
i here only. Xen. Hell. vi. 2. 30.
k constr., Acts xiv. 18 reff.
l = Acts xxv. 16 reff. Sir. iv. 5.
m 2 Cor. xi. 10. Gal. i. 21 only. (Judg. xx. 2 A Ald. compl.?)
n here only +. (-θεῖν, ch. i. 11.)
o constr., Acts xiv. 9 reff.
p Luke viii. 43.
q = Acts ix. 23 reff. Luke xxiii. 8 al.
r 2 Macc. i. 20.
s = 1 Cor. xi. 34. Phil. ii. 23.
t absol., Luke xviii. 36 (vi. 1. xiii. 22. Acts xvi. 4) only. Zech. ix. 8. Xen. Anab. ii. 2. 11.
u Acts xv. 3 reff.
v = Matt. ii. 22. John xi. 8. xviii. 3.
w ver. 15.
x = here (Luke i. 53. vi. 25. John vi. 12) only. Eccl. vi. 3. Polyb. i. 17. 3. see Acts xiv. 17.

21. απηγγελη C (238 ?): ανηγγελλη(sic) ℵ c h k^2 o. οψονται bef οις ανηγ. π. αυ. B m [copt].

22. for ενεκοπτομην, ενεκοπην DF. for τα πολλα, πολλακις BDF: txt ACL[P]ℵ rel Chr$_1$ Thdrt [Damasc].

23. [for μηκ., ουκετι P.] for 2nd εχων, εχω (*corrn of constr*) D^1F m o. om του A. rec (for ικανων) πολλων (*more usual exprn*), with ADFLℵ rel Chr$_1$ Thdrt: txt BC[P] m Damasc.

24. rec (for αν) εαν, with L rel Chr$_1$ Thdrt: txt AB C(appy) DF[P]ℵ Chr$_1$ Damasc. add ουν DF. πορευομαι DF[P] a^1 b^1 c f m^1 n [47 Euthal-ms]: -σομαι L 122^2: txt ABCℵ rel Chr$_1$ Thl. rec aft σπανιαν ins ελευσομαι προς υμας (*to fill up the aposiopesis: see note*), with Lℵ^3 rel syr [Euthal-ms] Thdrt Thl Œc: om ABCDF[P]ℵ^1 latt Syr copt æth arm Chr$_1$ Damasc [Orig-int$_2$] Ambrst Pel Sedul. om γαρ F latt Syr copt æth [arm Orig-int$_2$] (*videbo vos et a vobis deducar* Ambrst): ins ABCDL[P]ℵ syr [copt Euthal-ms] (Thdrt$_1$) Damasc Thl Œc: δε a^2 3. 5. 108^1-20 Chr-ms Thdrt$_1$. πορευομενος A 62 Damasc$_1$. rec (for αφ) υφ, with ACL[P]ℵ rel Chr$_1$ [Thdrt Damasc]: txt B(απο) DF [47. for προπεμφθ., πορευθηναι P.]

rule of Scripture: I determined to act in the spirit of these words, forming part of a general prophecy of the dispersion of that Gospel which I was preaching), &c. The citation is from the LXX, περὶ αὐτοῦ referring to ὁ παῖς μου, ver. 13, but being unrepresented in the Heb. Our E. V. renders: "That which had not been told them, shall they see: and that which they had not heard, shall they consider."

22.] **διό**, not, *because a foundation had been already laid at Rome by another:* this would refer to merely a secondary part of the foregoing assertion: διό refers to the *primary*, viz. his having been so earnestly engaged in preaching elsewhere. **τὰ πολλά, these many times:** not [*'for the most part,'* or], as Meyer, Fritz., *'the greater number of times,'*—which would suggest the idea that there had been other occasions on which this hindrance had not been operative.

23.] **μηκ. τόπ. ἔχων, I have no more occasion**, viz. of apostolic work. The *participial construction* prevails throughout, the participles standing as direct verbs. This not having been seen, the words ἐλεύσομαι πρὸς ὑμᾶς have been inserted to fill up what seemed an aposiopesis. **Now, however, I have no longer any business in these parts, but have had for many years past a desire to see you, whenever** (as soon as) **I journey into Spain.** Respecting the question whether this journey into Spain was ever taken, the views of Commentators have differed, according to their conclusion respecting the liberation of the Apostle from his imprisonment at Rome. I have discussed this in the Prolegg. to the Pastoral Epistles, § ii. The reader may see, on the side of the *completion of the journey*, Neander, Pfl. u. Leit., ed. 4, pp. 527—552,—and on the other side, Dr. Davidson, Introd. to N. T. vol. ii. pp. 96—132, and Wieseler, Chron. der Apost. Zeitalt., Excursus I., where a copious list of books on both sides is given. 24.] **ἀπὸ μέρους** is an affectionate limitation of ἐμπλησθῶ, implying that he would wish to remain much longer than he anticipated being able to do,—and also, as

ομαι εἰς Ἱερουσαλὴμ [y] διακονῶν τοῖς [z] ἁγίοις. 26 [a] εὐ- ABCD
δόκησαν γὰρ Μακεδονία καὶ Ἀχαΐα [b] κοινωνίαν τινὰ FL[P]א abcdf
ποιήσασθαι [c] εἰς τοὺς πτωχοὺς τῶν [z] ἁγίων τῶν ἐν Ἱερου- ghkl mno17
σαλήμ. 27 [a] εὐδόκησαν γάρ, καὶ [d] ὀφειλέται εἰσὶν αὐτῶν. [47]
εἰ γὰρ τοῖς [e] πνευματικοῖς αὐτῶν [f] ἐκοινώνησαν τὰ ἔθνη,
[g] ὀφείλουσιν καὶ ἐν τοῖς [h] σαρκικοῖς [i] λειτουργῆσαι αὐτοῖς.
28 τοῦτο οὖν [k] ἐπιτελέσας καὶ [l] σφραγισάμενος αὐτοῖς τὸν
[m] καρπὸν τοῦτον [n] ἀπελεύσομαι δι' ὑμῶν [n] εἰς Σπανίαν·
29 οἶδα δὲ ὅτι ἐρχόμενος πρὸς ὑμᾶς ἐν [o] πληρώματι [p] εὐλογίας χριστοῦ ἐλεύσομαι. 30 [q] παρακαλῶ δὲ ὑμᾶς,
[ἀδελφοί,] [q] διὰ τοῦ κυρίου ἡμῶν Ἰησοῦ χριστοῦ καὶ [q] διὰ
τῆς [r] ἀγάπης τοῦ [r] πνεύματος, [s] συναγωνίσασθαί μοι ἐν

y = 2 Tim. i. 18. Philem. 13. Heb. vi. 10. pres. part., Winer, edn. 6, § 45. 1. 2. *a*. Acts vi. 11. xv. 27.
z = Acts ix. 13 reff.
a = Luke xii. 32. 1 Cor. i. 21. Gal. i. 15. Ps. lxvii. 16.
b = 2 Cor. ix. 13. Heb. xiii. 16 only. (-νεῖν, ver. 27. ch. xii. 13.)
c = 1 Cor. xvi. 1 reff.
d ch. i. 14 reff.
e Paul (ch. i. 11. vii. 14. 1 Cor. ix. 11 al.) only, exc. 1 Pet. ii. 5, bis +.
f ch. xii. 13 reff.
g ver. 1 reff.
h = 1 Cor. ix. 11 (iii. 3 reff.).
i = here only. (Acts xiii. 2 reff.) 3 Kings i. 4. (-γία, 2 Cor. ix. 12. -γός, ver. 16.)
k 2 Cor. vii. 1. viii. 6, 11 bis. 1 Kings iii. 12. of sacred rites, Heb. ix. 6.
l see John iii. 33.
m = Gal. v. 22. Eph. v. 9. Heb. xii. 11. James iii. 18.
n = Matt. viii. 19. x. 5 al. fr. Josh. vi. 11.
o = Eph. iii. 19.
p ch. xvi. 18. 1 Cor. x. 16. 2 Cor. ix. 5 al. Ezek. xxxiv. 26.
q ch. xii. 1 reff.
r here only. see Col. i. 8.
s here only +. (ἀγων- Col. iv. 12.)

25. διακονησαι DF latt [Orig-int$_1$ Ambrst]: διακονησων א^1: txt ABCL[P]א^3 rel.
26. ευδοκησεν B 62. 120 Thdrt$_1$[(and ms$_1$) Chr-c$_1$]: G-lat has both (ηυδ. B^{1}א m [Chr-com]: so [A]א m Chr-ms in next ver). μακαιδονες και αχαιακοι F, D^1-lat also has μακαιδονες. των εν ιερ. αγιων D F[-gr].
27. for ευδοκ. γαρ και οφειλεται, οφειλ. γαρ DF Ambrst. rec αυτων bef εισι, with FL rel: txt ABCD[P]א vulg(with am &c agst fuld &c) spec Syr copt [arm Damasc Orig-int$_1$] Ambrst. om 2nd αυτων L.
28. aft τουτο ουν ins αρα F. σφραγισαμενοις(sic) א. om αυτοις B 76. 108. δι υμας F. rec ins την bef σπανιαν (*none om την in ver* 24), with CLא^3 rel: om ABDF[P]א^1 m Chr$_1$ [Damasc].
29. for οιδα δε, γινωσκω γαρ F. om ερχομενος F. πληροφορια D^{1}F. rec ins του ευαγγελιου του bef χριστου (*prob a gloss*), with Lא^3 rel vulg[-clem arm-mss] syrr Chr$_1$ Thdrt: om ABCDF[P]א^1 am(with demid harl [fuld tol]) copt æth arm[-ed](om χρ. also) Clem$_1$ [Orig-int$_4$ Ambrst].
30. om αδελφοι B 76 æth Chr$_1$: ins bef παρακ. υμ. a(in red) lectt (and C^3-marg); bef υμ., demid: add μου syrr copt (*the variations in posn are suspicious: but may not the word, characteristic as it is here, have been first rejected as unnecessary, and then noted in the margin, and variously inserted? Lachm retains it*). ins ονοματος του bef κυριου L a 74. 120 lectt.

Chrys. οὐδεὶς γάρ με χρόνος ἐμπλῆσαι δύναται, οὐδὲ ἐμποιῆσαί μοι κόρον τῆς συνουσίας ὑμῶν. **25.**] See Acts xix. 21; xxiv. 17; 2 Cor. viii. 19. **διακονῶν,** not the future, because he treats the whole action as already begun; see reff. **26.**] See 2 Cor. ix. 1, ff. **κοινων.**] See reff. Olsh. remarks, on **τοὺς πτωχοὺς τ. ἁγίων,** that this shews the community of goods in the church at Jerusalem not to have lasted long: cf. Gal. ii. 10. **27.**] The *fact* is re-stated, with a view to an inference from it, viz. that the εὐδόκησαν was not merely a matter of benevolence, but of *repayment*: the Gentiles being debtors to the Jews for spiritual blessings. This general principle is very similarly enounced in 1 Cor. ix. 11. It is suggested by Grot., al., that by this Paul wished to hint to the Romans the duty of a similar contribution. **28.**] **καρπόν,** hardly, as Calv., al., "proventum quem ex Evangelii satione ad Judæos redire nuper dixit:" more probably said generally,—*fruit of the faith and love of the Gentiles.* **σφραγισ.,** ὡς εἰς βασιλικὰ ταμιεῖα ἐναποθέμενος ὡς ἐν ἀσύλῳ κ. ἀσφαλεῖ χωρίῳ, Chrys. Hom. xxx. p. 739. **δι' ὑμῶν, through your city.** **29.**] **The fulness of the blessing of Christ** imports that richness of apostolic grace which he was persuaded he should impart to them. So he calls his presence in the churches a χάρις, 2 Cor. i. 15. See also ch. i. 11. **30—32.**] **τ. ἀγάπ. τ. πνεύμ.,** *the love shed abroad in the heart by the Holy Ghost;*—a love which teaches us to look not only on our own things, but on the things of others. **συναγων.**] "Ipse oret oportet, qui alios vult orare secum. Orare, *agon* est,

ταῖς [t]προσευχαῖς ὑπὲρ ἐμοῦ [t]πρὸς τὸν θεόν, 31 ἵνα
[u]ῥυσθῶ ἀπὸ τῶν [v]ἀπειθούντων ἐν τῇ Ἰουδαίᾳ, καὶ ἡ
[w]διακονία μου [x]ἡ εἰς Ἱερουσαλὴμ [y]εὐπρόσδεκτος τοῖς
[z]ἁγίοις γένηται, 32 ἵνα [a]ἐν χαρᾷ ἔλθω πρὸς ὑμᾶς [b]διὰ
[b]θελήματος [b]θεοῦ[, καὶ [c]συναναπαύσωμαι ὑμῖν]. 33 ὁ δὲ
[d]θεὸς τῆς [d]εἰρήνης [e]μετὰ πάντων ὑμῶν. ἀμήν.
XVI. 1 [f]Συνίστημι δὲ ὑμῖν Φοίβην τὴν ἀδελφὴν ἡμῶν,
οὖσαν [g]διάκονον τῆς ἐκκλησίας τῆς ἐν Κεγχρεαῖς, 2 ἵνα
[h]προσδέξησθε αὐτὴν [hi]ἐν κυρίῳ [k]ἀξίως τῶν [l]ἁγίων καὶ

t Acts xii. 5 reff. u = ch. vii. 24 reff. v = Acts xiv. 2 reff. w = Acts vi. 1 reff. x ellips., ch. ii. 8 al. fr. y ver. 16 reff. z = vv. 25, 26. a = 1 Cor. ii. 3 al. b 1 Cor. i. 1. 2 Cor. i. 1. viii. 5. Eph. i. 1. Col. i. 1. 2 Tim. i. 1 only. c here only. (see 1 Cor. xvi. 18. 2 Cor. vii. 13.) Isa. xi. 6 only. d ch. xvi. 20. 1 Cor. xiv. 33. 2 Cor. xiii. 11. Phil. iv. 9. 1 Thess. v. 23. Heb. xiii. 20. (2 Thess. iii. 16.) e ellips., Matt. i. 23. ch. xvi. 20 [24]. 1 Cor. xvi. 23, 24 al. f = 2 Cor. iii. 1. v. 12. (ch. iii. 5 reff.) 1 Macc. xii. 43. g = Phil. i. 1. 1 Tim. iii. 8, 12. fem., here only. h = Phil. ii. 29. i vv. 8, 12. 1 Cor. xvi. 19 al. k Eph. iv. 1. Phil. i. 27. Col. i. 10. 1 Thess. ii. 12. 3 John 6 only †. Wisd. vii. 15. xvi. 1. Sir. xiv. 11 only. l = Acts ix. 13 reff.

aft *προσευχαις* ins *υμων* DF [n²] vulg-ed(not am demid fuld harl² [mar]) [copt æth] Pel. om *υπερ εμου* F [D¹-lat Orig-int₂].

31. rec aft *και* ins *ινα*, with D²·³[-gr] Lℵ³ rel syr Chr₁ Thdrt [Thl Œc] : om AB C[appy] D¹F[P]ℵ¹ latt Syr copt arm Damasc [Orig-int₁] Ambrst Pel. for *διακονια*, *δωροφορια* (*corrn to avoid harshness of* *διακον. εις ιερ.*: *see below*) BD¹F, *remuneratio* D¹-lat, *munerum meorum ministratio* Ambrst : txt AC D²·³-gr Lℵ vss(*administratio* G-lat, *obsequii oblatio* vulg, *ministerium* D²-lat [Orig-int]) Chr₁ Thdrt Damasc Thl Œc. om 2nd *η* L[P] b¹ h m 73. 93. 122 Thdrt[-ms₂] Chr-ms. for *εις*, *εν* BD¹F : txt ACD³L[P]ℵ rel Chr-ms Thdrt₂ [Damasc] Thl. [for *ευπρος.*, *προσδεκτος* F.] rec *γενηται* bef *τοις αγιοις*, with DFL rel [(vulg) syr copt arm Chr₁ Thdrt Orig-int₁] : txt ABC[P]ℵ m.

32. *ελθων* AC ℵ¹ 17 [copt arm Orig-int₁ (of these] ℵ¹ [copt Orig-int have it] bef *χαρα*). for *θεου*, *κυριου ιησου* B [*domini* æth(" ut sæpe pro *θεος*," Tischdf] : *χριστου ιησου* D¹F [fuld] : *ιησου χριστου* ℵ¹ : txt ACD³L[P]ℵ³ rel [vulg syrr copt arm] Chr₁ Thdrt Damasc Thl Œc [Orig-int₁]. om *και συναναπαυσωμαι υμιν* B : ins (ACDF)L(ℵ) rel vss Chr₂ Euthal₁ Thdrt Damasc Thl Œc [(Orig-int) Ambrst] : om *και* ℵ¹[AC æth arm Damasc Orig-int].—*αναψυξω* D : *αναψυχω* F.—*μεθ υμων* DF latt.

33. ins *ητω* bef *μετα* D¹F latt Syr [æth arm Orig-int₁]. om *αμην* AF : ins BCDL[P]ℵ rel [vulg syrr copt æth arm] Chr₁ Thdrt Damasc Thl Œc [Orig-int₁].

Chap. XVI. **1.** om *δε* D¹F æth arm Sedul. *υμων* A F[-gr] P [k] Thl. aft *ουσαν* ins *και* BC¹ℵ³ 47.

2. rec *αυτην* bef *προσδεξησθε*, with ALPℵ rel vulg Chr₁ Thdrt [Euthal-ms Damasc Orig-int₁] Ambrst : txt BCDF d harl copt.

præsertim ubi *homines* resistunt." Bengel.

31.] Compare Acts xx. 22; xxi. 10—14. The exceeding hatred in which the Apostle was held by the Jews, and their want of fellow-feeling with the Gentile churches, made him fear lest even the ministration with which he was charged might not prove acceptable to them.

32.] **διὰ θελ. θεοῦ** = *ἐὰν ὁ κύριος θελήσῃ*, 1 Cor. iv. 19: otherwise in reff.

[κ. συναν. ὑμ., and may refresh myself together with you;—i. e. 'that we may mutually refresh ourselves, I after my dangers and deliverance, you after your anxieties for me.' But the text is in some confusion.] Chap. XVI. 1—16.] Recommendation of Phœbe: Greetings.

1, 2.] In all probability Phœbe was the bearer of the Epistle, as stated in the (rec.) subscription. **διάκονον**] **Deaconess.** See 1 Tim. iii. 11, note. Pliny in his celebrated letter to Trajan says, "necessarium credidi, ex duabus ancillis quæ *ministræ* dicebantur, quid esset veri et per tormenta quærere." A minute discussion of their office, &c., in later times may be found in Suicer, Thesaurus, sub voce; and in Bingham, book ii. chap. 22, § 8. Neander, Pfl. u. Leit., ed. 4, pp. 265—267, shews that the deaconesses must not be confounded with the *χῆραι* of 1 Tim. v. 3—16, as has sometimes been done. Kenchreæ, the port of Corinth (*τῶν Κορινθίων ἐπίνειον*, Philo in Flacc. § 19, vol. ii., p. 539: *κώμη τις τῆς Κορίνθου μεγίστη*, Theodoret, h. l.) on the Saronic gulf of the Ægean, for commerce with the east (Acts xviii. 18): seventy stadia from Corinth, Strabo viii. 380. Pausan. ii. 2, 3. Livy xxxii. 17. Plin. iv. 4. The Apostolical Constitutions (vii. 46, p. 1053, Migne) make the first bishop of the Cen-

m παραστῆτε αὐτῇ ἐν ᾧ ἂν ὑμῶν n χρῄζῃ πράγματι· καὶ
γὰρ αὐτὴ o προστάτις πολλῶν ἐγενήθη, καὶ ἐμοῦ αὐτοῦ.
3 Ἀσπάσασθε Πρίσκαν καὶ Ἀκύλαν τοὺς p συνεργούς
μου ἐν χριστῷ Ἰησοῦ, 4 q οἵτινες ὑπὲρ τῆς r ψυχῆς μου
τὸν ἑαυτῶν st τράχηλον su ὑπέθηκαν, οἷς οὐκ ἐγὼ μόνος
v εὐχαριστῶ ἀλλὰ καὶ πᾶσαι αἱ w ἐκκλησίαι τῶν ἐθνῶν,
5 καὶ τὴν xy κατ' οἶκον αὐτῶν x ἐκκλησίαν. ἀσπάσασθε
Ἐπαίνετον τὸν z ἀγαπητόν μου, ὅς ἐστιν a ἀπαρχὴ τῆς

ABCDF L[P]ℵ a b c d f g h k l m n o 17 [47]

m — 2 Tim. iv. 17 only. Jer. xv. 11. n Matt. vi. 32. Luke xi. 8. xii. 30. 2 Cor. iii. 1 only. Judg. xi. 7 B al. (only?). o here only †. (-της, 1 Chron. xxvii. 31. see Rom. xii. 8.) p Paul (vv. 9, 21. 1 Cor. iii. 9 al8.) only, exc. 3 John 8 †. 2 Macc. viii. 7. xiv. 5 only. (-γεῖν, ch. viii. 28.) q = Acts x. 41 reff. r = Acts xv. 26 reff. s here only. Sir. li. 26 (but not =). t Acts xv. 10 reff. u 1 Tim. iv. 6 only. v to *man*, here only. (ch. i. 8 reff.) w ver. 16 reff. x 1 Cor. xvi. 19. Col. iv. 15. Philem. 2. y Acts ii. 46 reff. z Acts xv. 25 reff. a ch. viii. 23 reff.

for προστατις to εμου, και εμου και αλλων προστατις εγενετο D; κ. ε. κ. α. παραστατεις [εγ.] F. rec αυτου bef εμου, with rel [arm] Chr-c$_1$-montf$_1$ Œc: και αυτου και εμου ℵ: txt ABC L(Treg, expr) P d m vulg [Syr] syr copt [æth] Chr-2-mss$_1$ Thdrt Damasc Thl [Orig-int$_1$], εμου τε αυτου A.

3. [ασπασθε F (so often below).] rec πρισκιλλαν (*corrn to Acts* xviii. 2, *&c*), with rel syrr æth Chr$_1$ Thdrt(τὴν γὰρ Πρίσκιλλαν ἢ Πρίσκαν, ἀμφότερα γάρ ἐστιν εὑρεῖν ἐν τοῖς βιβλίοις) Ambrst: txt ABCDFLPℵ d g h m [n] 17. 47 [vulg copt arm Euthal-ms Damasc Orig-int$_1$]. at end, instead of in ver 5, ins και τ. κατ. οικ. αυτ. εκκλ. D[1]F.

[4. εαυτον P c. υπεθ. bef τραχ. P.]

5. [om 1st clause P; see D[1]F, ver 3.] for απαρχη, απ' αρχης D[1]-gr, *in principio* D[1]-lat: *a principio* G-lat: om απαρχη της P[1].

chrean church to have been Lucius, consecrated by Paul himself (Winer, Realw.). The western port, on the Sinus Corinthiacus, was Leche (Paus.), Lecheæ (Plin.), or Lecheum (Strab., Ptol.). **2.**] **ἐν κυρίῳ**, *in a Christian manner*,—as mindful of your common Lord: **ἀξίως τ. ἁγίων**, '*in a manner worthy of saints*;' i. e. '*as saints ought to do*,'—refers to προσδέξησθε, and therefore to *their* conduct to her;—not, 'as saints *ought to be received*.' **παραστῆτε**] Her business at Rome may have been such as to require the help of those resident there. **προστάτις πολλῶν**] This may refer to a part of the deaconess's office, the attending on the poor and sick of her own sex. **κ. ἐμοῦ αὐτοῦ**] when and where, we know not. It is not improbable that she may have been, like Lydia, one whose heart the Lord opened at the first preaching of Paul, and whose house was his lodging. **3, 4.**] The form Prisca is also found 2 Tim. iv. 19. On Prisca and Aquila see note, Acts xviii. 2. They must have returned to Rome from Ephesus since the sending of 1 Cor.:—see 1 Cor. xvi. 19: and we find them again at Ephesus (?), 2 Tim. iv. 19. Their endangering of their lives for Paul may have taken place at Corinth (Acts xviii. 6 ff.) or at Ephesus (Acts xix.). See Neander, Pfl. u. Leit., p. 441. "**ὑποτιθέναι** est *pignori opponere*. Demosth. in Aphobum: ἀπέτισα τὴν λειτουργίαν, ὑποθεὶς τὴν οἰκίαν καὶ τἀμαυτοῦ πάντα. Æschines: ὑπέθησαν αὐτῷ τοῦ ταλάντου τὰς δημοσίας προσόδους." Wetst. The '*churches of the Gentiles*' had reason to be thankful to them, for having *rescued the Apostle of the Gentiles* from danger. It seems to have been the practice of Aquila and Priscilla (ref. 1 Cor.) and some other Christians (reff. Col., Philem.) to hold assemblies for worship in their houses, which were saluted, and sent salutations as *one body* in the Lord. Some light is thrown on the expression by the following passage from the Acta Martyrii S. Justini, in Ruinart, cited by Neander, Church Hist. i. 330, Rose's trans. "The answer of Justin Martyr to the question of the prefect (Rusticus) 'Where do you assemble?' exactly corresponds to the genuine Christian spirit on this point. The answer was; 'Where each one can and will. You believe, no doubt, that we all meet together in one place; but it is not so, for the God of the Christians is not shut up in a room, but, being invisible, He fills both heaven and earth, and is honoured every where by the faithful.' Justin adds, that when he came to Rome, he was accustomed to dwell in one particular spot, and that those Christians who were instructed by him, and wished to hear his discourse, assembled at his house. (This assembly would accordingly be ἡ κατ' οἶκον τοῦ Ἰουστίνου ἐκκλησία.) He had not visited any other congregations of the Church." **5.**] Epænetus is not elsewhere named. **ἀπαρχή**,

Ἀσίας [b] εἰς χριστόν. 6 ἀσπάσασθε Μαριάν, [c] ἥτις πολλὰ
[d] ἐκοπίασεν εἰς ὑμᾶς. 7 ἀσπάσασθε Ἀνδρόνικον καὶ
Ἰουνιᾶν τοὺς [e] συγγενεῖς μου καὶ [f] συναιχμαλώτους μου,
[c] οἵτινές εἰσιν [g] ἐπίσημοι ἐν τοῖς [h] ἀποστόλοις, οἳ καὶ πρὸ
ἐμοῦ γέγοναν [i] ἐν χριστῷ. 8 ἀσπάσασθε Ἀμπλίατον τὸν
[z] ἀγαπητόν μου ἐν κυρίῳ. 9 ἀσπάσασθε Οὐρβανὸν τὸν
[k] συνεργὸν ἡμῶν ἐν χριστῷ, καὶ Στάχυν τὸν [z] ἀγαπητόν

b see ch. xv. 26. c Acts x. 41 reff. d Matt. vi. 28. Acts xx. 35 al. Ps. cxxvi. 1. e ch. vi. 3. Luke i. 36, 58. Acts x. 24 al. Levit. xxv. 45. f Col. iv. 10. Philem. 23 only +. g Matt. xxvii. 16 only. Esth. v. 4. 3 Macc. vi. 1. Polyb. xviii. 38. 1. Jos. Antt. v. 7. 1. h see Acts xiv. 4 note. i 1 Cor. i. 30. Eph. ii. 13. 1 Pet. v. 14. k ver. 3 reff.

rec for ασιας, αχαιας, with $D^{2.3}$LP rel syrr Chr_2 Thdrt Thl Œc: txt $ABCD^1F$א latt(not harl[1]) copt æth arm Damasc $Orig\text{-}int_{1expr}$ Ambrst. (*The rec has prob been an error of the scribe, who had απαρχη της αχαιας, 1 Cor xvi. 15, in his mind. To suppose, with De Wette, that he altered αχ. here to ασ. to avoid the inconsistency of* two *persons being the first fruits of Achaia, is surely too far-fetched.*) for εις χριστον, εν χριστω DF latt syrr $Orig\text{-}int_1$.

6. rec μαριαμ, with DFLא rel Chr_1 Thdrt [Damasc] Thl: txt ABCP copt arm. rec εις ημας, with C^2L rel syr $Chr\text{-}comm_1$ Thdrt Damasc Thl Œc: εν υμιν D F[-gr] latt[(*in domino* F-lat) Orig-int-mss vary between *nobis* and *vobis*] Ambrst: txt ABC^1Pא Syr copt æth [arm].

7. ins τους bef συναιχμαλωτους B. om οι א[1] [Damasc]. for οι κ. προ εμ. γεγ., τοις προ εμου DF. rec γεγονασιν, with CLP rel: txt A B(sic: see table) א. aft χριστω add ιησου DF Ambrst Pel Jer.

8. rec αμπλιαν, with B^2 C(appy) D[-gr] LP rel syrr [arm] Chr_1 Thdrt Chron Damasc Thl Œc: txt A B^1(Tischdf) Fא latt copt æth [$Orig\text{-}int_1$ Ambrst].—om τον B^1. om μου B F[-gr](not G).

9. [υμων P.] for χριστω, κυριω CDF c m arm Chr-3-mss: txt ABLPא rel [am fuld &c] syrr æth [copt Chr-montf Thdrt Damasc] $Orig\text{-}int_1$ [Ambrst, *in Christo Jesu* vulg-clem].

the same metaphor being in the Apostle's mind as in ch. xv. 16,—*the first believer.*

On **Ἀσίας** see var. readd. **εἰς χρ.**, elliptical: the full construction would be τῆς προσφορᾶς εἰς χρ. **6.**] *None of the names occurring from ver.* 5—15 *are mentioned elsewhere* (except possibly Rufus: see below). De Wette remarks, that, notwithstanding the manuscript authority, εἰς ἡμᾶς is perhaps the more likely reading, (1) because the Apostle would hardly mention a service done to *themselves* as a ground of salutation from him, and (2) because κοπιᾶν without being expressly followed by λόγῳ (1 Tim. v. 17: see Phil. ii. 16; Col. i. 29), said of *women*, most likely implies acts of kindness peculiar to the sex.

7.] Ἰουνιᾶν may be fem. (Ἰουνίαν), from Ἰουνία (Junia), in which case she is probably the wife of Andronicus,—or masc., from Ἰουνιᾶς (Junianus, contr. Junias). It is uncertain also whether συγγενεῖς means *fellow-countrymen*, or *relations.* Aquila and Priscilla were Jews: so would Maria be, and probably Epænetus, being an early believer. If so, the word may have its strict meaning of '*relations.*' But it seems to occur vv. 11, 21 in a wider sense. **συναιχμ.**] When and where, uncertain. **ἐπίσημοι ἐν τ. ἀποστ.**] Two renderings are given: (1) '*of note among the Apostles,*' so that *they themselves are counted among* the Apostles: thus the Greek ff. (τὸ ἀποστόλους εἶναι, μέγα· τὸ δὲ καὶ ἐν τούτοις ἐπισήμους εἶναι, ἐννόησον ἡλίκον ἐγκώμιον, Chrys.), Calv., Est., Wolf, Thol., Kölln., Olsh., al.: or (2) '*noted among the Apostles,*' i. e. *well known and spoken of by* the Apostles. Thus Beza, Grot., Koppe, Reiche, Meyer, Fritz., De W. But, as Thol. remarks, had this latter been the meaning, we should have expected some expression like διὰ πασῶν τῶν ἐκκλησιῶν (2 Cor. viii. 18). I may besides remark, that for Paul to speak of any persons as *celebrated among the Apostles* in sense (2), would imply that he had more frequent intercourse with the other Apostles, than we know that he had; and would besides be improbable on any supposition. The whole question seems to have sprung up in modern times from the idea that οἱ ἀπόστολοι must mean *the Twelve only.* If the wider sense found in Acts xiv. 4, 14; 2 Cor. viii. 23; 1 Thess. ii. 6 (compare i. 1) be taken, there need be no doubt concerning the meaning.

οἳ καὶ . . . .] refers to Andr. and Jun., not to the Apostles. In the use of **γέγοναν**, there is a mixed construction—"who have been longer than me," and "who *were* before me." **8 ff.**] Ampliatus = Amplias: see v. r. **ἀγ. ἐν κυρ.** beloved in the bonds of Christian fellowship.

l ch. xiv. 18 reff. m see 1 Cor. i. 11. n ch. viii. 33 reff. o = Acts ix. 13 reff. p 1 Cor. xvi. 20. 2 Cor. xiii. 12. 1 Thess. v. 26. see 1 Pet. v. 14. q as above (p). Luke vii. 45. xxii. 48 only. Prov. xxvii. 6. Cant. i. 2 only. r plur., Acts xv. 41. xvi. 5. ver. 4. 1 Cor. vii. 17. xi. 16 al.

μου. 10 ἀσπάσασθε Ἀπελλῆν τὸν l δόκιμον l ἐν χριστῷ. ABCDF L[P]ℵ a b c d f g h k l m n o 17 [47]
ἀσπάσασθε τοὺς ἐκ m τῶν Ἀριστοβούλου. 11 ἀσπάσασθε
Ἡρωδίωνα τὸν e συγγενῆ μου. ἀσπάσασθε τοὺς ἐκ m τῶν
Ναρκίσσου τοὺς ὄντας ἐν κυρίῳ. 12 ἀσπάσασθε Τρύφαι-
ναν καὶ Τρυφῶσαν τὰς d κοπιώσας ἐν κυρίῳ. ἀσπάσασθε
Περσίδα τὴν z ἀγαπητήν, ἥτις πολλὰ d ἐκοπίασεν ἐν κυρίῳ.
13 ἀσπάσασθε Ῥοῦφον τὸν n ἐκλεκτὸν ἐν κυρίῳ, καὶ τὴν
μητέρα αὐτοῦ καὶ ἐμοῦ. 14 ἀσπάσασθε Ἀσύγκριτον, Φλέ-
γοντα, Ἑρμῆν, Πατρόβαν, Ἑρμᾶν, καὶ τοὺς σὺν αὐτοῖς
ἀδελφούς. 15 ἀσπάσασθε Φιλόλογον καὶ Ἰουλίαν, Νηρέα
καὶ τὴν ἀδελφὴν αὐτοῦ, καὶ Ὀλυμπᾶν, καὶ τοὺς σὺν e παν και τους...
αὐτοῖς πάντας o ἁγίους. 16 ἀσπάσασθε ἀλλήλους p ἐν ABCDF L[P]ℵ a b c d e f g h k l m n o 17 [47]
pq φιλήματι p ἁγίῳ. ἀσπάζονται ὑμᾶς αἱ r ἐκκλησίαι πᾶσαι
τοῦ χριστοῦ.

10. αριστοβολου (for -βουλου) B[1]F vulg [D[1]-lat].
11. συγγενην A B[1](Tischdf) D[1].
12. κοπιασας C. om from εν κυριω to εν κυριω AF(and G).
14. rec ερμαν π. ερμην, with D[3]L rel [vulg-clem demid] Syr syr(txt and mg-gr) arm Chr$_1$ Thdrt Chron$_1$ Ambrst : txt ABC D[1][and lat] FPℵ m am(with fuld harl flor mar [tol]) copt æth Orig-int$_1$.
15. ιουνιαν C[1]F. νηρεαν AF. [om 3rd και P c Ambrst.] ολυμπειδα F, *Olympiadem* latt Orig-int Ambrst : ολυμπιαν D[2] arm.
16. om ασπαζονται . . . χριστου DF, but aft συγγ. μου ver 21 read και αι εκκλ. πασαι του χρ. rec om πασαι (*see note*), with rel Chr$_1$ [Damasc] Thl Œc : ins ABC(DF)LPℵ m [vulg syrr copt æth arm] (Chr-comm ?) Cyr[-p$_2$] Thdrt Orig-int$_1$ Ambrst Pel Bede.

συνεργ. ἐν χρ., fellow-workman in (the work of) **Christ.** Origen and others have confounded Apelles with the well-known Apollos, but apparently without reason. Cf. Hor. Sat. i. 5. 100. **δόκιμ. ἐν χρ., approved** (by trial) **in** (the work of) **Christ.** It does not follow that either Aristobulus or Narcissus were *themselves Christians.* Only those of their *familiæ* (**τοὺς ἐκ τῶν**) are here saluted who were ἐν κυρίῳ: for we must understand this also after Ἀριστοβούλου. **συγγ.**, see above. Grot., Neander, al., have taken Narcissus for the well-known freedman of Claudius. But this can hardly be, for he was executed (Tac. Ann. xiii. 1) in the very beginning of Nero's reign, i. e. cir. 55 A.D., whereas (see Prolegg. § iv. 4, and Chronol. Table) this Epistle cannot have well been written before 58 A.D. Perhaps, as Winer (Realw.) suggests, the family of this Narcissus may have continued to be thus known after his death (?).

13.] Rufus may have been the son of Simon of Cyrene, mentioned Mark xv. 21: but the name was very common. **ἐκλεκτόν**—not to be softened, as De W., al., to merely 'eximium,' a sense unknown to our Apostle;—**elect**, i. e. one of the elect of the Lord. **καὶ ἐμοῦ** the Apostle adds from affectionate regard towards the mother of Rufus: 'my mother,' in my reverence and affection for her. Jowett compares our Lord's words to St. John, John xix. 27.

14.] These Christians of whom we have only the names, seem to be persons of less repute than the former. Hermas (= Hermodorus, Grot.) is thought by Origen (in loc. "Puto, quod Hermas iste sit scriptor libelli istius qui Pastor appellatur"), Eus. H. E. iii. 3, and Jerome, Catal. script. eccl., c. x., vol. ii., p. 846, to be the author of the 'Shepherd.' But this latter is generally supposed to have been the brother of Pius, bishop of Rome, about 150 A.D. The **σὺν αὐτοῖς ἀδελφοί** of ver. 14, and **σὺν αὐτοῖς πάντες ἅγιοι** of ver. 15, have been taken by De W. and Reiche to point to some separate associations of Christians, perhaps (De W.) assemblies as in ver. 5: or (Reiche) unions for missionary purposes.

16.] The meaning of this injunction seems to be, that the Roman Christians should take occasion, on the receipt of the Apostle's greetings to them, to testify their mutual love, in this, the ordinary method of salutation, but having among Christians a Christian and holy meaning, see reff. It became soon a custom in the churches at the celebration

17 [s]Παρακαλῶ δὲ ὑμᾶς, ἀδελφοί, [t]σκοπεῖν τοὺς τὰς
[u]διχοστασίας καὶ τὰ [v]σκάνδαλα [w]παρὰ τὴν [x]διδαχὴν ἣν
ὑμεῖς ἐμάθετε ποιοῦντας, καὶ [y]ἐκκλίνατε [y]ἀπ' αὐτῶν. 18 οἱ
γὰρ τοιοῦτοι τῷ κυρίῳ ἡμῶν χριστῷ οὐ [z]δουλεύουσιν,
ἀλλὰ τῇ ἑαυτῶν [a]κοιλίᾳ, καὶ διὰ τῆς [b]χρηστολογίας καὶ
[c]εὐλογίας [d]ἐξαπατῶσιν τὰς καρδίας τῶν [e]ἀκάκων. 19 ἡ
γὰρ ὑμῶν [f]ὑπακοὴ εἰς πάντας [g]ἀφίκετο· ἐφ' ὑμῖν οὖν
χαίρω, θέλω δὲ ὑμᾶς σοφοὺς εἶναι [h]εἰς τὸ [h]ἀγαθόν, [i]ἀκε-
ραίους δὲ εἰς [k]τὸ [k]κακόν. 20 ὁ δὲ [l]θεὸς τῆς [l]εἰρήνης

s = ch. xii. 1 reff.
t Luke xi. 35. 2 Cor. iv. 18. Gal. vi. 1. Phil. ii. 4. iii. 17 only †. 2 Macc. iv. 5 only.
u Gal. v. 20 only †. 1 Macc. iii. 29 only.
v = ch. xiv. 13 reff.
w = ch. i. 26 reff.
x = Acts ii. 42 reff.
y 1 Pet. iii. 11 (ch. iii. 12) only. Ps. xxxvi. 27.
z = Acts xx. 19 reff.
a = Phil. iii. 19. Prov. xxiv. 15.
b here only †.
c = here only. see note. (ch. xv. 29 reff.)
d ch. vii. 11 reff.
e = here (Heb. vii. 26) only. Prov. i. 4. viii. 5 al.
f ch. i. 5 reff.
g here only. Prov. i. 27. = Sir. xlvii. 16.
h ch. xiii. 4 reff.
i Matt. x. 16. Phil. ii. 15 only †.
k ch. ii. 9 reff.
l ch. xv. 33 reff.

17. for παρακαλω, ερωτω $D^{1.3}$, *rogo* latt. for σκοπειν, ασφαλως σκοπειτε DF Sing-cler. for παρα, περι D[1][-gr]. ins λεγοντας η bef ποιουντ. DF Sing-cler. εκκλινετε BCℵ[1] m Thdrt Damasc.

18. om τω F. rec ins ιησου bef χριστω, with L rel Syr copt æth-pl arm-mss Chr_1 [Damasc]: om ABCDFPℵ e m vulg syr æth-rom arm-ed $Orig\text{-}int_3$.—χρ. bef ημων DF. δουλευσουσιν F[-gr]. om και ευλογιας (*homœotel*) D[1]F 17 Chr-ms.

19. υπακοη bef υμων D-gr F. rec χαιρω ουν το εφ υμιν, with (DF)ℵ[3] rel vulg syrr copt (arm) Chr_1 Thdrt: το εφ' υμιν συνχαιρω, omg ουν, m(m[1] Treg): txt ABCLPℵ[1] Damasc $Orig\text{-}int_2$.—om το D[1]F d (arm). for θ. δε, και θελω D[1][and-lat] F Syr æth. rec aft σοφους adds μεν (*on account of* δε *follg ?*), with ACPℵ rel syr [Chr-montf$_1$] Thl Œc Aug_1: om BDFL [o] copt [æth arm] $Clem_1$ $Cæs_1$(but om also δε follg) Chr[-mss$_1$] Thdrt $Orig\text{-}int_1$.

of the Lord's Supper. See Suicer under ἀσπασμός and φίλημα, and Bingham, xv. 3. 3. **ἀσπάζ. ὑμ. αἱ ἐκκλ. π.**] This assurance is stated evidently on the Apostle's authority, speaking for the churches; not implying as Bengel, "quibuscum fui, c. xv. 26. His significarat, se Romam scribere," but vouching for the brotherly regard in which the Roman church was held by all churches of Christ. The above misunderstanding has led to the exclusion of πᾶσαι.

17—20.] Warning against those who made divisions among them. To what persons the Apostle refers, is not plain. Some (Thol., al.) think the Judaizers to be meant, not absolutely within the Christian pale, but endeavouring to sow dissension in it: and so, nearly, Neander, Pfl. u. Leit., p. 452. De W. thinks that Paul merely gives this warning *in case* such persons came to Rome. *Judging by the text itself*, we infer that these teachers were similar to those pointed out in Phil. iii. 2, 18; 1 Tim. vi. 3 ff.; 2 Cor. xi. 13, 20: *unprincipled and selfish persons, seducing others for their own gain:* whether Judaizers or not, does not appear: but considering that the great opponents of the Apostle were of this party, we may perhaps infer that they also belonged to it. **17.] σκοπεῖν** = βλέπειν, Phil. iii. 2. The διδαχή here spoken of is probably rather ethical than doctrinal; compare Eph. iv. 20—24. **18.]** **χρηστολογία**, κολακεία, Theophyl. Wetstein cites from Julius Capitolinus, in Pertinace, 13, "omnes, qui libere conferebant, male Pertinacem loquebantur, *chrestologum* eum appellantes, qui bene loqueretur et male faceret." **εὐλογίας, fairness of speech:** so Plato, Rep. iii. 400 D, εὐλογία ἄρα κ. εὐαρμοστία κ. εὐσχημοσύνη κ. εὐρυθμία εὐηθείᾳ ἀκολουθεῖ—or perhaps '*eulogies*' (flatteries), as Pind. Nem. iv. 8, οὐδὲ θερμὸν ὕδωρ τόσον | γε μαλθακὰ τεύχει | γυῖα, τόσσον εὐλογία φόρ | μιγγι συνάορος. **19.]** See ch. i. 8. Their obedience being matter of universal notoriety, is the ground of his confidence that they will comply with his entreaty, ver. 17. Some slight reproof is conveyed in χαίρω, θέλω δὲ κ.τ.λ. They were well known for obedience, but had not been perhaps cautious enough with regard to these designing persons and their pretended wisdom. See Matt. x. 16, of which words of our Lord there seems to be here a reminiscence. **20.]** ἐπειδὴ γὰρ εἶπε τοὺς τὰς διχοστασίας κ. τὰ σκάνδαλα ποιοῦντας, εἶπεν εἰρήνης θεόν, ἵνα θαρσήσωσι περὶ τῆς τούτων ἀπαλλαγῆς. Chrys. Hom. xxxii. p. 755: and so most Commentators. De W. prefers taking ὁ θ. τῆς εἰρ. more generally as 'the God of *salvation;*' and the usage of the expression (see reff.) seems to favour this. **συντρ. τ. σατ.** is a similitude from Gen. iii. 15.

^{m} συντρίψει τὸν σαταναν̂ ὑπὸ τοὺς πόδας ὑμῶν ^{n} ἐν ^{n} τάχει.
Ἡ χάρις τοῦ κυρίου ἡμῶν Ἰησοῦ [χριστοῦ] ^{o} μεθ' ὑμῶν.
21 Ἀσπάζεται ὑμᾶς Τιμόθεος ὁ ^{p} συνεργός μου, καὶ
Λούκιος καὶ Ἰάσων καὶ Σωσίπατρος οἱ ^{q} συγγενεῖς μου.
22 ἀσπάζομαι ὑμᾶς ἐγὼ Τέρτιος ὁ γράψας ^{r} τὴν ἐπιστολὴν
ἐν κυρίῳ. 23 ἀσπάζεται ὑμᾶς Γάϊος ὁ ^{s} ξένος μου καὶ
^{t} ὅλης τῆς ^{t} ἐκκλησίας. ἀσπάζεται ὑμᾶς Ἔραστος ὁ ^{u} οἰκονόμος τῆς πόλεως, καὶ Κούαρτος ὁ ἀδελφός. [24 Ἡ
χάρις τοῦ κυρίου ἡμῶν Ἰησοῦ χριστοῦ ^{o} μετὰ πάντων
ὑμῶν. ἀμήν.]

ABCDF L[P]ℵ a b c d e f g h k l m n o 17 [47]

m Matt. xii. 20. Mark v. 4. xiv. 3. Luke ix. 39. John xix. 36. Rev. ii. 27 only. Gen. xix. 9.
n Luke xviii. 8. Acts xii. 7. xxii. 18. xxv. 4. Rev. i. 1. xxii. 6 only. Deut. xxviii. 20.
o ellips., ch. xv. 33 reff.
p ver. 3 reff.
q vv. 7, 11 reff.
r see 1 Cor. v. 9 reff.
s = here only. Diod. Sic. xvii. 47. Xen. Anab. vii. 1. 4.
t Acts v. 11. xv. 22. 1 Cor. xiv. 23.
u = here only. (Luke xvi. 1, &c. 1 Cor. iv. 1, 2.) Esth. viii. 9. Jos. Antt. xi. 6. 12.

20. *συντριψαι* A 67^2 vulg(am demid harl F-lat agst fuld tol) G-lat spec Orig$_1$[-int$_2$] Thdrt-comm Ambr$_3$. *εν ταχει* bef *υπο τ. π. ημων* A [(Syr)]. om last clause D[not D-lat^3] F Sedul. om *χριστου* Bℵ. elz at end adds *αμην*, with [a(e sil)] m^2(Treg): om ABCLPℵ rel vss gr-lat-ff.

21. rec *ασπαζονται*, with D^{3}L rel Syr Thdrt Œc: txt ABCD^{1}FPℵ m latt syr copt [æth(*salutate* = *ασπαζετε*) arm Chr$_1$ Thl Orig-int$_1$ Ambrst. om 1st *μου* B 67^2. om 2nd *και* B [om *και ιασ.* 47]. at end D^{1}F add *και αι εκκλησιαι πασαι του χ̅υ̅* (see ver 16).

23. rec *τ. εκκλησιας* bef *ολης*, with L rel Chr$_1$ Thdrt: *ολαι αι εκκλησιαι* F æth: *ολη η εκκλησια* vulg[-clem(with demid)] copt(*eccl. omnis*): txt ABCDPℵ m am [fuld tol] syrr.

[**24.** om ver ABCℵ am(with fuld harl^1 &c) copt æth-rom [Orig-int$_1$]: ins DFL rel [vulg-ed demid tol harl^2 syr] Chr$_1$ Thdrt [Euthal-ms Damasc] Thl Œc Sedul Bede; and (but aft ver 27) P 17. 80 Syr æth-pl [arm] Ambrst.—for *ημων*, *υμων* L: om P [m].—om *ιησ. χρ.* F.]

συντρίψει, not as Stuart, 'for optative,' nor does it express any *wish*, but a prophetic assurance and encouragement in bearing up against all adversaries, that it would not be long before the great Adversary himself would be bruised under their feet. **ἡ χάρις κ.τ.λ.**] It appears as if the Epistle was intended to conclude with this usual benediction, but the Apostle found occasion to add more. This he does also in other Epistles: see 1 Cor. xvi. 23, 24; similarly Phil. iv. 20, and vv. 21—23 after the doxology,—2 Thess. iii. 16, 17, 18:—1 Tim. vi. 16, 17 ff.:—2 Tim. iv. 18, 19 ff. **21—24.**] Greetings from various persons.

21.] Lucius must not be mistaken for Lucas (= Lucanus),—but was probably Lucius of Cyrene, Acts xiii. 1, see note there. Jason *may* be the same who is mentioned Acts xvii. 5, 7, as the host of Paul and Silas at Thessalonica. A '*Sopater* (son) *of Pyrrhus of Berœa*' occurs Acts xx. 4, but it is quite uncertain whether this Sosipater is the same person. **οἱ συγγενεῖς**, see above, ver. 7. These persons may have been Jews; but we cannot tell whether the expression may not be used in a wider sense. **22.**] There is nothing strange (as Olsh. supposes) in this salutation being inserted in the first person. It would be natural enough that Tertius the amanuensis, inserting ἀσπάζεται ὑμ. Τέρτ. ὁ γρ. τ. ἐπ. ἐν κυρ., should change the form into the first person, and afterwards proceed from the dictation of the Apostle as before. Beza and Grot. suppose him to have done this on transcribing the Epistle. Thol. notices this irregularity as a corroboration of the genuineness of the chapter. On the supposed identity of Tertius with Silas see note on Acts xv. 22.

23.] Gaius is mentioned 1 Cor. i. 14, as having been baptized by Paul. **The host of the whole church** probably implies that the assemblies of the church were held in his house:—or perhaps, that his hospitality to Christians was universal. Erastus, holding this office (οἰκονόμος, the public treasurer, ὁ ἐπὶ τῆς δημοσίας τραπέζης, arcarius, Wetst., who quotes from inscriptions, Νείλῳ οἰκονόμῳ Ἀσίας,—Secundus, arkarius Reip. Armerinorum), can hardly have been the same who was with the Apostle in Ephesus, Acts xix. 22. It is more probable that the Erastus of 2 Tim. iv. 20 is identical with this than with that other. **ὁ ἀδελφός, our brother** [see 1 Cor. i. 1],—the generic singular; one among οἱ ἀδελφοί, '*the brethren.*' The rest have been specified by their services or offices. [**24.**] *The benediction*

25 Τῷ [v] δὲ δυναμένῳ ὑμᾶς [w] στηρίξαι κατὰ τὸ [x] εὐαγγέλιόν
[x] μου καὶ τὸ [y] κήρυγμα Ἰησοῦ χριστοῦ [z] κατὰ [za] ἀποκάλυψιν [b] μυστηρίου [c] χρόνοις [c] αἰωνίοις [d] σεσιγημένου 26 [e] φα-

v 1 Tim. i. 17. Jude 24.
w ch. i. 11. Luke xxii. 32 al. Ps. l. 12 (14).
x ch. ii. 16. 2 Tim. ii. 8 only. see 2 Cor. iv. 3. 1 Thess. i. 5. 2 Thess. ii. 14.
y (=) Matt. xii. 41 ‖ L. 1 Cor. i. 21. ii. 4. xv. 14. 2 Tim. iv. 17. Tit. i. 3 only. (2 Chron. xxx. 5. Prov. ix. 3.)
z Gal. ii. 2. Eph. iii. 3 only. a ch. viii. 19 reff. b ch. xi. 25. c 2 Tim. i. 9. Tit. i. 2 only. see Gen. ix. 12. dat. of duration, Luke viii. 29. ch. viii. 11. d = here only (Acts xii. 17 reff.). L.P. Ps. xxxi. 3. e ch. i. 19 reff.

25, 26, 27. These verses are variously placed: (I) in BCDℵ 16. 80. 137-76 latt Syr copt æth [Orig-int$_1$] Ambrst Pel Bede they stand here and here only: (II) they stand *aft ch xiv* 23 in L rel and about 192 others syr goth(appy) Chr Thdrt Damasc Thl Œc Theodul: (III) they are *omd altogether* in (D³?) F[-gr](a space is left aft xvi. 24) G(a space is left aft xiv. 23) Mcion(*penitus abstulit* accg to Orig(see Orig in Rom. lib. x. 43, vol. iv. p. 687) as also chaps xv. xvi.) some mss in Jer(appy): (IV) they occur in *both places* in AP 5. 17. 109-lat arm-zoh. (Sz reckons 246 mss of St. Paul. Here 16 are defective (see Sz, addg 126), 21 are unexamined (see Sz, addg 216. 239 to 246), 7 are not distinct mss (viz. 8. 10. 56. 60-1-6. 117), and 5 are included under "rel.")

25. [ημας m (and P in ch xiv.).] for το κηρυγμα, κυριου ℵ¹(txt ℵ-corr¹). χριστου bef ιησου B.

repeated; see above on ver. 20. The omission (see var. read.) has perhaps been by the caprice of the copyists.]

25—27.] Concluding doxology. The genuineness of this doxology, and its position in the Epistle have been much questioned. The external evidence will be found in the var. readings;—from which it is plain, that *its genuineness* as a part of the Epistle is *placed beyond all reasonable doubt.* Nor does the variety of position militate here, as in some cases, against this conclusion. For the transference of it to the end of ch. xiv. may be explained, partly from the supposed reference of στηρίξαι to the question treated in ch. xiv. (so Chrys., πάλιν γὰρ ἐκείνων ἔχεται τῶν ἀσθενῶν, κ. πρὸς αὐτοὺς τρέπει τὸν λόγον), partly from the supposed inappropriateness of it here after the benediction of ver. 24, in consequence of which that verse is omitted by mss. which have the doxology here,—partly from the unusual character of the position and diction of the doxology itself. This latter has been used as an internal argument against the genuineness of the portion. Paul never elsewhere ends with such a doxology. His doxologies, when he does use such, are simple, and perspicuous in construction, whereas this is involved, and rhetorical. This objection however is completely answered by the supposition (Fritz.) that the doxology was the effusion of the fervent mind of the Apostle on taking a general survey of the Epistle. We find in its diction striking similarities to that of the pastoral Epistles:—a phænomenon occurring in several places where Paul writes in a fervid and impassioned manner,—also where he writes *with his own hand;*—the inferences from which I have treated in the Prolegg. to those Epistles (vol. iii. Prolegg. ch. vii. § i. 30—33). That the doxology is made up of unusual expressions taken from Paul's other writings, that it is difficult and involved, are facts, which if rightly argued from, would substantiate, *not its interpolation, but its genuineness:* seeing that an interpolator would have taken care to conform it to the character of the Epistle in which it stands, and to have left in it no irregularity which would bring it into question. The construction is exceedingly difficult. Viewed superficially, it presents only another instance added to many in which the Apostle begins a sentence with one construction, proceeds onward through various dependent clauses till he loses sight of the original form, and ends with a construction presupposing another kind of beginning. And such no doubt it is: but it is not easy to say what he had in his mind when commencing the sentence. Certainly, ᾧ ἡ δόξα εἰς τ. αἰῶνας forbids us from supposing that δόξα was intended to follow the datives,—for thus this latter clause would be merely a repetition. We might imagine that he had ended the sentence as if it had begun ὁ δὲ δυνάμενος, κ.τ.λ. and expressed a wish that He who was able to confirm them, *might confirm them:* but this is prevented by its being evident, from the μόνῳ σοφῷ θεῷ, that the datives are still in his mind. This latter fact will guide us to the solution. The dative form is still in his mind, but not the reference in which he had used it. Hence, when the sentence would naturally have concluded (as it actually does in B: see digest) μόνῳ σοφῷ θεῷ, διὰ Ἰησοῦ χριστοῦ, ἡ δόξα εἰς τ. αἰῶνας,—a break is made, as if the sense were complete at χριστοῦ, and the relative ᾧ refers back to the subject of the sen-

νερωθέντος δὲ νῦν διά τε [f] γραφῶν [g] προφητικῶν κατ' [h] ἐπιταγὴν τοῦ [i] αἰωνίου [i] θεοῦ [k] εἰς [k] ὑπακοὴν [k] πίστεως εἰς πάντα τὰ ἔθνη [l] γνωρισθέντος,
27 [m] μόνῳ [m] σοφῷ [m] θεῷ, [n] διὰ Ἰησοῦ χριστοῦ, ᾧ ἡ [o] δόξα [p] εἰς τοὺς αἰῶνας. ἀμήν.

ABCDF L[P]ℵ a b c d e f g h k l m n o 17 [47]

ΠΡΟΣ ΡΩΜΑΙΟΥΣ.

f Acts xvii. 2. ch. i. 2 reff. g 2 Pet. i. 19 only †. h 1 Cor. vii. 6, 25. 2 Cor. viii. 8. 1 Tim. i. 1. Tit. i. 3. ii. 15 only †. P. Wisd. xiv. 16. i here only. Gen. xxi. 33. k ch. i. 5 (reff.). l 1 Cor. xii. 3 reff. m here only. (1 Tim. i. 17. Jude 25.) n see ch. ii. 16. o ch. xi. 36 reff. p ch. i. 25 reff.

26. om τε D vulg (syrr [æth]) arm Chr_1 $Orig\text{-}int_1$ Hil_1 [Ambrst]. aft προφητ. add και της επιφανειας(*adventum*) του κυριου ημων ιησ. χριστου $Orig_4$[not int_1] mss-in-Jer.
27. θεω bef σοφω D. χριστ. bef ιησ. B. [for ω, αυτω P(here) arm(here) Chr-2-mss:] om B [F-lat] Syr $Orig\text{-}int_1$. aft αιωνας add των αιωνων ADPℵ vulg [and F-lat] Syr copt æth arm Damasc [$Orig\text{-}int_2$ Hil_1 Ambrst] (but not AP arm xiv. 23). om αμην 49. 63 am [$Orig\text{-}int_1$.—add ver 24(see above) P 17. 80 Syr æth-pl arm Ambrst.]

SUBSCRIPTION: rec πρ. ρ. εγραφη απο κορινθου, with B² D-corr P(prefixing παυλου επιστολη) rel syrr[prefg ετελεσθη] copt [Euthal-ms(aft ρωμ. ins επιστ.)], adding δια φοιβης της διακονου της εν κεγχρεαις εκκλησιας, with rel copt (but a k [Euthal-ms] pref ἡ; a b d e f k m n 47 [syrr Euthal-ms] om της εν κεγχρ. εκκλ.; m om πρ. ρω.): του αγ. κ. πανευφημου αποστολου παυλου επισ. πρ. ρ. εγραφη απο κορινθου δια φοιβης της διακονου L: om F c g l 17: εγραφη απο κορινθου o: εγρ. δια φοιβης απο κορ. h: txt AB¹CD¹ G(adding ετελεσθη) ℵ.

tence preceding, thus imagined complete,—viz. to ὁ δυνάμενος—μόνος σοφὸς θεός. The analogy of the similar passage Acts xx. 32 would tempt us to supply with the datives παρατίθεμαι ὑμᾶς, or the like, as suggested by Olsh.;—but as De W. remarks, the form of a doxology is too evident to allow of this. After all, perhaps, the datives may be understood as conveying a *general ascription of praise for the mercies of Redemption detailed in the Epistle*, and then ᾧ ἡ δ. as superadded, q. d., **To Him who is able &c. . . . . be all the praise: to whom be glory for ever.**
25.] **κατά, in reference to,** i. e. 'in subordination to,' and according to the requirements of. **κήρυγμα Ἰησοῦ χρ.** can hardly mean, as De W. and Meyer, '*the preaching which Jesus Christ hath accomplished by me*' (ch. xv. 18),—nor again as Chrys., ὃ αὐτὸς ἐκήρυξεν,—**but the preaching of Christ,** i. e. making known of Christ, as the verb is used 1 Cor. i. 23; xv. 12 al. fr. So Calv., and most Commentators. **κατὰ ἀποκ.]** This second κατά is best taken, not as co-ordinate to the former one, and following στηρίξαι, nor as belonging to δυναμένῳ, which would be an unusual limitation of the divine Power,—but as subordinate to κήρυγμα,—**the preaching of Jesus Christ according to, &c.** The omission of τό before κατὰ ἀποκ. is no objection to this. **μυστ.]** The *mystery* (see ch. xi. 25, note) *of the gospel* is often said to have been thus *hidden from eternity* in the counsels of God—see Eph. iii. 9; Col. i. 26; 2 Tim. i. 9; Tit. i. 2; 1 Pet. i. 20; Rev. xiii. 8.

26.] See ch. i. 2. The prophetic writings were the storehouse out of which the preachers of the gospel took their demonstrations that Jesus was the Christ: see Acts xviii. 28;—more especially, it is true, *to the Jews,* who however are here included among πάντα τὰ ἔθνη. **κατ' ἐπιταγ.** may refer either to the *prophetic writings* being drawn up by the command of God,—or to the *manifestation of the mystery by the preachers of the gospel* thus taking place. The latter seems best to suit the sense. **αἰωνίου** refers back to χρ. αἰωνίοις [the word should have been kept scrupulously the same in English, not as here and in Matt. xxii. 46 rendered by two different English terms]. The first εἰς indicates the *aim*—in order to their becoming obedient to the faith:—the second, the *local extent* of the manifestation. **27.]** **διὰ Ἰησ. χρ.** must by the requirements of the construction be applied to μόνῳ σοφῷ θεῷ, and not (as Aug. [and E. V.]) to δόξα, from which it is separated by the relative ᾧ. The quantity of intervening matter, especially the datives μόνῳ σοφῷ θεῷ, prevent it from being referred (as Œc., Theophyl.) to στηρίξαι. It must then be rendered **to the only wise God through Jesus Christ,** i. e. Him who is revealed to us by Christ as such. On the construction of ᾧ see above. It cannot without great harshness be referred to *Christ,* seeing that the words μόνῳ σοφῷ θεῷ resume the chief subject of the sentence, and to them the relative must apply.

ΠΡΟΣ ΚΟΡΙΝΘΙΟΥΣ Α.

ABCDF LPℵ a b c d e f g h k l m n o 17. 47

I. 1 Παῦλος [[a] κλητὸς] ἀπόστολος χριστοῦ Ἰησοῦ [b] διὰ
θελήματος θεοῦ, καὶ Σωσθένης ὁ ἀδελφός, 2 τῇ [c] ἐκκλησίᾳ
τοῦ [c] θεοῦ, [d] ἡγιασμένοις [d] ἐν χριστῷ Ἰησοῦ, τῇ οὔσῃ ἐν

a Rom. i. 1, 6, 7. Jude 1 al. 2 Kings xv. 11.
b Rom. xv. 32 reff.
c Acts xx. 28. ch. x. 32. xi. 16, 22. xv. 9. 2 Cor. i. 1. Gal. i. 13. 1 Thess. ii. 14. 2 Thess. i. 4. 1 Tim. iii. 5, 15. Neh. xiii. 1.
d Rom. xv. 16 reff.

Title. Steph *η προς τους κορινθιους επιστολη πρωτη*: elz *παυλου του αποστολου η προς κορινθιους επ. πρ.*, with rel: *πρ. κορ. αρχεται ᾱ* F(but G om ᾱ): *του αγιου και πανευφημου αποστολου παυλου επιστολη πρ. κυρ. πρωτη* L: *προς κο. α′ επ.* h n: *πρ. κο. επ. πρ.* k: *παυ. επ. πρ. κορ. ᾱ* P: *πρ. κορ.* m: om D: txt A(appy: the title is nearly gone) BCℵ (l o) 17. 47 [and D at top of pages].

Chap. I. 1. om *κλητος* AD Cyr_1[-p] (*perhaps because it does not occur elsw in the openings of epp exc Rom* i. 1: *but it may have been* insd from there, *so I have left it doubtful*): ins BCFLPℵ rel [vulg fri syrr copt æth arm] Chr_2 $Thdrt_{2expr}$ Thl_{expr} $Œc_{expr}$ Orig-int_1 Ambrst Aug Bede. rec *ιησ.* bef *χρ.*, with ALPℵ rel [vulg-clem syrr copt æth arm Cyr_1 Euthal-ms] Thdrt Thl Œc Orig-int_1: txt BDF [m 17] am(with demid fuld tol [fri]) Chr_2 Hil[(Wetst) Ambrst Aug_1(ed Bened)].—*αυ* corrd to *ιῡ* $ℵ^1$. (C is defective in this and follg ver.)

2. rec *τη ουση εν κορ.* bef *ηγιασμ. εν χ. ι*, with AD^2LPℵ rel [vulg am &c syrr copt æth arm]: txt B $D^{1\cdot3}$[and lat] F [fuld-corr].

Chap. I. 1—3.] Address and greeting. 1.] It is doubtful whether **κλητός** is not spurious: see var. readd. The words **διὰ θελ. θεοῦ** point probably to the depreciation of Paul's apostolic authority at Corinth. In Gal. i. 1 we have this much more strongly asserted. But they have a reference to Paul himself also: "ratio auctoritatis ad ecclesias: humilis et prompti animi, penes ipsum Paulum." Bengel. Chrys., referring it to *κλητός*, says, *ἐπειδὴ αὐτῷ ἔδοξεν, ἐκλήθημεν, οὐκ ἐπειδὴ ἄξιοι ἦμεν*. Hom. i. p. 4. **Σωσθένης** can hardly be assumed to be identical with the ruler of the synagogue in Acts xviii. 17: see note there. He must have been some Christian well known to the church at Corinth. Thus Paul associates with himself Silvanus and Timotheus in the Epistles to the Thessalonians; and Timotheus in 2 Cor. Chrysostom attributes it to modesty: *μετριάζει, συντάττων ἑαυτῷ τὸν ἐλάττονα πολλῷ*. Some have supposed Sosthenes to be the *writer* of the Epistle, see Rom. xvi. 22. Possibly he may have been one *τῶν Χλόης* (ver. 11) by whom the intelligence had been received, and the Apostle may have associated him with himself as approving the appeal to apostolic authority. Perhaps some slight may have been put upon him by the parties at Corinth, and for that reason Paul puts him forward. **ὁ ἀδελφός**, as 2 Cor. i. 1, of Timothy, **our brother**,—one of *οἱ ἀδελφοί*. 2.] The remarks of Calvin on **τῇ ἐκκλ. τ. θεοῦ**, *κ.τ.λ.* are admirable: "Mirum forsan videri queat, cur eam hominum multitudinem vocet Ecclesiam Dei, in qua tot morbi invaluerant, ut Satan illic potius regnum occuparet quam Deus. Certum est autem, eum noluisse blandiri Corinthiis: loquitur enim ex Dei Spiritu, qui adulari non solet. Atqui inter tot inquinamenta qualis amplius eminet Ecclesiæ facies? Respondeo, . . . utcunque multa vitia obrepissent, et variæ corruptelæ tam doctrinæ quam morum, extitisse tamen adhuc quædam veræ Ecclesiæ signa. Locus diligenter observandus, ne requiramus in hoc mundo Ecclesiam omni ruga et

Κορίνθῳ, [a] κλητοῖς [e] ἁγίοις, [f] σὺν πᾶσιν τοῖς [g] ἐπικαλουμένοις τὸ ὄνομα τοῦ κυρίου ἡμῶν Ἰησοῦ χριστοῦ ἐν παντὶ
τόπῳ [h] αὐτῶν [τε] καὶ [h] ἡμῶν. 3 [i] χάρις ὑμῖν καὶ [i] εἰρήνη
ἀπὸ θεοῦ πατρὸς ἡμῶν καὶ κυρίου Ἰησοῦ χριστοῦ.
4 [k] Εὐχαριστῶ τῷ [k] θεῷ [k] μου πάντοτε περὶ ὑμῶν [l] ἐπὶ τῇ

ABCDF LPℵ a b c d e f g h k l m n o 17. 47

e Acts ix. 13 reff.
f Acts xxiii. 15. 2 Cor. i. 1. Phil. i. 1.
g = Acts ii. 21 reff.
h see Rom. xvi. 13 and ch. xvi. 18.
i Rom. i. 7.
k Rom. i. 8 (reff.).
l = Phil. i. 3 al.

om 1st ημων A 77. 109 fuld $Orig_1$[not int_3] Pel. om χριστου A. om τε (A^1 ?)$BD^1Fℵ^1$ 17 [vulg Syr copt Euthal-ms Damasc]: ins [A^2]$D^2LPℵ^3$ rel [syr æth arm Chr_2 Thdrt $Cyr\text{-}c_1$ $Phot\text{-}c_1$].
4. om μου $Bℵ^1$ æth: ins ACDFLP ℵ-$corr^1$ rel [vulg syrr copt arm $Orig\text{-}c_1$].

macula carentem: aut protinus abdicemus hoc titulo quemvis cœtum in quo non omnia votis nostris respondeant. Est enim hæc periculosa tentatio, nullam Ecclesiam putare ubi non appareat perfecta puritas. Nam quicunque hac occupatus fuerit, necesse tandem erit, ut discessione ab omnibus aliis facta, solus sibi sanctus videatur in mundo, aut peculiarem sectam cum paucis hypocritis instituat. Quid ergo causæ habuit Paulus, cur Ecclesiam Corinthi agnosceret? nempe quia Evangelii doctrinam, Baptismum, Cœnam Domini, quibus symbolis censeri debet Ecclesia, apud eos cernebat." On **τοῦ θεοῦ**, Chrys. remarks, οὐ τοῦδε καὶ τοῦδε, ἀλλὰ τοῦ θεοῦ,—and similarly Theophyl., taking the expression as addressed to the Corinthians to remind them of their position as a congregation belonging to God, and *not to any head of a party*. Perhaps this is too refined, the words ἡ ἐκκλ. τ. θεοῦ being so usual with St. Paul,—see reff. The harshness of the position of ἡγιασμένοις ἐν χρ. Ἰησ. is in favour of its being the original one:—**hallowed** (i. e. dedicated) **to God in** (in union with and by means of) **Jesus Christ.** **τῇ οὔσῃ**—'which exists,' 'is found, at Corinth.' So ἐν Ἀντιοχ. κατὰ τὴν οὖσαν ἐκκλησίαν, Acts xiii. 1. **κλητοῖς ἁγίοις**] See Rom. i. 7, note. **σὺν πᾶσιν** κ.τ.λ.] These words do not belong to the designations just preceding, = 'as are all,' &c., but form part of the *address* of the Epistle, so that these πάντες οἱ ἐπικαλ. are partakers with the Corinthians in it. They form a weighty and precious addition,—made here doubtless to shew the Corinthians, that membership of God's Holy Catholic Church consisted not in being planted, or presided over by Paul, Apollos, or Cephas (or their successors), but in *calling on the name of our Lord Jesus Christ*. The Church of England has adopted from this verse her solemn explanation of the term, in the 'prayer for all sorts and conditions of men:' "More especially, we pray for the good estate of *the Catholic Church;* that it may be so guided and governed by thy good Spirit, that *all who profess and call themselves Christians* may be led into the way of truth, and hold the faith in unity of spirit, in the bond of peace, and in righteousness of life." **ἐπικαλ.**] not '*calling themselves by*' (though in sense equivalent to this, for they who *call upon* Christ, *call themselves by* His Name): the phrase ἐπικαλεῖσθαι τὸ ὄνομα τοῦ κυρίου was one adopted from the LXX, as in reff.; the adjunct ἡμῶν Ἰησοῦ χρ. defines that Lord (Jehovah) on whom the Christians called, to be Jesus Christ,—and is a direct testimony to the divine worship of Jesus Christ, as universal in the church. The ὄνομα ἐπικληθὲν ἐφ' ὑμᾶς (James ii. 7) is not to the point, the construction being different. **ἐν παντὶ τόπ. αὐτ. [τε] κ. ἡμ.**] **In every place, both theirs** (in their country, wherever that may be) **and ours.** This connexion is far better than to join αὐτ. [τε] κ. ἡμ. with κυρίῳ, thereby making the first ἡμῶν superfluous. * **αὐτῶν** refers to the πάντες οἱ ἐπικαλ., **ἡμῶν** to Paul, and Sosthenes, and those whom he is addressing. Eichhorn fancied τόπος to mean '*a place of assembly:*' Hug, '*a party*' or '*division:*' Beza, al., would limit the persons spoken of to Achaia: others, to Corinth and Ephesus:—but the *simple meaning* and *universal reference* are far more agreeable to the spirit of the passage. I may as well once for all premise, that many of the German expositors have been constantly misled in their interpretations by what I believe to be a mistaken view of ver. 12, and the supposed Corinthian parties. See note there. **3.**] See introductory note to the Epistle to the Romans. Olsh. remarks, that εἰρήνη has peculiar weight here on account of the dissensions in the Corinthian Church.

4—9.] Thanksgiving, and expression of hope, on account of the spiritual state of the Corinthian church. There was much in the Corinthian believers for which to be thankful, and on account of which to hope. These things he puts in the foreground, not only to encourage them, but (as Olsh.) to appeal to their better selves,

mn χάριτι τοῦ θεοῦ τῇ n δοθείσῃ ὑμῖν ἐν χριστῷ Ἰησοῦ
5 ὅτι ἐν παντὶ o ἐπλουτίσθητε ἐν αὐτῷ, ἐν p παντὶ λόγῳ καὶ
p πάσῃ q γνώσει, 6 καθὼς · τὸ r μαρτύριον τοῦ χριστοῦ
s ἐβεβαιώθη ἐν ὑμῖν, 7 ὥστε ὑμᾶς μὴ t ὑστερεῖσθαι ἐν
μηδενὶ u χαρίσματι, v ἀπεκδεχομένους τὴν w ἀποκάλυψιν
τοῦ κυρίου ἡμῶν Ἰησοῦ χριστοῦ· 8 ὃς καὶ s βεβαιώσει
ὑμᾶς x ἕως x τέλους y ἀνεγκλήτους ἐν τῇ z ἡμέρᾳ τοῦ κυρίου
ἡμῶν Ἰησοῦ χριστοῦ. 9 a πιστὸς ὁ θεὸς b δι' οὗ ἐκλή-

m = Acts xi. 23 reff.
n Rom. xii. 3, 6. xv. 15. ch. iii. 10. 2 Cor. viii. 1. Gal. ii. 9. Eph. iii. 2, 8. iv. 7. 2 Tim. i. 9. James iv. 6.
o 2 Cor. vi. 10. ix. 11 only. Gen. xiv. 23 al.
p = Acts xx. 19 reff.
q = Rom. xv. 14 al fr.
r = ch. ii. 1. 2 Thess. i. 10. 1 Tim. ii. 6. 2 Tim. i. 8.
s Rom. xv. 8 reff.
t Luke xv. 14. Rom. iii. 23. Phil. iv. 12. Heb. xi. 37 al. Ps. xxii. 1.
u = Rom. xi. 29. xii. 6 (ch. xii. 4) al.
v Rom. viii. 19, 23, 25. Gal. v. 5. Phil. iii. 20. Heb. ix. 28. 1 Pet. iii. 20 only †.
w = Rom. viii. 19 reff.
x 2 Cor. i. 13 only. μέχρι τ., Heb. iii. 14. ἄχρι τ., Rev. ii. 26.
y Col. i. 22. 1 Tim. iii. 10. Tit. i. 6, 7 only †. 3 Macc. v. 31. ellips., Matt. xii. 13.
z = Acts ii. 20 (from Joel ii. 31). ch. iii. 13. iv. 3. v. 5. 2 Cor. i. 14. Eph. iv. 30. Phil. i. 6, 10. ii. 16.
a = ch. x. 13. 2 Cor. i. 18. 1 Thess. v. 24. 2 Thess. iii. 3. 2 Tim. ii. 13 al.
b = Rom. i. 5. 2 Cor. i. 11.

om του θεου A^1 39. 87 Cyr_2[(ins$_1$)-p].
5. εν (1st) is written twice but corrd by $\aleph^1$.
6. for χριστου, θεου B^1(but corrd, Tischdf) F n 46-7. 72. 109-20 lectt-8. 12 arm.
8. the ver is written twice by $\aleph^1$(corrd by ℵ-corr^1). for εως, αχρι DF. for ημερα(*in diem* fri), παρουσια DF Ambrst Cassiod$_1$; *die adventus* vulg Pel. om χριστου B.
9. om ὁ C^1. for δι, υφ D^1[-gr] F[-gr].

and to bring out the following contrast more plainly. **4. τ. θεῷ μου**] so in reff. Rom. Phil. **πάντοτε**] expanded in Phil. i. 4 into πάντοτε ἐν πάσῃ δεήσει μου. The ἡ χάρις ἡ δοθεῖσα = τὰ χαρίσματα τὰ δοθέντα (see below on ver. 7)—a metonymy which has passed so completely into our common parlance, as to be almost lost sight of as such. '*Grace*' is properly *in God*: the *gifts of grace* in us, given by that grace. **ἐν**] not, as Chrys., Theophyl., Œcum., for διά, [nor = *by* as E. V.,] but as usually in this connexion, **in Christ**,—i. e. *to you as members of Christ.* So also below. **5. ἐν παντί**] general: particularized by ἐν παντὶ λόγῳ κ. πάσῃ γνώσει, in **all teaching and all knowledge. λόγος** (obj.), *the truth preached.* **γνῶσις** (subj.), *the truth apprehended.* They were rich in the *preaching* of the word, had among them able preachers, and rich in the *apprehension* of the word, were themselves intelligent hearers. See 2 Cor. viii. 7, where to these are added πίστις, σπουδή, and ἀγάπη. **6. τὸ μαρτ. τ. χριστοῦ**] the witness concerning Christ delivered by me. **καθώς, as indeed**, 'siquidem.' **ἐβεβ., was confirmed**,—*took deep root*, among you; i. e. 'as was to have been expected, from the impression made among you by my preaching of Christ.' This confirmation was *internal*, by faith and permanence in the truth, not external, by miracles. * **7.**] **So that ye are behind** (others) **in no gift of grace**;—not, *lack no gift of grace*, which would be genitive. **χάρισμα** here has its widest sense, of *that which is the effect of* **χάρις**,—not meaning 'spiritual gifts' in the narrower sense, as in ch. xii. 4. This is plain from the whole strain of the passage, which dwells not on outward gifts, but on the inward graces of the Christian life. **ἀπεκδεχ.**] which is the greatest proof of maturity and richness of the spiritual life; implying the coexistence and co-operation of *faith*, whereby they believed the promise of Christ,—*hope*, whereby they looked on to its fulfilment,—and *love*, whereby that anticipation was lit up with earnest desire;—compare πᾶσιν τοῖς **ἠγαπηκόσιν** τὴν ἐπιφάνειαν αὐτοῦ, 2 Tim. iv. 8. ἀπεκδ. κ.τ.λ., is taken by Chrys.,—who understands χαρίσματα of miraculous powers,—as implying that *besides them they needed patience* to wait till the coming of Christ; and by Calv.,—"ideo addit *expectantes revelationem*, quo significat, non talem se affluentiam illis affingere in qua nihil desideretur; sed tantum quæ sufficiet usquedum ad perfectionem perventum fuerit." But I much prefer taking ἀπεκδεχομένους as parallel with and giving the result of μὴ ὑστ. κ.τ.λ. **8. ὅς**] viz. θεός, ver. 4, not **Ἰησοῦς** χριστός, in which case we should have ἐν τῇ ἡμέρᾳ **αὐτοῦ**. The καί besides shews this. **ἕως τέλ. ἀνεγκ.**] i. e. εἰς τὸ εἶναι ὑμᾶς ἀνεγκ.;—so ἀπεκατεστάθη ὑγιής, Matt. xii. 13. **To the end**, see reff.—i. e. to the συντέλεια τ. αἰῶνος,—not merely 'to the end of your lives.' **9.**] See ref. 1 Thess.; also Phil. i. 6. The **κοιν. τοῦ υἱ. αὐτ.**, as Meyer well remarks, is the δόξα τῶν τέκνων τοῦ θεοῦ, Rom. viii. 21; for they will be συγκληρονόμοι τοῦ χριστοῦ, and συνδοξασθέντες with Him,—see Rom. viii. 17, 23; 2 Thess. ii. 14. The mention of κοινωνία may perhaps have been

θητε εἰς [c] κοινωνίαν τοῦ υἱοῦ αὐτοῦ Ἰησοῦ χριστοῦ τοῦ
κυρίου ἡμῶν.
10 [de] Παρακαλῶ δὲ ὑμᾶς, ἀδελφοί, [f] διὰ τοῦ [f] ὀνόματος
τοῦ κυρίου ἡμῶν Ἰησοῦ χριστοῦ, [e] ἵνα τὸ αὐτὸ λέγητε
πάντες καὶ μὴ ᾖ ἐν ὑμῖν [g] σχίσματα, ἦτε δὲ [h] κατηρ-
τισμένοι ἐν τῷ αὐτῷ [i] νοῒ καὶ ἐν τῇ αὐτῇ [k] γνώμῃ.
11 [l] ἐδηλώθη γάρ μοι περὶ ὑμῶν, ἀδελφοί μου, ὑπὸ [m] τῶν
Χλόης, ὅτι [n] ἔριδες ἐν ὑμῖν εἰσιν. 12 [o] λέγω δὲ τοῦτο,
ὅτι ἕκαστος ὑμῶν λέγει Ἐγὼ μέν εἰμι [p] Παύλου, ἐγὼ δὲ

ABCDF LPℵ a b c d e f g h k l m n o 17. 47

c 2 Cor. vi. 1 reff. d Rom. xii. 1 reff. e constr., Matt. xiv. 36. ch. xvi. 12, 15, 16. 2 Cor. viii. 6. ix. 5. xii. 8. Col. iv. 8 al. f Acts iv. 30 reff. g = John vii. 43. ix. 16. x. 19. ch. xi. 18. xii. 25 (Mark ii. 21 ||) only +. (-μή, Isa. ii. 21.) h = Luke vi. 40. 2 Cor. xiii. 11. Gal. vi. 1. Heb. xiii. 21. 1 Pet. v. 10. Ezra iv. 13. i = Rom. i. 28. Eph. iv. 17. P. only, exc. Luke xxiv. 45. Rev. xiii. 18. xvii. 9. k = ch. vii. 25, 40. 2 Cor. viii. 10. P. or of P. (Acts xx. 3) only, exc. Rev. xvii. 13, 17 [bis]. 2 Macc. xiv. 20. l ch. iii. 13. Col. i. 8. Heb. ix. 8. xii. 27. 1 Pet. i. 11. 2 Pet. i. 14 only. Exod. vi. 3. m see Rom. xvi. 10, 11. n plur., 2 Cor. xii. 20. 1 Tim. vi. 4. Tit. iii. 9. -ιδες, here only. sing., Rom. i. 29. xiii. 13. ch. iii. 3. Gal. v. 20. Phil. i. 15 only +. Sir. xxviii. 11. xl. 5, 9 only. o = ch. x. 29. Gal. iii. 17. see ch. vii. 29. xv. 50. p gen., Acts ix. 2. Rom. xiv. 8. ch. iii. 23 al.

10. [αδελφοι bef παρ. υμ. (omg δε) C³ a 74.] ιησ. χρ. bef του κυρ. ημ. DF.—χρ. bef ιησ. D[-gr].—om του F(not G).
11. for μου, μοι B¹(sic) : om C¹(appy) D-lat Ambrst.

intended to prepare the way, as was before done in ver. 2, for the reproof which is coming. Chrys. remarks respecting vv. 1—9, σὺ δὲ σκόπει πῶς αὐτοὺς τῷ ὀνόματι ἀεὶ τοῦ χριστοῦ προσηλοῖ. καὶ ἀνθρώπου μὲν οὐδενός, οὔτε ἀποστόλου οὔτε διδασκάλου, συνεχῶς δὲ αὐτοῦ τοῦ ποθουμένου μέμνηται, καθάπερ ἀπὸ μέθης τινὸς τοὺς καρηβαροῦντας ἀπενεγκεῖν παρασκευάζων. οὐδαμοῦ γὰρ ἐν ἑτέρᾳ ἐπιστολῇ οὕτω συνεχῶς κεῖται τὸ ὄνομα τοῦ χριστοῦ· ἐνταῦθα μέντοι ἐν ὀλίγοις στίχοις πολλάκις, καὶ διὰ τούτου σχεδὸν τὸ πᾶν ὑφαίνει προοίμιον. Hom. ii. p. 10.

10—IV. 21.] Reproof of the party-divisions among them: by occasion of which, the Apostle explains and defends his own method of preaching only Christ to them. **10.]** **δέ** introduces the *contrast* to the thankful assurance just expressed. **διὰ τ. ὀν.**, as διὰ τῶν οἰκτιρμῶν τοῦ θεοῦ, Rom. xii. 1: "as the bond of union, and as the most holy name by which they could be adjured." Stanley. ἵνα (reff.) not only introduces the result of the fulfilment of the exhortation, but includes its import. **τὸ αὐτὸ λέγητε**—contrast to λέγει ἐγὼ μὲν . . . ἐγὼ δὲ . . . ἐγὼ δὲ . . . . ἐγὼ δέ of ver. 12,—but further implying the *having the same sentiments* on the subjects which divided them: see Phil. ii. 2. **ἦτε δέ]** δέ here implies **but rather**, as in Thuc. ii. 98, ἀπεγίγνετο μὲν αὐτῷ οὐδὲν τοῦ στρατοῦ, . . . προσεγίγνετο δέ. Hartung, Partikellehre, i. 171, gives many other examples. καταρτίζω is the exact word for the healing or repairing of the breaches made by the σχίσματα,—**perfectly united.** So Herod. v. 28, ἡ Μίλητος . . . . ἐπὶ δύο γενεὰς ἀνδρῶν νοσήσασα ἐς τὰ μάλιστα **στάσει**, μέχρι οὗ μιν Πάριοι **κατήρτισαν**. **νοΐ** (reff.), **disposition**,—**γνώμη** (do.), **opinion.**

11.] We cannot fill up τῶν Χλόης, not knowing whether they were *sons*, or *servants*, or other members of her family. Nor can we say whether Chloe was (Theophyl., al.) an *inhabitant of Corinth*, or *some Christian woman* (Estius) known to the Corinthians *elsewhere*, or (Michaelis, Meyer) *an Ephesian*, having friends who had been in Corinth. **12.] λέγω δὲ τοῦτο ὅτι,**—not, '*I say this because*,'—but (see reff.) **I mean this, that . . .** **ἕκαστ. ὑμ. λέγ.]** The meaning is clear, but the form of expression not strictly accurate, the ἕκαστος being a *different person in each case.* Accurately expressed it would run thus, ὅτι πάντες τοιοῦτό τι λέγετε, ἐγώ εἰμι Π., ἐγὼ Ἀπολ., ἐγὼ Κηφ., ἐγὼ χριστοῦ,—or as De W., ὅτι πάντες λ., ὁ μέν, ἐγώ εἰμι . . . . ὁ δέ, ἐγὼ κ.τ.λ.—Respecting the matter of fact to which the verse alludes, I have given references in the Prolegg. § ii. 10, to the principal theories of the German critics, and will only here restate the conclusions which I have there (ib. parr. 5—9) endeavoured to substantiate: (1) that these designations are *not used* as pointing to *actual parties formed and subsisting* among the Corinthians, but (2) as *representing the* spirit with which they contended *against one another*, being the sayings of *individuals*, and *not of parties* (ἕκαστος ὑμῶν λέγει): q. d. 'You are all in the habit of alleging against one another, some your special attachment to Paul, some to Apollos, some to Cephas, others to no mere human teacher, but barely to Christ, to the exclusion of us his Apostles.' (3) That these sayings, while they are not to be made the *

Ἀπολλώ, ἐγὼ δὲ Κηφᾶ, ἐγὼ δὲ χριστοῦ. 13 q μεμέρισται ὁ χριστός; μὴ Παῦλος ἐσταυρώθη ὑπὲρ ὑμῶν, ἢ r εἰς τὸ

q = Matt. xii. 25, 26 ||. (ch. vii. 34. Rom. xii. 3 reff.) 3 Kings xvi. 21. r = Acts viii. 16 reff.

13. for υπερ, περι BD[1]: txt ACD[2.3]FL[P]ℵ rel.

basis of any hypothesis respecting *definite parties* at Corinth, *do* nevertheless *hint at matters of fact,* and are *not merely* 'exempli gratia:' and (4) that this view of the verse, which was taken by Chrys., Theodoret, Theophylact, Calv., is *borne out,* and indeed *necessitated,* by ch. iv. 6 (see there). **ἐγὼ . . . Παύλου**] This profession, of being guided especially *by the words and acts of Paul,* would probably belong to those who were the first fruits of, or directly converted under, his ministry. Such persons would contend for his apostolic authority, and maintain doctrinally his teaching, *so far being right;* but, as usual with partisans, would magnify into importance practices and sayings of his which were in themselves indifferent, and forget that theirs was a service of perfect freedom under one Master, even Christ. With these he does not deal *doctrinally* in the Epistle, as there was *no need for it:* but involves them in the same censure as the rest, and shews them in ch. ii., iii., iv. that he had no such purpose of gaining personal honour among them, but only of building them up in Christ. **ἐγὼ Ἀπολλώ**] Apollos (Acts xviii. 24 ff.) had come to Corinth after the departure of Paul, and being eloquent, might attract some, to whom the bodily presence of Paul seemed weak and his speech contemptible. It would certainly appear that some occasion had been taken by this difference, to set too high a value on external and rhetorical form of putting forth the gospel of Christ. This the Apostle seems to be blaming (in part) in the conclusion of this, and the next chapter. And from ch. xvi. 12, it would seem likely that Apollos himself had been aware of the abuse of his manner of teaching which had taken place, and was unwilling, by repeating his visit just then, to sanction or increase it. **ἐγὼ Κηφᾶ**] All we can say in possible explanation of this, is, that as Peter was the *Apostle of the circumcision,*—as we know from Gal. ii. 11 ff. that his course of action on one occasion was reprehended by Paul, and as that course of action no doubt had influence and found followers, it is very conceivable that some of those who in Corinth lightly esteemed Paul, might take advantage of this honoured name, and cite against the Christian liberty taught by their own spiritual founder, the stricter practice of Peter. If so, these persons would be mainly found among the Jewish converts or Judaizers; and the matters treated in ch. vii.—xi. 1, may have been subjects of doubt mainly with these persons. **ἐγὼ δὲ χριστοῦ**] A rendering has been proposed (Estius, al.) which need only be mentioned to be rejected: viz. that Paul having mentioned the three parties, then breaks of, and adds, *in his own person,* ἐγὼ δὲ (Παῦλος), χριστοῦ (εἰμι) [not of any of these preceding]. Beza represents this as Chrysostom's view, but it is not: οὐ τοῦτο ἐνεκάλει, ὅτι τὸν χριστὸν ἑαυτοῖς ἐπεφήμιζον, ἀλλ' ὅτι μὴ πάντες μόνον. οἶμαι δὲ αὐτὸν καὶ οἴκοθεν αὐτὸ προστεθεικέναι βουλόμενον βαρύτερον τὸ ἔγκλημα ποιῆσαι, καὶ δεῖξαι οὕτω καὶ τὸν χριστὸν εἰς μέρος δοθέντα ἕν, εἰ καὶ μὴ οὕτως ἐποίουν τοῦτο ἐκεῖνοι:—(Hom. iii. p. 16 f.):—meaning by οἴκοθεν, not, as *his own sentiment,* but *of his own invention,* to shew them the inconsistency of their conduct. The words seem to apply to those who make a merit of *not being attached to any* human *teacher,*—who therefore slighted the apostleship of Paul. To them frequent allusion seems to be made in this and in the second Epistle, and more especially in 2 Cor. x. 7—11.

For a more detailed discussion of the whole subject, see Prolegg. as above, and Dr. Davidson's Introd. to the N. T. ii. 222 ff. **13.**] Some (Lachmann has so printed it) take μεμέρισται ὁ χρ. as an assertion,—'*Christ has been divided* (by you),'—or, as Chrys. mentions, διενείματο πρὸς ἀνθρώπους κ. ἐμερίσατο τὴν ἐκκλησίαν. But it is far better to take it, as commonly, interrogatively: **Is Christ** (the *Person* of Christ, as the centre and bond of Christian unity—not, the *Gospel* of Christ (Grot., al.),—nor the *Church* of Christ (Estius, Olsh.): nor the *power* of Christ (Theodoret), i. e. his right over all) **divided** (not in the primary sense (Meyer, ed. 1), against Himself, as Mark iii. 24, 25, where we have ἐφ' ἑαυτήν, but '*into various parts,* one under one leader, another under another,—which in fact would amount, after all, to a division against Himself)? The question applies to *all addressed,* not to the ἐγὼ χριστοῦ only, as Meyer, ed. 1. In that case μεμέρισται ὁ χρ. would mean 'Has Christ become the property of one part only?' as indeed Dr. Burton renders it. Meyer urges against the interrogative rendering, that the questions begin

s ver. 4. ὄνομα Παύλου r ἐβαπτίσθητε ; 14 s εὐχαριστῶ τῷ s θεῷ ὅτι ABCDF
οὐδένα ὑμῶν ἐβάπτισα, εἰ μὴ Κρίσπον καὶ Γάϊον, 15 ἵνα LPℵ a b c d e f g
t ch. iv. 2. 2 Cor. xiii. 11. 1 Thess. iv. 1. μή τις εἴπῃ ὅτι r εἰς τὸ ἐμὸν ὄνομα r ἐβαπτίσθητε. 16 ἐβά- h k l m n o 17.
u = Acts xix. 2 reff. πτισα δὲ καὶ τὸν Στεφανᾶ οἶκον· t λοιπὸν οὐκ οἶδα u εἴ 47
v constr., Acts xxvi. 17 reff. τινα ἄλλον ἐβάπτισα. 17 οὐ γάρ v ἀπέστειλέν με χριστὸς
w absol., Rom. xv. 20 reff. βαπτίζειν, ἀλλὰ w εὐαγγελίζεσθαι· οὐκ ἐν σοφίᾳ λόγου,

14. om τω θεω Bℵ[1] 67[2] [Chr-comm$_1$ Damasc-comm]. add μου A d g 17 vulg-sixt(with demid fuld harl[2]) Syr syr-w-ob copt arm Thdrt$_3$ Orig-int$_1$ Pel Sedul Bede. πρισκον ℵ[1].

15. rec (for εβαπτισθητε) εβαπτισα, with C[3]DFLP rel fri Syr [syr-txt] goth Thdrt Tert$_1$: txt ABC[1]ℵ a m 17 vulg syr-mg coptt arm Chr$_1$ Damasc Ambr-mss Pel Primas Bede.

16. for εβαπτισα, βεβαπτικα D[1][twice] F[1st]. ins το bef λοιπον F. om αλλον F fuld [D-lat].

17. for απεστειλεν, απεστα(. . .) A : απεσταλκε c. ins ο bef χριστος BF Thdrt: om ACDLPℵ rel [Orig-c$_2$] Chr$_1$ Thl Œc. (αλλα, so A(appy) BDℵ.) ευαγγελισασθαι B: txt ADFLPℵ rel. (C uncert.)

immediately after, with μή. But we may fairly set against this argument, that the μή introduces a new *form* of interrogation respecting a new individual, viz. Paul: and that it was natural, for solemnity's sake, to express the other question differently. In μεμέρισται **ὁ χριστός**, the Majesty of Christ's Person is set against the unworthy insinuation conveyed by μεμέρισται,—in μὴ Παῦλος ἐσταυρώθη ὑπὲρ ὑμ.,—the meanness of the individual, Paul, is set against the triumph of divine Love implied in ἐστ. ὑπ. ὑμῶν. Two such contrasts could hardly but be differently expressed.

μὴ Π. ἐστ. κ.τ.λ.] **Surely Paul was not crucified for you?** By repudiating all possibility of *himself* being the Head and ἐπώνυμος of their church, he does so *à fortiori* for Cephas and Apollos: for *he founded* the Church at Corinth. On εἰς τὸ ὄν. ἐβαπτ. see Matt. xxviii. 19.

14.] Olsh. characterizes it as surprising that Paul should not have referred to the *import of baptism itself* as a reason to substantiate his argument. He does not this, but tacitly assumes, between ver. 13 and 14, the probability that his having baptized any considerable number among the Corinthians would naturally have led to the abuse against which he is arguing.

εὐχ. τ. θ.] '*I am* (now) *thankful to God, who so ordered it that I did not,' &c.* Crispus, the former ruler of the synagogue, Acts xviii. 8. Gaius, afterwards the host of the Apostle, and of the church, Rom. xvi. 23.

15.] **ἵνα** represents the purpose, not of the Apostle's conduct at the time, but of the divine ordering of things: 'God so arranged it, that none might say,' &c.

16.] He subsequently recollects having baptized Stephanas and his family (see ch. xvi. 15, 17),—perhaps from information derived *from Stephanas himself*, who was with him:—and he leaves an opening for any others whom he may possibly have baptized and have forgotten it. The last clause is important as against those who maintain the *absolute omniscience* of the inspired writers on *every topic which they handle.*

17.] This verse forms the transition to the description of his preaching among them. His mission was *not to baptize*:—a trace already, of the separation of the offices of baptizing and preaching. ἄνθρωπον μὲν γὰρ κατηχούμενον λαβόντας καὶ πεπεισμένον βαπτίσαι, παντὸς οὑτινοσοῦν ἐστιν· ἡ γὰρ προαίρεσις τοῦ προσιόντος λοιπὸν ἐργάζεται τὸ πᾶν, καὶ ἡ τοῦ θεοῦ χάρις· ὅταν δὲ ἀπίστους δέῃ κατηχῆσαι, πολλοῦ δεῖ πόνου, πολλῆς τῆς σοφίας· τότε δὲ καὶ τὸ κινδυνεύειν προσῆν. Chrys. Hom. iii. p. 18. It is evident that this is said in no *derogation* of Baptism, for he did on occasion baptize,—and it would be impossible that he should speak lightly of the ordinance to which he appeals (Rom. vi. 3) as the seal of our union with Christ.

οὐκ ἐν σοφίᾳ λόγου] It seems evident from this apology, and other hints in the two Epistles, e. g. 2 Cor. x. 10, that the *plainness and simplicity of Paul's speech* had been *one cause* among the Corinthians of alienation from him. Perhaps, as hinted above, the eloquence of Apollos was extolled to Paul's disadvantage.

ἐν σοφ.] **in** (as the element in which: better than '*with*') **wisdom of speech** (i. e. the speculations of philosophy: that these are meant, and not mere eloquence or rhetorical form, appears by what follows, which treats of the *subject*, and not merely of the *manner* of the preaching) **in order that the Cross of Christ** (the great central point of his preaching; exhibiting man's guilt and God's love in their highest degrees and

ἵνα μὴ ˣ κενωθῇ ὁ ʸ σταυρὸς τοῦ χριστοῦ. 18 ὁ ᶻ λόγος
γὰρ ὁ τοῦ ʸ σταυροῦ τοῖς μὲν ᵃᵇ ἀπολλυμένοις ᶜ μωρία
ἐστίν, τοῖς δὲ ᵇᵈ σωζομένοις ἡμῖν ᵉ δύναμις θεοῦ ἐστιν.
19 γέγραπται γὰρ ᶠ Ἀπολῶ τὴν σοφίαν τῶν σοφῶν, καὶ
τὴν ᵍ σύνεσιν τῶν ʰ συνετῶν ⁱ ἀθετήσω. 20 ᵏ ποῦ σοφός;
ᵏ ποῦ ˡ γραμματεύς; ᵏ ποῦ ᵐ συνζητητὴς τοῦ ⁿ αἰῶνος ⁿ τούτου; οὐχὶ ᵒ ἐμώρανεν ὁ θεὸς τὴν σοφίαν τοῦ κόσμου;
21 ᵖ ἐπειδὴ γὰρ ἐν τῇ ᑫ σοφίᾳ τοῦ ᑫ θεοῦ οὐκ ʳ ἔγνω ὁ

x = Rom. iv. 14 reff.
y = Gal. v. 11. vi. 12, 14. Phil. iii. 18.
z = Acts xiii. 26 reff.
a = Rom. ii. 12. 2 Cor. ii. 15. iv. 3. 2 Thess. ii. 10. (1 Pet. i. 7.) Lev. xxiii. 30.
b dat., ch. ii. 14. viii. 6. ix. 2.
c vv. 21, 23. ch. ii. 14. iii. 19 only +. Sir. xx. 31. xli. 15 only. (-ρός, ver. 25.)
d pres., ch. xv. 2 reff.
e Acts viii. 10. Rom. i. 16. ver. 24.
f Isa. xxix. 14.
g Mark xii. 23. Luke ii. 47. Eph. iii. 4. Col. i. 9. ii. 2. 2 Tim. ii. 7 only. Prov. ii. 2.
h Matt. xi. 25. Luke x. 21. Acts xiii. 7 only. Prov. xvi. 21.
i = Mark vii. 9. Luke x. 16. John xii. 48. Gal. ii. 21 al. Isa. xlviii. 8.
k = Rom. iii. 27. Isa. xxxiii. 18.
l = Matt. xiii. 52. Epp., here only. Ezra vii. 6.
m here only +. (-τεῖν, Acts vi. 9. ix. 29. -τησις, Acts xv. 7.)
n Rom. xii. 2 reff.
o = Rom. i. 22 (reff.) only. Isa. xix. 11.
p Acts xv. 24 reff.
q ver. 24. Rom. xi. 33. Eph. iii. 10.
r Rom. i. 21. Gal. iv. 9. 1 John iv. 6, 7, 8. (Jer. xxxviii. [xxxi.] 34.)

18. om *γαρ* P b^1. om 2nd *ὁ* B a^1 Cyr-jer$_1$. *σωμενοις*(sic) ℵ. om *ημιν* F am^2 fuld^1 fri D-lat G-lat Iren-int$_1$ Tert Cypr$_1$ Hil$_1$ Ambrst Cassiod: *id est nobis* vulg Pel Sedul Bede.

19. om *γαρ* D^1[-gr(appy, Treg)] k [Orig-c$_1$].

20. rec aft *τ. κοσμ.* ins *τουτου* (*to correspond with του αι. τουτου above*), with C^{3}D^{3}FLℵ^3 rel [latt syrr copt goth arm-mss] Clem$_1$ Orig$_1$ Chr$_1$ Thdrt Tert$_1$: om ABC^1 D^1[-gr] Pℵ^1 a 17 [spec arm-ed Euthal-ms] Clem$_1$ Cyr[-p$_1$] Did$_1$ Damasc Thl Orig-int$_1$ Tert$_1$.

21. om *γαρ* F 3. 108-77 arm.

closest connexion) **might not be deprived of its effect.** This would come to pass rather by *philosophical speculations* than by *eloquence.* **18.] For** (explanation of the foregoing clause,—and that, assuming the *mutual exclusiveness* of the *preaching of the Cross* and *wisdom of speech,* and the * identity of *οἱ ἀπολλύμενοι* with the lovers of *σοφία λόγου*: q. d. 'wisdom of speech would nullify the Cross of Christ: for the doctrine of the Cross is to the lovers of that wisdom, folly.' The reasoning is elliptical and involved, and is further complicated by the emphatic position of *τοῖς ἀπολλ.* and *τοῖς σωζ.*) **the** [**preaching** (**speech,** or] **doctrine** "there is a word, an eloquence, which is most powerful, the eloquence of the Cross: referring to *σοφία λόγου.*" Stanley) **of the Cross is to the perishing** (those who are through unbelief on the way to everlasting perdition) **folly: but to us who are being saved** (Billroth (in Olsh.) remarks that *τ. σωζ. ἡμ.* is a gentler expression than *ἡμῖν τ. σωζ.* would be: the latter would put the *ἡμ.* into strong emphasis, and exclude the opponents in a more marked manner. **οἱ σωζόμενοι** are *those in the way of salvation:*—who by faith have laid hold on Christ and are by Him *being saved,* see reff.) **it is the power** (see ref. Rom. and note. Hardly, as Meyer,—*a medium* of divine Power,—etwas, wodurch Gott kräftig wirkt: rather, *the perfection* of God's Power—the Power itself, in its noblest manifestation) **of God. 19.] For** (continuation of reason for *οὐκ ἐν σοφίᾳ λόγου*: because it was prophesied that such wisdom should be brought to nought by God) **it is written, &c.** The citation is after the LXX, with the exception of *ἀθετήσω* for *κρύψω.* The Heb. is 'the wisdom of the wise shall perish, and the prudence of the prudent shall disappear.' (Lowth.) But Calv. says most truly, 'Perit sapientia, sed Domino destruente: sapientia evanescit, sed inducta a Domino et deleta.' **20.]** See ref. The question implies *disappearance* and *exclusion.* **σοφός, the wise,** *generally:* **γραμμ., the Jewish scribe** [**interpreter of the law**],—**συνζητ., the Greek disputer** [**arguer**] (reff.). **τοῦ αἰῶν. τ.** is best taken with the whole three,—**of this present** (ungodly) **world.** **ἐμώρανεν**] *μωρὰν ἔδειξεν οὖσαν πρὸς τὴν τῆς πίστεως κατάληψιν,* Chrys. **21.] For** (explanation of *ἐμώρανεν*) **when** (not *temporal,* but illative = 'since,' 'seeing that,'—so Plato, Gorg. p. 454, *ἐπειδὴ τοίνυν οὐ μόνη ἀπεργάζεται τοῦτο τὸ ἔργον, ἀλλὰ καὶ ἄλλαι . . .*; see Hartung, Partikellehre, i. 259) **in the wisdom of God** (*as part of the wise arrangement of God.* De W., Meyer, al., render it '*by the revelation of the wisdom of God,*' which was made to the Gentiles, as Rom. i., by creation, and to the Jews by the law,—thus connecting *ἐν* with *ἔγνω,* and making *τῇ σοφ. τ. θ.* the medium of knowledge:—Chrys. takes it for the wisdom manifest in His *works only*: *τί ἐστιν, ἐν τ. σοφ. τ. θ.; τῇ διὰ τῶν ἔργων φαινομένῃ, δι' ὧν ἠθέλησε γνωρισθῆναι.* But I very

s Rom. xv. 26 reff. t ver. 18. u Rom. xvi. 25 reff. v = Matt. xvi. 1. Isa. vii. 11 al. w Acts xvi. 29 reff. Lam. iv. 4. x = Matt. xii. 43 L. Prov. xiv. 6. y Acts viii. 5 reff. z = Rom. xiv. 13 reff. Rom. viii. 3. a see ch. v. 13. 2 Cor. iv. 17. viii. 8. b ver. 1 al. c ver. 18. d ver. 21. e neut., f Matt. vii. 26. ch. iii. 18. iv. 10 al. Deut. xxxii. 6. (-ρία, ver. 18.)

ABCDF LPℵ a b c d e f g h k l m n o 17. 47

κόσμος διὰ τῆς σοφίας τὸν [r] *θεόν,* [s] *εὐδόκησεν ὁ θεὸς διὰ*
τῆς [t] *μωρίας τοῦ* [u] *κηρύγματος σῶσαι τοὺς πιστεύοντας·*
22 [p] *ἐπειδὴ καὶ Ἰουδαῖοι* [v] *σημεῖα* [w] *αἰτοῦσιν καὶ Ἕλληνες*
σοφίαν [x] *ζητοῦσιν,* 23 *ἡμεῖς δὲ* [y] *κηρύσσομεν χριστὸν ἐσταυ-*
ρωμένον, Ἰουδαίοις μὲν [z] *σκάνδαλον, ἔθνεσιν δὲ* [t] *μωρίαν,*
24 [a] *αὐτοῖς δὲ τοῖς* [b] *κλητοῖς, Ἰουδαίοις τε καὶ Ἕλλησιν,*
χριστὸν θεοῦ [c] *δύναμιν καὶ θεοῦ* [d] *σοφίαν·* 25 *ὅτι* [e] *τὸ* [f] *μωρὸν*

ηυδοκ. C m [Ath$_1$] Chr$_1$ Damasc. for ο θεος, τω θεω F. πιστευσαντας L.

22. for επειδη και, επει F: om και fuld [harl[1]] Syr [(Clem$_1$) Tert$_1$ Cypr$_2$ Hil$_2$ Ambrst]. rec σημειον (*Meyer and De W think* σημεια *a corrn, because only the* sing *could present any difficulty: but Tischdf* (Ed. 7 [and 8]) *refers to such passages as Matt* xii. 39, xvi. 4 *al as having suggested the sing, which considg the immense weight of manuscript authority, seems, I own, more likely*), with L rel arm [Euthal-ms Cyr-p$_1$] Thl-txt Œc-txt: txt ABCDFPℵ 17 latt syrr copt goth [æth-pl] Clem$_2$ [Sevrn-c$_1$ Chr$_1$ Thdrt Damasc] Mcion-t Cypr$_2$ Hil. επιζητουσιν A.

23. rec (for εθνεσιν) ελλησιν (*to suit precedg and follg*), with C[3]D[3] rel [Syr(appy)] Clem$_2$ Orig-ms$_1$ Eus$_2$ [Euthal-ms Chr$_1$ Thdrt]: txt ABC[1]D[1]FLPℵ m 17 latt syr copt goth æth arm Orig$_1$[-int$_1$] Eus$_1$ Ath [Cyr-jer$_1$ Damasc] Cypr$_2$ Hil$_3$ [Ambrst].

24. [for αυτοις, αυτος C(sic, Tischdf).] om τοις F. om τε F k.

much doubt the legitimacy of this absolute objective use of *σοφία*, as = those things by which the *σοφία* is manifested. I cannot see with Olsh. why the interpretation given above is 'ganz unpaulinisch:' it is merely an expansion of *ἐμώρανεν*,—and agrees much better with Paul's use of the words *ἡ σοφία τ. θεοῦ* in reff. and in ch. ii. 7) **the world** (Jew and Gentile, see next verse) **by its wisdom** (as a means of attaining knowledge: or, but I prefer the other, "through the wisdom (of God) which I have just mentioned:" so Stanley) **knew not** (could not find out) **God, God saw fit by the foolishness of preaching** (lit., 'of the proclamation:' gen. of apposition,—by that preaching which is reputed folly by the world) **to save believers.** Rom. i. 16 throws light on this last expression as connected with *δύναμις θεοῦ* in our ver. 18, and with what follows here. There the two are joined: *δύναμις γὰρ θεοῦ ἐστιν (τὸ εὐαγ. τ. χρ.) εἰς σωτηρίαν παντὶ τῷ πιστεύοντι, Ἰουδαίῳ τε πρῶτον κ. Ἕλληνι.* **22.] ἐπειδή**, not as in ver. 21, but = 'siquidem,' and explains *τ. μωρίας τ. κηρ.* **καὶ—καί]** see Mark ix. 13, unite (De W.) things resembling each other in this particular, but else unlike. Jews and Gentiles both made false requirements, but of different kinds. **σημεῖα αἰτ.]** see Matt. xii. 38, xvi. 1; Luke xi. 16; John ii. 18, vi. 30. The correction *σημεῖον* has probably been made from remembering the *σημεῖον* of these passages. The sign required was not, as I have observed on Matt. xii. 38, a mere miracle, but some token from Heaven, substantiating the word preached. **23.]** Still the expansion of *ἡ μωρ. τ. κηρύγ.* Now, *σκάνδ.* as regards the Jews, and *μωρία* as regards the Gentiles, correspond to the general term *μωρία* before. The *δέ* after *ἡμεῖς* is that so often found in clauses following the temporal conjunctions *ἐπεί, ἕως, ὄφρα*, &c., in Homer, and *ὅς, ὡς, ὥσπερ, εἰ*, &c., in Attic writers: e. g. Od. ξ. 178, *τὸν* **ἐπεὶ** *θρέψαν θεοί, ἔρνεϊ ἶσον . . . , τοῦ* **δέ** *τις ἀθανάτων βλάψε φρένας ἔνδον ἐΐσας*,—and Xen. Cyr. viii. 5. 12, **ὥσπερ** *οἱ ὁπλῖται, οὕτω* **δὲ** *καὶ οἱ πελτασταὶ κ. οἱ τοξόται.* See many other examples in Hartung, Partikellehre, i. 184 f. It serves to give a slight prominence to the consequent clause, as compared with the antecedent one. **24.]** This verse plainly is a continuation of the opposition to ver. 22 before begun, but itself springs by way of opposition out of *Ἰουδ. μὲν σκάνδ., ἔθν. δὲ μωρίαν*,—and carries the thought back to vv. 18 and 21. **αὐτοῖς δὲ τ. κλητοῖς]** Not, '*but to the elect themselves,*' which would be either *αὐτοῖς δὲ κλητοῖς*, or *τοῖς δὲ κλητοῖς αὐτοῖς*;—but **to these, viz. the elect,**—the *αὐτοῖς* serving to identify them with the *σωζόμενοι* of ver. 18. There it was **ἡμῖν**,—here *αὐτοῖς*, because by the mention of *preaching* joined with *ἡμεῖς*, he has now separated off the *hearers*. **δύναμιν**, as fulfilling the requirement of the seekers after a *sign*:—**σοφίαν**,—of those who sought *wisdom*. The repetition of *χριστόν* gives solemnity, at the same time that it concentrates the *δύναμις* and *σοφία* in the Person of Christ; q. d.

τοῦ θεοῦ σοφώτερον τῶν [g] ἀνθρώπων ἐστίν, καὶ [e] τὸ
[h] ἀσθενὲς τοῦ θεοῦ [i] ἰσχυρότερον τῶν ἀνθρώπων ἐστίν.
26 [k] βλέπετε γὰρ τὴν [l] κλῆσιν ὑμῶν, ἀδελφοί, ὅτι οὐ πολλοὶ σοφοὶ [m] κατὰ [m] σάρκα, οὐ πολλοὶ [n] δυνατοί, οὐ πολλοὶ [o] εὐγενεῖς, 27 ἀλλὰ τὰ [f] μωρὰ τοῦ κόσμου [p] ἐξελέξατο
ὁ θεὸς ἵνα [q] καταισχύνῃ τοὺς σοφούς, καὶ τὰ [h] ἀσθενῆ τοῦ
κόσμου [p] ἐξελέξατο ὁ θεὸς ἵνα [q] καταισχύνῃ τὰ [r] ἰσχυρά,
28 καὶ τὰ [s] ἀγενῆ τοῦ κόσμου καὶ τὰ [t] ἐξουθενημένα [p] ἐξ-

g constr., Matt. v. 20. John v. 36. 1 John ii. 2.
h ch. iv. 10. xii. 22. Gal. iv. 9. Heb. vii. 18. Wisd. ii. 11.
i compar., Luke iii. 16 ||. xi. 22. ch. x. 22. Judg. xiv. 18.
k ch. x. 18. Phil. iii. 2.
l Rom. xi. 29 reff. Eph. iv. 1, 4 al.
m Rom. i. 3 reff. n Acts xxv. 5. o = Luke xix. 12 (Acts xvii. 11) only. Job i. 3. 2 Macc. x. 13 only. p Acts i. 2, 24 al. Deut. iv. 37. q = ch. xi. 4, 5, 22. 2 Kings xix. 5. r see above (i). Matt. xii. 29 bis ||. ch. iv. 10 al. s here only †. t = Rom. xiv. 3 reff.

25. εστιν bef των ανθρ. (both times) DF latt [Syr] arm Hil_2 [Ambrst, 2nd copt]. om 2nd εστιν Bℵ[1] o 17. 67[2] Orig_1 Eus_1.
26. for γαρ, ουν D[-gr] F æth (Pamph_1 [Orig_1 γουν]). om ου πολλ. δυν. F[-gr] copt.—ουδε D[1][-gr].
27. om from [1st] to [2nd] ινα A F[-gr] m[: from 1st θεος to θεος (next ver)] Orig[-gr_1]. rec τους σοφους bef καταισχυνη, with rel: txt BCDLPℵ k 17. 47 latt syrr copt æth arm Orig[$_{\text{sæpe}}$ Pamph_1 Cyr-p_1] Eus_2 Tert_1.
28. for αγενη, ασθενη ℵ[1](txt ℵ-corr[1]) Orig[-ms_1(txt_2-c_1)].

'*Christ even in His humiliation unto death, the power of God and wisdom of God.*' The use of δύναμις and σοφία here as applied to Him who was the greatest example of both, would not justify the absolute use of σοφία in this sense in ver. 21. 25.] **Because** (reason why Christ (crucified) is the power and wisdom of God) **the foolishness of God** (that act of God which men think foolish) **is wiser than men** (surpasses in wisdom, not only *all which they call* by that name, but *men*, all possible wisdom of mankind); **and the weakness of God** (that act of God which men think weak) **is stronger than men** (not only surpasses in might all which *they think powerful*, but *men themselves*,— all human might whatsoever. For the construction of the genitives, see reff.). The latter clause introduces a fresh thought, the way for which however has been prepared by δύναμις, vv. 18, 24. The Jews required a proof of *divine Might*: we give them *Christ crucified*, which is to them a thing ἀσθενές: but this ἀσθενὲς τοῦ θεοῦ is stronger than *men*. 26.] βλέπετε, imperative, as in reff. If taken indicatively, it loses the emphasis which its place in the sentence requires. It would thus be τὴν γὰρ κλῆσιν ὑμῶν βλέπετε. See a similar reminder on the part of the Apostle, 1 Thess. i. 4.
γάρ seems best to apply to what has immediately gone before. As a proof that the foolishness of God is wiser than men and the weakness of God stronger than men, he calls attention to the fact that the Christian church, so full of divine wisdom and strength by the indwelling Spirit of God, consisted for the most part, not of the wise or mighty among men, but of those whom the world despised. **κλῆσιν**, as in reff. the calling ἐν ᾗ ἐκλήθημεν—**the vocation** and standing of Christian men. **ὅτι οὐ πολλοὶ . . .]** **that not many of you are wise according to the flesh** ('significari vult sapientiam, quæ studio humano absque doctrina Spiritus Sancti potest acquiri,' Estius), **not many mighty** (no need to supply κατὰ σάρκα, which is understood as a matter of course), **not many noble.** This is far better than to supply (as E. V., and most Commentators) ἐκλήθησαν after εὐγενεῖς; and thus Vulg., Chrys., Beza, Meyer, De Wette, al. Olsh. observes: "The ancient Christians were for the most part slaves and men of low station; the whole history of the expansion of the church is in reality a progressive victory of the ignorant over the learned, the lowly over the lofty, until the emperor himself laid down his crown before the cross of Christ." **27, 28.]** **τὰ μωρά**, neut. for more generalization, but = τοὺς μωρούς. This is shewn by τοὺς σοφούς following, in that case it being necessary to use the masculine. **τοῦ κόσμ., of** (belonging to) **the world**: not *in the eyes of the world*, as Theodoret, Luth., Grot., Est., al.,—which would not fit τὰ ἀγενῆ τ. κόσμ., nor the *sense*: for they were not only *seemingly* but *really* foolish, when God chose them. **καταισχύνῃ**, by shewing to the wise and the strong, the foolish and the weak entering the kingdom of heaven before them.
τὰ ἀγενῆ, matter of *fact*—**the low-born**: **τὰ ἐξουθενημένα**, matter of *estimation*, **the despised.** Without the καί, which is certainly the true reading, τὰ μὴ ὄντα

ελέξατο ὁ θεός, τὰ [u] μὴ ὄντα, ἵνα τὰ ὄντα [v] καταργήσῃ,
29 ὅπως μὴ [w] καυχήσηται [x] πᾶσα σὰρξ [y] ἐνώπιον τοῦ θεοῦ·
30 [z] ἐξ αὐτοῦ δὲ ὑμεῖς ἐστὲ [a] ἐν χριστῷ Ἰησοῦ, ὃς [b] ἐγενήθη
σοφία ἡμῖν [c] ἀπὸ θεοῦ [d] δικαιοσύνη τε καὶ [e] ἁγιασμὸς καὶ

ABCDF LPℵ a b c d e f g h k l m n o 17. 47

u so Eur. Troad. 608, Ὁρῶ τὰ τῶν θεῶν, ὡς τὰ μὲν πυργοῦσ' ἄνω Τὰ μηδὲν ὄντα, τὰ δὲ δοκοῦντ' ἀπώλεσαν. v Paul (Rom. iii. 3, 31. ch. ii. 6. xiii. 8 al.) only, exc. Luke xiii. 7. Heb. ii. 14. Ezra iv. 21. w absol., ch. iv. 7. 2 Cor. xi. 16 al. 1 Kings ii. 3. x Acts ii. 17 reff. y = Acts xix. 9. 3 John 6. z = John vii. 22. Rom. xi. 36. a = Rom. viii. 1. xvi. 7, 11. 2 Cor. v. 17. Gal. i. 22. b = 2 Cor. vii. 14. 1 Thess. i. 5 al. c = Rom. xiii. 1. ch. iv. 5. vi. 19 al. d Rom. iii. 21, 25. e Rom. vi. 19 reff.

rec ins και bef τα μη οντα (*a mistaken supplement of the sense: see note*), with BC[3]D[3]LPℵ[3] rel vulg [F-lat spec] fri syrr copt [æth-pl arm $Pamph_1$] $Orig_{aliq}$ Eus_3 Chr_1 Thdrt [Damasc]: om AC[1] D[1][and lat] F[-gr] ℵ[1] 17 æth-rom $Orig_1$ [Euthal-ms] Iren-int $Tert_1$ Ambrst Tich.

29. Elz καυχησεται, with FP [b o]: txt ABCDLℵ rel $Orig_{[sæpe]}$ Eus_1. rec for του θεου, αυτου (*corrn, to avoid repetition, not observing the emphasis*), with C[1] vulg syrr arm-usc $Orig_1$ $Dial_1$ [$Sevrn\text{-}c_1$] Thdrt Ambrst: txt ABC[3]DFLPℵ[1] rel fri spec copt arm-zoh æth $Orig_3$[$-int_1$] Eus_1 $Ephr_1$ Bas Chr_1 Damasc Thl Aug $Tich_2$.—ℵ[3] began to write αυτου, but erased it.

30. rec ημιν bef σοφια, with L rel vulg-ed(with [harl[1]]) syrr copt arm $Orig_5$ Eus_6 Mac_2 Chr_1 Thdrt [$Cyr\text{-}p_2$ Damasc] $Ambr_2$ Aug: txt ABCDFPℵ m 17 am(with demid harl[2] [fuld tol]) $Orig_{sæpe}$ [$Dial_1$] Eus_2 Did_1 Cyr[$-p_1$] $Ambr_2$ Ambrst Jer_2. ημων B. for δικ. τε, και δικ. D[2][?]F $Orig_1$ [om τε D[1]].

may belong to all four, the μωρά, ἀσθενῆ, ἀγενῆ, and ἐξουθεν.,—but more probably it has reference only to the last two. Nothing (as e. g. μέγα τι) must be supplied after μὴ ὄντα: it means **as good as having no existence**: μή being subjective, and implying that the non-existence is not *absolute* but *estimative*. Were it absolute *matter of fact*, it would be expressed by τὰ οὐκ ὄντα, as in 1 Pet. ii. 10, οἱ οὐκ ἠλεημένοι, νῦν δὲ ἐλεηθέντες. See Hartung, Partikellehre, ii. p. 131; Winer, edn. 6, § 55. 5; and Phil. iii. 3; Eph. v. 4. Olshausen refines on the expression too much, when he explains it of those who have lost their old carnal life and have not yet acquired their new spiritual one: it more probably means, things (persons) of absolutely *no account* in the world, unassignable among men, which the ἀγενῆ and ἐξουθενημένα are. Meyer remarks that the threefold repetition of ἐξελ. ὁ θεός, with the three contrasts to σοφοί, δυνατοί, and εὐγενεῖς, announces the fact with a triumphant emphasis. **καταργ.**] 'reduce to the state of οὐκ ὄντα.' All the ὄντα, the *realities*, of the world, are of absolutely *no account*, unassignable, in God's spiritual kingdom. **29.**] **That all flesh may have no ground of boasting before God.** The negative in these clauses goes with the *verb*, not with the adjective; so that each word retains its proper meaning.

30.] **But** (contrast to the boasting just spoken of) **of Him are ye** (from Him ye, who once were as οὐκ ὄντα,—ἐστέ.—He is the author of your spiritual life) **in** (in union with) **Christ Jesus, Who was made** (not 'is made:' see reff. On γενήθη see 1 Thess. i. 5 note) **to us from God wisdom** (standing us in stead of all earthly wisdom and raising us above it by being ἀπὸ θεοῦ;—Wisdom—in His * incarnation, in His life of obedience, in His teaching, in His death of atonement, in His glorification and sending of the Spirit: and not only Wisdom, but all that we can want to purify us from guilt, to give us righteousness before God, to sanctify us after His likeness, **(and) both righteousness** (the source of our justification before God), **and sanctification** (by His Spirit; observe the **τε καί**, implying that in these two, δικαιοσ. and ἁγιασμ., the Christian life is complete—that they are so joined as to form one whole—**our righteousness as well as our sanctification.** As Bisping well remarks, "δικ. and ἁγ. are closely joined by the τε (καί) and form but one idea, that of Christian justification: δικαιοσύνη the negative side, in Christ's justifying work—ἁγιασμός the positive, sanctification, the imparting to us of sanctifying grace"), **and redemption** (by satisfaction made for our sin, reff.:—or perhaps *deliverance*, from all evil, and especially from eternal death, as Rom. viii. 23: but I prefer the other). The foregoing construction of the sentence is justified, (1) as regards ἀπὸ θεοῦ belonging to ἐγενήθη, and not to σοφία, by the position of ἡμῖν, which has been altered in rec. to connect σοφία with ἀπὸ θ., (2) as regards the whole four substantives being co-ordinate, and not the last three merely explicative of σοφία, by the usage of τε καί—καί, e. g. Herod. i. 23, διθύραμβον πρῶτον ἀνθρώπων τῶν ἡμεῖς ἴδμεν ποιήσαντά τε καὶ ὀνομάσαντα καὶ διδάξαντα, and Hom. Od. ο. 78, ἀμφότερον, κῦδός τε καὶ ἀγλαΐη καὶ ὄνειαρ,—so

[f] ἀπολύτρωσις, 31 ἵνα [g] καθὼς γέγραπται Ὁ [h] καυχώμενος
ἐν κυρίῳ [h] καυχάσθω.
II. 1 Κἀγὼ ἐλθὼν πρὸς ὑμᾶς, ἀδελφοί, ἦλθον οὐ [i] καθ'
[k] ὑπεροχὴν λόγου ἢ σοφίας [l] καταγγέλλων ὑμῖν τὸ [m] μαρτύριον τοῦ θεοῦ. 2 οὐ γὰρ [n] ἔκρινά τι εἰδέναι ἐν ὑμῖν, εἰ
μὴ Ἰησοῦν χριστόν, [o] καὶ τοῦτον ἐσταυρωμένον. 3 κἀγὼ
[p] ἐν [q] ἀσθενείᾳ καὶ [p] ἐν [r] φόβῳ καὶ [p] ἐν [rs] τρόμῳ πολλῷ

f Rom. iii. 24 reff.
g ch. ii. 9 reff.
h Rom. ii. 17 reff. 1 Kings ii. 10. Jer. ix. 24.
i = Phil. ii. 3. iii. 6.
k 1 Tim. ii. 2 only. 1 Kings ii. 3 A Ald. compl. 2 Macc. xiii. 6 only. (-έχειν, Rom. xiii. 1.)
l = Acts xiii. 5 reff. part. pres., Acts xv. 27.
m = ch. i. 6 reff.
n = Acts xv. 19 reff.
o Rom. xiii. 11. ch. vi. 6, 8 al.
p = Rom. xv. 32 al.
q = Rom. vi. 19. 2 Cor. xi. 30. xii. 5, &c. Heb. v. 2. vii. 28. Job xxxvii. 7.
r 2 Cor. vii. 15. Eph. vi. 5. Phil. ii. 12 only. Ps. liv. 5.
s as above (r). Mark xvi. 8 only.

Chap. II. 1. for *μαρτυριον*, *μυστηριον* (*appy a gloss from ver* 7) ACℵ¹ n fri Syr copt Ambrst[mss vary] $Ambr_2$ Aug_1 : txt BDFLPℵ³ rel vulg syr sah æth arm Orig[-c_2] Chr_2 Cyr[-p Damasc] Thl Œc [Pel] Jer Bede.

2. rec aft *εκρινα* ins *του*, with D²L rel Chr_1 Thdrt Thl Œc : om ABCD¹·³FPℵ a m 17 (Orig Ath) Chr_1 Cyr_1 $Antch_1$ Damasc. rec *ειδεναι* bef *τι*, with AD²FLℵ 47 latt [syrr coptt arm] Orig-c_1 Did_1 [Chr_1] Cyr_1 $Tert_1$ [Ambrst] : txt BC(D¹·³)P a m 17 Cyr_1 Bas_1 $Isid_1$ Chr_1 Tert Hil_1 Victorin Aug_1.—*τι εν υμιν ειδ.* D¹·³ : *του εν υμιν ειδ. τι* D². (*The posn of τι, and harshness of τι ειδεναι, seem to have occasioned the transposns, and του would be supplied from elsw, see Acts* xxvii. 1, 1 *Cor* vii. 37.) *χρ.* bef *ιησ.* F 109 am(with harl tol) Orig-int_3 Hil_1 [Ambrst] Aug_2.

3. rec *και εγω*, with DFL rel Chr_1 Thdrt Thl Œc : txt ABCPℵ a k m 17 $Orig_1$[-c_1] Bas_1 $Antch_1$ Damasc. om 2nd *εν* F 49 latt(exc D-lat) [Ambrst]. om 3rd *εν* DF 49. 119 latt [Ambrst].

that (see Hartung, Partikellehre, i. 103; Donaldson, Gr. Gram. 551) the words coupled by τε καί (compare the exegesis above) rank as *but one* with regard to those coupled to them by καί, compare **ἀμφότερον** above. Hence these *three* cannot be under one category, as explicative of σοφία, but must be thus ranged: σοφία δικαιοσύνη τε καὶ ἁγιασμός, καὶ ἀπολύτρωσις. **31.**] The construction is an anacoluthon, the citation being retained in the original imperative, though the ἵνα required a subjunctive. It is freely made from the LXX. This verse declaring, in opposition to ver. 29, the only true ground of boasting, viz. in God and His mercies to us in Christ, closes the description of *God's dealing* in this matter. He now reverts to the subject of *his own preaching*. **II. 1—5.**] *Accordingly, Paul did not use among them words of worldly wisdom, but preached Christ crucified only, in the power of the Spirit.* **1.**] **I also** (as one of the ἡμεῖς of ch. i. 23, and also with reference to the preceding verse, ὁ καυχ. ἐν κυρ. καυχάσθω) **when I came to you, brethren, came, not with excellency of speech or wisdom announcing** (pres. part., not fut.,—as in ref., and in Xen. Hell. ii. 1. 29, ἐς τὰς Ἀθήνας ἔπλευσεν ἀγγέλλουσα τὰ γεγονότα. The time taken in the voyage is overlooked, and the announcement regarded as beginning when the voyage began) **to you the testimony of** (concerning) **God.** **2.**] **For I did not resolve to know any thing** (hardly = ἔκρινα εἰδέναι οὐδέν, as E. V., but meaning, "*the only thing that I made it definitely my business to know, was*") **among you, except Jesus Christ** (His Person) **and Him** (as) **crucified** (His Office). It would seem that the historical facts of redemption, and especially the crucifixion of Christ, as a matter of offence, had been kept in the background by these professors of human wisdom. "We must not overlook, that Paul does not say 'to know *any thing of* or *concerning* Christ,' but to know Him Himself, to preach Him Himself. The *historical Christ* is also the *living Christ*, who is *with His own till the end of time*: He works personally in every believer, and forms Himself in each one. Therefore it is universally Christ Himself, the crucified and the risen One, who is the subject of preaching, and is also Wisdom itself: for His history evermore lives and repeats itself in the whole church and in every member of it: it never waxes old, any more than does God Himself;—it retains at this day that fulness of power, in which it was revealed at the first foundation of the church." Olshausen. **3.**] **κἀγώ, and I,** coupled to ἦλθον in ver. 1, and ἐγώ repeated for emphasis, the *nature of his own preaching* being the leading subject-matter here. The **weakness and fear and much trembling** must not be exclusively understood of his *manner of speech* as contrasted with the rhetorical preachers, for ὁ λόγος μου κ. τὸ κήρυγμά

t ἐγενόμην t πρὸς ὑμᾶς, 4 καὶ ὁ λόγος μου καὶ τὸ u κήρυγμά μου οὐκ v ἐν w πειθοῖς σοφίας λόγοις, ἀλλ' v ἐν
x ἀποδείξει y πνεύματος καὶ δυνάμεως, 5 ἵνα ἡ πίστις ὑμῶν
μὴ ᾖ p ἐν σοφίᾳ ἀνθρώπων, ἀλλ' p ἐν z δυνάμει θεοῦ.
6 Σοφίαν δὲ λαλοῦμεν ἐν τοῖς a τελείοις, σοφίαν δὲ οὐ

ABCDF LPℵ a b c d e f g h k l m n o 17. 47

t = ch. xvi. 10. 2 John 12. see Matt. xiii. 56. Mark xiv. 49. John i. 1, 2.
u Rom. xvi. 25 reff.
v Luke iv. 32.
w here only †.
x here only †. (-κνυσθαι, Acts ii. 22.)
y = ver. 13. Gal. v. 5, 16.
z ch. i. 18 reff.
a = ch. xiv. 20. Heb. v. 14 al. 1 Chron. xxv. 8.

4. for πειθοις, πειθοι b[1] e o 1. 18[1]. 48. 72. 106-8-53 D-lat G-lat am(with F-lat) Syr sah [æth-pl] arm Orig$_2$ Eus[-mss$_1$ Chr-mss$_1$] Ath$_1$ Ambr$_3$ Ambrst Sedul Leo. rec ins ανθρωπινης bef σοφιας (*explanatory gloss*), with ACLPℵ[3] rel vulg-ed(with demid [fuld[2]] agst am fuld[1] tol) syr copt Orig$_2$ Ath$_1$ Mac$_1$ [Eus-mss$_1$ Bas$_1$ (Cyr-p$_1$)] Cyr-jer$_2$ Thl Œc Ambrst-comm [Pel] Sedul Bede: ανθρωπινοις m 93: om BDFℵ[1] 17 latt Syr sah æth arm Orig$_7$[-int$_1$ Eus-mss$_1$] Nys Cyr-jer$_1$ Chr[-mss$_2$ Sevrn-c$_1$] Thdrt-ms$_1$ [Damasc Ambr$_2$] Jer$_2$. λογων Syr arm Orig$_1$, των λογων Orig$_1$, λογου [k] am D-lat sah, λογοις ℵ[1]: om F a 18[1]. 74 G-lat Orig$_1$ Ath$_1$ Ambrst-comm Sedul. αλλα B. for αποδειξει, αποκαλυψει D[1.3].
5. om ᾖ F c m. αλλα B.

μου follow in the next verse,—but partly of this, and principally of his *internal* deep and humble *persuasion* of his own weakness and the mightiness of the work which was entrusted to him. So in Phil. ii. 12, 13, he commands the Philippians, μετὰ φόβου κ. τρόμου τὴν ἑαυτῶν σωτηρίαν κατεργάζεσθε, θεὸς γάρ ἐστιν ὁ ἐνεργῶν ἐν ὑμῖν. The ἀσθένεια may have reference to the παρουσία σώματος ἀσθενής of 2 Cor. x. 10. Chrys., al., understand it of *persecutions*: but in the places to which he refers, it has a far wider meaning,—viz. *infirmities*, including those resulting from persecution. **4.] And** (not adversative, as Olsh., but following naturally on the weakness, &c., just mentioned—'as corresponding to it') **my discourse and my preaching** (**λόγος** of the *course of argument and inculcation of doctrine*, **κήρυγμα** of the *announcement of facts*. This (De W.) is better than with Olsh. to understand λ. as his *private*, κ. his *public* discourse: see Luke iv. 32, and ὁ λόγος τ. σταυροῦ, ch. i. 18) **was not in** (did not consist of, was not set forth in, see ref.) **persuasive** (πειθός = πιθανός, πειστήριος, πειστικός in Greek. The var. readings have been endeavours to avoid the unusual word, which however is analogically formed from πειθώ, as φειδός from φείδομαι, as Meyer) **words of wisdom** (ἀνθρωπίνης, a gloss, but a correct one. "Corinthia verba, pro exquisitis et magnopere elaboratis, et ad ostentationem nitidis," Wetst.), **but in demonstration of the Spirit and of power**: i. e. either, taking the genitives as objective, demonstration having for its object, *demonstrating, the presence or working of the Spirit and Power of God* (so Estius, Billroth, al., and the gloss ἀποκαλύψει):—or, taking them subjectively, demonstration (of the truth) *springing from the Spirit and Power of God* (so most Commentators. I prefer the latter. It can hardly be understood of the *miracles done by the Spirit through him*, which accompanied his preaching (Chrys., al., Olsh.), for he is here simply speaking of the *preaching itself*. **5.] ᾖ ἐν, may be grounded on**,—owe its origin and stability to. "The Spirit is the original Creator of Faith, which cannot be begotten of human caprice, though man has the capability of *hindering* its production: and it depends for its continuance on the same mighty Spirit, who is almost without intermission begetting it anew." Olshausen.

6—16.] *Yet the Apostles spoke wisdom among the perfect, but of a kind higher than the wisdom of this world; a wisdom revealed from God by the Spirit, only intelligible by the spiritual man, and not by the unspiritual* (ψυχικός). The Apostle rejects the imputation, that the Gospel and its preaching is *inconsistent* with *wisdom*, rightly understood: nay, shews that the wisdom of the Gospel is of a far higher order than that of the wise in this world, and far above their comprehension. **6.] δέ** contrasts with the foregoing. **λαλ.]** viz. '*we Apostles*:' not '*I Paul*,'—though he often uses the plur. with this meaning:—for, ch. iii. 1, he resumes κἀγώ, ἀδελφοί. **ἐν τ. τελείοις]** * **among the perfect**,—when discoursing to those who are not babes in Christ, but of sufficient maturity to have their senses exercised (Heb. v. 14) so as to discern good and evil. That this is the right interpretation the whole following context shews, and especially ch. iii. 1, 2, where a difference is laid down between the *milk administered to babes*, and the *strong meat to men*. The difference is in the *matter of the teaching itself*: there is a lower, and there is a

τοῦ [b] αἰῶνος [b] τούτου οὐδὲ τῶν [cd] ἀρχόντων τοῦ [bd] αἰῶνος
[b] τούτου τῶν [e] καταργουμένων, 7 ἀλλὰ λαλοῦμεν [f] θεοῦ
[f] σοφίαν [g] ἐν [h] μυστηρίῳ τὴν [i] ἀποκεκρυμμένην, ἣν [k] προώρισεν ὁ θεὸς [l] πρὸ τῶν [l] αἰώνων εἰς δόξαν ἡμῶν, 8 ἣν

b Rom. xii. 2 reff.
c = Acts xiii. 27 reff.
d here bis only.
e = ch. i. 28 reff.
f ch. i. 21 reff.
g = ver. 13. ch. xiv. 6.
h = Rom. xi. 25. xvi. 25. ch. iv. 1. Col. i. 26 al. Dan. ii. 18.
i Luke x. 25. Eph. iii. 9. Col. i. 26 only. 4 Kings iv. 27.
k Acts iv. 28. Rom. viii. 29, 30. Eph. i. 5, 11 only †.
l here only. Ps. liv. 19. see Eph. Col. as above (i). Jude 25.

6. om 1st *του* F[not G]. om from *αιων. τουτ.* to *αιων. τουτ.* F 114 lect-7 æth.
7. rec *σοφιαν* bef *θεου* (*corrn, the emphasis not being noticed*), with L rel Thdrt: txt ABCDFPא a k m 17 arm $Clem_2$ $Orig_4$ Eus_1 [Bas_1 Chr_1 Cyr-p_3].

higher teaching. So Erasm., Estius, Bengel, Rückert, Meyer, De Wette, al. On the other hand, Chrys., Theodoret, Theophyl., Calv., Grot., Olsh., al., understand the difference to be merely in the *estimate formed of the same* teaching according as men were spiritual or unspiritual, interpreting ἐν τ. τελείοις, '*in the estimation of* the perfect,' which is philologically allowable, but plainly irreconcileable with the whole apologetic course of the chapter, and most of all with the οὐκ ἠδυνήθην κ.τ.λ. of ch. iii. 1, where he asserts that *he did not* speak *this wisdom* to the Corinthians. We are then brought to the enquiry,—*what was this σοφία?* "Meyer limits it too narrowly to *consideration of the future kingdom of Christ.* Rückert adds to this, *the higher views of the divine ordering of the world* with respect to the unfolding of God's kingdom,—of the meaning of the preparatory dispensations before Christ, e. g. the law,—of the manner in which the death and resurrection of Christ promoted the salvation of mankind. According to ver. 12, the knowledge of the blessings of salvation, of the glory which accompanies the kingdom of God, belongs to this higher species of teaching. Examples of it are found in the Epistle to the Romans, in the setting forth of the doctrine of justification,—of the contrast between Christ and Adam,—of predestination (compare μυστήριον, Rom. xi. 25), and in the Epistles to the Eph. and Col. (where μυστήρ. often occurs) in the declarations respecting the divine plan of Redemption and the Person of Christ: nay, in our Epistle, ch. xv. Of the same kind are the considerations treated Heb. vii.—x.: cf. iv. 11 ff." De Wette. **But a wisdom not of this world,**—not, as E. V., "*not the wisdom of this world,*" which loses the peculiar force of the negative:—so in Rom. iii. 21, 22, we have δικαιοσύνη θεοῦ πεφανέρωται . . . . . δικαιοσύνη δὲ θεοῦ διὰ πίστ. Ἰησοῦ χρ. See instances of the usage in note there.
The ἄρχοντες are parallel with the σοφοί, δυνατοί, εὐγενεῖς, of ch. i. 26, and are connected with them expressly by the τῶν καταργουμένων, referring to ἵνα τὰ ὄντα καταργήσῃ, ch. i. 28. They comprehend *all in estimation and power*, Jewish or Gentile. ἄρχοντας δὲ αἰῶνος ἐνταῦθα οὐ δαίμονάς τινας λέγει, καθώς τινες ὑποπτεύουσιν· ἀλλὰ τοὺς ἐν ἀξιώμασι, τοὺς ἐν δυναστείαις, τοὺς τὸ πρᾶγμα περιμάχητον εἶναι νομίζοντας, φιλοσόφους κ. ῥήτορας κ. λογογράφους· καὶ γὰρ αὐτοὶ ἐκράτουν, κ. δημαγωγοὶ πολλάκις ἐγίνοντο. Chrys. Hom. vii. p. 50. **τῶν καταργ.**] **who are (being) brought to nought,** viz. by God making choice of the weak and despised, and passing over them, ch. i. 28: not said of *their transitoriness generally*, as Chrys., Theophyl., Rückert,—nor of *their power being annihilated at the coming of Christ* (Grot., Meyer, al.),—nor as Olsh., of *their having* indeed *crucified Christ,* but of their being καταργούμενοι *by His Resurrection and the increase of His Church.*
7.] **But we speak** God's **wisdom** (emphasis on θεοῦ:—the wisdom which *God* possesses and has revealed) **in a mystery** (ἐν μυστ. does not belong to τὴν ἀποκεκ., as Theodoret and Grot., which must be τὴν ἐν μυστ. ἀποκ.,—nor to σοφίαν, as Beza, Bengel, which though not absolutely, yet certainly here, seeing **τὴν** ἀποκεκρ. immediately follows, would require the art., τὴν ἐν μυστ.,—but to λαλοῦμεν,—'we *speak* God's wisdom *in a mystery,*' i. e. as handling a mystery, dealing with a mystery. So τὴν σύνεσίν μου ἐν τῷ μυστ. τ. χριστοῦ, Eph. iii. 4.
Estius and the Romanists, taking the connexion rightly, have wrested the meaning to support the *disciplina arcani* which they imagine to be here hinted at, explaining ἐν μυστ., "non propalam et passim apud omnes, quia non omnes ea capiunt, sed . . . secreto et apud pauciores, scilicet eos qui spirituales et perfecti sunt," Est.), **which has been** (hitherto) **hidden** (see Rom. xvi. 25; ref. Col.):—**which God foreordained** (nothing need be supplied, as ἀποκαλύπτειν, or the like, after προώρισεν) **before the ages** (of time) **to** (*in order to*, the purpose of this preordination) **our glory** (our participation in the things which He has prepared for them that love Him, ver. 9: δόξα, as contrasted with the bring-

οὐδεὶς τῶν [d] ἀρχόντων τοῦ [bd] αἰῶνος [b] τούτου ἔγνωκεν· εἰ
γὰρ ἔγνωσαν, οὐκ ἂν τὸν [m] κύριον τῆς [m] δόξης ἐσταύρω-
σαν· 9 ἀλλὰ [n] καθὼς γέγραπται [o] Ἃ ὀφθαλμὸς οὐκ εἶδεν
καὶ [p] οὖς οὐκ ἤκουσεν καὶ ἐπὶ [q] καρδίαν ἀνθρώπου οὐκ
[q] ἀνέβη, ὅσα [r] ἡτοίμασεν ὁ θεὸς τοῖς ἀγαπῶσιν αὐτόν,
10 ἡμῖν δὲ [s] ἀπεκάλυψεν ὁ θεὸς διὰ τοῦ πνεύματος [αὐτοῦ]·

ABCDF LPℵ a b c d e f g h k l m n o 17. 47

m James ii. 1. see Acts vii. 2. Eph. i. 17. Ps. xxviii. 3.
n Rom. xv. 3, 21. ch. i. 31.
o Isa. lxiv. 4. lxv. 17. see notes.
p Rom. xi. 8 reff.
q Acts vii. 23 reff.
r = Matt. xx. 23. xxv. 34. John xiv. 2, 3.
s = Matt. xi. 25. Rom. i. 17. ch. xiv. 30. Prov. xi. 13 al.

9. om *αλλα* A Pel. *ιδεν* C[P] 80 Clem-rom$_1$ Smyrn-ep$_1$ [Bas$_1$]. rec (for *οσα*) ἅ, with DFLPℵ rel Smyrn-ep$_1$ [Clem$_2$] Orig$_3$ Const$_1$ Eus$_4$ [Ps-]Ath$_2$ Epiph$_1$ Cyr[-p Mac$_1$ Euthal-ms] Chr$_1$ Thdrt [Damasc] Thl Œc, *quæ* latt [Orig-int$_4$] : txt AB C(appy) Clem-rom$_1$ Hip$_1$ [Epiph$_1$] Mac$_1$.

10. for *δε*, *γαρ* B m 39. 46. 57. 71-3. 93. 116 coptt Clem$_1$ [Bas$_2$ Euthal-ms Antch$_1$]. rec *ο θεος* bef *απεκαλυψεν* (*appy, as above, corrn from not noticing the emphasis*), with L rel syr sah Orig$_1$[-c] Chr$_1$ Thdrt [Damasc] : txt ABCDFPℵ a m 17 latt Syr copt æth arm Clem [Ath$_1$ Bas$_2$ Did$_1$-int$_1$ Epiph$_1$ Euthal-ms Mac$_1$ Cyr$_1$ Antch$_1$] Orig[-int$_5$ Hil]. om *αυτου* (*perhaps on acct of το πν. follg*) ABCℵ[1] 17(appy) copt Clem$_1$ Bas$_2$ Cyr[-p$_1$] : ins DFLPℵ[3] rel [latt syrr sah æth arm Ath$_1$] Did$_1$ Epiph$_1$ Mac$_1$

ing to nought of the ἄρχοντες).

8.] **ἥν** is in apposition with the former ἥν, and does not refer to δόξαν, as Tert. contra Marc. v. 6, vol. ii. p. 483,—"subjicit de gloria nostra, quod eam nemo ex principibus hujus ævi scierit . . . ," for this would be departing from the whole sense of the context, which is, that the *wisdom of God* was *hidden* from men. **εἰ γὰρ ἔγν.** κ.τ.λ., is a *proof from experience*, that the rulers of this world, of whom the Jewish rulers were a representative sample, were ignorant of the wisdom of God. Had they known it, they would not have put to a disgraceful death (ὁ σταυρὸς ἀδοξίας εἶναι δοκεῖ, Chrys.) Him who was the Lord of glory (reff.),—i. e. who possesses in his own right glory eternal, see John xvii. 5, 24.

These words are not a parenthesis, but continue the sense of the foregoing, completing the proof of man's ignorance of God's wisdom ;—even this world's *rulers* know it not, as they have shewn : how much less then the rest. **9 f.**] **But** (opposition to ver. 8) **as it is written, The things which eye saw not, and ear heard not, and which came not up** (reff.) **upon heart of man, how many things God prepared for them that love Him, to us God revealed through His Spirit.** There is no anacoluthon (as De W.) nor irregularity of construction, as some suppose, supplying after ἀλλά, λαλοῦμεν (Estius, &c.) or γέγονεν (Theophyl., Grot., al.); the δέ in the consequent clause after ὅς in the antecedent, which has occasioned these suppositions, is by no means unexampled ;—so Herod. iii. 37, ὃς δὲ τούτους μὴ ὀπώπεε, ἐγὼ δέ οἱ σημανέω,—and Soph. Philoct. 86, ἐγὼ μὲν οὓς ἂν τῶν λόγων ἀλγῶ κλύειν, Λαερτίου παῖ, τοὺς δὲ καὶ πράσσειν στυγῶ. See Hartung, Partikellehre, i. 184 f.

Whence is the citation made? Origen says, 'In nullo regulari libro invenitur, nisi in secretis Eliæ prophetæ,' a lost apocryphal book :—Chrys., Theophyl., give the alternative, either that the words are a paraphrase of Isa. lii. 15, οἷς οὐκ ἀνηγγέλη περὶ αὐτοῦ ὄψονται, κ. οἳ οὐκ ἀκηκόασι συνήσουσι, or that they were contained in some lost book, of which Chrys. argues that there were very many,—καὶ γὰρ πολλὰ διεφθάρη βιβλία, καὶ ὀλίγα διεσώθη. Jerome, Ep. lvii. (ci.), ad Pammachium, de optimo genere interpretandi, 9, vol. i. p. 314, says, "Solent in hoc loco apocryphorum quidam deliramenta sectari, et dicere quod de Apocalypsi Heliæ testimonium sumptum sit : cum in Esaia juxta Hebraicum ita legatur : A seculo non audierunt, nec auribus perceperunt, oculus non vidit, Deus, absque te, quæ præparas tu expectantibus te. Hoc LXX multo aliter transtulerunt : A seculo non audivimus, neque oculi nostri viderunt Deum absque te : et opera tua vera, et facies expectantibus te misericordiam. Intelligimus, unde sumptum sit testimonium : et tamen Apostolus non verbum expressit e verbo, sed παραφραστικῶς eundem sensum aliis sermonibus indicavit." I own that probability seems to me to incline to Jerome's view, especially when we remember, how freely St. Paul is in the habit of citing. The words of Isa. lxiv. 4, are quite as near to the general sense of the citation as is the case in many other instances, and the words ἐπὶ καρδίαν οὐκ ἀνέβη may well be a reminiscence from Isa. lxv. 17, not far from the other place, οὐ μὴ ἐπέλθῃ αὐτῶν ἐπὶ τὴν καρδίαν. Such minglings together of clauses from various parts are not unexampled with the Apostle, especially when, as here, he is not citing *as authority*, but merely *illus-*

τὸ γὰρ πνεῦμα πάντα [t] ἐραυνᾷ, καὶ τὰ [u] βάθη τοῦ θεοῦ.
11 τίς γὰρ οἶδεν ἀνθρώπων [v] τὰ [w] τοῦ ἀνθρώπου, εἰ μὴ τὸ
[x] πνεῦμα [w] τοῦ ἀνθρώπου τὸ ἐν αὐτῷ; οὕτως καὶ [v] τὰ τοῦ
θεοῦ οὐδεὶς ἔγνωκεν, εἰ μὴ τὸ πνεῦμα τοῦ θεοῦ. 12 ἡμεῖς δὲ
[y] οὐ τὸ [za] πνεῦμα τοῦ [z] κόσμου [a] ἐλάβομεν, ἀλλὰ τὸ πνεῦμα
τὸ ἐκ τοῦ θεοῦ, ἵνα εἰδῶμεν τὰ ὑπὸ τοῦ θεοῦ [b] χαρισθέντα
ἡμῖν, 13 ἃ καὶ λαλοῦμεν οὐκ [c] ἐν [d] διδακτοῖς [e] ἀνθρωπίνης

t = Rom. viii. 27 reff.
u (plur., Rev. ii. 24) see Rom. xi. 33 reff. Judith viii. 14.
v Matt. xvi. 23. Luke ii. 49. James iv. 14.
w gener. art., Matt. xv. 11.
x = Acts xvii. 16 reff.
y see Rom. viii. 15.
z here only.

a Acts viii. 15 reff. b pass., Acts iii. 14. Phil. i. 29. Philem. 22. L.P.† (2 Macc. iii. 33.) c = ver. 7. d here bis. John vi. 45 only, from Isa. liv. 13. see 1 Thess. iv. 9. e Acts xvii. 25 reff.

Chr$_1$ Thdrt [Damasc] Thl Œc Orig[-c$_1$]-int$_3$ Hil. (*ερ*αυνα, so AB[1]Cℵ.)

11. om *ανθρωπων* A 17 Ath$_1$ Cyr[-p$_2$(ins$_2$)]. om 2nd *του ανθρωπου* F arm-mss Orig$_2$[ins$_3$-int$_2$] Hil$_1$ Ambr$_1$[ins$_2$]. *το του θεου* D[1] : *τα εν τω θεω* F[-gr] lat-ff. rec (for *εγνωκεν*) *οιδεν* (*prob a corrn to corresp with previous clause*), with L rel Orig$_2$ [Ath$_2$] Chr$_1$ Thdrt: txt ABCDPℵ a d m 17 Orig$_1$ Ath$_2$ Cyr-jer$_1$ Bas$_{alic}$ *Cyr*[-p Euthal-ms] Antch$_1$ Damasc, *εγνω* F 23 Ath$_1$ Cyr-jer$_1$ Bas$_1$ Epiph$_1$, *cognovit* latt(but *scit* fri Aug$_{sæpe}$) Ambr$_1$. at end add *το εν αυτω* P [(Tert$_2$)].

12. aft *κοσμου* ins *τουτου* DF [vulg(not fuld harl[1]) copt arm Bas-ms$_1$] Cyr$_1$ [Orig-int$_2$ Hil$_2$(but mss vary) Ambrst]. *ιδωμεν* DFL[P d m (n)] Orig$_3$(elsw *ειδ*.). om last *του* P [(k) Orig$_1$].

13. om *ἅ* F[-gr].

trating his argument by O. T. expressions. **10. τὸ πνεῦμα**] the Holy Spirit of God—but working in us and with our Spirits, Rom. viii. 16. "Sufficiat nobis Spiritum Dei habere testem: nihil enim tam profundum est in Deo quo non penetret." Calvin. **ἐραυνᾷ**] a word of active research, implying accurate knowledge: so Chrys., *οὐκ ἀγνοίας, ἀλλ' ἀκριβοῦς γνώσεως ἐνταῦθα τὸ ἐρευνᾶν ἐνδεικτικόν.* **τὰ βάθη**] see reff. There is a comparison here between the *Spirit of God* and the *spirit of a man*, which is further carried out in the next verse. And thus as the *spirit of a man* knows the *βάθος* of a man, all that is in him, so the *Spirit of God* searches and knows *τὰ βάθη*, the manifold and infinite depths, of God—His Essence, His Attributes, His Counsels: and being *τὸ πνεῦμα τὸ ἐν ἡμῖν*, besides being *τὸ πν. τοῦ θεοῦ* (De Wette well observes that the Apostle purposely avoids using the expression *τὸ πνεῦμα* **τὸ ἐν αὐτῷ** of the *Spirit of God*, keeping the way open for the expression in ver. 12, *τὸ πν.* **τὸ ἐκ** *τοῦ θεοῦ*), *teaches us* according to our capacity, *those depths of God.* **11.] For who among** MEN **knoweth the things of a** MAN (*τοῦ ἀνθρώπου*, generic, see reff. The emphasis is on *ἀνθρώπων* and *ἀνθρώπου*, as compared with *θεοῦ*) **except the spirit of a man which is in him? Thus the things of God also none knoweth, except the Spirit of God.** We may remark, (1) that nothing need be supplied (as *βάθη*) after *τά* in each case, see reff. (2) that the comparison here must not be urged beyond what is intended by the Apostle. He is speaking of the impossibility of any but the *Spirit of God conferring a knowledge* of the *things of God.* In order to shew this, he compares human things with divine, appealing to the fact that none but the spirit of a man knows *his matters.* But further than this he says nothing of the *similarity of relation* of *God and God's Spirit* with *man and man's spirit:* and to deduce more than this, will lead into error on one side or the other. In such comparisons as these especially, we must bear in mind the constant habit of our Apostle, to contemplate the thing adduced, *for the time, only with regard to that one point* for which he adduces it, to the disregard of all other considerations. **12.] ἡμεῖς δέ** carries on the *ἡμῖν δέ* of ver. 10. **τὸ πν. τ. κόσμ.**] Not merely, the mind and sentiments of unregenerate mankind, 'sapientia mundana et sæcularis,' as Estius, al., but **the Spirit** (personally and objectively taken) **of the world,** = *τὸ πνεῦμα τὸ νῦν ἐνεργοῦν ἐν τοῖς υἱοῖς τῆς ἀπειθείας*, Eph. ii. 2, where it is strictly personal. **τὸ πν. τὸ ἐκ τ. θ.**] Not only, '*the Spirit of God*,' but **the Spirit which is** FROM **God,** —to shew that we have received it only by the will and imparting of Him whose Spirit it is. And this expression prepares the way for the *purpose* which God has in imparting to us His Spirit, **that we may know the things freely given to us by God,** i. e. the treasures of wisdom and of felicity which are the free gifts of the gospel dispensation, = *ὅσα ἡτοίμασεν ὁ θεὸς τοῖς ἀγαπῶσιν αὐτόν*, ver. 9. **13.] καί, also;** *τὰ χαρισθ. ἡμῖν*, we not only *know* by the teaching of the Holy Ghost, but

f ver. 4. g = ch. iii. 1. xiv. 37. Gal. vi. 1. h ch. x. 3, 4 reff. i 2 Cor. x. 12 (bis) only ‡. Gen. xl. 8. Num. xv. 34. j ch. xv. 44 (bis), 46. James iii. 15. Jude 19 only †. k = Luke viii. 13. Acts viii. 14. xi. 1. xvii. 11. 1 Thess. i. 6. ii. 13. James i. 21. Prov. iv. 10. l ver. 11 reff. m ch. i. 18 (reff.). n Rev. xi. 8 only †. o Acts iv. 9 reff.

ABCDF LPא a b c d e f g h k l m n o 17. 47

σοφίας λόγοις, ἀλλ' [e] ἐν [d] διδακτοῖς [f] πνευματος, [g] πνευματικοῖς [h] πνευματικὰ [i] συγκρίνοντες.
14 [j] ψυχικὸς δὲ ἄν-
θρωπος οὐ [k] δέχεται [l] τὰ τοῦ πνεύματος τοῦ θεοῦ· [m] μωρία
γὰρ [m] αὐτῷ ἐστιν, καὶ οὐ δύναται γνῶναι, ὅτι [n] πνευματικῶς [o] ἀνακρινεται.
15 ὁ δὲ [g] πνευματικὸς [o] ἀνακρίνει

"λογοις α rescript א[1]" Tischdf. rec aft πνευματος ins αγιου, with D[3]LP rel [fuld[2]] syr æth Eus$_1$ Chr$_1$ Thdrt: om ABCD[1]Fא 17 latt Syr copt arm Clem$_1$ Hip$_2$ Orig$_6$[-c$_1$] Eus$_1$ Epiph$_1$ [Damasc]. for πνευματικοις, πνευματικως B 17. 213. συνκρινομεν F[-gr]: συγκρινοντος P.

also *speak* them, **not in words** (arguments, rhetorical forms, &c.) **taught by human wisdom, but in those taught by the Spirit.** The genitives are governed by διδακτοῖς in each case: see ref., and cf. Pind. Olymp. ix. 153: τὸ δὲ φυᾷ κράτιστον ἅπαν. πολλοὶ δὲ διδακταῖς ἀνθρώπων ἀρεταῖς κλέος ὤρουσαν ἑλέσθαι· ἄνευ δὲ θεοῦ κ.τ.λ. **πνευμ. . . . πν. συγκρ.] interpreting spiritual things to the spiritual.** So Theophyl. altern., πνευματικοῖς ἀνθρώποις τὰ πνευματικὰ συγκρίνοντες καὶ διαλύοντες· οὗτοι γὰρ μόνοι δύνανται χωρεῖν ταῦτα. And very nearly so as regards συγκρίνοντες Chrysostom and Grotius; only they take πνευματικοῖς not masc. but neuter, 'by spiritual things:' ὅταν πνευματικὸν καὶ ἄπορον ᾖ, ἀπὸ τῶν πνευματικῶν τὰς μαρτυρίας ἄγομεν. οἷον λέγω, ὅτι ἀνέστη ὁ χριστός, ὅτι ἀπὸ παρθένου ἐγεννήθη. παράγω μαρτυρίας κ. τύπους κ. ἀποδείξεις, τοῦ Ἰωνᾶ, κ.τ.λ. Chrys. Hom. vii. p. 55. 'Exponentes ea quæ Prophetæ Spiritu Dei acti dixere, per ea quæ Christus suo Spiritu nobis aperuit.' Grot. Meyer denies that συγκρίνω ever means to interpret: but evidently the LXX do so use it in Gen. xl. 8, ἐνύπνιον εἴδομεν, καὶ ὁ συγκρίνων οὐκ ἔστιν αὐτό. See also ib. vv. 16, 22, and Dan. v. 12, Theodotion (where the LXX have συγκρίματα ἀπέδειξε). Erasmus, Beza, Calvin, De Wette, and Meyer render it, '*fitting*, or *attaching*, *spiritual words to spiritual things.*' And so I gave and defended it in my earlier editions. It seems to me now more natural to take πνευματικοῖς as masculine, and as leading to the introduction of the two men, the ψυχικός, and the πνευματικός, immediately after. **14.]** He now prepares the way for shewing them that he could not give out the depths of this spiritual wisdom and eloquence to *them*, because they were *not fitted for it*, being carnal (ch. iii. 1—4). **ψυχ. δὲ ἄνθ.]** The *animal* man, as distinguished from the *spiritual* man, is he, whose governing principle and highest reference of all things is the ψυχή, the *animal soul*, αἰτία κινήσεως ζωικῆς ζώων, Plato, Definit. p. 411. In him, the πνεῦμα, or *spirit*, being unvivified and uninformed by the Spirit of God, is *overborne* by the animal soul, with its desires and its judgments,—and is *in abeyance*, so that he may be said to have it not;—ψυχικοὶ πνεῦμα μὴ ἔχοντες, ref. Jude. The ψυχή is *that side* of the human soul, so to speak, which is *turned towards the flesh, the world, the devil:* so that the ψυχικός is necessarily in a measure σαρκικός (ch. iii. 3), also ἐπίγειος, and δαιμονιώδης, as in ref. James. This general interpretation of ψυχικός must be adhered to, and we must not make it merely *intellectual*, as Theodoret,—ὁ μόνοις τοῖς οἰκείοις ἀρκούμενος λογισμοῖς,—Grot. "qui humanæ tantum rationis luce ducitur:"—Chrys.: ὁ τὸ πᾶν τοῖς λογισμοῖς τῆς ψυχῆς διδούς, καὶ μὴ νομίζων ἄνωθέν τινος δεῖσθαι βοηθείας,—nor merely *ethical*, as Erasm., Rosenmüller ('qui cupiditatum sub imperio omnem vitam transigunt'), al.,—but embracing both these. **οὐ δέχεται, receives not**, i. e. *rejects*, see reff.,—not, *cannot receive*, '*non capax est*,' *understands not*, which is against the context,—for we may well *understand* that which seems folly to us, but we *reject* it, as unworthy of our consideration:—and it besides would involve a tautology, this point, of *inability to comprehend*, following by and by:—**and he cannot know them** (τὰ τοῦ πνεύματος, the matter of our spiritual teaching, itself furnished by the Spirit) **because they are spiritually** (by the πνεῦμα of a man exalted by the Spirit of God into its proper paramount office of judging and ruling, and inspired and enabled for that office) **judged of. 15.] But** (on the contrary) **the spiritual man** (he, in whom the πνεῦμα rules: and since by man's fall the πνεῦμα is overridden by the animal soul, and in abeyance, this *always presupposes* the infusion of the Holy Spirit, to quicken and inform the πνεῦμα—so that there is no such thing as an unregenerate πνευματικός) **judges of all**

[μὲν] πάντα, αὐτὸς δὲ ὑπ' οὐδενὸς °ἀνακρίνεται. 16 ᵖ τίς γὰρ ἔγνω ᵖ νοῦν κυρίου, ὃς ᵍ συμβιβάσει αὐτόν; ἡμεῖς δὲ ʳ νοῦν χριστοῦ ʳ ἔχομεν.

III. 1 Κἀγώ, ἀδελφοί, οὐκ ἠδυνήθην λαλῆσαι ὑμῖν

p Rom. xi. 34, from Isa. xl. 13. (compare Wisd. ix. 13.)
q Acts ix. 22. xvi. 10. xix. 33 v. r. Eph. iv. 16. Col. ii. 2, 19 only. L.P. Lev. x. 11.
r Rev. xiii. 18.

15. om ver א[1](ins א-corr[1]) harl[1]. om μεν ACD[1]F latt Syr copt arm ($Iren_1$) $Clem_1$ $Orig_5$ Meth $Thdrt_1$ lat-ff: ins BD[2.3]LP א-corr[1] rel syr $Orig_1$[-c Euthal-ms Did_2] Mac_2 Chr_1 $Thdrt_1$. (*Has μεν been insd on acct of the δε follg, as Meyer,—or omd on acct of the δε precedg, as De W?*) ins τα bef παντα ACD[1]P 17 Iren-ms $Orig_2$ Nys_1 Chr_1: om BD[2.3]FL א-corr[1] $Clem_1$ $Orig_5$ Meth Mac_2 $Thdrt_1$ [Damasc]. (*τα was prob a gloss to shew that παντα was not masc sing acc.*)

16. for χριστου, κυριου B D[1][-gr] F Thl-txt Ambrst Aug_1 Sedul. (*Mechanical repetn of νουν κυρ. above. So Meyer, rightly: addg, if any gloss had been written in marg on κυριου, it wd not have been χριστου, but θεου, seeing that the ref of the foregoing κυρ. is to* God.)

Chap. III. 1. rec και εγω, with L rel Thdrt Thl Œc: txt ABCDFPא a m 17 $Clem_2$ $Orig_1$[-c_1 Did_1 Euthal-ms] Chr_1 Damasc. εδυνηθην C. υμ. bef λαλ. D[2][-gr] LP a b c e f g h l n o vulg $Clem_1$ $Orig_3$[-c_1-int_2] Chr_1 Damasc [$Cypr_1$ Ambrst Pel].

things (Meyer, reading τὰ πάντα, interprets it, 'all *spiritual* things;' but the ordinary rendering, '*all things*,' is better: the Apostle is generalizing, and shewing the high position of the spiritual man, who alone can judge things by their true standard. The acceptation of πάντα as masc. sing.,—"convincere potest quemlibet profanum," as Rosenm.,—is against the context, which speaks of *things*, τὰ τοῦ πν.,—besides that πάντα would not be used absolutely, for 'every man,' but either πάντα ἄνθρωπον, as Col. i. 28, or τὸν πάντα), **but himself is judged of by none** (who is not also πνευματικός, see ch. xiv. 29; 1 John iv. 1, where such judgment is expressly attributed to Christian believers). καὶ γὰρ ὁ βλέπων, πάντα μὲν αὐτὸς καθορᾷ καὶ τοῦ μὴ βλέποντος, τὰ δὲ ἐκείνου τῶν μὴ βλεπόντων οὐδείς. Chrys. Hom. vii. p. 57. 16.] Proof of **αὐτὸς δὲ ὑπ' οὐδ. ἀνακρίνεται.** In order for an *unassisted man*, not *gifted from Christ*, to judge the πνευματικός, he must *know the* **νοῦς κυρίου**, the intent and disposition of Christ; *yea more*, must be *able to teach, to instruct, Christ*—being not, as the πνευματικός,—*taught by Him*, he must have an *independent wisdom of his own*, which Christ *has not*:—and *who is there, of whom this can be said?* **But we** (πνευματικοί, among whom he includes himself and the other Apostles) **have** (not a wisdom independent of Christ, nor do we know His mind, nor can we teach Him, but) **the mind of Christ**: the same mind, in our degree of apprehensiveness of it, by the imparting of His Spirit, which is in Him, and so can judge all things. The νοῦς κυρίου is *the spiritual intent* and designs of Christ. κυρίου in the prophecy is spoken of Jehovah; but in the whole of Isa. xl., the *incarnate Jehovah* is the subject. The meaning of συμβιβάζω, *to teach*, belongs to the LXX: in the N. T. it is *to conclude, to prove, to confirm*, see reff.

III. 1—4.] *He could not speak to them in the perfect spiritual manner above described, seeing that they were carnal, and still remained so, as was shewn by their divisions.* 1.] **κἀγώ, I also**; i. e. as well as the ψυχικός, was compelled to stand on this lower ground,—he, because *he cannot understand* the things of the Spirit of God: I, because *you could not receive* them. Or perhaps better, with Stanley, 'καὶ ἐγώ, as in ii. 1, "What I have just been saying, was exemplified in our practice."' σαρκίνοις is certainly the true reading, being, besides its manuscript authority, required by the sense. He was compelled to speak to them (this affirmative clause is to be supplied from the former negative one) **as to men of flesh**: not ὡς σαρκικοῖς, for that they *really were*, and he asserts them yet to be, ver. 3. I quite agree with Meyer (against De Wette) that the distinction between σάρκινοι and σαρκικοί is *designed* by the Apostle, and further regard it as implied in the very form of the sentences. Here, he says that he was compelled to speak to them *as if* they were *only of flesh*,—*as if* they were *babes*, using in both cases the material comparison, and the particle of comparison ὡς. But in ver. 3 he drops comparison, and asserts matter of fact—'Are ye not *still* σαρκικοί (= ὡς σάρκινοι), fleshly, carnal, living after the flesh, resisting the Spirit?'—q. d. 'I was obliged to regard you as mere *men of flesh*, without the Spirit: and it is not far different even now: ye are yet *fleshly*—ye retain the same character.' Both the σάρκινοι, the mere men of the flesh,

ὡς [s] πνευματικοῖς, ἀλλ' ὡς [t] σαρκίνοις, ὡς [u] νηπίοις ἐν ABCDF
χριστῷ. 2 [v] γάλα ὑμᾶς [w] ἐπότισα, οὐ [x] βρῶμα· οὔπω LPℵ a b c d e f g
γὰρ ἐδύνασθε. [yz] ἀλλ' [z] οὐδὲ ἔτι νῦν δύνασθε· 3 ἔτι γὰρ h k l m n o 17.
[a] σαρκικοί ἐστε. [b] ὅπου γὰρ ἐν ὑμῖν [cd] ζῆλος καὶ [ce] ἔρις, 47
οὐχὶ [a] σαρκικοί ἐστε καὶ [fg] κατὰ ἄνθρωπον [g] περιπατεῖτε;
4 ὅταν γὰρ λέγῃ [h] τὶς Ἐγὼ μέν εἰμι [i] Παύλου, [h] ἕτερος δὲ

s = ch. ii. 15. t Rom. vii. 14 reff. u = Matt. xi. 25 ‖ L. Rom. ii. 20. Eph. iv. 14. Heb. v. 13. Ps. xviii. 7. Pind. Pyth. iii. 148. v ch. ix. 7. Heb. v. 12, 13. 1 Pet. ii. 2 only. Gen. xviii. 8. w Rom. xii. 20 reff. x Matt. xiv. 15 ‖. Luke iii. 11. Rom. xiv. 15 al. Ezra iii. 7. y = 2 Cor. vii. 11. z = Acts xix. 2. ch. iv. 3 al. a here bis. Rom. xv. 27. ch. ix. 11. 2 Cor. i. 12. x. 4. 1 Pet. ii. 11 only. 2 Chron. xxxii. 8 compl. only. b = Heb. ix. 16. x. 18. James iii. 16. 2 Pet. ii. 11. c Rom. xiii. 13. 2 Cor. xii. 20. Gal. v. 20. Sir. xl. 5. d = Acts xiii. 45 reff. e ch. i. 11 reff. f Rom. iii. 5. ch. xv. 32. Gal. i. 11. iii. 15. 1 Pet. iv. 6. (see Rom. vi. 19.) g = Rom. viii. 4. Eph. ii. 2 al. h = Luke xi. 15, 16 al. i gen., ch. i. 12 reff.

rec *σαρκικοις* (*see notes*), with C³D³FLP rel Clem$_2$ Orig[-c$_1$] : txt ABC¹D¹ℵ 17 Clem-ms$_2$ Orig$_3$ Nys$_1$.

2. [*υμιν* L Orig-c$_1$.] rec ins *και* bef *ου βρωμα*, with DFL rel Syr æth arm (Orig$_1$) Cæs$_1$ Thl Œc: om ABCPℵ m 17 vulg fri syr copt Iren-gr$_1$ Clem$_3$ Orig[-c$_3$-int$_{sæpe}$ Dial$_1$] Eus$_1$ Did Cyr$_2$ Cypr$_2$ Hil$_2$ [Ambrst]. rec *ηδυνασθε*, with DL a c d k n 47 Iren$_1$ Orig$_1$ Cæs$_1$ Dial$_1$ [Did$_1$ Chr$_1$] Thdrt: txt A B(sic: see table) CFLP rel Clem$_3$ Orig$_3$[-c$_2$ Chr$_1$ Damasc]. rec *ουτε* (*see note*), with L rel Orig$_1$ Œc: txt ABCDFPℵ c d f k 17 Iren Clem$_3$ Orig$_2$[-c$_2$ Euthal-ms]. (om last clause m [æth].) om *ετι* B Orig-int$_1$ Cypr$_2$.

3. *σαρκινοι* (twice) D¹F Orig[1st$_1$, 2nd$_1$] (*error by repeatg σαρκιν. from ver* 1, *the difference not being noticed: see there*): txt ABCD³LPℵ rel Clem$_2$[1st$_1$] Orig[1st$_2$-c$_1$, 2nd$_1$ Chr$_1$]. 1st *εστε* bef 1st *σαρκ*. DF am(with demid harl tol) Clem$_1$ Orig$_1$ Nys Cypr$_2$ [Hil$_1$] Aug: txt ABCLPℵ rel [vulg-clem Clem$_1$] Orig$_2$[-c$_1$ Dial$_1$] Chr$_1$ Thdrt [Damasc]. *ημιν* F[-gr]. rec aft *ερις* ins *και διχοστασιαι* (*from Gal* v. 20), with DFL rel syrr Iren-gr$_1$ Chr$_1$ Thdrt Cypr$_2$: om ABCPℵ a vulg fri [spec] copt æth arm Clem$_2$ Dion Orig$_2$ Eus$_1$.—*ερεις* A F[-gr] L [e] n [Eus$_1$].

4. *τις* bef *λεγη* DF [vulg fri Ambrst]. for *ετερ. δε εγω*, *εγω δε* A c 23. 224 Chr$_1$: om *εγω* m.

and the *σαρκικοί*, the carnally disposed, are included under the more general *ψυχικοί*, which therefore, as Meyer observes, is not here used, because this distinction was to be made. **ὡς νηπ. ἐν χρ.**] The opposite term, *τέλειοι ἐν χρ.*, is found Col. i. 28, and in connexion with this, Heb. v. 13, 14. Schöttgen (on 1 Pet. ii. 2) and Lightfoot adduce the similar Rabbinical term תִּינוֹקוֹת, *sugentes*, used of novices in their schools. A recent proselyte also was regarded by them as a newborn infant.

He speaks of his first visit to Corinth, when they were recently admitted into the faith of Christ,—and excuses his merely elementary teaching by the fact that they then required it. *Not this*, but their *still requiring it*, is adduced as matter of blame to them. **2.**] See the same figure in Heb. v. 12. So also Philo de Agricult. § 2, vol. i. p. 301, *ἐπεὶ δὲ νηπίοις μέν ἐστι γάλα τροφή, τελείοις δὲ τὰ ἐκ πυρῶν πέμματα, καὶ ψυχῆς γαλακτώδεις μὲν ἂν εἶεν τροφαὶ κατὰ τὴν παιδικὴν ἡλικίαν . . . τέλειαι δὲ καὶ ἀνδράσιν* . . . . Basil, Hom. i. p. 403, ed. Paris, 1638, cited by Meyer, explains, *γάλα, τὴν εἰσαγωγικὴν κ. ἁπλουστέραν τοῦ εὐαγγελίου διδασκαλίαν*: see also Heb. vi. 1,—*τὸν τῆς ἀρχῆς τοῦ χριστοῦ λόγον*. On *ἐπότισα . . . . βρῶμα*, Wetst. quotes *νέκταρ τ' ἀμβροσίην τε, τά περ θεοὶ αὐτοὶ ἔδουσι*, Hes. Theogon. 640. See Hom. Il. *θ*. 546. Winer, edn. 6, § 66. 2. e. **οὔπω γὰρ ἐδύνασθε**] Either, **for ye were not yet able** (scil. *βρῶμα ἐσθίειν*),—or, **for ye were not yet strong**, *δύναμαι* being used absolutely, as in Demosth. 1187. 8, *δυνάμενος τῷ τε πράττειν κ. τῷ εἰπεῖν*, and 484. 25, *τῶν πολιτευομένων τινὲς δυνηθέντες*, and see other reff. in Meyer. In the former case, the ellipsis is harsh: the latter meaning seems preferable, though not found elsewhere in the N. T. **ἀλλ' οὐδὲ ἔτι νῦν, but neither even now** . . .; the *οὔτε* of the rec. is grammatically inadmissible,—see Winer, edn. 6, § 55. 6. **3.**] On **σαρκικοί**, see above, ver. 1. **ὅπου**, not = *ἐπεί*, but putting the assumption in a *local* form, see reff. **ζῆλος, emulation**, in a bad sense; or as in reff., '*angry jealousy*.' **κατὰ ἄνθρ.**, see reff., **according to the manner of** (unrenewed and ungodly) **man**, = *κατὰ σάρκα*, Rom. viii. 4; see note on ch. xv. 32.

4.] He names *but two* of the foregoing designations, ch. i. 12: intending, both there more fully, and here briefly, rather to give a *sample of the sectarian spirit* prevalent, than to describe, as matter of fact, any sects into which they were actually divided: see note there, and on ch. iv. 6. Meyer sees in the mention here of Paul and Apollos only, a reference to the

Ἐγὼ [i] Ἀπολλώ, οὐκ [j] ἄνθρωποί ἐστε; 5 τί[ς] οὖν ἐστιν
Ἀπολλώς; τί[ς] δέ ἐστιν Παῦλος; διάκονοι δι' ὧν
[k] ἐπιστεύσατε, καὶ [l] ἑκάστῳ ὡς ὁ κύριος ἔδωκεν. 6 ἐγὼ
[m] ἐφύτευσα, Ἀπολλὼς [n] ἐπότισεν, ἀλλὰ ὁ θεὸς [o] ηὔξανεν·
7 ὥστε οὔτε ὁ [m] φυτεύων ἐστίν [p] τι, οὔτε ὁ [n] ποτίζων, ἀλλ'
ὁ [o] αὐξάνων θεός. 8 ὁ [m] φυτεύων δὲ καὶ ὁ [n] ποτίζων [q] ἕν
εἰσιν, ἕκαστος δὲ τὸν ἴδιον [r] μισθὸν λήμψεται κατὰ τὸν

j see ver. 3.
k = Acts xix. 2 reff.
l constr., Rom. xii. 3. ch. vii. 17.
m ch. ix. 7. Matt. xv. 13. xxi. 33 ‖ al. Gen. ii. 8 al.
n Rom. xii. 20 reff.
o tr., here bis. 2 Cor. ix. 10 only. Gen. xvii. 6. mid. or pass., 2 Cor. x. 15. Col. i. 6, 10. 1 Pet. ii. 2 only. intr., Acts vi. 7 reff.
p = Acts v. 36. ch. x. 19. Gal. ii. 6. vi. 3, 15. Demosth. 582. 27.
q constr., John x. 30. xvii. 11, &c. Eph. ii. 14.
r = Rom. iv. 4 reff.

...θεος F[-gr] (and also G).

ABCDL PℵA b c d e f g h k l m n o 17. 47

rec ουχι (*corrn from ver* 3), with DFLPℵ[3] rel [Nyss$_1$] Chr$_1$ Thdrt Thl Œc: [ου b k Euthal-ms:] txt ABCℵ[1] 17 Damasc. rec for ανθρωποι, σαρκικοι (*corrn from ver* 3), with LPℵ[3] rel syrr [Nyss$_1$]: txt ABCDFℵ[1] 17 latt copt æth arm Damasc Origint$_1$ Ambrst Aug$_1$.—P adds at end και κ. ανθ. περιπατειτε (*also from ver* 3).

5. τι (twice) ABℵ[1] 17 latt æth [Euthal-ms Damasc Ambrst Aug$_{sæpe}$ Pel] (*prob corrn to suit the sense: the question being rather* qualis est *than* quis est): τις CDFLPℵ[3] rel syrr copt arm Chr$_1$ Thdrt Thl Œc. rec παυλος τις δε απολλως (*alteration of order, to suit ver* 4), with D[2][-gr] L rel syrr æth arm Chr$_1$ Thdrt Opt$_1$: txt ABC(D[1.3]F)Pℵ m 17 latt copt [Euthal-ms] Damasc Ambrst Aug$_1$ Pel.—rec om 2nd εστιν, with DFL latt copt arm Chr$_1$ Thdrt [Thl Œc]: ins ABCPℵ m 17 [Euthal-ms Damasc]. rec ins αλλ' η bef διακον. (*addition to complete the sense*), with D[2.3][-gr] LP rel syrr [Euthal-ms] Chr$_1$ Thdrt Thl Œc Opt$_1$: om ABC D[1][and lat] Fℵ vulg [fri] copt æth arm Damasc Ambrst Pel [Aug$_{sæpe}$]. om ως C tol[1].

6. (αλλα, so ABD[1]Fℵ. (for αλλα ο, ο δε f 17 [Orig$_1$].))

7. om 1st ουτε A. for 2nd ουτε, ουδε Cℵ[1]. αλλα D[1].

two methods of teaching which have been treated of in this section: but as I have before said, the German Commentators are misled by too *definite* a view of the Corinthian parties. **ἄνθρωποι**, i. e. walking *κατὰ ἄνθρωπον,—σαρκικοί.*

5—15.] *He takes occasion, by example of himself and Apollos, to explain to them the true place and office of Christian teachers: that they are in themselves nothing* (vv. 5—8), *but work for God* (vv. 9, 10), *each in his peculiar department* (ver. 10; cf. ver. 6), *each requiring serious care as to the manner of his working, seeing that a searching trial of its worth will be made in the day of the Lord* (vv. 10—15). **5.**] **οὖν** follows on the assumption of the truth of the divided state of things among them: '*Who then* (*What then*) . . . . , *seeing that ye exalt them into heads over you?*' The question is not asked by an objector, but by Paul himself; when an objector is introduced, he notifies it, as ch. xv. 35; Rom. ix. 19. **ἐπιστεύσατε**, as in reff.: **ye became believers.** **ἑκάστῳ ὡς . . .**, = ὡς ἔδωκ. ὁ κύρ. ἑκάστῳ, see reff. It refers, not to the *teachers*, but to the *hearers*, see below ὁ αὐξάνων θεός. In the rec. text, the question is carried on to the end of the verse by ἀλλ' ἤ, which is good Greek for 'nisi,' 'præterquam,'—so οὐδὲ χρησόμεθα ἐξηγητῇ ἀλλ' ἢ τῷ πατρῴῳ, Plato, Rep. p. 427, see Hartung, Partikellehre, ii. 44,—but seems to have been inserted from not observing the form of the sentence. **6.**] The similitude is to a *tilled field* (γεώργιον, ver. 9): the *plants* are the Corinthians, as members of Christ, vines bearing fruit: these do not yet appear in the construction: so that I prefer, with De Wette, supplying nothing after ἐφύτευσα and ἐπότισεν, regarding merely the *acts themselves*, as in E. V. If any thing be supplied, it must be ὑμᾶς, which would but ill fit ver. 7. Apollos was sent over to Corinth after Paul had left it (Acts xviii. 27), at his own request, and remained there preaching during Paul's journey through Upper Asia (ib. xix. 1). **7.**] **ἐστίν τι**, either '*is any thing to the purpose,*' as in λέγειν τι, &c., or absol. **is any thing**: which latter is best: compare εἰ καὶ **οὐδέν** εἰμι, 2 Cor. xii. 11. **ἀλλ' ὁ αὐξ. θεός**, scil. τὰ πάντα ἐστί,—to be supplied from the negative clauses preceding. Theophylact remarks: ὅρα πῶς ἀνεπαχθῆ ποιεῖ τὴν ἐξουδένωσιν τῶν προεστώτων ἐν Κορίνθῳ σοφῶν κ. πλουσίων, ἑαυτὸν κ. Ἀπολλὼ κατὰ τὸ φαινόμενον ἐξουδενώσας, κ. διδάξας, ὅτι θεῷ δεῖ μόνῳ προσέχειν, κ. εἰς αὐτὸν ἀνατιθέναι πάντα τὰ συμβαίνοντα ἀγαθά. **8.**] **ἕν**, in the nature of their ministry,—generically, κατὰ τὴν ὑπουργίαν· ἀμφότεραι γὰρ τῷ θείῳ διακονοῦσι βουλήματι. Theodoret. **ἕκαστος δὲ . . .**] Here he introduces a new element—the *separate* responsibility of *each minister*

ἴδιον [s] κόπον. 9 [t] θεοῦ γάρ ἐσμεν [tu] συνεργοί· θεοῦ [v] γεώργιον, θεοῦ [w] οἰκοδομή ἐστε. 10 κατὰ τὴν [x] χάριν τοῦ θεοῦ
τὴν [x] δοθεῖσάν μοι ὡς [y] σοφὸς [z] ἀρχιτέκτων [ab] θεμέλιον
[b] ἔθηκα, ἄλλος δὲ [c] ἐποικοδομεῖ. ἕκαστος δὲ [de] βλεπέτω
[d] πῶς [c] ἐποικοδομεῖ. 11 [ab] θεμέλιον γὰρ ἄλλον οὐδεὶς
δύναται [b] θεῖναι [f] παρὰ τὸν [g] κείμενον, ὅς ἐστιν Ἰησοῦς

ABCDL PℵA a b c d e f g h k l m n o 17. 47

s = 2 Cor. vi. 5 reff. t 1 Thess. iii. 2 only. u = Rom. xvi. 3 reff. v here only. Prov. xxiv. 30. xxxi. 16. (-γος, John xv. 1. -γεῖν, Heb. vi. 7.) w = Matt. xxiv. 1 || Mk. 2 Cor. v. 1. Eph. ii. 21 only. (Rom. xiv. 19 reff.) Ezek. xvii. 17. x ch. i. 4 reff. y = Exod. xxxv. 10. z here only. Isa. iii. 3. Sir. xxxviii. 27. 2 Macc. ii. 29 only. a masc., 2 Tim. i. 19. Rev. xxi. 19. = Rom. xv. 20. Heb. vi. 1. b Luke vi. 48. xiv. 29. c here &c., 4 times. Eph. ii. 20. Col. ii. 7. Jude 20 only. Num. xxxii. 38 Ald.(οἰκ., AB) only. see Rom. xv. 20. d Luke viii. 18. Eph. v. 15. e = Mark xiii. 5 al. fr. f = Luke iii. 13. Heb. xi. 4. i. 4 al. ἐποίει ἄλλα παρ' ἃ ἐνόμιζεν, Plato, Minos, 320. ἔχομέν τι παρὰ ταῦτα ἄλλο λέγειν, id. Phædo, 80. g Matt. v. 14.

8. om 2nd δε C 31 Syr[-ed]. for κοπον, τοπον C.
9. aft γεωργιον ins εστε D^2 vulg(not harl[1]) [F-lat] arm Chr_2 [Pel].
10. rec τεθεικα, with $C^3Dℵ^3$ rel [$Clem_1$] $Orig_1$[-c_1] ($Chr\text{-}mss_1$) Thdrt Thl Œc, τεθηκα LP f n 47: txt $ABC^1ℵ^1$ m[1] 17 (Chr_1). om 2nd δε D Chr Orig[-i nt_1] Gild.

for the results of his own labour, so that, though κατὰ τὴν ὑπουργίαν they are *one*,—κατὰ τὸ ἔργον (ib.) they are *diverse*. The stress is twice on ἴδιον.

9.] Proof of the last assertion, and introduction of *Him*, from Whom each λήμψεται. The stress thrice on θεοῦ:—**shall receive, &c.,—for it is of God that we are the fellow-workers** (in *subordination to Him*, as is of course implied: but to render it 'fellow workers *with one another*, under God,' as Estius prefers, and Olsh., al., maintain, is contrary to usage: see reff.;—and not at all required, see 2 Cor. v. 20; vi. 1), **of God that ye are the tillage, of God that ye are the building.** This last new similitude is introduced on account of what he has presently to say of the different kinds of teaching, which will be more clearly set forth by this, than by the other figure.

10.] **κατὰ τ. χάρ.** &c., as an expression of humility (reff.), fitly introduces the σοφός which follows. So Chrys.: ὅρα γοῦν πῶς μετριάζει. εἰπὼν γὰρ σοφὸν ἑαυτόν, οὐκ ἀφῆκεν αὐτοῦ τοῦτο εἶναι, ἀλλ' ὅλον ἑαυτὸν πρότερον ἀναθεὶς τῷ θεῷ τότε ἑαυτὸν οὕτως ἐκάλεσε. Hom. viii. p. 69. The **χάρις** is not *the peculiar grace of his apostleship*—for an apostle was not always required to lay the foundation, e. g. in Rome:—but that given to him in common with all Christians (ver. 5), only in a degree proportioned to the work which God had for him to do. **σοφός, skilful**, see reff., and many examples in Wetstein. The proof of this skill is given, in his *laying a foundation:* the unskilful master-builder *lays none*, see Luke vi. 49. The foundation (ver. 11) was and must be, Jesus Christ: the facts of redemption by Him (obj.), and the reception of Him and His work by faith (subj.). The mascul. form ὁ θεμέλιος (sc. λίθος) is said by Thomas Mag. (in Wetst.) to belong to the κοινὴ διάλεκτος—the Attic form is θεμέλιον, or, if in the plur., οἱ θεμέλιοι: —οἱ γὰρ θεμέλιοι παντοίων λίθων ὑπόκεινται, Thucyd. i. 93. **ἄλλος**, '*whoever comes after me*,'—another: not only Apollos. **ἐποικοδομεῖ**, *pres.*, as the necessary state and condition of the subsequent teacher, be he who he may. The *building on, over the foundation*, imports the carrying them onward in knowledge and intelligent faith. **πῶς**, emphatic, = here, *with what material*. De Wette imagines that it also conveys a caution not to *alter the foundations*, and that the **γάρ** in ver. 11 refers to this. But the identity of the foundation is surely implied in ἐποικοδομεῖ. On the γάρ, see below.

11. θ. γάρ] q. d. 'I speak of superimposing merely, for it is unnecessary to caution them respecting the foundation itself: there *can be but one*, and that one has already been (objectively, for all, see below) laid by God.' At the same time, in taking this for granted, he implies the strongest possible caution against attempting to lay any other. **δύναται**, strictly **can**,—not '*nemini licet*,' as Grot., al., nor as Theophyl., οὐ δύναται θεῖναι, ἕως ἂν μένῃ σοφὸς ἀρχιτέκτων, ἐπεὶ ὅταν μὴ ᾖ τις σοφ. ἀρχ., δύναται θεῖναι, κ. ἐκ τούτου αἱ αἱρέσεις:—for it is *assumed*, that **θεοῦ** οἰκοδομή is to be raised—and it *can* only be raised on this one foundation. All who build on other foundations are not συνεργοὶ θεοῦ, nor is their building θεοῦ οἰκοδομή at all. **ἄλλον . . . . παρά**, see reff. and cf. Thucyd. i. 23, πυκνότεραι παρὰ τὰ ἐκ τοῦ πρὶν χρόνου μνημονευόμενα. **κείμενον**] not, '*by me*,' but '*by God*,' for universal Christendom; but *actually laid in each place*, as regards *that church*, by the minister who founds it. De Wette denies this universal reference, as introducing a new element into the context. But surely the reference in ὁ θεμέλιος ὁ κείμενος is

χριστός. 2 εἰ δέ τις c ἐποικοδομεῖ ἐπὶ τὸν a θεμέλιον
[τοῦτον] χρυσόν, h ἄργυρον, i λίθους i τιμίους, k ξύλα,
l χόρτον, m καλάμην, 13 ἑκάστου τὸ ἔργον n φανερὸν n γενή-

h Matt. x. 9. Acts xvii. 29. James iv. 3. Rev. xviii. 12 only. Isa. lx. 9.
i Rev. xvii. 4. xviii. 12, 16. xxi. 11, 19. Ps. xviii. 10.
k = here only. Ezra v. 8.
l = here only. (Matt. vi. 30 al. fr. Gen. ii. 5.)
m here only. Exod. v. 12. xv. 7. Isa. v. 24.
n Mark vi. 14. Acts vii. 13. Phil. i. 13. Gen. xlii. 16.

11. rec ins *ο* bef *χριστος* [with Euthal-ms] : om ABCDLPℵ rel.—*χριστ. ιησ.* C³D vulg [F-lat] syr Orig$_1$[-int$_2$ Dial$_1$] Chr$_1$ Max Damasc Hil Jer Ambrst Aug$_{sæpe}$ Sedul : txt ABLPℵ rel Syr [coptt æth arm] Orig$_1$[-c$_1$-int$_1$] Marcell$_2$ Ath$_1$ [Eus$_3$ Bas$_1$ Did$_2$ Chr$_2$] Arnob : om *ιησ.* C¹. (*The rec ιησ. ο χρ. appears to have been a corrn to give a* doctrinal *meaning*—'Jesus (is) the Christ.' *χρ. ιησ. may have had the same intention, cf ch* xii. 3.)

12. om *τουτον* ABC¹ℵ¹ fuld¹ sah æth Ambr$_1$ (*perhaps from similarity of endgs ; or as unnecessary*) : ins C³DLPℵ³ rel latt syrr copt arm [Bas$_1$] Cyr-jer$_1$ Chr$_2$ Thdrt Thl Œc Orig[-int$_2$ Ambrst] Aug$_1$ Jer. *χρυσιον* Bℵ 73 Clem$_1$ [Bas-mss$_1$ Epiph$_1$ Damasc]. (C doubtful.) add *και* B 73 æth Clem [Orig$_1$]. *αργυριον* BCℵ 73 Clem.

13. for *εκαστου* to *γενησεται*, *ο ποιησας τουτο το εργον φανερος γενηται* (*see ch* v. 2)

too direct to the well-known prophecy of the divinely-placed foundation or corner-stone, to surprise any reader or divert his mind from the train of thought by a new element. **Ἰησοῦς χριστός**, THE PERSONAL, HISTORICAL CHRIST, as the object of all Christian faith. If it be read as in rec., Ἰησοῦς ὁ χριστός, it need not *necessarily* be, *that Jesus is the Christ*, but may be in this case also, JESUS THE CHRIST ; not any *doctrine*, even that of the Messiahship of Jesus, is the foundation, but JESUS HIMSELF (see var. readd.).

12.] The **δέ** implies that though there can be but one foundation, there are *many ways of building upon it*. To the right understanding of this verse it may be necessary to remark, (1) that the similitude is, not of *many buildings*, as Wetst. and Billroth,—but of *one*, see ver. 16,—and that [one,] raised *on Christ as its foundation;*—different parts of which are built by the ministers who work under Him,—some well and substantially built, some ill and unsubstantially. (2) That gold, silver, &c., refer to the *matter* of the ministers' teaching, *primarily ;* and by inference to those whom that teaching penetrates and builds up in Christ, who should be the living stones of the temple: not, as Orig., Chrys., Theodoret, Theophyl., Phot., Aug., Jer., &c., to the moral fruits produced by the preaching in the individual members of the church, —*εἴ τις κακὸν βίον ἔχει μετὰ πίστεως ὀρθῆς, οὐ προστήσεται αὐτοῦ ἡ πίστις εἰς τὸ μὴ κολάζεσθαι*, Chrys. Hom. ix. p. 77. (3) That the builder of the worthless and unsubstantial *is in the end* SAVED (see below): so that even *his* preaching was *preaching of Christ*, and *he himself was in earnest.* (4) That what is said does not refer, except by accommodation, to *the religious life of believers in general*—as Olsh., Schrader, see also the ancient Commentators above : —but to the DUTY AND REWARD OF TEACHERS. At the same time, such accommodation is legitimate, *in so far as each man is a teacher and builder of himself.* (5) That the various materials specified must not be fancifully pressed to indicate *particular doctrines or graces*, as e. g. Schrader has done, "Some build with the gold of faith, with the silver of hope, with the imperishable costly stones of love,—others again with the dead wood of unfruitfulness in good works, with the empty straw of a spiritless, ostentatious knowledge, and with the bending reed of a continually-doubting spirit." Der Apostel Paulus, iv. p. 66. This, however ingenious, is beside the mark, not being justified by any indications furnished in our Epistle itself. An elaborate résumé of the very various minor differences of interpretation may be seen in Meyer's Comm. ed. 2, in loc. Cf. also Estius's note; and Stanley's. **λίθους τιμίους**] Not '*gems*,' but '*costly stones*,' as marbles, porphyry, jasper, &c., compare 1 Kings vii. 9 ff. By the *ξύλα, χόρτον, καλάμην*, he indicates the various perversions of true doctrine, and admixtures of false philosophy which were current: so Estius, "doctrina non quidem hæretica et perniciosa, *talis enim fundamentum destrueret :* sed minus sincera, minusque solida ; veluti si sit humanis ac philosophicis, aut etiam Judaicis opinionibus admixta plus satis : si curiosa magis quam utilis; si vana quadam oblectatione mentes occupans Christianas." Comm. i. p. 268 B.

13.] **Each man's work** (i. e. that which he has built : *his part* in erecting the *οἰκοδομὴ θεοῦ*) **shall** (at some time) **be made evident** (shall not always remain in the present uncertainty, but be tested, and shown of what sort it is): **for the day shall make it manifest** (the *day of the Lord*, as Vulg., 'dies domini :' see reff.,—and so most Commentators, ancient and modern. The other interpretations are (1) '*the day*

σεται· ἡ γὰρ [o] ἡμέρα [p] δηλώσει, ὅτι ἐν πυρὶ [q] ἀποκαλύπτεται, καὶ ἑκάστου τὸ ἔργον [r] ὁποῖόν ἐστιν τὸ πῦρ αὐτὸ
[s] δοκιμάσει. 14 εἴ τινος τὸ ἔργον [t] μενεῖ ὃ [u] ἐποικοδό-
μησεν, [v] μισθὸν λήμψεται. 15 εἴ τινος τὸ ἔργον [w] κατακαήσεται, [x] ζημιωθήσεται· αὐτὸς δὲ σωθήσεται, [y] οὕτως δὲ

ABCDL Pℵ a b c d e f g h k l m n o 17. 47

o = ch. i. 8 reff. 1 Thess. v. 4. Heb. x. 25.
p ch. i. 11 reff.
q = Rom. i. 18 reff. see 2 Thess. i. 7, 8.
r Acts xxvi. 29 reff.
s = Luke xiv. 19. ch. xi. 28. 2 Cor. xiii. 5. 1 Pet. i. 7. Zech. xiii. 9.
t = Rom. ix. 11 reff.
u vv. 10, 12.
v ver. 8.
w Matt. iii. 12 || L. xiii. 30. Acts xix. 19 al. Gen xxxviii. 24. form also, 2 Pet. iii. 10. Rev. viii. 7. Isa. xlvii. 14 A.
x Matt. xvi. 26 ||. 2 Cor. vii. 9. Phil. iii. 8 only. Prov. xix. 19. xxii. 3.
y ch. iv. 1. ix. 26. Eph. v. 33. James ii. 12.

D[1][and lat] Ambrst. rec om *αυτο* (*as unnecessary: but see note*), with DLℵ rel [latt syr coptt æth arm] (Clem$_1$) Orig$_1$[-c$_1$-int$_2$ Cyr-p$_1$ Damasc] Chr-mss$_2$ Thdrt$_3$ Thl Œc [Ambrst]: ins ABC P(*αυτω*) m 17 Syr Orig$_1$[-c$_1$] Eus$_1$ Bas[-2-mss$_1$] Chr$_1$ Thdrt$_2$ Procop$_1$.
14. rec *επωκοδομησεν*, with B[2]C rel [Orig$_1$]: txt AB[1]DLPℵ [n] 17 [Bas$_1$].

of the destruction of Jerusalem,' which shall shew the vanity of Judaizing doctrines: so Hammond (but not clearly nor exclusively), Lightf., Schöttg., al.,—against both the context, and our Apostle's habit of speaking, and under the assumption, that nothing but Jewish errors are spoken of:—(2) '*the lapse of time*,' as in the proverb, '*dies docebit*;'—so Grot., Wolf, Mosheim, Rosenm., al., which is still more inconsistent with the context, which necessitates a definite *day*, and a definite *fire*:—(3) '*the light of day*,' i. e. of clear knowledge, as opposed to the present time of obscurity and night: so Calv., Beza, Erasm.:—but the fire here is not a *light-giving*, but a *consuming* flame; and, as Meyer remarks, even in that case the ἡμέρα would be that of the παρουσία, see Rom. xiii. 12:—(4) '*the day of tribulation*:'—so Augustine, Calov.: but this again is not definite enough: μισθὸν λήμψεται can hardly be said of mere abiding the test of tribulation);—**because it** (the *day*—not, the *work*, as Theophyl., Œcum., al., which would introduce a mere tautology with the next clause) **is** (to be) **revealed** (the present ἀποκαλύπτεται expresses the definite certainty of prophecy: or perhaps rather the *attribute* of that day, which is, to be revealed, &c., as in the expressions ὁ πειράζων, ὁ σπείρων, &c.) **in fire** ('accompanied,' 'clothed,' 'girt,' 'with fire;' i. e. fire will be *the element* in which the day will be revealed. Cf. 2 Thess. i. 8, and Mal. iii. 2, 3, iv. 1, to which latter place the reference is,—see LXX. But notice, that this is *not the fire of hell*, into which the gold, silver, and costly stones will never enter, but the *fire of judgment*, in which Christ will appear, and by which *all works will be tried*. This *universality* of trial by fire is equally against the idea of a *purgatorial fire*, which lucrative fiction has been mainly based by the Romanists on a perversion of this passage. See Aug. de Civ. Dei, xxi. 26. 4, vol. vii. p. 745, who mentions the idea with 'non redarguo, quia forsitan verum est.' See Estius, who does not maintain the allusion to Purgatory here; and Bisping, who does), **and each man's work, of what kind it is, the fire itself shall try** (this clause does not depend upon ὅτι, but ranges with the following futures. It is a question whether ἔργον is nom. or acc.,—*of what kind each man's work is* (Meyer),—or as above. In the only other places where Paul uses ὁποῖος, Gal. ii. 6, 1 Thess. i. 9 (see also Acts xxvi. 29), it commences a clause, as here if ἔργον be accus.;—we have a very similar expression, Gal. vi. 4, τὸ ἔργον ἑαυτοῦ δοκιμαζέτω ἕκαστος:—and it seems more natural that the *action of the fire* should be described as directly passing upon the work. For these reasons, I prefer the accus. τὸ πῦρ **αὐτό**, the fire itself, of its own power, being a πῦρ καταναλίσκον.

14.] **If any man's work shall remain** (i. e. stand the fire,—being of inconsumable materials. μενεῖ fut. (so latt syrr coptt), is better than the pres. of rec., as answering to εἰ . . . . κατακαήσεται below), **which he built on the foundation,—he shall receive wages** (as a builder;—i. e. 'shall be rewarded for his faithful and effectual work as a teacher'):

15.] **if any man's work shall be burnt up** (i. e. consist of such materials as the fire will destroy: Stanley adds, "It is possible that this whole image, as addressed to the Corinthians, may have been suggested, or at least illustrated, by the conflagration of Corinth under Mummius: the stately temples (one of them remaining to this day) left standing amidst the universal crash and destruction of the meaner buildings"), **he shall** [**suffer loss** (literally,) **be mulcted**. ζημιωθ., scil. τὸν μισθόν, see ref. Matt., and Herod. vii. 39, τοῦ δὲ ἑνός, τοῦ περιέχεαι μάλιστα, τὴν ψυχὴν ζημιώσεαι, and Plato, Legg., vi. p. 774, εἰς μὲν οὖν χρήματα ὁ μὴ θέλων γαμεῖν τοσαῦτα ζημιούσθω): **but he himself shall be saved** (having held, and built on, the true foundation Jesus Christ, he shall not be excluded from that salva-

[y] ὡς [z] διὰ πυρός. 16 [a] οὐκ [a] οἴδατε ὅτι [b] ναὸς θεοῦ ἐστε
καὶ τὸ πνεῦμα τοῦ θεοῦ [c] οἰκεῖ ἐν ὑμῖν; 17 εἴ τις τὸν [b] ναὸν
τοῦ θεοῦ [d] φθείρει, [d] φθερεῖ τοῦτον ὁ θεός· ὁ γὰρ [b] ναὸς τοῦ

F[-gr] (and also G) οικει.. ABCDF LPℵ a b c d e f g h k l m n o 17. 47

z see Isa. xliii. 2. Zech. xiii. 9.
a Rom. vi. 16. ch. v. 6 al.
b = ch. vi. 19. 2 Cor. vi. 16. (2 Thess. ii. 4 al.) Jer. vii. 4.
c Rom. vii. 17 reff.
d = here bis. ch. xv. 33. 2 Cor. vii. 2. xi. 3. Eph. iv. 22. 2 Pet. ii. 12. Jude 10. Rev. xix. 2 only. Isa. liv. 16. play on word, ch. vi. 12.

16. εν υμιν bef οικει BP m 17 [Bas_1] ($Tert_1$).
17. for φθερει, φθειρει D[-gr] F[-gr] P 47 am: φθειρεῖ L. for τουτον, αυτον (*corrn as more usual*) ADF Syr syr-mg arm [$Orig\text{-}c_1$], *illum* latt $Iren\text{-}int_1$ [$Orig\text{-}int_2$ $Tert_1$ Hil_1] $Cypr_1$: txt BCLPℵ rel syr[-txt] coptt æth Orig[$\text{-}c_2$] Eus_1 Mac_1 Did_2 $Amphil_1$ Chr_4 [$Cyr\text{-}p_1$ Damasc] Thdrt Thl Œc.

tion which is the *free gift* of God to all who believe on Christ, but shall get no *especial reward* as a faithful and effectual teacher. Cf. 2 John 8, βλέπετε ἑαυτούς, ἵνα μὴ **ἀπολέσητε ἃ εἰργασάμεθα**, ἀλλὰ **μισθὸν πλήρη** ἀπολάβητε. Meyer remarks, that our Lord hints at such persons under the name of ἔσχατοι, Matt. xx. 16; Mark x. 31), **but so, as through fire**:—i. e. as a builder whose building was consumed would escape with personal safety, but with the loss of his work. Chrys., Theophyl., Œc., strangely understand it, that he shall be burnt for ever in the fire of Hell, unconsumed: οὐχὶ καὶ αὐτὸς οὕτως ἀπολεῖται ὡς τὰ ἔργα, εἰς τὸ μηδὲν χωρῶν· ἀλλὰ μενεῖ ἐν τῷ πυρί, Chrys. σώζεται, τουτέστι, σῶος τηρεῖται. δίκας αἰωνίους ὑπέχων, Theophyl. But (1) the *fire of Hell* is quite alien from the context (see above),—and (2) the meaning given to σώζεσθαι is unexampled,—and least of all could be intended where the coming of the Lord is spoken of: cf. *inter alia*, ch. v. 5, παραδοῦναι κ.τ.λ. . . . . ἵνα **τὸ πνεῦμα σωθῇ ἐν τῇ ἡμέρᾳ τ. κυρίου.** Grot., Elsn., al., explain ὡς διὰ πυρός as a proverb, '*tanquam ex incendio*,' for 'with difficulty.' But this is needless here, as the *figure itself* is that of an 'incendium:' and ὡς is *not* '*tanquam*,' but belongs to οὕτως, see reff. The whole imagery of the passage will be best understood by carefully keeping in mind the *key*, which is to be found in the θεοῦ οἰκοδομή, and the ναὸς θεοῦ, as connected with the prophecy of Malachi iii. and iv. There, ἐξαίφνης ἥξει εἰς τὸν ναὸν ἑαυτοῦ κύριος . . . . αὐτὸς εἰσπορεύεται ὡς πῦρ χωνευτηρίου . . . καθιεῖται χωνεύων καὶ καθαρίζων ὡς τὸ ἀργύριον καὶ ὡς τὸ χρυσίον. . . . . διότι ἰδοὺ ἡμέρα (add κυρίου A) ἔρχεται καιομένη ὡς κλίβανος, κ. φλέξει αὐτούς, καὶ ἔσονται . . . καλάμη, κ. ἀνάψει αὐτοὺς ἡ ἡμέρα ἡ ἐρχομένη. The Lord thus coming to His temple in flaming fire, all the parts of the building which will not stand that fire will be consumed: the builders of them will escape with personal salvation, but with the loss of their work, through the midst of the conflagration.

16—23.] *The figure is taken up afresh and carried further: and made the occasion of solemn exhortation, since they were the temple of God, not to mar that temple, the habitation of His Spirit, by unholiness, or by exaltation of human wisdom: which last again was irrelevant, as well as sinful; for all their teachers were but their servants in building them up to be God's temple,—yea all things were for this end, to subserve them, as being Christ's, by the ordinance, and to the glory of God the Father.* **16.**] The foregoing figures, with the occasion to which they referred, are now dropped, and the οἰκοδομὴ θεοῦ recalled, to do further service. This *building* is now, as in Mal. iii. 1, and as indeed by implication in the foregoing verses, the *temple* of God (ναὸς θεοῦ, with emphasis on ναός, not θεοῦ ναός), the *habitation of His Spirit*. **οὐκ οἴδατε ὅτι—Are ye ignorant that . . .** an expression of surprise arising out of their conduct. **καὶ . . . ἐν ὑμῖν** = ἐν ᾧ, τουτέστιν, ἐν ὑμῖν. Meyer rightly remarks, that "ναὸς θεοῦ is *the temple* of God, not *a* temple of God: for Paul does not conceive (as Theodoret, al.) of the various churches as *various temples* of God, which would be inconsistent with a Jew's conception of God's temple, but of each Christian church as, sensu mystico, *the temple of Jehovah*. So there would be, not many temples, but many churches, each of which is, ideally, the same temple of God." And, we may add, if the figure is to be strictly justified in its widest acceptation, that all the churches are built together into one vast temple: cf. ἐν ᾧ **καὶ ὑμεῖς συνοικοδομεῖσθε**, Eph. ii. 22. **17.**] **φθείρει**, [destroys, or] **mars**, whether as regards its *unity and beauty*, or its *purity and sanctity*: here, the meaning is left indefinite, but the latter particulars are certainly hinted at,—by ἅγιος below. **φθερεῖ**, either by *temporal death* (Mey.), as in ch. xi. 30; or by *spiritual death*, which is more probable, seeing that the *figurative* temple is spoken of, not (as Mey.) the material temple:—and as *tem-*

θεοῦ ἅγιός ἐστιν, [e] οἵτινές ἐστε ὑμεῖς.
18 μηδεὶς ἑαυτὸν [f] ἐξαπατάτω· εἴ τις [g] δοκεῖ σοφὸς εἶναι ἐν ὑμῖν ἐν τῷ [h] αἰῶνι [h] τούτῳ, [i] μωρὸς γενέσθω, ἵνα γένηται σοφός.
19 ἡ γὰρ σοφία τοῦ κόσμου τούτου [k] μωρία [l] παρὰ [τῷ] θεῷ ἐστιν. γέγραπται γὰρ [m] Ὁ [n] δρασσόμενος τοὺς σοφοὺς ἐν τῇ [o] πανουργίᾳ αὐτῶν.
20 καὶ πάλιν Κύριος γινώσκει τοὺς [p] διαλογισμοὺς τῶν σοφῶν [q] ὅτι εἰσὶν [r] μάταιοι.
21 [s] ὥστε μηδεὶς [t] καυχάσθω [t] ἐν ἀνθρώποις· πάντα γὰρ [u] ὑμῶν ἐστιν,

ABCDF LPℵ a b c d e f g h k l m n o 17. 47

e = Rom. vi. 2. f Rom. vii. 11 reff. g = ch. viii. 2. xiv. 37. Gal. vi. 3. Phil. iii. 4. James i. 26. h Rom. xii. 2 reff. i ch. i. 25 reff. k ch. i. 18 reff. l Rom. ii. 13. Gal. iii. 11 al. m Job v. 13 (but καταλαμβάνων and φρονήσει). n here only. Levit. ii. 2. v. 12. Num. v. 26. (Ps. ii. 12, w. gen.) Herod. iii. 13. Jos. B. J. iii. 8. 6. Dion. Hal. ix. 21. o (=) Luke xx. 23. 2 Cor. iv. 2. xi. 3. Eph. iv. 14 only. Josh. ix. 4 (10). (-γος, 2 Cor. xii. 16.) p = Rom. i. 21. James ii. 4. Psa. xciii. 11. q constr., ch. xvi. 15 al. fr. Winer, edn. 6, § 66. 5. a. r Acts xiv 15. ch. xv. 17. Tit. iii. 9. James i. 26. 1 Pet. i. 18 only. Exod. xx. 7. s = ch. iv. 5. t ch. i. 31. Rom. ii. 17 reff. u gen., ch. i. 12. Rom. xiv. 8. 2 Tim. ii. 19.

18. aft εξαπατατω [απατατω 47] ins κενοις λογοις (*see Eph* v. 6) D 23-marg. 73. 118. εν υμ. ειναι σοφ. P.

19. rec ins τω bef θεω (*corrn: but art is unnecessary aft prepn*), with ABLPℵ rel $Orig_3$ $Dion_1$ Eus_1 Chr_1 [Euthal-ms Damasc] Thdrt: om CDF b¹ o $Clem_1$ $Orig_1$[-c_1]. om γαρ D¹[-gr]. om ὁ and τους F. [πανουργει F.]

21. ανθρωπω F [$Tert_1$ Ambrst Aug_1] (not Pel Bede).

poral death was the punishment for defiling the material temple (Exod. xxviii. 43. Levit. xvi. 2 al. fr.), so *spiritual death* for marring or defiling of God's spiritual temple. **ἅγιος**, the constant epithet of ναός in the O. T., see Ps. v. 7; x. 5 (LXX). Hab. ii. 20, and passim. **οἵτινες**, i. e. ἅγιοι, not, '*which temple are ye*,' which would be tautological after ver. 16, and would hardly be expressed by οἵτινες, '*ut qui*,' or '*quales*.' Meyer well remarks, that οἵτινές ἐστε ὑμεῖς is the minor proposition of a syllogism:—'Whoever mars the temple of God, him will God destroy, because His temple is *holy*; but ye also, as His ideal temple, are holy:—therefore, whoever mars you, shall be destroyed by God.'

18—20.] *A warning to those who would be leaders among them, against self-conceit.* 18.] **ἐξαπατάτω**, not, as Theophyl., νομίζων ὅτι ἄλλως ἔχει τὸ πρᾶγμα καὶ οὐχ ὡς εἶπον:—it is far more naturally referred to what follows, viz. thinking himself wise, when he must become a fool in order to be wise. **If any man [seemeth to be** (i. e.,**] thinks that he is) wise among you in this world** (ἐν τῷ αἰ. τούτῳ belongs to δοκεῖ σοφ. εἶν. ἐν ὑμ.,—to the whole assumption of wisdom made by the man, which as made in *this present world*, must be false: not (1) merely to σοφός, Grot., Rückert, al.,—as the arrangement of the words shews,—nor (2) to μωρὸς γενέσθω, Orig., Chrys., Luther, Rosenm., al., in which case, the stress being on μωρός, it must have been μωρὸς γενέσθω ἐν τῷ αἰῶνι τούτῳ), **let him become a fool** (by receiving the gospel in its simplicity, and so becoming foolish in the world's sight), **that he may become (truly) wise.** 19.] *Reason why this must be*:—shewn from Scripture. **παρὰ θ., in the judgment of God,** reff. **ὁ δρασσ.**] The sense of the Heb. is equally expressed by the Apostle and the LXX. The words are taken out of the context as they stand, which accounts for the participle, see Heb. i. 7. The sense is, 'If God uses the craft of the wise as a net to catch them in, such wisdom is in His sight folly, since He turns it to their confusion.' "**δρασσόμενος** (possibly a provincialism) is substituted for καταλαμβάνων, as a stronger and livelier expression for 'grasping,' or 'catching with the hand.'" Stanley. Cf. Judith xiii. 7. 20.] The LXX have ἀνθρώπων (Heb. אָדָם); the Psalmist however is speaking of the *proud*, ver. 2 ff., and such, when διαλογισμοί are in question, would be the *worldly wise*. 21—23.] *A warning to them in general, not to boast themselves in human teachers.* 21.] **ὥστε**, viz. seeing that this world's wisdom is folly with God: or perhaps as a more general inference from what has gone before since ch. i., that as the conclusion there was, ὁ καυχώμενος, ἐν κυρίῳ καυχάσθω,—so now, having gone into the matter more at length, he concludes, μηδεὶς καυχάσθω ἐν ἀνθρώποις. This *boasting in men* is explained in ch. iv. 6 to mean μὴ εἷς ὑπὲρ τοῦ ἑνὸς φυσιοῦσθαι κατὰ τοῦ ἑτέρου. **καυχάσθω** after ὥστε is a change of construction. A somewhat similar change occurred in the parallel ch. i. 31, ἵνα . . . . καυχάσθω: but there, by the citation being adduced in its existing form. **πάντα γὰρ ὑμ. ἐστ.**] 'For such boasting is a *degradation* to those who are *heirs of all things*, and *for whom all*, whether minis-

22 [v] εἴτε Παῦλος εἴτε Ἀπολλὼς εἴτε Κηφᾶς, εἴτε κόσμος
εἴτε [w] ζωὴ εἴτε [w] θάνατος, εἴτε [wx] ἐνεστῶτα εἴτε [wy] μέλλοντα,
πάντα [u] ὑμῶν, 23 ὑμεῖς δὲ [u] χριστοῦ, χριστὸς δὲ [u] θεοῦ.
IV. 1 [z] Οὕτως ἡμᾶς [a] λογιζέσθω [b] ἄνθρωπος, [z] ὡς [c] ὑπηρέτας
χριστοῦ καὶ [d] οἰκονόμους [e] μυστηρίων θεοῦ. 2 [f] ὧδε [g] λοι-

v so Rom. xii. 6. Col. i. 16.
w so Rom. viii. 38.
x see 2 Thess. ii. 2.
y = Acts xxiv. 25 reff.
z ch. iii. 15 reff.
a Rom. viii. 36 reff. ix. 8.
b = ch. xi. 28. Gal. vi. 1.
c = Acts xiii. 5 reff.
d = Tit. i. 7. 1 Pet. iv. 10. (Luke xii. 42. xvi. 1, &c.)
e ch. ii. 7 reff.
f = Col. iv. 9. Heb. xiii. 14.
g ch. i. 16 reff.

22. *απολλω* F 17. ins *δι'* bef *υμων* F[-gr]. *ημων*, and in ver. 23 *ημεις* B 48 Orig$_1$. rec at end ins *εστιν*, with D$^{2\cdot3}$L rel vulg [F-lat syrr copt arm Orig$_1$-int$_2$] Chr$_1$ Thdrt [Tert$_1$]: om ABC D^1[and lat] F[-gr] Pא 17 [æth] Dial$_1$ Ambrst Aug$_1$.

CHAP. IV. **1.** ins *του* bef *θεου* F.

2. rec ὃ *δε λοιπον*, with D^3[-gr] L rel Orig$_2$[-c$_1$] Chr$_1$ Thdrt Thl Œc: txt ABCD^{1}FPא

ters, or events, or the world itself, *are working together*: see Rom. viii. 28: and iv. 13. **22, 23.**] *Specification of some of the things included under πάντα: and first of those teachers in whom they were disposed to boast*,—in direct reference to ch. i. 12. But having enumerated Paul, Apollos, Cephas, he does not say *εἴτε χριστός*, but adding the world itself and its events and circumstances, he reiterates the *πάντα ὑμῶν* as if to mark the termination of this category, and changing the form, concludes with *ὑμεῖς δὲ* (not only one part of you) *χριστοῦ· χριστὸς δὲ θεοῦ* (see below). The expressions *ζωή, θάνατος, ἐνεστῶτα, μέλλοντα*, have nothing to do with the *teachers*, as Chrys., Theophyl., Grot.,—*ἡ ζωή, φησι, τῶν διδασκάλων δι' ὑμᾶς ἔστιν ἵνα ὠφελῆσθε διδασκόμενοι· κ. ὁ θάνατος αὐτῶν δι' ὑμᾶς· ὑπὲρ ὑμῶν γὰρ κινδυνεύουσι καὶ τῆς ὑμετέρας σωτηρίας*, Theophyl.,—and "*præsentia*, . . . linguarum et sanationum dona . . . . *futura*, ... rerum futurarum revelationes," Grot.,—but are perfectly general. **ἐνεστῶτα** is *things actually present*,—see note on 2 Thess. ii. 2. **23.**] On the change of the possessives, see above:—*Christ* is not *yours*, in the sense in which *πάντα* are,—not *made for and subserving you*—*but* (*δέ*) *you are His*,—and even that does not reach the Highest possession: He possesses not you *for Himself; but* (*δέ* again) *κεφαλὴ χριστοῦ ὁ θεός*, ch. xi. 3. CHRIST HIMSELF, the Incarnate God the Mediator, *belongs to* God, is subordinate to the Father, see John xiv. 28; and xvii. passim. But this mediatorial subordination is in no way inconsistent with His eternal and co-equal Godhead: see notes on Phil. ii. 6—9; and on ch. xv. 28, where the subjection of all things to Christ, and His subjection to the Father, are similarly set forth. There is a striking similarity in the argument in this last verse to that in our Lord's prohibition, Matt. xxiii. 8—10. See Stanley's beautiful note.

IV. 1—5.] *He shews them the right view to take of Christian ministers* (vv. 1, 2); *but, for his part, regards not man's judgment of him, nor even judges himself, but the Lord is his Judge* (vv. 3, 4). *Therefore let them also suspend their judgments till the Lord's coming, when all shall be made plain.*

1.] **οὕτως**, emphatic, preparatory to *ὡς*, as in ref. **ἄνθρωπος**, as E. V., **a man**, in the most general and indefinite sense, as '*man*' in German: not a Hebraism, nor = *ἕκαστος*. The whole is opposed to *καύχησις ἐν ἀνθρώποις*: the ministers of Christ are but subordinates to Him, and accountable to God. **ἡμᾶς**, *here*, not, '*us ministers generally*,' see below, ver. 6, but '*myself and Apollos*,' as a sample of such. **ὑπηρ. χριστοῦ**, see ch. iii. 5, 22, 23. But in **οἰκον. μυστ. θεοῦ** we have a new figure introduced. The Church, 1 Tim. iii. 15, is the *οἶκος θεοῦ*—and those appointed to minister in it are *οἰκονόμοι*, *stewards* and *dispensers* of the property and stores of the *οἰκοδεσπότης*. These last are the *μυστήρια*, hidden treasures, of God,—i. e. the riches of his grace, *now manifested* in Christ, ch. ii. 7; Rom. xvi. 25, 26, which *they* announce and distribute to all, having received them from the Spirit for that purpose. "Ea mysteria sunt incarnationis, passionis et resurrectionis Christi, redemptionis nostræ, vocationis gentium, et cætera quæ complectitur evangelica doctrina." Estius, who also, as a Romanist, attempts to include the *sacraments* among the *μυστήρια* in this sense. The best refutation of this is given by himself: "sed cum ipse Paulus dixerit primo capite, *Non misit me Christus baptizare, sed evangelizare*, rectius est ut mysteria Dei intelligantur fidei nostræ dogmata." It may be doubted, whether, *in the N. T. sense* of *μυστήρια*, the sacraments can be in any way reckoned

πὸν [h] ζητεῖται ἐν τοῖς [d] οἰκονόμοις ἵνα πιστός τις [i] εὑρεθῇ.
3 [k] ἐμοὶ δὲ [l] εἰς ἐλάχιστόν ἐστιν [m] ἵνα ὑφ' ὑμῶν [n] ἀνακριθῶ
ἢ ὑπὸ [o] ἀνθρωπίνης [p] ἡμέρας· [q] ἀλλ' [q] οὐδὲ ἐμαυτὸν [n] ἀνα-
κρίνω· 4 οὐδὲν γὰρ ἐμαυτῷ [r] σύνοιδα, ἀλλ' οὐκ [s] ἐν τούτῳ
[s] δεδικαίωμαι· ὁ δὲ [n] ἀνακρίνων με κύριός ἐστιν. 5 [t] ὥςτε

ABCDF LPℵ a b c d e f g h k l m n o 17. 47

h = 2 Cor. xiii. 3. (ch. i. 22.) i = Matt. i. 18. Acts v. 39. Rom. vii. 10. 2 Cor. v. 3. Phil. ii. 8. Neh. ix. 8. k dat., Rom. xiv. 14. l = Acts xix. 27. m constr., Matt. x. 25. xviii. 6. n Acts iv. 9 reff. o Acts xvii. 25 reff. p = ch. i. 8 reff. q = Acts xix. 2. ch. iii. 2. r Acts v. 2. xii. 12. xiv. 6 only. Lev. v. 1. Job xxvii. 6 only. 1 Macc. iv. 21 al. s Acts xiii. 39. Rom. v. 9. ch. vi. 11. Gal. ii. 17. iii. 11. v. 4. t = ch. iii. 21.

17 latt syrr copt æth arm Orig-int$_1$ [Ambrst Aug$_1$]. aft λοιπον ins τι ℵ^1(om ℵ-corr^1?). ζητειτε (*itacism?*) AC D[-gr] F[-gr(-τητε)] Pℵ f g n 17 [Eutha lms]: txt BL rel latt syrr [copt Orig$_3$-c$_1$-int$_1$]. τις ευρεθη bef πιστος D$^{1\cdot3}$[-gr]: [τις] bef πιστος D^2[-gr] F goth.

3. ημων A [o]. αλλα D^1. for ουδε, ουδ F.

4. for ουκ, ουδε P [*nec* Jer$_2$ Aug$_1$]. for δε, γαρ ℵ^1 Syr æth. at end ins θεος D^1[and lat].

as such: for μυστ. is a (usually *divine*) proceeding, *once hidden, but now revealed,* or *now hidden, and to be revealed;* under neither of which categories can the sacraments be classed. * **2.] Moreover, here (on earth)** (see var. readd. and reff. ὧδε is emphatic, and points to what follows, that though in the case of stewards enquiry was necessarily made *here below,* yet he, God's steward, awaited no such enquiry ὑπὸ ἀνθρωπίνης ἡμέρας, but one at the coming of the Lord. Lachmann, I cannot but think somewhat strangely, places ὧδε at the end of ver. 1: οἰκονόμους μυστηρίων θεοῦ ὧδε. Stanley takes ὧδε for 'in this matter,' and supports the meaning by Rev. xiii. 10, 18; xiv. 12; xvii. 9) **enquiry is made in the case of stewards** (or, *it is required* in the case of stewards), **in order that** (or *that,* the purport of the requirement expressed as its purpose) **a man may be found** (proved to be) **faithful** (emph.). **3.] But to me** (contrast to the case of the stewards into whose faithfulness enquiry is made ὧδε, here on earth) **it is** (amounts to) **very little** (Meyer compares ἐς χάριν τέλλεται, Pind. Ol. i. 122, and Theognis, 162, οἷς τὸ κακὸν δοκέον γίγνεται εἰς ἀγαθόν) **that I [should] be** (the ἵνα, here and always, is more or less the conj. of *purpose.* The construction is a mixed one in such clauses as this, compounded of ἐλάχιστόν ἐστιν ἀνακριθῆναι, and ἐλαχίστου ἂν πριαίμην, ἵνα ἀνακριθῶ) **judged** (enquired into, as to my faithfulness) **by you, or by the day of man** ([i. e., **of man's judgment,**] in reference to ὧδε above, and contrast to the ἡμέρα κυρίου, to which his appeal is presently made, ver. 5, and of which, as testing the worth of the labour of teachers, he spoke so fully ch. iii. 13—15. Jerome, Quæstiones ad Algasiam, Ep. xxxi. (cli.) 10, vol. i. p. 879, numbers the expression among the *cilicisms* of the Apostle. Estius, al., suppose it to be a Hebraism, referring to Jer. xvii. 16, which is irrelevant. All these are probably wrong, and the expression *chosen purposely* by the Apostle. Grot. compares 'diem dicere,' 'to cite to trial;' to which Stanley adds the English 'daysman' for arbiter (see Job ix. 33), and the Dutch 'dagh vaerden' and 'daghen,' to 'summon'),—**nay, I do not judge even** (hold not an enquiry on: lit. '*but neither do I,*' &c.) **myself:** **4.] for I [know nothing against myself** (i. e.)] **am conscious to myself of no** (official) **delinquency;** so Plato, Apol. p. 21, οὔτε μέγα οὔτε σμικρὸν ξύνοιδα ἐμαυτῷ σοφὸς ὤν,—ib., Rep. i. (Wetst.), τῷ δὲ μηδὲν ἑαυτῷ ἀδίκων ξυνειδότι ἡδεῖα ἐλπὶς ἀεὶ πάρεστι, and Hor., Epist. i. 1. 61, 'Nil conscire sibi, nulla pallescere culpa.' The E. V., 'I know nothing by myself,' was a phrase commonly used in this acceptation at the time; cf. Ps. xv. 4, Com. Prayer Book version, 'He that *setteth not by himself,*' i. e. is not wise in his own conceit. 'I know no harm by him' is still a current expression in the midland counties. See Deut. xxvii. 16; Ezek. xxii. 7, in E. V. So Donne, Serm. lvii., "If thine own spirit, thine own conscience, accuse thee of nothing, is all well? why, *I know nothing by myself, yet am I not thereby justified.*" This meaning of 'by' does not appear in our ordinary dictionaries), **but I am not hereby justified** (i. e. it is not *this circumstance* which clears me of blame—*this* does not decide the matter. There can be no reference (as Meyer) to *forensic justification* here, by the very conditions of the context: for he is speaking of that μισθός of the teacher, which may be lost, and yet personal salvation be attained, see ch. iii. 15); **but he that judges** (holds an enquiry on) **me is the Lord** (Christ, the judge). **5.] So then** (because the Lord is the sole infallible dijudicator) **decide nothing** (con-

μὴ [u] πρὸ [u] καιροῦ τι κρίνετε, ἕως ἂν ἔλθῃ ὁ κύριος, ὃς καὶ
[v] φωτίσει τὰ [w] κρυπτὰ τοῦ σκότους καὶ [x] φανερώσει τὰς
[yz] βουλὰς τῶν [z] καρδιῶν, καὶ τότε ὁ [a] ἔπαινος [b] γενήσεται
ἑκάστῳ [b] ἀπὸ τοῦ θεοῦ.
6 Ταῦτα δέ, ἀδελφοί, [c] μετεσχημάτισα εἰς ἐμαυτὸν καὶ
Ἀπολλὼ δι' ὑμᾶς, ἵνα [d] ἐν ἡμῖν μάθητε [e] τὸ μὴ [f] ὑπὲρ ἃ

u Matt. viii. 29 only. Sir. xxx. 24. v — 2 Tim. i. 10 only. Jos. Antt. viii. 5. 3. (John i. 9 al.) w Rom. ii. 16 reff. x Rom. i. 19 reff. y plur., here only. 2 Chron. xxii. 5 al. z Sir. xxxvii. 13. a Rom. ii. 29 (reff.). b ch. i. 30 reff. c 2 Cor. xi. 13, 14, 15. Phil. iii. 21 only †. 1 Kings xxviii. 8 Symm. Jos. Antt. vii. 10. 5. d = John xiii. 35. Gen. xlii. 33. e = Rom. viii. 26 reff. f = ch. x. 13. 2 Cor. xii. 6.

5. κρινεται (*itacism?*) APℵ 3. 17. 39. 48. 72. om ος D[1][and lat] F Aug$_{sæpe}$ (ins$_1$). om last του D l.

6. om δε ℵ[1](ins ℵ-corr[1]) arm. om εις F[-gr]. απολλων A B[1](απο πολλων B[2]) ℵ[1]: txt CDFLP ℵ-corr[1](?)[3] rel [Euthal-ms]. εν υμιν D[1][and lat[2]] l 17. 23. 115 syr copt Chr$_1$[txt$_2$] Antch$_1$. om το F 2. rec (for ἃ) ὃ, with DFL rel Syr goth arm Chr$_3$ Thdrt [Cyr-p$_1$ Damasc]: txt ABCPℵ 17 syr copt Ath$_1$ Chr-ms$_1$ Cyr[-p$_1$]. (*Meyer and De W. think that ἃ has been a corrn to suit ταυτα preceding. But I can hardly think this probable: is it not more likely that in a proverbial exprn the sing seemed most appropriate, and thus ἃ has been corrd to ὃ?*)

cerning us, of merit or demerit) **before the time, until the Lord shall have come** (explains πρὸ καιρ.), **who shall also** (καί, *inter alia:* as part of the proceedings of that Day: or both) **bring to light** (throw light on) **the hidden things of darkness** (general—*all things* which are hidden in darkness), **and shall make manifest the counsels of the hearts** (then first shewing, what your teachers really are, in heart), **and then shall the** (fitting) **praise accrue to each from God. ἔπαινος** is not a *vox media,* praise or blame, as the case may be, but strictly *praise.* Theophyl., Grot., Billr., Rück., Olsh., suppose the word to be used euphemistically, "unde et contrarium datur intelligi, sed mavult εὐφημεῖν," Grot.: Calv., Meyer, al., think that he speaks without reference to those who will obtain *no praise:* "hæc vox ex bonæ conscientiæ fiducia nascitur." Calv. But I agree with De Wette, in thinking that he refers to καυχᾶσθαι ἐν ἀνθρώποις:—they, their various parties, gave *exaggerated praise* to certain teachers: let them wait till the day when the *fitting* praise (be it what it may) will be adjudged to each from God; Christ as the Judge being the ὡρισμένος ὑπὸ τοῦ θεοῦ κριτής, Acts x. 42, and so His sentences being ἀπὸ θεοῦ. See also Acts xvii. 31, and Rom. ii. 16, κρινεῖ ὁ θεὸς τὰ κρυπτὰ τῶν ἀνθρώπων, . . . διὰ Ἰησοῦ χριστοῦ.

6—13.] *He explains to them* (ver. 6) *that the mention hitherto of himself and Apollos* (and by parity of reasoning, of Cephas and of Christ, in ch. i. 12) *has a more general design, viz. to abstract them from all party spirit and pride: which pride he then blames, and puts to shame by depicting, as a contrast, the low and afflicted state of the Apostles themselves.*

6.] **But** (transeuntis: he comes to the conclusion of what he has to say on their party divisions) **these things** (De Wette, Meyer, al., limit ταῦτα to what has been said since ch. iii. 5. But there surely is no reason for this. The Apostle's meaning here must on all hands be acknowledged to be, 'I have taken our two names as samples that you may not attach yourselves to and be proud of *any* party leaders, one against another.' And if these *two* names which had been last mentioned, why not analogously, *those four which he had also alleged in ch.* i. 12? There can be no reason against this, except the determination of the Germans to regard their Paulus-parthei, and Apollos-parthei, and Petrus-parthei, and Christus-parthei, as historical facts, and consequent unwillingness to part with them here, where the Apostle himself by implication repudiates them as such) **I transferred** (the epistolary aorist) **to myself and Apollos** (i. e. when I might have set them before you generally and in the abstract as applying to all teachers, I have preferred doing so by taking two samples, and *transferring to them* what was true of the whole. This is far more probable than the explanation of Chrys., al., that he put * in his own name and that of Apollos instead of those of the real leaders of sects, concealing them on purpose. On μετασχ., see reff. and cf. Plato, Legg. x. p. 903, μετασχηματίζων τὰ πάντα οἷον ἐκ πυρὸς ὕδωρ,—and p. 906, τοῦτο τὸ ῥῆμα μετεσχηματισμένον, Meyer) **on your account, that ye by us** (as your example: by having our true office and standing set before you) **might learn this, "Not above those things which are written"** (i. e. not to exceed in your estimate of yourselves and us, the standard of Scrip-

γέγραπται, [g] ἵνα μὴ [h] εἷς ὑπὲρ τοῦ [h] ἑνὸς [i] φυσιοῦσθε κατὰ
[k] τοῦ ἑτέρου. 7 τίς γάρ σε [l] διακρίνει; τί δὲ ἔχεις ὃ οὐκ
ἔλαβες; εἰ δὲ καὶ ἔλαβες, τί [m] καυχᾶσαι ὡς μὴ λαβών;
8 ἤδη [n] κεκορεσμένοι ἐστέ, ἤδη [o] ἐπλουτήσατε, χωρὶς ἡμῶν

ABCDF LPℵ a b c d e f g h k l m n o 17. 47

g w. indic. pres., Gal. iv. 17. Tit. ii. 4. 1 John v. 20. h 1 Thess. v. 11. i vv. 18, 19. ch. v. 2. viii. 1. xiii. 4. Col. ii. 18 only †. (-ωσις, 2 Cor. xii. 20.) k Rom. ii. 1 reff. l = here only. see Acts xv. 9 reff. m absol., ch. i. 29 reff. n Acts xxvii. 38 only. Deut. xxxi. 20 only. o 2 Cor. viii. 9. Rev. iii. 17, 18. Luke xii. 21. Hos. xii. 8.

rec aft γεγραπται ins φρονειν, with C(appy) D[3][-gr] LPℵ[3] rel syrr goth arm Chr_3 $Cyr[-p_2]$ Thdrt [$Antch_1$ Damasc]: om ABD[1]Fℵ[1] latt Orig[$-c_1$ Ambrst Aug]. om 2nd μη D. for υπερ, κατα F.

ture,—which had been already in part shewn to them in the citations ch. i. 19, 31; iii. 19. To refer γέγραπται to *what has been written in this Epistle*, as Luth., Calov., Calv. (altern.), is quite inadmissible, for, as Grot. remarks, "γέγραπται in his libris semper ad libros Veteris Testamenti refertur." But he (and Olsh.) refer the words to Deut. xvii. 20,—whereas it is far better to give them a perfectly general reference. Chrys., Theodoret, and Theophyl. refer it to *words of our Lord in the N. T.*, such as Matt. vii. 1, 3; xxiii. 12; Mark x. 43, 44, but these could not be indicated by γέγραπται,—cf. ch. vii. 10 and note. The ellipsis, as here, of the *verb* in prohibitory clauses, with μή, is common enough: thus, Aristoph. Vesp. 1179, μή μοί γε μύθους. Soph. Antig. 577, μὴ τριβὰς ἔτι, ἀλλά νιν κομίζετ' εἴσω. Demosth. Phil. i. p. 46, μή μοι μυρίους μηδὲ δισμυρίους ξένους. Hartung, Partikellehre ii. 153, where see more examples), **that ye may not one on behalf of another be puffed up against a third** (i. e. 'that you may not adhere together in parties to the detriment or disparagement of a neighbour who is attached to a different party'). There is a grammatical difficulty here, the occurrence of ἵνα with an indic. pres. This is variously explained. See Winer, edn. 6, § 41. *b.* 1. c. Some suppose that here, and in ref. Gal. St. Paul has commited a philological error in the formation of the subjunctive, and written the indic. for it. It is at least remarkable, that that other instance, ἵνα αὐτοὺς ζηλοῦτε, is *also* in the case of a contracted syllable in ου,—so that we might almost suppose that there was some provincial usage of forming the subj. of contracted verbs in οω, which our Apostle followed. At all events (especially considering that we have two other cases of ἵνα with an indic., see reff.) it is better to suppose a solecism or peculiar usage, than with Meyer to give ἵνα a local sense,—'*where*,' i. e. 'in which *case ye are not* (pres. for the future) *puffed up*,'—i. e. if you keep to the Scripture measure: the double ἵνα of the purpose being, as he himself observes, according to Paul's usage, Rom. vii. 13; Gal. iii. 14; iv. 5, al., and here being absolutely demanded by the sense. 7.] **For** (reason why this puffing up should be avoided) **who separates thee** (distinguishes thee from others? meaning, that all such conceits of pre-eminence are unfounded. That *pre-eminence*, and not merely distinction (Meyer), is meant, is evident from what follows)? **And** (δέ *connects interrogative clauses*, as Od. α. 225, τίς δαίς, τίς δὲ ὅμιλος ὅδ' ἔπλετο; and Il. ε. 704, ἔνθα τίνα πρῶτον, τίνα δ' ὕστατον ἐξενάριξεν; See Hartung, Partikellehre, i. 169) **what hast thou which thou receivedst not** ('*from God*'—not, 'from me as thy father in the faith')? **but if** (which I concede;—στέγαι δὲ εἰ καὶ ἡμῖν αὐτοῖς εἰσιν, ἀλλὰ μὰ Δί' οὐχ ἵπποις; Xen. Cyr. vi. 1. 14. Hartung, i. 140) **thou receivedst it**, &c. He speaks not only to the leaders, but to the members of parties,—who imagined themselves superior to those of other parties,—as if all, for every good thing, were not dependent on God the Giver.

8.] The admonition becomes ironical: 'You behave as if the trial were past, and the goal gained; as if hunger and thirst after righteousness were already filled, and the kingdom already brought in.' κωμῳδῶν αὐτοὺς ἔλεγεν Οὕτω ταχέως πρὸς τὸ τέλος ἐφθάσατε, ὅπερ ἀδύνατον ἦν γενέσθαι διὰ τὸν καιρόν. Chrys. Hom. xii. p. 138. The emphases are on ἤδη in the two first clauses, and χωρὶς ἡμῶν in the third. The three verbs form a climax. Any interpretation which stops short of the full meaning of the words as applied to the triumphant final state (so Grot., Est., Calvin., Wetst., al., interpreting them of *knowledge*, of *security*, of the *lordship of one sect over another*), misses the force of the irony, and the meaning of the latter part of the verse. **χωρὶς ἡμῶν**] 'because *we, as* your fathers in Christ, have ever looked forward to *present you*, as our glory and joy, in that day.' There is an exquisite delicacy of irony, which Chrys. has well caught: πολλὴ ἔμφασις ἐνταῦθα καὶ πρὸς τοὺς διδασκάλους κ. πρὸς τοὺς μαθητάς. καὶ τὸ ἀσυνείδητον δὲ αὐτῶν δείκνυται κ. τὸ

[p] ἐβασιλεύσατε. καὶ [q] ὄφελόν γε [p] ἐβασιλεύσατε, ἵνα καὶ
ἡμεῖς ὑμῖν [r] συμβασιλεύσωμεν. 9 [s] δοκῶ γάρ, ὁ θεὸς
ἡμᾶς τοὺς ἀποστόλους ἐσχάτους [t] ἀπέδειξεν ὡς [u] ἐπιθανατίους, ὅτι [v] θέατρον ἐγενήθημεν τῷ κόσμῳ καὶ ἀγγέλοις
καὶ ἀνθρώποις. 10 ἡμεῖς [w] μωροὶ διὰ χριστόν, ὑμεῖς δὲ
[x] φρόνιμοι ἐν χριστῷ· ἡμεῖς [w] ἀσθενεῖς, ὑμεῖς δὲ [w] ἰσχυροί·
ὑμεῖς [y] ἔνδοξοι, ἡμεῖς δὲ [z] ἄτιμοι. 11 [a] ἄχρι [b] τῆς [b] ἄρτι ὥρας
καὶ [c] πεινῶμεν καὶ διψῶμεν καὶ [d] γυμνιτεύομεν καὶ [e] κο-

p = Rom. v. 17. ch. xv. 25. Rev. v. 10. xx. 4, 6. xxii. 5.
q 2 Cor. xi. 1. Gal. v. 12. Rev. iii. 15 only. 4 Kings v. 3. Job xiv. 13. Ps. cxviii. 5 only.
r 2 Tim. ii. 12 only †.
s ch. iii. 18 reff.
t Acts ii. 22 reff. (-ξις, ch. ii. 4.)
u here only †. see note.
v = here (Acts xix. 29, 31) only †.
w ch. i. 25 reff. (see ch. ii. 3, 14.)
x Rom. xi. 25 al. Prov. xi. 12. iron., 2 Cor. xi. 19.
y Luke vii. 25. xiii. 17. Eph. v. 27 only. 1 Kings ix. 6 al.
z Matt. xiii. 57. Mark vi. 4. ch. xii. 23 only. Isa. liii. 3.
a Rom. viii. 22 reff.
b here only.
c Rom. xii. 20 reff.
d here only †.
e Matt. xxvi. 67 ‖ Mk. 2 Cor. xii. 7. 1 Pet. ii. 20 only †.

8. om *χωρ. ημ. εβασ.* (*hom*) A [om *και οφ. γε εβασ.* (*hom*) m n]. *ωφελον* D³L l. om *γε* D¹F. ins *συν* bef *υμιν* D¹.

9. rec aft *δοκω γαρ* ins *οτι*, with D³[-gr] LPℵ³ rel [vulg-clem fuld² harl syrr copt goth arm $Orig_1$] Chr_1 Thdrt $Ambr_1$ [Ambrst Pel] : om ABC D¹[and lat] Fℵ¹ am(with demid fuld¹ tol) $Clem_1$ Orig[-c_1-int_1] Damasc Thl $Tert_1$ [Hil_1].

11. for *αχρι της*, *εως* F. rec *γυμνητευομεν* (*see note*), with L rel [Euthal-ms] : txt A² B²(sic : see table) CD³FPℵ a g h m, *γυμνειτευομεν* B¹[D¹].—om *γυμν. και* A¹.

σφόδρα ἀνόητον. ὃ γὰρ λέγει, τοῦτό ἐστιν. ἐν μὲν τοῖς πόνοις φησὶν εἶναι πάντα κοινὰ καὶ ἡμῖν κ. ὑμῖν, ἐν δὲ τοῖς ἐπάθλοις κ. τοῖς στεφάνοις ὑμεῖς πρῶτοι. p. 99. The latter part of the verse is said *bonâ fide* and with solemnity: **And I would indeed** (γε strengthens the wish; so ἡ δ' εἵλεθ' . . . ὥς γε μήποτ' ὤφελεν λαβεῖν . . . Μενέλαον, Eur. Iph. Aul. 70. Hartung, i. 373. **ὄφελον** is used in LXX and N. T. as a particle, with the indic.: also with optative. See, for both, reff.) **that ye did reign** (that the kingdom of the Lord was actually come, and ye reigning with Him), **that we also might reign together with you** (that we, though deposed from our *proper place*, might at least be vouchsafed a humble share in your kingly glory). **9.**] **For** (and there is abundant reason for this wish in our present afflicted state) **I think,—God set forth** (before the eyes of the world,—the similitude is in θέατρον following) **us the Apostles** (meaning all the Apostles, principally himself and Apollos) **last** (the rendering of Erasm., Calv., Beza, al., *us who were last called to be Apostles*, q. d. τοὺς ἀπ. τοὺς ἐσχ., or τοὺς ἐσχ. ἀποστ.,—is ungrammatical. **ἐσχάτους**, *last and vilest*: not, 'respectu priorum,' *last, as the prophets were before us*, as Corn.-a-lap., and in part, Bengel) **as persons condemned to death** (ὡς καταδίκους, Chrys. Tertullian seems to define the meaning too closely when, De Pudic. 14, vol. ii. p. 1006, he interprets it '*veluti bestiarios.*' Dion. Hal. vii. 35, says of the Tarpeian rock, ὅθεν αὐτοῖς ἔθος βάλλειν τοὺς ἐπιθανατίους)—**for we are become a spectacle** (θέατρον = θέαμα: so Achilles Tatius, i. p. 55 (Kypke), and θέατρα ποιητῶν, Æschines, Dial. Socr. iii. 20:—see θεατριζόμενοι, Heb. x. 33) **to the world, as well to angels** (*good angels*: ἄγγελοι absol., never either includes, or signifies, *bad angels*) **as to men** (κόσμῳ being afterwards specialized into angels and men). **10.**] Again, the bitterest irony: 'how different our lot from yours! How are you to be envied—we, to be pitied!' There is a distinction in διὰ χριστόν and ἐν χριστῷ—q. d. **We are foolish for Christ's sake** (on account of Christ,—our connexion with Him does nothing but reduce us to be fools), **whereas you are φρόνιμοι ἐν χριστῷ**, have entered into full participation of Him, and grown up to be wise, subtle Christians. **ἀσθενεῖς—ἰσχυροί** are both to be understood *generally*: the ἀσθένεια is not here that of *persecution*, but that of ch. ii. 3: the *strength* is the high bearing of the Corinthians. **Ye are in honour** (in glorious repute, party leaders and party men, highly honoured and looked up to), **whereas we are despised** (without honour). Then ἄτιμοι leads him to enlarge on the disgrace and contempt which the Apostle met with at the hands of the world. **11—13.**] *He enters into the particulars of this state of affliction, which was not a thing past, but enduring to the present moment.*

11.] **ἄχρι τ. ἄρτι ὥρας** is evidently not to be taken strictly as indicative of the situation of Paul *at the time of writing* the Epistle, but as generally describing the kind of life to which, then and always, he and the other Apostles were exposed: οὐ παλαιὰ διηγοῦμαι πράγματα, ἀλλ' ἅπερ

λαφιζόμεθα καὶ [f] ἀστατοῦμεν, 12 καὶ [g] κοπιῶμεν [hi] ἐργαζόμενοι ταῖς ἰδίαις [i] χερσίν· [k] λοιδορούμενοι [l] εὐλογοῦμεν,
[m] διωκόμενοι [n] ἀνεχόμεθα, 13 [o] δυςφημούμενοι [p] παρακαλοῦ-
μεν· ὡς [q] περικαθάρματα τοῦ κόσμου ἐγενήθημεν, πάντων [r] περίψημα [s] ἕως [s] ἄρτι. 14 οὐκ [t] ἐντρέπων ὑμᾶς γράφω
ταῦτα, ἀλλ' ὡς τέκνα μου [u] ἀγαπητὰ [v] νουθετῶ. 15 ἐὰν

ABCDF LPℵ a b c d e f g h k l m n o 17. 47

f here only †. g Rom. xvi. 6, 12 reff. h = Acts xviii. 3 reff. i Eph. iv. 28. 1 Thess. iv. 11. Wisd. (iii. 14) xv. 17. k Acts xxiii. 4 reff. l = Rom. xii. 14 reff. m = Matt. v. 10, &c. ch. xv. 9. 2 Kings xxi. 5. n absol., 2 Cor. xi. 4. (Acts xviii. 14 reff.) o here only †. 1 Macc. vii. 41 only. (-μία, 2 Cor. vi. 8.) p absol., Luke iii. 18. Rom. xii. 8. 2 Cor. v. 20. 2 Tim. iv. 2 al. q here only. Prov. xxi. 18 only. r here only †. Tobit v. 18 (19) only. Jer. xxii. 28 Schol. ap. Tromm.[? Symm.] s Matt. xi. 12. John ii. 10. v. 17. xvi. 24. ch. viii. 7. xv. 6. 1 John ii. 9 only. t act., here only. = pass., 2 Thess. iii. 14. Tit. ii. 8 only. Ps. xxxiv. 26. (mid., Luke xviii. 2 al.) u Rom. i. 7 reff. v Acts xx. 31 reff. P.

12. λοιδορ. και ευλ. and διωκ. και ανεχ. F (Syr) Orig-int$_1$.

13. rec **βλασφημουμενοι** (*substitution of more usual word*), with BDFLℵ^3 rel [vulg] Orig$_2$[-int$_1$] Chr$_1$ Thdrt [Ambrst]: txt ACPℵ^1 17 Clem$_1$ Orig$_3$ Eus$_2$ Cyr[-p$_1$] Damasc. περικαθαρμα (for -ματα) D^1[-gr harl^1].

14. ταυτα bef γραφω DF k latt [lat-ff]. αλλα B(C doubtful). νουθετων ACPℵ 17 Thl-txt: txt BDFL rel latt [Chr$_1$ Thdrt Damasc Ambrst].

καὶ ὁ παρὼν μοι καιρὸς μαρτυρεῖ. Chrys. See, on the subject-matter, 2 Cor. xi. 23—27. **γυμνιτ.**] **are in want of sufficient clothing**: cf. ἐν ψύχει κ. γυμνότητι, 2 Cor. xi. 27. Meyer (after Fritzsche) believes γυμνιτεύομεν to be a mistake in writing the word, of very ancient date: but surely we are not justified, in such a conventional matter as the form of writing a word, to desert the unanimous testimony of the oldest MSS. And we have the forms γυμνίτης, and γυμνῖτις: why not then γυμνιτεύω? **κολαφ.**] **are buffeted**—see reff., there is no need to press the strict meaning. **ἀστατ.**] τουτέστιν, ἐλαυνόμεθα, φεύγομεν. Theophyl. **12.**] As testimonies to *Paul's* working with his own hands, see Acts xviii. 3; xx. 34; ch. ix. 6; 1 Thess. ii. 9; 2 Thess. iii. 8. That the other Apostles did the same, need not *necessarily* be inferred from this passage, for he may be describing the state of all by himself as a sample; but it is conceivable, and indeed probable, that they did. **λοιδ. . . . κ.τ.λ.**] 'So far are we from vindicating to ourselves places of earthly honour and distinction, that we tamely submit to reproach, persecution, and evil repute;—nay, we return blessing, and patience, and soft words.' **13.**] **παρακ.**, ἀντὶ τοῦ, πραοτέροις λόγοις κ. μαλακτικοῖς ἀμειβόμεθα. Theophyl. **ὡς περικαθάρματα**] A climax of disgrace and contempt, summing up the foregoing particulars. **We are become as it were the refuse of the world.** περικ. from περικαθαίρω, that which is removed by a thorough purification, the offal or refuse. So Ammonius (in Wetst.): καθάρματα, τὰ μετὰ τὸ καθαρθῆναι ἀποῤῥιπτόμενα:—Theophylact, ὅταν ῥυπαρόν τι ἀποσπογγίσῃ τις, περικάθαρμα λέγεται τὸ ἀποσπόγγισμα ἐκεῖνον: and similarly Œcum. Wetst. gives many examples of the metaphorical usage of the term κάθαρμα as a reproach, from Demosth., Aristoph., Lucian, al., and of *purgamentum* in Latin. περικαθάρματα is found in Arrian, Epict. iii. 22, Πρίαμος, ὁ νῦν γεννήσας περικαθάρματα. But Luther and very many Commentators suppose the word to imply *piacula*, as Schol., Aristoph. Plut. 454 (Wetst.), καθάρματα ἐλέγοντο οἱ ἐπὶ καθάρσει λοιμοῦ τινος ἤ τινος ἑτέρας νόσου θυόμενοι τοῖς θεοῖς, τοῦτο δὲ τὸ ἔθος καὶ παρὰ Ῥωμαίοις ἐπεκράτησε. Meyer well remarks that **περικαθάρματα** will hardly bear this meaning, and that περίψημα in the sing. would not suit it. Still we may remark, with Stanley, that **περικάθαρμα** is so used in ref. Prov., and **περίψημα** in ref. Tobit: and that Suidas says, περίψημα . . . ., οὕτως ἐπέλεγον τῷ κατ' ἐνιαυτὸν συνέχοντι τῶν κακῶν Περίψημα ἡμῶν γένου· ἤτοι, σωτηρία καὶ ἀπολύτρωσις· καὶ οὕτως ἐνέβαλον τῇ θαλάσσῃ ὡσανεὶ τῷ Ποσειδῶνι θυσίαν ἀποτίννυντες.

περίψ.] much the same as περικαθάρματα,—but the expression is more contemptuous:—the individual περικαθάρματα are generalized into one περίψημα, the τοῦ κόσμου is even further extended to πάντων,—see ch. iii. 22. **14—21.**] *Conclusion of this part of the Epistle:—in what spirit he has written these words of blame: viz. in a spirit of admonition, as their father in the faith, whom they ought to imitate. To this end he sent Timothy to remind them of his ways of teaching,—would soon, however, come himself,—in mildness, or to punish, as the case might require.* **14. οὐκ ἐντρέπων**] **not as one who shames you**, see reff., and ch. vi. 5; xv. 34,—and for the force of the participle, ch. ii. 1. **νουθετῶ** contrasts with **ἐντρέπων γράφω**, the construction being purposely adopted, to set in a more vivid light the paternal inten-

γὰρ [w] μυρίους [x] παιδαγωγοὺς ἔχητε ἐν χριστῷ, [y] ἀλλ᾽ οὐ
πολλοὺς πατέρας· ἐν γὰρ χριστῷ Ἰησοῦ διὰ τοῦ εὐαγγελίου ἐγὼ ὑμᾶς [z] ἐγέννησα. 16 [a] παρακαλῶ οὖν ὑμᾶς,
[b] μιμηταί μου γίνεσθε. 17 διὰ τοῦτο ἔπεμψα [c] ὑμῖν Τιμόθεον,
ὅς ἐστίν μου τέκνον [u] ἀγαπητὸν καὶ [d] πιστὸν ἐν [d] κυρίῳ, ὃς
ὑμᾶς [e] ἀναμνήσει τὰς [f] ὁδούς μου τὰς ἐν χριστῷ, καθὼς
[g] πανταχοῦ ἐν πάσῃ ἐκκλησίᾳ διδάσκω. 18 [h] ὡς μὴ ἐρχο-

w ch. xiv. 19. Matt. xviii. 24 only. Esther iii. 9.
x Gal. iii. 24, 25 only †.
y = Rom. vi. 5. ch. ix. 2. 2 Cor. xi. 6. xiii. 4. 1 Macc. ii. 19, 20.
z = Philem. 10.
a ver. 13.
b ch. xi. 1. Eph. v. 1. 1 Thess. i. 6. ii. 14. Heb. vi. 12 only †. (-μεῖσθαι, 2 Thess. iii. 7, 9.)
c dat., Acts xi. 29. Phil. ii. 19.
d see Eph. i. 1. Acts xvi. 15.
e Mark xi. 21. xiv. 72. 2 Cor. vii. 15. 2 Tim. i. 6. Heb. x. 32 only. Gen. viii. 1 Ed-vat. compl. [B def.] (-μνησις, ch. xi. 24.)
f = ch. xii. 31. see Acts xiii. 10 reff.
g Acts xvii. 30 reff.
h w. gen. abs., 2 Cor. v. 20. 2 Pet. i. 3. Soph. Œd. Tyr. 11. Winer, edn. 6, § 65. 9.

15. om *ιησου* B $Clem_1$ Pac_1 : ins ACDFL[P]ℵ rel vulg Syr $Orig\text{-}int_4$.
16. for *ουν*, *δε* D¹[-gr] F[-gr].
17. aft *τουτο* ins *αυτο* APℵ¹ 17 syr [Euthal-ms]. rec *τεκνον* bef *μου* (*corrn to more usual order*), with DFL rel latt Orig[-c_1] Thdrt Thl Œc lat-ff: txt ABCPℵ m 17 arm [Euthal-ms] Chr Damasc. **πιστος** F. A [has not] *χριστω* for *κυριω* [as Woide]. *αναμιμνησει*(sic) A a¹. for *χριστω*, *χρ. ιησου* C D²[-gr] ℵ b m o 17 vulg-ed [fuld harl arm] syr copt Chr_1 Damasc [Ambrst]: *κυριω ιησ.* D¹[and lat] F : txt AB D³[-gr] LP rel am(with demid [tol]) Syr Orig[-c_1] Thdrt Thl Œc.

tion:—**I am not writing these things** (vv. 8—13) **as shaming you,—but I am admonishing you as my beloved children.**

15.] Justification of the expression *τέκνα μου*. **μυρίους**, the greatest possible number—see reff. **παιδαγ.**] He was their spiritual *father:* those who followed, Apollos included, were but *tutors*, having the care and education of the children, but not the rights, as they could not have the peculiar affection of the father. He evidently shews by *μυρίους*, that these *παιδαγωγοί* were *more in number than he could wish*,—including among them doubtless the false and party teachers: but to refer the word *only* to them and their despotic leading (as Beza, Calvin, al., and De Wette), or to confine its meaning to the stricter sense of *παιδαγωγός*, *the slave who led the child to school*, is not here borne out by the facts. See ref. and note: and for the wider sense of *παιδαγ.*, examples in Wetst. **ἀλλ᾽ οὐ** brings out the contrast strongly, giving almost the sense of '*at non ideo:*' so Æsch. in Ctes. § 155, *καὶ γὰρ ἐὰν αὐτὰ διεξίῃ τὰ ἐκ τοῦ ψηφίσματος προστάγματα, ἀλλ᾽ οὐ τόγ᾽ ἐκ τῆς ἀληθείας αἰσχρὸν σιωπηθήσεται.* See Hartung, Partikellehre, ii. 40. **ἐν γὰρ χρ.**] **For in Christ Jesus** (as the spiritual element in which the begetting took place: so commonly *ἐν χριστῷ*, applied to relations of life, see ver. 17, bis,—not to be joined as De W. with *ἐγώ*, q. d. *ἐγὼ γὰρ ἐν χ. Ἰησοῦ δ. τ. εὐ. ὑμ. ἐγέννησα*) **by means of the gospel** (the preached word being the instrument) **I** (emphatic) **begat you** (there is also an emphasis on *ὑμᾶς*, as coming before the verb, q. d. in *your case, I* it was who begat you). **16.**] **οὖν**, because I am *your father*. **μιμηταί**, not only, nor perhaps chiefly, in the things *just mentioned*, vv. 9—13,—but as ver. 17, in *αἱ ὁδοί μου αἱ ἐν χρ.*, *my manner of life and teaching*. See reff. **17.**] **διὰ τοῦτο**,—in order that you may the better imitate me by being put in mind of my ways and teaching: not, as Chrys., Theophyl., al., *ἐπειδὴ ὡς παίδων κήδομαι, καὶ ὡς γεγεννηκώς*,—which would make ver. 16 a very harsh parenthesis, and destroy the force of what follows. On the *fact*, see Prolegg. to 2 Cor., § ii. 4. **τέκνον**] see 1 Tim. i. 2, 18; 2 Tim. i. 2. Meyer remarks, that by the strict use of the word *τέκνον* in this passage (vv. 14, 15) we have a certain proof that Timothy was *converted by Paul:* see Acts xiv. 6, 7 and note. "The phrase seems to be used here in reference to *τέκνα ἀγαπητά*, ver. 14: 'I sent Timotheus, who stands to me in the same relation that you stand (in).'" Stanley. **ἐν κυρίῳ** points out the spiritual nature of the relationship. **ἀναμνήσει**] Timothy, by being himself a close imitator of the Christian virtues and teaching of his and their spiritual father, would bring to their minds his well-known character, and way of teaching, which they seemed to have well-nigh forgotten. See 2 Tim. iii. 10. **καθώς** specifies what before was expressed generally: so Luke xxiv. 19, 20, *τὰ περὶ Ἰησοῦ . . . .* **ὅπως** *τε παρέδωκαν αὐτὸν οἱ ἀρχιερεῖς κ.τ.λ.*; and Thucyd. i. 1, *τὸν πόλεμον τῶν Πελ. κ. Ἀθ.*, **ὡς** *ἐπολέμησαν πρὸς ἀλλήλους*. **πανταχοῦ ἐν π. ἐκκλ.**] To shew the importance of this his manner of teaching, he reminds them of his *unvarying* practice of it: and as he was guided by the Spirit, by inference, of its

μένου δέ μου πρὸς ὑμᾶς [i] ἐφυσιώθησάν [k] τινες· 19 ἐλεύσομαι δὲ ταχέως πρὸς ὑμᾶς, [l] ἐὰν ὁ [l] κύριος [l] θελήσῃ,
καὶ γνώσομαι οὐ τὸν [m] λόγον τῶν [i] πεφυσιωμένων, ἀλλὰ
τὴν [m] δύναμιν· 20 οὐ γὰρ ἐν [m] λόγῳ ἡ [n] βασιλεία τοῦ [n] θεοῦ,
ἀλλ' [o] ἐν δυνάμει. 21 τί θέλετε; [pq] ἐν [qr] ῥάβδῳ ἔλθω πρὸς
ὑμᾶς, ἢ [p] ἐν ἀγάπῃ, [s] πνεύματί τε [t] πραΰτητος;

...ταχεως e.
ABCDF LPℵ a b c d f g h k l m n o 17. 47

i ver. 6 reff. k = 2 Cor. iii. 1. x. 2. Gal. i. 7. ii. 12. 1 Tim. i. 3, &c. l James iv. 15. Sir. xxxix. 6. m 1 Thess. i. 5. see Rom. xv. 18 reff. n = Rom. xiv. 17. o Rom. i. 4 reff. p = ch. v. 8. 2 Cor. ii. 1. Eph. i. 8. iii. 12. iv. 15, 17 al. q Rev. ii. 27. Isa. x. 24. r Matt. x. 10 ‖. Heb. i. 8 al. s Rom. xi. 8 reff. t Paul (2 Cor. x. 1. Gal. v. 23. vi. 1 al4.) only, exc. James i. 21. iii. 13. 1 Pet. iii. 15. Ps. xliv. 4.

18. om δε F latt copt lat-ff.

19. θελησει LP [f]. om ου D[1]. aft λογον ins αυτων F. τον πεφυσιωμενον L h m 3. 46[1]-9. 57. 109-16 lectt-7-12 $Orig_1$ (not $Clem_2$ Chr_1 Thdrt [$Sevrn\text{-}c_1$ Damasc] &c).

21. [πνευμα (for -ματι) D[1] (and lat).] rec πραοτητος, with DFLPℵ rel [Euthalms $Clem_1$ $Orig_1$ Chr_1 Thdrt]: txt ABC[1 or 2] 17 Damasc.

universal necessity in the churches.

18—20.] To guard against misrepresentation of the coming of Timothy just announced, by those who had said and would now the more say, 'Paul dare not come to Corinth,' *he announces the certainty of his coming, if the Lord will.* **18.**] **ὡς μὴ ἐρχομένου** forms *one* idea, and the δέ is in consequence placed after it all: so Thucyd. i. 6, ἐν τοῖς πρῶτοι δὲ Ἀθηναῖοι: Isocr. περὶ εἰρ., p. 160, ὅτι ἂν τύχῃ δὲ γενησόμενον. Hartung, Partikellehre, i. 190. ὡς expresses the assumption in their minds: the present part. ἐρχομένου refers to their saying—οὐκ ἔρχεται, as Meyer. **19.**] **ἐλεύσομαι** is prefixed, for emphasis, being the matter in doubt: as we say, 'Come I will.' **ταχέως**] *How* soon, see ch. xvi. 8. **γνώσομαι**] **I will inform myself of—not the words of those who are puffed up** (*those* I care not for), **but their power:** whether they are really mighty in the Spirit, or not. This general reference of δύν. must be kept, and not narrowed, as Chrys., Theophyl., to [the] *power of working miracles:* or "quantum apud vos sua scientia et doctrina quam jactant profecerint," Est.; or *virtuous lives* (Theodoret, al.), or *energy in the work of the gospel* (Meyer): he leaves it general and indefinite. **20.**] *Justification of this his intention by the* very nature *of that kingdom of which he was the ambassador.* **ἡ βασ. τ. θεοῦ,** *the Kingdom* (τ. οὐρ. Matt. iii. 2; iv. 17 and passim; τ. θ. Mark i. 15, al.) announced by the prophets, preached by the Lord and the Apostles, being now prepared on earth and received by those who believe on Christ, and to be consummated when He returns with His saints: see Phil. iii. 20, 21; Eph. v. 5. **ἐν λόγῳ . . . . ἐν δυνάμει . . . . is not** (i. e. does not consist in, has not its conditions and element of existence) **in** (mere) **word, but in power**—is a kingdom of *power.* **21.**] He offers them, with a view to their amendment, the alternative: 'shall his coming be in a judicial or in a friendly spirit?' as depending on themselves. **τί** not for πότερον (as Meyer, De W.), but general, and afterwards confined to the two alternatives: **What will ye** (respecting my coming) **? ἔλθω, must I come? ἐν ῥάβδῳ, with a rod;** but not *only* 'with,' as *accompanied with:* the prep. gives the idea of the element *in which,* much as ἐν δόξῃ: not only *with* a rod, but *in such purpose as to use it.* There is no Hebraism: see Passow under ἐν, No. 3 and 4. He speaks *as a father:* τί ἐστιν, ἐν ῥάβδῳ; ἐν κολάσει, ἐν τιμωρίᾳ, Chrys. **πνεύμ. τ. πραΰτητος**] Generally, and by De Wette, explained, *a gentle spirit,* meaning by πνεύμ, his own spirit: but Meyer has remarked, that in every place in the N. T. where πνεῦμα is joined with an abstract genitive, it imports the Holy Spirit, and the abstract genitive refers to the specific working of the Spirit in the case in hand. So πν. τῆς ἀληθείας (John xv. 26; xvi. 13; 1 John iv. 6), υἱοθεσίας (Rom. viii. 15), τῆς πίστεως (2 Cor. iv. 13), σοφίας (Eph. i. 17), ἁγιωσύνης (Rom. i. 4). (This does not however appear to be without exceptions: cf. πνεῦμα ἀσθενείας, Luke xiii. 11; δουλείας, Rom. viii. 15; κατανύξεως, Rom. xi. 8; δειλίας, 2 Tim. i. 7; τῆς πλάνης, 1 John iv. 6. We may indeed say, that in none of these cases is the πνεῦμα subjective, or the phrase a mere periphrasis: but the πνεῦμα is objective, a possessing, indwelling spirit, whether of God or otherwise.) And so Chrys., Theophyl.,—ἔνι γὰρ καὶ πνεῦμα αὐστηρότητος κ. τιμωρίας, ἀλλ' ἀπὸ τῶν χρηστοτέρων αὐτὸ καλεῖ· ὡς καὶ τὸν θεὸν οἰκτίρμονα κ. ἐλεήμονά φαμεν, ἀλλ' οὐ κολαστήν, καίτοιγε καὶ τοῦτο ὄντα. Theophyl.

V. 1—13.] CONCERNING A GROSS CASE OF INCEST WHICH HAD ARISEN, AND WAS

V. 1 u Ὅλως v ἀκούεται ἐν ὑμῖν w πορνεία, καὶ τοιαύτη
w πορνεία x ἥτις y οὐδὲ ἐν τοῖς ἔθνεσιν, ὥστε γυναῖκά τινα
τοῦ πατρὸς z ἔχειν· 2 a καὶ ὑμεῖς b πεφυσιωμένοι ἐστὲ καὶ
οὐχὶ μᾶλλον c ἐπενθήσατε, d ἵνα e ἀρθῇ f ἐκ f μέσου ὑμῶν ὁ

u Matt. v. 34. ch. vi. 7. xv. 29 only +. v = here only. 2 Macc. x. 13. see Acts xi. 22 reff. w Matt. v. 32. ch. vi. 13, 18 al. Gen. xxxviii. 24. x = Heb. ii. 3. y = Matt. vi. 29. ch. xiv. 21. Gal. ii. 5 al. z = Matt. xiv. 4. xxii. 28. ch. vii. 2, 29. Deut. xxviii. 30. a interrog., Luke x. 29. xviii. 26. John ix. 36. 2 Cor. ii. 2. b ch. iv. 6 reff. c Matt. v. 4. ix. 15. Mark xvi. 10. Luke vi. 25. 2 Cor. xii. 21. James iv. 9. Rev. xviii. 11, 15, 19 only. Isa. lxi. 2. d = John xi. 15. e = Matt. xiii. 12. Luke xi. 22. John ii. 16 al. Isa. lvii. 1, 2. f Acts xvii. 33 reff.

CHAP. V. 1. rec aft εθνεσιν ins ονομαζεται (*see note*), with LPℵ[3] rel syrr Chr_2 [Bas_1 $Cyr\text{-}p_1$ Damasc] Thdrt Cassiod: om ABCDFℵ[1] 17 latt copt æth arm Orig[$-c_1$-int_3 Euthal-ms] $Manes_1$ $Tert_1$ $Lucif_2$ [Ambrst]. του πατρος εχειν bef τινα DF.
2. for ουχι, ου F. rec ἐξαρθη (*corrn from ver* 13), with L rel Chr_1 [Bas_3

HARBOURED, AMONG THEM (vv. 1—8): AND QUALIFICATION OF A FORMER COMMAND WHICH HE HAD GIVEN THEM RESPECTING ASSOCIATION WITH GROSS SINNERS (9—13). The subject of this chapter is bound on to the foregoing by the question of ch. iv. 21: and it furnishes an instance of those things which required his apostolic discipline. **1.] ὅλως, actually,** 'omnino,' see reff.: in negative sentences, 'at all.' **ἀκούεται ἐν ὑμ. πορνεία**] another way of saying ἀκούουσί τινες ἐν ὑμ. πόρνοι,—**the character of πόρνος is borne (by some) among you,—fornication is borne as a character among you.** From missing this sense of ἀκούομαι, Commentators have gone wrong (1) as to ὅλως, rendering it *'commonly,'* to suit ἀκούεται, *'is reported,'*—(2) as to ἐν ὑμῖν, joining it with πορνεία, whereas it belongs to ἀκούεται,—(3) as to ἥτις οὐδὲ ἐν τ. ἔθν., see below. **καὶ τοιαύτ. π.**] **And fornication of such a sort** (the καί rises in a climax, there being an ellipsis of οὐ μόνον . . . , ἀλλὰ . . . . before it; so Aristoph. Ran. 116, ὦ σχέτλιε, τολμήσεις γὰρ ἰέναι καὶ σύ γε; see Hartung, Partikellehre, i. 134), **as (is) not** (borne as a character) **even among the heathen.** The ὀνομάζεται of the rec. is a clumsy gloss, probably from Eph. v. 3: the meaning being, that not even among the heathen does any one ἀκούει πόρνος in this sense, that it was a crime that they would not tolerate as a matter of public notoriety. **So that one among you has** (*as wife* most probably, not merely *as concubine:* the word ἔχω in such cases universally in the N. T. signifying *to possess in marriage:* and Meyer remarks that ὁ τὸ ἔργον τοῦτο ποιήσας (ver. 2), and τὸν οὕτως τοῦτο κατεργασάμενον (ver. 3) seem to point to a consummation of marriage, not to mere concubinage) **his father's wife** (i. e. his step-mother, see Lev. xviii. 8; οὐκ εἶπε μητρυιὰν ἀλλὰ γυναῖκα πατρός, ὥστε πολλῷ χαλεπώτερον πλῆξαι, Chrys. Hom. xv. p. 125). The Commentators generally refer to Cicero, Pro Cluentio, 5, 6, "Nubit genero socrus, nullis auspicibus, nullis auctoribus, funestis ominibus omnium omnibus. O mulieris scelus incredibile, et præter hanc unam, in omni vita inauditum," &c. It may seem astonishing that the authorities in the Corinthian church should have allowed such a case to escape them, or if known, should have tolerated it. Perhaps the universal laxity of morals at Corinth may have weakened the severity even of the Christian elders: perhaps, as has often been suggested, the offender, if a Jewish convert, might defend his conduct by the Rabbinical maxim that in the case of a proselyte, the forbidden degrees were annulled, a *new birth* having been undergone by him (see Maimon. in Wetst.). This latter however is rendered improbable by the fact that the Apostle says nothing of the *woman,* which he would have done had she been a Christian:—and that Jewish maxim was taxed with the condition, that a proselyte might marry any of his or her former relatives, *'modo ad Judaicam religionem transierint.'* The father was living, and is described in 2 Cor. vii. 12, as ὁ ἀδικηθείς;—and from the Apostle saying there that he did not write *on his account,* he was probably a Christian. **2.] καί** often introduces a question, especially one by which something inconsistent or preposterous is brought out,—see reff.: and note on 2 Cor. ii. 2. **πεφυσ. ἐστέ**] Not, which would be absurd,—*at the occurrence of this crime,* οὐκ ἐπὶ τῷ ἁμαρτήματι· τοῦτο γὰρ ἀλογίας. Chrys.: neither, as he proceeds,—ἀλλ' ἐπὶ τῇ διδασκαλίᾳ τῇ ἐκείνου, imagining the offender to have been some party teacher: so also Theophyl.:—but as before, with a notion of their own wisdom and spiritual perfection: the being puffed up is only *cum hoc,* not *propter hoc.* **ἐπενθήσατε**] **And did ye not rather mourn** (viz. when the crime became first known to you), **in order that** (your mourning would be *because of the existence* of the evil, i. e. with *a view to its removal*) **he who did this deed (the**

τὸ ἔργον τοῦτο ποιήσας; 3 ἐγὼ [g] μὲν [g] γὰρ [hi] ἀπὼν τῷ σώματι, [hj] παρὼν δὲ τῷ [k] πνεύματι, ἤδη [l] κέκρικα ὡς [j] παρὼν
τὸν οὕτως τοῦτο [m] κατεργασάμενον, 4 ἐν τῷ ὀνόματι τοῦ
κυρίου ἡμῶν Ἰησοῦ [n] συναχθέντων ὑμῶν καὶ τοῦ ἐμοῦ
[l] πνεύματος σὺν τῇ δυνάμει τοῦ κυρίου ἡμῶν Ἰησοῦ

ABCDF LPℵ a b c d f g h k l m n o 17. 47 vv 4 and 5 are cut away in C.

g = ch. xi. 18. h 2 Cor. x. 2, 11. xiii. 2, 10. Wisd. xi. 11. xiv. 17. i as above (h). Phil. i. 27. Col. ii. 5 only. P. Job vi. 13. Wisd. ix. 6 only. j Acts xii. 20. 2 Cor. xi. 8 al. k Acts xvii. 16 reff. Col. ii. 5. see ch. vii. 34. l = Acts xv. 19 reff. m Rom. ii. 9 reff. n epp., here only. = Acts xiv. 27. xx. 7, 8 al.

Damasc] Thdrt: txt ABCD[F]Pℵ a m 17 [Euthal-ms] Epiph$_1$. for *ποιησ.*, *πραξας* ACℵ m 17 [Euthal-ms] Epiph Bas$_1$: txt BDFLP rel Chr$_1$ [Bas$_3$ Damasc] Thdrt.

3. rec ins *ως* bef *απων* (*to corresp with ως παρων below, it being imagined that απων . . . . . πνευμ. was to be taken together: so Mey*), with D^2[and lat] FL rel syr Dial$_1$ Chr$_1$ [Bas$_1$ Damasc] Thdrt Thl Œc Lucif$_2$ Aug$_2$: om ABC D^1[-gr] Pℵ m 17 vulg [Syr æth] copt Manes[-in-]Epiph$_1$ Orig-int$_1$ [Hil$_1$ Ambrst Aug$_1$ Pel]. om *τουτο* F latt arm Lucif$_2$ [Ambr$_1$].

4. om 1st *ημων* Aℵ demid Lucif$_2$ Pac$_1$ [syr has it w-ast]. rec aft 1st *ιησ.* ins *χριστου*, with D^3[-gr] FLPℵ rel [vulg] Syr syr-w-ast copt goth [æth-pl] arm Dial$_1$ Chr Thdrt [Bas$_1$ Damasc Ambrst]: om AB D^1[and lat] æth-rom Lucif. (C doubtful.) [om 2nd *ημων* P am fuld tol harl Orig$_3$-int$_1$ Bas$_2$ Thdrt-ms$_1$ Lucif$_2$(ins$_1$). syr has it w-ast.] rec aft 2nd *ιησ.* ins *χριστου*, with D^3[-gr] FL rel [Syr syr-w-ast copt goth æth-pl arm] Orig$_2$[-int$_1$] Chr Thdrt [Damasc] Lucif$_1$ Aug$_1$ Pac: om AB D^1[and lat] Pℵ vulg syr-txt æth-rom Orig$_3$[-int$_1$] Dial$_1$ [Bas$_2$ Lucif$_2$].

past part. ποιήσας is *itself used from the past point of time* indicated by ἐπενθήσατε, and must therefore be expressed by the past) **might** (may) **be removed from among you** (viz. by your casting him out from your society)? **3—5.**] justifies the expression ἵνα ἀρθῇ just used, by declaring the *judgment which the Apostle, although absent, had already passed on the offender.* **3.**] ἐγὼ μὲν γάρ, **I for my part . . . . .** 'ego certe:' so Aristoph. Plut. 355, μὰ Δί', ἐγὼ μὲν οὔ: see Hartung, Partikellehre, ii. 413. **ὡς παρών, as if really present**, not, *as being present in spirit.* **τὸν οὕτως τοῦτο κατ.**] The *object* is put foremost for emphasis' sake, and after several intervening clauses, taken up again with τὸν τοιοῦτον, ver. 5. **οὕτως**, Meyer thinks, alludes to *some peculiarly offensive method* in which he had brought about the marriage, which was known to the Corinthians, but unknown to us. Olsh. understands it, '*under such circumstances*,' 'being such as he is, a member of Christ's body.' But this, being before patent, would hardly be thus emphatically denoted. Perhaps after all, τοῦτο κατεργασάμενον refers to πορνεία generally, οὕτως to **τοιαύτη** πορνεία, ver. 1.

4.] We may arrange this sentence in four different ways: (1) ἐν τῷ ὀν. may belong to συναχθέντων, and σὺν τῇ δυν. to παραδοῦναι,—so Beza, Calov., Billroth, Olsh., al.: (2) both ἐν τῷ ὀν. and σὺν τῇ δυν. may belong to συναχθέντων,—so Chrys., Theophyl. (altern.), Calvin (quoting for σὺν τῇ δυν. Matt. xviii. 20), Grot., Rückert: (3) both may belong to παραδοῦναι,—so Mosheim, Schrader, al.: or (4) ἐν τῷ ὀν. belongs to **παραδοῦναι**, and σὺν τῇ δυν. to συναχθέντων,—so Luther, Castal., Estius, Bengel, De Wette, Meyer, al. And this, I am persuaded, is the right arrangement. For according to (2) and (3), the balance of the sentence would be destroyed, no adjunct of authority being given to one member of it, and *both* to the other: and (1) is hardly consistent with the arrangement of the clauses, the parenthetical portion beginning far more naturally with the participle than with ἐν τῷ ὀν.,—not to mention that the common formula of the Apostles' speaking authoritatively, is ἐν τῷ ὀνόματι Ἰησοῦ χρ. or the like: see Acts iii. 16; xvi. 18; 2 Thess. iii. 6. The sentence then will stand:—(I **have decreed**),—**in the name of our Lord Jesus (when ye have been assembled together and my spirit with the power of our Lord Jesus)**, (i. e. 'I myself, in spirit, endowed by our Lord Jesus with apostolic power:' σὺν τῇ δυν. belongs to τοῦ ἐμοῦ πνεύμ., and is not, as in Chrys.,—see above —merely an element in the assembly) **to deliver such an one** (reff.) **to Satan for the destruction of his flesh, that his spirit may be saved in the day of the Lord.** *What does this sentence import?* Not, *mere excommunication*, though it is doubtless *included*. It was a delegation to the Corinthian church of a *special power, reserved to the Apostles themselves*, of *inflicting corporeal death or disease* as a punishment for sin. Of this we have notable examples in the case of Ananias and Sapphira, and Elymas, and another hinted at 1 Tim. i. 20. The congregation itself could αἴρειν ἐκ μέσου,—but it could not παραδοῦναι τῷ σατανᾷ εἰς ὄλεθρον τῆς σαρκός, without the authorized concur-

5 [op] παραδοῦναι τὸν [q] τοιοῦτον τῷ σατανᾷ [p] εἰς [r] ὄλεθρον
τῆς [s] σαρκός, ἵνα τὸ [s] πνεῦμα σωθῇ ἐν τῇ [t] ἡμέρᾳ τοῦ
κυρίου. 6 οὐ καλὸν τὸ [u] καύχημα ὑμῶν. οὐκ οἴδατε ὅτι
[vw] μικρὰ [vx] ζύμη ὅλον τὸ [vy] φύραμα [vz] ζυμοῖ; 7 [a] ἐκκαθά-
ρατε τὴν [b] παλαιὰν [w] ζύμην, ἵνα ἦτε νέον [y] φύραμα, καθώς

o = 1 Tim. i. 20. Luke xxiii. 25. 1 Chron. xii. 17. p Mark xiii. 12. Eph. iv. 19. Isa. liii. 12. q Acts xxii. 22 reff. r 1 Thess. v. 3. 2 Thess. i. 9. 1 Tim. vi. 9 only. Prov. xxi. 7. s Matt. xxvi. 41 || Mk. Rom. ii. 28, 29. viii. 4 al. t ch. i. 8 reff. u Rom. iv. 2 reff. v Gal. v. 9. w = John vii. 33 al. x Matt. xiii. 33. xvi. 6. Exod. xii. 15 al. y Rom. ix. 21 reff. = Exod. viii. 3. z (in N. T. alw. w. ὅλ.) as above (w). Matt. xiii. 33 || L. only. Hos. vii. 4. a 2 Tim. ii. 21 only. Deut. xxvi. 13. Judg. vii. 4 B al. [δοκιμ. A Ald. compl.] only. b Rom. vi. 6 reff. 2 Cor. iii. 14. 1 John ii. 7.

5. for *τον τοιουτ.*, *αυτον* F[-gr Syr syr-mg æth]. rec aft *κυριου* ins *ιησου*, with L$\aleph$ rel am(with tol [flor) æth] Chr_2[(and ms_1) Bas_1] Thl Œc Orig-int_1 Aug_3: *ιησ. χριστου* D demid [Ambrst]: *ημων ιησ. χρ.* AFP m 17 [vulg-clem fuld harl Syr] (*ημων* and *χρ.* syr-w-ast) [copt arm] $Orig_1$[-int_2 Chr_2 Thdor-mops-c_1] Thdrt [$Lucif_2$ $Ambr_2$ Pel]: om B $Orig_3$-int_1[-c_1 Eus_1] $Tert_2$ Hil_2 Aug_1 Pac_2. (*It seems evident that κυριον alone was the origl, and the other varr are additions.*)

6. for *ζυμοι*, *δολοι* D^1-gr Bas-ed Hesych(appy): *corrumpit* vulg D-lat $Iren_1$ Orig-int_2 $Lucif_1$ [Ambrst Aug_2]: txt ABC D^2-gr FLP$\aleph$ rel [$Orig_1$-c_2 $Chr_{sæpe}$ Bas_4 Cyr_1 Euthal-ms Thdrt Damasc].

7. rec aft *εκκαθαρατε* ins *ουν*, with CLP$\aleph^3$ rel syr [æth Cyr-p_1 Euthal-ms Damasc] Thdrt Thl Orig-int_1[-c_1]: om ABDF$\aleph^1$ 1 vulg Syr [copt goth spec] $Clem_1$ Bas_1 Chr_1 Œc Tert $Cypr_2$ $Lucif_1$ Ambrst [Pel].

rence of the Apostle's *πνεύματος, σὺν τῇ δυν. τ. κυρ. ἡμ. Ἰησοῦ.* What the *ὄλεθρος τ. σαρκός* was to be, does not appear: certainly more than the mere destruction of his pride and lust by repentance, as some (Estius, Beza, Grot., al.) suppose: rather, as Chrys., *ἵνα μαστίξῃ αὐτὸν ἕλκει πονηρῷ ἢ νόσῳ ἑτέρᾳ.* Hom. xv. p. 127. Estius's objection to this, that in 2 Cor. ii. and vii. we find no trace of such bodily chastisement, is not to the point,—because we have no proof that this *παράδοσις was ever inflicted*,—nor does the Apostle *command* it, but only describes it as his own determination, held as it were *in terrorem* over the offender. See note on ver. 13.
Obs., **σαρκός**, the offending element, not *σώματος*. Paul could not say *ὄλεθρον τοῦ σώματος*, seeing that the body is to partake of the salvation of the spirit;—but not the *σάρξ*, see ch. xv. 50. **5. ἵνα τὸ πν. σωθῇ]** The aim of the *ὄλεθρ. τ. σαρ.*,—which he said *ἤδη τῷ διαβόλῳ νόμους τιθεὶς, καὶ οὐκ ἀφιεὶς αὐτὸν περαιτέρω προβῆναι*, as Chrys. p. 128. Thus the proposed punishment, severe as it might seem, would be in reality a merciful one, tending to the eternal happiness of the offender. A greater contrast to this can hardly be conceived, than the terrible forms of excommunication subsequently devised, and even now in use in the Romish church, under the fiction of delegated apostolic power. The delivering to Satan *for the destruction of the spirit*, can belong only to those who *do the work of Satan*. Stanley remarks, "For the popular constitution of the early Corinthian church, see Clem. Rom. i. 44 (p. 297): where the rulers of that society are described as having been appointed *συνευδοκησάσης τῆς ἐκκλησίας πάσης.*"
6.] 'How inconsistent with your harbouring such an one, appear your high-flown conceits of yourselves!' **καύχημα, your matter of glorying. Are you not aware that a little leaven imparts a character to the whole lump?** That this is the meaning, and not, 'that a little leaven *will*, if not purged out, leaven the whole lump,' is manifest from the point in hand, viz. the inconsistency of their *boasting*: which would not appear by their *danger of corruption hereafter*, but by their *character* being *actually lost*. One of them was a fornicator of a fearfully depraved kind, tolerated and harboured: by this fact, the *character of the whole was tainted*. **7.]** The **παλαιὰ ζύμη** is not the *man*, but the *crime* attaching to their character as a church, which was a remnant of their unconverted state, their *παλαιὸς ἄνθρωπος*. This they are to purge out from among them. The *ἐκκαθάρ.* alludes to the careful 'purging out' from the houses of every thing leavened before the commencement of the feast of unleavened bread. Schöttgen, Hor. Hebr., in loc., gives a full account of the extreme care with which this was done. See also Stanley's note.
That ye may be a new lump (opposed to the *παλαιὸς ἄνθρωπος* of old and dissolute days), **as ye are** (normally and by your Christian profession) **unleavened** (i.e. dead to sin and free from it). This indicating the state by profession, the *normal state*, as a fact, and the *grounding of exhortations on it*, is common enough with our Apostle,—see Rom. vi. 3, 4: ch. iii. 16, al. freq.,

ἐστε [c] ἄζυμοι· καὶ γὰρ τὸ [de] πάσχα ἡμῶν [ef] ἐτύθη χριστός.
8 [g] ὥςτε [h] ἑορτάζωμεν μὴ [i] ἐν [w] ζύμῃ [b] παλαιᾷ μηδὲ [i] ἐν
[w] ζύμῃ [jk] κακίας καὶ [kl] πονηρίας, ἀλλ' [i] ἐν [c] ἀζύμοις [m] εἰλικρινείας καὶ [n] ἀληθείας.

ABCDF LPℵ a b c d f g h k l m n o 17. 47

c here bis. Matt. xxvi. 17. Mark xiv. 1, 12. Luke xxii. 1, 7. Acts xii. 3. xx. 6 only. Levit. ii. 4, &c.
d Matt. xxvi. 2, &c. ||. 4 Kings xxiii. 22.
e Mark xiv. 12. Luke xxii. 7. Exod. xii. 21.
f of Christ here only. = Acts xiv. 13 reff.
g = ch. xi. 33. xiv. 39. xv. 58. Phil. ii. 12. iv. 1.
h here only. Exod. v. 1. Deut. xvi. 15.
i = ch. iv. 21 reff.
j ch. xiv. 20 reff.
k Rom. i. 29.
l Acts iii. 26.
m 2 Cor. i. 12. ii. 17 only †. (-νής, Phil. i. 10.)
n = John iii. 21.

rec aft πασχ. ημων adds υπερ ημων (*a doctrinal gloss*), with C³L P(υμ.) ℵ³ rel syrr goth Hip_1 $Orig_1$ $Meth_1$ [$Cyr\text{-}p_1$] Thdrt Pseud-Ath_1 Thl Œc : om ABC¹DFℵ¹ 17 latt copt æth [arm] $Clem_1$ $Orig_{sæpe}$(mss $vary_3$) Mcion-e_2 [$Dial_1$ Eus_1] Archel Ath_1 Chr_1 Cyr_1 $Cypr_2$ $Tert_1$ Ambrst Jer [$Aug_{sæpe}$ Zeno]. elz εθυθη : txt ABDFLPℵ rel [syr-mg-gr]. (C is here illegible.) ins ο bef χριστος F.

8. εορταζομεν A D[-gr] P d [goth $Orig_1$] : txt BCFLℵ rel [latt syrr copt æth arm $Orig_2$-c_1-$int_{sæpe}$ &c]. παλαιας P. for μηδε, μη B $Orig_1$(txt_2-c_1). for πονηριας, πορνειας F[-gr]. (G-lat has both.)

and involves no tautology here, any more than elsewhere. An unfortunate interpretation has been given to these words,—'as ye are *now celebrating the feast of unleavened bread;*' and has met with some recent defenders, e. g. Wieseler,—and Conybeare, Life and Epistles of St. Paul, edn. 2, vol. ii. p. 40, note. But first, *the words will not admit it;* for ἄζυμοι cannot (as joined immediately with ἐν ἀζύμοις, ver. 8) without much harshness be applied in its literal sense to the *celebrators* of the feast, but must indicate the *material* which was unleavened, see reff.,—ἄρτον ζυμιτήν, ἄζυμον, Athenæus iii. 109, and Gen. xix. 3; Exod. xxix. 2. Secondly, the celebration of a Jewish feast would certainly not be predicated without remark of a whole mixed congregation of Gentiles and Jews, even supposing that the Gentile converts did celebrate it with the Jews. It is no answer to this, to cite passages (see Conyb. and Howson, ubi supra), where he seems to treat mixed churches, e. g. Gal. iv. 8; Rom. vii. 1; xi. 18, as if they belonged wholly to one or other of their component elements. For this is not a parallel case. He would here, as above, be distinctly *predicating,* as a fact, of the whole church, a practice which he himself would have been the first to deprecate. See Gal. iv. 10. Thirdly, it is not at all probable that the Apostle would either address the Corinthians as *engaged in a feast* which *he, at Ephesus,* was then celebrating, seeing that it would probably *be over before his letter could be delivered,*—or would *anticipate* their being engaged in it when they received his letter, if it were yet to come. For be it remembered, that in the sense required, they would only be ἄζυμοι during seven days. Here again, I do not see how the example of "a birth-day letter to a friend in India," adduced by Mr. Conybeare, as an answer to my objection, will apply. It seems to me that if strictly considered, in detail, it tells my way, not his. But, fourthly,—and even could all the other objections be answered, this would remain in its full force,—the reference is one *wholly alien from the habit and spirit of our Apostle.* The ordinances of the old law are to him *not points on whose actual observance to ground spiritual lessons,* but things passed away in their literal acceptance, and *become spiritual verities* in Christ. He thus regards the Corinthian church as (normally) *the unleavened lump* at the Passover; he beseeches them to put away the old leaven from among them, to correspond with this their normal state: **for,** he adds, it is high time for us to be ἄζυμοι in very deed (καὶ γάρ—so Xen. Anab. v. 8. 7, ἀκούσατε, ἔφη, καὶ γὰρ ἄξιον. It introduces a powerful reason, *for* (on other accounts and) *also.* See Hartung, Partikellehre, i. 137, 8), seeing that **our Passover was sacrificed** (see reff.: and cf. Heb. ix. 26, 28), **even Christ** (the days of unleavened bread *began* with the Passover-sacrifice): **therefore** (reff.) **let us keep the feast** (not the *actual* Passover, but the continued Passover-feast of Christians on whose behalf Christ has died. There is no change of metaphor: the Corinthians are the living ἄρτοι, as believers are the living stones of the spiritual temple) **not in** (as our element) **the old leaven** (general—our old unconverted state), **nor** (particular) **in the leaven of vice and wickedness** (the genitives are of apposition,—'the leaven which is vice and wickedness;' see Winer, edn. 6, § 59. 8. *a*), **but in the unleavenedness** (τὰ ἄζυμα, unleavened things, see Exod. xii. 15, 18) **of sincerity and truth.** The view here maintained is that of Chrys., καὶ αὐτὸς δὲ ἐπιμένει τῇ μεταφορᾷ, ἀναμιμνήσκων παλαιᾶς αὐτοὺς ἱστορίας, καὶ πάσχα καὶ ἀζύμων, καὶ τῶν εὐεργεσιῶν τῶν τότε καὶ τῶν νῦν, καὶ τῶν κολάσεων καὶ τῶν τιμωριῶν· ἑορτῆς ἄρα ὁ παρὼν καιρός. καὶ

9 [v]Ἔγραψα ὑμῖν ἐν [o] τῇ ἐπιστολῇ μὴ [p] συναναμίγνυσθαι
[q] πόρνοις· 10 οὐ [r] πάντως τοῖς [qst] πόρνοις τοῦ κόσμου τούτου ἢ τοῖς [su] πλεονέκταις καὶ [v] ἅρπαξιν ἢ [stw] εἰδωλολάτραις,
[x] ἐπεὶ [y] ὠφείλετε [x] ἄρα ἐκ τοῦ κόσμου ἐξελθεῖν· 11 νῦν δὲ

o (see note) compare Rom. xvi. 22 2 Cor. vii. 8. Col. iv. 16. 1 Thess. v. 27. 2 Thess. iii. 14.
p here bis. 2 Thess. iii. 14 only. Hos. vii. 8 A Ald. compl. (συμμίγν., B) only.
q as below (s, t). 1 Tim. i. 10. Heb. xii. 16. xiii. 4 only †. Sir. xxiii. 16, 17 only.
r see Rom. iii. 9 reff.
s ch. vi. 9. Eph. v. 5.
t as above (s). Rev. xxi. 8. xxii. 15.
u as above (s). here bis only †. Sir. xiv. 9 only.
v here bis. Matt. vii. 15. Luke xviii. 11. ch. vi. 10 only. Gen. xlix. 27 only.
w as above (s, t). here bis. ch. x. 7 only †. (-τρεία, ch. x. 14.)
x ch. vii. 14 only.
y Rom. xv. 1 reff.

10. rec ins *και* bef *ου παντως*, with D^{3}LP$\aleph^3$ rel syr Orig-c Chr Thdrt Thl Œc: txt ABCD^{1}F$\aleph^1$ 17 latt copt [goth] Orig[-int$_1$] Tert$_1$ Lucif$_1$ Ambrst Pel. *τουτου* bef *τ. κοσμ.* D. rec (for *και*) *ἢ* (*alteration to conform to the general context*), with D$^{2.3}$[-gr] L$\aleph^3$ rel [vulg E-lat syrr copt goth arm] Orig[-c$_1$-int$_1$ Bas$_1$ Damasc] Chr$_1$ Thdrt Lucif: txt ABC D^1[and lat] FP$\aleph^1$ m[*η και*] 17 æth. rec **οφειλετε** (*corrn from misunderstanding: see note*), with B^{2}P rel [Bas$_1$ Euthal-ms] Chr$_1$ Thdrt: txt AB^{1}CDFL$\aleph$ c n 17. 47 latt Damasc Tert$_1$ Lucif$_1$ [Ambrst].

11. rec *νυνι*, with CD$^{1.2}\aleph^1$ rel Orig[-c$_1$] Chr$_1$ Thl Œc: txt AB [D^3(Tischdf)] FLP$\aleph^3$ d k n 17 [Sevrn-c$_1$ Euthal-ms] Bas$_1$ Chr$_1$ Thdrt Damasc.

γὰρ εἰπὼν **ἑορτάζωμεν**, *οὐκ ἐπειδὴ πάσχα παρῆν, οὐδὲ ἐπειδὴ ἡ πεντηκοστή, ἔλεγεν, ἀλλὰ δεικνὺς ὅτι πᾶς ὁ χρόνος ἑορτῆς ἐστι καιρὸς τοῖς Χριστιανοῖς διὰ τὴν ὑπερβολὴν τῶν δοθέντων ἀγαθῶν.* Hom. xv. p. 128. With regard to the chronological superstructure which has been built (by Wieseler and others) on this passage, *that* the Epistle was written *shortly before Easter*, we cannot of course say that the approach of the Passover *may not* have *suggested* to the Apostle this similitude: and we know from ch. xvi. 8 that he was looking forward to Pentecost. But further than this it would not be safe to assume: see Prolegg. to this Epistle, § vi. 3, 4. 9—13.] *Correction of their misunderstanding of a former command of his respecting keeping company with fornicators.* 9.] **I wrote to you in my letter** (not *this present epistle*, which *τῇ ἐπιστολῇ might* mean, see reff.,—for there is nothing in the preceding part of this Epistle which can by any possibility be so interpreted,—certainly not either ver. 2 or ver. 6, which are commonly alleged by those who thus explain it—and *ἐν τῇ ἐπιστολῇ* would be a superfluous and irrelevant addition, if he meant the letter on which he was now engaged:—but, a *former epistle*, which has not come down to us:—cf. the similar expression, ref. 2 Cor. used with reference to *this Epistle*,—and see note on 2 Cor. i. 15, 16. So Ambrose, Calvin, Beza, Estius, Grot., Calov., Bengel, Wetst., Mosh., De Wette, Meyer: so also Lightfoot, understanding however an Epistle *committed to Timothy*, see ch. iv. 17: which could not be, as Timothy was not coming to them till after they had received this Epistle, ch. xvi. 10, and thus the words would be unintelligible to them:—on the other side are Chrys., Theodoret, Theophyl., Erasm., Corn.-a-lapide, Wolf, al. It has been suggested (see Stanley, in loc.) that the whole passage, ch. v. 9—vi. 8, may have been a postscript or note inserted subsequently to the rest of the Epistle, and referring especially to ch. vi. 9—20) **not to keep company with fornicators.** 10.] **οὐ πάντως** *limits the prohibition*, which perhaps had been complained of owing to its strictness, and the impossibility of complying with it in so dissolute a place as Corinth, and *excepts* the fornicators of *this world*, i. e. who are *not professing Christians*: **not under all circumstances with the fornicators of this world**: so Theophr. C. P. vi. 25, cited by Wetst. on Rom. iii. 9, *ποιεῖ γὰρ οὐ πάντως, ἀλλ' ἐὰν οὐλή τις ᾖ ὑπόκαυστος.* *οὐ*, not *μή*, because not the whole context of the prohibition is negatived, but only one portion of it, and thus *οὐ πάντως τ. π. τ. κόσ. τ.* stands together as one idea. So Thucyd. i. 51, *ὑποτοπήσαντες ἀπ' Ἀθηνῶν εἶναι* **οὐχ** *ὅσας ἑώρων ἀλλὰ πλείους.* See more examples in Hartung, Partikellehre, ii. p. 125, 6. **τοῦ κόσμ. τούτου**, *belonging to the number of unbelievers,—Christians* who were *πόρνοι* being *expressly excluded*. So Paul ever uses this expression, ch. iii. 19; (2 Cor. iv. 4;) Eph. ii. 2. **πλεονέκταις** and **ἅρπαξιν** are joined by *καί*, as belonging to the same class—that of *covetous* persons;—*πλεονέκτης* being an *avaricious* person, not a *lascivious* one, as sometimes rendered (e. g. Conybeare, vol. ii. p. 41, edn. 2), nor does it seem to have any where merely this meaning; see Eph. iv. 19 and note. Compare on the other side Stanley's note here, which however has not convinced me. The root of the two sins being the same, viz. lust or greed, they come often to be mentioned together and as if running into one another. See Trench, N. T. Syn. pp. 91, 2. On *ἅρπαξιν*, Stanley remarks, "It is difficult to see why it should be expressly

z ch. vi. 10 only. Prov. xxvi. 21. (-ρεῖν, ch. iv. 12. -ρία, 1 Tim. v. 14.)
a ch. vi. 10 only. Prov. xxiii. 21. xxvi. 9. Sir. xix. 1. xxvi. 8 only.
b ver. 5.
c Luke xv. 2. Acts x. 41. xi. 3. Gal. ii. 12 only. Gen. xliii. 32. Ps. c. 5 only.
d here only. (Mark v. 7. 2 Kings xvi. 10. Matt. viii. 29.) see Matt. xxvii. 4. John xxi. 22, 23.
e (Acts xxvi. 11. 2 Cor. iv. 16.) = here bis. Col. iv. 5. 1 Thess. iv. 12. Mark iv. 11 only. (cf. τοῖς ἐκτός, Sir. prol.)
f = John viii. 15. Rom. iii. 7.
g = here only. see Rom. vii. 22. 2 Cor. iv. 16. Eph. iii. 16. 3 Kings vi. 15.
h here only. Deut. xvii. 7, 12. xxiv. 7.
i see ch. i. 24.

ABCDF LPא a b c d f g h k l m n o 17. 47

ἔγραψα ὑμῖν μὴ [p] συναναμίγνυσθαι, ἐάν τις ἀδελφὸς
ὀνομαζόμενος ᾖ [qst] πόρνος ἢ [su] πλεονέκτης ἢ [stw] εἰδωλολά-
τρης ἢ [z] λοίδορος ἢ [a] μέθυσος ἢ [v] ἅρπαξ, τῷ [b] τοιούτῳ μηδὲ
[c] συνεσθίειν. 12 [d] τί γάρ [d] μοι [e] τοὺς [e] ἔξω [f] κρίνειν;
οὐχὶ [g] τοὺς [g] ἔσω ὑμεῖς [f] κρίνετε; 13 [e] τοὺς δὲ [e] ἔξω ὁ θεὸς
[f] κρίνει. [h] Ἐξάρατε τὸν πονηρὸν ἐξ ὑμῶν [i] αὐτῶν

Steph for ᾖ, ἦ, with (B[2] D-gr, perhaps) F-lat G-lat arm Aug$_4$: txt (not defined in the other uncials) vulg [D-lat] syrr copt goth æth Iren-int$_1$ Tert$_1$ [Lucif$_1$ Ambrst] Aug$_1$. πορν. η μεθ. η ειδ. η λοιδ. η πλ. η αρπ. C. ειδωλ. η πλεον. m [arm]. for μηδε, μη A 119 [Orig$_1$]: μητε F. (*non* aut *nec* G-lat.)

12. for τι, ει F[-gr]. rec aft μοι ins και, with D[-gr] L rel syr goth arm Chr$_6$ Thdrt Thl Œc: om ABCFPא 17 latt Syr copt æth Orig[-c$_1$] Chr$_1$ Tert$_1$ [Ambr$_1$]. υμας C[1]. κρινειτε א[1](txt א-corr[1]).

13. κρινεῖ [B[2] P(Tischdf)] a b d f g h k l o [vulg F-lat] arm lat-ff: txt L D-lat. (κρινει B[1] sed antea et mox κρειν. Verc.) rec (for εξαρατε) και εξαρειτε (και *insd as above more than once, for connexion: but the abruptness is characteristic*: -ρειτε *from* LXX-A), with D[3]L rel (*tollite autem* Syr, *et tollite* syr &c) [Orig-c$_1$] Chr(om και? and -ρατε ms$_1$ in Matthaï) Thdrt: και εξαρατε 17: txt ABCD[1]FPא d m latt copt goth arm [Bas$_2$ Euthal-ms].

introduced here, especially if πλεονέκτης has the meaning of sensuality." Certainly: but not, if πλ. retains its proper meaning, as containing the key to πορνεία on the one hand, and ἁρπαγή on the other. **ἐπεὶ ὠφ.] For in that case ye must go out of the world,**—as Chrys. and Theophyl., ἑτέραν οἰκουμένην ζητῆσαι. The past ὠφείλ., as ἔχρην, al., because the necessity would long ago have occurred and the act have passed. **11. νῦν δὲ ἔγραψα] But my meaning was . . .;**—'but, the case being so, that ye must needs consort with fornicators among the heathen, I wrote to you, not to consort, &c.' That this is the meaning and not 'But *now* I write (the epistolary aorist), &c.,' seems plain, from the use of ἔγραψα twice so close together, and therefore probably in the same reference,—from the fact noticed by Meyer, that if a contrast had been intended between ἐν τῇ ἐπιστολῇ and νῦν, ἐν τῇ ἐπ. must have *preceded* ἔγραψα:—and from the usage of νῦν δέ, of which Hartung, Partikellehre, ii. 25, gives examples, e. g. Plut. Protag. p. 347, νῦν δὲ σφόδρα γὰρ καὶ περὶ τῶν μεγίστων ψευδόμενος δοκεῖς ἀληθῆ λέγειν, διὰ ταῦτά σε ἐγὼ ψέγω,—and Lycurg. Leocr. p. 138, ἐβουλόμην δ' ἄν, ὦ ἄνδρες . . . . νῦν δὲ . . . See also Heb. xi. 16. Thus by the right rendering, we escape the awkward inference deducible from the ordinary interpretation,—that the Apostle had previously given a command, and now retracted it. **ἐάν τις] If one who is called a brother be, &c. Œcumenius, Augustine, Ambrose, Estius,** al., join ὀνομαζόμενος with πόρνος, and understand it either as = ὀνομαστός, '*be a notorious* πόρνος, *&c.*,' or '*be named a* πόρνος *&c.*' But ὀνομαζόμ. or even ὀνομαστός, in the bad sense, is hardly admissible,—and in either case Paul would have written ἀδελφός τις, the stress on ἀδελφός in that case requiring it to precede τις, as it now precedes ὀνομαζόμενος. **εἰδωλολάτρης]** One who from any motive makes a compromise with the habits of the heathen, and partakes in their sacrifices: Chrys. well remarks, προκαταβάλλεται τὸν περὶ τῶν εἰδωλοθύτων λόγον ὃν μετὰ ταῦτα μέλλει γυμνάζεσθαι. **μέθυσος** was, in pure Greek, not used of a man, but of a woman only. So Phrynichus, p. 151 (but see Lobeck's note), **μέθυσος ἀνὴρ** οὐκ ἐρεῖς, ἀλλὰ **μεθυστικός**· γυναῖκα δὲ ἐρεῖς μέθυσον κ. μεθύσην: and Pollux, vi. 25 (Wetst.), μέθυσος ἐπὶ ἀνδρῶν Μενάνδρῳ δεδόσθω. Seeing that μηδὲ συνεσθίειν must imply a *more complete separation* than μὴ συναναμίγνυσθαι, it cannot be applied to the ἀγάπαι (as Mosheim, al.), but must keep its general meaning,—**not even to sit at table with such an one.** This rule, as that in 2 Thess. iii. 14, regards only their *private* intercourse with the offending person: nothing is *here* said of public excommunication, though for some of these crimes it would be implied.

12.] *Ground of the above limitation.* **τί γάρ μοι . . . .] for what concern of mine is it . . . ?** So Ælian, Var. H. vi. 11, τοὺς δὲ ἄλλους ἐῶ. τί γάρ μοι κωφοῖς κ. ἀνοήτοις συμβουλεύειν τὰ

e εχων... ABCFL PℵabcdefghklmnO 17. 47

VI. 1 [k]Τολμᾷ τις ὑμῶν [l]πρᾶγμα [l]ἔχων [m]πρὸς [n]τὸν
[n]ἕτερον [o]κρίνεσθαι [p]ἐπὶ τῶν [q]ἀδίκων καὶ οὐχὶ [p]ἐπὶ τῶν

k = Acts v. 13. Rom. v. 7. 2 Cor. x. 12. Esth. vii. 5. l here only. Xen. Mem. ii. 9. 1. m = Acts xxiv. 19 reff. n Rom. ii. 1 reff. o = Matt. v. 40. Gen. xxvi. 21. Job ix. 3. p = Acts xxiii. 30 reff. q = here only. see Gal. ii. 15 reff.

Chap. VI. 1. ins εξ bef υμων A[P] a[1] d m 17 syrr Chr_1 Thdrt. προς τ. ετερ. bef πραγμα εχων DF [copt goth Chr_1] Thdrt Cypr [Ambrst Aug_2].—om τον B.

λυσιτελέστατα; see other examples in Wetst. **τοὺς ἔξω**] reff. It was among the Jews the usual term for the Gentiles. Cf. Schöttgen in loc. He means, 'this might have been easily understood to be my meaning: for what concern have I with pronouncing sentence on the world without, or with giving rules of discipline for *them*? I could only have referred to persons *among yourselves*.' **οὐχὶ τοὺς ἔσω**] "Ex eo, quod in ecclesia fieri solet, interpretari debuistis monitum meum, ver. 9. Cives judicatis, non alienos: quanto magis ego." Bengel. But I am not quite certain of this interpretation, which is also that of De Wette and Meyer, because it would more naturally correspond to οὐχὶ τοὺς ἔσω καὶ ὑμεῖς κρίνετε; A preferable way seems to be this; 'My judgment was meant to *lead your judgment*. This being the case, what concern had I with *those without*? Is it not on *those within*, that your judgments are passed?' The arrangement mentioned by Theophylact, and adopted by Knatchbull, Hammond, Michaelis, Rosenm., al., οὐχί· τοὺς ἔσω ὑμεῖς κρίνετε, '*No: those within do ye* (imper.) *judge*,'—is clearly wrong, for οὐχί is no answer to τί, and would require ἀλλά after it,—even supposing μοι τοὺς ἔξω κρίνειν and τοὺς ἔσω ὑμεῖς κρίνετε formed any intelligible logical contrast, which they do not. 13.] **But those who are without God judgeth.** The pres. κρίνει both expresses better the attribute and office of God, and answers better to the other *presents* than the future κρινεῖ. I have therefore retained it. The future perhaps came from Heb. xiii. 4. '*To judge those without, is God's matter*.' These remarks about *judging* form a transition point to the subject of the next chapter. But having now finished his explanation of the prohibition formerly given, and with it the subject of the fornicator among them, he gives, before passing on, a plain command in terms for the excommunication (but no more: *not the punishment* mentioned in vv. 3—5) of the offender. And this he does in the very words of Deut. xxiv. 7 (from which the reading καὶ ἐξαρεῖτε has come). **ὑμῶν αὐτῶν** is in Deut., but need not therefore lose its emphatic force: **from among your own selves.**

Chap. VI. 1—11.] Prohibition to settle their differ ces in the legal courts of the heathen: rather should these be adjudged among themselves (1—6): but far better not to quarrel—rather to suffer wrong, waiting for justice to be done at the coming of the Lord, when all who do wrong shall be excluded from his kingdom (6—11). 1.] On τολμᾷ, **Dares . . .**, Bengel remarks, "Grandi verbo notatur læsa majestas Christianorum." **τις**, no particular *individual*, but **any one**: for he proceeds in the plur., vv. 4, 7. **πρᾶγμα**] So ref. and Demosth. κατὰ Στεφ. α. p. 1120, τῷ μὲν υἱεῖ τῷ τούτου πολλῶν πραγμάτων ὄντων οὐ παρέστη πώποτε οὐδ' ἐβοήθησεν; **κρίνεσθαι**, reff., **to go to law.** So Eur. Med. 609, ὡς οὐ κρινοῦμαι τῶνδε σοὶ τὰ πλείονα,—and Anthol. ii. 30, δυσκώφῳ δύσκωφος ἐκρίνετο, καὶ πολὺ μᾶλλον ἦν ὁ κριτὴς τούτων τῶν δύο κωφότερος. Wetst. on Matt. v. 40. **ἐπί** (reff.), **before**, as judges. **τῶν ἀδίκων**] οὐκ εἶπεν, ἐπὶ τῶν ἀπίστων, ἀλλ' ἐπὶ τῶν ἀδίκων, λέξιν θείς, ἧς μάλιστα χρείαν εἶχεν εἰς τὴν προκειμένην ὑπόθεσιν, ὥστε ἀποτρέψαι κ. ἀπαγαγεῖν. ἐπειδὴ γὰρ περὶ δίκης αὐτῷ ὁ λόγος ἦν, οἱ δικαζόμενοι δὲ οὐδὲν οὕτως ἐπιζητοῦσιν, ὡς τὸ πολλὴν εἶναι πρόνοιαν τοῦ δικαίου παρὰ τοῖς δικάζουσιν, ἐντεῦθεν αὐτοὺς ἀποτρέπει, μονονουχὶ λέγων Ποῖ φέρῃ καὶ τί ποιεῖς, ἄνθρωπε, τοὐναντίον πάσχων ὧν ἐπιθυμεῖς, καὶ ὑπὲρ τοῦ τῶν δικαίων τυχεῖν ἀδίκοις ἐπιτρέπων ἀνθρώποις; Chrys. Hom. xvi. p. 137. The Rabbinical prohibitions against going to law before Gentiles may be seen in Wetst.: e. g. "Statutum est, ad quod omnes Israelitæ obligantur, eum qui litem cum alio habet, non debere eam tractare coram gentilibus." Tanchuma, xcii. 2. **καὶ οὐχὶ ἐπὶ τ. ἁγίων**] The Apostle does not mean that the Christians had their *courts of law*, but that they should submit their differences to *courts of arbitration* among themselves. Such courts of arbitration were common among the Jews. In Jos. Antt. xiv. 10. 17, there is a decree by which the Jews of Sardis are allowed the use of a σύνοδος ἰδία . . . . . καὶ τόπος ἴδιος, ἐν ᾧ τά τε πράγματα κ. τὰς πρὸς ἀλλήλους ἀντιλογίας κρίνουσι. Theodoret shews, ὡς οὐκ ἐναντία ταῦτα τοῖς πρὸς Ῥωμαίους γραφεῖ-

r = Acts ix. 13 reff. s vv. 9, 15, 16, 19. t John iii. 17 al. fr. u = Matt. xix. 28. Luke xxii. 30. see DAN. vii. 22. v Luke xi. 15. Acts xvii. 31. see note. w here only. Jer. xv. 19 Ed-vat. F Ald. compl.(not ABℵ1.) Sir. xxv. 8 (not ℵ) only. (-ίως, ch. xi. 27.) x here bis. James ii. 6 only. Judg. v. 10 B Ald. compl.

[r] ἁγίων; [2] ἢ [s] οὐκ οἴδατε ὅτι οἱ [r] ἅγιοι τὸν [t] κόσμον [tu] κρι-
νοῦσιν; καὶ εἰ [v] ἐν ὑμῖν [u] κρίνεται ὁ κόσμος, [w] ἀνάξιοί
ἐστε [x] κριτηρίων ἐλαχίστων; [3] [s] οὐκ οἴδατε ὅτι ἀγγέλους

ABCFL Pℵ a b c d e f g h k l m n o 17. 47

2. rec om ἤ, with D[3][-gr] L rel: ins ABC D[1][and lat] FPℵ a m 17 Syr syr-w-ast copt arm $Clem_1$ Chr_1 Damasc [Hil_1 Ambr Ambrst, *an nescitis* vulg F-lat Cypr Aug Pel]. for ει, εαν F: om D[1][and lat] k[1] Hil_2.

3, 4, 5, 6. om A (*homœotel, -ιστων ending ver 2, and also ver 6*).

σιν (Rom. xiii. 1 ff.):—*οὐ γὰρ ἀντιτείνειν κελεύει τοῖς ἄρχουσιν, ἀλλὰ τοῖς ἠδικημένοις νομοθετεῖ μὴ κεχρῆσθαι τοῖς ἄρχουσι.* See Stanley in loc., who thinks the existence of such courts is here implied. But his support of his view from the Ap. Constt. and the Clementines, cir. A.D. 150, would only go to shew that the Apostle's injunction here had been obeyed, and that those courts were the result. **2.**] **οὐκ οἴδατε** (reff.) appeals to an axiomatic truth. **οἱ ἅγιοι τ. κ. κριν.**] **that the saints shall judge the world?**—i. e. as assessors of Christ, at His coming: so Daniel vii. 22 (Theod.), *ἦλθεν ὁ παλαιὸς ἡμερῶν, καὶ* **τὸ κρίμα ἔδωκεν ἁγίοις ὑψίστου**; see also Matt. xix. 28. So Calv., Beza, Grot., Est., Wolf, Olsh., Billroth, Rückert, Meyer, De Wette. All attempts to elude this plain meaning of the words are futile: whether of Chrys., Theophyl., Theodor-Mops., Theodoret, Erasm.,—*κρινοῦσι δὲ οὐχὶ αὐτοὶ καθήμενοι κ. λόγον ἀπαιτοῦντες, ἀλλὰ κατακρινοῦσι* (Matt. xii. 41, 42), Chrys.—for this would be no parallel to the case in hand;—or of Lightf., Vitringa, Bengel (but only as a *prœludium futurorum*), al.,—'*quod Christiani futuri sint magistratus et judices in mundo,*'—Lightf., which does not satisfy ver. 3, nor agree with the Apostle's earnest persuasion (see 2 Cor. v. al., and note on 2 Thess. ii. 2) that the coming of Christ was near at hand: or of Mosheim, Ernesti, Rosenm., '*quod Christiani profanos judicare possint,*' Rosenm., in the sense of ch. ii. 15, 16,—for no such meaning can be conveyed by the *future,* which is fixed here by the following *κρινοῦμεν.* **καί** brings out an inconsequence or a contradiction between the members of the sentence, which it is the object of the question to remove: so Xen. Cyr. iv. 3. 11, *ἀλλ' εἴποι ἄν τις, ὅτι παῖδες ὄντες ἐμάνθανον. καὶ πότερα παῖδές εἰσι φρονιμώτεροι ὥστε μαθεῖν τὰ φραζόμενα κ. δεικνύμενα ἢ ἄνδρες;* see Hartung, Partikellehre, i. 147. **ἐν ὑμῖν**] Chrys. attempts by this prepos. to defend his view (see above),—*οὐ γὰρ εἶπεν, ὑφ' ὑμῶν, ἀλλ'* **ἐν ὑμῖν** ('exemplo vestro'). But in vain: nor as Grot., al., is *ἐν*, *by*:—for *κρίνεσθαι ἐν* is the expression for *to be judged before*, as judges: the judges being the *vehicle* of judgment, its conditioning element, as in ref. Acts. So Aristides, Platon. ii. p. 214 (Wetst.), *τινὲς ἤδη λέγονται τῶν ἡρώων ἐν θεοῖς δικασταῖς κριθῆναι,* and Polyb. v. 29. 6, *Πτολεμαῖον . . . . κρίνας ἐν τοῖς Μακεδόσιν ἀπέκτεινε.* See other examples in Wetst. Hence (Meyer) by this '*coram vobis*' it appears plainly, though it might be otherwise inferred from the context, that the Saints *are to be the judges,* sitting in judgment. **ἀνάξιοί ἐστε κριτ. ἐλαχ.**] **are ye unworthy of** (i. e. to hold or pronounce) **the smallest judgments?** *κριτήρια* cannot be, as usually rendered, '*matters to be judged:*' it signifies either (1) *criteria*, lit. or metaphor., which sense is irrelevant here: (2) *tribunals, courts of justice*:—so Glossar. *κριτήριον, δικαστήριον,* and Polyb. ix. 33. 12, *κοινὸν ἐκ πάντων τῶν Ἑλλήνων καθίσας κριτήριον,*—or (3) *judgments held* in such courts, *judicia,*—as Lucian. bis accus. (§ 25, p. 253, ed. Hagan. 1526); Hermes describes Pyrrhon as being not in court, *ὅτι οὐδὲν ἡγεῖται κριτήριον ἀληθὲς εἶναι:* to which *Δίκη* replies, *τοιγαροῦν ἐρήμην αὐτοῦ καταδικάτωσαν.* The last meaning suits both this place and ver. 4. So Cicero speaks of 'in privatis minimarum rerum judiciis.' Here, they are *ἐλάχιστα* in comparison with the weighty judgments which shall be held hereafter; = *βιωτικά*, ver. 4. **3.**] The same glorious office of Christians is again referred to, and even a more striking point of contrast brought out. **ἀγγέλους**] always, where not otherwise specified, *good angels:* and therefore here; the *λειτουργικὰ πνεύματα* of Heb. i. 14: but exactly *how* we shall judge them, is not revealed to us. Chrys., Theodoret, Œcum., Theophyl., and most Commentators interpret it of *bad angels,* or *of bad and good* together: and Chrys. as before, understands that the bad angels will be condemned by comparison with us, *ὅταν γὰρ αἱ ἀσώματοι δυνάμεις αὗται ἐλαττον ἡμῶν εὑρεθῶσιν ἔχουσαι τῶν σάρκα περιβεβλημένων, χαλεπώτερον δώσουσι δίκην.*

[u] κρινοῦμεν, [y] μήτι [y] γε [z] βιωτικά ; 4 [z] βιωτικὰ [a] μὲν οὖν
[x] κριτήρια ἐὰν ἔχητε, τοὺς [b] ἐξουθενημένους ἐν τῇ ἐκκλησίᾳ,
τούτους [c] καθίζετε. 5 [d] πρὸς [e] ἐντροπὴν ὑμῖν λέγω. [f] οὕτως

y here only †. z here bis. Luke xxi. 34 only †. a = ver. 7. ch. ix. 25. Phil. ii. 23. b Rom. xiv. 3 reff. c trans., Acts ii. 30. Eph. i. 20 only. 1 Kings xxx. 21. mid., Matt. xix. 28. d = ch. vii. 35 reff. e ch. xv. 34 only. Ps. xxxiv. 26. f = Matt. xxvi. 40. Mark vii. 18. John xviii. 22. Gal. iii. 3.

3. for *μητι γε, ποσω μαλλον* F vulg æth Pel. **4.** for *μεν ουν, γουν* F. **5.** for *λεγω, λαλω* B. (C doubtful.)

p. 138. But see above on ver. 2. **μήτι γε**, to say nothing of, '*ut omittam:*' so Demosth. p. 24. 23, *οὐκ ἔνι δ' αὐτὸν ἀργοῦντα οὐδὲ τοῖς φίλοις ἐπιτάττειν ὑπὲρ αὐτοῦ τι ποιεῖν, μή τί γε δὴ τοῖς θεοῖς.* See Hartung, Partikellehre, ii. 155. **βιωτικά**, matters relating to *ὁ βίος*, *a man's livelihood:* see ref. and Clem. Alex. Strom. vii. 12 [69], p. 873 P., *θλιβόμενον ἐπικουφίζει παραμυθίαις . . . , ταῖς βιωτικαῖς χρείαις ἐπικουρῶν.* It is a word of later Greek usage, see Lexx. In classic Greek it would be *τὰ τοῦ βίου.* The meaning here then will be **civil causes**, matters of *meum* and *tuum*, as De Wette. The sense is best with only a comma at *κρινοῦμεν*.

4.] *βιωτικά* is emphatically repeated, as being the only sort of *κριτήρια* which were in question here. Meyer compares Herod. vii. 104, *τὰ ἂν ἐκεῖνος ἀνώγῃ· ἀνώγει δὲ τὠὐτὸ ἀεί*, and Aristoph. Ran. 287 f. **μὲν οὖν**, '*immo vero*,' reff. (see below). It corrects a foregoing misapprehension: so Soph. Œd. Col. 31, "*ἦ δεῦρο προστείχοντα κἀξορμώμενον;*" "*καὶ δὴ μὲν οὖν παρόντα.*" Hartung, Partikell. ii. 400. See also Moulton's Winer, p. 556, note 2. **κριτήρια**, again, not *matters to be judged*, but **judgments**: the matters about which, are expressed in *βιωτικά*. The following words may be rendered in two ways: either, (α) '*Yea, rather* (so far from remembering your high prospect, of judging angels, your practice is), *if ye have in hand judgments concerning civil matters,—those men who are of no account in the church* (viz. the heathen), *those you set up* (place on the bench) *as judges*' (i. e. by bringing your causes before them, you set them up as judges over you). *καθίζω* occurs in this sense in Plato, Legg. ix. p. 873, *ἐὰν δὲ ἄψυχόν τι ψυχῆς ἄνθρωπον στερήσῃ, . . . δικαστὴν μὲν αὐτῷ καθιζέτω τῶν γειτόνων τὸν ἐγγύτατον ὁ προσήκων γένει*,—and Polyb. ix. 33. 12, cited above on *κριτήριον*. Thus, making *καθίζ.* indicative, Valla, Castal., Luther, Calov., Wolf, al., Schrader, Rückert, Olsh., De Wette, Meyer. But (β) Syr., Vulg., Chrys., Theodoret, Theophyl., Erasm., Beza, Calvin, Grot., Estius, Bengel, Wetst., al., take *καθίζετε* as *imperative*, and *τοὺς ἐξουθεν. ἐν τ. ἐκκλ.* as '*minimos de piorum plebe.*' So E. V.: **set them to judge who are least esteemed in the church.** And to this last interpretation I am inclined to accede, both from the context and from the arrangement of the words. The *context* is this: 'Your office is to judge *angels:*' mere business causes of this world are almost beneath your notice. If such causes arise among you (he continues in a lofty irony) set those to judge them who are of no account among you:—do not go out of your own number to others to have them judged: the meanest among you is capable of doing it. Let it be noticed that he is passing to ver. 7, where he insists on the impropriety of *βιωτικὰ κριτ.* between Christians *at all*, and is here depreciating them ironically. But the *arrangement* and *construction* of the words are even more strongly in favour of the imperative rendering. For (1) on the other, no account is given of the emphatic position of *βιωτικά.* (2) the *μὲν οὖν* is not so naturally rendered (see above) 'yea rather your course is,' as 'yea rather let your practice be:' it expresses more naturally a subjective correction, in the mind of the speaker, than an objective one: see below, ver. 7. (3) if the sentence had referred to their existing practice of going before heathen tribunals, it would have been expressed not *βιωτικὰ μὲν οὖν κριτ. ἐὰν ἔχητε*, but *β. μ. οὖν κρ. ἔχοντες*, as in ver. 1. (4) *οἱ ἐξουθενημένοι ἐν τῇ ἐκκ.* are much more naturally **the despised in** (within) **the church**, than *those who in* (the estimation of) *the church are held of no account.* Meyer argues against this that it would be in this case *τοὺς ἐξουθ. τοὺς ἐν τῇ ἐκκλ.*, but surely he can hardly be serious, or I do not understand him rightly. (5) *καθίζετε* applies much better to the *appointing* judges over a matter among themselves, than to *going before* judges *already appointed.* (6) as to the objection that on this rendering the word 'rather' must be inserted, *τούτους μᾶλλον καθίζετε*, it has no force, for no such supplement is required. The command is absolute, but given to shew them the absurdity of their going to law about *βιωτικά* at all, rather than *bona fide.*

5.] **πρὸς ἐντρ. ὑμ. λέγω** refers to the ironical command in ver. 4—**I say this to put you to shame.** **οὕτως**] **Is there so completely a lack of all wise men among you . . . .** He now suggests the more

οὐκ [g] ἔνι ἐν ὑμῖν οὐδεὶς σοφός, ὃς δυνήσεται [h] διακρῖναι
[i] ἀνὰ [i] μέσον τοῦ ἀδελφοῦ αὐτοῦ; 6 ἀλλὰ ἀδελφὸς
[k] μετὰ ἀδελφοῦ [kl] κρίνεται, [m] καὶ [m] τοῦτο [l] ἐπὶ [n] ἀπίστων.
7 ἤδη [o] μὲν οὖν [p] ὅλως [q] ἥττημα ὑμῖν ἐστιν ὅτι [r] κρίματα
ἔχετε μεθ' [s] ἑαυτῶν. [t] διὰ τί οὐχὶ μᾶλλον [u] ἀδικεῖσθε;
[t] διὰ τί οὐχὶ μᾶλλον [uv] ἀποστερεῖσθε; 8 ἀλλὰ ὑμεῖς ἀδικεῖτε
καὶ [v] ἀποστερεῖτε, [m] καὶ [m] τοῦτο ἀδελφούς. 9 ἢ [w] οὐκ οἴδατε

...απιστων, και ου επι αγιων F [-gr] (and also G).

ABCDL PℵA a b c d e f g h k l m n o 17.47

g Gal. iii. 28 (3ce). Col. iii. 11. James i. 7 only. see Luke xi. 41 +. h = here only. Ezek. xxxiv. 17, 20. i Matt. xiii. 25. Mark vii. 31. Rev. vii. 17 only. Exod. xi. 7. Isa. lvii. 5. constr., here only. k constr., Job ix. 3 A. 12, &c. x. 27. xiv. 22, &c. 2 Cor. vi. 14, 15. 1 Tim. v. 8. l ver. 1. m Rom. xiii. 11 reff. n = ch. vii. o ver. 4. p ch. v. 1 reff. q Rom. xi. 12 only. Isa. xxxi. 8 only. r = here only. Exod. xviii. 22. s = Eph. iv. 32. Col. iii. 13 (see note there). t Matt. ix. 14. Rom. ix. 32 (reff.) al. Num. xi. 11. u = here only. mid., cf. δογματίζεσθε, Col. ii. 20. v Mark x. 19. ch. vii. 5. 1 Tim. vi. 5. James v. 4 only. Mal. iii. 5. w vv. 2, 3.

rec (for ενι) εστιν, with DF m Ath_1 : txt BCLPℵ rel Orig[-c_2] Chr_1 Thdrt Damasc Thl Œc. rec σοφος ουδε εις (*Rom* iii. 10), with D[3]L rel vulg syr (Chr_1) Thdrt Thl Œc : [σοφ. ουδεις 137 Euthal-ms, *sapiens quisquam* vulg $Ambr_1$ Pel :] om ουδεις D[1][and lat] æth Orig[-c_1] Ath_1 : txt BCℵ 17 copt [Syr Orig-c_1] Damasc ; ουδε εις σοφ. FP a m [Ambrst] Aug_1. aft ος ins ου L. ανακριναι ℵ[1] n Orig[-c_2].

6. [κρινατε F-gr(not G).] for τουτο, ταυτα CD[2] syr-mg Thdrt. for επι, μετα D[1]. at end ins και ου επι αγιων F. (ου sic F and G.)

7. om ουν D[1]ℵ[1] a 17 latt copt arm Orig-int_1 [$Cypr_1$ Ambrst Aug_1], marked with an asterisk in syr. om ολως A Syr $Orig_1$[-c]. rec ins εν bef υμιν, with vulg F-lat [Damasc] Thl Orig-int_1 $Cypr_1$: om ABCDLPℵ rel syrr copt $Orig_1$[-c Euthal-ms] Bas_1 Chr_1 Thdrt $Antch_2$ Œc. κριμα ℵ [$Antch_2$ Damasc]. transp αδικεισθε and αποστερεισθε L [$Antch_2$].

8. transp αδικ. and αποστ. D. rec (for τουτο) ταυτα (*probably because two things*, αδικ. *and* αποστ., *are mentd*), with L rel syr arm Chr Thdrt [Bas_1 Damasc] : txt ABCDPℵ 17 latt copt $Orig_1$[-c Euthal-ms] $Antch_2$ $Cypr_1$.

Christian way of settling their differences, viz. *by arbitration:* and asks, 'Are you come to this, that you are obliged καθίζειν any δικαστάς at all,'—**have you no wise man among you** (the rec., οὐδὲ εἷς, would be 'quod est vehementius, cum sitis tam multi.' Erasm.) **who shall be able** (in such event) **to decide** (as arbitrator) **between his brother** (i. e. his brethren) **?** This last is a harsh method of expression, and apparently only to be accounted for by the singular form of οὐδεὶς σοφός having attracted the other into the singular likewise, so that instead of σοφοὶ οἳ δυνήσονται διακρ. ἀνὰ μέσον τῶν ἀδελφῶν αὐτῶν, we have σοφὸς ὃς δυνήσεται διακρ. ἀνὰ μ. τοῦ ἀδ. αὐτοῦ. But it is not without use: it prevents the apparent inference, which might be made if τῶν ἀδελφῶν αὐτοῦ were used, that *one wise man was to be appointed universal arbitrator,*—and confines the appointment of the arbitrator to each possibly arising case respectively. **6.**] (*It seems not to be so*): **nay,** &c., as implied in ver. 1. **ἀλλά** after a question passes rapidly on to the other alternative, the particle negativing the question being suppressed. So Xen. Mem. i. 2. 2, πῶς οὖν αὐτὸς ὢν τοιοῦτος ἄλλους ἂν ἀσεβεῖς . . . ἐποίησεν; 'Αλλ' ἔπαυσε μὲν τούτων πολλούς, ἀρετῆς ποιήσας ἐπιθυμεῖν. See Hartung, Partikellehre, ii. 37. **7.**] He gives his own censure of their going to law at all. **μὲν οὖν** as above, ver. 4. **ὅλως, altogether,** without the aggravation of ἐπὶ ἀπίστων. **ἥττημα, a falling short,** viz. of your inheritance of the kingdom of God—a hindrance in the way of your salvation: see ver. 9:—not as ordinarily understood (see especially Estius in loc.) a *moral delinquency* (cf. the usage in reff.), nor an ἡττᾶσθαι τῇ ὀργῇ, as Œcum. **κρίματα, matters of dispute,** leading to κρίνεσθαι; not = κρίσεις,—**μεθ' ἑαυτῶν, with one another** (reff.), as being brethren in Christ. **ἀδικεῖσθε** and **ἀποστερεῖσθε** not passives, but middle (cf. Bernhardy, Syntax, chap. viii. § 4, p. 346: Menander frag.: οὗτος κράτιστός ἐστ' ἀνήρ, ὦ Γοργία, ὅστις ἀδικεῖσθαι πλεῖστ' ἐπίσταται βροτῶν: Hesiod. ἔργ. 347, εὖ μὲν μετρεῖσθαι παρὰ γείτονος, εὖ δ' ἀποδοῦναι) —**allow yourselves to be wronged and defrauded.** See Matt. v. 39 ff. **8.**] cannot be, as Meyer, a continuation of the question, on account of the emphatic ὑμεῖς, which would thus be without meaning. The account of this emphatic ὑμεῖς is to be found in an ellipsis after ἀποστερεῖσθε to the effect, 'as our Lord commanded us His disciples,' or 'as it behoves the followers of Christ.' Then ὑμεῖς comes in contrast: YOU **on the contrary** (ἀλλά, see above ver. 6) **do wrong, and defraud, and that** (your) **brethren. 9.**] 'Ye *commit wrong:*' this looks as if you had forgotten

ὅτι ἄδικοι θεοῦ [x] βασιλείαν οὐ [xy] κληρονομήσουσιν ; [z] Μὴ
[z] πλανᾶσθε. οὔτε [a] πόρνοι οὔτε [b] εἰδωλολάτραι οὔτε [c] μοι-
χοὶ οὔτε [d] μαλακοὶ οὔτε [e] ἀρσενοκοῖται 10 οὔτε [f] κλέπται
οὔτε [b] πλεονέκται, οὐ [g] μέθυσοι, οὐ [g] λοίδοροι, οὐχ [b] ἅρπαγες, [x] βασιλείαν θεοῦ [xy] κληρονομήσουσιν. 11 καὶ
[h] ταῦτά τινες ἦτε· ἀλλὰ [i] ἀπελούσασθε, ἀλλὰ [k] ἡγιάσθητε,
ἀλλὰ [lm] ἐδικαιώθητε [m] ἐν τῷ ὀνόματι τοῦ κυρίου Ἰησοῦ
καὶ [m] ἐν τῷ πνεύματι τοῦ θεοῦ ἡμῶν.

x — Matt. xxv. 34. ch. xv. 50. Gal. v. 21. see James ii. 5.
y = Matt. v. 5.
z ch. xv. 33. Gal. vi. 7. James i. 16. Isa. xli. 10.
a ch. v. 9, 10, 11 reff.
b ch. v. 10, 11 (reff.).
c Luke xviii. 11. Heb. xiii. 4 only. Job xxiv. 15.
d = here (Matt. xi. 8 bis. Luke vii. 25) only ‡. (Prov. xxv. 15. xxvi. 22 only.)
e 1 Tim. i. 10 only †. see Levit. xviii. 22.
f Matt. vi. 19 al. Obad. 5.
g ch. v. 11 (reff.).
h see John xv. 17. 3 John 4.
i Acts xxii. 16 only. Job ix. 30 only. see Rev. i. 5.
k Rom. xv. 16 reff.
l = Rom. iii. 20, 30. v. 1 al.
m Acts xiii. 39 reff.

9. There is an erasure of two letters (οι ?) bef αδικοι in A. rec βασιλειαν bef θεου (*as below in ver* 10), with L rel latt Polyc$_1$ Clem$_1$ Chr$_1$ Thdrt [Antch$_2$ Damasc] Iren-int$_1$[some mss om *dei*] Tert$_1$ Cypr$_1$: txt ABC D[-gr] Pℵ m 17 [Orig-c$_1$ Euthal-ms]. om ου B^1(ins B-corr^1) o^1. ουδε (throughout vv. 9, 10) D^1.

10. πλεονεκται ουτε κλεπται D[-gr^2] L b c d e f g h l n o 47 syrr Clem$_2$ Chr$_1$ Thdrt Damasc Thl : om ουτε πλεονεκται k 3. 35. 42. 238. rec (for 1st ου) ουτε, with BD^{3}L rel [Clem$_1$ Ps-Ign$_1$ Meth$_2$(in Epiph) Euthal-ms] Ath$_1$ [Iren-int$_2$ Cypr$_1$] : ουδε D^1(as above) : txt AC[P]ℵ a 17 Clem$_1$ [Ps-Ath$_1$ Julian$_1$(in [Cyr]) Chr$_1$ Thdrt [Damasc]. transp. μεθ. and λοι. P [Ps-Ath$_1$]. θεου bef βασ. D^1[-gr]. rec ins ου bef κληρονομησουσιν (*prob from writing the* ου *of* θεου *twice over : the mistake being perpetuated, or even the readg occasioned, by the* ου κληρ. *of ver* 9. *This seems a more likely account than that a variation betw the two vv should have been sanctioned by perpetuating an accidental omn of the* ου), with LP rel Ign(but readg varies. Coteler has κληρονομησαι δυνανται, omg ου) [Clem$_2$ Orig$_1$-c$_1$] Ath$_1$ Ps-Ath$_1$ Cyr-jer$_1$ Chr-ms$_1$ Thdrt$_1$ Thl : om ABCDℵ l^1 17 Polyc$_1$ Orig[-c$_1$] Meth$_1$ Ath$_1$ Chr$_1$ Thdrt$_1$ Damasc$_1$.

11. (αλλα (3ce), so AB(D)[P]ℵ : C has αλλ' all three times ; D^1, the 1st time ; L m, the 2nd and 3rd times.) aft κυριου ins ημων B C(appy) P l m 17. 47 vulg [F-lat spec] Syr syr-w-ast copt æth arm Ath$_3$[-int$_2$ Ps-Ath$_2$ Chr$_1$ Euthal-ms Dial$_1$ Thdrt] Did$_3$ Epiph$_1$ Iren-int$_2$ Orig-int$_3$ Cypr$_1$: om ADLℵ rel [(Clem$_1$) Did$_1$ Cyr$_1$ Damasc Iren-int$_2$ Tert$_1$]. aft ιησου ins χριστου B C(appy) D^1[and lat] Pℵ l m 17 &c (as precedg) [and Cyr$_1$ Tert$_1$] : om AD^{3}L [Damasc] Thl Œc.

the rigid exclusion from the kingdom of God of *all wrong-doers* of every kind (included here under ἄδικοι) ; see Gal. v. 21. **μὴ πλανᾶσθε**] This caution would be most salutary and needful in a dissolute place like Corinth. It is similarly used, and with an express reference to ὁμιλίαι κακαί, ch. xv. 33. **πόρνοι** refers back to ch. v., and is taken up again, vv. 12 ff. **μαλακοί** = παθικοί (see in Wetst.). **μέθυσοι**, see on ch. v. 11. **11.**] 'These things were the *former state* of some among you : but ye are now in a far different state.' **These things** (I cannot think with Meyer that ταῦτα is used with an implication of contempt, *such a horde*, or *rabble* : it is rather '*of such a kind*,' see Winer, Gr. § 23. 5) **were some of you** (τινες limits the ὑμεῖς which is the suppressed subject of ἦτε) : **but ye washed them off** (viz. at your baptism. The 1 aor. mid. cannot by any possibility be passive in signification, as it is generally, for doctrinal reasons, here rendered. On the other hand the middle sense has no doctrinal import, regarding merely the fact of their having submitted themselves to Christian baptism. See ref. Acts), **but** (there is in the repetition of ἀλλά, the triumph of one who was under God the instrument of this mighty change) **ye were sanctified** (not in the dogmatic sense of *progressive* sanctification, but so that whereas before you were unholy, by the reception of the Holy Ghost you became *dedicated to God* and *holy*), **but ye were justified** (by faith in Christ, you received the δικαιοσύνη θεοῦ, Rom. i. 17), **in the Name of the Lord Jesus, and in the** (working of the) **Spirit of our God.** These two last clauses must not be fancifully (as Meyer, al.) assigned amongst the preceding. They belong to *all*, as De Wette rightly maintains. The spiritual washing in baptism, the sanctification of the children of God, the justification of the believer, are all wrought in the Name of the Lord Jesus, and are each and all the work of the Spirit of our God. By the ἡμῶν again, he binds the Corinthians and himself together in the glorious blessings of the gospel-state, and mingles the oil of joy with the mourning which by his reproof he is reluctantly creating.

12 [n] Πάντα μοι [no] ἔξεστιν, ἀλλ' οὐ πάντα [p] συμφέρει.
[n] πάντα μοι [no] ἔξεστιν, ἀλλ' οὐκ ἐγὼ [qr] ἐξουσιασθήσομαι ὑπό
τινος. 13 τὰ [s] βρώματα τῇ [t] κοιλίᾳ, καὶ ἡ [t] κοιλία τοῖς
[s] βρώμασιν· ὁ δὲ θεὸς καὶ [u] ταύτην καὶ [u] ταῦτα [v] καταργήσει. τὸ δὲ σῶμα οὐ τῇ [x] πορνείᾳ, ἀλλὰ τῷ κυρίῳ,
καὶ ὁ κύριος τῷ σώματι· 14 ὁ δὲ θεὸς καὶ τὸν κύριον

K και ταυτα... ABCDK LPℵab cdefg hklm no 17. 47

n constr., Mark ii. 24. ch. x. 23 bis.
o Acts xxi. 37 reff.
p constr., ch. x. 23. 2 Cor. viii. 10. Prov. xix. 10. Sir. xxxvii. 28.
q play on words, ch. iii. 17 al.
r Luke xxii. 25. ch. vii. 4 bis only. Eccl. ix. 17.
s plur., Matt. xiv. 15 ‖ L. Mark vii. 19. Luke iii. 11. 1 Tim. iv. 3. Heb. ix. 10. xiii. 9 only. Job vi. 5.
t = Matt. xv. 17. Rev. x. 9, 10. 2 Kings xx. 10. 2 Chron. xxi. 15, 18, 19.
u see ch. vii. 7.
v Rom. iii. 3 reff.
x ch. v. 1 reff.

12. om 2nd *μοι* C[1] Orig$_1$ Tert$_3$.

12—20.] Correction of an abuse of the doctrine of Christian freedom which some among them had made, that, as meats were indifferent, so was fornication (vv. 12—17). Strong prohibition of, and dissuasive from this sin (vv. 18—20). **12.**] *Statement of the true doctrine of Christian freedom.* **πάντα μοι ἔξεστιν** are *the bona fide words of the Apostle himself*, not, as some have understood them, the saying of an opponent cited by him. For (1) the sentiment is a true Christian axiom: *πάντα* being of course understood, as it evidently was even by the abusers of the doctrine, of things (supposed by them) *ἀδιάφορα*. (2) It is not introduced by any clause indicative of its being the saying of another, which is Paul's habit in such cases, see Rom. xi. 19. (3) The Apostle does not either deny or qualify the *ἔξεστιν*, but takes up the matter from another point of view, viz. the *συμφέρει*. The *μοι* is spoken in the person of Christians generally. "Sæpe Paulus prima persona singulari eloquitur quæ vim habent gnomes: in hac præsertim epistola, ver. 15, ch. vii. 7, viii. 13, x. 23, 29, 30, xiv. 11." Bengel. **συμφέρει**] **are advantageous**—in the most general sense: distinguished from *οἰκοδομεῖ*, ch. x. 23, where the words again occur. Meyer cites from Theodor. Mops., —*ἐπειδὴ γὰρ οὐ πάντα συμφέρει, δῆλον ὡς οὐ πᾶσι χρηστέον, ἀλλὰ τοῖς ὠφελοῦσι μόνοις.* **ἀλλ' οὐκ ἐγὼ ἐξ.**] Meyer thinks that the *ἐγώ* here has an emphasis, as meaning *the real I*, my moral personality. But this can hardly be so: the real emphasis is on *οὐκ*, and *ἐγώ* corresponds to *μοι*, expressed more to bring out the first person as the *sample of Christians in general*, than for any such formal distinction. **ἐξουσιασθήσομαι**] **I will not be deprived of my freedom by any practice**;—i. e. indulge in any practice which shall mar this liberty and render it no real freedom, making me to be one under *ἐξουσία*, instead of one exercising it. The play on *ἔξεστι* and *ἐξουσία* cannot be given in English. **13, 14.**] "a cibis ad venerem non valet consequentia." Bengel. The argument is,—meats (of which he doubtless had often impressed on them that *they were ἀδιάφορα*, whence the abuse) are expressly created for the belly, and the belly for them, by its organization being fitted to assimilate them; and both these are of a transitory nature: in the change to the more perfect state, God will do away with both. Therefore meats *are ἀδιάφορα*. But neither is the body *created for* fornication, nor can this transitoriness be predicated *of it*: the body is *for the Lord*, and the Lord (in his mediatorial work) for the body: and God raised up the Lord, and will raise up us (i. e. our bodies): so that the body is not perishable, and (resumed ver. 18) he that fornicates, sins *against his own body*. Therefore, fornication *is not* an *ἀδιάφορον*. It is very remarkable how these verses contain the germ of three weighty sections of the Epistle about to follow, and doubtless in the Apostle's mind when he wrote them, (1) the relation between the sexes: (2) the question of meats offered to idols: (3) the doctrine of the Resurrection of the Body. See Neander, Pfl. u. Leit. p. 401, note 21. **13.**] **τῇ κοιλ.**, scil. *ἐστιν*. The belly is their appointed receptacle—they, its appointed pabulum. Of course even this part of the argument must be understood within the limits of *οὐ πάντα συμφέρει.* **ὁ δὲ θ. . . . καταργ.**] viz. *at the appearing of the Lord:* when, ch. xv. 51, 52, we shall be changed from a *σῶμα ψυχικόν*, to be a *σῶμα πνευματικόν*: not, *at death*. **τῇ πορν.**] The body was not made for the practice of fornication. The reciprocal subserviency of the belly and meats is shewn by their coextensiveness in duration, and perishing together: but when *πορνεία* (and even that lawful use which is physically the same, but which is not *here* contemplated) shall have for ever passed away, the body shall be subserving *its real use*—that of being an instrument for the Lord's work.
κ. ὁ κύρ. τῷ σώμ.] not, *only* for the body: but **for the body**; to sanctify our bodies by His Spirit, and finally to glorify them for Himself, see Rom. viii. 11. This final

[Q is cited on ver 14.] F[-gr] (and also G) [η] ουκ οιδατε... ABCDF KLP$\aleph$ a b c d e f g h k l m n o 17. 47

[y] ἤγειρεν, καὶ ἡμᾶς [z] ἐξεγερεῖ διὰ τῆς δυνάμεως αὐτοῦ.
15 [a] οὐκ οἴδατε ὅτι τὰ σώματα ὑμῶν [b] μέλη χριστοῦ ἐστιν;
[c] ἄρας οὖν τὰ [b] μέλη τοῦ χριστοῦ [d] ποιήσω [e] πόρνης
[b] μέλη; [f] μὴ γένοιτο. 16 ἢ [a] οὐκ οἴδατε ὅτι ὁ [g] κολλώμενος τῇ [e] πόρνῃ ἓν σῶμά ἐστιν; Ἔσονται γάρ [h] φησιν

y = Matt. x. 8. xiv. 2. xvi. 21 al. Isa. xxvi. 19.
z = here only. (Rom. ix. 17 only. Judg. v. 12 al.) Dan. xii. 2 Theod.-B. &c. (not A).
a vv. 2, 3, 9.
b = Rom. xii. 4, 5 (vi. 13 reff.).
c = Matt. xxi. 21. John ii. 16. xi. 39. xx. 1. Eph. iv. 31.
d = Matt. iv. 19. John vi. 15 al. Gen. xlv. 9.
e Matt. xxi. 31, 32. Luke xv. 30 al. Gen. xxxiv. 31.
f Rom. iii. 4 reff.
g Acts v. 13 reff. see Matt. xix. 5.
h ellips., Heb. viii. 5. ch. xv. 27. (see Rom. iv. 3. ix. 17. 1 Tim. v. 18.)

14. elz υμας (*error? Mey thinks, perhaps from Rom* viii. 11), with arm: txt ABCDKLP$\aleph$ rel [vulg F-lat syrr copt æth] Polyc$_1$ [Meth$_1$ Euthal-ms] Iren-int$_1$ [Tert$_1$]. εξεγειρει A D[1][(and lat) Q]: εξεγειρεῖ P m: εξηγειρεν B 67[2]: *suscitavit* am [fuld] harl(but qu, for *-bit?*): txt (*see note*) C D[3][-gr] K(e sil) L$\aleph$ rel vulg-ed [F-lat arm] syrr copt æth Meth$_1$ Ath-mss$_1$ Chr$_1$ [Euthal-ms] Thdrt Iren-int$_1$ Archel$_1$ Tert$_1$, συνεξεγερει 47.

15. ins η bef ουκ F Meth$_1$. ημων A$\aleph^1$ 238. om εστιν F[-gr]. for αρας, αρα P [b[1] d e[2] g k] 47[2], η αρα F Orig$_1$[-c$_1$] Meth Tert. μελη bef πορνης DF latt [Antch$_1$] Iren-int$_1$ [Tert] Cypr Lucif.

16. om η D[-gr] KL rel syr Mcion-e$_2$ Dial$_1$ Thdrt-ms Damasc Tert$_1$: ins ABCFP$\aleph$ a[1] h m 17 [vulg D-lat Syr copt] Clem$_1$ Meth$_1$ Chr$_1$ [Euthal-ms] Œc Cypr$_1$ Lucif$_1$. om φησιν A Epiph$_1$ Cypr$_1$ Ambr$_{sæpe}$ (Tert$_1$): ins BCDFKL[P]$\aleph$ rel latt Dial$_1$ Mcion-e$_1$ [Meth$_1$ Euthal-ms] Chr Thdrt Lucif$_1$.

reference must not be *excluded* here, though it is not the principal thought:—rather, the redemption of the body from sin, and making it into a member of Himself by the Spirit. **14.**] So far from the case of the Lord and the body answering to the other, God **raised up the Lord** (Rom. viii. 11, al. fr.), **and will raise up us too by His power.** I cannot adopt here the reading (ἐξήγειρεν), or the view, of Meyer. He holds, that all reference to the *resurrection*, as a thing *future*, is out of place: that the Apostle refers to the virtual and proleptic resurrection which *has already taken place* in the case of the believer, as Eph. ii. 6; Col. ii. 12,—and thinks that the reading ἐξεγερεῖ has arisen from not seeing this. But how unnatural will the construction thus be—ὁ δὲ θεὸς καὶ τὸν κύριον ἤγειρεν, καὶ ἡμᾶς ἐξήγειρεν, διὰ τ. δυν. αὐτοῦ! I can conceive no account of such a sentence, except that some emphasis is meant to be laid on the distinction between ἤγειρεν and **ἐξήγειρεν**, which idea (maintained by Bengel, al.) Meyer himself very properly repudiates: see below. The future corresponds to καταργήσει, and is used with ἡμᾶς,—contrary to the usual practice of Paul, who expected to be alive at the παρουσία,—as the expression, in the first person, of the truth of the future *resurrection, not destruction* of the body. **ἤγειρεν**, viz. ἐκ νεκρῶν, Acts iii. 15; Rom. iv. 24, and passim: **ἐξεγερεῖ**, viz. ἐκ νεκρῶν. So that there is no real difference between the two words. **15.**] Resumption of τὸ σῶμα τῷ κυρίῳ κ. ὁ κύριος τῷ σώματι. The two are so intimately connected, that the Lord *is a mystical Body, of which our bodies,* parts of ourselves in our perfect organization, *are members.* This Christian axiom is introduced as before (reff.) by οὐκ οἴδατε ὅτι. **Having then** (οὖν, 'concesso,' that my body is a member = my members are members of Christ) **alienated** ([**or, taken away**] ἄρας is not merely pleonastic, '*Shall I take .... and make them ....*' as E. V. This is shewn by its position first in the sentence) **the members of Christ** (i. e. my own members) **shall I make them an harlot's members?** The expression πόρνης μέλη is put as coarsely and startlingly as possible, with the emphasis on **πόρνης**. **ποιήσω** may also be the aor. subj., '*must I, have I any right to, make them?*' But μὴ γένοιτο answers better to the future. **16.**] Explanation and justification of the expression πόρνης μέλη. **ἤ**, as De Wette well, "Do you think the expression ποιήσω πόρν. μέλη too strong?" **κολλ.** "üblicher Ausdruck für Geschlechtsvereinigung." De Wette. **τῇ πόρνῃ**] **with a harlot,** generic: or which in fact amounts to the same, with 'the harlot,' presupposed in the hypothesis. **ἓν σῶμα**, viz. '*with her.*' The full construction would be ὅτι ὁ κολλ. τῇ πόρ. καὶ ἡ πόρ. ἓν σ. εἰσιν, but he is here bringing out the criminality of the *fornicator*, and leaves the other out of view. The citation is spoken of *marriage;* but here as above (see on ver. 13) he is treating merely of the physical act, which is the same in both cases. **φησιν**, viz. GOD, Who is the speaker in the Scriptures: so in citing the same words, our Lord gives them to ὁ ποιήσας (αὐτοὺς) ἀπ' ἀρχῆς, Matt. xix. 5. They were spoken by the mouth of Adam, but prophetically, *divino afflatu.*

οἱ δύο [i] εἰς σάρκα μίαν· 17 ὁ δὲ [gj] κολλώμενος τῷ [j] κυρίῳ
ἓν πνεῦμά ἐστιν. 18 [k] φεύγετε τὴν [l] πορνείαν. πᾶν
[m] ἁμάρτημα ὃ ἐὰν [n] ποιήσῃ ἄνθρωπος, [o] ἐκτὸς τοῦ σώματός ἐστιν· ὁ δὲ [p] πορνεύων [q] εἰς τὸ ἴδιον σῶμα [q] ἁμαρτάνει. 19 ἢ [a] οὐκ οἴδατε ὅτι τὸ σῶμα ὑμῶν [r] ναὸς τοῦ
ἐν ὑμῖν ἁγίου πνεύματός ἐστιν, [s] οὗ ἔχετε ἀπὸ θεοῦ, καὶ
οὐκ ἐστὲ [t] ἑαυτῶν; 20 [u] ἠγοράσθητε γὰρ [v] τιμῆς. [w] δοξά-
σατε [x] δὴ τὸν θεὸν ἐν τῷ σώματι ὑμῶν.

ABCDF KLPℵ a b c d e f g h k l m n o 17. 47

i Gen. ii. 24. = Luke iii. 5. Rom. ii. 26. Gen. xv. 6. j = (Rom. xii. 9) Deut. x. 20. (xi. 22.) 4 Kings xviii. 6. Jer. xiii. 11. k = Paul only. ch. x. 14. 1 Tim. vi. 11. 2 Tim. ii. 22. Sir. xxi. 2. l ch. v. 1 reff. m Mark iii. 28, 29. Rom. iii. 26 only. Isa. lviii. 1. n = 2 Cor. xi. 7 reff. o = 2 Cor. xii. 2 [3 v. r.] ‡. (Acts xxvi. 22. ch. xv. 27 al. 3 Kings iv. 23.) p ch. x. 8 bis only in Epp. Rev. ii. 14, 20. xvii. 2. xviii. 3, 9 only. Ps. lxxii. 27. q Matt. xviii. 15. Luke xv. 18, 21. ch. viii. 12. Gen. xx. 6, 9. Xen. Hell. i. 7. 20. r ch. iii. 16 reff. s attr., Acts i. 1 reff. t gen., ch. i. 12. iii. 23. Rom. xiv. 8. u = ch. vii. 23. 2 Pet. ii. 1. Rev. v. 9. xiv. 3, 4. v Acts xix. 19 reff. w Rom. i. 21 reff. x = Luke ii. 15. Acts xiii. 2. xv. 36. Gen. xviii. 4.

18. for φευγ., φυγετε F. for εαν, αν D^1 17. 106 [Meth$_1$].

19. for το σωμα, τα σωματα (*corrn to suit* υμων) A-corr^1 L c d f g m n 17 syr copt arm Orig$_2$[-c$_2$-int$_1$] Meth$_1$ Did$_4$ [Cyr$_1$ Euthal-ms Hil$_1$] Jer Ambrst Aug Vig: *membra vestra* vulg [spec] Ambr Pel Fulg Bede: txt A^1(appy) BCDFKPℵ rel Syr [basm] Chr$_1$ Orig-int$_2$ Tert$_1$. πνευματος bef αγιου B vulg [F-lat spec Orig-int$_2$ Did-int$_1$ Ambrst]. ins του bef θεου Pℵ^3 [Orig-c$_1$ Did$_1$ Chr$_1$]. for εαυτ., αυτων ℵ^1.

20. (for δοξασατε δη, *glorificate et portate* vulg [F-lat] G-lat Cypr$_2$ [Lucif$_1$ Ambrst (but *clarificate* Cypr$_1$ Ambrst)]; *gl. et tollite* spec Tert, δοξασατε δη αρα Chr-txt(Sav and Matth's ms$_1$), δοξασατε δη αρατε Chr-txt(Montf and Matth's ms$_1$), δοξ. τ. θ. τουτεστιν αρατε τ. θ. Chr-txt(ms$_1$)—see Griesb, who adds "Cæterum in comm istud ἄρατε non attingit, præter hom. 4. in 1 Tim. hæc habet δοξάσωμεν δὴ τὸν θεὸν, ἄρωμεν τὸν θεὸν ἐν τῷ σώματι" &c.—om δη ℵ^1(ins ℵ-corr^1) [D-lat copt Orig-c$_1$ Did$_1$ Thdrt Iren-int$_1$].) rec at end adds και εν τω πνευματι υμων ατινα εστι του θεου (*insd appy with a view to make the exhortation complete. An ecclesiastical portion began at* δοξασατε), with C^3 D$^{2\cdot3}$[-gr] KLP rel syrr [arm-usc(and as far as υμων arm-zoh)] Chr$_1$ Thdrt$_2$: om ABC^{1}D^{1}Fℵ 17 latt copt [basm arm-ms] æth Orig[-c$_1$] Meth$_1$(in Epiph) Did$_2$ Cyr$_1$ [Euthal-ms] Max Damasc Iren-int$_1$ Tert$_2$ Cypr Lucif [Ambrst].

To render φησιν impersonal, 'it says,' 'heißt es,' though justified by classical usage, see Winer, edn. 6, § 58. 9, would, as Meyer remarks, be altogether without precedent in the citations of Paul. The words **οἱ δύο** are not in the Heb., but in the LXX and the Samaritan Pentateuch, and are found in the Rabbinical citations of the passage. See note on Matt. xix. 5.

17.] Union to God, His service, and His ways, is often expressed by this word (κολλ.) in the LXX (reff.): but here *that inner union with Christ in spirit* is meant, which is the normal state of every believer, and of which it may be said that he ἓν πν. ἐστιν with Christ. See John xvii. 21, and the parable of John xv. 1—7. Meyer rightly remarks, that the mystical marriage between Christ and His Church must not (as Olsh. from Eph. v. 23 ff.) be pressed here, as the relations of the compared are not correspondent. Still, however, the inner verity of that mystical relation is the *ground* of both passages.

18—20.] *Direct prohibition of fornication, and its grounds.*

18.] **φεύγετε** might be followed by οὖν, but is more forcible in this disconnected form. **πᾶν ἁμάρτ.**] The assertion, which has surprised many of the Commentators, is nevertheless *strictly true.* Drunkenness and gluttony, e. g. are sins done *in* and *by* the body, and are sins *by abuse of* the body,—but they are still ἐκτὸς τοῦ σώματος—introduced *from without*, sinful *not* in their *act*, but in their *effect*, which effect it is each man's duty to foresee and avoid. But fornication is the *alienating that body which is the Lord's, and making it a harlot's body*—it is sin *against a man's own body*, in its very nature,—against *the verity and nature* of his body; not an *effect on* the body from participation of things without, but a *contradiction of the truth* of the body, wrought *within itself*. When *man* and *wife* are one in the Lord,—united *by His ordinance*,—no such alienation of the body takes place, and consequently no sin.

19.] Justification of the εἰς τὸ ἴδ. σῶμ. ἁμαρτ. above,—and this by an amplification of the above σῶμα τῷ κυρίῳ, and ἓν πνεῦμά ἐστιν. **Your body** (i. e. the body of each man among you, but put singular, to keep, as in ch. iii. 16, the unity of the idea of God's temple, or perhaps because *the body* in its attributes is in question here) **is the temple** of (possessed by, as His residence: *the* temple, not a temple, see note on ch. iii. 16) **the Holy Spirit who is in you** (reminiscence of the reality of His indwelling), **whom ye have from God** (reminis-

VII. 1 Περὶ δὲ [y] ὧν ἐγράψατε, [z] καλὸν [a] ἀνθρώπῳ

y attr., Rom. xv. 18 reff. z = Rom. xiv. 21 reff. vv. 8, 26. a = Matt. xix. 5 (from Gen. ii. 24), 10.

Chap. VII. 1. rec aft εγραψατε ins μοι, with ADFKLP rel [vulg-clem] syrr copt [basm æth arm] Orig[-c_1] $Meth_1$ Chr_2 Thdrt Jer_1 $Ambrst_1$ Aug: om BCℵ 17 am fuld[1] [Euthal-ms] $Tert_2$.

cence, *whose* Spirit He is, and so preparation for the following inference), **and are not your own** (so that ye have no right to alienate your body, not being *yours*). **20.**] *Proof, that ye are not your own.* The *possession* of your body as His temple, by the Holy Ghost, is a *presumptive proof* that ye are not; but there is also a proof in *matter of fact:* **For ye were bought** (not, as E. V. *are bought*, which destroys the historic reference) **with a price** (viz. the *blood of Christ*, see 1 Pet. i. 18, 19; Matt. xx. 28; Gal. iii. 13,—not as Vulg. *pretio magno:* τιμῆς merely recalls the fact *here*, that *a price* was paid and so the purchase completed). This *buying* is here mentioned mainly with reference to the *right of possession*, which Christ has thereby acquired in us. In other places it is alleged as a freeing from other services: e. g. that of sin (Rom. vi. 17, 18), of the law and its curse (Gal. iii.), of Satan (Col. i. 13). **δοξάσ. δὴ . . . .**] **Glorify then** (δή, not exactly an inference from the foregoing, but = 'eja,' 'agedum,' tending to enforce and intensify the command: "as a cheering or hortatory expression," Stanley. So Od. *v.* 17, τέτλαθι δή, κραδίη; see Hartung, Partikellehre, i. 284 f.) **God** (i. e. not *praise* God, but glorify Him by your acts) **in your body** (not, *by means of* your body, but *in your body*, as the temple of God; see John xiii. 32).

Chap. VII. 1—40.] Reply to their enquiries respecting marriage; by which occasion is given for various collateral instructions and commands. In order to the right understanding of this chapter, it will be well to remember, that the enquiries in the letter of the Corinthians appear to have been made in *disparagement of marriage*, and to have brought into doubt whether it were not better to *avoid it where uncontracted*, and *break it off where contracted*, or this last at all events *where one of the parties was an unbeliever*. These questions he answers, vv. 1—16: and puts on their true grounds, vv. 17—24. They appear also to have asked respecting *virgins*, what was their duty and that of their parents, as to their contracting marriage. This he discusses in its various aspects of duty and Christian expediency, vv. 25—38. Then he concludes with an answer and advice, respecting the liberty of a woman to marry after the death of her husband. The *whole* is written under the strong impression (see on this, notes, Acts ii. 20; Rom. xiii. 11, and 2 Cor. v.: and Prolegg. to Vol. III. ch. v. § iv. 5—10) of the near approach of the end of this state of things (vv. 29—31), and as advising them under circumstances in which persecution, and family division for the Gospel's sake, might at any time break up the relations of life. The precepts therefore and recommendations contained in the chapter are to be weighed, as those in ch. viii. al., *with reference to change of circumstances;* and the meaning of God's Spirit in them with respect to the subsequent ages of the Church, to be sought by *careful comparison and inference*, not rashly assumed and misapplied. I may also premise, that in hardly any portion of the Epistles has the hand of correctors and interpolators of the text been busier, than here. The absence of all ascetic tendency from the Apostle's advice, on the point where asceticism was busiest and most mischievous, was too strong a testimony against it, to be left in its original clearness. In consequence, the textual critic finds himself in this chapter sometimes much perplexed between different readings, and in danger of on the one hand adopting, on overwhelming manuscript authority, corrections of the early ascetics,—and on the other excluding, from a too cautious retention of the rec. text, the genuine but less strongly attested simplicity of the original.

1, 2.] *Concession of the expediency* (where possible) *of celibacy, but assertion of the practical necessity of marriage, as a remedy against fornication.* **1.**] **δέ**, transitional, passing on to another subject. **καλὸν . . . .**] not, *morally good:* for in ver. 28 expressly *not sin*, but *inexpediency*, is the reason for not marrying: nor good in the sense of ὑπερέχον, as Jerome, adv. Jovin. i. 7, vol. ii. p. 246, 'si bonum est mulierem non tangere, malum ergo est tangere:' but **expedient**, generally: 'more for a man's best interests under present circumstances:' Angl. 'it is the best way,' in the colloquial sense: so also throughout the chapter: see the word qualified ver. 26, καλὸν . . . **διὰ τὴν ἐνεστῶσαν ἀνάγκην.** **ἀνθρώπῳ**] though of necessity by what follows, the *man* only is intended, yet ἀνθρώπῳ does not here or in reff. = ἀνδρί, but as Meyer remarks, regards the man not merely in his *sexual* but in his *human* capacity. Thus in its deeper reference, it

γυναικὸς μὴ [b] ἅπτεσθαι· 2 διὰ δὲ τὰς [c] πορνείας ἕκαστος
τὴν ἑαυτοῦ γυναῖκα ἐχέτω, καὶ ἑκάστη τὸν ἴδιον ἄνδρα
ἐχέτω. 3 τῇ γυναικὶ ὁ ἀνὴρ τὴν [d] ὀφειλὴν [e] ἀποδιδότω,
[f] ὁμοίως [f] δὲ [f] καὶ ἡ γυνὴ τῷ ἀνδρί. 4 ἡ γυνὴ τοῦ ἰδίου
σώματος οὐκ [g] ἐξουσιάζει, ἀλλὰ ὁ ἀνήρ· [f] ὁμοίως [f] δὲ [f] καὶ
ὁ ἀνὴρ τοῦ ἰδίου σώματος οὐκ [g] ἐξουσιάζει, ἀλλὰ ἡ γυνή.
5 μὴ [h] ἀποστερεῖτε ἀλλήλους, [i] εἰ [i] μή [i] τι ἂν [k] ἐκ [l] συμφώνου
[m] πρὸς [m] καιρόν, ἵνα [n] σχολάσητε τῇ [o] προσευχῇ καὶ πάλιν

ABCDF KLPℵ a b c d e f g h k l m n o 17. 47 [Q is cited on ver 3.]

b = Gen. xx. 6. Prov. vi. 29. c ch. v. 1 reff. abstr. plur., 2 Cor. xii. 20. Gal. v. 20. James ii. 1. Winer, edn. 6, § 27. 3. d Matt. xviii. 32. Rom. xiii. 7 only +. (-ημα, Rom. iv. 4.) e = Rom. xiii. 7. (xii. 17 reff.) f here bis. Matt. xxvii. 41 (|| Mk. v. r.). Luke v. 10. x. 32. James ii. 25 only. see Rom. i. 27. g ch. vi. 12 reff. h = here only. (ch. vi. 7, 8 reff.) Exod. xxi. 10. i Luke ix. 13. 2 Cor. xiii. 5 only. k = John iii. 34. 2 Cor. viii. 13. ix. 7. l here only. Eccl. vii. 14 Aℵ Ald. compl. (-νως B, -νεῖν C) only. (-νεῖν, Acts v. 9. -νησις, 2 Cor. vi. 15.) m Luke viii. 13 (1 Thess. ii. 17) only. Wisd. iv. 4. n Matt. xii. 44 (|| L. v. r.) only. Exod. v. 8, 17 bis. Ps. xlv. 10 only. o absol., Rom. xii. 12.

2. C [has not] τε [for δε, as in Tischdf's Codex Ephræmi]. την πορνειαν F vulg syrr Orig-int$_1$ Tert$_1$ Cypr$_1$ [Ambrst]. om και εκαστ. τ. ιδ. ανδ. εχ. (*homœotel*) F 48. 114-77 Tert$_1$.

3. om ὁ F(not G). rec (for οφειλην) οφειλομενην ευνοιαν (*see note*), with KL rel syrr [Anton$_1$ Damasc] Thdrt Thl Œc: txt ABCDFP[Q]ℵ[1] 17 latt copt [basm] æth arm Clem$_2$ Orig$_2$[-c$_1$] Meth$_1$ Chr$_2$ [Euthal-ms] Tert$_1$ Cypr$_1$ Ambrst. αποδιδετω A. om δε A 55 Syr copt [basm] arm Orig$_1$ Chr-mss$_1$ Cypr$_1$.

4. (αλλα(twice), so ABCℵ (2nd, D[1] 17).)

5. om αν B Orig$_1$ [Damasc$_1$]. rec σχολαζητε, with KL rel Meth$_1$ Chr$_3$ Thdrt [Damasc]: txt ABCDFPℵ Orig$_2$[-c$_1$ Euthal-ms Cyr$_1$] (Dion) Chr$_{aliq}$. rec ins τη νηστεια και bef τη προσευχη (*see note*), with KLℵ[3] rel syrr goth Chr$_2$[-txt-ed$_1$ Dion$_1$]

would embrace the other sex also. **απτεσθαι**] so in reff.; and in Latin *tangere, attingere, virgo intacta*. See examples in Wetst. This expression is obviously here used in the widest sense, without *present* regard to the difference between the lawful and unlawful use of the woman. The idea that the assertion applies to abstinence from intercourse in the *already married* (see again below), is altogether a mistake. **2.**] The former course is expedient—would avoid much trouble 'in the flesh:' but as a general rule *it may not be*, seeing that for a *more weighty reason* the contrary course is to be recommended. **But on account of [the] fornications** (the many instances of fornication current. The plur. of an abstract noun implies repetition, or varieties of the occurrence: so Herod. vii. 158, ὑμῖν μεγάλαι ὠφελίαι τε κ. ἐπαυρέσεις γεγόνασι: iii. 40, ἐμοὶ δὲ αἱ σαὶ μεγάλαι εὐτυχίαι οὐκ ἀρέσκουσι, see reff., and Kühner, Gramm. ii. 28 (§ 408, γ)) **let each man possess his own wife, and let each woman possess her own husband.** The ἐχέτω is (1) *not concessive*, but *imperative*; not '*habere liceat*,' but '*habeto*.' So the other expressions, γαμησάτωσαν ver. 9, μενέτω ver. 11, &c. (2) not here in the sense of '*utatur, eique commisceatur*,' as Estius, al., which does not come into consideration till the next verse. (3) not emphatic, let each *retain*, according to the mistaken idea mentioned on ver. 1, that he is speaking to the *married*, who though they are not to cohabit are yet to *remain together*. Had either of the two latter senses been meant, the sentence would rather have stood ἐχέτω ἕκ. τ. ἑαυτ. γυναῖκα, κ. ἐχέτω ἑκάστη τ. ἴδ. ἄνδρ. With regard to the assertion of Rückert, that the Apostle here gives a very low estimate of marriage, as solely a remedy against fornication, the true answer is, that Paul does not either here, or in this chapter at all, give any *estimate* of marriage in the abstract. His estimate, *when he does*, is to be found Eph. v. 25—32.

3, 4.] *The duty of cohabitation incumbent on the married.* This point was in all probability raised in the letter of the Corinthians. The Apostle's command is a legitimate following out of διὰ τὰς πορνείας above. **3. τὴν ὀφειλήν**] '*debitum tori*.' The rec. was perhaps an euphemism (we have also the varieties, ὀφειλομένην τιμήν, Chrysostom once: ὀφ. τιμὴν καὶ εὔνοιαν in the ms. 40) for the same thing. Meyer will not concede this, but thinks it arose from a mistaken interpretation of ὀφειλή as meaning *merely* '*benevolentia*:' thinking that not εὔνοια, but φιλότης would be the word in the other case. But some of the later examples in Wetst. seem to bear out this meaning of εὔνοια.

4.] The axiom is introduced without a γάρ, as frequently. **τοῦ ἰδίου . . . . οὐκ ἐξουσιάζει**] '*sui*, cum *potestatem non habet*, elegans facit paradoxon.' Bengel. The ground of this *being another's while they remain their own*, is to be found in the *oneness of body*, in which the marriage state places them. **5.] ἀποστερεῖτε**

[pq] ἐπὶ τὸ αὐτὸ [p] ἦτε, ἵνα μὴ [r] πειράζῃ ὑμᾶς ὁ σατανᾶς [s] διὰ
τὴν [t] ἀκρασίαν ὑμῶν. 6 τοῦτο δὲ λέγω κατὰ [u] συγγνώμην,
οὐ κατ' [v] ἐπιταγήν. 7 θέλω δὲ πάντας ἀνθρώπους εἶναι
ὡς καὶ ἐμαυτόν· ἀλλὰ ἕκαστος ἴδιον ἔχει [w] χάρισμα ἐκ
θεοῦ, ὁ μὲν [x] οὕτως, ὁ δὲ [x] οὕτως.

p Acts ii. 1, 44.
q Luke xvii. 35. Acts i. 15. ii. 47. ch. xi. 20. xiv. 23.
r Matt. iv. 1, 3. ch. x. 13. James i. 13. 3 Kings x. 1.
s = Rom. xiv. 15 reff.
t Matt. xxiii. 25 only +. Jos. Antt. viii. 7. 5. Xen. Mem. iv. 5, 6. (-τής, 2 Tim. iii. 3.)
u here only. Sir. iii. 13 only.
v Rom. xvi. 26 reff.
w = here only. (Rom. i. 11 reff.)
x see ch. vi. 13.

Thdrt: om ABCDFPא[1] 17 latt copt [basm] æth arm ($Clem_1$) $Orig_2$[$-c_2-int_2$] $Dion_1$ $Meth_1$ [$Epiph_1$ $Cyr-p_1$ Euthal-ms Damasc Ambrst] $Cypr_1$. [elz] (for ητε) συνερχεσθε (*gloss: see note*), with a c h $Meth_1$ Chr_1 $Thdrt_1$ Thl: [Steph] συνερχησθε[, with] KLP rel [copt basm] $Thdrt_1$: γινεσθε Tat[-in-]$Clem_1$: *revertimini* vulg [syrr goth arm $Cypr_1$]: txt ABC D[-gr] Fא 17 æth $Orig_1$[$-c_2-int_1$] $Dion_1$ Cyr_1 [Euthal-ms] $Damasc_2$ Aug(*estote*$_{sæpe}$). [πειραζει P(appy) 47[1].] om υμων B Tat(in Clem) Meth.

7. rec γαρ (*gloss, substituted for* δε, *as more appropriate*), with B $D^{2\cdot3}$[-gr] KLPא[3] rel [vulg-clem] syrr [æth arm] Chr_1 $Thdrt_2$ Thl Œc: txt AC D[1][and lat] Fא[1] d 17 am (with demid fuld) copt goth $Orig_1$[$-c_1$] Chr_1 Cyr_1 [Euthal-ms] Damasc [$Cypr_1$ Ambrst]. (αλλα, so BCD[1] 17.) rec χαρισμα bef εχει, with KL rel [vulg-clem harl] syrr goth arm $Ephr_1$ Chr_1 $Thdrt_2$ [Damasc Ambrst Aug$_{sæpe}$]: txt ABDF[P]א m 17 am (with [fuld] demid tol) $Clem_1$ $Orig_1$[$-c_1-int_1$] Cyr[$-p_1$ Euthal-ms] $Cypr_1$, C(appy) has εχει bef εκαστος [Tischdf, ed 8, suspects that it reads as txt]. ins του bef θεου DF c $Thdrt_1$. rec ὃς (twice), with KLא[3] [47(sic)] rel $Orig_1$[$-c_1$] Chr Thdrt [Damasc]: txt ABCDFPא[1] 17 $Clem_1$ Cyr[$-p_1$ $Orig-c_1$ Euthal-ms].

is applied by Meyer to τῆς ἐξουσίας,—by Billroth, al., to τῆς ὀφειλῆς; De Wette suggests τοῦ σώματος, but prefers, and rightly, leaving its reference indefinite, to be supplied in the reader's mind. **εἰ μή τι, unless perchance** (reff.). **ἄν**] "The verb is sometimes omitted after this particle, but always so that it can be supplied from a foregoing clause. So Eur. Alcest. 181, σὲ δ' ἄλλη γυνὴ κεκτήσεται, σώφρων μὲν οὐκ ἂν μᾶλλον, εὐτυχὴς δ' ἴσως." Hartung, Partikellehre, ii. 330. **ἐκ, according to**: the mutual agreement being the *ground*, and the *measure*, of the act. **ἵνα σχ.**] **in order that ye may have undisturbed leisure for prayer.** The pres. σχολάζητε of the rec. would refer to the *general habit*, and would thus make τῇ προς., 'your *ordinary prayers*,'—being thus inconsistent with the direction given πρὸς καιρόν: the *aorist* expresses this temporary purpose, and shews that the prayer meant is not ordinary but extraordinary,—*seasons of urgent supplication*. Both the alteration to the *present* and the addition of τῇ νηστείᾳ καί, shew how such passages as this have been tampered with by the ascetics: see also Mark ix. 29. **ἦτε,**—not συνέρχησθε as it has been amended (nor -εσθε as it has been re-amended), because εἶναι ἐπὶ τὸ αὐτό in this sense is the *normal state* of the married. For the expression see reff.

The subjunc. still depends on ἵνα—the aim of the temporary separation is *not that you may keep apart*, but for a certain end, and then *that you may be united again*. **ἵνα μὴ πειρ.**] Purpose of the re-union stated, by that which might happen did it not take place. πειράζῃ now is *present*, not *aor.*, as betokening the danger of a state of abstinence if continued. **ἀκρασία** here, not that from ἄκρᾱτος (˘˘¯˘),—which signifies *a bad mixture*, as ἄκρ. ἀέρος, 'insalubrity of the air:' but that from ἀκρᾰτής (˘˘˘¯),—**incontinence**; see reff. **διὰ τ. ἀκρ. ὑμ., on account of your incontinence,**—but hardly, as Meyer seems to think, with allusion to the proverbial fault of the Corinthians in this particular, which would be more definitely expressed, were it intended. The ὑμῶν is necessary to carry out the form of the sentence, corresponding to ὑμᾶς above.

6.] **But this I say by way of allowance** (for you), **not by way of command. τοῦτο** refers, not to ver. 2, as Beza, Grot., and De Wette, because the precept there given depends on a *reason* also given, διὰ τὰς πορνείας, from the nature of which reason it *must be* κατ' ἐπιταγήν: nor to the whole since ver. 2, as Billroth, Rückert, al.,—because the precept in ver. 3 depends on the general truth in ver. 4, and is also a command: nor to πρὸς καιρόν, as Theophyl.:—nor as the ascetics, Orig., Tert., Jerome, Estius (also Calvin), to ἐπὶ τὸ αὐτὸ ἦτε, because both these are but subordinate members of the preceding sentence:—still less to *what follows*, as Rosenm., al.:—but, as the context (ver. 7) shews, to the whole recommendation given in ver. 5. This recommendation all depended on the possibility of their being tempted by incontinence: he gives it not then *as a command* in all cases, but *as an allowance* for those to whom he was writing, whom he knew, and as-

8 Λέγω δὲ τοῖς ʸ ἀγάμοις καὶ ταῖς ᶻ χήραις, ᵃ καλὸν
αὐτοῖς ἐὰν μείνωσιν ὡς κἀγώ. 9 ᵇ εἰ δὲ ᵇ οὐκ ᶜ ἐγκρατεύονται, γαμησάτωσαν· ᵈ κρεῖσσον γάρ ἐστιν γαμῆσαι ἢ
ᵉ πυροῦσθαι. 10 τοῖς δὲ γεγαμηκόσιν ᶠ παραγγέλλω οὐκ

ABCDF KLPℵa bcdef ghkl mno 17. 47

y vv. 11, 32, 34 only †. z Luke iv. 25. Acts ix. 39 al. 2 Kings xiv. 5. a = ver. 1. b Matt. xxvi. 42. Rom. viii. 9. c ch. ix. 25 only. Gen. xliii. 31. 1 Kings xiii. 12 only. (-τής, Tit. i. 8. -τεια, Acts xxiv. 25.) d = Phil. i. 23. 1 Pet. iii. 17. 2 Pet. ii. 21. (ver. 38. ch. xi. 17. Heb. i. 4 al12.) Prov. iii. 14. e = here (2 Cor. xi. 29. Eph. vi. 16. 2 Pet. iii. 12. Rev. i. 15. iii. 18) only. (2 Macc. iv. 38. Ps. xi. 6.) f Acts xvi. 18 reff.

8. ins οτι bef καλον A [syrr]. rec aft αυτοις ins εστιν, with $D^{2\cdot3}$K(om αυτ.) L rel syr [basm] goth Thdrt [$Damasc_1$] Thl Œc: om ABCD¹FPℵ 17 Syr copt [arm] Orig[-c_2] $Meth_1$ $Epiph_1$ Chr_1 Cyr[-p_2 Cyr-jer_1 Euthal-ms] $Damasc_1$. for εαν, αν B. ins ουτως bef μεινωσιν C latt $Meth_1$ [Ambr Ambrst] Aug; bef ως m [basm]. και εγω DF $Meth_1$: εγω a.

9. for ουκ εγκρ., ου κρατευονται F. γαμειτωσαν F [f Epiph-ed_1] Chr-ed_1. κρειττον BDℵ a m 17. om εστιν D¹[-gr] F[-gr] c copt [basm] Orig[-c_1(txt_2)-int_1] $Meth_1$. γαμειν AC¹ℵ¹ 17 $Clem_1$ Orig[-c_1 Euthal-ms] $Damasc_2$.

sumes, to *be thus tempted.* The meaning '*by permission,*' E. V., is ambiguous, appearing as if it meant *by permission of the Lord* (*to say it*): that given by Hammond, al., κατὰ τὴν ἐμὴν γνώμην, is philologically inadmissible. 7.] **I rather** (δέ) **wish that all men were as I myself also am** (καί comparandi, so Xen. Anab. ii. 1. 22, καὶ ἡμῖν ταὐτὰ δοκεῖ ἅπερ καὶ βασιλεῖ. See Hartung, Partikell. i. 126)—viz., ἐν ἐγκρατείᾳ, which Chrys. seems to have read in the text; see below on ver. 8. **ἀλλὰ ἕκαστος . . .** said in the most general way, as a milder expression of 'all have not the gift of continence.' **οὕτως . . . . οὕτως**] both are said *generally,* not one *in the way in which I have it* (of continence), another *in the way of marrying* (i. e. though he have not *this,* and be therefore *better married,* yet has *some other*), which should be ἐκείνως,—but, **one thus, and another thus,**— i. e. 'one in one way, another in another.' 8, 9.] *Advice to the unmarried, that it is best so to remain, but better to marry than be inflamed with lust.*

8. λέγω δέ] taking up the former λέγω, ver. 6, and bringing this advice under the same category as ver. 7, viz. his own wish that all were as himself. The stress is on λέγω, not on τοῖς ἀγ. κ. ταῖς χ., which would in that case be placed first, as τοῖς γεγαμηκόσιν below. **τοῖς ἀγάμοις, the unmarried,** of both sexes: not as usually interpreted, *widowers,* or *unmarried males alone:* this is shewn by the contrasted term γεγαμηκόσιν, which embraces (see vv. 10, 11) *both sexes.* **καὶ ταῖς χήραις** may be added as singling out widows *especially;*—or more probably, because τοῖς ἀγάμοις would naturally be taken as those who *never were married,* and thus widows would not be understood to be included. **καλόν,** see on ver. 1, **it is good for them,** i. e. 'their best way.' **ὡς κἀγώ**] i. e. ἄγαμος. This brings the Apostle's own circumstances more clearly before us than ver. 7, which might be misunderstood: and there can be little doubt from this, that he *never was married.* Grot. says, "ex h. l. non improbabiliter colligitur, Paulo fuisse uxorem, quod et Clemens Alex. putat, sed cum hæc scriberentur, mortuam." But this rests on the mistaken interpretation of ἀγάμοις noticed above. The passage of Clem. Alex. (Strom. iii. [6.] 53, p. 535 P., alluded to in Euseb. iii. 30) is grounded on Paul's having in a certain epistle addressed τὴν αὐτοῦ σύζυγον, ἣν οὐ περιεκόμιζε, διὰ τὸ τῆς ὑπηρεσίας εὐσταλές. But the words σύνζυγε γνήσιε, Phil. iv. 3, certainly have no reference to a wife: see note there.

9.] **but if they are incontinent . . .** οὐκ must be joined not with εἰ, which would require μή, but with the verb. So reff. and Soph. Aj. 1131, εἰ τοὺς θανόντας οὐκ ἐᾷς θάπτειν παρών, '*vetas.*' See other examples in Hartung, Partikellehre, ii. 122 f. ἐγκρατεύω is said by Lobeck, ad Phryn. p. 44, not to be found except in the LXX and N. T. But both Phrynichus and Thom. Mag. say ἀκρατεύεσθαι μηδαμῶς εἴπῃς, ἀλλὰ οὐκ ἐγκρατεύεσθαι. See in Wetst. **γαμησάτ.**] Lobeck, in Phrynichus, p. 742, says, "post ἔγημα (ut ἔγηρα) ἐγάμησα invaluit quod non solum in N. T. libris, ut quidam putaverunt, sed etiam in ipsa Græcia reperitur, auctore, ut videtur, Menandro: ἐγάμησεν ἣν ἐβουλόμην ἐγώ, nihil impediente pedum modulatione quominus usitato uteretur aoristo." **πυροῦσθαι**] "melius nuberent quam urerentur, id est, quam occulta flamma concupiscentiæ in ipsa conscientia vastarentur." Aug. de sancta Virginitate, 34, vol. vi. p. 415. 10, 11.] *Prohibition of separation after marriage; or in case of separation, of another marriage.* These **γεγαμηκότες,** as the ἄγαμοι and χῆραι above, are *all Christians.* The case of *mixed marriages* he treats ver. 12 ff.

ἐγώ, ἀλλὰ ὁ κυριος, γυναῖκα ἀπὸ ἀνδρὸς μὴ [g] χωρισθῆναι.
11 ἐὰν δὲ καὶ [g] χωρισθῇ, μενέτω [h] ἄγαμος ἢ τῷ ἀνδρὶ
[i] καταλλαγήτω· καὶ ἄνδρα γυναῖκα μὴ [j] ἀφιέναι. 12 τοῖς
δὲ λοιποῖς λέγω ἐγώ, οὐχ ὁ κύριος, εἴ τις ἀδελφὸς
γυναῖκα ἔχει [k] ἄπιστον, [l] καὶ [m] αὕτη [n] συνευδοκεῖ [op] οἰκεῖν
[p] μετ' αὐτοῦ, μὴ [j] ἀφιέτω αὐτήν· 13 καὶ γυνὴ [q] ἥτις ἔχει
ἄνδρα [k] ἄπιστον, [l] καὶ [m] οὗτος [n] συνευδοκεῖ [op] οἰκεῖν [p] μετ'

[Q is cited on ver 13.]

g Matt. xix. 6. Judg. iv. 11.
h ver 8.
i Rom. v. 10 reff.
j = here 3ce only. Jos. Antt. xv. 7. 10.
k ch. vi. 6 reff.
l = 2 John 2. Luke xvii. 31.
m Acts ix. 20 reff.
n = and constr., here bis (Luke xi. 48. Acts viii. 1. xxii. 20. Rom. i. 32) only †. (1 Macc. i. 57. 2 Macc. xi. 24, 35 only.)
o Rom. vii. 17 reff.
p = here bis only ‡. (Gen. xxvii. 44.) Soph. Œd. Tyr. 990.
q = Acts x. 41 reff.

10. (αλλα, so AB C(appy) D[1]ℵ.) χωριζεσθαι ADF Orig[-c_1] $Epiph_1$ Bas_1 $Cæs_1$: txt BCKLPℵ rel $Clem_1$ Chr_1 [Euthal-ms] Thdrt.

11. μενειν αγαμον, and καταλλαγηναι F latt goth lat-ff. ins ιδιω bef ανδρι P.

12. rec εγω bef λεγω, with DFKL rel latt syr goth $Orig_1$[-int_1] Chr_1 Thdrt Iren-int_1 : txt ABCPℵ m 17 Syr copt æth Clem $Orig_1$.

13. for ητις, ει τις D[1]FPℵ b[1] h k latt Chr_1([and] ms_1) $Thdrt_1$ Thl-mss_2 [Damasc Ambrst Aug]. rec (for ουτος) αυτος, with D[3][-gr] KL rel syrr arm $Chr_{[sæpe]}$ Thdrt : txt ABCD[1]FP[Q]ℵ m latt copt goth Cyr_1 [lat-ff]. (17 def.) for συνευδ., ευδοκει B.

They are **those already married**.

10. οὐκ ἐγώ, ἀλλὰ ὁ κύριος] *Ordinarily*, the Apostle (ἐγώ) writes, commands, gives his advice, *under conscious inspiration of the Holy Spirit of God*. See ver. 40. He claims expressly, ch. xiv. 37, that the things ἃ γράφω ὑμῖν should be recognized as κυρίου (ἐντολή). But here he is about to give them a command resting, not merely on *inspired apostolic authority*, great and undoubted as that was, but on that of THE LORD HIMSELF. So that all supposed distinction between the Apostle's own writing *of himself* and *of the Lord*, is quite irrelevant. He *never* wrote *of himself*, being a vessel of the Holy Ghost, who ever spoke by him to the church. The distinction between that which is imperative, and that which is optional, that which is more and that which is less weighty in his writings, is to be made by the cautious and believing Christian, from a wise appreciation of the *subject-matter*, and of the *circumstances under which* it was written. ALL *is the outpouring of the Spirit*, but *not all for all time*, nor *all on the primary truths* of the faith. **Not I, but the Lord**, viz. in ref. Matt. See also Mark x. 12, where the *woman's* part is brought out. That *it* occupies the *principal place* here, is perhaps because the *Christian women* at Corinth may have been the most ready to make the separation: or perhaps, because the woman, from her place in the matrimonial union, may be more properly said ἀπὸ ἀνδρὸς χωρισθῆναι than the man ἀπὸ γυναικὸς χωρισθῆναι. **χωρισθ., be separated**, whether by *formal divorce* or *otherwise*; the καταλλαγήτω below, is like this, an *absolute passive*; undefined whether by her own or her husband's doing. **11.**] ἐάν to καταλλαγήτω is parenthetical. It supposes a case of *actual* separation, contrary of course to Christ's command: **if such** *have really taken place* (καί, veritably: see note on 2 Cor. v. 3, and Hartung, Partikell. i. 132), the additional sin of a new marriage (Matt. v. 32) must not be committed, but the breach healed as soon as possible. **καταλλ.**] see above on χωρισθῇ. **κ. ἄνδρ. γυν. μὴ ἀφ.**] The Apostle does not add the qualification παρεκτὸς λόγου πορνείας Matt. v. 32 (xix. 9), not found in Mark x. 11 or Luke xvi. 18. But we cannot hence infer that he was not aware of it. The *rule*, not the exception, here was in his mind: and after what had been before said on the subject of fornication, the latter would be understood as a matter of course. **12—16.**] *Directions for such Christians as were already married to Heathens. Such a circumstance must not be a ground* per se *of separation,—and why: but if the unbelieving party wished to break off the union, let it be so.* **12.**] **τοῖς λοιποῖς, the rest**, perhaps in respect of their *letter of enquiry*,—the *only ones not yet dealt with*. At all events, the meaning is plain, being those who are involved in mixed marriages with unbelievers. **ἐγώ, οὐχ ὁ κύρ.**] **I**, i. e. I Paul, in my apostolic office, under the authority of the Holy Spirit (see above on ver. 10), **not the Lord**, i. e. not Christ by any direct command spoken by Him: it was a question with which HE *did not deal*, in His recorded discourses. In the right arrangement of the words (txt) the stress is not on ἐγώ, but on λέγω: **But to the rest I say (I, not the Lord).** συνευδοκεῖ presupposes *his own* wish to continue united. **αὕτη**, not αὐτή, and **οὗτος**, not αὐτός, below,—see reff. **13.**] The change of construction καὶ γυνὴ ἥτις . . . καὶ οὗτος . ., is found frequently with καί: so Il. α. 78, ἦ γὰρ ὀΐομαι ἄνδρα χολωσέμεν, ὃς μέγα πάντων | Ἀργείων κρατέει καί οἱ πείθονται

r = Acts xx. 32. xxvi. 18. Exod. xxix. 37.
s ver. 12.
t = ch. xv. 22 reff. ἐν σοὶ πᾶσ' ἔγωγε σώζομαι, Soph. Aj. 519.
u ch. v. 10 only.
v = Acts x. 14 reff.

ABCDF KLPℵ a b c d e f g h k l m n o 17. 47

αὐτῆς, μὴ [j] ἀφιέτω τὸν ἄνδρα. 14 [r] ἡγίασται γὰρ ὁ ἀνὴρ
ὁ [s] ἄπιστος [t] ἐν τῇ γυναικί, καὶ [r] ἡγίασται ἡ γυνὴ ἡ
ἄπιστος [t] ἐν τῷ ἀδελφῷ· [u] ἐπεὶ [u] ἄρα τὰ τέκνα ὑμῶν
[v] ἀκάθαρτά ἐστιν, νῦν δὲ ἅγιά ἐστιν. 15 εἰ δὲ ὁ [s] ἄπιστος

rec (for τον ανδρα) αυτον (*corrn to conform to αυτην above, ver* 12), with KLP rel syr Chr_1 Thdrt [Damasc] $Tert_1$: αυτην (o^1 ?) 106 : txt ABCDF[Q] m 17 vulg Syr copt goth æth arm Cyr_1 [Euthal-ms] Jer Ambrst Aug Pel Bede : αυτον ανδρα ℵ, but αυ erased by $ℵ^{1 \text{ or } 3}$.

14. om γαρ P. aft γυναικι ins τη πιστη DF latt Syr Mart-Clem $Tert_1$. (om Aug-mss and expr.) (στος of 2nd απιστος is supplied in smaller letters by ℵ-$corr^1$.) rec (for αδελφω) ανδρι (*explanatory gloss, substituted as more appropriate : but* αδελφω *has peculiar force here*), with D^3[-gr] $KLℵ^3$ rel vulg syrr goth æth arm Chr_1 Thdrt [Euthal-ms Damasc] Thl Œc Iren[-int_1 $Tert_1$] (but add τω πιστω vulg Syr Iren-int Tert [Ambrst]): txt ABC D^1[and lat] $FPℵ^1$ 17 copt [Cyr-p_1] Aug_{expr}. νυνι D^1F Chr_1 [and ms]. [om εστιν A(appy). It reads νυν δε αγ . . . the end of the line being def).]

'Αχαιοί. See reff., and Kühner, ii. 526 (§ 799). Meyer remarks, that the Apostle uses the *vox media* ἀφιέναι here, of *both parties*, the husband and wife, not ἀπολύειν (as Matt. v. 31, &c.), which would apply only to the husband. In the E. V. this identity of terms is unfortunately neglected. The same word, part from, would well have expressed ἀφιέτω in both cases.

By the Greek as well as Roman customs the *wife had the power of effecting a divorce.* At Athens,—when the divorce originated with the wife, she was said ἀπολείπειν the house of her husband : when with the husband, ἀποπεμπέσθαι. At Rome, the only exception to the wife's liberty of effecting a divorce appears to have been in the case of a freedwoman who had married her patronus. See Smith's Dict. of Gr. and Rom. Antt. artt. Divortium, and ἀπολείψεως δίκη. Olsh. thinks that Paul puts both alternatives, because he regards the *Christian party* as the *superior one* in the marriage. But, as Meyer remarks, this would be inconsistent with the fundamental law of marriage, Gen. iii. 16, and with the Apostle's own view of it, ch. xi. 3, xiv. 34; Eph. v. 22, 23; 1 Tim. ii. 11, 12. **14.**] *Ground of the above precept.* **ἡγίασται**] The meaning will best be apprehended by remembering (1) that *holiness*, under the Gospel, answers to *dedication to God* under the law; (2) that the ἡγιασμένοι under the Gospel are the *body of Christian men*, dedicated to God, and thus become His in a peculiar manner : (3) that this being so, things belonging to, relatives inseparably connected with, the *people of God* are said to be *hallowed* by *their* ἁγιότης : so Theophylact, οὐχ ὅτι ἅγιος γίνεται ὁ Ἕλλην. οὐ γὰρ εἶπεν ὅτι **ἅγιός ἐστιν· ἀλλ', ἡγίασται·** τουτέστι, τῇ ἁγιότητι τοῦ πιστοῦ νενίκηται. Chrysostom well shews the distinction between this case and that in ch. vi. 15, that being a connexion κατὰ τὴν ἀσέβειαν,—in and under the condition of the *very state*, in which the other party is *impure :* whereas this is a connexion according to a pure and holy ordinance, by virtue of which, although the physical unity in both cases is the same, the *purity overbears the impurity*. **ἐν τῇ γ., ἐν τῷ ἀδελ.**] in, i. e. his or her ἁγιότης is *situated in*, rests in, *the other* (see reff.: and note, ch. vi. 2). **ἐπεὶ ἄρα**] as ref., but here elliptically : **since in that case** (i. e. as understood, the *other* alternative, —the *non-hallowing*). **ἐστιν**, not ἂν εἴη, nor ἦν [E. V.], but *pres.:* because the supposed case is *assumed*, and the ind. pres. used of what *has place* on its assumption. **ἅγια**] as ἡγίασται above : **holy to the Lord.** On this *fact, Christian children being holy*, the argument is built. This being so,—they being hallowed, because the children of Christians,—it follows that *that union out of which* they sprung, must *as such* have the same hallowed character ; i. e. that the *insanctity* of the one parent is in it *overborne* by the *sanctity* of the other. The *fact* of the children of Christians, God's spiritual people, *being holy*, is tacitly assumed as a matter of course, from the precedent of God's ancient covenant people. With regard to the bearing of *this verse* on the subject of Infant Baptism,—it seems to me to have *none*, further than this : that it establishes the analogy, so far, between Christian and Jewish children, as to shew, that if the initiatory rite of the old covenant was administered to the one,—that of the new covenant, in so far as it was regarded as corresponding to circumcision, would probably as a matter of course be administered to the other. Those, as Meyer, who deny any such inference, forget, as it seems to me, that it is not *personal*

[w] χωρίζεται, [w] χωριζέσθω. οὐ [x] δεδούλωται ὁ ἀδελφὸς ἢ
ἡ ἀδελφὴ ἐν [y] τοῖς τοιούτοις, [z] ἐν δὲ εἰρήνῃ [z] κέκληκεν
ἡμᾶς ὁ θεός. 16 [a] τί γὰρ [ab] οἶδας, γύναι, [bc] εἰ τὸν ἄνδρα

w vv. 10, 11. x Acts vii. 6 reff. see ver. 39. y neut., Rom. i. 32 al. masc., ver. 28. ch. xvi. 16, 18. Acts xxii. 22 reff. z = Gal. i. 6. Eph. iv. 4. 1 Thess. iv. 7. a here only ‡. b John ix. 25. 2 Kings xii. 22. Eccl. iii. 21 ABℵ compl.[εἶδε Ed-vat. Ald.] Joel ii. 14. Jonah iii. 9. c Acts xix. 2 (b) reff.

15. om ἡ FPℵ[1] [k[1]] m[Scr states that m omits ἡ] Chr-ms$_1$. υμας ACKℵ[1] copt (sic Treg) [Euthal-ms] Damasc Thl Pel Sedul Bede : txt BDFLℵ[3] rel latt syrr goth æth arm Nys$_1$ Chr$_1$ Thdrt Phot[-c$_1$] Œc Ambrst. (P def.)

holiness which is here predicated of the children, any more than of the unbelieving husband or wife, but *holiness of dedication*, by strict dependence on *one dedicated*. Notwithstanding this ἁγιότης, the Christian child is individually born in sin and a child of wrath; and individually needs the washing of regeneration and the renewing of the Holy Ghost, just as much as the Jewish child needed the typical purifying of circumcision, and the sacrificial atonements of the law. So that in this ἁγιότης of the Christian child there is nothing inconsistent with the idea, nor with the practice, of Infant Baptism. On **νῦν δέ**, see note, ch. v. 11. 15.] *But if the wish for separation* (implied by the *present* χωρίζεται,—**is for being separated**, see Winer, edn. 6, § 40. 2. a, and compare John x. 32, xiii. 6, 27) *proceed from the side of the* UNBELIEVER (emphasis on **ὁ ἄπιστος**), *let him* (or her) *depart* (be separated off). **οὐ δεδούλ.**] οὐκ ἔχει ἀνάγκην ὁ πιστὸς ἢ ἡ πιστὴ ἐν τοῖς ἀπίστοις τοιαύτην, οἵα αὐτῷ ἐπίκειται ἐπὶ τῶν πιστῶν. ἐκεῖ μὲν γὰρ παντὶ τρόπῳ, χωρὶς λόγῳ πορνείας, οὐκ ἔξεστιν ἀπ' ἀλλήλων τοὺς συναφθέντας χωρισθῆναι· ἐνταῦθα δέ, ἂν μὲν συνευδοκῇ τὸ ἄπιστον μέρος τῷ πιστῷ συνοικεῖν, δεῖ μὴ λύειν τὸ συνοικέσιον. ἂν δὲ στασιάζῃ καὶ τὴν λύσιν ἐκεῖνος ποιῇ, οὐ δεδούλωται ὁ πιστὸς εἰς τὸ μὴ χωρισθῆναι. Photius, in Œcumenius. **ἐν τοῖς τοιούτοις** may be taken as masc., *in the case of such persons*,—as above by Phot.:—but the ἐν seems harsh; it is better therefore to render it, **in such cases.**
ἐν δὲ εἰρ.] Not = εἰς εἰρήνην [E. V.], but signifying the moral element *in which* we are called to be: see reff. and ver. 22 below. The meaning is, 'let the unbeliever depart, rather than by attempting to retain the union, endanger that peace of household and peace of spirit, which is part of the calling of a Christian.'
Observe, (1) that there is no contradiction, in this licence of breaking off such a marriage, to the command of our Lord in Matt. v. 32,—because the Apostle expressly asserts, ver. 12, that *our Lord's words do not apply* to such marriages as are here contemplated. They were spoken to those *within the covenant*, and as such apply immediately to the wedlock of *Christians* (ver. 10), but *not to mixed marriages*. De Wette denies this, and holds that Paul is speaking only of the Christian's duty in cases where the marriage is *already virtually broken off*,—and by his remarks on Matt. v. 32, seems to take πορνεία in a wide sense, and to regard it as a justifiable cause of divorce *because it is such a breaking off*. This however appears hardly consistent with ver. 12; for, if it were so, there *would be* a command of the Lord regarding this case. At all events, we may safely assume that where the Apostle is *distinctly referring* to our Lord's command, and supplying what it did not contain, there can be *no real inconsistency*: if such appear to be, it must be in our apprehension, not in his words. (2) That the question of re-marrying after such a separation, is here *left open*: on this, see note on Matt. v. 32. (3) That not a word here said can be so strained as to imply any licence to *contract* marriages with unbelievers. Only those *already contracted* are dealt with: the ἑτεροζυγεῖν ἀπίστοις is expressly forbidden, 2 Cor. vi. 14, and by implication below, ver. 39.
16.] This verse is generally understood as a ground for *remaining united*, as ver. 13, in hope that conversion of the unbelieving party may follow. Thus ver. 15 is regarded as altogether parenthetical. But (1) this interpretation is harsh as regards the context, for ver. 15 is evidently *not parenthetical*,—and (2) it is hardly grammatically admissible (see below, for it makes εἰ = εἰ μή,—'What knowest thou . . . . whether thou shalt *not* save . . . . ?' Lyra seems first to have proposed the true rendering, which was afterwards adopted hesitatingly by Estius, and of late decidedly by Meyer, De Wette, and Bisping: viz. that the verse is *not* a ground for *remaining united*, in *hope*, &c.,—but a ground for *consummating a separation*, and not marring the Christian's peace for so uncertain a prospect as that of converting the unbelieving party. **τί οἶδας εἰ** thus preserves its strict sense, **What knowest thou** (about the question) **whether . . . . ?** and the verse coheres with the words immediately preceding, ἐν εἰρήνῃ κέκλ. ἡμᾶς ὁ θ. I may observe, in addition to Meyer and De W.'s remarks, that the position of the words

d σώσεις; ἢ a τί ab οἶδας, ἄνερ, bc εἰ τὴν γυναῖκα d σώσεις;
17 e εἰ μὴ f ἑκάστῳ ὡς g ἐμέρισεν ὁ κύριος, f ἕκαστον ὡς
h κέκληκεν ὁ θεός, οὕτως i περιπατείτω· καὶ οὕτως ἐν ταῖς
j ἐκκλησίαις πάσαις k διατάσσομαι. 18 l Περιτετμημένος
τις gm ἐκλήθη, μὴ n ἐπισπάσθω· ἐν o ἀκροβυστίᾳ h κέκληταί

d = Rom. xi. 14 reff. e = appy here only. see Gal. i. 7. 2 Cor. iii. 1 rec. f constr., ch. iii. 5. Rom. xii. 3. g = Mark vi. 41. Luke xii. 3. 2 Cor. x. 13. Heb. vii. 2. Josh. xiii. 7. h = ver. 15 reff. i = ch. iii. 3 reff. j plur., Rom. xvi. 16 reff. k = ch. xvi. 1 reff. l Luke i. 59. Acts vii. 8. Gal. ii. 3 al. L.P., exc. John vii. 22. Gen. xvii. 10 al. m hypothet. indic., ver. 27. James v. 13. n here only ‡. Isa. v. 18. o Rom. iii. 30 reff.

...ἐπι-σπασθω C.

ABDFK LPℵ a b c d e f g h k l m n o 17. 47

16. γυνη and ανηρ F. for η τι, ει τι A.

17. μεμερικεν Bℵ¹. [P def.] rec transp κυριος and θεος, with KL rel Syr Chr_1 Thdrt [Damasc]: θεος (twice) 32-3. 63. 93 goth: ο κς and ο κς ο θς G¹[and lat]: txt A B(sic: see table) CDFℵ m 17 latt Syr copt arm [Euthal-ms Ambrst].—ο κς bef εμερισεν A: ο θς εμερισεν and ο κς κεκληκεν k. (P def.) ins και bef εκαστον ως F [Syr]. πασαις bef ταις εκκλησιαις ℵ 17. 47 vulg [$Orig_1$(omg ταις)]. for διατασσομαι, διδασκω (*see ch* iv. 17) D¹F, *doceo* latt lat-ff.

18. εκληθη bef 1st τις D¹·³F [copt basm] goth. rec (for κεκληται τις) τις εκληθη (*conformation to former*), with D³KL rel Chr_1 Thdrt: txt ABPℵ a m 17 copt goth arm [Euthal-ms], τις κεκλ. D¹F [Damasc].

further establishes this rendering. If the *point* of the argument had been the importance, or the prospect, of saving (= converting) the unbelieving party, the arrangement would probably have been εἰ σώσεις τὸν ἄνδρα, and εἰ σώσεις τὴν γυναῖκα, whereas now the verb holds in both clauses a subordinate place, rather subjective to the person addressed, than the main object in the mind of the writer.

Those who take εἰ for εἰ μή, attempt to justify it by reff. 2 Kings, Joel, Jonah, where the LXX have for the Heb. מִי יוֹדֵעַ, τίς οἶδεν εἰ, to express *hope*: but (1) in every one of those passages the verb stands in the emphatic position, and (2) the LXX use this very expression to signify uncertainty, e.g. ref. Eccles., τίς εἶδε(οἶδεν ABℵ: add τό Aℵ³) πνεῦμα υἱῶν τοῦ ἀνθρώπου, εἰ ἀναβαίνει αὐτὸ (add εἰς ABCℵ) ἄνω; The rendering then of the verse will be as follows: (Let the unbeliever depart: hazard not for an uncertainty the peace in which you ought to be living as Christians): **for what assurance hast thou, O wife, whether thou shalt be the means of thy husband's conversion? Or what assurance hast thou, O husband, whether thou shalt be the means of thy wife's conversion?** "This interpretation is the only one compatible with the obvious sense of ver. 15, and of the expression (not τί οἶδας εἰ μή, but) τί οἶδας εἰ σώσεις; and is also in exact harmony with the general tenor of the Apostle's argument, which is not to urge a union, but to tolerate a separation." Stanley; the rest of whose note is deeply interesting as to the historical influence of the verse as commonly misunderstood. **17.] εἰ μή** takes an exception, by way of caution, to the foregoing motive for not remaining together (ver. 16). The Christian partner might carry that motive *too far*, and be tempted by it to *break* the connexion *on his own part*; a course already prohibited (vv. 12—14). Therefore the Apostle adds, **But** (q. d. only be careful not to make this a ground for *yourselves* causing the separation) **as to each** (ἑκάστ. ὡς = ὡς ἑκάστ., reff.) **the Lord distributed (his lot), as** (i.e. ᾗ κλήσει, ver. 20) **God has called each, so** (in that state, without change) **let him walk** (reff.). The **εἰ μή** has raised considerable difficulties. (1) some cursives, with syr-marg and Sevrn., read εἰ τὴν γυναῖκα σώσεις, ἢ μή;—and Knatchbull, al., join **εἰ μή** similarly to the foregoing; εἰ . . . . σώσεις,—εἰ μή. But as De W. remarks, this would be, as Matt. xxii. 17, ἢ οὔ: and then we should have the strictly parallel clauses of ver. 16 rendered unequal, by an appendage being attached to the second, which the first has not: besides that ver. 17 would be disjoined altogether. (2) Pott would supply χωρίζεται,—Mosheim, Vater, and Rückert, σώσεις, after εἰ μή. But so, to say nothing of the irrelevancy of the idea thus introduced, εἰ δὲ μή, or εἰ δὲ καὶ μή (as Meyer), would be required. (3) Theodoret, al., join all as far as κύριος to the foregoing: '*What knowest thou, &c., except in so far as the Lord has apportioned to each?*' But thus the evidently parallel members, ἑκάστ. ὡς ἐμ. ὁ κύρ., and ἑκάστ. ὡς κέκλ. ὁ θ., would be separated, and a repetition occasioned which, except in the case of intended parallelism, would be alien from St. Paul's habit of writing. **οὕτως . . . . διατ.]** τοῦτο εἶπεν, ἵνα τῷ ἔχειν καὶ ἄλλους κοινωνοὺς προθυμότεροι περὶ τὴν ὑπακοὴν διατεθῶσι. Theophyl.

18—24.] *Examples of the precept just given.* εἶτα συνήθως ἀπὸ τοῦ προκειμένου εἰς ἕτερα μεταβαίνει, πᾶσι νομοθετῶν τὰ

τις, μὴ [l] περιτεμνέσθω. 19 ἡ [p] περιτομὴ [q] οὐδέν ἐστιν,
καὶ ἡ [o] ἀκροβυστία [q] οὐδέν ἐστιν, ἀλλὰ [rs] τήρησις [st] ἐντολῶν [t] θεοῦ. 20 ἕκαστος ἐν τῇ [u] κλήσει ᾗ [h] ἐκλήθη, ἐν ταύτῃ
μενέτω. 21 δοῦλος [h] ἐκλήθης, μή σοι [v] μελέτω· ἀλλ' εἰ καὶ
δύνασαι ἐλεύθερος γενέσθαι, μᾶλλον [w] χρῆσαι. 22 ὁ γὰρ

p Paul only, exc. John vii. 22, 23. Acts vii. 8. x. 45. xi. 2. Gen. xvii. 13. Exod. iv. 26. Jer. xi. 16 only.
q = Matt. xxiii. 16, 18. John viii. 54. ch. xiii. 2. 2 Cor. xii. 11.
r = here (Acts iv. 2. v. 18) only †. Wisd. vi. 18 al. ellipt. constr., see ch. iii. 7.
s Sir. xxxv. (xxxii.) 23.
t Matt. xv. 3 ||. Rev. xii. 17. xiv. 12 only. Ezra x. 3.
u = Rom. xi. 29 (reff.).
v ch. ix. 9 reff.
w Acts xxvii. 17. ver. 31. ch. ix. 12, 15. 1 Tim. i. 8. v. 23. Prov. x. 26.

19. om 1st *η* F. om from *εστιν* to *εστιν* F. **20.** *τουτω* A.
21. *αλλα* D¹. om *και* F ms-of-vulg copt.

κατάλληλα. Theodoret. **18—20.**] *First example:* CIRCUMCISION.

18. ἐκλήθη] **Was any one called in circumcision,**—i. e. circumcised at the time of his conversion. **ἐπισπάσθω**] By a surgical operation; see Theophyl., Wetst.,—Winer, Realwörterbuch, art. Beschneidung,—Jos. Antt. xii. 5. 1; 1 Macc. i. 15; Celsus de Re Medica, vii. 25 (in Wetst.). The practice usually was adopted by those who wished to appear like the Gentiles, and to cast off their ancient faith and habits. Among the Christians a strong anti-Judaistic feeling might lead to it. **περιτεμνέσθω**] See Gal. v. 2, al. **19.**] See Gal. v. 6, where our *τήρησις ἐντολῶν θεοῦ* is expressed by *πίστις δι' ἀγάπης ἐνεργουμένη*; and Gal. vi. 15, where it is given by *καινὴ κτίσις*. Cf. an interesting note in Stanley, on the relation of these three descriptions. After **θεοῦ**, supply *τὰ πάντα ἐστίν*: see ch. iii. 7. **20.**] *Formal repetition of the general precept,* as again ver. 24. **κλῆσις** is not the *calling in life,* for it never has that meaning either in classical or Hellenistic Greek (in the example which Wetst. gives from Dion. Hal. Antt. iv. 20, *κλήσεις* is used to express the Latin '*classes,*'—**ἃς καλοῦσιν Ῥωμαῖοι** *κλήσεις*, and so is not a Greek word at all); but strictly **calling** ('vocatio') **by God,** as in ref. The *κλῆσις* of a circumcised person would be *a calling in circumcision,*—and by this he was to abide. **ἐν τῇ . . . ἐν ταύτῃ**] See ch. vi. 4: emphatic. **21—24.**] *Second example:* SLAVERY. **Wert thou called (converted) [being] a slave, let it not be a trouble to thee: but if thou art even able to become free, use it** (i. e. remain in slavery) **rather.** This rendering, which is that of Chrys., Theodoret, Theophyl., Œcum., Phot., Camerar., Estius, Wolf, Bengel, Meyer, De Wette, al., is required by the *usage of the particles, εἰ καί,*—by which, see Hartung, Partikellehre, i. 139, the *καί*, '*also,*' or '*even,*' does not belong to the *εἰ*, as in *καὶ εἰ*, but is spread over the whole contents of the concessive clause: so Soph. Œd. Tyr. 302, *πόλιν μέν,* **εἰ καὶ** *μὴ βλέπεις, φρονεῖς δ' ὅμως, οἵᾳ νόσῳ ξύνεστιν.* Plato, Rep. p. 337, **εἰ** *δ'* *οὖν* **καὶ** *μή ἐστιν ὅμοιον, φαίνεται δὲ τῷ ἐρωτηθέντι τοιούτων.* Aristoph. Lysistr. 254, *χώρει, Δράκης, ἡγοῦ βάδην,* **εἰ καὶ** *τὸν ὦμον ἀλγεῖς.* Thucyd. ii. 64, *μήτε ἐμὲ δι' ὀργῆς ἔχετε . . .* **εἰ καὶ** *ἐπελθόντες οἱ ἐναντίοι ἔδρασαν, ἅπερ εἰκὸς ἦν μὴ ἐθελησάντων ὑμῶν ὑπακούειν.* See more examples in Hartung. It is also required by the *context:* for the *burden* of the whole passage is, 'Let each man *remain* in the *state in which he was called.*' It is given in the Syr.: which has ܓܒܝ ܠܟ ܕܬܫܬܥܒܕ "choose for thyself that thou mayest serve," or simply, "prefer servitude:" not as Meyer from the erroneous Latin of Tremelius, "elige tibi potius quam ut servias" (I am indebted for this correction of some of my earlier editions to the kindness of the Rev. Henry Craik, of Bristol). The other interpretation,—mentioned by Chrys., and given by Erasm., Luther (Stanley is mistaken in quoting him as favourable to the other interpretation: his words are, "Bist du ein Knecht berufen, sorge der nicht: doch, kannst du frei werden, so brauche deß viel lieber"), Beza, Calvin, Grot., and almost all the moderns,—understands *τῇ ἐλευθερίᾳ* after *χρῆσαι*: '*but if thou art able to become free, take advantage of it rather.*' The objections to this are, (1) the position of *καί*, which in this case must have been after *δύνασαι*,—*εἰ δύνασαι καὶ ἐλεύθερος γενέσθαι*, or have been absent altogether. (2) The clause would hardly have begun with **ἀλλὰ** *εἰ*, but with *εἰ* **δέ**—so the alternative suppositions in vv. 9, 11, 15, 28, 36. The **ἀλλά** brings out a strong opposition to the **μελέτω**, and implies a climax which would ill suit a merely parenthetic clause, but must convey the *point* of the sentence. (3) The absence of a demonstrative pronoun after *χρῆσαι*, by which we are thrown back, not on the secondary subject of the sentence, *ἐλευθερία*, but on the primary, *δουλείᾳ*. (4) Its utter inconsistency with the general context. The Apostle would thus be giving two examples of the precept *ἕκαστος ἐν ᾧ ἐκλήθη ἐν τούτῳ με-*

x here only +. Jos. Antt. vii. 11. 2. Ign. ad Rom. § 4, p. 689. (-ρουν, Lev. xix. 20.)
y ch. vi. 20 (reff.).
z Acts xvii. 23 al.
a = here only (?). see Luke xviii. 27. John viii. 38.

ἐν κυρίῳ [h] κληθεὶς δοῦλος [x] ἀπελεύθερος κυρίου ἐστίν· ABDF
ὁμοίως ὁ ἐλεύθερος [h] κληθεὶς δοῦλός ἐστιν χριστοῦ. KLPℵa
23 [y] τιμῆς [y] ἠγοράσθητε· μὴ γίνεσθε δοῦλοι ἀνθρώπων. bcdef
24 ἕκαστος ἐν [z] ᾧ [h] ἐκλήθη, ἀδελφοί, ἐν [z] τούτῳ μενέτω ghkl
[a] παρὰ θεῷ. mno 17. 47

22. rec aft ομοιως ins και (*as being usual aft* ομοιως: *so also* δε και), with KL rel syr-w-ast copt æth arm Chr$_1$ Damasc Thl Œc Orig-int$_1$ Ambr$_1$: δε και DF l m(Treg) : om ABPℵ 17 vulg Syr goth Chr-ms$_1$ Thdrt Ambr$_1$ Ambrst Pel Bede. χριστου bef εστιν Fℵ^1 c copt.

24. αδελφοι bef εν ω εκληθη D(-θητε D^1) F Ambrst : om αδελφοι a^1 39. 120 (Chr$_1$) Thdrt$_2$. rec ins τω bef θεω, with A e k Œc : om BDFKLPℵ rel Thdrt$_1$ Damasc Thl.

νέτω, one of which would convey a recommendation of the contrary course. See this followed out in Chrysostom. (5) Its entire contradiction to ver. 22: see below. (6) It would be quite inconsistent with the teaching of the Apostle,—that in Christ (Gal. iii. 28) *freeman and slave are all one,*—and with his remarks on the urgency and shortness of the time in this chapter (ver. 29 ff.),—to turn out of his way to give a precept merely of worldly wisdom, that a slave should become free if he could. (7) The import of χράομαι in such a connexion, which suits better the remaining in, enduring, labouring under, giving one's self up to, an *already-existing* state, than the adopting or taking advantage of a *new* one; cf. such expressions as τοιούτῳ μόρῳ ἐχρήσατο ὁ παῖς, Herod. i. 117: συμφορᾷ, συντυχίᾳ, εὐτυχίᾳ, χρῆσθαι, often in Herod.: ἀμαθίᾳ χρῆσθαι, and the like. The instance quoted by Bloomfield for '*become free,*' ἑκὼν γὰρ οὐδεὶς δουλίῳ χρῆται ζύγῳ, Æsch. Agam. 953, tells just the other way. There χρῆται is used not of *entering,* but of *submitting* to, the yoke of slavery, as here. 22.] *Ground of the above precept.* **For the slave who was called in the Lord** (not, as E. V. and De Wette, '*He who is called in the Lord, being a slave,*' which would be δοῦλος κληθείς, see above, δοῦλος ἐκλήθης: **ἐν κυρίῳ,** as the *element in which* what is about to be stated takes place) **is the Lord's freedman** (" ἀπελεύθερος with genit. is not here in the ordinary sense of 'libertus alicujus,' 'any one's manumitted slave:' for the *former master* was *sin* or *the devil,* see on ch. vi. 20;—but only a *freedman belonging to Christ,* viz. freed by Christ from the service of another. This the reader would understand as a matter of course." Meyer): **similarly he that was called being free** (not here, κληθεὶς ἐλεύθερος, see above) **is the slave of Christ.** Christ's service is perfect *freedom,* and the Christian's *freedom* is the *service* of Christ. But here the Apostle takes, in each case, *one member* of this double antithesis from the *outer world, one* from the *spiritual.* The (actual) slave is (spiritually) free: the (actually) free is a (spiritual) slave. So that the two are so mingled, in the Lord, that the slave need not trouble himself about his slavery, nor seek for this world's freedom, seeing he has a more glorious freedom in Christ, and seeing also that his brethren who seem to be free in this world are in fact Christ's servants, as *he* is a servant. It will be plain that the reason given in this verse is quite inconsistent with the prevalent modern rendering of ver. 21. 23.] *Following out of* δοῦλός ἐστιν χριστοῦ, *by reminding them of the* PRICE PAID *whereby Christ* PURCHASED *them for His* (ch. vi. 20): *and precept thereupon,* BECOME NOT SLAVES OF MEN: i. e. 'do not allow your relations to human society, whether of freedom or slavery, to bring you into bondage so as to cause you anxiety to change the one or increase the other.' Chrys., al., think the precept directed against ὀφθαλμοδουλεία, and general regard to men's opinion. But it is better to restrict it (however it may legitimately *be applied* generally) to the case in hand. Hammond, Knatchbull, Michaelis, al., understand it as addressed to the *free,* and meaning that *they* are not to *sell themselves into slavery:* but this is evidently wrong: as may be seen by the change to the *second person plur.* as addressing *all his readers:* besides that a new example would have been marked as in vv. 18, 21. See Stanley's note.
24.] *The rule is again repeated,* but with the addition παρὰ θεῷ, reminding them of the relations of Christ's freedman and Christ's slave, and of the price paid, just mentioned: — of that relation to God in which they stood by means of their Christian calling. "The *usual* rendering, *Deo inspectante* (Grot.), i. e. 'perpetuo memores, vos in ejus conspectu versari' (Beza), does not so well suit the *local*

25 Περὶ δὲ τῶν [b] παρθένων [c] ἐπιταγὴν κυρίου οὐκ ἔχω, [de] γνώμην δὲ [e] δίδωμι ὡς [f] ἠλεημένος ὑπὸ κυρίου [g] πιστὸς εἶναι. 26 νομίζω οὖν τοῦτο [h] καλὸν [i] ὑπάρχειν διὰ τὴν [k] ἐνεστῶσαν [l] ἀνάγκην, ὅτι [h] καλὸν ἀνθρώπῳ τὸ [m] οὕτως εἶναι. 27 [n] δέδεσαι γυναικί, μὴ [o] ζήτει [p] λύσιν· [q] λέλυσαι

b Paul, here &c. (7 times and 2 Cor. xi. 2 only. Matt. i. 23 (from Isa. vii. 14) al. c Rom. xvi. 26 reff. d = ch. i. 10 (reff.). e 2 Cor. viii. 10. f pass., Rom. xi. 30, 31 reff. g = ch. iv. 2 al. fr. h = ver. 1. i Acts viii. 16 reff. k Rom. viii. 38. ch. iii. 22. Gal. i. 4. 2 Thess. ii. 2. 2 Tim. iii. 1. Heb. ix. 9 only. 1 Macc. xii. 44. (see note.) l = Luke xxi. 23. 2 Cor. vi. 4. xii. 10. 1 Thess. iii. 7. 1 Kings xxii. 2. m = ver. 40. n = Rom. vii. 2. ver. 39. o = Matt. vi. 33. Col. iii. 1. 1 Pet. iii. 11. 1 Macc. ii. 29. p here only. Eccl. vii. 30 (viii. 1). Wisd. viii. 8 only. q = Acts xxii. 30. Ps. cxlv. 7.

26. aft *οτι καλον* ins *εστιν* D^1F ⌈latt syrr⌉. om *το* F $Meth_1$.

word *μενέτω*." Meyer. **25—38.**] *Advice* (with some digressions connected with the subject) *concerning the* MARRIAGE OF VIRGINS. **25.**] **παρθένων** is not, as Theodor-mops., Bengel, Olsh., al., *unmarried persons of both sexes*, a meaning which, though apparently found in Rev. xiv. 4 (see note there), is perfectly unnecessary here, and appears to have been introduced from a mistaken view of vv. 26—28. The emphasis is on *ἐπιταγήν* —**command of the Lord have I none,** i. e. no *expressed precept:* so that, as before, there is no marked comparison between *ὁ κύριος* and *ἐγώ*. **πιστὸς εἶναι**] **to be faithful**, as in ref.,—as a steward and dispenser of the hidden things of God, and, among them, of such directions as you cannot make for yourselves, but require one so entrusted to impart to you. This sense, which has occurred in the estimate given of himself in this very Epistle, is better than the more general ones of *true* (Billroth, Rückert) or *believing* (Olsh., Meyer, De Wette). **26.**] The question of the marriage of *virgins* is one involving the expediency of contracting marriage *in general:* this he deals with now, on grounds connected with the then pressing necessity. **οὖν, then,** follows on *γνώμ. δίδωμι*, and introduces the *γνώμη*. **τοῦτο** indicates what is coming, viz. *τὸ οὕτως εἶναι*. **καλόν,** see note on ver. 1 : **the best way.**
τὴν ἐνεστῶσ. ἀνάγκ.] **the instant necessity:** viz. that prophesied by the Lord, Matt. xxiv. 8, 21, &c.: which shall precede His coming : see especially ver. 19 there : not, *the cares of marriage*, as Theophyl., *διὰ τὰς ἐν αὐτῷ δυσκολίας, κ. τὰ τοῦ γάμου ὀχληρά*: nor *persecutions*, as Photius in Œcum., al., which are only a *part* of the apprehended troubles. These the Apostle regards as *instant, already begun:* for this is the meaning of *ἐνεστῶσαν*, not *imminent, shortly to come:* see reff. and Jos. Antt. xvi. 6. 2, *τὸ ἔθνος τῶν Ἰουδαίων εὐχάριστον εὑρέθη, οὐ μόνον ἐν τῷ ἐνεστῶτι καιρῷ, ἀλλὰ καὶ ἐν τῷ προγεγενημένῳ*,—where *all time future* is evidently excluded. See note on 2 Thess. ii. 2, where this distinction is very important. **ὅτι καλ. ἀνθ. . . . . .**] De Wette takes *ὅτι* as *because*, understanding **τοῦτο** above = *τὸ παρθένον εἶναι*, '*that this* (virginity) *is best on account of the instant necessity, because it is* (*generally*) *best for a man so to be* (i. e. unmarried).' But this seems constrained, and tautological, and the only rescue of it from the charge of tautology is found in the word 'generally,' which is not in the text. Far better, with Meyer and most interpreters, to view the sentence as an anacoluthon, begun with one construction, *τοῦτο καλὸν ὑπάρχειν*, and finished, without regard to this, when on account of the intervening words it became necessary to restate the *καλόν*, with another construction, *ὅτι*, &c. Thus we shall have it, literally rendered : **I think then this to be the best way on account of the instant necessity, that it is the best way for a man thus to be.**
ἀνθρώπῳ, not as in ver. 1 (which in its *outward form* will not bear the wider meaning), but here purposely general, including those treated of, young females.
οὕτως = *ὡς κἀγώ* as ver. 8 ? or perhaps *ὡς ἐστίν*, which seems better on account of the following context, ver. 27. This, in the case of the *unmarried*, would amount to the other : and the case of *virgins* is now that especially under consideration.
27.] *τὸ οὕτως εἶναι restated* and *illustrated:* neither the married nor the unmarried are to *seek for a change.* The general recommendation here is referable alike to *all* cases of marriage, and does not touch on the prohibition of ver. 10,—only *dissuading from a spirit of change, in consideration of the* **ἐνεστῶσα ἀνάγκη.** It seems better to take the verse thus, than with Meyer and De Wette, to regard it as inserted to guard against misunderstanding of the preceding *γνώμη* of the Apostle. **λέλυσαι** does not imply *previous marriage*, but as Phot., *οὐχὶ πρὸς τοὺς συναφθέντας, εἶτα διαλυθέντας, . . . ἀλλ' ἁπλῶς πρὸς τοὺς μὴ συνελθόντας ὅλως εἰς γάμου κοινωνίαν, ἀλλὰ* **λελυ-**

ἀπὸ γυναικός, μὴ ° ζήτει γυναῖκα. 28 ἐὰν δὲ καὶ γαμήσῃς,
οὐχ ἥμαρτες, καὶ ἐὰν ʳ γήμῃ [ἡ] ᵇ παρθένος, οὐχ ἥμαρτεν·
ˢ θλῖψιν δὲ τῇ ᵗ σαρκὶ ˢ ἕξουσιν ᵘ οἱ τοιοῦτοι, ἐγὼ δὲ ὑμῶν
ᵛ φείδομαι. 29 ʷ τοῦτο δέ ʷ φημι, ἀδελφοί, ὁ καιρὸς ˣ συνεσταλμένος ἐστὶν τὸ ʸ λοιπόν, ἵνα καὶ οἱ ἔχοντες γυναῖκας

ABDFK LPℵ a b c d e f g h k l m n o 17. 47

r γαμέω, of the woman ver. 34. 1 Tim. v. 11, 14 only. of both, ver. 36 only. of the man, Matt. v. 32 al.† (2 Macc. xiv. 25 bis only.)
s John xvi. 33. Rev. ii. 10. Sir. li. 3.
t dat., 2 Cor. xii. 7.
u ver. 15.
v Rom. xi. 21 reff.
w = ch. xv. 50. see ch. i. 12.
x = here (Acts v. 6) only †. Sir. iv. 31. see Tobit xii. 13.
y — Matt. xxvi. 45. Heb. x. 13. (Eph. vi. 10 reff.)

28. rec for *γαμησης*, *γημης* (*to conform to the follg*), with KL rel Orig[-c_2] Chr_1 Thdrt [$Damasc_{h.l.}$]; *λαβης γυναικα* DF: *acceperis uxorem* latt [$Tert_1$ Ambrst]: *duxeris* $Tert_1$: txt A(-*ση*) B[P]ℵ m 17 Bas [Euthal-ms] Damasc. for *γημη*, *γαμη* D^1F. om *ἡ* BF: ins ADKLPℵ rel [Orig-c $Meth_1$ Bas_1]. ins *εν* bef *τη σαρκι* D^1[-gr] F[-gr].

29. elz ins *οτι* bef *ο καιρος* (*supplementary: see ch. xv. 50, where there is* no var readg), with DF d e h l (syrr) copt [basm arm Damasc] Thl Orig[-int_1] $Tert_1$: om ABKLPℵ rel vulg [spec] Eus_1 $Meth_1$ Bas_1 (Chr_1) Thdrt [$Tert_1$ Ambrst]. *συννεσταλμενον*(sic) ℵ. rec *το λοιπον* bef *εστιν*, with D^3KL rel Thdrt [Damasc] Thl: *εστιν· λοιπον εστιν* F 67^2 latt [($Clem_1$) Orig-int_3] $Tert_1$ Jer_1 [Ambrst $Aug_{sæpe}$]: txt AB $D^{1\cdot2}$(om *το* D^1) Pℵ a^1 m 17 (Syr ?) syr copt arm Eus-ms_1 Bas_2 [Euthal-ms]. There is great var in the punctn:—[elz] has *συν. το λ. εστιν·*, with L &c syrr copt [basm arm Chr_1 Damasc] Thdrt; [Steph] *συνεστ.· το λοιπον εστιν ινα*[, with] DF 67^2-8. 71 latt lat-ff (Aug_1: *το λοιπον* $twice_{aliq}$); *συνεστ. εστιν· το λοιπ.* B^2: *συνεστ. εστιν το λοιπον·* m. (*The varr have appy arisen from a desire to fix the connexion of το λοιπον more definitely.*)

μένους ὄντας τοῦ τοιούτου δεσμοῦ,—and Estius, "intelligit liberum a conjugio, sive uxorem aliquando habuerit, sive non."

28.] Not *sin*, but *outward trouble*, will be incurred by contracting marriage, whether in the case of the unmarried man or of the virgin; and it is *to spare them this*, that he gives his advice. **But if also** (*καί*, of the *other alternative*: see ver. 21) **thou shalt have married, thou didst not sin** (viz. when thou marriedst); **and if a virgin** (if the art. is to stand, it is generic) **shall have married, she sinned not; but such persons** (viz. *οἱ γήμαντες*) **shall have tribulation in the flesh** (it is doubtful, as Meyer remarks, whether the *dative* belongs to the substantive,—*trouble for the flesh*,—or to the verb,—*shall have in the flesh trouble*): **but I** (emphatic—*my* motive is) **am sparing you** (endeavouring to spare you this *θλῖψιν τῇ σαρκί*, by advising you to keep single).

29—31.] *He enforces the foregoing advice by solemnly reminding them of the shortness of the time, and the consequent duty of sitting loose to all worldly ties and employments.*

29.] **τοῦτο δέ φημι . . .** q. d. 'What I just now said, of marrying being no *sin*, might dispose you to look on the whole matter as indifferent: my motive, the sparing you outward affliction, may be underrated in the importance of its bearing: but I will add this solemn consideration.' **ὁ καιρ. συνεστ. ἐστ. τὸ λοιπόν] The time that remains is short**: lit., 'the time is shortened henceforth:'—i. e. the interval between now and the coming of the Lord has arrived at an extremely contracted period. These words have been variously misunderstood. (1) *ὁ καιρός* has been by some (Calvin, Estius, al.) interpreted '*the space of man's life on earth*:' which, however true it may be, and however legitimate this *application* of the Apostle's words, certainly was not in his mind, nor is it consistent with *his* usage of *ὁ καιρός*: see Rom. xiii. 11; Eph. v. 16,—or with that in the great prophecy of our Lord which is the key to this chapter, Luke xxi. 8; Mark xiii. 33. (2) *συνεσταλμένος* has been understood as meaning *calamitosus* (so Rosenm., Rückert, Olshausen, al.). But it never has this signification. In such passages as 1 Macc. iii. 6, v. 3; 2 Macc. vi. 12, *παρακαλῶ . . . . μὴ συστέλλεσθαι διὰ τὰς συμφοράς*: 3 Macc. v. 33, *τῇ ὁράσει . . . συνεστάλη*,—it has the meaning of *humbling, depressing*, which would be obviously inapplicable to *καιρός*. The proper meaning of *συστέλλεσθαι*, *to be contracted*, is found in Diod. Sic. i. 41, *διὸ καὶ τὸν Νεῖλον εὐλόγως κατὰ τὸν χειμῶνα μικρὸν εἶναι καὶ* **συστέλλεσθαι**. It is, as Schrader well renders it, 'in Kürzem stürzt die alte Welt zusammen.' *συστέλλεσθαι* and *συστολή* are the regular grammatical words used of the *shortening of a syllable* in prosody. (3) *τὸ λοιπόν* has been by some (Tertull. ad Uxorem i. 5 (vol. i. p. 1283), Jer. de perp. virg. B. V. M. adv. Helv. 20 (vol. ii. p. 227), on Ezek. vii. 13 (lib. ii., vol. v. p. 69), on Eccl. iii. (vol. iii. p. 410),—Vulg., Erasm., Luther, Calvin, Estius; also E. V. and Lachm.) *joined to what follows*; '*it remains that both they*,' &c.

ὡς μὴ ἔχοντες ὦσιν, 30 καὶ οἱ κλαίοντες ὡς μὴ κλαίοντες,
καὶ οἱ χαίροντες ὡς μὴ χαίροντες, καὶ οἱ [z] ἀγοράζοντες
ὡς μὴ [a] κατέχοντες, 31 καὶ οἱ [b] χρώμενοι τὸν κόσμον,
ὡς μὴ [c] καταχρώμενοι· [d] παράγει γὰρ τὸ [e] σχῆμα τοῦ
κόσμου τούτου. 32 θέλω δὲ ὑμᾶς [f] ἀμερίμνους εἶναι.

z ch. vi. 20 reff.
a = 2 Cor. vi. 10. Josh. i. 11.
b ver. 21 reff. acc., Wisd. vii. 14 Bא[1] &c. see note.
c ch. ix. 18 only †. Ep. Jer. 28 only. w. acc., 3 Macc. v. 22.
d intrans., Matt. ix. 9 (and always, exc. 1 John ii. 8, 17). Ps. cxliii. 4.
e Phil. ii. 8 only. Isa. iii. 17 only.
f Matt. xxviii. 14 only †. Wisd. vi. 15. vii. 23 only.

om ωσιν F arm.

30. for κλαιοντες (twice), κλεθοντες F.

31. rec (for τον κοσμον) τω κοσμω τουτω (*gramml corrn, and supplementary addn*), with $D^{2\cdot3}$KLPא[3] rel (vulg[F-lat spec] syrr) [Eus_1 $Ephr_1$ Bas_1 Chr_1 Euthal-ms $Sevrn\text{-}c_1$] Thdrt Thl [Damasc (Orig-int_2 $Tert_1$ $Cypr_2$ Ambrst)]: τον κοσμον τουτον D[1][and lat] F[-gr]: τω(sic, appy) κοσμον τουτον 17: txt ABא[1] coptt. for καταχρ., παραχρ. L Bas_1 $Thdrt_3$; χρωμενοι 121 latt [$Cypr_1$ Ambrst] (not $Tert_1$).

32. om δε F o 61 fuld D-lat [spec] $Meth_1$ [Ambrst]: γαρ 38 Clem.

But thus (α) the sense of ἵνα will not be satisfied—see below: (β) the usage of τὸ λοιπόν is against it, which would require it to *stand alone*, and the sense *not* to be carried on as it is in '*superest ut*,' τὸ λοιπόν, ἵνα . . . . ,—see reff. and Phil. iii. 1, iv. 8; (1 Thess. iv. 1;) 2 Thess. iii. 1. (γ) The continuity of the passage would be very harshly broken: whereas by the other rendering all proceeds naturally. We have exactly parallel usages of τὸ λοιπόν in reff. **ἵνα καὶ . . .**] *The end for which* the time has been (by God) thus gathered up into a short compass: **in order that both they,** &c.: i. e. in order that Christians, those who wait for and shall inherit the coming kingdom, may keep themselves loosed in heart from worldly relationships and employments: that, as Meyer, "the married may not fetter his interests to his wedlock, nor the mourner to his misfortunes, nor the joyous to his prosperity, nor the man of commerce to his gain, nor the user of the world to his use of the world." This is the only legitimate meaning of ἵνα with the subj. The renderings which make it = ὅτε, 'tempus . . . . futurum cum ei qui uxores habent pares futuri sint non habentibus,' Grot., or 'ubi' (local), are inadmissible. We may notice that according to this only right view of ἵνα, the clauses following are not *precepts of the Apostle*, but the *objects* as regards *us*, of the *divine counsel in shortening the time*. **30. ὡς μὴ κατέχοντες**] **as not possessing** (their gains). So in the line of Lucretius (iii. 984), "Vitaque mancupio nulli datur, omnibus usu." **31. χρώμενοι . . . . . καταχρώμενοι**] The κατά, as in κατέχοντες, appears here to imply that intense and greedy use which turns the legitimate use into a fault. This meaning is better than '*abuse*,' which is allowable philologically, and is adopted by Theodoret, Theophyl., Œc., Luther, Olsh., al., but destroys the parallel. I would render them, **and they who use the world, as not using it in full.** So, or merely 'as not using it,' regarding καταχρ. = χρ.,—Vulg., Calv., Grot., Estius, al., and Meyer and De Wette. χρῆσθαι with an acc. is found only here: never in classical Greek, and very rarely in Hellenistic. Almost the only undoubted instance (in ref. Wisd., A reads κτησάμενοι, and is supported by א[3a]. In Xen. Ages. xii. 11, we have τὸ μεγαλόφρον . . . ἐχρῆτο, but most edd. read τῷ μεγαλόφρονι) seems to be in a Cretan inscription, Boeckh, Corp. Inscr. ii. 400, καὶ τὰ ἄλλα πάντα χρήμενοι, ἐν δὲ τᾷ ὁδῷ τὰς ξενικὰς θοίνας. See Bornemann, note on Acts xxvii. 17, where βοηθείας is a var. read. in some mss. **παράγει γὰρ . . . .**] *gives a reason for* ὁ καιρ. συνεσταλμ. ἐστ. τὸ λοιπ., the clauses which have intervened being subordinate to those words: see above. Emphasis on **παράγει: for the fashion** (present external form, cf. Herodian i. 9, ἀνὴρ φιλοσόφου φέρων σχῆμα, and other examples in Wetst.) **of this world is passing away** (is in the act of being changed, as a passing scene in a play: cf. πάραγε πτέρυγας, Eur. Ion, 165). This shews that the time is short:—the form of this world is already beginning to pass away. Grot., al., according to the mistaken view of ver. 20, —'non manebunt, quæ nunc sunt, res tranquillæ, sed mutabuntur in turbidas. Theophyl. and many Commentators understand the saying of *worldly affairs in general*—ἄχρις ὀψεώς εἰσι τὰ τοῦ παρόντος κόσμου, καὶ ἐπιπόλαια:—but this is inconsistent with the right interpretation of ver. 29: see there. Stanley compares a remarkable parallel, 2 Esdr. xvi. 40—44, probably copied from this passage.

32—34.] *Application of what has been just said to the question of marriage.* **32. θέλω δὲ . . .**] **But** (i. e. since this is so—since the time is so short, and

g ver. 8.
h constr., ch. xii. 25. Phil. ii. 20. iv. 6 only. Exod. v. 9 (a).
i Rom. ii. 14 reff.
k Rom. viii. 8 reff.
l see ch. i. 13 reff.
m vv. 25, 28.

ὁ [g] ἄγαμος [h] μεριμνᾷ [i] τὰ τοῦ κυρίου, πῶς [k] ἀρέσῃ τῷ ABDFK
κυρίῳ· 33 ὁ δὲ γαμήσας [h] μεριμνᾷ [i] τὰ τοῦ κόσμου, πῶς LPℵ a b
[k] ἀρέσῃ τῇ γυναικί. 34 καὶ [l] μεμέρισται καὶ ἡ γυνὴ καὶ ἡ c d e f g
[m] παρθένος. ἡ [g] ἄγαμος [h] μεριμνᾷ [i] τὰ τοῦ κυρίου, ἵνα ᾖ h k l m
ἁγία καὶ τῷ [n] σώματι καὶ τῷ [n] πνεύματι· ἡ δὲ [o] γαμήσασα n o 17. 47

n 1 Thess. v. 23. see ch. v. 3 reff. o of the woman, see ver. 28 reff.

33. rec (for *αρεση* vv 32-3-4) *αρεσει*, with KLP 17(ver 33) rel $Clem_1$[ver 33] $Orig_1$ $Meth_1$ [Euthal-ms] $Epiph_4$ Cyr_1[ver 33] Ephr Thdrt Damasc Thl Œc: txt ABDFℵ 17 Eus_1 [$Meth_1$(and ms_1) Bas_1(but mss vary)]. for *κυριω*, *θεω* F vulg Orig Cypr.

34. rec om 1st *και*, with D[3][and lat] F[-gr] KL 47(Treg) rel [G-lat spec] Chr_1 $Thdrt_2$ [$Damasc_1$ $Tert_1$ $Ambr_1$ Ambrst mss-in-Jer] : ins AB D[1][-gr] Pℵ 6. 17. 31. 71-3 vulg [F-lat] syrr copt [basm æth arm] Eus_1 $Meth_1$ Bas_2 Cyr[-p_1 $Ephr_1$ Euthal-ms] Pel Jer_2 Aug Fulg Primas Bede. rec om 2nd *και*, with D[1] demid(and fuld) copt [basm arm spec] $Tert_1$ [$Ambr_1$ Ambrst mss-in-]Jer Aug: ins AB D[3][and lat] F[-gr] KLPℵ 6. 31. 71-3 rel vulg [am harl tol F-lat æth] syr Eus_1 $Meth_1$ Bas_2 Chr_1 [Euthal-ms] $Thdrt_2$ Damasc.—*μεμ. δε* 30, *μεμ. δε και* Syr. aft *η γυνη* ins *η αγαμος* (retaining it also after *παρθενος*) AF[2]ℵ 17 [Bas-ed Euthal-ms Aug_2]; so (but omg the 2nd) BP 6. 31. 71-3 vulg [coptt] Eus_1 [$Ambr_3$] Pel Jer_1. om *και* (bef *τω σωματι*) A D(sic, Treg)[-gr ?] P m 17 vulg-ed(with some mss, but agst am demid [fuld harl[2]]) Syr copt arm Did_2[-int_1 $Epiph_2$ Ps-]Ath_1 Orig[-int_1 Ath-int_1 Pel] Tert. rec om *τω* (bef *σωμ.* and bef *πνευμ.*), with DFKL rel ($Orig_1$) $Meth_2$ Did_2 [Bas_1] $Thdrt_2$ Thl: ins ABPℵ a

that, in order that we Christians may sit loose to the world) **I wish you to be without worldly cares** (undistracted). Then he explains how this touches on the subject. **πῶς ἀρέσῃ**—**how he may please**: *πῶς ἀρέσει*—'how he *shall* please.' The variety being not in reality a various reading, but only an itacism, I retain the form found in the most ancient MSS.

* **34.**] See var. readd.: I treat here only of the *text*. **Divided also is the** (married) **woman and the virgin** (i. e. *divided in interest* (i. e. in cares and pursuits) from one another: *οὐ τὴν αὐτὴν ἔχουσι φροντίδα, ἀλλὰ μεμερισμέναι εἰσὶ ταῖς σπουδαῖς*, Theophyl.: not merely, *different from one another*, as E. V., Chrys., Luth., Grot., al. *Divisa est mulier et virgo* D-lat G-lat Tert). It may be well to remark as to the reading, on which see Digest,—that Jerome testifies to this having been the reading of the old Latin copies, and himself sometimes quotes the passage in this form; but, when speaking of it critically, he states that it is not in the "apostolica veritas," i. e., it would seem, the Greek as understood by him. "*Nunc illud breviter admoneo in Latinis codicibus hunc locum ita legi:* 'Divisa est virgo et mulier;' *quod quamquam habent suum sensum, et a me quoque pro qualitate loci sic edissertum sit, tamen, non est apostolicæ veritatis. Siquidem Apostolus ita scripsit, ut supra transtulimus:* 'Sollicitus est quæ sunt mundi, quomodo placeat uxori, et divisus est.' *Et hac sententia definita transgreditur ad virgines et continentes et ait:* 'Mulier innupta et virgo cogitat quæ sunt Domini ut sit sancta corpore et spiritu.' *Non omnis innupta, et virgo est. Quæ autem virgo utique et innupta est. Quamquam ob elegantiam dictionis potuerit id ipsum altero verbo repetere,* 'mulier innupta et virgo:' *vel certe definire voluisse quid esset innupta, id est virgo: ne meretrices putemus innuptas, nulli certo matrimonio copulatas*" (Jer. contra Jovin. i. 13, vol. ii. p. 260). The sing. verb seems to be used, as standing first in this sentence, and because *ἡ γυνὴ κ. ἡ παρθ.* embraces the female sex as one idea: so e. g. Plato, Lys. p. 207, *φιλεῖ σε ὁ πατὴρ καὶ ἡ μήτηρ*: Herod. v. 21, *εἵπετο γὰρ δή σφι κ. ὀχήματα κ. θεράποντες καὶ ἡ πᾶσα πολλὴ παρασκευή*: q. d. 'There loves thee father and mother,'—'there followed them,' &c. See more examples in Kühner, ii. p. 58 (§ 433, exception 1):—Reiche thinks that one and the same woman is intended at different periods: but *ἡ δὲ γαμήσασα* is against this: it would be *γαμήσασα δέ* (Meyer). The judgment of marriage here pronounced by the Apostle must be taken, as the rest of the chapter, *with its accompanying conditions.* He is speaking of a pressing and quickly shortening period which he regards as yet remaining before that day and hour of which neither he, nor any man, knew. He wishes his Corinthians, during that short time, to be as far as possible *totally undistracted.* He mentions as an objection to marriage, that which is an *undoubted fact of human experience:* —which is necessarily bound up with that relation: and *without which the duties of the relation could not be fulfilled.* Since he wrote, the unfolding of God's providence

h μεριμνᾷ i τὰ τοῦ κόσμου, πῶς k ἀρέσῃ τῷ ἀνδρί. 35 τοῦτο
δὲ p πρὸς τὸ ὑμῶν αὐτῶν q σύμφορον λέγω, οὐχ ἵνα
r βρόχον ὑμῖν s ἐπιβάλω, ἀλλὰ p πρὸς τὸ t εὔσχημον καὶ
u εὐπάρεδρον τῷ κυρίῳ v ἀπερισπάστως. 36 εἰ δέ τις
w ἀσχημονεῖν x ἐπὶ τὴν y παρθένον αὐτοῦ z νομίζει, ἐὰν ᾖ
a ὑπέρακμος, καὶ οὕτως b ὀφείλει γίνεσθαι, ὃ θέλει ποιείτω·

p = ch. vi. 5. x. 11. xii. 7 al. q ch. x. 33 only †. Eccl. ii. 3 Symm. r here only. Prov. vi. 5. vii. 21. xxii. 25 only. s and constr., Mark xi. 7. Prov. xx. 26.

t Acts xiii. 50 reff. u here only †. (παρεδρεύειν, ch. ix. 13.) v here only †. Polyb. ii. 20. 11 al. (-στος, Wisd. xvi. 11. περισπᾶσθαι, Luke x. 40. Sir. xli. 2.) w ch. xiii. 5 only. Deut. xxv. 3. Ezek. xvi. 8. (-μων, ch. xii. 23. -μοσύνη, Rom. i. 27.) x Mark xv. 24 ‖ J. James v. 14. y = Eur. Iph. in Aul. 714, ἐκεῖσ' ἀπάξει σὴν ἐμήν τε παρθένον; Soph. Œd. Tyr. 1462, ταῖν ἀθλιαῖν οἰκτραῖν τε παρθένοιν ἐμαῖν. z and constr., Acts viii. 20 reff. a here only †. see Sir. xlii. 9. b = ch. v. 10. ix. 10. Heb. ii. 17. v. 3.

m 17 $Clem_1$ $Orig_1$ [Euthal-ms Ps-]Ath_1. om τα του κοσμου B [$Tert_2$(appy)].
35. rec συμφερον, with D³FKLPℵ³ m(sic, Treg) [47(sic)] rel $Meth_1$ Eus_1 Chr_1 [Bas_1 Euthal-ms $Damasc_2$] $Thdrt_2$: txt ABD¹ℵ¹ 17 Hesych. rec ευπροσεδρον, with K rel Chr_1 Œc : προσεδρον L : ευπροσεκτον [ευπροσδεκτον Tischdf, ed 8] 5. 6 : txt ABDFPℵ m 17 $Clem_2$ Eus_1 Bas[$_{sæpe}$ Chr-ms_1, απαρεδρυν o].
36. ασχημονει (for ασχημονειν) F[-gr]. εαυτου P [c]. om νομιζει F[-gr] : ins bef ε. τ. π. αυ. D¹ [latt (Syr) basm arm]. for ουτως, τουτο A. γενεσθαι F a $Meth_1$.

has taught us more of the interval before the coming of the Lord than it was given even to an inspired Apostle to see. And as it would be perfectly reasonable and proper to urge on an apparently dying man the duty of abstaining from contracting new worldly obligations,—but both unreasonable and improper, should the same person recover his health, to insist on this abstinence any longer: so now, when God has manifested His will that nations should rise up and live and decay, and long centuries elapse before the day of the coming of Christ, it would be manifestly unreasonable to urge,—except in so far as every man's καιρός is συνεσταλμένος, and similar arguments are applicable,—the considerations here enforced. Meanwhile they stand here on the sacred page as a lesson to us how to regard, though in circumstances somewhat changed, our worldly relations; and to teach us, as the coming of the Lord may be as near now, as the Apostle then believed it to be, to act at least in the spirit of his advice, and be, as far as God's manifest will that we should enter into the relations and affairs of life allows, ἀμέριμνοι. The duty of ver. 35 fin. is incumbent on all Christians, at all periods.

35.] *Caution against mistaking what has been said for an imperative order, whereas it was only a suggestion for their best interest.* **τοῦτο**] vv. 32—34. **πρὸς τὸ ὑμ. αὐτ. σύμ.**] **For your own** (emph.) **profit**,—i. e. not for my own purposes—not to exercise my apostolic authority: **not that I may cast a snare** (lit. 'a noose;' the metaphor is from throwing the noose in hunting, or in war; so Herod. vii. 85, ἡ δὲ μάχη τούτεων τῶν ἀνδρῶν ἥδε. ἐπεὰν συμμίσγωσι τοῖς πολεμίοις, βάλλουσι τὰς σειρὰς ἐπ' ἄκρῳ βρόχους ἐχούσας, ὅτευ δ' ἂν τύχῃ ἤντε ἵππου ἤντε ἀνθρώπου, ἐπ' ἑωϋτὸν ἕλκει· οἱ δὲ ἐν ἕρκεσι ἐμπαλασσόμενοι διαφθείρονται. See other examples in Wetst.) **over you** (i. e. entangle and encumber you with difficult precepts), **but with a view to seemliness** (cf. Rom. xiii. 13) **and waiting upon the Lord without distraction.** De W. remarks, that πρὸς τὸ παρεδρεύειν τῷ κ. ἀπερ. would be the easier construction. Stanley draws out the parallel to the story in ref. Luke. **36—38.**] For seemliness' sake: and consequently, if there be danger, by a father withholding his consent to his daughter's marriage, of *unseemly* treatment of her, let an exception be made in that case: but otherwise, if there be no such danger, it is better not to give her in marriage. **But** (introduces an inconsistency with εὔσχημον) **if any one** (any *father*) **thinks that he is behaving unseemly towards his virgin daughter** (viz. in setting before her a temptation to sin with her lover, or at least, bringing on her the imputation of it, by withholding his consent to her marriage. Or the reference may be to the supposed disgrace of having an unmarried daughter in his house), **if she be of full age** (for *before that* the imputation and the danger consequent on preventing the marriage would not be such as to bring in the ἀσχημοσύνη. The ἀκμή of woman is defined by Plato, Rep. v. p. 460, to be twenty years, that of man thirty. See Stanley's note [and ref. Sir.]), **and thus it must be** (i. e. and there is no help for it,—they are bent on it beyond the power of dissuasion:—depends not on ἐάν, as the indic. shews, but on εἰ. **οὕτως**, viz. that they must marry. Theophyl. takes

οὐχ ἁμαρτάνει, [c] γαμείτωσαν. 37 ὃς δὲ ἕστηκεν ἐν τῇ ABDFK
καρδίᾳ αὐτοῦ [d] ἑδραῖος, μὴ [e] ἔχων [e] ἀνάγκην, [fg] ἐξουσίαν LPℵ a b c d e f g
δὲ [f] ἔχει [g] περὶ τοῦ ἰδίου [h] θελήματος, καὶ τοῦτο [i] κέκρικεν h k l m n o 17. 47
ἐν τῇ ἰδίᾳ καρδίᾳ [k] τηρεῖν τὴν ἑαυτοῦ [y] παρθένον, [l] καλῶς
ποιήσει. 38 ὥςτε καὶ ὁ [m] [ἐκ]γαμίζων [τὴν ἑαυτοῦ παρθένον]
[l] καλῶς ποιεῖ, καὶ ὁ μὴ [m] [ἐκ]γαμίζων [n] κρεῖσσον ποιήσει.

c see ver. 28 reff. d ch. xv. 58. Col. i. 23 only †. Ps. lvi. 8 Symm. e = Luke xiv. 18. [xxiii. 17.] Heb. vii. 27. Jude 3. Jos. Antt. xvi. 9. 3. f Matt. vii. 29. ix. 6. Luke xii. 5. xix. 17. Acts ix. 14. Rom. ix. 21. 2 Thess. iii. 9. 1 Macc. x. 35. g here only. h of man, Luke xxiii. 25. John i. 13. ch. xvi. 12. Eph. ii. 3. 2 Pet. i. 21. 3 Kings v. 8. i = Acts xv. 19 reff. k = 1 Thess. v. 23. see John xii. 7. 1 Pet. i. 4. l = Acts x. 33. Phil. iv. 14. James ii. 8, 19. 2 Pet. i. 19. 3 Kings viii. 18. m [here bis.] Matt (xxii. 30 ‖ L. rec.) xxiv. 38 only †. (γαμίζ., Mark xii. 25. Luke xvii. 27 †.) n ver. 9 reff.

for γαμειτωσαν, γαμειτω D^{1}F [Syr arm] Epiph$_1$ Aug$_1$: *si nubat* vulg(including F-lat) D-lat [Ambrst].

37. rec εδραιος bef εν τη καρδια, with KLℵ^3 rel [Syr] Thdrt$_1$ Thl : om εδραιος F D-lat arm : txt AB D-gr Pℵ^1 a d m 17 vulg syr coptt Bas$_1$ Thdrt$_1$ [Ambr$_1$ Ambrst]. (*The transposn seems to have been made for perspicuity, to bring* εστηκεν *and* εδραιος *together.*) rec om αυτου, with KL rel syr Thdrt$_1$ Damasc Thl Œc : ins ABDFPℵ d m 17 [latt Syr coptt æth arm] Bas$_1$ Thdrt$_1$ [Euthal-ms Ambr$_{sæpé}$ Ambrst]. om de A [coptt]. rec (for ιδια καρδια) καρδια αυτου, with DFKL rel [Bas$_1$] Thdrt$_2$ Damasc : ιδια καρδια αυτου m : καρδια (alone) 67^2 : txt ABPℵ a. rec ins του bef τηρειν, with DFKL rel [Bas$_1$] Damasc Œc : om ABPℵ c d 17 [Euthal-ms]. rec (for ποιησει) ποιει, with DFKL[P] rel syrr æth Thdrt Damasc Thl Œc : txt ABℵ 6. 17. 67^2 coptt [Bas$_1$].

38. om ωστε to ποιει (*homœotel*) F b^1 d. rec εκγαμιζων (twice), with K^{2}LPℵ^3(2nd) rel [Chr$_2$ Thdrt$_1$] Thl Œc : [εγγαμ. K^1 Thdrt$_1$ Damasc :] γαμιζων ABD F(once) ℵ^1 17 Clem$_1$ Meth$_1$ Bas$_1$ [Euthal-ms]. rec om την εαυ. παρθ., with KL rel [Chr$_2$] Thdrt Damasc Aug$_{aliq}$: ins A[P]ℵ m 17 Meth$_1$ Bas$_1$: την παρθ. εαυ. BD vulg Syr syr-w-ob coptt [æth arm spec] Clem$_1$ Aug$_1$ [Ambrst Pel]. for ποιει, ποιησει B m 6. 67^2 [Bas$_1$] : txt ADKLPℵ 17 rel [vulg Clem$_1$ Meth$_1$ Chr$_2$ Euthal-ms Thdrt$_2$]. rec (for και ὁ) ὁ δε (*corrn for contrast*), with KLPℵ^3 rel syr æth [Chr$_2$] Thdrt Thl Œc : txt ABDFℵ^1 m 17 latt Syr coptt arm Clem Meth Bas$_1$ [Euthal-ms Ambrst Aug$_{sæpe}$]. rec (for ποιησει) ποιει, with DFKLP rel latt [Clem$_1$ Meth$_1$ Chr$_2$ Damasc] Thdrt$_2$: txt ABℵ m 6. 17. 67^2 [copt Bas$_1$ Euthal-ms].

the words for the beginning of the *consequent* sentence = οὕτως καὶ γενέσθω. But, as Meyer remarks, the words would thus be altogether superfluous, and after ὀφείλει, οὐχ ἁμαρτάνει would be inapplicable), **what he will** (as his determination on this νομίζειν), **let him do** (τὸ δοκοῦν πραττέτω, Theodoret), **he sinneth not** (ἁμαρτίας γὰρ ὁ γάμος ἐλεύθερος, Theodoret); **let them** (his daughter and her lover) **marry.** Some (Syr., Grot., al.) take ἀσχημονεῖν *passively*,—'*thinks that he is* (likely to be) *brought into disgrace as regards his daughter*,' viz. by her seduction, or by her being despised as unmarried. But this would require (1) the future ἀσχημονήσειν.—(2) ἐπί with a *dative*, the *acc.* shewing that the verb is one of *action* : Meyer compares ἀσχημονεῖν εἴς τινα, Dion. Hal. ii. 26. And (3) the active sense of the verb is found in this Epistle (ref.), the only other place where it occurs in the N. T.

37.] But he who stands firm in his heart (= *purpose*,—having no such misgiving that he is behaving unseemly), **not involved in any necessity** (no ὀφείλει γενέσθαι as in the other case; no determination to marry on the part of his daughter, nor attachment formed), **but has** (change of construction :—the clause is opposed to ἔχων ἀνάγκ.) **liberty of action respecting his personal wish** (to keep his daughter unmarried), **and has determined this in his own** (expressed, as it is a matter of private determination only) **heart** (**τοῦτο**, not stated *what*, but understood by the reader to mean, *the keeping his daughter unmarried* :—but this would not be in apposition with nor explained by **τοῦ τηρ. τ. ἑαυτ. παρθ.**, see below), **to keep** (in her present state) **his own virgin daughter** (the rec., **τοῦ τηρ.**, would express the *purpose* of the determination expressed in **κέκρικεν** : not (as commonly given) the explanation of τοῦτο, which would require τὸ τηρεῖν or τηρεῖν. It shews that the motive of the **κέκρικεν** is the feeling of a father, desirous of retaining in her present state his own virgin daughter. So Meyer, and I think rightly : see note on Acts xxvii. 1. De Wette, on the other hand, regards the words τοῦ τηρ. . . . , as merely a periphrasis for not giving her in marriage. Our present text merely explains the τοῦτο), **shall do well.**

38.] The latter καί has been altered to δέ because a contrast seemed to be required between καλῶς and κρεῖσσον. One account might

39 Γυνὴ [o] δέδεται [p] ἐφ' [p] ὅσον [p] χρόνον ζῇ ὁ ἀνὴρ αὐτῆς·
ἐὰν δὲ [q] κοιμηθῇ ὁ ἀνήρ, [r] ἐλευθέρα ἐστὶν ᾧ θέλει γαμηθῆναι, μόνον [s] ἐν κυρίῳ. 40 [t] μακαριωτέρα δέ ἐστιν, ἐὰν
[u] οὕτως μείνῃ, κατὰ τὴν ἐμὴν [v] γνώμην· [w] δοκῶ δὲ κἀγὼ
[x] πνεῦμα θεοῦ [x] ἔχειν.

VIII. 1 Περὶ δὲ τῶν [y] εἰδωλοθύτων, [z] οἴδαμεν [z] ὅτι

o — Rom. vii. 2. ver. 27. p Rom. vii. 1 reff. q — Matt. xxvii. 52. Acts vii. 60. xiii. 36. ch. xi. 30. xv. 6, &c. 1 Thess. iv. 13, 14. Isa. xiv. 8. r w. inf. here only. s = Rom. xvi. 2, 8, 11 al. t compar., here only †. see Acts xx. 35. u ver. 26. v = ch. i. 10 reff. w ch. iii. 18 reff. x Rom. viii. 9. Jude 19. y vv. 4, 7, 10. ch. x. 19. Acts xv. 29. xxi. 25. Rev. ii. 14, 20 only †. z = ch. vi. 2 al. fr.

39. [at beg ins η Coisl-oct-marg coptt Clem$_1$.] rec aft δεδεται ins νομω (*from Rom* vii. 2), with D$^{2\cdot3}$[-gr] FLPℵ^3 rel vulg-ed(with fuld F-lat) Syr syr [Epiph-ms$_1$] Chr$_{sæpe}$ Thdrt$_2$ Damasc$_2$ Ambrst$_1$: om AB D^1[and lat] ℵ^1 Coisl-oct-marg 17 am(with demid tol harl^2) coptt æth arm Clem$_1$ Orig$_2$[-c$_1$ Tert$_1$ Cypr$_1$ Ambr$_1$ Aug$_{alic}$]. om 1st ὁ F (not G). ins και bef κοιμηθη D^3 F[-gr(κεκοιμ.)] L a b e f h l o syr Thdrt$_1$ Œc: om ABD^{1}KPℵ rel Clem$_1$ Orig$_2$[-c$_1$ Chr$_5$]. for κοιμηθη, αποθανη A 73 syr-mg basm Clem Orig[-c$_2$ Epiph$_1$] Bas$_1$ Tert$_1$ [Jer$_3$]. rec aft 2nd ο ανηρ ins αυτης, with DFL a m 17. 47 vss (syr-w-ast) Orig$_1$ Damasc Thl lat-ff: om ABKPℵ Orig$_1$[-c$_2$ Chr$_1$] Bas Thdrt$_2$ Œc Vig$_1$. for γαμηθηναι, γαμηθη F latt [Tert$_1$ Cypr$_1$]: γαμησαι L^1(appy).
40. for 2nd δε, γαρ B m 4. 17. 67^2. 71-3. 116 tol syr(δε in marg) basm æth [Cyr$_1$ (txt-p$_1$)] Orig[-int$_1$(txt$_2$-c$_1$)] Ambr$_{[alic]}$ Ambrst Vig Sedul (not Tert$_3$ Aug Jer). εχω F Tert$_3$ Ambrst Aug.

be (as M. and De W.) that Paul had intended to write καλῶς ποι. twice, but *currente calamo*, intensified the expression to κρεῖσσον ποιήσει. Perhaps a better one will be found by referring the καί—καί to that which καλῶς and κρεῖσσον have in common: '*both he who gives in marriage does well, and he who gives not in marriage shall do well, even in a higher degree.*' I need hardly remind the tiro that 'both—and' here does not, as Bloomf. objects, represent τε καί,—each subject being accompanied by its own predicate. Observe the ποιήσει—ποιεῖ—ποιήσει; the pres., of the mere act itself, the fut., of its enduring results. **39, 40.**] *Concerning second marriages of women.* **39. δέδεται**] viz. τῷ ἀνδρί, or perhaps absolutely, **is bound**, in her marriage state. **γαμηθῆναι**] γαμηθῆναι and γαμῆσαι are later forms, reprobated by the grammarians: γαμεθῆναι and γαμέσαι being the corresponding ones in good Greek. See Lobeck on Phrynichus, p. 742. Meyer cites Schol. on Eur. Med. 593, γαμεῖ μὲν γὰρ ὁ ἀνήρ, γαμεῖται δὲ ἡ γυνή. But not invariably, see ver. 28. **μόνον ἐν κυρίῳ**] **only in the Lord**, i. e. within the limits of *Christian* connexion—in the element in which all Christians live and walk;—'*let her marry a Christian.*' So Tertull., Cypr., Ambrose, Jerome, Grot., Est., Bengel, Rosenm., Olsh., Meyer, De W. But Chrys. explains it μετὰ σωφροσύνης, μετὰ κοσμιότητος:—and so (but in some cases including in this the marrying of a Christian) Theodoret (τουτέστιν ὁμοπίστῳ, εὐσεβεῖ, σωφρόνως, ἐννόμως), Theophyl., Calv., Beza, Calov., al. This however seems flat, and the other much to be preferred; also as making a better limitation of ᾧ θέλει. **40. μακαριωτέρα**] [not merely happier, in our merely social secular sense, but including this] **happier**, partly by freedom from the attendant trials of the ἐνεστῶσα ἀνάγκη,—but principally for the reason mentioned verse 34. "To higher blessedness in heaven, which became attached to celibacy afterwards in the views of its defenders (Ambrose, Corn.-a-Lap., al.), there is no allusion here." Meyer. **δοκῶ δὲ κἀγώ**] This is modestly said, implying more than is expressed by it,—not as if there were any uncertainty in his mind. It gives us the true meaning of the saying that he is *giving his opinion*, as ver. 25: viz. not that he is speaking without inspiration, but that in the consciousness of inspiration he is giving that counsel which should determine the question. The rationalizing Grotius explains πνεῦμα θεοῦ, 'non revelationem, sed sincerum affectum Deo et piis serviendi,' referring to ch. iv. 21, where (1) the meaning is not this (see note); and (2) the expression is not πνεῦμα θεοῦ. **κἀγώ**] '*as well as other teachers.*' Whether said with a general or particular reference, we cannot tell, from not being sufficiently acquainted with the circumstances.

VIII. 1—XI. 1.] On the partaking of meats offered to idols, and assisting at feasts held in honour of idols.

Chap. VIII. 1—13.] Though (vv. 1—6) *for those who are strong in the faith, an idol having no existence, the question has no importance, this is not so with all* (ver. 7); *and the infirmities of the weak must*

a = vv. 7, 10, 11. Hos. iv. 6. see 1 Tim. vi. 20.
b ch. iv. 6 reff.
c = Acts ix. 31 reff.

πάντες [a] γνῶσιν ἔχομεν· ἡ [a] γνῶσις [b] φυσιοῖ, ἡ δὲ ἀγάπη [c] οἰκοδομεῖ.
2 εἴ τις [w] δοκεῖ ἐγνωκέναι τί, οὔπω ἔγνω

ABDF LPℵ a c d e f h k l n o 17 47

CHAP. VIII. 2. rec aft ει ins δε, with DFKL rel vulg[-clem] syr-w-ast (æth) Chr$_1$ Thdrt Thl Œc Jer: [aft τις m:] om ABPℵ [a[1]] 17 am(with fuld harl[1](appy) tol) coptt arm Clem$_1$ Orig[-c$_1$]-int$_1$ Nys$_1$ Melet$_1$ [Euthal-ms] Damasc Tert$_1$ Cypr$_1$ Ambrst. rec (for εγνωκεναι) ειδεναι, with KL rel Chr$_3$ Thdrt Thl Œc, *scire* vulg [F-lat Tert$_1$ Cypr$_1$ Ambrst]: txt ABDFPℵ m 17 coptt Clem$_1$ Orig[-c$_1$] Nys$_1$ [Chr$_1$ Euthal-ms] Thdrt$_2$ Damasc, *cognovisse* D-lat. (G-lat has both *cognoscere* and *scire*.) rec **ουδεπω**, with DFKL rel Chr$_3$ Thdrt$_4$ Damasc Thl Œc: om m: txt ABPℵ 17 Clem$_1$ Orig[-c$_1$] Melet$_1$ [Nys$_1$ Chr$_2$ Euthal-ms]. rec aft ου(δε)πω ins ουδεν, with D[-gr[2.3]] KL rel syrr Chr$_4$ Thdrt$_2$ Damasc Thl Œc: om ABD[1]FPℵ 17 latt coptt [æth arm] Clem Orig[-c$_1$-int$_1$] Nys Melet Thdrt$_2$ [Chr$_1$ Euthal-ms Tert$_1$ Cypr$_1$]. rec εγνωκεν, with D[3]KL rel Chr$_4$ Thdrt$_2$ Thl Œc: txt ABD[1]FPℵ a m Clem Orig[-c] Nys Melet [Euthal-ms] Thdrt$_2$ Damasc.—for ουπω εγνω καθως δει γνωναι, ουδεν εδει (= ᾔδει) καθως εδει 17.

in such a matter be regarded in our conduct (vv. 8—13). 1.] **δέ**, *transitional*, as in ch. vii. 1, al. fr. As regards the construction, we may observe, that περὶ δ. τῶν εἰδ., is *again taken up* ver. 4, περὶ τῆς βρώσ. οὖν τῶν εἰδ., after a parenthesis. We may also observe that in the latter case οἴδαμεν ὅτι is *restated*, bearing therefore, it is reasonable to suppose, the *same* meaning as before, viz. **we know, that.** This to my mind is decisive against beginning the parenthesis with ὅτι, and rendering ὅτι '*for*,' as Luther, Bengel, Valckn., al.:—'*we know* (*for we all have knowledge*),' *&c.* Are we then to begin it with πάντες, leaving περὶ . . . οἴδαμεν ὅτι broken off, corresponding to the words resumed in ver. 4? We should thus leave within the parenthesis a very broken and harsh sentence; πάντες γνῶσιν ἔχομεν (*what* γνῶσις? if γν. about the εἰδωλοθ., it should be joined with the preceding; if γν. *in general*, it should be τὴν γνῶσιν, see ch. xiii. 2, which would be absurd; if *some* γν. on *some subjects*, as σὺ πίστιν ἔχεις, James ii. 18, it would here be irrelevant), ἡ γν. φυσιοῖ, ἡ δὲ ἀγ. κ.τ.λ. The first *logical break* in the sense is where *the concrete* **γνῶσις**, *that* **περὶ τῶν εἰδ.**, *is forsaken, and the abstract* **ἡ γνῶσις** *treated of.* Here therefore, with Chrys., &c., Beza, Grot., Calv., Est., al., De Wette, and Meyer, I begin the parenthesis,—. . . **we are aware that we all** (see below) **have knowledge; knowledge,** &c.; not however *placing it in brackets*, for it is already provided for *in the construction* by the resumption of περὶ . . οὖν below; and is not a grammatical but only a logical parenthesis. The **εἰδωλόθυτα** were those portions of the animals offered in sacrifice which were not laid on the altar, and which belonged partly to the priests, partly to those who had offered them. These remnants were sometimes eaten at feasts holden in the temples (see ver. 10), or in private houses (ch. x. 27, f.), sometimes sold in the markets, by the priests, or by the poor, or by the niggardly. Theophrastus, Charact. xviii., describes it as characteristic of the ἀνελεύθερος,—ἐκδιδοὺς αὐτοῦ θυγατέρα, τοῦ μὲν ἱερείου, πλὴν τῶν ἱερῶν, τὰ κρέα ἀποδίδοσθαι. They were sometimes also reserved for future use; Theophr. mentions it as belonging to the ἀναίσχυντος,—θύσας τοῖς θεοῖς αὐτὸς μὲν δειπνεῖν παρ' ἑτέρῳ, τὰ δὲ κρέα ἀποτιθέναι ἁλσὶ πάσας. Christians were thus in continual danger of meeting with such remnants. Partaking of them was an abomination among the Jews: see Num. xxv. 2; Ps. cvi. 28; Rev. ii. 14; Tobit i. 10—12; and was forbidden by the Apostles and elders assembled at Jerusalem, Acts xv. 29; xxi. 25. That Paul in the whole of this passage makes no allusion to that decree, but deals with the question on its own merits, probably is to be traced to his wish to establish his position as an independent Apostle, endowed with God's Holy Spirit sufficiently himself to regulate such matters. But it also shews, *how little such decisions were at that time regarded as lastingly binding on the whole church*; and how fully competent it was, even during the lifetime of the Apostles, to Christians to open and question, on its own merits, a matter which *they* had, for a special purpose, once already decided.
There should be a comma at εἰδωλοθύτων, as the resumed sentence (ver. 4) shews.

πάντες γνῶσιν ἔχομεν] *Who are* **πάντες**? Meyer says, *Paul himself and the enlightened* among the Corinthians; Estius, al., *these latter alone*; and some think it said *ironically*, some *concessively*, of them: Grot., "pars maxima nostrum, ut Rom. iii. 12." But it is manifest from vv. 4—6, which is said in the widest possible reference to the faith of *all Christians*, that *all Christians* must be intended here also: and so Chrys., Theophyl., Œcum., Calov., al., and De Wette. But then, ver.

καθὼς δεῖ γνῶναι· 3 εἰ δέ τις [d] ἀγαπᾷ τὸν [d] θεόν, οὗτος
[e] ἔγνωσται ὑπ᾽ αὐτοῦ. 4 περὶ τῆς [f] βρώσεως οὖν τῶν
[g] εἰδωλοθύτων, [g] οἴδαμεν [g] ὅτι οὐδὲν εἴδωλον ἐν κόσμῳ,
καὶ ὅτι οὐδεὶς θεὸς [h] εἰ μὴ εἷς· 5 καὶ γὰρ εἴπερ εἰσὶν

d Matt. xxii. 37 ‖, and Luke x. 27, from Deut. vi. 5. Rom. viii. 28. 1 John iv. 20, 21. v. 2.
e = Gal. iv. 9. 2 Tim. ii. 19 (from Num. xvi. 5). Matt. vii. 23.
f Rom. xiv. 17 reff.
g ver. 1.
h = Matt. xii. 4. Gal. i. 19.

3. om υπ αυτου א[1] 17 $Clem_1$.

4. for π. της βρ. ουν, π. δε της βρ. D^2[Treg]·[3](and lat: D^1 has both δε and ουν(Treg, expr [in error, according to Tischdf ed 8, who says that D^1 has π. δε τ. γνωσεως, D^2 π. τ. βρ. ουν])) e 1. 17. 108-15 vulg (*autem* vulg al: *enim* spec: *ergo* F-lat) Aug_1.—for βρωσεως, γνωσεως D^1P 121. aft ουδεν ins εστιν F vulg Syr syr-w-[ob copt spec] Iren[-int_1] Orig-int_2 [Ambrst Aug_1]. rec aft θεος ins ετερος, with KLא[3] rel syrr Chr_2 Thdrt Damasc Thl Œc: om ABDFPא[1] 17. 47 latt copt [basm] æth arm Bas_1 Cyr_2 [Euthal-ms] Iren-int_1 [Ambrst Aug_1].

7, he says, **οὐκ ἐν πᾶσιν** ἡ γνῶσις [obviously pointing at the weak Christian brother]: and how are the two to be reconciled? By taking, I believe, the common-sense view of two such statements, which would be, in ordinary preaching or writing, that the first was said of what is *professed* and *confessed*,—the second of what is *actually and practically apprehended by each man.* Thus we may say of our people, in the former sense, '*all are Christians; all believe in Christ:*' but in the latter, 'all are *not* Christians; all do *not* believe.' **γνῶσιν**, scil. περὶ αὐτῶν. From ἡ γν. to end of ver. 3 (see above) is a *logical* parenthesis. **ἡ γνῶσις, knowledge,** abstract, —scil. when *alone*, or improperly predominant: it is the attribute of ἡ γνῶσις, '*barely*' [to puff up]. **ἡ ἀγάπη**] viz. '*towards the brethren,*' see Rom. xiv. 15, and ch. x. 23. **οἰκοδ.**] **helps to build up** (God's spiritual temple), ch. iii. 9.

2, 3.] The general deductions, (1) from a *profession of knowledge*, and (2) from the *presence of love*, in a man:—expressed sententiously and without connecting particles, more, as Meyer observes, after the manner of St. John in his Epistles. On the text, see var. readd. The case supposed is the only one which can occur where love is absent and conceit present: a man can then *only think he knows*,—no *real knowledge* being accessible without humility and love. Such a man **knows not yet, as he ought to know**: has had no real practice in the art of knowing.

But if a man loves God (which is the highest and noblest kind of love, the *source* of brotherly love, 1 John v. 2), **this man** (and not the wise in his own conceit) **is known by Him.** The explanation of this latter somewhat difficult expression is to be found in ref. Gal., νῦν δὲ γνόντες θεόν, **μᾶλλον δὲ γνωσθέντες ὑπὸ θεοῦ.** So that *here* we may fairly assume that he chooses the expression ἔγνωσται ὑπ᾽ αὐτοῦ *in preference* to that which *would have been*, had any object of knowledge but the Supreme been treated of, *the natural one*, viz. οὗτος ἔγνω αὐτόν. We cannot be said to *know* God, in any full sense (as here) of the word *to know.* But those who become acquainted with God by love, **are known by Him**: are the *especial objects of the divine Knowledge,*—their being is pervaded by the Spirit of God, and the wisdom of God is shed abroad in them. So in ref. 2 Tim., ἔγνω κύριος τοὺς ὄντας αὐτοῦ. See also Ps. i. 6. "Cognitionem passivam sequitur cognitio activa c. xiii. 12. Egregia metalepsis: cognitus est, adeoque cognovit." Bengel. γινώσκω does not seem, any more than יָדַע in Ps. i. 6, xxxvii. 18, for which the LXX have γινώσκω, to signify *to approve*, any further than personal knowledge of an intimate kind necessarily involves approval.

4.] The subject is resumed, and further specified by the insertion of τῆς βρώσεως. **οὖν** resumes a broken thread of discourse: so Plato, Apol. p. 29, ὥστε οὐδ᾽ εἴ με ἀφίετε . . . εἴ μοι πρὸς ταῦτα εἴποιτε, &c. . . . εἰ **οὖν** με, ὅπερ εἶπον, ἐπὶ τούτοις ἀφίοιτε . . . See Hartung, Partikellehre, ii. 22. **We know that there is no idol in the world,** i. e. that the εἴδωλα of the heathen (meaning not strictly the *images*, but the *persons represented by them*) *have no existence* in the world. That they who worship idols, worship devils, the Apostle himself asserts ch. x. 20; but that is no contradiction to the present sentence, which asserts that the deities imagined by them, Jupiter, Apollo, &c., have *absolutely no existence.* Of that subtle Power which, under the guise of these, deluded the nations, he here says nothing. The rendering of Chrys., Theodoret, Theophyl. Œcum., Vulg., E. V., Luther, Beza, Grot., Est., al. ('an idol is nothing in the world,' ch. x. 19; Jer. x. 3. Sanhedr. 63. 2 (Wetst.), "noverant utique Israelitæ idolum nihil esse"), is certainly wrong here, on account of the parallel οὐδεὶς θεὸς εἰ μὴ εἷς which follows. **And that there is no god, but One:** the insertion of ἕτερος has probably

i = 2 Thess. ii. 4. Eph. ii. 11. [i] λεγόμενοι θεοὶ εἴτε ἐν οὐρανῷ, εἴτε ἐπὶ γῆς, ὥσπερ
k = Acts xxv. 26. εἰσὶν θεοὶ πολλοὶ καὶ [k] κύριοι πολλοί, 6 [l] ἀλλ' [m] ἡμῖν εἷς
l = Col. ii. 5. m dat. = ch. i. 18 reff. θεὸς ὁ πατήρ, [n] ἐξ οὗ τὰ πάντα καὶ ἡμεῖς [n] εἰς αὐτόν,
n Rom. xi. 36. see Col. i. 16. καὶ εἷς κύριος Ἰησοῦς χριστός, [n] δι' οὗ τὰ πάντα καὶ
o Acts xiii. 15. 2 Cor. xi. 10. ἡμεῖς [n] δι' αὐτοῦ. 7 ἀλλ' οὐκ [o] ἐν πᾶσιν ἡ [p] γνῶσις· τινὲς
p ver. 1. q w. gen. obj., 1 Pet. ii. 19. δὲ τῇ * [q] συνειδήσει [r] ἕως [r] ἄρτι τοῦ εἰδώλου ὡς [g] εἰδωλόθυτον
Heb. x. 2. συνήθ., ch. xi. 16 reff. r ch. iv. 13 reff.

η γνωσις K. ABDF[illegible] PℵA b d e f g [illegible] k l m [illegible] o 17. 4[illegible]

5. ins οι bef λεγομενοι FK Iren[-int$_1$] Hil$_1$. om from εισιν to εισιν L. aft 1st θεοι ins και κυριοι D Ambrst. rec ins της bef γης, with rel [Chr$_1$ Damasc] Thdrt$_2$ Œc: txt ABDFKPℵ f g k l m n 17 Orig$_2$ Eus$_1$ Cyr-jer$_2$ Chr$_1$ Thdrt$_1$ Dion-areop.

6. om αλλ' B basm Eus$_1$ Iren[-int$_1$].—ημιν δε 17 copt [Cyr-jer$_1$(txt$_1$) Epiph$_1$ Ps-]Ath Cyr$_1$[-p(txt$_2$, αλλα$_1$)] Epiph$_1$ Orig-int$_2$. ins ο bef θεος F. om θεος ℵ[1](ins ℵ-corr[1]). om 1st τα D[1]. ins ο bef χρ. P. δι ον B æth.

7. * συνηθείᾳ ABPℵ[1] 17 syr-mg copt æth [Euthal-ms] Damasc: συνειδησει DFLℵ[3] rel latt syrr [arm] Chr$_1$ Thdrt Thl Œc Tert [Ambrst] Aug$_1$. rec του ειδωλου bef εως αρτι (*corrn for perspicuity*), with ALP rel syr [basm] Chr$_2$ [Euthal-ms Damasc] Thl Œc: txt BDFℵ m latt Syr [copt æth] arm Thdrt [Aug$_1$].

been occasioned by the first commandment, οὐκ ἔσονταί σοι θεοὶ ἕτεροι πλὴν ἐμοῦ.

5, 6.] *Further explanation and confirmation of ver. 4.* 5.] **For even supposing that** (εἴπερ makes an hypothesis, so that "in incerto relinquitur, jure an injuria sumatur," Herm. ad Viger., p. 834. See also Hartung, Partikellehre, i. 343, who gives many examples. **καὶ γὰρ εἰ,** as Eur. Med. 450, καὶ γὰρ εἰ σύ με στυγεῖς, οὐκ ἂν δυναίμην σοὶ κακῶς φρονεῖν ποτε; see Hartung, Partikellehre, i. 140 f.) **beings named gods** (not *those who are named gods,* **οἱ** λεγ. θ., i. esset, *all* who are so named) EXIST (*the chief emphasis is on* **εἰσίν**, *on which the hypothesis turns*), **whether in heaven, whether upon earth, as** (we know that) **there are** (viz. as being spoken of, Deut. x. 17, ὁ γὰρ κύριος ὁ θεὸς ὑμῶν, οὗτος θεὸς **τῶν θεῶν** καὶ κύριος **τῶν κυρίων**, see also Ps. cxxxv. 2, 3) **gods many, and lords many** (the **ὥσπερ** brings in an acknowledged fact, on which the possibility of the hypothesis rests—'*Even if some of the many gods and many lords whom we know to exist, be actually identical with the heathen idols . . .*' The Apostle does not *concede this,* but only *puts* it). This exegesis, which is Meyer's, is denied by De Wette, who takes εἴπερ as concessive, '*even though,*' and understands εἰσίν both times as only '*are,*'—*in the meaning of the heathen,*—imagining it impossible that Paul should have seriously said in an objective sense, '*there are gods many.*' But in the sense in which he uses θεοί (see above) there is no unlikelihood that he should assert this. Chrys. gives the following explanation: καὶ γὰρ εἴπερ εἰσὶ λεγόμενοι θεοί, ὥσπερ οὖν καὶ εἰσίν, οὐχ ἁπλῶς εἰσίν, ἀλλά, λεγόμενοι, οὐκ ἐν πράγματι, ἀλλ' ἐν ῥήματι τοῦτο ἔχοντες· εἴτε ἐν οὐρανῷ, εἴτε ἐπὶ γῆς· ἐν οὐρανῷ τὸν ἥλιον λέγων κ. τὴν σελήνην κ. τὸν λοιπὸν τῶν ἄστρων χορόν· καὶ γὰρ καὶ ταῦτα προσεκύνησαν Ἕλληνες· ἐπὶ γῆς δὲ δαίμονας, καὶ τοὺς ἐξ ἀνθρώπων θεοποιηθέντας ἅπαντας. Hom. xx. p. 172. And similarly Theodoret, Theophyl., Œcum., Calv., Beza, Calov., Estius, Schrader, al. See the various minor differences of interpretation, in Pool's Synopsis and De Wette: and a beautiful note in Stanley. There is a sentence in Herodotus (ix. 27) singularly resembling this in its structure: ἡμῖν δέ, εἰ μηδὲν ἄλλο ἐστὶ ἀποδεδεγμένον, ὥσπερ ἐστὶ πολλά τε καὶ εὖ ἔχοντα, . . . ἀλλὰ καὶ ἀπὸ τοῦ ἐν Μαραθῶνι ἔργου ἄξιοί ἐσμεν, κ.τ.λ. Cf. also Hom. Il. α. 81 f.; φ. 576 f.

6.] **Yet** (see reff. just given, and ch. iv. 15) TO US (emphatic: however that matter may be, *we* hold) **there is** ONE GOD, **the Father** (ὁ πατήρ answers to Ἰησοῦς χριστός in the parallel clause below, and serves to specify *what God*—viz. *the Father* of our Lord Jesus Christ), **of Whom** (as their Source of being) **are all things, and we unto** (i. e. for) **Him** (His purposes—to serve His will); **and one Lord Jesus Christ** (notice the εἷς θεός opposed to θεοὶ πολλοί, and εἷς κύριος to κύριοι πολλοί), **by Whom** (as Him by whom the Father made the worlds, John i. 3; Heb. i. 2) **are all things, and we** (but here secondly, we as his spiritual people, in the new creation) **by Him.** The inference from the foregoing is that, *per se,* the eating of meat offered to idols is a thing indifferent, and therefore allowed. The limitation of this licence now follows. 7.] **But** (sondern) **not in all is the knowledge** (of which we have been speaking: i. e. see above, is not in them in their individual apprehension, though it is by their profession as Christians): **but** (**aber**) **some through their conscious-**

ἐσθίουσιν, καὶ ἡ [s] συνείδησις αὐτῶν [t] ἀσθενὴς οὖσα [u] μο-
λύνεται. 8 [v] βρῶμα δὲ ἡμᾶς οὐ [w] παραστήσει τῷ θεῷ·
οὔτε ἐὰν μὴ φάγωμεν, [x] ὑστερούμεθα, οὔτε ἐὰν φάγωμεν,
[y] περισσεύομεν. 9 [z] βλέπετε δὲ [a] μή [a] πως ἡ [b] ἐξουσία ὑμῶν
αὕτη [c] πρόσκομμα γένηται τοῖς [t] ἀσθενέσιν. 10 ἐὰν γάρ
τις ἴδῃ σὲ τὸν ἔχοντα [p] γνῶσιν ἐν [d] εἰδωλείῳ [e] κατακείμενον, οὐχὶ ἡ [s] συνείδησις αὐτοῦ [t] ἀσθενοῦς ὄντος

s w. gen. subj., Rom. ii. 15. ix. 1. 2 Cor. i. 12 al.
t = here (3ce) only. (-νεῖν, Rom. xiv. 1. iv. 19 al.)
u Rev. iii. 4. xiv. 4 only. Isa. lxv. 4 al. = Sir. xxi. 28.
v Rom. xiv. 15 reff.
w Rom. xii. 1. xiv. 10. 2 Cor. iv. 14.
x ch. i. 7 reff.
y = ch. xiv. 12 al. (Rom. iii. 7 reff.)
z = Acts xiii. 40 reff.
a = Rom. xi. 21.
b = ch. vii. 37 al.
c Rom. ix. 32, 33 reff.
d here only †. Esdr. ii. 10. 1 Macc. i. 47. x. 83 only.
e = Mark ii. 15 ||. L. xiv. 3. Luke vii. 37 only ‡. (Prov. vi. 9.)

for εσθιουσιν, εστιν ℵ[1](txt ℵ-corr[1]).

8. **υμας** ℵ[1] c k l m 17 [Damasc]. rec παριστησι (*corrn to suit the follg pres tenses*), with DLPℵ[3] rel vulg Orig$_1$ Ath-4-mss Chr$_1$ [Bas$_2$ Euthal-ms] Thdrt Jac-nisib$_1$ [Tert$_2$ Cypr$_1$]: σινιστησιν F [συνιστ. G]: txt ABℵ[1] 17 coptt Clem$_2$ Orig$_2$ Ath$_1$ Damasc$_2$. rec aft ουτε ins γαρ, with DFLP rel latt syrr Clem$_1$ Orig$_2$ Chr$_1$ Thdrt [Bas$_1$ Damasc] Jac-nisib$_1$ Ambrst: om ABℵ 17 am(with tol) coptt æth arm Orig$_1$ [Bas$_1$ Euthal-ms] Cypr$_1$ Aug$_2$ (Tert$_1$). rec ουτε εαν φαγ. περισσευομεν bef ουτε εαν μη φαγ. υστερουμεθα (*appy to bring closer the clause* φαγωμ. περισ., *to* βρωμ. ου παριστ., *as being logically connected with it*), with DFLPℵ rel [vulg-clem fuld æth] syrr Clem$_1$ Orig$_3$ Chr$_2$ [Bas$_1$ Cyr$_1$-p Euthal-ms Damasc] Thdrt Jac-nisib Cypr$_1$ [Tert$_2$ Ambrst Aug]: εαν μη φαγωμεν περισσευομεν ουτε εαν φαγωμεν υστερουμεθα A[2](but in A "περισ. usque ad υστ. voces rescriptæ: quid olim non liquet") 17[1][om μη altogether 17[2]]: txt (A[1]?)B am(with demid flor mar tol) coptt arm Bas$_1$.—περισσευομε**θα** B Orig$_1$.

9. **ημων** P. rec ασθεν**ου**σιν (*appy corrn to suit* ασθενων *below, which however is gradually introduced,*—ασθενεσιν,—ασθενους οντος,—ασθενων), with L rel Chr$_1$ Thdrt [Antch$_1$] Thl Œc: txt ABDFPℵ 17 Clem$_2$ [Euthal-ms] Damasc$_1$.

10. **ειδη** A 17. om σε BF vulg Orig-int$_1$ [Ambrst Aug$_1$]: ins ADLPℵ rel syrr coptt goth arm [(Bas$_1$) Chr$_1$ Euthal-ms Thdrt Antch$_1$ Damasc]. γνωσιν bef εχοντα ℵ[1] 17 Orig-int$_1$. ειδωλιω (for -λειω) AB D[[1](Tischdf)] L[P]ℵ h k [l] m 17 (ιδωλ. AFℵ 17).

ness (or, according to the other reading, **habituation) to this day, of the** (particular) **idol** (i. e. through their having an apprehension to this day of the *reality* of the idol, and so being conscientiously afraid of the meat offered, as belonging to *him*: not wishing to be connected with him. τῇ συνειδήσει ἕως ἄρτι is not = τῇ ἕως ἄρτι συν., but ἕως ἄρτι stands separate, as above: so διὰ τῆς ἐμῆς παρουσίας πάλιν πρὸς ὑμᾶς, Phil. i. 26) **eat it as offered to an idol, and their conscience, in that it is weak, is defiled.** By **ἕως ἄρτι**, it is shewn that these ἀσθενεῖς must have belonged to the *Gentile* part of the Corinthian church: to those who had *once*, before their conversion, held these idols to be veritable gods. Had they been *Jewish* converts, it would not have been συνείδησις τοῦ εἰδώλου which would have troubled them, but apparent violation of the Mosaic law. **8.**] *Reason why we should accommodate ourselves to the prejudices of the weak in this matter: because* it is not one in which any spiritual advantage is to be gained, but one perfectly indifferent: not, with Calv., al., an objection of the *strong* among the Corinthians: no such assumption must be made, without a *plain indication in words* that the *saying of another is being cited*: see Rom. ix. 19; xi. 19; and as Meyer well remarks, if the *eaters* had said this, they would have expressed it, οὔτε ἐὰν **μὴ** φάγωμεν **περισσ.**, οὔτε ἐὰν φάγ., ὑστερ., as it has actually been corrected (see var. readd.) in some MSS., and adopted by Lachm. in his last edn. The δέ carries on the argument.

Bengel remarks (against the ordinary rendering, which takes παρίστημι = συνίστημι, 'commendo,' which meaning it will not bear) that παραστήσει is a verbum μέσον, after which may follow a good or a bad predicate:—**will not affect our** (future) **standing before God**;—and to this indifferent meaning of παραστήσει answers the antithetic alternative which follows. **9.**] **δέ**—q. d. "I acknowledge this indifference—this licence to eat or not to eat; *but* it is on that very account, *because* it is a matter indifferent, that ye must take heed," &c. The particular πρόσκομμα in this case would be, the tempting them to *act against their conscience*:—a practice above all others dangerous to a Christian, see below, ver. 11. **10.**] *Explanation how the* **πρόσκομμα** *may arise.* **τίς**, scil. (see below) ἀσθενὴς ὤν. **τὸν ἔχοντα γνῶσιν** seems to imply that the weak brother *is aware of this*, and *looks up*

[f] οἰκοδομηθήσεται εἰς τὸ τὰ [g] εἰδωλόθυτα ἐσθίειν, 11 καὶ
[h] ἀπόλλυται ὁ [i] ἀσθενῶν [k] ἐν τῇ σῇ [p] γνώσει, ὁ ἀδελφὸς
δι' ὃν χριστὸς ἀπέθανεν; 12 οὕτως δὲ [l] ἁμαρτάνοντες [l] εἰς
τοὺς ἀδελφοὺς καὶ [m] τύπτοντες αὐτῶν τὴν [n] συνείδησιν
[i] ἀσθενοῦσαν, [l] εἰς χριστὸν [l] ἁμαρτάνετε. 13 [o] διόπερ εἰ
[p] βρῶμα [q] σκανδαλίζει τὸν ἀδελφόν μου, οὐ μὴ φάγω [r] κρέα
[s] εἰς τὸν αἰῶνα, ἵνα μὴ τὸν ἀδελφόν μου [q] σκανδαλίσω.

IX. 1 Οὐκ εἰμὶ ἐλεύθερος; οὐκ εἰμὶ ἀπόστολος; οὐχὶ

K ουτως δε... ...συνειδησιν d. ABDFK LPℵ a b c e f g h k l m n o 17. 47

f = Acts ix. 31 reff. (iron., here only. see Mal. iii. 15.) constr., Eph. ii. 22. g ver. 1 reff. h Rom. xiv. 15 reff. i Rom. iv. 19 reff. k Matt. vi. 7. l constr., ch. vi. 18 reff. m = here only. 1 Kings i. 8. Prov. xxvi. 22. n ver. 7. o ch. x. 14 (xiv. 13 v. r.) only. p Rom. xiv. 15 reff. q Matt. xv. 12. xvii. 27. Rom. xiv. 21 +. Sir. ix. 5. xxiii. 8. xxxv. (xxxii.) 15 only. r Rom. xiv. 21 only. Gen. ix. 4 al. s Matt. xxi. 19. Mark iii. 29. John viii. 35. Deut. xv. 17.

εσθιειν bef τα ειδωλοθυτα DF [vulg syrr coptt æth] Orig-int [Ambrst] Aug.

11. for και απολ., απολ. γαρ Bℵ[1] 17 coptt goth Clem$_1$(elsw cites freely αλλα απ.) [Antch$_1$ (Thdrt$_1$)]: απολ. ουν AP: και απ. ουν 46 Damasc: txt DFLℵ[3] rel vulg syrr [æth arm Euthal-ms] Chr$_1$ Iren-int$_1$ [Ambrst] Jer. (*The sentence has prob been tampered with to get rid of the apparent awkwardness of the question being carried on through ver 11,—and* ουν *and* γαρ *have been attempts to break it off at* εσθιειν.) rec απολειται (*to suit the fut above*), with D[3][-gr] FL rel [vulg syrr æth arm] Chr$_1$ (edd and mss vary) Thdrt Thl Œc Iren-int$_1$ [Ambrst] Jer: txt AB D[1][and lat] Pℵ [a basm] copt goth Clem$_2$ Bas[(edd and mss vary) Euthal-ms] Antch$_1$ Thdrt$_1$ Damasc. (απολυται D[1], απολλυται D[2]: 17 illeg.) rec επι (= 'on account of,' *seems to have been a corrn for the more difficult* εν,—*see note*), with L rel Chr$_1$ [Antch$_1$] Thdrt Thl Œc: txt ABDFPℵ 17 Bas$_1$ Thdrt$_1$ [Euthal-ms Damasc]: *in* latt Iren-int [Ambrst] Jer: om εν Clem$_2$ (Orig$_1$). om σῃ B. rec αδελφος, omg art, bef εν τῃ σῃ γνωσει (*attempt to simplify, at the expense of the emphatic character of the sentence*), with LPℵ[3] rel fuld syr(αδ. ο ασθ.) [arm] Chr$_1$ Thdrt$_1$ [Antch$_1$ Damasc]: om αδελφος vulg-ms Syr: txt AB D[om ο D[2·3]] Fℵ[1] m(omg ὁ) 17 latt copt [basm] goth æth Bas$_1$ Iren-int$_1$ Ambrst Jer (Clem$_1$ has ο αδ. ασθ.: elsw$_1$ he cites απ. γαρ ο ασθ. τῃ σῃ γν.).

12. om τους F. om και F(including F-lat G-lat) D-lat [basm].

13. ins το bef βρωμα F. om μου (twice) F(including F-lat G-lat) Cypr$_1$; [D-lat[1]] goth Clem$_1$ also om 1st μου; D[1](and lat) Cypr$_1$ [Ambrst Aug$_1$ Sing-cler] om 2nd. κρεας ℵ[1].

Chap. IX. 1. rec transp ελευθερος and αποστολος (*possibly to bring the weightiest question into prominence,—or, as Mey,* ουκ ειμ. απ. *having been omd in mistake (as* 71. 178*), was re-insd first as the weightier and first treated, cf vv* 2, 3), with DFKL rel fuld syr basm goth Chr$_2$ [Euthal-ms] Thdrt Ambrst: txt ABPℵ m 17 vulg [am demid harl tol] Syr copt æth arm Orig$_1$ Tert$_1$ Ambr$_1$ Aug$_1$ Pel Cassiod Bede.

to thee as such. **ἐν εἰδωλείῳ κατ.**] See on εἰδωλοθ., ver. 1. εἰδωλεῖον, as Ποσειδεῖον, 'Απολλωνεῖον, 'Ισεῖον, &c. "**οἰκοδομηθήσεται** is not a *vox media*, as Le Clerc, Elsner, Wolf, al., nor is it *impelletur*, as Castal., Bengel, Kypke, al., nor *confirmabitur*, as Syr., Grot., Billroth, al." (Mey.), but as Meyer and De Wette, *ædificabitur*, not without a certain irony, seeing it is accompanied by ἀσθενοῦς ὄντος,—for thus the building up would be without solid foundation—a *ruinosa ædificatio*, as Calv. **11.**] . . . . **and (thus) the weak perishes** (hereafter: see the parallel, ref. Rom. and note) **in** (as the element in which,—he entering into it as his own, which it is not) **thy knowledge,—the brother, in whose behalf Christ died?** See again Rom. as above. **12.**] **οὕτως**, viz. as in vv. 10, 11. **καί** fixes and explains what is meant by ἁμαρτ. εἰς τ. ἀδ. **τύπτοντες**] smiting: τί γὰρ ἀπηνέστερον ἀνθρώπου γένοιτ' ἂν τὸν νοσοῦντα τύπτοντος; Chrys. p. 176 **13.**] *Fervid expression of his own resolution consequent on these considerations, by way of an example to them.* **βρῶμα, food,** i. e. *any* article of food, as ver. 8; purposely indefinite here; 'if such a matter as food . . . . ,' but presently particularized. **οὐ μὴ φάγω**, strong future, **I surely will not eat**; 'there is no chance that I eat.' **κρέα**] 'Quo certius vitarem carnem idolo immolatam, *toto genere* carnium abstinerem.' Bengel. **σκανδαλίσω**] **be the means of offending**; "commutatur persona: modo dixit *si cibus offendit.*" Bengel. "Non autem hoc dicit quod hoc aliquo casu opus sit, sed ut ostendat multo graviora quam de quibus hic agitur sustinenda pro proximorum salute." Grot. IX. 1—27.] *He digressively illustrates the spirit of self-denial which he professed in the resolution of ch. viii. 13,—by contrasting his rights as an Apostle with his actual conduct in*

Ἰησοῦν τὸν [t] κύριον ἡμῶν [t] ἑώρακα; οὐ τὸ ἔργον μου
ὑμεῖς ἐστε ἐν κυρίῳ; 2 εἰ [u] ἄλλοις οὐκ εἰμὶ ἀπόστολος,
[v] ἀλλά γε ὑμῖν εἰμι· ἡ γὰρ [w] σφραγίς μου τῆς [x] ἀποστολῆς ὑμεῖς ἐστε ἐν κυρίῳ. 3 ἡ ἐμὴ [y] ἀπολογία τοῖς ἐμὲ
[z] ἀνακρίνουσίν ἐστιν αὕτη. 4 [a] μὴ [a] οὐκ [b] ἔχομεν [b] ἐξου-

t John xx. 18, 25. (Acts xxii 15.) u dat. = ch. . 18 reff. v ch. iv. 15 reff. w = Rom. iv. 11 (reff.) only. x Acts i. 25. Rom i. 5. Gal ii. 8 only. Deut. xxii. 7. y w. dat., 1 Pet. iii. 15 only. see Acts xxii. 1 (xxv. 16 reff.). z Acts iv. 9 reff. a here bis. Rom. x. 18, 19. ch. xi. 22 only. P. b ch. vii. 37 reff.

rec aft ιησ. adds χριστον, with DKLP rel Syr syr-w-ast copt [goth æth-pl arm] Chr Thdrt: om ABא a am(with [fuld] harl tol) sah æth[-rom] $Orig_1$ [$(Tert_1)$] Ambrst: pref, F vulg-ed(with demid) $Tert_1$ Aug_1 [Pel]. (17 illeg.) εορακα B^1D^3F[P]א e.

2. om A (i. e. from εν κυριω to εν κυριω). rec (for μου της) της εμης, with DFKL rel Chr_1 [Euthal-ms] Thdrt, *apostolatus mei* vulg D-lat [Ambrst Aug_1]: txt (*Meyer objects to txt, that σφρ. μου is prob a corrn to suit εργ. μου above. This is surely improb*) BPא 17 $Orig_1$ [Damasc], *mei apostolatus* F-lat G-lat. om εν κυριω D^1(and lat) tol [Syr] goth Chr_2.

3. rec αυτη bef εστιν, with DFKL rel [vulg syr copt arm Euthal-ms] Thdrt Thl Œc: txt ABPא m 17 Chr_2 Damasc.

abstaining from demanding them (vv. 1—22). *This self-denying conduct he further exemplifies*, vv. 23—27, *for their imitation.* See Stanley's introductory note; and Conyb. and Howson, vol. i. pp. 61, 457, edn. 2. 1.] He sets forth, (1) his *independence* of men (contrast ver. 19); (2) his apostolic *office* (for the order, see var. readd.):—(3) his *dignity* as an Apostle, in having been vouchsafed a sight of Christ Jesus our Lord;—(4) his *efficiency* in the office, as having converted them to God. **ἐλεύθ.**] So that the resolution of ch. viii. 13 is not necessitated by any *dependence* on my part *on the opinion of others.* **ἑώρακα**] Not, during the life of our Lord on earth, as Schrader, nor is such an idea supported by 2 Cor. v. 16; see note there;—but, in the *appearance* of the Lord to him *by the way to Damascus* (Acts ix. 17; ch. xv. 8: see Neand. Pfl. u. Leit. p. 151, note); and also, secondarily, in those *other visions* and *appearances*,—recorded by him, Acts xviii. 9 (?), xxii. 18,—and possibly on other occasions since his conversion. οὐ μικρὸν δὲ καὶ τοῦτο ἀξίωμα ἦν, Chrys. Hom. xxi. p. 180. **ἐν κυρίῳ** is not a mere humble qualification of τὸ ἔργον μου, as Chrys. ib., τουτέστι τοῦ θεοῦ τὸ ἔργον ἐστίν, οὐκ ἐμοῦ,—but designates, as elsewhere, the *element, in which* the work is done: they were his work *as an Apostle*, **i. e.** *as the servant of the Lord enabled by the Lord*, and SO IN THE LORD. See ch. iv. 15. 2.] At least my apostleship cannot be denied by *you* of all men, who are its seal and proof. **εἰ . . . . οὐκ εἰμί**] **οὐκ**, because it belongs closely to the hypothesis: '*if I am no-Apostle*,' see ch. vii. 9. **ἄλλοις**, **to others**, i. e. *in the estimation of others.* **ἀλλά γε**, **yet at least**, is stronger than ἀλλά alone. The particle shews that the sentiment which it introduces has more weight than the other to which the ἀλλά is a reply. See Hartung, Partikellehre, i. 385. Meyer (after Klotz) remarks that "in the classics ἀλλά γε is never found without one or more words intervening:" those words being emphatic: e. g. Aristoph. Nub. 399, πῶς οὐχὶ Σίμων' ἐνέπρησεν . . . . . ἀλλὰ τὸν αὑτοῦ γε νεὼν βάλλει; **σφραγίς**] *as being the proof of his apostolic calling and energy, by their conversion*: better than,—by the signs and wonders which he wrought among them, as Chrys. (al.) from 2 Cor. xii. 11—13, and perhaps misled by the similarity of σημεῖον and σφραγίς. Their *conversion* was the great proof: so Theodoret, ἀπόδειξιν γὰρ τῶν ἀποστολικῶν κατορθωμάτων τὴν ὑμετέραν ἔχω μεταβολήν. **ἐν κυρ.**] belongs to the whole sentence, see above, on ver. 1. 3.] This belongs to the *preceding*, not to the *following* verses: **αὕτη**, viz. the *fact of your conversion*: this word is the *predicate, not the subject*—as in John i. 19; xvii. 3, and stands here in the emphatic place before the verb; referring to what went before. With ver. 4 a new course of questions begins, which furnish no ἀπολογία. **τοῖς ἐμὲ ἀνακρ.**] For the dat. see Acts xix. 33; 2 Cor. xii. 19:—**to those, who call me in question**: ἐμέ, emphatic, as Chrys. says, of ver. 2, κἂν βούληταί τις . . μαθεῖν ποθεν ὅτι ἀπόστολός εἰμι, ὑμᾶς προβάλλομαι, p. 181. 4.] He resumes the questions which had been interrupted by giving the proof of his Apostleship.
μὴ οὐκ ἔχ.] μή *asks the question*: οὐκ ἔχομεν is the *thing in question*: **Is it so, that we have not power . . . . ?** The plur. seems to apply to *Paul alone*: for though Barnabas is introduced momentarily in ver. 6, there can be no reference to him in ver. 11. It may perhaps be used as pointing out a matter of *right*, which any would have had on the same conditions (see ver.

c trans., here only. Ezek. xxxvii. 2. intrans., Acts xiii. 1 reff.
d = Acts xiv. 4 (note), 14.
e constr., Acts xiv. 9 reff.

σίαν φαγεῖν καὶ πεῖν; 5 [a] μὴ [a] οὐκ [b] ἔχομεν [b] ἐξουσίαν ABDF
ἀδελφὴν γυναῖκα [c] περιάγειν, ὡς καὶ οἱ λοιποὶ [d] ἀπόστο- LPℵ a
λοι καὶ οἱ ἀδελφοὶ τοῦ κυρίου καὶ Κηφᾶς; 6 ἢ μόνος c e f g
ἐγὼ καὶ Βαρνάβας οὐκ [b] ἔχομεν [b] ἐξουσίαν [[e] τοῦ] μὴ k l m
o 17. 47

4. (πειν, so B[1](Tischdf), πιν D[1]Fℵ[1].)

5. for αδελφην γυναικα, γυναικας F (Clem$_1$) Tert$_2$: αδελφας γυναικας arm(and mss mentioned by Jer): αδελφοι γυναικα lectt 8. 56: Sedul says, *in græco sorores, non mulieres, legitur: uxores* Helvid Cassiod: *mulierem sororem* vulg(with harl[1], [*sororem mulierem*] am demid fuld [Aug$_1$]). (*The variations shew, as in ch* vii., *how the sacred text was tampered with by the parties in the controversy on celibacy.*) om 2nd οἱ K [Damasc].

6. om του (*to conform to vv* 4 *and* 5) ABD[1]FPℵ 17 Orig[-c$_1$ Euthal-ms] Isid$_1$: ins D[3]KL rel [Bas$_1$] Chr$_1$ Thdrt Damasc Thl Œc.

11), and as thus not belonging personally to Paul, as do the things predicated in vv. 1, 2, 15. This however will not apply to ver. 12, where the emphatic ἡμεῖς is personal. **φαγεῖν κ. πεῖν]** **To eat and to drink,** sc. *at the cost of the churches:* not with any reference to the eating of things offered to idols (as Schrader, iv. 132), nor to Jewish distinctions of clean and unclean (as Billroth and Olshausen);—see below, vv. 6, 7. **5.] Have we not the power to bring about with us** (also to be maintained at the cost of the churches, for *this*, and not the power to marry, is here the matter in question) **as a wife, a (believing) sister** (or, '*to bring with us a believing wife:*' these are the only renderings of which the words are legitimately capable. Augustine, De Opere Monachorum, 4 (5), vol. vi. p. 552, explains it thus: "Ostendit sibi licere quod ceteris Apostolis, id est ut non operetur manibus suis, sed ex Evangelio vivat: . . . . ad hoc enim et fideles mulieres habentes terrenam substantiam ibant cum eis, et ministrabant eis de substantia sua," &c., and similarly Jerome adv. Jovin. i. 26, vol. ii. p. 277. So likewise Tertull., Theodoret, Œcum., Isid. Pelus., Theophylact, Ambrose, and Sedul. So too Corn.-a-Lap. and Estius. See Estius, and Suicer, γυνή, II. And from this misunderstanding of the passage grew up a great abuse, and such women are mentioned with reprobation by Epiphan. Hær. 78, vol. i. (ii. Migne), p. 1043, under the name of ἀγαπηταί. They were also called ἀδελφαί: and were forbidden under the name of συνείσακτοι by the 3rd Canon of the 1st Council of Nicæa. See these words in Suicer), **as also the other Apostles** (in the wider sense, not only the twelve, for ver. 6, Barnabas is mentioned. It does not follow hence that all the other Apostles *were married:* but that *all had the power*, and *some had used it*) **and the brethren of the Lord** (mentioned not *because distinct* from the ἀπόστολοι, though they were absolutely distinct from the *Twelve*, see Acts i. 14,—but as a further specification of the *most renowned persons*, who travelled as missionaries, and took their wives with them. On the ἀδ. τοῦ κυρ. see note, Matt. xiii. 55. They were in all probability the actual brethren of our Lord by the same mother, the sons of Joseph and Mary. The most noted of these was James, *the Lord's brother* (Gal. i. 19; ii. 9, 12, compare Acts xii. 17; xv. 13; xxi. 18), the resident bishop of the Church at Jerusalem: the others known to us by name were Joses (or Joseph), Simon, and Judas, see note on Matt. ib.), **and Cephas** (Peter was married, see Matt. viii. 14. A beautiful tradition exists of his encouraging his wife who was led to death, by saying μέμνησο, ὦ αὕτη, τοῦ κυρίου, Clem. Alex. Strom. vii. § 11 (63), p. 868 P. Euseb. H. E. iii. 30. Clem. Alex. Strom. iii. § 6 (52), p. 535 P., relates that he had children)? On a mistake which has been made respecting St. Paul's (supposed) wife, see note on ch. vii. 8. **6.] Or** (implying what the consequence would then be, see ch. vi. 2, 9: does not introduce a new ἐξουσία, but a consequence of the denial of the last two) **have only I and Barnabas** (why Barnabas? Perhaps on account of his former connexion with Paul, Acts xi. 30; xii. 25; xiii. 1—xv. 39; but this seems hardly enough reason for his being here introduced. It is not improbable that having been at first associated with Paul, who appears *from the first* to have abstained from receiving sustenance from those among whom he was preaching, Barnabas, after his separation from our Apostle, may have retained the same self-denying practice. "This is the only time when he is mentioned in conjunction with St. Paul, since the date of the quarrel in Acts xv. 39." Stanley) **not power to abstain from working** (i. e. power to look for our maintenance from the churches, without manual labour of our own. The Vulg. has '*hoc*

γα-εσθαι... ABCDF KLPℵ a bcefg hklm no 17. 47

[f] ἐργάζεσθαι; 7 Τίς [g] στρατεύεται ἰδίοις [h] ὀψωνίοις [i] ποτέ;
τίς [k] φυτεύει [l] ἀμπελῶνα, καὶ τὸν καρπὸν αὐτοῦ οὐκ
ἐσθίει; τίς [m] ποιμαίνει [n] ποίμνην, καὶ [o] ἐκ τοῦ [p] γάλακ-
τος τῆς [n] ποίμνης οὐκ [o] ἐσθίει; 8 μὴ [q] κατὰ ἄνθρωπον
ταῦτα λαλῶ, [r] ἢ [r] καὶ ὁ νόμος ταῦτα οὐ λέγει; 9 ἐν
γὰρ τῷ Μωυσέως νόμῳ γέγραπται Οὐ [s] κημώσεις βοῦν
[t] ἀλοῶντα. μὴ τῶν βοῶν [u] μέλει τῷ θεῷ, 10 ἢ δι' ἡμᾶς

f absol., Acts xviii. 3. Rom. iv. 4, 5. 2 Thess. iii. 8 al. Exod. v. 18.
g Luke iii. 14. 2 Cor. x. 3. 1 Tim. i. 18. 2 Tim. ii. 4. James v. 1. 1 Pet. ii. 11 only. Isa. xxix. 7.
h Luke iii. 14. Rom. vi. 23. 2 Cor. xi. 8 only +. Esdr. iv. 56. 1 Macc. iii. 28. xiv. 32 only. dat., ch. xi. 5. 2 Cor. i. 15 al.
i = Heb. i. 5, 13.
k ch. iii. 6 reff. Deut. xx. 6.
l Matt. xx. 1, &c. | al. in Gospp. elsw., here only. Isa. v. 1.
m = Luke xvii. 7. 1 Kings xxv. 16. see Acts xx. 28 reff.
n here bis. Matt. xxvi. 31. Luke ii. 8. John x. 16 only. Gen. xxxii. 16.
o = here only (ver. 13). 2 Kings xii. 3. see John vi. 26, 50, 51.
p ch. iii. 2 reff.
q Rom. iii. 5 reff.
r Luke xi. 11, 12. xviii. 11. Rom. ii. 15. ch. xvi. 6. 2 Cor. i. 13. Job ix. 26. interrog., Luke xii. 41. Rom. iv. 9.
s here only +. (-μός, Ps. xxxi. 9. Ezek. xix. 4, 9.) DEUT. xxv. 4.
t here bis. 1 Tim. v. 18 (from l. c.) only. 1 Chron. xxi. 20.
u constr., but ellipt., ch. vii. 21. Xen. Cyr. iii. 1. 30. gen., here only. usu. w. περί, Matt. xxii. 16 al.

7. rec (for τον καρπον) εκ του καρπου (*corrn to conform to the follg* εκ του γαλ.), with (C^3 ?)D$^{2\cdot3}$KLℵ^3 rel [syrr copt arm] Chr$_1$ [Bas$_1$ Euthal-ms] Thdrt, *de fructu* vulg-ed (with am fuld): εκ των καρπων (C^3 ?) Damasc: txt ABC^{1}D^{1}FPℵ^1 17 sah goth Orig-c$_1$, *fructum* G-lat flor(and harl tol) F-lat Bede. aft εσθιει ins και πινει DF. rec ins η bef τις ποιμ., with AC^{1}KLPℵ rel Syr copt [Bas$_1$ Cyr$_1$] Damasc Œc: txt B C^2(appy) DF latt syr sah goth arm Chr$_1$ [Euthal-ms] Thdrt Thl Ambrst Aug$_{[alic]}$. for της ποιμνης, αυτης D^{1}F [flor] sah æth Chr$_1$ Thl Ambrst Aug[has both readgs].
8. for λαλω, λεγω DF f. rec ins ουχι bef και ο νομος (omg ου bef λεγει), with KLP rel sah Dial$_1$ Chr$_1$ Thdrt [Cyr-p$_1$ Damasc]: simly, but ει instead of ουχι, F(*an si lex hæc dicit* lat) [arm]: *ecce etiam lex hæc dixit* Syr: txt ABCDℵ [vulg syr copt] Orig$_1$ Mcion-e$_1$ Epiph$_1$, *an et lex hæc non dicit* vulg. (17 def.)
9. γεγραπται γαρ, omg εν τω μωυσεως νομω, D^1(om γαρ D^2[-gr]) F Orig$_1$ Hil$_1$: txt ABCKLPℵ rel [vulg æth arm] Orig$_1$ [Dial$_1$ Euthal-ms Cyr$_1$] Aug$_1$. rec (for κημωσεις) φιμωσεις (*see* 1 *Tim* v. 18 *and* LXX), with AB^{2}CD$^{2\cdot3}$KLPℵ rel Orig$_4$ Dial$_1$ Cyr[-p$_2$ Euthal-ms Damasc] Thdrt$_1$: txt B^{1}D^{1}F Chr$_{[h.l.]}$ Thdrt$_1$. ins περι bef των βοων DF (vss[?]).

operandi,' so also Tertull., Ambrose, al., omitting μή, and against the usage of ἐργάζεσθαι, see reff.)? **7—12**] *Examples from common life, of the reasonableness of the workman being sustained by his work.* **7.**] *from the analogies of human conduct.* (1) *The soldier.* **ἰδίοις ὀψωνίοις**] with pay furnished out of his own resources,—the dativus modalis, see Winer, edn. 6, § 31. 7. **στρατεύομαι,** of the *soldier,* who serves in the army: **στρατεύω,** of the *general,* or the *nation,* that leads, or undertakes, the war. So Thucyd. iii. 101, of the states which joined the Peloponnesians, οὗτοι καὶ ξυνεστράτευον πάντες: but Xen. Cyr. viii. 4. 29, of the wife of Tigranes, ἀνδρείως ξυνεστρατεύετο τῷ ἀνδρί. See Kühner, ii. 18 (§ 398). (2) *The husbandman.* **τὸν καρπ. αὐτ. οὐκ ἐσθ.**] τὸν καρπόν, as Meyer observes, is simply objective: he does *eat the fruit,* though it may be only part of it. (3) *The shepherd.* Here it is ἐκ τοῦ γάλ., perhaps on account of the inappropriateness of τὸ γάλα . . . . ἐσθίει, and also of τὸ γάλα πίνει, milk being for the most part made into other articles of food, which sustain the shepherd partly directly, partly by their sale. **8.**] **Am I speaking these things merely according to human judgment of what is right? Or** (see note, ver. 6) **does the law too not say these things?** **9.**] (It does say them): **for in the law of Moses it is written, Thou shalt not** (on the fut. with an imperative meaning, 'Thou shalt not,' i. e. 'This I expect of thee, that thou wilt not,' common to all civilized languages, see Winer, edn. 6, § 43. 5. c; Kühner, § 446. 2) **muzzle** (the reading φιμώσεις probably came in from the similar place, 1 Tim. v. 18, and LXX. The verb κημόω occurs, with its substantive κημός, in Xen. de re equestri, v. 3, ἀεὶ ὅποι ἂν ἀχαλίνωτον ἄγῃ, κημοῦν δεῖ· ὁ γὰρ κημὸς ἀναπνεῖν μὲν οὐ κωλύει, δάκνειν δὲ οὐκ ἐᾷ) **an ox while treading out the corn** (in the *sense* = 'the ox that treadeth out:' but strictly that would require τὸν β. τὸν ἀλοῶντα)—"ἀλοᾷν dicuntur boves, quum grana ex aristis exterunt pedibus, qui mos Orientis, sed et Græciæ, ut ex Theophrasto et aliis discimus. Hic triturandi mos in Asia hodieque retinetur. Solent enim illarum regionum incolæ, postquam demessæ fruges sunt, non domum eas ex agris, more nostro, granis nondum excussis, in horrea convellere: sed in aream quandam sub dio comportare: deinde, sparsis in aream manipulis frugum, boves et bubalos immittunt, qui

v Acts xxi. 22 reff.
w ch. vii. 36 reff.
x Rom. iv. 18 reff.
y here bis. Luke xvii. 7 only. Deut. xxii. 10.
z Acts xiv. 9 reff.

[v] πάντως λέγει; δι' ἡμᾶς γὰρ ἐγράφη, ὅτι [w] ὀφείλει [x] ἐπ' ABCDF
ἐλπίδι ὁ [y] ἀροτριῶν [y] ἀροτριᾶν, καὶ ὁ [t] ἀλοῶν [x] ἐπ' ἐλπίδι KLPℵ a
[z] τοῦ [a] μετέχειν. 11 εἰ ἡμεῖς ὑμῖν τὰ [b] πνευματικὰ [c] ἐσπεί- b c e f g
ραμεν, [d] μέγα εἰ ἡμεῖς ὑμῶν τὰ [b] σαρκικὰ [e] θερισομεν; h k l m n o 17. 47

a here bis. ch. x. 17, 21, 30. Heb. ii. 14. v. 13. viii. 13 only. Prov. i. 18. Esdr. v. 40 al. b Rom. xv. 27 (reff.). c = Mark iv. 14 al. fr. d = 2 Cor. xi. 15 only. Gen. xlv. 28. Isa. xlix. 6. e Matt. xxv. 24, 26 ||. John iv. 36. 2 Cor. ix. 6. Ps. cxxv. 5.

10. rec επ' ελπιδι bef οφειλει ο αροτριων (*appy connected with the next var read,—to throw the 1st* επ ελπιδι *more into emphasis at the beginning, as the 2nd is at the end of the sentence*), with D²[-gr] KLℵ³ rel [Syr] Chr Thdrt$_1$[-ms$_1$] Thl Œc [Orig-int$_1$]: ο επ ελπ. αρ. οφ. D¹[-gr]: οφειλει ο εφ ελπ. αρ. οφειλει F[-gr]: *in spe qui arat debet arare* F-lat, so also D³(and lat): txt ABCPℵ¹ m 17 Orig$_3$ Dial$_1$ Eus$_1$ *Cyr*[-p Euthal-ms] Damasc, *debet in spe qui arat arare* vulg Aug$_1$ Pel Bede. rec (for επ ελπ. του μετεχειν) της ελπιδος αυτου μετεχειν επ ελπιδι, with D²·³KLℵ³ rel Chr$_1$ Thdrt Damasc Thl Œc: της ελπιδος αυτου μετεχειν D¹[and lat] F[-gr(and G-lat)]: txt ABCPℵ¹ 17 (vulg [F-lat]) syrr (copt) sah (æth) Orig$_2$[-c$_1$-int$_1$ Euthal-ms] Eus$_2$ Cyr$_2$ Aug$_2$. (*Meyer's account seems to be the right one, that, it being overlooked that* αλοαν *must be supplied aft* αλοων, μετεχειν *was supposed to be infin aft* οφειλει, *and so* του *altered to* αυτου; *then the sense bettered by insg* της ελπιδος *and transposing the original* επ ελπιδι *to the end.*)

11. ins ου bef μεγα D¹(and lat). θερισωμεν CDFLP c m latt Thdrt [lat-ff]: txt ABKℵ rel Chr$_1$ Cyr$_1$ Damasc Thl Œc.

vel pedibus calcantes (see Micah iv. 13), vel curruum quoddam genus trahentes super frumenta, ex aristis eliciunt grana." Rosenmüller. **Is it for OXEN** (generic) **that God is taking care?** We must not, as ordinarily, supply μόνον, *only* for oxen, and thus rationalize the sentence: the question imports, 'In giving this command, are the *oxen*, or those *for whom the law was given*, its objects?' And to such a question there can be but one answer. Every duty of *humanity* has for its ultimate ground, not the mere welfare of the animal concerned, but its welfare *in that system of which* MAN *is the head:* and therefore *man's* welfare. The good done to man's immortal spirit by acts of humanity and justice, infinitely outweighs the mere physical comfort of a brute which perishes. So Philo (de victimas offerentibus, § 1, vol. ii. p. 251) rightly explains the spirit of the law: οὐ γὰρ ὑπὲρ τῶν ἀλόγων ὁ νόμος, ἀλλ' ὑπὲρ τῶν νοῦν κ. λόγον ἐχόντων· ὥστε οὐ τῶν θυομένων φροντίς ἐστιν, ἵνα μηδεμίαν ἔχοι λώβην, ἀλλὰ τῶν θυόντων, ἵνα περὶ μηδὲν πάθος κηραίνωσι. **10.**] **Or** (the other alternative being rejected) **on OUR account** (δι' ἡμᾶς, emphatic—not on account of *men* generally, but as Estius, "propter nos evangelii ministros:" cf. the ἡμεῖς of vv. 11, 12, with which this ἡμᾶς is inseparably * allied) **altogether** (τὸ πάντως προσθείς, ... ἵνα μὴ συγχωρήσῃ μηδ' ὁτιοῦν ἀντειπεῖν τῷ ἀκροατῇ. Chrys. p. 183) **does it** (ὁ νόμος: or perhaps ὁ θεός, but better the former, as above, τῷ θεῷ being only incidentally introduced as the confessed Author of the law, and ὁ νόμος remaining the subject of the sentence) **say (this)?** (on our account): **for on our account it** (viz. οὐ κημώσεις κ.τ.λ., not, that which follows, q. esset γέγραπται) **was written: because** (argumentative, as the *ground* of ἐγράφη,—not, as in some of my earlier editions, containing the *purpose* of ἐγράφη, *expressed in its practical result*) **the plougher** (not literal but spiritual, see below) **ought to plough in hope, and the thresher** (*to thresh,* see var. readd.) **in hope of partaking** (of the crop). The words used in this sentence are evidently *spiritual,* and *not literal.* They are inseparably connected with δι' ἡμᾶς which precedes them: and according to the common explanation of them as referring to a mere maxim of agricultural life, would have no force whatever. But spiritually taken, all coheres. "The command (not to muzzle, &c.) was written on account of *us* (Christian teachers) because we ploughers (in the γεώργιον θεοῦ, ch. iii. 9) ought to plough in hope,—and we threshers (answering to the βοῦς ἀλοῶν) ought to work in hope of (as the ox) having a share." So Chrys. and Theophyl.: τουτέστιν, ὁ διδάσκαλος ὀφείλει ἀροτριᾷν, καὶ κοπιᾷν ἐπ' ἐλπίδι ἀμοιβῆς κ. ἀντιμισθίας. So also Meyer and De Wette: but by far the greater part of interpreters (also Stanley) take it literally; understanding ἡμᾶς of mankind in general, and ὁ ἀροτριῶν and ὁ ἀλοῶν of *labourers in agriculture.* No minute distinction must be sought between the ἀροτριῶν and the ἀλοῶν. The former is perhaps mentioned on account of the process answering to the breaking up the fallow ground of Heathenism:—the latter on account of its occurrence in the precept. **11.**] The **ἡμεῖς** (both times *strongly emphatic:*—we need sorely some means of marking in our English Bibles, for ordinary readers, *which words have the emphasis*) is categoric, but

12 εἰ ἄλλοι τῆς [f] ὑμῶν [g] ἐξουσίας [a] μετέχουσιν, οὐ μᾶλλον
ἡμεῖς; ἀλλ' οὐκ [h] ἐχρησάμεθα τῇ ἐξουσίᾳ ταύτῃ, ἀλλὰ
πάντα [i] στέγομεν, ἵνα μή τινα [j] ἐγκοπὴν [k] δῶμεν τῷ εὐαγγελίῳ τοῦ χριστοῦ. 13 [l] οὐκ [l] οἴδατε ὅτι οἱ τὰ [mn] ἱερὰ [no] ἐργαζόμενοι [τὰ] ἐκ τοῦ ἱεροῦ ἐσθίουσιν, οἱ τῷ [p] θυσιαστηρίῳ
[q] παρεδρεύοντες τῷ [p] θυσιαστηρίῳ [r] συμμερίζονται; 14 οὕτως

f posn., see 2 Cor. xii. 19 reff. and note.
g w. gen. obj., Matt. x. 1. John xvii. 2. Rom. ix. 21. Sir. x. 4. xvii. 2.
h ch. vii. 21 reff.
i ch. xiii. 7. 1 Thess. iii. 1, 5 only †. Sir. viii. 17 only.
j here only †. (-πτειν, Rom. xv. 22.)
k = 2 Cor. vi. 3.
l ch. vi. 2, &c.
m adj., 2 Tim. iii. 15 only. Josh. vi. 7.
n here only.
o = Jer. xxxvii. (xxx.) 9. (ἐργασία, 1 Chron. vi. 43. ix. 13. xxviii. 13.)
p ch. x. 18 reff.
q here only. Prov. i. 21 only. (εὐπάρεδρος, ch. vii. 35.)
r here only †.

12. rec εξουσιας bef υμων, with KL rel vulg Chr$_1$ Thdrt [Cyr$_1$ Damasc]: txt ABCDFPℵ m 17. 47 arm Chr$_1$. for ου, ουχι ℵ^3. ου κεχρημεθα A. for ταυ., αυτη F[-gr]. rec εγκοπην bef τινα, with D[-gr] F[-gr] KLP rel syr Chr$_1$ Thdrt [Cyr$_1$ Damasc]: txt ABCℵ 17 vulg D-lat [Euthal-ms] Tert Ambrst [Aug$_{alic}$]: om τινα F-lat G-lat sah arm Clem$_1$ Orig-int$_1$. εκκοπην D^{1}Lℵ a b^1 f g k o Orig[-c$_1$ Chr-ms$_1$ Euthal-ms Thdrt Damasc]: συνεκ. m.

13. rec om τα (bef εκ), with AC D^2[$^{\cdot 3}$-gr] KLP rel syrr arm [Chr$_1$ Thdrt Damasc]: ins B D^1[-gr] Fℵ 46 coptt, *quæ de sacrario sunt* vulg G-lat coptt [Aug$_{alic}$]. (F-lat omits *sacrario* and reads *quæ desunt* [Aug has *templo* for *sacr.*].) rec **προς**εδρευοντες (*see ch* vii. 35), with KLℵ^3 rel Chr$_1$ Thdrt Thl Œc: txt ABCD F[παρ**α**δρ., so Euthal-ms] Pℵ^1 17. 47 Eus$_1$ Damasc. [m^1 repeats προsεδρ. bef συμμερ.]

in fact applies to Paul alone. The secondary emphasis is on ὑμῖν . . . ὑμῶν. It is one of those elaborately antithetical sentences which the great Apostle wields so powerfully in argument. The ἡμεῖς—ἡμεῖς, being identical, stand out in so much the stronger relief against the triple antithesis, **ὑμῖν, πνευματικά, ἐσπείραμεν,**—and **ὑμῶν, σαρκικά, θερίσωμεν.** If we read the subjunctive, for the usage after εἰ, see Winer, edn. 6, § 41. b. 2, end; ch. xiv. 5; 1 Thess. v. 10; Kühner, § 818 A. 1. The usage is common in Homer, Od. α. 204, al. fr.,—doubtful in Herod. ii. 13; viii. 49, 118,—and hardly ever found in Attic writers. See Soph. Œd. Tyr. 198, εἴ τι νὺξ ἀφῇ, and Œd. Col. 1442, εἴ σου στερηθῶ. **πνευμ.** and **σαρκ.** (see Rom. xv. 27) need no explanation. The first are so called as belonging to the *spirit* of man (De W. and Meyer, as *coming from the Spirit of God;* but it is better to keep the antithesis exact and perspicuous), the second as serving for the nourishment of the flesh. **12.**] **ἄλλοι** does not necessarily point at the *false* teachers; others may have exercised this power. **ὑμῶν** is the objective genitive: **power over you,**—see reff. The second ἀλλά is not in apposition with the first, but in opposition to the idea implied in ἐχρ. τῇ ἐξ. ταύτῃ. Meyer compares Hom. Il. α. 24 f., ἀλλ οὐκ Ἀτρείδῃ Ἀγαμέμνονι ἥνδανε θυμῷ, Ἀλλὰ κακῶς ἀφίει. **στέγομεν**] The word was commonly used, as may be seen in Wetst., of vessels *containing, holding without breaking,* that which was put into them; thence of *concealing* or *covering,* as a secret; and also of *enduring* or *bearing up against.* In this last sense Diod. Sic. iii. 34, uses it literally of ice, στέγοντος τοῦ κρυστάλλου διαβάσεις στρατοπέδων κ. ἁμαξῶν ἐφόδους,—and (xi. 25, Wetst. but?) of a besieged fort, οὐ μήνγε τὴν ὁρμὴν . . . ἔστεγεν . . . τὸ . . . τεῖχος, . . . ἀλλὰ ὑπείκειν ἠναγκάζετο. So also Æsch. Sept. c. Theb. 216, πύργον στέγειν εὔχεσθε πολεμίων δόρυ. These last usages are very near akin to this of our text,—**We endure all things:** viz. labour, privations, hardships. The ἐγκοπαί (hindrances—so Diod. Sic. i. 32, speaks of the Nile as being πολλάκις διὰ τὰς ἐγκοπὰς ἀνακλώμενος) would arise from his being charged with covetousness and self-seeking, which his *independence of them* would entirely prevent. **13, 14.**] *Analogy of the maintenance of the Jewish priesthood from the sacred offerings, with this right of the Christian teacher, as ordained by Christ.* Meyer rightly remarks, that **οἱ τὰ ἱερὰ ἐργαζόμενοι** can only mean the *priests, not including the Levites:* and therefore that both clauses apply to the same persons. **ἐργάζεσθαι,** ἔρδειν, ῥέζειν, are technical words for the *offering of sacrifice.* See reff. to LXX. **ἱεροῦ** here, as θυσιαστηρίου is parallel with it below, is probably not '*the sacrifice,*' '*the holy thing,*' but **the temple**—'*the holy building.*' Similarly Jos. B. J. v. 13. 6, makes the Zealots say, δεῖ . . . τοὺς τῷ ναῷ στρατευομένους **ἐκ τοῦ ναοῦ τρέφεσθαι.** **παρεδρ.**] So Jos. contra Apion. i. 7, speaks of the priests as τῇ θεραπείᾳ τοῦ θεοῦ προσεδρεύοντας. On the practice referred to, see Num. xviii. 8 ff.; Deut. xviii. 1 ff. *No other priesthood but the Jewish* can have been in the mind of the Apostle. The Jew knew of no θυσιαστή-

καὶ ὁ κύριος [s] διέταξεν τοῖς τὸ εὐαγγέλιον [t] καταγγέλλουσιν, ἐκ τοῦ εὐαγγελίου [u] ζῆν. 15 ἐγὼ δὲ οὐ [v] κέχρημαι
οὐδενὶ τούτων· οὐκ ἔγραψα δὲ ταῦτα ἵνα οὕτως γένηται
[w] ἐν ἐμοί· [xy] καλὸν γάρ μοι [y] μᾶλλον ἀποθανεῖν ἢ τὸ
[z] καύχημά μου * [a] ἵνα τὶς [b] κενώσει. 16 ἐὰν γὰρ [c] εὐαγ-
γελίζωμαι, οὐκ ἔστιν μοι [z] καύχημα· ἀνάγκη γάρ μοι
[d] ἐπίκειται· [ef] οὐαὶ γάρ μοι [f] ἐστὶν ἐὰν μὴ [c] εὐαγγελίσωμαι.

ABCDF KLPℵ abcef ghklm no 17. 47

s constr. dat., Matt. xi. 1. Acts xxiii. 31. 3 Kings xi. 18. inf., Luke viii. 55 al. dat. and inf., here only. Dan. i. 5 Theod. t = Acts xiii. 5 reff. u = Matt. iv. 4 || L. (from Deut. viii. 3) only. v ch. vii. 21 reff. w Matt. xvii. 12. Luke xxii. 37. xxiii. 31. John xiv. 30. x = ch. vii. 1, 8, 26. Jonah iv. 3. y Mark ix. 42. constr., Acts xx. 35. z Rom. iv. 2 reff. Prov. xvii. 6. a arrang. of words, 2 Cor. ii. 4 reff. b Rom. iv. 14 reff. c absol., Rom. xv. 20 reff. d Acts xxvii. 20 reff. *κρατερὴ δ' ἐπικείσετ' ἀνάγκη*, Hom. Il. ζ. 458. e Paul, here only. epp., Jude 11 only. gospp. (but not John) and Rev. passim. f here only. Hos. ix. 12.

15. rec *ουδενι εχρησαμην τουτων*, with K rel Thdrt Thl Œc: *ουδενι τουτων εχρησαμην* c [Chr_2]: *ουκ εχρησαμην ουδενι τ.* ℵ[3] 23: *ουδενι ου κεχρημαι τ.* 80: *ουδενι κεχρημαι τ.* D[2] L[sic (Tischdf)]: txt ABCD[1.3]FPℵ[1] m 17 [Euthal-ms] Damasc. **οὐδεὶς* B D[1][and lat] ℵ[1] 17 sah Tert Ambrst-ed[and mss]: *ουθεις μη* A: *τις* F 26: *ινα τις ου μη* 109: *ινα τις* C D[2.3][-gr] KLPℵ[3] rel vulg(and F-lat) Chr[alic Bas_3] Thdrt Damasc Thl Œc Jer_2 Aug[alic]. rec *κενωσῃ*, with K rel Chr[alic Bas_3 Euthal-ms Damasc] Thdrt: txt ABCDFLPℵ k 17. 47[1].

16. *ευαγγελιζομαι* LP f k Damasc: *ευαγγελισωμαι*[*evangelizavero*] DF [vulg Aug alic]. for *καυχημα*, *χαρις gratia* DF ℵ[1](txt ℵ-corr[1]) Ambrst-ms. rec *ουαι δε* (*clumsy alteration, not seeing that γαρ explains αναγκη*), with KLℵ[3] rel syrr æth arm Chr_2 Thdrt [Damasc]: txt ABCDFPℵ[1] 17 latt coptt $Orig_1$-int_1 Ath_1 Chr_1 Cyr_1 [Euthal-ms Aug alic] Ambrst Jer. for 2nd *εστιν*, *εσται* (*alteration, to apply it better to the last day*) F Ambrst: *est aut erit* G-lat: om 119. rec *ευαγγελιζωμαι* (*from -ζωμαι above*), with AKℵ rel $Orig_1$ Ath_1 [Chr_3 Euthal-ms Thdrt Damasc]: *evangelizem* D-lat G-lat(2nd altern): *-ζομαι* LP f m [Cyr-p_1]: txt BCDF Chr_1: *evangelizavero* vulg(and F-lat) G-lat(1st altern) [Orig-int_1 Aug, *prædicavero evangelium* Ambrst].

ριον but *one:* and he certainly would not have proposed heathen sacrificial customs, even *in connexion with* those appointed by God, as a precedent for Christian usage: besides that the idea is inconsistent with *οὕτως καί*: see below. **14.**] **So also** (i. e. in analogy with that His other command) **did the Lord** (Christ; the Author by His Spirit of the O. T. as well as the New) **command** (viz. Matt. x. 10; Luke x. 7, 8) **to those who are preaching the gospel, to live of** (be maintained by. Themistius (Kypke) has *ζῆν ἐξ ἐργασίας*) **the gospel.** Observe, that here the Apostle is establishing an analogy between the rights of the *sacrificing priests* of the law, and of the *preachers of the gospel. Had those preachers been likewise sacrificing priests,* is it possible that all allusion to them in such a character should have been here omitted? But as all such allusion *is omitted,* we may fairly infer that no such character of the Christian minister was then known. As Bengel remarks on ver. 13: 'Si missa esset sacrificium, plane Paulus versu sequente apodosin huc accommodasset.' **15.**] **οὐδενὶ τούτων** is best explained of the different forms of *ἐξουσία*,—not, with Chrys. al., *τῶν πολλῶν παραδειγμάτων—πολλῶν γάρ μοι παρεχόντων ἐξουσίαν, τοῦ στρατιώτου, τοῦ γεωργοῦ, τοῦ ποιμένος, τῶν ἀποστόλων, τοῦ νόμου, τῶν παρ' ἡμῶν εἰς ὑμᾶς γενομένων, τῶν παρ' ὑμῶν εἰς τοὺς ἄλλους, τῶν ἱερέων, τοῦ προστάγματος τοῦ χριστοῦ, οὐδενὶ τούτων ἐπείσθην εἰς τὸ καταλῦσαι τὸν ἐμαυτοῦ νόμον, καὶ λαβεῖν.* Hom. xxii. p. 193. True, that each of these examples pointed to a form of *ἐξουσία*, and none of *these forms* had he *made use of.* See ref. on ch. vii. 21. **ἔγραψα** is the epistolary aorist—**I wrote** (write) **not these things however, that it may be thus** (viz. after the examples which I have alleged) **done to me** (in my case, see reff.):—**for it were good** (reff.) **for me rather to die** (or, *better for me to die,* see ref. Mark) **than that any one should make void** (the remarkable reading of the great MSS. appears to have arisen from the unnatural look of the future with *ἵνα*. It can only be explained by supposing an aposiopesis; the Apostle breaking off at *ἤ*, and exclaiming with fervour, *τὸ καύχημά μου οὐδεὶς κενώσει*) **my (matter of) boasting.** To understand *ἀποθανεῖν* as Chrys., Theophyl., Œc., Estius, Billroth, al., *ἀποθ.* **λιμῷ**, seems quite unnecessary. Further on, Chrys. himself expresses the true sense: *οὕτω καὶ ζωῆς αὐτῷ γλυκύτερον ἦν τὸ γινόμενον*:—and Calvin, "tantum Evangelii promovendi facultatem nimirum propriæ vitæ præferebat." **16 ff.**] The reason why he made so much of this *materies glori-*

17 εἰ γὰρ [g] ἑκὼν τοῦτο πράσσω, [h] μισθὸν ἔχω· εἰ δὲ
[i] ἄκων, [k] οἰκονομίαν [l] πεπίστευμαι. 18 τίς οὖν μού ἐστιν
ὁ [h] μισθός, ἵνα [c] εὐαγγελιζόμενος [m] ἀδάπανον [n] θήσω τὸ
εὐαγγέλιον, εἰς τὸ μὴ [o] καταχρήσασθαι τῇ ἐξουσίᾳ μου
ἐν τῷ εὐαγγελίῳ ; 19 [p] ἐλεύθερος γὰρ ὢν ἐκ πάντων,

d ινα . . . ABCDF KLPℵ abcde fghkl mno 17. 47

g Rom. viii. 20 only. Exod. xxi. 13 only. h = Matt. v. 12. vi. 1. Rom. iv. 4 reff. i here only. Job xiv. 17 only. k Luke xvi. 2, 3, 4. Eph. i. 10. iii. 2, 9. Col. i. 25. 1 Tim. i. 4 only. L.P. Isa. xxii. 19, 21 only. l = Rom. iii. 2 reff. m here only †. n constr., Matt. xxii. 44 ‖ (from Ps. cix. 1). Rom. iv. 17 (from Gen. xvii. 5). Gen. xxxii. 12. Wisd. x. 21. o ch. vii. 31 only †. Ep. Jer. 28 only. 3 Macc. v. 22. p w. ἐκ, here only. w. ἀπό, Rom. vii. 3.

18. rec (for 1st *μου*) *μοι*, with DFLPℵ³ rel syr Chr[alic Euthal-ms² Damasc] Thdrt Aug[alic] : txt A B(Tischdf [N. T. Vat(expr), not N. T. edd 7, 8]) CKℵ¹ n 17 vulg Syr coptt [Chr₁ Euthal-ms] Cyr₁ Ambrst Jer₁ Pel Bede.—*εσται*[*εστιν* D³-gr(and E)] *μοι* *erit mihi* D¹F. rec aft *το ευαγγελιον* ins *του χριστου* (*see ver* 12), with D²·³FKLP rel syrr Thdrt Jer : om ABCD¹ℵ a 17 vulg(not F-lat) D-lat coptt æth arm Chr₅ Cyr₁ [Euthal-ms] Ambrst Aug[alic] Pel Bede. *καταχρασθαι* A 17 [Orig-c₁]. *εν*(but marked for erasure) *τη εξ.* ℵ¹ : *την εξουσιαν* D¹F. for 2nd *μου*, *μοι* F[-gr] (not G). at end add *μου* D¹[-gr].

andi : viz. that his *mission itself* gave him no advantage this way, being an office *entrusted to him*, and for which he was solemnly accountable : but in this thing only had he an *advantage* so as to be able to boast of it, that he preached the gospel *without charge*. **οὐαὶ γάρ**—explains the *ἀνάγκη*. On *οὐαί ἐστιν*, see ref. Hos.

17.] **For** (illustration and confirmation of *οὐαὶ γὰρ κ.τ.λ.* above) **if I am doing this** (preaching) **of mine own accord** (as a *voluntary undertaking*, which in Paul's case was *not so*, as Chrys., *τὸ ἑκὼν κ. ἄκων ἐπὶ τοῦ ἐγκεχειρίσθαι καὶ μὴ ἐγκεχειρίσθαι λαμβάνων* : not, as E. V., al., *willingly*, for this *was so*), **I have a reward** (i. e. if *of mine own will* I took up the ministry, it might be conceivable that a *μισθός* might be due to me. That this was not the case, *and never could be*, is evident, and the *μισθός* therefore only hypothetical) : **but if involuntarily** (which *was* the case, see Acts ix. 15 ; xxii. 14 ; xxvi. 16), **with a** STEWARDSHIP (*οἰκ.* emphatic) **have I been entrusted** (and therefore from the nature of things, *in this respect* I have no *μισθός* for merely doing what is my bounden duty, see Luke xvii. 7—10 : but an *οὐαί*, if I fail in it. Chrys. observes well : *οὐδὲ γὰρ εἶπεν, εἰ δὲ ἄκων, οὐκ ἔχω μισθόν, ἀλλ'* **οἰκ. πεπίστ.** *δεικνὺς ὅτι καὶ οὕτως ἔχει μισθόν, ἀλλὰ τοιοῦτον, οἷον ὁ τὸ ἐπιταχθὲν ἐξανύσας, οὐχ οἷον ἐκεῖνος ὁ ἐκ τῶν ἑαυτοῦ φιλοτιμησάμενος κ. ὑπερβὰς τὸ ἐπίταγμα.* p. 194). The above interpretation, which is in the main that of Chrys., Theophyl., Œcum. (altern.) al., Meyer, and De Wette, is the only one which seems to me to satisfy, easily and grammatically, all the requirements of the sentence, and at the same time to suit the logical structure of the context. The other Commentators go *in omnia alia*, and adopt various forced and arbitrary constructions of the verse.

18.] Ordinarily, and even by De Wette, thus arranged and rendered : '*What then is my reward ?* (*It is*), *that in preaching I make the gospel to be without cost, that I use not my power in the gospel.*' But this, though perhaps philologically allowable (against Meyer,—see John xvii. 3,—*αὕτη ἐστὶν ἡ αἰώνιος ζωή, ἵνα γινώσκωσι* . . . . also John xv. 8 ; 1 John iv. 17 (?)), is *not true*. His making the gospel to be without cost, *was not his μισθός, but his καύχημα only :* and these two are *not identical*. The *καύχημα* was *present :* the *μισθός*, *future*. Meyer's rendering is equally at fault. He would make *τίς οὖν μού ἐστιν ὁ μισθός ;* a question implying a *negative* answer—'*What then is my reward ? None : in order that I preach gratuitously*,' &c. But thus he severs off (see below) the whole following context, vv. 19—23 : and as it seems to me, stultifies the *καύχημα*, by robbing it altogether of the coming *μισθός*. I am persuaded that the following is the true rendering : **What then is my reward** (in prospect) **that I** (*ἵνα*, like *ὅπως* in classical Greek, with a fut. indic., points to the actual realization of the purpose, with more precision than when followed by the subjunctive. So Xen. Cyr. ii. 4. 31, *Κῦρος, ὦ 'Αρμένιε, κελεύει οὕτω ποιεῖν σε,* **ὅπως** *ὡς τάχιστα ἔχων* **οἴσεις** *καὶ τὸν δασμὸν καὶ τὸ στράτευμα,*—Kühner, Gramm. ii. 490, where see more examples) **while preaching, render the gospel without cost** (i. e. what reward have I in prospect *that induces me to preach gratuitously*) **in order not to use** (as carrying out my design not to use) [**to the full**] (**καταχρ.** see ref. and note : not, to *abuse*, as E. V.) **my power in the gospel** (= *τῇ ἐξουσ. μου τῇ ἐν τῷ εὐαγγ.*, as often ; cf. *τοῖς κυρίοις κατὰ σάρκα*, Eph. vi. 5 ; *οἱ νεκροὶ ἐν χριστῷ*, 1 Thess. iv. 16, al. fr.) ? **19 ff.**] He now proceeds to *answer* the question, '*What prospect of reward could induce*

πᾶσιν ἐμαυτὸν q ἐδούλωσα, ἵνα r τοὺς r πλείονας s κερδήσω·
20 καὶ ἐγενόμην τοῖς Ἰουδαίοις ὡς Ἰουδαῖος, ἵνα Ἰουδαίους s κερδήσω· τοῖς t ὑπὸ νόμον ὡς t ὑπὸ νόμον, μὴ
ὢν αὐτὸς t ὑπὸ νόμον, ἵνα τοὺς t ὑπὸ νόμον s κερδήσω·
21 τοῖς u ἀνόμοις ὡς u ἄνομος, μὴ ὢν u ἄνομος θεοῦ
ἀλλ' v ἔννομος χριστοῦ, ἵνα s κερδάνω τοὺς u ἀνόμους.
22 ἐγενόμην τοῖς w ἀσθενέσιν w ἀσθενής, ἵνα τοὺς w ἀσθενεῖς

ABCDF KLPℵ a b c d e f g h k m n o 17. 47

q Acts vii. 6 reff. r (Luke vii. 43, sing.) Acts xix. 32. xxvii. 12. ch. x. 5. xv. 6 al. Exod. xxiii. 2 Ed-vat. &c. (om art. AB.) s = Matt. xviii. 15. 1 Pet. iii. 1. (Matt. xvi. 26 al. fr.†. Job xxii. 3 Symm. -δος, Phil. i. 21.) t Rom. vi. 14, 15. Gal. iv. 4, 5, 21. u = here 4 times. Acts ii. 23 only. Wisd. xvii. 2. (-μως, Rom. ii. 12.) v = here (Acts xix. 39) only †. w = Rom. v. 6.

19. ins εν bef πασιν D^1(and lat).

20. om και D^1(and lat) m coptt. om 1st ως F-gr 39. 67^2 (Clem) Orig$_3$[-int$_1$] Tert Sedul. (*ως quasi* G-marg.) [F-gr reads ιουδαιος ιουδαιοις, G^1 ιουδαιοις(-corr -*os*) ιουδαιοις, F-lat *judæis judæis.*] rec om μη ων αυτος υπο νομον (*i. e. from* νομον *to* νομον, *by oversight of copyist*), with D^3[-gr] K rel Syr copt æth Orig$_3$ Thdrt [Chr$_{alic}$ (Cyr$_1$) Thl Œc (Mar-merc$_1$(quoting Nest))]: ins ABCD^{1}FPℵ 17 latt syr sah goth arm Chr[-txt$_1$] Cyr$_1$ Damasc Orig-int$_1$[not ed Delarue].—om from κερδησω to κερδησω L [Euthal-ms].

21. rec θεω and χριστω (*confusion of vowels and not observing the constr: see note*), with D^3[-gr] KL rel sah [arm Cyr-p$_1$] Thdrt: txt ABCD^{1}FPℵ d m 17 latt syr copt [goth] Orig$_1$[-c$_1$] Did$_1$ Chr$_1$ Cyr[-p$_2$ Euthal-ms] Isid$_1$ Damasc Ath[-int$_1$ Ambrst-txt Aug$_3$ Mar-merc(quoting Nest)]. rec κερδησω (*from ver* 20), with DKLℵ^3 rel Orig$_1$[-c$_1$] Did$_1$ Chr$_1$ Thdrt [Cyr-p$_1$ Euthal-ms Isid$_1$ Damasc]: txt ABCFPℵ^1 [m] 17 (κερδανωμεν Clem$_1$), and m Orig$_2$[-c] in next verse.—τους ανομους bef κερδ. D. rec om τους (*probably to suit* ιουδαιους *above*), with FKLℵ^3 rel Chr Thdrt [Euthal-ms Isid Damasc]: ins ABCDPℵ^1 17 Orig$_2$ Did.

22. aft εγενομην ins δε και *autem et* F. ασθενουσιν DF. rec aft ασθενεσιν ins ως (*to tally with the three former*), with C D[-gr] FKLPℵ^3 rel [syrr coptt goth æth arm] Orig$_2$[-c] Chr$_3$ Thdrt [Euthal-ms Damasc] Thl: om ABℵ^1 vulg(not F-lat) D-lat Orig$_1$(retaining the three former) Orig-int$_3$ Cypr$_1$ Ambr$_{[alic]}$ Ambrst Aug Bede.

me to do this?' [**Yea** (literally] **For,** q. d. the reward must have been great and glorious in prospect) **being free from (the power of) all men, I enslaved myself** (when I made this determination: and have continued to do so) **to all, that I might gain** (not τοὺς πάντας, which he could not exactly say, but) **the largest number** (*of any:* that hereafter Paul's converts might be found to be οἱ πλείονες: see below on ver. 24). Bengel has remarked on **κερδήσω,** 'congruit hoc verbum cum consideratione *mercedis:*' but '*congruit*' is not enough: it is *actually* THE ANSWER *to the question* τίς μού ἐστιν ὁ μισθός; This '*lucrifecisse*' *the greater number* is distinctly referred to by him elsewhere, as *his reward* in the day of the Lord: τίς γὰρ ἡμῶν ἐλπὶς ἢ χαρὰ ἢ στέφανος καυχήσεως; ἢ οὐχὶ καὶ ὑμεῖς, ἔμπροσθεν τοῦ κυρίου ἡμῶν Ἰησοῦ ἐν τῇ αὐτοῦ παρουσίᾳ; ὑμεῖς γάρ ἐστε ἡ δόξα ἡμῶν καὶ ἡ χαρά. 1 Thess. ii. 19, 20. And it is for this reason that ἵνα . . . . κερδ. is *three times repeated:* and, as we shall presently see, that the similitude at the end of the chapter is chosen. **20—22.**] *Specializes the foregoing assertion* πᾶσιν ἐμ. ἐδούλωσα, by *enumerating various parties to whose weaknesses he had conformed himself, in order to gain them.*

20. τοῖς Ἰουδ. ὡς Ἰουδ.] See examples, Acts xvi. 3; xxi. 26. οὐκ εἶπεν, Ἰουδαῖος, ἀλλ' **ὡς** Ἰουδαῖος, ἵνα δείξῃ ὅτι οἰκονομία τὸ πρᾶγμα ἦν, Theophyl. after Chrys. The *Jews* here are not *Jewish converts,* who would be already *won* in the sense of this passage. **τοῖς ὑπὸ νόμον . . . .**] These again are not Jewish converts (see above); nor *proselytes,* who would not be thus *distinguished* from other Jews, but are much the same as Ἰουδαῖοι, only to the number of these the Apostle *did not belong,* not being himself (**αὐτός** contrasts with **ὡς** above) under the law, whereas he *was nationally a Jew.* **21. τοῖς ἀνόμοις ὡς ἄν.**] The ἄνομοι are *the Heathen:* hardly, with Chrys., *such as Cornelius,* fearing God but not under the law. Paul became as a Heathen to the Heathen, e. g., when he discoursed at Athens (Acts xvii.) in their own manner, and with arguments drawn from their own poets. **μὴ ὢν κ.τ.λ.**] **not being** (being conscious of not being, remembering well in the midst of my ἀνομία that I was not. This is implied by μή, which is subjective, giving the *conviction of the subject,* not merely the *objective fact,* as οὐκ ὢν would do) **an outlaw from God** (θεοῦ and χριστοῦ are genitives of dependence, as after κατήκοος, ἔνοχος, &c.) **but a subject-of-the-law of Christ** (the words seem inserted rather to put before the reader the true position of a Christian

[s] κερδήσω. [x] τοῖς [x] πᾶσιν γέγονα πάντα, ἵνα [y] πάντως
τινὰς [z] σώσω. 23 πάντα δὲ ποιῶ διὰ τὸ εὐαγγέλιον, ἵνα
[a] συγκοινωνὸς αὐτοῦ γένωμαι. 24 [b] οὐκ [b] οἴδατε ὅτι οἱ
ἐν [c] σταδίῳ τρέχοντες πάντες μὲν τρέχουσιν, εἷς δὲ
λαμβάνει τὸ [d] βραβεῖον; οὕτως [e] τρέχετε, ἵνα [f] καταλά-

x Rom. xi. 32 reff. P.
y Acts xxi. 22 reff.
z = Rom. xi. 14 reff.
a Rom. xi. 17. Phil. i. 7. Rev. i. 9 only. (-νεῖν, Eph. v. 11.)
b ch. vi. 2. ver. 13 al.
c — here (Luke xxiv. 13. John vi. 19. xi. 18. Rev. xiv. 20. xxi. 16) only. Polyb. xviii. 29. 4 al.
d Phil. iii. 14 only †.
e = Rom. ix. 16 reff.
f = Rom. ix. 30. Phil. iii. 12. Exod. xv. 9.

for γεγονα, εγενομην F Clem$_1$. rec ins τα bef παντα (*prob to suit τοις πασιν: but often when παντα occurs, τα is insd bef it in some mss*), with D$^{2\cdot3}$KLP rel Orig$_1$[-c$_1$] Mac$_1$ Chr$_2$ Thdrt [Cyr-p$_1$ Damasc]: txt ABCD^{1}Fℵ Clem$_1$ Orig$_1$ Naz$_2$ Chr$_2$ Cyr[-jer$_1$ Euthal-ms]. for παντως τινας, παντας (*conformation to the foregoing clauses*) DF latt lat-ff, τους παντας 17 Clem$_1$ Orig$_1$(but παντα$_1$ [Mac$_1$, παντας η τινας Orig-c$_1$]).

23. rec (for παντα) τουτο, with KL rel syrr goth Thdrt Damasc Thl Œc: txt ABCDFPℵ m 17 latt coptt æth arm Orig$_1$[-c] Naz$_1$ Chr$_1$(schol on 7) [Euthal-ms] Ambrst Pel.

24. aft βραβειον ins εγω δε λεγω υμιν *ego autem dico vobis* F.

with regard to God's law revealed by Christ, than merely with an apologetic view to keep his own character from suffering by the imputation of ἀνομία) **that I might gain those who had no law.** κερδανῶ (here only in N. T.) and κερδήσω are both found in the classics: see Matthiæ, § 239, and Lobeck on Phrynichus, p. 740. **22.**] The **ἀσθενεῖς** here can hardly be the *weak Christians* of ch. viii. and Rom. xiv., who were *already won*, but as in ref., *those who had not strength to believe and receive the Gospel.* This sentence then does not bring out a new form of condescension, but recapitulates the preceding two classes, τοῖς ὑπὸ νόμον . . . . τοῖς ἀνόμοις. **τοῖς πᾶσιν . . . .**] This sums up the above, and others not enumerated, in one general rule,—and the various *occasions* of his practising the condescension (aorists) in one general result (perfect). **To all men I am become all things** (i. e. to each according to his situation and prejudices) **that by all means** ('omnino:' or perhaps as Meyer, *in all ways:* but I prefer the other) **I may save some** (**τινάς** is emphatic: *some,* out of each class in the πάντες. It is said, as is the following verse, in extreme humility, and distrust of even an Apostle's confidence, to shew them the immense importance of the μισθός for which he thus denied and submitted himself). **23.**] **But** (q. d. 'not only this of which I have spoken, but *all*') **all things I do on account of the gospel, that I may be a fellow-partaker** (with others) **of it** (of the blessings promised in the gospel to be brought by the Lord at His coming).

24 ff.] 'This is my aim in all I do: but inasmuch as many run in a race, many reach the goal, but *one only* receives the prize,—I as an Apostle run *my course,* and *you* must so run *yours,* as each to labour not to be rejected at last, but to gain the glorious and incorruptible prize.' This, as compared with the former context, seems to be the sense and connexion of the passage. He was anxious, as an Apostle, to labour more abundantly, more effectually than they all: and hence his condescension (συγκατάβασις) to all men, and self-denial: accompanied with which was a humble self-distrust as to the great matter itself of his personal salvation, and an eager anxiety to secure it. These he proposes for their example likewise.

24.] The allusion is primarily no doubt to the Isthmian games [' celebrated under the shadow of the huge Corinthian citadel' (Stanley)]; but this must not be pressed too closely: the foot-race was far too common an element in athletic contests, for any accurate knowledge of its predominance in some and its insignificance in others of the Grecian games to be here supposed. Still less must it be imagined that those games were to be celebrated in the year of the Epistle being written. The most that can with certainty be said, is that he alludes to a contest which, from the neighbourhood of the Isthmian games, was well known to his readers. See Stanley's note: who, in following out illustrations of this kind, writes with a vivid graphic power peculiarly his own. **βραβεῖον**] Wetst. quotes from the Schol. on Pindar, Olymp. 1, λέγεται δὲ τὸ διδόμενον γέρας τῷ νικήσαντι ἀθλητῇ ἀπὸ μὲν τῶν διδόντων αὐτὸ βραβευτῶν βραβεῖον, ἀπὸ δὲ τῶν ἀθλούντων ἆθλον, and from the Etymol., βραβεῖον λέγεται ὁ παρὰ τῶν βραβευτῶν διδόμενος στέφανος τῷ νικῶντι. **οὕτως τρ.**] **Thus** (after this manner—viz. as they who run all, *each endeavouring to be the one who shall receive the prize:*—not, *as the one who receives it* (Meyer, De Wette),—for the others strive as earnestly as he: still less must we take ἵνα καταλάβητε for ὡς καταλαβεῖν, which is barely

βητε. 25 πᾶς δὲ ὁ [g] ἀγωνιζόμενος [h] πάντα [i] ἐγκρατεύεται· ABCDF KLPℵ a b c d e f g h k l m n o 17. 47
ἐκεῖνοι [k] μὲν οὖν ἵνα [l] φθαρτὸν στέφανον λάβωσιν, ἡμεῖς
δὲ [l] ἄφθαρτον. 26 ἐγὼ [m] τοίνυν [n] οὕτως τρέχω [n] ὡς οὐκ
[o] ἀδήλως, [n] οὕτως [p] πυκτεύω [n] ὡς οὐκ [q] ἀέρα [r] δέρων·

g Luke xiii. 24. John xviii. 36. Col. i. 29. iv. 12. 1 Tim. iv. 10 v. r. vi. 2. 2 Tim. iv. 7 only +. Sir. iv. 28 al. Dan. vi. 14 Theod. h constr., Acts xx. 35 reff. i ch. vii. 9 (reff.) only +. k ch. vi. 4 reff. l Rom. i. 23 (reff.). m Luke xx. 25. Heb. xiii. 13 (James ii. 24 v. r.) only. Isa. iii. 10. v. 13. n ch. iii. 15 reff. o here only +. (-λος, ch. xiv. 8. -λότης, 1 Tim. vi. 17.) p here only +. Xen. Rep. Lac. iv. 6. q Acts xxii. 23. ch. xiv. 9. Eph. ii. 2. 1 Thess. iv. 7. Rev. ix. 2. xvi. 17 only. Wisd. v. 11, 12. r Acts v. 40 reff.

25. om *ουν* K k 6. 119 arm $Clem_1$ $Iren[-int_1]$: insd in syr with an asterisk. (*α* at the beginning of *αφθαρτον* is written over the line by ℵ[1].)

allowable, and here would not suit the sense; the *οὕτως* being particularized presently by one point of the athletes' preparation being specially alleged for their imitation) **run** (not *καὶ ὑμεῖς τρέχετε*, because the evident analogy between the race and the Christian conflict is taken for granted. If, as Dr. Peile imagines, a contrast had been intended, between the stadium where *one only* can receive the prize, and the Christian race where *all* may, it must have stood *οὕτως δὲ ὑμεῖς τρέχετε, ὡς καὶ* (*πάντας?*) *καταλαβεῖν*. But such contrast would destroy the sense), **in order that ye may fully obtain** (the prize of your calling, see Phil. iii. 14. On *λαμβάνω* and **κατα***λαμβάνω* see note, ch. vii. 31). **25.**] The point in the **οὕτως**, *the conduct of the athletes in regard of temperance*, which he wishes to bring into especial prominence for their imitation:—as concerning the matter in hand,—*his own abstinence from receiving the world's pelf*, in order to save himself and them that heard him. The **δέ** specifies, referring back to *οὕτως*. The emphasis is on **πᾶς**, thus *shewing* **οὕτως** *to refer to the πάντες who τρέχουσιν*. **ἀγωνιζόμενος** is more general than *τρέχων*,—q. d. 'Every one who engages, not only in the *race*, but in *any athletic contest*,' and thus strengthening the inference. The art. (*ὁ ἀγων.*) brings out the man as an enlisted and professed *ἀγωνιζόμενος*, and regards him in that capacity. Had it been *πᾶς δὲ ἀγωνιζ.*, the sense would have been, 'Now every one, *while contending*,' &c., making the discipline to be merely accidental to his contending—which would not suit the spiritual antitype, where we are enlisted for life. Examples of the practice of abstinence in athletes may be seen in Wetst. in loc. I will give but two: (1) Hor. de Arte Poet. 412: "Qui studet optatam cursu contingere metam, Multa tulit fecitque puer, sudavit et alsit: Abstinuit venere et vino." (2) Epict. c. 35: *θέλεις ὀλύμπια νικῆσαι; κἀγὼ νὴ τοὺς θεούς, κομψὸν γάρ ἐστιν. ἀλλὰ σκόπει καὶ τὰ καθηγούμενα καὶ τὰ ἀκόλουθα, καὶ οὕτως ἅπτου τῶν ἔργων. δεῖ σ' εὐτακτεῖν, ἀναγκοτροφεῖν, ἀπέχεσθαι πεμμάτων, γυμνάζεσθαι πρὸς ἀνάγκην ἐν ὥρᾳ τεταγμένῃ, ἐν καύματι, ἐν ψύχει, μὴ ψυχρὸν πίνειν, μὴ οἶνον· ὡς ἔτυχεν ἁπλῶς, ὡς ἰατρῷ παραδεδωκέναι σαυτὸν τῷ ἐπιστάτῃ, εἶτα εἰς τὸν ἀγῶνα παρέρχεσθαι.* **ἐκεῖνοι**] scil. *ἐγκρατεύονται.* **μὲν οὖν**, 'immo vero' (reff.). The Schol. on Pind. Isthm. *ὑπόθεσις*, cited by Meyer, says: *στέφος δέ ἐστι τοῦ ἀγῶνος* **πίτυς**, *τὸ δὲ ἀνέκαθεν σέλινα καὶ αὐτοῦ ἦν ὁ στέφανος.* **ἡμεῖς δέ**, scil. *ἐγκρατευόμεθα ἵνα λάβωμεν στέφανον.* He takes for granted the Christian's temperance in all things, as his normal state. **26.**] **I then** (*ἐγώ* emphatic—recalls the attention from the incidental exhortation, and reminiscence of the Christian state, to the main subject, his own abstinence from receiving, and its grounds. **τοίνυν**, as distinguished from other particles which imply restriction of what has been generally said to some particular object, indicates the *dropping of minute or collateral points, and returning to the great necessary features of the subject*,—and this, as introducing some short and pithy determination or conclusion: see Hartung, Partikellehre, ii. 348. E. g.,—Xen. Cyr. vi. 3. 17, *τούτων μὲν τοίνυν ἅλις εἴη, ἃ δὲ καιρὸς ἡμῖν εἰδέναι, ταῦτα, ἔφη, διηγοῦ*) **so run as** (*οὕτως—ὡς*, see reff.) **not uncertainly** (reff.: cf. also Polyb. iii. 54. 5, *τῆς χιόνος ἄδηλον ποιούσης ἑκάστοις τὴν ἐπίβασιν*:—'*uncertainly*,' i. e. without any sure grounds of contending or any fixed object for which to contend; both these are included. Chrysostom rightly brings it into subordination to the main subject, the participation with idolaters:—*τί δέ ἐστιν, οὐκ ἀδήλως; πρὸς σκοπόν τινα βλέπων, φησίν, οὐκ εἰκῆ καὶ μάτην, καθάπερ ὑμεῖς, τί γὰρ ὑμῖν γίνεται πλέον ἀπὸ τοῦ εἰς εἰδωλεῖα εἰσιέναι, καὶ τὴν τελειότητα δῆθεν ἐκείνην ἐπιδείκνυσθαι; οὐδέν. ἀλλ' οὐκ ἐγὼ τοιοῦτος, ἀλλὰ πάντα ἅπερ ποιῶ, ὑπὲρ τῆς τῶν πλησίον σωτηρίας ποιῶ. κἂν τελειότητα ἐπιδείξωμαι, δι' αὐτούς· κἂν συγκατάβασιν, δι' αὐτούς· κἂν ὑπερβῶ Πέτρον ἐν τῷ μὴ λαμβάνειν, ἵνα μὴ σκανδαλισθῶσι· κἂν καταβῶ πλέον πάντων, περιτεμνόμενος καὶ ξυρώμενος, ἵνα μὴ ὑποσκελισθῶσι.* Hom. xxiii. p. 201); **so fight I, as not striking the air** (and not

27 ἀλλ' [s] ὑπωπιάζω μου τὸ σῶμα καὶ [t] δουλαγωγῶ,
[u] μή [u] πως ἄλλοις κηρύξας αὐτὸς [v] ἀδόκιμος γένωμαι.

s Luke xviii. 5 only †. (-πιον, Prov. xx. 30.) t here only †. Gen. xliii. 18 Symm. (Fischer, but not in Montf. or Bahrdt. [Field believes it to be from a scholium].) u ch. viii. 9 [Rom. xi. 21] al8. P. (exc. Acts xxvii. 29 v. r.) v Rom. i. 28 reff.

27. αλλα B m. υποπιεζω D^3(υπωπ-) e l^1 m^1(Treg [and Tischdf: m Scr]) 46. 113-marg $Clem_1$ Eus_1 Naz_1 Chr-ms_2 $Thdrt_1$: υποπιαζω FKLP a b^1 c f g^2 n o $Ephr_1$ Naz_2 Bas-2-mss_1 Chr-ms Cyr_1 [Euthal-ms] $Damasc_3$. (*castigo* vulg(and F-lat) G-lat(1st altern) Ambr[alic Ambrst] Aug; *lividum facio* D-lat G-lat(2nd altern) [spec] Iren-int_1 $Paulin_1$.) στομα F-gr. [Steph δουλαγαγω (not C).]

my adversary). The allusion is not to a *σκιαμαχία* or rehearsal of a fight with an *imaginary* adversary, as Chrys. (ἔχω γὰρ ὃν πλήξω), Theophyl. al. m., but to a fight with a *real* adversary (viz. here, *the body*) in which the boxer vainly hits into the air, instead of striking his antagonist. So Entellus in the pugilistic combat, Æn. v. 446, 'vires in ventum effudit,' when Dares 'ictum venientem a vertice velox Prævidit, celerique elapsus corpore cessit.' See examples both of what is really meant, and of the *σκιαμαχία*, in Wetst. Obs., in both places *οὐκ* is used and not *μή*, as importing the matter of fact, and joined closely with the adverb in one case and the verb in the other. 27.] **But I bruise my body** (**ὑπωπιάζω**, lit. to strike heavily in the face so as to render black and blue,—"ὑπώπια,—τὰ ὑπὸ τοὺς ὦπας τῶν πληγῶν ἴχνη, ut ait Pollux: sed latius dici sic cœpere ἀφ' οἱασδηποτοῦν πληγῆς τραύματα, ut ait Scholiastes ad Aristoph. Acharn., Cicero Tusc. 2, 'Pugiles cæstibus contusi,' i. e. ὑπωπιαζόμενοι." Grot. The *body* is the adversary, considered as the seat of the temptations of Satan, and especially of that self-indulgence which led the Corinthians to forget their Christian combat, and sit at meat in the idol's temple. The abuse of this expression to favour the absurd practice of the Flagellants, or to support ascetic views at all, need hardly be pointed out to the rational, much less to the Christian student. It is not even of fasting or prayer that he is here speaking, but as the context, vv. 19—23, shews, of breaking down the pride and obstinacy and self-seeking of the natural man by laying himself entirely out for his great work—the salvation of the greatest number: and that, denying himself "solatium" from without: "My hands have been worn away (cf. χεῖρες αὗται, Acts xx. 34) with the black tent-cloths, my frame has been bowed down with this servile labour (cf. ἐλεύθερος . . . . ἐδούλωσα, ver. 19)." Stanley) **and enslave it** ('etiam δουλαγωγεῖν a pyctis desumptum est; nam qui vicerat, victum (vinctum?) trahebat adversarium quasi servum.' Grot. But this seems to want confirmation. I can find no account of such a practice in any of the ordinary sources of information. Certainly Dares is not made the slave of Entellus in Æn. v.: and Virgil is generally accurate in such matters. I had rather give a more general meaning: that viz. of the necessary subjection, for the time, of the worsted to the prevailing combatant), **lest perchance having proclaimed** (κηρ. absolute [answering to our use of *preach*]: as in Æsch. Eum. 566, κήρυσσε, κῆρυξ, καὶ στρατὸν κατειργάθου (Peile). The subject of the proclamation might be the *laws of the combat*, or the *names of the victors* (Æn. v. 245), each by one in the capacity of *herald:* probably here the former only, as answering to the preaching of the Apostles. The nature of the case shews, that the Christian herald differs from the agonistic herald, in being himself *a combatant as well*, which the other was not: and that this is so, is no objection to thus understanding κηρύξας. "This introduces indeed a new complication into the metaphor: but it is rendered less violent by the fact, that . . . . sometimes the victor in the games was also selected as the herald to announce his success. So it was a few years after the date of this Epistle, in the case of Nero. Suet. Nero, c. 24." Stanley) **to others, I myself may prove rejected** (from the *prize:* not, as some Commentators, from the *contest altogether*, for he was already *in it*). An examination of the victorious combatants took place after the contest, and if it could be proved that they had contended unlawfully, or unfairly, they were deprived of the prize and driven with disgrace from the games. Such a person was called ἐκκεκριμένος, and ἀποδεδοκιμασμένος, see Philo de Cherub., § 22, vol. i. p. 152. So the Apostle, if he had proclaimed the laws of the combat to others, and not observed them himself, however successful he might apparently be, would be personally rejected as ἀδόκιμος in the great day. And this he says with a view to shew them the necessity of more self-denial, and less going to the extreme limit of their Christian liberty; as Chrys. εἰ γὰρ ἐμοὶ τὸ κηρῦξαι, τὸ διδάξαι, τὸ μυρίους προσαγαγεῖν οὐκ ἀρκεῖ εἰς σωτηρίαν, εἰ μὴ καὶ τὰ κατ' ἐμαυτὸν παρασχοίμην ἄληπτα,

X. 1 [w]Οὐ θέλω γὰρ ὑμᾶς [w]ἀγνοεῖν, ἀδελφοί, ὅτι οἱ
[x]πατέρες [x]ἡμῶν πάντες [y]ὑπὸ τὴν νεφέλην [y]ἦσαν καὶ πάντες [z]διὰ τῆς θαλάσσης [z]διῆλθον, 2 καὶ πάντες [a]εἰς τὸν
Μωυσῆν [a]ἐβαπτίσαντο ἐν τῇ νεφέλῃ καὶ ἐν τῇ θαλάσσῃ,
3 καὶ πάντες τὸ αὐτὸ [b]βρῶμα [c]πνευματικὸν ἔφαγον, 4 καὶ

w Rom. xi. 25 reff. x Acts v. 30 reff. y John i. 49. Acts iv. 12. ch. ix. 20. Gal. iv. 21. v. 18. z Acts ix. 32 reff. a Acts viii. 16 reff. b Rom. xiv. 15 reff. c Paul (here 3ce. Rom. i. 11. ch. ii. 13. xii. 1. xiv. 1 al.) only, exc. 1 Pet. ii. 5 bis †.

...ημων e. ABCDF KLPℵ a b c d f g h k l m n o 17. 47

CHAP. X. 1. rec (for γαρ) δε (*the connexion not being perceived or wrong word supplied aft omn at beg of lection*), with KLℵ[3] rel syrr Chr$_1$ Thdrt [Euthal-ms Damasc]: om goth arm: txt ABCDFPℵ[1] 17 latt coptt Clem$_1$ Orig$_1$ Mcion-e$_2$ Did$_1$ [Bas$_1$] Cyr$_1$ Iren-int$_1$ Cypr$_2$.

2. **εβαπτισθησαν** ACDFℵ 17 Dial$_1$ Bas$_2$ Did$_1$ Chr$_1$ *Cyr*[-p] Thdrt$_{aliq}$ Thl: txt BKLP rel Orig$_3$ Chr$_4$ Thdrt$_1$ Damasc Œc. (*Notwithstanding the strong manuscript evidence, the passive appears to have been a corrn to the more usual expression in the case of* Christian baptism.) transp νεφ. and θαλ. F.

3. om αυτο A C[1](appy) 46 æth [Did$_2$ Chr$_1$ Promiss$_2$]: om το αυτο ℵ[1]. πνευματικον bef βρωμα BC[2]Pℵ[1] 93 [Cyr$_1$ Euthal-ms]: πνευματικον εφαγον bef βρωμα A 17. 137 Mcion-e: txt (C[1]?)DFKLℵ[3] rel [latt syrr copt goth arm] Orig$_3$[-int$_3$] Dial$_1$ Chr$_4$ Thdrt [(Did$_2$) Damasc] Iren-int.

πολλῷ μᾶλλον ὑμῖν. p. 202. X. 1—22.] He proceeds, in close connexion with the warnings which have just preceded, to set before them the *great danger of commerce with idolatry*, and enforces this by *the example of the rebellions and rejections of God's ancient people*, who were under a dispensation analogous to and typical of ours (1—11); and by *the close resemblance of our sacrament of the Lord's Supper,—their eating of meats sacrificed,—and the same act among the heathen*, in regard of the UNION in each case of the *partakers* in *one act of participation*. So that THEY COULD NOT EAT THE IDOL'S FEASTS WITHOUT PARTAKING OF IDOLATRY = VIRTUALLY ABJURING CHRIST (vv. 15—22). 1.] **γάρ** joins to the preceding. He had been inculcating the necessity of *self-subduing* (ch. ix. 24—27), and now enforces it in the particular departments of *abstaining from fornication, idolatry, &c.*, by the example of the Jews of old. **οὐ θέλω . . . .**, see reff. **οἱ πατ. ἡμῶν**] He uses this expression, not merely speaking for himself and his Jewish converts, but regarding the Christian church as a continuation of the Jewish, and the believer as the true descendant of Abraham. **πάντες . . . πάντες . . . πάντες**, each time with strong emphasis, as opposed to τοῖς πλείοσιν, ver. 5. ALL had these privileges, as *all of you* have their counterparts under the Gospel: but *most of them* failed from rebellion and unbelief. **ὑπὸ τὴν νεφ. ἦσαν**] The pillar of cloud, the abode of the divine Presence, went before them, and was to them a *defence:* hence it is sometimes treated of as *covering* the camp, e. g. Ps. civ. 39, διεπέτασε νεφέλην εἰς σκέπην αὐτοῖς: and thus they would be *under* it. So also Wisd. x. 17, xix. 7,—ἡ τὴν παρεμβολὴν σκιάζουσα νεφέλη. See Exod. xiii. 21, xiv. 20. 2.] **εἰς τ. Μωυσ. ἐβαπτ.**, **received baptism** (lit. baptized themselves: middle, not passive, see var. read.) **to Moses**; entered by the act of such immersion into a solemn covenant with God, and became His church under the law as given by Moses, God's servant,—just as we Christians by our baptism are bound in a solemn covenant with God, and enter His Church under the Gospel as brought in by Christ, God's eternal Son; see Heb. iii. 5, 6. Others (Syr., Beza) explain it '*per Mosen*,' or (Calv., al.) '*auspiciis Mosis*,' which εἰς will not bear,—not to mention that the formula βαπτίζω εἰς was already fixed in meaning, see reff. **ἐν τῇ ν. καὶ ἐν τῇ θ.**] The cloud and the sea were both *aqueous;* and this point of comparison being obtained, serves the Apostle to indicate the outward symbols of their initiation into the church under the government of Moses as the servant of God, and to complete the analogy with our baptism. The allegory is obviously not to be pressed minutely: for neither did they *enter* the cloud, nor were they *wetted by the waters* of the sea; but they *passed under* both, as the baptized passes under the water, and it was said of them, Exod. xiv. 31, "*Then the people feared the Lord, and believed the Lord and his servant Moses.*" To understand, as Olsh., the *sea* and *cloud*, of *water* and the *Spirit* respectively, is certainly carrying the allegory too far: not to mention that thus the baptism by the Spirit would precede that by water.

3.] They had what answered to the one Christian sacrament, Baptism: now the Apostle shews that they were not without a

πάντες τὸ αὐτὸ [c] πνευματικὸν ἔπιον [d] πόμα· ἔπινον γὰρ ἐκ [c] πνευματικῆς ἀκολουθούσης πέτρας, ἡ πέτρα δὲ [e] ἦν ὁ

d Heb. ix. 10 only. Ps. ci. 9 only. Dan. i. 16 Theod.

e = Matt. xxvi. 26. xiii. 37. John xv. 1. Gen. xli. 26, 27. Exod. xii. 11. Ezek. xxxvii. 11.

4. om αυτο A 46 æth $Orig_1$[(ins_2-int_4) Chr_1]. rec πομα bef πνευματικον επιον (*to conform with the preceding*), with DFKL rel latt syrr [copt goth arm] $Orig_1$-int_3 $Dial_1$ Chr_4 Thdrt [Damasc] Iren-int_1 [Aug_2]: txt ABCPℵ 17. 137 $Orig_2$[-int_1 Did_2 Euthal-ms Mcion-in-]$Epiph_2$ Jer (επινον [m[2]] 137 $Orig_1$ [Did_1]: επιαν D[1]). rec δε bef πετρα (*not observing the emphasis*), with ACD[2]KLP rel Mcion[-e_2] $Orig_4$ Eus_3 Chr[alic Did_2 Cyr_1 Euthal-ms Damasc] Thdrt: txt BD[1.3]ℵ $Orig_5$ Eus_6.—πετρα δε, omg the ἡ preceding, F.

symbolic correspondence to the other, the Lord's Supper. The two elements in this Christian sacrament were anticipated in their case by the manna and the miraculous stream from the rock: these elements, in their case, as well as ours, symbolizing THE BODY AND BLOOD OF CHRIST. The whole passage is a standing testimony, incidentally, but *most providentially*, given by the great Apostle to the *importance* of the *Christian sacraments*, as *necessary to membership of Christ*, and *not mere signs or remembrances:* and an inspired protest against those who, whether as individuals or sects, would lower their dignity, or deny their necessity. **βρῶμα πνευματικὸν** κ.τ.λ.] The manna is thus called, from its being no mere physical production, but miraculously given by God—the work of His Spirit. Thus Isaac is called, Gal. iv. 29, ὁ **κατὰ πνεῦμα** γεννηθείς, in opposition to Ishmael, ὁ κατὰ σάρκα γεννηθείς. Josephus calls the manna θεῖον βρῶμα καὶ παράδοξον, Antt. iii. 1. 6: and in Ps. lxxvii. 24, it is said ἄρτον οὐρανοῦ ἔδωκεν αὐτοῖς. We can scarcely avoid recognizing in these words a tacit reference to our Lord's discourse, or at all events to the substance of it,—John vi. 31—58. "For the sense of πνευματικός, as '*typical*,' 'seen in the light of the spirit,' cf. Rev. xi 8, ἥτις καλεῖται πνευματικῶς Σόδομα." Stanley.

4.] It is hardly possible here, without doing violence to the words and construction, to deny that the Apostle has adopted the tradition current among the Jews, that the *rock followed the Israelites* in their journeyings, and gave forth water all the way. Thus Rabbi Solomon on Num. xx. 2: "Per omnes quadraginta annos erat iis puteus" (Lightf.): and Schöttgen cites from the Bammidbar Rabba, "Quomodo comparatus fuit ille puteus (de quo Num. xxi. 16)? Resp. Fuit sicut petra, sicut alveus apum, et globosus, et volutavit se, et ivit cum ipsis in itineribus ipsorum. Cum vexilla castra ponerent, et tabernaculum staret, illa petra venit, et consedit in atrio tentorii. Tunc venerunt Principes, et juxta illum steterunt, dicentes, 'Ascende, putee, &c.' (Num. xxi. 17) et ascendit." See other testimonies in Schöttgen. The only ways of escaping this inference are, (1) by setting aside the *natural* sense altogether, as Chrys. (οὐ γὰρ ἡ τῆς πέτρας φύσις τὸ ὕδωρ ἠφίει, ... ἀλλ' ἑτέρα τις πέτρα πνευματικὴ τὸ πᾶν εἰργάζετο, τουτέστιν ὁ χριστός, ὁ παρὼν αὐτοῖς πανταχοῦ, καὶ πάντα θαυματουργῶν· διὰ γὰρ τοῦτο εἶπεν, ἀκολουθούσης. p. 203), Theophyl.,—or (2) by taking πέτρα = τὸ ἐκ τῆς πέτρας ὕδωρ, as Erasm., Beza, Grot., Estius, Lightf. —and so Calvin, who says: "Quomodo, inquiunt, rupes quæ suo loco fixa stetit, comitata esset Israelitas? Quasi vero non palam sit sub petræ voce notari aquæ fluxum, qui nunquam populum deseruit." But against both of these we have the plain assertion, representing matter of physical fact, ἔπινον ἐκ πνευματικῆς ἀκολουθούσης πέτρας, **they drank from a** (or, after a preposition, *the*) [**spiritual, or**] **miraculous rock which followed them:** and I cannot consent to depart from what appears to me the only admissible sense of these words. How extensively the traditionary reliques of unrecorded Jewish history were adopted by apostolic men under the inspiration of the Holy Spirit, the apology of Stephen may bear witness. **ἡ πέτρα δὲ ἦν ὁ χριστός**] **But** (distinction between what *they* saw in the rock and what *we* see in it: they drank from it and knew not its dignity: *but* **the Rock was Christ.** In these words there appear to be *three allusions:* (1) to *the ideas of the Jews themselves:* so the Targum on Isa. xvi. 1: "Afferent dona Messiæ Israelitarum, qui robustus erit, propterea quod in deserto fuit RUPES ECCLESIA ZIONIS:" so also in Wisd. x. 15 ff., the σοφία θεοῦ (see note on John i. 1) is said to have been present in Moses, to have led them through the wilderness, &c. That the MESSIAH, the ANGEL OF THE COVENANT, was present with the church of the Fathers, and that His upholding power was manifested in miraculous interferences for their welfare, was a truth acknowledged no less by the Jew than by the Christian. (2) To *the frequent use of this appellation*, A ROCK, for the God of Israel. See, *inter alia*, Deut. xxxii. 4, 15, 18, 30, 31, 37; 1 Sam. ii. 2; 2 Sam. xxii. 2, and passim; xxiii. 3,

f Matt. iii. 17 || Mk. L. 2 Cor. xii. 10. [2 Thess. ii. 12.] Jer. xiv. 12.
g ch. ix. 19 reff.
h here only. Num. xiv. 16.
i = Rom. v. 14 ‡.

χριστός· 5 ἀλλ᾽ οὐκ [f]ἐν [g]τοῖς [g]πλείοσιν αὐτῶν [f]ηὐδό- ABCDF KLPℵ
κησεν ὁ θεός, [h]κατεστρώθησαν γὰρ ἐν τῇ ἐρήμῳ. abcdf ghklm
6 ταῦτα δὲ [i]τύποι ἡμῶν [k]ἐγενήθησαν, [l]εἰς τὸ μὴ εἶναι no 17. 47
ἡμᾶς [m]ἐπιθυμητὰς κακῶν, καθὼς κἀκεῖνοι [n]ἐπεθύμησαν.
7 μηδὲ [o]εἰδωλολάτραι γίνεσθε, καθώς τινες αὐτῶν, ὥσπερ

k plur., ver. 11 reff., but see note. l Rom. iv. 11 reff. m here only. Num. xi. 34 (only ?). n absol., Rom. vii. 7 reff. o ch. v. 10, 11 reff.

5. (ηυδοκησεν, so AB^1C $Clem_1$ $Mcion\text{-}e_2$ Chr_2 [Euthal-ms].)
7. ειδωλολατρας γινεσθαι F c k 3. 116-22 arm, *effici aut efficiamini* G-lat. aft καθως ins και D^1[-gr] Syr. ins εξ bef αυτων A [vulg D-lat (not Iren-int)]. rec (for ωσπερ) ως, with CD^1KP d k $Mcion\text{-}e_2$ [Euthal-ms]: καθως 17 $Mcion\text{-}e_1$: txt ABD^3Lℵ rel Chr_2 Thdrt Damasc Thl.—om καθως τινες αυτων ωσπερ F.

&c.; Psalms passim, and especially lxxviii. 20, compared with ver. 35: see also Rom. ix. 33; 1 Pet. ii. 8. Hence it became more natural to apply the term *directly to Christ*, as the ever-present God of Israel. (3) To *the sacramental import of the water* which flowed from the rock, which is the point here immediately in the Apostle's mind. As well in sacramental import as in upholding physical agency, *that rock was Christ*. The miraculous (spiritual) food was (sacramentally) the flesh of Christ: the miraculous (spiritual) drink was the blood of Christ: so that the Jews' miraculous supplies of food and drink were *sacramentally significant of the Body and Blood of Christ*, in kind analogous to the two great parts of the Christian Supper of the Lord. In the *contents* prefixed to the chapters in the E. V., we read as the import of these verses, "*The sacraments of the Jews are types of ours,*" which though perhaps correctly meant, is liable to be erroneously understood; inasmuch as no sacramental ordinance can be *a type of another*, but all alike, though in different degrees of approximation, and by different representations, *types of* Him, who is the fountain of all grace. The difference between their case and ours, is *generally*, that they were unconscious of the sacramental import, whereas we are conscious of it: "they knew not that I healed them," Hos. xi. 3: and *in this particular case*, that Christ has come to us "not by water only, but by water and blood," 1 John v. 6: His Death having invested our sacramental ordinance with another and more deeply significant character. To enter more minutely into the import of the words, '*the rock was Christ*,' would be waste of time and labour. The above reasons abundantly justify the assertion, without either pressing the verb ἦν beyond its ordinary acceptation, or presuming to fix on the Apostle a definiteness of meaning which his argument does not require. See in Meyer's note an example of the proceeding which I blame. 5.] **Howbeit with the more part of them** (in fact the exceptions were Joshua and Caleb only) **God was not well pleased.** **κατεστρ. γὰρ . . .**] The very words of the LXX, see ref. 6.] **Now** (δέ transitional; the contrast being, between the events themselves, and their application to us) **these things happened as figures** (not 'types' as we now use the word, meaning by type and antitype, the *material representation*, and the *ultimate spiritual reality*,—but *figures*, as one imperfect ceremonial polity may figure forth a higher spiritual polity, but still this latter may not itself be the ultimate antitype) **of us** (the spiritual Israel as distinguished from the literal),—**in order that we might not be** (God's purpose in the τύποι: of course an *ulterior* purpose, for they had their *own immediate purpose* as regards the literal Israel) **lusters** [the use of the substantive forcibly depicts the habit] **after evil things** (*generally*: no special reference yet to the Corinthian feasters, as Grot. supposes. So Theophyl. rightly: καθολικῶς περὶ πάσης κακίας λέγει, ἐπειδὴ καὶ πᾶσα κακία ἐξ ἐπιθυμίας. εἶτα καὶ κατ᾽ εἶδος τίθησι τὰς κακίας. Similarly Chrys.) **as they also** (καί, i. e. supposing us to be like them) **lusted.** The construction (ταῦτα . . . ἐγενήθησαν) may be a verb substantive attracted into the plur. (or sing.) by the predicate,—one often found: so Herod. i. 93, ἡ μὲν περίοδος, ... εἰσὶ στάδιοι ἕξ: and ii. 15, αἱ Θῆβαι Αἴγυπτος ἐκαλέετο: so in Latin, Ter. Andr. iii. 3. 23, 'Amantium iræ amoris integratio est:' see many other examples in Kühner, § 429: or, which is perhaps better, as in ver. 11, where see note. The rendering, '*Now in these things they were figures of us*' (I know not by whom suggested, but I find it in Dr. Peile's notes on the Epistles), is inconsistent both with the arrangement of the words,—in which ταῦτα has the primary emphasis,—and with ἐγενήθησαν, which should be ἦσαν. 7.] Now, the *special* instances of warning follow, coupled to the *general* by **μηδέ** in this

γέγραπται ᵖ Ἐκάθισεν ὁ λαὸς φαγεῖν καὶ πεῖν, καὶ ᵠ ἀνέστησαν ʳ παίζειν. 8 μηδὲ ˢ πορνεύωμεν, καθώς τινες αὐτῶν ˢ ἐπόρνευσαν καὶ ἔπεσαν [ἐν] μιᾷ ἡμέρᾳ εἰκοσιτρεῖς
χιλιάδες. 9 μηδὲ ᵗ ἐκπειράζωμεν τὸν κύριον, καθώς τινες

p Exod. xxxii. 6. abs., Acts xvi. 13 reff.
q Acts ix. 6 al. fr.
r here only. l. o. = Judg. xvi. 25. 2 Kings vi. 5 ‖ Chron. Jer. xxxviii. (xxxi.) 4. Hom. Od. θ. 251.
s ch. vi. 18 reff. Num. xxv. 1—6.
t Luke iv. 12 ‖ Mt. (from Deut. vi. 16). x. 25 [John viii. 4] only. Ps. lxxvii. 18.

(πειν, so B[1](Tischdf) D[1]F : πιν ℵ.) ανεστη F[-gr].
8. εκπορνευωμεν D[1]F. εξεπορνευσαν (*see* LXX) D[1]F 67[1] Chr_1[txt_4]. (επεσαν, so ABCD[1]FPℵ l m 17 $Chr\text{-}ms_1$ Thdrt Damasc.) om εν BD[1]Fℵ[1] Iren[$\text{-}int_1$].
9. εκπειρασωμεν F [-ζομεν KP : πειραζωμεν 17 $Epiph_1$(txt_1)]. rec (for κυριον) χριστον (*see note*), with DFKL rel latt syrr copt-wilk sah Thdrt $Mcion_2$(Epiph says: ὁ δὲ Μαρκίων ἀντὶ τοῦ κύριον χριστὸν ἐποίησεν) Chr_3 Œc Thl $Iren\text{-}int_1$(citing "Seniores") Ambr Ambrst Aug_1 Pel : θεον A 2 [Euthal-ms] : txt BCPℵ 17 syr-mg copt-ms æth arm [Syn-ep-ant] $Epiph_1$ Chr_1 Thdrt $Damasc_3$ Sedul $Cassiod_1$. rec aft καθως ins και, with D[3][-gr] KL rel Syr Chr_1 Thdrt : om ABCD[1]FPℵ a m n 17 [vulg syr coptt arm Syn-ep-ant Chr_3 Euthal-ms $Damasc_2$] $Iren\text{-}int_1$ [Ambrst].

negative sentence, as so often by καί in an affirmative one. Notice, that all four of these were brought about by the ἐπιθυμεῖν κακῶν, not distinct from it. This first instance is singularly appropriate. The Israelites are recorded to have sat down and eaten and drunken *at the idol feast of the golden calf* in Horeb: the very temptation to which the Corinthians were too apt to yield. And as the Israelites were *actually* idolaters, doing this *as an act of worship* to the image: so the Corinthians were *in danger of becoming such*, and the Apostle therefore puts the case in the strongest way, **neither be (become) ye idolaters.** **παίζειν**, צַחֵק, 'choreas agere,' 'saltare accinentibus tympanis vel cantoribus :' see reff., where the same word (or its cognate שִׂחֵק) occurs in the Heb. The dance was an accompaniment of the idol feast : see Hor. ii. 12. 19 : 'Quam nec ferre pedem dedecuit choris . . . . sacro Dianæ celebris die.' **8.**] Another prominent point in the sins of the Corinthian church. **εἰκοσιτρεῖς χ.**] The number was *twenty-four* thousand, Num. xxv. 9, and is probably set down here from memory. The subtilties of Commentators in order to escape the inference, are discreditable alike to themselves and the cause of sacred Truth. Of the principal ancient Commentators, Chrysostom and Theophyl. do not notice the discrepancy : Œcum. notices it, and says that some ancient copies εἰκοσιτέσσαρας ἔθεσαν here (so m tol syr-txt arm), but passes it without comment. Although the sin of Baal-peor was strictly speaking *idolatry*, yet the form which it exhibited was that of *fornication*, as *incident to idolatrous feasting*, see Num. xxv. 1, 2. Thus it becomes even more directly applicable to the case of the Corinthians. **9.**] **ἐκπειρ.**—**tempt beyond endurance**, 'tempt thoroughly.' Similarly ἐξαρνεῖσθαι, 'to persist in denying,' al., as Suidas, ἡ γὰρ ἐξ πρόθεσις, ἐπίτασιν δηλοῖ. See Musgr. on Eurip. Iph. Taur. 249, and cf. ἐκπληρόω, Acts xiii. 32. So also in Latin, 'oro' and 'exoro,' &c. **τὸν κύριον**] There may be two views taken of the internal evidence concerning the reading here. On the one hand it may be said that **χριστόν** being the original reading, it was variously altered to κύριον or θεόν by those who found a difficulty in supposing that the Jews of old tempted *Christ*, or even by those who wished to obliterate this assertion of His præ-existence : and so De Wette, al. On the other it may be said, that **κύριον** being the original, it was variously explained in the margin χριστόν and θεόν, as is often the case : and so Meyer. On comparing these, it seems to me that the latter alternative is the more probable. The inference that τινες αὐτῶν ἐπείρασαν requires τὸν χριστόν as an object, is not a necessary one, and hardly likely to have produced the alteration, closely connected as τ. χρ. is with the verb in the first person. I have therefore with Meyer adopted the reading κύριον. The *tempting of the Lord* was,—as on the other occasions alluded to Num. xiv. 22, where it is said that they *tempted God ten times*,—the *daring Him, in trying His patience by rebellious conduct and sin.* Cf. the similar use of πειράζω Acts v. 9; xv. 10. And he warns the Corinthians, that they should not in like manner provoke God by their sins and their partaking with idols. Chrys., Theophyl., and Œc. understand the temptation of God to be the *seeking for signs* : Theodoret, to be *in danger arising from those who spoke with different tongues*, ἐπείραζον δὲ κ. οἱ ταῖς διαφόροις κεχρημένοι γλώτταις, κατὰ φιλοτιμίαν μᾶλλον ἢ χρείαν ταύτας ἐπ' ἐκκλησίας προσφέροντες.

αὐτῶν ᵘ ἐπείρασαν καὶ ὑπὸ τῶν ᵛ ὄφεων ἀπώλοντο.
10 μηδὲ ʷ γογγύζετε, καθώς τινες αὐτῶν ʷ ἐγόγγυσαν καὶ
ἀπώλοντο ὑπὸ τοῦ ˣ ὀλοθρευτοῦ. 11 ταῦτα δὲ [πάντα]
ʸ τυπικῶς ᶻ συνέβαινον ἐκείνοις, ἐγράφη δὲ ᵃ πρὸς ᵇ νουθεσίαν ἡμῶν, εἰς οὓς τὰ ᶜ τέλη τῶν ᶜ αἰώνων ᵈ κατήντηκεν.
12 ὥστε ὁ ᵉ δοκῶν ᶠ ἑστάναι, ᵍ βλεπέτω μὴ ᶠ πέσῃ.

ABCDF KLPℵ abcd ghklm no 17. 47

u = Acts v. 9. xv. 10. Heb. iii. 9. Exod. xvii. 2, 7. v Mark xvi. 18. Luke x. 19 al. Num. xxi. 6. w here bis. Matt. xx. 11. Luke v. 30. John vi. 41, 43, 61. vii. 32 only. Exod. xvi. 7 A Ald. (διαγογ. B). Num. xiv. 29. x here only +. (-εύειν, Heb. xi. 28, from Exod. xii. 23. -ευσις, Josh. xvii. 13 A.) y here only +. z Acts iii. 10 reff. plur., ver. 6. Luke xxiv. 11. John xix. 31. James ii. 19. Rev. i. 19. iii. 2. Ps. cxlv. 10. a = ch. vii. 35 reff. b Eph. vi. 4. Tit. iii. 10 only +. Judith viii. 27 (23) Ald. compl. (-τησις, ABℵ). Wisd. xvi. 6 only. (-θετεῖν, Acts xx. 31.) c here only. see Matt. xiii. 39. xxviii. 20. Heb. ix. 26. d Acts xxvi. 7 reff. e ch. iii. 18 reff. f Rom. xiv. 4 (reff.). g = Acts xiii. 40 reff.

om αυτων ℵ^1 [αυτον L Syn-ep-ant]. εξεπειρασαν CD^{1}FPℵ a m 17 [Syn-ep-ant Euthal-ms Damasc$_1$(txt$_2$)]. απωλλυντο Bℵ [Cyr$_1$-p]. (A is doubtful.)

10. for γογγυζετε, γογγυζωμεν D F-gr ℵ 17 copt arm Orig$_1$[-c] Chr$_3$(txt$_{h.l.}$) Aug$_1$. rec aft καθως ins και, with KL rel Chr[$_{h.l.}$(but mss vary)]: om ABCDFPℵ a d m 17 latt syrr coptt [arm] Orig[-c$_1$-int$_1$] Eus [Bas$_2$ Chr$_4$ Euthal-ms Thdrt Damasc$_2$] Iren-int$_1$.—**καθαπερ** BPℵ 93 Orig[-c$_1$ Bas$_1$]. απωλλυντο A. ολεθρευτου D^1 : ολεθρου F-gr.

11. om παντα (*as ver* 6) AB 17 sah Mcion-e$_2$-t$_1$ Orig$_1$[-int$_1$] Dial$_2$ Hip$_1$ Cyr-jer$_2$ Cyr[-p$_2$ Bas$_2$ Chr$_1$ Iren-int-2-mss$_1$] Pac$_1$: ins CKLP rel [vulg D-lat syrr copt arm Chr$_1$ Euthal-ms Damasc] Thdrt$_2$ Thl Œc [Orig-int$_5$] Iren-int$_1$ Jer, and, but παντα δε ταυτα, D[-gr] Fℵ d æth Orig$_1$[-int$_1$] Chr$_2$ Iren-int-ms$_1$ Aug$_1$. rec τυποι (*as ver* 6), with DFL rel syr-txt coptt [Dial$_1$ Nyss$_1$ Chr$_1$] Thdrt$_3$(h. l. expressly: αντι του ως τυποι, and elsw expl ταυτα τυπικως εκεινοις συνεβη): txt ABCKPℵ d 17. 47^1 syr-mg Mcion-e$_2$ Orig$_4$ Hip$_1$ Eus$_1$ Mac$_1$ Cyr-jer$_1$ Chr$_2$ Cyr$_{sæpe}$[-p: *in figura* latt Iren-int-from-Sen$_2$ Orig-int$_4$ Ambrst Aug$_{alic}$: *figuraliter* Orig-int$_3$]. συνεβαινεν (*see note*) BCKPℵ d 17. 47 Mcion-e$_2$ Orig$_4$ Dial$_1$ Hip$_1$ Cyr-jer$_1$(εγενετο$_1$) Chr-2-mss$_2$ [Bas$_2$ Nyss$_1$ Cyr$_2$ Euthal-ms]: txt ADFL rel Dial$_1$ Chr$_1$ Thdrt$_3$ [Damasc]. for προς, εις ℵ^1 [Epiph$_4$]. rec κατηντησεν (*alteration of the perf into the aor, so common with the copyists*), with ACD^{3}KL rel Orthod Orig$_3$ Dial$_2$ Epiph$_1$ Chr$_3$ [Cyr-ms$_1$-p] Thdrt, -σαν P Hip$_1$ [Damasc]: txt BD^{1}Fℵ Hip$_1$ Orig$_1$[-c$_1$] Bas$_2$ Cyr$_3$[-p Euthal-ms].

ὑπὸ τῶν ὄφεων, by the (well-known) **serpents.** The art. is so often *omitted* after a preposition, that wherever it is *expressed,* we may be sure there was a reason for it. **10.**] **γογγύζετε** has been by Estius, Grot., al., and De Wette, understood of murmuring *against their teachers,* as the Israelites against Moses and Aaron, Num. xiv. 2; xvi. 41. But not to mention that this was in fact *murmuring against God,* such a reference would require something more specific than the mere word γογγύζετε. The warning is substantially the same as the last, but regards more the spirit, and its index the tongue. Theophyl.: αἰνίττεται δὲ αὐτοὺς καὶ διὰ τούτου, ὅτι ἐν τοῖς πειρασμοῖς οὐκ ἔφερον γενναίως, ἀλλ' ἐγόγγυζον λέγοντες Πότε ἥξει τὰ ἀγαθά, καὶ ἕως πότε αἱ κακώσεις; similarly Chrys. The destruction referred to must be that related Num. xvi. 41 ff. when the pestilence (which though it is not so specified *there,* was administered on another occasion by a destroying angel, 2 Sam. xxiv. 16, 17, see also Exod. xii. 23) took off 14,700 of the people. The punishment of the unbelieving congregation in Num. xiv., to which this is commonly referred, does not seem to answer to the expression ἀπώλοντο ὑπὸ τ. ὀλοθρευτοῦ, nor to the τινες, seeing that all except Joshua and Caleb were involved in it. **11.**] **τυπικῶς,** see var. readd., **by way of figure.** Meyer cites from the Rabbis, 'Quidquid evenit patribus, signum filiis.'

The plural συνέβαινον expresses the plurality of events separately happening: the singular ἐγράφη, their union in the common record of Scripture. Similarly 2 Pet. iii. 10, στοιχεῖα . . . λυθήσονται . . . τὰ ἐν αὐτῇ ἔργα κατακαήσεται. See reff. and Winer, edn. 6, § 58. 3. a. **δέ** conveys a slight opposition to συνέβαινον ἐκείνοις. **τὰ τέλη τ. αἰών.**] = ἡ συντέλεια τοῦ αἰῶνος of reff. Matt., and τὸ ἔσχατον τῶν ἡμερῶν τούτων of Heb. i. 1, where see note: **the ends of the ages** of this world's lifetime. So Chrys.: οὐδὲν ἄλλο λέγει ἢ ὅτι ἐφέστηκε λοιπὸν τὸ δικαστήριον τὸ φοβερόν. The form νουθεσία belongs to later Greek. The classical word is νουθέτησις or νουθετία: see Lobeck on Phrynichus, p. 512.

κατήντ.] **have reached.** The ages are treated as occupying space, and their extent as just coincident with our own time. See a similar figure in ch. xiv. 36. **12.**] **ἑστάναι,** viz. *in his place as a member of Christ's church,* to be recognized by him at His coming for one of His. To such an one the example of the Israelites is a warning to take heed that he fall not, as they did from their place in God's church.

13 [h] πειρασμὸς ὑμᾶς οὐκ [i] εἴληφεν εἰ μὴ [k] ἀνθρώπινος·
[l] πιστὸς δὲ ὁ θεός, ὃς οὐκ ἐάσει ὑμᾶς [m] πειρασθῆναι [n] ὑπὲρ
ὃ δύνασθε, ἀλλὰ ποιήσει σὺν τῷ [h] πειρασμῷ καὶ τὴν [o] ἔκβασιν [p] τοῦ δύνασθαι [q] ὑπενεγκεῖν. 14 [r] διόπερ, [s] ἀγαπητοί
μου, [t] φεύγετε ἀπὸ τῆς [u] εἰδωλολατρείας. 15 [v] ὡς [w] φρονίμοις λέγω· κρίνατε ὑμεῖς ὅ φημι. 16 [x] τὸ ποτήριον τῆς

h Luke xxii. 28. Acts xx. 19 al. Deut. iv. 34. i = Luke v. 26. vii. 16. Exod. xv. 15. k Acts xvii. 25 reff. l = ch. i. 9 reff. m ch. vii. 5 reff. n = ch. iv. 6. 2 Cor. xii. 6. o Heb. xiii. 7 only +. Wisd. ii. 17. viii. 8. xi. 14 only. ἡ ἔκβ. ἐκ τ. πολέμου, Polyb. iii. 7. 2. p Matt. xiii. 3. Acts iii. 2. xviii. 10. xxvi. 18. Rom. xi. 8, 10. Ps. cxlix. 7, 9. q 2 Tim. iii. 11. 1 Pet. ii. 19 only. Job ii. 10. Ps. liv. 12. Prov. vi. 33. r ch. viii. 13 (xiv. 13 v. r.) only. s Acts xv. 25 reff. t ch. vi. 18 reff. u Gal. v. 20. Col. iii. 5. 1 Pet. iv. 3 only +. (-τρης, ver. 7.) v = Acts xvii. 22. 2 Cor. vi. 13. w Matt. vii. 24. ch. iv. 10 al. Prov. xiv. 17. x attr., Matt. xxi. 42 (from Ps. cxvii. 22) al.

13. for *ουκ ειληφεν, ου καταλαβη* F; *non apprehendat* latt. for *εασει, αφησει* DF. *πειρασθηναι* bef *υμας* B [m]. ins *ου* bef *δυνασθε* F 123[2] D-lat, adding *υπενεγκειν* F Aug[$_3$(txt]$_{aliq}$). rec ins *υμας* bef *υπενεγκειν*, with K[*επεν.*] ℵ[3] rel Thdrt$_4$ Damasc Thl-ed Œc: aft, D[3][but erased]: om ABCD[1]FLPℵ[1] n 17. 47 [arm Orig$_1$] Mac$_2$ Bas$_2$ Chr-comm$_1$-and-2-mss$_1$ Cyr$_{sæpe}$ Thdrt$_1$ Thl-mss.
15. aft *φρονιμοις* ins *υμιν* D c (coptt). for *κρινατε υμεις ο φημι, κρινετε ουν φημι* D[1][-gr]. *υμας* ℵ[1](txt ℵ-corr[1]).

13.] There are two ways of understanding the former part of this verse. Chrys., Theophyl., Grot., Est., Bengel, Olsh., De Wette, al., take it as a *continuation, and urging of the warning of the verse preceding*, by the consideration that no temptation had *yet* befallen them but such as was ἀνθρώπινος, '*within the power of human endurance*:' but 'major tentatio imminet,' Beng.:—while Calvin, al., and Meyer regard it as a consolation, tending to shew them that βλεπέτω μὴ πέσῃ is within the limits of their power, seeing that their temptation to sin was nothing extraordinary or unheard of, but only '*according to man*:' and they might trust to God's loving care, that no temptation should ever befall them which should surpass their power to resist. This latter seems to me beyond doubt the correct view. For (1) in the parallel which they bring for the former sense, Heb. xii. 4, **οὔπω** is distinctly expressed,—and would have been here also, had it been intended. Besides, in that case, οὔπω, as having the primary emphasis, would have been *prefixed*, as in Heb. xii. 4: οὔπω πειρασμὸς ὑμᾶς εἴληφεν . . . . Then again (2) this restricts the sense of πειρασμός to *persecution*, which it here does not mean, but *solicitation to sin*, in accordance with the whole context. **εἴληφεν—has taken you**, not ἔλαβεν, 'took you,' shews that the temptation was *still soliciting* them. **ἀνθρώπινος**] not, as Piscator, al., and Olsh., *originating with man*, as opposed to other temptations originating with the devil, or even with God's Providence: but, as Chrys.: ξύμμετρος,—opposed to ὑπὲρ ὃ δύνασθε, **adapted to man.** **πιστός**] He has *entered into a covenant* with you by *calling* you: if He suffered temptation beyond your power to overcome you, He would be violating that covenant. Compare 1 Thess. v. 24, πιστὸς ὁ καλῶν ὑμᾶς, ὃς καὶ ποιήσει. **ὅς** = ὅτι οὗτος. **ποιήσει . . . καὶ τὴν ἔκβ.**] Then God *makes* the temptation too: arranges it in His Providence, and in His mercy will ever set open a door for escape. **τὴν ἔκβ.**] **the [way to] escape**, i. e. *which belongs to the particular temptation*: τὴν ἀπαλλαγὴν τοῦ πειρασμοῦ, Theophyl. **τοῦ δύν.**] **in order that you may be able to bear (it)**: obs., not, 'will *remove* the temptation:' but, 'will make an escape *simultaneously with the temptation*, to encourage you to *bear up against it*.'

14.] *Conclusion from the above warning examples*: IDOLATRY IS BY ALL MEANS TO BE SHUNNED; not tampered with, but *fled from*. **φεύγετε ἀπό** ('*fugiendo discedite a*,' Meyer) expressing even more strongly than the accus. with φεύγω, the entire avoidance. This verse of itself would by inference forbid the Corinthians having any share in the idol feasts; but he proceeds to ground such prohibition on further special considerations. **15—22.**] By the analogy of the *Christian participation in the Lord's Supper*, and the *Jewish participation in the feasts after sacrifices*, joined to the fact that the *heathens sacrifice* to *devils*, he shews that the partaker in the idol feast is a PARTAKER WITH DEVILS; which none can be, and yet be a Christian.

15.] An appeal to their own sense of what is congruous and possible,—as introducing what is to follow. **ὡς** expresses an assumption on the Apostle's part, that they *are* φρόνιμοι. De W. compares Plato, Alcib. i. 104, ὡς ἀκουσομένῳ λέγω. **λέγω** and **φημί** both refer to what follows, vv. 16—21. **ὑμεῖς** is emphatic—be YE **the judges of what I am saying.** **16.**] The analogy of the *Lord's Supper*, which, in both its parts,

[y] εὐλογίας ὃ [z] εὐλογοῦμεν, οὐχὶ [a] κοινωνία τοῦ [b] αἵματος
τοῦ [b] χριστοῦ ἐστιν; [x] τὸν ἄρτον ὃν [c] κλῶμεν, οὐχὶ [a] κοινωνία τοῦ [d] σώματος τοῦ [d] χριστοῦ ἐστιν; 17 ὅτι εἷς ἄρτος,
ἓν σῶμα [e] οἱ [e] πολλοί ἐσμεν· [f] οἱ γὰρ [f] πάντες ἐκ τοῦ ἑνὸς

ABCDF KLPℵ abcdf ghklm no 17. 47

y Gal. iii. 14. James iii. 10. Rev. v. 12, 13. vii. 12. Gen. xxviii. 4. z Matt. xxvi. 26 ‖ Mk. Luke ix. 16. xxiv. 30. ch. xiv. 16 al. 1 Kings ix. 13. a 2 Cor. vi. 14 reff. b (ch. xi. 25, 27.) Eph. ii. 13. Heb. ix. (12) 14. 1 Pet. i. 2. 1 John i. 7 al. c Acts ii. 46 reff. d Rom. vii. 4. (ch. xi. 24, 27, 29.) e Rom. v. 15 reff. f Rom. xi. 32 reff.

16. for ευλογιας, ευχαριστιας F 71. 80. 213 Syr. ηυλογουμεν D^1[-gr]. κοινωνιας ℵ^1(marked for correction by ℵ-corr^1). 1st εστιν bef τ. αιμ. τ. χρ. (*transposn to avoid the harshness of* εστιν *at the end*) ABP Syr coptt [arm(Tischdf)] Cyr$_2$[-p] Aug$_1$: txt CDFKLℵ rel latt syr goth Chr$_2$ Thdrt [Euthal-ms Damasc] Ambrst. 2nd εστιν bef τ. σωμ. τ. χρ. A Syr copt Cyr$_1$ Aug$_1$ (*see above*): om sah: txt BCDFKLPℵ rel [latt syr goth Chr$_1$ Euthal-ms Cyr-p$_1$ Thdrt Damasc]. for 2nd χριστου, κυριου D^1F 21 latt goth (Dial$_1$) Thdrt Ambrst Aug$_1$ (goth Thdrt Ambrst syr-mg κυριου before): αυτου n.
17. aft αρτου ins και του (ενος) ποτηριου DF vulg-sixt(with demid harl tol, not am) [goth] Ambrst Pel. (om ενος D[-gr].)

is a *participation* in Christ. The stress throughout to ver. 20, is on **κοινωνία**, and **κοινωνοί**. **τὸ ποτήριον** is the accus., by attr. corresponding to **τὸν ἄρτον**. **τὸ π. τῆς εὐλ.**] i. e. ὃ εὐλογοῦντες κατασκευάζομεν (Œc.), as explained immediately by ὃ εὐλογοῦμεν,—**over which we speak a blessing**, the Christian form of the Jewish כּוֹס בְּרָכָה, the cup in the Passover over which thanks were offered after the feast,—*in blessing of which cup*, our Lord instituted this part of the ordinance: see Lightfoot in loc., and note on the history in Matt. xxvi. The rendering of Olsh., al., the *cup which brings a blessing*, is wrong, as being against this analogy. **ὃ εὐλογοῦμεν**] **which we bless**, i. e. consecrate with a prayer of thanksgiving: not, as Erasmus, Beza, '*quod cum gratiarum actione sumimus*' (περὶ οὗ εὐχαριστοῦμεν). Observe, the first person plural is the *same throughout:* the blessing of the cup, and the breaking of the bread, the acts of consecration, were *not the acts of the minister, as by any authority peculiar to himself, but only as the representative of the* οἱ πάντες, *the whole Christian congregation* (and so even Estius, but evading the legitimate inference). The figment of sacerdotal consecration of the elements by transmitted power, is as alien from the apostolic writings as it is from the spirit of the Gospel. **κοινωνία**] **the participation** (i. e. that whereby the act of participation takes place) **of the Blood of Christ?** The strong literal sense must here be held fast, as constituting the very kernel of the Apostle's argument. The wine *is the Blood*, the bread *is the Body*, of Christ. (In *what sense* the Blood and the Body, does not belong to the present argument.) *We* receive into us, make by assimilation parts of ourselves, that wine, that bread: we *become* therefore, by participation of that Bread, *one Bread*, i. e. ONE BODY: hence the close and literal participation in and with Christ. If we are to render this ἐστιν, *represents* or *symbolizes*, the argument is made void. On the other hand it is painful to allude to, though necessary to reprobate, the caricature of this real union with Christ which is found in the gross materialism of transubstantiation. See further on ch. xi. 26, 27. **ὃν κλῶμεν**] probably already the *breaking* of the bread in the communion was part of the act of consecration, and done after the example of our Lord in its institution. See ch. xi. 24; Acts ii. 42, xx. 7, 11. For the rest, see above. **17.**] **Because we, the** (assembled) **many, are one bread** (by the assimilation of that one bread partaken: not 'one loaf'), **one Body** (by the κοινωνία of the Body of Christ, of which that bread is the vehicle); **for the whole of us partake of that one bread.** Meyer and De Wette and many other Commentators take εἷς ἄρτος alone, '*there is one bread;*' and impugn the interpretation given above by saying that it is evidently not so, because the following clause uses ἄρτος in its literal sense. But it is for *that very reason*, that I adhere to the interpretation given. By partaking of that bread, we become, not figuratively but literally, *one bread:* it passes into the substance of our bodies, and there is in every one who partakes, a portion of himself which *is that bread.* The *bread* which was *before*, is *now* ἡμεῖς. But that loaf, broken and blessed, is the medium of κοινωνία of the Body of Christ; we then, being that one bread, are *one Body; for* we all partake of that one bread. So that there is no logical inversion, and no arguing (Meyer) from the *effect* to the *cause*. The argument is a very simple and direct one;—the bread is the Body of Christ; we partake of the bread: therefore we partake of the Body of Christ. Of these propositions, the con-

ἄρτου [g] μετέχομεν. 18 [h] βλέπετε τὸν Ἰσραὴλ [i] κατὰ [i] σάρκα·
οὐχ οἱ ἐσθίοντες τὰς θυσίας, [k] κοινωνοὶ τοῦ [l] θυσιαστηρίου
εἰσίν; 19 τί οὖν φημι; ὅτι [m] εἰδωλόθυτόν [n] τί ἐστιν, ἢ ὅτι

g ch. ix. 10, 12 reff. h ch. i. 26. Phil. iii. 2. i Rom. i. 3 reff. k Matt. xxiii. 30. 2 Cor. i. 7. Heb. x. 33. 1 Pet. v. 1. Isa. i. 23. l ch. ix. 13 bis. Rom. xi. 3 (from 3 Kings xix. 10) al. m ch. viii. 1 reff. n = Acts v. 36. ch. iii. 7. Gal. ii. 6. vi. 3, 15. Demosth. 582. 27.

18. rec ουχι, with BD[3]KLPℵ[3] rel Thdrt [Euthal-ms Damasc]: txt ACD[1]FPℵ[1] 17 Chr_1. εσθοντες D[1].

19. rec transp ειδωλοθυτον and ειδωλον, with KL rel syrr goth Chr_1 Thdrt [Damasc]: ιδωλοθυτον twice F[-gr]; but G-lat has over the 1st *idolis immolatum sit*, and over the 2nd *idolum aut idolothitum*: ειδωλοθυτον, omg from τι εστιν to τι εστιν, AC[1]ℵ[1] (omg τι also) $Epiph_1$: ειδωλον, omg the other clause by homœotel, 17. 71: txt BC[2]DP ℵ-corr[1] m vulg(and F-lat) coptt æth arm [Euthal-ms] Ambrst Aug_1 Pel Bede. (*The received reading seems to have been adopted as the most natural order on the re-insertion of the omitted clause. For the remarks of Epiph and Aug, see Tischdf.*) εστιν bef τι (twice) D[1][only 1st D[1]-gr] F latt. for η οτι, ουχ οτι DF [spec] ($Tert_1$) Ambrst $Aug\text{-}mss_1$. (for 1st ὅτι, ουχ οτι [k] Chr[-4]-mss_1.)

clusion is implied in the form of a question in ver. 16: the minor stated in the latter clause of ver. 17; its connexion with the major producing the conclusion given in the former clause ὅτι . . . . ἐσμέν. The major itself, τοῦτό ἐστιν τὸ σῶμά μου, is suppressed, as axiomatic. The above remarks shew also the untenableness of the rendering of Calv., Beza, Bengel, al.,—"*because there is one bread* (antecedent), *we being many are one body*" (consequent): for this would parenthesize ver. 17, and take it altogether out of the argument, giving it a sense which, as occurring here, would be vapid—"obiter hoc dicit, ut intelligant Corinthii, externa quoque professione colendam esse illam unitatem quæ nobis est cum Christo," Calv. Meyer objects to rendering ἐκ τοῦ ἑνὸς ἄρτου μετέχομεν, *we partake of that one bread*: saying rightly that μετέχω is always found with a gen. or an acc., never with ἐκ. He would render, *for we all, by means of that one bread, partake* (viz. in the one Body: so μετέχ. is absol. ver. 30). This is exceedingly harsh, besides as it seems to me (see above) confusing the whole argument: and we may safely say would not have been thus expressed by the Apostle, leaving the most important words to be supplied from the context,—but would have been οἱ γὰρ πάντες ἐν τῷ ἑνὶ ἄρτῳ τοῦ ἑνὸς σώματος μετέχομεν. The usage of ἐκ, too, would, though perhaps *barely allowable*, be very harsh, especially when it is remembered that the ἄρτος is not (by the hypothesis) the ultimate, but only the mediate object of participation. None of the examples given in Bernhardy, Syntax, p. 230, which Meyer quotes for his sense of ἐκ, seem to justify it. They apply mostly to the subjective source, ἐκ προνοίας, or the circumstances originating, ὡς ἐκ τούτων,—not to the medial instrument, which it appears to me would require διά. (In a subsequent edn. Meyer seems to have slightly modified his view, rendering, *for from the one bread we all receive a portion.*) **18.**] Another example of κοινωνία, from *the Jewish feasts after sacrifice.* **τ. Ἰσρ. κατὰ σάρκα**] (= τ. Ἰσρ. **τὸν** κατὰ σάρκα: so we have τοῖς κυρίοις κατὰ σάρκα, Eph. vi. 5), **the actual** material **Israel**, as distinguished from ὁ Ἰσρ. κατὰ πνεῦμα, see Rom. ii. 29; Gal. iv. 29; and ὁ Ἰσρ. τοῦ θεοῦ, Gal. vi. 16. **οἱ ἐσθ. τ. θυσ.**] viz. those parts of the sacrifices which were not offered; see on ch. viii. 1. The parts to be offered are specified, Levit. iii. 3; the practice of eating the remainder of the meat sanctioned and regulated, ib. vii. 15—18. **κοινωνοὶ τοῦ θυσ.**] **partakers with the altar** (in a strict and peculiar sense,—the *altar* having *part* of the animal, the *partaker another part;* and by the fact of the *religious consecration* of the offered part, this connexion becomes a *religious connexion.* The question has been raised, and with reason, why the Apostle did not say κοινωνοὶ τοῦ **θεοῦ**? Meyer answers,—because the Jew was *already in covenant with God*, and the Apostle wished to express a *closer connexion*, brought about by the sacrifice in question:—De Wette,—because he was unwilling to ascribe so much to the mere act of sacrifice, see Heb. x. 1 ff.: and to this latter view I incline, because, as De W. remarks, θεοῦ would have *suited the analogy better* than θυσιαστηρίου, but Paul avoids it, and evidently is reluctant to use it. But to carry this view further, and suppose with Rückert that he would not concede to the Ἰσρ. κατὰ σάρκα any κοινωνία θεοῦ, is (Meyer) contradicted by Rom. ix. 4, 5. Still the inference lies open, to which our Saviour's saying points, Matt. xxiii. 20, 21. The altar is GOD'S *altar*). **19, 20.**] The inference from the preceding analogies would naturally be, that Paul was then representing the idols as *being in reality what the heathen sup-*

[o] εἴδωλόν [n] τί ἐστιν; 20 ἀλλ' ὅτι ἃ [p] θύουσιν [q] δαιμονίοις
καὶ οὐ θεῷ [p] θύουσιν, οὐ θέλω δὲ ὑμᾶς [k] κοινωνοὺς τῶν
[q] δαιμονίων γίνεσθαι. 21 οὐ δύνασθε [r] ποτήριον [r] κυρίου
πίνειν καὶ ποτήριον [q] δαιμονίων, οὐ δύνασθε [s] τραπέζης
κυρίου [g] μετέχειν καὶ [st] τραπέζης [qt] δαιμονίων. 22 [u] ἢ [v] παρα-
ζηλοῦμεν τόν κύριον; μὴ [w] ἰσχυρότεροι αὐτοῦ ἐσμεν;

e νασθε πο... ABCDF KLPℵ a b c d f g h k m n o 17 47

H εσμεν...

o Acts vii. 14. xv. 20. ch. viii. 4, 7. xii. 2. 2 Cor. vi. 16. 1 Thess. i. 9 al. Num. xxv. 2.
p absol., Acts xiv. 13. Exod. xxiii. 18. w. dat., Acts xiv. 18.
q Deut. xxxii. 17. Paul, here (4 times) and 1 Tim. iv. 1 only. gospp. passim. Acts xvii. 18. James ii. 19. Rev. ix. 20. xvi. 14 only.
r ch. xi. 27. s = Rom. xi. 9. Ps. lxxvii. 20. t see Isa. lxv. 11. u = ch. x. 22.
v Rom. x. 19 (from Deut. xxxii. 21). xi. 11, 14 only. w ch. i. 25 reff.

20. for αλλ οτι α, α δε D: αλλα α F[*sed quæ*] latt. rec (for θυουσιν, twice) θυει (*occasioned by the insn of* εθνη *below*), with KL rel Chr_1 Thdrt Damasc: txt ABC DFPℵ m 17 Mcion-e_3[1st; om 2nd] Eus_1 [Euthal-ms(1st θυσουσιν)]. rec aft 1st θυ. ins τα εθνη, with ACKPℵ rel vulg(and F-lat) G-lat syrr coptt goth æth arm Chr_1 Thdrt [Euthal-ms Damasc] Orig-int_1 Aug_3: aft οτι, L: om BD F[-gr] Mcion-e_3 Eus_1 $Tert_1$ Ambrst Aug_3($expr_1$) Aug-cit(*qui sacrificant*). rec 2nd θυ. bef και ου θεω, with DFKL rel [syrr coptt goth Chr Thdrt Damasc Aug_{alic}]: txt ABCPℵ m 17 [arm(Tischdf)] Eus_1 [Euthal-ms] Orig-int_1 Aug_3. δαιμονιων bef κοινωνους (omg των) $D^{1.3}$[and lat] F goth. for γινεσθαι, ειναι F.

posed them to be—and the eater of meats offered to them, as partaking with the idol. This objection he meets,—but with the introduction of a new fact to their consideration—that the things which the heathen sacrifice, they sacrifice really to *devils*.

19.] **τί οὖν φημι; what am I then assuming?** so Xen. Anab. i. 14. 4, τί οὖν κελεύω ποιῆσαι; **ὅτι εἰδωλόθ. τί ἐστιν] that a thing sacrificed to an idol is any (real) thing (so sacrificed)?** (i. e. *has any real existence as a thing sacrificed?* The accentuation τι ἔστιν; would come nearer to the sense of ch. viii. 4, ὅτι οὐδὲν εἴδωλον ἐν κόσμῳ,—'*that there is any* (such thing as an) *offering to an idol?*' and in a matter so ambiguous it is impossible to decide between the two) **or that an idol is any thing** (*real?* e. g. that Jupiter *is* Jupiter in the sense of a living power)? —(*Not so*:—this ellipsis of the negative, taken up by ἀλλά, is found in classical Greek: e. g. Xen. Mem. i. 2. 2, πῶς οὖν αὐτὸς ὢν τοιοῦτος ἄλλους ἂν ἀσεβεῖς . . . . . ἐποίησεν; ἀλλ' ἔπαυσε μὲν τούτων πολλούς, ἀρετῆς ποιήσας ἐπιθυμεῖν, &c. See Hartung, Partikellehre, ii. 37.) **But** (I say) **that the things which they** (i. e. the Gentiles) **sacrifice, they sacrifice to devils, and not to God** (δαιμ., not '*false-gods*,' nor in the sense in which it is used in the mouth of idolaters themselves, Acts xvii. 18, and Xen. Mem. i. 1. 1, *deities* (see Stanley's note, in which this idea is ingeniously combined with the Christian sense given below),—but, as always in LXX and N. T. when used by worshippers of the true God, 'DEVILS,' '*evil spirits*.' The words are from Deut. (ref.), see also Ps. xcv. 5 (Baruch iv. 7, θύσαντες δαιμονίοις κ. οὐ θεῷ). Heathendom being under the dominion of Satan (ὁ ἄρχων τοῦ κόσμου τούτου), he and his angels are in fact the powers honoured and worshipped by the heathen, however little they may be aware of it): **but** (the inference being suppressed 'and ye therefore by partaking in their sacrifices would be partakers with devils: but') **I would not have you become partakers with devils** (τῶν generic).

21.] *Reason of the* οὐ θέλω,—sententiously expressed without γάρ. **οὐ δύνασθε** applies of course to the *real spiritual participation* of the table of the Lord so as to profit by it: to *moral* possibility. The **ποτήριον δαιμονίων** is said as corresponding to the cup of which mention has been already made, not as Grot., al., and De Wette fancy, referring to the *libation* at an idol feast. **τράπεζα** is said by Pollux vi. 12 (Suicer) to be used in the sense of τὰ σιτία τὰ ἐπ' αὐτῶν τῶν τραπεζῶν τιθέμενα. Compare the description in Herod. iii. 18, of the Ἡλίου τράπεζα,—Polyb. iv. 35. 4, ὥστε περὶ τὸν βωμὸν κ. τὴν τράπεζαν τῆς θεοῦ κατασφαγῆναι τοὺς Ἐφόρους ἅπαντας,—and ref. Isa. From this passage probably, the τράπεζα κυρίου became an expression current in all ages of the Christian Church: see Suicer in voc.

22.] **Or are we provoking** (is it our wish to provoke, that He may assert His power) **the Lord** (Christ) **to jealousy** (by dividing our participation between Him and devils)?—see ref. Deut., which evidently is before the Apostle's mind:—**are we stronger than He** (are we then such, that we can afford to defy His power to punish)?

23—XI. 1.] Now that he has fully handled the whole question of partaking in idol feasts, and prepared the way for specific directions as about a matter no longer to be supposed indifferent, *he pro-*

23 Πάντα [x] ἔξεστιν, ἀλλ' οὐ πάντα [x] συμφέρει· πάντα
[x] ἔξεστιν, ἀλλ' οὐ πάντα [y] οἰκοδομεῖ. 24 μηδεὶς [z] τὸ ἑαυτοῦ
[a] ζητείτω, ἀλλὰ [z] τὸ [b] τοῦ ἑτέρου. 25 πᾶν τὸ ἐν [c] μακέλ-
λῳ [d] πωλούμενον ἐσθίετε μηδὲν [e] ἀνακρίνοντες διὰ τὴν
[f] συνείδησιν· 26 [g] Τοῦ κυρίου γὰρ ἡ γῆ καὶ τὸ [h] πλήρωμα
αὐτῆς. 27 εἴ τις [i] καλεῖ ὑμᾶς τῶν [k] ἀπίστων καὶ θέλετε
πορεύεσθαι, πᾶν τὸ [l] παρατιθέμενον ὑμῖν ἐσθίετε μηδὲν

x ch. vi. 12 (reff.).
y Acts ix. 31 reff.
z see Matt. xvi. 23.
a ver. 33. ch. xiii. 5. 2 Cor. xii. 14. Phil. ii. 21. Neh. ii. 10.
b Rom. ii. 1 reff.
c here only +.
d epp., here only. Matt. x. 29 al. Gen. xli. 56.
e = Acts iv. 9 reff.
f = ch. viii. 7. 2 Cor. i. 12.
g Psa. xxiii. 1. xlix. 12.
h = Mark viii. 20. Ps. xcv. 11.
i = Matt. xxii. 3, &c. John ii. 2 al. Esth. v. 12.
k = ch. vi. 6 reff.
l = Mark vi. 41. Acts xvi. 34 al. Gen. xliii. 31, 32.

23. rec (twice) ins μοι bef εξεστ. (*from ch* vi. 12), with C[3](1st time) HKL (P[once]) ℵ[3] rel (æth 1st time, demid goth, 2nd) syrr Chr$_1$ [Bas$_1$ Euthal-ms Damasc (1st)] Thdrt Orig-int$_1$ [Ambrst]: txt ABC[1]Dℵ[1](F 17, once) am(with fuld harl[1] lux tol) copt [sah] Clem$_2$ [Orig] Iren-int$_1$ [Ambr$_1$] Tert$_2$ Cypr$_2$.—om 2nd clause (*passing from* παντα *to* παντα) F: om 1st cl. P 17.

24. for το (twice), τα A 47 Antch$_1$ (Tert$_1$). rec aft ετερου ins εκαστος (*supplementary: perhaps, as Mey, a reminiscence of Phil* ii. 4), with D[2·3]KL rel syrr goth Chr$_1$ [Bas$_2$ Antch$_1$ Damasc] Thdrt: om ABCD[1]FHPℵ 17 latt coptt æth arm Clem [Euthal-ms Ambr$_1$ Ambrst].

25. διακρινοντες P [Thdrt$_1$].

26. rec γαρ bef κυριου (*transposn to more usual order, not observing the emphasis*), with AHKLP rel Chr$_1$ Thdrt [Euthal-ms Damasc]: txt BCDFℵ a 17.

27. rec aft ει ins δε (*for connexion; but thus perplexing the sense*), with CD[3]HKL rel (Syr) syr sah goth Thdrt$_1$ Damasc Thl Œc: [*et si* æth:] om ABD[1]FPℵ latt copt arm Antch Chr$_2$ [Euthal-ms] Thdrt$_1$ Jac-nisib$_1$ Ambrst Aug. aft απιστων ins εις δειπνον D[1][and lat] F fuld[1] Ambrst Pel Bede. παντα τα παρατιθευενα A coptt.

ceeds to give those *directions*, accompanying them with their reasons, as regards mutual offence or edification. **23.**] *He recurs to the plea of* ch. vi. 12;—*reasserts his modification of it*, with a view, after what has passed since, to shew its reasonableness, and to introduce the following directions. **οἰκοδομεῖ**] viz. *the Christian body:* tend to build up the whole, or the individual parts, of that spiritual temple, God's οἰκοδομή. **24.**] Further following out of οἰκοδομεῖ. This ought to be our object: the bringing on one another to perfection, not the pleasing ourselves, see Rom. xv. 2, 3. In the second clause, ἕκαστος must be supplied from μηδείς (hence it has found its way into the rec.): so Plato, Rep. ii. p. 366 D, οὐδεὶς ἑκὼν δίκαιος, ἀλλ' . . . . ψέγει τὸ ἄδικον,—i. e. ἕκαστος ψέγει. See Bernhardy, Syntax, p. 458. **25.**] The key to understanding this and the following verse is, to remember that **συνείδησις** is used in each case of the conscience of the *person spoken of*, i. e. in the two first cases, that of the *reader*,—in the third, as explained by the Apostle, that of the *weak brother:* see there. **Every thing which is being sold** (offered for sale) **in the flesh-market** (**μάκελλον** is adopted from the Latin. It was also used by the Rabbis, in the form מקולין. See Stanley, and examples in Wetst.), **eat, making no enquiry** (whether it is meat offered to idols or not), **on account of your conscience** (to be joined with ἐσθίετε μηδ. ἀνακ., not with ἀνακρίνοντες only,—as is shewn by the parallel below, ver. 28,—where the *reason given* is joined to ἐσθίετε). The meaning being,—'*eat without enquiry, that your conscience may not be offended.*' If you *made enquiry*, and heard in reply, that the meat *had been* offered to idols, *your conscience would be offended*, and you would eat διὰ προσκόμματος to *yourselves*. De Wette, al., understand τὴν συν., *all through*, of the *conscience of another*, and apply to all the explanation of ver. 29. But as Meyer well observes, no reader could possibly refer τὴν συνείδ. to any one but himself, *no other person having been mentioned*, until ver. 28, where ἐκεῖνον τὸν μηνύσαντα is introduced, and τὴν συνείδησιν is to be referred (but even then not without *special explanation given*) to the *new* subject. **26.**] *The principle on which such an eating ought to rest:* that *all is* GOD'S, and *for our use:* and where no subjective scruple is cast in, *all to be freely partaken of:* see 1 Tim. iv. 4. **27.**] The same maxim applied to their conduct at *a banquet given by a heathen*. A *miscellaneous banquet*, and not a sacrificial feast, is meant. At such, there might be meat which had been offered to idols. Grot. says well on θέλετε πορεύεσθαι, "Admonet tacite, melius forte facturos, si non eant: ire tamen non prohibet: supra,

[e] ἀνακρίνοντες διὰ τὴν [f] συνείδησιν· 28 ἐὰν δέ τις ὑμῖν
εἴπῃ Τοῦτο [m] ἱερόθυτόν ἐστιν, μὴ ἐσθίετε δι' ἐκεῖνον τὸν
[n] μηνύσαντα καὶ τὴν [f] συνείδησιν. 29 [f] συνείδησιν δὲ [o] λέγω
οὐχὶ τὴν [p] ἑαυτοῦ, ἀλλὰ τὴν [b] τοῦ ἑτέρου. [q] ἵνα τί γὰρ
ἡ [r] ἐλευθερία μου κρίνεται ὑπὸ [s] ἄλλης [f] συνειδήσεως;
30 εἰ ἐγὼ [t] χάριτι [u] μετέχω, τί [v] βλασφημοῦμαι [w] ὑπὲρ οὗ
ἐγὼ [x] εὐχαριστῶ; 31 [y] εἴτε οὖν ἐσθίετε εἴτε πίνετε εἴτε τὶ

...ελευθερια H. ABCDF KLPℵ a b c d e f g h k l m n o 17. 47

m here only +. n Luke xx. 37. John xi. 57. Acts xxiii. 30 only +. 2 Macc. iii. 7. vi. 11. xiv. 37 only. o = ch. i. 12 reff. p 2nd pers., 2 Cor. vii. 11 reff. q Paul, here only. Matt. ix. 4. xxvii. 46. Luke xiii. 7. Acts iv. 25. vii. 26 only. Gen. iv. 6. r = Gal. ii. 4. v. 1, 13 al. s = Job xix. 27 Bℵ Ald.[?] t = Rom. vi. 17 reff. dat., Rom. iv. 19, see note. u ch. ix. 10, 12 reff. v = Rom. iii. 8 reff. w ellips., ch. vii. 1 al. x = Rom. xiv. 6. i. 8 al. absol., ch. xi. 24 reff. y so ch. iii. 22 reff.

28. om *υμιν* F latt goth $Tert_1$ Aug_1[ins_1]. rec (for *ιεροθ.*) *ειδωλοθυτον* (*see notes*), with CDFKLP rel syr copt goth arm Chr_1 Thdrt [Euthal-ms Damasc $Tert_1$]: *immolaticium* D-lat F-lat [Ambrst] (in ver 19 *simulacro immolatum* D-lat, *idolis immolatum* F-lat vulg [Aug_1]): txt ABHℵ sah Eus (Clem) Orig [*de sacrificio* Syr (*victima idoli* ver 19)]. om *εκεινον τον μηνυσαντα και* F. aft *και* ins *δια* D Syr syr-w-ob. rec at end ins *του γαρ κυριου η γη και το πληρωμα αυτης* (*repetition from ver* 26: *see also on ver* 31), with H²KL rel syr goth Chr_1 [Euthal-ms] Thdrt Phot Thl Œc: om ABCDFH¹Pℵ 17 latt Syr coptt æth arm Damasc Ambrst Aug_1 Pel Bede.

29. for *ουχι*, *ου* D¹ 17. *εμαυτου* H m: *σεαυτου* D¹: *tuam* latt [(Syr) syr coptt Ambrst Aug]. for *αλλης*, *απιστου* F[-gr] D-lat G-lat goth Ambr Jer Sedul Primas (txt Ambrst Aug_1 Pel Bede).

30. rec aft *ει* ins *δε* (*supplementary, but disturbing the sense*), with Œc: om ABCD FKLPℵ rel [latt syrr coptt goth æth-pl(om vv. 29, 30 æth-rom) arm] $Clem_2$ Cyr_1 [Chr_1 Euthal-ms Damasc Aug_1].

cap. v. 10." On **διὰ τ. συνείδ.**, see above, ver. 25. **28.**] *Who is* the person supposed to say this? not, as Grot., al., think, the *host*, of whom **τις** could hardly be said, but it would stand ἐὰν δὲ ὑμῖν εἴπῃ: nor, as Chrys., Theophyl., al., and De Wette, —some *heathen guest*, by whom De W. imagines it said maliciously, or to put the Christian to the proof,—for his *συνείδησις* would hardly be so much taken into account in the matter; but, as Neander, Pfl. u. Leit. p. 399, and Meyer,—*some weak Christian*, wishing to warn his brother. **ἱερόθυτον** is apparently placed advisedly, to represent what would be said at a *heathen's* table. De W. supposes it on this very account to be a correction: but surely this is giving a corrector credit for more fineness of discrimination than they ordinarily shew. Much more probable is it, that the unusual and apparently incorrect **ἱερόθυτον** should give place to the ordinary and more exact term. **δι' ἐκ. τ. μην. . . .**] **On account of the man who informed you, and** (*καί specifying* the particular point or points to which the more general preceding clause applies: as, τῶνδε εἵνεκα, καὶ γῆς ἱμέρῳ . . . καὶ μάλιστα τῷ χρηστηρίῳ πίσυνος ἐών, καὶ τίσασθαι θέλων . . . . . Herod. i. 73. See Hartung, Partikellehre, i. 145) **conscience**: i. e. to spare the informer *being wounded in his conscience*. **29.**] Explanation of the last διὰ τὴν συνείδησιν, as meaning *not your own*, but *that of the informer*. True to his interpretation (see above), De W. supposes τοῦ ἑτέρου not to refer to τὸν μηνύσαντα, but to '*your weak Christian brother;*' but then how very harsh and clumsy are the various references to understood persons;—and how simple, on the other interpretation, is the reference in each case of τὴν συν. to the subject of the clause. **ἵνα τί γάρ**] **For why is my freedom judged by a conscience not mine own?**—i. e. '*Why should I be so treated* (hazard by my actions such treatment) *that the exercise of my Christian freedom, eating as I do and giving thanks, should become matter of condemnation to another, who conscientiously disapproves of it?*' **If** (no copula) **I partake thankfully** ([not, as E. V., '*by grace*'] dat. of the manner, cf. Soph. Antig. 616, σοφίᾳ γὰρ ἔκ του κλεινὸν ἔπος πέφανται,—and Bernhardy, Syntax, p. 101), **why am I to be spoken ill of for that for which I give thanks?** These words have been misunderstood. It has been generally supposed that the Apostle is *impressing a duty*, not to *give occasion* for the condemnation of their liberty by another's conscience. But the ground on which he is *here* arguing, is the unfitness, absurdity, *injustice to oneself* and the cause of God, ver. 31, of *so acting as to be condemned* for that in which a man not only allows himself, but for which he *gives thanks to God*. The sentiment is the same as in Rom. xiv. 16, μὴ βλασφημείσθω ὑμῶν τὸ ἀγαθόν. The emphasis is each time on ἐγώ. **31—XI. 1.**] *General conclusion of this part of the Epistle*,

ποιεῖτε, πάντα [z] εἰς δόξαν θεοῦ ποιεῖτε. 32 [a] ἀπρόσκοποι
καὶ Ἰουδαίοις γίνεσθε καὶ Ἕλλησιν καὶ τῇ [b] ἐκκλησίᾳ τοῦ
[b] θεοῦ· 33 καθὼς κἀγὼ [c] πάντα πᾶσιν [d] ἀρέσκω, μὴ [e] ζητῶν
τὸ ἐμαυτοῦ [f] σύμφορον, ἀλλὰ τὸ [g] τῶν [g] πολλῶν, ἵνα σωθῶσιν. XI. 1 [h] μιμηταί μου γίνεσθε, καθὼς κἀγὼ χριστοῦ.
2 [i] Ἐπαινῶ δὲ ὑμᾶς ὅτι [c] πάντα μου [k] μέμνησθε, καὶ
καθὼς [l] παρέδωκα ὑμῖν τὰς [m] παραδόσεις [n] κατέχετε.
3 [o] θέλω δὲ ὑμᾶς [o] εἰδέναι ὅτι παντὸς ἀνδρὸς ἡ κεφαλὴ ὁ

z Rom. iii. 7. ch. ii. 7. Eph. i. 6 al.
a Acts xxiv. 16. Phil. i. 10 only †. P. Sir. xxxv. (xxxii.) 21 only.
b ch. i. 2 reff.
c Acts xx. 35 reff.
d Rom. viii. 8 reff.
e ver. 24.
f ch. vii. 35 only †. Eccl. ii. 3 Symm.
g = Rom. v. 15 reff.
h ch. iv. 16 reff.
i Luke xvi. 8. Rom. xv. 11. vv. 17, 22 only. w. ὅτι, Eccles. viii. 15.
k = 2 Tim. i. 4. Heb. xiii. 3. Prov. xxxi. (xxiv.) 7.
l = Luke i. 2. Acts xvi. 4. ver. 23. ch. xv. 3. 2 Pet. ii. 21. Jude 3.
m = Matt. xv. 2. Gal. i. 14. 2 Thess. ii. 15. iii. 6 al.‡ Jer. xxxix. (xxxii.) 4. xli. (xxxiv.) 2 only.
n = Luke viii. 15. ch. xv. 2. 1 Thess. v. 21. Heb. iii. 6, 14. x. 23‡.
o Col. ii. 1.

31. 1st ποιειτε bef τι D[-gr] F[-gr]. om 2nd ποιειτε F [spec] Ambrst. at end add του γαρ κυριου η γη &c (as in ver 28) C³.

32. rec γινεσθε bef και ιουδαιοις, with DKL[P]ℵ³ rel [Bas$_1$ Chr$_2$ Thdrt Damasc$_2$ Orig-int$_1$]: γιν. ιουδ. τε F[-gr: *estote Judæis* vulg F-lat syrr coptt Hil$_1$ Ambrst]: txt ABCℵ¹ m 17 Orig$_1$ Did$_1$ Cyr[-p$_1$ Euthal-ms]. om του F: αυτου G[but αυ marked for erasure].

33. for παντα πασιν, πασιν κατα παντα [*omnibus omnia*] F [D-lat Orig-int$_2$ Tert$_1$ Cypr$_1$ Ambrst Aug$_{alic}$]: πα[σιν] παντα D[-gr goth]. rec συμφερον (*more usual*), with DFKLPℵ³ rel Orig$_1$[-c$_1$] Petr$_1$ [Bas$_1$ Chr$_1$ Euthal-ms Thdrt Damasc]: txt ABCℵ¹. om 2nd το F.

Chap. XI. **2.** rec aft υμας ins αδελφοι(*addition at beginning of a new section*), with DFKL rel [latt syrr(add μου) goth æth-pl] Thdrt [Damasc Ambrst]: om ABCPℵ a coptt æth-rom arm Ath$_1$ Cyr-jer$_1$ Bas$_1$ Chr$_2$ [Ors$_1$ Euthal-ms] Thl-comm. παντοτε P [Cyr-jer$_1$]. om και A¹ o 57. ins πανταχου bef παρεδωκα F D-lat Ambrst. (In F, *ubique* is not written in the Latin column but inserted over the Greek word.) παραδεδωκα ℵ: παραδωκα F. om υμιν F(and G-lat, not F-lat) Ambrst. aft παραδοσεις ins μου D¹F latt [Ambrst Pel]. ins ουτως bef κατεχετε C æth Ath$_2$ Chr$_3$.

3. om 1st δε F(and G-lat, not F-lat) syr Ambrst. om 1st ο B¹D¹F.

—*enforced by the example of himself.* **31.**] This εἴτε οὖν . . . ., passing from the special to the general, is not without reference to the last verse, in which the hypothesis is, that the *Christian and thankful act* of the believer is *marred* by the condemnatory judgment of his weak brother. All such hindrances to God's glory they are to avoid; and in all things, *eating* or *drinking*, or any other particular of *conduct* (τι, **any thing**, the stress being on ποιεῖτε,—**whether ye eat or drink, or do any thing**; not as E. V. *whatever ye do,—*ὅτιοῦν), *the glory of God is to be the aim,* self-regard being set aside: and so,— **32.**] *all offence is to be avoided* (it being understood that this refers to ἀδιάφορα, for in *other things,* both Jews and Greeks *must be offended,* see ch. i. 23), *whether to Jews or Heathens* (both these out of the Church), *or to the Church of God* (their own brethren). **33.**] *His own course of conduct*:—**As I in all things** (accus. of that on which the subject acts, or over which the quality predicated extends, as in ἀλγῶ τὴν κεφαλήν;—so τοῦ πάντ' εὐδαίμονος ὄλβου, Soph. Œd. Tyr. 1197. See Kühner, ii. 222. 4) **please** (' am pleasing:' as Meyer well remarks, not the *result,* but the *practice on Paul's part;* for πᾶσιν ἀρέσκειν τὸν συμβουλεύοντα κ. τὰ κοινὰ πράττοντα ἀδύνατον, Demosth. 1481. 4). **ἐμαυτοῦ** and **τῶν πολλῶν** are opposed: see ver. 24. **ἵνα σωθ.**, his great aim and end;—so ch. ix. 22.

XI. **1.**] **κἀγώ**, scil. μιμητὴς γέγονα. Compare on the sense, Phil. ii. 4, 5.

XI. **2—34.**] Reproofs and directions regarding certain disorders which had arisen in their assemblies: viz. (1) the not veiling of their women in public prayer (vv. 2—16): (2) the abuse of the **ἀγάπαι** (17—34). **2—16.**] *The law of subjection of the woman to the man* (2—12), *and natural decency itself* (13—16), *teach that women should be veiled in public religious assemblies.* **2.**] **δέ**, implying a distinction from the spirit of the last passage, which was one of *blame,* and exhortation to imitate him. He praises them for the degree in which they did this already, and expresses it by the slighter word μέμνησθε. **πάντα**, see above, on ch. x. 33. **And ye keep** (continue to believe and practise) **the traditions** (apostolic maxims of faith and practice, delivered either orally or in writing,

χριστός ἐστιν, κεφαλὴ δὲ γυναικὸς ὁ ἀνήρ, κεφαλὴ δὲ
τοῦ χριστοῦ ὁ θεός.
4 πᾶς ἀνὴρ [p] προσευχόμενος ἢ [q] προφητεύων [r] κατὰ [r] κεφαλῆς ἔχων [s] καταισχύνει τὴν κεφαλὴν

ABCDF KLPא abcde fghkl mno 17. 47

p absol., Matt. vi. 5, &c. Luke iii. 21. Acts vi. 6. x. 9, 30 al. Ezra x. 9. q — Acts xix. 6. ch. xiii. 9. xiv. 1, &c. r (Mark xiv. 3 rec.) and ellips., Esth. vi. 12. s = ch. i. 27. ver. 22.

[om 2nd δε P.] rec om του (bef χριστου), with CFKLP rel $Orig_1$ Eus_1 Chr_3 [$Cyr\text{-}p_1$] Thdrt Damasc Thl_2 $Œc_2$: ins ABDא m 17 Clem Eus_1 Chr_1 [Euthal-ms] Thl_1 $Œc_1$.

2 Thess. ii. 15), **according as** (according to the words in which) **I delivered** (them) **to you.** This was their *general practice :* the *exceptions* to it, or departures at all events from the *spirit* of those παραδόσεις, *now follow.* 3.] "It appears, that the Christian women at Corinth claimed for their sex an equality with the other, taking occasion by the doctrine of Christian freedom and abolition of sexual distinctions in Christ (Gal. iii. 28). The gospel unquestionably did much for the emancipation of women, who in the East and among the Ionian Greeks (not among the Dorians and the Romans) were kept in unworthy dependence. Still this was effected in a quiet and gradual manner; whereas in Corinth they seem to have taken up the cause of female independence somewhat too eagerly. The women overstepped the bounds of their sex, in coming forward to pray and to prophesy in the assembled church with uncovered heads. Both of these the Apostle disapproved,—as well their coming forward to pray and to prophesy, as their removing the veil: here however he blames the latter practice only, and reserves the former till ch. xiv. 34. In order to confine the women to their true limits, he reminds them of their subjection to the *man,* to whom again he assigns his place in the spiritual order of creation, and traces this precedence up to God Himself." De Wette. **παντὸς ἀνδρός**] 'of every *Christian* man' (as Chrys., al., Meyer, De W.), certainly,—and for such the Apostle was writing: but not *only* of every Christian man: the Headship of Christ is *over all things* to His Church, Eph. i. 22, and thus He is Head of **every man.** The word κεφαλή in each case means the head *next above.* This must be borne in mind, for Christ is THE HEAD of the Christian *woman,* as well as of the Christian *man.* God is the Head of Christ, not *only* according to His human Nature: the Son is, *in his Sonship,* necessarily *subordinate to the Father :* see ch. iii. 23, note, and ch. xv. 28. From χριστός, the order *descends* first: then, in order to complete the whole, *ascends* up to God. Observe that though (Gal. iii. 28) the distinction of the sexes is *abolished* in Christ, *as far as the offer of and standing in grace* is concerned, yet for *practical purposes,* and for *order* and *seemliness,* it *subsists* and *must be observed.* 4.] The case of the *man* here treated, was regarded by the ancient Commentators, Chrys., Theodoret, Theophyl., Œc., and Grot., Mosh., al., as an *actually occurring* one among the Corinthians:—but by recent ones, since Storr and Bengel, as *hypothetically put,* to *bring out* that other abuse which really *had occurred.* Had it been real, more would have been said on it below: but from ver. 5 onwards, attention is confined to the *woman.*

προσευχ. **praying in public:** **προφ.** **discoursing in the spirit;** see on ch. xii. 10. **κατὰ κεφ. ἔχων**] scil. τι. The Jews when praying in public put over their heads a veil, called the Tallith, to shew their reverence before God and their unworthiness to look on Him: Lightf., Hor. Heb. in loc. Grotius's note on the Greek and Roman customs is important:—"Apud Græcos mos fuit sacra facere capite aperto. Legendum enim apud Macrob. i. Saturn. 8, *Illic Græco ritu capite aperto res divina fit,* apparet ex loco ejusdem libri c. 10, ubi itidem de Saturno agitur, et *sacrum ei fieri* dicitur *aperto capite ritu peregrino;* et ex loco iii. 6, ubi Varronem ait dicere, Græci hoc esse moris, aperto capite sacrificare. ἀπαρακαλύπτῳ κεφαλῇ ait de ejusdem Saturni sacris agens Plutarchus in Romanis quæstionibus. *Lucem facere* id dici solitum Festus testatur. Eodem modo, id est aperto capite, etiam Herculi in ara maxima sacrum fieri solere testatur, præter Macrobium dicto libro iii. 6, Dion. Hal. lib. i., nimirum quia id sacrum institutum erat ab Evandro homine Græco. Sed Æneas (?) contrarium morem in Italiam intulit sacra faciendi velato capite, ne quod malum omen oculis aut auribus obveniret: ut Virg. nos docet Æn. iii. et ad eum Servius, et in Breviario Aurelius Victor: sed et Plutarchus in Romanis quæstionibus. Et ejus moris etiam Plautus meminit in comœdiis quibusdam: ut solet admiscere Romana Græcis. Paulus Græcis Corinthiis scribens Græcum præfert morem, et causas adfert quales ferebat negotii natura. Ex Pauli præscripto perpetuo hunc morem tenuere Christiani veteres. Tertul. Apologetico: 'Illuc suspicientes Christiani manibus expansis, quia innocui: capite

αὐτοῦ. 5 πᾶσα δὲ γυνὴ [p] προσευχομένη ἢ [q] προφητεύουσα
[t] ἀκατακαλύπτῳ τῇ κεφαλῇ [s] καταισχύνει τὴν κεφαλὴν
αὐτῆς· [u] ἓν γάρ ἐστιν [u] καὶ τὸ αὐτὸ τῇ [v] ἐξυρημένῃ. 6 εἰ
γὰρ οὐ [w] κατακαλύπτεται γυνή, καὶ [x] κειράσθω· εἰ δὲ
[y] αἰσχρὸν γυναικὶ [z] τὸ [x] κείρασθαι ἢ [v] ξυρᾶσθαι, [w] κατακαλυπτέσθω. 7 ἀνὴρ μὲν γὰρ οὐκ [a] ὀφείλει [w] κατακαλύπτε-
σθαι τὴν κεφαλήν, [b] εἰκὼν καὶ [c] δόξα θεοῦ [d] ὑπάρχων· ἡ

t ver. 13 only. Levit. xiii. 45 A Ald. compl. (there also w. κεφ.) only. Polyb. xv. 27. 2. dat., Winer, edn. 6, § 31. 7.
u ch. xii. (9) 11 only. constr., here only. see 1 Pet. v. 9.
v here bis. Acts xxi. 24 only. Num. vi. 9.
w here (3ce) only. Gen. xxxviii. 15 al.
x here bis. Acts viii. 32. xviii. 18 only. 2 Kings xiv. 26.
y ch. xiv. 35. Eph. v. 12. Tit. i. 11 only. P. Gen. xli. 3, &c. only.
z constr., Phil. i. 21.
a = Acts xvii. 29. Rom. xv. 1.
b Rom. viii. 29 reff. Gen. i. 26, 27.
c = Ps. xviii. 1.
d Acts viii. 16 reff.

..οφειλει n.
..κατακαλ. την b.

ABCDF KLPℵ a c d e f g h k l m o 17 47.

5. for πασα δε, και π. A Syr æth: om δε P. om τη D^1F. rec for αυτης, εαυτης (*see note*), with BD^3KL rel $Orig_1$: txt ACD^1FLPℵ a b^1 d g^2 h o 17 Chr_1 Thdrt [Euthal-ms Damasc].
6. aft κειρασθω ins η ξυρασθω B.
7. rec om ἡ (*conforming to the preceding and following*), with $CD^3KLℵ_1$ rel Chr_1

nudo, quia non erubescimus: denique sine monitore, quia de pectore oramus,' &c. Nihil huc pertinet mos Septentrionis in reverentiæ signum caput velandi, qui quanquam per Germanicas nationes late manavit, et Judæis tamen et Græcis, et veteri Italiæ fuit incognitus." **καταισχ. τ. κεφ. αὐτοῦ**] **dishonours his Head**, i. e. *Christ*: not, his *own head* literally,—except in so far as the literal and metaphorical senses are both included,—the (literal) head of the man being regarded as the representative of his spiritual Head. See this brought out in Stanley's note: for the head of the man *in this respect of honouring or dishonouring, has been, ver. 3, explained to be* Christ. Him he dishonours, by appearing veiled before men, thus recognizing subjection to *them* in an assembly which ought to be conformed to *Christian order*. **5.**] The case of the woman is just the converse. She, if she *uncovers* herself (on the manner of covering, see below ver. 15, note) in such an assembly, dishonours her head (*the man;* not, as Meyer and many others, literally, her *own head* (but see above): of *this kind of dishonour* there is no mention at all in our passage, and ver. 3 has *expressly guarded us against making the mistake*) by apparently casting off his headship: and if this is to be so, the Apostle proceeds, why not go further and cut off her hair, which of itself is a token of this subjection? But if this be acknowledged to be shameful (it was a punishment of adulteresses, see Wetst. in loc. and Tacit. Germ. 19), let the further decency of the additional covering be conceded likewise. The reading ἑαυτῆς may have arisen from fancying that her *own* head is meant.

ἓν . . . ἐστιν κ. τὸ αὐτό] *she:* not *it*, τὸ ἀκατακάλυπτον εἶναι. The neut. is used because the identity is generic, not individual: cf. Eur. Med. 928,—γυνὴ δὲ θῆλυ κἀπὶ δακρύοις ἔφυ, and other examples in Kühner, ii. 45 (§ 421). **6.**] the argument see above. **οὐ κατ.,**—**is to be unveiled**, the *pres.* indicating the *normal habit*. **καὶ κειρ.**, let her also, besides being unveiled, &c. **κείρ. ἢ ξυρ.**] 'plus est radi quam tonderi,' Grot.

7—9.] *A second reason for the same,—from the dependence of the man on God only, but of the woman on the man.*

7.] **γάρ** refers back to and gives a reason for κατακαλυπτέσθω, the difference between the sexes being assumed,—that one *should be* and the other should *not* be veiled. The emphasis is accordingly on **ἀνήρ**. **οὐκ ὀφείλει, should not, ought not**: see reff. **εἰκὼν θεοῦ**, ref. Gen. This the *man* is, having been created first,—*directly*, and in a special manner: the woman indirectly, only *through the man*. **κ. δόξα θ.**] **And the** (representative of the) **glory of God**: on account of his superiority and *godlike* attributes among other created beings. This is obviously *the point* here brought out, as in Ps. viii. 6: not, that he is *set to shew forth God's glory* (εἰς γὰρ δόξαν θεοῦ ὀφείλει ὁ ἀνὴρ ὑποτετάχθαι τῷ θεῷ, Phot. in Œcum.), however true that may be: nor, as Estius, from Augustine, '*quia in illo Deus gloriatur:*' nor is δόξα the representative of the Heb. דְּמוּת, Gen. i. 26 (ὁμοίωσις), as Rückert, al., suppose, because the LXX have rendered תְּמוּנָה, Num. xii. 8; Ps. xvii. 15, by δόξα: for, as Meyer observes, in so well-known a passage as Gen. i. 26, the Apostle could hardly fail to have used the LXX word ὁμοίωσις.

Man is *God's glory:* He has put in him His Majesty, and he represents God on earth: *woman* is *man's glory:* taken (ver. 8) from the *man*, shining (to follow out Grotius's similitude, "minus aliquid vero, ut luna lumen minus sole") not with light direct from God, but with light derived

e Rom. i. 25 reff. f = as ordinarily; e.g. Matt. x. 1 al. fr. g see note.

γυνὴ δὲ [c] δόξα ἀνδρός ἐστιν. [8] οὐ γάρ ἐστιν ἀνὴρ ἐκ
γυναικός, ἀλλὰ γυνὴ ἐξ ἀνδρός· [9] καὶ γὰρ οὐκ [e] ἐκτίσθη
ἀνὴρ διὰ τὴν γυναῖκα, ἀλλὰ γυνὴ διὰ τὸν ἄνδρα. [10] διὰ
τοῦτο [a] ὀφείλει ἡ γυνὴ [f] ἐξουσίαν [g] ἔχειν [g] ἐπὶ τῆς κεφαλῆς

H ανηρ. ÄBCDF HKLPℵ acdef ghklm o 17. 47

[Euthal-ms] Damasc: ins ABD¹FPℵ³ Isid₁ Thdrt. ins του bef ανδρος F. 8. om ver K. 10. η γυνη bef οφειλει H m 17.

from *man*, "τὸ θῆλυ, ἄῤῥεν ἀτελές, philosophis. Imperat materfamilias suæ familiæ, sed viri nomine." Grot. This of course is true only as regards her place in creation, and her providential subordination, not in respect of the dependence of every woman's individual soul directly on God, *not on man*, for supplies of grace and preparations for glory. The Apostle omits εἰκών, because anthropologically the woman is not the *image* of the man, on account of the difference of the sexes: and also perhaps because thus he would seem to deny to the woman the being created in the *divine* image, which she is as well as the man, Gen. i. 26, 27. The former reason appears the more probable: and so De W. and Meyer. "It may be observed that, whereas in Genesis the general character of man under the Hebrew name answering to ἄνθρωπος is the only one brought forward, here it is merged in the word ἀνήρ, which only expresses his relation to the woman." Stanley. **8.**] **γάρ** gives the reason of the former assertion γυνὴ δόξα ἀνδρός,—viz. that **the man is not** (emphasis on ἐστιν, which prevents the ἐκ having a figurative sense, of *dependence:* —'takes not his being,' in the fact of his *original creation.* The *propagation* of the species is not here in view) **out of the woman, but the woman out of the man** (compare Gen. ii. 23, κληθήσεται γυνή, ὅτι **ἐκ τοῦ ἀνδρὸς αὐτῆς ἐλήφθη**).
9.] **For also** (*parallel* with ver. 8—*another* reason: not *subordinate* to it, as Meyer, who renders ἐκ in ver. 8, 'dependent on,' and regards this verse as giving the reason) **the man was not created** (emphasis on ἐκτίσθη, as before on ἐστιν) **on account of the woman, &c.** In this verse, besides the *manner* of creation, **ἐκ** τοῦ ἀνδρός, the *occasion* of creation, **διὰ** τὸν ἄνδρα, is insisted on; see Gen. ii. 18 ff. **10.**] **διὰ τοῦτο**, *on account of what has just been said,* by which the subordination of the woman has been proved:—refers to vv. 7—9, not as Meyer, to ver. 9 only: for vv. 8, 9, give two parallel reasons for γυνὴ δόξα ἀνδρός, the inference from which proposition *has not yet been given,* but now follows, with **ὀφείλει** answering to **οὐκ ὀφείλει** above. **ὀφ. ἡ γ. ἐξουσίαν ἔχ. ἐπὶ τῆς κεφ.] The woman ought to have power** (the *sign of power* or *subjection;* shewn by the context to mean *a veil*). So Diodor. Sic. i. 47: εἰκόνα . . . . εἴκοσι πηχῶν, μονόλιθον, ἔχουσαν τρεῖς βασιλείας ἐπὶ τῆς κεφαλῆς, ἃς διασημαίνειν ὅτι καὶ θυγάτηρ καὶ γυνὴ καὶ μήτηρ βασιλέως ὑπῆρξε, where βασίλειαι evidently are *crowns,* the *tokens of kingdom.* And as there from the context it is plain that they indicated *participation* in the glory of the kingdoms, so here it is as evident from the context that the token of ἐξουσία indicates being *under* power: and such token is the covering. So Chrys. (τὸ καλύπτεσθαι, ὑποταγῆς κ. ἐξουσίας), Theodoret, Theophyl. (τὸ τοῦ ἐξουσιάζεσθαι σύμβολον), Œcum., Beza, Grot., Est., Bengel, Wolf, al., Billroth, Rückert, Olsh., Meyer, De Wette. To enumerate the various renderings would be impossible. Some of the principal are, (1) a sign of *power to pray and prophesy in public, bestowed on her by her husband.* So Schrader, iv. 158: but this would be quite irrelevant to the context. (2) Some suppose ἐξουσίαν actually to mean *a veil,* because the Heb. רְדִיד, 'a veil,' comes from the root רָדַד, '*subjecit.*' So Hammond, Le Clerc, al. But (see Lexx.) '*subjecit*' is not the primary, only a tropical meaning: the primary meaning, '*extendit, diduxit,*' is much more likely to have given rise to the substantive. It is certainly a curious coincidence that the Heb. *terms* should be thus allied,—and that alliance may have been *present to the Apostle's thoughts:* but this does not shew that he used ἐξουσία *for a veil.* (3) Kypke would put a comma after ἐξουσ., and render '*propterea mulier potestati obnoxia est, ita ut velamen* (*see ver.* 4) *in capite habeat.*' But the sense of ὀφείλειν τι would require (see Lexx.) ὑπακοήν, not ἐξουσίαν. (4) Pott renders, '*mulierem oportet servare jus* (*sive potestatem*) *in caput suum,* sc. *eo, quod illud velo obtegat.*' But this, though philologically allowable (see Rev. xi. 6; xx. 6; xiv. 18; and with ἐπάνω, Luke xix. 17), is entirely against the context, in which the woman has *no power* over her own head, and *on that very account is to be covered.* (5) Hagenbach (in the Stud. und Krit. 1828, p. 401) supposes ἐξουσία here to mean *her origin,* ἐξ-ουσία from ἐξ-εἰμι, as παρ-ουσία from παρ-εἰμι:—to shew that she (ver. 8) ἐστιν ἐξ ἀνδρός. But apart from other

διὰ τοὺς [h] ἀγγέλους. 11 [i] πλὴν οὔτε γυνὴ χωρὶς ἀνδρὸς

h = as ordinarily; so Ps. cxxxvii. 1. i — Matt. Luke passim (not Mark, John, nor Luke in Acts). Paul, Eph. v. 33. Phil. i. 18. iii. 16. iv. 14 only. Rev. ii. 25. Lam. iii. 3.

11. rec ανηρ χωρις γυν. ουτε γυνη χωρις ανδ. (*appy more natural order*), with D^2[-gr]

objections to this, it must thus be, **τὴν ἐξ.** or **τὴν ἐξ. αὐτῆς.** Other renderings and conjectures may be seen in Meyer's note, from which the above is mainly taken: and in Stanley's. **διὰ τοὺς ἀγγέλους**] **On account of the angels**: i. e. because in the Christian assemblies the holy angels of God are present, and delighting in the due order and subordination of the ranks of God's servants,—and by a violation of that order we should be giving offence to them. See ref. So Chrys. (*οὐκ οἶδας ὅτι μετ' ἀγγέλων ἕστηκας; μετ' ἐκείνων ᾄδεις, μετ' ἐκείνων ὑμνεῖς, καὶ ἕστηκας γελῶν;* cited by Hammond, but from what work of Chrys. I have not been able to find. In his commentary on this passage he is not clear, but seems to take this view,—*εἰ γὰρ τοῦ ἀνδρὸς καταφρονεῖς, φησί, τοὺς ἀγγέλους αἰδέσθητι,* Hom. xxvi. p. 234. In the Hom. on the Ascension, vol. ii. pt. ii. p. 443 (Migne), he says, *εἰ βούλει ἰδεῖν κ. μάρτυρας κ. ἀγγέλους ἄνοιξον τῆς πίστεως τοὺς ὀφθαλμούς, κ. ὄψει τὸ θέατρον ἐκεῖνο· εἰ γὰρ πῶς ὁ ἀὴρ ἀγγέλων ἐμπέπλησται, πολλῷ μᾶλλον ἡ ἐκκλησία . . . . ὅτι γὰρ ἅπας ὁ ἀὴρ ἀγγέλων ἐμπέπλησται, ἄκουσον τί φησιν ὁ ἀπόστολος, ἐντρέπων τὰς γυναῖκας ὥστε ἔχειν κάλυμμα ἐπὶ τῆς κεφαλῆς· "ὀφείλουσιν κ.τ.λ."*), Grot. (whose note see in Pool), Estius, Wolf, Rückert, Meyer, De Wette. (1) Others, with a modification of this rendering, take *τοὺς ἀγγέλους* as the *guardian angels,* appointed, one to take charge of each Christian. So Theophyl. (*τὸ ἀνακεκαλύφθαι ἀναισχυντίαν ἐμφαίνει· ἣν καὶ οἱ τοῖς πιστοῖς παρεπόμενοι ἄγγελοι βδελύσσονται*), Jerome (not Aug. de Trin. xii. 7, as Meyer, see below), Theodoret. But, though such angels *certainly do minister* to the heirs of salvation,—see Matt. xviii. 10, and note,—there does not appear to be any immediate allusion to them *here.* (2) Others again understand '*bad angels,*' who might *themselves* be lustfully excited; so Tertull. de Virg. Vel. 7, vol. ii. p. 899, "propter angelos: scilicet quos legimus a Deo et cœlo excidisse ob concupiscentiam fœminarum." See also cont. Marcion. v. 8, p. 488,—or might *tempt men so to be,* —Schöttgen, Mosh., al.,—or might *injure the unveiled themselves:* so, after Rabbinical notions, Wetst. But *οἱ ἄγγελοι, absol.,* never means any thing in the N. T. except *the holy angels of God.* See, in Stanley's note, a modification of this view, which is consistent with that meaning. (3) Clem. Alex. fragm. ix. *ὑποτυπ.* lib. iii. (p. 1004 P.) says, *ἀγγέλους φησὶ τοὺς δικαίους, κ. ἐναρέτους.* (4) Beza, the Christian *prophets,* "in cœtu loquentes ut Dei nuncios et legatos." (5) Ambrose, the *presidents of the assemblies.* (6) Lightf., the *angeli* or *nuntii desponsationum,* persons deputed to bring about *betrothals.* (7) Rosenm., Schrader, and many others,—*exploratores* vel *speculatores:* "Poterat nempe novæ consuetudinis notitia per *ἀπίστους* speculatores in publicum emanare, christianasque uxores tum Judæis, de isto mulierum habitu pessime existimantibus, tum Græcis quoque in suspicionem rei christianæ probrosissimam adducere." Rosenm. Against all these ingenious interpretations is the plain sense of *οἱ ἄγγελοι* (Matt. xiii. 49. Mark i. 13. Luke xvi. 22. chap. xiii. 1. Col. ii. 18. Heb. i. 4, 5, 7, 13, al.), which appears to me irrefragable. But still a question remains, WHY *should the Apostle have here named the angels, and adduced them as furnishing a reason for women being veiled in the Christian assemblies?* Bengel has given an acute, but not I believe the correct answer: "mulier se *tegat* propter angelos, i. e. quia etiam angeli teguntur. Sicut ad Deum se habent angeli: sic ad virum se habet mulier. Dei facies patet: velantur angeli: Esa. vi. 2. Viri facies patet: velatur mulier." Surely this lies *too far off* for any reader to supply without further specification. Aug. de Trin. xii. 7 (10), vol. viii. p. 1004, gives an ingenious reason: "Grata est enim sanctis angelis sacrata et pia significatio. Nam Deus non ad tempus videt, nec aliquid novi fit in Ejus visione atque scientia, cum aliquid temporaliter aut transitorie geritur, sicut inde afficiuntur sensus vel carnales animalium et hominum, vel etiam cœlestes angelorum." (He makes no mention,—see above,—of *guardian* angels.) I believe the account given above to be the true one, and the *reason* of adducing it to be, that the Apostle *has before his mind the order of the universal church,* and prefers when speaking of the assemblies of Christians, to adduce those beings who, as not entering into the gradation which he has here described, are conceived as *spectators* of the whole, delighted with the decency and order of the servants of God. Stanley thinks the most natural explanation of the reference to be, that the Apostle was led to it by a train of association familiar to his readers, but lost to us: and compares the intimations of a similar familiarity on their part with the subjects of which he

οὔτε ἀνὴρ χωρὶς γυναικὸς ἐν κυρίῳ· 12 ὥςπερ γὰρ ἡ γυνὴ
[k] ἐκ τοῦ ἀνδρός, οὕτως καὶ ὁ ἀνὴρ διὰ τῆς γυναικός, τὰ δὲ
[l] πάντα [l] ἐκ τοῦ θεοῦ. 13 ἐν ὑμῖν αὐτοῖς [m] κρίνατε· [n] πρέπον
ἐστὶν γυναῖκα [o] ἀκατακάλυπτον τῷ θεῷ προσεύχεσθαι;
14 οὐδὲ ἡ [p] φύσις αὐτὴ διδάσκει ὑμᾶς ὅτι ἀνὴρ μὲν ἐὰν
[q] κομᾷ, [r] ἀτιμία αὐτῷ ἐστιν, 15 γυνὴ δὲ ἐὰν [q] κομᾷ, δόξα
αὐτῇ ἐστιν; ὅτι ἡ [s] κόμη [t] ἀντὶ [u] περιβολαίου δέδοται

ABCDF HKLPℵ a c d e f g h k l m o 17. 47

k ver. 8. l ch. viii. 6. Rom. xi. 36. m = Luke vii. 43. Acts iv. 19. Ps. lvii. 1. n Matt. iii. 15 only. 1 Macc. xii. 11 only. (-πει, Eph. v. 3. 1 Tim. ii. 10. Tit. ii. 1. Heb. ii. 10. vii. 26 only. Ps. lxiv. 1.) constr., here only. o ver. 5. p = Rom. i. 26 (reff.). ii. 27. xi. 21, 24. see James iii. 7. q here bis only †. r Rom. i. 26 reff. s here only. Num. vi. 5. t = Luke xi. 11. u Heb. i. 12 (from Ps. ci. 26) only. Exod. xxii. 27. Job xxvi. 6. Ps. ciii. 6.

KL rel vulg syrr Chr_2 Thdrt Pel: txt ABC $D^{1.3}$[and lat] FHPℵ d m 17 coptt æth arm $Clem_1$ Bas-sel Damasc $Sing\text{-}cler_1$ Ambrst Aug_1.

12. om ὁ F(not G) 17[om η also]. for δια, εκ K [f]. om της H [Montf: e contra Tischdf].

13. for εν υμιν αυτοις, υμεις αυτοι D vulg(not tol [*vos autem* am]) lat-ff. προσευχ. bef τω θ. DF [latt syrr coptt æth arm(Tischdf)].

14. rec ins η bef ουδε (*addition to mark the* interrogation), with D^3KL rel syr-mg sah: om $ABCD^1$FHPℵ 17. 47 latt syrr copt arm [Euthal-ms] $Ambr_1$ Ambrst. rec αυτη bef η φυσις, with D^2KL rel Chr_1 Thdrt: om αυτη F[-gr] arm[?] $Tert_1$: txt $ABCD^{1.3}$HPℵ a m 17 [Euthal-ms] $Damasc_2$. aft μεν ins γαρ $ℵ^1$(but marked for erasure) copt. for εαν, αν D^1.

15. αυτη δεδοται CHP a d m vulg(with F-lat) syr $Damasc_2$ Ambr: om αυτη D F[-gr] KL e f h l [47] Chr_2 Thdrt Œc Tert.: δεδοται αυτη ABℵ c g k o 17 G-lat Syr coptt æth arm [Euthal-ms].

was treating in 2 Thess. ii. 5—7. **11.**] *Yet is neither sex insulated and independent of the other in the Christian life.* **ἐν κυρίῳ** is not the predicate (as Grot., &c.),—'neque viri exclusis mulieribus . . . participes sunt beneficiorum per Christum partorum:' nor does it mean *according to the ordinance of God*, as Chrys., Beza, Olsh.,—for the phrase ἐν κυρίῳ is well known as applying to the *Christian state*, **in the Lord**. See e. g. Rom. xvi. 2, 8, 11, 12 (bis), &c. **12.**] *And in this, the Christian life accords with the original ordinance of God.* **For** (proof of ver. 11) **as the woman is** (was taken, Gen. ii. 21 f.) **out of the man, so the man is** (is born, in the propagation of the human race) **by means of the woman; but all things** (both man and woman and all things else: a general maxim, see 2 Cor. v. 18) **are of** (as their source,—thus uniting in one great head both sexes and all creation) **God.** They are dependent on one another, but *both* on HIM: the Christian life therefore, which unites them in Christ, is agreeable to God's ordinance. **13.**] *Appeal to their own sense of propriety:* cf. ch. x. 15. **ἐν ὑμῖν αὐτ.**] Each man within himself, in his own judgment. **14.**] **ἡ φύσις αὐτή, nature herself**: i. e. the mere fact of *one sex* being *by nature unveiled*, i. e. having short hair,—the *other, veiled*, i. e. having long hair. This plainly declares that *man* was intended to be *uncovered*,—*woman, covered.* When therefore we deal with the proprieties of the *artificial* state, of *clothing the body*, we must be *regulated by nature's suggestion:* that which she has indicated to be left uncovered, we must so leave: that which she has covered, when we clothe the body, we must cover likewise. This is the argument. φύσις is not *sense of natural propriety*, but NATURE,—the *law of creation.* **κομᾷ**] So Eustathius, Il. γ. p. 288, in Wetst., κόμην δὲ ἔχειν, καὶ εὔκομον εἶναι, γυναικώτερόν ἐστιν. διὸ καὶ ὁ Πάρις ὀνειδίζεται ὡς κόμην ἔχων. On φύσις and κομᾷ Pool observes, 'locus est vexatissimus doctorum sententiis;' and gives a note of four folio columns; and Bengel has a long discussion on the lawfulness of wigs. The Apostle (see above) makes no allusion to the *customs of nations* in the matter, nor is even the mention of them relevant[: he is speaking of the dictates of nature herself.] **15.**] See on ver. 14: compare Milton, Par. Lost, iv. 304 ff. **περιβόλαιον**, properly a *wrapper*, or enveloping garment: see reff., and Eurip. Herc. fur. 549, and in a metaphorical sense, 1269. "In this passage," says Stanley, "the Apostle would refer to the 'peplum,' which the Grecian women used ordinarily as a shawl, but on public occasions as a hood also, especially at funerals and marriages." See a woodcut in Smith's Dict. of Antt. art. 'peplum.' **16.**] Cuts off the subject, already abundantly decided, with a settlement of any possible difference, by appeal to universal apostolic and ecclesiastic custom. **But if any man seems to be contentious** (i. e. 'if any arises who appears to dispute the matter, who

[αὐτῇ]· 16 εἰ δέ τις [v] δοκεῖ [w] φιλόνεικος εἶναι, ἡμεῖς τοιαύτην
[x] συνήθειαν οὐκ ἔχομεν, οὐδὲ αἱ [yz] ἐκκλησίαι τοῦ [z] θεοῦ.
17 Τοῦτο δὲ [a] παραγγέλλω οὐκ [b] ἐπαινῶν, ὅτι οὐκ [c] εἰς
τὸ [d] κρεῖσσον ἀλλὰ [c] εἰς τὸ [e] ἧσσον [f] συνέρχεσθε. 18 [g] πρῶ-

..θεου H. ABCDF KLPℵ a c d e f g h k l m o 17. 47

v = Luke xxii. 24. Gal. ii. 6. Prov. ii. 10. w here only. Ezek. iii. 7 only. (-κία, Luke xxii. 24. -κεῖν, Prov. x. 12.) x John xviii. 39. ch. viii. 7 v. r. only †. Prov. xvii. 9 Symm. [or -θης]. (-θης, 2 Macc. iii. 31.) y plur., Rom. xvi. 16 reff. z ch. i. 2 reff. a Acts i. 4 reff. b ver. 2. c see Rom. xiii. 4 reff. d ch. vii. 9 reff. e = here (2 Cor. xii. 15) only ‡. (Isa. xxiii. 8.) f = Acts i. 6 reff. g [Rom. iii. 2.]

17. rec παραγγελλων ουκ επαινω (*see vv.* 2 *and* 22), with C³(appy) D³(and lat) F[-gr] KLPℵ rel copt [sah-mnt] Chr₃ Thdrt [Sedul] : -λω ουκ -νω D¹[-gr] 137 sah[-woide Euthal-ms]: -λων ουκ -νων B d: txt AC¹ 17 latt syrr æth[appy] arm Ambrst Aug Pel Bede. (κρεισσον, so ABCD¹FPℵ 17 [Damasc].) (αλλα, so ABCD¹ℵ m¹ [Euthal-ms].) (ησσον, so ABCD¹ℵ [Euthal-ms]: ελαττον F Thdrt: ἴσον 17.)

seems not satisfied with the *reasons* I have given, but is still disputatious;'—this is the only admissible sense of δοκεῖ in this construction: see reff.:—for the meaning, '*if it pleases any one*,' &c. would require τινι δοκεῖ: and '*if any one thinks that he may*,' &c. would not agree with φιλονεικεῖν, which is in itself *wrong*). **ἡμεῖς**] declarative: **let him know that . . . .**; so, εἰ δὲ κατακαυχᾶσαι, οὐ σὺ τὴν ῥίζαν βαστάζεις, ἀλλ' ἡ ῥίζα σέ, Rom. xi. 18. **We,**—the Apostles and their immediate company,—including the women who assembled in prayer and supplication with them at their various stations, see Acts xvi. 13. **τοιαύτην συνήθειαν**] The best modern Commentators, e. g. Meyer and De Wette, agree with Chrys. in understanding this, τοιαύτ. συνήθ., ὥστε φιλονεικεῖν κ. ἐρίζειν κ. ἀντιτάττεσθαι. p. 235. And so Ambrose, Beza, Calvin, Estius, Calov., al. But surely it would be very unlikely, that after *so long a treatment of a particular subject*, the Apostle should wind up all by merely a censure of a fault *common* to their behaviour on *this and all the other* matters of dispute. Such a rendering seems to me almost to *stultify the conclusion*:—'If any will dispute about it still, remember that it is neither our practice, nor that of the Churches, *to dispute*.' It would seem to me, but for the weighty names on the other side, hardly to admit of a question, that the συνήθεια alludes to *the practice* (see ref. John) *of women praying uncovered*. So Theodoret, Grot., Michaelis, Rosenm., Billroth, Olsh., al., and Theophyl. altern. He thus cuts off all further disputation on the matter by *appealing to universal Christian usage*: and to make the appeal more solemn, adds **τοῦ θεοῦ** to αἱ ἐκκλ.,—the assemblies which are held in honour of and for prayer to God, and are *His own Churches*. Obs. **αἱ** ἐκκλησίαι, not **ἡ** ἐκκλησία. The *plurality of independent testimonies to the absence of the custom*, is that on which the stress is laid. This appeal, 'to THE CHURCHES,' was much heard again at the Reformation: but has since been too much forgotten. See, on the influence of this passage on the Christian church, the general remarks of Stanley, edn. 2, pp. 198—200. **17—34.**] *Correction of abuses regarding the Agapæ and the partaking of the Supper of the Lord.* **17.**] Refers back to what has been said since ver. 2, and forms a transition to what is yet to be said. **But this** (viz. *what has gone before*, respecting the *veiling of women*; not, as Chrys., Theophyl., Grot., Bengel, al., that which follows: see below) **I command you** (not '*announce to you*,' nor '*declare to you from report*,' which are senses of παραγγ. unknown to the N. T., where it only means '*to command*,'—'to deliver *by way of precept*:' see reff., and ch. vii. 10; 1 Thess. iv. 11; 2 Thess. iii. 4, 6, 10, 12. This makes it hardly possible to refer τοῦτο to *what follows*; for if so, some definite command should immediately succeed) **not praising** (refers to the ἐπαινῶ of ver. 2, and *excepts what has been said since* from that category); **because you come together not for the better** (so that edification results) **but for the worse** (so that propriety is violated, and the result is to the hindering of the faith). These last words ὅτι . . . συνέρχ. are introduced with a manifest view to include *more* than the subject hitherto treated, and to *prepare the way* for other abuses of their assemblies to be noticed. **18.**] **πρῶτον**—where is the *second* particular founda, nswering to this πρῶτον? Ordinarily, it is assumed that the σχίσματα are the *first* abuse, the disorders in the Agapæ (beginning with ver. 20), the *second*. But I am convinced, with Meyer, that this view is wrong. For (1) neither special blame, nor correction of abuse, is conveyed in vv. 18, 19: nor is it so much as intimated, on the ordinary hypothesis, what the character of these σχίσματα was. And (2) the words of ver. 22, ἐπαινέσω ὑμᾶς ἐν τούτῳ; οὐκ ἐπαινῶ, plainly refer back to ver. 17, and shew that the whole is continuous. Again (3) the οὖν of ver. 20, as so frequently,—see ch.

του [gh] μὲν [h] γὰρ [f] συνερχομένων ὑμῶν ἐν ἐκκλησίᾳ [i] ἀκούω ABCDF KLPℵ
[j] σχίσματα ἐν ὑμῖν [k] ὑπάρχειν, καὶ [l] μέρος τι [m] πιστεύω. acdef
19 [n] δεῖ γὰρ καὶ [o] αἱρέσεις ἐν ὑμῖν εἶναι, ἵνα [καὶ] οἱ [p] δό- ghklm o 17. 47

h = ch. v. 3. 2 Cor. ix. 1. i w. acc. and inf., John xii. 18 only. j ch. i. 10 reff. k Acts viii. 16 reff. al. fr. Job xxix. 24. l = here only. Thucyd. ii. 64. iv. 30. = ἐκ μέρους, ch. xiii. 9, &c. m = Matt. xxiv. 23, 26 n = Acts iv. 12 reff. o Acts v. 17 reff. p Rom. xiv. 18 reff.

18. rec ins τη bef εκκλησια (*the meaning being mistaken: see note*), with g h 47 [arm(Treg)] Thl Œc: om ABCDFKLPℵ rel Chr_1 [Euthal-ms] Damasc. υπαρχειν bef εν υμιν $D^{1.3}$F vulg-ed arm: om εν υμιν am(with demid fuld harl [tol]) Orig[$-int_1$] Ambrst Bede.

19. om 1st εν υμιν D^1F latt $Orig\text{-}int_1$ [($Tert_3$) $Cypr_2$ Ambrst Aug_1] (not $Orig_1$ [Chr_1 Euthal-ms Thdrt Damasc] Jer_1 Primas): ins aft ειναι D^3[-gr coptt] $Archel_1$.
aft ινα ins και B D^1(and lat) m 17 vulg sah Ambrst Pel Bede: om AC D^3[-gr] FKLPℵ rel syrr copt [arm] $Orig_1$[$-int_1$] $Epiph_1$ Chr_7 [Euthal-ms] Thdrt Damasc $Cypr_2$ [($Tert_2$) Jer_1]: και ινα και m^1.

viii. 4, and Hartung, Partikellehre, ii. 22, —*resumes the subject* broken off by καὶ μέρος . . . γέν. ἐν ὑμῖν. The **σχίσματα** before the Apostle's mind are, *specifically*, those occurring at the Agapæ,—but on the mention of them, he breaks off to shew that such divisions were to be no matters of surprise, but were ordained to test them,—and in ver. 20 he returns with the very words, συνερχομένων ὑμῶν,—to the immediate matter in hand, and treats it at length. See more on vv. 21 ff. But the question still remains, where is the *second* point, answering to this πρῶτον? Again with Meyer (and Macknight) I answer,—*at* ch. xii. 1. The ABUSE OF SPIRITUAL GIFTS, *which also created disorder in their assemblies*, ch. xiv. 23 al., and concerning which he concludes, xiv. 40, πάντα εὐσχημόνως κ. κατὰ τάξιν γινέσθω,—was the *other point* before his mind, when he wrote this πρῶτον. That he takes no notice in ch. xii. 1, by any ἔπειτα δέ or the like, of what has gone before, will be no objection to the above view to any one but the merest tiro in our Apostle's style.

There is a trajection of the ἀκούω, which, in the sense, precedes συνερχ., &c. **ἐν ἐκκλ.**] **in assembly**; not *local*, as E. V., '*in the church*,' but = ἐπὶ τὸ αὐτό, ver. 20. [In ver. 16, where the word is used of distinct bodies of Christians, it was not possible to keep the word *assemblies*, but it should be done whenever the sense admits it, and it suits the matter in hand]. **σχίσματα**] *of what sort*, is specified below; viz. that he does not here refer to the party dissensions of ch. i. 10, nor could he say of them μέρος τι πιστεύω, but strictly to σχίσματα which took place *at their meetings together*, viz. that each takes before other his own supper, &c. So Chrys.: οὐ λέγει, ἀκούω γὰρ μὴ κοινῇ ὑμᾶς συνδειπνεῖν· ἀκούω κατ' ἰδίαν ὑμᾶς ἑστιᾶσθαι, καὶ μὴ μετὰ τῶν πενήτων· ἀλλ' ὃ μάλιστα ἱκανὸν ἦν αὐτῶν διασεῖσαι τὴν διάνοιαν, τοῦτο τέθεικε, τὸ τοῦ σχίσματος ὄνομα, ὃ καὶ τούτου ἦν αἴτιον, Hom. xxvii. p. 241; and Theophyl., Œc., Est., Pisc., Grot., which last remarks, 'Accidebat jam illis temporibus, quod nostris multo magis evenit, ut res instituta ad concorporandos fideles in vexillum schismatis verteretur.' **κ. μέρος τι πιστ.**] Said in gentleness: q. d. "I am unwilling to believe *all* I hear concerning the point, but *some* (hardly '*much*,' '*in great* part,' as Stanley: nor do his testimonies from Thucyd. i. 23; vii. 30, bear out this meaning. It might, of course, lie beneath the surface, but is not given by μέρος τι) I cannot help believing." **19.**] **δεῖ**, in the divine appointment, the ἵνα which follows expressing *God's purpose* thereby. Our Lord had said ἀνάγκη ἐλθεῖν τὰ σκάνδαλα, Matt. xviii. 7:—and Justin Martyr, Tryph. 35, p. 132, quotes among His sayings prophetic of division in the church, ἔσονται σχίσματα κ. αἱρέσεις. From the pointed manner in which δεῖ γὰρ **καὶ αἱρέσεις** . . . is said, I should be inclined to think that the Apostle *tacitly referred to the same saying of our Lord*: **for there must be** (not only dissensions, but) **even heresies** (not in the ecclesiastical or doctrinal sense,—as Pelag., Est., Calv., Beza, —see reff., but indicating a further and more matured separation, where not only is there present dissension, as in the Agapæ, but a deliberate choice and maintenance of party distinction. It does not appear, in spite of all that has been written in Germany on the supposed parties of ch. i. 10, that such separations had yet taken place among the Corinthians. Nor even in Clement's Epistle, forty years after this, do we find any allusion to such, but only, as here, to a general spirit of dissension and variance, see chaps. iii. and xiv., pp. 213, 257. Chrys. would refer αἱρ. *only to the Agapæ*: οὐ ταύτας λέγων τὰς τῶν δογμάτων, ἀλλὰ τὰς τῶν σχισμάτων τούτων, p. 242,—and so Theophyl., Œc. But this hardly justifies the climax, δεῖ γὰρ καὶ αἱρ.) **among you, that the approved**

κιμοι [q] φανεροὶ [q] γένωνται ἐν ὑμῖν.
20 [fr] συνερχομένων οὖν ὑμῶν [rs] ἐπὶ τὸ αὐτὸ οὐκ ἔστιν [t] κυριακὸν [u] δεῖπνον φαγεῖν·
21 ἕκαστος γὰρ τὸ ἴδιον [u] δεῖπνον [v] προλαμβάνει [w] ἐν τῷ φαγεῖν, καὶ [x] ὃς μὲν [y] πεινᾷ, [x] ὃς δὲ [z] μεθύει.
22 [a] μὴ γὰρ οἰκίας [a] οὐκ ἔχετε [b] εἰς τὸ ἐσθίειν καὶ πίνειν; [c] ἢ τῆς [d] ἐκκλησίας τοῦ [d] θεοῦ [e] καταφρονεῖτε, καὶ [f] καταισχύνετε τοὺς

q Mark vi. 14. Luke viii. 17. Acts vii. 13. ch. iii. 13. xiv. 25. Phil. i. 13. Gen. xlii. 16. 1 Macc. xv. 9.
r ch. xiv. 23.
s Acts i. 15 reff.
t Rev. i. 10 only †.
u John xiii. 2, 4. xxi. 20 al. Dan. i. 16 (v. 1 Theod.) only.
v Mark xiv. 8. Gal. vi. 1 only †. Wisd. xvii. 17 only.
w Acts ix. 3 reff.
x = Matt. xiii. 8. Acts xxvii. 44. Rom. xiv. 5. 2 Cor. ii. 16 al.
y Matt. iv. 2. Rom. xii. 20 (from Prov. xxv. 21) al.
z Acts ii. 15 reff.
a Rom. x. 18, 19. ch. ix. 4, 5 only. P.
b Rom. iv. 11 reff.
c = ch. x. 22.
d ch. i. 2 reff.
e Matt. xviii. 10. Rom. ii. 4 al. Prov. xiii. 13.
f ch. i. 27. vv. 4, 5.

om 2nd εν υμιν C æth Orig_1[ins Delarue from Philocal] Chr_2[ins_7] Epiph_1 Damasc-comm_1 Jer_1.

20. om ουν D^1(and lat) F[not F-lat] Chr_1 : δε 17. for εστιν, ετι D^1[-gr] F(and G-lat) : om D-lat : *jam non est* vulg(and F-lat) [Ambrst]. φαγει ℵ[1].

21. προςλαμβανει A 46. 106-8-22[2]. for εν τω, επι τω D[-gr] F[-gr] : *ad* vulg (and F-lat) E-lat : εις τω (= το) 17, *in manducandum* G-lat : *in manducando* D-lat [Ambrst Aug_1].

22. for εις το εσθ. κ. πιν., φαγειν και πειν F.

[also] (i. e. as well as the other party, who would become manifest by their very conduct) **may be made manifest among you**; viz. through a better and nobler spirit being shewn by them, than by the contentious and separatists. **20.**] The same subject—resumed from the συνερχ. of ver. 18: see notes on πρῶτον. **When then ye come together** (*are assembling*, pres. and perhaps here, where he deals with particulars, to be pressed,—as their *intention* in thus assembling is blamed) **to one place** (reff. Acts) **it is not to eat** (*with any idea of eating* [or, **there is no eating**]. But Meyer, Bengel, and many others, render οὐκ ἔστιν here, '*non licet*,' as in οὐκ ἔστιν εἰπεῖν and the like: De Wette, after Estius, al., as E. V., '*this is not*,' 'cannot be called,'—'*id quod agitis, non est*.' But the greediness which is blamed, seems to refer οὐκ ἔστιν to the συνέρχεσθαι, and φαγεῖν to the motive = ἵνα φαγῆτε) **the Supper of the Lord** (emphasis on κυριακόν, as opposed to ἴδιον below). **κυρ. δεῖπν.**] '*the Supper instituted by the Lord*.' This was an inseparable adjunct, in the apostolic times, to their agapæ or feasts of love. Chrys. on ver. 17, and Tertull. Apol. § 39, vol. i. pp. 474 ff., give an ample description of these feasts, which were of the nature of ἔρανοι, or mutual contributions, where each who was able brought his own portion,—and the rich, additional portions for the poor. See Xen. Mem. iii. 14, in which the circumstances bear a remarkable similarity to those in the Corinthian church. Not *before* this feast, as Chrys. (μετὰ τὴν τῶν μυστηρίων κοινωνίαν ἐπὶ κοινὴν πάντες ᾔεσαν εὐωχίαν, p. 240), al.,—but *during* and *after* it, as shewn by the institution, by the custom at the Passover, by the context here, and by the remnants of the ancient custom and its abuse until forbidden by the council of Carthage,—the ancient Christians partook of the Supper of the Lord. The best account of this matter is to be found in the note in Pool's Synopsis on Matt. xxvi. 26. It was necessary for the celebration of the Lord's Supper that all should eat of the same bread and drink of the same cup; and in all probability, that a prayer should be offered, and words of consecration said, by the appointed ministers. Hence cessation of the feast itself, and solemn order and silence, would be necessitated even by the outward requirements of the ordinance. These could not be obtained, where each man was greedily devouring that which he had brought with him: where the extremes were seen, of one craving, and another being drunken. This being their practice, there could be [no possibility, and at the same time] *no intention* of celebrating the *Lord's* Supper,—no [provision for it, nor] discernment of the solemnity of it. On the whole subject, see Stanley's note.

21.] **προλ.**, as in E. V., **takes before another**, viz. during the feast (ἐν τῷ φ.), not, *at home*, before coming. Obviously the ἕκαστος must be limited to the *rich*: the poor had no ἴδιον δεῖπνον to take, and were the losers by the selfishness of the rich. **πεινᾷ**] **one is craving** (the poor), **another is drunken** (the rich. There is no need to soften the meaning of μεθύει: as Meyer says, "Paul draws the picture in strong colours, and who can say that the reality was less strong?").

22.] **For** (a reason for the blame in the foregoing: this should not be: for) **have you no houses, to eat, &c.**: meaning, '*at home* is the place to satiate the appetite, *not the assembly of the brethren*.' **Or do ye shew your contempt for** (pres.) **the**

g = Luke iii. 11. xxii. 36. Neh. viii. 10 (?). h ver. 2. i = ch. xv. 1, 3. Gal. i. 9, 12 al. j = ver. 2 reff. k = Rom. iv. 25 reff. Gospp. passim. l absol., Luke xxii. 19. Rom. i. (8 reff.) 21. ch. xiv. 17 al. + Wisd. xviii. 2 only. m Acts ii. 46 reff. n = ‖ Mt. Mk. L. Matt. xiii. 37. John xv. 1. ch. x. 4. Gen. xii. 26, 27. Exod. xii. 11. Ezek. xxxvii. 11. o ellips., here only? p = Matt. viii. 34. Mark i. 4. xiv. 9. q here bis. ‖ L. Heb. x. 3 only. Lev. xxiv. 7. r ‖ L. Matt. xxi. 30. Luke xx. 31. Rom. viii. 26. Prov. xxvii. 15.

ABCDF KLPℵ acdef ghklm o 17. 47

[g] μὴ ἔχοντας; τί εἴπω ὑμῖν; [h] ἐπαινέσω ὑμᾶς ἐν τούτῳ;
οὐκ [h] ἐπαινῶ.
23 ἐγὼ γὰρ [i] παρέλαβον ἀπὸ τοῦ κυρίου
ὃ καὶ [j] παρέδωκα ὑμῖν, ὅτι ὁ κύριος Ἰησοῦς ἐν τῇ νυκτὶ
ᾗ [k] παρεδίδετο ἔλαβεν ἄρτον,
24 καὶ [l] εὐχαριστήσας [m] ἔκλα-
σεν καὶ εἶπεν Τοῦτό μου [n] ἐστὶν τὸ σῶμα τὸ [o] ὑπὲρ
ὑμῶν· τοῦτο ποιεῖτε [p] εἰς τὴν ἐμὴν [q] ἀνάμνησιν.
25 [r] ὡς-

rec υμιν bef ειπω, with KL rel syr [arm-mss] Thdrt: om υμιν P æth-pl arm-ed: txt ABCDFℵ m 17 vulg Syr coptt goth [Bas$_1$ Cyr-p$_1$] Damasc lat-ff. for επαινεσω, επαινω (*conformation to the* pres *follg*) BF latt lat-ff: txt AC D[-gr] KLPℵ rel vss Chr$_1$ [Bas$_1$ Cyr$_1$ Euthal-ms] Thdrt Damasc.

23. for απο, παρα D [Bas-2-mss$_1$]. om του DF. for κυριου, θεου F(with G-lat, but not F-lat). om ιησους B 44. εν η νυκτι παρεδ. D^{1}F, *in qua nocte* latt [Cypr Ambrst]. rec παρεδιδοτο, with B^{2}LP rel Chr$_1$ Thdrt [Bas$_1$ Euthal-ms Damasc$_1$]: txt AB^{1}CDFKℵ [17] Damasc[h.l.]. ins τον bef αρτον D^{1}F.

24. rec aft ειπεν adds λαβετε φαγετε (*interpoln from Matt* xxvi. 26), with C^{3}KLP rel syrr goth [æth-pl] (Cyr-jer$_1$) Chr$_4$ [Euthal-ms] Thdrt Damasc Thl Œc, λ. και φ. vulg [demid harl tol] arm[-usc] Ambrst; λαβετε (alone) æth[-rom]: om ABC^{1}DFℵ 17 am(with fuld al) coptt arm(ed-1805) Bas$_1$ Cyr$_1$ (Ath$_1$) Cypr$_1$. rec aft υπερ υμων ins κλωμενον, with C^{3}D^{3}FKLPℵ^3 rel syrr goth [Bas$_1$ Chr$_3$ Euthal-ms] Thdrt$_{h.l.}$(elsw$_2$ διδομενον η κλωμενον κατα τον αποστ.) Damasc$_2$ Thl Œc; θρυπτομενον D^1; διδομενον coptt; *quod pro vobis tradetur* vulg Cypr$_1$ Ambrst-ed: om ABC^{1}ℵ^1 17. 67^2 [arm-zoh] Cyr$_1$ Ath$_1$ Fulg$_1$. om την F.

congregation of God (θεοῦ to express, as Bengel, 'dignitatem ecclesiæ.' This contempt was expressed by their *not sharing* with the congregation the portion which they brought),—**and put to shame those who have not** (houses to eat and to drink in, and therefore come to the daily ἀγάπαι to be fed. There is no reason for rendering with the majority of Commentators τοὺς μὴ ἔχοντας, 'the *poor;*' the μὴ ἔχοντας has a distinct reference to the ἔχετε before. Meyer refers in support of the meaning, 'the poor,' to Wetst. on 2 Cor. viii. 13, where nothing on the subject is found: De Wette, to Luke iii. 11, where the case is as here, the preceding ἔχων being referred to. The meaning is *allowable*, e. g. πρὸς γὰρ **τὸν ἔχονθ'** ὁ φθόνος ἕρπει, Soph. Aj. 157: πρὸς τῶν ἐχόντων, Φοῖβε, τὸν νόμον τίθης, Eurip. Alc. 57: πότε μὲν ἐπ' ἦμαρ εἶχον, εἶτ' οὐκ εἶχον ἄν, where however it is qualified by ἐπ' ἦμαρ)? **What must I say to you? Shall I praise you in this matter? I praise you not.** (See ver. 17.) 23—25.] To shew them the solemnity of the ordinance which they thus set at nought, *he reminds them of the account which he had before given them, of its* INSTITUTION BY THE LORD. MATT. xxvi. 26—29. MARK xiv. 22—25. LUKE xxii. 19, 20. 23.] **For I** (see ch. vii. 28; Phil. iv. 11) **received**
* **from the Lord** (*by special revelation*, see Gal. i. 12. Meyer attempts to deny that this revelation was made to Paul himself, on the strength of ἀπό meaning '*indirect*,' παρά '*direct*' reception from any one: but this distinction is fallacious: e. g. 1 John i. 5, αὕτη ἐστὶν ἡ ἐπαγγελία ἣν ἀκηκόαμεν ἀπ' αὐτοῦ. He supposes that it was made to Ananias or some other, and communicated to Paul. But the sole reason for this somewhat clumsy hypothesis is the supposed force of the preposition, which has no existence. If the Apostle had referred only to the Evangelic tradition or writings (?) he would not have used the first person *singular*, but παρελάβομεν. I may remark, that the similarity between this account of the Institution and that in Luke's Gospel, is only what might be expected on the supposition of a special revelation made to Paul, of which that Evangelist, being Paul's companion, in certain parts of his history availed himself) **that which I also delivered** (in my apostolic testimony) **to you,** (viz.) **that the Lord Jesus, &c.** **παρεδίδετο**] the imperf.: **He was being betrayed.** "There is an appearance of fixed order, especially in these opening words, which indicates that this had already become a familiar formula." Stanley. **ἄρτον**] not, as Meyer, '*a loaf*,' but **bread**: cf. the common expression, φαγεῖν ἄρτον. 24.] On **εὐχ. ἔκλασεν**, see note, Matt. xxvi. 26. Meyer well remarks, that "the filling up of τὸ ὑπὲρ ὑμῶν is to be sought in the foregoing ἔκλασεν." Hence the insertion of κλώμε-

αὕτως καὶ τὸ ποτήριον μετὰ τὸ [s] δειπνῆσαι, λέγων Τοῦτο
τὸ ποτήριον ἡ [t] καινὴ [t] διαθήκη ἐστὶν [u] ἐν τῷ ἐμῷ αἵματι·
τοῦτο ποιεῖτε, [v] ὁσάκις ἐὰν πίνητε, [p] εἰς τὴν ἐμὴν [q] ἀνάμνησιν. 26 [v] ὁσάκις γὰρ ἐὰν ἐσθίητε τὸν ἄρτον τοῦτον, καὶ
τὸ ποτήριον πίνητε, τὸν θάνατον τοῦ κυρίου [w] καταγγέλλετε, [x] ἄχρις οὗ ἔλθῃ. 27 ὥστε ὃς ἂν ἐσθίῃ τὸν ἄρτον ἢ
πίνῃ τὸ [y] ποτήριον τοῦ [y] κυρίου [z] ἀναξίως, [a] ἔνοχος ἔσται

b ενοχος ...

ABCDF KLPℵ abcde fghkl mo 17. 47

s || L. Luke xvii. 8 Rev. iii. 20 only. Prov. xxiii. 1. Tobit viii. 1 (not ℵ) only.
t ||. 2 Cor. iii. 6. Heb. viii. 8 (from Jer. xxxviii. [xxxi.] 31). ix. 15.
u = Heb. ix. 22, 25. x. 19. 1 John v. 6. Zech. ix. 11.
v here bis. Rev. xi. 6 only †. Xen. Mem. iii. 4. 3.
w = Acts xiii. 5 reff.
x constr., Rom. xi. 25. Gal. iii. 19 al.
y ch. x. 21.
z here only †. 2 Macc. xiv. 42 only. (-ιος, ch. vi. 2.)
a = and constr., Mark iii. 29. xiv. 64 || Mt. Heb. ii. 15. James ii. 10. (Matt. v. 21, 22 [3ce]) only. (Deut. xix. 10.)

25. for *εμω αιματι*, *αιματι μου* ACP m 17: txt BDFKLPℵ rel. homœotel in A, *οσακις* here and at beg of next ver. rec (for *εαν*) *αν*, with DFKL rel Chr$_1$ Cyr[-p$_1$ Nest-in-Cyr$_1$]: txt BCℵ 17 Orig$_1$ Thdrt Euthal-ms$_1$. (om *οσακις αν πινητε* P[appy] a d m [Bas$_1$ Euthal-ms$_1$ Damasc$_1$].)

26. om *γαρ* A (*cf homœotel above*) 238 goth æth arm. rec *αν*, with DFKLP rel: txt ABCℵ a 17. for *τουτον*, *τουτο* ℵ^1. rec aft *ποτηριον* ins *τουτο* (*for uniformity*), with [C^3]D$^{2\cdot3}$KLPℵ^3 rel tol syrr copt goth æth Chr$_1$ [Bas$_1$ Nest-in-Cyr$_1$] Thdrt Damasc$_1$ [Phot-c$_1$] Cypr$_1$: om ABC^{1}D^{1}Fℵ^1 c 17 latt sah arm Cyr$_1$ Damasc$_1$ Cypr$_1$ Ambrst Pel. *αχρι* B^{1}ℵ^1. rec aft *αχρις ου* ins *αν* (*to fill up the constr*), with D^{3}KLPℵ^3 [47(sic)] rel Thdrt: om ABCD^{1}Fℵ^1 17 Bas^I Chr-ms Cyr$_1$ Damasc.

27. *αισθειηται* and *πινηται* F. rec aft *τον αρτον* ins *τουτον* (*supplementary, or as above*), with KLP rel [vulg-clem] copt goth æth arm-mss Chr$_1$ [Euthal-ms]: om ABCDFℵ o 17 am(with demid fuld harl tol mar) [Syr] syr sah arm-ed Clem$_1$ Bas$_1$ Ps-Ath$_1$ Thdrt Damasc$_2$ Orig-int$_1$ Cypr$_4$ [Cassiod$_1$]. for *η*, *και* A 39. 46. 109 lect-1 syrr coptt æth Clem$_1$ Ps-Ath$_1$ Orig-int$_1$ Pel Cassiod$_1$: txt BCDFKLPℵ rel latt syr-mg goth Chr [Euthal-ms] Thdrt Damasc$_2$ Cypr$_4$ [Ambrst]. aft *του κυριου αναξιως* add *του κυριου* D^3[-gr] Lℵ e 47^1 syr goth.

νον. **τοῦτο ποι. . . .**] See note on Matt. ut supra. **25.**] See Luke xxii. 20. **ὡσαύτ. καὶ τὸ π.**] "viz. ἔλαβεν καὶ εὐχ. ἔδωκεν αὐτοῖς. These last words are implied in ἔκλασεν above." Meyer. **ἡ καιν. δ. ἐστὶν ἐν τῷ ἐμῷ αἵμ.**] **is the new covenant in** (ratified by the shedding of, and therefore *standing in*, as its conditioning element) **my blood:** = ἐστὶν ἡ καιν. δ. ἡ ἐν τῷ ἐμῷ αἵμ. The position of ἐστιν is no objection to this, nor the omission of the art. Meyer would render it, '*is the N. C. by means of my blood:*' i.e. by virtue of its contents, which are my blood: and this solely on account of the position of ἐστιν. But the meaning is as harsh, as the rendering is unrequired. **ὁσάκις ἐὰν πίν.**] Not a *general* rule for all common meals of Christians; but a precept that as often as *that cup* is drunk, it should be *in remembrance of Him:* on these last words is the emphasis: see below. **26.**] **γάρ** gives an explanatory reason for εἰς τ. ἐμὴν ἀνάμν., viz. that the act of eating and drinking is a *proclamation of the death of the Lord till His coming*. The rendering of καταγγέλλετε *imperative*, as Theophyl.?, Luth., Grot., Rückert, is evidently wrong. The Apostle is substantiating the application of the Lord's words by the acknowledged nature of the rite. It is a *proclamation of His death:* and thus is a *remembrance of Him.* It is so, by our making mention of in it, and seeing visibly before us and partaking of, *His body broken, and His blood shed.* **ἄχρις οὗ ἔλθῃ**] The καταγγ. is addressed *directly to the Corinthians*, not *to them and all succeeding Christians;* the Apostle regarding the coming of the Lord as near at hand, in *his own* time, see notes on 2 Cor. v. 1—10. Thdrt. remarks, μετὰ γὰρ τὴν αὐτοῦ παρουσίαν, οὐκέτι χρεία τῶν συμβόλων τοῦ σώματος, αὐτοῦ φαινομένου τοῦ σώματος· διὰ τοῦτο εἶπεν, ἄχρις οὗ (ἂν) ἔλθῃ.

The ἄν has been inserted from not being aware that its absence implies the *certainty* of the event. See examples in Lobeck on Phrynichus, pp. 15, 16, note.

27.] A *consequence*, from the nature of the ordinance being, *to proclaim the death of the Lord: the guilt of the unworthy participation of either of the elements.* The death of the Lord was brought about by the breaking of His body and shedding His blood: this Death we proclaim in the ordinance by the bread broken—the wine poured out, of which we partake: whoever therefore shall *either* eat the bread *or* drink the cup of the Lord unworthily (see below ver. 29) shall be guilty of the Body and Blood of the Lord: i. e. "*crimini et pœnæ corporis et sanguinis Christi violati obnoxius erit:*" Meyer. Such an one proclaims the death of Christ, and yet *in an*

b see ch. x. 16. c = ch. iii. 13 reff. d = ch. iv. 1. Gal. vi. 1. e = Rom. v. 12 reff. f = Rom. ii. 2, 3 reff. g Acts xv. 9. James ii. 4. Job xii. 11.

τοῦ [b] σώματος καὶ τοῦ [b] αἵματος τοῦ [b] κυρίου. 28 [c] δοκιμαζέτω δὲ [d] ἄνθρωπος ἑαυτόν, καὶ [e] οὕτως ἐκ τοῦ ἄρτου
ἐσθιέτω καὶ ἐκ τοῦ ποτηρίου πινέτω· 29 ὁ γὰρ ἐσθίων καὶ
πίνων [f] κρῖμα ἑαυτῷ ἐσθίει καὶ πίνει μὴ [g] διακρίνων τὸ
σῶμα. 30 διὰ τοῦτο ἐν ὑμῖν πολλοὶ ἀσθενεῖς καὶ [h] ἄῤῥω-

ABCDF KLPℵ a b c d e f g h k l m o 17. 47

h Matt. xiv. 14. Mark vi. 5, 13. xvi. 18 only. 3 Kings xiv. 5 A, Ald. &c. (see xii. 24 sq. B). Mal. i. 8. Sir. vii. 35 only. (-τεῖν, 2 Kings xii. 15. -τημα, Sir. x. 10. -τία, Ps. xl. 3.)

rec om *του* (bef *αιματος*) (*as unnecessary?*), with a^1 d h k 47[sic] Thl: ins ABCDFKLPℵ rel Clem Ps-Ath$_1$ Bas$_1$ Chr$_1$ Thdrt [Euthal-ms Damasc]. for *κυριου*, *χριστου* A 17 æth-rom Jer$_1$.

28. *εαυτον* bef *ανθρωπος* CDFP latt goth Damasc: *εαυτον εκαστος* 17, simly 4 Orig: txt ABKLℵ rel syrr (coptt) æth arm Clem$_1$ Orig$_1$ Cyr$_1$ [Bas$_1$ Thdrt Damasc$_{h.l.}$].—ins *ο* bef *ανθρ.* D^1. aft *εαυτ.* ins *πρωτον* ℵ^3 [Epiph$_1$].

29. rec aft *πινων* ins *αναξιως* (*gloss from ver* 27), with C^{3}DFKLPℵ^3 rel vulg syrr [copt goth æth-pl arm Bas$_4$ Chr$_3$(*αναξ. τ. κυρ.*$_3$) Euthal-ms Thdrt Damasc$_2$ Ambrst]: om ABC^{1}ℵ^1 17 sah æth-rom. rec aft *το σωμα* ins *του κυριου* (*gloss from ver* 27), with C^{3}DFKLPℵ^3 rel [vulg-clem am^2 demid fuld^2 harl^2 tol syrr copt goth arm Bas$_2$ Euthal-ms Damasc$_2$] Chr$_1$ Thdrt Ambrst: om ABC^{1}ℵ^1 17. 67^2 am^1(with fuld^1 harl^1) sah æth.

unworthy spirit—with no regard to that Death as *his* atonement, or a proof of Christ's love: he proclaims that Death *as an indifferent person*: he therefore *partakes of the guilt of it*. Chrysostom strikingly says, σφαγὴν τὸ πρᾶγμα ἀπέφηνεν, οὐκέτι θυσίαν, p. 247. But the idea ὡς καὶ αὐτὸς ἐκχέας τὸ αἷμα, Theophyl. (and Chrys., τί δήποτε; ὅτι ἐξέχεεν αὐτό, καὶ σφαγ., &c., as above), is irrelevant here, see ver. 29. The Romanists absurdly enough defend by this ἤ (the meaning of which is not to be changed to καί, as is *most unfairly* done in our E. V., and the completeness of the argument thereby destroyed) their practice of *communicating only in one kind*. Translated into *common language*, and applied to the ordinary sustenance of the body, their reasoning stands thus: 'Whoever eats to excess, *or* drinks to excess, is guilty of sin: *therefore* eating, without drinking, will sustain life.'

28.] The **δέ** implies an opposition to, and wish to escape from, the ἔνοχος ἔσται.

δοκιμ. ἑαυτ.] **prove himself**—examine τὴν διάνοιαν ἑαυτοῦ, as Theodor.-mops., in loc.: ascertain by sufficient tests, what his state of feeling is with regard to the death of Christ, and how far this feeling is evinced in his daily life—which are the best guarantees for a worthy participation. **καὶ οὕτως**] i. e. '*after examination of himself*.' The case in which the self-examination ends in an *unfavourable* verdict, does not come under consideration, because it is assumed that such a verdict will lead to repentance and amendment. **29.**] **For he who eats and drinks** (scil. of the bread and of the cup: certainly not, as Meyer, 'the *mere eater and drinker*, he who partakes as a mere act of eating and drinking,' which is harsh to the last degree, and refuted by the parallel, ver. 27. ἀναξίως is spurious, see var. readd.) **eats and drinks judgment to himself** (i. e. brings on himself judgment by eating and drinking. κρῖμα, as is evident by vv. 30—32, is not '*damnation*' (κατάκριμα), as rendered in our E. V., a mistranslation, which has done infinite mischief), **not appreciating** (*dijudicans*, Vulg. μὴ ἐξετάζων, μὴ ἐννοῶν ὡς χρή, τὸ μέγεθος τῶν προκειμένων, μὴ λογιζόμενος τὸν ὄγκον τῆς δωρεᾶς. Chrys. Hom. xxviii. p. 251) **the Body** (scil. of the Lord: here standing for the *whole* of that which is symbolized by the Bread and the Cup, *the Body and Blood*. The mystery of these, spiritually present in the elements, he, not being spiritual, *does not appreciate*: and therefore, as in ver. 27, falls under the divine judgment, as trifling with the death of Christ. The interpretation of Stanley, "not discerning that the body of the Lord is in himself and in the Christian society, and that it is as the body of the Lord, or as a member of that body, that he partakes of the bread," is surely somewhat far-fetched, after τοῦτό μου ἐστὶν τὸ σῶμα, ver. 24). **30.**] Experimental proof of the κρῖμα ἑαυτῷ, from the present sicknesses and frequent deaths among the Corinthian believers. Meyer distinguishes **ἀσθενεῖς**, *weaklings*, persons whose powers have failed spontaneously, from **ἄῤῥωστοι**, *invalids*, persons whose powers are enfeebled by sickness; and cites Tittmann, Synon. p. 76. **ἀσθ.** and **ἀῤῥ.** refer to *physical*, not (as Olsh., altern.) *moral* weaknesses. **31.**] **δέ** contrasts with this state of sicknesses and deaths: *it might be otherwise*. This **διεκρινόμεθα** (parallel with δοκιμαζέτω before) should be rendered by the *same word* as **διακρίνων**

στοι, καὶ [i] κοιμῶνται [k] ἱκανοί. 31 εἰ δὲ [l] ἑαυτοὺς [g] διεκρί-
νομεν, οὐκ ἂν [m] ἐκρινόμεθα· 32 [m] κρινόμενοι δὲ ὑπὸ [τοῦ]
κυρίου [n] παιδευόμεθα, ἵνα μὴ σὺν τῷ κόσμῳ [o] κατακριθῶ-
μεν. 33 [p] ὥςτε, ἀδελφοί μου, [q] συνερχόμενοι [r] εἰς τὸ φαγεῖν
ἀλλήλους [s] ἐκδέχεσθε. 34 εἴ τις [t] πεινᾷ, [u] ἐν [u] οἴκῳ ἐσθιέτω,
ἵνα μὴ [v] εἰς [w] κρῖμα [q] συνέρχησθε. τὰ δὲ λοιπὰ [x] ὡς ἂν
ἔλθω [y] διατάξομαι.

XII. 1 Περὶ δὲ τῶν [z] πνευματικῶν, ἀδελφοί, [a] οὐ θέλω

i = ch. vii. 39 reff. k = Acts xii. 12 reff. l 1st pers., Rom. viii. 23 reff. m = Acts xiii. 27. Rev. xviii. 8 al. n Luke xxiii. 16. Heb. xii. 7, 10. L.P.H., exc. Rev. iii. 19. 2 Chron. x. 11. Prov. xix. 18. o Matt. xxvii. 3. [John viii. 10.] Rom. ii. 1. Esth. ii. 1. p = ch. v. 8 reff. q ver. 17. r ver. 22. s Acts xvii. 16 reff. ‡ t ver. 21. u anarth., ch. xiv. 35. Deut. xi. 19. see Mark ii. 1. v ver. 17 reff. w ver. 29. x = Rom. xv. 24. Phil. ii. 23. y = ch. xvi. 1 reff. z = ch. x. 3, 4 reff. a Rom. i. 13. xi. 25. ch. x. 1. 2 Cor. i. 8. 1 Thess. iv. 13.

31. rec (for δε) γαρ, with CKLPא^3 rel syrr coptt arm Chr[$_{\text{sæpe}}$ Bas$_1$ Cyr$_1$ Euthal-ms Damasc$_2$] Thdrt Aug$_{[\text{alic}]}$: txt ABDFא^1 17 vulg goth æth Clem$_1$ Aug$_1$. εαυτον F(not G).

32. απο F. ins του bef κυριου BCא m 17 Clem$_1$ Damasc-txt: om ADFKLP rel Cæs$_1$ Chr$_2$ [Bas$_{\text{alic}}$ Cyr$_1$ Euthal-ms] Thdrt Damasc$_1$ Thl Œc. aft τω κοσμω ins τουτω F, simly latt lat-ff.

34. rec aft ει ins δε, with D$^{2\cdot3}$[-gr] KLPא^3 rel demid syrr arm Clem$_1$ [Chr$_2$] Thdrt Damasc Bede: om ABCD^{1}Fא^1 17 latt coptt æth [Euthal-ms] Cypr$_1$ Ambrst Pel. κρισιν K. διαταξωμαι ADF m 47.

Chap. XII. **1.** αγνοειν bef αδελφοι ου θ. υ. D^1[^{3}(Tischdf)] F latt æth [Did$_1$ Ath-int$_1$ Ambrst].

before, the idea being the same. '*Appreciate,*' if etymologically understood, is the nearest to the meaning: in Latin *dijudico*, which the Vulg. has, is an excellent rendering,—preserving also the 'judico,' so essential to the following clause. In the E. V. '*If we would judge ourselves, we should* * *not be judged,*' the tenses are wrong: it should be, '*If we had judged ourselves, we should not have been judged:*' 'no such punishments would have befallen us.' Thus I wrote in some former editions: and so also Stanley. But this collocation of the (imperfect) tenses may be rendered either way. Donaldson, Gr. Gr., p. 204, renders εἴ τι εἶχεν, ἐδίδου ἄν, '*si quid haberet, daret:*' and so we have it in Æschyl. Suppl. 244, καὶ τἄλλα πόλλ' ἐπεικάσαι δίκαιον ἦν, εἰ μὴ παρόντι φθόγγος ἦν ὁ σημανῶν: Æschin. Ctes. p. 86, εἰ δ' ἦν ἀναγκαῖον ῥηθῆναι, οὐ Δημοσθένους ἦν ὁ λόγος: and other places (Bernhardy, p. 376). But as certainly, we find the other sense: e. g. Herod. iii. 25, of Cambyses, εἰ . . . ἀπῆγε ὀπίσω τὸν στρατὸν . . . ἦν ἂν σοφὸς ἀνήρ. So that the E. V. may *here* be kept, if thought desirable. In John v. 46, our translators have adopted the other rendering: 'Had ye believed Moses, ye would have believed me:' but in ib. viii. 39, 42, have rendered as here.

32.] **But now that we are judged, it is by the Lord** (emph.) **that we are being chastised** (to bring us to repentance), **that we may not be** (eternally) **condemned with the** (unbelieving) **world.**

33.] *General conclusion respecting this disorder.* **So then** ('quæ cum ita sint'), **my brethren** (milder persuasive: as has been the assumption of the first person, vv. 31, 32), **when ye are coming together to eat, wait for one another** (contrast to ἕκαστος . . . . προλαμβάνει, ver. 21: as Theophyl.: οὐκ εἶπεν, ἀλλήλοις μετάδοτε, ἀλλ', ἐκδέχεσθε· δεικνύων ὅτι κοινά εἰσι τὰ ἐκεῖσε εἰσφερόμενα. καὶ δεῖ ἀναμένειν τὴν κοινὴν συνέλευσιν).

34.] The ἀγάπαι were not meals to satiate the bodily appetites, but for a higher and holier purpose: let the hungry take off the edge of his hunger at home: see ver. 22. **τὰ δὲ λοιπά**] viz. *things omitted* (probably matters of detail) *in the above directions.* Perhaps they had asked him questions respecting the most convenient time or manner of celebration of the Lord's supper: points on which primitive practice widely differed. **ὡς ἂν ἔλθω,** see reff., **whenever I shall have come.** ὡς ἄν, as ὅτ' ἄν, implies uncertainty as to the event anticipated: see Kühner, vol. ii. p. 535, § 807.

Chapp. XII.—XIV.] On the abuse of Spiritual Gifts: especially prophesying, and speaking with tongues. The *second particular requiring correction in their assemblies,* see ch. xi. 18, note. Chrys. well says: τοῦτο ἅπαν τὸ χωρίον σφόδρα ἐστὶν ἀσαφές· τὴν δὲ ἀσάφειαν ἡ τῶν πραγμάτων ἄγνοιά τε καὶ ἔλλειψις ποιεῖ τῶν τότε μὲν συμβαινόντων, νῦν δὲ οὐ γινομένων. Hom. xxix. p. 257.

XII.] On the nature,

b ch. x. 19 reff. c Acts viii. 32 reff. d = Mark vi. 56. Acts ii. 45. iv. 35. Gen. ii. 19. e Matt. xxvi. 57 al. Epp., here only. Deut. xxviii. 37.

ABCDF KLPℵ abcde fghkl mo 17. 47

ὑμᾶς [a] ἀγνοεῖν. 2 οἴδατε ὅτι ὅτε ἔθνη ἦτε, πρὸς τὰ
[b] εἴδωλα τὰ [c] ἄφωνα ὡς [d] ἂν ἤγεσθε [e] ἀπαγόμενοι. 3 διὸ

2. rec om οτε (*either a mistake, or a corrn to help the constr: the same of the omn of* οτι), with F[-gr K-marg(Tischdf)] b d l D-lat Syr copt Ambrst: om οτι K[1] m Thdrt[-ed Euthal-ms] Damasc Aug_2: txt ABC D[-gr] LPℵ rel vulg G-lat syr (sah) arm [æth(*olim cum*) Bas_1 Did_1 Chr_2 Thdrt-ms $Ath\text{-}int_1$ Vig_1 Pel]. for αφωνα, αμορφα F[-gr, *ad simulacrorum formationes* G-lat]. (ἀνήγεσθε B[2] G[-corr(appy, Tischdf)] m: *ascendebatis* Aug.)

INTENT, AND WORTH OF SPIRITUAL GIFTS IN GENERAL. 1—3.] *The foundation of all spiritual utterance is the confession of Jesus as the Lord:* and *without the Spirit, no such confession can be made.* 1.] **δέ** transitional. Some have thought that the Corinthians had referred this question to the Apostle's decision: but from the οὐ θέλω ὑμ. ἀγνοεῖν, it rather looks as if, like the last, it had been an abuse which he had *heard of,* and *of his own instance corrects.* **τ. πνευματικῶν**] Most likely *neuter,* as ch. xiv. 1, *spiritual gifts:* so Chrys., Theophyl., Œc., Beza, Calov., Est., al., De Wette, and Meyer: —not masc., as ch. xiv. 37: so Grot., Hammond, al., and Locke, who maintains that the subject of this section is not the *things,* but the *persons,* quoting ch. xiv. 5. But surely the *things* are the main subject, enounced here, vv. 4—11, and treated of through the rest of the chapter; the inspired *persons* being mentioned only incidentally to *them.* Others, as Storr, Billroth, Wieseler cited by Meyer, and De W., limit τὰ πν. to the *speaking with tongues,* which indeed is mainly treated of in the latter part of the section (see ch. xiv. 1): but *here* the gifts of the Spirit *generally* are the subject. **οὐ θέλω ὑμ. ἀγν.**] Theodor.-mops. cited by Meyer: θέλω ὑμᾶς καὶ τῶν πνευματικῶν χαρισμάτων εἰδέναι τὴν τάξιν, ὥστε βούλομαί τι καὶ περὶ τούτων εἰπεῖν. See reff. 2.] *Reason why they wanted instruction concerning spiritual gifts*—because *they once were heathen,* and could not therefore have any experience in spiritual things. Thus Meyer, and so far rightly: but the stress of this reason lies in the words ἄφωνα and ὡς ἂν ἤγεσθε, which he has not sufficiently noticed:—**Ye know (that) when ye were Gentiles** (the construction is an anacoluthon, beginning with οἴδατε ὅτι, and then as if οἴδατε ὅτι had been merely a formula for 'ye know,' passing into the construction so common, that of placing ὅτε after such verbs as μέμνημαι, οἶδα, ἀκούω, and the like, an ellipsis taking place of τοῦ χρόνου, as Lysias actually fills it up in one place, ἐκείνου τοῦ χρόνου μνησθέντας, ὅτε . . . . in Poliuch. (περὶ δημεύσεως κ.τ.λ.), p. 151, 34. Thus Il. ξ. 71, ᾔδεα μὲν γὰρ ὅτε πρόφρων Δαναοῖσιν ἄμυνεν: Plato, Menon, p. 79, μέμνησαι ὅτ' ἐγώ σοι ἄρτι ἀπεκρινάμην. See more examples in Kühner's Gr. Gramm. ii. 480) **led about** ([or, **carried away**] ἀπαγ. not necessarily, '*led wrong;*' and the context seems rather to favour the idea of being '*led at will,*' blindly transported hither and thither,—and so De W., and Estius, "qualitercunque, temere, pro nutu ducentium, et huc illuc illos circumagentium, abductos fuisse") **to idols which were without utterance** ('the God in whom you now believe is a living and speaking God—speaking by his Spirit in every believer: how should you know any thing of such spiritual speech or gifts at all, who have been accustomed to *dumb idols?*'), **just as ye happened to be led** (scil., *on each occasion:* the force of ἄν being to indicate the indefiniteness, i. e. in this case, the *repetition* of the act: so Xen. Anab. i. 5. 2: οἱ μὲν ὄνοι, ἐπεί τις διώκοι (whenever any followed them) προδραμόντες ἂν εἱστήκεισαν,—and Eurip. Phœn. 401: ποτὲ μὲν ἐς ἦμαρ εἶχον, εἶτ' οὐκ εἶχον ἄν. See other examples in Kühner, ii. 93, 94). These last words seem to me to imply the absence of all *fixed principle* in the oracles of Heathendom, such as he is about to announce as regulating and furnishing the criterion of the spiritual gifts of Christendom. This ὡς ἂν ἤγεσθε might take a man to *contradictory* oracles, the whole system being an imposture—their idols being void of all power of utterance, and they being therefore imposed on by the fictions of men, or *evil spirits,* who led them. Chrys., Œc., Theophyl., make this refer to the difference between the heathen μάντις, who was possessed by an evil spirit, and therefore εἵλκετο ὑπὸ τοῦ πνεύματος δεδεμένος, οὐδὲν εἰδὼς ὧν λέγει, and the Christian προφήτης,—which however is entirely unwarranted by the context. 3.] *The negative and positive criteria of inspiration by the Spirit of God:* viz. the *rejection,* or *confession,* of *Jesus as the Lord.* **διό,** '*because ye*

[f] γνωρίζω ὑμῖν ὅτι οὐδεὶς [g] ἐν [g] πνεύματι θεοῦ λαλῶν λέγει
[h] Ἀνάθεμα Ἰησοῦς· καὶ οὐδεὶς δύναται εἰπεῖν Κύριος
Ἰησοῦς, εἰ μὴ [g] ἐν [g] πνεύματι ἁγίῳ. 4 [i] διαιρέσεις δὲ [k] χαρισμάτων εἰσίν, τὸ δὲ αὐτὸ πνεῦμα· 5 καὶ [i] διαιρέσεις [l] διακο-
νιῶν εἰσίν, καὶ ὁ αὐτὸς κύριος· 6 καὶ [i] διαιρέσεις [m] ἐνεργη-

f Luke ii. 15. John xv. 15. Acts ii. 28. Rom. ix. 22, 23 al. Ezek. xliv. 23.
g Matt. xxii. 43. Luke ii. 27. iv. 1. Rev. i. 10 al. Mic. iii. 8.
h Rom. ix. 3 reff.
i here (3ce) only. 1 Chron. xxvi. 1. 2 Chron. viii. 14. Ezra vi. 18. (-ρεῖν, ver. 11.)
k = Rom. (v. 15. vi. 23. xi. 29) xii. 6 al.
l Acts i. 17. vi. 1 al.†
m ver. 10 only †.

3. om θεου P. om λαλων D F[-gr Hil$_2$ Victorin$_1$]. (insd by F-lat [vulg spec$_2$ Ambrst] Aug$_{alic.}$) rec ιησουν (*corrn to bring it into government by* λεγει, *whereas it is an* oratio directa), with D[G]KLP rel harl syr-mg-gr sah Orig$_2$ Chr$_1$ Thdrt Damasc Novat$_1$ Hil-ed$_1$: ιησου F 17[2] vulg [spec Ath-int$_1$ Did-int$_1$ Hil-ms Ambrst]: txt ABCℵ 17[1] syrr(appy) copt æth arm Cyr-p$_6$ [Euthal-ms]. rec κυριον ιησουν (*see above*), with D F[-gr] KLP rel syr [copt] arm Ath$_1$[-int$_1$ Bas$_2$(and mss$_1$) Dial-trin$_2$ Epiph$_2$] Mac$_1$ Chr$_2$ Thdrt [Damasc] Orig-int$_5$ Did-int$_1$ [Ambr$_{sæpe}$ Ambrst Aug$_2$] : txt ABCℵ 17 vulg(and F-lat) Syr sah æth Orig$_5$[-int$_1$(but mss vary)] Did-gr$_1$ Bas$_1$ Cyr$_3$ Epiph$_2$ Gennad [Euthal-ms Ambr$_1$ Aug$_1$ Tich$_1$].

4. for δε, δ B [Orig$_1$ Eus$_2$].

5. [om 1st και P.] for και ο, ο δε 17. 41. 73. 115-9 vulg D-lat [F-lat spec] Syr arm Eus$_1$ Ath$_1$[(but mss vary)-int$_1$ Bas$_1$ Chr$_1$] Epiph$_2$ Cyr Iren-int[-mss$_1$] Orig-int$_1$ [Hil$_1$(txt$_1$)] : om ο A[1][(corrd eadem manu, appy) k]: txt is cited by Orig$_1$ Thdrt$_1$ Damasc Œc Iren-int-mss Aug.

have been hitherto in ignorance of the matter.' **ἐν πν. θεοῦ—ἐν πν. ἁγ.**] The Spirit of God, or the Holy Ghost, is the *Power pervading* the speaker, the *Element in which* he speaks. So Schöttgen, on Matt. xxii. 43, quotes from the Rabbis, '*David* saw ברוח הקדש, in the Holy Spirit.' **λαλῶν λέγει**] On the difference of meaning between λαλῶ, 'to *discourse*,' 'to *speak*,' and λέγω, 'to *say*,' the former of the *act* of utterance absolutely, the latter having for its object that which is uttered, see note on John viii. 25. In all the seeming exceptions to this, λαλῶ may be justified as keeping its own meaning of 'to discourse:' we may safely deny that it is ever '*to say*' simply. **ἀνάθ. Ἰησ.**] **Jesus** (not *Christ*, the *Name of office*, itself in some measure the *object of faith*,—but Jesus, the personal Name,—the historical Person whose life was *matter of fact:* the curse, and the confession, are in this way far deeper) **is accursed** (see ref. Rom. note). So κύρ. Ἰησ., **Jesus is Lord** (all that is implied in **κύριος**, being here also implied: and we must not forget that it is the LXX verbum solenne for the Heb. Jehovah). By these last words the influence of the Holy Spirit is widened by the Apostle from the supernatural gifts to which perhaps it had been improperly confined, to the faith and confession of every Christian. It is remarkable that in 1 John iv. 1, 2, where a test to try the spirits is given, the *human* side of this confession is brought out,—Ἰησοῦν χριστὸν ἐν σαρκὶ ἐληλυθότα,—John having to deal with those who denied the reality of the Incarnation. Or also, as Bengel: "Paulus præbet criterium veri contra *gentes:* Johannes, contra *falsos prophetas.*" **4—6.**] **But** (as contrasted to this absolute unity, in ground and principle, of all spiritual influence) **there are varieties** (in reff. 2 Chron. and Ezra, used of the courses or divisions of the priests) **of gifts** (**χαρίσματα** = eminent endowments of individuals, in and by which the Spirit indwelling in them manifested Himself,—the φανέρωσις τοῦ πνεύματος in each man:—and these either *directly bestowed* by the Holy Ghost Himself, as in the case of healing, miracles, tongues, and prophesying, or *previously granted* them by God in their unconverted state, and now *inspired, hallowed, and potentiated* for the work of building up the church,—as in the case of teaching, exhortation, knowledge. Of all these gifts, *faith working by love* was the necessary substratum and condition. See Neander, Pfl. u. Leit. pp. 232 ff.), **but the same Spirit** (as their Bestower,—see the sense filled up in ver. 11) : **5.**] **and there are varieties of ministries** (appointed *services* in the church, in which as their channels of manifestation the χαρίσματα would work), **and the same Lord** (Christ, the Lord of the church, whose it is to appoint all ministrations in it. These διακονίαι must not be narrowed to the *ecclesiastical orders*, but kept commensurate in extent with the gifts which are to find scope by their means, see vv. 7—10) : **and varieties of operations** (effects of divine ἐνέργειαι : not to be limited to *miraculous* effects, but understood again commensurately with the gifts of whose working they are the results), **and the same God. Who works all of them in all persons** (all the χαρίσματα in all who are gifted). Thus

μάτων εἰσίν, καὶ ὁ αὐτὸς θεὸς ὁ [n] ἐνεργῶν [o] τὰ [op] πάντα ἐν
[p] πᾶσιν. 7 ἑκάστῳ δὲ δίδοται ἡ [q] φανέρωσις τοῦ πνεύματος
[r] πρὸς τὸ [s] συμφέρον. 8 [t] ᾧ μὲν γὰρ διὰ τοῦ πνεύματος δίδοται [u] λόγος [vw] σοφίας, [t] ἄλλῳ δὲ [u] λόγος [wx] γνώσεως [y] κατὰ

ABCDF KLPℵ a b c d e f g h k l m o 17. 47

n ver. 11. Rom. vii. 5 reff. o = ch. viii. 6 al. fr. p ch. xv. 25. Eph. i. 23. (Col. iii. 11.) q 2 Cor. iv. 2 only †. r = ch. vi. 5. vii. 35. x. 11 al. s Acts xx. 20 reff. t usage, here only. see Matt. xiii. 4 ‖ Mk. ch. iii. 4. ver. 28. u = and constr., Acts xiii. 26 reff. v = ch. ii. 6 al. w Prov. xxx. (xxiv.) 3. x = 2 Cor. xi. 6 al. y = καθὼς β., ver. 11.

6. rec ο δε αυτος (*corrn to express contrast. It can hardly have been altered to* και ο *to conform to the precedg clause, the first remaining* το δε), with AKLPℵ rel latt syrr sah arm Eus$_1$ Epiph$_2$ Cyr$_1$ [Ath$_1$-int$_1$ Did$_1$ Bas$_2$ Chr$_1$ Orig-int$_1$] Iren-int$_1$ Hil$_3$ [Ambrst Aug$_{alic}$], *deus hic idem est* copt; ο αυτος δε DF: txt BC m Orig$_1$ [Euthal-ms]. rec ins εστι bef θεος, with KLℵ^3 rel (syr) Orig$_1$ Thdrt Damasc; aft ενεργων B [Cyr-ms-p$_1$]; ins χριστος bef θεος c: om ACDFPℵ^1 m 17 latt (Syr) sah arm Eus$_1$ Ath$_1$[-int$_1$ Did$_1$ Epiph$_2$ Euthal-ms] Bas$_2$ Chr$_1$ Thl Iren-int Orig-int Hil. om τα D^1.

8. homœotel αλλω to αλλω next ver K.

we have God the Father, the First Source and Operator of all spiritual influence in all: God the Son, the Ordainer in His Church of all ministries by which this influence may be legitimately brought out for edification: God the Holy Ghost, dwelling and working in the church, and effectuating in each man such measure of His gifts as He sees fit. **7—11.**] *These operations specified in their variety, but again asserted to be the work of one and the same Spirit.* **7.**] **To each individual, however** (the emphasis on **ἑκάστῳ**, as shewing the character of what is to follow, viz. *individual distinction* of gifts. δέ again contrasted with the **ὁ αὐτός** of the last verse; though the workings of *One* God, *One* Lord, *One* Spirit, they are bestowed *variously* on each man), **is given the manifestation of the Spirit** (not, as Meyer, al., the *means of manifesting the Spirit which dwells in him* (gen. obj.): but, as De W., the *manifestation by which the Spirit acts* (gen. subj.); it is a general term including χαρίσματα, διακονίαι, and ἐνεργήματα) **with a view to profit** (with the profit of the whole body as the aim: see reff.).

8—10.] It has been disputed, whether or not any studied arrangement of the gifts of the Spirit is here found. The most recent and best advocates of the two views are Meyer and De Wette. Meyer gives the following arrangement: grounding it mainly on what he believes to be the intentional use of **ἑτέρῳ δέ** as distinguished from **ἄλλῳ δέ**, and pointing out a new category:—I. gifts having reference to *intellectual* power: (1) λόγος σοφίας. (2) λόγος γνώσεως. II. (ἑτέρῳ δέ) gifts, whose condition is *an exalted faith* (Glaubens-heroismus): (1) *faith* itself. (2) *practical* workings of the same, viz. (a) ἰάματα. (b) δυνάμεις. (3) *oral* working of the same, viz. προφητεία. (4) *critical* working of the same, the διάκρισις πνευμάτων. III. gifts having reference to the γλῶσσαι: (1) speaking with tongues: (2) interpretation of tongues. To this De Wette objects, (1) that ᾧ μέν, ἑτέρῳ δέ, ἑτέρῳ δέ, do not stand with any reference to one another, but ἑτέρῳ δέ is in each case opposed to the ἄλλῳ δέ which immediately precedes it, and followed by an ἄλλῳ δέ similarly opposed to it: therefore neither can the one betoken the genus, nor the other the species. (2) If any thing could be relied on as marking a division, it would be the repeated κατὰ τὸ αὐτὸ πν., ἐν τῷ αὐτ. πν., and the concluding πάντα δὲ ταῦτα ver. 11: but even thus we get no satisfactory partition, for in ver. 10 dissimilar gifts are classed together. (3) We must not look for a classification, for the catalogue is incomplete, see ver. 28. (4) The classification given is objectionable. Speaking with tongues is plainly more nearly allied to προφητεία than προφ. to gifts of healing: and the two, tongues and prophesying, are subsequently treated of *together*. Besides which, Kling (Stud. u. Krit. 1839, p. 482) rightly remarks, that both διάκρισις πν. and ἑρμηνεία γλ. have reference to the *understanding*. I am inclined to think that De W.'s objections are valid, as applied to a rigorous arrangement like Meyer's; but that at the same time there is a *sort of arrangement*, brought about not so much designedly, as by the falling together of similar terms,—λόγος σοφ., λόγος γν.,—γένη γλωσσῶν, ἑρμ. γλωσσῶν. Unquestionably, any arrangement must be at fault, which proceeding on *psychological* grounds, classes together the *speaking* with tongues and the *interpretation* of tongues: the *working of miracles*, and the *discernment of spirits*. I believe too that Meyer's distinction between ἑτέρῳ δέ and ἄλλῳ δέ is imaginary: see Matt. xvi. 14; Heb. xi. 35, 36. **8.**] **γάρ** appeals to *matter of fact*, as the ground of the assertion in ver. 7, both as to the δίδοται and as to the πρὸς τὸ συμφέρον. **ᾧ μὲν . . . ἄλλῳ δέ**, a loose construction, as in ver. 28.

τὸ αὐτὸ πνεῦμα, 9 [t] ἑτέρῳ [δὲ] πίστις [z] ἐν τῷ [a] αὐτῷ [z] πνεύματι, ἄλλῳ δὲ [b] χαρίσματα [c] ἰαμάτων [z] ἐν τῷ [a] ἑνὶ [z] πνεύματι,
10 ἄλλῳ δὲ [d] ἐνεργήματα [e] δυνάμεων, ἄλλῳ δὲ [f] προφητεία,
ἄλλῳ δὲ [g] διακρίσεις [h] πνευμάτων, ἑτέρῳ δὲ [i] γένη [k] γλωσ-

z ver. 3.
a see ver. 11.
b ver. 4.
c vv. 28, 30 only. Jer. xl. [xxxiii.] 6. (ἴασις, Acts iv. 22.)
d ver. 6 only †.
e = Acts viii. 13 reff.
f = Rom. xii. 6. ch. xiii. 2 al.
g Rom. xiv. 1. Heb. v. 14 only. Job xxxvii. 16 only. (-κρίνειν, ch. vi. 5.)
h = ch. xiv. 32. 1 Tim. iv. 1. 1 John iv. 1. 3 Kings xxii. 21.
i = Matt. xiii. 47. Mark ix. 29 [‖ Mt.]. ver. 28. ch. xiv. 10 only. (Acts iv. 6 al.) Gen. i. 11, &c.
k Acts ii. 4 reff.

9. om 1st δε BD^{1}Fℵ^1 [47] latt Syr [arm(ut sæpe, Treg)] Clem$_1$ Orig$_3$[-c$_1$-int$_1$] Eus$_2$ [Did-int$_1$ Hil$_2$ Ambrst Aug$_{alic}$] : ins AC D$^{2\cdot3}$[-gr] LPℵ^3 rel syr coptt Orig$_2$ Eus$_2$ Cæs$_1$ Cyr-jer$_2$ Chr$_1$ Thdrt$_4$ (Did$_1$[-int$_1$]) Damasc Thl$_1$ Hil$_1$ Aug$_1$. om 2nd δε DF latt Syr [arm] Eus$_2$ [Hil$_1$]. rec for ενι, αυτω (*conformation to foregoing*), with C^3 D[-gr] F[-gr] KLPℵ rel (syrr) copt Clem [Cyr-jer$_1$ Bas-ed$_1$] Chr$_1$ Thdrt [Hil-ms$_1$] : txt AB a 17 vulg(and F-lat, but over F-gr *eodem* is written) D-lat Did$_2$ [Bas-mss$_1$ Euthal-ms Damasc Hil$_1$(and ms$_1$) Ambr$_{sæpe}$ Aug$_{sæpe}$].—om εν τω ενι πν. C^1 Eus$_1$ Tert$_1$ Cassiod.

10. om 1st δε D^{1}F latt [arm] Clem$_1$ Hil$_2$. ενεργεια DF, *operatio* latt [Hil$_2$] (not Aug$_3$ al). δυναμεως DF. om δε (2nd, 3rd, and 4th) BDF latt Clem$_1$ [Tert$_1$ Ambrst] : om 4th δε Pℵ^1 1 Cæs : ins ACKLℵ^3 rel syrr copt [Eus$_2$ Bas$_1$ Cyr-jer$_1$ Euthal-ms] Chr$_1$ Thdrt Damasc. διακρισις C(?)D^{1}FPℵ 17 latt Syr [sah-mnt arm] Clem Orig[-c$_1$] Bas$_1$ [Tert$_1$ Hil]. om 5th δε D^1 latt [Tert$_1$ Hil$_{alic}$ (not Jer$_1$)].

λόγος σοφίας . . . λόγος γνώσεως] *What is the distinction?* According to Neander, **σοφία** is the *skill*, which is able to reduce the whole *practical* Christian life into its due order in accordance with its foundation principles (see Pfl. u. Leit. p. 247);—**γνῶσις**, the *theoretical insight* into divine things: and similarly Olsh. and Billroth. But Bengel, al., take them conversely, **γνῶσ.** for the practical, **σοφ.** for the theoretical. Both, as De W. remarks, have their grounds in usage: *σοφία* is *practical* Col. i. 9, as is *γνῶσις* Rom. xv. 14, but they are *theoretical* respectively in ch. i. 17 ff. and viii. 1. Estius explains **λόγος σοφίας**, 'gratiam de iis quæ ad doctrinam religionis ac pietatis spectant disserendi ex causis supremis,'—as ch. ii. 6 f.:—and **λόγ. γνώσεως**, he says, "gratia est disserendi de rebus Christianæ religionis, ex iis quæ sunt humanæ scientiæ vel experientiæ." Meyer says, "*σοφία* is the *higher Christian wisdom* (see on ch. ii. 6) in and of itself;—so that discourse which expresses its truths, makes them clear, applies them, &c. is *λόγος σοφίας*. But this does not necessarily imply the speculative penetration of these truths,—the philosophical treatment of them by deeper and more scientific investigation, in other words, *γνῶσις*: and discourse which aims at this is *λόγος γνώσεως*." This last view is most in accordance with the subsequently recognized meaning of *γνῶσις* and *γνωστικός*, and with the Apostle's own use of *σοφία* in the passage referred to, ch. ii. 6. **κατὰ τ. αὐ. πν.**] **according to** the disposition (see ver. 11) of **the same Spirit.** **9.**] **πίστις**, as Chrys.: *πίστιν οὐ ταύτην λέγων τὴν τῶν δογμάτων, ἀλλὰ τὴν τῶν σημείων, περὶ ἧς φησιν Ἐὰν ἔχητε πίστιν ὡς κόκκον σιν. κ.τ.λ.* (Matt. xvii. 20)· *καὶ οἱ ἀπόστολοι δὲ περὶ αὐτῆς ἠξίουν λέγοντες Πρόσθες ἡμῖν πίστιν* (Luke xvii. 5). *αὕτη γὰρ μήτηρ τῶν σημείων ἐστίν.* Hom. xxix. p. 263. This seems to be the meaning here; a faith, enabling a man to place himself beyond the region of mere moral certainty, in the actual realization of things believed, in a high and unusual manner. **ἐν τ. αὐτ. πν.**] in, i.e. by and through, as the effective cause and the medium. **χαρίσματα ἰαμάτων**] **gifts of** (miraculous) **healings;** plur., to indicate the different kinds of diseases, requiring different sorts of healing. **ἐν**, see above. **10. ἐνεργ. δυν.**] **operations of miraculous powers** (in general). **προφητεία**] **speaking in the Spirit.** Meyer gives an excellent definition of it: "discourse flowing from the revelation and impulse of the Holy Spirit, which, not being attached to any particular office in the church, but improvised,—disclosed the depths of the human heart and of the divine counsel, and thus was exceedingly effectual for the enlightening, exhortation, and consolation of believers, and the winning of unbelievers. The *prophet* differs from the *speaker with tongues* . . . . in that he speaks *with the understanding*, not ecstatically: from the *διδάσκαλος*, thus:—*ὁ μὲν προφητεύων πάντα ἀπὸ τοῦ πνεύματος φθέγγεται· ὁ δὲ διδάσκων ἐστὶν ὅπου καὶ ἐξ οἰκείας διαλέγεται*, as Chrys. on ver. 28." (Hom. xxxii. p. 286.) **διακρίσεις πν.**] **discernings of spirits:** i.e. the power of distinguishing between the operation of the Spirit of God and the evil spirit, or the unassisted human spirit: see 1 John iv. 1, and compare *προσέχοντες πνεύμασιν πλάνοις*, 1 Tim. iv. 1. The exercise of this power is alluded to ch. xiv. 29. **γένη**

σῶν, ἄλλῳ δὲ [l] ἑρμηνεία [k] γλωσσῶν· 11 πάντα δὲ ταῦτα
[m] ἐνεργεῖ τὸ [n] ἓν καὶ τὸ [n] αὐτὸ πνεῦμα, [o] διαιροῦν [p] ἰδίᾳ
ἑκάστῳ [q] καθὼς [r] βούλεται. 12 [s] καθάπερ γὰρ τὸ σῶμα
ἕν ἐστιν, καὶ [t] μέλη πολλὰ ἔχει, πάντα δὲ τὰ [t] μέλη τοῦ
σώματος, πολλὰ ὄντα, ἕν ἐστιν σῶμα, οὕτως καὶ ὁ χριστός. 13 καὶ γὰρ [u] ἐν ἑνὶ πνεύματι ἡμεῖς πάντες [v] εἰς ἓν
σῶμα [uv] ἐβαπτίσθημεν, εἴτε Ἰουδαῖοι εἴτε Ἕλληνες, [w] εἴτε
[wx] δοῦλοι [w] εἴτε [wx] ἐλεύθεροι, καὶ πάντες ἓν πνεῦμα [y] ἐποτίσθη-

ABCDF KLPℵ a b c d e f g h k l m o 17. 47

l ch. xiv. 26 only †. Sir. prol. & xlvii. 17 only. (-εύειν, Heb. vii. 2. -ευτής, ch. xiv. 28 v. r.)
m ver. 6. Rom. vii. 5 reff.
n ch. xi. 5 only. see ver. 9.
o Luke xv. 12 only. Josh. xviii. 5. (-ρεσις, vv. 4, 5, 6.)
p here only. 2 Macc. iv. 34 only. Xen. Cyr. vi. 2. 34.
q = Mark iv. 33. Acts xi. 29. Num. xxvi. 54.
r of God, Heb. vi. 17. James i. 18. 2 Pet. iii. 9 only. 1 Kings ii. 25.
s Rom. iv. 6 reff.
t Rom. vi. 13 reff.
u Matt. iii. 11. Acts i. 5. xi. 16.
v Acts viii. 16 reff.
w Eph. vi. 8.
x as above (w). Gal. iii. 28. Col. iii. 11. Rev. vi. 15. xiii. 16. xix. 18.
y Rom. xii. 20 reff. acc., see Mark x. 38. Luke xii. 47. 2 Thess. ii. 15. Heb. vi. 9. Rev. xvi. 9. Ps. lxviii. 21. Winer, edn. 6, § 32. 5.

om αλλω δε ερμηνεια γλωσσων (*homœotel*) BK d k [Eus$_1$]. **διερμηνεια** (*mistake occasioned by* δε? *Tischdf* (ed 7 [and 8]) *says* "*cf xii.* 30; *xiv.* 5, 13, 27, 28") A D^1(adds γενη): txt CD^{3}FKLPℵ rel Clem Cæs Cyr-jer Chr [Bas$_1$ Euthal-ms] Thdrt Damasc.

11. ταυτα δε παντα DF latt copt [Just$_1$ Did$_1$(txt$_2$) Ath$_2$(txt$_1$) Cyr$_1$ Chr$_2$(txt$_1$) Thdrt$_1$] Orig$_1$ Hil$_1$ [Ambrst]. om το (bef ἓν) D^{1}F arm Orig$_1$ Chr$_2$ [Sevrn-in-Chr$_1$]. om ιδια (D^1)F latt Syr [arm Bas$_2$] (Orig$_1$) Epiph$_3$ Orig-int$_1$ Did-int$_1$ Hil$_1$ [Jer$_{\text{sæpe}}$ Ambrst].—for διαιρουν ιδια, διερουμενα D^1.

12. om γαρ K a æth arm; d has it in red. for και μελη, μελη δε D^1(and lat) F[-gr] Hip$_1$ Hil Tich$_1$. rec εχει bef πολλα, with DFKL rel latt syrr goth Chr$_1$ Thdrt$_1$ [Damasc] Hil Ambrst: txt ABCPℵ m 17 Hip$_1$ Thdrt$_1$ Jer$_1$. **μεληλη**(sic) ℵ. ins εκ bef του σωμ. D^1(and lat) goth Hil Ambrst Tich. rec aft σωματος ins του ενος (*gloss*), with Dℵ^3 rel [sah-mnt] goth Chr$_1$ Thdrt$_1$ Damasc Œc Hil [Ambrst Tich]: om ABCFKLPℵ^1 d vulg syrr copt æth arm [Chr$_2$ Euthal-ms Thdrt$_{\text{h.l.}}$ Jer$_1$ Aug$_{\text{alic}}$]. (17 def [but there is not room for the addn].) for χρ., κυριος C.

13. om ενι F[-gr]. rec ins εις bef ἓν πνευμα (*appy to conform to the first member of the sentence*), with D^{3}KL rel vulg(and F-lat) Thdrt$_2$ Vig: om (A)BCD^{1}FPℵ d 17. 47 am(with demid [fuld] harl tol) D-lat syrr copt goth æth arm Ps-Ign$_1$ Ath$_2$ Did$_5$ Chr$_1$ [Euthal-ms Ambrst Aug$_1$]. for πνευμα εποτισθημεν, σωμα εσμεν A: for πνευμα, πομα a f g l syr-mg-gr: πν. **εφωτισθημεν** L. 21. 39. 116.

γλωσσῶν] **kinds of tongues**, i. e. the power of uttering, in ecstasy, as the mouthpiece of the Spirit, prayer and praise in *languages unknown to the utterer*,—or even in a *spiritual language unknown to man*. See this subject dealt with in the note on Acts ii. 4, and ch. xiv. 2 ff. **ἑρμηνεία γλωσσῶν**] the power of *giving a meaning to what was thus ecstatically spoken*. This was not always resident in the speaker himself: see ch. xiv. 13. **11.**] The Spirit is the universal worker in men of all these powers, and that according to His own pleasure: see above on vv. 4—6. **ἰδίᾳ**, '*seorsim*,' respectively, or '*severally*,' as E. V. This unity of the source of all spiritual gifts, in the midst of their variety, he presses as against those who valued some and undervalued others, or who depreciated them all. **12—30.**] *As the many members of the body compose an organic whole, and all belong to the body, none being needless, none to be despised; so also those who are variously gifted by the Spirit compose a spiritual organic whole, the mystical body of Christ.* First, however, vv. 12, 13, this likeness of the mystical Christ to a *body* is *enounced*, and *justified by the facts of our Baptism.*

12.] The *organic unity* of the various members in one body, is predicated also of CHRIST, i. e. *the Church as united in Him*, see ch. vi. 15. The γάρ confirms the preceding ἓν κ. τὸ αὐτὸ πνεῦμα, by an analogy. By the repetition,—τὸ σῶμα, ... τοῦ σώματος . . . , σῶμα, the unity of the members as an organic whole is more strongly set forth. **13.**] This shewn from our being *baptized into one* body, and *receiving one* Spirit. **For in** (see on ver. 9) **one Spirit also** (the emphasis on ἑνὶ πν., to which words καί belongs) **we all were baptized into one Body, whether Jews or Greeks, whether slaves or freemen; and we all were made to drink of one Spirit** (or, '*all watered by one Spirit*,' viz. the *water of baptism*, here taken as identical with the Spirit whose influence accompanied it). So (understanding the whole verse of *baptism*) Chrys., Theophyl., Œc., Rückert, Meyer, De Wette. Luther, Beza, Calv., Estius, Grot., al., refer the latter half to the *Lord's Supper*: and this is *mentioned* by Chrys. and Theophyl.:—Billroth and Olsh. to the abiding influence of the Spirit in strengthening and refreshing. But the aor. **ἐποτίσθημεν**, referring to a *fact gone by*, is

μεν. 14 καὶ γὰρ τὸ σῶμα οὐκ ἔστιν ἓν [t] μέλος, ἀλλὰ πολλά.
15 ἐὰν εἴπῃ ὁ πούς Ὅτι οὐκ εἰμὶ χείρ, οὐκ [z] εἰμὶ [z] ἐκ τοῦ
σώματος, οὐ [a] παρὰ τοῦτο οὐκ [z] ἔστιν [z] ἐκ τοῦ σώματος;
16 καὶ ἐὰν εἴπῃ τὸ [b] οὖς Ὅτι οὐκ εἰμὶ ὀφθαλμός, οὐκ [z] εἰμὶ
[z] ἐκ τοῦ σώματος, οὐ [a] παρὰ τοῦτο οὐκ [z] ἔστιν [z] ἐκ τοῦ σώματος; 17 εἰ ὅλον τὸ σῶμα ὀφθαλμός, [c] ποῦ ἡ [d] ἀκοή; εἰ
ὅλον [d] ἀκοή, [c] ποῦ ἡ [e] ὄσφρησις; 18 [f] νῦν δὲ ὁ θεὸς [g] ἔθετο
τὰ μέλη, [h] ἓν [h] ἕκαστον αὐτῶν ἐν τῷ σώματι [i] καθὼς ἠθέλησεν. 19 εἰ δὲ ἦν [[k] τὰ] [k] πάντα ἓν μέλος, [c] ποῦ τὸ σῶμα;
20 [f] νῦν δὲ πολλὰ μὲν μέλη, ἓν δὲ σῶμα. 21 οὐ δύναται δὲ

z of things, — here 4 times only. of pers., Matt. xxvi. 73. John i. 24. Acts xxi. 8 al. Obad. 11.
a = here bis only. Polyb. i. 32. 4, παρὰ τί νῦν σφαλείησαν. Demosth. 545. 22, ταῦτα πέπονθεν... παρὰ τὴν πενίαν. Winer, edn. 6, § 49 g. c.
b Rom. xi. 8 reff.
c ellips., Rom. iii. 27. ch. i. 20.
d = 2 Pet. ii. 8. Xen. Mem. i. 4. 6.
e here only +.
f = Luke xi. 39 al.
g = Acts xx. 28. ver. 28. Gen. xvii. 5.
h Acts xvii. 27 reff.
i ver. 11 reff.
k ver. 6.

15. for εστιν, ειμι(?) ℵ¹(but corrd).
16. om και D¹[and lat]. om οτι P [Chr-ms]. **17.** ins ὁ bef οφθαλμος D¹.
18. rec νυνι, with CD²·³KLPℵ rel Chr₂ [Euthal-ms] Thdrt Damasc Œc: txt ABD¹F l Thl. [ins εις bef εν εκαστον K.]
19. om τα BF 17: ins ACDKLPℵ rel [Chr₂ Euthal-ms Thdrt₂ Damasc].
20. νυνι FP 32. 47. 67, 80. 114 Chr₁ Thl. om μεν B D¹(and lat) 73. 114 goth [arm] Aug₂.
21. om δε (*as being in the way? but it brings out a contrast to the unity just insisted on*) ACFP d m 17. 47 fuld(and demid) Syr copt [æth arm] (Orig) Bas (Thdrt₁) [Euthal-ms Aug₁] Jer: ins BDKLℵ rel vulg syr goth Chr₂ Thdrt Damasc Thl Œc Ambrst Aug₁ Pel.

fatal to both these latter interpretations: besides that it would be *harsh* to understand even **εἰς** ἓν πν. ἐποτίσθ. (see var. readd.) and *impossible* to understand **ἓν πν. ἐποτ.**, of the cup in the Lord's Supper.

14.] *Analogy, by which this multiplicity in unity is justified*: it is even so in the *natural body*,—which, though *one*, consists of *many members*. The object of the continuation of the simile seems to be, to convince them that their various gifts had been bestowed by God on them as members of the Christian body, and that they must not, because they did not happen to possess the gifts of *another*, consider themselves *excluded* from the *body*,—in which the weaker as well as the stronger, the less comely as well as the more comely members were necessary. The student will remember the fable spoken by Menenius Agrippa to the mutinous plebs in Livy ii. 32. The passage is also illustrated by Seneca de Ira, ii. 31, 'Quid si nocere velint manus pedibus, manibus oculi? Ut omnia inter se membra consentiunt, quia singula servari totius interest: ita homines singulis parcent, quia ad cœlum geniti sumus: salva autem esse societas nisi amore et custodia partium non potest:'—and by Marc. Antonin. ii. 1, where in his morning meditations on the duty of repressing anger through the day, he says, *γεγόναμεν γὰρ πρὸς συνεργίαν, ὡς πόδες, ὡς χεῖρες, ὡς βλέφαρα, ὡς οἱ στοῖχοι τῶν ἄνω καὶ τῶν κάτω ὀδόντων· τὸ οὖν ἀντιπράσσειν ἀλλήλοις, παρὰ φύσιν.* See also id. vii. 13: Clem. ad Cor. c. xxxvii. p. 284: and other examples in Wetstein.

15.] The **ὅτι** is rightly rendered in E. V. **because.** **οὐ παρὰ τ. κ.τ.λ.**] These words [may be taken, here and in the next verse, "*it is not therefore not of the body.*" But they] are best taken as a question, appealing to the sense of the reader: they thus have more of the vigour of the Apostle's style. **παρά**, see reff. **ἐκ τ. σ., belonging to the body** as an aggregate; so εἷς ἐκ τῶν δώδεκα,—ἦσαν ἐκ τῶν Φαρισαίων. The double negation strengthens,—see Winer, edn. 6, § 55. 9 b (he takes the two, *in this case*, as destroying one another (?), see ib. a).

17.] *The necessity* of the members to *one another*, and to the *body*. Understand **ἦν** in each clause, which is indeed expressed in ver. 19. **18.**] **νῦν δέ, but as the case really stands**: see Hartung, Partikellehre, ii. 25. **τὰ μέλη**, generally,—**ἓν ἕκαστον αὐτῶν**, severally. **καθὼς ἠθέλ.** answers to καθὼς βούλεται, ver. 11.

19.] The *same 'reductio ad absurdum'* which has been made in the *concrete* twice in ver. 17, is now made in the *abstract*: **if the whole were one member, where would be the body** (which by its very idea μέλη ἔχει πολλά: see vv. 12, 14)? **20.**] Brings out the fact *in contrast to ver.* 19, as ver. 18 in contrast to ver. 17. **21—26.**] *And the spiritual gifts are also necessary to one an-*

ὁ ὀφθαλμὸς εἰπεῖν τῇ χειρὶ [l]Χρείαν σου οὐκ [l]ἔχω· ἢ
[m]πάλιν ἡ κεφαλὴ τοῖς ποσὶν [l]Χρείαν ὑμῶν οὐκ [l]ἔχω.
22 ἀλλὰ [n]πολλῷ [n]μᾶλλον τὰ [o]δοκοῦντα μέλη τοῦ σώματος
ἀσθενέστερα [p]ὑπάρχειν [q]ἀναγκαῖά ἐστιν, 23 καὶ ἃ [o]δοκοῦ-
μεν [r]ἀτιμότερα εἶναι τοῦ σώματος, τούτοις [s]τιμὴν [t]περισ- ...ειναι P ABCDF KLℵ a b c d e f g h k l m o 17. 47
σοτέραν [su]περιτίθεμεν, καὶ τὰ [v]ἀσχήμονα ἡμῶν [w]εὐσχημο-
σύνην [t]περισσοτέραν ἔχει. 24 τὰ δὲ [x]εὐσχήμονα ἡμῶν οὐ
[y]χρείαν [y]ἔχει· ἀλλὰ ὁ θεὸς [z]συνεκέρασεν τὸ σῶμα, τῷ
[a]ὑστερουμένῳ [t]περισσοτέραν δοὺς τιμήν, 25 ἵνα μὴ ᾖ
[b]σχίσμα ἐν τῷ σώματι, ἀλλὰ τὸ αὐτὸ ὑπὲρ ἀλλήλων
[c]μεριμνῶσιν τὰ μέλη. 26 καὶ εἴτε πάσχει ἓν μέλος, [d]συν-

l Matt. vi. 8. Luke v. 31 ||. Prov. xviii. 2. m = 2 Cor. x. 7. n Rom. v. 9, 10 reff. o = (1) Matt. xvii. 25 al. (2) ch. iv. 9 al. p Acts ii. 30 reff. q Acts xiii. 46 reff. r ch. iv. 10 reff. s Esth. i. 20. t Mark xii. 40. Luke xii. 4 +. Dan. iv. 33 (36) Theod. u = here (Matt. xxi. 33 || Mk. xxvii. 28 || Mk., 48 || Mk. J.) only. (Ruth iii. 3.) (-θεσις, 1 Pet. iii. 3.) v here only. Deut. xxiv. 1. (-μονεῖν, ch. vii. 36. -μοσύνη, Rom. i. 27.) w here only +. Polyb. x. 18. 7. x Acts xiii. 50 reff. (-μόνως, ch. xiv. 40.) y abs., Acts ii. 45 reff. z Heb. iv. 2 only +. 2 Macc. xv. 39 only. a ch. i. 7 reff. b ch. i. 10 reff. c Matt. vi. 25 al. fr. 2 Kings vii. 10. plur., ch. x. 11 reff. constr. acc., ch. vii. 32, &c. reff. w. ὑπέρ, here only. Ps. xxxvii. 18. d Rom. viii. 17 only +. 1 Kings xxii. 8 Symm.[? or Incert.]

rec om ὁ (*absorbed in the οφθαλμος follg ?*), with K e h o [arm Thdrt$_1$]: ins ABCDF LPℵ rel Orig$_1$ Bas$_1$ Chr$_1$ [Euthal-ms] Thdrt Damasc Thl-comm Œc.

23. ins μελη bef του σωματος D F[-gr] lat-ff[not Aug$_2$]; bef ειναι 17 [vulg F-lat Damasc].

24. aft εχει ins τιμης D F-gr Syr. (αλλα, so ABCDLℵ b e g m o.) συνεκερασεν bef ο θεος A. om το ℵ^1. rec υστερουντι (*appy corrn to more usual N. T. expression*), with DFKLℵ^3 rel Orig$_1$ Dial$_1$ Chr$_1$ [Euthal-ms Antch$_1$] Thdrt Thl Œc: txt ABCℵ^1 17 Melet$_1$(in Epiph) Damasc. for περισσοτεραν δους τιμην, τι περισσοτερον δους B(see table).

25. σχισματα D^1[-gr] F[-gr] Lℵ rel fuld arm Bas$_1$ Antch$_1$ Damasc Thl Aug$_4$ Sedul: txt ABCD^{2,3}K f h l m o 17 vulg(and F-lat) D-lat syrr copt Orig$_1$ [Chr$_1$ Thdrt Œc] Ambrst Aug$_1$. for το αυτο, τα αυτα D^1[-gr] F[-gr] arm Orig$_2$. μεριμνα DF Thl-marg.

26. for 1st ειτε, ει τι BF latt syr arm Ambrst Pel Cassiod Bede: txt AC D[-gr] KLℵ rel [Syr(*ut quando*) copt Bas$_1$ Euthal-ms] Chr$_2$ Thdrt Damasc Thl Œc [Cypr$_3$(*si*) Aug$_{saepe}$ (*quia si*)]. om 1st ἐν A (Orig$_1$).

other. This is spoken in reproof of the *highly endowed,* who imagined they could do without those less gifted than themselves, as the preceding to those of small endowment, who were discontented with their gifts. 22, 23.] Nay, the relation between the members is so entirely different from this, that the *very disparagement,* conventionally, of *any member,* is the *reason why more care should be taken of it.* I understand by the τὰ δοκοῦντα μέλη τοῦ σώματος ἀσθενέστερα ὑπάρχειν, those members which in each man's case appear to be *inheritors of disease,* or to have *incurred weakness.* By *this very fact,* their *necessity to him* is brought out much more than that of the others. 23.] So also in the case of the parts ἃ δοκοῦμεν ἀτιμότερα εἶναι—on which *usage has set the stamp of dishonour.* Perhaps he alludes (as distinguished from τὰ ἀσχήμ. below) to those limbs which we conceal from sight in accordance with custom, but in the exposure of which there would be no absolute indecency. So Chrys., καλῶς εἶπε **τὰ δοκοῦντα,** καὶ **ἃ δοκοῦμεν** (but I should draw a distinction between the two, in accordance with the above explanation of ἀσθενέστ., and render τὰ δοκοῦντα, **which appear to be** [of themselves], and ἃ δοκοῦμεν, **which we think** [conventionally]: notice also ὑπάρχειν and εἶναι, on which see Acts xvi. 20, note) δεικνὺς ὅτι οὐ τῆς φύσεως τῶν πραγμάτων, ἀλλὰ τῆς τῶν πολλῶν ὑπονοίας ἡ ψῆφος. Hom. xxxi. p. 278. **τιμ. περισσ. περιτίθ.**] viz. by *clothing* (*garments of honour,* as the Targ. of Onkelos on Gen. iii. 21): honouring them more than the face, the noblest part, which we do not clothe. **καὶ τὰ ἀσχ.**] Here there is *no* **ἃ δοκοῦμεν,** and no ambiguity. Chrys. (ibid.) says: . . ἀλλ' ὅμως πλείονος ἀπολαύει τιμῆς· καὶ οἱ σφόδρα πένητες, κἂν τὸ λοιπὸν γυμνὸν ἔχωσι σῶμα, οὐκ ἂν ἀνάσχοιντο ἐκεῖνα τὰ μέλη δεῖξαι γυμνά. 24.] The *comely* parts are in some measure *neglected,* not needing to be covered or adorned: **but** (opposed to χρείαν ἔχει) **God** (at the creation) **tempered the body together** (compounded it of members on a principle of mutual compensation),—**to the deficient part giving more abundant honour,** 25.] **that there be no disunion** (see ver. 21) **in the body, but that the members**

πάσχει πάντα τὰ μέλη· εἴτε [e] δοξάζεται [ἓν] μέλος, [f] συγχαίρει πάντα τὰ μέλη. 27 ὑμεῖς δέ ἐστε σῶμα χριστοῦ καὶ
μέλη [gh] ἐκ [h] μέρους. 28 καὶ [i] οὓς μὲν [k] ἔθετο ὁ θεὸς ἐν τῇ
[l] ἐκκλησίᾳ πρῶτον ἀποστόλους, δεύτερον [mn] προφήτας,
τρίτον [mo] διδασκάλους, ἔπειτα [p] δυνάμεις, ἔπειτα [q] χαρίσματα
[q] ἰαμάτων, [r] ἀντιλήμψεις, [s] κυβερνήσεις, [p] γένη [p] γλωσσῶν.

e = here only. f Luke i. 58. xv. 6, 9. ch. xiii. 6. Phil. ii. 17, 18 only. L.P. Gen. xxi. 6 only. g = ch. vii. 5 reff. h ch. xiii. 9 bis, 10, 12 only. (see Rom. xi. 25 reff. 1 Kings xxiii. 26.) i = ver. 8 al. see note. k = ver. 18. l absol., Acts xii. 1. Eph. i. 22 al. m Acts xiii. 1. Eph. iv. 11. n Acts xi. 27 reff. o 1 Tim. ii. 7. 2 Tim. i. 11. p = ver. 10. q ver. 9 (reff.). r here only. Ps. xxi. 19. Sir. xi. 12. 2 Macc. viii. 19. (-λαμβάνεσθαι, Acts xx. 35.) s here only. Prov. i. 5. xi. 14. (xx. 18 F compl.[? 21 Ald.]: Prov. xx. 14—22 is omd in ABℵ.) xxiv. 6 only.

om 2nd ἐν ABℵ[1].

27. σωμα bef εστε F[not F-lat] $Ambr_1$[txt_1]. for μερους, μελους (*perhaps error: perhaps, as Mey, εκ μερ. was not understood*) D[1](and lat) vulg [F-lat] syr(μερ. mg) arm $Orig_1$ Eus_1 $Epiph_1$ $Thdrt_1$ $Procl_1$ [$Sevrn\text{-}c_1$ Ambrst] (om εκ με. Hil_1 Aug_1): txt is supported by $Orig_2$(and int_2) Eus_7 Chr_1 [Bas_1 Euthal-ms] $Thdrt_2$ Damasc Thl Œc.

28. ins [και bef τριτ. m $Orig_1$(om_1-int_1) : add] δε D[1][-gr]. rec for 2nd επειτα, ειτα (*corrn as more usual, follg* επειτα : *the* omn *may be accounted for by a desire to throw all into one catalogue*), with KL rel Thdrt Thl Œc : om D F[-gr] Hil_1 $Ambr_3$: txt ABCℵ a 17 Bas_1 $Cyr\text{-}jer_1$ Chr_1 [Euthal-ms] Damasc. om γενη ℵ[1](ins above the line ℵ-corr[1]).

may have the same care (viz. that for mutual well-being) **for one another.** The verb is plur., on account of the personification of the individual members (Meyer).

26.] **καί, and accordingly,** in matter of fact: we see that God's *temperament* of the body has not failed of its purpose, for the members sympathize most intimately with one another. **πάσχει . . . συνπάσχει**] καὶ γὰρ τῇ πτέρνῃ πολλάκις προσπαγείσης ἀκάνθης, ὅλον τὸ σῶμα αἰσθάνεται καὶ μεριμνᾷ· καὶ νῶτος κάμπτεται, καὶ γαστὴρ καὶ μηροὶ συστέλλονται, καὶ χεῖρες καθάπερ δορυφόροι κ. ὑπηρέται προσιόντες ἀνέλκουσι τὸ παγέν, καὶ κεφαλὴ ἐπικύπτει, καὶ ὀφθαλμοὶ μετὰ πολλῆς ὁρῶσι τῆς φροντίδος. Chrys. p. 282. **δοξάζεται . . . συγχαίρει**] Chrys. again with equal beauty instances, στεφανοῦται ἡ κεφαλή, καὶ ἅπας ὁ ἄνθρωπος δοξάζεται· λέγει τὸ στόμα, καὶ γελῶσιν ὀφθαλμοὶ καὶ εὐφραίνονται (ibid.). But perhaps the analogy requires that we should rather understand δοξ. of those things which *physically* refresh or benefit the member, e. g. *anointing* or *nourishment*.

27.] *Application of all that has been said of the physical body, to the Corinthians as the mystical body of Christ:* and to *individuals* among them, as *members in particular,* i. e. each according to his allotted part in the body. *Each church* is said to be *the body of Christ,* as each is said to be *the temple of God* (see ch. iii. 16, note) : not that there are many bodies or many temples ; but that each church is an image of the whole aggregate,—a microcosm, having the same characteristics. Chrys. would understand ἐκ μέρους —ὅτι ἡ ἐκκλησία ἡ παρ' ὑμῖν μέρος ἐστὶ τῆς πανταχοῦ κειμένης ἐκκλησίας, καὶ τοῦ σώματος τοῦ διὰ πασῶν συνισταμένου τῶν ἐκκλησιῶν (Hom. xxxii. p. 285) : but this, though true, does not appear to have been here before the Apostle,—only *the whole Corinthian church as the body of Christ,* and its individual components as members, each in his appointed place.

28.] *The divine disposition of the members in the spiritual body.* **οὓς μέν** was apparently intended to be followed by οὓς (or ἄλλους) δέ, but meanwhile another arrangement, πρῶτον, δεύτ., τρίτ., occurs to the Apostle, and οὓς μέν is left uncorrected, standing alone. See Eph. iv. 11, where τοὺς μέν is followed by τοὺς δέ, regularly. **ἐν τῇ ἐκκλ.**] **in the (universal) church,** a sense more frequently found in the Epistle to the Ephesians, than in any other part of St. Paul's writings. **πρ. ἀποστόλους**] Not merely *the Twelve* are thus designated, but they and others who bore the same name and had equal power, e.g. Paul himself, and Barnabas, and James the Lord's brother: see also note on Rom. xvi. 7. **προφ.**] See above, on ver. 10. **διδασκάλους**] See reff. : those who had the gift of expounding and unfolding doctrine and applying it to practice,—the λόγος σοφίας and the λόγος γνώσεως. **δυνάμεις**] He here passes to the *abstract* nouns from the *concrete,*—perhaps because no definite class of persons was endowed with each of the following, but they were promiscuously granted to all orders in the church : more probably, however, *without any assignable reason;* as in Rom. xii. 6—8, he passes from the abstract to the concrete.
ἀντιλήμψεις] i. e. ἀντέχεσθαι τῶν ἀσθενῶν and the like, as Chrys. forming one department of the διακονίαι of ver. 5 : as do also

t Acts ii. 4. x. 46. xix. 6. ch. xiv. 2 &c.
u Luke xxiv. 27. Acts ix. 36. ch. xiv. 5, 13, 27 only †. 2 Macc. i. 36 only. (-νευτής, ch. xiv. 28.)
v = ch. xiv. 1, 39 (xiii. 4 al.) only. Sir. li. 18.
w ver. 4 reff.
x = ch. xiii. 13. xiv. 5.
y Rom. vii. 13 reff.
z ch. iv. 17. 1 Kings xii. 23. see Acts xiii. 10 reff.

ABCDF KL‎א a b c d e f g h k l m o 17. 47

29 μὴ πάντες ἀπόστολοι; μὴ πάντες [mn] προφῆται; μὴ
πάντες [mo] διδάσκαλοι; μὴ πάντες [p] δυνάμεις; 30 μὴ πάντες
[q] χαρίσματα ἔχουσιν [q] ἰαμάτων; μὴ πάντες [t] γλώσσαις
[t] λαλοῦσιν; μὴ πάντες [u] διερμηνεύουσιν;
31 [v] Ζηλοῦτε δὲ τὰ [w] χαρίσματα τὰ [x] μείζονα· καὶ ἔτι
[y] καθ' [y] ὑπερβολὴν [z] ὁδὸν ὑμῖν δείκνυμι. XIII. 1 ἐὰν ταῖς

31. om 1st τα F [2nd τα is written above the line]. rec for μειζονα, κρειττονα, with DFKL rel (-σσονα DF &c) latt copt(appy) arm $Orig_1$[-int_2] Sevrn-c_1 Chr_1 $Damasc_2$ $Phot_1$ Thl(οὐκ εἶπε τὰ μείζονα ἀλλὰ τὰ κρείττονα) [$Ambr_2$ Ambrst]: txt ABC‎א m 17. 73 am æth $Orig_3$ Thdor-cat_1 [Cyr_1 Euthal-ms] Thdrt-comm $Damasc_2$ Jer_3. om και F old-lat Syr. for ετι, ειτι D^1: ετει[G: ειτι] F. δεικ. bef υμιν F[-gr].

κυβερνήσεις, a higher department, that of the presbyters or bishops—the *direction* of the various churches. **γένη γλωσσῶν**] εἶδες ποῦ τέθεικε τουτὶ τὸ χάρισμα, καὶ πῶς πανταχοῦ τὴν ἐσχάτην αὐτῷ νέμει τάξιν; Chrys. p. 287. There certainly seems to be intention in placing this *last* in rank: but I am persuaded that we must not, with Meyer, seek for a *classified* arrangement: here, as above, vv. 7—11, it seems rather *suggestive* than *logical:* the χαρ. ἰαμ. naturally suggesting the ἀντιλήμψεις,—and those again, the assistances to carry out the work of the church, as naturally bringing in the κυβερνήσεις, the government and guidance of it.

29, 30.] *The application of the questions already asked* vv. 17—19.

29. δυνάμεις] not, as Meyer, al., *accusative,* governed by **ἔχουσιν**—which involves a departure from the parallelism, besides the harshness of construction:—but *nominative,* in apposition with πάντες. The Apostle has above placed the concrete, ἀπόστολοι, προφῆται, διδάσκαλοι, in apposition with δυνάμεις and χαρίσμ. ἰαμ., and now proceeds with the same arrangement till he comes to χαρίσματα ἰαμάτων, which being too palpably unpredicable of *persons,* gives rise to the change of construction,—μὴ πάντες χαρ. **ἔχουσιν** ἰαμάτων; In the last two questions, he departs from the order of the last verse, and takes in again one particular from the former catalogue, ver. 10. Meyer compares Hom. Il. ν. 726—734. See Stanley's note and excursus.

31.] **But** (he has been shewing that *all* gifts *have their value:* and that all are *set in the church by God: some* however are *more valuable* than *others*) **do ye aim at the greater gifts** (μείζ. is explained ch. xiv. 5). This exhortation is not inconsistent with ver. 11: but, as we look for the divine blessing on tillage and careful culture, so we may look for the aid of the Spirit on carefully cultivated powers of the understanding and speech;—and we may notice that the greater gifts, those of προφητεία and διδασκαλία, consisted in *the inspired exercise of the conscious faculties,* in which culture and diligence would be useful accessories. "Spiritus dat, ut vult (ver. 11): sed fideles tamen libere aliud præ alio possunt sequi et exercere, c. xiv. 26." Bengel. Compare also xiv. 39. There is thus no need to explain away ζηλοῦτε, as Grot. ("*agite cum Deo precibus ut accipiatis*") and others: or to depart from the known usage of χαρίσματα, and explain it to mean *faith, hope, and love,* as Morus, or the *fruits of love,* as Billroth. **καὶ ἔτι**] **And moreover**: besides exhorting you to emulate the greatest gifts.

καθ' ὑπ. ὁδ.] **An eminently excellent way,** viz. *of emulating the greatest gifts:*—so Theophyl.: καὶ μετὰ τούτων (τοῦτο γὰρ δηλοῖ τὸ καὶ ἔτι), ἐὰν ὅλως ζηλωταὶ ὑπάρχητε χαρισμάτων, δείξω ὑμῖν μίαν ὁδὸν καθ' ὑπερβολήν, τουτέστιν, ὑπερέχουσαν, **ἥτις φέρει ἐπὶ πάντα τὰ χαρίσματα·** τὴν ἀγάπην δὲ λέγει. **καθ' ὑπερβ.**] must not be joined with the verb,—'est adhuc via quam vobis diligentissime demonstro' (Pagnini's version, and some mentioned by Estius): see reff. and cf. ἡ μάλιστα ἀναγνώρισις, Arist. Poet. ii. 6,—μάλα στρατηγόν, Xen. Hell. vi. 2. 39,—εὖ πρᾶξις, Æsch. Agam. 262,—σφόδρα γυναικῶν, Plato, Legg. i. p. 639 c, and other examples in Bernhardy, Syntax, p. 338. The explanation of Estius and Billroth, that the way which he is about to shew them is 'multo excellentiorem iis donis de quibus hactenus egit' (Est.), is clearly wrong: the opening verses of ch. xiii. shewing, that he does not draw a *comparison between love and gifts,* but only shews that it is *the only* WAY, in which *gifts* can be made effectual in the highest sense. See also on ch. xiv. 1.

CHAP. XIII. **1—13.**] THE PANEGYRIC OF LOVE; *as the principle without which all gifts are worthless* (1—3): *its attributes* (4—7): *its eternity* (8—12): *its superior dignity to the other great Christian graces* (13). Meyer quotes from Valcknaer, p. 299: "Sunt figuræ oratoriæ, quæ hoc

[t] γλώσσαις τῶν [a] ἀνθρώπων [t] λαλῶ καὶ τῶν [a] ἀγγέλων,
ἀγάπην δὲ μὴ ἔχω, [b] γέγονα [c] χαλκὸς [d] ἠχῶν ἢ [e] κύμβαλον [f] ἀλαλάζον. 2 κἂν ἔχω [g] προφητείαν καὶ εἰδῶ τὰ
[h] μυστήρια πάντα καὶ πᾶσαν τὴν [i] γνῶσιν, κἂν [k] ἔχω πᾶσαν

a so ch. iv. 9. b = 2 Cor. xii. 11. c Mark vi. 8 || Mt. xii. 41. Rev. xviii. 12 only. Gen. iv. 22. d here (Luke xxi. 25 v. r.) only. Jer. xxvii. (l.) 42. (-χος, Acts ii. 2.) e here only. 1 Chron. xiii. 8. f Mark v. 38 only. Josh. vi. 20. g = Rom. xii. 6. ch. xii. 10. xiv. 22 al. (Rev. i. 3.) see Sir. xxiv. 33. h Matt. xiii. 11. ch. xv. 51. Dan. ii. 18 al. i = ch. viii. 1. xii. 8 al. Prov. xxx. (xxiv.) 3. k Acts xiv. 9 reff.

Chap. XIII. 1. homœotel in ℵ[1] from μη εχω to μη εχω next ver: supplied by ℵ-corr[1]. for γεγονα, ἐν ειμι D[1] F(addg ἥ), (*in*) *unum sum ut* old-lat(viz, D-lat E-lat G-lat spec) [Ambrst]. [χαλικος F.] αλαλαζων AD d [17].

2. rec (for κἂν) και εαν (twice in this ver and twice in next), with DF K(1st και αν) L(ℵ) rel(om 2nd εαν εχω 47 [Bas_1]) Chr_1 [Bas_1 $Ephr_1$ (Euthal-ms 1st and 2nd)] Thdrt, 1st (4th και αν) B, 4th 17 : txt AC [Cyr_1], 2nd and 3rd B [$Clem_1$], 1st 2nd and 3rd 17. for ειδω, ουδα (= οιδα) F : ιδω AD[1] 17. 47[1]. ins τα bef παντα F.

caput illuminant, omnes sua sponte natæ in animo heroico, flagrante amore Christi et huic amori divino omnia postponente." "It may," he adds, "without impropriety be called 'a Psalm of Love :' "—the שִׁיר יְדִידֹת of the New Test. (see Ps. xlv. title). "On each side of this chapter the tumult of argument and remonstrance still rages : but within it, all is calm : the sentences move in almost rhythmical melody: the imagery unfolds itself in almost dramatic propriety : the language arranges itself with almost rhetorical accuracy. We can imagine how the Apostle's amanuensis must have paused to look up in his master's face at the sudden change of his style of dictation, and seen his countenance lighted up as it had been the face of an angel, as the sublime vision of divine perfection passed before him." Stanley. **1.**] **ἐὰν λαλῶ** supposes a case which never has been exemplified : **even if I can speak,** or as E. V. **though I speak.** So Isocr. Areop. p. 142,—ἀλλ' ἐὰν μὲν κατορθώσωσι περί τινας πράξεις, ἢ διὰ τύχην, ἢ δι' ἀνδρὸς ἀρετήν, μικρὸν διαλιπόντες πάλιν εἰς τὰς αὐτὰς ἀπορίας κατέστησαν. See Matthiæ, § 523. 1. **ταῖς γλώσσαις τ. ἀνθρ. κ. τ. ἀγγ.**] ὅρα πόθεν ἄρχεται· πρῶτον ἀπὸ τοῦ θαυμαστοῦ δοκοῦντος εἶναι παρ' αὐτοῖς καὶ μεγάλου, τῶν γλωσσῶν. Chrys. p. 289. It is hardly possible to understand γλῶσσαι here of any thing but *articulate forms of speech* : i. e. *languages.* Meyer and De W., who deny that the speaking with tongues was ever in an articulate language, vehemently impugn such a rendering here. But their own rendering is to me undistinguishable from it, as far as the *sense* is concerned : '*tongues speaking in all possible ways,*' surely, in the common acceptation of words, must mean, *tongues speaking all possible languages*, and the use of the word indifferently for *the tongue* and *a tongue* (a language), when this very gift is spoken of, e. g. Acts ii. 4, compared with 11, and here as compared with ch. xii. 30, is one of the strongest proofs that λαλεῖν γλώσσαις is to speak in *languages* : see note on Acts ii. 4. **Of men** (generic) **and of angels** (generic) : i. e. 'of *all* men and *all* angels,' whatever those tongues may be. **ἀγάπην**] Love *to all,* in its *most general sense,* as throughout the chapter : no distinction being here drawn between love to *man* and to *God*, but the *general principle* dealt with, *from which both spring.* The '*Caritas*' of the Latin versions has occasioned the rendering '*charity*' in most modern versions. Of this word Stanley remarks, "the limitation of its meaning on the one hand to mere almsgiving, or on the other to mere toleration, has so much narrowed its sense, that the simpler term 'Love,' though too general exactly to meet the case, is now the best equivalent." **γέγονα**] **I am become**; the case supposed is regarded as present : '*if I can speak . . . I am become.*' **χαλκ. ἠχ.**] Brass, of any kind, struck and yielding a sound : i. e. ἀναίσθητόν τι κ. ἄψυχον. Chrys. No particular musical instrument seems to be meant. **κύμβαλον**] κύμβαλα ἦν πλατέα κ. μεγάλα χάλκεα, Jos. Antt. vii. 12. 3. The Heb. name is most expressive, צֶלְצְלִים. There appear to have been two sorts, mentioned in Ps. cl. 5, צִלְצְלֵי שָׁמַע and צ"תְרוּעָה, rendered by the LXX, κυμβάλοις εὐήχοις —and κ. ἀλαλαγμοῦ, as here. Winer thinks the former answered to our *castagnettes*, the latter to our *cymbals*. The larger kind would be here meant. See Winer, Realw. art. 'Becken.' **ἀλαλάζον**] see Ps. cl. cited above. **2.**] **τὰ μυστήρ. πάντα** are all *the secrets of the divine counsel,*—see Rom. xi. 25 (note); xvi. 25,—and reff. The knowledge of these would be the perfection of the gift of prophecy. The verb belongs to both μυστ. and γνῶσιν. The full construction would be εἰδῶ μυστ. and ἔχω γνῶσιν. **πᾶσαν τὴν πίστιν** hardly, as Stanley, implies '*all the faith in the world,*' but rather, 'all the faith required to,' &c. : or perhaps the art. conveys the allusion to our Lord's

τὴν [k] πίστιν ὥςτε [l] ὄρη [lm] μεθιστάνειν, ἀγάπην δὲ μὴ ἔχω,
[n] οὐθέν εἰμι. 3 κἂν [o] ψωμίσω πάντα τὰ [p] ὑπάρχοντά
μου, κἂν [q] παραδῶ τὸ σῶμά μου ἵνα καυθήσωμαι,
ἀγάπην δὲ μὴ ἔχω, οὐδὲν [s] ὠφελοῦμαι. 4 ἡ ἀγάπη [tu] μακροθυμεῖ, [uv] χρηστεύεται, ἡ ἀγάπη οὐ [w] ζηλοῖ, [ἡ ἀγάπη]
οὐ [x] περπερεύεται, οὐ [y] φυσιοῦται, 5 οὐκ [z] ἀσχημονεῖ, οὐ
[a] ζητεῖ τὰ [a] ἑαυτῆς, οὐ [b] παροξύνεται, οὐ [c] λογίζεται [d] τὸ

l Isa. liv. 10.
m -άνειν, here only +. (Luke xvi. 4. Acts xiii. 22. xix. 26. Col. i. 13 only. Judg. x. 16 A Ald. compl.)
n ch. vii. 19 reff.
o Rom. xii. 20 only. constr., here only. Num. xi. 4, 18 al.
p = Matt. xix. 21. xxiv. 47. Heb. x. 34 al. Gen. xii. 5. q = Acts xv. 26. Dan. iii. 28 (95). s Mark v. 26. Matt. xvi. 26. Prov. x. 2. t Matt. xviii. 26, 29. Luke xviii. 7. 1 Thess. v. 14. Heb. vi. 15. James v. 7 bis, 8. 2 Pet. iii. 9 only. Prov. xix. 11. (-μία, Rom. ix. 22. -μως, Acts xxvi. 3.) u see Rom. ii. 4. 2 Cor. vi. 6. v here only +. (not found elsewhere. Lexx.) w Acts vii. 9 reff. x here only +. see note. y ch. iv. 6 reff. z ch. vii. 36 only. Deut. xxv. 3. (-μοσύνη, Rom. i. 27. -μων, ch. xii. 23.) a ch. x. 24. Phil. ii. 21. b Acts xvii. 16 only (reff.). c = Rom. iv. 8, from Ps. xxxi. 2. d Rom. ii. 9 reff.

λογιζεται ... P ABCDF KLP א a b c d e f g h k l m o 17. 47

μεθισταναι BDF א-corr[1] m 17 Clem [Cyr$_1$] Thl: txt ACKL rel Orig$_3$ Chr$_1$ [Bas$_2$ Ephr$_1$ Euthal-ms] Thdrt Damasc$_2$ Œc. elz ουδεν, with D[1]F K[e sil] Clem$_1$ Meth$_1$ Mac$_1$ Chr$_1$ [Bas$_1$ Cyr$_1$] Thdrt: txt ABCD[3]Lא Clem$_1$ Eph$_2$ Bas$_1$[-mss$_1$ Euthal-ms] Mac$_1$ Damasc$_2$ Thl-comm Œc. for ειμι, ωφελουμαι A Ambr$_2$.

3. elz ψωμιζω (*corrn, the force of the aor not being perceived*), with K[e sil]: txt ABCDFLא rel. παραδωσω F. καυθησομαι DFL b[2] c d f h k 47 [Bas$_1$ Cyr$_1$ Euthal-ms] Max-conf$_1$: καυχησωμαι ABא 17 copt-ms æth[-rom] Ephr$_1$ Jer$_3$(from gr-mss asserts *apud Græcos ipsos ipsa exemplaria diversa esse,* but thinks, *ob similitudinem καυθησωμαι et καυχησωμαι apud Latinos errorem inolevisse*): txt CK rel Orig[-c$_1$ Ephr$_1$] Chr$_1$ Thdrt [Cyr$_1$: simly latt syrr copt-wilk goth æth arm Tert$_1$ Cypr$_2$ Rebapt$_1$ Ambrst Aug$_{sæpe}$] Jac-nisib. ουθεν Aא 17. 73 Bas-ms$_1$: txt BCDFKL rel Chr$_1$ [Ephr$_2$ Bas$_2$ Cyr$_2$ Euthal-ms] Thdrt.

4. om 3rd η αγαπη B a 17-9. 55. 73-4. 118-22[1] lect-17 vulg [F-lat] copt arm Clem$_1$ Ephr$_1$ Chr$_1$ [Bas$_1$ Cyr$_1$] Thl Orig-int$_2$ Tert$_1$ Cypr$_1$ Ambr Ambrst. περπορευεται A Ephr$_1$.

5. for τα εαυτης, το μη εαυτης B Clem$_1$[txt$_1$].

saying, Matt. xvii. 20; xxi. 21: 'all that faith,' so as, &c. **3.**] The double accus. after ψωμίζω is found in the reff. to LXX: but here the accus. of the *person* is omitted, and left to be supplied from the context: **If I bestow in food all my substance.** See the quotation from Coleridge in Stanley's note. **παραδ. τὸ σῶμ. μ. ἵνα καυθ.**] So ref. Dan., καὶ παρέδωκαν τὰ σώματα αὐτῶν εἰς ἐμπυρισμόν, LXX. πῦρ, Theod.: see also 2 Macc. vii. 37. He evidently means *in self-sacrifice:* for country, or friends. Both the deeds mentioned in this verse are such as ordinarily are held to be the fruits of love, but they may be done *without it,* and if so, are worthless. Stanley prefers καυχήσωμαι—and Lachmann has edited it. The objections to it seem to me to be, (1) It leaves παραδῶ standing in a very vague and undefined meaning—"deliver, *to what?*" (2) It introduces an irrelevant and confusing element, a *boastful motive,* into a set of hypotheses which put forward merely an act or set of acts on the one side, and the absence of love on the other: and indeed, worse still, (3) it makes an hypothesis which would reduce the self-sacrifice to nothing, and would *imply* the absence of love; and so would render ἀγάπην δὲ μὴ ἔχω unnecessary.

4—7.] *The blessed attributes of love.* **4.**] **μακροθυμεῖ** is the negative side, **χρηστεύεται** the positive, of a loving temper: the former, the withholding of anger; the latter, the exercise of kindness. **οὐ ζηλοῖ,** '*knows neither envy nor jealousy:*' both are included under the more general sense of ζῆλος. **περπερεύεται**] The word occurs in Cicero ad Attic. i. 14: 'Di boni! quomodo ἐπερπερευσάμην novo auditori Pompeio!' and Marc. Antonin. v. 5: ἀρεσκεύεσθαι, καὶ περπερεύεσθαι, κ. τοσαῦτα ῥιπτάζεσθαι τῇ ψυχῇ. Among the examples in Wetst. of πέρπερος and περπέρεια, is a good definition from Basil: τί ἐστι τὸ περπερεύεσθαι; πᾶν ὃ μὴ διὰ χρείαν, ἀλλὰ διὰ καλλωπισμὸν περιλαμβάνεται περπερείας ἔχει κατηγορίαν. And the Etymol. Mag.,—ἀντὶ τοῦ, ματαιοῦται, ἀτακτεῖ, κατεπαίρεται μετὰ βλακείας ἐπαιρόμενος. The nearest English expression would perhaps be **displays not itself.** See Wetst. **φυσ.,** see, for a contrast, ch. viii. 1. **5.**] **οὐκ ἀσχημονεῖ** seems to be *general,* without particular reference to the disorders in public speaking with tongues. **τὰ ἑαυτῆς**—Love is so personified, as here to be identified with the man possessing the grace, who does not seek τὰ ἑαυτοῦ: see ch. x. 33. **οὐ λογίζ. τὸ κακόν**] **imputeth not (the) evil:** οὐδὲν πονηρὸν οὐ μόνον οὐ κατασκευάζει ἀλλ' οὐδὲ ὑποπτεύει κατὰ τοῦ φιλουμένου, Chrys. Hom. xxxiii. p. 304: and so Theod., Theophyl., Estius,

[d] κακόν, 6 οὐ [e] χαίρει ἐπὶ τῇ ἀδικίᾳ, [f] συγχαίρει δὲ τῇ
[g] ἀληθείᾳ, 7 πάντα [h] στέγει, πάντα [i] πιστεύει, πάντα
ἐλπίζει, πάντα [k] ὑπομένει. 8 ἡ ἀγάπη οὐδέποτε [l] πίπτει.
[m] εἴτε δὲ [n] προφητεῖαι, [o] καταργηθήσονται· [m] εἴτε [p] γλῶσσαι,
[q] παύσονται· [m] εἴτε [n] γνῶσις, [o] καταργηθήσεται. 9 [r] ἐκ
[r] μέρους γὰρ γινώσκομεν καὶ [r] ἐκ [r] μέρους [s] προφητεύομεν·

...γλωσσαι C.

ABDFK LPℵ a b c d e f g h k l m o 17. 47

e constr., Matt. xviii. 13. Luke i. 14. Acts xv. 31. ch. xvi. 17. 2 Cor. vii. 13. Prov. xxiv. 19.
f ch. xii. 26 reff.
g = Col. i. 5. 2 Thess. ii. 12. Rom. i. 18. 2 Tim. iii. 8.
h ch. ix. 12. 1 Thess. iii. 1, 5 only +. Sir. viii. 17 only.
i acc., Acts xiii. 41 reff.
k constr., 2 Tim. ii. 10. Heb. x. 32. xii. 2, 3. James i. 12. Wisd. xvi. 22.
l — Luke xvi. 17. 1 Kings iii. 19. ἐκπ., = James i. 11. see note, and Acts xii. 7. Rom. ix. 6.
m so ch. xiv. 7. xv. 11. 2 Cor. viii. 23.
n ver. 2 (reff.).
o ch. i. 28 reff. 2 Cor. iii. 14.
p Acts ii. 4 reff.
q absol., Acts xx. 1. Exod. ix. 33, 34.
r ch. xii. 27 reff.
s ch. xi. 4, 5 reff.

6. om 1st τη F. **7.** B[1] repeats παντα στεγει.
8. om ἡ B. rec **εκπιπτει**, with C[3]DFKLPℵ[3] rel Clem$_2$ Orig$_3$ Mac$_1$ Chr$_1$ [Ephr$_2$ Bas$_1$ Cyr$_2$ Euthal-ms] Thdrt$_2$ Damasc Thl Œc [Tert$_1$ Cypr$_2$]: txt ABC[1]ℵ[1] 17. 47[1] Nys$_1$ Orig-int$_1$ Ambrst Aug$_{sæpe}$. om δε C[1]D[1]FKP latt copt arm Did$_1$ [Ambrst]: ins ABC[2] D[2.3][-gr] Lℵ rel syr goth [Chr$_2$ Thdrt Damasc Aug$_1$]. προφητεια καταργηθησεται B: προφητεια καταργηθησονται(*sic*) A. γνωσεις (or -σις) καταργηθησονται (*to conform to the preceding clauses*) A D[2][-gr] F[-gr] ℵ 17. 47 (Tert): γν. παυσεται P.
9. for γαρ, δε (*perhaps because this sentence was regarded not as rendering a reason for the last, but as* another *assertion of the imperfection of knowledge and prophecy*) KL rel Phot(in Œc: δὲ ἀντὶ τοῦ γάρ. αἰτία γάρ ἐστι τοῦ διὰ τὶ μέλλουσι καταργ. κ. παύσ.) Œc: om 67[2] goth æth[-rom] Orig$_3$ Eus$_1$ Melet$_1$ [Epiph$_1$] Chr$_1$: txt ABDF[P]ℵ m (17, e sil) 47[sic] latt [syrr copt æth-pl arm] Orig$_1$ [Did$_1$ Eus$_1$ Ath$_1$ Damasc] Thdrt Iren-int$_1$ Hil$_1$ [Ambrst].

Rückert, Meyer: and this is better and more accordant with the sense of λογίζεται, than the more general rendering '*thinketh no evil*.' And we must not overlook the article, which seems here to have the force of implying that the evil actually exists, '*the evil*' which is,—but Love does not impute it. So Theodoret, συγγινώσκει τοῖς ἐπταισμένοις, οὐκ ἐπὶ κακῷ σκόπῳ ταῦτα γεγενῆσθαι ὑπολαμβάνων.

6. οὐ χ. ἐπὶ τῇ ἀδ.] rejoices not at (the) iniquity, i. e. at its commission by others,—as is the habit of the unloving world. **συγχαίρει τῇ ἀλ.]** Most Commentators, as the E. V., altogether overlook the force of the verb and the altered construction, and render, '*rejoiceth in the truth*:' others, who respect the verb, make τῇ ἀληθ.=τοῖς εὐδοκιμοῦσι (Chrys.), those to whom, as in 3 John 12, μεμαρτύρηται ὑπ' αὐτῆς τῆς ἀληθείας. But Meyer's rendering is the only one which preserves the force of both words: **rejoices with the Truth,** ἡ ἀλήθ. being personified, and meaning especially *the spread among men* (as opposed to ἀδικία) of *the Truth of the Gospel*, and indeed of *the truth in general*,—in opposition to those who (ref. Rom.) τὴν ἀλήθειαν ἐν ἀδικίᾳ κατέχουσι,—who (ref. 2 Tim.) ἀνθίστανται τῇ ἀληθείᾳ. **7.] πάντα,**—i. e. all things which *can be borne with a good conscience*. So Bengel, of *all four*: 'videlicet, quæ tegenda vel credenda, quæ speranda et sufferenda sunt.' **στέγει] bears**: see note, ch. ix. 12. Hammond, Estius, Bengel (above),—'*covers*:' but the variation in sense from ch. ix. is needless. **πιστ.]** viz. without suspicion of another. **ἐλπίζ.]** viz., even against hope—hoping what is good of another, even when others have ceased to do so. **ὑπομ.]** viz. persecutions and distresses inflicted by others, rather than shew an unloving spirit to them.

8—12.] *The eternal abiding of Love, when other graces have passed away.*

8. πίπτει] The exact word is that of the E. V., **faileth**: so Theod.: οὐ διασφάλλεται, ἀλλ' ἀεὶ μένει βεβαία κ. ἀσάλευτος κ. ἀκίνητος, ἐς ἀεὶ διαμένουσα. τοῦτο γὰρ διὰ τῶν ἐπαγομένων ἐδίδαξεν. Of the two readings, we may illustrate **πίπτει** by Plato, Phileb., p. 22 E, ἀλλὰ μήν, ὦ Σώκρατες, ἔμοιγε δοκεῖ νῦν μὲν ἡδονή σοι πεπτωκέναι καθαπερεὶ πληγεῖσα ὑπὸ τῶν νῦν δὴ λόγων: and Polyb. x. 33. 4, κἂν ποτε πέσῃ τὰ ὅλα, "in case the whole plan should fail:" id. i. 35. 5: and **ἐκπίπτει** by Plato, Gorg. p. 517, εἰ οὗτοι ῥήτορες ἦσαν, οὔτε τῇ ἀληθινῇ ῥητορικῇ ἐχρῶντο (οὐ γὰρ ἂν ἐξέπεσον) οὔτε τῇ κολακικῇ: where Heindorf,—'proprie usurpatur de actoribus, citharœdis, aliisque, qui a spectatoribus exploduntur et exsibilantur:' and by the celebrated passage in Demosthenes περὶ στεφ. p. 315,—ἐτριταγωνίστεις, ἐγὼ δ' ἐθεώρουν. ἐξέπιπτες, ἐγὼ δ' ἐσύριττον: where also, by the way, ἔπιπτες is a various reading. By **εἴτε, εἴτε, εἴτε,** the *general* idea, **χαρίσματα,** is split into its *species*—**be there prophesyings,—be there** (speakings in) **tongues,—be there knowledge.** Chrys., al., understand the two first futures, **καταργ., παύσ.,** of the time when, the faith being every

10 ὅταν δὲ ἔλθῃ τὸ ᵗ τέλειον, τὸ ʳ ἐκ ʳ μέρους ᵒ καταργηθήσεται. 11 ὅτε ᵘ ἤμην ᵛ νήπιος, ἐλάλουν ὡς ᵛ νήπιος,
ʷ ἐφρόνουν ὡς ᵛ νήπιος, ˣ ἐλογιζόμην ὡς ᵛ νήπιος· ὅτε γέγονα ἀνήρ, ᵒ κατήργηκα ʸ τὰ τοῦ ᵛ νηπίου. 12 βλέπομεν
γὰρ ἄρτι δι' ᶻ ἐσόπτρου ἐν ᵃ αἰνίγματι, τότε δὲ ᵇ πρόσωπον

ABDF LPא a c d e f h k l m o 17. 47

t = ch. ii. 6. xiv. 20. Rom. xii. 2. James i. 4 bis. 1 John iv. 18. Ps. cxxxviii. 22. u gospp. and Acts, passim. Paul, Gal. i. 10, 22 only. Neh. ii. 15. ἤμεθα, Matt. xxiii. 30 bis. Acts xxvii. 37. Eph. ii. 3. v ch. iii. 1 reff. Gal. iv. 1, 3. w absol., here only. Isa. xliv. 18. x = Rom. ii. 3. y Rom. viii. 5 reff. z James i. 23 only †. Wisd. vii. 26. Sir. xii. 11 only. a here only. Num. xii. 8. Sir. xxxix. 3. b Gen. xxxii. 30. see 2 John 12. 3 John 14. Num. xii. 8.

10. rec ins τοτε bef το εκ μερους (*for emphasis and precision*), with D$^{2 \cdot 3}$[-gr] KL rel syrr Orig$_2$ Melet$_1$ Chr$_1$ Thdrt: om ABD^{1}FPא 17. 47 latt copt goth æth arm Orig$_5$ (-int$_4$) Eus$_1$ Ath$_1$ [Cyr-p$_2$ Euthal-ms Max$_1$] Damasc Iren-int. καταργηθησεται bef το εκ μερους D$^{1 \cdot 3}$F latt Syr goth Orig-int$_5$ [Ambrst] Jer. τα εκ μ. F[-gr] Iren-int$_1$.

11. aft 1st οτε ins δε D^1[-gr] fuld. rec ως νηπιος bef the verb (3 times), with D F[-gr(and G-lat)] KLP rel fuld syrr goth arm Orig[-c$_1$ Bas$_1$ Euthal-ms] Epiph$_1$ Chr$_1$ Thdrt$_1$ Thl Œc [(Tert$_1$) Aug$_{alic}$]; 1st time, m [Orig-int$_1$]: txt ABא 17 vulg [F-lat] copt æth Clem$_1$ Orig[-c$_1$]-int$_1$ Bas$_1$ Nys$_1$ (Did$_1$) Thdrt$_1$ Damasc Jer$_1$ Aug$_1$. rec aft 2nd οτε ins δε, with D^3[-gr] FKLPא^3 rel [vulg-clem fuld demid] syrr copt æth arm Orig [-c$_2$-int]$_{aliq}$ Meth Epiph$_1$ Chr$_1$ [Bas$_1$ Euthal-ms] Thdrt [Damasc Ambrst] Tert$_1$: om ABD^1(and lat) א^1 am(with harl^1 tol) goth Orig[$_1$-int$_2$] Did$_1$ Hil$_1$. for γεγονα, εγενομην B Orig[-c]$_1$. τα του νηπιου bef κατηργηκα D F[-gr(and G-lat)] syr goth [arm (Tischdf) Epiph$_1$] Bas Orig-int$_3$[(txt$_1$-c$_2$-int$_6$) Tert$_1$ Hil$_1$ Ambrst]. (not F-lat Aug$_{[sæpe]}$.)

12. [βλεπωμεν P 42: -ποιμεν m.] om γαρ D^{1}FP latt goth arm Clem$_1$ [Thdot$_1$] Tert Cypr Ambrst. ins ὡς bef δι εσοπτρου D-gr b g o Syr syr-w-ast arm Clem$_4$ Thdrt$_4$ [Orig-int$_1$(om$_{sæpe}$)] Tert$_1$. ins και bef εν αινιγματι LP f 63. 109-78 Orig$_{sæpe}$[-int$_{sæpe}$] Hil$_2$ Gaud$_1$ [om Orig$_1$-int$_1$ Hil$_1$ Gaud$_1$].

where dispersed, these gifts should be *no longer needed*. But unquestionably the time alluded to is that of *the coming of the Lord;* see ver. 12, and this applies to *all these*, not to the last (γνῶσις) only. The two first, **προφ.** and **γλῶσσ.**, shall be *absolutely* superseded: **γνῶσις**, *relatively:* the imperfect, by the perfect. **9, 10.**] *Reason given;*—that our knowledge, and our prophesying (utterance of divine things) are but *partial*, embracing *but a part:* but when that which is *perfect* (entire—universal) shall have come, this *partial* shall be abolished—superseded. See Eph. iv. 11—13, where the same idea is otherwise expressed. **11.**] *Analogical illustration of ver.* 10. **νήπιος** and **τέλειος** are used in contrast ch. ii. 6—iii. 1; xiv. 20. **ἐλάλουν, ἐφρόνουν, ἐλογιζόμην—I spoke, I [thought]** (felt, was minded), **I [reasoned** (or] **judged).** There can hardly be an allusion, as Theophyl., Œc., Bengel, Olsh., al., think, to the *three gifts*, of *tongues* (ἐλάλ.), *prophecy* (ἐφρόν., which suits but very lamely), and *knowledge* (ἐλογιζ.). **ὅτε γέγ. κ.τ.λ.] Now that I am become a man, I have brought to an end the ways of a child:** not, as E. V, '*when I became a man, I put away* . . . .,' as if it were done *on a set day*, and as if γέγ. and κατήργ. were aorists. For this use of ὅτε, cf. Demosth. Olynth. 1, init. ὅτε τοίνυν ταῦθ' οὕτως ἔχει, προσήκει προθύμως ἐθέλειν ἀκούειν: see Kühner, § 813. 2. **12.**] *Contrast between our present sight and knowledge,—and those in the future perfect state.* **γάρ** justifies the analogy of the former verse: for it is just so with *us*. **ἄρτι**, in our *present condition*, until the Lord's coming. **δι' ἐσόπτρου, through a mirror:** i. e. as Billroth, Meyer, and De W.—*according to the popular illusion*, which regards the object, really seen *behind* the mirror, as seen through it. We must think, not of our mirrors of glass, but of the imperfectly-reflecting metallic mirrors of the ancients. The idea of the *lapis specularis*, placed in windows, being meant, adopted by Schöttgen from Rabbinical usage (e. g. 'omnes prophetæ viderunt per specular obscurum, et Moses doctor noster vidit per specular lucidum' (Wetst.): and see numerous examples in his Hor. Hebr. i. 646 ff.), and followed by many Commentators, is inconsistent with the usage of **ἔσοπτρον**, which (Meyer) is *always a* MIRROR (Pind. Nem. vii. 20: Anacr. xi. 2; xx. 5. Lucian, Amor. xliv. 48: see also reff.): the window of *lapis specularis* being **δίοπτρα** (Strabo, xii. 2, p. 540). **ἐν αἰνίγματι**] There is a reference to ref. Num., στόμα κατὰ στόμα λαλήσω αὐτῷ ἐν εἴδει, καὶ οὐ δι' αἰνιγμάτων. Many take the words adverbially,—'*enigmatically*' (so E. V., '*darkly*' [and so we are almost obliged to do in an English version]): but this cannot be [the strict rendering], because αἴνιγμα is objective, not subjective: '*a dark hint given by words.*' I agree with Meyer, notwithstanding De Wette's strong objec-

[b] πρὸς [b] πρόσωπον· ἄρτι γινώσκω [r] ἐκ [r] μέρους, τότε δὲ
[c] ἐπιγνώσομαι [d] καθὼς καὶ [c] ἐπεγνώσθην. 13 [e] νυνὶ δὲ
[f] μένει πίστις ἐλπὶς ἀγάπη, τὰ τρία ταῦτα· [g] μείζων δὲ
τούτων ἡ ἀγάπη.

XIV. 1 [h] Διώκετε τὴν ἀγάπην, [i] ζηλοῦτε δὲ τὰ [k] πνευματικά, μᾶλλον δὲ ἵνα [l] προφητεύητε. 2 ὁ γὰρ [m] λαλῶν

c = Rom. i. 32. Matt. xi. 27 bis. Jer. v. 5. (absol., Acts ix. 30 only.)
d ch. xii. 11 reff.
e Rom. vi. 22. vii. 6, 17 al. Job xxx. 1, 9.
f = Heb. xiii. 1. see note.
g = ch. xii. 31. xiv. 5. comparat., Matt. xiii. 32. Luke ix. 46. ch. xv. 19.
h = Rom. ix. 30 reff. Ps. xxxiii. 14.
i = ch. xii. 31. ver. 39 only. Sir. li. 18.
k = ch. x. 3, 4 reff.
l ch. xi. 4, 5 reff.
m ch. xii. 30 reff.

in 2nd τοτε, τε is written over the line by ℵ-corr[1]. ins εγω bef επεγνωσθην F[-gr] D-lat G-lat tol $Cypr_1$.

13. for νυνι δε μενει, μενει δε F(μινει)[(not F-lat) D-lat] $Clem_1$ Hil_1 [Ambrst Aug_1].

tions, in believing ἐν αἰνίγματι to mean *'in a dark discourse,'* viz. *the revealed word,* which is *dark,* by comparison with our future *perfect knowledge.* So also Luther: in einem dunkeln Wort. Thus, as M. observes, ἐν will denote, as ἐν τῷ κρυπτῷ, Matt. vi. 4, the *local department, in which* the βλέπειν takes place. τότε = ὅταν ἔλθῃ τὸ τέλειον, ver. 10: *'at the Lord's coming, and after.'* **πρόσωπ. πρὸς πρόσωπ.]** **Face towards face,** i. e. by immediate intuition: so Heb. in reff. **I shall thoroughly know even as I was** (during this life: he places himself *in that state,* and uses the aor. as of a thing gone by) **thoroughly known.** In this life we *are known by* God, rather than *know* Him: see Gal. iv. 9; ch. viii. 3, note,—and cf. Philo de Cherub. 32, vol. i. p. 159, νῦν ὅτε ζῶμεν, κρατούμεθα μᾶλλον ἢ ἄρχομεν, κ. γνωριζόμεθα μᾶλλον ἢ γνωρίζομεν. The sense of this aor. ἐπεγνώσθην must not be forced, as in E. V., to a present, or to a future, as by some Commentators.

13.] *Superiority of Love to the other great Christian graces.* Some gifts shall pass away—but *these three* great graces *shall remain for ever*—FAITH, HOPE, LOVE. *This is necessarily the meaning,*—and *not that love alone shall abide for ever, and the other two merely during the present state.* For (1) **νυνὶ δέ** is not 'but *now,'* i. e. in this present state, as opposed to what has just been said ver. 12,—but *'rebus sic stantibus,' 'quæ cum ita sint,'* —and the inference from it just the contrary of that implied in the other rendering: viz. that *since tongues, prophesyings, knowledge, will all pass away,* we have left *but* THESE THREE. (2) From the position of **μένει,** it has a *strong emphasis,* and carries the weight of the clause, as opposed to the previously-mentioned things which καταργηθήσεται. (3) From τὰ τρία ταῦτα, a *pre-eminence* is obviously pointed out for *faith, hope, and love,* distinct from aught which has gone before. This being the plain sense of the words, how can *faith* and *hope* be said to endure to eternity, when faith will be lost in sight, and hope in fruition? With *hope,* there is but little difficulty: *but one place* has inscribed over its portals, "Lasciate ogni speranza, voi ch' entrate." New glories, new treasures of knowledge and of love, will ever raise, and nourish, blessed hopes of yet more and higher,—hopes which no disappointment will blight. But how can *faith* abide,—faith, which is the evidence of things *not seen,*—where all things once believed are seen? In the form of *holy confidence and trust,* faith will abide even there. The stay of all conscious created being, human or angelic, is *dependence on God;* and where the faith which *comes by hearing* is out of the question, the faith which *consists in trusting* will be the only faith possible. Thus *Hope* will remain, as anticipation certain to be fulfilled: *Faith* will remain, as trust, entire and undoubting:—the anchor of the soul, even where no tempest comes. See this expanded and further vindicated in my Quebec Chapel Sermons, Vol. i. Serm. viii. **μείζων τ.]** **The greater of these,**—not *'greater than* these.' "The greater," as De Wette beautifully remarks, "because it contains in itself the root of the other two: we believe only one whom we love,—we hope only that which we love." And thus the forms of Faith and Hope which will there for ever subsist, will be sustained in, and overshadowed by, the all-pervading superior element of eternal Love.

CHAP. XIV. 1—25.] *Demonstration of* THE SUPERIORITY OF THE GIFT OF PROPHECY OVER THAT OF SPEAKING WITH TONGUES. 1.] *Transition from the parenthetical matter of the last chapter to the subject about to be resumed.* **Pursue after Love** (let it be your great aim,—important and enduring as that grace has been shewn to be): **meantime however** (during that pursuit; making that the first thing, take up this as a second) **strive for spiritual gifts** [see note on ch. xii. 1], **but more** (more than πν. in general: i. e. more for this than for others[; **chiefly**]) **that ye may prophesy** (sc. ζηλοῦτε, ἵνα . . . *

n = Mark iv. 33. Gen. xi. 7. xlii. 23.
o = vv. 14, 15. Acts xvii. 16.
p ch. xiii. 2 reff.
q = Rom. xiv. 19 reff.
r = Rom. xii. 8 reff.
s here only †. Wisd. xix. 12 only. (-θιον, Phil. ii. 1. -θεῖσθαι, 1 Thess. ii. 11.)
t = Acts ix. 31 reff.
u = ch. xii. 31. xiii. 13.

ᵐγλώσσῃ οὐκ ἀνθρώποις λαλεῖ, ἀλλὰ [τῷ] θεῷ· οὐδεὶς ABDFK LP‎א a b c d e f g h k l m o 17. 47
γὰρ ⁿἀκούει, ᵒπνεύματι δὲ λαλεῖ ᵖμυστήρια· 3 ὁ δὲ ˡπρο-
φητεύων ἀνθρώποις λαλεῖ ᵠοἰκοδομὴν καὶ ʳπαράκλησιν
καὶ ˢπαραμυθίαν. 4 ὁ ᵐλαλῶν ᵐγλώσσῃ ἑαυτὸν ᵗοἰκοδομεῖ,
ὁ δὲ ˡπροφητεύων ἐκκλησίαν ᵗοἰκοδομεῖ. 5 θέλω δὲ πάντας
ὑμᾶς ᵐλαλεῖν ᵐγλώσσαις, μᾶλλον δὲ ἵνα ˡπροφητεύητε·
ᵘμείζων δὲ ὁ ˡπροφητεύων ἢ ὁ ᵐλαλῶν ᵐγλώσσαις, ᵛἐκτὸς
ᵛεἰ μὴ ʷδιερμηνεύῃ, ἵνα ἡ ἐκκλησία ᵠοἰκοδομὴν λάβῃ.
6 ˣνῦν δέ, ἀδελφοί, ἐὰν ἔλθω πρὸς ὑμᾶς ᵐγλώσσαις ᵐλαλῶν,

v ch. xv. 2. 1 Tim. v. 19 only. w ch. xii. 30 reff. x ch. xii. 18 al.

Chap. XIV. 2. **γλωσσαις** D-gr F-gr b o G²-lat arm Chr₁ [Ambr₁]. ουχ א (*see Acts* ii. 7 *digest*). ανθρωπους F[-gr] (so in ver 3). om τω (bef θεω) (*for conformity with ανθρ.* ?) BD¹FPא¹ l Chr-comm₁ : ins AD³KLא³ rel Thdrt Damasc Thl Œc. ουθις א. for πνευματι, πνευμα F-gr D-lat G[-lat] am² with(fuld flor) Pel Vig Bede.
3. for ο δε, ει γαρ ο F-gr G[-lat] ; *nam qui* vulg(and F-lat) D-lat [*qui enim* Ambrst].
4. for λαλων, λαλει F(G adds *aut* λαλων). **γλωσσαις** D 46 arm Mac₁. aft εκκλησιαν ins θεου F-gr G[-lat] vulg-ed [harl(appy)](not am demid fuld tol F-lat) Pel.
5. υμας bef παντας A Ambrst. γλωσσαις bef λαλειν A am Chr₁ Thl : om λαλειν k¹. for ινα προφητευητε, προφητευειν D¹[-gr F-lat] vulg Jer₁ Pel. rec (for δε aft μειζων) γαρ, with DFKLא³ rel [syrr æth arm] Chr₁ Thdrt [Damasc] Jer₁ Ambrst: txt ABPא¹ 39 copt [Euthal-ms]. add εστιν F. **διερμηνευει** (*the later mss confound* ει *and* η *to a very great extent : see the original collations passim*) L a b c d f g h k l o 47 Chr₁ Thl : διερμηνευων D¹[-gr], η ο διερμηνευων F-gr(and G[-lat]).
6. rec **νυνι**, with D³KL rel Chr₁ Thl Œc : txt ABD¹FPא Chr-ms [Euthal-ms] Thdrt

as the aim of your ζῆλος). **2—20.**] *Prophecy edifies the* BRETHREN *more than speaking with tongues.* **2.**] **For he that speaks in a tongue, speaks not to men but to God; for no one understands him** (so ἀκούω in reff. and Athen. ix. p. 382, ἔλεγεν ῥήματα ἃ οὐδὲ εἷς ἤκουσεν ἄν, i. e. as a *general rule*, the assembly do not understand him; some, who have the gift of interpretation of tongues, may,—but they are the exception), **but** (opposed to οὐδεὶς γὰρ ἀκούει) **in the spirit** (in his spirit, as opposed to in his understanding: his spirit is the organ of the Holy Ghost, but his understanding is unfruitful, see vv. 14, 15) **he speaks mysteries** (things which are hidden from the hearers, and sometimes also from himself): **3.**] **but** (on the other hand) **he who prophesies, speaks to men edification** (genus) **and** (species) **exhortation and** (species) **consolation.** See the definition of *prophecy* given on ch. xii. 10: and Stanley's excursus introductory to this chapter. **παραμυθία** occurs Plato, Axioch. p. 365,—ἀσθενῆ τὴν ψυχήν, πάνυ ἐνδεᾶ παραμυθίας: and Ælian, V. H. xii. 1, fin., παρεμυθήσατο Ἀρταξέρξην, κ. τὸ τῆς λύπης ἰάσατο πάθος, εἴξαντος τοῦ βασ. τῇ κηδεμονίᾳ, κ. τῇ παραμυθίᾳ πεισθέντος συνετῶς. **4.**] **ἑαυτ. οἰκ.** does not necessarily involve his *understanding* what he speaks: the *exercise of the gift* in accordance with the prompting of the Spirit may be regarded as an οἰκοδομή: the intensity of the feeling of prayer or praise in which he utters the words is edifying to him, though the words themselves are unintelligible. This view is necessary on account of what is said in ver. 5, that if he can *interpret*, he can edify not only himself but the church. **ἐκκλησίαν**] [i. e. the * assembled Christians: see note on ch. xi. 18] not, as Meyer, *a congregation*, but = τὴν ἐκκλησίαν: the art. being often omitted when a noun in government has an emphatic place before the verb: accordingly in ver. 5, it is ἡ ἐκκλ. which is edified. **5.**] He shews that it is from no *antipathy* to or *jealousy* of the gift of tongues that he thus speaks: but (force of the **δέ**) that he *wished them all to speak with tongues, but rather that they should prophesy.* The distinction between the acc. and inf. after θέλω, as the simple direct object of the wish, and ἵνα with the subj., as its higher and ulterior object, has been lost in the E. V. The second δέ is opposed to the subordinate λαλ. γλ., as in ver. 1 to τὰ πνευματικά. **μείζων δέ**] δέ is transitional. **μείζων**] see reff.,—superior *in usefulness*, and therefore *in dignity.* **ἐκτὸς εἰ μή** is a mixture of two constructions, ἐκτὸς εἰ, and εἰ μή. It is not a Hebraism, as Grot. supposes; Wetst. gives examples from Demosth., Aristides, Lucian, Sextus Empiricus: and from Thom. Mag., φαμέν, ἐκτὸς εἰ μὴ τόδε, καὶ ἐκτὸς εἰ τόδε. **διερμηνεύῃ**] viz. ὁ λαλῶν γλώσσῃ, not τις, as suggested by Flatt. On the subj. with εἰ,

τί ὑμᾶς ὠφελήσω, ἐὰν μὴ ὑμῖν λαλήσω ἢ [y] ἐν [z] ἀποκαλύψει ἢ [y] ἐν [a] γνώσει ἢ [y] ἐν [a] προφητείᾳ ἢ [y] ἐν [b] διδαχῇ;
7 [c] ὅμως τὰ [d] ἄψυχα φωνὴν [e] διδόντα, [f] εἴτε [g] αὐλὸς [f] εἴτε
[h] κιθάρα, ἐὰν [i] διαστολὴν τοῖς [k] φθόγγοις μὴ [e] δῷ, πῶς
γνωσθήσεται τὸ [l] αὐλούμενον ἢ τὸ [m] κιθαριζόμενον; 8 καὶ
γὰρ ἐὰν [n] ἄδηλον [o] φωνὴν [o] σάλπιγξ [e] δῷ, τίς [p] παρα-

y ch. ii. 7, 13. Matt. xiii. 3.
z = ver. 26. 2 Cor. xii. 1, 7. Gal. ii. 2. Rev. i. 1 ‡. (1 Kings xx. 30. Sir. xi. 27 al.)
a ch. xiii. 2 (reff.).
b Acts ii. 42 reff.
c John xii. 42. Gal. iii. 15 only. 2 Macc. xv. 5.
d here only †. Wisd. xiii. 17. xiv. 29 only.
e = Matt. xxiv. 29. Isa. xiii. 10. ἠχὼ διδοῦσα θόρυβον, Eur. Hec. 1093.
f ch. xiii. 8 reff.
g here only. 1 Kings x. 5 al. (-λητής, Matt. ix. 23.)
h Rev. v. 8. xiv. 2. xv. 2 only. Gen. iv. 21 al.
i Rom. x. 12 reff.
k Rom. x. 18 only, from Ps. xviii. 4. Wisd. xix. 18 only.
l Matt. xi. 17 || L. only †.
m Rev. xiv. 2 only. Isa. xxiii. 16.
n = here (Luke x. 44) only. (Ps. l. 6 [8].) 2 Macc. vii. 34 only. Polyb. viii. 3. 2, ἄδηλοι ἐλπίδες, and al. (-λως, ch. ix. 26. -λότης, 1 Tim. vi. 17.)
o Matt. xxiv. 31. Rev. i. 10. viii. 13. Exod. xix. 16, 19.
p Acts x. 10. 2 Cor. ix. 2, 3 only. Jer. xii. 5.

Damasc. [for υμας] υμιν P. om 1st ἢ ℵ c 17 [D-lat] syr copt [Thl]. om last εν D[1][-gr] F[-gr] ℵ[1] b tol harl[2]. (am [demid] D-lat om 2nd εν: am harl[2] [demid tol] F-lat D-lat om 3rd.)

7. μη bef διαστολην τ. φθογγ. D[1]F. for τοις φθογγοις, φθογγου B tol D-lat arm Ambrst. διδω D[3]LP rel Thdrt Damasc Thl: δωτε K: txt ABD[1][F]ℵ f Chr_1 [Euthal-ms] Œc. γνωσθη (for -θησεται) D[1]F [*scietur* latt].

8. σαλπ. bef φωνην APℵ d 17. 119 coptt $Orig_1$. δωη D[1].

giving a sense not distinguishable from the ind., see Winer, edn. 6, § 41. *b.* 2 end, and Herm., on Soph. Ant. 706. **6.**] *Example of the unprofitableness of speaking with tongues without interpreting,*—expressed in the first person as of himself. **νῦν δέ**] '*quod cum ita sit*'—viz. that there is no edification without interpretation. **ἐὰν ἔλθω**] Chrys. understands the first person to imply '*not even I myself* should profit you,' &c. But then αὐτὸς ἐγώ or some expression similarly emphatic would have been used. The second ἐάν is parallel to the first, not dependent on ὠφελήσω. It is the negative side of the supposition, as ἐὰν ἔλθω κ.τ.λ. was the affirmative. On this double apodosis Hermann remarks, Soph. Aj. 827,—'Est enim hæc verborum complexio ex eo genere, cujus jam apud Homerum exempla inveniuntur, quod duplicem habet apodosin, alteram præmissam, sequentem alteram: quæ ratio ibi maxime apta est, ubi in magno animi motu, quasi non satis sit id quod præmissum est, aliud infertur secunda apodosi, quod gravius sit et fortius.' **ἢ ἐν ἀποκ. . . . .**] It seems best here, with Estius, to understand 'duo juga, ut conjugata sint revelatio et prophetia, ac rursus conjugata scientia et doctrina.' So also Meyer, who observes that the ground of προφητεία is ἀποκάλυψις, and that of διδαχή, γνῶσις: the former being a *direct speaking in the Spirit,* and the latter a *laying forth by the aid of the Spirit* of knowledge acquired. Thus ἐν, as referred to ἀποκ. and γνώσ., denotes the *internal element:*—as referred to προφ. and διδ., the *external element,* of the spiritual activity. **7—11.**] *Instances to shew that unintelligible discourse profits nothing.* And first,—**7—9.**] *from musical instruments.* **7.**] **ὅμως** occurs here and in the two other places where * it is used in the N. T. (reff.) at the beginning of the sentence, out of its logical order, which would be before ἐὰν διαστολὴν . ., thus: **Things without life which yield sound, whether flute or harp, yet, if they do not,** &c. The renderings, '*even* things without life' (E. V.), or 'things which, though without life, yet give sound' (Winer, edn. 6, § 61. 5. f), are inadmissible,—the former because of the usage of ὅμως, the latter because no such idea as any surprise at a thing without life yielding sound is here in place. **φων. διδ.**] so δίδου φωνάν Pind. Nem. v. 93. **ἐὰν διαστ.**] **If they** (the ἄψυχα φ. δ.) **shall not have yielded a distinction** (of musical intervals) **in their tones, how shall be known that which is being played on the flute or that which is being played on the harp** (i. e. *what tune is played* in either case: the art. being repeated to shew that two distinct instances are contemplated, not necessarily '*one tune, either piped, or harped*' = τὸ αὐλούμενον ἢ κιθαριζόμενον;)? The observation of Meyer, that this example is decisive against *foreign languages* being spoken in the exercise of this gift, is shewn to be irrelevant by the next example, from which the contrary might be argued—the ἄδηλος φωνή of the trumpet being exactly analogous to an *unknown language,* not to an *inarticulate sound.* But the fact is that all such inferences, from pressing analogies close, are insecure. **8.**] **ἄδηλον, uncertain,** in its *meaning:* for a particular succession of notes of the trumpet then, as now, gave the signals for attack, and retreat, and the various evolutions of an army. The giving the signal for battle with the trumpet is called by Dio Cassius τὸ πολεμικὸν βοᾶν,

σκευάσεται εἰς πόλεμον; 9 οὕτως καὶ ὑμεῖς διὰ τῆς
γλώσσης [q] ἐὰν μὴ [r] εὔσημον λόγον [e] δῶτε, πῶς γνωσθήσεται τὸ λαλούμενον; ἔσεσθε γὰρ εἰς [s] ἀέρα λαλοῦντες.
10 τοσαῦτα, [t] εἰ [t] τύχοι, [u] γένη φωνῶν εἰσιν ἐν κόσμῳ, καὶ
οὐδὲν [v] ἄφωνον· 11 ἐὰν οὖν μὴ εἰδῶ τὴν [w] δύναμιν τῆς
φωνῆς, ἔσομαι τῷ λαλοῦντι [x] βάρβαρος, καὶ ὁ λαλῶν [y] ἐν
ἐμοὶ [x] βάρβαρος. 12 οὕτως καὶ ὑμεῖς ἐπεὶ [z] ζηλωταί ἐστε

ABDFK LPℵ a b c d e f g h k l m o 17. 47

q arrangt. of words, 2 Cor. ii. 4 reff. r here only ‡. Ps. lxxx. 3 only. s ch. ix. 26 reff. t ch. xv. 37 only. Philo de Mut. Nom. 26, vol. i. p. 600, μουσικὰ μὲν γάρ, εἰ τύχοι, κ. γραμματικά . . . . (Dion. Hal. iv. 19, μυρίων ἢ δισμυρ., εἰ τύχοι . . . . Galen. de usu part. vi., δέκα μέν, εἰ τύχοι. Wetst.) see ch. xvi. 6. u = ch. xii. 10 reff. v = here only. (Acts viii. 32 reff.) w = here only. Num. vi. 21. Dion. Hal., Antt. i. 68, τοῦ π μήπω γράμματος εὑρημένου, τῷ δ δηλοῦν τ. ἐκείνου δύναμιν τ. παλαιούς. Dio Cass. lv. 3, τοιοῦτον γὰρ ἡ δύναμις τοῦ ὀνόματος τούτου δηλοῖ. x Acts xxviii. 2, 4 reff. y = Rom. xi. 25. z Acts xxi. 20 reff.

παρασκευαζεται A Orig$_1$.

9. for ευσημον, ευσχημον D[1][-gr] 21-3[3]. 80. for δωτε, δω L. [at εαν μη . . . δωτε K-marg notes, αντι του· εαν μη διερμηνευοιτε.]

10. om τοσαυτα D[1] F(with G-lat). rec (for εισιν) εστιν (*gramml corrn: see note*), with KL rel Chr$_1$ Thdrt Œc: txt ABDFPℵ 47 Clem$_1$ Damasc Thl. ins τω bef κοσμω D[1]F b o, *hoc* vulg-ed ([fuld demid &c] and F-lat, not am) Ambrst Bede. rec aft ουδεν ins αυτων (*addn for precision*), with D[3]KLℵ[3] rel G-lat syrr Chr$_1$ Thdrt: om ABD[1]FPℵ[1] d 17 vulg E-lat coptt arm Clem$_1$ [Euthal-ms] Damasc Ambrst Bede. aft αφωνον ins εστιν D[1]F vulg [not E-lat: pref c].

11. for εαν, ει P. ιδω AD[1]L a m 17: γινωσκω F(*si ergo nesciero* F-lat, and so vulg [Ambrst]). om last clause (*homœotel*) L a[1]. om εν DF latt syrr copt arm Clem Chr$_{expr}$(ο εμοι λαλ. βαρβ.) Damasc [Ambrst].

by Ælian τὸ παρορμητικὸν ἐμπνεῖν: see Wetst., where many examples are to be found. **9.**] *Application of these instances.* **διὰ τ. γλώσσης** is most naturally understood *physically*, **by means of your tongue**, as answering to the utterance of the sound by the musical instruments. But the technical rendering, by means of *the tongue* (in the sense of γλώσσῃ λαλεῖν), is allowable. **ἔσεσθε . . . λαλ.**] This periphrasis of the future implies, **ye will be**, so long as ye speak, **speaking, . . .** On **εἰς ἀέρα**, see ref.: it implies the *non-reception by hearers* of what is said. **10, 11.**] *Another example of the unprofitableness of an utterance not understood.* **10.**] **εἰ τύχοι, if it should so happen,** i. e. **peradventure:**—it is commonly found with numerical nouns; but sometimes with hypothetical sentences in general, as in ch. xv. 37. See reff. and examples in Wetst. It will not bear the rendering '*for example*,' though in meaning it nearly approaches it. It belongs here to **τοσαῦτα**, itself representing some fixed number, but not assignable by the information which the writer possesses, or not worth assigning. See similar expressions, Acts v. 8,—and 2 Sam. xii. 8 in E. V. **γένη φωνῶν**] **kinds of languages**: the more precise expression would be γένη φωνῆς, or φωναί: we can hardly say, with Meyer, that each language is a γένος φωνῶν. The use of φωνῶν, and not γλωσσῶν, is no doubt intentional, to avoid confusion, γλῶσσα being for the most part used in this passage in a peculiar meaning: but no argument can be grounded on it as to the γλῶσσαι being languages or not. **εἰσίν** (plur.), because it is wished to distinguish them in their variety. **οὐδέν**, scil. γένος. Bleek renders, '*no rational animal is without speech*;' and Grot., reading as the rec. αὐτῶν, understands it as referring to *men*: others supply ἔθνος to οὐδέν. But the common rendering is both simpler, and better sense: **none of them is without signification**, as E. V.: or, **is inarticulate.** **11.**] **οὖν**, *seeing that* none is without meaning: for if any *were*, the imputations following would not be just. We assume that a tongue which we do not understand *has a meaning*, and that it is the way of expression of some *foreign nation.* **βάρβαρος,—a foreigner,** in the sense of one who is ignorant of the speech and habits of a people. So Ovid, Trist. v. 10,—'Barbarus hic ego sum, quia non intelligor ulli:' and Herod. ii. 158,—βαρβάρους δὲ πάντας οἱ Αἰγύπτιοι καλέουσι τοὺς μὴ σφισι ὁμογλώσσους. (Wetst.) The appellation always conveyed a certain contempt, and such is evidently intended here. So Ovid, in the next line,—'Et rident stolidi verba Latina Getæ.' **ἐν ἐμοί, in my estimation**: so Eurip. Hippol. 1335, σὺ δ' ἔν τ' ἐκείνῳ κἂν ἐμοὶ φαίνῃ κακός,—'in his judgment and in mine:' see Kühner, ii. 275. **12.**] *Application of the analogy*, as in ver. 9. The **οὕτως** is evidently meant as in ver. 9, but is rendered somewhat difficult by the change of the construction into a direct exhortation. It is best therefore to suppose an ellipsis; and

[a] πνευμάτων, [b] πρὸς τὴν [bc] οἰκοδομὴν τῆς ἐκκλησίας ζητεῖτε, ἵνα [e] περισσεύητε. 13 διὸ ὁ [f] λαλῶν [f] γλώσσῃ
[g] προσευχέσθω [g] ἵνα [h] διερμηνεύῃ. 14 ἐὰν γὰρ προσεύχω-
μαι γλώσσῃ, τὸ [i] πνεῦμά μου προσεύχεται, ὁ δὲ νοῦς

a = ch. xii. 10 reff.
b = Rom. xv. 2.
c Rom. xiv. 19 reff.
e absol., Matt. v. 20. ch. viii. 8.
f vv. 2 &c.
g Matt. xxiv. 20 || Mk. Mark xiv. 35. (ὅπως, Acts viii. 15.) Phil. i. 9. Col. i. 9. iv. 3. 2 Thess. i. 11. iii. 1.
h ch. xii. 30 reff.
i = Acts xvii. 16 reff.

12. πνευματικων P 23-mg 73 spec sah Ambr$_1$. (G-lat has both.) for περισσευητε, προφητευητε A 73 Ambrst.

13. rec διοπερ, with KLℵ[3] rel Chr$_1$ Thdrt Thl Œc: txt ABDFPℵ[1] 17 Damasc.

14. om γαρ B F[-gr G-lat] sah arm: ins ADKLPℵ rel vulg(and F-lat) E-lat syrr copt Chr$_1$ Thdrt Damasc Thl Œc Orig-int$_1$ Ambrst Aug$_1$ Pel Sedul Bede. (17 def [but om appy, Tischdf Treg].)

give to οὕτως the pregnant meaning, *after the lesson conveyed by this example.* Meyer's rendering, *since in such a manner* (i. e. so as to be barbarians to one another) *ye also are emulous,* &c., is very harsh, besides making the second clause, standing as it does without a μᾶλλον or any disjunctive particle, mean (and I do not see that it will bear any other meaning), *seek this βαρβαροφωνία to the edifying of the Church.* **Thus likewise ye** (i. e. after the example of people who would not wish to be barbarians to one another,—avoiding the absurdity just mentioned), **emulous as ye are of spiritual gifts** (reff.), **seek them to the edifying of the church, that ye may abound:** or *perhaps* (but I can find no instance of ζητῶ ἵνα thus used: ch. iv. 2 is no case in point, see note there) as in E. V. '*seek that ye may excel* (abound in them) *to the edifying of the church.*' 13.] *Hortatory inference from the foregoing examples.* There is some difficulty in the construction of this verse. **προσευχ. ἵνα διερμ.** is rendered by Chrys., Theodoret, Theophyl., Erasm., Beza, Calv., Grot., Estius, Wetst., Bleek, Rückert, Olsh., al., '*pray that he may interpret.*' But the next verse shews that this is untenable. For the act of προσεύχεσθαι γλώσσῃ is there introduced in strict logical connexion with this verse, so as to shew that the προσευχέσθω here must have the same meaning as there, viz., that of *praying in a tongue,* openly in the church. Seeing this, Luther, Rosenm., al., * render it, 'let . . . . . *so pray, that he may interpret:*' i. e. 'not pray, unless he can interpret.' But this rendering of ἵνα is hardly allowable even where οὕτω is expressed, see note on ch. ix. 24. The knot of the difficulty lies in the relation of ἵνα to verbs of this kind. It may be doubted whether in such expressions as προσεύχεσθαι ἵνα (see reff.), the conj. ever represents the mere *purport* of the prayer, as in our "to pray, that." The idea of *purpose* is inseparably bound up in this particle, and can be traced wherever it is used. Thus προσεύχ. ἵνα seems always to convey the meaning, "to pray, *in order that.*" At the same time, *prayer* being a *direct seeking* of the fulfilment of the purpose on account of which we pray,—not, like many other actions, *indirectly* connected with it,—the *purport* and *purpose* become *compounded in the expression.* This will be illustrated by γρηγορεῖτε κ. προσεύχεσθε, ἵνα μὴ εἰσέλθητε εἰς πειρασμόν: where it is plain enough that ἵνα μή represents the *ulterior object* of γρηγορεῖτε, and, *now that it is joined with* γρηγορεῖτε, of προσεύχεσθε: but had it been *merely,* προσεύχεσθε ἵνα μὴ κ.τ.λ., the above confusion would have occurred. Now this confusion it is, which makes the words προσευχέσθω ἵνα διερμηνεύῃ so difficult. Obviously, the προσευχέσθω is not *merely* used to express a *seeking by prayer* of the gift of interpretation, on account of the sense in the next verse: but as plainly, there is in προσευχέσθω *a sense* which passes on to ἵνα διερμηνεύῃ. The rendering of Meyer and De Wette, '*pray, with a view to interpret* (what he has spoken in a tongue),' is unobjectionable, but does not give any reason for the choice of **προσευχέσθω,** any more than εὐχαριστείτω, or the like. I believe the true rendering to be pointed out by the distinction in the next verse. If a man prays *in a tongue,* his *spirit prays,* but his *understanding is barren.* This prayer of *his spirit* is, the intense direction of his will and affections to God, accompanied by the utterance of sounds to him unintelligible. '*Let then him who speaks with a tongue, pray,* when he does pray, *with an earnest striving* (in this prayer of his spirit) *after the gift of interpretation.*' The meaning might be more strictly given thus in English: **wherefore let him who speaketh with a tongue, in his prayer** (or, **when praying**), **strive that he may interpret.** 14.] This verse has been explained above. It *justifies the necessity of thus aiming at the gift of interpretation.* **τὸ πν. μου,** not as in ver. 32, and Chrys. (Hom. xxxv. p. 325) τὸ χάρισμα τὸ δοθέν μοι καὶ κινοῦν τὴν γλῶσσαν, —but as in reff., **my** (own) **spirit,** taking

μου [k] ἄκαρπός ἐστιν. 15 [l] τί οὖν ἐστιν; προσεύξομαι τῷ ABDFK
[i] πνεύματι, προσεύξομαι δὲ καὶ τῷ νοΐ· [m] ψαλῶ τῷ [i] πνεύ- LPℵ a b
ματι, [m] ψαλῶ δὲ καὶ τῷ νοΐ. 16 ἐπεὶ ἐὰν [n] εὐλογῇς [i] πνεύ- c d e f g
ματι, ὁ [o] ἀναπληρῶν τὸν [p] τόπον τοῦ [q] ἰδιώτου πῶς ἐρεῖ h k l m
[r] τὸ [rs] ἀμὴν [t] ἐπὶ τῇ σῇ [u] εὐχαριστίᾳ, [v] ἐπειδὴ τί λέγεις οὐκ o 17. 47
οἶδεν; 17 σὺ μὲν γὰρ [w] καλῶς [x] εὐχαριστεῖς, ἀλλ᾽ [y] ὁ [y] ἕτε-

k Matt. xiii. 22 || Mk. Eph. v. 11. Tit. iii. 14. 2 Pet. i. 8. Jude 12 only. Jer. ii. 6. Wisd. xv. 4 only.
l Acts xxi. 22. ver. 26.
m here bis, Rom. xv. 9, from Ps. xvii. 49. Eph. v. 19. James v. 13 only.
n ch. x. 16 reff.
o = here (Matt. xiii. 14. ch. xvi. 17. Gal. vi. 2. Phil. ii. 30. 1 Thess. ii. 16) only ‡. (Gen. xxix. 28 al.) Jos. B. J. v. 2. 5, στρατιώτου τάξιν ἀναπληροῦν. Philo, Flacc. 12, vol. ii. p. 531, πρεσβευτοῦ τάξ. ἐκπλήσω. Tac. Ann. iv. 38, "locum principem impleam."
p = here only. Sir. xii. 12.
q Acts iv. 13 reff.
r 2 Cor. i. 20.
s = Rev. v. 14. Neh. v. 13. viii. 6 al.
t = Acts xi. 19. 2 Cor. xii. 21. Heb. viii. 1.
u Acts xxiv. 3 reff.
v Acts xv. 24 reff.
w ch. vii. 37 reff.
x abs., ch. xi. 24 reff.
y Rom. ii. 1 reff.

15. om τι ουν εστιν K. προσευξωμαι (twice) ADFP 47: -ξωμαι and -ξομαι ℵ: txt BKL rel $Orig_4$ Eus_2 [Chr_2 Euthal-ms Thdrt Damasc: *orabo* latt $Orig\text{-}int_2$ Ambr Ambrst] (*see note*). om 1st δε FKP 35. 46. 109-14 latt Syr sah arm $Orig_3$(om και $also_1$) [Euthal-ms] Damasc Orig-int[$_{sæpe}$ Ambrst]: ins ABDLℵ rel syr [copt] $Orig_2$ Eus_2 Chr_2 Thdrt Thl Œc. om τω (bef 2nd πνευματι) FP. om 2nd δε BF 46. 109 latt Syr sah æth arm $Orig_1$(where he has the 1st δε) $Cæs_1$ [Ath_1] $Ps\text{-}Ath_1$ Damasc Thl $Orig\text{-}int_3$ [Ambrst]: ins ADKLPℵ rel syr copt $Orig[\text{-}c]_1$ Eus_1 Ath_1 Chr_2 [Euthal-ms] Thdrt Œc (homœotel in 47 νοι to νοι).

16. rec ευλογησης, with FKL rel Chr_1 Thdrt Thl Œc; *benedixeris* latt: txt ABDPℵ b[1] o 17 [Euthal-ms] Damasc. rec ins τω bef πνευματι (*to conform to last ver: but see note*), with KL rel Chr_1 Thdrt: εν B(sic: see table) D[P]ℵ[3]: om AFℵ[1] 17 [Euthal-ms] Damasc. om το F. for επειδη, επει B. ουκ οιδεν bef τι λεγεις F(not F-lat) E-lat G-lat [Ambrst] Jer_1 Aug_1.

17. αλλα B l.

himself as an example, as above, ver. 6: a use of the word familiar to our Apostle, and here necessary on account of ὁ νοῦς μου following, 'When I pray *in a tongue*, my higher being, my *spirit*, filled with the Holy Ghost, is inflamed with holy desires, and rapt in prayer: but my *intellectual part*, having no matter before it on which its powers can be exercised, bears no fruit to the edification of others (nor of myself:' but this is not expressed in ἄκαρπος; cf. the usage of καρπός by Paul,—Rom. i. 13; vi. 21, 22; xv. 28; Gal. v. 22, al.).

15.] **What then is (the case)** (i. e. as our '*What then?*' Cf. τί οὖν, Rom. iii. 9; vi. 15. 'What is my determination thereupon?')? **I will pray** (on the reading προσεύξωμαι, see note on Rom. v. 1) **with the** (my) **spirit: I will pray also with my mind** (i. e. will interpret my prayer for the benefit of myself and the church), &c. This resolution, or expression of self-obligation, evidently leads to the inference, by and by clearly expressed, ver. 28, that *if he could not* pray τῷ νοΐ, he would *keep silence*. **ψαλῶ**] hence we gather that the two departments in which the gift of tongues was exercised were *prayer and praise*. On the day of Pentecost it was confined to the latter of these. **16.**] The discourse changes from the first person to the second, as De W. observes, because the hypothesis contains an imputation of folly or error. **ἐὰν εὐλ.**] **if thou shalt have blessed in spirit** (no art. now: the dat. is now merely of the *manner in which*, the *element*; not of the *specific instrument*, as in the last verse), **how shall he that fills** (i. e. is in) **the situation of a private man** (ἰδιώτης, in speaking of any business or trade, signifies a *lay person*, i.e. one unacquainted with it as his employment. Thus in state matters, it is one out of office—Δημοσθένει ὄντι ἰδιώτῃ, Thuc. iv. 2; in philosophy, one uneducated and rude—ἡμεῖς μὴν οἱ ἰδιῶται οὐ δεδοίκαμεν, ὑμεῖς δὲ οἱ φιλόσοφοι δειλιᾶτε, Diog. Laert. Aristipp. ii. 71, &c. &c. See examples in Wetst. So here it is, *one who has not the gift of speaking and interpreting*. The word **τόπον** is not to be taken literally, as if the ἰδιῶται had any *separate seats* in the congregation: the expression, as in ref., is figurative) **say the** Amen (the Amen always said: see Deut. xxvii. 15—26 Heb. and E. V. (LXX, γένοιτο); Neh. viii. 6. From the synagogue,—on which see Wetst., Schöttg. in loc., Winer, Realw., art. Synagogen, and Philo, Fragm. vol. ii. p. 630—συνεδρεύουσι . . . . οἱ μὲν πολλοὶ σιωπῇ, πλὴν εἴ τι προσεπιφημίσαι τοῖς ἀναγινωσκομένοις νομίζεται,—it passed into the Christian church; so Justin Mart. Apol. i. 65, p. 82, οὗ (scil. τοῦ προεστῶτος) συντελέσαντος τὰς εὐχὰς καὶ τὴν εὐχαριστίαν, πᾶς ὁ παρὼν λαὸς πανευφημεῖ λέγων, ἀμήν. See Suicer, sub voc. and Stanley's note here) **to** (at the end of) **thy thanksgiving, since what thou sayest he knows not?** This is, as Doddridge has remarked, decisive against the practice of praying and praising in an unknown tongue, as ridi-

ρος οὐκ [z] οἰκοδομεῖται. 18 [a] εὐχαριστῶ τῷ θεῷ, πάντων
ὑμῶν μᾶλλον [b] γλώσσῃ [b] λαλῶ· 19 ἀλλὰ ἐν ἐκκλησίᾳ [c] θέλω
πέντε λόγους τῷ νοΐ μου λαλῆσαι, ἵνα καὶ ἄλλους [d] κατ-
ηχήσω, [ce] ἢ [f] μυρίους λόγους ἐν γλώσσῃ. 20 Ἀδελφοί,
μὴ παιδία γίνεσθε ταῖς [g] φρεσίν· ἀλλὰ τῇ [h] κακίᾳ [i] νηπιά-
ζετε, ταῖς δὲ [g] φρεσὶν [k] τέλειοι γίνεσθε. 21 ἐν τῷ νόμῳ γέ-

z Acts ix. 31 reff. a Rom. i. 8 reff. b vv. 2, &c. c here only. 2 Macc. xiv. 42. d Acts xviii. 25 reff. e constr., Matt. xviii. 8, 9 || Mk. Luke xv. 7. xvii. 2. Gen. xxxviii. 26. f Matt. xviii. 24. ch. iv. 15 only. Esth. iii. 9. g here bis only. Prov. xviii. 2. h Rom. i. 29. ch. v. 8. Eph. iv. 31 al. Ps. li. 3 (5). i here only +. (-πιος, ch. xiii. 11.) k = ch. ii. 6. Heb. v. 14 al. 1 Chron. xxv. 8.

18. rec aft τω θεω ins μου (*addn from such places as ch* i. 4, *Rom* i. 8 *&c*: 38 æth arm *even further add* περι), with KL rel [vulg-clem demid harl] Thdrt[-ed] Damasc Ambrst Pel: om ABDFPℵ 17 E-lat G-lat am(with tol) syrr copt æth arm Chr$_1$ [Euthal-ms] Thdrt-ms Jer$_1$ Sedul Bede. (om [τω] θεω F-lat.) ins οτι bef παντων F latt syrr copt lat-ff. γλωσση bef μαλλον F[-gr(and G-lat)]: om μαλλον 41[1] D-lat Chr-ms. —*omnium vestrum lingua loquor* vulg(and F-lat). rec γλωσσαις, with BKLP rel syrr copt æth Chr$_1$ Thdrt Orig-int$_1$: txt ADFℵ 17 latt arm Damasc Ambrst Pel Bede. rec λαλων (*the* bare present *aft* ευχ. *was not understood, and thus some helped it with* οτι, *some by turning* λαλω *into* λαλων. *Or* λαλων *was understood to belong to* ευχαριστω, '*I give thanks, speaking,*' &c.), with KL rel Chr$_1$ [Euthal-ms] Thdrt Damasc: om A: txt BDFPℵ c 17 latt syrr copt arm Orig-int$_1$ lat-ff.

19. (αλλα, so ABD: om ℵ[1].) rec δια του νοος (*see note. If* τω νοι *had come from ver* 15, μου *would prob have been omd*), with KL rel D-lat syr Mac$_1$ Chr$_1$ Thdrt Max-conf$_1$ Phot[-c$_1$] Thl Œc: δια τον νομον (omg μου) Mcion-e$_2$, *per legem* Ambrst-txt [ed-ven]; *in lege* Paulin$_1$: txt AB D[-gr] (F)[P]ℵ m (17) vulg Syr copt [arm(omg μου)] Nys$_1$ Epiph$_2$ Damasc [Ambr$_1$].—τω ν. μ. bef π. λογ. 17.—λαλη ο μεν (sic) bef τω ν. μ. F.

20. ινα ταις φρ. τελ. γενησθε, omg δε, F D-lat Orig-int$_1$ Ambrst Aug Gaud.

21. aft νομω ins τι ℵ[1](ℵ[3] disapproving).

culously practised in the church of Rome. **17.**] **καλῶς** is not ironical, but concessive: it is not the act of *thanksgiving in a tongue* that the Apostle blames, for that is *of itself good*, being dictated by the Spirit: but the doing it *not to the edification of others*. **ὁ ἕτερος**, the ἰδιώτης spoken of before. **18, 19.**] *Declaration of his own feeling on the matter, highly endowed as he was with the gift.* **I thank God, I speak with a tongue** (have the gift of speaking with tongues) **more than you all.** This juxtaposition of two clauses, between which '*that*' is to be supplied in the sense, is not unusual: βούλει σκοπῶμεν: 'fac videas,'—Eur. Hippol. 567, ἐπίσχετ', αὐδὴν τῶν ἔσωθεν ἐκμάθω. Hom. Od. β. 195, Τηλεμάχῳ δ' ἐν πᾶσιν ἐγὼν ὑποθήσομαι αὐτός, Μητέρα ἣν ἐς πατρὸς ἀνωγέτω ἀπονέεσθαι. See Hartung, Partikell. ii. p. 134. **19.**] **ἐν ἐκκλησίᾳ, in** (the) **assembly**, 'in the congregation' [this is the better rendering here, and wherever there is a chance of the word *church* being mistaken as meaning a building],—not 'in *an* assembly,' as Meyer. The art. is omitted after a preposition: so Middleton, ch. vi. § 1; the logical account of which is, that the prep. serves to *categorize* the substantive following it, and so make it general instead of particular. **θέλω . . ., ἤ**, as βούλομαι, ἤ, Il. α. 117: similarly ἐπιθυμέω, ζητέω,—see Hartung, ii. p. 72. διὰ τοῦ νοός has probably been a correction, because **λαλεῖν τῷ νοΐ** was found harsh, the understanding being only the indirect instrument. **20.**] With this exhortation he concludes this part of his argument, in which he reproves the folly of displaying and being anxious for a gift in which there was no edification. '**ἀδελφοί** suavem vim habet,' Bengel. **ταῖς φρεσίν, in your understandings**, as this preference shews you to be. **τῇ κακίᾳ**—dat. of reference, **as regards vice**: see Winer, edn. 6, § 31. 6.

21—25.] By a citation from the O. T. he takes occasion to shew that tongues are a sign *to the unbelieving only*: and that *even for them* they are profitless in comparison with prophecy. **21.**] **ἐν τῷ νόμῳ**, as John x. 34; xii. 34; xv. 25;—where the *Psalms* are thus quoted. The passage stands in the LXX: διὰ φαυλισμὸν χειλέων, διὰ γλώσσης ἑτέρας ὅτι λαλήσουσι τῷ λαῷ τούτῳ . . . κ. οὐκ ἠθέλησαν ἀκούειν. The context is thus: The scoffers in Jerusalem (see ver. 14) are introduced as scorning the simplicity of the divine commands, which were line upon line, precept upon precept, as if to children (vv. 9, 10). Jehovah threatens them that, since they would not hear these simple commands, He would speak to them by men of other tongues, viz. the Assyrians, their captors. Here as in many other cases,

γραπται ῞Οτι ἐν [l] ἑτερογλώσσοις καὶ ἐν [m] χείλεσιν [n] ἑτέρων
λαλήσω τῷ λαῷ τούτῳ, καὶ [o] οὐδ' [p] οὕτως [q] εἰςακούσονταί
μου, λέγει κύριος. 22 ὥςτε αἱ [r] γλῶσσαι [s] εἰς [t] σημεῖόν
εἰσιν οὐ τοῖς πιστεύουσιν ἀλλὰ τοῖς [u] ἀπίστοις, ἡ δὲ [v] προφητεία οὐ τοῖς [u] ἀπίστοις ἀλλὰ τοῖς πιστεύουσιν. 23 ἐὰν
οὖν [wx] συνέλθῃ ἡ [y] ἐκκλησία [y] ὅλη [xz] ἐπὶ τὸ αὐτὸ καὶ πάντες

ABDFK LPℵ a c d e f g h k l m o 17. 47

l here only †. (Isa. xxviii. 11.) Ps. cxiii. 1 Aq. m = Matt. xv. 8 ‖ Mk. (from Isa. xxix. 13.) Rom. iii. 13. Heb. (xi. 12.) xiii. 15. 1 Pet. iii. 10 only. n = Acts ii. 4. Exod. xxx. 9. o = ch. v. 1 reff. p = Rom. v. 12 reff. q Matt. vi. 7. Luke i. 13. Acts x. 31. Heb. v. 7 only. Deut. i. 43. r Acts ii. 4 reff. s so εἰς μαρτύριον, &c. Matt. viii. 4 al. fr. Jer. ix. 22. t Rom. iv. 11 reff. u = ch. vi. 6 reff. v ch. xiii. 2 reff. w = Acts i. 3 reff. x ch. xi. 20. Josh. ix. 2. y Rom. xvi. 23 reff. z Acts i. 15 reff.

for ετερογλωσσοις, ετεραις γλωσσαις F lect-8 vulg copt goth $Tert_1$. rec ετεροις, with D[F]KLP rel [latt Syr(*lingua alia*) syr copt goth æth arm] $Orig_1$ $Constt_1$ Chr_1 [Cyr_1] Damasc Thl Œc [$Tert_1$ Ambrst]: txt ABℵ 17 [Cyr_1-ms_1-p]. (*Meyer thinks the dat a mere mechanical corrn to suit the other datives.*) for ουδ ουτως, ουδεπω F [not F-lat]. εισακουσεται F(not [F]-lat) 43. 113 lect-14.

22. for (2nd) πιστευουσιν, πιστοις F [vulg $Ambr_1$. (G-lat has both.)]

23. om ουν F[-gr] 67² old-lat goth $Ambr_1$ Ambrst. for συνελθη, ελθη BG¹. ολη bef η εκκλησια DF latt goth [Syr goth $Ambr_1$ Ambrst]. rec παντες γλωσσαις λαλωσιν, with [D²-gr] KL [47(-ουσιν)] rel vulg(and F-lat) syrr arm Chr-txt_1 [γλ. π. $λ._1$] Thdrt Damasc Œc Vict-vit Bede: λαλ. παν. γλ. copt æth Ambrst: λαλ. γλ. παν. D¹·³[and lat] goth: txt AB F[-gr(and G-lat)] Pℵ Bas_1 [Euthal-ms] Thl.

the historical sense is not so much considered, as the aptness of the expressions used for illustrating the matter in hand; viz. that belief would not be produced in the unbelieving by speaking to them in strange tongues. The ὅτι answers in the LXX to כִּי, '*for;*' or '*yea verily,*' as Louth. It forms part of the citation, not of the text. **ἐν ἑτερ.**] **in** (in the person of) **men of other tongues:** Heb. *with another tongue;*—and it is placed *second.* The Apostle personifies it and gives it the prominence. **ἐν χ. ἑτ.**] **in** (as speaking in, using as the organ of speech) **lips of others** (strangers, see reff.): Heb. *in* (by) *stammerers of lip:* Louth, *with a stammering lip.* **τῷ λαῷ τούτῳ**] in Isa., *the Israelites:* here taken generally for the unbelieving world. **οὐδ' οὕτως εἰςακούσ.**] This is the point of the passage for St. Paul's argument: see ver. 23:—"for them, and not for us: but *even for them,* profitless in the main:"—*not even under such circumstances will they listen to me: even this sign* will be for them ineffectual. **22.**] **ὥςτε,**—viz. according to the words of the foregoing prophetic passage. **αἱ γλ.**] **the tongues,** in the *then* acceptation of the term. He is not interpreting the prophecy, nor alluding to the tongues *there* spoken of, but returns back to the subject in hand—*the tongues* about which his argument was concerned. **εἰς σημ. εἰσίν**] **are for a sign:** but there is no emphasis on the words,—the meaning being much the same as if εἰς σημεῖον were omitted, and it stood ὥστε αἱ γλ. εἰσὶν οὐ τοῖς π. Not seeing this, Commentators have differed widely about the meaning of σημεῖον. So Chrys. (Hom. xxxvi. p. 335): εἰς σημεῖον, τουτέστιν, εἰς ἔκπληξιν:—Bengel: 'quo allecti auscultare debebant:'—Calvin: 'linguæ, quatenus in signum datæ sunt:' &c. &c. All dwelling on the word σημεῖον would introduce an element foreign to the argument, which is, *that tongues are* (a sign) *for the unbelieving, not for the believing.* **οὐ τ. πιστ.**] **not to men who believe, but to unbelievers,** i. e. 'men who do not believe:' not, as Neander, Billroth, Rückert, and in substance De Wette, 'men who *will* not believe:' ἄπιστος must be kept to the same sense through this whole passage, and plainly by ver. 23 it is *not one who* will *not believe,* but *an unbeliever open to conviction.* The mistake has been occasioned by regarding *those to whom the prophecy was directed,* and interpreting Paul by Isaiah, instead of by himself. **ἡ δὲ προφ.**] scil. ἐστίν, as Meyer, or εἰς σημ. ἐστίν, as De Wette: it seems to me to import little which we supply, seeing that εἰς σημ. is of so very slight weight in the preceding clause. If emphatic meaning had been attached to σημεῖον *as belonging to* αἱ γλ., we must not have supplied it here: but if it be a mere indifferent word, to be interpreted according to the sense in which αἱ γλ. and ἡ προφ. were σημεῖα, there can be no objection to it here: and the uniformity of construction seems to require it. Both here and above, **τοῖς ἀπίστ.** and the other are datives *commodi*—for, not **'*to,*' the unbelieving.** ἡ προφητεία *was* a sign *to* the unbelieving, see vv. 24, 25. Prophecy, i. e. *inspired and intelligent exposition of the word and doctrine,* was eminently *for* believers, but, as below, would

..εδιω-
αι P.

λαλῶσιν γλώσσαις, εἰςέλθωσιν δὲ [a] ἰδιῶται ἢ [u] ἄπιστοι, οὐκ
ἐροῦσιν ὅτι [b] μαίνεσθε; 24 ἐὰν δὲ πάντες [c] προφητεύωσιν,
εἰςέλθῃ δέ τις [u] ἄπιστος ἢ [a] ἰδιώτης, [d] ἐλέγχεται ὑπὸ πάντων, [e] ἀνακρίνεται ὑπὸ πάντων, 25 τὰ [f] κρυπτὰ τῆς καρδίας αὐτοῦ [g] φανερὰ [g] γίνεται, καὶ [h] οὕτως [i] πεσὼν ἐπὶ
[i] πρόσωπον [k] προσκυνήσει τῷ θεῷ, [l] ἀπαγγέλλων ὅτι [m] ὄν-

a ver. 16.
b Acts xii. 15 reff.
c ch. xi. 4, 5 reff.
d = John iii. 20. Ps. xlix. 21.
e Acts iv. 9 reff.
f Rom. ii. 16 reff.
g ch. xi. 19 reff.
h = ver. 21. Rom. v. 12 reff.
i Matt. xvii. 6. xxvi. 39. Luke v. 12. xvii. 16. Rev. xi. 16. Num. xvi. 4. xx. 6.
k Paul, here and Acts xxiv. 11 only. dat., Matt. ii. 2 al. fr. Ps. xxviii. 2.
l gospp. and Acts, passim. elsw., 1 Thess. i. 9. Heb. ii. 12. 1 John i. 2, 3 only. Gen. xiv. 13.
m = Mark xi. 32. Luke xxiii. 47. 1 Tim. v. 5 al. Num. xxii. 37 only.

om η απιστοι B[: *infideles et idiotæ*] Ambrst.
24. for 2nd δε, τε A Syr (æth). om ανακ. υ. π. (*homœot*) K.
25. rec ins και ουτω bef τα κρυπτα (*from below,—the result being imagined better to begin here; the follg κ. ουτως being by some omd, as Chr Ambr, by some carelessly left, or reintroduced without erasing this former. So Meyer*), with D^3[-gr] KL rel syr Chr_3 Thdrt [Damasc]: om $ABD^1F\aleph$ 17 latt (Syr) copt goth (æth arm) Orig[-c_1-int_2 Did_1] Bas_1 Chr_1 [Euthal-ms (Ambr). Syr æth arm Orig-int_1 Ambr ins και.] αναγγελλων F(not G),

be also profitable *to* unbelievers, furnishing a token that God was truly among his assembled servants. **23—25.**] *Instances given of the operation of both on the ungifted or the unbeliever.*

23.] **οὖν**, following up the axiom just laid down, by supposing a case = **if then . . . .** The first case put answers to the former half of ver. 22: the second, to the latter. The supposition is this: that all the (Corinthian) church is assembled, and all its members speak with tongues (not in a *tumultuary* manner—that is not part of the present hypothesis, for if it were, it must apply equally to ver. 24, which it clearly cannot:—but that all have the gift, and are *in turn* exercising it):—then ἰδιῶται, '*plain* believers,' persons unacquainted with the gift and its exercise, come in. It is obvious that the hypothesis of *all* being assembled, and *all* having the gift, must not be pressed to infer that no such ἰδιώτης could be found: no one hypothesizes thus rigidly. If any will have it so, then, as Meyer, we may suppose the ἰδιῶται to come *from another congregation:* but the whole difficulty seems to me mere trifling. The ἰδ. plainly cannot be, as De W. maintains, an *unbeliever*, for *his* case is separately mentioned. Such **plain men**, or perhaps a company of unbelievers, have come in:—they have no understanding of what is going on: the γλῶσσαι sound to them an unmeaning jargon; and they come to the conclusion, 'These men are mad;' just as men *did infer*, on the day of Pentecost, that the speakers were *drunken*. **24.**] **But if all** (see above) **prophesy** (i. e. intelligibly lay forth, in the power of the Spirit, the Christian word and doctrine) **and there enter any** (singular *now*, setting forth that this would be the effect *in any case:* plural *before*, to shew that however many there might be, *not one could appreciate the gift*) **unbeliever or plain man** (ἄπιστος *first now*, because the great stress is on the power of prophecy in its greatest achievement, the *conversion of the unbeliever;* but ἰδιῶται was first *before*, because the stress there was on the unprofitableness of tongues, *not only to the ἄπιστοι, but to the ἰδιῶται*), **he is convicted by all** (the inspired discourse penetrating, as below, into the depths of his heart,—by *all*, i. e. by each in turn), **he is searched into by all** (each inspired speaker opening to him his character), **the hidden things of his heart become manifest** (those things which he had never before seen are revealed,—his whole hitherto unrecognized personal character laid out. Instances of such revelations of a man to himself by powerful preaching have often occurred, even since the cessation of the prophetic gift): **and thus** (thus convicted, searched, revealed to himself:—in such a state of mind) **having fallen on his face, he will worship God, announcing** (*by that his act*, which is a public submission to the divine Power manifest among you: or, but not so well, *aloud*, by declaration of it in words) **that of a truth** (implying that previously he had regarded the presence of God among them as an idle tale; or, if a plain Christian, had not sufficiently realized it) **God is among you** (or in each of you: by His Spirit). In this last description the ἰδιώτης is thrown into the background, and (see above) the greater achievement of prophecy, the conviction and conversion of the ἄπιστος, is chiefly in view. "For a similar effect of the disclosure of a man's secret self to himself, compare the fascination described as exercised by Socrates over his hearers by the 'conviction' and 'judgment' of his questions in the Athenian market-place. Grote's Hist. of Greece,

τως ὁ θεὸς [n] ἐν ὑμῖν ἐστιν. 26 [o] Τί οὖν ἐστιν, ἀδελφοί;
ὅταν [w] συνέρχησθε, ἕκ ιστος [ὑμῶν] [p] ψαλμὸν ἔχει, [q] διδα-
χὴν ἔχει, [q] ἀποκάλυψιν ἔχει, γλῶσσαν ἔχει, [r] ἑρμηνείαν
ἔχει· πάντα [s] πρὸς [s] οἰκοδομὴν [t] γινέσθω. 27 εἴτε γλώσσῃ
τὶς λαλεῖ, [u] κατὰ δύο ἢ [v] τὸ [v] πλεῖστον τρεῖς, καὶ [w] ἀνὰ
[w] μέρος καὶ εἷς [x] διερμηνευέτω· 28 ἐὰν δὲ μὴ ᾖ [y] διερμηνευ-
τής, [z] σιγάτω ἐν ἐκκλησίᾳ, ἑαυτῷ δὲ λαλείτω καὶ τῷ θεῷ.
29 [a] προφῆται δὲ δύο ἢ τρεῖς λαλείτωσαν, καὶ οἱ ἄλλοι

ABDFK Lℵ a b c d e f g h k l m o 17. 47

n = 2 Cor. xiii. 5.
o Acts xxi. 22. ver. 15.
p = Eph. v. 19. Col. iii. 16 (Luke xx. 42. xxiv. 44. Acts i. 20. xiii. 33) only. Isa. lxvi. 20.
q ver. 6 (reff.).
r ch. xii. 10 only +. Sir. prol. & xlvii. 17 only. (-νεύειν, John i. 43.)
s ver. 12.
t = ver. 40. ch. xvi. 14.
u = Mark vi. 40. ἀνά, Luke ix. 3. x. 1. John ii. 6. καθ' ἕνα, Eph. v. 33. John xxi. 25. Xen. Anab. iv. 7. 8.
v here only. (Isa. ix. 3.)
w here only. ἀνὰ μ. ᾄδειν, Polyb. iv. 20. 10, and al. freq. see Rom. xi. 25 reff.
x ch. xii. 30 reff.
y here only +.
z Acts xii. 17 reff. change of subject, Luke xv. 15. xix. 4. Acts vi. 6. Winer, edn. 6, § 67. 1. c.
a Acts xi. 27 reff.

rec *ο θεος* bef *οντως*, with KL rel syr Chr_3 Thdrt [Bas_1 Damasc]: om *οντως* k 3. 32 Thdrt-comm: txt AB(DFℵ) h 17 latt Syr copt goth æth arm Orig-[c_1-]int_2 [Did_1 Chr_1 Euthal-ms $Ambr_1$].—om *ο* D[1]Fℵ[1] l[1] 109[1] $Orig[-c]_1$ Chr.

26. om *υμων* ABℵ[1] a 17 copt [Bas_1 Euthal-ms]: ins DFKLℵ[3] rel [latt syrr goth æth(appy) arm] Chr_1 Thdrt Damasc [Ambrst]. om *διδαχ. εχει* (*homœotel*) A k. rec *γλωσσαν εχει αποκαλυψιν εχει* (*the clauses dropped out by homœotel, and were then confusedly reinserted*), with L rel Chr_1 Thdrt Damasc: om *αποκαλυψιν εχει* m 35-9. 42-7. 63 arm Chr-mss: om *γλωσσαν εχει* K 35-9. 42-3. 57. 91[1]. 106-77. 238 [fuld[1]: *ερμ. εχει γλ. εχ.* goth:] txt ABDFℵ [d] 17 latt syrr coptt æth Bas_1 [Euthal-ms] Thl Œc-comm [Ambrst]. **διερμηνειαν** DF. rec *γενεσθω*, with Damasc: txt ABDFKLℵ rel Chr [Bas_2 Euthal-ms] Thdrt &c.

28. for *διερμ.*, *ερμηνευτης* BD[1]F, pref *δ* D[1]F. for *εαυτω*, *αυτω* F.

29. om *οι* D[1]FL l[1].

viii. 609—611." Stanley. **26—35.**] *Regulations respecting the exercise of spiritual gifts in the assemblies.* **26.**] The rule for *all*, proceeding on the fact of each having his gift to contribute when they come together: viz. that all things must be done with a view to edification. **τί οὖν ἐστιν**] See ver. 15. **ὅτ. συν.**] **whenever ye happen to be assembling together**: the *present* vividly describes each coming with his gift, eager to exercise it. **ψαλμόν**] most probably **a hymn of praise** to sing in the power of the spirit, as did Miriam, Deborah, Symeon, &c. See ver. 15. **διδαχήν**] **an exposition of doctrine** or moral teaching: belonging to the gift of *prophecy*, as indeed do also **ψαλμ.** and **ἀποκάλ.**, the latter being something revealed to him, to be prophetically uttered. **γλῶσσαν**] **a tongue**, i. e. an act of speaking in tongues: see vv. 18, 22. **ἑρμηνείαν**] See below, and ver. 5. **πάντ. πρ. οἰκ. γιν.**] THE GENERAL RULE, afterwards applied to the several gifts: and **27, 28.**] *to the speaking with tongues.* **εἴτε** begins the construction, but is not carried on, ver. 29, where *προφῆται δέ* answers to it. **27.**] **κατὰ δύο** (scil. let it take place), **by two** (at each time, i. e. in one assembly: not more than two or three might speak with tongues *at each meeting*) **or at the most three, and by turn** (one after another, not together): **and let one** (some one who has the gift,—and *not more than one*) **interpret** (what is said in the tongue). **28.**] **But if there be not an interpreter** (Wieseler, in the Stud. und Krit. for 1838, p. 720, would render it, '*if he be not an interpreter*,' viz. himself. But this would exclude the possibility of *others* interpreting, which we know from ch. xii. 10 might be the case. And thus the preceding *εἷς* could hardly bear its proper meaning. Wieseler tries to make it mean '*one at a time*.' Besides, the emphatic position of *ᾖ* seems to require more stress than this sense would give, which would be better expressed by *ἐὰν δὲ διερμηνευτὴς μὴ ᾖ*), **let him** (the speaker in a tongue, see reff.) **be silent in the church: but** (as if *σιγάτω* had been *μὴ λαλείτω*) **let him speak for himself and for God**: i. e. in private, with only himself and God to witness it. Chrys. *καθ' ἑαυτὸν φθεγγέσθω*: which Theophyl. enlarges to *τουτέστιν ἀψοφητὶ καὶ ἠρέμα καθ' ἑαυτόν*: which does not seem to agree with *λαλείτω*, the *speaking* being essential to the exercise of the gift. **29—33.**] *Similar regulations for* PROPHECY. **29.**] **δέ**, transitional. **δύο ἢ τρεῖς**, viz. *at one assembling*;—not *together*; this is plainly prohibited, ver. 30. There is no *τὸ πλεῖστον* as in the other case, because he does not wish to seem as if he were limiting this most edifying of the gifts. **οἱ ἄλλοι**, scil. *προφῆται*,—or perhaps, any

[b] διακρινέτωσαν· 30 ἐὰν δὲ ἄλλῳ [c] ἀποκαλυφθῇ καθημένῳ,
ὁ πρῶτος [z] σιγάτω. 31 δύνασθε γὰρ [u] καθ' ἕνα πάντες
[d] προφητεύειν, ἵνα πάντες μανθάνωσιν καὶ πάντες [e] παρα-
καλῶνται· 32 καὶ [fg] πνεύματα [ag] προφητῶν [a] προφήταις [h] ὑπο-
τάσσεται· 33 οὐ γάρ ἐστιν [i] ἀκαταστασίας ὁ [j] θεός, ἀλλὰ
[j] εἰρήνης, ὡς ἐν [k] πάσαις ταῖς [k] ἐκκλησίαις τῶν [l] ἁγίων.

b ch. vi. 5.
c ch. ii. 10 reff.
d ch. xi. 4, 5 reff.
e = Rom. xii. 8 reff.
f = ch. xii. 10 reff.
g Rev. xxii. 6.
h Luke ii. 51. Rom. viii. 7, 20 al. 1 Chron. xxix. 24.

i Luke xxi. 9. 2 Cor. vi. 5. xii. 20. James iii. 16 only. Prov. xxvi. 28. Tobit iv. 13 (not in ℵ) only. (-στατος, James i. 8.) j Rom. xv. 33 reff. k Rom. xvi. 16. ch. vii. 17. 2 Cor. viii. 18. xi. 28 only. l Rom. i. 7. Acts ix. 13 reff.

ανακρινετωσαν D^1F.

30. om δε D^1[and lat] F[-gr G-lat] Orig-int_1[: *et si* Syr: *quodsi* vulg F-lat] Ambrst. (κα in καθημενω is written over the line, **ο π** having been first written, and then marked for erasure by $ℵ^1$.)

31. παντες bef καθ ενα DF h^1 latt Syr arm: om παντες 17 Ambrst: εκαστοι 6. 67^2: εκαστοι παντες 38. 72.

32. for πνευματα, πνευμα D F[-gr(and G-lat)] 1. 43. 52. 67^2. 213 [fuld] Syr [$Epiph_1$] Thdrt Orig-int_1[-ed Did-int_1 $Novat_1$ Hil_1 Ambrst]: txt ABKLℵ rel vulg(and F-lat) syr copt [arm] $Orig_2$(and int_1) $Epiph_2$ Chr_1 [Euthal-ms] Thdrt-ms Damasc Thl Œc $Tert_1$. (*The plur was corrd to the sing because, One Spirit inspiring all the prophets,* πνευματα *was not understood.*) υποτασσονται L.

33. ο θεος bef ακαταστασιας A 57 Syr copt [Hip_1]: om ο F. (αλλα, so ABDℵ e g k 47 [Chr_1 Euthal-ms Damasc].) at end ins διδασκω (*from ch* iv. 17) F b o 2. 10. 39 vulg ([fuld demid harl tol:] not am) syr-w-ast [arm-ed] Chr_2: διατασσομαι Chr-ms_1 Damasc.

person possessing the gift of διακρίσεις πνευμάτων, mentioned ch. xii. 10 in immediate connexion with προφητεία. Such would exercise that gift, to determine *whether the spirit was of God*: see ch. xii. 3; 1 John iv. 1—3. **30.**] **But if a revelation shall have been made to another** (prophet) **while sitting by, let the first** (who was prophesying) **hold his peace** (give place to the other: but clearly, not as ejected by the second in any disorderly manner: probably, by being made aware of it and ceasing his discourse). The rendering of Grot., al., '*let him* (the second) *wait till the first has done speaking*,' q. d., '*let the first have left off*,' is ungrammatical. See also vv. 28, 34.

31, 32.] He shews that the ὁ πρῶτος σιγάτω is *no impossibility*, but *in their power to put into effect*. **For ye have the power** (the primary emphasis of the sentence is on δύνασθε, which is not merely permissive, as E. V., '*ye may*,' but asserts the *possession of the power*;—the secondary on καθ' ἕνα) **one by one all to prophesy** (i. e. you have power to bring about this result—you can be silent if you please), **in order that all may learn and all may be exhorted** (or, **comforted**): **32.**] **and** (not, *for*: but a parallel assertion to the last, 'ye have power, &c. *and*') **spirits of prophets** (i. e. *their own spirits*, filled with the Holy Spirit: so Meyer, and rightly: not, as De Wette, the Spirit of God within each: and so ver. 12: the inspired spirit being regarded as a **πνεῦμα** *in a peculiar sense*—from God, or otherwise. See the distinction plainly made 1 John iv. 2: ἐν τούτῳ γινώσκετε **τὸ πνεῦμα τοῦ θεοῦ.** πᾶν **πνεῦμα** κ.τ.λ. The omission of the art. generalizes the assertion, making it applicable to all genuine Christian prophets) **are subject to prophets** (i. e. to the men whose spirits they are. But very many Commentators, e. g. Theophyl.(alt.), Calvin, Estius, and more recently Bleek and Rückert, take προφήταις to signify *other prophets*—τὸ ἔν σοι χάρισμα, καὶ ἡ ἐνέργεια τοῦ ἔν σοι πνεύματος, ὑποτάσσεται τῷ χαρίσματι τοῦ ἑτέρου τοῦ κινηθέντος εἰς τὸ προφητεύειν (Theophyl.). But the command ὁ πρῶτος σιγάτω would be superfluous, if his gift was in subjection to *another*).

33.] *Reason of the above regulations.* The premiss, *that the church is God's church*, is suppressed. He is the God of peace, not confusion: therefore those assemblies which are His must be peacefully and orderly conducted. And this character of God is not one dependent for its truth on preconceived views of Him:—we have a proof of it wherever a church of the saints has been gathered together. '*In all the churches of the saints*, God is a God of peace: let Him not *among you* be supposed to be a God of confusion.' I am compelled to depart from the majority of modern critics of note, e. g. Lachmann, Tischendorf (ed. 7 [and 8]), Billroth, Meyer, De Wette, and to adhere to the common arrangement of this latter clause. My reason is, that taken as beginning the next paragraph,

m = & constr., Acts xxvi. 1 reff.
n Gen. iii. 16.
o ch. xi. 34 reff.
p Matt. xii. 10 al. fr. Epp., Rom. x. 20 (from Isa. lxv. 1) only.
q ch. xi. 6 reff.
r Acts xi. 1 reff.
s = Rom. x. 18 reff.
t Acts xxvi. 7 reff.
u = ch. iii. 18 reff.

34 Αἱ γυναῖκες ἐν ταῖς ἐκκλησίαις [z] σιγάτωσαν· οὐ γὰρ
[m] ἐπιτρέπεται αὐταῖς λαλεῖν, ἀλλὰ * [h] ὑποτάσσεσθαι, καθὼς
καὶ ὁ [n] νόμος λέγει. 35 εἰ δέ τι μαθεῖν θέλουσιν, [o] ἐν
οἴκῳ τοὺς ἰδίους ἄνδρας [p] ἐπερωτάτωσαν· [q] αἰσχρὸν γάρ
ἐστι γυναικὶ λαλεῖν ἐν ἐκκλησίᾳ. 36 ἢ ἀφ' ὑμῶν ὁ [r] λόγος
τοῦ [r] θεοῦ [s] ἐξῆλθεν, ἢ [t] εἰς ὑμᾶς μόνους [t] κατήντησεν; 37 εἴ
τις [u] δοκεῖ [a] προφήτης εἶναι ἢ [v] πνευματικός, [w] ἐπιγινωσκέτω

ABDF LℵA b d e f g k l m 17. 47

v ch. ii. 15 reff. w constr., Acts iii. 10. iv. 13. 2 Cor. i. 14. xiii. 5.

Vv. **34, 35** are placed aft ver **40** in DF 93 fuld² Ambrst Sedul.

34. rec aft γυναικες ins υμων, with DFKL rel Syr syr-w-ob Chr_2 Thdrt Œc $Ambr_2$ Ambrst Sedul: om ABℵ 17 vulg(and F-lat: *vestræ* is written over υμων in the gr column) coptt æth arm Orig[$-c_1$] Mcion-e_2 $Dial_1$ Nys_1 Damasc ($Cypr_1$) Pel. rec επιτετραπται (*'the sense of the perfect,* permissum est, *was more familiar to the transcribers.' Meyer*), with K rel syrr Mcion-e_1 Chr_1 Thdrt, επιτετρεπται L: txt ABDFℵ 17 [latt coptt arm Orig-c_1 Euthal-ms] Mcion-e_1 Damasc [$Ambr_2$ Ambrst]. (αλλα, so ABD'ℵ [Mcion-e_1 Euthal-ms].) * ὑποτασσέσθωσαν ABℵ 17 Syr coptt æth Mcion-e_3 [Euthal-ms] Damasc: υποτασσεσθαι DFKL rel latt syr arm $Dial_1$ Chr Thdrt Thl Œc [Ambr Ambrst]. add τοις ανδρασιν A.

35. ει τι δε *si quid autem* DF vulg Ambrst. μανθανειν A²ℵ¹ 17. 23-6. 31. 73 Nys_1. (A¹ doubtful.) θελωσιν A 73 Damasc. om εστιν B [Euthal-ms]. rec γυναιξιν (*to agree with plurals preceding*), with DFKLℵ³ rel syrr Orig[-c]$_1$ Chr-mss_1 Thdrt Ambrst: txt ABℵ¹ 17 vulg(and F-lat: *mulieribus* is written over γυναιξιν in gr column) coptt æth arm Orig[$-c_2$] Chr[$-ed_1$ (Euthal-ms)] Damasc Pel. rec εν εκκλησια bef λαλειν, with D(F)K(L) 47 syrr Orig[-c]$_1$ Chr_1 [Euthal-ms] Thdrt Ambrst: txt ABℵ m 17 vulg coptt æth $Orig_2$ Damasc Bede.—εκκλησιαις F[not F-lat] L 49. 69. 106-8 D-lat syr Thdrt.

36. κατηντ. bef μονους F[not F-lat] copt.

37. επιγιγνωσκετω D: γινωσκετω B Chr_1(addg ταυτα).

it is harsh beyond example, and superfluous, as anticipating the reason about to be given οὐ γὰρ κ.τ.λ. Besides which, it is more in accordance with St. Paul's style, to place the main subject of a new sentence first, see 1 Tim. iii. 8, 11, 12; and we have an example of reference to general usage coming in last, in aid of other considerations, ch. xi. 16: but it seems unnatural that it should be placed first in the very forefront of a matter on which he has so much to say. **34, 35.**] *Regulation prohibiting women to speak publicly in the church, and its grounds.* If **ὡς . . . ἁγίων** be placed at the beginning of this sentence, we must not, as Lachm. absurdly does, put a comma before τῶν ἁγίων, which would throw the emphasis on it and disturb the sense: and which besides would then be expressed ἁγίων γυναῖκες, or even ἁγίων αἱ γυναῖκες, but certainly not τῶν ἁγίων αἱ γυναῖκες. **34.**] **ἀλλὰ ὑποτάσσεσθαι,** scil. κελεύεται αὐταῖς. The same construction where a second verb must be supplied from the context, occurs 1 Tim. iv. 3. So Soph. Œd. Tyr. 236, τὸν ἄνδρ' ἀπαυδῶ τοῦτον . . . . . μήτ' εἰσδέχεσθαι μήτε προσφωνεῖν τινα, ὠθεῖν δ' ἀπ' οἴκων πάντας: Lucian, χάρων ἢ ἐπισκοποῦντες, line 49 from beg.,—σὲ δὲ καὶ αὐτὸν κωλύσει ἐνεργεῖν τὰ τοῦ θανάτου ἔργα, καὶ τὴν Πλούτωνος ἀρχὴν ζημιοῦν. See other examples in Kühner, § 852 κ. **ὁ νόμος**—ref. Their speaking in public would be of itself an act of *in*dependence; of teaching the assembly, and among others their own husbands. **35.**] This prohibits another kindred irregularity—their *asking questions* publicly. They might say in answer to the former σιγάτωσαν, 'But if we do not understand any thing, are we not to ask?' The stress is on μαθεῖν. **ἰδίους,** confining them to their *own husbands,* to the exclusion of other men. **αἰσχρόν**] See ref.: **indecent,** bringing deserved reproach. **36—40.**] General Conclusion: *the unseemliness and absurdity of their pretending to originate customs unknown to other churches, as if the word of God first went forth from them: and the enforcement of his apostolic authority.* Then, *a summary in a few words of the purport of what he has said on the spiritual gifts, and a repetition,* in another form, *of the fundamental precept,* ver. 26. **36.**] I cannot agree with Meyer in referring this only to the regulation concerning women which has preceded. It rather seems to refer to *all the points of church custom* which he has been noticing, and to be inseparably connected with what follows,—the recognition of *his* apostolic

ἃ γράφω ὑμῖν, [w] ὅτι κυρίου ἐστὶν [ἐντολή]· 38 εἰ δέ τις
[x] ἀγνοεῖ, [x] ἀγνοείτω. 39 [y] ὥςτε, ἀδελφοί [μου], [z] ζηλοῦτε
τὸ [a] προφητεύειν, καὶ τὸ [b] λαλεῖν μὴ [c] κωλύετε [b] ἐν [b] γλώσσαις, 40 πάντα δὲ [d] εὐσχημόνως καὶ κατὰ [e] τάξιν [f] γινέσθω.
XV. 1 [g] Γνωρίζω δὲ ὑμῖν, ἀδελφοί, τὸ εὐαγγέλιον ὃ

κωλυε- . . .

x = 2 Pet. ii. 12. Sir. v. 15. (pass., 2 Cor. vi. 9.) y = ch. v. 8 reff. z = ver. 1. a ch. xi. 4, 5. b ver. 19 only (ch. xii. 30 reff.). c = Matt. xix. 14. Luke xxiii. 2 al. Exod. xxxvi. 6. d Rom. xiii. 13. 1 Thess. iv. 12 only †. (-μων, ch. xii. 24.) e Luke i. 8. Col. ii. 5. Heb. v. 6, 10 & vi. 20 (from Ps. cix. 4), vii. 11, &c. only. L.P.H. Job xxxviii. 12. f = ver. 26. ch. xvi. 14. g ch. xii. 3 reff. 2 Cor. viii. 1.

rec ins του bef κυριου, with Thl: om ABDFKLℵ rel Orig$_2$ Chr$_1$ Thdrt Damasc Œc. for κυριου, θεου A copt Orig$_2$. rec εισιν εντολαι, with D$^{2.3}$[-gr] KL rel vulg(and F-lat) syrr basm Chr Thdrt Ambrst-ms: εντολαι εισιν m: εντολη εστιν ℵ^1: εστιν, omg εντολη, D^1(and lat) F[-gr(and G-lat)] Orig$_2$[-c$_1$-](int$_2$) Hil$_1$ Ambrst-ed: εστιν εντολη ABℵ^3 17 copt æth Aug$_2$.

38. for αγνοειτω, αγνοειται D^1(-τε) F(ηγν-) ℵ^1 17 Orig$_f$[-c$_1$(appy): simly coptt (engelbr)] and perhaps A^1(ω is written secunda manu, the original letter being erased): *ignoratur* D-lat: *ignorabitur* vulg [F-lat] G-lat Orig-int$_2$ [Ambr$_1$ Ambrst]: *non cognoscetur* Hil$_1$: txt A^{2}B D$^{2.3}$[-gr] KLℵ^3 rel syrr copt[-wilk] æth arm Orig[-c]$_2$ Chr$_1$ [Euthal-ms] Thdrt Damasc Thl Œc. (*There appears no reason why the indic should have been altered to the imperat; but the form of exprn in ch* viii. 2, 3 *may perhaps have occasioned an alteration of the imperat into the indic, esp if, as Meyer supposes, in writing* αγνοειτω ωστε, *one* ω *had dropped out, and left the last letter of* αγνοειτ. *to be supplied.*)

39. aft αδελφοι ins μου AB^1 D$^{2.3}$[-gr] ℵ c g m o syrr copt Chr$_1$ Thdrt Damasc [*nostri* æth]: om B^2(sic: see table) D^{1}FKL rel latt basm arm Ambrst Pel. om 1st το F. om 2nd το B 48. rec γλωσσαις bef μη κωλυετε, with DFKL rel latt syrr æth arm Chr$_1$ Thdrt Ambrst: txt ABPℵ m 17 [Euthal-ms] Damasc.—rec om εν (λαλ. γλ. *being the more usual exprn?*), with A D^3[-gr] KL[P]ℵ rel vulg(and F-lat) syrr [arm Euthal-ms] Chr Thdrt Ambrst: ins B D^1(and lat) F[-gr] G-lat coptt.

40. rec om δε (*because there appeared to be no contrast?*), with KL rel basm [Bas$_4$] Orig-int$_2$ Ambr$_1$: ins ABDFPℵ 17 a m vulg Syr copt arm Chr$_1$ [Euthal-ms Cyr$_1$] Thdrt Damasc Pel Bede.

Chap. XV. 1. (aft γνωριζω ℵ^1 has written α, but erased it.)

orders, as *those of God*. 37.] **πνευματικός**, one spiritually endowed: not quite as in ch. ii. 15. **ἃ γράφω**] **the things which I am writing**, viz. '*these regulations* which I am now making.' **κυρίου**, emphatic: **the Lord's (commandment)**: carrying His authority. No more direct assertion of inspiration can be uttered than this. "Paul stamps here *the seal of apostolic authority*: and on that seal is necessarily *Christ*." Meyer. 38. **ἀγνοείτω**] implying both the hopelessness of reclaiming such an one, and the little concern which his opposition gave the Apostle. The other reading, ἀγνοεῖται, gives a passable sense —'he is ignored,' scil. by God: cf. ch. viii. 2, 3; xiii. 12; Gal. iv. 9.

39.] **ζηλοῦτε** and **μὴ κωλύετε** express the different estimations in which he held the two gifts. 40.] **δέ, only provided, that . . .** **κατὰ τάξιν**] i. e. in right time, and due proportion.— Meyer compares Jos. B. J. ii. 8. 5, of the Essenes: οὔτε κραυγή ποτε τὸν οἶκον οὔτε θόρυβος μολύνει, τὰς δὲ λαλιὰς ἐν τάξει παραχωροῦσιν ἀλλήλοις. See Stanley, edn. 2, pp. 293 f.

Chap. XV.] Of the Resurrection of the Dead; which some in the Corinthian church denied. For the enquiry, who they were that denied the Resurrection, see note on ver. 12.

1—11.] The Apostle lays the foundation of his intended polemical argument in the historical fact of the Resurrection of Christ. But he does not altogether *assume* this fact. He deals with its *evidence*, in relating minutely the various appearances of the Lord after His Resurrection, to *others*, and to *himself*. Then, in ver. 12, the *proclamation* of Christ's Resurrection as the great fact attending the preaching of the gospel, is set against the denial of the Resurrection by some of them, and it is subsequently shewn that the two hang together, so that they who denied the one must be prepared to deny the other; and the consequences of this latter denial are pointed out. But it by no means follows, as De W. (in part) and Meyer have assumed, that the impugners were *not prepared* to deny the Resurrection of Christ. The Apostle writes not only for *them*, but for the rest of the Corinthian believers, shewing them the historical cer-

h constr. acc. & dat., Luke i. 19. ii. 10. Acts xiii. 32 [xvii. 18]. 2 Cor. xi. 7.
i = ch. xi. 23. Gal. i. 9, 12 al. see John i. 11.

h εὐηγγελισάμην ὑμῖν, ὃ καὶ i παρελάβετε, j ἐν ᾧ καὶ
j ἑστήκατε, 2 δι' οὗ καὶ k σώζεσθε, τίνι λόγῳ εὐηγγελισάμην ὑμῖν εἰ l κατέχετε, m ἐκτὸς m εἰ μὴ n εἰκῇ o ἐπιστεύσατε.
3 p παρέδωκα γὰρ ὑμῖν q ἐν q πρώτοις ὃ καὶ i παρέλαβον,

ABDFK LPℵ a b c d e f g h k l m o 17. 47

j John viii. 44. Rom. v. 2. (2 Cor. i. 24.) Col. iv. 12. k pres., Acts ii. 47. ch. i. 18. 2 Cor. ii. 15. 1 Pet. iii. 21. iv. 18. Isa. xlv. 20. l ch. xi. 2 reff. m ch. xiv. 5. 1 Tim. v. 19 only. n Rom. xiii. 4 reff. o = Acts xix. 2. Rom. xiii. 11. ch. iii. 5. Eph. i. 13. p = ch. xi. 2 reff. q here only. see note. Gen. xxxiii. 2.

ευαγγελισαμην D Orig-c. for εστηκατε, στηκετε[*statis*] D[1]F latt copt Ambrst.
2. aft λογω ins και D[1](and lat); *quod et sermone* Ambrst. for ει κατεχετε, οφειλετε κατεχειν D[1](and lat) F[not F-]lat lux Ambrst.

tainty, and vital importance of Christ's Resurrection, and its inseparable connexion with the doctrine which they were now tempted to deny. **1, 2.**] **δέ** transitional. **γνωρίζω**, not, as most Commentators, aft. Œc., *οἷον ὑπομιμνήσκω*, nor as Rück., '*I direct your attention to*' (both which meanings are inadmissible, from the usage of the word: see reff.),—but as E. V. **I declare**: i. e. '*declare anew*:' not without some intimation of surprise and reproach to them. **τὸ εὐαγγ.**] **the (whole) Gospel**: not merely the Death and Resurrection of Christ, which were *ἐν πρώτοις* parts of it; the reproach still continues; q. d. 'I am constrained to begin again, and declare to you the whole gospel which I preached to you.' **ὃ καὶ παρ.**] The thrice repeated *καί* indicates a climax:—**which ye also received** (see especially ref. John), **in which moreover ye stand, by means of which ye are even being saved** (in the course of salvation). **τίνι λόγ.**] **if ye hold fast, with what discourse** (not, as Moulton supposes me to interpret (in his Winer, Gr. Gr. p. 211, note 2,) = *the discourse with which*) **I preached to you**: the clause *τίνι λόγ.* being prefixed for emphasis' sake. **λόγος**, of the *import*, not the *grounds* of his preaching: for *of this* he reminds them below, *not of the arguments.* Some Commentators take *τίνι λόγῳ κ.τ.λ.* as a mere epexegesis of *εὐαγγέλιον*,—'*the gospel . . . ., with what discourse I preached to you*,' as *οἶδά σε, τίς εἶ.* But as Meyer has remarked, in that case,—(1) *σώζεσθε* and *εἰ κατέχετε* being altogether severed from one another, *εἰ κατέχετε* becomes the conditional clause to *γνωρίζω ὑμῖν*, with which it has no logical connexion: (2) *εἰ κατέχετε* would be inconsistent with *ἐν ᾧ καὶ ἑστήκατε*, which would thus be an *absolute assertion*: (3) the words *ἐκτὸς εἰ μὴ εἰκῇ ἐπιστ.* would have to be referred as a second conditional clause to *εἰ κατέχετε* (see below). **ἐκτὸς εἰ μὴ εἰκῇ ἐπιστ.**] The only chance, if you hold fast what I have taught you, of your missing salvation, is the hardly supposable one, that your *faith is vain*, and the gospel a fable; see ver. 14, of which this is an anticipation:—**unless** (perchance) **ye believed** (not as E. V. '*have believed*,' which confuses the idea: it is, '*became believers*,' see reff.) **in vain** (*εἰς κενόν*, as ver. 14). So Chrys., who remarks: *νῦν μὲν ὑπεσταλμένως αὐτό φησι, προϊὼν δὲ καὶ διαθερμαινόμενος· γυμνῇ λοιπὸν τῇ κεφαλῇ βοᾷ καὶ λέγει Εἰ δὲ χριστὸς οὐκ ἐγήγερται, κ.τ.λ.*, ver. 14. Hom. xxxviii. p. 352. This explanation of the words appears to me the only tenable one. Meyer, and in the main De W., understand them of a *vain and dead faith*, which the Apostle will not suppose them to have. But surely if the previously expressed condition of *κατέχετε* were fulfilled, their faith *could not be vain or dead*; and again the *aorist* is against this interpretation: **unless ye became believers in vain**, not, '*unless your faith has been a vain one.*' A still further reason is, the parallelism of *εἰκῇ ἐπιστεύσατε* here and *οὕτως ἐπιστεύσατε*, ver. 11: leading to the inference that *εἰκῇ* here relates, not to the subjective insufficiency of their faith, but to the (hypothetical) objective nullity of that on which their faith was founded. Œc., Theophyl., Theodoret, Luther, Calv., Estius, and De W. connect *ἐκτὸς εἰ μή* (see above) as a second conditional clause to *εἰ κατέχετε*, supplying between, *κατέχετε δὲ πάντως* (Theophyl.): but this is arbitrary and unnatural. **3—11.**] *A detail of the great facts preached to them, centering in* THE RESURRECTION OF CHRIST.

3. ἐν πρώτοις] *in primis*, with relation not to order of time (as Chrys.: *ἐξ ἀρχῆς*), but to *importance* (as Theophyl.: *οἱονεὶ γὰρ θεμέλιός ἐστι πάσης τῆς πίστεως*). So Plato, Rep. vii. 6, p. 522: *τοῦτο τὸ κοινὸν . . . . ὃ καὶ παντὶ ἐν πρώτοις ἀνάγκη μανθάνειν.* **ὃ καὶ παρέλαβον**] viz. (see ch. xi. 23 and note) *from the Lord himself*, by special revelation. Before his conversion he may have known the bare fact of the *death* of Jesus, but the nature and reason of that Death he had to learn from revelation:—the Resurrection he regarded as a fable,—but revelation informed him of its reality, and its accord- *

ὅτι χριστὸς ἀπέθανεν [r] ὑπὲρ τῶν [r] ἁμαρτιῶν ἡμῶν [s] κατὰ
τὰς [t] γραφάς, 4 καὶ ὅτι [u] ἐτάφη, καὶ ὅτι [v] ἐγήγερται τῇ ἡμέρᾳ
τῇ τρίτῃ [w] κατὰ τὰς [t] γραφάς, 5 καὶ ὅτι [x] ὤφθη Κηφᾷ, εἶτα
τοῖς δώδεκα. 6 ἔπειτα [x] ὤφθη [y] ἐπάνω πεντακοσίοις ἀδελφοῖς [z] ἐφάπαξ, ἐξ ὧν [a] οἱ [a] πλείονες [b] μένουσιν [c] ἕως [c] ἄρτι,

r Heb. v. 1. vii. 27. x. 12. Ezek. xlv. 22.
s Psa. xxi. 16. Isa. liii. 5. Dan. ix. 24. Zech. xiii. 7.
t plur., Acts xvii. 2.
u Matt. viii. 21, 22 ‖ L. xiv. 12. Luke xvi. 22. Acts ii. 29. v. 6, 9, 10 only. Gen. xxiii. 4.
v = Matt. x. 8. xiv. 2. xvi. 21 al. Isa. xxvi. 19.
w Psa. xv. 10. Isa. liii. 9, 10. Hosea vi. 2. Jon. i. 17 (ii. 1). see Matt. xii. 40.
x Acts ii. 3 reff. 1 Tim. iii. 16. in this ref., = ἐφάνη or ἐφανερώθη, (Mk. xvi. 9—20) John. See Stanley.
y = Mark xiv. 5 only. Exod. xxx. 14 al. elsw. of *place or authority*. See Winer, edn. 6, § 37. 5.
z = here (Rom. vi. 10. Heb. vii. 27. ix. 12. x. 10) only +.
a ch. ix. 19 reff.
b = John xxi. 22, 23. Phil. i. 25.
c ch. iv. 13 reff.

4. rec τη τριτη ημ. (*see Matt* xvi. 21; xvii. 23. *Here* τη ημ. τη τρ. *is solemn and emphatic*), with FKLP rel vulg Syr basm goth Mcion-e_2 $Dial_1$ Eus_1 [Cyr-jer_1] Chr_1 Thdrt [$Archel_1$ Damasc] Iren-int_1 $Tert_1$: txt ABDℵ m 17 syr copt Cyr-jer_1 Cyr[-p_3 Euthal-ms] Hil_1.

5. επειτα Aℵ m 17 Eus_2 Cyr-jer_1 Chr_1 [Euthal-ms $Hesych_1$]: και μετα ταυτα D¹F am goth [(Syr arm)]. for δωδεκα, ενδεκα D¹F nonnulli-codices-in-Aug latt syr-mg goth arm-usc [Eus_1] $Archel_1$ Damasc Phot [Ambrst] Jer.

6. rec πλειους, with KLP rel Eus_1 Chr_1 Thdrt Damasc: txt ABDFℵ k m 17 $Orig_1$ Eus_1 Cyr[(varies) Euthal-ms].

ance with prophecy. On the following clauses, 'the earliest known specimen of what may be termed the creed of the early Church,' see Stanley's notes, and [his] dissertation at the end of the section.

ὑπὲρ τ. ἁμ. ἡμ.] ON BEHALF OF OUR SINS: viz. to atone for them. Meyer makes the important remark, that this use of ὑπέρ with **τῶν ἁμαρτιῶν** ἡμ. shews, that when Paul uses it in speaking of Christ's sufferings with **ἡμῶν** *only*, he *does not mean by it* '*loco* nostri.' He also quotes from Buttmann (Index to Meidias, p. 188), on the distinction between ὑπέρ and περί: "id unum interest, quod περί usu frequentissimo teritur, multo rarius usurpatur ὑπέρ, quod ipsum discrimen inter Lat. præp. *de* et *super* locum obtinet." It may be noticed, that in 3 Kings xvi. 19, where it is said that Zimri ἀπέθανεν ὑπὲρ τῶν ἁμαρτιῶν αὐτοῦ ὧν ἐποίησεν, it is for his own sins, as their punishment, that he died. So that ὑπέρ *may* bear the meaning that Christ's death was the punishment of the sins of that our nature which he took upon Him. But its undoubtedly inclusive vicarious import in other passages where ὑπὲρ ἡμῶν and the like occur, seems to rule it to have that sense here also.

κατὰ τὰς γρ.] This applies to Christ's *Death, Burial*, and *Resurrection on the third day*: see reff.

4. ἐγήγερται] the perfect marks the continuation of the state thus begun, or of its consequences: so Herod. vii. 8, ἀλλ' ὁ μὲν τετελεύτηκε, καὶ οὐκ ἐξεγένετό οἱ τιμωρήσασθαι: see Kühner, § 441. 6.

5.] That the following appearances are related in chronological order, is evident from the use of the definite adverbs of sequence, εἶτα, ἔπειτα, ἔσχατον δὲ πάντων. See examples in Wetstein. Wieseler, Chron. Synops. der vier Evv. pp. 420 f., attempts to disprove this, but certainly does not succeed in getting over ἔσχατον πάντων, ver. 8.

ὤφθη Κηφᾷ] See Luke xxiv. 34.

τοῖς δώδεκα] used here popularly, as *decemviri*, and other like expressions, although the number was not full. The occasion referred to seems to be that in John xx. 19 ff.; Luke xxiv. 36 ff. Clearly we must not with Chrys., suppose *Matthias* to be included as possibly having seen Him *after His ascension*: for the appearance is evidently *one and the same*.

6.] He drops the construction with ὅτι, dependent on παρέδωκα, and proceeds in a direct narration. But evidently the *sense* of the former construction continues: he is relating what he had received and preached to them.

ἐπάνω πεντακ. ἀδ. ἐφάπ.] From Matt. xxviii. 17, it appears (see note there) that others besides the eleven witnessed the appearance on the mountain in Galilee. But we cannot say that it is the appearance here referred to:—nor indeed is it likely that so many as 500 believers in Jesus would have been gathered together in Galilee: both from its position in the list, and from the number who witnessed it, this appearance would seem rather to have taken place *at Jerusalem*, and before the dispersion of the multitudes who had assembled at the passover: for we find that the church of Jerusalem itself (Acts i. 15) subsequently contained only 120 persons.

ἐφάπαξ] not here in its commoner meaning of '*once for all*,' but **at once, at one and the same time**; as Theodoret, οὐ καθ' ἕνα, ἀλλ' ὁμοῦ πᾶσιν.

μένουσιν] **survive**; see reff. The circumstance of most of them remaining alive is mentioned apparently by way of strength-

d = ch. vii. 39 reff.
e adv., here only. Numb. xxxi. 2.
f neut., see Mark xii. 28, and note.
g here only †. Jos. Antt. iii. 7. 1. Diod. Sic. iii. 39.
h here only. Job iii. 16. Eccles. vi. 3 only.
i = Matt. iii. 11. 2 Cor. iii. 5. Exod. iv. 10. constr., 2 Tim. ii. 2.
j = Matt. v. 10, 11 al. fr. Ps. vii. 1. 2 Macc. v. 8.
k ch. i. 2 reff.
l 1 Pet. i. 10.

τινὲς δὲ [καὶ] [d] ἐκοιμήθησαν· 7 ἔπειτα [x] ὤφθη Ἰακώβῳ, ABDFK
ἔπειτα τοῖς ἀποστόλοις πᾶσιν. 8 [e] ἔσχατον δὲ [f] πάντων LPℵ a b c d e f g
[g] ὡσπερεὶ τῷ [h] ἐκτρώματι [x] ὤφθη κἀμοί. 9 ἐγὼ γάρ εἰμι ὁ h k l m o 17. 47
ἐλάχιστος τῶν ἀποστόλων· ὃς οὐκ εἰμὶ [i] ἱκανὸς καλεῖσθαι
ἀπόστολος, διότι [j] ἐδίωξα τὴν [k] ἐκκλησίαν τοῦ [k] θεοῦ·
10 χάριτι δὲ θεοῦ εἰμὶ ὅ εἰμι, καὶ ἡ [l] χάρις αὐτοῦ ἡ [l] εἰς ἐμὲ

aft δε ins εξ αυτων K. om και (*not perceiving its force or confusion from* ε και εκοι) A^1(perhaps) BD^1Fℵ^1 latt syr coptt goth arm [Ambrst Aug_1]: ins A^2 D^3[-gr] KLPℵ^3 rel (Syr) æth $Orig_1$ $Archel_1$ Eus_1 Chr [$Cyr\text{-}p_2$ Euthal-ms] Thdrt Damasc.

7. for 1st επειτα, ειτα D copt [Cyr_1]: txt ABFKLPℵ 17 rel $Orig_1$ [Eus_1 Euthal-ms] $Cyr\text{-}jer_1$ Chr Damasc. rec (for 2nd επειτα) ειτα, with BDLPℵ^3 rel Chr_1 Thdrt: txt AFKℵ^1 a c e g 17 $Orig_1$ Eus_2 [Cyr_1 Euthal-ms] Damasc.

8. ωσπερ (for -περει) D^1 Eus_1. om τω F lect-19 sah. και εμοι F.

10. om 2nd ἡ D^1F, *gratia ejus in me* latt lat-ff.

ening the evidence: q. d. "and can attest it, if required:"—hardly for the reason suggested by Stanley, that the dead among them would have been worse off even than others, if there were no resurrection, having been "tantalised by the glimpse of another world in the vision of their risen Lord." **7. Ἰακώβῳ]** Probably, from no distinguishing epithet being added, *the celebrated* James, *the brother of the Lord:* see Gal. i. 19. So Chrys.: ἐμοὶ δοκεῖ, τῷ ἀδελφῷ τῷ ἑαυτοῦ, p. 355. See notes on ch. ix. 5, Matt. xiii. 55, and the Prolegg. to the Epistle of James. On Wieseler's view that this is the appearance on the road to Emmaus, see note on Luke xxiv. 13. This appearance cannot however be identical with that traditional one quoted by Jerome (from the Gospel according to the Hebrews), Catal. Script. Eccles. ii. vol. ii, p. 831 f.: "Juraverat enim Jacobus, se non comesturum panem ab illa hora qua biberat calicem Domini, donec videret eum resurgentem a mortuis." This would imply that the appearance was very soon after the Resurrection, and before any of those to large collections of believers, in which James would naturally be present. **ἀποστ. πᾶσιν]** This is decisive for the much wider use of the term ἀπόστολος than as applying to the Twelve only: and a strong presumption that James, just mentioned, and evidently here and Gal. i. 19, included among the ἀπόστολοι, was not one of the Twelve. Chrys. (ubi supra) extends the term to the Seventy of Luke x, and others; ἦσαν γὰρ καὶ ἄλλοι ἀπόστολοι, ὡς οἱ ἑβδομήκοντα.

8.] **But last of all** (not *masc.*, as Meyer, who refers it to τῶν ἀποστόλων,—for others than the Apostles have already been mentioned,—but *neut.*, as in ref. and in the expression πάντων μάλιστα (Plato, Protag. p. 330)), **as to the abortively born** (τῷ pointing out the Apostles as a family, and himself as *the abortion* among them,—the one whose relation to the rest in point of worthiness, was as that of the immature and deformed child to the rest of the family. That this is the meaning is evident from ver. 9, which drops the figure. On ἔκτρωμα, see examples in Wetstein. It is not, as τινες in Theophyl., τὸ ὕστερον γέννημα, '*a weakling child of old age.*' The grammarians find fault with the term, and prefer ἄμβλωμα or ἐξάμβλωμα: but it occurs in Aristotle, de generatione animalium, iv. 5,—οὐ δύναται τελειοῦν, ἀλλὰ κυήματ' ἐκπίπτει παραπλήσια τοῖς καλουμένοις **ἐκτρώμασιν**. The suggestion of Valcknaer, al., that τῷ is τῳ for τινι, is equally inconsistent with usage and the sense of the passage), **He appeared to me also:** viz. *on the road to Damascus.* This, and this only, can here be meant; as he is speaking, not of a succession of visions, but of some one definite apparition.

9, 10,] Digressive, explanatory of ἐκτρώματι. **9. ἐγώ]** The stress is on ἐγώ, '*I, and no other.*' **ὅς]** '*ut qui:*' assigns the reason. **ἱκανός]** see reff. **καλεῖσθαι]** 'to bear the honourable name of an Apostle.' **10. χάρ. δὲ θεοῦ]** "With the humiliating conviction of his own unworthiness is united the consciousness of that higher Power which worked on and in him,—and this introduces his chastened self-consciousness of the extent and success of his apostolic labours." De Wette. The position of χάριτι δὲ θεοῦ, and the repetition of ἡ χάρις αὐτοῦ afterwards, shew the emphatic prominence which he assigns to the divine Grace. **ὅ εἰμι]** viz. in my office and its results. The church has admirably connected this passage, as Epistle for the 11th Sunday after Trinity, with that other speech of a Pharisee, Luke xviii. 11,—ὁ θεός, εὐχαριστῶ σοι ὅτι οὐκ εἰμὶ ὥς-

οὐ [m] κενὴ ἐγενήθη, ἀλλὰ [n] περισσότερον αὐτῶν πάντων
[o] ἐκοπίασα, οὐκ ἐγὼ δέ, ἀλλὰ ἡ χάρις τοῦ θεοῦ [p] σὺν
ἐμοί. 11 [q] εἴτε οὖν ἐγὼ [q] εἴτε ἐκεῖνοι, οὕτως [r] κηρύσσομεν,
καὶ οὕτως [s] ἐπιστεύσατε. 12 εἰ δὲ [t] χριστὸς [t] κηρύσσεται * ἐκ
[u] νεκρῶν ὅτι [uv] ἐγήγερται, [w] πῶς λέγουσιν ἐν ὑμῖν τινες ὅτι

m = Acts iv. 25 (from Ps. ii. 1). vv. 14, 58. 1 Thess. ii. 1. Deut. xxxii. 47.
n adv., Mark vii. 36. Heb. vi. 17. vii. 15.
o Matt. vi. 28. Acts xx. 35. Rom. xvi. 6, 12. Phil. ii. 16. Ps. cxxvi. 1.
p Acts xiv. 4.
q ch. xiii. 8 reff.
r absol., Matt. iii. 1, and passim. Exod. xxxii. 5.
s = ver. 2 reff.
t see Acts viii. 5 reff.
u Matt. xvii. 9. (ἠγ. ἀπὸ τ. ν., Matt. xiv. 2 al. not in Mk., who has ἐκ ν. ἀναστ., vi. 14.) Luke ix. 7. John ii. 22. xii. 1, 9, 17. xxi. 14. Acts iii. 15 al2. Paul, passim. Heb. xi. 19. 1 Pet. i. 21.
v = ver. 4 al. fr.
w = Rom. vi. 2. Gal. ii, 14. iv. 9.

for ου κενη εγενηθη, πτωχη ουκ εγενηθη D[1] : πτωχη ου γεγονεν F : *pauper*(*a*) *non fuit* D-lat G-lat [Ambrst] (not Jer$_{alic}$ Aug$_1$: *egena* [Ambr$_2$: simly goth]). om αυτων D[1]-gr L[1] : παντων bef αυτων a. **απαντων** (but α erased) ℵ. (αλλ**a**, so ABD[1]ℵ 17.) rec ins η bef συν (*see note*), with A D-corr([2 or 3 ?])[-gr] KLPℵ[3] rel sah æth arm [Bas$_2$ Ps-]Ath Chr$_1$ Cyr[-p$_2$ Euthal-ms] Thdrt$_2$ Damasc$_2$ Thl Œc Orig-int$_2$ Jer$_{[alic]}$: om BD[1]Fℵ[1] latt goth Orig(gr and int$_6$) [Ambrst].

11. for ουν, δε *autem* D[1]F goth Iren-int$_1$: *enim* vulg Tert$_1$. πιστευσατε ℵ[1].

12. *rec ὅτι ἐκ νεκρῶν, with AB D[2][-gr] KLPℵ rel Iren(gr and int) Chr$_1$ Thdrt [Cyr$_1$ Euthal-ms Damasc Tert$_1$ Ambrst : *quod resurrexit a mortuis*] vulg(and F-lat) : εκ νεκρων οτι D[1·3](and lat) F[-gr] G-lat Orig$_2$. rec τινες bef εν υμιν, with DFKL rel goth arm Epiph$_1$ Chr$_2$ Thdrt Ambrst Promiss$_1$: *quidam dicunt in vobis* latt [coptt] Tert$_1$: txt ABPℵ a 17 syrr Orig$_1$([-c$_1$]-int$_1$) Chr$_1$ [Cyr-p$_3$ Euthal-ms] Damasc.

περ οἱ λοιποὶ τῶν ἀνθρώπων : see note there. **ἡ εἰς ἐμέ**] **which was** (manifested) **towards me** : see ref. and Rom. viii. 18. **ἀλλά** opposed to κενὴ ἐγ.,—'*by means of God's grace*' being understood after ἀλλά, as afterwards explained. **περισσότερον**] adverbial, as in reff.: or perhaps neut. accus. governed by ἐκοπίασα. **αὐτῶν πάντων**] either, '*than any of them,*' or '*than they all,*' scil. *together*. Meyer prefers the latter, on account of τοῖς ἀπ. πᾶσιν, ver. 7. But it seems hardly necessary, and introduces an element of apparent exaggeration. **ἐκοπίασα**] Spoken of his apostolic work, in all its branches; see reff., especially Phil. **οὐκ ἐγὼ δέ**] explanatory, to avoid misapprehension: it had been implied (see above) in the ἀλλά:—**not I, however, but the Grace of God with me** (see var. readd.): scil. ἐκοπίασεν κ.τ.λ. That is,—the Grace of God worked with him in so overwhelming a measure, compared to his own working, that it was no longer the work of himself but of divine Grace. Augustine, de Grat. et Lib. Arb. § 5 (12), vol. x. p. 889, hardly expresses this: "Non ego autem, i. e. non solus, sed gratia Dei mecum : ac per hoc nec gratia Dei sola, nec ipse solus, sed gratia Dei cum illo :"—for he overlooks the *entire preponderance* of Grace, which Paul asserts, even to the exclusion of his own action in the matter. The right view of this preponderance of Grace prevents the misunderstanding of the words which has led to the insertion of the article, ἡ σὺν ἐμοί, whereby Grace becomes absolutely the *sole agent*, which is contrary to fact. On the coagency of the human will with divine Grace, but in subordination, see Matt. x. 20; 2 Cor. v. 20; vi. 1, and ch. iii. 9, note. **11.**] * He resumes the subject after the digression respecting himself:—**it matters not whether it were I or they** (the other Apostles) —SUCH **is the purport of our preaching**— SUCH **was your belief**:—οὕτως, after **this manner**, viz. *that Christ died, was buried, and rose again*, as vv. 3, 4.

12—19.] *On the fact of Christ's Resurrection, announced in his preaching, and confessed in their belief, he grounds* (*negatively*) *the truth of the general Resurrection :—If the latter be not to happen, neither has the former happened :—and he urges the results of such a disproof of Christ's Resurrection.* **12.**] introduces the argument for the resurrection, by referring to its denial among a portion of the Corinthian church. **δέ** belongs to the whole question, and is opposed to οὕτως κηρ. and οὕτ. ἐπιστ. of the foregoing verse. The position of χριστός before the verb gives it the leading emphasis, as an *example* of that which is denied by some among you: **But if** CHRIST **is preached** [not subjunctive, be preached: he is arguing from a matter of fact, not from a mere hypothesis] **that He is risen from the dead** (if an instance of such resurrection is a fact announced in our preaching), **how say some among you** (how comes it to pass that some say) **that a resurrection of the dead does not exist** (οὐκ ἔστ. as ver. 13)? If the *species* be *conceded*, how is it that some among you *deny* the *genus*? **τινες**] It is an interesting question, WHO *these* τινες *were*; and one which can only be answered by the indications which the argument in

ABDFK LPℵ a b c d e f g h k l m o 17. 47

^{x} ἀνάστασις ^{x} νεκρῶν οὐκ ἔστιν; 13 εἰ δὲ ^{x} ἀνάστασις ^{x} νεκρῶν οὐκ ἔστιν, οὐδὲ χριστὸς ^{y} ἐγήγερται· 14 εἰ δὲ χριστὸς
οὐκ ^{y} ἐγήγερται, ^{z} κενὸν ^{a} ἄρα καὶ τὸ ^{b} κήρυγμα ἡμῶν,
^{z} κενὴ καὶ ἡ πίστις ὑμῶν· 15 ^{c} εὑρισκόμεθα δὲ καὶ ^{d} ψευδο-

x Matt. xxii. 31 only in gospp. Acts xvii. 32 al4. Paul, Rom. i. 4. here &c. 4 times only. Heb. vi. 2. see Acts iv. 2 reff. x. 41 reff. y ver. 4. z ver. 10. a 2 Cor. v. 15. Gal. iii. 29. see Rom. vii. 3, 25. b Rom. xvi. 25 reff. c = ch. iv. 2 reff. d Matt. xxvi. 60 only †. see Acts vi. 13. (-ρεῖν, Mark x. 19. -ρία, Matt. xv. 19.)

13. om ει δε to εστιν (*homœotel*) [E] ℵ^1(ins ℵ-corr^1) a d 17 [Cyr$_1$].—for ει, εαν F.
14. om ει to εγηγ. (*homœotel*) D^1[and lat]. rec om 1st και (*as superfluous*), with BLℵ^3 rel [vulg F-lat syrr coptt æth arm] Ps-Ign$_1$ Constt Epiph$_1$ Cyr-jer$_1$ Chr$_1$ [Cyr-p$_2$] Thdrt Damasc Jac-nisib$_1$ [Iren-int$_1$ Tert$_1$ Ambrst]: ins AD F[-gr] KPℵ^1 d (e) f^2 l m 17. 47 G-lat basm goth Dial$_1$ [Euthal-ms] Œc. (D-lat [Iren-int] lat-ff express neither και nor αρα.) rec aft κενη ins δε, with D^3[-gr] KL [47(sic)] rel (am) syr Ps-Ign$_1$ Chr$_1$ Thdrt Thl Œc: om ABD^{1}FPℵ a^1 m 17 latt [Syr goth æth arm] coptt Cyr-jer$_1$ Dial$_1$ [Cyr$_1$ Euthal-ms] Damasc [Iren-int$_1$ Tert$_1$ Ambrst]. ημων BD^1 [17] 67^2. 73. 91. 106 sah goth Ps-Ign-2-mss Dial$_1$ Cyr-jer [Cyr-p$_2$] Œc Ruf$_1$ Arnob Bede.
15. om και D^1 goth arm Tert$_1$.

this chapter furnishes. (1) *Were they Sadducees?* If so, the Apostle would hardly have begun his argument with the fact of the Resurrection of Jesus. And yet we must remember that he is arguing not *with the deniers*, but with those who being as yet sound, were liable to be misled by them. But the opposition between Sadduceism and Christianity was so complete, that we have little reason to think that any leaven of the Sadducees ever found its way into the church. (2) *Were they Epicureans?* Probably not, for two reasons: (α) the Epicurean maxim, "Let us eat and drink," &c., is represented as a legitimate *consequence* of adopting their denial of the resurrection, not as an accompaniment of, much less as the ground of it: and (β) had the Epicurean element entered to any extent into the Corinthian church, we certainly should have had more notice of its exceedingly antichristian tenets. It is possible that the deniers may have been, or been in danger of being, *corrupted by mixture* with Epicureans *without*, from the warning of ver. 33. (3) *Were they Jews?* If not Sadducees, hardly Jews at all, or Judaizers: a strong tenet of Pharisaism was *this very one* of the Resurrection, see Acts xxiii. 6: and we know of no tendency of Essenism which should produce such a denial. (4) They must then have been *Gentile believers*, inheriting the unwillingness of the Greek mind to receive that of which a full account could not be given, see vv. 35, 36: and probably of a philosophical and cavilling turn. Meyer argues, from the antimaterialistic turn of the Apostle's counter-arguments, vv. 35 ff.,—that the objections were antimaterialistic also: De W. infers the very opposite, which certainly seems to me more probable. No trace whatever is found in the argument of an *allegorizing* character in the opponents, as was that of Hymenæus and Philetus, who maintained that the resurrection was past already, 2 Tim. ii. 17, 18,—as Olsh. after Grot. supposes. Whether the Apostle regarded the resurrection of the body as inseparably bound up with a future existence of the soul, does not very clearly appear in this chapter. From the use of the word ἀπώλοντο, ver. 18, which must refer, not to annihilation, but to *perdition*, it would seem that he admitted an independent existence of the soul; as also from Phil. i. 23. But from ver. 32, εἰ νεκροὶ οὐκ ἐγείρονται, φάγωμεν κ. πίωμεν, αὔριον γὰρ ἀποθνήσκομεν, it would seem that the Apostle regarded the denial of the resurrection as involving that of the future state and judgment. On the question, to which of the (supposed) Corinthian parties the opponents belonged, I have nothing to say, not recognizing the divisions into the Pauline, Apollonian, Petrine, and Christine parties as having any historical foundation; see note on ch. i. 12. **13.**] **δέ** is the **but** argumentandi, frequent in mathematical demonstrations. **ἀν. νεκ. οὐκ ἔστιν**] the words (οὐκ) of the deniers. **οὐδὲ χριστ. ἐγήγερται**] This inference depends, as Grot. observes, on the maxim, "Sublato genere tollitur et species;" the Resurrection of Christ being an *instance* of the *rule*, that dead *men* rise; inasmuch as *He is man*. This is enlarged on, vv. 20—22. **14.**] **δέ**, again introducing a new inference. **οὐκ ἐγ.**] Again repeating and using as matter of fact (οὐκ) the inference of the last verse; q. d. εἰ δὲ χρ. οὐκ-ἐγήγερται. **κενόν**] idle, 'empty,' 'without result:' placed first for emphasis. **ἄρα**] **then**: 'rebus ita comparatis' (Meyer). **καί**] **also**, q. d. "If Christ's Resurrection be gone, then also our faith is gone." Without the copula δέ, the clause is much more forcible:—**idle also is our preach-**

μάρτυρες τοῦ θεοῦ, ὅτι [e] ἐμαρτυρήσαμεν [f] κατὰ τοῦ θεοῦ
ὅτι [y] ἤγειρεν τὸν χριστόν, ὃν οὐκ [y] ἤγειρεν [g] εἴπερ ἄρα
νεκροὶ οὐκ [y] ἐγείρονται. 16 εἰ γὰρ νεκροὶ οὐκ [y] ἐγείρονται, οὐδὲ χριστὸς [y] ἐγήγερται· 17 εἰ δὲ χριστὸς οὐκ
[y] ἐγήγερται, [h] ματαία ἡ πίστις ὑμῶν, ἔτι ἐστὲ [i] ἐν ταῖς
[i] ἁμαρτίαις ὑμῶν· 18 ἄρα καὶ οἱ [k] κοιμηθέντες [l] ἐν χριστῷ
[m] ἀπώλοντο. 19 εἰ ἐν τῇ [n] ζωῇ ταύτῃ [o] ἐν χριστῷ [op] ἠλπικότες [q] ἐσμὲν μόνον, [r] ἐλεεινότεροι πάντων ἀνθρώπων ἐσμέν.

e = John i. 7, 8, 15. Acts xxiii. 11 al.
f = here only. Xen. Cyrop. i. 2. 16, ταῦτα μὲν δὲ κατὰ πάντων Περσῶν ἔχομεν λέγειν. Arist. Eth. Nic. i. 10. 7, ἀληθεύσεται κατ' αὐτοῦ.
g = Rom. viii. 9 (reff.), 17. 1 Pet. ii. 3.
h ch. iii. 20 reff. i John viii. 24 bis. ix. 34. k = ch. vii. 39 reff. l = 1 Thess. iv. 16. Rev. xiv. 13. m = Rom. xiv. 15 reff. n = Phil. i. 20. James iv. 14. 1 Pet. iii. 10, from Ps. xxxiii. 12. o 4 Kings xviii. 5. see Eph. i. 12. p perf., John v. 45. 2 Cor. i. 10. 1 Tim. iv. 10. v. 5. vi. 17 only. q constr., Acts xxv. 10 reff. r Rev. iii. 17 only †. compar., ch. xiii. 13 reff.

aft χριστον ins αυτου ℵ[1](ℵ[3] disapproving). om ειπερ to εγειρονται D 43 harl[1] Syr sah goth [Thdrt] Iren-int$_1$ [Tert$_1$ Archel$_1$ Ambrst]. ins οι bef νεκροι F.
16. om ει to εγειρ. (*homœotel*) P am(with fuld). ins ο bef χρ. P.
17. aft υμων ins εστιν BD[1] (vss (not arm)). ins και bef ετι Aℵ[1] Syr sah æth [copt(*etiam*) goth(Tischdf) arm-usc Euthal-ms] Damasc: [*adhuc enim*] Orig[-int$_1$ Ambrst].
19. rec ηλπικοτες εσμεν bef εν χριστω, with D[3][-gr] KLP rel [syrr coptt æth arm] Orig$_1$ Chr$_1$ Thdrt Œc: txt ABD[1]Fℵ m 17 latt goth (Orig$_1$)[-c$_1$] Chron$_1$ (Thl) Iren-int$_1$ Ambr$_2$ Ambrst. 2nd εσμεν bef παντων ανθρωπων D latt[(not G-lat) Syr arm] goth Orig[-c$_1$(txt$_2$) Ambr$_2$ Ambrst]: *omnibus sumus hominibus* Iren-int.

ing, idle also is your faith. Thus καί *both times* refers to the hypothesis, εἰ χρ. οὐκ ἐγήγ. 15.] Not to be joined with the former verse, as Lachm., al., and Meyer: for it does not depend on εἰ δὲ χρ. κ.τ.λ., but has its reason given below. **δὲ καί, moreover.** **ψευδ. τοῦ θ.] false witnesses concerning God** (gen. obj.), not '*belonging to God*' (gen. subj.), as Billroth: and false witnesses, as *bearing false testimony* (see below), not, as Knapp, as *pretending to be witnesses, and not being*:—there is no such distinction as Müller attempts to lay down (Diss. Exeget. de loco Paul. 1 Cor. xv. 12—19, cited by De Wette) between ψευδεῖς μάρτυρες, 'qui falsum testimonium dicunt,' and ψευδομάρτυρες, 'qui mentiuntur se esse testes:' see reff., and compare (De Wette) ψευδοδιδάσκαλος, ψευδοκατήγορος.
* **κατὰ τοῦ θεοῦ**] not, as commonly, and even Meyer, '*against God*:' but as E. V., **of, or concerning God**: see, besides ref., Plut. de Liberis Educandis, § 4:—ὃ κατὰ τῶν τεχνῶν κ. τῶν ἐπιστημῶν λέγειν εἰώθαμεν, ταὐτὸν καὶ κατὰ τῆς ἀρετῆς φατέον ἐστίν. ὡς εἰς τὴν παντελῆ δικαιοπραγίαν τρία δεῖ συνδραμεῖν, φύσιν, κ. λόγον, κ. ἔθος. **εἴπερ ἄρα] If in reality, as they assert, . . . ,** compare Plato, Protag. p. 319 (§ 27), ἦ καλόν, ἦν δ' ἐγώ, τέχνημα ἄρα κέκτησαι, εἴπερ κέκτησαι, and see Hartung, Partikellehre, i. 343. 16.] Repetition of the inference in ver. 13, for precision's sake. 17, 18.] Repetition of the consequence already mentioned in ver. 14, but fuller, and with more reference to its present and future calamitous results. 17. **ματαία**] from μάτην, and thus more directly pointing at the *frustration* of all on which faith relies as accomplished,—e. g. the removal of the guilt and power of sin;—and of all to which hope looks forward, e. g. bliss after death for those who die in Christ. This is so, because Christ's Resurrection *accomplished our justification* (Rom. iv. 25), and, through justification, our *future bliss*, even in the *disembodied state* (for that seems *here* to be treated of). 18. **ἄρα καί] then also.** **οἱ κοιμ.] those who fell asleep in Christ, perished** (i. e. passed into misery in Hades). He uses the aorists, speaking of the act of death, not of the continuing state: the act of falling asleep in Christ was to them ἀπώλεια. **ἐν χρ.**, in communion with, membership of Christ. On **κοιμηθέντες** Meyer quotes a beautiful sentence from Photius (Quæst. Amphiloch. 168 (al. 187 or 197), vol. i. p. 861, Migne): ἐπὶ μὲν οὖν τοῦ χριστοῦ **θάνατον** καλεῖ, ἵνα τὸ πάθος πιστώσηται· ἐπὶ δὲ ἡμῶν **κοίμησιν,** ἵνα τὴν ὀδύνην παραμυθήσηται. ἔνθα μὲν γὰρ παρεχώρησεν ἡ ἀνάστασις, θαῤῥῶν καλεῖ θάνατον. ἔνθα δὲ ἐν ἐλπίσιν ἔτι μένει, κοίμησιν καλεῖ. 19.] Assuming this ἀπώλεια of the dead in Christ, the state of Christians is indeed miserable. It has perhaps not been enough seen that there are here *two emphases*, and that μόνον belongs to the aggregate of both. According to the ordinary interpretation, 'If *in this life only* we have hope in Christ . . . ,' it

s = ch. xiii. 13 reff. t ver. 12. u Rom. viii. 23 reff. v Acts xv. 24 reff. w ver. 13 reff. x = Acts iv. 2. ch. iv. 6. vii. 14. 2 Cor. v. 19. Col. i. 16. Gal. ii. 17. Eph. i. 4. iii. 11. y Rom. iv. 17 reff.

20 [s] νυνὶ δὲ χριστὸς [t] ἐγήγερται [t] ἐκ νεκρῶν, [u] ἀπαρχὴ τῶν ABDFK
[k] κεκοιμημένων. 21 [v] ἐπειδὴ γὰρ δι᾽ ἀνθρώπου [ὁ] θάνατος, LPℵa b c d e f g
καὶ δι᾽ ἀνθρώπου [w] ἀνάστασις [w] νεκρῶν. 22 ὥσπερ γὰρ h k l m o 17. 47
[x] ἐν τῷ Ἀδὰμ πάντες ἀποθνήσκουσιν, οὕτως καὶ [x] ἐν τῷ
χριστῷ πάντες [y] ζωοποιηθήσονται. 23 ἕκαστος δὲ ἐν τῷ

20. for *νυνι*, *νυν* F Dial$_1$. ins *των* bef *νεκρων* F Damasc-comm. rec at end adds *εγενετο* (*supplemental gloss*), with D^3[-gr] KL rel syrr goth Thdrt Damasc Orig-int$_1$: *γενομενος* 80: om ABD^{1}FPℵ 17 latt coptt [æth] arm Orig[$_2$-c$_1$](and int$_1$) Dial$_1$ [Chr$_1$ Euthal-ms] Iren-int$_1$ Hil$_1$ [Ambrst].

21. *δια* (twice) F. om *ο* (bef *θανατος*) ABD^{1}Kℵ 17(appy) Orig$_1$ Dial$_1$ Ath$_1$ Ps-Ath$_1$ [Cyr-p$_2$ Euthal-ms] Damasc (*appy to conform to αναστ. below: this is more prob than to suppose with Meyer that it has been introd from Rom* v. 12): ins D$^{2.3}$FLP rel Orig[-c]$_1$ Eus$_1$ [Did$_1$ Cyr-p$_1$] Ath$_1$ Cyr-jer$_1$ Chr$_1$ Thdrt Euther$_2$. [Of these Eus Cyr-jer Chr Euther$_1$ have *η αναστ.* also.]

23. *δε* is written over the line by ℵ^1 [om Orig$_1$(-ins$_3$)].

would be implied that in reality we *shall have* hope in Christ in another state also, which would not agree with the perfect *ἠλπικότες ἐσμέν*. The right arrangement of the Greek gives the key to the sentence: *εἰ (ἐν τῇ ζωῇ ταύτῃ ἐν χριστῷ ἠλπικότες ἐσμὲν) μόνον*,—'if all we have done is merely *having hoped in Christ in this life*,' 'if it is there to end, and that hope have no result . . .' The perf. **ἠλπικότες ἐσμ.** implies the endurance of the hope through our lives. **ἐλεειν. πάντ.**] **We are most to be pitied** (most miserable) **of all men**; viz. because they, all other men, live at ease,—we on the contrary are ever exposed to danger and death: because our hope is more intense than that of all others, and leads us to forego more: and to be disappointed *in it*, would be the height of misery. **20—28.**] *Reassertion of the truth that Christ* IS RISEN *from the dead,—and prophetic exposition of the consequences of that great event.*

20.] **νυνί**, 'as matters now stand:' see reff. [and note.] **ἀπαρχ. τ. κεκοιμ.**] (as) (the) **first-fruit of them that sleep** (anarthrous, because categorematical). For the construction Meyer compares Eur. Or. 1098: *Ἑλένην κτάνωμεν, Μενελέῳ λύπην πικράν*. The sense is, 'Christ, in rising from the dead, is but the firstling or earnest of the resurrection of the whole number of those that sleep.' There does not appear to be any intended reference to the legal ordinance of the first-fruits (Lev. xxiii. 10, 11): but however general the application of the analogy may be, it can hardly fail to have been suggested to the mind of a Jew by the Levitical ordinances, especially as our Lord rose on the very morrow after the Paschal Sabbath, when (l. c.) the first-fruits were offered. **τῶν κεκοιμημένων**, from the logical connexion, should mean, not the dead *in Christ*, but *all the dead*; see next verse: but it is the *Christian dead* who are before the Apostle's mind, when he calls our risen Lord *ἀπαρχὴ τῶν κεκ.* **21.**] MAN *the bringer-in both of death and life: explanation* (not proof) *of Christ being the ἀπαρχὴ τ. κεκοιμ.*: and (1) *in that He is* MAN: it being necessary that the first-fruit should be *as* the lump. The verity lying at the root of this verse is, that *by* MAN ONLY can *general effects pervading the whole human race* be introduced. **δι᾽ ἀνθρώπου**, sc. *ἐστίν*.

22.] (2) *In that He is* (and here the fact of His being the Lord of Life and Righteousness, and the second and spiritual Head of our nature, is assumed) *to us the bringer-in of* LIFE, *as Adam was the bringer-in of* DEATH. **ἐν τῷ Ἀδ., ἐν τῷ χριστῷ**] **in community with**, as partakers in a common nature with, **Adam** and **Christ**: who are respectively the sources, *to the whole of that nature* (*πάντες*), of *death*, and *life*, i. e. (*here*) *physical death*, and *rescue from physical death.* The practice of Paul to *insulate the objects of his present attention* from all ulterior considerations, must be carefully here borne in mind. The antithesis is *merely* between the bringing in of death by Adam, and of life (its opposite) by Christ. No *consequence*, whether on the side of death or of life, is brought into consideration. That death physical involved death eternal—that life eternal (in its only worthy sense) involves bliss eternal, is not so much as thought of, while the two great opposites, Death and Life, are under consideration. This has been missed by many Interpreters, and the reasoning thereby marred. But the ancients, Chrys., Theophyl., Theodoret, Œcum., and Olsh., De Wette, and Meyer, keep to the *universal* reference. Theophylact's note is clear and striking: *αἰτίαν προστίθησι δι᾽ ἧς πιστοῦται τὰ εἰρημένα· ἔδει γάρ, φησιν, αὐτὴν*

ἰδίῳ [z] τάγματι· [u] ἀπαρχὴ χριστός, ἔπειτα [a] οἱ τοῦ χριστοῦ
[b] ἐν τῇ [bc] παρουσίᾳ αὐτοῦ, 24 εἶτα τὸ [d] τέλος, ὅταν [e] παρα-

z here only. 1 Kings iv. 10. 2 Kings xxiii. 13. a w. gen., see Rom. xvi. 10, 11. ch. i. 11. b = 1 Thess. ii. 19. iii. 13. v. 23. 1 John ii. 28. c = Matt. xxiv. 3, &c. James v. 7, 8 al. (ch. xvi. 17 reff.) d = Matt. xxiv. 6, 14. 1 Pet. iv. 7. e = Matt. xi. 27.

rec om του (bef χριστου) (*by a mistake appy*). ins οι bef εν τη παρουσια and add ελπισαντες F G-lat vulg-ed [Orig-int$_2$ Hil$_1$ Ambrst]. (*qui in adventu*(*m*) *ejus crediderunt* demid fuld [spec], *sperantes* is written over ελπ. in the gr column of F: on the other hand, am [tol] D-lat F-lat have *in adventu ejus*; fri Aug$_1$, *in præsentia ejus*.)

24. rec παραδω (*alteration to conform to* καταργηση, *the propriety of the pres being overlooked: see note*); with KL rel Orig$_2$ Eus$_1$ Chr$_1$ [Euthal-ms] Thdrt Damasc: παραδιδω ADPℵ Hip$_1$ [Marcell$_2$] Eus$_1$ Did$_1$ Bas[-mss$_2$] Nys$_2$: txt BF. (17 def.)

νικῆσαι τὴν ἡττηθεῖσαν φύσιν, καὶ τὸν καταβληθέντα, αὐτὸν ἐκνικῆσαι· καὶ γὰρ ἐν τῷ Ἀδάμ, τουτέστι διὰ τὸ τοῦ Ἀδὰμ πταῖσμα, πάντες τῷ θανάτῳ ὑπέπεσον· οὕτως οὖν ἐν χριστῷ πάντες ἀναστήσονται· τουτέστι διὰ τὸ εὑρεθῆναι τὸν χριστὸν ἀναμάρτητον κ. ἀνένοχον τῷ θανάτῳ, καὶ ἑκόντα μὲν ἀποθανεῖν, ἀναστῆναι δέ, καθὸ οὐκ ἦν δυνατὸν αὐτὸν κρατεῖσθαι ὑπὸ τῆς φθορᾶς, τὸν ἀρχηγὸν τῆς ζωῆς. See on the great antithesis, Rom. v. 12 ff., and notes.

23.] *But in this universal Resurrection*, ALL SHALL NOT HOLD THE SAME RANK. Chrys. rightly, εἶτα, ἵνα μὴ τὴν ζωοποίησιν κοινὴν ἀκούσας, καὶ τοὺς ἁμαρτωλοὺς νομίσῃς σώζεσθαι, ἐπήγαγεν **ἕκαστος δὲ** κ.τ.λ. Hom. xxxix. p. 367. **τάγμα** is not *order of priority*, but **rank**, or '*troop in an army*,' so Plut., Otho, p. 1072 (Wetst.): λεγεῶνες, οὕτω γὰρ τὰ **τάγματα** Ῥωμαῖοι καλοῦσιν ἐπίκλησιν. The three ranks are *mentioned in order of priority*, but this does not constitute their distinctive character:—Christ is the ἀπαρχή this is His ἴδιον τάγμα, see Col. i. 18:—οἱ τοῦ χριστοῦ follow at His coming, who are the φύραμα (as understood by the context, and implied by ἀπαρχή), in the proper and worthiest sense, made like unto Him and partaking of His glory; then (after how long or how short a time is not declared, and seems to have formed no part of the revelations to Paul, but was afterwards revealed,—see Rev. xx. 4—6: compare also 1 Thess. iv. 15—17) shall come THE END, viz. the resurrection of the rest of the dead, here veiled over by the general term τὸ τέλος,—that resurrection not being in this argument specially treated, but only that of Christians. *The key* to the understanding of this passage is to be found in the prophecy of our Lord, Matt. xxiv., xxv., but especially in the latter chapter. The resurrection and judgment of οἱ τοῦ χριστοῦ forming the subject of vv. 1—30 there, and τὸ τέλος,—the great final gathering of πάντα τὰ ἔθνη, of vv. 31—46. **ἀπαρχή**, therefore necessarily *the first* **τάγμα**: and hence the word stands first. **οἱ τοῦ χρ.**] = οἱ νεκροὶ ἐν χριστῷ, 1 Thess. iv. 16. No mention occurs here of any judgment of these his ἴδιοι δοῦλοι, as in Matt. xxv., for it does not belong to the present subject. **ἐν τῇ παρ. αὐτ.**] ἐν as *forming part of, involved in*, His appearing,—which, as the great event of the time, includes their resurrection in it. It ought to be needless to remind the student of the distinction between this παρουσία and the final judgment; it is here peculiarly important to bear it in mind.

24. εἶτα] **then**, next in succession, introducing the third τάγμα,—see above. **τὸ τέλος**] **the end** κατ' ἐξοχήν: not the end *of the resurrection*, as Meyer, after Theodoret, Œcum., Bengel, al.:—nor, *of this present world*, as Chrys., al.,—which properly happens at the παρουσία: nor exactly, *of the Kingdom of Christ*, as Grot. and Billroth: but *generally*, THE END, when all shall be accomplished, the bringing in and fulness of the Kingdom by the subjugation of the last enemy, the whole course of [the] mediatorial work of Christ, the salvation of the elect; the time indicated by Matt. xxv. ult.: καὶ ἀπελεύσονται οὗτοι εἰς κόλασιν αἰώνιον, οἱ δὲ δίκαιοι εἰς ζωὴν αἰώνιον. **ὅταν παραδιδοῖ**] **when He** (Christ) **gives up** (the pres., for that which is certainly attached to the event as its accompaniment—ὅταν indicating the uncertainty of the time when, and the verb being probably subjunctive: see Winer, Moulton's Trans. p. 360, note 2), **the Kingdom to God, and the Father** (reff.: to Him who is God and His Father)

Then the rest of the section as far as ver. 28, is in explanation of the giving up the kingdom. And it rests on this weighty verity: the KINGDOM OF CHRIST *over this world*, in its beginning, its furtherance, and its completion, has one great end,—THE GLORIFICATION OF THE FATHER BY THE SON. *Therefore*, when it shall be fully established, every enemy overcome, every thing subjected to Him, He will,—not, reign over it and abide its King, but DELIVER IT UP TO THE FATHER. Hence as in ver. 25, His reign will endure, not, like that of earthly kings, WHEN He shall have put all enemies under

f = Acts xx. 25 al. g see Rom. xv. 6 reff. h ch. i. 28 reff. i = Rom. viii. 38 (reff.). k = Rom. xiii. 1 &c. reff. l = Acts iv. 12 reff. m = ch. iv. 8 reff. n Matt. xxii. 44 ||, Acts ii. 35, & Heb. i. 13. x. 13, from Psa. cix. 1. ch. vi. 16 (reff.). o Rom. viii. 20 reff. Psa. viii. 6. p ellips.,

διδοῖ τὴν [f] βασιλείαν [g] τῷ θεῷ καὶ [g] πατρί, ὅταν [h] καταρ- ABDFK LPℵ a b c d e f g h k l m o 17. 47
γήσῃ πᾶσαν [i] ἀρχὴν καὶ πᾶσαν [k] ἐξουσίαν καὶ [i] δύναμιν.
25 [l] δεῖ γὰρ αὐτὸν [m] βασιλεύειν, ἄχρι οὗ [n] θῇ πάντας τοὺς
ἐχθροὺς ὑπὸ τοὺς πόδας αὐτοῦ. 26 ἔσχατος ἐχθρὸς
[k] καταργεῖται ὁ θάνατος. 27 Πάντα γὰρ [o] ὑπέταξεν ὑπὸ
τοὺς πόδας αὐτοῦ. ὅταν δὲ [p] εἴπῃ ὅτι πάντα [k] ὑποτέ-

του θυ ℵ[1]. [for πατρι, πνι F-gr(not G).]

25. rec αχρις, with B[2]DFKLℵ[3] rel: txt AB[1]Pℵ[1] 17 (Chr-c$_1$) [Euthal-ms] Damasc. rec aft αχρι ου ins αν (*perhaps from Matt* xxii. 42 ||, *or, as Meyer, from* LXX, *Ps* cix. 1), with D[2.3]KLℵ[3] rel Orig$_1$[-c$_1$?] Marcell$_1$ Cæs$_1$ [Did$_1$ Marc$_1$] Chr$_1$ Thdrt: om ABD[1]FPℵ[1] a[2] 17 Hip$_1$ Orig$_2$ Eus$_2$ Epiph$_{sæpe}$ [Euthal-ms] Damasc. aft εχθρους ins αυτου AF 17 Syr coptt goth æth Orig$_3$(-int$_5$) Marcell$_1$ Eus$_1$ Cæs$_1$ Cyr-jer$_2$ [Did$_1$ Marc$_1$] Tert$_2$ Hil$_1$: om BDKLPℵ rel vulg(with am demid [fuld tol], agst harl[1] F-lat [fri]) syr arm Hip$_1$ Orig$_3$(-int$_2$) Marcell$_1$ Eus$_3$ Ath$_1$ Chr$_1$ [Nys$_1$ Euthal-ms] Thdrt Damasc Iren[-int$_1$] Hil$_3$ [Ambrst]. om αυτου F(not F-lat).

26. This ver in D[1][and lat] ℵ-corr[1] tol harl[1] goth æth [Hil$_3$] Ambrst Jer stands after ποδας αυτου ver **27**: om ver **26** and 1st clause of ver **27** (*homœotel*) ℵ[1](ins (but see above) ℵ-corr[1.3]) 17. 92(sic).

27. om 1st οτι B vulg D-lat Hip$_1$ [Did$_1$ Chr$_1$] Iren[-int$_1$ Hil$_3$ Ambrst]. (not F-lat Aug$_1$.) ins τα bef 2nd παντα ℵ [Did$_1$].

His feet, but only TILL He shall have, &c.,—and then will be absorbed in the all-pervading majesty of Him for whose glory it was from first to last carried onward. It may be observed that the whole of this respects the mediatorial work and kingdom: the work of redemption,—and that Lordship over dead and living, for which Christ both died and rose. Consequently nothing is here said which can affect either (1) His coequality and coeternity with the Father in the Godhead, which is prior to and independent of this mediatorial work, and is not limited to the mediatorial kingdom; or (2) the eternity of His Humanity: for that Humanity ever was and is subordinate to the Father; and it by no means follows that when the mediatorial kingdom shall be given up to the Father, the Humanity, in which that kingdom was won, shall be put off: nay, the very fact of Christ in the body being the first-fruits of the resurrection, proves that His body, as ours, will endure for ever: as the truth that our humanity, even in glory, can only subsist before God *by virtue of* His Humanity, makes it plain that He will be VERY MAN to all eternity. **τὴν βασιλείαν**] That kingdom, which in its fullest sense is then *first* His. At this very time of τὸ τέλος, Matt. xxv. 34, He first calls Himself by the title of **ὁ βασιλεύς**. The name will no sooner be won, than laid at the feet of the Father, thus completing by the last great act of Redemption the obedience which He manifested in his Incarnation, and in his Death. **ὅταν καταργήσῃ**] (aor.) **when He shall have brought to nought,** &c.: see above. **πᾶσ. ἀρχ.** κ.τ.λ.] not *only*, as Meyer, &c., *hostile* power and government, but as the *context necessitates*, ALL power. Christ being manifested as universal King, *every* power co-ordinate with His must come under the category of *hostile*: all *kings* shall submit to Him: the *kingdoms* of the world shall become the kingdoms of the Lord and of His Christ:—and see the similar expressions Eph. i. 21, where speaking proleptically, the Apostle clearly indicates that *legitimate* authorities, all the powers that be, are included. Compare by all means Rev. xi. 15.

25.] See on the last verse:—this is the divine appointment with regard to the mediatorial kingdom,—that it should last *till*, and only till, all enemies shall have been subdued to it. **θῇ**, viz. *Christ*, not *the Father*, as Beza, Grot., Est., Billr., al.: it is parallel with καταργήσῃ, and included in the mediatorial acts of Christ, who in His world's course goes forth νικῶν καὶ ἵνα νικήσῃ, Rev. vi. 2. It is otherwise with ὑπέταξεν, ver. 27: see there.

26.] Connect **ἔσχατ. ἐχθρός** together; not as Bloomf., "last of all, the enemy Death is to be destroyed," which is ungrammatical. If ἔσχ. is to stand alone, ἐχθρὸς καταργεῖται must be "is destroyed as an enemy." Death is *the last enemy*, as being the *consequence of sin*: when he is overcome and done away with, the whole end of Redemption is shewn to have been accomplished. Death is personified, as in Rev. xx. 14. **καταργεῖται**,—pres., either as a prophetic certainty as παραδιδοῖ above,—or as an axiomatic truth. **27.**] *Scriptural proof of the above declaration.*

ταται, qr δῆλον q ὅτι s ἐκτὸς τοῦ o ὑποτάξαντος αὐτῷ τὰ
πάντα· 28 ὅταν δὲ o ὑποταγῇ αὐτῷ τὰ πάντα, τότε [καὶ]
αὐτὸς ὁ υἱὸς o ὑποταγήσεται τῷ o ὑποτάξαντι αὐτῷ τὰ
πάντα, ἵνα t ᾖ ὁ θεὸς t πάντα ἐν πᾶσιν. 29 ἐπεὶ u τί
u ποιήσουσιν οἱ βαπτιζόμενοι ὑπὲρ τῶν νεκρῶν; εἰ v ὅλως

q Gal. iii. 11 only. r as above (q) Matt. xxvi. 73 only. Num. xxvii. 21. s = Acts xxvi. 22. Isa. xxvi. 13. t = Col. iii. 11. (ch. xii. 6.) Herod. iii. 157, πάντα ἦν ἐν τοῖσι Βαβυλωνίοισι Ζώπυρος. Polyb. v. 26. 5, τὸ ὅλον αὐτοῖς ἦν καὶ τὸ πᾶν Ἀπελλῆς. u = Mark xi. 5. John xi. 47. Acts xxi. 13. v Matt. v. 34. ch. v. 1. vi. 7 only †.

aft υποτετακται ins αυτω ei F [vulg Syr copt arm] Hip_1 $Orig[-int_1]$ Hil_1 Ambr[st]; bef υπ., $[Cyr\text{-}jer_1]$ $Epiph_1$. om τα F[not G].

28. om 1st clause (homœotel) ℵ[1](ins ℵ-corr[1]) m [Hip_1 $Hil_2(\text{-}ms_3)$]. αυτω bef υποταγη D Eus_1 $Orig\text{-}int_2[txt_3]$ $Iren[-int_1]$. om και B D[1][and lat] F[-gr(and G-lat)] 17 am(with fuld harl mar tol) Syr $Orig_2$ $Marcell_4$ [Did_1] $Iren\text{-}int_1$ $Ps\text{-}Ath\text{-}int_1$ Hil_5 Jer: ins AD[3]KLPℵ [vulg-clem F-lat fri demid] rel syr coptt [æth arm] $Ps\text{-}Ign_1$ Hip_1 Eus_1 Ath_2 $Ps\text{-}Ath_2$ $Cæs_1$ $Cyr\text{-}jer_1$ Chr_1 [Bas_2 Nys_1 Euthal-ms] Thdrt Damasc $Orig\text{-}int_5$ $Tert_1$ Hil_2 [Ambrst]. θεος bef η D[1][and lat]. rec ins τα bef 3rd παντα, with D[3]FKLPℵ rel $Orig_4$ $Marcell_1$ Eus_2 Ath_1 [Did_1] Tit_1 $Epiph_1$ Cæs $Cyr\text{-}jer_1$ Chr_1 [Nys_1] Thdrt Damasc: om ABD[1] 17 ⌊arm] Hip ($Orig_2$) $Marcell_1$ Eus_2 [Euthal-ms].

29. ποιησωσιν m 47, ποιουσιν F. aft ολως ins οι P.

ὑπέταξ. viz., from the Psalm,—God, *the Father.* See on the Psalm itself, Heb. ii. 6 ff. notes. **εἴπῃ**, scil. ὁ θεός, the same subject as ὑπέταξεν. Meyer alone, as it seems to me, gives the right construction of ὅταν . . . ὑποτέτακται. "The aor. εἴπῃ must be rendered regularly, not in the *present* sense, but as a *futurum exactum:* see Luke vi. 26: Plato, Parm. p. 143, c (τί δ' ὅταν εἴπω οὐσία τε καὶ ἕν, ἆρα οὐκ ἀμφοτέρω;),—Ion, p. 535, b (ὅταν εὖ εἴπῃς ἔπη καὶ ἐκπλήξῃς μάλιστα τοὺς θεωμένους). The time referred to, is that when the as yet unfulfilled πάντα ὑπέταξεν shall be fulfilled and completed: hence it is no longer the aor., but the perf. ὑποτέτακται. The meaning then is: 'when God, who in Ps. viii. 6 has announced the ὑπόταξις, shall hereafter have declared that this ὑπόταξις is *come to pass,*' . . . This *form* of expression was suggested to the Apostle by his having already expressed himself in the words of a *saying of God.*" I render then, **But when God shall have declared that all things have been subjected to Him, it is evident that they have been subjected** (ellipsis of the predicate of the foregoing sentence after δῆλον ὅτι and οἶδ' ὅτι is common; so Plato, Gorg. p. 475, c, 'οὐκοῦν κακῷ ὑπερβάλλον τὸ ἀδικεῖν κάκιον ἂν εἴη τοῦ ἀδικεῖσθαι,'—'δῆλον δὴ ὅτι,'—scil. κάκιον ἂν εἴη. Kühner, § 852, d) **with the exception of Him who subjected all things to Him.** 28.] On the sense, see above. "The interpretations, that *subjection* is only an hyperbolical expression for the *entire harmony of Christ with the Father* (Chrys., Theophyl., Œc.):—the limitation of it to His human nature (Theodoret, Aug., Jerome, Est., Wolf, al.), with the *declarative* explanation, that it will then *become plain to all, that Christ even in regard of His kingship, is, on the side of His Humanity, dependent on the Father* (Flatt)—and the addition, *that Christ will then in His divine nature reign with the Father* (Calv.:—'regnum—ab humanitate sua ad gloriosam divinitatem quodammodo traducet');—the interpretation (of αὐτὸς ὁ υἱός!) as referring to Christ's *mystical Body,* i. e. *the Church* (Theodoret),—are idle subterfuges (leere Ausflüchte)." De Wette. The refutation of these and all other attempts to explain away the doctrine here plainly asserted, of the *ultimate subordination of the Son,* is contained in the three precise and unambiguous words, **αὐτὸς ὁ υἱός.** **ἵνα ᾖ ὁ θ. πάντα ἐν πᾶσιν**] **that God (alone) may be all things in all,**—i. e. recognized as sole Lord and King: 'omnia erunt subordinata Filio, Filius Patri.' Bengel. Numerous examples of πάντα in this sense (less commonly τὰ πάντα, Kühner, § 422) may be found in Wetst. 29—34.] Arguments for the reality of the resurrection, *from the practice* (1) *of those who were baptized for the dead,* (2) *of the Apostles, &c., who submitted to daily peril of death.* 29.] **ἐπεί** resumes the main argument, which has been interrupted by the explanation since ver. 23 of ἕκαστος ἐν τῷ ἰδίῳ τάγματι. After it is an ellipsis of 'if it be as the adversaries suppose.' **τί ποιήσουσιν**] There is in these words a tacit reprehension of the practice about to be mentioned, which it is hardly possible altogether to miss. Both by the third person, and by the art. before βαπτ., he indirectly separates himself and those to whom he is writing from participation in or approval of the practice:—the meaning being, **what will become of**—'what ac-

w ver. 4.
x here bis. [Rom. viii. 24.]
y Acts xix. 27 reff. (-νος, 2 Cor. xi. 26.)
z here only. Exod. xviii. 22, 26. Levit. xvi. 2.

νεκροὶ οὐκ [w] ἐγείρονται, [x] τί [x] καὶ βαπτίζονται ὑπὲρ ABDFK LPℵ a b c d e f g h k l m o 17. 47
αὐτῶν; 30 [x] τί [x] καὶ ἡμεῖς [y] κινδυνεύομεν [z] πᾶσαν [z] ὥραν;

rec (for αυτων) των νεκρων (*mechanical repetition of the above*), with D[3][-gr] L rel Syr Chr$_1$ Thdrt Thl Œc: αυτων των νεκρων m 43. 52: txt ABD[1]FKPℵ a d 17. 47 latt syr coptt goth arm Orig$_1$ Dial$_1$[but mss vary] Epiph$_1$ [Euthal-ms Isid$_1$ Damasc Jac-nisib$_1$ Ambrst].

count can they give of their practice?'

οἱ βαπτιζόμενοι] **those who are in the habit of being baptized**—not οἱ βαπτισθέντες. The distinction is important as affecting the interpretation. See below. **ὑπὲρ τῶν νεκρῶν**] **on behalf of the dead**; viz. *the same* νεκροί who are spoken of in the next clause and throughout the chapter as the subjects of ἀνάστασις—not νεκροί in any figurative sense. **τῶν** νεκρ., the art. marking the particular dead persons on behalf of whom the act took place. Before we pass to the exegesis, it will be well to go through the next question—εἰ ὅλως κ.τ.λ. **If dead men are not raised at all, why do they trouble themselves** (τί καί as in reff.) **to be baptized for them?** Thus much being said as to the plain meaning of the words used, there can be no doubt as to their interpretation. The *only legitimate reference* is, to a practice, not otherwise known to us, not mentioned here with any approval by the Apostle, not generally prevalent (**οἱ** βαπτ.), but in use by some, of *survivors allowing themselves to be baptized on behalf of* (believing?) *friends who had died without baptism.* With the subsequent similar practices of the Cerinthians (Epiph. Hær. xxviii. § 6, p. 114) and Marcionites (Chrys., Tertull. de resurr. 48, vol. ii. p. 864, adv. Marc. v. 10, p. 494 f.) this may or may not have been connected. All we clearly see from the text, is that it unquestionably *did exist.* With regard to the other interpretations, Bengel well says, "Tanta est interpretationum varietas, ut is, qui non dicam varietates ipsas, sed varietatum catalogos colligere velit, *dissertationem* scripturus sit." I will give a few of them, mostly in the words of their authors: Chrys. (Hom. xl. p. 379):—ὑπὲρ τῶν νεκρῶν, τουτέστι τῶν σωμάτων. καὶ γὰρ ἐπὶ τούτῳ βαπτίζῃ, τῇ τοῦ νεκροῦ σώματος ἀναστάσει, πιστεύων ὅτι (Migne reads τὴν τ. ν. σ. ἀνάστασιν πιστ., ὅτι) οὐκέτι μένει νεκρόν. καὶ σὺ μὲν διὰ τῶν ῥημάτων λέγεις νεκρῶν ἀνάστασιν· ὁ δὲ ἱερεύς, ὥσπερ ἐν εἰκόνι τινὶ . . . . δείκνυσί σοι . . . . διὰ τοῦ ὕδατος· τὸ γὰρ βαπτίζεσθαι κ. καταδύεσθαι, εἶτα ἀνανεύειν, τῆς εἰς ᾅδου καταβάσεως ἐστὶ σύμβολον κ. τῆς ἐκεῖθεν ἀνόδου. διὸ κ. τάφον τὸ βάπτισμα ὁ Π. καλεῖ (Rom. vi. 4),—Theophyl.: φησὶν οὖν, ὅτι οἱ πιστεύσαντες ὅτι ἔσται ἀνάστασις νεκρῶν σωμάτων, καὶ βαπτισθέντες ἐπὶ τοιαύταις ἐλπίσι, τί ποιήσουσιν ἀπατηθέντες; τί δὲ ὅλως καὶ βαπτίζονται ἄνθρωποι ὑπὲρ ἀναστάσεως, τουτέστιν ἐπὶ προσδοκίᾳ ἀναστάσεως, εἰ ν οὐκ ἐγ.; and so in the main, Pelag., Œcum., Phot., Corn.-a-Lap., Wetst.—Theodoret:—ὁ βαπτιζόμενός, φησι, τῷ δεσπότῃ συνθάπτεται, ἵνα τοῦ θανάτου κοινωνήσας καὶ τῆς ἀναστάσεως γένηται κοινωνός· εἰ δὲ νεκρόν ἐστι τὸ σῶμα, καὶ οὐκ ἀνίσταται, τί δήποτε καὶ βαπτίζεται; and so Castal., al. All these senses would require τί ποιήσετε βαπτισθέντες, to say nothing of the impossibility of thus understanding ὑπὲρ τῶν νεκρῶν. Estius explains ὑπὲρ τῶν νεκρ. as = '*jamjam morituri,*' and Calvin justifies this, 'baptizari pro mortuis erit sic baptizari *ut mortuis non vivis prosit.*' So too Epiph. (l. c.),—of catechumens who πρὸ τῆς τελευτῆς λουτροῦ καταξιοῦνται:—and Bengel:—"baptizantur super mortuis ii, qui mox post baptismum ad mortuos aggregabuntur." But against this ὑπὲρ **τῶν νεκρῶν** is decisive,—as is **ὑπέρ** against '*over* the dead,' i. e. over their sepulchres (Luth., al.): this local sense of ὑπέρ not being found in the N. T. Le Clerc, Hammond, Olsh., al., explain ὑπ. τ. νεκρ., '*to fill the place of the dead.*' But, as Meyer observes, such an idea can hardly be gathered from the words, but would want explaining in the context;—and besides, the *question would thus be irrelevant,* because, the place of the dead being supplied by their successors, it would be *no matter to them, whether the dead themselves rose or not:* whereas now, the benefits of baptism being supposed to be conveyed to the *dead* by the baptism of his substitute, the *proceeding would be stultified,* if the dead could never rise to claim those benefits. This, the only justifiable rendering, is adopted by Ambrose, and by Anselm, Erasmus, Grotius, al., and recently by Billroth, Rückert, Meyer, De Wette, al. The ordinary objection to it is, that thus the Apostle would be giving his sanction to a superstitious usage, or at all events mentioning it without reprobation. But this is easily answered, by remembering that if the above view of τί ποιήσουσιν is correct, he does *not* mention it without a slur on it;—and more completely still, as Rückert (in Meyer), "usurpari ab eo mo-

31 [a] καθ' ἡμέραν ἀποθνήσκω, [b] νὴ τὴν [c] ὑμετέραν [de] καύχησιν, ἀδελφοί, ἣν [e] ἔχω ἐν χριστῷ Ἰησοῦ τῷ κυρίῳ ἡμῶν.
32 εἰ [f] κατὰ ἄνθρωπον [g] ἐθηριομάχησα ἐν Ἐφέσῳ, τί μοι τὸ
[h] ὄφελος; εἰ νεκροὶ οὐκ [w] ἐγείρονται, [i] φάγωμεν καὶ πίωμεν·

a Acts ii. 46 reff.
b here only. Gen. xlii. 15, 16 only.
c = Rom. xi. 31. φόβῳ τῷ ὑμετέρῳ, Thucyd. i. 33. see Rom. xv. 4. note, and ch. iii. 3 reff.
d Rom. iii. 27 reff.
e Rom. xv. 17.
f see Job xv. 3 only.
g here only †.
h James ii. 14, 16 only.
i Isa. xxii. 13.

31. Steph ημετεραν, with A a (h[1] ?) k m 2[2]. 4. 44[1]. 51-6. 72[1]. 89. 120-2 lect-14 æth Orig[-c_1 Euthal-ms(ημεραν) $Thdrt_1$]: txt BDFKLP rel [latt syrr coptt goth arm $Dial_1$ (but mss vary) Chr_1 $Thdrt_1$ Damasc $Ambr_2$ Ambrst $Aug_{sæpe}$]. rec om αδελφοι, with DFL rel arm-zoh Orig[-c_2] Chr_1 Thdrt Damasc Ambrst: ins ABKPℵ m 17 vulg fri syrr coptt [goth] æth Dial [Cyr-p_2 Euthal-ms] $Aug_{[sæpe]}$ Pel Bede. om χρ. ιησ. τω and ημ. D[1](and lat) Ambrst.

32. om το D[1]F $Clem_1$.

rem, qui ceteroqui displiceret, ad errorem, in quo impugnando versabatur, radicitus evellendum; ipsius autem reprehendendi aliud tempus expectari." See a multitude of other interpretations in Pool's Synopsis and in Stanley's note. His concluding remarks are worth quoting: "On the whole, therefore, this explanation of the passage (*that given above*) may be safely accepted, (1) as exhibiting a curious relic of primitive superstition, which, after having, as the words imply (?), prevailed generally in the apostolical church, gradually dwindled away till it was only to be found in some obscure sects, where it lost its original significance: (2) as containing an example of the Apostle's mode of dealing with a practice, with which he could have no real sympathy; not condemning or ridiculing it, but appealing to it as an expression, however distorted, of their better feelings."

30.] *Not only the practice of those just spoken of, but his own, and that of those like him, who lived a life of perpetual exposure to death, were absurd, if there be no resurrection.* Observe that the argument *here* applies equally to the *future existence of the soul;* and so Cicero uses it, Tusc. Quæst. i. 15: "Nescio quomodo inhæret in mentibus quasi seculorum quoddam augurium futurorum . . . quo quidem demto, quis tam esset amens, qui semper in laboribus et periculis viveret?" **31.**] To **die daily** is a strong expression for to be daily in sight of death and expecting it. See 2 Cor. iv. 11. This he strengthens by an asseveration, grounded on his boast of them as his work in Christ: not that this is immediately or proximately at stake in the matter, but much as we should say, "As I love you, it is true." He would not think of deceiving those of whom he boasted before God in connexion with Christ. **ὑμετ.**] gen. obj., see reff. νή, the affirmative, as μά is the negative particle of adjuration: but ναὶ μά is often found in an affirmative sense: see Kühner, § 701.

32.] The stress of the first clause is on **κατὰ ἄνθρωπον**, and its meaning, **merely as man**, i. e. '*according to this world's views*,' 'as one who has no hope beyond the grave;' see ref. If *thus* only he fought, &c., where was his profit (seeing he despised all those things which κατὰ ἄνθρωπον might compensate for such a fight,—fame, praise, &c.)? The renderings, ὅσον τὸ εἰς ἀνθρώπους (Chrys. p. 381), i. e. 'so far as one can be said θηριομαχεῖν against men,'—and κατὰ ἀνθρώπων λογισμὸν θηρίων ἐγενόμην βορά (Theodoret),—'*exempli causa*' (Semler, Rosenmüller),—'*ut hominum more loquar*' (Estius and Bloomf.), are all constrained, and scarcely to be extorted from the words. **ἐθηριομάχησα**] **I fought with beasts** (aor. referring to *one special occasion*). How? and when? Most ancient and modern Commentators take the expression figuratively, as used in Appian, B. C. ii. p. 763 (Wetst.), where Pompey says, οἵοις θηρίοις μαχόμεθα,—and Ignat. ad Rom. 5, p. 689 f., ἀπὸ Συρίας μέχρι Ῥώμης θηριομαχῶ διὰ γῆς κ. θαλάσσης, δεδεμένος δέκα λεοπάρδοις, ὅ ἐστι στρατιωτικὸν τάγμα. So, of our text, Tertull. de Resurr. 48, vol. ii. p. 865: "Depugnavit ad bestias Ephesi, illas scilicet bestias Asiaticæ pressuræ."

And this explanation must be right: for his Roman citizenship would have precluded his ever being literally thrown to beasts: and even supposing him to have waived it, and been miraculously rescued, as Ambrst., Theodoret, Erasm., Luther, Calv., al. suppose, is it conceivable that such an event should have been altogether unrecorded in the Acts? Adopting the figurative rendering,—we cannot fix on any recorded conflict which will suit the words. His danger from Demetrius and his fellow-craftsmen (Acts xix.) had not yet happened (see Prolegg. § vi. 2): but we cannot tell what opposition, justifying this expression, the ἀντικείμενοι πολλοί of ch. xvi. 9 may ere this have made to his preaching. **εἰ νεκρ.**] **If dead men rise not**, i. e. '*if none of the dead rise*.' These words are best joined with

[k] αὔριον γὰρ ἀποθνήσκομεν. 33 μὴ [l] πλανᾶσθε. [m] φθείρου- ABDFK
σιν [n] ἤθη [o] χρηστὰ [p] ὁμιλίαι κακαί. 34 [q] ἐκνήψατε [r] δικαίως, LPℵ a b c d e f g
καὶ μὴ ἁμαρτάνετε· [s] ἀγνωσίαν γὰρ θεοῦ τινὲς ἔχουσιν. h k l m o 17. 47
[t] πρὸς [u] ἐντροπὴν ὑμῖν λαλῶ.

35 [v] Ἀλλ' [v] ἐρεῖ τις Πῶς [w] ἐγείρονται οἱ νεκροί; ποίῳ

k adv., Matt. vi. 30. Luke xii. 28. xiii. 32, 33. Acts xxiii. 20. xxv. 22. James iv. 13. Exod. viii. 29.
l ch. vi. 9 reff.
m = ch. iii. 17 reff.
n here only. Sir. xx. 26 only.
o = here (Matt. xi. 30. Luke v. 39. vi. 35. Rom. ii. 4. Eph. iv. 32. 1 Pet. ii. 3) only.
p here only. Exod. xxi. 10. Prov. vii. 21. Wisd. viii. 18 only.
q here only. Gen. ix. 24. 1 Kings xxv. 37. met., as here, Joel i. 5. ἀνανήφ., 2 Tim. ii. 26.
r || here (Luke xxiii. 41. 1 Thess. ii. 10. Tit. ii. 12. 1 Pet. ii. 23) only. see Deut. xvi. 20.
s 1 Pet. ii. 15 only. Job xxxv. 16. Wisd. xiii. 1 only.
t = ch. vii. 35. xiv. 12 al.
u ch. vi. 5 only. Ps. xxxiv. 26.
v James ii. 18.
w ver. 4.

33. rec χρησθ' (*to suit the metre*), with Clem_1: txt ABDFKLPℵ rel Clem-hom_2 Eus_1 Ath_1 Chr_1 [Cyr-p_2 Euthal-ms] Thdrt Damasc_2 Thl Œc.

34. rec λεγω (*negligence, the force of* λαλω *not being perceived*), with AFKL rel Chr_1 Thdrt [Damasc], *dico* flor(and F-lat) G-lat [spec Orig-int, simly Syr basm æth arm]: txt BDPℵ k m 17 Dial_1 [Euthal-ms], *loquor* vulg D-lat(and fri) Ambrst [simly syr copt goth].

35. αλλα BP Orig_1.

the following, as Chrys., Theophyl., Beza, Bengel, Griesb., Meyer, De Wette, al.—not with the preceding, as Theodoret, Grot., Est., Luther, al. [and E. V.] For **κατὰ ἄνθρωπον** already expresses their meaning in the preceding sentence; and the form of ver. 29 seems to justify this arrangement, besides that otherwise φάγ. κ. πίωμεν, &c., would stand awkwardly insulated. **φάγ. κ. πίωμεν . . .**] In Isa. the words represent the recklessness of those who utterly disregard the call of God to weeping and mourning, and feast while their time lasts. Wetst. has collected very numerous parallels from the classics. The most striking perhaps is Herod. ii. 78.

33.] The *tendency* of the denial of the resurrection, represented by the Epicurean maxim just quoted, leads him to hint that this denial was not altogether unconnected with a practice of too much intimacy with the profligate society around them.

μὴ πλαν., as in ref., introduces a warning against moral self-deception. **φθείρ. ἤθη . .**] These words (according to the reading χρῆσθ', which has, however, hardly any support) form an Iambic trimeter, and occur in this form in a fragment of the Thais of Menander; but Clem. Alex. Strom. i. 14 (59), p. 350 P., says, πρὸς γοῦν Κορινθίους . . ἰαμβείῳ συγκέχρηται **τραγικῷ**—but this may be a mere inaccuracy. Socrates, Hist. Eccl. iii. 16, quotes it as a sufficient proof that Paul was conversant with the tragedies of Euripides. "Perhaps," says Dr. Burton, "Menander took it from Euripides." The Apostle *may* have cited it merely as a *commonplace* current, without any idea whence it came;—and χρηστά seems to shew this. The plur. ὁμιλίαι, points out the repetition of the practice. Meyer quotes Plato, Rep. viii. p. 550, διὰ τὸ μὴ κακοῦ ἀνδρὸς εἶναι τὴν φύσιν, ὁμιλίαις δὲ ταῖς τῶν ἄλλων κακαῖς κεχρῆσθαι. **34. ἐκνήψ.**] **Awake out of** (your moral) **intoxication**, already possessing you by the influence of these men. **δικαίως**] either, **as is just,—as you ought** (Wahl, al.),—or, **in a proper manner** (Olsh., al.),—or, ἐπὶ συμφέροντι καὶ χρησίμῳ (Chrys. p. 382, al.), or *so as to be* **δίκαιοι** [i. e. so as to recover your righteousness, which you are in danger of losing], as E. V., **Awake to righteousness.** The last meaning is well defended by Dr. Peile from Thuc. i. 21: ἀπίστως ἐπὶ τὸ μυθῶδες ἐκνενικηκότα,—'so as to become incredible;'—and seems to be the best. The aor. imper. ἐκνήψατε marks the quick momentary awaking; the pres. imper. μὴ ἁμαρτάνετε, on the other hand, the enduring practice of abstinence from sin (Meyer). But that this must not always be rigidly pressed, see Kühner, § 445. 2. Anm. 1. **ἀγνωσίαν**] The stress is on this word: **for some** (the τινές of ver. 12, most probably, are hinted at, and the source of their error pointed out) **have** (are affected with) **ignorance** (an absence of all true knowledge) **of God.** See ref. to Wisd. **πρὸς ἐντ. ὑμ. λ.** shews that these τινές were ἐν ὑμῖν,—not the heathen without:—the existence of such in the Corinthian church was a disgrace to the whole. **λαλῶ**] **I am speaking**; not merely I **say this**; it refers to the spirit of the whole passage.

35—50.] *The argument passes from the* fact *of the resurrection, already substantiated, to the* MANNER *of it: which is indicated, and confirmed, principally by analogies from nature.* **35.**] The new difficulty is introduced in the form of a question from an objector. This is put first generally, **πῶς . . . ., In what manner,**—and next specifically, ποίῳ δὲ (δέ, 'what I mean, is . . . .') σώματι, **With what kind of body—ἔρχ.,** do **they** (pres. as transferring the action to that time,—as ἐγείρονται before: so Meyer and De W.:—or

σώματι ἔρχονται; 36 [x]ἄφρων, σὺ ὃ σπείρεις, οὐ [y]ζωο-
ποιεῖται, ἐὰν μὴ [z]ἀποθάνῃ· 37 καὶ ὃ σπείρεις, οὐ τὸ
σῶμα τὸ γενησόμενον σπείρεις, ἀλλὰ [a]γυμνὸν [b]κόκκον,
[c]εἰ [c]τύχοι, [d]σίτου ἢ τινος τῶν λοιπῶν· 38 ὁ δὲ θεὸς δίδωσιν
αὐτῷ σῶμα καθὼς ἠθέλησεν, καὶ ἑκάστῳ τῶν σπερμάτων
[e]ἴδιον σῶμα. 39 οὐ πᾶσα σὰρξ ἡ αὐτὴ σάρξ· ἀλλὰ ἄλλη

x Luke xi. 40. xii. 20 al. Ps. xciii. 8.
y Rom. iv. 17 reff.
z = John xii. 24.
a = here only.
b Matt. xiii. 31 ||. xvii. 20 ||. John xii. 24 only.
c ch. xiv. 10 only (reff.). opt., 1 Pet. iii. 17.
d John xii. 24. Acts xxvii. 38 al. epp., here only.
e = ver. 23. Acts i. 25 al.

36. rec αφρον, with KL rel $Orig_1$ [Dial $Epiph_1$ Chr_2 Euthal-ms Thdrt Damasc]: txt ABDFPℵ m 17. 47. for ζωοποιειται, ζωογονειται A 89. 108[1] $Epiph_1$, and(but not *ad loc*) Chr_1[-mss(txt_3)] $Thdrt_1$[txt_2]. aft ζωοπ. ins εις την (but marked for erasure) ℵ[1]. aft αποθανη ins πρωτον D[-gr]: pref, F latt(not fri) $Dial_1$ Iren[-int_1] Orig-int_1[(om $Orig_2$) Ambrst Aug_1].
37. om 2nd σπειρεις ℵ[1](ins ℵ-corr[1]). for ει, η A.
38. rec αυτω bef διδωσιν, with DFKL rel fri [spec] $Orig_1$ Chr_1 Thdrt Ambrst: txt ABPℵ b d m o 17 vulg(and F-lat) syrr (copt) $Orig_1$(-int_1) $Dial_1$ $Epiph_1$ [Euthal-ms] Damasc $Tert_1$. rec ins το bef ιδιον, with KLℵ[3] rel $Orig_1$ Chr Thdrt Damasc Thl Œc: om ABDFPℵ[1] 17 [arm] $Epiph_1$ [Euthal-ms].
39. om 2nd σαρξ F(not F-lat) Syr Chr-2-mss_1. om αλλα D[1][-gr] fri æth $Dial_1$ Chr_1 [Aug_{alic}]. rec aft αλλη μεν ins σαρξ, with Syr arm [copt $Dial_1$]: om ABDFKLPℵ rel [latt] syr æth [Chr Euthal-ms Thdrt Ambrst Aug_{alic}].

rather perhaps, as *assuming* for the moment the truth of the resurrection as a thing actually happening in the course of things) **come** (forth at that time)?

36—41.] *Analogies illustrative of the question just asked: and first, that of seed sown in the earth* (36—38). **36.**] Meyer would point this, ἄφρων σύ, ὃ σπείρεις . . ., because according to the common punctuation there is necessarily an emphasis on σύ, which the context does not allow. But on the other hand, it seems to me, there is an objection to the introduction of a new matter so lamely as by ὃ σπείρεις. Besides which, the emphatic σύ does not necessarily require any *other agency* to be emphatically set against it, but may imply an appeal to the objector's *own* experience (as Billr. in Dr. Peile):—'*thou* say this, who art continually witness of the process, &c.?' And let it be remembered that we *have* another σπείρειν below, vv. 42—44, which may be set against *thy sowing*. I retain therefore the stop at ἄφρων (nom. for voc. as freq. See Luke xii. 20; Mark ix. 25; Luke viii. 54, al., and Winer, edn. 6, § 29. 2), and the emphasis on σύ. The similitude was used by our Lord of His own Resurrection, ref. John. **οὐ ζωοποιεῖται**] Its life is latent in it; but is not developed into quick and lively action without the death of the deposited seed,—i. e. its perishing, disappearing from nature. The same analogy was used by the Rabbis, but to prove that the dead would rise *clothed*: 'ut triticum nudum sepelitur et multis vestibus ornatum prodit, ita multo magis justi,' &c.

37.] Before, the *death* of the seed was insisted on: now, the *non-identity of the seed with the future plant*. There is a mixture of construction, the words ὃ σπείρεις being *pendent*, as the sentence now stands. The two constructions as De W. observes are, εἴ τι σπείρεις, οὐ τὸ σ. τὸ γεν. σπείρεις,—and ὃ σπείρεις, οὐ τὸ σ. τὸ γεν. ἐστιν. He names the *plant* **τὸ σῶμα τὸ γενησόμενον**, having already in his eye the application to the Resurrection. **εἰ τύχοι**] **if it should so happen,—peradventure**: not, '*for example*.' See on ch. xiv. 10. **τῶν λοιπῶν**, scil. σπερμάτων. **38.**] **ἠθέλησεν**, *willed*, viz. at the creation: the aor. setting forth the *one act* of the divine Will giving to the particular seed the particular development at first, which the species retains: whereas θέλει would imply a fresh act of the divine Will giving to every individual seed (not ἑκάστῳ τῶν σπερμάτων, but ἑκάστῳ σπέρματι, or rather ἑκάστῳ κόκκῳ) his own body. But the *whole gift to the species* being God's, to continue or withhold, the pres. δίδωσιν still holds good. **ἑκάστ. τῶν σπερμ.**] **to each of the (kinds of) seed**; see above: τῶν is generic. **ἴδιον σῶμα**] **a body of its own.** Such then being the case with all seeds, why should it be thought necessary that the *same body* should rise *as was sown*, or that God cannot give to each a resurrection-body, as in nature? **39—41.**] And the more,—because we have examples from analogy of *various kinds of bodies*; viz. (1) in the *flesh* of animals (ver. 39): (2) in *celestial and terrestrial bodies* (ver. 40): (3) in the *various characters of light* given by the sun, moon, and stars.
σάρξ] *animal organism* (De W.). Dean Stanley's former rendering (corrected in his 3rd edn.) of οὐ πᾶσα σάρξ, ἡ αὐτὴ σάρξ, 'no flesh is the same flesh,' is contrary to the usage of the passages which he alleged to defend it, where *the negative*

μὲν ἀνθρώπων, ἄλλη δὲ σὰρξ ^{f}κτηνῶν, ἄλλη δὲ σὰρξ
^{g}πτηνῶν, ἄλλη δὲ ^{h}ἰχθύων.
40 καὶ σώματα ^{i}ἐπουράνια,
καὶ σώματα ^{k}ἐπίγεια· ἀλλὰ ^{l}ἑτέρα μὲν ἡ τῶν ^{i}ἐπουρα-
νίων ^{m}δόξα, ^{l}ἑτέρα δὲ ἡ τῶν ^{k}ἐπιγείων.
41 ἄλλη
^{m}δόξα ἡλίου, καὶ ἄλλη ^{m}δόξα ^{n}σελήνης, καὶ ἄλλη ^{m}δόξα
^{o}ἀστέρων· ^{o}ἀστὴρ γὰρ ^{o}ἀστέρος ^{p}διαφέρει ἐν ^{m}δόξῃ.
42 οὕτως καὶ ἡ ^{q}ἀνάστασις τῶν ^{q}νεκρῶν. ^{r}σπείρεται ἐν
^{s}φθορᾷ, ἐγείρεται ἐν ^{t}ἀφθαρσίᾳ·
43 ^{r}σπείρεται ἐν ^{u}ἀτιμίᾳ,

C μεν η... ABCDF KLPℵ a b c d e f g h k l m o 17. 47

f Luke x. 34. Acts xxiii. 24. Rev. xviii. 13 only. Num. xx. 4, 8, 11.
g here only +. Job v. 7 Aq. [and ed. sexta]. Xen. Cyr. i. 4. 11.
h Matt. vii. 10 al. epp., here only.
i John iii. 12. Phil. ii. 10 al. Ps. lxvii. 15. 2 Macc. iii. 39 only. Dan. iv. 23 (26) Theod-A Ald. compl. (οὐρ., BF.)
k here bis. John iii. 12. 2 Cor. v. 1. Phil. ii. 10. iii. 19. James iii. 15 only +.
l = here only. see Luke ix. 29.
m = Acts xxii. 11 reff.
n Epp., here only. Acts ii. 20 reff.
o Paul, here 3ce only. Matt. ii. 2, &c. xxiv. 29 ‖ Mk. Jude 13. Rev. i. 16 al13. Gen. i. 16.
p = and constr., Gal. iv. 1 only. (Rom. ii. 18 al.) Dan. vii. 3 (Theod.).
q ver. 12 reff.
r see ver. 36.
s = Rom. viii. 21. ver. 50. Gal. vi. 8. Col. ii. 22. 2 Pet. i. 4. ii. (12 bis) 19 only. Jonah ii. 7,
t Rom. ii. 7 reff.
u Rom. i. 26 reff.

ανθρωπου D^1[(and lat) spec] Syr Dial$_1$ Tert$_1$ [Ambrst]. om 3rd *σαρξ* D^{1}F 17 latt (exc fri) Syr Chr$_1$ Tert [Ambrst]: om 3rd clause K k m 47 harl^1. **κτηνους** D^1[and lat] F[-gr] Syr Tert [Ambrst]. om 2nd *δε* D^1[(and lat) vulg fri spec Ambrst]. rec om 4th *σαρξ*, with AKLP rel [vulg-clem fuld^2 harl^1 spec] fri syrr Chr Thdrt Aug$_{[alic]}$ Pel: ins BDFℵ (17) 47 am(with demid fuld harl^2 tol) copt [æth arm Euthal-ms] (Damasc) Thl Orig-int$_2$ Tert$_1$ Ambrst. [*πετεινων* D^{1}F a.] rec *ιχθυων αλλη δε πτηνων*, with FKL rel syr Thdrt Œc Orig-int$_1$: txt ABDPℵ 17. 47 vulg fri [spec] Syr copt æth arm Chr Thl Orig-int$_1$ Tert$_1$ [Ambrst.—Damasc Orig-int$_1$ transpose *κτηνων* and *πτηνων*].

40. om 2nd *σωματα* F(not F-lat) [æth] (Tert$_1$). (*αλλα*, so ABD^{1}P.)

41. aft 1st and 2nd *αλλη* ins *δε* F[not F-lat]: aft 2nd, lect-8(sic).—om 1st *και* F lect-8 vulg(and F-lat) fri copt Orig-int$_3$ [Archel$_1$ Ambrst] Jer. *αστερος* (for *-ρων*) K. om *γαρ* K Orig-int$_2$[-ins$_3$].

is always attached to the verb; οὐ δικαιωθήσεται πᾶσα σάρξ, Rom. iii. 20; Gal. ii. 16. See Matt. xxiv. 22 ‖; Acts x. 14; ch. i. 29; 1 John iii. 15; Rev. vii. 16; ix. 4. On the other hand, *where the negative is attached to* πᾶς, *as here,* the sentence is a particular negative, not an universal: e.g. Rom. x. 16, ἀλλ' οὐ πάντες ὑπήκουσαν: ix. 6, 7; Heb. iii. 16; Matt. vii. 21, οὐ πᾶς ὁ λέγων μοι κύριε κύριε εἰσελεύσεται εἰς τὴν βασιλείαν τῶν οὐρανῶν,—where the rendering in question would involve portentous consequences indeed. I observe that Conyb. also, although disapproving on the ground of the sense, adds, "the words of the Greek text no doubt admit of such a rendering."

κτηνῶν] properly (κτέανος, κτάομαι) animals *possessed by man:* but used in a wider sense for quadrupeds in general.

40. σώματα ἐπουράνια] not, according to our modern expression, *heavenly* * *bodies,*—for they are introduced first ver. 41, and if we apply these words to them, we must suppose the Apostle to have imagined the stars to be endowed with bodies in the literal sense: for he is here comparing not figurative expressions, but physical realities:—nor (as Chrys., al.) *the bodies of the righteous,* as opposed to those of the wicked; for in these there is no organic difference whatever: but, as Meyer and De Wette, '*the bodies of angels,*'—the only heavenly organisms of which we are aware (except indeed the Resurrection-Body of our Lord, and that of those few who have been taken into glory, which, as belonging to the matter *in question,* are not alleged) which will bear comparison with *bodies* on earth. **δόξα** belongs to the ἐπουράνια more strictly than to the ἐπίγεια. In Luke ix. 26, we have ἐν τῇ δόξῃ αὐτοῦ καὶ τοῦ πατρὸς **καὶ τῶν ἁγίων ἀγγέλων.** **41.**] This third analogy is suggested perhaps by δόξα just before. There is no allusion whatever here (as some have imagined,—even Chrys., Œcum., Theodoret, Calov., Estius, al.) to *different degrees of glorification* of the bodies of the blessed; the introduction of such an idea confuses the whole analogical reasoning: which is, that even various fountains of *light,* so similar in its aspect and properties, differ; the sun from the moon and the stars: the stars (and much more vividly would this be felt under the pure sky of the East than here) from one another: why not then a *body* here from a resurrection-*body,*—both *bodies,* but *different?* **42—44 a.**] *Application of these analogies to the doctrine of the Resurrection.* **42.**] **οὕτως, thus,** viz. in the entire diversity of that which is raised again from the former body.

σπείρεται] "Cum posset dicere *sepelitur,* maluit dicere *seritur,* ut magis insisteret similitudini supra sumtæ de grano." Grot. **ἐν φθορᾷ, ἐν ἀφθαρσίᾳ**] in

ἐγείρεται [v] ἐν [v] δόξῃ· [r] σπείρεται ἐν [w] ἀσθενείᾳ, ἐγείρεται
[x] ἐν [x] δυνάμει· 44 [r] σπείρεται σῶμα [y] ψυχικόν, ἐγείρεται σῶμα
[z] πνευματικόν. εἰ ἔστιν σῶμα [y] ψυχικόν, ἔστιν καὶ [z] πνευματικόν. 45 [a] οὕτως καὶ γέγραπται [b] Ἐγένετο ὁ πρῶτος
ἄνθρωπος Ἀδὰμ [b] εἰς ψυχὴν ζῶσαν, ὁ ἔσχατος Ἀδὰμ

v = Luke ix. 31. 2 Cor. iii. 7, &c. Phil. iv. 19. Col. iii. 4. 1 Tim. iii. 16 only. L.P.
w = ch. ii. 3 reff. (see note.)
x Rom. i. 4 reff.
y here 3ce. ch. ii. 14. James iii. 15. Jude 19 only †.
z = here 4 times only. (ch. x. 3, 4 reff.)
a = Matt. ii. 5. Luke xxiv. 46. Acts xiii. 47 al.
b Gen. ii. 7. constr., Acts v. 36 reff.

44. rec om ει, with $D^{2\cdot3}$[-gr] KL rel syrr [Chr_1] Thdrt Phot-cat_1 Jac-$nisib_1$: ins ABCD[1] Fℵ 17 latt copt æth arm Damasc [Ambrst] $Aug_{[alic]}$ Bede. (ι is written above the line by ℵ[1](?)[3].) [homœotel in P k spec Chr-2-mss Euthal-ms 1st to 2nd πνευματικον.]—rec και bef 2nd εστιν, with KL rel &c: txt ABCDFℵ 17 &c. [æth doubtful.]—rec ins σωμα bef [2nd] πνευματικον, with KL rel syrr (copt) æth [Chr] Thdrt Phot-cat Jac-$nisib_2$: om ABCDFℵ 17 latt arm [Damasc Ambrst Aug_{alic}]. (*Conformation to the foregoing assertions: or perhaps ει overlooked from εστιν following. The 2nd σωμα was a gloss.*)
45. for ουτως και, καθως F fuld [demid(*sicut et*) tol(*sicut enim*)] arm[-usc Aug_{alic}]. om ανθρωπος BK Did_1 Iren[-int_1] (Orig-int_1) [$Ambr_1$(txt_{alic}) Aug_1].

a state of corruption,—in a state of incorruptibility. **43. ἐν ἀτιμίᾳ, ἐν δόξῃ] in dishonour** (*τί γὰρ εἰδεχθέστερον νεκροῦ διαῤῥυέντος;* Chrys. Hom. xli. p. 390. Cf. Xen. Mem. i. 2. 53,—*τῆς ψυχῆς ἐξελθούσης, ... τὸ σῶμα τοῦ οἰκειοτάτου ἀνθρώπου τὴν ταχίστην ἐξενέγκαντες ἀφανίζουσιν*),—**in glory**: regarding, as throughout this argument (see on ver. 23), only the *resurrection of the just*: see Phil. iii. 21. **ἐν ἀσθενείᾳ] in weakness,**—the characteristic of the lifeless body, which is relaxed and powerless. Chrys. understands ἀσθ. of its *inability to resist corruption*: De Wette would refer it to the previous state of pain and disease: but it seems better to understand it of the *powerlessness* of the corpse, contrasted with **ἐν δυν., in vigour,** viz. the fresh and eternal energy of the new body free from disease and pain. "That which Grot. adds: 'cum sensibus multis, quos nunc non intelligimus,' is very likely in itself *true*, but is not implied in *ἐν δυνάμει*." Meyer. **44 a. σῶμ. ψυχ.] an animal body**, of which the *ψυχή*, the animal soul, was the acting and informing power. This soul having departed out of it, does not do away with the correctness of the predicate: its whole organism which still remains *when it is sown*, is arranged to suit this predominance of the animal soul. **σῶμα πνευματικόν]** Theophyl., having explained **σῶμα ψυχ.**,—*ἐν ᾧ ἡ ψυχὴ τὸ κῦρος καὶ τὴν ἡγεμονίαν ἔχει*,—proceeds *πνευματικὸν δέ, τὸ τὴν τοῦ ἁγίου πνεύματος καταπλουτοῦν ἐνέργειαν, καὶ ὑπ' ἐκείνου τὰ πάντα διοικούμενον. εἰ γὰρ καὶ νῦν ἐν ἡμῖν ἐνεργεῖ τὸ πνεῦμα, ἀλλ' οὐχ οὕτως, οὐδὲ ἀεί. ἀφίπταται γὰρ ἁμαρτανόντων. καὶ τοῦ πνεύματος δὲ παρόντος, ἡ ψυχὴ διοικεῖ τὸ σῶμα· τότε δὲ διηνεκῶς παραμενεῖ τοῖς σώμασι τῶν δικαίων τὸ πνεῦμα.* But this is not quite enough:—for thus the body might remain as it is, sin only being removed: whereas it shall be no longer a body in which the *ψυχή* predominates to the subordination of the higher part, the *πνεῦμα*, but one in which the *πνεῦμα*, and that informed fully by the Spirit of God, shall predominate,—its organism being conformed not to an animal, but to a spiritual life: see on ch. vi. 13. Some understood *πνευματικόν*, *ætherial, aery*, *κουφότερον καὶ λεπτότερον, καὶ οἷον καὶ ἐπ' ἀέρος ὀχεῖσθαι* (Chrys. p. 391), or as Origen, *ἀερῶδες κ. αἰθέριον* (see Theophyl.), but the other is certainly right.

44 b—49.] *Reassertion and Confirmation of the existence of the spiritual body.* **44 b.] If there exists an animal body, there exists also a spiritual**: i. e. it is no more wonderful a thing, that there should be a body fitted to the capacities and wants of man's highest part, his spirit, than (which we see to be the case) that there should be one fitted to the capacities and wants of his subordinate animal soul. The emphasis is both times on **ἔστιν**.

45.] Confirmation of this from Scripture. **οὕτως, thus,** viz. in accordance with what has been just said. The citation extends only to the words *ἐγένετο ὁ ἄνθρ. εἰς ψυχ. ζῶσαν*: *πρῶτος* and *Ἀδάμ* are supplied, as are also the concluding words, in which lies the real confirmation. The words quoted serve therefore rather for the illustration of man being a *ψυχή*, than for a proof of the existence of the spiritual body. **ἐγένετο]** by his creation,—by means of God breathing into him the breath of life. **εἰς ψ. ζῶσ.]** becoming thereby a *σῶμα ψυχικόν*. **ὁ ἔσχ. Ἀδάμ]** This expression was well known among the Jews as indicating the Messiah. The Rabbinical work Neve Shalom ix. 9 (Schöttgen), says: "Adamus postremus est Messias:" see other instances in Schöttg. ad loc. **ἔσχατος**, as being the *last* HEAD of humanity,—to be manifested in the *last times*: or merely in contrast to the

c ver. 36. Rom. iv. 17 reff.
d here (4 times) only +.
e ver. 40 reff.
f Rom. xiii. 4 reff.
g Rom. viii. 29 reff.
h = ch. vii. 29. see ch. i. 12.
i = Matt. xvi. 17. Eph. vi. 12. Heb. ii. 14. Sir. xiv. 18.
k ch. vi. 9, 10 reff.

[b] εἰς πνεῦμα [c] ζωοποιοῦν. 46 ἀλλʼ οὐ πρῶτον τὸ [z] πνευματικόν, ἀλλὰ τὸ [y] ψυχικόν, ἔπειτα τὸ [z] πνευματικόν.
47 ὁ πρῶτος ἄνθρωπος ἐκ γῆς [d] χοϊκός, ὁ δεύτερος
ἄνθρωπος ἐξ οὐρανοῦ. 48 οἷος ὁ [d] χοϊκός, τοιοῦτοι καὶ
οἱ [d] χοϊκοί, καὶ οἷος ὁ [e] ἐπουράνιος, τοιοῦτοι καὶ οἱ
[e] ἐπουράνιοι· 49 καὶ καθὼς [f] ἐφορέσαμεν τὴν [g] εἰκόνα τοῦ
[d] χοϊκοῦ, [f] φορέσομεν καὶ τὴν [g] εἰκόνα τοῦ [e] ἐπουρανίου.
50 [h] τοῦτο δέ [h] φημι, ἀδελφοί, ὅτι [i] σὰρξ καὶ [i] αἷμα [k] βασι-

ABCDF KLPℵ a b c d e f g h k l m o 17. 47

46. αλλα D[1].

47. aft *ο πρωτος ανθρωπος* add *αδαμ* C[1]. rec ins *ο κυριος* bef *εξ ουρ.* (*gloss*), with A D[-gr[2.]][3] KLPℵ[3] rel syrr goth [arm Hip-ed$_1$] Orig$_1$ Chr$_1$ [Bas$_1$ Euthal-ms] Cyr[-p$_4$(but mss and the old syr and lat translations vary)] Thdrt Ps-Ath$_1$ Damasc Thl Œc Tert$_1$ Maximin$_1$ (*the insertion is ascribed to Marcion by Tert and in Dial*) : om BCD[1]Fℵ[1] 17 latt copt æth arm[-marg] Orig$_1$(and int$_4$) Hip-ms$_1$ [Petr$_1$] Ath$_1$ Nys$_1$ Naz$_1$ Cyr[-p$_5$(but see above) Ps-Ath] Apollinarist-in-Epiph$_1$ Photin Tert$_1$ Cypr$_{sæpe}$ Hil [Ambr$_1$ Ambrst]. aft *ουρανου* add *ο ουρανιος* F vulg[-clem am[2] æth arm-marg Bas$_1$ (Ps-Ath$_1$)] Orig-int$_3$ [Cypr-ms$_1$ Ambr$_1$ Ambrst].

48. aft *τοιουτοι* ins *ουτοι* C. om 1st *και* F(not F-lat) [am[1]] Iren-int$_1$[but mss vary : ins$_1$]. for *επουρ.*, *ουρανιος* and *ουρανιοι* D[1]F.

49. [for 1st *και*, *αρα* F(and G-marg) Aug$_1$: om Orig-int$_1$ Cypr$_4$.] *φορεσωμεν* (*from a desire* (as Chrys below) *to turn what is really a physical assertion into an ethical exhortation : see note at Rom* v. 1) ACDFKLPℵ [17(sic)] rel latt copt goth Thdot$_1$[not ed Migne] Orig$_2$[-c$_2$](-int$_4$) Cæs$_1$ [Nys$_1$] Mac$_1$ Meth(pref *ινα*) Chr$_{expr}$(*τοῦτʼ ἔστιν, ἄριστα πράξωμεν. . . . συμβουλευτικῶς εἰσάγει τὸν λόγον*) Epiph$_1$ Ps-Ath$_1$ Damasc Iren-int$_2$ Tert$_{2expr}$ Cypr$_4$ Hil$_1$ [Ambr$_{alic}$ Ambrst] Jer : txt B a c g [æth(Tischdf)] arm Thdrt$_{expr}$(*τὸ γὰρ φορέσομεν προῤῥητικῶς, οὐ παραινετικῶς εἴρηκεν*) Thl$_{expr}$ Œc$_{expr}$.

50. for *δε*, *γαρ* D F[not F-lat] Iren[-int$_1$] Tert$_2$.

first. **εἰς πν. ζωοπ.**] scil. *ἐγένετο*—**became a quickening** (life-bestowing) **spirit.** *When?* This has been variously answered: see De Wette and Meyer. The principal periods selected are his *Incarnation*, his *Resurrection*, and his *Ascension*. But it seems to me that the question is not one to be pressed: in the union of the two natures, the second Adam *was constituted a life-bestowing Spirit*, and is such now in heaven, yet having the resurrection-body. The whole complex of his suffering and triumphant state seems to be embraced in these words. That His resurrection-state *alone* is not intended, is evident from *ἐξ οὐρανοῦ*, ver. 47. He was a *πνεῦμα ζωοποιοῦν*, even while in the *σῶμα ψυχικόν*; and is still such in the *σῶμα πνευματικόν*. The *life* implied in *ζωοποιοῦν*, is the *resurrection-life*: see John v. 21, 28; Rom. viii. 11. **46.**] But in the natural order, that which is *animal* precedes that which is *spiritual* (**τὸ ψυχ.**, **τὸ πνευμ.**, not *σῶμα*, but abstract and general): as in ver. 45, *ὁ πρῶτος*—*ὁ ἔσχατος*. **47.**] So exactly in Gen. ii. 7. God made man *χοῦν λαβὼν ἀπὸ τῆς γῆς*. Meyer has some excellent remarks here, with which I entirely agree:—"Since the body of Adam is thus characterized as a *ψυχικὸν σῶμα*, as ver. 45, and psychical organism involves *mortality* (ver. 44), it is clear that Paul treats of Adam *not as created exempt from death*: in strict accordance with Gen. ii. 7; iii. 19. Nor does this militate against his teaching that *death came into the world through sin*, Rom. v. 12. For had our first parents not sinned, they would have remained in Paradise, and would, by the use of the *Tree of Life*, which God *had not forbidden them* (Gen. ii. 16, 17), have become immortal (Gen. iii. 22). But they were driven out of Paradise, *ere yet they had tasted of this tree* (Gen. iii. 22), and so, according to the record in Genesis also, Death came into the world by sin." See also some striking remarks on the verse in Genesis in Stier, 'Andeutungen für glaübiges Schriftverständniss,' pp. 202, 3. **ἐξ οὐρανοῦ**] either, in this *glorified Body*, at his coming,—as Meyer: or, in his *whole Personality* (De W.) as the God-man: this latter seems more probable from John iii. 13, where *ὁ υἱὸς τοῦ ἀνθρώπου* is designated as *ὁ ἐκ τοῦ οὐρανοῦ καταβάς*.

48.] **ὁ χοϊκός**, *Adam*; **οἱ χ.**, *his posterity on earth*: **ὁ ἐπουρ.**, *Christ*; **οἱ ἐπ.**, *His risen people*. See, as admirably illustrating this verse, Phil. iii. 20, 21. **49.**] For the reason of keeping **φορέσομεν**, see var. readd. **As we** (Christians) **bore** in this life; the time imagined is when this life is *past*, and the resurrection *instant* . . .

λείαν θεοῦ [k] κληρονομῆσαι οὐ δύνανται, οὐδὲ ἡ [l] φθορὰ
τὴν [m] ἀφθαρσίαν [k] κληρονομεῖ. 51 ἰδοὺ [n] μυστήριον ὑμῖν
λέγω. πάντες οὐ [o] κοιμηθησόμεθα, πάντες δὲ [p] ἀλλαγησόμεθα, 52 ἐν [q] ἀτόμῳ, ἐν [r] ῥιπῇ ὀφθαλμοῦ, ἐν τῇ ἐσχάτῃ
[s] σάλπιγγι· [t] σαλπίσει γάρ, καὶ οἱ νεκροὶ [u] ἐγερθήσονται

M σαλπισει...

l ver. 42 reff. m Rom. ii. 7 reff. n = Matt. xiii. 11. Rom. xi. 25. Dan. ii. 18 al. o = ch. vii. 39 reff. p here bis. Acts vi. 14. Rom. i. 23 (from Ps. cv. 20). Gal. iv. 20. Heb. i. 12 (from Ps. ci. 26) only. Lev. xxvii. 33. q here only †. r here only †. Eur. Iph. Taur. 885. (-πίζειν, James i. 6.) s ch. xiv. 8 reff. 1 Thess. iv. 16. t Matt. vi. 2. Rev. viii. 6, &c. (6 times.) ix. 1, 13. x. 7. xi. 15 only. Num. x. 3—8. u ver. 4.

for κληρονομησαι ου δυνανται, ου κληρονομησουσιν (*see ch* vi. 9, *Gal* v. 21) F 42 copt Mac$_1$ Chr[and 2-mss] Iren[-int$_2$] Orig-int$_2$ Tert$_1$.—δυναται BPℵ k. κληρονομησει (*see as above*) C[1]D[1]F latt[(not am[1]) syrr] copt (Meth$_1$).

51. ins οι bef παντες, twice, A; but 2nd οι corrd into ου A[1]. rec aft παντες ins μεν (*on acct of the* δε *following*), with A[1]C[2] D[3][-gr] KLPℵ rel vulg syr copt Dial$_1$ Orthod$_1$ Cyr$_2$ [Ephr$_1$ Nys$_1$ Chr$_5$ Euthal-ms Thdrt Damasc] Cæs$_1$ Orig-int$_1$ Tert$_1$: μεν ουν A[2] (appy) F [17(Tischdf)] : δε k : om B(C?[1]) D[1](and lat) Syr æth [arm(Tischdf)] Orig$_1$(-int$_2$) Jer(on the testimony of the greek mss: for after stating that the lat mss read *omnes quidem resurgemus,* he says all the greek have either *omnes dormiemus* or *non omnes dormiemus*) Jac-nisib$_1$. for κοιμηθησομεθα, αναστησομεθα D[1](and lat) vulg(and F-lat) arm-marg lat-mss-mentioned-by-Jer-Aug-Pel-Gennad Jac-nisib$_1$ Hil$_3$ Ambr Aug. κοιμηθησομεθα bef ου (thus reading πάντες (μὲν) κοιμηθησόμεθα, οὐ πάντες δὲ ἀλλαγησόμεθα) A[1]C(D[1])Fℵ 17 and greek-mss-mentioned-by-[Max-conf]-Jer-Aug-Pel, also vulg æth[-rom] arm Orig$_1$(and int$_1$) Did[-in-Jer] : ου (? ουν) κοιμ. ου A, the 1st ου is written over the line in small letters A[1] : txt B D[2][appy]·[3] KLP rel and greek-mss-mentioned-by-[Max-conf]-Jer-Acac-Did-Pel, also syrr copt goth æth-pl [spec] Thdot Orig$_1$(int$_2$: also [once] more in Jer) Thdor-heracl Diod Apollin(these three in Jer) Dial-trin$_1$ Tit$_1$ Nys$_1$ Cæs$_1$ Chr$_5$ [Cyr$_1$ Euthal-ms] Thdrt$_3$ Andr$_1$ Damasc Thl Œc Tert Jer$_3$. (*The variation has prob arisen from the apparent difficulty of reconciling* παντες (μεν) ου κοιμ. *with the fact that St. Paul and his readers* had all died. *Hence the negative particle was transferred to the other clause, to the detriment of the sense.*)

52. ins ως bef εν ριπη C[1]. for ριπη, ροπη D[1]F 67[2] Dial[-ms$_1$ Nys$_1$] and greek-mss-mentioned-by-Jer(*ριπη s. ροπη utrumque enim legitur, et nostri interpretati sunt in ictu* [latt Ambrst], *s. in motu* [Tert$_{alic}$]). for εγερθ., αναστησονται ADFP Orig$_1$ Chr$_1$ Damasc Thl-marg : txt BCKLMℵ rel Orig$_6$ Dial$_1$ Chr$_{h.l.}$ Cyr[-p] Thdrt Cosm$_1$.

50—54.] *The necessity of the change of the animal body into the spiritual, in order to inherit God's kingdom. The manner of that change prophetically described: and the abolition of Death in victory consequent on it.* 50.] **τοῦτο δέ φ.**, see reff. It calls attention to something to be observed, and liable to be overlooked. Not only is the change of body *possible*, and according to natural and spiritual analogies,—but it is NECESSARY. **σὰρξ καὶ αἷμα**] = σῶμα ψυχικόν, the present organism of the body, calculated for the wants of the animal soul. τὴν θνητὴν φύσιν καλεῖ· ἀδύνατον δὲ ταύτην ἔτι θνητὴν οὖσαν τῆς ἐπουρανίου βασιλείας τυχεῖν. Theodoret. **ἡ φθορὰ . . . . τὴν ἀφθαρσίαν,** the abstracts, representing the impossibility of the φθαρτόν inheriting the ἄφθαρτον as one *grounded in* these qualities. **κληρονομεῖ,** *pres.,* sets forth the *absolute impossibility in the nature of things.* 51.] He proceeds to reveal to them something of the process of the change at the resurrection-day. This he does under the name of a **μυστήριον**, a *hidden doctrine* (see reff., especially Rom.).

πάντες οὐ κοιμ.] See var. readd. Meyer maintains that the only rendering of the words which is philologically allowable (the ordinary one, regarding πάντες (μὲν) οὐ as = οὐ πάντες (μέν),—we shall not all sleep, being inadmissible, here and in other instances where it has been attempted, see Winer, edn. 6, § 26. 1), is this, '*we all* (viz. as in 1 Thess. iv. 15, ἡμεῖς οἱ ζῶντες οἱ περιλειπόμενοι εἰς τὴν παρουσίαν τοῦ κυρίου, —in which number the Apostle firmly believed that he himself should be, see 2 Cor. v. 1 ff. and notes) *shall not sleep, but shall all be changed.*' But we may observe that this would commit the Apostle to the extent of believing that *not one Christian* would die before the παρουσία;—and that it is besides not necessary, for the emphasis is both times on πάντες—'(*All of us*) *shall not sleep, but* (*all of us*) *shall be changed :*' i.e. 'the sleep of death cannot be predicated of (all of us), but the resurrection-change *can.*' See also Winer, § 61. 5 f, and Moulton's note, p. 695. 52.] **ἐν ἀτόμῳ, in a point of time** *absolutely indivisible,* ἐν ῥιπήματι, Hesych. **ἐν τῇ ἐσχ.**

v Rom. i. 23 (reff.). w = Acts iv. 12 reff. x Rom. xiii. 12, 14. Eph. iv. 24. vi. 11. 2 Cor. v. 3. Col. iii. 10. Ps. cxxxi. 9. y Rom. vi. 12 reff. z here bis. 1 Tim. vi. 16 only +. Wisd. viii. 13 al4. a = Matt. v. 18. Mark xi. 23. b Isa. xxv. 8 (Heb., not LXX, but κατ. occ. there) = 2 Cor. (ii. 7.) v. 4 (Matt. xxiii. 24. Heb. xi. 29. 1 Pet. v. 8. Rev. xii. 16) only. c Matt. xii. 20 only. 2 Kings ii. 26. Job xxxvi. 7. d as above (c). here 3ce only. e here bis, Acts xxvi. 14. Rev. ix. 10 only. Hosea xiii. 14. f = Rom. vi. 17 reff.

v ἄφθαρτοι, καὶ ἡμεῖς p ἀλλαγησόμεθα.
53 w δεῖ γὰρ τὸ v φθαρτὸν τοῦτο x ἐνδύσασθαι m ἀφθαρσίαν καὶ τὸ y θνητὸν τοῦτο x ἐνδύσασθαι z ἀθανασίαν.
54 ὅταν δὲ τὸ v φθαρτὸν τοῦτο x ἐνδύσηται m ἀφθαρσίαν καὶ τὸ y θνητὸν τοῦτο x ἐνδύσηται z ἀθανασίαν, τότε a γενήσεται ὁ λόγος ὁ γεγραμμένος, b Κατεπόθη ὁ θάνατος c εἰς cd νῖκος.
55 Ποῦ σου, θάνατε, τὸ e κέντρον; ποῦ σου, θάνατε, τὸ d νῖκος;
56 τὸ δὲ e κέντρον τοῦ θανάτου ἡ ἁμαρτία, ἡ δὲ δύναμις τῆς ἁμαρτίας ὁ νόμος·
57 τῷ δὲ θεῷ f χάρις τῷ διδόντι ἡμῖν

I$_b$ τουτο... ABCDI$_b$KLMPℵ a b d e f g k l m o 17. 47

n θανατου... ABCDI$_b$KLMPℵ a b d e f g k l m o 17. 47

53. [for 1st τουτο, τουτον P k.] om 2nd τουτο F[not F-lat]. ins την bef αθανασιαν I$_b$.

54. om το φθαρτ. τουτ. ενδ. αφθ. και (i. e. το φθαρτ. to το θνητ.) C[1]I$_b$Mℵ[1](in supplying the omission ℵ[3] has written και το, το being superfluous) 64. 71 vulg copt goth æth arm Mcion-e$_1$ Ath[-4-mss$_1$] Iren-int$_1$(citing from *oportet enim*, ver 53, to *victoria tua*, ver 55) Hil$_1$ Ambrst Aug$_1$ Fulg Oros Bede.—in A arm, το φθ. to αφθαρσ. is put aft το θν. του. ενδ. αθανασ.—om κ. το θν. του. ενδ. αθαν. D[1](supplied in D-lat, a prima manu) 1. Orig$_1$: om αθανασ. to αθανασ. F. ins την bef αθανασιαν AI$_b$ℵ 17[also bef αφθαρσ.].

55. transp νικος and κεντρον (*see* LXX) BCI$_b$Mℵ[1] 17 vulg copt æth[-rom] arm[-zoh] Orig$_1$(-int$_2$) Eus$_1$ Ath$_1$ Did$_1$ Cyr-jer$_1$ Bas-sel$_1$ [Euthal-ms] Damasc$_1$ Iren-int$_1$ Tert$_1$ Ambr[$_{sæpe}$ Ambrst] Jer: txt A[2]DFKLPℵ[3] rel syrr goth æth-pl [arm-mss] Orig$_1$(and int$_1$) Eus$_1$ Ath$_1$ Cyr-jer$_1$ Chr$_2$ Thdrt Euther[-in-Thdrt] Iren-int$_1$ Tert$_3$ Cypr$_1$ Hil$_1$.—om που σου θ. το νικ. A[1].—(νεικος, here and in vv. 54, 57 (*confusion between* ει *and* ι *as constantly elsw*) BD[1]I$_b$(ℵ ver 57) m, *contentio* Tert$_1$[*victoria vel contentio*$_1$: Aug varies].) rec for 2nd θανατε, αδη (*so* LXX), with A[2] D[3][-gr](appy) KLMPℵ[3] rel syrr goth [æth-pl arm] Orig$_2$ Ath$_1$ [Did$_1$ Bas$_1$ Chr$_1$ Euthal-ms Thdrt] Euther$_1$: txt BC D[1][and lat] FI$_b$ℵ[1] vulg copt æth-rom Eus$_2$ Iren-int$_2$ [Orig-int$_3$] Tert$_4$ Cypr$_1$ Hil$_1$ Ambr$_{sæpe}$ Aug$_{sæpe}$.

56. ins εστιν bef η αμαρτ. A.

57. for διδοντι, δοντι D a b d l o [syrr(not syr-mg)] Ath-3-mss Chr$_1$ Œc.

σάλπ. **at** (in, as part of the events of) **the last trumpet-blowing.** The word ἐσχ. must obviously not be refined upon as some (τινές in Theophyl.—and Olsh.) have done, identifying it with the *seventh trumpet* of the Apocalypse;—nor pressed too closely as if there were necessarily no trump after it,—but is *the trump at the time of the end*, **the last trump**, in a wide and popular sense. See ref. 1 Thess. **σαλπίσει**] impersonal,—ὁ σαλπιγκτής, scil. So Od. φ. 142, ἀρξάμενοι τοῦ χώρου ὅθεν τέ περ οἰνοχοεύει (scil. ὁ οἰνόχοος): Herod. ii. 47, ἐπεὰν θύσῃ: Xen. Anab. i. 2. 17, ἐπεὶ ἐσάλπιγξε: iii. 4. 36, ἐκήρυξε: —vi. 5. 25, ἕως σημαίνοι τῇ σάλπιγγι. Kühner, § 414. 2. σαλπίσω for σαλπίγξω is reprobated by the grammarians: see Wetst. **ἡμεῖς**, see above [on ver. 51]. **53.**] Confirmation of **καὶ ἡμ. ἀλλαγ.**, by a re-statement of the necessity of putting on incorruptibility and immortality. **τὸ φθ. τοῦτο . . . τὸ θν. τοῦτο**] **this**, indicating *his own* body. **ἐνδύσασθαι**—see note on the force of the aor. as indicating that which is momentary, on ver. 34. Compare on the figure of *putting on*, 2 Cor. v. 3 and notes. **54.**] **ὅταν δέ**, &c. is a repetition, in a triumphant spirit, of the description of the glorious change. **γενήσεται**] **shall come to pass**—really *be*. The citation is from the Heb. with this difference, that the active, '*He* (*Jehovah*) *abolishes*,' בִּלַּע, is made passive, and לָנֶצַח, '*for ever*,' is rendered (as elsewhere by the LXX, e. g. ref. 2 Kings, but not here) εἰς νῖκος. **εἰς ν.** '*so as to result in victory*. Wetst. quotes from the Rabbis, 'In diebus ejus (Messiæ) Deus S. B. *deglutiet* mortem.'

55.] Triumphant exclamation *of the Apostle realizing in his mind that glorious time*: expressed nearly in the terms of the prophetic announcement of Hosea,—ποῦ ἡ δίκη σου, θάνατε; ποῦ τὸ κέντρον σου, ᾅδη; The figure of death as a *venomous beast* is natural, from the *serpent*, Gen. iii. Num. xxi. The souls in Hades being freed by the resurrection, Death's victory is gone: sin being abolished by the change of the animal body (the source of sin) to the spiritual, his sting is powerless. For a discussion of the quotation, see Stanley's note. **56.**] See above: and compare Rom. v. 12, and vii. **57.**] For this blessed con-

τὸ [d] νῖκος διὰ τοῦ κυρίου ἡμῶν Ἰησοῦ χριστοῦ. 58 [g] ὥςτε,
[h] ἀδελφοί μου [h] ἀγαπητοί, [i] ἑδραῖοι γίνεσθε, [k] ἀμετακίνητοι,
[l] περισσεύοντες ἐν τῷ [m] ἔργῳ τοῦ [m] κυρίου πάντοτε, εἰδότες
ὅτι ὁ [n] κόπος ὑμῶν οὐκ ἔστιν [o] κενὸς ἐν κυρίῳ.
XVI. 1 Περὶ δὲ τῆς [p] λογίας τῆς [q] εἰς τοὺς [r] ἁγίους,
ὥςπερ [s] διέταξα ταῖς [t] ἐκκλησίαις τῆς Γαλατίας, οὕτως καὶ
ὑμεῖς ποιήσατε. 2 [u] κατὰ [v] μίαν [w] σαββάτου ἕκαστος ὑμῶν
[x] παρ᾽ [x] ἑαυτῷ τιθέτω [y] θησαυρίζων ὅ τι ἂν [z] εὐοδῶται, ἵνα

g = ch. v. 8 reff. h address, Paul, here only. James i. 16, 19. ii. 5 only. (Eph. vi. 21. Col. iv. 7, 9. Philem. 16. 2 Pet. iii. 15.) i ch. vii. 37. Col. i. 23 only +. Ps. lvi. 8 Symm. k here only +. l Rom. iii. 7. Phil. i. 26. 1 Thess. iv. 10 al. Tobit iv. 16 [א om. vv. 6—18]. m ch. xvi. 10. (Phil. ii. 30.) n 2 Cor. vi. 5 reff. o ver. 10 reff. p here bis only +. q = Rom. xv. 26. 2 Cor. viii. 4. ix. 13. r Acts ix. 13 reff. Rom. xv. 26. s ch. vii. 17. Acts xviii. 2. L.P., exc. Matt. xi. 1. 3 Kings xi. 18. Dan. i. 5 Theod. t plur., Rom. xvi. 16 reff. u = Acts ii. 46 al. v Mark xvi. 2. Luke xxiv. 1. John xx. 1, 19. Acts xx. 7. w = Luke xviii. 12. Mark xvi. 9. x see Luke xxiv. 12 ; J. y Matt. vi. 19, 20. Luke xii. 21. Rom. ii. 5. 2 Cor. xii. 14. James v. 3. 2 Pet. iii. 7 only. 4 Kings xx. 17. z Rom. i. 10 (reff.). 3 John 2 (bis) only. Gen. xxxix. 3, 23.

ιησ. χρ. bef *τ. κυρ. ημ.* M.
58. ins *και* bef *αμετακινητοι* A [vulg F-lat Syr æth] Ambrst. for *εργω*, *οικω* P. om *του* I_b. *ουκ εστιν* bef *ο κοπ. υμων* F[not F-lat].

CHAP. XVI. 2. rec *σαββατων*, with KLMא[3] rel copt goth [arm Euthal-ms] Thdrt Damasc: *σαββατω* א[1] m[Scr]: txt ABCDFI_bP א-corr[1] 17 latt [syrr] Chr_1. *εαν* BI_bM.—*ὅτ᾽ ἂν* n(and so vv. 3, 5, 12) 47. *ευοδωθη* ACI_bKM א[3](-*δοθη*) [Euthal-ms] Damasc.

summation of victory over death, he breaks out in thanks to God, who gives it to us (*present*, as being certain) through our Lord Jesus Christ (the Name in full, as befits the solemnity and majesty of the thanksgiving). **58.**] *Conclusion of the whole by an earnest exhortation.* **ὥςτε**] '*quæ cum ita sint*,'—seeing that the victory is sure. **ἑδρ., ἀμετακίν.**] a climax (Mey.);—in reference, viz. to the doubt which is attempted to be raised among you on this matter. **ἐν τῷ ἔργῳ τοῦ κυρ.**] The *work of the Lord* is the *Christian life*, with its active and passive duties and graces,—the bringing forth the fruits of the Spirit. **εἰδότες**] **Knowing** (as you do—being convinced by what has been said), **that your labour** (bestowed on the *ἔργ. τοῦ κυρ.*) **is not vain** (which it would be, were there no resurrection: see reff.) **in the Lord.** These last words cannot belong to *ὁ κόπος ὑμ.*, nor very well to *οὐκ ἔστι κενός* (as Meyer), but are best taken with the whole sentence, *your labour is not in vain:* so ch. ix. 1.

CHAP. XVI.] VARIOUS DIRECTIONS AND ARRANGEMENTS (1—18). SALUTATIONS (19, 20). AUTOGRAPH CONCLUSION AND BENEDICTION (21—24). **1—4.**] *Directions respecting the collection and transmission of alms for the poor saints at Jerusalem.* **1.**] The construction is as in ch. vii. 1; viii. 1; xii. 1;—the *περὶ δὲ* . . . rather serves to introduce the new subject than to form any constructional part of the sentence. Similarly in ver. 12. **λογίας**] *λογία, συλλογή*, Hesych. *λογίαν, τὴν συλλογὴν τῶν χρημάτων καλεῖ*, Theodoret (Wetst.). The word is said in the Lexx. not to be found in classic writers. **εἰς τ. ἁγ.**] = *εἰς τοὺς πτωχοὺς τ. ἁγίων τῶν ἐν Ἰερουσαλήμ*, ref. Rom. See also 2 Cor. viii. 1 ff.; ix. 1 ff.: and on the poverty of the church at Jerusalem, note on Acts ii. 44. That poverty was no doubt increased by the continual troubles with which Jerusalem was harassed in this, the distressful close of the Jewish national history. See other causes in Stanley. That the mother church of Christendom should be thus, in its need, sustained by the daughter churches, was natural; and it is at the same time an affecting circumstance, to find *him* the most anxious to collect and bear to them this contribution, whose former persecuting zeal had doubtless (see Acts xxvi. 10) made not a few of those saints *widows and orphans.* **ὥςπερ διέτ.**] We do not find any such order in the Epistle to the Galatians: ch. ii. 10 there being merely incidental. It had probably been given during his journey among them Acts xviii. 23,—or perhaps by message (?) from Ephesus. Not as E. V., '*as I have given order*,' but **as I gave order.** He refers to the occasion, whatever it was, when that order was given. Bengel remarks: "Galatarum exemplum Corinthiis, Corinthiorum exemplum Macedonibus, Corinthiorum et Macedonum Romanis proponit. 2 Cor. ix. 2. Rom. xv. 26. Magna exemplorum vis." **2.**] **μίαν σαββ.**] For this Hebraism, and *σαβ.* in the singular, signifying *week*, see reff. On the observance of the first day of the week, see notes, Acts xx. 7, and Rom. xiv. 5. Here there is no mention of their *assembling*,

μή, ὅταν ἔλθω, τότε [p] λογίαι γίνωνται· 3 ὅταν δὲ [a] παραγένωμαι, οὓς ἐὰν [b] δοκιμάσητε, [c] δι᾽ ἐπιστολῶν τούτους
πέμψω [d] ἀπενεγκεῖν τὴν [e] χάριν ὑμῶν εἰς Ἱερουσαλήμ·
4 ἐὰν δὲ [f] ἄξιον ᾖ [g] τοῦ κἀμὲ πορεύεσθαι, σὺν ἐμοὶ πορεύ-
σονται. 5 ἐλεύσομαι δὲ πρὸς ὑμᾶς, ὅταν Μακεδονίαν
[h] διέλθω· Μακεδονίαν γὰρ [h] διέρχομαι· 6 [i] πρὸς ὑμᾶς δὲ
[k] τυχὸν [l] παραμενῶ [m] ἢ [m] καὶ [n] παραχειμάσω, ἵνα ὑμεῖς με

ABCDF I_bKLM Pℵ a b c d e f g h k l m n o 17. 47

a absol., Acts xvii. 10 reff. b = Rom. xiv. 22 reff. c = Rom. ii. 27. d Acts xix. 12 reff. e = 2 Cor. viii. 6, 7, 19. f = and constr., here only. g = Luke xxiv. 25. h Acts xiii. 6 reff. i — Matt. xiii. 56. John i. 1, 2. Gal. i. 18. 1 John i. 2. see ver. 10. ch. ii. 3. k here only. Xen. Anab. v. 9. 20. (see ch. xiv. 10.) l Phil. i. 25. Heb. vii. 23. James i. 25 only. Gen. xliv. 33. m ch. ix. 8 reff. n Acts xxvii. 12. xxviii. 11. Tit. iii. 12 only +.

3. [**οσους** K.] for εαν, αν BD[1]F. ιεροσολυμα A.
4. rec η bef αξιον, with D F[-gr] KLℵ[1] rel syr (goth) [arm Euthal-ms] Chr_1 Thdrt Damasc: txt A(ην) BCI_bMPℵ[3] a m 17 [latt(not G-lat) Syr copt].
5. for γαρ, δε F[-gr](not G) m.
6. for δε, γ(αρ) I_b. **κατα**μενω BM 67[2]: παραπομεινω F.—παραμ. bef τυχ[ων (sic)] P. om η F(not F-lat) 2. om και BM 3. 116 (Syr) Chr-2-mss. for ινα, ει μη F[not F-lat] D-lat.—ινα ει και παραχ. D[1][-gr].

which we have in Acts xx. 7, but a plain indication that the day was already considered as a special one, and one more than others fitting for the performance of a religious duty. **παρ᾽ ἑαυτῷ τιθ.**] **let each of you lay up at home** (reff.) **in store whatsoever he may by prosperity have acquired** (lit. '*whatsoever he may be prospered in:*' i. e. the pecuniary result of any prosperous adventure, or dispensation of Providence): not, as Bengel, al.: '*quod commodum sit,*'—a meaning which the word will not bear. **ἵνα μή, . .**] **that there may not, when I come,** THEN **be collections to be made.** His time would be better employed in imparting to them a spiritual benefit, than in urging them to and superintending this duty. **3.**] "Vide quomodo vir tantus nullam suspicioni rimam aperire voluerit." Grot. **δι᾽ ἐπιστολῶν** cannot belong to δοκιμάσητε (as Beza, Calv., Wetst., E. V.,—for what need of letters *from them* ὅταν παραγένωμαι, or before his coming, if the person recommended were *not to be sent off before his arrival?*), but is emphatically prefixed, as the safe and proper way of giving credentials to those *sent;*—τούτους πέμψω,—the alternative which follows, of himself accompanying them, being already in the mind of the Apostle. **ἐπιστολῶν**, plur.,—not of the category merely, meaning *one letter,*—but meaning, either that each should have his letter of credentials,—or more probably, that Paul would give them letters to several persons in Jerusalem. Meyer well remarks: "Hence we see how common in Paul's practice was the writing of Epistles. Who knows how many private letters of his, not addressed to churches have been lost? The only letter of the kind which remains to us (except the Pastoral Epistles), viz. that to Philemon, owes its preservation perhaps to the mere circumstance, that it is at the same time addressed to *the church in the house* of Philemon. See ver. 2." **χάριν**] see reff. Meyer compares Plato, Def. p. 113, E: χάρις, εὐεργεσία ἑκούσιος.

4.] **But if it** (the occasion,—dependent on the magnitude of your collection) **be worthy of my also taking the journey** (i. e. if your collection be large enough to warrant an apostolic mission in order to carry it,—not said for *security,*—nor to procure himself a fair reception at Jerusalem,—but with a sense of the dignity of an apostolic mission: "justa æstimatio sui non est superbia," Bengel), **they shall go in my company** (σὺν ἐμοὶ π. contrast to δι᾽ ἐπιστολῶν πέμψω, and observing the same order). This did apparently take place, see Acts xx. 4 ff.

5—9.] Taking up ὅταν παραγένωμαι, he *announces his plan of visiting them.*

5.] This plan was a *change from his former intention,* which had been (see 2 Cor. i. 15, 16, and note), to *pass through them to Macedonia,* and *again return to them from Macedonia,* and thence to Judæa. This he had apparently announced to them in the *lost Epistle* alluded to ch. v. 9 (or in some other), and he now tacitly drops this scheme, and announces another. For this he was charged (2 Cor. i. 17 ff.) with *levity of purpose:*—but his real motive was, *lenity towards them,* that he might not come to them in sorrow and severity (2 Cor. i. 23; ii. 1). The second plan *he adhered to:* we find him already in Macedonia when 2 Cor. was written (2 Cor. ii. 13; viii. 1; ix. 2, 4), and on his way to Corinth (2 Cor. xii. 14; xiii. 1);—and in Acts xx. 1, 2, the journey is briefly narrated. **Μακεδ. γ. διέρχ.** is not parenthetical, but διέρχ.

° προπέμψητε οὗ ἐὰν πορεύωμαι. 7 οὐ θέλω γὰρ ὑμᾶς ἄρτι
ἐν [p] παρόδῳ ἰδεῖν· ἐλπίζω γὰρ χρόνον τινὰ [q] ἐπιμεῖναι [i] πρὸς
ὑμᾶς, ἐὰν ὁ κύριος [r] ἐπιτρέψῃ. 8 [q] ἐπιμενῶ δὲ ἐν Ἐφέσῳ
ἕως τῆς [s] πεντηκοστῆς· 9 [tu] θύρα γάρ μοι [u] ἀνέῳγεν μεγάλη
καὶ [v] ἐνεργής, καὶ [w] ἀντικείμενοι πολλοί.
10 Ἐὰν δὲ ἔλθῃ Τιμόθεος, [x] βλέπετε ἵνα [y] ἀφόβως
[z] γένηται [z] πρὸς ὑμᾶς· τὸ γὰρ [ab] ἔργον [a] κυρίου [b] ἐργάζεται
ὡς κἀγώ· 11 μήτις οὖν αὐτὸν [c] ἐξουθενήσῃ, ° προπέμψατε

...ανεωγεν I_b. ABCDF KLMPℵ a b c d e f g h k l m n o 17. 47

o Acts xv. 3 reff. p here only. Gen. xxxviii. 14. Polyb. v. 68. 8. q Acts x. 48 reff. r Acts xxvi. 1 reff. Heb. vi. 3. Esth. ix. 14. s Acts ii. 1 reff. t 2 Cor. ii. 12 reff. u 2 Cor. vi. 11. v Philem. 6. Heb. iv. 12 only+. Polyb. xi. 23. 2. (-γεῖν, -γημα, ch. xii. 6. -γεια, Eph. i. 19.) w Luke xiii. 17. xxi. 15. Gal. v. 17. Phil. i. 28. 2 Thess. ii. 4. 1 Tim. i. 10. v. 14 only. L.P. Zech. iii. 1. x w. ἵνα, Col. iv. 17 only. (see 2 John 8.) w. πῶς, Luke viii. 18. ch. iii. 10. Eph. v. 15. y Luke i. 74. Phil. i. 14. Jude 12 only. Prov. i. 33. Wisd. xvii. 4 Bℵ Ald. (-βος, AC compl.) only. z ch. ii. 3 reff. a ch. xv. 58. b Acts xiii. 41 reff. c = Rom. xiv. 3 reff.

for εαν, αν D[1]F. πορευσομαι P; -σωμαι b[1] o [-ομαι LM f k 47].
7. for 1st γαρ, δε I_b: om Syr. rec (for 2nd γαρ) δε, with KL rel syr [æth] Thdrt: txt ABCDFI_bMPℵ 17 latt Syr copt goth Chr_1 Damasc [Euthal-ms Ambrst]. rec επιτρεπη (*the force of the aor not being perceived: see note*), with DFK rel [Thdrt Damasc, -πει L c f k[2]]: txt ABCI_bM P(-ψει) ℵ d m 17 Chr_1 Thl-mss, *permiserit* latt.
8. om εν F(not G). 9. om και αντ. πολ. L.
10. οφοβως B[1]: αφοβος P 47. rec και εγω, with DF rel Orig[-c]$_2$ Chr_1(καθως κ. εγ.): εγω, omg και, BM 67[2]: txt ACKLPℵ n 17 Thdrt Damasc.
11. om ουν D[1](and lat) F[not F-lat] goth arm Ambrst.

is opposed (by δέ) to παραμενῶ. The pres. implies, as in E. V., his *now matured plan*,—not, as in the erroneous subscription of the Epistle, that he was *on his way* through Macedonia, when he wrote the word. **6. παραμενῶ**] This, of which he speaks uncertainly, was accomplished; he spent (Acts xx. 3) three months, and those (ib. ver. 6) the three winter months, in Greece (at Corinth). **ὑμεῖς**, Meyer justly remarks, is emphatic, and conveys an affectionate preference, in his present plan, for them. **οὗ**, with a verb of motion. The account of this is that the ideas of motion and rest are both involved in the verb: rest, when the motion is accomplished. So Luke x. 1;—Soph. Trach. 40, κεῖνος δ' ὅπου βέβηκεν οὐδεὶς οἶδε:—Xen. Hell. vii. 1. 25, ὅπου βουληθεῖεν ἐξελθεῖν. See Kühner, § 623, Anm. 2. Whither he should go from Corinth, was as yet uncertain, see ver. 4. **7.**] **For I am not willing, this time to see you in passing.** There is a slight, but a very slight, reference to his change of purpose (see above); but we must not take ἄρτι with θέλω (which Meyer charges Neander with doing, but clearly in error, see Pfl. u. Leit. p. 415 note): rather the ἄρτι refers to the *occasion*, the news from 'them of Chloe,' which had made it advisable that he should not *now* pay them a mere passing visit. **γάρ**] ground of οὐ θέλω—but not the ultimate one, see above. **ἐπιτρέψῃ**] **shall have permitted me**, i. e. 'if it shall so turn out, in the Lord's direction of my work, that I shall then find my way open to do so.' **8, 9.**] *His present plan regarding his stay in Ephesus* (where he was writing). **τ. πεντηκ.**] viz. that *next coming*. This probably happened so, or nearly so, notwithstanding the tumult of Acts xix.: for he already (see there vv. 21, 22) was *meditating his departure*, and had sent on two of his company, when the tumult occurred. **θύρα**, see reff.: *an opportunity of action*. **μεγάλη** refers to the *extent* of the action thus opened before him: **ἐνεργής**, to its *requirements*: neither of them (though μεγάλη *may* be referred to θύρα) properly agreeing with the *figure*, but both with the *reality*. Meyer compares Plato, Phædr. p. 245, A: μουσῶν ἐπὶ ποιητικὰς θύρας ἀφίκηται. **ἀντικ. πολλ.**] See Acts xix. 9, 23 ff.

10, 11.] *Recommendation of Timothy to their good reception and offices.* He had preceded Paul (Acts xix. 22) in the journey to Macedonia. From **ἐὰν ἔλθῃ**, it would appear to have been *probable*, but not quite certain, that he would visit them. In ch. iv. 17, he is described as sent on *for that purpose*: so that the ἐάν may merely refer to the uncertainties of the journey. **10. βλ. ἵνα ἀφόβ. γ.**] There must have been some special reason for this caution respecting Timothy, besides that assigned by Meyer, al., that he would naturally be depreciated as only a subordinate of Paul, whom so many of them opposed. His *youth* occurs to us, mentioned 1 Tim. iv. 12: but even that is not enough, and would hardly be intended here, without some reference to it. De Wette's conjecture may not be without foundation, that he was perhaps of a *timid*

δὲ αὐτὸν [d] ἐν [d] εἰρήνῃ, ἵνα ἔλθῃ πρός με· [e] ἐκδέχομαι γὰρ
αὐτὸν μετὰ τῶν ἀδελφῶν.
12 Περὶ δὲ Ἀπολλὼ τοῦ ἀδελφοῦ, [f] πολλὰ [g] παρεκάλεσα αὐτόν, [g] ἵνα ἔλθῃ πρὸς ὑμᾶς μετὰ τῶν ἀδελφῶν·
καὶ [h] πάντως οὐκ [i] ἦν [ik] θέλημα [il] ἵνα νῦν ἔλθῃ, ἐλεύσεται
δὲ ὅταν [m] εὐκαιρήσῃ.
13 [n] Γρηγορεῖτε, [o] στήκετε ἐν τῇ πίστει, [p] ἀνδρίζεσθε,
[q] κραταιοῦσθε. 14 [r] πάντα ὑμῶν ἐν ἀγάπῃ [s] γινέσθω.
15 [t] Παρακαλῶ δὲ ὑμᾶς, ἀδελφοί· οἴδατε τὴν [u] οἰκίαν
Στεφανᾶ, [v] ὅτι ἐστὶν [w] ἀπαρχὴ τῆς Ἀχαΐας καὶ [x] εἰς [y] δια-

ABCDF KLMPℵ a b c d e f g h k l m n o 17 47

d Luke ii. 29. Acts xvi. 36 (reff.). ch. vii. 15. James ii. 16 al. Judg. xviii. 6 B (εἰς εἰρ. A Ald. compl.). e Acts xvii. 16 reff. f adv. (in gospp., Matt. ix. 14. Mark iii. 12 al5.) ver. 19. James iii. 2. Eccl. xii. 10 (?). g constr., ch. i. 10 reff. w. inf., Rom. xii. 1 reff. h Acts xxi. 22 reff. i Matt. xviii. 14. k of man, ch. vii. 37 reff. l see Matt. vii. 12. Mark vi. 25. ix. 30 al. m Mark vi. 31. Acts xvii. 21 (reff.) only. n = Mark xiii. 37. 1 Thess. v. 6 al. fr. (Jer. v. 6.) o Rom. xiv. 4 reff. p here only. Josh. i. 6. q Luke i. 80. ii. 40. Eph. iii. 16 only. Neh. ii. 18. (-ος, 1 Pet. v. 6.) r constr., here only. s = ch. ix. 15. xiv. 26, 40. t ver. 12. u = John iv. 53. Gen. 1. 8. v constr., ch. iii. 20. Gal. i. 11 al. w Rom. viii. 23 reff. x Acts xiii. 48 reff. y ch. xii. 5. Acts i. 17. vi. 1 al.†

for δε, ουν MP : om ℵ[1]. εμε BD[1]F Orig[-c_2](txt_2) Damasc. om μετα των αδελφ. B.

12. om απολλω ℵ[1](ins ℵ-corr[1]) æth. ins δηλω υμιν οτι bef πολλα D[1]Fℵ[1] latt [not am harl[2]] goth [Ambrst].

13. om τη F. ins και bef κραταιουσθε A D-gr vulg(and F-lat) Syr copt æth [Pel] : om BC F[-gr] KLPℵ rel D-lat(with G-lat fri) syr goth Chr_1 [Euthal-ms] Thdrt Damasc Thl Œc Ambrst. [M doubtful.]

15. om δε D[1]-gr ℵ[1] 71 goth æth arm. aft στεφανα ins και φορτουνατου Dℵ[3] am(with demid fuld harl) arm Thdrt Damasc Ambrst : και φορτ. και αχαϊκου C[1] F a vulg-ed(with [demid] tol F-lat) syr-w-ast(and mg-gr) (*additions from ver* 17). for εστιν, εισιν C[1](appy) DF [vulg arm] $Orig\text{-}int_1$.

disposition. Meyer objects that we have no historical trace of this: but I think some are to be found in 1 Tim.:—e. g. iii. 15; v. 22, 23. **τὸ ἔργον κυρ.**] see ref., note. **11. ἐν εἰρήνῃ**] χωρὶς μάχης καὶ φιλονεικίας, Theophyl., and similarly Chrys. **ἵνα ἔλθ.**] the aim of προπέμψ. **ἐκδέχ. γὰρ αὐτ.**] καὶ τοῦτο φοβοῦντος αὐτοὺς ἦν. ἵνα γὰρ εἰδότες, ὅτι πάντα εἰρήσεται πρὸς αὐτὸν ἅπερ ἂν πάθῃ, ἐπιεικέστεροι γένωνται, διὰ τοῦτο προσέθηκεν· **ἐκδ. γ. αὐτ.** Chrys. Hom. xliv. p. 407. Theophyl. adds, ἅμα δὲ καὶ αἰδεσιμώτερον αὐτὸν ποιῶν, εἴγε οὕτως ἀναγκαῖον τοῦτον ἔχει, ὥστε ἐκδέχεσθαι αὐτόν. By **μετὰ τῶν ἀδελφῶν** it would appear, comparing ver. 12, that more brethren besides Erastus (Acts xix. 22) accompanied Timotheus to Macedonia. It is hardly probable (as Calov. and De W., al.), that μετὰ τ. ἀδ. is to be taken with ἐκδέχομαι: '*I and the brethren* expect him.' **12.**] *Of Apollos: that he was not willing at present to go to them.* **δέ**, transitional.

On the construction of **περὶ . . . . ἀδ.**, see on ver. 1. **παρεκάλ. ἵνα ἔλθῃ**] ἵνα denotes the aim, not only the purport of the exhortation. See remarks on ch. xiv. 13. "Ideo excusat, ne suspicentur Corinthii ab eo fuisse impeditum . . . . Apud se quærere poterant: Cur hos potius quam Apollo nobis misit? Respondet, minime per se stetisse, &c." Calvin. Meyer remarks, perhaps the Corinthians had expressly desired that Apollos should be sent to them. **μετὰ τ. ἀδελφ.**] perhaps, those who went with Timotheus (see above): perhaps, those who were to bear this letter (ver. 17). **καί**] **and**, not, '*but*:' see John xvi. 32; Rom. i. 13. It merely couples the exhortation with its result. **θέλημα**] Evidently the *will of Apollos*, not, as Theophyl.: τουτέστιν, ὁ θεὸς οὐκ ἤθελεν. **ὅταν εὐκαιρ.**] The present καιρός not seeming to him a suitable one: apparently on account of the divisions hinted at in the beginning of the Epistle. **13.**] εἶτα δεικνὺς ὅτι οὐκ ἐν τοῖς διδασκάλοις, ἀλλὰ καὶ ἐν ἑαυτοῖς ὀφείλουσι τὰς ἐλπίδας ἔχειν τῆς σωτηρίας, φησί· **γρηγ. κ.τ.λ.** Chrys., who adds: διὸ λέγει, **γρηγορεῖτε**, ὡς καθευδόντων· **στήκετε**, ὡς σαλευομένων· **ἀνδρίζεσθε**, **κραταιοῦσθε**, ὡς μαλακιζομένων. **πάντα ὑμ. ἐν ἀγάπῃ γινέσθω**, ὡς στασιαζόντων. p. 407 f. **ἀνδρίζ.**] Aristot. Eth. iii. 6. 12:—ἅμα δὲ καὶ ἀνδρίζονται, ἐν οἷς ἐστιν ἡ ἀλκή, ἢ καλὸν τὸ ἀποθανεῖν. Wetst.: where see other examples. **15—18.**] *Recommendation of the family of Stephanas to their honourable regard: and by occasion, expression of his own joy at the presence of Stephanas and his companions.* **15.**] Some expositors (Erasm., Wolf, al.) take **οἴδατε** as *imperative*, and regard *it* as the command: but the imperative use of οἴδατε

κονίαν τοῖς [z] ἁγίοις [x] ἔταξαν ἑαυτούς· 16 [t] ἵνα καὶ ὑμεῖς
[a] ὑποτάσσησθε [b] τοῖς [b] τοιούτοις, καὶ παντὶ τῷ [c] συνεργοῦντι καὶ [d] κοπιῶντι. 17 [e] χαίρω δὲ [e] ἐπὶ τῇ [f] παρουσίᾳ
Στεφανᾶ καὶ Φορτουνάτου καὶ Ἀχαϊκοῦ, ὅτι τὸ [g] ὑμέτερον
[h] ὑστέρημα αὐτοὶ [i] ἀνεπλήρωσαν· 18 [k] ἀνέπαυσαν γὰρ τὸ
ἐμὸν [l] πνεῦμα καὶ τὸ ὑμῶν. [m] ἐπιγινώσκετε οὖν [b] τοὺς
[b] τοιούτους.

19 Ἀσπάζονται ὑμᾶς αἱ [n] ἐκκλησίαι τῆς Ἀσίας. ἀσπάζεται ὑμᾶς [o] ἐν [o] κυρίῳ [p] πολλὰ Ἀκύλας καὶ Πρίσκιλλα,

z Acts ix. 13 reff. Rom. i. 7.
a Rom. viii. 7, 20 reff.
b ch. vii. 15, 28.
c Mark xvi. 20. Rom. viii. 28. 2 Cor. vi. 1. James ii. 22 only†. Esdr. vii. 2. 1 Macc. xii. 1 only. (-γος, ch. iii. 9.)
d ch. xv. 10 reff.
e constr., ch. xiii. 6 reff.
f = 2 Cor. vii. 6, 7. Phil. i. 26. ii. 12 al.† Macc. viii. 12. xv. 21 only.
g = ch. xv. 31.
h 2 Cor. viii. 13, 14. ix. 12. xi. 9. Phil. ii. 30. Col. i. 24. 1 Thess. iii. 10. P., exc. Luke xxi. 4. Judg. xviii. 10.
i ch. xiv. 16 reff.
k = Matt. xi. 28. 2 Cor. vii. 13. Philem. 7, 20. 1 Chron. xxii. 9, 18.
l = Acts xvii. 16 reff.
m = 2 Cor. vi. 9. Deut. i. 17. xxxiii. 9. (see 1 Thess. v. 12.)
n Rom. xvi. 16 reff.
o Rom. xvi. 2, 8, 12 al.
p ver. 12 reff.

16. om 1st *και* M. aft *και κοπιωντι* ins *εν υμιν* F Ambrst.
17. rec *φουρτουνατου*, with KMP rel Chr-ed Thdrt-ed [Euthal-ms Damasc-ed] : txt ABCDFLℵ e m 17. 47. rec (for *υμετερον*) *υμων*, with AKLℵ rel Chr_1 [Euthal-ms] Thdrt Damasc : txt BCDF[M]P m 17. rec *ουτοι*, with BCKLPℵ rel [Euthal-ms] Thdrt Damasc : txt ADFM vulg Syr [syr] Chr_1 Œc (*illi* D-lat [fri] : *ipsi* [*aut*] *illi* G-lat : *ipsi* vulg [Ambrst]).
18. aft *γαρ* ins *και* D^1F latt goth Ambrst Pel Bede. *τοις τοιουτοις* P.
19. om A 34 [om 1st clause a m]. aft *αι εκκλησιαι* add *πασαι* CP 47 Syr Chr_1. rec *ασπαζονται* (for -ε-), with BFLM rel [latt &c Chr_1 Euthal-ms Thdrt Damasc] : txt C D[-gr] KPℵ c goth [Thdrt-c_1]. *πολλα* bef *εν κυριω* M a 17. 74 arm : om *εν κυρ.* 123 Ambrst. *ακυλας* bef *πολλα* D [fri]. for *πρισκιλλα*, *πρισκα* BMPℵ 17 am(with demid harl) fri copt goth arm Pel.

for ἴστε) seems to be without example. We must therefore understand it as indicative, and the construction is the well-known attraction, *οἶδά σε τίς εἶ* (Meyer). **ἀπαρχή**] See Rom. xvi. 5: *the first Achæan converts.* **ἔταξαν**, plur., referring to the noun of number, *οἰκία*. This family were among the few *baptized by Paul*, see ch. i. 16. **ἔταξαν ἑαυτούς**] So Demosth. de falsa legat.: *βούλομαι δὲ ὑπομνῆσαι εἰς τίνα τάξιν ἔταξεν ἑαυτὸν Αἰσχίνης*, Wetst.: where see other examples. The *ἑαυτούς* is not without meaning—they voluntarily devoted their services. **εἰς διακ. τοῖς ἁγίοις**] **to service for the saints**: in what way, does not appear: but perhaps, from the fact of Stephanas being at that time in Ephesus,—for journeys and missions. **16.**] **καὶ ὑμεῖς, you in your turn,**—in return for their self-devotion. **ὑποτάσσ.**] viz. in honouring their advice and being ready to be directed by them: there is an allusion to ἔταξαν ἑαυτούς above. **τοῖς τοιούτοις**] *to such persons*, meaning the individuals of Stephanas's family, whom they knew. See the usage of *ὁ τοιοῦτος* in reff. **συνεργοῦντι**] viz. with *τοῖς τοιούτοις*.

17.] Perhaps Fortunatus and Achaicus were members of the family of Stephanas. The Fortunatus mentioned by Clement at the end of his Ep. i. to the Corinthians (c. 59, p. 328) may be the same. **παρουσίᾳ**] viz. in Ephesus. **τὸ ὑμέτερον ὑστ.**] **The want of you** (ref.): i. e. of your society. Grotius interprets it, "Quod vos omnes facere oportuit, id illi fecerunt: certiorem me fecere de vestris morbis," and holds them to have been *οἱ Χλοῆς* of chap. i. 11. But it is very improbable that he should mention thus a family so distinguished as this: he names them just after, ch. i. 16, as the household of Stephanas:—and still more improbable that one of so fine feeling should add of the bearers of such tidings, *ἀνέπαυσαν κ.τ.λ.*, which would on that hypothesis be almost ironical.

18. καὶ ὑμῶν] this is a beautiful expression of true affection used in consciousness of the effect of this epistle on them: q. d. 'it is to their presence here that you owe much of that in this my letter which I know will refresh and cheer your spirits.' Theophyl. explains it: *ἔδειξεν αὐτοῖς ὅτι ἡ αὐτοῦ ἀνάπαυσις, αὐτῶν ἐστιν. ὥστε ἐπεί, ἐμοῦ ἀναπαυθέντος περὶ αὐτῶν, καὶ ὑμεῖς ἐκερδήσατε αὐτὸ τοῦτο, τὴν ἐμὴν ἀνάπαυσιν, μηδὲν ἄχαρι πρὸς αὐτοὺς τούτους ἐνδείξησθε*:—Grot., of the announcement which they would make on their return of Paul's love for the Corinthians. But this last can hardly be. **ἐπιγινώσκετε**] **know**, the prep. giving force, and slightly altering the meaning to that of *recognition.* Grot. and Theophyl.,—*ἐν τιμῇ αὐτοὺς ἔχετε.* **19, 20.**] *Salutations.*

19. ἐν κυρίῳ] see note, Rom. xvi. 2.

q Rom. xvi. 5. r Acts ii. 46 reff. s Rom. xvi. 16 reff. t Col. iv. 18. 2 Thess. iii. 17. u = (and Paul) as above (t) only. (gospp., Matt. xxiii. 7 ‖ al4.) + v as above (t). Gal. vi. 11. Philem. 19. w Rev. xiv. 11. x James v. 12. Ps. ciii. 31. 1 Macc. x. 31. y Rom. ix. 3 reff. z here only. a Rom. xvi. 20 [24]. Rev. xxii. 21 al. b gen. subj., Phil. i. 9. Col. i. 8. Philem. 5, 7. Rev. ii. 4, 19.

ABCDF KLMPℵ a b c d f g h k m n o 17 47

σὺν [q] τῇ [qr] κατ᾽ [r] οἶκον αὐτῶν [q] ἐκκλησίᾳ.
20 ἀσπάζονται ὑμᾶς οἱ ἀδελφοὶ πάντες. ἀσπάσασθε ἀλλήλους ἐν [s] φιλήματι ἁγίῳ.
21 Ὁ [tu] ἀσπασμὸς [tv] τῇ ἐμῇ [v] χειρὶ Παύλου.
22 [w] εἴ τις οὐ φιλεῖ τὸν κύριον, [x] ἤτω [y] ἀνάθεμα. [z] μαραναθά.
23 ἡ [a] χάρις τοῦ [a] κυρίου Ἰησοῦ [a] μεθ᾽ ὑμῶν.
24 ἡ ἀγάπη [b] μου μετὰ πάντων ὑμῶν ἐν χριστῷ Ἰησοῦ. [ἀμήν.]

ΠΡΟΣ ΚΟΡΙΝΘΙΟΥΣ Α.

... C d.

at end ins παρ οις(ους F) και ξενιζομαι DF latt[not am fuld harl(appy, Treg) fri] goth Pel.

21. om τη C.

22. rec aft κυριον ins ιησουν χριστον, with C^{3}DFLℵ^3 e g m 47 am [fuld harl] syr copt goth [Damasc Ambrst]: ημων ιησ. χρ. KP rel vulg-ed [demid] (Syr) [æth] Chr$_1$ (Victorin$_1$): om ABC^{1}Mℵ^1 17 fri Chr-ms [Euthal-ms] Cyr$_1$.

23. aft κυριου ins ημων ALP b f k m o-17 vulg ([fuld demid &c] not am) fri Syr copt Chr$_1$ [Euthal-ms] Thl Ambrst. rec aft ιησου adds χριστου, with ACD F[-gr] KLMPℵ^3 rel latt syrr copt æth arm Chr [Euthal-ms Damasc] Ambrst: om Bℵ^1 n 17. 47 am(with tol F-lat al) goth Thdrt.

24. om μου A 73. om αμην BFM 17 fuld(and tol) fri [Euthal-ms Ambrst]: ins ACDKLPℵ rel [vulg-clem am demid syrr copt goth æth arm Chr$_1$-txt Thdrt-txt Damasc-txt].

Subscription: rec adds εγραφη απο φιλιππων δια στεφανα και φουρτουνατου και αχαικου και τιμοθεου, with KL(first inserting επιστολη) a e f g k (m) n 47 [Euthal-ms], similarly (but for φιλιππων, εφεσου) d h: εγραφη απο εφεσου B^{2}P: εγραφη απο φιλιππων μακεδονιας D^2: εγραφη απο ασιας κ.τ.λ., omg (as does m) πρ. κορ. πρωτη, b o: om altogether M l: txt AB^{1}Cℵ 17, and D^1(adding επληρωθη) F(prefixing ετελεσθη).

On Aquila and Priscilla, see Rom. xvi. 3, 4; Acts xviii. 2. They had removed from Corinth (Acts xviii. 1) to Ephesus (ib. 26), and had there, as subsequently at Rome (Rom. xvi. 3, 5), an assembly of the faithful meeting in their dwelling. **οἱ ἀδ. πάντες**—the whole Ephesian church. **ἐν φιλ. ἁγ.**] see Rom. xvi. 16, note. 21—24.] *Autograph conclusion.* **ὁ ἀσπασμός** is the *final greeting,* which, according to ref. 2 Thess., was *always in his own hand,* the rest having been written (see Rom. xvi. 22) by an amanuensis. **Παύλου** is in apposition with ἐμοῦ implied in ἐμῇ, as Il. ρ. 226, ὑμέτερον δὲ ἑκάστου θυμὸν ἀέξω: ἐμὸς τοῦ ἀθλίου βίος, and the like. See Kühner, § 499. 4. 22.] He adds, as in Col. iv. 18; Eph. vi. 24, some exhortation, or solemn sentence, *in his own hand,* as having especial weight. On the distinction between φιλεῖν and ἀγαπᾶν see notes on John xxi. 15. The negation here of the feeling of personal affection, "has no love in his heart for," is worthy of note, as connected with the curse which follows. **ἤτω ἀνάθ.**] On ἀνάθεμα, see note, Rom. ix. 3:—let him be accursed. **μαραναθά**] An Aramaic expression, מָרַן אֲתָא or מָרָנָא אֲתָא the (or our) Lord cometh (or, is come, as Chrys., al., ὁ κυρ. ἡμ. ἦλθε: in 1 John iv. 2 the same Syriac form is used to express ἐληλυθότα): probably unconnected with ἀνάθεμα: and added perhaps (Mey.) as recalling some remembrance of the time when Paul was among them: at all events, as a weighty watchword tending to recall to them the nearness of His coming, and the duty of being found ready for it:—not added, as Rückert, to stamp genuineness on the letter,—for why here rather than in other Epistles, especially as those who were to bear it were so well known? See Stanley's note.

24. ἡ ἀγ. μου] Because the Epistle had contained so much that was of a severe character, he concludes it with an expression of affection; so Chrys.: μετὰ τοσαύτην κατηγορίαν οὐκ ἀποστρέφεται, ἀλλὰ καὶ φιλεῖ καὶ περιλαμβάνει πόῤῥωθεν αὐτοὺς ὄντας. Hom. xliv. p. 411. **ἐν χρ. Ἰησ.**] τουτέστιν, οὐδὲν ἀνθρώπινον ἢ σαρκικὸν ἡ ἀγάπη μου ἔχει, ἀλλὰ πνευματική ἐστι καὶ ἐν χριστῷ. Theophyl.

ΠΡΟΣ ΚΟΡΙΝΘΙΟΥΣ Β.

I. 1 Παῦλος ἀπόστολος χριστοῦ Ἰησοῦ [a] διὰ θελήματος
θεοῦ, καὶ Τιμόθεος ὁ ἀδελφός, τῇ [b] ἐκκλησίᾳ τοῦ [b] θεοῦ τῇ
οὔσῃ ἐν Κορίνθῳ [c] σὺν τοῖς [d] ἁγίοις πᾶσιν τοῖς οὖσιν ἐν
ὅλῃ τῇ Ἀχαΐᾳ. 2 [e] χάρις ὑμῖν καὶ [e] εἰρήνη ἀπὸ θεοῦ
πατρὸς ἡμῶν καὶ κυρίου Ἰησοῦ χριστοῦ.
3 [f] Εὐλογητὸς ὁ [g] θεὸς καὶ [g] πατὴρ τοῦ κυρίου ἡμῶν

C και ειρηνη... ABCDF KLMPℵ a b c e f g h k l m n o 17. 47

a Rom. xv. 32 reff.
b 1 Cor. i. 2 reff.
c = Acts xxiii. 15. 1 Cor. i. 2. Phil. i. 1.
d Acts ix. 13 reff.
e Rom. i. 7.
f Rom. ix. 5 reff.
g Rom. xv. 6 reff.

Title. Steph *η προς τους κορινθιους δευτερα*: elz *παυλου του αποστολου η προς κορινθιους επιστολη δευτερα*, with rel: *του αγιου αποστολου παυλου επιστολη προς κορ. β′* L (h): *αρχεται προς κορινθιους β′* D[1] F(*δευτερη*): [*η πρ. κορ. β′ επ. εκτεθεισα ως εν πινακι* M:] *επιστολη προς κορ. δευτερα* k l: txt ABKℵ m(*δευτ.*) n o 17. 47, and C at top of page. (P [def.])

Chap. I. 1. rec *ιησου* bef *χριστου*, with ADGKL rel [latt Syr copt goth æth arm] Chr_1 Damasc [Ambrst]: om *ιησ. χρ.* F(and lat): txt BMPℵ 17 hal(and mar al) syr [Euthal-ms] Thdrt.

Chap. I. 1, 2.] Address and Greeting. 1. **διὰ θελ. θεοῦ**] see 1 Cor. i. 1, note. **Τιμόθεος ὁ ἀδ.**] So of Sosthenes, 1 Cor. i. 1; '*one of οἱ ἀδελφοί*;'—but perhaps in this case with peculiar emphasis: see 1 Cor. iv. 17; 1 Tim. i. 2, 18; 2 Tim. ii. 1. On his being with Paul at this time, see Prolegg. to this Epistle, § ii. 4. **σὺν τ. ἁγ. πᾶσιν . . . .**] This, and the Epistle to the Galatians, were circular letters to all the believers in the respective countries: the variation of expression in the two cases (*ταῖς ἐκκλησίαις τ. Γαλατίας*, Gal. i. 2) being accounted for by the circumstance that the matter of this Epistle concerned *directly* the *church at Corinth*, and *indirectly* all the saints in the province,—whereas that to the Galatians, being to correct deep-rooted Judaizing error, directly concerned all the *churches* of Galatia. *Achaia* comprehended Hellas and Peloponnesus; the province was so named by the Romans because they became possessed of them by subduing the *Achæan* league, Pausan. vii. 16. 7. See Acts xviii. 12. **2.**] See 1 Cor. i. 3. **3—11.**] Thanksgiving for deliverance from great danger of his life: — his ability to comfort others in affliction. Commentators have endeavoured to assign a definite purpose to this opening of the Epistle. De Wette thinks that Paul had *no* definite purpose, except to pour out the thankfulness of his heart, and to begin by placing himself with his readers in a position of religious feeling and principle far above all discord and dissension. But I cannot agree with this. His purpose shews so plainly through the whole latter part of the chapter, that it is only consistent with vv. 12—24 to find it beginning to be introduced here also. I believe that Chrys. has given the right account: *ἐλύπει λίαν αὐτοὺς κ. ἐθορύβει τὸ μὴ παραγενέσθαι ἐκεῖ τὸν ἀπόστολον, καὶ ταῦτα ἐπαγγειλάμενον, ἀλλὰ τὸν ἅπαντα ἐν Μακεδονίᾳ ἀναλῶσαι χρόνον, καὶ δοκεῖν αὐτῶν ἑτέρους προτετιμηκέναι. διὰ τοῦτο πρὸς τοῦτο ἱστάμενος τὸ θορυβεῖν* (al. *ἀνθορμοῦν*), *λέγει τὴν αἰτίαν δι' ἣν οὐ παρεγένετο· οὐ μὴν ἐξ εὐθείας αὐτὴν τίθησιν, οὐδὲ λέγει ὅτι οἶδα μὲν ὑποσχόμενος ἥξειν, ἐπειδὴ δὲ διὰ τὰς θλίψεις ἐνεποδίσθην, σύγγνωτε, κ. μὴ καταγνῶτέ τινα ὑπεροψίαν ἢ ῥᾳθυμίαν ἡμῶν· ἀλλ' ἑτέρως αὐτὸ* (al.

h = Eph. i. 17. James i. 17.
i Rom. xii. 1. Phil. ii. 1. Col. iii. 12. Heb. x. 28 only. Isa. lxiii. 15.
j = Rom. xv. 4. Acts xv. 31 al. Ps. xciii. 19.
k = Luke xvi. 25. Acts xx. 12. ch. ii. 7, 8 al. Gen. xxiv. 67.
l = Mark xii. 17. Rom. v. 2. Matt. xiv. 14 al. fr.
m Acts iii. 19. vii. 19 al.
n constr., Rom. ii. 16.
o Rom. iii. 7 reff.
p Rom. vii. 5 reff. (see note.)
q = Rom. v. 15. viii. 18.
r = 1 Thess. iv. 2.
s constr., 1 Cor. xii. 26.
t = ch. iv. 8. vii. 5. 1 Thess. iii. 4. 2 Thess. i. 6, 7. 1 Tim. v. 10. Heb. xi. 37 (Matt. vii. 14. Mark iii. 9) only. Ps. cxix. 1.
u posn., see ch. xii. 19 reff. and note.

Ἰησοῦ χριστοῦ, ὁ [h] πατὴρ τῶν [i] οἰκτιρμῶν καὶ θεὸς πάσης
[j] παρακλήσεως, 4 ὁ [k] παρακαλῶν ἡμᾶς [l] ἐπὶ πάσῃ τῇ
θλίψει ἡμῶν, [m] εἰς τὸ δύνασθαι ἡμᾶς [k] παρακαλεῖν τοὺς
ἐν πάσῃ θλίψει διὰ τῆς [j] παρακλήσεως [n] ἧς [k] παρακαλούμεθα αὐτοὶ ὑπὸ τοῦ θεοῦ, 5 ὅτι καθὼς [o] περισσεύει τὰ
[p] παθήματα τοῦ χριστοῦ [q] εἰς ἡμᾶς, οὕτως [r] διὰ τοῦ
χριστοῦ [o] περισσεύει καὶ ἡ [j] παράκλησις ἡμῶν. 6 [s] εἴτε
δὲ [t] θλιβόμεθα, ὑπὲρ τῆς [u] ὑμῶν [j] παρακλήσεως καὶ σω-

ABCD KLMP abce ghkl no17.4

3. om 2nd ο F.

4. for επι, εν C 1 n Eus_1 Chr_1 $Antch_1$ $Procop_1$. (P [def.]) om ημων M Hil Ambr: υμων 3. for εις, ινα F [*ut possimus* latt]. ins και bef αυτοι D^1F latt $Ambr_1$ Bede (not fri Jer_1 Ambrst). (P [def.]) for υπο, απο F(not G) 109.

5. for τα παθηματα, το παθημα D^1 [D-gr, Tischdf: τα παθητα m]. aft ουτως ins και D^1F m 17. 80 latt copt goth. (vulg Damasc om και below.) rec om του (bef 2nd χριστου): ins ABCDFKM P(appy) ℵ rel $Orig_1$[om δ. τ. $χ._1$].—om from περισσ. to περισσ. L.

6. for ειτε δε, ει δε D^1[-gr] 32: om δε C. for 1st υμων, ημων L. om 1st

τοῦτο) κ. μεγαλοπρεπέστερον κ. ἀξιοπιστότερον κατασκευάζει, ἐπαίρων τῇ παραμυθίᾳ τὸ πρᾶγμα, ἵνα μηδὲ ἐρωτῶσι λοιπὸν τὴν αἰτίαν, δι᾽ ἣν ὑστέρησε. Hom. i. p. 420. Calvin, somewhat differently: "Incipit ab hac gratiarum actione, partim ut Dei bonitatem prædicet, partim ut animet Corinthios suo exemplo ad persecutiones fortiter sustinendas: partim ut pia gloriatione se efferat adversus malignas obtrectationes pseudapostolorum." But this does not touch the matter of *the postponed journey to Corinth*, which through the latter part of the chapter is coming more and more visibly into prominence, till it becomes the direct subject in ver. 23.

3.] εὐλ., Blessed (above all others) **is . . . . ὁ θ. κ. πατ. . . . .] The God and Father of our Lord Jesus Christ.** Here, as in ref. Rom., De Wette would render, '*God, and the Father*' . . . ., which grammatically is allowable; but I prefer the other rendering, on account of its greater verisimilitude and simplicity.

ὁ π. τ. οἰκτιρ.] οἰκτ. can hardly be the gen. of the *attribute*, as De W. and Grot., seeing that οἰκτ. is plural and refers to *acts* of mercy; but as Chrys., p. 421, ὁ οἰκτιρμοὺς τοσούτους ἐπιδειξάμενος: see ref. James. This meaning De W. himself recognizes in ὁ θ. πάσης παρακλ.,—'the God who works all (possible) comfort,' and refers to ὁ θεὸς τ. ἐλπίδος, Rom. xv. 13. **4.]** The Apostle in this Epistle uses mostly the *first person plur.*, perhaps as including Timothy, perhaps, inasmuch as he writes *apostolically* (cf. ἡμᾶς τοὺς ἀποστόλους, of himself and Apollos, 1 Cor. iv. 9), as speaking of the Apostles in common. This however will not explain all places where it occurs elsewhere: e.g. 1 Thess. ii. 18, ἠθελήσαμεν ἐλθεῖν πρὸς ὑμᾶς, ἐγὼ μὲν Παῦλος, καὶ ἅπαξ κ. δίς,—where see note. So that after all perhaps it is best to regard it merely as an idiomatic way of speaking, when often only the singular is intended.

In order that we may be able: not, 'so that we are able.' διὰ τοῦτο γὰρ παρεκάλεσεν ἡμᾶς, φησίν, ἵνα ἡμεῖς ἀλλήλους παρακαλῶμεν. Chrys. ib. "Non sibi vivebat Apostolus, sed Ecclesiæ: ita quicquid gratiarum in ipsum conferebat Deus, non sibi soli datum reputabat, sed quo plus ad alios juvandos haberet facultatis." Calv.

ἧς, attr. for ᾗ, or perhaps (Winer, edn. 6, § 24. 1) for ἣν (παράκλησιν παρακαλεῖν).

5.] 'As He is, so are we in this world:' 1 John iv. 17. **As the sufferings of Christ** (*endured by Christ*, whether in his own person, or in his mystical body the Church, see Matt. xxv. 40, 45) **abound towards us** (i. e. *in our case*, see reff.);—**even so through Christ our consolation also abounds.** The form of expression is altered in the latter clause: instead of ἡ παράκλησις τοῦ χριστοῦ περισ. we have ἡ παράκ. ἡμῶν περισσ. διὰ τοῦ χριστοῦ. And not without reason:—we *suffer*, because *we are His members*: we *are consoled* because *He is our Head*. There is no *comparison* (as Chrys., p. 422, οὐ γὰρ ὅσα ἔπαθε, φησίν, ἐπάθομεν μόνον, ἀλλὰ καὶ περισσά) between the personal sufferings of Christ, and theirs. **6.]** And all this for your benefit. **But whether we are afflicted,** (it is) **on behalf of your**

τηρίας τῆς [v] ἐνεργουμένης ἐν [w] ὑπομονῇ τῶν αὐτῶν [q] παθημάτων [x] ὧν καὶ ἡμεῖς πάσχομεν, καὶ ἡ [y] ἐλπὶς ἡμῶν
[z] βεβαία [a] ὑπὲρ ὑμῶν· [t] εἴτε [k] παρακαλούμεθα, ὑπὲρ τῆς
[u] ὑμῶν [j] παρακλήσεως καὶ σωτηρίας, 7 εἰδότες ὅτι ὡς
[b] κοινωνοί ἐστε τῶν [q] παθημάτων, οὕτως καὶ τῆς [j] παρακλήσεως. 8 [c] Οὐ γὰρ θέλομεν ὑμᾶς [c] ἀγνοεῖν, ἀδελφοί,
[d] ὑπὲρ τῆς θλίψεως ἡμῶν τῆς γενομένης ἐν τῇ Ἀσίᾳ,
ὅτι [e] καθ' [e] ὑπερβολὴν [f] ὑπὲρ δύναμιν [g] ἐβαρήθημεν, ὥστε

v Rom. vii. 5 reff.
w Rom. ii. 7 reff.
x attr., Acts i. 1 reff.
y constr., w. gen. of person, Acts xxviii. 20. Phil. i. 20.
z = Rom. iv. 16 (reff.). Heb. iii. 14. vi. 19. ix. 17.
a = Phil. i. 7.
b 1 Cor. x. 18, 20 reff.
c Rom. i. 13. xi. 25. 1 Cor. x. 1. xii. 1. 1 Thess. iv. 13.
d = John i. 30. ch. viii. 23. 2 Thess. ii. 1.
e Rom. vii. 13 reff.
f = Acts xxvi. 13 al.
g Matt. xxvi. 43 (‖ Mk. v. r.). Luke ix. 32. xxi. 34. ch. v. 4. 1 Tim. v. 16 only †. Isa. i. 4 Symm. [Aq., &c.?]

και σωτηριας B 17. 176. rec has ειτε παρακαλουμεθα υπερ της υμων παρακλησεως και σωτηριας bef και η ελπις ημων βεβαια υπερ υμων : ειτε παρακ. υπερ τ. υμ. παρακλησεως της ενεργουμενης εν υπομονη των αυτ. παθ. ων κ. ημ. π. και η ελπ., omg και σωτηριας, ACMPℵ am(with flor fuld[2] harl tol[1]) fri Syr copt æth (arm Ephr$_1$) Antch$_1$ [Ambrst (Jer$_1$)], and, but insg και σωτηριας, m fuld[1] : *sive consolamur pro vestra consolatione sive exhortamur pro vestra exhortatione et salute* vulg-ed(with demid): txt (BDFK)L rel syr[has της σωτηριας w-ast] goth Chr$_1$ Thdrt Damasc Phot Thl Œc.—om αυτων K : αυτου b c g k o.—ως D[1]F (G-lat has both).—for ημων, υμων B o.

7. rec (for ως) ωσπερ, with D[2.3][-gr] KL rel Chr$_1$ Thdrt: οι (= ει?) F[-gr], *si* D-lat Syr: om G-lat: *sicut* F-lat [vulg Ambrst]: txt ABC D[1][-gr] MPℵ 17 Orig$_1$ Ephr$_1$ Damasc. των παθηματων bef εστε DF latt goth. om ουτως F[not F-lat] D-lat Syr goth.

8. for υπερ, περι ACDFPℵ b m[2] o 17. 47 Orig[-c$_1$] Bas$_1$ Chr$_1$ Thdrt Antch$_1$ Tert: txt BKLM rel [Chr$_2$] Damasc Thl Œc. rec aft γεν. ins ημιν, with D[3][-gr] KLℵ[3] rel [syrr copt-wilk goth æth] Bas$_1$ Chr$_2$ Thdrt [Antch] Damasc Ambrst: om ABC D[1]FMPℵ[1] 17 latt [arm] Orig[-c$_1$ Euthal-ms] (Tert$_1$) Jer$_1$. for υπερ, παρα D[1.]F. rec εβαρηθημεν bef υπερ δυναμιν, with DFKL rel vulg syrr goth Chr$_1$ Thdrt [Antch] Damasc Tert Ambrst: txt ABCMPℵ m 17 fri arm [(Orig-c$_1$) Euthal-ms] Bas$_1$ Jer$_1$.

comfort (εἰς τὸ δύνασθαι κ.τ.λ. ver. 4, only now applied to the Corinthians) **and salvation** (the great end of the παράκλησις), **which** (viz. παράκλησις and σωτηρία) **is working** (not, as Chrys., Theophyl., Estius, Beza, al., '*being worked*:' the passive does not occur in St. Paul) **in the endurance of the same sufferings which we also suffer;—and our hope is stedfast on your behalf** (that you *will* endure hardness, and be consoled and saved); **—or whether we are comforted,** (it is) **for your comfort and salvation.** This place of the words καὶ—ὑμῶν agrees best with the sense, besides being in accordance with the best MSS. Their position has perhaps been altered to bring the two parts of the dilemma closer together, and because ἐλπὶς ἡμῶν seemed to suit the part. εἰδότες, and the future supposed to be implied after οὕτως καί (as in E. V.). The objection to this is (as De W.) that the ἐλπίς clearly must be referred to σωτηρία, which however is not hinted at in ver. 7. **7.**] **εἰδότες** refers back to παρακαλούμεθα:—**we are comforted with the assurance that,** &c. After οὕτως καί understand not ἔσεσθε, but ἐστε: he is speaking generally, of the community of consolation *subsisting* mutually between himself and the Corinthians; and it was this thought which helped to console him. **8.**] see var. read. It is generally supposed that the tribulation here spoken of was the danger into which Paul was brought by the tumult at Ephesus, related in Acts xix. This opinion has been recently defended by Neander, Wieseler, and Dr. Davidson, but impugned by De Wette, on the grounds, (1) that ἐν τῇ Ἀσίᾳ can hardly refer to Ephesus, which Paul generally *names*, 1 Cor. xv. 32; xvi. 8; (2) that he was not in danger of his life in this tumult. The first ground is hardly tenable: there would be an appropriateness in ἐν τῇ Ἀσίᾳ here, as he has in his mind an apologetic account of the reasons which hindered him from leaving those parts and coming to them. I own, however, that the strong expressions here used do not seem to me to find their justification in any thing which we know of that tumult or its consequences. I am unable to assign *any other event* as in the Apostle's mind: but the expressions seem rather to regard a *deadly sickness*, than a persecution: see below, vv. 9, 10. **καθ' ὑπερβ.** signifies the greatness of the affliction itself, objectively considered: **ὑπὲρ**

h ἐξαπορηθῆναι ἡμᾶς καὶ i τοῦ ζῆν· 9 ἀλλὰ αὐτοὶ ἐν
j ἑαυτοῖς τὸ k ἀπόκριμα τοῦ θανάτου l ἐσχήκαμεν, m ἵνα μὴ
no πεποιθότες n ὦμεν o ἐφ' j ἑαυτοῖς, ἀλλ' o ἐπὶ τῷ θεῷ τῷ
p ἐγείροντι τοὺς νεκρούς, 10 ὃς ἐκ q τηλικούτου r θανάτου
s ἐῤῥύσατο ἡμᾶς καὶ s ῥύσεται, t εἰς ὃν tu ἠλπίκαμεν ὅτι
καὶ ἔτι s ῥύσεται, 11 v συνυπουργούντων καὶ ὑμῶν ὑπὲρ

d ρυεται ... ABCDF KLMPℵ a b c d f g h k l m n o 17. 47

h ch. iv. 8 only. Ps. lxxxvii. 15 only. i constr., see Acts iii. 12 reff. j 1st pers., ch. iii. 1 reff. k here only +. l ch. ii. 13. vii. 5. m = John i. 31. n Heb. ii. 13, from Isa. viii. 17. o constr., as above (n). Mark x. 24. Luke xi. 22. xviii. 9 only. Ps. ii. 12. w. acc., ch. ii. 3 reff. p = 1 Cor. xv. 4 reff. q Heb. ii. 3. James iii. 4. Rev. xvi. 18 only +. 2 Macc. xii. 3. r = ch. xi. 23. Ps. lv. 13. (see ἀποθνήσκειν, 1 Cor. xv. 31.) s Rom. vii. 24 reff. t see Rom. xv. 12 reff. u perf., 1 Cor. xv. 19 reff. v here only +.

9. om εσχηκαμεν D^1. θεον τον εγειραντα F: εγειραντι b^1 l^1 o Cyr[-ms-p_1] Thdrt Thl.

10. for ερρυ., ερυσατο B^1. rec (for 1st ρυσεται) ρυεται (*see notes*), with D^3FKLM rel vulg-ed(with fuld F-lat) syr goth Orig[-c]$_2$(and int$_1$) Chr$_1$ Thdrt Thl Œc [Ambrst] Jer$_1$: txt BCPℵ 17. 47 G-lat am(with mar tol) copt (æth[-rom doubtful (Tischdf)]) arm (Ath$_1$) [Euthal-ms] Damasc.—om και ρυσεται A D^1[and lat] demid Syr æth-pl Chr$_{h.l.}$ om οτι B D^1[-gr] M: και bef οτι F[not F-lat]. om ετι D^2 F[not F-lat] h k [Chr$_1$] Ambrst Jer [goth æth om και also]. for 2nd ρυσ., ρυεται F[-gr] goth.

11. [for υμων] ημων A. for υπερ, περι D^1F. τη δεησει bef υπερ ημων C

δύν., the relation of it to our power of endurance, subjectively. **ὥστε ἐξ.**] **So that we utterly despaired even of life.** Such an expression surely would not be used of a tumult, where life would have been *the first thing* in danger, if Paul had been at all mixed up in it,—but to some wearing and tedious suffering, inducing despondency in minor matters, which *even reached* the hope of life itself.

9.] **ἀλλά, moreover,**—carries on and intensifies the description of his hopeless state. **We had in ourselves the response of death,** i. e. our answer within ourselves to the question, 'Life or Death?' was, 'Death.' So Vulg., Estius, Billroth, Rückert, Meyer, De Wette. **τ. ἀπόκρ.** may perhaps mean, the '*sentence*,' as Hesych.: ἀπόκριμα, κατάκριμα, ψῆφον,—and most Commentators. The perfect ἐσχήκαμεν is here (see also ch. ii. 12, 13) in a historical sense, instead of the aorist: which is unusual. Winer, edn. 6, § 40. 4 (see Moulton's note 4, p. 340), illustrates the usage by ἦλθεν καὶ εἴληφεν (τὸ βιβλίον), Rev. v. 7: see also Rev. viii. 5. **ἵνα μὴ . . .**] very similarly ch. iv. 7, ἔχομεν δὲ τὸν θησαυρὸν τοῦτον ἐν ὀστρακίνοις σκεύεσιν, **ἵνα** ἡ ὑπερβολὴ τῆς δυνάμεως **ᾖ τοῦ θεοῦ**, καὶ **μὴ ἐξ ἡμῶν**. **τῷ ἐγ. τ. νεκρούς**] Our thoughts were weaned from all hope of surviving in this life, and fixed on that better deliverance which God shall work when He raises us from the dead. To see in this expression merely a figure (De W.), and understand '*Who raiseth the dead*' as = '*Who delivers men from peril of their lives?*' because such peril is below and elsewhere (ch. xi. 23) called θάνατος,—is surely very forced. Understanding it literally as above, I cannot see how it can be spoken with reference to the Ephesian tumult. If it alludes to *any external danger*, I should be disposed to refer it to the same obscure part of Paul's history to which he alludes 1 Cor. xv. 32, where he also speaks of the *hope of the resurrection* as his great support. But there would be this objection, that these two passages can hardly refer to the *same* event; *this* evidently had taken place *since* the sending of the first Epistle.

10.] **Who rescued us from so great a death, and will rescue us,—on whom we hope that He will also continue to rescue us.** The rec. ῥύεται, has been substituted for the fut. ῥύσεται, as more appropriate. But *it* regards the *immediate* future,—the καὶ ἔτι ῥύσεται the *continuance* of God's help in time distant and uncertain. The whole verse (as De W. confesses, who although he repudiates the Ephesian tumult, yet interprets the passage as alluding to external danger) seems to favour the idea of *bodily sickness* being in the Apostle's mind.

11.] **συνυπουργούντων** — *with whom?* From the similar passage Rom. xv. 30, συναγωνίσασθαί μοι ἐν ταῖς προσευχαῖς ὑπὲρ ἐμοῦ, it would seem as if μοι should be supplied;—but he himself could hardly be said ὑπουργεῖν, though he well might ἀγωνίσασθαι. We must therefore understand the preposition either with Chrys., Hom. ii. p. 432, τουτέστιν, εὐχομένων πάντων ὑμῶν ὑπὲρ ἡμῶν,—or as merely signifying *coincidence with the purpose to be accomplished*, as in μὴ προσεῶντος ἡμᾶς τοῦ ἀνέμου, Acts xxvii. 7, where see note. **ἵνα ἐκ πολλῶν προσώπων . . .**]

ἡμῶν τῇ δεήσει, ἵνα [w] ἐκ πολλῶν [x] προσώπων τὸ [y] εἰς
ἡμᾶς [z] χάρισμα [a] διὰ πολλῶν [b] εὐχαριστηθῇ ὑπὲρ ἡμῶν.
12 Ἡ γὰρ [c] καύχησις ἡμῶν αὕτη ἐστίν, τὸ [d] μαρτύριον
τῆς [e] συνειδήσεως ἡμῶν, ὅτι ἐν [f] ἁγιότητι καὶ [g] εἰλικρινείᾳ
[h] τοῦ θεοῦ, οὐκ ἐν σοφίᾳ [i] σαρκικῇ, ἀλλ' ἐν [j] χάριτι θεοῦ,
[k] ἀνεστράφημεν ἐν τῷ κόσμῳ, [l] περισσοτέρως δὲ πρὸς ὑμᾶς.

w = ch. ii. 2. iii. 5.
x = here only. πρόςωπον ἀξιόχρεων τὸ προστησόμενον, Polyb. xv. 25. 8.
y = Acts xx. 21. xxiv. 24. ch. ii. 4 al.
z = Rom. v. 15, 16. vi. 23. xi. 29 al.+
a so 1 Cor. i. 9.
b 1 Cor. xi. 24 reff. constr., here only.
c Rom. iii. 27 reff.
d Matt. viii. 4 al. fr. Josh. xxiv. 27.
e = [John viii. 9.] Acts xxiii. 1. Rom. ii. 15 al. fr.‡ (Eccles. x. 20.) Wisd. xvii. 11 only.
f Heb. xii. 10 only+. 2 Macc. xv. 2 only.
g 1 Cor. v. 8. ch. ii. 17 only+. (-ής, Phil. i. 10.)
h so δικαιοσ. θεοῦ, Rom. iii. 21, 22.
i 1 Cor. iii. 3 reff.
j = Rom. i. 5. 1 Cor. iii. 10 al.
k = Eph. ii. 3. 1 Tim. iii. 15. 1 Pet. i. 17. 2 Pet. ii. 18. Ezek. xix. 6. see Matt. xvii. 22.
l ch. ii. 4 al[8]., Paul. Heb. ii. 1. xiii. 19 (Mark xv. 14 v. r.) only+. (-ρος, 1 Cor. xii. 23, 24.)

vulg copt Chr_2: om [*υπ. ημ.*] Sedul, syr has it with ast. for 1st *ημων*, *υμων* A [G-gr] ℵ[1](but corrd) e^2. *εν πολλω προsωπω* F[-gr] M 67^2 Chr_4[txt_1], *in multifacie* D-lat, *in multa facie* G-lat.—homœotel in P *πολλων* to *πολλων*. *υμας* 17. [for 2nd *ημων*] *υμων* BD^3 F[-gr(not G)] KLP c e^2 f g h l m n o [æth(appy, Treg)] Damasc Phot(in Œc).

12. for 2nd *ημων*, *υμων*(but corrd) ℵ[1]. rec (for *αγιοτητι*) *απλοτητι* (*see note, and Eph* vi. 5, *Col* iii. 22), with DFLℵ[3] latt syrr goth Chr_2 Thdrt Thl Œc Ambrst: txt ABCKMPℵ[1] m 17 copt arm $Clem_1$ $Orig_1$ [Euthal-ms] Antch $Damasc_2$. ins *εν* bef *ειλικρινεια* A. rec om *του*, with FKLPℵ[3a] rel $Orig_1$ Thl Œc: ins ABC DMℵ[1.3b] a m 17. 47 $Damasc_2$. ins *και* bef *ουκ* BM a m vulg(and F-lat) syr $Damasc_1$[om h.l.]. *σαρκινη* F.

"Three constructions of this verse are possible: (1) to take ἐκ πολλ. προsώπ. as well as διὰ πολλῶν with εὐχαριστηθῇ,—'*in order that the mercy shewn to me may be given thanks for on my behalf by many persons with many words*' (Storr, Opusc. ii. 253): but the rendering 'with many words,' is objectionable, see Matt. vi. 7:—(2) to take ἐκ πολλ. προsώπ. with εὐχαρ., and διὰ πολλῶν with τὸ εἰς ἡμ. χάρ.—'*in order that the mercy shewn to me by means of* (the intercession of) *many, may be given thanks for by many persons on my behalf*' (Theophyl., Billroth, Meyer, who explain ἐκ π. προsώπ. 'ex multis oribus:' Stanley, 'from many upturned *faces*'): but the position of the words is against this,—and it is more natural that the mention of the effect of the intercession should precede that of the thanksgiving. (3) Consequently, the best method is to take ἐκ πολλ. προsώπ. with τὸ εἰς ἡμ. χάρ., and διὰ πολλῶν with εὐχαρ. (Beza, Calov., Estius, Fritz., Rückert, al.):—**in order that the mercy shewn to us by the intercession of many persons, may by many be given thanks for on our behalf.**" De Wette. The emphasis of the whole being on the **ἐκ πολλῶν προsώπων**, he places it first, even before the art., after which it would naturally come. **προsώπων**, '*persons*,' a later meaning, which Phrynichus (see Wetst.) blames as used by οἱ ἀμφὶ τὰς δίκας ῥήτορες.

12—24.] Expression of his confidence in his integrity of purpose towards them (12—14), and defence of himself against the charge of fickleness of purpose in not having come to them (15—24). **12.**] **γάρ**, reason why they should help him with their united prayers. **καύχησις**] viewed in its ground and substance. But we must not say that it is *for* καύχημα: the Apostle regards the μαρτύριον and the καύχησις as coincident:—it is not the testimony, &c., *of which* he boasts, but *in which* his boasting itself consists. **ἁγιότ.**] ἁπλότητι seems to be a gloss from Eph. vi. 5:—**in holiness and sincerity of God**: i. e. either '*belonging to God*,' as ἡ δικαιοσ. αὐτοῦ, Matt. vi. 33, or '*which is the gift of God*,' as in ref. Rom.,—or better than either, as E. V., '*godly*,' i. e. maintained as in the service of and with respect to God. Calvin interprets it, '*coram Deo*.' See on ch. ii. 17; and on the senses of ἁγιότ. and ἁπλότ., Stanley's note. **οὐκ ἐν σοφ. σαρκ.**] which fleshly wisdom is any thing but holy and pure, having many windings and insincerities in order to captivate men. **ἀλλ' ἐν χάρ. θεοῦ**] **but in the grace of God**, i. e. in that χάρις which he had received (ref. Rom.) εἰς ὑπακοὴν πίστεως ἐν πᾶσιν τοῖς ἔθνεσιν—the grace of his apostleship. To this he often refers, see Rom. xii. 3, xv. 15; Eph. iii. 2, al. **περισσοτέρως**] "Non quod apud alios minus sincere conversatus fuisset; sed quia majora sinceræ suæ conversationis documenta apud Corinthios ostenderat: ut quibus gratis ac sine stipendio prædicasset evangelium, parcens eorum infirmitati." Estius. But perhaps

13 οὐ γὰρ ἄλλα γράφομεν ὑμῖν [m] ἀλλ' ἢ ἃ [n] ἀναγινώσκετε
[o] ἢ [o] καὶ [p] ἐπιγινώσκετε, ἐλπίζω δὲ ὅτι [q] ἕως [q] τέλους [p] ἐπιγνώσεσθε, 14 καθὼς καὶ [pr] ἐπέγνωτε ἡμᾶς [s] ἀπὸ [s] μέρους,
[r] ὅτι [t] καύχημα ὑμῶν ἐσμεν [u] καθάπερ καὶ ὑμεῖς ἡμῶν ἐν τῇ
[v] ἡμέρᾳ τοῦ κυρίου ἡμῶν Ἰησοῦ. 15 καὶ [w] ταύτῃ τῇ [x] πεποιθήσει ἐβουλόμην πρότερον πρὸς ὑμᾶς ἐλθεῖν, ἵνα δευτέ-

...ινα M. ABCDF KLdℵ a b c d e f g h k l m n o 17. 47

m Luke xii. 51. Num. xiii. 29. n Acts viii. 28 reff. o 1 Cor. ix. 8 reff. p Acts xxiii. 28 reff. q 1 Cor. i. 8 only (reff.). r constr., see 1 Cor. xiv. 37. s Rom. xi. 25 (reff.). xv. 15, 24. ch. ii. 5 only. t Paul (Rom. iv. 2 al8.) only, exc. Heb. iii. 6. Deut. x. 21 al. u Rom. iv. 6 reff. v 1 Cor. i. 8 reff. w dat., 1 Cor. ix. 7. xi. 5 al. x ch. iii. 4. viii. 22. x. 2. Eph. iii. 12. Phil. iii. 4 only. P. 4 Kings xviii. 19 only.

13. om αλλ' F. om ἢ ἃ A : om ἢ 4. [17] 219¹ Syr goth arm : om ἃ D¹. om η και επιγινωσκετε (*homœotel*) B o¹ 31. 41. 109. 238 Œc : om η FK 114 latt copt arm Ambrst. rec ins και bef εως, with D³[-gr] KLMP rel syr Chr₁ Thdrt [Antch₁] Thl Œc : om ABCD¹Fℵ 17 latt Syr copt goth arm Damasc [Euthal-ms Ambrst].

14. om καθ. κ. υμ. ημ. K. rec om last ημων, with ACD [K(e sil)] L rel goth Œc : ins BFMPℵ m 17 vulg Syr syr-w-ast copt æth arm Chr₁ Thdrt [Euthal-ms Antch₁ Damasc] Ambrst. aft ιησ. add χριστου D¹FMP ℵ³(but erased) b m o latt Syr syr-w-ast copt goth æth arm-ed Chr Antch Thl [Ambrst].

15. ελθειν bef προς υμας DFKL rel latt Syr copt goth Chr-ms Thdrt Thl [Ambrst] : txt ABCMPℵ (a) h m 17 syr [arm Euthal-ms] Chr Damasc.—rec προς υμας ελθειν bef προτερον, with (K h 47) copt Thdrt : ελθειν προτερον προς υμας a [Antch₁(το πρ.)] :

it may relate only to the longer time, and greater opportunities which he had had at Corinth for shewing his purity of purpose: so Calv., De W. **13, 14.**] *Confirmation of the foregoing assertion.* **For we do not write to you any other things, except those which ye read, or [even] acknowledge** (by experience of facts), **and I hope, shall [continue to] acknowledge to the end**:—i. e. 'my character in my writings is one and the same, not fickle and changing, but such as past facts have substantiated it to be, and as I hope future facts to the end of my life will continue to do.' ἀναγινώσκοντες γὰρ ἐπιγινώσκετε, ὅτι ἃ σύνιστε ἡμῖν ἐν τοῖς ἔργοις, ταῦτα καὶ ἐν τοῖς γράμμασι λέγομεν· καὶ οὐκ ἐναντιοῦται ὑμῶν ἡ μαρτυρία ταῖς ἐπιστολαῖς, ἀλλὰ συνᾴδει τῇ ἀναγνώσει ἡ γνῶσις, ἣν προλαβόντες εἴχετε (al. ἔχετε) περὶ ἡμῶν. Chrys., Hom. iii. p 443, who has the advantage of being able to express in his exposition the play of words in ἀνα- and ἐπι-γινώσκετε. **As also ye did partly** (that part of you, viz. which have fairly tried me: ἀπὸ μέρους, because they were divided in their estimate of him, and those who were prejudiced against him had shut their minds to this knowledge. Chrys. refers it to what follows: μετριάζων εἶπεν: Theophyl. to the not yet completed testimony of his ἐναρέτου βίου: Estius and Calvin, to their *inadequate estimation* of him, which he blames: but I much prefer the above. So most Commentators) **acknowledge us, that** (not '*because*,' putting a colon at μέρους, as Luth., Griesbach, and Scholz: nor is it to be joined with ἐπιγνώσεσθε, what follows being parenthesized, as Theophyl., al., Meyer, Olsh.) **we are your boast, [even] as ye [also] are ours, in the day of the Lord Jesus.** ἐσμεν, '*present*,' as of that which is a settled recognized fact. But this is no ground for its being joined with ἐπιγνώσεσθε, as Olsh. The experimental mutual knowledge of one another as a καύχημα was not confined to what should take place ἐν τῇ ἡμ. τ. κ. Ἰησοῦ, but regarded a present fact, which should receive its full completion at the day of the Lord. **15—24.**] *His defence of himself against the charge of fickleness of purpose for not having come to them.*

15.] **ταύτῃ τῇ πεπ.**, i. e. of my character being known to you as that of an earnest and sincere man. **πρότερον** belongs to ἐλθεῖν, not to ἐβουλόμην. **πρότερον,** viz. *before* he visited Macedonia, where he now was. **ἵνα δευτέραν χάριν σχῆτε**] **that you might have a second benefit** (effusion of the divine χάρις by my presence: not = χαράν as Chrys., see var. read.). **δευτέραν**, *second*, because there would thus have been opportunity for *two* visits, one in going towards Macedonia, the other in returning. This is the interpretation of De Wette, Bleek, and Wieseler, and I believe the only one which the words will bear. The other, according to which δευτέραν χάριν would mean 'a second benefit,' by my visiting you *for the second time*, is in my view unnatural, and would hardly have justified the use of δευτέραν at all. For *come when he would*, the χάρις of the *second visit* would be the δευτέρα χάρις, and the conferring a δευτέρα χάρις would have been of no signification in the present connexion, which is to state a purpose of paying them *two visits in one and the same journey*. The first *of these* he characterizes by πρότερον . . . ἐλθεῖν,—the second by δευτέρα χάρις, implying also the first. So

ραν [y] χάριν σχῆτε, 16 καὶ [z] δι᾽ ὑμῶν [za] διελθεῖν [a] εἰς Μακεδονίαν, καὶ πάλιν ἀπὸ Μακεδονίας ἐλθεῖν πρὸς ὑμᾶς καὶ
ὑφ᾽ ὑμῶν [b] προπεμφθῆναι εἰς τὴν Ἰουδαίαν. 17 τοῦτο οὖν
βουλόμενος μή τι [c] ἄρα τῇ [d] ἐλαφρίᾳ [e] ἐχρησάμην; ἢ
ἃ [f] βουλεύομαι [g] κατὰ [g] σάρκα [f] βουλεύομαι, ἵνα ᾖ [h] παρ᾽
ἐμοὶ τὸ [i] ναὶ ναί, καὶ τὸ [i] οὒ οὔ; 18 [k] πιστὸς δὲ ὁ θεός,

y = here only.
z Acts ix. 32 reff. Num. xx. 18, 20. (see Rom. xv. 28.)
a Mark iv. 35 ||. Acts xviii. 27. Rom. v. 12 only. Amos vi. 2.
b Acts xv. 3 reff.
c in interrog., Acts [vii. 1.] xxi. 38.
d here only +. (-φρός, ch. iv. 17.)
e = ch. iii. 12. (1 Cor. vii. 21 reff.)
f epp., here bis only. Acts v. 33. xxvii. 39. gospp., Luke xiv. 31. John (xi. 53 v. r.) xii. 10 only. Isa. iii. 9 al.
g Rom. i. 3 reff.
h = Rom. xii. 16 al.
i Matt. v. 37. James v. 12.
k — 1 Cor. i. 9 reff.

txt ABC(DFL)MP א-corr[1] m 17 (rel) latt syrr goth [arm Euthal-ms] Chr_1 Damasc [Ambrst].—**το** προτερον L rel [$Antch_1$] Thl Œc: το δευτερον K: om προτερον א[1]. χαραν B L(Tischdf(N. T. ed 7 [and 8])) Pא[3] 31. 71-3. 80. 115 $Thdrt_2$ [$Antch_1$]. (Chr says: χάριν δὲ ἐνταῦθα τὴν χαρὰν λέγει.) rec εχητε (*probably from similarity of* s *and* ε. *There is nothing in what Tischdf* (ed 7 [not 8]) *says against* σχῆτε *as being conformed to the tense of* ἐβουλόμην, *seeing that that word may be either imperfect or aor*), with ADFKL rel: txt BCPא $Thdrt_2$ [Euthal-ms $Antch_1$] Damasc.

16. δια F(not G). for διελθ., απελθειν A D[1][-gr] F[-gr P arm] copt Chr_1 Damasc: ελθειν a b o Œc [*proficisci* D-lat]: *proficiscerer aut transirem* G-lat: txt BC D[3][-gr] KLא rel vulg [F-lat] syrr Chr_2 Thdrt Thl [Euthal-ms Ambrst]. (*See Rom* xv. 28.) for υφ, αφ D[1]F b l o 47 Chr-mss Thdrt-ms, εφ 17.

17. for ουν, δε A; *vero igitur* goth. rec βουλευομενος, with DK rel G-lat syrr goth æth arm Thdrt Ambrst: βουλευσομενος L: txt ABCFPא a c h m o 17 vulg copt Chr_1 [Euthal-ms] Damasc. om τη F Thdrt. [εμου P b o.]

that I do not believe this passage to be relevant to the question respecting the number of visits which Paul *had made* to Corinth *previously* to writing these Epistles. See on that question, Prolegg. to 1 Cor. § v. **16.**] *If this is the same journey* which is announced in 1 Cor. xvi. 5, the idea of visiting them *in the way to* Macedonia as well as after having passed through it, must have occurred to him subsequently to the sending of that Epistle; or may even then have been a *wish*, but not expressed, from uncertainty as to its possibility,—the main and longer visit being there principally dwelt on. But perhaps the following is the more likely account of the matter. He had announced to them in the lost Epistle (see 1 Cor. v. 9) his intention, as here, of visiting them *on his way* to Macedonia: but the intelligence from "them of Chloe" had altered his intention, so that, in 1 Cor. xvi., he speaks of visiting them *after he should have passed through* Macedonia. For this he was accused of levity of purpose. Certainly, some intention of coming to them seems to have been mentioned in that lost Epistle: see 1 Cor. iv. 18. But the προπεμφθῆναι εἰς τὴν Ἰουδαίαν can hardly but be coincident with the alms-bearing scheme of 1 Cor. xvi. 4; in which case the two plans certainly are modifications of one and the same. **17.**] μή τι.. **Did I at all use levity (of purpose)? τῇ** ἐλαφ., as ἡ ἀρετή, ἡ πίστις,—the art. being generic. Olsh., De Wette, Billroth, take it to mean *'the levity of purpose which has been laid to my charge:'* Winer, *'the levity of purpose inherent in human nature.'* **Or those things which I plan, do I plan according to the flesh** (i. e. according to the changeable, self-contradictory, and insincere purposes of the mere worldly and ungodly man), **that there may be with me** (not, *so that there is* with me: he is speaking not merely of the result, but of the design: *'do I plan like the worldly, that I may shift and waver as suits me?'*) **the Yea, yea, and the Nay, nay** (i. e. both affirmation and negation concerning the same thing)? Chrys., Theodoret, Theophyl., Œc., Calv., Bengel, Billroth, Winer, al., take it thus: *'Or those things which I plan, do I plan after the flesh* (as fleshly men do), *so that my yea must* (at all events) *be yea, and my nay, nay?'* i. e. as worldly men who perform their promise at all hazards, and whatever the consequences, whereas I am under the guidance of the Spirit, and can only journey whither He permits. But this explanation is directly against the next verse, where ναὶ καὶ οὔ is clearly parallel to ναὶ ναὶ καὶ οὒ οὔ here, the words being repeated, as in ref. Matt., without altering the sense: and inconsistent with ver. 23 and ch. ii. 1, where he says that his alteration of plan arose *from a desire to spare them.* See the whole discussed in Stanley's note. **18.**] Such fickleness, you know, was not my habit in preaching to you. Chrys. gives the connexion well:

l constr., see Rom. xiv. 11. Judith xii. 4.
m 1 Tim. iii. 16.
n = Acts viii. 5 reff.
o constr., Matt. x. 14.
p Acts i. 4 reff.
q Matt. xix. 18. Mark ix. 23. Eph. iv. 9. Heb. xii. 27.
r see Rev. i. 7. xxii. 20.
s see Rom. xv. 7, 9. ch. iv. 15. viii. 19.

[l]ὅτι ὁ λόγος ἡμῶν ὁ πρὸς ὑμᾶς οὐκ ἔστιν [i]ναὶ καὶ [i]οὔ.
19 ὁ τοῦ θεοῦ γὰρ υἱὸς Ἰησοῦς χριστὸς ὁ [m]ἐν ὑμῖν δι'
ἡμῶν [mn]κηρυχθείς, δι' ἐμοῦ καὶ Σιλουανοῦ καὶ Τιμοθέου,
οὐκ ἐγένετο [i]ναὶ καὶ [i]οὔ, ἀλλὰ ναὶ ἐν αὐτῷ γέγονεν·
20 [o]ὅσαι γὰρ [p]ἐπαγγελίαι θεοῦ, ἐν αὐτῷ [q]τὸ [r]ναί, διὸ καὶ
δι' αὐτοῦ [q]τὸ [r]ἀμὴν [s]τῷ θεῷ πρὸς [s]δόξαν δι' ἡμῶν.

[O αυτου...] ABCDF KL[O] Pℵ a b c d e f g h k l m n o 17. 47

18. om *ημων* L[1][insd above the line a prima manu(appy, Tischdf)]. om *ο* (bef *προς*) D[1]. rec (for *εστιν*) *εγενετο* (*corrn to suit the supposed reference to the past?*), with D[-gr[2.]][3] KLℵ[3] rel Chr_1 Thdrt Damasc, *fuit* syrr: txt ABCD[1]FPℵ[1] 17 latt goth [copt arm Euthal-ms] Thl-marg [Ambrst].

19. rec *γαρ* bef *του θεου*, with D(F)KL rel Chr_1 Thdrt [Damasc]: txt ABCPℵ m 17 [(Euthal-ms)].—om *του* F. *χριστ.* bef *ιησ.* ACℵ[1], om *χρ.* 17. ins *ο* bef *δι' ημων* F[-gr], *qui per nos* D-lat G-lat fuld [Ambrst]. *σιλβανου* DF. for *εγενετο*, *εστι* C.

20. ins *του* bef *θεου* A f o 48. 72. 106 [Mcion-e_2(om_1)] Thdrt. rec (for *διο και δι' αυτου*) *και εν αυτω*, with D[2.3][-gr] KL rel syr Chr_1 Thdrt Thl Œc: *και δι' αυτου*, omg *διο*, D[1](and lat) $Epiph_1$(appy): txt ABCF [O(appy)] Pℵ m 17 vulg G-lat Syr copt goth arm Mcion-e_2 [Euthal-ms Thdrt-comm(appy)] Damasc Pel Fulg Bede. om 2nd *το* ℵ[1]. aft *δοξαν* ins *και τιμην* F. (not vulg nor F-lat, but *honorem per nos* over the greek in F.) om *δι* (bef *ημων*) CL[O] vulg.

καλῶς ἀντίθεσιν ἀνακύπτουσαν καταλύει. εἰ γὰρ ὑποσχόμενος, φησί, παραγενέσθαι ὑπερέθου, καὶ οὐκ ἔστι παρά σοι ναί, ναί (predicate in Chrys.'s interpretation; see above), καὶ οὔ, οὔ, ἀλλὰ νῦν ἃ λέγεις ἀνατρέπεις μετὰ ταῦτα, ὥσπερ ἐπὶ τῆς σῆς ἐπιδημίας ἐποίησας· οὐαὶ ἡμῖν, μή ποτε καὶ ἐν τῷ κηρύγματι τοῦτο γέγονεν. ἵν' οὖν μὴ ταῦτα ἐννοῶσι, μηδὲ θορυβῶνται, φησί· πιστὸς δὲ ὁ θεὸς κ.τ.λ. p. 446.

πιστ. δὲ ὁ θ., ὅτι] a form of asseveration: see reff. The δέ follows on the denial of the preceding question. **ὁ λόγ.]** **Our doctrine** (which we preached, cf. ὁ λόγος ὁ τοῦ σταυροῦ, 1 Cor. i. 18), **to you is not** (*present*, inasmuch as the character of the doctrine was present and abiding. The pres. has been altered in rec. to the easier ἐγένετο) **yea and nay** (i. e. inconsistent with itself). **19.]** *Confirmation of the last verse*, by affirming the same of the great Subject of that doctrine, as set before them by Paul and his colleagues. **χριστός**, personal—not for '*doctrina de Christo*'—HE HIMSELF is the centre and substance of all Christian preaching: see 1 Cor. i. 23, and note at ii. 2. **ὁ τοῦ θεοῦ υἱός** is prefixed for solemnity, and to shew how unlikely fickleness or change is in Christ, *being such as He is*. Cf. 1 Sam. xv. 29, 'the Strength of Israel will not lie nor repent.'

Σιλουανοῦ] so 1 Pet. v. 12; = Silas, see Acts xviii. 5 and al. He names his companions, as shewing that neither was he inconsistent with himself, nor were they inconsistent with one another. The Christ was the same, whether preached by different persons or by one person at different times. **ἀλλὰ ναὶ ἐν αὐτ. γέγ.]** 'Christus prædicatus, i. e. prædicatio nostra de Christo, facta est næ in *Ipso Christo*.' Bengel. This seems to me far better than with De Wette, al., to make ναί the subject, and γέγονεν predicatory. The absence of the art. before ναί, as well as the sense, stamps it as the predicate. 'Christ preached as the Son of God by us, **has become yea in Him**,' i. e. has been affirmed and substantiated as verity by the agency of the Lord Himself. **20.]** **ὅσαι γὰρ . . .** is an independent relative clause, as in ref.,—not the subject answering to ἐν αὐτῷ τὸ ναί as a predicate, as E. V.:—**For how many soever be the promises of God, in Him is the yea** (the affirmation and fulfilment of them all); **wherefore also through Him is the Amen, for glory to God by our** (the Apostles') **means.** This reading, which has the stronger external authority, *may* have arisen from an idea that the clause had reference to *the Amen uttered at the end of prayers*. So Theodoret, οὗ δὴ χάριν καὶ δι' αὐτοῦ τὸν τῆς εὐχαριστίας αὐτῷ προσφέρομεν ὕμνον, from which comment De Wette thinks the reading has sprung. The apparent objection to it is, that then **ἡμῶν** must mean ἡμῶν καὶ ὑμῶν, which without notice it perhaps could hardly do. In the next verse, when such is about to be its meaning, we have first **ἡμᾶς σὺν ὑμῖν**, and then in ver. 22, ἡμᾶς . . . ἡμῶν in the general sense: but here, without any such preparatory notice, δι' ἡμῶν must signify 'by means of *us Apostles*,' 'by our work in the Lord.' Thus **ἀμήν** will be merely a

21 ὁ δὲ [t] βεβαιῶν ἡμᾶς σὺν ὑμῖν εἰς χριστὸν καὶ [u] χρίσας
ἡμᾶς θεός, 22 ὁ καὶ [v] σφραγισάμενος ἡμᾶς καὶ [w] δοὺς
τὸν [x] ἀῤῥαβῶνα τοῦ πνεύματος [w] ἐν ταῖς καρδίαις ἡμῶν.
23 Ἐγὼ δὲ [y] μάρτυρα τὸν θεὸν [z] ἐπικαλοῦμαι [a] ἐπὶ τὴν
ἐμὴν ψυχήν, ὅτι [b] φειδόμενος ὑμῶν οὐκέτι ἦλθον εἰς Κόρινθον. 24 [c] οὐχ [c] ὅτι [d] κυριεύομεν ὑμῶν τῆς πίστεως,
ἀλλὰ [e] συνεργοί ἐσμεν τῆς χαρᾶς ὑμῶν· τῇ γὰρ [f] πίστει
[g] ἑστήκατε· II. 1 [h] ἔκρινα δὲ [i] ἐμαυτῷ [k] τοῦτο, [l] τὸ μὴ

t Rom. xv. 8 reff.
u Acts iv. 27 reff.
v = John vi. 27. Eph. i. 13. iv. 30. see Rev. vii. 3 &c. Dan. xii. 4, 9.
w = ch. viii. 16 reff. Ezek. xxxvi. 26.
x ch. v. 5. Eph. i. 14 only. Gen. xxxviii. 17, 18, 20 only.
y Rom. i. 9 reff.
z = here only. see Acts xxv. 11 al.
a = Luke ix. 5. Acts xiii. 51.
b Rom. xi. 21 reff.
c = John vi. 46. ch. iii. 5. Phil. iii. 12. iv. 11, 17. 2 Thess. iii. 9 only.
d Rom. vi. 9, 14 reff.
e Rom. xvi. 3 reff. constr., here only.
f dat., Acts xxi. 21.
g = Rom. v. 2. 1 Cor. xv. 1.
h = Acts xx. 16. 1 Cor. ii. 2. v. 3. vii. 37. Tit. iii. 12 al. 2 Macc. xi. 25.
i dat , Rom. xiv. 7 reff. Tit. ii. 14.
k so Rom. xiv. 13. 1 Pet. ii. 19. 2 Pet. iii. 8.
l art., Rom. xiv. 13 al.

21. υμας συν ημιν C a d o syr : *υμας συν υμιν* B 115 : *nos nobiscum* F-lat, so also b[1] [Ps-Just$_1$]. ins *ο* bef *και χρισας* D[1]. for 2nd *ημας*, *υμας* B[1].

22. om *ὁ* AC[1]KPℵ[1] a e m o 17 Syr(appy) copt goth Ps-Just Did Chr Damasc: *και* bef *ὁ* F [am fuld spec] tol demid [Ambr$_1$]. *αραβωνα* [A](F)Lℵ m [47] ; *-βονα* FP.

23. for *ουκετι*, *ουκ* F[not F-lat] latt Syr copt goth (æth).

24. *της πιστεως* bef *υμων* DF a latt Ambrst Aug.

Chap. II. **1.** for *δε*, *τε* D[1][-gr] æth : *γαρ* B m 17 syr copt.

strengthening of *ναί*—the *affirmation and completion* of God's promises. **21, 22.**] construction as in ch. v. 5, which in form is remarkably similar; **21.**] **ὁ δὲ βεβ.** . . . **ἡμᾶς** is the (prefixed) predicate, and **θεός** the subject. *βεβ. εἰς χριστόν* = *βεβ. τῇ πίστει εἰς χριστόν*, **confirmeth us** (in believing) **on Christ.** **χρίσας ἡμᾶς**, after **ἡμ. σὺν ὑμῖν** and the *καί*, cannot refer (as Meyer, al.) to any anointing of *the Apostles only*, but must be taken, as Chrys., al., of *all*, Apostles and Corinthians. —*δμοῦ προφήτας κ. ἱερεῖς κ. βασιλεῖς ἐργαζόμενος· ταῦτα γὰρ τὸ παλαιὸν ἐχρίετο τὰ γένη.* Chrys., p. 448. See 1 John ii. 20. "Observe the connexion of *χριστός* and *χρίσας.*" Stanley. **22.**] **σφραγ.** again cannot refer to the Apostles alone, nor is ref. John any ground for such a reference,—but as in the other N. T. reff., to *all*,—sealed by the Holy Spirit to the day of redemption. **καὶ δοὺς** . . . .] '*And assured us of the fact of that sealing:*' see Rom. viii. 16. **τ. ἀῤῥ. τ. πν.**] **the pledge or token of the Spirit**: genitive of apposition: the Spirit *is* the token. *ἀῤῥ.*, *πρόδομα*, Hesych. :—*ἡ ἐπὶ ταῖς ὠναῖς παρὰ τῶν ὠνουμένων διδομένη προκαταβολὴ ὑπὲρ ἀσφαλείας*, Etymol. in Wetst., where see examples. "It is remarkable that the same word עֵרָבוֹן, is used in the same sense in Gen. xxxviii. 17, 18, from עָרַב, to 'mix' or 'exchange,' and thence to 'pledge,' as Jer. xxx. 21 ; Neh. v. 3. It was therefore probably derived by the Greeks from the language of Phœnician traders, as 'tariff,' 'cargo,' are derived, in English and other modern languages, from Spanish traders." Stanley. **23, 24.**] *His reason for not coming to them.*

23. ἐπὶ . . . . ψυχ.] **against my soul,**—'cum maximo meo malo, si fallo.' Grot. **φειδόμενος ὑμ.**] **sparing you,**—out of a feeling of compassion for you. **οὐκέτι**, '*no more,*' viz. after the first time: see Prolegg. to 1 Cor. § v. 6. The following **οὐχ ὅτι κυρ.** seems to be added to remove any false inference which might have been drawn from *φειδόμενος* as seeming to assert an unreasonable degree of power over them. But why **ὑμῶν τῆς πίστεως** ? He *had power* over them, but it was in matters of *discipline, not of faith* : over matters of faith not even an Apostle has power ('fides enim prorsus ab hominum jugo soluta liberrimaque esse debet.' Calv.), seeing it is in *each man's faith* that he *stands before God.* And he puts this strongly, that in matters of faith he is only a fellow-helper of their joy (the *χαρὰ ἐν τῷ πιστεύειν*, Rom. xv. 13), in order to shew them the *real department* of his apostolic power, and that, however exercised, it would not attempt to rule their faith, but only to secure to them, by purifying them, joy in believing. He proceeds to say, that it was the probable disturbance of this joy, which induced him to forego his visit. **τῇ πίστει**, dat. of the state or condition in which : cf. Rom. xi. 20. So Polyb. xxi. 9. 3, *ἕστη τῇ διανοίᾳ.*

Chap. II. 1—4.] Further explanation on the reason of the postponement of his visit. **1.**] **δέ** is merely transitional, and does not imply any contrast with what has preceded. **ἐμαυτῷ**, not = *παρ' ἐμαυτῷ* (as most Commentators and E. V.), but 'dat. commodi,' **for my own sake**, as is evident by the considera-

πάλιν [m] ἐν λύπῃ πρὸς ὑμᾶς ἐλθεῖν. 2 εἰ γὰρ ἐγὼ [n] λυπῶ
ὑμᾶς, [o] καὶ τίς ὁ [p] εὐφραίνων με εἰ μὴ ὁ [n] λυπούμενος [q] ἐξ
ἐμοῦ; 3 καὶ ἔγραψα [r] τοῦτο [r] αὐτό, ἵνα μὴ ἐλθὼν [s] λύπην
[s] σχῶ [t] ἀφ' ὧν [u] ἔδει με χαίρειν, [v] πεποιθὼς ἐπὶ πάντας

ABCDF KL[O] Pℵ a b c d e f g h k l m n o 17. 47

m = 1 Cor. iv. 21 reff. n Matt. xix. 22 ‖. Rom. xiv. 15 al. act., ver. 5 (bis). ch. vii. 8 (bis). Eph. iv. 30 only. Job xxxi. 39. o interrog., 1 Cor. v. 2 reff. see Phil. i. 22. p Acts vii. 41 reff. act., here only. Prov. xv. 20. q = ch. i. 11. iii. 5. r see Acts xxiv. 15, 20. xxv. 25. ch. vii. 11 al. s John xvi. 21, 22. Phil. ii. 27 only. t constr., Phil. iv. 11. 1 Pet. ii. 12. iii. 16. Ezek. xiv. 4. u Acts xxvii. 21. v constr., Matt. xxvii. 43. 2 Thess. iii. 4. w. dat., ch. i. 9 reff.

rec ελθειν bef εν λυπη, with copt æth: ελθειν bef προς υμας DF latt Syr (goth) arm Chr$_1$ Thl [Ambr$_1$ Ambrst]: txt ABCKL[O]Pℵ rel syr [Euthal-ms] Thdrt Damasc.

2. (ε in ει is written over the line, and ο inserted before λυπω but erased, by ℵ^1.) rec aft και τις ins εστιν, with DFKL[O]Pℵ^3 rel latt Orig$_2$(-int$_2$) Chr$_1$ [Cyr-p$_1$] Thdrt: om ABCℵ^1 copt [Euthal-ms] Damasc$_2$. om με P.

3. rec aft εγραψα ins υμιν, with C^{3}DFKLℵ^3 rel latt syrr goth æth [arm ?] Chr$_1$ Thdrt Pel: om ABC^1[O]Pℵ^1 17 am copt [Euthal-ms] Damasc$_1$[ins$_1$] Ambrst. αυτο bef τουτο C[O Euthal-ms] Chr$_1$ Thl: om αυτο A copt arm Damasc$_1$[txt$_1$]: txt BDF KL[P]ℵ rel [latt goth Thdrt Ambrst]. τουτο αυτο bef εγραψα DF latt goth æth Pel. aft λυπην ins επι λυπην (*see Phil* ii. 27) DF a latt syr-w-ast [Euthal-ms] Pel. rec εχω, with CDFKLℵ^3 rel Thdrt Damasc: txt AB[O]Pℵ^1 a d 17 Chr$_1$ [Euthal-ms] Thl. (*See var read, ch* i. 15, *Phil* ii. 27.) for αφ', εφ' *de* F [vulg Pel].

tion in the next verse. **τοῦτο** refers to what follows: see reff. **τὸ μὴ πάλιν ἐν λύπῃ πρὸς ὑμᾶς ἐλθεῖν**] **not again to come to you in grief.** This is the only fair rendering of the words; implying, that *some former visit had been in grief.* Clearly the first visit Acts xviii. 1 ff., could not be thus described: we must therefore infer, that an *intermediate unrecorded visit* had been paid by him. On this subject, compare ch. xii. 14; xiii. 1 and notes: and see Prolegg. to 1 Cor. § v. **ἐν λύπῃ**] is explained in vv. 2, 3 to mean (so Estius, Bengel, Rückert, Olsh., De Wette, al.) **in mutual grief**: 'I grieving you (ver. 2), and you grieving me' (ver. 3): not, as Chrys., al., Paul's grief alone, nor, as Meyer, al., grief inflicted on them by Paul. **2.**] **γάρ**, reason why I would not come to you in grief: because I should have to grieve those who formed my proper material for thankfulness and joy. **ἐγώ** has a peculiar emphasis: 'If *I* cause you grief' .... implying, 'there are who cause you sufficient.' **καί** prefixed to a question denotes *inconsequence on*, or *inconsistency with*, the foregoing supposition or affirmation: so Eur. Med. 1388, ὦ τέκνα φίλτατα! "μητρί γε, σοὶ δ' οὔ." κἄπειτ' ἔκτας; see other examples in Hartung, Partikellehre, i. p. 147. It is best expressed in English by '*then*:' **who is he then, &c.** as in E. V. The explanation of Chrys., who has been followed by Erasm., Bengel, Olsh., al., is curious, and certainly inconsistent with the context: εἰ καὶ λυπῶ ὑμᾶς, χάριν μοι παρέχετε κἂν τούτῳ μεγίστην, ὅτι δάκνεσθε ὑπὸ τῶν παρ' ἐμοῦ λεγομένων. Hom. iv. p. 456. Some of these Commentators refer the *singular* to the offender, vv. 5—8. But however the words may *bear* the meaning, and however *true* the saying might be, it is pretty clear that it would be beside the subject: nay, would give a reason the other way,—why he *should* come to them.

3.] **ἔγραψα τοῦτο αὐτό, I put in writing this same thing**, viz. the τοῦτο which I ἔκρινα, ver. 1: the announcement of my change of purpose in 1 Cor. xvi. 7, which had occasioned the charge of fickleness against him. The theories of Commentators have given rise to various interpretations of τοῦτο αὐτό: Chrys. understands, *ch.* xii. 21 *of this same Epistle*:—Beza, Meyer, al., *my blame of you in the first Epistle*:—so Estius, especially 1 Cor. iv. 19, 21:—Bleek supposes *a lost Epistle* to be referred to: De Wette wavers, but is disposed with Erasm., Rückert, al., to render αὐτὸ τοῦτο '*on this account*,' as Plato, Protag. p. 310, ἀλλ' αὐτὰ ταῦτα καὶ νῦν ἥκω: but Meyer rejoins, that this idiom is foreign to the style of Paul. I imagine that *two meanings* are open to us: (1) as above, *the announcement* which caused the charge of fickleness: (2) *the reproaches in the* 1st *Epistle* which grieved them. Of these, specious as is the latter on account of the following context, I prefer the former because of the τοῦτο in ver. 1. * **ἀφ' ὧν**, ellipt. for ἀπὸ τούτων, ἀφ' ὧν, see reff. **πεποιθὼς ....**] **having trust in** (reposing trust on) **you all, that my joy is** (the pres. expressing the purport of the trust when felt) **that of all of you**: i. e. trusting that you too would feel that there was sufficient reason for the postponement, if it interfered with our mutual joy.

ὑμᾶς ὅτι ἡ ἐμὴ χαρὰ πάντων ὑμῶν ἐστιν. 4 [w] ἐκ γὰρ
πολλῆς θλίψεως καὶ [x] συνοχῆς καρδίας ἔγραψα ὑμῖν [y] διὰ
πολλῶν δακρύων, οὐχ ἵνα [z] λυπηθῆτε, ἀλλὰ [a] τὴν ἀγάπην
ἵνα γνῶτε ἣν ἔχω [b] περισσοτέρως [c] εἰς ὑμᾶς. 5 Εἰ δέ τις
[z] λελύπηκεν, οὐκ ἐμὲ [z] λελύπηκεν, ἀλλὰ [d] ἀπὸ [d] μέρους, ἵνα
μὴ [e] ἐπιβαρῶ, πάντας ὑμᾶς. 6 [f] ἱκανὸν [g] τῷ [g] τοιούτῳ ἡ
[h] ἐπιτιμία αὕτη ἡ [i] ὑπὸ [k] τῶν [k] πλειόνων, 7 ὥστε [l] τοὐναν-

w = 1 Cor. vii. 5 reff.
x Luke xxi. 25 only. Job xxx. 3.
y = Rom. ii. 27 reff. 2 Tim. ii. 2.
z ver. 2 reff.
a arrangt. of words, John xiii. 29. Acts xix. 4. Rom. xi. 31. 1 Cor. ix. 15. xiv. 9. Gal. ii. 10.
b ch. i. 12 reff.
c Acts xx. 21. xxiv. 24. ch. i. 11 al.
d Rom. xi. 25 reff.
e 1 Thess. ii. 9. 2 Thess. iii. 8 only †.
f Luke xxii. 38. Gen. xxx. 15.
g Acts xxii. 22 reff.
h here only †. Wisd. iii. 10 only. (-ιον, 2 Macc. vi. 13.)
i ellips., see 2 Pet. ii. 22.
k 1 Cor. ix. 19 reff.
l Gal. ii. 7. 1 Pet. iii. 9 only †. 3 Macc. iii. 22.

4. ινα γνωτε bef την αγαπην F l. for εις, προς F.
5. (αλλα, so ABCL[O]Pℵ rel [exc 17].) επιβαρων F.
6. om η υπο των πλειονων F(not F-lat) æth-rom.

Meyer well observes, that **πάντας** ὑμᾶς, in spite of the existence of an anti-pauline faction in the Corinthian church, is a true example of the love which πάντα πιστεύει, πάντα ἐλπίζει, 1 Cor. xiii. 7. **4.**] *Explanation* (γάρ) *that he did not write in levity of purpose*, but *under great trouble of mind*,—not to grieve them, but to testify his love. **ἐκ**, of the *inducement*— **διά**, *of the condition:* he wrote, **out of much tribulation** (inward, of spirit, not outward) **and anguish** (συνοχή, '*angustiæ*') **of heart, with** (q. 'through,'—the state being the vehicle of the action, see reff.) **many tears.** **τ. ἀγάπην**, before the conjunction ἵνα, for special emphasis: see reff. **περισσοτέρως**—'*than to other churches* (?)'—so Chrys. (referring to 1 Cor. iv. 15; ix. 2), Theophyl.: Estius thinks, the comparative is not to be pressed, but understood as [some take the adjective] in ver. 7,—'*exceedingly*.'

5—11.] Digressive reference to the case of the incestuous person, whom the Apostle orders now to be forgiven, and reinstated. From the λύπη of the former verses, to him who was one of the principal occasions of that grief, the transition is easy. **5.**] δέ, transitional. **Now if any one hath occasioned sorrow** (a delicate way of pointing out *the one* who had occasioned it), **he hath grieved, not me** (not,—'not *only* me,' which destroys the meaning,—'*I* am not *the aggrieved* person, but *you*'), **but,** [**in part** (i. e.] more or less, *partially:*' ref.), **that I be not too heavy on him** (refers to ἀπὸ μέρους, which qualifies the blame cast on the offender), **all of you.** The above punctuation and rendering is adopted by Chrys. (ἵνα μὴ βαρήσω ἐκεῖνον τὸν πορνεύσαντα, p. 459), Beza, Calvin (but not in his *text*), al., with Meyer, De Wette. But Theodoret, Vulg., Luther, Bengel, Wetst., al., join ἐπιβαρῶ πάντας ὑμ., thus: '*he hath not grieved me* (alone and principally) *but only in part* (having grieved you also), *that I may not lay the fault on all of you*,' which I should in this case do, by making myself the only person aggrieved, and classing you with the offender. But this can hardly be; ἀλλά must be εἰ μή. Another way is adopted by Mosheim, Billroth, and Olsh.,—to join πάντας with ἵνα μὴ ἐπιβ.,—'*but in part,—that I burden not all,—you:*'—ἐπιβαρῶ being variously understood, either (1) of including you in the blame of the offender, or (2) as Olsh., of extending to them all the burden of this sorrow;—he supposes it to be ironically spoken; their highest praise would have been that *all* had been troubled. But as Meyer remarks, irony is entirely out of place in this part of the Epistle. The meanings are well discussed in Stanley. **6.**] **ἱκανόν**, sc. either ἐστιν or ἔστω. **τῷ τοιούτῳ**] Meyer remarks on the expression as being used in mildness, not to designate any particular person: but the same designation is employed in 1 Cor. v. 5, παραδοῦναι τὸν τοιοῦτον τῷ σατανᾷ.

ἡ ἐπιτ. αὕτη] **This punishment** (= ἐπιτίμιον, see reff.): *what it was*, we are unable with certainty to say; but 1 Cor. v. seems to point to *excommunication* as forming at least a *part* of it. But it was not a formal and public, only a *voluntary individual abstinence from communion* with him, as is shewn by ὑπὸ **τῶν πλειόνων**: the anti-pauline party probably refusing compliance with the Apostle's command.

ἱκανόν] **enough,** not in *duration*, though that would be *the case*, but in *magnitude:* sufficient, as having produced its desired effect, penitence. **7.**] **so that** (conseq. on ἱκανόν) **on the contrary you** (should) [**rather** (than continue the punishment)] **forgive and comfort him,** &c. Meyer denies that δεῖν should be supplied, and makes ὥστε depend immediately on

τίον [μᾶλλον] ὑμᾶς [m] χαρίσασθαι καὶ [n] παρακαλέσαι,
[o] μή [o] πως τῇ [p] περισσοτέρᾳ λύπῃ [q] καταποθῇ [g] ὁ [g] τοιοῦτος.
8 διὸ [r] παρακαλῶ ὑμᾶς [s] κυρῶσαι εἰς αὐτὸν ἀγάπην. 9 [t] εἰς
τοῦτο γὰρ καὶ ἔγραψα, ἵνα γνῶ τὴν [u] δοκιμὴν ὑμῶν, εἰ
[v] εἰς πάντα [w] ὑπήκοοί ἐστε. 10 ᾧ δέ τι [m] χαρίζεσθε, κἀγώ·
καὶ γὰρ ἐγὼ ὃ [x] κεχάρισμαι, εἴ τι [x] κεχάρισμαι, δι' ὑμᾶς,
[y] ἐν [y] προσώπῳ χριστοῦ, 11 ἵνα μὴ [z] πλεονεκτηθῶμεν ὑπὸ
τοῦ σατανᾶ· οὐ γὰρ αὐτοῦ τὰ [a] νοήματα [b] ἀγνοοῦμεν.

ABCDF KL[O] Pℵ a b c d e f g h k l m n o 17. 47

m = Luke vii. 42, 43. ch. xii. 13. Col. ii. 13. iii. 13 (bis). L.P.† (Sir. xii. 3 al.)
n = ch. i. 4, &c. reff.
o 1 Cor. ix. 27 reff.
p = Mark xii. 40 || L. 1 Cor. xii. 23 †. Dan. iv. 33 (36) Theod.
q 1 Cor. xv. 54 reff.
r = w. inf., Rom. xii. 1 al. 2 Macc. iv. 34.
s Gal. iii. 15 only. Gen. xxiii. 20. Levit. xxv. 30 only.
t Rom. xiv. 9 reff.
u Rom. v. 4 reff.
v = ch. viii. 23. ix. 8. Gal. v. 10 al.
w Acts vii. 39 reff.
x act. signif., Acts xxvii. 24. Gal. iii. 18. 2 Macc. iii. 33.
y ch. iv. 6. Prov. viii. 30. see note.
z ch. vii. 2. xii. 17, 18. 1 Thess. iv. 6 only. P. Ezek. xxii. 27.
a ch. iii. 14. iv. 4. x. 5. xi. 3. Phil. iv. 7 only. P. † Baruch ii. 8 only.
b Acts xiii. 27.

7. om *μαλλον* AB Syr Aug_1: ins CKL[O]Pℵ rel syr copt arm Chr $Thdrt_{h.l.}$ Damasc Thl Œc [$Tert_1$] Ambrst, and aft *υμας* DF goth $Thdrt_1$.

9. aft *εγραψα* ins *υμιν* F (*υμων*(*sic*) *vobis* F and G) 31 copt æth Chr_2 [Euthal-ms] Thdrt Pel. ins *παντων* bef *υμων* F(not F-lat). for *ει*, *η* (ῆ ?) AB 17.

10. rec *και εγω*, with C¹F K[e sil] Lℵ³ᵃ rel Thdrt : txt ABC²D[O]Pℵ¹ a m 17. 47 $Epiph_1$ Chr_1 [Euthal-ms] Damasc. om *εγω* A. rec *ει τι κεχαρ. ᾧ κεχαρ.*, with D²KL rel syr Thdrt Thl Œc : txt ABC(D¹)F[O](P)ℵ latt [Euthal-ms] Damasc Ambrst.—om ὃ D¹[-gr (goth)] (æth-pl): *ω* D³P m g²(perhaps).

ἱκανόν,—'*enough, for you to forgive and console him.*' **τῇ περισσοτέρᾳ λύπῃ**] not, as E. V., '*by overmuch sorrow:*' but (as Meyer), **by the increase of sorrow** which will come on the continuance of his punishment. **καταποθῇ** does not set any definite result of the excessive sorrow before them, such as apostasy or suicide, but leaves them to imagine such possible. **8.**] **κυρῶσαι**, hardly (as usually understood) *to ratify by a public decree of the church:* if (see above) his exclusion was not by such a decree, but only by the abstinence of individuals from his society, the ratifying their love to him would consist in the majority making it evident to him that he was again recognized as a brother. **9.**] *Reason why* they should now be ready to shew love to him again,—the end of Paul's writing to them having been accomplished by their obeying his order. **For to this end I also wrote:** the **καί** signifying that my former epistle, as well as my present exhortation, tended to this, viz. the *testing your obedience.* Meyer (ed. 2) explains the *καί* as implying that other orders to the same effect were sent by word of mouth. He alludes beyond doubt to the former Epistle, ch. v. Yet the ancient Commentators, Chrys., &c., and Erasm., Wolf, Bengel, al. (not Olsh., as De Wette says), interpret it of *this Epistle:* which certainly is grammatically allowable (see 1 Cor. v. 9, note), but opposed to the context (see vv. 3, 4, besides the manifest sense here, that the object of his writing *had been accomplished*). **That I might know the proof of you, whether in all things** (emphatic) **ye are obedient.** This was that one among the various objects of his first Epistle, which belonged to the matter at present in hand, and which he therefore puts forward: not by any means implying that he had *no other* view in writing it. **10.**] *Another assurance to encourage them in forgiving and reinstating the penitent;*—that they need not be afraid of lack of apostolic authority or confirmation of their act from above—he would ratify their forgiveness by his sanction. **ᾧ δὲ . . .**] '*Your* forgiveness is *mine:*' not said *generally* (as Meyer), but definitely, pointing at the one person here spoken of and no other. **κἀγώ**, scil. χαρίζομαι. Then he substantiates this assurance, by further assuring them, that his forgiveness of any fault in this case, if it takes place, takes place *on their account.* Meyer's (former: now (4th edn.) abandoned) and Rückert's rendering of **κεχάρισμαι** as *passive*, disturbs the whole sense of the passage, besides being inconsistent with the N. T. usage of the word, see reff. **ἐν προσώπῳ χριστοῦ**] either '*in the presence of Christ,*' as in ref. Prov. (compare Matt. xxi. 42),—so Theodoret, Erasm., Beza, Calv., Olsh., De W.,—or, and far better, **in the person of Christ**, *acting as Christ*, in the same way as he had commanded the punishment ἐν τῷ ὀνόματι τοῦ κυρίου ἡμῶν Ἰησοῦ, 1 Cor. v. 4: so Vulg., Estius (who argues the matter at some length), Wetst., al. **11. ἵνα μὴ . . .**] follows out the δι' ὑμᾶς—**to prevent Satan getting any advantage over us** (the Church generally: or better, *us Apostles*), in robbing us of some of our people,—viz. in causing the

[... ii. 12. O.] 12 Ἐλθὼν δὲ εἰς τὴν Τρωάδα [v] εἰς τὸ εὐαγγέλιον τοῦ
χριστοῦ, καὶ [c] θύρας μοι [c] ἀνεῳγμένης ἐν κυρίῳ, 13 οὐκ
[d] ἔσχηκα [e] ἄνεσιν [f] τῷ πνεύματί μου, [g] τῷ μὴ εὑρεῖν με
Τίτον τὸν ἀδελφόν μου· ἀλλὰ [h] ἀποταξάμενος [i] αὐτοῖς,
[... μακεδον P.] [k] ἐξῆλθον [k] εἰς Μακεδονίαν. 14 Τῷ δὲ θεῷ [l] χάρις τῷ
πάντοτε [m] θριαμβεύοντι ἡμᾶς ἐν τῷ χριστῷ καὶ τὴν

c Acts xiv. 27. 1 Cor. xvi. 9. Col. iv. 3. Rev. iii. 8. Isa. xlv. 1.
d ch. i. 9. vii 5.
e Acts xxiv. 23 reff.
f Acts xvii. 16 reff.
g causal dat., here only. Xen. Cyr. iv. 5. 9. Winer, edn. 6, § 44. 5.
h Acts xviii. 18 reff.
i Acts viii. 5 reff.
k = Acts xi. 25 reff.
l Rom. vi. 17 reff.
m Col. ii. 15 only †.

12. **δια** το ευαγγελιον F Damasc: δια του ευαγγελιου D[-gr]: *propter evangelium* latt [Ambrst]. και θυρα μοι ην εωγμενη F: ηνεωγ. DP.
13. for 2nd τω, του C²ℵ¹: το LP f l¹ m n [Euthal-ms]: εν τω D 17. ευριϲκειν D¹. [om] αυτο[ι]ς K.

penitent offender to despair and fall away from the faith. Chrys. remarks: *πλεονεξίαν εἰκότως ἐκάλεσεν, ὅταν καὶ διὰ τῶν ἡμετέρων κρατῇ. τὸ γὰρ δι' ἁμαρτίας λαμβάνειν, ἴδιον αὐτῷ ἐστι· τὸ μέντοι διὰ μετανοίας, οὐκέτι· ἡμέτερον γάρ, οὐκ ἐκείνου, τὸ ὅπλον.* p. 462. The word has yet another propriety: the offender was to be delivered over *τῷ σατανᾷ εἰς ὄλεθρον τῆς σαρκός*—care must be taken lest we *πλεονεκτηθῶμεν ὑπὸ τοῦ σ.*, and his *soul perish likewise.* **οὐ γὰρ . . .**] **αὐτοῦ** before **τὰ νοήμ.** for emphasis:—such devices, *as coming from him*, are special matters of observation and caution to every Christian minister; much more to him who had the care of all the churches. See 1 Pet. v. 8. The personality and agency of the Adversary can hardly be recognized in plainer terms than in both these passages.

12—17.] He proceeds (after the digression) to shew them with what anxiety he awaited the intelligence from Corinth, and how thankful he was for the seal of his apostolic ministry furnished by it. The only legitimate connexion is that with vv. 1—4. **δέ** serves to resume the main subject after parenthetical matter: so Herod. viii. 67,—*ἐπεὶ ὦν ἀπίκατο ἐς τὰς Ἀθήνας πάντες οὗτοι πλὴν Παρίων· Πάριοι δὲ ὑπολειφθέντες ἐν Κύθνῳ ἐκαραδόκεον τὸν πόλεμον κῇ ἀποβήσεται·* **οἱ δὲ λοιποὶ** *ὡς ἀπίκοντο ἐς τὸ Φάληρον, κ.τ.λ.* See Hartung, Partikellehre, i. 174. **12.**] To *Troas*, viz. on his journey from Ephesus, Acts xx. 1, 2; 1 Cor. xvi. 5—9. "The art. perhaps indicates the region of 'the Troad,' rather than the city." Stanley. **εἰς τὸ εὐαγγ. τ. χρ.**] for (the purpose of preaching) **the Gospel of Christ.** He had been before at Troas, but the vision of a Macedonian asking for help prevented his remaining there. He now revisited it, purposely to stay and preach. On his return to Asia he remained there seven days, Acts xx. 6—12. **καὶ θύρας . . .**] **and an opportunity of apostolic action being afforded me; ἐν κυρίῳ** defines the *sort* of action implied, and to which the door was opened. It is remarkable that in speaking of this journey, though not of the same place, Paul uses this expression, 1 Cor. xvi. 9. Compare the interesting passage at Troas on his return from Europe the next spring, Acts xx. 6—13. **13. ἔσχηκα ἄνεσιν**] perf. in the sense of aorist, as ch. i. 9. **I had not rest for my spirit** (not, '*in* my spirit:' compare *οὐχ εὑροῦσα ἡ περιστερὰ ἀνάπαυσιν τοῖς ποσὶν αὐτῆς*, Gen. viii. 9). He could not with any tranquillity prosecute the spiritual duties opened to him at Troas. **τῷ μὴ εὑρ.**] **by** (reason of) **my not finding**: see reff.

Paul had sent Titus to Corinth, ch. xii. 18, partly to finish the collection for the saints, but principally to bring intelligence respecting the effect of the first Epistle. Probably it had been fixed that they should meet at Troas. **τ. ἀδελ. μου** implies a relation closer than merely that of Christian brotherhood—my *colleague* in the Apostleship. **αὐτοῖς**] the disciples there: understood from the context.

14—17.] *Omitting, as presupposed, the fact of his having met with Titus in Macedonia, and the nature of the intelligence which he brought,—he grounds on these a thanksgiving for that intelligence, and a magnification of his apostolic office.* It is evidently beside the purpose to refer this thanksgiving to the diffusion of the gospel in Macedonia (as Flatt), or in Troas (as Emmerling), or to general considerations (as Bengel):—both the context, and the language itself (see below), shew that its reference is to the effects of the apostolic reproof on the Corinthians. **14. θριαμβεύοντι**] **leading us in triumph**, see ref. *Two kinds of persons* were led in triumph: the *participators of the victory*, and the *victims of the defeat.* In Col. the *latter* are plainly meant; here, according to many Commentators (Calv., Elsner, Bengel, De Wette, al.), the *former*: which however is never elsewhere the reference of the word,

[n] ὀσμὴν τῆς γνώσεως [o] αὐτοῦ [p] φανεροῦντι δι' ἡμῶν ἐν
παντὶ τόπῳ. 15 ὅτι χριστοῦ [q] εὐωδία ἐσμὲν τῷ θεῷ [r] ἐν
τοῖς [s] σωζομένοις καὶ [r] ἐν τοῖς [t] ἀπολλυμένοις, 16 [u] οἷς
μὲν [n] ὀσμὴ ἐκ θανάτου [v] εἰς θάνατον, [u] οἷς δὲ [n] ὀσμὴ ἐκ

ABCDF KLℵ a b c d e f g h k l m n o 17. 47

n here 3ce. John xii. 3. Eph. v. 2. Phil. iv. 18 only. Exod. v. 21.
o gen. object., ch. x. 5.
p Rom. i. 19 reff.
q Eph. v. 2. Phil. iv. 18 only. Ezra vi. 10.
r ≏ 1 Cor. ii. 6.
s 1 Cor. xv. 2 reff.
t Rom. ii. 12 reff.
u 1 Cor. xi. 21 reff.
v = Acts xi. 18. Rom. v. 16 reff.

14. (*s* of *της* is written over the line by ℵ[1] or -corr[1].)
16. *οσμην* (twice) D[-gr]. rec om *εκ* (twice), with DFKL rel latt arm [Chr_3] $Thdrt_2$ Thl Œc Iren[-int_1 Ambrst $Aug_{sæpe}$]: ins ABCℵ m 17. 47[1st] copt [goth (2nd)] æth $Clem_1$ $Orig_1$(-int_2) $Dial_1$ Nys [Cyr-p_1 Euthal-ms] Hil_1.

but it always implies *triumphare de aliquo.* Wetst. quotes this sense, *βασιλεῖς ἐθριάμβευσε*, Plut. Rom. p. 38 D, and in four other places:—and the Scholiast to Hor. Od. i. 37. 31, who relates of Cleopatra, "invidens Privata deduci superbo Non humilis mulier triumpho," that she refused the terms offered her by Augustus, saying, *οὐ θριαμβευθήσομαι.* Meyer in consequence understands it in this sense here: **who ever triumphs over us,** i. e. 'who ceases not to exhibit us, His former foes, as overcome by Him:'—and adds in a note, "Remark the emphatic *πάντοτε*, prefixed, to which the similarly emphatic *ἐν παντὶ τόπῳ*, at the end, corresponds. God *began* His triumph over the *ἡμεῖς* at their conversion;—over Paul, at Damascus, where he made him a servant, from being an enemy. This triumph he ever continues, not ceasing to exhibit before the world these His former foes, by the results of their present service, as overcome by Him. This, in the case before us, was effected by Paul, in that (as Titus brought him word to Macedonia) his Epistle had produced such good results in Corinth." De W. objects to this as a strange way of expressing thankfulness for deliverance from our anxiety. But *is it so* to those who look beneath the surface? In our spiritual course, *our only true triumphs* are, *God's* triumphs over us. His defeats of *us*, are *our only* real victories. I own that this yet appears to me to be the *only admissible rendering.* We must not violate the known usage of a word, and invent another for which there is no precedent, merely for the sake of imagined perspicuity. Such is that of 'to make to triumph' (Beza, Estius, Grot., al.):—*μαθητεύειν*, Matt. xxviii. 19, and *βασιλεύειν*, 1 Kings viii. 22, are not cases in point, their sense being, to 'make a disciple,' 'to make a king,'—whereas that required for *θριαμβεύειν*, would be, '*triumphatorem* facere.' *χορεύειν*, for 'to make to dance,' is more to the point: *οὔπω καταπαύσομεν μούσας, αἵ μ' ἐχόρευσαν*, Eur. Herc. Fur. 688,—*τάχα σ' ἐγὼ μᾶλλον χορεύσω*, ib. 873:—but the Apostle's own usage in ref. Col., in my mind, decides the question. See also the following context. **ἐν τῷ χρ.**, as usually, **in our connexion with,** '*as members of,*' **Christ:** not, 'by Christ.' **τὴν ὀσμήν]** The similitude is not that of a *sacrifice*, but still the same as before: during a triumph, sweet spices were thrown about or burnt in the streets, which were *θυμιαμάτων πλήρεις*, Plut. Æmil. p. 272 (cited by Dr. Burton). As the fact of the triumph, or approach of the triumphal procession, was made known by these odours far and wide, so God diffuses by our means, who are the materials of His triumph, the sweet odour of the knowledge of Christ (who is the Triumpher, Col. ii. 15). **τῆς γνώσ.]** genit. of apposition: the *odour*, which in the interpretation of the figure, *is* the knowledge. **αὐτοῦ,**—*χριστοῦ*, cf. next verse. **15.]** Here the propriety of the figure is lost, and the source of the odour identified with the Apostles themselves. **For we are to God a sweet savour of Christ** (gen. object., of that which was diffused by the odour, viz. the *knowledge of Christ.* 'Instar fragrantis cujusdam unguenti, seu florum aut herbarum, famam nominis ejus, velut bonum et suavem odorem, ... spargimus apud omnes.' Estius) **among those who are being saved, and among those who are perishing** (*σωζ.* and *ἀπολλ.*, see note, 1 Cor. i. 18). *κἂν σώζωνταί τινες, κἂν ἀπολλύωνται, τὸ εὐαγγέλιον μένει ἔχον τὴν οἰκείαν ἀρετήν, κ. ἡμεῖς μένομεν τοῦτο ὄντες ὅπερ ἐσμέν*, Theophyl., mainly from Chrys., who proceeds *καὶ καθάπερ τὸ φῶς, κἂν σκοτίζῃ τοὺς ἀσθενεῖς, φῶς ἐστι, καίτοι σκοτίζον· κ. τὸ μέλι, κἂν πικρὸν ᾖ τοῖς νοσοῦσι, γλυκὺ τὴν φύσιν ἐστίν· οὕτω καὶ τὸ εὐαγγέλιον εὐῶδές ἐστι, κἂν ἀπολλύωνταί τινες ἀπιστοῦντες.* Hom. v. p. 467.

16 a.] **to the one** (the latter) **an odour arising from death and tending to death: to the others** (the former) **an odour arising from life and tending to life.** The odour was, CHRIST,—who to the unbelieving is *Death*, a mere announcement of a man crucified,—and working

ζωῆς [v] εἰς ζωην. καὶ [w] πρὸς ταῦτα τίς [w] ἱκανός; 17 οὐ
γάρ ἐσμεν ὡς [x] οἱ [x] πολλοὶ [y] καπηλεύοντες τὸν [z] λόγον τοῦ
[z] θεοῦ, ἀλλ' [a] ὡς ἐξ [b] εἰλικρινείας, ἀλλ' [a] ὡς ἐκ θεοῦ,
[c] κατέναντι [τοῦ] θεοῦ [d] ἐν χριστῷ λαλοῦμεν.

III. 1 Ἀρχόμεθα πάλιν [e] ἑαυτοὺς [f] συνιστάνειν; ἢ

w here only. Wisd. xviii. 12. Xen. Mem. i. 2. 15. see Col. i. 12.
x Rom. v. 15 reff.
y here only †. see note.
z Acts xi. 1 reff.
a = Matt. vii. 29. John i. 14.
b ch. i. 12 reff.
c Rom. iv. 17 reff.
d = 1 Thess. iv. 1.
e 1st pers., Rom. viii. 23. xv. 1. 1 Cor. xi. 31. ch. i. 9. iv. 2, 5. x. 12, 14. 1 Thess. ii. 8.
f (-άνειν) ch. v. 12. x. 12, 18 only. see Rom. iii. 5 reff.

[for ζωης] ζωην (but corrd) ℵ^1. [ος ταυτα is written over an erasure in C, the former writing being a little shorter.]

17. for πολλοι, λοιποι D F[-gr] L d e f g h l n syrr arm Chr$_1$ Thdrt: *plurimi* vulg (and F-lat); *ceteri aut plurimi* G-lat. αλλα (1st) B. om 1st ως F latt copt goth Iren-int [Ambrst]. om 2nd αλλ' F [D-lat] fuld(and demid) syr Iren-int$_1$ [Ambrst]. rec (for κατεναντι) κατενωπιον, with DFKL[ℵ^3(sic, Tischdf N. T. ed 8)] rel Bas$_1$ Chr$_1$ Thdrt Damasc: ενωπιον ℵ^3[so Tischdf Cod. Sin.]: txt ABCPℵ^1 m 17 Did$_1$ Chr-ms [Euthal-ms]. om του (bef θεου) (*to corresp with* εκ θεου *before: but the art here is significant as giving solemnity*) ABCD^{1}ℵ^1 m 17 Bas [Euthal-ms]: ins D$^{2\cdot3}$FKLPℵ^3 rel Chr Thdrt Damasc.

Chap. III. 1. for συνιστανειν, συνισταν BD^1 17: συνισταναι F Thdrt[-ms]: txt ACD$^{2\cdot3}$KLPℵ rel [Chr$_1$ Euthal-ms Thdrt-ed Damasc]. rec (for 1st ἢ) ει, with

death by unbelief: but to the believing, *Life*, an announcement of His Resurrection and Life,—and working in them life eternal, by faith in Him. The *double working* of the Gospel is set forth in Matt. xxi. 44; Luke ii. 34; John ix. 39.

16 b.] In order to understand the connexion, we must remember that the purpose of vindicating his apostolic commission is in the mind of Paul, and about to be introduced by a description of the office, its requirements, and its holders. This purpose already begins to press into its service the introductory and apologetic matter, and to take every opportunity of manifesting itself. In order then to exalt the dignity and shew the divine authorization of his office, he asks this question: **And** (see remarks at ver. 2) **for** (to accomplish) **these things** (this so manifold working in the believers and unbelievers,—this emission of the εὐωδία χριστοῦ every where), **who is sufficient?** He does not express the answer, but it is too evident to escape any reader,—indeed it is supplied in terms by ch. iii. 5, οὐχ ὅτι ἱκανοί ἐσμεν λογίσασθαί τι ἀφ' ἑαυτῶν ὡς ἐξ ἑαυτῶν, ἀλλ' ἡ ἱκανότης ἡμῶν ἐκ τοῦ θεοῦ. Meyer remarks that **πρὸς ταῦτα** is put first, in the place of emphasis, to detain the attention on its weighty import, and then τίς purposely put off till the end of the question, to introduce the interrogation unexpectedly; as in Herod. v. 33,—σοὶ δὲ κ. τούτοισι τοῖσι πρήγμασι τί ἔστι;—Plato, Symp. p. 204, ὁ ἐρῶν τῶν καλῶν τί ἐρᾷ;

17.] **οἱ πολλοί** here points definitely at those false teachers, of whom he by and by, ch. x.—xii., speaks more plainly. **ἐσμεν . . . καπηλεύοντες] are not in the habit of adulterating** (the word κάπηλος (Sir. xxvi. 29) originally signifies any kind of huckster or vender, but especially of wine,—and thence, from the frequency of adulteration of wine, καπηλεύω implied *to adulterate:* in Isa. i. 22, we have οἱ κάπηλοί σου μίσγουσι τὸν οἶνον ὕδατι: in the Etymol. (Wetst.) κάπηλος, ὁ οἰνοπώλης . . . ὁ δὲ Αἰσχύλος τὰ δόλια πάντα καλεῖ κάπηλα· 'κάπηλα προφέρων τεχνήματα:' in Lucian, Hermotim. 59 (ib.), ὅτι καὶ φιλόσοφοι ἀποδίδονται τὰ μαθήματα, ὥσπερ οἱ κάπηλοι, κεράσάμενοί γε οἱ πολλοί, καὶ δολώσαντες, καὶ κακομετροῦντες. See many more examples in Wetst. The same is expressed ch. iv. 2, by **δολοῦντες τ. λόγον τ. θεοῦ) the word of God, but as** ('ut qui') **from sincerity** (the subjective regard of the speakers), **but as from God** (the objective regard—a dependence on the divine suggestion) **we speak before God** (with a *consciousness* of His presence) **in Christ** (not '*in the name of Christ,*' Grot., al., nor '*concerning Christ,*'—Beza, al.: nor '*according to Christ,*' Calv.: but as usual, **in Christ**: as united to Him, and members of His Body, and employed in His work).

Ch. III. 1—VI. 10.] Beginning with a disowning of self-recommendation, the Apostle proceeds to speak concerning his apostolic office and himself as the holder of it, his feelings, sufferings, and hopes, partly with regard to his connexion with the Corinthians, but for the most part in general terms. 1—3.] *He disclaims a spirit of self-recommendation.* 1.] **ἀρχ., are we beginning? πάλιν**, alluding to a charge probably made

g Rom. xvi 2 reff. h = 1 Cor. iv. 18 reff. i here only †. Arrian, Epictet. ii. 3. k here bis. Luke x. 20 only †. 1 Macc. xiii. 40 only. l Acts viii. 28, 30 (reff.). m Rom. i. 19 reff. n John iii. 21. 1 John ii. 19. o pass., ch. viii. 19, 20. act., 2 Tim. i. 18. 1 Pet. i. 12. iv. 10. p = 2 John 12. 3 John 13 only ‡. q Acts xiv. 15 note. r here bis. Heb. ix. 4 only. Exod. xxxi. 18. s John ii. 6. Rev. ix. 20 only. Exod. l. c. al. t Rom. vii. 14 reff.

ABCDF KLPℵa bcdef ghklm no17.47

μὴ [g] χρῄζομεν ὥς [h] τινες [i] συστατικῶν ἐπιστολῶν πρὸς
ὑμᾶς, ἢ ἐξ ὑμῶν; 2 ἡ ἐπιστολὴ ἡμῶν ὑμεῖς ἐστε,
[k] ἐγγεγραμμένη ἐν ταῖς καρδίαις ἡμῶν, [l] γινωσκομένη καὶ
[l] ἀναγινωσκομένη ὑπὸ πάντων ἀνθρώπων, 3 [mn] φανερούμενοι
[n] ὅτι ἐστὲ ἐπιστολὴ χριστοῦ [o] διακονηθεῖσα ὑφ᾽ ἡμῶν, [k] ἐγγεγραμμένη οὐ [p] μέλανι, ἀλλὰ πνεύματι [q] θεοῦ [q] ζῶντος,
οὐκ ἐν [r] πλαξὶν [s] λιθίναις, ἀλλ᾽ ἐν [r] πλαξὶν καρδίαις [t] σαρ-

AKLP rel arm Chr$_1$ Damasc: txt BCDFℵ a f m [latt copt goth Euthal-ms] Thdrt [Pel]. ωσπερ AD^1 m. rec at end adds *συστατικων*, with DKLP rel syrr goth Thdrt-ms Damasc; *συστατικων επιστολων* F, the words *commendaticiis epistolis* are written over the greek in F(as also in G, the latin being there always so written): om ABCℵ 17 vulg(and F-lat) copt æth arm Chr$_1$ [Euthal-ms] Thdrt(exc ms$_1$) Ambrst. (*συν-* DF: *-στατικας* D^1.)

2. for 2nd *ημων*, *υμων* ℵ b k o 17 [demid æth-rom]. for *παντων*, *των* F[-gr(and G-lat). (*omnibus* vulg with F-lat.)

3. ins *και* bef *εγγεγραμμενη* B a^2 67^2. 74 vulg. rec *καρδιας* (*see note*), with FK rel latt Syr copt (goth) æth arm Orig$_1$(-int$_5$) Dial$_1$ Eus[-edd$_1$ Mac$_1$] Chr$_1$ Cyr$_1$ Thdrt Damasc Iren-int$_1$ Hil$_1$: txt ABCD[G]L[P]ℵ rel syr Eus-mss [Cyr-p$_1$ Euthal-ms].

against him of having done this in his former epistle: perhaps in its opening section, and in some passages of 1 Cor. v., ix. and xiv. 18; xv. 10 al.: see our ch. x. 18. **ἢ μὴ χρ.**] **Or do we want** (the *μή* gives an ironical turn to the question, which is more strongly expressed in the rec. reading *εἰ μή*,—'unless it be thought, that' . . . .) **as some** (so *τινες*, 1 Cor. iv. 18; xv. 12; Gal. i. 7, of the teachers who opposed him. Probably these persons had come recommended to them, by *whom* does not appear, whether by churches or Apostles, but most likely by the former (*ἐξ ὑμῶν*), and on their departure requested similar recommendations from the Corinthian church to others), **letters of recommendation to you** (*ἐπιστ. συστατικαί* are fully illustrated by Suicer, Thes. in voc. Among other passages he cites the 13th canon of the council of Chalcedon: *ξένους κληρικοὺς καὶ ἀγνώστους ἐν ἑτέρᾳ πόλει* **δίχα συστατικῶν γραμμάτων τοῦ ἰδίου ἐπισκόπου** *μηδὲ ὅλως μηδαμοῦ λειτουργεῖν*; and Epist. cclxxi. (al. xi.) of Basil, vol. iv. p. 417, which has this inscription: *Εὐσεβίῳ ἑταίρῳ συστατικὴ ἐπὶ Κυριακῷ πρεσβυτέρῳ*, "Eusebio sodali commendatitia Cyriaci presbyteri") **or from you?** The rec. *συστατικῶν* at the end, as well as *συστ. ἐπιστολῶν*, have probably been glosses, inserted (the ancient MSS. having no stops) to prevent *ἐξ ὑμ.* being taken with *ἡ ἐπιστ.* following. **2.**] **Ye are our epistle** (of commendation), **written on our hearts** (not borne in our hands to be shewn, but engraven, in the consciousness of our work among you, on our hearts. There hardly can be any allusion, as Olsh. thinks, to the twelve jewels engraven with the names of the tribes and borne on the breast-plate of the High Priest, Exod. xxviii. 21. The plural seems to be used, as so often in this Epistle,—see e. g. ch. vii. 3, 5,—of Paul himself only), **known and read** (a play on *γιν.* and *ἀναγιν.*, as at ch. i. 13) **by all men** (because all men are aware, what issue my work among you has had, and receive me the more favourably on account of it. But 'all men' includes the Corinthians themselves; his success among them was his letter of recommendation *to* them as well as to others *from* them), **3.**] **manifested to be** (that ye are) **an epistle of Christ** (i. e. *written by Christ*,—not, as Chrys. al., *concerning* Christ:—He is the Recommender of us, the Head of the church and Sender of us His ministers) **which was ministered** (aor.) **by us** (i. e. *carried about, served in the way of ministration* by us as tabellarii,—not, as Meyer and De W. and al., *written by us as amanuenses:* see below), **having been inscribed, not with ink, but with the Spirit of the living God** (so the tables of the law were *γεγραμμέναι τῷ δακτύλῳ τοῦ θεοῦ*, Exod. xxxi. 18), **not on stone tables** (as the old law, ib.), **but on** (your) **hearts** (which are) **tables of flesh** (Meyer calls the reading *καρδίαις a mistake of the pen.* But surely internal as well as external evidence is strong in its favour, the correction to *καρδίας* being so obvious to those who found the construction harsh). The apparent change in the figure in this verse requires explanation. The Corinthians are his Epistle of recommendation, both to themselves

κιναις. 4 [u] Πεποίθησιν δὲ τοιαύτην ἔχομεν διὰ τοῦ
χριστοῦ [v] πρὸς τὸν θεόν· 5 [w] οὐχ [w] ὅτι [x] ἱκανοί ἐσμεν
[y] λογίσασθαί τι [z] ἀφ' [za] ἑαυτῶν ὡς [b] ἐξ [a] ἑαυτῶν, ἀλλ' ἡ
[c] ἱκανότης ἡμῶν [b] ἐκ τοῦ θεοῦ, 6 ὃς καὶ [d] ἱκάνωσεν ἡμᾶς
[e] διακόνους [f] καινῆς [fg] διαθήκης, οὐ [h] γράμματος ἀλλὰ
[h] πνεύματος· τὸ γὰρ [h] γράμμα [i] ἀποκτέννει, τὸ δὲ [h] πνεῦμα

u ch. i. 15 reff. v = Rom. v. 1 reff. w ch. i. 24 reff. x ch. ii. 16. 1 Cor. xv. 19 reff. y = Rom. iii. 28. (Jer. xi. 19.) z Luke xii. 57. xxi. 30. John v. 19. x. 18. xvi. 13 al. a 1st pers., ver. 1. b = ch. i. 11. ii. 2. c here only †. d Col. i. 12 only †. e = Eph. iii. 7. Col. i. 23 al. f 1 Cor. xi. 25 ||. Heb. viii. 8 (from Jer. xxxviii. [xxxi.] 31). ix. 15. g Rom. ix. 4 reff. h Rom. ii. 29. vii. 6. i (-κτενν-) Matt. x. 28. Mark xii. 5. Luke xii. 4. Rev. vi. 11.

4. for *εχομεν*, *εχω* A.

5. *λογιζεσθαι* CDF l n. rec *αφ' εαυτων* bef *λογισασθαι τι*, with KL rel syr Did$_1$ Chr$_1$ Thdrt Damasc: bef *ικανοι εσμεν* BCℵ copt arm Bas$_1$ [Euthal-ms] Antch: bef *εσμεν* m (*attempts to connect* *ικανοι* and *αφ εαυτων*): om 17. 139 Syr: txt ADF(P) latt goth [(æth) Ambrst].—*τι* bef *λογ.* P [Chr$_1$]: om *τι* B. om *ως* C. for 2nd *εαυτων*, *αυτων* BF.

6. rec *αποκτεινει*, with B b d Orig[-ed$_2$ Bas-ed$_1$]: *αποκτενει* ACDL (*αποκτένει* D^{3}L) rel Orig-ms$_1$ [Euthal-ms] Cyr-p: txt F(*-κτηνναι*) KPℵ e f l m^2 17 Did$_1$ Chr-2-mss.

and others; *an Epistle, written* by Christ, *ministered* by Paul; the *Epistle itself* being now the subject, viz. the Corinthians, *themselves the writing of Christ*, inscribed, not on tables of stone, but on hearts, tables of flesh. The Epistle itself, written and worn on Paul's heart, and there known and read by all men, consisted of *the Corinthian converts*, on whose hearts Christ had written it by His Spirit. *I bear on my heart, as a testimony to all men, that which Christ has by His Spirit written in your hearts.* On the tables of stone and of flesh, see Exod. as above; Prov. iii. 3; vii. 3; Jer. xxxi. 31—34, and on the contrast, also here hinted at in the background, between the heart of stone and the heart of flesh, Ezek. xi. 19; xxxvi. 26.

4—11.] *His honour of his apostolic office was no personal vanity, for all the ability of the Apostles came from God, who had made them able ministers of the new covenant* (4—6), *a ministration infinitely more glorious than that of the old dispensation* (7—11). 4.] The connexion with the foregoing is immediate: he had just spoken of his consciousness of apostolic success among them (which assertion would be true also of other churches which he had founded) being his world-wide recommendation. It is *this confidence* of which he here speaks. **Such confidence however we possess through Christ towards God**: i. e. 'it is no vain boast, but rests on power imparted to us through Christ in regard to God, in reference to God's work and our own account to be given to Him:' 5.] **not that** (i. e. 'I mean not, that' . . . :—not, 'not *because*,' as Winer in his former editions: see edn. 6, § 61. 5. f) **we are of ourselves able to think any thing** (to carry on any of the processes of reasoning or judgment, or faith belonging to our apostolic calling: there is no ellipsis, 'any thing *great*,' or '*good*,' or the like) **of ourselves, as if from ourselves** (ἀφ' ἑαυτ. and ἐξ ἑαυτ. are parallel: the latter more definitely pointing to ourselves as the origin),—**but our ability** (λογίσασθαι τὰ πάντα) **is from** (as its source) **God,** 6.] **Who also** (='qui idem;' so Eur. Bacch. 572, ταῦτα καὶ καθύβρισ' αὐτόν, 'hæc eadem illi exprobravi.' See Hartung, Partikellehre, i. p. 132) **enabled us as ministers of the** (or, as Stanley, "a:" but not necessarily from the omission of the art.: cf. Heb. xii. 24, καὶ διαθήκης νέας μεσίτῃ Ἰησοῦ) **new Covenant** (i. e. the *gospel*, Eph. iii. 7; Col. i. 23, as distinguished from the *law*: see 1 Cor. xi. 25; Gal. iv. 24:—the πλάκες λίθιναι and σάρκιναι are still borne in mind, and lead on to a fuller comparison of the two covenants),—**not of** (governed by διακόνους, not by καινῆς διαθ.—'*ministers, not of*' . . . . .) **letter** (in which, viz. in formal and literal precept, the Mosaic law consisted), **but of Spirit** (in which, viz. in the inward guiding of the Spirit of God, the gospel consists. Bengel remarks: 'Paulus etiam dum hæc *scripsit*, non literæ, sed *spiritus* ministerium egit. Moses in proprio illo officio suo, etiam cum haud scripsit, tamen in litera versatus est'): **for the letter** (mere formal and literal precept, of the law) **killeth** (as in Rom. vii.,—brings the knowledge of sin, its guilt and its punishment. The reference is not, as Meyer, to *natural death*, which is the result of sin even where there is *no law*; nor as Chrys. to the law *executing punishment*), **but the Spirit** (of the gospel, i. e. God's Holy Spirit, acting in and through Christ, Who ἐγένετο εἰς **πνεῦμα ζωοποιοῦν**, 1 Cor. xv. 45. See also below, ver. 17) **giveth life** (not merely life eternal, but

[k] ζωοποιεῖ. 7 εἰ δὲ ἡ [l] διακονία τοῦ θανάτου ἐν [h] γράμματι
[m] ἐντετυπωμένη λίθοις ἐγενήθη [no] ἐν [op] δόξῃ, ὥςτε μὴ δύνασθαι [q] ἀτενίσαι τοὺς υἱοὺς Ἰσραὴλ εἰς τὸ πρόσωπον
Μωυσέως διὰ τὴν [p] δόξαν τοῦ προσώπου αὐτοῦ τὴν [r] κατ-
αργουμένην, 8 πῶς οὐχὶ μᾶλλον ἡ [l] διακονία τοῦ [p] πνεύματος ἔσται [no] ἐν [op] δόξῃ; 9 εἰ γὰρ ἡ [l] διακονία τῆς [s] κατακρίσεως δόξα, [t] πολλῷ [t] μᾶλλον [u] περισσεύει ἡ [lv] διακονία τῆς [v] δικαιοσύνης [p] δόξῃ. 10 καὶ γὰρ οὐ [w] δεδόξασται

ABCDF KLPℵ a b c d e f g h k l m n o 17. 47

k Rom. iv. 17 reff. l Acts i. 17 al. m here only †. n Luke iv. 32 al. Ps. xxviii. 4. o 1 Cor. xv. 43 reff. p = Acts xxii. 11 reff. q epp., here and ver. 13 only. Acts i. 10 reff. (Exod. xxxiv. 29, 30.) r 1 Cor. i. 28 reff. part. pres., ib. ii. 6. s ch. vii. 3 only †. Numb. xiii. 33 alius in Hexapl. [Montf. (not Fd.)] t Rom. v. 9, 10 reff. u = Rom. iii. 7 reff. constr., ch. viii. 7 (πίστει, κ.τ.λ.). Sir. xi. 12. v see ch. xi. 15. w = Rom. xi. 13. Judg. ix. 9.

7. for θανατου, θεου ℵ[1](txt ℵ-corr[1]). rec (for γραμματι) γραμμασιν (*see note*), with ACD[2.3]KLPℵ rel latt(*litteris aut littera* G-lat) syr copt goth $Orig_2$[-c_1](-int_3) Mac_1 Chr_1 Thdrt Damasc [Euthal-ms Ambrst]: ενγεγραμμενη 17: txt B D[1][-gr] F[-gr] Syr [arm]. for εντετ., τετυπωμενη F. rec ins εν bef λιθοις, with D[2.3]KLℵ[3] rel [latt arm] $Orig_1$(-int_3) Mac_1 Chr Damasc [Aug_3]: om ABC D[1][-gr] F[-gr] Pℵ[1] 17 G-lat $Orig_2$[-c_1 Euthal-ms] Did_2 Epiph Thdrt. for του, αυτου (but αυ erased) ℵ[1].

8. for ουχι, ουδι ℵ[1](but χ written above by ℵ[1] or -corr[1]).

9. for 1st η, τη AC D[1][and lat] F[-gr] ℵ a 17 am syrr æth $Orig_1$(-int_1) Cyr_1 Ambrst: txt B D[2][-gr] KLP rel vulg[-ed](and F-lat) G-lat copt goth Mac_1 Chr_1 Thdrt [$Antch_1$] Damasc Aug Pel. aft δοξα ins εστιν D[1]F [latt (Syr copt arm)] Orig-int_1[om $Orig_1$]. περισσευσει D-gr k o syrr Mac_1 Orig-int_1, *abundabit* G-lat Ambrst: *abundavit* D-lat. rec ins εν bef δοξη (*prob from* εν δ. *above, ver* 8, *and below, ver* 11), with DFKLPℵ[3] rel latt goth $Orig_1$(-int_1) Mac [Cyr_1 $Antch_1$] Ambrst: om ABC 17 tol Syr [Euthal-ms].—δοξα ℵ[1].

10. rec ουδε (*mistake, from* δε *being the first syllable of the next word*), with h latt Thdot-$ancyr_1$(ουδε γαρ) Thl-ed Orig-int_1: txt ABC D[-gr] F[-gr] KLPℵ rel copt goth

the *whole new life* of the man of God, see Rom. vi. 4, 11; viii. 2, 10). On the history of this meaning of γράμμα, see Stanley's note. **7—11.**] *And this ministration is infinitely more glorious than was that of Moses under the old Covenant.* He argues from the less to the greater: *from the transitory glory of the killing letter*, to the *abiding glory of the life-giving Spirit.* **7.**] **But** (passing to another consideration,—the comparison of the two διακονίαι) **if the ministration of death in the letter** (of that death which the law, the code of literal and formal precept, brought in. This not having been seen, it was imagined that γράμματι belonged to ἐντετυπωμένη, and hence it was altered, as more according to fact, into γράμμασιν, the received reading.

No art. is required before γράμματι, as Meyer objects,—on account of the preposition ἐν) **engraven on stones** (it seems strange that ἐντετ. λίθ. should be the predicate of διακονία; but the *ministration* is the *whole putting forth* of the dispensation, the purport of which was summed up in the decalogue, written on stones. The decalogue thus written was, as in ver. 3, διακονηθεῖσα ὑπὸ Μωυσέως) **was** (constituted) **in glory** (as its state or accompanying condition:—the abstract as yet, to be compared with the glory of the other: the concrete, the brightness on the face of Moses, is not yet before us), **so that the sons of Israel could not fix their eyes on** (they were afraid to come nigh him, Exod. xxxiv. 30—so that μὴ δύνασθαι is not said of physical inability, but of inability from fear) **the face of Moses, on account of the glory of his face, which was transitory** ('transitoria et modici temporis,' Estius;—supernaturally conferred for a season, and passing away when the occasion was over), **how shall not rather the ministration of the Spirit** (= ἡ διακονία τῆς ζωῆς ἐν πνεύματι, as formally opposed to the other:—but not so expressed, because the Spirit is the *principle of life*, whereas the Law only *led to* death) **be** (future, because the glory will not be *accomplished* till the manifestation of the kingdom: according to Billroth, 'esse invenietur si rem recte perpenderimus:' or as Bengel, 'loquitur ex prospectu veteris Testamenti in novum:' but I much prefer the above, as giving the contrast, by and by expressed, between τὸ καταργούμενον and τὸ μένον) **in glory?** **9.**] **For** (an additional reason 'a minori ad majus') **if the ministration of condemnation was** (or, is) **glory** (the change of ἡ διακονία to the dat. has been made apparently because a difficulty was found in the ministration itself *being glory*), **much more does the ministration of righteousness abound in glory.** The ministration

τὸ [x] δεδοξασμένον [y] ἐν τούτῳ τῷ [y] μέρει, εἵνεκεν τῆς [z] ὑπερ-
βαλλούσης δόξης. 11 εἰ γὰρ τὸ [r] καταργούμενον [a] διὰ δόξης, [t] πολλῷ [t] μᾶλλον τὸ [b] μένον, [no] ἐν [op] δόξῃ. 12 ἔχοντες
οὖν τοιαύτην ἐλπίδα πολλῇ [c] παῤῥησίᾳ [d] χρώμεθα, 13 καὶ
οὐ [e] καθάπερ Μωυσῆς ἐτίθει [f] κάλυμμα ἐπὶ τὸ πρόσωπον
αὐτοῦ [g] πρὸς τὸ μὴ [h] ἀτενίσαι τοὺς υἱοὺς Ἰσραὴλ εἰς

x Exod. xxxiv. 30.
y ch. ix. 3. Col. ii. 16 (1 Pet. iv. 16 v. r.) only.
z ch. ix. 14. Eph. i. 19. ii. 7. iii. 19 only. P.+ 2 Macc. iv. 13 al. (ὑπερβαλλόντως, ch. xi. 23. -βολή, ch. i. 8.)
a = ch. ii. 4. v. 7.
b = Heb. xii. 27. 1 Pet. i. 23, 25 (from Isa. xl. 8) al. fr.
c (Gospp. παῤῥησίᾳ, Mark viii. 32. John vii. 13 al6. ἐν π., John vii. 4. xvi. 29 only.) Acts ii. 29 al4. Paul, ch. vii. 4 al6. Heb. iii. 6 al3. 1 John ii. 28 al3. only. Prov. i. 20 al.
d ch. i. 17.
e Rom. iv. 6 reff.
f here 4 times only. Exod. xxxiv. 33—35.
g constr., = 1 Thess. ii. 9. (see note.)
h ver. 7.

æth arm $Orig_3$[-c_1] Mac_1 Bas Chr-2-mss [Euthal-ms] Jer_2 Aug_1. rec (for ειν.) ενεκεν, with CF¹KL rel $Orig_3$ [Mac Bas Chr Euthal-ms Thdot-anc Thdrt]: txt ABD F²GPא g m 47 Damasc, ἥνεκεν 17.

13. rec εαυτου, with DKא rel Chr_1 Thdrt: [om goth:] txt ABCFLP Frag-coisl a c d m 17. [47 Euthal-ms] Chr-2-mss Damasc.

of *condemnation*, because (Rom. vii. 9 ff.) the Law detects and condemns sin:—the ministration of *righteousness*, because (Rom. i. 17) therein the righteousness of God is revealed and imparted by faith.

10.] **For** (substantiation of the foregoing πολλῷ μᾶλλον) **even that which has been glorified** (viz. the διακ. τ. κατακρίσ., which was ἐν δόξῃ by the brightness on the face of Moses) **has not been glorified** (has lost all its glory) **in this respect** (i. e. when compared with the gospel,—κατὰ τὸν τῆς συγκρίσεως λόγον, Chrys. Hom. vii. p. 481. De W. takes ἐν τ. τῷ μέρ. with δεδοξασμένον, 'that which was in this particular glorified,' viz. in the brightness on the face of Moses:—but that would more naturally be τὸ ἐν τούτῳ τῷ μέρει δεδοξασμένον:—as it now stands I cannot divide otherwise than οὐ δεδόξασται | τὸ δεδοξασμένον | ἐν τούτῳ τῷ μέρει. Meyer takes τὸ δεδοξ. as *abstract*, and ἐν τούτῳ τῷ μέρει as pointing to the *concrete*: 'that which has been glorified (general and abstract) has in this particular department (concrete, viz. the διακ. τ. κατακρίσ. which was δεδοξασμ.) no glory: q. d. the glorified is unglorified in this case.' This may certainly be, and is ingenious: but the other is simpler) **on account of** (i. e. when we take into consideration) **the surpassing glory** (viz. of the other διακονία:—*present*, because spoken of qualitatively).

11.] **For** (a fresh ground of superiority in glory of the Christian over the Mosaic ministry) **if that which is transitory** (not here, as above, the brilliancy of the visage of Moses, for that *was* the δόξα, but *the ministry itself*, the whole purpose which that ministry served, which was parenthetical and to come to an end) **was with glory** (διά, see reff., of the condition or circumstances in which a thing takes place), **much more is that which abideth** (the everlasting gospel) **in glory.** Estius says, "*per gloriam* (διὰ δ.) innuere videtur aliquid momentaneum ac transitorium: *in gloria*, aliquid manens et stabile." Similarly, Olshausen: but it is quite in the style of our Apostle to use various prepositions to express nearly the same relation,—see Rom. iii. 22, 30; v. 10.

12, 13.] *From a consciousness of this superior glory of his ministration, the Apostle uses great plainness of speech, and does not, as Moses, use a vail.*

12. ἐλπίδα] viz. that expressed by ἔσται ἐν δόξῃ, ver. 8: the hope of the ultimate manifestation of exceeding glory as belonging to his ministration. **παῤῥησίᾳ**] πρὸς τίνα, εἰπέ μοι· πρὸς τὸν θεόν, ἢ πρὸς τοὺς μαθητάς; πρὸς ὑμᾶς τοὺς μαθητευομένους, φησί· τουτέστι, μετ' ἐλευθερίας πανταχοῦ φθεγγόμεθα, οὐδὲν ὑποστελλόμενοι, οὐδὲν ἀποκρυπτόμενοι, οὐδὲν ὑφορώμενοι, ἀλλὰ σαφῶς λέγοντες· καὶ οὐ δεδοίκαμεν μὴ πλήξωμεν ὑμῶν τὰς ὄψεις, καθάπερ Μωυσῆς τὰς Ἰουδαίων, Chrys. p. 482.

13.] **καὶ οὐ, and** (do) **not** (place a vail on our face,—so Mark xv. 8, ὁ ὄχλος ἤρξατο αἰτεῖσθαι (ποιεῖν) καθὼς ἀεὶ ἐποίει αὐτοῖς. See Winer, edn. 6, § 64, i. 1 b.) **as Moses placed a vail on his face, in order that** (see below) **the sons of Israel might not look on the termination of the transitory** (viz. his διακονία, see ver. 11, but spoken of as δεδοξασμένη: 'the glory of his ministration'). A mistake has been made with regard to the history in Exod. xxxiv. 33—35, which has considerably obscured the understanding of this verse. It is commonly assumed, that Moses *spoke* to the Israelites, *having the vail on his face*; and this is implied in our version—'till Moses had done speaking with them, he put a vail on his face.' But the LXX (and Heb.) gave a different account: καὶ **ἐπειδὴ κατέπαυσεν λαλῶν** πρὸς αὐτούς, ἐπέθηκεν ἐπὶ τὸ πρόσωπον αὐτοῦ κάλυμμα. He spoke to them *without* the vail, with his face shining and glorified: *when he had done speaking*, he

τὸ [i] τέλος τοῦ [h] καταργουμένου. 14 ἀλλ' [k] ἐπωρώθη τὰ [l] νοήματα αὐτῶν. [m] ἄχρι γὰρ τῆς [n] σήμερον [n] ἡμέρας

ABCDF KLPℵ a b c d e f g h k l m n o 17. 47

i see Rom. x. 4. k Rom. xi. 7 reff. l ch. ii. 11 reff. m = Rom. viii. 22 reff. n Matt. xxviii. 15. Acts xx. 26. Rom. xi. 8 only. Josh. v. 9. Jer. i. 18.

om το D¹F. for τελος, προσωπον A vulg(and F-lat) Ambrst. (*finem* is written over τελος in the greek column of F. *The mistake in* A *and* vulg *may have arisen from the eye of some scribe having passed to the* προσωπον *in the line above:* τελος *stands just below* προσωπον *in Matthæi's edn of* K.)

14. αλλα B. επωρωθησαν K (g¹ ?). rec om ημερας (*as unnecessary, see ver* 15), with KL rel [Syr æth] Archel$_1$ Did$_1$ Bas$_1$ Chr$_1$ Thdrt Damasc: ins ABCDFPℵ

placed the vail on his face: and that, not because they were afraid to look on him, but as here, *that they might not look on the end*, or the fading, *of that transitory glory;* that they might only see it as long as it was the credential of his ministry, and then it might be withdrawn from their eyes. Thus the declaration of God's will to them was not ἐν παῤῥησίᾳ, but was interrupted and broken by intervals of concealment, which ours is not. The opposition is twofold: (1) between the *vailed* and the *unvailed* ministry, quoad the mere fact of concealment in the one case, and openness in the other: (2) between the ministry which was *suspended* by the vailing, that its τέλος might not be seen, and that which proceeds ἀπὸ δόξης εἰς δόξαν, *having no termination.* On the common interpretation, Commentators have found an almost insuperable difficulty in πρὸς τὸ μὴ ἀτ. The usual escape from it has been to render it, 'so that the Israelites could not,' as in ver. 7. De Wette somewhat modifies this, and sees in it the *divine* purpose: 'in order that,' but not in the intention of Moses, but of God's Providence. But both these renderings are ungrammatical. πρὸς τό with an infinitive *never signifies the mere result*, nor, as Meyer rightly remarks against De Wette, the *objective* purpose, but always the *subjective purpose present to the mind of the actor:* he refers to Matt. v. 28; vi. 1; xiii. 30; xxiii. 5; Mark xiii. 22; Eph. vi. 11; 1 Thess. ii. 9; 2 Thess. iii. 8; James iii. 3 (rec.); and Matt. xxvi. 12 (see my note there). I may remark also, that the narrative in Exodus, the LXX version of which the Apostle here closely follows (see below on ver. 16), implies that the brightness of Moses's face had *place not on that one occasion only, but throughout his whole ministry* between the Lord and the people. *When he ceased speaking to them*, he *put on the vail;* but *whensoever he went in before the Lord* to speak to Him, the *vail was removed* till he came out, and *had spoken to the Israelites all that the Lord had commanded him*, during which speaking they saw that his face shone,—and after which speaking he *again put on the vail.* So that the vail was the symbol of concealment and transitoriness: the part revealed they might see: beyond that, they could not: the ministry was a broken, interrupted one; its end was wrapped in obscurity. In the τέλος τοῦ καταργ. we must not think, as some Commentators have done, of *Christ* (Rom. x. 4), any further than it may be hinted in the background that when the law came to an end, He appeared.

14—18.] *The contrast is now made between the* CHILDREN OF ISRAEL, *on whose heart this vail still is in the reading of the O. T., and* US ALL (Christians), *who with uncovered face behold the glory of the Lord.* This section is parenthetical. Before and after it, the *ministry* is the subject: in it, *they to whom the ministry is directed.* But it serves to shew the *whole spirit* and *condition* of the two classes, and thus further to substantiate the character of openness and freedom asserted of the Christian ministry.

14.] **But** (also) **their understandings were hardened** (on this, the necessary sense of **ἐπωρώθη**, see note, Eph. iv. 18). These words evidently refer, as well as what follows, not to the τέλος, which they *did not see*, but to that which they *did see:* to that which answers to the present ἀνάγνωσις τῆς παλαιᾶς διαθήκης, viz. the *word of God imparted by the ministration of Moses.* And by these words the transition is made from the form of similitude just used, to that new one which is about to be used; q. d. '*not only was there a vail on Moses's face, to prevent more being known, but also their understandings were darkened: there was, besides, a vail on their hearts.*' So that ἀλλά = **but also**, or **moreover.** To refer this ἀλλ' ἐπωρ. to παῤῥησίᾳ χρώμεθα, to the present hard-heartedness of the Jews under the freedom of speech of the Gospel, as Olsh., De W., al., is, in my view, to miss the whole sense of the passage. No reference whatever is made to the state of the Jews *under the preaching of the gospel*, but only as the objects of the O. T. ministration,—*then*, under the oral teaching of Moses,—*now*, in the reading of the O. T. In order to understand what follows, the change of similitude must be carefully borne in mind.

τὸ αὐτὸ [f] κάλυμμα [o] ἐπὶ τῇ [p] ἀναγνώσει τῆς [qr] παλαιᾶς
[q] διαθήκης μένει, μὴ [s] ἀνακαλυπτόμενον ὅτι ἐν χριστῷ
[t] καταργεῖται· 15 ἀλλ' [u] ἕως [u] σήμερον, [v] ἡνίκα ἂν [w] ἀνα-
γινώσκηται Μωυσῆς, [f] κάλυμμα [x] ἐπὶ τὴν καρδίαν αὐτῶν
κεῖται. 16 [v] ἡνίκα δ' ἂν [y] ἐπιστρέψῃ [y] πρὸς κύριον, [z] περι-

o = John iv. 27. ch. vii. 4. Heb. ix. 15, 26.
p Acts xiii. 15. 1 Tim. iv. 13 only. Neh. viii. 8.
q here only. see ver. 6.
r Rom. vi. 6. 1 Cor. v. 7, 8 al. Lev. xxv. 22.
s here bis only. Job xii. 22 and Isa. iii. 17 BN. (ἀποκ. A.)
t vv. 7 &c.
u here only. Sir. xlvii. 7. see Matt. xxvii. 8. Rom. xi. 8.
v here bis only. Exod. xxxiv. 34. Deut. vii. 12.
w constr., Acts viii. 28. (xiii. 27.) xv. 21.
x so Acts x. 17. xi. 11. Rev. iii. 20. v. 1. vii. 1. xx. 1.
y = 1 Thess. i. 9. (Acts ix. 40.) Amos iv. 6.
z Acts xxvii. 20 reff.

m 17 latt copt [syr goth arm] Clem$_1$ Cyr[-p Euthal-ms] Orig-int$_1$ [Cypr$_1$] Ambrst. for *επι*, *εν* DF Chr$_1$.

15. rec om *αν* (*from αν beginning αναγινωσκ.*?), with DFKL[P] rel (Orig[-c$_1$]) Eus$_1$ Cyr-jer$_1$ Cæs$_1$ Chr$_1$ Cyr$_2$ [Euthal-ms] Thdrt$_4$ Damasc: ins ABCℵ Orig$_2$ Cyr$_1$ Thdrt$_1$, *εαν* 17. rec *αναγινωσκεται*, with FKL rel vulg Eus$_1$ Cyr-jer$_1$ Cæs$_1$ Chr$_1$ Cyr$_3$[-ms$_2$-p] Thdrt$_1$ Damasc Orig-int$_2$: txt A B(see table) CDPℵ c m 17 Orig$_2$[-c$_1$] Chr-ms Cyr[-p$_2$-ms$_1$ Euthal-ms] Thdrt$_2$. from *καλυμμα* to *το* next ver is repeated by B[1]. *κειται* bef *επι την καρδ. αυ.* D[1.3]F latt [copt] goth æth.

16. for *ηνικα*, *οταν* F[*οτα*] Chr$_1$. *δε εαν* Aℵ[1] 17: om *αν* C k Mac Bas.

τὸ αὐτὸ κάλυμμα] 'the vail once on Moses's face,' is now regarded as laid on *their hearts.* It denoted the ceasing, the covering up, of his oral teaching; for it was put on *when he had done* speaking to the people. *Now,* his oral teaching has altogether ceased, and the *διακονία* is carried on by *a book.* But as when we *listen,* the speaker is the *agent,* and the hearers are *passive,*—so on the other hand, when we *read, we* are the *agents* and the book is *passive.* The book is the same to all: the difference between those who understand and those who do not understand is now a *subjective* difference—the vail is no longer on the face of the speaker, but on the *heart of the reader.* So that of necessity the form of the similitude is changed. **For** (answering to an understood clause, 'and remain hardened') **to the present day the same vail** (which was once on the face of Moses) **remains at the reading of the Old Testament** (*ἡ παλ. διαθ.* here, as we now popularly use the words, *the book comprising the ancient Covenant*), **the discovery not being made** (by the removal of the vail) **that it** (the O. T.) **is done away in Christ** (that the Old Covenant has passed away, being superseded by Christ). This I believe to be the only admissible sense of the words, *consistently with the symbolism of the passage.* The renderings, '*remains not taken away—for it* (i. e. the vail) *is done away in Christ,*' and (as E. V.) '*remaineth . . untaken away . . which vail* (*ὅ τι*) *is done away in Christ,*'—are inadmissible: (1) because they make **καταργεῖται**, which throughout the passage belongs to the *glory of the ministry,* to apply to the *vail:* and (2) because they give no satisfactory sense. It is not *because* the vail can only be done away in Christ, that it now remains untaken away on their hearts, but *because their hearts are hardened.* Besides, the Apostle would not have expressed it thus, but *ἐν χριστῷ γὰρ καταργ.* The word *ἀνακαλυπτόμενον* has been probably chosen, as is often the practice of the Apostle, on account of its relation to *κάλυμμα,* —**it not being unvailed to them that . . . .** 15.] **But** (reassertion of *μὴ ἀνακαλυπτόμενον,* with a view to the next clause) **to this day, whenever Moses is read, a vail lies upon their heart** (understanding. *κεῖται ἐπί* w. acc.,—pregn., involving the *being laid* on, *and remaining there*). 16.] Here, the tertium comparationis is, *the having on a vail, and taking it off on going into the presence of the Lord.* This *Moses did; and the choice* of the *same words* as those of the LXX, shews the closeness of the comparison; **ἡνίκα δ' ἂν** *εἰσεπορεύετο Μωυσῆς ἔναντι* **κυρίου** *λαλεῖν αὐτῷ,* **περιῃρεῖτο τὸ κάλυμμα.** This shall likewise be done in the case of the Israelites: **when it** (i. e. *ἡ καρδία αὐτῶν,*—not *Israel,* as Chrys., Theod., Theophyl., Erasm., al.,—nor *Moses,* as Calv., Estius,—nor *τίς,* as Orig., al.) **shall turn to the Lord** (here again *ἐπιστρέψῃ πρός* is carefully chosen, being the very expression of the LXX, when the Israelites, having been afraid of the glory of the face of Moses, returned to him after being summoned by him:—*ἐφοβήθησαν ἐγγίσαι αὐτῷ· καὶ ἐκάλεσεν αὐτοὺς Μωυσῆς, καὶ* **ἐπεστράφησαν πρὸς αὐτὸν** . . . . ,—and *κύριον* appears to be used for the same reason) **the vail is taken away** (not, *shall* be, because *ἡ καρδία* is the subject, and thus the *taking away* becomes an individual matter, happening whenever and wherever conversion takes place). Let me restate this,—as it is all-important towards the understanding of vv. 17, 18. 'When

a Acts viii. 39 reff.
b Rom. viii. 21. 1 Cor. x. 29. Gal. v. 1, 13. Lev. xix. 20.
c here only †. (see note.)
d Rom. viii. 29 reff.
e constr., here only, see Moulton's Winer, p. 538, note 1. Matt. xvii. 2 ‖ Mk. Rom. xii. 2 only †. Ps. xxxiii. 1 Symm.
f Rom. iv. 6 reff.
g = Acts ii. 22. James i. 13 al.

αιρεῖται τὸ [f] κάλυμμα.
17 Ὁ δὲ κύριος τὸ πνεῦμά ἐστιν· οὗ δὲ τὸ [a] πνεῦμα [a] κυρίου, [b] ἐλευθερία.
18 ἡμεῖς δὲ πάντες [s] ἀνακεκαλυμμένῳ προσώπῳ τὴν δόξαν κυρίου [c] κατοπτριζόμενοι, τὴν αὐτὴν [d] εἰκόνα [e] μεταμορφούμεθα ἀπὸ δόξης εἰς δόξαν, [f] καθάπερ [g] ἀπὸ κυρίου πνεύματος.

ABCDF KLPℵ a b c d e f g h k l m n o 17. 47

17. for οὗ, που F. for κυριου, το αγιον L. rec ins εκει bef ελευθερια (*see notes*), with D$^{2\cdot3}$FKLPℵ^3 rel latt syr goth æth arm Ath$_1$[-int$_1$] Epiph$_1$ Bas$_1$ Chr$_1$ Cyr$_2$ Thdrt Damasc Orig-int$_5$ Hil$_2$ [Novat$_1$ Ambrst]: om ABC D^1[-gr] ℵ^1 17 fri Syr copt Nys$_1$ [Cyr-p$_1$(in Cyr$_2$ both readings are found) Euthal-ms].

18. αποπτριζομενοι F: ενοπτριζομεθα Mac$_1$. μεταμορφουμενοι A 23 Orig$_1$(-int$_1$) Eus$_1$ Mac$_1$. καθωσπερ B.

their heart *goes in to speak with God*,—ceases to contemplate the dead letter, and begins to commune with the Spirit of the old covenant (the Spirit of God), then the vail is removed, as it was from the face of Moses.' **17.] Now** (δέ exponentis. τίς δὲ οὗτος πρὸς ὃν δεῖ ἀποβλέψαι; Theodoret) **the Lord is the Spirit**: i.e. the **κύριος** of ver. 16, is, the *Spirit*, whose word the O. T. is: the πνεῦμα,—as opposed to the γράμμα,—which ζωοποιεῖ, ver. 6. But it is not merely, as Wetst., 'Dominus *significat* Spiritum,' nor is πνεῦμα merely, as Olsh., *the spiritual sense of the law*: but, '*the Lord*,' as here spoken of, 'Christ,' '*is the Spirit*,' is identical with the Holy Spirit: not personally nor essentially, but, as is shewn by **τὸ πνεῦμα κυρίου** following, *in this department of His divine working*:—*Christ*, here, *is the Spirit of Christ*. The principal mistaken interpretation (among many, see Pool's Synops., Meyer, De Wette) is that of Chrys., Theodoret, Theophyl., Œcum., Estius, Schulz,—making τὸ πνεῦμα the subject, and ὁ κύρ. the predicate, which though perhaps (but would δέ then have had its present position?) allowable, is against the context, ὁ δὲ κύρ. being plainly resumed from ὁ κύρ. in ver. 16. The words are then used by them as a proof of the Divinity of the Holy Spirit.

But (δέ appealing to a known or evident axiom, as in a mathematical demonstration) **where the Spirit of the Lord** (see above) **is, is liberty** (ἐκεῖ has probably been inserted, as being usual after οὗ: but, as Meyer remarks, not in St. Paul's style, see Rom. iv. 15; v. 20). They are fettered in spirit as long as they are slaves to the letter, = as long as they have the vail on their hearts; but when they turn to the Lord the Spirit, which is not πνεῦμα δουλείας but πν. υἱοθεσίας, Rom. viii. 15,—and by virtue of whom οὐκ ἔτι εἶ δοῦλος, ἀλλὰ υἱός, Gal. iv. 7,—then they are at liberty. There can hardly be any allusion to a vail over the head implying subjection, as 1 Cor. xi. 10, (Erasm., Beza, Grot., Bengel, Fritz.,) for here the *covering of the head* with a vail is not thought of, but merely intercepting the sight.

18.] But (the sight of the Jews is thus intercepted; in contrast to whom) **WE all** ('*all Christians*:' not, as Erasm., Estius, Bengel, al. m., 'we Apostles and teachers: the contrast is to the υἱοὶ Ἰσραήλ above) **with unvailed face** (the vail having been removed at our conversion: the stress is on these words) **beholding in a mirror the glory of the Lord** (i. e. Christ: from vv. 16, 17. **κατοπτρίζω** is to *shew in a mirror, to make a reflexion in a mirror*; so Plutarch, de Placitis Philosophorum, iii. 5: Anaxagoras explained a rainbow to be the reflexion of the sun's brightness from a thick cloud, that always stands opposite τοῦ κατοπτρίζοντος αὐτὸ ἀστέρος. In the middle, it is '*to behold oneself in a mirror*:' so Diog. Laert., Plato, p. 115, τοῖς μεθύουσι συνεβούλευε κατοπτρίζεσθαι;—but also, *to see in a mirror*, so Philo, Legis Allegor. iii. 33, vol. i. p. 107, μὴ γὰρ ἐμφανισθείης μοι δι' οὐρανοῦ ἢ γῆς ἢ ὕδατος ἢ ἀέρος ἤ τινος ἁπλῶς τῶν ἐν γενέσει, μηδὲ κατοπτρισαίμην ἐν ἄλλῳ τινὶ τὴν σὴν ἰδέαν, ἢ ἐν σοὶ τῷ θεῷ. And such is evidently the meaning here: the gospel is this mirror, the εὐαγγέλιον **τῆς δόξης τοῦ χριστοῦ**, ch. iv. 4, and we, looking on it with unvailed face, are the contrast to the Jews, with vailed hearts reading their law. The meaning '*reflecting* the glory,' &c. as Chrys., Luth., Calov., Bengel, Billroth, Olsh., is one which neither the word nor the context (see above) will bear (see, however, Stanley's note), **are transfigured into the same image** (which we see in the mirror: the image of the glory of Christ, see Gal. iv. 19, which is more to the point than Rom. viii. 21, cited by Meyer, and 1 John iii. 3. But the change here spoken of is a *spiritual* one, not the bodily change at the Resurrection: it is going on here in the process of sanctification. No prep. need be understood before τὴν αὐτὴν *

IV. 1 διὰ τοῦτο ἔχοντες τὴν [h] διακονίαν ταύτην, καθὼς
[i] ἠλεήθημεν, οὐκ [k] ἐγκακοῦμεν, 2 ἀλλὰ [l] ἀπειπάμεθα τὰ
[m] κρυπτὰ τῆς [n] αἰσχύνης, μὴ [o] περιπατοῦντες [o] ἐν [p] πανουρ-

h = Acts xx. 24 reff. i Rom. xi. 30, 31 reff. k Luke xviii. 1. ver. 16. Gal. vi. 9. Eph. iii. 13. 2 Thess. iii. 13 only. L.P.+ Symm., Gen. xxvii. 46. Num. xxi. 5. Isa. vii. 16. l here only. 3 Kings xi. 2. Job x. 3 al. m and constr., Rom. ii. 16 reff. n Luke xiv. 9. Phil. iii. 19. Heb. xii. 2. Jude 13. Rev. iii. 18 only. Ps. lxxxviii. 45. o Rom. vi. 4. ch. x. 3. Eph. v. 2 al. Prov. viii. 20. p 1 Cor. iii. 19 reff.

CHAP. IV. 1. for ταυτην, αυτην F[-gr: om vulg-clem]. rec εκκακουμεν, with CD[3]KLP rel [Chr$_1$ Thdrt Damasc]: txt ABD[1]Fℵ m 17 [Euthal-ms].
2. (αλλα, so A(perhaps) BCDℵ c d e f g h k l n 47 [Damasc].) for κρυπτα, εργα K.

εἰκόνα—the passive verb indirectly governs the acc., as in ἀποτέμνομαι τὴν κεφαλήν and similar cases) **from glory to glory** (this is explained, either (1) '*from one degree of glory to another;*' so most Commentators and De Wette, or (2) '*from* (by) *the glory which we see, into glory,*' as Chrys. p. 486, ἀπὸ δόξης, τῆς τοῦ πνεύματος, εἰς δόξαν, τὴν ἡμετέραν, τὴν ἐγγιγνομένην,—Theodoret, Œcum., Theophyl., Bengel, Fritz., Meyer, al. I prefer the former, as the other would introduce a tautology, the sentiment being expressed in the words following) **as by the Lord the Spirit.** κυρίου πνεύματος = τοῦ κυρίου τοῦ πνεύματος,—the first art. being omitted after the preposition, the second to conform the predicate to its subject, as in ἀπὸ θεοῦ πατρός, Gal. i. 3,—and answers to ὁ δὲ κύριος τὸ πνεῦμά ἐστιν above. This seems the obvious and most satisfactory way of taking the words, and, from ver. 17, to be necessitated by the context; and so Theodoret, Luther, Beza, Calov., Wolf, Estius, al. The rendering upheld by Fritz., Billroth, Meyer, De Wette, '*the Lord of the Spirit,*' i. e. 'Christ, whose Spirit He is,' seems to me to convey very little meaning, besides being an expression altogether unprecedented. The transformation is effected *by the Spirit* (τοῦτο μεταμορφοῖ, Chrys.), the Author and Upholder of spiritual life, who 'takes of the things of Christ, and *shews them* to us,' John xvi. 14, see also Rom. viii. 10, 11,—who sanctifies us till we are holy as Christ is holy; the process of renewal after Christ's image is *such a transformation as may be expected by the agency of* (καθάπερ ἀπό, so Chrys., καὶ τοιαύτην οἵαν εἰκὸς ἀπὸ . . .) *the Lord the Spirit,*—Christ Himself *being the image,* see ch. iv. 4. The two other renderings are out of the question, as being inconsistent with the order of the words: viz.: (1) that of E. V. and of Vulg., Theophyl., Grot., Bengel, '*the Spirit of the Lord,*' and (2) that of Chrys., Theodoret, Calov., Estius, '*the Spirit who is the Lord.*' Meyer objects to the interpretation given above as inconsistent with the *self-evident connexion of the genitives.* How would he render ἀπὸ θεοῦ πατρός?

IV. 1—6.] *Taking up again the subject of his freedom of speech* (ch. iii. 12), *he declares his renunciation of all deceit, and manifestation of the truth to every man* (ver. 2), *even though to some the Gospel be hidden* (vv. 3, 4). *And this because he preaches, without any selfish admixture, only the pure light of the Gospel of Christ* (vv. 5, 6). **1.] διὰ τοῦτο** refers to the previous description of the freeness and unvailedness of the ministry of the Gospel, and of the state of Christians in general (ch. iii. 18). **ἔχοντες τ. δ. ταύτ.** further expands and explains διὰ τοῦτο. **καθὼς ἠλεήθ.] even as we received mercy** (from God, at the time of our being appointed; cf. ἠλεήθην, 1 Tim. i. 16): belongs to ἔχ. τ. δ. ταύτ., not to what follows, and is a qualification, in humility, of ἔχοντες—'possessing it, not as our own, but in as far as we were shewn mercy.' **οὐκ ἐγκακοῦμεν] We do not behave ourselves in a cowardly manner,** do not shrink from plainness of speech and action. ἐγκακέω is the opposite of παῤῥησιάζω. οὐκ ἐκκακοῦμεν would be, '*we do not give up through faintness or cowardice.*' It is hardly possible to decide satisfactorily between the two readings. ἐγκ. seems to be universal, except in the N. T. (rec. text) and the Fathers, which have ἐκκ. Did the Fathers borrow this form from the N. T., or was it the usual form of later Greek, and as such introduced into the text by the copyists? In such doubt, I have followed manuscript authority. **But** (cowardice alone prompting concealment in such a case, where it does not belong to the character of the ministry itself) **we have renounced** (so Herod. iv. 125, τῶν ἀπειπαμένων τὴν σφετέρην συμμαχίην: Ælian, N. H. vi. 1, τὴν ἀκόλαστον κοίτην ἀπείπατο παντελῶς πᾶσαν: and other examples in Wetst.) **the hidden things of shame** (the having any views, ends, or practices which such as have them hide through shame: not, as De Wette, *the hidden things of infamy* or *dishonesty.* αἰσχύνη is subjective, =, as Meyer, φόβος ἐπὶ προσδοκίᾳ ἀδοξίας, Plato Defin. p. 416. It is plain from the context that it refers, not to crimes and unholy practices, but to *crooked arts,* of which

γίᾳ, μηδὲ [q] δολοῦντες τὸν λόγον τοῦ θεοῦ, ἀλλὰ τῇ
[r] φανερώσει τῆς ἀληθείας [s] συνιστάντες [t] ἑαυτοὺς πρὸς
πᾶσαν [u] συνείδησιν ἀνθρώπων ἐνώπιον τοῦ θεοῦ. 3 [v] εἰ δὲ
[v] καὶ ἔστιν κεκαλυμμένον τὸ [w] εὐαγγέλιον [w] ἡμῶν, [x] ἐν τοῖς
[y] ἀπολλυμένοις ἐστὶν κεκαλυμμένον, 4 [z] ἐν οἷς ὁ [a] θεὸς τοῦ [H iv. 4 ...?]
[ab] αἰῶνος [b] τούτου [c] ἐτύφλωσεν τὰ [d] νοήματα τῶν [e] ἀπίστων, ABCDF [H]KL
[f] εἰς τὸ μὴ [g] αὐγάσαι τὸν [h] φωτισμὸν τοῦ [i] εὐαγγελίου τῆς Pא a b c d e f g h
[i] δόξης τοῦ χριστοῦ, ὅς ἐστιν [k] εἰκὼν τοῦ θεοῦ. 5 οὐ γὰρ k l m n o 17. 47

q here only. Ps. xiv. 3. xxxv. 2.
r 1 Cor. xii. 7 only †.
s = Rom. xvi. 1 reff. see ch. iii. 1.
t 1st pers., ch. iii. 1 reff.
u ch. i. 12 reff.
v ver. 16. ch. v. 16. vii. 8 al.
w 1 Thess. i. 5. 2 Thess. ii. 14. see Rom. ii. 16. xvi. 25. 2 Tim. ii. 8.
x = ch. ii. 15.
y Rom. ii. 12 reff.
z = 1 Cor. iv. 2, 6 al.
a here only. see John xii. 31. xiv. 30. Eph. ii. 2. vi. 12.
b Rom. xii. 2 reff.
c John xii. 40. 1 John ii. 11 only. Isa. xlii. 19 only.
d ch. ii. 11 reff.
e = Matt. xvii. 17 al. fr.
f Rom. iv. 11 reff.
g here only. Levit. xiii. 24, &c. xiv. 56 only. (-γή, Acts xx. 11.)
h here bis only. not in classics. Job iii. 9 Bא[3a] F &c. (not Aא[1].) Ps. xxvi. 1. xliii. 3. lxxvii. 14. lxxxix. 8 only.
i 1 Tim. i. 11 only.
k Col. i. 15. Rom. viii. 29. 1 Cor. xi. 7 al. Gen. i. 26, 27.

rec *συνιστωντες*, with D³KL rel: *συνισταvοντες* A(appy) BP 47. 67². 80: txt CD¹Fא 17 [Euthal-ms].

[3. *απολυμμενοις* F l (17).]

4. **διαυγασαι** A d 17 Eus$_1$ Archel$_1$[-ed$_1$] Cyr-jer$_2$ Damasc: **καταυγ.** CD[H] Orig$_1$ [Dial$_1$ Amphil$_1$] Eus$_1$ (*both glosses, further to particularize the simple verb*): txt BFKLPא rel Orig$_1$ [Archel-ms$_1$ Euthal-ms] Chr$_1$ Thdrt Damasc [Cyr-mss fluctuate hopelessly]. rec adds *αυτοις*, with D$^{2.3}$[-gr] KL[P] rel [vulg-clem spec syrr goth æth] Orig$_1$ Chr$_3$ [Amphil$_1$ Thdrt]: om ABCD¹F[H]א 17 old-lat am(with demid fuld harl [tol]) Orig$_1$ Eus$_1$ Cyr-jer Epiph$_2$ Cyr[-p Archel$_2$ Euthal-ms] Iren-int$_1$ [Aug$_1$]. for *χριστου*, *κυριου* C. for *ος*, *ο* F. aft *του θεου* ins *του αορατου* (*see Col* i. 15) LPא³ a f l m 47 syr [goth] arm: pref spec.

men *are ashamed*, and which perhaps were made use of by the false teachers), **not walking** (having our daily conversation) in **craftiness** (see ref.) **nor adulterating** (see ch. ii. 17, note) **the word of God, but by the manifestation of the truth** (as *our only means*, see 1 Thess. ii. 3, 4;—the words come first, as emphatic), **recommending ourselves** (a recurrence to the charge and apology of ch. iii. 1 ff.) **to** (with reference to,—the verdict of) **every conscience of men** (every possible variety of the human conscience; implying, there is no conscience but will inwardly acknowledge this, however loath some among you may be outwardly to confess it. So that the expression is not exactly = *πρ. τὴν συν. πάντων ἀνθρώπων*. We need hardly extend *ἀνθρ.* so wide as Chrys. (Hom. viii. p. 493), *οὐ . . πιστοῖς μόνον, ἀλλὰ καὶ ἀπίστοις ἐσμὲν κατάδηλοι*:—he is speaking as a *teacher*, and the men spoken of are naturally *his hearers and disciples*), **in the sight of God** (as ch. ii. 17; not *merely* to satisfy men's consciences, but with regard to God's all-seeing eye which discerns the heart).

3.] **But if** ('which I concede;'—see note, 1 Cor. iv. 7) **it is even so, that our gospel** (the gospel preached by us) **is vailed, it is among** (in the estimation of) **the perishing that it is vailed.** The allegory of ch. iii. is continued,—the hiding of the gospel by the vail placed before the understanding.

4.] **in whose case** (it is true, that) **the god of this world** (the Devil, the ruling principle in the men of this world, see reff. It is historically curious, that Irenæus (Hær. iv. 39. 2, p. 266), Origen, Tertull. (contra Marc. iv. 11, vol. ii. p. 499), Chrys., Augustine (c. advers. leg. ii. 7 (29), vol. viii. p. 655), Œcum., Theodoret, Theophylact, all repudiate, in their zeal against the Marcionites and Manichæans, the grammatical rendering, and take *τῶν ἀπίστων τοῦ αἰῶνος τούτου* together) **blinded** (the aor. of a purely historical event) **the understandings of the unbelieving** (i. e. who, the *ἀπολλύμενοι*, are victims of that blinding of the understandings of the unbelieving, which the Devil is habitually carrying on. Meyer well remarks, that if it had merely been *τὰ νοήματα*, it would have only expressed in the concrete the *νοήμ.* of those signified by *ἐν οἷς*,—whereas now, by the addition of *τῶν ἀπίστ.*, the blinding inflicted on the *ἀπολλ.* is marked as falling under its *category*. The rendering *τῶν ἀπίστων* 'so *that they believe not*,' Fritz., Billroth, is out of all question) **in order that the illumination of** (*shining from*, gen. subj.) **the gospel of the glory of Christ, who is the image of God** (recurrence to the allegory of ch. iii. 18;—Christ is the image of God, *ἀπαύγασμα τῆς δόξης αὐτοῦ*, Heb. i. 3, into which same image, *τὴν αὐτὴν εἰκόνα*, we, looking on it in the mirror of the gospel, are changed by the Spirit; but which glorious image is not visible to those who are blinded by Satan), **might not shine forth** ([see var. readd. The object of the god of this world was not merely to prevent *them* from being

[l] ἑαυτοὺς [m] κηρύσσομεν, ἀλλὰ χριστὸν Ἰησοῦν κύριον· [l] ἑαυτοὺς δὲ δούλους ὑμῶν [n] διὰ Ἰησοῦν. 6 ὅτι ὁ θεὸς ὁ [o] εἰπὼν [p] Ἐκ σκότους [pq] φῶς [q] λάμψει, ὃς [q] ἔλαμψεν ἐν ταῖς καρδίαις ἡμῶν [r] πρὸς [h] φωτισμὸν τῆς [s] γνώσεως τῆς [s] δόξης τοῦ θεοῦ [t] ἐν [t] προσώπῳ χριστοῦ.

[...iv. 7 H?] 7 Ἔχομεν δὲ τὸν [u] θησαυρὸν τοῦτον ἐν [vw] ὀστρακίνοις

l ch. iii. 1 reff. m Acts viii. 5 reff. n ver. 11. o = James ii. 11. p Job xxxvii. 15. q Acts xii. 7 (reff.). Isa. ix. 2. r = 1 Cor. vii. 35 reff. s see Hab. ii. 14. t ch. ii. 10. Prov. viii. 30. x. 21. Luke vi. 45 al3. Josh. vi. 19. u Epp., Col. ii. 3. Heb. xi. 26 only. Gospp., Matt. ii. 11 al8. Mark vi. 28. v 2 Tim. ii. 20. w as above (v) only. Levit.

5. *ιησ.* bef *χρ.* ACDא vulg syr goth [(æth) Aug_1, and but] om *κυρ.* P d: *κυρ. ιη. χρ.* F[not F-lat]: om *ιησ.* 47: txt B[H]KL rel Syr copt arm Mcion-e_1[and ms_1] Cyr-jer_1 Chr_1 [Cyr-p Euthal-ms] Thdrt Damasc Ambrst. *ημων*(sic) א 17. for 2nd *ιησουν*, *ιησου* A²Cא¹ 17 Mcion-e_2 [Cyr-p_1]: *χριστου* א-corr¹ 5 [Cyr-p_1].

6. om 1st *ὁ* B(sic: see table) n [Mcion-e-ms_1(ins_2)]. aft *ειπων* ins *ο* (but erased) א¹. rec *λαμψαι*, with CD³F[H]KLPא³ rel latt goth Mcion-e_3 $Orig_1$ $Dial_1$ Mac_1 [Ps?-]Ath_2 Chr_2 *Cyr*[-p Euthal-ms] Thdrt Damasc [$Tert_1$]: txt AB D¹[-gr] א¹ $Clem_1$. om *os* D¹F old-lat demid(and harl) Chr_2 $Tert_1$ Ambrst [Aug_1]. *υμων* C 3. 47 Chr_2. for *του θεου*, *αυτου* C¹ D¹[and lat] F[(not F-lat) fri] æth $Dial_1$ *Cyr*[-p] $Tert_2$: txt ABC³D³[H]KLPא rel [vulg F-lat syrr copt goth arm] ($Orig_4$) Ath_1 Chr [Euthal-ms] Thdrt Damasc $Ambr_2$ Ambrst. (*του θεου is certainly original; for, as Meyer observes, had αυτου been origl, it is hardly possible that του θεου should have been a gloss on it, as ο θεος occurs just before.*) rec ins *ιησου* bef *χρ.*, with C[H]KLPא rel tol [syrr copt goth arm-ed] $Orig_1$ [Euthal-ms] Thdrt Damasc: aft *χρ.*, DF latt Cyr_1 [Ambr Ambrst Aug]: om AB 17 arm-mss $Orig_2$ $Dial_1$ Ath_1 Chr_2 [Cyr-p_1-ms_1] $Tert_3$.

illuminated, but to stop the shining forth altogether]:—the rendering, '*that they might not see*,' Grot., al., is inadmissible). 5, 6.] *We have no reason to use trickery or craft, having no selfish ends to serve: nor concealment, being ourselves enlightened by God, and set for the spreading of light.* 5.] **For we preach not** (the subject of our preaching is not) **ourselves** (Meyer understands *κυρίους*, 'as lords;' but as De W. observes, this would anticipate the development of thought which follows, the contrast between *χρ. Ἰησοῦν* as *κύριον*, and ourselves as your *δούλους*, not being yet raised),—**but Christ Jesus as Lord, and ourselves as your servants for Jesus' sake** (on account of Him and His work). 6.] **Because** (explains and substantiates the last clause,—that we are your servants for Jesus' sake) (*it is*) **God, who said Out of** (not, '*after* the darkness;' this meaning of *ἐκ*, though allowable, e.g. *ἐκ κυμάτων γὰρ αὖθις αὖ γάλην' ὁρῶ*, does not occur in N. T.) **darkness light shall shine** (allusion to Gen. i. 3: the change to *λάμψαι* appears to have been made because the words cited are not the exact ones spoken by the Creator), **who shined** (Grot., Fritz., Meyer, would render *ἔλαμψεν*, 'caused light to shine,' using the verb in the *factitive* sense, as *ἀνατέλλω*, Matt. v. 45, and *ὦ λάμπουσα πέτρα πυρὸς δικόρυφον σέλας*, Eur. Phœn. 226. But this usage of the word seems entirely poetical, and the intransitive sense would as well express the divine act) **in our hearts** (the physical creation bearing an analogy to the spiritual) **in order to the shining forth** (to others) **of the knowledge** (in us) **of the glory of God in the face of Christ** (= *τῆς δόξης τ. θεοῦ τῆς ἐν προσώπῳ χρ.*, 'the glory of God manifested in Christ'). The figure is still derived from the history in ch. iii., and refers to the brightness on the face of Moses:—the only true effulgence of the divine glory is from the face of Christ. Meyer contends for the connexion of *ἐν προσώπ. χρ.* with *φωτισμόν*, but his explanation fails to convey to my mind any satisfactory sense. He says that when the *γνῶσις* is imparted by preaching, it shines, and its brightness illuminates *the face of Christ*, because it is His face whose glory is looked on in the mirror of preaching. But I cannot think that any thing so very far-fetched would be in the Apostle's mind. As to the necessity of the art. *τῆς* before *ἐν*, none will assert it who are much versed in the many varieties of expression in such sentences in the Apostle's style. 7—18.] *This glorious ministry is fulfilled by weak, afflicted, persecuted, and decaying vessels, which are moreover worn out in the work* (7—12). *Yet the spirit of faith, the hope of the resurrection, and of being presented with them, for whom he has laboured, bears him up against the decay of the outer man, and all present tribulation* (13—18). We are not justified in assuming with Calvin, Estius, al., that a definite reproach of personal meanness had induced the Apostle to speak thus. For he does not deal with any

x Acts ix. 15 reff.
y Rom. vii. 13 reff. Joseph. Antt. i. 13. 4. ii. 2. 1.
z = ch. vi. 4. vii. 5, 11. viii. 7. xi. 6.
a ch. i. 6 reff.
b ch. vi. 12 (bis) only. Josh. xvii. 15. Isa. xxviii. 20. xlix. 19 only. (-ρία, Rom. ii. 9.)
c Acts xxv. 20 reff.
d ch. i. 8 only. Ps. lxxvii. 15 only.
e = 1 Cor. iv. 12 reff.
f Matt. xxvii. 46 ‖ Mk. Acts ii. 27 (from Ps. xv. 10), 31. 2 Tim. iv. 10, 16. Heb. xiii. 5. 1 Chron. xxviii. 20.
g = here (Heb. vi. 1) only. 4 Kings iii. 19.
h = Matt. ii. 13 al. fr.
i Rom. iv. 19 only †.

ABCDF KLPℵ bcdeghklmno 17. 47

[v] [x] σκεύεσιν, ἵνα ἡ [y] ὑπερβολὴ τῆς δυνάμεως ᾖ τοῦ θεοῦ
καὶ μὴ ἐξ ἡμῶν· 8 [z] ἐν [z] παντὶ [a] θλιβόμενοι ἀλλ᾽ οὐ [b] στενοχωρούμενοι, [c] ἀπορούμενοι ἀλλ᾽ οὐκ [d] ἐξαπορούμενοι,
9 [e] διωκόμενοι ἀλλ᾽ οὐκ [f] ἐγκαταλειπόμενοι, [g] καταβαλ-
λόμενοι ἀλλ᾽ οὐκ [h] ἀπολλύμενοι, 10 πάντοτε τὴν [i] νέκρωσιν

9. εγκαταλιμπανομενοι F Eus$_1$ Chr$_2$ Max$_1$.

such reproach here, but with matters common to all human ministers of the word. All this is a following out in detail of the οὐκ ἐγκακοῦμεν of ver. 1, already enlarged on in *one of its departments*,—that of *not shrinking from openness of speech*, —and now to be put forth in *another*, viz. *bearing up against outward and inward difficulties.* If *any* polemical purpose is to be sought, it is the setting forth of the abundance of sufferings, the glorying in weakness (ch. xi. 23, 30), which substantiated his apostolic mission: but even such purpose is only in the background; he is pouring out, in the fulness of his heart, the manifold discouragements and the far more exceeding encouragements of his office. **7.] τὸν θησ. τοῦτ.**, viz. '*the light of the knowledge of the glory of God*, ver. 6. ἐπειδὴ γὰρ πολλὰ καὶ μεγάλα εἶπε περὶ τῆς ἀποῤῥήτου δόξης· ἵνα μή τις λέγῃ Καὶ πῶς τοσαύτης δόξης ἀπολαύοντες μένομεν ἐν θνητῷ σώματι; φησὶν ὅτι τοῦτο μὲν οὖν αὐτὸ μάλιστά ἐστι τὸ θαυμαστόν, καὶ δεῖγμα μέγιστον τῆς τοῦ θεοῦ δυνάμεως, ὅτι σκεῦος ὀστράκινον τοσαύτην ἠδυνήθη λαμπρότητα ἐνεγκεῖν, καὶ τηλικοῦτον φυλάξαι θησαυρόν. Chrys. p. 496. Some (Calv., al.) think the θησ. to be the whole διακονία: but it seems simpler to refer it to that which has immediately preceded, in a style like that of Paul, in which each successive idea so commonly evolves itself out of the last. The **σκεῦος** is the *body*, not the whole personality; the ὁ ἔξω ἄνθρωπος of ver. 16; see ver. 10. And in the troubles of the body the personality shares, as long as it is bound up with it here. The similitude and form of expression is illustrated by Wetst. from Artemidorus vi. 25, θάνατον μὲν γὰρ εἰκότως ἐσήμαινε τῇ γυναικὶ τὸ εἶναι ἐν ὀστρακίνῳ σκεύει,—Arrian, Epict. iii. 9, ταῦτα ἔχω ἀντὶ τῶν ἀργυρωμάτων, ἀντὶ τῶν χρυσωμάτων· σὺ χρυσᾶ σκεύη, ὀστράκινον δὲ τὸν λόγον, and Herod. iii. 96, τοῦτον τὸν φόρον θησαυρίζει ὁ βασιλεὺς τρόπῳ τοιῷδε. ἐς πίθους κεραμίους τήξας καταχέει, πλήσας δὲ τὸ ἄγγος περιαιρέει, ἐπεὰν δὲ δεηθῇ χρημάτων, κατακόπτει τοσοῦτον, ὅσου ἂν ἑκάστοτε δέηται. **ἡ ὑπερβ. τῆς δυν.** not = ἡ ὑπερβάλλουσα δύναμις, but, the δύναμις contemplated on the side of its ὑπερβολή,—the power consisting in the effects of the apostolic ministry (1 Cor. ii. 4), as well as in the upholding under trials and difficulties. The passage commonly referred to (even by Stanley) to prove the hendiadys, may serve entirely to disprove it: Jos. Antt. i. 13. 4, μαθὼν δὲ αὐτοῦ τὸ πρόθυμον κ. τὴν ὑπερβολὴν τῆς θρησκείας: "the readiness and surpassingness of his obedience." **ᾖ τοῦ θεοῦ] may belong to** (i. e. be seen to belong to) **God.** Tertull., Vulg., and Estius, render it 'ut sublimitas sit virtutis Dei, non ex nobis,' which is hardly allowable, and disturbs the sense by confusing the antithesis between ὁ θεός and ἡμεῖς. **8—10.]** He illustrates the expression, 'earthen vessels,' in detail, by *his own experience and that of the other ministers of Christ.*

8.] in every way (see reff.) **pressed, but not** (**inextricably**) **crushed** (στ. 'angustias h. l. denotat tales, e quibus non detur exitus,' Meyer, from Kypke);—**in perplexity but not in despair** (a *literal* statement of what the last clause stated *figuratively*: as Stanley, "bewildered, but not benighted"):—**persecuted but not deserted** (ἐγκαταλειπόμενοι, see reff., used of desertion both by God and by man. Hammond, Olsh., Stanley, al., would refer διωκόμ. . . . . to the foot-race, and render it '*pursued, but not left behind*,' as Herod. viii. 59, οἱ δέ γε ἐγκαταλειπόμενοι οὐ στεφανοῦνται,—but the sense thus would be quite beside the purpose, as the Apostle is speaking not of rivalry from those who as runners had the same end in view, but of troubles and persecutions): **struck down** (as with a dart during pursuit: so Xen. Cyr. i. 3. 14, θηρία . . . . τοξεύων καὶ ἀκοντίζων καταβαλεῖς. It is ordinarily interpreted of a fall in wrestling; but *agonistic figures* would be out of place in the present passage, and the attempt to find them has bewildered most of the modern Commentators), **but not destroyed:**

10.] always carrying about in our body (i. e. ever in our apostolic work having our body exposed to and an example of: or perhaps even, as Stanley, "bearing with us, wherever we go, the burden of the

τοῦ Ἰησοῦ [j] ἐν τῷ [j] σώματι [k] περιφέροντες, ἵνα καὶ ἡ [l] ζωὴ
τοῦ Ἰησοῦ ἐν τῷ σώματι ἡμῶν [m] φανερωθῇ· 11 ἀεὶ γὰρ
ἡμεῖς οἱ ζῶντες [n] εἰς θάνατον [n] παραδιδόμεθα [o] διὰ Ἰησοῦν,
ἵνα καὶ ἡ [l] ζωὴ τοῦ Ἰησοῦ [m] φανερωθῇ ἐν τῇ [p] θνητῇ
σαρκὶ ἡμῶν. 12 ὥστε ὁ θάνατος ἐν ἡμῖν [q] ἐνεργεῖται, ἡ δὲ

j Gal. vi. 17. k Mark vi. 55. Eph. iv. 14 [Heb. xiii. 9, and Jude 12 v. r.] only. Prov. x. 24. Eccl. vii. 8. 2 Macc. vii. 27 only. l = Rom. v. 10. m Rom. i. 19 reff. n Matt. x. 21. Mark xiii. 12. Isa. liii. 12 a. o ver. 5. p Rom. vi. 12 reff. q Rom. vii. 5 reff.

10. rec ins *κυριου* bef 1st *ιησου*, with KL rel [flor] syr goth Chr_1 Thdrt Damasc $Tert_2$ Ambrst-ms : om ABCDFPℵ 17 (latt) Syr copt æth arm $Orig_{sæpe}$ [Eus_1 Nys_1 Euthal-ms] Cyr_2 $Iren\text{-}int_1$ $Tert_2$.—*χριστου* D[1]F(and their lat) [æth] $Orig\text{-}int_2$ $Tert_1$: *χρ. ιησ.* D[2] $Tert_1$. aft 1st *σωματι* ins *ημων* DF [latt(not am[1]) Syr copt arm] $Iren\text{-}int_1$ $Orig\text{-}int_3$ [$Tert_2$ Ambrst]. aft 2nd (*του*) *ιησ.* ins *χριστου* D[1](and lat) F[not F-lat] (spec) Iren-int $Orig\text{-}int_3$ [$Ambr_1$].—om *του* F. *τοις σωμασιν* [2nd] ℵ vulg [fri] $Orig_1$. *φανερωθη* bef *εν τω σωματι ημων* A vulg(not am fuld demid [tol]) [copt $Cyr\text{-}p_1$] $Tert_5$.

11. for *αει*, *ει* F k [Syr] $Tert_1$ Ambrst. for *παραδιδ.*, *διδομεθα* F[-gr]. om *και* C o 3 $Tert_1$. for *του ιησ.*, *ιησ. χριστου* D[1](and lat) F[not F-lat] : *του χρ.* C.

12. [om] *ο* [ℵ[1](insd] over the line [eadem manu,] appy) [Damasc]. rec ins *μεν* bef *θανατος* (*to correspond to δε below*), with KL rel syr-w-ob Thl Œc Ambrst-ms : om ABCDFPℵ 17 latt copt (goth) arm Chr_1 [Euthal-ms] Thdrt Damasc lat-ff.

dead body." But see below) **the killing** (the word seems only to occur besides, in ref. Rom., where it signifies, figuratively, utter lack of strength and vital power, in a fragment of the Oneirocritica of Astrampsychus (Meyer), *νεκροὺς ὁρῶν, νέκρωσιν ἕξεις πραγμάτων*, where the sense is also figurative, and in its primary physical sense in the medical works of Aretæus and Galen. But here the literal sense, '*the being put to death*,' must evidently be kept, and the expression understood as 1 Cor. xv. 31, and as Chrys.: *οἱ θάνατοι οἱ καθημερινοί, δι' ὧν καὶ ἡ ἀνάστασις ἐδείκνυτο.* Hom. ix. p. 498. The rendering, 'the *deadness* of Jesus to the flesh, as opposed to the vitality, *ἡ ζωὴ τοῦ Ἰησοῦ* below,'—see Dr. Peile's Annotations on the Epistles, i. 383,—is beside the present purpose, and altogether inconsistent with *ἀεὶ εἰς θάνατον παραδιδόμεθα διὰ Ἰησοῦν*, ver. 11. See Stanley's note) **of Jesus** (as *τὰ παθήματα τοῦ χριστοῦ*, ch. i. 5 :—not 'ad exemplum Christi,' as Grot., al.), **in order that also the life of Jesus may be manifested in our body**: i. e. 'that in our bodies, holding up against such troubles and preserved in such dangers, may be shewn forth that mighty power of God which is a testimony that Jesus lives and is exalted to be a Prince and a Saviour :'—not, 'that our repeated deliverances might resemble His Resurrection, as our sufferings His Death,' as Meyer, who argues that the literal meaning must be retained, as in the other member of the comparison, owing to *ἐν τῷ σώματι ἡμ.* But, as De W. justly observes, the bodily deliverance is manifestly a subordinate consideration, and the *ζωή* of far higher significance, testified indeed by the body's preservation, but extending far beyond it. **11.**] Explanation and confirmation of ver. 10. **For we who live** (**ζῶντες** asserting that to which death is alien and strange, an antithesis to *εἰς θάνατον παραδ.*, as in the other clause *ζωή* to *ἐν τῇ θνητῇ σαρκί*. No more specific meaning for *ζῶντες* must be imagined, as '*tantis mortibus superstitem*,' Bengel, Estius, al.,—or '*as long as we live*,' Beza, al.,—or '*qui adhuc vivimus, qui nondum ex vita excessimus ut multi jam Christianorum*,' as Grot.) **are alway being delivered to death** (in dangers and persecutions, so ch. xi. 23, *ἐν θανάτοις πολλάκις*) **on account of Jesus** (so in Rev. i. 9 John was in Patmos *διὰ τὸν λόγον τοῦ θεοῦ κ. διὰ τὴν μαρτυρίαν Ἰησοῦ*), **that also the life of Jesus may be manifested in our mortal flesh** (the antithesis is more strongly put by *θνητῇ σαρκί* than it would be by *θνητῷ σώματι*, see Rom. viii. 11, the *flesh* being the very pabulum of decay and corruption). By this antithesis, the wonderful greatness of the divine power, *ἡ ὑπερβολὴ τῆς δυνάμεως*, is strikingly brought out: God exhibits DEATH in the *living*, that He may exhibit LIFE in the *dying*. **12.**] By it is also brought out that which is here the immediate subject,—the vast and unexampled trials of the apostolic office, all summed up in these words: **So that death works in us, but life in you; i. e.** '*the trials by which the dying of Jesus is exhibited in us, are exclusively and peculiarly* OUR OWN,—*whereas* (and this is decisive for the *spiritual* sense of *ζωή*) *the life, whereof we are to be witnesses, extends beyond ourselves, nay finds its field of action and energizing* IN YOU.' Estius, Grot., and apparently Olsh., take *ἐνεργεῖ-*

r = & constr., Rom. viii. 15 reff. (xi. 8 reff.)
s Psa. cxv. 1. (cxiv. 10.)
t 1 Cor. xv. 4 and passim. Isa. xxvi. 19.

l ζωὴ ἐν ὑμῖν. 13 ἔχοντες δὲ τὸ αὐτὸ r πνεῦμα τῆς πίστεως
κατὰ τὸ γεγραμμένον s Ἐπίστευσα, διὸ ἐλάλησα, καὶ
ἡμεῖς πιστεύομεν, διὸ καὶ λαλοῦμεν, 14 εἰδότες ὅτι ὁ
t ἐγείρας τὸν [κύριον] Ἰησοῦν καὶ ἡμᾶς σὺν Ἰησοῦ t ἐγερεῖ

...γεγραμμενον A BCDFK LPℵ a b c d e f g h k l m n o 17. 47

13. aft 1st διο ins και Fℵ syrr goth arm [Epiph$_1$ Aug$_1$(om$_1$)].
14. om κυριον B 17. 71-3 vulg(with am fuld demid al, agst tol F-lat) arm Chr-comm$_1$ Tert$_1$ Pel Sedul Bede: ins CDFKLPℵ rel D-lat(and G-lat, but not fri) [Chr$_1$ Euthal-ms Thdrt Damasc Ambrst]. rec (for συν) δια (*corrn, on account of the difficulty found in σ ὺ ν Ἰησοῦ being joined to a future verb, His Resurrn being past*), with D^3[-gr] KLℵ^3 rel syrr goth [Chr$_1$] Thdrt Damasc: txt BCD^{1}FPℵ^1 17 latt copt æth arm [Euthal-ms] (Tert$_1$) Ambr$_1$ Ambrst(not ed rom) Pel Bede.—In ℵ a superfluous ι has been written and erased before ιῡ. εγιρει D^{1}F [εγειρει P], *suscitat et constituit* goth.

ται passively, 'is wrought' ('mors agitur et exercetur . . . perficitur vita.' Est.): but it is never so used in N. T. Chrys., Calv., al., take the verse ironically, τὰ μὲν ἐπικίνδυνα ἡμεῖς ὑπομένομεν, τῶν δὲ χρηστῶν ὑμεῖς ἀπολαύετε,—but such a sentiment seems alien from the spirit of the passage. Meyer, as unfortunately, limits ζωή to *natural* life, whereas (as above) the context plainly evinces *spiritual life* to be meant, not merely natural. In Rom. viii. 10, 11, the vivifying influence of His Spirit who raised Jesus from the dead is spoken of as extending to the body also; *here*, the upholding influence of Him who delivers and preserves the body, is spoken of as vivifying the whole man: LIFE, in both places, being *the higher and spiritual life, including* the lower and natural. 'And, in our relative positions,—of this *life*, YE are the examples,—a church of believers, alive to God through Christ in your various vocations, and not called on to be θεατριζόμενοι [cf. 1 Cor. iv. 9; Heb. x. 33] as WE are, who are (not indeed excluded from that *life*,—nay it flows from us to you, —but are) more especially examples of conformity to the *death* of our common Lord:—in whom DEATH WORKS.'

13—18.] ENCOURAGEMENTS: and (1) FAITH, which enables us to go on preaching to you. Meyer connects this verse with ἡ δὲ ζωὴ ἐν ὑμῖν: for, he says, by means of πιστεύομεν διὸ καὶ λαλοῦμεν, is that ζωὴ ἐν ὑμ. ἐνεργεῖται, wrought. But, not to mention that thus the context is strangely disturbed, in which *we and our trials* form the leading subject, it would surely be very unnatural that ἔχοντες δέ should apply not to the principal but to the subordinate clause of the foregoing verse. **But** (contrast to the foregoing state of trial and working of death in us) **having the same spirit of faith** (not *distinctly* the *Holy Spirit*,—but as in reff., not merely a *human disposition*: the indwelling Holy Spirit penetrates and characterizes the whole renewed man) **with that described in the Scriptures** (τὸ αὐτὸ κατὰ τὸ γεγρ., i. e. either as Billroth, τὸ αὐτὸ (ἐκείνῳ) περὶ οὗ γέγραπται, or as De W., = τὸ αὐτὸ ὡς γέγρ., ὥσπερ being sometimes found after ὁ αὐτός, ἴσος, and the like, and κατὰ here being equivalent to it. I prefer the former: but at all events the connexion of τὸ αὐτό and κατὰ τὸ γεγρ. must be maintained, and we must not, with Meyer, connect κατὰ τὸ γεγρ. . . . with καὶ ἡμεῖς πιστεύομεν, which makes the Apostle say that *his faith* is *according to the words of the citation*, and thus confuses the whole process of thought), **I believed, wherefore I spoke** (the connexion of the words in the Psalm is not clear, nor the precise meaning of כִּי, rendered by the LXX διό. See Pool's Synopsis in loc. for the various renderings), **we too believe, wherefore we also speak** (continue our preaching of the gospel, notwithstanding such vast hindrances within and without):

14.] **knowing** (fixes and expands in detail the indefinite πιστεύομεν, and thus gives the *ground* of λαλοῦμεν,—not as commonly understood, the *matter* of which we speak) **that He who raised up** (from the dead) **the Lord Jesus, will raise up us also** (*from the dead hereafter*, see 1 Cor. vi. 13, 14:—not in a figurative resurrection from danger, as Beza, who afterwards changed his opinion, al., and lately Meyer, whose whole interpretation of this passage is singularly forced, and his defence of it unfair, see below) **with Jesus** (σὺν Ἰησοῦ is not necessarily figurative, as Meyer; even in the passages where a figurative sense is the prevailing one, it is only as built upon the fact of a *literal* 'raising with Christ,' to be accomplished at the great day: see Eph. ii. 6; Col. iii. 1, 3; 1 Thess. v. 10) **and present us with you** (i. e. as in Jude 24, τῷ δυναμένῳ . . . στῆσαι κατενώπιον τῆς δόξης αὐτοῦ ἀμώμους ἐν ἀγαλλιάσει . . ., and in reff., *at the day of His coming*). Meyer's objection to the meaning above given,—that the Apostle could not thus speak of the resurrection,

καὶ [u] παραστήσει σὺν ὑμῖν. 15 τὰ γὰρ πάντα δι᾽ ὑμᾶς, ἵνα
ἡ [v] χάρις [v] πλεονάσασα διὰ [w] τῶν [w] πλειόνων τὴν [x] εὐχαριστίαν [y] περισσεύσῃ εἰς τὴν δόξαν τοῦ θεοῦ. 16 διὸ οὐκ
[z] ἐγκακοῦμεν, ἀλλ᾽ [a] εἰ [a] καὶ ὁ [b] ἔξω ἡμῶν [b] ἄνθρωπος
[c] διαφθείρεται, ἀλλ᾽ [d] ὁ [d] ἔσω[θεν] ἡμῶν [e] ἀνακαινοῦται

u = ch. xi. 2. Eph. v. 27. Col. i. 22, 28.
v Rom. v. 20 (reff.).
w 1 Cor. ix. 19 reff.
x Acts xxiv. 3 reff.
y transit., ch. ix. 8. Eph. i. 8. 1 Thess. iii. 12 only ‡. intr., Rom. v. 15 al.
z ver. 1.
a ver. 3.
b here only. see Rom. vii. 22 reff.
c Luke xii. 33. 1 Tim. vi. 5. Rev. viii. 9. xi. 18 only. 2 Kings i. 14. Dan. vii. 14 Theod.
d see 1 Cor. v. 12 reff. [-θεν, = Luke xi. 39, 40 only.]
e Col. iii. 10 only †. (-νίζειν, Heb. vi. 6. Ps. cii. 5.)

15. B^1 wrote ταρ [for τα γαρ] (whence Mai gives an omn of τα) but corrd perhaps eadem manu.

16. rec εκκακουμεν (*see ver* 1), with CD^3KLP rel: txt BDFא e m. εξωθεν $D^{1 \cdot r}$ 73. 137 $Bas_1[txt_3]$ $Thdrt_1(txt_2)$. for διαφθειρ., φθειρεται KL a^2 d 46^1-7. 114. εσω (*for uniformity ?*) BCD^1FPא d m 47 $Orig_2$ Ath_1 Chr_1 [Bas_3 Euthal-ms] $Thdrt_1$ Damasc: εσωθεν D^3KL rel [Nys_1 Bas_1] $Thdrt_2$ Thl Œc. (17 def.) rec om [1st] ημων, with KL rel latt(not G-lat) Syr copt goth $Orig_1$[-$int_{sæpe}$] Ath Chr [Euthal-ms] $Thdrt_1$ Thl Œc $Tert_2$ Lucif Ambrst: ins (*for uniformity ?*) B C[αλλ ει to ημων is written over an erasure, C^1 having appy omd ημων] D[-gr] F[-gr] א [m] syr æth arm $Thdrt_1$.

because he expected (1 Cor. xv. 51, 52; i. 8; ch. i. 13, 14) to be *alive* at the day of Christ, is best refuted by this very passage, ch. v. 1 ff., where *his admission of at least the possibility of his death* is distinctly set forth. The fact is that the ἐγερεῖ here, having respect rather to the contrast of the future glory with the present suffering, does not necessarily imply one or other side of the alternative of being quick or dead at the Lord's coming, but embraces all, quick and dead, in one blessed resurrection-state. This confidence, of being presented at that day σὺν ὑμῖν, is only analogous to his expressions elsewhere; see ch. i. 14; 1 Thess. ii. 19, 20; iii. 13. 15.] Explanation of σὺν ὑμῖν as a ground of his trust: with reference also to ἡ δὲ ζωὴ ἐν ὑμῖν, ver. 12; viz. that all, both the sufferings and victory of the ministers, are *for the church*: see the parallel expression, ch. i. 6, 7. **For all things** (*of which we have been speaking*; or perhaps hyperbolically, ALL THINGS, the whole working and arrangements of God, as in 1 Cor. iii. 22, εἴτε ἐνεστῶτα εἴτε μέλλοντα, πάντα ὑμῶν) **are on your behalf, that Grace, having abounded by means of the greater number** (who have received it), **may multiply the thanksgiving** (which shall accrue), **to the glory of God.** Such (1) is the rendering of Meyer, and, in the main, of Chrys., Erasm., al., and recently, Rückert and Olshausen. *Three other ways* are possible; (2) '*that Grace, having abounded, may, on account of the thanksgiving of the greater number, be multiplied* ('πλεονάζω habet vim positivi: περισσεύω, comparativi,' Bengel) *to the glory of God.*' So Luther, Beza, Estius, Grot., Bengel, al.:—(3) '*that Grace, having abounded, may, by means of the greater number, multiply the thanksgiving to the glory of God.*' So Emmerling and De Wette:—(4) '*that Grace having multiplied* (see 1 Thess. iii. 12, for the transitive sense) *by means of the greater number the thanksgiving, may abound to the glory of God.*' This last has not been suggested by any Commentator that I am aware of, but is admissible. I prefer (1), as best agreeing with the position of the words, and with the emphases. If (2) had been intended, I should have expected ἵνα πλεονάσασα ἡ χάρις,—πλεονάσασα in its present position standing awkwardly alone. The same remark applies to (3), and this besides, that in that case I should expect πλειόνων, and not τῶν πλ., in which the art. rather regards the *matter of fact*, the many who *have received* the grace, or who give thanks, than the intention, to multiply the thanksgiving by the (possible) greater number of persons. If (4) had been intended, I should have looked for ἵνα ἡ χάρις τὴν εὐχαριστίαν πλεον. διὰ τῶν πλει., περισσ. κ.τ.λ. By adopting (1), we keep the words and emphases just where they stand: ἵνα ἡ χάρις, πλεονάσασα διὰ τῶν πλειόνων (not διὰ τ. πλ. πλεον., which would give an undue prominence to διὰ τῶν πλειόν., whereas those words only particularize πλεονάσασα), τὴν εὐχ. περισσεύσῃ, εἰς τὴν δόξαν τ. θεοῦ. As to the *sense*, (see the very similar sentiment, ch. i. 11,) *thanksgiving* is the highest and noblest offering of the Church to God's glory (θυσία αἰνέσεως δοξάσει με, Ps. xlix. 23, LXX): *that this may be rendered*, in the best sense, as the result of the working of grace which has become abundant by means of the many recipients, is the great end of the Christian ministry. 16—18.] *Second ground of encouragement*—HOPE.

16.] **Wherefore** (on account of the hope implied in the faith spoken of ver. 14, which he is about to expand) **we do not**

f here only. (see note.) g neut., 1 Cor. i. 25 &c. reff. h here only. Ps. lxix. 3. Tobit iv. 14 only [ℵ omits vv. 6—19]. i Matt. xi. 30 only. Exod. xviii. 26. (-φρία, ch. i. 7.)

[f]ἡμέρᾳ [f]καὶ [f]ἡμέρᾳ. 17 [g]τὸ γὰρ [h]παραυτίκα [i]ἐλαφρὸν τῆς BCDFK
θλίψεως ἡμῶν [kl]καθ' [kl]ὑπερβολὴν [k]εἰς [k]ὑπερβολὴν αἰώνιον LPℵ a b
[m]βάρος [n]δόξης [o]κατεργάζεται [p]ἡμῖν, 18 μὴ [q]σκοπούντων c d e f g
[p]ἡμῶν τὰ [r]βλεπόμενα ἀλλὰ τὰ μὴ [r]βλεπόμενα· τὰ γὰρ h k l m r
[r]βλεπόμενα [s]πρόςκαιρα, τὰ δὲ μὴ [r]βλεπόμενα αἰώνια. o 17. 47

k here only. l Rom. vii. 13 reff. m = here only. (Acts xv. 28 reff.) n = Rom. ii. 7 reff. o = Rom. iv. 15 reff. p constr., see Acts xxi. 17 reff. q = Phil. ii. 4. (Rom. xvi. 17 reff.) r = Rom. viii. 24. s Matt. xiii. 21 ‖ Mk. Heb. xi. 25 only †.

17. ins προςκαιρον και bef ελαφρον D^1F latt (Syr) goth arm Orig-int$_2$ [Ambrst Aug$_{alic}$]. (Thdrt says: διὰ τοῦ παραυτίκα ἔδειξε τὸ βραχύ τε καὶ πρόςκαιρον.) om ημων BC^2 (appy: see Tischdf's Cod Ephr) [Syr] Chr$_1$. om εις υπερβολην $C^1Kℵ^1$(ins ℵ-corr^1) 38. 80 [syr copt goth æth arm].

18. for σκοπ. ημων, σκοπουντες D^1 F[not F-lat] D-lat. aft προςκαιρα ins εστιν F, so also latt [D-lat aft αιων.] Orig-int$_7$[(om$_1$) Ambrst].

shrink (as in ver. 1: but *now*, owing to *despair*), **but** (on the contrary) **though even** (not '*even if*,' putting a *case*; εἰ καί with ind. asserts the *fact*, as in εἰ καὶ σπένδομαι, Phil. ii. 17) **our outward man is** [**being**] **wasted away** (i. e. our *body*, see Rom. vii. 22, *is*, by this continued νέκρωσις and ἐνέργεια τοῦ θανάτου, *being worn out*:—he is not as yet speaking of dissolution by death, but only of gradual approximation to it), **yet** (ἀλλά in the apodosis after a hypothetic clause, introduces a strong and marked contrast:—so Hom. Il. α. 81,—εἴπερ γάρ τε χόλον γε καὶ αὐτῆμαρ καταπέψῃ, ἀλλά τε καὶ μετόπισθεν ἔχει κότον, ὄφρα τελέσσῃ: see other examples in Hartung, Partikellehre, ii. 40) **our inner** (**man**) **is** [**being**] **renewed** (contrast, subordinately to διαφθείρεται, but mainly to ἐγκακοῦμεν) **day by day** (ἡμ. καὶ ἡμ., so Hebr. יוֹם וָיוֹם, Esth. iii. 4; an expression not found (Meyer) even in the LXX): i. e. 'our spiritual life, the life which testifies the life of Jesus, even in our mortal bodies (ver. 11), is continually fed with fresh accessions of grace:' see next verse. So Chrys.,—πῶς ἀνακαινοῦται; τῇ πίστει, τῇ ἐλπίδι, τῇ προθυμίᾳ, τὸ λοιπὸν δεῖ (al. τῷ λοιπὸν) κατατολμᾷν τῶν δεινῶν. ὅσῳ γὰρ ἂν μυρία πάσχῃ τὸ σῶμα, τοσούτῳ χρηστοτέρας ἔχει τὰς ἐλπίδας ἡ ψυχή, καὶ λαμπροτέρα γίνεται, καθάπερ χρυσίον πυρούμενον ἐπιπλέον. p. 500. **17, 18.**] *Method of this renewal.* **For the present light** (**burden**) **of our affliction** (the adject. use of παραυτίκα is common with Thucyd., e. g. ii. 64, ἡ παραυτίκα λαμπρότης, καὶ ἐς τὸ ἔπειτα δόξα: viii. 82, τήν τε παραυτίκα ἐλπίδα: vii. 71, ἐν τῷ παραυτίκα, where Schol. ἐν τῷ ἐνεστῶτι τότε χρόνῳ;—and with his imitator Demosthenes, e. g. p. 72. 16, ἡ παραυτίχ' ἡδονὴ κ. ῥᾳστώνη μεῖζον ἰσχύει τοῦ ποθ' ὕστερον συνοίσειν μέλλοντος;—see also pp. 34. 24; 215. 10: and more examples in Wetst. **ἐλαφρόν** as a substantive, contrasted with βάρος; see reff.), **works out for us** ('*efficit*,' 'is the means of bringing about') **in a surpassing and still more surpassing manner** (καθ. ὑπ. εἰς ὑπερ. must belong to the *verb*, as Meyer and De W.; for otherwise it can only qualify αἰώνιον, the idea of which forbids such qualification, not βάρος, which is *separated from it by the adjective*:—i. e. so as to exceed beyond all measure the tribulation) **an eternal weight of glory** (αἰώνιον βάρος opposed to παραυτίκα ἐλαφρόν). **18.**] *Subjective condition under which this working out takes place.* **While we regard not** ('propose not as our aim,' 'spend not our care about,'—reff.) **the things which are seen** (ref. = τὰ ἐπίγεια, Phil. iii. 19. Chrys. strikingly says, ubi sup., τὰ βλεπόμενα πάντα, κἂν κόλασις ᾖ, κἂν ἀνάπαυσις· ὥστε μήτε ἐκεῖθεν χαυνοῦσθαι, μήτε ἐντεῦθεν βιάζεσθαι), **but the things which are not seen** ('aliud significat ἀόρατα, *invisibilia*, nam multa quæ non cernuntur, erunt visibilia, confecto itinere fidei.' Bengel. **μὴ** βλ., not οὐ, perhaps because μή stands with participles in clauses of a subjective character, so στήκετε . . . . μὴ πτυρόμενοι ἐν μηδενὶ . . . , Phil. i. 27, 28. Winer, edn. 6, § 55. 5. g. β,—or rather perhaps, as ib. α, as hypothetic (see also Moulton's note, p. 606. 1): τὰ **οὐ** βλεπόμ. would be the things which *as a matter of fact* at *any given time* we do not see, cf. οἱ οὐκ ἠλεημένοι, 1 Pet. ii. 10: τὰ **μὴ** βλ., *generally* and *hypothetically*, the things not seen. So ὁ μὴ ὢν μετ' ἐμοῦ, Matt. xii. 30, in a case indefinite and hypothetical. This amounts to much the same as when in the ordinary account of such clauses, we say that μή belongs to the *subject*, οὐ to the *predicate*,—but is a better explanation, inasmuch as that account gives only the logical *fact*,—*this*, the logical *reason* of the usage): **for the things which are seen are temporary** (not '*temporal*,' belonging to time,' but '*fleeting*,' 'only for a time,' see reff.;—i. e. till the day of Christ): **but**

V. [1] [t]οἴδαμεν γὰρ [t]ὅτι ἐὰν ἡ [u]ἐπίγειος ἡμῶν [w]οἰκία τοῦ
[x]σκήνους [y]καταλυθῇ, [z]οἰκοδομὴν ἐκ θεοῦ ἔχομεν [w]οἰκίαν
[a]ἀχειροποίητον αἰώνιον ἐν τοῖς οὐρανοῖς. [2] καὶ γὰρ ἐν

t Rom. vii. 14 reff. u 1 Cor. xv. 40 reff. w = Job iv. 19. (xxx. 23.) x here bis only †. Wisd. ix. 15 only. (-νωμα, Acts vii. 46. -νοῦν, John i. 14). y = Matt. xxvi. 61 ||. Acts vi. 14. Ezra v. 12. z = 1 Cor. iii. 9 reff. a Mark xiv. 58. Col. ii. 11 only †.

Chap. V. 1. ins οτι bef οικοδομην DF latt goth Chr_1[om_2] $Cypr_1$ Ambrst Pel Sedul (not fri [$Orig\text{-}int_1$] Tert Aug al). ins ουκ bef αχειροποιητον F(*non manufactam* [latt]).

the things which are not seen are eternal. Chrys. again: κἂν βασιλεία, κἂν κόλασις ᾖ πάλιν· ὥστε καὶ ἐκεῖθεν φοβῆσαι, καὶ ἐκεῖσε (al. ἐντεῦθεν) προτρέψασθαι, ib. Seneca, Ep. 59 (Wetst.), has a very similar sentiment: 'ista imaginaria sunt, et ad tempus aliquam faciem ferunt. Nihil horum stabile nec solidum est . . . Mittamus animum ad ea, quæ æterna sunt.'

Chap. V. 1—10.] *Further specification of the hope before spoken of, as consisting in anticipation of an eternity of glory after this life, in the resurrection-body: which leads him evermore to strive to be found well pleasing to the Lord at His coming: seeing that all shall then receive the things done in the body.* 1.] **For** (gives the reason of ch. iv. 17,—principally of the emphatic words of that verse, καθ' ὑπερβολὴν εἰς ὑπερβ.,—shewing how it is that so wonderful a process takes place) **we know** (as in ch. iv. 14,—are convinced, as a sure matter of hope) **that if** ('*supposing;*' —not = κἄν, 'etiamsi,' but indefinite and doubtful: if this delivering to death continually should end in veritable death. The case is hypothetical, because many will be glorified without the κατάλυσις taking place: see 1 Cor. xv. 51, 53) **our earthly tabernacle-dwelling** (τοῦ σκήνους is gen. of apposition. The similitude is not derived from the wandering of the Israelites in the wilderness, nor from the tabernacle, but is a common one with Greek writers, see examples in Wetstein. "The whole passage is expressed through the double figure of a house or tent, and a garment. The explanation of this abrupt transition from one to the other may be found in the image which, both from his occupation and his birthplace, would naturally occur to the Apostle,—the tent of Cilician haircloth, which might almost equally suggest the idea of a habitation and of a vesture." Stanley. Chrys. observes: εἰπὼν οἰκίαν σκήνους, καὶ τὸ εὐδιάλυτον καὶ πρόσκαιρον δείξας ἐντεῦθεν, ἀντέθηκε τὴν αἰωνίαν· τὸ γὰρ τῆς σκηνῆς ὄνομα τὸ πρόσκαιρον πολλάκις δείκνυσι. Hom. x. p. 506) **were dissolved** ('mite verbum,' Bengel: i. e. '*taken down,*' 'done away with:' but '*dissolved,*' as well as the vulg. 'dissolvatur,' is right), **we have in the heavens** (as Meyer rightly remarks, the *present* is used of the time at which the dissolution shall have taken place. But even then the dead have it not in *actual possession,* but only prepared by God for them against the appearing of the Lord: and therefore they are said to have it *in the heavens.* Chrys., &c., Beza, Grot., al., join ἐν τοῖς οὐρ. with οἰκίαν, which can hardly be: it would be either ἐπουράνιον or ἐξ οὐρανοῦ. The E. V. according to the present punctuation, yields no sense: '*not made with hands, eternal in the heavens*') **a building** (no longer a σκῆνος) **from God** ('in an especial manner prepared by God,' '*pure from God's hands:*' not as *contrasted* with our earthly body, which, see 1 Cor. xii. 18, 24, is also *from* God), **a dwelling not made with hands** (here again, not as contrasted with *the fleshly body,* for *that too* is ἀχειροποίητος, but with other οἰκίαι, which are χειροποίητοι. Remember again the Apostle's occupation of a tent-maker), **eternal.** A difficulty has been raised by some Commentators respecting the *intermediate disembodied state,*—how the Apostle here regards it, or whether he regards it at all. But none need be raised. The οἰκία which in this verse is said, *at the time of dissolution,* to be ἐν τοῖς οὐρανοῖς, is, *when we put it on,* in the next verse, our οἰκητήριον τὸ ἐξ οὐρανοῦ. Thus the intermediate state, though lightly passed over, as not belonging to the subject, is evidently in the mind of St. Paul. Some Commentators, Photius, Anselm, Thomas Aq. (in Estius), Wolf, Rosenm., al., understand *these words themselves* (οἰκ. ἀχειρ. αἰών. ἐν τ. οὐρ.) of the *intermediate state of absence from the body;* Usteri and Flatt, of an *immediate glorified body in heaven,* to be united with the body of the resurrection. Calvin hesitates: "Incertum est, an significet statum beatæ immortalitatis, qui post mortem fideles manet, an vero corpus incorruptibile et gloriosum, quale post resurrectionem erit. In utrovis sensu nihil est incommodi: quanquam malo ita accipere, ut initium hujus ædificii sit beatus animæ status post mortem: consummatio autem sit gloria ultimæ resurrectionis." But if this be so, (1) the parallel will not hold, between the οἰκία in one case, and the οἰκία in the other,—and (2) the language of ver. 2 is

τούτῳ [b] στενάζομεν, τὸ [c] οἰκητήριον ἡμῶν τὸ ἐξ οὐρανοῦ [d] ἐπενδύσασθαι [e] ἐπιποθοῦντες· 3 * [f] εἴ [f] γε καὶ [g] ἐνδυσάμενοι

BCDFK LPℵ a b c d e f g h k l m n o 17. 47

b Rom. viii. 23 reff. c Jude 6 only. (Jer. xxxii. [xxv.] 30 Ald.) d here bis only +. (-δύτης, John xxi. 7.) e w. inf., Rom. i. 11 reff. f Gal. iii. 4. Eph. iii. 2. iv. 21. Col. i. 23 only. εἴπερ, Rom. viii. 9 reff. g 1 Cor. xv. 53, 54 reff.

3. * εἴπερ BDF 17 mss-in-Chr_2(τινὲς δέ φασιν, ὃ καὶ μάλιστα ἐγκριτέον, Εἴπερ καὶ ἐνδυσάμενοι. So also Œc) $Max\text{-}conf_1$: ει γαρ 52 : *si tamen* latt Aug_1 Pel : *si quidem* $Tert_2$ Ambrst : ει γε CKLPℵ rel $Clem_1$ Did_1 Mac_1 Chr_3 [Euthal-ms $Antch_1$] Thdrt Damasc Thl Œc. εκδυσαμενοι (*see notes*) D^1[and lat] spec Chr_1(explaining it κἂν ἀποθώμεθα τὸ σῶμα)[txt_4] $Tert_2$ Ambr $Paulin_1$ Primas Quæst, εκλυσαμενοι *expoliati* F. (*vestiti* vulg with F-lat, *expol.* is written over the Greek in F.) γυμνον D^1.

against it, see below. **2.] For also** (our knowledge, that we possess such a building of God, even in case of our body being dissolved, is testified by the *earnest desire* which we have, to put on that new body *without such dissolution taking place.* See the similar argument in Rom. viii. 18, 19) **in this** (viz. σκήνει, as Beza, Meyer, Olsh., al. The rendering ἐν τούτῳ, '*wherefore*,'—some referring it to the foregoing,—'propter hoc quod dictum est,' Est., some to the following,—is inconsistent with ὄντες ἐν τῷ σκήνει, which is parallel with it, ver. 4. The stress is not necessarily on **ἐν**, '*in* this,' as contrasted with 'out of this,' as Meyer, who joins καί with ἐν τούτῳ; but see above) **we groan** (see Rom. viii. 23), **longing** (i. e. because we desire, the reason of στενάζομεν. ἐπιποθ., not *ardently* desire: the prep. does not intensify, but denotes the direction of the wish, as ἀνέμου μὴ προσεῶντος, Acts xxvii. 7) **to put on over this** ('*superinduere*:' viz. *by being alive at the day of Christ*, and *not* dissolved as in ver. 1:—see on ver. 4 below. The similitude is slightly changed: the *house* is now to be *put on*, as an outer garment, *over the fleshly body*) **our dwelling-place** ('οἰκία est quiddam magis absolutum,—οἰκητήριον, domicilium, respicit *incolam*:' Bengel. So Eur. Orest. 1113,—ὥσθ' Ἑλλὰς αὐτῇ σμικρὸν οἰκητήριον) **from heaven** (i. e. = ἐκ θεοῦ ver. 1, but treated now as if *brought with* the Lord at His coming, and put upon us who are alive and remain then. 'Itaque,' says Bengel, 'hoc domicilium *non est cœlum ipsum*'): **3.] seeing that** (**εἴ γε** (see var. readd.) is used 'de re, quæ jure sumta creditur:' **εἴπερ**, when 'in incerto relinquitur, utrum jure an injuria sumatur.' Herm. ad Viger., p. 834. So Xen. Mem. ii. 1. 17, ἀλλὰ γάρ, ὦ Σ., οἱ εἰς τὴν βασιλικὴν τέχνην παιδευόμενοι, ἣν δοκεῖς μοι σὺ νομίζειν εὐδαιμονίαν εἶναι, τί διαφέρουσι τῶν ἐξ ἀνάγκης κακοπαθούντων, **εἴ γε** πεινήσουσι κ. διψήσουσι, κ.τ.λ.,—'*if they are to hunger and thirst*, &c.' and for **εἴπερ**, Æsch. Ag. 29 f. εἴπερ Ἰλίου πόλις ἑάλωκεν, ὡς ὁ φρυκτὸς ἀγγέλλων πρέπει, '*if, that is, the city*, &c.') **we shall really** (καί, '*in very truth*:' so Soph. Antig. 766, ἄμφω γὰρ αὐτὰ καὶ κατακτεῖναι νοεῖς; '*dost thou intend verily to kill them both?*' and Æsch. Sept. Theb. 810, ἐκεῖθι κῆλθον; '*have they really come to that?*' See more examples in Hartung, Partikellehre, i. 132) **be found** (shall prove to be) **clothed** ('*having put on clothing*,' viz. *a body*), **not naked** (*without a body*—"ἐνδυσ., οὐ γυμν., as γάλα, οὐ βρῶμα, 1 Cor. iii. 2 and often, cf. ver. 7." Meyer. See Stanley's note). The verse *asserts strongly*, with a view to substantiate and explain ver. 2, the *truth of the resurrection* or *glorified body*; and, with Meyer, I see in it a reference to the deniers of the resurrection, whom the Apostle combated in 1 Cor. xv.: its sense being this: "*For I do assert again, that we shall in that day prove to be clothed with a body, and not disembodied spirits.*" Several other renderings have been given:—(1) '*Si nos iste dies deprehendet cum corpore, non exutos a corpore*,—si erimus inter mutandos, non inter mortuos,' Grot.: Estius, Bengel, Conyb., al. To this there are *three* objections,—that **εἴγε** should be **εἴπερ** (the force of this objection is however much weakened by the amount of authority which can be adduced for εἴπερ),—that καί is *not rendered at all*,—and that ἐνδυσάμενοι, the *aor. mid.*, should be ἐνδεδυμένοι, the *perf. pass.* (2) The same objections apply to Billroth's rendering, '*If we, having been once clothed* (with the earthly body), *shall not be found naked*' (without the body). (3) De Wette renders: '*seeing that when we are also* (really) *clothed, we shall not be found naked*:' i. e. 'setting down for certain as we do, that that heavenly dwelling *will also be a body*.' To this Meyer rightly objects, that it is open to the difficulty of making ἔνδυσις and γυμνότης, and that in the *very sense* in which they are *opposites*, to co-exist;—*no clothing but that of a body* is thought of here, or else οὐ **σώματος** γυμνοί must have been expressed. (4) This latter objection applies to the rendering of Chrys., Theodoret, Theophyl., Œcum., al., who take ἐνδυσάμενοι = σῶμα ἄφθαρτον λαβόντες, and γυμνοί to mean γυμνοὶ δόξης. Similarly Anselm explains γυμνοί, 'nudi *Christo*;'

οὐ [h] γυμνοὶ [i] εὑρεθησόμεθα. 4 καὶ γὰρ οἱ ὄντες ἐν τῷ
[x] σκήνει [b] στενάζομεν [j] βαρούμενοι, [k] ἐφ' ᾧ οὐ θέλομεν [l] ἐκ-
δύσασθαι, ἀλλ' [d] ἐπενδύσασθαι, ἵνα [m] καταποθῇ τὸ [n] θνητὸν
ὑπὸ τῆς ζωῆς. 5 ὁ δὲ [o] κατεργασάμενος ἡμᾶς εἰς [p] αὐτὸ
[p] τοῦτο θεός, ὁ δοὺς ἡμῖν τὸν [q] ἀῤῥαβῶνα τοῦ πνεύματος.

h so Plato, Cratyl. p. 277 c, ἡ ψυχὴ γυμνὴ τοῦ σώματος. see 1 Cor. xv. 37.
i = 1 Cor. iv. 2 reff.
j ch. i. 8 reff.
k Rom. v. 12. see Matt. xix. 9. Acts iii. 16.
l Matt. xxvii. 28, 31 ‖ Mk. Luke x. 30 only. Gen. xxxvii. 23.
m = 1 Cor. xv. 54 (reff.), from Isa. xxv. 8.
n Rom. vi. 12 reff.
o Rom. ii. 9 reff. constr., here only.
p Acts xxiv. 15 reff.
q ch. i. 22. Eph. i. 14 only. Gen. xxxvii. 17, 18, 20 only.

4. aft σκηνει ins τουτω DF d [syrr copt goth æth Euthal-ms] Chr$_3$ Thdrt$_1$ Thl Orig-int$_2$[: pref vulg spec Aug$_1$] Tert$_1$ Ambrst : om BCKL[P]ℵ rel am arm Orig$_5$ Eus$_2$ [Chr$_2$] Thdrt$_{h.l.}$ Damasc Œc Tert$_1$. βαρυνομενοι D[1]F Orig-ms$_1$ Thl. Steph (for εφ ω) επειδη, with rel: txt BCDFKL P(o) ℵ c Eus$_3$. αλλα ℵ. aft θνητον ins τουτο F[-gr](and G-lat spec) copt goth Tert$_1$ [Ambrst].
5. κατεργαζομενος DF latt(exc fuld) Iren-int$_1$ Ambrst. (καταργασ. C.) ins ὁ bef θεος ℵ[1] Orig$_1$. rec ins και bef δους (*cf ch* i. 22), with D[2.3][-gr] KLℵ[3] rel syr goth Iren-gr$_1$ Chr$_1$ Thdrt Damasc(και διδους, omg ο [as do 17(δους) Euthal-ms]) Ambrst: txt BCD[1]FPℵ[1] latt Syr copt æth arm Orig$_1$ Iren-int Aug$_1$ Pel Sedul Bede. αραβωνα Dℵ m o 47. (P [def.])

Pelagius, Hunnius, and Baldwin, 'vacui *fide*:' Erasm. Paraphr. 'si tamen hoc exuti corpore non omnino nudi reperiamur, sed ex bonæ vitæ fiducia spe immortalitatis amicti:' in part too Calvin,—restricting it however to the faithful only,—'if at least we, having put on Christ in this life, shall not be found naked then.' Olshausen too takes οὐ γυμνοί as an expansion of ἐνδυσάμενοι, 'provided that we shall be found clothed with the robe of righteousness, not denuded of it.' Of all these we may say, that if the Apostle had meant by γυμνοί to hint at *any other* kind of γυμνότης than that which the similitude obviously implies, he would have certainly indicated it. (5) The rendering of εἰ '*utinam*,' 'utinam etiam induti, non nudi reperiamur!' as Knatchbull and Homberg, need hardly be refuted. (6) Another class of renderings arise from the reading **ἐκδυσάμενοι** in a few cursives, which in connexion with εἴπερ was evidently adopted in consequence of the views of expositors. It stood as a *conditional* sentence,—'*provided, that is, that*' . . ., and in the idea that it referred to the *time after putting off* the mortal body, **ἐν** was altered to **ἐκ**. For much of the reference to opinions in this note I am indebted to Meyer and De Wette.

4.] *Confirmation and explanation of ver.* 2. **For also** (a reason, why we ἐπιποθοῦμεν ἐπενδύσασθαι . . . . as in ver. 2) **we who are in the tabernacle** (before spoken of, i. e. of the body), **groan, being burdened** (not by *troubles and sufferings*, nor by the *body itself*, which would be directly opposite to the sense: but for the reason which follows), **because** (ἐφ' ᾧ as in ref. Rom.) **we are not willing to divest ourselves** (of it), **but to put on** (that other) **over it, that our mortal part may** (not, die, but) **be swallowed up by life** (absorbed in and transmuted by that glorious principle of life which our new clothing shall superinduce upon us). The feeling expressed in these verses was one most natural to those who, as the Apostles, regarded the coming of the Lord as *near*, and conceived the possibility of their living to behold it. It was no terror of death as to its *consequences*—but a natural reluctance to undergo the *mere act of death as such*, when it was within possibility that this mortal body might be superseded by the immortal one, without it. **5.**] This great end, the καταποθῆναι τὸ θνητὸν ὑπὸ τῆς ζωῆς, is justified as the object of the Apostle's fervent wish, seeing that it is for this very end, that this may ultimately be accomplished, that God has wrought us (see below) and given us the pledge of the Spirit;—**But** (and this my wish has reason: for) **He who wrought us out** (prepared us, by redemption, justification, sanctification, which are the qualifications for glory) **unto this very purpose** (viz. that last mentioned—τὸ καταποθῆναι τὸ θνητὸν ἡμῶν ὑπὸ τ. ζωῆς, —not τὸ ἐπενδύσασθαι, a mere accident of that glorious absorption: see below) **is God, who gave unto us** (a sign that our preparation is of Him: '*quippe qui dederit*' . . . . .) **the earnest** (reff. and note) **of** (gen. of apposition) **the (Holy) Spirit.** The Apostle in this verse, is no longer treating exclusively of his own wish for the more summary swallowing up of the mortal by the glorified, but is shewing that *the end itself*, which he individually, or in common with others then living, wishes accomplished in this particular form of ἐπενδύσασθαι, *is*, *under whatever form brought about*, that for which all the preparation, by grace, of Christians, is carried on, and to which the earnest of the Spirit

r (-ῤῥ-) here bis. ch. vii. 16. x. 1, 2. Heb. xiii. 6 only. P.H. Prov. i. 21 (xxxi. 11 א Ald. [-ρσ- AB compl.]) only. part. constr., ch. vii. 5. 2 Pet. i. 17. Lev. iv. 5. Winer, edn. 6, § 45. 6. *b.* s here (each 3ce) only †. see ch. viii. 19. t ch. xii. 2, 3. Heb. xiii. 3. u Rom. ii. 27 reff. v Rom. vi. 4. Acts xxi. 21 reff. w Luke iii. 22. ix. 29. John v. 37. 1 Thess. v. 22 only. Exod. xxiv. 17. x = Rom. xv. 26 reff. y Rom. xv. 20. 1 Thess. iv. 11 only †.

BCDFK LPא a b c d e f g h k l m n o 17. 47

6 ^r θαῤῥοῦντες οὖν πάντοτε, καὶ εἰδότες ὅτι ^s ἐνδημοῦντες
^t ἐν τῷ ^t σώματι ^s ἐκδημοῦμεν ἀπὸ τοῦ κυρίου· 7 ^u διὰ πίστεως
γὰρ ^v περιπατοῦμεν, οὐ ^u διὰ ^w εἴδους· 8 ^r θαῤῥοῦμεν δὲ
καὶ ^x εὐδοκοῦμεν μᾶλλον ^s ἐκδημῆσαι ἐκ τοῦ σώματος καὶ
^s ἐνδημῆσαι πρὸς τὸν κύριον. 9 διὸ καὶ ^y φιλοτιμούμεθα,

6. for *ενδ.*, *επιδημουντες* D[1] F[*επιλημ.*]. for *εκδ.*, *αποδημουμεν* D F[*απολημ.*] Chr_1. for *απο*, *υπο* F. for *κυρ.*, *θεου* D F[not F-lat] old-lat copt (not [vulg $Cypr_1$] $Tert_2$ Lucif &c).
7. ins *και* bef *ου* F vulg.
8. *θαρρουντες* (*see ver* 6) א 17 $Orig_1$ $Tert_1$ Ambrst. for *δε*, *ουν* F(*ουν δε ergo* aut *autem* G) 17 : om b[1] d o 67[2] $Orig_1$. for *εκ*, *απο* m : om א[1] a[2]. for *κυρ.*, *θεον* D[1][-gr] 17 am arm Clem Ambrst.

points forward. Meyer would limit this verse entirely to the wish expressed in the last: but he is *certainly wrong:* for it forms a note of transition to *θαῤῥοῦντες οὖν πάντοτε* in the next: see below.

6—8.] *He returns to the confidence expressed in ver.* 1; that *however this may be,* whether this wish is to be fulfilled or not, *he is prepared to accept the alternative of being denuded of the body, seeing that it will bring with it a translation to the presence of the Lord.* **Being confident then** (because it is God's express purpose to bring us to glory, as in last verse) **always** (either *under all trials :* or, *always, whether this hope of ἐπενδύσασθαι, or the fear of the other alternative, be before us,*—which latter I prefer), **and knowing** (not as the *ground of our confidence,* as Calv., al., nor as *an exception* to it, '*though we know,*' as Est., Olsh., al.,—but *correlative with it,* and the *ground of the* **εὐδοκοῦμεν** below) **that while in our home in the body, we are absent from [our home in] the Lord** (the similitude of the body as our *οἰκία* being still kept up: see similar sentiments, respecting our being wanderers and strangers from our heavenly home while dwelling in the body, Phil. iii. 20; Heb. xi. 13; xiii. 14),—**for** (proof of our *ἐκδημία ἀπὸ τ. κυρ.*) **we walk** (the usual figurative sense,—'go on our Christian course,'—not literal, as of pilgrims) **by means of** (not '*in a state of,*' nor '*through,*' as the element through which our life moves, Meyer; who is thereby necessitated to interpret the two prepositions differently, see below) **faith, not by means of appearance** (*εἶδος cannot possibly be subjective,* as rendered in E. V. and by many Commentators; see reff.—i. e. 'faith, not the actual appearance of heavenly things themselves, is the means whereby we hold on our way,' a sure sign that we are *absent from* those heavenly things),—**notwithstanding (I say)** (he resumes the *θαῤῥοῦντες*, which was apparently at first intended to belong to *εὐδοκοῦμεν*,—by the *indicative,* inserting the *δέ* because the last clause seemed something like a *dash* to that confidence) **we are confident, and are well pleased rather to go from (out of) [our home in] the body and come to our home with the Lord:** i. e. 'if (as in ver. 1) a dissolution of the body be imminent,—even that, though not according to our wish, does not destroy our confidence: for so sensible are we that dwelling in the body is a state of banishment from the Lord, that we prefer to it even the alternative of dissolution, bringing us, as it will, into His presence.' Meyer regards *ἐκδημ.* and *ἐνδημ.* as equivalent to the *putting off of the mortal* (but how?) and *putting on the immortal body* at the coming of the Lord:—but surely by this the whole sense is destroyed. The Apostle, it seems to me, carefully chooses the words, new to the context, *ἐκδημεῖν* and *ἐνδημεῖν*, to *avoid* such an inference, and to express, as he does in Phil. i. 23, then in the actual prospect of death, that *τὸ ἀναλῦσαι* is equivalent to *σὺν χριστῷ εἶναι*: for *here* is no hint of the new house from heaven, only of a certain indefinite *ἐνδημία πρὸς τὸν κύριον*, which is all that is revealed to us, and it would seem was all that was revealed to *him,* of the *disembodied state* of the blessed. I may remark that Meyer, whose commentary on this Epistle is most able and thorough, has been misled in this passage by an endeavour to range the whole of it under the specific wish of vv. 2—4.

9, 10.] **Wherefore** (this being so,—our confidence, in event whether of death, or of life till the coming of the Lord, being such)—**it is also** (besides our confidence) **our aim, whether present** (dwelling in the body) **or absent** (from the body at the time of His appearing),

εἴτε [s] ἐνδημοῦντες εἴτε [s] ἐκδημοῦντες, [z] εὐάρεστοι αὐτῷ
εἶναι. 10 [a] τοὺς γὰρ [a] πάντας ἡμᾶς [b] φανερωθῆναι [c] δεῖ
[d] ἔμπροσθεν τοῦ [de] βήματος τοῦ [d] χριστοῦ, ἵνα [f] κομίσηται
ἕκαστος [g] τὰ διὰ τοῦ σώματος, [h] πρὸς ἃ ἔπραξεν, εἴτε
ἀγαθὸν εἴτε κακόν. 11 Εἰδότες οὖν τὸν [ij] φόβον τοῦ [j] κυρίου, ἀνθρώπους [k] πείθομεν, θεῷ δὲ [l] πεφανερώμεθα· ἐλπίζω

z Rom. xii. 1, 2 reff.
a Rom. xi. 32 reff.
b = (see note). Col. iii. 4. 1 Pet. v. 4. 1 John ii. 28.
c = Acts iv. 12 reff.
d Acts xviii. 17.
e Acts xii. 21 reff.
f = Eph. vi. 8. Col. iii. 25 al. Ps. xxxix. 15. 2 Macc. viii. 33.
g constr., Eph. Col. as above (f).
h = Luke xii. 47. Gal. ii. 14.
i not = Rom. xiii. 3.
j Acts ix. 31 only. φ. θεοῦ, Rom. iii. 18. ch. vii. 1. φ. χριστοῦ, Eph. v. 21.
k = Acts xii. 20. Gal. i. 10. 1 Kings xxiv. 8.
l = Mark iv. 22. John iii. 21 al.

10. א[1] has written ε bef *κομισηται*, but marked it for erasure. for *τα*, *ἅ*, omg *προς α*, D[1]F.—om *τα δ. τ. σ.* L. for *κακον*, *φαυλον* Cא d m 17 $Orig_6$[-c_1] Eus_2 $Ephr_1$ Ath_1 Bas_1 Cyr[-p Euthal-ms] $Damasc_1$: txt BDFKLP rel $Clem_1$ $Orig_1$[-c_1] Eus_1 Chr_1 [Bas_1 $Antch_1$] $Thdrt_{sæpe}$ $Damasc_{h.l.}$
[**11.** *πειθωμεν* P Œc-comm(altern). for *πεφαν.*, *φανερουμεθα* K : *φανερωμεθα* m.]

to be well pleasing to Him, i. e. '*whether He find us ἐνδημ. or ἐκδημ., to meet with His approval in that day.*' That this is the sense, the next verse seems to me to shew beyond question. For there he renders a reason for the expressions, and fixes the participles as belonging to the time of His coming. But this meaning has not, that I am aware, been seen by the Commentators, and in consequence, the verse has seemed to be beset with difficulties. The ordinary rendering is represented by Chrys., p. 508, τὸ . . ζητούμενον τοῦτό ἐστι, φησίν. ἄν τε ἐκεῖ ὦμεν, ἄν τε ἐνταῦθα, κατὰ γνώμην αὐτοῦ ζῆν·—the objection to which of course is, that when *there with Him*, there will be *no striving* to be εὐάρεστοι αὐτῷ, the acceptance *having taken place.* Nor is De Wette's interpretation free from objection —'*whether we live till His coming, or we die :*' because no sufficient account is given of the present participles. Of all renderings, Meyer's is in this place the most absurd, misled as he is by his interpretation of ver. 8. He would make ἐνδημοῦντες and ἐκδ. here *merely literal*, the similitude being dropped :—'*whether at home, or on travel.*' But, all else aside, can he tell us *where Paul's home was*, subsequently to Acts ix. ? For this would be necessary, though he shrinks from any 'geographische Bestimmung.' **10.**] **For** (explanation and fixing of εὐάρεστοι αὐτῷ εἶναι, as to *when*, and *how testified*) **we all** (and myself among the number) **must be made manifest** (not merely '*appear*' = παραστῆναι [which is a most unfortunate rendering of the E. V., giving to the reader merely the idea of "appearing before" as when summoned to a magistrate], but '*appear in our true light*,' appear as we have never done before, as in reff., where the word is used of our Lord Himself: see also 1 Cor. iv. 5) **before the judgment-seat** (on **βῆμα**, see Stanley's note) **of Christ, that each may receive** (the technical word for *receiving wages*) **the things** (done) **through the body** (as a medium or organ of action. Meyer cites τῶν ἡδονῶν αἱ διὰ τοῦ σώματός εἰσιν, Plato, Phædo, p. 65, and αἰσθήσεις αἱ διὰ τοῦ σώματος, Phædr. p. 250), **according to the things which he did** (in the body), **whether** (it were) **good, or bad** (singular, as abstract). I may observe that no more definite inference must be drawn from this verse as to the place which the saints of God shall hold in the general judgment, than it warrants; viz. that they as well as others, shall be manifested and judged by Him (Matt. xxv. 19): *when*, or *in company with whom*, is not here so much as hinted. I cannot pass on, without directing the student to the passage on this verse in Chrysostom's tenth Homily, p. 510 ff., as one of the grandest extant efforts of human eloquence. **11—13.**] *Having this* **φιλοτιμία**,—*being a genuine fearer of God* (see below)—*he endeavours to make his plain dealing* EVIDENT TO MEN, *as it* IS EVIDENT TO GOD. *He will give the Corinthians whereof to boast concerning him in reply to his boastful adversaries : this his conduct being, whatever construction may be put on it, on behalf of God and them.* **11.**] **Being then conscious of** ('*no strangers to:*' so Homer freq., e. g. ἀθεμίστια εἰδώς) **the fear of the Lord** (not, as Chrys. and most of the ancient Commentators = τὸ φοβερὸν τ. κυρ.,—so also Beza and Estius, '*terrorem* Domini,' and E. V., 'the terror of the Lord;'—but as Vulg., '*timorem* Domini,' —this wholesome fear of Christ as our Judge: see reff. The expression is particularly appropriate for one who had been suspected of double dealing and insincerity : he was inwardly conscious of the principle of the fear of God guiding and leading him),—**we persuade men** (the stress on ἀνθρώπους, '*it is* MEN *that we*

m 1 Cor. iii. 7, &c. reff. n ch. iii. 1 reff. o Rom. xvi. 1 reff. p 1 Tim. v. 14 only. Polyb. xxvii. 6. 10. ἀφ. λαμβ., Rom. vii. 8, 11. q as above (p). ch. xi. 12 (bis). Gal. v. 13 only. P. Ezek. v. 7 only. r Rom. iv. 2 reff. s see σχῶ τί γράψω, Acts xxv. 26. t 1 Thess. ii. 17. u constr., ch. i. 6. 1 Cor. xii. 26. v Paul, here only. = Mark iii. 21. Acts viii. 11. x. 45. xii. 16. Jer. ii. 12. w Rom. xii. 3 reff.

δὲ καὶ ἐν ταῖς [m] συνειδήσεσιν ὑμῶν [l] πεφανερῶσθαι. 12 οὐ πάλιν [n] ἑαυτοὺς [no] συνιστάνομεν ὑμῖν, ἀλλὰ [pq] ἀφορμὴν [p] διδόντες ὑμῖν [r] καυχήματος ὑπὲρ ἡμῶν, ἵνα [s] ἔχητε πρὸς τοὺς ἐν [t] προσώπῳ καυχωμένους, καὶ [t] οὐ [t] καρδίᾳ. 13 [u] εἴτε γὰρ [v] ἐξέστημεν, θεῷ· [u] εἴτε [w] σωφρονοῦμεν, ὑμῖν· 14 ἡ γὰρ

BCDFK LPℵ a b c d e f g h k l m n o 17. 47

12. rec aft ου ins γαρ, with D³[-gr] KLP rel Damasc Thl Œc: [*et non* æth:] om BCD¹Fℵ [latt syrr copt goth arm Euthal-ms] Chr₁ Thdrt Ambrst Pel Bede. for 2nd υμιν, ημιν B¹, *nobis* D-lat. υμων Bℵ 17 G-lat æth. for ου, μη εν Bℵ m 17 [Euthal-ms]: ουκ εν D¹F: txt CD³KLP rel syr goth Chr Damasc.

attempt to persuade.' *Of what?* Beza, Grot., al., *of the truth of Christ's religion; win them to Christ*, which however suits the rendering '*terrorem* Domini,' better than the right one:—Chrys., Theodoret, Theophyl., '*of our own integrity,*' and so in the main, Estius, Bengel, Olsh., De Wette,—and Meyer, though he seems to object to it, for he connects the words with the φιλοτιμία of ver. 9:—Erasm., Luther, Wolf, Hammond, al., understand πείθομεν of the *endeavour to make ourselves acceptable to men;* Cornel.-a-Lapide, Le Clerc, al., '*eundem hunc timorem* hominibus suademus.' But from the context, it must have reference to *ourselves;* and I therefore agree with Chrys., al., as above [I may remind the English reader that there are few texts so much perverted as this one, owing to the rendering of the E. V. It is frequently understood and preached upon, as if it meant, "*Knowing how terrible God is, we persuade others to fear Him:*" a meaning as far as possible from the Apostle's mind]), **but to God we are already manifested** (we have no need to persuade HIM of our integrity, for He knows all things);—**and I hope** (am confident) **that we have been manifested** (Meyer remarks, that ἐλπίζω in the N. T. elsewhere has only the inf. aor.; here however the inf. perfect is logically necessary. He hopes, that the manifestation *is complete.* Cf. Acts xxvii. 13, δόξαντες τῆς προθέσεως κεκρατηκέναι, and Hom. Il. ο. 110, ἤδη γὰρ νῦν ἔλπομ' Ἄρηΐ γε πῆμα τετύχθαι) **in your consciences also.**

12.] **We are not recommending ourselves again to you** (see ch. iii. 1), **but [are] giving you an occasion for matter of boasting** (καύχημα,—not = καύχησις as De W.,—'a source, whence matter of boasting may be derived') **on our behalf** (of us, as your teachers, and to the upholding of our ministry), **that ye may have it** (viz. καύχημα, matter of boasting) **against those who boast in face** (fair **outward appearance**), **and not in heart** (i. e. in those things which they *exhibit*, and *are outwardly* = κατὰ τὴν σάρκα, ch. xi. 18, not in matters which are *in their hearts:* implying that their hearts are indifferent about the matters of which they boast).

13.] **For** (ye have good reason to boast of me as your teacher; seeing that) **whether we have been mad** (there is no need to soften the meaning to '*inordinately praise ourselves,*' as Chrys., al.; or '*act foolishly,*' as others; or '*ultra modum agimus,*' as Bengel, Luther:—μαίνῃ, Παῦλε, was once said, Acts xxvi. 24, and doubtless this charge was among the means taken to depreciate his influence at Corinth), **it was to God** (in God's work and to His glory): [or] **whether we be of sound mind, it is for you** (on your behalf). 'So that you have reason to glory in us either way; if you will ascribe to us madness, it is a holy madness, *for God:* if you maintain and are convinced of our sobriety, it is a soundness *in your service.*' On the interpretation of Chrys. above, he explains the last clause,—ἄν τε μέτριόν τι κ. ταπεινὸν (φθεγξώμεθα), δι' ὑμᾶς, ἵνα μάθητε ταπεινοφρονεῖν. Hom. xi. p. 513. But he gives our interpretation also, as an alternative: μαίνεσθαί τις ἡμᾶς φησί; διὰ τὸν θεὸν τοιαῦτα μαινόμεθα.

14—19.] *And his constraining motive is the love of Christ; who died for all, that all should live to Him; and accordingly the Apostle has no longer any mere knowledge or regards according to the flesh, seeing that all things are become new in Christ by means of the reconciliation effected by God in Him, of which reconciliation Paul is the minister.*

14.] **For** (reason of his devotion under all reports and circumstances, θεῷ and ὑμῖν, as in last verse) **Christ's love** (not, *love to Christ*, as Œc., Beza, al.,—but *Christ's love to men*, subjective, as most Commentators; as shewn in *His Death*, which is the greatest proof of love, see Rom. v. 6—8. Meyer remarks that the gen. of the person after ἀγάπη is with Paul *always*

[x] ἀγάπη τοῦ [x] χριστοῦ [y] συνέχει ἡμᾶς,
15 [z] κρίναντας τοῦτο, ὅτι εἷς ὑπὲρ πάντων ἀπέθανεν, [a] ἄρα [b] οἱ [b] πάντες [c] ἀπέθανον· καὶ ὑπὲρ πάντων ἀπέθανεν, ἵνα οἱ ζῶντες μηκέτι [d] ἑαυτοῖς ζῶσιν, ἀλλὰ [d] τῷ ὑπὲρ αὐτῶν ἀποθανόντι καὶ [e] ἐγερθέντι.
16 ὥστε ἡμεῖς [f] ἀπὸ τοῦ νῦν οὐδένα οἴδαμεν

x = Rom. viii. 35. Eph. iii. 19.
y = Luke xii. 50. Acts xviii. 5. Phil. i. 23 (L.P., exc. Matt. iv. 24). Job xxxi. 23.
z = Acts xv. 19.
a 1 Cor. xv. 14. Gal. iii. 29. see Rom. vii. 3, 25.
b ver. 10.
c = Rom. vi. 8.
d dat., Rom. vi. 2, 10, 11. xiv. 7 al.
e 1 Cor. xv. 4, and passim. Isa. xxvi. 19.
f Acts xviii. 6 (Paul) reff.

14. for χριστου, θεου CP 17. 39. 42-6. 120. 238 syr Chr $Thdrt_1$($txt_{b.l.}$) Thl-marg.
15. κριναντες F: -νοντας 17. rec ins ει bef εἷς, with C[1]ℵ[3] rel vulg(and F-lat) copt arm Ath-mss Chr_3 Cyr_1[-p Bas_1-ms_1 Euthal-ms] Thl Aug_2(elsw mss vary) Bede: om B(sic: see table) C[2]DFKLPℵ[1] d e l n 17. 47 syrr goth æth Ath-edd_1 Chr_1 Cyr_1[-p Bas-edd_1] Thdrt Damasc. for απεθανον, απεθανεν ℵ[1]. aft 2nd απεθανεν ins χριστος F vulg(not am harl [fuld tol) arm $Cypr_1$ Ambrst].

subjective,—Rom. v. 5, 8; viii. 35, 39; ch. viii. 24; xiii. 13; Eph. ii. 4; Phil. i. 9 al. (but see his own note on 2 Thess. iii. 5, where he maintains the objective sense), whereas with John it is not always so, 1 John v. 3. Paul usually expresses love *of*, i. e. *towards*, by εἰς, Col. i. 4; 1 Thess. iii. 12) **constraineth us** (a better word could not be found: the idea of συνέχω is that of *forcible limitation*, either in a good or a bad sense,—of *confining to one object*, or *within certain bounds*, be that one object a painful or glorious one,—those bounds the angustiæ of distress, or the course of apostolic energy, as here. '*Constraineth us*,' generally:—limits us to one great end, and prohibits our taking into consideration any others. 'Metaphora est in verbo *constringendi*: qua notatur, fieri non posse, quin, quisquis mirificum illum amorem quem testatus est nobis Christus morte sua, vere expendit et reputat, quasi ei alligatus, et arctissimo vinculo constrictus, se in illius obsequium addicat.' Calv. The varieties of interpretation, some as Meyer, urging more the sense *cohibendi*, others as Chrys., that *excitandi*, οὐκ ἀφίησιν ἡμᾶς ἡσυχάζειν, all in fact amount to one—that of the *forcible compression* of his energies to one line of action),
15.] [**having judged this** (i. e.] **because we formed this judgment**, viz. at our conversion:—learned to regard this as a settled truth) **that One died on behalf of all** (not only, for the *benefit* of all, as Meyer,—but *instead of* all, suffered death in the root and essence of our humanity, as the second Adam. This death on behalf of *all men* is the absolute objective fact: that *all* enter not into the benefit of that Death, is owing to the non-fulfilment of the subjective condition which follows), —**therefore all died** (i. e. therefore, in the death of Christ, *all, the* all for whom He died, οἱ πάντες, *died too*: i. e. see below, became planted in the likeness of His death,—died to sin and to self, that they might live to Him. This was true, *objectively*, but *not subjectively* till such death to sin and self is realized in each: see Rom. vi. 8 ff.). The other renderings,—'*ought to die*,' as Thomas Aq., Grot., Estius, al., —'*were under sentence of death*,' as Chrys., Theodoret, Beza, al.;—'*as good as died*, Flatt;—are shewn to be erroneous by carefully noticing the construction, with or without εἰ. The *verb* is common to both members of the sentence; the correspondent emphatic words in the two members being (1) **εἷς ὑπὲρ πάντων**, (2) **πάντες**: * '(*One on behalf of all*) died, therefore (*all*) died: if *One* died the death of (belonging to, due from) all, then all died (in and with Him).' Meyer's rendering of ὅτι *because*, can hardly be right as it would leave κρίναντας τοῦτο standing awkwardly alone. **And He died for all, in order that they who live** (in *this life*, see ἡμεῖς οἱ ζῶντες, ch. iv. 11; = in sense, '*as long as they are in this state*,' as De W.:—not, 'those who live *spiritually*,' as Beza, Flatt, which would altogether strike out the sense, for it is, *that they may* live spiritually, &c.: nor, '*superstites*,' they whom He left behind at His death, ζῶντες in contrast with Him who ἀπέθανεν, as Meyer;—for, not to insist on the more general reference to *all time*, many to whom the Apostle was now writing were *not born at the time of His Death*) **should no longer** (now that His Death has taken place: or, as they did before they apprehended that Death as theirs,—but I prefer the former, see ἀπὸ τοῦ νῦν below) **live to themselves** (with *self* as their great source and end of action, to please and to obey) **but to Him that died and rose again for them** (ὑπέρ, not merely even as connected with ἐγερθέντι '*for the benefit of*,' as Meyer again; but strictly '*in the place of*:' as the Death of Christ is *our death*, so His Resurrection is *our resurrection*). **16.**] **So that** (*accordingly*,—consistently with our judg-

g Rom. i. 3 reff.
h 1 Cor. i. 30 reff.
i Gal. vi. 15.
k Acts xv. 7 reff. = Isa. xliii. 18.
l = Matt. v. 18. xxiv. 35 al. see Acts xxvii. 9 reff.

[g] κατὰ [g] σάρκα· εἰ καὶ ἐγνώκαμεν [g] κατὰ [g] σάρκα χριστόν,
ἀλλὰ νῦν οὐκ ἔτι γινώσκομεν.
17 ὥςτε εἴ τις [h] ἐν χριστῷ,
[i] καινὴ [i] κτίσις· τὰ [k] ἀρχαῖα [l] παρῆλθεν, ἰδού, γένονεν

BCDFK LPℵ a b c d e f g h k l m n o 17. 47

16. rec aft ει ins δε, with C^2 $D^{2.3}$[-gr] (K)LPℵ^3 rel syr (copt goth) Chr_2 [Cyr-p_3 Euthal-ms] $Thdrt_2$ Damasc : και bef ει F latt [Syr Orig-int_{alic} Dind-int_1 Ambrst $Aug_{sæpe}$] : txt B D^1[-gr] ℵ^1 17 [arm] $Orig_4$ Eus_1 [Nys_1]. (C^1 uncert.)—om και K 115 copt goth [Cyr_1 Orig-int_1]. χριστον bef κατα σαρκα D æth $Orig_2$(-$int_{sæpe}$) Jer_{alic}. aft γινωσκομεν ins κατα σαρκα D^1[and lat] F Jer_1. (not vulg F-lat.)

ment expressed ver. 15) **we** (in opposition to our adversaries, the false teachers: not *general*, of *all Christians*, as De W.,—but as yet spoken, as the emphatic position of ἡμεῖς shews, of the Apostle himself (and his colleagues?)) **from this time** (since this great event, the Death of Christ) **know no man according to** (as he is in) **the flesh** (Meyer well remarks: "Since all are (ethically) dead, and each man is bound to live only to Christ, not to himself, our knowledge of others must be altogether independent of that which they are κατὰ σάρκα,—must not be regulated κατὰ σάρκα. And the connexion of ver. 16 with ver. 15 shews that we must not take κατὰ σάρκα as the *subjective* rule of οἴδαμεν,—so that the explanation would be, 'according to mere human knowledge,' 'apart from the enlightening of the Holy Spirit,' cf. ch. i. 17; 1 Cor. i. 26,—but as the *objective* rule, cf. ch. xi. 18; John viii. 15; Phil. iii. 4,—so that εἰδέναι τινὰ κατὰ σάρκα = '*to know any one according to his mere human individuality*,'—'to know him as men have judged him by what he is in the flesh,' not by what he is κατὰ πνεῦμα, as a Christian, as καινὴ κτίσις, ver. 17. He who knows no man κατὰ σάρκα has, e. g. in the case of the Jew, entirely lost sight of his Jewish origin,—in that of the rich man, of his riches,—in that of the learned, of his learning,—in that of the slave, of his servitude, &c., cf. Gal. iii. 28"): **if even we have** (εἰ καί *concedes* what follows: πόλιν μέν, εἰ καὶ μὴ βλέπεις, φρονεῖς δ' ὅμως, οἵᾳ νόσῳ ξύνεστι, Soph. Œd. Tyr. 302,—but also, as distinguished from καὶ εἰ, *introduces no climax*, and distributes the force of the καί over the whole concessive clause, whereas in καὶ εἰ it is confined to the conditional particle εἰ,—see Hartung, Partikellehre, i. 139) **known Christ according to the flesh, now however we know Him (thus) no longer.** The fact alluded to in the concessive clause, is, not any personal knowledge of the Lord Jesus while He was on earth, but that view of Him which Paul took *before his conversion*, when he knew Him only according to His outward apparent standing in this world, *only as Jesus of Nazareth.* **χριστόν** is not = τὸν χριστόν, '*the* Christ,' but merely as a proper name designating Him whom he now knew as Christ. Observe, the stress is *not on* χριστόν, q. d. 'If we have known *even Christ* after the flesh,' &c., as usually understood;—the position of χρ. forbids this, which would require εἰ καὶ χριστὸν ἐγν. κ. σάρ.,—but on **ἐγνώκαμεν**, as belonging to the *past*, contrasted with our *present* knowledge. Observe likewise, that the position of κατὰ σάρκα, as above also, forbids its being taken as the subjective qualification of ἐγνώκαμεν, as = εἰ καὶ κατὰ σάρκα ἐγν. χρ., or εἰ κ. ἐγν. χρ. κ. σάρκ., and fixes it as belonging to χριστόν,—'*Christ according to the flesh.*' St. Paul now, since his conversion, knew Him no longer as thus shewn, but as ὁρισθέντα υἱὸν θεοῦ ἐν δυνάμει, κατὰ πνεῦμα ἁγιωσύνης. At that time, εὐδόκησεν ὁ ἀφορίσας με . . . **ἀποκαλύψαι τὸν υἱὸν αὐτοῦ** ἐν ἐμοί, Gal. i. 15, 16. See by all means Stanley's remarks, on the absence of all local and personal recollections of our Lord's life, in the apostolic age. **17.**] **So that** (additional inference from what has gone before: hardly as Meyer, from ver. 16 *only*: the *death* of ver. 15, as well as the new knowledge of ver. 16, going to make up the καινὴ κτίσις) **if any man is in Christ** (far better than 'whoever is in Christ.' See note on Phil. iv. 8. '*In Christ*,' i. e. in union with Him: Christ being 'the element in which by faith we live and move,' as Meyer), **he is a new creature** (κτίσις, '*creation*,'—the act, implying here the result of the act. See ref. and Col. iii. 10, 11; Eph. ii. 10; iv. 23.

'He has received,' 'passed into,' 'a new life,' John iii. 3): **the old things** (of his former life—'all the old selfish and impure motives, views, and prejudices,'—De Wette) **have passed away** (there does not appear to be any allusion, as in Chrys., Theophyl., to the passing away of Judaism, but only to the *new birth*, the antiquation of the former unconverted state, with all that belonged to it); **behold** (a reminiscence of Isa. xliii. 18, 19—μὴ μνημονεύετε τὰ πρῶτα, καὶ τὰ ἀρχαῖα μὴ συλλογίζεσθε· ἰδού, ἐγὼ ποιῶ καινά), **they have become new** (see var. readd.). The arrangement of the sentence followed by

καινά. 18 τὰ δὲ [m] πάντα [m] ἐκ τοῦ θεοῦ τοῦ [n] καταλλάξαν-
τος ἡμᾶς ἑαυτῷ διὰ χριστοῦ καὶ δόντος ἡμῖν τὴν
[o] διακονίαν τῆς [p] καταλλαγῆς, 19 [q] ὡς [q] ὅτι θεὸς ἦν [r] ἐν
χριστῷ κόσμον [n] καταλλάσσων ἑαυτῷ, μὴ [s] λογιζόμενος
αὐτοῖς τὰ [t] παραπτώματα αὐτῶν, καὶ [u] θέμενος ἐν ἡμῖν
τὸν [v] λόγον τῆς [p] καταλλαγῆς. 20 ὑπὲρ χριστοῦ οὖν

m 1 Cor. xi. 12 reff.
n Rom. v. 10 reff.
o Acts xx. 24 reff.
p here bis. Rom. . 11. xi. 15 only. Isa. ix. 5. 2 Macc. v. 20 only.
q = here (ch. xi. 21. 2 Thess. ii. 2) only.
r 1 Cor. xv. 22 reff.
s = Rom. ii. 26. iv. 4, 8 al. fr. Num. xviii. 27.
t Rom. iv. 25 reff.
u Ps. civ. 27. (Amos v. 7.)
v Acts xiii. 26 reff.

17. rec aft *καινα* ins *τα παντα*, with D[2.3][-gr] KLP rel syr goth æth-pl [arm-mss] Orig$_1$ Constt$_1$ Did$_1$ Chr$_3$ Damasc Tert$_1$: bef *καινα* b d f k o 17. 46. 67[2] vulg-ed (Syr) Ath$_1$[-ed$_2$] Dial$_1$ Meth$_1$ Cyr[-p$_5$ Ephr$_1$ Euthal-ms] Thdrt Procl$_1$ Orig-int$_3$ [Ambr$_1$] Ambrst Jer Salv: om BCD[1]Fℵ latt copt æth-rom arm(1805) Clem$_1$ Ath-ms$_2$ Cyr[-p$_3$ Ambr$_1$] Hil$_1$ Aug$_1$ Promiss.
18. om 1st *του* D[1]F. rec ins *ιησου* bef *χριστου*, with D[3][-gr] KL rel Thdrt Damasc: om BCD[1]FPℵ 17 latt syrr copt goth æth arm Chr$_1$ [Euthal-ms] Hil Ambrst Aug$_1$.
19. ins *ο* bef *θεος* FK b[1] o Chr$_1$ Thdrt. *καταλασσων*(sic) ℵ e f h[1] k. add *εν* D[1][corrd eadem manu]. for *λογ.*, *αστιζομενος* F. [*εαυτοις* (but corrd) D[1].] om 2nd *εν* K f h l[1] n 47. ins (*του*) *ευαγγελιου* bef *τον λογον* D[1] F[not F-lat]: *adnuntiationem* D-lat, *evangelii* G-lat(and so over the greek in F).—om *του* F.
20. for *υπερ χρ. ουν*, *ον υπερ χριστου* D[1] F[-gr]; *pro quo Christo* D-lat; *quod pro*

the Vulg., al., 'Si qua ergo in Christo nova creatura, vetera transierunt,' is inadmissible, because the second member would be a mere reassertion of the first.

18.] **And all things** (in this new creation: he passes to a more general view of the effects of the death of Christ—viz. our *reconciliation to God*) **are from God** (as their source), **who reconciled us** (*all men*, from next verse, where *κόσμον* is parallel with it) **to Himself by means of Christ** (as an atonement, an expiatory sacrifice, ver. 21, for sin which made us *ἐχθροὶ θεοῦ*, see Rom. v. 10), **and gave** (committed) **to us** (Apostles, not mankind in general; for had it been so,—in the next verse, which is parallel, *ἐν αὐτοῖς*, not *ἐν ἡμῖν*, must have stood, after *αὐτοῖς* and *αὐτῶν* just preceding) **the ministration of the reconciliation** (the duty of ministering in that office, whose peculiar work it is to proclaim this reconciliation: so *διακονία τῆς δικαιοσύνης*, ch. iii. 9. Observe, that the reconciliation spoken of in this and the next verse, is that of *God to us*, absolutely and objectively, through His Son: that whereby He can complacently behold and endure a sinful world, and receive all who come to Him by Christ. This, the subjective reconciliation,—*of men to God*,—follows as a matter of exhortation, ver. 20),

19.] **how that** (the *ὡς* imports that the proposition following it, introduced by *ὅτι*, is matter of indirect reference. So Xen. Hell. iii. 2. 14, *εἰπὼν τῷ Φάρακι ὡς ὅτι ὀκνοίη μὴ ὁ Τισσαφ. κ.τ.λ.*, and argum. Isocr. Busir. p. 520 (cited by Winer, edn. 6, § 65. 9), *κατηγόρουν αὐτοῦ, ὡς ὅτι καινὰ δαιμόνια εἰσφέρει*) **God in Christ was reconciling the world to Himself** (**ἦν καταλλάσσων** not exactly = *κατήλλασσεν*, any more than *ἦν κηρύσσων* Luke iv. 44 = *ἐκήρυσσεν*: in both cases the habitual state is more emphatically implied than could be done by the imperfect merely: the shade of difference can, however, hardly be expressed in English. **ἦν** cannot, as in Erasm., Luther, Calv., Beza, al., and E. V., belong to *ἐν χριστῷ*, 'God *was in Christ*, reconciling' &c.,—partly on account of the position of *ἐν χρ.*, which would thus probably be before *ἦν*, but principally (Meyer) because of incoherence with *θέμενος ἐν ἡμῖν κ.τ.λ.*: for in that case the two latter clauses must express the *manner* of reconciliation by Christ, which the second of them does not. **κόσμον**,—without the article, as governed words placed for emphasis before their verbs often are—it would not be *καταλλάσσων κόσμον*, but *τὸν κόσμον*,—**the whole world**,—*man, and man's world, entire, with all that therein is*, see Col. i. 20, but considered, cf. *αὐτῶν* below, as *summed up in man*),—**not reckoning to them their trespasses** (*present*: on the expression see reff.), **and having placed in us** (*past*:—not merely = '*committed to us*,' but '*laid upon us*,' as our office and charge, and, besides, '*empowered us for*,' '*put in our souls by His Spirit*.' '*Us*,' viz. Apostles and teachers) **the word of the reconciliation** (as *ὁ λόγος ὁ τοῦ σταυροῦ*, 1 Cor. i. 18).

20, 21.] *He describes his office as that of an ambassador for Christ, consisting in beseeching them*, ON THEIR PART, *to be reconciled to God; and that, in consideration of the great Atonement which God has provided by Christ.* **On Christ's**

w Eph. vi. 20 only †. (-εία, Luke xiv. 32.) x w. gen. abs., 1 Cor. iv. 18 reff. y absol., 1 Cor. iv. 13 reff. z = Eccles. viii. 5.

[w] πρεσβεύομεν, [x] ὡς τοῦ θεοῦ [y] παρακαλοῦντος δι' ἡμῶν· δεόμεθα ὑπὲρ χριστοῦ, [n] καταλλάγητε τῷ θεῷ. 21 τὸν μὴ [z] γνόντα ἁμαρτίαν ὑπὲρ ἡμῶν ἁμαρτίαν ἐποίησεν, ἵνα ἡμεῖς γενώμεθα [a] δίκαιοσύνη [a] θεοῦ ἐν αὐτῷ. VI. 1 [b] συνερ-

BCDFK LPℵ a b c d e f g h k l m n o 17. 47

a = Rom. i. 17 reff. (Phil. iii. 9.) b Mark xvi. 20. Rom. viii. 28. 1 Cor. xvi. 16. James ii. 22 only †. 1 Macc. xii. 1. Esdr. vii. 2 only. (-γος, 1 Cor. iii. 9.)

Christo G-lat. δεομενοι D[1](and lat) F[-gr] Chr-ms Hil$_1$ Ambrst(not [Orig-int$_3$ Jer$_1$] Aug$_{sæpe}$); *orantes aut obsecrantes* G-lat. καταλλαγηναι D[1](and lat) F[not F-lat] syr-mg goth, *reconciliari* G-lat [Hil$_1$ Ambrst Aug$_{sæpe}$]. om τω F.

21. rec aft τον ins γαρ (*see note*), with D[3][-gr] KLPℵ[3] rel syrr goth æth arm Chr$_1$ Euther$_1$ Thdrt$_3$ Damasc: om BCD[1]Fℵ[1] 17 latt copt Orig$_2$ Eus$_2$ Ath$_1$ [Cyr-p$_3$ Euthal-ms] Thdrt$_1$ Did[-int$_1$] Hil$_1$ Ambrst Aug Pel Alcim. rec γινωμεθα: txt BCDKPℵ rel Orig$_1$ Eus$_3$[-ms$_1$ Cyr-p$_2$] Chr$_1$ Thdrt$_{sæpe}$ Damasc Thl Œc, [γενομ. L Euthal-ms,] ενωμια F. θεου bef δικαιοσυνη KP d 93. 109. 219 Eus$_1$(txt$_3$) Sev Chr Thdrt$_3$: om θεου 46. 114 Thdrt$_1$.

behalf then (i. e. in pursuance of the imposition on us of the λόγος τῆς κατ.) **we are ambassadors, as if God were exhorting by us: we beseech** (*'you,'* but not uttered as an integral part of the present text, not a request *now made and urged*, as Rom. xii. 1; he is *describing the embassage;* we are ambassadors, and in our embassage it is our work to beseech—*'Be ye,'* &c.) **on Christ's behalf, Be reconciled to God:— καταλλ.** strictly *passive:* 'God was the Reconciler—let this reconciliation *have effect on you*—enter into it by faith.' Our E. V., by inserting the word *'ye,'* has given a false impression, making it appear as if there were an emphasis on it, corresponding to *God* being reconciled to *us*, as if it had been καταλλάγητε καὶ ὑμεῖς τῷ θεῷ,—whereas it is the simple *being reconciled* in that reconciliation in which *God was, in Christ, the Reconciler.* **21.**] *States the great fact on which the exhortation to be reconciled is grounded:*—viz. the *unspeakable gift* of God, to bring about the reconciliation. It is introduced without a γάρ (which has been supplied), as still forming part of the λόγος τῆς καταλλαγῆς. **Him who knew not sin** (τὸν οὐ γνόντα would merely assert *the fact*, that up to the time of ἐποίησεν, He was ignorant of sin. * But μή with a participle, as has been observed since the doctrine of the particles has been more accurately studied, always denies *subjectively*, i. e. in reference to the view of some person who is the subject, or to the hypothesis of some person who is the direct or indirect utterer of the assertion. Cf. note on ch. iv. 18. With what reference then is the particle here used? Fritz. (in Meyer) thinks, to *the Christian's necessary idea* of Christ, "quem talem virum mente concipimus, qui sceleris notitiam non habuerit:" Meyer, and Winer, edn. 6, § 55. 5. β, to *God's judgment* of Him. I much prefer to either regarding it as subjective with reference to *Christ Himself*, Who said, John viii. 46, τίς ἐξ ὑμῶν ἐλέγχει με περὶ ἁμαρτίας; He was thus ὁ μὴ γνοὺς ἁμαρτίαν (see Hartung, Partikellehre, ii. 131, who gives among other examples, one very similar, from Thucyd. i. 118, ἡσύχαζόν τε τὸ πλέον τοῦ χρόνου, **ὄντες** καὶ πρὸ τοῦ **μὴ ταχεῖς** ἰέναι ἐς τοὺς πολέμους),—*'knew not,'* i. e. by contact, by personal experience, *'sin.'* See, for the *sense*, 1 Pet. ii. 22; Heb. vii. 26), **on our behalf** (or, *instead of us:* I prefer here the former, because the purpose of the verse is to set forth how great things God has done *for us:*—the other, though true, does not seem so applicable. The words ὑπὲρ ἡμ. are emphatic) **He made** (to be) **sin** (not, *'a sin-offering,'* as Augustine, Ambros., Œcum., Erasm., Hammond, Wolf, al., for the word seems *never to have the meaning*, even in the LXX (see however the remarkable reading of the Codex A at Lev. vi. 25); and if it had, the former sense of the same word in this same sentence would preclude it here: nor = ἁμαρτωλός, as Meyer, al.: but, as De Wette, al., Sin, abstract, as opposed to Righteousness which follows; compare κατάρα, Gal. iii. 13. He, on the Cross, was *the Representative of Sin,*—of the sin of the world), **that we might become** (the present, γινώμ. as in rec., would signify, as Stallbaum, Crito, p. 43 (Meyer)—'id quod propositum fuerit, nondum perfectum et transactum esse, sed adhuc durare.' The aor., which is supported by all the MSS., also yields the best sense, as joining the whole justification of all God's people, as one act accomplished, with the Sacrifice of Christ) **the righteousness of God** (see above: representatives of the Righteousness of God, endued with it and viewed as *in it*, and *examples of it*) **in Him** (in union with Him, and by virtue of our standing in Him).

γοῦντες δὲ καὶ [c] παρακαλοῦμεν, μὴ [d] εἰς [de] κενὸν τὴν χάριν
τοῦ θεοῦ δέξασθαι ὑμᾶς 2 (λέγει γὰρ Καιρῷ [f] δεκτῷ [g] ἐπ-
ήκουσά σου, καὶ ἐν [h] ἡμέρᾳ σωτηρίας [i] ἐβοήθησά σοι. ἰδοὺ
νῦν καιρὸς [j] εὐπρόςδεκτος, ἰδοὺ νῦν [h] ἡμέρα σωτηρίας·)
3 μηδεμίαν [k] ἐν [k] μηδενὶ [l] διδόντες [m] προςκοπήν, ἵνα μὴ

c Rom. xii. 1 reff. d Gal. ii. 2. Phil. ii. 16 bis. 1 Thess. iii. 5 only. Isa. lxv. 23. e 1 Cor. xv. 10 reff. f Isa. xlix. 8. Luke iv. 19, 24. Acts x. 35. Phil. iv. 18 only. g here only l. c. Ps. xix. 1. h = 1 Cor. i. 8 reff. i Acts xvi. 9 reff. j Rom. xv. 16 reff. k ch. vii. 9. Phil. i. 28. Amos i. 4. see ver. 4. l 1 Cor. ix. 12. m here only +. διδόναι ἀφορμὰς προςκοπῆς, Polyb. xxvii. 6. 10. (-κομμα, Rom. ix. 32.)

Chap. VI. 1. παρακαλουντες D[1][and lat] F[not F-lat] goth. om υμας D[1]: ημας Cℵ[1](txt ℵ-corr[1.3]) 4. 17. 89 æth.
2. καιρω γαρ λεγει D[1](and lat) F(not F-lat) [goth] Sedul. (κτω of δεκτω are supplied by ℵ-corr[1].) for σοι, σου F(not G). for ευπροςδεκτος, δεκτος F.

Chap. VI. 1—10.] *He further describes his apostolic embassage, as one of earnest exhortation not to receive the grace of God in vain* (vv. 1, 2), *and of approving himself, by many characteristics and under various circumstances, as the minister of God* (vv. 3—10). 1.] **συνεργοῦντες**, viz. τῷ θεῷ, Whose representatives they were, and Whose grace they recommended. This is implied not only in what went before, but in the τοῦ θεοῦ of our verse itself. Meyer makes it τῷ χριστῷ, referring it to the ὑπὲρ χρ. above: Chrys., Theodoret, Bengel, Olsh., al., ὑμῖν, which certainly would have been *expressed*, and does not suit the sense, nor Paul's habit of speaking of the ministry, see 1 Cor. iii. 9. Flatt and Emmerling would make the σύν imply, working *with our exhortations*, aiding them by our example: which sense, though occasionally belonging to σύν and πρός in composition, could hardly have place here without some plainer indication in *what went before*, of that to which the preposition refers,—and would not suit the καί, which severs συνεργ. from παρακαλ.

The δέ is one of transition, introducing a new feature. **Moreover, while working with God, we also exhort, that you** (when preaching to *you*,—or others, when preaching to others: he still is *describing his practice* in his ministry, not using a direct exhortation to the Corinthians) **receive not** ('recipiatis;'—not 'rece*peritis*,' 'that ye will not *have received*,' i. e. 'will not by apostasy shew that ye have received . . .' as Erasm., al., and De Wette. This mistake arises mainly from regarding the words as *directly addressed* to the Corinthians instead of a *description of his apostolic practice*) **the grace of God** (i. e. the reconciliation above spoken of) **to no purpose** (i. e. unaccompanied by sanctification of life; so Chrys., ἵνα . . μὴ νομίσωσιν ὅτι τοῦτό ἐστι καταλλαγὴ μόνον, τὸ πιστεῦσαι τῷ καλοῦντι, ἐπάγει ταῦτα, τὴν περὶ τὸν βίον σπουδὴν ἀπαιτῶν. Hom. xii. p. 521.)
2.] *Ground of the exhortation*: viz. the importance of the present time as the day of acceptance,—shewn by a Scripture citation. **For he** (God, with whom we συνεργοῦμεν and whose grace we recommend) **saith, 'In an accepted time** (Heb. בְּעֵת רָצוֹן, '*in a season of grace*') **I heard thee, and in the day of salvation I helped thee:' behold** (inserted for solemnity—to mark the importance of what follows), **now is the favourably accepted time** (εὐπρόςδεκτος, a far stronger term than δεκτός, q. d. the *very* time of *most favourable* acceptance, said from the fulness of his feeling of the greatness of God's grace),—**behold, now is the day of salvation.** ὁ γὰρ ἐν τοιούτῳ καιρῷ ἀγωνιζόμενος, ἐν ᾧ τοσαύτη κέχυται δωρεά, ἐν ᾧ τοσαύτη χάρις, εὐκόλως ἐπιτεύξεται τῶν βραβείων. Chrys. p. 522. The prophecy is one directly of the Lord Jesus, as the restorer and gatherer of his people; and the time of acceptance is the interval of the offer of the covenant to men, conceded to Him by the Father. 3—10.] *And this doing, he approves himself as the minister of God by various characteristics, and under manifold circumstances in life.* 3.] **διδόντες**, resumed from συνεργοῦντες, ver. 1: ver. 2 being parenthetic. It, and all the following participles, vv. 9, 10, qualify παρακαλοῦμεν, shewing the pains and caution used by him to enforce this exhortation by his example as well as his precept. So Grot.: 'ostendit enim, quam serio moneat, qui, ut aliquid proficiat, nullis terreatur incommodis, nulla non commoda negligat.' But evidently, before the list is exhausted, he passes beyond the mere confirmation of his preaching, and is speaking generally of the characteristics of the Christian ministry. **ἐν μηδενί, in nothing**, compare ἐν παντί, below: not, '*in no man's estimation*,' as Luther. μηδεμ.,—μηδενί, are not = οὐδεμ.—οὐδενί, but, see on ch. v. 21, subjectively said—**we exhort, being such as give, &c.**: so 1 Cor. x. 33, ἐγὼ πάντα πᾶσιν ἀρέσκω, μὴ ζητῶν κ.τ.λ. **προσκοπή** = σκάνδαλον, or πρόσκομμα, Rom. xiv. 13.

[n] μωμηθῇ ἡ [o] διακονία, 4 ἀλλ' [p] ἐν [p] παντὶ [q] συνιστάντες
[q] ἑαυτοὺς ὡς θεοῦ διάκονοι, ἐν [r] ὑπομονῇ πολλῇ, ἐν [s] θλίψεσιν, ἐν [t] ἀνάγκαις, ἐν [s] στενοχωρίαις, 5 ἐν [uv] πληγαῖς,
ἐν [uv] φυλακαῖς, ἐν [w] ἀκαταστασίαις, ἐν [vxy] κόποις, ἐν [yz] ἀγρυπνίαις, ἐν [ya] νηστείαις, 6 ἐν [b] ἁγνότητι, ἐν [c] γνώσει, ἐν [d] μα-

BCDFK LPℵ a b c d e f g h k l m n o 17. 47

n ch. viii. 20 only. Prov. ix. 7. Wisd. x. 14 only. (-μος, 2 Pet. ii. 13.)
o = Acts i. 17. xx. 24 (reff.). Rom. xi. 13 †.
p = ch. iv. 8 reff.
q ch. iii. 1. iv. 2. v. 12. vii. 11. x. 12.
r Rom. ii. 7 reff.
s Rom. ii. 9 (reff.).
t = 1 Cor. vii. 26 reff.
u Acts xvi. 23.
v ch. xi. 23.
w 1 Cor. xiv. 33 reff.
x as above (v). 1 Cor. iii. 8. xv. 58 al. Gen. xxxi. 42.
y ch. xi. 27.
z as above (y) only †. 2 Macc. ii. 26. (-πνεῖν, Eph. vi. 18.)
a as above (y) (1 Cor. vii. 5 v. r.) only in Paul. [Matt. xvii. 21 ‖ Mk.] Luke ii. 37. Acts xiv. 23. xxvii. 9 only. 2 Kings xii. 16.
b ch. xi. 3 only †. (-νός, ch. vii. 11.)
c = 1 Cor. i. 5. xii. 8 al.
d Rom. ii. 4 (reff.).

3. μωθη(sic) B^1 f: μωμωθη D^1. aft η διακονια ins ημων DF d 66^2. 73 latt syrr sah [goth] Chr_1 Thdrt [$Antch_1$(pref)] Thl Œc-comm Ambrst Aug_1 Pel[, υμων æth].
4. rec συνιστωντες, with $D^3KLℵ^3$ rel Chr_1 Thdrt [$Antch_1$] Damasc h.l.: συνιστοντες f: συνισтανοντες BP 31. 73 $Damasc_1$: txt $CD^1Fℵ^1$ 17 $Clem_1$ Cyr_1 [Euthal-ms]. διακονους D^1[-gr] vulg [F-lat Ambrst Aug_1]: *ministros* aut *-i* G-lat.

μωμηθῇ] μωμᾶσθαι, *'to reproach'* (see Winer, edn. 6, § 38. 7. a, and Moulton's note), is one of those deponent verbs which have an aorist passive: so διαλέγεσθαι, βούλεσθαι, δύνασθαι, σπλαγχνίζεσθαι, &c. The διακονία, the office itself, would be reproached, if cause of offence were found in the character of its bearers. **4.**] Meyer well remarks the position of συνιστ. ἑαυτούς. When the words signified 'to recommend *ourselves*,' in a bad sense, ch. iii. 1, v. 12, —ἑαυτ. *preceded* the verb: but here and ch. iv. 2, where used in a good sense, and without any stress on ἑαυτούς, it *follows* the verb. This is only one of continually occurring instances of the importance of the collocation of words with regard to the emphasis. **διάκονοι**] not διακόνους: **recommending ourselves, as ministers of God should do.** The ambiguity of the E. V. might have been avoided by a different arrangement of words: *'in all things, as the ministers of God, approving ourselves.'* The following datives are a specification of παντί; but not all of the same sort: some signify *instruments by which*, some, *situations in which*, some *both these*. Bengel remarks: "Insignis gradatio. Sequuntur ter tria patienda (i.e. from θλίψεσιν to νηστείαις), quibus *patientia* (ὑπομονή) exercetur; *pressuræ,—plagæ,—labores.* Primus ternarius continet *genera*, secundus, *species* adversorum: tertia *spontanea*" (but qu?: see below). So that the ὑπομονὴ πολλή belongs to vv. 4, 5, and ver. 6 goes on to other points. **στενοχ.**] See ch. iv. 8, note. **5.**] On **πληγ.**, see reff. **φυλακ.**] At Philippi only *as yet*, as far as we know from the narrative of the Acts; —but there must have been many other occasions, see ch. xi. 23. He *may* have been imprisoned at Antioch in Pisidia, Acts xiii. 50, and at Lystra, xiv. 19, and at Corinth, xviii. 12, 14: and we cannot tell what may have befallen him during his journeys, Acts xv. 41; xvi. 6; xviii. 23. **ἐν ἀκαταστ.**] **in tumults**, see Acts xiii. 50; xiv. 5, 19; xvi. 22; xvii. 5; xviii. 12, and above all, xix. 23–41. The sense given by Chrys. (p. 522), al., τὸ μηδαμοῦ δύνασθαι στῆναι ἐλαυνόμενον, is philologically allowable, cf. Demosth. 383. 7, ἀκατάστατον ὥσπερ ἐν θαλάττῃ πνεῦμα, and James i. 8, and Polyb. xxxi. 13. 6, ὑποδεικνύων αὐτοῖς τὴν ἀκαταστασίαν τῆς βασιλείας,—but not found in N. T. **ἐν κόποις**] usually, and here, signifies *'labour in the Lord,'* for his sake, see reff. So also κοπιάω, Rom. xvi. 6, 12 (bis), and reff. Chrys., al., interpret it of his manual work, 1 Cor. iv. 12; and ἀστατοῦμεν and κοπιῶμεν occurring there together certainly gives some semblance to the view: but see ch. xi. 23, where this can hardly be; it is most probable that the *weariness of his excessive apostolic labour* was in his mind. **ἀγρυπνίαις**] Chrys. says, p. 523, τὰς νύκτας ἐν αἷς ἐδίδασκεν, ἢ ὅτι καὶ ἐν αὐταῖς εἰργάζετο. But I would rather believe the ἀγρυπνίαι to have been *watchings through anxiety* for the churches. **ἐν νηστείαις**] This is generally, and by De W. against Meyer, taken to refer to involuntary hunger and thirst. But, as the latter remarks, the word does not appear to be ever so used; and in ch. xi. 27, Paul himself distinguishes ἐν νηστείαις from ἐν λιμῷ κ. δίψει. The meaning of **fastings** must therefore be retained. So Chrys., Theodoret, and Calvin. **6.**] The nine preceding datives (see on ver. 4) have expanded ὑπομονῇ. We now resume the main catalogue, with **ἐν ἁγνότητι, in purity**: which is variously explained: of *bodily chastity*, Grot.:—of *unselfishness*, Theodoret, and Chrys., as an alternative (ἢ

κροθυμίᾳ, ἐν [d] χρηστότητι, ἐν πνεύματι ἁγίῳ, ἐν ἀγάπῃ
[e] ἀνυποκρίτῳ, 7 ἐν [f] λόγῳ [f] ἀληθείας, ἐν [g] δυνάμει [g] θεοῦ,
διὰ τῶν [h] ὅπλων τῆς δικαιοσύνης τῶν [i] δεξιῶν καὶ
[ik] ἀριστερῶν, 8 διὰ [l] δόξης καὶ [m] ἀτιμίας, διὰ [n] δυςφημίας
καὶ [o] εὐφημίας, ὡς [p] πλάνοι καὶ [q] ἀληθεῖς, 9 ὡς [r] ἀγνοού-

e Rom. xii. 9 reff.
f Eph. i. 13 2 Tim. ii. 15. James i. 18.
g = 1 Cor. i. 18 reff.
h = ch. x. 4. John xviii. 3 (Rom. vi. 13 bis. xiii. 12) only. Nah. iii. 3.
i (see note.) Matt. vi. 3. Mark x. 37. Luke xxiii. 33 only. 1 Chron. xii. 2.
k N. T. as above (i) only. Gen. xiv. 15.
l = John v. 41, 44 al.
m Rom. i. 26 reff.
n here only †. 1 Macc. vii. 38. Esdr. i. 43 [40] Ald. (δυσσέβεια, AB &c.) only. (-μεῖν, 1 Cor. iv. 13.)
o here only †. Ps. xcix. 2 Symm. (-μος, Phil. iv. 8.)
p Matt. xxvii. 63. 1 Tim. iv. 1. 2 John 7 (bis) only. Job xix. 4. Jer. xxiii. 32 only.
q subj., Matt. xxii. 16. John iii. 33. Rom. iii. 4 ‡.
r 1 Cor. xiv. 38. Gal. i. 22. 2 Pet. ii. 12 al.

σωφροσύνην . . . ἢ τὴν ἐν ἅπασι καθαρότητα, ἢ τὸ ἀδωροδόκητον, ἢ καὶ τὸ δωρεὰν τὸ εὐαγγ. κηρύττειν. ib.):—I prefer the second of Chrys.'s meanings, *general purity of character*, εἰλικρίνεια, — unblamableness of life, and singleness of purpose. **ἐν γνώσει]** **knowledge of the Gospel**, in a high and singular degree; see 1 Cor. ii. 6 ff. So Chrys.: σοφίᾳ τῇ παρὰ τοῦ θεοῦ δεδομένῃ. **χρηστότητι]** **kindness**: a kind and considerate demeanour. **ἐν πν. ἁγίῳ]** **in the Holy Spirit**, as the Power by Whom all these motives are wrought. The omission of the article, aft. ἐν, constitutes no objection to this rendering, as Bp. Middleton (in loc.) supposes: cf. διὰ πν. ἁγίου τοῦ δοθέντος ἡμῖν, Rom. v. 5,—and the very same words as these, 1 Thess. i. 5,—in both which places the meaning is undoubted; neither of which, however, is noticed by Middleton. The words do not appear to hold any *logical* place in the list, any more than ἐν δυν. θεοῦ below. **7. ἐν λόγ. ἀληθ.]** is taken by De W., Meyer, al., as subjective,—'in speaking, or teaching truth'—'*in discourse, the contents whereof were truth*:' but their objection against the sense **in the word of truth**, = ἐν τῷ λόγῳ τῆς ἀληθείας, as it is expressed Col. i. 5, is not valid, on account (1) of the government by a preposition, which would make the insertion of the article optional,—(2) of the whole catalogue being anarthrous, which would cause the article to be omitted for uniformity's sake. **ἐν δυν. θεοῦ]** viz. the Power spoken of ch. iv. 7,—the power manifested in every part of our apostolic working,—not merely in miracles. **διὰ τ. ὅπλ. τ. δικ.]** **By means of** (ἐν is changed for διά, first apparently *on account of* τὰ ὅπλα, marking them more distinctly as *instruments*,—and then continued) **the weapons of righteousness** (*belonging to*,—or as Meyer, *furnished by, the righteousness which is of faith*. That panoply, *part of which* only in the more particular specification of Eph. vi. 13—17, viz. the θώραξ, is allotted to δικαιοσύνη,—is here *all* assigned to it.

Some of the ancient Commentators,—Chrys., Œcum., al., and Grot., Estius, al., understand by ὅπλα, '*instruments*,' as in Rom. vi. 13, and interpret these instruments to be, *situations and opportunities of life*, whether prosperous, δεξιά, or adverse, ἀριστερά: but the other interpretation is in better accordance with the Apostle's habit of comparison,—see ch. x. 4; Eph. vi. 13 ff.; 1 Thess. v. 8). **τῶν δεξ. κ. ἀριστ.]** **which are on the right and left**: i.e. encompassing and guarding the whole person. Grot., Bengel, and most recent Commentators, even De W. and Meyer, explain it, both *right-handed*,—i. e. of *attack*, the sword and spear,—and *left-handed*,—i. e. of *defence*, the shield: but it seems to me that this would require τῶν δεξιῶν καὶ τῶν ἀριστερῶν: whereas now, no article being inserted before ἀριστ., it is implied that *the panoply* (τὰ ὅπλα) is *on both sides* (δεξιὰ κ. ἀριστερά) of the person. On the interpretation *prosperity* and *adversity*, see above. **8.]** Perhaps the *instrumental* signification of διά need not be strictly retained. The preposition, once adopted, is kept for the sake of parallelism, though with various shades of meaning. I would understand it in διὰ δοξ., &c., as in διὰ πολλῶν δακρύων, as pointing out the *medium through which*. Thus understood, these two pairs in ver. 8 will form an easy transition from instrumental, through medial, to the passive characteristics which follow. **ὡς πλάνοι]** From speaking of *repute*, he passes to the *character* of the repute. In all these capacities and under all these representations or misrepresentations, we, as ministers of God, recommend ourselves. But in these following clauses a new point is perhaps brought out, viz. the difference of our *real state* from our *reputed one*. That this is the case with ὡς ἀποθν. κ. ἰδοὺ ζῶμεν and all following, is of course clear. But is it so with the two clauses preceding that one? Do they mean, '*as deceivers, and yet true, as unknown, and yet well known*,' or,—'*as deceivers, and as true men, as unknown, and as well known?*' I own I am not clear on **this point.** The words καὶ ἰδοὺ ζῶμεν

μενοι καὶ [s] ἐπιγινωσκόμενοι, ὡς ἀποθνήσκοντες καὶ ἰδοὺ
ζῶμεν, ὡς [t] παιδευόμενοι, καὶ μὴ [u] θανατούμενοι,
10 ὡς [v] λυπούμενοι ἀεὶ δὲ χαίροντες, ὡς πτωχοὶ πολλοὺς δὲ
[w] πλουτίζοντες, ὡς μηδὲν ἔχοντες καὶ πάντα [x] κατέχοντες.
11 Τὸ [y] στόμα ἡμῶν [yz] ἀνέῳγεν πρὸς ὑμᾶς, Κορίνθιοι,

BCDFK LPℵ a b c d e f g h k l m n o 17. 47

s Acts xxiii. 28 reff. t Luke xxiii. 16, 22. Heb. xii. 7, 10. 2 Chron. x. 11. Prov. xix. 18. u Rom. vii. 4 reff. v ch. ii. 2 reff. w 1 Cor. i. 5. ch. ix. 11 only. Gen. xiv. 23 al. x = 1 Cor. vii. 30. Josh. i. 11. y see Eph. vi. 19. Sir. xxii. 22. z pres., 1 Cor. xvi. 9.

9. αποθνησκομυντεsνοι(sic) F. for ιδου, ετι F. for παιδευομενοι, πειραζομενοι D¹ F[-gr] (*temptati* D-lat G-lat [æth] Ambrst).
11. ins ω bef κορινθιοι F vulg [copt Orig-int$_1$(om Orig$_1$)]. for 2nd ημων, υμων Bℵ.

may be an indication how the Apostle would have the previous two clauses understood; but they also *may be a transition,* altering the previous reference of the second member of the clause, now that the subject is no longer matter of rumour, as πλάνοι and ἀγνοούμενοι, but matter of fact, as ἀποθνήσκοντες, and the following. If the latter alternative be taken, the two clauses will serve as a transition to the subsequent ones, thus: having said, διὰ δυσφημίας κ. εὐφημίας, he proceeds ὡς πλάνοι (answering to δυσφ.) καὶ ἀληθεῖς (answering to εὐφ.),—ὡς ἀγνοούμενοι (still having δυσφ. in view,—as '*unknown,*' of obscure reputation), καὶ ἐπιγινωσκόμενοι (still looking back at εὐφ., seeing that the ἐπίγνωσις would lead to good repute): then, having by the *participles* of the latter clause expressed more a matter of fact than did the adjectives of the former one, he passes to ὡς ἀποθνήσκοντες, which has no longer its main reference to the *repute of others,* but to the *fact,* see ch. iv. 7 ff., as exhibited in himself. I confess that on the whole this rendering recommends itself to my mind.

9.] **καὶ ἰδοὺ ζῶμεν** is much stronger, more triumphant, than καὶ ζῶντες. There is *something* still of the idea of *one reputed dead and found to be alive;* though I would not say with Meyer that ὡς ἀποθν. altogether refers to a supposd triumph of his adversaries, "Now it is all over with him! His course is ended!" **ὡς παιδ.**] Surely we must now drop altogether the putative meaning of the ὡς. The sense has been (see above) some time verging that way, and in the clauses which follow, the ὡς expresses just what it does in ὡς θεοῦ διάκονοι, viz. 'quippe qui simus.' Ps. cxvii. 18, LXX, seems to have been in his mind: παιδεύων ἐπαίδευσέ με ὁ (om ὁ ℵ) κύριος, καὶ τῷ θανάτῳ οὐ παρέδωκέ με . . .

10.] Here even more clearly than before, the first member of the clause ὡς λυπ. ἀεὶ δὲ χαίρ. cannot express the opinion of his adversaries. For however παιδευόμενος might be wrested to signify 'a man under the chastisement of God' as a ground of reproach, **λυπούμενος** will surely not bear the meaning 'ſolcher der nach gewöhnlicher menſchlicher Anſicht traurig ſeyn mußte,' 'one in such a situation, that according to ordinary human estimation he must be wretched,' as De Wette,—but must point to the matter of fact, that he is really '*afflicted.*' See reff. **πτωχοί** again can hardly have been a *reproach,* but sets forth the *fact*—**as poor men, but enriching** (not by distribution of alms, as Chrys., Theodoret, Estius, but by imparting spiritual riches, see 1 Cor. i. 5) **many:—as having nothing** (in the sense in which οἱ ἔχοντες are ὡς μὴ ἔχοντες, 1 Cor. vii. 29,—in the improper sense of '*to possess*' in which we here use the word—*thus,* we have nothing, are destitute), **but possessing** (finally and as our own, our inheritance never to be taken away; in that sense of the word '*to possess*' which this world's buyers are *not* to use—οἱ ἀγοράζοντες, ὡς μὴ **κατέχοντες**, 1 Cor. vii. 30) **all things.** See a similar 'possession of all things,' 1 Cor. iii. 22: though this reaches further than even that,—to the boundless riches of the heavenly inheritance.

11—VII. 1.] EARNEST EXHORTATIONS TO SEPARATION FROM UNBELIEF AND IMPURITY. 11—13.] These verses form *a conclusion to the preceding outpouring of his heart with regard to his apostolic ministry,* and at the same time *a transition to the exhortations* which are to follow.

11.] **Our** (my) **mouth is open** (not *past:* the use of ἀνέῳγα for ἀνέῳγμαι is common in later Greek: see Palm and Rost's Lex., and ref. 1 Cor. Rückert takes it as past, and renders, 'I have begun to speak with you, I have not concealed my apostolic sentiments—I cannot shut my mouth, but must go on speaking to you yet further.' The word seems to refer to the free and open spirit shewn in the whole previous passage on the ministry, in which he had so liberally imparted his inner feelings to them) **towards you, Corinthians** (καὶ ἡ προσθήκη δὲ τοῦ ὀνόματος φιλίας πολλῆς, καὶ διαθέσεως καὶ θερμότητος· καὶ γὰρ

ἡ καρδία ἡμῶν [a] πεπλάτυνται·
12 οὐ [b] στενοχωρεῖσθε ἐν ἡμῖν, [b] στενοχωρεῖσθε δὲ ἐν τοῖς [c] σπλάγχνοις ὑμῶν·
13 τὴν δὲ αὐτὴν [d] ἀντιμισθίαν ([e] ὡς τέκνοις λέγω) [a] πλατύνθητε καὶ ὑμεῖς.
14 Μὴ [f] γίνεσθε [g] ἑτεροζυγοῦντες [h] ἀπί-

a here bis, Matt. xxiii. 5 only. Psa. cxviii. 32. 1 Kings ii. 1. b here bis. ch. iv. 8 only. Josh. xvii. 15. Isa. xxviii. 20. xlix. 19 only. c = ch. vii. 15. Phil. i. 8. Philem. 20. Prov. xii. 10. d Rom. i. 27 only †. e Acts xvii. 22. 1 Cor. x. 15. f w. particip. = Heb. v. 12. Rev. iii. 2. Mic. ii. 1. see Acts ii. 5 reff. g here only †. (-γος, Lev. xix. 19.) see 1 Cor. xiv. 21. h = 1 Cor. vi. 6 reff.

12. om δε C a l. **13.** υμας F.
14. ins και bef μη F(and F-lat G-lat) D-lat Syr æth arm [$Ambr_1$] Ambrst. for απιστοις, μετα απιστων F latt [Cypr Lucif Ambr Ambrst Aug].

εἰώθαμεν τῶν ἀγαπωμένων συνεχῶς γυμνὰ τὰ ὀνόματα περιστρέφειν, Chrys. Hom. xiii. p. 530 f. See Phil. iv. 15; Gal. iii. 1, which last is written under a very different feeling),—**our** (my) **heart has become enlarged.** These last words are very variously explained. Chrys., Theodoret, Œc., al., understand them of the *expansive effect of love* on the heart: Luther, Estius, al., of *dilatio gaudii,* which does not however agree with πλατύνθητε καὶ ὑμεῖς below: nor with the general context, either of what precedes or of what follows: for to refer it to ch. vii. 4, as Estius, is evidently far-fetched, the intermediate matter being of such a different character. Alii aliter. Meyer holds with Chrys., and refers it to the preceding passage, during which his heart became expanded in love to them. De Wette takes it, '*I have poured out, enlarged and diffused, my heart to you,*' viz. by speaking thus open-hearted to you. I believe the precise sense will only be found by taking into account the πλατύνθ. κ. ὑμεῖς below, and the occurrence of the expression in the Psalm (reff.: cf. ἐν πλατυσμῷ, ib., ver. 45). Some light is also thrown upon it by χωρήσατε ἡμᾶς, ch. vii. 2. The *heart* is considered as a *space,* wherein its thoughts and feelings are contained. We have seen the same figure in our expression 'narrow-minded.' In order to *take in a new object* of love, or of desire, or of ambition, the heart must be *enlarged:* ὁδὸν ἐντολῶν σου ἔδραμον, ὅταν ἐπλάτυνας τὴν καρδίαν μου. The Apostle has had his heart *enlarged* towards the Corinthians: *he could and did take them in,* with their infirmities, their interests, their Christian graces, their defects and sins: but *they did not and could not take him in* (χωρῆσαι αὐτόν): he was misunderstood by them, and his relation to them disregarded. This he here asserts, and deprecates. He assures them of *their* place in *his* heart, which is *wide enough for,* and *does contain them;* and refers back to this verse in ch. vii. 3, thus, προείρηκα ὅτι **ἐν ταῖς καρδίαις ἡμῶν ἐστε** . . . . He tells them, ver. **12.**] that they are not straitened in *him,* i. e. that any constraint which they may feel towards him, any want of confidence in him and persuasion of his real appreciation of their state and interests, arose, not from *his* being *really* unable to appreciate *them,* and love them, and advise them,—but from *their own* confined view of *him,* of his love, his knowledge of and feeling for them.

13.] **τὴν αὐτὴν ἀντιμ.,** as τὸν ὅμοιον τρόπον, Jude 7, κλισίας, Luke ix. 14, not governed by κατά understood, but in fact an accus. of a *remoter object,* answering in many cases exactly to the *further removed of the two accusatives* in the *double accusative* government. The sense seems to be compounded of τὸν αὐτὸν τρόπον, and ἀντιμισθίαν, **In the same manner, as a return for my largeness of heart to you.**

ὡς τέκνοις λ. explains ἀντιμισθίαν,—it being naturally expected of children that they should *requite* the love and care of their parents, by corresponding love and regard. **14—VII. 1.**] *Separate yourselves from unbelief and impurity.* On the nature of the connexion, Stanley has some good remarks. He now applies to circumstances which had arisen among the Corinthians the exhortation which in ver. 1 he described himself as giving in pursuance of his ministry of reconciliation. The following exhortations are *general,* and hardly to be pressed as applying only to *partaking of meats offered to idols,* as Calv., al., or to *marriage with unbelievers,* as Estius,—but regard all possible connexion and participation,—all leanings towards a return to heathenism which might be bred by too great familiarity with heathens. **Become not** ('ne *fiatis,* molliter pro: ne *sitis,*' Bengel: rather, perhaps, as expressing, 'do not enter into those relations in which you must become') **incongruous yokefellows** (the word and idea from ref. Levit. Hesych.: ἑτερόζυγοι· οἱ μὴ συζυγοῦντες. Grot. explains it, '*alteram partem jugi trahere,*' but this does not give the force of **ἑτερο-**:—Theophyl., μὴ ἀδικεῖτε τὸ δίκαιον ἐπικλινόμενοι κ. προσκλινόμενοι οἷς οὐ θέμις: so making the simile that of an unequal balance: but this could hardly be without more precise noti-

στοις· τίς γὰρ [i] μετοχὴ δικαιοσύνῃ καὶ [k] ἀνομίᾳ, ἢ τίς
[l] κοινωνία φωτὶ πρὸς σκότος; 15 τίς δὲ [m] συμφώνησις
χριστοῦ πρὸς [n] βελίαρ, ἢ [o] τίς [op] μερὶς [q] πιστῷ μετὰ [h] ἀπίστου; 16 τίς δὲ [r] συγκατάθεσις [s] ναῷ [s] θεοῦ μετὰ [t] εἰδώλων;
ὑμεῖς γὰρ [s] ναὸς [s] θεοῦ ἐστε [t] ζῶντος, καθὼς εἶπεν ὁ θεὸς
ὅτι [u] ἐνοικήσω ἐν αὐτοῖς καὶ [v] ἐμπεριπατήσω, καὶ ἔσομαι
αὐτῶν θεός, καὶ αὐτοὶ ἔσονταί μοι λαός. 17 διὸ [w] ἐξέλθατε

BCDFK LPℵ a b c d e f g h k l m n o 17. 47

i here only. Ps. cxxi. 3 ℵ Ed-vat. F &c. (not A. B def.) only. (-χος, Heb. i. 9.)
k Rom. iv. 7 reff.
l 1 Cor. i. 9. x. 16. Gal. ii. 9 al. Lev. vi. 2.
m here only †. (-νος, 1 Cor. vii. 5.)
n here only †. see note.
o 3 Kings xii. 16. p Acts viii. 21 reff. q Acts x. 45 reff. r here only †. (-τίθεσθαι, Exod. xxiii. 1. Luke xxiii. 51.) s = 1 Cor. iii. 16. vi. 19. Jer. vii. 4. t 1 Cor. x. 19 reff. Acts xiv. 15 and note. u Rom. viii. 11. Col. iii. 16. 2 Tim. i. 5, 14 only. (not l. c.) Lev. xxvi. 32 al. v here only. LEVIT. xxvi. 12. w Acts xvii. 33. ISA. lii. 11 (free).

δικαιοσυνης και αδικιας D[1], also (but *-νη κ. -ια*) D[3]: *δικαιοσυνης μετα* (*και* Orig$_1$ [Tert$_1$ Cypr$_1$]) *ανομιας* F latt arm Orig$_1$(and int$_1$) [Lucif Ambrst Aug$_{alic}$]. rec (for *η τις*) *τις δε*, with K rel syr æth Chr$_1$ Thdrt Cosm$_1$ Thl Œc Tert$_1$: txt BCDFLPℵ d m 17 latt Syr syr-mg copt goth arm Clem$_2$ Orig$_1$(and int$_1$) [Ephr$_1$ Bas$_1$ Euthal-ms] Damasc$_2$ Cypr Lucif Ambrst Jer. **φωτος** (addg *η*) D[1][and lat] Cypr Lucif$_1$ Hil.

15. rec *χριστω* (*prob corrn for conformn to φωτι preceding*), with D-gr F-gr KL rel [G-lat syrr goth] Clem-ed$_1$ Orig$_1$(and int$_1$) Can-apost-ed [Chr$_1$ Nys$_1$ Bas$_1$ Euthal-ms Thdrt Damasc$_1$] Tert$_2$: txt BCPℵ 17 vulg(and F-lat) D-lat copt Clem$_1$(-ms$_1$) Orig$_2$ Can-apost-mss$_1$ Damasc[h.l. Ephr$_1$ Procop$_1$ Lucif$_1$ Ambrst Aug$_{alic}$]. elz **βελιαλ**, with vulg [F-lat] G-lat Clem$_1$[-ed] Tit-ed$_1$ Orig-int$_1$ Tert$_1$ Lucif$_1$: *βέλιαν* D-gr K m 47 syr-mg-gr goth(*Beliam*) many-mentioned-by-Jer("corrupte") Thdrt$_1$: *βελιαβ* F[-gr] D-lat: txt BCLPℵ rel fuld(and harl[1]) syr copt æth arm Orthod$_1$ Clem$_1$[-ms$_1$?] Orig$_4$ Nys$_1$ [Cyr-p$_1$] Bas$_2$ Ephr$_1$ Chr$_1$ [Euthal-ms] Thdrt$_2$ Damasc. **πιστου** B 17 8-pe copt.

16. *ημεις* and **εσμεν** BD[1]LPℵ[1] 17 D-lat copt [æth] (Clem$_1$) Did$_2$ Aug$_1$: txt C D[3][-gr] FK(ℵ[3]) rel vulg syrr goth arm Ath$_1$ Chr$_1$ [Euthal-ms] Thdrt Damasc Orig-int$_1$ Lucif$_1$ Tert$_1$ [Ambrst].—*ναοι* ℵ[1] Clem$_2$.—*εστε* bef *θεου* ℵ[3] for *καθως ειπεν*, *λεγει γαρ* D[1](and lat) F[not F-lat], *dicit enim* G-lat goth Tert$_1$ Aug$_1$. for *αυτων*, *αυτοις* F(and G-lat) P Orig$_2$. for *μοι*, *μου* BCPℵ m 17 arm [Clem$_1$ Orig$_1$] Eus$_2$ Damasc: txt DFKL rel [latt syrr copt goth] Orig$_1$[-ms$_1$-int$_1$ Eus$_1$] Ath$_1$ Cyr-jer$_1$ Thdrt [Tert Lucif].

17. (**εξελθατε**, so BCFℵ 17. 47 [Euthal-ms] Damasc.)

fication) **with unbelievers** (Winer explains the construction, edn. 6, § 31. 10, Remark 4, thus, *μὴ γίν. ἑτεροζυγοῦντες, καὶ οὕτως ὁμοζυγοῦντες ἀπίστοις*: better, as De W., *μὴ γίν. ὁμοζ. ἀπίστοις κ. οὕτως ἑτεροζυγοῦντες*). **μετοχή**] '*share in the same thing*,' **community**. **δικαιοσ.** is the state of the Christian, being justified by faith: he is therefore excluded from **ἀνομία**, the *proper fruit of faith* being *obedience*. **φωτί**, of which we are the children, 1 Thess. v. 5, and not of darkness. Meyer remarks, that the fivefold variation of the term to express partnership,—*μετοχή, κοινωνία, συμφώνησις, μερίς, συγκατάθεσις*, shews the Apostle's command of the Greek language. The construction of *κοινωνία* with a dat. and *πρός*, is illustrated by Wetst. from Stobæus, S. 28, *εἰ δέ τις ἔστι κοινωνία πρὸς θεοὺς ἡμῖν*,—and Philo, leg. ad Caium, § 14, vol. ii. p. 561, *τίς οὖν κοινωνία πρὸς Ἀπόλλωνα, τῷ μηδὲν οἰκεῖον ἢ συγγενὲς ἐπιτετηδευκότι;* **15.**] After a question beginning with *πῶς, τίς*, and the like, a second question is regularly introduced by *δέ*. Thus Hom. Od. α. 225, *τίς δαίς, τίς δὲ ὅμιλος, ὅδ' ἔπλετο;* see Hartung, Partikellehre, i. 169. **βελίαρ**] Heb. בְּלִיַּעַל, '*contemptibleness*,' '*wickedness*:' found 1 Sam. ii. 12 al., and variously translated by the LXX. Theod. has retained the original form in Judg. xix. 22. It appears to have been subsequently personified, and used, as here, for a name of the Evil One (see Stanley). The termination *-αρ* is stated by Meyer to have arisen from the frequent permutation of *λ* and *ρ* in the dialect of the Grecian Jews. **16.**] **συγκατάθ.**, '*agreement in opinions*;' see reff., and cf. Plato, Gorg. § 122, *σὺ δὲ δὴ πότερον συγκατατίθεσαι ἡμῖν περὶ τούτων τὴν αὐτὴν δόξαν ἢ ἀντιφῂς;* **ναῷ θεοῦ**, **between you, the Church of God**,—see below, and 1 Cor. iii. 16;—**εἰδώλων**, **idols**, as the lords and *ἐπώνυμοι* of the heathen world. **ὑμεῖς γάρ**] explanation of *ναῷ θεοῦ* as applying to them, and justification of it by a citation from the prophetic Scriptures. The words cited are compounded of Levit. xxvi. 12, and Ezek. xxxvii. 26, 27. **17.**] The necessity of

[w] ἐκ μέσου αὐτῶν καὶ [x] ἀφορίσθητε, λέγει κύριος, καὶ
[y] ἀκαθάρτου μὴ ἅπτεσθε· κἀγὼ [z] εἰςδέξομαι ὑμᾶς. 18 καὶ
[a] ἔσομαι ὑμῖν [a] εἰς πατέρα, καὶ ὑμεῖς [a] ἔσεσθέ μοι [a] εἰς υἱοὺς
καὶ θυγατέρας λέγει κύριος [b] παντοκράτωρ. VII. 1 ταύτας οὖν ἔχοντες τὰς [c] ἐπαγγελίας, [d] ἀγαπητοί, [e] καθαρί-
σωμεν [f] ἑαυτοὺς ἀπὸ παντὸς [g] μολυσμοῦ [h] σαρκὸς καὶ [h] πνεύματος, [i] ἐπιτελοῦντες [j] ἁγιωσύνην ἐν [k] φόβῳ [k] θεοῦ.
2 [l] Χωρήσατε ἡμᾶς· οὐδένα ἠδικήσαμεν, οὐδένα [m] ἐφθεί-

x Acts xix. 9 reff.
y = Acts x. 14 reff. l. c.
z here only. Ezek. xx. 34. Zeph. iii. 20.
a Matt. xix. 5 ||. Luke iii. 5. (Rev. xxi. 7.) 2 Kings vii. 14. Jer. xxxviii. (xxxi.) 33.
b here only, exc. Rev. i. 8 al8. 2 Kings vii. 8.
c Acts i. 4 reff.
d Rom. xii. 19. ch. xii. 19. Phil. iv. 1. 1 Pet. ii. 11. 1 John ii. 7 al.
e Acts xv. 9 reff.
f 1st pers., ch. iii. 1 reff.
g here only. Jer. xxiii. 15. Esdr. viii. 83 (80). 2 Macc. v. 27 only. (-ύνειν, 1 Cor. viii. 7.)
h so Matt. xxvi. 41 || Mk.
i ch. viii. 6 reff.
j Rom. i. 4 (reff.). 1 Thess. iii. 13 only.
k Rom. iii. 18 (reff.).
l = Matt. xix. 11, 12. (Gen. xiii. 6.)
m 1 Cor. iii. 17 reff.

Chap. VII. 2. υμας F[-gr](not G) [add *fratres mei* Syr].

separation from the heathen enforced by another citation,—Isa. lii. 11,—freely given from memory; κἀγὼ εἰσδέξ. ὑμ. being moreover substituted, from Ezek. xx. 34, for προπορεύσεται γὰρ πρότερος ὑμῶν κύριος, κ. ὁ ἐπισυνάγων ὑμᾶς θεὸς Ἰσραήλ. The ἀκάθαρτον must be understood of the *pollutions of heathenism generally*, not of any one especial polluted thing, as meat offered to idols. **18.**] The citation continues, setting forth the blessings promised to those who do thus come out from heathendom. Various passages of the O. T. are combined. In 2 Kings vii. 14 (LXX), we have ἐγὼ ἔσομαι αὐτῷ εἰς πατ., κ. αὐτὸς ἔσται μοι εἰς υἱόν·—the expression οἱ υἱοί μου and αἱ θυγατέρες μου is found Isa. xliii. 6: and τάδε λέγει κύριος παντοκράτωρ begins the section from which the former clauses are taken, 2 Kings vii. 8 (LXX). **VII. 1.**] *Inference from the foregoing citations:—seeing that we have such glorious* (ταύτας in the position of emphasis) *promises, we are to purify ourselves* (not merely, 'keep ourselves pure:' *purification* belongs to *sanctification*, and is a *gradual* work, even after conversion). **σαρκός**, as the actual instrument and suggester of pollution: **πνεύματος**, as the recipient through the flesh, and when the recipient, the retainer and propagator, of uncleanness. The exhortation is *general:* against impure acts and impure thoughts. **ἐπιτελ. ἁγιωσ.**, as De W. remarks, gives the *positive* side of the foregoing *negative* exhortation: every abnegation and banishing of impurity is a positive advance of that sanctification, in the fear of God (as its element) to which we are called.

2—16.] Concerning the effect on them, and results in their conduct, which his former Epistle had produced. **2—4.**] He introduces the subject by a friendly assurance of *his* love and bespeaking of *theirs*, as before in ch. vi. 11—13. **2.**] **χωρήσ.**, see above on ch. vi. 13; δέξασθε ἡμᾶς πλατέως, κ. μὴ στενοχωρώμεθα ἐν ὑμῖν. Theophyl. De Wette, after Bengel, al., renders it, '*understand us rightly*,' referring to ref. Matt.: but even there the meaning is '*to take in*,' and only 'to understand rightly,' because τὸν λόγον τοῦτον follows. And as Meyer observes, there could not well be any *misunderstanding* as to what he here says. **οὐδένα ἠδ., κ.τ.λ.**] *Reasons why they should make room for him in their hearts:* **We** (when he dwelt among them,—the aorists refer to a set time, not to his course hitherto) **wronged no man** (in outward acts, namely,—in the exercise of his apostolic authority, or the like),—**we ruined no man** (this probably also of outward conduct towards others, not as Calv., al., of corrupting by false doctrine),—**we cheated no man.** To understand, with Rückert, these verbs as applying to the contents of the former Epistle, is very forced. If ἠδικ. had really referred to the severe punishment of the incestuous person,—ἐφθείρ. to the delivering him over to Satan,—and ἐπλεον. to the power which Paul gained over them by this act of authority,—surely we should have found more express indication of such reference in the text. But no allusion has *as yet* been made to the former Epistle; and therefore it is much better to understand the words generally of the time when he resided among them. "In how many ways of which history says nothing, may such ruining of others have been laid to the charge of Paul? How easily might his severe visitation of sin, his zeal for eleemosynary collections, his habit of lodging with members of the churches, and the like, have been thus unfavourably characterized!" Meyer: who remarks, that the emphatic position of οὐδένα thrice repeated is no confirmation of Rückert's view.

n ch. ii. 11 reff. o = 1 Cor. vii. 35 reff. p ch. iii. 9 only †. Num. xiii. 33. alius in Hexapl. [Montf. (not Fd.)]. q ch. xiii. 2 reff. r Phil. i. 7. s Rom. iv. 11 reff. t Mark xiv. 31. 2 Tim. ii. 11 only †. Sir. xix. 10 only. u Rom. vi. 8. 2 Tim. ii. 11 only †.

ραμεν, οὐδένα [n] ἐπλεονεκτήσαμεν.
3 [o] πρὸς [p] κατάκρισιν οὐ λέγω· [q] προείρηκα γὰρ ὅτι ἐν ταῖς [r] καρδίαις ἡμῶν ἐστε [s] εἰς τὸ [t] συναποθανεῖν καὶ [u] συνζῆν.
4 πολλή μοι [vw] παῤῥησία [v] πρὸς ὑμᾶς, πολλή μοι [x] καύχησις ὑπὲρ ὑμῶν· [y] πεπλήρωμαι τῇ [z] παρακλήσει, [a] ὑπερπερισσεύομαι τῇ χαρᾷ [b] ἐπὶ πάσῃ τῇ θλίψει ἡμῶν.
5 καὶ γὰρ ἐλθόντων ἡμῶν εἰς Μακεδονίαν οὐδεμίαν [c] ἔσχηκεν [d] ἄνεσιν ἡ σὰρξ ἡμῶν, ἀλλ' [e] ἐν παντὶ [f] θλιβόμενοι· [gh] ἔξωθεν [i] μάχαι,

BCDFK LP‭א a b c d e f g h k l m n o 17. 47

v = Rom. v. 1 reff. w ch. iii. 12 reff. x = ver. 14. 1 Cor. xv. 31. (Rom. iii. 27 reff.) y constr., Luke ii. 40. Rom. i. 29 only. 2 Macc. vii. 21. z = ch. i. 3, &c. reff. a Rom. v. 20 only †. (-ῶς, Mark vii. 37.) b = ch. iii. 14 reff. c ch. i. 9 reff. d Acts xxiv. 23 reff. e ch. iv. 8 reff. f ch. i. 6 reff. part. constr., ch. v. 6 reff. g Matt. xxiii. 25, 27, 28 al. h see Deut. xxxii. 25. i 2 Tim. ii. 23. Tit. iii. 9. James iv. 1 only. = Gen. xiii. 7.

3. rec *ου* bef *προς κατακρισιν*, with DFKL rel vss [Chr$_2$ Thdrt Damasc Ambrst]: txt BCP‭א 17(appy, from the space after *κατακρι . .*) [Euthal-ms]. aft *οτι* ins *εστε* (but marked for erasure) ‭א^1. *υμων* ‭א^1. om *εστε* B.

4. aft *προς υμας* ins *εστιν* D^1(and lat). [*υπερπερισσευμαι* (for *-ευομαι*) L d e 47.] ins *εν* bef *τη χαρα* B(sic in cod). om 3rd *τη* F: aft *παση τη* ins *πολλη* D^1[-gr]. for *ημων*, *υμων* F[-gr](not G) K b c o. (so F[-gr] K ver 5.)

5. for *εσχηκεν*, *εσχεν* BFK: txt CDLP‭א rel Chr$_1$ [Euthal-ms] Thdrt$_2$ Damasc$_2$. *ανεσιν* bef *εσχ*. CF d [17 syrr] latt Thdrt$_2$ [Tert$_1$ Ambr$_1$ Ambrst]. *θλιβομενος* D^1[*tribulatio* D-lat].

3.] **I do not say it** (ver. 2) **for condemnation** (with a condemnatory view, in a spirit of blame: there is no ὑμῶν expressed, nor should it be supplied. He means, 'I do not say ver. 2 in any but a loving spirit'): **for** (and this shews it) **I have said before** (viz. ch. vi. 11 f. see note there) **that ye are in our hearts** (this was implied in ἡ καρδία ἡμῶν πεπλάτυνται, vi. 11. In the qualifying words, εἰς τὸ συν. κ.τ.λ., Paul, as Meyer says, is his own commentator), **to die together and live together.** This is ordinarily understood, '*so that I could die with you or live with you*,'—as Hor., 'Tecum vivere amem, tecum obeam libens,' Od. iii. 9. 24: which Meyer controverts, owing to ὑμεῖς being the subject of the sentence, and renders, 'in order to die and to live with us:' i. e. 'if our lot is to die, *in death*,—and if our lot is to live, *in life*, never to be torn from our hearts.' But to this I would reply, that though ὑμεῖς is the subject of ἐν ταῖς καρδ. ἡμ. ἐστε, it is but an accidental and secondary subject as regards the *whole sentence*; that *they* are present in *his* heart, is a sign, not of their state of mind, but of *his*: therefore the purpose, **εἰς τό**, must refer logically to *him*, the main subject, of *whom only* the *purposes* can come into consideration. **4.**] **παῤῥησία**, as in reff., **confidence**, which leads to and justifies καύχησις: not here *liberty of speech*,' as Chrys., al. **καύχ.**, *to others*, in speaking of them. **τῇ παρ.**, **the consolation** (which I have received), viz. that furnished by the intelligence from you. Though this is anticipating what follows vv. 7, 9, I cannot but believe it to have been already before the Apostle's mind, and to have been referred to by the articles before παρακλ. and χαρ. On the construction of πληρόω with an instrumental dative, see reff., and Winer, edn. 6, § 31. 7. So Eurip. Herc. Fur. 372, πεύκαισιν χέρας πληροῦντες,—and Bacchæ 18, μιγάσιν Ἕλλησι βαρβάροις θ' ὁμοῦ πλήρεις ἔχουσα καλλιπυργώτους πόλεις. **ὑπερπ.**] **I am made exceedingly to abound**, see Matt. xiii. 12. The pres. indicates the *abiding* of the effect. **τῇ χαρᾷ, with the joy**; see above. **ἐπὶ πάσ. τῇ θλ. ἡμ., in** (reff.) **all our tribulation**: refers to *both* preceding clauses. What θλῖψις he means, is explained in the next verse. **πάσῃ** here not of *all tribulation, at all times*, which the special reference of παρακλ. and χαρά forbids: but of *various sorts* of tribulation as specified (ἐν παντί) below. **5—7.**] *The intelligence received from them through Titus, and its comforting effect on the Apostle's mind.* **5.**] γάρ gives a reason for θλίψει above: καί connects with ch. ii. 12, 13, where he has spoken of the trouble which he had before leaving Troas. **For also, after our coming to Macedonia, our flesh had no rest** (there is a slight, but very slight, distinction from οὐκ ἔσχηκα ἄνεσιν τῷ πνεύματί μου, ch. ii. 12. Titus *was now present*, so that that source of inquietude was removed; but the outward ones of fightings generating inward fears (but see below), yet remained. No further distinction must be drawn—for **ἔσωθεν φόβοι** evidently

[g] ἔσωθεν φόβοι. 6 ἀλλ' ὁ [kl] παρακαλῶν τοὺς [lm] ταπεινοὺς
[k] παρεκάλεσεν ἡμᾶς ὁ θεὸς [n] ἐν τῇ [o] παρουσίᾳ Τίτου·
7 οὐ μόνον δὲ [n] ἐν τῇ [o] παρουσίᾳ αὐτοῦ, ἀλλὰ καὶ [n] ἐν τῇ
παρακλήσει ᾗ [k] παρεκλήθη [p] ἐφ' ὑμῖν, [q] ἀναγγέλλων ἡμῖν
τὴν ὑμῶν [r] ἐπιπόθησιν, τὸν ὑμῶν [s] ὀδυρμόν, τὸν ὑμῶν
[t] ζῆλον ὑπὲρ ἐμοῦ, ὥςτε με [uv] μᾶλλον [v] χαρῆναι. 8 ὅτι εἰ
καὶ [w] ἐλύπησα ὑμᾶς ἐν [x] τῇ ἐπιστολῇ, οὐ [y] μεταμέλομαι, εἰ
καὶ [y] μετεμελόμην· βλέπω γὰρ ὅτι ἡ ἐπιστολὴ ἐκείνη εἰ καὶ

k = ch. i. 4 reff.
l Isa. xlix. 13.
m Matt. xi. 29. Luke i. 52. Rom. xii. 16. ch. x. 1. James i. 9. iv. 6 & 1 Pet. v. 5 (from Prov. iii. 34) only.
n = ch. iv. 8.
o = 1 Cor. xvi. 17. Phil. i. 26. ii. 12 al.† 2 Macc. viii. 12. xv. 21 only.
p = 1 Cor. xiii. 6. xvi. 17. 1 Thess. iii. 7. Judg. xxi. 15 B Ald.
q Acts xiv. 27 reff.
r ver. 11 only †. Ezek. xxiii. 11 Aq. (-εῖν, Rom. i. 11. -ητος, Phil. iv. 1.)
s Matt. ii. 18 only, from Jer. xxxviii. (xxxi.) 15. 2 Macc. xi. 6 only.
t = Rom. x. 2 reff.
u compar., Acts xxv. 10 reff.
v ver. 13.
w ch. ii. 2 reff.
x see 1 Cor. v. 9 reff.
y here bis. Matt. xxi. 29, 32. xxvii. 3. Heb. vii. 21 (from Ps. cix. 4) only. Prov. xxv. 8. see ver. 10.

6. om 2nd *ο* C 4. for *ημ.*, *υμας* F[-gr](not G). for *εν*, *επι* C Chr_1 Thl-marg.
7. *ην παρεκληθην* D[1][-gr]. for *εφ*, *εν* L. for *ημ.*, *υμιν* D[1]א[1] (b[1] ?). om *υπερ εμου* K. *με* aft *μαλλον* D Thdrt: aft *χαρηναι* F: om K m 31-5-9. 109-14 lect-13.
8. aft *επιστολη* ins *μου* D[1][and lat] F. for 2nd *ει και*, *ει δε και* B. om *γαρ* B D[1](and lat) Ambrst-ms: *videns quod* vulg. (*The varr arise from attempts to clear the constr, making ει δε και μ. the beginning of a new sentence, and βλεπω, without γαρ, the apodosis,—or βλεπων κ.τ.λ. a qualifying clause: see also notes.*) om *η* F.

shews that *σάρξ* must be taken in a wide sense); **without, fightings** (the omission of *ἦσαν* renders the description more graphic), **within, fears.** Chrys., *ἔξωθ. μάχαι· παρὰ τῶν ἀπίστων· ἔσωθ. φόβοι· διὰ τοὺς ἀσθενεῖς τῶν πιστῶν.* Hom. xiv. p. 539. So Calv., Grot., Wetst., al., slightly varying in their assignment of each class. But it is better, as Paul speaks of *ἡ σὰρξ ἡμῶν*, to understand **ἔξωθεν** of the *state of things without him* [personally], contentions with adversaries either within or without the church, and **ἔσωθεν** of *that within* [*him* personally], fears, for ourselves, for others, or for *you*, how you might have received our letter.

6.] **τοὺς ταπεινούς**, generally, **those that are low: ἡμᾶς**, as belonging to that class. It was [the] *not finding Titus* which had given him such uneasiness in Troas, ch. ii. 12. **ἐν**, not '*by*,' but **in**, as the conditional element or vehicle of the consolation. So also [twice] in next verse. **7. ἀλλὰ καὶ . . . .**] **not only . . . . but also with the comfort with which he was comforted concerning you**: i. e. 'we shared in the comfort which Titus felt in recording to us your desire,' &c. see ver. 13. *He* rejoiced in announcing the news: *we* in hearing them. There is no inaccuracy of construction, as De W. supposes.

ἐπιπόθησιν, either longing *to see me*, or longing *to fulfil my wishes*. The former is the more simple. **ὀδυρμόν**,—*ἐπὶ τῇ ἐπιτιμήσει μου τῇ ἐν τῇ πρώτῃ ἐπιστολῇ*, as Œcum. **ζῆλον ὑπὲρ ἐμοῦ**] The art. is omitted after *ζῆλον*, as in *τῶν ἀδελφῶν μου τῶν συγγενῶν κατὰ σάρκα*, because the words *ζῆλον ὑπὲρ ἐμοῦ* cohere in the sense, and form as it were but one,—see Col. i. 4 (iv. 13, v. r.): and Winer, edn. 6, § 20. 2. **μᾶλλον**, viz. 'than before, at the mere coming of Titus.' The emphasis is on *μᾶλλον* from its position.

8—11.] *He expresses his satisfaction at the effect produced on them, as superseding his former regret that he had grieved them.* **8.**] **For** (reason of the *χαρῆναι*) **though I even grieved you in** (by means of) **my epistle, I do not** (now) **repent** (having written it), **though I even did repent it** (before the coming of Titus). Erasm., al., take *εἰ καὶ μετεμ.* for '*even supposing I repented it before, which was not the case*:' Calv., al. think 'verbum *pœnitendi* improprie positum pro *dolorem capere*.' The reason of these departures from grammatical construction and the meaning of words, is, for fear the Apostle should seem to have *repented of* that which he did under the inspiration of the Holy Spirit. But there is no difficulty even on the strictest view of inspiration, in conceiving that the Apostle may have afterwards regretted the severity which he was guided to use; we know that Jonah, being directed by inspiration to pronounce the doom of Nineveh, endeavoured to escape the unwelcome duty: and doubtless St. Paul, as a man, in the weakness of his affection for the Corinthians, was tempted to wish that he had never written that which had given them pain. But the result shewed that God's Spirit had ordered it well, that he should thus write: and this his repentance was *repented of again*.

βλέπω γὰρ κ.τ.λ.] **For I see that that letter, though but for a time, did grieve you.** This seems the only admissible rendering of the words. Chrys. sees in them *the*

ᶻ πρὸς ὥραν ʷ ἐλύπησεν ὑμᾶς· 9 νῦν χαίρω, οὐχ ὅτι
ʷ ἐλυπήθητε, ἀλλ᾽ ὅτι ʷ ἐλυπήθητε ᵃ εἰς μετάνοιαν· ʷ ἐλυπήθητε γὰρ ᵇ κατὰ θεόν, ἵνα ᶜ ἐν ᶜ μηδενὶ ᵈ ζημιωθῆτε ἐξ ἡμῶν.
10 ἡ γὰρ ᵇ κατὰ θεὸν λύπη ᵉ μετάνοιαν εἰς σωτηρίαν
ᶠ ἀμεταμέλητον ᵍ ἐργάζεται, ἡ δὲ τοῦ κόσμου λύπη θάνατον
ʰ κατεργάζεται. 11 ἰδοὺ γὰρ ⁱ αὐτὸ ⁱ τοῦτο ᵏ τὸ ᵇ κατὰ
θεὸν ʷ λυπηθῆναι [ὑμᾶς] πόσην ᵛ κατειργάσατο ὑμῖν

BCDFK LPא a b c d e f g h k l m n o 17. 47

z (=) John v. 35. Gal. ii. 5. Philem. 15 only. see 1 Thess. ii. 17.
a Matt. iii. 11. Rom. x. 10 al.
b = Rom. viii. 27. see ch. xi. 17.
c ch. vi. 3 reff.
d 1 Cor. iii. 15 reff.
e = Mark i. 4 al. fr.
f Rom. xi. 29 only †.
g = Rom. ii. 10 reff.
h = Rom. iv. 15. v. 3. ch. iv. 17 al.
i Acts xxiv. 15 reff.
k = Rom. viii. 26 reff.

υμας bef ελυπησεν F.
9. om νυν D[1](and lat) Syr. om αλλ οτι ελυπηθητε א[1](ins א-corr[1 obl]) tol[1].
10. rec **κατεργαζεται**, with FKLא[3] rel Orig$_1$ [Bas$_1$ Antch$_1$] Thdrt Thl Œc: txt BCDPא[1] m Clem$_1$ (Orig$_2$) Chr-mss [Cyr-p$_3$ Euthal-ms] Damasc. (om last clause (*homœotel*) K 17. 31. 108[1]-14-78.)
11. om υμας (*as unnecessary,* υμιν *occurring below: and to express, as above, the* abstract *and not the* concrete) BC F[not F-lat] א[1] 17 [Bas$_3$ Euthal-ms] Ambrst: ins DKL[P]א[3] rel Clem$_1$ Bas$_1$ Chr$_1$ Thdrt Damasc Thl Œc. κατηργ. B[1]D k[1] m.
ins εν bef υμιν CFPא[3] c d 47 vulg [Syr] syr Bas$_3$[-2-mss$_1$] Chr Thdrt Thl [Ambrst]: om BDKLא[1] rel [arm (copt Euthal-ms)] Clem$_1$ Damasc Œc.

reason of οὐ μεταμέλομαι, and adds (Hom. xv. p. 543) τὸ μὲν γὰρ λυπηρὸν βραχύ, τὸ δὲ ὠφέλιμον διηνεκές. It appears then that he would render εἰ καὶ πρὸς ὥραν, '*if even for a season,*' = '*scarcely for any time.*' Rinck (lucubr. crit. p. 162) would begin a new sentence with εἰ καὶ μετεμελόμην, and parenthesizing βλέπω . . . . ὑμᾶς, regard **νῦν χαίρω**, κ.τ.λ. as the *apodosis.* But this is very unnatural, with so abrupt a beginning as εἰ καί. It would certainly have been εἰ δὲ καί: and the *present,* βλέπω, would give no reason for the *past,* μετεμελόμην, which had passed away. The best sense, as well as the most legitimate rendering, is to regard βλέπω . . . . ὑμᾶς as the epexegesis of ἐλύπησα, as above. 9.] **νῦν,** emphatic, as distinguishing χαίρω from μετεμελόμην: *now* that I know not only of your grief, but of its being grief which worked repentance. **κατὰ θεόν]** as E. V., **after a godly sort**: '*with reference to God,*' see ref. Rom. and note: "*secundum,* hic significat sensum animi Deum spectantis et sequentis," Bengel. αὕτη γὰρ ἡ καλὴ λύπη, ὡς τό γε κατ᾽ ἄνθρωπον λυπεῖσθαι κακόν. Œcum. Cf. κατὰ ἄνθρωπον, 1 Cor. xv. 32. **ἵνα, κ.τ.λ.]** **in order that ye might in nothing be damaged by us**: not ἐκβατικῶς, *so that ye did not* . . . ., as many Commentators:—the *divine purpose* of their grief is indicated; 'God so brought it about, in order that your grief occasioned by me might have, not an injurious, but a beneficial effect.' 10.] *How* 'grief according to God' *produces such an effect.* **For grief according to God works** (brings about, promotes, see ref.) **repentance unto salvation never to be regretted.** **ἀμεταμέλητον** best belongs to σωτηρίαν, as Vulg., Theophyl., Aug., Est., Fritzsche, Meyer, De Wette; not to μετάνοιαν, as most Commentators:—not necessarily however from the position of the words, as Meyer and De Wette maintain: for what more common than for the predicate of a substantive (εἰς σωτηρίαν) to be placed between it and a qualifying adjective?—but on account of the *sense,* and the fact that not ἀμετανόητον, but ἀμεταμέλητον is chosen, so that the play in E. V., '*repentance not to be repented of,*' does not seem to have been intended. De W. well explains σωτηρία ἀμεταμέλητος—'*salvation which none will ever regret*' having attained, however difficult it may have been to reach, however dearly it may have been bought. **ἡ τ. κόσμου λύπη]** τί δέ ἐστι, κατὰ κόσμον; ἐὰν λυπηθῇς διὰ χρήματα, διὰ δόξαν, διὰ τὸν ἀπελθόντα. Chrys. ib. **τοῦ κόσμ.** is *subjective*: '*the grief felt by the children of this world.*' **θάνατον]** **Death eternal,** as contrasted with **σωτηρίαν**: not '*deadly sickness,*' or '*suicide,*' as Theophyl. (in part, πάντως μὲν τὸν ψυχικόν, πολλάκις δὲ καὶ τὸν σωματικόν), al. The grief which contemplates nothing but the blow given, and not the God who chastens, can produce nothing but more and more alienation from Him, and result in eternal banishment from His presence. So that **ἐργάζ.** is rather **works,** '*contributes to,*' and **κατεργάζ., works out,** '*results in.*' 11.] *The blessed effects of godly grief on themselves, as shewn by fact.* **αὐτὸ τοῦτο, this very thing,** *of which I have been speaking.* **σπουδήν, earnestness,** as contrasted with your former *carelessness* in the matter. **ἀλλά]** nay, not σπουδήν merely,—that is

[l] σπουδήν, [m] ἀλλὰ [n] ἀπολογίαν, [m] ἀλλὰ [o] ἀγανάκτησιν,
[m] ἀλλὰ φόβον, [m] ἀλλὰ [p] ἐπιπόθησιν, [m] ἀλλὰ [q] ζῆλον,
[m] ἀλλὰ [r] ἐκδίκησιν. [s] ἐν [s] παντὶ [t] συνεστήσατε [u] ἑαυτοὺς
[v] ἁγνοὺς εἶναι [w] τῷ [w] πράγματι.
12 ἄρα εἰ καὶ ἔγραψα
ὑμῖν, οὐχ ἕνεκεν τοῦ [x] ἀδικήσαντος οὐδὲ ἕνεκεν τοῦ
[x] ἀδικηθέντος, ἀλλ' ἕνεκεν τοῦ [y] φανερωθῆναι τὴν [l] σπουδὴν ὑμῶν τὴν ὑπὲρ ἡμῶν πρὸς ὑμᾶς [z] ἐνώπιον τοῦ θεοῦ.
13 διὰ τοῦτο [a] παρακεκλήμεθα. ἐπὶ δὲ τῇ [b] παρακλήσει

l — Rom. xii. 8, 11 reff. m — 1 Cor. iii. 2. n = 1 Cor. ix. 3. (Acts xxv. 16 reff.) Wisd. vi. 10 only. o here only †. (-τεῖν, Matt. xx. 24.) p ver. 7 only †. q — ver. 7. r Rom. xii. 19 reff. s ch. iv. 8 reff. t = ch. vi. 4 reff. u 2nd pers., Matt. iii. 9. Rom. vi. 11, 13, 16. xii. 19. ch. xiii. 5. v ch. xi. 2. Phil. iv. 8. 1 Thess. v. 22. Tit. ii. 5. James iii. 17. 1 Pet. iii. 2. 1 John iii. 3 only. Prov. xx. 9. (-νῶς, Phil. i. 17. -νότης, ch. vi. 6.) w see 1 Thess. iv. 6. x Eur. Med. 267. y = ch. ii. 14. iii. 3, &c. constr., here only. z = Acts iv. 19 reff. Rom. xii. 17. a = ch. i. 4, &c. reff. b ch. i. 3, &c. reff.

ανακτησιν (so 17) and *επιποθιαν* א[1]. (*αλλα* (last), so BD[1]FLPא a b d f m o 17. 47 [Clem$_1$ Bas$_3$ Thdrt].) rec ins *εν* bef *τω πραγματι*, with D[2.3][and lat] KLP rel [arm Bas$_2$] Chr$_1$ Thdrt Ambrst : txt BC D[1][-gr] Fא 17 vulg goth Clem$_1$ [Euthal-ms] Damasc$_1$ Pel Bede.

12. (*ενεκεν* (3ce), so BCDFK L(2nd and [3rd]) Pא a d f k 17.) [D[1]-gr transposes *αδικησαντος* and *αδικηθεντος*.] ins *αλλ'* bef *ουδε* Bא[3] m 73. elz *ημων την υπερ υμων* (*see notes*), with d 47 vulg(and F-lat) goth arm-usc Chr$_1$ Thdrt Ambrst : *υμ. τ. υπ. υμ.* D[1][-gr] F-gr א : *ημ. τ. υπ. ημ. nostram quæ est pro nobis* G [D[1]-lat] : txt BCD[2.3]KLP rel D[2]-lat E-lat syrr copt æth [arm-zoh Euthal-ms] Damasc.

saying too little;—**but . . . ἀπολογίαν**] viz. to Paul by means of Titus,—asserting their innocence in the matter; see below. **ἀγανάκτησιν**] πρὸς τὸν πεπορνευκότα. Theophyl. **φόβον**] 'ne cum virga venirem,' Bengel: fear *of Paul:* not here *of God.* The context is brought out well by Chrys. and Theophyl. The latter says, on **ἐπιπόθησιν**,—πρὸς ἐμέ. εἰπὼν δὲ **φόβον**, ἵνα μὴ δόξῃ αὐθεντεῖν, συντόμως διωρθώσατο, **ἐπιπόθησιν** εἰπών· ὅπερ ἐνδεικτικὸν ἀγάπης, οὐκ ἐξουσίας. **ζῆλον**] *on God's behalf,* to punish the offender;—**ἐκδίκησιν** being the *infliction of justice itself.* Bengel remarks, that the six accusatives preceded by ἀλλά fall into three pairs: ἀπολογ. and ἀγανάκτ., relating to *their own feelings* of shame,—φόβ. and ἐπιπόθ. to *Paul,*—ζῆλ. and ἐκδίκ. to the *offender.* **ἐν παντί** must be understood only of participation of *guilt:* by their negligence, and even refusal to humble themselves (1 Cor. v. 2), they had in some things made common cause with the offender. Of this, now that they had shewn so different a spirit, the Apostle *does not speak.* **συνεστήσατε**] **have commended yourselves by proving that ye are**; a pregnant construction. **τῷ πρ.**, the dat. of regard: see Rom. vi. 20, and Winer, edn. 6, § 31. 1. *k*,—**the matter,**—perhaps, as in ref., not only, 'of which I have been speaking,'—but with allusion to the *kind of sin* which was in question. **ἁγνούς, pure of stain.** **12.**] *He shews them that to bring out this zeal in them was the real motive of his writing to them, and no private considerations.* **ἄρα, accordingly,**—'in accordance with the result just mentioned.' **εἰ καὶ ἔγραψα ὑμ.** is parallel with εἰ καὶ ἐλύπησα ὑμᾶς, ver. 8,—**though** (i. e. *assumed that*) **I wrote** (severely) **to you.** The **ἀδικηθείς** would be the *father* of the incestuous person, who γυναῖκα τοῦ πατρὸς εἶχεν, 1 Cor. v. 1. Theodoret imagines it to mean the *stepmother,* who was the adulteress; and thinks that the *father* was dead. But there is no ground for this in 1 Cor. v., and the *masculine* participle, though not decisive against it, is at least more naturally explained on the other view. Others (as Wolf, Bleek, al.) suppose *Paul himself* to be meant, which however would be in direct contradiction to ch. ii. 5: * Bengel, al., the *Corinthians,* 'singularis pro plurali, per euphemiam,' which is forced: Theophyl., al., both the persons concerned (—ἀμφότεροι γὰρ ἀλλήλους ἠδίκησαν):—and Neander, al., take τοῦ ἀδικηθέντος as = τοῦ ἀδικήματος, '*the fault committed*:'—which however would not be true, for the Apostle certainly *did* write *on account of the committal* of the fault. It would be easy for any of the Apostle's adversaries to maintain that the reproof had been administered from private and interested motives. **ἀλλ' ἕνεκεν . . .**] *But he wrote, in order to bring out their zeal on his behalf* (i. e. to obey his command), *and make it manifest to themselves in God's sight.* The other reading, ἡμῶν τὴν ὑπὲρ ὑμῶν, has been an alteration owing to not understanding τ. σπουδ. ὑμ. τ. ὑπ. ἡμ., and is *inconsistent with the fact:* it was not to exhibit to them *his* zeal for them that he wrote, but to make manifest to (πρός '*among,*' '*chez*' them,

c ch. i. 12 reff. double compar., Mark vii. 36. Phil. i. 23.
d ver. 7.
e 1 Cor. xiii. 6 reff.
f = Acts xiv. 3. ch. i. 9 al.
g = 1 Cor. xvi. 18 reff.
h = Acts ii. 22 reff.
i constr., ch. ix. 2 (xii. 5).
k Rom. v. 5. ix. 33. x. 11 al. Ps. cxviii. 116.
l ver. 4.
m w. gen. = Acts xxiii. 30 reff.

ἡμῶν [c] περισσοτέρως [d] μᾶλλον [e] ἐχάρημεν [ef] ἐπὶ τῇ χαρᾷ BCDFK LPℵ a b c d e f g h k l m n o 17. 47
Τίτου, ὅτι [g] ἀναπέπαυται τὸ [g] πνεῦμα αὐτοῦ [h] ἀπὸ πάντων
ὑμῶν· 14 ὅτι εἴ τι [i] αὐτῷ [i] ὑπὲρ ὑμῶν [i] κεκαύχημαι, οὐ
[k] κατῃσχύνθην, ἀλλ᾽ ὡς πάντα ἐν ἀληθείᾳ ἐλαλήσαμεν
ὑμῖν, οὕτως καὶ ἡ [l] καύχησις * ὑμῶν ἡ [m] ἐπὶ Τίτου ἀλήθεια
[n] ἐγενήθη, 15 καὶ τὰ [o] σπλάγχνα αὐτοῦ [c] περισσοτέρως
[p] εἰς ὑμᾶς ἐστιν [q] ἀναμιμνησκομένου τὴν πάντων ὑμῶν
[r] ὑπακοήν, ὡς [s] μετὰ [t] φόβου καὶ [t] τρόμου ἐδέξασθε αὐτόν.
16 χαίρω, ὅτι [u] ἐν [u] παντὶ [v] θαῤῥῶ ἐν ὑμῖν.

n = 1 Cor. i. 30. o = ch. vi. 12 reff. p = ch. viii. 13, 14 reff.
q 1 Cor. iv. 17 reff. r Rom. i. 5 reff. s = Matt. xxviii. 8. Mark iii. 5. 1 Chron. xxix. 22.
t 1 Cor. ii. 3 reff. u ch. iv. 8 reff. v ch. v. 6, 8 reff.

13. rec places δε aft περισσοτερως (*appy to conform to the* εχαρημεν επι *below, by joining* παρακεκλ. επι : *then also the change of* ημ. *into* υμ. *became necessary*), with rel æth Œc: om e 32-6-9. 71 [arm Euthal-ms] Thdrt: txt BCDFKLPℵ d 17 latt syrr copt goth Chr-comm$_1$(and Mtt's ms$_1$) Damasc(has επειδη for επι δε) Thl$_1$ [Ambrst]. rec υμων, with F-gr KL rel syr-w-ast copt Chr$_1$ Thdrt [Euthal-ms Damasc] Bede: txt BCDGKPℵ 17 latt syrr goth æth arm Ambrst Pel.

14. αυτων ℵ. κεκαυχημαι bef υπερ υμων F[(not F-lat) Syr copt] Chr$_1$ Thl. αλλα C. παντοτε C F[-gr] syr copt Chr[-txt$_1$], *omnia aut omnino* G-lat. υμιν bef εν αλ. ελαλ. CDP vulg goth (æth) [Ambrst]: om υμιν ℵ[1](txt ℵ-corr[1 obl]).
* rec ἡμῶν (*see note*), with DGKLPℵ rel latt syrr goth [arm Euthal-ms] Chr$_1$ Thdrt [Damasc] Ambrst: υμων B F-gr c copt Thl. (C def.) om last ἡ Bℵ[1] 115-9[1] [Euthal-ms]. for επι τιτου [so syr-mg], προς τιτον *ad Titum* DFP m [latt syrr] Damasc.

15. om παντων ℵ[1].

16. elz aft χαιρω ins ουν, with m syr-mg goth arm: om BCDFKLPℵ rel latt Syr copt [Euthal-ms Thdrt Damasc Ambrst].

to bring out among them, *their zeal to regard and obey him.* **13.**] **On this account** (on account of the fulfilment of this purpose) **we are comforted: but in addition to** (or, on the occurrence of) **our comfort, we rejoiced very much more** (reff.) **at the joy of Titus, because his spirit has been refreshed by you all.** A similar declaration to that in ver. 7, where not only the arrival of Titus, but his comfort wherewith he was comforted by them, is described as the ground of the Apostle's joy. According to the received reading, the sense is: '*Therefore we are consoled on account of your consolation* (either gen. subj., 'that which you feel on account of the good issue of the affair,'—or gen. object., 'the consolation received from you'): *but we rejoiced very much more,*' &c. This however would hardly represent the real state of things.

14.] This increased joy was produced by the verification which my former boasting of you to Titus now received. **εἴ τι . .**] see one particular in which he boasted of them, ch. ix. 2. **οὐ κατῃσχ.**] **I was not put to shame,** viz. by being shewn, on Titus's coming to you, to have boasted in vain. **ἀλλ᾽ ὡς . . .**] 'But *truthfulness* was shewn to be my constant rule of speech, to whomsoever I spoke.' **But as we spoke** (*generally,* not merely in our teaching, as Theodoret, al.) **all things in truth** (truthfully) **to you, so also our boasting concerning you** (gen. obj.: the rec. ἡμῶν agrees better with the comparison, of '*our words*' in general, with '*our boasting*' in particular: but on that very account it is probably an alteration: and this is the implied meaning at all events) **before Titus was** (was proved to be: *was,* as shewn by proof) **truth.** De W. suggests that the Apostle had described (by anticipation) to Titus in glowing terms the affection and probable prompt obedience of the Corinthians, as an encouragement to his somewhat unwelcome journey. **15.**] enlarges ἀλήθεια ἐγενήθη. **And his heart is more abundantly** (turned) **toward you, remembering as he does the obedience of you all, how** (i. e. which was shewn in the fact, that) **with fear and trembling ye received him.** 'Fear and trembling,' i. e. 'lest ye should not pay enough regard to my injunctions, and honour enough his mission from me.' **16.**] **I rejoice** (more expressive than with a connecting particle) **that in every thing I am (re)-assured by you;** 'am of good courage, in contrast to my former dejection, owing to your good conduct.' The ordinary rendering, '*I can have confidence in you,*'

VIII. 1 [w] Γνωρίζομεν δὲ ὑμῖν, ἀδελφοί, τὴν [x] χάριν
τοῦ θεοῦ τὴν [xy] δεδομένην [y] ἐν ταῖς [z] ἐκκλησίαις τῆς Μακεδονίας, 2 ὅτι ἐν πολλῇ [a] δοκιμῇ θλίψεως ἡ [b] περισσεία
τῆς χαρᾶς αὐτῶν καὶ ἡ [c] κατὰ [cd] βάθους [e] πτωχεία αὐτῶν
[f] ἐπερίσσευσεν [f] εἰς τὸ [g] πλοῦτος τῆς [h] ἁπλότητος αὐτῶν,
3 ὅτι [i] κατὰ δύναμιν [k] μαρτυρῶ καὶ [lm] παρὰ [m] δύναμιν,
[n] αὐθαίρετοι, 4 [o] μετὰ πολλῆς [p] παρακλήσεως δεόμενοι
ἡμῶν τὴν [q] χάριν καὶ τὴν [r] κοινωνίαν τῆς [s] διακονίας τῆς
[t] εἰς τοὺς [u] ἁγίους, 5 καὶ οὐ καθὼς ἠλπίσαμεν, ἀλλ' ἑαυτοὺς
ἔδωκαν πρῶτον τῷ κυρίῳ καὶ ἡμῖν [v] διὰ θελήματος θεοῦ,

w 1 Cor. xii. 3 reff. xv. 1.
x 1 Cor. i. 4 reff.
y ver. 16 reff.
z plur., Rom. xvi. 16 reff.
a Rom. v. 4 reff.
b Rom. v. 17. ch. x. 15. James i. 21 only. Eccles. i. 3 al.
c here only. Strabo ix. 419. Winer, edn. 6, § 51. 2.
d Rom. xi. 33 reff.
e ver. 9. Rev. ii. 9 only. Job xxx. 27.
f Rom. iii. 7 reff.

g neut., Eph. i. 7. ii. 7. iii. 8, 16. Phil. iv. 19. Col. i. 27. ii. 2. h Rom. xii. 8 reff. i Matt. xxv. 15. 1 Chron. xxix. 2. k Rom. x. 2. Gal. iv. 15. Col. iv. 13. l = Luke xiii. 2, 4. Rom. xiv. 5. Heb. xi. 11. Ps. cxxxiv. 5. m here only. παρὰ δύν. μετέχειν, Thucyd. iii. 54. ὑπὲρ δ., ch. i. 8. n ver. 17 only †. Exod. xxxv. 5 Sym. (-τως, 2 Macc. vi. 19.) o = ch. vii. 15 reff. p = Rom. xii. 8 reff. q = Acts xxiv. 27. xxv. 3, 9. Sir. xxx. 6. r ch. vi. 14 reff. s Acts vi. 1 reff. t = 1 Cor. xvi. 1 reff. u = Acts ix. 13 reff. v Rom. xv. 32 reff.

CHAP. VIII. 2. βαθος (for -θους) D[1] [(k)] o. rec τον πλουτον, with DFKLℵ[3] rel: txt BCPℵ[1] 17. 31.

3. rec (for παρα) υπερ (*see ch* i. 8), with KLP rel Chr_1 Thdrt [Damasc]: txt BCDFℵ 17 [Euthal-ms].—homœotel in 47 δυν. to δυν.

4. ins της bef παρακ. C[1](appy). rec at end adds δεξασθαι ημας, with [b[2]] h k: aft κοινωνιαν ins δεξασθαι c: om BCDFKLPℵ rel latt syrr copt [æth Chr_1 Euthal-ms Thdrt Damasc $Orig\text{-}int_1$ Aug_1].

5. ηλπικαμεν B 80. αλλα CD[1] 17: και 47.

is wrong in not giving the indic. θαῤῥῶ, and still more, in making θαῤῥεῖν ἐν mean '*to have confidence in*,' which is unexampled. Meyer, who remarks this, does not notice, that the strongest reason against it is not mere want of usage, but the psychological meaning of θαῤῥεῖν, which is not like πεποιθέναι, descriptive of a *relative*, but of an *absolute* state of mind,—**to be of good courage**: and this admits only of qualification as to the *ground* of that good courage; thus we have θαῤῥεῖν ὑπέρ, περί, ἐπί, in the sense of 'rejoicing at,' 'feeling confident concerning:' but θαῤῥεῖν ἐν for '*to trust in*,' as πεποιθέναι ἐν, would, I think, be inadmissible. Meyer quotes ἐν σοὶ πᾶσ' ἔγωγε σώζομαι, Soph. Aj. 519, where, as here, ἐν gives the *ground* of the verb as *in* the person spoken of.

CHAP. VIII. 1—IX. 15.] SECOND PART OF THE EPISTLE: CONCERNING THE COLLECTION FOR THE SAINTS. 1—6.] *He informs them of the readiness of the Macedonian churches to contribute for the poor saints (at Jerusalem), which led him also to beg of Titus to complete the collection at Corinth.* See some interesting geographical and historical notices in Stanley's introduction to this section, edn. 2, pp. 479 f. 1.] **δέ** is transitional,—passing on to new matter: so 1 Cor. vii. 1; viii. 1 al. fr. **χάριν**] For every good gift and frame of mind comes by divine grace, not by human excellency: and this occasion was most opportune for resting the liberality of the Macedonian churches on God's grace, that he might not be extolling *them* at the expense of the Corinthians, but holding out an example of the effusion of that grace, which was common to the Corinthians also, if they sought and used it. It is a mistake, with Orig., Erasm., al., to understand ἐμοί or ἡμῖν after δεδομένην 'quemadmodum adfuerit mihi Deus in ecclesiis:' see the construction διδόναι ἐν, in reff.:—**given among,—shed abroad in,** the churches of Macedonia. **2.**] **how that** (depends on γνωρίζομεν) **in much proof of tribulation** (though they were put to the proof by much tribulation) **(was) the abundance of their joy** (i. e. their joy abounded), **and their deep poverty** (κατὰ βάθους, lit. '*down into the depth*,' as καθ' ὅλου, 'throughout the whole') **abounded to** ('abunde cessit in,' as Meyer, &c. or rather perhaps, 'abounded,' produced abundant fruit, 'so as to bring about' . . . .) **the riches** (τὸ πλ. the riches which have actually become manifest by the result of the collection **of their liberality** (see ref. Rom. and note). 3—5.] *Proof of this.* There is no difficulty, and no ellipsis, in the construction. **For according to their power, I testify, and beyond their power, voluntarily, with much exhortation beseeching of us the grace and fellowship of the ministry to the saints** (i. e. to allow them a share in that grace and fellowship), **and not as we expected** (i. e. far beyond our expectation),

w = ch. vii. 3. Heb. xi. 3.
x 1 Cor. i. 10 reff.
y ver. 10 only +. ἐναρχ., Gal. iii. 3. Phil. i. 6.
z Rom. xv. 28. ch. vii. 1. Gal. iii. 3. Phil. i. 6. 1 Kings iii. 12.
a = 1 Cor. xvi. 3. ver. 19.
b = Mark xvi. 7. Luke vii. 7. Acts ix. 6. x. 20. xxvi. 16.
c ch. iv. 8 reff.

6 [w] εἰς τὸ [x] παρακαλέσαι ἡμᾶς Τίτον, [x] ἵνα καθὼς [y] προενήρ- BCDFK
ξατο, οὕτως καὶ [z] ἐπιτελέσῃ εἰς ὑμᾶς καὶ τὴν [a] χάριν LPℵ a b c d e f g
ταύτην. 7 [b] ἀλλ' ὥσπερ [c] ἐν [c] παντὶ [d] περισσεύετε, πίστει h k l m n o 17. 47
καὶ [e] λόγῳ καὶ [e] γνώσει καὶ [f] πάσῃ [g] σπουδῇ καὶ τῇ ἐξ
ὑμῶν [h] ἐν ἡμῖν ἀγάπῃ, ἵνα καὶ ἐν ταύτῃ τῇ [a] χάριτι
[d] περισσεύητε. 8 οὐ κατ' [i] ἐπιταγὴν λέγω, ἀλλὰ διὰ τῆς
ἑτέρων [g] σπουδῆς, καὶ [k] τὸ τῆς ὑμετέρας ἀγάπης [kl] γνήσιον
[m] δοκιμάζων 9 (γινώσκετε γὰρ τὴν χάριν τοῦ κυρίου ἡμῶν
Ἰησοῦ χριστοῦ, ὅτι δι' ὑμᾶς [n] ἐπτώχευσεν πλούσιος ὤν,

d = 1 Cor. xv. 58. Col. ii. 7. 1 Thess. iv. 1. e 1 Cor. i. 5. f = Acts xx. 19 reff. g Rom. xii. 8, 11 reff. h see 1 John iv. 9. (John xvii. 26?) i Rom. xvi. 26 reff. k neut., 1 Cor. i. 25, &c. reff. l Phil. iv. 3. 1 Tim. i. 2. Tit. i. 4 only +. Sir. vii. 18 only. (-ως, Phil. ii. 20.) m Rom. xiv. 22 reff. n here only. = Judges vi. 6. Ps. xxxiii. 10. lxxviii. 8. Prov. xxiii. 21. Tobit iv. 21.

6. for προεν., ενηρξατο B : προηρξ. 47.
7. περισσευητε CP Chr-montf$_1$. ins εν bef πιστει ℵ^1(ℵ^3 disapproving). εξ ημων εν υμιν B a b m 31. 73-4. 80. 238 Syr (copt) arm Orig-int$_1$: εξ υμ. εν υμ. n o: εξ υμων εις ημας 17: txt CDFKLPℵ rel [latt syr goth æth Chr Euthal-ms Thdrt Ambrst-mss Aug]. περισσευσητε D^{1}F.
8. δια τὴν ετ. σπουδην D : *propter* D-lat G-lat Ambrst Aug$_1$. elz ημετερας [with k^1(?)] : txt BCDFKLPℵ rel. δοκιμαζω D^1[-gr] F[-gr] Chr-ms.
9. om χριστου B Ambr$_1$. ημας CK a k l^1 m o 19. 41. 55. 65. 74. 89. 93. 109-15. 238 arm-mss Orig$_1$(-int$_1$) Eus$_4$.

but themselves they gave first (i. e. *above all* : as the inducing motive : not first in point of *time*, but in point of *importance*, see Rom. ii. 9, 10) **to the Lord, and to us by the will of God** (the Giver of grace, who made them willing to do this : not = κατὰ τὸ θέλ. τ. θ., which only *expresses* (whatever it may imply) *consonance with* the divine will : **διὰ τοῦ θελ. τ. θ.** makes the divine will the *agent*). **6.**] **So that we besought Titus** (not, Titus besought *us*, see ver. 17), **that** (the aim, and purport as well, of our request), **as he had previously** (before the Macedonians began to contribute: 'during his visit from which he had now returned') **begun it, so he would also complete among you** (the construction is pregnant—ἔλθῃ εἰς ὑμᾶς καὶ ἐπιτελέσῃ) **this grace also** (this act of grace or mercy, reff. **καί,**—as well as other things which he had to do among them. It does not belong to ταύτην, '*this* grace also, as well as other *graces*,' but to τὴν χάριν ταύτην altogether). **7—15.**] *Exhortations and inducements to perform this act of charity.* **7.**] ἀλλά marks the transition to an exhortation, as in reff. It at the same time implies, as Herm. ad Viger. p. 812 (in Meyer), 'satis argumentorum allatum esse.' **πίστει,** see ch. i. 24. **λόγῳ κ. γνώσει,** see ref. and for γν., 1 Cor. viii. 1. **πάσῃ** σπουδῇ, because σπουδή may be manifold even in a good sense. Grot. well explains it, 'studium ad agendas res bonas.' **τῇ ἐξ ὑμ. ἐν ἡμ. ἀγ.**] your **love to us;**—the love which, arising **from you, has us for its object:** see reff. According to the reading, ἐξ ἡμῶν ἐν ὑμ., the only meaning agreeing with the context is, '*the love* (to God and man) *which, arising from our teaching, is planted in you*.' **ἵνα καὶ κ.τ.λ.**] the sense is *imperative,*—κελεύω, or βούλομαι,—(or βλέπετε, see 1 Cor. xvi. 10,)—being omitted. So Soph. Œd. Col. 156, ἀλλ' ἵνα τῷδ' ἐν ἀφθέγκτῳ, μὴ προσπέσῃς νάπει. See Hartung, Partikellehre, ii. 148, 9. **ταύτῃ** is emphatic here, although ταύτην is not in ver. 6: '*this* grace also;'—other graces having been enumerated. Grotius remarks, 'non ignoravit Paulus artem rhetorum, movere laudando.' **8.**] Lest his last words should be misunderstood, he explains the spirit in which they were said : not as a command, but by way of inducement, by mention of the earnestness of others, and to try the genuineness of their love. **κατ' ἐπιτ.**] not, '*in consequence of a command from God*,' as Dr. Burton,—but, **by way of command** (1 Cor. vii. 6). **διὰ τῆς** is not = διὰ τήν, '*by occasion of*,' as E. V. :—but treats the ἑτέρων σπουδή as the *instrument by which*, in the way of emulation, the effect was to be produced. The participial construction is as in 1 Cor. iv. 14. **9.**] Explanation of 'trying the genuineness of your love,' by upholding His example in the matter, Whom we ought to resemble. **τ. χάριν, the** (act of) **grace :—the beneficence. ὅτι**] **consisting in this, that . . . πλ. ὤν**] The participle refers to the time when

ἵνα ὑμεῖς τῇ ἐκείνου [o] πτωχείᾳ [p] πλουτήσητε) 10 καὶ [qr] γνώμην ἐν τούτῳ [r] δίδωμι. τοῦτο γὰρ ὑμῖν [s] συμφέρει, [t] οἵτινες
οὐ μόνον τὸ ποιῆσαι ἀλλὰ καὶ τὸ θέλειν [u] προενήρξασθε
[v] ἀπὸ [v] πέρυσι· 11 νυνὶ δὲ καὶ τὸ ποιῆσαι [w] ἐπιτελέσατε,

o ver. 2 reff. p = Rev. iii. 18. (Luke xii. 21. 1 Cor. iv. 8.) q = 1 Cor. i. 10 (reff.). r 1 Cor. vii. 25. s 1 Cor. vi. 12 reff. t = Acts x. 41 reff. Rom. i. 25 al. u ver. 6. v ch. ix. 2 only †. πρὸ πέρυσι, Demosth. 467. 14. w ver. 6 reff.

[τη εκ. πτ. bef υμεις D[1 3] F latt Ambrst. for εκεινου, αυτου D-gr F-gr Orig$_1$ Eus$_4$, *illius* latt.]
10. for οιτινες, οτι F Syr. for προεν., ενηρξασθε D[1]F.

the historic act implied in the aorist ἐπτώχευσεν took place. **He, being rich, became poor**:—not, as De W., merely by His renunciation of human riches during His life on earth, but *by His exinanition of His glory* (Phil. ii. 6, 7), when, as Athanas. (contra Apol. ii. 11, vol. ii. (Migne), p. 757), τὴν πτωχεύσασαν φύσιν ἐν ἑαυτῷ ἀνελάβετο. The stress is on **δι' ὑμᾶς**, to raise the motive of gratitude the more effectually in them. **τῇ ἐκ. πτωχ. πλουτήσητε**] **that by His poverty** (as the efficient cause) **ye might become rich**: viz. with the same wealth in which He was rich,—the kingdom and glory of Heaven, including τὰ μυρία ἅπερ παρέσχεν ἡμῖν ἀγαθά, as Chrys. (Hom. xvii. p. 559): who had just before said, εἰ μὴ πιστεύεις, ὅτι ἡ πτωχεία πλούτου ἐστὶ ποιητική, ἐννόησόν σου τὸν δεσπότην, καὶ οὐκέτι ἀμφιβάλῃς (al. -λεῖς). See the various possible meanings discussed in Stanley's note. **10.**] ver. 9 was parenthetic: he now resumes the οὐ κατ' ἐπιταγὴν λέγω . . . . **And I give my opinion** [not '*judgment*,' as rendered in the Version of the Five Clergymen, which is objectionable here, as conveying the very idea which the Apostle wishes to negative, that of an authoritative decision] **in this matter**, the stress being on **γνώμην**, as distinguished from ἐπιταγήν. **τοῦτο γὰρ . . . .**] **For this** (viz. '*my giving my opinion, and not commanding*,'—as Billroth and Meyer. De Wette controverts this, and would make τοῦτο refer to the *proof of their love* in the act of charity, contending that τοῦτο must refer to the same as ἐν τούτῳ. But Meyer rightly answers that this need not be, for ἐν τούτῳ is altogether unemphatic and insignificant, and the whole sense of the clause is in the words γνώμην δίδωμι) **is expedient for you** (better than "*befitting*," or "*suitable*," as suggested by Bloomf. after the Schol. ἁρμόζει, συνᾴδει. This sense of συμφέρει is not found in the N. T., and is very doubtful elsewhere. See Palm and Rost's Lex.), **seeing that you** ('quippe qui;' οἵτινες is decisive for the above meaning of τοῦτο. 'My giving my opinion, rather than commanding, is expedient for you, who have already shewn yourselves so willing.' A *command* from me would be a *lowering* of you, and depreciation of your zeal) **began before them** (the Macedonian churches, see below) **not only the act, but also the mind to act, from a year ago**: i. e. 'not only were you before them in the deed itself, but also in the will to do it.' The sense has been missed by many of the Commentators, from not observing the *comparison* implied in **προενήρξασθε**, and applying it only to the *Corinthians themselves* beginning. In that case, as the *will* comes before the *deed*, to say, you began *not only to do, but also to will*, would be unmeaning. Some, in consequence, as Grot., al., and the Peschito, have arbitrarily assumed an *inversion of terms*, so that '*non solum facere, sed velle*' should = '*non solum velle, sed facere*.' Others, as Chrys., Theodoret, al., Erasm., Calv., Beza, al., Billroth, Olsh., Rückert, al. m., have taken θέλειν = '*to do with a good will*,' which is certainly not its sense in ver. 11. The above explanation is that of Cajetan, Estius, De Wette, Winer, Meyer, and Wieseler, and puts the climax in its right order, making it a backward one of comparison. For as Wieseler remarks (Chron. Apost. Zeit. p. 364, note), there are *three steps* in the collection for the saints,—the wishing it (θέλειν), the setting about it (ποιῆσαι), and the completion of it (ἐπιτελέσαι). And the Corinthians had begun *not only the second*, but *even the first* of these, before the Macedonians. Long employed as they had then been in the matter, it was more creditable to them to receive *advice* from the Apostle, than *command*. "**θέλειν** is not a historic act like **ποιῆσαι**, but a permanent state: hence the pres. inf." Meyer.

In saying **ἀπὸ πέρυσι** '*from last year*,' it seems probable that Paul would speak as a Jew, regarding the year as beginning in Tisri. **11.**] **But** (contrast of your former zeal with your present need to be reminded of it) **now complete the act itself also** (καί can hardly apply to the whole τὸ ποι. ἐπιτ., as De Wette, but must be taken with ποιῆσαι; *now* shew not only the completion of a ready will in the act begun, but complete *the act also*,—

ὅπως [x] καθάπερ ἡ [y] προθυμία [z] τοῦ θέλειν, οὕτως καὶ τὸ BCDFK
[w] ἐπιτελέσαι [a] ἐκ τοῦ ἔχειν. 12 εἰ γὰρ ἡ [y] προθυμία [b] πρό- LPℵ a b c d e f g
κειται, [c] καθὸ ἐὰν ἔχῃ [d] εὐπρόσδεκτος, οὐ [c] καθὸ οὐκ ἔχει. h k l m n o 17. 47
13 οὐ γὰρ ἵνα ἄλλοις [e] ἄνεσις, ὑμῖν [δὲ] θλῖψις, ἀλλ' [f] ἐξ
[g] ἰσότητος, ἐν τῷ [h] νῦν [h] καιρῷ τὸ ὑμῶν [i] περίσσευμα [k] εἰς
τὸ ἐκείνων [l] ὑστέρημα, 14 ἵνα καὶ τὸ ἐκείνων [i] περίσσευμα
γένηται [k] εἰς τὸ ὑμῶν [l] ὑστέρημα, ὅπως γένηται [g] ἰσότης.
15 καθὼς γέγραπται [m] Ὁ τὸ πολὺ οὐκ [n] ἐπλεόνασεν, καὶ ὁ
τὸ ὀλίγον οὐκ [o] ἠλαττόνησεν.

x Rom. iv. 6 reff.
y Acts xvii. 11. ver. 19. ch. ix. 2 only †. Sir. xlv. 23 only. (-μος, Rom. i. 15.)
z constr., Acts xiv. 9 reff.
a = John iii. 34.
b Heb. vi. 18. xii. 1, 2. Jude 7 only. Levit. xxiv. 7 al.
c here bis. Rom. viii. 26. 1 Pet. iv. 13 only. Levit. ix. 5 B.
d Rom. xv. 16 reff.
e Acts xxiv. 23 reff.
f = 1 Cor. vii. 5 reff.
g here bis. Col. iv. 1 only. Job xxxvi. 29. Zech. iv. 7 only.
h Rom. iii. 26 reff.
i epp., here bis only. Matt. xii. 34 || L. Mark viii. 8 only. Eccles. ii. 15 (only ?).
k = Rom. iii. 22. Gal. iii. 14. Eph. i. 8. iii. 2.
l 1 Cor. xvi. 17 reff.
m and constr., Exod. xvi. 18. Winer, edn. 6, § 64. 4.
n Rom. v. 20 reff.
o here only. l. c. trans., Prov. xiv. 34.

11. for *του*, *το* D¹.
12. for *εαν*, *αν* D¹FLℵ f Chr-ms Damasc. for *εχη*, *εχει* L f [Euthal-ms]. rec adds *τις*, with C²L rel [syr-w-ast copt Chr_1]: om BC¹DFKPℵ 17 latt [syr-txt] goth æth arm $Clem_1$ [Chr_1 Euthal-ms Thdrt Damasc $Cypr_1$ Ambrst]. (so D[-gr] F [not F-lat] aft *εχει*.)
13. om *δε* BCℵ¹ 17 D-lat æth [Euthal-ms]. om *νυν* F[-gr(and G²)].
14. (the *τ* of 1st *το* is written over the line by ℵ¹(appy).) *εμον* K.
15. om 2nd *ὁ* F b g¹ h k o 47. 80. 93. 106-14-15-22. 238.

as Meyer), **that, as (there was)** (with you) **readiness of will, so (there may) also (be) completion according to your means** (**ἐκ τοῦ ἔχειν**, not '*out of that which ye have*,' as E. V., but '*after the measure of your* property,' as in ref. The verbs substantive must be supplied, as in ver. 13). **12.**] Explanation of **ἐκ τοῦ ἔχειν**,—that on it, *προθυμία* being presupposed, and not on absolute quantity, acceptability depends. **For if a willing mind is present,—according to what it may happen to possess, it is acceptable, not according to what it possesseth not.** The construction of the sentence is simple enough: *προθυμία* being the subject throughout, quasi-personified: readiness in God's service is accepted, if its exertion be commensurate with its means,—and is not measured by an unreasonable requirement of what it has not. **13—15.**] *Further explanation that the present collection is not intended to press the Corinthians καθὸ οὐκ ἔχουσι.* **For** (it is) **not** (the collection is not made) **that there may be to others** (the saints at Jerusalem) **relief, and to you distress** (of poverty): **14.**] **but that by the rule of equality** (*ἐξ* as in *ἐκ τοῦ ἔχειν*, above), **at this present time** (of their need: the stress is on *ἐν τῷ νῦν καιρῷ* as suggesting that this relation may hereafter be altered) **your abundance may subserve** (*γένηται*, see next clause. *γίνεσθαι εἰς*, 'to be extended to,' see ref. Gal.) **their deficiency; that also** (supposing circumstances changed) **their abundance may subserve your want.** The reference is **still**, as is evident from the next verse, to the supply of *temporal wants*, in respect of which there should be a mutual relieving and sharing among Christians. But the passage has been curiously misunderstood to mean, '*that their* (the Jewish Christians') *abundance in spiritual things may be imparted to you to supply your deficiency.*' Thus Chrys., al.,—the *ancients* regarding this imparting as the *Gospel-benefit received from them by the Gentiles* (which however was *past*, not future, and is urged as a *motive for gratitude*, see Rom. xv. 27), and the modern Romanists introducing the monstrous perversion of the attribution of the merits of the saints to others in the next world. So Estius: "Locus hic apostoli contra nostræ ætatis hæreticos ostendit, posse Christianos minus sanctos meritis sanctorum adjuvari etiam in futuro sæculo. Denique notanda virtus eleemosynæ, quæ facit hominem participem meritorum ejus in quem confertur."
15.] **that there may be equality, as it is written** (i. e. according to the expression used in the Scripture history: *παράγει παλαιὰν ἱστορίαν*, Chrys.,—of the gathering of the manna) **He that (gathered) much, did not exceed** (the measure prescribed by God): **and he that (gathered) little, did not fall short** (of it). The fact of *equality* being the only point brought into comparison as between the Israelites of old and Christians now, it is superfluous to enquire minutely *how* this equality was wrought among the Israelites. The quotation is according to the reading of the LXX generally supported by MSS.; except that *ἔλαττον* appears for *ὀλίγον* in A *a secunda manu.* Grabe (not F) and the

16 [p] Χάρις δὲ τῷ θεῷ τῷ [q] διδόντι τὴν αὐτὴν [r] σπουδὴν
ὑπὲρ ὑμῶν [q] ἐν τῇ καρδίᾳ Τίτου, 17 ὅτι τὴν μὲν [s] παράκλησιν [t] ἐδέξατο, [u] σπουδαιότερος δὲ [v] ὑπάρχων [w] αὐθαί-
ρετος [x] ἐξῆλθεν πρὸς ὑμᾶς. 18 [y] συνεπέμψαμεν δὲ μετ'
αὐτοῦ τὸν ἀδελφόν, οὗ ὁ [z] ἔπαινος [a] ἐν τῷ εὐαγγελίῳ διὰ
[b] πασῶν τῶν [bc] ἐκκλησιῶν· 19 [d] οὐ μόνον δέ, [d] ἀλλὰ καὶ
[e] χειροτονηθεὶς ὑπὸ τῶν [c] ἐκκλησιῶν [f] συνέκδημος ἡμῶν,
ἐν τῇ [g] χάριτι ταύτῃ τῇ [h] διακονουμένῃ ὑφ' ἡμῶν, [i] πρὸς

p = Rom. vi. 17 reff.
q constr., John iii. 35. ch. i. 22. ver. 1. Ezra vii. 10 B Ald. see Luke i. 17.
r vv. 7, 8.
s = Rom. xii. 8 al.
t = John iv. 45
u ver. 22 (bis). 2 Tim. i. 17 only. Ezek. xli. 25. (-ως Luke vii. 4. Phil. ii. 28. Tit. iii. 13.)
v Acts viii. 16 reff. w ver. 2 only (reff.). x = but w. εἰς, Acts xi. 25 reff. y ver. 22 only †. z Rom. ii. 29 reff. a Rom. i. 9. ch. x. 14 al. b 1 Cor. vii. 17. xiv. 33. ch. xi. 28. c plur., Rom. xvi. 16 reff. d Rom. v. 3. viii. 23 al. e Acts xiv. 23 only †. f Acts xix. 29 only †. (ἐκδημεῖν, ch. v. 6, 8, 9.) g = vv. 6. 7. 1 Cor. xvi. 3. h ch. iii. 3 reff. i = Acts iii. 10. ch. x. 4. xi. 8. 1 Tim. i. 16 al.

16. for διδοντι, δοντι DFLℵ[3] 47 syrr [arm] Chr$_1$, *dedit* vulg D-lat: *danti* G-lat. C tol[1] copt add ημιν.
18. τον αδελφον bef μετ αυτου Pℵ[1] c [copt].
19. for 1st ημων, υμων F[-gr](not G). add εγενετο D[-gr] b 91. 177 arm. rec (for εν) συν, with D F[not F-lat] KLℵ rel goth [Clem$_1$] Thdrt Aug: txt BCP d m 17. 47 vulg copt æth [arm Euthal-ms] Damasc Ambrst Aug Pel. om 1st τη C. υφ υμων C b[2] l 55. 73. 177. 238. homœotel in 17 from υφ' υμων in this ver to υφ' υμων in next.

Aldine edition have ᾧ τὸ πολύ and ᾧ τὸ ὀλίγον, probably a correction. The context supplies συλλέξας from the συνέλεξαν in the preceding verse,—and is presumed by the Apostle to be familiar to his readers. **16—24.**] *Of Titus and two other brethren whom Paul had commissioned to complete the collection.* **16.**] The sense is taken up from ver. 6. διδόντι ἐν, see reff. **τὴν αὐτ. σπ.**, viz. '*as in myself.*' This is evident from ὑπὲρ ὑμῶν. **17.**] *Proof of this;* that Titus *received indeed* (μέν) Paul's exhortation to go to them (said, to shew his subordination,—or perhaps to authenticate his authorization by the Apostle), but in reality (δέ) was *too ready to go, to need any exhortation;*—and therefore *went forth* (the past tense of the epistolary style,—as '*dabam,*' &c., indicating things which *will have passed* before the letter is received) *of his own accord to them.* **18—21.**] *Commendation of a brother sent with Titus.* **18.**] **ὁ ἀδελφός** cannot surely be, as some Commentators (Heumann, Rückert) have understood, '*the brother of Titus:*' the delicate nature of the mission would require that there should be at least no family connexion between those sent to fulfil it. This and the other are called in ver. 23, ἀδελφοὶ ἡμῶν, and were unquestionably *Christian brethren* in the usual sense. *Who this was,* we know not. Chrys., Theodoret, Œcum., Luther, Calvin, suppose *Barnabas* to be meant; but there is no historical ground for this, and we can hardly suppose him put under Titus. Baronius and Estius suppose, *Silas;* to whom this last objection would also apply; besides that he was well known to the Corinthians, and therefore would not need this recommendation. Orig., Jerome, τινές in Chrys., Ambrose, Pelagius, Primasius, Anselm, Cajetan, Grot., Olsh., al., suppose *Luke:*—and of these all before Grot. (who pointed out the mistake; which however I see reproduced in Mr. Birks's Horæ Apostolicæ, p. 242 f.) suppose οὗ ὁ ἔπαινος ἐν τῷ εὐαγγελίῳ to refer to his *gospel,*—διὰ τὴν ἱστορίαν ἥνπερ ἔγραψε, Chrys. Hom. xviii. p. 564;—but this is altogether without proof, as is the assumption that it was *Mark* (Lightfoot, Storr). It may have been *Trophimus,* who (Acts xx. 4) accompanied Paul into Asia, and (xxi. 29) to Jerusalem: so De Wette, Wieseler. If the expression **whose praise in** (the matter of) **the Gospel is throughout all the Churches,** is to be compared with any similar eulogium, that of Gaius in Rom. xvi. 23 seems to correspond most nearly: Γάϊος ὁ ξένος μου **καὶ ὅλης τῆς ἐκκλησίας**: but he was *resident at Corinth,* see 1 Cor. i. 14. A Gaius, a Macedonian, is mentioned Acts xix. 29, as one of the συνέκδημοι of Paul, as here, together with Aristarchus, which latter we know accompanied him to Jerusalem (but see below on ch. ix. 4). It must then rest in uncertainty. **19.**] parenthetical (see on ver. 20) adding to his general commendation a particular qualification for this office. **οὐ μόν. δέ,**—**and not only so** (i. e. praised in all the churches), **but who was also appointed** ('suffragiis designatus,' see ref. and note; and Stanley here) **by the churches** (of Macedonia? see ver. 1) **as our fellow-traveller** (to Jerusalem, from what follows) **in** (the matter of) **this charity which is being ministered by us,**

τὴν τοῦ κυρίου δόξαν καὶ [k] προθυμίαν ἡμῶν· 20 [l] στελ-
λόμενοι τοῦτο, μή τις ἡμᾶς [m] μωμήσηται [n] ἐν τῇ [o] ἁδρότητι
ταύτῃ τῇ [p] διακονουμένῃ ὑφ' ἡμῶν. 21 [p] προνοοῦμεν γὰρ
[p] καλὰ οὐ μόνον [p] ἐνώπιον κυρίου, ἀλλὰ καὶ [p] ἐνώπιον
ἀνθρώπων. 22 [q] συνεπέμψαμεν δὲ αὐτοῖς τὸν ἀδελφὸν
ἡμῶν, ὃν [r] ἐδοκιμάσαμεν [s] ἐν πολλοῖς πολλάκις [t] σπουδαῖον ὄντα, νυνὶ δὲ πολὺ [t] σπουδαιότερον [u] πεποιθήσει
πολλῇ τῇ [v] εἰς ὑμᾶς· 23 [w] εἴτε [x] ὑπὲρ Τίτου, [y] κοινωνὸς
ἐμὸς καὶ [v] εἰς ὑμᾶς [z] συνεργός· [w] εἴτε ἀδελφοὶ ἡμῶν, [a] ἀπόστολοι ἐκκλησιῶν, [b] δόξα χριστοῦ. 24 τὴν οὖν [c] ἔνδειξιν

BCDFK LPℵ a b c d e f g h k l m n o 17. 47

k vv. 11, 12 reff. l 2 Thess. iii. 6 only. Mal. ii. 5. m ch. vi. 3 reff. n := 1 Tim. v. 10. Heb. xi. 2. o here only †. (-ρός, Jer. v. 5.) p Rom. xii. 17 (reff.). Prov. iii. 4. q ver. 18 only. r = 2 Cor. iii. 13 reff. (1 Cor. xvi. 3.) s see ch. iv. 8. vi. 3 reff. t ver. 17 reff. u ch. i. 15 reff. v = ch. ii. 9, 12. ix. 8. Gal. v. 10 al. w so 1 Cor. xiii. 8. xv. 11. x ch. i. 8 reff. y 1 Cor. x. 18, 20 reff. z Rom. xvi. 3 reff. a = John xiii. 16. Phil. ii. 25. (3 Kings xiv. 6 A, &c. [B def.]) only. b = 1 Thess. ii. 20. c Rom. iii. 25, 26. Phil. i. 28 only †.

rec ins *αυτου* bef *του κυριου*, with $D^{2.3}$[-gr] Kℵ rel syrr Chr Thdrt Damasc: *αυτην* P a 6. 43. 67^2. 74 [fuld]: om BCD¹FL d latt copt goth æth arm [Euthal-ms Ambrst Aug_1]. rec (at end) **υμων**, with F[-gr] d: txt BCDGKL[P]ℵ rel latt syrr copt goth [æth arm Chr Euthal-ms Thdrt Damasc]. add *τελουσιν* D¹.

20. **υποστελλομενοι** F: *συστελλ.* 93: *devitantes* latt. **υμας** F[-gr] b g h m o 73. for *μωμησηται*, *μωμηται* C²(C¹ uncert).

21. rec *προνοουμενοι*, with CKL rel copt goth $Clem_1$ Chr-ms [Cyr_1 Euthal-ms] Thdrt Damasc: txt BDFPℵ f latt syrr arm Chr_1 [Ambrst Aug_1]. rec om *γαρ*, with KL rel Thdrt Damasc Thl: ins BCDFPℵ m 17. 47 latt syrr copt goth arm $Clem_1$ Chr [Cyr_1 Euthal-ms Ambrst Aug]. (*Meyer thinks* προνοουμενοι *to have been a mere mistake originally, arising from* στελλομενοι *above: and thus the* γαρ *which was at first retained from oversight, as in* C, *was at last erased. Probably* προνοουμενοι *was introduced from Rom* xii. 17, *where the same words occur.*) om 2nd *ενωπιον* ℵ¹.

22. **υμων** F(not G: so ver. 23). om *πολλη* F[not F-lat] 67^2-9: pref *δε* B. for *εις*, *προς* K c.

23. *συνεργος* bef *εις υμας* D [Syr] copt goth Ambrst. for *χρ.*, *κυριου* CF [æth: *dei* tol].

—**in order to subserve the glory of the Lord and our readiness** (this clause refers not to *διακον. ὑφ' ἡμ.* as usually interpreted, but to the *fact related*, the union of this brother with Paul in the matter of the alms, which was done to avoid suspicions detrimental to Christ's glory, and to the zeal of the Apostle): **20.**] **taking heed of this** ('*devitantes*,' Vulg.—*ὑποπτεύσαντες κ. δεδοικότες*, Theophyl.: —the participle belongs to *συνεπέμψαμεν*, ver. 19 being parenthetical) **that no one blame us** (ref.) **in the matter of this abundance** (of contributions) **which is being ministered by us.** On *ἁδρότης*, Meyer observes, "from *ἁδρός*, 'compact,' 'solid;'—is used in Homer (Il. *χ*. 363, *π*. 857, *ω*. 6) of a firm and succulent habit of body. Later, we have it in all the various references of the adjective, e. g. of abundance—of plants and fruits (Theophr.), of discourse (Diog. Laërt. x. 83), of tone (Athen. x. p. 415 A), &c. *What kind* of abundance is meant, the context therefore alone determines." Wetst. says, "*ἁδρότης* apud Zosimum quater pro *ingenti largitione*." **21.**] 'And such caution is in accordance with our general practice.' See reff. Rom. and Prov. **22.**] Still less can we determine who this *second* brother is. Every possible person has been guessed. Several would answer to the description, '*whom we have many times in many matters proved to be earnest.*' By our uncertainty in these two cases, we may see *how much* is required, to fill up the apostolic history at all satisfactorily. **πεποιθήσει . . .**] **through the great confidence which he has towards you**: belongs to *σπουδαιότερον*, and to the brother, not to *συνεπέμψαμεν* and to Paul. The brother had, by what he had heard from Titus, conceived a high opinion of the probable success of their mission. **23.**] *General recommendation of the three.* **εἴτε ὑπ. Τίτου**] **Whether concerning Titus** (we may supply *λέγω* or *γράφω*, or as in E. V., 'any enquire:' or we need not supply any thing), **he is my partner and** (especially) **my fellow-worker towards you: whether our brethren** (be in question:—viz. the two mentioned—but generalized by the absence of the article—'*whether* [*any*] *brethren of ours*'), **they are Apostles** (in the more general sense of Acts xiv. 14; 1 Thess. ii. 6; Phil. ii. 25) **of the churches** (i. e. 'are of the churches,

τῆς ἀγάπης ὑμῶν, καὶ ἡμῶν [d] καυχήσεως ὑπὲρ ὑμῶν, εἰς
αὐτοὺς [e] ἐνδεικνύμενοι [f] εἰς [f] πρόσωπον τῶν ἐκκλησιῶν.
IX. 1 περὶ [g] μὲν γὰρ τῆς [h] διακονίας τῆς [h] εἰς τοὺς [h] ἁγίους [i] περισσόν μοι ἐστὶν τὸ γράφειν ὑμῖν· 2 οἶδα γὰρ τὴν
[k] προθυμίαν ὑμῶν [l] ἣν [m] ὑπὲρ ὑμῶν [lm] καυχῶμαι [m] Μακεδόσιν, ὅτι Ἀχαΐα [n] παρεσκεύασται [o] ἀπὸ [o] πέρυσι· καὶ ὁ
[[p] ἐξ] ὑμῶν [q] ζῆλος [r] ἠρέθισεν [s] τοὺς [s] πλείονας. 3 ἔπεμψα δὲ

d Rom. iii. 27 reff.
e = Rom. ii. 15. ix. 22 al. (Gen. l. 15, 17.) constr., see note.
f = here (ch. xi. 20) only. see Num. xx. 6.
g so 1 Cor. v. 3. xi. 18.
h ch. viii. 4.
i = Matt. v. 47. Prov. xiv. 23. 2 Macc. xii. 44 B, F (not A) &c.
k ch. viii. 11, 12 reff.
l constr., ch. xi. 30. Prov. xxvii. 1.
m constr., ch. vii. 14.
n here bis. 1 Cor. xiv. 8. Acts x. 10 only. Jer. xii. 5.
o ch. viii. 10 only (ref.).
p = ch. viii. 7. see Luke xi. 13. ch. v. 2.
q Rom. x. 2 reff.
r Col. iii. 21 only. Prov. xix. 7.
s 1 Cor. ix. 19 reff.

24. (ν of την is written above the line by ℵ[1] or -corr[1].) υπερ ημων D[1][-gr] G. rec (for ενδεικνυμενοι) ενδειξασθε, with CD[2·3]KLPℵ rel vulg(and F-lat) syrr copt arm [æth Chr_1 Euthal-ms Thdrt Damasc Ambrst] : txt B D[1][and lat] F[-gr] 17 goth. rec ins και bef εις προσωπον: om BCDFKLPℵ rel latt syrr copt goth æth arm gr-lat-ff.

CHAP. IX. 1. om γαρ C 2. 41. 115 arm. εμοι B. om το C 17. 73: του F 109 Thdrt-ms Damasc. ημιν F(not G).
2. παραεσκευασται(but corrd) ℵ[1]. for ὁ, το Bℵ 17. for περυσι, περσυ D[1]F: περισυ D[2] [c] 17. (simly ch viii. 10.) om εξ BCPℵ a 17 vulg(and F-lat) Syr copt arm [Euthal-ms] $Orig-int_1$ Ambrst Pel: ins D F[-gr] KL rel fuld syr goth Chr Thdrt Damasc.
3. επεμψαμεν D-gr arm [demid copt Pel] Aug_1.

what we are of the Lord'—persons sent out with authority), **the glory of Christ** (i. e. men whose work tends to Christ's glory). **24.] Shew then to them the proof of your love** ('to us,' or perhaps, '*to your poor brethren*' (Meyer):—but the word has not been so used throughout this passage, see verse 7: χάρις has been the word), **and of our boasting concerning you, in the sight of the churches.** I may remark, (1) that the participial construction is elliptic, as in Rom. xii. 16 al. (2) That πρόσωπον τῶν ἐκκλησιῶν does not actually *import* 'the representatives of the churches,' as Meyer (which would be τὸ πρόσωπον or τὰ πρόσωπα, without εἰς), but as above, it being *implied* that they, being the ἀπόστολοι τ. ἐκκλ., *are such representatives.* And this is all that Theodoret seems to mean, whom Meyer quotes in support of his view:— τὸ πρόσωπον γὰρ τῶν ἐκκλησιῶν ἐπέχουσιν οὗτοι τῶν πεμψασῶν αὐτούς.

IX. 1—5.] *He recurs to the collection itself, and prays them that they would make good before the brethren his boasting of them, and prepare it before his own coming.* 1.] The **μὲν γάρ** connects with the last verse, thus, 'I beseech you to receive the brethren whom I send, courteously; for concerning the *duty of ministration to the saints*, it is surely superfluous for me to write to you who are so prompt already.' No new subject begins, as some have supposed; nor is there any break in the sense at all. Some obscurity has been introduced unnecessarily, by taking τῆς διακ. τ. εἰς τ. ἁγ. for *merely this collection which is now making*: whereas the Apostle chooses such general terms as a mild reproof to the Corinthians, who, well aware as they were of the duty of ministering to the saints, were yet somewhat remiss in this particular example of the duty. There is an emphasis on γράφειν: 'nam testes habebitis præsentes,' Bengel. Theophyl. well remarks: τοσαῦτα καὶ πρότερον εἰπὼν καὶ πάλιν μέλλων εἰπεῖν, ὅμως περιττὸν αὐτῷ λέγει τὸ περὶ τούτων γράφειν. σοφῶς δὲ τοῦτο ποιεῖ, ὥστε μᾶλλον αὐτοὺς ἐπισπάσασθαι. αἰσχυνθήσονται γὰρ εἴ γε τοιαύτην ὑπόληψιν περὶ αὐτῶν ἔχοντος τοῦ Παύλου, ὅτι οὐ δέονται συμβουλῆς πρὸς τὸ ἐλεεῖν, εἶτα φανῶσιν ἐλάττους τῆς ὑπολήψεως. **2.] For** (ground of περισσόν ἐστι) **I am aware of your readiness of which** (reff.) **I am in the habit of boasting concerning you to Macedonians** (Bengel remarks on the pres., 'adhuc erat Paulus in Macedonia') **that Achaia** (not ὑμεῖς—he relates his own words to the Macedonians) **has been ready** (viz. to *send off the money:* καὶ οὐδὲν λείπει εἰ μὴ τὸ ἐλθεῖν τοὺς δεξομένους τὰ χρήματα, Theophyl. The Apostle, judging by their readiness, had made this boast concerning them, supposing it was really so. That this is the sense is shewn by ἀπαρασκευάστους below, ver. 4) **from last year** (reff.):—**and the zeal which proceeds from you** ('which has its source in you and whose influence goes forth from you:' so ὁ ἐκ Πελοποννήσου πόλεμος, οἱ ἐκεῖθεν, and the like) **stirred up the greater number of them** (but not *only* the example of your zeal: see ch. viii. 1). **3.] But** (contrast, not to μέν in ver. 1, but to καυχῶμαι above;

τοὺς ἀδελφούς, ἵνα μὴ τὸ [t] καύχημα ἡμῶν τὸ ὑπὲρ ὑμῶν
[u] κενωθῇ [v] ἐν [v] τῷ [v] μέρει τούτῳ, ἵνα καθὼς ἔλεγον [uw] παρ-
εσκευασμένοι [w] ἦτε, 4 [x] μή [x] πως, ἐὰν ἔλθωσιν σὺν ἐμοὶ Μακε-
δόνες καὶ εὕρωσιν ὑμᾶς [y] ἀπαρασκευάστους, [z] καταισχυν-
θῶμεν ἡμεῖς (ἵνα μὴ λέγωμεν ὑμεῖς) ἐν τῇ [a] ὑποστάσει
ταύτῃ. 5 [bc] ἀναγκαῖον οὖν [cd] ἡγησάμην [e] παρακαλέσαι τοὺς
ἀδελφούς, [e] ἵνα [f] προέλθωσιν εἰς ὑμᾶς, καὶ [g] προκαταρτί-
σωσιν τὴν [h] προεπηγγελμένην [i] εὐλογίαν ὑμῶν ταύτην
ἑτοίμην εἶναι [j] οὕτως [j] ὡς [i] εὐλογίαν καὶ μὴ ὡς [k] πλεονεξίαν.

BCDFK LPℵ a b c d e f g h k l m n o 17. 47

t Rom. iv. 2 reff. u Rom. iv. 14 reff. v ch. iii. 10 reff. w constr., Acts xxv. 10 reff. x 1 Cor. ix. 27 reff. y here only †. z ch. vii. 14 reff. w. ἐν, here only. a = ch. xi. 17. Heb. (i. 3.) iii. 14. xi. 1 only. Ps. xxxviii. 7. b Acts xiii. 46 reff. c Phil. ii. 25. 2 Macc. ix. 21. d = Acts xxvi. 2 reff. e 1 Cor. i. 10 reff. f Acts xx. 5, 13. Gen. xxxiii. 14. g here only †. h Rom. i. 2 only †. i = Rom. xv. 29. xvi. 18. Ezek. xxxiv. 26. j 1 Cor. iii. 15 reff. k = here only. (Rom. i. 29 al.)

for ημων, υμων B¹(see table) om το υπερ υμων F[not F-lat] 45 Chr₁. ελεγεν(appy: but corrd) ℵ¹.

4. om πως D¹ [latt Ambrst Aug₁]. om εαν BD² Syr: αν D¹. ευρουσιν F. ins και bef καταισχυνθωμεν D¹·²(and lat) L (Syr) arm. for λεγωμεν, λεγω C¹D F[not F-lat] goth Ambrst Aug₁: om ινα μη λεγ. υμ. K. for υμεις, ημεις B¹ [Euthal-ms]. rec at end adds της καυχησεως (*see ch* xi. 17), with D³KLPℵ³ rel syrr goth arm [Chr Thdrt Damasc]: om BCD¹Fℵ¹ 17 latt copt æth [Euthal-ms] Ambrst Aug₁ Pel.

5. προσελθωσιν F[-gr] 48 Thdrt-ms. for εις, προς BDF m: txt CKLℵ rel [Euthal-ms] Thdrt Damasc Thl Œc. (P uncert.) rec προκατηγγελμενην (*occasioned probably by* προκαταρτ. *above*), with KL rel Thdrt Damasc Œc: txt BCDFPℵ d 17 vulg arm [Euthal-ms] Thl Ambrst Aug Pel. om υμων D¹(and lat) vulg [spec] Pel. om ταυτην F[not F-lat] arm (Chr). om και Fℵ¹ 52 latt Syr Chr-comm₁ [Ambrst Aug₁]. rec (for 2nd ως) ωσπερ, with b l: txt BCDFKLPℵ rel [Chr Euthal-ms Thdrt Damasc].

implying fear lest he should have been making a vain boast concerning them) **I sent** (epistolary past, as in ch. viii. 18, 22) **the brethren, in order that our matter of boasting concerning you** (καύχημα, our *whole* 'materies gloriandi,' not = καύχησις) **may not in this particular be proved empty** (ἐν τῷ μέρει τούτῳ does not belong to καύχημα, but to κενωθῇ—'that our boast of you, so ample and various—ch. vii. 4, may not break down in this one department.' Estius, in marg., well calls it 'acris cum tacita laude exhortatio apostolica'); **that, as I said** (when? in ver. 2? or, in his boasting to the Macedonians? or, in 1 Cor. xvi. 1? Most naturally, *in ver.* 2. If he had meant, *to the Macedonians,* it would probably have been λέγω, as καυχῶμαι above: if *in* 1 *Cor.* xvi., it would have been more clearly expressed. If so, ἔλεγον refers merely to the *word* παρεσκ.), **ye may be prepared,** (see above on ver. 2), **4.] lest perchance if Macedonians should come with me** (to you:—to bring me on my way, or to bear the Macedonian collection. We may infer from this expression, that neither of the two brethren above mentioned, ch. viii. 18, 22, was a Macedonian), **and should find you unprepared** (with your collection, see ver. 2) **we** (who have boasted), **not to say you** (who were boasted of), **should be put to shame, in the matter of this confidence** (respecting you. **ὑπόστασις,** as elsewhere in N. T. and LXX, see reff., *subjective:* the attempt to give it here the meaning of '*foundation,*' '*matter boasted of,*' as Chrys., Theophyl., Erasm., Grot., al., Rück., Olsh., is unnecessary, and has probably been induced by the gloss τῆς καυχ. inserted from ch. xi. 17: but see there also). **5.] I therefore** (because of ver. 4) **thought it necessary to exhort the brethren** (Titus and the two others) **that they would go before** (my coming) **to you, and previously prepare your long announced beneficence** (i. e. long announced by me to the Macedonians, ver. 2. **εὐλογία, blessing;** not used only of a blessing in *words,* but of one expressed by a *present,* as Gen. xxxiii. 11; Judg. i. 15. (See Stanley.) But beware of the blunder of connecting it with εὖ and λογία, '*a good collection.*' This sense of *blessing,* combined with the primitive sense, affords the Apostle an opportunity for bringing out the true spirit in which Christian gifts should be given), **that this same may be ready** (the construction is unusual: ταύτην refers back to εὐλ. and the inf. must have ὥστε supplied. De W. compares Heb. v. 5. Perhaps the nearest is Col. iv. 6) **in such sort as beneficence, and not as covetousness** (i. e. as the fruit of blessing, poured out from a beneficent mind, not of a sparing

6 [l] τοῦτο δέ, ὁ [m] σπείρων [n] φειδομένως [n] φειδομένως και
[m] θερίσει, καὶ ὁ [m] σπείρων [o] ἐπ᾽ εὐλογίαις [o] ἐπ᾽ εὐλογίαις
καὶ [m] θερίσει. 7 ἕκαστος καθὼς [p] προήρηται τῇ καρδίᾳ,
μὴ [q] ἐκ λύπης ἢ [qr] ἐξ [r] ἀνάγκης· [s] ἱλαρὸν γὰρ [t] δότην
ἀγαπᾷ ὁ θεός. 8 [u] δυνατεῖ δὲ ὁ θεὸς πᾶσαν [v] χάριν [w] περισ-

l see 1 Cor. vii. 29 reff.
m 1 Cor. ix. 11. Gal. vi. 7. Prov. xxii. 8.
n here bis only †. (-νος, Job xvi. 14.)
o = Rom. v. 14.
p here only. Prov. xxi. 25 al.
q = 1 Cor. vii. 5 reff.
r Heb. vii. 12 only.
s here only. Prov. xxii. 8. (-ότης, Rom. xii. 8.)
t here only. l. c. only.
u Rom. xiv. 4. ch. xiii. 3 only †.
v Acts xi. 23 reff.
w trans., ch. iv. 15. Eph. i. 8. 1 Thess. iii. 12 only ‡.

6. for 1st επ ευλογιαις, εν ευλογια *in benedictione* D[1][and lat] F[(not F-lat) spec] fuld copt goth Orig-int$_1$[(txt Orig$_1$) Ambrst Aug$_1$]. for 2nd επ ευλ., εξ ευλογιας D[1](and lat) fuld goth Orig-int$_1$[(txt Orig$_1$) Ambrst] Cypr$_1$: επ ευλογια F(not F-lat) copt Aug. om [last] και D[1][-gr] æth.

7. rec προαιρειται, with D[-gr] KL rel Chr$_1$ [Euthal-ms Antch$_1$] Thdrt Damasc$_2$: txt BC(FP)א (17) Chr-ms(Wtst) (προειρεται F[1], προειρητ. F[2]G 17 : προηριτ. P): *proposuit* [D-lat spec Cypr$_1$ Aug$_1$, *destinavit* vulg F-lat, *propositum habet* Jer$_1$].

8. rec δυνατος (*see notes*), with C[2]D[2·3]KLP rel [Chr] Thdrt Damasc [*potens est* latt(not G-lat) Ambrst Aug$_1$] : txt BC[1]D[1]Fא. for δε, γαρ D[1][-gr] 109-78 demid tol Syr.

covetous spirit which gives no more than it need. There is no need to alter the primitive meaning, or to make the *word signify* 'tenacity,' as Calv., De Wette, al.: he who defrauds the poor by stinting them πλεονεκτεῖ, in the literal sense. Still less must we with Chrys., al., refer πλεονεξ. to the Apostle,—μὴ νομίσητε, φησίν, ὅτι ὡς πλεονεκτοῦντες αὐτὴν λαμβάνομεν, Hom. xix. p. 573,—which is inconsistent with the interpretation φειδομένως below, and with εὐλογίαν, the corresponding word, which applies to the *spirit* of the givers).

6, 7.] *He enforces the last words by an assurance grounded in Scripture and partly cited from it, that as we sow, so shall we reap.* **τοῦτο**] Some supply φημί, as in ref.: others, as Meyer, would take it as an accus. absol., '*as regards this*,' viz. what has gone before. But I would rather take it as an imperfect construction, in which τοῦτο is used merely to point at the sentiment which is about to follow:—**But this**—(is true), or **But** (notice) **this** . . . **ἐπ᾽ εὐλογίαις**] **with blessings**: ἐπί denoting the accompanying state or circumstances, as in ref.: not, '*with a view to blessings*,' which will not suit the *second* ἐπ᾽ εὐλ.: nor as Theophyl., Œc., and E. V. μετὰ δαψιλείας, *bountifully*: which gives indeed the *sense*, but misses the meaning of the expression: see above. It refers to the *spirit* of the giver, who must be ἱλαρὸς δότης, not giving murmuringly, but *with blessings*, with a beneficent charitable spirit: such an one shall reap also with blessings, abundant and unspeakable. The only change of meaning in the second use of the expression is that the εὐλογίαι are *poured on him*, whereas in the first they *proceeded from him*: in both cases they are the element in which he works. So, we *bestow* the seed, but *receive* the harvest. The spirit with which we *sow*, is of ourselves: that with which we *reap*, depends on the *harvest*. So that the change of meaning is not arbitrary, but dependent on the nature of things. **7.**] Not, as Meyer and De W., a *limitation* of the foregoing, or else it would be expressed by some connecting particle,—but a continuation of the thought:—φειδομένως and ἐπ᾽ εὐλογίαις referred to the *spirit* of the giver; so does this verse,—ἐκ λύπης ἢ ἐξ ἀν. corresponding to φειδομένως,—ἱλαρός, to ἐπ᾽ εὐλογίαις. **καθὼς προήρηται**] **as he hath determined in his heart**; supply, 'so let him give:' i. e. let the προαίρεσις, the full consent of the free will, go with the gift; let it not be a reluctant offering, given **ἐκ λύπης**, out of an annoyed and troubled mind at having the gift extorted, nor ἐξ ἀνάγκης, out of necessity,—because compelled. Such givers,—that is implied,—God does *not* love. **δότης** is not a classical word. δότηρ, δωτήρ and (Hes. Op. 353) δώτης, are used (Meyer). **8—11.**] *He encourages them to a cheerful contribution by the assurance that God both can* (vv. 8, 9), *and will* (vv. 10, 11) *furnish them with the means of performing such deeds of beneficence.* **8.**] **δυνατεῖ** has the emphasis. I adopt the reading because after all it is difficult to imagine how so easy a construction as δυνατὸς ὁ θεός, should have been altered to δυνατεῖ, as Meyer supposes, or why the transcriber need have written δυνατός **ἐστιν** if the latter were a correction for δυνατεῖ, seeing that the verb substantive is just as frequently omitted in such clauses as inserted. **πᾶσαν χάριν**, 'etiam in bonis externis,' Bengel,—to which here the reference is: not excluding however the wider meaning of '*all* grace.' **περισσεῦσαι, to make to abound,**—reff.

σεῦσαι [x] εἰς ὑμᾶς, ἵνα [y] ἐν [y] παντὶ πάντοτε [z] πᾶσαν [a] αὐτάρ- BCDFK LPℵ a b
κειαν ἔχοντες [b] περισσεύητε [b] εἰς πᾶν [c] ἔργον [c] ἀγαθόν, c d e f g h k l m n
9 καθὼς γέγραπται [d] Ἐσκόρπισεν, ἔδωκεν τοῖς [e] πένησιν, o 17. 47
ἡ δικαιοσύνη αὐτοῦ [f] μένει [f] εἰς τὸν αἰῶνα. 10 ὁ δὲ [g] ἐπι-
χορηγῶν σπέρμα τῷ [i] σπείροντι καὶ ἄρτον εἰς [k] βρῶσιν
[l] χορηγήσει καὶ [m] πληθυνεῖ τὸν [n] σπόρον ὑμῶν καὶ [o] αὐξήσει
τὰ [p] γενήματα τῆς δικαιοσύνης ὑμῶν. 11 [q] ἐν [q] παντὶ [r] πλου-
τιζόμενοι εἰς [s] πᾶσαν [t] ἁπλότητα, [u] ἥτις [v] κατεργάζεται δι'
ἡμῶν [w] εὐχαριστίαν τῷ θεῷ, 12 ὅτι ἡ [x] διακονία τῆς [y] λει-

x = ch. ii. 9, 12. viii. 23. Gal. v. 10 al.
y ch. iv. 8 reff.
z = Acts xx. 19 reff.
a 1 Tim. vi. 6 only †. (-κης, Phil. iv. 11. -κεῖν, Deut. xxxii. 10.)
b Rom. iii. 7 reff.
c Acts ix. 36 reff.
d Matt. xii. 30 ‖ L. John x. 12. xvi. 32 only. 2 Kings xxii. 15. Psa. cxi. 9.
e here only. l. c. Exod. xxiii. 6 al. fr.
f John viii. 35 bis. xii. 34. Heb. vii. 24. 1 Pet. i. 25, from Isa. xl. 8. 1 John ii. 17 only.
g Gal. iii. 5. Col. ii. 19. 2 Pet. i. 5, 11 only †. Sir. xxv. 22 only. (-γία, Eph. iv. 16. Phil. i. 19.)
i ver. 6. Isa. lv. 10.
k Rom. xiv. 17 reff. Isa. l. c.
l 1 Pet. iv. 11 only. 3 Kings iv. 7. Sir. xxxix. 33.
m Acts vi. 7 reff.
n epp., here only. Mark iv. 26, 27. Luke viii. 5, 11 only. Deut. xi. 10.
o trans., 1 Cor. iii. 6, 7 reff.
p (γενν.) Matt. iii. 7 ‖ L. xii. 34. xxiii. 33. xxvi. 29 ‖ Mk. L. Luke xii. 18 only. Deut. xiv. 22. Hosea x. 12.
q ch. iv. 8 reff.
r ch. vi. 10. 1 Cor. i. 5 only. Gen. xiv. 23 al. participial constr., Acts xxiv. 10 reff.
s = Acts xx. 19 reff.
t Rom. xii. 8 reff.
u = Acts x. 41 reff.
v = Rom. iv. 15 reff.
w = Acts xxiv. 3 reff.
x Acts vi. 1 reff.
y Luke i. 23. Phil. ii. 17, 30. Heb. viii. 6. ix. 21 only. Num. viii. 22.

om *παντοτε* F(not F-lat) 7.

9. at end ins *του αιωνος* FK 238 vulg(not am demid [fuld]) æth.

10. for *σπερμα*, *σπορον* (*corrn from σπορον below*) BD[1]F. *σπειραντι* L m 47. rec *χορηγησαι πληθυναι αυξησαι* (*prob, as Meyer, corrns, in the idea that a* wish *was intended, and so the futures have been changed to* optatives: *for such they are, not* infinitives: *cf* 1 *Thess* iii. 11, 12; 2 *Thess* ii. 17; iii. 5,—*and var readd, Rom* xvi. 20), with D[3][-gr] Kℵ[3] rel syr goth Chr [Cyr$_1$] Thdrt Damasc: *χορηγησαι* and *πληθυναι* F[-gr]: *χορηγησαι* and *αυξησαι* L: txt BCD[1]Pℵ[1] m 17 [latt] copt æth arm [Euthal-ms] Cypr$_1$ Ambrst Aug$_1$. rec *γεννηματα*, with c k: txt BCDFKLPℵ rel Chr-mss [Cyr$_2$ Euthal-ms].

11. ins *ινα* bef *εν παντι* F Chr$_1$[(and-2-mss) Aug$_1$]. *υμων* C[2]P 66[2]-7. 71-4. 91. 119-20 syr-mg Damasc. for *τω θ.*, *θεου* B: om *τω* D[1].

ἵνα κ.τ.λ.] **in order that, having at all times in every thing all sufficiency** (of worldly substance; αὐτάρκ. is objective; not *contentedness*, subj.) **ye may abound towards** ('have an overplus for;' which is not inconsistent with αὐτάρκεια, seeing that αὐτ. does not *exclude* the having *more*, but only the having *less* than is sufficient: the idea of a man's having at all times and in all things a sufficiency, would presuppose that he had somewhat to spare) **every good work:** 9.] **as it is written** (i. e. fulfilling the character described in Scripture),—**He scattered abroad** (metaph. from *seed*: μετὰ δαψιλείας ἔδωκε, Chrys.), **he gave to the poor: his righteousness remaineth for ever.** In what sense is δικαιοσύνη used? Clearly in the only one warranted by the context—that of '*goodness proved by beneficence*,'—'a righteous deed, which shall not be forgotten,—as a sign of righteousness in character and conduct.' To build any inference from the text inconsistent with the great truths respecting δικαιοσύνη ever insisted on by Paul (as Chrys., p. 574, καὶ γὰρ δικαίους ποιεῖ (ἡ φιλανθρωπία), τὰ ἁμαρτήματα καθάπερ πῦρ ἀναλίσκουσα, ὅταν μετὰ δαψιλείας ἐκχέηται) is a manifest perversion. 10.] *Assurance that God will do this.* **But** (introduces the new assurance) **He that ministers seed to the sower and bread for eating** (in the physical world:—from ref. Isa., LXX. The Vulg., E. V., Luther, Calv., Grot., al., commit the mistake of joining κ. ἄρτον εἰς βρῶσιν with χορηγῆσαι, or -ει. **βρῶσις**, *the act of eating*: not = βρῶμα), **shall supply and multiply your seed** (i. e. the money for you to bestow,—answering to σπέρμα τῷ σπείροντι), **and will increase the fruits of your righteousness** (from ref. Hos.—the everlasting reward for your bestowals in Christ's name, as Matt. x. 42;—answering to ἄρτον εἰς βρῶσιν, which is the *result* of the sower's labours). 11.] *Method in which you will be thus blessed by God.* **In every thing being enriched** (the construction is an anacoluthon, as in ref. and in ch. i. 7 al.: nothing need be supplied) **unto all liberality** (i. e. in order that you may shew all liberality. On ἁπλ. see note, Rom. xii. 8), **which** (of a sort which) **brings about by our means** (as the distributors of it) **thanksgiving** (from those who will receive it) **to God.** 12.] *Explanation of the last clause.* **Because the ministration** (not on *our* part who distribute, though it might at first sight seem so: the next verse decides διακονία to mean, '*your administering by contribu-*

τουργίας ταύτης οὐ μόνον [z] ἐστὶν [a] προσαναπληροῦσα τὰ
[b] ὑστερήματα τῶν [c] ἁγίων, ἀλλὰ καὶ [d] περισσεύουσα διὰ
πολλῶν [w] εὐχαριστιῶν τῷ θεῷ· 13 διὰ τῆς [e] δοκιμῆς τῆς
[x] διακονίας ταύτης [f] δοξάζοντες τὸν θεὸν [f] ἐπὶ τῇ [g] ὑποταγῇ
τῆς [h] ὁμολογίας ὑμῶν [i] εἰς τὸ εὐαγγέλιον τοῦ χριστοῦ
καὶ [j] ἁπλότητι τῆς [kl] κοινωνίας [lm] εἰς αὐτοὺς καὶ [m] εἰς
πάντας, 14 καὶ αὐτῶν δεήσει ὑπὲρ ὑμῶν [n] ἐπιποθούντων
ὑμᾶς διὰ τὴν [o] ὑπερβάλλουσαν χάριν τοῦ θεοῦ ἐφ᾽ ὑμῖν.
15 [p] χάρις τῷ θεῷ [q] ἐπὶ τῇ [r] ἀνεκδιηγήτῳ αὐτοῦ [s] δωρεᾷ.

z constr., see Acts ii. 5 reff.
a ch. xi. 9 only †. Wisd. xix. 4 only.
b 1 Cor. xvi. 17 reff.
c Acts ix. 13 reff.
d Acts xvi. 5 reff.
e Rom. v. 4 reff.
f Luke ii. 20. Acts iv. 21. participial constr., ver. 11 al.
g Gal. ii. 5. 1 Tim. ii. 11. iii. 4 only †. (-τάσσειν, Rom. x. 3.)
h (=) 1 Tim. vi. 12, 13. Heb. iii. 1. iv. 14. x. 23 only. P.H.‡ (Deut. xii. 17.) gen. of reference, Rom. vii. 2 reff.
i = Acts xx. 21. j ver. 11. k Rom. xv. 26 reff. l Phil. i. 5.
m 1 Cor. xvi. 1 reff. n Rom. i. 11 reff. James iv. 5. constr., Phil. i. 8. ii. 26. 1 Pet. ii. 2. Ps. cxviii. 174. o ch. iii. 10 reff. p Rom. vi. 17. vii. 25. 1 Cor. xv. 57. ch. ii. 14. viii. 16.
q so ver. 13 reff. r here only †. s John iv. 10. Acts ii. 38 al. † Wisd. vii. 14. xvi. 25. 2 Macc. iv. 30 only. (Dan. ii. 6. v. 17 Theod.)

12. for θεω, χριστω B 46: *in Domino* vulg [F-lat].
13. ins και bef δια B. εαυτ. P.
14. for υμων, ημων B ℵ¹(but with υ written above) [ιμων F-gr(not G)]. aft υμας ins ιδιν ℵ³ [Ambrst, pref ιδειν 17].
15. rec aft χαρις ins δε, with C² D²·³[-gr] KLPℵ³ rel [syrr copt arm Chr₁ Euthal-ms] Ambrst Sedul: om BC¹D¹Fℵ¹ a 17 latt goth Aug₁ Pel Bede.

tion,' as in ver. 1) **of this public service** (**λειτ.** here seems to approach more nearly to its proper sense, serving the public by furnishing the means of outfit for some necessary purpose) **not only serves the end of supplying by its help the wants of the saints, but of abounding** (**περισσ.** *may be* transitive as in ver. 8, not only filling up, but '*causing to overflow*,' what were ὑστερήματα. But the usual intransitive sense is preferable. The emphasis is on προσαναπλ. and περισσεύουσα) **by means of many thanksgivings to God** (τῷ θεῷ with εὐχαρ., as in ver. 11, not with περισσεύουσα, which would not, as Meyer observes, give the sense of abounding *towards God*,—this would be εἰς τ. θεόν, see Rom. v. 15, or εἰς τ. δόξαν τ. θεοῦ, as in ch. iv. 15,—but the objectionable one of περισσεύει μοί τι, as John vi. 13; Luke ix. 17); **13.**] **they** (the recipients) **glorifying God** (the participle as in ver. 11, an anacoluthon) **by means of** (the proof, &c., is *the occasion, by means of which*) **the proof** (i. e. the tried reality —the substantial help yielded by) **of this** (your) **ministration, for the subjection of your confession as regards the Gospel of Christ** (i. e. that your ὁμολογία, (= 'you who confess Christ,') 'is really and truly subject in holy obedience, as regards the gospel of Christ.' But εἰς must not be joined with ὑποταγῇ, as '*obedience to*,' or (E. V.) '*subjection unto*,'—which is unexampled, and would more naturally have the art., τῇ εἰς: it is **towards**, '*in reference to*,' as in ref.) **and liberality of your contribution as regards them and as regards all men** (the same remarks apply to εἰς as above). Meyer would render ἁπλότητι τῆς κοινωνίας, '*the genuineness of your fellowship*:' but see note on Rom. xii. 8, and Rom. xv. 26. He also makes τῇ ὑποταγῇ τῆς ὁμολ., 'your subjection *to* your confession,' which perhaps *may be*, but disturbs the parallel of ἁπλότητι τ. κοιν. **14.**] The construction is very difficult. δεήσει may depend on περισσεύουσα, ver. 12 (but then we should expect διά as there),—or on δοξάζοντες (but then it should also depend on ἐπί—and they could not be said to glorify God *for* their own prayers. If on δοξάζοντες as the instrument whereby, it seems strange that αὐτῶν should be expressed), or αὐτῶν δεήσει ὑπὲρ ὑμ. ἐπιπ. ὑμ. may be (as Meyer) a gen. absol., '*while they desire you in prayers for you*' (but this seems forced, and as De W. observes, would require τῇ either before or after δεήσει). In the midst of these difficulties I see no way but this: the datives preceding, ὑποταγῇ and ἁπλότητι, have occasioned this also to be expressed in the dative, as though it depended on ἐπί, whereas it is in reality parallel with διὰ πολλῶν εὐχαριστιῶν and dependent on περισσεύουσα. Again, the words in another point of view are parallel with τῇ ὑποταγῇ and ἁπλότητι, inasmuch as these are ὑμῶν, and this δέησις is αὐτῶν. Amidst such complicated antitheses and attracted constructions, it may suffice if we discover the *clue* to the original formation of the sentence: the *meaning* is obvious enough, viz. that **glory also accrues to God by the prayers of the recipients, who are moved with the desire of Christian love**

X. 1 Αὐτὸς δὲ ἐγὼ Παῦλος [t] παρακαλῶ ὑμᾶς [t] διὰ
τῆς [u] πραΰτητος καὶ [v] ἐπιεικείας τοῦ χριστοῦ, ὃς [w] κατὰ
[w] πρόσωπον μὲν [x] ταπεινὸς ἐν ὑμῖν, [y] ἀπὼν δὲ [z] θαῤῥῶ εἰς
ὑμᾶς· 2 δέομαι δὲ [a] τὸ μὴ [y] παρὼν [z] θαῤῥῆσαι τῇ [b] πεποι-

BCDFK LPℵab cdefg hklmn o 17. 47

t Rom. xii. 1 reff.
u 1 Cor. iv. 21 reff.
v Acts xxiv. 4 (reff.) only +.
w ver. 7. Luke ii. 31. Acts iii. 13. 2 Chron. xiii. 8.
x Rom. xii. 16 reff.
y 1 Cor. v. 3 reff.
z ch. v. 6, 8 reff.
a constr., 1 Cor. iv. 6. Phil. ii. 6. Winer, edn. 6, § 44. 3. *b*.
b ch. i. 15 reff.

Chap. X. 1. rec πραοτητος, with CDKLℵ[3] rel: txt BFPℵ[1] 17. for εις, δι' B. for εις υμας, εν υμιν P [*in vobis* latt].
2. aft τη πεποιθησει ins ταυτη C[2](hence to οπλα της, ver 4, C is rewritten) copt.

(reff.) **to you, on account of the grace of God which abounds eminently towards** (over) **you** (**ἐφ' ὑμ.** belonging to **ὑπερβ.** not to **χάριν**, which would, but not of absolute necessity, require *τήν*).

15.] Having entered, in the three last verses, deeply into the thankful spirit which would be produced in these recipients of the bounty of the Corinthians, *he concludes with an ascription*, in the spirit also of a thankful recipient, *of unfeigned thanks to Him, who hath enriched us by the gift of His only Son, which brings with it that of all things else* (Rom. viii. 32), and is, in all its wonders of grace and riches of mercy, truly *ineffable*, ἀνεκδιήγητος. It is impossible to apply such a term, so emphatically placed as here, to any gift short of THAT ONE. And the ascription, as coming from Paul's fervent spirit, is very natural in this connexion. This interpretation is preferred by Chrys. Hom. xx. p. 579 f. (δωρεὰν δὲ ἐνταῦθα λέγει καὶ τὰ τοσαῦτα ἀγαθὰ τὰ διὰ τῆς ἐλεημοσύνης γινόμενα καὶ τοῖς λαμβάνουσι καὶ τοῖς παρέχουσιν· ἢ τὰ ἀπόῤῥητα ἀγαθὰ τὰ διὰ τῆς παρουσίας αὐτοῦ τῇ οἰκουμένῃ πάσῃ μετὰ πολλῆς δωρηθέντα τῆς φιλοτιμίας· ὃ καὶ μάλιστά ἐστιν ὑποπτεῦσαι. ἵνα γὰρ καὶ καταστείλῃ, καὶ δαψιλεστέρους ἐργάσηται, ὧν ἔτυχον παρὰ τοῦ θεοῦ, τούτων αὐτοὺς ἀναμιμνήσκει. καὶ γὰρ μέγιστον τοῦτο εἰς προτροπὴν ἀρετῆς ἁπάσης· διὸ καὶ ἐνταῦθα τὸν λόγον κατέκλεισεν), and Thl. (who, after beginning as Chrys., proceeds: ἢ καὶ τῶν ἀγαθῶν ἀναμιμνήσκει ὧν ἠξιώθημεν διὰ τῆς σαρκώσεως τοῦ χριστοῦ, ὡσανεὶ τοιαῦτα λέγων Μηδὲν μέγα νομίσητε ὑμεῖς ποιεῖν· ἀνεκδιήγητα γάρ εἰσι τὰ ἀγαθὰ ἃ ἐλάβομεν παρὰ θεοῦ· καὶ εἰ ὀλίγα καὶ φθαρτὰ δῶμεν, τί μέγα;) It is also given by Bengel ("Deus nobis dedit abundantiam bonorum internorum et externorum, quæ et ipsa est inenarrabilis, et fructus habet consimiles"), Meyer, al. The other explanation (see Chrys. above) is that of Calv., Grot., Est., al.

Chap. X. 1—XIII. 13.] Third Part of the Epistle. Defence of his apostolic dignity, and labours, and sufferings, against his adversaries: with announcement of his intended course towards them on his ensuing visit.

X. 1—6.] *He assures them of the spiritual nature, and power, of his apostolic office: and prays them not to make it necessary for him to use such authority against his traducers at his coming.*

1.] **δέ** marks the transition to a new subject,—and **αὐτός** points on to the personal characteristics mentioned below, 'Ego idem Paulus, qui . . . ;' the words **ἐγὼ Παῦλος** setting his Apostolic dignity in contrast with the depreciation which follows. Sometimes however we have *αὐτός* used, where the only object seems to be to *bring out the personality more strongly*: so 1 Thess. iii. 11; iv. 16; v. 23; 2 Thess. ii. 16; iii. 16. See also Rom. vii. 25: and ch. xii. 13:—and such may be the case here:—but the *ὅς* rather favours the former interpretation. **διὰ τ. πρ. κ. ἐπ.**] as in Rom. xii. 1, using *the meekness and gentleness of Christ* (Matt. xi. 29, 30) as *a motive whereby he conjures them*. And most appropriately: he beseeches them by the gentleness of Christ, not to compel him to use towards them a method of treatment so alien from that gentleness: "Remember how gentle my Master was, and force not me His servant to be otherwise towards you." "πραΰτης, lenitas, virtus magis absoluta: ἐπιείκεια, æquitas, magis refertur ad alios," Bengel. See many examples in Wetst. **ὃς κατὰ πρόσ.**] **Who in personal appearance indeed** (am) **mean among you** (he appropriates concessively, but at the same time with some irony,—so Chrys. Hom. xxi. p. 583, κατ' εἰρωνείαν φησί, τὰ ἐκείνων φθεγγόμενος,)—the imputation by which his adversaries strove to lessen the weight of his letters. **κατὰ πρ.** is not a Hebraism: Wetst. quotes several instances of its usage by Polybius), **but when absent am bold** (severe, *outspoken* in blame) **towards you;** 2.] **but** (however this may be, assuming this character of me to be true or not, as you please;—or, notwithstanding that I may have been hitherto *ταπεινός* among you) **I pray** (you) (not, *God*, as Bengel (1), al.) **that I may not** (**τὸ μή** sets the object of *δέομαι* in a stronger light, see reff.) **when present** ('as I intend to be:'—'*at my next visit*') **have to be bold** (see above) **with the con-**

θήσει ᾗ [c] λογίζομαι [d] τολμῆσαι ἐπί τινας τοὺς [e] λογιζομέ-
νους ἡμᾶς [e] ὡς [fg] κατὰ [fg] σάρκα περιπατοῦντας. 3 [h] ἐν
[h] σαρκὶ γὰρ [i] περιπατοῦντες οὐ [g] κατὰ [g] σάρκα [j] στρατευό-
μεθα· 4 τὰ γὰρ [k] ὅπλα τῆς [l] στρατείας ἡμῶν οὐ [m] σαρκικά,
ἀλλὰ δυνατὰ [n] τῷ θεῷ [o] πρὸς [p] καθαίρεσιν [q] ὀχυρωμάτων·
5 [r] λογισμοὺς [s] καθαιροῦντες καὶ πᾶν [t] ὕψωμα [u] ἐπαιρόμενον κατὰ τῆς γνώσεως [v] τοῦ θεοῦ, καὶ [w] αἰχμαλωτίζον-
τες πᾶν [x] νόημα εἰς τὴν [y] ὑπακοὴν τοῦ χριστοῦ, 6 καὶ

c = here only. 1 Kings xviii. 25. λογιζόμενοι ἥξειν ἅμα ἡλίῳ δύνοντι, κ.τ.λ., Xen. Anab. ii. 2. 13.
d = ch. xi. 21 bis. Il. κ. 232.
e Rom. viii. 36. 1 Cor. iv. 1. Amos vi. 5.
f Rom. viii. 4.
g Rom. i. 3 reff.
h = Gal. ii. 20. Phil. i. 22, 24. Col. ii. 1. 1 Tim. iii. 16. Philem. 16.
i ch. iv. 2 reff.
j 1 Cor. ix. 7 reff.
k = ch. vi. 7 (reff.).
l 1 Tim. i. 18 only †.
m 1 Cor. iii. 3 reff.
n dat., Acts vii. 20 reff.
o = ch. viii. 19 reff.
p ver. 8 reff.
q here only. Prov. xxi. 22. 1 Macc. v. 65.
r Rom. ii. 15 only. Prov. vi. 18. Jer. xi. 19.
s = Acts xix. 27. Lam. ii. 2.
t Rom. viii. 39 only. Job xxiv. 24. Judith x. 8. xiii. 4 only.
u = ch. xi. 20. Ezra iv. 19. Dan. xi. 14 Theod.
v gen. object., ch. ii. 14.
w Rom. vii. 23 reff.
x ch. ii. 11 reff.
y and constr., Rom. i. 5 reff.

om τινας C².

3. περιπατουντας F.

4. στρατιας (for -ειας) [B¹?(Tischdf)] CDFKLPℵ e l¹ m n 47: txt B[-corr(appy, Tischdf] 17.

5. καθαιρουντων D¹ Orig$_1$[?](and int$_3$: txt$_4$) Meth$_1$. om 2nd και F[(not F-lat) D-lat spec]. at end ins αγοντες D F[not F-lat] goth.

fidence (official peremptoriness, and reliance on my authority) **with which I reckon** (*am minded:* not passive, '*am reckoned,*' as Vulg., Luther, Beza, Estius, Bengel, al., which, as Meyer remarks, would naturally require ἀπών with τολμῆσαι) **to be bold towards [against] some, (namely) those who reckon (of) us as walking according to the flesh** (περιπατεῖν κατὰ σάρκα is well explained by Estius, 'hoc est, secundum carnales et humanos affectus vitam et actiones instituere . . . . . . Putabant enim Paulum, quando præsens erat, sive captandæ gratiæ causa, sive quod timeret offendere, vel simili affectu humano prohibitum fuisse, ne potestatem exerceret, quam absens per literas venditabat'). **3.**] The **γάρ** here shews that this verse is not the refutation of the charge κατὰ σάρκα περιπατεῖν, but a reason rendered for the δέομαι above; and ἐν σαρκί and κατὰ σάρκα *allude* only to the charge just mentioned. This indeed is shewn by the use, and enlargement in vv. 4—6, of στρατευόμεθα, instead of περιπατοῦμεν:—they who accuse us of walking after the flesh, shall find that we do not *war* after the flesh: therefore compel us not to use our weapons. **ἐν σαρ. γ. περιπ.**] **Although we walk in the flesh,** i. e. are found in the body,—yet we do not take our apostolic weapons from the flesh—do not make its rule our rule of warfare.

4.] *Enlargement of the idea in* **στρατευόμεθα.** If the warfare were according to the flesh, its weapons would be carnal; whereas now, as implied, they are spiritual, **δυνατὰ τῷ θεῷ,—powerful in the sight of God** (i. e. '*in His estimation,*' '*after His rule of warfare.*' It is not a Hebraism; see on ref. Acts; and for the dat., Winer, edn. 6, § 31. 4. Some render it, '*by means of God,*'—Beza, Grot., Estius, Bengel, al.: others, '*for God,*'—God's means of shewing his power,—Billroth, al., but wrongly) **in order to pulling down of strongholds** (see ref. Prov. So Philo de Abrah. § 38, vol. ii. p. 32, τὸν ἐπιτειχισμὸν τῶν ἐναντίων δοξῶν καθαιρεῖν,—see also de Confus. ling. § 26, vol. i. p. 424. Cf. Stanley: who thinks that recollections of the Mithridatic and piratical wars may have contributed to this imagery. The second of these, not more than sixty years before the Apostle's birth, and in the very scene of his earlier years, was ended by the reduction of 120 strongholds, and the capture of more than 10,000 prisoners). **5.**] The nom. καθαιροῦντες refers to ἡμεῖς, the implied subject of ver. 4;—this verse carrying on the figure in **ὀχυρωμάτων.** By **λογισμούς** he means, as Chrys., p. 585, τὸν τῦφον τὸν Ἑλληνικόν, καὶ τῶν σοφισμάτων κ. τῶν συλλογισμῶν τὴν ἰσχύν:—but not only these:—every towering conceit κατὰ σάρκα is also included. **κ. πᾶν ὕψ.**] **And every lofty edifice** (fortress or tower) **which is being raised** (or, raising itself) **against the knowledge of God** (i. e. the true knowledge of Him in the Gospel; not subjective here, but taken objectively, the *comparata* being *human knowledge*, as lifted up against the *knowledge of God*, i. e. the Gospel itself), **and leading captive every intent of the mind** (not '*thought,*' as E. V.: not *intellectual* subjection *here*, but that of the *will*, is intended) **into subjection to Christ** (in the figure he treats ἡ ὑπακοὴ τ. χριστοῦ, the new state into which the will is brought by its subjection, as the *country into which*

z ἐν z ἑτοίμῳ z ἔχοντες a ἐκδικῆσαι πᾶσαν b παρακοήν, ὅταν
c πληρωθῇ ὑμῶν ἡ d ὑπακοή.
7 Τὰ e κατὰ e πρόσωπον βλέπετε; εἴ τις f πέποιθεν
ἑαυτῷ g χριστοῦ εἶναι, τοῦτο h λογιζέσθω i πάλιν j ἀφ'
ἑαυτοῦ, h ὅτι καθὼς αὐτὸς χριστοῦ, οὕτως καὶ ἡμεῖς.
8 ἐάν k [τε] k γὰρ lm περισσότερόν m τι καυχήσωμαι περὶ

BCDFK LPℵ a b c d e f g h k l m n o 17. 47

z here only. Polyb. ii. 34. 2. (-ως ἔχειν Acts xxi. 13 reff.)
a Rom. xii. 19 reff.
b Rom. v. 19. Heb. ii. 2 only†. (-ούειν, Matt. xviii. 17.)
c = John iii. 29. al. fr. Dan. viii. 23.
d w. gen. subj., Rom. v. 19. xv. 18. xvi. 19 al.
e ver. 1.
f constr. dat., Phil. i. 14. Philem. 21. Prov. xiv. 16. Isa. xxviii. 17. inf., Rom. ii. 19.
g = 1 Cor. i. 12. iii. 23.
h constr., Rom. ii. 3 reff.
i = 1 Cor. xii. 21.
j ch. iii. 5 reff.
k = Rom. i. 26. vii. 7.
l ch. ii. 7 reff.
m Luke xii. 4 only.

6. for *εν ετοιμω*, *ετοιμως* D^1 Orig$_1$. aft *πληρωθη* ins *προτερον* C 39 fri Aug$_1$. *η υπακοη* bef *υμων* D$^{1\cdot3}$ F[(not F-lat) Ambrst Aug].—*ημων* D^1 F(not G).

7. for *πεποιθεν*, *δοκει πεποιθεναι* B. aft *χριστου* ins *δουλος* D^{1}F flor fuld Ambrst-ms. *παλιν* bef *λογιζεσθω* P [d]. for *αφ*, *εφ* BLℵ; *apud* vulg D-lat F-lat; *intra* G-lat. rec aft *ημεις* ins *χριστου*, with D^3[-gr] KL rel copt-wilk Damasc Œc: om BCD^{1}FPℵ 17 latt syrr goth æth arm Chr [Euthal-ms] Thdrt Thl Ambrst Pel.

8. om *τε* BF d 17 [arm] Chr Thl: ins CDKLPℵ rel [syr æth] Thdrt Damasc Ambrst. rec ins *και* bef *περισσοτερον*, with D^3[-gr] KLℵ^3 rel Syr syr-mg Chr Thdrt Damasc: om BCD^{1}FPℵ^1 c latt copt goth æth arm [Euthal-ms Ambrst]. *τι* bef *περισσ.* F[(not F-lat) D-lat] Ambrst Vig$_1$: om *τι* m^1 arm Sedul. *καυχησομαι* LPℵ c f k Thl: *-σωμεθα* 17.

it is led captive: compare Luke xxi. 24). **6.**] But perhaps some will not thus be subjected. In that case we are ready to inflict punishment on them: but not till every opportunity has been given them to join the ranks of the obedient; **when your obedience** (stress on *ὑμῶν*) **shall have been completed.** He does not mention any *persons*—not the *disobedient*, but **every** (case of) **disobedience**, and throws out *ὑμεῖς* into strong relief, as charitably embracing all, or nearly all, those to whom he was writing. Lachmann, strangely, and as it seems to me most absurdly, puts a period at *παρακοήν*, and joins *ὅταν πληρωθῇ ὑμ. ἡ ὑπακοή, τὰ κατὰ πρόσωπον βλέπετε*. More complete ignorance of the Apostle's style, and non-appreciation of the fine edge of his hortatory irony, can hardly be evinced, than this.

7—XII. 21.] *A digression, in which he vindicates his apostolic dignity, his fruitfulness in energy and in sufferings, and the honour put on him by the Lord in revelations made to him.* **7—11.**] He takes them on their own ground. They had looked on his outward appearance and designated it as mean. Well then, he says: '*do ye regard outward appearance?* even on that ground I will shew you that I am an Apostle—I will bear out the severity of my letters: I will demonstrate myself to be as much Christ's, as those who vaunt themselves to be especially His.' This rendering suits the context best, and keeps the sense of *κατὰ πρόσωπον* in ver. 1. The imperative rendering of Vulg., Ambrose, Theophyl., Billr., Rück., Olsh., De Wette, al.,—'*look at the things before your eyes,*' is objectionable (Meyer), (1) from altering the meaning of *κατὰ πρόσωπον*: (2) because it gives too tame a sense for the energy of the passage: (3) because *βλέπετε* generally in such sentences, in Paul's style, comes first, see 1 Cor. i. 26; x. 18; Phil. iii. 2 (3ce); Col. iv. 17. Another way, is to take it as said without a question, but indicatively. So Chrys., Calvin, 'Magni facitis alios qui magnis ampullis turgent,—me, quia ostentatione et jactantia careo, despicitis.' But in that case, surely some further intimation would have been given of such a sentiment than merely these words,—the break after which, without any connecting particle, would thus be exceedingly harsh. Others again fancifully mix up with *κατὰ πρόσωπ.* the supposed characteristics of the (?) *Christ-party*, the having seen Christ in the flesh: the being headed by James the brother of the Lord, &c. &c.

εἴ τις . . . .] **If any one believes himself to belong to Christ** (lit. '*trusts in himself to belong.*' From 1 Cor. i. 12, it certainly was one line taken by the adversaries of the Apostle to boast of a nearer connexion with, a more direct obedience to, Christ, in contradistinction to Paul: and to this mind among them he here alludes), **let him reckon this again out of his own mind** (i. e. let him think afresh, and come to a conclusion obvious to any one's common sense (*ἀφ' ἑαυτοῦ*) and not requiring any extraneous help to arrive at it), **that as he is Christ's, so also are we** (that whatever intimate connexion with or close service of Christ he professes, such, and no less, is mine). **8.**] This is shewn to be so. Even more boasting than he had ever yet made of his apostolic

τῆς [n] ἐξουσίας ἡμῶν [o] ἧς [p] ἔδωκεν ὁ κύριος εἰς [q] οἰκοδομὴν
...υμων C. καὶ οὐκ εἰς [r] καθαίρεσιν ὑμῶν, οὐκ [s] αἰσχυνθήσομαι, 9 ἵνα
BDFKL Pℵ a b c μὴ δόξω [t] ὡς [t] ἂν [u] ἐκφοβεῖν ὑμᾶς διὰ τῶν ἐπιστολῶν.
d e f g h 10 ὅτι αἱ μὲν ἐπιστολαί [v] φησιν [w] βαρεῖαι καὶ [x] ἰσχυραί, ἡ
k l m n o 17. 47 δὲ [y] παρουσία τοῦ σώματος [z] ἀσθενὴς καὶ ὁ λόγος [a] ἐξουθενημένος. 11 [b] τοῦτο [b] λογιζέσθω [c] ὁ [c] τοιοῦτος, [b] ὅτι οἷοί

n see 1 Cor. ix. 4, and passim. = ch. xiii. 10.
o attr., Acts i. 1 reff.
p so Matt. x. 1 al. fr.
q = Rom. xiv. 19 reff.
r ver. 4. ch. xiii. 10 only †. 1 Macc. iii. 43 only. (-ρεῖν, ver. 5.)
s Luke xvi. 3. Phil. i. 20. 1 Pet. iv. 16. 1 John ii. 28 only. Ps. xxxiv. 4.
t w. inf., here only. μεγάλα χρήματα ὡς ἂν εἶναι Ῥοδώπιος, Herod. ii. 135.
u here only. Levit. xxvi. 6. (-βος, Mark ix. 6.)
v see note.
w = Matt. xxiii. 23. Acts xxv. 7 (reff.).
x 1 Cor. i. 25 reff. iv. 10,
y 1 Cor. xvi. 17 reff.
z see 1 Cor. i. 25.
a Rom. xiv. 3 reff.
b ver. 7.
c Acts xxii. 22 reff.

om ημων C[1]P [115-9] Syr copt Chr. for κυριος, θεος D[1](and lat) F(-gr and lat) G-lat fri [Vig]. rec adds ημιν, with D[3][-gr] F[-gr] KLℵ[3] rel goth Thdrt [Damasc]: μοι Syr copt Chr[1] Thl: pref ημιν P 73 [vulg-clem F-lat am[2] syr arm Ambrst Vig]: om BC D[1](and lat) ℵ[1] 17 am[1](with tol al) æth [Euthal-ms]. for υμ., ημων F[-gr](not G).

9. δοξωμεν D[1][and lat] F(not F-lat) Ambrst. om ως αν D[1][-gr]. εκφοβουντες D G-lat(altern): εκφοβων P.

10. επιστ. bef μεν Bℵ[1]. φασιν B latt(exc D-lat) syrr goth. εξουδενημενος B.

power, would not disgrace him, but would be borne out by the fact. **For if we were to boast** (ἐάν is not concessive, but hypothetical, as in 1 Cor. xiii. 1. τε γάρ generally has a corresponding clause following, with τε, καί, δέ, or ἤ, as Eur. Phoen. 1313, ἐμός τε γὰρ παῖς γῆς ὄλωλ' ὑπερθανών, ... βοᾷ δὲ δῶμα πᾶν, so in reff. and Thucyd. i. 12 bis,—but sometimes the corresponding clause is wanting, being understood, or, as apparently here and in Heb. ii. 11, allowed to pass out of mind while following out the thought of the first clause. See Hartung, Partikellehre, i. 115. 5) **somewhat more abundantly** (than we have ever done: or than in vv. 3–6) **concerning our power which the Lord has given for building you up and not for pulling you down** (καὶ πῶς φησι, λογισμοὺς καθαιροῦντες; ὅτι αὐτὸ τοῦτο μάλιστα οἰκοδομῆς εἶδός ἐστι, τὸ τὰ κωλύματα ἀναιρεῖν, καὶ τὰ σαθρὰ διελέγχειν, καὶ τὰ ἀληθῆ συντιθέναι ἐν οἰκοδομῇ. Chrys. Hom. xxii. p. 589), **I shall not be put to shame** (οὐ δειχθήσομαι ψευδόμενος οὐδὲ ἀλαζονευόμενος, Chrys. ib.).

9.] follows on ver. 8, but requires some clause to be supplied such as 'And I say this,' or the like. Meyer would join it *immediately* to αἰσχυνθ., and regard it as the purpose to be served by *the fact verifying his boast*. But as De W. observes, a *particular* result like this can hardly be bound on to a *general* assertion like that of ver. 8. To suppose the *purpose* of Paul's boast of apostolic power being borne out, to be merely ἵνα μὴ δόξω, &c., would be out of keeping with the importance of the fact. So that ἵνα μὴ δόξω is much better taken *subjectively*—**I say this, because I wish not to seem, &c.** **ὡς ἄν**,—as Vulg. 'tanquam terrere vos.' It takes off the harshness of ἐκφοβεῖν. "ὡς ἄν in later (? see ref.) Greek, has the sense of 'quasi, tanquam,'—ἄν losing its proper force, in a commonly current expression; and the sense is much the same as that of ὡς alone." Meyer. Winer takes ὡς ἂν ἐκφοβεῖν as = ὡς ἂν ἐκφοβοῖμι, edn. 6, § 42. 6 (but see Moulton's note, p. 390, 1, who prefers the account given above), and is followed by Olsh., but this, in the presence of the above idiom, is unnecessary. **διὰ τῶν ἐπιστολῶν**] He had written *two* before this, see 1 Cor. v. 9; but this is not necessarily here implied: for he may reckon this which he is now writing. Still less can we infer hence that a *third* had been written before this (Bleek).

10.] **φησίν**, taken by Winer (edn. 6, § 58. 9. *b*. [β.]), De W., and Meyer, as impersonal —heißt es, '*men say*:' but why should not the τις of ver. 7, and ὁ τοιοῦτος of ver. 11, be the subject? **βαρεῖαι**] see in Wetst., definitions from the rhetoricians of βαρύτης in discourse. Among other illustrations of it, Aristides mentions ὅταν τι ἄτοπον ἑαυτῷ καταράσῃ· οἷον, τεθνάναι μᾶλλον ἢ ταῦτ' εἰρηκέναι βούλομαι (see 1 Cor. ix. 15), and ὅταν εἰς κρίσιν ἀγάγῃς τῶν τεθνεώτων ἐνδόξων, ... οἷον, πηλίκον ἂν στενάξαιεν οἱ πρόγονοι (see 1 Cor. xv. 18). **παρουσία . . . . ἀσθενής**] No countenance is given by these words to the idea that Paul was of weak physical constitution, or short in stature. His own explanation of them is sufficient as given in 1 Cor. ii. 1 ff. It is, that when he was present among them, he brought, not the strength of presence or words of the carnal teachers, but abjured all such influence and in fear and trembling preached Christ crucified. It was this, and not weakness of voice, which made his λόγος to be ἐξουθενημένος. At the same time, the contrast being between his *epistles* and his *word of mouth*, **his authority**

ἐσμεν [d] τῷ λόγῳ δι' ἐπιστολῶν [e] ἀπόντες, τοιοῦτοι καὶ
[e] παρόντες [d] τῷ ἔργῳ. 12 οὐ γὰρ [f] τολμῶμεν [g] ἐγκρῖναι ἢ
[h] συγκρῖναι [i] ἑαυτοὺς τισὶν τῶν [j] ἑαυτοὺς [j] συνιστανόντων·
ἀλλὰ αὐτοὶ [k] ἐν ἑαυτοῖς ἑαυτοὺς [kl] μετροῦντες, καὶ [h] συγκρίνοντες ἑαυτοὺς ἑαυτοῖς οὐ [m] συνιᾶσιν. 13 ἡμεῖς δὲ οὐκ

BDFK LPℵ a b c d e f g h k l m n o 17. 47

d Rom. xv. 18. Col. iii. 17. 1 John iii. 18. (see 1 Cor. iv. 19, 20. 1 Thess. i. 5.)
e 1 Cor. v. 3 reff.
f = 1 Cor. vi. 1 reff.
g here only †. Jos. B. J. ii. 8. 7, εἰς τὸν ὅμιλον ἐγκρίνεται.
h here bis. 1 Cor. ii. 13 only ‡. Gen. xl. 8 al. = Wisd. vii. 29. xv. 18.
i 1st pers., ch. iii. 1 reff.
j ch. iii. 1 (reff.).
k Matt. vii. 2 bis. Mark iv. 24 bis only.
l as above (k). Luke i. 38. Rev. xi. 1, 2. xxi. 15, 16, 17 only. Exod. xvi. 18.
m Rom. xv. 21 reff.

12. τολμω (for -μωμεν) B: τολμων m. for εγκρ., κριναι F n. add εαυτους D[1][and lat]. om τισιν D[1][-gr]. αλλ' D[1]L a m 17 [Chr_1]. om 3rd εαυτους ℵ[1](ins ℵ-corr[1 obl]). 2nd εαυτοις bef 4th εαυτους DK m Chr_1 Thdrt. rec συνιουσιν, with D[3]KLP rel: συνισασιν ℵ[1] [93]: txt B ℵ-corr[1·3] m 17 [Euthal-ms] Thdrt-ed.—om ου συνιασιν ημεις δε D[1](and lat) F vulg[but ins ημ. δε] Ambrst $Singcler_1$ Sedul Vig_1. (*Perhaps the transcriber's eye passed from ου above to ουκ follg, and so omitted all between: or perhaps on acct of the difficulty of the words. See the readings discussed in Stanley's note.*)

13. om ημεις δε [see above] D[1]F. rec ουχι, with D[3] rel Œc: txt BD[1]FKLPℵ

as *unaccompanied* or *accompanied* by his presence, it must be assumed, that there was *something* (see on ch. xii. 7) which discommended his appearance and delivery. See the traditional authorities for the Apostle's personal appearance, in Winer's Realw. vol. ii. p. 221, note. **11.] λογιζέσθω**, as in ver. 7. **ὁ τοιοῦτος**, viz. who thus speaks. The introduction of the verse without any connecting particle gives force and emphasis. After **παρόντες** supply ἐσμεν, not ἐσόμεθα. Not only the conduct of the Apostle on his next visit, but his *general character*, is in question.

12—18.] The difficulty of this passage is universally acknowledged. In early times Theodoret wrote: ἀσαφῶς ἅπαν τὸ χώρημα τοῦτο γέγραφεν, and adds as a reason, ἐναργῶς ἐλέγξαι τοὺς αἰτίους οὐ βουλόμενος. He substantiates what has just been said, by shewing *how unlike he is to those vain persons who boast of other men's labours;*—for he *boasts of what God had really done among them by him, and hopes that this boast may be yet more increased.*

12.] disclaims resemblance to those false teachers who made *themselves* their only standard. **For we do not venture** (ironical;—"dum dicit quod non faciat, notat quid isti faciant." Bengel) **to number ourselves with** (συναριθμῆσαι, Theophyl., Œcum., 'inserere,' Vulg.: see examples of this usage, with εἰς principally, but also with μετά and ἐπί w. gen., in Wetst.), **or compare ourselves with** (συγκρίνειν is properly, in classical Greek, '*to compound*,' or '*unite*:' but in later Greek, '*to compare*:' ὁ συγκριτικὸς τρόπος, with the grammarians, is the *comparative degree*) **some of those who commend themselves** (the charge made against *him*, ἑαυτὸν συνιστάνει, see ch. iii. 1; v. 12, he makes as a true one against the false teachers);—**but (they), themselves measuring themselves by themselves, and comparing themselves with themselves, are not wise.** The renderings are *very various.* Chrys. al., read συνιοῦσιν, and make it a particip., τουτέστι, μὴ αἰσθανομένοις πῶς εἰσὶ καταγέλαστοι τοιαῦτα ἀλαζονευόμενοι, p. 590: and see again below. Others, reading the same, take it rightly, as = συνιᾶσιν, but make μετροῦντες, &c., the object of συνιοῦσιν: '*know not that they are measuring,*' *&c.*: but the corresponding sentence, ἡμεῖς δὲ κ.τ.λ., shews that this sense would be irrelevant; for the Apostle does not oppose their *ignorance of* their foolish estimate of themselves to his own practice, but that foolish estimate itself.

Others again, as Emmerling and Olshausen, take ἀλλὰ—συνιοῦσιν (or -ᾶσιν) to apply to the *Apostle himself*, as contrasted with the τινές: '*We do not venture, &c.,—but we ourselves measure* (supply ἐσμεν, 'are in the habit of measuring') *ourselves by ourselves* (i. e. as ver. 18, by what the Lord has really made us to be), *and compare ourselves with ourselves, foolish as we are* (reputed to be:—συνιοῦσιν being a participle). *But foolish we are not: we will not boast ourselves,*' &c. But (1) this rendering would absolutely require the article before οὐ συνιοῦσιν, which, anarthrous, would imply, not an imputation, but *the fact:* (2) the mode of expression (αὐτοὶ ἐν ἑαυτοῖς ἑαυτ. μετρ.) would be a most extraordinary one to convey the meaning supposed:—and (3) the meaning itself would be irrelevant when obtained. Another variety of this rendering is to take (as Bos, Schrader, al.) ἑαυτοῖς, οὐ συνιοῦσιν, = ἑαυτοῖς, οὐ **τοῖς** συνιοῦσιν—with ourselves, not with the wise: which is also inadmissible.

Others again (see var. read.) would omit οὐ συνιᾶσιν (or -οῦσιν)· ἡμεῖς δέ,—which has been an evident correction, on the suppo-

M -σο-μεθα... BDFKL MP‎ℵ ab c d e f g h k l m n o 17. 47

ⁿ εἰς τὰ ᵒ ἄμετρα ⁿ καυχησόμεθα, ἀλλὰ κατὰ τὸ μέτρον τοῦ
ᵖ κανόνος ᑫ οὗ ʳ ἐμέρισεν ἡμῖν ὁ θεὸς ʳ μέτρου ˢ ἐφικέσθαι
ᵗ ἄχρι καὶ ὑμῶν. 14 οὐ γὰρ ὡς μὴ ˢ ἐφικνούμενοι εἰς
ὑμᾶς ᵘ ὑπερεκτείνομεν ᵛ ἑαυτούς, ᵗ ἄχρι γὰρ καὶ ὑμῶν
ʷ ἐφθάσαμεν ˣ ἐν τῷ εὐαγγελίῳ τοῦ χριστοῦ· 15 οὐκ

n = ver. 16. ch. xii. 6. ἐπαινεῖν εἰς . . . , Plato, Alc. i. p. 111. o here bis only†. (-τρητος, Isa. xxii. 18.) p vv. 15, 16. Gal. vi. 16. (Phil. iii. 16 v. r.) only. Mic. vii. 4. Judith xiii. 6 only. = Job xxxviii. 5 Aq. (σπαρτίον, LXX.) q attr., (ver. 8.) 1 John ii. 25. r Rom. xii. 3 (reff.). s here bis only†. Sir. xliii. 27 C Ed-vat. compl. 30 Ed-vat. &c. (C def. ἀφ. ABℵ) only. t = Acts xi. 5 reff. u here only†. v 1st pers., ver. 12. w Rom. ix. 31 reff. 2 Chron. xxviii. 9. Dan. viii. 7 Theod. x Rom. i. 9. ch. viii. 18 al.

c m 17 Chr_1 [Euthal-ms] Thdrt Damasc Thl. το αμετρον D[1]F : *immensum* (and so ver 15) latt. καυχωμενοι F Sing-cler : om D[1](and lat). οσου M [67[2]]. for εμερισεν, εμετρησεν M a 49. 64-7[2]. 74 [so latt(exc fri) Sing-cler Vig]. om ημιν F[not F-lat] L. for θεος, κυριος D $Epiph_1$ Vig_1. αφικεσθαι F 109 [$Epiph_1$] Chr-ms.

14. for ου γαρ ως, ως γαρ B 114-6 : ου γ. μη ως P [Chr]. for εφικνουμενοι, αφικν. K : αφικομενοι F : αφικουμενοι 106 : εφικομενοι Chr_1. om 2nd γαρ ℵ[1](ins ℵ-corr[1]) d.

sition that ἀλλὰ αὐτοὶ κ.τ.λ. belonged to *the Apostle*, to expunge words so much in the way of such an interpretation.

I may observe that much of the difficulty has arisen from taking αὐτοί with ἀλλά as the subject to οὐ συνιᾶσιν, whereas it belongs to what follows, ἀλλὰ αὐτοὶ ἐν ἑαυτ. ἑαυτ. μετρ. κ.τ.λ., as in the version given above: the subject of συνιᾶσιν being to be supplied, and the construction being an inaccurate one. Calvin well illustrates the *sense*, by the reputation which any moderately learned man gained among the ignorant monks of his day—"Si quis tenuem modo gustum elegantioris literaturæ habeat, . . . spargitur de eo mirabilis fama, adoratur inter sodales . . . . Inde præcipue monachis insolentissimus ille fastus quod se metiuntur ex se ipsis: quum in eorum claustris nihil sit præter barbariem, illic nihil mirum, si regnet luscus inter cæcos. Tales erant isti Pauli æmuli: sibi enim intus plaudebant, non considerantes quibus virtutibus constaret vera laus, quantumque a Pauli et similium excellentia distarent." **13.] But we** (opposed to those spoken of in last verse) **will not** (ever: will never allow ourselves to) **boast without measure** (lit. '*boast as far as to things unmeasured.*' **εἰς** with an adj. and the art. is used to signify the *extent to which;* so Herod. vii. 229, κατεκέατο ἐν Ἀλπηνοῖσι ὀφθαλμιῶντες ἐς τὸ ἔσχατον: as ἐπί with the same denotes the *direction towards which*, as ἐπὶ τὸ μεῖζον κοσμοῦντες, . . . ἐπὶ τὸ μυθῶδες ἐκνενικηκότα, Thucyd. i. 21,—**without measure,** scil. as they do who compare themselves with themselves and measure themselves by themselves,—for there is no standard for, no limit to, a man's good opinion of himself. The plur. τὰ ἄμετρα, instead of τὸ ἄμετρον, seems to be chosen to generalize the negative—'we adopt no such vague standard for our boasting'), **but according to the measure of the rule** (τὸ μέτρ. τοῦ καν.—'the measure *pointed out by* the rule,' gen. subj.) **which God apportioned to us as a measure, to reach as far as to you**—οὗ ἐμέρισεν ἡμῖν ὁ θ. μέτρου = ὃν ἐμέρ. ἡμ. ὁ θ. μέτρον, **which** (κανών) **God apportioned to us as a measure,**—or, as De W., τοῦ μέτρου ὃ ἐμέρ. ἡμ. ὁ θ., in which latter case μέτρου is in appos. with κανόνος: but I prefer the former. Mr. Green, Grammar of the N. T. dialect, p. 269, makes μέτρου governed by ἐφικέσθαι, as in οὕτω τάρβους ἀφικόμην, Eur. Phœn. 361; τοῦ βίου εὖ ἥκοντι, Herod. i. 30. My objections to this construction are, (1) that ἐφικνούμενοι εἰς ὑμᾶς is used absolutely in the very next clause, which makes it probable that the same usage is found here:—(2) that an unnecessary harshness is introduced, which I cannot persuade myself that the Apostle would have used, and which is apparent even in Mr. G.'s English, 'of advancing in standard as far as even you.' See Stanley's note. **ἐφικέσθαι** is the inf. of the purpose, **that we should reach**: or perhaps (but not so well) of the result, '*so that we reach.*' **14.]** Further explanation of ἐφικ. ἄχρι κ. ὑμ. **For we are not stretching ourselves beyond** (our bounds), **as** (we should be doing) **if we did not reach to you** (not, as if we *had not* reached to you, as Luth., Beza: the pres. betokens the *allotment* of the field of apostolic work as his own, 'ut si non perveniamus.' The μή shews that the case is only a *supposed* one: so also 1 Cor. iv. 18, but compare 1 Cor. ix. 26, ὡς **οὐκ** ἀέρα δέρων, where the case is the *real* one; see Winer, edn. 6, § 55. 1 [a]): **for even as far as** [**unto**] **you did we advance** (the *proper* meaning of φθάνω must hardly be pressed here: the Apostle would not introduce a

y Rom. ii. 17 reff. z Rom. xiv. 4 reff. a ch. vi. 5 reff. b = Matt. xiii. 32. Mark iv. 8. Col. i. 6, 10. 1 Pet. ii. 2 only. Exod. i. 7. trans., 1 Cor. iii. 6 reff. c = Matt. xxiii. 5. Luke i. 58 (Acts x. 46 reff.) only. Gen. xix. 19. d ver. 13 reff. e Rom. v. 17. ch. viii. 2. James i. 21 only. Eccles. i. 3 al.

BDFKL MPℵ a b c d e f g h k l m n o 17. 47

ⁿ εἰς τὰ ᵒ ἄμετρα ʸ καυχώμενοι ʸ ἐν ᶻ ἀλλοτρίοις ᵃ κόποις, ἐλπίδα δὲ ἔχοντες ᵇ αὐξανομένης τῆς πίστεως ὑμῶν ἐν ὑμῖν ᶜ μεγαλυνθῆναι κατὰ τὸν ᵈ κανόνα ἡμῶν εἰς ᵉ περισσείαν,
16 ᶠ εἰς τὰ ᵍ ὑπερέκεινα ὑμῶν ᶠ εὐαγγελίσασθαι, οὐκ ἐν ᶻ ἀλλοτρίῳ ᵈ κανόνι ʰ εἰς τὰ ἕτοιμα ʰ καυχήσασθαι.
17 ⁱ ὁ δὲ καυχώμενος ʸ ἐν κυρίῳ ʸ καυχάσθω·
18 οὐ γὰρ ὁ ἑαυτὸν ᵏ συνιστάνων, ˡ ἐκεῖνός ἐστιν ᵐ δόκιμος, ἀλλ' ὃν ὁ κύριος ᵏ συνίστησιν.

XI. 1 ⁿ Ὄφελον ᵒ ἀνείχεσθέ μου ᵖ μικρόν ᵖ τι ᑫ ἀφροσύ-

f 1 Pet. i. 25. see Heb. ii. 3. g here only †. h ver. 13. i Jer. ix. 24. 1 Cor. i. 31. k -άνειν, ver. 12. -άναι, Rom. iii. 5 reff. l so Mark vii. 15. John i. 18, 33 al. m = Rom. xiv. 18 reff. n 1 Cor. iv. 8 reff. o = Acts xviii. 14. 2 Tim. iv. 3. Heb. xiii. 22. Job vi. 26. p ver. 16 only. see Heb. ii. 7. q Mark vii. 22. vv. 17, 21 only. Job iv. 6.

15. om δε LM c l n. for υμων, ημων B d. for ημων, υμων ℵ.
18. for ου γαρ ο, ο γαρ (but corrd) ℵ[1]. rec (for συνιστανων) συνιστων, with D[3]KL rel Eus$_1$ Dial$_1$ Mac$_1$ Chr$_1$: συνισταν d: txt BD[1]FMPℵ m 17 Orig$_1$ Ephr$_1$ [Euthal-ms Antch$_1$] Thdrt Damasc[and ms$_2$]. δοκιμος bef εστιν Dℵ[1] [latt]: εστιν ο δοκ. F. αλλα B M[appy].

Chap. XI. 1. ωφελον D[3]FKL m n 17 [47 Euthal-ms] Chr-ms Œc: txt B D[1](οφιλον) MPℵ rel Chr$_2$ Thdrt Damasc Thl. elz ηνειχεσθε, with Chr-ed$_1$ Thl: ανεχεσθε K d m n[1] Chr-ms [Euthal-ms] Thdrt: txt B(Tischdf, expr) DFLMPℵ rel Chr-2-mss$_2$ Damasc Œc Thl-ms. μου aft μικ. τι αφρ. F latt [Lucif$_1$ Ambrst]. Steph om τι, with F[-gr] KLP rel D-lat(with G-lat fri) Chr$_3$ [Euthal-ms] Thdrt Damasc Œc Lucif [Ambrst]: ins B D-gr Mℵ n 17 vulg(and F-lat) goth [syr Chr$_1$] Thl. elz ins της bef αφροσυνης, with F a d [Chr$_1$] Thl: om BDPℵ n 17.—Steph τη αφροσυνη, with

distinct thought by a word of secondary importance in the sentence) **in the gospel** (the element in which our advance was made: 'the *gospel*'='the *promulgation of the gospel*'). 15.] in apposition with *οὐ γὰρ κ.τ.λ.* ver. 14, and carrying out the thought. **Not boasting without measure in other men's labours** (the element of the boasting), **but having a hope if** (or, *as*) **your faith grows, to be enlarged** (not as many Commentators, '*celebrated*:' the metaphor of *measure* still remains) **among you** (so Chrys., Theophyl., Est., Meyer. *ἐν ὑμ.* is not to be joined with *αὐξ.*, as Luth., Calv., Beza, Olsh., De W., in which case it would be superfluous) **according to our rule** (i. e. *our apportionment of apostolic work*, for we seek not *ὑπερεκτείνειν ἑαυτούς*) **unto abundance** ('so as to abound more than we now do,' viz. as ver. 16 explains), 16.] [**so as**] (with a view) **to preach the gospel as far as** (see on *εἰς τὰ ἄμ.*, ver. 15) **the parts beyond you** (Wetstein quotes from Thomas Magister, **ἐπέκεινα** *ῥήτορες* **λέγουσι . . . . ὑπερεκεῖνα** δὲ *μόνοι οἱ σύρφακες, la canaille*),—**not** (with a view) **to boast ourselves within another man's line** (*κανών* throughout seems to be used of a measuring *line*: according to the metaphor so common among us, 'in his line,'—i. e. 'within the line which Providence has marked out for him') **with regard to** (or, '*to the extent of*;' 'to extend our boasting to') **things ready made to our hands.** 17.] *He sets forth to them*, in contrast (δέ) to this boasting themselves in another's line, which was the practice of his adversaries, *wherein the only legitimate boasting must consist*: viz. *in the Lord*, the Source of all grace and strength and success in the ministry; see 1 Cor. xv. 10. 18.] The reason of this being, that *not the self-commender but he whom the Lord commends*, by selecting him as His instrument, as He had the Apostle, and giving him the *ἐπιστολὴ συστατική*, to be known and read by all men, of souls converted and churches founded, is **δόκιμος, approved**, i. e. really and in the end abiding the test of trial. **ἐκεῖνος** brings out the *distinction* of the man who is *δόκιμος*, —see reff. and Winer, edn. 6, § 23. 4. We have the usage in English in affirmative sentences, e. g. 'The Lord, he is the God,' 1 Kings xviii. 39: but not in negative ones. XI. His boasting of himself: and 1—4.] *apologetic introduction of it, by stating his motive,—viz. jealousy lest they should fall away from Christ.* 1.] **ἀνείχεσθε** is the Hellenistic form,—ἠνείχ. the Attic, not 'utinam *tolerassetis*,' as Calv., al.: the imperfect is put after *εἴθε, αἰ, ὄφελον*, &c., 'ubi optamus eam rerum conditionem, quam non

νης. ἀλλὰ καὶ [o] ἀνέχεσθέ μου. 2 [r] ζηλῶ γὰρ ὑμᾶς [s] θεοῦ
[s] ζήλῳ· [t] ἡρμοσάμην γὰρ ὑμᾶς ἑνὶ ἀνδρὶ [u] παρθένον [v] ἁγνὴν
[w] παραστῆσαι τῷ χριστῷ· 3 [x] φοβοῦμαι δὲ [xy] μή [xy] πως, ὡς
ὁ [z] ὄφις [a] ἐξηπάτησεν Εὖαν [b] ἐν τῇ [b] πανουργίᾳ αὐτοῦ,
[c] φθαρῇ τὰ [d] νοήματα ὑμῶν [e] ἀπὸ τῆς [f] ἁπλότητος καὶ
τῆς [g] ἁγνότητος τῆς [h] εἰς τὸν χριστόν. 4 εἰ μὲν γὰρ ὁ

r = Gal. iv. 17 bis. Zech. i. 14.
s Rom. x. 2. see Acts xxii. 3.
t here only. Prov. xix. 14.
u see Rev. xiv. 4. (1 Cor. vii. 25 reff.)
v = Tit. ii. 5. 1 Pet. iii. 2. Prov. xix. 13. (ch. vii. 11 reff.)
w = Luke ii. 22. Rom. vi. 13, 16, 19. xii. 1. ch. iv. 14. Ps. v. 3.
x ch. xii. 20. Gal. iv. 11.
y 1 Cor. ix. 27 reff.
z Rev. xii. 9. xx. 2. Gen. iii. 1 ff.
a Rom. vii. 11 reff.
b = 1 Cor, iii. 19 (reff.).
c 1 Cor. iii. 17 reff.
d ch. ii. 11 reff.
e = Rom. vii. 2. ix. 3 (reff.).
f Rom. xii. 8 reff.
g ch. vi. 6 only †.
h = ch. viii. 22. Eph. i. 15 al.

KL rel copt [Chr$_4$ Euthal-ms Thdrt Damasc Œc]. (M def.) αvασχεσθε ℵ.

3. om δε L. for πως, ποτε F a Chr-comm$_3$[txt$_{alic}$] : om D^1(and lat) vulg fri Clem$_1$ Lucif$_1$ [Ambrst Jer$_1$]. om ως L. rec ευαν bef εξηπατησεν, with DKL rel vulg(and F-lat) fri syr [goth arm] Clem$_1$ [Chr$_2$ Thdrt] Orig-int$_1$ Lucif$_1$ [Ambrst]: txt BFMP(ℵ) m 17 (Syr) copt æth Clem$_2$ Orig$_1$(-int$_1$) Eus$_1$ Damasc [Euthal-ms Gaud$_1$] Jer$_2$.—for ευαν, υμιν ℵ^1, but ευαν written above by ℵ$^{1 \text{ or } 3}$. om εν D^1·gr vulg F-lat fri Orig-int$_3$ Lucif [Ambrst Aug$_{sæpe}$]. rec ins ουτω bef φθαρη, with D$^{2\cdot 3}$[-gr] KLM rel vulg(and F-lat) syrr Orig$_1$(-int$_3$) Chr$_2$ Thdrt Damasc Archel$_1$ [Ambrst Aug$_{sæpe}$]: om BD^{1}FPℵ old-lat copt [goth] arm Clem$_2$ Eus$_2$ [Euthal-ms] Gaud$_1$ Lucif$_1$. rec om και της αγνοτ., with D^{3}KLMP rel vulg(and F-lat) Syr Clem$_2$ Orig$_1$(-int$_2$) Eus$_1$ Chr$_2$ Thdrt [Euthal-ms (Lucif$_1$ Ambrst) Jer$_2$]: ins BF ℵ^1(ℵ^3 has it in brackets) a 17 tol syr-w-ast copt goth æth Archel$_1$ [Damasc] Aug$_{sæpe}$, and (but transp απλ. and αγν.) D^1(with lat) Epiph$_1$. (*The omission appy arose from the similarity of endgs. Meyer and De Wette suppose* αγν. *to have been a gloss, to explain* απλ., *and afterwards to have found its way into the text.*) om τον FMℵ d 80-9.

esse sentimus:' Klotz ad Devar. p. 516, cited by Meyer. **μου** and **ἀφροσύνης** are not both genitives after *μικρόν τι*, as Meyer: nor is it so in the passage quoted by him, Job vi. 26, LXX: *οὐδὲ γὰρ ὑμῶν φθέγμα ῥήματος* (*φθέγματος ῥήματος ὑμῶν*, A) *ἀνέξομαι*. In both cases the personal pronoun is *governed by the verb*, as indeed here in *ἀνέχεσθέ μου* immediately following—and *μικρόν τι ἀφροσύνης* is the accusative of remote reference, as in the double accus. construction. **ἀλλὰ κ.**] **But** (why need I request this? for (**you really** (see note, ch. v. 3) **do bear with me.** The indicative is much better than the imperative rendering (as Vulg., Beza, Calvin, Grot., Estius, Bengel, al.),—which, after *ὄφελον ἀνείχ.*, is very flat, and gives no account of the *καί*. He says it, to shew them that he does not express the wish as supposing them void of tolerance for his weakness, but as having *experienced some* at their hands, and now *requiring more.* **2.**] 'That forbearance which you do really extend to me, and for more of which I now pray, is due from you, and I claim to have it exercised by you, because I have undertaken to present you to Christ as a chaste bride to her husband, and (ver. 3) I am jealous for fear of your falling away from Him.' **θεοῦ ζήλῳ**] so *εἰλικρινείᾳ τοῦ θεοῦ*, ch. i. 12: **a godly jealousy**: see note there. Meyer after Chrys., Estius, al., would render it, '*with God's jealousy*,' 'with such a jealousy as God has.' But though *θεοῦ ζήλῳ* and *τῷ τοῦ θεοῦ ζήλῳ* are for most purposes identical, I cannot but think that the latter expression would have been chosen to express such an idea as '*with the zeal which God has.*' And the rendering, 'with a *godly* zeal,' i. e. one which *has God's honour at heart*, satisfies well what follows: see below. **ἡρμοσάμην**] **I betrothed you** (viz. at your conversion: *προμνήστωρ ὑμῶν ἐγενόμην καὶ τοῦ γάμου μεσίτης*, Theodoret. Ordinarily, the *father*, or the *bridesman* (*παρανύμφιος*) is said *ἁρμόζειν*: the *middle* voice is used of the bridegroom only. So among other examples in Wetst.,—*εἶχεν ἐν δόμοις Αἴγισθος, οὐδ' ἥρμοζε νυμφίῳ τινί*, Eur. Electr. 24,—and *ἁρμοσαμένου Λευτυχίδεω Πέρκαλον τὴν Χίλωνος θυγατέρα, καὶ σχὼν γυναῖκα . . .*, Herod. vi. 65. But in Philo we have *γάμος ὃν ἁρμόζεται ἡδονή*, de Abr. § 20, vol. ii. p. 15) **to one husband, to present** (i. e. in order that I may present in you[, present you as]) **a chaste virgin to Christ** (viz. *at His coming*: *ὁ μὲν οὖν παρὼν καιρὸς μνηστείας ἐστίν· ὁ δὲ μέλλων τῶν γάμων, ὅτε κραυγὴ γίνεται, ἰδοὺ ὁ νυμφίος.* Theophyl.) **τῷ χρ.** is not in constructive apposition with *ἑνὶ ἀνδρί*, but explains and fixes it: the emphasis being on *παρθένον ἁγνήν*. **3.**] *But he fears their being seduced from their fidelity to Christ.* **ὁ ὄφις**] He takes for granted that the Corinthians recognized the agency of Satan in the (well-known) serpent: see vv. 13—15, where his *μετασχηματισμός* for the sake of deceit is alluded to. **ἐν τῇ παν. αὐτοῦ**] in

[i] ἐρχόμενος ἄλλον [k] Ἰησοῦν [k] κηρύσσει ὃν οὐκ ἐκηρύξαμεν,
ἢ [l] πνεῦμα [m] ἕτερον [l] λαμβάνετε ὃ οὐκ ἐλάβετε, ἢ εὐαγγέλιον [m] ἕτερον ὃ οὐκ ἐδέξασθε, καλῶς [n] ἀνέχεσθε.
5 [o] λογίζομαι [p] γὰρ μηδὲν [q] ὑστερηκέναι τῶν [r] ὑπερλίαν

BDFKL MP℞ a b c d e f g h k l m n o 17. 47

i particip., Gal. v. 8, 10. 1 Thess. v. 24.
k Acts ix. 20 reff.
l Acts viii. 15 reff.
m = Gal. i. 6 al.
n ver. 1.
o constr., Rom. xiv. 14 reff.
p Acts xxiv. 5. 2 Tim. ii. 7.
q constr., Rom. iii. 23. (ch. i. 7 reff.)
r ch. xii. 11 only †.

4. for ιησ., χριστον F 4[1] vulg arm Ambrst Pel. for ελαβετε, εδεξασθε F. in ℵ the 2nd ετερον is written twice, but marked for erasure by ℵ[1] or corr[1]. add λαμβανετε F[not F-lat]. rec ηνειχεσθε (*see ver* 1), with rel Chr_2-ed Thdrt-ed : ανειχεσθε D[3]GKLMPℵ b[1] e f g m o $Chr\text{-}ms_1$ [Euthal-ms] Damasc, ενειχεσται F : txt B[D[1]] 17 Cyr_1, *patimini* fri.
5. for γαρ, δε B 178 arm. aft υστερηκεναι ins εν υμιν D[1](and lat) fri(with fuld tol).

(i. e. *by means of*, as the *element* in which the deed was done) **his versatility** (or subtlety),—**so** (οὕτω has been a gloss from the margin) **your thoughts** ('*sentiments*,' ref. and ch. x. 5) **be corrupted from** (pregnant construction, = be corrupted, and seduced from) **your simplicity** (singleness of affection) **and your chastity towards Christ** (**εἰς χρ.** is not = ἐν χριστῷ, as Vulg., E. V., Beza, Calvin, al.).

4, 5.] The thought here seems to be this:—'If these new teachers had brought with them a *new Gospel*, superseding that which I preached, they might have some claim to your regard. But, since there is *but one* gospel, that which I preached to you, and which they pretend to preach also, I submit that *in that one* no claim to regard is prior to mine.' Observe, that *the whole hypothesis is ironical:* it is fixed and clear that *there can be no such new gospel:* therefore the inference is the stronger. **For** (the whole sentence is steeped in irony:—'the serpent deceived Eve by *subtlety:* I fear for you, but not because the new teachers use such subtlety—if they did, if the temptation were really formidable, there would be some excuse.' All this lies in the γάρ) **if indeed** (εἰ μέν introduces a *reality*, and is full here of deep irony. Cf. Il. α. 135, ἀλλ' εἰ μὲν δώσουσι γέρας μεγάθυμοι Ἀχαιοί : 'if the Achæans shall really give me another gift;' and μ. 138—142, εἰ μὲν δὴ Ἀντιμάχοιο δαΐφρονος υἱέες ἐστὸν . . . νῦν μὲν δὴ τοῦ πατρὸς ἀεικέα τίσετε λώβην . . . , 'if ye really are, &c., . . . ye verily will.' . . . . See Hartung, Partikellehre, ii. 414) **he that cometh** (viz. the false teachers generically thus designated: but here too perhaps there is irony: ὁ ἐρχόμενος was a ῥῆμα σεμνόν) **is preaching** (the indicative pres. carries on the ironical assumption, so λαμβ. below) **another Jesus whom we preached not, or ye are receiving a different Spirit** (ἄλλος, distinctive of individuality, ἕτερος of kind), **which ye received not** (from us), **or another gospel which ye accepted not** (ἐλάβ., ἐδέξ.,—'verba diversa, rei apta. Non concurrit voluntas hominis in accipiendo Spiritu, ut in recipiendo evangelio.' Bengel. But singularly enough, in English, usage has attached the *voluntary act* to the verb '*accept*') **ye with reason bear with him** (irony again: for they not only bore with, but preferred them to their father in the faith. The sense is: "there seems to be some excuse in that case,—but even in that, really there is none,—for your tolerating him." On the rec., Bengel remarks: 'Ponit conditionem, ex parte rei, impossibilem: ideo dicit in imperfecto, *tolerаretis:* sed pro conatu pseudapostolorum, non modo possibilem, sed plane præsentem: ideo dicit in præsenti, *prædicat*.' Similarly Meyer. See Winer, edn. 6, § 42. 2. That the rendering above given is right, seems to me beyond question. It is the only one which reaches the depth of the exquisite irony of the sentence, at the same time that it satisfies all grammatical requirements.

5.] See above. 'Seeing that there is *but one* gospel, and they and I profess to preach *one* Jesus and impart *one* Spirit, they have no such claim: mine is superior'): **for I reckon that in no respect do I fall short of** (the perf. sets forth the *past and present* truth of the fact) **these overmuch Apostles.** **τῶν ὑπερλίαν ἀποστ.** has very commonly been taken to mean bona fide '*the greatest Apostles*,' i. e. Peter, James, and John, or perhaps *the Twelve:* but (1) this hardly seems to suit the expression ὑπερλίαν, in which I cannot help seeing, with De W., some bitterness: (2) it would be alien from the spirit of the passage, in which he institutes no comparison whatever between himself and *the other Apostles*, but only between himself and *the false teachers*. (3) had any such comparison been here intended, the 'punctum comparationis' would not have been, *personal eminence in fruits of apostolic work and sufferings*, still less, seeing that the other Apostles were unlearned also, the distinction which immediately follows, between an ἰδιώτης, and one pretending to more skill,—but priority of arrival and

ἀποστόλων. 6 εἰ δὲ καὶ [s] ἰδιώτης τῷ [t] λόγῳ, [u] ἀλλ' οὐ τῇ
[v] γνώσει, ἀλλ' [w] ἐν [w] παντὶ [x] φανερώσαντες [y] ἐν [y] πᾶσιν εἰς
ὑμᾶς. 7 [z] ἢ [a] ἁμαρτίαν [ab] ἐποίησα, ἐμαυτὸν [cd] ταπεινῶν ἵνα
ὑμεῖς [ce] ὑψωθῆτε, ὅτι [f] δωρεὰν τὸ τοῦ [g] θεοῦ [g] εὐαγγέλιον
[h] εὐηγγελισάμην ὑμῖν; 8 ἄλλας [i] ἐκκλησίας [k] ἐσύλησα λαβὼν

s Acts iv. 13 reff. t = 1 Cor. ii. 1. u 1 Cor. iv. 15 reff. v = 1 Cor. xii. 8. w ch. iv. 8 reff. x = Col. iv. 4. y masc., 1 Cor. viii. 7. see Phil. iv. 12. Heb. xiii. 4. z so 1 Cor. vi. 2. a John viii. 34. James v. 15. 1 Pet. ii. 22. 1 John iii. 4, 8, 9. 3 Kings xvi. 19. b so 1 Cor. vi. 18. Gen. xxxix. 9. c Matt. xxiii. 12 bis. Luke xiv. 11 bis. xviii. 14 bis. James iv. 10. 1 Pet. v. 6. Ps. lxxxvii. 15. d as above (c). Matt. xviii. 4. Luke iii. 5, from Isa. xl. 4. ch. xii. 21. Phil. ii. 8. iv. 12 only. e Acts ii. 23. xiii. 7 al. Deut. xvii. 20. f = Rom. iii. 24 reff. g Rom. xv. 16 reff. h constr., 1 Cor. xv. 1 reff. i plur., Rom. xvi. 16 reff. k here only +. Ep. Jer. 18 only. see Acts xix. 37. Rom. ii. 22. Col. ii. 8. (-εύειν, Exod. iii. 22 Symm.? [rather Aq.])

6. om δε D[1](and lat) am(with demid [tol] F-lat G-lat) copt goth arm. aft ιδιωτης ins ειμι D[1](and lat) G-lat [demid (Ambrst)]. rec φανερωθεντες, with D[3][-gr] KLPℵ[3] rel fri syrr copt Chr, Thdrt [Euthal-ms Damasc] Sedul(*manifesti sumus* [so vulg-clem harl tol]): φανερωθεις (*manifestus* or *-status sum*) D[1·2](and lat) G-lat(altern) am(with demid flor F-lat) lat-ff: -ρωθεντι 1. 108: txt B F[-gr] ℵ 17 and, adding εαυτους, M 108[2] 8-pe goth arm: φανερωσαι εαυτους 67[2]. (*The variety appears to have arisen from the difficulty of* φανερωσαντες, *which became* φαν. εαυτους, *and then* -ρωθεντες.) om εν πασιν F vulg fri Syr Ambrst [Pel].
7. aft ἢ ins μη F vulg fri [Ambrst Pel]. for εμαυτον, εαυτον DFLP h 93.

teaching in Corinth. (4) the expression **ψευδ**απόστολος ver. 13, seems to me to refer to, and give the plain sense of, this ironical designation of ὑπερλίαν ἀπόστολοι. (5) the same expression ch. xii. 11 appears even more plainly than here to require this explanation. The above explanation is that of Beza, Michaelis, Schulz, Fritzsche, Billroth, Rückert, Olsh., Meyer, De Wette.

ὑπερλίαν is not found in classic Greek: but Wetstein cites from Eustath. Od. α. p. 27, 35: ἔστι γάρ ποτε καὶ τῷ λίαν κατὰ τὴν τραγῳδίαν χρᾶσθαι καλῶς, καθ' ὃ σημαινόμενον λεγομέν τινα ὑπερλίαν σοφόν. Meyer instances as analogous, ὑπεράγαν (2 Macc. x. 34), ὑπέρευ (ὑπέρευ πεπολίτευμαι, Demosth. 228. 17), and the frequent use by Paul of compounds of ὑπέρ. It has been the practice of Protestant Commentators (e. g. Bengel, Macknight) to adduce this verse against the primacy of Peter, and of the Romanists (e. g. Corn.-a-Lapide) to evade the inference by supposing the pre-eminence to be only in gifts and preaching, not in power and jurisdiction. All this will fall to the ground with the supposed reference to the other Apostles. **6.**] Explains that, *though in one particular he may fall short of them,* viz. in *rhetorical finish* and *word-wisdom,* yet *in real knowledge, not so.* **ἰδιώτης**] a laic,—a man not professionally acquainted with that which he undertakes, see reff. The Apostle disclaims mere rhetorical aptitude and power in 1 Cor. ii. 1 ff. **ἀλλά** brings out the contrast, see reff.:—εἴ τοι σύ γε σεωϋτοῦ μὴ προορᾷς, ἀλλ' ἡμῖν τοῦτό ἐστι οὐ περιοπτέον, Herod. v. 39. **τῇ γνώσει**] the depth of his knowledge of the mystery of the gospel, see Eph. iii. 1—4.

ἀλλ' ἐν παντί] **But in every matter we made things manifest** (i. e. *the things of the gospel,* thereby shewing our γνῶσις;—not, τὴν γνῶσιν. Meyer and De W. suppose φανερώσαντες to have been a gloss for φανερωθέντες, especially as it is followed in some mss. by ἑαυτούς, and to have been the more readily received into the text, because it might easily be taken with γνῶσιν. But how improbable that the easy φανερωθέντες should have been replaced by the harsh -σαντες. Much rather would the latter be replaced by φανερωθέντες from ch. v. 11) **before all men** (ἐν πᾶσιν, being separated from ἐν παντί by the verb, cannot be coupled with it, as in ref. Phil., but must mean *among all*) **unto you** (i. e. with a view to your benefit: not = '*to you,*' in which sense the *dative* is always found after φανερόω: see Rom. iii. 21, πεφανέρωται . . . . . εἰς πάντας κ. ἐπὶ πάντας . . . .). **7.**] Another particular in which he was not behind, but excelled, the ὑπερλίαν ἀπόστολοι; viz. *the gratuitous exercise of his ministry among them.* On the sense, see 1 Cor. ix. 1 ff. and notes. The supposition is one of sharp irony. **ἐμ. ταπεινῶν**] See Acts xviii. 3. The exaltation which *they received* by *his demeaning himself* was that of *reception into the blessings of the gospel,* which was more effectually wrought thereby: not merely, their being thus more favoured temporarily, or in comparison with other churches. **ὅτι δωρ.,** &c., is epexegetical of ἐμαυτὸν ταπεινῶν;—**in that I gratuitously, &c.**:—not, as Meyer, ἁμαρτ. ἐποίησα ὅτι, making ἐμαυτὸν . . . ὑψωθ. parenthetical. It was his wish to preach to them gratuitously, which necessitated his ταπεινοῦν ἑαυτόν,

l Luke iii. 14. Rom. vi. 23. 1 Cor. ix. 7 only +. Esdr. iv. 56. 1 Macc. iii. 28. xiv. 32 only. m = ch. viii. 19 reff. n = 2 Tim. iv. 11. Heb. i. 14. o Acts xii. 20. Gal. iv. 18, 20 only. p = Luke xv. 14. Phil. iv. 12. Heb. xi. 37. Sir. xiii. 4. q ch. xii. 13, 14 only +. (ναρκᾷν, Gen. xxxii. 25, 32. Job xxxiii. 19.) r 1 Cor. xvi. 17 reff. s ch. ix. 12 only +. Wisd. xix. 4 only. t ch. iv. 8 reff. u here only +. v = 1 Tim. v. 22. James i. 27. Wisd. x. 5. w Acts xiii. 15. 1 Cor. viii. 7. 1 John i. 8. x see Rom. iii. 7. xv. 8. y Rom. iii. 27 reff. z Rom. iii. 19. Heb. xi. 33 only. Hos. ii. 6. (ἐμφράττ., Dan. vi. 22 Theod.) a Rom. xv. 23 reff. b Rom. ix. 32 reff.

BDFKL MPℵ a c d e f h k l m o 17. 47

[l] ὀψώνιον [m] πρὸς τὴν ὑμῶν [n] διακονίαν, καὶ [o] παρὼν [o] πρὸς
ὑμᾶς καὶ [p] ὑστερηθεὶς οὐ [q] κατενάρκησα οὐθενός 9 (τὸ γὰρ
[r] ὑστέρημά μου [s] προσανεπλήρωσαν οἱ ἀδελφοὶ ἐλθόντες
ἀπὸ Μακεδονίας)· καὶ [t] ἐν [t] παντὶ [u] ἀβαρῆ ἐμαυτὸν ὑμῖν
[v] ἐτήρησα καὶ [v] τηρήσω. 10 [w] ἔστιν [x] ἀλήθεια [x] χριστοῦ [w] ἐν
ἐμοί, ὅτι ἡ [y] καύχησις αὕτη οὐ [z] φραγήσεται εἰς ἐμὲ ἐν
τοῖς [a] κλίμασιν τῆς Ἀχαΐας. 11 [b] διὰ τί; ὅτι οὐκ ἀγαπῶ

8. (ουθενος, so BMPℵ m 17 [Euthal-ms] Damasc(appy).)
9. rec υμιν bef εμαυτον, with D-gr FLℵ[3] rel [goth arm Thdrt Damasc]: om υμιν K m[1] Syr: txt BMPℵ[1] m[2] 17 vulg D-lat [F-lat Euthal-ms].
10. Steph (for φραγησεται) σφραγισεται, with d: σφραγησεται 14. 74. 238: txt BD FKLMPℵ rel. for εις εμε, εν εμοι F a[1] 2. 120. om της F.
11. om οτι B om ὁ D[1] Thdrt. (M uncert.)

i. e. not exercising the apostolic power which he might have exercised, but living on subsidies from others, besides (which he does not here distinctly allude to) his working with his own hands at Corinth. See Stanley. 8.] The '*other churches*' were the Macedonian, cf. ver. 9. Among them the Philippians were probably conspicuous, retaining as doubtless they did, their former affection to him; see Phil. iv. 15, 16. ἐσύλησα is hyperbolic, to bring out the contrast, and shame them. **ὀψ.**, see reff., **wages**; more properly here **subsidy**. **πρὸς τ. ὑμ. διακ.**] **in order to** (to support me in) **my ministration to you**, gen. obj. **ἄλλας** and **ὑμῶν** stand in the emphatic positions, as contrasted. In the former sentence, he implied that he *brought with him* from Macedonia supplies towards his maintenance at Corinth: λαβὼν . . . **πρὸς τ.** ὑμ. διακ.: here, he speaks of a new supply during his residence with the Corinthians, *when those resources failed*. **κατενάρκησα**] apparently = κατεβάρησα, ch. xii. 16. Hesych. interprets it ἐβάρυνα. Jerome, Ep. cxxi. (cli.) ad Algasiam, quæst. 10, vol. i. p. 879, says, 'multa sunt verba, quibus juxta morem urbis et provinciæ suæ familiarius Apostolus utitur: e quibus ex. gr. pauca ponenda sunt . . . . Et, οὐ κατενάρκησα ὑμᾶς, hoc est, non gravavi vos . . . quibus et aliis multis usque hodie utuntur Cilices.' Theophylact and Œcum. mention a rendering, οὐκ ἠμέλησα, ἢ ῥαθυμοτέρως πρὸς τὸ κήρυγμα γέγονα: and Beza, following the etymology, interprets οὐκ ἐνάρκησα κατ' οὐδενός, '*cum cujusquam incommodo.*' But the former meaning suits the context better. The word is found no where else in Greek. ἀποναρκάω occurs in Plutarch, de Liber. Educatione, p. 8, F (Wetst.), ἀποναρκῶσι κ. φρίττουσι πρὸς τοὺς πόνους. On the government of the genitive by verbs compounded with κατά, see Matthiæ, § 376.

9.] **For** (reason why he burdened no one) **the brethren** (*who*, he does not say: their names were well known to the Corinthians. Possibly, Timotheus and Silas, Acts xviii. 5) **when they came from Macedonia** (not as E. V., '*which came*,' οἱ ἐλθόντες) **brought a fresh supply of my want** (or perhaps προσαν. is used without the idea of *additional* supply, as in ch. ix. 12, the πρός merely denoting *direction*): **and in every thing I kept myself** ('*during my residence*:' not, '*have kept myself*,' as E. V.) **unburdensome to you, and will keep myself.** **10.**] **The truth of Christ is in me, that . . .**; i.e. '*I speak according to that truth of which Christ Himself was our example, when I say, that . . .*;'—there is no oath, nor even asseveration, as E. V. and most Commentators introduce. The expression is exactly analogous to Rom. ix. 1. **ἡ καύχ. . . . .**] **this boasting** (not = καύχημα, here or any where else) **shall not be stopped** (supply τὸ στόμα, which is not expressed, because καύχησις being itself a matter of *utterance*, suits the sense of the verb without it) **as regards** (or **against**) **me** (καύχ. is as it were personified—shall not have its mouth stopped as regards me) **in the regions of Achaia** (where the καύχησις is imagined as *being* and *speaking*).

11.] He *presupposes*, and *negatives*, a *reason* likely to be given for this resolution; viz. that he *loves them not*, and *therefore* will be under no obligation to them:

ὑμᾶς; ὁ [c] θεὸς [c] οἶδεν. 12 ὃ δὲ ποιῶ, καὶ ποιήσω, ἵνα
[d] ἐκκόψω τὴν [e] ἀφορμὴν τῶν θελόντων [e] ἀφορμήν, ἵνα [fg] ἐν
ᾧ [g] καυχῶνται [h] εὑρεθῶσιν καθὼς καὶ ἡμεῖς. 13 [i] οἱ γὰρ
[i] τοιοῦτοι [k] ψευδαπόστολοι, [l] ἐργάται [m] δόλιοι, [n] μετασχη-

c ch. xii. 2, 3. Josh. xxii. 22. d Rom. xi. 22, 23 reff. e Rom. vii. 8 reff. f ellips., Matt. xx. 23 al. g Rom. ii. 17 reff. h = 1 Cor. iv. 2 reff. i Acts xxii. 22 reff. k here only †. see Rev. ii. 2. l Matt. ix. 37 al.† Wisd. xvii. 17 al. = Phil. iii. 2. m here only. Prov. xii. 6. (-ιοῦν, Rom. iii. 13.) n here 3ce. 1 Cor. iv. 6. Phil. iii. 21 only †. 1 Kings xxviii. 8 Symm. Jos. Antt. vii. 10. 5.

12. υμεις F[-gr(not G)] d.
13. for οι, ου F[-gr]. ψευδοαπ. D¹. om εις F.

for we willingly incur obligations to those whom we love. **οἶδεν**, scil. ὅτι ὑμᾶς ἀγαπῶ. **12.**] *The true reason:*—**But that which I do, I will also continue to do** (καὶ ποιήσω must not, as Erasm., be coupled to ποιῶ, and διὰ τοῦτο ποιῶ supplied before ἵνα,—because it is for his resolution respecting the *future* that the reason is especially given) **in order that I may cut off the occasion** (**τήν**, which would be furnished if I did not so) **of those who wish for an occasion** (viz. of depreciating me by misrepresenting my motives if I took money of you). Many (Chrys., Theophyl., Calv., Grot., Billroth, al.) take this *occasion* to be one of aggrandizing themselves above Paul *if all took money*, assuming that the false teachers, as well as Paul, *took none:* which is extremely unlikely, from the prominence which he gives to the boast of his own abstinence in this point,—and seems directly opposed to ver. 20 and to 1 Cor. ix. 12. **ἵνα ἐν ᾧ κ.τ.λ.**] **that, in the matter of which they boast, they may be found even as we.** Such appears generally acknowledged to be the *rendering;* but as to the *meaning*, there is great variety of opinion. (1) Many of the ancient Commentators assume that they *taught gratis*, and were proud of it,—and that Paul would also teach gratis, to put both on an equality and take this occasion of boasting from them. This would suit the sense of the *present verse*, but seems (see above) at variance with the fact. (2) Theodoret, whom Meyer, al., follow, supposes them to have *pretended* to the credit of self-denial, while really making gain, and that Paul means, that he will *reduce them from pretended to real* self-denial. But this too is inconsistent with the context. Paul's boast of disinterested teaching was peculiarly *his own*, and there is nothing to shew that the false teachers ever professed or made any boast of the like. His resolution did not spring out of an actual comparison instituted by them between their own practice and what they might falsely allege to be his, but was adopted even before his coming to Corinth, arguing *a priori* that it was best to cut off any possible occasion of such depreciation of him from his probable adversaries. (3) Others, Cajetan, Estius, after Aug. de Serm. Dom. in Monte ii. 16 (54), vol. iii. p. 1292,—also Bengel,—join ἵνα . . . . ἡμεῖς with ἀφορμήν,—'*occasion that they may be found even as we*,' and explain ἐν ᾧ καυχ. as a parenthesis, '*that they may be found (a point in which they boast) even as we:*' i. e. 'that in point of selfishness and covetousness, we may be both on a level.' But this meaning would require rather εὑρεθῶμεν καθὼς καὶ αὐτοί, '*we* may be reduced to *their* level.' (4) Olsh., adopting in the main the last interpretation, would understand ἐν ᾧ καυχῶνται of the *taking of money of which they boasted*, accounting it an apostolic prerogative. But to this the last stated objection applies even more forcibly: and besides, the supposition is wholly arbitrary. (5) De Wette, believing the second ἵνα to be parallel with the first, as in (1) and (2), understands ἐν ᾧ καυχῶνται as applying to *their boast of apostolic efficiency:* 'that they may, in their apostolic work which they vaunt with such pretension, be found even as we,' and thinks the transition to what follows thus made easy. But the objection to this is, that the *punctum comparationis* in the rest of the chapter is *not apostolic efficiency*, but rather matters κατὰ σάρκα. (6) I cannot adopt any one of the above accounts of the sentence, for the negative reasons already given, and because all of them seem to me to have missed the clue to the meaning which the chapter itself furnishes. This clue I find in vv. 18 ff. The καυχῶνται is there taken up, described as being κατὰ σάρκα: the καθὼς καὶ ἡμεῖς is taken up by Ἑβραῖοί εἰσιν; κἀγώ &c. From this it is manifest to me, that his meaning in our present clause is, '*that in the matter(s) of which they boast they may be found even as we;*' i. e. 'we may be on a fair and equal footing:' 'that there may be no adventitious comparisons made between us arising out of misrepresentations of my course of procedure among you, but that in every matter of boasting,

o Rev. xvii. 6 only. Job xvii. 8. xviii. 20 only.
p see Eph. v. 8. 1 Thess. v. 5 al.
q = 1 Cor. ix. 11 only. Gen. xlv. 28. Isa. xlix. 6.
r see Gal. ii. 17.
s see ch. iii. 9.
t = Rom. vi. 21 reff.
u Rom. ii. 6. Rev. xx. 12, 13. Ps. xxvii. 4.
v = 1 Cor. iii. 18 reff.

[R xi. 14...] BDFKL MP[R]ℵ a b c d e f g h k l m n o 17. 47

ματιζόμενοι εἰς ἀποστόλους χριστοῦ. 14 καὶ οὐ [o] θαῦμα·
αὐτὸς γὰρ ὁ σατανᾶς [n] μετασχηματίζεται εἰς ἄγγελον
[p] φωτός· 15 οὐ [q] μέγα οὖν εἰ καὶ οἱ διάκονοι αὐτοῦ [n] μετα-
σχηματίζονται ὡς [rs] διάκονοι [s] δικαιοσύνης, ὧν τὸ [t] τέλος
ἔσται [u] κατὰ τὰ ἔργα αὐτῶν. 16 Πάλιν λέγω, μή τις με
[v] δόξῃ [w] ἄφρονα εἶναι· [x] εἰ [x] δὲ [x] μήγε, [y] κἂν ὡς [w] ἄφρονα
[z] δέξασθέ με, ἵνα κἀγὼ [a] μικρόν [a] τι [b] καυχήσωμαι. 17 ὃ
λαλῶ, οὐ [c] κατὰ [c] κύριον λαλῶ, ἀλλ' [d] ὡς [d] ἐν [e] ἀφροσύνῃ,

w Luke xi. 40. Rom. ii. 20 al. L.P., exc. 1 Pet. ii. 15. Prov. passim. x Matt. vi. 1. ix. 17. Luke v. 36, 37. x. ?. xiii. 9. xiv. 32 only. y Acts v. 15 reff. z see Matt. x. 14. ch. vii. 15 al. a ver. 1. b absol., 1 Cor. i. 29. iv. 7 al. c see ch. vii. 9—11. d so John vii. 10. e ver. 1 reff.

14. rec (for *θαυμα*) *θαυμαστον*, with $D^{2\cdot3}$KLM rel : txt BD^1FP[R]ℵ a 17 $Orig_1$ [Euthal-ms Damasc-ms]. for *εις αγγελον*, *ως αγγελος* D^1(and lat) Orig-int-mss_1 Cypr $Lucif_1$ Ambrst [Promiss].
15. om *ουν* D^1(and lat) spec Syr goth arm $Lucif_1$. om *διακονοι* K. *εαυτου* K. for *εσται*, *εστιν* D^1(and lat) [spec] Lucif.
16. om *γε* D^1. rec *μικρον τι* bef *καγω*, with syr Œc : txt BDFKLMP[R]ℵ rel latt Syr goth æth arm [Euthal-ms Thdrt Damasc]. *καυχησομαι* DKLP[R] d^1 [Euthal-ms].
17. rec *λαλω* bef *κατα κυριον*, with DLM rel vulg(not F-lat) fri syr copt goth : txt BFKP[R]ℵ a d (m[*κ. ανθρωπον*]) 17. 47 Syr æth arm [Bas_1] Chr_1 Damasc.

we may be fairly compared and judged by facts.' And then, before the *γάρ* of ver. 13 will naturally be supplied, 'And this will end in their discomfiture: *for* realities they have none, no weapons but misrepresentation, being *false Apostles*,' &c. **13.**] **For** (see above: the *γάρ* implying also that the choice of the above line of conduct has been made in a conviction of their falsehood and its efficacy to detect it) **such men are false Apostles** (not, as Vulg. and most expositors, '*such false Apostles are* **ἐργ. δόλ.**,' which destroys the whole emphasis of the sentence, wherein the **ὑπερλίαν** *ἀπόστολοι* of ver. 5 are pronounced now to be **ψευδαπόστολοι**: and besides, suggests an irrelevant comparison between *οἱ* **τοιοῦτοι** *ψ.* and *ψ.* of some other kind. On the sense, see Rev. ii. 2. **ὁ τοιοῦτος** is a familiar designation with the Apostle, see reff.),—**dishonest workmen** (in that they pretend to be teachers of the Gospel, and are in the mean time subserving their own ends),—**changing themselves into** (in appearance: the pres. participle indicates their *habit* and continual endeavours to assume the shape) **Apostles of Christ.** By a *fair* comparison between us, this mask will be stript off;—by the abundance of my sufferings, and distinctions vouchsafed by the Lord, my Apostolicity will be fully proved, and their Pseudapostolism shewn. **14, 15.**] **οὐ θαῦμα**—so Aristoph. Plut. 99, *καὶ θαῦμά γ' οὐδέν, οὐδ' ἐγὼ γὰρ ὁ βλέπων.* **αὐτὸς γὰρ ὁ σ.**] If any definite allusion is here intended, it is perhaps to Job i. 6, &c.: but I would rather suppose the *practice* of Satan in tempting and seducing men to be intended.

14. ἄγγ. φωτός] God is light, and inhabits light, and His angelic attendants are surrounded with brightness, see Acts xii. 7; Ps. civ. 4: whereas Satan is the Power of *darkness*, see reff. and Luke xxii. 53. **15.**] **εἰ καί, if also**, i. e. *as well as himself*, or perhaps better applying to the whole sentence, if, also . . . **μετασχ. ὡς**, i. e. *μετασχ. καὶ γίνονται ὡς*:—so Rom. ix. 29, *ὡς Γόμοῤῥα ἂν ὡμοιώθημεν.* *
αὐτός, the father of falsehood and wrong (John viii. 44), is directly opposed to *δικαιοσύνη θεοῦ*, Matt. vi. 33, that manifestation of God by which He is known to us in the Gospel, Rom. i. 17. **ὧν τὸ τέλ.**] **Of whom** (notwithstanding this disguise) **the end shall be correspondent to their works** (not to their pretensions). **16—21.**] *Excuses for his intended self-boasting.* **16.**] **πάλιν**—referring to ver. 1, not *repeating* what he had there said, but again *taking up the subject*, and expanding that request. The *ἀνέχομαι* of ver. 1 in fact implies both requests of this verse:—the not regarding him as a fool for boasting, or *even if they did* (*εἰ δὲ μήγε* after a negative sentence implies '*but if it cannot be so*,' 'if you will not grant this,' see reff. **κἄν** elliptical: the full construction would be *κἂν ὡς ἄφρονα δέξασθαι δέῃ, δέξασθέ με*: so in reff.) *as a fool* (i. e. yielding to me the toleration and hearing which men would not refuse even to one of whose folly they were convinced) *receiving him.* **κἀγώ**, *as well as they.* **17.**] Proceeding on the *ὡς ἄφρονα*, he disclaims for this self-boasting the character of inspiration—or of being said in pursuance of his

ἐν ταύτῃ τῇ [f] ὑποστάσει τῆς [g] καυχήσεως. 18 ἐπεὶ πολλοὶ
[b] καυχῶνται [h] κατὰ [h] τὴν [h] σάρκα, κἀγὼ [b] καυχήσομαι.
19 [i] ἡδέως γὰρ [k] ἀνέχεσθε τῶν [w] ἀφρόνων, [l] φρόνιμοι ὄντες·
20 [k] ἀνέχεσθε γάρ, εἴ τις ὑμᾶς [m] καταδουλοῖ, εἴ τις [n] κατεσ-
θίει, εἴ τις [o] λαμβάνει, εἴ τις [p] ἐπαίρεται, εἴ τις [q] εἰς [q] πρόσωπον ὑμᾶς [r] δέρει. 21 [s] κατὰ [t] ἀτιμίαν λέγω [u] ὡς [u] ὅτι ἡμεῖς

[...iii. 18(appy) R.]

f = ch. ix. 4. Heb. (i. 3.) iii. 14. xi. 1 only. Ps. xxxviii. 7.
g Rom. iii. 27 reff.
h John viii. 15 only. see Rom. i. 3 reff. Gal. vi. 8.
i Mark vi. 20. xii. 37 only. Prov. iii. 24. ix. 17. (-διστα, ch. xii. 9.)
k ver. 1.
l Rom. xi. 25 al. Prov. xv. 21. iron., 1 Cor. iv. 10.
m Gal. ii. 4 only. Gen. xlvii. 21.
n Mark xii. 40 || L. Gal. v. 15. Rev. xi. 5 only. Isa. ix. 12.
o = ch. xii. 16.
p = ch. x. 5 reff.
q see Matt. xxvi. 67.
r Acts v. 40 reff.
s = 1 Cor. vii. 6.
t Rom. i. 26 reff.
u ch. v. 19. 2 Thess. ii. 2.

18. for πολλοί, ολοι P[1]. om την D[1]F[R]א[1] 17 Chr$_1$ Damasc.
20. rec υμας bef εις προσωπον, with D[2][-gr] KLM rel am[*in vos faciem*(sic, Tischdf)] Syr goth arm Chr$_1$ Thdrt: txt BD[1.3]FPא m o 17 latt syr æth [Euthal-ms] Damasc Orig-int$_1$ [Ambrst].

mission from the Lord. **κατὰ κύρ.**] as in reff., **after the** (mind of the) **Lord**, in pursuance, i. e. *in this case*, of θεοπνευστία from above: not as in 1 Cor. vii. 10, 25, 40. **ὡς ἐν ἀφρ.**] **as it were in folly**, i. e. 'putting myself into the situation, and speaking the words of a foolish man vaunting of himself.' **ὑποστάσει**, as ch. ix. 4, **in this present confidence**, not as Chrys. '*subject*,'—'*this* subject of boasting,' ἵνα μὴ νομίσῃς **πανταχοῦ** ἀνοηταίνειν αὐτόν, (Hom. xxiv. p. 607)—and so al.: but the sense would be insipid in the last degree: nor could such a meaning well be expressed without γε,—ἐν ταύτῃ γε τῇ ὑπ. De Wette also renders ὑπ. '*subject-matter*,' and understands, '*since we are come to boasting*;' but here again γε would be more naturally found. He objects to '*confidence*,' that the boasting was *not begun*: but as Meyer replies, it is *conceived of as having begun in Paul's mind*, by the use of the present λαλῶ, **I am speaking**.
18.] **Since many** (viz. the false teachers, but not only they:—'since it is a common habit,'—for he is here speaking as εἷς τῶν ἀφρόνων, see Job ii. 10) **boast according to the flesh** (not = ἐν σαρκί, as Chrys., al., but 'in a spirit of fleshly regard,'—'having regard to their extraction, achievements, &c.' as below vv. 22 ff.), **I also will boast** (scil. κατὰ τὴν σάρκα. Rückert thinks these words are omitted purposely, thereby to imply that the Apostle's boasting *was not* fleshly; but this is distinctly contradicted by the context: he is speaking as one of the πολλοί of οἱ ἄφρονες, see next verse). **19.**] Bitterly ironical. They were φρόνιμοι—as 1 Cor. iv. 8, κεκορεσμένοι—so full of wisdom as to be able to tolerate complacently, looking down from the 'sapientum templa serena,' the follies of others. This, forsooth, encourages him to hope for their forbearance and patronage. Compare the earnestness of 1 Cor. iii. 1—4. And the irony does not stop here: it is not only matter of presumption that they *would* tolerate fools with complacency, but the matter of fact testified it: they *were doing this: and more*.
20.] **for** (proof that they could have no objection to so innocent a man as a *fool*, when they tolerated such noxious ones as are adduced) **ye endure (them), if** (as is the case) **one brings you into slavery** (the mere abstract act as regarded *them*, not the man's own selfish view, being in the Apostle's mind, the *active*, not the *middle*, is used. Thucyd. iii. 70, uses the active similarly: λέγοντες τοὺς Ἀθηναίους τὴν Κέρκυραν καταδουλοῦν. But the enslaving understood, is *to the man himself*, not to the *law*;—see ref. Gal.), **if one devours you** (by exaction on your property, see reff. Mk. L. So Hom. Od. γ. 315: μή τοι κατὰ πάντα φάγωσι κτήματα, and Plaut., Ter., and Quintil., in Wetstein), **if one catches you** (as with a snare, ref.: not, '*takes from you*'), **if one uplifts himself** (so freq. in Thucyd., e. g. vi. 11, χρὴ μὴ πρὸς τὰς τύχας τῶν ἐναντίων ἐπαίρεσθαι. See other examples in Wetst.), **if one smites you on the face** (in insult, see 1 Kings xxii. 24: Matt. v. 39; Luke xxii. 64; Acts xxiii. 2. This is put as the climax of forbearance. "That such violence might literally be expected from the rulers of the early Christian society, is also implied in the command in 1 Tim. iii. 3, Tit. i. 7, that the 'bishop' is not to be 'a striker.' Even so late as the seventh century the council of Braga (c. 7), A.D. 675, orders that no bishop at his will and pleasure shall *strike* his clergy, lest he lose the respect which they owe him." Stanley).
21.] **By way of disparagement** (κατ' ἀτιμ.,—so κατὰ λῃΐην ἐκπλώσαντες, Herod. ii. 152; κατὰ θέαν ἥκεν, Thucyd. vi. 31) **I assume that** (ὡς ὅτι, see ch. v. 19, note,—does not positively state a fact, but assumes one, or states the import of a saying) **WE** (emphatic) **were weak** (when we were among you). An ironical reminiscence of his own abstinence when among

v = Rom. iv. 19 reff.
w ver. 12.
x = ch. x. 2.
y ver. 17.
z Acts vi. 1. Phil. iii. 5 bis only. Gen. xxxix. 14 al.
a John i. 48. Acts ii. 22. Rom. xi. 1 al.
b Rom. ix. 7 reff.
c Col. i. 7. 1 Tim. iv. 6. see ch. vi. 4.
d here only. Zech. vii. 11 only. (-νία, 2 Pet. ii. 16.)
e as adv., here only. Winer, edn. 6, § 50, Remark 2.

BDFKL MPℵa b c d e f g h k l m n o 17. 47

[v] ἠσθενήσαμεν· [w] ἐν ᾧ δ' ἄν τις [x] τολμᾷ, ([y] ἐν [y] ἀφροσύνῃ
λέγω) [x] τολμῶ κἀγώ. 22 [z] Ἑβραῖοί εἰσιν; κἀγώ. [a] Ἰσραηλ-
ῖταί εἰσιν; κἀγώ. [b] σπέρμα Ἀβραάμ εἰσιν; κἀγώ. 23 [c] διάκονοι [c] χριστοῦ εἰσιν; ([d] παραφρονῶν λαλῶ) [e] ὑπὲρ ἐγώ· ἐν

21. ησθενησαμεν bef ημεις F[not F-lat]: ησθενηκαμεν Bℵ m [17(Griesb)] 80 [Euthal-ms].—add εν τουτω τω μερει D vulg-ed [demid](not am fuld [tol]) Ambrst. om δ' D[1](and lat) vulg syrr Ambrst. τολμω καγω bef εν αφρ. λεγω F[not F-lat].—om 2nd λεγω ℵ[1](ins ℵ-corr[1] obl).

them from all these acts of self-exaltation at their expense, q. d. (ironically), 'I feel that I am much letting myself down by the confession that *I* was too weak ever to do any of these things among you.' This I believe with Schrader, De Wette, and Meyer, to be the only satisfactory rendering. See also Stanley. Most expositors (1) refer λέγω back to ver. 20, '*I say it*,'—'*I speak*,' as E. V. So Chrys., Theophyl., Theodoret, Pelag., Erasm., Calv., al. (Chrys. remarks on ὡς ὅτι,—ἀσαφὲς τὸ εἰρημένον. ἐπειδὴ γὰρ φορτικὸν ἦν, διὰ τοῦτο οὕτως αὐτὸ τέθεικεν, ἵνα κλέψῃ τὴν ἐπάχθειαν τῇ ἀσαφείᾳ, p. 609), and (2) understand κατὰ ἀτιμ., 'to *your shame*,' and (3) ὡς ὅτι, '*as though*.' But (1) can hardly be, seeing that λέγω below and λαλῶ ver. 23 have a forward reference: (2) would require ὑμῶν, and even then would be exceedingly harsh,—cf. the similar meaning 1 Cor. xv. 34, where we have πρὸς ἐντροπὴν ὑμῖν λαλῶ: and (3) it may be doubted whether ὡς ὅτι ever can mean '*as though*,' even in ref. 2 Thess., where Winer, edn. 6, § 65. 9 (see German edn.), renders it by wie daß: it is pleonastic, answering to our expression '*how that*'—'I told him, how that' . . . . Winer, in a *former edition*, instances the use of wie daß in a somewhat similar way: wie daß ich gehört habe, ... where either wie or daß would be enough. Besides the instances given on ch. v. 19, Meyer quotes from Dion. Hal. ix. (with no further ref.) ἐπιγνούς, ὡς ὅτι ἐν ἐσχάτοις εἰσὶν οἱ κατακλεισθέντες. **ἐν ᾧ δ' ἄν**] **But in whatsoever matter any one** (the τις of ver. 20) **is bold** (the ἄν signifies habit, recurrence: so Soph. Philoct. 290, ταῦτ' ἂν ἐξέρπων τάλας ἐμηχανώμην· εἶτα πῦρ ἂν οὐ παρῆν, and Eur. Phœn. 412, ποτὲ μὲν ἐπ' ἦμαρ εἶχον, εἶτ' οὐκ εἶχον ἄν, where see Porson). Throughout this passage, compare by all means Stanley's interesting notes. **ἐν ἀφρ.**] see ver. 17. **22.**] "The three honourable appellations with which the adversaries magnified themselves,—resting on their Jewish extraction, are arranged so as to form a *climax*: so that Ἑβραῖοι refers to the *nationality*,—Ἰσραηλῖται to the *theocracy* (Rom. ix. 4 ff.), and σπέρμα Ἀβρ. to the *claim to a part in the Messiah* (Rom. ix. 7; xi. 1, al.)." Meyer. The interrogative form of the sentence is much more lively and consistent with the spirit of the context than the affirmative, as given by Erasm., Luther, Estius, al. **23.**] Meyer remarks, that all three points of Judaistic comparison, of so little real consequence in the matter, were dismissed with the short and contemptuous κἀγώ,—'*that am I too*.' But that is not enough, now that we are come to the *great* point of comparison; the consciousness of his real standing, and their nullity as ministers of Christ requires the ὑπὲρ ἐγώ, and the holy earnestness of this consciousness pours itself forth as a stream over the adversaries, so as to overwhelm their conceited aspirations to apostolic dignity.

παραφρ. λ.] stronger than ἐν ἀφροσ. λέγω: —**I say it as a madman.** Hardly, as Meyer, spoken from a consciousness of the verdict παραφρονεῖ which the opponents would pronounce on this ὑπὲρ ἐγώ,—but rather, as De W., from a deep sense of his own unworthiness, and conscious how utterly untrue was ὑπὲρ **ἐγώ**, in any boasting sense. He therefore repudiates it even more strongly than the τολμῶ κἀγώ.

ὑπὲρ ἐγώ must not be misunderstood. He *concedes* to them their being διάκ. χρ., and assumes (παραφρονῶν) for himself, *something more*, if more abundant labours and sufferings are to be any criterion of the matter. That this is the sense is obvious from the comparison being in the *amount* of labours and sufferings,—and not (as Meyer), that he denies to them the διάκ. χρ. and merely puts it hypothetically. 'Well, then, if *they* are to be considered διάκ. χρ., *I* must be *something more*.' If so, the comparison would be not in the *degree* of ministerial self-sacrifice, but in the *credentials of the ministry itself*. *Both* are now assumed to be ministers: but if so, Paul is a minister in a much higher degree, more faithful, more self-denying, richer in gifts and divine tokens, than they. The preposition is used ad-

[fg] κόποις [h] περισσοτέρως, ἐν [fi] φυλακαῖς [h] περισσοτέρως, ἐν
[fk] πληγαῖς [l] ὑπερβαλλόντως, ἐν [m] θανάτοις πολλάκις.
24 ὑπὸ Ἰουδαίων πεντάκις [n] τεσσεράκοντα [o] παρὰ μίαν
ἔλαβον, 25 τρὶς [p] ἐραβδίσθην, ἅπαξ [q] ἐλιθάσθην, τρὶς
[r] ἐναυάγησα, [s] νυχθήμερον ἐν τῷ [t] βυθῷ [u] πεποίηκα·
26 [v] ὁδοιπορίαις πολλάκις, [w] κινδύνοις [x] ποταμῶν, [w] κιν-

f ch. vi. 5.
g 1 Cor. iii. 8. xv. 58 al. Gen. xxxi. 42.
h ch. i. 12 reff.
i Matt. xxv. 36, &c. Heb. xi. 36.
k Luke x. 30. xii. 48. Acts xvi. 23, 33. Deut. xxv. 2.
l here only. Job xv. 11 only. (-βάλλειν, ch. iii. 10.)
m = ch. i. 10. Ps. lv. 13. see 1 Cor. xv. 31. προαποθνήσκω πολλοὺς θανάτους ὑπομένων ἀνθ' ἑνὸς τοῦ τελευταίου, Philo, Flacc. § 20, vol. ii. p. 542.
n ellips. of πληγ., see Luke xii. 47, 48.
o = here only. Herod. ix. 33.
p Acts xvi. 22 only‡. Judg. vi. 11.
q Acts v. 26 reff.
r 1 Tim. i. 19 only†.
s here only†.
t here only. Exod. xv. 5. Ps. cvi. 24. (-θίζειν, Luke v. 7.)
u — Acts xv. 33 reff.
v John iv. 6 only†. 1 Macc. vi. 41. (-ρεῖν, Acts x. 9.)
w here (8 times) and Rom. viii. 35 only. Ps. cxiv. 3. (-νεύειν, 1 Cor. xv. 30.)
x gen., = 1 Pet. i. 2, ῥαντ. αἵμ.

23. for λαλω, λεγω DF e Did$_1$. κονοις F(not G). rec εν πληγαις υπερβ. bef εν φυλακαις περισσ., with D^2[-gr] KLMℵ^3 rel syrr copt arm Orig$_1$ Chr$_1$ Thdrt Damasc, and F[-gr(and G-lat)] ℵ^1 Orig$_1$ [Hil$_1$], which (and P) put περισσ. with πληγ. and υπερβ. with φυλ.: om εν πλ. υπ. Clem [Euthal-ms] Tert: txt B D^1(and lat) (P) [17] vulg(and F-lat) goth æth Orig$_1$ [Ambrst Aug$_1$]. πολλοις D^1[-gr].

25. rec εραβδ., with M rel Chr [Thdrt Damasc]: txt BDFKLPℵ [a c d f k m n o] 17. 47 Orig$_2$ Eus$_1$ Chr-ms Thl Œc.

26. for πολλακις (and in next ver), πολλαις D^1(with lat); so also vulg [F-lat Syr] in ver 27 [twice].

verbially, see reff. **ἐν κόποις περισ.**] **By** (the ἐν is instrumental [in (the matter of) or, by (virtue of)]:—the direct dative is adopted ver. 26:—these facts *are proofs of the* **ὑπὲρ ἐγώ**,—not as Estius, al., *parallel with it*, which would only apply to the comparatives and not to ἐν θανάτοις πολλάκις) **labours** (occurring) **more abundantly** (the adverbs belong to the substantives in each case and are used adjectively; so τὴν ἐμὴν ἀναστροφήν ποτε, Gal. i. 13: τῆς ἐμῆς παρουσίας πάλιν, Phil. i. 26),—**by prisons** (imprisonments) **more abundantly** (but *one* such is mentioned in the Acts (xvi. 23 ff.) previous to the writing of this Epistle. Clement, in the celebrated passage of his 1st Epistle to the Corinthians (c. v. p. 220) on the labours of Paul, describes him as ἑπτάκις δεσμὰ φορέσας. This whole catalogue should shew the chronologists of the Apostle's life and epistles how exceedingly unsafe it is to build *only* on the history in the Acts for a complete account of his journeys and voyages), **by stripes more exceedingly** (particularized below), **by deaths often** (see reff. and ch. iv. 10. Such was the danger escaped at Damascus, Acts ix. 23, at Antioch in Pisidia, xiii. 50, at Iconium, xiv. 5, 6, at Lystra, ib. 19, at Philippi, xvi., at Thessalonica, xvii. 5 f., at Berœa, ib. 13, and doubtless many others of which we know nothing. See below).

24, 25.] are parenthetical, explaining some of the foregoing expressions: the construction is resumed, ver. 26. **At the hands of the Jews five times received I forty save one** (in Deut. xxv. 3, it is prescribed that not more than forty stripes should be given, 'lest thy brother should seem vile unto thee.' For fear of exceeding this number, they kept within it. This seems a more likely account of the thirty-nine stripes than that given by Wetst.,—that thirteen were inflicted on the breast, and the same number on each shoulder, and the fortieth omitted, lest one part of the body should receive more than another. See the Rabbinical authorities in Wetst., and cf. Joseph. Antt. iv. 8. 21 and 23, and Stanley's note here. He calls it τιμωρία αἰσχίστη: and Meyer remarks that Paul might well number it among the θάνατοι, for it was no rare occurrence for the criminal to die under its infliction. None of these scourgings are mentioned in the Acts),—**thrice was I beaten with rods** (scil. by the Roman magistrates, see Acts xvi. 22, 23, which is the only occasion mentioned in the Acts), **once was I stoned** (Acts xiv. 19), **thrice I suffered shipwreck** (*not one* of these shipwrecks is known to us. Thus we see that perhaps three, perhaps two, voyages of Paul, but certainly one,—previous to this time, must be somewhere inserted in the history of the Acts: see Prolegg. ch. iii. § v. 5), **a night and day have I spent** (reff.) **in the deep** (i. e. the sea: probably on some remnant of a wreck after one of his shipwrecks alone or with others. To understand ὁ βυθός, as Thl. (τινὲς δέ φασιν ἔν τινι φρέατι μετὰ τὸν ἐν Λύστροις κίνδυνον κατακρυφθείς, **βύθῳ** λεγομένῳ, νῦν τοῦτο λέγει), seems to be taking it out of its connexion here. Wetst. gives from Ælian, H. An. viii. 7, ἀθέατον νήχεσθαι ἐν βυθῷ. Still less must we think of the characteristic interpretation

y Epp., here only. Matt. xxi. 13 ‖ (from Jer. vii. 11) al.
z = Acts xviii. 2 reff. absol., 2 Macc. xii. 31.
a Matt. xv. 33 ‖ Mk. Heb. xi. 38 only. Ezek. xxxv. 4.
b Gal. ii. 4 only †.

δύνοις [xy] λῃστῶν, [w] κινδύνοις ἐκ [z] γένους, [w] κινδύνοις ἐξ
ἐθνῶν, [w] κινδύνοις ἐν πόλει, [w] κινδύνοις ἐν [a] ἐρημίᾳ,
[w] κινδύνοις ἐν θαλάσσῃ, [w] κινδύνοις ἐν [b] ψευδαδέλφοις,
27 [cd] κόπῳ καὶ [ce] μόχθῳ, ἐν [d] ἀγρυπνίαις πολλάκις, ἐν
[fg] λιμῷ καὶ [gh] δίψει, ἐν [d] νηστείαις πολλάκις, ἐν [i] ψύχει καὶ
[fgk] γυμνότητι. 28 [l] χωρὶς τῶν [m] παρεκτὸς ἡ [n] ἐπίστασίς

BDFKI MPℵ a c d e f hklm o 17. 4

c 1 Thess. ii. 9. 2 Thess. iii. 8 only. d ch. vi. 5 (reff.). e as above (c) only. Num. xxiii. 21. f Deut. xxviii. 48 only. g Rom. viii. 35. h here only. Exod. xvii. 3. i John xviii. 18. Acts xxviii. 2 only. Gen. viii. 22. k as above (f, g). Rev. iii. 18 only. l = Matt. xiv. 21. (Heb. iv. 15.) Gen. xxvi. 1. m Matt. v. 32. Acts xxvi. 29 only †. Deut. i. 36 Aq. constr., here only. n Acts xxiv. 12 only †. = 2 Macc. vi. 3? (only.) ἐπισύσ., (Acts as above, v. r.) Num. xxvi. 9.

27. rec ins *εν* bef *κοπω*, with KLMP ℵ-corr[1](?)[3] rel vulg(and F-lat) $Orig_2$(-int_1) [Bas_1 Chr_1 Euthal-ms Thdrt Damasc Ambrst Aug_1]: om BD F[-gr] ℵ[1] goth. *διψη* B[1] g[2] l [$Orig_1$].

28. rec *επισυστασις*, with KLMP rel Chr_1(explaining it: *οἱ θόρυβοι, αἱ ταραχαί, αἱ πολιορκίαι τῶν δήμων καὶ τῶν πόλεων ἔφοδοι.* So also Thdrt al) Damasc: txt BDFℵ

of Estius: "Subjunxit aliud periculum marinum longe gravius, nempe quod demersus fuerit ex naufragio in profundum maris, ubi tamen divina ope fuerit servatus incolumis noctem et diem, atque inde postea liberatus"). **26.**] The construction is resumed from ver. 23, but now with the instrumental dative without the preposition. **By journeys frequently, by perils of rivers** (the genitives denote the *material* of the perils; rivers and robbers being the things and persons actually attacking. Winer, edn. 6, § 30. 2 [*a*], renders it *perils on rivers*, justifying it by *κ. ἐν πόλει*: but in my view a *distinction* is pointed out by the variety of construction. Wetst. quotes *κινδ. θαλασσῶν* from Heliod. ii. 4. The 'perils of rivers' might arise from crossing or fording, or from floods. The crossing of the rocky and irregular torrents in Alpine districts is to this day attended with danger, which must have been much more frequent when bridges were comparatively rare. And this is the case with a road, among others, frequently traversed by Paul, that between Jerusalem and Antioch, crossed as it is by the torrents from the sides of Lebanon. Maundrell says that the traveller Spon lost his life in one of those torrents: see Conybeare and Howson, edn. 2, vol. i. p. 502, note: and Stanley in loc.), **by perils of robbers** (see note on Acts xiii. 14), **by perils from my kindred** (the Jewish nation, *ἐκ*, *arising from:* they not being always the direct agents,—but, as in many cases in the Acts, setting on others or plotting secretly: or *γένους*,—and *ἐθν.* below,—imports generically the *source*, or quarter whence the danger arose), **by perils from the Gentiles** (not merely "*from Gentiles*," as Stanley: this would be *ἐξ ἐθνικῶν*. The art. is omitted after the preposition, the word being thus categorized in Greek; but it must be supplied in our English idiom), **by perils in the city** (in Damascus, Acts ix. 23 f.,—Jerusalem, ib. 29,—Ephesus xix. 23 ff., and many other places), **by perils in the desert** (the actual desert? or merely the solitude of journeys as contrasted with 'the city?' but any how, not '*in solitude:*' the art. must be supplied as in *ἐν πόλει*), **by perils in the sea** (not, as De W., a repetition from ver. 25: there are many perils in the sea short of shipwrecks), **by perils among false brethren** (*who were these?* Grot., al., suppose, 'qui Christianos se simulabant, ut res Christianorum perdiscerent, deinde eos proderent,'—and so apparently Chrys., &c. But Paul's use of this compound leads us rather to persons who *bona fide* wished to be thought *ἀδελφοί*, but *were not*, scil. in heart and conduct, and were opponents of himself personally, rather than designed traitors to the Christian cause. Cf. *ψευδαπόστολοι* above, ver. 13); **27.**] **by labour and weariness, by watchings** (see on ch. vi. 5) **frequently** (the *ἐν* is here resumed, perhaps arbitrarily, perhaps also because *κόπος* and *μόχθος* are more directly instrumental,—*ἀγρυπν.*, &c., more conditionally), **by hunger and thirst, by fastings frequently** (voluntary fastings, 'ad purificandam mentem et edomandam carnem,' as Estius, see also ch. vi. 5 note. De W. here too (see also Stanley) holds to 'involuntary fastings;' but he is clearly wrong, for *νηστ.* is distinguished from *λιμ. κ. δίψ.*), **in cold and nakedness** (insufficient clothing:—or, literally, when thrust into prison after his scourgings,—or after his shipwrecks). **28.**] He passes from particulars, omitting others which might have been specified, to the weight of apostolic care and sympathy which was on him. **Not to mention those** (afflictions) **which are besides** (these) (the Vulg., E. V., Beza, Estius, Bengel, under-

μοι ἡ [o] καθ' ἡμέραν, ἡ [p] μέριμνα [q] πασῶν τῶν [q] ἐκκλησιῶν.
29 τίς [r] ἀσθενεῖ, καὶ οὐκ [r] ἀσθενῶ; τίς [s] σκανδαλίζεται,
καὶ οὐκ ἐγὼ [t] πυροῦμαι; 30 Εἰ [u] καυχᾶσθαι δεῖ, [vw] τὰ [v] τῆς

o Acts ii. 46 reff. p and constr., Matt. xiii. 22 ‖ (Luke xxi. 34. 1 Pet. v. 7) only. Sir. xlii. 9. q ch. viii. 18 reff. r = Acts xx. 35, or Rom. xiv. 1. s 1 Cor. viii. 13 reff. t 1 Cor. vii. 9 reff. u absol., vv. 16, 18. v constr., Rom. xiv. 19 al. w constr., ch. ix. 2. Prov. xxvii. 1.

k 17 [Euthal-ms]. rec (for *μοι*) *μου*, with D[-gr] KLMPℵ[3] rel vulg[(and F-lat) Ambrst]: txt B F[-gr] ℵ[1] 17 [Euthal-ms, *in me* D-lat Aug_3]. om 1st *η* F[1] (not G). for *καθ. ημ. η*, *καθημερινη* F.

stand *παρεκτός* as = *ἔξωθεν*, '*the things that are without*,'—a meaning which it never has, always implying *exception*, see reff. Chrys., al., join *χωρ. τ. παρεκτ.* with the foregoing, and put a period after *παρεκτ.*, interpreting it rightly, *πλείονα τὰ παραλειφθέντα τῶν ἀπαριθμηθέντων*, Hom. xxv. p 613:—but this seems to break the connexion too abruptly, besides giving a strange and unlikely termination to the long sentence preceding),—**my care** (*ἐπίστ.* may be either 'delay,' 'hindrance,' as Soph. Antig. 225, *πολλὰς γὰρ εἶχον φροντίδος ἐπιστάσεις*, and Xen. Anab. ii. 4. 26, *ὅσον δ' ἂν χρόνον τὸ ἡγούμενον τοῦ στρατεύματος ἐπιστήσειε, τοσοῦτον ἦν ἀνάγκη χρόνον δι' ὅλου τοῦ στρατεύματος γίγνεσθαι τὴν ἐπίστασιν*,—or, as very frequently in Polybius, see Schweigh., Lex. Polyb.,—'care,' 'attention,' 'matter of earnest thought:' e. g. *τὴν ὑπὲρ τῶν ὅλων ἐπίστασιν κ. διάληψιν*, viii. 30. 13, 'curam summæ rei,'—*οὐκ ἐκ παρέργου, ἀλλ' ἐξ ἐπιστάσεως*, iii. 58. 3,—*ἄγειν τινὰ εἰς ἐπίστασιν*, 'attentionem alicujus excitare,' ix. 22. 17, al. The rec. reading, **ἐπισύστασις** (which has perhaps been introduced from *ἐπίστασις* not being understood (see digest here and on ref. Acts) and then *μοι* has been altered to *μου* as easier; but substantives derived from verbs which govern a dative are sometimes followed by this case, see Winer, edn. 6, § 31. 3, and Moulton's note), can only mean *concursus*, in a hostile sense, see ref. and examples in Wetst.: and so Chrys. (see var. readd.), &c., take it here: others metaphorically, as Beza, 'agmen illud in me quotidie consurgens, i. e. sollicitudo de omnibus ecclesiis:'—somewhat similarly De W.,—'that which sets upon me, importunes me, daily:' and so E. V. Stanley, with Est. al., renders it, 'the concourse of people to see me:' but this is doubtful, as departing from the hostile sense. In Beza's sense, there is something Pauline in the rec., "the daily outbreak against me," and the reading cannot be considered certain) **day by day, (viz.) my anxiety for all the churches** (the construction is an anacoluthon: not, as Meyer, *ἐπίστ.* the subject and *μέριμνα* the predicate, which would be a very flat sentence,—'*my daily care is, anxiety &c.*' As it stands, *ἡ ἐπίστ.* is general, and *ἡ μέριμν.* particularizes it. Nothing need be supplied. *ἡ ἐπίστ.* occurs to the Apostle's mind, and is uttered, in the nominative, the construction being disregarded).

29.] 'Cura certe *συμπάθειαν* generat: quæ facit, ut omnium affectus in se suscipiat Christi minister, omnium personas induat, quo se accommodet omnibus,' Calv. Olsh., after Emmerling, strangely understands, '*Who is weak, if I am not weak?*' i. e. 'Who can be called weak, if I am not so?' The **ἀσθένεια** of the *τις* may be in various ways; in *faith*, as Rom. xiv. 1 al., or in *purpose*, or in *courage*: that of the Apostle, see 1 Cor. ix. 22, was a sympathetic weakness, a leaning to the same infirmity for the weak brother's sake, but also a veritable *θορυβοῦμαι κ. ταράσσομαι* (as Chrys., p. 614) in himself, on the weak brother's account. **τίς σκανδ.**] "Non priore, sed hac versiculi parte addit *ego*: nam illic infirmo se accommodat: hic dissimilem se scandalizantis fatetur, partes a scandalizante neglectas scandalizati causa *ipse* suscipiens. Partes a scandalizante neglectæ sunt amor, prudentia, &c. Idem tamen Paulus etiam partes scandalizati, sive incommodum quod scandalizatus sentit, in se suscipit." Bengel. **πυροῦμαι**,—with zeal, or with indignation. **30.**] partly refers back to what has passed since ver. 23. The *ἀσθένεια* not being that mentioned in a different connexion in ver. 29, but that of ver. 21, to which all since has applied. But the words are not without a forward reference likewise. He will boast of his weaknesses—of (*τὰ τῆς ἀσθ.*) *those things which made him appear mean and contemptible* in the eyes of his adversaries. He is about to adduce an instance of escape from danger, of which this is eminently the case: he might be scoffed at as *ὁ σαργανοφόρητος*, or the like—but he is carried on in his fervency of self-renunciation amidst his apparent self-celebration, and he will even cast before his enemies the *contemptible* antecedents of his career, boasting in being despised, if only for what Christ had done in him. The asseveration in ver. 31 *may* be applied to the whole, but I had rather view it as connected with the strange history about to be related:—'I will glory in my weaknesses

[x] ἀσθενειας μου [w] καυχήσομαι· 31 ὁ [yz] θεὸς καὶ [y] πατὴρ τοῦ BDFKL
κυρίου Ἰησοῦ [z] οἶδεν, ὁ ὢν [a] εὐλογητὸς [a] εἰς τοὺς [a] αἰῶνας, MPℵ a b c d e f g
ὅτι οὐ [b] ψεύδομαι. 32 ἐν Δαμασκῷ ὁ [c] ἐθνάρχης Ἀρέτα h k l m n o 17. 47
τοῦ βασιλέως [d] ἐφρούρει τὴν πόλιν Δαμασκηνῶν [e] πιάσαι
με [θέλων], 33 καὶ διὰ [f] θυρίδος ἐν [g] σαργάνῃ [h] ἐχα-
λάσθην [h] διὰ τοῦ [h] τείχους καὶ [i] ἐξέφυγον τὰς χεῖρας αὐτοῦ.
XII. 1 [k] * Καυχᾶσθαι δὴ οὐ [l] συμφέρει μοι· ἐλεύσομαι

x Rom. vi. 19. 1 Cor. ii. 3 reff.
y Rom. xv. 6 reff.
z so ver. 11.
a Rom. ix. 5 reff. and note.
b Rom. ix. 1 reff.
c here only †. 1 Macc. xiv. 47. xv. 1, 2 only. Jos. Antt. xiv. 7. 2 al.
d Gal. iii. 23. Phil. iv. 7. 1 Pet. i. 5 only †. Judith iii. 6.
e Acts xii. 4 reff.
f Acts xx. 9 only. Josh. ii. 15, 18.
g here only †.
h Acts ix. 25 (reff.).
i Rom. ii. 3 reff.
k absol., ch. xi. 16, 18, 30.
l constr., but w. aor. inf., Matt. xix. 10. Esth. iii. 8.

30. om *μου* B.

31. rec aft *κυριου* ins *ημων*, with DMP rel vulg(with [demid] fuld F-lat) Syr copt arm Thdrt [Euthal-ms Ambrst] Aug[alic] : om BFKLℵ e g h l m n 17 am syr goth æth Chr_1[and 2-mss] Damasc. rec aft *ιησ.* ins *χριστου*, with DKLMP rel vulg(with [demid] fuld F-lat) Syr copt æth Thdrt [Euthal-ms Damasc Ambrst] Aug: om BFℵ m 17 am syr goth arm Chr[and ms].

32. rec *δαμασκηνων* bef *πολιν*, with D^2[-gr] KLM rel Chr_1 Thdrt Damasc: txt $BD^{1.3}$FPℵ a m 17 [latt arm]. om *θελων* B D^1(and lat) vulg(and F-lat) Syr arm $Procop_1$ Ambrst Pel: ins D^3[-gr] KLMPℵ rel goth Chr_1 [Euthal-ms Damasc] Thdrt, and (but bef *πιασαι με*) F[-gr(and G-lat)] syr copt æth.

33. om *εν σαργανη* F[-gr].

Chap. XII. 1. * *καυχᾶσθαι δεῖ οὐ συμφέρον μὲν ἐλευσομαι δὲ* B(see table) F(ℵ) 17 vulg: so, but *συμφερει*, P: *καυχασθαι δη ου συμφερει μοι ελευσομαι γαρ* (D)KL rel Chr Thdrt [Thl] Œc.—ins *ει* bef *καυχ.* $ℵ^3$ 39 lect-17 vulg(and F-lat) [Euthal-ms Ambrst].—*δει* (*on the confusion between η and ει cf Tischdf N. T.* (ed. 7) *prolegg.* p. xxxvii) B D^3[and lat] FLP d e f g m n o [17] vulg syrr goth [Euthal-ms Ambrst]: *δε* D^1[-gr] ℵ copt Thl: *δη* KM 47 Ath_1 Chr Thdrt Damasc [Œc].—om *μοι* D^1[-gr] Syr goth. (M uncert.)—add *και* B 213.

—yea, and I will yet more abase myself—God knows that I am telling sober truth—&c.' If the solemnity of the asseveration seem out of proportion to the incident, the fervid and impassioned character of the whole passage must be taken into account. It will be seen that I differ from all Commentators here, and cannot but think that they have missed the connexion. Meyer supposes that vv. 32, 33 were only *the beginning of a catalogue of his escapes*, which he breaks off at ch. xii. 1: and that the asseveration was meant to apply to the whole catalogue: but surely this is very unnatural.

32, 33.] On the *fact*, and *historical difficulty*, see note, Acts ix. 24. **32.**] **ἐν Δαμ.** followed by *Δαμασκηνῶν* is pleonastic, but the pleonasm is common enough, especially when for any reason, our words are more than usually precise and formal. **ἐθνάρχης**] **Prefect**, or **governor**, stationed there by the Arabian king. The title appears to have been variously used. The High Priest Simon, as a vassal of Syria, is so named in reff. 1 Macc., and Jos. Antt. xiii. 6. 7. It was bestowed by Augustus on Archelaus after his father's death, Jos. Antt. xvii. 11. 4; B. J. ii. 6. 3. The presidents of the seven districts into which Egypt was divided under the Romans, bore it (Strabo, xvii. 798): as did a petty prince of the Bosporus under Augustus (Lucian, Macrob. 17). Also the chief magistrates of the Jews living under their own laws in foreign states had this title (Jos. Antt. xiv. 7. 2; xiv. 8. 5. B. J. vii. 6. 3). But apparently it must here be taken in its wider sense, and not in this latter: for the mere *chief magistrate of the Jews* would not have had the power of guarding the city. Doubtless he was *incited* by the Jews, who would represent Paul as a malefactor. **σαργάνη**, *κόφινος*, Hesych.;—*οἱ μέν, σχοινιόν τι, οἱ δὲ πλέγμα τι ἐκ σχοινίου.* Suidas (see Wetst.), = *σπυρίς*, Acts ix. 25. Probably it is, as Stanley, a "rope-basket;" a net.

Chap. XII. 1—10.] *He proceeds to speak of visions and revelations vouchsafed to him, and relates one such, of which however he will not boast, except in as far as it leads to fresh mention of infirmity, in which he will boast, as being a vehicle for the perfection of Christ's power.* In order to understand the connexion of the following, it is very requisite to bear in mind the burden of the whole, which runs through it —*ἐν ταῖς ἀσθενείαις καυχήσομαι.* There is no break between this and the last chapter. He has just mentioned a passage of his history which might expose him to con-

γὰρ εἰς [m] ὀπτασίας καὶ [n] ἀποκαλύψεις κυρίου. 2 οἶδα ἄνθρωπον ἐν χριστῷ [o] πρὸ ἐτῶν δεκατεσσάρων (εἴτε [p] ἐν

m Luke i. 22. xxiv. 23. Acts xxvi. 19 only. L.P.‡ Mal. iii. 2. Sir. xliii. 2, 16 only. = Dan. ix. 23 al. Theod. n = 1 Cor. xiv. 6 reff. w. gen. subj. (see note), Rev. i. 1 (Gal. i. 12 ?) only. (obj., 1 Cor. i. 7. 2 Thess. i. 7. 1 Pet. i. 7, 13. Sir. xlii. 1.) o see 2 Tim. i. 9. Tit. i. 2. John xii. 1. Amos i. 1. iv. 7. p ch. v. 6. Heb. xiii. 3.

aft εις ins τας P: τα(sic) F. for κυρ., χριστου F[not F-lat]. (P uncert.)

tempt and ridicule—this was one of the ἀσθένειαι. He now comes to *another:* but that other inseparably connected with, and forming the sequel of, a glorious revelation vouchsafed him by the Lord. This therefore he relates, at the same time repudiating it as connected with *himself*, and fixing attention only on the ἀσθένεια which followed it. 1.] (I have in recent editions *suspended* the very difficult question of this reading, not finding it possible to decide whether of the two deserves a place in the text. Meantime, the rec. is left in, and on it the following note is written.) Let only the two readings καυχᾶσθαι δὴ οὐ συμφέρει μοι, ἐλεύσομαι γάρ, and καυχᾶσθαι δεῖ, οὐ συμφέρον μέν· ἐλεύσομαι δέ, be compared, and it would certainly seem as if the former more resembled the nervous elliptic irony of the great Apostle, and the latter the tame conventional propriety of the grammatical correctors. The other variations, δέ for δή, and the prefixing of εἰ, are too palpable emendations to require critical treatment. The difficulty however is considerably lessened, when the right connexion is borne in mind. **To boast, verily, is not to my advantage: for** (i. e. it will be shewn to be so, by the following fact of a *correction administered to me* ἵνα μὴ ὑπεραίρωμαι) (on the other reading, **I must boast, though it is not to my advantage: but) I will proceed to visions and revelations of the Lord.** δή in this sense implies a *consciousness of a reason why the assertion is true*, and is therefore naturally followed by γάρ, if the sentence is completed. The same sense is found in Plato, Phæd. p. 60, ὦ Σώκρατες, ὕστατον δὴ σε προσεροῦσι νῦν οἱ ἐπιτήδειοι, καὶ σὺ τούτους,—the completion of the sense being,—'for you are to die to-night:'—πολλοὶ κακῶς πράσσουσιν, οὐ σὺ δὴ μόνος, Eur. Hec. 464: i. e. οὐ σὺ δὴ μόνος κακῶς πράσσεις, πολλοὶ γὰρ ἄλλοι . . . . (See Hartung, Partikellehre i. 270, who however explains δή in these examples somewhat differently.) The force of it here then, is: "*I am well aware that to boast is not good for me: for I will come to an instance in which it was so shewn to me.*" **εἰς ὀπτ. κ. ἀπ. κυρ.**] q. d. '*and the instances I will select are just of that kind in which, if boasting ever were good, it might be allowed:*' thus the γάρ gives a more complete proof. **ὀπτασία** is the form or manner of receiving ἀποκάλυψις, the revelation. There can hardly be an ὀπτασία without an ἀποκάλυψις of some kind. Therefore Theophylact's distinction is scarcely correct, ἡ ἀποκάλυψις πλέον τι ἔχει τῆς ὀπτασίας· ἡ μὲν γὰρ μόνον βλέπειν δίδωσιν· αὕτη δὲ καί τι βαθύτερον τοῦ δρωμένου ἀπογυμνοῖ. **κυρίου,** gen. subj, **vouchsafed me by the Lord,**—not obj., '*of* [i. e. revealing] *the Lord*' [as the subject of the vision], for such is not that which follows. No particular polemical reason, as the practice of particular parties at Corinth to allege visions, &c. (Baur), need be sought for the narration of this vision: Paul's object is *general*, and the means taken to attain it are simply subordinate to it, viz. the vindication of his apostolic character. 2—4.] *An example of such a vision and revelation.* The adoption of the third person is remarkable: it being evident from ver. 7 that *he himself* is meant. It is plain that a contrast is intended between the *rapt and glorified person* of vv. 2, 4,—and *himself*, the weak and afflicted and almost despairing subject of the σκόλοψ τῇ σαρκί of vv. 7 ff. Such glory *belonged not* to *him*, but the weakness *did*. Nay, so far was the glory from being *his*, that he knew not whether he was in or out of the body when it was put upon him: so that the ἐγὼ αὐτός, compounded of the νοῦς and σάρξ (Rom. vii. 25), clearly was not the subject of it, but as it were another form of his personality, analogous to that which we shall assume when unclothed of the body.

It may be remarked in passing, as has been done by Whitby, that the Apostle here by implication *acknowledges the possibility of consciousness and receptivity in a disembodied state.* Let it not be forgotten, that in the context, this vision is introduced not so much for the purpose of making it a ground of boasting, which he does only passingly and under protest, but *that he may by it introduce the mention of the* **σκόλοψ τῇ σαρκί**, *which bore so conspicuous a part in his* **ἀσθένειαι**, TO BOAST OF WHICH *is his present object.*

2.] **I know** (not, '*knew*,' as E. V.: which [is a mistake in grammar, and] introduces serious confusion, making it seem as if the πρὸ ἐτῶν δεκατ. were the date of the *knowledge*, not, as it really is, of the *vision*) **a man in Christ** (ἐν χρ. belongs to ἄνθρ., not to οἶδα, as Beza; ἄνθ. ἐν χρ. =

q 1 Cor. vi. 18 reff.
r ch. xi. 11, 31. Josh. xxii. 22.
s = John vi. 15. Acts viii. 39. 1 Thess. iv. 17. Rev. xii. 5.
t Acts xxii. 22. 1 Cor. v. 5, 11. ch. ii. 5, 6. x. 11.

p σώματι οὐκ οἶδα, εἴτε q ἐκτὸς τοῦ σώματος οὐκ οἶδα, ὁ r θεὸς r οἶδεν) s ἁρπαγέντα t τὸν t τοιοῦτον u ἕως τρίτου u οὐρανοῦ. 3 καὶ οἶδα t τὸν t τοιοῦτον ἄνθρωπον (εἴτε p ἐν p σώματι εἴτε v χωρὶς τοῦ σώματος οὐκ οἶδα, ὁ r θεὸς r οἶδεν) 4 ὅτι s ἡρπάγη εἰς τὸν w παράδεισον καὶ ἤκουσεν

BDFKL MPℵ a b c d e f g h k l m n o 17. 47

u so Matt. xi. 23. Luke x. 15. Deut. iv. 11. v = John i. 3 al. w Luke xxiii. 43. Rev. ii. 7 only. Gen. ii. 8, and fr.

2. ins τω bef σωματι D¹. (P uncert.) om του bef σωματος B d [so al next ver]. ins του bef τριτου F. (for τριτου ℵ¹ wrote τουτου, which he then altered to τρυτου.)

3. rec (for χωρις) εκτος (*from ver* 2), with D²·³FKLMPℵ [Chr₁ Euthal-ms Thdrt Damasc: *extra* latt]: txt BD¹ Meth₁. om ουκ οιδα B Meth₁.

'a Christian,' 'a man whose standing is in Christ:' so οἳ καὶ πρὸ ἐμοῦ γέγοναν ἐν χριστῷ, Rom. xvi. 7),—**fourteen years ago** (belongs not to οἶδα, nor to ἐν χρ. as Grot.: 'hominem talem, qui per 14 annos Christo serviat;'—but to ἁρπαγέντα. On the *idiom* see reff.,—the *date* probably refers back to the time when he was at Tarsus waiting for God to point out his work, between Acts ix. 30 and xi. 25. See the chronological table in the Prolegomena), **whether in the body, I know not, or out of the body, I know not: God knoweth** (if *in the body*, the idea would be that he was taken up *bodily*: if *out of the body*, to which the alternative manifestly inclines,—that his spirit was rapt from the body, and taken up disembodied. Aug. de genesi ad litteram xii. 2—5 (3—14), vol. iii. pp. 455 ff., discusses the matter at length, and concludes thus,—'Proinde quod vidit raptus usque in tertium cœlum, quod etiam se scire confirmat, proprie vidit, non imaginaliter. Sed quia ipsa a corpore alienata utrum omnino mortuum corpus reliquerit, an secundum modum quendam viventis corporis ibi anima fuerit, sed mens ejus ad videnda vel audienda ineffabilia illius visionis arrepta sit, hoc incertum erat,—ideo forsitan dixit, "sive in corpore sive extra corpus, nescio, Deus scit."' And similarly Thom. Aq. and Estius: not, as Meyer thinks, making the alternative consist between *reality* and a *mere vision*, but between the *anima*, the *life*, being rapt out of the body, leaving it dead, and the *mens*, the *intelligence* or *spirit*, being rapt out of the body, leaving it 'secundum modum quendam vivens'); **such an one** (so τὸν τοιοῦτον *resumes* after a parenthesis, 1 Cor. v. 5), **rapt** (snatched or taken up, reff.) **as far as the third heaven.** *What is the third heaven?* The Jews knew no such number, but commonly (not universally: Rabbi Judah said, "Duo sunt cœli, Deut. x. 14") recognized *seven* heavens: and if their arrangement is to be followed, the third heaven will be very low in the celestial scale, being only the *material clouds*. That the threefold division into the *air* (nubiferum), the *sky* (astriferum), and the *heaven* (angeliferum), was in use among the Jews, Meyer regards as a *fiction* of Grotius. Certainly no Rabbinical authority is given for such a statement: but it is put forward confidently by Grotius, and since his time adopted without enquiry by many Commentators. It is uncertain whether the *sevenfold* division prevailed so early as the Apostle's time: and at all events, as we must not invent Jewish divisions which never existed, so it seems rash to apply here, one about whose date we are not certain, and which does not suit the context:—for to be rapt only to the clouds, even supposing ver. 4 to relate a further *assumption*, would hardly be thus solemnly introduced, or the preposition ἕως used. The safest explanation therefore is, *not to follow any fixed division*, but judging by the evident intention of the expression, to understand a *high degree* of celestial exaltation. I cannot see any cogency in Meyer's argument, that 'the third heaven must have been an idea well known and previously defined among his readers,' seeing that in such words as τρὶς μακάριος, &c. it is manifestly inapplicable.

3, 4.] *A solemn repetition of the foregoing, with the additional particular of his having had unspeakable revelations made to him.* Some, as Clem. Strom. v. 12 (80), p. 693 P., Iren. ii. 30. 7, p. 162, Athan. Apol. 20, vol. i. p. 263, Orig. (or his interpreter) on Rom. xvi. lib. x. 43, vol. iv. p. 688, Œcum., al., think that this was a *fresh assumption*, ἕως τρίτου οὐρανοῦ κἀκεῖθεν εἰς τὸν παράδεισον, and with these Meyer agrees: but surely had this been intended, some intimation would have been given of it, either by καί, or by placing εἰς τὸν παράδεισον (as the stress would be then no longer on the fact ἁρπαγῆναι as before, but on the *new place to which* ἡρπάγη) in the place of emphasis before ἡρπάγη;—or, by both combined,—ὅτι καὶ εἰς τὸν παράδεισον ἡρπάγη. As it is,

[x] ἄῤῥητα ῥήματα ἃ οὐκ [y] ἐξὸν ἀνθρώπῳ λαλῆσαι. 5 [z] ὑπὲρ
[t] τοῦ [t] τοιούτου [z] καυχήσομαι, [z] ὑπὲρ δὲ ἐμαυτοῦ οὐ [z] καυχήσομαι, εἰ μὴ ἐν ταῖς [a] ἀσθενείαις [μου]. 6 ἐὰν γὰρ
θελήσω καυχήσασθαι, οὐκ ἔσομαι [b] ἄφρων· [c] ἀλήθειαν
γὰρ ἐρῶ· [d] φείδομαι δέ, μή τις [ef] εἰς ἐμὲ [f] λογίσηται [g] ὑπὲρ
ὃ βλέπει με, ἢ ἀκούει [τι] ἐξ ἐμοῦ. 7 καὶ τῇ [h] ὑπερ-

...μου M. A και τη ... ABDFK LPℵ a b c d e f g h k l m n o 17. 47

x here only †. Lev. xviii. 23 Symm. y Matt. xii. 4. Acts ii. 29 only. Esth. iv. 2. z ch. vii. 14. ix. 2. a ch. xi. 30. b ch. xi. 16, 19 reff. c Rom. ix. 1. Eph. iv. 25. Ps. xiv. 2. d = here only. (Rom. xi. 21 reff.) Isa. liv. 2. Xen. Cyr. i. 6. 19, 35. (μὴ φείδου διδάσκειν, Eur. Orest. 387.) e = ch. x. 13, 16 b. f = here only. (Hos. vii. 15.) g = 1 Cor. iv. 6. x. 13. h Rom. vii. 13 reff. Jos. Antt. i. 13. 4. ii. 2. 1.

[4. ανθρωπων L b 47.]

5. om του M. for 2nd υπερ, περι D[1]. om ου (*from preceding termination*) ℵ[1](corrd by ℵ[1] appy). τοις ασθενημασιν D[1]. om μου B D[1](and lat) 17 syrr copt arm: ins (*from ch* xi. 30?) D[3][-gr] FKLMPℵ rel vulg goth æth Ath, [Euthal-ms] Thdrt Damasc [Ambr$_2$ Ambrst].

6. for γαρ, δε K: γαρ και P [arm(Tischdf) Chr$_2$]. om τι (*as superfluous*) B D[3][-gr] F[-gr(and G-lat)] ℵ[1] m 17 am(with demid fuld[1] tol harl[2]) [(Syr copt)] æth arm Orig$_2$(-int$_1$) [Euthal-ms]: ins D[1](and lat) KLℵ[3] rel [vulg-clem F-lat harl[1]] syr goth Chr$_{[alic]}$ Thdrt Damasc Thl Œc Ambrst.

with the verb *preceding* in both clauses, and therefore no prominence given to the places as distinguished from one another, I must hold ἕως τρίτου οὐρ. to be at least so far equivalent to εἰς τὸν παράδεισον, as to be a general local description of the situation in which ὁ παράδεισος is found. The *repetition* of εἴτε . . . . οἶδεν is equally accountable on either explanation, being made for solemnity and emphasis. The **παράδεισος** cannot here be the Jewish Paradise, the blissful division or side of Hades (Scheol), where the spirits of the just awaited the resurrection, see note on Luke xvi. 22,—but the Paradise of which our Lord spoke on the Cross,—the place of happiness into which He at His Death introduced the spirits of the just: see on ref. Luke. **ἄῤῥητα ῥήματα,** i. e. as explained below, **words which it is not lawful to utter** :—as Vulg., "*arcana verba, quæ non licet homini loqui.*" The interpretation, "*quæ dici nequeunt,*" as Beza, Estius, Calov., Olsh., al., is hardly consistent with the narrative; for in that case, as Bengel remarks, 'Paulus non potuisset audire.' The passages adduced by Wetst. mostly refer to the *mysteries,* or some secret rites: e. g. Demosth. contra Neæram, p. 1369, αὔτη ἡ γυνὴ ὑμῖν ἔθυε τὰ ἄῤῥητα ἱερὰ ὑπὲρ τῆς πόλεως, καὶ εἶδεν, ἃ οὐ προσῆκεν αὐτὴν ὁρᾶν ξένην οὖσαν. **ἃ οὐκ ἐξόν] which it is not lawful for a** MAN **to utter** (see above):—imparted by God, but not to be divulged to others: and therefore, in this case, intended, we may presume, for the Apostle's own consolation and encouragement. *Of what kind* they were, or *by whom* uttered, we have no hint given, and it were worse than trifling to conjecture. "Sublimitatis certe magnæ fuere: nam non omnia cœlestia sunt ineffabilia, v. gr. Ex. xxxiv. 6, Isa. vi. 3, quæ tamen valde sublimia." Bengel. 5.] Of such a man he will boast, but not (see above on ver. 1) of himself, except it be in his infirmities. **τοῦ τοιούτου** must be *masc.* as before, *not neuter,* as Luth., al., take it. This is shewn by ὑπέρ, used of *the person respecting whom* (reff.), whereas ἐν is said of the *thing on account of which,* a man boasts. He strikes here again the key-note of the whole—*boasting in his infirmities.* He will boast of such a person, so favoured, so exalted; but this merely by the way: it is not his subject: it was introduced, not indeed *without reference* to the main point, but principally to bring in the infirmity following. 6.] **For** (supply the sentence for which γάρ renders a reason: '*Not but that I might boast concerning myself if I would*')—**if I shall wish to boast** (ὑπὲρ ἐμαυτοῦ), **I shall not be a fool** (I shall not act rashly or imprudently, for I shall not boast without solid ground for it): **for I shall speak the truth:—but I abstain** (reff.), **that no one may reckon of me** (reff. and add εἰς μαλακίαν σκώπτων, Demosth. 308. 18) **beyond** (by a standard superior to that furnished by) **what he sees me** (to be), **or hears** (if τι form part of the text, **or hears any thing**: a pleonastic construction = ἢ εἴ τι ἀκούει) **from me.** Lest he should seem to undervalue so legitimate a subject of boasting, he alleges the reason why he abstains: not that he had not this and more such exaltations, truly to allege: but because he wished to be judged of by what they really had seen and heard of and from himself in person. 7—10.] He now comes to that for which the foregoing was mainly alleged: the *infirmity in his flesh,* which above others hindered his personal efficiency in the apostolic

βολῇ τῶν [i] ἀποκαλύψεων [διὸ] [k] ἵνα μὴ [l] ὑπεραίρωμαι, ἐδόθη μοι [m] σκόλοψ [n] τῇ σαρκί, ἄγγελος σατανᾶ ἵνα με [o] κολαφίζῃ [[p] ἵνα μὴ [l] ὑπεραίρωμαι]. 8 [q] ὑπὲρ τούτου

ABDFK LPℵ a b c d e f g h k l m n o 17. 47

i ver. 1. k arrangement of words, ch. ii. 4 reff. l [here bis.] 2 Thess. ii. 4 only. Ps. lxxi. 16. m here only. = Num. xxxiii. 55. Ezek. xxviii. 24. n dat., 1 Cor. vii. 28. see Gal. iv. 14. o Matt. xxvi. 67 || Mk. 1 Cor. iv. 11. 1 Pet. ii. 20 only †. p pleonasm., Rev ii. 5. Matt. v. 18. Winer, edn. 6, § 65. 6. q = ver. 5

7. rec om *διο*, with DKLP rel [vulg F-lat syrr goth arm] Ath$_1$ Chr$_2$ Thdrt$_2$ [Damasc] Iren-int$_1$ [Orig-int$_2$ Ambrst] Aug: ins AB F[-gr(and G-lat)] ℵ 17 [Euthal-ms]. *υπεραιρομαι* DLP m. (so P m [Damasc-ms] below.) aft *σαρκι* ins *μου* F vulg Orig-int$_1$ [Bas-int$_1$] Cypr$_1$. rec (for *σατανα*) *σαταν*, with A^{2}D$^{2\cdot3}$KLP ℵ^3(appy) rel syr-mg-gr Orig$_1$ Ath$_1$ Mac$_2$ Chr$_2$ [Euthal-ms] Thdrt Damasc[and ms]: txt A^{1}BD^{1}Fℵ^1 17^1(sic, Treg) (Orig$_2$ *του σατανα*) [*satanæ* latt]. om 2nd *ινα μη υπεραιρωμαι* (*as superfluous: but the repetition has special emphasis*) ADFℵ^1 17 latt æth Chr$_5$ Iren-int Tert$_1$ Aug: ins BKLPℵ^3 rel syrr copt goth [arm] Orig$_2$ Mac$_1$ [Chr$_1$ Euthal-ms] Thdrt$_3$ Damasc Bas[-int$_1$ Tert$_1$ Cypr$_2$ Hil$_1$ Ambrst].

8. ins *και* bef *υπερ* A Orig Thdrt$_2$ Iren-int$_1$. *τον κυρ.* bef *τρις* D^1[and lat] copt æth.

ministry. **7.**] **And that I might not, by the abundant excess of revelations** (made to me), **be uplifted** (the order of the words is chosen to bring *τῇ ὑπερβ. κ.τ.λ.* into the place of foremost emphasis: see reff. The *διό* can hardly stand with the present punctuation. If it forms part of the text, it must begin the sentence, and we must with Lachmann join *καὶ τῇ ὑπερβ. τῶν ἀποκ.* to the foregoing, as in apposition with *ἀσθενείαις*. But thus a very strange sense would be given), **there was given me** ('*by God:*' certainly not, as Meyer, al., by *Satan*, of whom such an expression as *ἐδόθη* would surely hardly be used: cf. *ἡ χάρις ἡ δοθεῖσά μοι*, so often said by the Apostle,—Rom. xii. 3, 6; xv. 15 al., and the absolute use of *ἐδόθη* for *bestowed, portioned out by God*, 1 Cor. xi. 15; xii. 7, 8; Gal. iii. 21; James i. 5) **a thorn** (the word may signify a *stake*, or *sharp pointed staff*, *ξύλον ὀξύ*, Hesych.,—so in Hom. Il. *σ*. 176, *κεφαλὴν . . . πῆξαι ἀνὰ σκολόπεσσι*; but in the LXX, reff., it is '*a thorn*,' and such is the more likely meaning here. Meyer cites from Artemid. iii. 33, *ἄκανθαι καὶ σκόλοπες ὀδύνας σημαίνουσι διὰ τὸ ὀξύ* (compare ref. Ezek., *σκόλοψ πικρίας καὶ ἄκανθα ὀδύνης*). See however Stanley's note, who rejects the meaning '*thorn*,' and supposes the figure to refer to the punishment of impalement) **in my flesh** (the expression used Gal. iv. 14 of this same affliction, *τὸν πειρασμὸν ὑμῶν ἐν τῇ σαρκί μου*, seems decisive for rendering the dative thus, and not as a dativus incommodi: see also ref. 1 Cor.), **the** (or an) **angel of Satan** (even if we read *σατᾶν*, it can only be the genitive. If taken as the nom., the expression would mean either, *a hostile angel*, which would be contrary to the universal usage of Satan, as a proper name: or, *the angel Satan*, which is equally inconsistent with N. T. usage, according to which Satan, though once an angel, is now *ἄρχων τῆς ἐξουσίας τοῦ ἀέρος*, Eph. ii. 2, and has his own angels, Matt. xxv. 41), **that he** (*the angel of Satan*,—not the *σκόλοψ*, which would be an unnecessary confusion of metaphors. 'The continuation of a discourse often belongs to the *word in apposition*, not to the main subject,' Meyer) **may buffet me** (*κολαφίζῃ* is best thus expressed, in the *present*. The aorist would denote merely *one* such *act* of insult. Thus Chrys.: . . *ὥστε* . . **διηνεκοῦς** *δεῖσθαι τοῦ χαλινοῦ· οὐ γὰρ εἶπεν, ἵνα κολαφίσῃ, ἀλλ' ἵνα κολαφίζῃ*,—Theophyl., *οὐχ ἵνα ἅπαξ με κολαφίσῃ, ἀλλ' ἀεί*,—and similarly Œcum.), **that I may not be uplifted** (the repetition gives force and solemnity,—expressing his firm persuasion of the divine intention in thus afflicting him). As regards the *thorn itself*, very many, and some very absurd conjectures have been hazarded. They may be resolved into three heads, the two former of which are, from the nature of the case, out of the question (see below): (1) that Paul alludes to *spiritual solicitations of the devil* ('injectiones Satanæ'), who suggested to him blasphemous thoughts,—so Gerson, Luther (how characteristically!), Calov.,—or remorse for his former life, so Osiander, Mosheim, &c.: or according to the Romanist interpreters, who want to find here a precedent for their monkish stories of temptations,—*incitements to lust*,—so Thom. Aq., Lyra, Bellarmin, Estius, Corn.-a-Lapide, al. (2) that he alludes to *opposition from his adversaries*, or *some one adversary* *κατ' ἐξοχήν*; so many ancient Commentators, Chrys., Theophyl., Œcum., Theodoret,—Calvin, Beza, al., and more recently, Fritzsche, and Schrader. (3) that he points to *some grievous bodily pain*, which has been curiously specified by different Commentators. The ancients (Chrys., Theophyl., Œcum., Jerome on Gal. iv. 14 (lib. ii. 4, vol. vii. p. 460)) mention *κεφαλαλγία*: some

τρὶς τὸν κύριον [r] παρεκάλεσα [s] ἵνα [t] ἀποστῇ ἀπ᾽ ἐμοῦ.
9 καὶ εἴρηκέν μοι [u] Ἀρκεῖ σοι ἡ χάρις μου· ἡ γὰρ δύναμις
ἐν [v] ἀσθενείᾳ [w] τελεῖται. [x] ἥδιστα οὖν μᾶλλον [y] καυχήσομαι [y] ἐν ταῖς [v] ἀσθενείαις μου, ἵνα [z] ἐπισκηνώσῃ ἐπ᾽ ἐμὲ ἡ
δύναμις τοῦ χριστοῦ. 10 διὸ [ab] εὐδοκῶ [b] ἐν [v] ἀσθενείαις, ἐν

r = Matt. xviii. 32. xxvi. 53. Luke xv. 28. Acts xxv. 2. s 1 Cor. i. 10 reff. t = Acts v. 38 reff. u = Matt. xxv. 9. John xiv. 8 (Luke iii. 14. 1 Tim. vi. 8. Heb. xiii. 5. 3 John 10) only. Num. xi. 22. v = ch. xi. 30. w = here only. (See Luke ii. 39. Rom. ii. 27.) Eur. Bacch. 90. x ver. 15 only †. (-δέως, ch. xi. 19. -διον, Sir. xxii. 11.) y Rom. ii. 17 reff. z here only †. ἐπισκ. ἐπὶ τὰς οἰκίας, Polyb. iv. 18. 8. a ch. v. 8. Rom. xv. 26, 27 reff. b 1 Cor. x. 5 reff.

9. for ειρηκεν, ειπεν F Chr$_2$. rec aft δυναμις ins μου (*see note*), with A^2 D$^{2\cdot3}$[-gr] KLPℵ^3 rel syrr Orig$_1$[-c$_1$ Ath$_1$ Euthal-ms] Chr$_4$ Thdrt Pallad [Damasc]: om [A^1]BD^{1}Fℵ^1 [latt] goth æth Archel$_1$ Orig-int$_3$ Iren-int$_1$ Bas[-int$_1$] Tert$_1$ Cypr$_1$ Ambrst Jer. rec τελειουται, with D^{3}KLPℵ^3 rel Orig$_1$[-c$_1$ Iren$_1$] Ath [Chr$_4$ Euthal-ms Thdrt-p]: txt ABD^{1}Fℵ^1. om μου B 67^2. 71 harl syr copt [arm] Iren$_1$(gr and int).
10. aft ασθενειαις ins μου F vulg(not am [demid harl tol] F-lat).

have supposed *hypochondriac melancholy*, which however hardly answers the conditions of a σκόλοψ, in which *acute pain* seems to be implied; alii aliter, see Pool, Synops. ad loc.; and Stanley's note, which is important in other respects also, and full of interest. On the whole, putting together the figure here used, that of a *thorn*, occasioning pain, and the κολαφισμός, *buffeting* or *putting to shame*, it seems quite necessary to infer that the Apostle alludes to *some painful and tedious bodily malady, which at the same time put him to shame* before those among whom he exercised his ministry. Of such a kind *may* have been the disorder in his eyes, more or less indicated in several passages of his history and Epistles (see notes on Acts xiii. 9; xxiii. 1 f.:—and Gal. iv. 14 (15?); vi. 11 (?)). But it may also have been something besides this, and to such an inference probability would lead us; disorders in the eyes, however sad in their consequences, not being usually of a very painful or distressing nature *in themselves*. **8.**] **In respect of this** (*angel of Satan*, not σκόλοψ, see below) **I thrice** (τρίς, not indefinite as Chrys., Hom. xxvi. p. 621, τουτέστι, πολλάκις. Meyer well observes, 'At his first and second request, no answer was given to him: on the third occasion, it came; and his faithful resignation to the Lord's will prevented his asking again') **besought the Lord** (Christ, see ver. 9) **that he might depart from me** (the angel of Satan, see Luke iv. 13 [Acts xxii. 29]): **9.**] **And He said to me** (this perf. can hardly in English be represented otherwise than by the historical aorist; in the Greek, it partakes of its own proper sense—'*He said, and that answer is enough*:' '*He hath said*,'—but this last would not contain reference enough to the *fact* itself. The poverty of our language in the finer distinctions of the tenses often obliges us to render inaccurately, and fall short of, the wonderful language with which we have to deal. *How* this was said, whether accompanied by an appearance of Christ to him or not, must remain in obscurity), **My grace** (not,—'My favour generally;'—'*My imparted grace*') **is sufficient for thee** (**ἀρκεῖ**, spoken from the divine omniscience, '*suffices, and shall suffice*:' q. d. '*the trial must endure, untaken away: but the grace shall also endure, and never fail thee*'), **for** (the reason lying in My ways being not as man's ways, My Power not being brought to perfection as man's power is conceived to be) **(My) Power is made perfect** (has its full energy and complete manifestation) **in** (as the element in which it acts as observable by man) **weakness.** See ch. iv. 7, and 1 Cor. ii. 3, 4,—where the influence of this divine response on the Apostle, is very manifest. If I mistake not, *the expression* **τῆς δυνάμεως**, *there*, favours the omission of μου here, as in our text, and makes it probable that it was inserted for perspicuity's sake, and to answer to ἡ δύν. τοῦ χρ. below. **Most gladly therefore will I rather** (than that my affliction should be removed from me, which before that response, I wished) **boast** (καυχ. is in the emphatic place,—I will rather *boast* in mine infirmities. Had μᾶλλον signified '*rather than in revelations*,' or '*rather than in any thing else*,' it would have been μᾶλλον ἐν ταῖς ἀσθενείαις μου καυχήσομαι) **in my infirmities, that** (by my ἀσθένειαι being not removed from me, but becoming my glory) **the Power of Christ may have its residence in me** (see ref. Polyb.—'may carry on in me its work unto completion,' as above). **10.**] **Wherefore** (because of this relation to human weakness and divine power) **I am well content** [cf. the same expression Matt. iii. 17] **in infirmities** (four kinds of which are then specified, —all coming also, as well as ἀσθ. *proper*,

c = here (Acts xxvii. 10, 21) only. Prov. viii. 13 al.
d = 1 Cor. vii. 26 reff. plur., ch. vi. 4.
e Mark iv. 17 ‖ Mt. x. 30. Acts viii. 1. xiii. 50. Rom. viii. 35. 2 Thess. i. 4. 2 Tim. iii. 11 bis only. Prov. xi. 19. Lam. iii. 19. 2 Macc. xii. 23 only.

ABDFK LPא a b c d e f g h k l m n o 17. 47

c ὕβρεσιν, ἐν d ἀνάγκαις, ἐν e διωγμοῖς, ἐν f στενοχωρίαις,
ὑπὲρ χριστοῦ· ὅταν γὰρ g ἀσθενῶ, τότε δυνατός εἰμι.
11 h Γέγονα i ἄφρων· ὑμεῖς με k ἠναγκάσατε. ἐγὼ γὰρ
l ὤφειλον ὑφ᾽ ὑμῶν m συνίστασθαι· οὐδὲν γὰρ n ὑστέρησα
τῶν o ὑπερλίαν ἀποστόλων, εἰ καὶ p οὐδέν εἰμι. 12 τὰ
μὲν q σημεῖα τοῦ ἀποστόλου r κατειργάσθη ἐν ὑμῖν ἐν
s πάσῃ t ὑπομονῇ, u σημείοις τε καὶ uv τέρασιν καὶ uw δυνάμεσιν. 13 τί γάρ ἐστιν x ὃ y ἡσσώθητε z ὑπὲρ τὰς λοιπὰς

f Rom. ii. 9 reff. g = Rom. iv. 19 reff. h = 1 Cor. xiii. 1. i ch. xi. 16, 19 reff. k Acts xxvi. 11 reff. l = Acts xvii. 29. 1 Cor. xi. 7, 10. m = Rom. iii. 5 reff. n constr., Rom. iii. 23. ch. xi. 5. (i. 7 reff.) o ch. xi. 5 only †. p 1 Cor. vii. 19 reff. q = Luke ii. 12. 2 Thess. iii. 17 al. r Rom. ii. 9 reff. s = Acts xx. 19 reff. t Rom. ii. 7 reff. u Acts ii. 22. Heb. ii. 4. v Acts vii. 36 reff. w = Matt. vii. 22. 1 Cor. xii. 10 al. x constr. acc., as Matt. xvi. 26. y here only. (-ττᾶσθαι, 2 Pet. ii. 19, 20. Isa. viii. 9. xx. 5.) z = ver. 6.

for εν αναγκαις, και εναγκαις א¹ (corrd by origl scribe to [κ.] αναγκ. [so Orig$_1$], by א³ to txt). om εν διωγμοις A. for 5th εν, και Bא¹: και εν a [arm(Tischdf)]: txt ADFKL [P]א³ rel. οτε F. δυνατω (for -τος ειμι) F[not F-lat, G-lat has both].

11. rec aft αφρων ins καυχωμενος, with LP rel syrr goth [Chr$_1$ Thdrt Damasc]: om ABDFKא 17 latt coptt æth arm Orig[-c$_1$ Euthal-ms Ambr$_1$ Ambrst]. ημεις F[-gr]. om υφ B¹(Tischdf) D¹[-gr]. υφ ημων A. for ουδεν, ου F[not F-lat]. aft ουδεν γαρ ins τι B.

12. at beg ins αλλα F [37(omg μεν)]. κατηργασθη B¹F d: κατηργασθην D. rec ins εν bef σημειοις (*mechanical repetition from the foregoing*), with D³[-gr] KLP rel vulg-ed(with demid) Thdrt; και F[-gr(and G-lat)] Syr Chr$_1$: τε א³: om AB D¹[and lat] א¹ a 17 am(with fuld tol [F-lat]) syr goth arm [Euthal-ms] Damasc Ambrst. rec om τε, with ADFKLP א-corr¹ rel: ins Bא¹ a 17 [Euthal-ms] Damasc.

13. (ησσωθητε, so BD¹א¹ 17[ισωθ.]: ελατωθηται F.) for υπερ, παρα D.

under the category of ἀσθένειαι, as *hindrances and bafflings of human strength*),—**in insults, in necessities, in persecutions, in distresses,—on behalf of Christ: for whenever I am weak** (applying to all five situations above), **then I am mighty.** Wetst. quotes from Philo, Vita Mosis, i. 13, vol. ii. p. 92, μὴ ἀναπίπτετε. τὸ ἀσθενὲς ὑμῶν δύναμίς ἐστι. 11—18.] *He excuses his boasting, and is thereby led to speak of the signs of an Apostle wrought among them, and to reassert his disinterestedness in preaching to them, on occasion of his past and intended visits.*

11.] **I am** BECOME (the emphasis on γέγονα,—I am verily *become* a fool, viz. by this boasting, which I have now concluded. 'Receptui canit:' Bengel. But it is still ironical, spoken from the situation of his adversaries) **a fool: ye compelled me** (ὑμεῖς emphatic). **For I** (ἐγώ also emphatic, but more with reference to what has passed: *'ye compelled me*, it was no doing of *mine*, for *I* &c.' The meaning is not, as De W., "*I*, not mine adversaries," who are an element foreign to the present sentence) **ought to have been recommended by you** (emphatic, by *you*, *not by himself*): **for I was nothing behind** (when I was with you) **these overmuch Apostles** (see on ch. xi. 5: but here even more plainly than there, the expression cannot be applied to the other Apostles, seeing that the aor. would in that case be inconsistent with the fact—the Corinthians never having had an opportunity of comparing him with them), **even though I am nothing** (see similar expressions of humility, 1 Cor. xv. 9—11).

12.] *Confirmation of the* **οὐδὲν ὑστέρησα . . . . The signs indeed** (the μέν is elliptical,—see Hartung, Partikellehre, ii. 411,—corresponding to a suppressed ὅμως δὲ . . . .; '*in this case, the signs indeed* &c., *but, notwithstanding, I am not recommended by you.*' So Soph. Œd. Col. 526, ἤνεγκον κακότατ᾽, ὦ ξένοι, ἤνεγκ᾽, ἀέκων μέν, θεὸς ἴστω. It always throws out into strong emphasis the noun, pronoun, or verb to which it is attached, as here σημεῖα) **of an Apostle** (τοῦ generic,—'ejus qui Apostolus sit,' Bengel) **were wrought out among you** ("the Apostle's own personality as the worker is modestly veiled behind the passive." Meyer) **in all** (possible) **patience** (endurance of opposition, which did not cause me to leave off working. **ὑπομονή** is *not one of* the σημεῖα, as Chrys., Hom. xxvii. p. 627: θέα ποῖον πρῶτον τίθησι, τὴν ὑπομονήν. τοῦτο γὰρ ἀποστόλου δεῖγμα, τὸ φέρειν πάντα γενναίως,—but *the element in which* the σημεῖα were wrought out), **by signs and wonders** (σημ. not as above, but as constantly found with τέρασι, as an intensitive synonym) **and mighty works** (see ref. Heb.). 13—15.] *His disinterestedness, shewn in his past, and resolved in his future dealings with them.*

[a] ἐκκλησίας, εἰ μὴ ὅτι αὐτὸς ἐγὼ οὐ [b] κατενάρκησα ὑμῶν;
[c] χαρίσασθέ μοι τὴν [d] ἀδικίαν ταύτην. 14 ἰδοὺ [e] τρίτον
[[e] τοῦτο] [f] ἑτοίμως [f] ἔχω ἐλθεῖν πρὸς ὑμᾶς, καὶ οὐ [b] κατα-
ναρκήσω· οὐ γὰρ [g] ζητῶ τὰ ὑμῶν, ἀλλὰ ὑμᾶς. οὐ γὰρ
[h] ὀφείλει τὰ τέκνα τοῖς γονεῦσιν [i] θησαυρίζειν, ἀλλ' οἱ
γονεῖς τοῖς τέκνοις· 15 ἐγὼ δὲ [k] ἥδιστα [l] δαπανήσω καὶ [m] ἐκδαπανηθήσομαι ὑπὲρ τῶν [n] ψυχῶν ὑμῶν, εἰ [o] περισσοτέρως

a plur., Rom. xvi. 16 reff. b ch. xi. 8 only (reff.). c = ch. ii. 7, 10 reff. d = here only. Thuc. iii. 66. e ch. xiii. 1 reff. f Acts xxi. 13 reff. g 1 Cor. x. 24 reff. h ver. 11. i 1 Cor. xvi. 2 reff.
k ver. 9. l Acts xxi. 24 reff. m here only †. Polyb. xxv. 8. 4, ἐκδαπανᾳν τὰς προσόδους. n = Heb. xiii. 17. 1 Pet. ii. 11. o ch. i. 12 reff.

om οτι K 47. εγω bef αυτος F m latt goth. αμαρτιαν F[-gr].

14. rec om τουτο, with KLP rel Thdrt Œc: ins ABFℵ a b c d m o 17. 47 latt syr goth æth Chr_1 [Euthal-ms Thdrt] Damasc Thl Ambrst Pel, and (but bef τριτον) D[-gr] 93 (Syr?) copt [arm] Did_1. (*see note.*) rec aft καταναρκησω ins υμων (*from above; had* υμων *been in the text origly, it would never have been ejected, leaving the verb standing alone. This is further shewn by the var* υμας), with $D^{2\cdot3}$KLP rel [latt syrr coptt goth arm Chr_1 Thdrt]; υμας D^1F: om ABℵ 17 æth [Euthal-ms] Damasc. (αλλα(1st), so ABDFLPℵ a d e f k m n 47 [Euthal-ms Damasc].) αλλα(2nd) Aℵ 17.

15. aft δαπανησω add και εκδαπανησω D^1(and lat) Ambrst. om ει D^1(and lat) G-lat Ambrst. rec aft ει ins και (*to give* (*mistaken*) *emphasis: see notes*), with $D^{2\cdot3}$[-gr] KLPℵ^3 rel syrr [æth] arm Chr Thdrt Damasc Pel: om AB D^1[and lat] Fℵ^1 17 coptt goth [*licet* vulg F-lat].

The question τί γὰρ κ.τ.λ. is asked in bitter irony. It is an illustration of ἐν πάσῃ ὑπομονῇ, and of the distinction conferred on them by so long manifestation of the signs of an Apostle among them. '*Was this endurance of working which I shewed, marred by the fact that I worked gratuitously among you?*' ἡσσ. **ὑπέρ** does not imply that all churches suffered loss, and that the *loss* of the Corinthians was only not greater than that of other churches: but the comparative, implied in ἡσσ. is carried out by the ὑπέρ,—'*ye suffered loss in comparison with the other Churches.*' **13. εἰ μὴ ὅτι**] except *that one point*, in which of all others they had *least* reason to complain. This one is put forward to indicate their deep ingratitude, if they did complain, seeing that the only point of difference in their treatment had been a preference: 'die tief gekränkte Liebe redet,' Meyer. On **κατενάρκ.** see ref. **χαρ. μ. τ. ἀδ. ταύτην**] The irony here reaches its height. **14.**] **τρίτον** (the τοῦτο, though so strongly attested, can hardly have been *omitted*, had it ever been in the text, and therefore has probably been inserted from ch. xiii. 1) **ἑτ. ἔχω ἐλθ.**, must, *from the context*, mean, **I am ready to come the third time**;—not, '*I am the third time ready to come*,' i. e. 'this is the third time that I have been *ready to come* to you.' This latter meaning has been adopted by Beza, Grot., Estius, al., Paley, al., and even De Wette, hesitatingly, in order to evade the difficulty of supposing Paul to have been before this twice at Corinth. But on this see Prolegomena to 1 Cor. § v. Here, the context has absolutely nothing to do with his *third preparation* to come, which would be a new element, requiring some explanation, as in 1 Thess. ii. 18. The natural, and, I am persuaded, only true inference from the words here is, 'I am coming to you a third time,—and I will not burden you this time, any more than I did at *my two previous visits*.' Our business in such cases is, not to wrest plain words to fit our preconceived chronology, but to adapt our *confessedly uncertain and imperfect history of the Apostle's life*, to the data furnished by the plain honest sense of his Epistles.

οὐ γὰρ ζητῶ . . . .] Wetst. quotes Cicero de Fin. ii. 26: 'Me igitur ipsum ames oportet, non mea, si veri amici futuri sumus.'—μείζονα ἐπιζητῶ, ψυχὰς ἀντὶ χρημάτων, σωτηρίαν ἀντὶ χρυσίου, Chrys., p. 629. **οὐ γὰρ ὀφείλει . . .**] Paul was the *spiritual father* of the Corinthian Church, 1 Cor. iv. 14, 15: he does not therefore want to be *enriched by them*, his children, but rather to *lay up riches for them*, seeking to have *them* as his treasure, and thus to *enrich them*, as a loving father does his children. The θησαυρός is left indefinite: if pressed strictly, it cannot be *earthly* treasure in the *negative* part of the sentence, *heavenly*, in the *positive*;—cf. next verse.

Notice, ὀφείλει is not impersonal, but the common verb to τέκνα and γονεῖς, agreeing by proximity with the former. **15.**] ἐγὼ δὲ τῶν φύσει πατέρων καὶ πλέον τι ποιεῖν ἐπαγγέλλομαι, Theodoret: and similarly Chrys. and Theophyl. They *lay up* treasures: *I* will *spend* them:—καὶ τί

ὑμᾶς ἀγαπῶν [p] ἧσσον ἀγαπῶμαι. 16 Ἔστω δέ, ἐγὼ οὐ [q] κατεβάρησα ὑμᾶς. ἀλλὰ [r] ὑπάρχων [s] πανοῦργος [t] δόλῳ ὑμᾶς [u] ἔλαβον. 17 μή [v] τινα ὧν ἀπέσταλκα πρὸς ὑμᾶς, [v] δι' αὐτοῦ [w] ἐπλεονέκτησα ὑμᾶς; 18 [x] παρεκάλεσα Τίτον, καὶ [y] συναπέστειλα [z] τὸν ἀδελφόν· μή τι [w] ἐπλεονέκτησεν ὑμᾶς Τίτος; οὐ τῷ αὐτῷ [a] πνεύματι [a] περιεπατήσαμεν; οὐ τοῖς αὐτοῖς [b] ἴχνεσιν;

19 [c] Πάλαι δοκεῖτε ὅτι [d] ὑμῖν [e] ἀπολογούμεθα. [f] κατ-

ABDFK LPℵ a b c d e f g h k l m n o 17. 47

p = here (1 Cor. xi. 17) only. 2 Macc. iv. 40.
q here only †. (-ρύνειν, Mark xiv. 40. 2 Kings xiii. 25.)
r Acts viii. 16 reff.
s here only. = Job v. 12. (good sense, Prov. xiii. 1. xxviii. 2.) (-γία, ch. xi. 3.)
t Acts xiii. 10 reff.
u = ch. xi. 20.
v constr., Luke xxi. 6. Rom. viii. 3. Gal. i. 20.
w ch. ii. 11 reff.
x = 1 Cor. xvi. 12. ch. viii. 6.
y here only. Exod. xxxiii. 2, 12. Esdr. v. 2 only.
z see ch. viii. 18, 22.
a constr., Acts xxi. 21 reff.
b Rom. iv. 12 reff.
c = (see note) Mark xv. 44 (Matt. xi. 21. Luke x. 13. Heb. i. 1. 2 Pet. i. 9. Jude 4) only ‡. (Isa. xxxvii. 26 only.)
d dat., see 1 Cor. ix. 3.
e Acts xix. 33 reff.
f = ch. ii. 17. Rom. iv. 17 only. (Luke xix. 30 al.) Exod. xxxii. 11 A Ald.

for *αγαπων*, *αγαπω* ℵ[1] b[1] d 17 [coptt(Tischdf)]. (**ησσον**, so ABD[1]Pℵ[1] 17[*ισον*]: *ελασσον* F.)

16. aft *εγω* ins *δε* F[not F-lat] syr Thl. *ουκ εβαρησα υμας* D[1] : *ου κατεναρκησα υμων* Fℵ (a) 20-3[1]. 39. 57. 73 Chr_1 [Euthal-ms]. (**αλλα**, so ABD[1]FLPℵ a m 47 [Euthal-ms Damasc].)

17. om *δι αυτου* F. **18.** *ημας* L.

19. rec (for *παλαι*) *παλιν*, with D-gr KLPℵ[3] rel G-lat harl[1] syrr copt goth arm Chr_1 Thdrt [Damasc] : txt ABFℵ[1] 17 vulg D-lat [Euthal-ms] Ambrst-comm Pel.

λέγω, χρήματα δαπανήσω; αὐτὸς ἐγὼ ἐκδαπανηθήσομαι· τουτέστι, κἂν τὴν σάρκα δέῃ δαπανῆσαι ὑπὲρ τῆς σωτηρίας τῶν ψυχῶν ὑμῶν, οὐ φείσομαι, Theophyl. Cf. Hor. Od. i. 12. 38: 'animæque magnæ prodigum Paullum.' **εἰ** is less strong than *εἰ καί*, which has been apparently a gloss on it. It assumes the case, but does not bring out the contrast between the course of action and the state of circumstances so strongly. *Here*, it appears as if ἧσσον ἀγαπῶμαι were by the *εἰ* connected with ἐκδαπανηθήσομαι,—'*and will be spent*, used up, *in the service of your souls, if, the more abundantly I love you, the less I be loved*:' implying, that such a return for his love was leading to, and would in time accomplish, the ἐκδαπανηθήσομαι.

16—18.] *He refutes a possible*, perhaps an actual *calumny*,—*that though he had acted disinterestedly towards them himself, he had some side-way of profiting by them, through others.* **16.**] **ἔστω δέ**—'but let us suppose the former matter dismissed:' let the fact be granted, that I myself (emphatic) did not burden (= *κατενάρκησα*) you. Then the sense breaks off, and the force of the concession goes no farther, the following words making a new hypothesis. **Nevertheless, being** (by habit and standing, *ὑπάρχ.*) **crafty** (unprincipled, and versatile in devices), **I caught you with guile** (with some more subtle way. *Caught* you, in order to practise upon you for my own ends; but ἔλαβον is not ἐπλεονέκτησα, as Chrys., Hom. xxviii. p. 633:—see ref. and note). **17, 18.**] *Specification, in refutation, of the ways in which this might be supposed to have taken place.* The construction *τινα ὧν . . . δι' αὐτοῦ* is an anacoluthon. He sets *τινα ὧν ἀπέστ. πρ. ὑμ.* forward in the place of emphasis; how intending to govern *τινα*, is not plain: but drops the construction, and proceeds, *δι' αὐτοῦ κ.τ.λ.* See examples of the same in reff., and Winer, edn. 6, § 63. i. 2. d. **18.**] **παρεκάλεσα**, scil. '*to go to you*:' see reff. This journey of Titus cannot, of course, be the one spoken of ch. viii. 6, 17, 22, 24; but some previous mission to them before this Epistle was written: probably that from which he returned with the report of their penitence to Paul in Macedonia, ch. vii. 6 ff. We certainly have not elsewhere any hint of ὁ ἀδελφός having accompanied him on this journey: but this is no reason why it should not have been so. **τὸν ἀδελφόν**—perhaps, one of the two mentioned ch. viii. 18, 22: some other, well known to the Corinthians, but absolutely unknown to us: but not, *a brother*, as in E. V. It is plain from this and from what follows, that this brother was quite subordinate to Titus in the mission. **τῷ αὐτῷ πνεύμ.**] dat. of the *manner*; see ref. The Spirit in which they walked was *the Holy Spirit*: τῷ αὐτῷ πνευματικῷ χαρίσματι· χάρισμα γὰρ καλεῖ τὸ στενούμενον μὴ λαβεῖν, Theophyl. **τοῖς αὐτ. ἴχν.**] in the same footsteps, viz. each as the other: οὐδὲ μικρόν, φησί, παρεξῆλθον τὴν ἐμὴν ὁδόν, Theophyl. The dative ἴχνεσιν, as in ref. = ἐν ἴχνεσιν: see also Acts xiv. 16; Jude 11. Meyer cites Pind. Pyth. x. 20,—ἐμβέβακεν ἴχνεσιν πατρός, and Nem. vi. 27, ἴχνεσιν ἐν Πραξιδάμαντος ἐὸν πόδα νέμων. Cf. also Philo de Caritate, § 2,

έναντι θεοῦ [g] ἐν χριστῷ λαλοῦμεν· τὰ δὲ πάντα, [h] ἀγαπητοί, [i] ὑπὲρ τῆς [j] ὑμῶν [k] οἰκοδομῆς. 20 [l] φοβοῦμαι γὰρ [l] μή
[l] πως ἐλθὼν οὐχ οἵους θέλω [m] εὕρω ὑμᾶς, κἀγὼ [m] εὑρεθῶ
[n] ὑμῖν οἷον οὐ θέλετε· [l] μή [l] πως [opq] ἔρεις, [p] ζῆλος, [pqr] θυμοί,
[ps] ἐριθεῖαι, [t] καταλαλιαί, [u] ψιθυρισμοί, [v] φυσιώσεις, [w] ἀκατα-
στασίαι· 21 μὴ πάλιν ἐλθόντος [x] μου [y] ταπεινώσει [x] με ὁ [z] θεός

g Rom. ix. 1. Eph. iv. 17. h ch. vii. 1 reff. i = ch. i. 6. j posn., 1Cor. ix. 12. ch. i. 6 bis, 24. vii. 7 3ce. viii. 13, 14. xiii. 9. Phil. . 19, 25. ii. 30. Col. i. 8. 1 Thess. iii. 7 (Rom. xvi. 19. 1 Cor. vii. 35. ch. vii. 15) only. k Rom. xiv. 19 reff. l ch. xi. 3. m = 1 Cor. iv. 2 reff. n dat., Luke xxiv. 35 al. o 1 Cor. i. 11 reff. p Gal. v. 20. q as above (p). Rom. xiii. 13. 1 Cor. iii. 3. Sir. xl. 5. r = Eph. iv. 31 al. plur., Gal. v. 20 only. (Wisd. vii. 20.) s Rom. ii. 8 reff. t 1 Pet. ii. 1 only †. Wisd. i. 11 only. (-λος, Rom. i. 30.) u here only. Eccles. x. 11 only. (-στής, Rom. i. 29.) v here only †. (-σιοῦν, 1 Cor. iv. 6 al.) w 1 Cor. xiv. 33 reff. x constr., Acts xxi. 17 reff. y ch. xi. 7 reff. constr., Col. ii. 8. z Rom. i. 8 reff.

rec (for κατεναντι) κατενωπιον, with DKLP rel [Bas_1] Thdrt Thl Œc: txt ABFℵ m 17 [Euthal-ms] Damasc. rec ins του bef θεου, with D[2.3]KLℵ[3] rel: om ABD[1]FPℵ[1] m(θεω) 17 [Bas_1 Euthal-ms]. for αγαπ., αδελφοι P.

20. και εγω F. ερις (*itacism?*) Aℵ b d f g h k 17 Syr arm Chr Thl: txt BDFKLP rel latt syr coptt goth [Euthal-ms $Antch_1$] Thdrt Damasc [Œc] Ambrst. rec ζηλοι, with D[2.3]KLPℵ rel latt syr coptt Chr Thdrt [Euthal-ms Ambrst]: txt AB D[1][-gr] F[-gr] 17 Syr goth arm [$Antch_1$] Damasc.

21. rec ελθοντα με (*grammatical correction*), with DKLℵ[3] rel goth [Chr_1 $Thdrt_3$ Damasc]: txt ABFPℵ[1] [Euthal-ms]. rec ταπεινωση (*gramml corrn* or *itacism?*), with AKℵ rel [Chr Thdrt Damasc]: txt BDFLP (c?) d f g k n [Euthal-ms] Œc. rec om με, with D[3]KL rel: ins ABD[1]F[P]ℵ d.

vol. ii. p. 385, τοῖς αὐτοῖς ἴχνεσιν ἐπακολουθῆσαι. **19—21.**] *He refutes the notion which might arise in the minds of his readers, that he was vindicating himself* BEFORE THEM *as judges*, see 1 Cor. iv. 3; *and assures them that he does all for their good, fearing in what state he might find them on his arrival.* **19.**] **πάλαι** was misunderstood, and πάλιν appears to have been a conjectural emendation, from ch. iii. 1; v. 12. **πάλαι** does not suit the *interrogative* form of the sentence, which would throw it out into too strong emphasis. Lachmann, Tischdf. (ed. 7 [and 8]), Meyer, De Wette read it as in text:—**Ye have been some time imagining** (i.e. during this my self-defence) **that it is to you that I am defending myself.** Then the answer follows: the assumption being made, and elliptically answered, as in ver. 16. **κατ. θεοῦ** is emphatic, and opposed to ὑμῖν. **ἐν χρ. λαλοῦμεν**, as in ch. ii. 17, which see. **τὰ δὲ πάντα**] supply either λαλοῦμεν, or better understand τὰ πάντα as '*all our things*' (1 Cor. xvi. 14), i.e. our words and deeds, and supply γίνεται, as there. Grot., Griesbach, Scholz, and Olsh., would read τάδε πάντα, and join with λαλοῦμεν. But (1) Paul never uses the pronoun ὅδε; and (2) if he did, it must apply to what follows, not to what has preceded. The insertion of the personal pronoun between the article and the noun, as in **τῆς ὑμ. οἰκοδομῆς**, occurs, as A. Buttmann has correctly remarked (see Moulton's Winer, p. 193, note 4), in Paul only (see reff.), and with no other pronoun than ὑμῶν. **20.**] 'Edification, of which you stand in need, for, &c.' He here completely and finally throws off the apologist and puts on the Apostle, leaving on their minds a very different impression from that which would have been produced had he concluded with the apology. **Lest, when I arrive, I should find you not such as I wish** (in οὐχ οἵους θέλω is an *indefinite* possibility of aberration from οἵους θέλω, presently *particularized*, μή πως ἔρεις, κ.τ λ.), **and I should be found by you** (ὑμῖν merely the dative of the agent after the passive verb. Meyer makes it '*in your judgment*,' but I much prefer the other: the passive form is adopted to bring out the ἐγώ into emphatic contrast), **such as ye wish not** (not οὐχ οἷον θέλετε, because there is now no indefiniteness; *his* disposition towards them in such a case could be but of *one* kind, viz. *severity:* τουτέστι, τιμωρὸς κ. κολαστής, Theophyl. Chrys., p. 634, brings out another point,—οὐκ εἶπεν, οἷον οὐ **θέλω**. ἀλλὰ πληκτικώτερον,—οἷον οὐ βούλεσθε).

What follows, viz. μή πως . . . ἔπραξαν, is an epexegesis of the last sentence, but in it the definiteness is on the side of the οὐχ οἵους θέλω, the indefiniteness on that of οἷον οὐ θέλετε, which latter is only hinted at by the mild expressions of *being humbled, and lamenting the case of the impenitent.* **μή πως**, scil. ὦσιν (or εὑρεθῶσιν) ἐν ὑμῖν. "The vehemence of his language has caused him to omit the verb." Stanley. **ἐριθεῖαι, self-seekings**, see note on ref. Rom. **ψιθ. secret malignings,—καταλ. open slanders. ἀκαταστ.**, see reff. and note. **21.**]

[z] μου [a] πρὸς ὑμᾶς, καὶ [b] πενθήσω πολλοὺς τῶν [c] προημαρτηκότων καὶ μὴ [de] μετανοησάντων [ef] ἐπὶ τῇ [g] ἀκαθαρσίᾳ καὶ

ABDFK LPℵ a b c d e f g h k l m n o 17. 47

a = (? see note) 1 Cor. xvi. 6 reff. b 1 Cor. v. 2 reff. constr., here only. Gen. xxxvii. 34 al. c ch. xiii. 2 only +. d epp., here only. Acts ii. 38 reff. e here only. Joel ii. 13. Amos vii. 3. f = 1 Cor. xiv. 16. g Rom. i. 24 reff.

[προς υμ. bef ταπ. με ο θεος D Syr copt Thdrt$_2$. om 3rd και D[1](and lat) goth Tert$_1$.]

μή carries on the μή πως . . . μή πως, but with more precision, dropping the indefinite πως. The sentence loses much in force and, indeed, becomes inconsistent with the context, if with Lachmann (and Lücke, Conjectanea exeget. i. De W.) it be made interrogative (which it may be grammatically with either reading, ταπεινώσει or -σῃ), in which case the answer would be *negative*. **πάλιν** here, as Meyer observes, must belong to the whole ἐλθόντος μου ταπεινώσει με ὁ θ. μ. πρὸς ὑμ., because, ἐλθών having been used without πάλιν just before, the emphatic situation of πάλιν as applying to it would be unmeaning: see also the very different way in which it is connected with ἔλθω, ch. xiii. 2.

ταπεινώσει] 'Nihil erat quo magis exultaret apostolus, quam prospero suæ prædicationis successu (1 Thess. ii. 20): contra nihil erat, unde tristiore et demissiore animo redderetur, quam quum cerneret, se frustra laborasse,' Beza (Meyer). The fut. (ref.) indicates an assumption that the supposed case will really be. That this *humbling*, and *not* that of *being obliged to punish*, is intended, seems evident: the exercise of judicial authority being no humiliation, but the contrary, and humiliation being the natural result of want of success. **ὁ θεός μου** expresses the conviction that whatever humiliation God might have in store for him would be a part of His will respecting him. **πρὸς ὑμᾶς**] **among you**, as the generality of interpreters: '*in regard to you*,' *in my relation to you*, as Meyer. Either may be meant: but if we take the former, we must not join it, as Grot., al., with ἐλθόντος: it belongs at all events to ταπεινώσει.

πενθήσω] Theophyl. explains, μὴ ἐλθὼν κολάσῃ αὐτούς, καὶ πενθήσῃ διὰ τοῦτο· τουτέστι, τὰ ἔσχατα λυπηθῇ: so also al. and Billroth, Rückert, Olsh., and De Wette. But *punishment* seems out of place in this verse, which expresses his fear lest he should be humbled for, and have to lament the case of the impenitent,—and then, as he declares ch. xiii. 2, be forced to proceed to discipline; but this point is not yet introduced. I much prefer therefore taking it as Chrys., p. 635, —τοὺς μὴ μετανοοῦντας πενθεῖ, τοὺς τὰ ἀνίατα νοσοῦντας, τοὺς ἐν τῷ τραύματι μένοντας. ἐννόησον τοίνυν ἀποστολικὴν ἀρετήν, ὅταν μηδὲν ἑαυτῷ συνειδὼς πονηρόν, ὑπὲρ ἀλλοτρίων θρηνῇ κακῶν, καὶ ὑπὲρ τῶν ἑτέροις πλημμελημένων ταπεινῶται. τοῦτο γὰρ μάλιστα τοῦ διδασκάλου, τὸ οὕτω συναλγεῖν ταῖς τῶν μαθητῶν συμφοραῖς, τὸ κόπτεσθαι καὶ πενθεῖν ἐπὶ τοῖς τραύμασι τῶν ἀρχομένων. Similarly Calvin: 'veri et germani Pastoris affectum nobis exprimit, quum luctu aliorum peccata se prosequuturum dicit. Et sane ita agendum est, ut suam quisque Pastor Ecclesiam animo inclusam gestet, ejus morbis perinde ac suis afficiatur, miseriis condolescat, peccato lugeat.' So Estius, but perhaps too minutely fixing the meaning of πενθεῖν to mourning them as "Deo mortuos:" and Calovius (Meyer): "non de *pœna* hic Corinthiorum impœnitentium, sed de mœrore suo super impœnitentia:" and so likewise Meyer. **πολλ. τ. προημ.**] Why πολλούς? Why not *all*? I believe he uses πολλοὺς τῶν προημαρτηκότων as a *mild expression* for τοὺς πολλοὺς τοὺς προημαρτηκότας, and that we must not therefore press too closely the enquiry as to what the genus οἱ προημ. is, of which the πολλοί are the species. Lücke (as above) cited by Meyer, explains—"Cogitavit rem ita, ut primum poneret Christianorum ex ethnicis potissimum τῶν προημ. κ. μὴ μετανοησάντων genus universum, cujus generis homines essent ubique ecclesiarum, deinde vero ex isto hominum genere multos eos qui Corinthi essent, designaret definiretque." But this seems travelling quite out of the way. Meyer explains the *genus* to be all the sinners spoken of in ver. 20, the *species* (πολλούς) those designated by ἀκαθαρσ., πορν., and ἀσελγ. But this again is unnatural; and does not accurately fit ver. 20, in which not so much the προημαρτημένα as the present state at the Apostle's coming, is the subject. The distinction between the two participles, προημ. and μετανοησάντων, should be observed. As Meyer well remarks, the perf. προημαρτηκότων denotes the permanence of the state from the time of the committal of the sin: whereas the aor. μετανοησάντων has the sense of the 'futurum exactum,' —"and who at my coming shall not have repented." *To what does* προ- *refer?* to the time before their conversion? Hardly so: for the sins, of the incestuous person 1 Cor. v., and of these also, which would give the Apostle such pain, must be conceived to have been committed *in their Christian state*: being in fact those against which we find such repeated cautions in

[h] πορνείᾳ καὶ [i] ἀσελγείᾳ [k] ᾗ ἔπραξαν. XIII. 1 [lm] Τρίτον
[m] τοῦτο ἔρχομαι πρὸς ὑμᾶς. [n] ἐπὶ στόματος δύο μαρτύρων
καὶ τριῶν [o] σταθήσεται πᾶν ῥῆμα. 2 [p] προείρηκα καὶ

h 1 Cor. v. 1 reff.
i Mark vii. 22. Rom. xiii. 13. 2 Pet. ii. 2 al.† Wisd. xiv. 26 only.
k attr., Acts i. 1 reff.
l 1 Cor. xii. 28 reff.
m [ch. xii. 14.] John xxi. 14. Num. xxii. 28, 32. Judg. xvi. 15.
n Matt. xviii. 16. 1 Tim. v. 19. Deut. xix. 15. see Heb. x. 28.
o l. c. A Ald. compl. Rom. xiv. 4.
p Matt. xxiv. 25 ∥ Mk. ch. vii. 3 al.†. 2 Macc. iii. 28 al.

Chap. XIII. 1. ins ιδου bef τριτον (*from ch* xii. 14) A$\aleph^3$ a b c d f o 17 vulg æth Damasc Pel Aug$_1$ Bede. for ερχομαι, ετοιμως εχω ελθειν (*from ch* xii. 14) A Syr. ins ινα bef επι $\aleph^1$ 35 G-lat syrr [arm(Tischdf)]. for και, η ℵ 32. 46 vulg [F-lat arm(Tischdf)] Dial$_1$.

2. [aft προειρ. ins] γαρ D^1 o 4^2. 113-marg [demid] Ambrst Pel Sedul Bede.

1 Cor., e.g. ch. v. 11; vi. 15, 18; x. 8; xv. 33, 34. I would therefore understand the προ- *indefinitely*, almost pleonastically—pointing to *the priority of sin implied in the idea of repentance.* **μεταν. ἐπί**] Meyer would join together πενθήσω . . . ἐπί, and indicates this as the natural connexion of *verb, object*, and *ground*. But to say nothing of the harshness of πενθήσω πολλοὺς ἐπί, and the almost necessarily *reflective* form of μετανοησ. ἐπὶ τῇ ἀκ. . . . ᾗ ἔπραξαν,—I conceive the *aorist* **ἔπραξαν** to be fatal to this arrangement. Thus taken, it would make the Apostle lament over these impenitents, on account of the impurity, &c., which they ἔπραξαν—i. e. once practised, but which is now gone by. The sense would require πεπράχασι. Whereas if connected with μετανοησάντων, the aorist expresses 'and shall not have (repented of the ἀκ., &c., which they practised),' and would thus come rightly after **μετανοησ.**, implying the removal of the former state of sin. **μεταν.** is usually constructed with ἀπό, Acts viii. 22 (Heb. vi. 1), or ἐκ, Rev. only,—ii. 21 f.; ix. 20 f.; xvi. 11: but as Paul only uses the word this once, and as the construction with ἐπί is perfectly legitimate and highly expressive (see reff. LXX), there can be no objection to it here. Chap. XIII. 1—10.] *He warns them of the severity which on his arrival, if such be the case, he will surely exercise, and prove his apostolic authority. To this proof, however, he exhorts them not to put him.* 1.] **This third time I am coming to you**: i. e. '*this is the third visit, which I am now about to pay you.*' Had not chronological theories intervened, no one would ever have thought of any other rendering. The usual one, 'This is the third time that I have been intending to come to you,' introduces here, as also in ch. xii. 14, an element not only foreign to, but detrimental to, the purpose. The Apostle wishes to impress on them *the certainty* of this coming, and to prepare them for it by solemn self-examination; and in order to this, he (*on this interpretation*) uses an expression which would only remind them of the charge of **ἐλαφρία** which had been brought against him, and tend to *diminish the solemnity of the warning.* As another chronological refuge, Beza, al., suppose his *two Epistles* to be meant by the two former '*profectiones ad illos.*' In answer to *all* attempts to give here any but the obvious sense, we may safely maintain that had any other been meant, we should certainly have had more indication of it, than we have now. On τρίτον τοῦτο, Meyer compares Herod. v. 76, τέταρτον δὴ τοῦτο . . . . ἀπικόμενοι: see also reff.: and on Paul's visit to Corinth, the Prolegomena to 1 Cor. § v. **ἐπὶ στόμ.**] i. e. 'I will not now, as before, be with you ἐν πάσῃ ὑπομονῇ as regards the offenders: but will come to a regular process, and establish the truth in a legal manner,' see reff. This explanation, however, has not been the usual one: Chrys., Calvin, Estius, al., and recently Neander and Olsh. and Stanley, understanding the two or three witnesses, of Paul's *two or three visits*, as establishing, either (1) the truth of the facts, or (2) the reality of his threats: so Chrys., Hom. xxix. p. 639 f.: ἅπαξ εἶπον κ. δεύτερον, ὅτε παρεγενόμην· λέγω καὶ νῦν διὰ γραμμάτων. καὶ μὴν ἐὰν ἀκούσητέ μου (al. ἐὰν μὲν ἀκούσητε), ὅπερ ἐπεθύμουν γέγονεν. ἐὰν δὲ παρακούσητε, ἀνάγκη λοιπὸν στῆσαι τὰ εἰρημένα, καὶ ἐπαγαγεῖν τὴν τιμωρίαν,—and Theophyl., πᾶν ῥῆμα **ἀπειλητικὸν** κατασταθήσεται. But it is decisive against the whole interpretation, as Meyer remarks, that thus the sins committed *since the Apostle's last visit* would remain altogether unnoticed. Another view, connected with the rendering of ἔρχομαι '*am intending to come*,' is given by Wetstein: "Spero jam denique mihi successurum, ut vobis demonstrem, serio me desiderasse ad vos venire: sicut ea quæ trium hominum testimonio probantur, in judicio fidem faciunt." Similarly Grotius and Le Clerc. But it is fatal to this, that according to it, the **δύο** μάρτυρες *had failed* to establish it. **καὶ** τρ., not for ἢ τρ.,—**two** (where only two can be had), **and three** (where so many can be obtained): '*two and three respectively.*' μαρτύρων, the dual number not occurring in the N. T. 2.] **I**

q Gal. v. 21. 1 Thess. iii. 4 only. Isa. xli. 26 only.
r 1 Cor. v. 3 reff.
s Jude 5. (Gen. xxvii. 36).
t ch. xii. 21 only †.
u here only. see Lidd. and Scott, sub εἰς, ii. 2.

ABDFK LP‍א a b c d e f g h k l m n o 17. 47

q προλέγω, ὡς r παρὼν s τὸ s δεύτερον καὶ r ἀπὼν νῦν, τοῖς
t προημαρτηκόσιν καὶ τοῖς λοιποῖς πᾶσιν, ὅτι ἐὰν ἔλθω
u εἰς τὸ u πάλιν οὐ v φείσομαι· 3 ἐπεὶ w δοκιμὴν x ζητεῖτε τοῦ
ἐν ἐμοὶ λαλοῦντος χριστοῦ, ὃς εἰς ὑμᾶς οὐκ y ἀσθενεῖ,
ἀλλὰ z δυνατεῖ ἐν ὑμῖν. 4 καὶ γὰρ ἐσταυρώθη ἐξ a ἀσθε-

v = 2 Pet. ii. 4, 5. Acts xx. 29. Ezek. xxxvi. 21. w Rom. v. 4 reff.
x = 1 Cor. iv. 2. y = Rom. viii. 3. z Rom. xiv. 4. ch. ix. 8 only †. a 1 Cor. ii. 3 reff.

om ως D[1](and lat) syr arm. rec aft νυν ins γραφω, with D[3][-gr] KLP rel syrr goth arm Chr_1 Thdrt Damasc Ambrst; λεγω copt æth-pl: om ABD[1]Fא 17 latt æth-rom [Euthal-ms] Aug_1 Sedul Bede. om εις το F arm.

3. for επει, οτι F $Ambr_1$ Aug_{alic}: ει $Orig_4$ Mac_1 [$Cyr\text{-}p_7$] $Thdrt_1$: ἤ $Orig_2$ Dial [$Cyr\text{-}p_2$] $Thdrt_3$: *an* [vulg F-lat] $Orig\text{-}int_2$ [$Aug_{sæpe}$: *quia* D-lat Aug_1: *quia aut quoniam* G-lat: *quoniam* $Ambr_1$]: *quid* $Ambr_1$: *quomodo* Ambrst: for επει δοκιμην, επ οικοδομην 93. λαλουντος bef εν εμοι F[not F-lat].

4. rec aft 1st και γαρ ins ει (*see notes*), with A D[3][-gr] Lא[3] rel vulg(and F-lat) syrr goth [arm] Chr_1(και γαρ ημ. ει Chr-ms) $Thdrt_{h.l.}$ Œc $Orig\text{-}int_3$ $Ps\text{-}Ath\text{-}int_1$ [Hil_2]: om B D[1][and lat] FK[P]א[1] l[1] 17 copt æth Eus_1 [$Cyr\text{-}p_2$ Euthal-ms] Damasc Thl Paulin.

have forewarned you, and I now forewarn you, as (I did, προείρηκα) **when present the second time, so also** (I do) **now** (προλέγω) **when absent.** It certainly seems to me that this is the only natural way of taking the words. Grot., Est., Bengel, al., and De Wette, take ὡς παρὼν τὸ δεύτ. to mean, '*as if I were present the second time,*' meaning *this next time.* But is it possible that the Apostle should have written so confusedly, as to have said in the same sentence τρίτον τοῦτο ἔρχομαι, and ὡς παρὼν τὸ δεύτερον, *both,* according to these interpreters, with reference to *the same journey?* And would he not have even on such an hypothesis have said τὸ δεύτερον τοῦτο? But if we render as above, the **προείρηκα** (perf. because the warning yet endured in force) refers to his *second* visit (παρὼν τὸ δεύτ.), and the **προλέγω** to his present condition of absence (ἀπὼν νῦν), **ὡς** being **as** ('*I did*' or '*do,*' for it applies to both clauses), and **καί** the simple copula. **τοῖς προημ.**] the same persons as are thus designated above, ch. xii. 21. It is not necessary to fix the προ- any more accurately. **τοῖς λοιποῖς πᾶσιν**] **all the rest of you,** who may not have actually sinned, but still require warning, on account of your own personal danger, connexion with the προημαρτηκότες, &c. **ἐὰν ἔλθω εἰς τὸ π.**] **at my next coming.** This was what he προείρηκεν when he was last there, and now προλέγει. **3.**] **ἐπεί** gives the reason why he will not spare: they required the exertion of discipline; and they challenged him to the proof of his apostolic authority. **δοκιμὴν . . . χριστοῦ**] The genitive is either objective, **a proof of Christ speaking in me,** i. e. 'that Christ speaks in me,'—or subjective, **a proof given by Christ speaking in me**—'a token of my authority vouchsafed by Christ speaking in me.' This latter meaning is more suited to what follows, where *Christ* becomes the *subject.* Such proof would be, the immediate execution, by divine power, of some punishment denounced by Paul's word, as in Acts xiii. 11. **ὅς,** i. e. Christ: see above. **δυνατεῖ,** to answer to ἀσθενεῖ, refers both to gifts and miracles, and to the Power of Christ which He would exert in punishment—εἰς ὑμᾶς and ἐν ὑμῖν differ—the εἰς being hypothetical,—the ἐν, matter of fact. The assertion tends to remind them of the danger of provoking Christ, who spoke by Paul. **4.**] *Confirmation of the foregoing* οὐκ ἀσθενεῖ, ἀλλὰ δυνατεῖ. The rec. text, καὶ γὰρ εἰ, would be quite beside the purpose, and would mean, '*For even if He were crucified,*' 'for even putting the case that He was crucified:' καὶ εἰ cannot be = εἰ καί, *though,* as in Vulg. 'etsi,'—and E. V. Hartung, Partikellehre i. 139, shews that in καὶ εἰ, the climax belongs only to the hypothetical particle εἰ, not as in εἰ καί, to the fact presupposed: '*even if,*' not '*if even,*' or '*although.*' Examples of καὶ εἰ are Plato, Sympos. 185, καὶ ἐὰν τοῦτο ποιήσῃς ἅπαξ ἢ δίς, καὶ εἰ πάνυ ἰσχυρά ἐστι, παύσεται. Eur. Androm. 266, καὶ γὰρ εἰ πέριξ σ' ἔχει τηκτὸς μόλυβδος, ἐξαναστήσω σ' ἐγώ. Sappho, καὶ γὰρ αἰ φεύγει, ταχέως διώξει. See more in Hartung, l. c. **For he was even crucified** (that καὶ γάρ always means '*for . . . even*' . . ., or '*for . . . also,*' and never simply '*for,*' see Hartung, i. 137 f., where he has collected many examples, e. g.: Il. α. 63, καὶ γάρ τ' ὄναρ ἐκ Διός ἐστιν,—Herod. i. 77, καὶ γὰρ πρὸς τούτους αὐτῷ ἐπεποίητο συμμαχίη) **from** (as the source,—the conditional element,—by which His crucifixion became possible)

νείας, [b] ἀλλὰ ζῇ ἐκ δυνάμεως θεοῦ· καὶ γὰρ ἡμεῖς
[c] ἀσθενοῦμεν ἐν αὐτῷ, ἀλλὰ [d] ζήσομεν σὺν αὐτῷ ἐκ
[e] δυνάμεως [e] θεοῦ [εἰς ὑμᾶς]. 5 [f] ἑαυτοὺς [g] πειράζετε εἰ
ἐστὲ [h] ἐν τῇ [h] πίστει, [f] ἑαυτοὺς [i] δοκιμάζετε· [k] ἢ οὐκ [l] ἐπι-
γινώσκετε [f] ἑαυτούς, ὅτι Ἰησοῦς χριστὸς [m] ἐν ὑμῖν [ἐστιν]; [n] εἰ [n] μή [n] τι [o] ἀδόκιμοί ἐστε.
6 ἐλπίζω δὲ ὅτι γνώσεσθε ὅτι
ἡμεῖς οὐκ ἐσμὲν [o] ἀδόκιμοι. 7 [pq] εὐχόμεθα δὲ [q] πρὸς τὸν

b = 1 Cor. iv. 15 reff. c ch. xi. 31, 29. d = 1 Thess. iii. 8. e 1 Cor. i. 18 reff. f 2nd pers., ch. vii. 11 reff. g = Rev. ii. 2. iii. 10. Ps. xxv. 2. see Heb. xi. 17. h 1 Cor. xvi. 13. i = 1 Cor. iii. 13 reff. k 1 Cor. vi. 2, 9, 16, 19. l constr., 1 Cor. xiv. 37 reff. m 1 Cor. xiv. 25. n Luke ix. 13. 1 Cor. vii. 5 only. o Rom. i. 28 reff. p Acts xxvii. 29 reff. q here only. Num. xi. 2.

om 2nd γαρ F[-gr] 112 [Syr] arm. [elz] ins και bef ημεις (*appy, as Meyer, the* και γαρ *was taken as merely* = namque, *and thus another* και *added to give the emphasis*), with f g copt Chr$_1$: [ει K tol :] txt ABD F[-gr(and G-lat)] L[P]א rel latt syrr goth[mss vary] Cyr[-p$_1$ Euthal-ms] Thdrt Damasc Thl Œc lat-ff. for εν, συν AFא Syr copt goth. rec ζησομεθα, with D^{3}KL rel Chr$_1$ Thdrt : txt ABD^{1}א 17 Damasc[, -σωμεν F Euthal-ms].—om αλλα ζησ. συν αυτω P. for συν, εν D^1(and lat) 17 Chr$_2$(mss vary). om εκ δυναμεως θεου F[not F-lat] : om θεου K. om εις υμας BD^3 flor arm Chr$_2$ Sedul : *in vobis* joined with follg *ipsis* in D-lat (so also D^1-gr [simly G-lat]) : ins AD^{1}FKL[P]א rel (bef εκ δυναμ. θῡ g : ημας c d) [latt syrr copt goth Cyr-p$_1$ Euthal-ms Thdrt Damasc].

5. om εαυτους δοκιμαζετε A. om ἢ א^1 : ει P o. χριστος bef ιησους AFPא vulg copt arm Clem$_1$ [Euthal-ms] Damasc Ambrst Bede : txt BDKL rel [tol] syrr goth Thdrt Jer$_1$. om εστιν B D^1[-gr] 17 æth Clem Chr-comm$_3$: ins AD^{2,3}FK LPא rel latt goth arm [Chr-txt$_1$ Euthal-ms] Thdrt.

6. for δε, γαρ F[-gr(om F-lat : G-lat has both]. (aft ημεις ε is written but marked for erasure by א^1.)

7. rec ευχομαι (*conformation to* ελπιζω, *ver* 6 ?), with D^3[-gr] KL rel Syr goth Chr$_1$ Thdrt Ambrst Cassiod$_1$: txt ABD^{1}FPא m 17 latt syr copt æth arm [Euthal-ms] Isid$_1$ Damasc Aug$_1$.

weakness, yet He lives by (source [of His life]) **the Power of God** (which raised Him from the dead, Rom. vi. 4; viii. 11; Eph. i. 20; Phil. ii. 9). **For we also are weak in Him** (i. e. *in Him*, in our communion with and imitation of Christ, we, as He did, lay aside our power and spare you: we partake of His voluntary abnegation of power which we might have used. The context requires this explanation, and refutes that of Chrys., p. 644, *τί ἐστιν, ἀσθ. ἐν αὐτῷ; διωκόμεθα, ἐλαυνόμεθα, τὰ ἔσχατα πάσχομεν*, so Theodoret, Theophyl., Grot., Estius, al.), **but shall live** (exercise our apostolic authority, in contrast to the ἀσθένεια above) **with Him** (as He now exercises His power in His glorified resurrection life) **from** (source) **the power of God [with respect to you** (εἰς ὑμᾶς, if genuine, may belong either to δυνάμεως θεοῦ, = δυνάμ. θεοῦ **τῆς** εἰς ὑμᾶς, the art. being often omitted in such constructions, —or to ζήσομεν, '*we shall live with respect to you*,' which agrees better with the parallelism, but not so well with the arrangement of the sentence. The sense seems to require the *latter* interpretation, for the δύναμις θεοῦ **εἰς ὑμ.** would be rather the *result*, than the *source* of the apostolic energy indicated by ζήσομεν)]. I have taken ζήσομεν, as the context plainly requires, figuratively (see ref.): but many Commentators take it literally, of *the resurrection*: e. g. Grot.—'vitam consequemur immortalem.'

5.] "You want to prove *Christ* speaking in me;—if you necessitate this proof, it will be given. But I will tell you *whom rather to prove*. **Prove** YOURSELVES; *there* let your attention be concentrated, if you will apply tests." Notice the prominently emphatic ἑαυτούς: so Chrys., ib.: τί γὰρ λέγω περὶ ἐμοῦ τοῦ διδασκάλου, φησί . . . . ὑμᾶς γὰρ αὐτοὺς ἐὰν βουλήθητε ἐξετάσαι . . . . , ὄψεσθε ὅτι καὶ ἐν ὑμῖν ὁ χριστός. **εἰ ἐστὲ ἐν τῇ π.**] 'Whether you maintain your Christian place and standing in Christ, which will be shewn by the power of Christ's Spirit present and energizing among you.' **ἐπιγιν. ἑαυτ., ὅτι**] for the construction see reff. and Winer, edn. 6, § 66. 5. 1. a. **εἰ μή τι**, unless indeed . . . . see reff. **ἀδόκιμοι**, '*not abiding the proof*,' **worthless**,—i. e. in this case, 'mere pretended Christians.'

6.] **But** (however it may fall out with your proof of *yourselves*) **I hope** (or perhaps better, expect) **that ye shall know that we are not worthless** (unable to abide the proof to which you put us. The verse is said, as Theodoret, ἀπειλητικῶς;—and Chrys. remarks, ib., ἐπειδὴ γὰρ ἐντεῦθεν βούλεσθε, φησί, διὰ τῆς εἰς ὑμᾶς κολάσεως τὴν

r Rom. xiv. 18 reff. s = Rom. vii. 18, 21 reff. t constr., Mark ix. 22. Luke xii. 26. u ellips., 1 Cor. iii. 1. v = ch. xi. 21. w posn., see ch. xii. 19 reff. and note. x here only †. (-τίζειν, ver. 11. -τισμός, Eph. iv. 12.) y ver. 2. z Tit. i. 13 only †. Wisd. v. 22 only. (-μία, Rom. xi. 22.) a constr., Esth. i. 19. ix. 27. (Acts xxvii. 3.) iv. 1. 2 Tim. iv. 8. b ch. x. 8 reff. see above (x). c 1 Cor. i. 16. iv. 2. 1 Thess. d = 1 Cor. i. 10 reff. e = ch. i. 4 &c. reff.

θεὸν μὴ ποιῆσαι ὑμᾶς κακὸν μηδέν, οὐχ ἵνα ἡμεῖς [r] δόκι- ABDFK LP**א** a b c d e f g h k l m n o 17. 47
μοι φανῶμεν, ἀλλ' ἵνα ὑμεῖς τὸ [s] καλὸν ποιῆτε, ἡμεῖς δὲ
ὡς [o] ἀδόκιμοι ὦμεν.
8 οὐ γὰρ [t] δυνάμεθά τι κατὰ τῆς
ἀληθείας, [u] ἀλλὰ ὑπὲρ τῆς ἀληθείας.
9 χαίρομεν γὰρ
ὅταν ἡμεῖς [v] ἀσθενῶμεν, ὑμεῖς δὲ δυνατοὶ ἦτε· τοῦτο καὶ
[p] εὐχόμεθα, τὴν [w] ὑμῶν [x] κατάρτισιν.
10 διὰ τοῦτο ταῦτα
[r] ἀπὼν γράφω, ἵνα [y] παρὼν μὴ [z] ἀποτόμως [a] χρήσωμαι
κατὰ τὴν [b] ἐξουσίαν ἣν ὁ κύριος [b] ἔδωκέν μοι εἰς [b] οἰκοδομὴν καὶ οὐκ εἰς [b] καθαίρεσιν.
11 [c] Λοιπόν, ἀδελφοί, χαίρετε, [d] καταρτίζεσθε, [e] παρα-

for ουχ ινα, ινα μη KL [ut non D-lat]. for υμ., ημεις **א**¹(txt **א**-corr¹(?)³) [m(Treg)]. ποιειτε KL**א** d [Euthal-ms].

8. om της (twice) F. (αλλα, so D¹F**א**. (homœotel in d 17 [47].))

9. om γαρ D³K 46. 108¹-16 arm. οτε F. rec ins δε bef και, with D³[-gr] KL**א**³ rel Syr [Chr₁] Thdrt: om ABD¹FP**א**¹ 17 latt copt æth arm Damasc [Euthal-ms Ambrst].

10. μη bef παρων DF c 47 latt: μη π. μη m. χρησομαι DFP c d k¹ 47. rec εδωκε μοι bef ὁ κυριος, with KL rel syrr æth arm Chr₁ Thdrt Thl Œc: txt ABDFP**א** a² m 17 latt copt goth Damasc [Euthal-ms Ambrst].

11. ins το bef λοιπ. D² f [Chr₁ Thl]: add ουν P. χαιρεσθε P. add και L [Syr].

δοκιμὴν λαβεῖν, οὐκ ἀπορήσομεν τοῦ δοῦναι ὑμῖν τὴν ἀπόδειξιν). **7.**] Yet he prays God rather that they may require no such demonstration of his apostolic power, even though he lose in reputation by it. **μὴ ποιῆσ. ὑμ. κακ. μηδ.**] Not, as Grot., al., *'that I may not have to inflict on you any evil'* (an extraordinary rendering of κακὸν ποιεῖν), but **that ye may do no evil,** corresponding to **ἵνα ὑμεῖς τὸ καλὸν ποιῆτε** below. **οὐχ ἵνα . . . .**] 'And the purpose of this my prayer is not to gain any repute by your Christian graces, but that you may be highly endowed with them, and (if it so happen) we may be as of no repute ('hominum scilicet judicio,' Beza).' That this is the sense, and that **δόκιμοι** is not in this verse to be applied to *substantiation of power by punishment,* is necessitated by the construction,—it being plainly shewn by the infin. after εὐχόμ., that ἵνα is not here meant to apply, even in part, to the *purport* of the prayer (as in Col. i. 9; 2 Thess. i. 11; see note on 1 Cor. xiv. 13), but to its *purpose.* And that being settled,—**we pray . . . . not in order that we may appear δόκιμοι,**—it follows that the *appearing* **δόκιμοι** would be a result of the *fulfilment of the prayer,* viz. of your *doing no evil,* and this it could only be by their *doing no evil* bringing credit on the Apostle's ministry. It is not *for this end* that we pray that you may do no evil, but *for your own good,* even if that tend to the non-exercise, and so depreciation, of our apostolic power. **8.**] **For we have no power against the truth** (of the Gospel, as Meyer; not *of the facts,* as Chrys., al., and De Wette, which might suit κατὰ τῆς ἀλ., but comes in very lamely with ὑπὲρ τῆς ἀλ.—'If you walk in the truth, we shall be at one with you and so have no opportunity of shewing our power') **but** (only) **on behalf of** (in furtherance of the cause and spread of) **the truth.** **9.**] **For** (*confirmation of ver.* 8 *by the still stronger assertion,* WHEREIN *his joy consists, and for what he prays*) **our joy is, when we are weak** (have no opportunity for shewing our power in punishment) **but ye are mighty** (in Christian graces, and requiring no exercise of our authority): **this** (viz. that the state of the case may be as just mentioned) **we also pray for, viz. your perfection** (generally,—in all good things, see καταρτισμόν, Eph. iv. 12: not, as Bengel, 'ne opus sit quenquam de corpore rescindere;' the reference here being far more general).

10.] **διὰ τοῦτο,** *'because I wish and pray for your perfection.'* **ταῦτα,** *'this Epistle.'* **ἀποτ., sharply. χρήσ.,** scil. ὑμῖν. See in reff. similar omissions of the dative. βούλομαι γὰρ ἐν τοῖς γράμμασι κεῖσθαι τὴν ἀποτομίαν, ἀλλὰ μὴ ἐν τοῖς πράγμασι. Chrys., Hom. xxx. p. 649. **κατὰ τ. ἐξ. ἣν . . . .**] gives the reason why he did not wish to act ἀποτόμως,—*because the power would seem to be exercised in*

καλεῖσθε, [f] τὸ αὐτὸ [fg] φρονεῖτε, [h] εἰρηνεύετε, καὶ [ij] ὁ θεὸς
τῆς [i] ἀγάπης καὶ [j] εἰρήνης ἔσται μεθ' ὑμῶν. 12 [k] ἀσπάσασθε ἀλλήλους [k] ἐν ἁγίῳ [k] φιλήματι. ἀσπάζονται ὑμᾶς
οἱ [l] ἅγιοι πάντες.
13 Ἡ χάρις τοῦ κυρίου Ἰησοῦ χριστοῦ καὶ ἡ [m] ἀγάπη
τοῦ [m] θεοῦ καὶ ἡ [n] κοινωνία τοῦ ἁγίου πνεύματος μετὰ
πάντων ὑμῶν.

ΠΡΟΣ ΚΟΡΙΝΘΙΟΥΣ Β.

f Rom. xii. 16. xv. 5. Phil. ii. 2. iv. 2.
g Rom. viii. 5 reff.
h Mark ix. 50. Rom. xii. 18. 1 Thess. v. 13 only. 2 Chron. xiv. 5. Sir. vi. 6.
i here only.
j Rom. xv. 33.
k Rom. xvi. 16 (reff.).
l = Acts ix. 13 reff. Rom. i. 7 al. fr.
m Rom. v. 5. viii. 39.
n = 1 Cor. i. 9. Phil. ii. 1 al.

om το αυτο φρονειτε A. transp ειρηνης and αγαπης DL m vulg(with fuld, agst am [demid] tol [F-lat]) goth arm Thdrt Thl Ambrst Pel: om αγαπης και F[-gr(and G-lat)] 17 æth-rom.—aft last και ins της DL a d f h k m.

12. φιληματι bef αγιω AFL e g m n vulg Chr_1 Thl [Euthal-ms Ambrst], φιληματι αγαπης f: txt BDKPא rel Thdrt Damasc Œc.

13. om χριστου B k^2 [Cyr_1]. om υμων P. rec at end ins αμην, with DKP$א^3$ rel vulg syrr copt goth arm-zoh [Chr_1 Damasc] Thdrt Ambrst: om ABFL[?]$א^1$ 17 $harl^1$ [spec arm-usc] æth Chr-mss [Euthal-ms].

Subscription. rec προς κορ. δευτερα εγραφη απο φιλιππων της μακεδονιας δια τιτου κ. λουκα, with K Syr copt Thdrt-ed Œc, and omg της μακεδ. L a f g n 47: πρ. κορ. β' εγραφη απο φιλιππων B^2 (d), and (adding στιχων φη) P: εγραφη απο φιλιππων δια τιτου κ. λουκα b k m o: πρ. κορ. β. εγρ. απο φιλ. δια τιτου βαρναβα κ. λουκα h 44. 106-8-33: om l: προς κορ. β' επληρωθη· αρχεται πρ. γαλ. D: ετελεσθη πρ. κορ. β' αρχεται προς γαλ. F: txt AB^1 17, and (adding στιχων χιβ) א.

a direction contrary to that intended by Him who gave it. 11—13.] Conclusion. 11.] *General exhortations.* "Severius scripserat Paulus in tractatione; nunc benignius, re tamen ipsa non dimissa." Bengel. **χαίρ., rejoice,** scil. *in the Lord,* as Phil. iii. 1; iv. 4. So also 1 Thess. v. 16. **καταρτ.,** τέλειοι γίνεσθε καὶ ἀναπληροῦτε τὰ λείποντα, Chrys., ib.: amend "yourselves," Stanley. **παρακαλ., take comfort;** a recurrence in the end of the Epistle to the spirit with which it began; see ch. i. 6, 7, and, for the need they had of comfort, ch. vii. 8—13. This is better than '*comfort* (or '*exhort*') *one another,*' which would more naturally be expressed by παρακαλεῖτε ἀλλήλους, or ἑαυτούς, see 1 Thess. iv. 18; v. 11; Heb. iii. 13; also Heb. x. 25 and note. **τὸ αὐτὸ φρ.** belongs to ἀγάπη, **εἰρηνεύετε** to εἰρήνη. **καί,** 'and then.' 12.] *Concluding greetings.* **ἐν ἁγ. φιλ.**] See on Rom. xvi. 16. **οἱ ἅγ. πάντες**] viz. in the place whence the Epistle was written. 13.] *Concluding benediction;* remarkable for the distinct recognition of the Three Persons in the Holy Trinity, and thence adopted by the Christian Church in all ages as the final blessing in her Services. **The grace of our Lord Jesus Christ** is put first; "nam per gratiam Christi venitur ad Patris amorem." Bengel. **κοινων. τ. ἁγ. πν.**] **communion,—fellowship,** gen. obj.—not '*communicatio activa,*' gen. subj.—τουτέστι τὴν μετοχὴν αὐτοῦ κ. τὴν μετάληψιν, καθ' ἣν ἁγιαζόμεθα, τῇ ἐφ' ἡμᾶς ἐπιφοιτήσει τοῦ παρακλήτου κοινωνοὶ αὐτοῦ γενόμενοι, καὶ πνεῦμα καὶ αὐτοί, οὐκ οὐσίᾳ, ἀλλὰ μεθέξει, ὄντες, Theophyl., and similarly Œcum. Chrys. adds, p. 652, οὕτω τὰ τῆς τριάδος ἀδιαίρετα· καὶ οὗ τοῦ πνεύματός ἐστιν ἡ κοινωνία, εὑρέθη τοῦ υἱοῦ· καὶ οὗ τοῦ υἱοῦ ἐστιν ἡ χάρις, καὶ τοῦ πατρὸς κ. τοῦ ἁγίου πνεύματος. **μετὰ πάντων ὑμῶν**] "And this blessing he invokes, not on a few individuals, or on any one section of the Corinthian Church, but expressly on every portion and every individual of those with whom, throughout these two Epistles, he had so earnestly and so variously argued and contended. As in the first, so in the second Epistle, but still more emphatically, as being here his very last words, his prayer was, that this happiness might be 'with them all' (μετὰ πάντων ὑμῶν)." Stanley. Compare, for the same emphatic πᾶς, Rom. i. 5, 8; iv. 16; [xvi. 24,] &c.: and for πᾶς following its substantive and unemphatic, ib. viii. 32, 37; 1 Cor. vii. 17; x. 1, &c.

REVISIONS

The references in this revision to Arndt and Gingrich are to Arndt, William F., and Gingrich, F. Wilbur. *A Greek-English Lexicon of the New Testament and Other Early Christian Literature.* The University of Chicago Press, Chicago, 1957. (This is a translation and adaptation of Walter Bauer's *Griechisch-Deutsches Worterbuch zu den Schriften des Neuen Testaments und der ubrigen urchristlichen literatur.*)

Matt. 3:14, 15. διεκώλυεν—the conative use of the imperfect. John sought earnestly to prevent Him (from submitting Himself for baptism).

δικαιοσύνην—a doing of what God requires. However, the reference is not solely to baptism (for a righteous ordinance is δικαίωμα) but to the whole area of obedience to the divine will.

Matt. 6:13. "Lead us not into temptation." Worth consideration is the suggestion that the petition has in view not the exemption from temptation as an experience, but the desire to be kept from tempting God, such as would be the case if one were to ask a sign. This is a mark of doubt, not faith (see G. F. Allan's remarks in *The Expository Times,* Dec., 1955, p. 66)

Matt. 10:1ff. Alford does not comment on the change from disciples (v. 1) to apostles (v. 2). It should be noted that, practically speaking, the Gospels avoid using the word apostle save in connection with this sending forth (ἀποστελλεῖν) on a certain specific occasion. When we see these men taking the leadership in the early Church, however, they are recognized as the authoritative appointees of Christ (Acts 1:2, 26; cf. Eph. 4:11).

Matt. 10:4. Oscar Cullmann in *The State in the New Testament* (p. 15) has made the suggestion that since no town of Kerioth is known, "we may therefore quite properly consider whether Iscariot may not be a Semitic transcription of the Latin word *sicarius*." By identifying him thus with the zealots, Cullmann finds it easier to explain his betrayal of Christ.

Matt. 11:12. This difficult verse may possibly be illumined if we assume that Jesus has in mind the zealots who were seeking to make use of the kingdom of God in order to work their own purpose in the area of the state. Recall that there were those who would take Jesus by force and make Him a king (John 6:15).

Matt. 16:28. The claim that these words are fulfilled in the destruction of Jerusalem is strange in view of the precise language —"see the Son of man coming. . . ." This explanation would have more basis if the text read, "See the coming of the kingdom of the Son of man." No explanation of the passage is without its difficulty.

Matt. 17:5. The words *hear ye him* are doubtless not intended for the future only, but have special relevance to the incident at Caesarea Philippi, where Peter had been unwilling to hear the Lord and insisted on contradicting Him. The words constitute a rebuke as well as direction for the future.

Matt. 21:3. The most natural interpretation refers ὁ κύριος to Jesus. Jesus used κύριος of Himself in prophetic contexts (Matt. 7:21, 22; 24:42). Here the title, though used by Jesus of Himself, reflects the current employment of it by the circle of disciples, to which the owner of the colt belonged. The use of the definite article is less favorable to a reference to Jehovah than to Jesus (cf. Matt. 27:10).

Matt. 23:8. The conjecture that ὁ διδάσκαλος points to the Holy Spirit is highly improbable. The noun is not used of the Spirit anywhere in the New Testament. Jesus' references to the Spirit's teaching activity (John 14-16) look on to the future. Here the words of the Master are of immediate application. He Himself was commonly addressed as Teacher.

Matt. 26:17. Alford was convinced that the Synoptists represent the Lord as eating the Passover at the usual time, but that this is not the case in John's Gospel. The difficulty is created not

John 1:12. *Right* or *authority* comes closer to the idea for ἐξουσία than *power*. The latter is more accurately expressed by δύναμις.

John 1:18. The statement, "We should be introducing great harshness into the sentence, and a new and strange term into Scripture, by adopting Θεός," is somewhat misleading, for Θεὸς has already been used of the Logos in 1:1 and μονογενὴς in 1:14. Most translators have shown reluctance to follow the strong manuscript backing for Θεὸς which caused Westcott and Hort (Nestle also) to insert it in the text. Exceptions are Helen Barrett Montgomery and Williams.

John 1:18. The assertion that εἰς τὸν κόλπον is not equal to ἐν τῷ κόλπῳ must be set aside in view of the present day knowledge of the *koine*, where the two prepositions often have the same sense. See A. T. Robertson *Grammar* (pp. 592, 593); J. H. Moulton, *Prolegomena* (pp. 234, 235; note on p. 63).

John 2:4. To refer *my hour* to the time for working miracles is strange in view of the fact that Jesus proceeded immediately to work one. It would seem better to refer the hour to His death, in keeping with the other references in John (so Sir Edwyn Hoskyns in *The Fourth Gospel*, p. 188; also C. K. Barrett in *The Gospel According to St. John*, p. 159).

John 3:13. The words, "who is in heaven," are probably not part of the original text. Alford suggests that the manuscripts which omit them did so possibly out of misunderstanding or carelessness. But they are our leading manuscripts. Furthermore, the words are not congruent with Jesus' previous statement. Having come down from Heaven, He is in position to reveal heavenly things. It is true that there is some difficulty in accounting for the words if they are not genuine, but may have been introduced as a scribal addition based on John 1:18.

John 3:15. In view of this being the solitary instance of such a construction in the Fourth Gospel, it is customary today to join ἐν αὐτῷ with the verb ἔχῃ rather than with ὁ πιστεύων.

John 4:26. Jesus could announce Himself as Messiah in Samaritan territory with little fear of stirring up popular enthusiasm of a political sort. On Jewish soil this was impossible, hence His reluctance to use the term *Messiah* of Himself in public. A revolutionary movement could only defeat the spiritual purpose of His mission.

John 4:30. The imperfect tense of ἤρχοντο is better explained as picturing the steady stream of arrivals in the presence of Jesus.

John 5:39. Most expositors today prefer the indicative sense, which agrees better with the following words. Jesus' hearers were in the habit of searching the Scriptures because of their assumption that they would learn the secret of eternal life there. He finds fault with them, not for their searching, but for their failure to be prepared thereby for receiving Him.

John 13:2. The cumbersome explanation would be unnecessary if the other and superior reading were adopted. δείπνου γινομένου carries the meaning, "while supper was in progress."

John 14:16. These two aspects of the work of the Paraclete are readily understood when it is realized that one may give help to another directly (such is the Spirit's work of strengthening and instruction) and also indirectly. Such is the Spirit's work of intercession and advocacy.

John 20:17. Regarding the sense of Μή μου ἅπτου, though Alford rules out "a laying hold of to *retain*" as transgressing the proper sphere of meaning belonging to another word, κρατεῖν, research suggests that this is indeed the meaning here. J. H. Moulton (*Vocabulary of the Greek Testament*) cites an inscription from the second century B.C. where the word means, "lay hold of," "appropriate." For a conspectus of the modern literature on the problem, see Arndt and Gingrich.

Acts 2:5. Under 2:1 Alford discusses the significance of κατοικοῦντες and feels compelled to understand the language as referring to temporary sojourn. This is contrary to the force of the word and to its use throughout the book, in fact, throughout the New Testament generally. See Acts 13:27, where the identical phrase is used of those who condemned Jesus. Alford is heavily influenced by 2:9, but this may well mean former residents of Mesopotamia, etc., who had now come to dwell in the holy city. Not only lexicography but the broad context favors the idea of permanent dwelling, not temporary sojourn. Peter is able to presume full knowledge on the part of his hearers concerning the death of Christ and the events attending it. Further, those who respond to his preaching do not return to the places mentioned here, but continue with the apostles. Nor is there any indication of a return in subsequent days. The writer treats these converts as though they belonged to the community.

Acts 2:44. The claim that the greater part of the three thousand must have returned to their homes by this time is without foundation. The language of this verse suggests that the believers in question were the very ones saved on the day of Pentecost, the very ones who continued in the apostles' teaching. All confusion is avoided by giving κατοικοῦντες in 2:5 its proper force.

Acts 2:45. The community of goods was not a disavowal of the rights of private property. Believers did not surrender their possessions in one decisive resignation. From the imperfect tense of the verbs it is clear that the giving into the common fund took place as the need arose from time to time (cf. Acts 5:4).

Acts 2:47. The emphasis does not seem to be on the process of salvation as in I Corinthians 15:2, but on the fact that from time to time, even daily, people were being saved. Their being added to the saved community was strictly parallel to their being saved.

Acts 3:26. There is no good reason for resisting the idea that εὐλογοῦντα, though a present participle, expresses purpose. (See Robertson *Grammar*, pp. 1128, 1129).

Acts 7:56. On the meaning of Stephen's use of the title "Son of man," William Manson writes, "Stephen grasped and asserted the more-than-Jewish-Messianic sense in which the office and significance of Jesus in religious history were to be understood. More clearly than others, and indeed uniquely in that first age of Christianity, he perceived the universal range and bearing of the Christ-event, by which the call of God had passed from the Jewish people to embrace humanity at large" (*The Epistle to the Hebrews*, p. 31).

Acts 7:58. ἐλιθοβόλουν. The imperfect is inceptive in force—"they began to stone him." The same form in the following verse pictures the repetition of the process.

Acts 8:1. It may be that we are to understand that the persecution fell upon the Hellenists, of which group Stephen was acknowledged leader, rather than upon the Hebraists, to which group the apostles belonged. The latter were not prepared to break with Judaism in every respect. They observed the hours of prayer in the temple and were careful to honor the customs of the Jews. James the Lord's brother, though not one of the Twelve, personified this attitude, which was bound to commend him to the Jews (cf. Acts 15:13-21; 21:18ff.).

Acts 9:7. For Alford's view on inspiration, see reviser's Introduction.

Acts 10:2. The term, *proselyte of the gate,* which is here used by Alford, is seldom employed today because it is somewhat misleading. The term *proselyte* should be reserved for those Gentiles who became Jews by circumcision and assumption of the yoke of the law. Gentiles who manifested an interest in Judaism but who stopped short of the decisive step of incorporation into the commonwealth of Israel are properly designated as God-fearers. Cornelius belonged to this class (10:2, 35).

Acts 10:25. The use of τοῦ with the infinitive in a subject relation, where one would expect τό, lacks classical authority, but it is common in the LXX, and Luke has several examples. (See Robertson *Grammar,* pp. 1066-1068.)

Acts 13:1. The word σύντροφος may mean foster brother in the literal sense, but the word is also found in the inscriptions in the sense of associate or intimate friend of a royal figure. *Courtier* gets at the idea quite well. J. H. Moulton and George Milligan in *The Vocabulary of the New Testament* (p. 615) note that the word means "companion" in modern Greek. For a full discussion see A. Deissmann in *Bible Studies* (pp. 310-312).

Acts 13:32. ἀναστήσας can hardly be regarded as certainly a reference to the resurrection from the dead, despite the fact that both verses 30 and 34 contain clear references to this event. It should be observed that in the passage before us the words ἐκ νεκρῶν are lacking. Therefore it is quite possible that Jesus' emergence in history is thought of here. R. B. Rackham in *The Acts of the Apostles* (p. 216) tries to combine both ideas.

Acts 15:11. Note how strong Peter's statement is. We might have expected a broad statement that salvation is open to Gentiles as well as Jews, but this was not the real point at issue. Peter insists that both Jews and Gentiles are saved *in the same manner*, that is, apart from legal considerations, by grace alone. To underscore the point, he asserts that Jews are saved in the same manner as Gentiles, not vice versa. Instead of the Gentile being obliged to become a Jew to become saved, the Jew is obliged to become as a Gentile, putting aside circumcision and the law as irrelevant to the issue of salvation. (Cf. Paul's argument in Rom. 4:9-12.)

Acts 16:6-9. Alford is here adopting the so-called North Galatian theory. After his time Ramsay popularized the South Galatian theory, that the churches of Galatia are, in fact, the churches founded on the first missionary journey. This has become the dominant view, although a number of German scholars still prefer the North Galatian theory. Each side is able to muster cogent arguments.

Acts 16:12. The meaning here assigned to πρώτη is not likely in view of the ἥτις ἐστὶν preceding it. See the long note on this word in *The Beginnings of Christianity* by F. J. Foakes Jackson and Kirsopp Lake, *in loco*. They favor the interpretation, "a leading city."

Acts 16:13. The reading ἐνομίζετο, followed by Alford, is not as well attested as ἐνομίζομεν, "we were supposing."

Acts 17:19. Ramsay adduced evidence showing the local practice in Athens was to use the term *Areopagus* when designating the Court of Areopagus. It is probable that Luke intends us to think of the Court rather than the hill on which the group formerly had its meetings. In Paul's day it met in the Agora, near the scene of his discussions with the philosophers. (See Ramsay, *Bearing of Recent Discovery on the Trustworthiness of the New Testament*, pp. 102-105.)

Acts 18:5. The imperfect συνείχετο may well have inceptive force—"he began to be engrossed" (in the ministry of the word) with fresh intensity. Others prefer the rendering, "was wholly absorbed in preaching," considering the verb passive in force and descriptive of what was going on even before the arrival of Paul's associates.

Acts 19:29. For a picture of the ruins of the theater and other data on Ephesus see article by M. M. Parvis in the *Biblical Archaeologist* (Sept., 1945).

Acts 19:31. On the Asiarchs, see H. J. Cadbury, *The Book of Acts in History* (p. 42).

Acts 21:5. There is good authority for the meaning *complete* for ἐξαρτίσαι. (See Arndt and Gingrich, *A Greek-English Lexicon of the New Testament.*)

Acts 21:21. The aorist κατηχήθησαν need not refer to a certain fixed time, but may be rendered, "They have been informed." (See Moulton, *Prolegomena*, pp. 135, 136.)

Acts 22:20. The meaning *martyr* should not be imputed to the word at this stage. Stephen had borne witness to the Lord and particularly to his vision of the exalted Christ. In the apostolic age people died because they were faithful witnesses; they did not become μάρτυρες because they died. This belongs to a later development.

Acts 22:28. On the question of Paul's Roman and Tarsian citizenship, see Cadbury, *The Book of Acts in History* (pp. 65-82).

Acts 23:1. The suggestion that ἀτενίσας is to be connected with infirmity of sight is hardly borne out either by the usage of the word or our knowledge of Paul's physical condition. Ramsay comments: "The theory which makes Paul a permanent sufferer in his eyes, unable to see distinctly persons quite near him, and repulsive to strangers on account of their hideous state (Gal. 4:13f.), is hopelessly at variance with the evidence of Luke. In that word, as he uses it, the soul looks through the eyes" (*St. Paul the Traveler and the Roman Citizen*, p. 39).

Acts 23:5. Rather than tie in the explanation with Paul's alleged poor vision, which cannot be sustained by the ἀτενίσας in verse 1, it is better to understand that Paul had not learned of the change which placed Ananias in the office of high priest. His absence from the city for some time sufficiently accounts for this ignorance.

Acts 23:23. A conjecture on the meaning of δεξιολάβους is that they may have been bowmen or slingers (Arndt and Gingrich, *A Greek-English Lexicon of the New Testament*).

Acts 24:6-8. On the textual problem see the discussion in F. J. Foakes Jackson and Kirsopp Lake in *The Beginnings of Christianity*, Vol. IV (pp. 299, 300).

Acts 26:10. Alford speaks too positively when he says that κατήνεγκα ψῆμον can hardly be taken figuratively. (See comment by F. J. Foakes Jackson and Kirsopp Lake in *The Beginnings of Christianity*, Vol. V, p. 317.)

Acts 26:28. A. T. Robertson in *Word Pictures in the New Testament*, Vol. III (p. 453), accepting the better attested πείθεις, makes it conative in force—you are trying to persuade.

Acts 27:1. On the Augustan Cohort, see F. J. Foakes Jackson and Kirsopp Lake in *The Beginnings of Christianity*, Vol. V (pp. 443, 444).

Rom. 1:10. εὐοδωθήσομαι—Hellenistic usage commonly carries the meaning of *succeed.* (See Arndt and Gingrich.)

Rom. 1:17. While the word *order* favors joining ἐκ πίστεως εἰς πίστιν to ἀποκαλύπτεται, other considerations make plausible a combination with δικαιοσύνη. See the somewhat similar construction in 3:22.

Rom. 1:30. The active sense of θεοστυγεῖς may now be allowed. (See Arndt and Gingrich for references.)

Rom. 3:9. On this difficult verse, see the discussion in Arndt and Gingrich under προέχω.

Rom. 3:22. The words καὶ ἐπὶ πάντας should be omitted from the text as lacking sufficient attestation.

Rom. 3:23. The meaning of the words ὑστεροῦνται τῆς δόξης τοῦ Θεοῦ is quite uncertain. As a consequence of sin, men are destitute of the glory of God. One wonders if approbation is the proper sense here. It is rare in Paul. In II Corinthians 3:9 δόξα is associated with righteousness, which is the central issue here in the Romans' passage. This possibility ought not to be overlooked in the interpretation.

Rom. 3:31. Alford's interpretation rests on the assumption that νόμος has the same meaning without the article as with it. A glance at 3:21 will be instructive. When referring to the Pentateuch which enshrined the legislation God gave to Israel, Paul uses νόμος with the article. Yet in the same verse we find νόμος used without the article; apparently meaning law as law, that is, law in its distinctly legal aspects, apart from narrative, promise, etc. Rather than connect 3:31 with chapter 4, it is better to see it as the conclusion of the chapter in which it stands. God's method of justification does not void law, but rather establishes and vindicates it, for the law makes impossible any easy-going method of justification. Its full claims must be met. That they are met has been made plain in 3:25, 26.

Rom. 4:6-8. It is likely that the case of David is introduced not merely as a second example of justification by faith, but as illustrating an aspect of justification not so clearly obvious in Abraham's situation. David sinned as a justified man, but God refused to impute his sin to him so as to make him forfeit his justification. Nothwithstanding, he was obliged to bear the temporal consequences of his sin.

Rom. 4:13. In line with the context, it is better to take "heir of the world" in a spiritual sense only. Abraham was to have a great inheritance among those who believe, among those who would follow him in his faith, whether they be Jews or Gentiles.

Rom. 4:25. The parallel construction involved in the two διά clauses ought not to be put aside lightly. The resurrection of Christ attested the fullness of the satisfaction made for our sins. Our justification may be said to rest on the death of Christ as an objective fact (cf. 5:9), however much we need the resurrection for our faith in a subjective sense.

Rom. 5:1. The choice between ἔχομεν and ἔχωμεν is notoriously difficult. Erwin Nestle in *Novum Testamentum Graece,* after adopting the subjunctive, has gone back to the indicative (from the seventeenth edition on). In this case MS authority may have to yield to other factors, such as the possibility of confusion between ο and ω, even in dictation (Hans Lietzmann in *An die* Römer [*Handbuch zum Neuen Testametn,* p. 58]), and the strong impression that the remainder of the paragraph makes on the reader in the direction of stating benefits conferred rather than exhorting to a certain response.

Rom. 5:2. The access is not strictly treated as a thing past, but as gained in the past and currently operative. "We have obtained and continue to have" expresses the idea of the verb.

Rom. 6:5. It is quite possible that ἐσόμεθα is an ethical future, expressing logical necessity rather than futurity, in which case the resurrection here refers to the present walking in newness of life (v. 4) rather than the future bodily resurrection of believers which comes into view in verse 8.

Rom. 8:10. The alternative view is deserving of serious consideration, namely, that the sin here is Adam's sin which has brought death (cf. 5:12), and the righteousness is the imputed righteousness of God (cf. 5:18).

Rom. 10:3. On the rendering of ὑπετάγησαν see Moulton, *Prolegomena* (p. 163).

Rom. 10:4. Consult Sanday and Headlam (*I.C.C. Commentary on Romans*) for a strong statement of the interpretation of τέλος as meaning termination, not objective.

Rom. 10:6-8. Alford's comments here seem to stray from the course of Paul's argument, which is not that the Gospel is anticipated in the law, for the method of righteousness under law and under grace has just been declared to be utterly different (vv. 5, 6). The difficulty stems from a questionable interpretation of τέλος in verse 4.

Rom. 10:9. Jesus as Lord is alone defensible, κύριον being in a predicate relation to Ἰησοῦν. A similar construction occurs in II John 2:7, where ἐρχόμενον means *as coming.* The absence of the article in such constructions is all-important. Order of words makes no real difference (see I Cor. 12:3). On the other hand, when the article is present, we must translate *the Lord* as in Acts 11:20; 16:31.

Rom. 11:26. Alford's note in explanation of the force of *and thus* might seem to be open to objection that οὕτως does not have in it any notion of time. That is true of the word itself, but a context may lend a temporal aspect to it. Such is the case, for example, in I Corinthians 11:28.

Rom. 11:26. For the force of ἐκ Σιών, see Psalm 14:7.

Rom. 12:1. The remarks under *your bodies* suggest that the intended purpose of the presentation is the sanctification of the body. But the analogy of sacrifice suggests that the body must be holy in order to be offered. It is holy because redeemed (cf. I Cor. 6:19, 20). Emphasis on the body here seems to have in view the whole active life of the Christian which is covered in the remaining chapters. Alford's statement seems to involve some confusion between body and flesh. The latter is the seat of sin in Paul's teaching. It calls for crucifixion, not presentation to God.

Rom. 12:8. ὁ ἐλεῶν is better rendered, *He who performs acts of mercy.* Charitable activity is in view in the widest sense.

Rom. 14:1. Rather, faith is used in this chapter as a conviction regarding the extent of Christian liberty which one has in the realm of *adiaphora.* The presence of the article does not at all demand the rendering, *the faith.*

Rom. 14:5. It is doubtful that Paul is discussing days from the standpoint of observance by the Christian body for worship, but rather from the standpoint of the subject under discussion. Hence the days refer to feasting and fasting, special days. (Cf. Gal. 4:10, 11; Col. 2:16, 17.)

I Cor. 1:2. *Theirs and ours.* To relate this phrase to place is both needless and pointless, but to relate it to *Lord* has significance in view of the need of inculcating a catholic spirit in this sectarian-ridden church.

I Cor. 1:7. It is doubtful that there is any thought of comparison with other believers, though this is defensible if the construction be a middle (see Archibald Robertson and Alfred Plummer in *A Critical and Exegetical Commentary on the First Epistle of St. Paul to the Corinthians*, p. 6). Taken as a passive, it means "to be lacking," "be short of."

I Cor. 1:12. Alford's view on the parties at Corinth seems contradicted by verses 14, 15 and is not demanded by 4:6. Almost universally today the presence of these groups within the church is accepted in the literal sense, i.e., they did make use of these very names and ranged themselves under these respective banners. See the discussion in H. A. W. Meyer's *Critical and Exegetical Handbook to the Epistles to the Corinthians* (pp. 19, 20); also in J. P. Lange's *Commentary on the Holy Scriptures—Corinthians* (p. 28). Theodor Zahn (*Introduction to the New Testament*, Vol. I, p. 299) is very strong in his rejection of this view of Alford's.

I Cor. 1:18. The preposition ἀπὸ adds something to the force of the participle. It conveys a perfectivizing emphasis. "Strongly durative though the verb is, we see perfectivity in the fact that the goal is *ideally* reached: a complete transformation of its subjects is required to bring them out of the ruin implicit in their state" (Moulton, *Prolegomena*, pp. 114, 115).

I Cor. 1:30. In line with the context, wisdom is the central thought. The other three terms are explanatory of the content of that wisdom. (See Archibald Robertson and Alfred Plummer in *A Critical and Exegetical Commentary on the First Epistle of St. Paul to the Corinthians*, p. 27.)

I Cor. 2:6. Who are the τέλειοι? We ought not to anticipate the discussion in 3:1, where two types of believers are in contrast. Here the implied contrast is with those who have only worldly wisdom. R. C. H. Lenski in *The Interpretation of St. Paul's First and Second Epistles to the Corinthians* (p. 95) describes the τέλειοι here as "those who have reached Christ crucified as the goal." See F. W. Grosheide in *Commentary on the First Epistle to the Corinthians* (The New International Commentary on the New Testament, p. 63, in loco), and Karl Heim, *Die Gemeinde des Auferstandenen*, (p. 25.)

I Cor. 4:2. In the *koinê* ἵνα often has merely declaratory force and does not involve purpose. Such is the case here. Only because Alford lived before the era of Deissmann could he say, as he does under the following verse: "The ἵνα, here and always, is more or less the conjunction of *purpose*."

I Cor. 4:6. The view of Chrysostom, which Alford criticizes, is sounder and more widely accepted today than his own.

I Cor. 6:7. "Utterly a defeat" is the best rendering for ὅλως ἥττημα. ἀδικεῖσθε and ἀποστερεῖσθε are examples of the so-called permissive middle. (See H. E. Dana and Julius R. Mantey in *A Manual Grammar of the Greek New Testament*, p. 160.)

I Cor. 6:12. Not the words of an opponent, to be sure, but they may well be the words of the Corinthians who proposed to carry over much of their pagan morality into the Christian life. Paul may be quoting them in order to find a starting point, then proceeding to show wherein this is true and wherein it needs to be qualified.

I Cor. 7:21. The more probable interpretation sees the apostle recommending the use of freedom if it is obtainable. (See the two reasons for adopting this view given by Archibald Robertson and Alfred Plummer in *A Critical and Exegetical Commentary on the First Epistle of St. Paul to the Corinthians,* pp. 147, 148.

I Cor. 7:29. Again Alford goes astray by insisting that ἵνα can only denote purpose. The last six lines of his comment need revision, because ἵνα here denotes result rather than purpose. (See Robertson, *Grammar,* p. 997.)

I Cor. 7:34. The arrangement of the text adopted here is open to question. Certainly the interpretation which makes μεμέρισται mean "divided from one another," i.e., different from one another, is highly improbable. This would call for the verb διαφέρω. See the Nestle text for the preferable reading and punctuation.

I Cor. 9:10. πάντως preferably means *certainly, by all means* in this passage. Otherwise, Paul would be ignoring the plain, literal meaning of the Old Testament saying rather than building upon it. (See Arndt and Gingrich.)

I Cor. 9:17. It is perhaps better to understand the apostle as saying that if he pursues his ministry in a glad and willing spirit (which he does) he is entitled to a reward (which he is), but if he carries on his ministry in an unwilling spirit, simply because he has been pressed into service, the obligation to serve remains, but the ground for reward is removed.

I Cor. 11:23. It is not necessary to hold that a special revelation to Paul is meant. There are good reasons for holding that Paul simply means to designate the ultimate source of the tradition. (See J. Jeremias, *The Eucharistic Words of Jesus,* pp. 128-131; Oscar Cullmann, *The Early Church,* pp. 63, 64.)

I Cor. 11:31. The problem of syntax raised here needs clarification. It cannot be said that either construction is correct. In con-